# THE OXFORD ENGLISH
# DICTIONARY

# THE OXFORD ENGLISH DICTIONARY

BEING A CORRECTED RE-ISSUE

WITH AN

INTRODUCTION, SUPPLEMENT, AND BIBLIOGRAPHY

OF

# A NEW ENGLISH DICTIONARY

## ON HISTORICAL PRINCIPLES

FOUNDED MAINLY ON THE MATERIALS COLLECTED BY

The Philological Society

## VOLUME XI

## T–U

WITHDRAWN

OXFORD

AT THE CLARENDON PRESS

SAN BRUNO PUBLIC LIBRARY

*Oxford University Press, Amen House, London E.C.4*
GLASGOW NEW YORK TORONTO MELBOURNE WELLINGTON
BOMBAY CALCUTTA MADRAS KARACHI KUALA LUMPUR
CAPE TOWN IBADAN NAIROBI ACCRA

FIRST PUBLISHED 1933
REPRINTED 1961

PRINTED IN GREAT BRITAIN
AT THE UNIVERSITY PRESS, OXFORD
BY VIVIAN RIDLER, PRINTER TO THE UNIVERSITY

# KEY TO THE PRONUNCIATION.

## I. CONSONANTS.

b, d, f, k, l, m, n, p, t, v, z *have their usual values.*

g as in *go* (gōu).
h ... *ho!* (hōu).
r ... *run* (rɒn), ter*r*ier (te·riəɹ).
ɹ ... he*r* (həɹ), farthe*r* (fā·ɹðəɹ).
s ... *see* (sī), *cess* (ses).
w ... *wen* (wen).
hw ... *wh*en (hwen).
y ... *yes* (yes).

þ as in *th*in (þin), ba*th* (bɑþ).
ð ... *th*en (ðen), ba*the* (bēið).
ʃ ... *sh*op (ʃǫp), di*sh* (diʃ).
tʃ ... *ch*op (tʃǫp), di*tch* (ditʃ).
ʒ ... vi*si*on (vi·ʒən), dé*j*euner (deʒöne).
dʒ ... *j*u*dge* (dʒɒdʒ).
ŋ ... si*ng*i*ng* (si·ŋiŋ), thi*n*k (þiŋk).
ŋg ... fi*ng*er (fiŋgəɹ).

(FOREIGN.)
ṅ as in *French nasal*, envir*on* (aṅvīroṅ).
lʸ ... It. sera*gl*io (serā·lʸo).
nʸ ... It. si*gn*ore (sinʸō·re).
χ ... Ger. a*ch* (aχ), Sc. lo*ch* (loχ, loχʷ).
χʸ ... Ger. i*ch* (iχʸ), Sc. ni*ch*t (nėχʸt).
γ ... Ger. sa*g*en (zā·γĕn).
γʸ ... Ger. le*g*en, re*g*nen (lē·γʸĕn, rē·γʸnĕn)

## II. VOWELS.

ORDINARY.

a as in Fr. *à la* mode (a la mǫd').
ai ... aye = *yes* (ai), Is*a*iah (əizai·ă).
æ ... m*a*n (mæn).
ɑ ... p*a*ss (pɑs), ch*a*nt (tʃɑnt).
ɑu ... l*ou*d (lɑud), n*ow* (nɑu).
ɒ ... c*u*t (kɒt), s*o*n (sɒn).
e ... y*e*t (yet), t*e*n (ten).
e ... surv*ey* sb. (sɒ·ɹve), Fr. attach*é* (ataʃe).
‖ę ... Fr. ch*e*f (ʃęf).
ə ... ev*e*r (evəɹ), nat*io*n (nēi·ʃən).
əi ... *I*, *eye*, (əi), b*i*nd (bəind).
‖ə ... Fr. eau d*e* vie (ō də vī).
i ... s*i*t (sit), myst*i*c (mistik).
i ... Psych*e* (səi·ki), r*e*act (ri,æ·kt).
o ... ach*o*r (ēi·koɹ), m*o*rality (moræ·lĭti).
oi ... *oi*l (oil), b*oy* (boi).
o ... her*o* (hīə·ro), z*o*ology (zo,ǫlŏdʒi).
ǫ ... wh*a*t (hwǫt), w*a*tch (wǫtʃ).
ǫ, ǫ̇* .. g*o*t (gǫt), s*o*ft (sǫ̇ft).
‖ö ... Ger. K*ö*ln (köln).
‖ö ... Fr. p*eu* (pö).
u ... f*u*ll (ful), b*oo*k (buk).
iu ... d*u*ration (diurēi·ʃən).
u ... *u*nto (ɒ·ntu), fr*u*gality (fru-).
iu ... Matth*ew* (mæ·þiu), virt*ue* (vɜ·ɹtiu).
‖ü ... Ger. M*ü*ller (mü·lĕr).
‖ü ... Fr. d*u*ne (dün).
ə (see īə, ēə, ōə, ūə) }
ⁱ, ᵘ (see ēⁱ, ōᵘ) } see Vol. I, p. xxiv, note 3.
' as in able (ēⁱb'l), eaten (ī·t'n) = voice-glide.

LONG.

ā as in *a*lms (āmz), b*ar* (bāɹ).

ɒ̄ ... c*u*rl (kɒ̄ɹl), f*u*r (fɒ̄ɹ).
ē (ēə)... th*e*re (ðēəɹ), p*ea*r, p*a*re (pēəɹ).
ē (ēⁱ)... r*ei*n, r*ai*n (rēⁱn), th*ey* (ðēⁱ).
ę̄ ... Fr. f*ai*re (fę̄r').
ɜ ... f*i*r (fɜɹ), f*e*rn (fɜɹn), *ea*rth (ɜɹþ).

ī (īə)... b*ie*r (bīəɹ), cl*ea*r (klīəɹ).
ī ... th*ie*f (þīf), s*ee* (sī).
ō (ōə)... b*oa*r, b*o*re (bōəɹ), gl*o*ry (glōə·ri).

ō (ōᵘ)... s*o*, s*ow* (sōᵘ), s*ou*l (sōᵘl).
ǭ ... w*a*lk (wǭk), w*a*rt (wǭɹt).
ǭ ... sh*o*rt (ʃǭɹt), th*o*rn (þǭɹn).
‖ō ... Fr. c*oeu*r (kōr).
‖ō ... Ger. G*ö*the (gōtĕ), Fr. j*eû*ne (ʒōn).
ū (ūə).. p*oo*r (pūəɹ), m*oo*rish (mūə·riʃ).
iū, ⁱū... p*u*re (piūəɹ), l*u*re (lⁱūəɹ).
ū ... tw*o* m*oo*ns (tū mūnz).
iū, ⁱū... f*ew* (fiū), l*u*te (lⁱūt).

‖ü ... Ger. gr*ü*n (grün), Fr. j*us* (ʒü).

OBSCURE.

ă as in *a*mœb*a* (ămī·bă).

æ̆ ... *a*ccept (æ̆kse·pt), mani*a*c (mēⁱ·niæ̆k).

ɒ̆ ... dat*u*m (dēⁱ·tɒ̆m).
ĕ ... mom*e*nt (mōᵘ·mĕnt), sev*e*ral (se·vĕrăl).
ĕ ... separ*a*te (*adj.*) (se·părĕt).

ė ... add*e*d (æ·dėd), *e*state (ėstēⁱ·t).

ĭ ... van*i*ty (væ·nĭti).
ĭ ... r*e*main (rĭmēⁱ·n), b*e*lieve (bĭlī·v).
ŏ ... the*o*ry (þī·ŏri).

ǒ ... vi*o*let (vəi·ŏlėt), par*o*dy (pæ·rŏdi).
ǫ̆ ... *au*thority (ǫ̆þǫ·rĭti).
ǫ̆ ... c*o*nnect (kǫ̆ne·kt), amaz*o*n (æ·măzǫ̆n).

iŭ, ⁱŭ verd*u*re (vɜ·ɹdiŭɹ), meas*u*re (me·ʒⁱŭɹ).
ŭ ... altogether (ǫltŭge·ðəɹ).
iŭ ... circ*u*lar (sɜ·ɹkiŭlăɹ).

* ǫ̇ the *o* in s*o*ft, of medial or doubtful length.

‖ Only in foreign (or earlier English) words.

---

In the Etymology,

OE. *e*, *o*, representing an earlier *a*, are distinguished as *ę*, *ǫ* (having the phonetic value of *ę* and *ǫ*, or ǫ, above); as in *ęnde* from *andi* (OHG. *anti*, Goth. *andei-s*), *mǫnn* from *mann*, *ǫn* from *an*.

# LIST OF ABBREVIATIONS, SIGNS, &c.

a. [in Etymol.] … = adoption of, adopted from.
*a* (as *a* 1300) = *ante*, before.
*a.*, *adj.*, adj. = adjective.
*absol.*, absol. = absolutely.
abst. = abstract.
acc. = accusative.
ad. [in Etymol.] = adaptation of.
*adv.*, adv. = adverb.
advb. = adverbial, -ly.
AF., AFr. = Anglo-French.
*Anat.* = in Anatomy.
*Antiq.* = in Antiquities.
aphet. = aphetic, aphetized.
app. = apparently.
Arab. = Arabic.
*Arch.* = in Architecture.
*arch.* = archaic.
*Archæol.* = in Archæology.
assoc. = association.
*Astr.* = in Astronomy.
*Astrol.* = in Astrology.
*attrib.* = attributive, -ly.
bef. = before.
*Biol.* = in Biology.
Boh. = Bohemian.
*Bot.* = in Botany.
*Build.* = in Building.
*c* (as *c* 1300) = *circa*, about.
c. (as 13th c.) = century.
Cat. = Catalan.
*catachr.* = catachrestically.
Cf., cf. = *confer*, compare.
*Chem.* = in Chemistry.
cl. L. = classical Latin.
cogn. w. = cognate with.
*collect.* = collective, -ly.
*colloq.* = colloquially.
comb. = combined, -ing.
*Comb.* = Combinations.
*Comm.* = in commercial usage.
comp. = compound, composition.
compl. = complement.
*Conch.* = in Conchology
*concr.* = concretely.
*conj.* = conjunction.
cons. = consonant.
Const., *Const.* … = Construction, construed with.
*Cryst.* = in Crystallography.
(D.) = in Davies (Supp. Eng. Glossary).
Da. = Danish.
dat. = dative.
def. = definite.
deriv. = derivative, -ation.
dial., *dial.* = dialect, -al.
Dict. = Dictionary.
dim. = diminutive.
Du. = Dutch.
*Eccl.* = in ecclesiastical usage.
*ellipt.* = elliptical, -ly.
e. midl. = east midland (dialect).
Eng. = English.
*Ent.* = in Entomology.
erron. = erroneous, -ly.
*esp.*, esp. = especially.
etym. = etymology.
*euphem.* = euphemistically.
exc. = except.
f. [in Etymol.] … = formed on.
f. (in subordinate entries) = form of.
fem. (*rarely* f.) … = feminine.
*fig.* = figurative, -ly.
F., Fr. = French.
freq. = frequently.
Fris. = Frisian.
G., Ger. = German.
Gael. = Gaelic.
gen. = genitive.
*gen.* = general, -ly.
*gen. sign.* = general signification.
*Geol.* = in Geology.
*Geom.* = in Geometry.
Goth. = Gothic (= Mœso-Gothic).
Gr. = Greek.
*Gram.* = in Grammar.
Heb. = Hebrew.
*Her.* = in Heraldry.
*Herb.* = with herbalists.
*Hort.* = in Horticulture.
*imp.* = Imperative.
*impers.* = impersonal.
impf. = imperfect.
*ind.* = Indicative.
indef. = indefinite.
*inf.* = Infinitive.
infl. = influenced.
*int.* = interjection.
*intr.* = intransitive.
It. = Italian.
J., (J.) = Johnson (quotation from).
(Jam.) = in Jamieson, Scottish Dict.
(Jod.) = Jodrell (quoted from).
L. = Latin.
(L.) (in quotations) = Latham's edn. of Todd's Johnson.
lang. = language.
LG. = Low German.
lit. = literal, -ly.
Lith. = Lithuanian.
LXX. = Septuagint.
Mal. = Malay.
masc. (*rarely* m.) = masculine.
*Math.* = in Mathematics.
ME. = Middle English.
*Med.* = in Medicine.
med.L. = mediæval Latin.
*Mech.* = in Mechanics.
*Metaph.* = in Metaphysics.
MHG. = Middle High German.
midl. = midland (dialect).
*Mil.* = in military usage.
*Min.* = in Mineralogy.
mod. = modern.
*Mus.* = in Music.
(N.) = Nares (quoted from)
n. of action = noun of action.
n. of agent = noun of agent.
*Nat. Hist.* = in Natural History.
*Naut.* = in nautical language.
neut. (*rarely* n.) = neuter.
NF., NFr. = Northern French.
N. O. = Natural Order.
nom. = nominative.
north. = northern (dialect).
N. T. = New Testament.
*Numism.* = in Numismatics.
obj. = object.
*Obs.*, *obs.*, obs. … = obsolete.
occas. = occasional, -ly.
OE. = Old English (= Anglo-Saxon).
OF., OFr. = Old French.
OFris. = Old Frisian.
OHG. = Old High German.
OIr. = Old Irish.
ON. = Old Norse (Old Icelandic).
ONF. = Old Northern French.
*Opt.* = in Optics.
*Ornith.* = in Ornithology.
OS. = Old Saxon.
OSl. = Old Slavonic.
O. T. = Old Testament.
OTeut. = Original Teutonic.
orig. = original, -ly.
*Palæont.* = in Palæontology.
pa. pple. = passive or past participle.
*pass.* = passive, -ly.
pa. t. = past tense.
*Path.* = in Pathology.
perh. = perhaps.
Pers. = Persian.
*pers.* = person, -al.
pf. = perfect.
Pg. = Portuguese.
*Philol.* = in Philology.
phonet. = phonetic, -ally.
*phr.* = phrase.
*Phren.* = in Phrenology.
*Phys.* = in Physiology.
pl., *pl.* = plural.
*poet.* = poetic.
pop. = popular, -ly.
*ppl. a.*, ppl. adj. … = participial adjective.
pple. = participle.
Pr. = Provençal.
prec. = preceding (word or article).
*pref.* = prefix.
*prep.* = preposition.
*pres.* = present.
*Prim. sign.* = Primary signification.
priv. = privative.
prob. = probably.
*pron.* = pronoun.
pronunc. = pronunciation.
prop. = properly.
*Pros.* = in Prosody.
pr. pple. = present participle.
*Psych.* = in Psychology.
q.v. = *quod vide*, which see.
(R.) = in Richardson's Dict.
R. C. Ch. = Roman Catholic Church.
refash. = refashioned, -ing.
*refl.*, refl. = reflexive.
reg. = regular.
repr. = representative, representing.
*Rhet.* = in Rhetoric.
Rom. = Romanic, Romance.
sb., *sb.* = substantive.
Sc. = Scotch.
sc. = *scilicet*, understand or supply.
*sing.* = singular.
Skr. = Sanskrit.
Slav. = Slavonic.
Sp. = Spanish.
sp. = spelling.
*spec.* = specifically.
subj. = subject, subjunctive.
*subord. cl.* = subordinate clause.
subseq. = subsequently.
subst. = substantively.
suff. = suffix.
superl. = superlative.
*Surg.* = in Surgery.
Sw. = Swedish.
s.w. = south western (dialect).
T. (T.) = in Todd's Johnson.
*techn.* = technical, -ly.
*Theol.* = in Theology.
tr. = translation of.
*trans.* = transitive.
*transf.* = transferred sense.
*Trig.* = in Trigonometry.
*Typog.* = in Typography.
ult. = ultimate, -ly.
unkn. = unknown.
U.S. = United States.
*v.*, vb. = verb.
*v. str.*, or *w.* = verb strong, or weak.
*vbl. sb.* = verbal substantive.
var. = variant of.
wd. = word.
WGer. = West Germanic.
w. midl. = west midland (dialect).
WS. = West Saxon.
(Y.) = in Col. Yule's Glossary.
*Zool.* = in Zoology.

---

Before a word or sense.
† = obsolete.
‖ = not naturalized.

In the quotations.
* sometimes points out the word illustrated.

In the list of Forms.
1 = before 1100.
2 = 12th c. (1100 to 1200).
3 = 13th c. (1200 to 1300).
5–7 = 15th to 17th century. (See General Explanations, Vol. I, p. xx.)

In the Etymol.
* indicates a word or form not actually found, but of which the existence is inferred.
:— = extant representative, or regular phonetic descendant of.

The printing of a word in SMALL CAPITALS indicates that further information will be found under the word so referred to.

# T.

**T** (tī), the twentieth letter of the English and other modern alphabets, the nineteenth of the ancient Roman alphabet, corresponding in form to the Greek Τ (*tau*), from the Phœnician (and ancient Semitic) + ✕ X X (*tau*), in Phœnician, and originally also in Greek, the last letter of the alphabet. It represents the point-breath-stop consonant of Bell's 'Visible Speech', or surd dental mute, so called, but in English is gingival or alveolar rather than dental. Several varieties of a *t*-sound occur in different languages, according as the flow of the breath is stopped by bringing the tip or front of the tongue into contact with different points between the edge of the upper teeth and the roof of the palate. Thus, contact of the tip of the tongue with the teeth gives the true dental *t*, which is common in continental European languages, very distinct in Anglo-Irish, and heard in north-western English dialects before *r*, where it is often represented in dialect specimens by spelling *thrue* or *t'hrue* for *true*, and the like (though the consonant is not actually *th* or *þ*). The Indian languages, Aryan as well as Dravidian, distinguish two kinds of *t*, the dental, and the retracted or 'cerebral' (*mūrdhanya*), in Sanskrit त and ट, of which the latter is formed by contact of the retracted tip of the tongue with the roof of the palate. The English *t* is formed between these two extreme positions, the contact being with the back of the gum or the front margin of the palate; its sound is much closer to the cerebral than to the dental, and in the Tamil or Telugu representation of English words, the cerebral is regularly put for English *t*. In the Roman transliteration of Indian words it is usual to write *t* for the dental, and to distinguish the cerebral as *ṭ*, as is done in this dictionary. The Semitic languages also distinguish two *t*-sounds, one, the Hebrew *tau* (ת), Arabic *ta* (ت) dental; the other, Hebrew *teth* (ט), Arabic *ṭa* (ط), said to be formed by contact of the blade of the tongue with the palate; this also has been romanized as *ṭ*, though distinguished in Urdū from the cerebral *ṭ*.

In modern English, besides its proper sound as above described, *t* in the combinations *-tion*, *-tious*, *-tial*, *-tia*, *-tian*, *-tience*, *-tient*, after a vowel or any consonant except *s*, has the sound of *sh* (ʃ), in which the following *i* is absorbed, as in *nation* (nēⁱ·ʃən), *factious* (fæ·kʃəs), *partial* (pā·ɹʃăl), *militia* (mili·ʃă), *patience* (pēⁱ·ʃĕns); but in *-ia*, *-ian*, *i* is sometimes more or less preserved, especially in proper names, as in *inertia*, *Portia*, *Gratian*, *Dalmatian*. In these combinations Latin (t) became (ts), usually written *z*, and then (s), written *c*, in French, as in L. *grātia*, It. *grazia*, F. *grâce*, L. *nātiōnem*, It. *nazione*, OF., Sp. *nacion*. In French and English spelling the Latin *t* was subsequently in most cases restored, e. g. *nation*; but the living sound was (s), and it is this *s* which combining with the following *i* (= *y* consonant) as (sy-), passed in English into (ʃ), in the same way as written *c* or *s* has done in *gracious*, *Asia*, *emersion*: see S the letter, par. 4. Strictly, therefore, what we have is not *ti* pronounced as (ʃ), but (ʃ) derived from *ci*, spelt *ti* after its Latin source. After *s*, the original sound of *t* has remained, as in *bestial*, *Christian*, *Erastian*, *question*.

A much more recent change, as yet scarcely recognized by orthoepists, is the development in southern England of the sound *ch* (tʃ) from *t* followed by *u* with its diphthongal or name sound (y*u*, i*u*, ⁱ*u*), in such combinations as *-tual*, *-tue*, *-tuous*, and especially *-ture*, as in *nature* (nēⁱ·tiŭɹ), whence (nēⁱ·tyəɹ, nēⁱ·tʃəɹ). In those English dialects in which *u* has not become (yū), the original *t* remains, as in 'critter' = *creature*, 'pictur' = *picture*. In rapid speech *ti* after *s* often passes similarly into tʃ, as (kwe·stʃən) for (kwe·styən).

T between *s* and syllabic *l* or *n* (*en*), as in *bustle*, *castle*, *epistle*, *christen*, *fasten*, *hasten*, is now usually mute; so between *s* and *m* in *Christmas*, and between *f* and syllabic *n* in *often*, *soften*.



TH is a consonantal digraph representing two simple sounds (þ, ð), for which the Roman alphabet has no simple symbols, and is thus phonetically a distinct letter (or two letters), inserted between TE- and TI-, where see its history and pronunciation.

**I. 1.** The letter and its sound. The plural is variously written t's, *t*'s, *ts* (tīz). See also TEE *sb.*[1]

*c* **1000** [see B]. *c* **1374** CHAUCER *Boeth.* I. pr. i. 2 (Camb. MS.) Abouen þat lettre in the heyeste bordure a grekyssh t þat singnifieth the lyf contemplatyf. **1487** *Act 4 Hen. VII*, c. 13 Every Person so convicted..for any other Felony..to be marked with a T in the same Place of the Thumb. **1736** AINSWORTH *Lat.-Eng. Dict.* s. v., With a design to hang T on her own gibbet, as Lucian jocosely says. **1847** *Proc. Philol. Soc.* III. 45 Thus the Aztecs of Mexico, though able to pronounce an *l* in the middle of a word, at the commencement find it necessary to prefix a *t*-sound to the liquid. **1859** *Life E. Henderson* vi. 353 Before the little inmate of the Linn could have known a T from a craw's tae. **1861** DICKENS *Gt. Expect.* xvi, Everything producible that began with a T, from tar to toast.

**b.** In phrase *to cross the* t'*s*: to make the horizontal stroke of *t* (often omitted in hasty writing); *fig.* to be minutely exact or particular in one's account; to make the meaning more distinct; to particularize and emphasize the points. Cf. *to dot the* i'*s* in I (the letter) 1.

**1865** E. C. CLAYTON *Cruel Fortune* II. 220 To ascertain whether it was..properly spelt, and had all the i's dotted, and the t's crossed. **1882** MRS. HOUSTOUN *Recomm. to Mercy* xx, Please not to cross the t's. **1885** DUNCKLEY in *Manch. Exam.* 15 June 6/2 To dot his i's and cross his t's and polish up his manuscript.

**c.** Phr. *To a T* (also *to a tee*): exactly, properly, to a nicety.

[The original sense of T here has not been ascertained. Suggestions that it was the *tee* at Curling, or at Golf, or a T square, appear on investigation to be untenable; it has also been suggested that it referred to the proper completion of a *t* by crossing it (see b); or that it was the initial of a word; in reference to this it is notable that *to a tittle* (i. e. to a prick, dot, jot) was in use nearly a century before 'to a T', and in exactly the same constructions: see TITTLE.]

**1693** *Humours Town* 102 All the under Villages and Towns-men come to him for Redress; which he does to a T. **1700** *Labour in Vain* VIII. in *Harl. Misc.* (1810) X. 473 Harry cajoled my inquirer, and fitted his humour to a t—. **1771** J. GILES *Poems* 155 I'll tell you where You may be suited to a tee. **1815** *Zeluca* I. 385, I knew my man to a T. **1828** *Life Planter Jamaica* 161, I understand the practice to a tee. **1840** R. H. DANA *Bef. Mast* xxii. 66 The yards were squared 'to a T' by lifts and braces. **1856** MRS. STOWE *Dred* ii, All these old-fashioned goings on would suit you to a T.

**2.** The shape of the letter; an object having the shape Τ. See also TEE *sb.*[1], TAU. Also short for *T beard*, *T iron*, *T rail*: see 3.

*a* **1619**, *a* **1654** [see 3 b]. **1707** MORTIMER *Husb.* (1721) II. 262 Slit the Bark or Rind about an Inch long, in form of a T. **1733** TULL *Horse-Hoeing Husb.* xxii. 330 Made..with a Head like a T. **1875** SIR T. SEATON *Fret-Cutting* 69 Then see whereabouts to put them through the upright part or T of the bracket. **1891** *Daily News* 27 Apr. 2/5 Plate iron, angles, T's, and bars for railway waggon building are in large request. **1891** *Scott. Leader* 21 Sept. 3 Inquiries for old material are reviving, rails being chiefly in demand. Some holders are now asking 21 dols. for old T's. **1893** F. ADAMS *New Egypt* 237 The tongue of this inverted T, *i. e.*, the entrenchments, had been carried out some two miles.

**3.** *attrib.* (sometimes hyphened): Shaped like the letter Τ; having a cross piece at the top; as *T bandage*, *bar*, *chain*, *end*, *fish*, *handle*, *head*, *hinge*, *iron*, *joint*, *key*, *pattern*, *piece*, *spot*, *tap*, *tube*, *wharf*. Also comb., as *T-formed*, *-headed*, *-shaped* adjs. See also TEE *sb.*[1], TEE-PIECE, etc.

**1783** BENTLEY in *Med. Commun.* (1784) I. 257 The canula ..was left in the puncture, secured with a double *T bandage. **1882** NARES *Seamanship* (ed. 6) 84 Secured by a *T chain. **1841** *Penny Cycl.* XX. 465/2 The *T-formed or arrow-shaped bone [of the Saurians]. **1778** [W. MARSHALL] *Minutes Agric.* 20 Apr. an. 1775, A light beam of seven feet long, drawn by a *T handle, by one man, walking backwards. **1844** STEPHENS *Bk. Farm* III. 849 They are always attached..by a *T headed nail and spike. **1844** *Ibid.* I. 198 The inside doors should be hung with *T hinges, 18 inches long. **1838** *Civil Eng. & Arch. Jrnl.* I. 126/1 The roof.. is further supported and braced by strutts of *T iron and suspension rods. **1906** *Westm. Gaz.* 16 Mar. 8/1 The main cable..is always connected with the consumer's house by means of a *T-joint, which is enclosed in a box filled with bitumen. **1895** PARKES *Health* 54 Lead *T pieces, as they are called [in water-pipes] must be used. **1860** *Biog. & Crit. fr. 'The Times'* 235 *T-shaped traps for the wheatear. **1896** *Farrier's Price List*, *T taps and other tools. **1881** TYNDALL *Floating Matter of Air* III. xviii. 188 One end..of a glass *T-tube was connected with an air-pump.

**b.** *Special Combs.* (sometimes hyphened). †**T beard**, a beard worn in the 17th c., grown or cut in the form of a T. **T branch**, in piping, a right-angled joint of a small pipe to a main; a T joint. **T cart**, an open phaeton, so called from its ground-plan resembling the letter T. **T cloth**, a plain cotton cloth exported to India, China, Africa, etc., so called from the large letter T stamped on it. **T rail**, a railway metal or rail having a T section. **T square**, a square of the form of a Τ or rather ⊢ (with a long stem), used by mechanics and draughtsmen for drawing lines parallel, or at right angles, to each other. (See also TEE *sb.*[1]) **T-totum**: see TEETOTUM.

*a* **1619** FLETCHER, etc. *Q. Corinth* IV. i, Strokes his beard, Which now he puts i' th' posture of a T, The Roman T, your *T beard is the fashion. [*a* **1654** J. TAYLOR (Water P.) *Superb. Flagellum*, [Beards] Some with the hammer-cut, or Roman T.] **1873** MISS BROUGHTON *Nancy* II. 24 The butler took the housekeeper a driving-tour in my *T-cart, and threw down one of my best horses. **1882** *Daily News* 30 May 3/1 Stanhope phaetons (generally called by the absurd name of T cart). **1883** F. M. CRAWFORD *Dr. Claudius* xvi, A very gorgeous conveyance, called in America a T-cart, and resembling a mail phaeton in build. **1865** *Manch. Guard.* 2 Mar., *T cloths, 9*d.* and long-cloths, 6*d.* to 1*s.* per piece. **1880** *Plain Hints Needlework* 72 'T cloths' are lengths of 20 yards of calico, specially used as barter with native tribes in Africa. **1837** *Civil Eng. & Arch. Jrnl.* I. 39/2 The pattern..is by American engineers called the inverted *T rail. **18..** WHITMAN *To Working Men* vi, The strong, clean-shaped T-rail for railroads. [**1701** MOXON *Math. Instr.* 19 *Tee*, a double Square in the form of a T.] **1785** PEACOCK in *Phil. Trans.* LXXV. 369 A common *T square..will answer most purposes. **1861** SMILES *Engineers* II. 76 His trace, his T square, his augers, his gouges, and his engraving tools.

**II. 4.** Used like the other letters of the alphabet to denote serial order: applied e. g. to the twentieth (or more usually the nineteenth) of any series, to the nineteenth sheet of a book, etc.

**5.** A mediæval symbol for the numeral 160, and with a stroke over it (Τ̄) for 160,000.

**6.** Abbreviations: for various proper names, as Thomas, Timothy, Titus, Theresa, etc.; officially stamped on a letter, = *taxed*, i. e. postage to be paid; in music, = tasto, tempo, tenor, tutti; in a ship's log-book, = thunder; in *Math.*, = time, terms, etc.

**1724** *Short Explic. For. Wds. in Mus. Bks.*, The Letter T. is often used as an Abbreviation of the Word *Tutti.* **1743** EMERSON *Fluxions* 15, *t* = Number of Terms in V.. Continu'd to *t* Terms. **1871** TAIT & STEELE *Dynamics of Particle* (ed. 3) iii. § 80 Let *P* be the position of the particle at any time *t*. *Ibid.* § 86 If *T* be the time of descent down *AC*. **1894** *Westm. Gaz.* 12 Oct. 3/2 'England' stamps these cards with a 'T', an initial which, with St. Martin's-le-Grandiose conciseness stands for 'taxed'.

**III. 7.** T at the end of a word has sometimes been attached to the word following when this begins with a vowel: hence *the* To, *the* TONE, *the* TOTHER; cf. also *'tis*, *'twas*, etc. in 'T. The final *t* of *Saint* has in several cases been popularly prefixed to the name, as in *Tandrew*, *Tandry* = St. Andrew; *Tann* = St. Ann, hence *Tanswell*; *Tantolin* = St. Antholin; *Tooly* = St. Olave; see also TANTON, TANTONY, TAWDRY.

*c* **1450** *Mankind* 75 in *Macro Plays* 4, I gyff no force, by Sent Tanne! **1673** HICKERINGILL *Greg. F. Greyb.* 264 Our Tantlin Lectures. **1726** F. HOWGRAVE *Stamford* 53 The Corruption that has been made of *St. Anthony* into *Tantony*, and *St. Olave* into *Tooly*. **1872** HARDWICK *Trad. Lanc.* 269 Cakes baked for the lace-makers' feasts in honour of St. Andrew ..are locally termed '*Tandry Cakes*'. **1880** *W. Cornw. Gloss.*, *'T Andrew's dance*, St. Vitus' dance.

**8.** In early ME., *t* took the place of initial *þ*, *th*, after a word ending in a dental or *s*, esp. in the demonstratives *the*, *that*, *this*, *tha*, *there*, *then*, *thus*, etc., and the 2nd personal pronoun *thou* and its cases. Already in OE., *þæt þe* became *þætte*, THAT.

*c* **1200** ORMIN 325 Þiss streon þatt tuss wass sibb Wiþþ preostess & wiþþ kingess. *Ibid.* 12760 Nu shallt tu ben nemmnedd Cefas. *a* **1240** *Wohunge* in *Cott. Hom.* 271 Hwa is ta largere þen þu. *c* **1400** *Rule St. Benet* 23 Þis sais sain benet, þat ta þat ere of elde and vnderstandis, þai sal haue þaire mesur.

**T'**[1], shortened form of To, before a vowel, formerly in use, often combined with the following word, as *tabandon* to abandon, *tabyde* to abide; so *taxe* to ask, *tescape*, *t'attempt*; also, with omission of *h*, *tave*, *tafe*, to have, *ta* to hae, to have; *tadwellyd* to have dwelt, *talyved* to have lived, etc.

*c* **1200** ORMIN 3879 Þatt doþ uss tunnderrstanndenn. *c* **1330** R. BRUNNE *Chron. Wace* (Rolls) 4334 Ffair folk to fighte, Cesar tabyde. **1426** LYDG. *De Guil. Pilgr.* 1019–22 He gaff to hem..Talyved euere,.. Neuer tave had necessyte Off deyyng. *Ibid.* 9392 Taxe and lerne, thow art wys. *Ibid.*

9422 And tadwellyd Immutable. *Ibid.* 16962 Tescape Eche Trybulacion. **1559** *Mirr. Mag.* (1563) B vij, I forced the Frenchemen tabandon theyr bowers. **1592** in Tytler *Hist. Scot.* (1864) IV. 343 Proved cares and assured love aught,.. tafe the upperhand. **1706** E. Ward *Hud. Rediv.* I. III. 27 T' attempt some Massacre or Treason. **1746** Francis tr. *Hor., Sat.* II. iii. 117 Staberius thus compell'd his heirs t' engrave On his proud tomb what legacies he gave.

**T'** [2], north Eng. dial. form of *the*, before a vowel or consonant: as in *t'airm, t'bairn, t'bottle, t'faarm, t'heart, t'man, t'measter*; sometimes also written without apostrophe, *tman, tnail, trasps, twasp*. See The.

**'t,** shortened form of *it*, initially or finally, as in *'tis, 'twas, 'twere, 'twill, 'twould; do't, see't, on't*; formerly often written without apostrophe as one word: see It.

**-t,** *suffix* [1], formative of the pa. pple. in some weak verbs, for earlier *-d* and *-ed* (see -ed [1]), due usually to the devocalization of *d* after a breath consonant, as in *nipped, nip'd, nipt*. In some verbs the use of *t* for *-ed* goes back to OTeut., esp. in app. contracted or irregular verbs, as *bought, brought, might, thought, wrought* (Goth. *bauht, brâht, maht, þâht, waurht*); in others it appears in WGer., as *sought* (Goth. *sôkid*, OS. and OE. *sôht*); in others only in OE. as *laught* (læht), *taught* (tæht, taht). But in the majority of cases the *t* is of later appearance, arising from the reduction of *-ed* to *-'d, -d* in Middle or Mod. Engl., with consequent devocalization of *d*, not only after breath consonants, as in *dropt, nipt, crept, slept, swept, left, lost, tost, past*, but, in certain cases, after liquids and nasals, as in *felt, spelt, spilt, dreamt, burnt, meant, pent*; also in contracted formations, such as *built, bent, lent, sent, spent, girt, cast*. But in many words where the pronunciation has *t*, the current spelling is *-ed*, e.g. *blessed, dropped, hushed, passed* for *blest, dropt, husht, past*. See the article -ed *suffix* [1].

**-t,** *suffix* [2], formative of the pa. t. of some weak verbs, for earlier *-te, -de, -ede* (:—*da, -ida, -eda*). Parallel in formation to the prec., and generally going along with it in ME., and identical in form in mod.E.; but in OE. a pa. t. in *-te* was sometimes used where the pa. pple. retained the fuller *-ed*, as in *cyssan* to kiss, *cyste, cyssed, settan* to set, *sette, seted* (and *sett*). In mod.Eng. on the contrary the spelling in *t* is more frequent in the pa. pple., esp. when used adjectivally, than in the pa. t.: cf. *tempest-tost*, the wind *tossed* the ship; in time *past*, he *passed* his time. In some cases even the form in *-ed* is a mere modern fashion of spelling, at variance with both the pronunciation and the history; thus, *kissed* was in OS. *kusta*, OE. *cyste*, ME. *kist*, as actually pronounced; it has come to be spelt *kissed*, because in other verbs *-ed* is pronounced *-t*.

**-t,** *suffix* [3]. A formative of sbs. **a.** from verbs, going back to OTeut., and answering variously to the Indo-Eur. suffixes *-tos, -tā, -tis, -tus*, the *t* of which remained in Teutonic, when preceded by a guttural, labial, or *s*; e.g. *draught, drift, flight, frost, gift, heft, might, plight, shaft, shrift, slaught, thirst, thought, thrift, weft*, etc. (in some of which the formation is later and imitative). In a few cases the *t* is a later Eng. change of *-þ* after *h, ȝ*, as in *sight* (OE. *siehþ*), in which *þ* normally represented Indo-Eur. *t*. See -th.

**b.** from adjs. (or sbs.), changed from earlier *-þ, -th* (in *length*, etc.) after *h, ȝ*, as *height* (Goth. *hauhiþa*, OE. *hiehþo*, ME. *heiȝþe, highth*); *sleight* (ON. *slægþ*, ME. *sleiȝþe*); *theft* (OE. *þiefþ*, ME. *þiefþe*); *dreight* (for *dreighth*, from *dreiȝ*, Dree): here the suffix was OTeut. *-iþô*: *-iðô*: Indo-Eur. *-tā*. See -th. Also *dought* (OE. *dugup*:—**dugunþ*), *drought* (OE. *drûgup*, Sc. *drouth*), where the OE. suffix *-uþ* was for *-unþ*:—Indo-Eur. *-ntis*.

**Ta** (tā), *int.* Also 9 **taa.** An infantile word expressing thanks.

**1772** Mrs. Delany in *Life & Corr.* (1861) I. 457 You would not say 'Ta' to me for my congratulation. **1807** W. Irving *Salmag.* (1824) 363 How her ten weeks old baby will laugh and say taa! **1892** Zangwill *Childr. Ghetto* I. 117 Give it me. I'll say 'ta' so nicely.

**Ta,** obs. and dial. form of The, Thee, Thou.

**1597** Shaks. 2 *Hen. IV*, II. i. 63 Thou wot, wot ta? do, do, thou rogue! *a* **1619** Fletcher *Mad Lover* IV. v, Who art ta? **1814** Scott *Wav.* xxix (*Celt speaks*), 'It was either ta muckle Sunday..or ta little government Sunday that they ca'd ta fast'. *a* **1825** Forby *Voc. E. Anglia* 338 *Ta, te, to, art.* or *pron.* the, this, that, it. **1864** Tennyson *North. Farmer* xi, Done it ta-year I mean 'd.

**Ta,** dial. form of To *prep.* and sign of *inf.*

**1340–70** *Alex. & Dind.* 475 We sen selkouþe þing; þat is ta sain heuene. **1825** Jamieson, *Ta, Ti, To*; the sign of the *inf.* **1898** B. Kirkby *Lakel. Wds.* (E.D.D.), Allus royen an drinken is t'way ta neea spot.

**Ta, taa,** early ME. form of *þa, tha*; see T 8.

**Ta, taa,** in *the ta*, early ME. and north. form of To *adj.*, in *the to* for *that o* = the one: see T 7.

**Ta, taa,** obs. forms of Toe *sb.*, Take *v.*

**Taa-,** in various words: earlier spelling of Ta-.

**Taal** (tāl). *S. Africa.* [a. Du. *taal* language, speech, MDu. and MLG. *tāle* language, speech, tale, = OE. *talu* tale, story, account: see Tale.] The Dutch word for language, speech (*de Nederlandsche taal*, the Netherlands or Dutch language): in English, 'the taal', spec. applied to the Cape Dutch, or Dutch patois spoken in South Africa.

**1896** *Westm. Gaz.* 8 Jan. 8/1 He speaks the Taal better than a Hollander can, and can understand the Boers better. **1897** Bryce *Impressions S. Afr.* 480 It [Boer Dutch] differs widely from the cultivated Dutch of Holland, .. having become vulgarised into a dialect called the Taal. *Ibid.* 511 Except some of the men from Cape Colony, they could not speak the Boer Taal. **1900** *Spectator* 6 Oct. 460 One of the first results..was to establish the Taal, the Cape patois, as an official language.

*attrib.* and *Comb.* **1898** *Johannesburg Star* 4 June, Sundry clever and humorous volumes of taal-verse. **1901** *Daily Chron.* 22 July 5/3 An epitome of all the more unattractive qualities of the taal-speaking Dutch.

**Taal,** obs. f. Tale. **Taald,** obs. pa. pple. of Tell *v.* **Taar,** obs. f. *tare*, pa.t. of Tear *v.*; obs. f. Tar. **Taarge, Taart(e, Taas, Taast,** obs. ff. Targe, Tart, Tass, Taste. **Taas,** obs. 2 pers. sing. pres. ind. of Take *v.*

**Tab** (tæb), *sb.* Also 7 **tabb,** 8 **tabe.** [Origin obscure. At first, and still largely, a dialect word. Not in Johnson. In some senses it may be short for *tablet*; in others it interchanges with *tag*.]

**I. 1.** A short broad strap, flat loop, or the like, attached by one end to an object, or forming a short projecting part by which a thing can be taken hold of, hung up, fastened, or pulled; in various applications: see quots.

**1607** Markham *Caval.* III. (1617) 83 How the horse is girt.. and by some speciall markes or obseruations about the tabs to know how his garths do hold. **1611** Cotgr., *Contre-sanglot*, a Tab; the leather whereto a girth is fastened; a girth-leather. *Ibid.*, *Crampon de cuir*, a loope, or tab, of leather. **1629** *Pittington Vestry Bks.* (Surtees) 298 For tabbs to the bells, iiij*d.* [Cf. 1618 *Ibid.* 293 For 2 tagges for the belstrings, 6*d.*] **1664** in *Archæol. Æl.* XVII. 127 For broomes and a tab for yᵉ bell 2*d.* **1688** R. Holme *Armoury* III. xviii. (Roxb.) 126/1 The tab at the end of a belt. **1846** Brockett *N. C. Gloss.*, *Tab*..a strap. **1879** Rutley *Stud. Rocks* v. 40 It [a geologist's bag] should have a little tab by which it can be loosely attached to a button. **1894** Maskelyne *Sharps & Flats* 90 The 'tab' or loop at the back of the..boot. **1896** C. D. Waldo *Ban of the Gubbe* 144 If there were tabs to pull up the lid, why should there ever have been a knob or handle? **1904** *Eng. Dial. Dict.*, *Tab*... 5. The loop by which a garment is hung up. *Sc.* **1905** *Daily News* 27 Sept. 6 Strong leather tabs are being fastened to the backs of the volumes of the brobdingnagian catalogues [in the British Museum Library].

**b.** *spec.* A shoe latchet, for fastening with a buckle, button, or thong. Chiefly *dial.*

**1674** Ray *N. C. Words* 47 The *Tab* of a Shooe, the Latchet of a Shooe. **1731** in Bailey. **1775** in Ash. **1904** in *Eng. Dial. Dict.* [from North of Eng. to E. Anglia].

**c.** A short strap attached at one end to one side of a coat, jacket, vest, etc., and having a button-hole at the free end for fastening across.

Such a *tab* is often ornamented with a button at the attached end, so as to be symmetrical, and may become purely ornamental as in 2 c.

**d.** The metal end of a lace, etc.; = Tag *sb.*[1] 3; a shoe-string. *dial.*

*a* **1825** Forby *Voc. E. Anglia*, *Tab*...2. The end of a lace, commonly, and perhaps more properly called a *tag*. **1904** in *Eng. Dial. Dict.* [Cumbld. to Oxford, and E. Anglia]. *Ibid.*, *Tab*..a shoe-string [Hampsh.].

**e.** The tongue of a shoe or boot. *dial.*

**1866–** in *Eng. Dial. Dict.* from midland counties.

**2.** As an ornament of dress: Each of the projecting square pieces formed by cutting out the lower edge of a jacket or other article of dress, or sewn on to its uncut edge, and usually embellished with buttons, embroidery, etc.

*c* **1880** Mrs. G. M. E. Campbell *Let. to Editor*, A series of small squares cut out of the edge of a cape or sleeve and the intermediate pieces left hanging by way of fringe or ornament, is known by the name of Tabs. **1883** *Truth* 31 May 768/2 This brocade was cut out in deep tabs over a skirt of copper-coloured satin. **1887** *Illustr. Lond. News* 6 Aug. 151/1 The edges of the loose fronts [of the bodice] were..cut out in tabs.

**b.** A similar piece sewn by its upper edge on the surface of dress, so as to hang loose; or **c.** in recent use, sewn on entirely, and variously adorned with buttons, beads, embroidery, etc., sometimes simulating that described in 1 c.

**1834** Planché *Brit. Costume* xviii. 275 Towards the close of James [I]'s reign, however,..short jackets or doublets,with tabs and false sleeves hanging behind, succeed to the long-waisted doublets. **1882** *Daily News* 30 Aug. 3/1 Tabs are a favourite trimming for tunics. **1883** C. D. Warner *Roundabout Journ.* 39 Some of them have a black rosette on the shoulder, and a tab hanging from it tipped with ermine. **1909** *Civ. Serv. Store Catal.* 353 [Lady's] coat, 30 inches long, trimmed satin, with satin tabs and buttons.

**3.** *transf.* A small piece of some substance, e.g. of sod or turf.

**17..** E. Smith *Compl. Housew.* (1750) 365 Take..three or four tabes of the whitest goose-dung; put all in a quart of strong beer. **1893** Q. [Couch] *Delect. Duchy* 43 The boys ..could toss tabs of turf down her chimney.

**4.** *techn.* **a.** One of the revolving arms which lift the beaters of a fulling-mill (Knight *Dict. Mech.* 1877). **b.** A narrow projecting strip of metal along the inside of a hollow calico-printing roller to secure it to its mandrel by means of a slot in the latter.

**5.** A tie-label, a luggage label (cf. Tag *sb.*[1] 8).

**1904** *Eng. Dial. Dict.*, *Tab* 3, a label affixed to goods for sale; a luggage label. *Warwick.*

**II. 6.** *U.S. colloq.* A table, an account [cf. Tablet 1 c]; a check; esp. in phr., *to keep (a) tab.*

**1889** *Washington Post* 11 Feb., Every man keeps a mean little tab in his head on his fellows. **1890** *Voice* (N. Y.) 31 July, A generous mother in.. Michigan has been keeping tab in her family [on the baking for a year]. **1897** H. Porter *Campaigning with Grant* x. 159 You can't get away because he [the captain] is always keeping tab on you. **1907** *Daily News* 26 Aug. 7 Being subsequently shown the work tabs with the Salvation Army prices. **1907** W. James *Pragmatism* v. 172 To use this as a tally by which we 'keep tab' on the impressions that present themselves.

Hence **Tab** *v. trans.*, to furnish or ornament with tabs: see Tabbed.

**Tabac** (tăbæ·k), *a.* [f. F. *tabac* Tobacco.] Of a deep shade of brown; tobacco-coloured.

**1894** *Westm. Gaz.* 26 Apr. 3/2 A very stylish costume..in dark tabac canvas. **1900** *Ibid.* 6 Sept. 3/3 Brown, a dark tabac shade, is by some assigned the place of honour.

**Tabaccho, tabacco, tabaco,** obs. ff. Tobacco.

**Tabachir,** var. spelling (properly French) of Tabasheer.

‖**Tabacosis** (tæbăkōᵘ·sis). *Path.* [f. mod.L. *tabac-um* Tobacco + -osis.] Disease of the lungs produced by the inhalation of tobacco dust.

**1879** Buck *Hygiene* II. 43 There are but two autopsies of tobacco-workers on record which could be considered cases of tabacosis. **1898** *Syd. Soc. Lex.*, *Tabacosis*,..produced by the inhalation of dry vegetable fibre (especially cotton). Properly the form due to inhalation of tobacco dust.

**Tabagane,** obs. form of Toboggan.

‖**Tabagie** (tàbaʒī). [F. irreg. deriv. of *tabac* tobacco (1612 in Hatz.-Darm.).] A group of smokers who meet in club fashion; a 'tobacco-parliament'.

**1819** (*title*) The Englishman's Mentor. The Picture of the Palais Royal; describing its spectacles, gaming rooms, coffee houses, restaurateurs, tabagies [etc.]. **1858** Carlyle *Fredk. Gt.* v. vii. (1872) II. 114 Friedrich Wilhelm..had his *Tabaks-Collegium*, Tobacco-College, Smoking Congress, *Tabagie*. *Ibid.* 115 Tabagies were not uncommon among German Sovereigns of that epoch. **1885** *Daily News* 28 Nov. 5/3 (Stanf.) A sort of tabagie (to use a word which Mr. Carlyle has made familiar to English readers) or Tobacco Parliament.

‖**Taban** (tæ·băn). The Malay name of the tree, *Isonandra Gutta* (or *I. Taban*), that yields gutta-percha. Hence *taban-tree*.

**1861** Bentley *Man. Bot.* 588 *Isonandra Gutta*, the Gutta Percha or Taban-tree..a native of Singapore, Borneo, and other Malay Islands. **1874** Garrod & Baxter *Mat. Med.* (1880) 299 Gutta-Percha,..the inspissated juice of Isonandra gutta, the Gutta-percha or Taban tree.

**Tabanid** (tæ·bănid), *a.* and *sb.* [f. L. *tabānus* a gad-fly or horse-fly (adopted by Linnæus as a generic name) + -id [3].] **a.** *adj.* Belonging to the family *Tabanidæ* of flies, of which *Tabanus* is the typical genus. **b.** *sb.* A fly of this family, a gad-fly.

**1891** in *Cent. Dict.* **1895** *Bulletin Illinois Labor. Nat. Hist.* 197 As restless as a tabanid larva. *Ibid.* 199 It was, perhaps, this that the tabanids were feeding upon.

So **Taba·niform** *a.*, having the form of a gad-fly (Mayne *Expos. Lex.* 1860).

**Tabard** (tæ·bǎɹd). Forms: 4– **tabard**; also 4 (9) **tabart,** 4–5 **tabbard,** 4–6 **tabarde,** 4–8 **tabert,** 5 **taberde,** 5–7 **taberd,** 6 **tabarte,** *Sc.* **tawbart, talbart, -ert.** [a. OF. *tabart* (12th c. in Godef.), *tabar* (13–14th c.) = Sp. *tabardo*, It. *tabarro*: ulterior derivation unknown: see Diez.]

†**1.** A garment of coarse material; 'a loose upper garment without sleeves' (Jam.); formerly worn out of doors by the lower classes, also by monks and foot-soldiers. *Obs.*

*c* **1300** in *Langtoft's Chron.* in *Pol. Songs* (Camden) 303 He haves overhipped, His typeth is typed, hise tabard es tome. **13..** *E. E. Allit. P.* B. 41 His taberde to-torne and his totez oute. **1362** Langl. *P. Pl.* A. v. 111 A toren Tabart of twelue Wynter Age. *c* **1386** Chaucer *Prol.* 541 A Plowman ..In a tabard he rood vpon a Mere. **1389** in *Eng. Gilds* (1870) 81 Noman come be-forn yᵉ alderman..in tabard ne in cloke. **1513** Douglas *Æneis* I. v. 80 Than with the glitterand volf skyn ouer his array, Cleid in his nwreis talbart glaid and gay. **1523** Ld. Berners *Froiss.* I. xii. 12 Syr Thomas Wage caused syr Hewe Spencer to be fast bound on yᵉ best and leuiest hors of al yᵉ host, and caused hym to were on a tabarte, suche as traytours and theues were wont to were. **1568** Grafton *Chron.* II. 213. [**1866** Rogers *Agric. & Prices* I. xxii. 582 Tabards, that is short gowns, with or without sleeves, probably without an opening in front, but drawn over the head like a round frock.]

*transf.* **1423** Jas. I *Kingis Q.* cx, Vnlike the cukkow [is] to the phylomene; Thaire tabartis ar noght bothe maid of array.

**2.** A short surcoat open at the sides and having

short sleeves, worn by a knight over his armour, and emblazoned on the front, back, and sleeves with his armorial bearings. Now only *Hist.*

*c* **1450** *Brut* cc. 228 (MS. O.), After he lete him vnclopе of his furrede tabard and of his hood, and..saide vnto him ..now art þow no kny3t, but a knaue. **1562** LEIGH *Armorie* (1597) 96 Gentlewomen vnder the degree of a countesse, haue armes on Taberts. **1603** DRAYTON *Bar. Wars* II. xxiii, Ferrer his Taberd, with rich Verry spred, Well knowne in many a Warlike Match before. **1843** JAMES *Forest Days* I. ii, His sword peeped from under his tabard.

**3.** The official dress of a herald or pursuivant; a coat or jerkin having short sleeves, or none, and emblazoned with the arms of the sovereign.

**1598** STOW *Surv.* 238 Now these Tabardes are onely worne by the Heraults, and bee called their coates of Armes in seruice. **1633** B. JONSON *Love's Welcome* Wks. (Rtldg.) 661/1 As witnesseth the brief taberd or coat-armour he carries. **1724** *Lond. Gaz.* No. 6307/1 The Heralds..invested with Taberts of the Sovereign's Arms. **1808** SCOTT *Marm.* I. xi, Two pursuivants, whom tabarts deck, With silver scutcheon round their neck. **1864** BOUTELL *Her. Hist. & Pop.* xiii. 132 The Tabard remains in use as the Official Habit of Heralds.

†**4.** (?)

**1526** *Rutland MSS.* (1905) IV. 264 Leyeng tabardes for your chapell roff, and takyng down the olde ledde.

**5.** *Comb. tabard-fashion, -wise*; *tabard-like* adj.

?*a* **1500** *Assemb. Ladies* 523 In tabard-wyse the slevës hanging doun. **1890** DOYLE *White Comp.* xviii, An air of masterful dignity, which was increased by his tabardlike vesture. **1903** *Daily Chron.* 31 Mar. 9/1 Those [S. African natives] that don a coat wear it behind before, or slung round their shoulders, tabard-fashion.

Hence **Ta·barded** *a.*, wearing a tabard.

**1837** *Old Commodore* II. 12 The tabarded official most submissively replied, That if such right existed [etc.].

**Tabarde**, obs. var. TABARD, TABRET.

**Tabarder**: see TABERDAR.

**Tabaret** (tæ·băret). [mod. trade name, prob. f. TABBY: cf. TABINET.] A fabric of alternate satin and watered silk stripes used in upholstery.

**1851** MAYHEW *Lond. Lab. & Poor* I. 427/1 A composition to remove stains from silks, muslins, bombazeens, cords, or tabarets of any kind or colour. **1866** *Times* 23 Apr. Advt., 450 yards rich damasks and tabarets. **1883** [see TABBAREA].

**Tabaret**, obs. form of TABRET.

**Tabarte**, obs. form of TABARD, TABRET.

**Tabasco** (tăbæ·sko). [From Tabasco, name of a river and state of Mexico.] More fully *Tabasco (pepper) sauce*: A very pungent sauce made from the pulp of the ripe fruit of a variety of *Capsicum annuum*. Also *fig.*, a story 'highly-spiced'. *Tabasco allspice*, name for *Pimenta officinalis*, var. *Cumarensis* (formerly *Myrtus Tabasco*), Sp. *Pimienta de Tabasco*.

**1898** *Missouri Bot. Garden, 9th Rept.* 59. **1900** *Westm. Gaz.* 5 Dec. 8/2 He..was..seized and forced to swallow a large dose of Tabasco sauce mixed with ketchup and cayenne pepper. **1902** *Ibid.* 26 Apr. 2/1 Mix with due assiduity, and finally add from three to six drops of tabasco. **1903** *Agric. News* (Barbados) XI. 227 There seems to be no reason for supposing that the Tabasco allspice enters into the preparation of Tabasco pepper. **1908** *Times* 30 July 3/3 He had written 'Sultry Stories—Peppery Paragraphs—Tabasco Tales'. Tabasco was a hot sauce.

‖ **Tabasheer** (tæbăʃiə·ɹ). Also 6–7 (fr. Pg.) tabaxir, 8 (fr. Fr.) tabachir. [Arab., Pers., Urdū تباشير *tabāshīr* chalk, mortar.] A siliceous substance, white or translucent, occasionally formed in the joints of the bamboo; also called *bamboo salt*; used medicinally in the East.

**1598** W. PHILIP *Linschoten* 104/2 These Mambus have a certain matter within them..a very medicinable thing.. much sought for by the Arabians, Persians, and Moores, that call it Tabaxiir. **1662** J. DAVIES tr. *Mandelslo's Trav.* II. 149 A sort of Canes..in which the Tabaxir is found. **1790** P. RUSSELL in *Phil. Trans.* Abr. XVI. 653 (*heading*) Account of the Tabasheer. **1826** BREWSTER *Let.* in *Home Life* ix. (1869) 129, I have enclosed some specimens of Tabasheer, a substance of extreme rarity. **1829** *Nat. Philos.* I. Gloss. (Usef. Knowl. Soc.), *Tabasheer*..is, originally, a transparent fluid in the jointed cavities of the bamboo cane. This fluid thickens,..until..it is converted into a white, or a bluish white solid, something like a small fragment of a shell.

‖ **Tabatière** (tàbatyę̄r). [F. for *tabaquière*, f. *tabac* TOBACCO (Hatz.-Darm.).] A snuff-box. (Rare in Eng. use.)

**1823** SCOTT *Quentin D.* Introd., The marquis was somewhat disconcerted, and had recourse to his *tabatière*. **1841** LADY BLESSINGTON *Idler in France* I. xi. 253 A pinch of snuff from the *tabatière* of the Marquise de Rambouillet.

**Tabbarea** (tæbărī·ă). = TABARET.

**1843** W. C. TAYLOR in *Statistical Jrnl.* Dec. 353 It is generally believed that an ancestor of the present..family of the Latouches commenced the weaving of tabinets or poplins and tabbareas in the liberties of Dublin, about the year 1693. **1883** R. HALDANE *Workshop Receipts* Ser. II. 146/1 Tabaret or Tabbarea.—This may be cleaned and finished in the same manner as described for silk damasks.

**Tabbed** (tæbd, tæ·bĕd), *a.* [f. TAB + -ED.] Having a tab or tabs; furnished or adorned with tabs, as an article of dress.

**1872** J. DRUMMOND in Campbell *Rec. Argyll* (1884) 482 His attendant wears hose tabbed at the top. **1884** G. H. BOUGHTON in *Harper's Mag.* Sept. 533/2 Tabbed jackets, short skirts and buckled shoes. **1901** *Daily Chron.* 5 Oct. 8/3 A pretty blouse, with tabbed fronts bound with stitched white taffetas.

**Tabber, Tabbern**, obs. ff. TABOR, TABORN.

**Tabbied** (tæ·bid), *ppl. a.* [f. TABBY *v.* + -ED[1].] Having a wavy or streaky appearance.

**1861** THORNBURY *Turner* (1862) I. 279 They have..a 'tabbied' or 'mackerel' sky.

**Tabbinet**, variant of TABINET.

**Tabbor, Tabborer**, obs. ff. TABOR, TABORER.

**Tabby** (tæ·bi), *sb.* and *a.* Also 7 **taby**. [In sense 1, a. F. *tabis*, earlier *atabis* (both 14th or early 15th c. in Godef.), Sp., Pg., It. *tabi*, med.L. *attābi* (M. Devic in Littré), app. a. Arab. عتابى *ʿattābiy*, name of a quarter of Bagdad in which this stuff was manufactured, named after *'Attāb*, great-grandson of Omeyya. Of this quarter Yule cites from an Arab writer of the 12th c. 'Here are made the stuffs, called *'Attābīya*, which are silks and cottons of divers colours'.

The connexion of the other senses is not very clear. *Tabby cat*, instanced in 1695, is generally held to have been so named from the striped or streaked colour of its coat. The simple *tabby*, in the same sense, is much later (1774). *Tabby*, old maid, is usually associated with *tabby* a cat; but it appears earlier, and may have originated as the familiar contraction of *Tabitha* (cf. *Abby* for *Abigail*), as an old-fashioned female name, and have become humorously associated with *tabby cat*. It is possible that *tabby* in the sense of she-cat originated in *Tabby* for *Tabitha*; otherwise it is difficult to see any sense-connexion between she-cat and brindled cat, since a tom-cat may also be brindled or striped. Sense 4 of the sb. prob. arose from resemblance to the markings of the tabby cat; the origin of sense 5 is very uncertain, and sense 6 may be a different word, though it may also have originated in a fancied resemblance of colour to that of the tabby cat.]

**A.** *sb.*

**1.** A general term for a silk taffeta, app. originally striped, but afterwards applied also to silks of uniform colour waved or watered.

**1638** [see B. 1]. **1647** HERRICK *Noble Numb., New-Yeeres Gift*, Let others looke for pearle and gold, Tissues or tabbies manifold. **1648** — *Hesper., Life is the Bodies Light* 3 Those counter-changed Tabbies in the ayre, (The Sun once set) all of one colour are. **1654** WHITELOCKE *Jrnl. Swed. Emb.* (1772) II. 153 The bride and bridegroome were both clothed in white tabby. **1662** J. DAVIES tr. *Olearius' Voy. Ambass.* 23 One piece of silver'd Taby, with flowers of Gold. **1696** *Lond. Gaz.* No. 3228/4 Lost.., a Child's Mantle, of a Sky-colour Tabby. **1720** SWIFT *Song* Wks. 1755 IV. I. 29 Brocados and damasks, and tabbies and gawses. **1727** BAILEY vol. II, *Tabby*, a Sort of Silk, waved or watered. **1736** *Ibid.* (folio), *Tabby*, a kind of coarse Silk taffety watered. **1745** POCOCKE *Descr. East* II. I. viii. 125 The manufactures they [of Damascus] export, are chiefly burdets of silk and cotton, either striped or plain, and also plain silks like tabbies. **1760** H. WALPOLE *Let. to Earl of Strafford* 7 June, The Duke of York, who was dressed in a pale blue watered tabby. **1868** HAWTHORNE *Amer. Note-Bks.* (1879) II. 61 His lady in crimson tabby. **1888** W. MORRIS *Arts & Crafts Catal.* 19 A different tone is obtained by the figure and the ground being woven with a longer or shorter twill: the tabby being tied by the warp very often, the satin much more rarely.

**b.** Short for *tabby gown* or *dress*.

*a* **1727** MRS. DELANY in *Life & Corr.* (1861) I. 124 To alter my white tabby and my new clothes. **1786** MME. D'ARBLAY *Diary* 29 Sept., I wore my memorable present-gown this day...It is a lilac tabby. **1881** BESANT & RICE *Chapl. of Fleet* II. 58 A watered tabby would become you.

**2.** Short for *tabby cat* (see B. 2): A cat having a striped or brindled coat.

**1774** GOLDSM. *Nat. Hist.* (1862) I. IV. iii. 423 The civet varies in its colour, being sometimes streaked, as in our kind of cats called tabbies. **1874** GORDON STABLES *Cats* i. 8 *Brown Tabby.* Colour to be rich brown, striped and marked with black...They are the true English cats. *Ibid.* 9 *Blue or Silver Tabby.* Colour to be blue, or silver grey, striped and marked with black. *Ibid.* 12 *Red and White Tabby.* Colour to be reddish or sandy, marked with white. **1903** *Daily Chron.* 28 Oct. 3/1 Among silver tabbies,..Sweet William and..Dame Fortune were particularly noteworthy.

**b.** Also, A she-cat: correlative to *tom-cat*.

**1826–8** *Townley's High Life below Stairs* (acting ed.), Your cat has kittened—two Toms and two Tabbies. **1903** *Speaker* 14 Feb. 486/2 Where is the centurion who has ever commanded a tom-cat, the astronomer who predicted the movements of a tabby?

**3.** An old or elderly maiden lady: a dyslogistic appellation; often with a half-humorous attribution of certain qualities of the cat; sometimes applied to any spiteful or ill-natured female gossip or tattler: cf. also CAT *sb.*[1] 2.

[**1748**: see B. 3]. **1761** G. COLMAN *Jealous Wife* II. iii, I am not sorry for the coming in of these old tabbies. **1782** ELIZ. BLOWER *Geo. Bateman* I. 222 A delightful ground-work, on which the tabbies of Clairfield embroidered a thousand different anecdotes. **1785** GROSE *Dict. Vulg. Tongue, Tabby*, an old maid; either from Tabitha, a formal antiquated name; or else from a tabby cat, old maids being often compared to cats. **1824** SCOTT *St. Ronan's* xxxiii, Why should not I pay my respects to Lady Penelope, or any other tabby of quality? **1843** LEVER *J. Hinton* xiii, I was playing whist with the tabbies when it occurred. **1894** [see TABLEAU 2 c].

**4.** A collector's name for two Pyralid moths, the Tabby, *Aglossa pinguinalis*, and the Small Tabby, *A. cuprealis*, both with fore wings greyish brown, clouded with a darker colour.

**1819** G. SAMOUELLE *Entomol. Compend.* 427 *Pyralis capreolalis*...The small Tabby. *pinguinalis*...The Tabby. *Ibid.* 435 The tea Tabby. **1859** STAINTON *Man. Butterfl. & Moths* II. 135 *Aglossa pinguinalis* (Tabby)...Abundant everywhere. *A. cuprealis* (Small Tabby).

†**5.** Padding or quilting to improve the figure. *Tabbies*, padded or quilted stays. *Obs.*

**1748** FOOTE *Knights* II. i, Ward, at the Cat and Gridiron, Petticoat-lane, makes tabby all over for people inclined to be crooked; and, if he was to have the universal world for making a pair of stays, he could not put better stuff in them. **1752** — *Taste* I. i, *Lady Pentweazel.* Bless me, Mr. Carmine, don't mind my shape this bout; for I am only in jumps. Shall I send for my tabbies?

**6.** A concrete formed of a mixture of lime with shells, gravel, or stones in equal proportions, which when dry becomes very hard. Orig. *tabby work.*

**1802** A. ELLICOTT *Jrnl.* (1803) 267 A small battery of tabby work (as it is called in that country [Georgia]), which is a composition of broken oyster shells and lime. **1836** SMART, *Tabby*..a mixture of stone or shell and mortar. **1887** *Cassell's Encycl. Dict.* cites WEALE.

**B.** *adj.* (attrib. use of sb.)

**1.** Made or consisting of tabby (see A. 1).

**1638** T. VERNEY in *V. Papers* (1853) 197 First, for one good cloth sute, and one taby or good stuff sute. **1661** PEPYS *Diary* 13 Oct., This day..put on..my false taby waste-coate with gold lace. *a* **1712** W. KING *Art of Love* 1043 If she in tabby waves encircled be,..If by her the purpureal velvet's worn. **1748** H. WALPOLE *Lett.* (1846) II. 224 A new sky-blue watered tabby coat. **1863** LE FANU *Ho. by Church-yard* III. 127 Mrs. Sturk..sat in a dingy old tabby saque.

**2.** Of a brownish, tawny, or grey colour, marked with darker parallel stripes or streaks; brindled: primarily and especially in **tabby cat** or **tabby-cat**, a cat of this coloration, or (by extension) of other colour similarly marked: see A. 2. In quot. 1789 *ellipt.* = tabby coloration.

[**1665**: cf. *tabby-coloured* in C.] *c* **1689** PRIOR *Ld. Buckhurst playing w. Cat* 21 On her tabby rival's face She deep will mark her new disgrace. **1695** CONGREVE *Love for L.* II. iii, I can bring witness that..you suckle a young devil in the shape of a tabby-cat. **1698** FRYER *Acc. E. India & P.* 176 It was a Tigre..of a light Yellow, streaked with Black, like a Tabby Cat. **1702** POPE *Wife of Bath* 142 The Cat, if you but singe her tabby skin, The chimney keeps. **1747** GRAY *Let. to Walpole* in Mason *Life* (1775) 188 Then as to your handsome Cat,..it must be the tabby one that had met with this sad accident. **1747** — *Cat* 4 Demurest of the tabby kind. **1789** MRS. PIOZZI *Journ. France* I. 347 Cats..in the woods are all of the uniformly-streaked Tabby. **1796** STEDMAN *Surinam* (1813) II. xviii. 62 The spotted cat [fish] is called so from its tabby color and long whiskers. **1903** *Longm. Mag.* Sept. 450 It had been brought up from infancy with a tabby kitten.

*fig.* (cf. A. 3). **1874** MRS. H. WOOD *Mast. Greylands* xv, A meddling, tattling, tabby-cat set of women!

**b.** *Tabby-cat striation*, 'the appearance presented in extreme fatty degeneration of muscle' (*Syd. Soc. Lex.*).

**1897** *Allbutt's Syst. Med.* II. 871 The heart..often shows some fatty degeneration of the myocardium (tabby-cat striation). **1898** *Ibid.* V. 530 The musculi papillares..are nearly always variegated by wavy whitish streaks—the 'tabby-cat striation' of Quain.

**3.** Of or pertaining to a tabby, in sense A. 3.

**1748** RICHARDSON *Clarissa* (1811) VI. lv. 227 The two antiques only bowed their tabby heads.

**C.** *attrib.* and *Comb.*, as *tabby weaving* (see A. 1); *tabby-coloured* adj.; **tabby-cat** (see B. 2); **tabby-waterer**, one who waters or tabbies silk by a process of calendering; **tabby work**: see A. 6.

**1665** SIR T. HERBERT *Trav.* (1677) 304 Cats..very large they are and tabby-coloured, streakt like those of Cyprus. **1867** SMILES *Huguenots Eng.* (1880) 373 [He] carried on the business of a calenderer and Tabby Waterer. **1879** A. BARLOW *Weaving* 89 A piece of plain woven cloth is represented ..as it would be drawn by the designer, and it is generally called 'tabby' or plain weaving.

**Tabby** (tæ·bi), *v.* [f. prec.]

**1.** *trans.* To give a wavy appearance to (silk, etc.) by calendering. Hence **Ta·bbying** *vbl. sb.*

**1728** CHAMBERS *Cycl.* s. v. *Roll*, Tis also between two Rollers that the Waves are given to Silks, Mohairs, and other Stuffs proper to be tabied. **1839** URE *Dict. Arts* 1225 Tabbying, or Watering, is the process of giving stuffs a wavy appearance with the calender.

**2.** To stripe or streak in parallel lines with darker markings. Usually in pa. pple. **Ta·bbied.**

**1860** *All Year Round* No. 37. 260 They [mackerel] were tabbied with indigo tattooings. **1870** THORNBURY *Tour Eng.* II. xix. 49 The beautiful fish, shining like solid lumps of rainbow, tabbied with dark veins.

**Ta·bbyhood.** [f. TABBY *sb.* + -HOOD.] The condition of being an old maid: see TABBY *sb.* 3.

**1793** J. GIFFORD *Resid. France* (1797) I. 357, I venture to add a word in defence of Tabbyhood. **1824** *Blackw. Mag.* XV. 115 He..married a wife verging on her tabbyhood.

†**Tabe.** *Obs.* [ad. L. *tābēs* (see TABES) or *tābum* corruption, infectious or pestilent disease.] Gradual wasting away; = TABES.

**1614** T. ADAMS *Fatal Banquet* II. Wks. 1861 I. 191 They put a pleurisy into their bloods, a tabe, and consumption into their states. **1633** — *Exp. 2 Peter* ii. 2 He doth work a tabe and consumption into his fellows' virtues.

**Tabe**, obs. variant of TAB.

†**Tabefact**, *a. Obs. rare*[−1]. [ad. L. *tābefact-us*: see next.] Wasted, corrupted.

*c* **1425** tr. *Arderne's Surgery* (E. E. T. S.) 43, I perceyued þe bone of þe fynger to be tabefacte, i. corrupte.

**Tabefa·ction.** *rare*[−0]. [n. of action from late L. *tābefacĕre*, pa. pple. *tābefactus*: see TABEFY.] The action or process of tabefying; the wasting away or consumption of the body.

1658 PHILLIPS, *Tabefaction*, a melting, corrupting, or consuming [1706 (ed. 6) *adds* or wasting away]. 1890 BILLINGS *Nat. Med. Dict.*, *Tabefaction*, emaciation.

**Tabefical**, erron. f. TABIFICAL (infl. by *tabefy*).

**Tabefy** (tæ·bǐfəi), *v. rare.* [a. obs. F. *tabéfier* (Paré *c* 1570), ad. late L. *tābefacĕre* (Vulgate), to cause to waste (f. *tābē-re* to waste, melt + *facĕre* to make): see -FY; cf. also late L. *tābificāre* (Cassiod.) in same sense (f. *tābific-us* TABIFIC), whence F. *tabifier* (Cotgr., Oudin).]

**1.** *trans.* To waste away, consume; to emaciate; †to melt down (*obs.*).

1656 BLOUNT *Glossogr.*, *Tabefy*, to corrupt, consume or melt. 1657 TOMLINSON *Renou's Disp.* 78 Out of these [Anacards] thus tabefied proceeds a liquor. 1666 G. HARVEY *Morb. Angl.* (1672) 79 Meat eaten in greater quantity than what is convenient tabefyes the body.

**2.** *intr.* To waste away gradually, become emaciated. *rare.* 1891 in *Cent. Dict.*

Hence **Ta·befied** *ppl. a.*, affected with tabes, decayed, consumptive.

1666 G. HARVEY *Morb. Angl.* i. 4 Whole families.. descended from tabefyed ancestors.

**Tabel, -ele, -ell(e**, obs. forms of TABLE.

**Tabelet(te, tabellet(t**, obs. forms of TABLET.

‖ **Tabe·lla.** *Pharm.* Pl. **-æ**. [L. dim. of *tabula* TABLE.] = TABLET 3.

1693 tr. *Blancard's Phys. Dict.* (ed. 2), *Tabella*, a solid Medicine taken inwardly, made of Powder, and three or four times as much Sugar..made into little round Cakes upon a Marble Stone. 1706 PHILLIPS (ed. 6). 1890 *Allen & Hanbury's Advt.* in *Lancet* 25 Oct. 74 It..renders our Compressed Tabellæ the most eligible form for the administration of several important medicines.

† **Tabella·rious**, *a. Obs. rare*$^{-0}$. [f. L. *tabellāri-us* (see next) + -OUS.]

1656 BLOUNT *Glossogr.*, *Tabellarious*, belonging to carriers or auditors.

† **Tabellary**, *sb. Obs. rare*$^{-0}$. [ad. L. *tabellārius* letter-carrier, courier, f. *tabella* tablet, writing-tablet.]

1656 BLOUNT *Glossogr.*, *Tabellary*, a carrier of letters; an auditor, a scrivener. 1658 in PHILLIPS.

† **Ta·bellary**, *a. Obs. rare*$^{-1}$. [ad. L. *tabellārius* of or pertaining to voting tablets, f. *tabella* tablet.] Pertaining to the use of voting tablets; *tabellary liberty*, liberty of voting by tablets.

1613 T. GODWIN *Rom. Antiq.* III. III. v. 142 Cœlius Trib. Pl. established a law, that..in taintments of treason against any person of State,..or against the Common-weale, this Tabellary libertie should have place, when the people should iudge thereof.

† **Tabe·llion.** *Obs.* Also 5 -ioun, -yo(u)n. [ad. L. *tabellio*, *-ōnem*, one who draws up written instruments, a notary, scrivener, f. *tabella* tablet, letter, etc.] A scrivener, a kind of subordinate notary; *esp.* in the Roman Empire, and in France till the Revolution, an official scribe having some of the functions of a notary. In 17–18th c. used at a recognized designation of a vocation in England and New England.

1413 *Pilgr. Sowle* (Caxton) I. xxi. (1859) 21, I my self wyl only be wryter and tabellyon of al that he wyl sey. 1469 *Sc. Acts Jas. III* (1814) II. 95 His hienes may mak notaris & tabellionis. 1622 MALYNES *Anc. Law-Merch.* 198 A Notarie is called a Tabellion, Scriuenor, or a publike seruant. 1656 in *Thurloe St. Papers* V. 401 We do certify that Rob. Wickenden..is notary and tabellion public in this port of Dover. 1735 in Carol. Hazard *Life T. Hazard* (1893) 229, I Joseph Marion Notary and Tabellion Publick Dwelling in Boston in New England. 1755 MAGENS *Insurances* II. 71 To make the Assurance before a Justice, Notary, Tabellion, or other public Person. 1909 SHARPE *Cal. Let. Bk. I Lond.* p. xxviii *note*, We find him formally appointing a notary public and tabellion throughout the Roman Empire.

**Taber, Taberd**, obs. ff. TABOR, TABARD.

**Taberdar** (tæ·bəɹdāɹ). Also 7 **taubator, tabitter**, 8 **tabiter**, 7–8 **taberder**, 7– **tabardar.** [f. *taberd*, TABARD.] *lit.* One who wears a tabard; a name formerly given to certain scholars of Queen's College, Oxford, from the gown they wore; still surviving in the name of some of the scholarships at that college.

[1566 *Register of Queen's Coll.* 5 Apr., Electio Taberdorum habita 5º die mensis Aprilis Anno Elizabethe Regine 8º. 1569 *Ibid.* 29 Jan., Electio Taberdiorum.] 1648 in Burrows *Reg. Visitors Univ. Oxf.* (Camden) 177 Oct. 30 Avery Tompson, Tho. Collinson, Taubators. 1660 WOOD *Life* Dec. (O. H. S.) I. 352 The Taberder sings the aforesaid song. 1691 — *Ath. Oxon.* I. 348/2 After he [Henry Airay] was Bachelaurs standing, in 1583, he was made *Pauper Puer*, or *Tabardus* or *Tabardarius*; that is, a Tabarder or Tabitter, (so called because anciently they wore Coats or upper Gowns, much according to the fashion of those belonging to Heralds). 1769 *De Foe's Tour Gt. Brit.* II. 243 (Queen's College, Oxford.) The Society consists of a Provost, 16 Fellows, 16 Scholars, 2 Chaplains, 8 Taberders ..and 40 Exhibitioners. 1882 *Stat. Queen's Coll.* III. i. in *Stat. Univ. Oxford* 336 The eight holders of Open Scholarships who are highest in seniority from the time of their election shall always be called Taberdars.

† **Ta·bere.** *Obs.* [perh. var. of TABARD.] A hood for a hawk.

1467 *Mann. & Househ. Exp.* (Roxb.) 431 Paid for a tabere for the hawke, ij. s. iiij. d.

**Taberer(e, -et(t(e**, obs. ff. TABORER, TABRET.

**Tabergite** (tā·bəɹgəit). *Min.* [Named (in Ger.) 1847 from Taberg in Sweden: see -ITE [1].] A mineral of the chlorite group.

1868 DANA *Min.* (ed. 5) 496 *Tabergite*, from Taberg, Wermland..is a bluish-green or green chlorite. 1896 CHESTER *Dict. Names Min.*, *Tabergite*... a chlorite-like mineral, classed with both clinochlore and penninite, probably a mixture of one of these with phlogopite.

† **Ta·bern.** *Obs.* Also 5 **tabyrn.** [ad. L. *taberna* hut, booth, shop, tavern.] An obsolete doublet of the word TAVERN, variously used in the senses 'shop, tavern, cellar, cupboard'.

14.. *Voc.* in Wr.-Wülcker 729/40 *Hec taberna*, a tabyrn. *c* 1590 MARLOWE *Faust.* viii. 21, I can make thee drunk with ippocras at any tabern in Europe for nothing. 1605 WILLET *Hexapla Gen.* 281 Food..commonly vendible in their tabernes. 1657 TOMLINSON *Renou's Disp.* 472 In the ..angle of the kitchin .. may be made a Tabern. 1674 RAY *N. C. Words* 47 A *Tabern*, a Cellar.

**Tabernacle** (tæ·bəɹnæk'l), *sb.* Forms: 3– **tabernacle**; also 5–6 **taburn-**, 6 **tabarn-**; 4 **-acil**, 4–5 **-akile**, 4–6 **-akil(l**, **-akle**, 5 **-akille**, **-akyl(le.** [a. F. *tabernacle* (12th c. in Hatz.-Darm.), ad. L. *tabernāculum* tent, booth, shed, dim. of *taberna* hut, booth. Used first in special sense 2, from Old Test. history.]

**1.** A temporary dwelling; generally movable, constructed of branches, boards, or canvas; a hut, tent, booth.

1382 WYCLIF *Num.* xxiv. 5 How feyr thi tabernaclis, Jacob, and thi tentis, Yrael. — *Mark* ix. 4 Maistir.. make we here thre tabernaclis, oon to thee, oon to Moyses, and oon to Helye. 1483 CAXTON *Gold. Leg.* 66/2 Dauid toke the heed of Golye and brought it in to Jherussalem and his armes he brought in to his tabernacle. 1535 COVERDALE *Heb.* xi. 9 By faith was he a straunger in the londe of promes..& dwelt in tabernacles [WYCLIF litel housis]. 1598 HAKLUYT *Voy.* I. 54 Some of these Tabernacles [of the Tartars] may quickely be taken asunder, and set together againe. *c* 1618 MORYSON *Itin.* IV. I. (1903) 44 When his Tents were once pitched, then all the Army..pitched their Tents or Tabernacles about him, in a huge Circuite of grounde. 1756–7 tr. *Keysler's Trav.* (1760) II. 433 Frescati ..derives its name from the arbours or tabernacles built by the inhabitants of Tusculum, when their city was demolished ..A.D. 1191. 1860 PUSEY *Min. Proph.* 223 The tabernacle was originally a rude hut, formed of intertwined branches. 1864 BURTON *Scot Abr.* I. iii. 109 Some of them..would as soon have sought Kamschatka, as a place wherein to pitch their tabernacle and pursue their fortune.

**b.** *Feast of Tabernacles*: a Jewish festival, commemorating the dwelling of the Israelites in tents during their sojourn in the wilderness, held from the 15th to the 23rd of Tisri (October). It was also called the Feast of Ingathering, and was observed as a thanksgiving for the harvest.

1382 WYCLIF *Lev.* xxiii. 34 The fiftenthe day of this seuenthe moneth shulen be the cesynge dayes of the tabernacles [1388 the feries of tabernaclis]. — *Deut.* xvi. 13 The solempte of the tabernaclis. — *Zech.* xiv. 16 That thei ..halewe the feest of tabernaclis. 1535 COVERDALE *John* vii. 2 The Iewes feast of Tabernacles [TINDALE the iewes tabernacle feast] was at hande. 1860 PUSEY *Min. Proph.* 79 The feast of tabernacles was the yearly remembrance of God's miraculous guidance and support of Israel through the wilderness. 1896 *Westm. Gaz.* 25 Sept. 3/2 More than any of the other Jewish festivals, Tabernacles claims to be a holyday distinctly commemorative of the harvest.

**2.** *spec.* in *Jewish Hist.* The curtained tent, containing the Ark of the Covenant and other sacred appointments, which served as the portable sanctuary of the Israelites during their wandering in the wilderness and afterwards till the building of the Temple. Also called *tabernacle of the congregation* (or *meeting*), *of testimony*, and *of witness*.

*c* 1250 *Gen. & Ex.* 3174 Gold and siluer he hauen vt-broȝt, Ðe tabernacle ðor-wið wurð wroȝt. 1340 *Ayenb.* 236 Aaron and his children þet serueden ine þe tabernacle. 1535 COVERDALE 2 *Chron.* v. 6 And yᵉ Leuites toke the Arke, & broughte it vp with the Tabernacle of witnesse, and all the holy vessels that were in the Tabernacle. 1642 FULLER *Holy & Prof. St.* III. xxiv. 219 The Tabernacle was a moveable Temple. 1862 STANLEY *Jew. Ch.* (1877) I. vii. 142 The most remarkable vestige of the nomadic state of the nation was the Tabernacle or Tent..the shelter of the Ark.

**b.** Applied to a portable shrine used in heathen or idolatrous worship.

1382 WYCLIF *Amos* v. 26 And ȝe han born tabernaclis to Moloch, ȝour god. [Also in later versions.]

**c.** Transferred to the Jewish temple, as continuing the sacred functions and associations of the earlier tabernacle.

1388 WYCLIF *Heb.* xiii. 10 We han an auter, of which thei that seruen to the tabernacle, han not power to ete. 1535 COVERDALE *Ps.* lxxv[i]. 2 At Salem is his tabernacle, & his dwellinge in Sion. 1653 MILTON *Hirelings* Wks. 1851 V. 345 The Levitical and Ceremonial service of the Tabernacle ..which is now abolish'd.

**3.** *fig.* In phraseology chiefly of biblical origin: A dwelling-place. **a.** *spec.* The dwelling-place of Jehovah, or of God.

Orig. with reference to the Jewish tabernacle or temple.

*a* 1340 HAMPOLE *Psalter* xiv. 1 Lord wha sall won in þi tabernakile? *Ibid.* xxvi. 9 He hid me in his tabernakill in day of illis. 1382 WYCLIF *Rev.* xxi. 3 Lo! the tabernacle of God [is] with men, and he shal dwelle with hem. 1567 *Gude & Godlie B.* (S. T. S.) 90 O Lord quha sall in heuin dwell with the, In thy tryumphant throne and Tabernakil? 1831 LANDOR *Guzman & Son* 17 Wks. 1846 II. 610 The brave man's breast Is God's pure tabernacle.

**b.** *gen.* A dwelling-place, a dwelling, a place of abode.

1382 WYCLIF *Job* xii. 6 The tabernaclis of reueres abounden. 1526 *Pilgr. Perf.* (W. de W. 1531) 13 b, For euery good chrysten man and woman a tabernacle of glory. 1635 PAGITT *Christianogr.* I. iii. (1636) 105 They deserue to be receiued into the eternall Tabernacles. 1845 MAURICE *Mor. & Met. Philos.* in *Encycl. Metrop.* (1847) II. 572/1 The portion from the encompassing whole, which hath taken up its tabernacle in these our bodies. 1860 HAWTHORNE *Marb. Faun* (1879) II. viii. 84 How undesirable it is to build the tabernacle of our brief lifetime out of permanent materials. 1891 F. TENNYSON *Niobe* Poems 346 And all The crowned Gods in their high tabernacles Sigh unawares.

**c.** Applied to the human body regarded as the temporary abode of the soul or of life.

*c* 1374 CHAUCER *Boeth.* II. pr. iii. 26 (Camb. MS.) Arthow now comen fyrst A sodeyn gest in to the shadwe or tabernacle of this lyf? 1382 WYCLIF 2 *Peter* i. 14 The puttyng off of my tabernacle is swift. 1557 N. T. (Genev.) 2 *Cor.* v. 1 We knowe that if the tabernacle of this our earthy howse shalbe destroyed, we haue a building geuen of God..eternal in heauen. 1596 SPENSER *Hymn Hon. Beautie* 142 Many a gentle mynd Dwels in deformed tabernacle drownd. 1671 MILTON *P. R.* IV. 599 True image of the Father,..enshrin'd In fleshly Tabernacle, and human form. 1746–7 HERVEY *Medit.* (1818) 118 These earthly tabernacles will be transformed into the likeness of Christ's glorious body. 1841 JAMES *Brigand* i, The spirit was busy in its tabernacle dealing with high thoughts.

**4.** † **a.** An ornate canopied structure, as a tomb or shrine; in quot. *c* 1430, an ornate structure in a pageant. *Obs.*

1297 R. GLOUC. (Rolls) 466 Tours þe gode kniȝt .. Brut let bringe an erþe .. & let vair tabernacle in honur of him rere. *c* 1394 *P. Pl. Crede* 181 Tombes opon tabernacles tyld opon lofte, Housed in hirnes harde set abouten. *c* 1400 *Destr. Troy* 8813 When this taburnacle atyrit was..Thai closit hit full clanly, all with clene ambur. *c* 1430 LYDG. *Min. Poems* (Percy Soc.) 10 In Cornhille..To do plesaunce to his majesté, A tabernacle surmontyng of beauté Ther was ordeyned. ? *a* 1500 *Maundevile & Sultan of Egypt* 95 in *Rel. Ant.* II. 115 Than the body they bryng unto that place Wher he salle ly armet in his wede, In a tabernacle or a case, Right preciose.

**b.** A canopied niche or recess in a wall or pillar, to contain an image.

*c* 1384 CHAUCER *H. Fame* III. 100 But many..Babewinnes and pinacles, Imageries and tabernacles, I saw. 1389 *Eng. Gilds* (1870) 51 An ymage of seynt Wylyam, standyng in a tabernakle, in þe chirche of seynt Margarete of Lenne. 1487–8 *Rec. St. Mary at Hill* 142 Maistres Agnes Breten did do gilte & paynte the tabernacle of owr lady with in þe queer. 1536 *Reg. Riches* in *Antiq. Sarisb.* (1771) 194 A Tabernacle of Ivory, standing upon four feet, with two leaves, and an ymage of our Lady in the middle. 1862 BARING-GOULD *Iceland* (1863) 237 On either side are tabernacles or niches, containing figures.

† **c.** A canopy of tabernacle-work over a throne or stall, esp. the abbot's stall in a choir. *Obs.*

*c* 1400 *Destr. Troy* 1671 For the souerayn hym selfe was a sete rioll, .. Attyret with a tabernacle of Eyntayill fyn. *a* 1400–50 *Alexander* 5645 A tabernacle ouir þe trone tildid vp on loft.

**5.** *Eccl.* An ornamented receptacle for the pyx containing the consecrated host.

1487–8 *Rec. St. Mary at Hill* 131 Rynges and hookes to henge the clothe for the newe tabernacle. 1546 BALE *Eng. Votaries* I. (1548) 19 b, Pranked vp with tabernacles & lyghtes, sensynges & massinges. *a* 1615 *Brieue Cron. Erlis Ross* (1850) 17 He brought home [for the kirk] an tabernacle. 1716 in J. O. Payne *Recs. Eng. Cath. of* 1715 (1889) 130 A tabernacle of silver belonging to yᵉ Altar. 1853 DALE tr. *Baldeschi's Ceremonial* 301 He .. opens the Tabernacle, genuflects, and takes out the ciborium. 1885 *Cath. Dict.* 717/1 In most English [R. C.] churches the tabernacle with the Blessed Sacrament is placed over the chief altar.

**6.** A place of worship distinguished in some way from a church. **a.** A temporary place of worship; esp. applied to the structures temporarily used during the rebuilding of the churches destroyed by the Fire of London in 1666.

1693 EVELYN *Diary* 19 Feb., The Bp. of Lincoln preach'd in the afternoon at the Tabernacle neere Golden Square, set up by him. 1695 SIR J. BRAMSTON *Autobiog.* May (Camden) 389 She [Lady Dyke] was at morninge or euening prayer in the church or tabernacle daily. 1711 *Jrnl. Ho. Com.* XVI. 582 Allowing the 18 chapels or tabernacles to be capable of receiving as many persons as 8 churches. 1739 *Act 12 Geo. II*, c. 7 *Preamble*, The parishioners [of Ealing] were obliged to assemble for Divine worship in a slight Timber Tabernacle.

**b.** Applied frequently to the meeting-houses or places of worship of Protestant Nonconformists, esp. when not of ecclesiastical architecture.

Sometimes part of the title, as *Whitefield's Tabernacle* in Tottenham Court Road, London, and the *Metropolitan Tabernacle* built for Mr. Spurgeon. Now chiefly so used by Baptists and some Methodists. In Scotland, early in the 19th century, commonly applied to the places of worship of the Independents or Congregationalists ('Tabernacle-people'). Otherwise, the name is mostly applied in contempt.

1768 GOLDSM. *Good-n. Man* I. i, I believe she would spread a horse laugh through the pews of a tabernacle. 1796 MORSE *Amer. Geog.* II. 116 A great number of methodist tabernacles. 1805 J. BROWN (Gartmore) *Vind. Presbyt. Ch. Govt.* ii. 13 *note*, The tabernacle-churches in Scotland require their members to stand in singing. 1820 SOUTHEY *Wesley* II. 357 They called it [the shed built as a preaching place for Whitefield] a Tabernacle in allusion to the moveable place of worship of the Israelites. *a* 1878 SIR G. G. SCOTT *Lect. Archit.* (1879) I. 182 Pewing which would disgrace a tabernacle of the last century. *c* 1880 ALLEN *Guide to Nottingham* 33 The next building on the main road of any note is known as *The Tabernacle*..and is a Baptist Chapel.

**c.** *fig.* Applied to the 'edifice' which for the time enshrines the principles of a party.

1902 Sir H. Campbell-Bannerman *Sp. at Leicester* 19 Feb., I do not know down to this moment whether Lord Rosebery speaks to us from the interior of our political tabernacle or from some vantage-ground outside. 1902 Ld. Rosebery in *Times* 21 Feb. 6/1 Speaking pontifically within his 'tabernacle' last night, he [Sir H. C.-B.] anathematised my declarations on the 'clean slate' and Home Rule... I remain, therefore, outside his tabernacle, but not, I think, in solitude. 1902 *Westm. Gaz.* 26 Feb. 6/3 Dr. Heber Hart.. is convinced that the principles of the League can be effectively advocated only by those who remain within the tabernacle of the party, whoever may be the Chief Rabbi for the time being.

**7.** *Naut.* An elevated socket or step for the mast of a river-boat, or a post to which the mast is hinged, that it may be lowered to pass bridges.

1877 in Knight *Dict. Mech.* 1886 *Field* 13 Feb. 209/3 The mizen mast to be stepped in a tabernacle on a false transom in front of the rudder head. 1889 H. M. Doughty *Friesland Meres* 356, I watched the tabernacle anxiously; the strain must be enormous; we must have shrouds set up. 1892 — *Wherry in Wendish L.* 15 Her one mast, very far forward, is as high nearly as her length, and balanced in a tabernacle with a ton and more of lead.

†**8.** An alleged term for a company of bakers.

1486 *Bk. St. Albans* f vj b, A Tabernacle of bakers.

**9.** *attrib.* and *Comb.* **Tabernacle-niche**, a niche having a canopy of tabernacle-work over it; **tabernacle roof**, a roof which slopes at the ends, as well as the sides, to a central ridge shorter than the side-walls; **tabernacle-spire**, a spire ornamented with many tabernacles or canopied niches; **tabernacle-work**, (*a*) the ornamental carved work or tracery usual in canopies over niches, stalls, or pulpits, and in the carved screens of churches; (*b*) architectural work in which tabernacles form the characteristic feature.

1526 Tindale *John* vii. 2 Tabernacle feast [see 1 b, quot. 1535]. 1774 Pennant *Tour Scot. in* 1772, 2 The tabernacle work in the choir is very neat. 1815 J. Smith *Panorama Sc. & Art* I. 133 The ornamental open work over the stalls is called tabernacle work. 1842 *Civil Eng. & Arch. Jrnl.* V. 121/2 The Tabernacle-spire also is one of which there is no example in this country. 1886 Willis & Clark *Cambridge* III. 286 A central tabernacle-niche, and on each side of it a narrow square-headed window.

**Ta·bernacle**, *v.* [ad. med.L. *tabernāculā-re* (1342 in Du Cange: rendering Gr. σκηνοῦν in John i. 14), f. *tabernāculum*: see prec.]

**1.** *intr.* To occupy a tabernacle, tent, or temporary dwelling, or one that can be shifted about; to dwell for a time, to sojourn: usually *fig.*, in devotional or poetical language, said of the sojourning of Christ on earth or 'in the flesh', and of the indwelling of the Spirit of Christ; also of men as spiritual beings dwelling in the 'fleshly tabernacle' of the body.

1653 Collinges *Caveat for Prof.* xiv. 69 The Evangelist Saint John, Joh. i. 14 saith, He tabernacled amongst us. 1667 I. Pennington *Quest. to Prof. Chr.* 20 Is it the flesh and blood of him, who took, tabernacled and appeared in the Body? 1677 Gale *Crt. Gentiles* II. iv. 91 That of Paul 2 Cor. xii. 9..that the power of Christ might tabernacle or dwel on me. 1847 Chr. Rossetti *Face of Deep* (1892) 454 Not with the sparrow building here a house; But with the swallow tabernacling so As still to poise alert to rise and go. 1872 Liddon *Elem. Relig.* iii. 94 It is..as personal spirits, tabernacling in bodily forms, that we men are capable of religion. 1876 C. M. Davies *Unorth. Lond.* 188 Tabernacling first in a room in Burton Street. 1881 N. T. (R.V.) *John* i. 14 And the Word became flesh, and dwelt [*marg.* tabernacled: Gr. ἐσκήνωσεν] among us.

**2.** *trans.* To place in a tabernacle; to enshrine.

1822 Milman *Mart. Antioch* iii. 116 In thee the light, Creation's eldest born, was tabernacled. 1891 *Tablet* 21 Nov. 825 In any church in this land in which Jesus is tabernacled and has found a home. 1896 *Cath. News* 25 Apr. 6/6 The real presence of God..tabernacled in yon loving place.

Hence **Ta·bernacling** *vbl. sb.*, dwelling in a tabernacle or tent; sojourning; temporary abode.

1685 J. Scott *Chr. Life* (1696) V. 246 It is no note of distinction between these two dwellings or tabernaclings of Christ. 1856 Ruskin *Mod. Paint.* IV. v. vi. § 9. 89 This tabernacling of the unendurable sun with men. 1866 J. G. Murphy *Comm. Exod.* xxiii. 16 The feast of tabernacles, because the tabernacling of the people in the wilderness was then commemorated.

**Ta·bernacled** (-ækl'd), *ppl. a.* [f. Tabernacle *sb.* + -ed [2], perh. after a med.L. **tabernāculātus*.] Made with tabernacle-work, having a carved canopy.

c 1468 in *Archæol.* (1846) XXXI. 333 Over the court gate.. was a riche healme, richelye tabernacled of golde, subtilie gravin things in pinacles. 1905 *Athenæum* 23 Dec. 874/3 A good fifteenth-century tabernacled font cover, 5 ft. high.

**Ta·bernacler.** *rare.* [f. Tabernacle *sb.* + -er [1].] One who worships in a 'tabernacle'.

1810 Coleridge in *Lit. Rem.* (1839) IV. 371 The Ebenezerites.., and their..fellow Methodists, the Tabernaclers.

**Tabernacular** (tæbəɹnæ·kiŭlăɹ), *a. rare.* [f. L. type **tabernāculār-is*, f. *tabernācul-um*: see above and -ar [1].] Of or pertaining to a tabernacle.

**1.** Of the style or character of an architectural tabernacle; constructed or decorated with open-work and tracery.

1678 Wood *Life* 28 June (O. H. S.) II. 411 An antient carved peice of tabernacular worke. 1774 Warton *Hist. Eng. Poetry* (1840) II. xxiii. 300 Cloisters..fronted with tabernacular or open work.

**2.** Savouring of the language of a 'tabernacle' or conventicle. *contemptuous.*

1847 De Quincey *Protestantism* Wks. 1858 VIII. 89 The word 'shortcomings'..being horridly tabernacular, and such that no gentleman could allow himself to touch it without gloves. 1858 Bailey *Age* 171 But you condemn all verse of solemn vein As canting, tabernacular in strain.

†**Taberna·culous**, *a. Obs. rare.* [f. L. *tabernācul-um* Tabernacle + -ous: cf. *miraculous.*] = Tabernacular.

1696 Brookhouse *Temple Open.* 34 As his [Solomon's] Temple was the Perfection of the Tabernacle, so this City [the New Jerusalem] is the Perfection of the last Tabernaculous Dispensation of [the apocalyptic] Babylon.

†**Taberna·rious**, *a. Obs.* $rare^{-0}$. [f. L. *tabernāri-us* belonging to booths or shops, vulgar, low + -ous.]

1656 Blount *Glossogr.*, *Tabernarious*, belonging to Shops or Taverns.

**Taberne**, obs. form of Taborn.

**Taberner**, obs. form of Taborner, Taverner.

**Tabert, Tabertte**, obs. ff. Tabard, Tabret.

‖**Tabes** (tē·bīz). [L. *tābēs* wasting away, dissolution, consumption.] **1.** *Path.* Slow progressive emaciation of the body or its parts; consumption.

Common in medical Latin names of specific diseases, as *tabes dorsalis*, locomotor ataxia, *tabes mesenterica*, tuberculosis in the mesenteric glands, etc.

1651 Biggs *New Disp.* § 258 In Tabes, or Consumptions, distempers of the lungs, head, eyes. 1681 tr. *Willis' Rem. Med. Wks.* Vocab., *Tabes dorsalis*, the mourning of the chine; a wasting or consumption of the back. 1706 in Phillips. 1899 *Allbutt's Syst. Med.* VII. 125 General paralysis is a 'tabes of the brain'.

**2.** Decay of trees or other plants caused by disease or injury.

1832 *Libr. Usef. Knowl., Husb.* III. *Planting* 70 Spontaneous bleeding, or great loss of sap, generally ends in the disease termed *tabes*. *Ibid.* 71 *Tabes*, or the wasting of trees, is brought on not unfrequently by parasitical plants.

**Tabescent** (tăbe·sĕnt), *a.* [ad. L. *tābēscent-em*, pr. pple. of *tābēscĕre*, inceptive of *tābēre* to waste away: see -escent.] Wasting away.

1890 in Billings *Nat. Med. Dict.* 1898 in *Syd. Soc. Lex.* So **Tabe·scence**, emaciation. 1890 in Billings.

**Tabetic** (tăbe·tik), *a.* and *sb.* [irreg. f. L. *tābēs, tābi-*, on false analogy of words etymologically in *-etic*, as *diabetic.*] **A.** *adj.* Of, pertaining to, or affected with tabes or emaciation.

1847 Webster, *Tabetic*, tabid, affected with tabes. 1897 J. Hutchinson in *Arch. Surg.* VIII. No. 31. 232 The patient..has no bladder symptoms, nor any characteristic tabetic pains. 1899 *Allbutt's Syst. Med.* VII. 100, I have met with cases which began with tabetic symptoms and ended in general paralysis.

**B.** *sb.* One who suffers from tabes.

1899 *Allbutt's Syst. Med.* VI. 808 [He] has found the labyrinth and auditory nerve normal in tabetics with defective hearing. *Ibid.* VII. 110 Tabetics, who did not show Romberg's sign.

‖**Tabi** (tā·bi). [Japanese.] Cotton stockings having the toes separate, worn by Japanese women.

1895 Holland *Jap. Wife* 18 The curious *tabi* of white cotton, shoes and stockings all in one, with separated toes. 1902 *Daily Chron.* 22 Nov. 3/2 When the whole people celebrate the rites of Shintoism..men and boys exchange their customary black foot-gear for the white *tabi* of women.

**Ta·bic**, *a. rare.* [irreg. f. L. Tabes + -ic.]

1895 in *Funk's Stand. Dict.* 1898 *Syd. Soc. Lex.*, *Tabic*, same as *Tabetic*.

**Tabid** (tæ·bid), *a.* Now *rare.* [ad. L. *tābid-us* wasting, declining, f. *tābēre* to waste: see -id. Perh. through F. *tabide* (1545 in Hatz.-Darm.).]

**1.** *Path.* Affected with tabes; wasted by disease; consumptive; marcid.

1651 Biggs *New Disp.* § 232 Whosoever within fourty daies are not perfectly cured, grow tabid. 1672 Sir T. Browne *Let. Friend* § 20 Consumptive and tabid Roots sprout more early. 1713 W. Cheselden in *Phil. Trans.* XXVIII. 281 A Man, who died Hydropic and Tabid. 1822–34 *Good's Study Med.* (ed. 4) IV. 88 Sinking..into a premature and tabid old age.

†**2.** Corrupted, decomposed. *Obs.*

1650 Bulwer *Anthropomet.* i. (1653) 24 All other Creatures were produced from the tabid Carcasses by the Celestiall influx without seed. 1657 Tomlinson *Renou's Disp.* 91 These, kept in a moyst place, become tabid.

**3.** Causing consumption, wasting, or decline.

1671 R. Bohun *Wind* 140 Dry and tabid mists, which corrupt the lungs. 1895 Quiller Couch *Wand. Heath* 92 The tabid Curse Brooded over Pelops' hearse.

**4.** Of the nature or character of tabes; characterized by wasting away.

1747 tr. *Astruc's Fevers* 136 A simple tabid fever is not so dangerous as a suppurative one. 1765 Sterne *Tr. Shandy* VII. xiv, A gradual and most tabid decline. 1822–34 *Good's Study Med* (ed. 4) IV. 92 The salacity of age..often wears away the hoary frame to the last stage of a tabid decline.

Hence **Ta·bidly** *adv.*, in a tabid manner, consumptively; **Ta·bidness**, emaciation, tabes.

1672 Sir T. Browne *Let. Friend* § 4 He that is *tabidly inclined were unwise to pass his days in Portugal. 1668 *Phil. Trans.* III. 699 How it [Sugar] intenerates the flesh, and disposeth to *tabidness. 1700 C. Leigh *Nat. Hist. Lanc.* ii. ii. § 2. 62 A tabidness of the Flesh, hot and cold fits alternately succeeding.

†**Ta·bid**, *v. Obs.* $rare^{-1}$. [f. prec.] *trans.* To make tabid or consumptive; = Tabefy 1.

1661 Feltham *Resolves* ii. lxxxv. 374 Slender Hairs..as nets to catch the dust and moats, which..we should else draw in, and tabid all our Lungs.

**Tabific** (tăbi·fik), *a. rare.* [ad. L. *tābific-us*, f. Tabes: see -fic. Cf. mod.F. *tabifique* (Littré).] Causing tabes; consumptive, emaciating, wasting.

1669 *Address hopef. yng. Gentry Eng.* 14 Whose souls languish under the irreparable decays of tabific inactivity. 1684 tr. *Bonet's Merc. Compit.* xiv. 492 The Tabifick Matter deposited in the Lungs [in Phthisis]. 1774 T. West *Antiq. Furness* p. xvii, The younger sort amongst the fair sex.. have been carried off by tabific complaints.

†**Tabi·fical**, *a. Obs.* [f. as prec. + -al: see -ical.] = prec.

1608 Topsell *Serpents* (1658) 636 So great is the tabifical effect of this poyson of Asps. 1620 Venner *Via Recta* viii. 192 [They] that are affected with tabeficall [*ed.* 1650 tabifical] passions, as sorrow, anxietie of minde [etc.]. 1657 Tomlinson *Renou's Disp.* 465 When compounded of others, its vertue is more tabifical.

**Tabil, -ill(e**, obs. forms of Table.

**Tabillette**, obs. form of Tablet.

†**Tabine.** *Obs.* App. the same as Tabby *sb.* 1, the cloth: cf. next.

1611 *Bk. of Rates* (Jam.), Tabins [*ed.* 1670 tabies] of silke, the elle v l. 1626 Middleton *Quiet Life* ii. ii. 6 Cloth of tissue or tabine That like beaten gold will shine.

**Tabinet** (tæ·binėt, -et). Also tabb-, -ette. [app. an arbitrary trade-term from Tabby, or perhaps rather from Tabine.] A watered fabric of silk and wool resembling poplin: chiefly associated with Ireland.

1778 *Phil. Surv. S. Irel.* 201 Poplins, some of which, called tabinets, have all the richness of silk. 1796 *Hist. Ned Evans* I. 162 A gown of the most beautiful Irish tabbinet. 1842–3 Thackeray *Fitz-Boodle's Confess.* Pref., Yonder she marches..in her invariable pearl-coloured tabinet. 1883 R. Haldane *Workshop Receipts* Ser. ii. 148/1 Irish Poplins and Tabinets are to be cleaned with camphine.

*attrib.* and *Comb.* 1818 Lady Morgan *Autobiog.* (1859) 294, I am still in my Dublin tabinette gowns. 1866 *Lond. Rev.* 6 Jan. 6/1 The Lord Lieutenant of Ireland..holds.. levées which serve to demoralize the middle classes into dire extravagance, and a tabinet gentility. 1886 Rosa Mulholland *Marcella Grace* i, Tabinet-weaving..is now on the wane.

**Tabiter, tabitter**, obs. forms of Taberdar.

**Ta·bitude.** $rare^{-0}$. [ad. L. *tābitūdo*, f. stem of *tābēs, tābēre, tābidus* (see Tabes, Tabid) + -tude.] The state of being affected with tabes; marasmus.

1623 Cockeram, *Tabitude*, a consumption. 1847 in Webster; and in mod. Dicts.

**Tablature** (tæ·blătiŭɹ). Also 6 tabli-, 6–9 table-, 7–9 tabulature. [app. a. F. *tablature* (1553 in Hatz.-Darm.), f. L. *tabula* table; prob. in imitation of It. *tavolatura* 'any kind of Prick-song' (Florio), f. *tavolare* to board, plank, enclose with boards; also 'to set in Musike or Prick-song' (Florio): cf. late and med.L. *tabulāre* to plank, board over (Quicherat *Addenda*; also in Du Cange) and the L. derivatives *tabulātus* boarded, *tabulātio* boarding, flooring, implying the vb.]

**1.** *Mus.* An old name for musical notation in general, esp. for systems differing from the ordinary staff notation; *spec.* a peculiar form of notation used for the lute and other stringed instruments, in which the lines of the stave denoted the several strings, and letters or figures were placed upon them to indicate the points at which they were to be 'stopped' with the fingers; also, a similar notation for the flute and other wind instruments, in which the lines denoted the several holes, and dots or dashes were placed upon them to indicate those which were to be stopped. *Obs.* exc. *Hist.*

1574 (*title*) A briefe and plaine instruction, to set all Musicke of 8 diuers Tunes in Tableture for the Lute. 1587 Golding *De Mornay* xiv. (1617) 216 The plaine and sweet Harmonie of his [the Lute player's] Tablature, as they terme it. 1596 (*title*) A new Booke of Tabliture.. shewing howe to attain the knowledge to guide and dispose thy Hand to play on sundry Instruments... Whereunto is added, an Introduction to prickesong. 1603 Holland *Plutarch's Mor.* 1046 The propositions described in the Tablature of musicians, which consisteth of five tetrachords. 1641 Evelyn *Diary* Aug., One..play'd all sorts of compositions [on a chime of bells] from the tablature before him, as if he had fingered an organ. 1724 *Short Explic. For. Wds. in Mus. Bks.*, *Tabulatura*, or *Tablature*, is the old Way of writing Musick with Letters instead of Notes. 1898 Stainer & Barrett *Dict. Mus. Terms* 426 Organ Tablature was a system of writing the notes without the stave by means of letters... Figured bass has also been called Tablature.

*fig.* 1649 Lovelace *Poems* (1864) 121 Sound all my thoughts, and see exprest The tablature of my large brest. 1656 — *Ibid.* 247 What means this stately tablature, The ballance of thy streins?

**2.** A tabular formation or structure bearing an inscription or design; a tablet. *Obs.* or *arch.*

1606 Ford *Honour Triumph.* iii. (1843) 25 Whose shames, were they enameled in the tableture of their foreheads, it would be a hideous visour. 1641 *Arminian Nunnery* in R. Brunne *Chron.* (1725) I. p. cxxxi, On the Chimney-peice ..there was a Manuscript Tableture with this Inscription following [etc.]. **1786** MURPHY *Braganza* Prol., A tableture of honour. **1820** MOIR in *Blackw. Mag.* VII. 493 Behind the massy tablatures of death. **1844** *Ibid.* LVI. 586 Ranges of headstones showed, Each on its hoary tablature,..The sculptured leer of that hyena face.

*fig.* **1633** FORD *Love's Sacr.* I. ii, You set before you, in the tablature Of your remembrance, the becoming griefs Of a most loyal lady. **1856** DOVE *Logic Chr. Faith* Introd. 15 The..same method..would obliterate them from the tablature of human knowledge.

†**3.** A painting; a picture; *spec.*: see quot. 1711.

**1711** SHAFTESB. *Charact.* (1737) III. 348 In Painting we may give to any particular Work the name of Tablature, when the Work is in reality 'a Single Piece, comprehended in one View,..which constitutes a real Whole'. **1739** MELMOTH *Fitzosb. Lett.* (1763) 188 Influenced in his censure or applause of the whole tablature, by the predominancy or deficiency of his favorite beauty. **1762** KAMES *Elem. Crit.* (1774) II. xxv. 487 He prefers the Saracen's head upon a sign-post before the best tablature of Raphael. **1767** S. PATERSON *Another Trav.* I. 86 This is the subject of the third tablature.

**b.** *collectively.* Work consisting or of the nature of paintings or pictures. ? *Obs.*

**1714** *Fr. Bk. of Rates* 44 Images painted on Wood or Linen pay as Tableture per 100 Weight. **1762-9** FALCONER *Shipwr.* III. 340 The roof, where storied tablature appear'd. **1819** *Blackw. Mag.* V. 219 To dazzle us with the tablature of splendid hues and imposing forms.

**c.** *fig.* A 'picture' formed by description or in fancy; (*pl.*) the 'pictures' or representations of memory, or the faculty of retaining these.

**1779** SHERIDAN *Critic* I. ii, Yielding a tablature of benevolence and public spirit. **1779** *Hist. Mod. Europe* II. lxx. 490 The transactions of this turbulent period I propose to comprehend in two extensive tablatures. **1860** *Bacon's Mor. & Hist. Wks., Wisd. Anc.* (Bohn) 254 How beautifully and elegantly the fable has drawn two reigning characters in human life, and given two examples, or tablatures of them, under the persons of Prometheus and Epimetheus.

**4.** *Arch.* = ENTABLATURE 1. *rare.*

**1869** A. W. WARD tr. *Curtius' Hist. Greece* II. II. iv. 84 The columns rise to bear the tabulature of marble.

†**5.** *Anat.* The tabulate structure of the skull: cf. TABLE *sb.* 16. *Obs.*

**1706** PHILLIPS (ed. Kersey), *Tablature*...In Anatomy, it signifies a Division, or parting of the Scull-bones. **1727-41** CHAMBERS *Cycl.*, *Tablature*, in anatomy, a division or parting of the scull into two tables.

**Table** (tēⁱ·b'l), *sb.* Forms: 1 **tabule, tabula,** 3 **tabele,** 5 **tabel, -yl(e, -ule,** 5-6 **-ell(e, -il, -ill(e, -ull(e, -yll(e,** 6 **-ul;** 2- **table.** [In OE. *tabule* wk. fem. (already *a* 900), later also *tabele*, ad. L. *tabula*. In ME. *table* (*a* 1200), a. F. *table* (11th c.), ad. L. *tabula* a flat board, a plank, a board to play on, a writing tablet, a written tablet, a writing, a list, an account, a painted tablet, a painting, a votive tablet, a flat piece of ground, prob. from same root as *taberna* TAVERN.

L. *tabula* became by ordinary phonetic progression in Romanic, *tavola* (as in It.), **tav'la*, *taula* (in Pr.), *tavle*, *taule* (in OF.), *tôle* (F. = sheet of metal); but in most of the langs. these phonetic forms were superseded by others assimilated to the L., as F. *table*, Sp. *tabla*, Pg. *taboa*. The word entered Teutonic at different stages; app. bef. 400 in WGer. as **tabal*, repr. by OHG. *zabal*, ON. *tafl*, board for a game, and OE. *tæfl*, *tæfel* die, tablet, ME. TAVEL, q. v.; also later, influenced by L., OHG. *tavala*, *-ela* (MHG. *tavel(e*, MLG., MDu. *tāfele*, *tāvele*, Ger., Du. *tafel*, Da. *tavle*, Sw. *tafel*) table; OE. beside *tabule* had *tabul* masc. and *tablu* fem.]

**I.** Ordinary senses. **A flat slab or board.*

**1.** A flat and comparatively thin piece of wood, stone, metal, or other solid material (usually shaped by art); a board, plate, slab, or tablet; as a slab forming the top of an altar, or part of a pavement, etc., or a tablet used for ornament or other purpose; also applied to natural formations, as the laminæ of a slaty rock. *Obs.* exc. in special applications: see also senses 2-4.

*a* **900** tr. *Bæda's Hist.* v. xi. § 2 (Camb. MS.; see ed. Miller, pp. 416, 523), Hæfdon hi mid him ȝehalȝode fato and ȝehalȝode tabulan [*MS. B.* ȝehalȝode tablu, *O.* ȝehalȝodne tabul] on wiȝbedes wrixle [L. *tabulam altaris vice*]. **13..** *E. E. Allit. P.* A. 1003 Þe calsydoyne..In þe þryd table con purly pale. *c* **1440** *Alphabet of Tales* 39 He layed hym downe before þe ya[tt], & knokkid with his tables as lepre men duse. **1447** BOKENHAM *Seyntys* (Roxb.) 35 In tablys of marbyl coryously wrout. **1507** *Acc. Ld. High Treas. Scot.* III. 253 Item, for ane tabil of gold to the Kingis bonet. **1530** PALSGR. 278/2 Table for an auter, *table dautel.* **1585** T. WASHINGTON tr. *Nicholay's Voy.* II. xx. 57 The inner part of the temple is altogether plastered and couered with great tables of Porphyre. **1672** JOSSELYN *New Eng. Rarities* 100 A fair Table curiously made up with Beads likewise, to wear before their Breast. **1687** A. LOVELL tr. *Thevenot's Trav.* II. 75, I observed by the ways side several Rocks of black Stone..which were all divided into Tables, hardly thicker than blew Slates,..but joyned very close together. **1730** W. WARREN *Collect.* in Willis & Clark *Cambridge* (1886) I. 225 A Marble Table for yᵉ Side-board on a Mohogany Stand. **1849** RUSKIN *Sev. Lamps* iii. § 17. 83 The dark, flat, solid tables of leafage. **1889** *Philos. Mag.* May 409 Strata which..lie in their original horizontal position. These parts are called 'tables' by Suess.

†**b.** A board or plank (in quots., a plank used as a raft after shipwreck); hence *fig. Obs.*

**1390** GOWER *Conf.* III. 296 He..broghte him sauf upon a table, Which to the lond him hath upbore. *c* **1440** *Gesta Rom.* lxv. 293 (Harl. MS.) Þerfor seiyth Ierome, *Penitencia est secunda tabula post naufragium*, Penaunce is the secunde table after naufragie. *a* **1533** LD. BERNERS *Huon* lvii. 194 We saued vs on a table of wode. **1617** *Janua Ling.* 6 Contrition of heart is a second table after shipwracke.

**2.** *spec.* **a.** A tablet bearing or intended for an inscription or device: as the stone tablets on which the ten commandments were inscribed, a memorial tablet fixed in a wall, a votive tablet, a notice-board, etc. *arch.*

*c* **1050** *Byrhtferth's Handboc* in *Anglia* VIII. 327 Þæra ȝeara ȝetæl hæfð seo tabule þe we mearkian willað. *c* **1175** *Lamb. Hom.* 11 Efter þan drihten him bi-tahte twa stanene tables breode on hwulche godalmihti heofde iwriten þa ten laȝe. *c* **1250** *Gen. & Ex.* 3535 And gaf to tabeles of ston, And .x. bodeword writen ðor-on. *a* **1300** *Cursor M.* 6541 Þe tables þat in hand he [Moses] bare To pees he þam brak right þar. *c* **1400** MAUNDEV. (1839) ii. 10 The table abouen his heued..on the whiche the tytle was writen, in Ebreu, Greu, and Latyn. **1543** N. HEATH *Injunctions* in Frere *Use of Sarum* II. 236 Certain prayers..conteyned in Tabylles sett in the grammer scole. **1641** EVELYN *Mem.* 4 Oct., Divers votive tables and relics. **1720** OZELL *Vertot's Rom. Rep.* I. VI. 311 The last Laws of the Decemvirs engraved upon Tables of Brass. **1849** JAMES *Woodman* viii, As stern as the statue of Moses breaking the tables.

†**b.** A small portable tablet for writing upon, esp. for notes or memoranda; a writing-tablet. Often in phr. *a pair* (*of*) *tables. Obs.*

*Rased table* = *tabula rasa*: see TABULA 1 b.

*a* **1300** *Cursor M.* 11087 Þam asked þan sir zachari Tables and a pontel tite. **1382** WYCLIF 1 *Macc.* xiv. 17 Thei wryten to hym in brasen tablis. **1387** TREVISA *Higden* (Rolls) VI. 257 Charles..bare a peyre of tables for to write ynne. **1451** CAPGRAVE *Life St. Aug.* 25 He took a peyre tables, and wroot in þe wax al his desir. **1555** EDEN *Decades* 51 Rased or vnpaynted tables are apte to receaue what formes soo euer are fyrst drawen theron. *a* **1592** GREENE *Jas. IV* Wks. (Rtldg.) 193 Draw your tables, and write what wise I speak. **1614** B. JONSON *Barth. Fair* IV. iii, I saw one of you buy a pair of tables, e'en now. **1656** STANLEY *Hist. Philos.* v. (1701) 184/1 These things are imprinted and form'd in her as in a Table.

**c.** *fig.* (from a or b). *Obs.* or *arch.*

**1382** WYCLIF 2 *Cor.* iii. 3 Writun..not in stoony tablis, but in fleischly tablis of herte. **1599** DAVIES *Immort. Soul* cccxxxv, All these true notes of Immortalitie In our Hearts Tables we shall written find. **1602** LD. MOUNTJOY *Let.* 25 Feb. in Moryson *Itin.* II. (1617) 268, I should..sooner and more easily..haue made this Countreye a rased table, wherein shee might haue written her owne lawes. **1693** BENTLEY *Serm.* (J.), The mighty volumes of visible nature, and the everlasting tables of right reason.

**d.** *Anc. Hist.* (*a*) *pl.* The tablets on which certain collections of ancient Greek and Roman laws were inscribed; hence applied to the laws themselves; esp. *the Twelve Tables*, drawn up by the decemviri B.C. 451 and 450, embodying the most important rules of Roman law, and forming the chief basis of subsequent legislation. (*b*) *New tables* (tr. L. *novæ tabulæ*): see quot. 1727-38.

**1726** AYLIFFE *Parergon* 33 By the Law of the twelve Tables, only those were called unto the Legal or Intestate Succession of their Parents, that were in the Parent's power at the time of his Death. **1727-38** CHAMBERS *Cycl.* s. v., *New Tables, Tabulæ novæ*, an edict occasionally published, in the Roman commonwealth, for the abolishing all kinds of debts, and annulling all obligations. **1788** GIBBON *Decl. & F.* xliv. (1790) VIII. 8 In the comparison of the tables of Solon with those of the Decemvirs, some casual resemblance may be found. **1847** GROTE *Greece* II. x. (1849) III. 156 There occurred at Rome several political changes which brought about new tables or at least a partial depreciation of contracts. **1875** MAINE *Hist. Inst.* i. 10 The Roman law..is descended from a small body of Aryan customs reduced to writing in the fifth century B. C., and known as the Twelve Tables of Rome.

**e.** *First, second table*: the two divisions of the decalogue, relating to religious and moral duties respectively, held to have occupied the two 'tables of stone'. Hence *attrib.*

**1560** *Maitl. Club Misc.* III. 249 Committing..adultery brekand the third command of the Second table. **1605** JAMES I *Gunpowder Plot* in *Harl. Misc.* (Malh.) III. 6 All the impieties and sins, that can be devised against both the first and second table. **1672** G. NEWTON in *Life J. Alleine* iv. (1838) 37 He was a second table man, a man of morals. **1873** H. ROGERS *Orig. Bible* i. 21 The great commands of the 'Second Table' are ultimately based on the relations in which all creatures stand to Him who demands our homage in the 'First Table'.

†**3.** A board or other flat surface on which a picture is painted; hence, the picture itself. *Obs.*

**1387** TREVISA *Higden* (Rolls) V. 399 Þe baner of þe cros wiþ a crucifix i-peynt in a table [L. *in tabula depicti*]. *a* **1425** *St. Eliz. of Spalbeck* in *Anglia* VIII. 110/5 A tabil, ful wele depeynte with an ymage of oure lorde crucifyed. **1538** STARKEY *England* I. ii. 28 Aftur the sentence of Arystotyl, the mynd of Man fyrst of hyt selfe ys as a clene and pure tabul, wherin ys no thyng payntyd or carvyd. **1538** CROMWELL in Merriman *Life & Lett.* (1902) II. 120 That he may also take the Phisionomie of her that he may ioine her sister and her in a faire table. **1606** PEACHAM *Art Drawing* 7 Cesar..redeemed the tables of Ajax and Medæa for eighty talents. **1688** R. HOLME *Armoury* III. 145/1 On this Frame [an easel] Painters set their Cloth or Table while it is in working. **1700** T. BROWN *Amusem. Ser. & Com.* 74 My Picture is not yet dry: I will bring you this Table some Months hence. *fig. c* **1600** SHAKS. *Sonn.* xxiv, Mine eye hath play'd the painter and hath steeld, Thy beauties forme in table of my heart.

†**4. a.** The 'board' on which chess, draughts, backgammon, or any similar game is played. *Obs.*

*c* **1470** *MS. Ashmole* 344 (Bodl.) lf. 22 This is a Iupertie that may neuer be mated out of the medylle of the table. **1474** CAXTON *Chesse* I. iii. (1883) 14 Then the philosophre began..to shewe hym the maner of the table of the chesse borde. **1519** HORMAN *Vulg.* lf. 280/1, I have bought a playing tabull, with xii poyntes on the one syde, and chekers on the other syde. **1688** R. HOLME *Armoury* III. 67/2 Those men as break through the other and come to the opposite side of the table, are then made kings. **1801** STRUTT *Sports & Past.* IV. ii. 437 The table for playing at goose is..divided into sixty-two small compartments arranged in a spiral form.

**b.** Each of the two folding leaves of a backgammon board (*inner* and *outer table*); hence in *pl.* (often *pair of tables*), a backgammon board (*obs.*). Also, the half of each leaf in relation to the player to whom it belongs.

**1483** *Cath. Angl.* 376 A paire of Tabyls *tabelle.* **1573** L. LLOYD *Marrow of Hist.* (1653) 136 The art of dicing and playing divers kinds of games upon tables. **1611** COTGR., *Damier*, a Chesse-boord; or, paire of Tables. **1657** *North's Plutarch, Add. Lives* (1676) 10 Necessitated to cast up the Cards, to shut the Tables, and to resign the Game. **1745** HOYLE *Backgam.* 22 Two Fours, two of them are to take your Adversary's Cinq Point in his Tables. **1779** MACKENZIE in *Mirror* No. 11 ¶ 13 [He] snatched up the tables and hit Douglas a blow on the head. **1870** HARDY & WARE *Mod. Hoyle* 141 The object of the game is to bring the men round to your own 'home', or inner table.

**c.** Phr. *To turn the tables*: to reverse the relation between two persons or parties, so as to put each in the other's place or relative condition; to cause a complete reversal of the state of affairs. In the active voice, one of the parties is said *to turn the tables* (*upon* the other), in passive, *the tables are turned* (sometimes †*the tables turn*).

(A metaphor from the notion of players reversing the position of the board so as to reverse their relative positions.)

**1634** SANDERSON *Serm.* II. 290 Whosoever thou art that dost another wrong, do but turn the tables: imagine thy neighbour were now playing thy game, and thou his. **1647** DIGGES *Unlawf. Taking Arms* iii. 70 The tables are quite turned, and your friends have undertaken the same bad game, and play it much worse. **1682** *Enq. Elect. Sheriffs* 31 Whensoever the Tables shall so far turn, as that we have a Mayor who will..drink to one of the contrary and opposite Party. **1713** ADDISON *Guard.* No. 134 ¶ 4 In short, Sir, the tables are now quite turned upon me. **1889** JESSOPP *Coming of Friars* iii. 165 Suppose the men of the thirteenth century could turn the tables upon us [etc.]. **1893** SELOUS *Trav. S. E. Africa* 33 They had won the first match, though I hoped I might yet turn the tables on them in the return.

** *A raised board at which persons may sit.*

**5.** An article of furniture consisting of a flat top of wood, stone, or other solid material, supported on legs or on a central pillar, and used to place things on for various purposes, as for meals (see 6), for some work or occupation, or for ornament.

The specific use is often indicated by a qualifying word, as in *billiard-table*, *dining-table*, *writing-table*, *work-table*, etc.: see these words. *Table dormant*, *dormant table*: see DORMANT A. 3 b. See also ROUND TABLE.

*a* **1300**, *c* **1330**, etc. [see ROUND TABLE 1 a]. *c* **1386** Table dormant [see DORMANT *a.* 3 b]. **1393** LANGL. *P. Pl.* C. XIX. 158 Crist..over-turnede in þe temple here tables and here stalles. *c* **1450** *Brut* 446 Next þaim, at the same table syttyng, þe Iustices. *a* **1562** G. CAVENDISH *Wolsey* (1893) 227 My Lord's great crosse of sylver accustumably stode in the corner, at the table's end. **1611** COTGR. s.v. *Table*, Round tables take away contention; one being as neere his meat as another. **1625** BACON *Ess., Counsel* (Arb.) 329 A long Table, and a square Table, or Seats about the Walls. **1719** DE FOE *Crusoe* I. 78 To make such necessary things as I found I most wanted, as particularly a Chair and a Table. **1853** W. IRVING in *Life & Letters* (1864) IV. 131, I see you are in the midst of hocus pocus with moving tables [etc.].

**b.** Phr. *Upon the table*: under consideration or discussion. *To lay on* or *upon the table*: of a legislative or deliberative body, to leave (a report, proposed measure, etc.) for the present, subject to its being considered or called up at any subsequent time; hence, sometimes, to defer its consideration indefinitely: so *to lie on the table.*

**1645** R. BAILLIE *Anabaptism* (1647) 163 The question of dipping and sprinkling never came upon the Table. **1817** EVANS *Parl. Deb.* 336 The petition was ordered to lie on the table. **1884** RIDER HAGGARD *Dawn* xlii, The facts are, so to speak, all upon the table, and I will merely touch upon the main heads of my case.

**6.** *spec.* An article of furniture as described in 5 upon which food is served, and at or around which persons sit at a meal; often in phr. *at table*, at a meal or meals; *for the table*, for eating at a meal, for food. (Often passing into c.)

**1377** LANGL. *P. Pl.* B. x. 101, I haue yherde hiegh men etyng atte table. *c* **1386** CHAUCER *Prol.* 100 He..carf biforn his fader at the table. *c* **1430** LYDG. *Min. Poems* (Percy Soc.) 67 Nat gredy at the table. *c* **1500** *Doctr. Gd. Servaunts* (Percy Soc.) 8 Ye servauntes that wayte upon the table. **1577** B. GOOGE *Heresbach's Husb.* IV. (1586) 163 They are a very good dishe for the table. **1638** JUNIUS *Paint. Ancients* 164 You doe consecrate your tables, by setting salt-sellers and images of Gods upon the boord. **1706** E. WARD *Wooden World Diss.* (1708) 18 He never deigns to discourse at Table with any below a Brother Captain. **1785** HOLCROFT *Tales of Castle* (ed. 2) I. 65 Just as the family were sitting down to table. **1842** S. LOVER *Handy Andy* ii, He shared in the hospitality of all the best tables in the county. **1855** DELAMER *Kitch. Gard.* (1861) 19 The greening [of potatoes]..renders them unfit for table.

†**b.** A board (cf. sense 1) upon which food is served, placed on trestles or supports (the whole constituting a 'table' in the existing sense), and

'taken up' or removed at the conclusion of the meal. *Obs.*

[**1390** *Earl Derby's Exp.* (Camden) 49/18 Pro j tabula comensali cum j pare tresteles.] *c* **1440** *Promp. Parv.* 485/1 Table, mete boord that ys borne a-wey whan' mete ys doon, *cillaba.* **15..** *Adam Bel* 569 in Hazl. *E. P. P.* II. 162 Take vp the table, anone he bad: For I may eate no more. **1612** SHELTON *Quix.* I. IV. vi. 358 Dinner being ended, and the table taken vp.

**c.** *transf.* Provision of food for meals; supply of food; fare; = BOARD *sb.* 7; entertainment of a family or guests at table; eating, feasting.

*c* **1400** *Langl.'s P. Pl.* C. XVII. 322 Hus wone is to wende in pilgrymages, Ther poure men and prysouns beþ, and payeþ for here lyflode [*v.rr.* fode, table]. **1426–7** *Rec. St. Mary at Hill* 67 Also payd for Elymesfordes table ix dayes, euery day ij d. **1602** *2nd Pt. Return fr. Parnass.* II. v. (Arb.) 30 My father..keepes an open table for all kinde of dogges. **1611** COTGR., *Tenir bonne table*, to keepe a good table, to fare well. **1672** SIR C. LYTTELTON in *Hatton Corr.* (Camden) 97 The King allowes mee..10li a weeke for a table. **1722** B. STAR tr. *Mlle. de St. Phale's Mem.* i. 4 My Mother..entertained thoughts of placing me in a Convent, paying for my Table. **1882** *Harper's Mag.* LXV. 598 Boarding at four dollars a week, and not a very good table at that. *Mod.* Too much addicted to the pleasures of the table.

**7.** Usually with defining word, as *the Lord's table, the holy table*: (*a*) In a church, that upon which the elements are placed at the Communion; the communion table: esp. when the rite is not regarded as a sacrifice (cf. ALTAR 2 b). (*b*) *transf.* The Communion.

**1340** *Ayenb.* 236 Godes table is þe wyeued. Þe coupe is þe chalis. **1526** TINDALE 1 *Cor.* x. 21 Ye cannot be parte takers off the lordes table, and off the table off devyls. **1548–9** (Mar.) *Bk. Comm. Prayer, Communion*, Not suffering them to bee partakers of the Lordes table untill he knowe them to bee reconciled. **1550** *Acts Privy Counc.* (1891) III. 170 That it was convenyent to take downe the aultars as thinges abused, and in liewe of them to sett up tables as thinges moste meete for the Supper of the Lorde, and most agreable to the first constitution. **1552** *Bk. Com. Prayer, Communion*, The Table hauyng at the Communion tyme a fayre white lynnen clothe vpon it. **1678** EVELYN *Diary* 22 Mar., Now was our communion table plac'd altar-wise. *a* **1711** KEN *Edmund* Poet. Wks. 1721 II. 203 Just in the midst was th' Holy Table plac'd, Where it the Past'ral Chair directly fac'd. *a* **1751** DODDRIDGE *Hymn*, My God, and is Thy table spread? **1890** BP. W. W. HOW *Holy Communion* II. 66 You will now have some little space of time for private prayer and meditation,..before you go up to the Holy Table. **1902** T. M. LINDSAY *Ch. & Min. in Early Cent.* vi. 254 After the celebration the faithful, who all remained in the church, came forward to the 'Table'.

**b.** In Presbyterian churches, applied also to each dispensing of the Sacrament on a Communion Sabbath.

Formerly, it was usual to have three or more 'tables', one after another; it is still common to have two. *To fence the tables*: see FENCE *v.* 9.

**1709** [see FENCE *v.* 9]. **1714** T. BOSTON *Mem.* 24 Aug., I communicated at the fourth table. **1840** R. McCHEYNE in *Mem.* v. 133 At the last table every head seemed bent like a bulrush while A. B. spoke.

**8.** *transf.* A company of persons at a table.

*c* **1330–1485** [see ROUND TABLE 1 c]. **1532** MORE *Confut. Tindale* III. 177 Lyke a iugler that conuayeth his galles so craftely, that all the table spyeth them. **1890** DOYLE *White Company* ix, King Arthur and all his table could not have done more.

**b.** The company at dinner or at a meal.

**1602** SHAKS. *Ham.* v. i. 211 Your flashes of Merriment that were wont to set the Table on a Rore. **1750** JOHNSON *Rambler* No. 75 ⁋ 15 He..carries me the first dish, in defiance of the frowns and whispers of the table. **1778** *Phil. Surv. S. Irel.* 424 His flashes of wit and humour keep the table in a roar.

**c.** An official body of persons who sit at a table for the transaction of business; = BOARD *sb.* 8 b. *Obs.* exc. in special connexions.

*The Tables* in *Sc. Hist.*, the permanent committees formed in 1638, to defend the Presbyterian system, by whom the *National Covenant* was framed. *Table of Magnates* and *of Deputies*, the two divisions of the Hungarian Diet.

**1606** BRYSKETT *Civ. Life* 8, I my selfe can testifie with how good contentment of all the table you did serue so many yeares. **1640–1** *Kirkcudbr. War-Comm. Min. Bk.* (1855) 40 For the foirsaid ryot,..and for the upbraiding of the table, by saying that he was committit to ward without ane fault. **1647** CLARENDON *Hist. Reb.* III. § 52 Committees of dexterous men have been appointed out of the Table to do the business of it. **1654** H. L'ESTRANGE *Chas. I* (1655) 149 In despight of the Kings Proclamation, [they] erected Four Tables, one of the Nobility, another of the Gentry, a third of the Burroughs, a fourth of the Ministers; these four were to prepare and digest what was to be propounded at the General Table. **1665** *Nicholas Papers* (Camden) II. 336 Impositions without parliament, committments by councell table. **1673** *Essex Papers* (Camden) 96 There were then two elections in being, one made by ye Lord Mayor in ye presence & wth ye consent of a Table of Aldermen & Sheriffs, & another by ye Lord Mayor singly, in ye presence of a Table of Aldermen & Sheriffs. **1890** BLAIR *Bellesheim's Hist. Cath. Ch. Scot.* IV. 5 The National Covenant..was framed by four committees called the Tables.

**9.** A table on which some game of chance is played; a gaming-table; also, the company of players at such a table.

**1750** JOHNSON *Rambler* No. 15 ⁋ 11, I perpetually embarrassed my partner, and soon perceived the contempt of the whole table gathering upon me. **1770** FOOTE *Lame Lover* II. Wks. 1799 II. 80 Lady Cicely..has six tables every Sunday. **1826** DISRAELI *Viv. Grey* v. xiii, The plan will be for two to bank against the table. **1879** W. COLLINS *Haunted Hotel* iii. 21 A gambler at every 'table' on the Continent.

**** A tabulated arrangement or statement.*

**10.** An arrangement of numbers, words, or items of any kind, in a definite and compact form, so as to exhibit some set of facts or relations in a distinct and comprehensive way, for convenience of study, reference, or calculation. Now chiefly applied to an arrangement in columns and lines occupying a single page or sheet, as the multiplication table, tables of weights and measures, a table of logarithms, astronomical tables, insurance tables, TIME-TABLES, etc. But formerly sometimes merely: An orderly arrangement of particulars, a list.

*c* **1386** CHAUCER *Frankl. T.* 545 Hise tables tolletanes forth he brought Ful wel corrected ne ther lakked nought. *c* **1391** — *Astrol.* II. § 45 So many ȝeris, monythis, & dayes entere in-to thy tabelis of thy mene mote. *c* **1400** *Prymer* (1891) 13 In this table men mowe knowe..what day schal be Ester day. **1553** EDEN *Treat. Newe Ind.* (Arb.) 8 The most parte of Globes and mappes are made after Ptolomeus Tables. **1617** MORYSON *Itin.* To Rdr., A briefe Table expressing the value of the small Coynes most commonly spent. **1660** J. MOORE *Arith.* II. 5 All decimal Arithmetick is brought to that scale or degree..as appears by the Table in the beginning of my other Book. **1674** The multiplication-table [see MULTIPLICATION 6]. **1712** ADDISON *Spect.* No. 421 ⁋ 8 A Table of the principal Contents in each Paper. **1758** REID tr. *Macquer's Chem.* I. 159 Explanation of the Table of Affinities. **1808** PIKE *Sources Mississ.* III. 221 A statistical table, on which he had in a regular manner taken the whole province of New Mexico,..giving latitude, longitude, and population. **1858** BUCKLE *Civiliz.* (1864) II. ii. 182 Tables of mortality. **1863–72** WATTS *Dict. Chem.* I. 464 Table of Atomic Weights.

†**b.** *absol.* = *Table of contents* (CONTENT *sb.*[1] 2 b): a concise and orderly list of contents, or an index; in quot. 1460 applied to a concordance. *Obs.*

**1460** CAPGRAVE *Chron.* (Rolls) 154 He was eke the first begynner of the Concordauns, which is a tabil onto the Bibil. *c* **1550** H. LLOYD *Treas. Health*, The table of this boke. **1583** (*title*) The Newe Testament..with a Table or Concordance, Englished by L. Tomson. **1614** SELDEN *Titles Hon.* Pref. B iij, Out of the Title, Table, and Contents of the Chapters..the Summe and Method discouer themselues. **1707** MORTIMER *Husb.* (1721) I. 393 A Table to the First Volume. **1824** J. JOHNSON *Typogr.* I. 317 The Work contains three Prologues and a Table, which occupy nine leaves.

†**c.** A statement of particulars or details in a concise form, so as to be exhibited at one view, as in a broadside; a synoptical statement; a document embodying such a statement. In quot. *a* 1577 *fig.* a sketch, plan, scheme. *Obs.*

**1560** DAUS tr. *Sleidane's Comm.* XVIII. 260 b, *margin*, The Protestauntes answer to the table of outlawery. *a* **1577** SIR T. SMITH *Commw. Eng.* (1609) 134 This being as a project or table of a Commonwealth truly laid before you. **1593–4** (Mar. 20) *Proclam. Privy Counc.* in Arb. *Garner* I. 299 In this brief Table is set down the punishment appointed for the offenders. **1599** MASSINGER, etc. *Old Law* II. i, He bought a table, indeed, Only to learn to die by 't.

†**d.** *Geographical table*: a map or chart. *Obs.*

**1610** HOLLAND *Camden's Brit.* (1637) 106 A chorographicall table or mappe of Britaine. **1654** tr. *Martini's Conq. China* A iij b, I thought it good to prefix a little Geographical table of the Countries, and chief Cities, which might serve as a guide to conduct the eye of the understanding.

**e.** *Tables*: the common arithmetical tables, as the multiplication table and those of money, weights, and measures, esp. as learnt at school.

**1828** MISS MITFORD *Village* Ser. III. 125 (*Village Schoolmistress*) She is going to be a governess..and it's to be hoped the little ladies will take kindly to their tables. **1893** K. GRAHAME *Pagan Papers* (1894) 127 He had 'gone into tables', and had been endowed with a new slate.

**II.** Special and technical senses (chiefly arising out of sense 1).

†**11.** *pl.* **Tables**, formerly the ordinary name of BACKGAMMON (*Obs.* since *c* 1750); app. orig. the 'men' or pieces used in playing early forms of this game: cf. med.L. *tabulæ*, OF. *tables*, ON. *tafla*, pl. *töflur*, in same sense.

Chiefly in the phr. *to play at* (*the*) *tables*, OF. *juer as tables* (*Chans. Rol.* 11th c.). In this application the name has in later use been often associated with sense 4 b.

[*a* **700** *Epinal Gl.* 6 *Alea* teblae. *c* **725** *Corp. Gl.* 110 *Alea* tebl.] **1297** R. GLOUC. (Rolls) 3965 Wiþ pleynge atte tables oþer atte chekere. *a* **1300** *Cursor M.* 28338 (Cott.), I ha me liked..til idel gammes, chess and tablis. **1330** R. BRUNNE *Chron. Wace* (Rolls) 11392 Somme pleide wyþ des & tables. *c* **1386** CHAUCER *Parson's T.* ⁋ 719 Now comth hasardrie with hise apurtenances as tables and Rafles. **1472** *Surtees Misc.* (1888) 25 John Coke suffers men to play in his hous at the tablez for mony by nyghtes. *a* **1548** HALL *Chron., Hen. VIII* 149 b, A proclamacion..against al vnlawfull games..in all places, Tables, Dice, Cardes, and Boules, were taken and brent. **1665** PEPYS *Diary* 21 Sept., After losing a crowne betting at Tables, we walked home. **1700** S. L. tr. *Fryke's Voy. E. Ind.* 10 Tables & Draughts are allowed, yet must they not play at them for Money. **1808** SCOTT *Marm.* I. xxii, Full well at tables can he play, And sweep at bowls the stake away.

**12.** *Arch.* **a.** A general term for a horizontal projecting course or moulding, as a cornice; a string-course. Usually with defining word, as *base-table, bench-t., corbel-t., earth-t., grass-t., ground-t., water-t.*: see these words.

**13..** *Gaw. & Gr. Knt.* 789 Ande eft a ful huge heȝt hit haled vpon lofte, Of harde hewen ston vp to þe tablez. **1447–8** Corbel table [see CORBEL *sb.* 3]. **1640** Ground-table [see GROUND *sb.* 18]. **1688** R. HOLME *Armoury* III. 472/1 The Foot Table, is a Square Corner standing out at the bottom, or middle sides of the Gable end. **1845** PARKER *Gloss. Archit.* (ed. 3) 357 The word table, when used separately without any adjunctive term to point out its position, appears to have signified the cornice, but it is very usually associated with other epithets which define its situation, as *base-table, earth-table*, or *ground-table, bench-table, corbel-table*, &c. *Ibid.*, *Earth Table*, or *Ground Table*, and *Grass Table*, the plinth of a wall.., or lowest course of projecting stones immediately above the ground.

**b.** A member consisting of a flat vertical surface, usually of rectangular form, plain or ornamented, sunk in or projecting beyond the general surface of a wall, etc.; a panel.

**1678** MOXON *Mech. Exerc.* No. 6. 113 In Plate 6. *s* is the Table. **1703** MAUNDRELL *Journ. Jerus.* (1721) 37 A large Table plain'd in the side of the Rock. **1727–41** CHAMBERS *Cycl.* s. v. *Pedestal*, The generality of architects..use tables or pannels, either in relievo or creux, in the dyes of pedestals. **1823** P. NICHOLSON *Pract. Build.* 594 Table, projecting or raised. *Ibid.*, Table, raking; one not perpendicular to the horizon. **1876** GWILT *Archit.* Gloss. s. v., When the surface is rough, frosted, or vermiculated, from being broken with the hammer, it is called a *rusticated table*.

**13.** †**a.** A plot of ground for planting; a bed. Cf. TABLEMEAL. *Obs. rare.*

*c* **1440** *Pallad. on Husb.* I. 810 Mark oute thi tables [*gloss* beddes], ichon by hem selve. *Ibid.* II. 99 [heading *De tabulis vinearum*] The tables for thi vynes maist thou make..as the list, or as thi lande Wol axe.

**b.** A flat elevated tract of land; a table-land, plateau; a flat mountain-top; also *Geol.* applied to a horizontal stratum.

**1587** HARRISON *England* I. i. 1/2 Albeit the continent hereof..lieth as it were a long table betweene the two seas. **1607** TOPSELL *Four-f. Beasts* (1658) 428 There was a Region, called by Ptolemeus, *Randa marcostra*, wherein he placeth the eleventh Table of Asia. **1634** SIR T. HERBERT *Trav.* 13 The ascent to the Sugar-loafe and Table [Table Mountain], two Hils so named. **1869** TOZER *Highl. Turkey* I. 155 A valley..nearly..filled up from side to side by a level table of land. **1888** J. D. WHITNEY *Names & Places* 181 (Cent. D.) The flat summits of mountains are sometimes called 'tables', and especially in California, where there are several 'table mountains'..capped usually with horizontal or table-like masses of basalt.

**c.** A flat hedge-bank: see quot. *dial.*

**1844** STEPHENS *Bk. Farm* II. 574 The hedger lays them, with the grass side downwards, upon the edges of the set-sods,..pushing them under and as if to support the thorn roots with them. These..are called the *table*.

**14.** *Palmistry.* The quadrangular space between certain lines in the palm of the hand: see quots., and cf. *table-line* in 22.

*c* **1460** METHAM *Wks.* 86 The fourthe lyne ys the tabyl lyne, for that parte off the hand ys clepyd the tabyl the qwyche ys be-twene the myd lyne and the tabyl lyne. **1596** SHAKS. *Merch. V.* II. ii. 167 If anie man in Italie haue a fairer table which doth offer to sweare vpon a booke, I shall haue good fortune. **1625** SHIRLEY *Love Tricks* v. i. (1631) 63 In this table Lies your story; 'tis no fable, Not a line within your hand But I easily vnderstand. **1653** R. SANDERS *Physiogn.* 87 This space is called the Table of the hand, which hath on the one side the Mensal Line, on the other the middle Natural Line. **1883** FRITH & HERON-ALLEN *Chiromancy* 138 The Quadrangle is that portion of the human hand comprised between the line of the Head and the line of the Heart, and between the line of Fate and the line of Apollo. It is sometimes called the table of the Hand.

**15.** †**a.** A small cake of some drug or confection: = TABLET *sb.* 3. *Obs.*

**1580** FRAMPTON *Monardi's Dial. Yron* 162 Then take a small table of rosade of a sweete smel. **1621** VENNER *Tobacco* (1650) 410 Tables made with an Ounce or two of fine Sugar dissolved in Fennell water.

**b.** A large flat circular disk, plate, or sheet of crown-glass, being the form in which it is made.

**1688** R. HOLME *Armoury* III. 385/2 A *Table* is a broad peece of Glass neere a yard, some more, square, it is also called a Tablet. **1727–41** CHAMBERS *Cycl.* s. v. *Glass*, The number of tables annealed at a time. *Ibid.*, Ratcliff crown glass..the tables being of a circular form, about three foot six inches in diameter. **1823** P. NICHOLSON *Pract. Build.* 420 The glass is bought by the crate, which consists of twelve tables. **1890** W. J. GORDON *Foundry* 144 The 'table' of crown glass is from four to five feet across.

**c.** A crystal of flattened or short prismatic form.

**1796** KIRWAN *Elem. Min.* (ed. 2) I. 362 Crystallized in rhomboidal tables. **1805–17** R. JAMESON *Char. Min.* (ed. 3) 106 Table..is but a very short prism. **1857** MILLER *Elem. Chem.* (1862) III. 542 The acid benzoate of potash..in colourless, pearly tables,..sparingly soluble in water.

**d.** A sheet (of lead).

**1809** BAWDWEN *Domesday Bk.* 294 These manors paid in King Edward's time..five cartloads of lead of fifty tables [orig. *v plaustratas plumbi de l tabulis*].

**16.** *Anat.* Each of the two dense bony layers of the skull, separated by the diploë.

**1612** WOODALL *Surg. Mate* Wks. (1653) 3 If a Fracture happen in the Cranium, with contusion and depression of both the Tables thereof. **1799** HOOPER *Med. Dict.*, *Diploe* ..the spongy substance between the two tables of the skull. **1898** *Syd. Soc. Lex.* s. v., The inner or vitreous table is compared to porcelain, and is close-grained and brittle.

**17.** A flat plate, board, or the like, forming part of a mechanism or apparatus.

†**a.** The face or dial-plate of a clock or watch.

*a* **1677** HALE *Prim. Orig. Man.* IV. iv. 326 To fit the Table with Divisions suitable to the Hours. *Ibid.* vi. 341 The Wheels, and the Ballance, and the Case, and Table.

**b.** In various manufactures, A flat metal plate

(often movable or adjustable) for supporting something to be operated upon, etc.; the plate with a raised rim on which plate-glass is made.

1727-41 CHAMBERS *Cycl.* s. v. *Glass*, The table of glass is now in its last perfection...When taken out, they lay it on a table of copper. 1832 G. R. PORTER *Porcelain & Gl.* 200 Another essential part of the apparatus consists in flat tables whereon the plates of glass are cast. 1833 J. HOLLAND *Manuf. Metal* II. 238 By turning the wheel, the table E is drawn between the cylinders, the counterpoise F rising accordingly. 1839 URE *Dict. Arts* 590 Whenever the melted glass is poured out, two men spread it over the table. 1877 KNIGHT *Dict. Mech.* 2477/2 The shaping-machine..has two tables for holding work both of which are movable up and down..and longitudinally. 1892 [see *table-loader* in 22].

**c.** (See quot.)

1763 MILLS *Pract. Husb.* I. 332 M. Duhamel's drill is fastened to the fore-carriage of a common plough. The hind part consists of a plank..at least three inches thick, which is called the table.

**d.** In an organ: (*a*) The upper part of the sound-board, above the sound-board bars and grooves, perforated with holes for admitting air to the pipes. (In quot. 1852 applied to the sound-board bars.) (*b*) The upper board of the bellows.

1852 SEIDEL *Organ* 52 These partitions are called *grooves*, and the ledges..by which they are separated, *tables*. 1881 C. A. EDWARDS *Organs* 49 The top of the sound-board, technically called the table. 1881 W. E. DICKSON *Organ-Build.* vi. 72 Organ-bellows..consist of three main boards, namely, the middle board, the top board or table [etc.].

**e.** 'The board or bar in a draw-loom to which the tails of the harness are attached' (Knight, 1877).

**f.** *Shipbuilding.* = COAK *sb.* 1, q. v.

Cf. TABLE *v.* 6, TABLING *vbl. sb.* 7.

**g.** *Plain table* (surveying instrument): see PLANE-TABLE.

**18. a.** The upper horizontal surface of a table diamond or a brilliant. **b.** Short for TABLE DIAMOND; also applied to other precious stones cut in a similar form.

1530 *Lett. & Pap. Hen. VIII*, IV. No. 6789 (P. R. O.), iiij diamantes wherof ij poynted and ij tables. 1538 *Acc. Ld. High Treas. Scotl.* VII. 14 Ane grete diamand sett in table for the quenis spousing ring. 1703 *Lond. Gaz.* No. 3929/4 Two single Stone Diamond Rings, Tables. 1751 D. JEFFERIES *Treat. Diamonds* (ed. 2) Explan. Techn. Terms, The Table is the large horizontal plane, or face, at the top of the Brilliant. 1861 W. POLE in *Macm. Mag.* III. 184/2 The apex of the upper pyramid is cut off to a considerable extent, and the large facet thus formed is called the *table*. 1904 *19th Cent.* July 136 A necklace of carnelian, 'cut in tables', is deemed worthy of being handed down to posterity as an heirloom.

**19.** *Perspective.* A name for the perspective plane, or 'plane of the picture': see PLANE *sb.*[3] 1 d. (Cf. sense 3.) ? *Obs.*

1727-41 CHAMBERS *Cycl.*, *Table*, in perspective, denotes a plain surface, supposed to be transparent, and perpendicular to the horizon. 1876 in GWILT *Archit.* Gloss.

**20.** = TABULA 2.

1891 in *Cent. Dict.*

**III.** *attrib.* and *Comb.*

**21. a.** Simple attrib.: in sense 5, 'of a table': as *table-drawer*, *-head*, *-leg*; in sense 6, 'of the dinner-table': as *table-companion*, *-fellow*, (*-fellowship*), *-friend*, *-guest*, *-jester*, *-mate*, *-parasite*, *-patron*, †*-peer* (= -companion), *-servant*, *-steward*; *table argument*, *collection*, *conference*, *conversation*, *fellowship*, *gratification*, *manner*, *philosophy*; of implements, etc. used at table, as *table-fork*, *-furniture*, *-garnish*; of articles of food or drink, consumed or adapted for consumption at table, as *table ale*, *beer*, *bird*, *cider*, *dainty*, *delicacy*, *drink*, *fish*, *fruit*, *honey*, *mustard*, *potato*, *salt*. **b.** Objective, etc., as *table-jogging*, *-serving*, *-setting*, etc. **c.** Having the form of a table; having a wide horizontal surface on which things may be placed, as *table-cabinet*, *-screen*, *-stage*, etc.; *table-formed*, *table-like* adjs.

1547 SALESBURY *Welsh Dict.*, *Ailcwrwf*, *table ale. 1848 DICKENS *Dombey* xviii, Mrs. Wickam..takes more table-ale than usual. 1632 *Star Chamb. Cases* (Camden) 100 It is hard I confesse to call in question for all that is spoaken at table; and yet this should not have been a *table argument. 1643 in *10th Rep. Hist. MSS. Comm.* App. IV. 435, 2 hogsheades of stronge beere, 1 hogshead of *table beere. 1830 M. DONOVAN *Dom. Econ.* I. 207 Table-beer should have the characters of an ale, not of porter. 1884 *St. James' Gaz.* 22 Aug. 4/2 The capercailzie..as a *table bird..will prove a disappointment. 1851 MANTELL *Petrifact.* iii. § 1. 136 The floor [of a room in Brit. Mus.] being occupied by twenty-six *Table-cabinets. 1902 *Daily Chron.* 17 May 6/4 There are many families who make it a habit to have a *table collection each week for some religious or philanthropic work. 1656 BLOUNT *Glossogr.*, *Commensal*, a *Table-companion. 1861 THACKERAY *Four Georges* iv. (1876) 107 His next set of friends were mere table companions. 1712 ADDISON *Spect.* No. 495 ¶ 9 This shuts them out from all *Table Conversation. 1802 WOLCOTT (P. Pindar) *Ld. Belgrave & Motions* Wks. 1812 IV. 523 Every *table-dainty, flesh and fish. *c* 1813 MRS. SHERWOOD *Stories Ch. Catech.* xvi. 137 To look in the *table-drawer, for a little book. 1817 LADY MORGAN *France* I. (1818) I. 65 The *table-drink of the poorest peasantry. 1592 G. HARVEY *Four Lett.* Wks. (Grosart) I. 208 The *Table-fellow of Duke Humfrey, & Tantalus, might learne of him to curse Iupiter. 1863 HAWTHORNE *Our Old Home* (1879) 356, I was meditating in what way this grisly featured table-fellow might..be accosted. 1903 *Hibbert Jrnl.* Mar. 614 James's scruples about *table-fellowship between Jewish and Gentile believers in Gal. ii. 12. 1897 *Outing* (U. S.) XXX. 435/2 Pickerel were better *table-fish. 1842 J. AITON *Domest. Econ.* (1857) 110 The scones should be pricked with a *table-fork or small pointed wooden pin. *a* 1843 SOUTHEY *Comm.-pl. Bk.* (1849) IV. 408 The mountains are *table-formed. 1586 T. B. *La Primaud. Fr. Acad.* I. (1594) 135 We must shun such parasites, who are but saluting and *table friends. 1707 MORTIMER *Husb.* (1721) II. 293 The Fig-apple is a good *Table-Fruit. 1861 *Our Eng. Home* 11 The *table garnish was not very extensive, a few wooden platters, some knives and spoons ..were the principal articles. 1773 MELMOTH *Remarks on Cato* 229 (Jod.) A moderate indulgence..in the *table gratifications. *a* 1592 GREENE *Jas. IV*, Wks. (Rtldg.) 188 1, I found *table-guests to eat me and my meat. 1733 SWIFT *On Poetry* 264 Battus from the *table-head,..Gives judgment with decisive air. 1865 KINGSLEY *Herew.* xix, At the table-head..sat..the new Lord of Bourne. 1571 GOLDING *Calvin on Ps.* xxxv. 16 Ye *tablejesters, which gave their verdict of his death among the cups. 1891 *Pall Mall G.* 29 Oct. 2/1 There was a certain amount of *table-jogging and spilling of liquors. *c* 1870 TENNYSON in *Daily News* 1 Mar. (1898) 7/5, I am convinced that God and the ghosts of men would choose something other than mere *table-legs through which to speak to the heart of man. 1904 *Daily Chron.* 28 July 4/7 What the Americans would call his '*table-manners'. 1624 GATAKER *Mariage Praier* 19 [Woman] was..giuen to man, not to be a play-fellow, or a bed-fellow, or a *table-mate, onely with him,..but to be a yoake-fellow, a worke-fellow, a fellow-labourer with him. 1797 *Encycl. Brit.* (ed. 3) XIII. 192/1 Leaving a cake behind, fit for making the common *table-mustard. 1751 WARBURTON in *Pope's Wks.* (1806) IV. 7 A detected Slanderer, a *Table-Parasite, a Church-Buffoon, and a Party-Writer. 1576 FLEMING *Panopl. Epist.* 14, I knowe you are no *table patrones. 1605 SYLVESTER *Du Bartas* II. iii. *Law* 843 God's pensioner, and Angel's *Table-peer, O Israel! 1576 R. JOHNES (*title*) The Schoolemaster; or Teacher of *Table Philosophie. 1593 G. HARVEY *Pierce's Super.* Wks. (Grosart) II. 34 It is another Table-Philosophy, that I fansie. 1807 VANCOUVER *Agric. Devon* (1813) 200 The produce of the *table potatoe crop seldom falls short of 350 bushels. 1878 GURNEY *Crystallogr.* 84 Common *table salt crystallises in this form. 1881 A. C. GRANT *Bush Life Queensl.* I. vii. 85 The fleece, gathered carefully with both hands is conveyed to a long *table-screen. 1882 FLOYER *Unexpl. Baluchistan* 163 He had appointed himself *table servant. 1907 *Philippine Education* Sept. 46/1 We had a few lessons in *table-setting. 1867 J. HOGG *Microsc.* I. ii. 88 Below the *table-stage is the secondary or sub-stage.

**22.** Special Combs.: **table-allowance**, an allowance of money for provisions (= *table money* (*a*)); **table-almanac**, an almanac on a single sheet or card; **table-anvil**, 'a small anvil adapted to be screwed to a table for bending plates of metal or wires, making small repairs, etc.' (Knight 1877); †**table balas**: see BALAS, and cf. TABLE DIAMOND, RUBY; **table-bat** [BAT *sb.*[2] 11], ? a horizontal stratum of 'bat' or shale in a bed of coal; **table-bed**: see quot.; **table-bell**, a small hand-bell placed upon the table for summoning attendants; **table-bit**: see quot.; †**table-carpet**, a woollen table-cloth (see CARPET *sb.* 1); **table-centre**, a piece of embroidery, decorated work, etc., for the centre of a table, placed over the table-cloth; **table-churn**, a churn placed upon a table; **table-clamp**, a clamp for fastening something to a table; **table-clock**, a clock that is or may be placed on a table; **table-couch**, a couch for reclining on at table; **table-counter**, a counter of the form of a table; **table-cover**, a cloth of wool or other fabric used for covering a table permanently or when not in use for meals (= TABLE-CLOTH b); †**table-coverer**, an attendant who 'covered' the table, i. e. laid the cloth, etc. for a meal (see COVER *v.*[1] 2 d); **table-crumb**, a crumb that falls from the table at a meal; †**table-decker** = *table-coverer*; **table-discourse**, discourse at table, table-talk; **table-faced** *a.* = TABLE-CUT (see sense 18); **table-flap**, a hinged flap or 'leaf' at the end or side of a table, which can be raised so as to extend the surface; †**table-gesture** [GESTURE *sb.* 2], posture or attitude at table, i. e. at a meal; **table-glass**, (*a*) glass made in 'tables' (see 15 b), crown-glass; (*b*) a glass (drinking-vessel) for use at table; †**table-gospeller**, one who makes table-talk of the gospel; one whose religion is mere talk; **table-grinder**, 'a form of grinding-bench' (Knight *Dict. Mech.* 1877); **table-ground**, flat elevated ground (cf. TABLE-LAND); **table-knife**, a knife used at table, esp. one of the shape or size used in cutting the meat small; **table-knight**, a knight who sits at some one's table, *spec.* at the ROUND TABLE; **table-lathe**, a small lathe clamped to a table when in use; **table-leaf** [LEAF *sb.* 12 c], (*a*) = *table-flap*; (*b*) any additional piece which can be inserted so as to extend the surface of a table; also *attrib.* **table-leaf joint**, the form of joint, with one part convex and the other concave, used in a hinged table-leaf; **table-lifting**, the lifting of a table by supposed spiritual agency (cf. TABLE-TURNING); **table-line**, in *Palmistry*, a line running from beneath the little finger to the base of the index-finger, forming the upper boundary of the 'table'; **table-linen**, linen for use at table, as table-cloths and table-napkins; **table-loader**, one who loads the hoist-table of a lift; **table-maid**, a domestic servant who lays the table and waits at meals; **table-maker**, a joiner who makes tables; **table-matter** (*Printing*) = *table-work*; **table-money**, (*a*) an extra allowance of money made to the higher officers in the British army and navy for table expenses; (*b*) a charge made in some clubs for the use of the dining-room; also, an extra charge in some restaurants; †**table-monument**, a monument consisting of a 'table' (sense 2 a); a monumental tablet; **table-mountain**, a flat-topped mountain; *spec.* the name of the mountain which rises behind Cape Town; **table-moving**, the moving of a table by supposed spiritual agency (cf. TABLE-TURNING); **table-music**, music in parts, so printed (as in some early books of madrigals, etc.) that the performers, sitting at opposite sides of a table, can read their respective parts from the same page or opening; **table-napery** = *table-linen*; **table-napkin**, a napkin used at meals to protect the clothes from being soiled, to wipe the fingers, etc.; **table-pew**, a large pew containing the communion-table, as formerly usual in some Presbyterian and other churches; †**table-picture**, a picture painted on a 'table' (sense 3); **table-plain**, an elevated plain, a table-land; **table-plane**, a plane for making rule-joints in table-flaps, etc.; **table-plank**, a plank serving as a table when placed upon supports; cf. 6 b; **table-plate**, (*a*) articles of plate (PLATE *sb.* 15), for use at meals; (*b*) a plate (usually of earthenware) from which food is eaten at table; (*c*) a flat metal plate on which pulverized gold or silver ore is treated with mercury in the process of amalgamation; †**table-play**, play at 'tables' or backgammon; so †**table-player**, †**tables-playing**; **table-prayers**, a name for the communion service, or a part of it, read at the communion-table, but without administration; †**table-rent**: see quot.; **table-rock**, a flat-topped rock; †**table-room**, room or place at table, i. e. at meals; board; **table-saw**, a small saw fitted to a table and worked by a treadle; **table-service**, (*a*) the Communion service (in Presbyterian churches); (*b*) service or attendance at table; (*c*) a set of utensils for the table, as a dinner-service; **table-shore**, *Naut.*, a low level shore; **table-sod**, in hedging, one of the sods forming the 'table' (sense 13 c); **table-song**, (*a*) *Gr. Antiq.*, a song sung by the guests at a banquet in turn; (*b*) a part-song such as is sung in a German *liedertafel* or choral society (*Cent. Dict.*); **table-spar**, a name for WOLLASTONITE, also called *tabular spar*, occurring in 'tables' or flat crystals; **table-sport**, sport or play at table; in quot., an object of sport or mockery at table, the butt or laughing-stock of a company; **table-tapping** = TABLE-RAPPING; **table-tennis**, a parlour game resembling lawn-tennis, played upon a table: = PING-PONG; **table-tilting**, **-tipping**, the tilting or tipping of a table by supposed spiritual agency (cf. TABLE-TURNING); so **table-tipper**, one who practises table-tipping; **table-tomb**, a tomb in the Roman catacombs containing a burial-chest with a flat cover; any tomb in some way resembling a table; **table-top**, (*a*) the upper surface of a table; (*b*) a flat top of a hill, rock, etc.; **table-topped** (-tǫpt) *a.*, having a flat top like that of a table; **table-tree**, an adjustable table-like rest mounted on a lathe; **table-turf** = *table-sod*; **table-vessel**, a vessel for use at table; † such vessels collectively (*obs.*); **table-water**, water (*esp.* a mineral water) suitable for drinking at table; **table-wheel**: see quot.; **table-work** (*Printing*), the setting up of tables (sense 10), or of matter between column rules; *concr.* printed matter of this kind, as distinguished from ordinary letter-press. See also TABLE-BOARD, -BOOK, -CLOTH, etc.

1810 WELLINGTON in Gurw. *Desp.* (1838) V. 598, I beg that you will draw a *table allowance of thirty shillings a day. 1621 *Stationers' Register* (Arb.) IV. 11 *Table almanacke on a sheet of paper. 1530 *Lett. & Papers Hen. VIII*, IV. No. 6789 (P.R.O.) A goodly carkeyn with a fayr *table balasse. 1712 F. BELLERS in *Phil. Trans.* XXVII. 542 The *Table-Bat, next under the Rubble Iron-Stone. 1773 JOHNSON, **Tablebed*, a bed of the figure of a table. 1858 SIMMONDS *Dict. Trade*, **Table-bell*, a small hand-bell for summoning domestics or office attendants. 1843 HOLTZAPFFEL *Turning* II. xxiv. 539 The spoon-bit..the *table-bit, for making the holes for the wooden joints of tables, [is] of this kind. 1715 J. CHAPPELOW *Rt. Way Rich* (1717) 144 *Table-carpets or bed-coverlets. 1901 *Lady's Realm* X. 616 This white satin *table-centre is decorated with ribbon, lace, braid, and embroidery. 1844 STEPHENS *Bk. Farm* III. 906 For this purpose, there is perhaps none better than the *Table-churn. 1774 *Chron.* in *Ann. Reg.* 121/1 A *table-clock, a silver spoon, and a silk gown. 1877 C. Geikie *Christ* lviii. (1879) 704 Lazarus reclined with him on the *table-couch. 1667 in Pettus *Fodinæ Reg.* (1670) 36 One *Table-counter with Cupboards, Shelves, etc. 1851 Mayhew *Lond. Labour* I. 388 Sellers of Japanned *table-covers.. The glazed table-covers. 1864 Webster, *Table-cover*, a cloth for covering a table, especially at other than meal-times. 1737 J. Chamberlayne *St. Gt. Brit.* (ed. 33) ii. iii. 220 *Table-Coverer to the Chaplains. 1726–46 Thomson *Winter* 255 Till, more familiar grown, the *table-crums Attract his [the redbreast's] slender feet. 1804 J. Grahame *Sabbath* (1808) 34 Where little birds..Light on the floor, and peck the table-crumbs. 1737 J. Chamberlayne *St. Gt. Brit.* (ed. 33) ii. iii. 228 *Table-Deckers. 1843 Macaulay *Ess., Mme. d'Arblay* (1887) 755 The whole Palace from Gold Stick in Waiting down to the Table-Deckers. 1611 Cotgr. s. v. *Table*, *Table-discourse is an excellent Schoole-maister. 1659 *Burton's Diary* (1828) IV. 395 It is their table discourse that we shall be ruined. 1877 W. Jones *Finger-ring* 366 The other ring is also of gold, with a square *table-faced diamond. 1858 Simmonds *Dict. Trade*, **Table-flap*, the leaf of a folding-table. 1641 Sanderson *Serm.* (1681) II. 8 They, using the liberty of that power, had appointed sitting or standing, rather than kneeling, as judging either of them a more proper *table gesture than it. 1646 Sir T. Browne *Pseud. Ep.* 241 Many..(though they concede a table-gesture) will hardly allow this usuall way of Session. 1727–41 Chambers *Cycl.* s. v. *Glass*, The same for window, or *table glass, as for round glass. 1815 J. Smith *Panorama Sc. & Art* II. 208 White flint, or English crystal, generally used for table-glasses. 1610 Boys *Wks.* (1630) 374 O that the *table-gospellers of our time..would consider aright this terrible judgement. 1850 R. G. Cumming *Hunter's Life S. Afr.* (1902) 157/1, I had the satisfaction to discover the spoor of three bucks on a piece of rocky *table-ground on the highest summit of the range. c 1460 J. Russell *Bk. Nurture* 334 in *Babees Bk.*, Take a loofe of trenchurs in þy lifft hande, þan take þy *table knyfe. 1810 *Sporting Mag.* XXXV. 282 To work..at his business, as a table-knife cutler. c 1865 G. Gore in *Circ. Sc.* I. 235/2 This tendency is sometimes manifested in depositing silver upon table-knives and forks. 1675 J. Smith *Chr. Relig. App.* i. 18 In his erecting of that strange Order of *Table-Knights,..instituted..in contempt of Apollo. 1871 Tennyson *Last Tourn.* 69 Some hold he was a table-knight of thine..the Red Knight, he. 1883 *Proc. Soc. Psych. Research* I. 248 He would have really 'exploded the whole non-sense' of *table-lifting. c 1460 *Tabyl lyne [see sense 14 above]. 1611 Cotgr., *Mensale*, the Table-line in the hand; (a tearme of Palmistrie). 1653 R. Sanders *Physiogn.* 45 He that hath the Table-line broad and well-coloured he is jocund and couragious. 1680 *Lond. Gaz.* No. 1500/4 A large black Trunk filled with Diaper-*Table-Linnen and Sheets. 1855 Mrs. Gaskell *North & S.* xxvi, Continuing her inspection of the table-linen. 1892 *Labour Commission Gloss.*, **Table-loaders*, synonymous with 'lift-loaders'. 1895 *Cath. News* 16 Nov. 2 She had been *tablemaid to a clergyman. c 1515 *Cocke Lorell's B.* (Percy Soc.) 10 *Table makers, sylke dyers, and shepsters. 1771 Luckombe *Hist. Print.* 283 *Table-matter is generally braced in, when it wants driving out in width. 1866 *Cornh. Mag.* Oct. 467 The old screw..saves half his *table-money, and gives you stuff to drink only fit to send down the scuppers. 1901 *Daily News* 13 Dec. 7/1 In the lower-priced restaurants it is called 'table money', and in the higher-priced ones placed under the captivating heading of *couvert*. 1761 *Biogr. Dict.* IV. 200 A handsome *table monument of blue marble was raised over his [Drayton's] grave. [1791 *Encycl. Brit.* (ed. 3) VIII. 16/2 On approaching the Cape, a very remarkable eminence may..be discovered..called the *Table-mountain from its appearance.] 1822 G. Young *Geol. Surv. Yorks. Coast* (1828) 67 Extensive flats, nearly level, as in what are called Table mountains. 1886 A. Winchell *Walks Geol. Field* 95 When the erosion cuts the lava-sheet along parallel lines, it gives rise to the forms known as 'table-mountains'. 1853 *Ann. Reg.* 66 The faith in question is termed '*Table-moving'. 1862 B. Taylor *Home & Abr.* Ser. ii. vii. 442 Circles began to be formed in my native town, for the purpose of table-moving. 1875 Stainer & Barrett *Dict. Mus. Terms*, **Table music*, compositions intended to be sung by several persons sitting at a table. 1859 Mrs. Gaskell *Round Sofa* 331 Some fine yarn she was having spun for *table-napery. 1564 *Will J. Smyth* (2 Morrison & Crimes, Somerset Ho.), A fine *table napkin with blewe clowdes. a 1649 Drumm. of Hawth. *Hist. Jas. IV*, Wks. (1711) 74 Girded about him with a towel or table-napkin, of a comely and reverend aspect. 1828 Scott *F. M. Perth* xxviii, A handful of soft moss served the purposes of a table-napkin. 1897 Spurgeon *Autobiog.* iv. 26 In front of the pulpit, was the *table-pew, wherein sat the elders of the congregation. 1610 Healey *St. Aug. Citie of God* ii. (1620) 7 Gazing upon a *table picture. 1835 Willis *Pencillings* I. xxiii. 166 A graceful slope..swells up to a broad *table-plain on the mountain. 1626 in *Mem. Fountains* (Surtees) 365 One bed of wainscott..and also three *table plankes. 1669 W. Montagu in *Buccleuch MSS.* (Hist. MSS. Comm.) I. 446 The Queen's *table plate. 1705 tr. *Bosman's Guinea* 272 As broad as a common Table-Plate. 1877 Raymond *Statist. Mines & Mining* 329 Amalgamation in batteries, on table-plates, in pans, and on a second set of table-plates on a floor below. 1550 Crowley *Last Trump.* 490 Thy tauerne gate, and *table playe, thy cardes, thy dyce. 1586 T. B. *La Primaud. Fr. Acad.* (1589) 317 Plato compared our life to table-play. 1631 R. Byfield *Doctr. Sabb.* 152 Let no Table-play carry away the mind. c 1450 *Medulla* (Cath. Angl. 376), *Aliator*, a *tabyl pleyare. 1631 *Celestina* i. 15 Your Table-players, and other Gamesters never lose, but they peale foorth her prayses. 1577 Northbrooke *Dicing* (1579) 55 *Table playing and Chesse playing may be vsed of any men moderately. 1862 *Union* 11 Apr., Anything more dreary than '*Table prayers' at eleven o'clock we cannot conceive. 1701 *Cowell's Interpr.*, **Table-Rents*, *Redditus ad mensam*, rents paid to Bishops or Religious Prelates, reserv'd or appropriated to their Table or House-keeping. 1853 Mrs. Moodie *Life in Clearings* 365 The fall of that large portion of the *table-rock has made the alteration. 1607 Tourneur *Rev. Trag.* iv. ii, For *table-roome, I feed on those that cannot be rid of me. 1823 Chalmers in Hanna *Mem.* (1849) II. xv. 395 She allowed me..to continue the *table-service in the way I had found to be most convenient. 1846 Mrs. Gore *Eng. Char.* (1852) 99 In table-service his attendance was impartial. 1891 *Cent. Dict.* s. v. *Service*[1], *Table-service*, a set of utensils for the table. 1896 *Daily News* 6 Apr. 2/5 The President..handed to him the handsome table service which he had given to be run for. 1864 Webster, **Table-shore, Naut.*, a low, level shore. 1871 Tennyson *Last Tourn.* 461 As the crest of some slow-arching wave, Heard in dead night along that table-shore, Drops flat. 1844 Stephens *Bk. Farm* II. 575 The assistant throws the parings of the sides and bottom of the ditch upon the hedge-bank, immediately behind the *table-sod. 1847 Grote *Greece* ii. xxix. IV. 109 [Archilochus] was the earliest popular and successful composer of *table-songs or Skolia. 1836 Brande *Chem.* (ed. 4) 860 There are some minerals, and among them *table-spar or Wollastonite ..which are silicates of lime. 1598 Shaks. *Merry W.* iv. ii. 169 Let me for euer be your *Table-sport. 1854 J. G. MacWalter (*title*) The Modern Mystery of *Table-Tapping. 1901 *Daily Chron.* 16 Dec. 8/2 The *table tennis or 'ping-pong' tournament..concluded on Saturday night at the Royal Aquarium. 1903 *Westm. Gaz.* 2 Mar. 7/1 We tried spiritualism..first by *table-tilting. 1865 Lowell *Lett.* I. 386, I translate by direct inspiration of a scholiast turned *table-tipper. 1855 Smedley, etc. *Occult Sc.* 201 If the *table-tipping be made to answer as a code of signals. 1876 E. Venables in *Encycl. Brit.* V. 209/2 In the *table-tomb the recess above, essential for the introduction of the corpse, is square, while in the arcosolium, a form of later date, it is semi-circular. 1807 Vancouver *Agric. Devon* (1813) 293 He reached and ascended the *table top of Haldon. 1886 A. Winchell *Walks Geol. Field* 95 It..projects like a table-top beyond the gravel. 1834 Ld. Houghton *Mem. Many Scenes, Tempe* Introd. (1844) 35 A line of rugged crags, peaked or *table-topped. 1897 *Daily News* 3 May 7/4 A..valley lying between high, sharply scarped table-topped hills. 1853 O. Byrne *Artisan's Handbk.* 63 A miniature lathe-head mounted on a wooden *table-tree. 1805 R. W. Dickson *Pract. Agric.* I. 119 Care being taken..to raise the ground where they are placed with two or three *table turfs. 1594 Plat *Jewell-ho.* 14 One masse, whereof they make our drinking Glasses, and all sortes of *Table-vessell. 1895 *Westm. Gaz.* 23 Oct. 5/2 The Rosbach *table-water, a fresh sparkling table-water. 1794 *Rigging & Seamanship* I. 57 **Table-wheel*, to lay ropes, from a six-thread ratline to a two-inch and half rope, is fixed in the wheel-house. 1771 Luckombe *Hist. Print.* 272 Divisions are used instead of rules, in *Table-work of narrow Columns. 1832 Babbage *Econ. Manuf.* xxi. (ed. 3) 207 Work with irregular lines and many figures, and what the printers call rules,..is called *table-work*. 1879 [see Tabular 2 c].

**Table**, *v.* [f. Table *sb.* In some senses representing F. *tabler* (1544 in Godef.) or med.L. *tabulāre* (Du Cange).]

**1.** *trans.* To enter in a table or list; to tabulate (now *rare*); † to appoint (a person) to some duty by entering his name in a table or list (*obs.*).

c 1450 in Aungier *Syon* (1840) 324 The secunde and thryd antemes and matens schal be bygon of them that be tabled unto them. 1550 *Rec. Elgin* (New Spald. Cl.) I. 105 That the baillies..tabill certane honest men for gadering of Sanct Gelis lycht. 1611 Shaks. *Cymb.* i. iv. 6 Though the Catalogue of his endowments had bin tabled by his side. c 1630 Sir T. Hope *Minor Practicks* (1726) 5 There can be no Protestation granted upon the Copy, till the Copy be tabled. 1838 [implied in Tabling *vbl. sb.* 1].

**2. a.** To entertain at table as a guest, or for payment; to provide with meals, or *gen.* with food; = Board *v.* 8. Now *rare.*

1457–8 *Cal. Anc. Rec. Dublin* (1889) 297 Every of the Baylyfys to tabyll one of them. 1553 in *10th Rep. Hist. MSS. Comm.* App. v. 414 Every Maior..shall tabull and vittaill towe massons or carpinders in his own housse. 1583 Stubbes *Anat. Abus.* ii. (1882) 75 They haue..ten pound a yeere..and table themselues also of the same. 1610 Holland *Camden's Brit.* ii. 166 He entertained the Freers and tabled them at his owne charge. 1715 Brokesby *Life Dodwell* 306 Mr. Cherry..procured a Place for him where he might be tabled. 1903 *Westm. Gaz.* 12 Sept. 8/1 At ten o'clock the establishment is closed, after having often tabled between four and five hundred persons.

**b.** *intr.* (for *refl.*) To have a meal, to dine; to take one's meals habitually (at a specified place or with a specified person); = Board *v.* 9. Now *rare* or *Obs.*

1562 *Child Marr.* 139 He came to Schole to Northerden,.. and tablid at Withinshawe, with James Barlowe. 1602 Rowlands *Greene's Ghost* 14 Comming to Ordinaries about the Exchange where Merchants do table for the most part. 1748 Richardson *Clarissa* (1810) IV. lvi. 370 O that,..as she boarded there, she had oftener tabled with them! 1857 J. Raine *Life J. Hodgson* I. 14 It seems to be pretty clear that Hodgson had tabled with this talkative but hearty man.

**3.** *trans.* **a.** To picture, depict, represent as in a picture: cf. Table *sb.* 3. *Obs.* (or *rare arch.*)

1607–8 Bacon *Let. to Matthew* in Spedding *Life & Lett.* (1868) IV. 10 This last Powder Treason, fit to be tabled and pictured in the chambers of meditation, as another hell above the ground. 1852 Bailey *Festus* (ed. 5) xx. 326 That we, in the dark chamber of the heart,..see the world tabled to us.

**b.** To fix as on a tablet. *rare*$^{-1}$.

1852 Bailey *Festus* (ed. 5) xxxi. 530 Thine the stars Tabled upon Thy bosom like the stones Oracular of light, on the priest's breast.

**4.** To place or lay upon a table.

**a.** To lay (an appeal, proposal, resolution, bill, etc.) on the table of a deliberative or legislative assembly; hence, to bring forward or submit for discussion or consideration. In the *U. S. Congress*, to lay on the table as a way of postponing indefinitely; to shelve: cf. Table *sb.* 5 b.

1718 *Wodrow Corr.* (1843) II. 378 Another act was passed ..that all appeals should be brought up and tabled before the Bills, within three days after the Assembly sit down. 1726 *Ibid.* III. 245 Provost Campbell's appeal..was tabled, and the President and others moved a committee might be named to take it up. 1862 *Star & Dial* 14 Mar., Mr. Walpole has tabled a set of resolutions devised in the true Conservative spirit. 1866 *Daily Tel.* 30 Jan., To table a resolution has nearly the same effect in America as the order to read a bill 'this day six months' has in England. 1887 *Pall Mall G.* 3 Jan. 11/1 If any more 'Old Residents' wish to be heard they must table their names.

**b.** With other implications: *esp.* to pay down (money); to throw down or play (a card).

1827 Carlyle *Germ. Rom.* III. 224 Could he tell what to ..table [for the lackey]? 1832 — *J. Carlyle* 45 A refreshment of ale, for which he too used to table his twopence. 1837 — *Fr. Rev.* II. iii. vi, Royalty has always that sure trump-card in its hand;..yet never tables it, still puts it back again. 1878 Bayne *Purit. Rev.* v. 177 When the Short Parliament of 1640 refused to grant supplies, Laud's clergy in Convocation tabled their money. 1892 *Gard. Chron.* 27 Aug. 248/2 The nurserymen and florists tabled a large and fine assortment of cut flowers.

**5.** To furnish (a room) with tables. *nonce-use.*

1844 Dickens *Mart. Chuz.* xxvii, The offices were..newly tabled.

**6.** *Carpentry.* To join two pieces of timber firmly together by means of flat oblong projections (called 'tables' or 'coaks': see Table *sb.* 17 f, Coak *sb.* 1) in each alternately, fitting into corresponding recesses in the other. Also *intr.* for *pass.*

1794 *Rigging & Seamanship* I. 23 Cheeks..sometimes table on to the mast-head thus. 1794–c 1850 [see Tabling *vbl. sb.* 7]. 1797 *Encycl. Brit.* (ed. 3) XVII. 402/1 The customary way of putting them together is to table them; and the length of the tablings should be one-half more than the depth of the beam.

**7.** *Sailmaking.* To make a broad hem or 'tabling' on the edge of (a sail), to strengthen it in that part which is sewed to the bolt-rope (see Tabling *vbl. sb.* 8).

1794 *Rigging & Seamanship* I. 89 *Tabled*, the edges turned over and sewed down. 1797 in *Encycl. Brit.* (ed. 3) XVII. 433/1 That the lower side of the band may be tabled upon or sewed over the end of the buntline pieces. *Ibid.*, The buntline cloths and top-linings are carried up to the lower side of the middle band, which is tabled on them.

**8.** To sift (shot): see quot.

1858 Greener *Gunnery* 436 About three different sizes come out through one pan. These are separated by the aid of riddles, or tabled, as the process is termed.

‖ **Tableau** (tàblō·). *sb.* Pl. **tableaux** (-ō·z). [F. *tableau* (tàblo), OF. *tablel*, dim. of *table*.]

**1.** A picture; usually *fig.* a picturesque or graphic description.

1699 Lister *Journey to Paris* 39 The History of Maria of Medicis is Painted by Rubens... The Allegoric assistants in all the Tableaux are very airy and fancifully set out. 1801 Fuseli in *Lect. Paint.* iii. (1848) 429 The Massacre of the Innocents by Baccio Bandinelli..is a complicated tableau of every contortion of human attitude. 1855 H. R. Schoolcraft in *Longfellow's Life* (1891) II. 301 Exhibiting these fresh tableaux of Indian life. 1886 F. Harrison *Choice Bks.* iii. 54 They epitomise civilisation in a regular series of striking tableaux of the past.

**2.** A group of persons and accessories, producing a picturesque effect.

1813 Sir R. Wilson *Pr. Diary* II. 458 [In the battle of Leipzig] the whole arrangement and execution were perfect, presenting the grandest tableau ever contemplated. 1867 Baker *Nile Tribut.* viii. (1872) 130 All now halted, and gazed stedfastly in our direction, forming a superb tableau.

**b.** = *Tableau vivant*: see 4.

1828 W. Irving *Life & Lett.* (1864) II. 276 We had afterwards a tableau of a Sybil by Mademoiselle F. 1862 Baroness Bunsen in Hare *Life* II. vii. 318 After all possible singing and toasting two tableaux were given.

**c.** Used elliptically to express the sudden creation of a striking or dramatic situation, a 'scene', which it is left to the reader to imagine.

1885 *Pall Mall G.* 12 Nov. 11/1 A delay occurs in the working of the machinery [of the guillotine], when in rushes Miss Rorke, and tableau. 1894 *Westm. Gaz.* 18 Oct. 5/2 She overheard a gentleman ask another, pointing to two of the witnesses, 'Which of those old cats is Mrs. C.?' Mrs. C. leaned over and said 'That particular tabby, sir, is behind you'. Tableau!

**3.** A table, a schedule; an official list. (A common use in Fr.)

1798 T. W. Tone *Autobiog.* (1828) 266, I was carried on the tableau of the Armée d'Angleterre. 1863 Lepsius *Stand. Alphabet* 75 Comprise the seven classes in a general tableau. 1838 *Harper's Mag.* May 924/1 Those who, belonging to the fourteen grades of the tchin, or official tableaux of rank, are exempt from certain degrading penalties.

**4. Tableau vivant** (tàblō vivaṅ), pl. **tableaux vivants** (same pron.), lit. 'living picture'; a representation of a personage, character, scene, incident, etc., or of a well-known painting or statue, by one person or a group of persons in suitable costumes and attitudes, silent and motionless; *transf.* a picturesque actual scene. (In quot. 1883, applied to a group of statuary.)

1817 Moore *Lalla R.* Pref. (1850) 15 The different stories ..were represented in *Tableaux Vivans* and songs. 1837 Sir F. Palgrave *Merch. & Friar* (1844) 4 The intellectual amusement of a *tableau vivant*. 1844 Warburton *Crescent & Cross* (1845) I. xii. 106 The rich colouring, the antique attitudes, the various complexions that continually present themselves, form an unceasing series of *tableaux vivans* in an Eastern city. 1883 C. C. Perkins *Ital. Sculpt.* 385 Upon canvas the group would be counted a masterpiece, in clay it is a *tableau vivant*.

Hence **Ta·bleau** *v.*, *trans.* to put into a tableau.
**1903** *Contemp. Rev.* Dec. 873 'Tableaued' year by year in the popular Christmas Crib,..the Ass and the Ox, have become only less familiar than the Shepherds.

**Ta·ble-board.**
†1. A board for backgammon or any similar game: = TABLE *sb.* 4 a, BOARD *sb.* 2 c. *Obs.*
**1483** *Cath. Angl.* 376/1 A Tabylle burde, *tabella.* **1540** HYRDE tr. *Vives' Instr. Chr. Wom.* F ij, What a foule thing is it, to see a woman in steade of her woolbasket, to handle the tablebourd. **1623** WEBSTER *Devil's Law-Case* II. i, Shaking your elbow at the table-board. **1905** [see TABLE-MAN 1].
2. A board forming the top of a table; also a table (*obs.* or *dial.*).
*a* **1603** in H Hall *Soc. Eliz. Age* vii. (1886) 99 Table-bordes, formes, and a countinge table. **1668** CLARENDON *Vind.* Tracts (1727) 33 Walnut-tree..of which I made some table-boards and frames for chairs. **1731** W. HALFPENNY *Perspective* p. iv, The Table-Board fixed on the three Legs. **1847–78** HALLIWELL, *Table-board*, a table. *Cornw.*
3. Board, i. e. meals, without lodging. *U. S.*
**1884** *N. York Herald* 27 Oct. 2/3 First class table Board. **1895–6** *Cal. Univ. Nebraska* 177 Table board ranges from $1.50 to $2.50 per week.

**Ta·ble-book.**
†1. A book composed of tablets for memoranda; a pocket note-book or memorandum-book. *Obs.*
**1596** NASHE *Saffron Walden* Wks. (Grosart) III. 67 Registers..busie with their Table-books..to gather phrases. **1602** SHAKS. *Ham.* II. ii. 136. **1616** *Trav. Eng. Pilg.* in *Harl. Misc.* (Malh.) III. 332 Writing my notes out of my table-book. **1667** PEPYS *Diary* 10 May, Found in the dead man's pocket.. a table-book, wherein were entered the names of several places where he was to go. **1711–12** SWIFT *Jrnl. to Stella* 22 Jan., He thanked me for telling him, and immediately put his name in his table-book. **1816** SINGER *Hist. Cards* 276 He was observed to busy himself by writing in his table book.
2. A book of arithmetical or other tables; a Ready Reckoner or the like.
**1827** G. DARLEY *Sylvia* 28 He cannot count his fingers Without a table-book.
3. An ornamental book for a drawing-room table.
**1845** (*title*) George Cruikshank's Table-Book. **188.** *Lit. World* (Cent. Dict.), The Christmas table-book has well nigh disappeared, and well-illustrated editions of famous works are becoming more and more popular.
Hence †**Ta·ble-book-wi·se** *adv. Obs.*, in the manner of a table-book (sense 1).
**1642** HOWELL *For. Trav.* (Arb.) 27 Some do use to have a small leger booke fairely bound up table-book-wise.

**Table-cloth** (tēi·b'l,klǫþ, -klǫþ; for pl. see CLOTH *sb.*). A cloth for covering a table.
**a.** A white cloth, usually of linen, spread upon a table in preparation for a meal, and upon which the dishes, plates, etc. are placed.
**1467** *Mann. & Househ. Exp.* (Roxb.) 409 My mastyr paid there for a tabylle clothe ij. s. vj. d. **1496–7** *Rec. St. Mary at Hill* 34 Item, ij dyapre Tableclothis for the high Auter. **1575** in Willis & Clark *Cambridge* (1886) III. 363 If either fellowe or pensioner do wipe his hande or finger of the table clothe he shall pay for every time j$^{d}$. **1586** B. YOUNG *Guazzo's Civ. Conv.* IV. 185 Y$^{e}$ table cloathes wer spread. **1610** HOLLAND *Camden's Brit.* (1637) 481 Table clothes and linnen used at the solemne Coronation. **1855** MRS. GASKELL *North & S.* xxvi, Clothes-basket[s]..full of tablecloths and napkins. **1885** *Manch. Exam.* 9 Sept. 3/1 Equal to the task of instructing a laundress in the ironing of a tablecloth.
**b.** A cloth, usually of woollen material and often of ornamental design, used to cover a table permanently or when not in use for meals; = *table-cover* (TABLE *sb.* 22).
**1610** in *Eng. Wom. Dom. Mag.* (1862) IV. 109 If the green table-cloth be too little I will make a pair of warm stockings of it. **1879** CROCKETT *Kit Kennedy* xlix. 358 The letter was laid down on the tablecloth, with a fast-falling rain of tears falling upon it.
**c.** *fig.* Name for a cloud covering the flat top and hanging down over the edge of Table Mountain at the Cape of Good Hope.
[**1791** *Encycl. Brit.* (ed. 3) VIII. 16/2 The Table Land or Mountain is sometimes suddenly capped with a white cloud, by some called the 'spreading of the Table-cloth'.] **1836** *Lett. fr. Madras* (1843) 29 When the cloud that they call the Table-cloth comes down, people are often lost in the fog. **1898** *Westm. Gaz.* 13 Oct. 1/3, I had no time to spare for the ascent of Table Mountain, and the tablecloth of clouds indeed forbade me to attempt it.
Hence **Ta·ble-clo:thing** (-klǫþiŋ), linen for table-cloths; **Ta·ble-cloth-wi:se** *adv.*, in the manner of a table-cloth; **Ta·ble-clo:thy** (-klǫþi) *a.*, resembling or suggesting a table-cloth.
**1859** GEO. ELIOT *A. Bede* xxxi, I'm having linen spun, an' thinking all the while it'll make sheeting and table-clothing for her when she's married. **1891** KIPLING *Life's Handicap*, *End of Passage* 159 Clouds of tawny dust..flung themselves tablecloth-wise among the tops of the parched trees, and came down again. **1866** HOWELLS *Venet. Life* iii, Where the marble is carven in vast and heavy folds..to simulate a curtain..it has..a harshness decidedly table-clothy.

**Ta·ble-cut,** *a.* (*sb.*) [f. TABLE *sb.*, used adverbially + CUT *ppl. a.* or *sb.*[2]] Of a diamond or other precious stone: Cut in the form of a 'table': see TABLE *sb.* 18 and TABLE DIAMOND.
**1688** *Lond. Gaz.* No. 2320/4 Lost.., a Diamond Ring, Table Cut. **1704** *Ibid.* No. 4046/4, 8 Rings, one a Diamond with 7 Stones, Table-cut. **1905** A. LANG in *Longm. Mag.* Apr. 566, I could not tell what stones the table-cut stones were.
**b.** *sb.* The style of cutting a precious stone as described in A. **1891** in *Cent. Dict.*

So **Ta·ble-cutter,** a lapidary who cuts precious stones in 'tables'; **Ta·ble-cutting** = B.
**1877** E. W. STREETER *Precious Stones* iv. 23 A little later [than 1373] the so-called 'table-cutters' at Nürnberg, and all other stone-engravers, formed themselves into a guild. **1877** KNIGHT *Dict. Mech.* 2478/1 Table-cutting is adopted with flat thin gems, which have not sufficient protuberance to be cut as rose diamonds or brilliants.

**Tabled** (tēi·b'ld), *a.* [f. TABLE *sb.* and *v.*]
1. Made in or into the form of a table or flat surface; shaped like a table; *spec.* = TABLE-CUT *a.*
**1382** WYCLIF *Exod.* xxxv. 11 The tabernacle, and the roof of it, and the coueryng; rynges, and the tablid sides. **1575** LANEHAM *Let.* (Ballad Soc.) 51 Diamons, EmeraudS, Rubyes, and Saphyres: poynted, tabld, rok, and roound. **1832** J. BREE *St. Herbert's Isle* 95 Mountains with tabled heads. **1853** M. ARNOLD *Empedocles on Etna* II. 177 Sitting on a tabled stone.
2. ? Pictured, depicted. *rare.*
**1848** BAILEY *Festus* (ed. 4) viii. 84 The mornlit revel and the shameless mate, The tabled hues of darkness and of blood.
3. Entered on a list; listed. *Sc.*
*c* **1630** SIR T. HOPE *Minor Practicks* (1726) 9 The Keeper ..was obliged to affix on the Tolbooth-wall the Roll of the tabled Causes.
4. Having a table or tables: in *comb.*, as *double-tabled* adj., having two 'tables', leaves, or tablets (cf. TABLE *sb.* 2 e).
**1848** BAILEY *Festus* (ed. 4) xix. 216 The bright universe, The double tabled book of Heaven and earth.

‖**Table d'hôte** (tābl,dōt). [Fr., = host's table.] A common table for guests at a hotel or eating-house; a public meal served there at a stated hour and at a fixed price; an ordinary. Also *attrib.* as *table d'hôte dinner.*
**1617** MORYSON *Itin.* III. 60 Neither at this time was there any ordinarie Table (which they call *Table de l'hoste*, the Hosts table). *a* **1667** COWLEY *Ess. Verse & Prose, Liberty* Wks. (1684) 83 All this is but Tabl'd Host, 'tis crowded with people for whom he cares not. **1759** H. WALPOLE *Let. to H. S. Conway* 19 Sept., Mrs. Howe, who rides a fox-chase, and dines at the *table d'hôte* at Grantham. **1816** *Gentl. Mag.* LXXXVI. I. 198/2 At Dunkirk..I found a good table d'hote, a luxury which foreign travellers do not find in England. **1838** *Murray's Handbk. N. Germ.* 300/1 The table-d'hôte dinner..takes place at 2 o'clock.

**Ta·ble di·amond.** [f. TABLE *sb.* 18 + DIAMOND.] A diamond cut with a table or large flat upper surface surrounded by small facets; esp. a thin diamond so cut having a flat under surface.
**1470** *N. C. Wills* (Surt. 1908) 56 A ringe of gold with table dyamond. **1519** *Lett. & P. Hen. VIII*, III. No. 463 (P.R.O.) A black carkeyn with a syphre.. garnysshed with three table diamauntes, oon losenge diamaund, oon great poynted diamaunt. **1607** in *Heriot's Mem.* App. VII. (1822) 212 A ringe, with a table diamond on the head. **1750** D. JEFFRIES *Diamonds & Pearls* 58 The manufacture of Table and Rose Diamonds. **1833** *Encycl. Brit.* VIII. 6 The forms into which the diamond is cut are the brilliant, the rose, and the table. **1877** W. JONES *Finger-ring* 379 A ring with seventy-five table-diamonds, set in gold.

**Tableful** (tēi·b'lful). [f. TABLE *sb.* + -FUL.] The amount or number that a table will hold or accommodate. **a.** As many (persons) as can be seated at a table; a company seated at a table and occupying all the seats around it.
**1535** COVERDALE *Mark* vi. 39 He commaunded them all to syt down by table fulles vpon the grene grass. **1774** ABIGAIL ADAMS in *Fam. Lett.* (1876) 35 We make a table-full at meal times. **1858** O. W. HOLMES *Aut. Breakf.-t.* iii, One man who is a little too literal can spoil the talk of a whole tableful of men of *esprit.*
**b.** As many (things) as a table will hold.
**1886** *Philadelphia Times* 9 Jan. (Cent.), Three large tablefuls of housekeeping things.

†**Table·ity.** *Obs. nonce-wd.* [f. TABLE *sb.* + -ITY; rendering Erasmus's L. *mensеitās* for Gr. τραπεζότης (Diog. Laertes). Cf. CUPPEITY.] The abstract quality of a table.
**1542** UDALL *Erasm. Apoph.* 123 b, Hauyng in his mouth.. the said forged vocables of the Idees, as for exaumple, tablietees, for the facion of table. *Ibid.* 124 b [see CUPPEITY]. **1656** STANLEY *Hist. Philos.* VII. (1701) 287/1 Plato answered, it is true indeed, you have Eyes by which the *Table* and *Cup* are seen; but not an Intellect, by which *Tableity* and *Cuppeity* are seen. **1702** LOCKE *Defence* App. *Pers. Identity* (1769) 41 Personality therefore may be ranked among the whole scholastick terms of corporeity, egoity, tableity, etc.

**Ta·ble-land.** [f. TABLE *sb.* + LAND *sb.*] An elevated region of land with a generally level surface, of large or considerable extent; a lofty plain; a plateau.
**1697** DAMPIER *Voy.* I. xix. 531 The most remarkable Land at Sea is a high Mountain, steep to the Sea, with a flat even top, which is called the Table Land [at the Cape of Good Hope]. **1774** COOK *Voy. S. Pole* III. iv. (1777) II. 50 At sun-rise we discovered a high table land (an island) bearing E. by S. **1824** MISS MITFORD *Village* Ser. I. 70 (*Lucy*) The common.. is one of a series of heathy hills, or rather a high table land, pierced in one part by a ravine of marshy ground. **1899** BARING-GOULD *Bk. of West* I. x. 155 The great irregular tableland of Dartmoor, over a thousand feet above the sea.
**b.** Without *a* or *pl.*: Elevated level ground.
**1836** W. IRVING *Astoria* (1849) 248 These lofty plats of table-land seem to form a peculiar feature in the American continents. **1869** TOZER *Highl. Turkey* II. 190 One long line of table-land.., half mountain, half plain.
**c.** *fig.*
**1820** HAZLITT *Lect. Dram. Lit.* 12 He [Shakspere] indeed overlooks and commands the admiration of posterity, but he does it from the table-land of the age in which he lived. **1876** GEO. ELIOT *Dan. Der.* III. xxii, A healthy Briton on the central table-land of life.

**Tableless** (tēi·b'l,lès), *a.* [-LESS.] Without a table; unfurnished with a table.
**1887** H. KNOLLYS *Sk. Life Japan* 183, I am..conducted into the enlarged partition in a doll's house, clean as a match-box, but tableless and chairless. **1895** *Strand Mag.* Oct. 451/1 The tableless, curtainless, carpetless, chestless apartment.

†**Ta·bleman.** *Obs.* Pl. -men.
1. One of the 'men' or pieces used in any game played on a board, esp. backgammon.
**1483** *Cath. Angl.* 376/1 A Tabylle man, *scaccus.., calculus.* **1534** *Camden Misc.* (1855) 39 One paire of tables of peerle, ..withoute table men. **1626** BACON *Sylva* § 158 A Soft Body dampeth the Sound...And therefore..in Colleges they use to line the Tablemen. **1641** HINDE *J. Bruen* xl. 123 He saw everywhere Cards and Dise, Tables and Tablemen. **1725** SLOANE *Jamaica* II. 136 The wood [Guaiacum] is..good for bowls, tables, table-men, and cabinets. **1905** FISKE *Chess in Iceld.* 89 The list of chess boards and chessmen, table-boards and table-men in the king's possession.
2. Applied in contempt to a gamester.
**1608** DEKKER *Lanthorne & Candlel.* D j b, Knowing that your most selected Gallants are the only Table-men that are plaid withal at Ordinaries. **1609** — *Gvlls Horne-bk.* Introd. 2 All the painted table-men about you, take you to be heires apparant to rich Midasse.

†**Ta·blemeal,** *adv. Obs. rare*$^{-1}$. [f. TABLE *sb.* (sense 13 a) + -MEAL: rendering L. *tabulātim.*] By 'tables'; bed by bed.
*c* **1440** *Pallad. on Husb.* III. 148 Thi vynes olde eke graffe hem table mele.

**Tablement** (tēi·b'lmĕnt). [f. TABLE *v.* + -MENT, after L. *tabulāment-um*, f. *tabulāre.*]
1. *Arch.* = TABLE *sb.* 12 a; also, a foundation or basement.
*a* **1300** *Cursor M.* 1678 A schippe be-houes þe to dight... Fiueten [ellen] on heght, þat es þentent, Fra grund vnto þe tabulment. **13..** *E. E. Allit. P.* A. 993 Vch tabelment watz a serlypez ston. **1489** CAXTON *Faytes of A.* II. xxxv. 147 An edyfyce made of grete tymber and of tablementes with many loftes and stallages. **1601** HOLLAND *Pliny* (1634) II. 604 Stones larger than small tablements of pillars or counting-bourds. **1603** — *Plutarch's Mor.* 1196 We sat us downe upon the tablements on the South side of the temple. **1853** PARKER *Turner's Dom. Archit.* II. v. 218 So that a decent stone tablement be made on the wall.
†2. A wooden frontal for an altar: = TABULA 2.
**1445** *Yatton Churchw. Acc.* (Som. Rec. Soc.) 86 Payde to W. Stubbe rydyng to Brystowe to see the tabylment. **1500** in *Wiltsh. Archæol., etc., Mag.* (1855) II. 310 Pd. for making of the tabullment of the High Altar. **1552** *Inv. Ch. Goods Berksh.* 24 A clothe to hange before the tablement.
†3. A tabulation, list, catalogue. *Obs. rare.*
**1551** RECORDE *Pathw. Knowl.* Ep. to King, And thus will I omit this great tablement of vnhappie hap.

†**Ta·bler**[1]. *Obs.* Also 4 tablere, 5 tabelere. [In sense 1, a. OF. *tablier* (12–13th c. in Godef.) = L. *tabulārium*, in one of its mediæval senses, f. *tabula* table: cf. TABLE *sb.* 4.]
1. A backgammon board; hence, the game of backgammon or 'tables'. Also, a chess-board.
**1303** R. BRUNNE *Handl. Synne* 1041 To pley at þe ches or at þe tablere. *c* **1400** *Lanfranc's Cirurg.* 247 Wiþinne a monþe he mi3t se to pleie at þe tabler. **1426** LYDG. *De Guil. Pilgr.* 17272 Squar as ys a Tabler. **14..** *Metr. Voc.* in Wr.-Wülcker 626/13 *Scaccarium* checure, *alea* tabelere, *decius* dyce. **1474** CAXTON *Chesse* IV. i. (1883) 161 Wherfore y$^{e}$ ther ben in the tabler as many poynts wyde as ben full.
2. (? A table-cloth or a towel: med.L. *tablerium.*)
**1392** *Earl Derby's Exp.* (Camden) 178 Graunsom bastard pro j tabler per ipsum empt' ibidem pro domino, xij scot. **1393** *Ibid.* 281 Pro iiij lb. cotoni et j matte..pro j tablerio.

**Tabler**[2] (tēi·blər). Now *rare.* [f. TABLE *sb.* and *v.* + -ER: in sense 1 = OF. *tableour*; in other senses = OF. *tablier.*]
†1. A player at backgammon. Cf. TABLING *vbl. sb.* 2. *Obs.*
**1561** BP. PARKHURST *Injunctions* 19 Dycers, tablers, carders, swearers or vehemently suspected therof. **1571** GRINDAL *Injunctions* § 23 Rem. (Parker Soc.) 130 Nor any of you shall be..a hunter, hawker, dicer, carder, tabler.
†2. Rendering Gr. τραπεζίτης, a money-changer.
*c* **1550** CHEKE *Matt.* xxv. 27 You schold yeerfoor haav put out mi moni to y$^{e}$ tablers.
3. **a.** One who gets his meals at another's table for payment; = BOARDER 1. *Obs.* or *rare.*
**1598** FLORIO *Ital. Dict.*, *Comensale*, a fellow boorder, a fellowe commoner, a fellow tabler. **1641** HINDE *J. Bruen* iii. 10 He was sent..to be taught and trained up under one James Roe..where he continued a Scholler and Tabler for the space of three yeares. *a* **1714** M. HENRY *Life F. Tallents* Wks. 1853 I. 624 He left off house-keeping, and went to be a tabler. **1755** JOHNSON, *Boarder*, a tabler; one that eats with another at a settled rate.
†**b.** One who boards persons. *Obs.*
**1665** BRATHWAIT *Comment Two Tales* 8 We are to suppose him to be a Lodger or Tabler of Scholars and other Artists, for their Chamber and weekly Commons.
4. Possible in senses 4–8 of TABLE *v.*; as in 'the tabler of the resolution', etc.

**Ta·ble-ra·pping.** The production of raps or knocking sounds on a table without apparent physical means; by spiritualists ascribed to the agency of departed spirits, and used as a supposed means of communication with them.
**1858** HAWTHORNE *Fr. & It. Note-Bks.* II. 141 He made his communication by means of table-rapping. **1860** *All*

*Year Round* No. 64. 328 His aunt, who almost made a profession of table-rapping, who kept a journal of her spiritual experiences.

**Table Round,** = ROUND TABLE *sb.*

**Ta·ble ru·by.** A ruby cut with a large flat upper surface surrounded by small facets: cf. TABLE *sb.* 18, TABLE DIAMOND.

**1529** in *Wills Doct. Com.* (Camden) 18 One ring with a table rubye. **1660** F. BROOKE tr. *Le Blanc's Trav.* 285, I gave a fair table Rubie to my Sister. **1901** *Westm. Gaz.* 31 Dec. 1/1 The Coronation ring..will probably take the form of a plain gold ring set with a large table ruby on which is engraved a plain or St. George's Cross.

**Ta·ble-spoon.** A spoon (larger than a dessert-spoon) used for taking soup, and, in a larger size, for serving vegetables, puddings, etc. at table.

**1763** *Brit. Mag.* IV. 275 The villain stole two large table-spoons. **1865** DICKENS *Mut. Fr.* I. ii, Like a face in a table-spoon.

Hence **Ta·blespoo·nful,** as much as a table-spoon holds.

**1772** HIGGINS in *Phil. Trans.* LXIII. 140 Half a table-spoonful of the..solution. **1856** KANE *Arct. Expl.* I. xvi. 198 Brandy..served out in tablespoonful doses. **1894** WALSH *Coffee* (Philad.) 240 Add half tablespoonful of powdered chicory to two tablespoonfuls of ground coffee.

**Ta·ble-stone.**

†**1.** *Arch.* A flat stone, a stone tablet; also, a horizontal stone. *Obs.*

*c* **1467–9** *Durham Acc. Rolls* (Surtees) 641 Pro..nova operacione et posicione tabilstonys [in the walls of a church]. **1554** *Aberdeen Regr.* (1844) I. 281 Findand sufficient hewyn stanes to the haill wark with the tabill stane of the gavillis and makand the said tolbuith vattirthicht.

**2.** *Archæol.* **a.** A flat stone supported by two or more upright stones; a cromlech or dolmen; also, the horizontal stone forming the top of this.

**1840** T. A. TROLLOPE *Summ. Brittany* II. 88 These dolmens, or table-stones, consist..of one large flat mass, supported by several upright stones. **1880** JEFFERIES *Gr. Ferne F.* 150 He crawled right under the table-stone of the dolmen.

**b.** A small flat round stone supposed to have been used in a game resembling draughts.

**1851** D. WILSON *Preh. Ann.* (1863) II. IV. vi. 335 Table-stones, or draughtsmen, are found alongside the weapons and other relics buried with the warrior.

**Tablet** (tæ·blėt), *sb.* Forms: 4–6 tablette, 5 tabulette, -elet(te, (taplet), 5–6 tablett, tabellet(t, 6 tabillette, *Sc.* teblet, tabullatte, 6– tablet. [a. OF. *tablete* (13th c.), F. *tablette*, dim. of *table*, = Pr. *tauleta*, Sp. *tableta*, Pg. *taboleta*, It. *tavoletta*, med.L. *tabuleta* (1376 in Du Cange): see TABLE *sb.* and -ET, -ETTE.]

**1.** A small, flat, and comparatively thin piece of stone, metal, wood, ivory, or other hard material, artificially shaped for some purpose; a small slab.

**a.** A small slab of stone or metal bearing or intended to bear an inscription or carving, *esp.* one affixed to a wall as a memorial; also applied to a flat surface cut in a rock for the same purpose.

*c* **1315** SHOREHAM iii. 67 Ope two tablettes of ston..He hys [= them] wrot, Moyses by-tok. **1447** BOKENHAM *Seyntys* (Roxb.) 254 A taplet of marbyl [he] held in hys honde. **1649** G. DANIEL *Trinarch., Hen. V* cclxi, His single Honour needs noe Fret of Names..To glimer ore the Tablet. **1700** PRIOR *Carmen Sæculare* 167 When..The pillar'd marble, and the tablet brass, Mouldering, drop the victor's praise. **1851** LAYARD *Pop. Acc. Discov. Nineveh* Introd. 13 The most important trilingual inscriptions hitherto discovered are those..in the rock tablet of Behistun. *Ibid.* vii. 163 Four tablets have been cut in the rock. **1870** F. R. WILSON *Ch. Lindisf.* 30 The mural tablets are also numerous.

**b.** A slab or panel, usually of wood, for a picture or inscription. *Votive tablet*: an inscribed panel anciently hung in a temple in fulfilment of a vow, e.g. after deliverance from shipwreck or dangerous illness. Chiefly *arch.* or *Hist.*

**1581** PETTIE *Guazzo's Civ. Conv.* I. (1586) 30 b, Others, with Tablets and pictures use to represent men and women in some infamous and dishonest act. *a* **1700** DRYDEN (J.), Through all Greece the young gentlemen learned..to design upon tablets of boxen wood. **1782** V. KNOX *Ess.* lxiii. 274 Apelles used to say, that Protogenes knew not when to take his hand from the tablet which he was painting. **1851** D. WILSON *Preh. Ann.* (1863) II. III. ii. 40 A votive tablet in honour of the Legate. **1869** LECKY *Europ. Mor.* I. iii. 382 The votive tablets of those who escaped are suspended in the temple, while those who were shipwrecked are forgotten.

**c.** A small smooth inflexible or stiff sheet or leaf for writing upon; usually, one of a pair or set hinged or otherwise fastened together; anciently, of wood, or other material, covered with wax, written upon with a style, and used for correspondence, legal documents, etc.; in later times, of ivory, cardboard, or the like, carried in the pocket and used for memoranda; hence sometimes, in pl. *tablets*, applied vaguely to a note-book. Formerly called *tables* (TABLE *sb* 2 b).

**1611** SHAKS. *Cymb.* v. iv. 109 This Tablet lay vpon his Brest, wherein Our pleasure, his full Fortune, doth confine. **1780** MME. D'ARBLAY *Diary* 29 Apr., Had I not kept memorandums in my tablets, I could not possibly give any account of our proceedings. **1836** MARRYAT *Japhet* xl, I took out my tablets, and wrote down the address. **1860** RAWLINSON *Herodotus* VII. § 239 IV. 196 Demaratus..took a pair of tablets, and clearing the wax away from them, wrote what the king was purposing to do upon the wood. **1883** *Chamb. Jrnl.* 28 Apr. 266/2 There were unearthed nearly forty thousand inscribed tablets of unbaked clay. **1885** BIBLE (R. V.) *Isa.* viii. 1 Take thee a great tablet, and write upon it with the pen of a man.

**d.** In general or various applications, as a slab or tile, used in roofing or flooring, a flat piece in some mechanism, etc.; in quot. 1782 applied to playing-cards.

*c* **1440** *Pallad. on Husb.* VI. 195 Now brode and thynne Tilette or tabulette of marbul stoon. **1698** FRYER *Acc. E. India & P.* 395 A Bed made..on the Tablets upon the Tops of their Houses. **1782** COWPER *Progr. Err.* 170 The painted tablets, dealt and dealt again. **1842** I. WILLIAMS *Baptistery* I. (1874) 1 Quaint tablets rang'd some antique hearth around, Blue Holland porcelain, all rudely wrought.

†**2.** An ornament of precious metal or jewellery of a flat form, worn about the person. *Obs.* [Cf. med.L. *tabula* and *tabuletus* in Du Cange.]

*c* **1400** MAUNDEV. (1839) 234 Euerych of hem bereth a tablett of Iaspere or of Iuory or of cristall. **1504** *Will Goodyear* (Somerset Ho.), My tablet of golde that I was wonte to were abowte my nek. **1542** *Acc. Lord H. Treas. Scotl.* VIII. 58 Chenȝeis, tabullattis, tergattis, bracelattis, ringis. **1546** *Inv. Ch. Goods* (Surtees) 86 A great tablett of golde havyng in yt the ymage of Our Lady. **1583** GOLDING *Calvin on Deut.* cxxvi. 774 These great lords & braue lads which wil needs weare tablets at their neckes y^t is to say sumptuous Iewels for folke to gase at a great way off. **1611** BIBLE *Exod.* xxxv. 22 And they came both men and women, ..and brought bracelets, and earerings, and rings, & tablets, all iewels of gold. *c* **1620** Z. BOYD *Zion's Flowers* (1855) 31 The tablets and the rings made for the eare.

**3.** A small flat or compressed piece of some solid confection, drug, or the like; a lozenge of flattened (originally rectangular) form; a flat cake of soap.

**1582** HESTER *Secr. Phiorav.* I. xxix. 34 Giuing them euery mornyng one dragme of good Sope in tablettes accordyng to our inuention. **1626** BACON *Sylva* § 970 It is yet in use, to wear little bladders of quicksilver, or tablets of arsenic, as preservatives against the plague. **1655** CULPEPPER *Riverius* I. ii. 15 You may often use..these Tablets or Lozenges following. **1704** J. HARRIS *Lex. Techn.* I, *Tablets*, or solid Electuaries, are much the same with Lozenges. **1890** *Lancet* 1 Nov. 39 (Advt., B. W. & Co.) The Bicarbonate of Potash and Bicarbonate of Soda 'Tablets' or 'Tabloids' prove efficacious in dyspepsia. **1898** *Allbutt's Syst. Med.* V. 996 [Trinitrine may be administered] in the form of tablets. **1902** *Times* 30 Mar. 12/3 At this date the plaintiffs had used the word 'tablet' to denote compressed drugs,..but Mr. Wellcome set about finding a new word, and invented the word 'tabloid'. *Mod.* A tablet of chocolate; a tablet of soap.

**b.** Hence, *Sc.* (*taiblet*), hardbake or almond toffy made in tablets.

*c* **1900** *Wee Macgregor* i. 2, I want taiblet. *Ibid.* 5.

†**4.** Short for *tablet diamond*: see sense 8. *Obs.*

**1519** *Lett. & Pap. Hen. VIII*, III. No. 463 (P.R.O.) Having an owche at the eend wherin is sett a fair table balas with iiij fair diamauntes wherof ij great poynted dyamaundes, oon tablet and oon losenge. *Ibid.*, iiij diamauntes wherof ij poynted and ij tablettes.

**5.** *Glass-making.* = TABLE *sb.* 15 b. ? *Obs.*

**1688** [see TABLE *sb.* 15 b].

**6.** *Arch.* = TABLE *sb.* 12 a, b.

**1823** P. NICHOLSON *Pract. Build.* 444 A Tablet is a projection, fixed in a wall, with one face parallel to the surface. **1875** LEWIS & STREET in *Encycl. Brit.* II. 390/1 The crowning tablet or fillet [of an Egyptian pylon or portico] is quite plain and unornamented.

**7.** *Anat.* = TABLE *sb.* 16. **1891** in *Cent. Dict.*

**8.** *attrib.* and *Comb.*: **tablet-book**, a set of tablets for writing on; **tablet check**, in *Telegraphy*: see quot.; †**tablet diamond** = TABLE DIAMOND; †**tablet jewel**, ? = sense 2; **tablet-letter**, an ancient letter written on a tablet; **tablet tea**, tea made up in tablets (sense 3); **tablet-writing**, writing on tablets.

**1896** BOSCAWEN *Bible & Mon.* v. 110 The series of tablets when complete consisted of twelve *tablet-books. **1876** PREECE & SIVEWRIGHT *Telegraphy* 293 Every circuit..is supplied with a form called a '*Tablet check,' upon which each message as it goes off is ticked. **1530** *Lett. & Pap. Hen. VIII*, IV. No. 6789 (P.R.O.) Rynges..oon with a *tablet dyamount. [Cf. sense 4 above.] **1598** YONG *Diana* 91 Two iewels curiously enchased with tablet Diamonds. **1599** MINSHEU *Sp. Dict.*, *Dial.* 15 Chaines of Ieat, Amber, or such like, *tablet Iewels, girdles [etc.]. **1899** T. NICOL *Archæol. & Bible* v. 186 Seven of the *tablet-letters are from the Governor of Jerusalem. **1891** *Daily News* 5 June 5/6 '*Tablet tea' and 'brick tea', so familiar in Russia,..are apt to be confounded by outsiders. The former..is made of the finest tea-dust procurable...It is manufactured by steam machinery, with the aid of steel moulds, under great pressure. **1905** J. ORR *Probl. O. T.* Notes 525 Cuneiform tablet-writing probably in some measure continued after the settlement in Canaan.

**Tablet** (tæ·blėt), *v.* [f. prec. sb.]

**1.** *trans.* To furnish with a tablet (esp. one bearing an inscription); to affix a tablet to.

**1864** *Reader* 11 June 750 A large series of Irish and British fossils, about 17,000 specimens..named and tableted. **1883** G. H. BOUGHTON in *Harper's Mag.* Apr. 698/2 About the square were numbers of..old houses, with elaborately adorned gables, crow-stepped,..and tableted. **1894** *Westm. Gaz.* 28 June 2/2 [The] chapel tableted with the names of some who have died in their country's service.

**b.** To inscribe on a tablet.

**1878** *Masque of Poets* 152 And tableted above Him Still we read 'Love taught the smith to paint'.

**2.** ? *trans.* To make into a tablet; or ? *intr.* To make tablets.

**1889** *Sci. Amer.* 7 Dec. 363/1 A formula for the preparation of liquid glue for tableting purposes, which can be applied cold and which will retain its elasticity.

**Table-talk** (tē^i·b'l,tǭ·k). Talk at table; familiar conversation at meals.

In a general sense including ordinary conversation or gossip at the dinner-table; but now usually applied to the social conversation of famous men or of intellectual circles, esp. as reproduced in literary form; cf. the *Colloquia Mensalia* of Luther, first publ. 1567, Engl. transl. 1652, 1846.

*a* **1569** KINGESMYLL *Godly Advise* (1580) 11 Suche verelie is the Table-talk emongst the Gentiles the gentlemen. **1596** SHAKS. *Merch. V.* III. v. 93 *Ies.* Nay, let me praise you while I haue a stomacke? *Lor.* No pray thee, let it serue for table talke. **1608** BP. HALL *Char. Virtues & V., Busie-bodie* Wks. (1627) 188 Himselfe begins table-talke of his neighbour at anothers boord; to whom he bears the first newes, and adiures him to conceale the reporter. **1811** SIR G. JACKSON *Diaries & Lett.* (1873) I. 192 This little episode..started some table talk.

**1689** (*title*) Table-Talk: being the Discourses of John Selden Esq.; or his Sence of Various Matters of Weight and High Consequence. **1791** BOSWELL *Johnson* Introd. (1831) I. 55 The small portion which we have of the table-talk and other anecdotes of our celebrated writers. **1838–9** HALLAM *Hist. Lit.* IV. IV. vii. § 31. 314 One group has acquired the distinctive name of Ana; the reported conversation, the table-talk of the learned. **1846** (*title*) The Table Talk of Martin Luther, translated and edited by W. Hazlitt.

**b.** *transf.* A subject for table-talk; a theme for general conversation.

**1579–80** NORTH *Plutarch* 775 Antonius commanded him at the Table to tell him what wind brought him thither, he answered, That it was no Table-talk, and that he would tell him to morrow morning fasting. **1781** COWPER *Table Talk* 151 To be the Table Talk of clubs up stairs.

**c.** *attrib.*

**1581** SIDNEY *Apol. Poetrie* (Arb.) 29 Not speaking (table talke fashion..) words as they chanceably fall from the mouth. **1614** JACKSON *Creed* III. xviii. § 2 Acquainted with none but table-talke Diuinity.

So **Ta·ble-talker,** one who talks or converses at table; esp. a person of high conversational powers.

**1846** WORCESTER, *Table-talker*, one who converses at table. *Month. Rev.* **1880** *Q. Rev.* Jan. 101 He was the best of table-talkers.

**Tabletary** (tæ·blėtări). *a. rare.* [f. TABLET *sb.* + -ARY [1]; cf. *planetary*.] Of, pertaining to, or contained in a tablet or tablets.

**1880** *Libr. Univ. Knowl.* (N. Y.) II. 186 s. v. *Bank & Banking*, No. 2 dated at Babylon..597 B. C., bears tabletary evidence, attested by three witnesses, of the loan of 2 minas.

‖ **Tablette** (tæble·t, tæ·blėt). [a. mod.F. *tablette*: see TABLET.]

**1.** = TABLET *sb.* 1 c.

**1728** H. HERBERT tr. *Fleury's Eccl. Hist.* I. 536 He came out with the tablette in his hand and read it. **1860** W. COLLINS *Wom. White* ep. i. narr. W. H. vii, I made some entries in my tablettes this morning. Find my tablettes.

**2.** = TABLET *sb.* 3.

**1725** *Bradley's Fam. Dict.*, *Tablette*, or Lozenge, a Term in Pharmacy,..a solid Electuary..cut into the form of small, round or square Boards. **1890** *Harper's Mag.* Jan. 230/2 Some *tablettes* of grated cocoa candied in liquid sugar.

**3.** *Arch.* = TABLET *sb.* 6, TABLE *sb.* 12 a; *spec.* in *Fortif.* (see quot. 1853).

**1723** CHAMBERS tr. *Le Clerc's Treat. Archit.* I. 124 Balusters with their Rail, serving as a Tablette or Rest to the Elbows. **1853** STOCQUELER *Milit. Encycl.*, *Tablette*, a flat coping-stone, generally two feet wide and eight inches thick, placed at the top of the revêtement of the escarp, for the purpose of protecting the masonry from the effects of the weather, and also to serve as an obstacle to the besiegers when applying the scaling-ladders.

**Tableture,** obs. or erron. form of TABLATURE.

**Ta·ble-tu·rning.** The action of turning or moving a table without the use of any apparently adequate means, as by a number of persons placing their hands or fingers upon it; such movements being ascribed by some to spiritual agency (cf. TABLE-RAPPING). So **Ta·ble-tu·rner,** one who practises table-turning.

**1853** *Ann. Reg.* 67 When the apparatus was kept in sight it proved to possess a corrective power over the mind of the table-turner. **1855** SMEDLEY, etc. *Occult Sc.* 200 Faraday explains table-turning by involuntary muscular action. **1860** JEAFFRESON *Bk. about Doctors* II. 38 The vagaries of..electro-biologists, spirit-rappers, and table-turners. **1861** HOOK *Lives Abps.* I. vii. 421 The superstitions of the age, ranking with our mesmerism and table-turning.

**Tableware** (tē^i·b'lwē^ə.ɪ). Ware for the service of the table; a collective term for the articles which are used at meals, as dishes, plates, knives, forks, etc.

**1832** G. R. PORTER *Porcelain & Gl.* 16 The principal inventions of Mr. Wedgwood were—1. His table ware. **1897** *Outing* (U. S.) XXX. 376/2 Each member of the party should provide his own tableware...A cup, plate, and spoon of tin, knife and fork. **1904** *Times* 26 July 7/3 The mayor ..presented him on behalf of the city with a magnificent service of tableware.

**Tablewise** (tē^i·b'lwəiz), *adv.* [f. TABLE *sb.* + -WISE.] In the manner or form of a table: in various senses. †**a.** ? In a rectangular shape. *Obs.*

*c* **1425** *Found. St. Bartholomew's* 10 The Chirche he made of cunly stoonewerke tabylwyse.

**b.** In tabular form; tabularly: cf. TABLE *sb.* 10.

**1611** SPEED *Hist. Gt. Brit.* v. v. 27 It shal not..be amisse in this place once for all, tablewise to lay down the same. **1812** G. CHALMERS *Dom. Econ. Gt. Brit.* 463 A Comparative State, tablewise, of our domestic, and foreign trade. **1816** BENTHAM *Chrestom.* Wks. 1843 VIII. 7/2 The matter of the text being thus treated Table-wise.

**c.** Said in reference to the holy table when placed in the body of the church or chancel with its length in the direction of that of the church; opp. to *altarwise*.

**1637** J. WILLIAMS *Holy Table* 10 Your Communion-Table, when it is not used, should stand in the upper end of the Chancell, not Altar-wise but Table-wise. **1654** EVELYN *Diary* 12 July, To Magdalen College [Oxf.], where we saw the Library and Chapell, which was likewise in pontifical order, the altar onely I think turn'd table-wise. *c* **1710** CELIA FIENNES *Diary* (1888) 71 Their alter stood tablewise for ye Comunion just in ye middle of ye Chancell. **1881** W. R. W. STEPHENS *Dioc. Hist. Chichester* 194 In some it [the altar] was placed altarwise, in others tablewise.

**d.** In reference to a precious stone: Cut as a 'table' (see TABLE *sb.* 18, TABLE-CUT).

**1727-41** CHAMBERS *Cycl.* s.v. *Table*, A diamond cut Table-wise.

**e.** In the form of a table as a piece of furniture, i. e. (placed) horizontally on supports.

**1902** *Munsey's Mag.* XXVI. 622/2 It was a flat, plain slab of dark gray stone, placed on pillars tablewise.

‖ **Tablier** (tabli*e*). [Fr. *tablier*: see TABLER [1].]

† **1.** A chess-board; = TABLER [1] 1. *Obs. rare*—[1].

**1474** CAXTON *Chesse* IV. i. I vij, For to represente the mesure of this cyte, in whiche this playe or game was founden, the philosopher that fond hit first ordeyned a tablier conteynyng lxiiij poyntes square.

**2.** A part of a lady's dress resembling an apron; the front of a skirt cut or trimmed in the form of an apron.

**1835** *Court Mag.* VI. p. xvii/2 The skirts of these latter are closed before, and trimmed with folds in the form of a *tablier*. **1862** *Eng. Wom. Dom. Mag.* IV. 236/1 The dress..ornamented in front with a *tablier* of white satin. **1885** *Pall Mall G.* 29 Jan. 9/1 The bride..wore a dress of striped white satin with pearl tablier in front and net veil. **1903** *Daily Chron.* 30 May 8/4 At the edge of the tablier skirt that falls loosely over the deep flounce. **1908** *Ibid.* 4 Aug. 7/5 [The gown] has what the French call a 'tablier', that is a plain breadth let in down the front of the skirt.

**3.** Name for the enlarged *labia pudendi* characteristic of Hottentot women.

**1893** *Edin. Rev.* Apr. 294 The tablier is usual among their women and believed to be a mark of race.

**Tabling** (tē^i·bliŋ), *vbl. sb.* [f. TABLE *v.* and *sb.* + -ING [1].]

**1.** The action of setting down or entering in a table; tabulation. Now *rare*.

*c* **1450** in Aungier *Syon* (1840) 361 To her settyng hygher or lower,..tabulyng and assygnementes, alle owe redyly to obey. **1561** *Reg. Privy Council Scot.* I. 179 Without ony continuatioun, dyet or tabling of uther summondis. **1607** COWELL *Interpr.*, *Tabling of Fines*, is the making of a table for euery countie, where his Maiesties writ runneth, conteining the contents of euery fine, that shall passe in any one terme [etc.]. **1624** *3rd Rep. Hist. MSS. Comm.* 30/2 An Act concerning the fees to be taken in cities, boroughs, towns, &c., and the tabling thereof. **1838** W. BELL *Dict. Law Scot.*, Tabling of a Summons. At the institution of the College of Justice (1537), there was appointed a table, in which were set down all summonses, to be called in their turns.

† **2.** Playing at 'tables' or backgammon. Cf. TABLER [2] 1. *Obs.*

**1553** *Ord. Voy. Cathay* in Hakl. (1886) III. 19 Neither dicing, carding, tabling, nor other divilish games to be frequented. **1583** BABINGTON *Command.* iv. (1599) 166, I require..that..they better weigh whether carding, dising, and tabling.. be exercises commanded of God for the sabaoth day or no. **1608** WILLET *Hexapla Exod.* 411 Vsurie, carding, tabling and such like.

**3.** The action of providing or fact of being provided with meals; provision of food; boarding, board. Cf. TABLE *v.* 2. Now *rare* or *Obs.*

*a* **1553** in Cole *Hen. VIII's Scheme Bishopricks* (1838) 117 Borde and tabelyng frely in the late Monasterie to one scolemaster. **1587** HARRISON *England* II. vi. (1877) I. 142 To spend their time in large tabling and bellie cheere. *a* **1639** W. WHATELEY *Prototypes* II. xxxiv. (1640) 165 He would have left the matter of his tabling to him. **1725** *Postmaster* 16 Apr. 6 Lodgings, furnish'd or unfurnish'd, with good Tabling or without. **1830** J. HODGSON in J. Raine *Mem.* (1858) II. 154 *note*, You can have a bed and tabling here.

**4.** Material for table-cloths; table-linen. (Cf. *bedding*.)

**1640** in Entick *London* (1766) II. 167 Diaper for tabling. **1721** C. KING *Brit. Merch.* II. 347, 10281 Yards Diaper Tabling, at 2s. **1812** J. SMYTH *Pract. of Customs* (1821) 131 Diaper Tabling, of the manufacture of Silesia.

**5.** Tables collectively; accommodation of tables.

**1892** *Gard. Chron.* 27 Aug. 254/3 The length of tabling filled with products must have reached fully half a mile. **1902** *Westm. Gaz.* 21 Mar. 8/1 Supposing we had to put up tabling, the capacity of the hall would be reduced at once from 3,000 to 800.

**6.** *Arch.* The making of a 'table' or horizontal projecting course (see TABLE *sb.* 12 a); *concr.* such a course itself; *spec.* a coping.

**1411** in J. R. Boyle *Hedon* (1875) App. 168 In ij. bussellis calcis emptis pro dictis fenestris et pro tabelyng de les wykes ibidem, iiij. d. **1671** in Holmes *Pontefract Bk. Entries* (1882) 103 Item, for corbells, rigginge and tableinge I. 13. 4. **1870** F. R. WILSON *Ch. Lindisf.* 21 There was the corbel tabling, showing the old height. **1876** GWILT *Encycl. Archit.* Gloss., *Tabling*, a term used by the Scotch builders to denote the coping of the walls of very common houses.

**7.** *Carpentry* and *Shipbuilding*. See TABLE *v.* 6, and quots.

**1794** *Rigging & Seamanship* I. 11 *Tabling* is the uniting of pieces together in a manner similar to the chain-coak, but broader. *c* **1850** *Rudim. Navig.* (Weale) 155 *Tabling*, letting one piece of timber into another by alternate scores or projections from the middle, so that they cannot be drawn asunder either lengthwise or sidewise.

**8.** *Sailmaking*. A broad hem made at the edge of a sail to strengthen it: see TABLE *v.* 7.

**1769** FALCONER *Dict. Marine* (1776), *Tabling, lander*, a sort of broad hem formed on the skirts and bottoms of a ship's sails, to strengthen them in that part which is attached to the bolt-rope. **1794** *Rigging & Seamanship* I. 89. **1882** NARES *Seamanship* (ed. 6) 11 *Tabling*, the double part of a sail, close to the bolt-rope.

**9.** In hedging: see quot., and cf. TABLE *sb.* 13 c.

**1843** J. SMITH *Forest Trees* 24 Give the hedge what is called a tabling, that is to collect the earth..that has been taken away from the roots,..and place it again in its original position.

**10.** *Anat.* = TABLATURE 5. **1891** in *Cent. Dict.*

**11.** *attrib.*, as † **tabling-den**, a low-class gaming-house; † **tabling school**, a boarding-school.

**1886** H. HALL *Soc. Eliz. Age* viii. 105 The towns were flooded with tippling-houses, bowling-alleys, tabling-dens. **1660** C. HOOLE *New Disc. old Art Teaching Schoole* vi. 282 The shutting of children up..into a dark room, and depriving them of a meals meat, or the like (which are used in some Tabling Schools)..cannot be commendably..used in our greater Schooles.

† **Ta·bling-house.** *Obs.* [f. prec. (sense 2) + HOUSE *sb.*] A house of resort for playing 'tables' or other games; a gambling-house.

The sense 'boarding-house', alleged in mod. Dicts. (app. founded on Halliwell's casual remark in Nares (ed. 1859) on quot. 1577), is not certainly supported by any quot.

**1577** NORTHBROOKE *Dicing* (1843) 128 They alledge, that there is none but common gamehouses and tabling houses that are condemned, and not the playing sometimes in their own private houses. **1598** FLORIO *Ital. Dict.*, *Ridotto*,..a gaming or tabling house. **1605** *Play Stucley* in Simpson *Sch. Shaks.* (1878) I. 165 Gods me, my masters father! Now my master He's at the Tabling-house too!

‖ **Tablinum** (tăbləi·nŏm). *Rom. Antiq.* Pl. **tablina.** [L. *tablīnum*, *tabulīnum*, as in definition, also a floored place in the open air, a picture-gallery, f. *tabula* TABLE.] An apartment or recess in an ancient Roman house, opening out of the *atrium* opposite the principal entrance, and containing the family archives, statues, etc.

**1828-9** J. NARRIEN *Arch.* in *Encycl. Metropol.* (1845) V. 292/2 The *tablinum*, or repository for the archives and records of the family. **1832** GELL *Pompeiana* I. viii. 159 The tablinum itself, so called from being closed with planks. **1862** E. FALKENER *Ephesus*, etc. II. iv. 259. **1890** *Athenæum* 23 Aug. 265/2 In the central block [of a Roman villa] are the principal rooms, such as the *tabulinum* and *triclinium*.

**Tabliture**, obs. form of TABLATURE.

**Tabloid** (tæ·bloid). [A term registered on 14 March, 1884, by Messrs. Burroughs, Wellcome & Co., as a trade-mark applied to chemical substances used in medicine and pharmacy prepared by them, and afterwards for other goods; held by the Court of Appeal to be a 'fancy word' as applied to the goods for which it is registered, and legally restricted to the preparations of the firm named.]

The figurative, transferred, and sometimes humorous use, chiefly *attrib.* or as *adj.*, illustrated below has relation mostly to the compressed or concentrated form of the drugs sold by the firm under the name: see quot. 1903.

**1898** *Natural Science* Feb. 112 This presumed tabloid condition [of the flints] is brought about by a presumed extreme cold. **1901** *Westm. Gaz.* 1 Jan. 9/3 He advocated tabloid journalism. **1902** *Ibid.* 1 Apr. 10/2 The proprietor intends to give in tabloid form all the news printed by other journals. **1902** *Encycl. Brit.* XXXI. 574/2 The untouched cells below the cut grow larger..with the formation of tabloid cork-cells. **1903** Nov. 20–Dec. 14 Mr. JUSTICE BYRNE in *Repts. Patent & Trade Mark Cases* XXI. 69 The word Tabloid has become so well-known..in consequence of the use of it by the Plaintiff firm in connection with their compressed drugs that I think it has acquired a secondary sense in which it has been used and may legitimately be used so long as it does not interfere with their trade rights. I think the word has been so applied generally with reference to the notion of a compressed form or dose of anything. **1906** *Westm. Gaz.* 3 Jan. 3/1 Five short tableaux of drama which ..might be described brutally as five tabloids of melodrama.

**Taboggan, taboggnay**, var. ff. TOBOGGAN.

**Taboo, tabu** (tăbū·), *a.* and *sb.* Also tapu, tambu, tabou. [ad. Tongan *ta·bu* (see A).

*Ta·bu* is also the form in several languages of Melanesia and Micronesia, as in some of the New Hebrides, Banks Is., Gilbert Is., Papua (South Cape), etc. The general Polynesian and Maori form (also in some of the New Hebrides) is *ta·pu*, in Hawaiian *ka·pu*. Some of the Melanesian langs., as those of Fiji, and some of the Solomon Is., have *ta·mbu*, New Britain *ta·bu* and *ta·mbu*. Various cognate forms occur in Melanesian and cognate langs. The Tongan form was that first met with by Captain Cook, in 1777, from the narrative of whose voyages the custom with its name became known in England. In Fr. spelt *tabou*. The accentuation *taboo*, and the use of the word as sb. and vb., are English; in all the native langs. the word is stressed on the first syllable, and is used only as adj., the sb. and vb. being expressed by derivative words or phrases.]

**A.** *adj.* (chiefly in predicate). **a.** As originally used in Polynesia, Melanesia, New Zealand, etc.: Set apart for or consecrated to a special use or purpose; restricted to the use of a god, a king, priests, or chiefs, while forbidden to general use; prohibited to a particular class (esp. to women), or to a particular person or persons; inviolable, sacred; forbidden, unlawful; also said of persons under a perpetual or temporary prohibition from certain actions, from food, or from contact with others.

**1777** COOK *Voy. to Pacific* II. vii. (1785) I. 286 [At Tongataboo] Not one of them would sit down, or eat a bit of any thing...On expressing my surprize at this, they were all *taboo*, as they said; which word has a very comprehensive meaning; but, in general, signifies that a thing is forbidden. Why they were laid under such restraints, at present, was not explained. *Ibid.* ix. 338 As every thing would, very soon, be *taboo*, if any of our people, or of their own, should be found walking about, they would be knocked down with clubs. *Ibid.* xi. 410 When any thing is forbidden to be eat, or made use of, they say, that it is *taboo*. **1826** SCOTT *Diary* 24 Oct. in *Lockhart*, The conversation is seldom excellent amongst official people. So many topics are what Otaheitians call taboo. **1845** J. COULTER *Adv. in Pacific* xiii. 171 As soon as ever the anchor is down, if the ship is not a taboo or restricted one, she will be at once boarded, not by a few, but hundreds of women. **1873** TROLLOPE *Austral. & N. Z.* II. 419 Priests are *tapu*. Food is very often *tapu*, so that only sacred persons may eat it, and then must eat it without touching it with their hands. Places are frightfully *tapu*, so that no man or woman may go in upon them. **1888** C. M. WOODFORD in *Proc. Roy. Geog. Soc.* New Monthly Ser. X. 372 The human heads..are reserved for the canoe-houses. These..are tambu (tabooed) for women —i.e., a woman is not allowed to enter them, or indeed to pass in front of them.

**b.** *transf.* and *fig.*

**1826** MISS MITFORD *Village* Ser. II. 63 (*Touchy Lady*) The mention of her neighbours is evidently taboo, since..she is in a state of affront with nine-tenths of them. **1891** *Spectator* 2 May 611/2 A..pledge that that Wednesday should not be absorbed by the Government, but should be taboo. **1901** R. GARNETT *Ess.* viii. 224 The legendary history of Ireland is..taboo to the serious historian.

**B.** *sb.* **1.** The putting of a person or thing under prohibition or interdict, perpetual or temporary; the fact or condition of being so placed; the prohibition or interdict itself. Also, the institution or practice by which such prohibitions are recognized and enforced; found in full force in the islands of the Pacific when first visited by Europeans, and still prevailing in some of them, as also, under other forms and names, among many other races in early stages of culture.

The institution is generally supposed to have had a religious or superstitious origin (certain things being considered the property of the gods or superhuman powers, and therefore forbidden to men), and to have been extended to political and social affairs, being usually controlled by the king or great chiefs in conjunction with the priests. Some things, acts and words were permanently taboo or interdicted to the mass of the people, and others specially to women, while temporary taboo was frequently imposed, often apparently quite arbitrarily.

**a.** As originally used in Polynesia, New Zealand, Melanesia, etc.

**1777** COOK *Voy. to Pacific* II. xi. (1785) I. 410 When the *taboo* is incurred, by paying obeisance to a great personage, it is thus easily washed off. *Ibid.*, Old Toobou, at this time, presided over the *taboo*. **1778** KING in *Cook's Voy.* III. xii. (1785) II. 249 The *taboo* also prevails in Atooi, in its full extent, and seemingly with much more rigour than even at Tongataboo. **1779** — *Ibid.* v. iv. III. 81 The *taboo*, which Eappo had laid on it [the bay at Hawaii] the day before, at our request, not being yet taken off. **1817** SOUTHEY in *Q. Rev.* XVII. 14 This taboo was now to be taken off, by a large slaughter of hogs. **1831** *Tyerman & Bennet's Voy. & Trav.* I. xix. 423 The priests [in Oahu] recommended a ten days' tabu, the sacrifice of three human victims [etc.]. *Ibid.* xx. 440 A pole, ten feet high, on which was suspended a bit of white stick,..having remnants of the bones of a fowl attached to it. This..was a tabu, prohibiting any body from stealing the canes growing there. **1851** MRS. R. WILSON *New Zealand*, etc. 24 But chiefly thou, mysterious Tapû, From thy strange rites a hopeful sign we draw. **1862** M. HOPKINS *Hawaii* 89 One of the great instruments used by both king and priests for maintaining their power and their revenue, was the system of 'tabu' or 'taboo'. **1870** H. MEADE *New Zealand* 319 A tambu has been laid on the trees for a certain number of years.

**b.** Extended, as a general term of anthropology, to similar customs among other primitive races.

**1883** A. LANG in *Contemp. Rev.* Sept. 417 The hero Cuchullain..came by his ruin after transgressing this totemistic taboo. **1896** F. B. JEVONS *Introd. Hist. Relig.* vii. 72 The very conception of taboo, based as it largely is on the association of ideas, is one peculiarly liable to extension by analogy. *Ibid.* viii. 89 The irrational restrictions, touch not, taste not, handle not, which constitute formalism, are essentially taboos. **1905** *Athenæum* 21 Jan. 87/1 Tabus connected with animals and plants are common, and such tabus are part of totemism. **1906** *Ibid.* 17 Mar. 332/1 There are many tabous on food which are certainly not totemic in origin.

**2.** *transf.* and *fig.* Prohibition or interdiction generally of the use or practice of anything, or of social intercourse; ostracism.

**1833** R. MUDIE *Brit. Birds* (1841) I. 366 There are subjects which appear to be under the taboo of nature. **1852** LYTTON *My Novel* XI. ix, Under what strange taboo am I placed? **1853** S. WILBERFORCE in R. G. Wilberforce *Life* (1881) II. v. 190 To labour hardest as a Bishop is to incur certain taboo. **1894** MRS. FR. ELLIOT *Roman Gossip* 281 French officers.. found themselves placed in such a painful taboo at Rome.

**3.** *attrib.* and *Comb.*

**1870-4** ANDERSON *Missions Amer. Bd.* II. i. 6 Interwoven with the tabu system. **1896** F. B. JEVONS *Introd. Hist. Relig.* vi. 66 Before a great feast, a taboo-day or days are proclaimed. *Ibid.* vii. 78 They remove their hair before entering on the taboo-state. *Ibid.* viii. 88 The terror..with which he viewed the taboo-breaker. **1897** *Edin. Rev.* July 238 The taboo custom, which is a prohibition with a curse.

**1903** R. Kipling in *Windsor Mag.* 368/2 Remember you're a tabu girl now.

Hence **Tabooism,** the system of taboo; **Tabooist,** one who practises or believes in taboo.

**1885** J. Fitzgerald tr. *Schultze's Fetichism* iii. ad fin., Here is the fetichist become a tabooist, supposing that the description of tabooism heretofore given is correct.

**Taboo, tabu** (tăbū·), *v.* [f. prec.]

**1.** *trans.* To put (a thing, place, action, word, or person) under a (literal) taboo: see Taboo *sb.* 1.

**1777** Cook *Voy. to Pacific* II. ix. (1785) I. 359 He had been discovered..with a woman who was *taboo'd.* **1779** King *Ibid.* v. iv. III. 81 Eappo was dismissed with orders to *taboo* all the bay; and, in the afternoon, the bones [of Captain Cook] were committed to the deep with the usual military honours. **1799** *Naval Chron.* I. 305 Having tabooed one side of the ship in order to get all the canoes on the starboard side. **1831** *Tyerman & Bennet's Voy. & Trav.* II. xxix. 40 There are many houses which, having been built, or occupied, or entered casually by him [King Pomare], are thus tabued, and no woman dare sit down or eat in them. **1865** Tylor *Early Hist. Man.* vi. 144 In the South Sea Islands, words have been tabued, from connexion with the names of chiefs. **1896** F. B. Jevons *Introd. Hist. Relig.* vi. 65 On the day of a chief's decease work is tabooed.

**2.** *transf.* and *fig.* **a.** To give a sacred or privileged character to (a thing), which restricts its use to certain persons, or debars it from ordinary use or treatment; † (*a*) with stress on the privilege: To consecrate, set apart, render inviolable (*obs.*); (*b*) with stress on the exclusion: To forbid, prohibit *to* the unprivileged, or to particular persons.

(*a*) **1832** *Blackw. Mag.* Apr. 582/2 The silks and the veils, &c., which some years ago were as exclusively tabooed, and set apart to the use of the mistress as pearls or rubies, are now familiarly worn by the servant. **1846** R. Bell *G. Canning* viii. 218 Slavery was cruel...But it was a sacred institution..tabooed by the consecrating hand of time.

(*b*) **1825** *Blackw. Mag.* XVII. 161 The 'King's highway' seems Tabooed to these individuals. **1839** T. Hook in *New Monthly Mag.* LV. 439 There were no splendid couches taboo'd against the reception of wearied feet. **1854** H. Miller *Sch. & Schm.* xiv. (1860) 151 Such of the gentlemen ..as taboo their Glen Tilts, and shut up the passes of the Grampians. **1870** Lowell *Study Wind.* 67 That sacred enclosure of respectability was tabooed to us.

**b.** To forbid or debar by personal or social influence the use, practice, or mention of, or contact or intercourse with; to put (a person, thing, name, or subject) under a social ban; to ostracize, boycott.

**1791** [see Tabooed]. **1822** Southey *Lett.* (1856) III. 305 He has tabooed ham, vinegar, red-herrings, and all fruits. **1850** Kingsley *Alton Locke* xxx, The political questions which I longed to solve..were tabooed by the well-meaning chaplain. **1860** H. Gouger *Imprisonm. in Burmah* xii. 126, I found myself as strictly tabooed as if I had been a leper. **1862** Maurice *Mor. & Met. Philos.* IV. x. § 18. 664 Their names were tabooed by Whig and Tory coteries. **1888** Bryce *Amer. Commw.* I. xii. 161 You cannot taboo a man who has got a vote.

Hence **Tabooed** (tăbū·d) *ppl. a.*

**1791** Burke *App. Whigs* Wks. VI. 106 A plain declaration, that the topick of France is *tabooed* or forbidden ground to Mr. Burke. **1841** J. Mackerrow *Hist. Secession Ch.* xxi. 767 Perpetual bickerings between the favoured and tabooed sects. **1849** C. Bronte *Shirley* xxi. 310 The gentlemen..regarded me as a 'tabooed woman'. **1906** *Athenæum* 17 Mar. 332/2 We doubt whether M. Reinach is entirely aware of the difficulty and complexity of the problem of the taboued animals in Leviticus.

**Tabor, tabour** (tēi·bəɹ), *sb.*$^1$ Now *rare.* Also 4 **tabre**, 4–5 **tabur**, 5 **-yr**, 5–6 **taboure**, 4–8 **taber**, 6–9 **tabber.** See also Taborn. [a. OF. *tabur* (11th c.), *tabour* (13–16th c.), beside *tanbor*, *tambur* (14–15th c.), *tambour* (16th c.–) = Pr. *tabor*, *tanbor*, Sp. *tambor* (OSp. *atambor*), It. *tamburo*: the relations between the forms in *ta-* and those in *tam-*, *tan-* have not been clearly determined. The word is held to be of Oriental origin, and has been compared with Pers. تبیره *tabīrah*, and تبوراك *tabūrāk*, both meaning 'drum', and with Arab. طنبور *ṭanbūr* a kind of lute or lyre. The actual history is uncertain: see Dozy, and Devic in Littré; also Gaston Paris in *Romania*, 1902.]

**1.** The earlier name of the drum; in later use (esp. since the introduction of the name *drum* in the 16th c.), A small kind of drum, used chiefly as an accompaniment to the pipe or trumpet; a taborin or tabret. Now *Hist.*, *arch.*, or *poetic.*

*c* **1290** *Beket* 1851 in *S. Eng. Leg.* I. 159 Of bellene and of tabours so gret was þe soun. **1297** R. Glouc. (Rolls) 8166 Of trompes & of tabors þe sarazins made þere So gret noyse. *c* **1300** *Havelok* 2329 Þe gleymen on þe tabour dinge. **1399** Langl. *Rich. Redeles* I. 58 Men myȝtten as well haue huntyd an hare with a tabre. **14..** *Voc.* in Wr.-Wülcker 616/28 *Timpanum*, a taber, or a tymbre. **14..** in *Hist. Coll. Citizen London* (Camden) 220 He stode a-pon an hylle wyth hys tabyr and hys pype. *c* **1460** *Emare* 389 Ther was myche menstralse, Trommpus, tabours, and sawtre. **1523** Ld. Berners *Froiss.* I. cxlvii. 176 Than the kyng mounted on his horse, and entred into the towne with trumpets, tabours. **1587** Fleming *Contn. Holinshed* III. 1553/2 Singing of psalmes, marching about their fiers with tabber and pipe. **1610** Shaks. *Temp.* IV. i. 175 Then I beate my Tabor, At which like vnback't colts they prickt their eares. **1624** Capt. J. Smith *Virginia* IV. 155 Will any goe to catch a Hare with a Taber and a Pipe? **1693** *Humours Town* 2 The Clamours of a Country-Mob..is no more than the beating of a Tabour. **1766** Goldsm. *Vic. W.* iv, The whole neighbourhood came out to meet their minister,..preceded by a pipe and tabor. **1843** Lytton *Last Bar.* I. ii, A marvellous horse that beat a tabor with his fore feet. **1880** in Grove *Dict. Music* II. 754/2 The tabor was a diminutive drum, without snares, hung by a short string to the waist or left arm, and tapped with a small drumstick. **1907** *Ibid.* III. 750/2 The pipe and tabor, for a long time very popular throughout Europe, are now obsolete in this country.

*fig.* **1601** Hakewill *Van. Eye* xvii. (1615) 87 The Duke of Vandosme, the common tabour of the French wits. **1624** Quarles *Job* xi. 69, I am become a By-word, and a Taber, To set the tongues, and eares of men, in labour.

**b.** *transf.* The drummer (with his drum).

**1362** Langl. *P. Pl.* A. II. 79 Taberes & tomblers & tapesters fele. **1789** Burney *Hist. Mus.* III. iii. 254 As a new married couple went out of the church the violins and tabors attended them.

†**2.** The tympanum or drum of the ear. *Obs.*

**1594** T. B. *La Primaud. Fr. Acad.* II. 84 The aire.. moueth the litle hammer of the eares,..and so maketh a sound by meanes of the litle taber, through whose sounde the spirites of hearing are awakened. **1615** Crooke *Body of Man* 592 The first cauity of the stony bone, which before we called the Tympane, that is the drume or Taber.

**3.** *attrib.* and *Comb.*, as *tabor-beating*; *tabor-like* adj. or adv.; **tabor-stick**, a drumstick.

**13..** *K. Alis.* 2158 (Bodl. MS.) Now rist grete tabor betyng, Blaweyng of pypes, & ek trumping. **1486** *Bk. St. Albans, Hawking* d j b, With yowre hande or with yowre tabur styke becke yowre hawke to come to you. **1698** Fryer *Acc. E. India & P.* 27 The whole Fabrick..covered atop Taber-like.

‖ **Ta·bor,** *sb.*$^2$ Also **tabour.** [Boh., Polish, Serv. *tabor*, Magyar *tábor*, a. Turkish *tabor* camp (anciently a camp of nomads formed by a circle of wagons or the like).] An encampment.

**1877** *Daily News* 25 Oct. 5/4 At Podgoritza..15 tabors of Nizams and four tabors of troops of the reserve are being concentrated preparatory to offensive operations against Montenegro.

**Tabor, tabour** (tēi·bəɹ), *v.* Now *rare.* Forms: see Tabor *sb.*$^1$ [f. Tabor *sb.*$^1$, or a. OF. *taborer* (13th c. in Godef.).]

**1.** *intr.* To perform upon or beat the tabor; to drum. Also *to tabor it.*

**13..** *K. Alis.* 924 (Bodl. MS.) Þer was trumpyng & tabouryng Lepyng of stedes & nayȝeyng. **1377** Langl. *P. Pl.* B. XIII. 230, I can noither tabre ne trompe. **1413** *Pilgr. Sowle* (Caxton) II. xliv. (1859) 50 They floyted and they tabered; they yellyd, and they cryed. *c* **1440** *Promp. Parv.* 485/2 Tabowryn, *timpaniso.* **1530** Palsgr. 746/1, I will tabour, play thou upon the flute therwhyles. **1591** Nashe *Pref. Sidney's Astr. & Stella* in G. G. Smith *Eliz. Crit. Ess.* (1904) II. 226 Nor hath my prose any skill to imitate the Almond leape verse, or sit tabring..nothing but 'to bee, to hee', on a paper drum. **1694** Motteux *Rabelais* IV. xiv. (1737) 56 Trudon Pip'd it and then Taber'd it like mad. **1902** *Speaker* 5 Apr. 10/1 The inevitable 'tambourinaire' fifes and tabors away.

**b.** *transf.* and *fig.* To beat as upon a tabor; to drum.

**1579–80** North *Plutarch* (1676) 72 This brought the common rumor to taber on his [Solon's] head. **1611** Bible *Nahum* ii. 7 Her maids shall leade her..tabring vpon their breasts. **1653** Dorothy Osborn *Lett., to Sir W. Temple* (1903) 179 His humour was to rise in the night, and with two bedstaves tabour upon the table an hour together. **1692** L'Estrange *Fables* ccccxvii. (1714) 451 He [the Ass] went.. Tabring with his Feet all the Way. **1719** D'Urfey *Pills* VI. 265 With Hammer on Kettle he tabbers all Day. **1859** F. E. Paget *Curate of Cumberworth* 356 Mrs. Soaper.. re-echoed her husband's words, and tabbered with her fingers on the table, expectant of my reply.

**2.** *trans.* To beat (a tune, etc.): cf. Drum *v.* 8.

*c* **1385** Chaucer *L. G. W.* Prol. 354 (Fairf. MS.) In youre courte ys many a losengeour and many a queynt totelere accusour That tabouren [*v. rr.* taboryn, tauburn] in youre eres many a swon.

†**3.** To beat, thump (anything); to thrash. *Obs.*

**1624** Quarles *Job* xviii. 63 Marke with what pride his horny hoofes doe tabor The..Earth. *a* **1625** Fletcher *Woman's Prize* II. v, I would tabor her, Till all the legions that are crept into her, Flew out with fire i' th' tails. **1655** tr. *Com. Hist. Francion* III. 55 Beating the Switzers march upon their buttocks; and..they fell to tabour mine to the same tune.

Hence **Ta·boring** *vbl. sb.*

**13..** [see sense 1]. **1603** Holland *Plutarch's Mor.* 98 Of his drumming, tabouring, and other enormious indignities, under the colour of religion. **1867** Morris *Jason* VIII. 360 Bear back the fleece Along our streets..with much scattered flowers and tabouring.

**Ta·borer.** *Obs.* exc. *Hist.* Also 5–7 **taberer**, 6 **tab(b)orer, tabourier, tabrer(e.** [f. Tabor *v.* or *sb.* + -er$^1$. Cf. OF. *taboreor* (14th c.).] One who tabors; a drummer; a performer on the tabor.

*c* **1400** *Song Roland* 918 Trumpetis and taberers, sothe to say. *c* **1430** Lydg. *Min. Poems* (Percy Soc.) 170 Tabourers withe theyr mokkes and false dupplicité Please more these dayes. *c* **1537** *Thersytes* in *Four O. Pl.* (1848) 79 The tryflinge tabborer trowbler of tunys. **1579** Spenser *Sheph. Cal.* May 22 Before them yode a lusty Tabrere, That to the many a Horne pype playd. **1610** Shaks. *Temp.* III. ii. 160, I would I could see this Taborer. **1885** *Newcastle Chron.* 25 May, The squire and his dame..attended by piper and taborer, looking on condescendingly.

**Taboret, -ete,** obs. forms of Tabret.

†**Ta·borin.** *Obs.* Also 6 **-oryn, taberyne,** 7–8 **tabourin(e,** 9 **-orine.** [a. F. *tabourin* (1482 in Godef. *Compl.*, and in Dict. Acad. 1690), deriv. of *tabour* Tabor; cf. med.L. *taborīnus* in sense = *tympanista* taborer (1497 in Du Cange). In mod. F. *tambourin*, Pr. *tamborin*, It. *tamburino.*] A kind of drum, less wide and longer than the tabor, and struck with one drumstick only, to accompany the sound of a flute which is played with the other hand. (In quot. 1871, used for Tambourine.)

*c* **1500** *Three Kings' Sons* 40 Thorugh all the cristen navee they made to blowe trompettes, claryons & taberynes. **1507** *Justes Moneths May & June* 150 in Hazl. *E. P. P.* II. 119 Of taboryns and of many a douce lute The mynstrelles were proprely clade in sute. **1512** *Helyas* in Thoms *Prose Rom.* (1858) III. 31 Pipes, taborins, doucimers. **1606** Shaks. *Tr. & Cr.* IV. v. 275 Beate lowd the Taborins, let the Trumpets blow. **1765** Sterne *Tr. Shandy* VII. xliii, 'Tis the fife and tabourin, said I. **1871** R. Ellis *Catullus* lxiii. 8 With a snowy palm the woman took affrayed a taborine.

**Taborite** (tæ·bŏrəit). [ad. G. *Taboriten* pl., ad. Boh. *taborzhina*, f. *tabor* Tabor *sb.*$^2$; so called from their encampment on a craggy height, now the town of Tabor in Bohemia.] A member of the extreme party or section of the Hussites led by Zizska.

**1646** Bp. Maxwell *Burd. Issach.* in *Phenix* (1708) II. 313 We might..add the Remainder of the Waldenses and Albigenses in Piedmont, and the Parts adjoining; or of the Taborites in Bohemia. **1786** A. Maclean *Christ's Comm.* III. (1846) 250 Exterminating the Taborites or Vaudois. **1861** J. Gill *Banished Count* vi. 68 The Calixtines might be styled the Gallicans of Bohemia, and the Taborites the Protestants.

†**Ta·born, tabroun,** *sb. Obs.* Forms: 4 **taborne,** 4–5 **taburn(e,** 5–6 *Sc.* **taberne,** 6 *Sc.* **tabro(u)n, tabberone,** 7 **tabern,** *Sc.* **tabbern;** also *Sc.* 4 **tawburn,** 5 **tawberne, talburn,** 6 **tau-, tawbron, tawbern, talbrone.** [A by-form of Tabor, chiefly north. Eng. and Sc., in med.L. *tabornum* (Du Cange). The inserted *n* appears also in OF. *taborner*, *tabourner* vb. (see next). (The Sc. spellings *taw-*, *tal-* stand for a broad *ā*.)] = Tabor *sb.*$^1$, tabour, a drum.

*a* **1340** Hampole *Psalter* cl. 4 Taburn is made of a dryid scyn. **13..** *E. E. Allit. P.* B. 1414 Tymbres & tabornes, tulket among. *c* **1400** Maundev. (Roxb.) xxxi. 138 Noyse as it ware of trumppes and tawburnez. *a* **1400–50** *Alexander* 1385 Now tynkyll vp taburnes. *c* **1450** Holland *Howlat* 760 The trumpe, and the talburn, the tympane but tray. **1513** Douglas *Æneis* IX. x. 66 Wyth tympanis, tawbronis [*ed.* **1555** tawbernis], ȝe war wont to heyr. **1533** Bellenden *Livy* II. xxvi. (S. T. S.) I. 238 With þe noyiss of swasche and tawberon. **1544** *Acc. Ld. H. Treas. Scotl.* VIII. 278 Twa men..quhilkis had thair tabronis brokin. **1552** Lyndesay *Monarche* I. 2505 With talbrone, troumpet, schalme, and clarioun. **1561** *Burgh Rec. Edinb.* (1875) III. 114 At the sound of the common bell, trumpet or tabroun. **1559–60** J. Wood *Let.* in Sir R. Sadler *St. Papers* (1809) II. 156 When they cam nere the towne, hard the commen bell and tabbern. **1688** R. Holme *Armoury* III. xvi. (Roxb.) 57/1 The pipe belonging to the Tabern is much longer then the whisell or Flajalett.

†**Ta·born,** *v. Obs.* Also 5 **taburne.** [f. prec. or ad. OF. *taborner*, *tabourner* (12–14th c. in Godef.) = *taborer.*] = Tabor *v.*, to drum.

**13..** *K. Alis.* 1042 (Bodl. MS.) At þe fest was harpyng And pipyng & tabournyng. *c* **1400** *Langl.'s P. Pl.* B. XIII. 230 (MS. C), I can neither taborne ne trompe. **1483** *Cath. Angl.* 376/2 To Taburne, *timpanizare.*

†**Ta·borner.** Chiefly *Sc. Obs.* [Agent-n. f. Taborn *v.* = OF. *taborneur* (1317 in Godef.).] By-form of Taborer, a drummer.

**14..** *Nom.* in Wr.-Wülcker 696/36 *Hic timpanizator*, a taberner. **1483** *Cath. Angl.* 376/2 A Taburner (*A.* Tabernar), *timpanista.* **1518** *Acc. Ld. High Treas. Scotl.* V. 157 To þe Franche Talbanaris and Menstralis .. in aile, viij s. **1560** *Burgh Rec. Edinb.* (1875) III. 74 The sax tabroneris that playit thre sundrie dayis at the parliament. **1688** R. Holme *Armoury* III. 156/2 *Taberner*, a Man playing on the Tabern and Pipe.

**Tabougin,** var. Toboggan.

**Tabour, -er,** var. Tabor *sb.* and *v.*, Taborer.

**Tabouret** (tæ·bŏret, *or as Fr.*). Also 8 **tabret.** [a. F. *tabouret* (taburę), in sense 2 (1442 in Hatz.-Darm.); orig. a small tabor or drum, a Tabret, dim. of *tabour*, Tabor, drum.]

†**1.** The same as Tabret, q. v. *Obs.*

**2.** A low seat or stool, without back or arms, for one person: so called originally from its shape. *Privilege of the tabouret*: see quot. 1656.

**1656** Blount *Glossogr.*, *Tabouret*, a pincase; also a little low stool for a childe to sit on. In France the priviledge of the Tabouret is of a stool for some particular Ladies to sit in the Queens presence. **1679** tr. *Marie Mancini's Apol.* 30, I had the priviledge of sitting on a Tabourette in the Queens presence. *a* **1711** Ken *Hymnotheo* Poet. Wks. 1721 III. 191 Soon as a Stranger comes, she'll him embrace, Near her proud Person, on a tabret Place. **1858** Masson *Milton* (1859) I. 704 A studied slight put upon Lady Scudamore by refusing her the honour of the *tabouret*,—i.e. the right of being seated—on the occasion of a visit of ceremony to the French queen. **1899** Morrow *Bohem. Paris* 60 He had bought a new easel and two rush-bottomed tabourets.

†**3.** A pin-case or needle-case. *Obs.*

**1656** [see sense 2]. **1891** in *Cent. Dict.*

**4.** A frame for embroidery, a tambour-frame.

**1858** Simmonds *Dict. Trade*, *Tabouret*,..an embroidery frame. **1891** in *Cent. Dict.*

**Tabourin(e,** variant of Taborin *Obs.*

**Tabre, Tabrer(e,** obs. ff. Tabor, Taborer.

**Tabret** (tæ·brėt). Forms: *α.* 4–5 **taberett,** 5 **-ette,** 5–6 **-et,** 5– **tabret,** (6 **-ette,** 7 **tabberet,**

tabaret); β. 6 tabertte, -erde, -arte, -arde; γ. 5 taborete, 6–7 tabouret. [f. TABOR + -ET.]

**1.** A small tabor; a timbrel. *Hist.* or *arch.*

α. **1464** *Mann. & Househ. Exp.* (Roxb.) 264 Item, for a hedstalle for the taberet iiij d. **1489** CAXTON *Faytes of A.* III. xiv. 198 He had lost hys pype and hys tabret. **1535** COVERDALE *Gen.* xxxi. 27 That I might haue brought the on the waye with myrth,..with tabrettes and harpes. **1607** TOPSELL *Four-f. Beasts* (1658) 134 A Hare..was seen in England..playing with his former feet upon a tabberet. **1683** PETTUS *Fleta Min.* II. 12 Choice Instruments of Musick.. also the Tabaret. **1748** RICHARDSON *Clarissa* (1810) IV. xxvi. 147 Not a tabret, nor the expectation of a new joy to animate him on! **1879** STAINER *Music of Bible* 155 The tabret has now been excluded from sacred buildings, having given place to the more solemn and imposing drum.

β. **1556** *Chron. Gr. Friars* (Camden) 27 With trompettes, shalmes, and taberttes in the best maner. **1570** LEVINS *Manip.* 31/1 A Tabarde, *timpanum.* **1575** TURBERV. *Falconrie* 191 The Falconer muste haue with him a little drumme or Taberde fastened to the pommell of his saddle. ? **1600** *Chester Pl., Banns* 118 Get mynstrilles to that shewe, pipe, tabarte, and flute.

γ. **1599** BP. HALL *Sat.* IV. i. 78 Or Mimoes whistling to his tabouret. **1676** DUGDALE *Baronage Eng.* II. 107/2 So shalle they departe the Manoir..with Trompets, Tabouretts, and other manoir of Mynstralce [*orig. c* 1500]. **1885** H. C. McCOOK *Tenants Old Farm* 299 In the katydid..the musical instruments are a pair of taborets.

**b.** *fig.* **1610** BOYS *Expos. Dom. Epist.* Wks. (1622) 443 Making their infirmities and sinnes our tabret and delight.

†**2.** *transf.* A performer on a tabret. *Obs.*

*a* **1377** in *Househ. Ord.* (1790) 4 Mynstrelles—Taberett 1. **14..** in *Hist. Coll. Citizen London* (Camden) 220 On manly man..that was a taberette..stode a-pon an hylle wyth hys tabyr and hys pype. **1464** *Mann. & Househ. Exp.* (Roxb.) 239, I delyverd my taborete the same day a new gowen, and iij.d. **1540** in *Vicary's Anat.* (1888) App. xii. 241 Item, for John Buntanus, tabret—xljs. iiij d. **1634** SIR T. HERBERT *Trav.* 67 Amongst the horse were aboue fortie Kettle-drummes and Tabrets.

**Tabret,** obs. form of TABOURET.

**Tabro(u)n, Tabronar,** etc.: see TABORN, -ER.

**Tabu,** variant spelling of TABOO.

**Tabul,** obs. form of TABLE.

‖ **Tabula** (tæ·biŭlă). Pl. **-æ** (-ī). [The L. word *tabula* TABLE, used in particular senses.]

**1.** An ancient writing-tablet; also *transf.* a body of laws inscribed on a tablet: see TABLE *sb.* 2 b, d, TABLET *sb.* 1 c.

**1881** E. HÜBNER in *Encycl. Brit.* XIII. 124/1 Instruments or charters, public and private (styled by the Romans first *leges,* afterwards *instrumenta* or *tabulæ*). **1904** C. WORDSWORTH *Old Service Bks.* 264 The Tabula or Wax-brede was of the nature of a service-paper rather than of a service-book.

**b.** *Tabula rasa* [L. = scraped tablet], a tablet from which the writing has been erased, and which is therefore ready to be written upon again; a blank tablet: usually *fig.*

**1535** LYNDESAY *Satyre* 224 Because I haue bene, to this day, Tanquam tabula rasa. **1607** SIR T. BODLEY in *Cabbala* II. (1654) 76 For that were indeed to become *Tabula rasa,* when we shall leave no impression of any former principles, but be driven to begin the world again. **1662** SOUTH *Serm.* (1727) I. 52 Aristotle..affirms the Mind to be at first a mere *Rasa Tabula.* **1875** JOWETT *Plato* (ed. 2) III. 73 The artist will do nothing until he has made a tabula rasa. **1893** *Nation* (N.Y.) 1 June 403/1 France had become a *Tabula rasa,* and everything had to be reorganized.

**2.** *Eccl.* A wooden or metal frontal for an altar.

**1845** PARKER *Gloss. Archit.* s.v. *Table,* The most remarkable example of the *tabula,* destined for the front of the Altar, is preserved in Westminster abbey; it is formed of wood, elaborately carved, painted, and enriched with a kind of mosaic work of coloured glass superficially inlaid.

**3. a.** *Anat.* = TABLE *sb.* 16.

**1857** DUNGLISON *Med. Dict., Table, Tabula, Tabella, Tabulatum,*..a name given to the plates of compact tissue, which form the bones of the cranium. Of these, one is external; the other internal, and called *Tabula vitrea,* on account of its brittleness.

**b.** *Palæont.* Name for the horizontal dissepiments in certain corals: cf. TABULATE *a.* 3.

**1855** LYELL *Elem. Geol.* xxv. (ed. 5) 407 The *lamellæ* are seen around the inside of the cup;..and large transverse plates, called *tabulæ,* divide the interior into chambers. **1859** MURCHISON *Siluria* (ed. 2) x. 243 The development of the transverse plates or tabulæ, in the body of the coral.

**Tabular** (tæ·biŭlăɹ), *a.* [ad. L. *tabulār-is* of or relating to a board or plate, f. *tabula*; now used in reference to many senses of TABLE.]

**1.** Having the form of a 'table', tablet, or slab; flat and (usually) comparatively thin; consisting of, or tending to split into, pieces of this form, as a rock; of a short prismatic form with flat base and top, as a crystal; flat-topped, as a hill.

*Tabular spar,* a name for WOLLASTONITE, as occurring in masses of tabular structure, or rarely in tabular crystals.

**1656** BLOUNT *Glossogr., Tabular,* wherof boards, plancks, or tables may be made, long and large. **1688** R. HOLME *Armoury* II. 296/1 The Persian Pye..of a dusky color: the Feet bluish, with black tabular scales. *a* **1728** WOODWARD *Fossils* (1729) I. 34 Nodules..that are tabular and plated. **1796** KIRWAN *Elem. Min.* (ed. 2) I. 36 The tabular [form] which consists of plates that grow thinner and sharp at the extremities. **1802** PLAYFAIR *Illustr. Hutton. Th.* 295 A bed or tabular mass of whinstone..interposed between strata. **1821** JAMESON *Man. Mineral.* 229 Associated with quartz, tabular-spar, and iron-ore. **1826** KIRBY & SP. *Entomol.* IV. xlvi. 332 When it is elevated on a footstalk above the dorsolum, and forms a tabular or flat surface. **1830** LINDLEY *Nat. Syst. Bot.* 210 The apex..is connected by a common tabular dilated stigma. **1850** R. G. CUMMING *Hunter's Life S. Afr.* (1902) 144/2 Mr. Livingstone pointed out to me a range of tabular hills. **1875** HUXLEY in *Encycl. Brit.* I. 130/2 Horizontal plates..which..constitute tabular dissepiments.

**b.** Painted on a 'table' or panel. *rare.*

**1859** GULLICK & TIMBS *Paint.* 305 The uses to which the tabular or wooden pictures were applied.

**2. a.** Entered in, or calculated by means of, a table or tables, as a number or quantity.

**1710** *Lond. Gaz.* No. 4737/3 In this Book you have above forty thousand Tabular Numbers. **1806** HUTTON *Course Math.* I. 40 Hence, by the rule..·1 the tabular height. This being found in the first column of the table, the corresponding tabular area is ·04088. **1837** WHEWELL *Hist. Induct. Sc.* (1857) II. 224 Uranus still deviates from his tabular place.

**b.** Of the nature of, or pertaining to, a table, scheme, or synopsis; arranged in the form of a table; set down in a systematic form, as in rows and columns.

**1816** BENTHAM *Chrestom.* 242 By means of a set of systematic and tabular diagrams. **1830** HERSCHEL *Study Nat. Phil.* II. vi. (1851) 182 A list of them in tabular order. **1832** BABBAGE *Econ. Manuf.* xix. (ed. 3) 183 A tabular view of the time occupied by each process. **1876** C. M. DAVIES *Unorth. Lond.* 67 Carefully elaborated tabular statements.

**c.** *Printing.* (*a*) Applied to matter set up in the form of tables (see *table-work,* TABLE *sb.* 22).

**1771** LUCKOMBE *Hist. Printing* 283 The curious method of Tabular Writing..is practised in England to greater perfection than in any other Nation. **1879** *Lond. Compositors' Sc. Prices,* Tabular and Table Work is matter set up in three or more columns and reading across the page. **1899** *Daily News* 11 Sept. 9/5 Compositor.—All-round jobbing, book, and tabular hand.

† (*b*) (Printing) from wooden blocks or tablets, on which the matter is cut. *Obs. rare.*

**1816** SINGER *Hist. Cards* II. 75 As far as regards tabular printing, there is no reason to doubt that the Europeans derived their knowledge of printing from the Chinese.

† **Tabula·rious,** *a. Obs. rare*$^{-0}$. [f. L. *tabulāri-us* of or belonging to written documents (f. *tabula* table) + -OUS.] (See quot.)

**1656** BLOUNT *Glossogr., Tabularious,* pertaining to writings or accounts; also belonging to tables, or good for them.

**Ta·bularize,** *v.* [f. TABULAR + -IZE.] *trans.* To put into a tabular form, to tabulate. Hence **Ta:bulariza·tion.**

**1853** MORFIT *Tanning & Currying* 332, I have carefully collected and tabularized..the following statistics. **1864** WEBSTER, *Tabularization.*

**Ta·bularly,** *adv.* [f. as prec. + -LY [2].] In a tabular form or manner; in a table.

**1862** SIR H. HOLLAND *Ess., Meteors* 302 The details..are ..given tabularly. **1875** JEVONS *Money* (1878) 246 The amount of interest being tabularly stated on the form.

**Tabulary** (tæ·biŭlări), *sb. Rom. Antiq.* [ad. L. *tabulārium* a record-office, archives, f. *tabula* table, tablet: see -ARIUM.] A place where the public records were kept in ancient Rome; hence, in other places.

**1656** BLOUNT *Glossogr., Tabulary,* a chest or place wherein Registers, or Evidences are kept in a City; the Chancery or Exchequer office. **1835–8** S. R. MAITLAND *Dark Ages* xii. (1844) 196 The charter cited..from the tabulary of the monastery of St. Maur. **1858** in W. SMITH *Dict. Grk. & Rom. Antiq.*

**Ta·bulary,** *a.* Now *rare.* [ad. L. *tabulār-is,* f. *tabula* table: see -ARY [2].]

**1.** Of, pertaining to, contained in, or of the nature of a table: = TABULAR 2 a, b.

**1594** BLUNDEVIL *Exerc.* II. (1636) 130 Then subtract the lesser tabulary Sine from the greater. **1674** JEAKE *Arith.* (1696) 104 [The Obolus] is all one with the Sextans, according to the Tabulary Division. **1865** CARLYLE *Fredk. Gt.* XXI. ii. (1873) IX. 268 Much documentary and tabulary raw-material.

†**2.** ? Pictorial. *Obs. rare.*

**1716** M. DAVIES *Athen. Brit.* III. 106 Whereunto Fabretti appendicularizes a Tabulary Representation of the Destruction of Troy, and a Description of Fucinus, now call'd the Lake of Celano in the Kingdom of Naples.

†**3.** Made or recorded upon a 'table' or tablet.

**1716** M. DAVIES *Athen. Brit.* VI. *Diss. Physick* 29 Even the Original Prescriptions of King Mithridates..were.. thought to be owing chiefly to some of those Empyrical Recipe's recorded in those tabulary Experiences.

**Tabulate** (tæ·biŭlĕt), *a.* (*sb.*) Also 6 *Sc.* -et. [ad. L. *tabulāt-us* boarded, planked, in med.L. also panelled, f. *tabulāre*: see next.]

†**1.** Formed of 'tables' or panels: panelled. *Obs.*

**1596** DALRYMPLE tr. *Leslie's Hist. Scot.* (S.T.S.) I. 295 The inner parte of this tour al of tabulet [L. *tabulato*] Wark curiouslie caruet.

**2.** Formed like a tablet; thin and flat: = TABULAR 1.

**1826** KIRBY & SP. *Entomol.* IV. 349 Postfrænum. 1. Tabulate (*Tabulatum*): When it forms a broad pannel or table on each side the postscutellum. Ex. Most *Coleoptera.*

**3.** *Palæont.* Having *tabulæ* or horizontal dissepiments, as the corals of the group *Tabulata.*

**1862** DANA *Man. Geol.* vi. 618 The interior of the coral divided by horizontal partitions (a characteristic called *tabulate* by Edwards). **1879** NICHOLSON (*title*) On the Structure and Affinities of the 'Tabulate Corals' of the Palæozoic Period.

**B.** *sb.* = TABLET 3. *rare.*

**1834** SOUTHEY *Doctor* xxiv. (1848) 58/1 For all faintness.. a cordial was prepared in tabulates, which were called *Manus Christi.*

**Tabulate** (tæ·biŭleit), *v.* [f. late L. *tabulāt-*, ppl. stem of *tabulāre* (*Onom. lat. gr.* in Quicherat *Addenda*) to board, plank, floor; in other senses directly from mod. senses of TABLE.]

†**1.** *trans.* (See quot.) *Obs. rare*$^{-0}$.

**1656** BLOUNT *Glossogr., Tabulate,* to board a floore or other place, to make a thing of boards.

**2.** To put into the form of a table, scheme, or synopsis; to arrange, summarize, or exhibit in a table; to draw up a table of.

**1734** J. KIRKBY tr. *Barrow's Math. Lect.* Pref. 29 That we rightly..tabulate, and calculate scattered ranks of numbers, and easily compute them. **1804** W. TAYLOR in *Ann. Rev.* II. 357 The result of this writer's enquiries and speculations are thus tabulated. **1869** FARRAR *Fam. Speech* ii. (1873) 70 *note,* We may tabulate the Italic family as follows.

†**3.** To enter on the roll. *Sc. Obs.* (Pa. pple. **tabulat**(e.)

*c* **1630** SIR T. HOPE *Minor Practicks* (1726) 5 If the principal Cause be of that Nature, which requires to be tabulate.

¶ **4.** 'To shape with a flat surface' (Todd). Only in TABULATED *ppl. a.,* q. v.

Hence **Ta·bulating** *vbl. sb.* and *ppl. a.*

**1757** LD. KAMES *Stat. Law Scot.* 357 Tabulating of summons. **1901** *Daily Tel.* 8 Mar. 10/7 The tabulating staff..are admitted on the ordinary examinations.

**Tabulated** (tæ·biŭleitĕd), *ppl. a.* [In sense 1, f. TABULATE *a.* + -ED [1]; in 2, pa. pple. of TABULATE *v.*]

**1.** Shaped with or having a flat upper surface; flat-topped: cf. TABULAR 1. Also, composed of thin parallel layers.

**1681** GREW *Musæum* III. I. iv. 282 Many..of the best [diamonds] are pointed with six Angles..and some Tabulated, or Plain, and Square. **1794** SULLIVAN *View Nat.* I. 435 The zoned or tabulated form of the onyx. **1886** A. W. GREELY *Arct. Service* I. vi. 62 The remarkable tabulated masses of land in the neighbourhood of Cape Alexander.

**2.** Arranged or exhibited in the form of a table, scheme, or synopsis: cf. TABULAR 2.

**1802** (*title*) Copy of a Letter from Citizen Talleyrand to Citizen Fauvelet at Dublin, with a Tabulated List of Questions on the Commercial and Maritime Affairs of that Country. **1862** BP. FORBES in *Ecclesiologist* XXIII. 34 We propose giving a tabulated scheme of the different calendars of the Scottish Church. **1862** M. HOPKINS *Hawaii* 369 *note,* A tabulated statement issued by authority.

**Tabulation** (tæbiŭlēi·ʃən). [n. of action from TABULATE *v.*; cf. L. *tabulātio* a flooring over, a floor or story.]

†**1.** See quot. *Obs. rare*$^{-0}$.

**1658** PHILLIPS, *Tabulation,* (lat.) a fastning together of planks or boards, a making a floor.

**2.** The action or process of tabulating; arrangement in the form of a table or orderly scheme.

**1837** WHEWELL *Hist. Induct. Sc.* (1857) III. 101 The value of such a tabulation was immense. **1867** BRANDE & COX *Dict. Sc.* etc., *Tabulation of chronology,* the arrangement of historical or professedly historical events according to their real or supposed dates is sometimes spoken of under this name. **1883** *Stubbs' Merc. Circular* 10 Oct. 902/1 If the collection and tabulation of these Statistics were entrusted simply to one department.

**3.** *Arch.* Division into successive stages of height by 'tables' or horizontal mouldings, etc.

**1886** WILLIS & CLARK *Cambridge* I. 103 The new design of that front..is..contrived so as to accommodate itself at the angle to the ancient lines of tabulation.

**Tabulator** (tæ·biŭleitəɹ). [Agent-n. from TABULATE *v.*: see -OR.] One who tabulates, or draws up a table or scheme. **b.** A machine or apparatus for this purpose; also, an attachment to a typewriter for typing columns of figures.

**1885** *Athenæum* 14 Nov. 639/3 This..means a corresponding increase in the work of the tabulators. **1892** *Daily News* 6 June 5/5 It is these cards that are passed through the electrical tabulator, which, by ingenious contrivances, records the answers on a number of dials. **1901** *Phonetic Jrnl.* 28 Sept. 611/1 Mr. F. P. Gorin, inventor of the tabulator bearing his name.

**Tabulatory** (tæ·biŭlĕtəri), *a. rare.* [f. L. *tabulāt-*, ppl. stem of *tabulāre* to TABULATE + -ORY [2].] Relating to or consisting in tabulation. Hence **Ta·bulatorily** *adv.,* in relation to tabulation or tables.

**1900** *Daily News* 20 Oct. 7/1 Her occasional historical and tabulatory excursuses may require a skip here and there. **1900** *Words Eyewitness* (1902) 282 The British nation is giving the lie to all history and all rules. Its 'life'—from the insurance-office point of view—is a marvel. Tabulatorily speaking, it is a monstrosity.

**Tabulature,** variant of TABLATURE.

**Tabule** (tæ·biul). [mod. ad. L. *tabula* table, tablet.] A medicine or drug prepared in a flattened form; = TABLET *sb.* 3.

**1893** *Advt.,* Tabules for dyspepsia, headache &c. **1898** *Westm. Gaz.* 28 Nov. 9/2 Witnesses who had been in communication with the prisoner in regard to tabules.

**Tabule, -ull(e,** obs. forms of TABLE.

**Tabulette,** obs. form of TABLET.

**Tabuliform** (tæ·biŭlifǭɹm), *a.* [f. L. *tabula* table + -FORM.] Having the form of a 'table' or tablet; = TABULAR 1.

**1848** LINDLEY *Introd. Bot.* II. 148 A single tabuliform cell of the upper cuticle.

† **Ta·bulous,** *a. Obs. rare.* [f. as prec. + -OUS.] Divided into compartments by tabulæ.

1733 MASSEY in *Phil. Trans.* XXXVIII. 191 A Tabulous Shell divided into several Cavities.

**Tabur, Taburn,** obs. ff. TABOR, TABORN.

† **Ta·burnister.** *Obs. rare.* In 4 -yster, -ystir. [f. *taburn,* TABORN + -STER: feminine corresp. to TABORNER.] A female player on the tabor.

*a* 1340 HAMPOLE *Psalter* lxvii. 27 Bifor come prynces ioyned til syngand: in myddis of wenchis taburnystirs [L. *iuuencularum tympanistriarum*]. *Ibid.*, Taburnysters.

**Taby, Tabyl, tabyll(e, Tabyr,** obs. forms of TABBY, TABLE, TABOR. **Tac**: see TAKE *v.*

**Tacamahac** (tæ·kămăhæk), **tacamahaca** (tæ:kămăhā·kă). Also 7–8 **tacamahacca,** 8 **tacamahack,** 8 **taccamahac, tacamacha, tacka mohacca.** [ad. obs. Sp. *tacamahaca,* in Hernandez 1614 *thecomahaca,* ad. Aztec *tecomahiyac*; mod. Sp. *tacamaca.* Cf. Monardes 1579 'ex Nova Hispania . . ab Indis *tacamahaca* vocatum'. In F. *tacamaque. Tacamahac* is the more usual form, and that recognized in North America in sense 2.]

**1.** An aromatic resin, used for incense, and formerly extensively in medicine. **a.** *orig.* That yielded by a Mexican tree, *Bursera* (*Elaphrium*) *tomentosa.* **b.** Extended in the West Indies and S. America to similar resins obtained from other species of *Bursera* and the allied genus *Protium,* and subsequently to resins imported from Madagascar, Bourbon, and the East Indies, chiefly the product of species of *Calophyllum.*

1577 FRAMPTON *Joyful News* I. 3 Gumme called Tacamahaca. 1616 BULLOKAR *Eng. Expos., Tacamahaca,* a Rosin brought out of the West Indies, of great vertue against any cold humours [etc.]. 1703 *Lond. Gaz.* No. 3898/3 The Cargo of the Galeon.., consisting of..Jollop, Gum Elemni, Tacka Mohacca, .. &c. 1714 *Fr. Bk. of Rates* 92 Gum call'd Tacamacha *p.* 100 Weight 05 05. 1718 QUINCY *Compl. Disp.* 137 Tacamahack is a resinous Gum, from the West Indies. 1747 WESLEY *Prim. Physick* (1762) 108 Apply to the Cheek Gum Tacamahac spread on Silk. 1802 *Naval Chron.* VIII. 150 (I. of France) Tacamahaca, stinking wood. 1846 LINDLEY *Veg. Kingd.* 460 Tacamahac from *Elaphrium tomentosum. Ibid.* 401 The true East India Tacamahaca is produced by *Calophyllum Calaba.*

**2.** The resin of the buds of the N. American Balsam Poplar, *Populus balsamifera*; hence a name of this tree.

1739 MILLER *Gard. Dict.* (ed. 3) II. *Addenda* s.v., The Tacamahaca. This Tree grows spontaneously on the Continent of America. 1759 *Ibid.* (ed. 7) s.v. *Populus,* The Buds of this Tree are covered with a glutinous Resin, which smells very strong, and this is the Tacamahacca used in the Shops. 1786 J. ABERCROMBIE *Arrangem.* in *Gard. Assist.* 32/1 Tacamahacca, or great balsam poplar. 1842 SELBY *Brit. Forest Trees* 213 The list of Tacamahacs mentioned by Loudon. 1846 LINDLEY *Veg. Kingd.* 255 Poplar buds, especially those of *P[opulus] nigra, balsamifera,* and *candicans,* are besmeared in winter with a resinous..exudation, which [passes] under the name of Tacamahac. 1881 tr. *Verne's Fur Country* 95 Jaspar also noticed the tacamahac, a species of poplar which grows to a great height.

‖ **Tac-au-tac** (takotā·k). *Fencing.* [F. *tac-au-tac,* lit. clash for clash, f. *tac* echoic word.] In *tac-au-tac riposte,* the return stroke after parrying with opposition: see quot. 1889 and RIPOSTE *sb.* 1.

[1889 POLLOCK, etc. *Fencing* (Badm. Libr.) 75 [The riposte] may be delivered in two ways:..[secondly], quitting the steel after a clean, smart parry...This is called..the *riposte du tac-au-tac.*] 1907 *Daily Chron.* 20 Nov. 8/2 The retort was in the nature of the tac-au-tac riposte beloved of the skilled swordsman.

‖ **Tacca** (tæ·kă). *Bot.* [mod.L. a. Malay.] Name of a small genus of tropical herbs with tuberous roots, the type of a natural order *Taccaceæ.* The tubers of *T. pinnatifida* yield the starch known as South-sea arrow-root.

1866 *Treas. Bot.* 1119/1 *Tacca* chiefly differs from its ally *Ataccia* in having a one-celled instead of a three-celled fruit.

Hence **Ta·ccad,** any plant of the N.O. *Taccaceæ.*

1846 LINDLEY *Veg. Kingd.* 149 Order xliii. Taccaceæ.—Taccads. 1855 E. SMITH *Bot.* in *Orr's Circ. Sc.* 187 *Narcissales*..(N.O.) 43 Taccaceæ or Taccads.

‖ **Taccada** (tăkā·dă). [Sinhalese *takkada.*] The Malayan rice-paper plant, *Scævola Lobelia* (or *Kōnigii*), an erect shrub found on the sea-shores of tropical Asia, Australia, and Polynesia; its young stems have a pith resembling that of the rice-paper plant (*Aralia papyrifera*), and used by the Malays for making artificial flowers, etc.

1866 *Treas. Bot.* 1027/2 *S[cævola] Lobelia* (alias *S. Kōnigii* and *S. Taccada*), the Taccada of India and Ceylon. 1887 MOLONEY *Forestry W. Afr.* 376 Taccada of India and Ceylon (*Scævola Lobelia,* L.).—Shrubby plant.

‖ **Tace** (tē·sĭ). [L. *tacē,* imper. of *tacēre* to be silent.] The Latin for 'Be silent'. *Tace is Latin for a candle,* a humorously veiled hint to any one to keep silent about something.

[Cf. 1605 CAMDEN *Rem.* 162 (*Impresses*) Edmund of Langley..asked..his sonnes..what was Latine for a fetter-locke: Whereat when the yong gentleman studied, the father said, '..I will tell you, *Hic hæc hoc taceatis*', as advising them to be silent and quiet.] 1697 *Dampier's Voy.* 356 Trust none of them for they are all Thieves, but Tace is Latin for a Candle. 1752 FIELDING *Amelia* I. x, '*Tace,* Madam', answered Murphy, 'is Latin for a candle'; I commend your prudence'. 1821 SCOTT *Fam. Lett.* 24 Feb. (1894) II. 115 *Tace* shall be hereafter with me 'Latin for a candle'.

**Tace,** = *tas,* obs. 3 sing. pres. of TAKE *v.*; obs. form of TASSE.

‖ **Tacenda** (tăse·ndă), *sb. pl.* [L., gerundive neut. pl. of *tacēre*: see next.] Things to be passed over in silence; matters not to be mentioned.

1883 *Blackw. Mag.* Feb. 274 Topics..regarded as tacenda by society.

† **Ta·cent,** *a. Obs. rare.* [ad. L. *tacēnt-em,* pr. pple. of *tacēre* to be silent.] Silent.

1652 KIRKMAN *Clerio & Lozia* 179 There was a fair Tragedy, whose subject I will be tacent of.

‖ **Tacet** (tē·set). *Mus.* [L., = 'is silent', from *tacēre* to be silent.] A direction that the voice or instrument is to be silent for a time.

1724 *Short Explic. For. Wds. in Mus. Bks., Tace* or *Tacet,* to hold still, or keep Silence. 1789 REES *Chambers' Cycl., Tacet,* in the Italian Music, is often used to denote a long rest, or pause. 1823 in CRABB *Techn. Dict.*, etc.

**Tache** (†tætʃ, ‖taʃ), *sb.*[1] Forms: 4 **teiche,** 4–5 **tech(e, tecch(e, techch(e, tacch(e,** 4–7 **tatch(e,** 4–8 **tach,** 5 **tetch(e, taich(e, tachch(e,** 6–9 **tash,** 5– **tache.** [a. OF. *teche* (11th c.), *tesche, tece, tecce, taiche, teiche, teke, teqe* (Godef.); also F. *tache* (12th c. in Godef. *Compl.*), † *tasche.*

The Fr. word is of uncertain origin, but, according to Hatz-Darm., is to be distinguished from the radical *tac* of TACHE *sb.*[2], ATTACH, etc., with which earlier etymologists have associated it.]

† **1.** A spot, blotch, blot. *Obs.* exc. as in b.

13.. *St. Erkenwolde* 85 in Horstm. *Altengl. Leg.* (1881) 268 Wemles were his wedes with-outen any teiche. 13.. *Gaw. & Gr. Knt.* 2436 How tender hit is to entyse teches of fylþe. *a* 1450 *Knt. de la Tour* (1906) 163 A stone so clere and faire that there is no tache therein.

‖ **b.** In modern scientific use only as French.

1893 W. R. GOWERS *Dis. Nervous Syst.* (ed. 2) II. 339 The well-known *tache cérébrale,* in which cutaneous irritation is followed by unusually vivid and enduring congestion of the skin [etc.]. 1898 *Syd. Soc. Lex., Tache,* congenital discolorations, or freckles, or spots. Blemish.

† **2.** *fig.* A moral spot or blemish; a fault or vice; a bad quality or habit; in quots. 1340–70, 1541, a physical blemish. *Obs.*

*c* 1330 R. BRUNNE *Chron. Wace* (Rolls) 3899 Alle his wykked tecches he left. 1340 *Ayenb.* 32 Vor opre zix vices ..þet byeþ techches of kuead seriont. 1340–70 *Alisaunder* 282 Hee made a uery uow auenged too beene Of þat teenefull tach [the loss of an eye] þat hee tooke þere. 1377 LANGL. *P. Pl.* B. IX. 146 If þe fader be false and a shrewe, Þat somdel þe sone shal haue þe sires tacches. 1422 tr. *Secreta Secret., Priv. Priv.* 188 Vices and ewil taichis thou shalt enchue. *c* 1430 LYDG. *Min. Poems* (Percy Soc.) 256 Snybbyd of my frendys such techechys for t'amende. 1483 CAXTON *Gold. Leg.* 261 b/2 She that neuer had tatche ne spot of corrupcion. 1541 [see TACHE *v.*[1]]. 1577 HELLOWES *Gueuara's Chron.* 106 He had therewith a tache or a fault. 1602 WARNER *Alb. Eng.* XIII. lxxvii. 318 Of whom euen his Adorers write euill Taches many an one.

**b.** An imputation of fault or disgrace; a stain; a stigma. *Sc. Obs.* or *rare.*

*c* 1610 SIR J. MELVIL *Mem.* Author to Son (1683) b iij, Her marrying a Man commonly judged her Husbands murtherer would leave a Tash upon her name. 1692 SIR W. HOPE *Fencing-Master* 162 If you can by any means (without puting a tash upon your honour). ? *c* 1716 in Wodrow *Hist. Church Scotl.* (1829) III. 227/1, I have made this reflection, not as a tach upon the persons who suffered. 1723 R. HAY (*title*) A Vindication of Elizabeth More from the Imputation of being a Concubine; and her Children from the Tache of Bastardy. 1862 M. NAPIER *Visct. Dundee* II. 218 The only tache upon his military fame.

† **c.** A smack, slight taste or flavour. *Obs. rare.*

1607 *Barley-Breake* (1877) 28 Their grazing feast will haue a wearish tatch.

**3.** A distinctive mark, quality, or habit; a trait, a characteristic, good or bad. [So in OF.] *Obs.* exc. *dial.* (tetʃ).

*a* 1400–50 *Alexander* 4390 Oure techis haue we schawid, Oure dedis & of oure disciplyne. 1470–85 MALORY *Arthur* VII. xx. 244 Wel maye he be a kynges sone for he hath many good tatches on hym. 1539 TAVERNER *Erasm. Prov.* (1545) 75 It is theyr owne maners, theyr owne qualities, tetches, condicions, and procedynges that shape them this fortune. 1598 BARRET *Theor. Warres* IV. i. 119 Euery braue man of warre beareth a tatch of ambition and of aspiring minde. 1780 BERRIDGE *Lett.* (1864) 400 Is any tache wanting, you could wish to see in a young man designed for the ministry? 1886 ELWORTHY *W. Somerset Word-bk., Tetch,* habit, gait. 'Tis a tetch her've a-got.

**Tache, tach** (tætʃ), *sb.*[2] Now *rare.* Also 6–7 **tatch.** [a. OF. *tache* fibula (14th c.), also a large nail: cf. Genevese *tache,* Languedoc *tacho* nail with broad round head, hob-nail, tack, tacket, Sp. *tacha* a kind of nail; also (from OF.) MDu. *taetse,* Du. *taats,* a round-headed nail, an iron pin. A doublet of TACK *sb.*[1]. The root is also that of F. *attacher, détacher,* Eng. ATTACH, DETACH. See Diez and Littré. Sense 2 may be in origin a different word.]

**1.** A contrivance for fastening two parts together; a fibula, a clasp, a buckle, a hook and eye, or the like; a hook for hanging anything on. *Obs.* or *arch.*

14.. *Voc.* in Wr.-Wülcker 583/10 *Fibula,* a tache or a laas [or a botun]. 1452 *Maldon, Essex, Crt. Rolls* (Bundle 31, No. 2 b), A tache of sylver..for a monkis hode. *c* 1500 *Melusine* 304 Thenne geffray cutte the taches of the geant helmet, and after cutte of his heed. 1530 PALSGR. 279/1 Tache for a gowne, *atache.* 1535 in *Ripon Ch. Acts* (Surtees) 359, j tach with j ruby ston. 1535 COVERDALE *Num.* xxxi. 50 Brynge we a present vnto the Lorde what euery one hath,..bracelettes, rynges, earinges and taches. 1582 STANYHURST *Æneis* IV. (Arb.) 99 With gould tache thee vesture purple is holden. 1611 BIBLE *Exod.* xxvi. 6 Thou shalt make fiftie taches [1885 *R.V.* clasps] of gold, and couple the curtaines together with the taches. 1641 EVELYN *Diary* Aug., A lamp..hanging loose upon a tach in the middst of a beame. 1668 WILKINS *Real Char.* II. vii. 184 Hook, Crook, Clasp, Hasp, Tatches. 1867 H. MACMILLAN *Bible Teach.* xiv. (1870) 274 Taches of gold connecting together the curtains of the tabernacle.

† **b.** A band or strap that may be fastened round anything. *Obs. rare.*

1610 HOLLAND *Camden's Brit.* I. 287 It came into [K. Richard's] mind to draw upon the legs of certaine choise Knights of his a certaine Garter or tach of leather. 1611 SPEED *Theat. Gt. Brit.* xiv. (1614) 27/2 K. Richard the First ..girt the legs of certaine choise knights with a tache of leather, which promised a future glory to the wearers.

**c.** *fig.* A means of attachment, a link, a bond of connexion.

1701 J. LAW *Counc. Trade* (1751) 225 Here is no such bar or tache, as either to hinder or discourage a thief of any sort from returning to his duty. 1860 FARRAR *Orig. Lang.* ii. 47 Finally, the word became a middle term of reminiscence, a tach between the external object and the inward impression.

**2.** *techn.* A rest for the shank of a punch or drill: see quots. Now *dial.*

1683 MOXON *Mech. Exerc., Printing* xii. ¶ 9 The Tach is ..to rest and hold the Shank of a Punch steady..while the Work-man Files. *Ibid.* 392 *Tache,* a small Board with Notches in its Fore-edge..to rest the Shank of a Punch in. 1829 in J. HUNTER *Hallamshire Gloss.* 1888–90 *Sheffield Gloss., Tache* (taiche)..has been defined for me as 'a stake or rest used by silversmiths, and fixed in the workbench'.

**3.** *Comb.,* as † *tach-hook,* † *tach-nail.*

1592 R. D. *Hypnerotomachia* 50 The Veluet brought downe to the frame of the Settles..fastened to the same with tatch Nayles of Golde. 1623 tr. *Favine's Theat. Hon.* II. xiii. 224 Their long Cloak, or Houpe-land,..tied with a Tach-hooke of Wood.

**Tache** (tætʃ), *sb.*[3] Forms: 7–9 **tach, tatch,** 8 **tetch,** 8–9 **tatche,** 9 **teache, taych, tache.** [app. a. obs. or dial. F. *tache, têche* plate of iron (Godef.), in Walloon *tak* 'plaque de fer qu'on applique au fond d'une cheminée' (Littré), which in F. dictionaries is usually identified with *tache,* TACHE *sb.*[1]]

**1.** *Sugar-boiling.* Each pan of the series through which the juice of the sugar-cane is passed in evaporating it; *esp.* the smallest and last of these, called specifically the *striking-tache.*

1657 R. LIGON *Barbadoes* 84 The Coppers, in which the Sugar is boyled, of which, the largest is called the Clarifying Copper, and the least, the Tatch. *Ibid.* 90 To throw in some of the liquor of the next Copper, to keep the tach from burning. 1740 *Hist. Jamaica* xii. 321 The least is called the Tach, where it boils longest. 1756 P. BROWNE *Jamaica* 131 The juice will often begin to granulate in the second tetch. 1839 URE *Dict. Arts,* etc. 1202 The term striking is also applied to the act of emptying the teache. 1871 KINGSLEY *At Last* xi, I flung it, sugar and all, into the tache. 1885 LOCK *Workshop Receipts* Ser. IV. 163/2 The earliest and crudest system of evaporation was the 'copper wall', or 'battery' of open pans called 'teaches' (taches, tayches, &c.).

† **2.** Applied to the flat iron pan in which tea-leaves are dried. *Obs.*

1701 J. CUNNINGHAM in *Phil. Trans.* XXIII. 1206 The Bing Tea is the second growth in April: and Singio the last in May and June, both dry'd a little in Tatches or Pans over the Fire. 1802 *Nat. Hist.* in *Ann. Reg.* 764/2 Then they [tea leaves] are tatched; this is done by throwing each time about half a catty of leaves into the tatche, and stirring them with the hand twice, the tatche being very hot. [*Foot-note*] Tatche is a flat pan of cast iron.

† **Tache,** *sb.*[4] *Obs. rare*[—1]. Also 5 **tach, tacche, tasche, tasshe.** [Origin obscure.] Touch-wood, tinder.

1393 LANGL. *P. Pl.* C. xx. 211 Bote þou haue tache [*v. rr.* tach, tasche, tasshe, B. XVII. 245 towe] to take hit with tunder and broches, Al þy labour is lost.

**Tache** (tætʃ, taʃ), *v.*[1] Now *dial.* Forms: (4 tass), 5–6 **tatch,** 6–7 **tach(e,** 7– *Sc.* **tash.** [a. F. *tacher,* OF. *tachier* to stain, soil, f. *tache,* TACHE *sb.*[1]] *trans.* To stain or taint, esp. with moral defilement, or with the imputation of guilt or shameful conduct; to stigmatize; rarely (quot. 1541), to infect physically. *Obs.* or *Sc. dial.*

1390 GOWER *Conf.* III. 242 The wyde world merveileth yit, That he [Solomon]..With fleisshly lustes was so tassed [*rime* passed]. 1495 *Trevisa's Barth. De P. R.* VI. v. (W. de W.) m v b, Al chyldern ben tatchyd wyth euyll maners. 1502 ATKYNSON tr. *De Imitatione* III. xxxiv. 223 What shall I say, that am tached thus with tribulacions. 1541 R. COPLAND *Guydon's Quest. Chirurg.* Q ij b, To be scalled, or tached with suche infecte dyseases, or that he bere some tache vpon hym. 1596 WARNER *Alb. Eng.* X. lviii, Otherwise a worthy Prince, nor tache we him but so. *Ibid.* XI. lxv. (1612) 280 Though she did obserue his soone Reuolt.. And him thereof had tacht. 1598 BARRET *Theor. Warres* II. i. 28 Infamous, or tatched with foule crimes. *a* 1649 DRUMM. OF HAWTH. *Hist. Jas. V,* Wks. (1711) 104 At the least to leave him suspected and tached with this treason. 1747 in *Ann. Gen. Assemb. Ch. Scot.* (1838) 105 His character ought not to be tashed. 1827 J. WATT *Poems* 101 (E.D.D.) Their frien's gat word an' gather roun' Determin'd sair to tease an' tash.

**b.** To blemish, deface; to tarnish or spoil slightly by handling or use; to make the worse for wear; *tashed,* tarnished, worn, weather-beaten. *Sc.*

17.. in Ritson *Sc. Songs* (1794) I. 214 They're tashed like, and sair torn, And clouted sair on ilka knee. **1863** ALEX. SMITH *Dreamthorp* 18 They [books] are tashed as roses are tashed by being frequently handled or smelt. **1895** W. C. FRASER *Whaups* xiii. 189 An indoor face. no tashed wi' the weather, but sair blotched wi' the dram. **1903** GLAISER in *Co-op. News* 16 May 567 (E.D.D.) If thet isna Miss Thorpe's new body slip...Go and get it off afore yo' tash it any worse.

**Tache** (tætʃ), *v.*² *Obs.* or *dial.* Also 4–5 **tacche**, 5–7 **tatche**, 5–9 **tatch**. [f. TACHE *sb.*², or from the same root. In sense 2 (and sometimes in 1), app. aphetic from *atache*, ATTACH.]

**1.** *trans.* To fasten, attach, fix, secure (a person or thing). Also *fig.*

*a* **1310** in Wright *Lyric P.* xxv. 70 Thy love sprenges tacheth me. *c* **1315** SHOREHAM *Poems* ii. 101 Þo þy chyld was an-honge, Itached to þe harde tre Wyþ nayles grete and longe! *c* **1330** R. BRUNNE *Chron. Wace* (Rolls) 12056 Ropes ..to tache & teye. **1483** *Cath. Angl.* 376/2 To Tache, *attachiare.* **1530** PALSGR. 746/1, I tache a gowne or a typpet with a tache. **1575** *Gamm. Gurton* II. iii, To seeke for a thonge Therwith this breech to tatche & tye. **1609** R. BARNERD *Faithf. Sheph.* To Rdr. 7 Tatching matter together with dependancie.

**2.** To lay hold of (a person); *esp.* to arrest, apprehend by legal authority; = ATTACH *v.* 1 a.

*c* **1400** *Laud Troy Bk.* 5690 Thei scholde for euere him haue tached, Ne hadde ben duk Menescene. *c* **1440** *Jacob's Well* 24 Alle þat malycyously tachyn, arestyn, or endyten.. men of holy cherch. *c* **1470** HENRY *Wallace* VII. 304 Thar folowed him fyfteyn Wicht, wallyt men..to tach him to the law. **1528** *Tyball's Confess.* in Strype *Eccl. Mem.* (1721) I. App. xvii. 35 The same day..that Sir Richard Fox was tached. **1530** PALSGR. 746/1, I tache a thefe, I laye handes upon hym. ?*a* **1635** FORBES *Disc. Pervers Deceit* 6 (Jam.) A cunning and long covered thiefe tatched with innumerable fanges [plunder].

Hence **Ta·ching** *vbl. sb.* and *ppl. a. Taching end*, a shoemaker's waxed thread pointed with a hog's bristle.

*c* **1440** *Promp. Parv.* 485/2 Tachynge, or a-restynge, *arestacio.* *c* **1485** *E. E. Misc.* (Warton Club) 73 Grynd hem togedyre a longe tyme one a stone, tylle hit be somdele tacchynge. *c* **1535** BYGOD *Impropriations* in *Lever's Serm.* (Arb.) Introd. 13 Snatchynge and scratchinge, tatchynge and patchynge, scrapinge and rakynge togyther of almost all the fatte benefyces. **1611** COTGR., *Ligneul*, shoomakers thread; or, a tatching end. *a* **1763** SHENSTONE *Ess.*, *Men & Manners* (1765) 187 A cobler with ten or a dozen children dependent on a tatching end. **1858** H. AINSWORTH *Mervyn Clitheroe* i. 15 Canes..tied with tatching end to prevent them from splitting. **1881** *Leicestersh. Gloss.* s.v., Every piece of 'tachin-end' used in joining has a hog's bristle fixed at each end so as to act as a kind of flexible needle.

† **Tache**, *v.*³ *Obs.* [Perh. the same in origin as TACHE *v.*²; cf. OF. *atachier* in sense 'to attack', It. *attaccare* to attach, to attack, and see note to ATTACH *v.*] *intr.* To make a (hostile) charge or attack; to charge.

*a* **1400–50** *Alexander* 2622 Kniȝtis on cursours kest þan in fewtire, Taches [*Dubl. MS.* tachyng] in-to targetis tamed þaire brenys [*v.r.* brynnes]. *c* **1400** *Sege Jerusalem* 656 Quarels & arwes.. Toysen at þe toures: tachen on þe Jewes. *c* **1400** *Destr. Troy* 6717 Telamon hym tacchit on with a tore speire. *Ibid.* 6783 Deffibus the doughty,.. Tachit vpon Teutro, a full tore dynt. *Ibid.* 8297 Then Diamede..On Troiell with tene tachet belyue.

† **Tache, tatch**, *v.*⁴ *Obs. rare.* [f. TACHE *sb.*³] *trans.* To dry (tea) in a 'tache' or shallow pan.

**1802** *Nat. Hist.* in *Ann. Reg.* 765/1 Bohea tea is gathered, sunned in baskets, rolled with the hand, and then tatched, which completes it. *Ibid.*, Tatching seems to give the green colour to the leaves of the tea trees.

**Tache**, early ME. var. of TEACH *v.*

† **Ta·ched**, *a. Obs.* Also 5 **techyd, tacched.** [f. TACHE *sb.*¹ + -ED ².] Having qualities of a specified kind; (well- or ill-) mannered or conditioned.

*c* **1400** tr. *Secreta Secret.*, *Gov. Lordsh.* 116 He þat hauys a lityll ffete..ys wycked, and euyl-techyd, deceyuant, and dronkelew. *a* **1450** *Knt. de la Tour* (1906) 18 All gentilwomen and nobill maydenes..ought to be goodli, meke, wele tached, ferme in estate, behauing, and maners. *c* **1450** *Merlin* 88 The trewest of this londe and beste tacched. **1532** MORE *Confut. Tindale* Wks. 556/2 An euil tached horse shaketh of sometime the bridle and runneth out at large.

† **Ta·cheless**, *a. Obs. rare*⁻¹. In 4 **teccheles.** [f. TACHE *sb.*¹ + -LESS.] Stainless, faultless.

**13..** *Gaw. & Gr. Knt.* 917 Now schal we semlych se sleȝtez of þewez, & þe teccheles termes of talkyng noble.

**Tacheometer** (tækiˌǫ·mĭtəɹ). [a. F. *tachéomètre*, f. Gr. ταχε-, obl. stem of ταχύ-ς quick, swift, τάχος swiftness + -METER: see also TACHYMETER.] A name given to instruments (of which there are various kinds) for the rapid location of points on a survey; = TACHYMETER. Hence **Tacheome·tric** *a.*, pertaining to a tacheometer or tacheometry; **Tacheo·metry**, surveying by means of a tacheometer.

**1876** *Catal. Sci. App. S. Kens.* 425 The Tacheometer of Gentilli...The means by which it measures the distance is an apparatus which obliges the lunette to traverse an unvarying angle. **1888** B. H. BROUGH *Mine Surveying* 204 The aim of tacheometry is to survey and level simultaneously a tract of ground with the greatest possible accuracy in the least possible time. **1900** *Nature* 11 Oct. 571/2 Suggestions on possible methods of utilising existing transit theodolites for tacheometric work. **1905** MAJOR CLOSE *Text Bk. Surveying* v. 51 Tacheometry (called also in American books Tachymetry or Tachyometry) a system of 'rapid measuring'..includes all the eight variations just mentioned. The system was first largely employed in Italy in 1820, but had been used in the eighteenth century in England. *Ibid.* 55 The term 'tacheometer' is best confined to instruments which have this optical arrangement [a converging lens between the object-glass and the diaphragm of a theodolite].

† **Tache·tte.** *Obs. rare*⁻¹. [dim. of TACHE *sb.*¹, a spot: see -ETTE.] A stud.

**1688** R. HOLME *Armoury* III. xix. (Roxb.) 166/1 *Tachettes*, the buttons or round naile heads which are set about the skirts or the Armour to adorn and set it out, resembling little spots.

**Tachistoscope** (tæki·stǒskoup). [mod. f. Gr. τάχιστο-ς swiftest + -SCOPE.] An instrument by means of which objects may be presented to the eye for a brief measured period, a fraction of a second; one of its principal applications being the measurement of 'the span of apprehension', that is, the amount of detail that can be apprehended by a single act of attention or apperception.

**1909** C. S. MYERS *Text-bk. Exper. Psychol.* 415 The essentials of a good tachistoscope.

† **Ta·chment, ta·chement.** *Obs.* [Aphetic f. ATTACHMENT.]

**1.** Something attached; an appurtenance.

?*a* **1400** *Morte Arth.* 1568, I ȝif the for thy tyþandez [*MS.* thyȝandez] Tolouse þe riche, The tolle and þe tachementez, tavernez and oþer.

**2.** A judicial seizure or apprehension of one's person or goods; *ellipt.* the writ authorizing such seizure: = ATTACHMENT 1, 2.

**14..** *Customs Malton* in *Surtees Misc.* (1888) 58 Noo othyr Balyffe schal make no tachement nor somond. **1467–9** *Paston Lett.* II. 296 Be the wey of tachements owte of the Chauncer. **1545** BRINKLOW *Compl.* 41 Ye haue a parcyall lawe in making of tachmentys, first come, first seruyd.

**Tachometer** (tækǫ·mĭtəɹ). [f. Gr. τάχος speed + -METER: cf. *barometer.*] **a.** An instrument by which the velocity of machines is measured. **b.** An instrument for measuring the velocity of a moving body of water, a current-measurer.

**1810** DONKIN in *Trans. Soc. Arts* XXVIII. 185 An instrument of my invention for indicating the velocity of machines, and which may not improperly be called a Tachometer. **1825** J. NICHOLSON *Operat. Mechanic* 42 The method of putting the tachometer in motion whenever we wish to examine the velocity of the machine. **1864** WEBSTER, *Tachometer*,..(*b.*) an instrument for measuring the velocity of running water in rivers, canals, &c. **1875** L. D'A. JACKSON *Hydraulic Man.* I. 84 The tachometer of Brünings is the best instrument of this type.

So **Tacho·metry**, the scientific use of a tachometer; the measurement of velocity.

**1891** in *Cent. Dict.*

**Tachy-** (tæ·ki), combining form of Gr. ταχύ-ς swift, used in the formation of some scientific terms. **Tachhydrite, Tachydrite,** *Min.* [ad. Ger. *tachhydrit* (Rammelsberg 1856), contr. for **tachyhydrit*, f. Gr. ὕδωρ water + -ITE ¹: from its property of deliquescing readily], a chloride of calcium and magnesium found at Stassfurt in Prussian Saxony. **Ta·chydida:xy** [Gr. δίδαξις teaching]: see quot. **Ta·chydrome** [Gr. -δρομ-ος -running, -runner, δρόμος a race-course], anglicized form of *Tachydromus*, Illiger's name for the ornithological genus *Cursorius*, a small group of birds allied to the Plovers; = COURSER ³; so **Tachydro·mian,** a bird of this group; **Tachy·dromous** *a.*, of the tachydromes; cursorial. **Ta·chygen,** *Biol.* [-GEN ¹], the sudden appearance of an organ in evolution; the part so appearing (Webster *Suppl.* 1902); so **Tachyge·nesis** [GENESIS], acceleration in development by the shortening or suppression of intervening stages; **Tachygene·tic** *a.*, of or exhibiting tachygenesis; **Tachyge·nic** *a.*, appearing or developing suddenly (Webster *Suppl.* 1902). **Tachyglo·ssal** *a.*, *Zool.* [Gr. γλῶσσα tongue], of a tongue: capable of being quickly thrust forth and retracted, as that of the ant-eater; so **Tachyglo·ssate** *a.*, having a tachyglossal tongue; pertaining to the *Tachyglossidæ*, a family of aculeate monotrematous mammals, of which the typical genus *Tachyglossus* contains the Echidna or porcupine ant-eater of Australia; **Tachyglo·ssid,** an animal of this family. **Tachyi·ater** [Gr. ἰατρός healer], 'one who cures speedily' (*Syd. Soc. Lex.* 1898); hence **Tachyi·atry,** the art of quick healing (*ibid.*). **Tachy·petous** *a.* [πετ-, stem of πέτεσθαι to fly + -OUS], swift-flying (Mayne *Expos. Lex.* 1860). **Tachypnœa** (tækipnī·ă) [Gr. -πνοια, f. πνέ-ειν to breathe], hurried or unusually rapid respiration. **Ta·chyscope** [-SCOPE], a kind of kinetoscope, in which a series of representations of an object in successive phases of motion are rapidly revolved, so as to present the appearance of actual motion. **Tachytha·natous** *a.* [Gr. θάνατος death + -OUS], killing quickly, rapidly fatal. **Tachy·tomy, tachyo·tomy** [Gr. τομή a cutting], the art of rapid surgical or anatomical operation.

**1866** BRANDE & COX *Dict. Sci.*, etc. II. 532/3 *Tachydrite. **1868** DANA *Min.* 119 *Tachhydrite*...Color yellowish. Transparent to translucent. Very deliquescent on exposure. **1846** WORCESTER, **Tachydidaxy*, a short method of teaching. *Scudamore.* **1842** BRANDE *Dict. Sci.*, etc. **Tachydromians*, the name of a family of wading birds, of which the genus Tachydromus is the type. **1860** MAYNE *Expos. Lex.* 1247/1 Having the *Tachydromus* for their type: *tachydromous. **1893** HYATT in *Proc. Boston Soc. Nat. Hist.* 77 Thus, from Cope's point of view, *tachygenesis is the law of progression, and retardation is the law of retrogression, and they are both essential parts of his law of acceleration and retardation. *Ibid.* 79 Normal types in which tachygenesis occurs in a marked way might be called *tachygenetic. **1891** *Cent. Dict.*, *Tachyglossal, *Tachyglossate. **1898** *Syd. Soc. Lex.*, *Tachypnœa. **1899** *Allbutt's Syst. Med.* VIII. 109 There is an hysterical dyspnœa, or rather tachypnœa; the respirations are hurried. **1889** *Sci. Amer.* 16 Nov. 310/1 Mr. Anschuetz has invented apparatus by means of which these [animated] pictures may be exhibited in a very perfect manner. This instrument..is known as the 'electrical *tachyscope'. **1860** MAYNE *Expos. Lex.*, *Tachythanatous. **1890** in BILLINGS *Nat. Med. Dict.* **1898** *Syd. Soc. Lex.*, *Tachyotomy, *Tachytomy.

‖ **Tachycardia** (tækikā·ɹdiă). *Path.* [mod.L. f. Gr. ταχύ-ς swift + καρδία heart.] 'Abnormal paroxysmal rapidity of the heart's action' (*Syd. Soc. Lex.*).

**1889** *Lancet* 2 Mar. 442/1 Those nerve cells and fibres which are concerned in the production of the tachycardia. **1891** *Ibid.* 2 May 1012/1 Dr. Wood proposes the restriction of the name 'tachycardia' to those cases in which very violent heart action occurs without obvious reason. **1898** *Allbutt's Syst. Med.* V. 813 Tachycardia..is improperly applied in the sense of mere rate; it is the name of a particular disease.

So **Tachyca·rdiac** [cf. CARDIAC], **a.** *adj.*, of or pertaining to tachycardia; **b.** *sb.* a person subject to or affected with tachycardia.

**1898** *Allbutt's Syst. Med.* V. 828 The tachycardiac attacks have been the cause of this disposition. *Ibid.* 832 One of my tachycardiacs began to ride a bicycle two years ago, and with much advantage.

**Tachygraph** (tæ·kigrɑf). [a. F. *tachygraphe*, ad. Gr. ταχυγράφος a swift writer, a scribe, f. ταχύ-ς swift + -γράφος writing, writer.]

**1.** One who practises tachygraphy; a writer of shorthand, a stenographer; *spec.* one of the shorthand writers of the ancient Greeks and Romans.

**1810** *Hist. Europe* in *Ann. Reg.* 114/2 If all the speeches ..were faithfully represented by the bench of tachygraphes. **1865** M. PATTISON *Ess.* (1889) I. 87 Of Greek scribes there were two kinds, the tachygraph (ταχυγράφος), and the calligraph (καλλιγράφος). **1895** FARRAR *Gather. Clouds* II. 142 The other tachygraph, Phocas, had also reported this sermon.

**2.** A tachygraphic writing. (In mod. Dicts.)

Hence **Tachy·grapher, Tachy·graphist,** a shorthand writer, a stenographer; = sense 1.

**1887** *Cassell's Encycl. Dict.*, *Tachygrapher.* **1891** in *Cent. Dict.* **1895** FARRAR *Gather. Clouds* II. 151 That you..may injure my reputation as a tachygraphist.

**Tachygraphic** (tækigræ·fik), *a.* [f. as prec. + -IC: cf. GRAPHIC.] Of or pertaining to the art of tachygraphy or rapid writing; *spec.* applied to a cursive or running handwriting as opposed to one having separate and fully-formed letters, also to writing with many contractions, ligatures, and compendia.

*a* **1763** BYROM *Robbery Cambr. Coach* xii, 'No Help!' said I, 'No Tachygraphic Pow'r, To interpose in this unequal Hour!' — *Art Eng. Poetry* vi, To learn the truly tachygraphic Plan. **1852** H. ROGERS *Ecl. Faith* (1853) 38 Amuse yourself (I know your old tachygraphic skill)..by jotting down some fragments of our absurdities. **1879** RENOUF *Hibbert Lect.* 14 The Egyptians had from the earliest times used a tachygraphic or cursive character which is a rough and abridged form of the hieroglyphic. **1890** E. M. THOMPSON in *Classical Rev.* May 220/1 Thus was introduced into the Greek writing of the middle ages a new set of compendia commonly called tachygraphic signs.

So **Tachygra·phical** *a.* [see -ICAL] = prec.

**1764** JEFFERSON *Let.* Writ. 1892 I. 356, I will send you some of these days Shelton's Tachygraphical Alphabet, and directions. **1882–3** *Schaff's Encycl. Relig. Knowl.* III. 2556/1 The old character..was altered..and assumed somewhat of a cursive, or tachygraphical form.

**Tachygrapho·meter.** [See TACHYGRAPH and -METER.] (See quot. 1900.)

**1891** *Rep. U. S. Coast & Geodetic Survey* App. 16. **1900** H. M. WILSON *Topogr. Surveying* xiii. 280 There are two forms of this instrument [Wagner-Fennel Tachymeter]... The first of these..corresponds to a transit, and the second to an alidade. The latter called a tachygraphometer, for use with the plane-table.

**Tachygraphy** (tæki·grăfi). [f. Gr. ταχύ-ς swift + -GRAPHY.] 'The art or practice of quick writing' (J.); variously applied to shorthand, and (in palæography) to cursive as distinguished from angular letters, to the Egyptian hieratic, and to the Greek and Latin writing of the Middle Ages with its many abbreviations and compendia.

**1641** SHELTON (*title*) Tachygraphy. The most exact and compendious methode of short and swift writing. **1656** BLOUNT *Glossogr.*, *Tachygraphy*, the art or description of swift writing. **1778** KIPPIS *Biog. Brit.* (ed. 2) I. 538 *note*, Thomas Shelton became famous..for his Tachygraphy; or easy, exact, and speedy short writing. **1826** *Edin. Rev.* XLV. 145 The Hieratic..is immediately derived from the hieroglyphic, of which it is merely a tachygraphy. **1890** E. M. THOMPSON in *Classical Rev.* May 220/1 The twofold system of tachygraphy, if it may be so termed, in use among the scribes of the middle ages.

**Tachylite, -lyte** (tæ·kiləit). *Min.* [ad. Ger. *tachylit* (Breithaupt 1826), f. Gr. ταχύ-ς swift + λυτός soluble, in reference to its easy fusibility.] 'A black basaltic glass, formerly regarded as a homogeneous mineral' (Chester *Dict. Min.*).

*Tachylyte basalt*, a variety of basalt having glassy selvages, and a highly microlithic basis.

**1868** DANA *Min.* 245 The species may be the same with tachylyte. **1879** RUTLEY *Stud. Rocks* x. 113 A proceeding analogous to that which seems to have taken place in some tachylytes. **1888** G. A. J. COLE in *Q. Jrnl. Geol. Soc.* XLIV. 300 On some additional occurrences of Tachylite. *Ibid.*, This tachylite adhered more firmly to the contact rocks than to the mass from which it was developed.

Hence **Tachyli·tic, -ly·tic** *a.*, of the nature of, composed of, or containing tachylite.

**1888** G. A. J. COLE in *Q. Jrnl. Geol. Soc.* XLIV. 303 The vein..showed thin tachylitic selvage.

**Tachymeter** (tæki·mĭtəɹ). Also **tachyometer**. [mod. f. Gr. ταχύ-ς swift + -METER; so F. *tachymètre* (a form more on Gr. analogies than TACHEOMETER).] Name of a surveying instrument, adapted to the rapid location of points on a survey. So **Tachyme·tric** *a.*, **Tachy·metry**, the use of such an instrument.

**1860** MAYNE *Expos. Lex.*, *Tachymeter*, term for an instrument for quickly measuring level surfaces. **1891** BUFF & BERGER *Handbk. Engin. & Surv. Instr.* 109 The name Tachymeter, or rapid measurer, has been applied for many years, in Europe, to instruments of this description. *Ibid.*, Tachymetry. **1900** H. M. WILSON *Topogr. Surveying* xii. 236 Tachymetry, or, as it is sometimes called, tachyometry..enables the operator, by a single observation upon a rod, to obtain the necessary horizontal and vertical data for the determination of the three elements of position of a point on the surface of the earth. *Ibid.*, There are practically two systems of tachymetric measurement: The angular or tangential system; and The stadia, telemeter, or subtend system. *Ibid.* xiii. 282 A most satisfactory tachymeter, both for filling in details on large-scale maps, and for carrying on rough geographic or exploratory surveys.

† **Ta·cid**, *a.* *Obs. rare.* [f. L. *tacēre* to be silent + -ID[1]; cf. *acid* from L. *acēre*.] = TACIT.

**1651** J. F[REAKE] *Agrippa's Occ. Philos.* 119 Whence also the tacid consents of animals seem to agree with divine bodies. **1659** T. PECKE *Parnassi Puerp.* 38 In the Chest.. lockt up, of your most Tacid Breast.

Hence † **Ta·cidly** *adv.* = TACITLY.

**1640** G. SANDYS *Christ's Passion* III. 255 Nor Loaves, so tacidly increast, Againe so many thousands feast.

**Tacit** (tæ·sit), *a.* Also 7-8 **tacite**. [ad. L. *tacit-us*, pa. pple. of *tacēre* to be silent. Cf. F. *tacite* (14th c. in Hatz.-Darm.).]

**1.** Unspoken, unvoiced; silent, emitting no sound; noiseless, wordless.

**1605** BACON *Adv. Learn.* I. i. § 1 Without the interruption of tacite obiections. **1628** LE GRYS tr. *Barclay's Argenis* 73 With a tacit vpbraiding she put them in mind. **1798** LANDOR *Gebir* II. 238 With a long and tacit step..He looked and tottered on a black abyss. **1824** W. IRVING *T. Trav.* I. 113 A tacit thankfulness in his looks, as if he felt grateful to me. **1854** J. S. C. ABBOTT *Napoleon* (1855) II. xviii. 329 One of those tacit prayers to which no language can give adequate expression.

**b.** Saying nothing; still, silent.

**1604** R. CAWDREY *Table Alph.*, *Tacite*, still, silent, saying nothing. **1651** HOBBES *Govt. & Soc.* xv. § 3. 238 Gods lawes are declar'd after a threefold manner: first, by the tacit dictates of Right reason, next by immediate revelation [etc.]. **1804** WELLINGTON in Gurw. *Desp.* (1837) III. 497 If the British Government had remained..a tacit spectator of events. **1866** CARLYLE *Remin.*, *Irving* (1881) I. 221 Edward Strachey was..a man rather tacit than discursive.

**2.** Not openly expressed or stated, but implied; understood, inferred. *Tacit mortgage*, a lien in the nature of a mortgage created by operation of law. *Tacit relocation*: see RELOCATION.

[*c* **1575** *Balfour's Practicks* (1754) 208 *Tacita relocatio*.] **1637-50** ROW *Hist. Kirk* (Wodrow Soc.) 251 This tacite approveing of these commissioners, men so highlie guiltie,.. argues a great decay of zeall, and courage. **1681** STAIR *Instit. Law Scot.* I. x. § 61. 149 In the tacite legal hypothecation, [our custom] hath only allowed a few. **1690** LOCKE *Hum. Und.* III. ii. § 8 Common use, by a tacit Consent, appropriates certain Sounds to certain Ideas in all Languages. **1705** ADDISON *Italy*, *Monaca* (1733) 23 A tacit Acknowledgment that Monarchy is the more honourable. **1881** *Spectator* 30 Apr. 573 Locke's doctrine of a tacit social compact.

**Taciteau** (tæsitī·ăn), *a.* [f. the name of the Roman historian Tacitus (*c* 54–117): see -AN.] Pertaining to Tacitus, or resembling his pregnant sententious style. So **Ta·citist**, a student or follower of Tacitus; **Ta·citize** *v.*, *intr.* to write in the style of Tacitus.

**1890** LOWELL *Milton's Areop.* Lat. Lit. Ess. (1891) 101 He [Milton] is never weary of insisting on the *Tacitean distinction between liberty and license. **1907** *Athenæum* 7 Sept. 265/3 Accurate scholarship, especially in matters of Tacitean diction. **1656** EARL MONM. tr. *Boccalini's Advts. fr. Parnass.* I. xxiii. (1674) 24 He might like a *Tacitist have written the Civil Wars of Flanders. **1833** ROSCOE tr. *Pellico's Ten Years' Imprisonm.* xxxvi, With all my admiration for the genius of Tacitus, I had never much faith in the justice of *tacitising as he does.

**Tacitly** (tæ·sitli), *adv.* [f. TACIT *a.* + -LY[2].]

**1.** Without speaking; silently; quietly.

**1643** PRYNNE *Rome's Master-Piece* (ed. 2) 24 The secular Iesuites have bought all this street, and have reduced it into a quadrangle, where a Iesuiticall Colledge is tacitly built. **1751** EARL ORRERY *Remarks Swift* (1752) 88 Here a reflection naturally occurs, which..leads me tacitly to admire, and confess the ways of Providence. **1866** GEO. ELIOT *F. Holt* i, To be no longer tacitly pitied by her neighbours for her lack of money.

**2.** Without stating or expressing it; by implication: cf. TACIT *a.* 2.

**1635** EARL STRAFFORD *Lett.* (1739) I. 471 Not tacitely or by way of Consequence, but even in express and binding Terms. **1660** STANLEY *Hist. Philos.* III. I. 30 He tacitely implyed that the rest of mankind were but beasts. **1735** BERKELEY *Free-think. in Math.* § 21 There are certain points tacitly admitted by mathematicians. **1825** MCCULLOCH *Pol. Econ.* II. iv. 179 If, as M. Sismondi has tacitly assumed, the machines cost nothing.

**Ta·citness.** *rare.* [f. TACIT *a.* + -NESS.] The quality of being tacit; silence.

**1657** W. MORICE *Coena quasi Κοινὴ* xxxii. 298 To instruct ..our brethren, who by our tacitnesse might be scandalized. **1885** PATER *Marius the Epicurean* I. 15 That inward tacitness of mind esteemed so important by religious Romans.

**Taciturn** (tæ·sitɒ̄ɹn), *a.* [ad. L. *taciturn-us*, f. *tacit-us*, TACIT.] Characterized by silence or disinclination to conversation; reserved in speech; saying little; uncommunicative.

**1771** SMOLLETT *Humph. Cl.* 26 June, Grieve..was very submissive, respectful, and remarkably taciturn. **1816** *Remarks Eng. Mann.* 61 The people in Europe who partake most with us in this taciturn propensity, are the Dutch. **1849** MACAULAY *Hist. Eng.* vi. II. 68 Godolphin, cautious and taciturn, did his best to preserve neutrality. **1876** BRISTOWE *The. & Pract. Med.* (1878) 875 The patient becomes apathetic, morose or taciturn, or irritable.

Hence **Ta·citurnist**, one who practises habitual silence or reserve; **Ta·citurnly** *adv.*, in a taciturn manner; with habitual reserve.

**1887** *Congregationalist* (U.S.) 10 Feb. (Cent. Dict.) His [von Moltke's] more than eighty years seemed to sit lightly on 'the great *taciturnist'. **1847** WEBSTER, **Taciturnly*, silently, without conversation. **1902** A. AUSTIN *Ld. Kitchener* in *Standard* 12 July 5/2 Honours he needs not, for about his brow He bears them clustered, taciturnly great.

**Taciturnity** (tæsitɒ̄·ɹnĭti). Also 5 -**te**(e, 6 -**ty**(e, 6-7 -**tie**. [a. F. *taciturnité* (14th c.), or ad. L. *taciturnitās*, f. *taciturn-us*: see prec. and -ITY.]

**1.** Habitual silence or disinclination to conversation; reservedness in speech; a taciturn character or state.

*c* **1450** tr. *De Imitatione* III. xli. 112 Oþer whiles he aunsuerde, lest by his taciturnite occasion of offendynge mi3t haue be yoven. **1491** CAXTON *Vitas Patr.* (W. de W. 1495) I. l. 99 b/2 In the sayde monasterie was so grete tacyturnytee and scylence. **1576** FLEMING *Panopl. Epist.* 145, I cannot in this poinct vse taciturnitie and silence. **1606** SHAKS. *Tr. & Cr.* IV. ii. 75 The secrets of nature Haue not more gift in taciturnitie. **1711** ADDISON *Spect.* No. 261 ¶ 1 My natural Taciturnity hindered me from shewing my self to the best Advantage. **1809** W. IRVING *Knickerb.* III. viii. (1861) 107 Our ancestors were noted as being men of truly Spartan taciturnity. **1856** MISS MULOCK *J. Halifax* ix, After which brief reply John relapsed into taciturnity.

**2.** *Sc. Law.* The silence of the creditor occasioning the extinction of an obligation in a shorter period than forty years' prescription: it being presumed that the creditor would not have been so long silent if the debt had not been paid or the obligation implemented.

**1765-8** ERSKINE *Instit. Law Scot.* III. vii. § 29 (1773) 533 No general rule can be laid down, at what precise times actions may be lost by taciturnity. **1838** W. BELL *Dict. Law Scot.* 967/2 The only cases in which extinction by such taciturnity has been recognised were those of bills of exchange, prior to the introduction of the sexennial prescription.

† **Tacitu·rnous**, *a.* *Obs. rare*$^{-0}$. [f. L. *taciturn-us* TACITURN + -OUS.] = TACITURN.

**1727** BAILEY *Dict.* vol. II, *Taciturnous*, silent, saying nothing, making no Noise.

**Tack** (tæk), *sb.*[1] Forms: 4-6 **tak**, **takk**(e, 5-7 **tacke**, 6 **take**, (pl. **tax**), 5- **tack**. [TACK *sb.*[1] and *v.*[1] go together, and are doublets of TACHE *sb.*[2], *v.*[2] (q.v.), though forms in *k* or *q* are not recorded in OF., and the etymological history is obscure. For the ulterior etymology Diez compares Ger. *zacken* prong, MHG. *zacke*, Du. *tak* bough; so also Kluge. (The occurrence of Ir. *taca*, Gael. *tacaid* nail, tack, peg, Breton *tach* small nail, has suggested a Celtic origin for the root *tac-*, but this Thurneysen rejects.) App. most of the senses of the sb., including sense 5, were derived from the vb., but the nautical senses of the vb. arose out of sense 5 of the sb., and in their turn gave rise to senses 6 and 7.]

**I.** That which fastens or attaches, etc.

**1.** That which fastens one thing to another, or things together: applied to a fibula or clasp, a buckle, a hook or stud fitting into an eye or loop, a nail, or the like. *Obs.* exc. as in senses 2, 3.

**13..** *Minor Poems fr. Vernon MS.* iii. 410 He bot a bite þat made vs blak, Til fruit weore tied on treo wiþ tak; O fruit for anoþer. *c* **1440** *Promp. Parv.* 485/2 Takke (*H.*, *P.* or botun), *fibula*, *fixula*. **1500-20** DUNBAR *Poems* lxxii. 69 Unto the crose of breid and lenth, Syne tyit him on with greit irne takkis. **1617** MINSHEU *Ductor*, A tacke or hooke, vid. *Buckle*, *Clasp*. **1670** EACHARD *Cont. Clergy* 70 The tackes put into the loops did couple the curtains of the tent, and sew the tent together. **1696** *Lond. Gaz.* No. 3228/4 Lost.., 3 pair of black Stays,..one with black Buckles, in black Tacks and black Loops.

**b.** The frænum of the tongue (in a tongue tied person).

**1671** LIVINGSTON *Let.* in *Wodrow Soc. Sel. Biog.* (1845) I. 247 The sight of the father's danger brake the tack of a son's tongue who was tongue-tacked from birth.

**2.** *spec.* (perh. orig. short for *tack-nail*: see 12 a.) A small sharp-pointed nail of iron or brass, usually with a flat and comparatively large head, used for fastening a light or thin object to something more solid, especially in a slight or temporary manner, so as to admit of easy undoing.

Tacks are distinguished according to their use, as *carpet-tack*, one used for fixing a carpet on the floor; their action, as *thumb-tack*, one pushed in with the thumb, as a drawing-pin; their material, as *brass tack*, *iron tack*, TIN-TACK.

[**1463**, etc.: see *tack-nail* in 12 a.] **1574** in Feuillerat *Revels Q. Eliz.* (1908) 237 Tackes One Thowsand. *a* **1585** POLWART *Flyting w. Montgomerie* 558 His lugs..That to the Tron hes tane so many a tacke. **1601** HOLLAND *Pliny* XXXIV. xiv. 514 Yron..for nailes, studs, and tackes, emploied about greeves and leg-harneis. **1688** R. HOLME *Armoury* III. 292/1 Two sorts of tacks used by [shoemakers], the Sole Tack..and the Heel Tack. **1703** MOXON *Mech. Exerc.* 53 Drive in a small Tack on each side. **1745** P. THOMAS *Jrnl. Anson's Voy.* 259 The Scale..is made of Bambo, the Divisions distinguished by small Brass Tacks. **1851** D. JERROLD *St. Giles* xvi. 168 At his work, driving tin tacks into a baby's coffin.

**b.** (See quot.)

**1847-78** HALLIWELL s. v., A wooden peg for hanging dresses on is sometimes called a tack.

**3.** *Technical uses.* **a.** *Gardening.* A fastening for shoots, etc., consisting of a strip or band secured at each end to a wall or the like. **b.** *Plumbing.* A strip of lead having one end soldered to a pipe, and the other fastened to a wall or support.

**1545** *Rates of Customs* a vj, Corke takkes the thousande x.s. **1615** W. LAWSON *Country Housew. Gard.* (1626) 7 To plant Apricockes, Cheries, and Peaches, by a wall, and with tacks, and other meanes to spread them vpon, and fasten them to a wall. **1658** EVELYN *Fr. Gard.* (1675) 34 They do extreamly ill, when they fagot, and bundle together a great many small twiggs, in one tack. **1693** — *De la Quint. Compl. Gard.* II. 41. **1823** P. NICHOLSON *Pract. Build.* 408 Two broad pieces of lead, called tacks, are attached to the back lap-joints and spread out, right and left, for fastening the [socket] pipes to the wall by means of wall-hooks of iron. **1877** S. S. HELLYER *Plumber* ii. 33 When there are no chases, and the pipes are fixed on tacks, the tacks should be strong.

**4.** An act of tacking or fastening together, now esp. in a slight or temporary way; a stitch, *esp.* a long slight stitch used in fastening seams, etc., preparatory to the permanent sewing; a very slight fastening or tie, by which a thing is loosely held, as *hanging by a tack*.

**1705** VANBRUGH *Confed.* v. ii, If dear mother will give us her blessing, the parson shall give us a tack [cf. TACK *v.*[1] 1 c]. **1808** JAMIESON s. v., *It hings by a tack*, it has a very slight hold. **1878** DICKINSON *Cumbld. Gloss.*, *Teck*, *Tack*, a stitch. 'A teck i' time seavvs nine'. *Mod.* Give it a tack, to hold it together until there is time to stitch it.

**b.** Adhesiveness, tackiness; esp. in *Bookbinding*, 'a slight stickiness remaining in leather before the varnish or dressing is quite dry' (C. Davenport).

**1908** *Academy* 11 Apr. 656/1 It is very cunningly reproduced, even to the extent of a suggestion of a slight 'tack' belonging to old leather.

**II.** Nautical and derived senses. (Sense 5 is a special application of 1, and is the origin of sense 7 of the vb., whence again comes sense 6 here.)

**5.** A rope, wire, or chain and hook, used to secure to the ship's side the windward clews or corners of the courses (lower square sails) of a sailing ship when sailing close hauled on a wind; also the rope, wire, or lashing used to secure amidships the windward lower end of a fore-and-aft sail.

*To bring, get, haul*, or *put the tacks aboard* (= to the board), to haul the tacks into such a position as to trim the sails to the wind, to set sail. *To bring* or *have the starboard* or *port tacks aboard*, to set the sails to, or sail with, the wind on the side mentioned. Also *transf.* used allusively in reference to travelling by land.

**1481-90** *Howard Househ. Bks.* (Roxb.) 111 My Lord paid him for iij. hausers, a peir takkes, a ratling line for Chewdes..xv.s. **1486** *Naval Accts. Hen. VII* (1896) 13 A payre of takkes & a payr of shets weying DCCXlj lb. **1582** L. WARD in Hakluyt *Voy.* III. 757 Wee brought our tacks aboord, and stoode along West by North and West larboord tacked. **1611** COTGR., *Coytes*, Tackes; great Ropes vsed about the (maine) sayle of a ship. **1626** CAPT. SMITH *Accid. Yng. Seamen* 28 The wind veares, git your star-boord tacks aboord. **1627** — *Seaman's Gram.* v. 23 Tackes are great ropes which hauing a wall-knot at one end seased into the clew of the saile, and so reeued first thorow the chestres, and then commeth in at a hole in the ships sides, this doth carry forward the clew of the saile to make it stand close by a wind. **1688** J. CLAYTON in *Phil. Trans.* XVII. 984 They must there bring the contrary Tack on Board [*i.e.* to put the vessel on the other tack]. **1747** *Gentl. Mag.* 521 The wind shifted 3 or 4 points, which obliged us to tack, and make more sail, by hauling our main tack on board. **1825** H. B. GASCOIGNE *Nav. Fame* 52 To set each Course the Tacks they Haul on Board, Then drag the Sheets aft, as they can afford. **1846** YOUNG *Naut Dict.*, *The tack of a fore and aft sail* is the rope which keeps down its lower forward clue; and of a studding sail that which keeps down its lower outer clue. The tack of a lower studding-sail is called the Out-Haul.

*transf.* **1780** S. CURWEN *Jrnl. & Lett.* 22 June (1864) 277 Discouraged from proceeding further by water,..and taking, as the sailors phrase it, our London tack on board, [we] proceeded the next stage of fifteen miles. **1820** A. GIFFORD *MS. Acc.* 7 Sept., We took our land tacks on board of our waggon, and directed our course west souwest for New London.

**b.** The lower windward corner of a sail, to which the tack (rope or chain) is attached.

**1769** FALCONER *Dict. Marine* (1789), *Aboard main tack!* the order to draw the main-tack, i. e. the lower corner of the main-sail, down to the chess-tree. **1851** KIPPING *Sailmaking* (ed. 2) 5 In all triangular sails and in those four-sided sails wherein the head is not parallel to the foot, the foremost corner at the foot is called the tack. **1904** F. T. BULLEN *Creatures of Sea* xvii. 232 The peak of the sail is dropped and the tack hoisted; in sea parlance, the sail is 'scandalised'.

†**c.** *Tack of a flag*: see quot. *Obs.*

**1794** *Rigging & Seamanship* I. 176 *Tack of a Flag*, a line spliced into the eye at the bottom of the tabling, for securing the flag to the haliard.

**6.** An act of tacking (TACK *v.*[1] 7); hence, the direction given to a ship's course by tacking; the course of a ship in relation to the direction of the wind and the position of her sails; a course or movement obliquely opposed to the direction of the wind; one of a consecutive series of such movements to one side and the other alternately made by a sailing vessel, in order to reach a point to windward.

A ship is said to be *on the starboard* or *port tack* as the wind comes from starboard or port. At each change of tack, the relative positions of the tack and sheet of the courses are reversed.

**1614** SIR R. DUDLEY in *Fortesc. Papers* (Camden) 9 Being fare more swyfte then the gallie..(espetiallye uppon a tacke). **1666** PEPYS *Diary* 4 July, Even one of our flag-men in the fleete did not know which tacke lost the wind, or which kept it, in this last engagement. **1676** *Lond. Gaz.* No. 1108/1 Their Admiral was lost by accident, or rather neglect of the Seamen, who omitting upon a Tack to fasten the Guns, they run all to one side, and over-set the ship. **1694** NARBOROUGH, etc., in *Acc. Sev. Late Voy.* I. 165 Before the Ship could Ware and bring to upon the other Tack, She struck. **1749** CAPT. STANDIGE in *Naval Chron.* III. 207 We kept working the Ship in the wind's eye, tack and tack. **1779** KING *Cook's Voy. Pacific* VI. ix. (1785) III. 418 During the afternoon, we kept standing on our tacks, between the island of Potoe, and the Grand Ladrone. **1804** W. LAYMAN in Nicolas *Disp. Nelson* (1845) V. 496 Turning to the Westward, against the wind, some tacks do not exceed one mile. **1836** MARRYAT *Midsh. Easy* xiii, That they should make short tacks with her, to weather the point. **1885** *Law Times Rep.* LIII. 54/1 The *J. M. Stevens* was proceeding under all sail close-hauled on the port tack.

**b.** *fig.* and *transf.* A zigzag course on land.

**1788** J. MAY *Jrnl. & Lett.* (1873) 31, I..advanced as fast as possible to finish my land tacks. **1813** *Salem Gaz.* 22 Oct. 3/2 Saw 2 four horse wagons, standing abreast, upon their larboard tacks, head towards us. **1854** J. L. STEPHENS *Centr. Amer.* 363, I could not walk, so I beat up making the best tacks I could, and stopping every time I put about. **1893** Q. [COUCH] *Delect. Duchy* 305 Bontigo's Van..scaling the acclivity..in a series of short tacks.

**7.** *fig.* A course or line of conduct or action; implying change or difference from some preceding or other course.

**1675** V. ALSOP *Anti-Sozzo* i. 29 No man more reall when he offers an Injury, nor more complemental in his Courtesies; for he's just now standing upon a Tack. **1697** COLLIER *Ess. Mor. Subj.* II. (1709) 72 His Business will be to follow the Loudest Cry, and make his Tack with the Wind. **1795** BURKE *Let. to Ld. Auckland* Wks. IX. Pref. 22 Through our publick life, we have generally sailed on somewhat different tacks. **1811** T. CREEVEY in *Cr. Papers* (1904) I. vii. 140 They are upon a new tack in consulting publick opinion. **1901** *Scotsman* 8 Mar. 6/5 The bill..seemed to proceed upon the wrong tack.

**b.** A circuitous course of conduct.

**1869** BALLANTYNE *Deanhaugh* 117 (E.D.D.) Your nephew ..canna be up to sae mony shifts an' tacks as you.

**III.** That which is tacked on or appended.

**8.** Something tacked on or attached as an addition or rider; an addendum, supplement, appendix; *spec.* in parliamentary usage, A clause relating to some extraneous matter, appended, in order to secure its passing, to a bill, esp. a bill of supply.

**1705** in Hearne *Collect.* 10 Oct. (O. H. S.) I. 54 All the World's a general Tack Of one thing to another. Why then about one Honest Tack Do Fools make such a Pother? **1712** SWIFT *Jrnl. to Stella* 10 May, The parliament will hardly be up till June. We were like to be undone some days ago with a tack. *a* **1715** BURNET *Own Time* VII. (1823) V. 177 Some tacks had been made to money-bills in king Charles's time. **1768** LD. HILLSBOROUGH in *North Car. Col. Rec.* VII. 868 Appointed by a Law..especially passed for that purpose, and not by way of Tack to a Law for other purposes. **1787** *Minor* I. xiv. 52 My mother to this added the following tack. **1879** MINTO *Defoe* v. 64 The Lords refused to pass the Money Bill till the tack was withdrawn.

**b.** *Tack-on*: the act of tacking something on, or that which is tacked on or added. *colloq.*

**1905** *Outlook* 11 Nov. 664/1 She has not the passion for a tack-on which is general in this country.

**9.** *dial.* (some doubtfully belonging here). **a.** A hanging shelf: see quot. 1847–78. **b.** Each of the two nibs or handles of a scythe. **c.** *Coal-mining.* A temporary prop or scaffold: see quots.

**a.** **1446** *Yatton Churchw. Acc.* (Som. Rec. Soc.) 85 It. y payde to Hurneman for ij takys v[d]. *c* **1730** J. POYNTER *Dorset Voc.* in *N. & Q.* 6th Ser. VIII. 45/2 *A tack*, a shelf. **1847–78** HALLIWELL, *Tack*,..a shelf. A kind of shelf made of crossed bars of wood suspended from the ceiling, on which to put bacon, &c. **1862** T. HUGHES in *Macm. Mag.* V. 245/1 An ther wur beacon upon rack An plates to yet it upon tack. **b.** *a* **1825** FORBY *Voc. E. Anglia*, *Tack*,..the handle of a sithe. **1892** P. H. EMERSON *Son of Fens* 131 Some on 'em fitting new sticks to the scythes, some on 'em putting in tacks. **c.** **1849** GREENWELL *Coal-trade Terms Northumb. & Durh.*, *Tack*, a small prop of coal, sometimes left..to support it until the kirving is finished, except knocking out the tack. **1883** GRESLEY *Coal Mining Gloss.*, *Tack*..(Som[erset].) A wooden scaffold put into a pit-shaft for temporary purposes.

**IV.** As a quality.

**10.** Hold; holding quality; adherence, endurance, stability, strength, substance, solidity. Now *dial.*

**1412–20** LYDG. *Chron. Troy* II. 1868 Who þat geynstryueth schal haue litel tak. *c* **1425** *Cast. Persev.* 2987 in *Macro Plays* 166 Tresor, tresor, it hathe no tak. **1573** TUSSER *Husb.* (1878) 168 What tacke in a pudding, saith greedie gut wringer. **1583** GOLDING *Calvin on Deut.* lxvi. 404 There will neuer bee any holde or tacke in it. **1651–66** CARYL *Expos. Job* xxii. 25 (1676) 2255 He should find..that there was tack in it, that it was solid silver, or silver that had strength in it. **1884** *Cheshire Gloss.*, *Tack*,..hold, confidence, reliance. There is no tack in such a one, he is not to be trusted.

**b.** Adhesive quality, stickiness: cf. TACKY *a.*

**18..** *Gilder's Man.* 28 (Cent. Dict.) Let your work stand until so dry as only to have sufficient tack to hold your leaf.

†**11.** Phrases. **a.** *To hold*, rarely *have*, *tack with* (*to*), to hold one's own with, hold one's ground with, keep up with; to be even with or equal to; to match. *Obs.*

**1412–20** LYDG. *Chron. Troy* I. 4259 Here lith on ded, þer a-noþer wounded, So þat þei myȝt with them haue no tak. *a* **1518** SKELTON *Magnyf.* 2084 A thousande pounde with Lyberte may holde no tacke. **1600** W. WATSON *Decacordon* (1602) 71 Secular Priests, whom no English Iesuit is able to hold tacke withall. **1652** URQUHART *Jewel* Wks. (1834) 227 The incomparable Crichtoun had..held tack to all the disputants. **1658** J. HARRINGTON *Prerog. Pop. Govt.* I. xii. Wks. (1700) 317 Fourteen Years had their Commonwealth held tack with the Romans, in Courage, Conduct, and Virtue. *c* **1695** in Curwen *Hist. Booksellers* (1873) 29 To make the parallel hold tack, Methinks there's little lacking.

†**b.** *To hold* (a person, etc.) *tack* (*to tack*): to be a match for; to hold at bay. *Obs.*

**1555** W. WATREMAN *Fardle Facions* II. vi. 150 Thei [Parthians] helde the Romaines suche tacke, that in sondrie warres they gaue them great ouerthrowes. **1606** *Sir G. Goosecappe* III. i, I am sure our Ladies hold our Lords tacke for Courtship, and yet the French Lords put them downe. **1612** DRAYTON *Poly-olb.* xi. 48 Faire Chester, call'd of old Carelegion,..the faithfull station then, So stoutly held to tack by those neere North-Wales men. **1615** HOBY *Curry-combe* i. 3 As if I haue not a good dish of Oysters, and a cold pye at home to hold you tacke. **1706** MRS. CENTLIVRE *Basset-Table* II. Wks. (1723) 221 Ay, give me the woman that can hold me tack in my own dialect. *a* **1825** FORBY *Voc. E. Anglia* s.v. *Hold*, Phr. 'to hold one tack', to keep him close to the point.

†**c.** *To bear*, *hold tack*, to be substantial, strong, or lasting; to hold out, endure, hold one's own.

**1573** TUSSER *Husb.* (1878) 28 And Martilmas beefe doth beare good tack, when countrie folke doe dainties lack. **1600** W. WATSON *Decacordon* (1602) 164 It serueth to hold tacke, till by inuasion or otherwise the Iesuits may worke their feate. **1663** BUTLER *Hud.* I. III. 277 If this twig be made of Wood That will hold tack. **1673** R. HEAD *Canting Acad.* 19 With good Milk pottage I held tack.

†**d.** *To hold, keep tack, stand to tack*: see quots.

**1611** COTGR., *Ester à vne chose conuenuë*, to keepe touch; hold tacke, stand to a bargaine. **1686** F. SPENCE tr. *Varillas' Ho. Medicis* 305 The correspondence he had in that place not keeping tack at the time prefixt.

†**e.** *To be half tack with*: (?) to be midway between in position or quality. *Obs.*

**1567** MAPLET *Gr. Forest* 60 Reede is halfe tack with the Herbe and tree, but in force or growth, aboue the Herbe. And nothing in strength to the tree his comparison.

**V. 12.** *attrib.* and *Comb.* **a.** in sense 2: **tack-claw, -extractor, -lifter, -puller**, a tool for extracting tacks or small nails from a carpet, etc.; **tack-comb**, a row of tacks cast in the form of a hair-comb for use in a shoe-making machine; **tack-driver**, a machine which automatically places and drives a series of tacks; also = *tack-hammer*; **tack-hammer**, a light hammer for driving tacks; **tack-mill**, a factory for making tacks; †**tack-nail**, a tack, tacket, or hob-nail; **tack-rivet**, a small metal rivet; **tack work**: see quot.

**1889** TALMAGE in *Voice* (N. Y.) 28 Feb., Much [church work] amounts to..a *tack-hammer smiting the Gibraltar. **1890** 'R. BOLDREWOOD' *Miner's Right* (1899) 11 Which made the heavy tool tremble in my grasp like a tack hammer. **1858** SIMMONDS *Dict. Trade*, **Tack-lifter*, a tool for taking up tacks from carpets on a floor. **1884** H. D. LLOYD in *N. Amer. Rev.* June 546 The *tack-mills in the combination run about three days in the week. **1463** in Rogers *Agric. & Pr.* III. 556/3, 1 c. *taknail 4*d.* **1519** HORMAN *Vulg.* 237 Set some tacke naylis, or racke naylis arowe. **1591** PERCIVALL *Sp. Dict.*, *Broca*, a shooemakers tacke naile. **1874** THEARLE *Naval Archit.* 71 The side plates, or bars, are connected to the vertical plate by..small rivets, termed '*tack rivets'. **1879** C. HIBBS in *Cassell's Techn. Educ.* IV. 299/2 '*Tack work', which means brass-headed nails, hooks, sash and drawer knobs, and little things of that sort.

**b.** in sense 5: *tack-block, -earing, -end, -lashing, -piece* (see quot.), *-tackle*; **tack-pins**, belaying pins of the fife-rail (Smyth *Sailor's Word-bk.* 1867).

**1777** COOK *Voy.* III. ii. II. 17 When they change tacks they throw the vessel up in the wind, ease off the sheet, and bring the heel or *tack-end of the yard to the other end of the boat, and the sheet in like manner. **1865** MACGREGOR *Rob Roy in Baltic* (1867) 296 The tack end of the boom is made fast to the mast by a flat piece of leather. **1711** W. SUTHERLAND *Shipbuild. Assist.* 164 **Tack-piece*, that to which the Fore-sail is tack'd down. **1769** FALCONER *Dict. Marine* (1776), **Tack-tackle*, a small tackle used occasionally to pull down the tack of the principal sails of a ship to their respective stations. **1882** NARES *Seamanship* (ed. 6) 82 *Tack tackle*..a tackle from the tack of the spanker to the deck.

**Tack** (tæk), *sb.*[2] Chiefly *Sc.* and *north. Eng.* Forms: 4–6 **tak**, 5–6 **takk** (*pl.* **tax**), 6–8 **tacke**, 6– **tack**. [f. *tac, tak*, TAKE *v.*; cf. TAKE *sb.*; also ON. *tak* taking, seizure, etc., *taka* a taking, seizure, capture, revenue, tenure (Vigf.), OSw. *tak* taking, hold, *taka man* collector.]

**I.** †**1.** A customary payment levied by a ruler, feudal superior, or corporation. *Obs.*

*a* **1300** *Cursor M.* 28438 Toll and tak, and rent o syse, Withalden i haue wit couettise. **1564** *Reg. Privy Council Scot.* I. 295 To mak and deliver to the saidis Margaret and Alexander infeftmentis of the saidis landis..likwyise..in all pointis without takkis. *a* **1578** LINDESAY (Pitscottie) *Chron. Scot.* (S.T.S.) I. 322 He dressit the said bischope.. for certaine teindis and tax that the bischope gaif him.

**2.** Tenure or tenancy, of land, benefice, etc.: *esp.* leasehold tenure, e. g. of a farm, mill, or the like; the period of tenure. *Sc.* and *north. Eng.* (Cf. ON. *taka* tenure (of land).)

**1423** *Charters, etc. of Edinb.* (1871) 55 To have thair corne grundin at the saide millis..durand the saide tak. **1424** *Coldstream Chartul.* (1879) 43 Ye said priores and ye conuent sal enter in ye tak of ye said land at Qwitsonday. **1449** *Sc. Acts Jas. II* (1814) II. 35 Suppos the lordis sel or analy þai landis þ[t] þe takaris sall remayne with þare takis, on to þe ische of þare termes. **1526** *Lanc. Wills* (Chetham Soc.) I. 15, I will that Dorothe my wyff shall have all such takks leysses and graunts as I now have by the graunts of the Abbot of Qhalley. **1571** PLOWDEN *Reports* 169 b, Cesty qe prist lease pur ans dun ferme en le Northe paiz, appelle ceo Tacke. **1671** in *Proc. Soc. Ant. Scot.* (1892) XXVI. 194 We..Stewart Principall Justiciare and Admirall of Orknay and Zetland, having power be vertue of my tack therof to nominat and appoynt bailyies [etc.]. **1701** J. LAW *Counc. Trade* (1751) 40 That the present farm or tack of the customs be broken, and that the said impositions of foreign excise and entry-money may never hereafter be leased out, or let to farm. **1885** J. G. BERTRAM in *Brit. Alm. Comp.* 77 The 'tack' [of a deer forest] may be for a period of years, or it may be for 'the season'. **1887** *S. Chesh. Gloss.* s. v., 'It's the best tack as ever I seid',..i. e. the farm in question was taken on the best conditions.

**b.** Sometimes more or less concretely: A leasehold tenement, a farm. *Sc.*

*c* **1470** HENRYSON *Mor. Fab.* XII. (*Wolf & Lamb*) xviii, How durst thow tak on hand..To put him fra his tak, and gar him thig? **1508** KENNEDIE *Flyting w. Dunbar* 365 Thow has a tome purs, I haue stedis and takkis. **15..** DUNBAR *Poems* xvii. 21 Sum takis vthir menis takkis. **1515** in *Fam. Rose Kilravock* (Spalding Club) 185 Aucht oxin to plenys ane tak.

**c.** *fig.* A period, a spell (*of* some condition). *Sc.* Cf. 'lease' of life, etc.

*a* **1758** RAMSAY *Masque* 189 Thou'lt grant them a lang tack of bliss. **1821** GALT *Ann. Parish* xii, There came on a sudden frost, after a tack of wet weather. **1887** SERVICE *Dr. Duguid* xxi. 138 We had a lang tack of very wat weather.

**3.** *transf.* An agreement or compact. *Sc.*

(Cf. prec. 11 d.)

*a* **1758** RAMSAY *Clout the Caldron* iv, I've a tinkler under tack, That's us'd to clout my caldron. **1786** BURNS *Earnest Cry & Prayer* vi, In gath'rin' votes you were na slack; Now stand as tightly by your tack.

**4.** Pasture for cattle let on hire. *dial.*

**1804–12** DUNCUMB *Hist. Heref.* I. 214 A *tack*, grass or clover for horses and cattle, hired by the week, month, or quarter. **1863** MORTON *Cycl. Agric.*, *Tack*, hired pasturage. **1873** *Berrow's Worcester Jrnl.* Apr. (E.D.D.), Horses or horned cattle will be taken into Westwood Park to tack or ley. **1877** *Birmingham Weekly Post* 22 Dec. 1/1 It is..a common expression where a farmer turns his cattle out on the lands of another to say they are out at 'tack'. **1879–81** MISS JACKSON *Shropsh. Word-bk.* s. v., 'Yo'n got a power o' stock fur yore farm'...'Aye, I mus' get some out on tack'.

**II. 5.** A take of fish; a catch, draught, haul: = TAKE *sb.* 5. Also *fig.* *Sc.* and *north. Eng.*

**1596** DALRYMPLE tr. *Leslie's Hist. Scot.* I. 40 Gif in ony place quhair a tak of herring is..ony scheding of manis blude aryse..thay ar said to abhor frome that place. **1597** SKENE *De Verb. Sign.* s. v. *Assisa*, An thousand herring of ilk tack that halds. **1678** W. ADAMS *Dedham Pulpit* 68 Whence a great tack of souls to Christ hath followed. **1772** *Hartford Merc., Suppl.* 18 Sept. 3/2 There is at present the finest tack of herrings ever known, which are now selling on the shore at sixteen-pence the hundred. **1888** VAN HARE *Fifty Years Showman's Life* 2 When they draw their net it's called a tack; if there are plenty of fish in the net they call it a good tack, or if there are very few fish they call it a bad tack.

**III. 6.** *attrib.* and *Comb.*, as **tack-duty**, the rent reserved on a lease; the rent paid by a tacksman or farmer of the customs; **tack-money**, payment for pannage or pasture; †**tack-swine**, hogs paid in rent; **tack-work**: see quot.

**1680** (Dec. 23) *St. Andrew's Town Council Minute-bk.* 86 Impouring him quarterlie to receave from the taxmen of Costomes the *tak deutie payable for the saidis Costomes. *a* **1722** FOUNTAINHALL *Decis.* (1759) I. 8 Had he not paid the tack-duty for tiends and all. **1809** TOMLINS *Jacob's Law Dict.*, *Tack-Duty*, the rent reserved on a lease. **1876** GRANT *Burgh Sch. Scotl.* II. xiv. 457 In 1680 the council of St. Andrews allocated the tack duties of the customs of the city towards paying the schoolmaster's stipend. **1688** R. HOLME *Armoury* III. 75/1 An Agistor, is an Officer of the Forest, that takes in to Feed the Cattel of Strangers, and receives for the Kings use all such *Tack-Money as becomes due from those Strangers. **1523** FITZHERB. *Surv.* viii. 8 Where as the tenauntes pay *tacke swyne by custome,..or a halfpeny for euery swyne, as the custome is vsed. **1879–81** MISS JACKSON *Shropsh. Word-bk.*, **Tack-work*, work done by contract.

**Tack,** *sb.*3 *Obs.* or *dial.* [Origin uncertain; in sense 1, it appears to be a doublet of TACHE *sb.*1; cf. Picard *taque* = Fr. *tache* spot; but cf. also F. *tac* 'a kind of rot among sheepe; also, a Plague-spot' (Cotgr.), which Hatz.-Darm. think possibly borrowed from L. *tactus* found in the sense of infection, contagious disease. Sense 2 is possibly transf. from 1, but may be of different origin.]

†**1.** A spot, a stain; a blemish; = TACHE *sb.*1 1, 2.

*c* **1425** *Cast. Persev.* 2178 in *Macro Plays* 142 In sory synne had he no tak & ȝyt for synne he bled blody ble. *a* **1603** T. CARTWRIGHT *Confut. Rhem. N. T.* (1618) 467 The witnesse of the other hath often a wrest and tacke of her corruption.

**2.** A smack, taste, or flavour (*of* something); *esp.* an alien, peculiar, or ill flavour; = TACHE *sb.*1 2 c. Also *fig.*

**1602** R. T. *Five Godlie Serm.* 146 Superstitious ceremonies, without anie smacke or tacke of anie sound Christian doctrine. **1611** COTGR. s. v. *Piquer*, *Le poisson pique*, begins to haue a tacke, or ill tast. **1622** DRAYTON *Poly-olb.* xix. 130 Or cheese which our fat soil to every quarter sends, Whose tack the hungry clown and plow-man so commends. **1868** ATKINSON *Cleveland Gloss.* s. v., If two articles of food are cooked together, and the stronger flavoured one communicates a taste to the other, it is said to 'have a tak o' t'ither'. **1884** *Cheshire Gloss.* s. v., Ale which has been put into a musty cask is said to have a tack, or a tack of the cask.

† **Tack,** *sb.*4 *Obs. rare.* [Origin uncertain.] A billiard-cue: see quot.

**1688** R. HOLME *Armoury* III. 262/1 On each side [the billiard table] standeth a Man with a Tack in his hand, to push the Ball into an Hassard, or Hole. *Ibid.* xvi. (Roxb.) 69/1 In the base of this quarter, is the figure of the Tack or a Stick used at the Billiard table for the strikeing of an Ivory ball.

**Tack,** *sb.*5 [Origin obscure: perh. from TACK *sb.*1 10; but cf. also TACKLE *sb.* sense 8.] Food-stuff; chiefly in HARD-TACK, ship's biscuit, SOFT-TACK; also *gen.* stuff, often in depreciatory sense. Cf. TACKLE *sb.* 8.

**1833** MARRYAT *P. Simple* xxviii, The..steward..came back with a basket of *soft-tack*, i. e. loaves of bread. **1841** LEVER *C. O'Malley* lxxxviii, No more hard tack thought I, no salt butter. **1864** *Daily Tel.* 5 Nov., Horses stopped to graze, and the men..began quietly munching a hard tack. **1889** D. C. MURRAY *Dang. Catspaw* 129 He knows Lord Byron from beginning to end, but his head's that full of that kind of tack there's no room for anything else. **1894** — *Making of Novelist* 42, I thought the canteen tack the nastiest stuff I had ever tasted.

**Tack,** *sb.*6 *rare.* [Echoic. Cf. *tack* sb., clap, *tack* vb., to slap, clap, in *Eng. Dial. Dict.*; F. *tac* in *tac-au-tac*.] The sound of a smart stroke.

**1821** SCOTT *Kenilw.* x, Now, hush and listen,..you will soon hear the tack of a hammer.

**Tack,** *v.*1 [Doublet of TACHE *v.*2; cf. TACK *sb.*1]

**I.** To attach.

†**1.** *trans.* To attach, fasten (one thing to another, or things together). *Obs.* except as in 3.

**1387** TREVISA *Higden* (Rolls) III. 173 He..made hem sprede and takkede þe skyn aboute þe chayer [orig. *sellæ judiciariæ circumponi*] þere þe iuge schulde sitte in plee forto deme. *c* **1400** *Brut* 103 Kyng Alurede hade þat boke in his warde, and..lete hit faste bene tackede to a piler, þat men myȝt hit nouȝt remeve. **1483** *Act* 1 *Rich. III*, c. 8 § 16 Without tacking or sowing of any Bulrushes..upon the Lists of the same. **1530** PALSGR. 746/1 Tacke it faste with a nayle. *a* **1616** BEAUM. & FL. *Scornf. Lady* II. iii, Peace, or I'le tack your tongue up to your roof. **1696** BP. PATRICK *Comm. Exod.* xxvi. (1697) 506 The Loops were..tackt to the Selvage of the outermost of them. **1713** STEELE *Englishm.* No. 26. 172 He dried and tacked together the Skins of Goats. **1843** LE FEVRE *Life Trav. Phys.* II. I. xviii. 153 We often tacked on twelve horses to a small vehicle.

**b.** *transf.* and *fig.* To attach.

*a* **1533** LD. BERNERS *Gold. Bk. M. Aurel.* xliii. (1535) 83 b, Al the vnderstandynges are tacked to one free wyll. **1653** tr. *Hales' Dissert. de pace* in *Phenix* (1708) II. 376 The Fathers did, with ingenious comments, tack the mysteries of their philosophy to the Word of God. **1695** PRIOR *Taking Namur* ix, With Eke's and Also's tack thy Strain, Great Bard. **1791** GILPIN *Forest Scenery* II. 187 He who works without taste..tacks one part to another, as his misguided fancy suggests.

†**c.** To join in wedlock. *slang. Obs.*

**1732** FIELDING *Debauchees* III. xiv, We will employ this honest gentleman here, to tack our son and daughter together. **1775** SHERIDAN *Duenna* III. iv, I' faith, he must tack me first; my love is waiting. **1821** *Sporting Mag.* VIII. 105 A Curate..Had brought to the altar a pair to be tack'd.

†**2.** To connect or join by an intervening part.

**1639** FULLER *Holy War* II. xii. (1840) 65 It [Tyre]..was tacked to the continent with a small neck of land. **1645** EVELYN *Diary* June, The numberless Islands tacked together by no fewer than 450 bridges. **1762–71** H. WALPOLE *Vertue's Anecd. Paint.* (1786) I. 186 They..have tacked the wings to a house by a colonade.

**3.** To attach in a slight or temporary manner; *esp.* to attach with tacks (short nails or slight stitches), which can be easily taken out.

*c* **1440** *Promp. Parv.* 485/2 Takkyn', or some what sowyn' to-gedur,..*consutulo*. **1642** FULLER *Holy & Prof. St.* III. x. 175 If agitation..jog that out of thy head, which was there rather tack'd then fastned. **1696** J. F. *Merchant's Ware-ho.* 8 The Hamborough is rowled up very hard, and either tacked with Thred, or tyed about with Tape. **1703** MOXON *Mech. Exerc.* 53 Drive in a small Tack on each side..or you may Tack down two small thin boards on either side. **1830** in Cobbett *Rur. Rides* (1885) II. 348 The wretched boards tacked together, to serve for a table. **1853** KANE *Grinnell Exp.* xxxiii. (1856) 295, I copy the play-bill from the original..tacked against the main-mast. **1894** *Times* 3 Mar. 11/3 He had 'tacked' the cloth down to the stage. **1896** *Allbutt's Syst. Med.* I. 434 They [jackets] are lined with a layer of cotton-wool neatly tacked in. *Mod.* The sleeves are tacked in to try how they fit.

**b.** *spec.* †(*a*) *Gardening.* To fasten with tacks (TACK *sb.*1 3 a). *Obs.*

**1693** J. EVELYN *De la Quint. Compl. Gard.* II. 41 In Tacking for the first time after the Pruning.

(*b*) *Metal-working.* To keep (a metal plate, etc.) in place by small lumps of solder until the soldering is completed.

**1886** in *Cassell's Encycl. Dict.*

(*c*) *Plumbing.* To secure (a pipe) with tacks (TACK *sb.*1 3 b). **1895** in *Funk's Stand. Dict.*

**4.** To join together (events, accounts, etc.) so as to produce or show a connected whole; to bring into connexion. (Often implying arbitrary or artificial union.)

**1683** DRYDEN *Vindic. Duke of Guise* Dram. Wks. 1725 V. 325 Mr. Hunt has found a rare Connection, for he tacks them together, by the Kicking of the Sheriffs. **1695** J. EDWARDS *Perfect. Script.* 434 Many expositors labour to tack this text to the immediately foregoing one. **1699** BENTLEY *Phal.* 166 The Gentleman..tacks these two accounts together. **1712** J. JAMES tr. *Le Blond's Gardening* 128 The foregoing Practices..being but Things detached and separate,..there is still a farther Difficulty to tack them together, so as to make one Piece. **1720** WATERLAND *Eight Serm.* 221 One might suspect that there had been two Versions of the same words, and Both, by degrees, taken into the Text, and tack'd together. **1844** LINGARD *Anglo-Sax. Ch.* (1858) I. App. B. 326 Traditionary tales, tacked together without regard to place or chronology.

**5.** To attach or add as a supplement; to adjoin, append, annex; *spec.* in parliamentary usage: see quots. and cf. TACK *sb.*1 8.

**1683** ROBINSON in *Ray's Corr.* (1848) 137 Thus far your queries as to France, to which I will tack an observation to fill up. **1692** LUTTRELL *Brief Rel.* (1857) II. 365 A committee of the lords sat..to search presidents about tacking one bill to another. **1700** EVELYN *Diary* Apr., The greate contest betweene the Lords and Commons concerning the Lords power of..rejecting bills tack'd to the money bill. **1757–8** SMOLLETT *Hist. Eng.* (1759) IX. 296 The lords had already resolved by a vote, That they would never pass any bill sent up from the commons, to which a clause foreign to the bill should be tacked. **1791** 'G. GAMBADO' *Ann. Horsem.* ix. (1809) 107 As it's a fact, you may tack my name to it. **1855** MACAULAY *Hist. Eng.* xxii. IV. 771 A strong party in the Commons..proposed to tack the bill which the Peers had just rejected to the Land Tax Bill. **1863** H. COX *Instit.* I. viii. 114 The return is made by indenture..is signed and sealed, and returned to the Crown office in Chancery, tacked to the writ itself. **1902** L. STEPHEN *Stud. Biog.* IV. v. 179 So prosperous a consummation was never tacked to so dismal a beginning. **1909** [see TACKING *vbl. sb.* b].

**6.** *Law.* To unite (a third or subsequent incumbrance) to the first, whereby it acquires priority over an intermediate mortgage.

**1728** SIR J. JEKYLL in Peere Williams *Reports* (1793) II. 491 If a judgment creditor..buys in the first mortgage..he shall not tack or unite this to his judgment and thereby gain a preference. **1818** CRUISE *Digest* (ed. 2) II. 225. **1841** *Penny Cycl.* XIX. 361/2 Now if..D pays off B, and takes an assignment of his mortgage and of the outstanding term; if, to use the technical phrase, he 'tacks' B's security to his own, he unites in himself equal equity with C, and also the legal right which the term gives him. **1883** *Encycl. Brit.* XVI. 849/1 In addition to the risk of a third mortgagee tacking.

**II.** Nautical senses. (From TACK *sb.*1 5.)

**7.** *intr.* To shift the tacks and brace the yards, and turn the ship's head to the wind, so that she shall sail at the same angle to the wind on the other side; to go about in this way; also *tack about*. Hence, to make a run or course obliquely against the wind; to proceed by a series of such courses; to beat to windward: often said of the ship itself.

**1557** in A. Jenkinson *Voy. & Trav.* (Hakl. Soc.) I. 8 The rest of the shippes shall tacke or take of their sailes in such sort as they may meete and come together, in as good order as may be. **1595** *Drake's Voy.* (Hakl. Soc.) 22 They had the winde of us, but we soone regained it upon them, which made them tacke about. *c* **1600** CHALKHILL *Thealma & Cl.* (1683) 19 His Ketch Tackt to and fro, the scanty wind to snatch. **1748** *Anson's Voy.* II. iv. 163 We tacked and stood to the N.W. **1777** ROBERTSON *Amer.* (1783) III. 217 These..could veer and tack with great celerity. **1834** *Nat. Philos.* III. *Navigation* II. v. § 55. 26 (Usef. Knowl. Soc.) When the wind blows from any point within six points of the bearing of a port for which a vessel is bound, she must tack or ply to windward. **1873** *Daily News* 21 Aug., The little craft was caught by a sudden squall when tacking, or, as sailors say, 'in stays,' taken aback, and capsized in a moment. **1886** E. L. BYNNER *A. Surriage* i. 16 Two or three..ketches were tacking up before the brisk off-shore breeze to make the anchorage.

**b.** Said of the wind: To change its direction.

**1727** *Philip Quarll* (1816) 32, I was hurried on board, the wind having tacked about and fair for our departure. *Mod.* [A sailor said] The wind was tacking all over the place.

**8.** *intr.* **a.** *transf.* To make a turning or zigzag movement on land.

**1700** T. BROWN *Amusem. Ser. & Com.* 34, I Tack'd about, and made a Trip over Moor-fields. **1716** B. CHURCH *Hist. Philip's War* (1865) I. 97 They..tack'd short about to run as fast back as they came forward. **1787** 'G. GAMBADO' *Acad. Horsem.* (1809) 37 [The Massilians] Without a bridle on the bare back, Make with a stick their horse or mare tack. **1854–6** PATMORE *Angel in Ho.* I. ii. IV. (1879) 184 But he who tacks and tries short cuts Gets fool's praise and a broken shin.

**b.** *fig.* To change one's attitude, opinion, or conduct; also, to proceed by indirect methods.

**1637** POCKLINGTON *Altare Chr.* 169 He will..tacke about for other considerations..if hee bee well put to it. **1663** PEPYS *Diary* 24 June, He hath lately been observed to tack about at Court, and to endeavour to strike in with the persons that are against the Chancellor. **1791–1823** DISRAELI *Cur. Lit.*, *Dom. Hist. Sir E. Coke*, Bacon..tacked round, and promised Buckingham to promote the match he so much abhorred. **1860–70** STUBBS *Lect. Europ. Hist.* II. ii. (1904) 166 He is not for a moment diverted, although he sometimes consents to tack.

**9.** *trans.* To alter the course of (a ship) by turning her with her head to the wind (sometimes said of the ship); opposed to WEAR *v.* Also, to work or navigate (a ship) against the wind by a series of tacks. Also *fig.*

**1637** POCKLINGTON *Altare Chr.* 152 No man that has not his understanding tackt and the eye thereof turned after the humour of the men of Gr[antham]. **1747** in *Col. Rec. Pennsylv.* V. 115 They then tacked the Ship and stood out to Sea. **1805** *Naval Chron.* XIV. 16 She tacked Ship. **1860** E. STAMP in *Merc. Marine Mag.* VII. 279 All hands were turned up to tack ship. **1906** *Temple Bar Mag.* Jan. 72 It is sung sometimes when tacking ship in fair weather.

**Tack,** *v.*2 *dial.* [f. TACK *sb.*2]

**1.** *trans.* To take a lease of (a farm, etc.). *Sc. rare.*

**1882** JAMIESON, *Tack*, to take, to lease.

**2. a.** To put *out* (cattle) to hired pasture. **b.** To take (cattle) to pasture for hire.

**1839** [SIR G. C. LEWIS] *Heref. Gloss.*, He has tacked out his cattle. **1863** MORTON *Cycl. Agric.*, *Tacking out*, putting cattle upon hired pasturage. **1879–81** MISS JACKSON *Shropsh. Word-bk.* s. v., Mary Cadwallader 'as sent half-a-crown for tackin' the donkey, an' wants to know if you'll tack 'im a week or nine days longer.

**Tack** (tæk), *v.*3 *Obs.* exc. *dial.* [f. TACK *sb.*3: cf. F. *tac* there.] *trans.* To taint, infect; ? to tinge, stain; *dial.* to give a smack or tang to.

**1601** HOLLAND *Pliny* XVI. xliv, In case any of the sheep were deeply tackt and infected with the rot. **1643** TRAPP *Comm. Gen.* xxxi. 19 She was somewhat tackt with her fathers superstition. *Ibid.* xxxiv. 28 All the Corinthians were tackt with..the incestuous mans offence. **1868** ATKINSON *Cleveland Gloss.*, *Takt*, adj. Having a marked flavour; usually applied in the case of an acid liquid.

**Tack,** *v.*4, aphetic f. ATTACK *v.*; cf. *tack* sb. short for *attack* in *Eng. Dial. Dict.*

**1720** H. CAREY *Poems* 56 But if they once Tack you, They certainly Back you. **1731** PEYTON *Catastr. Ho. Stuarts* 42 As if a Partridge being near to a Faulcon..might peck and tack her, yet would not she yield to a small Bird.

**Tack,** obs. form of TAKE *v.*

**Tacked** (tækt), *ppl. a.* [f. TACK *v.*1 + -ED 1.] Attached, appended, etc.: see TACK *v.*1

**1596** WARNER *Alb. Eng.* XII. lxxiii. (1612) 303 Hence Dispensations, Iubilees, Pardons, and such tack't geere, Were had at Rome. **1687** T. LUDFORD in *Magd. Coll.* (O.H.S.) 75 His answer..was drawn up in tacked schedules. **1692** LUTTRELL *Brief Rel.* (1857) II. 363 After a long debate about the tackt clause, [the lords] adjourned it further till Munday. **1693** DRYDEN *Juvenal's Sat.* (1697) p. xxxvi, Laws were also call'd *Leges Saturæ*; when they were of several Heads and Titles; like our tack'd Bills of Parliament. **1904** *Westm. Gaz.* 9 Sept. 3/2 The tacked-on happy conclusion of 'Merely Mary Ann'.

**Tacker**1 (tæ·kəɹ). [f. TACK *v.*1 + -ER 1.]

**1.** One who tacks: in various senses.

**a.** *Eng. Hist.* One who favoured the tacking of other bills in parliament to money-bills, in order to secure their passage through the House of Lords; *esp.* in early 18th c., one who advocated tacking the bill against occasional conformity, 1704, to a money-bill.

**1704** SIR H. MACKWORTH (*title*) A Letter..Giving a short Account of the Proceedings of the Tackers, upon the Occasional and Self-denying Bills [etc.]. **1705** (*title*) Daniel the Prophet no Conjurer, or his Scandal Club's Scandalous Ballad, called the Tackers, answer'd Paragraph by Paragraph. **1705** HEARNE *Collect.* 27 Oct. (O.H.S.) I. 59 He was a Tacker, and a true Friend of ye Church. **1711** *Medley* No. 35. 384 A very bold Attempt was made upon the Civil and Religious Rights of our Fellow-Subjects, by certain Men call'd Tackers or High-Church-men. **1727** *Brice's Week. Jrnl.* 25 Aug. 2 One of the Gentlemen distinguished by the Name of a Tacker in the Reign of King William III. **1859** W. CHADWICK *De Foe* v. 280 Every kind of rascality was attempted to be passed through the Lords by its being tacked to a money bill, and by its being called a money bill; whence the term *tacker*.

**b.** In various trades, One who tacks or fastens articles or parts of things; also, a machine for putting or driving in tacks.

**1727** BAILEY vol. II, *Tacker*, one who fastens or fixes one Thing to another by Tacks, or by Sewing, etc. **1884** E. SIMCOX in *19th Cent.* June 1041 A preparer of collars and wristbands, known as a 'tacker and turner' [in shirt-making]. **1892** *Labour Commission Gloss.*, *Tacker*, one who puts in the tacks used in 'lasting'. **1895** *Daily News* 16 Mar. 6/5 Works..fitted with the latest types of machinery for all purposes, except the magnetic tacker.

**2.** *dial.* A small child.

**1885** *Reports Provinc.* (E.D.D.), Ever since I was a little

2–2

tacker. **1893** Q. [Couch] *Delect. Duchy* 220 I've [not] a-zet eyes 'pon the young man since he was a little tacker.

† **Tacker**$^{2}$, **takkar.** *Sc. Obs.* [f. Tack *sb.*$^{2}$ + -er$^{1}$.] One who grants a tack or lease; a lessor.

**1551** *Recds. Elgin* (1903) I. 109 All to be eschet to the takkar.

**Tacket** (tæ·kėt), *sb.* Now *dial.* Forms: 4–6 **taket(e, -ett(e,** 5–6 *Sc.* **tak(k)at(e,** 6– **tacket.** [f. Tack *sb.*$^{1}$ + -et.] A nail; in later use, a small nail, a tack: cf. Tack *sb.*$^{1}$ 1, 2; now, in *Sc.* and *north. dial.*, a hob-nail with which the soles of shoes are studded.

**1316** in Rogers *Agric. & Prices* II. 524/2 Takets [*ibid.* I. 546 tackets..seem to be cart or strake-nails]. *c* **1330** *Coldingham Priory* Inv. 10 In xviij barres ferri ad fenestras, wegges, et taketes. **1345–6** *Ely Sacr. Rolls* (1907) II. 133 In takettis empt. pro mappis emendandis—4½d. **1483** *Cath. Angl.* 377/2 A Taket, *claviculus.* **1512** *Acc. Ld. High Treas. Scot.* IV. 298 Item, for v$^{c}$ takkatis. **1532** *Lett. & Pap. Hen. VIII*, V. 448 Pyne nails and English tacketts for nailing up the said buds and leaves. **1542** *Acc. Ld. High Treas. Scot.* VIII. 132 Twa hankis wyre..to wyre the caisis of the windois..v$^{c}$ small takettis deliverit to him thairto. **1617** Minsheu *Ductor*, A *Tacket*, or *tache.* Vid. *Naile.* **1698** R. Thoresby in *Phil. Trans.* XX. 207 Curiously nailed with two rows of very small Tackets. **1789** Burns *Capt. Grose's Peregrinations* vi, Rusty airn-caps and jinglin jackets, Wad haud the Lothians three in tackets. **1859** J. Brown *Rab & Fr.* (1862) 25 Heavy shoes, crammed with tackets, heel-capt and toe-capt.

*attrib.* and *Comb.* **1888** Grant *Keckleton* 63 'The tackit-mackers..can barely supply the deman' for tackits'. **1896** Keith *Indian Uncle* xvii. 274 He envied the tacket-soled boots that gave his quarry the advantage. **1897** — *Bonnie Lady* xvi. 171 Wearing his strongest tacket boots.

Hence **Ta·cket** *v. trans.*, to stud (shoes) with tackets; whence **Ta·cketed** *ppl. a.*, hob-nailed.

**1896** Setoun *R. Urquhart* i, Thick-soled blucher boots tacketed for rough roads. **1899** *Westm. Gaz.* 31 Jan. 1/3 'Tacketed' boots, and clothes,..impervious to the rain.

**Tackety** (tæ·kėti), *a. Sc.* [f. prec. + -y.] Of a shoe: Studded with tackets.

**1864** Latto *Tam Bodkin* ix. (1894) 95 The neb o' Andra's tackety shoe. **1888** Barrie *Auld Licht Idylls* (1892) 5 My feet encased in stout 'tackety' boots.

**Ta·ckiness.** [f. Tacky *a.*$^{2}$ + -ness.] The quality of being tacky or slightly adhesive.

**1883** R. Haldane *Workshop Receipts* Ser. ii. 184/2 This varnish .. retains sufficient tackiness to hold powdered graphite on its surface. **1908** *Installation News* II. 55/1 No doubt the 'tackiness' of the enamel also helps to hold the tube in place.

**Ta·cking,** *vbl. sb.* [f. Tack *v.*$^{1}$ + -ing$^{1}$.] The action of Tack *v.*$^{1}$ in various senses.

**a.** Joining or fastening together, now esp. in a slight or temporary manner; also, that which is tacked or joined on.

**1713** Derham *Phys. Theol.* iv. viii. (1714) 159 The Muscles, their curious Structure, the nice tacking them to every Joynt. **1880** A. Arnold *Free Land* 133 As to mortgages, Mr. Joshua Williams described that nefarious dealing.. known as 'tacking'. **1888** Mrs. H. Ward *R. Elsmere* xiv, You don't know anything about tacking or fixing, or the abominable time they take. **1887** Saintsbury *Hist. Elizab. Lit.* ix. (1890) 351 [In Hobbes's *Human Nature*] the terse phrasing, the independence of all after-thoughts and tackings-on, manifest themselves at once.

**b.** The attaching to a money-bill in parliament of a measure for some other purpose.

**1700** Evelyn *Diary* Apr., This tacking of bills is a novel practice, suffer'd by K. Cha. II. who..let any thing pass rather than not have wherewith to feed his extravagance. *a* **1745** Swift *Four last Y. Q. Anne* iii. Wks. (Bohn) I. 471/2 The reasonableness of uniting to a money-bill one of a different nature, which is usually called tacking, hath been likewise much debated, and will admit of argument enough. **1909** A. Grant in *Contemp. Rev.* Nov. 540 The argument that the Finance Bill of this year is an instance of 'tacking', that is, of the inclusion in a Money Bill of clauses not dealing with Finance.

**c.** *Naut.* The action of making a tack or a series of tacks (Tack *sb.*$^{1}$ 6).

**1675** tr. *Camden's Hist. Eliz.* iii. 414 Ships fit for Fight, Good Sailers, and nimble and tight for tacking about which way they would. **1806** A. Duncan *Nelson* 86 The damage..prevented him from tacking. **1868** E. Edwards *Ralegh* I. vii. 111 [The] great galleons..had to encounter the quick fire and the deft tacking of the smaller..ships of England.

**d.** *attrib.*, as *tacking-cotton, -needle, -thread.*

**1880** *Plain Hints Needlework* 57 'Basting' or 'tacking cotton'. **1898** *Westm. Gaz.* 7 Apr. 3/2 Then run a tacking cotton (no back stitches) all round the four sides...Press the fold of lace till it is nearly dry before you take out the tacking threads. *Ibid.* 8 Oct. 4/1 A sailor's tacking needle.

**Ta·cking,** *ppl. a.* [f. as prec. + -ing$^{2}$.] That tacks; that joins or connects: cf. prec.

**1705** Hickeringill *Priest-cr.* ii. Wks. 1716 III. 126 If they get..a Tacking Parliament, to make Acts of Uniformity and Conformity to their Models and little Ways. *Ibid.* iv. 40, I never yet in all our Chronicles met with a Parliament stigmatized with the Name of the *Tacking Parliament.*

**Tackle** (tæ·k'l), *sb.* Forms: 3–6 **takel,** 4–6 *Sc.* **takil(l,** 4–8 **tacle, takle,** 5 **takul(l,** 5–6 **takell, -yl, -yll, tackyl (tickell),** 6–7 **tackel, -ell,** 6–8 *Sc.* **taikle,** (8 **teakle,** *Sc.* **-kil),** 6– **tackle.** [app. of Low German origin: cf. MLG. *takel* equipment generally, e.g. of a horseman, spec. of a ship, hoisting apparatus, LG. *takel*, also early mod.Du. *takel* strong rope, hawser, pulley, mod. Ger. *takel*, Sw. *tackel*, Da. *takkel* tackle; f. MLG. *taken*, MDu. *tacken* to lay hold of, grasp, seize, with instrumental suffix *-el*: see -le 1.]

**1.** Apparatus, utensils, instruments, implements, appliances; equipment, furniture, gear.

*c* **1250** *Gen. & Ex.* 883 And tol and takel and orf he [Abram] dede Wenden hom to here oȝen stede. **13..** *Minor Poems fr. Vernon MS.* xxviii. 32 Vr takel, vr tol, þat we on trowe. **1464** *Mann. & Househ. Exp.* (Roxb.) 248 Payd ffor my masterys takelys, ij.d. **1539** *Will L. Godsman* (Somerset Ho.), Item I give all my tickell..to the chapell of Saynt James to the making of the Northe Ille. **1626** B. Jonson *Staple of N.* Epil., We'are sorry that haue so mis-spent Our Time and Tackle. **1669** Penn *No Cross* i. iv. § 10 To transport themselves, or tackle in a Journey. **1717** Derham in *Buccleuch MSS.* (Hist. MSS. Comm.) I. 365, I am sorry my tackle was not ready when you would have favoured me with your company. **1815** Mme. D'Arblay *Diary* (1876) IV. 295 As I had no writing tackle, I sent him..to procure me proper implements at the stationer's. **1889** J. K. Jerome *Three Men in Boat* 64 George wanted the shaving tackle.

**2.** The rigging of a ship: in early use often in wider sense of 'equipment' or 'gear' as in 1; in later use *spec.* the running rigging or ropes used in working the sails, etc., with their pulleys; passing into sense 3. *Ground tackle*, anchors, cables, etc., by which a ship is made fast to the ground.

*a* **1300** *Cursor M.* 24944 Ful fair bicome þat see to sight, And þai bigan þair takel dight. **1390** Gower *Conf.* I. 312 The reyni Storm fell doun algates, And al here takel made unwelde. **1450–1530** *Myrr. our Ladye* 226 Dresseth surely the ropes and shyp tacle. **1481** Caxton *Godeffroy* 261 They ..bare away cordes, cables and saylles, and the other takle, and leyde it in the fortresse. **1585** T. Washington tr. *Nicholay's Voy.* i. xxi. 27 b, Vpon all the gallies..and other vessels all along vpon the takels, yardes, and other ropes and poupes.., aboue 300 candels. **1633** Sir J. Boroughs *Sov. Brit. Seas* (1651) 125 To brooke the seas, and to know the use of the tackles, and compasse. **1671** Milton *Samson* 717 With all her bravery on, and tackle trim, Sails fill'd, and streamers waving. *a* **1687** Sir W. Petty *Pol. Arith.* (1690) 14 Holland is..for keeping Ships in Harbour with small expence of Men and ground Tackle. **1745** P. Thomas *Jrnl. Anson's Voy.* 282 The Second Shot..carry'd away.. our Fore-stay Tackle. **1885** Sir J. C. Matthew in *Law Times Rep.* LII. 265/1 The vessel..was sold as she lay with her gear and tackle.

**b.** Cordage; a rope used for any purpose.

**1529** *Act 21 Hen. VIII*, c. 12 § 1 Diuers..persons..provide Hemp, and thereof make Cables, Ropes,.. Traces, Halters, and other Tackle. **1542** *Aberdeen Regr.* (1844) I. 185 For vij stane of takkillis..for bynding of the gunnis. **1570** Levins *Manip.* 6/11 A Tackle, *capulum.* **1712** Steele *Spect.* No. 454 ¶ 4 The Tackle of the Coach-window is so bad she cannot draw it up again.

*fig.* **1893** Stevenson *Heathercat* iii, The circle of faces was strangely characteristic; long, serious, strongly marked, the tackle standing out in the lean brown cheeks.

**3.** An arrangement consisting of a rope and pulley-block, or more usually a combination of ropes and blocks, used to obtain a purchase in raising or shifting a heavy body.

**1539–40** in *Devon. N. & Q.* Oct. (1903) 238 Ropys, poleys and other takle to hawse uppe the ledde uppon the Castell. **1626** Capt. Smith *Accid. Yng. Seamen* 16 Sheeps feet is a stay in setling a top mast, and a guie in staying the tackles when they are charged with goods. **1722** in *Hist. Brechin* (1867) 133 Item for a big teakil, being double the hight of the small steeple £40 Scots. **1731** Desaguliers in *Phil. Trans.* XXXVII. 292 The Machine consists of three Pullies (two upper and one lower, or a Tackle of Three). **1769** Fitz Gerald in *Phil. Trans.* LX. 78 It would not be difficult, with a proper teakle, to raise a barometer of this kind ..as high as 200 feet. **1796** Morse *Amer. Geog.* I. 507 The cannon were raised by large brass tacles..from rock to rock. **1830** Kater & Lardner *Mech.* xv. 198 A combination of blocks, sheaves, and ropes is called a *tackle.* **1859** F. A. Griffiths *Artil. Man.* (1862) 107 A simple tackle consists of one or more pulleys rove with a single rope.

**b.** A windlass and its appurtenances, used for hoisting ore, etc.; also, generally, the apparatus of cages or kibbles, with their chains and hooks, for raising ore or coal.

**1874** J. H. Collins *Metal Mining* (1875) 79 The first machine used in mining operations for raising ore or deads is usually the tackle or windlass. **1881** Raymond *Mining Gloss.*, *Tackle* (Corn.), the windlass, rope, and kibble.

†**4.** Implements of war, weapons; *esp.* arrows; also, a weapon; an arrow. *Obs.*

*c* **1375** *Sc. Leg. Saints* v. (*Johannes*) 486 It [a bow] suld hafe bene sone out of pyth To schot ony takil vith. *c* **1386** Chaucer *Prol.* 106 A sheef of pecok arwes bright and kene..Wel koude he dresse his takel yemanly. *c* **1400** *Rom. Rose* 1729 Shette att me so wondir smert, That thorough myn eye unto myn hert The takel smote, and depe it wente. *c* **1440** *Promp. Parv.* 485/2 Tacle, or wepene, *armamentum.* **1513** Douglas *Æneis* ix. x. 78 His bow.. bend hes he, Tharin a takyll set of sovyr tre. *a* **1550** *Christis Kirke Gr.* x, Ane hasty hensure, callit Hary..Tilt up a taikle withouten tary. **1663** Butler *Hud.* i. iii. 823 This said, she to her Tackle fell, And on the Knight let fall a peal Of Blows so fierce.

†**b.** Phr. *To stand* (or *stick*) *to one's tackle*: cf. Tackling *vbl. sb.* 3. *Obs.*

**1577–87** Holinshed *Chron.* I. 119/1 The Englishmen would in no wise giue ouer, but did sticke to their tackle. **1586** J. Hooker *Hist. Irel.* in *Holinshed* II. 9/2 To incourage his people to stand to their tackle, and valiently to withstand Mac Morough. **1724** De Foe *Mem. Cavalier* (1840) 187 Two regiments of country militia..stood to their tackle better than well enough [in defence of a town]. **1828** E. Irving *Last Days* 230 You would have armed the house against him, and stood to your tackle all the night.

**5.** Apparatus for fishing; fishing-gear, fishing-tackle.

**1398** Trevisa *Barth. De P. R.* xi. viii. (Tollem. MS.), Aristotel sayeþ þat fischeres heldeþ hoot water on here instrumentes and takles, þat þey be þe raþer frore. *Ibid.* xiii. xxix, [The fish] comeþ ofter in to newe tacle þat is set for hem, þan in to olde. **1711** Gay *Rural Sports* i. 181 The Peacock's plumes, thy tackle must not fail. **1783** Johnson 20 Apr. in *Boswell*, I indeed now could fish, give me English tackle. **1850** *Act* 13 & 14 *Vict.* c. 88 § 1 The word 'net' shall..include all descriptions of tackle, trawl, trammel, stake, bag, coghill, eel, haul, draft, and seine nets. **1867** F. Francis *Angling* i. (1880) 27 Use the very neatest tackle which you can afford for roach.

**6.** The equipment of a horse; harness.

**1683** Burnet tr. *More's Utopia* (1685) 115 Take off both his Saddle, and all his other Tackle. **1725** T. Thomas in *Portland Papers* VI. (Hist. MSS. Comm.) 133 [The] coach ..I thought could hardly have been able to get over.. without some loss either to the poor beasts, or the tackle. **1728** Vanbrugh & Cib. *Prov. Husb.* i. i, Our Tackle was not so tight as it should be. **1890** 'R. Boldrewood' *Col. Reformer* (1891) 102 I've backed two a week since I came, and have three in tackle, in the yard now.

† **7.** A mistress. *Obs. slang.*

**1688** Shadwell *Sqr. Alsatia* iv. Wks. 1720 IV. 85 Oh my dear Blowing, my Convenient, My tackle. *a* **1700** B. E. *Dict. Cant. Crew*, *Tackle*, a Mistress.

**8.** Victuals; food or drink; 'stuff'. *slang.*

**1857** Hughes *Tom Brown* i. iv, The purl warms the cockles of Tom's heart...'Rare tackle that, sir, of a cold morning', says the coachman. **1900** G. Swift *Somerley* 113 Do you think ladies usually eat that stodgy tackle?

**9.** [from the vb.] *Football.* **a.** The act of tackling: see Tackle *v.* 5.

**1901** *Scotsman* 11 Mar. 4/8 Neill, by a plucky tackle.. prevented a break away. **1905** *Oxford Mag.* 22 Feb. 215/1 One of his tackles was excellent.

**b.** In American football: Each of two players (right and left) stationed next to the end rusher or forward in the rush-line.

**1894** *Outing* (U.S.) XXIV. 281/1 Every one knew he had been a famous tackle on one of the football teams. **1905** *McClure's Mag.* (U.S.) June 123/2 Captain and right-tackle of the Yale eleven.

**10.** *attrib.* and *Comb.*, as *tackle-box, -chain, -dealer, -hook, -maker, -shop*; **tackle-block,** = Block *sb.* 5; **tackle-board,** a frame, placed at the end of a rope-walk, containing the whirls to which the yarns are attached to be twisted; **tackle-fall,** = Fall *sb.*$^{1}$ 26; **tackle-man,** a man who works the tackle, e.g. of a gun. See Tackle-house, -porter.

**1793** Smeaton *Edystone L.* § 122 A pair of *tackle-blocks. **1905** *Daily Chron.* 26 July 4/7 Banks..lined with seedy, quiet, elderly men with *tackle-boxes, evening papers, and roach-poles. **1865** S. Ferguson *Lays West. Gael* 119 The windlass strains the *tackle chains, the black mound heaves below. **1698** in *MSS. Ho. Lords* (1905) III. 338 We were forced to unreeve our *tackle-falls to make lanyards for our lower shrouds. **1769** Falconer *Dict. Marine* (1789), *Garant*, a tackle-fall, or the part upon which the labourers pull in hoisting. **1857** Hughes *Tom Brown* i. ix, The little *tackle-maker..would soon have made his fortune had the rage lasted. **1859** F. A. Griffiths *Artil. Man.* (1862) 207 Traversing *tacklemen..7 and 8. **1873** *Routledge's Yng. Gentl. Mag.* Jan. 79/2 The 'rear tackleman'..held the end of the tackle. **1909** *Nation* (N. Y.) 3 Oct. 12/1 Flies.. bought at a *tackle-shop.

**Tackle** (tæ·k'l), *v.* Forms: see sb. [f. prec. So Da. *takle*, Sw. *tackla* to tackle, to rig a ship.]

[In the following, a MS. variant of *tagild*: see Tagle *v.*

*a* **1340** Hampole *Psalter, Cant.* 512 Þaire affeccioun s ere ay takild with sum luf þat draghis þaim fra godis luf.]

†**1.** *trans.* To furnish (a ship) with tackle; to equip with the necessary furnishings. *Obs.*

*c* **1400** *Destr. Troy* 12313 To gyffe..Tho shippes to shilde o þe shyre whaghes,..And tyrn hom to takle, & trusse for the sea. **1486** *Naval Acc. Hen. VII* (1896) 74 The same Ship so takled & aparailled was deliuered..to Rauf Astry. **1530** Palsgr. 752/1 My shyppe is takylled and talowed, and redy to hoyse up the sayle. **1550** Nicolls *Thucyd.* 5 Althoughe the shyppe be..well garnished and tacled with sayle and ballast. **1653** F. G. tr. *De Scudery's Artamenes*, etc. (1655) IV. vii. ii. 99 At the same time, they trimmed and tackled up a great company of Ships. **1686** J. Dunton *Lett. fr. New-Eng.* (1867) 26 He is a pitch'd Piece of Reason, calckt and tackl't, and only studied to dispute with Tempests.

†**b.** To handle or work the tackle of a ship.

**1513** Douglas *Æneis* iii. ii. 119 The noyis wpsprang of mony marynair Besy at thair werk, to takilling euery tow Thair feris exhorting. **1549** *Compl. Scot.* vi. 41 Quhen the schip vas taiklit, the master cryit, boy to the top. **1579–80** North *Plutarch* (1676) 7 Scirus..gave to Theseus..another marriner to tackle the sails, who was called Phœas. *a* **1642** Sir W. Monson *Naval Tracts* ii. (1704) 253/2 There are so few Sailors to tackle their Ships, that they will be taken upon the Stays.

†**c.** *intr.* To tack, or sail across the wind. *Obs.*

**1632** Lithgow *Trav.* (1906) 288 Seven weekes crossed with Northerly Windes, ever Tackling and boarding from the Affricke Coast, to the Carminian shoare. **1669** in Sturmy *Mariner's Mag.* i. ii. 20 In this unease Of Tackling Boards, we so the way make short.

†**2.** To raise or hoist with tackle. *Obs. rare.*

**1711** W. Sutherland *Shipbuild. Assist.* 6 A Portland.. Stone, may be wrought to its exact Shape before it be tackled up on St. Paul's Church.

**3.** To harness (a horse) for riding or draught. Also *absol.* with *up.*

**1714** S. Sewall *Diary* 5 Apr. (1879) II. 432 Our Horses were forced to leap into the Sea. By that time had tackled them [it] was duskish. **1770** Mrs. E. Smith in *Lett. Jas. Murray* (1901) 130 Wednesday her coach and chaise was tackled for us to take an airing and see all the curiositys of Kelso. **1787** 'G. GAMBADO' *Acad. Horsem.* (1809) 7 How to chuse a horse, how to tackle him properly, in what sort of dress to ride him, how to mount and manage him. **1826** P. POUNDEN *France & It.* 7 Five untrimmed little horses, tackled to with ropes. **1869** MRS. STOWE *Old Town Folk* xx, I shall jest tackle up and go over and bring them children home agin. **1890** 'R. BOLDREWOOD' *Col. Reformer* (1891) 93 I'll get a spare saddle and bridle, and will tackle him.

**4.** *colloq.* **a.** To grip, lay hold of, take in hand, deal with; to fasten upon, attack, encounter (a person or animal) physically.

**1828** WEBSTER s. v., A wrestler tackles his antagonist; a dog tackles the game. This is a common popular use of the word in New England, though not elegant. **18..** *Dial. Northampton*, The dog tackled the sheep in the field and almost killed one. **1872** BESANT & RICE *Ready-Money Mort.* vii, Smith's a big man; but I think I can tackle him. **1887** JESSOPP *Arcady* ii. 58 The people seem to have been afraid to tackle them [otters].

**b.** To 'come to grips with', to enter into a discussion or argument with; to attack; to approach or question on some subject.

**1840** DICKENS *Barn. Rudge* i, That John Willet was in amazing force to-night, and fit to tackle a Chief Justice. **1858** MASSON *Milton* (1859) I. iv. 168 The Respondent having stated and expounded his theses, was then tackled by a series of Opponents. **1887** R. BUCHANAN *Heir of Linne* iii, I'll tackle the laird myself. **1901** *Scotsman* 13 Mar. 12/2 He too was tackled on the question, but when he explained it ..he found the electors..reasonable.

**c.** To grapple with, to try to deal with (a task, a difficulty, etc.); to try to solve (a problem).

**1847** E. FITZGERALD *Lett.* (1889) I. 171 There was no difficulty at all in coming to the subject at once, and tackling it. **1871** L. STEPHEN *Playgr. Eur.* iv. II. 320 Learn..how most effectually to tackle any little difficulty that occurs. **1897** D. HAY FLEMING in *Bookman* Jan. 118/1 Has any previous writer ever tackled a work of such difficulty and magnitude among similar surroundings?

**d.** To attack, fall upon, begin to eat (food).

**1889** J. K. JEROME *Three Men in Boat* xii, We tackled the cold beef for lunch. **1890** 'R. BOLDREWOOD' *Col. Reformer* (1891) 132 A strong man gets over it in a day or two, and tackles his bread and meat, and his work, pretty much as usual.

**e.** *intr.* To set *to*; to grapple *with* something.

**1867** TROLLOPE *Chron. Barset* I. xxxii. 273 We'll tackle to? Very well; so be it. **1867** *Country Wds.* No. 17. 262 Tackle to't reet while yo're yung. *a* **1868** S. LOVER (Ogilvie), The old woman..tackled to for a fight in right earnest. *Mod. dial.* (E.D.D.) Ah tackled wi' t' badger.

**5.** *Football.* (*a*) In *Rugby*, To seize and stop (an opponent) when in possession of the ball; (*b*) In *Association*, To obstruct (an opponent) with the object of getting the ball away from him. Also *absol.*

**1884** *Daily News* 23 Dec. 5/5 He..tackled well, kicked judiciously, and as captain of the team gave every satisfaction. **1891** *Lock to Lock Times* 24 Oct. 13/1 (*Association*) He now plays half-back, and is exceedingly useful in that position, tackling and kicking in great style. **1897** *Sportsman* 16 Dec., He was tackled close to his own quarter line. **1899** *Badm. Libr., Football* 121 (*Assoc.*) Practically the best general rule is for the half-back to tackle the man with the ball, and the back to be near up ready to intercept a pass. **1901** *Scotsman* 11 Mar. 4/8 Those who questioned his ability to tackle..must have got a surprise when they saw the manner he dealt with his opponent.

†**6.** (?) To enclose or fortify. *Obs. rare*$^{-1}$.

Perh. some error, or a different word.

*c* **1645** HOWELL *Lett.* I. vi. lvii, The moralist tells us that a quadrat solid wise man should involve and tackle himself within his own vertue, and slight all accidents that are incident to man, and be still the same.

**Tackled** (tæ·k'ld), *a.*, *ppl. a.* [f. TACKLE *sb.* and *v.* + -ED.]

†**1.** Made of tackle or ropes: cf. TACKLING 6.

**1592** SHAKS. *Rom. & Jul.* II. iv. 201 My man shall..bring thee Cords made like a tackled staire.

**2.** Furnished with a tackle or harness.

**1542** *Will Sir C. Storke, Newton Seynt-lo, Somerset* 18 Apr., Wm. Becke a tackled heyfar.

†**Ta·ckle-house.** *Obs.* [f. TACKLE *sb.* + HOUSE.] app. either, A house in which porters employed in loading and unloading ships kept their tackle; or, A house having a tackle or pulley for hoisting heavy goods; a warehouse for lading and unlading merchandise going or coming by sea.

In London each of the twelve great Merchant Companies had formerly the right to have its own tackle-house, with its porter or porters, and in some of them the titular office of 'tackle-house porter' or 'tackle-porter' still survives: see quot. 1851 in b, TACKLE-PORTER quot. 1909. The tackle-houses at Southwold were on the quay of a creek, evidently for the loading and unloading of vessels lying there; those at London may have been on the river's brink.

**1562** *Will* in T. Gardner *Acc. Dunwich*, etc. (1754) 215 My Tackle House at the Woods-End [Southwold]. **1579** *Act Com. Council London* 15 Aug. (Jrnl. 20, II. lf. 506), It is thought convenient yt no other tacklehouses or companie of porters shall hereafter be erected without the especiell licence of ye L. Maior, his brethren, and the Counsell. **1606** *Ibid.* 27 June (Jrnl. 27, lf. 52 b), Complaintes..by freemen porters of the Tacklehouses of the said citie against others streete porters workinge in the said citie, for interdealinge with worke..touchinge shippinge and unshippinge of goodes ..with which business the said street porters have not presumed to deal untill of late time. **1607** in *Remembrancia* (City of London) II. 288 The peticion enclosed..by the Porters of the Tackell Houses of this Cittie, prayinge.. Assistance for the preventinge of much inconvenience to growe uppon them through the erection of an newe Office to be established for the ladinge and unladinge..of all Marchantes goodes not free of the twelve Companies. [The petition follows, entitled in margin] 'A Peticion concerninge the Tacle Porters'. **1618** in T. Gardner *Acc. Dunwich*, etc. (1754) 215 (*Southwold*) One entire Place, Key or Wharfe, the whole abutting and bounding against..the Tackle-House at the South-East End. **1754** T. GARDNER *ibid.* 214 The antient Key stood in the Woods-End-Creek; near thereto were Dwelling-Houses, Warehouses, Tackle-Houses, the Blubber-Pans and Carters-Grounds for Ship-Building. **1842–51** [see b].

**b.** *attrib.* **Tackle-house porter,** *orig.* A porter belonging to or employed at a tackle-house; later (usually shortened to *tackle-porter*: see next) a porter authorized to act as such by one of the London Companies having this right, as distinguished from a *ticket-porter* who was licensed by the corporation.

**1606** *Act Com. Council London* 27 June in Mayhew *Lond. Labour* (1861) III. 365/1 Tackle-house porter, porter-packer of the gooddes of English merchants, streete-porter, or porter to the packer for the said citie for strangers' goods. **1646** *Act Com. Council conc. Tackle-house Porters* (1712) 9 Whereas divers Controversies and Differences have heretofore been between the Tacklehouse-Porters of this City, and the Ticket-Porters, otherwise called the Street-Porters of this City in and about several Matters [etc.]. **1842** PULLING *Treat. Laws & Customs London* 502 The Tackle-house Porters, who, with their subordinates the Packers' Porters, originally formed a part of the establishment of the principal trading companies, and were attached to their respective tackle-houses, are employed in lading and unlading goods not subject to metage. *Ibid.* 504 The tackle-house porters are composed of a few persons appointed by the twelve principal companies, to each of which the privilege belonged of having a tackle-house for lading and unlading goods. Each of the companies appoint one person as their tackle-house porter, and some of them two. **1851** MAYHEW *Lond. Labour* (1861) III. 366/1 The tackle-house porters that are still in existence, I was told, are gentlemen. One is a wharfinger, and claims and enjoys the monopoly of labour on his own wharf.

**Ta·ckle-po·rter.** Short for *tackle-house porter*: see preceding.

**16..** [see quot. 1607 s.v. TACKLE-HOUSE]. **1648** *Minutes Goldsmiths' Co.* 8 Nov., It was moved by Mr Ashe that this Company might have some tackle porters waiting at the Customs House as the Fishmongers and other Companies do. **1851** MAYHEW *Lond. Labour* (1861) III. 365/2 There were 24 tackle-porters appointed; each of the 12 great city companies appointing two. **1909** SIR W. PRIDEAUX in *Let.* 23 Dec., The [Goldsmiths'] Company used to appoint two tackle porters, but for many years past only one has been appointed. There is no salary or emolument of any kind attached to the office. The present Lord Mayor is tackle porter of this Company.

**Tackler** (tæ·klə). [f. TACKLE *v.* + -ER[1].] One who tackles, in various senses. †**a.** (?). *Obs.* **b.** An overlooker of power-loom weavers. **c.** One who tackles in football. **d, e:** see quots.

**a.** **1686** BLOME *Gentl. Recreat.* II. 62 *Hack Hawk*, that is a Tackler. **b.** **1864** RAMSBOTTAM *Phases Distress* 34 Tackler Tom con stond it o'. **1882** *Standard* 7 Sept. 2/3 Power-loom overlookers, or 'tacklers', and carders and strippers followed. **1901** *Speaker* 20 July 439/1 Each 'tackler' or overlooker has a certain number of looms assigned to his care. *Ibid.*, While the tacklers 'drive' the weavers, the manager in turn 'drives' the tacklers. **c.** **1891** *Lock to Lock Times* 24 Oct. 13/1 He is a rare tackler, and his famous rushes have warded off many an attack on the Marlow goal. **d.** **1891** *Labour Commission Gloss.*, *Tackler*, one who puts in the tacks used in 'lasting'. **e.** **1881** RAYMOND *Mining Gloss.*, *Tacklers* (Derb.), small chains put around loaded *corves*.

**Ta·ckless,** *a.* [f. TACK *sb.*[1] 2 + -LESS.] Having no tacks; made (as a sewn shoe) without tacks.

**1907** *Westm. Gaz.* 4 Nov. 8/4 A boot or shoe..being tackless throughout, is much more flexible than would otherwise be possible. **1907** *Daily Chron.* 5 Nov. 8/2 A patent 'lasting' machine with which boots can be made without the aid of tacks or other metal fastening is shown by the Tackless and Flexible Shoe Machinery Company.

**Tackling** (tæ·kliŋ), *vbl. sb.* Also 5–6 tak(e)-lyng, 6 taclyng. [f. TACKLE *v.* + -ING[1].]

†**1.** The furnishing of a vessel with tackle. *Obs.*

**1486** *Naval Acc. Hen. VII* (1896) 17 The wages of xxx marriners..for the Rigging and takeling of the same Ship.

†**b.** *concr.* The rigging of a ship; the tackle.

*c* **1422** HOCCLEVE *Jereslaus's Wife* 914 Our taklynge brast and the ship claf In two. **1526** TINDALE *Acts* xxvii. 19 The thyrde daye we cast out with oure awne hondes the tacklinge [1885 (R.V.) *marg.* or furniture] of the shippe. **1529** *Act 21 Hen. VIII*, c. 12 § 1 The great Cables, Halsers, Ropes, and all other Tackling .. for your Royal Ships. *c* **1615** BACON *Adv. Sir G. Villiers* v. § 9 For tackling, as sails and cordage,..we are beholden to our neighbours for them. **1676** HUBBARD *Happiness of People* 12 If the Mast be never so well strengthened, and the Tackline never so well bound together. **1696** *London Gaz.* No. 3176/1 Abundance of Lanthorns were hung upon the Tackling of the Ships. **1769** FALCONER *Dict. Marine* (1789) Uu ij b, Unless we adopt the obsolete word *Tackling*, which is now entirely disused by our mariners.

*fig.* **1601** SIR W. CORNWALLIS *Ess.* xvi. K iij b, Graue, wise, sober, temperate men,..meete to bee part of the tacklings of a Commonwealth. **1655** FULLER *Ch. Hist.* I. i. § 11 A relation as ill accoutred with tacklings, as their Ship; ..unrigged in respect of time, and other circumstances.

†**2.** Gear, furnishings, fittings, accoutrements, outfit, baggage, etc.; = TACKLE *sb.* 1. *Obs.*

**1558** *Ludlow Churchw. Acc.* (Camden) 86 Takelynges and nayles for the great belle. **1637** B. JONSON *Sad Sheph.* I. ii, Here's Little John hath harbord you a Deere, I see by his Tackling. *a* **1659** *Lond. Chanticleers* ix. in Hazl. *Dodsley* XII. 345 Meet me here two hours hence with all your tacklings. I'll see this bundle shall be safe. **1695** J. EDWARDS *Perfect. Script.* 120 This sort of country tackling is call'd threshing-instruments. **1718** S. SEWALL *Diary* 25 July, I give her two Cases with a knife and fork in each; one Turtle shell tackling; the other long, with Ivory handles. **1749** C. CAMPBELL in *Scots Mag.* Sept. (1753) 454/2 Remember Lady Ardsheil's discharges, and all your other tackling. **1813** SIR R. WILSON *Pr. Diary* II. 244 It is necessary that I should feast myself into a little more *embonpoint*, for otherwise I shall not have sufficient carcase to suspend my tackling upon.

†**b.** A horse's harness. *Obs.*

*c* **1645** HOWELL *Lett.* (1650) III. 14 If he wanted money to mend his plow or his Cart, or to buy tacklings for his horses. **1726** *Boston News-Let.* 14 July, To be sold..two good carts, four good horses, and tackling compleat for the same. **1787** 'G. GAMBADO' *Acad. Horsemen* (1809) 45 Let me entreat you to examine your tackling well at setting out..: see that your girths are tight.

†**3.** Arms, weapons, instruments; also *fig.*, esp. in phr. *to stand* or *stick to one's tackling*, to 'stand to one's guns', to hold one's ground, to maintain one's position or attitude: cf. TACKLE *sb.* 4 b; so *to hold tackling* (cf. *to hold tack*, TACK *sb.* 11); also *to give over one's tackling*, to 'lay down one's arms', surrender, give in. *Obs.*

**14..** *Voc.* in Wr.-Wülcker 565/36 *Armamentum*, take-lyng. **1529** MORE *Dyaloge* IV. Wks. 278/2 Than would he haue them abide by their tackeling like mighty champions. *a* **1548** HALL *Chron., Hen. VI* 160 b, Perceiuyng the kentishmen, better to stande to their taclyng, then his imagination expected. **1551** T. WILSON *Logike* (1580) 61 b, Thus the aunswerer..maie..force the apposer to giue ouer his tacklyng, without any aduauntage gotten. **1576** FLEMING *Panopl. Epist.* 362 Your brother..tolde me..that you haue forsaken your booke...I wishe you to..sticke still to your tackling: and as you haue begonne, so proceede. **1593** in Abp. Bancroft *Daung. Posit.* IV. iii. 141, I thinke it a great blessing of God, that hath raised vp Martin to hold tackling with the Bishops. *a* **1635** CORBETT *Poems* (1807) 23 Reader, unto your tackling look, For there is coming forth a book Will spoyl Joseph Barnisius The sale of *Rex Platonicus*. **1679** *Hist. Jetzer* 29 An ambition to be accounted and Canonized for a Saint, which by standing stoutly to his tackling he hoped for.

†**4.** Fishing tackle. *Obs.*

**1548** ELYOT *Dict.*, *Alopex marina*..a fysshe of the sea, whyche perceyuynge the hooke to bee fastened in his bealy, byteth of the lyne aboue the taklyng, and so escapeth. **1653** WALTON *Angler* 53, I will sit down and mend my tackling. *Ibid.* 105 Sure, Master, yours is a better Rod, and better Tackling. **1727** *Philip Quarll* (1816) 7 Having ..caught a..dish of fish, we put up our tackling.

**5.** The action of the vb. TACKLE in mod. senses (in quots., in sense 5).

**1893** *Daily News* 14 Dec. 2/6 Cambridge's tackling stood them in great capital defence. **1900** *Westm. Gaz.* 12 Dec. 7/3 A strong Cambridge attack was foiled by the splendid tackling of the Oxford men.

**6.** *Comb.* †**Tackling-ladder,** a rope-ladder.

**1680** OTWAY *Caius Marius* III. i, My man shall meet thee there; And bring thee cords made like a tackling-ladder.

**Tackman** (tæ·kmæn). *dial.* [f. TACK *sb.*[2] 4 + MAN.] One who looks after horses or cattle which are grazed on tack.

**1885** *Athenæum* 10 Oct. 467/2 With constables, tackmen, and pinders we are familiar. **1891** *Sportsman* 14 Feb. 1/1 (Advt.) Wanted, by Young Man, a Situation as Tackman or Helper in a racing stable.

**Tacksman** (tæ·ksmæn). *Sc.* Also 6–9 tax-, 7 taxs-. [f. *tack's*, poss. of TACK *sb.*[2] + MAN.] One who holds a tack or lease of land, a water-mill, coal-mines, fisheries, tithes, customs, or anything farmed or leased; a lessee; esp. in the Highlands, a middleman who leases directly from the proprietor of the estate a large piece of land which he sublets in small farms.

**1533** *Aberdeen Regr.* (1844) I. 148 Gif thair be ony takkismen of the tovne that dissentis to the paiment of thir settis, that thai salbe discharged of thair takkis. **1563** *Inchaffray Reg.* (Bann.) 83 Our lait cousing David Lord Drummond and Dame Lilias Ruthven his spous as takismen of the Abbacie of Inchaeffray. **1627** *Rep. Parishes Scotl.* (Bann.) 2 William Erle of Angus taxman off the haill personag teinds of the Barronj. **1630** in *Proc. Soc. Ant. Scot.* (1896) XXX. 58 The takismen and custumeris of the saidis impostis of wynnes. **1680** [see TACK *sb.*[2] 6] **1775** JOHNSON *W. Isl., Ostig*, Next in dignity to the laird is the Tacksman. **1791** NEWTE *Tour Eng. & Scot.* 125 The Tacksmen of the Highlands were usually descendants of those heads of families of whom they held their lands. **1794** *Sporting Mag.* III. 50 Mr. Richard Graham, tacksman of the fishery of J. C. Curwen. **1814** SCOTT *Wav.* xx, Tacksmen, as they were called, who occupied portions of his estate as..lessees. **1887** *Times* (weekly ed.) 25 Feb. 9/3 In Munster or Connaught, the tacksmen who covenanted directly with the lairds might deal as they pleased with their sub-tenants.

So **Ta·ckswo·man,** a female holder of a tack.

**1585** *Exch. Rolls Scotl.* XXI. 583 The dewtie of the kirk of Kinros awand be Agnes Leslie, ledie Lochlewin, taxiswoman thairof.

**Tacky** (tæ·ki), *sb.* and *a.*[1] *local U.S.* Also tackey. [Origin obscure.]

**A.** *sb.* **a.** A degenerate 'weedy' horse: see quot. 1884. **b.** A poor white of the Southern States from Virginia to Georgia.

**1884** E. EGGLESTON in *Cent. Mag.* Jan. 444/2 The scrubby little 'tackeys' still taken in the marshes along the North Carolina coast are descendants of the wild horses of the colony. **1888** *Ibid.* Sept. 799/2 If Mr. Catlett will come to Georgia and go among the 'po' whites' and 'piney-wood tackeys'. **1889** FARMER *Americanisms*, *Tackey*, in the South, a jade of a horse; a sorry beast; and idiomatically a man neglectful of personal appearance. **1896** *Peterson Mag.* Jan. 84/2 Here..is a native of the Virginia wilds, a specimen of the genus 'tacky'.

**B.** *adj.* Dowdy, shabby. *U. S. colloq.*

**1893** L. J. RITTENHOUSE in *Chicago Advance* 22 June, She looks so tacky in her shabby dress.

**Tacky** (tæ·ki), *a.*[2] [f. TACK *sb.*[1] 4 b + -Y.] Slightly sticky or adhesive: said of gum, glue, or varnish nearly dry.

**1788** G. SMITH in *Lond. Mag.* 624 The moistened gum.. must not be waterish but something tacky or clammy. **1822** IMISON *Sc. & Art* II. 244 If left in the damp, it remains tacky..a long time. **1897** *Complete Cyclist* (Isthmian Libr.) 188 Sufficient time must be given to allow the solution to become dry, or, as it is technically known, 'tacky'.

**Tackyl, tacle,** obs. ff. TACKLE.

‖ **Taclobo** (tăklōᵘ·bo). [Native name in Philippines.] A bivalve mollusc, of great size, the Giant Clam (*Tridacna gigas*) of the Indian and China seas.

**1885** BALFOUR *Cyclop. India* (ed. 3) s.v. *Kima*, The shells of the taclobo, or gigantic Philippine oyster, are used as fonts in the churches of that group. **1885** *Encycl. Brit.* XVIII. 750/2 The 'taclobo' shell sometimes weighs 200 lb., and is used for baptismal fonts.

**Ta·c-lo:cus.** *Geom.* [f. L. *tac-tus* touch + LOCUS.] The locus of the points of contact of two curves of different families, or of two non-consecutive curves of the same family.

**1873** CAYLEY *Math. Papers* VIII. 533.

**Tacnode** (tæ·knōᵘd). *Geom.* [f. L. *tac-tus* touch + NODE.] A point at which two parts of the same curve have ordinary contact.

**1852** CAYLEY *Math. Papers* (1889) II. 28 The tacnode is a double point where two branches touch. **1873** SALMON *Higher Plane Curves* 207 Two nodes may coincide, giving rise to the singularity called a tacnode; this is in fact an ordinary (two-pointed) contact of two branches of the curve.

*attrib.* **ta·cnode-cu·sp**, the singularity of a curve which arises when a cusp and an immediately following tangency of the two branches coalesce.

**1873** SALMON *Higher Plane Curves* (1879) 207.

**Taconic** (tăkǫ·nik), *a. Geol.* See quot. 1865.

**1849** LYELL *2nd Visit U. S.* (1850) II. 354, I believe the formations called Taconic, in the United States,..to be simply Silurian strata much altered, and often quite metamorphic. **1865** PAGE *Geol. Terms, Taconic*, a term applied by the late Professor Emmons to the rocks east of the Hudson (from the Taconic range lying along the western slope of the Green Mountains),..which consist of slates, quartz-rock, and lime-stones of Lower Silurian or perhaps more properly of Upper Cambrian age.

‖ **Tacsonia** (tæksōᵘ·niă). *Bot.* [mod.L. (Jussieu 1789), f. Peruvian name *tacso*.] A genus of West Indian and Central American shrubs, N.O. *Passifloraceæ*, closely allied to the Passion-flowers.

**1869** DARWIN *Life & Lett.* III. 279 The long pendent tube and valve-like corona which retains the nectar of Tacsonia.

**Tact** (tækt). [ad. (immed. or ult.) L. *tactu-s* touch, f. ppl. stem of *tangĕre* to touch: cf. F. *tact* (14th c. in sense 1), Ger. *tact, takt* (1619 in sense 4).]

**I. 1.** The sense of touch; touch. In quot. 1809 *transf.* [So in L.; F. *tact* (14th c. in Littré).]

[*c* **1200** *Vices & Virtues* 17 Ða fif wittes.. þat is, *visus, auditus, gustus, odoratus, et tactus*, þat is ȝesihthe, ȝeherhþe, smac, and smell, and tactþe.] **1651** A. ROSS *Arcana Microcosm.* II. xxi. 110 Of all the creatures, the sense of tact is most exquisite in man. **1809** KENDALL *Trav.* III. 102 Such is the delicacy of their [divining or mineral rods'] tact, that the weakest power is sufficient to determine them. **1865** GROTE *Plato* (1867) II. xxvi. 370 The various Percepta or Percipienda of tact, vision, hearing—sweet, hot, hard, light—have each its special bodily organ. **1881** LE CONTE *Sight* 77 Sight is a very refined tact.

**b.** *fig.* A keen faculty of perception or discrimination likened to the sense of touch.

**1797** W. TOOKE *Life Catherine* II. 206 It was from his genius alone that he had seized the character of other nations, and it shews a niceness of tact exceedingly rare. **1802** COLERIDGE *Lett., to W. Sotheby* (1895) 397 You..must needs have a better tact of what will offend that class of readers. **1842** MANNING *Serm.* ii. (1843) I. 22 To..deaden the keen tact of conscience. **1876** GREEN *Stray Stud.* 120 The popular voice showed a singular historical tact in its mistake.

**2.** Ready and delicate sense of what is fitting and proper in dealing with others, so as to avoid giving offence, or win good will; skill or judgement in dealing with men or negotiating difficult or delicate situations; the faculty of saying or doing the right thing at the right time. [a. F. *tact* (Voltaire 1769).]

[**1793** D. STEWART *Outl. Mor. Philos.* I. x. § 87 (1855) 48 The use made in the French tongue of the word *Tact*, to denote that delicate sense of propriety which enables a man to feel his way in the difficult intercourse of polished society.] **1804–6** SYD. SMITH *Mor. Philos.* xii. (1850) 154 We have begun, though of late years, to use the word *tact.* **1837** CARLYLE *Fr. Rev.* (1872) II. I. iv. 22 A most delicate task; requiring tact. **1875** HELPS *Ess., Secrecy* 55 Few persons have tact enough to perceive when to be silent, and when to offer you counsel or condolence. **1892** R. B. BRETT in *19th Cent.* Jan. 22 That fine instinct in the management of men which is commonly called tact.

†**3.** The act of touching or handling; an instance of this, a touch. *Obs. rare.* [So in L.]

**1801** JEFFERSON *Writ.* (1830) III. 467, I judged from a tact of the southern pulse. **1823** J. BADCOCK *Dom. Amusem.* 64 Others that are harmless in tact.

**II. 4.** *Mus.* A stroke in beating time; = BEAT *sb.*[1] 4: see also quot. 1891. [= (Germ.) L. *tactus*, Adam v. Fulda 1490; Ger. *tact*, Prätorius 1619.]

**1609** J. DOULAND *Ornith. Microl.* 46 *Tact* is a successive motion in singing, directing the equalitie of the measure. **1614** T. RAVENSCROFT *Brief Disc.* 20 Tact, Touch or Time, is, a certaine Motion of the hand (whereby the Quantity of Notes and Rests are directed) by an equall Measure. [**1777** R. DONKIN *Military Coll.* 161 Count Saxe recommends the *tact*, or marching *en cadence.*] **1828** WEBSTER, *Tact*,.. formerly the stroke in beating time in music. **1891** *Cent. Dict., Tact*..in music, a beat or pulse; especially, the emphatic down-beat with which a measure begins; hence, also, a measure.

†**Ta·ctable,** *a. Obs.* [f. L. *tact-* (see TACTIC *a.*[2]) + -ABLE.] Capable of being touched; tangible.

**1611** CHAPMAN *May-Day* I. i. Plays 1873 II. 331 Alas good soules, women of themselves are tractable and tactable enough. **1656** STANLEY *Hist. Philos.* VI. (1701) 257/1 Whatsoever is gustable, is tactable, and humid.

†**Tacta·tion.** *Obs. rare.* [f. as prec. + -ATION.] The act of touching.

**1688** R. HOLME *Armoury* II. 387/1 A Tactation, or a touching, is that whereby we discern the difference of objects, and the nature of things.

**Tactful** (tæ·ktfŭl), *a.* [f. TACT + -FUL.] Full of or endowed with tact; of actions, displaying or inspired by tact.

**1864** *Lond. Soc.* VI. 497, I never heard a better, more tactful speech in my life. **1884** *Macm. Mag.* Nov. 28/1 With a tactful Governor to show them the way. **1894** *Educ. Rev.* VII. 310 An eloquent, tactful and persuasive appeal.

Hence **Ta·ctfully** *adv.*, in a tactful manner.

**1880** MISS BIRD *Japan* II. 72 Ito very tactfully neither gave it [the message] nor told me of it. **1889** *Tablet* 21 Dec. 980 To both deputations Mr. Chaplin replied tactfully.

**Tactic** (tæ·ktik), *sb.*[1] [ad. 17th c. L. *tactic-a*, a. Gr. τακτική (sc. τέχνη) the art of arrangement or tactics, fem. of τακτικός, TACTIC *a.*[1], = F. (*la*) *tactique* (sometimes used in Eng.). In sense 2, ad. Gr. τακτικός (sc. ἀνήρ) tactician.]

**1.** A system of tactics; = TACTICS 1.

[**1570** J. DEE *Math. Pref.* a iv b *margin*, The difference betwene Stratarithmetrie and Tactice [*printed* Tacticie].] **1766** *Misc.* in *Ann. Reg.* 171/2 What is commonly called Tactick, or the formation of battalions. **1801** in Nicolas *Disp. Nelson* (1845) IV. 303 He alluded..to the total want of *tactique* among the Northern Fleets. **1838–42** ARNOLD *Hist. Rome* II. xxix. 143 The arms and tactic of both armies were precisely similar.

**b.** A piece of military tactics.

**1868** FREEMAN *Norm. Conq.* II. ix. 389 Ralph required his men to practise an unusual and foreign tactic.

**c.** *transf.* and *fig.*

**1791** BURKE *App. Whigs* Wks. VI. 206 By a divine tactick. **1817** *Sporting Mag.* L. 8 Great coquettes have another tactic. **1860** M. PATTISON in *Ess. & Rev.* 314 Lord Chesterfield, seeing what advantage the High-church party derived from this tactic, endeavoured to turn it against them.

†**2.** A tactician. *Obs.*

**1638** JUNIUS *Paint. Ancients* 128 A Tactike shall never know how to set his men in aray, unlesse he doe first trie the case by designe. *a* **1641** BP. MOUNTAGU *Acts & Mon.* ii. (1642) 81 Removes, *ambulante exercitu*, as Tacticks phrase it.

**3.** *Math.* (See quots.)

**1861** SYLVESTER in *Phil. Mag.* 374, I have given the general name of *Tactic* to the third pure mathematical science, of which order is the proper sphere, as are number and space of the other two. **1864** CAYLEY *Math. Papers* V. 294 The two great divisions of Algebra are Tactic and Logistic. **1883** *Ibid.* XI. 433 We have a large enough subject, including the partition of numbers, which Sylvester has called Tactic.

**Tactic** (tæ·ktik), *a.*[1] [ad. mod.L. *tactic-us* (17th c.), a. Gr. τακτικός of arrangement or tactics, f. τακτός ordered, vbl. adj. of τάσσειν to set in order. Cf. F. *tactique* (1690 in Furetière).]

†**1.** Of or pertaining to military (or naval) tactics; = TACTICAL *a.* 1. *Obs.*

**1604** EDMONDS *Observ. Cæsar's Comm.* II. 129 The maner of our moderne training, or tacticke practise. **1635** DAVENANT *Madagascar* (1638) 5 Men so exact, In Tactick Arts, both to designe and act. **1652** C. B. STAPYLTON *Herodian* 141 Skilfull in both parts of War, Tactick and Stratagematick. **1775** *Chron.* in *Ann. Reg.* 107/2 To..follow the tactic rules of the other European powers. **1831** CAMPBELL *Power Russia* vii, The Russ will woo..All murder's tactic arts.

**2.** Of or pertaining to arrangement or order.

**1811–31** BENTHAM *Logic* Wks. 1843 VIII. 218/2 In the works of Aristotle..the tactic was scarcely considered in any other light than that of an instrument employed in carrying on the disputatious branch. **1871** SIR W. THOMSON in *Daily News* 3 May, Visible or invisible..according to circumstances, not only of density, degree of illumination, and nearness, but also of tactic arrangement, as of a flock of birds. **1909** J. W. JENKINSON *Experim. Embryol.* 272 Herbst classifies organic reactions to stimuli as either directive or formative. The former are..tactic when the response is some locomotion of a freer body.

**Ta·ctic,** *a.*[2] (*sb.*[2]) *rare.* [f. L. *tact-*, ppl. stem of *tangĕre* to touch + -IC; in sense 2 akin to TACT 4.]

**1.** Of, belonging or relating to touch; tactual.

**1625** JACKSON *Creed* v. xii. § 3 Touch is but an apprehension or feeling of its own tactick qualities being actually moved by other of the same kind. **1886** T. ARNOLD in *Amer. Ann. Deaf & Dumb* Apr. 125 Exercises to increase the tactic sensibility.

†**2.** Of or pertaining to the beating of time: cf. TACT *sb.* 4. *Tactic song* (absol. *tactic*), a song to keep rowers in time.

**1779** FORREST *Voy. N. Guinea* 25, I found Tuan Hadjee in high spirits, cheering up the rowers with a certain Tactic song, to which a man beat time with two brass timbrels. *Ibid.* 303 In rowing..they have always a song as a kind of tactic, and beat on two brass timbrels to keep time.

**Tactical** (tæ·ktikăl), *a.* [f. Gr. τακτικ-ός (see TACTIC *a.*[1], *sb.*[1]) + -AL: see -ICAL. (This appears to be the earliest in use of the words of the group.)]

**1.** Of or pertaining to (military or naval) tactics.

*Tactical point*: a point or place of importance in the disposition of forces. *Tactical unit*: see quot. 1879.

**1570** DEE *Math. Pref.* a iv b, Stratarithmetrie..differreth from the Feate Tacticall, *De aciebus instruendis*, bycause, there, is necessary the wisedome and foresight, to what purpose he so ordreth the men: and Skillfull hability, also, for any occasion, or purpose, to deuise and vse the aptest and most necessary order, array and figure of his Company and Summe of men. **1706** PHILLIPS, *Tactical*, belonging to Martial Array. **1777** W. DALRYMPLE *Trav. Sp. & Port.* lvi, Military books had been bought up in all languages for the use of this tactical school. **1836** *Fraser's Mag.* XIV. 453 We have actually seen them form a hollow square ..with the most perfect tactical accuracy. **1879** *Soldiering* in *Cassell's Techn. Educ.* IV. 320/1 The largest number of men..to whom one man can issue personal orders..called in infantry the 'tactical unit' or unit of manœuvre. **1884** *Mil. Engineering* (ed. 3) I. II. 14 The first and second lines would be taken from the same tactical unit, each battalion having half a battalion in the front line.

**2.** Of or relating to arrangement, esp. the arrangement of procedure with a view to ends.

**1876** TAIT *Rec. Adv. Phys. Sc.* xii. (ed. 2) 302 Each in the same tactical order. **1881** *Nation* (N. Y.) XXXII. 367 With an admirable temper and manners..he combines a good deal of tactical craft. **1893** *Times* 26 Apr. 9/4 To arrive at an understanding upon tactical details.

**b.** Relating to the construction of a sentence. *rare.* **1698** [see TAGHMICAL].

**3.** Of a person, his actions, etc.: Characterized by skilful tactics; skilful in devising means to ends.

**1883** *Manch. Exam.* 26 Nov. 5/3 The address of the French Ambassador was admirably tactical. **1884** *Ibid.* 20 May 5/1 Those who knew M. Ferry as a practical and tactical statesman. **1899** SIR W. LAWSON in *Daily Chron.* 7 Feb. 4/7 All that we want is..an able, an honest, a tactical leader.

**4.** *Math.* Of or pertaining to TACTIC (sense 3): opposed to LOGISTICAL.

**1864** CAYLEY *Math. Papers* V. 293 A tactical operation is one relating to the arrangement in any manner of a set of things.

Hence **Ta·ctically** *adv.*, in a tactical manner; in reference to tactics.

**1871** *Standard* 23 Jan., The Prussians..seem to have outmanœuvred the French both strategically and tactically. **1890** W. STEBBING *Peterborough* ix. 176 The obstinately brave and tactically skilful but uninspired Huguenot [Earl of Galway].

**Tactician** (tækti·ʃăn). [f. as TACTIC *sb.*[1] + -IAN. So mod.F. *tacticien* (1812 in Hatz.-Darm.).] One versed or skilled in the science or art of tactics.

**1798** LD. AUCKLAND *Corr.* (1862) III. 386 An armed nation, composed, perhaps, of ignorant tacticians, but steady and brave. **1838** *Sparks' Biog.* IX. *Steuben* 23 Trained under so expert a tactician as the great Frederic. **1877** GREEN *Hist. Eng. People* I. 426 Edward..had shewn himself as consummate a strategist in the campaign as a tactician in the field.

*transf.* **1842** MIALL in *Nonconf.* II. 505 The lubricity of the clever tactician. **1880** 'OUIDA' *Moths* I. 143 She was a clever tactician.

Hence **Tacti·cianize** *v. nonce-wd.*, to play the tactician; **Tacti·tionary** *a.*, **Tacti·tionist** (bad formations, confusing *-ician* with *-ition*).

**1868** *Guardian* 12 Aug. 905 He does not tacticianize morning, noon, and night. **1881** *Philad.* (U. S.) *Record* No. 3467. 2 Mr. Wheeler has never been a tactitionist in his party. **1890** SIR J. FERGUSON in *Standard* 1 May 2/2 But that [legislation] was altogether artificial and tactitionary. **1890** *Sat. Rev.* 3 May 519/2 The possibly useful, but not blessed, word 'tactitionary'.

**Tactics** (tæ·ktiks). [pl. of TACTIC *sb.*[1], rendering mod.L. (17th c.) *tactica* pl., Gr. τὰ τακτικά, lit. 'matters pertaining to arrangement': see -IC 2.]

**1.** The art or science of deploying military or naval forces in order of battle, and of performing warlike evolutions and manœuvres.

As an art or science often construed as *sing.*; as carried out in practice usually as *pl.*

**1626** GOUGE *Serm. Dignity Chivalry* § 4 Martiall discipline, Artillery tacticks, and Military trainings are matters of moment. **1646** SIR T. BROWNE *Pseud. Ep.* 31 Claudius Ælianus..flourished not long after in the raigne of Trajan, unto whom he dedicated his Tacticks. **1710** J. HARRIS *Lex. Techn.* II, *Tacticks*, is the Art of Disposing any Number of Men into a proper Form of Battle. **1782** V. KNOX *Ess.* I. xix. 94 Tactics and fortification..must be studied, as essentially necessary to the military and naval officer. **1853** J. H. NEWMAN *Hist. Sk.* (1873) II. I. iv. 190 Their tactics by sea was a sort of land engagement on deck. **1876** FREEMAN *Norm. Conq.* V. xxiii. 265 At Tinchebrai, though the chiefs are Norman, the tactics are English.

**b.** *transf.* and *fig.*

**1763** SIR W. JONES *Caissa* Wks. 1799 VI. 502 The chief art in the Tacticks of Chess consists in the nice conduct of the royal pawns. **1842** MIALL in *Nonconf.* II. 305 We have seen principle strangled by tactics so often. **1856** EMERSON *Eng. Traits* v. 83 In parliament, the tactics of the Opposition is to resist every step of the Government by a pitiless attack.

†**2.** Arrangement, disposition. *Obs. rare*⁻¹.

**1650** FULLER *Pisgah* 392 So strange a posture, that scarcely either Jewish or Christian Tacticks of Temple-implements, will admit thereof.

**Tactile** (tæ·ktil, -əil), *a.* [ad. L. *tactilis* tangible, f. *tact-*, ppl. stem of *tangĕre* to touch; cf. F. *tactile.*]

**1.** Perceptible to the touch; tangible.

**1615** H. Crooke *Body of Man* 717 Beside the Sapour it hath also many Tangible or Tactile qualities. **1706** Phillips (ed. 6) s. v., The chief Tactile Qualities are Heat, Cold, Driness, Moistness, and Hardness. **1898** *Allbutt's Syst. Med.* V. 789 Certain visible and tactile signs.

**2.** Of or pertaining to touch; relating to the sense of touch.

**1657–83** Evelyn *Hist. Relig.* (1850) I. 34 The tactile, auditory, and olfactory senses. **1855** Bain *Senses & Int.* II. ii. § 2 (1864) 155 That high tactile sensibility distinguishing the tip of the tongue. **1874** Carpenter *Ment. Phys.* I. i. § 10 (1879) 11 Our own Tactile Sense (under which general head may be combined the Sense of Touch, the Sense of Muscular Exertion, and the Mental Sense of Effort). **1876** Foster *Phys.* III. iv. (1879) 532 The tactile sensation is..a symbol to us of some external event. **1899** *Allbutt's Syst. Med.* VII. 299 Tactile anæsthesia over..the whole of the left side.

**b.** Of organs: Endowed with the sense of touch.

**1768** Tucker *Lt. Nat.* (1834) I. 388 The gustatory papillæ of the tongue and tactile papillæ of the fingers. **1859** Darwin *Orig. Spec.* vii. (1878) 172 The external ears of the common mouse..no doubt serve as tactile organs. **1873** A. Flint *Nerv. Syst.* i. 39 The name tactile corpuscles implies that these bodies are connected with the sense of touch.

**Tactility** (tækti·lĭti). [f. after L. type **tactilitās*, f. *tactilis* Tactile: see -ity.] The quality or condition of being tactile.

**1659** Stanley *Hist. Philos.* XIII. (1701) 565/2 There are others [qualities] which depend upon these; as Flexility, Tactility, Ductility, and others, from Softness. **1727** Bailey vol. II, *Tactility*, capableness of being touched. **1899** *Allbutt's Syst. Med.* VIII. 169 Contrast the commonest seat of pain in subjective tactility.

**b.** Sensitiveness, touchiness. *nonce-use.*

**1831** Syd. Smith *Mem. & Lett.* cccxxi. (1855) II. 331 You have a little infirmity,—tactility, or touchiness.

**Ta:ctinva·riant.** *Math.* [f. L. *tactu-s* touch + Invariant.] (See quots.)

**1856** Cayley *Math. Papers* II. 320 The function which, equated to zero, expresses the result of the elimination is an invariant which (from its geometrical signification) might be termed the Tactinvariant of the two quantics. **1873** Salmon *Higher Plane Curves* iii. (1879) 80 The condition that two curves U, V, should touch (which condition is called their tact-invariant).

**Taction** (tæ·kʃən). [ad. L. *tactiōn-em*, n. of action from *tangĕre* to touch. Cf. F. *taction* (17th c.).] The action of touching; contact.

**1623** Cockeram, *Taction*, a touching. **1668** *Phil. Trans.* III. 689 The First Part of it handles the Taction of Circles. **1726** Swift *Gulliver* III. ii, They neither can speak nor attend to the discourses of others, without being roused by some external taction upon the organs of speech and hearing. **1866** Shuckard *Brit. Bees* 346 It is possibly from some taction of this instrument that she discerns the sizes of the eggs.

† **Ta·ctive,** *a. Obs. rare.* [ad. L. type **tactīvus*, f. *tact-*, ppl. stem (see Tact and -ive).] Of or characterized by touching; = Tactile *a.* 2.

**1634** T. Johnson *Parey's Chirurg.* I. x. (1678) 15 That [Spirit] which is carried to the instruments of Touching, is termed the Tactive. **1644** Bulwer *Chirol.* 171 Although this touching vertue or tactive quality be diffused through the whole body within and without.

**Tactless** (tæ·ktlės), *a.* [f. Tact + -less.] Destitute of tact; awkward.

**1847** in Webster. **1875** *Fam. Herald* 17 July 181/2 'But ..' laughed Doris, quickly answering this tactless speech. **1886** M. Moorsom *Thirteen all Told* 26 A glance of warning, which he was too dull and tactless to take.

Hence **Ta·ctlessly** *adv.*, **Ta·ctlessness.**

**1893** *Academy* 21 Oct. 333/3 Severe and just, but somewhat tactlessly contrived, measures against the Jewish usurers. **1882** Beresf. Hope *Brandreths* III. xxxviii. 73, I should not have to blame my own tactlessness for the result.

**Tactor** (tæ·ktǫı, -əı). [a. L. *tactor*, agent-n. from *tangĕre* to touch.] A feeler; an organ of touch.

**1817** Kirby & Sp. *Entomol.* xxiii. (1818) II. 312 Some woodlice..use them as tactors, touching the surface on each side with them, as they go along. **1835** Kirby *Hab. & Inst. Anim.* II. xvii. 113 Cuvier regards them [barbs of some fishes] as a kind of tactors.

**Tactual** (tæ·ktiuăl), *a.* [f. L. *tactu-s* touch + -al: cf. *visual.*] Of or pertaining to touch; of the nature of or due to touch.

**1642** H. More *Song Soul* II. III. I. xxi, Her sight is tactuall, The sunne and all the starres that do appear She feels them in herself. **1678** Cudworth *Intell. Syst.* I. iv. § 36. 549 A kind of Tactual Union..with the Centre of the Universe. **1833** Carlyle *Misc. Ess., Cagliostro* (1872) V. 68 Thy existence is wholly an Illusion and optical and tactual Phantasm. **1871** Tyndall *Fragm. Sc.* (1879) II. ix. 185 In the lowest organisms we have a kind of tactual sense diffused over the entire body.

Hence **Tactua·lity,** tactual quality; **Ta·ctually** *adv.*, in a tactual manner or way.

**1858** W. R. Pirie *Inq. Hum. Mind* vii. 398 It is not improbable that we have even a sense of tactuality, if we may so speak, in the secondary sensations. **1855** H. Spencer *Psychol.* (1872) I. III. vi. 332 When the combined appliances of touch and muscular sense are fully developed ..an immense variety of textures can be known tactually.

† **Ta·cture.** *Obs.* [ad. L. type **tactūra*, f. *tact-*, ppl. stem of *tangĕre* to touch: see -ure.] Touch, taction, contact.

**1597** A. M. tr. *Guillemeau's Fr. Chirurg.* 9 b/1 Yet..with the tacture, or the eyes, we can not espye the fissure or rente. **1650** T. Bayly *Herba Parietis* 122 Berontus tooke his Amarissa by the hand, whose sprightly behaviour answered the tacture, with like affection. **1727** Earbery tr. *Burnet's St. Dead* I. 15 The Soul has no Manner of Action either in itself or externally, by Tacture or Impulse, but what proceeds from the force of Thinking.

† **Tactu·riency.** *Obs. nonce-wd.* [f. L. type **tactūrīre*, desiderative vb. f. *tangĕre*, *tact-*, to touch + -ency.] The desire of touching.

**1652** Urquhart *Jewel* Wks. (1834) 236 The visuriency of either, by ushering the tacturiency of both, made the attrectation of both consequent to the inspection of either.

**Tadcheese, Tadde, tade:** see Toad.

**Taddy, tadee, tadie,** obs. forms of Toddy.

**Tadpole** [1] (tæ·dpōul). Also 5 **taddepol, tadpolle,** 6 **tadpal,** 7 **tod-, toad-pole, toad-poll.** [f. ME. *tāde, tadde*, Toad + (app.) Poll *sb.*[1], head, round head. The latter element has been questioned, on the ground of the apparent inappropriateness of the name 'toad-head'; but cf. the dialectal synonym *pollhead* or *polehead* (in Sc. and north. Eng. *powheid*), app. = head-head.]

**1.** The larva of a frog, toad, or other batrachian, from the time it leaves the egg until it loses its gills and tail. Chiefly applied in the early stage when the animal appears to consist simply of a round head with a tail.

**14..** *Voc.* in Wr.-Wülcker 569/7 *Brucus*, a taddepol. *c* **1475** *Pict. Voc.* ibid. 766/20 *Hic lumbricus*, a tadpolle. **1519** Horman *Vulg.* 277 b, This water is full of tadpollys. **1598** Sylvester *Du Bartas* II. ii. III. *Colonies* 411 After a sweltring Day, some sultry showr Doth in the Marshes heaps of Tadpals pour. **1605** Shaks. *Lear* III. iv. 135 Poore Tom, that eates the swimming Frog, the Toad, the Todpole. **1681** Hickeringill *Char. Sham-Plotter* Wks. 1716 I. 212 A Sham-Plotter..is the Spawn of a Papist, as a Toad-Poll of a Toad. **1774** Goldsm. *Nat. Hist.* IV. 47 The egg, or little black globe which produces the tadpole. **1886** Ruskin *Præterita* I. ix. 293 Without so much water anywhere as..a tadpole could wag his tail in.

**b.** *transf.* and *fig.* (In quot. 1588, a black infant.)

**1588** Shaks. *Tit. A.* IV. ii. 85 Ile broach the tadpole on my Rapiers poynt, Nurse giue it me, my sword shall soone dispatch it. **1881** *Macm. Mag.* XLIV. 475 Such pale tadpoles,..with listless ways, and few games.

**2.** Sometimes applied to the tailed larva of a tunicate, the swimming tail of which is afterwards dropped or absorbed.

**1880** E. R. Lankester *Degeneration* 42 The egg of *Phallusia* gives rise to a tadpole. **1909** W. Hatchett Jackson *Let. to Editor*, The ascidian or tunicate tadpole.

**3.** A local name in U.S. of a water-fowl, the Hooded Merganser, *Lophodytes cucullatus*, apparently from the size of its head, or from the patch of white on its crest. **1891** in *Cent. Dict.*

**4.** *attrib.* and *Comb.*, as *tadpole form*, *state*, etc.; *tadpole-like* adj.; **tadpole fish, -hake,** a ganoid fish of the North Atlantic, *Raniceps raninus.*

**1682** Dryden *Medal* 304 Frogs and Toads and all the Tadpole Train. **1682** S. Pordage *Medal Rev.* 30 The Tadpole-Priests, Shall lift above the Lords, their Priestly Crests. **1768** G. White *Selborne* xvii, Frogs are as yet in their tadpole state. **1832** Johnston in *Proc. Berw. Nat. Club* I. No. 1. 7 Of the tadpole fish [*Raniceps trifurcatus*, Flem.], I had the pleasure of exhibiting to you a living specimen. **1847** Carpenter *Zool.* § 980 The young animal [ascidian] has..a large tadpole-like tail. **1856** Gosse *Marine Zool.* II. 27 At first it has a tadpole-like form.

Hence (chiefly *nonce-wds.*) **Ta·dpoledom, Tadpolehood, Ta·dpolism,** the state of being a tadpole; also *fig.*; **Ta·dpolewa:rd** *adv.* [see -ward].

**1863** Kingsley *Let.* 29 May, in *Life* (1879) II. 157 Little beggars an inch long, fresh from water and *tadpoledom. **1891** C. L. Morgan *Anim. Sk.* 222 Little Froggies which have just emerged from *tadpole-hood. **1897** G. C. Bateman *Vivarium* 296 Many of the Batrachians, during a portion of their tadpolehood, are vegetable feeders. **1897** *Voice* (N. Y.) 8 Apr. 3/1 Degeneration is involution through self *tadpoleward. **1883** Baring-Gould *J. Herring* III. lix. 293 All previous existence would be *tadpolism.

**Tadpole** [2]. In *Tadpole and Taper*, names of two political schemers in Disraeli's *Coningsby*; hence allusively, in the sense 'professional politicians, the hacks of a political party'. Hence *Tadpole and Taperism.*

[**1844** Disraeli *Coningsby* II. ii, Mr. Tadpole and Mr. Taper were also there; they too had lost their seats since 1832; but being men of business, and accustomed from early life to look about them, they had already commenced the combinations which..were to bear them back to the assembly where they were so missed.] **1885** *Manch. Exam.* 3 June 5/4 The tadpoles and the tapers of the party demand a cry. **1904** A. Birrell in *Contemp. Rev.* Apr. 475 A book further removed from such Tadpole and Taperism is not in the library. **1905** W. Churchill in *Daily Chron.* 13 May 5/6 The Cabinet was packed with nonentities, Tadpoles and Tapers from the Whips' room. **1908** F. Harrison in *Trans. Roy. Hist. Soc.* Ser. III. III. 45 The reasons why he [Chatham] would never take office again [etc.]..all this has greatly exercised the Tadpoles and Tapers of his age and of our own.

**Tae,** Sc. form of Toe *sb.*; **Tae'd,** toed.

**Tae,** in *the tae*, Sc. dial. f. To *adj.* in *the to* = the one, Tone; mod. Sc. dial. form of To *prep.*

**Tædium,** obs. form of Tedium.

**Tael** (tēl). Also 7 **taile, tayel, tayl,** 7–9 **tale,** 8 **tahel;** 7 **tay, taye,** *pl.* 6 **taes.** [a. Pg. *tael* (pl. *taeis*), ad. Malay *tahil*, *taïl* weight. The early *tay*, *taes*, etc. represent the Pg. plural.]

**1.** The trade name for the Chinese *liang* or 'ounce', a weight used in China and the East.

In Chinese use the *liang* varies according to local custom, and to the commodity weighed; but the weight of 1⅓ oz. avoirdupois is fixed by treaty for commercial purposes.

**1598** W. Philip *Linschoten* 44 A Tael is a full ounce and a halfe Portingale weight. **1613** J. Saris *Voy. to Japan* (1900) 222 Bezar stones are there bought by the Taile.. which is one Ounce, and the third part English. **1699** Dampier *Voy.* II. I. 132, 5 Tale make a Bancal, a weight so called. **1854** in R. Tomes *Amer. in Japan* (1857) 410 The Japanese have a decimal system of weight, like the Chinese, of catty, tael, mace, candareen, and cash, by which articles in general are weighed; but gold and silver are not reckoned above taels. **1908** Morse *Trade Chinese Emp.* 149 It is necessary always to bear in mind the distinction between the tael of value and the tael of weight.

**2.** Hence, A money of account, originally a tael (in weight) of standard silver, the value of which fluctuates with the price of the metal.

The *Haikwan tael*, i. e. the tael accepted by the Chinese Foreign Custom-house in payment of duties, is the equivalent of 584·85 grains of pure silver (Morse 152). From 1745 to 1860 its value was between 6*s.* and 7*s.*, in 1864 6*s.* 8*d.*, in 1900 about 3*s.*, in 1904 2*s.* 10*d.*

**1588** Parke tr. *Mendoza's Hist. China* III. iv. 61 They giue him foure million..Taes. **1598** J. Davis *Voy.* (Hakl. Soc.) 152 Foure Masses makes a Perdaw. Foure Perdawes makes a Tayel. **1613** J. Saris *Voy. to Japan* (1900) 97 Bantam Pepper..was worth here [Japan] at our comming tenne Tayes the Peecull...A Taye is five shillings sterling with them. **1726** Shelvocke *Voy. round World* 457 They demanded 6000 Tahel. **1745** P. Thomas *Jrnl. Anson's Voy.* 215 Taëls, each of which in our Money comes to about six Shillings and Threepence. **1800** *Chron.* in *Asiat. Ann. Reg.* 62/2 His wealth, which..is said to have amounted at the lowest computation, to eighty millions of tales, near twenty-seven millions of pounds sterling. **1901** *Empire Rev.* I. 394 The land tax is levied upon the cultivable land, and may be put at half a tael or 1*s.* 6*d.* per acre. **1908** Morse *Trade Chinese Emp.* 151 The Haikwan tael.. is a purely fictitious and non-existent currency...At no Custom House does any merchant tender Haikwan taels in payment of duties.

**Ta'en,** contr. f. *taken*, pa. pple. of Take *v.*

‖ **Tænia, tenia** (tī·niă). Pl. **-æ, -as.** [L. *tænia*, a. Gr. ταινία a band, fillet, ribbon.]

**1.** *Archæol.* A headband, ribbon, or fillet.

**1850** Leitch tr. *C. O. Müller's Anc. Art* § 340 (ed. 2) 406 The twisted fillet of the athletes and of Hercules consists of several tæniæ of different colours. **1857** Birch *Anc. Pottery* (1858) I. 412 A wreath or branch, which is exchanged on the later vases for the *tainia* or fillet.

**2.** *Arch.* In the Doric order, A band separating the architrave from the frieze. (So in Vitruvius.)

**1563** Shute *Archit.* C j b, The Architraue..ye shal deuide into 6. parts wherof Tenia, to be the sixte part. **1704** J. Harris *Lex. Techn.* I, *Tænia*..is a Member of the Dorick Capital, which resembles the Shape of a square Fillet. **1817–48** Rickman *Archit.* (ed. 5) 32 The fillet of the tenia of the architrave is very nearly as large as the ogee under it.

**3.** *Surg.* A long narrow ribbon used as a ligature. **1882** in Ogilvie (Annandale).

**4.** *Anat.* A ribbon-like structure; applied *esp.* to the bands of white nervous matter in the brain and the longitudinal muscles of the colon.

**1882** Ogilvie (Annandale), *Tænia hippocampi*, in anat. the plaited edges of the processes of the fornix. **1890** Billings *Med. Dict.*, *Tænia*, a tape; in anatomy applied to tape- or band-like structures.

**5.** *Zool.* A tapeworm [so in L.]; *spec.* a genus of cestoid worms, including the common tapeworm. Also *fig.*

[**1693** tr. *Blancard's Phys. Dict.* (ed. 2), *Tænia*, broad Worms.] **1706** Phillips, *Tænia.* **1753** Chambers *Cycl. Supp.* s. v. *Tape-worm*, A fragment of the jointed tænia, sometimes voided..in separate pieces. **1836–9** *Todd's Cycl. Anat.* II. 121/1 The species of Tænia infesting the intestines of other animals are extremely numerous. **1861** Hulme tr. *Moquin-Tandon* II. II. 60 The Tænias and similar animals. **1869** Browning *Ring & Bk.* XI. 1606 Unbrokenly lay bare Each taenia that had sucked me dry of juice.

**6.** *Comb.* **Tænia-chain,** the whole series, or a number of the consecutive joints of a tapeworm; **tænia-head,** the scolex of a tapeworm, the worm itself without the proglottides or deutoscolices.

**1878** Bell *Gegenbaur's Comp. Anat.* 130 A process of gemmation, the product of which is the Tænia-chain.

Hence **Tænian** (tī·niăn) *a.*, pertaining to tapeworms; **Tæ·niate** *a.*, tænioid, tæniiform.

**1897** *Allbutt's Syst. Med.* II. 1114 Conditions which favour the entrance of the tænian ova into man or the domestic herbivora. **1860** Mayne *Expos. Lex.*, *Tæniatus*.. teniate. **1891** *Cent. Dict.*, Tæniate.

**Tænii-** (tīni,i), combining form of L. *tænia* ribbon, often contracted to **tæni-** (also *erron.* **tænia-**). **Tæniipho·bia** [-phobia], morbid fear of tapeworm. **Tæ·ni(i)cide** (also **tæniacide**) [-cide [2]], a destroyer of tapeworms, a tænifuge. **Tæ·ni(i)form** *a.* [-form], having the form of a tape or ribbon, tænioid. **Tæ·nifuge** (also **tæniafuge**) [-fuge], *sb.* a substance used to expel tapeworms from the body; *adj.* expelling tapeworms.

**1897** *Allbutt's Syst. Med.* II. 1020 The belief that a worm is present either where no worm had ever existed, or after its complete expulsion—a sort of *tæniaphobia. **1857** Dunglison *Med. Dict.* 898/2 *Tæniacide..Tænicide. **1885**

*Lancet* 26 Sept. 568 A Canadian doctor has recently advocated the use of glycerine as a tæniacide. **1872** H. C. Wood *Fresh-water Algæ* (1874) 101 Conjoined in filiform or *tæniform fascia. **1857** Dunglison *Med. Dict.* 898/2 *Tæniafuge..Tenifuge. **1866** A. Flint *Princ. Med.* (1880) 575 The male fern (filix mas) is a taenifuge. **1881** tr. *Trousseau & Pidoux' Treat. Therap.* (ed. 9) III. 353 Experiments upon the tæniafuge virtues of the [pomegranate-root] bark.

**Tænio-** (tīˑniˌo), combining form of Gr. ταινία ribbon, used in the formation of some zoological terms. **Tæ:niobra·nchiate** *a.* [Gr. βράγχια gills + -ate[2]], having tæniate gills; pertaining to the *Tæniobranchia*, a division of ascidians. **Tæ:nioglo·ssate** *a.* [Gr. γλῶσσα tongue], in Mollusca, having upon the lingual ribbon one median tooth between three admedian teeth on either side. **Tænio·pterine** *a.* [Gr. πτερόν wing + -ine[1]], belonging to the *Tæniopterinæ*, a sub-family of tyrant-birds. **Tæ·niosome** [Gr. σῶμα body], one of the sub-order *Tæniosomi* of teleocephalous fishes; a ribbon-fish; so **Tæ:nioso·mous** *a.*, having a ribbon-like body; pertaining to the ribbon-fishes.

**1891** *Cent. Dict.*, *Tæniobranchiate. **1883** E. R. Lankester in *Encycl. Brit.* XVI. 660/2 The Pneumonochlamyda.. have..a complex rhipidoglossate or *taenioglossate radula.

**Tænioid** (tīˑniˌoid), *a.* (Also *erron.* tænoid.) [f. Tænia + -oid.] Of a ribbon-like shape; related to the tapeworms.

**1836–9** *Todd's Cycl. Anat.* II. 410/2 The Tænioid Sterelmintha furnish us one of the simplest examples of this arrangement. **1867** J. Hogg *Microsc.* 363 The anterior extremity of a taen[i]oid worm is usually called the head. **1875** C. C. Blake *Zool.* 327 The name Echinococcus is given to the hydatid cyst filled with the larvæ of tænioid worms.

‖ **Tæniola** (tīniˑolă). *Zool.* Also anglicized tæ·niole. [mod. L. *tæniola*, dim. of *tænia* band, ribbon.] One of the radial partitions in the body of some acalephans.

So **Tæ·niolate** *a.*, belonging to the division *Tæniolata* of hydroids.

**1884** *Proc. Boston Soc. Nat. Hist.* 114 Such a form would differ from a tæniolate Hydrozoon.

**Tænite** (tīˑnəit). *Min.*

† **1.** [f. Gr. ταινία ribbon + -ite[1]: named 1841.] A variety of feldspar occurring in striped crystals.

**1841** E. Hitchcock *Rep. Geol. Mass.* II. 676 Some have proposed for it the name *taenite*..on account of its resemblance to a ribbon.

**2.** [ad. Ger. *tänit*, Reichenbach 1861, f. Gr. ταινία ribbon, from the shape of its crystals.] Nickeliferous iron found in meteorites.

**1868** Dana *Min.* 16 Reichenbach has named..that [alloy of iron and nickel] approaching probably the formula $Fe_4Ni_3$, Tænite. **1883** *Science* I. 464/2 Meteorite fragments are composed of nickeliferous iron, magnetic pyrites, taenite, and silicates.

**Tafe,** = *to have*: see T' [1] and Have *v.*

**Taffel, -il.** *Sc. Obs.* or *dial.* Also 9 tafil. [prob. ad. Du. *tafel*, MDu., MLG. *tafele, taffele*, = Ger. *tafel*, OE. *tæfl* Tavel, Table.] A table.

**1633** Dell in *Cerem. Coronat. Jas. I* (1685) 16 The Regal, Crown,..and Spurs are laid down on a Taffel besides the Altar. *a* **1670** Spalding *Troub. Chas. I* (1850) I. 38 The Erll of Erroll sat..at ane four nvkit taffill..coverit with grein claith. **1884** C. Rogers *Soc. Life Scot.* I. vii. 242 Potatoes were tossed from the saucepan on the tafil or dinner-board.

**Tafferel** (tæˑfĕrĕl, tæˑfrĕl). Also 7 taffer(r)ell, 8 -eral, -eril, -rill, 8–9 -arel, 9 -aril, -rel. [a. Du. *tafereel* panel, picture, dim. of *tafel* Table (for *tafeleel, with dissimilation of *l* .. *l* to *r* .. *l*). The 19th c. corruption to *taffrail*, with accompanying change of sense, shows confusion of the ending *-rel* with Rail *sb.*: cf. quot. 1704.]

† **1.** A panel: *esp.* a carved panel. *Obs.*

**1622–3** in *Brit. Mag.* (1833) III. 655 Item paid to John James a carver for cutting a Tafferell with a deathes head vpon it which is sett vpp at the entraunce..to our parish Church 00 15 00. **1632** in E. B. Jupp *Carpenters' Co.* (1887) 302 Carpenters..haue allwaies vsed to haue..the cutting of ballesters, hances, tafferrells, pendants and piramides.

**2.** *Naut.* The upper part of the flat portion of a ship's stern above the transom, usually ornamented with carvings, etc. In later use including, and now applied to, the aftermost portion of the poop-rail, and spelt Taffrail.

**1704** J. Harris *Lex. Techn.* I, *Tafferel*, is the uppermost Part, Frame, or Rail of a Ship abaft over the Poop. **1705** *Lond. Gaz.* No. 4116/3 Only her Hull from the Taffrill to the Midships remained above Water. **1750** *Minutes Bd. of Admiralty* 1 Jan. (P. R. O.), To cause the Taffarel and Quarter Pieces of the Model of the *Victory* at the Royal Academy at Portsmouth to be carved agreeably to the ornaments of that Ship. **1833** M. Scott *Tom Cringle* ix. (1859) 179 He again attempted to drag me away from my hold on the Tafferel. *c* **1850** *Rudim. Navig.* (Weale) 155 *Taffarel* or *taffrail*, the upper part of the ship's stern, usually ornamented with carved-work or mouldings, the ends of which unite to the quarter-pieces. **1857** Wilkinson *Egypt. Pharaohs* 113 Boats had..one rudder turning on the taffrel.

**b.** *Comb.* Tafferel-rail = Taffrail.

**1846** Young *Naut. Dict.* 244 *Taffrail* or *Tafferel-Rail*, the rail over the heads of the stern timbers.

**Taffeta, taffety** (tæˑfĕtă, -ĕti). Forms: *α.* 4 tapheta, 4–6 tafeta, 4–8 taffata, 5–6 tafata, 5–7 taffatas, 6–7 taffita, (6 -yta), 6– taffeta, -as. *β.* 5–8 taffaty, 6 tafete, -ie, 6 *Sc.* taffate, -ati, -atis, -eti, -etti, -ete, -etee, tapheit, -ite, -ettye, taftais, -teis, teffites, 6–7 taffatie, -etie, -itie, 6–8 -ity, 6– taffety. [a. OF. *taffetas, taphetas* (1317 in Hatz.-D.) or med.L. *taffata*, etc. (Du Cange) = It. *taffetà*, Pg. *tafeta*, Sp. *tafetan*; ultimately a. Pers. تافته *tāftah*, (*a*) silken cloth, (*b*) linen clothing, subst. use of *tāftah*, pa. pple. of تافتن *tāftan* 'to shine', also 'to twist, to spin'.] A name applied at different times to different fabrics. In early times apparently a plain-wove glossy silk (of any colour); in more recent times, a light thin silk or union stuff of decided brightness or lustre. In the 16th c. mention is also made of 'linen taffety'. In recent times the name has been misapplied to various mixtures of silk and wool, and even cotton and jute, thin fine woollen material, etc.

*a.* **1373** in *Exch. Rolls Scotl.* II. 440 In empcione vnius pecie de taffata. *c* **1386** Chaucer *Prol.* 440 A Doctour of Phisik..In sangwyn and in pers he clad was al Lyned with Taffata [*Lansd. MS.* tafeta] and with Sendal. *c* **1425** *Cast. Persev.* 239 in *Macro Plays* 84 With tapytys of tafata I tymbyr my towris. **1530** Palsgr. 279/1 Tafata a maner of sylke, *taffetas*. **1561** *Burgh Rec. Edinb.* (1875) III. 122 Sum brawf abulyement of taffate or vther silk. **1604** *Lismore Papers* Ser. II. (1887) I. 106 One ell iij qu^trs^ of taffita to line y^e^ same Dublett and faice it. **1634** Sir T. Herbert *Trav.* 182 Taffataes of transparant finenesse. **1650** Fuller *Pisgah* IV. vi. 129 Riddling oracles..like changeable taffata (wherein the woofe and warpe are of different colours), seems of several hues, as the looker on takes his station. **1773** Brydone *Sicily* viii. 83 We are melting with heat, in thin suits of taffeta. **1836–41** Brande *Chem.* (ed. 5) 156 Trials were made with raw silk, ravelings of white taffeta, and of common sewing silk. **1884** *Girl's Own Paper* Aug. 682/1, I must mention the return of the ancient challis, which is now called a woollen taffetas. **1903** *Times* 12 Feb. 5/3 In silks..it is noted that taffetas are becoming less asked for. **1908** *Let. to Editor, Chiffon-taffeta*, a bright, lustrous, softly finished thin glacé silk, now much worn for ladies' blouses or dresses.

*β.* **1515** *Acc. Ld. High Treas. Scot.* V. 9 Twa elne of goldin hewit taffity, to be thame quaiffs. **1541** *Ibid.* VIII. 42, v elnis blak teffites of Janis. **1539** *Aberdeen Regr.* (1844) I. 161 Ane blak bonat, with ane typpat of taphite. **1550** Lyndesay *Sqr. Meldrum* 125 Of yallow taftais wes hir sark. **1573** *Inv. Roy. Wardrobe* (1815) 189 (Jam.) Freinzeit with gold and lynit with reid tafteis. **1583** Stubbes *Anat. Abus.* II. (1882) 108 They must weare silkes .. grograms, taffeties, and the like. **1630** Capt. Smith *Trav. & Adv.* xvi. 31 A white mares taile with a peece of greene taffity, on a great Pike, is carried before him [the Chan] for a standard. **1766** *Chron.* in *Ann. Reg.* 103/2 An additional duty on the importation of silks, crapes, and taffaties. **1865** E. C. Clayton *Cruel Fort.* I. 248 Dressed in the costume of 1827 or 1828—a gown of taffety with gigot sleeves, and a muslin canezon spencer.

**b.** *fig.* Florid language; = Fustian 2.

**1821** Byron *Jrnl.* 12 Jan. in Moore *Life* III. 102 There is a good deal of taffeta in some of Tom's prefatory phrases.

**B.** *attrib.* and as *adj.*

**1.** Of taffeta; of the nature of taffeta.

**1552–3** *Inv. Ch. Goods Staffs.* in *Ann. Lichfield* (1863) IV. 38 Itm. ij vestements, on of blewe chamblet, thother of taffeta silke. **1561** *Burgh Rec. Edinb.* (1882) IV. 122 Doubletis of saterne,..tafetie hatis. *a* **1586** Sidney *Arcadia* I. (1622) 51 Her bodie..couered with a light Taffeta garment. **1602** Dekker *Satirom.* Wks. 1873 I. 260 Horace did not weare the Badge of gentlemens company, as thou doost thy Taffetie sleeves. *c* **1645** Howell *Lett.* (1688) II. 316 Full of Taffity Silks and Sattins. **1725** *Bradley's Fam. Dict.* s.v. *Ointment*, Searce it thro' a Taffety Sieve. **1849** Jas. Grant *Kirkaldy of Gr.* xxvii, Captain Lambie, he of the taffety standard celebrity. **1883** *Glasgow Herald* 21 Apr. 8/3 Taffeta Silk Gloves. **1903** *Daily Chron.* 26 Sept. 8/6 Evening gowns..made of soft light-blue taffetas silk.

**2.** *fig.* Florid, bombastic; over-dressed; dainty, delicate, fastidious: *taffety cream*, ? velvet cream.

**1588** Shaks. *L. L. L.* v. ii. 406 Taffata phrases, silken tearmes precise. **1621** Middleton *Span. Gipsy* IV. iii, Can taffeta girls look plump without pampering? **1653** Urquhart *Rabelais* I. v, O the fine white wine,..it is a kind of taffatas wine. **1719** D'Urfey *Pills* VI. 124 With Taffity-Tarts and Pies. **1773** Goldsm. *Stoops to Conq.* II. i, A shaking pudding, and a dish of tiff—taff—taffety cream. **1840** Miss Yonge (Heard in Hampshire), The old sow won't eat that stuff, she's so very taffety.

**3.** *Comb.*, as *taffeta-bordered, -covered* adjs.

**1889** Doyle *Micah Clarke* 115 Dame Hobson's best taffata covered settee. **1908** *Westm. Gaz.* 8 Feb. 13/2 A crown of taffeta with a taffeta-bordered brim of crinoline straw and other such blendings of straw and fabric.

**Taffey, taffia,** variants of Tafia.

**Taffrail** (tæˑfrĕl). *Naut.* Also tafrail. [A 19th c. alteration of Tafferel, due to false etymology, the termination *-rel* being taken as Rail.] The aftermost portion of the poop-rail of a ship.

**1814** *Chron.* in *Ann. Reg.* 176/2 We crossed his stern, our jib-boom passing over his tafrail. **1823** Scoresby *Jrnl. Whale Fish.* 39, I stood on the taffrail as the ship was turned before the wind. **1840** R. H. Dana *Bef. Mast* xxxiii. 126 With her head for the equator, and Cape Horn over her taffrail, she went gloriously on. **1899** Bullen *Log Sea-waif* 187 She dipped her stern right under, taking a sea in over the taffrail that filled the decks fore and aft.

**Taffy** [1] (tæˑfi). The earlier form of Toffee, now Scotch, North Eng., and American.

**1.** A sweetmeat made from sugar or treacle, with butter, etc.: see Toffee.

**1817** R. Wilbraham *Cheshire Gloss.*, *Taffy*,.. treacle thickened by boiling and made into hard cakes. **1819** R. Anderson *Cumbld. Ball.* (*c* 1850) 51 Now heaps o' treagle chaps brong in, An taffey suin they meade us. **1825** Jamieson, *Taffie*, treacle mixed with flour, and boiled till it acquire consistency; a sweetmeat eaten only on Hallowe'en. **1864** Webster, *Taffy*, a kind of candy made of molasses boiled down and poured out in shallow pans. **1884** W. H. Rideing in *Harper's Mag.* Mar. 522/1 Is Everton taffy a myth? **1890** S. J. Duncan *Social Departure* vii. 57 The steward made almond-taffy, or toffee, as Orthodocia had been brought up to pronounce it.

**2.** *U. S. slang.* Crude or vulgar compliment or flattery; 'soft soap'; blarney.

**1879** *Tribune* (N. Y.) 16 Sept. (Cent. Dict.), There will be a reaction, and the whole party will unite in an offering of taffy. **1894** Howells *Traveller from Altruria* 180 'If we learn anything at all from him, it will be because you have taught us how.' She could not resist this bit of taffy. **1901** *N. Amer. Rev.* Feb. 172 At this point..we should throw in a little trade-taffy about the Blessings of Civilization.

**3.** *attrib.* and *Comb.*, as *taffy stand, stick*; **taffy-join**, a reunion of young people for the making of taffy to which each contributes.

**1854** Taffy-join [remembered in use]. **1878** *Cumberland Gloss.*, *Taffy joinin'*.. young people in the country sometimes assemble on a winter evening and subscribe a few pence each to buy treacle for making 'taffy'. **1881** T. E. Brown *Fo'c's'le Yarns* (1889) 151 My lad with the taffystick in his fist. **1894** Hall Caine *Manxman* v. x, Break up every taffy stand in the fair, if you can't find anything better.

**Taffy** [2] (tæˑfi). [An ascribed Welsh pronunciation of *Davy* or *David*, in Welsh *Dafydd*.] A familiar nickname for a Welshman: cf. *Paddy*, *Sawney*, etc.

*a* **1700** B. E. *Dict. Cant. Crew*, *Taffy*, a Welshman or David. *Taffy's Day*, the first of March. **1708** *Brit. Apollo* No. 98. 2/2 Welch-men are called *Taffies* from the Corruption of the word *David*. **1893** *Sun* 26 July 2/7 Cheers echoed over the Surrey hills when it was known that for the first time a Taffy had gained the Queen's.

‖ **Tafia** (tæˑfiă). Also 8 taffia, taffey, -fy. [Origin uncertain: given in 1722 as native name in West Indies (Labat *Voy. aux Iles de l'Amér.* III. 410 L'eau-de-vie qu'on tire des cannes est appelée guildive [see Kill-devil]; les sauvages et les nègres l'appellent *tafia*): but *tāfia* is also given in Malay dicts. as 'a spirit distilled from molasses'. The word appears therefore to be widely diffused in east and west.] A rum-like spirituous liquor obtained from the lower grades of molasses, refuse brown sugar, etc.

**1777** (Apr. 10) in *Illinois Hist. Collect.* (1903) I. 296 The person that intoxicated them with Rum or Taffia. **1779** in W. H. English *Conq. Northwest* (1896) I. 375, $7\frac{1}{2}$ gallons of taffey at sixty-four dollars per gallon. **1779** G. R. Clark *Campaign Illinois* (1869) 79, I..gave them..Taffy and Provisions to make merry on and left them. **1793** Trapp tr. *Rochon's Madagascar* 189 Over which he poured some *tafia* or rum. **1799** *Naval Chron.* I. 173 A sloop laden with taffia. **1880** G. W. Cable *Grandissimes* xxviii. 197 From the same sugar-cane comes sirop and tafia. **1889** *Harper's Mag.* Nov. 851 Sugar is very difficult to ship; rum and tafia can be handled with less risk.

**Taft** (toft), *sb. Plumbing.* A widening-out of the end of a lead pipe into a broad thin flange. So **Taft** *v. trans.*, to expand and turn outwards at a sharp angle the end of (a lead pipe) so as to form a wide edge or fastening flange.

**1877** Hellyer *Plumber* i. 21 The soil pipe can be 'tafted' at the end. *Ibid.* ii. 33 When the pipe is tafted back at right angles,..the lower pipe is liable to break away at the taft.

**Taftais, -eis,** obs. Sc. forms of Taffeta.

**Tag** (tæg), *sb.*[1] Also 5–6 tagge, 6 tagg, tage. [Known shortly after 1400: origin obscure. In senses 1, 2 a, and 3, it is synonymous with Dag *sb.*[1], which appears to have been the earlier form: if so, *tag* may have been influenced by association with Tack. Some compare Sw. *tagg* 'prickle, point, tooth', but evidence of historical connexion is wanting.

The evidence at hand for the early history is deficient, the earliest quot. for the group being *c* 1380 in Tagged 1, a deriv. of the sb. in sense 1.]

**1.** Originally, one of the narrow, often pointed, *laciniæ* or pendent pieces made by slashing the skirt of a garment; hence, any hanging ragged or torn piece; also, any end or rag of ribbon or the like.

**1402** *Pol. Poems* (Rolls) II. 69 Of suche wide clothing, tateris and tagges, it hirtith myn hert hevyly. *c* **1500** *Rowlis Cursing* 135 in Laing *Anc. Poet. Scotl.*, Ruffy Ragmen [a devil] with his taggis Sall ryfe thair sinfull saule in raggis. **1500–20** Dunbar *Poems* xxvi. 115 Thae tarmegantis, with tag and tatter, Ffull lowd in Ersche begowth to clatter. **1542** Udall *Erasm. Apoph.* 313 The skyrtes of his goune all pounced in cuttes and tagges. **1840** Thackeray *Paris Sk. Bk.* (1872) 7 Crumpled tags of ribbon. **1884** *St. James's Gaz.* 10 May 6/1 The tags of drapery and other accessories. **1889** *Cornh. Mag.* Feb. 124 With tags of ribbon sticking out in unexpected places.

**2.** A small pendent piece or part hanging from, or attached more or less loosely to the main body of anything. With numerous specific applications, e.g.

**a.** A matted lock of wool on a sheep; a tag-lock; a twisted or matted lock of hair. **b.** A shred of animal tissue. **c.** A shred of metal in a casting: see quot. **d.** A final curl, twirl, or flourish added to a letter, sometimes used as a mark of contraction. **e.** *fig.* An appendage; the tail-end (of any proceeding).

a. *c* 1640 J. Smyth *Lives Berkeleys* (1883) I. 157 What money was..made by sale of the locks, belts and tags of Sheep. 1888 *Harper's Mag.* June 137/2 Her reddish-brown hair, which grew in a fringe below her crown, was plaited into small tags or tails. b. 1724 Ramsay *Health* 186 Bones corrupt and bare, Through ulcerated tags of muscles stare. 1897 J. Hutchinson *Arch. Surg.* VIII. No. 31. 214 Under atropine the pupils dilated, but shewed numerous tags of adhesion. 1897 *Allbutt's Syst. Med.* III. 716 They [adhesions] are then seen as filamentous tags on the outside of the intestine. 1899 *Ibid.* VII. 612 A small tag of fibrin from the valve. c. 1863 Lyell *Antiq. Man* ii. 10 Some of the moulds in which the bronze instruments were cast, and 'tags' as they are called, of bronze, which are formed in the hole through which the fused metal was poured. d. 1867 Furnivall *Percy Fol.* I. 18 *note*, To many of the final s is a tag, which often means nothing, and often means s. e. 1703 Steele *Tender Husb.* I. i, Seem to have come into the World only to be Taggs in the Pedigree of a Wealthy House. 1882 Holland *Logic & Life* (1885) 317 Death is but the tag of this life.

**3.** A point of metal or other hard substance at the end of a lace, string, strap, or the like, primarily used to facilitate its insertion through an eyelet-hole, as in a boot-lace or stay-lace, but when externally visible often made ornamental, as on the 'points' in use before buttons; an aglet.

(The first two quots. are of doubtful sense.)

[1501–2 *Acc. Ld. High Treas. Scot.* II. 33 Item, for taggis to ane Franch sadill and mending of it xij d. 1507 *Ibid.* III. 270 Item, for taggis, bukkilles, and small graith to thaim, xv. s.] 1570 Levins *Manip.* 10/19 Ye Tag of a poynt, *ferrétrum.* 1580 Hollyband *Treas. Fr. Tong*, *Vn fer d'aiguillette*, a tagge. 1592 Lyly *Gallathea* v. i. 70 Thy Maister could make silver pottes of tagges of poynts. 1648 Gage *West Ind.* 56 With long silver or golden Tags hanging down before. *a* 1734 North *Exam.* III. viii. § 15 (1740) 593 Now comes the Tag to this fine Lace. 1832 Babbage *Econ. Manuf.* iv. (ed. 3) 31 The simple art of making the tags of boot-laces. 1861 Wright *Ess. Archæol.* I. vii. 133 The object..is part of the metal tag at the end of the belt.

**b.** *fig.*

*c* 1572 Gascoigne *Fruites Warre* lxi, Is witte nowe wente so wandring from thy minde? Are all thy points so voide of Reasons taggs? 1611 Middleton *Roaring Girl* III. i, Here's the point [*Draws her sword*] That I untruss; 't has but one tag, 't will serve though To tie up a rogue's tongue.

†**c.** Phrases. *To hold tag*, to keep a person engaged in conversation: cf. *to buttonhole*. *To a tag*, to the minutest point, exactly; cf. *to a T*. *Obs.*

1567 Drant *Horace, Epist.* v. C vij, Scotfree we may hould tagge In frendly chat this sommers night. 1679 V. Alsop *Melius Inquir.* Introd. 20 To hang on a string only with those who jump in with our own Points to a Tag. 1682 N. O. *Boileau's Lutrin* IV. 318 At Trent, when Concord in a Bag Came Post from Rome, they hit it to a Tag!

**4.** An ornamental pendant; a tassel; a ribbon bearing a jewel, etc.

1570 Levins *Manip.* 10/20 Ye Tag of a purse, *appendix.* 1686 *Lond. Gaz.* No. 2132/4 Lost.., a black laced Palatin with Diamond Tags upon black Ribon. 1762–71 H. Walpole *Vertue's Anecd. Paint.* (1786) I. 230 The first lady has tags of a particular form, exactly like those on the dress of my duchess of Suffolk. 1848 Thackeray *Van. Fair* vi, Our good child..passed in review all her gowns, fichus, tags, bobbins, laces, silk stockings, and fallals. 1890 *Spectator* 14 June 834/2 The sculptor..has filled up part of the arch with long heavy tassels hanging from the saddle-cloth. Throughout the work there seems to be an excess of tag and small decoration.

**b.** *pl.* A footman's shoulder-knots.

1837 J. Morier *Abel Allnutt* xxx. 175 A stout footman staggering under a long cane and matted tags, and with difficulty waddling in his stiff plushes. 1844 Dickens *Mart. Chuz.* ix, With such great tags upon his liveried shoulder.

**5.** A catkin of a tree. *rare.*

1597 Gerarde *Herbal* I. xv. § 2. 17 The catkins or tags which grow on nut trees and aller trees. 1878 Mrs. Stowe *Poganuc P.* xvii. 147 The tremulous tags of the birches and alders shook themselves gaily out in the woods.

**6.** The tip of the tail of an animal, esp. when distinct in colour or otherwise; the tail-piece of an angler's fly. (Much earlier in Tagged *a.* 3.)

1681 Chetham *Angler's Vade-m.* xxxv. § 1 (1689) 222 Some Red warp'd in for the tag of the Tail. 1787 Best *Angling* (ed. 2) 106. 1863 Kingsley *Water-Bab.* i. 37 A great brown sharp-nosed creature with a white tag to her brush. 1867 F. Francis *Angling* xiii. (1880) 472 Tie on the tag, which is usually a bit of tinsel. 1886 *Field* 27 Feb. 268/1 The fox ..gets the credit of being a vixen; but his snowy tag has only to be seen in order to dispel that notion. 1902 *Encycl. Brit.* XXV. 449/1 Two of the best grayling flies are a very small apple-green dun and the red tag.

**7.** The strip of parchment bearing the pendent seal of a deed.

1688 R. Holme *Armoury* III. xv. (Roxb.) 21/1 A writt sealed vp, haueing two taggs or Labells Or, in a feild Gules. 1872 C. Innes *Lect. Scotch Leg. Antiq.* v. 235 A small piece of the seal shall stick at the tag of the brief. 1887 J. B. Sheppard in *Lit. Cantuar.* (Rolls) I. 341 *note*, The originals have now both lost their seals, although the slits for the tags remain.

**8.** A tab or tie-label attached by one end to a package, to luggage, etc.; also, a label pinned on as a badge, etc. Orig. and chiefly *U.S.*

1864 Webster, *Tag*..2. Any slight appendage..; specifically, a direction card or label. 1891 *Cent. Dict.*, *Tag*..2 (c). A strip of leather, parchment, strong paper, or the like, loose at one end, and secured to a box, bag, or parcel, to receive a written address or label. 1908 *Times* 26 Dec. 10/2 A new system of street collecting for public charities by means of tags or labels,..tried at San Francisco recently on behalf of the Children's Hospital...The advent of 'tag day' is well advertised. *Mod. Price List*, Tags with strings in packets Extra large tags with ruled lines.

**b.** Sometimes applied to a tab or loop by which a coat or the like is hung up.

**9.** Something appended or added to a writing or speech, esp. by way of ornament or improvement, e.g. the moral of a fable, etc.

*a* 1734 North *Exam.* II. v. § 74 (1740) 360 To avoid the Fastidium of noting all the Author's Tags joined to his Relations of this Time. 1872 Minto *Eng. Prose Lit.* I. ii. 134 A tag of statistics is very chilling. 1874 L. Stephen *Hours in Library* (1892) II. v. 151 [Massinger] is fond of adding little moral tags..to the end of his plays. 1885 *Manch. Exam.* 13 Oct. 4/7 Each paragraph..would serve.. as a tag by way of peroration to a debating club harangue.

**b.** A brief and usually familiar quotation added for special effect; a much used or trite quotation.

1702 S. Parker tr. *Cicero's De Finibus* I. 5 With Tags of Metre translated from the Greek..we can dispense well enough. 1866 Geo. Eliot *F. Holt* xvii, I don't talk in tags of Latin, which might be learned by a schoolmaster's footboy. 1893 Jessopp *Stud. Recluse* vii. 225 Putting in tags and rags of French..to conceal poverty of style. 1897 *Sat. Rev.* 18 Dec. 701 The Latin tag holds: 'Quem Deus vult perdere, prius dementat.' 1902 Buchan *Watcher by Thresh.* 175 Stories from Procopius and tags of Roman law.

**c.** The refrain or catch of a song or poem; the last words of a speech in a play, etc.

1793 H. Walpole *Let. to Agnes Berry* 18 Oct., They have brought to my recollection the tag of an old song. 1815 Scott *Let. to Miss J. Baillie* 12 Nov. in *Lockhart*, I am ..anxious to store the heads of my young damsels with something better than the tags of rhymes. 1830 H. Lee *Mems. Manager* II. viii. 104 The tag; which is the technical phrase for the last lines of any play. 1876 *N. Amer. Rev.* CXXIII. 480 And, to borrow the tag of an old story, 'There —my lord—I leave you'.

†**10.** The rabble, the lowest class of people. *Obs.*

1607 Shaks. *Cor.* III. i. 248 Will you hence, Before the Tagge returne? *a* 1825 Forby *Voc. E. Anglia*, *Tag*, the rabble.

†**b.** *esp.* in collocation with Rag *sb.*[1] 3 b: *Tag and rag*, a contemptuous expression for all the components of the rabble, of the lower classes, or of an assemblage of people held in small esteem; all and any, every man Jack, everybody, Tom, Dick, and Harry. *Obs.* See also Tag-rag.

*c*1535 Bygod *Impropriations* (K.O.), Your fathers were wyse, both tagge and rag. 1553–4 Machyn *Diary* (Camden) 50 Huntyd, and kyllyd tage and rage with honds and swords. 1566 J. Partridge *Plasidas* 1041 To walles they go, both tagge and rage, their Citie to defende. 1610 Cooke *Pope Joan* in *Harl. Misc.* (Malh.) IV. 95 That you have made Levites..of the scurvy and scabbed, of the lowest of the people, tag and rag. *a* 1626 Bp. Andrewes *Serm.* (1641) 181 This is the time when all hypocrites, atheists, tag and rag come. 18.. Southey *Devil's Walk* xxiii, With music of fife and drum, And a consecrated flag, And shout of tag and rag, And march of rank and file. 1809 W. Irving *Knickerb.* VI. ix. (1861) 231 Every tag having his rag at his side, to finish his pipe..and laugh at his flights of immortal dulness.

**11.** In servants' vocabulary: A lower servant.

1857 T. Wright *Dict.*, *Tag*, one who assists another at work in a secondary character. *Northampt.* 1860 *Athenæum* 17 Nov. 664 Servants..with their own distinction of ranks, the 'Pugs' and the 'Tags'.

**12.** A disease in sheep; = *tag-sore* (13): see quots. (Cf. Tagged 5 a, which is evidenced much earlier.)

1741 *Compl. Fam.-Piece* III. (ed. 3) 494 Of the Tag or Belt in Sheep. Sheep are said to be tagged or belt, when they have a Flux, or continued running of Ordure, which lighting upon the Tail, the Heat of the Dung, by its scalding, breeds the Scab. 1756 *Compl. Body Husb.* 694 The Tag is situated in the inner part of the Tail; it consists of Scabs and Sores. 1807 *Essays Highland Soc.* III. 434 A disease..affecting the tail, has been denominated *Tag*.

**13.** *attrib.* and *Comb.*, as *tag-like* adj.; tag alder, *U.S. local*, name for some species of alder, esp. *Alnus incana*, *A. serrulata*, and (on the Pacific coast) *A. rubra*; **tag-belt**, = *tag-sore*; **tag-boat**, *U.S. local*, a boat towed behind a small steamer or sailing vessel; a tender, cockboat; **tag-end**, the last part or remnant of anything; a remaining scrap or fragment; = Fag-end; **tag-fastener, -holder**, a device for attaching tags or labels; **tag-lock**, a matted lock of sheep's wool, esp. one of those about the hinder parts; = Dag-lock; **tag-machine**, a machine for making tags or labels; **tag-needle**, a needle for attaching labels to bags, bales, etc.; **tag-sore**, pustular excoriation of a sheep's tail set up by the irritation of diarrhœal flux; **tag-tail**, a worm with a yellow tag or tail; also, a parasite, a hanger-on; **tag-wool**, wool made from tag-locks; **tag-worm**, = *tag-tail*.

1891 *Lancet* 3 Oct. 772/1 *Tag alder. 1832 Boucher *Gloss. Obs. & Prov. Wds.*, *Tagbelt, excoriation brought on by diarrhoea. 1893 Sarah Jewett *Deephaven* 128, I got into the schooner's *tag-boat quick. 1818 Coleridge *Diss. Sc. Method* ii. 40 Not made up of miserable clap-traps, and the *tag-ends of mawkish Novels, and endless sermonizing. 1900 *Westm. Gaz.* 8 Nov. 3/2 The mania for gold embroidering and braiding and the gold tag ends of present-day fashions. 1897 *Allbutt's Syst. Med.* IV. 160 Ragged sloughy material, which often projects in *tag-like pieces into the abscess cavity. 1615 T. Adams *Lycanthropy* 17 They will plucke our fleeces; leave us nothing but the *tag-locks. 1884 *Century Mag.* Feb. 519/2 The tag-locks and pulled wool were mostly worked up in the..small factories into stocking-yarn [etc.] for the farmer's use. 1828 Webster, *Tag-sore, a disease in sheep. *Cycl.* 1653 Walton *Angler* iv. 95 There are..divers other kindes of worms..as the marsh-worm, the *tag-tail,..the gilt-tail. 1681 Chetham *Angler's Vade-m.* iv. § 5 (1689) 32 Tag-tail is a worm of ..a pale Flesh colour, with a yellow Tag on his Tail. 1875 'Stonehenge' *Brit. Sports* I. v. xi. § 3. 312 The Tagtail is common in good strong clays which are well-manured for turnips, mangold-wurzel, &c. 1864 Webster, *Tag-tail*..a person who attaches himself to another against the will of the latter; a dependent; a sycophant; a parasite. 1602 Carew *Cornwall* 26 His baites are flies and *Tag-wormes, which the Cornish English terme Angle-touches. 1839 Hofland *Brit. Angler's Man.* ii. (1841) 10 The little gilt-tail, or tag-worm, Is of a pale yellow towards the tail.

**Tag** (tæg), *sb.*[2] Also 8 tagg. [Origin obscure.] A children's game in which one player pursues the others until he touches one of them, who in turn becomes pursuer; = Tig.

1738 *Gentl. Mag.* VIII. 80/1 In Queen Mary's Reign, Tag was all the Play; where the Lad saves himself by touching of cold Iron. 1760–72 H. Brooke *Fool of Qual.* (1809) I. v. 67 After they were cloyed with hide and seek, they all played tagg, till they were well warmed. 1864 *Louie's last term* (N. Y.) 179 There's Eva Leonard beckoning to me to come and play Tag. 1903 *Smart Set* IX. 78 The merry hornet played a game Of tag about my head.

**Tag**, var. of Teg, a young sheep.

**Tag** (tæg), *v.*[1] [f. Tag *sb.*[1]]

**1.** *trans.* To furnish or mark with or as with a tag (in various senses).

[1436, 1503: see Tagging.] 1627 W. Hawkins *Apollo Shroving* II. i. 20 What did you giue me? Nothing but a dozen of rotten silke points. You must tagge them better ere I trusse vp your request. 1630 Davenant *Just Ital.* Wks. (1673) 455, I must e'en go tag Points in a Garret. 1705 *Hudibras Rediv.* IV. vi, Their Hair tagg'd with Pearls of Sweat. 1707 in W. McDowall *Hist. Dumfries* (1873) 461 The expense of tagging, tongueing, transporting and hanging of the said three bells. 1800 Watkins *Biog. Dict.* s. v. *Bobart*, Mr. Granger says that on rejoicing days he used to tag his beard with silver. 1842 Tennyson *St. Sim. Styl.* 31 All my beard Was tagg'd with icy fringes in the moon. 1899 Conan Doyle *Duet* iv. 41 The dim watery..sunlight.. tagged all her wandering curls with a coppery gleam.

**b.** To furnish with a tag, tab, or label; to label. (In quot. 1907 to patch, as with a label.)

1883 *Fisheries Exh. Catal.* 203 Photographs..showing.. the..tagging the fish, and the process of manipulation of the eggs and young fish at the hatchery. 1896 *Daily News* 30 Jan. 3/7 After inspection each animal will be tagged and described so that identification will be easily made upon landing. 1907 *Macmillan's Mag.* May 540 The..cloak of brown sackcloth, sometimes tagged here and there with red and green. 1908 *Daily Chron.* 26 Feb. 8/5 They should be..wrapped in tissue paper and tagged, so that their covering need not be disturbed in a search for any particular colour.

**c.** To furnish (a speech or composition) with a verbal tag, or tags, as quotations; to supply (prose or blank verse) with rimes.

1687 *Reflect. on Hind & Panther* 32 He hath put them into an unusual dress, and hath tagg'd 'em with Rhimes. 1690 *Waller's Poems* II. Pref., Really Verse in those days was but down-right prose, tag'd with rhymes. *a* 1695 Aubrey *Lives* (1898) II. 72 (*Milton*) Dreyden..went to him to have leave to putt his Paradise Lost into a drama in rhymne. Mr. Milton recieved him civilly, and told him he would give him leave to tagge his verses. 1714 Pope *Wife of Bath* 109 And tag each sentence with My life! my dear! 1823 *Examiner* 705/2 Canning tags his speeches with poetry. 1841 D'Israeli *Amen. Lit.* (1867) 369 The Scriptures..were tagged with rhymes for ballads.

**2.** To append as an addition or afterthought; to fasten, tack on, or add as a tag *to* something. (Chiefly of things non-material.)

1704 Swift *Tale Tub* ii. (1709) 39 To this system of Religion were tagged several Subaltern Doctrines. 1785 Martyn *Rousseau's Bot.* (1794) 10 The barbarous custom ..of tagging new names to the old ones. 1833 M. Scott *Tom Cringle* i. 1 Before the time when a gallant action or two tagged half of the letters of the alphabet to a man's name like the tail of a paper kite. 1839–40 W. Irving *Wolfert's R.* vi. (1855) 87 They could not help expressing their wonder..why the duke should have tagged this supernumerary day to the end of the year. 1848 Thackeray *Van. Fair* (Bef. Curtain), I have no other moral than this to tag to the present story of 'Vanity Fair'.

†**3.** To fasten, stitch, or tack together; to join. Also *fig.* *Obs.* (exc. as in b.)

1681 T. Flatman *Heraclitus Ridens* No. 34 (1713) I. 222 He..has a great share of the Joyner's Trade in tagging Ends of Sedition. 1697 Dryden *Æneid* III. 777 His clothes were tagg'd with thorns; and filth his limbs besmear'd. 1706 De Foe *Jure Div.* VII. 140 Tagging Fig-leaf-Vests, To hide his Body from the Sight of Beasts. 17.. Swift (J.), Resistance, and the succession of the house of Hanover, the whig writers perpetually tag together.

**b.** To join or string together (verses, rimes).

1720 Mrs. Manley *Power of Love* (1741) p. viii, Adjusted into proper Periods, with necessary Monosyllables to tag them together. 1752 Fielding *Amelia* VIII. v, I have been sometimes longer in tagging a couplet, than I have been in writing a speech. 1849 C. Bronte *Shirley* III. vii. 159 He writes verses,—tags rhymes. 1887 Lowell *Democr.* 207 It shows a pretty knack at tagging verses.

**c.** *intr.* To serve as a tag (in a verse, etc.).

1878 Browning *Poets Croisic* lxxiv, Thetis, who Is either Tethys or as good—both tag.

**4.** *intr.* To trail or drag behind; to follow closely, follow in one's train.

1676 Wycherley *Pl. Dealer* I. i, I hate a harness, and will not tag on in a faction, kissing my leader behind, that another slave may do the like to me. 1768 Tucker *Lt. Nat.* (1834) I. 596 They range the world with a boisterous rabble tagging at their heels. *c* 1794 *Search after Perfect.* I. iv. in *New Brit. Theatre* (1814) III. 55 Why should a nurse and child come tagging after her? **1902** Eliz. L. Banks *News-paper Girl* 24 I'm an American girl and can take care of myself, and I won't have anybody tagging round after me.

**b.** *trans.* To follow closely, to dog.

**1884** C. H. Farnham in *Harper's Mag.* Feb. 394/1 The Indians are wandering.., tagged at their heels by death and starvation.

†**5.** *intr.* To hang down or trail like a tag. *Obs.*

**1617** J. Moore *Mappe Mans Mortalitie* II. viii. 153 They which weare long garments..doe take and gird them vp, lest they should tag in the way.

**6.** *trans.* To cut off tags from (sheep).

**1707** Mortimer *Husb.* (1721) I. 243 Before they are shorn, great care ought to be taken to tag them, as they call it, which is to clip away the Wooll of their Tails, and behind, that the Dung may not hang on it. *a* **1890** [implied in Tagging].

**Tag,** *v.*$^2$ [f. Tag *sb.*$^2$] *trans.* To touch or hit (a person), as in the game of tag; = Tig *v.*

**1891** in *Cent. Dict.*

**Tagarene** (tægărīˑn). *north. dial.* Also **tag(a)-reen.** [Origin uncertain: perh. arbitrary formation on Tag *sb.*$^1$] More fully *tagarene shop*: An old clothes or rag shop; a marine store. Hence **tagarene-man**, the keeper of a marine store, *esp.* one who visits ships in dock or harbour with a boatful of wares for exchange.

**1855** Robinson *Whitby Gloss.* s. v., 'They keep a tagreen shop', an old clothes store; an old rope and rag depôt. **1894** *Northumb. Gloss.* s. v., A 'tagareen man' has a floating shop which he rows about the tiers of ships, announcing his presence by a bell. **1900** F. W. Bullen *With Christ at Sea* xi. 285 The skipper arrived with his crony the 'tagarene' man and a large supply of brandy.

**Tagged** (tægd, tæˑgėd), *ppl. a.* [f. Tag *sb.*$^1$ and *v.*$^1$ + -ed.] Furnished with a tag or tags.

**1. a.** Of a garment: Slashed. **b.** Tattered. **c.** Bearing or wearing a tag or label; labelled.

*c* **1380** *Antecrist* in Todd *Three Treat. Wyclif* (1851) 128 Men to kerve here morsellis wiþ tagged cloþes & crakowe pykis. **1570** Levins *Manip.* 49/21 Tagged, *laciniatus, infulatus.* **1631** Gouge *God's Arrows* I. § 57. 98 The Father of the Prodigall seeing his sonne afarre off ragged and tagged. **1908** *Times* 26 Dec. 10/2 By 10 o'clock every man, woman, and child..were wearing at least one tag, and among the younger men there was competition to be the most 'tagged' person in the city [San Francisco].

**2.** Of a lace or point: Having a tag or aglet.

**1645** Evelyn *Diary* June, Knots of points richly tagged about their shoulders. **1714** *Fr. Bk. of Rates* 45 Laces silk tagg'd per Pound 00 12. **1828** H. Best *Italy as it is* 228 The tagged ends of the ribs of whalebone by which these [parasols] are distended. *a* **1859** Macaulay *Biogr.*, *Bunyan* (1860) 37 He learned to make long-tagged thread laces.

**3.** Of cattle: Having the tail tipped with white (or other distinctive colour); also, furnished with a bob or brush.

**1458** *Will* in *Ripon Ch. Acts* 75 Unum bovem vocatum taggyd ox. **1544** in *Knaresborough Wills* (Surtees) I. 42 One taged whye. **1588** *Wills & Inv. N. C.* (Surtees) II. 33 *note*, A black tagged cow. **1640** Sir J. Lessley in *Antiq. Rep.* (1809) IV. 436, I maun hae the tag'd tail'd trooper [horse] that stands in the staw. **1680** *Lond. Gaz.* No. 1482/4 One red taged Bullock. **1852** Mundy *Our Antipodes* (1857) 87 With a white-tagged brush peeping out of his pocket, the dingo's head hanging from the whipper-in's saddle.

**4.** Of wool or hair: Hanging in matted locks.

**1757** Dyer *Fleece* I. 369 Skill..which trims their tails, of filth and tagged wool.

**5. a.** Of sheep: Having the disease known as tag.

**1614** Markham *Cheap Husb.* III. xvii. (1668) 91 A sheep is said to be Tag'd or Belt, when by a continual squirt..he berayeth his tail in such wise, that..it scaldeth, and breedeth the scab therein. **1741** [see Tag *sb.*$^1$ 12].

**b.** Of wheat: see quot.

**1892** *Chamb. Jrnl.* 10 Sept. 591/1 Wheat..discoloured at the tip of the kernel by smut, 'tagged' as it is called.

**Tagger**$^1$ (tæˑgəɹ). [f. Tag *v.*$^1$ or *sb.*$^1$ + -er$^1$.]

**1.** One who tags: see the verb.

**1648** *Pair of Spectacles for City* 11 We bound him to a Tagger of Points. **1785** R. Graves *Eugenius* I. ii. 6 Our orators are mere praters—and our poets taggers of rhime. **1883** *Sat. Rev.* 12 May 592/1 The Scotch seem to have entertained a mistaken theory that the taggers of rhymes to the prose version of the Psalms were inspired.

†**2.** A tag, a projecting part. *Obs.* ? *misuse.*

*a* **1687** Cotton *Burlesque Gt. Frost* Poems (1689) 98 Comparing Hedg-hogs, or Porcupine's small Taggers, To their more dang'rous Swords and Daggers.

**3.** A device for tagging a sheep: see Tag *v.*$^1$ 6.

**1891** in *Cent. Dict.*

**4.** *pl.* Very thin sheet-iron, usually coated with tin. (Also **taggar.**) [Probably so called from being used to make tags of laces.]

**1834** McCulloch *Dict. Comm.* II. 1160 Taggars 14 by 10 inches, £2 5*s.* **1853** *Lardner's Cab. Cycl.*, *Manuf. Metals* III. 43 Tinned Taggers, Black Taggers. **1858** Simmonds *Dict. Trade*, *Taggers*, a very thin kind of tin-plates used for coffin-plate inscriptions and tops of umbrellas. **1879** P. W. Flower *Hist. Tin Trade* xiii. (1880) 156 A sheet of taggers, as thin as paper itself. **1894** *U. S. Tariff, Schedule Rates* § 121 Sheets or plates of iron or steel, or taggers iron or steel, coated with tin or lead..and commercially known as tin plates, terne plates, and taggers tin.

**Tagger**$^2$ (tæˑgəɹ). *U. S.* [f. Tag *sb.*$^2$ or *v.*$^2$ + -er$^1$.] The pursuer in the game of tag.

**1891** in *Cent. Dict.*

**Taˑggery.** *nonce-wd.* [f. Tagger$^1$: see -ery$^1$.] The work of a tagger; the tagging of rimes.

**1845** *Blackw. Mag.* LVII. 376 Had Milton lived to hear their taggery, wrathful fire would have been in his eyes.

**Tagging** (tæˑgiŋ), *vbl. sb.* [f. Tag *v.*$^1$ and *sb.*$^1$ + -ing$^1$.] The action of Tag *v.*$^1$

**1503** *Acc. Ld. High Treas. Scot.* II. 202 For ane curpal and ane tee to the harnes sadill, tagging..of the samyn. **1572** in Feuillerat *Revels Q. Eliz.* (1908) 159 For Tagging of Laces iiij$^d$. **1693** Dennis *Imp. Crit.* v. 50 'Tis not the tagging of the Acts with a Chorus, that properly makes a Tragedy one Body, but the Unity of the Action. **1779** Mme. D'Arblay *Diary* 11 Jan., What trouble and tagging we had! *a* **1890** *New Amer. Farm Bk.* 436 (Cent. Dict.) Tagging or clotting is the removal of such wool as is liable to get fouled when the sheep are turned on to the fresh pastures. **1906** *Athenæum* 2 June 664/3 An occasional..tagging-out of a line.

**b.** *attrib.*, as †**tagging iron**, a tailor's tool for tagging cloth.

**1436** *Exch. Rolls Scotl.* IV. 681 Certis ferris scissorum dictis taging irynnis.

†**Taˑghmical,** *a. Heb. Gram. Obs. rare.* [f. Heb. טַעַם *ṭaʿam* taste, discernment, judgement, in later Heb. explanation, meaning, and then the ordinary word for accentual mark (in reference to the functions of the Heb. accents) + -ical. (The Heb. ע is here represented by *gh*: cf. *Gaza, Gomorrah.*)] Of or pertaining to the Hebrew written accents as determining the syntactical structure and hence the meaning of passages (as understood by the Masoretes).

**1698** W. Cross (*title*) The Taghmical Art: or the Art of Expounding Scripture By the Points usually called Accents, But are really Tactical. **1730** T. Boston *Mem.* x. (ed. Morrison) 301 What Mr. Cross calls the Taghmical Art; viz. the sacred stigmatology or accentuation of the Hebrew Bible. **1859** *Life E. Henderson* iii. 119 *note*, The idea broke in upon him when reading Cross's Taghmical Art.

**Taght,** obs. f. *taught*: see Teach *v.*

**Tagil**: see Tagle *v.*

**Tagilite** (tæˑgiləit). *Min.* [f. *Tagilsk* (see def.) + -ite$^1$.] A name given by R. Hermann to a hydrous phosphate of copper occurring in monoclinic crystals at Nischni Tagilsk, in the Urals.

**1868** Dana *Min.* 567 Hermann's tagilite was in reniform concretions.

†**Tagle, tagil, tagyl,** *v. Obs.* [Known in northern ME. only in Hampole; app. the same as mod. Sc. Taigle, q.v. Prob. of Scand. origin, and cognate with Sw. dial. (Bornholm) *taggla* to disarrange, bring into disorder.

In the quots. from the *Prose Treatises* of Hampole only *tagil, tagyl* are cited. In the *Psalter* (ed. Bramley 1884), in Ps. xxxix. 16, 2 MSS., including N., which best represents the original, have *tagild*; 8 later MSS. have *tangild, -gyld, -glyd, -glid, -gled, -geled.* In *Ibid., Abacuc* 31, MS. N. again has *tagild*; 3 MSS. have *takyld, takild*, 2 *tackid*, 2 *tangild, tanglid.* Evidently, *tagild* was the original word, *takild* perh. a scribal, and *tangild* a nasalized phonetic variant. *Tagil* appears to be preserved in the Sc. Taigle *v.*; the nasalized form remains in Tangle *v.*, q. v.]

*trans.* To entangle, to involve or engage in things that embarrass or encumber.

*a* **1340** Hampole *Ps.* xxxix. 16 (MS. N.) Na man may wit hou many vices ar þat men ar tagild with. [*So MS. S.*; *MSS. U. & L.* tangild; *Laud* 321 tangyld, *Magd. Coll.* 52 *& Laud* 418 tanglid, *Bodl.* 953 tanglyd, *Tanner* 1 tangled, *Univ. Coll.* LVI tangeled; *Bodl.* 467 snaryd.] *Ibid., Abacuc* 31 (N.) Swa þaire affecciouns ar ay tagild with som lufe þat drawes þame fra godds lufe. [*MSS. U.* & *Laud* 286 takild, *S.* takyld; *Tanner* 1 tanglid, *Laud* 448 tangild, *Bodl.* 288 & 877 tackid, *Bodl.* 953 medelid.] *c* **1340** — *Prose Tr.* 12 All delytes of all thyngez þat mane may be tagyld with in thoghte or dede. *Ibid.* 13 Withowttene tagillynge of oþer thynges.

**Taglet** (tæˑglėt). *rare.* [f. Tag *sb.*$^1$ + -let.] A small tag: *spec.* **a.** A tendril; **b.** A catkin.

**1578** Lyte *Dodoens* v. lxxx. 650 The vine..putteth foorth ..certayne tendrelles, or clasping caprioles, & tying tagglets, wherewith al it taketh hold vpon trees. *Ibid.* 651 The same tagglettes or clasping tendrelles of the vine. **1698** Fryer *Acc. E. India & P.* 405 Out of Taglets of Willows they make a compound Cool-Water, very sweet smelling and refreshing. **1864** in Webster; and in mod. Dicts.

[**Taglia,** the Italian word for a pulley, or system of pulleys: in some recent Eng. dicts. from Brande, but not known in Eng. use.]

**Tagliacotian**: see Taliacotian.

†**Taglioni** (talyōˑni). *Obs.* [Named after a family of ballet-dancers in the early 19th c.] A kind of overcoat in use in the first half of the 19th c.

**18..** Scott (Webster), He ought certainly to exchange his *taglioni* or comfortable great-coat for a cuirass of steel. **1837** Thackeray *Ravenswing* iii. (1887) 167 A rhubarb-coloured coat of the sort which, I believe, are called Taglionis, and which have no waist-buttons. *a* **1845** Barham *Ingol. Leg.* Ser. III. *Blasphemer's Warn.*, I've brought to protect myself well, a Good stout Taglioni and gingham umbrella. **1847** *Man in Moon* Apr. I. 201 White Taglioni, with four-in-hand drags on the buttons.

‖**Tagma** (tæˑgmă). *Veg. Physiol.* Pl. **tagmata.** [a. Gr. τάγμα something arranged, f. τάσσειν to set in order.] A term applied by Pfeffer (in German, 1877) to the aggregates of molecules of which the structure of a plant is supposed to consist.

**1885** Goodale *Physiol. Bot.* § 588. 213 *note*, Pfeffer applies a general term, *Tagma*, to all aggregates of molecules, thus bringing under one head the pleon, micella, and micellar aggregate; and he applies the name *Syntagma* to all bodies made up of tagmata. **1889** Burdon-Sanderson in *Nature* 26 Sept. 524 That an element of living material, is not equivalent to a molecule, however big or complex, but must rather be an arrangement or phalanx of molecules of different kinds. Hence the word tagma, first used by Pfeffer, has come to be accepted as best expressing the notion.

‖**Tagnicati** (tanʸīkāˑti). Also **tañi-.** [a. Guarani and Sp. *tañicati*; in F. *tagnicati.*] The native name in Guarani of the White-lipped Peccary of Paraguay, also called Tayassu.

**1827** Griffith tr. *Cuvier's Anim. Kingd.* III. x. 334 Here may be placed..the Tagnicati, Taitetou, Tajassou, etc. (*Dicotyles labiatus*, Cuv.). **1868** J. E. Gray in *Proc. Zool. Soc.* 45 *Dicotyles labiatus.* Black-brown, varied with yellowish; no neck-bands; lower jaw white...Tagnicati, Azara, Paraguay i. 25. **1888** Wood *Illustr. Nat. Hist.* 753 The Tagnicati, or white-lipped Peccary..derives its name from a band of white hairs that crosses the upper jaw, and covers nearly the whole of the lower.

**Tag-rag** (tæˑgˌræg), *sb.*, *a.*, *adv.* [Orig. two words, = both *tag* and *rag*: cf. Tag *sb.*$^1$ 10 b; at length taken as expressing one notion, and hyphened or written as one word, **tag-rag, tagrag.**]

**A.** *sb.* The rabble, the riff-raff; also (with *pl.*) a member of the rabble; a low or despicable person. Now *rare* exc. as in D.

**1609** Eburne *Maintenance Ministerie* 173 Then the ministerie was filled vp with Tag, rag, such as the time would yeeld. **1638** Ford *Lady's Trial* II. i, Tag, rag, or other, hogen-mogen vanden, Skip-jacks or chouses. **1650** A. B. *Mutat. Polemo* 15 A company of lamentable Tag-rags ..going under the names of Colonels, Majors, and Captains. **1706** E. Ward *Wooden World Diss.* (1708) 85 If ever he prays, it's..to some Tag-Rag, to fetch him a little Ship-Beer. **1826** Moore *Canonization of St. B-tt-rw-rth* xi, Call quickly together the whole tribe of Canters, Convoke all the serious Tag-rag of the nation.

**b.** With reference to Tag *sb.*$^1$, senses 9 and 1, and Rag: A ragged tag or appendage.

**1827** Carlyle *Richter* in *Misc. Ess.* (1872) I. 11 No story proceeds without the most erratic digressions and voluminous tagrags rolling after it. **1831** — *Sart. Res.* I. iv, Sentences..buttressed-up by props (of parentheses and dashes), and ever with this or the other tagrag hanging from them. **1885** Lang *Custom & Myth* 18 A rude imitation of the human shape..dressed in some tag-rags of finery.

**B.** *adj.* †**a.** Of or belonging to the rabble. *Obs.* **b.** Consisting of tags and rags of dress, etc.; dressed in rags, ragged.

**1601** Shaks. *Jul. C.* I. ii. 260 If the tag-ragge people did not clap him, and hisse him,..I am no true man. **1675** Cotton *Scoffer Scoft* 90 Tag-rag Plebeans. **1805** W. Taylor in *Ann. Rev.* III. 303 Clad in the tagrag garb of democracy. **1897** *Daily News* 1 Nov. 6/3 Love for his dear, tag-rag, genial, happy-go-lucky green isle!

†**C.** *adv.* (for *tag and rag.*) All to tags and rags; also, pell-mell; one and all; in a mingled crowd or heap, promiscuously. *Obs.*

**1582** Stanyhurst *Æneis* I. (Arb.) 21 Thee northen bluster aproching Thee sayls tears tag rag, to the sky thee waues vphoysing. **1610** B. Jonson *Alch.* v. ii, Men and women, And of all sorts, tag-rag, [have] beene seene to flock here. **1737** Ozell *Urquhart's Rabelais* I. iv. I. 150 After Dinner they all went tag-rag together to the willow-grove.

**D. Tag, rag, and bobtail** [orig. an extension of *tag and rag* (Tag *sb.*$^1$ 10 b); see also Bobtail. Now sometimes **tagrag and bobtail.**] A contemptuous term for a number of persons of various sorts and conditions, all and sundry, especially of the lower classes.

**1645** *Just Defence John Bastwick* 16 That rabble rout tag ragge and bobtaile. **1660** Pepys *Diary* 6 Mar., They all went down into the dining-room, where it was full of tag, rag, and bobtail, dancing, singing, and drinking. **1692** L'Estrange *Fables* clxxxv. (1714) 198 Jupiter Invited all Living Creatures, Tag, Rag, and Bob-tail, to the Solemnity of the Wedding. **1728** Byrom *Jrnl. & Lit. Rem.* (1856) I. I. 287 Here's thy good health..and all thy little tag, rag, and bobtails. **1785** Wolcott (P. Pindar) *Odes to R.A.'s* II. 1 Tagrags and Bobtails of the sacred Brush. **1840** Dickens *Barn. Rudge* xxxv, 'We don't take in no tagrag and bobtail at our house, sir', answered John. **1883** Ld. R. Gower *My Remin.* I. xiii. 251 The mounted police charged the crowd..and our party had to fly before them along with tag, rag, and bob-tail.

**b.** *attrib.*

? **1730** *Royal Remarks* 53 The Dramatis Personæ,..a Tag-Rag and Bob Tail Crew. **1849** Thackeray *Pendennis* vii. (1885) 71 Fancy..your house filled with her confounded tag-rag-and-bobtail relations! **1890** *Guardian* 15 Oct. 1597/1 Inspectors belonging to 'the tag-rag and bobtail class'.

Hence *tag, rag, and bobtailry*; and variations *tag, rag, and long-tail*; *tag, rag, and rascality.*

**1701** *New Jersey Arch.* (1881) II. 414 At ye disposall of ye tag, rag, and Rascality. **1719** D'Urfey *Pills* IV. 113 To make a Match with Tag-rag, and Long-tail. **1858** F. E. Paget *Curate Cumberworth* (1859) 248 A tag, rag, and bobtailry..gathered together..for electioneering purposes.

**Taˑgraˑggery.** [f. Tag-rag + -ery, collective. (Chiefly Carlylese.)] A tag-rag collection or assemblage; a mass of trumpery odds and ends.

**1837** Mrs. Carlyle *Lett.* I. 66 When one is delivered from the tag-raggery of printers' devils. **1845** Carlyle *Cromwell* App. xi. (1871) V. 188 *note*, Antiquarian tagraggeries. **1858** — *Fredk. Gt.* IV. vii. I. 454 Was there ever seen such a travelling tagraggery of a Sovereign Court before? **1887** *Sat. Rev.* 30 July 139/1 The 'inventing fiend'..has upset the war-ship so utterly, and has pestered it about with such a tag-raggery of small machines.

‖**Tagua** (tæˑgwă). [Native name in Colombia.] The ivory-palm, *Phytelephas macrocarpa*, which produces the ivory-nut or corozo-nut; also in *Comb.*, as *tagua-nut, -palm, -plant.*

**1830** LINDLEY *Nat. Syst. Bot.* 285 Buttons are turned from the hard albumen of Phytelephas, or the Tagua plant. **1883** JAGO in *Knowledge* July 52/1 Cellulose .. occurs in an approximately pure state in the 'tagua-nut'. **1901** KEANE *S. Amer.* I. 132 The tagua, whose melon-shaped pods contain the hard grains known as Vegetable Ivory.

‖ **Taguan** (tæ·gwăn). [app. native name in the Philippines.

Said by Pallas, *Miscell. Zoolog.* 1766, on the authority of Valentyn *Lettres édif. ex Epist. Jesuit.*, to be so called 'a Philippinensium insularum incolis'.]

The Malayan Flying Squirrel, *Pteromys petaurista.* (Sometimes erroneously applied to other species.)

**1807** BARR tr. *Buffon's Nat. Hist.* VII. 169 It was taken upon the Malabar coast, where they are very common, as well as in the Philippine Islands, and other parts of India, where they are called taguans, or great flying squirrels. **1826** SYD. SMITH in *Edin. Rev.* Feb. 309 The taguan knocks you down with a blow of his paw, if suddenly interrupted, but will run away, if you give him time to do so. **1901** CORNISH *Living Anim. World* 149 The taguan, a large squirrel of India, Ceylon and the Malacca forests.

‖ **Tagus** (tē^i·gɒ̆s). *Gr. Hist.* [Latinized form of Gr. ταγός ruler, leader, f. stem ταγ- of τάσσ-ειν to arrange, order.] A commander, leader, ruler, chief; *spec.* the title of the chief of the confederation of Thessaly.

**1839** THIRLWALL *Greece* V. xxxviii. 55 The first step which he had to take was to acquire the title of tagus, and to unite all Thessaly under his legitimate authority. **1846** GROTE *Greece* II. iii. II. 373 A chief or Tagus was nominated to enforce obedience. **1849** *Ibid.* II. liii. VI. 542 The federal authority or power of the tagus, which bound together the separate cities [of Thessaly], was generally very weak.

**Tah** (tā), *int.* An exclamation expressing lightness of humour, unconcern, or the like.

*a* **1688** VILLIERS (Dk. Buckhm.) *Rehearsal* (1714) 73 But you should be light and easie, tah, tah, tah.

**Tah** = *þah*, early form of THOUGH: see T 8.

‖ **Taha** (tā·hā). [Native (? Bechuana) name.] A South African species of weaver-bird, *Euplectes taha* of Sir A. Smith, now *Pyromelana taha*, the male of which is chiefly yellow and black.

**1836** SIR A. SMITH *Rept. of Explor. Exped.* **1906** *Times* 14 Aug. 2/6 Captain B. R. Horsbrugh .. serving in the Orange River Colony .. presented to the Zoological Society .. the taha weaver.

† **Ta ha**, *int. Obs.* A derisive exclamation.

*a* **1529** SKELTON *Replyc.* 75 Se where the heretykes go, Wytlesse wandring to and fro! With, Te he, ta ha, bo ho, bo ho!

‖ **Tahalli** (tăha·lli). Erron. tahali. [Arabic تحلّي *taχallī* ornamenting.] Decoration.

**1833** LONGF. *Outre-Mer* Prose Wks. 1886 I. 166 Moorish knights gayly arrayed .. with scarfs of blue and jewelled tahalies. **1904** J. PARKINSON *Lays Love & War* 47 What ho! my spear, My mail, and helm, and gleaming tahali.

‖ **Tahona** (tăhōu·nă). *U.S.* [Sp.] See quots.

**1840** *Civil Eng. & Arch. Jrnl.* III. 129/1 To devise some simple and efficient means of working the 'tahonas', or grinding mills used in the reduction of the silver ore in the mining districts. **1875** J. H. COLLINS *Metal Mining* 113 All the washings .. are then ground fine in the 'arrastre' or 'tahona', a rude mill of rough stones worked by mules.

**Tahr**, var. TEHR, a Himalayan wild goat.

‖ **Tahsildar** (tɒχsī·ldār). *E. Indies.* Also 8 **tisheldar**, 9 **tehsildar**, **tuhseeldar**, **tusseeldar**, **taxildar**. [Urdū, f. Arab., Pers. تحصيل *taḥṣīl* collection + Pers. دار *dār*, agential suffix.] The chief revenue-officer of a subdivision of a district under the Mogul rule; retained by the British; formerly sometimes applied to the cashier in a business house.

**1799** SIR T. MUNRO *Let.* in Gleig *Life* (1830) I. 215 He [Tippoo] divided his country into 37 Provinces under Dewans .. and subdivided these again into 1025 inferior districts, having each a Tisheldar. **1801** WELLINGTON *Suppl. Desp.* (1858) II. 564 Accounts since received from the tahsildar of the Currup talook. **1808** in *5th Rep. Sel. Comm. on E. I. Company* (1812) 583 (Y.) He continues to this hour tehsildar of the petty pergunnah of Sheopore. **1810** CAPT. T. WILLIAMSON *E. Ind. Vade-m.* I. 209 The *sircar*, or *tusseeldar* (cash-keeper) receiving one key, and the master retaining the other. **1849** *Direct. Rev. Off. N. W. Prov.* 188 Great care should be taken to maintain the respectability of the Tuhseeldars. **1871** MATEER *Travancore* 72 [The provinces] are subdivided into thirty-two counties, with a Tahsildar, or magistrate, at the head of each.

**Taich(e**, obs. ff. TACHE *sb.*[1], spot, stain.

**Taicoon, taikun**, var. ff. TYCOON.

**Taigle** (tē^i·g'l), *v. Sc.* Also 7 teagle. [app. mod. Sc. form of ME. *tagil, tagyl*, TAGLE, q. v.]

1. *trans.* To entangle, impede, or hinder in course or action; to keep back, retard, detain, delay.

[*c* **1340**: see TAGLE.]

**1635** DICKSON *Writings* (1845) I. 194 He .. forgot all things which might teagle him in the way. *Ibid.*, Forget things past that would teagle us. **1684** PEDEN in *Life & Prophecies* (1868) 56 Tell all the Lords people to try by mourning and prayer to teagle Him. **1895** FRASER *Whaups* ii. 23 Others cunningly stretched out their legs to taigle the wrathful dominie. **1895** CROCKETT *Men of Moss-Hags* 64 Ye hae taigled us overly long already.

2. To 'catch' or entangle in talk; to embarrass.

**1865** in *Beeton's Bk. Anecd.* 24 Two graceless young fellows who had determined, as they said, to taigle their minister.

3. *intr.* To linger, tarry, delay; to dally, loiter.

**17..** *Laird o Ochiltree Wawis* ix. in Child *Ballads* VII. ccxvii. 196/1 Kind maister, ye've taiglit lang. **1823** GALT *R. Gilhaize* xxvi. (E.D.D.), Robin Brown taigled more than two hours for me. **1895** CROCKETT *Men of Moss-Hags* xi. 87 'Make haste', they said, 'we haena time to taigle wi' ye'.

4. *intr.* To walk slowly or heavily, to drag oneself, to trudge.

**1886** STEVENSON *Kidnapped* xviii, Ay, man, ye shall taigle many a weary foot, or we get clear! **1893** — *Catriona* vii. 74 A man that comes taigling after a Macgregor's daughter. *Ibid.* xix. 223 Her two sisters had to taigle home by theirselves.

‖ **Taigu** (tai·gu). [Native name in Guarani.] In taigu wood, also called *lapacho wood*: see quots. Hence **Taigu·ic** *a. Chem.* in *taiguic acid*, an acid obtained from this wood.

**1868** WATTS *Dict. Chem.* V. 655 *Taigu wood*, a wood from Paraguay, resembling guaiacum-wood in appearance and specific gravity. *Ibid.*, *Taiguic acid* .. occurs in the cold alcoholic extract of taigu wood. **1892** MORLEY & MUIR *Watts' Dict. Chem.* III. 119 Lapachic acid, $C_{15}H_{14}O_3$; Oxy-amenyl-naphtho-quinone; Taiguic acid .. a yellow colouring matter present in the 'lapacho' wood of a genus of the *Bignoniaceæ*.

**Taik(e**, obs. forms of TAKE *v.*

**Taiken, -in**, obs. Sc. forms of TOKEN.

**Taikle**, obs. Sc. form of TACKLE.

**Tail** (tēl), *sb.*[1] Forms: 1 tæᵹel, tæᵹl, 3 teil, 3– tail; also 3–8 tayl, 4 taille, 4–6 tayll(e, 4–7 taile, tayle, 5–6 taill; *Sc.* 4–6 tale. [Com. Teut.: OE. *tæᵹel, tæᵹl*, = ON. *tagl* a horse's tail (Sw. *tagel* horse-hair of tail or mane); OHG. *zagel*, MHG. *zagel*, dial. *zail, zeil*, tail of animal, etc., mod.Ger. dial. *zagel, zâl, zael* tail; LG. *tagel* a twisted scourge or whip of thongs or ropes, a rope-end, rope (Brem. Wbch.), Goth. *tagl* hair (of the head, of the camel). Ulterior etymology uncertain; but the evidence appears to show that the primary sense was either 'hair' or 'hairy tail', as of the horse, ox, fox, etc., whence it was extended to the tails of other animals. Already in OE. it was applied to the tails of 'worms' or reptiles, and to the sting of the bee. In OE. the tail was also called *steort*, START. = Du. *staart*.]

1. The posterior extremity of an animal, in position opposite to the head, either forming a distinct flexible appendage to the trunk, or being the continuation of the trunk itself behind the anus. Also, a representation or figure of this part.

In most vertebrate animals, consisting of a number of gradually attenuated coccygeal vertebræ covered with flesh and integument; in quadrupeds often clothed with hair, in birds with feathers (see also PEACOCK'S TAIL), and in fishes bearing the caudal fin; in invertebrate animals, sometimes a distinct and well-marked member, at other times not distinctly marked off from the rest of the body.

*a* **800** *Laws of Ine* c. 59 Oxan tæᵹl bið scill[inges] weorð. *a* **1023** WULFSTAN *Hom.* xlii. (1883) 200 Eᵹeslice mycele deor .. hi habbaþ tæᵹlas ðam wyrmum ᵹelice. *c* **1200** *Vices & Virtues* 151 Ðat ðe tail ware on auriche netene. *c* **1205** LAY. 29557 Heo .. nomen tailes of rehᵹen and hangede on his cape. *a* **1225** *Ancr. R.* 254 Sansumes foxes .. weren bi þe teiles iteied ueste .. And in euerich ones teile a blase berninde. *c* **1290** *S. Eng. Leg.* I. 363/38 And teiden him sethþe to a wilde hors at þe taile bihinde. **1340** HAMPOLE *Pr. Consc.* 4419–23 He says, 'with his tayle he droghe don even þe thred part of þe sternes of heven,' .. Þis was þe taille of þe dragon. *c* **1391** CHAUCER *Astrol.* II. § 4 The tail of the dragoun, is in [þe] hows of the assendent. **1413** *Pilgr. Sowle* (Caxton) I. xix. (1859) 19 No body had he under this hede, but only a tayl whiche semyd the tayle of a worme. **1470–85** MALORY *Arthur* v. iv. 163 The bore .. whiche was x foote large fro the hede to the taylle. **1483** CAXTON *Gold. Leg.* 174 b/2 Castyng on hym the tayles of thornback or like fisshes. **1486** *Bk. St. Albans* b ij b, The federis of the wynges and of the taylle. *a* **1548** HALL *Chron., Hen. VII* 30 Thinkyng to haue gotten God by the foote, when she had the deuell by the tayle. **1600** J. PORY tr. *Leo's Africa* IX. 341 Others affirmed that they had seene one of those tailes [of a sheep] of an hundred and fiftie pounds weight. *a* **1604** HANMER *Chron. Irel.* (1633) 125 This reformation was but a sweeping of a house with a Foxes tayle. **1626** YATES *Ibis ad Cæsarem* I. 6 Though the head of this Hydra was cut off, yet it had still a frigling taile. **1690** LOCKE *Hum. Und.* III. ii. § 3 A Child .. applies the Word Gold only to his own Idea of that Colour, and nothing else; and therefore calls the same Colour in a Peacock's Tail, Gold. *a* **1727** NEWTON *Chronol. Amended* i. (1728) 83 The Tayl of the South Fish [constellation]. **1826** KIRBY & SP. *Entomol.* III. xxxiii. 389 *Cauda* (the Tail). Where the abdomen grows suddenly slenderer, and terminates in a long jointed tail, as in *Scorpio* and *Panorpa*. **1861** HULME tr. *Moquin-Tandon* II. III. iii. 96 The abdomen [of the Crayfish], improperly termed the tail. **1894** NEWTON *Dict. Birds* 701 The so-called 'tail' of the Peacock is formed not by the rectrices or true tail-feathers, but by the singular development of the tail-coverts.

**b.** The tail of a horse, of which one, two, or three were borne before a pasha as insignia of rank: see PASHA (note), and HORSE-TAIL 1 b.

**1717** LADY M. W. MONTAGU *Let. to Abbé Conti* 17 May, The pashas of three tails have those ensigns .. placed in a very conspicuous manner before their tents. **1820** HUGHES *Trav. Sicily* II. i. 23 It was governed by beys, and pashas of two tails, sent by the Porte. **1836** *Penny Cycl.* V. 231/1 Bosnia .. is governed by a pasha of three tails, to whom the governors of the six sandshaks, who are pashas of two tails, are subordinate.

† **c.** *Contemptuously*: expressing exhaustive clearance: cf. HOOF 3. *Obs.*

*c* **1330** R. BRUNNE *Chron.* (1810) 214 Of þe aliens ilk taile þe lond voided clere. **1525** LD. BERNERS *Froiss.* II. xlix. 171 There shall not one tayle of them retourne agayne into fraunce.

2. A thing, part, or appendage, resembling the tail of an animal in shape or position.

**a.** In general sense. **b.** The luminous train usually extending from the 'head' of a comet. †**c.** The germinating sprout of barley; = COME *sb.*[2] *Obs.* **d.** The stalk or peduncle of a fruit (*obs.*); the stalk of a mushroom (*dial.*). **e.** The attenuated part of a muscle at its insertion. **f.** A twisted or braided tress of hair; a queue, pig-tail. **g.** In writing and printing, A stroke or loop forming the lower portion of certain letters and figures, and usually passing below the line. **h.** In musical notation, The line proceeding from the head of a note; the stem. **i.** A kind of wooden lever at the back of a windmill by which it is turned to the wind; also, a vane for the same purpose. **j.** The long handle of an implement, as a rake. **k.** = QUEUE *sb.* 3; in phrase *in tail* rendering the Fr. *en queue*.

**a.** **1523** FITZHERB. *Husb.* § 14 The roughe otes .. be very lyghte, and haue longe tayles, wherby they wyll hange eche one to other. **1666** G. HARVEY *Morb. Angl.* xxxv. 112 The Distill'd water of those tails that hang on Willow Trees. **1683** TRYON *Way to Health* xix. (1697) 416 To see .. a Man, (according to the Vulgar Proverb) appear like an Onion with a Gray Head and a Green Tail. **1776** WITHERING *Brit. Plants* (1796) II. 499 Flowers naked; seeds without tails. **1808** CURWEN *Econ. Feeding Stock* 54 Turnips .. with the tops and tails cut off. **1883** R. HALDANE *Workshop Receipts* Ser. II. 255/1 Be careful not to leave clouds or tails where the brush leaves the roof after the stroke. **1883** KNIGHT *Cruise Falcon* (1887) 125 Some tails of strong black tobacco. **1884** W. C. SMITH *Kildrostan* I. iv. 253, I .. cannot rise Without it .. More than the kite without its load of tail. **1901** *Daily Chron.* 12 Aug. 3/3 The Kallima butterfly .. generally rests upon the trunk of a tree .. with the 'tails' on the hind wings directed upwards.

**b.** [**1297** R. GLOUC. (Rolls) 8604 Þe taylede sterre men clupeþ. Vor þer comþ fram hire a lem suiþe cler & briᵹte, As a tayl oþer a launce.] **1572** T. SMITH in Ellis *Orig. Lett.* Ser. III. IV. 7 The new faire Starre, or Comett, but without beard or taile, which hath appeared here this three weekes. **1690** LEYBOURN *Curs. Math.* 451 Kepler is of Opinion, that the Tail of a Comet is only enlightened by the Sun's Beams. **1738** *Gentl. Mag.* VIII. 244/2 They .. terrify the gazing Nations, who from their glaring Tail and hideous Aspect forbode the worst of Consequences. **1849** HERSCHEL *Outl. Astron.* § 557 The tail is .. by no means an invariable appendage of comets.

**c.** **1594** PLAT *Jewell-ho.* I. 49 The duste and tailes of the malt, which are left in malting. **1763** *Museum Rust.* (ed. 2) I. 114 In what manner to make a profitable use of malt-dust; that is, the dust, tails, &c. which fall off in the screening. **1805** R. W. DICKSON *Pract. Agric.* I. 223 The dust which is screened from malt, mixed with the tails, .. may be converted to the purpose of manure.

**d.** **1613** PURCHAS *Pilgrimage* (1614) 184 If the tayle or woodden substance, whereby it groweth, be on it [an apple].

**e.** **1719** QUINCY *Lex. Physico-Med.* (1722) 5 The Tendon formed by the Tails of several Muscles. **1877** ROSENTHAL *Muscles & Nerves* (1881) 13 The ends are spoken of as the head and tail, of the muscle.

**f.** **1799** in *Spirit Pub. Jrnls.* III. 320 Club nor queue, nor twisted tail Nor e'en thy chatt'ring, barber! shall avail. **1840** MARRYAT *Poor Jack* vii, In a minute the tail was off. **1852** MRS. STOWE *Uncle Tom's C.* xx, Her woolly hair was braided in sundry little tails. **1877** A. B. EDWARDS *Up Nile* xxii. 701 They wore their hair .. plaited in long tails behind.

**g.** **1599** MIDDLETON, etc. *Old Law* III. i. 76 The cipher is turned into 9 by adding the tail. **1676** MOXON *Print. Lett.* 16 Describe the Arch for the inside of the Tail of a. **1771** LUCKOMBE *Hist. Printing* 280 The J .. should run to the depth of three lines, on account of its tail. **1852** MRS. STOWE *Uncle Tom's C.* iv, Uncle Tom laboriously brought up the tail of his *g* the wrong side out. **1893** FURNIVALL *Capgrave's Life S. Kath.* (E.E.T.S.) p. xxxix *note*, Hart's *e* has a curl or tail under it.

**h.** *c* **1325** in *Rel. Ant.* I. 292 Ther is a streinant, with to longe tailes. **1597** MORLEY *Introd. Mus.* 9 If your first note lack a tayle. **1674** PLAYFORD *Skill Mus.* I. viii. 28 Semiquavers are Tyed together by a long stroke on the top of their Tails. **1879** GROVE *Dict. Mus.* s. v. *Crotchet*, But *croche* is a quaver .. and is so called on account of the hook at the end of its tail.

**i.** **1712** J. JAMES tr. *Le Blond's Gardening* 192 Turning themselves to the Wind, by means of a Tail in Form of a Ship's Rudder, which turns about every way. **1892** P. H. EMERSON *Son of Fens* xxxii. 336, I .. got hold of the rope and pulled the gripe up, and made that fast round the tail so that wouldn't jerk her off.

**k.** **1837** CARLYLE *Fr. Rev.* I. VI. iv, Long strings of purchasers, arranged in tail so that the first come be the first served. *Ibid.*, In time we shall see .. the art .. of standing in tail become one of the characteristics of the Parisian People, distinguishing them from all other Peoples.

†**l.** A piece or 'slip' of irregularly bounded land jutting out from a larger piece. *Sc. Obs.*

Represented in med.L. by *cauda*, e.g. 1546–80 in *Regr. of Great Seal of Scott.* No. 268 Croftam seu caudam; *Exch. Rolls of Scott.* VII. 169 Cauda de Lekkok *vel* tale de Lekkok.

**1472** *Rental Bk. Cupar Angus* (1879) I. 162 With the twa talis of land left and made to ws be the last perambulatioun. **1541** *Records of Elgin* (New Spald. Cl. 1903) I. 64 Mr Thomas Gaderar .. complenit vpon Robert Mawar for cassin ane stank upon ane taill pertynyng to the said Mr Thomas. **1550** *Ibid.* 100 Ane taill of land lyand on the north syid of the said burgh. **1690** *Ibid.* 349 Croftis, taillis, yairdis and utheris lyabill in paying the teynd scheaff.

3. The train or tail-like portion of a woman's dress (now *colloq.*); the pendent posterior part of a man's dress-coat or a peasant's long coat; the loose part of any coat below the waist; (often in *pl.*) the bottom or lower edge of a gown, a skirt, etc., which reaches quite or nearly to the ground. Also *dial.* the skirt of a woman's dress; *tails*, skirts.

**1297** R. GLOUC. (Rolls) 2513 Þis maide .. side drou hire tail Akne to þe king 30 sede, Louerd king, washayl. *a* **1450**

*Knt. de la Tour* 30 Her hodes, taylles, and sleues be not furred ynowgh after the shape that rennithe now. **1500–20** DUNBAR *Poems* xiv. 73 Sic fowill tailis, to sweip the calsay clene, The dust vpskaillis. **1532** *Acc. Ld. High Treas. Scotl.* VI. 80 Ane doublat with ane taile, to the Kingis grace. **1560** ROLLAND *Crt. Venus* IV. 541 And Venus taill twa Ladeis vp it beiris. **1690** CROWNE *Eng. Friar* v. Wks. 1874 IV. 111 Madam, speak to the ladies now I am here, to let down their trains; 'tis not manners in the presence of a man o' my quality, to cock up their tails. **1762** FOOTE *Lyar* I. Wks. 1799 I. 277 The draggled tail of my tatter'd academical habit. **1857** HUGHES *Tom Brown* I. viii, His friends at home..hadn't put him into tails. **18..** *St. Nicholas* (U.S.) XIV. 406 (Cent. D.) Once a boy [at Harrow] has reached the modern remove, he puts on his tails, or tailed coat. **1888** *Century Mag.* May 128/1 He crossed the room, stepping over the tails of gowns, and stood before his old friend. **1890** PARNELL *Sp. Ho. Comm.* 14 Feb., To go about like the traditional Irishman at Donnybrook Fair, and exclaim 'Will nobody tread on the tail of my coat?'

**4.** The lower or hinder extremity of anything; the part opposite to what is regarded as the head. **a.** in general application.

**1362** LANGL. *P. Pl.* A. v. 19 Beches and brode okes weore blowen to þe eorþe, And turned vpward þe tayl. **1731** MORTIMER in *Phil. Trans.* XXXVII. 107 They [packthreads] are all spread on a Cross-piece fastened to two Staples: These are called the Tail of the Mounture. **1778** PRYCE *Min. Cornub.* IV. ii. 234 The stony coarse poorer part settles..on the tail or lower end of the boards. **1805** R. W. DICKSON *Pract. Agric.* I. 296 The tail, or terminating part of the strata. **1859** F. GRIFFITHS *Artill. Man.* (1862) 114 The gun is at the tail of the platform. **1872** ELLACOMBE *Ch. Bells Devon*, etc. ii. 217 Bells are sometimes chimed..by hitching the rope round the flight or tail of the clapper. **1887** D. A. LOW *Machine Draw.* (1892) 6 The head already formed on the rivet, and called the tail, is then held up, and the point is hammered or pressed so as to form another head. **1890** BILLINGS *Nat. Med. Dict.*, *Tail of epididymis*, the lower pointed extremity. **1898** in *Daily News* 8 Nov. 6/1 [Mr. Gladstone] would prefix the address and affix his signature, writing (as he called it) the 'head and the tail'.

**b.** The terminal or concluding part of anything, as of a text, word, or sentence (cf. HEAD *sb.* 19), of a period of time, or something occupying time, as a storm, shower, drought, etc.

**1377** LANGL. *P. Pl.* B. III. 347 And þat is þe taille of þe tixte. *a* **1450** MYRC *Par. Pr.* 1889 Cotte þow not þe wordes tayle. **1579** FULKE *Heskins's Parl.* 258 Here M. Hesk. choppeth off yᵉ taile [of the sentence]. **1613** SIR H. NEVILL in *Buccleuch MSS.* (Hist. MSS. Comm.) I. 131 The tail of this storm fell a little upon my Lord himself. **1771** SMOLLETT *Humph. Cl.* 20 Apr., I now sit down to execute the threat in the tail of my last [letter]. *a* **1774** FERGUSSON *Sandie & Willie* Poems (1789) II. 4 It's wearin' on now to the tail o' May. **1833** HT. MARTINEAU *Loom & Lugger* I. i. 16 At the tail of their conversation. **1872** BLACK *Adv. Phaeton* xx. 278 The tail of a shower sometimes overtaking us.

**c.** The rear-end of an army or marching column, of a procession, etc. (Cf. HEAD *sb.* 18 a.)

**1565** COOPER *Thesaurus* s. v. *Agmen*, They cutte of the tayle of the armie, or kyll them that are behynde. **1610** HOLLAND *Camden's Brit.* (1637) 43 They attempted to cut off the taile of our armie. **1800** WELLINGTON in Gurw. *Desp.* (1837) I. 197 Colonel Stevenson is after them, and will cut off part of the tail, I hope. **1858** O. W. HOLMES *Aut. Breakf.-t.* iii. 19 The wit knows that his place is at the tail of a procession. **1899** BALDOCK *Cromwell* 231 The King with the head of his column reached Harborough in safety, the tail quartering as far back as Naseby.

**d.** The hinder part of a cart, plough, or harrow; = PLOUGH-TAIL. (Cf. HEAD *sb.* 18 c.)

**1466** AGNES PASTON *Will* in *P. Lett.* II. 286 Withouȝt they shuld hold the plowe to the tayle. **1526** R. WHYTFORD *Martiloge* 114 b, They were tyed unto the tayles of cartes, & so drawen thrugh bushes, breres, & thornes unto deth. **1547** (15 Nov.) *City of Lond. Rep.* in *Vicary's Anat.* (1888) App. iii. 174 John Launder..& John Croydon..beggers.. shall..be whypped naked att A Cartes Taylle. **1563–87**, etc. [see CART'S-TAIL]. **1577** B. GOOGE *Heresbach's Husb.* I. (1586) 21 The partes of the Plowe, are the Tayle, the Shelfe, the Beame [etc.]. **1887** JESSOPP *Arcady* iv. 117 Their sturdy sons will push their way, but not..at the plough's tail.

†**e.** The stern of a ship or boat. (Cf. HEAD *sb.* 21.) *Obs.*

**1553** BRENDE *Q. Curtius* T viij, Swimming at the boates tailes. **1645** EVELYN *Diary* June (1827) I. 312 These vessells [gondolas] are built very long and narrow, having necks and tailes of steele. **1709** *Lond. Gaz.* No. 4510/7 The Hoy Burthen 9 or 10 Tun, very full built forward, with a clean Tail.

**f.** The part of a mill-race below the wheel; the tail-race; the lower end of a pool or stream.

**1533–4** *Act* 25 *Hen. VIII*, c. 7 Any other engine..at the taile of anie mille or were. **1613** J[OHN] D[ENNYS] *Secr. Angling* II. xxvi, See some standing..at the Tayles of Mills and Arches small. **1725** DE FOE *Voy. round World* (1840) 288 The water..had made a pit under it with the fall, like the tail of a mill. **1829** *Nat. Philos.* I. *Hydraulics* iii. 26 (Usef. Knowl. Soc.) To permit a portion of the upper water to flow down into the tail or lower stream immediately in front of the wheel. **1867** F. FRANCIS *Angling* i. (1880) 40 The tail of a pool is a favourite place for them. **1886** *Q. Rev.* Oct. 341 The tail of a swift stream, where it broadens out before another white rapid.

**g.** The spit or extremity of a reef or sandbank, where it slopes under the water.

**1761** *Chron.* in *Ann. Reg.* 149/2 The Actaeon ran aground on the tail of the Pall-Bank. **1799** *Hull Advertiser* 6 Apr. 3/1 The cutter got up as far as the tail of the bank. **1817** *Sporting Mag.* L. 172 At what sailors call the 'Tail' of the land, there is always a turbulent sea, or rather Race. **1858** *Merc. Marine Mag.* V. 225 Ships..should pass as close as possible to the tail of the Reef.

**h.** The reverse side of a coin; esp. in phr. *head(s or tail(s*: see HEAD *sb.* 3 b.

**1684** OTWAY *Atheist* II. i, As Boys do with their Farthings ..go to Heads or Tails for 'em. **1764** BRIDGES *Burlesque Homer* (1774) 115 (Farmer) 'Tis heads for Greece, and Tails for Troy...Two farthings out of three were Tails. **1801** STRUTT *Sports & Past.* IV. ii. (1810) 296 The reverse of the head being called the tail without respect to the figure upon it. **1884** *Punch* 16 Feb. 73/1 A sovereign, a half sovereign,..or farthing, so long as it has a 'head' one side, and..a 'tail' the other. **1893** F. ADAMS *New Egypt* 267 The goddess who sits on the 'tails' side of our bronze currency.

**i.** The lower, inner, or subordinate end of a long-shaped block or brick; the bottom or visible part of a roofing slate or tile.

**1793** SMEATON *Edystone L.* § 82 The tail of the header was made to..bond with the interior parts. **1856** S. C. BREES *Gloss. Terms*, *Tail*,..the lower end of the slate or tile.

**j.** *Surg.* Either end of an incision, which does not go through the whole thickness of the skin.

**1846** BRITTAN tr. *Malgaigne's Man. Oper. Surg.* 5 The bistoury must be repeatedly passed over the same course, so as to divide layer by layer. Here 'tails' are inevitable; but this inconvenience is light in comparison to the advantages to be sometimes derived from this mode of operating.

**k.** *Printing* and *Bookbinding.* The lower edge of a page or cover. (Cf. HEAD *sb.* 13.)

**1865** HANNETT *Bibliopegia* (ed. 6) 234 The head being cut, the book is taken out of the press, and the quantity to be taken off the tail marked with the compasses. **1895** ZAEHNSDORF *Hist. Bookbinding* 25 *Headbander*, the person who works the fine silk or cotton ornament at head or tail of the book as a finish to the edge.

**l.** *Tail of the eye*, the outer corner of the eye. *Out of, with the tail of the eye*, with a sidelong or furtive glance.

**1802** R. ANDERSON *Cumberld. Ball.* 45 But I only made luive thro' the tail o' my e'e. **1824** GALT *Rothelan* II. v. iii. 203 'Sir Gibrel', cried the lady, at the same time winking to him with the tail of her eye. **1859** READE *Love me little* xiv, Miss Lucy noticed this out of the tail of her eye. **1888** J. PAYN *Myst. Mirbridge* (Tauchn.) II. xvii. 187 Mrs. Westropp watched him with the tail of her eye as she talked to Lady Trevor.

**5.** The lower and hinder part of the human body; the fundament, posteriors, buttocks, backside. *Tail over top* = *top over tail*: see TOP *sb.* Now *dial.* or *low colloq.*

**1303** R. BRUNNE *Handl. Synne* 5416 Þarfor shul þey..Go to helle, both top and tayle. *c* **1330** — *Chron.* (1810) 70 Into þe waise þam fro he tombled top ouer taile. *c* **1400** *Land Troy Bk.* 16727 He bar him tayl ouer top, That he lay ther as a sop. ?*a* **1500** *Chester Pl.* (Shaks. Soc.) II. 176 Thou take hym by the toppe and I by the tayle. **1530** PALSGR. 279/1 Tayle or arse, *queue* or *cul.* **1542** UDALL *Erasm. Apoph.* 81 He was forbidden to sitte on his taille & was charged to stand vpon his feete. **1686** tr. *Chardin's Trav. Persia* 97 They go Barefoot, and all in Tattars that hardly cover their Tails. **1889** J. M. DUNCAN *Dis. Wom.* xxxii. (ed. 4) 268 Ever since that time she has had pain, in what she calls her tail.

**b.** *At* († *after*) *the tail of*, at the back of, in the rear of, following; *in the tail of*, in the train of; so † *to follow the tail of*. Cf. 6.

**13..** *K. Alis* 2142 (Bodley MS.) Siweþ me after [*Weber* at] my taile. **1471** RIPLEY *Comp. Alch.* v. xxviii. in Ashm. *Theatr. Chem. Brit.* (1652) 155 Folys doe folow them at the tayle. **1542** UDALL *Erasm. Apoph.* 283 b, After his taille should come his owne souldyours. *a* **1547** SURREY *Æneid* IV. 207 The skies gan rumble sore, In tail thereof a mingled showr with hayle. **1549** LATIMER *2nd Serm. bef. Edw. VI* (Arb.) 66 That ye wyll geue youre byshoppes charge yer they go home ..to se your maiesties iniunctions better kepte, and sende youre visitours in theyr tayles. **1614** RALEIGH *Hist. World* IV. ii. § 4. 147 In the taile of these Horses the Regiment of foot marched. **1848** THACKERAY *Van. Fair* xxiii, Peggy with the infantine procession at her tail. **1891** HALL CAINE *Scapegoat* vii, She..had..come to Morocco at the tail of a Spanish embassy.

**c.** Sexual member; penis or (oftener) pudendum.

**1362** LANGL. *P. Pl.* A. III. 126 Heo is Tikel of hire Tayl.. As Comuyn as þe Cart-wei to knaues and to alle. *c* **1450** *Cov. Myst.* (Shaks. Soc.) 134 Suche a ȝonge damesel..Of hire tayle oftetyme be lyght. **1483** *Cath. Angl.* 377/1 A Tayle, *penis equi est.* *c* **1515** *Cocke Lorell's B.* (Percy Soc.) 14 Many whyte nonnes with whyte vayles, That was full wanton of theyr tayles. *a* **1744** POPE *To Mr. J. Moore* iv. **1785** GROSE *Dict. Vulg. T.* s. v. *Cab.*

**6.** A train or band of followers; a following; a retinue. Also *fig.*

**1297** R. GLOUC. (Rolls) 10774 Hiderward Þe kinges conseilors londes hii destruede mid hor tayle. **1362** LANGL. *P. Pl.* A. II. 160, I haue no tome to telle þe Tayl [B. II. 185 taille] þat hem folweþ. *c* **1420** ? LYDG. *Assembly of Gods* 754 Of vngracious gastes he bryngeth a long tayll. **1578** *Reg. Privy Council Scot.* III. 15 To draw eftir thame a large taill of ignorant personis. **1633** B. JONSON *Tale Tub* II. i, Why should her worship lack Her tail of maids? **1675** M. CLIFFORD *Hum. Reason* in *Phenix* (1708) II. 540 If Errors in Belief draw so ill a Tail after them as the Devils and Damnation. **1814** SCOTT *Wav.* xvi, The Chief with his tail on..that is, with all his usual followers. **1838** [MISS MAITLAND] *Lett. fr. Madras* (1843) 180 Everybody has a tail, consisting of poor followers, flappers, and flatterers... When head walks abroad, tail walks after him at a respectful distance. **1862** *Sat. Rev.* 15 Mar. 286 The glorious days when O'Connell's tail supplied Lord Melbourne's Cabinet with the means of protracting a miserable existence.

**7.** (Also *pl.*) The inferior, less valuable, or refuse part of anything; foots, bottoms, dregs, sediment. Also *fig.* Cf. TAILING *vbl. sb.*[1] 2.

**1542** BOORDE *Dyetary* x. (1870) 256 It [ale] must haue no weft nor tayle. **1642** ROGERS *Naaman* 71 Abandoning the refuse and taile that remained. **1674** RAY *Collect. Words, Prepar. Metals, Tin* 123 The wast Tin that falls hindmost in the Buddle and Wreck, which they call the tail. **1778** PRYCE *Min. Cornub.* IV. i. 221. *Ibid.* Gloss. 329/1 *Tails*, the roughest refuse of stampt Tin thrown behind the tail or end of the buddle. **1890** *Science* 5 Sept. 129 The tails or faints, as well as the still less volatile or ordinary fusel oil, are mixtures of several alcohols and fatty acid ethers.

**b.** (Also in *pl.*) Short for *tail corn*, etc.: see 12 b, and cf. TAILING *vbl. sb.*[1] 2 a.

**1778** [W. MARSHALL] *Minutes Agric.* 14 Oct. an. 1775, Last year, we made a bushel of tail to every fifteen bushels of head. **1801** *Farmer's Mag.* Apr. 215 After grinding [it] produced 483 lb. English of barley meal, 3 lb. and a half of tails, and 40 lb. and a half of bran. **1880** JEFFERIES *Gt. Estate* 110 He had a bushel of the 'tail', or second flour, from the mill.

**8.** The inferior, least influential, or least skilful members of a body; e. g. of a profession, a political party, a cricket team, etc.

**1604** HIERON *Wks.* I. 493 Those that are but the refuse, and (as I may so speake) the taile of an honest profession. **1780** BURKE *Corr.* (1844) II. 385, I will say nothing about that tail which draggles in the dirt, and which every party in every state must carry about it. **1855** MACAULAY *Hist. Eng.* xv. III. 553 These Whigs..belonged, not to the main body of the party, but either to the head or to the tail. **1876** GRANT *Burgh Sch. Scotl.* II. xiii. 357 The more talented and industrious scholars are impeded for the sake of the tail of the class. **1892** *Pall Mall G.* 30 May 1/3 It would seem as if Sussex has a very bad 'tail' indeed this year, the last seven batsmen being good for 35 only in the first innings and for but 37 in the second.

**b.** *spec.* The inferior animals of a flock or herd.

**1844** STEPHENS *Bk. Farm* II. 39 The lambs, dinmonts, or wethers, that are drafted out of the fat stock, are called the sheddings or tails. **1886** C. SCOTT *Sheep-Farming* 88 With overstocking..not only is there a greater 'tail' among the lambs, but the death rate is higher.

**9.** In various figurative uses.

**1340** *Ayenb.* 61 Zuyche byeþ ycleped ine writinge: tayles. Vor hi wreþ þe uelþes of zenne of riche men uor zom timlich guod, hueruore hi byeþ anlicned to þe tayle of þe uoxe. **1382** WYCLIF *Deut.* xxviii. 13 The Lord thi God shal sett thee into heed, and not into tayl [1388 the taill]. **1579** TOMSON *Calvin's Serm. Tim.* 1036/1 That the worde of God is a truth, a truth without a taile (as wee say). **1630** LENNARD tr. *Charron's Wisd.* I. xx. § 8 (1670) 73 To swell and to be puffed up for every good and profitable action, is to shew his tail while he lifts up his head. **1742** *Col. Records Pennsylv.* IV. 555 The names of 'Imposter,..Invader of the Liberties of the People' (with a Tail of et cetera's). **1786** COWPER *Let. to W. Unwin* 24 Aug., I catch a minute by the tail and hold it fast, while I write to you. **1895** MRS. B. M. CROKER *Village Tales* (1896) 64 One of the last joints in the tail of precedence.

**10.** Short for *tail-ill*: see 14. *Obs.* or *dial.*

**1577** B. GOOGE *Heresbach's Husb.* III. (1586) 133 A disease which they call the Woolfe, others the Taile, which is perceiued by the loosenesse or softnesse betwixt the iointes. **1741** *Compl. Fam.-Piece* III. 472 The Disease called the Tail, is by some Farmers called the Wolf.

**11.** Phrases. † **a.** *Tail on end*, said lit. of some beasts when running with the tail erect; hence *attrib.* headlong; precipitate(ly). **b.** *With the tail between the legs*, lit. of a dog or other beast; *fig.* with a cowed and dejected demeanour. † **c.** *Tail and top*, = *top and tail*: see TOP *sb.* **d.** *To turn tail* (orig. a term of falconry), to turn the back; hence, to run away, take to flight.

*Crag and tail*: see CRAG *sb.*[1] 1 b. *Cut and long tail*: see CUT *ppl. a.* 9. *Head and (or, nor) tail*: see HEAD *sb.* *To twist the lion's tail*: see LION *sb.* 2 g. *To put salt on the tail*: see SALT *sb.*[1] 2 c. *Top over tail*: see TOP *sb.*, and cf. sense 5.

**a.** **1790** R. TYLER *Contrast* II. ii, I was glad to take to my heels and split home, right off, tail on end. **1850** R. G. CUMMING *Hunter's Life S. Afr.* (ed. 2) I. 98 *note*, Hunted on horseback, and ridden down by a long, severe, tail-on-end chase. *Ibid.* 120 The oryx leading me a cruel long chase due north, tail-on-end, from my waggons. **b.** *c* **1400** *Lanfranc's Cirurg.* 59 A wood hound..renneþ hidirward & þidirward..wiþ..his tail bitwene hise leggis. **1884** W. E. NORRIS *Thirlby Hall* xii, We shall have you back here very soon..with your tail between your legs. **1897** *Westm. Gaz.* 22 Jan. 2/3 If this sneaking tail-between-the-legs policy is persisted in no more Church votes for the Union! **c.** **1558** PHAER *Æneid* v. N j b, Headlong down in dust he ouerturnyd tayle and topp.

**d.** *a* **1586** SIDNEY *Arcadia* II. (1629) 109 Would shee..turne taile to the Heron, and flie out quite another way. **1587** GREENE *Euphues his Censure* Wks. (Grosart) VI. 192 To cast out no lure to such a haggarde as would turne taile to a full fist. **1589** PUTTENHAM *Eng. Poesie* III. xxiv. (Arb.) 300 Such as retire from the Princes presence, do not by and by turne tayle to them as we do, but go backward or sideling for a reasonable space. **1611** MARKHAM *Countr. Content.* I. v. (1668) 34 Short winged Hawks..will many times neither kill their Game, nor flie their mark; but will give it over.. and (as Faulconers term it) turn tail to it. **1639** LAUD in Rushw. *Hist. Coll.* (1721) II. II. 899 For him to turn tail against my Lord Deputy must needs be a foul Fault. **1719** DE FOE *Crusoe* (1840) I. xx. 360 The wolves turned tail. **1807** E. S. BARRETT *Rising Sun* II. 128 Ashamed to avow that you are going to turn tail on your former principles.

**12.** *attrib.* or as *adj.* **a.** Forming or situated at the tail, bottom, or rear, hindmost; as *tail decoy*, *half*, *hound*, *van*; coming from the rear, as *tail-wind.* **b.** Forming the lowest or most inferior quality, as *tail barley*, *corn*, *flour*, *meal*, *wheat.*

**a.** **1673** S. C. *Rules Civility* 104 Flounders, Place, or the like;..the tail-half is the best. **1857** HUGHES *Tom Brown* I. vii, The tail hounds all straining to get up with the lucky leaders [in hare-and-hounds]. **1874** J. W. LONG *Amer. Wildfowl* xxv. 257 Wait until they are over the 'tail' decoys. **1891** *Daily News* 23 Oct. 5/8 When the last train, with two engines, got through..the tail van is said to have been floating on the water. **1897** *Westm. Gaz.* 1 Mar. 8/1 With a strong tail wind birds have accomplished more than sixty miles in the hour.

**b.** **1765** *Museum Rust.* IV. lxiii. 282 For tail barley.. *ol.* 14*s.* 3*d.* **1851** *Jrnl. R. Agric. Soc.* XII. I. 133 The light or tail corn goes a considerable length in feeding the horses upon a farm. **1887** O. CRAWFURD *Beyond Seas* 35 The enemy's army but riff-raff and tail-corn fellows.

**13.** General combs.: **a.** attributive, as *tail-blotch, -cap, -feather. -fin, -flap* (FLAP *sb.* 4 d), *-fur, -plumage, -pocket, -quill, -ring, -spot, -stroke, -temptation, -tip*, etc.; **b.** objective and obj. gen., as *tail-raiser*; *tail-chasing, -pulling, -spreading, -switching, -wagging* sbs. and adjs.; **c.** instrumental and locative, as *tail-cropped, -decorated, -docked, -joined, -tied* adjs.; *tail-fisher, -fishing*; also *tail-like* adj; *tail-first, -foremost* advbs.

**1872** COUES *N. Amer. Birds* 99 *Tail-blotches small or obscure. **1891** MORGAN *Anim. Sk.* 198 Each successive moult [of the rattlesnake] leaves an additional *tail-cap of dried skin and these constitute the rattle. **1892** KIPLING *Cleared* xv, *Barrack-r. Ball.* 186 The *tail-cropped heifer's low. **1774** GOLDSM. *Nat. Hist.* (1776) V. 97 The common eagle..the *tail feathers white, blackening at the ends. **1681** GREW *Musæum* I. v. i. 85 The *Tail-Finn, as it were half a Finn, being ½ a foot high. **1835–6** *Todd's Cycl. Anat.* I. 562/2 The horizontal position of the tail-fin..distinguishes the cetacean from the fish. **1886** STEVENSON *Kidnapped* xviii. 171 Alan's morals were all *tail-first; but he was ready to give his life for them. **1904** *Blackw. Mag.* June 818/2 A spaniel ..dragged tail-first upstairs and downstairs by a child. **1865** TYLOR *Early Hist. Man.* xii. 355 To proceed now to the story of the *Tail-Fisher. *Ibid.* 357 The curious mythic art of *Tail-fishing. **1847–8** H. MILLER *First Impr.* v, Her [female lobster's] dorsal plates curve round from the joint at the carapace till the *tail-flap rests on her breast. **1875** MORRIS *Æneid* VIII. 210 Which same..*Tail-foremost dragged he to his den. **1902** *Daily Chron.* 18 Oct. 8/3 Ermine, spotted with the tips of the *tail-fur. **1649** G. DANIEL *Trinarch.* To Rdr. 172 *Tayle-Ioyn'd foxes hurrying Sylla's Nose, A Brand to wast the ffeilds. **1835–6** *Todd's Cycl. Anat.* I. 208/2 The last segment of the *tail-like abdomen. **1849** D. J. BROWNE *Amer. Poultry Yd.* (1855) 153 A well-developed *tail plumage. **1848** THACKERAY *Van. Fair* xiii, The head of the family thrust his hands into the great *tail-pockets of his great blue coat. **1681** GREW *Musæum* I. IV. iii. 75 The two *Tail-Quills of the same [Tropick Bird]. **1894** NEWTON *Dict. Birds* 705 In some [penguins] the tail-quills, which are very numerous, are also long. **1907** *Macm. Mag.* July 673 His [a tiger's] *tail rings were very finely marked. **1872** COUES *N. Amer. Birds* 101 Wing-bars and *tail-spots ordinary. **1891** MORGAN *Anim. Sk.* 138 The vigorous *tail-strokes..often leave their mark on the smooth surface of the water. **1905** R. GARNETT *Shakespeare* 97 *Tail-switching Lucifer, Hell's emperor. **1690** C. NESSE *O. & N. Test.* I. 25 The Son of God..broke the serpents head, and leaves only *tail-temptations for us. **1904** B'NESS VON HÜTTEN *Pam* 135 If the proverbial worm had not only turned, but risen on its *tail-tip. **1869** PLATTS tr. *Ikhwanu-s-Safa* 70 If watching, barking, and *tail-wagging are required there, I am the one for it.

**14.** Special combinations: † **tail-band,** = CRUPPER *sb.* 1; **tail-bandage,** a bandage divided into strips at the end; **tail-bay,** (*a*) the space between a girder and the wall: cf. BAY *sb.*[3]; (*b*) in a canal-lock, the narrow water-space just below the lock, opening out into the lower pond: see quot.; **tail-beam,** a beam that is tailed in, as to a wall; a tail-piece; † **tail-bearer,** a train-bearer; **tail-binder**: see quot.; **tail-block,** (*a*) *Naut.*: see quot. 1769; (*b*) in a sawmill carriage, a support of the log at the end where the cut ends; (*c*) in a lathe = *tail-stock*; **tail-bond,** *Building*, a stone placed with its greatest length across a wall, serving as a tie to hold the face to the interior; **tail-bone,** any one of the caudal vertebræ in animals; also applied to the coccyx, when anchylosed into one bone; **tail-box**: see quot.; † **tail-castle,** the poop of a ship; **tail-coat,** a coat with tails; *esp.* a dress or swallow-tailed coat; hence **tail-coated** *a.*; **tail-coverts** (**-covers**), *sb. pl.*, *Ornith.*, the feathers that cover the rectrices or quill-feathers of the tail in birds; divided into upper and lower, according to their position on the dorsal or ventral surface; **tail-crab** (cf. CRAB *sb.*[1] 7): see quot.; **tail-cut**: see CUT *sb.*[2] 20 a; **tail-dam,** *Sc.*, the tail-race of a mill; **tail-drain**: see quot. 1805; **tail-ducat** (Ger. *Schwanzdukaten*), a Prussian gold coin of Frederick William I (1713–40), worth about 10*s.* sterling, bearing the king's head with a queue; **tail-dust**: see quot.; **tail-fan,** in macrurous crustacea, the tail-end formed by the sixth pair of pleopods with the telson; **tail-flower,** a W. Indian araceous plant of the genus *Anthurium*; from its tail-like spicate inflorescence; **tail-fly,** *Angling*, the fly at the end of the leader; a stretcher-fly; **tail-gate,** (*a*) the lower gate or pair of gates of a canal-lock; the aft-gate; (*b*) *U.S. local*, the tail-board of a wagon; **tail-grape,** a name for the species of *Artabotrys*, N.O. *Anonaceæ*, shrubs of tropical Africa and the East Indies; so called from the hook-like form of the flower-stalks, by the aid of which the fruit is suspended; **tail-head,** the root of an animal's tail; **tail-hook,** *Angling*, the hook of a tail-fly; **tail-hounds,** the hounds in the tail of a pack; **tail-house**: see quot.; **tail-ill,** a name for palsy, supposed to be caused by looseness between the tail-joints; **tail-joist,** a joist tailed into the wall, a tail-piece; **tail-knife**: see quot.; **tail-lamp, tail-light,** the (usually red) light or lights carried at the rear of a train, motor-car, etc.; **tail-lobe,** either of the two lobes of the caudal fin present in most fishes; **tail-lock,** a lock at the exit or lower end of a dock; **tail-mill** = *tail-house*; **tail-muscle,** any muscle in the tail of an animal; a caudal or coccygeal muscle; **tail-piles**: see quot.; **tail-pin,** † (*a*) some part of an ancient gun or its carriage; † (*b*) a pin for the tail of a woman's gown; (*c*) the centre in the tail-spindle of a lathe; **tail-rime** = *tailed rime* (TAILED[1] 1 d); hence **tail-rimed** *a.*; **tail-rod,** a continuation of the piston-rod, which passes through the back cover of the cylinder, and serves to steady the piston and rod by giving the former a double bearing; **tail-rot** = *tail-ill*; **tail-screw,** in a lathe, the screw which moves the back centre tail-spindle to and fro: the tail-piece; **tail-seed,** the small ill-developed part of a quantity of seed; **tail-shaft,** in screw steamships, that section of the shaft nearest the propeller; **tail-slip** = *tail-ill*; **tailsman,** *rare*, a ploughman; **tail-soaked** *a.*: see quot.; **tail-spindle,** the spindle in the *tail-stock* of a lathe; **tail-stern,** the tail-piece of a musical instrument; **tail-stock** = DEAD-HEAD 2 b: see quot.; **tail-tackle,** a handy tackle consisting of a double and a single block, or two double blocks, having the strop of one of the double blocks lengthened as in a tail-block; **tail-trimmer,** *Building*: see quot.; **tail-twisting,** the twisting of a tail or tails; (*a*) *lit.* in the fur-trade; (*b*) in political slang, the act of 'twisting the lion's tail': see LION 2 g; hence **tail-twist** *v.*, **tail-twister**; **tail-valve,** (*a*) the air-pump valve in some forms of condenser; (*b*) = SNIFTING-VALVE; **tail-van,** the last van of a train; **tail-vice,** a small hand-vice with a tail or handle to hold it by (Webster 1864); **tail-water,** the water in a mill-race below the wheel, or in a canal or navigable channel below a lock; **tail-worm** = *tail-ill*; **tail-worts,** a name given by Lindley to plants of the N.O. *Triuridaceæ*.

**1483** *Cath. Angl.* 377/1 A *Taylbande (*A.* Taylle bande), *caudile, subtela.* **1856** S. C. BREES *Gloss. Terms*, **Tail bays*, a name given to common joists when one end is framed in a girder and the other rests on a wall. **1875** KNIGHT *Dict. Mech.* s.v. *Lock*, The tail bay or aft-bay, below the lock-chamber. **1598** MARSTON *Sco. Villanie* II. v, Codrus my well-fac't Ladies *taile-bearer (He that ..play'th Flauias vsherer). **1828** *Craven Gloss.*, **Tail-binder*, a long stone..which rests upon the corner stone,.. to bind, or give strength to the wall. **1769** FALCONER *Dict. Marine* (1776), **Tail-block*, a small single block, having a short piece of rope attached to it, by which it may be fastened to any object..either for convenience, or to increase the force applied to the said object. **1829** MARRYAT *F. Mildmay* viii, A tail block was attached to the boom-iron. **1881** YOUNG *Ev. Man his own Mechanic* § 591 The tail-block [of a lathe] has a sliding spindle worked by the screw and wheel. **1776** G. SEMPLE *Building in Water* 141 The Headers, Stretchers and *Tail-bonds. **1548–77** VICARY *Anat.* ix. (1888) 74 Three *cartilaginis* spondels of *Ossa caude*, called the *tayle bone. **1898** *Syd. Soc. Lex.*, *Tail-bone*, the coccygeal vertebræ; coccyx, or os coccygis. **1895** RAYMOND *Smoke of War* 22 The *tail-box—one part of that revolving dome at the head of a stone [wind-] mill by which the sails are brought to face an ever-shifting wind. **1585** HIGINS *Junius' Nomenclator* 222/1 *Puppis, la poupe*, the hind decke, or *taile castell. **1847** ALB. SMITH *Chr. Tadpole* ix. (1879) 86 He was..going to put on a *tail-coat for the first time. **1879** STEVENSON *Trav. Cevennes* (1895) 16 A tall peasant.. arrayed in the green tail-coat of the country. **1889** HICKSON *Naturalist in N. Celebes* 10 The visitor must assume a black tail-coat, a white shirt with a black tie,..and, pro forma, a hat. **1850** LYNCH *Theo. Trinal* xi. 211 How he was born, cradled, schooled, *tailcoated, colleged, and the like. **1861** DU CHAILLU *Equat. Afr.* xvi. 306 Its back, *tail-cover, and very long flowing tail are pure milk-white. **1815** STEPHENS in Shaw *Gen. Zool.* IX. I. 6 *Tail-coverts grey. **1849** D. J. BROWNE *Amer. Poultry Yard* (1855) 21 The wing coverts on the shoulders, and the tail coverts are dark-greyish. **1883** GRESLEY *Coal Mining Gloss.*, **Tail crab*, a crab for overhauling and belaying the tail rope in pumping gear. **1791** *Rep. Nav. Thames & Isis* 12 A *tail Cut from a Lock on River Navigations should be as short as possible. **1903** LUMSDEN *Toorle* v. i. 100 His speech rusht out o' the mou' o' him like water out o' a *tail dam. **1805** R. W. DICKSON *Pract. Agric.* II. 923 **Tail-Drain*, the principal ditch which conveys the water out of the meadow. **1842** J. AITON *Domest. Econ.* (1857) 183 Taking the levels, and laying off the main feeders, the floating gutters, the tail drains,..and the main drain to carry away the whole water. **1864** CARLYLE tr. *Linsenbarth* (1750) in *Fredk. Gt.* XVI. v, A Secretary came..told down on the table five *Tail-ducats (*Schwanz-dukaten*), and a Gold Friedrich under them. **1764** *Museum Rust.* III. lxi. 281 The *tail-dust, which falls through the screen whilst the malt is cleaning before it is put up in sacks,..may be applied to a better use. **1893** STEBBING *Crustacea* xi. 146 Except in the Lithodidæ, that [pair of pleopods] belonging to the sixth segment is always present, this pair with the telson forming the *Rhipidura* or *tail-fan. **1884** MILLER *Plant-n.* 161 *Anthurium*, Banner-plant, Flamingo-plant, *Tail-flower. **1883** *Century Mag.* XXVI. 378 For a stretcher or *tail-fly. **1875** KNIGHT *Dict. Mech.* s.v. *Lock*, The head-gate and *tail-gate, which, with the side-walls, inclose the lock-chamber. **1886** E. EGGLESTON *Graysons* xxiii. 345 The two were picking near together and throwing corn over the tail-gate of the wagon. **1884** MILLER *Plant-n.* 163 *Artabotrys*, *Tail-grape. **1704** *Lond. Gaz.* No. 4018/4 A pretty large white Hound Bitch, with..a Tann'd Spot on her Fore-head, and another on the *Tail-head. **1844** STEPHENS *Bk. of Farm* II. 164 The first point..handled is the end of the rump at the tail head. **1901** *Westmorld. Gaz.* 26 Oct. 5/3 Lost, three Ewes and two Lambs,..ewes marked across tail-head. **1888** GOODE *Amer. Fishes* 8 Use a '*tail-hook' to avoid the risk of losing the minnow without gaining the Perch. **1852** R. S. SURTEES *Sponge's Sp. Tour* (1893) 50 The last of the *tail-hounds are flying the fence out of the first field. **1881** RAYMOND *Mining Gloss.*, **Tail-house, Tail-mill*, the buildings in which tailings are treated. **1824** MACTAGGART *Gallovid. Encycl.* s.v. *Yirb-wives*, When a cow takes the *Tailill, or is Elfshot, these females are sent for to cure them. **1846** J. BAXTER *Libr. Pract. Agric.* (ed. 4) II. 134 This complaint is traced to a most ridiculous cause. The original evil is said to be in the tail; and all maladies of this kind, involving the partial or total loss of motion of the hind limbs of the animal, are classed under the name of *tail-ill*, or *tail-slip*. **1667** PRIMATT *City & C. Build.* 80 Observe that the Carpenter doth pin all his *Tayl-Joynts, they being apt to slip. **1820** SCORESBY *Acc. Arctic Reg.* II. 233 A '*tail-knife',..used for perforating the fins or tail of a dead whale. **1891** *Cent. Dict.*, *Tail-lamp. **1908** *Westm. Gaz.* 17 Nov. 5/2 Side lamps, tail lamp, head-light with separate generator. **1844** *Illustr. Lond. News* 14 Dec. 374 Each train..is provided with..red *tail lights. **1903** *Westm. Gaz.* 28 Jan. 5/1 He did not slow even when the red tail-lights of the standing local train were seen. **1907** J. E. EWART in *Q. Rev.* Apr. 558 At the base of the long dock there is no vestige of a *tail-lock. **1891** *Cent. Dict.*, *Tail-muscle. **1898** *Syd. Soc. Lex.*, *Tail muscle*, coccygeus, depressor of the tail. **1837** in *Civil Eng. & Arch. Jrnl.* I. 6/1 The component parts of a groin are piles, planking, land-ties,..*tail-piles and keys, and screw-bolts. *Ibid.* 6/2 The relative proportions of the component parts are, four piles, one land-tie with tail-piles and keys [etc.]. **1497** *Naval Acc. Hen. VII* (1896) 84 Lymores with boltes forlokkes kayes lynces and a *taile pynne for the said Curtowe. *c* **1540** HEYWOOD *Four P. P.* in Hazl. *Dodsley* I. 351 The trimming and pinning up their gear; Specially their fiddling with the tail-pin. **1887** *Cassell's Encycl. Dict.*, *Tail-pin*, the back-centre pin of a lathe. **1886** SCHMIRGEL in *Sir Beues* (E.E.T.S.) App. xlv, Romances with *tail-rhymed stanzas. **1894** *Times* 26 June 12/1 Rods, which pass through the covers of the low-pressure cylinders after the manner of a *tail rod. **1896** KIPLING *Seven Seas* 43 Yon orchestra sublime Whaur-to .. the tail-rods mark the time. **1847** W. C. L. MARTIN *Ox* 139/2 Palsy, or paralysis. This disease..bears among farmers and cow-leeches the ridiculous names of joint-yellows, *tail-rot, tail-ill, or tail-slip. **1786** *Young's Ann. Agric.* V. 114 (E.D.D.) *Tail-seed from my seed-mill. **1897** *Westm. Gaz.* 8 July 5/2 The *tail-shaft got bent and could not be rectified, consequently the ship became disabled. **1901** *Scotsman* 5 Mar. 7/8 Accidents principally of the kind known as tail-shaft breakages. **1846** *Tail-slip [see *tail-ill*]. **1867** D. G. MITCHELL *Rural Stud.* 121 Every man who can use a hoe or a pitchfork is supposed to be a competent *tailsman for the plow. **1766** *Compl. Farmer*, **Tail-soaked*, a disease incident to cows, by which the joint of the tail near the rump, will, as it were, rot away. **1864** WEBSTER, **Tail-stock*, the sliding block or support, in a lathe, which carries the tail-screw and adjustable center. **1859** F. GRIFFITHS *Artil. Man.* (1862) 318 If the moveable block of a tackle be strapped with a tail, it is called a *tail*, or *jigger block*: and the tackle a **tail*, or *jigger tackle*. **1823** P. NICHOLSON *Pract. Build.* 594 **Tail-trimmer*, a trimmer next to the wall, into which the ends of joists are fastened. **1898** *Westm. Gaz.* 9 Dec. 7/1 He was..in the hands of clerks and restless explorers who longed to *tail-twist and otherwise annoy. **1839** EDWARDES *Sardinia* 375 A terrible amount of *tail-twisting, kicking and anathematization. **1896** *Westm. Gaz.* 4 Nov. 1/3 If the temper of the British lion is at all affected by the tail-twisting process, he must be in a rage just now and roaring loudly. Tail-twisting seems to be the principal employment of the New York Bryanites. **1902** *Daily Chron.* 13 May 10/6 Fur Trade.—Girls wanted, used to boa and tail twisting. **1839** R. S. ROBINSON *Naut. Steam Eng.* 131 It will have to pass through the blow-through, or *tail valve. **1885** C. G. W. LOCK *Workshop Receipts* Ser. IV. 99/2 It is usual to fix an extra valve, called a 'tail' valve, to prevent the water from running out of the pipe when not in use. **1759** SMEATON in *Phil. Trans.* LI. 138 An overshot [wheel], whose height is equal to the difference of level, between the point where it strikes the wheel and the level of the *tail-water. **1825** J. NICHOLSON *Operat. Mechanic* 103 When the water in the mill-tail will not run off freely, but stands pent up in the wheel-race, so that the wheel must work or row in it, the wheel is said to be tailed, or to be in back-water or tail-water. **1905** *Westm. Gaz.* 17 Mar. 9/1 At Molesey Lock the tail water was almost five feet above the summer level. **1811** G. S. KEITH *Agric. Surv. Aberdeen* 491 The *tail-worm is also cured by cutting off a few inches of the tail, which bleeds pretty freely. **1816** TOWNE *Farmer & Grazier's Guide* 67 Tail Worm. In that Part of the Tail which is affected..the Spine appears deprived of Sensibility. **1846** LINDLEY *Veg. Kingd.* 213 *Triuridaceæ.* *Tailworts.

**Tail** (tēl), *sb.*[2] Forms: 4–6 **tayle, tayll, taill,** 4–8 **taille, taile,** 5–7 **taylle,** (5 **tayille,** 6 **tall**), 4– **tail.** [a. OF. *taille* cut, cutting, division, partition or assessment of a subsidy or impost, tax (12th c. in Hatz.-Darm.), vbl. sb. f. *taillier* to cut, TAIL *v.*[2] But, in sense 4, OF. *taille* was perh. :— L. *tālea*, med.L. *tālia* stick, rod: cf. TALLY.

*Tail* in *K. Alisaunder* 2217 (Weber) appears to be a scribal error; MS. Bodley, Laud Misc. 622, has 'among the toyle Hardapilon'.]

**I.** † **1.** Shape, fashion, bodily form or appearance. [F. *taille*; cf. CUT *sb.*[2] 16.] *Obs. rare.*

*c* **1300** *Cursor M.* 11855 (Cott.) Yee se he has na mans taill [*v.rr.* taille, tale, taile] þar-for yee sai me your consaill. *c* **1325** *Poem Times Edw. II* 282 in *Pol. Songs* (Camden) 336 A newe taille of squierie is nu in everi toun.

**II. †2.** The individual assessment of a subsidy or tallage levied by the king or lord; a tax, impost, due, duty, or payment levied. *Obs.*

**1340** *Ayenb.* 38 Kueade lordes..þet be-ulaȝeþ þe poure men: þet hi ssolden loki, be tayles, be tornees. **1375** BARBOUR *Bruce* XII. 320 Gif ony deis in this battaill, His air, but ward, releif, or taill, On the first day his land sall weild. *a* **1450** *Knt. de la Tour* (1906) 89 That quene..dede mani aduersiteez to the pepille, by tailez and subsidiez. **1456** SIR G. HAYE *Law Arms* (S.T.S.) 93 Kirk men suld pay tailles, tributis and imposicionis to seclere kingis. *c* **1460** FORTESCUE *Abs. & Lim. Mon.* i. (1885) 109 [The king] mey sett vppon thaim tayles and other imposicions, such as he wol hym self, with owt thair assent. *a* **1577** SIR T. SMITH *Commw. Eng.* (1633) 59 The Yeoman or Husbond man is no more subject to taile or taxe in England. **1645** MILTON *Tetrach.* Wks. 1851 IV. 254 Not the drudging out a poore and worthlesse duty forc't from us by the taxe, and taile of so many letters.

‖ **b.** Now only as Fr., in form *taille.* A tax formerly levied upon the unprivileged classes in France.

*a* **1533** LD. BERNERS *Huon* lx. 210 He hath reysyd vp in all his londes new taylles & gables & impossessyons. **1554** WOTTON *Let.* 29 July in *State Pap. Mary, Foreign* IV. 193 (P. R. O.) The priuiledges of nobilite, emonge the which one is that the gentlemen pay nothing to the ordinarye taylles, which alle Fraunce payeth continuallye to the king. **1682** WARBURTON *Hist. Guernsey* (1822) 48 They should be exempted from all gendarmeries, tailles. **1792** A. YOUNG *Trav. France* 30 The money is raised by tailles, and, in making the assessment, lands held by a noble tenure are so much eased, and others by a base one so burthened, that 120 arpents..held by the former, pay 90 liv. and 400 possessed by a plebeian right..is, instead of that, assessed at 1400 liv. **1863** KIRK *Chas. Bold* I. v. 216 The *taille* and the *gabelle* levied on the villain burghers. **1877** MORLEY *Crit. Misc.* II. 200 The great fiscal grievance of old France was the *taille*, a tax raised..only on the property and income of the unprivileged classes.

**III. 3.** *Law.* The limitation or destination of a freehold estate or fee to a person and the heirs of his body, or some particular class of such heirs, on the failure of whom it is to revert to the donor or his heir or assign. [Cf. TAIL *a.*, TAIL *v.*[2] 5; = TAILYE *sb.* 3.] Hence phrase *in tail*, as *estate in tail, tenant in tail, heir in tail,* i.e. within or under the limitation in question.

[**1321–2** *Rolls of Parlt.* I. 394/2 C'est son droit par vertu de la taille avantdit [i.e. an entail to heirs of the body of the spouses].] **1373–5** in *Calr. Proc. Chanc. Q. Eliz.* (1830) I. Pref. 59 An olde dede..comprisynge the wordes of a tayll made in Kynge Edwardes tyme the second. **1439** in *E. E. Wills* (1882) 125 And aftir him and his issue, to Iohn his brother, and his issue in the taile. *c* **1460** FORTESCUE *Abs. & Lim. Mon.* xi. (1885) 136 To some parte þeroff the eyres off thaim þat some tyme owed it be restored; some bi reason off tayles, some bi reason off oþer titles. **1479** in *Bury Wills* (Camden) 52 And after the decess of the seid Alice, I will that the seid maner shall remayne to the issues of my body lawfully begoten accordyng to the tayle therof made. **1523** FITZHERB. *Surv.* 11 If the gyfte were in the tayle and no remaynder in fe euer, nowe the reuercyon resteth styll in yͤ donor. **1607** COWELL *Interpr., Taile,..* is vsed for the fee, which is opposite to fee simple: by reason that it is so..minced, or pared, that it is not in his free power to be disposed,..but is..tyed to the issue of the Donee...This limitation, or taile, is either generall, or speciall. **1718** PRIOR *Chameleon* 7 As if the Rain-bow were in Tail Settled on him [a Chameleon] and his Heirs Male. **1766** BLACKSTONE *Comm.* II. vii. 115 The incidents to a tenancy in tail. **1796** MORSE *Amer. Geog.* I. 463 All estates given in tail..shall become fee simple estates to the issue of the first donee in tail [cf. quot. 1876]. **1868** ROGERS *Pol. Econ.* xiii. (1876) 177 The defendant a donee in tail, i.e. a person in whose behalf an estate tail had been created. **1876** BANCROFT *Hist. U.S.* V. xv. 516 All donees in tail, by the act of this first republican legislature of Virginia, were vested with the absolute dominion of the property entailed. **1893** MARY CHOLMONDELEY *D. Tempest* iii, You're in the tail, I suppose?

**b.** With qualifying adjective: *tail general*, limitation of an estate to a man and the heirs of his body lawfully begotten; *tail special,* limitation of an estate to a special class of heirs, e.g. to a man and his wife and the heirs of their bodies lawfully begotten; *tail male* (or *female*), limitation of an estate to male (or female) heirs.

**1495** *Rolls of Parlt.* VI. 485/1 Seised, in his or their Demeane as of Fee, Fee Tayll generall or speciall, or any other astate. **1503** HAWES *Examp. Virt.* xiv. 10 To whome heuen by tayll generall Entayled is by a dede memoryall. **1642** tr. *Perkins' Prof. Bk.* v. § 302. 134 If Tenant in generall taile, take a wife and enfeoff a stranger, and take back an estate unto him and his wife in speciall taile. **1710** *Lond. Gaz.* No. 4735/4 Then to his first Son in Tail Male, then to his Daughter in Tail general. **1766** BLACKSTONE *Comm.* II. vii. 113. **1796** MORSE *Amer. Geog.* I. 707 They agreed to grant their lands in tail male in preference to tail general. **1844** WILLIAMS *Real Prop.* (1877) 35 An estate in tail male cannot descend to any but males, and male descendants of males. *Ibid.*, Tail female scarcely ever occurs.

**IV. †4.** = TALLY *sb.*[1] 1; hence, a score, an account. *By tail*, by means of tallies; on credit. (Cf. *on tick.*) *Obs.* [Cf. Cotgr. '*Taille*..also, a tallie, or score kept on a peece of wood'.]

[**1114–18** *Leges Henrici I.* c. 56 § 1 Si..controuersia oriatur, siue de taleis agatur siue de supplecione in ipso manerio. **1312** *Rolls of Parlt.* I. 284/1 Les gentz ount diverses acquitaunces, les unes par tailes & par brefs, & les unes par diverses fraunchises.] *a* **1325** tr. *Estatuz del Eschekere* (MS. Rawl. B. 520 lf. 36 b), ȝif ani bringe taille ase of paie imad ate chekere. **1362** LANGL. *P. Pl.* A. IV. 45 He ..bereþ awei my whete, And takeþ me bote a tayle [B. IV. 58 taile, taille] of Ten quarter oten. *c* **1386** CHAUCER *Prol.* 570 Wheither that he payde, or took by taille [*v.rr.* taile, tayle]. **1443** HEN. VI *Let.* in Ellis *Orig. Lett.* Ser. III. I. 81 Ther shall be made and delivered..sufficient assignement for your repaiement therof by tailles to be rered at the said Eschequier. **1512** *Earl Northumberland's Househ. Bk.* (1770) 172 The stok of the Tail to be delivert to the Brewar ande the Swatche to the Butler. **1530** PALSGR. 184 *Vnes taylles*, a payre of taylles, suche as folke use to score upon for rekennyng. *Ibid.* 644/1, I nycke, I make nyckes on a tayle, or on a stycke, *je oche.* **1556** WITHALS *Dict.* 56 a/2 A score or tayle to marke the dette vpon, *tessera, vel tessella.* **1607** COWELL *Interpr.* s.v., Taile in the other signification, is what we vulgarly call a Tallie;..a clouen peece of wood to nick vp an accompt vpon. **1647** *City Law London* 49 A Taile of debt ensealed by usage of the city, is as strong as an obligation. **1677** CARY *Chronol.* I. I. I. i. 2 These were the Tailles (as I may so say) by which they marked..the Signal Occurrences of their Life.

**† b.** *fig.* Account, reckoning. *Obs.*

*c* **1330** R. BRUNNE *Chron. Wace* (Rolls) 896 Wyþoute seriauntz & oþer pytaille Þat ar nought for to sette in taille. *Ibid.* 1316 Þre hundred schipes þer was in taille, And foure mo. **1421** *Coventry Leet Bk.* 24 Hit is do the maiour to witt þat tauerners haue sold wyne to certen men of hur alye, by Tailes maid bytwen them, derre than þe maiour hathe ordenyd hit to be sold.

**5.** *Comb.* **† tail-maker,** (?) one who fashioned the tallies used in the Exchequer; **† tailstick,** a tally-stick. *Obs.*

**1235–52** *Rentalia Glaston.* (Som. Rec. Soc.) 217, j porcellum et taylstich' cujuslibet porci necati provenientis de sua custodia. *a* **1577** SIR T. SMITH *Commw. Eng.* (1609) 71 Other officers are Tellers, Auditors, Collectors, rentgatherers, tailemakers.

**Tail** (tēil), *a. Law.* [a. AF. *taylé, tailé* = OF. *taillié, taillé,* pa. pple. of *taillier* to cut, shape, hence, to fix the precise form of, to limit, TAIL *v.*[2]; the final *e* having become mute in ME. as in *assign, avowe* sbs., and some other legal terms.]

Of a fee or freehold estate (= AF. *fee taylé*, med. Anglo-L. *feodum tāliātum*): Limited and regulated as to its tenure and inheritance by conditions fixed by the donor: thus distinguished from *fee simple* or absolute ownership: see quot. 1592. See also FEE-TAIL, CONDITIONAL *a.* 7.

[**1284** *De Banco Roll*, Mich. 11–12 Edw. I. m. 70 d. Quod predicta Emma non habuit in predictis tenementis nisi feodum talliatum secundum formam donacionis predicte. **1285** *Stat. Westm.* II. (13 Edw. I.) c. 4 Tenentes in maritagium per Legem Anglie, vel ad terminum vite, vel per feodum talliatum. [*tr.* 1543 tenantes in free maryage, by the lawe of Englande, or for terme of lyfe, or in fee taile.] **1292** BRITTON II. iii. § 9 Des queus douns aucuns sount condicionels et dount le fee est taylé et en pendaunt jekes autaunt qe cele chose aveigne ou cele. **1294** *Year bks.* 21–2 *Edw. I* (Rolls 1873) 641 Kar le estatut 'quia emptores terrarum &c.' est entendu la ou home feffe un autre en fee pur, e nent de fee tayle.] **1473** *Rolls of Parlt.* VI. 81/1 That this Acte..extend not..to Sir Thomas Bourghchier Knyght, ne to his heires masles of his body lawfully begoten,..duryng the seid astate Taille, of, to, or for any Graunte or Grauntes unto hym made. **1473–5** in *Calr. Proc. Chanc. Q. Eliz.* (1830) II. Pref. 58 To make and delyvere unto her a lawefull estate tayle of alle the forseid landes. **1592** WEST *1st Pt. Symbol.* § 40 B, A perticuler estate of inheritance, is an estate taile or limited: that is an estate expressing in certaine, whose issue and of what Sexe shall inherite; and it is generall or speciall. **1628** COKE *On Litt.* 26 If lands bee giuen to the husband & the wife, and to the heires which the husband shall beget on the body of the wife, in this case both of them haue an estate taile. **1766** BLACKSTONE *Comm.* II. vii. 112. **1818** CRUISE *Digest* (ed. 2) I. 90 Estates tail, like estates in fee simple, have certain incidents annexed to them, which cannot be restrained by any proviso or condition whatever. **1895** POLLOCK & MAITL. *Hist. Eng. Law* II. II. iv. § 1. 19 In 1285 the first chapter of the Second Statute of Westminster, the famous *De donis conditionalibus*, laid down a new rule. The 'conditional fee' of former times became known as a fee tail (Lat. *feodum talliatum*, Fr. *fee taillé*)..and about the same time the term *fee simple* was adopted to describe the estate which a man has who holds 'to him and his heirs'.

**Tail** (tēil), *v.*[1] [f. TAIL *sb.*[1]; in various unconnected senses.]

**I.** Transitive uses.

**1.** To furnish with a tail or final appendage.

(In early use only in the pa. pple.: see TAILED *ppl. a.*[1] 1.)

**1817** COLERIDGE *Satyrane's Lett.* ii. 211 The cap behind tailed with an enormous quantity of ribbon. **1876** PREECE & SIVEWRIGHT *Telegraphy* 224 A double shackle is fixed, and each side is first 'tailed', that is to say, a wire is passed round the porcelain and bound in the ordinary way, leaving one end projecting to a distance of from eighteen inches to two feet. **1879** BARING-GOULD *Germany* I. ii. 46 In England now anyone adopts arms, and tails his name with esquire, whether he have a right or not to these distinctions.

**2.** To grasp or drag by the tail.

† *To stave and tail*, to take part in bear-baiting or bull-baiting, by staving the bear or bull, or tailing the dogs.

**1663** BUTLER *Hud.* I. II. 163 Lawyers, lest the Bear Defendant, And Plaintiff Dog should make an end on't, Do stave and tail with Writs of Error, Reverse of Judgment, and Demurrer. *Ibid.* III. 134 First Trulla stav'd, and Cerdon tail'd, Until their Mastives loos'd their hold. **1867** F. FRANCIS *Angling* i. (1880) 12 Tailing a fish out is more often employed on salmon. **1892** MRS. J. GORDON *Eunice Anscombe* 177 One..dived forward in a vain attempt to 'tail' the otter. **1893** *Field* 11 Mar. 360/2 Grasp it [the fish] above the tail—'tail it', to employ the technical phrase.

**3.** To dock the tail of (a lamb, etc.); to cut or pull off that which is regarded as the tail, esp. of a plant or fruit. (Cf. TOP *v.*)

**1794** *Rigging & Seamanship* I. 61 Hemp..should be well topt, and tailed; that is, both ends cleared by the hatchell. **1824** L. M. HAWKINS *Mem., Anecd.,* etc. II. 52 A gentleman..was topping and tailing gooseberries for wine. **1844** STEPHENS *Bk. Farm* II. 42 Another worker..tops and tails the turnips. **1886** C. SCOTT *Sheep-Farming* 88 The number of lambs castrated and tailed.

**4.** To form the tail or last member of (a procession, etc.); to terminate. (Cf. HEAD *v.* 10.)

**1835** *Fraser's Mag.* XI. 465 A male author heads and a male author tails the procession. **1890** *Pall Mall G.* 9 June 4/2 The quaint little procession headed..by the officially-robed Lord Chancellor, and tailed by the blue-gowned Common Councilmen. **1894** R. H. DAVIS *Eng. Cousins* 117 The boat which is to tail the procession.

**5.** In Australia: To follow, drive, or tend (sheep or cattle).

**1844** *Port Phillip Patriot* 5 Aug. 3/6, I know many boys from the age of nine to sixteen years tailing cattle. **1852** MUNDY *Our Antipodes* I. x. 314 The stockman..considers 'tailing sheep' as an employment too tard'grade for a man of action and spirit. **1890** 'R. BOLDREWOOD' *Col. Reformer* (1891) 239 The cattle..being..'tailed' or followed daily as a shepherd does sheep.

**6.** *U. S. local.* (See quots.)

**1792** BELKNAP *Hist. New Hampsh.* III. 106 In descending a long and steep hill, they have a contrivance to prevent the load from making too rapid a descent. Some of the cattle are placed behind it; a chain..attached to their yokes is brought forward and fastened to the hinder end of the load, and the resistance which is made by these cattle checks the descent. This operation is called *tailing.* **1851** *Harper's Mag.* III. 518 In this manner the load is tailed down steeps where it would be impossible for the tongue-oxen to resist the pressure of the load.

**7.** To attach to the tail or hind end of something else; to join on behind, annex, subjoin *to.*

**1523** LD. BERNERS *Froiss.* I. xci. 113 They toke foure Englysshe shyppes..and tayled them to their shyppes. **1589** PUTTENHAM *Eng. Poesie* II. xii. (Arb.) 128 Wordes monosillables,..if they be tailed one to another, or th'one to a dissillable or polyssillable. **1633** J. CLARKE *2nd Praxis* 44 *Ne* is alwayes tayled to the first word of the Interrogation. **1681** RYCAUT tr. *Gracian's Critick* 224 They met great Mules tailed one to the other. **1685** J. SCOTT *Chr. Life* II. 155 What is this but to tail one folly to another? **1851** MAYHEW *Lond. Labour* II. 161/2 Each new row of houses tailed on its drains to those of its neighbours.

**8.** *Building.* To insert the tail or end of (a beam, stone, or brick) *into* a wall, etc.; to let in, dovetail.

**1823** P. NICHOLSON *Pract. Build.* 365 Party-walls may also be cut into for the purposes of tailing-in stone steps. *c* **1850** *Rudim. Navig.* (Weale) 155 To *tail*, or *dovetail*, to let one piece of timber into another.

**9.** *passive.* Of a mill-wheel: To be clogged by tail-water (q. v., s. v. TAIL *sb.*[1] 14, quot. 1825).

**II.** Intransitive uses.

**10.** Of a ship: To run *aground* stern foremost.

**1725** DE FOE *Voy. round World* (1840) 147 She tailed aground upon a sand bank. **1799** *Naval Chron.* I. 258 The Formidable..tailed on the..mud. *c* **1850** *Rudim. Navig.* (Weale) 117 It is to..preserve the main post, should the ship tail aground.

**11.** Of water, flame, etc.: To flow or creep back against the current; to run back, recoil.

**1799** *Trans. Soc. Arts* XVII. 349 Floods are very apt to dam or tail-back, and thereby impede or clog the..wheel. **1883** GRESLEY *Coal Mining Gloss.* s.v., When fire-damp ignites..and the flame..creeps backwards against the current of air..it is said to tail back into the workings.

**12.** Of a moving body of men or animals: **a.** To lengthen out into a straggling line, as in hunting, racing, etc.; to drop behind, fall away.

**1781** W. BLANE *Ess. Hunting* (1788) 116 [The hounds] not being of equal speed..will be found to tail, which is an inconveniency. **1862** WHYTE MELVILLE *Ins. Bar* x. **1864** TREVELYAN *Compet. Wallah* (1866) 134 As down towards Barton Wold we sail, The Cockneys soon began to tail. **1897** THORNTON *Remin. Clergyman* i. 2 Then straggling, tailing, as the fox-hunters phrase it, up came the field.

**b.** To move or proceed in the form of a line or tail; to fall into a line or tail.

**1859** KINGSLEY *Misc.* (1860) I. 160 If ten men tail through a gap. **1882** MOZLEY *Remin.* I. xix. 128 The congregation ..came down the road in a dense black mass, but obliged to tail a little. **1899** ANNIE E. HOLDSWORTH *Valley Gr. Shadow* x, The procession was tailing to Bergstein.

**13.** To take a position in which the tail or rear is directed away from the wind. current, etc.

**1849** DANA *Geol.* ii. (1850) 115 In more moderate weather the vessel tails out against the wind. **1860** MAURY *Phys. Geog. Sea* ii. 29 Sea-weed always 'tails to' a steady or a constant wind. **1867** SMYTH *Sailor's Word-bk.* s.v., *To tail up* or *down a stream*, when at anchor in a river, is as a ship's stern swings.

**14.** *Building.* Of a beam, stone, or brick: To have its end let into a wall, etc.: cf. 8.

**1842–76** GWILT *Archit.* Gloss. s.v., Where the end of a timber lies or tails upon the walls. **1892** MIDDLETON *Rome* I. 62 Blocks of tufa..tailing 3 to 5 inches into the concrete backing.

**15.** Of a stream: To flow or fall *into.* (Cf. HEAD *v.* 7.)

**1889** *Blackw. Mag.* Apr. 456 *note*, The Dorak canal, which tails into the Jarrahi river. **1900** *Westm. Gaz.* 10 July 2/2 All the channels and spills tailed into the Ziraf.

**16.** Of a fish: To show its tail at the surface.

**1892** in *Daily News* 21 May 5/2 The Man sees there is no fly up. The Man sees the fish are tailing. **1908** *Edin. Rev.*

Apr. 391 When trout are 'tailing' they break the surface with their caudal fin as they grub with their noses for water shrimps.

**17.** *Calico-printing.* Of a colour, etc.: To spread beyond its proper limits in a tail-like blur.

**III.** With adverbs.

**18. Tail away.** *intr.* To fall away in a tail or straggling line; to die away.

**1860** RUSSELL *Diary India* II. xix. 369 They were, however, tailing away fast, as we afterwards discovered. **1905** HICHENS *Garden Allah* vii, The arid, sunburnt tracts, where its life centred and where it tailed away into suburban edges not unlike the ragged edges of worn garments.

**19. Tail off** (out). **a.** *trans.* To cause to fall away gradually towards the end; to taper off.

**1827** STEUART *Planter's G.* (1828) 304 They [artificial hillocks] should be well 'tailed out', as the workmen call it,.. letting their hard outline imperceptibly disappear, and, as it were, die away in the outline of the adjoining surface. **1842** S. LOVER *Handy Andy* v, He..finished it in a gentle murmur—tailed it off very taper, indeed.

**b.** *intr.* To fall away in a tail; to diminish and cease; to come gradually to an end; to subside.

**1854** HOOKER *Himal. Jrnls.* I. xvii. 396 It tailed off abruptly at the junction of the rivers. **1862** *Lond. Soc.* II. 86 Already the weaker horses are weeded out, and the poorer spirited are tailing off. **1898** *Allbutt's Syst. Med.* V. 977 The dull sound of valvular tension may be heard to precede it [a cardiac bruit], when it 'tails off' from the first sound. **1905** F. YOUNG *Sands of Pleasure* I. iv, His voice tailed off into a sigh.

**c.** *intr.* To turn tail, take to flight, go or run off; to withdraw. *colloq.*

**1841** F. E. PAGET *S. Antholin's* vii. 146 Mrs. Spatterdash ..tailed off at last to a dissenting chapel. **1868** — *Lucretia* 102 He ducked his head; made a slouching bow; tailed off to his pigs. **1877** KINGLAKE *Crimea* VI. vi. 376 Some.. even tailed off. **1885** RIDER HAGGARD *K. Solomon's M.* xvi, I was tailing out of it as hard as my legs would carry me.

**d.** *trans* To pass and leave behind (other competitors in a race, etc.).

**1852** BATEMAN *Aquatic Notes* 52 They got close to them at Grassy [corner], but were tailed-off in the Long Reach. **1907** *Times* 6 June 4/3 He was..one of the leaders for half a mile, but afterwards he was tailed off.

**20. Tail on.** **a.** *trans.* To add on as an appendage. **b.** *intr.* To join on in the rear.

**1825** (Jan. 3) CAPT. B. HALL in Lockhart *Scott*, Anxious to tail on a branch from Melrose to meet the [projected railway from Berwick to Kelso]. **1862** MAYHEW *Boyhood Luther* i. (1863) 11 As the long train swept by, the peasants and villagers tailed on to the rest. **1874** BURNIE *Mem. Thomas* 451 A superb passenger car which tails on to the trucks. **1880** CLARK RUSSELL *Sailor's Sweetheart* xiv, All hands tailing on, we ran it [a boom] through the bowsprit cap.

**Tail** (tēil), *v.*2 Forms: 4-5 taille, 4-6 taylle, tayle, taile, (6 talle, tale), 6- tail. [ME. *taile*, a. OF. *taillier*, 3 sing. pres. *taille* (S. Leger *a* 1000), to cut, shape by cutting, determine the form of, limit, etc.; in mod.F. *tailler* to cut, etc.; = Pr. *talhar*, *talar*, Cat. *tallar*, Sp. *tajar*, Pg. *talhar*, It. *tagliare*, to cut:—late pop. and med.L. *tāliāre*, *talliāre*, f. *tal(l)ia*, in cl. L. *tālea* rod, twig, cutting: see TALLY *sb*1 OF. *taillier* gave *taille* vbl. sb., TAIL *sb*2, whence again *taillier* vb. to impose a tax on, to tax: see sense 6 below.]

**I.** In literal and connected senses.

†**1.** *trans.* To cut, esp. to a certain size or shape; to shape, fashion; *well tailed*, well shaped or fashioned. See also TAILED *ppl. a.*2 1. *Obs.*

*c* **1400** *Laud Troy Bk.* 3154 Thenne by-gan this clerkes to tayle Parchemyn and lettres dite. **1422** tr. *Secreta Secret., Priv. Priv.* 227 Thay that haue the shuldres hangynge downe-ward and welle taillet, bene fre and lyberall. **1558** *Acc. Fratern. Holy Ghost, Basingstoke* (1882) 9 Paide.. for fellinge the oke..Item payde..for tallinge and sawinge of the same.

†**2.** To cut up, cut to pieces, slaughter. *Obs.*

*c* **1330** R. BRUNNE *Chron. Wace* (Rolls) 14136 Arthur sey þe day gan faille, He bod & stynte his folk to taille. [*Taile* in *K. Alisaunder* 2133 (Weber) is a scribal error; MS. Bodley, Laud Misc. 622 has (l. 2137) 'Bigynneþ 3oure fomen coile Alto slei3te & nou3th to spoyle'.]

†**3.** To put into shape, trim, make ready. (Cf. OF. *metre en taille.*) *Obs.*

*c* **1330** R. BRUNNE *Chron.* (1810) 115 Dauid of Scotland hasted to þe bataile, Walter Spek ros on hand, þe folk to forme & taile. *c* **1330** — *Chron. Wace* (Rolls) 12081 Mariners dighte þem..þer takel for to righte & taille. *c* **1375** *Sc. Leg. Saints* xxiii. (*vii Sleperis*) 237 þai..bad malchus he suld hyme taile, & pas to þe towne fore vitale.

**II.** [a. AF. *tailler*, OF. *taillier* in sense 'to determine, fix, appoint': cf. the Sc. form TAILYE. But, in sense 5, in later use app. f. TAIL *sb.*2 3.]

†**4.** To decide or determine in a specified way; to settle, arrange, or fix (a matter).

[OF. *taillier*: cf. *c* 1250 in Godef. 'Puis fu la pais ensi taillie que..'.]

*c* **1315** SHOREHAM *Poems* vii. 817 And was þat conseyl so y-tayled, Þat hyt ne my3te habbe faylled To bote of manne. **1375** BARBOUR *Bruce* XVIII. 238 (Edin. MS.) At that tyme he wald him taile, To dystroy wp sa clene the land, That nane suld leve tharin liffand. *Ibid.* XIX. 188 (MS. C) [see TAILYE *v.* 2]. *c* **1425** WYNTOUN *Cron.* VIII. 5309 (Cotton MS.) Had þe Talbot, as talyt [*Wemyss MS.* tal3eit] was, Iustit, he had suelt in þat plasse. **1472–3** *Rolls of Parlt.* VI. 24/1 Yf the seid William Lord Berkeley and Johan his wyfe.. cause or suffre any recovere to be had or tayled ayenst theym ..by their covyne or assent.

**5.** *trans. Law.* To limit (an estate of inheritance) to the donee and his heirs general or special; to grant in tail (TAIL *sb.*2 3); to tie up by entail; to ENTAIL.

[**1292** BRITTON II. iii. § 9: see TAIL *a.*] **1425** in *E. E. Wills* 64 My lande þat is tayled to him. **1425** *Rolls of Parlt.* IV. 274/2 By cause ye name of Duc of Norffolke is tailled to me, and to my heirs males of my body commyng: and ye name of Erel of Norffolke is tailled to me, and to my heirs of my body commyng generaly. **1483** *Ibid.* VI. 253/1 Hereditaments, that were tailled to hym, or to eny other of his Auncesters, by dede or withoute dede. **1501** *Plumpton Corr.* (Camden) 152 If Mr. Eleson can fynd any of your lands talled to the here male, send copies therof; I thinke none be. **1647** N. BACON *Disc. Govt. Eng.* I. xli. (1739) 66 In latter times this estate was also tailed, or cut out sometimes to the Sons and Daughters severally. **1864** SERJT. MANNING in *Athenæum* 27 Feb. 302/2 The great landholders..obtained an Act of Parliament, called the statute *de donis*, which directed that thenceforth the will of the donor should be strictly observed. Upon this the lands so tailed (appointed) became inalienable.

**III.** Related to *tail* tax, impost (TAIL *sb.*2 2).

†**6.** *trans.* To impose a 'tail' or tax upon; to tax. [OF. *taillier*, med.L. *tāl(l)iare*, Du Cange.] *Obs.*

*c* **1330** R. BRUNNE *Chron. Wace* (Rolls) 2382 Þe Duk of Cornewaille, Al þe souþ tyl hym gan taylle. *Ibid.* 16550 Ffro Scotland vntil Cornewaille, Al þe lond gan þey [the Saxons] taille. **1474** *Rolls of Parlt.* VI. 165/1 That the Maier, Bailyfs and Cominalte..to xx li only..shulden be assessed, taxed and tailed. **1525** LD. BERNERS *Froiss.* II. lxii. [lxv.] 210 Nowe they tayle theyr people at theyr pleasure. *a* **1577** SIR T. SMITH *Commw. Eng.* (1633) 263 In France the Lords doe taile them whom they call their subjects at their pleasure and cause them to pay summes of money.

**IV.** Related to *tail* a tally (TAIL *sb.*2 4).

†**7.** *trans.* To mark or record on a tally; to charge (a person) with a debt; *transf.* to make a mark on, to mark. *Obs.*

**1377** LANGL. *P. Pl.* B. v. 429 3if I bigge and borwe it, but 3if it be ytailled [*v.r.* tailled, **1393** C. VIII. 35 y-tayled] I for3ete it as 3erne. ? *a* **1500** *Chester Pl.* vii. 410 Nay, he come by night—all things lafte—Our tuppes with tar to tayle. **1655** FULLER *Ch. Hist.* XI. i. § 10 His bond of two thousand pounds wherewith he was tailed, continued uncancelled, and was called on the next Parliament.

†**8.** *intr.* To deal by tally, or on credit. *Obs.*

**1514** SIR R. JERNEGAN *Let.* in Strype *Eccl. Mem.* (1721) I. App. v. 10 They [of the garrison] had offered the victualers to taylle with them and to set it upon scores:..for mony they had none. **1570** FOXE *A. & M.* (ed. 2) 413/1 He was in great debt..dryuen to tale [*so edd.* 1576–83; *ed.* 1596 tallie] for his owne cates.

†**9.** *trans.* To tally or agree with; to equal; = TALLY *v.*1 5. *Obs.*

**1638** FORD *Lady's Trial* III. iii, Sure this bulk of mine, Tails in the size! a tympany of greatness, Puffs up too monstrously my narrow chest.

**Tail,** *v.*3 [Local variant of TILL *v.*] *trans.* To set (a trap or snare); to bait (a trap).

**1862** *Telegram* (Yeovil) 15 Feb., The defendant..proceeded some distance lower, and tailed another trap. **1899** C. K. PAUL *Memories* 250 To tail a trap, to set or bait it. **1901** *Blackw. Mag.* Nov. 691/1 There are the traps to tail.

**Tail, Tailage,** obs. ff. TALE, TALLAGE *sb.*1

†**Tai·lard.** *Obs.* In 4 taylard. [f. TAIL *sb.*1 + -ARD.] One with a tail.

An opprobrious epithet founded on a legend told first of St. Augustine at Dorchester (or Rochester), and later of Thomas a Becket in Kent, in which the people of these places were said to be cursed with tails for indignities done by attaching a tail to these holy men. See Layamon 29535–86, Fuller *Ch. Hist.* II. ii. § 22, Lambarde *Kent* 400, Stanley *Hist. Mem. Cant.* (1872) I. 53, and references in the last. On the continent, tails used to be ascribed to Englishmen generally. Cf. TAILED 1 and LONG-TAIL 2 a.

**13..** *Coer de L.* 724 The kyng callid Rychard be name, And clepyd hym taylard, and sayde hym schame. *Ibid.* 1996. *Ibid.* 2112 The emperour..cried, as uncourteys: Out, taylards, of my paleys! Now go and say your tayled king That I owe him no thing.

**Tail-board** (tēi·lbōəɹd). [f. TAIL *sb.*1 + BOARD.] **1.** The board at the hinder end of a cart, barrow, van, etc.; usually one attached to the bottom by a hinge, and capable of being suspended at various angles for convenience in loading, etc.

**1805** *Chron.* in *Ann. Reg.* 376/1 She was crushed between the tail-board of the cart and the house. **1847** ALB. SMITH *Chr. Tadpole* xlvi. (1879) 405 Have you..a shutter, or the tail-board of a cart..you can carry him on? **1881** YOUNG *Ev. Man his Own Mechanic* § 1072 The parts which compose the barrow may be enumerated as the two sides, the front, the tail board, the bottom, the wheel, and the legs.

**2.** (See quot.)

**1841** TOTTEN *Naval Textbk.* (U.S.) 411 *Tailboards*, in shipbuilding, the carved work between the cheeks, fastened to the knee of the head.

**Tailed** (tēild), *a.* and *ppl. a.*1 Also 4–5 ytailed. [f. TAIL *sb.*1 and *v.*1 + -ED.]

**1.** Having, or furnished with, a tail or tails; in *Zool.* and *Bot.* = CAUDATE. Often in parasynthetic comb., as *long-tailed*, *white-tailed*, etc.

**1297** R. GLOUC. (Rolls) 8821 Men ieie iwis þe tailede sterre, þat gret bodiinge is. *c* **1330** R. BRUNNE *Chron.* (1810) 158 What haf I to do with Inglis tayled kyng? *a* **1400** *R. Glouc.'s Chron.* (Rolls) App. T. 10 3ute libbeþ of þe kunde ytailed mani3e so. **1413** *Pilgr. Sowle* (Caxton) I. xx. (1859) 20 Thenne answered this tailed worm. **1594** BLUNDEVIL *Exerc.* v. xii. (1636) 556 He is eared and tailed like a Rat. **1601** HOLLAND *Pliny* (1634) I. 352 Panthers are not after the same manner tailed. **1767** GOOCH *Treat. Wounds* I. 147 That called the tailed-bandage, used in compound fractures. **1848** DICKENS *Dombey* v, [A] blue baize tailed coat. **1890** JULIA BALLARD *Among Moths* 17 The hinder wings tailed.

†**b.** Of cattle: = TAGGED 3. *Obs.*

**1539** *Will H. Myrth of Puriton, Somerset* 26 Oct. (MS.), To John Hore a taylyd heffer. **1543** *Will J. Popyll, Shapwick, Som.* 9 Jan., ij steyres a taylyd & a sterryd.

†**c.** Of malt: Containing the tails. *Obs.*

**1742** *Lond. & Country Brewer* I. (ed. 4) 75 This Caution against using tailed or dusty Malt.

**d.** *Tailed rime* (rarely *tail-rime*), rendering of F. *rime couée*, med.L. *rithmus caudātus* (see COUWEE), applied to a couplet, triplet, or stanza with a tail, tag, or additional short line, either unrimed or riming with another tag further on.

**1890** *Cent. Dict.* s.v. *Rime*1, Tailed rime. **1893** TRAILL *Soc. Eng.* I. iv. 448 [Verses] in *rime couée.* *Note*, Or tail-rime [ed. **1898** (also called tailed-rime)]: a stanza where some lines, usually the third and sixth, are shorter (*e.g.* Chaucer's Rime of Sir Thopas).

**2.** *ppl. a.* Deprived of the tail or tails.

**1550** *Proclam. Edw. VI* 20 Oct., Wheate..of the meanest sorte, not cleane or tailed. **1844** STEPHENS *Bk. Farm* II. 8 Topped and tailed turnips.

**Tailed** (tēild), *ppl. a.*2 [f. TAIL *v.*2 + -ED 1.]

†**1.** Cut; *esp.* cut to a special shape or size.

*c* **1430** *Two Cookery-bks.* 55 Take Roysonys of coraunce.. & taylid Datys y-kyt a-long. *a* **1552** LELAND *Itin.* V. lf. 66 Mr. Brainton..dyd fetch much tayled Stone there toward his buildinges.

**2.** *Law.* Of lands and tenements: Granted, settled, or held in tail (see TAIL *v.*2 5); = ENTAILED. *Obs.* or *arch.*

**1430–31** *Rolls of Parlt.* IV. 378/1 Toward eny tailled land. *c* **1475** *Harl. Contin. Higden* (Rolls) VIII. 502, I.. condempne..alle thy londes taylede and not taylede to be applyede to the use of the kynge for ever. **1523** FITZHERB. *Surv.* 18 b, Another forme of landes tayled with a remayndre ouer. **1593** *Calr. Laing Charters* (1899) 309 Outwith the teylit land and toftis presentlie occupiit.

**Tail-end** (tē·iˌle·nd). [f. TAIL *sb.*1 + END *sb.*]

**1.** The hindmost or lowest end of anything; that part which is opposite the head: cf. TAIL *sb.*1 4.

**1837** M. DONOVAN *Dom. Econ.* II. 277 A tail-end of a rump of beef, weighing 12¾ lb., when boiled gave 1½ lb. of bone. **1871** MORRIS in Mackail *Life* (1899) I. 255 Two or three tail-ends of glaciers dribbled over them [cliffs]. **1880** L. WALLACE *Ben Hur* IV. vii, A dray with low wheels and broad axle, surmounted by a box open at the tail-end.

*attrib.* **1904** *Westm. Gaz.* 11 Jan. 2/1 Fielder bowled very well indeed at the tail-end men of the Victorian eleven.

†**b.** *spec.* The backside, rump: = TAIL *sb.*1 5.

**1377** LANGL. *P. Pl.* B. v. 395 Were I brou3te abedde, but if my taille-ende it made, Sholde no ryngynge do me ryse, ar I were rype to dyne. **1401** *Pol. Poems* (Rolls) II. 50 Quenching of torches in 3ou tayl-ende.

**c.** *fig.*; *esp.* the concluding part of an action, period of time, etc.: cf. TAIL *sb.*1 4 b.

**1845** DARWIN in *Life & Lett.* (1887) II. 31, I am sorry to say I have not even the tail-end of a fact in English Zoology to communicate. **1872** BLACK *Adv. Phaeton* xxii, The tail-end of a shower caught us. **1887** *Spectator* 17 Sept. 1240 At the tail-end of the Session.

**2.** The end or tip of a tail. *rare.*

**3.** = TAILING *vbl. sb.*1 2 a.

**1859** GEO. ELIOT *A. Bede* vi, Everybody 'ud be wanting bread made o' tail-ends.

Hence **Tail-e·nder**, one that is at the tail-end.

**1895** *Outing* (U.S.) XXVI. 31/1 Six teal flew across the water, and I downed the tailender. **1908** *Daily Chron.* 8 Jan. 5/7 The Australians..failed because they could not get our tail-enders out.

**Tailer** (tēi·ləɹ). *Angling.* [f. TAIL *v.*1 + -ER 1.] A fish that tails: see TAIL *v.*1 16.

**1899** BUXTON in *19th Cent.* Jan. 120 A moderate performer with the rod..will often..pick up a grubber under the bank, a bulger here, a tailer there. **1899** *Daily News* 22 Apr. 8/3 Now, like a fan, the broad, waving tail of a 'tailer' shows yellow in upper air.

**Tailet** (tēi·lėt). *rare.* [f. TAIL *sb.*1 + -ET.] A minute tail or tail-like appendage.

**1817** KIRBY & SP. *Entomol.* xxiii. (1818) II. 346 Though the wings are the principal instruments of the flight of insects, yet there are others subsidiary to them...These are winglets, tailets, hooklets.

**Tailing** (tēi·liŋ), *vbl. sb.*1 [f. TAIL *v.*1 + -ING 1.]

**1.** The action of TAIL *v.*1, in its various senses.

**1703** MOXON *Mech. Exerc.* 267 You must Cement pieces to the ends of your bricks for tailing, or to make them longer. **1781** P. BECKFORD *Hunting* (1802) 70 *note*, The tailing of them [hounds' ears] is usually done before they are put out. **1829** *Nat. Philos.* I. *Hydraulics* iii. 26 (Usef. Knowl. Soc.) The tailing of mill-streams only occurs in the winter seasons, or at times when there is a profusion of water. **1840** HOOD *Up Rhine* 44 Short as the course was, it led to a great deal of what the turfmen call tailing. **1854** SCOFFERN in *Orr's Circ. Sc., Chem.* 494 Mercury, holding but a slight portion of any impurity, dissolved, loses its property of cohering into globular drops.., and assumes the ..appearance designated by the..term *tailing*, that is to say each..aggregation is..an irregularly elongated bar or tail. **1858** O. W. HOLMES *Aut. Breakf.-t.* iv. 86 They will not get up again in the race,..And the rest of them, what a 'tailing off!' **1860** *Merc. Marine Mag.* VII. 327 Moored in 6 fathoms..clear from tailing into shoal water.

**2.** *pl.* A name for the inferior qualities, leavings, or residue of any product; foots, bottoms.

**a.** Grain or flour of inferior quality; tail grain, etc. **b.** *Mining.* The residuum after most of the valuable ore has been extracted. **c.** A decomposed outcrop of a vein or bed. **d.** *Tanning*: see quot. **e.** General.

**a. 1764** *Museum Rust.* III. xii. 40, I supposed..that they would go to the tailing, or off-fall corn. **1846** *Osborne Times* 24 Aug., For a bushel of best wheat they pay 7s., for first tailings they pay 6s. for second tailings 5s. the bushel. **1883** *Harper's Mag.* June 76/2 All that is left—no longer *wheat*—is divided into 'middlings' and 'tailings'. **b.** **1864** WESTGARTH *Colony Victoria* xi. 222 His people were content with 'tailings', and places abandoned by the colonists. **1874** RAYMOND *Statist. Mines & Mining* 20 In the river-beds ..are large accumulations of 'tailings', rich in gold, which escaped under the primitive processes of washing formerly in use. **1901** *Scotsman* 3 Apr. 6/7, 1570 tons of tailings produced by cyanide process yielded 138 ozs. **c.** **1881** RAYMOND *Mining Gloss.*, *Blossom*, the oxidized or decomposed outcrop of a vein or coal-bed, more frequently the latter...Called..tailing. **d.** **1885** C. T. DAVIS *Manuf. Leather* x. (1897) 174 In one of these [methods] the tanning-liquor which has been in use for some time, is made use of under the name of 'tailings', or sour liquor. **e.** **1889** *Daily News* 28 Feb. 7/2 We fancy that out of the rejected mass of papers there are very few 'tailings' worth sifting.

**3.** The end or latter part: cf. TAIL *sb.*[1] 4.

**1646** SIR J. TEMPLE *Irish Rebell.* II. 53, I shall hope to get the rest of my tailing together, and make such further provision of..materialls as may enable mee to goe through with the same. **1896** KIPLING *Seven Seas* (1897) 30 Good Lord, they slipped behind us In the tailing of our wake!

†**b.** *spec.* = TAIL *sb.*[1] 4 g. *Obs.*

**1684** I. MATHER *Remark. Provid.* (1856) 43 The vessel was driven on the tailings of a ledge of rocks, where the sea broke violently.

**c.** *Arch.* See quot.: cf. TAIL *sb.*[1] 4 i.

**1842** GWILT *Archit.* Gloss., *Tailing*, the part of a projecting stone or brick inserted in a wall. **1856** S. C. BREES *Gloss. Terms* s. v., The stone steps of a staircase have a tailing of about 9 inches, in order to support them.

**d.** *Surg.* = TAIL *sb.*[1] 4 j. *rare.*

**1864** in WEBSTER.

**4.** In calico-printing: A fault of impression, in which the colours are blurred: see TAIL *v.*[1] 17.

**5.** *attrib.* and *Comb.*, as *tailing-assay*, *-barley*, *-corn*, *-heap*, *-sand*, *-wheat*; *tailings-man*, *-mill*; **tailing-mob**, a herd of cattle regularly tailed or herded; **tailing-rope**, *Naut.* = TAIL-ROPE 2 a.

**1877** RAYMOND *Statist. Mines & Mining* 106 Yielding..a little over $7.15 per ton, exclusive of their *tailing-assay of $3.76 per ton. **1747** *Gentl. Mag.* 311 The *tailing corn may soon be cleaned. *c* **1830** *Glouc. Farm Rep.* 29 in *Libr. Usef. Knowl.*, *Husb.* III, Their food..in winter [is] raw potatoes, with tailing corn, whey, and skimmed milk. **1899** *Daily News* 13 Oct. 3/1 The immense *tailing heaps thrown up by the various companies have proved an excellent means of defence, forming earthworks which command the town [Kimberley] from every side. **1885** MRS C. PRAED *Head Station* 266 The beasts were..made to join what was called the '*tailing mob', or those which had been constantly herded. **1495** *Naval Acc. Hen. VII* (1896) 197 *Taylyng Ropes for the Mayne sayle..vj; Crane lynes for the Mayne Toppe..j. **1890** *Goldf. Victoria* 21 Recent assays of the *tailing sand. **1877** RAYMOND *Statist. Mines & Mining* 40 The remainder comprising 9 trammers, 6 mill-men, 1 *tailings-man [etc.]. *Ibid.* 180 The silver or *tailings mill has not undergone any change. **1862** *Q. Rev.* Apr. 286 When.. the..*tailing-wheat or 'gristing' is sound and of good quality.

† **Tai·ling**, *vbl. sb.*[2] *Obs.* Also 4 -ende. [f. TAIL *v.*[2] + -ING [1].] ? Tallying, reckoning.

**1362** LANGL. *P. Pl.* A. IX. 74 Ho is..Trewe of his tonge ..And trusti of his taylende [B. VIII. 82 tailende, taylyng] takeþ bote his owne.

**Tailing** (tē^i·liŋ), *ppl. a.* [f. TAIL *v.*[1] + -ING [2].] That tails.

**1899** BUXTON in *19th Cent.* Jan. 121 There is the 'tailing' fish [trout], feeding on caddis snail or shrimp, breaking the surface. **1903** *Edin. Rev.* Apr. 391 Offering the 'tailing' fish a floating fly.

**Taillable, Taillage,** obs. ff. TALLIABLE, TALLAGE.

‖ **Taille.** [F. *taille* (formerly tāl^y, ta^ly', now tāy') (12th c.) cut: see TAIL *sb.*[2]]

**1.** Cut, shape, form; shape of the bust from the shoulders to the waist; figure, build, make. In *Dress-making*, the waist or bodice of a gown; the style or fit of this.

**1663** PEPYS *Diary* 13 July, Mrs. Stewart,..with her sweet eye, little Roman nose, and excellent taille, is now the greatest beauty I ever saw. **1697** VANBRUGH *Relapse* IV. vi, You would not think it impossible a person of a worse taille than mine might be a modern man of quality.

**2.** In old French law, a tax: see TAIL *sb.*[2] 2 b.

**Taille,** obs. f. TAIL, TALE, TALLY.

‖ **Taille-douce** (tāy'dus). *Obs.* Also 7 taledoux, 8 tali-douce. [Fr., = soft cutting.] Engraving on a metal plate with a graver or burin, as distinguished from work with the dry point, and from etching.

**1650** EVELYN *Diary* 21 June, A booke of statues..by which one may discover many errors in the taille douce of Perrier. **1657** in *Burton's Diary* (1828) II. App. 541 That no printers..imprint, or cause to be imprinted any work or works, book or books, taledoux or taledouxes. **1675** *Lond. Gaz.* No. 980/4 He already hath 108 Plates..cut in *Taille Douce.* **1718** A. NISBET *Ess. Armories* Index Terms, *Sable*, Black, is known in Tali-douce by perpendicular and horizontal Hatches. **1810** *Q. Rev.* III. 203 Plates engraved, as Malte-Brun tells us, in *taille douce.*

**Tailless** (tē^i·l,lės), *a.* [f. TAIL *sb.*[1] + -LESS.] Having no tail; deprived of a tail.

**15..** *Songs Costume* (Percy Soc.) 88 Elsse our horse and mayres shal be All taylesse at the Cart. **1781** PENNANT *Quadrupeds* I. 109 Tailless D[eer]. *Ibid.* II. 405 Tailless M[armot]. **1837** MARRYAT *Dog-fiend* xxxvi, He beheld Snarleyyow..tailless. **1854** OWEN *Skel. & Teeth* in *Orr's Circ. Sc.*, *Org. Nat.* I. 189 The frog and other tail-less batrachians. **1874** T. HARDY *Madding Crowd* xxvi, Never did a fragile tailless sentence convey a more perfect meaning. **1887** *Field* 2 July 7/1 Tailless schipperkes. **1893** [see next].

Hence **Tai·llessness.**

**1892** *Pall Mall G.* 24 Feb. 3/1 Our universal taillessness. **1893** *Westm. Gaz.* 22 Sept. 1/2 The little black Schipperkes, the tailless dogs of the Belgian bargees;..their taillessness was a fraud.

‖ **Tailleur**: see TALLIER. **Taillie,** variant of TAILYE. **Taillour**: see next.

**Tailor** (tē^i·ləɹ), *sb.* Forms: see below. [ME. a. AF. *taillour* = OF. *tailleor*, *-eur* (oblique case of *tailler(r)e*); in mod.F. *tailleur* = Pr. *talador* (nom. *talaire*), Cat. *tallador*, Sp. *tallador* engraver, *tajador* cutter, It. *tagliatore* cutter:—late L. or Com. Romanic *tāliātōr-em* (nom. *tāliātor*) cutter, agent-n. from *tāliāre* to cut: see TAIL *v.*[2] In Fr. the word had, and still has, the general sense of cutter, hewer, sculptor (*tailleur de pierre, de bois, de cuir, d'images*, etc.), but already in the 13th c. was used absolutely for *tailleur d'habits, de robes*, med.L. *tāliātor vestium, robārum*, cutter out or fashioner of clothes, tailor. The latter use is found in Eng. from the 14th c., the general sense 'cutter' being rare and doubtful: cf. 1297, *c* 1412, in sense 1.]

**A.** Illustration of Forms.

*α.* 3 [taylur], tailor, 4–5 taillour, 4–7 taylour, 4–9 taylor, 5 taylere, tayller, 5–7 tayler, tailour, 6– tailor.

[**1296** in *Fenland N. & Q.* (1905) July 210 Dilecto nobis in Xpo Ricardo de Masham dicto le Taylur.] **1297** Tailor [see B. 1]. **1318–19** in *Trans. Shropsh. Arch. Soc.* Ser. III. III. 54 Ricardus le taylor de Luytel Shrowardyn. **1362** LANGL. *P. Pl.* A. XI. 181 Trewe tiliers on erþe taillours [*v. r.* taliour] & souteris. **14..** *Voc.* in Wr.-Wülcker 629/1 Taylere, *scissor.* **1484** CAXTON *Fables of Alfonce* xiii, A tayller..as good a workman of his craft, as ony..at that tyme in alle the world. **1573–80** BARET *Alv.* T 10 A Tailour, *sutor vestiarius.* [See also B. 1.]

*β.* chiefly *north. dial.* and *Sc.* 4–5 taliour, 5 talȝer, -ȝour, -yowr, 5–6 tailȝour, taylȝor, -your, -eȝour, taill-, tayllyour, 6 talȝear, -yeor, tailȝeour, -eȝour, -yeour, -yeur, tel-ȝ(e)our, -yeour, 9 *dial.* taylior, teaylear.

**1415** in *York Myst.* Introd. 26 Taillyoures. *c* **1425** *Voc.* in Wr.-Wülcker 650/20 *Hic sissor*, tayleȝour. **14..** *Nom.* ibid. 685/25 *Hic sissor*, a taylȝor. *c* **1440** *Promp. Parv.* 486/1 Talyowre, *scissor.* **1442** *Aberdeen Regr.* (1844) I. 9 The talȝoures sal fynd [etc.]. **1474** *Acc. Ld. High Treas. Scot.* I. 24 To a tailȝour that makis the Kingis hos. **1483** *Surtees Misc.* (1888) 23 On Breyerton, talȝer. **1483** *Cath. Angl.* 377/1 A Taylyour (*A.* Taylȝore), *sartor, scissor.* *c* **1500** *Songs Costume* (Percy Soc.) 62 Tailyeouris and sowtaris, blist be ye. **1530** PALSGR. 279/1 Tayllyour, *cousturier.* **1549** *Compl. Scot.* xvii. 150 Thy father vas ane mecanyc tailȝour. *a* **1568** *Satir. Poems Reform.* xlvi. 64 Ane nobill telȝeour in this toun. **1573** *Ibid.* xxxix. 202 Thay socht na taileȝours for to busc thair breikis. **1580** J. HAY *Cert. Demandes* vii. in *Cath. Tractates* (S.T.S.) 37 Tailyeours, skinnars and wther artisans. **1583** *Leg. Bp. St. Androis* 567 He causit an talyeor turne it.

**B.** Signification.

**1.** 'One whose business is to make clothes' (J.); a maker of the outer garments of men, also sometimes those of women, esp. riding-habits, walking costumes, etc. See also MERCHANT-TAILOR.

(Although historically the *tailor* is the *cutter*, in the trade the 'tailor' is the man who sews or makes up what the 'cutter' has shaped.)

**1297** R. GLOUC. (Rolls) 6391 A robe he let him ssape uerst of blod red scarlet þere þe ssarpe stones bi þe stret is tailors were..þe tailors corue so moni peces uor is robe ne ssolde powȝe. *c* **1412** HOCCLEVE *De Reg. Princ.* 472 The taillours ..moot heer-after soone Shape in þe feeld. **1466** *Mann. & Househ. Exp.* (Roxb.) 354 Herry Galle taylour,..axsethe for makenge of a longe gowne of pewke, ij. s. **1504** WRIOTHESLEY *Chron.* (Camden) I. 5 This yeare the Taylors sued to the Kinge to be called Marchant taylors. **1530** PALSGR. 68 A tayllours wyfe or a woman tayllyour. **1595** SHAKS. *John* IV. ii. 195, I saw a Smith..With open mouth swallowing a Taylors newes. **1597** — *2 Hen. IV*, III. ii. 164 *Shal.* What Trade art thou Feeble? *Feeble.* A Womans Taylor sir...*Fal*...But if he had beene a mans Taylor, he would haue prick'd you. **1611** RICH *Honest. Age* (Percy Soc.) 34, I doe see the wisedome of women to be still ouerreached by Taylers, that can euery day induce them to as many new fangled fashions as they please to inuent. **1663** PEPYS *Diary* 25 May, Into the Coach again, and taking with me my wife's taylor. **1704** J. PITTS *Acc. Mohammetans* iii. (1738) 21 They all sit down cross-legg'd, as Taylors do. **1751** JOHNSON *Rambler* No. 123 ⁋ 5, I..sent for my taylor; ordered a suit..and..staid at home till it was made. *a* **1774** TUCKER *Lt. Nat.* (1834) II. 416 Our London company of tailors have a better title to the dignity of merchant by their magnificent hall. **1845** JAMES *A. Neil* II. i, Did you ever see a tailor cut out a coat?

**b.** In proverbial and allusive phrases; often implying disparagement and ridicule.

**1605** SHAKS. *Lear* II. ii. 60, *Kent.* A Taylor made thee. *Cor.* Thou art a strange fellow, a Taylor make a man? **1607** DEKKER *Northward Hoe* II. i, They say three Taylors go to the making vp of a man, but Ime sure I had foure Taylors and a halfe went to the making of me thus. **1625** B. JONSON *Staple of N.* I. i, Believe it, sir, That clothes do much upon the wit,..and thence comes your proverb, The tailor makes the man. **1651** CLEVELAND *Poems* 23 Like to nine Taylors, who if rightly spell'd, Into one man, are monysyllabled. **1663** BUTLER *Hud.* I. II. 22 Compos'd of many Ingredient Valors Just like the Manhood of nine Taylors. **1819** SCOTT *Let.* 26 July in Lockhart, They say it takes nine tailors to make a man—apparently, one is sufficient to ruin him. **1908** H. B. WALTERS in *Church Bells* 96 'Nine Tailors make a man', is *said* to be really 'nine tellers', 'tellers' being the strokes for male, female, or child, in a funeral knell or passing bell. 3×3 for male. [In Dorset these strokes are said to be called tailors: *Acad.* 11 Feb. 1899, 190/1.]

**2.** A name given to several kinds of fish, as **a.** The tailor-herring and the tailor-shad: see 6. **b.** The Silversides. **c.** The Bleak **d.** The Australian Skipjack, *Temnodon saltator* (New South Wales).

**1676** *Phil. Trans.* XI. 625 In the Creeks are great store of small fish, as Perches, Crokers, Taylors, Eels. **1860** BARTLETT *Dict. Amer.*, *Tailor*, a fish resembling the shad, but inferior to it in size and flavor...On the Potomac, the Blue fish is called a Salt-water tailor. **1880** *Rep. Roy. Comm. Fisheries N. S. Wales* 22 The 'Tailor', is well known in Port Jackson. The young fish are constantly making their appearance in shoals in the summer season. **1883** *Fisheries Exhib. Catal.* (ed. 4) 176 Schnapper, Mullet, Jew-fish, Taylor, Travalley, Black-fish. **1888** [see 6]. **1890** *Fishing Gaz.* 18 Jan. 32/1 All Thames anglers know that bleak are nick-named tailors.

**3.** Short for TAILOR-BIRD, *proud tailor* (see PROUD *a.* 10).

**1848** *Zoologist* VI. 2138 Goldfinches...That bird is in fact here [Leicestershire] known solely as a 'proud-tailor', though for brevity's sake..they..speak of it simply as a teelor.

**4. a.** *dial.* A kind of caterpillar. **b.** A *tipula* or daddy-long-legs.

**1682** LISTER *Gœdart Of Insects* 131 A creature furnished with 2 wings and 6 long Feet called by us when boyes, the Tayler. **1816** *Sporting Mag.* XLVIII. 96 The variegated hairy caterpillar called 'the Tailor'. **1840** WESTWOOD tr. *Cuvier's Anim. Kingd.* 619 These insects are well known under the names of *Daddy long-legs*, *Tailors*, &c.

**5.** *attrib.* and *Comb.* General, as *tailor-craft*, *-man*, *-proprietor*, *-shears*; = tailor-made, as *tailor-costume*, *-frock*, *-gown*, *-skirt*, *-stitching*, *-suit*; *tailor-built*, *-cut*, *-suited* adjs.; also *tailor-like* adj. and adv.; TAILOR-MADE, q. v.

**1905** *Daily Chron.* 27 May 3/7 With the hoop, the *tailor-built dress will disappear. **1897** *Westm. Gaz.* 22 Apr. 3/1 A *tailor costume destined for hard wear. *c* **1400** MAUNDEV. (Roxb.) xxvi. 122 All maner of craftez,..*talyour craft and sowter craft and swilk oþer. **1835** J. P. KENNEDY *Horse Shoe Rob.* xxiv, [It] did but little credit to the tailor-craft employed in its fabrication. **1886** G. R. SIMS in *Daily News* 4 Dec. 5/5 Her heavy *tailor-cut walking costume. **1891** 'J. S. WINTER' *Lumley* ix, Mrs. Hope made her appearance in another smart *tailor-frock. **1882** MISS BRADDON *Mt. Royal* III. vi. 106 A well grown..young woman, in a severe *tailor-gown of undyed homespun. **1630** *R. Johnson's Kingd. & Commw.* 557 Sitting..with their legges acrosse, *Taylor-like. **1899** *Daily News* 27 Feb. 6/6 One such costume..which some *tailor-man introduced as a novelty this season. **1483** *Act 1 Rich. III*, c. 12 § 1 No merchaunt Straungier..brynge..to be sold any manner Gurdels..*Taillour-shires, Scisors [etc.]. **1545** *Rates of Customs* cvij, Tayler sheres the dossen vj.s. viij.d. **1896** *Godey's Mag.* Apr. 443/1 Two straight flaps..finished with several rows of *tailor-stitching. **1907** *Westm. Gaz.* 12 Apr. 13/1 We do not soar beyond the new *tailor-suit for a week or two longer. **1906** *Ibid.* 13 Oct. 13/1 *Élégantes* of Paris who were *tailor-suited.

**6** Special combinations and collocations: †**tailor-fly** = sense 4 a; **tailor-herring**, a clupeoid fish, *Pomolobus mediocris*, of the Atlantic coast of N. America; also called *fall-herring* and *mattowacca*; **tailor-legged** *a.*, having the knees bent by sitting cross-legged; **tailor-shad** = *tailor-herring*; **tailor-tartan** *dial.*, a daddy-long-legs or crane-fly; **tailor-warbler** = TAILOR-BIRD; *spec* the long-tailed tailor-bird, *Sutoria longicauda.*

**1682** LISTER *Gœdart Of Insects* 131 These *Tayler Flyes are very Leacherous. **1767** *Poetry in Ann. Reg.* X. 250 A *taylor-legg'd Pompey, Cassius, shall you see, And the ninth part of Brutus strut in me! **1888** GOODE *Amer. Fishes* 405 [Hickory Shad or Mattowacca] *Clupea mediocris.* In the Potomac the species is called the '*Tailor Shad' or the 'Freshwater Tailor', in contradistinction to the bluefish, which is called the 'Salt-water Tailor' [*Tomatomax saltatrix*]. **1895** N. MUNRO *Lost Pibroch* (1902) 64 On the weedy stones the *tailor-tartans leaped like grass hoppers. **1783** LATHAM *Gen. Synops. Birds* IV. 515 *Tailor W[arbler]. This is a small species, being only three inches in length.

**b.** Also with *tailor's*: **tailor's block, tailor's dummy**, a lay figure on which to fit or display clothes; also *transf.* (*contemptuous*); **tailor's blow**: see quot.; **tailor's chair**, a legless seat with back and knee rest, used by tailors; **tailor's cramp**, 'a spasmodic affection of the muscles of the thumb, forefinger and forearm, occurring in tailors' (*Syd. Soc. Lex.* 1898); **tailor's friend**: see quot.; **tailor's muscle**, the SARTORIUS; **tailor's spasm**, 'a neurosis affecting the muscles of the hands of tailors' (*Syd. Soc. Lex.*); **tailor's twist**, stout silk thread used by tailors; **tailor's wagon**: see quot.; **tailor's yard**, the cloth-yard; **tailor's yard (-band)**, a popular appellation of Orion's Belt.

**1896** MRS. CAFFYN *Quaker Grandmother* 117 She's a bit too good for that *tailor's block. **1673** HICKERINGILL *Greg. F. Gregb.* 175 A *tailors blow, a knock with a thimble. **1889** DOYLE *Micah Clarke* 394 Away, away, you *tailor's dummy! **1904** *Woollen Draper's Terms* in *Tailor & Cutt.* 4 Aug. 480/1 **Tailors' Friend*, a rather soft make of canvas used for vest interlining, made in white and black, and colours. **1727–41** CHAMBERS *Cycl.*, *Sartorius*, in anatomy, the *Taylor's muscle. **1758** J. S. *Le Dran's Observ. Surg.* (1771) Cc viij, The Taylor's Muscle, so called because it brings the Legs across. **1894** *Westm. Gaz.* 27 Feb.

6/3 What is known as the 'tailor's muscle' running across the thigh and lifting the leg. **1818** *Sporting Mag.* II. 232 *Tailors' Waggons, as we used to call..those great, cumberous, four wheeled chaises. **1547** in Willis & Clark *Cambridge* (1886) II. 727, xx$^{tie}$ *taylors yerdes from the northe ende of the old Brewhouse. *a* **1548** HALL *Chron., Hen. VI* 186 b, They came not nere the Southermen by .xl. taylors yerdes. **1827** CLARE *Sheph. Cal.* 111 The *Tailor's Yard-band, which hangs streaming high.

**Tailor** (tēˑləɹ), *v.* [f. prec. sb.]

**1.** *intr.* To do tailor's work; to make clothes; to follow the calling of a tailor.

**1662** [see TAILORING *vbl. sb.*]. **1719** DE FOE *Crusoe* I. ix. 158, I set to work a Tayloring, or rather indeed a Botching. **1863** W. B. JERROLD *Signals Distr.* 99 Under their superintendence half a dozen boys..are sewing and tailoring. **1882–3** *Schaff's Encycl. Relig. Knowl.* 2249 [Stilling] taught school two days a week, and tailored four.

**2.** *trans.* To make or fashion (a garment, etc.) by tailor's work. Hence **Tailored** *ppl. a.*, tailor-made.

**1856** KANE *Arct. Expl.* I. xxviii. 366 My buffalo-robes already tailored into kapetahs on their backs. **1862** W. STORY *Roba di R.* (1863) I. iii. 38 He disdains the tailored skirts of a fashionable coat. **1888** *Daily News* 30 Apr. 2/7 A coat selling at 2*l.* 2*s.* was sewn and completely tailored for 4*s.* 6*d.* **1908** *Newspr.*, A tailored suit of tabac brown.

**3.** To fit or furnish (a person) with clothes; to apparel, to dress. Also *fig.*

**18..** BENTHAM *Fragm. Govt.* (ed. 2) Pref., Wks. 1843 I. 249/2 If tailoring a man out with God's attributes..is blasphemy, none was ever so rank as Blackstone's. **1885** D. C. MURRAY *Rainbow Gold* II. ii, The country tradesmen who tailored him had sleepless nights. **1893** *Westm. Gaz.* 24 July 1/2 He wore a frock coat, and seemed faultlessly tailored.

**b.** *intr.* To have dealings with tailors; to run up bills with tailors. *colloq.*

**1861** HUGHES *Tom Brown at Oxf.* xxviii, You haven't hunted or gambled or tailored much.

**4.** *trans.* To shoot at (birds) in a bungling manner, so as to miss or merely damage them. *slang.*

**1889** *Blackw. Mag.* CXLVI. 475 They ought to wait when a bird rises in this manner and tailor him accordingly. **1903** *Westm. Gaz.* 29 Sept. 4/2 One of them..letting birds past him untouched, knocking out tail feathers, and generally 'tailoring' his pheasants.

**Tailorage.** *rare.* [See -AGE.] Tailor's work.

**1858** CARLYLE *Fredk. Gt.* II. vii. (1873) I. 95 [Ottocar] in great pomp of tailorage. **1865** *Ibid.* XXI. viii. X. 152 A King supremely indifferent to small concerns; especially to that of shirts and tailorages not essential.

**Tailor-bird** (tēˑləɹbɜːd). [f. TAILOR *sb.* + BIRD.] One of a number of species of Asiatic passerine singing birds, belonging to the genera *Orthotomus*, *Prinia*, *Sutoria*, etc., which stitch together the margins of leaves with cotton, etc., so as to form a cavity for their nest. Originally applied to a particular species (*Motacilla sutoria* of Pennant, now variously called *Orthotomus sutorius*, *Sutoria longicauda*, or *S. sutoria*) of India and Ceylon.

**1769** PENNANT *Ind. Zool.* 7 Motacilla Sutoria. The Tailor Bird. **1813** J. FORBES *Oriental Mem.* I. 49 The tailor-bird of Hindostan; so called from its instinctive ingenuity in forming its nest, it..gathers cotton from the shrub, spins it to a thread by means of its long bill and slender feet, and then, as with a needle, sows the leaves neatly together to conceal its nest. **1870** GILLMORE tr. *Figuier's Reptiles & Birds* 183 The nest of the Tailor Bird is placed in a large leaf, the margins of which are sewn together so as to form a bag. **1876** GRANT *Hist. India* I. xxxii. 170/1. **1895** NEWTON *Dict. Birds* 943 Species of Tailor-birds more or less nearly allied are found throughout the greater part of the Indian Region.

**Tailordom** (tēˑləɹdəm). [See -DOM.]

**1.** The state, condition, or fact of being a tailor; *humorously*, the domain or realm of tailors.

**1861** G. MEREDITH *E. Harrington* I. iii. 32 Preserve him from tailordom—from all contact with trade—they must. **1873** MAYO *Never Again* iv. 43 With a punctuality unusual in tailordom the clothes were finished. **1901** *Blackw. Mag.* Jan. 44/1 They do for literary art what M. Planché's books ..have done for tailordom.

**2.** = TAILORING *vbl. sb.* b, TAILORY 3.

**1895** RASHDALL *Univ. Europe Mid. Ages* II. 644 The sobriety of hue characteristic of modern clerical tailordom.

**Tailoress** (tēˑlərés), *sb.* [f. TAILOR *sb.* + -ESS.] A woman who works as a tailor; a woman tailor.

**1654** GAYTON *Pleas. Notes* IV. ix. 234 The Protean Tayloresse ..could never be found in the same shape above once. **1771** *Boston Gaz.* 11 Nov. 3/1. **1837** HAWTHORNE *Twice-told T.* (1851) II. i. 9 At one of the back windows I observed some pretty tailoresses, sewing, and chatting. **1860** *Macm. Mag.* II. 46 There are sweaters' dens in London where living wages are utterly out of the reach of the poor tailoress. **1891** *Times* 2 Nov. 5/3.

Hence **Taiˑloress** *v.*, *nonce-wd.*, *intr.* to follow the occupation of a tailoress.

**1865** MRS. WHITNEY *Gayworthys* xxiii. (1879) 231 It's nice to get a glimpse of Eunice when she isn't tailoressing. **1888** [see TAILORING *vbl. sb.*].

**Taiˑlorhood.** *rare.* [See -HOOD.] The condition of a tailor; tailorly condition.

**1847** HELPS *Friends in C.* (1851) I. ii. 32 A creature clipt and twisted and tortured into tailorhood.

**Tailoring** (tēˑləriŋ), *vbl. sb.* [f. TAILOR *v.* + -ING [1].] The action or business of a tailor; the making of garments.

**1662** PETTY *Taxes* xv. Tracts (1769) 83 The value of wool, clothing, and tayloring, even to the thread and needles might be comprehended. **1831** CARLYLE *Sart. Res.* I. v, Neither in tailoring nor in legislating does man proceed by mere Accident. **1888** *Queen* 7 Apr. 425 Tailoring for Ladies (and not Tailoressing) is carried on at Ulster House. **1899** *Allbutt's Syst. Med.* VI. 704 Unable to follow her occupation of tailoring.

**b.** The production of the tailor; tailor's work.

**18..** WHITTIER *Pr. Wks.* (1889) II. 239 Priests, stripped of their sacerdotal tailoring, were in his view but men, after all. **1899** WHITEING 5 *John St.* xxiv. 246 In all the glory of the best tailoring in town.

**c.** *attrib.*

**1850** KINGSLEY *Cheap Clothes* in *Alt. Locke* (1881) II. 101 The means of reducing prices in the tailoring trade. **1886** C. E. PASCOE *Lond. of To-day* xli. (ed. 3) 352 The most finished examples of the tailoring art.

**Tailoring** (tēˑləriŋ), *ppl. a.* [-ING [2].] That does tailor's work. In quot. *fig.*

**1737** M. GREEN *Spleen* 520 These Tayl'ring artists for our lays Invent cramp'd rules, and with strait stays..Emaciate sense, before they fit.

**Taiˑlorism.** [See -ISM.] **a.** Tailor's work; a tailor-made dress or garment. **b.** Mode of expression or action characteristic of tailors.

**1839** *Fraser's Mag.* XIX. 121 Enrobed in the panoply of unpaid-for tailorism. **1850** L. HUNT *Autobiog.* I. vii. 288 The paternal and inextinguishable tailorism of old Rapid, in a 'Cure for the Heart-Ache'. **1904** *Westm. Gaz.* 14 Apr. 4/2 A short coat with a short skirt and a long coat with a long skirt,..both being popular tailorisms.

**Taiˑlorize,** *v.* [See -IZE.] **a.** *trans.* To treat as a tailor; to reduce to tailorhood. **b.** *intr.* To do tailor's work, to act the tailor; to sit cross-legged like a tailor.

**1829** SCOTT *Let. to Mrs. Hughes* 24 Aug., Here I am *tailorizing* as my good mother would have said, that is capeing, collaring [etc.]. **1831** CARLYLE *Sart. Res.* I. viii, Our Clothes-thatch, and how..it tailorises and demoralises us. **1832** *Blackw. Mag.* XXXI. 469 Did not Lord Melbourne—for we have not heard that he had been tailorized into humble submission—did he not kick him? **1873** LELAND *Egypt. Sketch-Bk.* 228 On the bunk where they all seem to be tailorising on their cross legs all day.

Hence **Tailorizaˑtion**, acting as a tailor, tailoring.

**1853** KANE *Grinnell Exp.* xl. (1856) 365 We have worn out all our flimsy wardrobes, and have of late resorted to domestic tailorization.

**Taiˑlorless,** *a.* [See -LESS.] Without a tailor.

**1885** MRS. INNES in *Athenæum* 12 Dec. 764 Our butcherless, bakerless, tailorless, cobblerless,..comfortless jungle. **1889** PROF. HUNTINGTON in *Chicago Advance* 24 Jan., What is barbarism but a tailorless state of society?

**Taiˑlorly,** *a.* [f. TAILOR *sb.* + -LY [1].] Pertaining to, like, or befitting a tailor; sartorial.

**1836** *Fraser's Mag.* XIV. 242 Their boots and their hats, and all tailorly ingredients of appearance,..are irreproachable. **1887** SMILES *Life & Lab.* 200 Samuel Pepys—a man of gossipy and tailorly turn of mind.

**Taiˑlor-maˑde,** *a.*

**1.** Made by a tailor; esp. said of women's garments of a heavier type, close-fitting, and plain in style, properly when made by a tailor (as distinguished from a dressmaker); hence ellipt. as *sb.*

**1873** *Punch* 20 Sept. 112/1, I shuddered to behold these words, 'Tailor-made costumes for ladies'. **1882** MISS BRADDON *Mt. Royal* II. x. 221 Gowns of dark brown serge which simulated the masculine simplicity of tailor-made garments. **1892** *Daily News* 29 Mar. 2/4 Braid is the favourite trimming for tailor-mades, now that fur is almost out of season. **1906** *Daily Chron.* 1 Sept. 4/7 If 'tailor-made' means anything, it means..distinct from dressmaker-made on the one hand and factory-made on the other.

**2. a.** *fig.* Made such by the tailor, i. e. by one's dress. **b.** *transf.* Dressed in tailor-made garments.

**1832** CARLYLE in *Fraser's Mag.* V. 386/1 If such worship for real God-made superiors showed itself also as worship for apparent Tailor-made superiors. **1896** *Westm. Gaz.* 1 May 8/2 Some severely tailor-made ladies were waiting in the entrance-hall. **1904** *Daily Chron.* 28 May 8/1 The 'tailor-made girl', like the 'frilly girl', has her opportunities upon the river.

Hence **Taiˑlor-maˑdeness**; so **Taiˑlor-make.**

**1898** *Daily News* 22 Jan. 6/5 Almost all the gowns of tailor-make were turned back in front with white, red, or cream-colour. **1900** MRS. BANKS in *19th Cent.* XLVIII. 790 A perfectly fitting gown, elegantly 'smooth', though plain in its tailor-made-ness.

**Taiˑlorship.** [See -SHIP.] The function or performance of a tailor; tailoring.

**1830** *Blackw. Mag.* XXVII. 118 Anxious thus early to announce the fact of Tailorship. **1838** *Fraser's Mag.* XVIII. 381 Far better..had it been to have taken to..tailorship or cobblership. **1896** *Daily News* 10 Nov. 2/1 From the day they were turned out spick and span with their fine tailorship to this ninth of November.

**Tailory** (tēˑləri). Also 5 talarie, tailloury, 6 (9) tailery, 7 taylorie, -ery. [f. TAILOR *sb.* + -Y: cf. -ORY.]

**1.** The art, craft, or occupation of a tailor.

*c* **1449** PECOCK *Repr.* I. x. 49 Euen as sadelarie and talarie been ij dyuerse facultees and kunnyngis. **1598** R. HAYDOCKE tr. *Lomazzo* I. 1 The art of Weaving and Tailery. **1639** in *T. Lechford's Note-Bk.* (1885) 91 Co-partners in the trade of Taylery. **1823** in *Spirit Pub. Jrnls.* 151 A student in tailory, or 'a tailor's apprentice', as the ancients used to say.

**2.** A tailor's workshop or establishment.

**1480** *Wardr. Acc. Edw. IV* (1830) 146 Coleyn threde delivered into the Tailloury. **1897** J. W. CLARK *Observ. Priory Barnwell* p. lxxiv, The Chamberlain is to..see that they [garments] are properly made in the tailery (*sartrinum*).

**3.** Tailors' work, tailors' wares; costumery.

**1610** GUILLIM *Heraldry* IV. vii. (1611) 205 Heereto we will annex some few examples of Taylorie. **1854** THACKERAY *Leech's Pictures* Wks. 1900 XIII. 489 Mr. Leech has as fine eye for tailory and millinery as for horse-flesh. **1891** *Pall Mall Gaz.* 11 July 2/2 How much time the Kaiser has to spend in the various changes from uniform to uniform... An eighth of his Majesty's time consumed in tailory!! *Sartor resartus*, indeed!

**4.** *attrib.*

**1901** *Westm. Gaz.* 9 May 3/1 What we call the tailory hat. **1906** *Ibid.* 8 Sept. 13/1 The little interregnum till the tailory clothes are ready.

**Tail-piece** (tēˑlpīs).

**1.** The piece of anything forming its tail or end; the piece at the end. Also *fig.*

Among technical uses are: the tail-pin of a lathe; in Mining, the perforated end of the tail-pipe of a pump, a snore-piece; in Stereotyping by the paper process, a piece of card-board or the like used to prevent the flow of the metal under the tail-end of the matrix; in Building, a piece inserted by tailing, a floor-timber of which one end rests on the wall; the last sclerite of the pygidium of an invertebrate.

**1601** HOLLAND *Pliny* I. 243 In other fishes the taile-peece is in greatest request. **1843** *P. Parley's Ann.* IV. 282 The chimney ended, as all chimneys do, with the sky for a tail-piece, and when Gibbo put his head out at the top, he.. looked around him, and drew in a few breathings of pure air. **1847** WEBSTER, *Tail-piece*.., in a violin, a piece of ebony at the end of the instrument to which the strings are fastened. **1869** OUSELEY *Counterp.* xxii. 177 It is called the 'coda', or 'tail-piece', of the fugue. **1876** G. F. CHAMBERS *Astron.* 635 A tube sliding easily within the tube to which the rack and pinion is attached, and called the tail-piece, is employed for first getting an approximate focus. **1890** *Spectator* 31 May, Toplady's hymn ['Rock of Ages'] was written as a tail-piece to a controversial article, in which Toplady discussed John Wesley's doctrines in the matter of faith and works.

**2.** *Printing.* A small decorative engraving placed at the end of a book, chapter, etc.

**1707** HEARNE *Collect.* 14 Apr. (O.H.S.) II. 5 In the..Bible ..are Curious..tayl-pieces. **1762–71** H. WALPOLE *Vertue's Anecd. Paint.* (1786) IV. 188 Frontispiece and tailpiece to the catalogue of pictures exhibited in 1761. **1862** ANSTED *Channel Isl.* I. vi. (ed. 2) 124 A view of this wreck..forms a tail-piece to the present chapter. **1895** C. R. B. BARRETT *Surrey* iv. 101 My tail-piece to the last chapter has for its subject the back gables of..the Hall.

**Taiˑl-pipe,** *sb.* The suction pipe of a pump.

**1883** GRESLEY *Coal Mining Gloss.*, *Tail-pipe*. **1889** WELCH *Text Bk. Naval Archit.* xi. 124 A suction-box or valve chest..is fitted beneath the pump and connected to the bottom thereof by the tail pipe shown.

**Taiˑl-pipe,** *v.* [The original implication of the second element seems lost.] *trans.* To tie a tin can or the like to the tail of (a dog, etc.) to distress and frighten him. Hence **Taiˑl-piped** *ppl. a.*

**1815** *Sporting Mag.* XLV. 256 A party of men and boys ..having tail-piped a dog for the humane purpose of making sport of its agonies. **1857** KINGSLEY *Two Y. Ago* ii, Even 'the Boys'..tail-piped not his dog. **1881** BLACKMORE *Christowell* liv, He..rushed away headlong, like a tail-piped dog, carrying our men after him.

**Tail-race** (tēˑlrēˑs). [Cf. RACE *sb.*[1] 8 c.] The part of a mill-race below the wheel, the tail-water; = TAIL *sb.*[1] 4 f.

**1776** C. CARROLL *Jrnl. Miss. Canada* in B. Mayer *Mem.* (1845) 54 The water ran through this passage about as swift as it does through your tail race. **1820** *Aberdeen Jrnl.* 2 Aug. (Jam. s. v. *Hack*), To put proper hecks on the tail-races of their canals. **1873** *Act* 36 & 37 *Vict.* c. 71 § 17 No person shall catch..any salmon..in the head race or tail race of any mill.

**b.** *Mining.* (See quot. 1881.)

**1881** RAYMOND *Mining Gloss.*, *Tail-race*, the channel in which tailings, suspended in water, are conducted away. **1890** *Melbourne Argus* 16 June 6/2 A value of gold equal to the amount now saved was run into the tail-race and lost.

**Tail-rope** (tēˑlrōᵘp).

†**1.** That part of a horse's harness near the tail, as a breeching or crupper. *Obs.*

*c* **1325** *Gloss. W. de Bibbesw.* in Wright *Voc.* 168 E à la koue un analuer [*gloss*] a tayl-rop [*Camb. MS.* Vauner, *glossed* taylrop]. *c* **1350** *Nominale Gall.-Angl.* 884 Esteles, *trays, et valuere*, Harnys, trays, taylerope. *c* **1425** *Voc.* in Wr.-Wülcker 665/35 *Hec postela*, taylerape.

**2.** A rope forming or attached to the tail, or the hinder or lower end of anything; in various technical applications: e. g.

†**a.** *Nautical.* (Also *tailing-rope*.) A sheet. *Obs.* **b.** One of several hand-ropes attached to the end of a main rope, as in a bell-rope which requires more than one ringer. **c.** A rope attached to the rear of a train of carriages or wagons to draw them back again, or to retard their speed in running down an incline. **d.** *Coal Mining*: see quot. 1883. **e.** A rope for moving a pulley-case in a slide.

**a.** **1495** *Naval Acc. Hen. VII* (1896) 206, iij hausers of Normandye.. abought makyng of vj tayle ropes for the Mayne sayle and a craynelyne for the mayne Toppe. **b.** **1656** HEYLIN *Surv. France* 97 There are no lesse then four main ropes, besides their severall tale ropes, to ring it [a bell at Notre Dame, Paris]. **c.** **1838** STEPHENSON & BIDDER in *Civil Eng. & Arch. Jrnl.* I. 110/2 We should propose to work this line by what is called a tail rope; that is, a rope attached to the train, by which it is drawn on the return journey. **1867** W. W. SMYTH *Coal & Coal-mining* 157 If the inclination of a down-brow be..less than 1 in 28, the empty tubs..must be provided with a tail-rope passing round a sheave at the bottom of the incline, by which they will be hauled down again. **1874** J. H. COLLINS *Metal Mining* 73 In the iron mines of the North of England and South Wales..'tail-rope haulage' is exceedingly common. **1900** *Engineering Mag.* XIX. 724 A main rope which pulls the full trams out, and a tail rope which tails after the full trams, and which then becomes the haulage rope to pull out the empty trams. **d.** 1883 GRESLEY *Coal Mining Gloss., Tail Rope,..*2. A round wire rope attached to cages as a balance. 3. A round hemp rope used for moving pumps in shafts. **e.** 1844 STEPHENS *Bk. Farm* II. 293 The pulley-case is moved in the slide, either by a long screw or by a tail-rope, which, when the case is adjusted, is fastened to a cleat.

**Tailsman,** ploughman: see TAIL *sb.*[1] 14.

**Tailward(s** (tē[i]·lwǭɹd(z), *adv.* [f. TAIL *sb.*[1] + -WARD(S.] Toward the tail; also quasi-*sb.* (with *to, from*), the direction in which the tail is.

1617 PURCHAS *Pilgrimage* v. vii. § 2. 590 Their faces to the taile-wards. 1665 HOOKE *Microgr.* 162 The finger being rubb'd from the tail-wards towards the head. 1851 MAYNE REID *Scalp Hunt.* l. 384 We were set astride on the bare backs [of the mules], with our faces turned tailwards.

**Tailwise** (tē[i]·lwaiz), *adv.* [f. TAIL *sb.*[1] + -WISE.] In the manner of a tail; also, with the tail foremost, i. e. backward.

*a* 1845 HOOD *To Dymoke* xi, When he [a horse] waddled tail-wise with the cup to his stall. 1899 WHITING 5 *John St.* 33 A ridiculous fag-end..sticks tailwise out behind.

**Tailye, tailzie, taillie** (tē[i]·lyi, tē[i]·li), *sb. Sc.* Forms: *α.* 4–5 talȝe, 5 taylyhe, 5–6 tailȝe, 6 taylie, tailye, tailze. *β.* 4– taillie, 5– tailyie, tailȝie, 6 talȝie, taillȝie, 6– tailzie. (In Sc. *lȝ* was the regular representative of F. *ll* mouillé (lʸ); this after 1500 was sometimes printed *ly* or *lyh* according to the sound, but more usually *lz* from the similarity of written *z* to *ȝ*.) [In *α* form *talȝe, tailȝe, tailyhe*, a. OF. *taille* cutting, = TAIL *sb.*[2] In *β* form *tailȝie*, a. OF. *tailliee, taillée, taillie* (13th c. in Godef.) = Pr. *talhada*, It. *tagliata* :—late L. or Comm. Romanic **tāliāta*, sb. fem. from pa. pple. of *tāliāre* to cut: see TAIL *v.*[2] and -ADE. In OF., *taille* and *tailliee* were in some senses synonymous, and in Sc. spelling the *α* and *β* forms ran together, the *β* forms in *-ie* at length prevailing.]

†**1.** A cut piece; a cut or slice (of meat). [prop. *tailȝie* = OF. *tailliée*.] *Obs.*

*c* 1470 HENRYSON *Mor. Fab.* II. (*Town & C. Mouse*) xvi, Muttoun and beif strukkin in tailyeis greit. 1513 DOUGLAS *Æneis* I. iv. 92 Rent furth the entralis, sum in tailȝeis schair. *Ibid.* XIII. ii. 18 Syne hakkin thaime [sacrificial beasts] in talȝeis. 1819 W. TENNANT *Papistry Storm'd* (1827) 185 They denner'd weil, wi' cheirfu' hearts, On tailyies fat and fine.

†**2.** Arrangement, fixture. [prop. *tailȝe* = OF. *taille.*] *Obs.*

*c* 1425 WYNTOUN *Cron.* IX. 1137 For bathe þai war be certane tailȝe Oblist to do þat deid, sauff failȝe. *Ibid.* 1144 De Lyndissay and de Wellis þa, On hors ane agane a noþir ran, As þar tailȝe was ordande þan.

**3.** *Sc. Law.* A legal disposition regulating the tenure and descent of an estate or dignity; = TAIL *sb.*[2] 3, ENTAIL *sb.*[2] 1. [prop. *tailȝe.*]

1375 BARBOUR *Bruce* XX. 134 (MS. E.) And at this tailȝe [*MS. C.* tale] suld lelely Be haldin, all the lordis swar. *c* 1375 *Sc. Leg. Saints* xxxvi. (*Baptista*) 1038 Þane wes antypater wa, Þat his fadir sic a talȝe can ma. 1391 in Fraser *The Lennox* (1874) II. 43 To the fulfilling of this taillie the forsaid Erl of Fife sal purches the kingis assent. 1473–4 *Acc. Ld. High Treas. Scot.* I. 6 Certane landis..to be gevin agane to his sone in talȝe. 1535 STEWART *Cron. Scot.* (Rolls) III. 393 And gif of him the airis maill did falze, Robert his bruther the narrest of the tailze. 1578 *Reg. Privy Council Scot.* II. 693 All taillies from the airis generall to the airis maill. 1676 W. ROW *Contn. Blair's Autobiog.* xii. (1848) 452 Desiring that the tailzie of the estate of Buccluch might be broken. 1769 *De Foe's Tour Gt. Brit.* IV. 53 By an Act 20 Geo. II..Heirs of Tailzie are allowed to sell Lands to the Crown [cf. quot. 1747 in TAILYE *v.* 3]. 1814 SCOTT *Wav.* x, In direct contravention of an unrecorded taillie. 1818 — *Hrt. Midl.* xii, Didna ye get baith liberty and conscience made fast, and settled by tailzie on you and your heirs for ever? 1832 AUSTIN *Jurispr.* (1879) II. li. 865 The fetters of a Scotch deed of tailzie. 1868 *Act* 31 & 32 *Vict.* c. 101 § 104 His heirs, whether of line, conquest, taillie, or provision.

†**4.** An account or reckoning. *Obs.*

1497 *Acc. Ld. High Treas. Scot.* I. 361 Giffin to the quareouris of the est quarel for schort tailȝee,..xiijs. iiij*d.* 1508 KENNEDIE *Flyting w. Dunbar* 446 A pak of flaskynnis, fynance for to mak the, Thow sall ressaue, in Danskyn, of my tailye.

**Tailye, tailzie** (tē[i]·lyi, tē[i]·li), *v. Sc.* Forms: 4 talȝe, 5 tailȝe, -ȝee, tayllie, 6 tailze, -zee, tailye, 8–9 tailzie (with z for ȝ = y, yh, in print after 1500). [Early Sc. *talȝe, tailȝe*, a. F. *taille*, infl. of *tailler* to cut, etc.; = corresp. English TAIL *v.*[2] The mod. *tailzie* is, as in the sb., an erroneous form for *tailȝe* or *tailye.*]

†**1.** *trans.* To cut; to cut to shape. *Obs.*

1581 *Satir. Poems Reform.* xliv. 200 Thou..I vene, The peperit beif can tailȝe be the threid. 1589 *Reg. Privy Council Scot.* IV. 421 Twa talyeit rubyis in chattonis, and three rubyis caboshon,..being of his Majesteis jowellis.

†**2.** To determine, settle, appoint, arrange. *Obs.*

1375 BARBOUR *Bruce* XIX. 188 And eftir syne war trewis tane Betuix the twa kyngis, that wer Talit [*v. r.* tailȝeit] to lest for thretten ȝheir. *c* 1375 *Sc. Leg. Saints* xxi. (*Clement*) 346 Sic fortone sal ȝe haf nedlinge, As was ȝow talȝet in ȝoure getting. 1456 SIR G. HAYE *Law Arms* (S. T. S.) 269 The bataill be tane under certane condicioun of tayllid strakis.

**3.** *Sc. Law.* To determine or tie up the succession to (an estate); to entail; = TAIL *v.*[2] 5.

1536 BELLENDEN *Cron. Scot.* (1821) II. 395 King Robert set ane parliament at Ayre, in the quhilk..he gat the croun of Scotland tailyet to him and the aris-male gottin of his body. *a* 1557 *Diurn. Occurr.* (Bannatyne Cl.) 24 The lord Erroll marijt the erle of Lennox sistar, quha bure him ane daughter; his landis was tailyeit. 1747 *Act* 20 *Geo. II*, c. 50 § 14 It shall and may be lawful for any Person.. possessed of a Tailzied Estate in Scotland, to sell, dispone, or resign..any Part thereof, which his Majesty..shall think fit to purchase, for erecting of Buildings, or making Settlements within the same. 1806 FORSYTH *Beauties Scotl.* IV. 150 In 1315 Thomas de Loch Orr is in the parliament at Air that tailzied the crown. 1832 AUSTIN *Jurispr.* (1879) II. li. 864 Proprietors were enabled to tailzie their lands, that is, to make a destination of their estates so as effectually to fetter the power of alienation of future proprietors.

†**4.** To keep account or tally of. *Obs.*

1497 *Acc. Ld. High Treas. Scot.* I. 351 Thome Foret, to remane in Dunbar to resaue and store and tailȝee the lyme, sand and othir gere. 1539 *Ibid.* VII. 217 George Balglavy for awayting and keiping and tailȝeing of the said tymmer, lyme, send, and stane.

Hence **Tai·lyed, tai·lzied** *ppl. a.*, cut to shape; appointed, fixed, arranged; entailed.

1456 [see 2]. 1589 [see 1]. 1747 [see 3].

**Tailyeour, -ȝour,** obs. ff. TAILOR.

†**Tailyevey,** *v. Sc. Obs. rare.* In 6 tailȝevey, taillȝewe. [Origin obscure.] *intr.* To reel from side to side, move to and fro. Hence †**Tailȝevey** *sb.*, a reeling or rocking from side to side.

1513 DOUGLAS *Æneis* v. xiv. 77 Quhow that the schip did rok and tailȝevey For lak of a gud sterisman on the se. *a* 1568 in *Satir. Poems Reform.* xlvi. 8 Scho will sale all the wintrinight, And nevir tak a telȝevie. *c* 1579 MONTGOMERIE *Misc. Poems* xlviii. 157 Betuixt the tua [Charybdis and Scylla] we tuik sik taillȝeweis, At hank and buick we skippit syndrie seis.

**Taim, Taime:** see THEM, TEAM.

**Tain** (tē[i]n), *sb.* [a. F. *tain* tinfoil, altered from F. *étain* tin. Cf. also ME. TEYNE.] (See quot.)

1858 SIMMONDS *Dict. Trade, Tain*, a thin tinplate; tinfoil for mirrors.

†**Tain,** *v. Obs. rare.* In 6 teyne, taygne. [Short for *obtain*, or ad. L. *tenēre*, F. *tenir*, on the analogy of the compounds *attain, maintain, obtain*, etc.] **a.** *trans.* To obtain, get. **b.** *intr.* To obtain, maintain itself, prevail.

1501 *Plumpton Corr.* (Camden) 156 Bryng with you money convenient for your expenses, for as yet..here be now rent teyned. *c* 1530 tr. *Erasmus' Serm. Ch. Jesus* (1901) 21 Enuyes, simulations, and the other vicyes, which especyally taygne in olde men.

**Tain,** obs. form of THANE.

**Tain, taine,** obs. ff. *taken*, pa. pple. of TAKE *v.*

**Tainchell,** obs. variant of TINCHEL.

**Tainct, -ure,** obs. ff. TAINT, TAINTURE.

†**Tai·nder.** *Obs. rare*[−1]. In 5 teyndre. Aphetic form of ATTAINDER.

1469 *Rolls of Parlt.* VI. 231 Afore the seid atteyndre or teyndres.

**Taing,** dial. variant of TANG *sb.*[1]

**Taings,** Sc. form of TONGS.

†**Tai·ning.** *Obs.* Some kind of device for catching fish in rivers.

1533–4 *Act* 25 *Hen. VIII*, c. 7 No..persone..shall..take.. in..any..nett, berd net of heare, tainyng, lepe, hyve, crele,.. the yonge frye..of any kynde of Salmon. 1558 *Act* 1 *Eliz.* c. 17 § 1 No Person..withe any..Net, Weele, Butt, Tayning, Kepper, Lyme, Crele..shall take..Spawne or Frye of Eeles, Salmon, Pyke or Pyckerell.

**Taint** (tē[i]nt), *sb.* Forms: 4–6 taynte, 5 teynt, 5–7 taynt, 6 tainte, teinte, 7 tainct, 6– taint. [Here, as in the vb., two words of distinct origin, being identical in form, appear to have run together in the formation of later senses. The original words are placed under A and B, the blended senses under C.]

**A.** [Aphetic form of ATTAINT *sb.*]

†**1.** A 'hit' in tilting; = ATTAINT *sb.* 1. Also *fig.*

*c* 1400 *Melayne* 1387 Bot me sall neuer be-tyde that taynte. 1494 in *Letters of Rich. III & Hen. VII* (Rolls) I. 397 Sir Edward A Borough..brake a spere well brokyn, the ij[de] better, with a teynt. 1543 GRAFTON *Contn. Harding* 596 He ..gaue so many teintes y[e] euery man maruayled at his wonderfull feetes. *Ibid.* 599 At euery coursse he brake a speare or gaue a taynt. 1551–2 EDW. VI *Lit. Rem.* (Roxb.) II. 389 Ther was a match..at tilt. Theis [the earl of Warwick, etc.] wane by 4 taintes. 1602 SEGAR *Hon. Mil. & Civ.* III. xxxviii. 168 At the last meeting the French Taint was so strong, as the Englishman was wel-neere borne downe: and so they departed. *c* 1611 CHAPMAN *Iliad* III. 374 This taint he follow'd with his sword, drawn from a silver sheath.

†**b.** *transf.* A knock, a blow. *Obs.*

*c* 1410 *Master of Game* (MS. Digby 182) vii, If grehoundes gyf hym [the fox] mony tayntes and ouersette hym.

**2.** A disease in horses; = ATTAINT *sb.* 3.

1565 BLUNDEVIL *Horsemanship* IV. cxix. (1580) 55 Of a nether taint...This is a little bladder full of iellie, much like vnto a wind-gall, not apparant to the eie, but to the feeling, growing in the midst of the pasterne, somewhat aboue the frush. It commeth by a straine, or else by some wrench, or by an ouerreach. 1844 STEPHENS *Bk. Farm* II. 672 His observations are particularly applicable to the *curl*, still they will apply equally well to the *taint*.

†**3.** A conviction; *spec.* the conviction of a jury for having given a false verdict; = ATTAINT *sb.* 4.

1530 PALSGR. 279/1 Taynte, *condamne* [sb.]. 1607 COWELL *Interpr., Taint*..signifieth either substantiuely a conviction, or adiectiuely a person conuicted of felonie or Treason &c. See *Attaint*. 1609 SKENE *Reg. Maj.* I. 13 Gif the assisors sall happin to be convict as mensworne in the court, be ane Taynt; that is, be probation of twentie foure loyall men. 1706 PHILLIPS (ed. Kersey), A *Taint*, a Conviction.

†**B.** [a. OF. *teint, taint* (12th c.):—L. *tinctu-s* (*u*-stem), and *teinte* (13th c.):—late and med.L. *tincta*, sb. fem. from *tinct-us*, pa. pple. of *tingĕre* to TINGE. Cf. the later doublets TINCT and TINT.] Colour, hue, tint; tinge; dye. *Obs.*

1567 DRANT *Horace, Epist.* II. ii. H vj, Pearles, stones, iewels, pictures, with costelie kynde of tainte. 1589 PUTTENHAM *Eng. Poesie* III. i. (Arb.) 150 The crimson tainte, which should be laid vpon a Ladies lips, or right in the center of her cheekes. *a* 1592 GREENE *Hexametra Alexis in laudem Rosamundæ* 6 Face rose-hued, cherry-red, with a silver taint like a lily. *c* 1593 EARL OXFORD *Sheph. Commend. Nimph* vii, This pleasant Lilly white, This taint of roseate red.

**C.** [Senses app. combining A and B.]

**1.** A stain, a blemish; a sullying spot; a touch, trace, shade, tinge, or tincture of some bad or undesirable quality; a touch of discredit, dishonour, or disgrace; a slur.

1601 SHAKS. *Twel. N.* III. iv. 390, I hate ingratitude more in a man, Then..any taint of vice. *a* 1637 B. JONSON *Underwoods* xiii, A hallowed temple, free from taint Of ethnicisme. 1643 CHAS. I. *Proclam.* Wks. 1662 II. 350 Free from the foul Taint of High Treason. 1682 OTWAY *Venice Pres.* II. i, They leave a Taint, a Sully where they've past. 1706 PHILLIPS (ed. Kersey), A *Taint*..a Blur, Spot, or Blemish in one's Reputation. 1742 FIELDING *Jos. Andrews* II. iv, His temper was..without the least taint of moroseness. 1781 COWPER *Expost.* 150 Free from every taint but that of vice. 1819 KEATS *Eve St. Agnes* xxv, She knelt so pure a thing, so free from mortal taint. 1838 PRESCOTT *Ferd. & Is.* (1846) II. xx. 211 A slight taint of pedantry. 1851 BRIMLEY *Ess., Wordsworth* 103 There is no taint upon his robe. 1883 SIR J. BACON in *Law Rep.* 25 Ch. Div. 316 For good consideration and without taint of suspicion.

†**b.** A flaw or blemish in the feathers of hawks from improper feeding; = HUNGER-TRACE(S. *Obs.*

1486 *Bk. St. Albans* B ij b, The tayntys that be vppon her tayll and her Wengys wiche tayntys com for lacke of fedyng when thay be Eyes. *Ibid.*, A Taynt is a thyng that gooth ouerwarte the federis of the wynges, and of the tayll lyke as and it were eetyn with wormys.

**2.** A contaminating, corrupting, or depraving influence, physical or moral; a cause or condition of corruption or decay; an infection.

1613 SHAKS. *Hen. VIII*, v. iii. 28 What followes then?..a generall Taint Of the whole State. 1692 LOCKE *Educ.* § 68 Keep him from the Taint of your Servants, and meaner People. 1735 BOLINGBROKE *On Parties* ii. 15 That epidemical Taint, with which King James infected the Minds of Men, continued upon us. 1828 MACAULAY *Ess., Hallam* (1887) 93 A deep and general taint infected the morals of the most influential classes. 1832 HT. MARTINEAU *Ireland* vi. 93 The health..was affected by the taint the marsh gave to the atmosphere.

**b.** A trace or tinge of disease in a latent state.

1615 W. LAWSON *Country Housew. Gard.* (1626) 16 It is a great signe of a taint, and next yeeres death. 1639 T. DE GRAY *Compl. Horsem.* 347 If you doe perceive a taint in his winde. 1804 *Med. Jrnl.* XII. 414 How often does latent venereal taint produce glandular obstructions? 1875 H. C. WOOD *Therap.* (1879) 410 Diseases of the bones, dependent upon or resulting from a scrofulous taint. 1879 *Spon's Encycl. Manuf.* I. 9 It is also essential that there shall be no dry rot or 'taint' present [in the wood]. 1899 *Allbutt's Syst. Med.* VIII. 116 Both diseases own a common origin, namely hereditary nervous taint.

†**3.** (Also **tant.**) Short for TAINT-WORM; also, a small red spider (see quot. 1646). *Obs.*

1577 B. GOOGE *Heresbach's Husb.* III. (1586) 134 b, If he swell of the taint, or stingworme. 1646 SIR T. BROWNE *Pseud. Ep.* III. xxvii. 176 There is found in the Summer a kind of spider called a Tainct of a red colour...This by Countrey people is accounted a deadly poison unto Cowes and Horses; who, if they suddenly die, and swell thereon, ascribe their death hereto, and will commonly say, they have licked a Tainct. 1656 in BLOUNT *Glossogr.* *a* 1705 RAY *Hist. Insects* (1710) 41 Araneus exiguus coccineus, vulgo Anglicè a *Tant or Taint.*

**4.** *Comb.* as **taint-free** *a.*, free from taint.

1663 *Flagellum, or O. Cromwell* 205 Nor were most of his Relations taint free of those principles.

†**Taint,** *ppl. a. Obs. rare.*

**1.** [Aphetic form of ATTAINT *ppl. a.*] **a.** Attainted, convicted. **b.** Affected, seized, struck. **c.** Exhausted.

*c* 1330 R. BRUNNE *Chron. Wace* (Rolls) 5164 Recreaunt & teynt. *Ibid.* 10903 Ful of yre, wyþ colour [=choler] teint. *c* 1380 *Sir Ferumb.* 2822 Gyoun þanne was teynt & paal; so longe he hadde yuaste. 1496 *Dives & Paup.* (W. de Worde) II. xvii. 129/1 He sholde be taken as a conuycte and a taynt [*perh.* ataynt] traytour. 1706 PHILLIPS (ed. Kersey), *Taint*, Convicted of a Crime, as Treason, Felony, etc.

**2.** [Shortened pa. pple. of TAINT *v.*] = TAINTED; infected, corrupt.

1620 QUARLES *Jonah* ix. *Medit.* H ij b, Their seruice is vnsweet, and foully taint. 1743 *Lond. & Country Brew.* IV. (ed. 2) 330 Such casks..will grow furry, taint, and stinking.

**Taint,** *v.* Forms: 4–6 taynte, 5–6 taynt, 6–7 teint, 5– taint. Pa. pple. **tainted**; also formerly contr. **taint** (**teint**, etc.). [Here, as in the sb., there are two words of distinct origin, A and B, and a series of senses C, in which both appear more or less to blend.]

**A.** [Aphetic form of ATTAINT *v.*]

**I.** †**1.** *trans.* To convict, prove guilty; = ATTAINT *v.* 3. *Obs.*

*c* **1375** *Sc. Leg. Saints* xxxi. (*Eugenia*) 603, & þu with þis dede is wele taynt, Þat makis na ansuere to þis plant. *c* **1400** MAUNDEV. (Roxb.) xxvi. 122 All thefez and robbours þat er taynted þeroff. *c* **1400** *Destr. Troy* 8109 Now art þou trewly hor traitour, & tainted for fals. *c* **1440** *York Myst.* xxvi. 6 Traytoures tyte will I taynte. **1603** HOLLAND *Plutarch's Mor.* 485 Apollo commanded them, that if they were all tainted with the said murder, they should all depart out of the citie Chios.

†**2.** To prove (a charge); = ATTAINT *v.* 4. *Obs.*

**1424** *Sc. Acts Jas. I* (1814) II. 6/1 And quhar it beis tayntyt þt þai [rukis] bige and þe birdis be flowin and þe nestis be fundyn in þe treis at beltane, þe treis salbe forfaltit to þe king.

†**3.** To subject to attainder; = ATTAINT *v.* 6. *Obs.*

**1732–8** NEAL *Hist. Purit.* (1822) I. 71 Elizabeth's blood being tainted by act of parliament.

†**4.** To accuse of crime or dishonour; = ATTAINT *v.* 7. *Obs.*

*a* **1619** FLETCHER *Bonduca* I. i, 'Tis dishonour, And, follow'd, will be impudence, Bonduca, And grow to no belief, to taint these Romans.

**II.** †**5.** To touch, strike, hit; esp. in tilting; = ATTAINT *v.* 1. *Obs.*

**1525** LD. BERNERS *Froiss.* II. clxviii. [clxiv.] 470 They ran togider, & tainted eche other on ye helmes, but their speres grated not. **1582** STANYHURST *Æneis* III. (Arb.) 80, I doe liue, I assure thee, thogh dangers sundrye me taynted. **1583** STOCKER *Civ. Warres Lowe C.* IV. 65 b, The Enemie ..tainted fower of them with the Shot of one Harquebouze. **1590** MARLOWE *2nd Pt. Tamburl.* I. iii, Tilting at a glove, Which, when he tainted with his slender rod, He [etc.].

†**b.** To break (a lance, staff) in tilting, etc. *Obs.*

**1599** B. JONSON *Every Man out of Hum.* II. i, He can sit a great horse; hee will taint a staffe well at tilt. **1624** MASSINGER *Parl. Love* IV. iii, Do not fear. I have A staff to taint, and bravely.

**B.** [a. AF. *teinter* (1409–10), f. *teint*, pa. pple. of OF. *teindre* to dye, colour:—L. *tingĕre* to dye, TINGE; cf. ATTAINT, PAINT.]

†**1.** *trans.* To colour, dye, tinge. *Obs.*

[**1409–10** *Act* 11 *Hen. IV*, c. 6 Qe certeins marchantz aliens..achatent..Mill draps de blanket fyne, ou pluis, & les font teintrere [*v.r.* teinter] de lour grayn demesne en Scarlet ou Sangwyne.] **1471** RIPLEY *Comp. Alch.* I. vi. in Ashm. *Theatr. Chem. Brit.* (1652) 130 Able to tayne [? taynt] with colour whych wyll not vade. *a* **1533** LD. BERNERS *Huon* cxxxviii. 513 With the blode of yᵉ dede sarasyns theyr swordys were all tayntyd red. **1589** GREENE *Menaphon* (Arb.) 54 At this, the pore swaine tainted his cheeks with a vermillion die. **1725** *Bradley's Fam. Dict.* s.v. *Butter*, As to that [Butter] which they taint with Eel-pouts, besides that it deceives the Sight it is very often disagreeable to the Taste. [*a* **1839** PRAED *Poems* (1864) II. 57 Bid faith and beauty die, and taint Her heart with fraud, her face with paint.]

†**b.** To dip, bathe. *Obs. rare.*

**1594** MARLOWE *Dido* I. i, And Phoebus, as in Stygian pools, refrains To taint his tresses in the Tyrrhene main.

†**2.** To apply tincture, balm, or ointment to (a wound, etc.). *Obs.*

**1579** LYLY *Euphues* (Arb.) 65 If it be ripe it shalbe lawnced, if it be broken it shalbe tainted. **1580** — *Euphues & Eng.* (Arb.) 314 Whether dost thou wade Philautus in launcing the wound thou shouldest taint. **1607** TOPSELL *Four-f. Beasts* (1658) 274 If you slit his [a horse's] fore-head, and loosening the skin from the bone, taint it with Turpentine and Sallet-oyl, it will undoubtedly help him. **1639** T. DE GRAY *Compl. Horsem.* 95 Annoynt, wash, bathe and taint (if need be) the sorance.

**C.** [Senses in which A and B appear to blend.]

**1.** *trans.* To affect (esp. in a slight degree); to touch, tinge, imbue slightly (usually *with* some bad or undesirable quality).

**1591** SHAKS. 1 *Hen. VI*, V. iii. 183 A pure vnspotted heart, Neuer yet taint with loue, I send the King. **1593** — 3 *Hen. VI*, III. i. 40 Nero will be tainted with remorse. **1605** R. CAREW in *Lett. Lit. Men* (Camden) 99, I am tainted with a sparcke of Envye. **1710** BERKELEY *Princ. Hum. Knowl.* Pref., Those who are tainted with Scepticism. **1761–2** HUME *Hist. Eng.* lxix. (1806) V. 198 Nowise tainted with enthusiasm. **1850** LYELL *2nd Visit U. S.* II. 115 The French or Spanish creoles here would shrink..from intermarriage with one tainted, in the slightest degree, with African blood. **1884** *Law Rep.* 26 Ch. Div. 124 It does not follow that all the subsequent payments were tainted with the original infirmity.

†**2.** To affect injuriously; to cause detriment to; to hurt, injure, impair. *Obs.*

**1601** SHAKS. *Twel. N.* III. iv. 13 Sure the man is tainted in's wits. *a* **1623** BEAUMONT *Ode Blessed Trin.* ii, No cold shall thee benumme, Nor darknesse taint thy sight.

†**b.** To sully, stain, tarnish (a person's honour).

**1613** SHAKS. *Hen. VIII*, III. i. 56 We come not by the way of Accusation, To taint that honour euery good Tongue blesses. **1710** STEELE *Tatler* No. 183 ᴘ 1 Any Occasion which he thinks may taint his own Honour. **1722** — *Conscious Lovers* IV. i, The honour of a Gentleman is liable to be tainted by as small a Matter as the Credit of a Trader.

†**3.** To affect with weakness; to cause to lose vigour or courage. *Obs.*

**1600** HOLLAND *Livy* XXVIII. xv. 679 [They] being thus tainted, as well in courage of heart, as in bodily strength, gave ground and reculed. *c* **1611** CHAPMAN *Iliad* XIII. 449 Fear taints me worthily, Though firm I stand, and show it not.

†**b.** *intr.* To lose vigour or courage; to become weak or faint; to wither, fade. *Obs.*

**1605** SHAKS. *Macb.* V. iii. 3 Till Byrnane wood remoue to Dunsinane, I cannot taint with Feare. **1639** HORN & ROB. *Gate Lang. Unl.* xi. § 106 Failing of that moisture it flags, tainteth (withereth), and by and by drieth away.

**4.** *trans.* To infect with pernicious, noxious, corrupting or deleterious qualities; to touch with putrefaction; to corrupt, contaminate, deprave.

**1573** *Durham Deposit.* (Surtees) 252 The said Bell is a great lyer, and taintyd of his tounge. **1592** SHAKS. *Rom. & Jul.* I. iv. 75 Ladies lips..Which oft the angry Mab with blisters plagues, Because their breath with Sweet meats tainted are. **1602** MARSTON *Antonio's Rev.* II. ii, Why tainst thou then the ayre with stench of flesh? **1667** MILTON *P. L.* XII. 512 The truth With superstitions and traditions taint. **1770** *Junius Lett.* xxxviii. (1820) 186 The poison of their doctrines has tainted the natural benevolence of his disposition. **1861** THACKERAY *Four Georges* ii. (1862) 116 One..who tainted a great society by a bad example.

**b.** *intr.* To become putrefied, corrupted, or rotten; to tarnish.

**1601** SHAKS. *Twel. N.* III. iv. 145 Nay pursue him now, least the deuice take ayre, and taint. **1637** T. MORTON *New Eng. Canaan* (1883) 117 Fish and Flesh both will taint in those partes, notwithstanding the use of Salt. **1641** H. L'ESTRANGE *God's Sabbath* 26 The putrefaction which Manna contracted by procrastination on other dayes..was the greater miracle..because it tainted against nature. **1766** *Museum Rust.* III. 239 The natural humidity of the plant ..which sometimes..is retained so long as to cause the heads to taint, and become rotten.

Hence **Tai·nting** *vbl. sb.* and *ppl. a.*

**1593** NASHE *Foure Lett. Confut.* Wks. (Grosart) II. 220 Yet tainting is no infamous surgerie for him that hath beene in so many hote skirmishes. **1598** FLORIO, *Macca*, a bruse, a spot, a tainting. **1611** SHAKS. *Cymb.* I. iv. 148 If you buy Ladies flesh at a Million a Dram, you cannot preserue it from tainting. **1632** *Star Chamb. Cases* (Camden) 109 These words were very foule and dishonorable: it is a tainting of all honor. **1842** MANNING *Serm.* xi. (1848) I. 156 All the tainting, stupifying power of its original sin.

**Taint,** obs. variant of TENT *sb.*

**Taintable** (tē^i·ntăb'l), *a.* [f. TAINT *v.* + -ABLE.] Liable to taint or be tainted.

**1864** BLACKMORE *Clara Vaughan* xxxii, We got all that was taintable into the little yard.

**Tainted** (tē^i·ntêd), *ppl. a.* [f. TAINT *v.* + -ED¹.]

**1.** Stained, tinged; contaminated, infected, corrupted; touched with putrefaction or incipient decay; affected with some corrupting influence.

**1577** B. GOOGE *Heresbach's Husb.* I. (1586) 43 He thinkes it better to let that [corn] alone that is alredy corrupted, and..when so euer ye neede to occupie it, to take away that is taynted, and to vse the rest. *a* **1619** FLETCHER, etc. *Knt. Malta* IV. ii, Treason and tainted thoughts are all the gods Thou worship'dst. **1630** B. JONSON *New Inn* II. ii, *Host.* ..And speakes a little taynted, fly-blowne Latin, After the Schoole. *Bea.* Of Stratford o' the Bow. For Lillies Latine, is to him vnknow. **1709** SWIFT *Adv. Relig.* Wks. 1755 II. I. 99 Women of tainted reputations. **1712** ADDISON *Hymn*, '*How are Thy Servants blest*', Thro' burning Climes I pass'd unhurt, And breath'd in tainted Air. **1821** WORDSW. *Sonn.*, *Virgin*, Woman! above all women glorified, Our tainted nature's solitary boast. **1837** M. DONOVAN *Dom. Econ.* II. 243 In what manner charcoal boiled with tainted meat can affect the interior. **1883** SIR W. B. BRETT in *Law Rep.* 11 Q. Bench Div. 454 That these statements were tainted evidence, because they came from accomplices.

**b.** Having a taint of disease; infected with latent disease. Cf. TAINT *sb.* C. 2 b.

**1596** SHAKS. *Merch. V.* IV. i. 114, I am a tainted Weather of the flocke, Meetest for death. **1697** DRYDEN *Virg. Past.* I. 70 Nor fear a Rott from tainted Company. **1897** *Allbutt's Syst. Med.* II. 924 Children of parents engaged in the manufacture of matches and tainted with phosphorism.

**2.** Imbued with the scent of an animal (usually a hunted animal). (Cf. BLEMISH *sb.* 4.) *Obs.* or *arch.*

**1704** ADDISON *Campaign* 122 So the stanch Hound the trembling Deer pursues, And smells his footsteps in the tainted dews. **1732** POPE *Ess. Man* I. 214 What modes.. Of smell, the headlong lioness between, And hound sagacious on the tainted green. **1810** SCOTT *Lady of L.* I. ii, [The stag] A moment snuffed the tainted gale.

†**3.** Tinted, stained. *Obs. rare.*

**1797** *Encycl. Brit.* (ed. 3) XIII. 715/2 They also use a kind of paper for drawing, which is called tainted paper.

**Tainter,** *sb.* and *v.*, obs. f. TENTER. **Taint-hook,** obs. f. TENT-HOOK. **Tainting**: see under TAINT *v.* **Taintingly** (in Shaks.): see TAUNTINGLY.

**Taintless** (tē^i·ntlės), *a.* Chiefly *poet.* [f. TAINT *sb.* + -LESS.] Free from taint; without stain or blemish; immaculate, clean, pure, innocent.

**1590** MARLOWE *2nd Pt. Tamburl.* IV. i, To flesh our taintless swords. **1602** MARSTON *Antonio's Rev.* IV. iii, Heaven permits not taintlesse bloode be spilt. **1776** MICKLE tr. *Camoens' Lusiad* 333 His loyalty as taintless snow. **1863** KINGSLEY *Water-Babies* i. 44 To the golden sands, and the leaping bar, And the taintless tide that awaits me afar. **1893** in Barrows *Parl. Relig.* I. 725 A pure, taintless, lofty, elevating..faith.

Hence **Tai·ntlessly** *adv.*, without taint.

**1846** in WORCESTER. **1847** in WEBSTER; and in mod. Dicts.

**Tai·ntment.** *rare.* [f. TAINT *v.* + -MENT.]

†**1.** = ATTAINTMENT, ATTAINT. *Obs.*

**1613** T. GODWIN *Rom. Antiq.* (1658) 217 Taintments of treason against any person of state.

**2.** Contamination, defiling tincture.

**1633** T. ADAMS *Exp. 2 Peter* ii. 14 That is a rare eye..that can mingle itself with sordid corruptions, and receive no taintment.

**Taintor, -our.** [Agent-n. from TAINT *v.*]

†**1.** [Cf. TAINT *v.* A.] One who brings legal evidence against another for conviction of some crime; an accuser, informer. *Obs.*

**1451** *Sc. Acts Jas. II* (1814) II. 40/2 Þat na man haf out of þe Realme gold bulȝeone or siluer vnder þe payn of escheite þareof, þe tane half to þe king & þe toþir half to þe tayntour & þe takar.

**2.** [a. AF. *teintour* = OF. *teintor, -ur, -eur.*] A dyer. *rare.*

**1889** MCANALLY in *Pop. Sci. Monthly* Oct. 812 The cloth ..finished and ready for the Dyer, Litter, or Lister, or the Norman Taintor or Taintur.

**Tainture** (tē^i·ntiŭɹ). Now *rare.* Also 5–7 taynt-, 6–7 tainct-.

**I.** [a. OF. *tainture, teinture* colouring (13th c.), ad. L. *tinctūra* dyeing, TINCTURE; in sense 2 as in TAINT *v.* C.] †**1.** Colouring. *Obs.*

**1490** CAXTON *Eneydos* vi. 24 We wryte the grete and firste capytall lettres..wyth the taynture of reed coloure.

**2.** Tainting, staining, stain, defilement, infection.

**1593** SHAKS. 2 *Hen. VI*, II. i. 188 Gloster, see here the Taincture of thy Nest, And looke thy selfe be faultlesse, thou wert best. **1609** RAWLINSON *Fishermen* 11 To keepe it from the corruption and tainture of sin. **1634** T. JOHNSON tr. *Parey's Chirurg.* XVIII. ix. (1678) 419 There are..three distinct causes of gout: A tainture from the Parents [etc.]. **1645** USSHER *Body Div.* (1647) 126 It shining in him without tainture or blemish. **1681** RYCAUT tr. *Gracian's Critick* 227 Others have always retained some tainture and favour of their former condition. **1854** *Fraser's Mag.* L. 667 Who Neerland's blood feel nobly flow, From foreign tainture free.

**II.** †**3.** Aphetic form of ATTAINTURE. *Obs.*

**1621** G. SANDYS tr. *Ovid's Met.* I. (1626) 20 Asham'd that such a tainture should be lay'd Vpon my blood, that could not be gayn-said.

**Tai·nt-worm.** *arch.* [f. TAINT *sb.* + WORM.] A worm or crawling larva supposed to taint or infect cattle, etc.: cf. TAINT *sb.* C. 3.

**1573** TUSSER *Husb.* (1878) 150 Doo taint wormes good, that lurke where ox should eat? **1637** MILTON *Lycidas* 46 As killing as the Canker to the Rose, Or Taint-worm to the weanling Herds that graze. **1840** BROWNING *Sordello* VI. 158 Study the corpse-face thro' the taint-worms' scurf.

‖ **Tai-ping** (tai,piŋ). Also **Taé-ping.** [Chinese *T'ai-p'ing*, i. e. *t'ai* great, *p'ing* peace.] The name given to the adherents of a great rebellion which arose in Southern China in 1850, under the leadership of Hung-siu-tsuen, styled *Tien-wang*, Heavenly Prince, and *T'ai-p'ing-wang*, Prince of great peace, who claimed a divine commission to overthrow the Manchu dynasty and establish one of native origin, to be called the *T'ai-p'ing Chao* or Great Peace Dynasty. Also *attrib.* Hence **Tai-pingdom, Tai-pingism.**

The war which ensued devastated some of the most fertile provinces of China for a number of years; partly by means of English help the Tai-pings were finally routed and dispersed in 1865.

**1860** *All Year Round* No. 71. 504 A Taiping's head is paid for, at the rate of one tael. *Ibid.*, He succeeded in forcing back the Taipings when they menaced the Pekin Canal. *Ibid.*, Of these alternatives, piracy pays the best, Taipingism being decidedly the least lucrative. **1883** *Chambers's Encycl.* IX. 274/1 The confusion and expense of the Tae-ping rebellion. **1884** A. FORBES *Chinese Gordon* xi, The Imperialist generals had hemmed Tai-pingdom within certain limits in the lower valley of the Yantsze.

**Tair,** obs. Sc. f. TEAR *v.* **Taira,** var. TAYRA, a Brazilian weasel-like animal. **Tairge,** obs. and dial. f. TARGE. **Tairn,** obs. f. TARN. **Tais,** obs. Sc. f. TASS, *takes* (see TAKE *v.*), *toes* (pl. of TOE).

**Tais, -e,** var. TEISE *sb.* and *v. Obs.*

‖ **Taisch, taish** (taiʃ). *Gaelic Folklore.* [a. Gaelic *taibhs* (taivʃ, taiʃ):—OIr. *taidbse*, MIr. *tadhbais*, phantasm.] The phantom or apparition of a living person who is about to die; also, in more general sense, a phantom or vision of second sight.

**1775** JOHNSON *Western Isles, Ostig*, By the term *second sight*, seems to be meant a mode of seeing, superadded to that which nature generally bestows. In the Erse it is called *Taisch*; which signifies likewise a spectre, or a vision. **1785** BOSWELL *Tour to Hebrides* 7 Sept., Some women said to him, they had heard two taischs, that is, two voices of persons about to die; and what was remarkable, one of them was an English taisch, which they never heard before. **1792** *Statist. Acc. Scotl., Ross* III. 380 The ghosts of the dying, called *tasks*, are said to be heard, their cry being a repetition of the moans of the sick...The corps follow the tract led by the tasks to the place of interment. [Here *task* appears to be Gael. *tasg* 'ghost', erroneously taken in sense of *taibhs*, taisch.] **1902** J. G. CAMPBELL *Witchcraft & Second Sight* 159 Some time after [the taish was seen] a ship was wrecked in the east end of Tiree, and one of the sailors whose dress, when his body was found, corresponded to that of the taish, was taken and buried in Kirkapool.

**Taisel, taissel,** obs. and Sc. ff. TASSEL.

**Taishes, taisses**: see TASSE, thigh-armour.

**Taist, Taister,** obs. Sc. ff. TASTE, TESTER.

†**Tait,** *a.* *ME.* and *Sc. Obs.* Also 4 **teyte,** tayt. [a. ON. *teitr* glad, cheerful, corresp. to a doubtful OE. *tǽtan* to gladden, cheer, from an adj. **tát*, and in form to OHG., MHG. *zeiz* tender, dear, pleasing.] Cheerful, lively, active, nimble.

*c* **1300** *Havelok* 1841 Þe laddes were kaske and teyte. **13..** *E. E. Allit. P.* B. 871, I schal biteche yow þo two þat tayt arn & quoynt. **13..** *Gaw. & Gr. Knt.* 1377 Techez hym to þe tayles of ful tayt bestes. *c* **1470** HENRYSON *Mor. Fab.* VII. (*Lion & Mouse*) xiii, Sua come ane trip of myis out of thair nest, Richt tait and trig. **1500–20** DUNBAR *Poems* xiv. 49 Our all the gait sa mony thevis sa tait. **1513** DOUGLAS *Æneis* XII. Prol. 184 Litill lammis Full tait and trig socht bletand to thar dammis.

**Tait**, Sc. variant of Tate.

†**Taite.** *Obs.* Also 4 tayt. [a. ON. *teiti* gladsomeness, joy, cheerfulness, f. *teitr* adj.: see Tait.] Gladness, alacrity.

13.. *E. E. Allit. P.* B. 889 Þenne vch tolke tyȝt hem þat hade of tayt fayled, & vchon roþeled to þe rest þat he reche moȝt. *a* **1400–50** *Alexander* 1208 Þus ȝede þai furthe..And trottes on toward Tyre with taite [*v.r.* ioy] at þaire hertis.

**Taith**, variant of Tath *sb.* and Tathe *v.*

**Taiver, Taivert**, var. Taver, Tavert.

**Tajaçu, tajassu**: see Tayassu.

**Takable, Takar**: see Takeable, Taker.

**Take** (tēⁱk), *v.* Pa. t. **took** (tuk); pa. pple. **taken** (tēⁱ·k'n). Forms: see below. [Late OE. *tacan*, *tóc*, **tacen*, a. ON. *taka*, *tók*, *tekinn* (OSw. *taka*, Sw. *taga*, Da. *tage*), to grasp, grip, seize, lay hold of, take, which appears *c* 1100, in late parts of the OE. Chron., first in MS. D, and then *a* 1150 also in E, and elsewhere, but may have been in use in the Dane-law district *a* 1000. In ME. it gradually superseded the OE. *niman* (see Nim *v.*), and has been, during the later ME. and the whole mod.Eng. period, the simplest and most direct word for the general notion expressed by Da. *tage*, Sw. *taga*, Ger. *nehmen*, Du. *nemen*, Fr. *prendre*, It. *prendere*, Sp., Pg. *tomar*, L. *capĕre*, *sumĕre*, Gr. λαμβάνειν, Russ. брать, взять, Heb. לקח *lāqaχ*, etc. ON. *taka* was app. cognate with MDu. and mod.EFris. *tāken* to lay hold of, grasp, seize, catch; it was also in ablaut-relation to Goth. *têkan*, *taitôk*, *têkans* to touch (with the hands, etc.). With the sense in Gothic cf. ON. *taka á*, late OE. *tacan on* to touch.]

**A.** Illustration of Forms and Inflexions.

*Take* is, like *shake*, *forsake*, a strong vb. of the 6th ablaut series. In northern ME. the *k* and following short vowel in *take*, *takes*, *taken* were often suppressed, leaving the forms *ta*, *tas*, *tan*, of which *ta*, *tay*, survives in Eng. dialects, *tane* in Sc. and many Eng. dialects, *ta'en* in Eng. poets. The reduction of the pa. t. to *tō* is obs., rare, and doubtful. A weak pa. t. *taked* occurs from 13th c., and is, with *tayed*, *teaed*, *tade*, still dialectal. For the pa. pple *taken*, the pa. t. *took* has been common since 16th c. in vulgar speech and in dialects, which have also *tooken*, *tooked*. In the pa. pple., *ton(e* for the northern *tan(e* occasionally appears. See *Eng. Dial. Dict.*

**1.** *Infin.*, and *Pres.* **a.** 2 **tacan** (**tæcen**), 3–5 **taken, -yn**; 4 **tac**, 4–5 (6– *Sc.*) **tak**, 5 **taake**, 6 **taik(e**, *Sc.* **tack**; 3– **take**.

*c* **1100** *O. E. Chron.* an. 1076 (MS. D) Ac se kyngc..hine let syððan tacan. *a* **1154** *Ibid.* an. 1140 On þis gær wolde þe king Stephne tæcen Rodbert. *a* **1272** *Luue Ron* 64 in *O. E. Misc.* 95 Al deþ hit wile from him take. **13..** *K. Alis.* 1799 (Bodl. MS.) Þat he shulde of þe werlde & þee Taken tol. **13..** *Cursor M.* 568 (Cott.) Þe god to tak and leue þe ill. *Ibid.* 2812 (Gött.) His mohwes..þat suld his dohutris tac. *c* **1380** Wyclif *Wks.* (1880) 367 Þai schal taake no þinge ellis. *c* **1400** *Lay Folks Mass Bk.*, *Bidding Prayer* ii. 64 Ensaumpil for to tak. *c* **1440** *Promp. Parv.* 485/2 Takyn, or receyvyn. **1538** Kath. Bulkeley in *Lett. Suppress. Monasteries* (Camden) 230 He..will not taike my answere. **1546** *Yorks. Chantry Surv.* (Surtees) II. 454 No man will taik yt. **1562** Winȝet *Cert. Tractatis* iii. Wks. (S. T. S.) I. 34 That this tumult tak rest. **1573** Tyrie *Refut.* in *Cath. Tractates* (S. T. S.) 14 He culd nocht tack tent to sic trifflis. **1785** Burns *To the Deil* xxi, O wad ye tak a thought an' men'!

*β. contr.* 4 (5–6 *Sc.*) **ta, taa**, 4–6 (9 *dial.*) **tay, tae**, 5 **tan**.

*c* **1340** *Cursor M.* 1250 (Gött.) Hugat þu sal ta [*Cott.* tak; *Fairf.*, *Trin.* take] þi right way. **1375** Barbour *Bruce* x. 610 And thair abaid thair aynd to ta. *c* **1375** *Sc. Leg. Saints* iii. (*Andreas*) 11 Sanct Andrew his way can tay. *c* **1400** *Laud Troy Bk.* 1742 Thelaman..nold her not to his spouse tan. *c* **1560** A. Scott *Poems* (S. T. S.) ii. 153 Quhen thay saw Sym sic curage ta. **1570** in J. Redford *Mor. Play Wit & Sc.*, etc. (Shaks. Soc.) 91 Eche swete corde eche ere woolde tay. **1865** Waugh *Besom Ben* vii, Wheer are yo beawn to tay mo too?

**2.** *Imper.* **a.** 3–4 **tac**, 4–5 (6– *Sc.*) **tak**, 4– **take**; *pl.* 3 **takez**, 4 **-es, -is**, 5 **takeþ**. *β. contr.* 4–6 **ta**, *pl.* **tas** (4 **tatz**).

*c* **1200** Ormin 8355 Josæp, ris upp & tacc þe child & tacc þe childess moderr. *c* **1230** *Hali Meid.* 7 Tac þe to him treoweliche. **13..** *Cursor M.* 15233 (Cott.) Takes and etes o þis bred. **13..** *E. E. Allit. P.* B. 735 Tatz to non ille, ȝif I mele a lyttel more. **13..** *Gaw. & Gr. Knt.* 413 Ta now þy grymme tole to þe. *Ibid.* 1396 Tas yow þere my cheuicaunce. *c* **1386** Chaucer *Pars. T.* ⁋ 77 Tak reward of þy value. *c* **1425** *Cursor M.* 661 (Trin.) Beþ war & takeþ good entent. *a* **1510** Douglas *King Hart* ii. 149 First witnes thow me ta. **1816** Scott *Old Mort.* xliii, This is the way; follow me,..sir, but tak tent to your feet.

**3.** *Pres. Indic.* (special forms). **a.** *2nd pers. sing.* **a.** 4 **takes**, 4–5 **-is**, 5 **-yst**, 5– **takest**. *β. contr.* 4 **tas**, 5 **taas**.

**13..** *Cursor M.* 18358 (Cott.) Þou þat..fra þi folk þair sinnes takes [*Gött.* takis; *c* **1425** *Trin.* takest, *Laud* takyst]. *Ibid.* 27132 (Cott.) Þou þi bising tas be oþer men. *c* **1430** *Christ's own Compl.* 464 in *Pol. Rel. & L. Poems* (1866) 197 No tent þou taas. *c* **1470** Henry *Wallace* ii. 85 To quhom takis thow this thing?

**b.** *3rd pers. sing.* **a.** 2 **tæcþ**, 3–4 **takeþ**, **-eð**, 4–5 **takith**, 4–7 (8– *arch.*) **taketh**; 4– **takes**, (6 *Sc.* **takis, tekis**).

*a* **1150** *MS.* 303 *Corp. Chr. Coll. Cambr.* 178 (Napier) Swa hwæt swa hit on tæcþ. *c* **1275** Lay. 3361 And takeþ hit his child. *c* **1350** *Will. Palerne* 3193 Þe comli quen þan takeþ meliors by þe hande. **13..** *Cursor M.* 29274 (Cott.) On þam þis cursing stede first takes That [etc.]. **1382** Wyclif *Matt.* x. 38 He that takith nat his crosse. **1484** Caxton *Fables of Æsop* v. xiii, He is not wyse whiche..taketh debate or stryf. **1571** *Satir. Poems Reform.* xxix. 41 The Duvill..tekis forme of Angell bryte.

*β. contr.* 4–5 **tas** (4 **tath**), 4–6 *Sc.* **tais**, 5 **tase, tace**.

*c* **1375** *Sc. Leg. Saints* xviii. (*Egipciane*) 270 Gret dowt in his hart he tais. **1390** Gower *Conf.* II. 129 He therof his part ne tath. *a* **1400–50** *Alexander* 1666 He..Tas him to his tresory. *c* **1430** *Brut* 406 Thanne Vmfreuyle, his leue he tace [*rime* space]. *a* **1450** *Le Morte Arth.* 956 Sir Gawayne..to conselle he tase [*rimes* was, case, has].

**c.** *pl.* **a.** 4 **taken**, 5 **-yn**; *β. contr.* 4 **tas**.

**1340–70** *Alex. & Dind.* 566 Of hure tenful tach ȝe taken ensample. **1357** *Lay Folks Catech.* 244 What thing so we gete, or tas.

**4.** *Past Indic.* (and *Subj.*). **a.**[1] ? 1 **tóc**, 2–3 **toc**, 3–4 **tock**, 3–5 **tok**, 3–6 **toke**, (4 **toek**, ? **to**), 5–7 **tooke**, 4– **took**. *pl.* ? 1 **tócon**, 2 **tocan**, 3–5 **token**, 4 **tokene, tooken**, 5 **tokyn**.

*c* **1100** *O. E. Chron.* (MS. D) an. 1075, He..tóc [*MS. E* nam] swilce ȝerihta swa he him ȝelaȝade. *c* **1200** Ormin Pref. 9 Crist toc dæþ o rodetre. *c* **1275** Lay. 54 He..þane hilke boc tock us to bisne. **1297** R. Glouc. (Rolls) 5864 As me him drinke tok. *Ibid.* 6651 Þis erl..toc hire þe castel of bruges. **13..** *Cursor M.* 13152 (Cott.) To þe bure sco tok hir pas. *Ibid.* 16454 Quen þai þe fine gold forsoke, And to [*v.r.* toke] þam to þe lede. **1377** Langl. *P. Pl.* B. (MS. Rawl.) xvi. 269 + 3 He softe ȝede, Þat he toek vs as tit. **1393** *Ibid.* C. iv. 47 Mede..took hym a noble For to be hure bedman. *c* **1420** (?) Lydg. *Assembly of Gods* 421 She toke hym by the hande. *Ibid.* 1888, I..myn hert to me tooke. **1579** Lyly *Euphues* (Arb.) 80 Lucilla..toke him by the hand. **1641** Hinde *J. Bruen* xlviii. 156 A little before hee tooke his Chamber.

*c* **1100** *O. E. Chron.* (MS. D) an. 1076, And [hi] tócon þær inne mycele æhta. **1154** *Ibid.* (MS. E) an. 1136, Þa tocan þa oðre & helden her castles aȝenes him. *c* **1200** Ormin 6492 Þeȝȝ tokenn nihhtess reste þær. *c* **1250** *Gen. & Ex.* 3194 Alle ðe bones ðe he ðor token. **1297** R. Glouc. (Rolls) 3987 A lettre hii toke þe kinge. **13..** *S. Erkenwolde* 57 in Horstm. *Altengl. Leg.* (1881) 267 Quen tithynges tokene to þe tone. *c* **1380** *Lay Folks Catech.* (Lamb. MS.) 1211 Whan we tok cristyndom. **1382** Wyclif *John* i. 5 Derknessis tooken not it. *c* **1400** *Destr. Troy* 4696 Þai..tokyn the tresure. *c* **1449** Pecock *Repr.* ii. ii. 145 To hem whiche token and helden tho ymagis to be her Goddis.

**a.**[2] (*Sc.* and *n. dial.*) 4–9 **tuk**, 5–9 **tuke**, (5 **twke**, 6 **twik, tuike**), 6– **tuik**.

*c* **1375** *Sc. Leg. Saints* i. (*Petrus*) 36 He hym tuk to be hym by In his transfiguracion. *c* **1470** Henry *Wallace* i. 78 King Eduuard than it tuk in gret greuance. **1533** Gau *Richt Vay* (S. T. S.) 32 The sone..twik apone hyme our natur. *c* **1560** Rolland *Seven Sages* (1837) A ij, I..tuke gude nicht. **1596** Dalrymple tr. *Leslie's Hist. Scot.* i. (S. T. S.) 100 He tuke thame, he eit thame rawe. *Ibid.* x. 320 His recreatioune he tuike in Caris hous. *Mod. Sc.* We tuik them wi' us.

*β.* 3 **takede**, 5– **taked**. (See *Eng. Dial. Dict.*)

*c* **1205** Lay. 3333 Þe we swa takede him on. **1485** *Waterf. Arch.* in *10th Rep. Hist. MSS. Comm.* App. v. 318 That spoiled, robbed, or taked ony of the Kyngs liege men.

**5.** *Past pple.* **a.** 2–4 **itaken**, 4 **ytakyn**; 4– **taken**, (4–5 **takin, -yn**, 5 **-yne, -on, -un**, 6 **takne, taking**; 7 **taiken**, *Sc.* **taikin**).

*c* **1175** Itaken [see B. 14]. *c* **1205** Itaken [see *take on*: 84 i]. *c* **1320** *Cast. Love* 202 Þe blisse of lyf he haþ forsaken, And to deolful deþ him taken. *c* **1330** *Assump. Virg.* (B. M. MS.) 625 When þi lord was ytakyn. *c* **1375** *Cursor M.* 4875 (Fairf.) Qua-so ys takin wiþ stollyn þinge. *a* **1380** *S. Bernard* 612 in Horstm. *Altengl. Leg.* (1878) 51/2 Wiþ seknesse stronge He was itaken. *c* **1400** *Destr. Troy* 1512 His towne was takon. *c* **1449** Pecock *Repr.* ii. iv. 159 Weel takun of wise men. **1537** Wriothesley *Chron.* (Camden) I. 60 The sayd Halam was takne. **1552** Lyndesay *Monarche* 5539 Quhilkis salbe taking, but warnyng. **1629** *Reg. Privy Council Scotl.* Ser. ii. III. 25 We..have taikin thame.

*β. contr.* 3–5 **itake**, 4–5 **ytake**; 4–7 **take**, 5 (6 *pseudo-Sc.*) **tak**.

**1297** R. Glouc. (Rolls) 6106 Nou adde heyemen of þe lond itake..His fader ostage god ynou. **1340–70** *Alex. & Dind.* 721 Ȝe schullen..offren to venus A ful derworþe douue on his den take. **1377** Langl. *P. Pl.* B. xi. 254 So is..pouerte or penaunce pacientlyche ytake. **1387** Trevisa *Higden* (Rolls) VIII. 79 At Turon he was i-take wiþ a fevere. **1423** Jas. I *Kingis Q.* cxciii, Sche hath me tak, hir humble creature. *c* **1425** *Cursor M.* 928 (Trin.) Þat erþe þou were of take. *c* **1440** *Pallad. on Husb.* iii. 906 To graffe a quynce is diuers tyme ytake. *c* **1450** *Merlin* 296 And his wif [was] also I-take. **1559** *Mirr. Mag.* (1563) I j, Shortly after was Kyng Henry take, And put in pryson. **1605** Take [see B. 49].

*γ. contr.* 4 **y-tan**; 4–5 **tan**, 4–8 **tane**, (4 **tene**, 4 (6 *Sc.*) **tain**, 4–5 **tayn**, 5–6 *Sc.* **tayne**, 6 **taan**, **teyne**, *Sc.* **teine**, 6–7 **taine**, 7 **taen**), 7–8 **ta'ne**, 9 (*poet.* and *dial.*) **ta'en**; (*erron.*) 5 **ton**, 5 (6 *pseudo-Sc.*) **tone**.

*c* **1320** *Sir Tristr.* 1000 Now haþ tristrem y tan Oȝain moraunt to fiȝt. *c* **1340** Hampole *Prose Tr.* (1866) 1 Ihesu the Worde of God has tane manes kynde. **13..** *Cursor M.* 4896 (Cott.) Lok þai alle be tain [*v. rr.* tan, tane, take] and bonden. *Ibid.* 16058 (Cott.) Þai him had tene [*v. rr.* tane, taken] al wit tresun. *c* **1400** *Rule St. Benet* 2112 Þen sall þis rewel eft furth be ton [*rime* gon]. *c* **1470** Henry *Wallace* ii. 400 Wallace..Apon the crag with his suerd has him tayne. **1500–20** Dunbar *Poems* xlvi. 102 That he..nocht in the feindis net be tone [*rime* allone]. *c* **1520** Nisbet *N. T. in Scots*, *Acts* i. 11 Quhilk is taan vp fra you into heuen. **15..** *Sir A. Barton* in *Surtees Misc.* (1888) 68 Where that Scoott hath teyne frome the a grootte. *a* **1578** Lindesay (Pitscottie) *Chron. Scot.* (S. T. S.) I. 197 Gif he had teine it. **1597** Shaks. *2 Hen. IV*, iv. v. 160 The Prince hath ta'ne it hence. **1602** — *Ham.* i. iii. 107 That you have tane his tenders for true pay. *a* **1631** Drayton *Triumph David* 805 The sword taen from the giant's side. *c* **1645** Howell *Lett.* v. 30 He hath taine such a habit of it. **1653** *Nissena* 43 From the time she had taen upon her the yoke of marriage. **1875** Tennyson *Q. Mary* v. v, The Holy Father Has ta'en the legateship from our cousin Pole.

*δ.* 6–7 **tooke**, 7–8 (9 *dial.* and *illit.*) **took**; 7–9 **tooken.**

**1592** Kyd *Sol. & Pers.* iii. i. 5 My brothers ghoasts..would now haue tooke their rest. **1610** Donne *Pseudo-martyr* 353 The Popes haue tooken order..to enact [etc.]. **1633** P. Fletcher *Pisc. Ecl.* v. ix, Thus many a Nymph is took. *a* **1667** Jer. Taylor *Rev. to Altar* Wks. 1849 V. 323 God hath tooke seisure of it. **1790** *Cook's Voy.* V. 1808 Having took our departure from Prince William's Sound. **1899** Betham-Edwards *Lord of Harv.* 155 Mr. Flindell..has took you up in his gig.

*ε.* 6 **taked.**

**1512** *Helyas* in Thoms *Prose Rom.* (1828) III. 24 My sonne..hath taked the quene Beatrice..to his wife. **1581** Rich *Farew. Milit. Prof.* (1846) 207 Till he had taked his firste fruites.

**B.** Signification.

The earliest known use of this verb in the Germanic languages was app. to express the physical action 'to put the hand on', 'to touch'—the only known sense of Gothic *têkan*. By a natural advance, such as is seen in English in the use of 'lay hands upon', the sense passed to 'lay hold upon, lay hold of, grip, grasp, seize'—the essential meaning of Old Norse *taka*, of MDu. *taken*, and of the material senses of *take* in English. By the subordination of the notion of the instruments, and even of the physical action, to that of the result, *take* becomes in its essence 'to transfer to oneself by one's own action or volition (anything material or non-material)'. This becomes then the general or ordinary sense of the verb, which falls into two main divisions, *take* in the sense of 'seize, grip', hence 'appropriate', and *take* in the sense of 'receive or accept what is handed to one'. Subordinate to these are the non-material senses of 'assume, adopt, apprehend, comprehend, comprise, contain'. For the common element of all these notions *take* is the simple and proper term, for which no simpler can be substituted. It is one of the elemental words of the language, of which the only direct explanation is to show the *thing* or *action* to which they are applied.

*Take* also enters into a great number of idiomatic phrases, which are often difficult to analyse. Many of these are parallel to, and influenced by French phrases with *prendre*: see F. H. Sykes, *French Elements in ME.*, Oxford 1899.

*General arrangement of senses*: I. To touch. II. To seize, grip, catch. III. Ordinary current sense, **i.** with material obj.; **ii.** with non-material obj. IV. To choose, take for a purpose, into use. V. To derive, obtain from a source. VI. To receive, accept, admit, contain. VII. To apprehend mentally, comprehend. VIII. To undertake, perform, make. IX. To convey, conduct, deliver, apply or betake oneself, go. X. Idiomatic uses with special obj. XI. Intransitive uses with preposition. XII. Adverbial combinations = compound verbs. XIII. Idiomatic phrases, and *Phrase-key*.

**I.** †**1.** To touch (*intr.* with *on*, also *trans.*: = ON. *taka á*, and *taka*). *Obs.*

*a* **1150** *MS.* 303 *Corp. Chr. Coll. Cambr.* 178 (Napier) Soðlice þæt ilce ele is swa mihtiȝ & swa strange þæt swa hwæt swa hit on tæcþ, þærrihtes hit eall forbærnð. *Ibid.* 179 Sona swa þæt ele toc on þæt wæter, þa aras þær upp swiðe mycel fyr. *c* **1250** *Gen. & Ex.* 3456 Abute ðis munt ðu merke make, If erf or man ðor-one take, It dead ðolen. *c* **1250** *Old Kent. Serm.* in *O. E. Misc.* 31 Ure lord him seide and spredde his hond, and tok his lepre. *a* **1300** *Cursor M.* 10969 (Cott.), I and mi wijf on ald tas. **1340** *Ayenb.* 91 Be zyȝþe, be hyerþe, be smellinge, be zuelȝynge, and be takynge.

**II.** To seize, grasp, capture, catch, and related senses. * *in literal and physical sense.*

**2.** *trans.* To lay hold upon, get into one's hands by force or artifice; to seize, capture, esp. in war; to make prisoner; hence, to get into one's power, to win by conquest (a fort, town, country). Also, to apprehend (a person charged with an offence), to arrest; to seize (property) by legal process, as by distraint, etc. See also *take by* Storm.

*c* **1100** *O. E. Chron.* an. 1072 (MS. D), Se kyng nam heora scypa & wæpna,..& þa menn ealle he toc, & dyde of heom þæt he wolde. *Ibid.* an. 1076, Ac se kyngc..hine let syððan tacan. **1154** *Ibid.* an. 1140 (Laud MS.), And te Lundenissce folc hire wolde tæcen. *c* **1200** Ormin 5948, & tatt he siþþenn takenn wass All gilltelæs & bundenn & naȝȝledd uppo rodetre. *a* **1300** *Cursor M.* 4896 Lok þai alle be tain and bonden. *Ibid.* 18554 Als prisun þai him tok for-þi. *c* **1400** *Rom. Rose* 5894 My modir is of gret prowesse; She hath tan many a fortresse. *c* **1450** *Merlin* 13 The Iuges made hir to be taken, and brought hir be-fore them. *c* **1460** *Brut* 524 Þei londed & come to Sandwych..& toke the town, & ryfled & dispoyled it. **1526** Tindale *Matt.* iv. 12 When Iesus had herde that Ihon was taken, he departed in to Galile. **1600** E. Blount tr. *Conestaggio* 184 Hauing quietly taken the other two gallions, they entred within the Porte. **1658** Cokaine *Trappolin* i. i, He is your brothers prisoner..That in the wars of Mantoa was took. **1736** Lediard *Life Marlborough* I. 180 The English took about 200 Prisoners. **1803** *Pic Nic* II. No. 8. 61, I was taken into custody. **1854** J. S. C. Abbott *Napoleon* (1855) II. 372, I took two guns and retook two.

**b.** To catch, capture (a wild beast, bird, fish, etc.); also of an animal, to seize or catch (prey).

*c* **1200** Ormin 13504 Rihht alls an hunnte takeþþ der Wiþþ hise ȝæpe racchess. *c* **1250** *Gen. & Ex.* 3323 Ðor miȝte euerilc man fuȝeles taken. *c* **1400** Maundev. (Roxb.) v. 15 Þai take wylde bestes riȝt wele. **1509** Hawes *Past. Pleas.* xxxi. (Percy Soc.) 154 Wo worth the beaute which toke me in snare. **1563** B. Googe *Sonnets* (Arb.) 82 By hydden hooke, the symple fole is tane. **1648** *Hunting of Fox* 23 They keep packs of dogs, or Beagles, on purpose to take them by hunting. **1801** Strutt *Sports & Past.* i. ii. 33 The present methods of taking fish. **1892** *Longm. Mag.* Nov. 87 They are readily taken by nets. **1899** Rider Haggard *Swallow* iii, The women and the little ones..were taken by wild beasts.

**c.** *subj.* in imprecations.

*a* **1533** Ld. Berners *Huon* lvii. 192 Mahounde take his soule! **1600, 1749** [see Devil *sb.* 17]. **1850** *Tait's Mag.* XVII. 298/1 Here he comes again!—deuce take him. **1856** Reade *Never Too Late* I, The devil take the hindmost.

**d.** In various games, as chess, cards, etc.: To capture (an adversary's piece, card, etc.) so as to put it out of play; also (*Cards*) to gain possession of (a trick): see Trick *sb.* (Also said of the piece, card, etc., by which the taking is effected).

14.. *Beryn* 1812 The next drauȝt aftir, he toke a roke for nauȝte. *c* **1440** *Gesta Rom.* xxi. 71 (Harl. MS.) Whenne he [the pawn at chess] goth aside, he takith anoþer. **1562** Rowbothum *Play Cheasts* B iv b, Thou shalt take his knight with thy Quene. **1735** Bertin *Chess* 55 The king takes the queen. **1840** *P. Parley's Ann.* I. 263 A pawn takes the enemy angularly.

**e.** *Cricket.* To catch (the ball) off the bat so as to put the batsman 'out' (also with the batsman as obj.); of the bowler, To 'capture' (a wicket) by striking it with the ball (or otherwise).

**1882** *Daily Tel.* 17 May, A minute or two later Walker was smartly taken at the wicket off Garrett. *Ibid.* 24 June, Lucas, who had been fielding at long-off, running at full speed, managed to take it [the ball]. **1883** *Ibid.* 15 May 2/7 He was..taken at cover-point by Woof. **1890** *Field* 10 May 672/2 Studd..was then beautifully taken at long-off.

**3.** To lay hold of, grasp (with the hand, arms, etc.); to seize and hold. *To take in one's arms*, to embrace. Often const. *by* the hand, head, horns, tail, etc.: see Hand *sb.* 46, Bull *sb.*[1] 1 c. Cf. also *take hold* in Phrases below (69).

*a* **1225** *Juliana* 70 He rende his claðes ant toc him seoluen bi þe top. *a* **1300** *Cursor M.* 2364 (Cott.) Ta loth þi broþer sun in hand, To chanaan ȝee most now drau. **1387** Trevisa *Higden* (Rolls) III. 147 To my Crist, whos riȝt hond I haue i-take. **1393** Langl. *P. Pl.* C. xxii. 170 Crist..took thomas by þe hand. *c* **1425** *Cursor M.* 4357 (Trin.) She toke him aboute þe necke wiþ þis And profered hir mouþ to kis. ?*c* **1500** in *Joseph Arim.* 30 He toke me by the hande and so ledde me in myn house. **1600** W. Watson *Decacordon* (1602) 117 He tooke him by the sleeve, as they were in going over a stile. **1709** Steele & Addison *Tatler* No. 114 ¶ 1 He took me by the Hand. **1825** *New Monthly Mag.* XIV. 361, I took her hand and kissed her. **1890** F. Barrett *Betw. Life & Death* III. 106 He took her in his arms.

**4.** *intr.* Of a hook, a mechanical device, etc.: To catch, engage: usually const. *into*.

*c* **1435** *Torr. Portugal* 1608 Sith he pullith at his croke, So fast in to the flesh it toke. **1729** Desaguliers in *Phil. Trans.* XXXVI. 197 The Pall or Lever.. does so communicate with the Catch, that..the Catch always takes. **1797** *Encycl. Brit.* (ed. 3) IX. 9 The teeth of these four wheels take alternately into the teeth of four racks. **1825** J. Nicholson *Operat. Mechanic* 310 The next tooth of the pinion will take into the gap in the end of the rack. *Ibid.* 513 These pins take into holes in the plate, made exactly to fit them. **1856** Kane *Arct. Expl.* II. xxvi. 262 A floe, taking upon a tongue of ice.., began to swing upon it like a pivot.

**b.** *trans.* Of a mechanical appliance, etc.: To 'lay hold of'; to act upon by contact, adhesion, or the like.

**1659** Leak *Waterwks.* 25 So as the Saws may take the said peece again. **1849** Pellatt *Curios. Glass Making* 94 The punty takes the flat end by adhesion. **1894** *Harper's Mag.* July 191/2 The blades no longer take the water together.

**5.** *trans.* To strike, hit, impinge upon (a person, etc.), usually *in*, *on* (*across*, *over*, etc.) some part; also with the part as obj.; = Catch *v.* 11.

[The notion here seems to have been originally to catch or get at a person by means of the part named, which catches the blow that otherwise might have passed.]

*c* **1400** *Destr. Troy* 8224 Ector turnet with tene, toke hym on þe hed. *c* **1470** Henry *Wallace* I. 403 Wallas with it [the poutstaff] fast on the cheik him tuk. *Ibid.* III. 175 As he glaid by, aukwart he couth hym ta. **1509** Hawes *Past. Pleas.* xl. (Percy Soc.) 202 Unto me than he came full softely, And with his staffe he toke me on the brest. **1594** Shaks. *Rich. III*, I. iv. 159 Take him on the Costard, with the hiltes of thy Sword. **1670** Cotton *Espernon* II. v. 201 He was..taken upon the head with a stone. **1719** De Foe *Crusoe* (1840) I. iii. 52 The blow taking my side and breast, beat the breath, as it were, quite out of my body. **1748** *Anson's Voy.* I. x. 104 A mountainous..sea took us upon our starboard quarter. **1795** *Hist.* in *Ann. Reg.* 70/1 A masked battery took them in flank. **1806–7** J. Beresford *Miseries Hum. Life* (1826) vi. Introd., The kick of a horse..took me across the ribs. **1891** *Blackw. Mag.* CL. 651/2 When a sheep runs amuck, he is..a living catapult, that, if he took you fair, would knock the life out of you. **1893** *Chamb. Jrnl.* 3 June 350/1 The ball took him squarely between the eyes.

**b.** With double obj.: e.g. *to take any one a blow*.

**1448** *Paston Lett.* (1901) IV. 19 He..toke his master on the hepe suche a strok that..brake his hepe. *c* **1590** Marlowe *Faust.* vii. 96 Cursed be he that took Friar Sandelo a blow on the pate! **1596** Shaks. *Tam. Shr.* III. ii. 165 This mad-brain'd bridegroome tooke him such a cuffe. **1603** — *Meas. for M.* II. i. 189 If he tooke you a box o'th'eare. **1781** C. Johnston *Hist. J. Juniper* II. 161 Taking him a blow full in the pit of his stomach. *Mod. colloq.* The ball took me an awful whack on the chest.

**6.** *absol.* or *intr.* **a.** Of a plant, seed, or graft: To 'get hold' of that on which it grows; to take root, 'strike', germinate, begin to grow.

*c* **1440** *Pallad. on Husb.* II. 153 In reed erthe ek a vyne is hard to take. *Ibid.* III. 576 But euery day me most hit delue & wete Vntil hit take. **1530** Palsgr. 747/1 A yonge plante or sette begynneth to take whan it groweth up. **1661** J. Childrey *Brit. Baconica* 14 Fruit fails in one countrey, and takes in another. **1712** J. James tr. *Le Blond's Gardening* 184 The Oak being in its own Nature very difficult to take again. **1802** Forsyth *Fruit Trees* i. (1824) 2 The cherry and plum will never take upon each other..but the apricot will take upon all sorts of plums. **1891** *Cosmopolitan* XII. 87/2 Patches where the seed has failed to take. **1892** *Field* 10 Dec. 883/3 We planted a thousand cedars of Lebanon, with shoots 6 in. high, and we have no doubt that they will take well.

**b.** Of ink, etc.: To adhere to the paper, parchment, etc.

**1883** R. Haldane *Workshop Receipts* Ser. II. 192/1 The use of ox-gall, which makes the ink 'take', has also the disadvantage of making it frequently 'run'.

** *with either the action or the agent non-material.*

**7.** *trans.* Of a disease, a pain, an injurious or destructive agency, natural or supernatural, magical, etc.; also of a notion, fancy, feeling, etc.: To affect, seize, lay hold of, attack. Also in imprecations, as 'pest' or 'plague take him'.

*a* **1300** *Cursor M.* 11823 (Cott.) Wit þe crache him tok the scurf [*Trin.* þe ȝicche toke him sikerly]. *a* **1325** *Prose Psalter* xlvii [i]. 5 Drede toke hem. **1450–80** tr. *Secreta Secret.* 31 Than mayst thou ete..as thyn appetit takith the. *a* **1533** Ld. Berners *Huon* lvii. 194 For a colyke that hath taken me in the ryght syde. *a* **1553** [see Mischief 9 b]. *a* **1566** [see Plague 3 d]. **1581** Pettie *Guazzo's Civ. Conv.* I. (1586) 12 b, Moued by some sodaine toie which taketh them in the head. **1598** Shaks. *Merry W.* IV. iv. 32 He blasts the tree, and takes the cattle. **1604** E. G[rimstone] *D'Acosta's Hist. Indies* VII. xxiii. 565 Fire tooke the Temple. **1661** Cowley *Disc. Govt. O. Cromwell* Wks. 1710 II. 664 Now the Freak takes him. **1707** Mortimer *Husb.* 173 No Beast will eat sour Grass till the Frost hath taken it. **1889** *Temple Bar Mag.* Dec. 451 An intense weariness of life took him. **1892** *Cassell's Fam. Mag.* Aug. 515/2 What in the name of wonder has taken the girl? **1893** *National Observer* 7 Oct. 542/2 He admired as the humour took him. *absol.* **1602** Shaks. *Ham.* I. i. 163 Then no planets strike, No fairy takes, nor witch hath power to charm.

**b.** *pass.* To be seized, attacked, or affected (*with* disease, a fit, fancy, etc.); to 'have an attack' of something.

*a* **1300** *Cursor M.* 8915 (Cott.) Sco es wode and wit warlagh tan [*Trin.* wiþ fende Itake]. **1387** Trevisa *Higden* (Rolls) VI. 157 He was i-take with sikenesse and deyde. *c* **1440** *Promp. Parv.* 261/2 Infectyn..as menne take wythe pestylence. **1526** Tindale *Matt.* iv. 24 All sicke people, that were taken with diuers diseases and gripinges. *a* **1533** Ld. Berners *Huon* xlviii. 162 He was taken in loue. **1578** Lyte *Dodoens* 609 The astonied members, or limmes taken with colde. **1680** Dryden *Spanish Friar* III. i, I am taken on the sudden with a grievous swimming in my Head. **1865** Dickens *Mut. Fr.* IV. xiii, Mrs. Boffin was then taken with a laughing fit of clapping her hands, and clapping her knees. **1888** Florence Warden *Witch of Hills* I. xiii. 273, I was going to be taken with a fit.

**c.** *pass.* (*ellipt.*) To have a seizure or attack; to be seized with sudden illness, pain, disease, numbness, or other affection (physical or mental). ? *Obs.* exc. *dial.*

**1450–1530** *Myrr. our Ladye* 29 Where the soule was take a non & sore tormented longe tyme togidre. **1568** Turner *Herbal* III. 40 Good for membres that are num or taken. **1607** Markham *Caval.* VII. (1617) 11 A horse that is taken our common Farriers say to be planet strooke. *c* **1642** Ld. Herbert in *Life* (1770) 45 Others..standing stiff and stark.. seem as if they were taken in their joynts.

**d.** *pass.* with complemental adj., as *to be taken ill* (formerly *blind*, *hoarse*, *lame*), to be seized or struck with illness, etc. Rarely in *active*: see quot. 13... Also humorously (quot. 1838).

13.. *E. E. Allit. P.* A. 1157 No thyng myȝt me dere To fech me bar & take me halte. **1588** Parke tr. *Mendoza's Hist. China* 48 Whatsoeuer children be borne a creeple.. or by sicknes be taken lame. **1657** W. Rand tr. *Gassendi's Life Peiresc* I. 64 Being soon after taken blind. **1662** J. Wilson *Cheats* v. iii, Being taken very ill of a sudden. **1711** Steele *Spect.* No. 96 ¶ 2 Master Harry was taken very ill of a Fever. **1802** Mar. Edgeworth *Moral T.* (1816) I. iv. 21 She was taken ill in the night. **1838** Dickens *Nich. Nick.* xxviii, 'Oh, charming!' interrupted Kate's patroness, who was sometimes taken literary. **1891** *Harper's Mag.* Apr. 750/1 He was taken hoarse at the last moment.

**e.** *intr.* for *pass.*, with *compl.*, as *to take ill* = to be taken ill, to fall or become ill. Also humorously (quot. 1890[2]). *colloq.* and *dial.*

**1674** N. Fairfax *Bulk & Selv.* 131 A woman..who took with child in the very fit of a Third Ague. **1822** J. Hodgson in Raine *Mem.* (1857) I. 400 My father-in-law took ill. **1890** Healy *Insula Sanct.* 317 He took sick and died in the island. **1890** *Illustr. Lond. News* 29 Nov. 686/3 Then, too, he took studious, and..pored over great tomes and learned things. **1903** Trevelyan in *Independent Rev.* Dec. 409 Mr. William Pitt..took ill and died after Austerlitz.

**f.** *intr.* To catch, catch hold: *esp.* of fire, to seize upon combustible substances, to be kindled, begin burning; also of a condition, humour, fancy, etc. (cf. 10 c). Now *rare.*

**1523** Ld. Berners *Froiss.* I. clviii. 192 All the base court was afyre, so that the fyre..toke into the coueryng of a great towre couered with rede. **1634–5** Brereton *Trav.* (Chetham Soc.) 43 The fire first took in rape-oil. **1639** S. Du Verger tr. *Camus' Admir. Events* 110 Rottennesse takes sooner in apples, which are bruised. **1700** T. Brown *Amusem. Ser. & Com.* 52 When any Humour Takes in London. **1803** *Ann. Rev.* II. 189/1 The tinder was ready, and the spark took.

**8.** *trans.* To 'catch' or come upon (any one) *in* some action or situation; *fig.* to catch or detect *in* (†*with*) a fault or error. *To take tardy*: see Tardy.

The first two quotations connect this with sense 2.

[**1387** Trevisa *Higden* (Rolls) III. 227 Pomphilia..was i-take into [*v.r.* in] leccherie. *c* **1400** *Apol. Loll.* 6 Many popis han synnyd, and ben snybbid; and sum tan in heresy and deposid.] **1577** Hanmer *Anc. Eccl. Hist.* (1663) 85 By reasoning with this old Apelles, I took him with many falshoods. **1597** Morley *Introd. Mus.* 95 In which fault you haue beene nowe thrise taken. **1602** *Narcissus* (1893) 91 What was that I tooke you all a gabling tother day? **1607** R. Johnson *Pleas. Conceites Old Hobson* (Percy Soc.) 15 His man seeing himselfe so taken napping, for a time stood amazed. **1652** Gaule *Magastrom.* 331 The poore astrologers, who had already been taken with so many lies. **1668** Shadwell *Sullen Lovers* I. i, I am glad I've taken you within, I come on purpose to tell you the news, d'ye hear it? **1885** Mrs. Harrison ('Lucas Malet') *Col. Enderby's Wife* VII. ii, The doctor was not easily taken off his guard.

**b.** To come upon suddenly, overtake, catch. *Obs.* or *arch.* exc. in certain phrases: see *take* Short, *take by* Surprise, *take at* Unawares.

[13.. *Gaw. & Gr. Knt.* 1811 Iche tolke mon do as he is tan, tas to non ille, ne pine.] *a* **1533** Ld. Berners *Huon* xlviii. 161 At last a wynd toke them whether they wolde or not. **1568** Grafton *Chron.* II. 210 A tempest toke them on the sea, that put them so farre out of their course. **1611** Bible *Ecclus.* xxxvi. 26 A man that..lodgeth wheresoeuer the night taketh him. **1890** Clark Russell *Ocean Trag.* II. xxi. 181 We were at breakfast when the first of the wind took us.

**9.** †**a.** To take to task; to reprehend, rebuke. *Obs.* **b.** To check, 'pull up', interrupt. *dial.* (Cf. *take up*, 90 m, n.)

*c* **1250** *Old Kent. Serm.* in *O. E. Misc.* 32 Þo a-ros up ure lord and tok þane wynd and þo [*MS.* to] see; and al-so raþe hit was stille. *a* **1586** Sidney *Arcadia* IV. (1622) 415 And therewith taking himself.. said hee. **1637** Rutherford *Lett.* xcviii. (1862) I. 251 But this is my infirmity. By His grace I take myself in these ravings.

**10.** To catch the fancy or affection of; to excite a liking in; to captivate, delight, charm; to 'fetch'.

**1605** [see Taking *ppl. a.* 2]. **1609** B. Jonson *Sil. Wom.* I. i, Such sweet neglect more taketh me, Than all th' adulteries of art. **1623** B. Jonson *To the memory of Shaks.* 76 Those flights vpon the bankes of Thames, That so did take Eliza, and our Iames! **1656** Earl Monm. tr. *Boccalini, Pol. Touchstone* (1674) 289 With a readiness that much took all the Literati. **1686** W. de Britaine *Hum. Prud.* iv. (ed. 3) 15 Take the Vulgar by your Civilities. **1830** Tennyson *To the Owl* II. i, Thy tuwhoos..Which upon the dark afloat, So took echo with delight. **1890** F. Barrett *Betw. Life & Death* II. xxi. 78 You took the whole audience. **1891** Galton *La Fenton* I. viii. 193 Scarcely the man to take the fancy of a very young girl.

**b.** *pass.* const. *with*, less usually *by*.

**1535** Coverdale *Prov.* vi. 25 Lest thou be taken with hir fayre lokes. **1622** Bacon *Hen. VII* 153 King James.. taken by Perkins amiable and alluring behaviour..entertained him..as became the person of Richard Duke of Yorke. **1641** W. Mountagu in *Buccleuch MSS.* (Hist. MSS Comm.) I. 286 The King and Queen seemed to be much taken with ..the entertainment. **1798** Charlotte Smith *Yng. Philos.* IV. 110, I was quite taken with the spirit and beauty of the young gentlewoman. **1867** Carlyle *Remin.* (1881) II. 23 He was much taken with my little Jeannie, as he well might be.

**c.** *absol.* or *intr.* *To take* = to take the fancy, win favour, gain acceptance; *esp.* to win popular favour, become popular.

*a* **1635** Naunton *Fragm. Reg.* (Arb.) 16 It took best with the people. **1654** H. Vaughan *Silex Scint.* Pref. (1900) 13 Nothing takes (as they rightly phrase it) like a Romance. **1762–71** H. Walpole *Vertue's Anecd. Paint.* (1786) I. 237 The whim took; he repeated the practice. **1817** Miss Mitford in L'Estrange *Life* (1870) II. i. 4 The new melodrame ..takes mightily.

**d.** *trans.* To attract and hold, to 'catch' (a person's eye or attention).

**1754** Richardson *Grandison* (1781) V. i. 6 We..took the Bishop's eye. He came to us. **1842** Whewell in *Life* (1881) 279, I am not surprised that your attention was taken by the examination papers. **1881** *Scribner's Mag.* XXI. 268/1 Some one took Horton's attention for a moment. **1889** *Eng. Illustr. Mag.* Dec. 268 My eye was taken by something bright.

**11.** *intr.* Of a plan, operation, etc.: To have the intended result; to succeed, be effective, take effect, 'come off'. Now *rare.* (See also 10 c.)

**1622** Bacon *Hen. VII* 63 The temporarie Fruit of the Parliament in their aide and aduice giuen for Britaine, tooke not, nor prospered not. **1625** Massinger *New way* v. i, It may be, Sweetheart, my project took. **1646** H. Lawrence *Comm. Angells* 98 This temptation tooke. **1658** *Hist. Christina Queen Swedland* 287 This machine was full of fire-workes, which took very handsomly. **1701** W. Wotton *Hist. Rome* 356 The design took and the Fellow got away. **1800–24** Campbell *Ritter Bann* xxxi, The treachery took: she waited wild.

†**b.** In weakened or indefinite sense: To have a result of some kind; to turn out, eventuate. *Obs.*

*a* **1625** Fletcher *Hum. Lieutenant* III. vii, Did I not tell you how 'twould take? **1648** C'tess Lindsey in *Buccleuch MSS.* (Hist. MSS. Comm.) I. 309 My son Paston is in town about a match for his son; how it will take I know not.

**c.** Of a medicine, inoculation, etc.: To take hold, take effect, prove operative or effective.

**1626** B. Jonson *Staple of N.* v. iii, If all succeed well, and my simples take. **1853** *Jrnl. R. Agric. Soc.* XIV. I. 253

To see if the previous inoculation would still take. **1897** S. L. HINDE *Congo Arabs* 61 The vaccine from Europe,—unfortunately none of it took.

**III.** Weakened sense of 'seize', with elimination of the notion of force or art: the ordinary current sense. **i.** With a material object.

* *with physical action distinct.*

**12.** *trans.* To perform the voluntary physical act by which one gets (something) into one's hand or hold; to transfer to oneself by one's own physical act. (Now the main sense.)

**a.** with the instrumentality of the hand or hands explicitly or implicitly indicated.

*c* **1200** ORMIN 135 He toc hiss reclefatt onn hand, & ȝede innto þe temmple. *a* **1300** *Cursor M.* 1374 Þou sal tak þis pepins thre, Þat I toke o þat appel tre. *c* **1375** *Ibid.* 21529 (Fairf.) Siþen he toke [*Cott.* & *Gött.* nam] a spade in hande. **1387** TREVISA *Higden* (Rolls) VII. 77 Anoon as he hadde i-take þe knyf all þe ymages gonne to grucche and to aryse. *c* **1391** CHAUCER *Astrol.* II. § 29 Tak thanne thyn Astrolabie with bothe handes. **1450** W. LOMNER in *Four C. Eng. Lett.* (1880) 4 And toke a rusty sword. **1471** CAXTON *Recuyell* I. Pref., [I] forthwith toke penne and ynke and began [etc.]. *a* **1533** LD. BERNERS *Huon* lix. 207 Take thy vyall, and geue vs a songe. **1608** TOPSELL *Serpents* (1658) 595 If a man take a Snake or a Serpent into his handling. **1611** BIBLE *John* xxi. 13 Iesus then commeth, and taketh bread, and giueth them. **1799** WORDSW. *Lucy Gray* vi, He plied his work;—and Lucy took The lantern in her hand. **1833** T. HOOK *Parson's Dau.* I. ii, He could take his hat and go.

**b.** with the instrumentality not expressed or considered.

*c* **1200** ORMIN 1338 Þe preost .. toc & snaþ þatt oþerr bucc Drihhtin þærwiþþ to lakenn. *a* **1300** *Cursor M.* 5646 Þar-for moyses was his nam, For he was o þe water tan. **1470–85** MALORY *Arthur* XXI. v. 849 Syr Bedwere toke the kyng vpon his backe and so wente wyth hym to that water syde. **1584** R. SCOT *Discov. Witchcr.* XII. xviii. (1886) 222 Take a cup of cold water, and let fall thereinto three drops of the same bloud. **1611** BIBLE *Gen.* ii. 22 The rib which the Lord God had taken from man, made hee a woman. **1685** BOYLE *Effects of Mot.* Postscr. 155 Take .. of the Arsenical Loadstone well pulverised two ounces. **1771** MRS. HAYWOOD *New Present* 77 Take a quart of shrimps. **1882** SOUTHWARD *Pract. Print.* xi. 444 While the roller [= pressman's assistant] is taking ink, the pressman should employ the time in looking over the heap.

†**c.** To take and put (a garment) *on* one, wrap *about* one. *Obs.*

*a* **1300** *Cursor M.* 9746 Fader, i sal on me for-þi, O thral tak clething sothfastli. *Ibid.* 10419 Sco tok on hir cleþing o care. **1530** PALSGR. 746/2 Take this mantell aboute you, *affullez ce manteau.* *a* **1604** *Song* in Shaks. *Oth.* II. iii. 99 And take thy awl'd Cloake about thee.

**13.** To receive into one's body by one's own act; to eat or drink, to swallow (food, drink, medicine, opium, etc.); to inhale (snuff, tobacco-smoke, etc.). (For tobacco, the ordinary expression is now *to smoke.*)

*c* **1200** ORMIN 7545 Þatt tokenn aȝȝ wiþþ mikell mæþ & aȝȝ unnorne fode. **13..** *Cursor M.* 16762+16 He tast it with tonge, Bot þer-of toke he noght. *c* **1400** *Apol. Loll.* 103 Þe meyt comendiþ vs not to God,..but frely it may be tan, & frely left. **1509** BARCLAY *Shyp of Folys* (1570) 34 Wine ne ale hurteth no maner creature But sharpeth the wit if it be take in kinde. **1601** HOLLAND *Pliny* XX. iv, The best way to take it [the juice of the radish], is at the end of a meale with the last meat. **1617** MORYSON *Itin.* II. 46 He tooke Tobacco abundantly,..which I thinke preserved him from sicknes. **1654–66** EARL ORRERY *Parthen.* (1676) 683 My Soldiers having..taken a little refreshment. **1675** BAXTER *Cath. Theol.* II. I. 298 It was then a crime with them to take Tobacco, and now it is none: thus custome changes the matter. **1732** BERKELEY *Alciphr.* v. § 7 Those..will take his physic. **1771** FOOTE *Maid of B.* I. Wks. 1799 II. 210 Mr. Flint and I, most evenings take a whiff here. **1784** *Unfortunate Sensibility* II. 70 To take a good drink of raw brandy. **1807** SOUTHEY *Espriella's Lett.* II. 219 We took an early breakfast. **1852** FITZGERALD *Euphranor* (1904) 73 No doubt he took his glass with the rest. **1875** JOWETT *Plato* (ed. 2) I. 429 He died by taking poison. **1879** MORLEY *Milton* 108 He died at Spa, where he was taking the waters, in September 1653. **1891** *Murray's Mag.* Apr. 532 Inordinately given to taking snuff. **1893** *Times* 22 Apr. 7/5 The Queen..took tea at the Cabanon on the sea shore.

**b.** To expose oneself to (air) so as to inhale it or get the physical benefit of it; chiefly in phr. *to take the air*, to walk out in the open air (now *rare* or *arch.*): see AIR *sb.* 5. So *to take a bath*, to bathe, esp. in a place or vessel prepared for the purpose; but the phrase is also used in sense 52 (cf. BATH *sb.*[1] 6, 1).

**1375** BARBOUR *Bruce* VI. 304 The kyng..of his basnet than had tane, To tak the air, for he wes hate. *c* **1450** *St. Cuthbert* (Surtees) 1078 His seruands..Bare him with oute to take þe ayre. **1470–85** MALORY *Arthur* VII. xvii. 239 Eyther of hem vnlaced his helme, and toke the cold wynde. **1594** BARNFIELD *Affect. Sheph.* I. xx, Abroad into the fields to take fresh ayre. **1711** ADDISON *Spect.* No. 123 ¶ 1 As I was Yesterday taking the Air with my Friend Sir Roger. **1777** SHERIDAN *Sch. Scand.* II. ii, Lady Betty..was taking the dust in Hyde Park. **1837** [see BATH *sb.*[1] 1]. **1866** HOWELLS *Venet. Life* 295 When the faire Venetians go out in their gondolas to 'take the air'. **1879** EDNA LYALL *Won by Waiting* xxxi, Her father..was to take a course of baths [in Germany]. **1890** *Cornh. Mag.* July 7 The English people hurry forth to take the morning air.

**c.** Phr. *Not to be taking any..*: not to be in the mood for; to be disinclined for. *slang.*

**1900** *Daily News* 10 Mar. 2/1 In the language of the hour, 'nobody was taking any.' **1905** *Daily Chron.* 20 Dec. 3/4 As one of her fellow countrywomen might have said, Frances was not 'taking any' pessimism just then.

** *with physical action subordinated to the relation produced.*

**14.** To bring, receive, or adopt (a person) into some relation to oneself (e.g. into one's service, protection, tuition, care, companionship, favour). *To take to (into) mercy*: see MERCY *sb.* 5.

*c* **1175** *Lamb. Hom.* 27 Þesne mon ic habbe itaken to mine aȝene bihofþe. *a* **1300** *Cursor M.* 2792, 'I haue', [loth] said, 'doghtres tua, Tas and dos your will wit þaa.' **13..** *Ibid.* 20106 (Gött.) Þan tok [*Cott.* name] þe apostel sone on-ane In-tille his keping, þat maidane. **1388** WYCLIF *Ps.* xxvi[i]. 10 For my fadir and my modir han forsake me; but the Lord hath take me. **1428** in *Surtees Misc.* (1888) 5 Þat tha tuke hym to þair grace. *c* **1477** CAXTON *Jason* 17 b, The fayr Myrro..toke Jason so in her good grace that vnto the deth she louyd him. **1531** in *Sel. Cas. Crt. Requests* (1898) 34 The said abbott..was greaitly laborid to taike to service the said Roger. **1643** BURROUGHES *Exp. Hosea* (1652) 147 If God takes them to mercy we must be ready willingly to take them into brotherly society. **1654** EARL MONM. tr. *Bentivoglio's Warrs of Flanders* 54 Being then tane into pay by the Princes. **1794** in J. O. Payne *Old Eng. Cath. Missions* (1889) 14 Took into the Church William Fawcett Grange. **1878** *Scribner's Mag.* XVI. 135/1 He would freely take them into his confidence. **1885** *Law Times* LXXX. 6/2 None were allowed to let their rooms or take lodgers. **1891** E. PEACOCK *N. Brendon* I. 120 He took pupils to increase his income.

**b.** *spec.* in reference to marriage or cohabitation; often in phr. *to take to wife, in marriage.*

*c* **1200** ORMIN 19593 Þat tiss Herode King..haffde takenn all wiþþ woh Filippess wif hiss broþerr. *a* **1300** *Cursor M.* 12667 A man in mariage hir tok, Hight alpheus. *c* **1386** CHAUCER *Melib.* ¶ 590 (Harl. MS.) If a neet-hurdes douȝter.. be riche, sche may cheese of a þousand men which she wol take to hir housbonde. ? *a* **1400** *Punishm. Adultery* 63 in Horstm. *Altengl. Leg.* (1881) 369 He rouȝt not what woman he toke. *c* **1477** CAXTON *Jason* 97 b, That they shold take eche other by mariage. **1560** DAUS tr. *Sleidane's Comm.* 35 b, They bidde him take a Leman lest he attempt to defile honest women. **1687** BURNET *Cont. Reply to Varillas* 77 He professed himself a Lutheran, and took a Wife. **1771** SMOLLETT *Humph. Cl.* 18 July, A young lady..who agreed to take me for better or worse. **1891** *Cornh. Mag.* Dec. 664 He took unto himself a village maid, and settled in Lyndhurst.

**15.** To transfer by one's own direct act (a thing) into one's possession or keeping; to appropriate; to enter into possession or use of. See also *take in possession*, s. v. POSSESSION *sb.* 1 c; *take possession* in Phrases below (71).

*c* **1200** *Trin. Coll. Hom.* 167 Þe deuel..þan toc his [Job's] oȝen lichame and þer one brohte swo michel sicnesse. *c* **1300** *Harrow. Hell* 103 Heouene ant erþe tac to þe, Soules in helle lef þou me. *c* **1450** *Godstow Reg.* 416 To entre the forsaid tenement and to take and hold all maner of goodes and catallis I-founde in the same. **1535** COVERDALE *Josh.* xix. 47 And the children of Dan..toke it in possession, & dwelt therin. **1611** BIBLE *John* x. 17, I lay downe my life that I might take it againe. **1683** *Pennsylv. Archives* I. 55, I desire thee take the towne of Salem into thy lott. **1795** *Fate of Sedley* I. 189, If he dare to take a bone which they had given to their dogs. **1818** CRUISE *Digest* (ed. 2) IV. 378 The question was, whether the heirs of S. Morris took any estate under this appointment. **1883** *Law Times Rep.* XLIX. 155/1 The undertakers..had power to take lands compulsorily.

**b.** *absol.* To take possession; *spec.* in *Law*, to enter into actual possession.

*c* **1407** LYDG. *Reason & Sens.* 6486 The hunger..gredy, and in-saturable Of wommen for to Acroche and take. **1642** tr. *Perkins' Prof. Bk.* i. § 52. 24 There is one named in the Lease who may take immediately. **1706** E. WARD *Wooden World Diss.* (1708) 33 But if he gives, he takes too sometimes. **1803** WORDSW. *Rob Roy's Grave* 39 The good old rule..the simple plan, That they should take, who have the power, And they should keep who can. **1818** CRUISE *Digest* (ed. 2) VI. 298 The testator intended, that when Francis was dead without issue, the eldest son should take. **1894** *Daily News* 29 June 5/2 The will of December, 1888, they find, was duly executed...The Royal Academy therefore take.

**c.** To secure beforehand by payment or contract; e.g. *to take a house*, etc., to engage (a house or other place) for the purpose of occupying it.

**1604** E. G[RIMSTONE] *D'Acosta's Hist. Indies* IV. vi. 223 Many Spaniardes..came thither to take mines. **1670** LADY MARY BERTIE in *12th Rep. Hist. MSS. Comm.* App. v. 22 My brother Norreys tooke a box and carryed my Lady Rochester and his mistresse and all us to. **1693** *Humours Town* 8, I have within these few days taken a Lodging. **1743** BULKELEY & CUMMINS *Voy. S. Seas* 196 To take a House in the Country at our own Expence. **1803** *Pic Nic* No. 11 (1806) II. 143 She has now taken a thirty years lease of a house. **1848** THACKERAY *Van. Fair* xli, Colonel Crawley and his wife took a couple of places in the same old High-flyer coach. **1850** *Tait's Mag.* XVII. 719/1 When he took his farm, it was well cultivated.

**d.** To get or procure regularly by payment (something offered to the public, as a periodical, a commodity). See also *take in*, 82 c.

**1593** *Acct. Bk. W. Wray* in *Antiquary* XXXII. 119 May the 28 we begun to take milke of Ann Smith for a halfe penneworth of the day. **1808** ELEANOR SLEATH *Bristol Heiress* III. 40 A morning paper, which Lady Harcourt constantly took. **1852** DE MORGAN in Graves *Life Sir W. R. Hamilton* (1889) III. 426 You take the Philosophical Magazine, I think. **1897** *N. & Q.* 8th Ser. XII. 354/1 In my boyhood I 'took' the *Penny Magazine.*

**ii.** With a non-material object.

* *To take to oneself, assume, an attribute, quality, character.*

**16. a.** To assume (a form, nature, character, name, or other attribute); sometimes, to assume the part or character of. *To take on oneself*, to put on.

*c* **1200** ORMIN 85 He sennde uss..Hiss Sune..To takenn ure mennisscleȝȝe. *a* **1300** *Cursor M.* 14464 Þai said þat crist suld ta manhede Of a maiden and of þair sede. *c* **1385** CHAUCER *L. G. W.* 1142 *Dido*, That Cupido..Hadde the liknesse of the child I-take. *c* **1440** *Alphabet of Tales* 57 At þe laste he tuke his spiritt vnto hym. **1546** LANGLEY *Pol. Verg. De Invent.* II. xv. 61 God..toke on him the shape of Man as Abraham sawe him. **1548–9** (Mar.) *Bk. Com. Prayer, Collect Christmas Day*, Almyghtye God, whiche haste geuen us thy onlye begotten sonne to take our nature upon hym. **1605** SHAKS. *Macb.* III. iv. 102 Take any shape but that, and my firme Nerues Shall neuer tremble. **1697** DRYDEN *Virg. Georg.* IV. 329 [They] take the Forms his Prescience did ordain. **1711** ADDISON *Spect.* No. 35 ¶ 4 An Impostor..who takes upon him the Name of this young Gentleman. **1810** SCOTT *Lady of L.* III. vii, The mountain mist took form and limb. **1844** *Fraser's Mag.* XXX. 532/2 Liddy was really taking the woman upon her in earnest, since she had attained the matronly age of seventeen. **1887** *Times* (weekly ed.) 9 Dec. 16/2 France cannot take the offensive, but she can paralyse Germany and Italy.

†**b.** To adopt (a law or custom); to undertake or begin to follow or observe. *Obs.*

*c* **1200** ORMIN Ded. 7 Broþerr min..Þurrh þatt witt hafenn takenn ba An reȝhellboc to folȝhenn. *a* **1300** *Cursor M.* 19540 Quen þe apostels þan hard sai Samaritans had tan þair wai [*other MSS.* lay]. *c* **1375** *Ibid.* 2700 (Fairf.) Abraham.. was .v. skore bot ane þat day quen þai toke [*Cott.* vnder-fang] þe new lay. **1474** CAXTON *Chesse* II. i. 21 The peple of tarante toke for a custome that the dronken men shold be punysshyd. *a* **1533** LD. BERNERS *Huon* xlv. 151 He thretenethe to slee me by cause I wyll not take on me his law.

**c.** To assume, adopt (a symbol or badge, or something connected with and denoting a function): in phrases having specific meanings, as:

*To take the crown, the throne*, to assume sovereignty; *to take the habit*, to become a monk; *to take the gown*, to become a clergyman; *to take the ball* (at cricket), to assume the position of bowler; *to take an oar*, to begin to row. See also CROSS *sb.* 4 c, SILK, VEIL *sb.*

*c* **1330** [see CROSS *sb.* 4 c]. *a* **1380** *St. Bernard* 287 in Horstm. *Altengl. Leg.* (1878) 46 Whon Bernard hed taken his abyt. *c* **1450** *St. Cuthbert* (Surtees) 6620 Þe abyte he toke, as bede of him wryte. **1568** GRAFTON *Chron.* II. 112 He had taken on him a little before the lyuery of the crosse. **1605** CAMDEN *Rem.* (1637) 344 John of Gaunt Duke of Lancaster ..took a red Rose to his device. **1784** J. POTTER *Virtuous Villagers* II. 135, I have now taken the gown. **1855** BROWNING *Protus* 39 John the Pannonian..Came, had a mind to take the crown. **1860** *All Year Round* No. 66. 384 'Take an oar, sir', said Philip. **1883** *Daily Tel.* 15 May 2/7 The champion took the ball, vice Penn.

** *To charge oneself with, undertake, discharge.*

**17.** To assume, charge oneself with, undertake (a function, responsibility, etc.). See also *take charge* (66 below), *take in charge* (CHARGE 13 b), *take in* or *on hand* (HAND 42); also 18 a, b.

*c* **1200** ORMIN 10896 Sannt Iohann..toc þatt wikenn þohh Þa siþþen, whanne he wisste [etc.]. **13..** *Cursor M.* 12390 Trein beddes was he wont to make And þar-for his seruis to take. *c* **1425** *Ibid.* 4795 (Trin.) Lo I am al redy boun Oure aller nedes to take in place. *c* **1450** *Merlin* 3 This feende that toke this enterprise ne taried not. **1647** JER. TAYLOR *Lib. Proph.* 193 That every man must take his adventure. **1847** MARRYAT *Childr. N. Forest* xviii, I think..I would take it [the post] on trial. **1863** KINGLAKE *Crimea* I. vi. 88 The plan of taking engagements upon possible eventualities. **1890** TOUT *Hist. Eng. from* 1689, 133 Grenville refused to take office without Fox. **1890** LANE-POOLE *Barbary Corsairs* I. xii. 124 He took service as a boy in the Turkish fleet. **1892** *Speaker* 3 Sept. 279/1 Captain Mayer..was compelled by circumstances to take the responsibility.

**b.** To subject oneself to (an oath, vow, pledge, or the like): see also OATH *sb.* 1, DICK *sb.*[5]

**1511–** [see OATH *sb.* 1]. **1599** SHAKS. *Much Ado* II. iii. 26 Ile take my oath on it. *a* **1715** BURNET *Own Time* an. 1678. III. (1724) I. 435 A bill..requiring all members of either House..to take a test against Popery. **1803** *Pic Nic* No. 4 (1806) I. 140 She has taken the monastic Vow. **1897** 'SARAH GRAND' *Beth Bk.* xlvi. (1898) 438 I'll take my dick he'll not trouble us with a bill for the next six months.

†**c.** *To take it*: to make oneself responsible for a statement; to affirm, asseverate. Const. *on* (one's death, honour: see ON *prep.* 12). *Obs.*

**1595** SHAKS. *John* I. i. 110 Vpon his death-bed he..tooke it on his death That this my mothers sonne was none of his. **1598** — *Merry W.* II. ii. 12, I took't vpon mine honour thou hadst it not. **1631** WEEVER *Anc. Fun. Mon.* 379 Guiltlesse of any offence..as he tooke it vpon his death.

**18.** *To take on* or *upon oneself.*

**a.** To charge oneself with, undertake (an office, duty, or responsibility); to make oneself responsible for. In quot. *c* 1470 *absol.*

*a* **1300** *Cursor M.* 20790 He wil noght tak þe cark [*MS. F.* charge] on him, Quar [*F.* queþer] þat it be sua soght or nai. **1432** *Paston Lett.* I. 34 The said Erle hath take upon him the governance of the Kinges persone. *c* **1470** HENRY *Wallace* VI. 355 Be caus we wait he is a gentill man, Cum in my grace, and I sall saiff him than, As for his lyff, I will apon me tak. *a* **1533** LD. BERNERS *Huon* xliii. 143 He wyll take on hym this bateyll ayenst the gyant. **1611** BIBLE *Num.* xvi. 7 Yee take too much vpon you [Cov. make to moch a doo], ye sonnes of Leui. *a* **1648** LD. HERBERT *Hen. VIII* (1683) 253 That..he should persuade her to enter a Monastery, and take on her a Religious life. **1728** in Picton *L'pool Munic. Rec.* (1886) II. 86 Occasioned by.. Mr. Hughes's taking upon him the office of Mayor. **1883** *Century Mag.* XXVI. 608/1 Helen took the blame upon herself.

**b.** With *inf.* To undertake; to assume the right, presume, make bold (*to do* something).

*c* **1275** *Passion of our Lord* 619 in *O. E. Misc.* 54 Vre louerd him tok on To schewen his apostles þet he wes god and mon. **1449** *Rolls of Parlt.* V. 151/2 Daren not take uppon hem to labour ayenst suche Felons. *c* **1489** CAXTON

*Sonnes of Aymon* xxii. 481, I shall take vpon me to make amendes for hym. **1523** LD. BERNERS *Froiss.* I. cclxxv. 411 To desyre him to take on him to be the Constable of France. **1648** THORPE *Charge at York Assizes* (1649) 26 If any Person take upon him to be a Badger of Corn. **1724** DE FOE *Mem. Cavalier* (1840) 234, I took upon me..to go to Leeds. **1837** HALLAM *Hist. Lit.* (1847) I. I. i. § 90. 78 Some took on them to imitate what they read. **1885** LD. COLERIDGE in *Law Rep.* 14 Q. B. Div. 825 The judgment, which the plaintiff has taken upon himself to sue out and to enter, is wrong.

†**c.** To profess, claim *to do* something; to assume, presume *that*.. (with implication that the claim or assumption is unwarranted). *Obs.*

?*a* **1500** *Wycket* (1828) p. viii, Hypocrites that take on them to make oure Lordes bodye. **1560** DAUS tr. *Sleidane's Comm.* 29 b, As thoughe I toke vpon me that I could not erre. **1653** GATAKER *Vind. Annot. Jer.* 31 The time whereof both of them, contrary to our Saviors avouchment take upon them to determine.

†**d.** To affect, feign, pretend, make believe, *to do* something. *Obs.*

**1571** tr. *Buchanan's Detection* E j b, Though thay tuke upon tham as if thay regardit nat these thynges, yet sometyme the rumors.. merely prickit them to the quick. **1597** SHAKS. 2 *Hen. IV*, II. ii. 123 How comes that, sayes he that takes vpon him not to conceiue. **1606** — *Tr. & Cr.* I. ii. 153 Shee takes vpon her to spie a white haire on his chinne.

†**e.** *absol.* or *intr.* To assume authority or importance; sometimes in good sense, to behave bravely or valiantly (quot. *c* 1470), to put oneself forward, assert oneself (quot. 1720); usually in bad sense, = to take too much upon one, to behave presumptuously or haughtily, assume airs. *Obs.*

*c* **1470** HENRY *Wallace* v. 43 Wallace so weill apon him tuk that tide, Throw the gret preys he maid a way full wide. **1530** PALSGR. 747/1, I take apon me, lyke a lord or mayster, *je fais du grant.* **1581** PETTIE tr. *Guazzo's Civ. Conv.* II. (1586) 109 b, It shalbe the part of a straunger, being in another mans house, not to take vpon him presumptuously. **1637** T. MORTON *New Eng. Canaan* (1883) 306 This man.. tooke upon him infinitely: and made warrants in his owne name. **1667** PEPYS *Diary* 3 June, But, Lord! to see how Duncomb do take upon him is an eyesore. **1720** DE FOE *Capt. Singleton* xiii. (1840) 233, I found it was time to take upon me a little.

**f.** *trans.* See 16.

**19. a.** To undertake and perform, conduct, or discharge (a part, function, duty, service, or the like). See also PART *sb.* 23.

**1411** *Rolls of Parlt.* III. 650/1 A Loveday taken bytwen the same parties by William Gascoigne Chief Justice of the forsaid Benche. **1596** [see PART *sb.* 23 b]. **1874** MICKLETHWAITE *Mod. Par. Churches* 60 Each priest..may take those parts of the service designed to him from time to time. **1885** MARY LINSKILL *Lost Son* iv. 58 Will you favour us by taking the tenor? **1889** *Cornhill Mag.* Dec. 623 The female parts in plays being taken by boys and men. **1890** *Pictorial World* 15 May 616/1 She would take the grammar class at ten and the arithmetic class at eleven. *Mod.* The assistant master who takes duty also takes preparation. The canon who was taking residence that day.

**b.** Phr. *To take pains, take trouble* (also formerly *take labour, toil*, etc.): to take upon oneself and exercise these activities and qualities; to exercise care and diligence: see also PAIN *sb.*[1] 5, 6, TROUBLE *sb.*

**13..** *Cursor M.* 4789 (Gött.) Loke quilk of ȝu sal take on hand For vs all take þis trauaile. **1528** *Impeachm. Wolsey* in Furnivall *Ballads from MSS.* I. 360 Whoo hathe þis matyr so playnly declaryd, or hathe the labowur Take. *a* **1533** LD. BERNERS *Huon* lxxxiii. 262 Ye shall not nede to take the laboure. **1600** TOURNEUR *Transf. Metamorph.* lv, But (Knight) believe me, I have t'ane much toile. **1794** MARQ. BUCKINGHAM in *14th Rep. Hist. MSS. Comm.* App. v. 489, I am sure you have taken every pains to do whatever you imagined might best forward my wishes. **1893** LIDDON, etc. *Life Pusey* I. xviii. 420 His unlimited capacity for taking trouble.

*** *To adopt or assume as one's own.*

**20.** To adopt as one's own (a part or side in a contest, controversy, etc.), to range oneself on, ally oneself with (a side or party); see PART *sb.* 23 c, PARTY *sb.* 5, SIDE *sb.*

*c* **1420**, etc. [see PART *sb.* 23 c]. **1530** PALSGR. 750/1, I take ones parte, I holde with hym in a mater, *je prens partye.* **1606** G. W[OODCOCKE] *Hist. Ivstine* XXXVI. 114 Shewed in derision to the people that had tooke part with him. **1751** ELIZA HEYWOOD *Betsy Thoughtless* II. 199 To take the party, which would best become his honour and reputation. **1820** L. HUNT *Indicator* No. 15 (1822) I. 118 No wonder that the Queen of France took part with the rebels against..her husband.

**b.** *absol.* or *intr.* in same sense: *to take against*, to oppose; *to take for*, to support, back up, side with. *rare.* (See also *take with*, 75 d.)

*c* **1330** R. BRUNNE *Chron. Wace* (Rolls) 15312 And for Englische mennes sake, Ageyn þe oughte we to take. **1770** FOOTE *Lame Lover* II. Wks. 1799 II. 70 A wise man should well weigh which party to take for. **1892** *Longm. Mag.* Mar. 558 'You are not taking against me?' he exclaimed suspiciously.

**21.** To assume as if one's own, to appropriate or arrogate to oneself (credit, etc.); to assume as if granted, e. g. *to take leave, liberty*, etc.: see also LIBERTY *sb.* 5 b. *To take for granted*: see 48.

**1525** LD. BERNERS *Froiss.* II. xxi. 46 Wherfore this Kyng Iohan toke tytell to make warr. **1611** BEAUM. & FL. *Philaster* I. i, Kissing your white hand [Mistress] I take leave, To thank your royal father. **1625**– [see LIBERTY *sb.* 5 b]. **1627–77** FELTHAM *Resolves* I. xxxi. 53 Hamans thirst was Honor: Achitophel took the glory of his Counsel. **1820** *Examiner* No. 612. 7/1 We would take leave to recommend..an alteration. **1850** *Tait's Mag.* XVII. 564/1 Voltaire took all sorts of liberties with his mother tongue. **1870** ROGERS *Hist. Gleanings* Ser. II. 93 He took credit to himself that..her son remained stanch.

**22.** *Gram.* Of a word, clause, or sentence: To have by right or usage, either as part of itself or with it in construction (a particular inflexion, accent, case, mood, etc.) as the proper one.

**1818** BLOMFIELD tr. *Matthiae's Grk. Gram.* I. 208 Verbs ..which are derived from compound adjectives, take the augment at the beginning. *Ibid.* 472 The following verbs ..take the genitive of the thing. **1860** GOODWIN *Grk. Moods & Tenses* 220 Causal sentences regularly take the Indicative. **1876** KENNEDY *Publ. Sch. Lat. Gram.* § 20 All Declensions take the Ending *m* for Masc. and Fem. Nouns. **1881** CHANDLER *Grk. Accentuation* § 767 The following take the accent on the penultimate.

**IV.** Pregnant senses related to III.; usually including a notion of choice, purpose, use, employment, treatment, or occupation.

* *Connoting choice.*

**23.** To pick out from a number: either by chance, at random; or with intention, to select, choose.

*c* **1275** LAY. 12176 Ten þusend cnihtes tock Gracien forþrihtes [*c* 1205 he chæs.. ten þusend cnihten]. **1382** WYCLIF 1 *Sam.* xiv. 42 Saul seith, Leyeth lot betwix me and Jonathan my sone. And Jonathas is taken. **1535** COVERDALE *ibid.*, Saul sayde: Cast the lot ouer me and my sonne Ionathas. So Ionathas was taken. **1612** *Two Noble K.* II. iii. 70 [*Peasant*] Thou wilt not goe along? *Arc.* Not yet, sir. [*P.*] Well, sir, take your owne time. **1625** BACON *Ess., Ambition* (Arb.) 225 Good Commanders in the Warres, must be taken, be they neuer so Ambitious. **1742** FRANCIS tr. *Hor. Sat.* I. iv. 31 Take me a man, at venture, from the crowd. **1769** JOHNSON 29 Oct. in *Boswell*, I'll take you five children from London, who shall cuff five Highland children.

** *Connoting purpose, use, employment.*

**24.** To adopt or choose in order to use in some way; to adopt in some capacity (const. *as, for*); hence, to employ for a purpose, to have recourse to, avail oneself of, proceed to use (a means or method); to seize (an opportunity, etc.). See also *take day* in Phrases below (67), ADVANTAGE *sb.* 5 b, MEASURE *sb.* 21, OCCASION *sb.*[1] 1.

**13..** *Cursor M.* 29177 For a reule þis sal þou take. **1471** SIR J. PASTON in *P. Lett.* III. 15 Thys next terme I hope to take on [= one] weye with hyr or other. **1483–4** *Act 1 Rich. III*, c. 2 § 1 That suche exaccions..afore this tyme takyn be take for no example to make suche or any lyke charge..hereafter. **1561** [see OCCASION *sb.*[1] 1]. **1579** FULKE *Heskins' Parl.* 316 He taketh times and occasions at his pleasure. **1605** SHAKS. *Macb.* III. i. 23 We should haue else desir'd your good aduice..In this dayes Councell: but wee'le take to morrow. **1667** DRYDEN *Sir Martin Mar-all* III. i, If thou wilt have a foolish word to lard thy lean discourse with, take an English one. **1686** tr. *Chardin's Coronat. Solyman* 122 He knew..how to take his Measures to the ruine of his Competitors. **1728** RAMSAY *Bonny Chirsty* iv, He wisely this white minute took, And flang his arms about her. **1729** BP. WADDINGTON in *Lardner's Wks.* (1838) I. p. lxiii, You have certainly took a very proper and christian way with him. **1758** S. HAYWARD *Serm.* Introd. 11 What special methods could be taken to stem the tide of immorality? **1789** *Triumphs Fortitude* I. 101, I shall take the first opportunity of sending the books I promised. **1820** *Examiner* No. 614. 39/1 That great genius is taken as the standard of perfection. **1867** HOWELLS *Ital. Journ.* 118 We raised our sail, and took the gale that blew for Capri. **1890** *Blackw. Mag.* CXLVIII. 442/2 Every possible means is now taken to conceal the truth.

**b.** To take into use, to use, have recourse to (one's hands, a tool, weapon, etc.) for doing something. *To take a stick* (etc.) *to*, to use it to beat (a person, etc.). (Sometimes with mixture of sense 12.)

**1768** STERNE *Sent. Journ.* (1778) II. 25, I took both hands to it. **1888** STEVENSON *Black Arrow* IV. ii. 208 He had ta'en his belt to me, forsooth! **1889** 'LEWIS CARROLL' *Sylvie & Bruno* iv. 53 'Take a stick to him!' shouted the Vice-Warden.

**c.** *esp.* To take into use or employment, to have recourse to as a means of progression (a vehicle, ship, horse, one's limbs, etc.); to enter or mount for a journey or voyage. Often without article, as *to take boat, coach, ship*, etc.: see also *take to* (74 b), *take horse* (70 a); HEEL *sb.*[1] 19, LEG *sb.* 2 b, WING *sb.* (Cf. 25.)

*c* **1450** [see 70 a]. **1517** TORKINGTON *Pilgr.* (1884) 46 We toke our assys at the Mownte Syon, .. and rode the same nyght to Bethlem. **1530** PALSGR. 751/1, I take shyppe or the see, *je monte sur la mer*..Where toke they shyppyng, *ou est ce quilz monterent sur la mer.* **1576** [see BOAT *sb.* 1 d]. **1654** tr. *Scudery's Curia Pol.* 19 If the Duke of Guise..had speedily taken post, and fled from Blois. **1672** SIR C. LYTTELTON in *Hatton Corr.* (Camden) 86, I am..just taking coach to give his R[ll] Highnesse y[e] paru bien after his late danger. **1721** DE FOE *Col. Jack* (1840) 199, I took the packet-boat, and came over to England. **1844** *Fraser's Mag.* XXX. 603/1 He takes ship for Ireland. **1885** 'ANSTEY' *Tinted Venus* viii. 95 I've a good mind to take the tram to the Archway. **1892** *Monthly Packet* Apr. 444 They..took train to London.

**25.** To gain the aid or help of (a place) by betaking oneself to it; to gain, reach, repair to, go into, enter (esp. for refuge or safety); to get into or on to: = *take to*, 74 c. Often in special phrases: see FIELD, GROUND, INN, LAND, REFUGE, SANCTUARY, SEA, WALL, WATER, etc.

*c* **1205** LAY. 7976 He droh in ane hælue & toc þan [*c* 1275 tock to] herberwe. *c* **1330** R. BRUNNE *Chron. Wace* (Rolls) 5397 Hauene he tok at Porcestre. *c* **1400** *Laud Troy Bk.* 10501 Thei token the toun with mychel spede..To saue her lyues. **1461** *Paston Lett.* II. 52 The Duc of Excestre and th'erle of Pembrok are floon and taken the mounteyns. **1480** CAXTON *Chron. Eng.* clxx. 155 They that myght take the bridge escaped. **1485** — *Paris & V.* 43 He took the ryuer wyth hys hors. **1512** *Act 4 Hen. VIII*, c. 2 § 2 If any murderer ..hadde taken any Church or Churchyerd or murder. **1565** STAPLETON tr. *Bede's Hist. Ch. Eng.* 169 Beinge vysited with syeknesse he toke his bedde. **1583** *Reg. Privy Council Scot.* III. 600 Constraning him to tak his hous for the saifty of his lif. **1618** ROWLANDS *Night Raven* (1620) 12 A cruell Beare, which forc'd him take a tree. **1831** *Examiner* 443/2 Vipers occasionally take the water. **1852** R. F. BURTON *Falconry Valley Indus* v. 61 *note*, The first falcon..caused the quarry to take the air. **1868** STANLEY *Westm. Abbey* v. 364 But the right of asylum rendered the whole precinct a vast 'cave of Adullam' for all the distressed and discontented of the metropolis who desired, according to the phrase of the time, to 'take Westminster'. **1880** T. STEVENSON in *Encycl. Brit.* XI. 455 A harbour which may be easily taken and left in stormy weather.

**b.** To adopt and enter upon (a road, way, path, course, etc., *lit.* or *fig.*); to betake oneself to, begin to go along or by: sometimes with mixture of sense 'to choose, select' (23). See also COURSE *sb.* 11 b, 21, WAY *sb.*

*a* **1300** *Cursor M.* 17643 To ierusalem he tok þe strete. **1375** BARBOUR *Bruce* II. 146 All him alane the way he tais. *c* **1380** *Sir Ferumb.* 3152 Þus othere toke þat cors an haste. **1513** DOUGLAS *Æneis* VI. viii. 1 With all his speid fra thens he tuke the gait. *a* **1533** LD. BERNERS *Huon* xxi. 63, I counsell you to take the long way. **1590** SPENSER *F. Q.* I. i. 10 So many pathes,..That which of them to take in diverse doubt they been. **1697** DRYDEN *Virg. Georg.* III. 459 Pleas'd I am, no beaten Road to take. **1749** FIELDING *Tom Jones* VII. x, Which way must we take? **1827** HALLAM *Const. Hist.* (1876) I. iii. 115 Elizabeth had taken her line as to the Court of Rome. **1895** *Law Times Rep.* LXXIII. 22/1 The court..left the parties to take their own course.

**c.** *To take* (*a place* or *person*) *in* (*on*) *one's way*, to touch at or visit in one's journey; to include in one's route.

*a* **1622** R. LAYNE in Capt. Smith *Virginia* I. 8, I..sent Pemissapan word I was going to Croatan, and tooke him in my way. **1676** WOOD *Life* (O.H.S.) II. 342 Wee went home and took Pershore in the way. **1701** W. WOTTON *Hist. Rome, Marcus* vi. 85 He did not take Rome in his way. **1837** LOCKHART *Scott* xliv, Scott..asked me to walk home with him, taking Ballantyne's printing office in our way.

*** *Connoting treatment.*

**26.** To proceed or begin to deal with or treat in some way or do something to; hence, to 'take in hand', 'tackle', deal with, treat.

See also *take at advantage* (ADVANTAGE *sb.* 5 c), *take it easy* (EASY B. 4), *take in turns* (TURN *sb.*). (In quot. 1671, to settle, adjust, make up: = *take up*, 90 u.)

**1523** [see ADVANTAGE *sb.* 5 c]. **1596** HARINGTON *Metam. Ajax* (1814) 12 He will take a weak man at the vantage. **1607** TOPSELL *Four-f. Beasts* 418 This disease.., if it be taken in any time, it is easie to be holpen. **1671** H. M. tr. *Erasm. Colloq.* 62 They themselves will better take this difference among themselves. **1720** MRS. MANLEY *Power of Love* (1741) 281 Being taken at such disadvantage; his Valour would have signify'd little. **1734** POPE *Ess. Man* IV. 227 Men in their loose unguarded hours they take, Not that themselves are wise, but others weak. **1737** BRACKEN *Farriery Impr.* (1756) I. 169 The Business is to take the Distemper in its first Stage. **1812** JEFFERSON *Writ.* (1830) IV. 176 To fight two enemies at a time, rather than to take them by succession. **1896** *Law Times* C. 438/2 Admiralty Appeals with Assessors will be taken in Appeal Court I on Wednesday. **1896** *Daily News* 30 May 8/4, I shall not take physiology next year, but I shall give some teaching on the subject in the way of object lessons in hygiene.

**b.** To use, deal with, or treat (a name or word) in some way. *To take in* IDLE, in VAIN.

*c* **1200** ORMIN 4402 Þatt tu ne take nohht wiþþ skarn, Wiþþ hæþinng, ne wiþþ idell Þe name off ure Laferrd Crist. *c* **1315** SHOREHAM III. 91 Honury þou schelt enne god..Take nauȝt hys name in ydelschepe. *c* **1386** [see IDLE B. 1 b].

**c.** To proceed to deal with mentally; to consider; to reckon. So *to take into* or *under consideration*, to proceed to consider (see CONSIDERATION 2 c). See also *take together*, 89 c.

*c* **1200** ORMIN 325 Tacc nu þiss streon þatt tuss wass sibb Wiþþ preostess & wiþþ kingess. *Ibid.* 335, 339. **1589** PUTTENHAM *Eng. Poesie* III. xix. (Arb.) 236 For example ye may take these verses. **1602** SHAKS. *Ham.* I. ii. 197 He was a man, take him for all in all: I shall not look vpon his like againe. *a* **1635** SIBBES *Confer. Christ & Mary* (1656) 66 Take a good Christian at the worst, he is better than another at the best. **1747** W. HORSLEY *Fool* (1748) II. 319 Take one Man with another now in Prison. **1820** *Examiner* No. 615. 51/1 If the Chamber were to take the petitions into its consideration. **1836** BRANDE *Chem.* (1841) 138 Let us take a fresh-water lake as an example. **1892** *Cassell's Fam. Mag.* Aug. 516/1 This, taken with his secretaryship,..left him but little leisure.

**** *Connoting occupation.*

**27.** To proceed to occupy, enter on the occupation of (a place or position, *lit.* or *fig.*). See also CHAIR *sb.*[1] 9, FLOOR *sb.*[1] 4, GROUND *sb.* 11 c, PLACE *sb.* 13 b, 27, POST *sb.*[3] 2, PRECEDENCE 3, 4, SEAT, STAND, etc.

*c* **1205** LAY. 7976 He droh in ane hælue & toc þan herberwe. *a* **1300** *Cursor M.* 11443 Þai toke þair gesting in þe tun. **1390** GOWER *Conf.* III. 293 This yonge Prince, as seith the bok, With hem his herbergage tok. **1430–40** LYDG. *Bochas* IX. xxxi. (Bodl. MS. 263) lf. 432/2 The ground Itake of wilful pouerte. **1605** SHAKS. *Lear* III. vi. 38 Thou robed man of justice, take thy place. **1711** ADDISON *Spect.* No. 165 ¶ 5 They took Post behind a great Morass. **1750** GRAY *Long Story* 111 She curtsies, as she takes her chair. **1807–8** W. IRVING

*Salmag.* iv. (1811) I. 71 The latter has taken his winter quarters..in the corner room, opposite mine. **1883** FARGUS *Cardinal Sin* xii, It was soon her turn to take the stage. **1888** *Scottish Leader* 27 July 6/7, I took the chair at a meeting to promote the candidature of a Radical as a member for Parliament.

† **b.** *intr.* ? ellipt. for *take place*, to occur. *rare.*

*c* **1374** CHAUCER *Troylus* IV. 1534 (1562) And yf so be þat pes her-after take As alday happeþ after anger game.

**28.** To use, occupy, use up, consume (so much material, space, time, energy, activity, etc.): = *take up*, 90 w (*b*). Sometimes nearly = 'need' or 'require'. Hence (*colloq.*) to require (a person or thing of so much capacity or ability) *to do* something.

*To take (one's) time*: to allow oneself sufficient time (to do something); hence (sarcastically), to be 'quite long enough', i. e. too long: to loiter.

*a* **1578** LINDESAY (Pitscottie) *Chron. Scot.* (S. T. S.) I. 251 This scheip..tuik so mekill timber that scho waistit all the wodis in Fyfe. **1590** SHAKS. *Mids. N.* I. i. 83 Take time to pause. *c* **1710** CELIA FIENNES *Diary* (1888) 239 At ye ffeete of the bed that tooke ye Length of the roome. **1713** BERKELEY *Hylas & Phil.* i. Wks. 1871 I. 284, I will take time to solve your difficulty. **1753** CHAMBERS *Cycl. Supp.* s.v. *Lime*, Lime-stone generally takes sixty hours in burning. **1858** GLENNY *Gard. Every-day Bk.* 134/1 They take less room on than off. **1890** *Field* 8 Mar. 364/1 Any ignoramus can construct a straight line, but it takes an engineer to make a curve. **1893** *Nat. Observer* 7 Oct. 541/2 The remainder of the Life will take two more volumes.

**b.** A person is said to *take* a particular size *in* gloves, boots, collars, etc., implying that that is the size which fits.

**1897** FLO. MARRYAT *Blood Vampire* ii, [She] informed me the other day that her Mamma took nines in gloves.

**29.** To begin or start afresh after leaving off, or after some one else; to resume; = *take up*, 90 r, s. (Also *absol.*) *To take the word*, to begin to speak, esp. after or instead of some one else: see WORD *sb.*

*c* **1400** *Destr. Troy* 747 Now turne to our tale, take þere we lefte. **1500** [see WORD]. *a* **1547** SURREY *Æneid* IV. 144 Quene Juno then thus tooke her tale againe. **1697** DRYDEN *Virg. Georg.* IV. 219, I must forsake This Task; for others afterwards to take. **1825** SCOTT *Betrothed* xix, Eveline remained silent. The abbess took the word.

**V.** To obtain from a source, to derive.

**30.** To get, obtain, or derive by one's own act from some source (something material or non-material); to adopt, copy, 'borrow' (also *absol.*, quot. 1493); to take example of, 'get' or 'learn' *from* some one (quot. 1544). See also ENSAMPLE *sb.* 2 b, EXAMPLE *sb.* 6 c.

*c* **1200** ORMIN 14470, ȝiff þu bisne takenn willt Off þise tweȝȝenn breþre. *c* **1330** R. BRUNNE *Chron. Wace* (Rolls) 5273 Þre þousand pound ylka ȝer.. Of alle þe lond gedered & tan. **13..** *Cursor M.* 17288+175 Cott. (*insert.*) To haf mercy of synful men Ensaumple at him he toke. *c* **1386** CHAUCER *Wife's Prol.* 183 Rede it in his Almageste and take it there. *c* **1460** FORTESCUE *Abs. & Lim. Mon.* x. (1885) 131 Þat we now serch how the kyng mey haue such livelod; but ffirst, off what comodities it mey best be take. **1493** *Festivall* (1515) 145 b, [Luke] loked what Marke and Mathewe had wryten, and so toke at them. **1544** BALE *Chron. Sir J. Oldcastell* in *Harl. Misc.* (Malh.) I. 269 Of them [Annas & Caiaphas] onely haue ye taken it to iudge Chrystes members, as ye do. **1606** G. W[OODCOCKE] *Hist. Ivstine* XXX. 101 Schollers which from him as their tuter had tane theyr practise. **1732** BERKELEY *Alciphr.* III. § 9 The proportions of the three Grecian orders were taken from the human body. **1766** GOLDSM. *Vicar W.* xvii, All the ladies of the continent would come over to take pattern from ours. **1878** H. H. GIBBS *Ombre* 8 The Frontispiece.. is taken from Seymour's 'Compleat Gamester'.

**b.** *spec.* To obtain from its natural source (e. g. stone from a quarry), to get; to pluck, gather (plants, a crop). Now *rare.*

*c* **1477** CAXTON *Jason* 121 b, And thenne she was..borne into alle the Regyons of the world where she gadred and toke many herbes of dyuerce facons and condicions. **1585** T. WASHINGTON tr. *Nicholay's Voy.* II. xi. 46 Mines whereof are taken great quantity of stone. **1844** *Jrnl. R. Agric. Soc.* V. I. 174 In taking the crop reaping is universal.

**31.** To derive, 'draw' (origin, name, character, or some attribute or quality) from some source. Const. *from*, *in*, *of*.

*c* **1200** ORMIN 16340 Adam..Off whamm I toc mi bodiȝlich. *c* **1205** LAY. 29410 Brutaine hit wes ihaten of Bruttin nom taken. **13..** *Cursor M.* 36 Ilk a frouit..takes fra þe rote his kinde. *Ibid.* 20085 He þat toke of hir his fless..hang a tre þar nailed to. **1432-50** tr. *Higden* (Rolls) II. 255 Men of Assiria toke theire name of Assur, men of Hebrewe of Heber. **1474** CAXTON *Chesse* III. i. (1883) 77 We were first formed and toke our begynnyng of the erthe. **1586** W. WEBBE *Eng. Poetrie* (Arb.) 56 Ryme, taken from the Greeke worde Ρυθμος. **1660** BLOOME *Archit.* A j, The..Columnes called Dorica, taking beginning of Dorus, Prince of Achaia and Peloponnesus. **1772** SIR W. JONES *Ess.* i. Poems, etc. (1777) 186 The Turks..took their numbers, and their taste for poetry from the Persians. **1855** MACAULAY *Hist. Eng.* xxii. IV. 776 No English title had ever before been taken from a place of battle lying within a foreign territory.

† **b.** To infer, deduce; to obtain as a result.

*c* **1380** WYCLIF *Wks.* (1880) 343 But hou shulde men take of þis to roune wiþ prestis & þus to be assoiled? *c* **1391** CHAUCER *Astrol.* II. § 25 Adde thanne thilke declinacion to the altitude of the sonne at noon and tak ther the heuedes of aries & libra & thin Equinoxial. *c* **1449** PECOCK *Repr.* 54 Of which..text thei taken that whoeuer is a persoon of Saluacioun schal soone understonde the trewe meenyng of Holi Scripture.

**32.** To get as a result or product by some special process. **a.** To get (information, evidence, etc.), or ascertain (a fact), by inquiry, questioning, examination, or the like; also *transf.* to perform or carry on (an examination or the like) in order to ascertain something (cf. 52).

**1460** *Rolls of Parlt.* V. 388/1 By Inquisitions tane uppon ychone of the same Wyrtes. **1511-12** *Act* 3 *Hen. VIII*, c. 21 Preamble, An untrue Inquysicion taken before your Eschetoure in the seid Countie. **1583** STOCKER *Civ. Warres Lowe C.* I. 68 b, Information which was taken by the Inquisitours here aboutes. **1596** SHAKS 1 *Hen. IV*, IV. i. 133 Let vs take a muster speedily. **1600** in *Shaks. Cent. Praise* (1879) 35 The examination of Sr Gelly merick Knyght taken the xvijth of Februarij, 1600. **1697** DRYDEN *Virg. Georg.* IV. 626 Himself their Herdsman, on the middle Mount, Takes of his muster'd Flocks a just Account. **1705** *Lond. Gaz.* No. 4139/5 The King..took a Review of the Forces. **1768** BLACKSTONE *Comm.* III. iv. 59 A commission of assise, directed to the judges and clerk of assise, to take assises; that is, to take the verdict of a peculiar species of jury called an assise. *Ibid.* vii. 101 [The judge] takes information by hearing advocates on both sides, and thereupon forms his interlocutory decree or definitive sentence at his own discretion. **1817** MAR. EDGEWORTH *Harrington* ii. (1832) 21 He hastened down to the country to take the sense of his constituents. **1863** H. COX *Instit.* III. vii. 698 He never disposes of any important preferments without taking the pleasure of the Crown. **1890** *Cornhill Mag.* Sept. 276 Tests are taken to see if the cable has sustained any damage. **1893** *National Observer* 7 Oct. 524/1 A Bill on which it dare not take the country's opinion.

**b.** To get or ascertain by measurement or scientific observation; also *transf.* to make, perform (a measurement, an observation). See also MEASURE *sb.* 2 c, 3 a.

*c* **1430** [see MEASURE *sb.* 2 c]. *c* **1470** HENRYSON *Mor. Fab.* x. (*Fox & Wolf*) v, Bot Astrolab, Quadrant, and Almanak, ..The mouing of the heuin this Tod can tak. **1579** GOSSON *Sch. Abuse* (Arb.) 38 The height of Heauen is taken by the staffe. **1598** PHILIP tr. *Linschoten* I. xciii. 170/1 Taking the hight of the Sunne, we found ourselues to be under 37 degrees. **1622** MASSINGER *Virg. Mart.* III. iii, Misery taking the length of my foot, it boots not me to sue for life. **1663** BUTLER *Hud.* I. I. 122 For he by Geometrick Scale Could take the Size of Pots of Ale. **1697** COLLIER *Ess. Mor. Subj.* I. (1703) 111 The Taylor should take measure of their quality as well as of their limbs. **1847** TENNYSON *Princ.* III. 153 That afternoon the Princess rode to take The dip of certain strata to the North. **1887** WESTALL *Capt. Trafalgar* xviii. 236 Isn't it about time for taking the sun?..it is four days since we knew our position. **1900** LÜCKES *Gen. Nursing* xii. (ed. 2) 147 The temperature has to be taken every hour. *Mod.* The weather was too cloudy to take any observations.

† **c.** To measure off (a length or distance). *Obs.*

**1660** BARROW *Euclid* I. ii. Schol., The line AG might be taken with a pair of compasses. **1669** STURMY *Mariner's Mag.* I. ii. 32 Take with your Compasses the Line C. **1831** BREWSTER *Optics* iv. 38 From a scale on which *hm* is 1·500, take in the compasses '1'.

**33. a.** To obtain in writing, write down, make (notes, a copy, etc.); to write down (spoken words), report in writing (a speech, etc.).

**1591-1875** [see NOTE *sb.*² 13 b]. **1601** SHAKS. *All's Well* IV. iii. 130 His confession is taken, and it shall bee read to his face. **1653** H. COGAN tr. *Pinto's Trav.* xv. 48 Taking an inventory of this prize. **1708** in *Burton's Diary* (1828) III. 93 His Majesty sent for Mr. Rushworth, the Clerk, whom he observed to take his speech in character. **1712** F. T. *Shorthand* p. vi, 'Tis by Short-Hand that all Speeches, Homilies, Tryals, Sermons, &c. are..taken. *a* **1715** BURNET *Own Time* ann. 1672 (1823) I. 538 He would not let me take a copy of it. **1732** BERKELEY *Alciphr.* IV. § 1 To stand by,.. and take notes of all that passeth. **1776** *Trial of Nundocomar* 22/1 The Monshy took the copy by my directions. **1883** M. D. CHALMERS *Local Govt.* iii. 41 Minutes of the meeting must be taken. **1901** S. PAGET *Mem. Sir J. Paget* iii. (ed. 2) 61 He had no clinical clerks, and his cases were not taken.

**b.** To obtain by drawing, delineating, etc.; to make, execute (a figure or picture, now esp. a photograph, of some object); also *transf.* to obtain or make a figure or picture of, to portray; now *esp.* to photograph. Also (*colloq.*) *intr.* for *pass.* (with qualifying adv.) of a person: To be a (good or bad) subject for photographing.

**1607** TOPSELL *Four-f. Beasts* 757 Another picture..which he tooke by another of these Cats in the possession of the Duke of Saxony. **1664** WOOD *Life*, etc. (O. H. S.) II. 20, I went to the castle [Bampton]..and took the ruins thereof. **1751** T. HOLLIS in *Lett. Lit. Men* (Camden) 379 A Scheme for taking and publishing the Antiquities existing at Athens. **1766** GOLDSM. *Vic. W.* xvi, A limner, who travelled the country, and took likenesses for fifteen shillings a head. **1789** MRS. PIOZZI *Journ. France* I. 150 Her portrait ..will not be found difficult to take. **1859** REEVE *Brittany* 48 Mr. Taylor took the view three times before he quite satisfied himself as to the quality of the negative. **1889** MALLOCK *Enchanted Isl.* 230, I took a photograph of their church. **1889** BLANCHE HOWARD *Open Door* ix. 145 The photographers..say a woman 'takes' better standing. **1899** F. V. KIRBY *Sport E.C. Africa* xxviii. 310, I wished for my camera, for never was there a better chance of 'taking' one of these animals. *Mod.* A snap-shot taken by an amateur.

**VI.** To take something given or offered; to receive, accept, exact, and related senses.

* *To receive what is given or bestowed.*

**34.** To receive, get (something given, bestowed, or administered); to have conferred upon one (*spec.* a sacrament, office, order of merit, degree, etc.); to win, or receive as won (a prize, reward); to gain, acquire (experience, etc.; see also *to take success*, s.v. SUCCESS). Also *absol.*

*c* **1200** ORMIN 5378 Forr to takenn hæle att himm Off iwhillc unntrummnesse. **13..** *Cursor M.* 12755 (Gött.) In water baptist he alle þa þat come til him baptim to ta. *c* **1375** *Ibid.* 19531 (Fairf.) Simon.. toke þe sacrement of hali kirk. **1382** WYCLIF *Matt.* vii. 8 Eche that axith, takith. — 1 *Cor.* xi. 24 For the Lord Ihesu..took breed ..and brak, and seide, Take ȝe and ete ȝe. *c* **1435** *Torr. Portugal* 2168 And ye now will liston a stound How he toke armes of kyng Calomond. [Cf. ARM *sb.*² 15.] *c* **1450** *St. Cuthbert* (Surtees) 5412 Þar he toke tonsure brade. *c* **1450** tr. *De Imitatione* III. lix. 250 It is more blessyd to gyue than take. **1617** MORYSON *Itin.* I. 29 In the house where the Doctors, and other Graduates take their degrees. **1689** T. R. *View Govt. Europe* 74 The Nations round about submitted and took Laws from him. **1766** ENTICK *London* IV. 31 The will is to be proved, and administration is to be taken. **1805** SCOTT *Last Minstr.* IV. xxvi, Knighthood he took of Douglas' sword. **1888** MRS. H. WARD *R. Elsmere* iv. 50, I don't feel as if I should ever take orders.

**b.** To receive (something inflicted); to have (something) done to one; to suffer, undergo, submit to.

*c* **1200** ORMIN Pref. 90 Þatt he toc dæþ o rode. **1303** R. BRUNNE *Handl. Synne* 12626 God graunte vs grace,..for oure synne swyche penaunce [to] take, Þat we be neuer more a-teynt. **13..** [see PENANCE *sb.* 2]. *a* **1425** *Cursor M.* 16290 (Trin.) Wiþ his hond a buffet he ȝaf ihesus ful sore ..'take þat to teche þe lore'. **1485** CAXTON *Chas. Gt.* 220 To the ende that they shold not take deth that day. **1581** RICH *Farewell* (Shaks. Soc.) 212, I will not see her take a manifest wrong. **1663** BUTLER *Hud.* I. II. 947 He took the Blow upon his Arm. **1748** G. WHITE *Serm.* (MS.), He had much rather take, than do, wrong. **1869** FREEMAN *Norm. Conq.* III. xii. 162 The mere senseless love of giving and taking blows without an object. **1879** MISS YONGE *Cameos* Ser. IV. iii. 39 He professed himself ready to take his trial.

**c.** To receive (something said to one); to receive information of, to hear; in *imper.* often = 'let me tell you'. Somewhat *arch.*

**1595** SHAKS. *John* I. i. 21 Then take my Kings defiance from my mouth. **1596** — *Tam. Shr.* II. i. 191 Take this of me, Kate of my consolation,..My selfe am moou'd to woo thee for my wife. **1609** HEYWOOD *Brit. Troy* XII. lxiv, After they had tooke and given the Time of Day. **1671** MILTON *Samson* 1570 Then take the worst in brief, Samson is dead. **1805** SCOTT *Last Minstr.* IV. xxvi, Take our defiance loud and high. **1846** W. E. FORSTER in Reid *Life* I. vi. 186 The fact is, they will soon wear nothing. There; take that!

**35.** To enter into the enjoyment of (pleasure, recreation, rest, or the like). See also EASE *sb.* 2, NAP *sb.*² b. (Cf. 13.)

**13..** *Cursor M.* 6317 (Gött.) Þat niht he ȝede and tok his rest. *c* **1350** *Will. Palerne* 2488 [Þei] hiȝed hem homward fast..& token redli here rest. **1530** PALSGR. 749/2, I take my rest. **1549** LATIMER *Serm. Ploughers* (Arb.) 38 In the meane tyme the Prelates take theyr pleasures. **1597** BEARD *Theatre God's Judgem.* (1612) 328 Before any other should take tast thereof. **1752** MRS. LENNOX *Fem. Quix.* I. i, Sometimes he took the diversion of hunting. **1779** *Mirror* No. 60 One of the company proposed that they should take a game at cards. **1897** MRS. RAYNER *Type-writer Girl* x. 108 So perforce I took holiday.

** *To receive what is due or owing; to exact.*

**36.** To receive or get in payment, as wages, etc., or by way of charge or exaction as a fine, tribute; sometimes with connotation 'accept' (cf. 39), or 'charge, exact, demand' (cf. 37, 38).

*a* **1300** *Cursor M.* 16485 'Tas', he said, 'your penis here A felun folk er yee'. **13..** *Ibid.* 28405 Agains will i lent my thing, And quilum tok þar-for okeryng. **1427-8** *Rec. St. Mary at Hill* 68 Also for a carpenter iiij dayes..takyng vj d & his mete a day. *c* **1489** CAXTON *Sonnes of Aymon* ix. 216 Straunge knyghtes that were come vnto hym to take wages. **1579** LYLY *Euphues* (Arb.) 133 This olde miser asking of Aristippus what he woulde take to teache and bring vp his sonne. **1684** *Contempl. State Man* I. vi. (1699) 64 What would he now take for all the Honours of this World. **1708** in Picton *L'pool Munic. Rec.* (1886) II. 83 For takeing greater interest..than by law is allow'd. **1842** BROWNING *Pied Piper* ix, A thousand guilders! Come, take fifty! **1896** *Act* 59 & 60 *Vict.* c. 59 § 2 (*b*), Provided always ..that no money for admission be taken at the doors.

**37.** To exact (satisfaction or reparation) for an offence; hence, to execute, inflict (vengeance, revenge; † punishment, † justice). Const. *on*, † *of.*

*a* **1300** *Cursor M.* 5862 Þat suerd apon hus tak na wrak. *Ibid.* 6094 O þam mi wengeance sal i take. *c* **1330** R. BRUNNE *Chron. Wace* (Rolls) 202 Whan God took wreche of Kaymes synne. **1474** CAXTON *Chesse* II. v. (1883) 68, I wold take vengeance and turmente the. **1533** BELLENDEN *Livy* I. ix. (S.T.S.) 52 Þat he mycht Iustlie tak punycioun of all þe Albane pepill. **1607** TOPSELL *Four-f. Beasts* (1658) 127 His fellowes take punishment of him, and fall on him, biting and rending his skin. **1633** [see REVENGE *sb.* 4]. *a* **1774** GOLDSM. tr. *Scarron's Com. Romance* (1775) II. 118 The counsellor.. had need of all his good sense to prevent him from taking immediate justice on a man, who sought to injure him so capitally. **1779** FORREST *N. Guinea* 313 To take satisfaction..for the death of Fakymolano's brother at Ramis.

† **38.** To receive, exact, or accept (a promise, engagement, oath, or the like); hence, to administer or witness (an oath). *To take an oath of*, *To take* (any one) *sworn*: see OATH *sb.* 1, SWORN *ppl. a.*

*c* **1450, 1593, 1599** [see OATH *sb.* 1]. **1560** DAUS tr. *Sleidane's Comm.* 55 b, Then began he to take stipulation of them. *a* **1715** BURNET *Own Time* an. 1672 (1823) I. 538 He took a solemn engagement of her, that, if scruples should arise in her mind, she would let him know them. **1833** *Act* 3 & 4 *Will. IV*, c. 74 § 82 [He] shall be competent to take the acknowledgment of any married woman wheresoever she may reside. **1873** *Act* 36 & 37 *Vict.* c. 66 § 84 Commissioners to take oaths and affidavits in the Supreme Court.

*** *To accept.*

**39.** To receive (something offered), not to refuse or reject; to receive willingly; to accept.

*c* 1200 ORMIN 4828 ȝiff þatt we takenn bliþeliȝ Att Godd all þatt iss sellþe. *c* 1330 *Amis & Amil.* 1112 Y schal for the take bataile. *c* 1400 *Prymer* (1895) 50 Take oure preier, & late þe merci of þi pitee assoile hem þat ben boundun wiþ þe cheyne of synnes. *a* 1500 in C. Trice-Martin *Chanc. Proc. 15th C.* (1904) 3 To thentent that she shuld not be taken to bayle, but kept still in prisone. 1534 MORE *Treat. Passion* Wks. 1281/1 Such as wil take the benefite. 1591 SHAKS. *Two Gent.* III. i. 100 Take no repulse, what euer she doth say. 1697 in *N. & Q.* 10th Ser. (1908) IX. 378/2 There was not one of the House of Commons but..would take a bribe. 1837 DICKENS *Pickw.* ii, Gentleman says he'll not detain you a moment, sir, but he can take no denial. 1848 THACKERAY *Van. Fair* xxii, She held out her hand with so frank and winning a grace, that Osborne could not but take it. 1904 STANLEY WEYMAN *Abbess of Vlaye* iii, There's a party ringing at the gate, my lord, and —and won't take no!

**b.** Of a female animal: To admit (the male). See also *take horse* in Phrases, 70 c.

1577 [see 70 c]. 1759 BROWN *Compl. Farmer* 65 Neither can they suckle their young, till they have taken buck. 1845 *Jrnl. R. Agric. Soc.* VI. II. 363, I..set down..the Ewes as they take the ram. 1864 *Ibid.* XXV. I. 254 The number of hours during which they take the bull varies from 24 to 48.

**c.** Of fish (with mixture of sense 2 b): To seize (the bait). Also *absol.*

1863 W. C. BALDWIN *Afr. Hunting* vi. 205 They take admirably, but we have only crooked pins for hooks, and cannot catch many. 1867 F. FRANCIS *Angling* v. (1880) 162 Sometimes fish rise quickly and take quickly. 1889 MRS. E. KENNARD *Landing a Prize* III. i. 6 Fish always take best after rain.

**40.** To accept (a wager, or the person who offers to lay the wager). So also in reference to a proposal, etc.: see also *to take any one at his* WORD.

1602 ROWLANDS *Greene's Ghost* 49, I take you, sayd one or two, and the wager being layd, awaie they went. 1719 DE FOE *Crusoe* (1840) II. xiii. 268, I was for taking him at that proposal. 1850 *Tait's Mag.* XVII. 678/2 I'll take ten to one on it. 1890 *Field* 24 May 757/1, 800 to 100 was taken about him. 1890 CLARK RUSSELL *Ocean Trag.* I. vi. 123 He bet me a sovereign...I took him.

**b.** *To take one's death* (upon a thing): to stake one's life upon it.

1553 BECON *Reliques Rome* (1563) 59 He tooke hys death thereon, that he was neuer giltye. 1593 SHAKS. 2 *Hen. VI*, II. iii. 90, I will take my death, I neuer meant him any ill.

**41.** To accept and act upon (advice, a hint, warning, etc.).

*c* 1300 *St. Margarete* 136 þ^t maide..seide..goþ fram me anon; Anoþer consail ich haue itake, ich forsake ȝou echon. *c* 1400 *Destr. Troy* 12869 The troiens full tite token his rede. 1605 [see ADVICE 5]. 1610 SHAKS. *Temp.* II. i. 288 They'l take suggestion, as a Cat laps milke. 1611 [see HINT *sb.* 1]. 1718 LADY M. W. MONTAGU *Let. to Lady Rich* 10 Oct., They..took the first hint of their dress from a fair sheep newly ruddled. 1877 MISS YONGE *Cameos* Ser. III. xxxiv. 363 Would that France had taken to itself the teaching! 1892 *Punch* 29 Oct. 196/2 [He] begged others to take warning by his fate. 1899 *Tit-Bits* 28 Oct. 109/2 'Come along, dear, take your call', said he, pulling back the heavy curtains.

**b.** To accept as true or correct; to believe (something told to one). (Cf. 34 c.) Also, to accept mistakenly as trustworthy, to be deceived by (quot. 1728): cf. *take in*, 82 o.

*c* 1200 ORMIN 2824 Forr þatt tu toc wiþþ trowwþe þatt word. 1587 in W. M. Williams *Ann. Founders' Co.* (1867) 69 He givinge his fayth promyse to Mr. Alderman...Mr. Alderman tooke his worde, and rose, and went his ways. 1605 SHAKS. *Lear* IV. vi. 144, I would not take this from report. 1622 MASSINGER *Virg. Mart.* II. i, We have not been idle, take it upon my word. 1728 ELIZA HEYWOOD tr. *Mme. de Gomez's Belle A.* (1732) II. 142 The King seeing that they had took the Feint, said at Night,..Ghent is invested, and we must go anon to raise the Siege. 1889 PHILIPS & WILLS *Fatal Phryne* II. iii. 76 You may take it from me that the pot means what it says.

**42.** To accept with the mind or will in some specified way (*well, ill, in earnest*, etc.). See also *to take to heart* (HEART *sb.* 44), *take in good* (etc.) *part* (PART *sb.* 26 b), *take in* SCORN, *take in* SNUFF.

*c* 1200 ORMIN 7390 Biforenn þa þatt tākenn all Onn hæþinng þatt we spellenn. *a* 1300 *Cursor M.* 4619 Nai, sir, tas noght in despite. *Ibid.* 16396 Quen [Pilate] sagh þat al his soigne þai tok it al to ill. *c* 1386 CHAUCER *Wife's T.* 342 To hym that taketh it in pacience. *c* 1450 *St. Cuthbert* (Surtees) 1049 þir wordes cuthbert wysely toke. 1530 PALSGR. 747/1, I take a thyng a mysse, *je mesprens.* 1553 LATIMER *Serm., on Twelfth Day* (1635) 293 b, There is a common saying amongst us.., Every thing is (say they) as it is taken, which indeed is not so: for every thing is as it is, howsoever it be taken. 1577 B. GOOGE *Heresbach's Husb.* IV. (1586) 182 b, They take it ill, and presently leaue working. 1579 W. WILKINSON *Confut. Familye of Loue* Bij, Take this brief ..aunswere..in good part. 1671 LADY MARY BERTIE in *12th Rep. Hist. MSS. Comm.* App. v. 22, I take it very ill that none of my nephews would drawe mee. 1728 MORGAN *Algiers* I. Pref. 26 Multitudes of People..would take it in excessive Dudgeon to be thought unfashionable. 1758 JOHNSON *Let. to Miss Porter* 1 Mar., I shall take it very kindly if you write to me. 1872 BLACK *Adv. Phaeton* x. 145 The Lieutenant took the matter very coolly. 1888 MRS. J. K. SPENDER *Kept Secret* III. i. 15, I did not mean you to take me in earnest.

**b.** To accept without objection, opposition, or resentment; to be content with; to put up with, tolerate, 'stand'.

1470–85 MALORY *Arthur* XX. vi. 805 Ye shalle take the wo with the wele, and take hit in pacyence, and thanke god of hit. 1535 COVERDALE 2 *Kings* xiv. 10 Take the prayse, and byde at home. 1595 MAYNARDE *Drake's Voy.* (Hakl. Soc.) 18 He resolved to departe, and to take the winde as God sent it. *c* 1779 R. CUMBERLAND in *Lett. Lit. Men* (Camden) 410, I take events as they fall without murmur or complaint. 1809 MALKIN *Gil Blas* v. i. ⁋ 38, I had the good sense to take things as I found them. 1896 WILLS in *Law Times Rep.* LXXIII. 689/1 If he does not conform to their law, he must take the consequences.

**43.** To face and attempt to get over, through, up, etc. (something that presents itself in one's way), or actually to do so; to clear (an obstacle, as a fence, ditch, wave, space, etc.); to mount (a slope), get round (a corner), clear (the points on a railway line), etc.

1579 TOMSON *Calvin's Serm. Tim.* 912/2 To take hedge and ditch, and go on forwards through brambles and briers. 1632 MASSINGER & FIELD *Fatal Dowry* IV. i, I look about, and neigh, take hedge and ditch. 1838 *Civil Eng. & Arch. Jrnl.* I. 139/2 The tendency to..friction in passing round curves, and the difficulty of taking the points. 1843 R. J. GRAVES *Syst. Clin. Med.* xxxi. 428 He ..is able to run up, taking two of the large stone stair-steps at each spring. 1859 GEO. ELIOT *A. Bede* xii, Nothing like 'taking' a few bushes and ditches for exorcising a demon. 1864 *Good Words* 628/1 His pony 'takes timber' without asking a question. 1892 *Graphic* 9 Apr. 467/1 The proper course to steer is for Craven Cottage Point, which can be taken rather closely.

**** *To admit, absorb, include.*

**44. a.** To admit, let in; to receive something fitted into it (quot. 1793): = *take in*, 82 a.

1674 tr. *Martiniere's Voy. Northern C.* 27 A small hole in the Keel, which took a little water. 1793 SMEATON *Edystone L.* § 244 The cavities cut on the under side..to take the upper half of each cube. 1890 *Temple Bar Mag.* Mar. 371 The *Anonyma*..several times took more water than we liked.

**b.** To absorb or become impregnated with (something detrimental, as moisture); to be affected injuriously by; to contract (disease, infection, injury, etc.); to fall into (a fit or trance). See also AIR *sb.* 11, COLD *sb.* 4 a, b, WIND.

13.. *Cursor M.* 23089 (Gött.) Of nakedhede quen i toke [*Cott.* drogh] harm ȝe gaf me clething wid to warm. 1387 TREVISA *Higden* (Rolls) I. 109 þat þe water..takeþ no defoul, but is clene i-now [etc.]. 1513 *Act 5 Hen. VIII*, c. 4 § 1 (3) If the same Worsted..taketh any Wet, incontinent it will shew spotty and foul. 1530 PALSGR. 747/2, I take colde, *je me morfons.* 1547 *Reg. Privy Council Scot.* I. 78 Personis that..takis seikness in our Soverane Ladyis army. 1555 EDEN *Decades* 16 The vytayles corrupted by taking water. 1597 SHAKS. 2 *Hen. IV*, v. i. 85 As men take diseases, one of another. 1639 N. N. tr. *Du Bosq's Compl. Woman* II. 22 That lampe of the Romans, which..went out as soone as it tooke Aire. 1712 HEARNE *Collect.* (O. H. S.) III. 301 The Book hath taken wet, and the Letters..are hardly visible. 1864 *Jrnl. R. Agric. Soc.* XXV. II. 559 Both sheep took the disease. 1885 MRS. LYNN LINTON *Chr. Kirkl.* III. x. 309 A man who takes all the epidemics afloat.

**c.** To absorb, contract, become impregnated with (a dye, colour, quality, salt, etc.); to receive, become affected by (an impression, a polish, or the like).

1592 SHAKS. *Ven. & Ad.* 354 His tendrer cheeke receiues her soft hands print, As apt as new falne snow takes any dint. 1601 HOLLAND *Pliny* XXXV. vi, It will take colour and be marked verie well. *a* 1642 SIR W. MONSON *Naval Tracts* II. (1704) 264/1 No Flesh in the Indies will take Salt. 1697 COLLIER *Ess. Mor. Subj.* II. (1703) 122 To see the cheeks take the dye of the passions thus naturally. 1727 A. HAMILTON *New Acc. E. Ind.* I. xxii. 260 The Flesh was not so savoury.. nor would it take Salt kindly. 1865 *Reader* 1 Apr. 371/2 It takes dyes admirably—much better than cotton. 1877 W. R. COOPER *Egypt. Obelisks* i. (1878) 3 A granite, or hard sandstone, capable of..taking a high polish.

**d.** *absol.* or *intr.* To become affected in the required or desired way: in various applications, as: to catch fire, kindle; to become coated or impregnated with something; to become inoculated; to become frozen; to catch the wind.

1599 SHAKS. *Hen. V*, II. i. 55, I can take, and Pistols cocke is vp, And flashing fire will follow. 1683 MOXON *Mech. Exerc., Printing* xxiv. ⁋ 10 He trys if his Balls will Take, that is..: If he finds the Inck sticks to it equally all about.., it Takes. 1793 *Regal Rambler, or, Devil in Lond.* 40 Our hero laid in a large cargo of fresh fuel, ready to touch and take like phosphorus. 1846 DICKENS *Cricket on Hearth* 30 Vaccinated just six weeks ago-o! Took very fine-ly! 1890 WHITELEGGE *Hygiene* xii. 264 Many [people] 'take' readily within five years [of vaccination].

**†45.** *trans.* To include, comprise; to contain: = *take in*, 82 k. *Obs.*

*c* 1200 ORMIN 15076 þa fetless tokenn, seȝȝþ Goddspell, Twinne mett, oþerr þrinne. *a* 1637 B. JONSON *Hymn on Nativity* ii, He whom the whole world could not take,.. Was now laid in a manger.

**b.** Of water: *To take* (one) *up to* (the ankles, knees, shoulders), *over* (the head), to submerge (one) to that depth. Now *Sc.*

1654 Z. COKE *Logick* To Reader, Truths that before delug'd you, will now take you but up to the Ancles. 1818 SCOTT *Rob Roy* xxx, Mountain torrents, some of which took the soldiers up to the knees. 1878 SAXON *Galloredian Gossip* 15 The sea took him abune the knees. *Mod. Sc.* There's a deep hole there, that will take a man over the head.

**VII.** Senses related to VI, denoting intellectual action.

* *To apprehend mentally, to conceive, understand, consider.*

**46.** To receive and hold with the intellect; to grasp mentally, apprehend, comprehend, understand: = *take in*, 82 l. (Now only in reference to the meaning of words.)

1382 WYCLIF *John* i. 5 And the liȝt schyneth in derknessis, and derknessis tooken [1388 comprehendiden] not it. *c* 1450 *St. Cuthbert* (Surtees) 4656 Goddis wisdome þat none may take [L. *incomprehensibilis*]. 1551 ROBINSON tr. *More's Utopia* II. (1895) 214 Thys kynde of learnynge..they toke so muche the souner. 1666 PEPYS *Diary* 30 July, The girl do take musick mighty readily. 1737 BRACKEN *Farriery Impr.* (1757) II. 278 The Reader will easily take the Meaning. 1860 THACKERAY *Round. Papers* i. (1899) 170 You take the allegory? Novels are sweets. 1893 *National Observer* 11 Mar. 413/2 An audience..quick to take his points.

**b.** *transf.* To apprehend the meaning of, understand (a person, i. e. what he says).

1513 DOUGLAS *Æneis* I. Prol. 318 Quha takis me nocht, go quhair thai haue ado. 1622 BACON *Holy War* Wks. 1879 I. 525/2 You take me right, Eupolis. 1707 J. STEVENS tr. *Quevedo's Com. Wks.* (1709) 350 Do you take me Sir? 1810 CRABBE *Borough* x. iii. Wks. 1834 III. 180, I spoke my thought—you take me—what I think. 1882 STEVENSON *New Arab. Nts.* (1884) 219, I am not in this affair for him. You take me?

**47. a.** With *adv.* or *advb. phr.* To understand or apprehend in a specified way. Also with person as obj. In quot. *a* 1300, 'to understand to be meant': cf. 48 b.

*a* 1300 *Cursor M.* 1379 [God] þe fader in cedre þou sal take, A tre of heght, þat has na make. 13.. *Ibid.* 28974 Chastiyng o flex[e]s foure fald to tak In praier, fasting, wand, and wak. *c* 1460 R. ROS *La Belle Dame* 582 And so must he be take in every place. 1552 *Bk. Com. Prayer, Communion* (*at fin.*), Leste yet the same kneelyng myghte be thought or taken otherwyse. 1642 tr. *Perkins' Prof. Bk.* viii. § 522 So was the law taken in Anno 4. H. 3. 1665 BUNYAN *Holy Citie* 164, I the rather take it thus,..Because [etc.]. 1721 BRADLEY *Philos. Acc. Wks. Nat.* 155 If we take the Story of it right.

**† b.** With *simple compl.* To understand as, suppose to be, consider as: = *take for*, 48; also, to understand to mean: = 48 b. *Obs.*

13.. *Cursor M.* 28121 (Cott.) And titter wald i lesyng make þan man my worde vn-treu to take. *c* 1400 *Apol. Loll.* 35 þo hous of God her is tane þe congregacoun of feiþful men. 1538 *Treat. Bps. Rome Supremacy* i, In times past the Bishop of Constantinople tooke himself highest of all bishops. 1660 MILTON *Free Commw.* Wks. 1851 V. 421 They took themselves not bound by the Light of Nature or Religion to any former Covnant. 1709 STEELE *Tatler* No. 1 ⁋ 9, I take my self obliged in Honour to go on.

**c.** With *dependent clause*: To suppose, apprehend, assume as a fact, be of opinion (*that*..). Usually *take it.*

*c* 1380 WYCLIF *Wks.* (1880) 460 Cristenmen taken ouer þat petre was cristis viker, & suyde hym in maner of lif. 1429 *Rolls of Parlt.* IV. 346/1 So take that the saide Cominaltes been no Cominaltes corporat. 1538 AUDLEY in *Lett. Suppress. Monasteries* (Camden) 240, I take it that your lordshypp ys at appoynt for me to have it. 1596 SHAKS. *Merch. V.* I. i. 63, I take it your owne busines calls on you. 1603 — *Meas. for M.* IV. ii. 110 As I take it, it is almost day. 1642 tr. *Perkins' Prof. Bk.* v. § 354 It is commonly taken, that if a wife run away from her husband..shee shall loose her dower. 1709 STEELE & ADDISON *Tatler* No. 93 ⁋ 4 Within this Height I take it, that all the fighting Men of Great Britain are comprehended. 1842 TENNYSON *Edwin Morris* 43, I take it, God made the woman for the man, And for the good and increase of the world. 1885 *Law Times* LXXX. 118/2 The learned counsel might take it that this court overruled the objection.

**d.** With *inf.* To understand, consider, suppose, imagine, assume (*to be* or *to do* something).

1548 UDALL *Erasm. Par. John* 16 b, Men toke him to be mine inferiour. 1663 BUTLER *Hud.* I. II. 889 For Men he [the Bear] always took to be His Friends, and Dogs the Enemy. *a* 1677 BARROW *Serm.* Wks. 1716 III. 72 He that taketh himself to have enough, what doth he need? 1719 DE FOE *Crusoe* (1840) II. vi. 151, I take that man to be a..penitent. 1878 HUXLEY *Physiogr.* 63 It may be taken roughly to represent one inch of rain.

**48.** *To take..for.* **a.** To suppose to be, consider as; often, with implication of error, to suppose to be (what it is not), to mistake for; also † to esteem or repute as (*obs.*: cf. 49); to assume to be. *Take for granted*: see GRANTED 2 b.

*c* 1435 *Torr. Portugal* 1333 Gret lordys..for a doughty knyght hym tase. *c* 1515 *Cocke Lorell's B.* 3 A man wolde take hym for a shrewe I trowe. 1579 GOSSON *Sch. Abuse* (Arb.) 65, I am not so childishe to take euery bushe for a monster. 1607 TOPSELL *Four-f. Beasts* (1658) 388 We will take it for granted that it pertaineth not to that rank or order. 1632 LITHGOW *Trav.* IX. 396 An Eagle taking his bald pate for a white rocke, let a shell-fish fall on it. 1693 TATE *Juvenal* xv. 178 So soft his Tresses..You'd doubt his Sex, and take him for a Girl. 1712 ADDISON *Spect.* No. 289 ⁋ 1, I have been sometimes taken..for a Parish Sexton. 1889 STEVENSON *Master of B.* x. 267 Do you take me for a fool?

**b.** To understand to mean, to interpret as. Now *rare* or *Obs.* † In quots. *c* 1200, 1340 in converse sense: To reckon or count as, to include in the meaning of (*obs.*).

*c* 1200 ORMIN 19029 Tacc nu þe sawle forr þatt mann þatt cumeþþ her to manne. 1340 HAMPOLE *Pr. Consc.* 2818 Alle þir four stedes..for helle þai may alle be tane, Of whilk four purgatory es ane. 1596 HARINGTON *Metam. Ajax* (1814) 24 Which word many of the simple hearers and readers take for a precious stone. 1684 J. P. tr. *Frambresarius' Art Physic* iii. 95 Generally the Word Aposteme is taken for any Tumor which is preternatural. 1697 EVELYN *Architects* Misc. Writ. (1825) 379 Otherwhiles it [the astragal] again is taken for the hoop, cincture or collar next the hypotrachelium.

**49.** To regard, consider, hold, esteem (*as*); to estimate, reckon (*at* so much).

1531–2 *Act 23 Hen. VIII*, c. 3 That any Utlarie..pleded

or alleged..shalbe taken but as voide plee. **1534** WHITINTON *Tullyes Offices* I. (1540) 49 He was take as a gret and a famous man. **1605** CAMDEN *Rem.* 36 This is to be take as a granted veritie. **1820** *Examiner* No. 620. 130/2 We are to take the word *liberal*..as a piece of irony. **1893** *Eng. Illustr. Mag.* X. 310/2 An average length of stroke may be taken at about six yards.

† **b.** *pa. pple.* (with qualifying adv.) Reputed, esteemed. *Obs.*

**1518** in Ld. Berners *Froiss.* (1812) Pref. 17 Sir John Style ..well beloued and well takyn in theis partes. **1526** TINDALE *Rom.* xvi. 7 Andronicus and Junia my cosyns.. which are wele taken amonge the apostles. **1535** COVERDALE *Judith* xvi. 21 Iudith was..right honorably taken in all the londe of Israel. **1597–8** BACON *Ess., Followers & Fr.* (Arb.) 34 A thing ciuile, and well taken euen in Monarchies.

** *To conceive and exercise.*

**50.** To begin to have or be affected by (a feeling or state of mind); to conceive; hence, to experience, entertain, feel (*delight, pleasure, pride*, etc.).

See also DELIGHT *sb.* 1 b, FRIGHT *sb.* 1, HUFF *sb.* 2 b, INTEREST *sb.* 7, OFFENCE *sb.* 5 c, PET *sb.*[2], PLEASURE *sb.* 5 f, PRIDE *sb.*[1] 4, UMBRAGE, etc.

*c* **1200** ORMIN 19558 Þatt tatt Farisewisshe follc Strang wraþþe takenn haffde. *a* **1300** *Cursor M.* 448 Agains him [God] he tok a pride. **1390**- [see OFFENCE *sb.* 5 c]. **1390** GOWER *Conf.* II. 100 Wherof the king gret hevynesse Hath take. **1470–85** MALORY *Arthur* IV. i. 119 Take none heuynesse, said Merlyn. *Ibid.* VI. xv. 207 She took suche sorou that shee dyed. **1535** COVERDALE *Ezek.* xxxvi. 31 Ye shal take displeasure at youre owne selues, by reason of youre synnes and abhominacions. *a* **1553** [see GRIEF *sb.* 4 b]. **1694** *Acc. Sev. Late Voy.* Introd. 6 Upon some disgust taken at his Master. **1773** *Life N. Frowde* 15 Persons to whom I had taken so much Dislike. **1888** LESTER *Hartas Maturin* III. ii. 41 Women do take prejudices.

**b.** *absol.* or *intr.* To take a fancy or liking: cf. *take to*, 74 g, *take with*, 75 c.

**1600** DYMMOCK *Treat. Irel.* (1841) 6 They are quicke and capable, kind harted where they take. **1874** HARDY *Madding Crowd* xviii, Mistress and man were engaged in the operation of making a lamb 'take', which is performed whenever a ewe has lost her own offspring, one of the twins of another ewe being given her as a substitute.

† **c.** *To take on oneself*: to become distressed or disturbed in mind: = *take on*, 84 j. *Obs.*

**1632** J. HAYWARD tr. *Biondi's Eromena* 121 The Prince,.. because he found him not, tooke on him like a mad man.

**51.** *trans.* **a.** To conceive and adopt with the will (a purpose, resolution, etc.), or with the intellect (an estimate, view, etc.); to form and hold in the mind. See also PURPOSE *sb.* 2 b, REDE *sb.*[1] 2 b.

*a* **1300** *Cursor M.* 11151 He..tok his redd al for to fle, Priuelik and latt hir be. **1375**- [see PURPOSE *sb.* 2 b]. **1513** DOUGLAS *Æneis* V. i. 10 The Troianis in thare breistis tuk ane ges Quharfor it was. **1652** NEEDHAM tr. *Selden's Mare Cl.* 37 A conclusion [was] taken to refer all to their several Princes. **1660** BARROW *Euclid* Pref. (1714) 2, I took a Resolution to make use of most of the Schemes of the said Book. **1749** FIELDING *Tom Jones* VII. ii, Having taken a resolution to leave the Country. **1891** *Law Times* XC. 462/2 We do not take the alarmist view of our correspondent.

**b.** To conceive and exercise (*courage, heart*, etc.; † *mercy* (obs.), *pity*, etc.); to form in the mind and exhibit in action. (Sometimes nearly coinciding with sense 16 a, to assume: cf. also branch VIII.) See also COURAGE *sb.* 4 d, HEART *sb.* 49, HEART OF GRACE, PITY *sb.* 2.

**13..** *Guy Warw.* (A.) 4656 Now, sir, take þerof pite. **13..**, **1530** [see HEART *sb.* 49]. **13..** *Cursor M.* 27136 Quen þou tas to þe baldhede O gretter mans sinful dede. **1483** CAXTON *G. de la Tour* A viij, Wherfore God took mercy on them. *c* **1490–1841** [see COURAGE *sb.* 4 d]. **1530–1890** [see HEART OF GRACE]. **1593** ABP. BANCROFT *Daung. Posit.* II. vii. 54 They haue taken greater boldnesse, and growen more rebellious. *a* **1715** BURNET *Own Time* an. 1672 (1823) I. 538 No popish priest had ever taken the confidence to speak to her of those matters. **1888** *Times* (weekly ed.) 18 May 3/4 The Arabs would have taken fresh heart.

**c.** To exercise with the mind, in thought (*note, notice*, † *intent*, etc.), or with the mind and will, in action (*care, heed*, † *diligence*, etc.). Cf. branches VIII, IX. See also CARE *sb.* 3 c, HEED *sb.* 1 b, INTENT *sb.* 2, KEEP *sb.* 1, 2, NOTE *sb.*[2] 20 b, NOTICE *sb.* 6, 7, REGARD *sb.* 6 b, TENT *sb.*[2], THOUGHT *sb.*

*a* **1225** *Leg. Kath.* 1379 Þe deore Drihtin areaw us, & toc read to ure alde dusischipes. *a* **1300**- [see KEEP *sb.* 1, 2]. *c* **1305**- [see HEED *sb.* 1 b]. **13..** *Cursor M.* 27228 Ilk man þat will ta ȝeme. *c* **1368** CHAUCER *Compl. Pite* 82 But ye the rather take cure To breke that periouse alliaunce. *c* **1375** *Cursor M.* 12592 (Fairf.) Hamward þai went & to ihesu toke nane entent. *c* **1425** *Ibid.* 7937 (Trin.) Son he seide take good gome ȝyuen þou hast þin owne dome. *c* **1475** *Songs & Carols 15th C.* (Percy Soc.) 54 To here song then tok I intent. **1564–5** *Reg. Privy Council Scot.* I. 320 Quhairunto hir Hienes and hir Counsall mon tak ee and regard. **1588**- [see CARE *sb.* 3 c]. **1592**- [see NOTICE *sb.* 6, 7]. **1596**- [see NOTE *sb.*[2] 20 b]. **1784** R. BAGE *Barham Downs* I. 230, I took no concern about any of them.

**VIII.** Various senses, nearly = make, do, perform (some action). (See also senses 19, 37, 51 b, c.)

**52.** To perform, make, do (an act, action, movement, etc.): usually with some notion of undertaking or taking upon one, and carrying out or carrying on; sometimes with that of getting.

Often it forms with the object merely a periphrastic equivalent of the cognate vb.: e. g. *to take a leap* = *to leap* (*once*), *to take a look* = *to look* (*once*), *to take one's departure* = *to depart*. (See also *take aim* in Phrases, 64; ACTION 7, JOURNEY *sb.* 3, STEP *sb.*, TURN *sb.*, WALK *sb.*)

*c* **1380** *Sir Ferumbras* 4029 To-morwe let ous our iorne take, Hamward aȝen to ryde. *c* **1412** HOCCLEVE *De Reg. Princ.* 3400 The kyng took a laghtre, and wente his way. *c* **1449** PECOCK *Repr.* 156 At which men mowe lawȝe and take bourde for her symplenes. **1477** EARL RIVERS (Caxton) *Dictes* 1, I determyned me to take that voyage. **1483** CAXTON *Cato* C vj b, Thou oughtest not to stryue ne take noyse wyth them that ben ful of superfluous wordes. *c* **1489** — *Sonnes of Aymon* xiv. 341 Thei toke grete debate for me wyth Charlemagn wythin his pavylion. **1491** *Churchw. Acc. St. Dunstan's, Canterb.*, They took an axion ageynst the executores of Wyllyam Belser. **1556** *Chron. Gr. Friars* (Camden) 13 Thys yere the kynge..toke his viage towarde Normandy. **1590** SPENSER *F. Q.* III. xi. 42 Like a winged horse he [Neptune] tooke his flight. **1617** *Acc. Bk. W. Wray* in *Antiquary* XXXII. 214 King James..tooke his progresse towards Scotland. **1678** BUNYAN *Pilgr.* I. 43 How many steps have I took in vain. **1693** *Humours Town* 3 Take a last farewel-look of this overgrown City. *Ibid.* 6 You might take a survey of the Rarities. **1711** BUDGELL *Spect.* No. 77 ⁋ 1 We took a turn or two more. **1719** DE FOE *Crusoe* (1840) II. xiv. 287 Without measuring the windings and turnings it takes. *Ibid.* xv. 315 He takes a great circuit about. **1766** GOLDSM. *Vic. W.* xxviii, My wife, my daughter and herself were taking a walk together. **1845** M. PATTISON *Ess.* (1889) I. 24 When Queen Brunchilde took her departure from Rouen. **1867** AUG. J. E. WILSON *Vashti* xxiv, I came to-day to beg you to take a trip somewhere, by sea or land. **1889** MRS. E. KENNARD *Landing Prize* III. viii. 148 The salmon took a great leap. **1893** J. ASHBY STERRY *Naughty Girl* vii, I'll just take a turn down to the club and see what's going on.

† **b.** *To take beginning*: to begin, start, commence. (See also 31.) *Obs.* [= ON. *taka upphaf*, to begin.]

*a* **1300** *Cursor M.* 12887 Þe ald testament hir-wit nu slakes, And sua þe neu bigining takes. **1557–75** *Diurnal Occurr.* (Bann. Club) 61 Vpoun the first day of August, the Parliament tuke begyning. **1601** DOLMAN *La Primaud. Fr. Acad.* (1618) III. 641 We must all beleeue..that time tooke beginning with the world.

**53.** *To take counsel* († *advice*, † *advisement*): to get advice, to consult, deliberate; † to devise; † to decide: see ADVICE 4, ADVISEMENT 3, COUNSEL 1.

*a* **1300** *Cursor M.* 4790 Þar of es god we ta consail. *c* **1386** CHAUCER *Melib.* ⁋ 760 Thanne Dame Prudence..delibered and took auys in hir self. **1480** CAXTON *Chron. Eng.* cxcvii. 173 The barons token counceyll bytwene hem. **1483** — *G. de la Tour* D iv b, Withoute takyng ony counceylle of her husbond. **1537** T. CUMPTUN in Ellis *Orig. Lett.* Ser. II. II. 92 After that they had communiked together and taken avisement. **1609** BIBLE (Douay) *Judg.* xx. 32 Who..tooke advise to draw them away from the citie. **1879** M. J. GUEST *Lect. Hist. Eng.* xxxvi. 359 She took counsel with witches and magicians.

† **b.** *intr.* ? ellipt. for *take advisement. Obs.*

*c* **1400** *Emare* 799 Grete lordes toke hem be-twene, That þey wolde exyle þe quene.

† **54.** *trans.* To arrange, fix, agree upon, conclude (a truce, peace, league, etc.). [Cf. OF. *prendre treve*, 13th c.] *Obs.*

**1375** BARBOUR *Bruce* XIV. 96 Quhill trewis at the last tuk thai. *c* **1400** *Laud Troy-Bk.* 8474 It was seyde to the Emperoure..How ffight was taken hem be-twene. *c* **1400** *Destr. Troy* 9072 The Troiens to the tenttes tristy men send, For a tru to be tan. *c* **1470** [see PEACE *sb.* 1 b]. **1523** LD. BERNERS *Froiss.* I. xxxiii. 48 So yᵗ they wolde take no peace, nor truse, with yᵉ kyng of Englande. *c* **1600** SHAKS. *Sonn.* xlvii. 1 Betwixt mine eye and heart a league is tooke. **1656** S. HOLLAND *Zara* (1719) 135 Having taken a Truce with his Enemy, he would not be the first should break it.

**55.** *To take adieu, farewell*: to bid farewell, say good-bye, take one's leave. Const. *of.* Cf. *to take leave*: see LEAVE *sb.* 2. So † *to take good night* (*obs.*).

*c* **1560** ROLLAND *Seven Sages* Prol. ii, I..tuke gude nicht, and said gude schirs adew. **1617** J. TAYLOR (Water-P.) *Trav.* (1872) 2 We all went to the Christopher where we took a Bacchanalian farewell one of another. **1665** PEPYS *Diary* 28 Aug., I think to take adieu to-day of the London Streets. **1700** DRYDEN *Cock & Fox* 256 Last he drew A piteous sigh, and took a long adieu. **1821** SCOTT *Kenilw.* vii, Thus saying, he at length took farewell. **1840** THIRLWALL *Greece* VII. 195 [He] besought Demosthenes to forgive his temporary estrangement, ..and took a last farewell of him.

**56.** To lay hold of, raise, put forth, make (an objection, an exception, a distinction, etc.). See also EXCEPTION *sb.* 7 c, OBJECTION 1 b.

**1542**- [see EXCEPTION *sb.* 7 c]. **1830** HERSCHEL *Nat. Phil.* 7 The objection which has been taken. **1830** MONK *Life R. Bentley* (1833) I. 303 Instead of doing so, they take a dilemma, and intimate a belief that either by the old statutes, or by the 40th of Elizabeth's, the Master is subject to the jurisdiction of the Bishop of Ely. **1849** MACAULAY *Hist. Eng.* vii. II. 265 Between punishments and disabilities a distinction was taken. *Ibid.* x. 556 The distinction which they took was..ingenious. **1864** BP. WILBERFORCE *Sp. Missions* (1874) 46, I know well the objections men can take.

**IX.** Senses denoting movement or removal (lead, convey, remove, deliver, etc.), and related senses.

* *To convey, carry, conduct, remove.*

**57. a.** To carry, convey; to cause (a person or animal) to go with one, to conduct, lead, escort. Also said of a vehicle, etc.: To convey, carry (a person) to some place. Also of a road, way, etc.: = LEAD *v.*[1] 6; so of a journey, etc.

*c* **1200** ORMIN 8355 Josæp, ris upp & tacc þe child, & tacc þe childess moderr. *a* **1300** *Cursor M.* 5117 Tas Ruben þan wit yow. *Ibid.* 23814 Es þar na wai..Cun tak us better. *a* **1400–50** *Alexander* 4886 Syne tas he with him titly his twelue tried prince[s]. **1503** in *Trans. Roy. Hist. Soc.* (1902) 153 Walter Robardes tooke this Alexʳ apart. **1590** SHAKS. *Com. Err.* IV. i. 36 Take the stranger to my house. **1665** MANLEY *Grotius' Low C. Warres* 832 Taking through the marshy Fields of Cazant Twelve hundred Walloons and Irish with him. **1719** DE FOE *Crusoe* (1840) I. xiv. 246, I took my man Friday with me. **1848** THACKERAY *Van. Fair* xlviii, Being obliged to take four of us in his carriage to wait upon His Majesty. **1878** *Scribner's Mag.* XV. 897/1 The second stage of the journey takes the traveler through Egypt. **1908** *Betw. Trent & Ancholme* 55 A yard or two further takes us to the N.E. corner. *Mod.* Will this road take me to Abingdon?

**b.** To carry or bear (a thing) with one; to carry to some place or person. In quot. 1883, to draw (something) *through* a liquid.

**1390** GOWER *Conf.* III. 217 [Eche] hath A pot of Erthe, in which he tath A lyht brennende in a kressette. *a* **1400** *Sir Perc.* 478 He..Tuke with hym his schorte spere. *c* **1470** HENRY *Wallace* II. 85 Thow Scot, to quhom takis thow this thing? **1590** SHAKS. *Com. Err.* IV. i. 37 And with you take the Chaine. **1605** — *Macb.* V. iii. 19 Take thy face hence. **1768** J. BYRON *Narr. Patagonia* (ed. 2) 221 They will take from the ground a glove or handkerchief. **1858** RAMSAY *Scot. Life & Char.* V. (1870) 118 She went out and did not take the door with her [*i. e.* shut it after her]. **1883** R. HALDANE *Workshop Receipts* Ser. II. 227/1 Take [the yarn] through dilute sulphuric acid, and wash very well.

**c.** *fig.* To induce (a person) to go; to be the cause of his going. (Cf. BRING *v.* 1 c.)

**1848** THACKERAY *Van. Fair* lxvii, 'Particular business', she said, took her to Bruges. **1856** J. H. NEWMAN *Callista* (1890) 114 What takes you into the city this morning? **1883** P. GREG *Sanguelac* II. xi. 223 What took you out so late? *Mod.* The business that took me to London.

**58.** With *from, off* (hence sometimes *simply*): To carry away, to remove; to extract; to deprive or rid a person or thing of (with various shades of connotation): = *take away*, 78 a, *take off*, 83 a, *take out*, 85 a: see also *take out of*, 86.

*To take off one's feet*: to carry off one's feet by force, as a wind or wave; also *fig.* So *to take off one's balance*, etc.

*a* **1272** *Luue Ron* 64 in *O. E. Misc.* 95 Al deþ hit wile from him take. *a* **1300** *E. E. Psalter* i. 5 Als duste þat winde þerthe tas fra. *a* **1400** *Cursor M.* 29546 (Cott. Galba) It takes [*Cott.* steres] his cristendom him fra. *c* **1489** CAXTON *Sonnes of Aymon* 19 Saying, that they should take the head from the body of hym. **1535** COVERDALE *Ps.* l[i]. 11 Take not thy holy sprete fro me. **1567** *Gude & Godlie B.* (S.T.S.) 147 He fra me my Sin hes tane. **1610** HOLLAND *Camden's Brit.* (1637) 73 He..tooke from the towne the benefit of their haven. **1655** SIR E. NICHOLAS in *N. Papers* (Camden) II. 235 His decree is annulled and taken of yᵉ file. **1678** BUTLER *Hud.* III. III. 693 The Law severely contrabands Our taking business off Mens hands. **1818** SCOTT *Hrt. Midl.* xv, The doing so would..take the case from under the statute. **1825** J. NICHOLSON *Operat. Mechanic* 560 A plane, which takes a thin shaving off the surface of the wood. **1867** TROLLOPE *Chron. Barset* i, John did take his eyes off his book. *Mod.* The sea was so rough when I was bathing that the waves took me off my feet.

**b.** *To take the life of*: to deprive of life, to kill.

[**13..** *Cursor M.* 25831 His lijf þan sal be fra him tane. *c* **1489** CAXTON *Sonnes of Aymon* xii. 306, I praye you..that yourselfe wyl take the liff fro me, and cut of my hede.] **1591** SHAKS. 1 *Hen. VI*, III. i. 22 Thou layd'st a Trap to take my Life. **1766** GOLDSM. *Vic. W.* xxx, You imagine, perhaps, that a contempt for your own life gives you a right to take that of another. **1847** TENNYSON *Princ.* V. 397 Take not his life: he risk'd it for my own.

**c.** To remove by death.

**1552** *Bk. Com. Prayer, Burial of Dead*, Forasmuche as it hath pleased almightie God of his great mercie to take vnto hym selfe the soule of our dere brother here departed, we therefore commit [etc.]. **1593** SHAKS. 3 *Hen. VI*, I. iv. 167 Hard-hearted Clifford, take me from the World. **1616** S. MOUNTAGU in *Buccleuch MSS.* (Hist. MSS. Comm.) I. 247 God hath taken to himself my brother Walter Mountagu. **1632** HEYWOOD *1st Pt. Iron Age* v. i. Wks. 1874 III. 338 Since the Fates Haue tane him from vs. **1864** TENNYSON *North. Farmer* iii, 'The amoighty's a taäkin o' you to 'issén, my friend', a said.

**d.** To subtract, deduct.

**1611** SHAKS. *Cymb.* II. i. 60 This her Sonne, Cannot take two from twenty for his heart, And leaue eighteene. **1806** HUTTON *Course Math.* (1827) I. 8, 6 − 2, denotes that 2 is to be taken from 6. **1876** E. JENKINS *Blot Queen's Head* 28 Every one took 50 per cent. off Bobby's expletives. **1890** *Sat. Rev.* 16 Aug. 192/1 Twopence in the pound was taken off the tea-duty.

**e.** *absol.* with *from*: To detract from, lessen, diminish. Cf. 78 c, 83 k.

**1625** MASSINGER *New Way* IV. i, [Ne'er] sullied with one taint or spot That may take from your innocence and candour. *a* **1700** DRYDEN (J.), It takes not from you, that you were born with principles of generosity. **1891** *Temple Bar Mag.* Oct. 254 It takes greatly from the pleasure.

**f.** *intr.* for *pass.* (with adv. or advb. phr.) To be capable of being, or adapted to be, taken *off, out, to pieces*, etc.; to be removable, detachable, etc.

So, by extension, *to take in and out* = to be capable of being put in and taken out; so *to take on and off.*

**1669** STURMY *Mariner's Mag.* II. ii. 53 A Brass pair of Compasses..and four Steel Points to take in and out. **1703** MOXON *Mech. Exerc.* 227 The Stop-screw, to take out when the Hollow Axis moves in the Moving-Coller. **1881** GREENER *Gun* 78 Guns..so constructed as to take to pieces and stow away in a small compass. **1892** *St. James' Gaz.* 8 Feb. 6/2 Yours [i. e. hair] takes off at night.

**59.** in various *fig.* senses. **a.** To carry, draw, or lead in thought, etc.; with *from, off*, to distract.

**1611** SHAKS. *Wint. T.* IV. iv. 356 Your heart is full of something, that do's take Your minde from feasting. **1670** COTTON *Espernon* II. v. 238 An accident fell out that soon took the Duke off all thoughts of that Solemnity. **1742** *Lond. & Country Brew.* I. (ed. 4) 41 These deluded People are taken into an Approbation of indeed an Ignis fatuus. **1890** *Murray's Mag.* VII. 65 Love..took her out of herself, and soothed her sorrows.

† **b.** *To take* (a person) *with one*: to speak so

that (he) can 'follow' or apprehend one's meaning; to enable (him) to understand one; to be explicit. (Usu. in *imper.*) *Obs.*

**1592** SHAKS. *Rom. & Jul.* III. v. 142 Soft, take me with you, take me with you, wife. **1695** CONGREVE *Love for L.* v. ii, Ay, but pray take me along with you, sir.

†**c.** *To take* (a thing) *with one*: to bear in mind, keep in remembrance, take note of. *Obs.*

**1599** MASSINGER, etc. *Old Law* II. ii, Oh! you are too hot, sir; Pray cool yourself, and take September with you. **1610** HOLLAND *Camden's Brit.* 715 Yet take here with you, that which William Newbrigensis..writeth. **1746** CHESTERF. *Lett.* (1792) I. 295 Take this along with you that the worst authors are always most partial to their own works. **1828** SCOTT *F. M. Perth* v, Take it with you that I will never listen to them.

†**d.** To render, translate. *Obs. rare.*

*c* **1430** *Syr Gener.* (Roxb.) 25 A clerk itt in to latyn tooke Att hertford out of a booke.

**e.** To bring or convey to a higher or lower degree; to raise or lower; to advance or put back. See also *take down*, 80; PEG *sb.*[1] 3.

**1589**– [see PEG *sb.*[1] 3]. **1890** *Field* 24 May 750/3 By steady play the score was taken to 18.

** *To deliver, give, commit, give up.*

†**60.** *trans.* To deliver, hand over; to give; to give in charge, commit, entrust. (= BETAKE 1, 1 b, 2.) Const. *to* or dative. *Obs.*

[In Layamon, in the early version rarely (2 instances), but in the later very commonly (22 instances), *bitake* is used as equivalent to *bitæche, biteche* (BETEACH, to deliver); in 19 cases *biteche* of the earlier text becomes *bitake* in the later. In 4 cases the later version has in the same sense the simple *take*; this became from 1300 to 1530 quite established, and continued in some writers to *c* 1560. This use was not in Norse, and is absent from northern ME. For the history see BETAKE *v.*]

*c* **1275** LAY. 54 He..wrot..And þane hilke boc tock us to bisne. *Ibid.* 3361 And takeþ [*c* 1205 bitachet] hit his child. *Ibid.* 22378 And ich wolle..To hostage take þe mine sone [*c* 1205 biteche þe mine þreo sunen]. *c* **1290** *S. Eng. Leg.* I. 99/254 To Ihesu crist ich habbe al-so al min heorte i-take. **1297** R. GLOUC. (Rolls) 2027 Some sede þat him betere were take is neueu conan þe kinedom of þis lond. **1340** *Ayenb.* 171 Þe castel of his herte and of his bodye þet god him heþ ytake to loki. **1377** LANGL. *P. Pl.* B. xv. 575 Owre lorde wrote it hym-selue In stone...And toke it moyses to teche men til Messye com. **1387** TREVISA *Higden* (Rolls) II. 323 Moyses..took his wif [*uxori tradidit*] þe ryng of forȝetnesse. *c* **1400** *Prymer* (1894) 78 We biseche þee þat þe soule of þi seruaunt..be not take in-to þe hondis of oure enemy. *c* **1425** *Cursor M.* 15411 (Trin.) In to ȝoure hondes I shal him take [*earlier MSS.* teche]. **1436** *Let.* in Burton & Raine *Hemingbrough* 393, I writte no more..at this tyme, so I tak ȝow to þe Holy Trinite. *c* **1440** *Promp. Parv.* 485/2 Takyn, or delyueryn a thynge to a-nother, *trado.* *c* **1440** *Gesta Rom.* xlvi. 183 (Add. MS.) Take me the Ryng, and I shalle kepe it as my lyf. *a* **1533** LD. BERNERS *Huon* lxvi. 226 Al that ye take me to kepe shalbe sauely kept to your behoue. **1533** MORE *Answ. Poysoned Bk.* Wks. 1063/1 When he tooke them the bread and bode them eate it. *a* **1553** UDALL *Royster D.* I. v. (Arb.) 31 Who tooke thee thys letter?

†**61.** *refl.* **a.** To commit or devote oneself (to God, to Christ, etc.); also, to commit or betake oneself *to* one's legs, heels, weapons, or other means of protection or safety. *Obs.* exc. as in b.

*c* **1200** ORMIN 356 Aȝȝ fra þatt Adam Godd forrlet & toc himm to þe deofell. *c* **1220** *Bestiary* 98 in *O. E. Misc.* 4 He..forsaket ðore satanas,..Takeð him to ihesu crist. *a* **1300** *Cursor M.* 23046 Þat al þis werld welth for-sok, And anerli to godd þam tok. *c* **1475** *Rauf Coilȝear* 938, I will forsaik Mahoun, and tak me to his micht. **1530** PALSGR. 749/1, I take me to my legges, I flye a waye. **1548** [see HEEL *sb.*[1] 19]. **1606** G. W[OODCOCKE] *Hist. Ivstine* VIII. 38 Which people perceiuing them selues entrapped..fearefully tooke them to their weapons. **1607** TOPSELL *Four-f. Beasts* (1658) 19 The Gyants..took them to their heels and so were overcome.

**b.** *refl.* To devote or give oneself up; to betake or apply oneself *to* (some pursuit, action, or object).

*a* **1300** *Cursor M.* 4032 Þir breþer tuain þam tok to red To dele þair landes þam bi-tuixs. *c* **1425** *Ibid.* 13429 (Trin.) Of wif forsoke he hondbonde And toke [*earlier MSS.* turned] him to þe better honde. *c* **1440** *Alphabet of Tales* 350 He lefte all his gude and tuke hym to pouertie. **1530** PALSGR. 749/1, I take me to relygyon, or any other Kynde of Lyvynge wherein I must contynue. **1570** T. WILSON tr. *Demosthenes' Olynth.* Epist. *j b, Such are contented..to weare our Countrie cloth, and to take themselues to hard fare. **1576** GASCOIGNE *Steel Gl.* (Arb.) 67 Art thou a craftsman? take thee to thine arte. **1707** *Curios. in Husb. & Gard.* 296 One of these Leaves..took it self to walking as soon as he touch'd it. **1888** SOPHIE VEITCH *Dean's Daughter* I. viii. 155, I..took myself to the Chase. **1890** E. L. ARNOLD *Phra* v, She would not eat and would not speak, and at last took her to crying.

**c.** *intr.* with *into*: To give oneself up to: = *take to*, 74 e. *rare.*

**1756** J. CLUBBE *Misc. Tracts* (1770) I. 105 Men had better read but few books at large, than take into this short and fallacious method of attaining..imperfect knowledge. **1765** *Ibid.* II. 10 Some men taking into life of pleasure, others into an easy chair of sleep and indolence. **1864** CARLYLE *Fredk. Gt.* xv. vi. (1872) VI. 25 Taking deeply into tobacco.

*** *To set oneself, begin, to apply oneself.*

**62.** *intr.* with *inf.* To set oneself, to begin (*to do* something). [After ON. *taka at*, e. g. *taka at ganga* to begin to go.] *Obs.*

**1154** *O. E. Chron.* (Laud MS.) an. 1135, Dauid king of Scotland toc to uerrien him. *c* **1200** ORMIN 223 [Zacariȝe] toc to becnenn till þe follc. *Ibid.* 4772 Swa..þatt hiss bodiȝ toc To rotenn bufenn eorþe. *Ibid.* 8332 Off þa fowwre riche menn þatt tokenn þa to rixlenn. *c* **1320** *Sir Tristr.* 1000 Now haþ tristrem y-tan Oȝain moraunt to fiȝt.

**b.** In later use, To apply oneself *to* a habitual action (cf. 61 b and 74 e).

**1677** YARRANTON *Eng. Improv.* 157 Since the Welsh took to break up their Mountains, and sow them with Corn, they have Corn sufficient for themselves. **1839** *Times* 5 Oct., He took to cultivate his genius by reading political economy. **1856** FREEMAN in W. R. W. Stephens *Life* (1895) I. iv. 232, I have taken to write a little in a penny paper called the *Star.* **1890** *Blackw. Mag.* CXLVII. 262/2 Their taking to smoke tobacco. **1891** G. MEREDITH *One of our Conq.* III. xi. 233 She has taken to like him.

†**c.** *refl.* in same senses. *Obs. rare.*

**1489** CAXTON *Sonnes of Aymon* i. 54 The duke Beues toke hym selfe for to wepe strongly. **1605** VERSTEGAN *Dec. Intell.* vi. (1628) 165 They tooke themselues first to rob vpon the sea coastes. *a* **1677** BARROW *Serm.* Wks. 1716 II. 63 A state..which they took themselves peculiarly to enjoy.

**** *To take one's course, to go.*

**63.** *intr.* To make one's way, go, proceed; = NIM *v.* 2, FANG *v.* 7. In early use chiefly with *to*; in later use with any prep. or adv. of direction: usually implying prompt action, cf. 'start', 'strike'.

See also *take to*, 74 b; *take away*, 78 d, *take back*, 79 e, *take in*, 82 p, *take off*, 83 n.

*c* **1250** *Gen. & Ex.* 1751 He toc, and wente, and folwede on. *c* **1330** R. BRUNNE *Chron. Wace* (Rolls) 13566 So harde þe parties to-gidere tok. **13..** *St. Erkenwolde* 57 in Horstm. *Altengl. Leg.* (1881) 267 Quen tithynges tokene to þe tone [= town]. ?**13..** *Cast. Love* 1686 In good tyme the[i] were i-bore, That to that feste mowe takyn [F. *peuent venir*]. *a* **1400** *Gosp. Nicod.* 1122 (Cott. Galba) On þe morn furth gan þai pas, to þaire iorne þai ta. *c* **1435** *Torr. Portugal* 598 A lytyl whyll before the day, He toke into a Ryde Wey. *c* **1489** CAXTON *Sonnes of Aymon* ix. 224 Whan they were all mounted, they toke on theyr way. **1606** G. W[OODCOCKE] *Hist. Ivstine* III. 19 They tooke on their way to seeke a new place of habitation. **1615** G. SANDYS *Trav.* 193 Turning backe, we tooke vp the said streete to the West. **1622** MABBE tr. *Aleman's Guzman d'Alf.* II. 282 They tooke downe through a groue of Alder trees. *c* **1645** T. TULLY *Siege of Carlisle* (1840) 5 Most of the fugatives took streight for Carlisle. **1707** FREIND *Peterborow's Cond. Sp.* 221 My Lord took along the edge of the Hills. **1801** tr. *Gabrielli's Myst. Husb.* III. 74, I took across some fields for the nearest way. **1863** W. C. BALDWIN *Afr. Hunting* vi. 212 He [the elephant] gave chase, and I took up the hill. **1892** MRS. E. STEWART in A. E. Lee *Hist. Columbus, Ohio* I. 264 A gang of wolves took after her.

**b.** *intr.* Of a road, a river, etc.: To proceed, go, run, strike off (in some direction). *Obs.* or *dial.*

**1610** HOLLAND *Camden's Brit.* (1637) 731 Where it [the high road] taketh Northward, it leadeth by Caldwell and Aldburgh. **1865** CARLYLE *Fredk. Gt.* XVIII. ii. (1872) VII. 110 [The river] Moldau..takes straight to northward again. **1894** CROCKETT *Raiders* 175 At this point the drove-road took over the Folds Hill.

**c.** *refl.* In same sense as a; also = to betake oneself, repair, resort *to.* See also *take off*, 83 c.

**1470–85** MALORY *Arthur* I. viii. 45 He took hym to a strong towre with v c good men with hym. *c* **1489** CAXTON *Sonnes of Aymon* xvi. 385 After all thyse wordes, they toke theym selfe on their waye. **1822** BYRON *Werner* I. i. 600 He will take himself to bed. **1865** TROLLOPE *Belton Est.* xxx, I am to pack up, bag and baggage, and take myself elsewhere.

**X.** In idiomatic phrases with special obj.

**64. Take aim.** To direct a missile at something with intention to strike it; to aim.

**1590** [see AIM *sb.* 3]. **1697** DRYDEN *Æneid* x. 479 The Sabine Clausus came, And, from afar, at Dryops took his aim. **1719** DE FOE *Crusoe* (1840) II. iv. 92 He took a sure aim. **1850** *Tait's Mag.* XVII. 546/1 He was in the act of taking aim with a carbine.

**65. Take alarm.** To accept and act upon a warning of danger; hence, to become alarmed or roused to a sense of danger.

**1624, 1772** [see ALARM *sb.* 8]. **1689** T. R. *View Govt. Europe* 38 The people took the Alarm, and clamour'd for a Parliament. **1825** *New Monthly Mag.* XIII. 398 His *amour propre* takes the alarm. **1893** *Nat. Observer* 7 Oct. 535/2 The pirate took the alarm in time.

**66. Take charge.** To assume the care or custody *of*; to make oneself responsible.

**1389** [see CHARGE *sb.* 13]. **1495** *Act 11 Hen. VII*, c. 22 § 1 A maister Ship Carpenter taking the charge of the werke. **1613** SHAKS. *Hen. VIII*, I. iv. 20 Place you that side, Ile take the charge of this. **1848** THACKERAY *Van. Fair* xli, The Baronet promised to take charge of the lad at school.

†**67. Take day.** To appoint or fix a day for the transaction of some business; to make an appointment; to put off to another day. Also *fig.*

*a* **1400** *Octouian* 1499 They..toke day at the monthys ende Of playn batayle. *c* **1477** CAXTON *Jason* 123 She accorded to her this request and toke daye for to do hit. **1523** LD. BERNERS *Froiss.* I. xxxii. 46 Then they toke day to come agayn a thre wekes after the Feast of saynt John. **1565** STAPLETON tr. *Bede's Hist. Ch. Eng.* 171 To make quick confession of their sinfull actes and not to take dayes with God. **1642** FULLER *Holy & Prof. St.* II. xix.* 126 He had rather disburse his life at the present, then to take day, to fall into the hands of such remorslesse creditours.

**68. Take fire. a.** *lit.* To become kindled or ignited; to begin to burn, to kindle, ignite: = *catch fire* (CATCH *v.* 44).

**1526** *Pilgr. Perf.* (W. de W. 1531) 263 b, At the last they take fyre & brenne. **1590** SIR J. SMYTH *Disc. Weapons* 21 Through the moystnes of the weather..the powder will take no fire. **1669** STURMY *Mariner's Mag.* v. 89 Dip therein one end of your short Pieces, least they take Fire at both ends together. **1771** SMOLLETT *Humph. Cl.* 4 July, The soot took fire. **1885** *Cent. Mag.* XXIX. 874/1 These..chimneys..often took fire.

**b.** *fig.* To become 'inflamed' with some emotion or the like; to become excited, esp. with anger; to become enraged, to 'fire up'.

**1607** G. WILKINS *Mis. Inforced Marr.* I. in Hazl. *Dodsley* IX. 473 On which tinder he soon takes fire, and swears you are the man. **1608** *Merry Devil of Edmonton* ibid. X. 239 How this jest takes fire. **1761** HUME *Hist. Eng.* III. liv. 171 The Commons took fire, and voted it a breach of privilege. **1844** THIRLWALL *Greece* VIII. lxii. 177 Cleomenes took fire at the affront. **1890** *Temple Bar Mag.* June 17 Lithgow's soul took fire with sympathy.

**69. Take hold. a.** To get something by one's own act into one's (physical) hold; to grasp, seize: = *catch hold* (CATCH *v.* 45), *lay hold* (LAY *v.* 22). Const. *of*; *on, upon* (arch.). Also said of things.

**1530** PALSGR. 748/2, I take holde apon one, *jempoygne.* **1611** *Vestry Bks.* (Surtees) 161 To picke forth the ould lyme and morter that the new might better take hold. **1613** PURCHAS *Pilgrimage* (1614) 19 [The Indian] Figge-tree..whose branches..doe bend themselves downewards to the earth, where they take holde, and with new rooting multiply. **1754** SHEBBEARE *Matrimony* (1766) II. 193 [She] fell on her Knees..taking hold on the Skirt of his Coat. **1816** [see HOLD *sb.*[1] 2].

**b.** *fig.* To get a person or thing into its (or one's) 'hold' or power; usually with *of* (*on, upon* arch.); of a feeling, a disease, etc.: to seize and affect forcibly and more or less permanently; of fire, to 'lay hold' *of* (something), begin to burn. Also, to seize, avail oneself of (an opportunity).

**1577** HARRISON *England* II. vi. (1877) I. 164 A thing latelie sproong vp, when pampering of the bellie began to take hold. **1605** SHAKS. *Lear* IV. vi. 238 Hence, Least that th'infection of his fortune take Like hold on thee. **1708** J. C. *Compl. Collier* (1845) 23 Another dangerous sort of bad Air, but of a fiery Nature like Lightning,..if it takes hold of the Candle. **1725** N. ROBINSON *Th. Physick* 292 When the Disease has taken any Hold of the Patient. **1889** M. GRAY *Reproach Annesley* III. vi, A sense of her bitter bereaval took hold of her.

**c.** (with *of*) To take possession and management of, take under one's control. ? *U. S.*

**1877** RAYMOND *Statist. Mines & Mining* 222 They..know that a company of moneyed men taking hold of their camp will have to spend a considerable amount of money before they can expect to recoup their investment. **1897** KIPLING *Captains Courageous* ix, No, I only capt—took hold of the 'Blue M.' freighters—Morgan and M'Quade's old line—this summer.

†**d.** To attach itself, take root. *Obs. rare*[−1].

*a* **1300** *Cursor M.* 9350 It tok neuer in þer hertes hald. **13..** *Ibid.* 10009 (Gött.) Þat er four vertus principalys,.. All oþer vertus of þaim tas [*Cott.* has] hald.

**e.** To apply oneself to action; to set to; to take an active part. *dial.* and *U. S.*

**1868** ATKINSON *Cleveland Gloss.*, *Tak' hold*, to undertake; an office, or specified performance or duty. **1870** MISS ALCOTT *Old-fashioned Girl* xi, I'm in despair, and shall have to take hold myself, I'm afraid. **1888** BRYCE *Amer. Commw.* III. IV. lxxxvi. 153 To believe that things will come out right whether he 'takes hold' himself or not.

**70. Take horse. a.** To mount a horse; to get on horseback (esp. for a journey): see sense 24 c.

[*c* **1450** *Brut* (E. E. T. S.) 450 On þe morow he toke hys hors and rode to Wyndysore vn-to our Kyng. *c* **1475** *Harl. Contin. Higden* (Rolls) VIII. 544 He toke his hors with a pryvy meyney. *a* **1533** LD. BERNERS *Huon* vii. 18 After masse [they] toke theyr horsses.] **1675** BROOKS *Gold. Key* Wks. 1867 V. 10 Bajazet,..Tamerlane took prisoner,..and used him for a footstool when he took horse. **1743** WESLEY *Jrnl.* (1749) 9 Just as I was taking horse, he return'd. **1889** *Univ. Rev.* Oct. 263 The princes..took horse and fled.

**b.** *Mining.* (See quot.) *local.*

**1855** J. R. LEIFCHILD *Cornwall Mines* 88 When a lode divides into branches, the miners say it has taken horse.

**c.** Of a mare: see sense 39 b, and HORSE *sb.* 1 c.

**1577** B. GOOGE *Heresbach's Husb.* III. (1586) 118 The Mare will not take the Horse. **1688** *Lond. Gaz.* No. 2378/4 A brown bay Filly,..being locked from taking Horse.

**71. Take possession. a.** To get something by one's own act into one's possession; to enter into possession. With *of*: to take into one's possession, make oneself possessor of, take for one's own, appropriate: see POSSESSION *sb.* 1 c.

**1535** COVERDALE 1 *Kings* xxi. 15 Vp, and take possession of the vynyarde of Naboth the Iesraelite. **1591** SHAKS. *Two Gent.* v. iv. 130 Take but possession of her, with a Touch. *a* **1641** BP. MOUNTAGU *Acts & Mon.* i. (1642) 21 They entred upon, and took possession of the Land of Promise. **17..** *Rem. Reign Will. III* in *Harl. Misc.* (1809) III. 359 The troops..would, in all likelihood, have took possession of White-hall. **1852** MRS. STOWE *Uncle Tom's C.* xxxiv, Then he came, the cursed wretch! he came to take possession.

**b.** *fig.* (with *of*) To begin to 'possess', dominate, or actuate: cf. POSSESSION *sb.* 5, 6.

**1595** SHAKS. *John* IV. i. 32 His words do take possession of my bosome. **1849** MACAULAY *Hist. Eng.* vi. II. 63 Another fatal delusion had taken possession of his mind.

**72.** In many other phrases, as *to take* ACCOUNT, ACQUAINTANCE, ARMS, BREATH, *the* CAKE, *one's* CHANCE, *the* CHANGE *out of*, CHRISTENDOM, COUNT, *one's* CROSS, EFFECT, END, FLIGHT, FORCE, HEAD, HEELS, *the* INITIATIVE, KNOWLEDGE, *the* LAW, *the* LEAD, LEAVE, ORDER, RECORD, RISE, ROOT, SHARE, STOCK, WITNESS, etc., for which see the sbs. (See also 91.)

**XI.** Intransitive uses in idiomatic combination with prepositions.

**73. Take after —. a.** To follow the example of;

to imitate; hence, to resemble (a parent, ancestor, predecessor, superior, etc.) in nature, character, habits, appearance, or other quality.

**1553** T. WILSON *Rhet.* (1580) 112 If the Nurse be of a noughtie nature, the childe must take thereafter. **1657** HEYLIN *Ecclesia Vind.* Gen. Pref., His Followers all take after him in this particular. **1678** PHILLIPS (ed. 4) s.v. *Imitatives, Patrissare*, to take after the Father, or imitate his actions, humor, or fashion. **1892** *Gd. Words* Nov. 784/2, I take after my mother's family.

† **b.** ? To conceive a desire for or inclination to.

**1707** *Curios. in Husb. & Gard.* 6 Men take strangely after this their first Imployment.

**Take against** —, **take for** — (= take part against, with): see 20 b.

**74. Take to** —. (See also 62, 63.)

**a.** To undertake, take in hand; to take charge of, undertake the care of. *Obs.* exc. *dial.*

[*Tóc tó þe rice* in quot. 1154 is the equivalent of the earlier *feng tó* (*þam*) *rice* of the Chronicle: cf. anno 488, Her Esc feng to rice; 1066 Her forðferde Eaduuard king, and Harold eorl feng to ðam rice. Cf. also 62 with inf.]

**1154** *O. E. Chron.* an. 1140 (MS. E), & te eorl of Angæu wærd ded, & his sune Henri toc to þe rice. *c* **1230** *Hali Meid.* 5 He wile carien for hire þat ha haueð itaken to of al þat hire biheoueð. *c* **1375** *Cursor M.* 5639 (Fairf.) Þis wommon bleþely toke þer-to [to þe childe; *Cott. & Gött.* it vnderfang] & fedde hit. *c* **1430** *Freemasonry* 120 That the mayster take to no prentysse, But he have good seuerans to dwelle Seven ȝer with hym. **1863** KINGSLEY *Water-Bab.* v. 199 All the little children whom the good fairies take to, because their cruel mothers and fathers will not. [See *Eng. Dial. Dict.* s.v.]

**b.** To betake oneself to, have recourse to (esp. some means of progression, as in *take to the boats, take to flight, take to wing, to one's heels* (HEEL *sb.*[1] 19); also (now *dial.*) *to* some resource or means of subsistence).

(The intr. use here and in c comes close in sense to the *refl.* use in 61 a, 63 c, and the trans. in 24 c, 25 a.)

*c* **1205** LAY. 23688 He hit wende þat Arður hit wolde forsaken And nawiht to þan fehte taken. *c* **1400** *Melayne* 1148 At þe laste þay tuke to flyinge. *a* **1450** *Le Morte Arthur* 1380 Madame, how may thou to us take? **1591** SHAKS. *Two Gent.* IV. i. 42 Haue you any thing to take to? *Val.* Nothing but my fortune. **1596** DANETT tr. *Comines* (1614) 32 The King tooke to barge and returned to Paris. **1693** J. DRYDEN, jun. *Juvenal* xiv. 98 The callow Storks..soon as e'er to Wing they take, At sight those Animals for Food pursue. **1708** *Lond. Gaz.* No. 4453/2 They took to their Oars, and got from us. **1761** HUME *Hist. Eng.* II. xxvii. 130 They immediately took to flight. **1786** tr. *Beckford's Vathek* (1883) 121 They all without ceremony took to their heels. **1873** HOLLAND *A. Bonnic.* i. 19, I should have alighted and taken to my feet.

**c.** To betake oneself to (a place); to repair, resort, or retire to; to take refuge in; to enter.

*c* **1275** LAY. 7976 He droh to on oþe[r] half and tock to herboreȝe. *c* **1425** *Cursor M.* 2832 (Trin.) No dwellyng here þat ȝe make Til ȝe þe ȝondir feld to take. **1707** FREIND *Peterborow's Cond. Sp.* 211 Take to the Mountains on the right. *a* **1851** MOIR *Bass Rock* iii, The rabbit..Took to its hole under the hawthorn's root. **1879** MISS YONGE *Cameos* Ser. IV. ix. 110 He took to his bed and there lay almost without speaking. [Cf. 25, and BED 6 c.]

† **d.** To attach oneself to, become an adherent of; to direct itself to. *Obs.* (Also with *till, unto.*)

*c* **1205** LAYAMON 29188 Crist seolue he for-soc and to þan wursen he tohc. *c* **1330** R. BRUNNE *Chron.* (1810) 96 Þe maistres of þe portes for gyftes tille him toke. *c* **1425** *Cursor M.* 17533 (Trin.) Raþer shulde þei to vs take, Þen to ihesu for oure sake. **1625** BACON *Ess., Goodness* (Arb.) 201 If it [goodness] issue not towards Men, it will take vnto Other Liuing Creatures.

**e.** To devote or apply oneself to; to adopt or take up as a practice, business, habit, or something habitual: cf. 61 b, c. See also ROAD *sb.* 5 b.

*a* **1300** *Cursor M.* 14114 O mani thing sco [Mary] tok til an, Wit-vten quam es beute nan. **1382** WYCLIF *Gen.* xxxviii. 14 The which, the clothis of widewhed don down, toke to [Vulg. *assumpsit*] a roket. *c* **1430** *Freemasonry* 462 Aȝayn to the craft they schul never take. **1610** HOLLAND *Camden's Brit.* (1637) 692 Clothing (a trade which they tooke to). **1707** J. STEVENS tr. *Quevedo's Com. Wks.* (1709) 319 If you take to Begging, I will take to give nothing. **1834** LYTTON *Pilgr. Rhine* vi, He has since taken to drinking. **1843** *Fraser's Mag.* XXVIII. 203 She..took to wearing caps. **1845** FORD *Handbk. Spain* I. 199 In Madrid..the men have taken to..Parisian *paletots*. **1887** [see DRINK *sb.* 3]. **1893** *Scribner's Mag.* Aug. 227/2 She has taken to society as a duck takes to water.

**f.** To apply oneself (*well, kindly*); to adapt oneself: leading to sense g.

*c* **1375** *Cursor M.* 8436 (Fairf.) Þen was þis childe sette to boke; Ful wele I wis þer-to [*Cott.* þar-wit] he toke. **1625** BACON *Ess., Parents & Childr.* (Arb.) 277 Thinking they will take best to that, which they haue most Minde to. **1766** J. W. BAKER in *Compl. Farmer* s.v. *Turnip*, [The bullock] took kindly to the turnips. **1820** *Examiner* No. 637. 413/2 A tree which is late transplanted seldom takes well to the soil. **1885** in *Manch. Weekly Times* 6 June 5/5 The new members may not take kindly to the work.

**g.** To take a liking to, conceive an affection for. (For absolute use: see 50 b.)

**1748** H. WALPOLE *Corr.* (1837) II. 239, I took to him for his resemblance to you. **1796** LAMB *Let. to Coleridge* 3 Oct., They, as the saying is, take to her very extraordinarily. **1844** LADY FULLERTON *Ellen Middl.* (1884) 23 To use a familiar expression, we took to each other instantaneously. **1885** *Manch. Exam.* 22 July 3/2 When first the idea was suggested, Doré did not take to it.

**75. Take with** —. † **a.** To receive, to accept; = sense 39. [= ON. *taka við* to receive.] *Obs.*

**1127** *O. E. Chron.* (Laud MS.), Þet landfolk him wið toc. *c* **1200** ORMIN 104 To ȝarrkenn follc onnȝæness Crist To takenn wiþþ hiss lare. *Ibid.* 1516 Hu wel he takeþþ aȝȝ wiþþ þa þatt sekenn Godess are. *a* **1300** *Cursor M.* 820 For-þi yett wald he wit him tak. *Ibid.* 5977 Vr lauerd wil tak na wirscip wiþ þat man him dos in cursd kyth. **1456** SIR G. HAYE *Law Arms* (S.T.S.) 68 The barnis..will nocht tak with the doctryne of the faderis. **1538** BALE *God's Promises* in Dodsley *O. Pl.* (1780) I. 9 Yet shall they not with hym take.

† **b.** To take up with; to have to do with. *Obs.*

**1597** BACON *Ess., Followers & Friends* (Arb.) 36 It is better to take with the more passable, then with the more able.

**c.** To be pleased with, put up with. ? *dial.* Cf. 50 b; also *take up with* 90 z (*c*).

**1632** RUTHERFORD *Lett.* (1862) I. 97 The silly stranger, in an uncouth country, must take with a smoky inn and coarse cheer. **1638** BRATHWAIT *Barnabees Jrnl.* II. (1818) 59 Thence to Ridgelay, where a black-smith, Liquor being all hee'd take with, Boused with me. **1825** JAMIESON s.v. *Tak with*, 'How does the laddie like the wark?' 'Indeed ..he taks unco ill wi't'. **1844** STEPHENS *Bk. Farm* II. 609 In a little time she [a ewe] will take with both [twin lambs].

† **d.** To take part with, agree with. Cf. 20 b.

**1654** J. BRAMHALL in *Ussher's Lett.* (1686) 612 Those of the King's Party asking some why they took with the Parliament's side. **1828** SCOTT *F. M. Perth* xxix, I would MacGillie Chattachan would take [*later edd.* agree] with me ..instead of wasting our best blood against each other.

† **e.** To admit, acknowledge, own. *Obs.*

*a* **1653** BINNING *Serm.* (1845) 607 Few of you will take with this, that ye seek to be justified by your own works. **1786** A. GIB *Sacr. Contempl.* I. VII. i. 157 A person is therefore brought to see and take with this sin, only when his conviction issues in conversion.

**f.** To contract or become affected by; to catch (fire), absorb (water): = 44 b, c (cf. also d). *dial.*

**1822** GALT *Steam-boat* xvi. 347 The kill took low, and the mill likewise took wi't,..and nothing was left but the bare wa's. **1847** *Jrnl. R. Agric. Soc.* VIII. II. 380 When it [the flax] begins to ferment, or 'take with the water', the latter becomes turbid and discoloured.

**XII.** In combination with adverbs, forming the equivalents of compound verbs, chiefly transitive.

**76. Take aback** *trans.*: see ABACK *adv.* 3 (*lit.* and *fig.*).

**1748** *Anson's Voy.* II. vii. 215 We were obliged to ply on and off..and were frequently taken aback. **1796** in Nicolas *Disp. Nelson* (1846) VII. p. xxxix, At ¼ past 8 taken flat aback with a strong wind and a high sea from the N.E.b.E. **1844** J. T. HEWLETT *Parsons & W.* liii, I never saw a man more 'taken aback' as the sailors say. **1889** J. K. JEROME *Three Men in Boat* xvii, Blest if it didn't quite take me aback.

**77. Take again.** **a.** *trans.* To resume: see simple senses and AGAIN *adv.* † **b.** To withdraw, recall: = *take back*, 79 b: cf. AGAIN *adv.* 3. *Obs.*

**1474** CAXTON *Chesse* III. i. (1883) 78 He began to take agayn his vertuous werkis and requyred pardoun and so retourned to god agayn. **1728** RAMSAY *Bob of Dunblane* ii, Lest I grow fickle, And take my word and offer again.

**78. Take away.** **a.** *trans.* To remove, withdraw, abstract; to remove by death; to subtract: see sense 58 and AWAY *adv.*

*a* **1300** *Cursor M.* 297 If þou ta þe light awai. **1388** WYCLIF *Ps.* l. 13 [li. 11] Take thou not awei fro me thin hooli spirit. **1415** SIR T. GREY in 43 *Dep. Kpr. Rep.* 583 A sefenneghte after that Murdok of Fyche was take awey. **1477** EARL RIVERS (Caxton) *Dictes* 75 To cut the vynes & take awey the euil branches therof. **1509** HAWES *Past. Pleas.* xliv. (Percy Soc.) 215 Do not I, Tyme, take his lyfe away? **1585** T. WASHINGTON tr. *Nicholay's Voy.* IV. xxxiii. 156 To take away or mittigate some of [these laws]. *c* **1600** *Timon* III. i, Yee theeues, restore what yee have tane away! **1736** LEDIARD *Life Marlborough* I. 131 It pleased God to take away His Majesty. **1886** AD. SERGEANT *No Saint* ix, It took away his appetite. **1890** *Jrnl. Educ.* 1 June 341/1 Take away 4 cows from 17 cows.

**b.** *absol.* To clear the table after a meal.

*c* **1450** *Bk. Curtasye* 820 in *Babees Bk.* 326 Whenne þay haue wasshen and grace is sayde, Away he takes at a brayde. **1768** STERNE *Sent. Journ.* (1775) II. 118 *Mon Dieu!* said Le Fleur,—and took away. **1809** MALKIN *Gil Blas* XI. v. (Rtldg.) 402 The servants..had taken away and left us to ourselves. **1872** S. BUTLER *Erewhon* viii. 64 She returned in about an hour to take away.

**c.** *absol.* To detract *from*: = 58 e, 83 k.

**1875** FREEMAN *Venice* (1881) 257 The slight touch of Renaissance in some of the capitals..in no sort takes away from the general purity of the style. **1889** STEVENSON *Master of B.* iv, This takes away from the merit of your generosity.

**d.** *intr.* To go away, make off: see 63.

**1850** R. G. CUMMING *Hunter's Life S. Afr.* (1902) 125/1 They set the dogs after him, when he took away up the river.

**79. Take back.** **a.** *trans.* To take possession of again, resume: see simple senses and BACK *adv.*

*a* **1771** GRAY *Dante* 68 Take back, what once was yours. **1908** *Daily Chron.* 26 Oct. 4/6 Molière never said, 'I take my goods where I find them', but 'I take back my goods where I find them'.

**b.** To withdraw, retract, recall, unsay (a statement, promise, etc.): cf. BACK *adv.* 7.

**1775** ABIGAIL ADAMS in *Fam. Lett.* (1876) 86, I had..made some complaints of you, but I will take them all back again. **1873** M. COLLINS *Squire Silchester* I. ix. 131, I shall take back my yes if you are troublesome.

**c.** To carry back in thought to a past time; cf. BACK *adv.* 4.

**1889** MALLOCK *Enchanted Isl.* 251 These churches took me back to the crusaders. **1890** *Temple Bar Mag.* May 43 The boy's letter has taken me back ten years.

**d.** = *take aback* (fig.): see ABACK *adv.* 3. ? *dial.*

? *a* **1860** MRS. H. WOOD *Ho. Halliwell* (1890) II. i. 6 Hester was never so taken back in her life. *Ibid.* v. 116 She was 'taken back', as the saying runs.

**e.** *intr.* To go back, return. ? *Obs.* exc. *dial.*

**1674** N. FAIRFAX *Bulk & Selv.* To Rdr., Being quite lost in a wilde and a frightful on and on, I e'en took back again where I was. **1889** STEVENSON *Master of B.* xi. 284 Having ..forgot my presence, he took back to his singing.

**80. Take down.** **a.** *trans.* To remove from a higher to a lower, or from an upright to a prostrate, position; to lower; to carry down; to cut down, fell (a tree); to pull down (a house, etc.: implying also 'take to pieces'); to distribute (type).

*a* **1300** *Cursor M.* 11664 'Ioseph', sco said, 'fain wald I rest'..Son he stert and tok hir dun. *c* **1435** *Torr. Portugal* 1426, I rede we take down sayle & rowe. **1548** in E. Green *Somerset Chantries* (1888) 116 One of theis ij churches maye well be spared and taken downe. *a* **1653** BINNING *Serm.* (1845) 425 It taketh down the tabernacle of mortality. **1751** LABELYE *Westm. Br.* 81 Whilst the Arches were unbuilding and taking down. **1818** in Willis & Clark *Cambridge* (1886) I. 573 Taking down three trees. **1886** *Troy* (U.S.) *Daily Times* 2 Jan. 1/3 A boat's crew..was taken down by a whale near the Cape Verde islands. **1909** R. RENWICK in Marwick *Edinb. Guilds* Pref. 6 The printers, seeing no early prospect of the release of their type.., took it down.

**b.** With various implications: (*a*) to swallow; † (*b*) to cause (a speaker) to sit down (*obs.*); (*c*) in *Falconry*, to cause (a hawk) to fly down; (*d*) in a school, to get above (another scholar) in class; so of a boat in a race, to get in front of (another boat); (*e*) to lead (a lady) down to dinner at a party.

**1607** B. JONSON *Volpone* III. v, I will take down poison, Eat burning coals, do any thing. **1656** in *Burton's Diary* (1828) I. 45 Captain Hatsel was speaking to have the debate put off till Monday, but Colonel Purefoy took him down. **1667** FAIRFAX in *Phil. Trans.* II. 549 Mr. Morley..was advised by some to take down a spoonfull of good English Honey. **1828** SIR J. S. SEBRIGHT *Observ. Hawking* 36 They are always taken down after having flown unsuccessfully at their game. **1844** DICKENS *Mart. Chuz.* xix, I took him down once, six boys, in the arithmetic class. **1848** THACKERAY *Van. Fair* v, Dobbin..was 'taken down' continually by little fellows. **1887** MRS. J. H. PERKS *Heather Hills* II. xviii. 308 A quiet dinner-party, with a nice, sensible man to take you down.

**c.** *fig.* To abase, humble, humiliate, abate the pride or arrogance of. In quot. 1562, ? to rebuke, reprimand.

**1562** *Child-Marriages* 112 She had spoken to the said Custance, and taken her downe for the same. **1593** PEELE *Chron. Edw. I*, Wks. (Rtldg.) 395 I'll take you down a button-hole. **1608** TOPSELL *Serpents* (1658) 755 For revenge, and taking down the pride of this young man. **1796** MRS. M. ROBINSON *Angelina* II. 27 He seems to experience..satisfaction in what he calls taking me down. **1857** MAURICE *Ep. St. John* i. 4 Whatever takes down a young man's conceit must be profitable to him.

**d.** To lower, diminish, lessen, abate, reduce; to lower in health or strength, bring low, depress. Now *Sc.* and *north. dial.*

**1697** DRYDEN *Virg. Georg.* III. 209 As for the Females,.. Take down their Mettle, keep 'em lean and bare. **1719** BAYNARD *Health* (ed. 2) 22 By Degrees take down your Heat. **1811** *Self Instructor* 539 Olive colours..are first put in green, and taken down again with soot. **1836–7** SIR W. HAMILTON *Metaph.* (1877) I. xviii. 342 Taken down with a bilious fever. [See *Eng. Dial. Dict.*]

**e.** To write down so as to use or preserve (what is said); to take a written report or notes of.

**1712** W. ROGERS *Voy.* 248, I took down the Names of those that had any. **1793** *Trans. Soc. Arts* (ed. 2) V. 121 The precision with which you took down their answers. **1883** MORFILL *Slavonic Lit.* iii. 48 These ballads had been taken down about the middle of the eighteenth century. **1885** C. H. EDEN *G. Donnington* I. xii. 240 Reporters would take down the speeches.

**81. Take forth.** **a.** *trans.* To lead forth, conduct out of a place; to bring forth, take out of a receptacle, produce; *fig.* to further, advance.

*a* **1300** *Cursor M.* 2693 (Cott.) Abram tok forth his men. *c* **1460** *Battle of Otterburn* xxxvi. in Child *Ballads* III. 297/1 The letters fayre furth hath he tayne. **1530** PALSGR. 748/1, I take forthe a man, I avaunce hym. **1890** BESANT *Demoniac* xv, When he [Damien] was taken forth to have his flesh wrenched off with red-hot pincers.

† **b.** *Take forth* one's *way*: to go forth, set forth (see 25 b); also *absol.*, to proceed. *Obs.*

**1523** LD. BERNERS *Froiss.* I. x. 10 On the iiii. day they toke forth their way. **1674** N. FAIRFAX *Bulk & Selv.* 187 We shall take forth to our last.

† **c.** To learn; *transf.* to teach: = *take out*, 85 f.

**1530** PALSGR. 748/1, I take forthe, as a childe, or a scoler dothe a newe lesson, *je apprens*..Take hym forthe a newe lesson. **1549** T. SOME *Latimer's 2nd Serm. bef. Edw. VI* To Rdr. (Arb.) 50 The gettynge of goodes and rytches, before thou hast well learned and taken furth of the lesson, of well vsyng the same. **1581** SAVILE *Tacitus, Hist.* II. lxxxiv. (1591) 102 Taught by ill masters, hee tooke foorth [L. *didicit*] a bad lesson.

**82. Take in.**

* *trans.* **a.** To take, draw, or receive into itself, or into something (see simple senses and IN *adv.*); to admit, absorb, imbibe; to receive as a tributary; to eat or drink, to swallow; to breathe in, inhale; to take on board (a ship). In quot. 1583 *absol.* to admit or let in water, to leak.

**13..** *Cursor M.* 6066 (Cott.) Siþen sal ilk hus in take A clene he-lambe, wit-vten sake. *c* **1400** MAUNDEV. (Roxb.) i. 4 It takes in to him xl. oþer ryuers. **1495** *Trevisa's Barth.*

*De P. R.* XVII. ii. (W. de W.) N j b/2 Full of holys to take in ayre. **1583** *Leg. Bp. St. Androis* Pref. 104 in *Sat. P. Ref.* (S.T.S.) 350 He lattis his scheip tak in at luife and lie. **1585** T. WASHINGTON tr. *Nicholay's Voy.* I. x. 12 b, We took in fresh water out of a wel. **1610** HOLLAND *Camden's Brit.* (1637) 547 The River Trent..taking in the River Soure from the field of Leicester. **1737** BRACKEN *Farriery Impr.* (1757) II. 103 The first of these takes in their Nourishment by their external..Absorbent Vessels. **1777** HAMILTON *Wks.* (1886) VII. 510 The ships are taking in water and provisions for two months. **1890** *Chamb. Jrnl.* 10 May 292/1 She took in amazingly little water. **1892** *Harper's Mag.* Sept. 596/2 It..readily takes in and yields moisture.

**b.** To receive (money) in payment, subscriptions, etc.; to receive and undertake (work) to be done in one's own house for pay.

**1699** in *Millington's Sale Catal. Skinner & Hampden Libraries*, Subscriptions are taken in by John Hartley, over against Gray's-Inn in Holborn. **1832** *Examiner* 403/1 She took in washing only for her amusement. **1889** MRS. E. KENNARD *Landing Prize* II. xii. 209 We supported ourselves..by taking in plain needle-work. **1892** *Idler* June 547 He was taking in more money than he had ever taken in before.

**c.** To subscribe for and receive regularly (a newspaper or periodical): = sense 15 d.

**1712** ADDISON *Spect.* No. 488 ⁋ 2 Their Father having refused to take in the Spectator. **1779** MACKENZIE in *Mirror* No. 2 ⁋ 3 A coffee-house, where it is..taken in for the use of the customers. **1891** *Blackw. Mag.* CL. 704/1 Many of them take in the French paper just as they buy 'Punch'.

**d.** *Cards.* To take (a card) into one's hand from the pack.

**1879** 'CAVENDISH' *Card Ess.*, etc. 69 The holder of the ace of trumps ruffed, i. e. he put out four cards and took in the stock. **1891** *Field* 28 Nov. 843/1 If the non-dealer takes in the king, he ought..to lead it.

**e.** To lead or conduct into a house, room, etc.

*c* **1450** *Cov. Myst.* xxvii. (Shaks. Soc.) 268 Take hym in, serys, be the honde. **1893** *Temple Bar Mag.* XCVIII. 469 John took Miss Everard in to supper.

**f.** To receive or admit as inmate or guest.

**1539** BIBLE (Great) *Matt.* xxv. 35, I was herbourlesse, and ye toke me in [WYCL. herboriden me: TINDALE, *Geneva*, lodged me]. **1562** J. MOUNTGOMERY in *Archæologia* XLVII. 231 Hospitalles..then the poore souldior..shoulde be taken yn, cured,..and healed. **1702** ROWE *Tamerl.* IV. i, Why stand thy..Doors still open To take the wretched in? **1840** *Jrnl. R. Agric. Soc.* I. III. 265 Invalid horses are taken in ..and treated at the hospital. **1849** *Ibid.* X. II. 413 No tenant-cottager shall take in any lodger.

†**g.** To receive or accept into some relation (e. g. into surrender, or as hostage or ally). *Obs.*

**1602** LD. MOUNTJOY *Let.* in Moryson *Itin.* II. (1617) 214 By the generall advice of the Counsell I tooke in Turlough mac Henry. **1606** MARSTON *Sophonisba* II. i, Her father.. on suddain shall take in Revolted Syphax.

†**h.** To capture, take prisoner, conquer (in war); to 'take' a town. Cf. sense 2. *Obs.*

**1387** TREVISA *Higden* (Rolls) VI. 285 Leo..wente to Seynt Peter..wiþ þe letayne, and his eyȝen i-put out, and his tonge i-kut of. **1535** COVERDALE *Jer.* xlix. 1 Why hath youre kynge then taken Gad in? **1684** *Scanderbeg Rediv.* v. 109 His Majesty took in Raskaw, a Considerable place on the Deinster. **1709** H. FELTON *Diss. Classics* (1718) 10 Open Places are easily taken in.

**i.** To bring into smaller compass, draw in, reduce the extent of, contract, make smaller; to shorten, narrow, or tighten; to furl (a sail).

*Take in a reef*: to roll or fold up a reef in a sail so as to shorten the sail: see REEF *sb.*[1] 1.

*c* **1515** *Cocke Lorell's B.* 12 Mayne corfe toke in a refe byforce. **1641** J. JACKSON *True Evang. T.* II. 153 But I must contract my selfe, and take in this saile of speech. *a* **1800** COWPER *Horace* II. Ode x. vi, If fortune fill thy sail.. Take half thy canvas in. **1837** DICKENS *Pickw.* ix, Strapping a buckle here, and taking in a link there. **1841** R. H. DANA *Seaman's Man.* ix. [*heading*] Making and taking in sail. **1848** THACKERAY *Van. Fair* xliii, Sure every one of me frocks must be taken in,—it's such a skeleton I'm growing. **1889** DOYLE *Micah Clarke* xxvii. 281, I took in one hole of my sword-belt on Monday. **1897** *Outing* (U.S.) XXX. 255/1 Take in leaders when about a team's length from corner; then take in wheelers a bit, off-wheeler more than near—in fact, many only take in off-wheel rein a couple of inches.

**j.** To enclose (a piece of land, etc.); to take into possession (a territory, a common), or into cultivation (a waste); to include; to annex.

*c* **1539** in G. J. Aungier *Syon Mon.* (1840) 131 To dyche in and take in our comyn. **1633** G. HERBERT *Temple, Sunday* vi, Christ hath took in this piece of ground, And made a garden there. **1697** in Picton *L'pool Munic. Rec.* (1883) I. 288 Others have a design to take in some Commons near Mosse Lake. **1845** *Jrnl. R. Agric. Soc.* VI. II. 301 Numerous waste patches along the sides of wide roads have been taken in. **1893** *Nat. Observ.* 5 Aug. 290/2 France is determined to take in all Siam. **1897** D. SLADEN in *Windsor Mag.* Jan. 278/1 A new alcove [has been] formed by taking in one of the..landings.

**k.** To admit into a number or list; to include, comprise, embrace; *spec.* to include in the consideration, take into account (quot. 1752); to include in a journey or visit (*U.S.*).

**1647** HAMMOND *Power of Keys* iii. 23 He hath taken in all the antient Church-writers into his catalogue. **1697** DRYDEN *Virg., Life* (1721) I. 30 Virgil was a great Mathematician, which, in the Sense of those times, took in Astrology. **1752** HUME *Ess. & Treat.* (1777) I. 106 In the former case, many circumstances must be taken in. **1870** FREEMAN *Norm. Conq.* (ed. 2) I. App. 712 Writers who..did not understand that his jurisdiction took in Kent. **1879** LUBBOCK *Addr. Pol. & Educ.* iii. 55 Attention will be concentrated on the four subjects taken in. **1883** BACON *Dict. Boston, Mass.* 359 The out-of-towner who fails to take-in a trip to Taft's.

**l.** To receive into or grasp with the mind; to apprehend, comprehend, understand, realize; to absorb or imbibe mentally, to learn; to conceive.

*a* **1677** HALE *Prim. Orig. Man.* I. i. 12 A created Understanding can never take in the fulness of the Divine Excellencies. **1685** BAXTER *Paraphr. N. T.* Matt. xiii. 18–19 By not understanding is meant also, Not considering it to take it in. **1711** STEELE *Spect.* No. 79 ⁋ 5 There is no end of Affection taken in at the Eyes only. **1810** LADY GRANVILLE *Lett.* (1894) I. 16 She plays..on the pianoforte, and takes in science kindly from Mr. Smart. **1877** FREEMAN *Norm. Conq.* (ed. 3) I. App. 731 Writers who do not take in the position of an Earl of the West-Saxons. **1887** BARING-GOULD *Gaverocks* III. li. 140 Sluggish minds..require time to take in new notions.

**m.** To comprehend in one view (physical or mental); to perceive at a glance.

**1727–41** CHAMBERS *Cycl.* s. v. *Eye*, In man..the eye is.. so ordered, as to take in nearly the hemisphere before it. **1800–24** CAMPBELL *View St. Leonard's* 18 The eagle's vision cannot take it in. **1878** *Scribner's Mag.* XV. 583/2 We..turned our heads from side to side,..the better to take in the full force of the effect.

**n.** To believe or accept unquestioningly.

**1864** *Spectator* No. 1875. 640 The Undergraduates took it all in and cheered Lord Robert Cecil as their future representative. **1888** FARJEON *Miser Farebrother* II. xiii. 169 Jeremiah listened and took it all in.

**o.** To deceive, cheat, trick, impose upon. *colloq.*

**1740** tr. *De Mouhy's Fort. Country-Maid* (1741) I. 132 The Griparts were never taken in yet, and what's more never will. **1745** FIELDING *True Patriot* No. 9 Wks. 1775 IX. 310 They are fairly taken in, and imposed upon to believe we have..as much money as ever. **1754** E. MOOR in *World* No. 96 III. 234, I am almost of opinion that (in the fashionable phrase) he is 'taking me in'. **1809** W. IRVING *Knickerb.* v. iv. (1849) 277 A contest of skill between two powers, which shall overreach and take in the other. **1846** LANDOR *Imag. Conv.* Wks. II. 228/1 Nobody shall ever take me in again to do such an absurd and wicked thing. **1884** GEO. DENMAN in *Law Rep.* 29 Ch. Div. 473 The Plaintiff has..been taken in and misled.

**p.** To offer (a subject) for examination.

*a* **1890** LIDDON *Life Pusey* (1893) I. 20 The poets and historians who, at that time, were taken in by candidates for Classical Honours at Oxford.

** *intr.* †**q.** To go in, 'put in', enter. *Obs.*

**1654** H. L'ESTRANGE *Chas. I* (1655) 88 Taking in at a Cooks shop where he supt. **1677** JOHNSON in *Ray's Corr.* (1848) 127 Great shoals of salmon, which often take in at the mouths of our rivers.

†**r.** *Take in with*: to take part with, side with, agree with. *Obs.*

**1597–8** BACON *Ess., Faction* (Arb.) 80 It is commonly seene that men once placed, take in with the contrarie faction to that by which they enter. **1646** SIR T. BROWN *Pseud. Epid.* I. vii. (1686) 20 Justinian took in with Hippocrates and reversed the decree. **1647** N. BACON *Disc. Govt. Eng.* I. xxxiv. (1739) 51 Kings doubting to lose their Game, took in with the weaker. *a* **1734** NORTH *Lives* (1826) I. 3 If he had acted in these mens measures, and betraying his master, took in with them.

**83. Take off.** * *transitive senses.*

**a.** To remove from the position or condition of being *on* (with various shades of meaning); to lift off, pull off, cut off, rub off, detach, subtract, deduct: see simple senses and OFF *adv.*

*a* **1300** *Cursor M.* 14318 He bad..Of þe tumb tak of þe lidd. **1495** *Ledger-bk. A. Halyburton* 40 Som of that sek, the bat of-tan is 17li. 15s. 2. *c* **1530** H. RHODES *Bk. Nurture* in *Babees Bk.* 67 With your Trenchour knyfe take of such fragmentes. **1644** WINTHROP *Hist. New Eng.* (1825) II. 199 He took off all her commodities, but not at so good rates as they expected. **1703** *Art & Myst. Vintners* 57 Take off the skim, and beat it together with 6 Eggs. **1709** STEELE *Tatler* No. 5 ⁋ 8 A Cannon Ball took off his Head. **1780** COXE *Russ. Disc.* 267 M. Engel..takes off twenty-nine degrees from the longitude of Kamtchatka, as laid down by the Russians. **1852** *Jrnl. R. Agric. Soc.* XIII. I. 80 Repeated crops of hay are taken off without any return. *Mod.* Isn't his name on the list? No, it has been taken off.

(*b*) *spec.* To remove from the person, divest oneself, or another, of, doff (a garment, etc.).

*a* **1300** *Cursor M.* 9070 (Cott.) 'Tas of', he said, 'mi kinges croun.' **13..** *Ibid.* 8116 (Gött.) Wiþ þis þe king tok of his gloue. **1485** CAXTON *Chas. Gt.* 212 He..took of hys clothes. *a* **1548** HALL *Chron., Edw. IV* 234 He toke of hys cappe, and made a lowe and solempne obeysance. **1662** J. DAVIES tr. *Olearius' Voy. Ambass.* 140 A little Cap like a Callotte..they never take off. **1736** LEDIARD *Life Marlborough* III. 422 The Armour was taken off. **1850** *Tait's Mag.* XVII. 465/1 She took off her shawl. **1891** *Murray's Mag.* Apr. 531 He never takes off his boots and spurs.

(*c*) To remove or convey (a person) from on shore, from a rock, or from on board ship.

**1883** BUCHANAN *Love me for Ever* v. ii. 261 He had arranged..to be taken off one night, and to sail with them right away. **1889** *Eng. Illustr. Mag.* Dec. 267, I might be able to support life on board of her until the *Ruby* took me off. **1890** *Standard* 12 Dec. 5/7 The passengers were taken off and landed safely.

(*d*) *absol.* To clear the table after a meal: = *take away*, 78 b. (*e*) *intr.* for *pass.*: see sense 58 f.

**1828** J. T. SMITH *Nollekens* I. 91 Nor do I think wine was even mentioned until the servants were ordered to 'take off'.

**b.** *trans.* To drink to the bottom, or at one draught; to drink off, 'toss off'.

**1613** PURCHAS *Pilgrimage* III. xv. 271 She dranke to him a cup of poysoned liquor: and hauing taken off almost halfe, she reached him the rest. **1662** J. DAVIES tr. *Olearius' Voy. Ambass.* 83 Many Muscovian women took off their Cups as smartly as they [their husbands] did. **1724** RAMSAY *Steer her up*, etc. ii, See that shining glass of claret..Take it aff, and let's have mair o't. **1850** HAWTHORNE *Scarlet L.* iv, And, that thou mayest live, take off this draught.

**c.** To lead away summarily; *refl.* to go away, take one's departure, be off.

**1838** DICKENS *O. Twist* xxiv, He..took himself off on tiptoe. **1850** *Tait's Mag.* XVII. 609/1 The guilty parties had taken themselves off. **1894** PARRY *Stud. Gt. Composers, Schubert* 230 In dread of being taken off as a soldier. *Mod.* He was arrested and taken off to prison. The child was taken off to bed.

**d.** To lead away or draw off (in *fig.* sense); to divert, distract, dissuade; †to free, rid (const. *from*); †to remove the opposition of by bribery or corruption, to buy off (*obs.*).

**1605** SHAKS. *Macb.* II. iii. 36 It makes him, and it marres him; it sets him on, and it takes him off. *a* **1626** BACON *New Atl.* (1900) 24 And hee..in great Courtesie tooke us off, and descended to aske us Questions of our Voyage and Fortunes. **1670** H. STUBBE *Plus Ultra* 11 This Philosophy..taking us off from the Pedantism of Philology. **1702** tr. *Le Clerc's Prim. Fathers* 27 Having not undertaken to take them off from this Opinion. *a* **1704** *Compl. Servant-Maid* (ed. 7) 58 You must endeavour to take off your Mistress from all the care you can. *a* **1715** BURNET *Own Time* (1823) I. 467 The chief men that promoted this were taken off (as the word then was for corrupting members). **1890** FENN *Double Knot* vii, The conversation took off his attention.

**e.** To remove or withdraw from office, or from some position or relation; to dismiss; to withdraw (a coach, train, etc.) from running.

**1745** WARD in *Lett. Lit. Men* (Camden) 369 Whom the Emperor had appointed governour..but afterwards..designed to have taken him off. **1768** J. BYRON *Narr. Patagonia* (ed. 2) 189 The centinel was taken off, and we were allowed to look about us a little. **1858** *Jrnl. R. Agric. Soc.* XIX. I. 144 My early calves..I allow to suck the cows for a fortnight, then take them off. **1892** *Field* 28 May 779/3 The coaches..will be taken off for one or more days. *Mod.* Several trains will be taken off on Bank Holiday.

**f.** To remove by death, put to death, kill, 'carry off', cut off: said of a person (esp. an assassin), of disease, devouring animals, etc.

**1605** [see TAKING *vbl. sb.* 6]. **1608** SHAKS. *Per.* IV. Prol. 14 To take off by treasons knife. **1618** BOLTON *Florus* (1636) 224 Himselfe taken off by sudden death. **1683** BURNET tr. *More's Utopia* Pref., The hiring of Assassinates to take off Enemies. **1701** W. WOTTON *Hist. Rome, Alex.* ii. 487 Diseases..took off very many of them. **1770** LANGHORNE *Plutarch* (1879) II. 828/2 Ptolemy of Cyprus..took himself off by poison. **1832** *Examiner* 6/2 Up to the 20th of November about thirty people had been taken off by cholera. **1840** *Jrnl. R. Agric. Soc.* I. III. 258 The mangold-wurzel was..taken off early by the fly.

**g.** To remove (something imposed), esp. so as to relieve those subject to it.

**1593** SHAKS. *Rich. II*, III. iii. 135 Oh God, oh God, that ere this tongue of mine, That layd the Sentence,..should take it off againe. **1660** INGELO *Bentiv. & Ur.* II. (1682) 147 You think to take off this Inconvenience. **1726** 'PHILALETHES' in J. Ker *Mem.* p. iii, If he would agree to the taking off the Penal Laws. **1737** *Gentl. Mag.* VII. Mar. 172/1 To give immediate Ease to his Majesty's Subjects, by taking off some of the Taxes which are most burthensome to the Poor. **1840** *Penny Cycl.* XVII. 399/2 The ecclesiastical courts may..take off the penance. **1879** M. J. GUEST *Lect. Hist. Eng.* xiv. 127 He pleased the people greatly by taking off a heavy tax. **1889** M. GRAY *Reproach Annesley* III. ii, The three months' embargo was now taken off.

**h.** To remove or do away with (a quality, condition, etc.).

**1605** SHAKS. *Macb.* v. viii. 71 Who..by selfe and violent hands, Tooke off her life. **1611** — *Cymb.* v. ii. 2 The heauinesse and guilt within my bosome, Takes off my manhood. **1652** FRENCH *Yorksh. Spa* x. 90 They..should take the water a little warm'd first..the cold being just taken off. **1691** CONSET *Pract. Spir. Crts.* (1700) To Rdr., Which thing.. may..take off the Edge of Detraction. **1737** BRACKEN *Farriery Impr.* (1756) I. 227 One or two Purges will take off the Running at his Mouth. **1885** MRS. LYNN LINTON *Chr. Kirkland* II. vi. 189 The smartest and prettiest kind of cap..took off the severity of her smoothly braided hair.

†(*b*) To do away with, disprove, confute. *Obs.*

**1630** PRYNNE *Anti-Armin.* 147, I must needs take off two principall daring obiections. **1682** CREECH tr. *Lucretius* (1683) Notes 26 After that I shall take off his exceptions against Providence. **1695** J. EDWARDS *Perfect. Script.* 478 To take off this seeming argument.

**i.** (*a*) To make or obtain (an impression) from something; to print off. In quot. 1660, to receive as an impression (in *fig.* sense).

**1660** tr. *Amyraldus' Treat. conc. Relig.* III. viii. 489 Those [languages] which live..take off better the impression and graces of the language of the Prophets. **1707** HEARNE *Collect.* 24 Jan. (O. H. S.) I. 320 The Stationers were obliged ..to take off 200 Copies of any Book. **1817** G. ROSE *Diaries* (1860) I. 19 *note*, He had an impression of 500 taken off. **1825** *New Monthly Mag.* XV. 234/1 The expedient..of taking off an impression in some soft substance.

(*b*) To make (a figure of something); *transf.* to draw a likeness of, to portray: = sense 33 b.

*a* **1719** ADDISON (J.), Take off all their models in wood. **1835–40** HALIBURTON *Clockm.* (1862) 306 A native artist of great promise..that is come to take us off. **1855** THACKERAY *Newcomes* xliv, Then Clive proposed..to take his head off; and made an excellent likeness in chalk of his uncle. **1890** 'R. BOLDREWOOD' *Col. Reformer* (1891) 182 A young lady who could take off a horse like that—the dead image of him —could do anything.

(*c*) To measure off; to determine or mark the position of: cf. sense 32 c.

**1793** SMEATON *Edystone L.* § 97 In this way I took off 35 ..of the most remarkable points,..These 35 primary points having been determined as above.

**j.** To imitate or counterfeit, esp. by way of

mockery; to mimic, caricature, burlesque, parody; to make a mock of. *colloq.*

**1750** CHESTERF. *Lett.* (1792) III. 85 He has since been taken off by a thousand authors: but never really imitated by any one. **1760–72** H. BROOKE *Fool of Qual.* (1809) II. 120 He so perfectly counterfeited or took off, as they call it, the real Christian, that many looked to see him..taken alive into Heaven. **1789** MRS. PIOZZI *Journ. France* I. 240 At the hazard of being taken off and held up for a laughing-stock. **1809** MALKIN *Gil Blas* II. vii. ¶ 20, I can take off a cat to the life: suppose I was to mew a certain number of times? *a* **1845** HOOD *Faithless Nelly Gray* v, She made him quite a scoff; And when she saw his wooden legs, Began to take them off! **1879** MINTO *Defoe* 40 One of the pamphlets which he professed to take off in his famous squib.

**k.** *absol.* with *from*: To detract from, diminish, lessen: = 58 e, 78 c.

**1701** W. WOTTON *Hist. Rome* 264 This gradual Advancement took off from the Obscurity of his Birth. **1753** CHAMBERS *Cycl. Supp.* s. v. *Sal*, A defect or flaw, which took off very much from the value of the gem. **1773** [J. RICHARDSON] tr. *Wieland's Agathon* Pref. 14 There are many allusions in it to modern customs..which take off in a great measure from the antique cast.

**l.** To close the stitches in knitting; to knit off. Also *absol.*

**1849** ESTHER COPLEY *Knitting-bk.* 12 By reversing the right hand pin, so inserting it in two stitches, not in front but at the back of the left hand pin, and knitting them off as one. This [way of reducing the number of stitches] is called 'taking off at the back'.

** *intr.* **m.** To abate, grow less, decrease; (of rain) to cease.

**1776** COOK in *Phil. Trans.* LXVI. 447, I judged it was about high water, and that the tides were taking off, or decreasing. **1854** H. MILLER *Sch. & Schm.* xxi. (1858) 463 No sooner had it [the hurricane] begun to take off than I set out for the scene of its ravages. **1878** STEVENSON *Inland Voy.* 20 The rain took off near Laeken. **1899** F. T. BULLEN *Log Sea-waif* 93 The breeze now began to take off a bit, and more sail was made.

**n.** To go off, start off, run away; to branch off from a main stream. (Cf. 63, 63 b.)

*c* **1813** MRS. SHERWOOD *Stories Ch. Catech.* xiii. (1873) 112 Dick ran out..and took off into the great bazar. **1825** WATERTON *Wand. S. Amer.* III. iv. 265 The Indian took off into the woods. **1888** *19th Cent.* Jan. 44 The second [head-water of the Hugli] takes off from the Ganges about forty miles eastward from the Bhagirathi.

(*b*) To start in leaping; to commence a leap. (Opp. to LAND *v.* 8 b.)

**1814** *Sporting Mag.* XLIII. 287 The spot where the horse took off to where he landed, is above eighteen feet. **1889** *Boy's Own Paper* 7 Sept. 780/3 Competitors should be encouraged to take-off with accuracy. **1892** *Strand Mag.* III. 633/2 The last attitude one would imagine a horse to adopt in 'taking off' for a jump.

(*c*) *Croquet.* To make a stroke from contact with another ball so as to send one's own ball nearly or quite in the direction in which the mallet is aimed: cf. TAKE-OFF *sb.* 4.

**1872** PRIOR *Notes on Croquet* 48 It were an improvement ..to tether a ball in the centre of the ground, which at starting should be hit by the players from a spot in the middle of the left-hand boundary. Taking off from this tethered ball, they might go to any part of the lawn.

**84. Take on.** **transitive senses.*

**a.** See simple senses and ON *adv.*: in quot. 1877, to take on board (opp. to *take off*, 83 a (*c*)).

*c* **1579** MONTGOMERIE *Misc. Poems* xlviii. 140 Tak on ȝour babert luifabuird. **1839** URE *Dict. Arts* 258 (Cards, Playing) The ink or colour..is..laid on the types and blocks..and the impressions [are] taken-on to thick drawing paper by means of a suitable press. **1877** *Scribner's Mag.* XV. 14/1 He took on the passengers who stood clustered on the wharf.

(*b*) †To put on, don (clothing, etc.) *obs.*; to 'put on' or add (flesh, etc.): see PUT *v.* 46 f (*a*).

**1389** in *Eng. Gilds* (1870) 56 Þe den xal warn alle þe gylde breþeren þ[t] be in toune, for to takyn on here hodis..and comen to messe. *c* **1489** CAXTON *Sonnes of Aymon* xxii. 494 Thenne they went, & toke on the beste clothyng that they had. **1583** *Satir. Poems Reform., Life Bp. St. Androis* 1069 On a gray bonnet he tackis. **1847** *Jrnl. R. Agric. Soc.* VIII. II. 392 Sheep..thrive very well and take on flesh rapidly. **1850** *Ibid.* XI. II. 600 The animal being thus gradually prepared to take on that increased amount of muscle and fat.

† (*c*) To take up (arms); to arm oneself: see 90 a (*c*). *Sc. Obs.*

**1565** *Reg. Privy Council Scot.* I. 355 Thair rebellis ar planelie conspyrit togidder, takin on arms. **1567** *Ibid.* 524 Thai have takin on armes to puneis the authouris of the said cruell murthour.

**b.** To assume, 'put on' (a form, quality, etc.) = sense 16 a: to assume, begin to perform (an action or function) (cf. 17); to contract, begin to be affected by, 'catch' (cf. 44 b, c).

**1799** KENTISH in Beddoes *Contrib. Phys. & Med. Knowl.* 258 He took on that peevish irritability so unhappy for the individual. **1842** *Jrnl. R. Agric. Soc.* III. II. 331 The blanched leaves soon take on the appearance of frost-bitten celery. **1869** G. LAWSON *Dis. Eye* (1874) 41 The ulcer.. took on a healing action, and soon cicatrized. **1893** M. GRAY *Last Sentence* III. v, The deep, mysterious eyes would take on a deeper charm.

(*b*) To adopt (an idea, etc.); to accept mentally.

**1890** *Pict. World* 4 Sept. 298/2 That belonged to the days before its author 'took on religion', as the Methodists term it. **1893** *Nat. Observ.* 23 Sept. 472/2 He is prepared to throw over all his convictions pretty much as he took them on.

(*c*) To apprehend with the senses; to perceive, 'catch'. *rare.*

**1827** D. JOHNSON *Ind. Field Sports* 45, I have heard the natives assert that they take on the scent of the deer many hours after they have passed.

**c.** To take (a person) into one's employment, or upon one's staff, to engage (also *fig.*); to accept in marriage; to receive into fellowship.

**1611** G. BLUNDELL in *Buccleuch MSS.* (Hist. MSS. Comm.) 97 If Holland take any companies on. **1625** MASSINGER *New Way* II. iii, I'll not give her the advantage..To..say she was forced To buy my wedding-clothes, and took me on With a plain riding-suit and an ambling nag. **1826** *Examiner* 631/1 The large manufacturers are about taking on a considerable number of hands. **1893** J. B. THOMPSON in *Chicago Advance* 20 July, A number of catechumens were taken on during the year.

**d.** To undertake; to begin to handle or deal with, to 'tackle'.

[*c* **1325** *Spec. Gy Warw.* 267 Allas! what sholen hij onne take, þat wolden here her god forsake þurw sinne of fleschly liking?] **1422** [see TAKING *vbl. sb.* 6]. **1885** *Graphic* 3 Jan. 11/3 He..so frightened the other..cowards that..they did not care to 'take him on'. **1898** *Daily News* 10 Mar. 7/1 We cannot take on both jobs. **1900** SIR R. BULLER *ibid.* 12 Nov. 3/4, I had taken on a task, and I was bound to see it through.

**e.** To undertake the management of (a farm, etc.), esp. in succession or continuance.

**1861** *Temple Bar Mag.* III. 474 When I was twenty-two, my father died, and I took on the farm. **1889** MRS. COMYNS CARR *Marg. Maliphant* II. xix. 70, I want him to take on another small farm. **1892** *Cornh. Mag.* Oct. 346 It will be quite impossible for me to take on the lease again.

†**f.** To assert, asseverate (cf. 17 c). *Obs. rare.*

**1583** STUBBES *Anat. Abus.* II. (1882) 26 Yet will they sweare, protest, and take on wonderfully, that it is very new, fresh and tender. *Ibid.* 48 If they sell you a cow,.. will protest and take on woonderfullie, that hee is but this olde, and that olde.

**g.** To buy on credit. *Sc.*

**1808** JAMIESON, *To tak on*, to buy on credit, to buy to accompt. **1866** J. H. WILSON *Our Father in Heaven* (1869) 180, I have heard of young people..going to shops and 'taking on' things, as it is called.

†**h.** To begin, commence (with *inf.*, or *intr.*); = sense 62. *Obs.*

*c* **1200** ORMIN 2553 Ȝho toc onn ful aldeliȝ To fraȝȝnenn Godess enngell. *Ibid.* 11260 Ȝiff þu takesst onn att an & tellesst forþ till fowwre.

** *intransitive senses.*

†**i.** To act, proceed, behave, 'go on'. *Const.* dative, to a person. *Obs.*

*c* **1205** LAY. 3333 Ȝef ferrene kinges hiherde þa tidinde, þe we swa takede him on. *Ibid.* 5592 Þat word come to Belinne..heo he hauede itaken on. *Ibid.* 10175 Þa þis wes al idon þa token heo oðer weise on. *Ibid.* 31619 Whæt Penda king hafueð iseid and hu he wulle taken on. *c* **1305** *Pilate* 149 in *E. E. Poems* (1862) 115 Ou liþere man,..haþ he itake on so, Assentede he to þe gywes? **1362** LANGL. *P. Pl.* A. III. 76 For toke þei on trewely þei timbrede not so hye. *c* **1450** LOVELICH *Grail* lvi. 505 And thus these lyowns Gonnon On to take Til the tyme that Cam Lawncelot de lake.

*reflexive.* *c* **1205** LAY. 30680 On alle wissen he toc him on swulc he weore a chepmon.

**j.** To 'go on' madly or excitedly; to rage, rave; to be greatly agitated; to make a great fuss, outcry, or uproar; now *esp.* to distress oneself greatly. Now *colloq.* and *dial.*

*c* **1430** *Syr Gener.* (Roxb.) 5200 That yondre knight on the white stede Taketh on as a deuel in dede. **1472** *Paston Lett.* III. 57 My modyr wepyth and takyth on mervaylously. **1530** PALSGR. 750/1, I take on lyke a madde man, *je menraige*. **1535** COVERDALE *Num.* xiv. 1 Then the whole congregacion toke on and cryed, and the people wepte. **1600** HOLLAND *Livy* II. xxvii. 61 All this while Appius raged and tooke on, inveying bitterly against the nicetie and popularitie of his brother Consul. **1668** PEPYS *Diary* 8 Apr., Her mother and friends take on mightily. **1767** *Woman of Fashion* I. 157 You'll make me cry too, if you take on in this Manner. **1830** GALT *Lawrie T.* I. ix, He took on like a demented man. **1852** THACKERAY *Esmond* II. i, She took on sadly about her husband.

**k.** To assume airs; to behave proudly or haughtily; to presume; to take liberties. (Cf. 18 e.)

**1668** R. STEELE *Husbandman's Calling* vi. (1678) 143 If a worm should take on, lift up itself, and be proud, then anything may be proud. **1851** *Beck's Florist* 180 'Pride goeth before destruction, and a haughty spirit before a fall'. I began to take on; and if the squire gave me any orders, I did not take 'em as I ought to have done.

**l.** To take service or employment, to engage oneself; to enlist.

*a* **1670** SPALDING *Troub. Chas. I* (1851) II. 335 Diuerss daylie took on [to serve in the army]. **1748** SMOLLETT *Rod. Rand.* xvi, If you take on to be a soldier. **1778** FOOTE *Trip to Calais* III. Wks. 1799 II. 377, I am engaged to take on with Miss Lydy. **1890** *Lippincott's Mag.* Mar. 336 At the end of their term of enlistment [they] would refuse to 'take on' again in D Troop. **1892** *Field* 7 May 698/3 'Then', replied one of the men, 'I will take on at 4*s*.'

(*b*) With *with*: to engage oneself to; to begin to associate with, to consort with; = *take up with*, 90 z; to adopt as a practice, etc.

**1737** BRACKEN *Farriery Impr.* (1757) II. 51 Such a Drake has been more used to a Hen when he was young, and.. will the sooner take on with her when he grows older. **1844** *Fraser's Mag.* XXX. 104/1 The misthress is going to take on with Mister Jowles the praacher. **1886** M. GRAY *Silence Dean Maitland* i, I liked Charlie Judkins well enough before he took on with this love-nonsense. **1894** G. MOORE *Esther Waters* 154 His young woman must be sadly in want of a sweetheart to take on with one such as him.

**m.** To 'catch on', become popular: = sense 10 c. *colloq.*

**1897** 'OUIDA' *Massarenes* xvii, He saw how greatly these musical entertainments 'took on'.

**85. Take out.** *trans.* **a.** To remove from within a place, receptacle, or inclosure; to extract, withdraw, draw forth: see simple senses and OUT *adv.*

**13..** *Cursor M.* 20564 (Gött), I toke þaim vte on [*v.r.* with] mi right hand. **1382** WYCLIF *Ps.* lxviii. 15 [lxix. 14] Tac me out fro clei, that I be not inficchid. *c* **1450** *Merlin* i. 1 Whan that oure lorde..had take oute Adam and Eve, and other [from hell]. **1597** SHAKS. 2 *Hen. IV*, IV. v. 206 Their stings, and teeth, newly tak'n out. **1711** ADDISON *Spect.* No. 94 ¶ 9 He had only dipped his Head into the Water, and immediately taken it out again. **1889** F. M. CRAWFORD *Greifenstein* II. xx. 280 Rex took out his purse and gave him a gold piece. *Mod.* I asked for the book at the library, but it had been taken out the day before.

(*b*) To remove, extract (a stain, etc.).

**1727** GAY *Begg. Op.* I. ix, Money..is the true fuller's earth for reputation, there is not a spot or a stain but what it can take out. *Mod.* Ammonia will take out the grease-spots.

(*c*) *intr.* for *pass.* See sense 58 f.

**b.** *trans.* To withdraw from a number or set (actually or mentally); to leave out, except, omit.

*c* **1200** ORMIN 8601 Þatt ȝer þatt he wass takenn ut þurrh Drihhtin Godd fra manne. *c* **1315** SHOREHAM *Poems* i. 552 Þaȝ he ne toke iudas out, þe worste man on erþe. *Mod.* There are 91 festivals in the Prayer Book Calendar; but if you take out those that have no special Collects, there are only 24.

**c.** To lead or carry out or forth: with various special implications, as: to lead (a partner) out from the company for a dance; to summon (an opponent) to a duel, to 'call out'; to lead (a person or animal) into the open air for exercise, etc.

**1613** SHAKS. *Hen. VIII*, I. iv. 95, I were vnmannerly to take you out, And not to kisse you. **1665** PEPYS *Diary* 13 Apr., When the company begun to dance, I came away, lest I should be taken out. **1749** FIELDING *Tom Jones* VII. xiii, When a matter can't be made up, as in a case of a blow, the sooner you take him out the better. **1811** JANE AUSTEN *Lett.* 29 May, Mrs. Welby takes her out airing in her barouche. **1877** *Scribner's Mag.* XV. 65/1 He had even promised to take her out on the ice. **1893** J. ASHBY STERRY *Naughty Girl* ii, It was awfully good of you to take the children out, Charlie. *Mod.* Take the dog out for a run.

(*b*) *Cricket.* *To take out one's bat*: said of a batsman who is 'not out' at the end of the innings.

**1890** *Standard* 9 May 3/8 He was batting nearly four hours and eventually took out his bat for 90. **1892** *Sat. Rev.* 16 July 63/2 The captain..took out his bat for 60.

†**d.** (*a*) To give vent to, utter. (*b*) To announce, give out (a text). *Obs.*

**1678** DRYDEN *All for Love* Pref., Ess. (Ker) I. 197 He took out his laughter which he had stifled. **1697** BURGHOPE *Disc. Relig. Assemb.* 6 They will take care to come before the text is taken out.

**e.** To make a copy from an original; to copy (a writing, design, etc.); *esp.* to extract a passage from a writing or book.

**1530** PALSGR. 750/1, I take out a writyng, I coppy a mater of a boke, *je copie*. **1573** *Art of Limming* 11 A pretie deuise to take out the true forme & proporcion of any letter, knott, flower, Image, or other worke. **1604** SHAKS. *Oth.* III. iii. 296, I am glad I haue found this Napkin:..Ile haue the worke tane out. *Ibid.* III. iv. 180 Take me this worke out..I would haue it coppied. *Mod.* To read a book and take out quotations for the dictionary.

(*b*) To extract from data.

**1881** *Times* 10 Nov. 4/2 The surveyor employed..to take out the quantities on the architect's plan—that is, to estimate the quantities of materials and labour which will be required to carry out the proposed plans. **1896** [see QUANTITY 13].

†**f.** To learn (a lesson); *transf.* to teach. (See also 81 c.) *Obs.*

*a* **1591** H. SMITH *Wks.* (1866) I. 499 If we be negligent and slack, and never take out his lessons, but stand at a stay. **1629** EARLE *Microcosm.* lxv. (Arb.) 89 He hath taken out as many lessons of the world, as dayes. **1642** *Strangling Gt. Turk*, etc., in *Harl. Misc.* (1745) IV. 37 The Discipline of War must take you out other Lessons of Fury.

**g.** To apply for and obtain (a licence, patent, summons, or other official document) in due form from the proper authority.

**1673** *Essex Papers* (Camden) I. 93 Y[e] vacating their charter, & forcing them to take out a new one. **1687** BURNET *Cont. Reply to Varillas* 76 The Bishops were obliged to take out new Commissions from the King..for holding their Bishopricks. **1726** BERKELEY *Let. T. Prior* 27 Jan., Wks. 1871 IV. 123, I have not yet taken out letters of administration. **1840** *Jrnl. Roy. Agric. Soc.* I. III. 351 Patents have been recently taken out for supposed improvements. **1892** *Sat. Rev.* 30 Apr. 497/1 [He] took out a summons against him.

**h.** To obtain or enjoy completely. ? *Obs.*

**1631** *Celestina* 217, I will goe downe and stand at the doore, that my Master may take out his full sleepe.

**i.** To obtain, receive, use up, spend, the value of (something) *in* another form. Const. *in.*

**1631** HEYWOOD *Fair Maid of West* Wks. 1874 II. 280 Because of the old proverbe, What they want in meate, let them take out in drinke. **1763** FOOTE *Mayor of G.* I. Wks. 1799 I. 168 When he frequented our town of a market day, he has taken out a guinea in oaths. **1828** *Examiner* 794/1 [He] has no objection, when a poor tradesman cannot advance the fee, to take it out in goods. **1891** *Review of Rev.* 15 Sept. 236/2 The prize was one guinea, which had to be taken out in books.

**86. Take out of.** *trans.* **a.** To withdraw or remove from within (*lit.* and *fig.*); to extract (a stain) from: see simple senses and OUT OF.

*To take the words out of one's mouth*: see MOUTH *sb.* 3 l.

*c* **1200** ORMIN Ded. 209 To täkenn ut off helle wa þa gode sawless alle. **1387** TREVISA *Higden* (Rolls) II. 133 While he dwellede longe in Fraunce..Chedde was i-take out of his abbay of Lestynge. *c* **1425** *Cursor M.* 16442 (Trin.) Þe monsleer þat barabas was take out of prisoun. **1535** STEWART *Cron. Scot.* (Rolls) II. 660 [He] Out of the erth his deid bodie hes tone. **1659** in *Burton's Diary* (1828) IV. 451 Take heed you take not the thorn out of another's foot, and put it in your own wholly. **1771** MRS. HAYWOOD *New Present* 246 To take Ink out of Linen. **1882** MISS BRADDON *Mt. Royal* III. iv. 59 He took the cartridges out of the case himself.

**b.** To get, derive, or obtain from.

**1579** W. WILKINSON *Confut. Familye of Loue* B iv, Out of their knowledge, whiche they take out of the Scriptures. **1650** J. FRENCH tr. *Paracelsus' Nat. Things* II. 17 Any flint taken out of River water. **1821** SCOTT *Kenilw.* i, There were as good spitchcocked eels on the board as ever were ta'en out of the Isis.

**c.** To subtract or deduct from. Now *rare.*

**1593** FALE *Dialling* 14, I take the complement of the Elevation, which is 38d. out of the reclination of the plat which is 55d., and there remain 17d. **1703** MOXON *Mech. Exerc.* 127 A setting off of 8 Foot broad and 10 Foot long taking out of the Yard.

**d.** To deprive a person or thing of (some quality, etc.); *spec.* to deprive of (energy or the like); usu. *to take it out of*, to exhaust, fatigue.

**1847** S. WILBERFORCE in *Life* (1879) I. 402 There is so much of interest in a Confirmation, that it takes a great deal out of one. **1858** HAWTHORNE *Fr. & It. Note-Bks.* II. 68 Rome..takes the splendor out of all this sort of thing elsewhere. **1884** H. SMART *Post to Finish* xxxii, Now you say you cannot come, and all the salt is taken out of my holidays. **1890** MRS. LAFFAN *L. Draycott* II. i, The sort of day that takes it out of a man.

**e.** To remove from the jurisdiction of; to prove not to come under (a statute).

**1885** SIR C. S. C. BOWEN in *Law Rep.* 29 Ch. D. 810 The burthen of taking the case out of the Statute of Limitations rests on the Appellant. **1891** *Law Times* XCII. 105/2 All lawyers are familiar with the doctrine of part performance to take a case out of the statute.

**f.** To take (something) from a person in compensation: *to take it out of*, to exact satisfaction from.

**1851** MAYHEW *Lond. Labour* I. 31/2, I take it out of him on the spot. I give him a jolly good hiding. **1888** MCCARTHY & PRAED *Ladies Gallery* I. iv. 91 What we have to miss in sight-seeing we try to take out of the people in the cars. **1901** *Scotsman* 29 Nov. 8/2 In the olden days the villages 'took it out' of each other with club and spear.

**87. Take over.** *trans.* †**a.** = OVERTAKE I. *Obs.*

*c* **1330** *Arth. & Merl.* 7163 The paiens token ouer our men, And fast leyd upon hem then.

**b.** To take by transfer from, or in succession to another; to assume possession or control of (something) from or after some one else.

**1884** A. FORBES *Chinese Gordon* ii. 36 The army whose command he took over in its headquarters. **1887** WESTALL *Capt. Trafalgar* xiv, [He] took service with us when we took over the *Eureka*. **1890** H. S. MERRIMAN *Suspense* viii, Brenda took over all the smaller household duties. **1891** *Law Reports, Weekly Notes* 43/1 The..company was formed..for the purpose of taking over the business..carried on by the plaintiff.

**c.** To carry or convey across, to transport. *Mod.* The ferry-boat will take you over.

**88. Take to.** In passive *to be taken to* = to be taken aback: see 76. *dial.*

**1865** MRS. H. WOOD *Mildred Arkell* xxxii, Mr. Van Brummel, considerably taken-to at being addressed individually, lost his head completely. **1872** *Argosy* Sept. 183 Mr. T. might possibly have been slightly taken to.., but there was no symptom of it in his voice. [See *Eng. Dial. Dict.*]

**89. Take together.**

**a.** *trans.* See simple senses and TOGETHER.

†**b.** To collect: cf. PULL *v.* 30 b. *Obs.*

*c* **1489** CAXTON *Sonnes of Aymon* xix. 429 But he toke togyder his strengthes, & stode vpryghte.

**c.** To consider or reckon together (cf. 26 c), or as a whole; to reckon as a group or collection.

**1678** CUDWORTH *Intell. Syst.* I. iv. § 14. 258 Plato in his Cratylus taking these two words, Ζῆνα and Δία, both together, etymologizeth them as one. **1742** RICHARDSON *Pamela* IV. 107 Numps, his Son, is a Character, take it all together, quite of Nature and Probability. *Mod.* Taken together, there cannot be more than a dozen.

**90. Take up.** **transitive senses.*

**a.** To lift, raise (from the ground, etc., or from a lying or prostrate position); to pick up; also, to lift or raise (something hanging down) so as to expose what is covered by it. Somewhat *arch.*

*a* **1300** *Cursor M.* 3064 (Cott.) Drightin has herd þi barn cri, Rise and tak it up for-þi. **1382** WYCLIF *John* v. 9 The man is maad hool, and took vp his bed, and wandride. *c* **1420–30** *Prymer* (1895) 9 Þi riȝthond took me vp. **1596** SHAKS. *Tam. Shr.* III. ii. 164 The Priest let fall the booke, And as he stoop'd againe to take it vp [etc.]. **1610** HOLLAND *Camden's Brit.* (1637) 278 The garter..which fell from her as she daunced, and the King tooke up from the floor. **1720** DE FOE *Capt. Singleton* v. (1906) 83 Ten men with poles took up one of the canoes and made nothing to carry it. **1844** HOOD *Bridge of Sighs* 5 Take her up tenderly, Lift her with care. **1890** *Univ. Rev.* Feb. 232 Martin..had taken up a stone to throw at him.

(*b*) *spec.* To raise or lift from some settled position, e. g. (plants) out of the ground, (a corpse) out of the grave, (a carpet) from the floor, etc.; to break up the surface of (a field, road, etc.).

† *To take up the table*: to clear the table after a meal (*orig.* to remove the board off the trestles: see TABLE *sb.* 6 b). *Obs.*

**13..** *Cursor M.* 8045 (Cott.) Quen þe king þam [þaa tres] had vp-tan, His ost þam honurd þan ilkan. **15..** [see TABLE *sb.* 6 b]. **1513** MORE in Hall *Chron., Rich. III* (1548) 27 b, Some saye that kynge Richard caused the priest to take them vp,..and to put them in a coffyne. **1585** T. WASHINGTON tr. *Nicholay's Voy.* I. xxi, The table being taken vp, the Ambassador..entred into the pauilion. **1612** [see TABLE *sb.* 6 b]. **1625** MASSINGER *New Way* I. ii, 'Tis not twelve o'clock yet, Nor dinner taking up. **1836–9** DICKENS *Sk. Boz, Sentiment*, The carpet was taken up. **1841** *Jrnl. R. Agric. Soc.* II. II. 229 The turnips were taken up and carted. **1895** *Times* 5 Feb. 8/2 That would mean taking up all the streets in South London.

(*c*) With special obj., implying a purpose of using in some way: as, *to take up one's pen*, to proceed or begin to write; *to take up a book* (i. e. with the purpose to read): *to take up the* (or *one's*) *cross* (see CROSS *sb.* 4, 10): *to take up* ARMS, *the* CUDGELS, *the* GLOVE, *the* HATCHET (see the sbs.).

*c* **1420** *Brut* ccxlii. 355 Þay waged batayle & cast doun her gloues; & þanne þey were take vp and seled. **1481, 1579** [see GLOVE *sb.* 1 d]. **1590–** [see GAUNTLET *sb.*[1] 1 c]. **1621** T. WILLIAMSON tr. *Goulart's Wise Vieillard* A ij b, I tooke up my Pen againe, and at starts and tymes finished it. **1660** tr. *Amyraldus' Treat. conc. Relig.* II. iv. 216 He took up arms for the conservation of his Country. **1712** STEELE *Spect.* No. 514 ¶ 1 Not finding my self inclined to sleep, I took up Virgil to divert me. **1816** SCOTT *Old Mort.* xxx, That the cause of his country, and of those with whom he had taken up arms, should suffer nothing from being entrusted to him. **1866** G. MACDONALD *Ann. Q. Neighb.* i, A man had to take-up his cross.

(*d*) To raise, lift (one's hand, foot, head, etc.). Now of a horse or other beast.

*c* **1425** *Cursor M.* 15227 (Trin.) Vp he toke his holy hond & ȝaf þe benesoun. *c* **1489** CAXTON *Sonnes of Aymon* ix. 249 Rycharde that lay a grounde thus wounded..toke up his hede, and sayd [etc.]. **1737** BRACKEN *Farriery Impr.* (1757) II. 73 He steps boldly, and takes up his Fore-Feet pretty high. *Ibid.* 77 A Horse should take up his Feet moderately high.

(*e*) To take (a person) from the ground into a vehicle, or on horseback, etc. Said of a person, or of the carriage, horse, train, etc. Also *absol.* of a vehicle, a train, etc. To take up its occupants.

**1689** *Lond. Gaz.* No. 2511/4 A Hackney-Coachman took up 3 Persons at Mark-Lane-end. **1710** *Ibid.* No. 4735/4 A Hackney Coach..that took up his Fair in Southwark. **1831** SCOTT *Ct. Robt.* xiii, We should not criticise the animal [elephant] which kneels to take us up. **1857** TROLLOPE *Barchester T.* x, Carriages..were desired to take up at a quarter before one. **1893** *Eng. Illustr. Mag.* X. 257/2 Our coach..duly took us up, and set us down. **1898** *Westm. Gaz.* 27 June 10/1 All carriages will take up on the Embankment and Savoy-hill. **1909** *Bradshaw's Railway Guide* Aug. 21 Stops to take up 1st class Passengers for London. *Ibid.*, Stops to take up for Reading or beyond.

† (*f*) *fig.* To 'raise' (a siege). *Obs. rare.*

*c* **1489** CAXTON *Sonnes of Aymon* xxiii. 493 Charlemagne.. receyued theim honourably, and toke vp his siege, and went agen to parys.

**b.** To lead, conduct, convey, or carry (a person or thing) to a higher place or position.

*a* **1300** *Cursor M.* 17547 (Cott.) Þat helias in ald dais, Was taken up als vnto heuen. **1526** TINDALE *Acts* i. 9 Whyll they behelde he was taken vp, and a cloude receaued hym vp out of their sight. **1748** *Anson's Voy.* II. viii. 219 The taking up oysters from great depths..by Negro slaves. *Mod.* He took me up into the belfry. You needn't walk up the stairs; they will take you up in the lift.

(*b*) *spec.* To bring (a horse, ox, etc.) from pasture into the stable or stall.

**1482** *Cely Papers* (Camden) 122 Lette hym [a horse] ron in a parke tyll Hallowtyd and then take hym wpe and ser hym and lette hym stand in the dede of whynter. **1688** R. HOLME *Armoury* III. xix. (Roxb.) 184/2 Take vp your horse, is to take him from grasse to be kept in the stable. **1844** *Jrnl. R. Agric. Soc.* V. I. 75 Calves..are taken up at night about the latter end of October. **1846** *Ibid.* VII. II. 394 Sixteen polled beasts..were taken up.

**c.** To pull up or in, so as to tighten or shorten; to make fast in this way, as a dropped stitch. In quot. 1882 *intr.* for *pass.* to become shortened, shrink.

**1804** MAR. EDGEWORTH *Pop. Tales, To-Morrow* 340 This operation of taking up a stitch..is one of the slowest. **1882** NARES *Seamanship* (ed. 6) 226 The longer the rope the more it takes up. **1891** MISS DOWIE *Girl in Karp.* iii. 33 Each girth was altered to its last hole, the stirrup-leather taken up half a yard, but nowhere could it grip the little beast. **1892** *Field* 8 Oct. 545/3 The direction to the groom would be 'take up' (or 'let down', as the case may be) the near-side horse's coupling rein.

(*b*) To tie up or constrict (a vein or artery); 'to fasten with a ligature passed under' (J.).

**1565** BLUNDEVIL *Horsemanship* IV. iii. (1580) 2 b, Most diseases are healed either by letting of bloud, by taking vp of vaines, by purgation, or else by cauterisation. **1737** BRACKEN *Farriery Impr.* (1757) II. 41 The Absurdity of taking up the Veins for the Cure of Spavins. **1840** *Jrnl. R. Agric. Soc.* I. III. 322 Should any considerable [blood] vessel be opened, it will be necessary to take it up by passing a thread underneath it, and tying it tightly.

**d.** To take into one's possession, possess oneself of; with various shades of meaning, as: to purchase wholesale, buy up; to get, receive, or exact in payment; to levy; to borrow (at interest); to hire.

**1421** *Coventry Leet Bk.* 29 Þat no maner of fresche fysher by, ne take up, no maner of fresche fysche of men of the contrey by way of regratry. *c* **1440** *Jacob's Well* 40 And þou apeyryst & lessyst þat tythe in takyng vp þi cost, here þou makyst þe cherche thrall. **1528** *Bill* in R. G. Marsden *Sel. Pl. Crt. Adm.* (1894) I. 41, I Thomas Thorne..have taken up by exchange of Thomas Fuller merchaunt..the sum of lxli sterling. **1589** PUTTENHAM *Eng. Poesie* III. xii. (Arb.) 179 He that standes in the market way, and takes all vp before it come to the market in grosse and sells it by retaile. **1655** tr. *Com. Hist. Francion* IV. 23, I must buy me a Cloak lined with plush, or take one up at the Brokers. **1760–72** H. BROOKE *Fool of Qual.* (1809) II. 130 He took up all the money he could, at any interest. **1838** T. MITCHELL *Aristoph. Clouds* 6 Strepsiades had for the purchase taken up money with two usurers, Pasias and Amynias. **1890** *Pict. World* 2 Jan. 11/3 The whole of the limited edition.. was taken up by the booksellers on the day of publication.

(*b*) To take (land) into occupation; to begin to occupy, settle upon. Cf. also v (*b*).

**1478** *Acta Dom. Conc.* (1839) 6/1 He occupijt and tuke vp sa mekle of þe said landis of þe ȝeris forsaide. **1682** S. WILSON *Acc. Carolina* 16 Rent to commence in two years after their taking up their Land. **1890** 'R. BOLDREWOOD' *Col. Reformer* (1891) 76 Persons..could 'take up', that is merely mark out and occupy, as much land as they pleased.

(*c*) To accept or pay (a bill of exchange); to advance money on (a mortgage); to subscribe for (stock, shares, a loan) at their original issue.

**1832** *Examiner* 283/1 It was not convenient for her husband to take up the bill. **1847** C. G. ADDISON *On Contracts* II. v. § 1 (1883) 771 A person who takes up a bill *supra protest* for the benefit of a particular party to the bill succeeds to the title of the party from whom..he receives it. **1873** SPENCER *Stud. Sociol.* x. 251 Not one of the thousand shares was taken up. **1888** RIDER HAGGARD *Col. Quaritch* xi. 84, I am disposed to try and find the money to take up these mortgages. **1890** *Chamb. Jrnl.* 10 May 294/1 Sums of money could be remitted for the purpose of taking up bills on the last day of grace. **1891** *Harper's Mag.* Nov. 946/2 He persuaded the citizens to take up the Queen's loans themselves.

(*d*) To make (a collection). *Sc.* and *U. S.*

**1892** 'MARK TWAIN' in *Idler* Feb. 15 They take up a collection and bury him. **1908** *Daily Chron.* 21 Dec. 4/7 The tambourine..still serves its notable purpose for 'taking up', as the Scotch say, a collection.

†**e.** To obtain or get from some source; to adopt, 'borrow' (= sense 30); to apprehend with the senses, perceive (quot. 1607); to deduce, infer (= 31 b); to contract, 'catch' (= 44 b). *Obs.*

**1607** TOPSELL *Four-f. Beasts* (1658) 454 Presently the wilde beasts take it [the scent] up, and follow it with all speed they can. **1628** EARLE *Microcosm.* ii. (Arb.) 22 Notes of Sermons, which taken vp at St. Maries, hee vtters in the Country. **1662** STILLINGFL. *Orig. Sacr.* III. ii. § 5 That the general conclusions of reason..were taken up from the observation of things as they are at present in the world. **1700** DRYDEN *Pref. Fables* Ess. (ed. Ker) II. 255, I find..I have anticipated already and taken up from Boccace before I come to him. **1848** *Jrnl. R. Agric. Soc.* IX. II. 360 We can conceive that an animal..should take up the disease, and afterwards communicate it to others.

† (*b*) ? To receive, get, have accorded to one.

**1639** FULLER *Holy War* v. xxvi. (1647) 274 A chronologer of such credit that he may take up more belief on his bare word than some others on their bond.

**f.** To receive into its own substance or interstices; to absorb (a fluid); to dissolve (a solid); also, to receive and hold upon its surface (quot. 1840).

**1682** *Art & Myst. Vintners* xxxviii. 20 Dip in it [*printed* it in] so many cloaths as will take it up, and put the cloaths in your Hogshead. **1737** BRACKEN *Farriery Impr.* (1757) II. 105 Nutritive Juices, taken up by the absorbent Vessels. **1758** REID tr. *Macquer's Chym.* I. 47 An acid cannot take up above such a certain proportion thereof as is sufficient to saturate it. **1805** W. SAUNDERS *Min. Waters* 29 Water, at a moderate temperature, will readily take up its own bulk of carbonic acid gas. **1840** GOSSE *Canadian Nat.* xvi. 251 Capable of taking up and holding a large quantity of water. **1877** *Scribner's Mag.* XV. 141/2 The elastic roller thus takes up the color from the pores of the wood. **1892** *Cornh. Mag.* Sept. 257 Water will take up 2 lb. 10 oz. of salt to the gallon.

**g.** To grasp with the mind; to apprehend, understand: = sense 46; *take in*, 82 l. Also with the speaker as obj. (= 46 b). *Obs.* exc. *Sc.* in general sense; now only in restricted sense: To apprehend, appreciate (points in discourse, etc.).

**1659** W. GUTHRIE *Christian's Gt. Interest* viii. (1724) 88 A Man may take up his gracious State by his Faith, and the Acting thereof on Christ. **1741** WATTS *Improv. Mind* I. vi. § 6 A student should never satisfy himself with bare attendance on the lectures of his tutor, unless he clearly takes up his sense and meaning. **1825** JAMIESON s. v., He taks up a thing before ye have half said it. **1867** N. MACLEOD *Starling* I. v. 55, 'I do not take you up, sir', replied the Sergeant. *Mod.* He is a humorous speaker, and his jokes were well taken up by the audience.

**h.** To accept. †(*a*) To accept mentally (*upon credit* or *trust*), believe without examination, take for granted. *Obs.* (*b*) To accept (anything offered, esp. a challenge, a bet: also the person who offers it). Cf. 40. See also GAUNTLET *sb.*[1] 1 c, GLOVE *sb.* 1 d: see a (*c*).

**1626** BACON *Sylva* § 34 It is strange how the ancients took up experiments upon credit, and yet did build great matters upon them. **1662** STILLINGFL. *Orig. Sacr.* I. iv. § 8 Greek writers..took up things upon trust as much as any people in the world did. **1711** ADDISON *Spect.* No. 126 ¶ 9 Notwithstanding he was a very fair Bettor, no Body would take him up. **1880** G. MEREDITH *Tragic Com.* xviii, Marko..had taken up Alvan's challenge. **1892** *Sat. Rev.* 8 Oct. 403/2 Mr. Stanley (on taking up the freedom of Swansea) spoke very vigorously on the subject. **1893** *Temple Bar Mag.* XCVII. 21 It don't concern you who takes up the bets.

**i.** To take (a person) into one's protection, patronage, or other relation; to adopt as a *protégé* or associate; to begin to patronize.

**1382** WYCLIF *Luke* i. 54 He, hauynge mynde of his mercy, took vp Israel, his child. **1482** *Monk of Evesham* (Arb.) 35 That worshipfull olde fader the whiche..had take me vp to be a felow with him of his wey. **1530** PALSGR. 751/2, I take up, as a man taketh up his frende that maketh hym curtesye. *a* **1635** NAUNTON *Fragm. Reg.* (Arb.) 26 The blow falling on Edward late Earl of Hereford, who to his cost took up the divorced Lady, of whom the Lord Beauchamp was born. **1848** THACKERAY *Van. Fair* li, When the Countess of Fitz-Willis..takes up a person, he or she is safe. **1877** *Scribner's Mag.* XV. 62/2 He is just the man to take up a girl whom everybody neglected. **1892** *Black & White* 10 Dec. 679/1 A great art patron took him up and he became 'the fashion'.

†**j.** To levy, raise, enlist (troops). *Obs.*

**1560** DAUS tr. *Sleidane's Comm.* 219 b, He toke vp all that were able to weare armure. **1597** SHAKS. 2 *Hen. IV*, II. i. 199 You are to take Souldiers vp, in Countries as you go. **1632** LITHGOW *Trav.* III. 91 He was taken vp as a souldier.

† (*b*) *intr.* for *refl.* To enter (military or naval) service; to enlist; = *take on*, 84 l. *Obs.*

**1689** SHADWELL *Bury F.* I. ii, The top of their fortune is to take up in some Troop.

**k.** *trans.* To capture, seize. † (*a*) *Chess.* = sense 2 d. *Obs.*

*c* **1440** *Gesta Rom.* xxi. 71 (Harl. MS.) Þe rook..holdith length & brede, and takith vp what so is in his way. *c* **1470** *Treat. Chess* (MS. Ashmole 344 lf. 5), Then he takith hym vpp with his knight.

(*b*) *Falconry.* To bring under restraint (a young hawk 'at hack') in order to train it: see quot. and HACK *sb.*[2] 1. Cf. b (*b*).

**1826** J. SEBRIGHT *Observ. Hawking* 8 When..[Hawks] have omitted to come for their food at the accustomed hour, for two or three successive days,..it will be necessary to take them up, or they would in a short time go away altogether. **1881** E. B. MICHELL in *Macm. Mag.* Nov. 40 An experienced falconer will 'take up' a young merlin from hack and have him trained in three or four days.

† (*c*) *To take up for hawks*: (app.) to seize and slaughter (an old or useless horse) as meat for hawks; hence allusively, *taken up for hawks* = done for, ruined. *Obs.*

**1471** J. PASTON in *P. Lett.* III. 7, I beseche yow, and my horse..be not takyn up for the Kynges hawkys, that he may be had hom and kept in your plase. *a* **1553** UDALL *Royster Doyster* III. iii, Ye were take vp for haukes, ye were gone, ye were gone. [Cf. **1632** BROME *Northern Lasse* I. iv, 'Slid I'le marrie out of the way; 'tis time I think: I shall be tane up for Whores meat else.]

**l.** To seize by legal authority, arrest, apprehend; in quot. 1821, to summon as a witness.

**1596** SPENSER *State Irel.* Wks. (Globe) 679/1 Though the sherriff have this authoritye..to take up all such stragglers, and imprison them. **1682** WOOD *Life* 25 Nov. (O.H.S.) III. 31 Duke of York hath brought an action against one Arrowsmith..upon the statute of *Scandalum magnatum*, who is taken up for it. **1796** SOUTHEY *Lett.fr. Spain* (1799) 303 The Alcayde took up all the inhabitants of the village where it happened. **1821** GALT *Ann. Parish* xii, It was thought she would have been taken up as an evidence in the Douglas cause. **1861** *Temple Bar Mag.* II. 358 [He] was taken up for sacrilege, and brought before a magistrate.

†**m.** To arrest the progress or action of; to check, stop, 'pull up'. *Obs.*

**1631** WEEVER *Anc. Fun. Mon.* To Rdr. 7, I haue beene taken vp in diuers Churches by the Churchwardens..and not suffered to write the Epitaphs. **1699** DAMPIER *Voy.* II. I. iv. 78 For a small piece of Money a man may pass quiet enough, and for the most part only the poor are taken up.

**n.** *intr.* for *refl.* To check oneself, stop short, 'pull up'; to slacken one's pace; to restrain oneself; to reform, mend one's ways. *Obs.* exc. *dial.*

**1613** FLETCHER, etc. *Captain* IV. iii, Take up quickly; Thy wit will founder of all four else, wench, If thou hold'st this pace: take up, when I bid thee. **1661** PEPYS *Diary* 13 Nov., My expensefull life..will undo me, I fear,..if I do not take up. *a* **1700** B. E. *Dict. Cant. Crew* s. v. *Oats*, One that has sown his wild Oats,..begins to take up and be more Staied. **1832** *Examiner* 611/1 She longs to make her fortune by her trade, that she may 'take up and live godly'. **1868** ATKINSON *Cleveland Gloss.*, *Tak' up*,..to reform one's ways.

(*b*) Of weather: To improve, mend, become fair.

**1845** *Jrnl. R. Agric. Soc.* VI. II. 570 The weather took up immediately afterwards. **1889** FROUDE *Two Chiefs Dunboy* xiv, On the second evening the weather began to take up.

(*c*) '*Mech.* To close spontaneously, as a small leak in a steam-pipe or water-pipe' (*Cent. Dict.*).

**o.** *trans.* To check (a person) in speaking; to interrupt sharply, esp. with an expression of dissent or disapproval; to rebuke, reprove, or reprimand sharply or severely. Also *to take up short*: see SHORT.

**1530** PALSGR. 750/1 It pityed my herte to here howe he toke hym up. **1573** L. LLOYD *Marrow of Hist.* (1653) 241 His wife Xantippe began to take her husband up with taunting and opprobrious words. **1645** T. COLEMAN *Hopes Deferred & Dashed* 2 [He] rebukes him sharply, takes him up roundly. **1768** TUCKER *Lt. Nat.* (1834) I. 80 Those, who would find fault with us for attributing colour, heat, and cold, to inanimate bodies, take us up before we were down. **1885** 'ANSTEY' *Tinted Venus* i. 14 'You do take one up so', he complained! 'I never intended nothing of the sort'. **1886** H. CONWAY *Living or Dead* xxv, She wondered why the master took her up so short when she had mentioned his name.

†**p.** 'To oppose, encounter, cope with' (Schmidt *Shaks. Lex.*). *Obs.*

**1597** SHAKS. 2 *Hen. IV*, I. iii. 73 His diuisions..Are in three Heads: one Power against the French, And one against Glendower: Perforce a third Must take vp vs. **1607** — *Cor.* III. i. 244 *Corio.* On faire ground, I could beat fortie of them. *Mene.* I could my selfe take vp a Brace o'th' best of them. **1641** BAKER *Chron.* (1660) 274 King Henry..in June kept a solemn Just at Greenwich, where he and Sir Charles Brandon took up all commers.

†**q.** (?) To touch up; to urge on, incite. *Obs.*

**1565** STAPLETON tr. *Bede's Hist. Ch. Eng.* V. vi. 158 But when I sawe them take their horses vppe with the spurres [L. *concitatis..equis*].

†**r.** To begin, commence (an action); *esp.* to begin to utter, set up, raise (laughter, lamentation, etc.). *Obs.* In quot. 1689 with *inf.* (obs.); in 1878 *absol.* (*dial.*).

*c* **1400** *Brut* 131 The Kyng his hondes lifte vp an hye, and a grete laughter toke op. *c* **1425** *Cursor M.* 15990 (Trin.) Þe cok toke vp his fli3t. *c* **1500** *Merch. & Son* 103 in Hazl. *E. P. P.* I. 139 The goste toke up a gresely grone, with fendys awey he glode. *a* **1610** HEALEY *Theophrastus* (1636) 70 Then hee would take up a great laughter, as if some prodigy or ominous thing had happened. **1689** AUBREY *Lives* (1898) I. 150 (*2nd Ld. Falkland*) 'Twas not long before he tooke-up to be serious. **1878** *Scribner's Mag.* XV. 653/1 Meanwhile the 'animal show' at the appointed time 'took up', as the country people expressed it.

† (*b*) To start, raise, or begin a song; hence (*Sc.*) to lead the singing of (a psalm) in church. *Obs.* (Cf. also *to take up one's parable*: PARABLE *sb.* d.)

*a* **1380** *Minor Poems fr. Vernon MS.* xxiii. 1089 We han taken vp þe song Of Iubilacion. **1577** *Burgh Rec. Edinb.* (1882) IV. 60 The oulklie pentioun of ten schillingis appoyntit to Edwerd..Hendersoun, for all the dayis of his lyfe for taikin vp of the spalmes. **1637** in Cramond *Ann. Cullen* (1888) 39 To read in the kirk and take up the psalm every Sabbath. **1825** JAMIESON s. v., 'He tuke up the psalm in the kirk', he acted as precentor.

**s.** *trans.* To begin afresh (something left off, or begun by another); to enter anew upon; to resume.

**1654–66** EARL ORRERY *Parthen.* (1676) 692 With Atasernes I joyfully took up our way to the Camp. **1712** ADDISON *Paraphr. Ps. xix*, Soon as the evening shades prevail, The moon takes up the wondrous tale. **1833** HT. MARTINEAU *Manch. Strike* i. 5 When at last she lost her voice..he took up the word. **1850** *Tait's Mag.* XVII. 482/2 Mr. Ward's diary takes up the history..just where Lord Malmesbury's memoirs leave it. **1879** M. PATTISON *Milton* xii. 161 He took up all the dropped threads of past years. **1902** O. WISTER *Virginian* xxxii, We took up our journey, and by the end of the forenoon we had gone some distance.

**t.** To adopt (a practice, notion, idea, purpose, etc.); to assume (an attitude, tone, etc.); to engage in, 'go in for' (a study, profession, business, etc.).

*a* **1450** *Knt. de la Tour* (1906) 64 She wolde not take hede to abyde unto her neygheboures..haue taken up the guyse or array that she wold haue. **1589** PUTTENHAM *Eng. Poesie* II. xii. (Arb.) 122 They of late yeares haue taken this pastime vp among them. **1611** BIBLE *Transl. Pref.* 6 To haue the Scriptures in the mother-tongue is not a quaint conceit lately taken vp. **1660** tr. *Amyraldus' Treat. conc. Relig.* II. ii. 163 He seem'd to have took up a resolution of trampling upon those superstitions. **1712** ARBUTHNOT *John Bull* I. iv, Lewis Baboon had taken up the trade of Clothier. **1821** SOUTHEY in *Q. Rev.* XXV. 289 Whatever part indeed Cromwell took up would be well maintained. **1890** *Sat. Rev.* 20 Sept. 355/1 Those parts of the Ethics which they are obliged to take up for 'Greats'.

(*b*) To take in hand, proceed to deal practically with (a matter, question, etc.); to interest oneself in, espouse, embrace (a cause).

**1502** *Star Chamber Proc.* Michaelm. 18 Hen. VII, The said late Shireffes..caused two of her frendes to take up this haynouse matier betuix theym as arbitrours. **1771** MRS. HARRIS in *Priv. Lett. Ld. Malmesbury* I. 221 This [conflict with the City] was taken up yesterday in the House; the Speaker gave a detail of the fact. **1820** *Examiner* No. 618. 109/1 How generous to take up the cause of the afflicted! **1869** FREEMAN *Norm. Conq.* III. xiii. 312 The cause of William was eagerly taken up. **1892** *Law Times* XCIII. 459/2 Mr. Bros..suggested that the Public Prosecutor should take the matter up.

†**u.** To make up, settle, arrange amicably (a dispute, quarrel, etc.). In quot. 1666, to make up temporarily, 'patch up'. *Obs.*

**1560** DAUS tr. *Sleidane's Comm.* 21 b, He had done as much as lay in him that the matter might be taken vp. **1600** SHAKS. *A. Y. L.* V. iv. 104, I knew when seuen Iustices could not take vp a Quarrell. **1605** *Lond. Prodigal* II. ii, If you come to take up the matter between my master and the Devonshire man. **1666** PEPYS *Diary* 24 Oct., The thing is not accommodated, but only taken up.

† (*b*) To make up, make good. *Obs.*

**1662** GURNALL *Chr. Arm.* III. 302 If you be hindred of your rest one Night by business, you will take it up the next.

**v.** To proceed to occupy (a place or position, *lit.* or *fig.*); to station or place oneself in; = sense 27.

**1565** STAPLETON tr. *Bede's Hist. Ch. Eng.* 86 Taking vpp his inne, and finding the neighbours of the parish at feast with the oste. **1589** PUTTENHAM *Eng. Poesie* II. v. (Arb.) 88 He taketh vp his lodging, and rests him selfe till the morrow. *a* **1672** WOOD *Life* (O. H. S.) I. 109 When they were going to their..beds, two or 3 houres after he had taken up his rest. **1736** WESLEY *Wks.* (1872) I. 26 Mr. Delamotte and I took up our lodging with the Germans. **1840** THIRLWALL *Greece* lviii. VII. 307 He cleared the defiles and took up his quarters for the rest of the winter at Celænæ. **1888** McCARTHY & PRAED *Ladies' Gallery* II. ii. 29, I did not accept his invitation to take up my residence in his house. **1893** TRAILL *Soc. Eng.* Introd. 15 We may take up a position from which we can survey the entire array.

† (*b*) To engage or hire (a lodging) for the purpose of occupying; = sense 15 c. Cf. d (*b*). *Obs.*

**1602** MARSTON *Antonio's Rev.* I. ii, Twere best you tooke some lodging up, And lay in private till the soile of griefe Were cleard your cheeke. **1709** STRYPE *Ann. Ref.* I. xv. 188 The Bp. of London's palace, and the Dean of Paul's house,..were taken up for the French ambassadors.

(*c*) *Take up house*: †to take or rent a house (*obs.*); to start housekeeping; become a householder. *Sc.*

**1612** *Shetland Act* in *Scotsman* 29 Jan. (1886) 7/2 It sall not be lesum for servile persones not worth..72 punds Scottis to tak up houssis. **1850** *Tait's Mag.* XVII. 13/1 He was unwilling to incur the expense of taking up house. **1876** SMILES *Sc. Natur.* i, John Edward and his wife 'took up house' in the Green, one of the oldest quarters of the city.

† (*d*) *absol.* or *intr.* To take up one's quarters, lodge, 'put up'. *Obs.*

**1625** B. JONSON *Staple of N.* IV. ii, How much 'twere better, that my Ladies Grace Would here take vp Sir, and keepe house with you. **1662** PEPYS *Diary* 14 Oct., To Cambridge.., whither we come at about nine o'clock, and took up at the 'Beare'. **1724** DE FOE *Mem. Cavalier* (1840) 14, I was..forced to take up at a little village.

**w.** *trans.* To occupy entirely; to occupy the whole of, fill up (space, time, etc.); to occupy exclusively (quot. 1615); to occupy so as to hinder passage, to obstruct (quots. 1607, 1631). Cf. 28.

**1607** SHAKS. *Cor.* III. ii. 116 My throat of Warre be turn'd ..into a Pipe.., and Schoole-boyes Teares take vp The Glasses of my sight. **1610** HOLLAND *Camden's Brit.* (1637) 633 It tooke up in compasse above a mile. **1615** G. SANDYS *Trav.* 69 The men take them [the public baths] up in the morning, and in the afternoone the women. **1631** WEEVER *Anc. Fun. Mon.* 11 Tombes are made so huge great, that they take vp the Church, and hinder the people from diuine Seruice. **1640** S. D'EWES in *Lett. Lit. Men* (Camden) 167 Some petitions..tooke upp our time a great parte of the morning. **1705** tr. *Bosman's Guinea* 490 The sixteen Red Cliffs, which take up in all about three Miles in length. **1719** DE FOE *Crusoe* (1840) I. v. 85 The 7th..I took wholly up to make me a chair. **1825** *New Monthly Mag.* XIV. 392 The first quatrain..is taken up with a list of rivers. **1885** MRS. LYNN LINTON *Christ. Kirkland* II. ix. 274 It took up his time and bored him.

(*b*) To use up, consume (labour, material): cf. 28. ? *Obs.*

**1679** MOXON *Mech. Exerc.* viii. 142 The Fraiming work will take up more labour. **1712** J. JAMES tr. *Le Blond's Gardening* 121 You may fill up the Holes to the Level of the Ground.., to take up the Earth that may possibly remain to be disposed of. **1719** DE FOE *Crusoe* (1840) I. iv. 80 The prodigious deal of time and labour which it took me up to make a plank or board.

(*c*) To occupy or engage fully, engross (a person, his attention, mind, etc.). Chiefly in *pass.* (const. *with*, sometimes *in*); also in *Sc.* and *north. dial.* = to be taken with, take an absorbing or engaging interest in.

**1599** B. JONSON *Cynthia's Rev.* V. ii, He is taken up with great persons. *a* **1617** BAYNE *Lect.* (1634) 201 To take our selves up with some behoofefull duty. **1624** MASSINGER *Renegado* IV. i, I am so wholly taken up with sorrow. **1712** BUDGELL *Spect.* No. 301 ¶ 8, I was wholly taken up in these Reflections. **1832** HT. MARTINEAU *Hill & Valley* v. 76 She is taken up with making her husband comfortable. **1886** RUSKIN *Præterita* I. vi. 174, I was extremely taken up with the soft red cushions of the armchairs. **1892** MRS. H. WARD *D. Grieve* II. vii, I think he feels he must make his way first. His business takes him up altogether.

*** intransitive senses.*

(See also subordinate uses in j (*b*), n, n (*b*, *c*), r, v (*d*).)

**x.** *Take up for*: to stand up for, take the part of, side with. *U. S.* Cf. *to take for*, 20 b.

**1878** *Scribner's Mag.* XV. 769/2 To Amanda's surprise her father took up for Mark. *Ibid.* XVI. 627/2 Twonnet thought..that it was a shame for..Mr. Whittaker to take up for Bonamy.

**y.** † *Take up in*, to interest oneself or itself in, concern itself with, have reference to. *Obs.*

**1665** J. SPENCER *Vulg. Proph.* 120 Hath not the World out-grown the follies of Auguries..and took up in the resolves of Reason, as the best Oracle to consult in a civil business? *c* **1666** SOUTH *Serm.*, *John* vii. 17 (1697) I. 246 The former Articles, that took up Chiefly in Speculation and Belief.

**z.** *Take up with.* (Cf. *take with*, 75 a–c.) (*a*) To associate with (a person); to begin to keep company with; to consort with (esp. with a view to marriage). Cf. i.

*a* **1619** FLETCHER *Wit without M.* I. i, He's taken up with those that woo the Widow. **1693** *Humours Town* 28 The man of Mode takes up with a damn'd Jilt. **1815** SCOTT *Guy M.* xi, To see his daughter taking up with their son. **1824** *Examiner* 250/2 Having..absconded and taken up with another woman. **1887** MISS E. MONEY *Dutch Maiden* (1888) 329 If you cannot marry her, you won't care to take up with another.

(*b*) To adopt, espouse (esp. as a settled practice); to assent to, agree with, accept. *arch.*

**1692** BENTLEY *Boyle Lect.* 58, I could as easily take up with that senseless assertion of the Stoicks. **1724** A. COLLINS *Gr. Chr. Relig.* 275 Taking up with all manner of false proofs in behalf of Christianity. **1825** FROUDE in *Rem.* (1838) I. 178 My lately having taken up with reading sermons. **1885** J. MARTINEAU *Types Eth. Th.* I. 127 We take up at once with the belief that the space around us is empty.

† (*c*) To be satisfied with; to content oneself with, put up with, tolerate. *Obs.*

**1609** HOLLAND *Amm. Marcell.* 394 Never doe wee find that he tooke up with any mild correction and punishment. **1633** BP. HALL *Hard Texts* 395 (*Jer.* xxii.) I will not take up with the old and meane buildings of my Ancestors. **1726** BUTLER *Serm., Love God* Wks. 1874 II. 186 Nature teaches and inclines us to take up with our lot. **1736** — *Anal.* II. viii. ibid. I. 300 The unsatisfactory nature of the Evidence, with which we are obliged to take up. **1825** *New Monthly Mag.* XIII. 588 The book-sellers..buy all the good books, and the joint stock company must take up with the refuse of the market.

†(*a*) To betake oneself to: = *take to*, 74 c. *Obs.* **1785** MISS FIELDING *Ophelia* I. iv, At night he again took up with his Couch.

**XIII. 91.** In various idiomatic phrases (besides those mentioned under the senses to which they belong), as *take into* ACCOUNT, *in* (*into*) *one's* HEAD, *in* (*to*) PIECES, *to* TASK, *in* TOW, *upon* TRUST, *in* VAIN, *to* WITNESS, *at one's* WORD, *in* WORTH, etc., for which see the sbs.

☞ Key to phrases treated under the senses.

Not including the adverbial combinations 76–90, nor all phrases referred to the sb. or other leading word in them; see also 72, 91.

*Take* an accent 22, *t* adieu 55, *t* after 73, *t* against 20 b, *t* aim 64, *t* the air 13 b, *t* alarm 65, *t* assizes 32, *t* the attention 10 d, *t* a bath 13 b, *t* beginning 52 b, *t* blind 7 d, *t* one a blow 5 b, *t* buck, bull 39 b, *t* the chair 27, *t* charge 66, *t* in charge 17, *t* cold 44 b, *t* with compasses 32 c, *t* credit 21, *t* at cards, at chess 2 d, *t* the crown 16 c, *t* day 67, *t* one's death 40 b, *t* a degree 34, *t* one's dick 17 b, *t* diligence 51 c, *t* a disease 44 b, *t* drink 13, *t* in earnest 42, *t* end 72, *t* an examination 32 a, *t* the eye 10 d, *t* farewell 55, *t* a fence 43, *t* fire 68, *t* flight 72, *t* to flight 74 b, *t* food 13, *t* for 20 b, 48, *t* form 16 a, *t* fright 50, *t* in good part 42, *t* good-night 55, *t* the gown, the habit 16 c, *t* to a habit 74 e, *t* by the hand 3, *t* in *or* on hand 17, *t* a hint 41, *t* hoarse 7 d, *t* hold 69, *t* horse 39 b, 70, *t* house 15 c, *t* in idle 26 b, *t* ill 7 d, e, 42, *t* an inflexion 22, *t* inn 25, *t* inquisition 32 a, *t* intent 51 c, *t* interest 50, *t* into 4, *t* it 17 c, 47 c, *t* a journey 52, *t* knighthood 34, *t* labour 19 b, *t* lame 7 d, *t* a lease 15 c, *t* leave 21, 72, *t* leg 24 c, *t* the life of 58 b, *t* in marriage 14 b, *t* medicine 13, *t* mercy 51 b, *t* to mercy 14, *t* minutes 33 a, *t* an oar 16 c, *t* an observation 32 b, *t* an obstacle 43, *t* off one's feet 58, *t* on 50 c, 84, *t* on oneself 16, 18, *t* a paper, periodical 15 d, *t* a photograph, picture 33 b, *t* the points 43, 46, *t* possession 71, *t* punishment 37, *t* a resolution 51 a, *t* salt 13, 44 c, *t* satisfaction 37, *t* ship 24 c, *t* short 8 b, *t* a size (in gloves, etc.) 28 b, *t* snuff 13, *t* in snuff 42, *t* (so much) 28, *t* one's stand 27, *t* a step 52, *t* a stick to 24 b, *t* temperature 32 b, *t* thought 51 c, *t* to 74, *t* one's time 28, *t* toil 19 b, *t* a trip 52, *t* trouble 19 b, *t* truce 54, *t* a turn 52, *t* upon oneself 18, *t* the way 25 b, *t* on one's way 25 c, *t* well 42, *t* (to) wife 14 b, *t* wing 24 c, *t* to wing 74 b, *t* with 75, *t* with one 59 b, c.

**Take** (tēik), *sb.* Also 6 tayke, 9 *Sc.* and *north. dial.* tak, takke: cf. TACK *sb.*[2] [f. TAKE *v.*]

**1.** †**a.** = TACK *sb.*[2] 2, a lease of land or of a farm for a term of years. *Obs.*

**1511** *Test. Ebor.* (Surtees) V. 24, I will that my wif & my childre have my take in my fermhold in Kendale. **1542** *Ibid.* VI. 157 Also I give to my wif my take of yeres of the parsonadge of Kellyngton. **1599** *Knaresb. Wills* (Surtees) I. 220 All the tayke of my farmehold to bringe up my children withall.

**b.** The act of taking or leasing (land); the land taken; a holding; cf. TACK *sb.*[2] 2 b. *dial.*

**1805** DICKSON *Pract. Agric.* I. 80 The quantity of land he must till, would occupy so much of his time, that the *take* would..be injurious to him. *c* **1850** *Northampt. Dialect*, This is my neighbour's take that we are on now, and that yonder is Lord B.'s. **1896** *Daily News* 19 Sept. 2/5 A few new 'takes' have been at less money, but old tenants have had to be content with a 10, 5, and..1 per cent. allowance. **1905** TUCKWELL *Remin. Radical Parson* xi. 157 He..will increase his take, build a cottage on it through a building society [etc.].

**2.** That which is taken or received in payment, or as proceeds of some business or transaction; *pl.* takings, receipts. In quot. 1654, ? impost, contribution imposed.

**1654** *Nicholas Pap.* (Camden) II. 41 The take off 200,000 crownes is now sett, and the Emperor declared his present shallbe apart. **1891** *Daily News* 14 Sept. 2/1 Confident of large 'takes' for to-day and Sunday. **1892** STEVENSON *Across the Plains* 193 [They] depart, if the 'take' be poor, leaving debts behind them. **1905** *Westm. Gaz.* 15 June 11/1 The current [railway] returns include the long-distance Whitsuntide takes.

†**3.** A seizure; a spell of magic or witchcraft; enchantment. *Obs. rare.*

[Cf. TAKE *v.* 7, quot. 1598.] **1678** *Quack's Academy* 7 He has a Take upon him, or is Planet-struck.

**4.** 'Taking' or captivating quality, charm. *rare.*

**1794** MRS. A. M. BENNETT *Ellen* IV. 179 Her face..had that kind of harmony and take in it, which when it has once pleased, will not cease to do so.

**5.** An act of taking or capturing an animal, or (usually) a number of animals (esp. fish) at one time; also the quantity so caught; a catch.

**1753** *Scots Mag.* Aug. 422/1 There was a great take of herrings. **1851** MAYHEW *Lond. Labour* (1861) II. 60/1 The yearly 'take' of larks is 60,000. **1854** BADHAM *Halieut.* 339 Of late years..greater takes have been effected off those of New England alone, than from the great fishery of Newfoundland itself. **1859** BAIN *Emotions* x. 189 The pleasure of each successful throw..rendering it easy [for the angler] to go on for a long time without a take. **1876** SMILES *Sc. Natur.* vi. 101 The weather..gave promise of an abundant 'take' of moths. **1883** *Daily Tel.* 25 June 7/1 Small boats being used to ferry the takes of fish to the smacks or steamers.

**b.** The action or process of catching fish, etc.

**1854** H. MILLER *Sch. & Schm.* iii. (1858) 43 We..became knowing..about the take and curing of herrings. **1881** A. LANG *Library* 11 The 'take', as anglers say, is 'on' from half-past seven to half-past nine a.m.

**6.** An act, or the action, of taking (in general).

**1816–** [see GIVE AND TAKE 2, 3]. **1885** *Times* 25 May 9 At each take there is a certain amount of waste.

**b.** *Chess*, etc. The taking of a piece or pieces.

**1870** HARDY & WARE *Mod. Hoyle, Draughts* 107 Such a dashing 'take' as this would not be likely to happen in actual play. **1903** *Times, Lit. Suppl.* 31 July 236/3 A good problem seldom commences with a check or take.

**7.** *Printing.* A portion of copy taken at one time by a compositor to be set up in type; = TAKING *vbl. sb.* 5 c.

**1864** in WEBSTER. **1871** *Printers' Register* 6 Nov., The first 'take' of copy which fell to our share was about two and a half pages of 12 mo Long Primer. **1882** J. SOUTHWARD *Pract. Print.* (1884) 146 The compositor is bound to write his name on his copy, with a mark showing where he began to set..Each of these portions is..called a 'take'. **1890** W. J. GORDON *Foundry* 192 In the small hours of the morning..the last speech is coming in on relays of flimsy telegrams, and the compositors are working short 'takes' of half a dozen lines apiece.

**b.** The amount taken down at one time by each one of a staff of reporters.

**1872** J. S. JEANS *West. Worthies* 98 The take of reporters became very much shortened, until they now seldom exceed a quarter of an hour or twenty minutes.

[**Take**, error for FAKE, a coil of rope.

**1658** in PHILLIPS, whence in various later dicts.]

**Take-**, the verb-stem in combinations and phrases used as sbs. or adjs. (mostly *nonce-wds.*): **take-all**, local name in Australia for a disease in wheat; **take-down**, an act of taking down (in quot. in sense 80 b (*d*)); **take-downable** *a.*, capable of being taken down; **take-for-granted** *a.*, that takes something for granted, involving unproved assumptions; †**take-heed**, the action of taking heed, caution; a warning to take heed, a caution; **take-it-easy** *a.*, that takes things easily, easy-going; adapted for making oneself at ease, comfortable; **take-it-or-leave-it** *a.*, allowing acceptance or rejection; showing indifference; **take-leave**, *a.* of or pertaining to taking leave, parting, 'farewell'; *sb.* an act of taking leave, leave-taking; **take-on**, a state of 'taking on' (TAKE *v.* 84 j) or mental agitation, a 'taking'. See also TAKE-IN, TAKE-OFF, TAKE-UP.

**1880** *Silver's Handbk. Australia* 72 That terrible foe to wheat known as the *take-all in South Australia, has spread beyond the Adelaide plains. **1893** *Westm. Gaz.* 12 June 6/3 In the second division [of Cambridge boat-races] as many as six *take-downs were effected, First Trinity III going sandwich boat instead of Christ's [etc.]. **1815** LAMB *Let. to Southey* 6 May, It will be a *take-downable book on my shelf. **1833** COLERIDGE *Lett., to T. H. Green* (1895) 767, I feel a *take-for-granted faith in the dips and pointings of the needle. **1853** LYNCH *Self-Improv.* ii. 26 You must talk of many things in a take-for-granted style in order to talk at all to the purpose. **1611** COTGR., *Mesgarde*,..carelesnesse, lacke of good-*take-heed. **1622** FLETCHER & MASSINGER *Span. Curate* IV. v, I know ye want good diets,..And, in your pleasures, good take-heed. **1648** WARD (*title*) Mercurius Anti-Mechanicus, or the Simple Coblers Boy, with his Lap-full of Caveats (or Take-heeds). **1872** *Routledge's Ev. Boy's Ann.* 500/2 The good-humoured *take-it-easy South-Sea Island nature. **1897** *Westm. Gaz.* 24 June 4/2 The walls and roofs of this take-it-easy room were draped with broad stripes of scarlet and white bunting. **1897** MARY KINGSLEY *W. Africa* 251, I affected an easy *take-it-or-leave-it-manner, and looked on. **1902** *Monthly Rev.* Aug. 155 England..sets out her exhibits with a 'take-it-or-leave-it' air, with a disregard of their possibilities which seems almost wilful. **1799** MRS. J. WEST *Tale of Times* II. 93 In his *take-leave visit he made some further discoveries. *c* **1815** JANE AUSTEN *Persuas.* v, Going to almost every house in the parish, as a sort of take-leave. **1837** *Lett. fr. Madras* (1843) 81, I was prevented from finishing this..by take-leave visits, &c. **1893** *Cornh. Mag.* June 566 The governor is in a dreadful *take on about you. **1894** BARING-GOULD *Kitty Alone* III. 142 Zerah's..in a fine take-on.

**Takeable, takable** (tēi·kăb'l), *a.* [f. TAKE *v.* + -ABLE.] Capable of being taken; that may or can be taken; in various senses; in first quot., comprehensible, intelligible (see TAKE *v.* 46).

*c* **1449** PECOCK *Repr.* I. ii. 11 Which..is not takeable of mannis witt. **1665** BOYLE *Occas. Refl.* II. vi. (1675) 116 Necessary to the rendring these Medicines takable by me. **1803** *Hist. Europe* in *Ann. Reg.* 21/1 In the last war we had taken every thing that was takeable. **1826** *Examiner* 772/1 Every take-able seat in the house had been taken. **1893** *Temple Bar Mag.* XCVII. 608 It is the only one takable, and I take it.

**Take-in** (tēi·kˌiˈn), *sb.* (*a.*) *colloq.* [The verbal phrase *take in* used as sb. or adj.] An act of taking in (TAKE *v.* 82 o); a cheat, swindle, deception; a thing or person that takes one in, a 'fraud'.

**1778** MISS BURNEY *Evelina* (1791) I. xxi. 105, I find it's as arrant a take-in as ever I met with. **1814** JANE AUSTEN *Mansf. Park* v, What is this but a take in? **1818** *Blackw. Mag.* II. 398 There are..at least twenty take-ins (as they are called) for one true heiress. **1858** LYTTON *What will he do* I. xii, Comedians are such takes in.

**b.** *attrib* or *adj.* That takes in; deceptive.

**1819** *Metropolis* III. 119 Tales of a take-in match and a vicious mother-in-law.

**Takel, -ell**, obs. forms of TACKLE.

**Taken** (tēi·k'n), *ppl. a.* [pa. pple. of TAKE *v.*, where see Forms.] In various senses corresponding to those of TAKE *v.*, q. v.

*a* **1340** HAMPOLE *Psalter, Cant.* 522 Þe lyknyng of takyn prysuns. **1535** STEWART *Cron. Scot.* III. 430 The tane men als the takaris did exceid. **1561** *Reg. Privy Council Scot.* I. 177 Greit partis of the takin gudis wer disponit in Argyle. **1659** MILTON *Civ. Power* Wks. 1851 V. 331 If any man be offended at the conscientious liberty of another, it is a taken scandal not a given. **1742** YOUNG *Nt. Th.* v. 987 Some..stumble, and let fall the taken prize. **1831** SCOTT *Ct. Robt.* xxviii, Did not my heart throb in my bosom with all the agitation of a taken bird?

**b.** With adv. or advb. phr., as *taken-for-granted*, *taken-in*, *taken-on*, etc.: see TAKE *v.*

*a* **1586** SIDNEY *Arcadia* III. (1622) 377 Keeping still her late taken-on grauitie. **1585–7** T. ROGERS 39 *Art.* (Parker Soc.) 186 Our liturgies..they call foolishness of taken-on services. **1901** *Daily Chron.* 24 Dec. 7/1 The bitter cry of the average taken-in tenant, emitted from a chilly residence, mean in furniture. **1907** *Morn. Post* 12 Aug. 2/3 Many of our taken-for-granted notions are seen to be meaningless.

**Taken**, OE. and obs. northern f. TOKEN.

**Ta·ke-note.** A licence empowering the holder to explore for gold in a defined district.

**1889** *Daily News* 18 July 7/1 The cost of the take-note amounted altogether to 5*l.* It gave the licensee the right to explore for gold in a certain area for one year. **1895** *Westm. Gaz.* 4 Nov. 6/1 (Gold found in Wales) 'Take notes' of various areas have been secured.

**Take-off** (tēi·kˌǫ·f), *sb.* and *a.* [The verbal phrase *take off* (see TAKE *v.* 83) used as sb. or adj.]

**A.** *sb.* **1.** A thing that 'takes off' or detracts from something (see TAKE *v.* 83 k); a drawback.

**1826** MISS MITFORD *Village* Ser. II. 214 (*French Emigrants*) Notwithstanding these take-offs, our good duchess had still the air of a lady of rank. **1868** LD. R. GOWER *Remin.* (1883) I. xvi. 304 The only take-off to being perfectly happy is the state of my dearest mother's health.

**2.** An act of 'taking off' or mimicking (see TAKE *v.* 83 j); a mimic; a caricature. *colloq.*

**1855** ROBINSON *Whitby Gloss.*, A *tak off*, a descriptive burlesque...A mimic, or satirical person. **1884** G. H. BOUGHTON in *Harper's Mag.* Sept. 526/1 He trotted beside the car.., roaring with glee at his 'take off'.

**3.** The act of 'taking off', or springing from the ground, in leaping (see TAKE *v.* 83 n (*b*)); usually *transf.* a place or spot from which one takes or may take off. Also *fig.*

**1869** BLACKMORE *Lorna D.* x, Is she able to leap sir? There is a good take-off on this side of the brook. **1889** *Boy's Own Paper* 7 Sept. 780/3 It..also encourages the habit of judging the take-off with accuracy. **1905** *Westm. Gaz.* 15 May 4/1 The true basis of offensive strategy is to ensure a sound 'take-off'. **1906** *Ibid.* 27 Aug. 4/1 The Great Western adopted Milford Haven as the 'take-off' for its service of steamers to Ireland.

**4.** *Croquet.* A stroke made from contact with another ball so as to send one's own ball nearly or quite in the direction of aim, the other ball being moved only slightly or not at all.

**1874** J. D. HEATH *Croquet-Player* 39 This is a take-off, and a sharp tap is made. The direction C, in which the mallet is aimed, has approached very near to B, the direction to be taken by the striker's ball Y. *Ibid.* 57 When the latter either is likely to miss his partner, or will have a long take-off to separate you.

**B.** *attrib.* or *adj.* **1.** From which one 'takes off' or makes the spring in leaping: cf. A. 3.

**1889** *Boy's Own Paper* 7 Sept. 780/3 The ground on the further side of the take-off line. **1896** *Harper's Mag.* Apr. 731 It was a species of hurdle-racing, with the softest of take-off and landing sides [snow].

**2.** Applied to a part of mechanism for taking something off. *Take-off board*: see quots.

**1896** *British Printer* 138 The sheets should not be allowed to accumulate on the take-off board. **1907** *Cambr. Mod. Hist. Prospectus* 97 So soon as the whole sheet is clear of the take-off drum, flyers..waft the sheet through a semi-circular arc, and drop it on to the take-off board..fixed at the end of the press opposite that from which the sheet started.

**Taker** (tēi·kəɹ). Also 4–6 *Sc.* takar (5 -are, 6 taikar, takkar); 6 takere, tacker. [f. TAKE *v.* + -ER[1].] One who or that which takes.

**1.** One who takes, in various senses of the verb.

**1486** *Act* 3 *Hen. VII*, c. 2 Where Wymmen..been oft tymes taken by mysdoers [etc.] and after maried to such mysdoers..Such mysdoers, takers, and procuratours to the same [etc.]. **1514** in *Eng. Hist. Rev.* (1900) XV. 450 The payne sessed as well to the Taker as to the gever. **1552** ABP. HAMILTON *Catech.* (1884) 11 Takaris of our mekil mail or farme, to the herschipe of the tenentis. **1579–80** NORTH *Plutarch* (1676) 203 We read of Alcibiades, that he was a great taker, and would be corrupted with Money. **1602** MARSTON *Ant. & Mel.* I. Wks. 1856 I. 13 A great tobacco taker too. **1615** G. SANDYS *Trav.* 66 The Turkes are also incredible takers of Opium. **1737** CHAMBERLAYNE *St. Gt. Brit.* (ed. 33) II. 93 Layers and takers of paper on and from the rolling-presses. **1875** JOWETT *Plato* (ed. 2) I. 101 The best taker to pieces of words of this sort. **1885** *Law Times* 7 Feb. 266/1 The taker of a railway ticket must know what is on the face of it.

**2.** *spec.* †**a.** One who takes another into his protection, etc.: cf. TAKE *v.* 14. *Obs.*

*a* **1325** *Prose Psalter* xlv[i]. 7 Þe Lord of vertuz ys wyþ vs; our taker [Vulg. *susceptor*] ys God of Jacob. *Ibid.* liii[i]. 4 Our Lord is taker of my soule.

**b.** One who captures or seizes; a captor, seizer, catcher, apprehender: cf. TAKE *v.* 2.

*c* **1375** *Sc. Leg. Saints* xxxi. (*Eugenia*) 512 [A lynx] Quhen hir qwhelpis are tan hir fra, To chas þe takaris, þaim to sla. **1454** *Cal. Anc. Rec. Dublin* (1889) 281 Halfe of that ransom to the takerys, and the othir halfe to the courte. *c* **1511** *1st Eng. Bk. Amer.* (Arb.) Introd. 35/1 They be good takers of fysshe. **1611** SPEED *Hist. Gt. Brit.* IX. xv. (1623) 785 The King..had promised a thousand marks to his taker. *c* **1650** DENHAM *Old Age* 196 Takers of cities, conquerors in war. **1807** G. CHALMERS *Caledonia* I. III. iv. 451 A searcher, and taker of thieves, and limmers. **1884** I. BLIGH in *Lillywhite's Cricket Ann.* 7 Principal takers of wickets.

†**c.** An officer who took or exacted supplies of necessaries for the sovereign: = PURVEYOR 3. *Obs.*

1444 *Rolls of Parlt.* V. 115/1 That no man of this Roialme have Takers but oonlye the Kyng and the Quene. 1519 *Interl. Four Elements* in Hazl. *Dodsley* I. 24 As for capons ye can get none, The king's taker took up each one. 1596 Nashe *Saffron Walden* 62 Let all the droppings of my pen bee seazed vpon by the Queenes Takers for Tarre to dresse ships with. 1619 Dalton *Country Just.* xliv. (1630) 103 Offences of Purveyors, Takers,..or other ministers for the King's Majestie.

**d.** One who takes something from another by force or wrongfully; a robber, thief, plunderer, pilferer; hence, a literary plunderer, a plagiarist. *Obs.* or merged in the general sense.

1500–20 Dunbar *Poems* xvii. 43 Grit men for taking and oppressioun Ar sett full famous at the Sessioun, And peur takaris ar hangit hie. 1561 T. Norton *Calvin's Inst.* Pref., As euell as a violent taker or (if you will) a robber. 1609 Rowlands *Dr. Merrie-man* 3 Sirrah sayes one, stand, and your Purse deliuer; I am a taker, thou must be a giuer. 1687 M. Clifford *Notes Dryden* ii. 6 Pray hear what Famianus Strada says of such Takers as Mr. Dryden. 1818 Scott *Hrt. Midl.* xxix, Robin Hood's dead and gwone, but there be takers yet in the vale of Bever.

**e.** (*a*) One who takes possession, esp. of land: often with *first* or *next*.

1766 Blackstone *Comm.* II. i. 9 Property, both in lands and moveables, being thus originally acquired by the first taker, ..it remains in him, by the principles of universal law, till such time as he does some other act which shews an intention to abandon it. *Ibid.* xviii. 275 The next taker is entitled to enter regularly. 1884 Sir J. W. Chitty in *Law Rep.* 26 Chanc. Div. 548 The absolute interest which the sixth Earl, as first taker, acquired.

(*b*) One who takes a lease of a farm, a mine, etc.; a lessee or tenant.

1778 Pryce *Min. Cornub.* 188 When the adventurers thus set a Mine to farm, they oblige the Taker or Tributor to keep the Mine in good repair. 1805 Forsyth *Beauties Scotl.* I. 535 The takers grant bill with a surety for the rent.

(*c*) In *Derbyshire Lead Mines*, A miner who takes possession of a mere, after the 'founder' has taken his mere (cf. *taker-mere* in 4 b).

1601 *High Peak Art.* in Mander *Derbysh. Min. Gloss.* (1824) 130 Where any Miner doth take and possess any fresh ground.., and does work the same to the knowledge of any other, who before such takers aforesaid were or pretended to be possessed of the same ground as taker of a Forefield for an old founder. 1747 Hooson *Miner's Dict.*, *Taker* [is] He that takes a Mear or Mears, from him that is the Founder; several Men may take one after another, if they think it may be worth their while, and then the Mears so taken go by some Name or other, as A's Taker Mear, or B's Taker Mear, or their second or third Taker Mear, to distinguish them from the Founders, and one Taker from another. 1753 Chambers *Cycl. Supp.*, *Next taker*, among miners, is he that hath the next meer in possession.

**f.** One who accepts a bet.

1810 *Sporting Mag.* XXXV. 245 Two to one were offered ..but there were no takers. 1873 *Standard* 30 Sept., The betting gradually veered round with even money offered on W. Beckwith with no takers.

**g.** *Foreign taker*: a former officer of the City of London appointed to supervise some of the markets held in the open streets and to attend to their clearing up. *Obs.* exc. *Hist.*

*c* 1690 in Bohun *Privil. Lond.* (1723) 136 Richard Robinson the present Foreign taker and Yeoman of Newgate Market. 1720 Strype *Stow's Surv. Lond.* II. 398 Formerly, before the great Fire..there were these Officers, viz. a Serjeant and Yeoman of the Channel, and Yeoman of Newgate Market, and Foreign Taker, whose Office was to sweep and make clean the said Streets, where the Market People resorted, and to carry away the Soil thereof, and to furnish the Market People with Boards and such like Accommodations. ..But since Markets are removed out of the Streets..these Officers retain only the Names.

†**3.** Applied to the nippers or claws of a scorpion, etc. *Obs.*

1608 Topsell *Serpents* (1658) 752 A flamant Scorpion.. hath tongs and takers very solid and strong, like the Gramnel or Crevish. 1688 R. Holme *Armoury* II. 199/1.

**4.** *Comb.* **a.** With adverbs, forming compound agent-nouns corresponding to adverbial combinations of the verb (see Take *v.* 76–90), as *taker-away*, *-down*, *-out*, etc.: **taker-in**, one who takes in, in various senses (see Take *v.* 82); also, an apparatus which takes in or receives something, e.g. the cotton in a carding-machine (quot. 1879); **taker-off**, one who takes off, in various senses (see Take *v.* 83); also, an apparatus for taking something off, in a machine (cf. Take-off, B. 2); **taker-up**, one who or that which takes up, in various senses (see Take *v.* 90); *spec.* †(*a*) one who takes another under his charge or protection, a patron, guardian (*obs.*); †(*b*) one who 'raises' the psalm in church, a precentor (*Sc. obs.*); †(*c*) a member of a gang of swindlers: see quot. 1591 [2] (*obs.*); (*d*) a purchaser or purveyor of commodities; (*e*) a receiver of money paid, as rent, etc.; (*f*) one who takes possession of an estate; (*g*) a labourer who gathers up the grass just mown; (*h*) something that occupies time, space, etc.

*a* 1804 W. Gilpin *Serm.* II. xxxvii. (R.), God..the giver, and *taker away of all earthly things. 1848 Mrs. Gaskell *M. Barton* xxiii, The taker-away of life. 1836 T. Hook *G. Gurney* I. 105 A practised *taker-in of credulous men. 1839 C. Bronte in Mrs. Gaskell *Life* viii. (1857) 127 A straw-bonnet maker, or a taker-in of plain work. 1879 J. Robertson in *Cassell's Techn. Educ.* IV. 273/2 Apart from the slight degree of combing..the only duty required of the 'taker-in' is indicated in its name. 1902 Cutcliffe Hyne *Thompson's Progr.* 70 'Who measured the pieces?' 'The taker-in'. 1825 J. Nicholson *Operat. Mechanic* 380 K is the doffer or *taker-off, having affixed to it the steel comb called the doffing-plate. 1830 G. Colman *Random Rec.*, *Dr. Graham*, A spurious kind of imitation which may account for the number of takers-off at secondhand. 1888 J. Southward in *Encycl. Brit.* XXIII. 706/1 The [printed] sheets are removed singly by an attendant called a taker-off, or by a mechanical automatic arrangement called a flyer. 1883 S. C. Hall *Retrospect* I. 255 A taker-off of peculiarities, he never sought to make a mock of deformity. 1388 Wyclif *Ps.* xli[i]. 10 [9] Y schal seie to God: Thou art my *takere vp [Vulg. *susceptor*]. 1550 *Act* 3 & 4 *Edw. VI*, c. 16 § 10 Such childe to be vsed..to what labor..soeuer the said taker vp or Mr or Maistres shall appointe him. 1578 in Spottiswood *Hist. Ch. Scot.* VI. (1677) 297 Takers up of Psalms, and other Officers of the Church. 1591 Percivall *Sp. Dict.*, *Recogedor*, a gatherer, a taker vp, *collector*, *receptor*. 1591 Greene *Disc. Coosnage* (1859) 8 Foure persons were required to performe their coosning commodity. The Taker up, the Verser, the Barnard, and the Butter...The Taker up seemeth a skilful man in al things, who hath by long travail learned..to insinuate himselfe into a man's acquaintance. 1603 *Eng. Mourn. Garm.* in *Select. fr. Harl. Misc.* (1793) 205 One of her own servants, a taker-up of provision. 1620 E. Blount *Horæ Subs.* 120 It is..a taker vp of time that may be better disposed. 1622 Malynes *Anc. Law-Merch.* 390 The Taker vp of the money at London, payeth for twelue pence the said marke of 13¾ pence, at two or three moneths Time in Scotland. *a* 1649 Drumm. of Hawth. *Hist. Jas. III*, Wks. (1711) 50 Taker up of the rents of that earldom. 1715 *Maryland Laws* vi. (1723) 20 The said Commissioners..shall..invest the Taker up, and Builder..with an Estate of Inheritance, in the said Lot. 1848 *Jrnl. R. Agric. Soc.* IX. II. 501 The takers-up follow the mower.

**b.** *attrib.* **Taker-mere**, in *Derbysh. Lead-mines*, a 'mere' or portion of ground allotted to a 'taker' (2 e (*c*); cf. *founder-meer* s. v. Founder *sb.*[5] 3).

1653 Manlove *Lead Mines* 46 But yet a difference may be taken clear, Betwixt a founder, and a taker meer. 1747 [see 2 e (*c*) above]. 1851 Tapping *Gloss. to Manlove* s. v. *Meer*, A *taker meer* was the meer formerly allotted by custom to any person who chose to have one set out to him after those of the founder and farmer had been allotted.

**Take-up** (tē̆·kʌ̆p), *sb.* (*a.*) [The verbal phrase *take up* (see Take *v.* 90) used as sb. or adj.] The act of taking up, or a contrivance for taking up.

**1.** The act of 'taking up' or drawing together the stuff so as to form 'gathers' in a dress; *concr.* one of such 'gathers'.

1825 Jamieson, *Tak-up*, *Take-up*, the name given to a tuck in female dress. 1880 *Plain Hints Needlework* 19 The take-up of each gather should be..neatly done.

**2. a.** A device in a machine for tightening a band, rope, etc. **b.** A device in a sewing-machine for drawing the thread so as to tighten the stitch.

1877 Knight *Dict. Mech.* 2483/2 The independent take-up is one which acts in its own time without being actuated by the needle-bar. 1888 *Sci. Amer.* 3 Mar. 138/2 A sewing machine, and a take up and tension for sewing machines, form the subject of three patents.

**3.** In a loom or other machine, the process of winding up the stuff already woven or treated; *concr.* the part of the mechanism by which this is done. Also *attrib.* or *adj.*, as in *take-up motion*.

1877 Knight *Dict. Mech.* 2483/2 The let-off is the paying off of the yarn from the beam, and proceeds coincidently with the take-up. 1884 *Ibid.* Suppl., *Take Up Motion*.., a device for automatically winding the tissue on to the cloth beam.

**4.** The part between the smoke-box and the bottom of the funnel of a marine engine boiler.

1838 *Civil Eng. & Arch. Jrnl.* I. 225/1 If the pressure continues..the water rises through the take-up into the fire, and extinguishes it. 1888 A. E. Seaton *Marine Eng.* (ed. 7) 365 The part between the smoke-box and funnel is called the 'uptake' or 'take-up'.

**Takil, -ill**, obs. Sc. forms of Tackle.

‖**Takin** (tā·kin). [Native name in Mishmi.] A horned ruminant (*Budorcas taxicolor*) of south-eastern Tibet on the northern frontier of Assam.

1850 B. H. Hodgkin in *Jrnl. Asiat. Soc. Bengal* XIX. 65 The large, massive and remarkable animal, denominated Tákin by the Mishmis, and Kin by the Khamtis, is one of the group of Bovine Antelopes. 1893 Lydekker *Horns & Hoofs* iv. 142 No English sportsman has ever shot a takin. 1909 *Daily Chron.* 23 June 5/5 The Zoological Society has just received..a fine young example of the takin, which, next to the okapi, is the rarest and least known of the ruminants... Takins are heavily built and powerful animals, an adult male standing three and a half feet high at the shoulder.

**Takin**, obs. Sc. form of Token.

**Taking** (tē̆·kiŋ), *vbl. sb.* [f. Take *v.* + -ing [1].]

**I.** Simple senses. * *The action or condition expressed by the verb* Take.

†**1.** Touching, touch: see Take *v.* 1. *Obs. rare.*

1340 [see Take *v.* 1].

**2.** Capture, seizure (in warfare, etc.); apprehension, arrest; catching (of fish or other animals): see Take *v.* 2, etc.

*c* 1330 R. Brunne *Chron.* (1810) 222 After þe takyng of Kilyngworth castelle. 1456 Sir G. Haye *Law Arms* (S.T.S.) 53 He herd the newis..of his brothir taking. 1494 *Act* 11 *Hen. VII*, c. 23 The same heryinges..shuld be of on tyme taking and salting. 1534 in 10th *Rep. Hist. MSS. Comm.* App. v. 406 If the Kinges Bayleffe be present at the takinge of the same dettor. 1628 Sir S. D'Ewes *Jrnl.* (1783) 43 Portsmouth (where he was imprisoned immediatelie upon his taking). 1748 *Anson's Voy.* III. viii. 370 The taking of the Manila galeon. 1869 Tozer *Highl. Turkey* II. 228 The taking of Adrianople by the Turks.

†**b.** A seizure or attack of disease, *esp.* a stroke of palsy or the like; also, enchantment; blasting, malignant influence: see Take *v.* 7, *sb.* 3. *Obs.*

1533 Elyot *Cast. Helthe* (1541) 50 Palseys, called of the vulgare people, takynges. 1559 Morwyng *Evonym.* 332 The same resisteth the taking, as they cal it, or inchantment. 1605 Shaks. *Lear* III. iv. 61 Blisse thee from Whirle-Windes, Starre-blasting, and taking. 1639 T. de Gray *Compl. Horsem.* 69 The takings, sleeping-evill, madnesse, and the like.

**3.** The physical act of possessing oneself of anything, of receiving, accepting, and related senses: see Take *v.* 12, etc.

13.. *Cursor M.* 28578 (Cott.) Þirkin sinnes..ar..for-giuen, Wit worthi takyng o þe fode O godds aun fles and blode. *c* 1380 Wyclif *Sel. Wks.* III. 345 Aftir takyng of þe Holi Goost. *c* 1460 Fortescue *Abs. & Lim. Mon.* xiii. (1885) 142 Wich maner off takynge is callid robbery. 1500–20 Dunbar *Poems* xvii. 1, 5 Eftir geving I speik of taking... In taking sowld discretioun be. 1505 *Sel. Cas. Crt. Star Chamber* (Selden) 221 The Town of Glowcestre is fre of all customs and takynges at Worcestre aforeseide. 1526 *Pilgr. Perf.* (W. de W. 1531) 54 Be not dronken through ouermoche takyng of wyne. 1651 Hobbes *Leviath.* II. xxii. 122 A taking of the Sword out of the hand of the Soveraign. 1656 H. Phillips *Purch. Patt.* (1676) 1 The letting and taking of Leases. 1660 Wood *Life* Dec. (O. H. S.) I. 359 Their taking of notes at sermons. 1714 Mandeville *Fab. Bees* (1725) I. 415 The taking of Snuff and smoaking of Tobacco. 1893 Hodges *Elem. Photogr.* (1907) 115 The taking of portraits. 1896 *Law Times* C. 408/1 The date of the taking of the census..was correctly stated.

**b.** Mental apprehension or perception (*obs.*); mental acceptance or reception; estimation.

1398 Trevisa *Barth. De P. R.* II. x. (1495) b vj b/1 God..is aboue vnmateryall & aboue worldly takynge. 1568 in *Liturg. Serv. Q. Eliz.* (1847) 517 With pacient takinge and quiett acceptation of this syckness. *a* 1639 Whateley *Prototypes* I. xxi. 253 Manifested in his sorrowful taking of her death.

**4. a.** Condition, situation, state, plight (in unfavourable sense). Only in phr. *in*, † *at* (*a*) *taking*, often with defining adj. *Obs.* exc. *Sc.*

1522 Skelton *Why not to Court* 933 He is at suche takynge. 1542 Udall *Erasm. Apoph.* 158 Wheras thou art in suche takyng, canst fynd in thyn herte to liue? 1592 Lyly *Midas* I. ii, These boyes be droonk! I would not be in your takings. 1635 R. Bolton *Comf. Affl. Consc.* iii. (ed. 2) 15 In what a taking was Job. 1662–3 Pepys *Diary* 12 Jan., The poor boy was in a pitiful taking and pickle. 1715 *Wodrow Corr.* (1843) I. 26 Persons, who have real scruples at oaths, are in a miserable taking. 1837 Mrs. Carlyle *Lett.* (1883) I. 65 We are all in sad taking with influenza.

**b.** *spec.* A disturbed or agitated state of mind; excited condition, passion. (Const. as in a.)

1577 Hanmer *Anc. Eccl. Hist.* (1619) 317 Valens, vnderstanding of this, was in a sore taking. 1581 Pettie tr. *Guazzo's Civ. Conv.* III. (1586) 159 b, Manie excellent and worthie men..comming before princes..haue plainely shewed in what troublesome taking they haue bene in. 1598 Shaks. *Merry W.* III. iii. 191. 1676 Etheredge *Man of Mode* III. iii, By this time your Mother is in a fine taking. 1797–8 Jane Austen *Sense & Sens.* xxxvii, Lord! what a taking poor Mr. Edward will be in when he hears of it. 1874 T. Hardy *Madding Crowd* xxx, You must not notice my being in a taking just now.

** *That which is taken.*

**5. a.** That which is received or gained; *esp.* in *pl.*, the receipts or earnings of merchants, tradesmen, or workmen.

1632 Massinger *City Madam* II. i, Some needy shopkeeper who surveys His every-day takings. 1662 Gurnall *Chr. in Arm.* III. verse 18. I. lii. (1669) 417/2 To mend their takings in their shop. 1851 Mayhew *Lond. Labour* I. 120/2 The weekly 'takings' of the ten thousand men and their families. 1885 G. Denman in *Law Rep.* 29 Ch. Div. 469 A charge upon the property, or the takings, or the profits of the concern.

**b.** That which is captured; *esp.* the fish or other animals caught at one time, a capture, a catch.

1809 Malkin *Gil Blas* v. i. ⁋ 67 Heyday! madam, your third husband dispatched already? You must be a most deadly taking. 1855 Robinson *Whitby Gloss.* s. v., 'A rare takking o' fish', a good catch, or a heavy haul.

**c.** *Printing.* = Take *sb.* 7.

1808 C. Stower *Printer's Gram.* 467 When the companionship are ready for their first takings of copy. 1875 *Ure's Dict. Arts* III. 640 The MS...is then handed to a clicker, or foreman of a companionship, or certain number of compositors, each of whom has a taking of copy, or convenient portion of MS., given to him, to be set up in type.

**II.** Combinations.

**6.** With adv. or advb. phr., expressing the action of similar combinations of the verb in various senses (see Take *v.* 76–90): as *taking away*, *back*, *down*, *for granted*, *in*, *off* (also attrib., esp. in sense 83 n (*b*) of the verb), *on* (in quot. = undertaking, enterprise: cf. Take *v.* 84 d), *out*, *up* (in quot. 1683 *concr.* that which is taken up).

1382 Wyclif *Isa.* xlii. 22 Thei ben maad in to raueyn,.. in to *taking awei [1388 in to rauyschyng]. 1617 Hieron *Wks.* II. 249 Those gifts..are lyable to taking away. 1629 W. Bedell in *Ussher's Lett.* (1686) 402 Mr. Usher's sudden taking away,..admonishes me to work while the day lasts. 1487–8 *Durham Acc. Rolls* (Surtees) 651 Pro le *takyngdowne et le riddyng fundi dicti cancelli, xxiijs. iiij*d*. 1864 *Gd. Words* 317/2 One hour of taking down makes about six hours' work in copying. 1876 Lowell *Among my Bks.* Ser. II. 174 A childlike simplicity and *taking-for-granted which win our confidence. 1879 Chr. G. Rossetti *Seek & F.* 248 Sloth, with its vicious allies of unpunctuality,..half measures, baseless taking for granted, guess-work. 1598 B. JONSON *Ev. Man in Hum.* III. i, The best leaguer that ever I beheld..except the *taking in of—what do you call it? 1603 KNOLLES *Hist. Turks* (1638) 184 Neither is this taking in of the country of Carasina to be accounted a small conquest. 1707 MORTIMER *Husb.* (1721) I. 27 Parcels of Land that would pay well for the taking in. 1605 SHAKS. *Macb.* I. vii. 20 His Vertues Will pleade like Angels, Trumpet-tongu'd against The deepe damnation of his *taking off. 1683 MOXON *Mech. Exerc., Printing* xxii. ⁋ 3 Having Destributed that Taking off he makes another Taking off as before. 1719 DE FOE *Crusoe* (1840) I. iv. 67 Thou art not worth..the taking off of the ground. 1755 *Connoisseur* No. 57 ⁋ 3 Imitations of..well-known characters..to which they have given the appellation of taking-off. 1852 SURTEES *Sponge's Sp. Tour* ix, [The] horse..had scrambled out of the brook on the taking-off side. 1881 *Times* 14 Feb. 4/2 The taking off at the jumps was awkward, and the landing more ugly still. 1894 H. NISBET *Bush Girl's Rom.* 180 If a man or woman was to be spared it was..because their taking off was a waste of powder and lead. 1898 L. STEPHEN *Stud. of Biogr.* I. vii. 230 A mere taking-off place for a flight into the clouds. 1422 tr. *Secreta Secret., Priv. Priv.* 180 That tokenyth hardynesse of herte, grete *takynge on, and stowtesse. 1466 *Paston Lett.* II. 268 To the glaser for *takyn owte of ii. panys of the wyndows. 1565 *Taking up [see TAKE *v.* 90 c (*b*)]. *a* 1649 DRUMM. OF HAWTH. *Declar.*, etc., Wks. (1711) 208 The treaty..discharging all taking up of arms against the kingdom. 1683 MOXON *Mech. Exerc., Printing* xxii. ⁋ 3 Now he has his Taking up in his Hand, with the Face of his Letter towards him. 1798 in Picton *L'pool Munic. Rec.* (1886) II. 224 A constant yearly taking up of money upon new bonds. 1841 *Civil Eng. & Arch. Jrnl.* IV. 318/1 Gearing for producing..the 'taking-up' or traversing motion' of the plank during the operation of sawing.

**7.** Attributive Combs., as *taking-day*; *taking-screen* (see TAKE *v.* 33 b).

1836 R. FURNESS *Astrologer* I. Wks. (1858) 139 On Takindays, when wit and ale were free. 1897 *Pop. Sc. Monthly* Nov. 138 The viewing [screens] differ from the taking screens. 1907 *Westm. Gaz.* 24 Aug. 14/2 This positive is then mounted in contact with a viewing-screen ruled in precisely the same way as the taking-screen.

**Ta·king**, *ppl. a.* [f. as prec. + -ING [2].] That takes, in various senses: see the verb.

**1.** Seizing, receiving; getting something into one's possession; rapacious. *rare.*

1483 *Cath. Angl.* 377/2 Takynge, *capax, accipiens, & cetera.* 1598 *Fam. Vict. Hen. V*, ii. 16, I dare not call him theefe, but sure he is one of these taking fellowes. 1835 *Court Mag.* VI. 168/2 There were taking men, who imposed upon him at pleasure; for he did not prosecute.

**2.** That takes the fancy or affection; captivating, engaging, alluring, fascinating, charming, attractive. (The most usual sense: now *colloq.*)

1605 B. JONSON *Volpone* I. i, That colour Shall make it much more taking. 1665 BOYLE *Occas. Refl.* VI. x. (1848) 376 He will ever consider the taking'st Notions he can frame of vertue, more as Engagements to it, than Arguments of it. *a* 1721 PRIOR *Songs* xv. 11 Phillis has such a taking way, She charms my very soul. 1757 FOOTE *Author* I. Wks. 1799 I. 137 You must provide me with three taking titles for these pamphlets. 1824 DIBDIN *Libr. Comp.* 771 The plates ..are bright, spirited, and very 'taking'. 1882 PEBODY *Eng. Journalism* xix. 143 The secret of immediate success in a public writer is said to be mediocre ideas and a taking style.

**3.** Seizing or affecting injuriously; † blasting, pernicious (*obs.*); infectious, 'catching'. *rare.*

1605 SHAKS. *Lear* II. iv. 166 Strike her yong bones, You taking Ayres, with Lamenesse. *a* 1620 FLETCHER & MASSINGER *False One* IV. iii, I am yet too taking for your company. 1636 FEATLY *Clavis Myst.* xvii. 220 The diseases of the mind are more taking than the diseases of the body.

**4.** With adverbs, as *taking-away, -in, -off*, etc.: see TAKE *v.* 76–90. (Here often blending with the vbl. sb.)

1530 PALSGR. 279/1 Takyng away, *ablatif.* 1841 SAVAGE *Dict. Printing* 791 Boys are employed in machine printing to take away the sheets as they are printed..; this is also styled Taking-off, and the boys taking-off boys. 1882 *Worc. Exhib. Catal.* iii. 38 Printing Machine with..automatic taking-off apparatus. 1884 SOUTHWARD *Pract. Printing* 462 When printed,..[the sheets] are deposited in a pile on the taking-off board. 1886 J. PATON in *Encycl. Brit.* XX. 845/1 The twisted twine is drawn off..and is wound on taking-up bobbins.

Hence **Ta·kingly** *adv.*, in a taking manner; engagingly, alluringly, attractively; **Ta·kingness**, taking quality or character, engagingness, alluringness, attractiveness.

1607 BEAUMONT *Woman Hater* IV. ii, I will gather my self together with my best phrases, and so I shall discourse in some sort *takingly. 1681 FLAVEL *Meth. Grace* xxix. 510 This will represent religion very beautifully and takingly to such as are yet strangers to it. *a* 1711 KEN *Psyche* Poet. Wks. 1721 IV. 161 Verse, by which Lust is takingly instill'd. 1656 *Artif. Handsom.* 41 Outward adornings..have something in them of a complaisance and *takingnesse. 1890 J. H. STIRLING *Philos. & Theol.* i. 18 A simple takingness that is divine.

**Takk, takke,** obs. forms of TACK *sb.*[1, 2], *v.*[1]

**Takle, takul(l, -yl(l,** obs. forms of TACKLE.

**Taknyn, -ys, -yt,** etc.: see TOKEN *v.*

**Taky** (tē¹·ki), *a. colloq.* [f. TAKE *v.* (sense 10) + -Y: cf. *shaky*.] = TAKING *ppl. a.* 2.

1854 W. COLLINS *Hide & Seek* I. ix, Those two difficult and delicate operations in art, technically described as 'putting in taky touches, and bringing out bits of effect'.

**Takyn, -yng,** obs. forms of TOKEN.

**Tal,** obs. f. TALE, TALL. **Talagalla,** var. TALEGALLA. **Taland, -e**: see TALENT, TALON.

‖ **Talapoin** (tæ·lăpoin). Forms: 6 **tallipoie,** 7–8 **tallapoi(e,** 7 **talapoi, talopoy, talipoy, telapoi**; 8 **talopoin,** 9 **telapoon,** 7– **talapoin.** [ad. Pg. *talapão*, ad. Talaing (Old Peguan) *tala pôi* 'my lord', the title of a Buddhist monk, corresponding (in use) to Burmese *p'ôngyî*. (Sir R. C. Temple in *Indian Antiq.* XXXIX. 159.)]

**1.** A Buddhist monk or priest, properly of Pegu; extended by Europeans to those of Siam, Burmah, and other Buddhist countries.

1586 R. FITCH in Hakl. *Voy.* (1599) II. 261 There are..many goodly houses for the Tallipoies to preach in. 1613 PURCHAS *Pilgrimage* (1614) 464 They..hidde themselues in woods and wildernesses, and some turned Talopoyes: so they call their religious persons. 1634 SIR T. HERBERT *Trav.* 195 The Priests [of Pegu] are called Tallapois. 1696 OVINGTON *Voy. Surat* 593 These Religious they call Telapoi, who are not unlike Mendicant Fryers, living upon the Alms of the People. 1713 BERKELEY *Guard.* No. 3 ⁋ 3 The Talapoins of Siam have a book of scripture written by Sommonocodom. 1752 HUME *Ess. & Treat.* (1809) II. 463 The excessive penances of the Brachmans and Talapoins. 1800 *Misc. Tr.* in *Asiat. Ann. Reg.* 43/1 Those philosophical begging monks, known under the name of Talapoins, who, in the first century of the Christian æra, emigrated from India, and introduced the religion of Buddha, or Goutama, in Pegu, Siam, China, and Japan. 1858 BP. BIGANDET *Life Gaudama* (1866) 483 The Phongies, or Budhist Monks, sometimes called Talapoins.

**2.** *Zool.* (In full *talapoin monkey*.) A small West African monkey, *Cercopithecus talapoin*.

1774 GOLDSM. *Nat. Hist.* (1776) IV. 234 The eighth is the Talapoin;..distinguished..by its beautiful variety of green, white, and yellow hair. 1827 GRIFFITH tr. *Cuvier's Anim. Kingd., Syn. Mam.* 11 The Talapoin Monkey..inhabits Africa. 1868 *Museum Nat. Hist.* I. 30 The mone (*Cercopithecus Mona*) is a species nearly allied to the talapoin. 1896 *List Anim. Zool. Soc.* 7 *Cercopithecus talapoin*.. Talapoin Monkey. *Hab.* West Africa.

**Talar** (tē¹·lăɹ). [ad. L. *tālār-is*, f. *tālus* ankle: see -AR. So Ger. *talar*.] A long garment or robe, reaching down to the ankles.

1738 [G. SMITH] *Curious Relat.* II. 363 A Blackmore on Horseback, dress'd in white Sattin, with a Scarlet Velvet Talar, embroidered with black Velvet. 1850 LEITCH tr. *C. O. Müller's Anc. Art* § 351 *note*, Zeus..has, like an Asiatic monarch, a sceptre and a broad magnificent talar. 1864 ENGEL *Mus. Anc. Nat.* 334 He who led their devotions was a young man in a Polish talar.

‖ **Talaria** (tălē³·riă), *sb. pl. Anc. Rom. Mythol.* Also 7 in Eng. form **talaries.** [L., neut. pl. of *tālāris*: see prec.; *lit.* things pertaining to the ankles.] Winged sandals or small wings attached to the ankles of some of the deities, esp. Mercury. Hence **Tala·ria'd** *a.*, wearing talaria.

1593 G. HARVEY *Pierce's Super.* Wks. (Grosart) II. 253 Euerlasting shooes, like the talaria of Mercury. 1656 BLOUNT *Glossogr.*, *Talaries*, shooes with wings, which Mercury wore, as Poets feigne. 1866 J. B. ROSE tr. *Ovid's Metam.* 26 Doffed the talaria and the helm, retains Caduceus to his aid. *Ibid.* 324 Thence sprung Autolychus, ingenious thief, To the talaria'd god.

† **Tala·rian,** *a. Obs. rare.* [f. L. *talāri-s* (see TALAR) + -AN.] Of or pertaining to the ankles; reaching down to the ankles.

1671 H. M. tr. *Erasm. Colloq.* 436 Prelates did ordain that Clergy men should wear Talarian coats, that is, coats hanging down to their ancles. *a* 1693 *Urquhart's Rabelais* III. vii, A colour never used in Talarian garments.

**Talaric** (tălæ·rik), *a.* [irreg. f. as prec. + -IC.] = prec.

1853 W. B. BARKER *Lares & Penates* 200 A draped female figure, apparently Venus, in a talaric tunic. 1887 B. V. HEAD *Hist. Numorum* 177 A woman clothed in a sleeveless talaric chiton with diploïs.

**Talaunde, Talaunt(e,** obs. ff. TALON, TALENT.

**Talbanar, Talbart, -bert, Talberone,** obs. Sc. ff. TABORER, TABARD, TABORN.

**Talbot** (tǭ·lbət). [Understood to be derived from the ancient Eng. family name *Talbot*: see quot. 1906 in sense 1; but evidence is wanting.

Chaucer has *Talbot* as the name of an individual dog; and in quot. *c* 1449, John Talbot, Earl of Shrewsbury, is called 'Talbott oure goode dogge' (in allusion to the badge of the family: see sense 2); but it is not clear what is the nature of the connexion between these applications, or which of the senses 1 and 2 was the earlier.

*c* 1386 CHAUCER *Nun's Pr. T.* 562 Colle oure dogge, and Talbot and Gerland. *c* 1449 in *Pol. Poems* (Rolls) II. 222 He is bownden that oure dore shuld kepe, That is Talbott oure goode dogge.]

**1.** Name of a variety of hound, formerly used for tracking and hunting; a large white or light-coloured hound, having long hanging ears, heavy jaws, and great powers of scent.

1562 LEIGH *Armorie* 96 b, A Talbot with coller and Lyame, these houndes pursue the foote of pray, by sente of yᵉ same, orels by yᵉ bloud thereof. 1615 MARKHAM *Country Contentm.* I. 5 The black hound, the black laund,..or the milk white, which is the true Talbot, are best for the string or lyam, for they doe delight most in blood, and haue a naturall inclination to hunt dry-foot. 1654 WASE tr. *Gratii Falisci Cynegeticon* B ij b, Then match them well; and thus a noble seed Derive, these parents will your Talbot [L. *Metagonta*] breed. 1668 CHARLETON *Onomast.* 23 *Sagax*, a Blood-hound, or Talbot. 1706 PHILLIPS (ed. Kersey), *Talbot*, a kind of Hound or Hunting-Dog. 1735 SOMERVILLE *Chase* I. 290 The bold Talbot kind Of these the prime, as white as Alpine snows. 1870 BLAINE *Encycl. Rur. Sports* § 1428 The talbot..is supposed to be the original stock from whence all the varieties of the scent hunting hounds are derived. 1906 *Blackw. Mag.* Sept. 381/1 The same white hounds were brought to England by the head of the Talbot family, and rapidly gaining credit for their qualities in the chase of the stag..were known as Talbots.

**2.** A representation of a hound or hunting-dog; *esp.* in *Her.* that which has been borne for many centuries by the Talbot family.

1491 *N. C. Wills* (Surtees 1908) 62 A standing cupp of silver parcell gilt with talbottes at the fete. 1537 *Will Geo. Talbot, Earl Shrewsbury* Ibid. 145, ij paier of pottes with flatt Talbottes upon the cover, ij paier of pottes with standing Talbottes upon the cover. 1562 [see 1]. 1603 DRAYTON *Bar. Wars* II. xxvii, Behold the Eagles, Lyons, Talbots, Beares, The Badges of your famous Ancestries. 1610 GUILLIM *Heraldry* III. xvi. 147 Hee beareth Or, a Fesse Dauncette, betweene three Talbottes passant, Sable, by the name of Carrick. 1688 R. HOLME *Armoury* II. 184/2 He beareth Gules, a Talbott, (or Blood-hound, or hunting hound) Or. 1884 *Mag. Art* Jan. 102 Another drinking vessel..is in form of a 'talbot', or dog, seated, and richly collared.

† **3.** Name of a dish in cookery. *Obs.*

*c* 1430 *Two Cookery Bks.* 19 Talbottys.—Take an Hare, an fle hem clene; þen take þe blode, & Brede, an Spycery, an grynde y-fere, & drawe it vppe with þe brothe [etc.].

**4.** *Comb.* as *talbot-like* adj.

1615 MARKHAM *Country Contentm.* I. 5 A large, heauy, slow, true Talbot-like hound.

**Talbotype** (tǭ·lbŏtəip), *sb.* Also **Talbot-type.** [f. *Talbot*, name of the inventor + TYPE *sb.*] The process of photographing on sensitized paper, patented by W. H. Fox Talbot in 1841: = CALOTYPE; also, a picture produced by this process.

1846 *Art-Union Jrnl.* June 143 In September 1840, Mr. Talbot discovered the process first called Calotype (but the name has since been changed by some of his friends into *Talbotype*). 1875 tr. *Vogel's Chem. Light* iv. 35 Thus the Talbot-type, which at first seemed hardly worth notice compared with the process of Daguerre,..ultimately took precedence of Daguerre's. 1883 *Hardwich's Photogr. Chem.* (ed. Taylor) 261 The original Talbotype process, in which the latent image is formed upon Iodide of Silver, produces, next to Collodion, the most stable image.

Hence **Ta·lbotype** *v.*, to photograph by this process.

1887 FRITH *Autobiog.* I. xx. 246 Photography, or as it was then [1852] called, Talbotyping, was tried.

**Talboy**: see TALLBOY.

**Talbrone, talburn,** variants of TABORN *Obs.*

**Talc** (tælk), *sb.* Also 6–7 **talke,** 7–8 **talck,** 7–9 **talk.** [a. F. *talc* (Palissy *a* 1590) or ad. med.L. *talcum*, = Pg., It. *talco*, Sp. *talco, talque*, ad. Arab. طلق *talq*, mentioned A.D. 869 by Jahiz of Bassora, and by Serapion the elder (Syriac and Arabic), Rhazi, Avicenna, Ibn-el-Beithar † 1248, etc. Held by Arabic scholars to be from Persian, where the form is تلك *talk*. So Ger., Da., Sw. *talk*; Du. *talk, talksteen*.

In med.L., Matth. Silvaticus *Pandectarum Opus*, *c* 1317, has *talk*; later writers have *talcum*; Matthiolus *Comment. in Dioscoridem*, 1549, has *talchus*; Agricola, 1546, *talk*.]

A name applied by the Arabs and mediæval writers to various transparent, translucent, or shining minerals, as talc proper, mica, selenite, etc. Now restricted to the following:

**1.** In popular and commercial use, (loosely) applied to (or including) MICA or Muscovy glass.

1601 HOLLAND *Pliny* XXI. xiv. (1634) II. 95 Many haue made them [bee-hives] of Talc [orig. *speculari lapide*], which is a kind of transparent glasse stone, because they would see through them how the Bees do worke and labor within. 1644 DIGBY *Nat. Bodies* XXVIII. 252 The gallery windows of my cabin..were of light moscovia glasse or talke. 1780 COXE *Russ. Disc.* 216 The windows..on account of the dearness of glass and Russian talk are generally of paper. 1866 LIVINGSTONE *Last Jrnls.* (1873) I. vi. 157 Granite with large flakes of talc. 1867 J. HOGG *Microsc.* I. i. 7 He fitted them on a little plate of talc, or thin-blown glass.

**b.** With *a* and *pl.* A plate of mica used as a microscopic slide.

1761 STILES in *Phil. Trans.* LV. 254 Many of the rings were broke..by some confinement of the talks. *Ibid.* 255 A third observation was made..of some blood dropped upon a single talk. *c* 1790 IMISON *Sch. Art* I. 223 'Tis proper to have some sliders furnished with talcs.

**2.** *Min.* A hydrated silicate of magnesium, usually consisting of broad flat laminæ or plates, white, apple-green, or yellow, having a greasy feel, and shining lustre, translucent, and in thin plates often transparent; it exists in three varieties—foliated, massive (*steatite* or *soapstone*), and indurated (*talc slate* or *schist*).

1610 B. JONSON *Alch.* II. v, With the calce of egge-shels, White marble, talck. 1668 WILKINS *Real Char.* 62 Fissil, into Flakes,..Selenite, Muscovia glass, Isinglass, Sparr. Talc. 1681 GREW *Musæum* III. I. v. 308 A piece thus figur d, I call A Crystal of Talk. 1770 COOK *Voy. round World* II. vi. (1773) 401 Some particular place where they [the Indians] got the green talc or stone of which they make their ornaments and tools. 1811 PINKERTON *Petralogy* I. 177 The mica may pass into talc or steatite, or siderite, as on the summit of Mont Blanc. 1862 DANA *Man. Geol.* § 66. 61 Talc.—In-foliated masses; folia flexible but not elastic; also compact, massive, very soft, and having a greasy feel. 1865 BRISTOW *Figuier's World bef. the Deluge* ii. 38 The Serpentine rocks are a sort of compact talc. 1867 BRANDE & COX *Dict. Sci.*, etc., s. v., Talc forms the basis of the rouge used by ladies; it is also employed by tailors for marking lines on cloth, and in a powdered state for making gloves and boots slip on easily, and to diminish the friction of machinery.

**b.** A species or variety of talc, or a mineral so called.

1794 SULLIVAN *View Nat.* II. 93 We see crystals,..even metals, talks and asbestos, growing from stony substances. 1796 MORSE *Amer. Geog.* I. 460 Talcs of various kinds, white, brown, and chocolate coloured crystals.

† **c.** *Oil of talc*, a preparation formerly used as a cosmetic, reputed to be obtained from talc. *Obs.*

1582 HESTER *Secr. Phiorav.* III. lxxxiii. 110 If this [verjuice] bee mixed with Oile of Talke, it will restore the sight vnto those that are almost blinde. 1610 B. JONSON *Alch.* III. ii, You restore [her face] With the oyle of Talck. 1639 J. MAYNE *City Match* II. i. in Hazl. *Dodsley* XIII. 225 Who Do verily ascribe the German War..to curling, False teeth, and oil of talc. [1678 PHILLIPS (ed. 4), *Talc*, a squamous, white, and lucid stone, of which is made an oil, with which Women that are curious to preserve their beauty use to wash their faces.] 1727-41 CHAMBERS *Cycl.* s.v., Some chymists..pretend to draw from it that precious oil..called Oil of Talc, which is supposed a wonderful cosmetic.

**3.** *attrib.* and *Comb.*, as (from 2) *talc crystal, earth, rock, stone; talc-like* adj.; esp. in names of mineral substances consisting partly of talc or containing magnesia, as *talc-alum, -apatite, -chlorite, -garnet, -gneiss, -iron-ore, -ironstone, -spar, -steatite*; **talc powder**, powdered talc, *talcum powder*: see TALCUM; **talc schist, talc slate**, a schistose rock consisting largely of talc; (from 1) **talc light**, a window glazed with mica, or a lantern with mica instead of glass; so *talc-windowed*.

1868 WATTS *Dict. Chem.* V. 656 **Talc-alum*, a term sometimes applied to magnesio-aluminic sulphate. *Ibid.*, **Talc-apatite*, a variety of apatite containing magnesia. *Ibid.*, **Talc-chlorite*, syn. with Clinochlore. 1681 GREW *Musæum* III. I. v. 310 A Diamond-square, i.e. with unequal Angles, and equal sides; whereas in a *Talk-Crystal, both are unequal. 1861 H. W. BRISTOW *Gloss. Mineral.*, *Talc earth, Native. 1868 WATTS *Dict. Chem.* V. 656 **Talc-garnet*, magnesian garnet from Arendal in Norway. *Ibid.*, **Talc-iron-ore*, Magnesian Iron-ore,..an iron-ore..consisting..of ferrous oxide with much magnesia. *Ibid.*, **Talc-ironstone*, Breithaupt's name for a magnetic iron-ore from Sparta in New Jersey. 1808 PIKE *Sources Mississ.* III. 207 In one or two houses there were *talc lights. 1866 BLACKMORE *Cradock Nowell* li, The rim of dazzled vision whitened to a *talc-like glimmer. 1895 *Syd. Soc. Lex.* s.v. *Powder*, *Talc powder. 1681 GREW *Musæum* III. I. v. 309 A lump of the *Talk-Rock near Spiral, in the upper Carinthia. 1839 URE *Dict. Arts* 747 It is..among the oldest *talc-schists and clay slates, that it usually occurs. 1866 LAWRENCE tr. *Cotta's Rocks Class.* (1878) 244 Talc-schist is almost always stratified, and forms alternating beds with other crystalline schists. 1832 MACGILLIVRAY tr. *Humboldt's Trav.* xxvi. (1836) 392 A primitive clay-slate passing into *talc-slate. 1834-5 J. PHILLIPS *Geol.* in *Encycl. Metrop.* VI. 560/2 Gneiss rocks..include among them many gradations, chlorite slate, talc slate, hornblende slate [etc.]. 1681 GREW *Musæum* III. I. v. 309 A Green *Talk-Spar..brittle as Glass. 1756-7 tr. *Keysler's Trav.* (1760) IV. 407 A kind of yellow green and whitish *talc-stone dug about Bern. 1888 LEES & CLUTTERBUCK *B. C.* 1887 xix. (1892) 206 An evil-smelling, *talc-windowed American stove.

**Talc**, *v.* Pa. t. and pple. **talcked** (incorrectly **talced**). [f. prec. sb.] *trans.* To treat with talc; to coat (a photographic plate) with talc. Hence **Talcked** (tælkt) *ppl. a.*

1888 *Engineer* LXVI. 334 A glass plate is first cleaned, talced, and collodionized. 1891 *Anthony's Photogr. Bull.* IV. 274 If the wet prints be squeegeed down upon talced glass, a glossy enamelled surface is obtained.

**Talca gum** (tæ·lkă gɒm). Also **talha, talka**. [According to Schweinfurth, from *talch*, Arabic name of *Acacia stenocarpa*.] An inferior kind of gum arabic of brownish colour, obtained in tropical Africa from *Acacia stenocarpa* and *Acacia Seyal*. Also called *Suakin gum*.

1867 FLÜCKIGER & HANBURY *Pharmacogr.* 206 Suakin Gum, Talca, or Talha Gum..is remarkable for its brittleness, which occasions much of it to arrive in the market in a semi-pulverulent state.

**Talch**, obs. form of TALLOW.

**Talcite** (tæ·lsəit). *Min.* [f. TALC *sb.* + -ITE 1 2.] **a.** Kirwan's name for the compact scaly variety of talc. **b.** Name given to a white muscovite from Wicklow. **c.** (See quot. 1888.)

1796 KIRWAN *Elem. Min.* (ed. 2) I. 149 Talcite. Colour, reddish or greenish white, or leek green. 1836 T. THOMSON in *Thomson's Rec. Gen. Sci.* III. 334 The specimens of talcite from Ireland are from the county of Wicklow, where it occurs crystallized in granite. 1888 *Nature* 20 Sept. 506/2 This upper group—that of the talcites (talc-schists)—contains talc only as an accessory constituent.

**Talcke**, obs. form of TALK.

**Talcky** (tæ·lki), *a.* Also 7-9 **talky**, (8-9 incorrectly **talcy**). [f. TALC *sb.* + -Y: cf. *colicky*.] Pertaining to, of the nature of, or consisting of talc.

1676 *Phil. Trans.* XI. 615 Some are marly..; some bolar, some sandy, some talky, some limy. 1709 *Ibid.* XXVI. 384 A foliated or talky Earth. 1733 *Ibid.* XXXVIII. 66 At last by encreasing the Fire to the highest Degree, there sublimed some white Talcky [*printed* Talckly] Flowers. 1746 DA COSTA *ibid.* XLIV. 405 Most of the talcy Bodies are of a fibrous Nature. 1799 W. TOOKE *Russ. Emp.* I. 118 There rises a talcky micaceous schistus out of the trapp. 1852 TH. ROSS *Humboldt's Trav.* III. xxv. 58 The micaceous and talky slates of his country.

**Talco-** (tæ·lko), combining form of med. and mod.L. *talcum* talc, in adjs. describing substances of which talc is an element; as *talcochlori·tic*, containing talc and chlorite; so *talcomica·ceous, talcoqua·rtzous*.

1839 DE LA BECHE *Rep. Geol. Cornw.* ii. 29 These talcomicaceous slates of the Lizard. 1860 MAYNE *Expos. Lex.*, *Talcoquarzosus*,..talcoquartzous.

**Talcoid** (tæ·lkoid), *a.* and *sb.* [See -OID.]
**A.** *adj.* Resembling or having the form of talc. 1891 in *Cent. Dict.*
**B.** *sb.* [a. Ger. *talkoid* (Naumann 1859).] A variety of talc: see quot.

1868 DANA *Min.* 454 Talcoid..is a snow-white, broadly foliated talc of Pressnitz.

**Talcose** (tæ·lkōᵘs), *a.* [f. TALC *sb.* + -OSE.] Abounding in or consisting largely of talc.

1796 KIRWAN *Elem. Min.* (ed. 2) I. 382 Talcose Argillite. 1802 PLAYFAIR *Illustr. Hutton. Th.* 224 A schistus, which is talcose rather than micaceous. 1854 F. C. BAKEWELL *Geol.* 22 When talc is an ingredient, the mineral is called talcose granite. 1893 BARKER *Wand. South. Waters* 195 With schist, talcose slate and fragments of quartz.

**Talcous** (tæ·lkəs), *a.* [f. TALC + -OUS.] Of the nature of talc; talcose.

1735 *Phil. Trans.* XXXIX. 40 Shining Talcous Laminæ are to be seen in the Liquor. 1777 G. FORSTER *Voy. round World* I. 149 A kind of brown talcous clay-stone. 1852 TH. ROSS *Humboldt's Trav.* III. xxv. 65 A gneiss passing into micaceous and talcous slate.

‖ **Talcum** (tæ·lkɒm). Also 6 **talchum**. [med.L.] = TALC. *Talcum powder*, a preparation of powdered talc or French chalk.

1558 W. WARDE tr. *Alexis' Secr.* I. 73 b, The poulder of Talchum. 1567 MAPLET *Gr. Forest* 21 Talchum the stone is like to Glasse. 1682 WHELER *Journ. Greece* VI. 451 Some sparkle like Walls of Diamond; which being broken splitteth into Talcum. 1901 *19th Cent.* Oct. 601 The gloves are boiled, then dusted inside with talcum powder.

**Tale** (tēᵊl), *sb.* Forms: 1 talu, *infl.* tale, 2- tale; also 3-5 talle, 3-6 tayle, 4 tayl, taal(e, 4-5 taille, 4-7 tail, 5 tayll(e, 5-6 taill, taile (6 tell(e), 6-9 *dial.* teale. *β.* 1-2, 4 tal, 4 tall. [OE. *talu*, infl. *tale*, = OFris. *tale*, OS. *tala*, MDu., MLG. *tāle*, Du. *taal* speech, LG. *tāl*, OHG. *zala*, MHG. *zal*, Ger. *zahl* number, ON. *tala* talk, speech, tale, number, Da. *tale* speech, discourse; all :—OTeut. **talā* strong fem., from verbal stem *tal-*, in *taljan*, to mention things in their natural or due order, to relate, enumerate, reckon: see TELL *v.* The ONorthumb. *tal* and early ME. *tal, tall* in sense 6, may represent the ON. *tal* neut. (Sw. *tal* speech, number, Da. *tal* number), or the OE. *getæl* reckoning, number.]

**I.** †**1.** The action of telling, relating, or saying; discourse, conversation, talk. *Obs.*

c 1000 ÆLFRIC *Saints' Lives* (1890) II. 210 Seo modor sæt geornlice hlystende hire tale. a 1225 *Ancr. R.* 66 Eue heold..longe tale mid te neddre. a 1250 *Owl & Night.* 3, Iherde ich holde grete tale An hule and one niȝtingale. 13.. *Gaw. & Gr. Knt.* 638 As tulk of tale most trewe. c 1400 *Destr. Troy* 1941 He turnyt hym tyte withouten tale more. a 1547 SURREY *Æneid* IV. 144 Quene Iuno then thus tooke her tale againe. 1592 SHAKS. *Rom. & Jul.* II. iv. 99 Thou desir'st me to stop in my tale against the haire.

†**b.** An enumeration, a list. *Obs. rare.*

c 1050 *Gloss.* in Wr.-Wülcker 437/34 *Laterculus*, talu.

†**2.** Speech, language. *Obs. rare.* (Cf. TAAL.)

c 1250 *Gen. & Ex.* 450 Bigamie is unkinde ðing, On engleis tale, twie-wifing. *Ibid.* 2526 God schilde hise sowle fro helle bale, Ðe made it ðus on engel tale.

**3.** That which one tells; the relation of a series of events; a narrative, statement, information.

*Thereby hangs a tale* (and such phrases): = 'about that there is something to tell'. *To tell one's tale*: see TELL *v.*

a 1060 *Charter of Godwine & Leofwine* in Kemble *Cod. Dipl.* IV. 266 Ða ða him seo talu cuð wæs, ða sende he ȝewrit. c 1205 LAY. 24439 Ne mai hit na mon suggen on his tale [c 1275 in tale]. a 1300 *Cursor M.* 24887 (Edin.) Þe angel þus he tald his talle. 13.. *Ibid.* 8697 (Cott.) O þiskin tall [*Gött.* playnt] him thoght sel-cut[h], Als of a cas þat was vncuth. 1382 WYCLIF *Mark* i. 28 And the tale [*gloss* or tything; 1388 fame; Vulg. *rumor*] of hym wente forth anoon in to al the cuntree of Galilee. 1412-20 *Lydg.'s Chron. Troy* (Roy. MS.) Rubric bef. l. 1701 Vlixes taile to Achile. c 1460 *Towneley Myst.* xx. 105 Vnto vs he takys no tent, bot ilk man trowes vnto his tayll [*rimes* dayll (= dale), hayll, avayll]. c 1470 HENRYSON *Mor. Fab.* x. (*Fox & Wolf*) ix, Ane leill man is not tane at half ane taill. 1523 SKELTON *Garl. Laurel* 1200 Yet, thoughe I say it, therby lyeth a tale. 1535 COVERDALE 1 *Kings* i. 14 While thou..talkest with the kynge, I wyll come in after the, and tell forth thy tayle. 1583 *Leg. Bp. St. Androis* 363 Sua he..brocht the teale bravelie about. 1596 SHAKS. *Tam. Shr.* IV. i. 60 *Gru.* Out of their saddles into the durt, and thereby hangs a tale. *Curt.* Let's ha't, good Grumio. 1600 HOLLAND *Livy* v. xxi. 194 But hereto longeth a tale. 1601 WEEVER *Mirr. Mart.* A iij b, One tale is good, untill another's told. 1722 DE FOE *Col. Jack* i, It was a good while before we ever heard tale or tidings of him. 1878 BROWNING *La Saisiaz* 181 Then my fellow takes the tale up. 1891 E. PEACOCK *N. Brendon* I. 117 Mr. Tournay told his tale without comment.

† **b.** The subject of common talk; the 'talk' (of the town, etc.). *Obs.*

c 1230 *Hali Meid.* 33 Vpbrud in uuel muð tale bimong alle. 1596 DRAYTON *Leg.* iii. 576, I was the Tale of every common Tongue.

**c.** *pl.* Things told so as to violate confidence or secrecy; reports of private matters not proper to be divulged; idle or mischievous gossip; esp. in *to tell* (*bear, bring, carry*) *tales*; *tales out of school* (see SCHOOL *sb.*¹ 1 e).

c 1350 *Will. Palerne* 334 Be no tellere of talis bur trewe to þi lord. c 1450 *Cov. Myst.* (Shaks. Soc.) 353 Now we have golde No talys xul be tolde. 1552 HULOET, Tales to brynge or tell, *perfero*. 1639 MASSINGER *Unnat. Combat* I. i, Peace, infant! Tales out of school! Take heed, you will be breeched else. 1737 L. CLARKE *Hist. Bible* (1740) I. I. 73 Joseph..told tales of them to his father. 1838 JAMES *Robber* vi, Dead men tell no tales. 1903 *Westm. Gaz.* 12 Feb. 2/3 Telling tales is reprobated by English public-school boys—rightly, in so far as the condemnation is directed against getting others into trouble for your own profit or pleasure.

**d.** *In the same tale, in a* (= *one*) *tale*, in the same enumeration, statement, or category; hence, in agreement; so *in two tales. arch.*

c 1375 *Cursor M.* 683 (Fairf.) Þe bestes were in samen tale [*Cott.* war samer-tale] Wit-outen hurt in herde ay hale 1577 HOLINSHED *Chron.* II. 1656/1 Thou art a false knaue to be in two tales, therfore said he, hang him vp. 1599 SHAKS. *Much Ado* IV. ii. 33 'Fore God they are both in a tale. 1642 R. CARPENTER *Experience* I. v. 14 Truth must needs be one ..and can never be found in two contrary tales. 1860 READE *Cloister & H.* lv, Which did accuse heavenly truth of falsehood for not being in a tale with him. 1887 LANG *Myth, Ritual & Relig.* II. 333 The Wesleyan missionary..is in the same tale with the Jesuit.

**4.** A story or narrative, true or fictitious, drawn up so as to interest or amuse, or to preserve the history of a fact or incident; a literary composition cast in narrative form.

c 1200 *Trin. Coll. Hom.* 101 We nime ȝeme of þre þing on þis tale. c 1275 *Passion our Lord* 1 in *O. E. Misc.* 37 Ihereþ nv one lutele tale..As we vyndeþ hit iwrite in þe godspelle. c 1290 *Beket* 1 in *S. Eng. Leg.* I. 106 Wolle ȝe nouþe i-heore þis englische tale? 1340-70 *Alex. & Dind.* 190 Tendeþ how þis tale is titeled. 1375 BARBOUR *Bruce* IX. 576 [He] tald me this taill as I sall tell. c 1386 CHAUCER *Prol.* 792 That ech of yow, to shorte with oure weye, In this viage shal telle tales tweye. *Ibid.*, *Pard. Prol.* 109 For lewed peple louen tales olde. 1483 CAXTON *G. de la Tour* F vij, I wold..that ye knewe..the tale of a quene of Fraunce whiche had to name Brunehault. 1546 J. HEYWOOD *Prov.* (1867) 67 A good tale yll tolde, in the tellyng is marde. 1606 *Sir G. Goosecappe* III. i. E ij, Indeed Sir the best Tales in England are your Canterburie tales I assure ye. a 1771 GRAY *Dante* 19 Hates the Tale of Troy for Helen's Sake. 1821 SCOTT *Kenilw.* xvii, They are spoken in a mad tale of fairies, love-charms, and I wot not what besides.

**5.** A mere story, as opposed to a narrative of fact; a fiction, an idle tale; a falsehood.

c 1250 *Gen. & Ex.* 321 He [Satan]..Wente into a wirme, and tolde eue a tale. 1382 WYCLIF 2 *Pet.* i. 16 Sotheli we not suynge vnwijse taales, han maad knowun to ȝou the vertu and prescience..of oure Lord Jhesu Crist. 1529 MORE *Dyaloge* IV. Wks. 269/2 Therfore it is but a tale to saye that faith draweth alway good workes with it. 1553 *Respublica* 727 Vaine woordes beeth but tales. 1619 *Let.* in *Eng. & Germ.* (Camden) 206 The report of the Marquis of Ansbach his having defeated Coronell Fulkes his regiment (which proves altogeather a tale). 1722 DE FOE *Plague* 85 There was more of tale than of truth in those things. 1867 *London Herald* 23 Mar. 222/2 If he had had the sense to..pitch them a tale, he might have got off.

**b.** In phrases, as *a Canterbury Tale, old wives' tales, pipers' tales, travellers' tales, a tale of Robin Hood, of a roasted horse, of a tub* (see TUB), etc.

1532 MORE *Confut. Tindale* Wks. 576/1 Thys is a fayre tale of a tubbe tolde vs of hys electes. c 1549 CRANMER *Serm. Rebellion* Wks. (Parker Soc.) II. 198 If we take it for a Canterbury tale, why do we not refuse it? 1575 GASCOIGNE *Cert. Notes Instruct.* in *Steele Gl.*, etc. (Arb.) 36 The verse that is to easie is like a tale of a rosted horse. c 1590 MARLOWE *Faust.* v. 133 Tush, these are trifles and mere old wives' tales. 1591 HARINGTON *Orl. Fur.* XLV. cv, This is a tale indeed of Robinhood, Which to beleeue, might show my wits but weake. 1608 TOPSELL *Serpents* (1658) 778 To interpret these to be either fables and Canterbury tales, or true historicall narrations. 1611 COTGR. s.v. *Cicogne, Contes de la cicogne*, idle histories; vaine relations; tales of a tub, or, of a rosted horse. a 1641 BP. MOUNTAGU *Acts & Mon.* iii. (1642) 170 Fained leasings and tales of Robin hood. 1724 DE FOE *Mem. Cavalier* (1840) 97 Having entertained the fellow with a tale of a tub.

**c.** A thing now existing only in story; a mere matter of history or tradition; a thing of the past.

1780 BURKE *Sp. at Bristol* Wks. III. 413 No power..could have prevented a general conflagration; and at this day London would have been a tale. 1855 B. TAYLOR *Poems Orient, On the Sea*, The world we leave is a tale untold.

**II. 6.** Numerical statement or reckoning; enumeration, counting, numbering; number.

c 1200 ORMIN 4324-5 Ȝiff þu þise taless kannst Inntill an tale sammnenn. c 1205 LAY. 7397 Swa fele þat nuste na man þe tale. 1297 R. GLOUC. (Rolls) 8100 Folc also wiþoute tale. c 1375 *Sc. Leg. Saints* xxvi. (*Nycholas*) 237 Þe quhet delieueryt hale in quantyte, mesur & tale. c 1450 *Hymns Virg.* 122/165 Alle the stonys grett and smale Thatt byth in erthe withoutyn tale. 1594 CAREW *Tasso* (1881) 15 Equall in tale, nor lesse in value tride. 1674 N. FAIRFAX *Bulk & Selv.* 39 Nothing with-holds, but that from an infinite tale of finites there may at length arise an infinite. 1691 LOCKE *Lower. Interest* Wks. 1727 II. 53 If you make your Money less in Weight, it must be made up in Tale. 1697 DRYDEN *Virg. Past.* III. 51 Once she takes the tale of all the Lambs. 1722 DE FOE *Plague* 97 An exact tale of the dead bodies. 1780 JOHNSON *Let. to Mrs. Thrale* 1 May, There were..Lord Monboddo, and Sir Joshua, and ladies out of tale. 1826 G. S. FABER *Diffic. Romanism* (1853) p. liii, The goodly tale of folios..which now decorate or crowd my *penetralè*. 1862 TROLLOPE *N. Amer.* I. xi. 249 By measures of forty bushels each, the tale is kept.

*β.* c 950 *Lindisf. Gosp.* Matt. xiv. 21 Ðæra etendra..tal [*manducantium numerus*]. *Ibid.* John vi. 10 ȝesetton uutudlice ueras of tal suelce fifo ðusendo. a 1300 *Cursor M.* 7174 O þat heþen folk he feld A thusand þat wit tal was teld.

**b.** *By tale*: as determined by counting individual objects or articles; by number; as distinguished from *by weight*, *by measure*.

*c* **1205** LAY. 27606 Fif hundred bi tale. *c* **1300** *Havelok* 2026 He weren bi tale sixti and ten. **13..** *Guy Warw.* (A.) 3430 Bi tale .xx. thousend hauberks of stiel. **1470–85** MALORY *Arthur* XIII. ix. 623 Thenne fond they by the tale an honderd and fyfty. **1529** MORE *Dyaloge* III. iv. Wks. 212 To way them rather then take them by tale. **1594** PLAT *Jewell-ho.* III. 75 Where oysters are..sold by tale. **1776** ADAM SMITH *W. N.* I. iv. (1869) I. 27 This money..was, for a long time, received at the exchequer by weight and not by tale. **1855** MACAULAY *Hist. Eng.* xxii. IV. 695 The second of May, had been fixed..as the last day on which the clipped crowns..were to be received by tale in payment of taxes.

**7.** The number or amount made up, or to be made up or accounted for; the number all told; the complete sum, enumeration, or list.

*a* **1225** *Ancr. R.* 42 And siggen þenne hire tale of auez. *c* **1250** *Gen. & Ex.* 2891 Hem-seluen he fetchden ðe chaf,.. And ðoȝ holden ðe tiȝeles tale. *a* **1300** *Cursor M.* 18627 Four thusand yere, þat was þe tale, And four hundret and four al hale. **1387** TREVISA *Higden* (Rolls) IV. 427 For Nero somtyme wolde wite þe tale and þe nombre of Iewes þat were at Ierusalem. **1539** BIBLE (Great) *Exod.* v. 18 Yet shal ye delyuer the hole tale of brycke. **1584** FENNER *Def. Ministers* (1587) 10 In generall and whole tale, we will allowe that, part whereof in the particular and seuerall parcelles wee will gayn-say. **1611** BIBLE 1 *Sam.* xviii. 27 They gaue them in full tale to the king. *a* **1732** T. BOSTON *Crook in Lot* (1805) 98 The one has multiplied the tale of their good works. **1790** BURKE *Fr. Rev.* 196 He will hardly be able to make up his tale of thirty millions of souls. **1864** SIR F. PALGRAVE *Norm. & Eng.* III. 70 They had a fair tale of children. **1884** MAY CROMMELIN *Brown-Eyes* xiii, Saddened at the increasing tale of years and months.

† **8.** An account, a reckoning of numbers (of money given and received, etc.). *Obs.*

**1401** *Pol. Poems* (Rolls) II. 73 Ȝe wolden that there where oon lesse, Ȝe ȝaue neuer tale. **1483** CAXTON *Gold. Leg.* 197 b/1 They moche doubted that they shold not fynde theyr counte ne tale. **1573** TUSSER *Husb.* (1878) 173 Giue tale and take count, is a huswifelie point. **1602** CAREW *Cornwall* I. 33 They keepe a iust tale of the number that euery hogshead contayneth. **1755** SMOLLETT *Quix.* (1803) II. 8 The tale and account of what was both sowed and reaped, passed through my hands. **1806–7** J. BERESFORD *Miseries Hum. Life* (1826) vi. 116 You might just as well require me to deliver in a tale of all the pores in my skin.

† **9.** Reckoning of value; account, estimation, esteem, regard; in phrases, as *to hold* (*make, give, tell*) *no tale of*: to hold of no account. *Obs.*

*c* **1175** *Lamb. Hom.* 147 Þet he telle swa lutel tale þer of; þet he hit nawicht ne luuie. *c* **1205** LAY. 12764 Þæt nis [*MS.* mis] þer bileued wel neh nan Þæt auere beo æi [*c* 1275 eni] tale on. *a* **1300** *Cursor M.* 7554 Quen golias on him bi-held, Ful littel tale of him he teld [*Trin.* litil he set bi him]. *Ibid.* 10980 He sale Bicum a man of mikel tale [*Trin.* a greet mon]. **1362** LANGL. *P. Pl.* A. I. 9 Of oþer heuene þen heer holde þei no tale. *c* **1400** *Laud Troy Bk.* 3923 Dyomedes ȝaf no tale Off alle that sat there In that sale. **1496** *Dives & Paup.* (W. de W.) I. vii. 38/2 The goodes of this worlde ..they gaaf no grete tale thereof.

**III. 10.** *attrib.* and *Comb.*: attrib., as *tale-book*, *-faculty*, *-monger*, *-story*; obj. and obj. gen., as *tale-forger*, *-gatherer*, *-maker*, *-writer*; *tale-gathering*, *-spinning*, *-writing* sbs. and adjs.; also **tale-carrier** = TALEBEARER; † **tale craft**, numeration, arithmetic; † **tale-fish**, a fish of such size as to be sold by tale; **tale-hearer**, a willing listener to scandal or gossip; **tale-master**, the authority for a report; † **tale-money**, money reckoned by the tale, i. e. by counting pieces or coins taken at their nominal value, not by weight; **tale-piet**, a chattering 'magpie'; a tell-tale (*dial.*); **tale-wright**, a constructor or maker of tales. See also TALEBEARER, TALE-TELLER, etc.

**1628** PRYNNE *Brief Suruay* Epist. A ij, For the inhibiting and suppressing of all scurrilous and prophane Play-books, Ballads, Poems, and *Tale-bookes whatsoeuer. **1552** HULOET, Tale bearer or *carier, *rumigerulus*. **1592** NASHE *P. Penilesse* 35 Spirits called spies and tale-carriers. **1643** PRYNNE *Sov. Power Parl.* App. 32 Common Tale-carriers, and accustomed to talke of trifling matters. **1674** N. FAIRFAX *Bulk & Selv.* 110 Nothing better is it, than pumping two out of one, or taking the greater number out of the rest, in *Talecraft or Arithmetick. **1677** W. HUGHES *Man of Sin* III. iii. 100 Forraign Authors have not the Monopoly of the *Tale-faculty neither. **1482** *Rolls of Parlt.* VI. 222/1 That *tale fissh shuld not be pakked with the lesse fissh called Grilles,..and that the same tale fissh shuld conteigne in lengeth..xxvi ynches. **1553** BECON *Reliques of Rome* (1563) 198 It is a harde thing for lyers and *taleforgers to agree. **1711** SHAFTESB. *Charac.* (1737) I. 350 We may often see a philosopher, or a wit, run a *tale-gathering in those idle desarts. **1647** TRAPP *Comm. Matt.* xviii. 16 The tale-bearer and the *tale-hearer are both of them abominable, and shut out of heaven. **1810** *Splendid Follies* I. 183 The variety of grimaces exhibited by the tale-bearer and the tale-hearers. **1483** *Cath. Angl.* 377/2 A *Tale maker, *fabulo*. **1897** *Q. Rev.* July 107 The sale-processes of *tale-makers. *a* **1661** FULLER *Worthies, General* xxiii. (1662) 64, I tell you my Tale and my *Tale-master, which is essential to the begetting of credit to any Relation. **1758** JOS. HARRIS *Coins* II. ii. 50 Increasing the quantity of *tale-money, by giving the old names to smaller pieces of silver. *Ibid.* 70 All artificial methods of increasing tale-money are..pernicious. **1613** *Answ. Uncasing of Machivils Instr.* E ij, Rather for thy quiets sake, liue with bread, Then mongst *talemongers seeke to be fed. **1796** W. MARSHALL *Yorksh.* (ed. 2) Gloss., *Teyl-peyat, or *Tel-pie*, a tell-tale..one who divulges secrets; spoken chiefly of children. **1816** SCOTT *Antiq.* iv, Never mind me, sir, I am no tale-pyet. **1895** CROCKETT *Men of Moss-Hags* xiii, A Gordon—Covenant or no Covenant—is no tale-piet. *a* **1661** FULLER *Worthies, Wilts.* (1662) III. 158 Such a Medly Cloth is the *Tale-story of this Clothier. **1570–76** W. LAMBARDE *Peramb. Kent* (1826) 326 This Clerkly μυθοπλάστης, this *Talewright (I say) and Fableforger. **1904** *Daily Chron.* 11 May 4/6 A *tale-writer who moves through the magazines. **1837** HT. MARTINEAU *Soc. Amer.* III. 213 *Tale-writing is her forte.

**Tale** (tēⁱl), *v.* Now *rare.* Forms: 1 **talian**, 3 **talie(n**, 4 **talen**; 3– **tale.** [OE. *talian* to reckon, impute, enumerate, = OS. *talôn* to reckon (MDu. *tālen* to speak, Du. *talen* to ask), OHG. *zalôn* to number, reckon (MHG. *zalen, zaln*, Ger. *zahlen* to pay), ON. *tala* (Sw. *tala*, Da. *tale*) to speak, talk, discourse:—OTeut. **talôjan*, f. stem *tal-*: see TALE *sb.*]

**I.** † **1.** *trans.* To account, reckon, consider (something) to be (so and so). *Obs.*

*c* **897** K. ÆLFRED *Gregory's Past. C.* xxxiii. 226 [He] hit ðonne swiðe unaberendlic talað. *a* **900** tr. *Bæda's Hist.* V. xiii. § 3 Nis ðis seo hel, swa ðu talest and wenest. *c* **950** *Lindisf. Gosp.* Matt. xxvi. 53 Ðu tales..þæt ic ne mæge ȝebidda fader min. *c* **1000** WULFSTAN *Hom.* vii. (Napier) 52 He talaþ..hine sylfne wærne and wisne. *c* **1000** *Sax. Leechd.* II. 208 Se man..talaþ, þæt he þonne hal sie. *c* **1400** *Cato's Mor.* 100 in *Cursor M.* p. 1670 (Fairf.) Þai þat talis miche riches maste in nede and bisines beggis in þis life.

† **2.** To lay to the account of some one, to charge or impute (a thing) *to.* Only OE.

*a* **900** tr. *Bæda's Hist.* II. ix. § 4 Ne tala þu me, þæt ic ne cunne þone intingan þinre unrotnisse. *c* **1000** ÆLFRIC *Hom.* (Thorpe) I. 114 Ne taliȝe nan man his yfelan dæda to Gode.

† **3.** To reckon, enumerate, relate. Only OE.

*c* **950** *Lindisf. Gosp.* Matt., Pref. (1887) 5/7 Ðæt æt ægiptum ..& ða æfterra..to talanna longsum is.

**4.** To count up; to deal *out* by number.

(In quot. 1626 the sense is not clear: cf. TALLY *v.*[1] 1.)

**1626** B. JONSON *Staple of N.* I. iii. Stage Direct., He tales the bils, and puts them vp in his pockets. **1828** W. IRVING *Columbus* (1849) III. 135 He..ordered the brawling ruffian to be rewarded with a hundred lashes, which were taled out roundly to him upon the shoulders. **1881** MISS JACKSON *Shropsh. Word-bk.*, *Tale*, to count. 'I tale them ship [=sheep] to forty—'ow many bin a?'

**II.** † **5.** *trans.* To say, speak, utter, tell. *Obs.*

*c* **1205** LAY. 787 Nan swa unwitti þat word talie..ær he ihere minne horn. *c* **1420** *Chron. Vilod.* 2157 And when þis blessud virgyn had talyd tys. *Ibid.* 3677 Bot he couthe nowther tale ny telle What þat euer was in his þouȝt. **1593** Q. ELIZ. *Boethius* III. Met. xi. 69 If Platoes Musis tales the trueth.

† **6.** *intr.* To discourse, talk, gossip; to tell (*of*); to tell tales. *Obs.*

*c* **1205** LAY. 3800 He[o] taleden wið Morgan. *a* **1225** *Leg. Kath.* 795 Þis meiden..toc on toward þeos fif siðe tene to talien o þis wise. *a* **1225** *Ancr. R.* 356 Þet is eadie scheome þet ich of talie [*MS. T* spekie]. *c* **1374** CHAUCER *Troylus* III. 182 (231) Al þat glade nyght By Troilus he lay with mery chere To tale. **1390** GOWER *Conf.* III. 329 The toun therof hath spoke and taled. *c* **1400** *Laud Troy Bk.* 14524 Priamus ran to halle a-valed, Ther these kynges to-gedur taled. *a* **1500** *Chaucer's Dream* 1896 [They] gan reherse Each one to other that they had seene And taling thus [etc.].

† **b.** To shout. *Obs.*

*c* **1205** LAY. 20857 Hunten þar talieð; hundes þer galieð. **13..** *K. Alis.* 1415 (Bodl. MS.) Þe maryneres crieþ & taleþ, Ancres in to shippe þai haleþ.

**Tale**, variant of TAEL; obs. form of TAIL.

**Talebearer** (tēⁱ·lˌbēᵊːrəɹ). [f. TALE *sb.* + BEARER.] One who officiously carries reports of private matters to gratify malice or idle curiosity.

**1478** *Maldon, Essex, Court Rolls* (Bundle 50, No. 8), Isabella Aylemer est a taleberer betuyx man and man. **1560** DAUS tr. *Sleidane's Comm.* 21 b, He admonisheth him to gyue no credit to talebearers. **1641** HINDE *Life J. Bruen* lii. 173 He would shut his eares against tale-bearers, being the very seed-men of strife. **1774** MRS. DELANY in *Life & Corr.* Ser. II. (1862) II. 75 We have heard nothing by the newspapers, but they are false talebearers. **1855** MACAULAY *Hist. Eng.* xii. III. 207 These words were spoken in private; but some talebearer repeated them to the Commons.

**Talebearing** (tēⁱ·lˌbēᵊːriŋ). The carrying of injurious or malicious reports. Also *attrib.*

**1571** GOLDING *Calvin on Ps.* lii. 2 He by his wicked talebearing kindled yᵉ Tyrants rage. **1680** ALLEN *Peace & Unity* 27 To forbear all hard speeches..especially talebearing, back-biting, and whispering. **1857** HUGHES *Tom Brown* I. iii, He was the great opponent of the tale-bearing habits of the school.

**Taledge** = *t' aledge*: see T' [1] and ALLEGE *v.*

**Taledoux**, obs. var. TAILLE-DOUCE.

**Taleful** (tēⁱ·lfŭl), *a.* [f. TALE *sb.* + -FUL 1.] Full of tales; making a long story; talkative.

**1726–46** THOMSON *Winter* 90 The cottage-hind Hangs o'er th' enlivening blaze, and taleful there Recounts his simple frolic.

‖ **Talegalla** (tæligæ·lă). *Ornith.* Also **talagalla, talegallus.** [mod.L. *talegalla* (F. *talégalle*), arbitrarily formed by Lesson from Malagasy *talèva* the porphyrio, and L. *gallus* cock, as a name for the species *Talegalla cuvieri*, the brush-turkey of Western New Guinea, discovered by him.

**1828** R. P. LESSON *Manuel d'Ornithol.* II. 186 Un oiseau ..qui retrace quelques-unes des formes des talèves ou porphyrions. C'est pour rappeler ces analogies que nous avons forgé le mot hybride *talégalle*. *Ibid.* 295 Talève ou poule-sultane. (Talève, nom malgache usité à Madagascar.)]

A genus of megapod birds inhabiting Australia, New Guinea, etc. As English, chiefly applied to *T. lathami*, the Brush-turkey of Australia.

*a* **1842** J. GOULD *Birds Australia* (1848) V. pl. 77 *Talegalla Lathami*, Wattled Talegalla; Brush-Turkey of the Colonists. *Ibid.*, The term *Alecturo* having been previously employed for a group of Flycatchers, and the present bird possessing all the characters of M. Lesson's genus *Talegalla* which was published prior to Mr. Swainson's *Catheturus*, I feel that I ought to accept that appellation...It is known to inhabit various parts of New South Wales from Cape Howe on the south to Moreton Bay in the north. **1842** *Penny Cycl.* XXII. 4 Mr. Gould describes *Talegalla Lathami*, or the *Wattled Talegalla* as a gregarious bird. **1890** LUMHOLTZ *Cannibals* 97 The mounds of the jungle-hen are larger than those of the talegalla.

**Talen**, obs. and dial. form of TALON.

**Talent** (tæ·lĕnt), *sb.* Forms: 1 **talente**; 3– **talent** (4 **taland(e**, 4–6 **-ente, -ant**, 6–7 **tallent**). [In OE. *talente, -an*, = OHG. *talenta* str. fem., ad. L. *talenta*, pl. of *talentum*, ad. Gr. τάλαντον balance, weight, sum of money (f. verbal root ταλ-, τλα- to bear). In ME., a. OF. *talent* will, desire, lust, appetite, = Pr. *talant, talen*, Sp., It. *talento* (OSp., Pg. *talante*), med.L. *talentum* (1098 in Du Cange), in a Com. Romanic sense 'inclination of mind, leaning, wish, desire'. Branch III (also in mod.F. and It.) originated in a fig. use of the word in sense 1 b, taken from the parable of the talents, Matt. xxv. 14–30.]

**I.** An ancient weight, a money of account (L. *talentum*).

**1.** A denomination of weight, used by the Assyrians, Babylonians, Greeks, Romans, and other ancient nations; varying greatly with time, people, and locality.

The Royal Babylonian talent averaged about 29·87 kilograms or 65 lb. 13 oz.; the chief Greek varieties were the Old Æginetan talent of 40·3 kilog. (88 lb. 12 oz.), the later Æginetan or emporetic Attic, 36·4 kilog. (80 lb. 4 oz.), and the Solonic or later Attic, 25·8 kilog. (56 lb. 14 oz., or a little over half a hundredweight).

*c* **893** K. ÆLFRED *Oros.* IV. vi. § 1 Hanna..him ælce ȝeare ȝesealde twa hund talentana siolfres: on ælcere anre talentan wæs lxxx punda. **1382** WYCLIF *Exod.* xxxviii. 26 An hundryd talentes of siluer. — *Zech.* v. 7 Lo! a talent of lede was born. — *Rev.* xvi. 21 And greet hayl as a talent cam doun fro heuen. **1494** FABYAN *Chron.* VI. ccvi. 218 There be thre maner of talentes; the firste & grettest is of yᵉ weyghte of .vi. xx. li. weyght. **1552** HULOET, Talent, or certayne poyse or weyght, *talentum*. **1697** DRYDEN *Æneid* IX. 352 With two great Talents of the finest Gold. **1800** *Suppl. to Chron.* in *Asiat. Ann. Reg.* 149/2 They afterwards advanced to deliver their presents, consisting of talents of gold and silver. **1807** ROBINSON *Archæol. Græca* V. xxvi. 551 Grecian weights reduced to English Troy weight:.. Talent = 65 lb., 12 dwt., 5⁴³/₁₉ grains. **1838** THIRLWALL *Greece* III. xix. 121 The statue of Athene in the Parthenon alone contained forty talents weight of pure gold.

**b.** The value of a talent weight (of gold, silver, etc.): a money of account.

The Babylonian silver talent was equal to 3000 shekels; the Greek talent contained 60 minæ or 6000 silver drachmæ, and the value of the later Attic talent of silver, with pure silver at 4*s.* 9*d.* an oz. troy, has been estimated at £200; at a higher value of silver, at £243 15*s.*

*c* **893** K. ÆLFRED *Oros.* IV. vi. § 18 Eac him ȝesealden þæronufan III. M talentana ælce ȝeare. **1382** WYCLIF *Matt.* xviii. 24 Oon was offrid to hym, that owȝte to hym ten thousand talentis. *Ibid.* xxv. 15 As a man goynge fer in pilgrimage, clepide his seruantis, and bitoke to hem his goodis; and to oon he ȝaue fyue talentis, forsothe to an other two. **1387** TREVISA *Higden* (Rolls) III. 5 Of þe whiche richesse.. Hircanus þe bisshop ȝaf Anthiochus, Demetrius his sone, þre þowsand talentis. **1530** PALSGR. 279/1 Talent a somme of money, *talent*. **1607** SHAKS. *Timon* II. i. 201 My occasions haue found time to vse 'em toward a supply of mony: let the request be fifty Talents. **1761** RAPER in *Phil. Trans.* LXI. 468 This way of reckoning 100 Drachms to the Mina, and 60 Minas to the Talent, was common to all Greece. **1879** FROUDE *Cæsar* xv. 228 He brought 7,000 talents—a million and a half of English money—to the Roman treasury.

† **c.** *Her.* Used as = BEZANT 3. *Obs.*

**1486** *Bk. St. Albans, Her.* E iij, It is not necessari here to expres the colowre of the talentis or besantis: for thay be euer of golde.

† **d.** *fig.* Treasure, riches, wealth, abundance.

*a* **1400–50** *Alexander* 1666 (Dubl. MS.) Takez hym to hys tresory, talentes hym shewys. *a* **1555** LATIMER in Foxe *A. & M.* (1563) 1311/1 All hayle holy crosse which hath deserued to beare the precious talent of the worlde. **1597** SHAKS. *Lover's Compl.* 204 And Lo behold these tallents of their heir, With twisted mettle amorously empeacht. *a* **1600** *Ballad Stucley* in Simpson *Sch. Shaks.* (1878) I. 146 Many a noble gallant—sold both land and talent. **1635** J. HAYWARD tr. *Biondi's Banish'd Virg.* 66 On her therefore spent he all the talent of his hatred.

**II.** Inclination, disposition (OF. *talent*).

† **2.** Inclination, propension, or disposition for anything; 'mind', 'will', wish, desire, appetite.

[**1292** BRITTON V. i. § 1 Pur doner meillour talent a femmes de amer matrimoigne.] *a* **1300** *Cursor M.* 3913 Þan bigan þam tak talent [*v.rr.* talande, taland] To wend in to þair aun land. *c* **1325** *Metr. Hom.* (Vernon MS.) in Herrig's *Archiv* LVII. 263 But hedde he no talent to chase. **1340** HAMPOLE *Pr. Consc.* 8459 To what thyng þe saule has talent, To þat þe body salle, ay, assent. **1375** BARBOUR *Bruce* III. 694 The wynd wes wele to thar talent. **1398** TREVISA *Barth. De P. R.* XII. vi. (Tollem. MS.) To make hem haue talent to mete. *c* **1440** *Promp. Parv.* 486/1 Talent, or lyste,..*appetitus, delectacio*. *c* **1450** *Bk. Hawkyng* in *Rel. Ant.* I. 306 The which schall..make here have a talente to hire mete. *c* **1460** *Towneley Myst.* ix. 157 Yis, lord, I am at youre talent. **1485** CAXTON *Paris & V.* 7 Grete talent and desyre she had to knowe hym. **1530** PALSGR. 279/1 Talent or lust, *talent*.

† **3.** An evil inclination, disposition, or passion; esp. and usually, anger: cf. MALTALENT, 'ill talent', ill-will (which occurs somewhat earlier). *Obs.*

[*c* **1320**: see MALTALENT.] *a* **1380** *St. Ambrose* 698 in Horstm. *Altengl. Leg.* (1878) 19 An officer greued Ambrose sore..And sende word to him wiþ gret talent. *c* **1386** CHAUCER *Man of Law's T.* 1039 Hym ne moeued outher conscience Or Ire or talent or som kynnes affray, Enuye, or pride. *c* **1412** HOCCLEVE *De Reg. Princ.* 2326 Al his angir and his irrous talent Refreyned he. **1622** BACON *Henry VII* 68 One that had of a long time borne an ill Talent towards the King. **1652** EARL MONM. tr. *Bentivoglio's Hist. Relat.* 41 Their tallent is alike evil against the Archduke Albertus and his wife. **1695** TEMPLE *Hist. Eng.* (1699) 581 Several Writers shew their ill Talent to this Prince.

† **4.** Disposition or state of mind or character.

*c* **1330** *Arth. & Merl.* 5882 To geuen the other gode talent. *a* **1400** *Lybeaus Disc.* 612 Elene..ladde her ynto the greves ..Wyth well good talent. **1450-80** tr. *Secreta Secret.* 15 The talent of man takith thereof gret strengthe and corage in alle manhode.

† **b.** *transf.* Quality (of taste or flavour). *rare.*

**1562** J. HEYWOOD *Prov. & Epigr.* (1867) 118 The talent of one cheese in mouthes of ten men, Hath ten different tasts. **1606** G. W[ODDCOCKE] *Hist. Ivstine* Pref., As with a tun of Wine, which..doth take an euill talent of the Caske.

**III.** Mental endowment; natural ability.

[From the parable of the talents, Matt. xxv. 14-30, etc.]

**5.** Power or ability of mind or body viewed as something divinely entrusted to a person for use and improvement: considered either as one organic whole or as consisting of a number of distinct faculties; (with *pl.*) any one of such faculties.

*c* **1430** LYDG. *Min. Poems* (Percy Soc.) 240 Who shal me save Fro feendys daunger, t'acounte for my talent? **1526** *Pilgr. Perf.* (W. de W. 1531) 12 They be the talentes that god hath lent to man in this lyfe, of the whiche he wyll aske moost strayte accounte. **1574** J. DEE in *Lett. Lit. Men* (Camden) 39 That this florishing Kingdome may long enjoye the great Talent committed to your Lordship (from above). **1586** T. B. *La Primaud. Fr. Acad.* (1589) 353 Hide not this talent, but teach it others, and giue thy selfe an example vnto them of well doing. **1607** HEYWOOD *Fayre Mayde* Wks. 1874 II. 60 His industry hath now increas'd his talent. **1671** WOODHEAD *St. Teresa* II. ii. 10 Our Lord having herein given him an extraordinary talent. **1697** COLLIER *Ess. Mor. Subj.* II. (1709) 178 We should presume People have understood their Opportunities, and managed their Talent, and their Time to advantage. **1781** COWPER *Conversat.* 1 Though Nature weigh our talents, and dispense To every man his modicum of sense. **1842** KINGSLEY *Lett.* (1878) I. 59 Remember that your talents are a loan from God.

**6.** A special natural ability or aptitude, usually for something expressed or implied; a natural capacity for success in some department of mental or physical activity; † an accomplishment (*obs.*).

**1600** W. WATSON *Decacordon* (1602) 336 Silly bodies and sorie fellowes of no talent gift or ability. **1635** J. HAYWARD tr. *Biondi's Banish'd Virg.* Ep. Ded., He alone having the talent of both conceiving and expressing himselfe. **1644** EVELYN *Diary* 4 Jan., He would needes perswade me to goe with him..to the Jesuites Colledge, to witness his polemical talent. **1685** DRYDEN *Sylvæ* Pref., Ess. (ed. Ker) I. 266 He is chiefly to be considered in his three different talents, as he was a critic, a satirist, and a writer of odes. **1693** CONGREVE *Old Bach.* IV. xiii, Where did you get this excellent talent of railing? **1774** CHESTERF. *Lett.* I. x. 36 To write letters well..is a talent which unavoidably occurs every day of one's life. **1846** GREENER *Sc. Gunnery* 398 They seem to possess a 'talent' for this sort of thing. **1849** MACAULAY *Hist. Eng.* ii. I. 199 He had shown..two talents invaluable to a prince, the talent of choosing his servants well, and the talent of appropriating to himself the chief part of the credit of their acts.

**b.** *pl.* Aptitudes or faculties of various kinds; mental powers of a superior order; abilities, parts.

**1654** EVELYN *Diary* 12 July, Mr. Gibbon..giving us a taste of his skill and talents on that instrument [the double organ]. **1656** BLOUNT *Glossogr.* s. v., We say, a man of good talents, i. of good parts or abilities. **1731** FIELDING *Letter Writer* II. i, Love and war I find still require the same talents. **1771** GOLDSM. *Hist. Eng.* II. 259 The duke of Buckingham, a man of talents and power. **1796** MRS. M. ROBINSON *Angelina* I. 69 She is the only unaffected woman of talents I have met with. **1866** WHITTIER *Marg. Smith's Jrnl.* Prose Wks. 1889 I. 92 What avail great talents, if they be not devoted to goodness? **1895** N. W. SIBLEY in *Law Times* XCIX. 476/2 It requires the talents of a Boileau, Molière, or La Fontaine to play the part of a *flâneur* with any success.

**c.** collective *sing.* (without *a* or *pl.*). Mental power or ability; cleverness.

**1622** MABBE tr. *Aleman's Guzman d'Alf.* I. (1623) 193 Other poore rogues of lesse talent. **1670** CAPT. J. SMITH *Eng. Improv. Reviv'd* 6 As much as their Talent and Capacity will amount to. **1749** MRS. BELFOUR in *Richardson's Corr.* (1804) IV. 259 Your talent may be universal; I believe it is. **1764** GOLDSM. *Trav.* 354 And talent sinks, and merit weeps unknown. **1771** SMOLLETT *Humph. Cl.* 2 June, Without principle, talent, or intelligence. **1800** SOUTHEY *Let. to J. Rickman* 9 Jan., We have men of talent here also. **1809** COLERIDGE *Own Times* 655 The aristocracy of talent. **1821** SYD. SMITH *Wks.* (1850) 313 A work in which great and extraordinary talent is evinced. **1847** EMERSON *Repr. Men, Goethe* Wks. (Bohn) I. 390 In England and in America, there is a respect for talent. **1877** MORLEY *Crit. Misc.* Ser. II. 149 He was a person of no talent, his friends allowed.

**d.** Talent as embodied in the talented; sometimes approaching or passing into the sense: Persons of talent or ability collectively; rarely, as sing., a person of talent. By the sporting press, applied to backers of horses, as distinguished from the 'layers' or bookmakers, the implication being that those whose investments make a horse a 'favourite' are supposed to be 'the clever ones'.

(*Administration of*) *All the Talents* (*Eng. Hist.*), an ironical appellation of the Ministry of Lord Grenville, 1806-7, implying that it combined in its members all the talents.

[**1809** SCOTT *Fam. Lett.* 15 Feb., Yet the aggregate talent from which assistance is expected is very formidable. **1838** MACAULAY *Ess., Temple* (1887) 452 Clarendon..seems to have taken a sort of morose pleasure in slighting and provoking all the rising talent of the kingdom. **1885** J. K. JEROME *On the Stage* 17 Selfish fellows who wanted to keep young talent from the stage.]

**1856** G. DAVIS *Hist. Sk. Stockbridge & Southbr.* 213 It summoned to its investigation the first talents of the nation. **1883** *Daily News* 21 July 6/5 Xarifa was the most in demand, and the talent again proved correct in their choice, Mr. Valentine's filly winning a capital race by a neck. **1885** *Field* 3 Oct. 489/1 All the talent were discomfited, though; as they often are in Nurseries. **1886** H. HALL *Soc. in Eliz. Age* vii. 100 Throughout the summer there were always two ..of the local 'talent' engaged in fishing upon the manor. **1888** H. JAMES in *Fortn. Rev.* May 651 M. Pierre Loti is a new enough talent for us still to feel something of the glow of exultation at his having not contradicted us, but [etc.]. **1861** KNIGHT *Pop. Hist. Eng.* VII. xxvi. 463 The ministry of 'All the Talents' was accepted without any hesitation on the part of the king. **1895** OMAN *Hist. Eng.* xxxviii. 608 The short Fox-Grenville cabinet, which contemporary wits called the ministry of 'All the Talents', on account of its broad and comprehensive character. **1897** MORLEY *Guicciardini* in *Misc.* Ser. IV. (1908) 79 Cabinets of all the Talents have sometimes been cabinets of all the blunders.

† **7.** The characteristic disposition or aptitude of a person or animal. (App. blending 4 and 6.) *Obs.*

**1669** DRYDEN *Tempest* Pref., Wks. 1883 III. 105 This is certainly the talent of that nation. **1697** COLLIER *Immor. Stage* i. (1698) 7 Obscenity in any Company is a rustick uncreditable Talent; but among Women 'tis particularly rude. **1697** VANBRUGH *Prov. Wife* II. ii, Besides, 'tis my particular talent to ridicule folks. **1701** SWIFT *Contests Nobles & Com.* Wks. 1755 II. I. 46 It is the talent of human nature to run from one extreme to another. **1741** RICHARDSON *Pamela* I. xxx. 116 Pride is not my Talent. **1774** GOLDSM. *Nat. Hist.* (1776) IV. 159 Its talents are entirely repressed in solitude, and are only brought out by society.

**b.** The good points or qualities of a horse. ? *Obs.*

**1725** *Bradley's Fam. Dict.* s. v. *Horse*, If your Horse's Talent be Speed, all that you can do is to wait upon the other Horse, and keep behind till you come almost to the Stand, and then endeavour to give a Loose by him.

**8.** *attrib.* and *Comb.*, as *talent-hiding*; **talent-money**, a bonus or gratuity given to a professional athlete, etc. for specially meritorious performance.

**1623** LISLE *Ælfric on O. & N. Test.* Pref. 7, I thought it a shame, and the great fault also of talent-hiding, to lead all my life in study. **1896** LD. HAWKE in *Westm. Gaz.* 25 Nov. 5/3 Whilst they were pleased to congratulate the one who made 100, [or] a bowler who earned talent money. **1896** *Daily Chron.* 5 May 5/8 Briggs..saw Sugg earn his 'talent money' after the latter had been batting fifty minutes.

**Ta·lent,** *v. rare.* Also 5 -awnt. [f. TALENT *sb.*]

† **1.** *trans.* To fill with desire; = ENTALENT *v.*

**1486** *Bk. St. Albans* C j b, That shall talawnt hir wele, and cause her to haue goode appetide.

**2.** To endow with talent or talents. Chiefly in *pa. pple.* **talented.**

*a* **1633** ABP. ABBOT in Rushw. *Hist. Coll.* (1659) 449 When one talented but as a common person, yet by the favour of his prince, hath gotten that interest. **1702** C. MATHER *Magn. Chr.* III. 103 So Great an Ability, as that wherewith Mr. Rogers was Talented. *Ibid.* IV. (1853) II. 18 In his peculiar opportunities, with which the free grace of Heaven hath talented him to do good unto the public. *a* **1774** TUCKER *Lt. Nat.* (1834) II. 589 We were neither born nor talented for ourselves alone; we are citizens of the universe.

**Talent(e,** obs. and dial. forms of TALON.

**Ta·lented,** *a.* [f. TALENT *sb.* + -ED [2].]

**I.** From obs. senses of TALENT *sb.*

† **1.** Naturally inclined or disposed *to* something.

**1422** tr. *Secreta Secret., Priv. Priv.* 228 Tho that haue grete Noosys lyghtely bene talentid to couetise, and bene desposyd to concupiscence.

† **2.** *Her.* = BEZANTY. *Obs. rare.*

**1486** *Bk. St. Albans, Her.* E iij, A certan bordure talentit as here, and it is not necessari here to expres the colowre of the talentis or besantis: for thay be euer of golde.

**II.** From existing sense of TALENT *sb.*

**3.** Endowed with talent or talents; possessing talent; gifted, clever, accomplished.

[*a* **1633**-: see *Talented* as *pa. pple.* in TALENT *v.* 2.]

**1827** LYTTON *Falkland* I. 16, I smiled at the kindness of the fathers who, hearing I was talented..looked to my support. **1828** SOUTHEY in *Corr. w. C. Bowles* (1881) 134 Unprincipled people, too many of them talented and clever and most agreeable. **1829** HERSCHEL *Ess.* (1857) 515 Those numerous and talented individuals throughout the continent, and in England. **1830** W. TAYLOR *Hist. Surv. Germ. Poetry* III. 406 His eye, though indicating a talented mind, was restless and unsteady. **1832** COLERIDGE *Table-t.* 8 July, I regret to see that vile and barbarous vocable *talented*, stealing out of the newspapers into the leading reviews and most respectable publications of the day. **1842** PUSEY *Crisis Eng. Ch.* 99 A talented writer, who has been one great instrument in its restoration. **1853** WHITTIER *Prose Wks.* (1889) II. 418 A successful advocate at the bar, talented, affable, eloquent.

**Talented,** obs. variant of TALONED.

† **Ta·lenter.** *Obs. rare.* [f. *talent*, obs. f. TALON *sb.* or *v.* + -ER [1].] A bird of prey with talons, as a hawk.

**1620** MIDDLETON & ROWLEY *World Tost at Tennis* Induct., The feather'd talenter to the falling bird.

† **Ta·lentive,** *a. Obs.* In 4-5 -if. [a. OF. *talentif* desirous (12th c. in Godef.), f. *talent*, TALENT *sb.* 2: see -IVE.] Desirous.

**13..** *Gaw. & Gr. Knt.* 350 Þaȝ ȝe ȝour-self be talenttyf to take hit to your-seluen. *c* **1450** *Merlin* xx. 352 Thei after that were full talentif hem to sle, yef thei myght hem take.

**Talentless** (tæ·lĕntlės), *a.* [f. TALENT *sb.* + -LESS.] Devoid of talent; not mentally gifted.

**1831** *Fraser's Mag.* IV. 180 'Misapplied talent', cry the talentless. **1846** H. W. TORRENS *Rem. Milit. Hist.* 78 The Romans, whose talentless leaders in the early wars of the republic seem to have been prone to depend on the soldier rather than themselves. **1898** *Westm. Gaz.* 11 May 3/2 Dreadful daubs, showing nothing but talentless ambition.

‖ **Tales** (tē·līz). *Law.* [L. pl. of *tālis* such, in the phrase *tales de circumstantibus* 'such (or the like) persons from those standing about', occurring in the order for adding such persons to a jury; whence used as a sb.]

Originally, in plural, Persons taken from among those present in court or standing by, to serve on a jury in a case where the original panel has become deficient in number by challenge or other cause, these being persons *such* as those originally summoned; loosely applied in Eng. as a singular (*a tales*) to the supply of men (or even one man) so provided. Also contextually applied to the order or act of supplying such substitutes, as *to pray, grant, award a tales.* In English use now restricted to such summoning of common jurors to serve on a special jury; orig. and still in U. S. in general use (including criminal jurisdiction).

[*c* **1250** BRACTON 238 b (Rolls IV. 8). **1345** *Year-Bk.* 19 *Edw. III* (Rolls) 146 Ou le panel par le *Habeas corpora* et *Octo Tales* fuit retourne devant luy. **1346** *Ibid.*, 20 *Edw. III* 490 Par quei il avoit briefe a Vicounte de feire venir præter les deux que furent jurez XII tales. **1370** *Ibid.*, 44 *Edw. III* Mich. pl. 62 f. 25 Pur que il [the counsel] pria XII tales et les serjeants d'autre part disoient que a autrefois il avoit ewe X tales. **1479** *Year-Bk.* 18 *Edw. IV* Pasch. pl. 31 p. 6 Home n'avera XII tales en nul cas forsque in appeal tantum. **1531** *Registr. omn. Brev. Judic.* (Rastell) 75.]

**1495** *Act* 11 *Hen. VII*, c. 21 Upon every tales graunted, the seid Maire and Aldermen shall impanell the seid Persones. **1607** COWELL s. v., A supply of men empaneled vpon a iury or enquest, and not appearing, or at their apparance, chalenged by..either partie..the Iudge vpon petition graunteth a supply to be made by the Shyreeue of some men there present, equall in reputation to those that were impaneled. And herevpon the very act of supplying is called a *Tales de Circumstantibus.* *Ibid.*, The first Tales must be vnder [*i. e.* fewer than] the principall panell, except in a cause of Appeale, and so euery Tales lesse then other. *a* **1680** BUTLER *Rem.* (1759) II. 69 He is chosen..like a Tales in a Jury, for happening to be near in Court. **1768** BLACKSTONE *Comm.* III. xxiii. 364 Either party may pray a *tales.* A *tales* is a supply of *such* men as are summoned upon the first panel, in order to make up the deficiency. **1837** DICKENS *Pickw.* xxxiv, It was discovered that only ten special jurymen were present. Upon this, Mr. Sergeant Buzfuz prayed a *tales*; the gentleman in black then proceeded to press into the special jury two of the common jurymen. **1863** H. COX *Instit.* II. iii. 355 In criminal cases it is not the practice to award a *tales.*

**b.** *Comb.* **Tales-book**, a name for the entry-book of persons summoned on a tales: see quots.

[**1604** COKE *Reports* IV. 93 b, Le liuer appel les Tales. **1607** COWELL, *Tales*, is the proper name of a booke in the Kings bench office [citing *Coke*].] **1670** BLOUNT *Law Dict.*, *Tales*, is also the name of a Book in the Kings Bench Office Of such Jury-men as were of the Tales.] **1823** CRABB *Techn. Dict.*, *Tales-book.* Hence in mod. Dicts.

**Tales, Taleshide**: see TALLITH, TALSHIDE.

**Talesman** [1] (tē·līz-, tē·lzmæn). *Law.* [f. TALES + MAN *sb.*[1]] A member of the tales impanelled to complete a jury: see TALES.

**1679** LUTTRELL *Brief Rel.* (1857) I. 18 There was a good jury impanelled, but they were never summoned; so that there were talesmen there ready who did the work. **1770** *Chron.* in *Ann. Reg.* 129/1 Only seven of the special jury attended, so that five talesmen were allowed to be taken out of the box. **1825** *Act* 6 *Geo. IV*, c. 50 § 37 Where a special jury shall have been struck the talesmen shall be such as shall be impanelled upon the common jury panel. **1891** 'OCTAVE THANET' *Otto the Knight, Trusty* 236 One of those court-room hangers-on always ready to the sheriff's hand either for jurors or talesmen. **1906** *Westm. Gaz.* 19 Oct. 14/1 In a murder case now being heard in Albany [N.Y.]. After the expenditure of a whole fortnight in the examination of 522 talesmen, only ten of the number have qualified as jurors.

† **Talesman** [2] (tē·lzmæn). *Obs.* [f. *tale's*, genitive of TALE *sb.* + MAN *sb.*[1]] The teller of a tale, the author of a story; a relater, a narrator.

*a* **1568** *Henryson's Credence of Titlaris* 12 (Bann. MS.) Ane worthy lord sowld wey ane taill wyslie..gif the tailisman [*Maitl. MS.* tellar] abyd at It he wald. **1570-76** LAMBARDE *Peramb. Kent* (1826) 358 Polydore might well have spared to magnifie Becket with this lie,..unlesse he had brought his Talesman with him. **1613** PURCHAS *Pilgrimage* I. ix. 44 Yet the Tales-man shall be Set by the Tale, the Authors name annexed to his Historie. *a* **1700** B. E. *Dict. Cant. Crew*, I tell you my Tale, and my Talesman, or Author. **1768** ROSS *Helenore* 29 Baith tale an' tales-man I to you shall tell.

So † **Ta·les-ma·ster**, in the same sense: cf. *tale-master*, s. v. TALE *sb.* 10.

**1656** HEYLIN *Extraneus Vapulans* 53 Without producing his Tales-master to make it good, he only says that he hath been told.

**Ta·le-te:ller.** [f. TALE sb. + TELLER.]
1. A teller of tales or stories; a narrator.
1387 TREVISA Higden (Rolls) I. 337 Beda knew neuere þat ilond wiþ his eyȝe; bot some tale tellere [L. relator] tolde hym suche tales. 1530 PALSGR. 279/1 Taletellar, embouchevr, diseur de fables. 1623 COCKERAM III, Bebeus, a notable Tale-teller. 1728–30 POPE in Spence Anecd. Bks. & Men I. (1820) 19 Chaucer..is the first Tale-teller in the true and enlivened natural way. 1871 MORRIS in Mackail Life (1899) I. 263 Thou tale-teller of vanished men.
2. A talebearer; a tell-tale. Also fig.
1377 LANGL. P. Pl. B. xx. 297 Alle taletellers and tyterers in ydel. 1494 FABYAN Chron. VII. ccxxvi. 254 By ill tale tellers .. this brotherlye loue was after desolued. 1583 BABINGTON Commandm. ix. (1622) 87 To be a taleteller and false witnesse. 1619 in Ferguson & Nanson Munic. Rec. Carlisle (1887) 277 Slandering Robert James to be comon tayle teller to Mr. Chancelor. 1896 BLACK Briseis xix, How quick a tale-teller is the expression of your face, to one who has the skill to remark.
3. One who tells a 'tale' or made-up story with the object of deceiving or misleading.
1894 Daily News 28 Mar. 5/5 Persons who had not backed horses on the recommendation of a 'tale-teller'.
So **Ta·le-te·lling** sb., the telling of tales, story-telling; a., that tells tales or stories.
1556 OLDE Antichrist 116 Thus the harlot bewrayeth him self in his owne tale telling. 1743 FRANCIS tr. Hor., Odes I. xviii. 16 The broad-glaring eye of the tale-telling day. 1833 HT. MARTINEAU Charmed Sea iv. 54 One is winked at for a tale-telling traveller, if one says what I am saying now. 1898 SAINTSBURY Short Hist. Eng. Lit. x. i, The wild stories which float through mediæval tale-telling.

†**Taleva·ce.** Obs. Also 4 talvace, talvas. [a. OF. talevas, talvas (12th c. in Godefroy), held to be transposed from *tavelas, ad. It. tavolaccio a great table, or target of boards, a wooden buckler, augm. of tavola, L. tabula table.] A large shield or buckler, properly of wood.
c1300 Havelok 2323 Buttinge with sharpe speres, Skirming with taleuaces, that men beres. 13.. Sir Beues (A.) 3960 And after mete .. þe children pleide at þe taluas. c1400 Ywaine & Gaw. 3158 Aither broght unto the place A mikel rownd talvace, And a klub, ful grete and lang.

†**Ta·lewise,** a. Obs. Also 4 talwis, talewys, 5 -wijs, 6 -wes. [f. TALE sb. + -wīs, from OE. -wīs, from wise, WISE sb., manner, way; cf. rihtwīs RIGHTEOUS.] Given to tales or talking; addicted to gossip; loquacious, garrulous, blabbing.
c1200 Trin. Coll. Hom. 193 Talewise men þe speches driuen, and maken wrong to rihte, and riht to wronge. 1362 LANGL. P. Pl. A. III. 126 Heo is Tikel of hire Tayl, Talewys [1377 B. III. 130 talwis] of hire tonge. c1430 How Wise Man tauȝt his Son 26 in Babees Bk. (1868) 49 Be not to tale-wijs bi no wey. 1520 Treat. Galaunt (W. de Worde) 17 Talewes and talkynge, and drynkynge ataunte.

**Talewod, -wood**: see TALWOOD.

**Talgh, -e,** obs. forms of TALLOW.

**Taliacotian** (tæliăkōu·ʃiăn), a. Surg. Also Taglia-, erron. Tali-. [f. Taliacoti-us, latinized form of It. Tagliacozzi + -AN.] Of, pertaining to, or named after Tagliacozzi, a surgeon of Bologna (1546–99); esp. in Taliacotian operation, a plastic operation described by him for restoration of the nose by means of tissue taken from another part.
1656 BLOUNT Glossogr., Tagliacotian nose (an inhabitant of Bruxiels had his nose cut off in a cumbate, and a new one of another mans flesh set on in its sted, by Taliacotius .. of Bononia), a nose of wax. 1657 W. MORICE Coena quasi Κοινὴ x. 120 In a Talicotian way of cure, to..cut off one mans flesh to salve anothers deformity. 1821 Blackw. Mag. IX. 178 The talicotian operation, whereby a nose, almost as good as the old one, lost in battles.., was formed from the skin of the forehead carefully peeled down. 1857 DUNGLISON Dict. Med. s.v. Rhinoplastic, The Tagliacotian operation..consists in bringing down a portion of flesh from the forehead, and causing it to adhere to the anterior part of the remains of the nose.
So **Taliaco·tify** v. trans., to perform the Taliacotian operation on (a person).
a1843 SOUTHEY Comm.-pl. Bk. (1851) IV. 589/1 The Chev. Saint Thoan found a silver nose so inconvenient that he submitted to be Taliacotified.

**Taliage,** obs. form of TALLAGE.

**Taliar,** variant of TALLIAR, Indian watchman.

†**Ta·liary,** a. Obs. rare$^{-1}$. [f. L. tāli-s such, the like (with reference to tālio) + -ARY.] Of or pertaining to TALION.
1620 FORD Linea V. (1843) 44 So much, it is to bee presumed, the verie taliarie law may require, and obtaine.

†**Talia·tion.** Obs. exc. Hist. [n. of action f. L. tāli-s such, the like, as if from a vb. *tāliāre: cf. late L. retāliāre to RETALIATE.] A return of like for like; retaliation; = TALION$^{1}$.
[c1485 tr. Act 37 Edw. III, c. 18 (MS. Harl. 4999, lf. 67) That ther thei fynden suerte to pursue their Suggestiouns and to incurre and renne the same peyne this that the other shulde have if he were atteynt, in cas that his suggestioun be founde fals and of malice.] 1591 LAMBARDE Archeion (1635) 123 The Commons of the Realme assented..in the Parliament 37. Edward 3. cap. 18. that these Petitioners should put in Suerties of Taliation. 1648 J. BEAUMONT Psyche XVII. xxvi, Just Heav'n this Taliation did decree, That Treason Treason's deadly Scourge should be. a1677 HALE True Relig. III. 43 If men..justifie it by the Law of Taliation,..a Spirit of Revenge, an Eye for an Eye, a Tooth for a Tooth, is..against the Doctrine of Christ. 1769 BLACKSTONE Comm. IV. i. 14 After one year's experience [of 37 Edw. III, c. 18], this punishment of taliation was rejected, and imprisonment adopted in it's stead.

**Tali-douce, -duce,** obs. var. TAILLE-DOUCE.
1683 J. REID Scots Gard. I. ii. 7 If your draught be a Taliduce, Mapps or the like.

‖**Taliera** (tæli,ēᵊ·ră). [Bot. L. f. Bengālī tālier, f. Skr. tālī, f. tāla fan-palm; cf. TALIPOT. (In Hindī tarra, tara.)] An East Indian palm, Corypha Taliera, allied to and resembling the talipot, but not nearly so high.
1814 ROXBURGH Hortus Bengal., Corypha Taliera, Skr. Talee. 1837 Penny Cycl. VIII. 74/1 The Tara or Talliera, Corypha talliera, is an elegant stately species inhabiting Bengal. Its trunk is about thirty feet high...The leaves are used by the natives..to write upon with their steel stiles.

**Ta·ling,** vbl. sb. Now rare. [f. TALE v. + -ING$^{1}$.] Telling of tales, talking, gossiping; also, a tale.
1382 WYCLIF Ps. cxviii[i]. 85 Wicke men tolden to me talingus; but not as thi lawe. c1430 Pilgr. Lyf Manhode II. cxxviii. (1869) 124 As flaterye heeld me thus with talinge,..and told me hire doinges. 1617 HIERON Wks. II. 84 Gaming, and taling, and reading of merry stories. 1628 WITHER Brit. Rememb. 211 Among the poore are many wicked things..scolding, fightings, cursings, taleing, lies.

‖**Talio** (tē·lio). [L. tālio, f. tālis such, the like.] A requiting of like for like, retaliation; = next.
1611 SPEED Hist. Gt. Brit. IX. xvi. § 2 God obseruing a talio and parilitie. 1631 GOUGE God's Arrows III. § 60. 296 In case of talio, or requiting like for like. 1704 HEARNE Duct. Hist. (1714) I. 226 Talio was a punishment in the same kind, as an Eye for an Eye, a Tooth for a Tooth. 1874 tr. Lange's Comm. Zeph. 25 The judgment is talio.

**Talion**$^{1}$ (tæ·liən). Also 5 talyon, talyoune. [a. F. talion (14th c. in Godef. Compl.), ad. L. tāliōn-em, nom. tālio: see prec.] = RETALIATION; esp. in the Mosaic, Roman, and other systems of Law, the Lex talionis, or †talion law, the principle of exacting compensation, 'eye for eye, tooth for tooth'; also, the infliction of the same penalty on the accuser who failed to prove his case as would have fallen upon the accused if found guilty.
1412–20 LYDG. Chron. Troy II. 3066 Vp-on Grekis for her offencioun, To parforme vp þe peyne of talioun. 1456 SIR G. HAYE Law Arms (S. T. S.) 273 He suld have the payne of talyoune.., that sik punycioun as the tothir suld have [had] that the crime is put on, sik punycioun sall he have. 1563 J. MAN Musculus' Commonpl. 33 b, According to the equitie of the Talion law. 1646 GAULE Cases Consc. 174 It is just Talion to deliver such up to Satan that have already given themselves unto him. 1738 WATTS Holiness of Times 77 The Talion Law of punishment for injuries received amongst the Jews. 1879 ROLLIN-TILTON tr. Amicis' Morocco (1882) 294 She..demanded that in virtue of the law of talion, he should order the English merchant's two front teeth to be broken. 1880 MUIRHEAD Gaius III. § 223 By the Twelve Tables the penalties of personal injury were,—for destruction of any of the members, talion.

†**Talion**$^{2}$. Obs. rare$^{-1}$. [a. OF. taillon cutting, deriv. of taille, or L. tālea: see TAIL sb.$^{2}$] A shoot or scion, such as is used in grafting.
c1440 Pallad. on Husb. III. 990 The croppe or talions to graffe is speed, But talions the better me shal fynde On either half maad smoth, vnhurt the rynde.

**Talionic** (tæliǫ·nik), a. rare. [f. L. tāliōn-em (see TALION$^{1}$) + -IC.] Of or pertaining to the law of talion, or to the rendering of like for like.
1886 G. MACDONALD What's Mine's Mine v, The growing talionic regard of human relations—that, namely, the conditions of a bargain fulfilled on both sides, all is fulfilled between the bargaining parties.

**Taliped** (tæ·liped), a. Path. and Zool. [f. mod. L. tāliped-em: see next.] 'Club-footed, as a result of disease; or as a natural condition, as in the sloth' (Syd. Soc. Lex. 1898).

‖**Talipes** (tæ·lipīz). [mod.L. tālipēs, -pedem, f. L. tālus ankle + pēs foot: cf. tālipedāre to walk on the ankles, to be weak in the feet, to walk lamely.]
1. Path. Club-foot; clubfootedness. Also attrib.
1857 in DUNGLISON Dict. Med. 1878 A. M. HAMILTON Nerv. Dis. 240 The primary forms are those which are seen in talipes of both kinds. 1879 St. George's Hosp. Rep. IX. 615 All cases of talipes have been submitted to subcutaneous tenotomy. 1898 P. MANSON Trop. Diseases xiv. 245 Foot-drop should be counteracted by Phelps's talipes splint.
2. Zool. A twisted disposition of the feet, occurring naturally in sloths. 1891 in Cent. Dict.

**Talipot** (tæ·lipǫt, -pət). Forms: 7–8 tallipot, -pat, 7–9 talipat, 9 talipot, -put, talpat. [a. Sinh. talapata, Malayālim tālipat = Hindī tālpāt:—Skt. tālapattra, leaf of the tāla, palmyra, or fan-palm, Borassus flabelliformis; transferred in Ceylon and Southern India to the leaf of Corypha umbraculifera.] A South Indian fan-palm, Corypha umbraculifera, native in Ceylon and Malabar, noted for its great height, and its enormous fan-shaped leaves, which are much used as a material to write on.
1681 R. KNOX Hist. Ceylon 15 The first is the Tallipot; It is as big and tall as a Ships Mast, and very streight, bearing only Leaves. 1837 J. MACCULLOCH Proofs Attrib. God III. xliv. 162 The Bamboo has been ordained for his dwelling and the Talipot to shelter him from the rains. 1859 TENNENT Ceylon I. I. iii. 109 The most majestic and wonderful of the palm tribe is the talpat or taliput, the stem of which sometimes attains the height of 100 feet, and each of its enormous fan-like leaves, when laid upon the ground, will form a semicircle of 16 feet in diameter.
b. attrib., as talipot-leaf, -palm, -tree.
1681 R. KNOX Hist. Ceylon Pref., A Fan made of the Talipat-Leaf. 1720 DE FOE Capt. Singleton xviii. (1840) 306 Two great tallipat leaves for tents. 1803 SYD. SMITH Wks. (1859) I. 44/2 A leaf of the talipot tree is a tent to the soldier,..and a book to the scholar. 1834 H. CAUNTER in Oriental Ann. vii. 75 [We] had the gratifying opportunity of seeing a talipât palm in blossom.

†**Ta·lish,** a. Obs. [f. TALE sb. + -ISH$^{1}$.] Of the nature of a tale or story; fabulous.
1530 PALSGR. 327/1 Talysshe, full of lyes, fabuleux. 1540 — Acolastus Z ij b, All thynges whiche menne telle or reporte of hell, be but talyshe .i. be but fables or tales.

†**Talisman**$^{1}$. Obs. Also 7 talasumany, talsuman; pl. 6–7 talismani, -manni, -mans. [= F. talisman, of uncertain history; occurring in Fr. and Eng. considerably earlier than TALISMAN$^{2}$. It appears to be a corrupt or mistaken form of some Arabic, Persian, or Turkish spoken word, imperfectly caught by early travellers. See Note below.]
A name formerly applied to a Turk learned in divinity and law, a Mullah; sometimes to a lower priest of Islam, a religious minister, a muezzin.
1599 HAKLUYT Voy. II. I. 208 This..Mosquita hath .. 5 steeples, from whence the Talismani call the people to the Mosquita. 1615 SANDYS Trav. 31 Turrets, exceeding high, and exceeding slender..from whence the Talismanni with elated voices (for they vse no bels) do congregate the people. c1618 MORYSON Itin. IV. (1903) 19 They are instructed by old Talismans called Cozza, as it were doctors of the law. 1632 LITHGOW Trav. IV. 142 The Talasumany, which is the chiefe Priest. Ibid. VIII. 369 To maintaine them, and a hundred Totsecks and preaching Talsumans..extendeth to two hundred Duccats a day. 1638 SIR T. HERBERT Trav. (ed. 2) 267 The Talismanni regard the houres of prayer by turning the 4 hour'd glasse. The Muyezini crie from the tops of Mosques. 1668 RYCAUT Pres. St. Ottoman Emp. II. vii. 114 Imams or Priests, Doctours of their Law, Talismans and others, who continually attend there for the Education of youth.
[Note. Professor Margoliouth suggests that the word intended may possibly have been طيلسان ṭailasān, a form of hood thrown over the head and shoulders, especially by preachers, but also used by doctors of law and others (see Dozy Dict. Noms de Vêtements Arabes 278). The wearer of this might be designated ṭailasānī, and this corrupted into talismānī. But evidence is wanting.]

**Talisman**$^{2}$ (tæ·lizmăn). [= 17th c. F., Sp., Pg. talisman, It. talismano, ultimately representing Arab. طلسم ṭilsam, in same sense, ad. Gr. τέλεσμα TELESM. The final -an is not accounted for.
An Arabic pl. ṭilsamān, alleged by Diez s.v., and thence in various recent dictionaries, is an error: no such form exists in Arabic, Persian, or Turkish. The only Arabic form at all similar would be a relative adj. *ṭilsimānī (one) dealing with talismans, if this were in use. The identity of talisman with τέλεσμα was first pointed out by Salmasius, Hist. Augusta 1620.]
1. A stone, ring, or other object engraven with figures or characters, to which are attributed the occult powers of the planetary influences and celestial configurations under which it was made; usually worn as an amulet to avert evil from or bring fortune to the wearer; also medicinally used to impart healing virtue; hence, any object held to be endowed with magic virtue; a charm.
In quot. 1638 applied to the telesms or consecrated statues set up in Egypt, and later in Greece, to protect the city or community: see TELESM. Among Moslem nations, the potent principle is held to be contained in verses from the Koran engraved on the charm.
1638 JUNIUS Paint. Ancients 137 The inaugurated statues, which now adays by them that are curious of such things are called Talisman. 1652 GAULE Magastrom. 41 To serve as a Talisman; as their Astrologers think, to aucupate the favour of Venus and the Moon against the influences of Scorpio and Mars. 1656 BLOUNT Glossogr., Talismans, images, or figures made under certain constellations. 1663 BUTLER Hud. I. I. 530 For mystic learning, wondrous able In magic, talisman, and cabal. 1682 WHELER Journ. Greece III. 270 This Inscription is a kind of Talisman, or Charm. 1798 Loves of Triangles I. 84 in Anti-Jacobin 23 Apr., Each scribbled Talisman, and smoky spell. 1825 SCOTT Talism. xviii, Know, then, that the medicine..is a talisman, composed under certain aspects of the heavens. 1875 STUBBS Const. Hist. II. xiv. 45 He had stolen from Henry..a Talisman, which rendered its wearer invulnerable.
2. fig. Anything that acts as a charm, or by which extraordinary results are achieved.
1784 COWPER Task VI. 98 Books are not seldom talismans and spells By which the magic art of shrewder wits Holds an unthinking multitude enthralled. 1834 PRINGLE Afr. Sk. xiv. 479 Let us subdue savage Africa by Justice, by Kindness, by the talisman of Christian Truth. 1908 H. A. L. FISHER Bonapartism vi. 123 Bonapartism can never again stand as the..talisman of victory.
†3. Applied to a person: see quot. Obs.
1646 J. GREGORY Notes & Obs. (1650) 38 One Debborius a Talisman (τελεστής) to prevent the falling of the city in case an earthquake should happen againe, set up this pillar and upon that a marble Pectorall inscribed ΑΣΕΙΣΤΑ ΑΠΤΩΤΑ. Ibid. 41 Moses the Talisman (so they would account him) sat it up upon a pole in the wilderness.
†4. (? Cf. tailasān in note to prec.) Obs.
1678 BUTLER Hud. III. II. 1555 On whom, in Equipage and State, His Scarecrow Fellow-Members wait,..Each in a tatter'd Talismane, Like Vermine in Effigie slain.

**Talismanic** (tælizmæ·nik), a. [f. TALISMAN$^{2}$ + -IC. Cf. F. talismanique (1625 in Hatz.-Darm.).]

Of, pertaining to, or of the nature of a talisman; occult, magical, potent.

**1678** BUTLER *Hud.* III. i. 432 Swore you had broke and robb'd his House, And stole his Talismanique Louse. **1761** STERNE *Tr. Shandy* III. xli, The word *siege*, like a talismanic power,..walting back my uncle Toby's fancy,..he open'd his ears. **1816** T. L. PEACOCK *Headlong Hall* ix, Spellbound by the talismanic influence of the coin. **1877** W. JONES *Finger-ring* 95 A remarkable gold talismanic ring..of Hindu workmanship.

**Talisma·nical,** *a.* [See -ICAL.] = prec.

**1650** CHILMEAD tr. Gaffarel (*title*) Unheard of Curiosities concerning the Talismanical Sculpture of the Persians. **1661** FELTHAM *Resolves* II. lxi. 313 There is a kinde of Talismanical influence in the soul of such. **1775** R. CHANDLER *Trav. Asia M.* (1825) I. 182 A kind of talismanical protection. **1844** KITTO *Pict. Hist. Palestine* I. iv. I. 110/2 The talismanical scarabæus of the Egyptians.

**Talisma·nically,** *adv.* [f. prec. + -LY [2].] In a talismanic manner; by or as by the influence of a talisman; magically.

**1831** *Fraser's Mag.* III. 230 We find the fear talismanically opening heaven's tollgate. **1864** *Realm* 9 Mar. 2 All is talismanically changed.

**Ta·lismanist.** *rare.* [f. TALISMAN [2] + -IST.] One who uses or believes in talismans.

**1706** PHILLIPS (ed. 6), *Talismanist*, one that makes Talismans or that gives Credit to them. **1720** DE FOE *D. Campbell* Ep. Ded. (1840) 15 Such was even the great Paracelsus, ..and such were all his followers..that are talismanists.

**Talisma·ntic,** *a. nonce-wd.* [irreg. f. TALISMAN [2], after *necromantic*, etc.] Talismanic.

**1814** *Sporting Mag.* XLIV. 67 The talismantic influence of his pencil.

**Talit, talith,** variants of TALLITH.

**Talk** (tǭk), *sb.* Forms: see the vb. [f. TALK *v.*] The action or practice of talking.

**I. 1.** Speech, discourse; *esp.* the familiar oral intercourse of two or more persons; conversation (of a familiar kind).

*c* **1475** *Rauf Coilȝear* 90 Into sic talk fell thay Quhill thay war neir hame. **1585** T. WASHINGTON tr. *Nicholay's Voy.* I. xvii. 19 The talke betweene them was for this time not very long. **1697** DRYDEN *Virg., Ess. Georg.* (1721) I. 205 Nothing which is a Phrase or Saying in common Talk, shou'd be admitted into a serious Poem. **1728** RAMSAY *Bonnie Chirsty* v, Time was too precious now for tauk. **1783** JOHNSON in *Boswell* (1816) IV. 202 We had talk enou h, but no conversation; there was nothing discussed. **1847** HELPS *Friends in C.* I. 1, I do not, however, love good talk the less for these defects of mine.

**b.** With *a* and *pl.* An instance of this; a conversation.

**1548** UDALL, etc. *Erasm. Par. Luke* ix. 88 Their thoughtes and their priuie talkes behynd his backe wer not hydden.. to hym. **1566** ABP. PARKER *Corr.* (Parker Soc.) 268 What speeches and talks be like to rise in the realm. **1658** A. FOX *Würtz' Surg.* I. ii. 3 It is not enough to be full of talks. **1871** L. STEPHEN *Playgr. Eur.* x. (1894) 250, I had many talks with him on the hills. *Mod.* I had a long talk with him on the matter.

**2.** A more or less formal or public oral interchange of views, opinions, or propositions; a conference. **b.** A palaver, a pow-wow with savages; also a verbal message to or from these.

**1550** BALE *Eng. Votaries* II. (1551) 88 At the lattre they came to talkes and to nyghte metynges. **1560** DAUS tr. *Sleidane's Comm.* 229 Themperoure had appoynted a talke of learned men at Regenspurge. *Ibid.* 441 b, Assaied by talcke and conference of learned men. **1760** *St. Papers* in *Ann. Reg.* 231/1 He [Amer. Indian] told the governor he would give his talk the next day; he said he had come with a good talk. **1768** *Chron.* ibid. 89/1 Captain Paterson had sent a talk to the great island, to disclaim the murders, and to pacify the Indians. **1791** W. BARTRAM *Carolina* 210 The talks (or messages between the Indians and white people) were perfectly peaceable and friendly...Bad talks from the Nation is always a very serious affair. **1837** W. IRVING *Capt. Bonneville* III. 114 Indians generally are very lofty, rhetorical, and figurative in their language at all great talks, and high ceremonials.

**3.** Mention (of a subject); making of statements and remarks; rumour; gossip; an instance of this.

**1560** DAUS tr. *Sleidane's Comm.* 370 b, In the Emperors court was..no talcke of it, and made as they knew not therof. **1577** *F. de L'isle's Legendarie* A viij b, His brother ..who, as the talke went, was sore ouerlayed with Anabaptistes. **1677** WOOD *Life* Apr. (O.H.S.) II. 372 Easter Week, great talk of a comet appearing in England. *a* **1768** ABP. SECKER *Serm., Tit.* ii. 6 (1770) III. iii. 68 It will not raise so early or so great a Talk about you. **1866** MRS. GASKELL *Wives & Dau.* xlviii, That would make a talk. **1887** GOLDW. SMITH in *Contemp. Rev.* July 3 A High Commissioner..has been sent to England, and there is talk of sending another to Washington.

**4.** The subject, theme, or occasion of topical conversation, esp. of current gossip or rumour.

**1624** MASSINGER *Parl. Love* IV. v, Live to be the talk Of the conduit and the bakehouse. **1703** CONGREVE *Tears Amaryllis* 107 Wert thou not..The Joy of Sight, the Talk of ev'ry Tongue? **1849** MACAULAY *Hist. Eng.* viii. II. 325 Just when these letters were the talk of all London. **1871** R. ELLIS *Catullus* xliii. 6 Thou the beauty, the talk of all the province?

**II. 5.** Utterance of words, speaking (to others), speech; = TALKING *vbl. sb.*; also, contemptuously, empty words, verbiage.

*Big talk, tall talk*, speaking in a boastful or exaggerated style; see also SMALL TALK.

**1539** TAVERNER *Erasm. Prov.* 19 As the man is, so is his talke. **1560** DAUS tr. *Sleidane's Comm.* 363 b, Seldie had the talk, and..propoundeth questions. **1651-7** T. BARKER *Art of Angling* (1820) 6 That is but talk. **1848** THACKERAY *Van. Fair* xxx, But these were mere by-gone days and talk. **1858** LYTTON *What will he do* I. iii, It is I who have all the talk now. **1869** [see TALL *a.* 8 b]. **1871** L. STEPHEN *Playgr. Eur.* xiii. (1894) 308 Tall talk is luckily an object of suspicion to Englishmen. **1895** *Pall Mall G.* 8 Oct. 1/3 There is nothing like big talk to draw contributions from a credulous peasantry.

**b.** Applied to writing of the nature of familiar or loose speech.

**1552** ASCHAM in *Lett. Lit. Men* (Camden) 13 Purposing elsewhan to troble yow with the taulk of longer lettres. **1884** *Chr. Commonwealth* 14 Feb. 416/1 Columns of wild, inflammatory, and dangerous talk are appearing in most of our newspapers. **1887** RUSKIN *Præterita* II. i. 1 This second volume must, I fear, be less pleasing...The talk must be less of other persons, and more of myself.

**c.** *fig.*

**1868** HAWTHORNE *Amer. Note-Bks.* II. 218 With so vivid a talk of countenance that it was precisely as if she had spoken. **1879** STEVENSON *Trav. Cevennes* (1886) 130 The indescribable quiet talk of the runnel over the stones.

**6.** Ordinary manner of speech; way of speaking; native language or dialect; lingo.

*a* **1788** T. RITSON in Mrs. Wheeler *Cumbld. Dial.* (1821) App. 2 Yan cudnt tell thare toke be geese. **1890** *Jrnl. Anthrop. Instit.* Feb. 396 [If they do not] speak the same language..the man stays in his own island, and the woman learns his 'talk'.

**7.** *Comb.*: †**talk-stuff**, matter for conversation.

**1598** MARSTON *Sco. Villanie* III. xi. 22 [He] For want of talk-stuffe, fals to foinery, Out goes his rapier.

**Talk** (tǭk), *v.* Forms: 3 talkien, -kin, 4 -ken, 4-7 talke, 4- talk, (6 talcke, taulk(e, tawlke; also *Sc.* 5 tawke, 6 tak, 8 tauk, tawk). [ME. *talkien, talken*: a deriv. vb. from TALE *sb.* or TELL *v.* Cf. EFris. *talken* to talk, chatter, prattle, speak quietly, whisper; also other deriv. vbs. in *-k*, with a diminutive or frequentative force, as *stalk, walk, lurk.*]

**I.** Intransitive senses.

**1.** To convey or exchange ideas, thoughts, information, etc. by means of speech, especially the familiar speech of ordinary intercourse; 'to speak in conversation' (J.); to converse.

*Talk about...*, often used *colloq.* to contrast something already mentioned with something still more striking.

*a* **1225** *Ancr. R.* 422 Auh talkeð mid ouer meidenes. *a* **1225** *St. Marher.* 13 Ich leote ham talkin ant tauelin of godlec, ant treowliche luuien ham. *a* **1300** *Cursor M.* 11743 (Cott.) Als þai to-gedir talked sua. **1377** LANGL. *P. Pl.* B. XVII. 82 To ouertake hym and talke to hym. *c* **1440** *Promp. Parv.* 486/1 Talkyn, *fabulor, colloquor, confabulor, sermocinor.* **1535** STEWART *Cron. Scot.* (Rolls) II. 123 Thai culd tak and tell of mony thing. **1560** DAUS tr. *Sleidane's Comm.* 125 He hath talked herein with the Dukes of Bavier. **1651** HOBBES *Leviath.* III. xl. 252 The Mountain where God talked with Moses. **1819** *Metropolis* III. 51 My mother and I talked at large on the subject. **1858** HAWTHORNE *Fr. & It. Note-Bks.* I. 180, I doubt whether I have ever really talked with half a dozen persons in my life. **1891** E. ROPER *By Track & Trail* xi. 157 Talk about English people being fond of eating, that Canadian party beat all I had ever seen.

**b.** By extension: To convey information in some other way, as by writing, with the fingers, eyes, etc.

**1705** ADDISON *Italy* 459 The Natural Histories of Switzerland talk very much of the Fall of these Rocks.

**2.** *Talk of*: to speak of, about, or in reference to (anything); often in indirect pass., *to be talked of. To talk of* (doing something), to speak somewhat vaguely, so as to suggest a notion, or express one's probable intention, of doing it. *Talking of...*, apropos of...

*c* **1230** *Hali Meid.* 17 ȝif ȝe þrafter þenne speken togedere folliche & talkeð of unnet. *c* **1375** *Cursor M.* 8035 (Fairf.) Hit is meruaile of ham to talke. *c* **1470** HENRY WALLACE I. 295 Tawkand thus of materis that was wrocht. *a* **1555** LATIMER *Serm. in Lincoln* ix. 142 Hearing them taulke of the wonderfull workes which Christ our Sauiour did. **1596** SHAKS. *Merch. V.* I. ii. 45 He doth nothing but talke of his horse. **1661** BOYLE *Style of Script.* (1675) 180 Erostratus, that Fir'd Diana's Temple to be Talk'd of for having done so. **1672**, etc. [see DEVIL *sb.* 22 l]. **1759** JOHNSON *Idler* No. 71 ¶ 15 [He] talked..volubly of pettifoggers. **1821** SCOTT *Kenilw.* viii, The day was long talked of. **1857** DICKENS *Let. to Miss Hogarth* 15 Sept., [Wilkie Collins] talks of going to the theatre tonight in a cab. **1886** J. PAYN *Heir of Ages* i, Talk of an angel and we hear the flutter of her wings. *Mod.* Talking of Switzerland—have you ever been there in winter?

**b.** *To talk over*: see 9 c.

**3.** To exercise the faculty of speech; to speak, utter words, say things; often contemptuous: to speak trivially, utter empty words, prate. *To talk to*, to address words to; *colloq.* to rebuke, scold, reprimand. *To talk at* RANDOM, *at* ROVERS: see these words.

**13..** *E. E. Allit. P.* B. 154 Þen þe lorde..talkez to his tormenttoures. *c* **1400** *Destr. Troy* 6136 Than Troilus tomly talket agayne. **1508** DUNBAR *Tua Mariit W.* 246 Now tydis me for to talk; my taill it is nixt. *a* **1586** SIDNEY *Ps.* IV. iv, Talk with yor heart and yet be still. **1592** SHAKS. *Ven. & Ad.* 427 What canst thou talke (quoth she), hast thou a tong? **1670** COTTON *Espernon* III. IX. 427 How comes it to pass you are not gone out to meet the Duke of Espernon? he'l talk with you for this when he comes. **1721** RAMSAY *Keitha* 22 Wha 've heard her sing or tauk. **1729** BUTLER *Serm.* Wks. 1874 II. 42 A disposition to be talking for its own sake. **1875** JOWETT *Plato* (ed. 2) V. 36 Be assured that I shall be glad to hear you talk as much as you please. **1878** W. S. GILBERT *H. M. S. Pinafore* II. (1881) 295 I'll talk to Master Rackstraw in the morning.

**b.** To say something as a rumour or matter of gossip; hence, to indulge in idle or censorious gossip. (Formerly also *trans.* with *obj. cl.*)

**1461** *Paston Lett.* II. 7 Item, som men talke Lord Wellys, Lord Wyllouby, and Skales ben on lyve. **1669** LADY CHAWORTH in *12th Rep. Hist. MSS. Comm.* App. v. 12 They talk heere as if the King would goe a northerne progresse this summer. **1719** RAMSAY *Prol. to 'The Orphan'* 15 But let them tauk. **1849** MACAULAY *Hist. Eng.* vi. II. 154 The king said..that it was difficult to prevent people from talking, and that loose reports were not to be regarded.

**c.** *To talk big, tall*, etc., to talk boastfully; to indulge in inflated language. *colloq.* or *slang. To talk down* (*to* an audience), to lower one's discourse to the assumed level of their intelligence.

**1699** R. L'ESTRANGE *Erasm. Colloq.* (1725) 236, I talk big, and wherever I find an hungry Buzzard I throw him out a Bait. **1702** *Eng. Theophrast.* 336 Some people think they need only talk loud and big and be very positive, to make all the World of their Opinion. **1841** THIRLWALL *Lett.* (1881) I. 175 We are able to talk big about light and freedom. **1888** BRYCE *Amer. Commw.* VI. cx. (1889) 669 On the Fourth of July..the speaker feels bound to talk 'his very tallest'.

**d.** *To talk at*, to make remarks intended for some one but not directly addressed to him.

**1837** MARRYAT *Olla Podr.* xxxiii, They talked at us, and not to us. **1838** DICKENS *Nich. Nick.* xxi, Mr. and Mrs. Wititterly, who had talked rather at the Nicklebys than to each other. **1894** MRS. DYAN *All in a Man's K.* (1899) 210 He had had no intention..of..talking at her, but the words had struck home.

**4.** To utter words, or the sound of words, unconsciously, mechanically, or imitatively, as *to talk in one's sleep*, etc.

**1591** SHAKS. *Two Gent.* III. i. 333 Item, she doth talke in her sleepe. **1704** NORRIS *Ideal World* II. iii. 120 That..we may not be supposed to talk like parrots. **1890** *Spectator* 4 Oct., The raven is the largest creature except man that can 'talk'.

**5.** *fig.* Of inanimate things: To make sounds or noises resembling or suggesting speech.

**1832** *Blackw. Mag.* XXXI. 508 She [a ship] began to slip through the water at a rapid rate and to talk. **1883** STEVENSON *Treas. Isl.* v. xxiii, The ship was talking, as sailors say, loudly, treading the innumerable ripples with an incessant weltering splash. **1885** W. L. CARPENTER *Soap & Candles* vi. 161 [The bubbles] make so much noise in their escape that, in the language of the soap-boiler, 'the soap talks'. **1900** *Daily News* 2 Jan. 6/1 It is to be hoped that they will not lose their heads when the rifles begin to talk in earnest.

**II.** Transitive senses.

**6.** To utter or speak in familiar language (words, a tale, etc.); to express in talk or speech (matter, opinions, etc.). †Also with *obj. cl.*: see 3 b. *To talk out*, to utter freely, give full utterance to.

*c* **1205** LAY. 788 Þat nan ne beo so wilde..þat word talie ne talkie mid speche. **13..** *Cursor M.* 17288 + 332 (Cott.) What wordez are þos..þat ȝe to-gedir talk? **13..** *Gaw. & Gr. Knt.* 2133 Bot I wyl to þe chapel..& talk wyth þat ilk tulk þe tale þat me lyste. **1445** in *Anglia* XXVIII. 269 The modrys of eloquence the musys ix..wisely talke dytees ful delectable. **1533** MORE *Debell. Salem* xiv. Wks. 966/2 To heare heresyes talked and lette the talkers alone. **1682** T. FLATMAN *Heraclitus Ridens* No. 52 (1713) II. 78 Let's leave him..and talk a little News that's common to the rest of the World. **1715** DE FOE *Fam. Instruct.* II. i. (1841) I. 174 Why, you talk blasphemy almost. **1775** ABIGAIL ADAMS in *Fam. Lett.* (1876) 115, I have written many things to you that..I never could have talked. **1848** THACKERAY *Van. Fair* xxxiv, They could not talk scandal in any tongue but their own. **1861** HUGHES *Tom Brown at Oxf.* iv, An old friend to whom he could talk out his mind.

**b.** To use as a spoken language, to speak conversationally; as *to talk French, German, Somerset, slang.* So *to talk sailor* (= to use nautical language), etc. *To talk Greek, Hebrew, Double-Dutch, gibberish*, etc., to use language unintelligible to the hearer.

**1859** *Habits of Gd. Society* (new ed.) 89 We..would not have him talk slang. **1869** F. W. NEWMAN *Misc.* 146 A single race, whose ancestors once talked a common language. **1886** *Manch. Exam.* 3 Nov. 5/6 Hundreds of young women who can talk French and German fluently. **1881** *Cent. Mag.* XXIII. 126/2, I..could talk sailor like an 'old salt'. **1903** *Daily Chron.* 12 Feb. 3/1 Englishmen who have visited America will remember their gratification at being invited to 'talk United States'.

**7.** To discourse about, speak of, discuss. Now *colloq. To talk shop*, to talk about matters pertaining to one's own business or profession.

**1387** TREVISA *Higden* (Rolls) IV. 359 He..talkede wiþ hym fiftene dayes þe gospel [*conferens cum eo evangelium*]. **1660** INGELO *Bentiv. & Ur.* II. (1682) 179 He desired to talk some things with him privately. **1667** MILTON *P. L.* III. 483 That Crystalline Sphear whose ballance weighs The Trepidation talkt. **1819** SHELLEY *Julian & Maddalo* 179 Aye, if we were not weak...You talk Utopia. **1821** BYRON *Diary* 29 Jan., They talk Dante —write Dante—and think and dream Dante. **1854** EMERSON *Soc. Aims* Wks. (Bohn) III. 181 Never 'talk shop' before company. **1870** MISS BRIDGMAN *Rob. Lynne* I. ix. 129 He threw all his ardour into talking business. **1871** M. COLLINS *Mrq. & Merch.* I. x. 302 Talking horse, and playing billiards. **1888** *Times* (weekly ed.) 3 Feb. 2/3 'Talking shop'..means talking of the interests of the work which you do, or the profession to which you belong. **1898** P. WHITE *Millionaire's Dau.* xxxi, We talked 'Oxford', the dean addressing his remarks to me.

**8.** To bring or drive (oneself or another) into some specified state by talking.

1599 SHAKS. *Much Ado* II. i. 369 They would talke themselues madde. 1613 — *Hen. VIII*, I. iv. 45 Talke vs to silence. 1816 SCOTT *Let. to Morritt* 21 Aug. in *Lockhart*, I talked them to death.

**9.** With *adv.* or *prep.*: To influence, move, or affect by talking; as *to talk down*, to put down by talking; to out-talk; *to talk out*, to talk to the end of; to carry on the discussion of (a bill in Parliament, etc.) till the time for adjournment is reached, and so frustrate its progress by preventing its being put to a vote; *to talk* (a person) *over* or *round*, to win over, or into compliance, by talking; *to talk* (a thing) *up*, to talk strenuously in support of, to 'crack up'; *to talk* (a person) *into* or *out of*, to persuade into, or dissuade from (something) by talking; *to talk* (a person) *up to*, to bring (him) up to the point or level of (something) by talking.

a 1658 FORD, etc. *Witch Edmonton* I. ii, Why Mr. Thorney, d'ye mean to talk out your dinner? 1697 COLLIER *Ess.* II. (1703) 64 A friend who relates his success talks himself into a new pleasure. 1706 VANBRUGH *Mistake* III. i. Wks. (1840) 449/1 [I have] told him the secret, and then talked him into a liking on't. 1719 DE FOE *Crusoe* (1840) II. vi. 152 He talks himself into a..convert. *Ibid.* xii. 262, I would be talking myself up to vigorous resolution. 1722 — *Col. Jack* (1840) 304, I failed not to talk up the gallantry..of his..majesty. 1797-8 JANE AUSTEN *Sense & Sens.* xxxv, You shan't talk me out of my satisfaction. 1847 TENNYSON *Princ.* v. 284 Her that talk'd down the fifty wisest men. 1862 LATHAM *Channel Isl.* III. xvi. (ed. 2) 377 He..was talked-over by Prince Maurice, whom, unless he meant to be talked-over, he had no occasion to meet. 1865 H. KINGSLEY *Hillyars & Burtons* lvi, He talked over Trevittick, who sulkily acquiesced. 1865 KINGSLEY *Herew.* vi, You need not try to talk this out of my head. 1873 *Punch* 19 July 22/2 Mr. Beresford Hope 'talked out' the Bill. 1883 *Cent. Mag.* XXV. 527/2 'Talk him into taking a little rest', said Helen. 1885 C. C. HARRISON in *Harper's Mag.* Mar. 546/1 He must be talked into it. 1894 MISS COBBE *Life* I. 341, I do believe I could walk down anybody and perhaps talk down anybody too. 1900 *Westm. Gaz.* 6 Mar. 9/3 Clever talkers are kept..to 'talk up' the patients to the highest possible fee. 1903 *Speaker* 21 Nov., Suppl. 3 Give Mr. Chamberlain time to talk himself out.

**b.** To spend or pass *away* (time, and the like) in or by talking.

1676 COTTON *Walton's Angler* II. i. (1881) 245 We have already talked away two miles of your journey. 1702 ADDISON *Dial. Medals* Misc. Wks. 1736 III. 12, I am very well content to talk away an evening with you on the subject. 1890 CLARK RUSSELL *Ocean Trag.* III. xxxiv. 242 Thus idly would we talk away the days.

**c.** *To talk* (a thing) *over*, *to talk over* (a matter): to discuss it in familiar conference or conversation.

1734 WATTS *Reliq. Juv.* (1789) 218 When I have talked my diseases all over to them. 1810 SCOTT *Let. to Morritt* 2 Mar. in *Lockhart*, We talked over this subject once while riding on the banks of Tees. 1847 MARRYAT *Childr. N. Forest* xxiii, We will talk over the matter as we go. 1851 FITZGERALD *Euphranor* (1904) 78 They could talk the matter over.

**Talkable** (tǭ·kăb'l), *a.* [f. TALK *v.* + -ABLE.]

**a.** Of a thing: That can or may be talked of or about. **b.** Of a person: Ready to converse; affable.

a 1800 GEN. PAOLI in P. Fitzgerald *Life J. Boswell* (1891) I. viii. 91 So cheerful, so witty, so gentle, so talkable. 1830 *Blackw. Mag.* XXVIII. 893 All speak—talk—whisper.. of all the speakable, talkable, whisperable..interesting affairs, incidents and occurrences.

**Talka·tion.** *nonce-wd.* [f. TALK *v.* + -ATION.] A talking. (Usually dyslogistic.)

1800 in *Spirit Pub. Jrnls.* IV. 155 It was no discourse.. but a kind of talkation (if I may be allowed the expression). 1898 B. GREGORY *Side Lights Confl. Meth.* 204 A tangled, wearisome talkation then ensued.

**Talkative** (tǭ·kătiv), *a.* [f. TALK *v.* + -ATIVE.] Given to talking; inclined to talk; chatty, loquacious; garrulous, 'full of prate' (J.).

1432-50 tr. *Higden* (Rolls) VI. 469 Hit is a fowle vice in a kynge to be talkatyve [orig. *dicacem fore*; TREVISA to iangle moche] in a feste. 1529 MORE *Dyaloge* III. Wks. 243/1 The more foole the more talkatife of great doutes and hygh questions of holy Scripture. 1552 HULOET, Talcatiue, or full of talkynge and pratlynge, *fabularis*. 1665 GLANVILL *Def. Van. Dogm.* 51 One Author will not reckon him among the slight and talkative Philosophers. 1866 GEO. ELIOT *F. Holt* ii, [He] became very talkative over his second bottle of port.

**b.** Said of personal qualities, etc.; also *fig.*

14.. *Craft of Lovers* iv. in *Chaucer's Wks.* (1561) 341 Your peinted eloquence, So gay, so freshe, and eke so talcatife. 1509 BARCLAY *Shyp of Folys* (1570) 54 Sophistrie nor Logike with their arte talcatife. 1644 BULWER *Chirol.* 1 The Hand, that busie instrument, is most talkative. 1719 STEELE *Plebian* Wks. (1790) 293 Nothing is so talkative as misfortune. 1778 MISS BURNEY *Evelina* (1791) II. xxxvii. 257 So little talkative is the fulness of contentment. 1860 TYNDALL *Glac.* I. vii. 47 This..is the most talkative glacier I have ever known.

Hence **Ta·lkatively** *adv.*, in a talkative way.

1589 WARNER *Alb. Eng.* VI. xxx. (1612) 150 For slaunder set on foote, though false, is talkatiuely dome. 1727 BAILEY vol. II, *Talkatively*, after a talkative Manner. 1847 in WEBSTER; and in mod. Dicts.

**Talkativeness** (tǭ·kătivnės). [f. prec. + -NESS.] The quality or state of being talkative.

1609 W. M. *Man in Moone* (1849) 48 Talkativeness, or much babling. 1674 *Govt. Tongue* vi. 73 We use to call this Talkativeness a Feminine vice. 176. WESLEY *To Children* 2 Wks. 1811 IX. 92 Talkativeness before any person has the appearance of disrespect. 1840 DICKENS *Old C. Shop* xiv, There was a clinking of wine-glasses and a great talkativeness on the part of everybody.

**Talked** (tǭkt), *ppl. a.* [f. TALK *v.* + -ED[1].] Spoken familiarly: chiefly in *talked-of*, familiarly or vaguely spoken about.

1841 COL. HAWKER *Diary* (1893) II. 208 Our long-talked-of trip. 1865 RUSKIN *Sesame* I. (1897) 16 A book is essentially not a talked thing, but a written thing. 1890 *Spectator* 31 May 764/1 To make himself the observed of all observers, and the talked-of among all talkers.

**Talkee.** *colloq.* = next 2.

1885 *Illustr. Lond. News* Christmas No. 7/1 Of our five hours' talkee..a few words are worth recording.

**Talkee-talkee** (tǭ·ki,tǭ·ki). [A reduplicated derivative of TALK, with dimin. ending.]

**1.** The name given to the imperfect or broken English of some native races; *esp.* the lingua franca of negro slaves in the West Indies.

1808 *Edin. Rev.* XII. 413 The *talkee-talkee*, or negro jargon, is now chiefly English. 1810 SOUTHEY *Let. to J. May* 5 Dec., The talkee talkee of the slaves in the Sugar Islands, as it is called, will prevail in Surinam. 1828 *Life Planter Jamaica* 13 Ignorant of the negro corrupted dialect, or the talkee talkee language. 1856 J. H. NEWMAN *Callista* i. (1890) 8 Not without parallel in the talkee-talkee of the West Indian negro.

**2.** Small-talk; petty or childish talk, chatter; continuous talk or prattle. (*contemptuous.*)

1812 MAR. EDGEWORTH *Vivian* x, There's a woman, now, who thinks of nothing living but herself!—all talkee talkee! 1840 *Fraser's Mag.* XXII. 55 The usual nothings which make up talkee-talkee. 1890 *Nature* 6 Mar. 410/2 That 'talkee-talkee' so often forced into books of this kind.

*attrib.* 1869 HUXLEY in *Life* (1900) I. xxiii. 309 The discourses are to [be] lessons and not talkee-talkee lectures.

**Talker** (tǭ·kəɹ). [f. TALK *v.* + -ER[1].] One who talks or is given to talking; a speaker, a conversationalist; a talkative person.

c 1386 CHAUCER *Pars. T.* ⁋ 304 Eke if..he be a talker of ydel wordes of folye or vileynye. 1470-85 MALORY *Arthur* x. lvi. 508 The meryest knyghte..and the maddest talker. 1648 MILTON *Observ. Art. Peace* Wks. 1851 IV. 564 The overworne objection of every triviall Talker. 1701 W. WOTTON *Hist. Rome* i. 15 Great Talkers should always be mistrusted. 1815 JANE AUSTEN *Emma* xli, I am rather a talker; and now and then I have let a thing escape me which I should not. 1861 CRAIK *Hist. Eng. Lit.* II. 248 Bolingbroke..was one of the most brilliant orators and talkers.

**b.** *Comb.*, as **talker-down**, one who talks down; so **talker-out**; **talker-seer**, a seer who is also a talker.

1833 MRS. BROWNING *Prometheus Bound* Poet. Wks. 1889 I. 205 The talker-down Of scorn by scorn. 1884 GOSSE in *Fortn. Rev.* Dec. 784 Such later talker-seers as Coleridge, De Quincey, and Carlyle. 1901 *Daily Chron.* 22 May 7/7 Mr. Banbury, the professional talker out of the House.

**† Ta·lkful**, *a. Obs. rare.* [f. TALK *sb.* + -FUL.] Full of talk, talkative, garrulous.

1598 SYLVESTER *Du Bartas* II. ii. I. *Ark* 611 Phrenzie that makes..The talkfull blab, cruel the violent.

**Talking** (tǭ·kiŋ), *vbl. sb.* [f. TALK *v.* + -ING[1].] The action of the verb TALK; speaking, discoursing. *Talking to* (*colloq.*), a reprimand, an admonition.

a 1300 *Cursor M.* 14760 It es bot foli al þi talking. 13.. *Ibid.* 27792 O suernes [*F.* slauþe] cums..vnnait talckhing. c 1386 CHAUCER *Can. Yeom. Prol.* 131 Whil this yeman was thus in his talkyng This Chanon drough hym neer. c 1450 tr. *De Imitatione* III. lvii. 134 Þi consolacions are not as mannes talkinges or confabulacions. 1503 HAWES *Examp. Virt.* viii. 155 Of whome I oft haue herd grete talkynge. 1667 JER. TAYLOR *Dissuas. Popery* II. II. vi. 144 The superstitious talkings and actings, of their Priests. 1781 COWPER *Conversat.* 8 Words learn'd by rote a parrot may rehearse, But talking is not always to converse. 1884 CLARK RUSSELL *Jack's Courtsh.* xvii, A person capable of giving a seaman a talking to.

**b.** *attrib.* and *Comb.*, as **† talking-craft** (see CRAFT *sb.* 6 c); **talking-house**, a house where people meet for conversation; **† talking-stock**, a subject of talk.

1548 UDALL *Erasm. Par. Luke* xxiv. 189 A common talkyng stocke to all peoples. 1562 WINȜET *Cert. Tractatis* i. Wks. (S.T.S.) I. 8 Vtheris..makis of the Gospell ane talkin craft. 1681 OWEN *Apostasy* Wks. 1852 VII. 256 This makes..misspense of time in talking-houses.

**Talking** (tǭ·kiŋ), *ppl. a.* [f. TALK *v.* + -ING[2].] That talks; loquacious.

1562 J. HEYWOOD *Prov. & Epigr.* (1867) 177 One talkyng tung. 1699 R. L'ESTRANGE *Erasm. Colloq.* (1711) 92 This is the talkingst Place that ever I set my Foot in. 1710 STEELE *Tatler* No. 197 ⁋ 3 The talking Creatures we meet in publick Places. 1770 GOLDSM. *Des. Vil.* 14 The hawthorn bush, with seats beneath the shade, For talking age and whispering lovers made. 1870 M. D. CONWAY *Earthw. Pilgr.* xiii. 171 Man has been defined as the talking animal.

Hence **Ta·lkingly** *adv.*, in a talking manner.

1895 H. B. M. WATSON in *Chap-Bk.* III. 489 At the word, spoken very talkingly, and with such an absence of offense, my dudgeon vanished.

**Talky** (tǭ·ki), *a.* [f. TALK *sb.* + -Y.] Inclined to or abounding in talk; talkative, loquacious.

1862 CARLYLE *Fredk. Gt.* XII. vii. (1873) IV. 172 The King is somewhat talky. 1884 A. A. PUTNAM *Ten Yrs. Police Judge* xii. 101 One of the talky attorneys dispels all their hopes.

Hence **Ta·lky-ta·lky** *a.*, abounding in (mere) talk; not rising above the level of talk.

1883 *Sat. Rev.* 10 Feb. 189/2 These Essays..are very 'talky-talky'. 1884 G. ALLEN *Philistia* II. 301 A social leader, of the ordinary commonplace talky-talky sort.

**Talky**, variant form of TALCKY *a.*

**Tall** (tǭl), *a.* Also 4-7 tal, 4-6 talle, 6 tawl(l)e. [Of obscure history. Most prob. repr. (with loss of prefix) OE. *ge-tæl* (pl. *ge-tale*) swift, prompt = OHG. *gizal*, MHG. *gezal* quick. Cf. Goth. *untals* unaccommodating, uncompliant, disobedient, ONorthumb. *untal* evil, improper. For the phonology, cf. *small*:—OE. *smæl*.

The sense-development is remarkable, but is paralleled more or less by that of other adjs. expressing estimation, as *buxom*, *canny*, *clean*, *clever*, *cunning*, *deft*, *elegant*, *handsome*, *pretty*, *proper*; Ger. *klein*, as compared with Eng. *clean*, presents the antithesis to mod. *tall* as compared with *tall* in early ME.

It has been conjectured that in the sense 'high of stature' it is a different word, adopted from Welsh *tal* in same sense; but the latter is, according to Prof. Rhŷs, merely a 16th c. borrowing of the Eng. word (in Owen Pughe's Dictionary erroneously mixed up with the genuine Welsh sb. *tal* end, brow, forehead, with which it has no possible connexion). The 15th c. instance of the adj. cited by Pughe is prob. from sense 2 or 3 below.]

**I. † 1.** Quick, prompt, ready, active. *Obs. rare.*

But the sense in both quots. is doubtful; in quot. c 1374, *tall* has been taken by some as = 'meek, docile'; quot. 1542 may belong to sense 2.

[c 1000 *Ags. Ps.* lvi. 5 (Th.) Wæron hyra tungan ȝetale teonan ȝehwylcre.] c 1374 CHAUCER *Compl. Mars* 38 (Harl. MS. 7333) Sche [Venus] made him [Mars] at hir lust [*v. r.* list] so humble & talle [*v. rr.* tal, tall; *Fairf. MS.* humble and calle; *Tan. MS.* humble in alle]. 1530-1600 [see 4]. 1542 UDALL *Erasm. Apoph.* 51 For lesse money..myght I bye a bondeman, that should dooe me tall & hable seruice.

**† 2.** Meet, becoming, seemly, proper, decent. *Obs.*

[Cf. c 1350-c 1440 s. v. TALLY *adv.*] c 1400 *Destr. Troy* 3098 Ho tentit not in tempull to no tall prayers, Ne no melody of mouthe made at þe tyme. c 1440 *Promp. Parv.* 486/1, Tal, or semely, *decens*, *elegans*.

**† b.** Comely, goodly, fair, handsome; elegant, fine. Cf. PROPER *a.* 8. *Obs.*

c 1450 *Cov. Myst.* xxiii. (1841) 215 A fayre ȝonge qwene.. Bothe ffresche and gay upon to loke, And a talle man with her dothe melle. 1451 *Paston Lett.* I. 224 On of the tallest younge men of this parysch lyth syke. 1530 PALSGR. 327/1 Talle..*bel*, as *bel home*. c 1592 MARLOWE *Jew of Malta* IV. iv, That such a base slave as he should be saluted by such a tall man as I am, from such a beautiful dame as you. 1656 H. MORE *Enthus. Tri.* 31 He was a tal proper man.. but of a very pale wasted melancholy countenance.

**† 3.** Good at arms; stout or strong in combat; doughty, brave, bold, valiant. Cf. PRETTY 3 a.

c 1400 *Destr. Troy* 8574 Mageron..macchet with Achilles, Wold haue takon the talle kyng, & to toun led. a 1518 SKELTON *Magnyf.* 821 *Cou. Ab.* I waraunt you I wyll not go away. *Cra. Con.* By Saynt Mary, he is a tawle man. *Clo. Col.* Ye, and do ryght good seruyce he can. a 1529 — *Agst. Garnesche* I. 5 Syr Frollo de Franko was neuer halfe so talle. a 1548 HALL *Chron.*, *Hen. VI* 159 This capitayn [Jack Cade]..assembled together a great company of talle personages. a 1553 UDALL *Royster D.* IV. viii, Now sirs, quite our selues like tall men and hardie. 1577 NORTHBROOKE *Agst. Dicing* (1843) 8 If he can kil a man,..he is called a tall man, and a valiant man of his hands. 1591 GREENE *Art Conny Catch.* III. (1592) 16 He that had done this tall exploit, in a place so open. 1598 J. DICKENSON *Greene in Conc.* (1878) 137 With her tongue she was as tall a warriouresse as any of hir sexe. a 1604 HANMER *Chron. Irel.* (1633) 126 Both sides lost many a tall man. a 1613 OVERBURY *Ess. Valour* in *Wife*, etc. (1630) Q vj b, It makes a little fellow to be called a Tall man. 1641 PRYNNE *Antip.* 16 He like a tall fellow, thereupon interdicted the King, with the whole Realme. 1670 MILTON *Hist. Eng.* II. Wks. (1847) 492/2 Telling the tall champions as a great encouragement, that with the Britons it was usual for women to be their leaders. 1820 W. IRVING *Sketch-Bk.*, *John Bull* (1865) 390 The old fellow's spirit is as tall and as gallant as ever. 1825 SCOTT *Betrothed* i, Beloved among the 'tall men', or champions, of Wales.

**† 4.** Phrase *tall of* (*his*) *hand*(*s*: sometimes, (cf. sense 1) Ready, active, deft, skilful with (his) hands; dexterous, handy; sometimes, (cf. sense 3) Stout of arm, formidable with weapons. So *tall of tongue*. stout of speech or argument. *Obs.*

1530 PALSGR. 784/1 He is a tall man of his handes,..*cest vng habille homme de ses mains*. 1589 R. HARVEY *Pl. Perc.* (1590) A iij, They were neuer tall fellows of their hands that were such hacksters in the street. 1598 FLORIO, *Manesco*, readie, nimble, or quicke-handed..a tall man of his hands. 1600 HOLLAND *Livy* II. xxxiii. 65 A Noble yoong gentleman, right politicke of advise, active besides, and tall of his hands [L. *promptus manu*]. *Ibid.* III. lxx. 136 Agrippa being a tall man of his handes [L. *viribus ferox*] and young withall,..caught the ensignes from the ensigne-bearers, advanced them forward his owne selfe. *Ibid.* XXI. xl. 415 Stout in heart, and tall of hand [L. *vigens corpore*]. 1607 MARSTON *What you will* Induct., Goe stand to it; shew thyselfe a tall man of thy tongue. 1632 HOLLAND *Cyrupædia* 46 Swift I am not of foot, nor yet a tall man of my hands.

**† 5.** Big, large, bulky. *Obs. rare.*

c 1430 LYDG. *Min. Poems* 200 This fair floure of womanheed Hath too pappys also smalle, Bolsteryd out of lenghth and breed, Lyche a large campyng balle; There is no bagpipe halff so talle,..Whan they been full of wynde at alle.

**II. 6.** Of a person: High of stature; of more than average height. Usually appreciative. Also of animals, as a giraffe, stag, or the like. (Cf. ELEGANT *a.* 2 b = tall of stature.)

1530 PALSGR. 327/1 Talle or hye..*hault*. 1538 ELYOT, *Procerus*, longe, talle. 1552 HULOET, Talle or verye hyghe in personage aboue other. 1599 HAKLUYT *Voy.* II. 256 The men are tall and slender. 1697 DRYDEN *Virg. Past.* VII. 54 Fair Galatea,..Tall as a Poplar, taper as the Bole. 1719 YOUNG *Paraphr*, *Job* Wks. 1757 I. 215 Will the tall Reem ..Low at the crib, and ask an alms of thee? 1796 H. HUNTER tr. *St.-Pierre's Stud. Nat.* (1799) I. 398 Tall as giants, hairy like bears. **1858** CARLYLE *Fredk. Gt.* v. I. 579 One Hohmann, a born Prussian, was so tall, you could not..touch his bare crown with your hand. **1861** HULME tr. *Moquin-Tandon* I. ii. 14 A man..is called tall when he is above 5.754 feet in height. **1886** RUSKIN *Præterita* I. vii. 210 A tall, handsome, and very finely made girl.

**b.** Having a specified or relative height; measuring in stature (so much): without implication of great height. (Cf. *big, broad, high*, etc.)

**1588** SHAKS. *L. L. L.* IV. i. 47 *Costard.* Which is the greatest Lady, the highest? *Princess.* The thickest, and the tallest. **1685** BAXTER *Paraphr. N. T.* Matt. vi. 27 All your care cannot make you any taller of stature. **1732** MACKY *Mem., Charac.* (ed. 2) 47 [Marquis of Hartington was] taller than a middle Stature. **1744** SARAH FIELDING *David Simple* II. iii, If a Man could make himself happy by imagining himself six Foot tall, tho' he was but three. **1845** JAMES *Arrah Neil* ii, A good deal taller than his companion. **1853** VISCT. S. DE REDCLIFFE in Lane-Poole *Life* II. 242 He is..6 ft. 3 in. tall. *Mod.* How tall are you? He is a little taller than his brother, but both are dwarfs.

**c.** *absol.* as *sb. nonce-use.*

**1903** MAX PEMBERTON *Dr. Xavier* i, They want 'talls' for the first row and she's just the height.

**7.** Of things, as ships, trees, mountains: High, lofty; esp. of things high in proportion to their width, as *a tall chimney, column, house, mast, spire.*

*a* **1548** HALL *Chron., Hen. IV* 32 b, Talle shippes furnished with vitayles municions and all thynges necessary. **1562** TURNER *Herbal* II. 6 There are two kyndes of ashes [trees], of yᵉ whiche the one is verye high & tawlle. **1582** M. PHILLIPS in Hakl. *Voy.* (1589) 579 Two good tall ships of warre. **1615** G SANDYS *Trav.* 220 To be imbargued in two tall Ships, and a great Gallion. **1655** STANLEY *Hist. Philos.* III. (1701) 106/1 Above the tallest Hill or Wood. **1702** ROWE *Tamerl.* I. i, Yon tall Mountains That seem to reach the Clouds. **1715–20** POPE *Iliad* XIII. 493 The mountain-oak, or poplar tall, Or pine, fit mast for some great admiral. **1784** COWPER *Task* I. 450 Upon the ship's tall side he stands, possess'd With visions prompted by intense desire. **1852** JAMES *Agnes Sorel* i, A tall house in the city of Paris. **1856** KANE *Arct. Expl.* I. xviii. 222 Its tallest summit near the water at thirteen hundred [feet]. **1908** MISS FOWLER *Betw. Trent & Ancholme* 18 Where..the Fuchsias grow tall, up to the eaves.

**b.** Of more than average length measured from bottom to top, as a *tall copy* of a book, a *tall folio*. *Tall hat*, a silk hat with high cylindrical crown.

**1608** TOPSELL *Serpents* (1658) 747 Very like a small and vulgar Lizard, except..their legs taller, and their tail longer. **1613** SHAKS. *Hen. VIII*, I. iii. 30 The faith they haue in Tennis and tall Stockings, Short blistred Breeches, and those types of Trauell. *a* **1704** T. BROWN *Lett. fr. Dead* II. i. Wks. 1720 II. 160, I..was to write Bills as tall as the Monument. **17..** *John o' Hazelgreen* v. in Child *Ballads* V. 163 Wi arms tall, and fingers small—He's comely to be seen. **1819** SCOTT *Let. to Miss Edgeworth* 21 July in *Lockhart*, A second edition of Walter Scott, a tall copy, as collectors say, and bound in Turkey leather. **1847** L. HUNT *Men, Women & B.* II. vi. 78 The charms of vellums, tall copies, and blind tooling. **1890** 'OUIDA' *Syrlin* xiv, They would go to Eton and wear ridiculous jackets and tall hats.

**c.** Applied distinctively to species or varieties of plants which grow higher than other species.

**1835** HOOKER *Brit. Flora* (ed. 3) 50 *Festuca elatior*, Tall Fescue grass. **1846** J. BAXTER *Libr. Pract. Agric.* (ed. 4) I. 371 Tall oat-like soft grass, *Holcus avenaceus.* **1850** KINGSLEY *Alt. Locke* xiv, The tender green of the tall rape, a plant till then unknown to me. **1861** MISS PRATT *Flower. Pl.* IV. 79 Tall Broom-rape..growing on the roots of the Great Knapweed. **1897–8** BRITTON & BROWN *Amer. Flora*, Tall moss, *Sedum acre.*

**d.** *absol.* as *sb.*

**1909** *19th Cent.* Jan. 76 Two thirds gave plants divided into 'talls' and dwarfs.

**8.** *fig.* †**a.** Lofty, grand, eminent. *Obs.*

**1655** STANLEY *Hist. Philos.* I. (1701) 45/1 Who in tall Corinth and Pirene dwell. **1686** W. DE BRITAINE *Hum. Prudence* xix. 88 Princes may bestow the tallest Preferments, but they cannot make Men truly Honourable. **1701** WATTS *Horæ Lyr.* III. *Death T. Gunston* 187 The tall titles, insolent and proud. **1827** LAMB *Let. to B. Barton* in *Final Mem.* viii. 260 Thine briefly in a tall friendship, C. Lamb.

**b.** Grandiloquent, magniloquent; high-flown; esp. in *tall talk* (TALK *sb.* 5). *colloq.*

**1670** EACHARD *Cont. Clergy* 39 Others..whose parts stand not so much towards tall words and lofty notions, but consist in..besprinkling all their sermons with plenty of Greek and Latin. **1864** *Spectator* No. 1884. 911 The somewhat tall title of 'Analysis and Synthesis in Painting'. **1869** *Routledge's Ev. Boy's Ann.* 518 What the Yankees call 'tall talk'. **1876** C. M. DAVIES *Unorth. Lond.* 55 Then succeeded the minister herself, whose prayer was 'taller' than the young girl's. **1890** *Spectator* 3 May 628/1 The diction is as impetuous as Niagara, as 'tall' as the Eiffel Tower.

**c.** Exaggerated, highly coloured. *U.S. colloq.*

**1846** T. B. THORPE *Backwoods, Big Bear Arkansaw* (Bartlett), The live Sucker from Illinois had the daring to say that our Arkansaw friend's stories smelt rather tall. **1870** *Zoologist* V. 2350 The producers of what is called 'tall writing'. **1891** *N. York Times* 26 Jan. (Cent. Dict.), A tall yarn about the Jews wanting to buy the Vatican copy of the Hebrew Bible. **1897** *Dublin Rev.* Oct. 267 'Tall stories' are the perquisite of every traveller. **1902** ELIZ. L. BANKS *Newspaper Girl* 279 Nor do I think that there is anything 'tall' in this statement.

**d.** Large in amount, big. *slang* (*orig. U.S.*).

**1842** DICKENS *Amer. Notes* (1850) 131/2 We were a pretty tall time coming that last fifteen mile. **1884** I. BLIGH in *Lillywhite's Cricket Ann.* 4, G. B. Studd's 19 including some tall hits. **1893** F. ADAMS *New Egypt* 128 It's a tall order, but it's worth trying, isn't it? **1902** *Westm. Gaz.* 13 Feb. 12/2 America is the land of 'tall' things, and this is certainly a 'tall' drink for twenty-five persons. **1905** *Sat. Rev.* 24 June 825 Usurping the functions of the King is rather a 'tall order' for a private M.P.

†**9.** *fig.* Great, eminent (*at* something). *Obs.*

**1591** LODGE *Diogenes in his Singularitie* (Hunter. Cl.) 29 Verie earnest to prooue himselfe a tall *a b c* Clearke, he read on [etc.]. **1646** G. DANIEL *Poems* Wks. (Grosart) I. 83 A hundred Rhiming Fellowes, that have bin Tall Men at Meeter. **1662** COKAINE *Trag. Ovid* IV. vi, Though she's but little, she's a tall woman at a Trencher.

**b.** Great in quality, excellent, good, first-class. (*U.S. slang.*)

**1835–40** HALIBURTON *Clockm.* (1862) 530 Won't it be tall feedin' at Queen's table, that's all. **1847** ROBB *Squatter Life* (Bartlett), I didn't estimate him very tall. **1852** MRS. STOWE *Uncle Tom's C.* xxxvii, They..make jist the tallest kind o' broth and knicknacks.

**B.** quasi-*adv.* In a tall manner; elatedly, proudly; *to walk tall*, to carry one's head high. Also *comb.*, as *tall-talking*.

**1846** T. B. THORPE *Myst. Backwoods* 131 (Bartl.), I will walk tall into varmint and Indian. **1860** THACKERAY *Round. Papers, De finibus* (1862) 282 The sin of grandiloquence, or tall-talking. **1869** MRS. STOWE *Oldtown Folks* vi. (1870) 65 I'm 'mazing proud on 't. I tell you I walk tall.

**C.** *Comb.*: parasynthetic, as *tall-bodied* (having a tall body), *-elmed, -masted, -necked, -sceptred, -tussocked, -wheeled*, etc.; quasi-*advb.*, as *tall-growing, -sitting*; † **tall-sail** (**tal-sail**) = TOPSAIL.

**14..** *Siege Jerus.* 289 Þey ty3ten vp tal-sail [*v.r.* topsaill], whan þe tide asked, Hadde byr at þe bake, & þe bonke lefte. *c* **1725** ARMSTRONG *Imit. Shaks.* 6 Misc. 1770 I. 147 A blast so shrewd makes the tall-bodied pines Unsinew'd bend. **1855** BAILEY *Spiritual Leg.* in *Mystic*, etc. 105 Tall-sceptred law, and loin-girt liberty. **1877** FURNIVALL *Leopold Shaks.* Introd. 117 You ride through Charlecote's tall-elmd park. **1886** P. S. ROBINSON *Valley Teet. Trees* 63 The tall-tussocked grass of the waste lands. **1897** *Westm. Gaz.* 6 July 2/1 A very tall-sitting lady, with a tremendous matinée hat, sat down in front of me. **1908** MISS FOWLER *Betw. Trent & Ancholme* 203 Sun-flowers, and other succulent tall-growing things.

**Tall**, obs. variant of TAIL *sb.*[2], *v.*[2]

**Tallage** (tæ·lédʒ), *sb.*[1] Forms: *α.* 3–8 **taillage**, 4–5 **taylage**, 4–7 **tailage**, 5 **tayllage** (7–8 **tailliage**). *β.* 4–5 **taliage**, 4–6 **talage**, 4–9 **talliage**, 5 **tal(l)yage**, 4– **tallage**. *γ.* 6 **talenge**. [a. OF. *taillage* (1170 in Godef.), f. *tailler*, TAIL *v.*[2]: see -AGE. Hence med.L. *talliagium, tallagium* (*taillagium, taliagium*), *a* 1087 in Du Cange.]

Orig., in *Eng. Hist.*, An arbitrary tax levied by Norman and early Angevin kings upon the towns and the demesne lands of the Crown; hence, a tax levied upon feudal dependants by their superiors; also, by extension, a municipal rate; a toll or customs duty; a grant, levy, imposition, aid.

By the articles of 1297, the Latin version of which is commonly cited as the Statute *De Tallagio non concedendo*, an attempt was made to restrict the right of tallage, which was finally surrendered by the king in the act of 1340.

[**1154–7** *Calr. Charter Rolls* III. 385. **1190** *Pipe Roll I Rich. I* (1844) 230 De toto tallagio quod Rex Henricus pater fecit.] *c* **1290** *Beket* 402 in *S. Eng. Leg.* I. 118 A taillage it is, and sumdel with vnri3te i-take. [**1292** BRITTON III. vii. § 5 Des vileyns, et de villenages..lour rentes, lour services, lour taillages, et lour custumes. **1302** *Rolls of Parlt.* I. 266/2 Ad assidendos tallagium nostrum in Civitatibus, Burgis, & Dominicis nostris.] *c* **1330** R. BRUNNE *Chron.* (1810) 44 Now comes Suane..Þe lond leid to taliage so mykelle on ilk a toun. *c* **1374** CHAUCER *Former Age* 54 No lord, no taylage by no tyranye. **1387** TREVISA *Higden* (Rolls) II. 97 Hydage, taylage of hydes of lond. Danegeld, taylage i-3eue to þe Danes. *c* **1420** *Chron. Vilod.* 224 He granted þo to þe Pope Leo such a talage Offe euery howse in his kyndam a peny by 3ere. **1440** J. SHIRLEY *Dethe K. James* (1818) 7 The saide kynge of Scottes..ordeynd that tallage..upon his people. **1481** CAXTON *Godeffroy* 277 To helpe..the cristen men of Iherusalem to paye the cruel taillages that the turkes had sette vpon them. **1534** MORE *Comf. agst. Trib.* III. Wks. 1212/1 With occasions of his warres, he pilleth them with taxes and tallages vnto the bare bones. **1556** *Chron. Gr. Friars* (Camden) 38 A rysynge in Lyngcolshere of the comons for taske and talenge of ane abbé there. **1610** HOLLAND *Camden's Brit.* II. 141 [The elected chief of every Irish county] had a generall tallage or cutting high or low at his pleasure upon all the inheritance. **1622** F. MARKHAM *Bk. War* V. vi. 183 It is..the Office of the Treasurer to receiue all Tribuits, Taxes, Tailliages and Impositions. **1642** *Declar. Ho. Parlt.* in Rushw. *Hist. Coll.* (1692) III. I. 665 The Law there declared was, That none could be compelled to contribute to any Tax, Tallage, Aid, or other like Charge but by Consent in Parliament. **1762** HUME *Hist. Eng.* I. App. ii. 413 The king..levied heavy tailliages at pleasure on the inhabitants. **1776** ADAM SMITH *W. N.* III. ii. (1869) I. 396 The taille, as it still subsists in France, may serve as an example of those ancient tallages. It is a tax upon the supposed profits of the farmer, which they estimate by the stock that he has upon the farm. **1874** STUBBS *Const. Hist.* I. xiii. 585 The donum, auxilium, or tallage, which Henry [II] imposed in lieu of the ancient Danegeld, was assessed by the officers of the Exchequer.

*fig.* **1303** R. BRUNNE *Handl. Synne* 9254 Ianglyng longeþ to sacrylage, Þar-of takeþ þe fende taylage.

†**Tallage**, *sb.*[2] *Obs.* Also 5–6 **talage**, 6 **-e(d)ge**, 7 **talang**. [app. corruption of TARAGE *sb.*[1]] Taste, savour (*lit.* and *fig.*); = TARAGE *sb.*[1]

**14..** [see TARAGE *sb.*[1]]. **1502** ATKYNSON tr. *De Imitatione* I. xxv. 178 To haue a spirituall tallage in god. **1528** PAYNELL *Salerne's Regim.* B b, Very nere the talage of water. **1542** BOORDE *Dyetary* xii. (1870) 266 Chese..must be of good sauour & taledge. **1601** HOLLAND *Pliny* VIII. xxxii. 213 Their first milke must haue a taste and talang of those two hearbs. **1617** J. MOORE *Map Mans Mortalitie* II. vii. 147 Wherein..there rests some taste and tallage of the former corruptions.

**b.** The sense of taste.

**1557** *Primer, Prayer after receiving Sacrament*, So to order the talage and taste of my heart, that I never fele other swetenes but thee. **1600** HOLLAND *Livy* V. v. 183 Some kinde of meat or drinke..to please his palate and to content his talage.

**Ta·llage**, *v.* [f. TALLAGE *sb.*[1]] *trans.* To impose tallage upon; to tax.

*c* **1460** *Godstow Reg.* 102 Whan the kyng tallagith his demaynes thurgh Englond. **1520** *Caxton's Chron. Eng.* VI. 77 b/2 The Archebysshop wolde not graunte hym to talenge the chirches at his wyll. **1523** LD. BERNERS *Froiss.* I. ccxxxii. 319 Without taxyng or talagyng any of your subgettes or countre. **1738** *Hist. Crt. Excheq.* ii. 17 None were tallaged, (i. e. taxed by the King or his Justices) but Ancient Demesnes and Burroughs holding of the Crown. **1890** GROSS *Gild Merch.* I. 57 The king tallaged his boroughs whenever he pleased. **1898** MAITLAND *Township & Borough* 66 He was tallaged along with the other men of the town.

**Tallageable** (tæ·lédʒăb'l), *a.* [f. prec. + -ABLE.] Liable to be tallaged or taxed. Hence **Tallageabi·lity**, liability or ability to be tallaged.

**1777** *Misc.* in *Ann. Reg.* 181/1 The other burgesses..were still talliageable at will. **1888** *Nation* (N.Y.) 31 May 443/3 These lists served to give the King a clue as to the tallageability of the Jews.

†**Ta·llager.** *Obs. rare*[−1]. In 5 **taylagier.** [f. TALLAGE *sb.*[1] + -ER[2] 2: see -ER[1] I.] One who assessed or collected tallage; a tax-gatherer.

*c* **1400** *Rom. Rose* 6811 But se what gold han usurers, And silver eke in garners, Taylagiers, & these monyours, Bailifs, bedels, provost, countours.

†**Ta·llagie.** *Obs.* [ad. med.L. *tallagi-um.*] = TALLAGE *sb.*[1]

**1444** *Rolls of Parlt.* V. 113/2 Custumes, Subsides, Tallagies. **1488–9** *Act 4 Hen. VII*, c. 5 Gathryng of dismes taxes tallagies or eny other subsidies.

**Tallance, -and, -aunt**, obs. var. TALON.

†**Tallant.** *Obs.* = FILANDER[1].

**1580** HOLLYBAND *Treas. Fr. Tong*, *Filandres*, are certaine stringes sharp as nedles growing in Hauks that are fed with euill meate, and cause him to die; tallants.

**Tallapoi(e**, obs. form of TALAPOIN.

**Tallat**, variant of TALLET.

**Tallboy** (tǭ·lboi). [f. TALL *a.* + (app.) BOY.]

**1.** A tall-stemmed glass or goblet. Now *local.*

**1676** D'URFEY *Mad. Fickle* II. i, *Bella*...Where shall we meet at night? *Maul.* At Lambs with the Fidles and a Talboy. **1694** MOTTEUX *Rabelais* V. xliii. 195 Cups, Goblets, and Talboys of Gold, Silver, and Cristal. *a* **1700** B. E. *Dict. Cant. Crew*, *Tall-boy*, a Pottle or two Quart-pot full of Wine. **1881** MISS JACKSON *Shropsh. Word-bk.* s. v., The Maister wants a jug o' ale..an' two tumbler-glasses—'e said not to sen' them tall-boys, kigglin' [= tottering].

**2.** A tall chest of drawers (often raised on legs), usually in two parts, one standing on the other, the lower sometimes projecting beyond the upper; sometimes applied to a chest of drawers or a bureau standing on a dressing-table. Also *attrib.*

**1769** *Dublin Merc.* 16–19 Sept. 2/2 Chamber chest, tallboy, dining tables, two side-boards. **1884** *W. Sussex Gaz.* 25 Sept., Mahogany tallboy chest of drawers. **1906** *Westm. Gaz.* 28 June 3/3 Tall-Boys .. those double chests of drawers which are to be found in nearly all old-fashioned houses. **1909** *Civ. Serv. Stores Assoc.* May 451, 18th century Mahogany Tall Boy Chest, with pull-out-tray in centre.

**3.** A kind of tall chimney-pot.

**1884** *Daily Tel.* 28 Jan. (Cassell), Scores of pots, tallboys, cowls..swept from the chimney-stacks of the Metropolis on Saturday night. **1904** *Daily Chron.* 21 June 3/5, I was fixing her some 'tallboys' on the chimneys.

**4.** *humorous.* ? A great man, a 'big pot'.

**1820** *Examiner* No. 644. 513/2 To play the coxcomb, pedant, and tall-boy. *Ibid.* No. 651. 629/2 The Imperial Tall-boy of Russia.

**Talld(e**, obs. f. *told*: see TELL *v.* **Talle**, obs. f. TAIL *v.*[2], TALE, TALL. **Tallen, tallent**, obs. ff. TALON. **Talles**: see TALLITH.

**Tallet, tallat** (tæ·lət). *dial.* Also 7 **tavelett**, 9 *dial.* **tallot, -ut, -art.** [A West-of-England word, used from Cornwall to Berkshire, from Gloucestersh. to Cheshire, and in English-speaking parts of S. Wales; a. Welsh *taflod* or *taflawd* fem. (ta·vlǫd, *dial.* ta·lǫd), loft, roof, in OIr. *taibled* a story, ad. med.L. *tabulāta* a boarded structure, a flooring, f. *tabulāre* to board, floor.] A loft formed by laying boards on the joists over a stable, cowshed, or the like, commonly used as a hay-loft (*hay-tallet*); also 'the unceiled space beneath the roof in any building; an attic' (E.D.D.).

**1586** *Will I. Palfrye, Ilminster* (Tanner), I..bequeath.. one tallett of barke which is the tallett now over my myllhouse. **1607** J. NORDEN *Surv. Dial.* V. 238 Some kind of lofts or hay tallets, as they call them in the West, that are not boorded. **1681** PH. HENRY *Diaries & Lett.* (1882) 307 From yᵉ lower Haybay & Tavelett they pitcht it & carry'd it on Pikehils to yᵉ Carts. **1791** *Life B. M. Carew* (1802) 87 Let me lie and die in some hay-tallet. **1850** SIR T. DYKE ACLAND in *Jrnl. R. Agric. Soc.* XI. II. 745 The humidity of the climate...One of the peculiarities resulting from this cause is the building of a second storey or loft over all bullock-sheds; it is called a 'tallat'. **1876** T. HARDY *Ethelberta* II. xlvi, Now up in the tallet with ye..and down with another lock or two of hay.

**b.** *Comb.* **Tallet-ladder**, the ladder giving access to the tallet.

1882 BLACKMORE *Christowell* xv, For the girls there was a tallat ladder.

**Talliable** (tæ·liăb'l), *a.* Now *Hist.* Also 6–7 taillable. [a. OF. *taillable* (13th c. in Hatz.-Darm.), f. *tailler*, TAIL *v.*[2]; assimilated to TALLY *v.*] Subject to tallage, liable to be 'tailed' or taxed.

[1321–2 *Rolls of Parlt.* I. 410/1, Qe lur tenaunz..ne seient geldables ne taillables.] 1531 in W. H. Turner *Select. Rec. Oxford* (1880) 98 They be tallyable with the Burgesses. 1575 *Ibid.* 371 Persons..talliable with scotte, lotte, and other charges as like occupiers. 1554 WOTTON *Let.* 29 July in *State Pap. Mary, Foreign* IV. 193 (P.R.O.) The king [of France] pronounced their sentences..somme..to be degraded from their nobilite..they were..pronounced to be taillable as anye other villaine. 1600 HOLLAND *Livy* XXXV. xvi. 897 Having..been made tributarie and taillable, he chalengeth of them the auncient rights & duties due from them. 1720 STRYPE *Stow's Surv.* II. v. xxvii. 359/2 They understood, that they of the City of London were not talliable. 1759 HURD *Dialogues* (1760) 270 The great towns and cities that before were royal demesnes, part of the king's private patrimony, and talliable by him at pleasure.

**Talliage**, etc., obs. ff. TALLAGE *sb.*[1], etc.

‖ **Talliar** (tæ·liăɹ). Also 7 tarryar, taliar, 9 *erron.* taliary. [ad. Tamil *talaiyāri*.] A village watchman in Southern India.

1680 *Fort St. George Consns.* 10 Feb. (Y.), The Peons and Tarryars sent in quest of two soldiers who had deserted. 1693 in Wheeler *Madras in Old. Time* (1861) I. 267 Taliars and Peons appointed to watch the Black Town. 1707 *Ibid.* II. 74 Resolving to march two hundred and fifty soldiers, two hundred talliars, and two hundred peons. 1858 J. B. NORTON *Topics* 204 The taliary, or watchman, guards it from being taken away by the owners.

**Talliate** (tæ·li,eit), *v.* [f. med.L. *talliāt-*, ppl. stem of *talliāre* to impose a subsidy or tax: see TAIL *v.*[2] 5.] *trans.* = TALLAGE *v.*; to tax.

1754 HUME *Hist. Eng.* (1761) I. xiii. 316 *note*, The king had not only the power of talliating the inhabitants within his own demesnes, but that of granting to particular barons the power of talliating the inhabitants within theirs. 1826 LINGARD *Hist. Eng.* (ed. 4) III. 190 *note*, It was proved from the records in the chancery and exchequer that they [citizens of London] had been talliated in the years 1214, 1223 [etc.]. 1892 *Yorksh. Inquisitions* I. 81.

† **Tallia·tion.** *Obs. rare.* [ad. med.L. *talliātio* (Du Cange), n. of action from *talliāre*: see prec.] The action of talliating; tallage.

1531 in W. H. Turner *Select. Rec. Oxford* (1880) 98 So alwey that they be tallyable with the Burgesses of the..Towne, the same tallyac[i]on to be assessed.

‖ **Tallicoona** (tælikū·nă). [corr. of F. *touloucouna* = *tulukuna*, native name in Wolof lang. of Fr. Senegambia; in the cognate Serer lang. *tulukuni*. (Thence by contraction *kunda*, COONDA, also *coondi*.)] A West African tree, *Carapa guineensis*. *Tallicoona oil*, a fixed oil expressed from the seeds of this.

[1832 GUILL. & PERR. *Fl. Seneg. Tent.* I. 128 Vulgo dicitur Touloucouna ab incolis...On obtient par expression de ses amandes une huile fixe connue dans le pays sous le nom d'Huile de Touloucouna.] 1866 *Treas. Bot.* 221 *Carapa guineensis* is a native of Senegal, and scarcely differs from the last [*C. guianensis*, the source of Carap or Crab oil]. Its seeds yield Tallicoonah or Coondi oil, which, besides being used for the same purposes as Crab oil, is employed as a purgative and anthelmintic.

**Tallied** (tæ·lid), *ppl. a.* [f. TALLY *v.*[1] + -ED[1].]

†**1.** Cut, scored, marked. *Obs.*

c1440 *Promp. Parv.* 486/1 Talyyd, *talliatus, dicatus, anticopatus*.

**2.** Made to tally or correspond with each other.

1895 DRIVER in *Expositor* Oct. 289 It is not sufficient for him to show that tallied speeches can exhibit marks of lateness.

† **Ta·llier.** *Cards. Obs.* Now only in Fr. form tailleur (taˈyör). Also 8 talliere, -ieur. [Agent-n. from TALLY *v.*[3], and from F. *tailler* to deal (at cards).] In rouge-et-noir and similar card-games, the name of the dealer or banker.

1709 *Cotton's Compl. Gamester* 178 (Stanf.) The *Talliere* is he that keeps the Bank. 1715 LADY M. W. MONTAGU *Basset-table* 1 The Bassette-Table spread, the Tallier come;..Rise, pensive nymph! the tallier waits for you. 1793 *Faro & Rouge et Noir*, Tailleur...The dealer, either the banker or a person he has employed to deal. 1794 *Sporting Mag.* IV. 43 The office of the tallieur is to deal and settle the game of the punters on each side of him. 1825 HOR. SMITH *Gai. & Grav.* II. 243 The Inspector, the Croupier, the Tailleur. 1877 READE *Woman Hater* ix, The *tailleur* dealt, and the croupier intoned.

**Tallingite** (tæ·liŋəit). *Min.* [Named 1865 after R. Talling: see -ITE[1].] Hydrous chloride of copper, akin to atacamite.

1865 A. H. CHURCH in *Jrnl. Chem. Soc.* XVIII. 214. 1865 *Athenæum* 25 Mar. 426/2 The new mineral Tallingite.

**Tallipat, -pot, -put**, var. of TALIPOT.

**Tallish** (tǭ·liʃ), *a.* [f. TALL *a.* + -ISH[1].] Inclining towards tallness; rather tall.

1748 RICHARDSON *Clarissa* (1810) VI. xxxvi. 132 He is a thin, tallish man. 1858 MASSON *Milton* (1859) I. vi. 467 According to Aubrey, he [Waller] was of tallish and rather slim make. 1882 *Garden* 11 Feb. 90/1 A big clump of tallish trees.

‖ **Tallith** (tæ·liþ, ‖tal,lī·þ). Also 7– talith, 7 talles, 9 talit, tales. [Rabb. Heb. טַלִּית *tallīþ*, with Spanish Jews *talit*, Ger. Jews *tallis*, f. טלל *ṭāla·l*, to cover, shelter, akin to צלל *tsāla·l*, to grow dark, whence *tsēl*, shade (H. Gollancz).] The garment or mantle (in modern times frequently assuming the form of a scarf) worn by Jews at prayer; formerly, and in some countries still, used in place of or in addition to the canopy at weddings, i. e. to cover the heads of bride and bridegroom.

Its religious significance is solely derived from the 'fringes' attached to the four corners in accordance with Numbers xv. 38 and Deut. xxii. 12.

1613 PURCHAS *Pilgrimage* (1614) 194 They call this garment *Talith*. *Ibid.* 210 The Priest draweth his *Talles* (a large cloth made of haires) before his eyes, and pronounceth the blessing. 1649 PRYNNE *Demurrer to Jews' Remitter* 35 Every Jew after he is past 7. years of age, shall carry a sign ..in his chief garment; that is to say in form of two Talles of yellow taffety. 1839 BEATON tr. *Jews in East* I. v. 152 Every one wore a talit. 1842 BONAR & M'CHEYNE *Mission to Jews* iv. (1843) 237 There were about thirty in the synagogue, all wearing the *Tallith* or shawl with fringes, and the *Tephillin* or phylacteries. 1886 FARRAR *Hist. Interpr.* iii. 126 To unite the Pallium of Japheth with the tallith of Shem. 1892 ZANGWILL *Childr. Ghetto* I. ii. 62, I have not the wherewithal..to make him a Talith-bag.

† **Ta·llman.** *Obs. Cant.* [f. TALL *a.* + MAN, after HIGHMAN.] In *pl.* Dice loaded so as to turn up high numbers.

1592 KYD *Sol. & Pers.* II. i, *Pist.* Heere are tall men and little men. *Iul.* Hie men and low men, thou wouldst say. 1592 *Nobody & Someb.* I ij b, Fulloms and gourds; heeres tall-men and low-men.

**Tallness** (tǭ·lnės). [f. TALL *a.* + -NESS.] The quality of being tall; greatness of stature.

1535 COVERDALE 1 *Sam.* xvi. 7 Loke not vpon his countenaunce ner vpon the tallnesse of his person. 1576 FLEMING *Panopl. Epist.* 276 Poplar trees, of notable talnesse. 1630 tr. *Camden's Hist. Eliz.* IV. an. 1592. 41 They soone desisted, being terrified with the tallnesse of the ship. a1661 FULLER *Worthies* (1840) I. xxiv. 101 It plainly proveth the properness of their parts, and tallness of their industry. 1870 SPURGEON *Treas. Dav.* Ps. xliv. 3 What mattered the tallness of the sons of Anak?

†**b.** *His tallness*, humorous for 'his highness'.

1656 I. S. *Picture New Courtier* 3 An Emissary, employed by his Talnesse to ensnare the plain-hearted.

**Tallow** (tæ·lo[u]), *sb.* Forms: *α.* 4 talȝ, talwgh, 4–5 talwȝ, 5 talgh(e; *Sc.* 5–6 talch, 6 tawlche, tawche, tauche, tawcht, 6–7 tauch, 7–8 taulch, 9 taugh. *β.* 4 talowȝ, 4–6 talow(e, 5 talogh, -ough, -owgh, talwhe, talwe, 5–6 talugh(e, talo, 5–7 tallo, tallowe, 6– tallow. *γ.* *Sc.* 5–6 tallone, -own(e, 5–7 -on, -oun(e, 9 *dial.* tallan, -in. [ME. *talȝ, talgh*, known first in 14th c.; corresponds to MLG. *talg, talch*, LG. *talg*, in early mod.Du. *talg, talch* (16th c.), Du. *talk* fem. and Ger. *talg*, in 1572 *talck* masc.; MIcel. (14th c.) *tólg, tólk*, MDa. (13th c.) *talgh, talwh*, MSw. *talgh(er)*, mod.Icel. *tólg*, Norw., Da., Sw. *talg*, Norw. dial. *tolg, taag, taalg, tǫlg*, Fær. *tálg*.

These forms indicate a common origin, but nowhere has the word yet been found before the 13th c. In the Scandinavian langs. a great diversity of gender suggests that the word is borrowed from MLG.; the ME. may have had a similar origin, but the parallelism of Eng. *sallow*, Sc. *sauch*, :—OE. *sealh*, Anglian *salh*, suggests for Eng. *tallow*, Sc. *tauch*, an OE. * *tealh*, * *talh*, = OLG. * *talg*, *talh*. Ulterior etymology unknown.]

**1.** The fat or adipose tissue of an animal, esp. that which yields the substance described in 2; suet.

*α.* 1382 WYCLIF *Ecclus.* xlvii. 2 As talȝ [1388 ynnere fatnesse] seuered fro the flesh. 14.. *Med. Receipts* in *Rel. Ant.* I. 53 Fresch talgh of a schepe. c1440 *Promp. Parv.* 486/1 Talwhe (*Pynson* talowe), *cepum*. 15.. *Aberdeen Regr.* XXI. (Jam.), Scheip tawcht & nolt tawcht. 1871 WADDELL *Ps. in Scottis* xvii. 10 They're theekit about wi' their ain taugh.

*β.* 1382 WYCLIF *Exod.* xxiii. 18 [Thow] shal not leeue the talowȝ of my solempnete vnto the morwen. c1400 *Lanfranc's Cirurg.* 60 Take schepis talow [*B. M. MS.* schepys talwȝ]. c1425 *Voc.* in Wr.-Wülcker 660/37 *Hoc sepum*, tallo. 1486 *Bk. of St. Albans* F ij, All beestis that beere talow and stonde vpright. 1518 *Cov. Leet Bk.* 663 That no bocher sell eny of his tallowe aboue ij s. the ston. 1613 MARKHAM *Eng. Husb.* II. II. vii. (1635) 90 Hee feeds fast, and his tallow wonderfully increaseth. 1787 HUNTER in *Phil. Trans.* LXXVII. 389 Ruminating animals have that species of fat called tallow. 1897 G. H. CLARK in *Outing* (U.S.) XXIX. 338/1 A much needed lunch of delicious reindeer tallow.

†**b.** *fig.* 'Fatness', richness. *Obs.*

c1380 WYCLIF *Wks.* (1880) 104 For þei [prelatis] ben so chokid wiþ talow of worldly goodis.

**2.** A substance consisting of a somewhat hard animal fat (esp. that obtained from the parts about the kidneys of ruminating animals, now chiefly the sheep and ox), separated by melting and clarifying from the membranes, etc., naturally mixed with it; used for making candles and soap, dressing leather, and other purposes. In quot. 1590, dripping.

*α.* 13.. *Coer de L.* 1552 And wex sumdel caste thertoo, Talwgh and grese menge alsoo. c1350 *Usages Winchester* in *Eng. Gilds* (1870) 359 Eueych sellere of grece and of smere and of talwȝ. c1440 tr. *Pallad. on Husb.* I. 444 Thorgh the ston, yf that the water synke, Take picche & talgh, as need is the to spende. 1449 *Aberdeen Regr.* (1844) I. 402 That na man by talch mar than may suffice his houss. 14.. (MS. a1600) *Iter Camerar.* c. 22 in *Scotch Acts* (1844) I. App. iv. 700/1 Þai suld gif þair lethir gude oyle and tauch [1609 SKENE tauch]. 1505 *Burgh Rec. Edinb.* (1869) I. 107 It is..forbidden that any maner of persoun melt or rynde thair tawlche in fore housis on the hie gaitt. 1544 *Aberdeen Regr.* I. 207 Selling of tauch. 1548 *Burgh Rec. Edinb.* II. 141 [To] by na kitchein fie nor paynsche tawche.

*β.* 1391 *Earl Derby's Exped.* (Camden) 71 Pro grees et talowe..emptis ibidem. 1413 *Pilgr. Sowle* (Caxton) II. lxi. (1859) 58 Wax smelleth wors after it is quenchid, than doth ony talowe. 1496 *Naval Acc. Hen. VII* (1896) 177 Talowgh. Also payed .. for DCC weight Talowe. 1529 *Supplic. to King* (E.E.T.S.) 32 A candell (which for lacke of talowe.. can not geue light). 1541 *Lanc. Wills* (Chetham Soc.) I. 81 Hole cakes of rendred tallow. 1590 SHAKS. *Com. Err.* III. ii. 100 Her ragges and the Tallow in them, will burne a Poland Winter. 1623 WHITBOURNE *Newfoundland* 98 Diuersities of the ground..that hath come in the Tallo, on the end of the Lead. 1727–41 CHAMBERS *Cycl.* s.v., There are scarce any animals but a sort of Tallow may be prepared from. 1839 URE *Dict. Arts*, etc., *Tallow*..of the ox consists of 76 parts of stearine, and 24 of oleine. 1884 *Harper's Mag.* July 299/1 'Prime' tallow is made from the kidney and caul fat only, while 'regular' tallow is made from the other fat, bones, and trimmings.

*γ.* 1482 in *Charters, etc. Edinb.* (1871) 169 Buttir, vynagir, flesch, or tallone. 1497 *Acc. Ld. High Treas. Scotl.* I. 349 Item for xxiij pund of talloune to Mons. 1498 *Reg. Privy Seal Scotl.* I. 23/1 Gold, siluer, tallon and al uther gudis that ar forbiddin to be had furth of the realme. 1529 *Rec. Edinb.* (1871) 6 At na candilmakir melt thair tallone on the foirgait. 1542 *Acc. Ld. High Treas. Scotl.* VIII. 77 For viij dusane..girthis putt upon the talloun puncheonis.

**3.** Applied to various kinds of grease or greasy substances, e. g. those obtained from plants. *Mineral tallow* = HATCHETTITE: see MINERAL *a.* 5.

1745 P. THOMAS *Jrnl. Anson's Voy.* 185 Of all the Trees that grow in China, that which produces Tallow is in my Opinion the most surprizing. 1860 [see BAYBERRY 2].

**b.** (See quot.) *local.*

1876 WOODWARD *Geol. Eng. & Wales* vii. 185 Beautiful plumose stalactites are often found in the fissures of the rock, and are called by the workmen..tallow.

**4.** Elliptical for TALLOW CANDLE.

1823 *Blackw. Mag.* XIII. 97 A little pair of tallows unsnuffed before him.

**5.** *attrib.* and *Comb.* **a.** *attrib.* Made or consisting of tallow, as *tallow-ball, -cake, -dip* (DIP *sb.* 7), *-grease, -soap*; of, pertaining to, containing, or dealing in tallow, as *tallow-can, -crap* (CRAP *sb.*[1] 3), *-cup, -leaf* (LEAF *sb.* 9), *-light, -man*. **b.** objective, instrumental, similative, etc., as *tallow-boiler, -melter*; *tallow-caked* (obs.), *-coloured, -hued, -lighted, -like, -pale, -white* adjs.

1856 KANE *Arct. Expl.* I. xxxii. 448 A few rats chopped up and frozen into the *tallow-balls. 1907 *Westm. Gaz.* 10 Dec. 9/2 The *tallow-boiler, the soap manufacturer, and a vast number of other dependent trades have been hard hit. 1599 *West Riding Sessions Rolls* (Yorks. Rec. Series III.) 135 One *tallowe cake..felonice cepit. 1577 tr. *Bullinger's Decades* (1592) 165 With face of *tallow caked hew. 1877 KNIGHT *Dict. Mech.*, **Tallow-can*, a vessel to hold melted tallow for lubricating purposes. 1822 SCOTT *Nigel* x, His cheek was still pale and *tallow-coloured as before. 1828 *Craven Gloss.*, **Tallow-craps*, the refuse or cracklings of tallow or hog's lard, after being rendered. 1863 HOLME LEE *Annie Warleigh* III. 224 To eat us out o' house an' home, an' keep Magsie doing for iver wi' biscuit, an' tallow-crap. 1877 KNIGHT *Dict. Mech.*, **Tallow-cup*, a lubricating device for journal-boxes, etc., in which tallow is employed as the lubricant. 1835 G. A. MCCALL *Lett. fr. Frontiers* (1868) 274, I set down the *tallow-dip upon the table. 1768 TUCKER *Lt. Nat.* (1834) I. 640 The unhappy negro..is thrown into a stinking hold, kept upon rotten pease besmeared over with *tallow grease. 1824 MACTAGGART *Gallovid. Encycl.* s.v., When an ox or a sheep has a gude *tallow-leaf, it is considered to have fed weel, and to be deep on the rib. 1633 P. FLETCHER *Purple Isl.* VII. xxxvii, *Tallow lights live glitt'ring, stinking die. 1825 CONSTABLE in Lockhart *Scott* lxii, I have hitherto been thinking only of the wax lights, but before I'm a twelvemonth older I shall have my hand upon the tallow. 1879 G. J. ROMANES in *19th Cent.* Sept. 401 The *tallow-lighted blackness of our mines. 1843 R. J. GRAVES *Syst. Clin. Med.* xxv. 326 Frequently they were combined with small *tallow-like sloughs of the mucous membrane at the angles of the mouth. 1860 EMERSON *Cond. Life, Beauty* Wks. (Bohn) II. 435, I have noticed a block of spermaceti lying about..mantelpieces for twenty years.., simply because the tallowman gave it the form of a rabbit. 1815 *Chron.* in *Ann. Reg.* 34/2 A very alarming fire broke out at Mr. Dunkin's, *tallow-melter, in Aldersgate Street. 1596 GOSSON *Pleas. Quippes Upst. Gentlew.* 98 in Hazl. *E. P. P.* IV. 254 But on each wight now are they seene, The *tallow-pale, the browning-bay. 1906 *Daily Chron.* 23 Oct. 5/2 The use of the old-fashioned *tallow soaps. 1853 KANE *Grinnell Exp.* xxxiv. 303 His nose was *tallow-white.

**c.** Special Combs.: **tallow-berry**, the edible fruit of a small malpighiaceous tree (*Byrsonima lucida*) of the West Indies and Florida Keys; also called *glamberry* (*Cent. Dict.* 1891); also, the tree; **tallow-cut** *a.*, = *tallow-topped*; **tallow-drop**, chiefly *attrib.*, describing a style of cutting precious stones, by which one side is made smooth and convex, the other similarly convex, or flat, or concave; **tallow-gourd**, an E. Indian climbing cucurbitaceous plant, *Benincasa cerifera* (*B. hispida*), so called from the waxy substance which exudes from its fruit when ripe; also called *wax-gourd, white gourd*; **tallow-loaf**, † (*a*) a lump of tallow; also *fig.*; (*b*) *attrib.* applied to a kind of cabbage (cf. LOAF *sb.* 5), also called DRUMHEAD (4); **tallow-nut**, a thorny tree, *Ximenia americana* (N.O. *Olacaceæ*), native of tropical America, bearing a plum-like fruit containing a white seed or 'nut'; also called HOG-PLUM, MOUNTAIN-*plum*; **tallow-nutmeg**, a species of nutmeg-tree, *Myristica* *sebifera*, native of tropical S. America, whose seed yields a concrete oil known as American nutmeg-oil, or virola-tallow; **tallow-oil**, oil expressed from tallow; **tallow-shrub**, a N. American shrub, *Myrica cerifera*, also called BAYBERRY (2), CANDLEBERRY (a), or *wax-myrtle*, whose fruit yields a wax-like substance (*bayberry tallow*) used for candles; **tallow-top**, a precious stone cut in *tallow-drop* fashion; also *attrib.*; hence **tallow-topped** adj.; **tallow-wood**, a large Australian tree, *Eucalyptus microcorys*, which yields a very hard greasy wood. See also TALLOW CANDLE, -CHANDLER, etc.

**1855** tr. *Labarte's Arts Mid. Ages* iv. 111 *Tallow-cut, that is, rounded and polished, in a convex shape, like the modern carbuncle. **1898** *Athenæum* 17 Sept. 391/2 A stone cut *en cabochon*—or tallow-cut, as the old term had it. **1798** GREVILLE in *Phil. Trans.* LXXXVIII. 411 Stones..of the common India polish and form, *en cabochon*, which is often called *tallow drop, from the French..term *goutte de suif*. **1891** KIPLING *Naulahka* vi, It's a tallow-drop emerald. **1483** *Cath. Angl.* 377/2 A *Talghe lafe (*A.* A Tallow lafe), *congiarium*. **1596** NASHE *Saffron-Walden* Wks. (Grosart) III. 183 The verie guts and garbage of his Note-book he hath put into this tallow loafe. **1780** *Lett. & Pap. Bath Soc.* I. 17 The sort principally raised is the tallow-loaf, or drum-head cabbage. **1805** R. W. DICKSON *Pract. Agric.* II. 682 Known in some districts by the name of the tallow loaf cabbage. **1891** *Cent. Dict.*, *Tallow-nut. *Tallow-nutmeg. **1866** *Treas. Bot.*, *Tallow-shrub, *Myrica cerifera*. **1884** F. J. BRITTEN *Watch & Clockm.* 208 Finishers generally use the old English screw head tool for producing the beautiful '*tallow top' screws used in English work. **1865** EMANUEL *Diamonds*, etc. 144 The old English expression, '*tallow-topped, which means cut, not in facets, but with a flat or hollow base, and a smooth convex top. **1889** J. H. MAIDEN *Usef. Plants Australia* 493 In Queensland it is known as 'Peppermint'... But its almost universal name is *Tallow Wood...Used..for flooring, *e.g.* in ball-rooms. **1897** *Melbourne Argus* 22 Feb. 5/4 (Morris) That the New South Wales black butt and tallow wood were the most durable and noiseless woods for street-paving.

**Ta·llow**, *v.* Forms: see prec. [f. prec. sb.]

1. *trans.* To smear or anoint with tallow; to grease (formerly esp. the bottom of a ship or boat).

*a* **1400–50** *Alexander* 4208 Quen it [a barge] was done.. pickid & taloghid. **1463** *Mann. & Househ. Exp.* (Roxb.) 220 To the schypmen that talluyd the shyp boot, vj.d. for wyne. *c* **1490** *Promp. Parv.* 486/1 (MS. A) Talwyn (*Pynson* talowyn), *sepo*. **1495** *Naval Acc. Hen. VII* (1896) 225 Talowe occupied abought talowying of the seid ship. **1497** *Acc. Ld. High Treas. Scotl.* I. 378 Item, for pyk to hir and to talloune hir. **1530** PALSGR. 752/1 Tallowe your shyppe or you go, it shall forther you moche on your waye. **1589** WARNER *Alb. Eng., Prose Add.* (1612) 336 Commaund..that thy Shippes be secretly calked, tallowed, ballaced. **1706** E. WARD *Wooden World Diss.* (1708) 84 There's near as much Stuff drops from his Carcase every Day, as would tallow the Ship's Bottom. **1806** PIKE *Sources Mississ.* (1810) 89 Tallowed my boats with our candles and launched them. **1886** J. K. JEROME *Idle Thoughts* vii, I..tallowed my nose, and went to bed.

†b. *intr.* (for *refl.*) *Obs.*

**1666** *Lond. Gaz.* No. 28/3 The *Forrester* having washed and tallowed here, is gone to her station. **1720** DE FOE *Capt. Singleton* xiv. (1840) 240 The sloop washed and tallowed also.

2. a. *intr.* Of cattle, etc.: To form, produce, or yield tallow.

*a* **1722** LISLE *Husb.* (1752) 262 Old cows generally tallowed best withinside. *Ibid.*, Very rarely [for a young cow] to tallow well on the inside. **1796** BURKE *Let. Noble Ld.* Wks. VIII. 63 Their only question will be..how he [the Duke of Bedford] cuts up? how he tallows in the cawl or on the kidneys? *a* **1843** SOUTHEY *Comm.-pl. Bk.* (1851) IV. 400/2 [Cattle] famous for..tallowing within in the first degree.

b. *trans.* To cause (cattle, etc.) to form tallow; to fatten. (Cf. TALLOWED 2.)

**1765** *Museum Rust.* IV. xliv. 190 The largest pasture.. will neither skin nor tallow, or, in other words, is fit for nothing but young stock. **1828** WEBSTER, *Tallow*,..to cause to have a large quantity of tallow; as, to tallow sheep.

Hence **Ta·llowing** *vbl. sb.* and *ppl. a.*

**1495** [see sense 1]. **1828** in WEBSTER.

**Ta·llow ca·ndle**, *sb.* A candle made of tallow.

**1452** in *Berks, Bucks & Oxon Archæol. Jrnl.* Oct. (1903) 78 Item for j lb. & a hafe of talowcandell..j d. ob. **1496–7** *Rec. St. Mary at Hill* 33 Item, iiij Candylstykes of laton with braunches for Talough candell. **1545** in *Shropsh. Parish Documents* (1903) 79 For talo candyllys. **1660** BOYLE *New Exp. Phys. Mech.* x. 74 We took a Tallow-Candle of such a size that eight of them make about a pound. **1886** RUSKIN *Præterita* I. vii. 229 My parents..used only tallow candles in plated candlesticks.

Hence **Tallow-candle** *v.* (*nonce-wd.*), *trans.* to smear or rub with a tallow candle.

**1894** BLACKMORE *Perlycross* 48 The nap of his old velvet-coat where a wicked boy had tallow-candled it.

†**Tallow catch.** *Obs.* A phrase applied in Shakspere (so in quartos and folios) to Falstaff, as a very fat man.

By Hanmer taken as = *tallow ketch* 'tub of tallow': see *ketch* 'tub or barrel', a Gloucestershire and West-of-England word, in Eng. Dial. Dict. By Johnson explained as *tallow keech* 'lump or mass of tallow' (see KEECH *sb.*), an explanation adopted by Steevens. See notes in critical editions.

**1596** SHAKS. 1 *Hen. IV*, II. iv. 252 *Prince.* Thou Knotty-pated Foole, thou Horson obscene greasie Tallow Catch.

**Ta·llow-cha·ndler.** [See CHANDLER 2.] One whose trade is to make or sell tallow candles.

**1406** *Close Roll* 7 *Hen. IV* b, Simon atte Holke, Talogh-chaundeler. **1431** *Cal. Pat. Rolls* 9 *Hen. VI* 96 Henry Pollard, citizen and talghchaundeler of London. *c* **1515** *Cocke Lorell's B.* 9 Talowe chaundelers, hostelers, and glouers. **1683** TRYON *Way to Health* 595 Neither does a Tallow-Chandler smell those horrible Scents and pernicious Fumes that old Tallow sends forth when it is melted. *a* **1763** LD. GRANVILLE in Boswell *Johnson* an. 1780, A letter, expressed in terms not good enough for a tallow-chandler to have used. **1876** L. STEPHEN *Hist. Eng. Th. 18th C.* I. III. v. 163 He was early apprenticed to a tallow-chandler.

Hence **Tallow-cha·ndlering**, also **Tallow-cha·ndling** (cf. *market-gardening*), the operation or business of a tallow-chandler.

**1837–8** THACKERAY *Yellowplush Corr.* i, Her father being a bankrup in the tallow-chandlering way. **1876** L. STEPHEN *Hist. Eng. Th. 18th C.* I. III. v. 163 The exception to his tallow-chandling was a short residence with Sir Joseph.

**Ta·llow-cha·ndlery.** [f. prec.: see -ERY.] a. The business or trade of a tallow-chandler. b. The place of work of a tallow-chandler.

**1864** in WEBSTER. **1866** *Routledge's Every Boy's Ann.* 71 His own tallow-chandlery business.

**Tallowed** (tæ·loud), *a.* Forms: see TALLOW *sb.* [f. TALLOW *sb.* and *v.* + -ED.]

1. Smeared or anointed with tallow, greased: said esp. of a ship's bottom.

*c* **1440** *Promp. Parv.* 486/2 Talwyd, *cepatus*. **1513** DOUGLAS *Æneis* IX. ii. 97 The tallownit burdis kest a pyky low [= the tallowed boards emitted a pitchy flame]. *a* **1547** SURREY *Æneid* IV. (1557) F j b, Now fleetes the talowed kele. **1716** *Lond. Gaz.* No. 5412/2 A clean-tallowed French Snow. **1804** NELSON in Nicolas *Disp.* (1846) VI. 283 She would require a clean tallowed bottom every six weeks.

†2. Of cattle, etc.: (Well) furnished with fat or tallow; in grease. *Obs.*

**1523** FITZHERB. *Husb.* § 57 And se the oxe haue a greate codde,..for than it shulde seme, that they shuld be wel talowed. **1613** MARKHAM *Eng. Husbandman* II. II. vii. (1635) 81 A..signe that the beast is very well tallowed within.

**Ta·llower.** *rare*—⁰. [f. TALLOW *sb.* and *v.* + -ER [1].] (See quots.)

**1828** WEBSTER, *Tallower*, an animal disposed to form tallow internally. *Cyc.* **1882** OGILVIE (Annandale), *Tallower*, a tallow-chandler.

**Ta·llow-face.** Now *rare* or *Obs.* A pale, yellowish-white face; hence, a person having such a face: a term of contempt.

**1592** SHAKS. *Rom. & Jul.* III. v. 158 Out you baggage, You tallow face. **1616** R. C. *Times' Whistle* v. 2237 O, 'tis Fumoso with the tallow-face. **1638** SIR T. HERBERT *Trav.* (ed. 2) 127 The entrance..neer which is hung a mirrour whether to admire their tallow faces in, or internal deformities, I know not.

So **Ta·llow-faced** *a.*, having a tallow-face.

**1592** GREENE *Disput.*, etc. 17 The Paynters coulde not.. make away theyr Vermiglion, if tallowe facde whoores vsde it not for their cheekes. **1621** BURTON *Anat. Mel.* III. ii. IV. i. (1651) 519 Every Lover admires his Mistress, though she be..pale, red, yellow, tand, tallow-faced. **1681** W. ROBERTSON *Phraseol. Gen.* (1693) 446 A deformed, thin, tallow-faced fellow, he looks like a Ghost. **1883** STEVENSON *Treas. Isl.* II. viii, It was the tallow-faced man.

**Ta·llowiness.** [f. TALLOWY + -NESS.] The quality of being tallowy.

**1832** S. WARREN *Diary Physic.* I. xiii. 291 The tallowiness of her complexion.

**Tallowish** (tæ·lo͡uiʃ), *a.* [f. TALLOW *sb.* + -ISH [1] 2.] Of the nature of or resembling tallow; tallow-like, tallowy.

**1552** HULOET, Tallowyshe, or lyke to tallow, *seuiosus*. **1598** FLORIO, *Songioso*, fattie, lardie, greasie, tallowish. **1731** MEDLEY *Kolben's Cape G. Hope* II. 65 The Fat [of Cape sheep] is not so tallowish as that of European Mutton; and the poorer Sort..use it in the Place of Butter. **1838** GRANVILLE *Spas Germ.* 378 The cheeks, formerly tallowish and saffrony, became ruddy.

**Tallow keech, ketch**: see TALLOW CATCH.

**Ta·llow-tree.** A name given to various trees yielding substances resembling tallow; *spec.* a. *Stillingia sebifera*, a euphorbiaceous tree of China, cultivated also in India and the warmer parts of America for the fatty covering of its seeds; b. *Pentadesma butyracea*, a guttiferous tree of Sierra Leone, also called *butter and tallow tree* (BUTTER *sb.*[1] 5); c. *Vateria indica* (N.O. *Dipterocarpaceæ*) of Malabar; d. = *tallow-wood* (TALLOW *sb.* 5 c).

**1704** PETIVER *Gazophyl.* IV. xxxiv, *Ricinus Chinensis Sebifera*..China Tallow-tree. **1851** *Art Jrnl. Illustr. Catal.* II. p. vi/1 The tallow-tree of China, the seeds of which furnish a fatty matter manufactured .. into candles. *c* **1865** LETHEBY in *Circ. Sc.* I. 95/1 A solid oil.. is obtained from the tallow-tree of Java—probably a species of *Bassia*. **1887** MOLONEY *Forestry W. Afr.* 279 Butter or Tallow tree of West Africa (*Pentadesma butyracea*, Don). —Fruits yield a yellow greasy juice when cut, which is mixed by the Negroes with their food.

**Tallowy** (tæ·lo͡u,i), *a.* Also *Sc.* **taughy.** [f. TALLOW *sb.* + -Y.]

1. Having the nature or properties of tallow; sebaceous.

*c* **1440** *Promp. Parv.* 486/1 Talwy, *ceposus*. **1530** PALSGR. 327/1 Talowye, *grasseux*. **1594** T. B. *La Primaud. Fr. Acad.* II. 112 Oyle, or some other tallowy and moyst matter. **1771** SMOLLETT *Humph. Cl.* 8 June, The tallowey rancid mass called butter. **1904** FARRER *Garden Asia* 130 The tallowy noisomeness of the temple smells.

b. Smeared with tallow; greasy.

**1867** N. MACLEOD *Starling* xxiv, I assure you he has a taughy fleece to scoor in this parish!

2. Resembling tallow in colour or complexion.

**1832** [implied in TALLOWINESS]. **1847** LE FANU *T. O'Brien* 170 A tallowy sensual face. **1883** STEVENSON *Treas. Isl.* I. ii, He was a pale, tallowy creature. **1899** *Allbutt's Syst. Med.* VIII. 677 The integument became dense, tallowy in colour and otherwise changed.

3. Of a beast: Abounding in tallow, fat.

**1495** *Trevisa's Barth. De P. R.* IX. xix. (W. de W.) 357 In Nouembre beestes wexen fatte and talowy and namely swyne. **1818** *Blackw. Mag.* III. 528 The bullock..lays himself down, with a lengthening groan, once more into his tallowy laziness.

**Tally** (tæ·li), *sb.*[1] Forms: 5–6 taly(e, 6 tallye, tallee, tale, 6–7 talie, tallie, talle, 7–9 talley, 6– tally. [In 15th c. *talye* = AF. (14th c.) *tallie* = Anglo-L. *tālea*, *tālia*, *tallia*, in same sense, L. *tālea*, cutting, rod, stick. The doublet *taille*, *taile*, TAIL *sb.*[2], from French *taille*, was in earlier use, and did not become obsolete till 17th c.]

1. A stick or rod of wood, usually squared, marked on one side with transverse notches representing the amount of a debt or payment. The rod being cleft lengthwise across the notches, the debtor and creditor each retained one of the halves, the agreement or tallying of which constituted legal proof of the debt, etc. Cf. TAIL *sb.*[2] 4.

[**1189** (Aug.) GERVASE OF CANT. *Op. Hist.* (Rolls) I. 453 Videlicet ut conventus Monachos tres vel quatuor ad custodiendas villas ordinaret, qui redditibus omnibus thesaurariis a conventu constitutis per taleas responderent. **1203** in *Placit. Abbrev.* (1811) 38/2 Eustacius..inde producit sectam et talliam ostendit quam fecerunt. **1321–2** *Rolls of Parlt.* I. 401/1 Illoques pristrent des biens..pur lour sustenaunce saunz paiement fere ou tallie al gardeyn du dit leu.]

*c* **1440** *Promp. Parv.* 486/1 Taly, or talye,..*talia, tallia*. **1545** BRINKLOW *Compl.* vi. (1874) 19 Ye shal not haue hir redy mony neyther, but a taly. **1552** HULOET, Talye or tale vsed in receypte, *tessera*,..*tesserula*,..*dimin.* a lyttle or shorte tallye. **1557** *Order of Hospitalls* H ij, The Tallyes of the same Baker and Bruer shalbe in the custodie and keping of the Thresorer. *a* **1628** PRESTON *New Covt.* (1634) 323 There is a law in the mind within, answerable to the law of God without;..it answers as Tallie answers to Tallie. **1756** *Gentl. Mag.* XXVI. 606/1 Harry, who ought to have minded the Tallies of the milk-score. **1790** PALEY *Horæ Paul.* xiv, It is like comparing the two parts of a cloven tally. **1881** WHITEHEAD *Hops* 62 In some cases the very old fashioned method prevails of cutting notches upon wooden tallies, one part kept by the picker, the counterpart by the measurer.

b. Such a cloven rod, as the official receipt formerly given by the Exchequer for a tax, tallage, etc. paid, or in acknowledgement of a loan to the sovereign.

[**1166** *Pipe Roll* 12 *Hen. II* (1888) 2 Et x. li. in II talliis. **1178** *Dialogus de Scaccario* v, Quid ad factorem talearum. **1284** *Provis. Exch.* (St. Rec. Comm. I. 69/1), Omnes illi qui habent tallias de scaccario de debitis suis vel antecessorum suorum.] *a* **1604** HANMER *Chron. Irel.* (1633) 208 Calmagh burnt all the rolles and tallyes of that countie. **1626** CHAS. I in *Buccleuch MSS.* (Hist. MSS. Comm.) I. 264 Acquittances to be given you, which shall be your warrant for striking tallies and for repayment hereafter. *a* **1692** POLLEXFEN *Disc. Trade* (1697) 70 When any Tax or Imposition is granted by Parliament, Tallies, Exchequer Notes or Bills, issued out upon the same, for the supplying of the Government with Ready Money till the Duties be paid. **1697** *Lond. Gaz.* No. 3328/4 Lost..a Talley of 300 l. on Wines and Tobacco, Dated the 11th of March, 1695, No. 2329. **1738** *Hist. Crt. Excheq.* v. 91 To pay in their Rents into the Exchequer, and take Tallies from thence. **1776** ADAM SMITH *W. N.* II. ii. (1869) I. 319 In 1696, tallies had been at forty, and fifty, and sixty per cent. discount, and bank notes at twenty per cent. **1847** J. FRANCIS *Hist. Bank Eng.* iv. 59 Tallies lay bundled up like Bath faggots in the hands of brokers, and stock-jobbers. **1848** WHARTON *Law Lex.* s.v., The use of tallies in the Exchequer was abolished by 23 Geo. III c. 82, and the old tallies were ordered to be destroyed by 4 & 5 Wm. IV c. 15. **1896** ANSON *Law & Cust. Constit.* II. vii. II. i. 329 *note* 2, In 1834..orders were given to destroy the tallies. They were used as fuel in the stoves which warmed the Houses of Parliament; they overheated the flues and burned down the Houses.

†c. *Tally of pro* (i. e. *pro*, for or in favour of some one), *tally of sol* (i. e. *solutum*, paid): see quot. 1843. *Obs.*

**1691** W. LOWNDES *Acc. Revenue Eng.* 88 (MS) The Tally of Pro called also the Tally of Assignement Imports on the same Stick both a Receipt and payment. **1696** *Lond. Gaz.* No. 3157/4 Lost..a Tally of Pro, dated the 18th of May 1695, in the Name of John Richards, Esq; for 300 l. struck on the Commissioners of His Majesty's Hereditary and Temporary Revenues of Excise. *Ibid.* No. 3244/4 Lost a Talley of 100 l. upon the Temporal Excise, struck the 5th of Aug. 1696, pro Edvardo Nicholas. **1697** *Ibid.* No. 3308/4 Lost.., a Talley of Pro No. 90. struck Aug. 6, 1696, in the Name of Edward Nicholas Esq; for 100 l. in part of 35000 l. by him Lent the 2d of July, 1696, upon the Hered' and Temp' Excise. **1703** *Ibid.* No. 3933/4 The Tallies of Pro, levied upon the Surplus of the Duties on Malt. **1843** *Fourth Rep. Dep. Kpr.* App. II. 166 The Tally of *Sol*..whereon the word *sol* was written, to show that the money..had been paid into the Exchequer. *Ibid.*, The Tally of Pro..operated as a modern cheque on a banker, being given forth in payment from the Exchequer, as a charge upon some public accountant, for him to pay the sum expressed thereon, out of the revenues in his hands. **1896** ANSON *Law & Cust. Constit.* II. vii. II. i. 329.

d. *transf.* Any tangible means of recording a payment or amount.

**1863** FAWCETT *Pol. Econ.* II. x. (1876) 258 Each customer, when he makes a purchase, receives certain tin tickets or tallies, which record the amount of his purchases.

†2. The record of an amount due; a score or shot, an account. *Obs.*

**1573** TUSSER *Husb.* (1878) 170 In buieng of drinke, by the firkin or pot, The tallie ariseth, but hog amendes not. **1828** *Life Planter Jamaica* 55 Keep tally of their number. **1833** HT. MARTINEAU *Brooke Farm* vii, To measure the milk and keep the tally.

† **b.** *Naut. Petty tally*, a petty account kept of a ship's provisions, orig. of a certain portion; hence *transf.* provisions. *Obs.*

**1626** CAPT. SMITH *Accid. Yng. Seamen* 39 How to keep his Petty Tally. **1627** — *Seaman's Gram.* xv. 74 A Commander at Sea should doe well..to consider..how to..prouide his petty Tally. *Ibid.* 75 There is neither..Grocer, Poulterer,..nor Butchers shop, and therefore the vse of this petty Tally is necessary. *a* **1642** SIR W. MONSON *Naval Tracts* vi. (1704) 519/2 Beer, Cask, Bread, and Petty-Talley ..12*l.* **1678** PHILLIPS (ed. 4), *Petty-Tally*, in Navigation is a competent proportion of edible and potable commodities in a Ship, according to the number of the Ships company. **1823** in CRABB *Technol. Dict.* **1847** in CRAIG.

† **c.** *Upon the tally*: on credit, 'on tick'; by running up a score. *Obs.*

**1807** *Sporting Mag.* XXIX. 185 To buy goods upon the Tally. (This term Tally, Mr. Garrow said, was not much known to the public.)

**3.** *fig.* (from 1 and 2). Reckoning, score, account. Now *rare*.

**1614** RALEIGH *Hist. World* II. (1634) 214 Ordinary occurrences, that are to be numbred by a shorter Tally [than by the year]. **1628** WITHER *Brit. Rememb.* IV. 1807 Left they upon thy Tally all that sin. **1648** C. WALKER *Hist. Independ.* I. 96 He that hath a Tally of every mans faults but his own hanging at his Girdle. **1649** G. DANIEL *Trinarch., Rich. II*, xxxviii, He threatened To weare it worthy, and a Tally make Of slaughter, to outvye his shop-board's Chalke. **1822** HAZLITT *Table-t.* (1870) I. i. 14 It is stamped on his brain, and lives there thenceforward, a tally for nature, and a test of art.

**4.** Each of the two corresponding halves or parts of anything; a thing, or part, that exactly fits or agrees with another thing or corresponding part; a counterpart; *fig.* an agreement, correspondence.

**1651** CLEVELAND *Mixt Assembly* 35 Whose Members being not tallies, they'l not own Their fellows at the Resurrection. *a* **1700** DRYDEN (J.), So suited in their minds and persons That they were fram'd the tallies for each other. **1816** JEFFERSON *Writ.* (1830) IV. 297 If histories so unlike..can ..be brought to the same tally, no line of distinction remains between fact and fancy. **1833** J. HOLLAND *Manuf. Metal* II. 266 The bit of which key is so cut or shaped as to form a complete tally with the interior machinery. **1906** *Edin. Rev.* Jan. 207 Here he will find again the tally between proportion and thought.

**b.** *To live* (*on*) *tally*, to live in concubinage, to cohabit without marriage. *slang.*

**1877** 5 *Years' Penal Servitude* iii. 246, I never took to a moll except on tally. *Ibid.* vi. 377 A man she was then living 'tally' with. **1890** *N. & Q.* 7th Ser. X. 297/2 To 'live tally' is quite a common expression amongst the working classes in Lancashire, as is also tally-woman. **1901** MABEL PEACOCK in *Folk-Lore* June 174 He had for years been 'living tally' with a woman—that is in cohabitation without marriage.

**5.** A number, group, series, lot, tale; *esp.* a certain number or group (of things or persons) taken as the unit of computation. Also, 'a company or division of voters at an election' (*Eng. Dial. Dict.*): see quot. 1774.

**1674** N. FAIRFAX *Bulk & Selv.* 56 Every tally by which we tell things must be either even or odd. **1683** KENNETT tr. *Erasm. on Folly* 102 When they tone out their daily Tally of Psalms. **1725** *Bradley's Fam. Dict.* s. v. *Wall*, Some Bricks..are broken, in every Load or 500 Bricks; and the Tally or Tale, is, for the most part,..too little. **1774** BURKE *Sp. Concl. Poll* Wks. III. 16 Mr. Brickdale opened his poll, it seems, with a tally of those very kind of freemen, and voted many hundreds of them. **1843** LEVER *J. Hinton* xvii. (1878) 123 We told them off by tallies as they marched on board. **1886** *Pall Mall G.* 4 June 14/1 Some few years ago..Victoria was well ahead of New South Wales in the tally of her people. **1889** *19th Cent.* Nov. 755 Though we had three deaths during the passage, as we also had three births, our tally remained correct. **1890** *Science* 12 Dec. 323 All the Indians..were drawn up in tallies, and arranged according to families. **1892** *Labour Commission Gloss.*, *Tally*, a check account made by a person receiving goods; ..used for the number of bricks or tons of other goods carried on canal boats and river barges.

**b.** *spec.* In market-gardening, Five dozen (cabbages, bunches of turnips, etc.).

**1851** MAYHEW *Lond. Labour* I. 92, I buy turnips by the 'tally'. A tally's five dozen bunches. **1883** *Daily News* 6 Sept. 2/7 Cauliflowers, 5s. per tally. **1891** *Times* 28 Sept. 4/2 Cabbages, 1s. 6d. to 2s. 6d. per tally;..marrows, 2s. 6d. to 3s. 6d. per tally.

**c.** *spec.* In hop-picking, A specified number of bushels that have to be picked for one shilling: see quot. 1904, and cf. quot. 1881 in 1.

**1868** *A Hop-sketch* in *Derby Mercury* 12 Feb., Back at the 'tally' to play your part. **1891** *Scott. Leader* 24 Sept. 7 A strike has occurred among the hop-pickers..owing to alleged 'excessive measure and high tally'. **1904** *Daily Chron.* 29 Aug. 8/3 The pay is..at the rate of 1s. for a certain number of bushels, called the 'tally', which varies from five to eight or nine, according to the growth of the hops.

**d.** The last of a specified number forming a unit of computation, on the completion of which the tally-man calls 'tally' and notes it down.

**1886** P. CLARKE *New Chum in Australia* xii. 175 As a 'hundred' is called, one of us calls out 'tally', and cuts one notch in a stick. **1894** *Northumbld. Gloss.* s.v., If the articles are counted singly, they are called out up to the nineteenth; but instead of..'twenty', the word tally is substituted; thus 'eighteen, nineteen, *tally*'..In counting articles that can be lifted in groups the tale is thus made—'five, ten, fifteen, *tally*'.

† **6.** A mark (such as the notch of a tally) representing a unit quantity, or a series or set of units.

**1719** D'URFEY *Pills* (1872) III. 314 In Courts had all their Heart's desire, For every Kiss a Tally. *Ibid.* IV. 264 He notcht his Arse with Tallies. **1807** CRABBE *Parish Reg.* I. 252 Where chalky tallies yet remain in rows.

**7.** A distinguishing mark on a bale or case of merchandise, etc., corresponding to one in a list, for the purpose of comparison or identification; hence, a mark, label, ticket, or tab, used for this purpose, or to denote the weight and contents, etc.

**1860** MAURY *Phys. Geog. Sea* vi. § 324 But the air is invisible; and it is not easily perceived how either marks or tallies may be put on it, that it may be traced. **1865** *Morning Star* 27 Jan., I entered the weights in the landing-book, and marked them in the tallies..and I saw a great number of the tallies afterwards put on the bales.

**b.** *Coal-mining.* (See quots.)

**1883** GRESLEY *Coal Mining Gloss.*, *Tally*, a mark or number placed by a collier upon every tub of coals loaded.. They are usually little bits of tin having a number stamped upon them. **1890** *N. & Q.* 7th Ser. X. 297/2 At many pits it is customary to send the tubs of coals to bank with tin tallies attached...This tally is so that the banksmen and weighmen may place the coals to the credit of the men working in the banks below, the banks and tallies bearing the same numbers.

**c.** *spec.* in *Gardening*, A tab or label of wood, metal, etc., on which are inscribed the name, class, etc. of the plant or tree to which it is attached, or beside which it is stuck in the ground.

**1822** LOUDON *Encycl. Gard.* III. IV. 1190 Every plant [in a Botanical Garden] ought to have its name painted on strong cast-iron talleys. **1842** *Penny Cycl.* XXIV. 17/1 Many different kinds of tally are used in gardens and arboretums, to bear either numbers referring to a catalogue, or the names of the plants near which they are placed. **1870** THORNBURY *Tour Eng.* I. i. 23 The..gray stone, the tally to mark a seed plot in Death's neglected garden. **1881** *Encycl. Brit.* XII. 234/2 Tallies of wood [in horticulture] should be slightly smeared with white paint and then written on while damp with a black-lead pencil.

**d.** A tie-label, tab, or tag for luggage, etc.

**1909** *Advt.*, Temple Tower Tallies, 1*d.* per packet, strung ready for use.

¶ **8.** Used as = TAIL *sb.*[2] 2 b. *Obs.*

**1609** OVERBURY *Observ. St. France* Wks. (1856) 238 The gentrie are the onely entire body there, which participate with the prerogatives of the crowne; for from it they receive..supply to their estates, by governments and pensions, and freedome from tallies upon their owne lands. **1642** HOWELL *For. Trav.* (Arb.) 74 When one hath seene the Tally and taillage of France,..the Assise of Holland, the Gabels of Italy,..hee will blesse God, and love England better ever after.

**9.** *attrib.* and *Comb.* **a.** Simple attrib. and obj. gen., as (from 1, 1 b) *tally-broker*, *-court*, *-cutter*, *-office*, *-stick*; (from 2, 2 b) *tally-book*, *-check*, *-keeper*, *-table*; **b.** in reference to the instalment or petty credit system (cf. 2 c) worked by the TALLYMAN, as *tally-business*, *-draper*, *-master*, *-packman*, *-room*, *-shop*, *-system*, *-trade*. **c.** Special combs.: **tally-board**, a board on which an account is notched or chalked; e.g. one on which the record of a weaver's work is kept (*Eng.Dial.Dict.*); **tally-clerk**, one who checks merchandise with a list in loading or discharging cargo; also (*U.S.*), one who assists in counting and recording votes; **tally-husband** (*slang*), a man who 'lives tally' (4 b) with a woman; **tally-mark** = sense 7; **tally-pot**, a vessel in which records of a counting or voting are placed (*Funk's Stand. Dict.* 1895); **tally-room** (Ireland), a committee-room at an election; **tally-sheet**, a score-sheet, esp. (*U.S.*) in recording votes; **tally-shouter** (*Mining*), see quot.; **tally-stick**, a stick used as or like a tally (sense 1); **tally-writer**, formerly, the clerk who wrote the description and amount of the payment on two opposite sides of the exchequer tallies. See also TALLYMAN, WOMAN.

**1849** JAMES *Woodman* vii, You have not got the *tally board so completely in your hand, my friend. *a* **1716** SOUTH *Serm.* (1717) IV. 154 Such a Money-Monger, such a *Tally-Broker, and Cheater of the Publick. **1851** *Tally-business [see *tally-master*]. **1862** MISS BRADDON *Lady Audley* xxvii, You're not connected with—with the tally business, are you, sir? **1884** *Times* (weekly ed.) 10 Oct. 13/4 Rudely inscribed potsherds..*tally-checks scrawled with entries of time-labour and food-wages. **1890** *Daily News* 13 Sept. 6/4 A large number of ships' *tally clerks,..have not had a day's work for weeks. **1902** *Westm. Gaz.* 25 Feb. 2/1 There is a duplicate of this board, but on a small scale, placed on the desk of the tally-clerk, so that the record of the votes is constantly before his eyes. **1684** E. CHAMBERLAYNE *Pres. St. Eng.* II. (ed. 15) 105 In the *Tally Court—the *Tally-cutter attends. **1786** *St. Paper* in *Ann. Reg.* 193/1 The tally writer..takes an account of the sum, and writes it on both sides of the tally delivered to him, with the sum cut upon it in notches by the tally-cutter. **1883** GILMOUR *Mongols* xviii. 247 Ocher..threw up his office of *tally-keeper. **1851** MAYHEW *Lond. Labour* I. 383/2 The 'travellers' ..are occasionally shopmen, for a 'large' *tally-master not unfrequently carries on a retail trade in addition to his tally-business. **1631** SIR S. D'EWES *Jrnl. Parlt.* (1783) 52 That unjust and rare recorde called Domesdei in the *tallie-office of the Exchequer. **1851** MAYHEW *Lond. Labour* I. 381/1 The pedlar or hawking tallyman travels for orders... The great majority of the *tally-packmen are Scotchmen. **1842** S. LOVER *Handy Andy* xvii, The popular tunes..in the *tally rooms, while the fellows are waiting to go up. **1910** *Daily News* 24 Jan. 8 Mr. Wood could neither show himself in the place nor get a tally-room, as they call their committee-rooms there [Lisburn]. **1889** *Century Mag.* Feb. 622/1 The growing disposition [in U.S.] to tamper with the ballot-box and the *tally-sheet. **1893** *Scribner's Mag.* June 779/2 To call her attention to a tally-sheet, covering a period of three calendar months. **1851** MAYHEW *Lond. Labour* I. 32/1 The poor,..pawnbrokers, loan-offices, *tally-shops, dolly-shops, are the only parties who will trust them. **1870** *Public Opinion* 16 July, [He] described from personal inspection the low quality of the provisions supplied in the tally-shops. **1883** GRESLEY *Coal Mining Gloss.*, *Tally-shouter*, one who shouts out the numbers on the tallies to the weigher. **1895** HOFFMAN *Beginnings of Writ.* 140 Several tribes of Indians, in California, employed a variety of *tallysticks to record transactions in business. **1897** MARY KINGSLEY *W. Africa* 49 They hopefully notched away the moons on their tally-sticks. **1851** MAYHEW *Lond. Labour* I. 372/2 Some had been unsuccessful as tallymen when shopkeepers, or travellers for tally-shops, and have resorted to hawking or street-trading,..blending the *tally system with the simple rules of sale for ready money. **1829** COBBETT *Adv. Yng. Man* ii. 60 The '*Tally-trade' by which household goods, coals, clothing, all sorts of things are sold upon credit, the seller keeping a tally, and receiving payment..little by little. **1851** MAYHEW *Lond. L.* I. 383/1 Establishments, 'doing largely' in the tally-trade. **1786** *Tally writer [see *tally-cutter*].

† **Tally**, *sb.*[2] *Cards. Obs.* [f. TALLY *v.*[3]: cf. F. *taille* from *tailler* to deal.] At faro, basset, etc., A deal.

**1706** MRS. CENTLIVRE *Basset Table* IV. 53 *Captain*...Pray count the Cards, I believe there's a false Tally. *Sir James.* ..No, they are Right, Sir (Sir James counts em). **1760** FOOTE *Minor* III. (1781) 65 A most infernal run. Let's see (Pulls out a card) Loader a thousand, the Baron two, Tally—Enough to beggar a banker.

**Ta·lly**, *sb.*[3] *rare.* Short for TALLY-HO. So **Tally** *v.*, to signal with *tally-ho!*

**1886** FORTESCUE *Stag Hunting on Exmoor* (1887) 180 Another hundred yards of slow hunting, and then a loud tally proclaims a fresh find. *Ibid.* 182 The farmer is half inclined to fear he has tallied a fresh hind.

**Tally** (tæ·li), *v.*[1] Forms: see TALLY *sb.*[1] [f. TALLY *sb.*[1] Cf. also med.L. *talliāre* to cut (wood); also, to conform or cause to correspond in number or measure: see Du Cange.

(Some of the uses may have been influenced by association with L. *tālis* such, *tālio* giving like for like.)]

**I. 1.** *trans.* † To notch (a stick) so as to make it a tally (*obs.*); hence, to mark, score, set *down* or enter (a number, etc.) on or as on a tally; *transf.* to record, register.

*c* **1440** *Promp. Parv.* 486/1 Talyyn, or scoryn' on taly, *tallio, dico.* **1632** *Star Chamb. Cases* (Camden) 94 M^rs Jennet Carrier had a knife in her hand,..to tally a sticke to shewe how many dishes full there were. **1633** FORD *Broken H.* IV. i, So provident is folly in sad issue, That afterwit, like bankrupt's debts, stands tallied, Without all possibilities of payment. *a* **1640** W. FENNER *Sacr. Faithf.* (1648) 53 There is not one of them that God tallies down, or reckons for a praier. **1706** E. WARD *Wooden World Diss.* (1708) 18 At every tenth Call perhaps you may tally down a Sailor. **1890** *Century Mag.* June 205/2 These [field judges] measure and tally the trials of competitors in jumps, pole vaults [etc.].

**b.** *spec.* To identify, count, and enter each bale, case, article, etc. of a cargo or lot of goods in loading or discharging.

**1812** J. SMYTH *Pract. of Customs* (1821) 7 Goods paying Duty by Tale, are, at the delivery, to be tallied at 1, 10, 20, &c. according to the nature thereof. **1886** *Pall Mall G.* 29 Jan. 5/2 Upon the mates of ships..falls the bulk of the work and responsibility entailed in getting a ship ready to receive cargo, in 'tallying' the cargo, in preparing her to leave port [etc.]. **1899** F. T. BULLEN *Log Sea-waif* 226 No pretence was made of tallying in the cargo.

**c.** To furnish (a bale of goods, etc.) with a tally or identifying label; to distinguish, mark, or identify by or as by a tally: see TALLY *sb.*[1] 7.

**1837** MARRYAT *Dog-Fiend* xxxiv, Leaving his people to mark and tally the bales. **1860** MAURY *Phys. Geog. Sea* (Low) vi. § 332 We have tallied the air, and put labels on the wind. **1865** *Morn. Star* 27 Jan., If a number of bales were tallied as having arrived by a vessel called the Onwards, the label with the mark 'Onwards' on it was taken off and another marked the 'City of Dublin' placed in its stead.

**2.** To count or reckon *up*, to number.

**1542** BECON *Pathw. Prayer* vi. C viij, Some..vpon theyr bedes taly vp I cannot tel howe many lady Psalters. **1585** W. WEBBE *Eng. Poetrie* (Arb.) 62 The first or the first couple hauing twelue sillables, the other fourteene, which versifyers call Powlters measure, because so they talle their wares by dozens. **1598** *Wills & Inv. N. C.* (Surtees) II. 335 Two men, to serve..att the pitt, to take the reckoninges, the one..who doth tallee the horses. **1648** BP. HALL *Breath. Devout Soul* iv. 5, I have not kept even reckonings with thee; I have not justly tallied up thy inestimable benefits. **1660** *Col. J. Okie's Lament.* 10, I must now tally the Account of our State Stinking Beer. **1885** A. MUNRO *Siren Casket* (1889) 85 They anchor'd at morning to tally their spoil.

**b.** *fig.* To reckon, estimate (with *obj. cl.*). *colloq. rare.*

**1860** HOLLAND *Miss Gilbert* xix, You can't hardly tally how she's coming out because she ain't exactly a woman yet.

† **3.** *intr.* To deal on tally or credit; to open or have a credit account *with* any one. *Obs.*

**1596** [see TAIL *v.*[2] 8, quot. 1570]. **1724** SWIFT *Drapier's Lett.* Wks. 1755 V. II. 25 Several gentlemen have been forced to tally with their workmen, and give them bits of cards sealed and subscribed with their names.

**II.** † **4.** *trans. fig.* To cause (things) to correspond or agree; to 'match'; *pa. pple.* matched, suited, adapted. *Obs.*

1627 Bp. Hall *Holy Observ.* Wks. 50 Morall philosophy [teacheth] that tallying of iniuries is iustice; diuinitie, that good must be returned for ill. *c* 1717 Prior *Epitaph* 16 They seem'd just tallied for each other. *a* 1745 Pope (J.), They are not so well tallied to the present juncture. 1812 Jefferson *Writ.* (1830) IV. 177 Peculiarly tallied in interests, by each wanting exactly what the other has to spare.

†5. To compare, as tallies, for the purpose of verifying an account, etc. *Obs.*

1702 *Lond. Gaz.* No. 3827/4 These are to give Notice to all the Fortunate in Sydenham's Land-Lottery..to bring their Prize Tickets, in order to have the same Tallied. 1703 *Ibid.* No. 3963/4 All Persons, whose Tickets in the late Land-Lottery have not been tallied and reported.

† b. *fig.* To bring into comparison, compare.

1773 J. Ross *Fratricide* vi. 478 (MS.) What but a shadow is this mortal life When tally'd with eternity?

6. *intr.* To agree, as one half of a cloven tally with its fellow; to correspond or answer exactly; to accord, conform, fit. Const. †*to* (obs.), *with.* (The chief current sense.)

1705 Addison *Italy* 227, I found pieces of Tiles that exactly tally'd with the Channel. 1720 *Lett. Lond. Jrnl.* (1721) 64 The Courage and Understanding of her [the High Church's] Passive Sons Tally to each other. 1727 Swift *Gulliver* iv. xii, Neither shall I ever be able to comprehend how such an animal [Yahoo], and such a vice [pride], could tally together. 1738 Warburton *Div. Legat.* I. 271 A Theory that does not exactly tally with fact. 1757 Da Costa in *Phil. Trans.* L. 229 The impressions of ferns, grasses, &c. are easily recognizable, they so minutely tally to the plants they represent. 1779 J. Moore *View Soc. Fr.* (1789) I. xxiv. 188 High hills, whose opposite sides tally so exactly. 1891 E. Peacock *N. Brendon* II. 82 It tallies exactly with what the others have said.

III. (?Connected with Tales.)

7. *trans.* (?) To summon or empanel as a juryman.

1776 in Stonehouse *Axholme* (1839) 145 None of the Lord's tenants, either freehold or copyhold, to be tallied out of the Manor, to the Assizes, Sessions, or Sheriff's Court.

**Ta·lly,** *v.*[2] *Naut.* Now *rare.* [Origin obscure.]

1. *trans.* To haul taut (the fore or main lee-sheets). Hence **Tallied** *ppl. a.*

*c* 1450 *Pilgrim's Sea-Voy.* 19 in *Stacions Rome* (1867) 37 A boy or tweyn Anone up styen, And ouerthwart the sayle-yerde lyen;—'Y how! taylia!' the remenaunt cryen, And pulle with alle theyr myght. *a* 1625 *Nomenclator Navalis* (Harl. MS. 2301), When they hale aft the Sheate of Maine or Fore-Saile, they saie Tallee aft the Sheate. 1627 Capt. Smith *Seaman's Gram.* ix. 39 Get your Starboord tacks aboord, and tally or hale off your Lee-Sheats. 1762–9 Falconer *Shipwr.* ii. 212 Taught aft the sheet they tally, and belay. 1769 — *Dict. Marine* (1789), *Border les écoutes tout plat,* to tally the sheets flat aft. 1836 E. Howard *R. Reefer* xxx, By hauling along tallied bights of rope.

2. *intr.* To catch hold or 'clap' *on* to a rope.

1840 R. H. Dana *Bef. Mast* xxviii. 97 All hands tallied on to the cat-fall. *Ibid.* xxxv. 133 All hands tally-on to the main tack. 1896 Kipling *Seven Seas* 93 Heh! Tally on. Aft and walk away with her! Handsome to the Cathead now; O tally on the fall!

†**Tally,** *v.*[3] *Cards. Obs.* Also 8 (**taillé**), **tailly.** [ad. F. *tailler* to cut, esp. to deal at cards, etc.: see Tail *v*[2]] *intr.* At faro, basset, and similar games, To be banker (i. e. to deal).

[1701 Farquhar *Sir H. Wildair* i. i, The French marquis, you know, constantly taillés. *Ibid.* ii. ii, I relied altogether on your setting the cards; you used to taillé with success.] 1706 Mrs. Centlivre *Basset Table* iv. 52 *Lady R.* Sir James, pray will you Tally? *Sir J.* With all my Heart, Madam. (Takes the Cards and shuffles them.) 1715 Lady M. W. Montagu *Basset-table* 68 Wretch that I was, how often have I swore When Winnall tally'd, I wou'd Punt no more? 1716 — *Let. to C'tess of Mar* 17 Dec., The duke taillys at basset every night. 1748 H. Walpole *Let. to Mann* 26 Dec., I don't know whom your Highness will get to tally to you; you know I am ruined by dealing.

**Tally,** *v.*[4]: see Tally *sb.*[3]

**Tally** (tǭ·l,li), *adv.* Now *rare* or *Obs.* [f. Tall *a.* + -ly [2].] In a tall manner.

†1. In a seemly manner; becomingly, elegantly; fairly, well; bravely. *Obs.*

*c* 1350 *Will. Palerne* 1706 Sche..borwed boiȝes cloþes, & talliche hire a-tyred tiȝtli þer-inne. *c* 1400 *Destr. Troy* 8813 When this taburnacle atyrit was tally to end, Thai closit hit full clanly, all with clene ambur. *c* 1440 *Promp. Parv.* 486/1 Tally,..in semely wyse, *decenter, eleganter.* 1450 *Anc. Deed* A. 8559 (P.R.O.) in *Catalogue* IV. 327 [Proctour should come to the] Hall of Broghton and ther tawly besek John of Broghton [es]qwier to be his gode master.

2. Highly, loftily.

1611 Cotgr., *Hautement,* highly, tally. 1613 Fletcher, etc. *Captain* ii. ii, You Ludovick That stand so tally on your reputation You shall be he shall speak it.

**Tallydiddle,** variant of Taradiddle.

**Tally-ho** (tæ:li,hōᵘ·), *int.* and *sb.* Also 8–9 **tallio,** 9 **tally-o, talleyho.** [app. an altered form of the Fr. *taïaut* (Molière, *Les Fâcheux* 1662), *tayau, tayaut* (Furetière), used in deer-hunting; earlier Fr. equivalents were *taho, tahou, theau, theau le hau, tielau, thialau,* and *thia hillaud* (Godef.).

The various Fr. forms appear to be meaningless exclamations. Much conjecture has been spent in vainly trying to put a French meaning into the English form by finding in it *taillis* coppice, *est allé* is gone, *hors* out, etc.]

1. The view-halloo raised by huntsmen on catching sight of the fox. **a.** as *int.*

[Cf. 1756 Foote *Englishman returned fr. Paris,* Sir Toby Tallyho (name of a roistering character).] 1772 R. Graves *Spir. Quixote* (1783) I. 68 Jerry..with the utmost vociferation, in the fox-hunters' language, cries out, 'Tallio! Tallio! Tallio!' 1815 W. H. Ireland *Scribbleomania* 19 Then at it, my Pegasus, here's whip and rein, Tally ho! Tally ho! dash it bold o'er the plain. 1835 *Encycl. Brit.* (ed. 7) XI. 752 The view holloa of the hare is, 'Gone away'; of a fox, 'Tallyho'. 1859 *Art Taming Horses,* etc. x. 168 When a fox breaks cover near you,..don't be in a hurry to give the 'Tally-a-e-o!' *Ibid.* 169 When he [the fox] is well away through the hedge of a good-sized field, halloo..'Tally-o aw-ay-o-o!' giving each syllable very slowly...If the fox makes a short bolt and returns, it is 'Tally-o *back*!' with the '*back*' loud and clear. If the fox crosses the side of a wood when the hounds are at check, the cry should be 'Tally-o over!'

**b.** as *sb.*

1787 *Generous Attachment* I. 115 One of his tallios would have sent them screaming out of their senses. 1830–83 R. Eg.-Warburton *Hunt. Songs* (ed. 7) xxvii. i, Beasts of the chace that are not worth a Tally-ho! 1860 *All Year Round* No. 71. 485 How the glad tally-hos, triumphant who-whoops,..come from the very hearts of the farmers.

**c.** *attrib.*

1857 H. Breen *Mod. Eng. Lit.* 138 Perhaps the most characteristic style of all is the tally-ho, or Nimrodian style.

2. Originally, the proper name given to a fast day-coach between London and Birmingham, started in 1823; subsequently appropriated by other fast coaches on this and other roads, and treated somewhat as a common noun. Also *tally-ho coach.*

1831 T. Attwood 9 Oct. in *Life* xii. (1885) 184, I prefer your coming by the Safety Tally ho, because it puts up at the most convenient inn. 1857 Hughes *Tom Brown* i. iv, Tally-ho coach..don't wait for nobody. *Ibid.,* His father.. had resolved that Tom should travel down by the Tally-ho, which..passed through Rugby itself. 1866 Geo. Eliot *F. Holt* Introd., The mail still announced itself by the merry notes of the horn; the hedge-cutter..might still know the exact hour by the..apparition of the pea-green Tally-ho or the yellow Independent. 1903 C. G. Harper *Stage-coach & Mail* II. ix., x., xiii. [much historical information].

**b.** *U. S.* A large four-in-hand coach or drag.

1882 Howells in *Longm. Mag.* I. 55 There was a tally-ho coach which had been driven out from Boston. 1885 W. P. Breed *Aboard & Abroad* 127 Who could..not take a tour of eight or ten hours in tallyho or wagonette? 1895 *Nebraska State Jrnl.* 18 June 4/2 A talleyho ride was taken by a large party of young people Friday afternoon.

**Tally-ho·,** *v.* [f. prec.]

1. *trans.* To salute or make known the presence of (a fox) by the cry of 'tally-ho'.

1812 *Sporting Mag.* XXXIX. 230 A fox was tallyho'd breaking covert, and the dogs laid on him. 1825 *Ibid.* XV. 363 The servant..tallyho'd the fox.

2. *intr.* To cry or utter 'tally-ho' or a similar call.

1826 J. Wilson *Noct. Ambr.* Wks. 1855 I. 137 A troop o' ..tallyhoin' 'wild and wayward humourists'. 1829 Hood *Epping H.* lxxiv, And milkmen tally-ho'd! 1904 H. Sutcliffe in *Westm. Gaz.* 1 Dec. 2/3 Oh, up to the saddle, the horn tally-ho-ing, Up to the tops of the hills o' Craven!

**Tallying** (tæ·li,iŋ), *vbl. sb.* [See -ing [1].] The action of Tally *v.*[1], in various senses.

*c* 1440 *Promp. Parv.* 486/1 Talyynge, *talliacio.* 1632 Le Grys tr. *Velleius Paterc.* 168 The tallying up of the names of these able wits. 1893 *Daily News* 14 Apr. 5/7 Superseding ship's officers in the work of tallying.

**b.** *spec.* Exact correspondence.

1845–6 Trench *Huls. Lect.* Ser. i. iv. 69 The curious tallying of the Old with the New. 1895 Stalker in *Expositor* Sept. 203 The tallying of events with the..predictions.

**Ta·llying,** *ppl. a.* [See -ing [2].] That tallies; corresponding.

1854 Owen *Skel. & Teeth* in *Orr's Circ. Sc.* I. *Org. Nat.* 179 Such names, when applied to the tallying bones in lower animals, losing that significance.

**Tallyman** (tæ·limæn). [f. Tally *sb.*[1] + Man.]

1. One who carries on a tally-trade, or supplies goods on credit, to be paid for by instalments.

1654 Gayton *Pleas. Notes* iv. xi. 242 Brewers, Clerks, Bakers, and all Tally-men. 1678 *Four for Penny* in *Harl. Misc.* (ed. Park) IV. 148 The unconscionable Tally-man..lets them have ten-shillings-worth of sorry commodities,..on security given to pay him twenty shillings by twelve-pence a week. *a* 1700 B. E. *Dict. Cant. Crew, Tally-men,* Brokers that let out Cloths at moderate Rates to wear per Week, Month, or Year. 1851 Mayhew *Lond. Labour* I. 380/2 The pedlar tally-man is a hawker who supplies his customers with goods, receiving payment by weekly instalments, and derives his name from the tally or score he keeps with his customers.

**b.** (See quot.)

1889 *Academy* 29 June 440/1 In the tailoring trade the worst paid work is that of the 'tallyman', who takes orders direct from the actual wearer without the intervention of any contractor.

2. One who tallies, or keeps account of, anything; *spec.* a clerk who tallies or checks a cargo in loading or discharging.

1888 Roosevelt in *Century Mag.* Apr. 862/1 With the voice of a stentor the tally-man shouts out the number and sex of each calf. 1889 Doyle *Micah Clarke* 190, I reckon them to be..mayhap five thousand two hundred foot. I have been thought a good tally man on such occasions. 1897 Kipling *Capt. Courageous* ix, I'm tally-man for the schooner.

3. One who 'lives tally' with a woman. *slang.*

1890 *N. & Q.* 7th Ser. X. 297/1 The terms *tally-man* and *tally-woman,* indicating a man and woman living together without marriage, are used in mining districts.

¶4. Erroneously for Talesman. *Obs.*

1682 *Enq. Elect. Sheriffs* 10 A company of Mercenary fellows, that used to serve as Tallymen in Guild-hall for their Groats a Cause; who..would, to recover their Four-pence a Trial, sell the Charter and all the Priviledges of this honourable Corporation.

Hence **Ta·llymanning, Ta·llymanship** (*nonce-wds.*), the business or occupation of a tallyman.

1844 J. T. Hewlett *Parsons & W.* xxxiv, The nature and objects of tallymanship. *Ibid.,* He talked of nothing but tally-maning.

**Ta·llywoman.** [f. Tally *sb.*[1] + Woman.]

**a.** A woman who sells goods on credit: cf. Tallyman 1. **b.** *slang.* A woman who 'lives tally' with a man (see Tally *sb.*[1] 4 b): correlative to Tallyman 3.

1727 Gay *Begg. Op.* iii. v, Mrs. Diana Trapes, the Tally-Woman. 1890 *Leeds Mercury* 11 Aug., in *N. & Q.* 7th Ser. X. 229/1, I thought she was his tally-woman lately. 1890 [see Tallyman 3]. 1894 *Daily Chron.* 11 June (Funk), Her dress she gets by paying a small weekly sum of 2*d.* or 3*d.* to what is called a 'tallyman' or 'tallywoman'.

**Talm,** *v. Obs.* exc. *dial.* Forms: *α.* 4–5 **talme.** *β.* 6–7 **tawme,** 7–9 **tawm,** 8–9 **taum.** [Akin to ON. *talma* to hinder, obstruct, MLG. *talmen* to trouble with speaking, LG. *talmen* to be slow in speech and at work, to linger, dawdle (*Brem. Wbch.*), EFris. *talmen* to plague, worry, solicit tiresomely, Du. *talmen* to linger, dawdle, loiter.] *intr.* To become exhausted; to fail, tire, faint, swoon.

*α.* *c* 1325 *Song on Learning Music* in *Rel. Ant.* I. 292, I donke upon David til mi tonge talmes. ? *a* 1400 *Morte Arth.* 2581 Thow trowes with thy talkynge þat my harte talmes! *c* 1440 *Le Bone Florence* (Ritson) 769 Hur fadur nere hande can [= gan] talme, Soche a sweme hys harte can swalme.

*β.* 1566 Drant *Wail. Hierim.* K iv, (*Lam.* ii. 11) My babes dyd faynt, And sucklynges tawmed in the streetes. 1674 Ray *N. C. Words* 47 To *Tawm*; to swoon. 1684 Meriton *Yorksh. Dial.* 169 Ise like to tawme, this day's seay [= so] varry warme. 1787 Grose *Provinc. Gloss.* Suppl., *Taum,* To swoon. 1828 *Craven Gloss., Taum,* to swoon, to fall sick; generally, 'to taum over'.

Hence **Talm** *sb.,* faintness, exhaustion; in mod. dial. (**tawm**), 'a fit of faintness or sickness (E.D.D.).

*c* 1375 *Cursor M.* 20758 (Fairf.) Ga to þa men þat lijs in talme [*Cott.* & *Gött.* sualm(e, *Trin.* qualm], And touche ham..And þai salle baþ haue hele & witte.

**Talma** (tæ·lmă). Pl. **-as.** [Named after François Joseph Talma, French tragedian (1763–1826).] A cape or cloak worn by men, and also by women in the 19th c.

1860 Hawthorne *Marb. Faun* i, If a lion's skin could have been substituted for his modern talma. 1894 *Times* 17 Aug. 9/3 [U.S. tariff] On cloaks, dolmans, jackets, talmas, ulsters, or other outside garments for ladies and children's apparel.

**Talman,** variant of Talisman [1] *Obs.,* mullah.

**Talmi** (tæ·lmi), **talmi-gold.** [a. Ger. *talmi-gold,* a fancy designation for trade purposes.] An alloy of copper, zinc, and tin, plated with gold, used for cheap jewellery.

(See *Monatsblatt des Gewerbe-Vereins für Hannover* July —Aug. 1863, *Deutsche Industrie-Zeitung,* 28 Sept. 1871.)

1868 Watts *Dict. Chem.* V. 657 *Talmi gold,* an alloy used for the manufacture of trinkets, contains .. 86·4 per cent. copper, 12·2 zinc, 1·1 tin, and 0·3 iron. 1890 A. H. Hiorns *Mixed Metals* 109 § 31 Talmi or Talmi Gold.—Also termed Abyssinian gold.

†**Talmou·se.** *Obs.* [a. obs. F. *talmouse* (talmū·z), also *talemouse* (14th c. in Hatz.-Darm.), of uncertain origin; see conjectures in Littré.] 'A Cheese-cake; a Tart, or cake made of egges, and cheese' (Cotgr.); a piece of sugared pastry, containing cream, cheese, and eggs (Littré).

1600 Surflet *Countrie Farme* v. xxii. 723 Some make with butter, cheese and yolkes of egges,..cheese cakes, talmouses and little lenten loaues.

‖**Talmud** (tæ·lmɒ̆d, talmū·d). Also 6 **Thalmood,** 6–8 **Thalmud.** [a. late Heb. תלמוד *talmūd* instruction (*c* 130 a.d.), f. למד *lāmad* to instruct, teach. So med.L., F., Ger., etc. *talmud.*

From its primary sense of 'teaching, instruction, learning', the word was applied to the teaching or instruction contained in a biblical text, and to the body of traditional learning possessed by a particular Rabbi; but it came to be applied distinctively to the discussion, explanation, and illustration of the body of traditional law contained in the Mishnah, and so to the concrete collection of this teaching.]

In the wide sense, The body of Jewish civil and ceremonial traditionary law, consisting of the Mishnah or binding precepts of the elders, additional to and developed from the Pentateuch, and the later Gemara or commentary upon these, forming a complement, explanatory, illustrative, and discursive, to the Mishnah. The term was originally applied to the Gemara, of which two recensions exist, known respectively as the Jerusalem (or Palestinian) and the Babylonian Talmud; to the latter of which the name is in strictest use confined.

The precepts of the Mishnah were collected and codified about a.d. 200; the redaction of the Jerusalem Talmud had reached almost its present form by a.d. 408; that of the Babylonian Talmud extended from a.d. 400 to 500.

1532 More *Confut. Tindale* Wks. 679/2 As the Iewes had set vp a boke of their Talmud to destroye the sense of the scripture. 1580 G. Gilpin *Beehive Rom. Ch.* 74 The Iewes Rabbines...with their Caballa and with their Thalmood. 1636 Weemse *Treat.* 4 *Degenerate Sons* 349 They say that the text of the Scriptures is like water, and Mishna like wine, and the Talmud like spiced wine...So they compare the Law to salt, Mishna to pepper, and the Talmud to spices. **1665** BOYLE *Occas. Refl.* v. vii. (1848) 322 He must devour the tedious and voluminous Rhapsodies that make up the Talmud, in many of which he can scarce learn any thing but the Art of saying nothing in a multitude of words. **1727-41** CHAMBERS *Cycl.* s. v., When they [the Jews] say simply the Talmud, they always mean this [the Babylonian Talmud]. **1867** DEUTSCH in *Q. Rev.* Oct., Between the rugged boulders of the law which bestrew the pass of the Talmud there grow the blue flowers of romance and poetry, in the most catholic and Eastern sense. *attrib.* **1892** ZANGWILL *Childr. Ghetto* I. 123 Mr. Moggid, you're a saint and a Talmud sage.

**Talmudic** (tælmū·dik, talmʊ·dik), *a.* (*sb.*) [f. prec. + -IC.] Of or pertaining to the Talmud.

**1611** H. BROUGHTON *Require Agreement* 73 My next demaund, Rabbi, shall trie your Thalmudique skill. **1618** J. PAGET *Arrow agst. Brownists* Title-p., An Admonition tovching Talmudique and Rabbinical allegations. **1677** GALE *Crt. Gentiles* II. III. 167 Corrupt imitamens of Pythagorean and Talmudic Traditions and Canons. **1831** CARLYLE *Sart. Res.* I. v, Its..depth of Talmudic and Rabbinical lore. **1854** MILMAN *Lat. Chr.* IV. i. *note*, Sale has traced..the fables in the Korân to their Talmudic or Rabbinical sources.

†**B.** *sb.* = TALMUDIST. *Obs. rare.*

**1624** R. SKYNNER in *Ussher's Lett.* (1686) 351 It is observable how Christ disputing against the Jews about the Resurrection, doth prove the Resurrection out of the sayings of their own Talmudicks. *a* **1656** BP. HALL *Revelation Unrevealed* viii. Wks. 1837 VIII. 540 Those carnal pleasures..dreamed of by those sensual Turks and Talmudiques [*printed* -iges].

Hence †**Talmudi·cian**, *sb.* = TALMUDIST c.; *a.* = TALMUDIC. *rare.*

**1575** T. ROGERS *Sec. Coming Christ* 6/1 Many things in those Thalmudician books.

**Talmu·dical**, *a.* [f. as prec. + -AL.] Of, pertaining to, or contained in the Talmud; of the nature of or characteristic of the Talmud.

**1605** CAMDEN *Rem.* (1637) 169 Whether this Cabala is more ancient than the Talmudicall learning. **1693** J. EDWARDS *Author. O. & N. Test.* 352 The wisest of all the Talmudical doctors. **1748** HARTLEY *Observ. Man* II. ii. 122 There are many Passages in the Talmudical Writings which afford Confirmation to the New Testament. **1867** *Q. Rev.* Oct. 437 Household words of talmudical Judaism, to which Christianity gave a higher and purer meaning.

**Ta·lmudism.** *rare.* [f. TALMUD + -ISM.] Belief in or practice of the teaching of the Talmud.

**1883** *Illinois Mission News* Nov. 132 The temporal effects of Talmudism may be..judged upon its own merits. **1896** *Nation* (N.Y.) 16 July 54/1 Talmudism and ritualism and Christian exclusion and repression have endowed him [the Jew] with a second nature which is mistaken for his fundamental character.

**Talmudist** (tæ·lmʊdist, talmū·dist). [f. TALMUD + -IST.] **a.** One of the authors of the Talmud. **b.** One who accepts or believes in the authority of the Talmud. **c.** One learned in the Talmud; a Talmudic scholar.

**1569** J. SANFORD tr. *Agrippa's Van. Artes* 6 b, There is a great contention of the Hebrewe tounge and Carracter, betwene the Thalmudistes. *c* **1645** HOWELL *Lett.* (1650) II. 10 The Jews at this day are divided to three sects. The first, which is the greatest, are call'd the Talmudists, in regard that, besides the holy scriptures, they embrace the Talmud. **1742** BISCOE *On Acts* (1829) 86 The Talmudists frequently speak of the transmigration of the souls of good men. **1882** *American* III. 186 Dr. Joseph Barclay, Bishop of Jerusalem, an eminent Talmudist. **1882** *Century Mag.* XXIV. 49 All [orthodox] Jews with whom Americans and Europeans are acquainted are Talmudists.

Hence **Talmudi·stic**, **Talmudi·stical** *adjs.* = TALMUDICAL. So **Ta·lmudize** *v. trans.*, to make Talmudic; to allegorize or mix with fable.

**1593** NASHE *Christ's T.* (1613) 76 With Th'almudisticall dreames. **1642** CUDWORTH *Disc. Lord's Supper* 30 Besides these Talmudisticke Jewes, there is another Sect..that reject all Talmudicall Traditions. **1781** WARTON *Hist. Eng. Poetry* lx. (1840) III. 386 The name Ariel came from the Talmudistic mysteries. **1839** R. PHILIP *Life W. Milne* ix. (1840) 246 There are facts in his itinerary although Talmudized. **1860** W. W. WEBB in *Med. Times* 1 Dec. 537/1 Talmudistical commentators on clinical medicine, whose patients seem to be immortal.

**Talo-** (tē¹lo), combining form of L. *tālus* ankle-bone, forming a few adjectives in anatomy, in sense 'pertaining to the ankle-bone', as **Talo-calca·neal** [CALCANEAN, heel-bone]. **Talo-fi·bular** [FIBULA], **Talo-sca·phoid** [SCAPHOID], **Talo-ti·bial** [TIBIA].

**1887** *Cassell's Encycl. Dict.*, Talo-scaphoid. **1890** BILLINGS *Nat. Med. Dict.*, *Talo-calcaneal*,.. *Talo-calcaneal articulation*... *Talo-fibular ligaments*,..anterior and middle fascicles of external lateral ligament of ankle-joint... *Talo-scaphoid articulation*.. *Talo-tibial ligaments*,.. passing between the internal malleus and astragalus.

**Talon** (tæ·lən), *sb.* Forms: *α.* 4-5 **taloun(e**, **5 -owne**, **5-7 tallon**, **7 tal(l)en**, *pl.* **tallance**, **5- talon.** *β.* **5-6 talente**, **talaunt(e**, **tala(u)nde**, **5-7 talland**, **6 tallaunt(e**, **6-7 talant(e**, **tallent**, **6-7** (**9** *dial.*) **tallant**, **6-8** (**9** *dial.*) **talent.** [ME. a. OF. *talon* heel of a man, or of a shoe, hinder part of the foot of a quadruped = Pr. *talo*, Sp. *talon*, Pg. *talão*, It. *talone* heel, heel-piece:—late pop. L. or Com. Romanic *tālo*, *tālōn-em* heel, deriv. form of *tālus* ankle. With the *β* forms *talant*, *talent*, cf. *ancient*, *margent*, *parchment*, *peasant*, *tyrant*, etc.: see -ANT ³. The sense-development shows the stages: ankle; heel of man (of a shoe, etc.); heel or hinder part of the foot of a beast; hinder claw of a bird of prey; any claw (usually in pl. the claws) of a bird, a dragon, an ungulate beast, an insect, etc. The extension to a bird of prey, and subsequent stages, are peculiar to English.]

**I.** †**1.** The 'heel' or hinder part of the foot of certain quadrupeds, as swine and deer, or of the hoof of a horse. *Obs.*

*c* **1410** *Master of Game* (MS. Digby 182) xxiv, A gret boore shall haue longe traces and þe clees rounde before and brode sooles of þe feete and a good talowne and longe bones. **1611** COTGR., *Argot*,..the deaw-clawe of a dog, &c.; the heele, or talon of a hog. **1639** T. DE GRAY *Expert Farrier* II. xvii. 298 [The Quitter-bone] causeth a hard round swelling upon the cronet of the hoofe, betwixt the heele and the quarter of the long talent. [**1688**, **1725**: cf. *talon-nail* in 5.]

†**b.** The hallux or hinder claw of a bird. *Obs.*

**1486** *Bk. St. Albans* a viij, The grete Clees [of a hawk] behynde..ye shall call hom Talons. **1530** PALSGR. 279/1 Talant of a byrde the hynder-clawe, *talon*, *argot.* **1552** HULOET, Talent or clawe of a hawke, *vngula.* **1577** B. GOOGE *Heresbach's Husb.* IV. (1586) 157 b, Let therefore your Henne be of a good colour, hauing..her tallons euen. *Ibid.* 158 Your Cockes..of colours, as I tolde you for the Hennes, and the like number of tallons.

**2.** *pl.* The claws (or less usually in *sing.* any claw) of a bird or beast. **a.** *spec.* The powerful claws of a bird of prey, or of a dragon, griffin, etc.

*α.* ? *a* **1400** *Morte Arth.* 800 The dragone..Towchez hym wyth his talounez, and terez hys rigge. *c* **1400** MAUNDEV. (1839) xxvi. 269 [The Griffon] hath his talouns so longe and so grete as þough þei weren hornes of grete oxen. *a* **1661** HOLYDAY *Juvenal* 250 Lubin..understands not how the pygmie should be snatch'd-up by the crane..in his crooked talens, when as the crane's talents are not crooked. **1671** MILTON *P. R.* II. 403 With sound of Harpies wings, and Talons heard. **1727** SWIFT *Gulliver* II. v, A kite..would have certainly carried me away in his talons. **1884** PAE *Eustace* 137 We must see and take the Falcon from the talons of the French eagle.

*β.* **1432-50** tr. *Higden* (Rolls) II. 369 Bryddes hauenge wynges and talandes. *Ibid.* VIII. 37 Thre [young eagles].. did bete the egle with theire talauntes and wynges. *a* **1533** LD. BERNERS *Gold. Bk. M. Aurel.* xxviii. (1535) 47 b, He sawe two kytes ioninge to gyther with their talantes. **1579** GOSSON *Sch. Abuse* (Arb.) 20 The Harpies haue Virgins faces, and vultures Talentes. **1635** R. JOHNSON *Hist. Tom a Lincolne* (1828) 104 The nailes of his fingers were as the tallents of eagles. **1760-72** H. BROOKE *Fool of Qual.* (1809) IV. 151 What would become of my..dove, within the talents of such a vulture? **1893** SALISBURY *S. E. Worc. Gloss.*, *Local Pronunc.*, *Talents*, talons.

**b.** The claws (or in *sing.* any claw) of a wild beast, of an insect, etc.

*α.* *a* **1591** H. SMITH *Jonah's Punishm.* II. (1602) B viij, Like Lions, which will be gentle vntill their tallons grow. **1664** POWER *Exp. Philos.* I. 5 The other four legs are cloven and arm'd with little clea's or tallons (like a Catamount). *a* **1667** COWLEY *Sylva*, *Ret. out of Scotl.*, Let spotted Lynces their sharp Talons fill, With Chrystal fetch'd from the Promethean Hill. **1873** HOLLAND *A. Bonnic.* xi. 184 Sheathed within the foot of velvet was hidden a talon of steel.

*β.* **1432-50** tr. *Higden* (Rolls) I. 83 Men hauenge hedes lyke dogges, whiche be callede Cynocephali,..y-armede with teithe and talaundes, lyffenge by hawkenge and huntenge. **1571** GOLDING *Calvin on Ps.* x. 10 The talantes and teethe of the Lyon. **1628** GAULE *Pract. The. Panegyr.* 47 It sufficeth, that wee discerne this Lyon, by his Talent.

**c.** Allusively applied to the grasping fingers or hands of human beings. (Cf. CLAW.)

**1588** SHAKS. *L. L. L.* IV. ii. 64 If a talent be a claw, looke how he clawes him with a talent. **1594** ? GREENE *Selimus* Wks. (Grosart) XIV. 264, I can scarce keep her talents from my eies. **1600** J. PORY tr. *Leo's Africa* III. 142 They haue..neither kniues or spoones but only their ten talons. **1818** SCOTT *Hrt. Midl.* xviii, An I had ye amang the Frigate Whins, wadna I set my ten talents in your wuzzent face for that very word? **1860** HAWTHORNE *Marb. Faun* xvi, Still he washed his brown, bony talons.

**d.** *fig.*

**1586** MARLOWE *1st Pt. Tamburl.* II. vii, Now doth ghastly Death With greedy talents gripe my bleeding heart. **1600** SURFLET *Countrie Farme* III. xxxiv. 497 The oliue tree being once seased in his tallance of a good peece of ground, contenteth it selfe. **1748** JOHNSON *Van. Hum. Wishes* 168 Rebellion's vengeful talons. **1751** — *Rambler* No. 113 ⁋ 7 Nothing should have torn me from her but the talons of necessity. **1774** BURKE *Corr.* (1844) I. 451 That they may yet be able to save something from the talons of despotism.

**II. 3.** *transf.* A heel-like part or object. [In a, b, c = F. *talon.*] **a.** *Naut.* The curved back of a ship's rudder. ? *Obs.* **b.** *Arch.* An ogee moulding: = OGEE 2. **c.** The 'heel' of a blade, as of a sword. **d.** A part of the shell of a bivalve; cf. HEEL *sb.*¹ 7 h. **e.** The projection on the bolt of a lock against which the key presses (Knight *Dict. Mech.* 1877). **f.** (See quot.)

**a.** **1485-6** *Naval Acc. Hen. VII* (1896) 14 For a pece of tymbre..spent in makyng of a talland for the same Rother. **1867** SMYTH *Sailor's Word-bk.*, *Tallant*, the upper hance, or break of the rudder abaft. **b.** **1704** J. HARRIS *Lex. Techn.* I. s. v., The Talon consists of two Portions of a Circle, one without, and the other within; and when the Concave Part is uppermost, it is called Reversed Talon. **1753** HOGARTH *Anal. Beauty* xii. 172 That ornamental member called by the architects 'cyma recta', or talon. **1810** *Rudim. Anc. Archit.* (1821) 41 The ovolo and talon are always employed as supporters to the essential members of the composition, such as the modillions, denteles, and corona. **1842-76** GWILT *Archit.* Gloss., *Talon*, the name given by the French to the ogee. **c.** **1854** WOODWARD *Mollusca* II. 276 Umbones elongated, progressively filled up with shell, and forming an irregular 'talon' in front of the fixed valve. **d.** **1869** BOUTELL *Arms & Arm.* ix. (1874) 180 From the *talon*, or heel of the blade, on the opposite side, is a hollow indent, intended to hold the thumb. **f.** **1898** *Syd. Soc. Lex.*, *Talon*, a heel or low cusp of a tooth.

**4.** *fig.* **a.** *Cards.* The remainder of the pack after the hands have been dealt. *Cent. Dict.* 1891. **b.** *Comm.* See quot. 1882. (So both in Fr.)

**1882** BITHELL *Counting-Ho. Dict.* (1893) s. v., A Talon, as most commonly known in commerce, is the last portion of a sheet of coupons.., and contains on its face an intimation that if it is presented at the house or office indicated, a new sheet of coupons will be given in exchange for it... The Talon is also a name applied to the marginal appendage of a Spanish coupon, and..payment of the coupon is refused if such talon or appendage happens to have been cut off.

**5.** *attrib.* and *Comb.*, as *talon-like*, *-tipped* adjs.; †**talon-nail**, in *Farriery*, a shoeing-nail driven into the back part of the hoof.

**1688** R. HOLME *Armoury* III. 89/2 *Tallon Nail*, is that Nail driven in the shooe towards the Horse heel. **1725** *Bradley's Fam. Dict.* s. v. *Shoeing of horses*, The two Talon nails must be drove first, then look whether the shoe stands right or not. **1894** *Outing* (U. S.) XXIV. 195/1 And talon-tipped hands toss him kisses. **1897** *Allbutt's Syst. Med.* II. 52 The nails are often split and break, or are changed into talon-like appendages.

Hence † **Ta·lon** *v. trans.*, to tear with the talons; to claw. In quot. *fig.*

**1685** F. SPENCE tr. *Varillas' Ho. Medicis* 306 When they came to talon them with an usurpation.

**Taloned** (tæ·lənd), *a.* Also 7 **ta(l)lented.** [f. TALON *sb.* + -ED ².] Furnished with talons.

**1611** COTGR., *Empiété*, pawed, pounced, clawed, talented. **1611** BIBLE *Jer.* xii. 9 A speckled [*marg.* tallented] bird. **1706** WATTS *Horæ Lyr.* II. *To Mitio* I. 119 A speedier prey To talon'd faulcons. **1838** S. BELLAMY *Betrayal* 164 One talon'd hand appear'd. **1840** CARLYLE *Heroes* v. (1858) 315 As if you should overturn the tree, and..show us ugly taloned roots turned-up into the air.

**Talook, -dar**, etc.: see TALUK, TALUKDĀR.

‖ **Talpa** (tæ·lpă). [L. *talpa* mole.]

**1.** *Zool.* The genus typified by the common mole (*Talpa europæa*).

[**1398** TREVISA *Barth. De P. R.* XVIII. cii. (Bodl. MS.), The wonte [*v.r.* molle] hiȝt *Talpa.*] **1706** PHILLIPS (ed. 6), *Talpa*, (Lat.) the Mole or Want.

**2.** *Path.* An encysted cranial tumour; a wen.

**1693** tr. *Blancard's Phys. Dict.* (ed. 2), *Talpa*, a Tumor, so called, because that as a Mole..creeps under ground; so this feeds upon the Scull under the Skin. **1726** QUINCY *Lex. Phys.-Med.* (ed. 3), *Talpæ* and *Nates*, are Tumours generally confined to the Head. **1857** DUNGLISON *Med. Lex.*, *Talpa*,..a tumour on the head, which has been supposed to burrow like a mole. **1890** BILLINGS *Nat. Med. Dict.*, *Talpa*,..abscess in superior and posterior part of head.

**Talpat**, variant of TALIPOT.

† **Talpe.** *Obs. rare*⁻¹. [f. L. *talpa*, or a. OF. *talpe*, *taulpe* (F. *taupe*) mole.] A mole.

*c* **1440** *Pallad. on Husb.* I. 931 Either shall thees talpes voide or sterve.

**Talpi-**, combining form of L. *talpa* mole, as in † **Ta·lpicide** [see -CIDE 2], the killing of moles; **Ta·lpiform** *a.*, mole-shaped; **Ta·lpify** *v. trans.* (*nonce-wd.*), to make mole-like (in allusive use). So **Ta·lpid** *Zool.* [f. mod.L. *Talpid-æ*], an animal of the family *Talpidæ*, a mole; **Ta·lpine** *a.*, pertaining to the moles, of the sub-family *Talpinæ*; **Ta·lpoid** [-OID, so F. *talpoïde*], *a.* having the form or structure of a mole; *sb.* an animal allied to the mole.

**1656** BLOUNT *Glossogr.*, **Talpicide*, the taking or killing moles or woants. **1660** S. FISHER *Rusticks Alarm* Wks. (1679) 326 But J. O. is so totally *talpified, that..he can't see that Jewish Idolatry nearer home. **1860** MAYNE *Expos. Lex.*, *Talpiformis*, applied by Latreille to a Family ..which resemble the Talpa: *talpiform. **1890** BILLINGS *Nat. Med. Dict.*, *Talpiform*, shaped like a mole. **1860** MAYNE *Expos. Lex.*, *Talpinus*,..*talpine.

† **Ta·lright**, *a.* *Obs. rare*⁻¹. [f. TALL *a.* + RIGHT *a.*] Upright and tall; lofty.

**1582** STANYHURST *Æneis* I. (Arb.) 34 On back her quiuer shee bears, and highlye the remnaunt Of Nymphs surpassing with talright quantitye mounting.

**Ta·lshide.** *Obs.* exc. *Hist.* Also 5 **talschide**, **-shed**, 6-7 **taleshide**, 7 **talshid.** [f. OF. *tail* cutting, cut + SHIDE: cf. TALWOOD.] A shide or piece of wood of prescribed length, either round, or split in two or four, according to thickness, for cutting into billets for firewood.

*Talshides* were classed from No. 1 to No. 7 according to girth: No. 1 contained round timber of 16 in. girth, half-round of 19 in., quarter-cleft of 18½; No. 2 contained round 23 in., half-round 27 in., quarter-cleft 26 in.; No. 3 round 28 in., half-round 33 in., quarter-cleft 32 in.; No. 4 round 33 in., half-round 39 in., quarter-cleft 38 in., and so on: see Act 43 Eliz. c. 14.

**1444-5** in Willis and Clark *Cambridge* (1886) I. 391 In prostracione, fissura, et factura CCC di Tal-chides apud Langley. **1447-8** *Ibid.* 388 Pro prostracione, sicatione, fissura, et factura, xiiij^m Talshides apud Snowdenhill. **1502** ARNOLDE *Chron.* (1811) 98 Item euery taleshide of one be in gretnes in the middis xx. ynches of assise. **1526** in *Househ. Ord.* (1790) 162 A Duke or a Dutchess for their Bouche of Court..[was to have] one torch, one pricket, two sises, one pound of white lights, ten talshides, eight faggotts. **1664** EVELYN *Sylva* 99 Every Taleshide to be four foot long, besides the carf; and if nam'd of one, marked one, to contain 16 inches circumference, within a foot of the middle.

|| **Taluk, taluq** (tălu·k). *East Ind.* Also 8–9 talook, 9 talooka, -ah. [a. Urdū تعلّق *taʿalluq* estate, tract of proprietary land, f. Arab. علق *ʿalaqa* to adhere, be affixed.] *orig.* A hereditary estate belonging to a native proprietor; also, more usually, a subdivision of a *zillah* or district, comprising a number of villages, placed for purposes of revenue under a native collector; a collectorate. Also *attrib.*

1799 WELLINGTON *Suppl. Desp.* (1858) I. 370 He may hereafter plunder the remainder of that talook. 1802 CLOSE in Owen *Wellesley's Desp.* (1877) 235 Such exchanges of talooks or lands shall be made hereafter..as the completion of the said purpose may require. 1839 *Lett. fr. Madras* (1843) 258 Let there be four schools at Madras..; one, at the principal station of every Zillah; and one in every Talook. *Ibid.* 259 In the Talook schools English would be unnecessary. 1880 C. R. MARKHAM *Peruv. Bark* 352 The taluq or district of Wainad is a plateau, averaging an elevation of 3000 feet above the sea. 1905 A. ANDREW *Indian Probl.* 21 It is not possible for the President of a Taluk Board to attend to the schools in his charge.

|| **Talukdār, taluqdār** (tălu·kdāɹ). *East Ind.* [f. prec. + *-dār*, Pers. agential suffix.] The holder of a taluk or hereditary estate, or the officer who has charge of the district so called. Hence **Talukdārī, -daree** (talookdarry), the office or position of a talukdār.

1798 WELLESLEY in Owen *Desp.* (1877) 170 Orders shall.. be issued to all talookdars on the frontiers. 1801 R. PATTON *Asiat. Mon.* 116 By acquiring a larger extent of the same species of hereditary possession, they became what are called talookdars. *Ibid.* 147 A grant of talookdarry of thirty-eight villages 'which lay contiguous to their factory in Bengal'. 1893 *Nation* (N.Y.) 27 July 70/2 The 'landlords' (or 'talookdars', as they were called in that district). 1904 *Times* 5 Oct. 8/6 Proposals respecting the education and training of the Oudh taluqdars put forward by Raja Ali Mahomed.

**Talus**[1] (tē·lǒs, || talü·). Also 7 talu, talud. [a. F. *talus* (16th c.), in Dict. Acad. 1696 *talut*, OF. (12th c. in Hatz.-Darm.) *talu* slope:—late pop. L. **tālūt-um*, deriv. of *tālus* ankle (taken in sense of F. *talon* heel): cf. next.]

1. A slope; *spec.* in *Fortification*, the sloping side of a wall or earthwork, which gradually increases in thickness from above downwards.

1645 N. STONE *Enchiridion Fortif.* 3 On the inward side they gave them [the walls] a *Talud* or slooping which increased them in thicknesse towards the bottom. 1672 *Phil. Trans.* VII. 4081 The first Wall..being much broader below by reason of the *Talu* or slope. 1704 J. HARRIS *Lex. Techn.* I, *Talus*, or *Talut*, properly signifies any Thing that goes sloping, as the Talus of a Wall in Masonry. ..In Fortification, the Talus of a Bastion or Rampart, is the Slope allowed to such a Work whether it be of Earth or Stone. 1762 STERNE *Tr. Shandy* VI. xxi, To determine the depths..of the ditches,—the talus of the glacis, and the precise height of the..parapets. 1862 WRAXALL tr. *Hugo's Misérables* III. vii, The enemy's guns had opened a break from the parapet to the talus.

†b. The sloping side of a trench or the like.

1727 *Bradley's Fam. Dict.* s.v. *Garden*, There must be one on the Brink of the Trench to spread the Dung upon the Talus.

2. *Geol.* A sloping mass of detritus lying at the base of a cliff or the like, and consisting of material which has fallen from its face; also, the slope or inclination of the surface of such a mass.

1830 LYELL *Princ. Geol.* I. II. xx. 266 It is only at a few points that the grassy covering of the sloping talus marks a temporary relaxation of the erosive action of the sea. 1863 — *Antiq. Man* xvii. 343 Huge taluses of fallen drift. 1865 LIVINGSTONE *Zambesi* vii. 171 The talus of each portal, keeping close together northwards, makes a narrow, upright-sided trough from the cataract up to Pajodze. 1876 PAGE *Adv. Text-bk. Geol.* xv. 275 The cemented fragments of a terrestrial talus or scree. 1881 DARWIN *Veg. Mould* 279 An old talus of chalk-fragments (thrown out of a quarry) which had become clothed with turf.

*attrib.* and *Comb.* 1867 H. MACMILLAN in *Macm. Mag.* No. 99. 256/2 Great talus-heaps of débris. 1904 *Daily Chron.* 24 Mar. 3/1 There was no stratification as might be expected if it were a talus-formation. 1906 *Ibid.* 20 Feb. 4/2 The water getting into the talus rock, a mass of soft stuff without any regular drainage.

b. A descending slope of a mountain, etc., without reference to its mode of formation.

1830 SIR T. D. LAUDER *Moray Floods* 230 We found an extensive marl bank reposing on the inclined talus at the foot of the hill. 1853 KANE *Grinnell Exp.* xv. (1856) 108 One of these bergs presented a long inclined talus, which was evidently part of an original slope, unaltered by after changes in equilibrium. 1856 — *Arct. Expl.* I. xv. 169 A slide down an inclined plane, whose well-graded talus gave me ample time to contemplate the contingencies at its base. 1865 LIVINGSTONE *Zambesi* ii. 61 One point of view on the talus of mount Morumbwa. 1868 LOCKYER tr. *Guillemin's Heavens* (ed. 3) 100 Beyond the second ridge a talus slopes gradually down northwards to the general level of the lunar surface.

|| **Talus**[2] (tē·lǒs). Pl. tali. [L. *tālus* ankle.]

1. The ankle-bone or astragalus; also applied to an analogous part in birds and insects.

1693 tr. *Blancard's Phys. Dict.* (ed. 2), *Talus*, see *Astragalus*. 1706 PHILLIPS (ed. 6), *Talus*, (lat.) the Ancle or Huckle-Bone, otherwise call'd Astragalus; the Pastern of a Beast; also a Die to play with. 1826 KIRBY & SP. *Entomol.* III. 385 *Talus* (the Ankle), the apex of the Tibia [of an insect], where it is united to the Tarsus. 1899 *Allbutt's Syst. Med.* VI. 556 The capsule of the ankle-joint was loose and lax, the talus smooth and oblique.

2. *Path.* A variety of clubfoot in which the toes are drawn up, the heel resting on the ground.

1864 in WEBSTER. 1887 in *Cassell's Encycl. Dict.*

3. A nodular concretion somewhat resembling an astragalus bone.

*a* 1728 WOODWARD *Nat. Hist. Fossils* (1729) I. I. 81 Of the Septa, or Partitions, that parcel out this Body into various Masses or Tali.

**Talvace, -vas**, variants of TALEVACE *Obs.*

**Talvett**, variant of TOVET, two-peck measure.

**Talwar**: see TULWAR, Indian sabre.

**Ta·lwood.** *Obs.* exc. *Hist.* Also 4–5 talwode, tallwod(e, (taleghwode, tallowood), 5–9 tallwood, 6 tal(e)wod, talewood, tallwodde, tallewode, 6–7 tall wood. [A rendering of OF. *bois de tail* 'bois en coupe' (Godef.), f. *tail* cutting, cut.] Wood for fuel, cut up usually to a prescribed size: cf. TALSHIDE.

[1268– Tallwood: cited in Rogers *Agric. & Prices* I. 393 et seq.] 1350 in Riley *Mem. Lond.* (1868) 254 Talwode. 1373 *Ibid.* 369 Taleghwode. 1424 *Will Stawell* (Somerset Ho.), Centum de talwode. 1497 *Naval Acc. Hen. VII* (1896) 227 M[1] tallowood occupyed & spent abought hetyng of pitche Talowe Tarre & Rosyn. 1502 ARNOLDE *Chron.* (1811) 97 The Ordinaunce for the Assise of Talewod and Belet in the Cyte of London. 1530 PALSGR. 279/2 Tallwodde pacte wodde to make byllettes of, *taillee*. 1552–3 *Act 7 Edw. VI*, c. 7 All talwoode, billet, fagot and coles..shall kepe thassises hereafter expressed. [A statement of sizes and prices follows.] 1573 TUSSER *Husb.* (1878) 133 Pile tallwood and billet, stacke all that hath band. 1674 JEAKE *Arith.* (1696) 68 Fuel contains Billets, Cordwood, Faggots, Talwood, and Coals. 1859 PARKER *Turner's Dom. Archit.* III. iv. 101 It was the duty of the grooms of the chamber to procure a regular supply of tallwood and fuel for the fire.

**Tam**, abbreviation of TAM-O'-SHANTER.

1895 *Daily News* 8 Apr. 6/7 The 'Tams' as the Tam O'Shanters are now universally called by shopkeepers, are favourites for windy weather. 1896 *Godey's Mag.* Feb. 224/2 The headgear is a coquettish white Tam with a white quill. 1899 ANNIE E. HOLDSWORTH *Valley Gt. Shadow* x, I'll put on your tam—there!

**Tamable**, variant spelling of TAMEABLE.

**Tamahauke**, obs. form of TOMAHAWK.

|| **Tamal** (tămā·l). Also tamaul, *erron.* tamale. [Mexican Sp. *tama·l*, pl. *tamales* (-ā·les).] A Mexican delicacy, made of crushed Indian corn, flavoured with pieces of meat or chicken, red pepper, etc., wrapped in corn-husks and baked.

1856 OLMSTED *Texas* (Bartl.), This [crowd] attracts a few sellers of whiskey, tortillas, and tamaules. 1860 BARTLETT *Dict. Amer.*, Tamal, or Tamauli. 1884 *Boston* (Mass.) *Jrnl.* 16 Feb. 2/2 A queer article of food, known as 'tamales', is sold in the streets of San Francisco at night by picturesquely clad Spaniards. 1893 KATE SANBORN *Truthf. Wom. S. California* 29 A *tamale* is a curious and dubious combination of chicken hash, meal, olives, red pepper, and I know not what, enclosed in a corn-husk.

|| **Tamandua** (tămæ·nduă). Also 7 tamendoa. [Pg. *tamandua* (in Gandavo *Historia*, 1576, *tamendoa*), a. Tupi *tamanduà*. (See J. Platt in *Athenæum* 19 Oct., 1901, 525.) So F. *tamandua* (1694 in Hatz.-Darm.), Sp. *tamándoa*.]

†a. Originally, a name for the Brazilian Ant-eaters generally, including the Great Ant-eater or Ant-bear, *Myrmecophaga jubata* (in Tupi *tamandua guaçu*).

1614 PURCHAS *Pilgrimage* IX. IV. (ed. 2) 835 The Tamendoas are as big as a Ram, with long and sharp snouts, a taile like a squirrell, (twice as long as the body and hairy). 1693 *Phil. Trans.* XVII. 851 The *Tamandua* or Ant-bear. [1753 CHAMBERS *Cycl. Supp.*, *Tamandua*,..called in English the ant-bear, and by the Brasilians *tamandua-guaçu*.] 1774 GOLDSM. *Nat. Hist.* (1776) IV. 338 The larger tamandua, the smaller tamandua, and the ant eater.

b. Now generally restricted by naturalists to the smaller *Tamandua tetradactyla*, and its congeners.

1834 *Penny Cycl.* II. 65/1 The *Tamandua* (*Myrmecophaga tamandua*, Cuvier,) or second species of ant-eater, is an animal much inferior to the great ant-bear in point of size, being scarcely so large as a good-sized cat. 1849 [see next]. 1851 OWEN in *Phil. Trans.* CXLI. 744 In the Tamandua (*Myrmecophaga Tamandua*)..all the cervical vertebræ have spinous processes except the atlas. 1896 *List Anim. Zool. Soc.* 198 *Tamandua tetradactyla*, Tamandua Ant-eater. 1903 *Westm. Gaz.* 17 Feb. 10/2 A new and interesting arrival at the Zoological Gardens is the Tamandua ant-eater, ..a native of the forests of tropical America, where it leads an entirely arboreal life.

|| **Tamanoir** (tamanwār). [F. corrupt form of Carib *tamanoà*, = Tupi *tamanduà*: see prec.] The French name of the Ant-bear: see prec. a.

1849 *Sk. Nat. Hist., Mammalia* IV. 212 In the general plan of its osteology the tamandua agrees with the tamanoir, but the bones of the muzzle are shorter than the cranial portion. *Ibid.* 213 In its manners the tamandua agrees with the tamanoir, with this difference, that it often climbs trees.

|| **Tamanu** (ta·mānū). Also -no. Tahitian name of the tree *Calophyllum Inophyllum* (see POON, TACAMAHAC); also *attrib.*, as *tamanu-resin, -tree.*

1839 T. BEALE *Nat. Hist. Sperm Whale* 349, I..engraved my name in the bark of a large tamanu tree. 1866 *Treas. Bot.*, *Tamanu*, a green heavy resin from the Society Islands, obtained from *Calophyllum Inophyllum*. 1897 *Daily News* 22 Mar. 8/2 The mountain forest of 'tamanu'. 1902 R. LOVETT *Chalmers* v. 142 A fine tamano tree grew close by.

**Tamarack** (tæ·măræk). Also -ac, -ach (*erron.* tamarisk). [app. a native Indian name in Canada.] a. Properly, The American Larch or HACKMATACK (*Larix americana*), growing in moist situations in British North America and the northern U.S.; also, the timber of this tree. b. Also applied to the Black or Ridge-pole Pine (*Pinus Murrayana*) of dry inland regions of western N. America, and app. sometimes to the Scrub Pine (*P. contorta*) of the coast (*Cent. Dict.*).

[*a* 1817 T. DWIGHT *Trav. New Eng.*, etc. (1821) I. 36 Hacmontac, or Tamarisk.] 1841 F. COOPER *Deerslayer* xxiii, The tamarack is healthiest in the swamp. 1842 G. BARSTOW *Hist. N. Hampsh.* 453 Boughs of the tamarac and spruce overhang the road. 1855 LONGF. *Hiaw.* VII. 48 Give me of your roots, O Tamarack! 1874 COUES *Birds N. W.* 152 Nesting in th tamarack swamps and windfalls of Minnesota.

||**Tamarau** (ta·mărau). Also -ao. [Native name.] A diminutive black buffalo, *Bubalus mindorensis*, peculiar to the island Mindoro, in the Philippines.

1898 *Guide Mammalia* 68 Attention may likewise be directed to the small Philippine Buffalo..,or Tamarau. 1902 *Geogr. Jrnl.* XIX. 622 The Tamarao, the remarkable anoa-like animal peculiar to Mindoro.

**Tamaric, -ice, -i(c)k,** obs. forms of TAMARISK.

**Tamarin** (tæ·mărin). [a. F. *tamarin* (La Condamine 1745), a. native name in the Galibi or Carib dial. of Cayenne.] A name for several species of the genus *Midas* of South American marmosets or squirrel-monkeys.

[1745 LA CONDAMINE *Relat. Voy. Amér. Mérid.* 165 On les nomme *Pinches* à Maynas, et à Cayenne, *Tamarins*.] 1780 SMELLIE tr. *Buffon's Nat. Hist.* (1791) VIII. 203 *note*, In Cayenne, there are very small monkeys called *tamarins*, which are extremely beautiful. They exceed not the size of a squirrel. 1797 *Encycl. Brit.* (ed. 3) XVII. 500/1 The tamarin, *Sagoinus Midas*, or great-eared monkey. 1854 H. G. DALTON *Brit. Guiana* (1855) II. 452 The Marakina or Silky Tamarin. 1881, 1896 Negro tamarin [see NEGRO 7]. 1882 Red-handed tamarin [see RED-HANDED *a.* 2]. 1899 *Daily News* 21 Nov. 5/1 The exceedingly rare monkey from South America, known as the red-bellied tamarin.

**Tamarind** (tæ·mărind). Forms: 6–7 tamarinde, 7 -ynd, tamerind, thamarind, 8 tamarinth, 7– tamarind; also 6 (from Pg.) tamarindo, *pl.* -os, 6–7 (It.) *pl.* tamarindi, 7 (from F.) *pl.* tamarines. [= Sp., Pg., It. *tamarindo*, med.L. *tamarindus*, ultimately ad. Arab. تمر هندي *tamr-hindī*, i.e. date of India, whence in the early herbalists and physicians *tamar indi*, in Marco Polo (Fr. version) *tamarandi*; in 13th c. F. *tamarindes* pl. (Hatz.-Darm.), mod.F. *tamarin* (15th c. in Hatz.-Darm.).]

1. The fruit of the tree *Tamarindus indica* (see 2), a brown pod containing one to twelve seeds embedded in a soft brown or reddish-black acid pulp, valued for its medicinal qualities, and also used in cookery as a relish, etc. In *Commerce, Med.*, etc. *tamarinds* means this pulp.

1533 ELYOT *Cast. Helthe* (1539) 60 Pourgers of choler... Tamarindes, halfe an ounce in a decoction. 1582 N. LICHEFIELD tr. *Castanheda's Conq. E. Ind.* I. xl. 94 They haue greate store of Ginger, Cardamomon, Tamarindos..and such lyke. 1612 WOODALL *Surg. Mate* Wks. (1653) 165 The Tamarinds brought from the Indies. 1652 FRENCH *Yorksh. Spa* ix. 82 Some Lenitive, as..Manna, Tamarines,..syrop of Roses. 1732 ARBUTHNOT *Rules of Diet* in *Aliments*, etc. 244 Tamarinds, cooling, astringent, yet laxative to the lower Belly. 1812 J. SMYTH *Pract. of Customs* (1821) 252 The Tamarind is a pod resembling a bean-cod, containing two, three, or four seeds. 1872 OLIVER *Elem. Bot.* II. 166 Tamarinds, as imported, are the pulp of the fruit of *Tamarindus*, preserved in syrup.

2. A large tree, *Tamarindus indica*, N.O. *Leguminosæ*, supposed to be a native of the E. Indies, but now cultivated in warm climates generally, bearing dark-green pinnate leaves and racemes of fragrant yellow flowers streaked with red, and producing the fruit described in 1, also a hard and heavy timber.

1614 PURCHAS *Pilgrimage* V. vii. (ed. 2) 483 Ouer the said Temple grow many Tamarinds. 1698 FRYER *E. India & P.* 126 A Grove of Mangoes and Thamarinds. 1727–46 THOMSON *Summer* 667 Lay me reclined Beneath the spreading tamarind. 1753 HANWAY *Trav.* (1762) I. VII. xcv. 438 A table of tamarinth,..half the diameter of the tree which produced it. 1872 OLIVER *Elem. Bot.* II. 165 The streaked wood of the Tamarind..used in cabinet work.

3. Applied to various trees (or their fruits) which resemble the tamarind in some respect: e.g. in New South Wales and other parts of Australia, a species of *Cupania*; usually with defining words. **Bastard tamarind**, *Acacia trichophylloides*, of Jamaica (Miller *Plant-n.* 1884). **Black, Black-crown, Brown,** or **Velvet tamarind**, a small leguminous tree, *Codarium acutifolium* or *Dialium guineense*: see quots. **Manilla tamarind**: see quot. 1866. **Wild tamarind**, applied to various leguminous trees or shrubs, as, in the W. Indies, *Pithecolobium filicifolium*; in Jamaica, *Acacia arborea*; in Trinidad, *Pentaclethra filamentosa* (Miller). **Yellow tamarind** of tropical America, *Acacia villosa*.

1833 M. SCOTT *Tom Cringle* vii. (1859) 130 Overshadowed by a magnificent wild Tamarind. 1857 HENFREY *Bot.* 280 The Tamarinds of Sierra Leone,..are species of *Codarium*. 1866 *Treas. Bot.* 898/2 P[ithecolobium] *dulce*, a large tree native of the hot regions of Mexico..is now planted..in the Madras Presidency, where the fruit is known as Manilla

Tamarinds. *Ibid.* 397/2 *D[ialium] acutifolium*, the Velvet Tamarind of Sierra Leone.. The pod, about the size and form of a filbert, is covered with a beautiful black velvet down. **1887** MOLONEY *Forestry W. Afr.* 332 Velvet Tamarind of Sierra Leone, Black Tamarind... The pulp surrounding the seeds is pleasantly acid and commonly eaten.

**4.** *attrib.* and *Comb.*, as *tamarind-pod, -pot, -pulp, -seed, -stone, -tree*; also **tamarind-fish**, a relish made from various kinds of Indian fish preserved with the acid pulp of the tamarind fruit; †**tamarind-palmetto**, some species of palmetto; **tamarind-plum**, an E. Indian tree, *Dialium indicum*, or its fruit: see quots.; **tamarind tea, tamarind water**, an infusion of tamarinds, used as a cooling drink; **tamarind-whey**: see quot.

**1858** SIMMONDS *Dict. Trade*, *Tamarind-fish. **1865** FR. DAY *Fishes Malabar* Introd. 9 The best Tamarind fish is prepared from the Seir fish and from the *Lates calcarifer*. **1698** FRYER *Acc. E. India & P.* 16 [The island of Johanna] The outwart Coat of which is embroidered with *Thamarind Palmetto. **1846** LINDLEY *Veg. Kingd.* 549 *Dialium indicum*, also called the *Tamarind Plum. **1857** HENFREY *Bot.* 280 Besides the Tamarind, other fruits, less acid, are eaten, as the Tamarind Plum. **1866** *Treas. Bot.* 1121/1 The *tamarind-pods imported from the East Indies vary in length from three to six inches, and are slightly curved. They consist of a brittle brown shell, within which is a soft acid brown pulp, traversed by strong woody fibres. **1850** THACKERAY *Pendennis* li, He knew the way to the *tamarind-pots. **1836** BRANDE *Chem.* (ed. 4) Index, *Tamarind pulp, 1062. **1844** H. H. WILSON *Brit. India* II. II. iv. 163 The Hindus endeavoured to appease the cravings of nature with.. bruised *Tamarind stones, and the leaves of trees. **1883** *Chambers' Encycl.* IX. 283/1 *Tamarind tea is made by infusing tamarinds in boiling water. **1681** R. KNOX *Hist. Ceylon* IV. i. 118 [He] sat down under a *Tamarind Tree. **1825** *Hone's Every-day Bk.* I. 678 According to some botanists, the tamarind-tree enfolds within its leaves the flowers or fruit every night. **1885-8** FAGGE & PYE-SMITH *Princ. Med.* (ed. 2) I. 150 For beverages he may be allowed to choose among barley-water, toast-and-water, lemonade, *tamarind-water, .. and cold weak tea. **1883** *Chambers' Encycl.* IX. 283/1 *Tamarind whey is prepared by boiling one ounce of tamarinds with a pint of new milk, and straining.

† **Tamarine.** *Obs. rare*—[1]. Some kind of cloth.

**1691** *Lond. Gaz.* No. 2675/4 A Piece of Ash-coloured woolly Tamarine striped with black.

**Tamarisk** (tæ·mărisk). Forms: α. 5 **thamarike, -yke,** 6 **tamarice,** 6–8 **-ic, -ik, tamerick,** 7 **tamricke.** β. 5–7 (in L. form) **tamariscus**, pl. **-i**; 6– **tamorisck**e 6–7 **tamar-,** 7 **tameriske, tamriske,** 6– **tamarisk.** [ad. late L. *tamariscus* (Palladius), var. of *tamarix, -īcem*, whence F. *tamaris* (13th c.), also in 16th c. *tamarisc, tamarix*. Ulterior source of the L. name unknown.]

A plant of the genus *Tamarix*, esp. *T. gallica*, the Common Tamarisk (called in L. *myrīca*, in Gr. μυρίκη), a graceful evergreen shrub or small tree, with slender feathery branches and minute scale-like leaves, growing in sandy places in S. Europe and W. Asia, and now much planted by the sea-shore in the south of England. Several other species, some with trunks 6 or 7 feet in girth, occur in the Mediterranean region.

*German Tamarisk*, the allied *Myricaria germanica*.

*c* **1400** *Lanfranc's Cirurg.* 220 Make him a gargarism of liquiricie, yreos, & tamarisci. *c* **1440** *Pallad. on Husb.* XII. 316 Atte gynnyng of this moone, of thamarike And other floures wilde, useth the bee Hony .. to pike. **1548** TURNER *Names of Herbes* s.v. *Myrica*, The scholemaisters in Englande haue of longe tyme called myrica heath, or lyng, but so longe haue they bene deceyued al together. It maye be called in englishe, Tamarik. **1562** — *Herbal* II. 59 Yͤ Cypres tre and the Tamarisk haue carnose or fleshy leues. **1599** HAKLUYT *Voy.* II. I. 165 The Archbishop of Canterburie Edmund Grindall, after he returned out of Germany, brought into this realme the plant of Tamariske from thence. *c* **1611** CHAPMAN *Iliad* XXI. 18 On the shore, the Worthy hid, and left his horrid lance Amids the Tamriskes. **1715–20** POPE *Iliad* VI. 49 His headlong steeds.. Rush'd on a tamarisk's strong trunk, and broke The shatter'd chariot from the crooked yoke. **1794** MRS. RADCLIFFE *Myst. Udolpho* iv, They sauntered over hillocks covered with lavender, wild thyme, juniper, and tamarisk. **1827** *Gentl. Mag.* XCVII. II. 34 Say, wilt thou court the tamarisk's lowly shade, And tune to strains of love thy dulcet reed? **1864** GILBERT & CHURCHILL *Dolomite Mount.* 68 Clumps of alder and willow, interspersed with bushes of the tamarisk (*Myricaria germanica*).

†**b.** A decoction or other preparation of the leaves of this plant, formerly used in medicine. *Obs.*

**1579** LANGHAM *Gard. Health* (1633) 627 Tamariske: it is a medicine of excellent power and vertue against the stopping & hardnes of the milt, if it be but drunke out of, being made into a vessell to drinke it. **1621** BURTON *Anat. Mel.* II. iv. I. v. (1651) 374 The wines ordinarily used to this disease are Wormewood-wine, Tamarisk and Buglossatum. **1718** QUINCY *Compl. Disp.* 139 Tamarisk.. attenuates, opens and absterges.

**c.** *attrib.* and *Comb.*, as *tamarisk-bough, -branch, -bush, -jungle, -stem, -tree, -twig*; *tamarisk-fringed, -grown* adjs.; **tamarisk salt**, salt found adhering to the trunk of *Tamarix orientalis* in edible quantity (*Cent. Dict.*); hence *tamarisk-salt-tree*; **tamarisk ware**, vessels or dishes made from the wood of the tamarisk.

*c* **1611** CHAPMAN *Iliad* X. 395 He hung them vp aloft, vpon a *Tamricke bow. **1863** M. L. WHATELY *Ragged Life Egypt* xx. 202 The school-room had been swept neatly and decorated with tamarisk-boughs and a few flowers. **1816** H. G. KNIGHT *East. Sk.* Pref. (1830) 36 *Tamarisk bushes, stunted acacia trees,.. complete the produce of the choicest spots in the Deserts [of Arabia]. **1899** F. C. GOULD in *Westm. Gaz.* 6 Sept. 1/3 The *tamarisk-fringed white-dusted road. **1712** tr. *Pomet's Hist. Drugs* I. 64 From this Wood is made a white Chrystal Salt, called *Tamarisk Salt. **1578** LYTE *Dodoens* VI. xv. 677 Swine which haue bene dayly fedde out of a trough.. made of *Tamarisk tree or timber, haue bene seene to haue no milt at al. [Cf. PLINY *N. H.* 24. 9. 41.] *c* **1611** CHAPMAN *Iliad* VI. 37 Low-growne Tamricke trees. **1876** *Oxford Bible-Helps* 116 Of the tamarisk-tree seven species exist in Palestine. **1614** PURCHAS *Pilgrimage* IV. vii. (ed. 2) 371 Muttering their prayers, holding a bundle of small *Tameriske-twigs. **1712** tr. *Pomet's Hist. Drugs* I. 64 They.. make little Casks, Cups, and Dishes of it, which are call'd *Tamarisk Ware.

¶ Erron. used for TAMARACK, q.v. (quot. *a* 1817).

**Tamarugite** (tămæ·rugəit). *Min.* ['f. the pampas del Tamarugal' (Chester); see -ITE [1] 2 b.] Hydrous sulphate of aluminium and sodium; a sodium alum.

**1890** *Amer. Jrnl. Sci.* Ser. III. XL. 258 One of these [sulphates] is *tamarugite*: this occurs in massive forms, colourless and with a radiated structure.

‖ **Tamasha** (tāmā·ʃā). *East Ind.* [a. Arab., Pers., Urdū تماشا *tamāʃā* walking about for recreation or amusement, an entertainment, f. 6th conj. of مشى *mašā(y)* to walk.] An entertainment, show, display, public function.

[**1687** A. LOVELL tr. *Thevenot's Trav.* II. 90 They stop at the meanest thing, to do that which they call *Tamacha*, (that's to say,) to consider and admire it.] **1872** MRS. VALENTINE *Let.* in *Mem.* viii. (1882) 135 The usual tamashas went on. **1889** *Pall Mall G.* 9 May 7/1 The people say to the Christian missionaries: 'Yours is a very dull religion; there is not enough tamasha (that is, show or function) about it'. **1892** *Sat. Rev.* 18 June 700/2 That very funny tamasha which is called a Convention in American politics. **1904** *Blackw. Mag.* June 835, I thought the tamasha had begun and turned out to look. **1906** *Athenæum* 26 May 635/1 The serious business of life.. at.. Khapallu.. seems to be polo and tamashas.

‖ **Tambac**, a native Indian name of agalloch or aloes wood.

**1727–51** CHAMBERS *Cycl.* s. v. *Aloes*, The heart, or innermost part [of Aloes] called *tambac*.. is more valued by the Indians than gold itself.

**Tambac, tambayack**, obs. var. TOMBAC.

‖ **Tambagut** (tæ·mbăgʊt). [Native name, from its cry, in the Philippines.] The Crimson-breasted Barbet of the Philippines (*Megalæma hæmacephala*). (*Cent. Dict.*)

**Tamberbase**: see TAMBOUR *sb.* 1 b.

**Tamberlaine, -lane**: see TAMERLANE.

**Ta·mbo.** [Negro abbrev. of *tambourine*: cf. BANJO.] The tambourine-player in a negro minstrel troupe.

**1884** *Sat. Rev.* 7 June 740/1 A single row of negro minstrels seated on chairs.. at the ends are Bones and Tambo.

**Tamboo**, variant of TABOO.

**Tambor** (tæ·mbǫɹ). [var. of TAMBOUR *sb.*]

**a.** See TAMBOUR *sb.* 3. **b.** *Tambor-oil*: see quot.

**1890** BILLINGS *Nat. Med. Dict.*, *Tambor oil*, an oil obtained from the seeds of *Omphalea oleifera*.. of Central America; said to be purgative without griping.

‖ **Tambouki** (tambū·ki), *a.* Also **tambookie, -bootie.** [S. Afr. Du., f. *Tembu*, tribal name + dim. ending *-kje*, also *-tje*.] Of or belonging to Tembu-land, as in **Tambouki grass, Tambouki wood**, a wild grass and timber of S. Africa.

**1858** SIMMONDS *Dict. Trade*, *Tambookie-wood*, a hard handsome furniture-wood: when powdered it is used by the Zulus of Africa as an emetic. **1885** RIDER HAGGARD *K. Solomon's Mines* iv, Dry tambouki grass.. is made into a bed. **1899** ALICE WERNER *Capt. of Locusts*, etc. 80 Open glades with bushes and clumps of tambootie-grass scattered about. **1905** *Blackw. Mag.* Sept. 382/1 [The grass] was dashed aside by some large object that came rapidly towards him, but was concealed beneath the long tambouki.

**Tambour** (tæ·mbuᵊɹ, -bǫɹ), *sb.* [a. F. *tambour* drum: see TABOR.]

**1.** A drum; *spec.* the great or bass drum.

**1484** CAXTON *Fables of Æsop* (1889) 95 Of his skynne he dyd doo make tambours, whiche ben euer bete. **1706** PHILLIPS (ed. 6), *Tambour*, a Drum, an Instrument of Martial Musick. **1745** POCOCKE *Descr. East* II. I. xvi. 156 One of them played on a tambour, and sung a Curdeen song. **1810** SOUTHEY *Kehama* I. xiv, And still with overwhelming din The tambours and the trumpets sound. **1812** — *Lett.* (1856) II. 307 A tambour is an outlandish drum, not such as soldiers use. **1879** STAINER *Music of Bible* 140 As they [cymbals] became reduced in size it was found possible to insert several pairs under the rim of the tambour.

‖ **b. Tambour de basque** (also 7 **tamber de base, tamberbase,** 9 **tamborbasque**) [F. *tambour de basque*, † *de Biscaye*], a tambourine.

**1688** R. HOLME *Armoury* III. xvi. (Roxb.) 85/1 He beareth sable, a Tamber de Base, or Tamber-base, Or... This is a kind of Instrument, vsed among the auncient Jews, and now by the Turkes. **1780** BECKFORD *Italy* (1834) I. iv. 34 *Tambours de basque* at every corner. **1840** *Encycl. Brit.* (ed. 7) XXI. 72/2 *Tambour de Basque*, a well-known kind of small drum, commonly called a tambourine. It is much used among the Biscayans.

**2.** An instrument for recording pulsations, as in respiration: see quots.

**1877** FOSTER *Phys.* I. iv. § 2 Each bag communicates by a separate air-tight tube with an air-tight tambour on which a lever rests; so that any pressure on either bag is communicated to the cavity of its respective tambour, the lever of which is raised in proportion. *Ibid.* II. ii. § 1 The movements of the column of air in the trachea are transmitted to the tambour, the consequent expansions and contractions of which are transmitted by means of a lever resting on it to the recording drum. **1890** BILLINGS *Nat. Med. Dict.*, *Tambour*, drum; used to collect and transmit movements in graphic registering apparatus.

**3.** (Also **tambor.**) A fish which makes a drumming noise, or which resembles a drum in form; as a fish of the genus *Pogonias*, a drum-fish; a globe-fish, swell-fish, or puffer; also the red rock-fish, *Sebastodes ruber*, of the coast of California.

[**1683–4** ROBINSON in *Phil. Trans.* XXIX. 480 Many Tamburo's or Drum-Fishes.] **1854** BUSHNAN in *Orr's Circ. Sc.* I. *Org. Nat.* 151 The pogonias, on account of the sounds which it produces, has been named the tambour. **1891** *Cent. Dict.*, Tambor.

**4.** A circular frame formed of one hoop fitting within another, in which silk, muslin, or other material is stretched for embroidering. Cf. TAMBOURING-*machine*.

**1777** SHERIDAN *Sch. Scand.* II. i, When I saw you first sitting at your tambour, in a pretty figured linen gown. **1781** MME. D'ARBLAY *Diary* Mar., Portraits of the three beautiful Lady Waldegraves,.. at work with the tambour. **1818** TODD, *Tambou'r*. **1841** BORROW *Zincali* I. viii. § 1. 131 Intertwining with their sharp needles the gold and silk on the tambour.

**b.** A species of embroidery in which patterns are worked with a needle of peculiar form on material stretched in a tambour-frame; now superseded by pattern-weaving; in recent use = *tambour-lace*: see 7.

**1813** *App. to Chron.* in *Ann. Reg.* 252/1 A bounty upon the exportation of stuffs, of silk ornamented with embroidery, tambour, needle work, lace or fringe. **1859** GREEN *Oxf. Stud.* ii. § 7 (O. H. S.) 94 A French master of tambour and similar accomplishments. **1883** *Standard* 26 June 3/3 The.. Limerick production is of four kinds: Tambour, the simplest and commonest. **1898** *Cent. Mag.* Jan. 365/1 My sisters and I covered it [the frock] with embroidered buds and roses, done in tambour. **1908** *Westm. Gaz.* 25 Apr. 13/2 Then there is the imitation of old Tambour.

**c.** A kind of fine gold or silver thread.

**1899** W. G. P. TOUNSEND *Embroidery* v. 82 Gold and Silver Passing and Tambour.—Fine kind of threads. *Ibid.* vi. 106 How tambour gold is used over cardboard. **1901** DAY & BUCKLE *Needlework* xxix. (ed. 2) 245 For stitching through, there is a finer [gold] thread, called 'tambour'.

**5.** *Arch.* **a.** The core of a Corinthian or Composite capital. **b.** Any one of the courses forming the shaft of a cylindrical column. **c.** The wall of a circular building surrounded with columns. **d.** A round exterior building surrounding the base of a dome or cupola; also the circular vertical part of a cupola. **e.** A lobby or vestibule enclosed with folding doors and ceiling, as within the porch of a church, to prevent the direct passage of air, etc. **f.** A projecting part of the wall of a tennis court: see quot. 1816.

**1706** PHILLIPS (ed. 6), *Tambour*... In Architecture, the Vase or Ornament in the Chapiter of Pillars of the Corinthian Order: Also the Name of part of a Tennis-Court. **1727–41** CHAMBERS *Cycl.*, *Tambour*, in architecture,.. applied to the Corinthian and Composite capitals, as bearing some resemblance to a drum... *Tambour* is also used for a little box of timber-work, covered with a cieling, withinside the porch of certain churches... *Tambour* also denotes a round course of stone, several whereof form the shaft of a column, not so high as a diameter. **1816** *Encycl. Perth.* XXII. 220/2 On the right hand side of the [tennis] court from the dedans is the tambour, a part of the wall which projects, and is so contrived in order to make a variety in the stroke. **1823** P. NICHOLSON *Pract. Build.* Gloss., *Tambour*,.. also the wall of a circular temple, surrounded with columns. **1838** *Civil Eng. & Arch. Jrnl.* I. 338/2 An iron clamp was fastened on the shoulder of the capital, and another on the lowest tambour of the column. **1841** *Penny Cycl.* XX. 73/1 If the dome [of the Pantheon] had sprung immediately from the upper cornice, so as to present a perfect hemisphere on the outside, the rotunda itself would have looked merely as a tambour to it. **1864** *Athenæum* 27 Feb. 304/2 Above the roofs will rise (in the centre) a bold tambour pierced with windows and inclosing the lower portion of the dome.

**6.** *Mil.* A small defensive work formed of palisades or earth, usually in the form of a redan, to defend an entrance or passage.

**1834** J. S. MACAULAY *Field Fortif.* 91 These small redoubts or tambours, though weak in themselves, are of use when nothing better can be done. *Ibid.* 140 Tambours are constructed with timbers 10 feet long, and about 6 inches square, which are planted touching each other, and sunk 3 feet into the earth. **1853** STOCQUELER *Milit. Encycl.*, *Tambour*,.. a work formed.. so that, when finished, it may have the appearance of a square redoubt cut in two... Tambours are also solid pieces of earth which are made in that part of the covert-way that is joined to the parapet. **1895** *Chapters in Adventurous Life* 340 There was a chapel of St. George some little distance inland of this point, around which a tambour of loose stones had been raised.

**7.** *attrib.* and *Comb.*, as (in sense 1) *tambour-peal*, (in sense 4) *tambour-cotton, -embroidery, -school, -sprig, -waistcoat, -work, -worker*; also **tambour-frame**, = sense 4; **tambour-lace**, a modern lace resembling tambour (4 b), consisting of needlework designs on machine-made net; **tambour-needle**, the needle used in tambour-work, a small steel hook set in a handle; **tambour-stitch**, the loop-stitch used in tambour-work; also a stitch used in crochet, by which a pattern of ridges intersecting at right angles is produced; so **tambour-stitcher.**

1798 *Tambour-frame [see *tambour-needle*]. 1803 MAR. EDGEWORTH *Emilie de Coulanges* (1832) 157 She would rather see Emilie guillotined at once, than condemned..to work like a galley-slave at her tambour-frame for her bread. 1884 *Bookseller* 6 Nov. 1190/1 She..added to their slender earnings by her skill at the tambour frame. 1899 *Westm. Gaz.* 28 Dec. 3/2, I would recommend the charming and inexpensive *Tambour lace for this design. 1798 EDGEWORTH *Pract. Educ.* (1811) I. 103 A lady who is learning to work with a *tambour needle puts her head down close to the tambour frame. 1863 JANET HAMILTON *Poems & Ess.* 196 The daughter plied the tambour-needles. 1823 MRS. HEMANS *Siege Valencia* v, The Moor is on his way! With the *tambour-peal and the tecbir-shout. 1799 J. ROBERTSON *Agric. Perth* 382 At Callander the weaving of cotton goods and a *tambour-school have been lately introduced. 1779 SHERIDAN *Critic* I. i, Tropes and flowers suit the general coarseness of your style, as *tambour sprigs would a ground of linsey woolsey. 1883 *Art Jrnl.* 150/2 Done by Turkish workers, and Chinese and Indian *tambour- titchers. 1778 MME. D'ARBLAY *Diary* 23 Aug., A *tambour waistcoat, worked in green silk. 1806–7 J. BERESFORD *Miseries Hum. Life* (1826) II. Sigh xiii, After having consumed three years on a piece of *tambour-work. 1879 *Temple Bar Mag.* Oct. 218 Her needle went to and fro through her tambour work. 1780 *Chron.* in *Ann. Reg.* 201/2 They were *tambour workers.

**Tambour** (tæ·mbuəɹ, tæmbūə·ɹ), *v.* [f. prec. sb.]

**1.** *trans.* To work or embroider in a tambour-frame; to ornament with tambour-work.

1774 *Westm. Mag.* II. 166 The waistcoats tamboured with coloured silks only, or interspersed with gold and silver. 1840 MRS. GAUGAIN *Lady's Assist. Knitting*, etc. I. 189 Join it up..by tambouring it together about 2½ inches at each side, and draw it up at each end. 1885 *Birmingham Daily Post* 5 Jan. 6/6 Some [fabrics] are embossed, and some tamboured in gold, or otherwise treated.

*fig.* 1830 *Blackw. Mag.* XXVII. 171 A coarse..web of words..—tamboured with clusters of fantastic figures.

**2.** *intr.* To work at a tambour-frame; to do tambour-work.

*a* 1845 BARHAM *Ingol. Leg.* Ser. III. *Knight & Lady*, She sat herring-boning, tambouring, or stitching. 1863 JANET HAMILTON *Poems, Tambourer*, She who tambours, tambours, tambours for fifteen hours a day Would have shoes on her feet and dress for church, had she a third of our pay.

Hence **Tamboured** *ppl. a.*, ornamented with tambour-embroidery; worked, as a design, on the tambour-frame.

1799 *Hull Advertiser* 30 Nov. 1/1 Some remarkably elegant..tamboured..muslins. 1830 SCOTT *Demonol.* i. 30 This personage, with tamboured waistcoat. 1885 *Manch. Exam.* 2 Mar. 4/6 Business..in tamboured cloths for Spain is also dull.

‖ **Tamboura** (tæ·mbŭră, tæmbūə·ră). Also 6 **tambora**, 7 **tamera**, 9 **tumboora**. [app. ad. Pers. طنبور *ṭanbūr*, Arab. *ṭunbūr*, in same sense.] An oriental musical instrument of the lute family, resembling the guitar, with wire strings struck by a plectrum.

1585 T. WASHINGTON tr. *Nicholay's Voy.* III. i. 69 b, A thing very like vnto a Cittern, which they call Tambora. 1662 J. DAVIES tr. *Olearius' Voy. Ambass.* 276 He would needs play on the *Tamera*,..an Instrument us'd by the Persians instead of the Lute. 1828 *Asiatic Costumes* 13 The tumboora in shape resembles the guitar more than any other instrument. 1864 ENGEL *Mus. Anc. Nat.* 51 The tamboura ..is at present in use, especially in Persia, Hindoostan, and Asiatic Turkey.

**Tambourer** (see the verb). [f. TAMBOUR *v.* + -ER [1].] One who does tambour-work.

1833 BREWSTER *Nat. Magic* xi. 287 A tambourer of ordinary skill could not..earn more than five or six shillings a week by constant application. 1845 *New Statist. Acc. Scotl.* VI. 294 English women taught the tambourers here the art. 1863 JANET HAMILTON *Poems, Tambourer*, Still the tambourer bends wearily over the frame.

**Tambouret** (tæ·mburet). ? *Obs. rare.* Also 7 **tamburet.** [f. TAMBOUR + -ET: cf. TABOURET.]

†**1.** = TABOURET 2. *Obs. rare*—[1].

1658 tr. *Hist. Christina A. Q. of Swedland* II. 75 The tamburet [orig. *tamburetto*], which is a less seat, granted usually by Queenes to Princesses of great quality, was given to the Dutchesses of Ascot, of Auray, and the Princess of Ligni.

**2.** A small drum; a TABRET or TABORIN. ? *Obs.*

1776 HAWKINS *Hist. Music* I. II. ix. 248 The *Tympanum leve*, an instrument yet known by the name of the *Tambouret*. 1839 ADM. PAGET *Autobiog.* ii. (1896) 59 This stirring [Bohemian] song, accompanied..with guitars and tambourets.

**Tambourin** (‖ tãnbu*rẽ*, tæ·mburin). [mod. F. (Voltaire 1769) = Pr. *tamborin*, It. *tamburino*, dim. of *tambour* drum: the earlier Fr. form down to 1700 was *tabourin*: see TABORIN.]

**1.** The long narrow drum or tabor used in Provence (see TABORIN); applied also to 'a bottle-shaped drum used in Egypt' (*Cent. Dict.*).

1833 BREWSTER *Nat. Magic* viii. 205 He holds in one hand a flageolet, and in the other the stick with which he beats the *tambourin*. 1907 RICKERT *Gold. Hawk* xxxix. 296 The music was pipe and tambourin, of course, how else should one dance in Provence?

**2.** A Provençal dance, originally accompanied by the tambourin. **b.** A piece of music for such a dance, in duple rhythm and quick time.

1797 *Encycl. Brit.* (ed. 3) XVIII. 305/1 *Tambourin*,..name of a dance performed on the French stage. The air is lively, and the movements are quick. 1884 W. B. SQUIRE in Grove *Dict. Mus.* IV. 55 *Tambourin*, an old Provençal dance, in its original form accompanied by a Flute and Tambour de Basque [*error for* Tambourin].

Hence **Ta·mbourin** *v.*, to play on the tambourin; **Ta·mbourina·de** [after *serenade*, etc.; see -ADE], a performance on the tambourin.

1884 J. PAYNE *Tales fr. Arabic* II. 234 They gave not over..tambourining and piping till the night waned. 1893 E. H. BARKER *Wand. South. Waters* 27 Every morning at five the tailor..awoke the echoes of the gorge with a long and furious tambourinade.

**Tambourine** (tæmbŭrī·n), *sb.* Forms: 6 **tamburin**, 7 **-ine**, **timburine**, 9 **tambourin**, **-borine**, 8- **tambourine.** [app. ad. F. *tambourin*, dim. of *tambour* (see prec.), but used not in the sense of that word, but in that of F. *tambour de basque*.]

**1.** A musical instrument consisting of a wooden hoop having skin or parchment stretched over one side, and pairs of small cymbals, called jingles, placed in slots round the circumference, small bells being sometimes fastened to the edge. It is played by shaking, striking with the knuckles, or drawing the fingers across the parchment.

The earlier names for this or a similar instrument mentioned in the Bible were *timbre* and *timbrel*. It is not clear what Spenser and Jonson meant by *tamburin*, *timburine*; the word was known to Blount 1661 only from Spenser; the modern use was unknown to Bailey, to Johnson, and to Ash (1775); it is certain in quot. 1782; but as it does not agree with that of F. *tambourin* it is difficult to know how it arose.

1579 SPENSER *Sheph. Cal.* June 59, I sawe Calliope wyth Muses moe..Theyr yuory Luyts and Tamburins forgoe. *Ibid.* Gloss., *Tamburines*, an olde kind of instrument, which of some is supposed to be the Clarion. 1637 B. JONSON *Sad Sheph.* I. iii, Though all the Bels, Pipes, Tabors, Timburines ring. 1661 in BLOUNT *Glossogr.* [giving Spenser's gloss]. 1791 WALKER *Dict.*, *Tambarine*, a tabour, a small drum. 1782 W. F. MARTYN *Geog. Mag.* I. 17 The tambourine.. which is well known in the streets of this metropolis,..being a hoop covered with parchment, and furnished with small pieces of metal hanging to the edges of it. 1821 CLARE *Vill. Minstr.* I. 38 To join the dance where gipsy fiddlers play, Accompanied with thumping tambourine. 1884 V. DE PONTIGNY in Grove *Dict. Mus.* IV. 55 *Tambourine* (Fr. *Tambour de Basque*)..consists of a wooden hoop, on one side of which is stretched a vellum head, the other side being open. 1899 KIPLING *Absent-Minded Beggar* i, Will you kindly drop a shilling in my little tambourine For a gentleman in khaki ordered South? [Refers to its use as a collecting dish.]

*Comb.* 1840 DICKENS *Barn. Rudge* xli, Some black tambourine-player, with a great turban on.

**2. Tambourine pigeon** (also ellipt. *tambourine*): an African species of pigeon, so called from the resonance of its note.

1891 *Cent. Dict.*, Tambourine. 1896 *List Anim. Zool. Soc.* 466 *Tympanistria bicolor*, Tambourine Pigeon.

Hence **Tambouri·ne** *v. intr.*, to play the tambourine.

1891 *Daily News* 5 Sept. 3/3 The jingle of the tambourining poke-bonnetted lass [i.e. member of the Salvation Army].

**Tambouring,** *vbl. sb.* [f. TAMBOUR *v.* + -ING [1].] The action of the verb TAMBOUR; embroidery done by this method. Also *attrib.*, as *tambouring-engine*, *-machine*, a machine for doing this work.

1775 ASH Suppl., *Tambouring*, the act of ornamenting with a kind of particoloured needlework. 1815 SIMOND *Jrnl. Tour Gt. Brit.* I. 285 The tambouring or embroidering mill. 1830 GALT *Lawrie T.* III. i, His wife had been bred to the tambouring. 1833 *Encycl. Brit.* (ed. 7) VII. 407/2 *margin*, Tambouring machine. 1872 *Routledge's Ev. Boy's Ann.* 223/2 The movements of the tambouring engine. 1908 *Daily Chron.* 21 Oct. 7/5 Some of the finer embroidery, called tambouring, is still worked by hand on a frame.

‖ **Tambreet** (tæmbrī·t). [Mallangong lang. of New South Wales.] A native name of the Duckbilled Platypus.

1840 *Penny Cycl.* XVII. 28/1 The Duckbill, or Duckbilled Platypus..; Mallangong, Tambreet,.. Water-mole of the English colonists. 1864 in WEBSTER; and in mod. Dicts.

**Tamburlain(e**: see TAMERLANE.

**Tame** (tēⁱm), *a.* Forms: 1, 4 **tam**, 3- **tame**, 4–5 *Sc.* **tayme**; 1 **tǫm**, 2–3 **tom**, 4 **tome.** [OE. *tam* (*tǫm*) = OFris. (EFris.) *tam*, OLG. **tam* (MLG., LG., MDu., Du. *tam*), OHG., MHG. *zam* (Ger. *zahm*), ON. *tamr*:—OTeut. **tamoᶻ* (evidenced in Goth. only by the deriv. vb. *tamjan* to tame). The Teut. stem *tam-* is cognate with that of L. *domāre*, Gr. δαμ-ᾶν to tame, subdue. The OE. variant *tǫm* was retained in southern Early ME. down to *c* 1300; the existing *tame* represents the inflected forms of *tam*: cf. also TAME *v.*[1]]

**1.** Of animals (rarely of men): Reclaimed from the wild state; brought under the control and care of man; domestic; domesticated. (Opp. to *wild.*)

*c* 888 K. ÆLFRED *Boeth.* xxxv. § 6 Wildu ðior..woldon.. standon swilce hi tame wæron. *c* 1000 ÆLFRIC *Saints' Lives* (1900) II. 326 Se wulf folgode..swylce he tam wære. *c* 1000 *Ags. Gloss.* in Wr.-Wülcker 481/22 *Subjugalis*, tam. *c* 1250 *Gen. & Ex.* 174 He made on werlde al erue tame. *Ibid.* 1482 Esau wilde man huntere, And Iacob tame man tiliere. *a* 1300 *Cursor M.* 25430 (Cott.) Of all þin sandes wild and tam, Man þou scop and gaf him nam. *c* 1375 *Sc. Leg. Saints* xxix. (*Placidas*) 318 Wyld hors & tayme. 1526 TINDALE 2 *Pet.* ii. 16 The tame and dom beast speakynge with mannes voyce. 1653 WALTON *Angler* ii. 44 I'll try if I can make her [a young otter] tame. 1660 F. BROOKE tr. *Le Blanc's Trav.* 166 They have also tame Lions. 1698 FRYER *Acc. E. India & P.* 271 From a Salvage Prince rendred himself a tame Follower of the Patriarch. 1772 PRIESTLEY *Inst. Relig.* (1782) I. 32 Small and tame animals breed fast. 1844 H. H. WILSON *Brit. India* II. 372 The beasts of the forest, or the scarcely tamer human beings. 1859 H. KINGSLEY *G. Hamlyn* xxviii, A tame black belonging to us. He is great at all sorts of hunting.

**b.** *humorously*, of a person: Domestic; kept or supported for domestic or private use.

1711 ADDISON *Spect.* No. 47 ¶ 2 It was formerly the Custom for every great House in England to keep a tame Fool dressed in Petticoats. 1895 *Westm. Gaz.* 13 Mar. 8/1 At the Treasury..A tame bookbinder receives £105 a year. *Mod.* They endow 'tame professors' to advocate their views.

**2.** Applied to plants, also (in *U.S.*) to land: Cultivated, improved by culture; garden- as opposed to *wild*. *Obs.* in ordinary use since *c* 1650.

*Tame hay*, hay made from specially sown grasses or forage plants; cf. *wild hay*. (Western U.S.)

1551 TURNER *Herbal* I. C v b, I haue not sene yet the right tame Anemone. 1562 — *Herbal* II. 112 Tame or gardin radice. 1578 LYTE *Dodoens* III. lix. 399 The tame Hoppe hath rough branches. 1604 E. G[RIMSTONE] *D'Acosta's Hist. Indies* IV. xxxi. 295 Cherries, both wilde and tame have not prospered well at the Indies. 1629 PARKINSON *Paradisus* (1904) 420 Any Rose either wilde or tame. 1885 tr. *Hehn's Wand. Plants & Anim.* (1887) 94 Herodotus makes the oracle speak of the tame olive. 1887 *Buck's Handbk. Med. Sc.* V. 9/2 The careful pioneer..had his corral..where the land had become 'tame'.

*fig.* 1855 THACKERAY *Newcomes* xlviii, His lordship sowed tame oats now after his wild ones.

**3.** Having the disposition or character of a domesticated animal; accustomed to man; not showing the natural shyness, fear of, or fierceness to man; familiar; also of persons, their disposition, etc.: made tractable, docile, or pliant.

*c* 888 K. ÆLFRED *Boeth.* xxv. § 1 Seo leo, ðeah hio wel tam se. *a* 1000 *Gnom. Verses* 142 Til mon tiles & tomes meares. *a* 1225 *Ancr. R.* 144 Noðing ne aweldeð wilde uleschs ne ne makeð hit tommure þen deð muche wecche. *a* 1225 *Leg. Kath.* 1318 Þet he ne talde him al tom ear he turnde from us. *a* 1250 *Owl & Night.* 1444 Hwich beo þe gome Þat of þe wilde makeþ tome. *a* 1300 *Cursor M.* 11628 Al þe bestes þat ar wild For me most be tame and mild. *c* 1302 *Pol. Songs* (Camden) 194 Alas! thou seli Fraunce, for the may thunche shome, That ane fewe fullaris maketh ou so tome. *c* 1374 CHAUCER *Compl. Mars* 278 The pruddest of yow may be made ful tame. *c* 1430 *Hymns Virg.* (1867) 63 Y wole þee leere To make þi lord to þee tame. 1526 *Pilgr. Perf.* (W. de W. 1531) 39 Go home mekely & tame to thy place. 1785 GROSE *Dict. Vulg. Tongue* s. v., To run tame about a house, to live familiarly in a family with which one is upon a visit. 1908 *Betw. Trent & Ancholme* 26 It [a gull] became tame enough to watch its food being dug.

**b.** *Tame cat*: One who is on the footing of the domestic cat; a person who is made a convenience by his friends. So †*tame-fellow*, †*tame goose* (*obs.*). (Cf. 1 b.)

1605 *Case is Altered* (Halliw.), Utterly cast away upon a noddy, a ninny-hammer, a tame-goose. *a* 1700 B. E. *Dict. Canting Crew*, *Tame-fellow*, tractable, easy, manageable. [1878 MRS. H. WOOD *Pomeroy Abb.* I. 255 Here has he been in the house continually like a tame cat.] 1885 *World* 9 Sept. 9 It sheds the gentle glamour of romance over the tame cat himself and the household where he is always welcome. 1900 *Daily News* 16 Jan. 3/2 He is the tamest of tame cats amongst local officials.

†**c.** *poet.* applied to a thing with which one is familiar. *Obs.*

1606 SHAKS. *Tr. & Cr.* III. iii. 10 All That time, acquaintance, custome and condition, Made tame, and most familiar to my nature.

**4.** Subdued as by taming; submissive; meek; poor-spirited, pusillanimous; servile.

1563 B. GOOGE *Eglogs*, etc. (Arb.) 87 The countnaunce sad The drowping Courage tame. 1654 WARREN *Unbelievers* 235 They are a company of tame Souldiers. 1715 POPE *Iliad* I. 168 Shall I my prize resign With tame content, and thou possess'd of thine? 1761–2 HUME *Hist. Eng.* (1806) V. lxx. 269 They should expose themselves..to public contempt, on account of their tame behaviour. 1769 *Junius Lett.* xi. (1820) 47 Never hope that the freeholders will make a tame surrender of their rights. 1849 MACAULAY *Hist. Eng.* ix. II. 422 The tribunal lately so insolent, became on a sudden strangely tame.

**5.** Lacking animation, force, or effectiveness; deficient in striking features; weak, spiritless, insipid, dull.

1602 SHAKS. *Ham.* III. ii. 18 Be not too tame neyther: but let your owne Discretion be your Tutor: suit the action to the word. 1651 JER. TAYLOR *Serm. for Year* I. v. 63 He that is cold and tame in his prayers, hath not tasted of the deliciousness of Religion, and the goodness of God. 1766 GOLDSM. *Vic. W.* xv, The tame correct paintings of the Flemish school. 1850 ROBERTSON *Serm.* Ser. I. xvi. (1866) 266 These words fall short: they are too tame and cool. 1860 TYNDALL *Glac.* I. xxvii. 217 My delight..was tame compared with that of my companions. 1894 PARRY *Stud. Gt. Composers, Schubert* 232 The tamer style of his instrumental works was probably owing to the same causes which made his song-writing so very remarkable.

**b.** Of scenery: Wanting boldness; having no striking features.

1807 SIR R. C. HOARE *Tour Irel.* 186 On descending..the scenery..becomes tamer. 1894 MRS. H. WARD *Marcella* I. 16 A broad expanse of tame arable country.

**6.** *Comb.*, as *tame-spirited*, *-witted*, etc.

1596 NASHE *Saffron-Walden* Wks. (Grosart) III. 72 Poore tame-witted silly Quirko. *Mod.* One could not expect the nation to be so tame-spirited.

**Tame** (tēⁱm), *v.*[1] [ME. *tamen*, f. TAME *a.*,

taking in the 14th c. the place of the earlier TEME:—OE. *tęmian*, f. *tam* adj.]

**1.** *trans.* To bring (a wild animal) under the control or into the service of man; to reclaim from the wild state, to domesticate. Also *fig.*

c1315 SHOREHAM *Poems* vi. 65 Þat vnicorn þat was so wyld..Þou hast y-tamed [hyt], and i-styld. 1390 GOWER *Conf.* II. 161 Hou men hem scholde ryde and tame. c1440 *Promp. Parv.* 486/2 Tamyn, or make tame, *domo.* 1593 SHAKS. *Lucr.* 956 To tame the vnicorne, and Lion wild. 1710 STEELE *Tatler* No. 222 ¶ 3 As People tame Hawks and Eagles, by keeping them awake. 1863 LYELL *Antiq. Man* 24 At a later period..the lake-dwellers succeeded in taming that formidable brute the *Bos primigenius*, the Urus of Cæsar. 1877 E. R. CONDER *Bas. Faith* i. 23 Or tames the lightning to be his newsmonger and his lamplighter.

†**b.** To bring (a wild plant) under or into cultivation; to reclaim or improve (land) by cultivation.

1601 DOLMAN *La Primaud. Fr. Acad.* (1618) III. 795 Many great personages..haue taken paines to tame them, and cause them to grow in gardens. 1697 DRYDEN *Virg. Georg.* I. 144 For he with frequent Exercise Commands Th' unwilling Soil, and tames the stubborn Lands. a1722 LISLE *Husb.* (1757) 100 (E.D.D.) By that time the ground will be tamed. 1746 W. DUNKIN in Francis *Horace, Ep.* II. ii. 280 Another shall..tame the savage Soil.

**2.** To overcome the wildness or fierceness of (a man, animal, or thing); to subdue, subjugate, curb; to render gentle, tractable, or docile.

1382 WYCLIF *Dan.* ii. 40 Hou yrun brekith to gydre alle thingus, and dauntith [*gloss* or tamith]. c1400 *Destr. Troy* 2194 Soche tyrandes to tame, þat vs tene wirkes. 1526 TINDALE 1 *Cor.* ix. 27 But I tame my body and brynge hym into subjeccion. a1548 HALL *Chron., Hen. IV* 23 The prince..had tamed & brideled the furious rage of the wild and sauage Welshemen. 1667 MILTON *P. L.* XII. 191 This River-dragon tam'd at length submits To let his sojourners depart. 1748 GRAY *Alliance* 43 Industry and gain..Command the Winds, and tame th' unwilling Deep. 1783 CRABBE *Village* II. 165 To tame the fierce grief and stem the rising sigh. 1838 DICKENS *Nich. Nick.* ix, She hoped she had tamed a high spirit or two in her day. 1852 MRS. STOWE *Uncle Tom's C.* xix, I took him in hand, and in one fortnight I had him tamed down as submissive and tractable as heart could desire. 1859 *Art Taming Horses*, etc. i. 20 Mr. Rarey had tamed Cruiser, the most vicious stallion in England. 1863 [see sense 1].

**b.** *intr.* To become tame; to grow gentle, submissive, or sedate. Also with *down.*

1646 SHIRLEY *Narcissus* lxxiii, All wilde shall tame before thee as thou go'st. 1655 H. VAUGHAN *Silex Scint.* I. *Disorder & Frailty* iii, My weak fire..after all my height of flames, In sickly expirations tames. 1853 MISS YONGE *Heir of Redclyffe* xii, She had..tamed down into what gave the promise of a sensible woman.

**3.** *trans.* To reduce the intensity of; to tone *down*; to temper, soften, mellow; also, to render dull or uninteresting.

?a1500 *Chester Pl.* vii. 78 Hemlockes, and herif..With Tarboyst most bene all tamed. 1697 DRYDEN *Virg. Georg.* III. 836 Nor cou'd Vulcanian Flame The Stench abolish, or the Savour tame. 1700 — *Baucis & Philemon* 69 This in the pot he plung'd without delay To tame the flesh, and drain the salt away. 1847 H. ROGERS *Ess.* I. v. 221 The first editors had tamed down some of the more startling statements of Pascal. 1871 PALGRAVE *Lyr. Poems, Brecon Bridge*, Manhood's colours tamed to gray.

**4.** Combs. (sb. or adj.) of the verb-stem with a sb. (as obj.), as **tame-grief**, *sb.* that which subdues grief, or *adj.* that subdues grief; **tame-horse** = tamer of horses (tr. Gr. ἱππόδαμος); **tame-poison**, a name of *Vincetoxicum officinale* (also called *Asclepias* or *Cynanchum Vincetoxicum*), the root of which was used as an antidote to poisons.

1605 SYLVESTER *Du Bartas* II. iii. I. *Vocation* 151 Soule's remedy! O contrite heart's restorer! Tears-wiping tame-griefe! c1611 CHAPMAN *Iliad* II. 16 Sleepes the wise Atreus-tame-horse sonne? 1785 MARTYN *Rousseau's Bot.* xvi. (1794) 216 Common Swallow-wort or Tame poison. 1866 *Treas. Bot.* 1217 The root..was formerly in some repute as a medicine;..as an antidote to poisons—whence it has been named Contrayerva Germanorum and Tame-poison.

Hence **Tamed**, **Ta·ming** *ppl. adjs.*

1552 HULOET, Tamed, *domesticus*, .. *domitus*. 1582 STANYHURST *Æneis* II. (Arb.) 55 Tamde men haue one saulfty. 1697 DRYDEN *Virg. Georg.* III. 227 Let 'em run at large; and never know The taming Yoak. 1836 J. H. NEWMAN in *Lyra Apost.* (1849) 217 Time hath a taming hand! 1894 A. WHYTE *S. Rutherford* xi. 87 Tamed and softened..by that taming and softening book.

**Tame** (tēɪm), *v.*$^2$ Now *dial.* Also 6 tayme. [Aphetic f. ATTAME, ENTAME *v.*]

**1.** *trans.* To pierce, cut into (in fighting or carving); to cut or break into, so as to use.

c1400 *Laud Troy Bk.* 7405 Her woundes bledde, her flesch was tamet, The holest of hem ful sore was lamet. 1470–85 MALORY *Arthur* II. xviii. 97 Balan..smote hym thorow the shelde and tamyd his helme. 1513 *Bk. Kervynge* in *Babees Bk.* (1868) 265 Tayme that crabbe. 1642 FULLER *Holy & Prof. St.* II. xviii. 118 Then he tameth his stacks of corn, which..providence hath reserv'd for time of need. 1840 H. AINSWORTH *Tower Lond.* xxxix, In the old terms of his art, he leached the brawn,..tranched the sturgeon,..tamed the crab, and barbed the lobster. 1847–78 HALLIWELL, *Tame*, to cut; to divide. *West.* 1904 in *Eng. Dial. Dict.* s. v., *S. Dev.* We shall have to tame the rick.

†**b.** To broach (a cask, bottle, etc.); also with the liquor as obj. *Obs.*

?a1412 LYDG. *Two Merchants* 701 Who that wil entren to tamen of the sweete, He mvst as weel..To taste the bittir. c1440 *Promp. Parv.* 486/2 Tame, or attame vessellys wythe drynke .., *attamino.* 1483 *Vulgaria abs Terentio* 15 b, I haue tamed or set a broche all my pypys or tunnys. 1681 W. ROBERTSON *Phraseol. Gen.* (1693) 1205 To tame a vessel, i. e. to tap or broach it.

†**2.** *fig.* To enter upon, broach (a subject); to take upon oneself; to begin upon; begin *to do* something. *Obs.*

c1386 CHAUCER *Nun's Pr. Prol.* 52 (Harl. MS.) And right anoon he haþ his tale tamyd [*v.r.* attamed]. c1407 LYDG. *Reson & Sens.* 5636 He wolde ha tamyd Tan [= t'han, *i.e.* to have] touched yonge Rosis new.

†**3.** To injure, hurt. *Obs.*

c1430 *Hymns Virg.* (1867) 55 Þouȝ ȝe drinke poisoun, it schal not ȝou tame. c1480 *Life St. Kath.* (MS. Cott. Titus A xxvi) 180 Neyþer clothys ne theyr here was tamyd with þe fire.

**Tameable, tamable** (tēɪ·măb'l), *a.* [f. TAME *v.*$^1$ + -ABLE.] Capable of being tamed.

1552 HULOET, Tameable, *domitalis, e.* 1576 FLEMING *Caius' Dogs* Preamble, In the second Order of milde and tamable beasts. 1648 WILKINS *Math. Magick* II. *Dædalus* vii. (1707) 118 Great Fowl, of a strong lasting Flight, and easily tameable. *Mod.* Tameable if taken young.

Hence **Ta·meableness, Tameabi·lity** (tama-), the quality of being tameable.

1821 SYD. SMITH in Lady Holland *Mem.* (1855) II. 213 The kingdom is in the hands of an oligarchy, who..are too cunning, and too well aware of the tameability of mankind to give it up. 1828 WEBSTER, Tamableness. 1898 E. P. EVANS *Evol. Ethics* vi. 218 The tamability of an animal is simply its capability of adapting itself to new relations in life.

†**Ta·mehed.** *Obs. rare*$^{-1}$. [f. TAME *a.* + -HEAD.] Tameness, domesticity, docility.

c1250 *Gen. & Ex.* 1485 Ðe fader luuede esau wel,..ðe moder, iacob for tamehed.

**Tameless** (tēɪ·mlės), *a.* [f. TAME *v.*$^1$ + -LESS.] That has never been tamed; that cannot be tamed; untamed, untameable.

1597–8 BP. HALL *Sat.* II. i. 49 The tame-lesse steed could well his wagon wield, Through downes and dales of the vneuen field. a1604 HANMER *Chron. Irel.* (1809) 369 The bones of him they Noble Meler call, Who was the tamelesse tamer of the Irish nation all. 1801 SOUTHEY *Thalaba* v. vii, And Tigris bore upon his tameless stream Armenian harvests to her multitudes. 1890 'R. BOLDREWOOD' *Col. Reformer* (1891) 129 A playful touch with the spurs .. caused that tameless steed to jump on one side.

Hence **Ta·melessness.**

1815 BYRON *Parisina* xiii, From thee—this tamelessness of heart. 1883 JEFFERIES *Story of my Heart* i. 9 The age, tamelessness, and ceaseless motion of the ocean.

**Tamely** (tēɪ·mli), *adv.* [f. TAME *a.* + -LY $^2$.] In a tame manner, in any of the senses of TAME *a.*; e. g. like a tame animal; submissively, tractably, quietly, passively; without resistance; without spirit or animation; without bold features.

1597 SHAKS. 2 *Hen. IV*, IV. ii. 42 True Obedience..[may] Stoope tamely to the foot of Maiestie. a1631 DONNE *Annuntiation & Passion* 1 Tamely fraile flesh, abstaine to day; to day My soule eates twice. 1651 JER. TAYLOR *Serm. for Year* I. v. 63 Our prayers upbraid our spirits when we beg coldly and tamely for those things for which we ought to dye. 1770 *Junius Lett.* xxxvi. (1820) 172 The English people will not tamely submit to this unworthy treatment. 1839 DARWIN *Voy. Nat.* i. (1879) 2 A kingfisher, which tamely sits on the branches of the Castor-oil plant. 1869 PHILLIPS *Vesuv.* vii. 172 Slopes not tamely identical but harmoniously diverse. 1885 *Manch. Exam.* 28 Jan. 3/4 An example rather of tamely edifying expatiation than of penetrative or stimulating thought.

**Tamendoa**: see TAMANDUA.

**Tameness** (tēɪ·mnės). [f. TAME *a.* + -NESS.] The quality or condition of being tame, in any sense; e. g. domesticated condition, absence of wildness; lack of spirit or courage; absence of animation or variety; commonplace quality.

1530 PALSGR. 279/1 Tamenesse, *priueur.* 1585 T. WASHINGTON tr. *Nicholay's Voy.* II. viii. 41 b, These Partriges.. become wild, forgetting their tamenes. a1633 AUSTIN *Medit.* (1635) 152 So that they lose not their fervour in Tamenesse, nor in preposterous zeale forget their Gentlenesse. 1655 *Nicholas Papers* (Camden) II. 177 Iff our dull countrymen will not fly to theire swords, they will suffer the deserved punishment of theire tameness. 1759 JOHNSON *Idler* No. 47 ¶ 12 He laughs at the letters..for their tameness of expression. 1774 GOLDSM. *Nat. Hist.* (1776) II. 310 The difference between animals in a state of nature and domestic tameness is so considerable, that [etc.]. 1781 COWPER *Alex. Selkirk* ii, They are so unacquainted with man, Their tameness is shocking to me. 1851 *Beck's Florist* 195 The monotony and tameness of a villa-garden. 1855 MACAULAY *Hist. Eng.* xix. IV. 370 This tameness was merely the tameness with which a tiger, caught, caged, and starved, submits to the keeper who brings him food.

**Tamer** (tēɪ·məɹ). [f. TAME *v.*$^1$ + -ER $^1$.] One who or that which tames.

1530 PALSGR. 279/1 Tamar of a horse, *courtier de chevaulx.* 1610 HEALEY *St. Aug. Citie of God* 139 Scipio..the tamer of Carthage. 1742 GRAY *Adversity* 2 Thou tamer of the human breast. 1859 *Art Taming Horses*, etc. vi. 77 The moment the horse moves the tamer draws the strap tight round the body of the horse.

**Tamera, Tamerick**, obs. ff. TAMBOURA, TAMARISK.

**Ta·merla·ne, Ta·mburlai·ne.** European corruptions of *Timur lenk* = lame Timur, appellation of Timur, the great Tartar conqueror 1335–1405, the title-character of Marlowe's tragedy *Tamburlaine* 1586, and of Rowe's *Tamerlane* 1702. Used allusively for a person like Timur, a conqueror, a scourge, a despot. Also *attrib.* and *comb.*, as *Tamerlane-like* adj. or adv. Hence **Ta·merlanism** *nonce-wd.*

a1579 T. HACKET tr. *Amadis of Fr.* XII. 306 (Stanf.) A number of Califes, Souldans, Tamberlanes. 1593 G. HARVEY *New Letter* Wks. (Grosart) I. 297 The graund Dissease ..smiling at his tamberlaine contempt, Sternely struckhome the peremptory stroke. 1596 NASHE *Saffron-Walden* Wks. S iv b, Tamburlain-like, hee braues it indefinently in her behalfe. 1598 E. GILPIN *Skial.* (1878) 32 It is the scourge, the Tamberlaine of vice, The three square Tyborne of impieties. c1618 MORYSON *Itin.* IV. (1903) 322 The German language..sounding better in the mouth of Tamberlin, than of a Civill man. 1632 MASSINGER *Maid of Hon.* II. ii, *Page*...I'll make Thy back my footstool. *Sylli.* Tamberlane in little! 1843 CARLYLE *Misc.* (1872) VII. 30 Out of it had come Napoleonisms, Tamerlanisms.

**Tamil, Tamul** (tæ·mĭl, -əl). Also 8 Tamoul. [ad. *Tamiṛ, Tamiḻ*, native name (known in 8th c.) of the people and language; in Pāli and Prākrit *Damiḷa, Daviḷa, Daviḍa*, Sinhalese *Demaḷa*, Skr. *Dramiḷa, Dramiḍa, Draviḍa* (whence Dr. Caldwell's term *Dravidian* for the Tamulic or Tamil family of languages). So Pg., Du., Ger. *Tamul*, F. *Tamoul.*]

One of a non-Aryan race of people belonging to the Dravidian stock, inhabiting the south-east of India and part of Ceylon. **b.** The language spoken by this people, the leading member of the Dravidian family. Also *attrib.* or as *adj.*

[1579 (*title*) Doctrina Christam .. feita em Portugal .. Tresladada em lingua Malavar ou Tamul. [Cochin].] 1734 (*title*) A Grammar of the Damul or Tamul Language. [Tranquebar.] 1778 (*title*) A Grammar for learning the Principles of the Malabar Language, properly called Tamul or the Tamulian Language. (Wepery.) 1788 *Encycl. Brit.* (ed. 3) I. 494/1 s. v. *Alphabet*, From this Shanscrit are derived the sacred characters of Thibet, the Cashmirian, Bengalese, Malabaric, and Tamoul. 1807 F. BUCHANAN *Jrnl. fr. Madras* II. 441 In the Tamul language it is called *Shuri cull*, or itch-stone. 1811 T. S. MOODELLIAR (*title*) A Tamil Expositor. [Madras.] 1842 W. C. TAYLOR *Anc. Hist.* xviii. (ed. 3) 575 By the persecution of the Buddhists..a great portion of the literature of India has been lost, and in particular,..all the ancient literature of the people that speak the Tamul language. 1864 M. C. SWAMY in *Reader* 12 Mar. 336/2 The Tamils [of Ceylon belong]..to the Dravidian race...Their religion is Sivaism, and their language the Tamil. 1902 *Daily Chron.* 30 Aug. 8/1 To expel from the British Empire the Tamil-speaking tribes who presume to influence its policy.

Hence **Tami·lian** (**Tamu·lian**) *a.*, Tamulic; *sb.* a member of the Tamil people; **Tamu·lic** *a.*, pertaining to the Tamils or their language, Tamil.

1764 *Ann. Reg.* 114 Dr. Francke, in Germany had sent them a number of Tamulian types..the government having erected a printing-office in the city of Madrass. 1863 LEPSIUS *Standard Alph.* 226 The four letters..which the Tamulians have added to the Sanscrit alphabet. 1800 *Misc. Tracts* in *Asiatic Ann. Reg.* 81/1 The Tamulic termination *en*..creates a striking resemblance between Pooden and the Wooden of the Goths. 1872 MORRIS *Eng. Accidence* i. 12 The Dravidian or Tamulic [groups], including Tamul, Telegu, Malabar, Canaries.

†**Tamin.** *Obs.* Also 7–8 -ine. [app. aphetic deriv. of F. *étamine* (in OF. *estamine*) STAMIN.] A thin woollen stuff: = STAMIN. Also *attrib.*

1552 in J. C. Jeaffreson *Middlesex County Rec.* (1886) I. 8 Unum par manicarum de serico vocato tamin [*pr.* tawin] damaske ad valenciam v.s. 1611 COTGR., *Estamine*, the stuffe Tamine; also, a strayner, searce, boulter, or boulting cloth. 1625 MASSINGER *New Way* III. ii, I took her up in an old tamin gown. 1653 URQUHART *Rabelais* I. lvi, Their stockins were of tamine [F. *estamet*] or of cloth-serge. 1714 *Fr. Bk. of Rates* 366 Cloth-Rash and Tamine common. [1822 NARES, *Tamine*, a sort of woollen cloth; probably the same that is now called *tammy*.]

¶ **b.** A strainer or bolter, of this stuff; = TAMIS 1.

1847 in WEBSTER. Hence in later dicts.; perh. never in use.

**Taming** (tēɪ·miŋ), *vbl. sb.* [f. TAME *v.*$^1$ + -ING $^1$.] The action of TAME *v.*$^1$ Also *attrib.* **Ta·ming-stick**, a kind of yoke for newly captured slaves.

c1440 *Promp. Parv.* 486/2 Tamynge fro wyyldenesse, *domesticacio.* a1533 FRITH *Disput. Purgat.* (1829) 137 What thou shalt do to the profit of thy neighbour, and taming of thy flesh. 1596 SHAKS. *Tam. Shr.* IV. ii. 54 Faith he is gone vnto the taming schoole..and Petruchio is the master. 1866 LIVINGSTONE *Last Jrnls.* (1873) I. iv. 107 Nearly all were in the taming-stick.

†**Taminy.** *Obs.* Prob. a misprint or misreading of TAMIN or TAMMY *sb.*$^1$

1737 *Ochtertyre House Bks.* (1907) 77 For six yeards of yellow taminy £0. 6. 0. 1755 JOHNSON, *Taminy*, a woollen stuff. Hence in ASH, and recent Dicts.

†**Ta·mis.** *Obs.* Also 7 tamise, 9 tammis: see also TAMMY *sb.*$^2$ [a. F. *tamis* (tàmi) a sieve (of wire, silk, hair, etc.) (12th c. in Littré) = Pr. *tamis*, Sp. *tamiz*, It. *tamigio*, Ven. *tamiso*, med.L. *tamisium* (Du Cange), identical in origin with WGer. *tamisjo-, the source of OE. and MLG. *tęmes* sieve, MDu. *tęmse*, OHG. *zemisa*: see TEMSE.]

**1.** A sieve; a strainer or bolting-cloth; also *tamis-bolter, -cloth.*

1601 HOLLAND *Pliny* XVIII. xi. I. 567 The best bread is of the finest wheat floure, which hath passed through a small tamis bulter. *Ibid.* XXII. xxv. II. 142 If they be halfe sodden in water..then let passe through a tamise, that the brans might be separate. 1698 M. LISTER *Journ. to Paris* (1699) 141 This Stone is beat to Powder, and sifted through a fine

Tamis. **1801** MOLLARD *Art of Cookery* (1836) 169 Rub them through a tamis cloth or sieve. **1817** W. KITCHINER *Cook's Oracle* (1818) 244 Strain it through a tammis into a clean stewpan. *Ibid.* 280 *note*, A *Tammis* is a worsted cloth, .. made on purpose for straining sauces. [Cf. p. 230, a tammy, or fine sieve.]

**2.** A name for an anther. (? from its scattering pollen.)

**1665** REA *Flora* I. ix. 51 Six chives [in the tulip], tipt with pendents (which are those after the French we call Tamis). **1688** R. HOLME *Armoury* II. 65/1 The Agot Tulip is of a sad Isabella colour, with..a dark bottom, and large black Tamis. **1725** *Bradley's Fam. Dict.* s.v. *Tulip*, The bottom and Tamis blue. **1775** ASH, *Tamis* [erroneously explained].

**3.** *attrib.*, as *tamis-bolter*, *-cloth* (see 1); **tamis-bird**, the Guinea-fowl (? from its speckled or powdered appearance).

**1774** GOLDSM. *Nat. Hist.* (1862) II. III. vi. 75 They [Guinea-hens] are by some called the Barbary-hen: by others the Tamis bird.

**Tamisage** (tæ·misėdʒ). *Math.* [ad. F. *tamisage* sifting: see TAMIS and -AGE.] Applied by Sylvester to a method of finding invariants.

**1882** CAYLEY *Math. Papers* XI. 409 *heading*, Note on an exceptional case in which the Fundamental Postulate of Professor Sylvester's theory of Tamisage fails.

**Tamkin**, obs. var. TAMPION, plug.

**Tammany** (tæ·măni). The name of the central organization of the Democratic party in the City (formerly also in the State) of New York, located in *Tammany Hall*, in 14th Street, New York. In English use the name has become esp. associated with the political and municipal corruption which at various times has characterized the government of New York.

*Tamanen*, *Tamene*, *Taminent*, *Taminy* was the name of an Indian chief with whom W. Penn had transactions for land 1683 and 1697. Some time prior to 1771 the name became 'canonized', and from 1772 for about twenty years 'Saint' (or 'King') *Tamina*, *Tamany*, *Tammany* (generally identified with the chief of Penn's time) was regarded as the tutelar saint of Pennsylvania and other northern colonies or States, and the day assigned to him, May 1st (Old Style), May 12th (New Style), appropriated to popular celebrations, festive gatherings (often with some benevolent object), etc. From 1782 the name became associated with Societies established on a more or less permanent basis, of which that organized in New York is mentioned in 1787. The one which in 1790 is recorded as the 'Society of St. Tammany' and 'the Sons of St. Tammany and Columbian Order', and which in its constitution is claimed to be 'founded on the true principles of patriotism, and has for its motives charity and brotherly love', soon developed strong political activity, and by *c* 1810 had become the head-quarters of the Democratic Party (then called the Republican Party) in the State and City of New York. (From notes supplied by Mr. A. Matthews, Boston, Mass.)

**1683** in *Pennsylv. Archives* (1852) I. 62, I, Tamanen..for me and my heirs and assignes doe graunt and dispose of all my Lands Lying betwixt [etc.]. **1683** PENN *Wks.* (1782) IV. 305. **1771** W. EDDIS *Lett. fr. Amer.* (1792) 115 The Americans on this part of the continent have..a Saint.. The first of May is..set apart to the memory of Saint Tamina. **1772** *Pennsylv. Chron.* 4 May VI. 63/2 On Friday..a number of American Gentlemen, Sons of King Tammany, met at the House of Mr. Bryn, to celebrate the Memory of that truly noble Chieftain... It is hoped..a Society may be formed of great Utility to the Distressed; as this meeting was more for the purpose of promoting Charity and Benevolence, than Mirth and Festivity. *Ibid.* 15 June VI. 85/1 The Sons of St. George, St. Patrick, St. Andrew, St. David, and King (or Saint) Tamany. **1773** in *Pennsylv. Mag. Hist. & Biogr.* (1902) XXV. 446 The natives..have adopted a great warrior sachem and chief named Tammany..to be the tutelar Saint of this Province [Pennsylvania]. **1779** *New Jersey Jrnl.* 4 May in *N. J. Archives* Ser. II. III. 310 Saturday last being the anniversary of St. Tamany, the titular St. of America. **1785** WASHINGTON *Diary* 2 May in *Pennsylv. Mag.* (1893) XVIII. 412 Accepted an invitation to dine with the Sons of Saint Taminy [at Richmond, Virginia]. **1787** *New York Jrnl.* 3 May 3/1 Tuesday last, being St. Tammany's Day (the Tutelar Saint of America) the St. Tammany Society of this City held their Anniversary Meeting, at the Wigwam at Halls. **1790** *Ibid.* 11 May 3/3 To-morrow..the annual feast of St. Tammany will be celebrated by the Sons of St. Tammany and Columbian Order, at their wigwam on the banks of the Hudson. **1805** (*title*) An Act to incorporate the Society of Tammany, or Columbian Order, in the City of New York. Passed April 9, 1805. **1838** W. IRVING in *Life & Lett.* (1866) III. 126 Yesterday I had a full deputation from Tammany Hall..informing me that I had been .nominated as Mayor. **1850** WHITTIER *W. Leggett* Pr. Wks. 1889 II. 200 The democratic committee issued its bull against him from Tammany Hall.

**b.** *attrib.* and *Comb.*, as *Tammany-organization*, *-ring*, *-tariff*, *-ticket*; *Tammany-ridden* adj.

**1871** *Harper's Weekly* 11 Nov. XV. 1056 The Tammany Tiger Loose.—What are you going to do about it? **1872** O. W. HOLMES *Poet Breakf.-t.* vi. (1885) 155 The Tammany Ring..is to take the place of the feudal lord. **1872** RUSKIN *Fors Clav.* II. xiv. 10 A complete Tammany Ring and lowest circle in the Inferno of the Worst. **1887** J. CHAMBERLAIN in *Times* (weekly ed.) 14 Oct. 3/1, I cannot accept as desirable..the degradation of the great city of Belfast and the province of Ulster to a Tammany ring in Dublin. **1894** *Daily News* 5 July 5/6 'The Tammany Tariff'..appears to refer to the rates at which certain abuses and violations of the law have in that city been able to enjoy a practical immunity. **1899** *Ibid.* 29 May 6/7 Even Tammany-ridden New York has made up its mind to construct a new underground system. **1901** *Scotsman* 7 Nov. 4/2 His opponent..was backed by the immensely powerful Tammany organisation.

Hence (chiefly *nonce-wds.*) **Tamma·nial** *a.*, of or belonging to (St.) Tammany; **Ta·mmanify, Ta·mmanize, Ta·mmany** *vbs.*, *trans.* to influence or dominate by, or as by, Tammany; whence **Ta·mmanied** *ppl.a.*, **Ta·mmanifica·tion, Tammaniza·tion**; also **Ta·mmanyism**, the system or principles of Tammany; **Ta·mmanyite**, one who adopts the methods and principles of Tammany, an adherent of Tammany.

**1791** J. PINTARD in *Amer. Daily Reg.* (N. Y.) 16 May, Before them was borne the cap of Liberty; after following seven hunters in Tammanial dress, then the great standard of the society. **1793** (May 15) in G. Meyers *Hist. Tammany Hall* (1901) 10 At Tammanial Hall in Broad street. **1882** *Tribune* (N. Y.) 5 Apr., A resolution striking the names of the Tammanyites from the caucus roll. **1893** in *Westm. Gaz.* 1 Nov. 3/1 For a section of the Press to Tammany London in the interests of the contractors and themselves. **1898** *Daily News* 28 Mar. 7/2 The charge brought against the Progressives of Tammanyfying London. **1899** *Westm. Gaz.* 14 Feb. 2/3 From all accounts Tammanied New York is anything but an ideal place in which to live. **1903** *Daily Rec. & Mail* 11 Nov. 4/3 A charge of paving the way for Tammanyism. **1909** *Sat. Rev.* 24 Apr. 518/1 To prevent the Tammanisation of London.

† **Ta·mmel.** *Obs. rare.* App. an alteration of STAMMEL, on analogy of *tamin* for *stamin*.

**1616** *Trial C'tess Somerset* in *Relat. Poysoning Sir T. Overbury* (1651) 106 The Prisoner..being attired in black Tammel, a Cyprus Caperoon, a Cobweb Lawn Ruff and Cuffs. **1668** *Flemings in Oxford* 9 Apr. (O. H. S.) I. 437 Paid unto Dr Smith which my Lady had disbursed for Tammell for my wife 01 05 00.

**Tammie** (tà·mi). *Sc.* [Sc. f. TOMMY.]

**1.** Name of a loaf of home-baked bread, used in Edinburgh and the surrounding district.

**1828** MOIR *Mansie Wauch* xviii, Their usual rations of beef and tammies. **1890** *Anent Old Edinburgh* 83 The pay was [1807] 6*d.* a day and a coarse roll called a 'tammie'.

**2. Tammie-norie.** A local name in Scotland for the Puffin, *Fratercula arctica*; also *Tommy Noddy*.

**1701** J. BRAND *Descr. Zetl.* viii. (1703) 119 Each kind or sort do Nestle by themselves; as the Scarfs by themselves, so the Cetywaicks, Tominories, Mawes, etc. **1816** SCOTT *Antiq.* vii, 'Did I not hear a halloo?' 'The skreigh of a Tammie Norie', answered Ochiltree, 'I ken the skirl weel'. **1841** R. CHAMBERS *Pop. Rhymes Scotl.* (1870) 190 The Puffin. Tammie Norie o' the Bass Canna kiss a bonny lass. **1896** NEWTON *Dict. Birds* 943 *Tammy-Norie*, a northern form of Tom-Noddy, and a name for the Puffin.

**Tammy** (tæ·mi), *sb.*[1] Also 7 **tammey**, 8 **tamy**. [Appears to be identical with obs. F. *tamise* 'étoffe de laine lustrée' cited by Littré from a letter patent of 22 July, 1780 (cf. *cerise*, *cherry*); but this may have been an adaptation of the Eng. word, which was in use a century earlier. It has also been suggested to be a corruption of TAMIN, or a deriv. of F. *estame* worsted, *estamet* cloth-rash (Cotgr.).] A fine worsted cloth of good quality, often with a glazed finish.

Much mentioned in 17th and 18th centuries, but app. obs. before 1858. The name has been recently revived as a trade-term: see quot. 1876.

**1665** in Strype *Stow's Surv.* (1754) II. v. xviii. 380/2 All other Kersies, Bayes, Tammies, Sayes, Rashes [etc.]. **1675** OGILBY *Brit.* 146 Stow market... Its chiefest Trade is making of Tammeys, and the Town affords several good Inns for Entertainment. **1706** PHILLIPS (ed. Kersey), *Tamy*, a kind of Stuff. **1730** BAILEY (folio), *Tammy*, a Sort of Worsted-Stuff, which lies cockled. **1757** DYER *Fleece* III. 481 Cheyney, and bayse, and serge, and alepine, Tammy, and crape, and the long countless list Of woollen webbs. **1758** *Chron.* in *Ann. Reg.* I. 119/1 Her riding dress a light drab, lined with blue tammy. **1770** *Gentl. Mag.* XL. 221 An account of a new loom, for weaving tamies, serges, stuffs and worsted cloaths. **1797** *Monthly Mag.* III. 34 Bradford is a manufacturing town for tammies, and other worsted stuffs. **1812** J. BIGLAND *Beauties Eng. & Wales* XVI. 805. **1858** SIMMONDS *Dict. Trade*, *Tammies*, a commercial name formerly given to Scotch camlets; a worsted fabric resembling bunting, but closer and finer. **1876** T. C. ARCHER *Wool & Applications* 46 Tammies are now made of wool with cotton warp. They are highly glazed and dyed in bright colours, and are still favourite fabrics.

**b.** *attrib.*, as *tammy gown*, *lining*, *warp*.

**1666** WOOD *Life* June (O. H. S.) II. 80, I bought of Mr. Fifield an English Tammy gowne which cost me, out of the shop, 2*li.* 4*s.* I had 18 yards and an half, at 2*s.* (a) yard. **1678** *Lond. Gaz.* No. 1329/4 A brown cloth wastecoat, a red tammy petticoat. **1719** J. ROBERTS *Spinster* 346 Many woollen stuffs..are quite lost,..such as..worsted tammy draughts. **1835** URE *Philos. Manuf.* 159 The hardest twisted worsted is called tammy warp. **1883** R. HALDANE *Workshop Receipts* Ser. II. 147/1 Tammy lining may also be cleaned with camphine.

**Ta·mmy**, *sb.*[2] [app. a. F. *tamis* (tàmi) TAMIS, assimilated to prec., perh. with the notion that it was made of that material.] A strainer.

**1769** J. SKEAT *Art Cookery* 27 Then strain or rub them through a tammy into another clean stewpan. **1796** MRS. GLASSE *Cookery* v. 44 Strain it off through a tammy. **1883** 'ANNIE THOMAS' *Mod. Housew.* 49 These vegetables can.. be boiled to pulp and passed through a tammy.

*attrib.* **1839** URE *Dict. Arts* 106 It must be equalised still more by passing through a tammy cloth, or a sieve.

Hence **Ta·mmy** *v.*, *trans.* to strain through a tammy.

**1903** *Daily Chron.* 14 Mar. 8/5 Then tammy or rub through a fine sieve with a wooden spoon.

**Tammy** (tæ·mi), *sb.*[3] Short for *Tammy Shanter*, corruption of next.

**1894** MRS. L. B. WALFORD *Matchmaker* xliv, The letter was found inside the inner brim of his 'Tammy'. **1896** *Westm. Gaz.* 26 Sept. 7/2 The Burns Statue... The poet stands in an easy attitude... He wears the 'tammy', the ploughman's coat and breeches, and the rough Scotch stockings.

**Tam o' Shanter** (tæmǒʃæ·ntəɹ). [f. the name of the hero of Burns's poem of that name (i.e. *Tom of Shanter*).] In full, *Tam o' Shanter bonnet*, *cap*: A soft woollen bonnet with flat circular crown, the circumference of which is about twice that of the head, formerly worn by Scottish ploughmen, etc.; introduced, in a modified form, *c* 1887 as a head-dress for girls and young women. Abbreviated TAM, TAMMY.

**1840-50** [Remembered in use]. **1884** *West. Daily Press* 29 May 3/7 The Tam o' Shanter is still occasionally worn [by men]. **1887** *Scott. Leader* 24 Sept. 5 Mr. O'Brien..was wearing an overcoat and a Tam o' Shanter, for the morning air was chilly. *Ibid.* 19 Oct. 4 The head-dress [adopted by Dundee factory girls] is the modest one of either a single or double-peaked cap or a Tam o' Shanter bonnet, and those workers who have adopted this..have been jeered at, and in some cases mobbed, while passing along the street. **1887** J. ASHBY STERRY *Lazy Minstrel* (1892) 26 Or if you think it right or wrong—I'll wear my Tam o' Shanter. **1888** BLACK *Adv. House-Boat* vi, A grey Tam o' Shanter..impervious to the wet. **1895** [see TAM].

Hence **Tam o' Shantered** *a.*, wearing a Tam o' Shanter.

**1894** DU MAURIER *Trilby* I. 81 He married the..tartaned and tam-o'-shantered barmaid at the Montagnards Ecossais.

**Tamp** (tæmp), *v.* [app. a 19th c. workmen's word; perh. a back-formation from *tampin* (var. of TAMPION) taken as = *tamping*.]

**1.** *trans. Mining.* **a.** To stop up (a bore-hole) with clay, sand, etc., rammed in upon the charge before firing the shot; also, to pack up (a gallery of a military mine) before firing it, in order to concentrate the effect. **b.** To ram home (the charge) in a bore-hole. Also *absol.*

**1819** FARADAY in B. Jones *Life* (1870) I. 301 Men..employed in making holes, tamping and blasting the rock. **1834** J. S. MACAULAY *Field Fortif.* 203 Then tamp strongly and carefully the ends of the gallery, leaving the space intended to be demolished void. **1838** *Civil Eng. & Arch. Jrnl.* I. 292/1 The hole is tamped with dry clay to the top. **1843** *Ibid.* VI. 165/1 To form these chambers the rock was perforated.., and the different proportions of powder were introduced..and 'tamped up' close. **1860** RUSSELL *Diary India* I. 199 The mines will soon be tamped, and the whole nest of temples [over the river at Cawnpore] will leap into the air amid fire and thunder. **1899** *Westm. Gaz.* 4 Dec. 2/1 All charges should be 'tamped'—that is, pressed or secured in position with stones or other material wedged around them—wherever possible.

**2.** To stop up with clay or loamy earth the issues of a blast-furnace (Knight *Dict. Mech.* 1877).

**3.** To ram down hard, so as to consolidate (earth, gravel, etc.); to pun; = POUND *v.*[1] 6; also to pack (anything) round with earth so rammed down.

**1879** L. STOCKBRIDGE *Investig. Rainfall* (Boston, U. S.) 5 [The lysimeter] was finished by throwing back and tamping in the earth which had been excavated on three sides. **1890** T. C. CLARKE in *Railways Amer.* 38 The track is raised, the gravel tamped well under the ties, and the track is ready for use. **1909** *Installation News* III. 63 If the conductor is tamped round with granulated carbon.

**4.** *Comb.*, as **tamp-work**, a surface made hard by tamping.

**1855** R. F. BURTON *El-Medinah* I. xiii. 370 He sees a plain like tamp-work, where knobs of granite act daisies.

Hence **Tamped** (tæmpt) *ppl. a.*, made hard and solid by pounding; **Ta·mper**, one who tamps a boring, etc.; also, a tamping-bar.

**1864** WEBSTER, *Tamper*, 1. One who tamps, or prepares for blasting... 2. An instrument used in tamping; a tamping-iron. **1875** R. F. BURTON *Gorilla L.* (1876) II. 204 The flooring is hard, tamped clay. **1878** H. M. STANLEY *Dark Cont.* II. iii. 83 The compact clay and tamped floor.

‖ **Ta·mpan.** Also tanpan. [?Sechuana name.] A South African species of acarus remarkable for the venom of its bite.

**1880** P. GILLMORE *On Duty* 295 Bitten all over by 'tampans', an insect synonymous to the 'jigger' of the West Indies. **1883** J. MACKENZIE *Day-dawn in Dark Places* 157 The mother was annoyed in her house by 'tanpans', insects whose bite is more distressing than that of mosquitoes.

**Tampeon**, obs. form of TAMPION, plug.

**Tamper**, *sb.*: see TAMP *v.*

**Tamper** (tæ·mpəɹ), *v.*[1] Also 4–7 **temper.** [Before 1600 mostly spelt *temper*, and app. originating in TEMPER *v.*, as used in reference to clay. The trans. use *to temper clay* appears to have become absol. *to temper*, and then intr. *to temper in clay*; hence fig. *to temper* or *tamper in* or *with* any business or matter. *Tamper*, which appears in reference to clay in 1573, was prob. a dial. or workmen's pronunciation, which became at length established, so as to differentiate this vb. from TEMPER.

For a development of sense very similar to that shown in *temper* and *tamper*, cf. MEDDLE *v.*]

**I.** †**1. a.** *intr.* To work in clay, etc. so as to mix it thoroughly. **b.** *trans.* To temper (clay). *Obs.*

**1573** TUSSER *Husb.* (1878) 37 A fork and a hooke, to be tampring in claie, A lath hammer, trowel, a hod, or a traie. **1766** *Compl. Farmer* s.v. *Spiky-roller*, Where..the clay grows dry, and will not admit of being duly tampered for use without great pains in breaking it.

**II. 2.** *intr.* To work or busy oneself for some end; to machinate, scheme, plot. Const. *in* some practice, *for* something, *to do* something.

*a.* **1596** DRAYTON *Leg.* iv. 289 Here first to worke my busie brayne was set,..To temper in so dangerous assayes. **1611** SPEED *Hist. Gt. Brit.* VIII. vii. § 17. 404 Howsoeuer Edward and he had tempered for the Kingdome.

*β.* **1613** FLETCHER, etc. *Captain* IV. ii, You have been tampring any time these three days, Thus to disgrace me. *a* **1661** FULLER *Worthies, Yorks.* (1662) II. 191 Tampering too soon and too openly, to derive the Crown in his wives right to himself. **1674** *Essex Papers* (Camden) I. 196 Yt I might discover whether Ormond was tampering, wth ye assistance of Duke, to give Essex his place. **1678** BUTLER *Hud.* III. II. 269 Others tamper'd For Fleetwood, Desborough, and Lambert. **1709** STRYPE *Ann. Ref.* I. xxxii. 328 The provost of Paris, being here in London, was especially tampering in treasonous practices against the Queen. **1736** CHANDLER *Hist. Persec.* 355 He tamper'd..to introduce some ceremonies bordering upon superstition. **1768** H. WALPOLE *Hist. Doubts* 77 The queen dowager tampered in this plot. **1823** SCOTT *Peveril* vii, You shall..[not] tamper..amongst my servants, with impunity.

**3.** *intr.* To try to deal or enter into clandestine dealings *with* (a person), *about* or in order *to* some design; often with the connotation of meddling or interfering improperly with a person.

*a.* **1567** HARMAN *Caveat* 70 For often hee hath bene tempering with me [a woman], and yet haue I sharpely sayde him naye. **1584** R. SCOT *Discov. Witchcr.* II. ii. (1886) 16 If they should first be committed to prison the divell would temper with them and informe them what to doo. **1599** SANDYS *Europæ Spec.* (1632) 108 After that the Pope was once againe admitted, and had libertie to temper with his partie at pleasure. **1603** KNOLLES *Hist. Turks* (1621) 71 Shortly after he began also to temper with Guy, perswading him to resigne unto him that little right.

*β.* **1649** MILTON *Eikon.* iii. 23 Tampering both with the English and the Scotch army to come up against the Parlament. **1683** KENNETT tr. *Erasm. on Folly* 65 Another had been tampering with his neighbours wife. **1741** RICHARDSON *Pamela* (1824) I. 58 When he withdrew, I began to tamper with the farmer and his wife. **1748** — *Clarissa* (1811) III. vii. 60 Joseph,..by tampering with Will, got all my secrets. **1790** BEATSON *Nav. & Mil. Mem.* II. 2 A small squadron.. was detached after them, who found them busy in tampering with the natives. **1840** DICKENS *Barn. Rudge* xxxii, She has been tampered with, and most treacherously deceived. **1852** MISS YONGE *Cameos* II. ii. 17 He was trafficking with her enemies and tampering with her friends. **1870** DISRAELI *Lothair* ix, Their secret organisation is tampering with the people and tampering with the priests.

**4.** *intr.* To have to do or interfere *with* improperly; to meddle *with* (a thing).

*a.* **1601** HOLLAND *Pliny* II. 220 Hee would needs be handling and tempering with the weapons of his said guest.

*β.* **1636** *Divine Tragedie lately Acted* 12 [He] spied a Gun over the chimney..and fell a tampearing with it, and first levelled at the mayds. **1655** FULLER *Ch. Hist.* I. ii. § 11 Humane Policy seldome proves prosperous, when tampering with Divine Worship. **1684** BUNYAN *Pilgr.* II. 85 This Boy has been tampering with something that lies in his Maw undigisted. **1789** W. BUCHAN *Dom. Med.* x. (1790) 119 There is no passion with which people are so ready to tamper as love. **1826** SCOTT *Jrnl.* 29 Dec., The son.. tampers with phrenology. **1868** FARRAR *Silence & V.* ii. (1875) 40 What was first tampered with, then yielded to, then persisted in, is next justified.

†**b.** *spec.* To meddle *with* medically. *Obs.*

**1655** CULPEPPER *Riverius* Printer to Rdr., Not that every Fool should turn Physition, or that every Reader should tamper with him or her self. **1677** G. MOUNTAGU in *Buccleuch MSS.* (Hist. MSS. Comm.) I. 326, I beseech you tamper not too much, nor let blood too much this cold season. **1706–7** FARQUHAR *Beaux' Strat.* IV. i, I have been a tampering here a little with one of your Patients. **1784** COWPER *Task* v. 668 Vain tamp'ring has but foster'd his disease.

**5.** *intr.* To meddle or interfere *with* (a thing) so as to misuse, alter, corrupt, or pervert it.

*a.* **1593** SHAKS. *3 Hen. VI*, IV. vi. 29 Your Grace..may seeme as wise as vertuous, By spying and auoiding Fortunes malice, For few men rightly temper with the Starres. **1641** 'SMECTYMNUUS' *Answ.* Post. (1653) 89 Peckam Archbishop of Can. in a Synod was tempering with the Kings liberties.

*β.* **1610** COOKE *Pope Joan* 38 Some paltry fellow hath bene tampering with his writings. **1722** DE FOE *Moll Flanders* (1840) 302 To have her up for tampering with the evidence. **1769** SIR W. DRAPER in *Junius Lett.* xxvi. (1820) 122 It is highly unbecoming the dignity of peers to tamper with boroughs. **1860** *All Year Round* No. 65. 354 His pistols, which Marcel had previously tampered with, miss fire. **1862** MAURICE *Mor. & Met. Philos.* IV. vii. § 80. 413 Those had in his judgment tampered with truth. **1888** BRYCE *Amer. Commw.* v. lxxxviii. 379 A large number of persons accused of..tampering with ballot boxes.

**b.** *trans.* To put *off* or do away with by tampering or clandestine dealing. *rare.*

**1817** KEATINGE *Trav.* II. 217 No putting off trials..until prosecutions are wearied off, or tampered off.

†**6.** *trans.* To bias, affect, influence, sway (a person, his mind, passions, etc.); to disaffect. *Obs.* ? for *tamper with*, or = TEMPER *v.* 6.

**1687** R. L'ESTRANGE *Answ. Diss.* 43 The Worst Way of Tampering Peoples Minds, and Spiriting away their Hearts from their Sovereign. **1692** — *Josephus, Antiq.* XIV. xx. (1733) 381 If he could but steal him away into Judæa, the Jews might be tamper'd to a Revolt.

Hence **Ta·mpered** (also *tampered-with*), **Ta·mpering** *ppl. adjs.*

**1681** DRYDEN *Abs. & Achit.* I. 809 The tampering world is subject to this curse, To physic their disease into a worse. **1856** MRS. BROWNING *Aur. Leigh* IV. 474 And kept her safe from tampering hands. **1869** *Daily News* 30 Aug., You have allowed yourself to be tampered with..You appear before us as a tampered witness. **1895** G. TYRRELL in *Month* Nov. 361 The tampered-with fragments in the Christian Fathers.

† **Ta·mper,** *v.*[2] *Obs. rare.* [Known only in Ph. Holland; ? suggested by L. *temperāre*.] *intr.* To beat lightly, to tap; to continue tapping, to TABOR.

**1606** HOLLAND *Sueton.* Annot. 15 The maner of these priestes..was to beat the Taber or tamper upon the Timbril, which is expressed here in these words, *Orbem digito temperat. Ibid.* 29 It will sound like a taber or drum, if one tamper upon it.

**Tamperer** (tæ·mpərəɹ). [f. TAMPER *v.*[1] + -ER[1].] One who tampers; a schemer; a meddler.

**1599** SANDYS *Europæ Spec.* (1632) 88 Yea there are not wanting some temperers among them, that have beene talking a long while..of a Generall solemne Conference. **1681** H. MORE *Exp. Dan.* Pref. 93 Unfaithful Tamperers with the Souls of men. **1854** DICKENS *Child's Hist. Eng.* xxxii. III. 157 He..was surrounded in the Tower by tamperers and traitors. **1906** *Athenæum* 3 Feb. 131/3 Modern tamperers with the ecclesiastical architecture.

**Ta·mpering,** *vbl. sb.* [f. TAMPER *v.*[1] + -ING[1].] The action of the verb TAMPER, in various senses: † plotting; meddling, improper interference.

*a* **1625** FLETCHER *Nice Valour* V. i, There is no tampering with these Cupids longer. **1738** BIRCH *Milton* M.'s Wks. I. 32 By reason of his continual Studies and the Head-ach,..and his perpetual tampering with Physic, his Eyes had been decaying for twelve Years before. **1822** W. IRVING *Braceb. Hall* xx, There is something strangely pleasing in these tamperings with the future. *a* **1854** H. REED *Lect. Eng. Lit.* iv. (1878) 153 It has come down from a remote antiquity, and has..escaped the tampering of modern hands.

**Tampicin** (tæ·mpisin). *Pharm. Chem.* [f. *Tampico* + -IN[1]: in F. *tampicine*.] The resin, $C_{68}H_{108}O_{28}$, obtained from Tampico jalap, the tuberous root of *Ipomæa simulans.*

**1890** in BILLINGS *Nat. Med. Dict.* **1898** in *Syd. Soc. Lex.*

**Tampin,** obs. variant of TAMPION.

**Tamping** (tæ·mpiŋ), *vbl. sb.* [f. TAMP *v.* + -ING[1].] The action of the verb TAMP: the plugging or filling up of a blast-hole above the charge; the packing of the part of a military mine nearest the charge with earth or other material.

**1828** J. M. SPEARMAN *Brit. Gunner* (ed. 2) 301 The stoppage or tamping of a mine. **1845** *Encycl. Metrop.* XVI. 303/1 The sand-bags used for tamping should not be filled up to the top.

**b.** *concr.* The material used for this purpose.

**1828** in WEBSTER. **1843** *Civil Eng. & Arch. Jrnl.* VI. 120/2 It would have found vent by blowing out the tamping. **1909** *Installation News* III. 63 The upper casting, to which the cable or tape is electrically connected by lead tamping.

**c.** *attrib.* and *Comb.*, as *tamping material*; **tamping-bar, -iron,** = STEMMER: see quot. 1877; **tamping-machine**: see quot.; **tamping-plug,** a plug or stopper used to block up a bore-hole.

**1838** *Civil Eng. & Arch. Jrnl.* I. 292/1 Drawings of the jumpers, the *tamping bar, the needle, and the discharging reed. **1891** C. ROBERTS *Adrift Amer.* 75 It was pick and shovel and tamping bar day in and day out. **1864** WEBSTER, **Tamping-iron.* **1877** KNIGHT *Dict. Mech., Tamping-iron,* a tool, prudently made of copper, by which the tamping is wadded down upon the cartridge or charge in a hole, for blasting. *Ibid.*, **Tamping-machine*.., a machine for packing clay or the material for artificial stone into a mold. **1839** URE *Dict. Arts* 836 Dry sand is sometimes used as a *tamping material. **1877** KNIGHT *Dict. Mech.*, **Tamping-plug*,..it usually consists of a cone with barbs, or of a set of wedge-shaped blocks, which jam by the pressure from beneath. **1884** *Mil. Engineering* (ed. 3) I. II. 116 Sandbags ready filled for *tamping purposes should be provided.

**Tampion, tompion** (tæ·mpiən, tǫ·mp-), *sb.* Forms: *a.* 5 tampyne, 5–6 -on, -ond, -yon, 6 -ioun, 6–8 -in, 7 -eon, 5– **tampion**; 6–7 tampkin, 7–8 tamkin; (7–9 tampoon). *β.* 7 tomping, 8–9 -ion, 9 -eon; 7 tomking, 7–8 -kin, **tompkin.** [a. F. *tampon*, in same senses (1440 in Godef. *Compl.*), a nasalized var. of F. *tapon* (1382 in Hatz.-Darm.) a piece of cloth to stop a hole, etc., deriv. of *tape* plug; cf. *tamper*, nasalized var. of *taper* vb. to plug. The original form *tampon* has undergone many corruptions in Eng.: cf. *pompon*, POMPION, PUMPKIN. The form *tampoon* (cf. *dragoon*, etc.) appears to be confined to dictionaries (from Phillips downwards). *Tompion* is a frequent form in all senses. See also TAMPON.]

†**1.** A plug for stopping an aperture: e.g. a bung for a cask, etc. *Obs.*

*c* **1460** J. RUSSELL *Bk. Nurture* 68 in *Babees Bk.* (1868) 121 With fawcet & tampyne redy to stoppe when ye se tyme. **1504** *Cal. Anc. Rec. Dublin* (1889) 393, viii. *d.* to hym that skowre the tamponds of the pypes. *Ibid.*, The skowryng of the tampones of the pypes. *c* **1512** in *Archæologia* (1902) LVIII. 302 A susp[i]rall with a tampioun to clense the home pype. **1594** PLAT *Jewell-ho.* I. 37 You must suffer the water to passe away by some tampion. **1658** PHILLIPS, *Tampoon*, or *Tampkin*, a small piece of wood serving for a bung. **1729** SHELVOCKE *Artillery* IV. 174 The Globe..shall be filled..and then stopped with a Tompion that has been steeped in hot Pitch. [**1882**: see 3 *fig.*]

†**b.** *Farriery.* A seton; a tent; a pessary: cf. TAMPON *sb.* I. *Obs.*

**1565** BLUNDEVIL *Horsemanship* IV. lxvi. (1580) 27 Make two stiffe long rowles, or tampins, of linnen clowtes, or such like stuffe, sharpe pointed like Suger loues:..thrust them vp into the Horses nostrils. **1610** MARKHAM *Masterp.* II. cxi. 395 Put therto a tampin made of the inner rinde of Elder barke. *Ibid.* clvii. 464 Take a tampin of horse haire twound together.

†**2.** A disk-shaped or cylindrical piece of wood made to fit the bore of a muzzle-loading gun, and rammed home between the charge and the missile, to act as a wad. *Obs.*

**1481–90** *Howard Househ. Bks.* (Roxb.) 40 Item ij. c. tampons xvj. d. **1485** *Naval Acc. Hen. VII* (1896) 69 Gonne Tampeyons..ccc. **1497** *Ibid.* 105 Tampons for gonnes.. xijml c. *Ibid.* 340 Tampiones..ccc shotte. **1489** CAXTON *Faytes of A.* II. xxvi. 139 Cartes laden with Elme wode for to make the said tampons. **1530** PALSGR. 279/1 Tampyon for a gon, *tampon.* **1582** STANYHURST *Descr. Liparen* in *Æneis*, etc. (Arb.) 137 Slinging Stoans, and burlye bulets, lyke tamponds. **1588** *Acts Privy Counc.* (1897) XVI. 25 Arrowes for the said muskettes with tampkines of eche 1,000. **1688** R. HOLME *Armoury* III. xviii. (Roxb.) 142/1 Of charging..a Morter peece..put in the Tampkin..a round peece of soft wood put into the mouth of the chamber. **1692** *Capt. Smith's Seaman's Gram.* II. iii. 92 Wedges, Tomkings, Priming-Irons. *Ibid.* xxi. 134 Draw out the Ladle, and with the Tampion at the other end of the Staff, thrust home the Powder. **1727–41** CHAMBERS *Cycl.*, *Tampion, Tompion, Tamkin*, or *Tomkin*, a kind of plug or stopple..to keep down the powder in a fire-arm. **1828** SPEARMAN *Brit. Gunner* (ed. 2) 307 In the larger mortars,..the chamber should be filled with powder, a tompeon of wood placed over it, and both the tompeon and shell surrounded with sifted earth or sand.

†**b.** Applied to the bottom plate of grape-shot, which serves as a wad to the charge. *Obs.*

**1802** JAMES *Milit. Dict.* (1816), *Tampions*, in sea-service artillery, are the iron bottoms to which the grape-shot are fixed. **1823** CRABB *Techn. Dict.*, *Tompions*. [Hence in various later Dicts.]

**3.** A block of wood fitting into the muzzle of a gun, and serving to exclude rain, sea-water, etc.

*a* **1625** *Nomenclator Navalis* (Harl. MS. 2301), Tampkin is a small peece of Wood turned fitt for the mouth of anie peece which is putt in..to keepe out the raine or Sea water, from washing in, when the Peeces lie without Bord. **1627** CAPT. SMITH *Seaman's Gram.* xiv. 68 A Tomkin is a round peece of Wood put into the Peeces mouth and couered with Tallow. **1662** J. DAVIES tr. *Olearius' Voy. Ambass.* 27 The Tampion, which they had forgotten to take out of one of the pieces, pass'd very near me. **1748** SMOLLETT *Rod. Rand.* lxv, He commanded..the tompions to be taken out of the guns. **1835** MARRYAT *Pirate* xiv, Clear away the starboard guns, and take out the tompions. **1904** FITCHETT *Commander of Hirondelle* 157 The wooden tompions were still lying harmlessly within their iron lips.

*fig.* **1756** *Gentl. Mag.* XXVI. 398 Take out the tompkin of your mouth, and fire away loud as thunder. **1864** BLACKMORE *Clara Vaughan* lxxii, She commenced an active bombardment, pulling out the tompions from every gun of mock religion. **1882** G. MACDONALD *Castle Warlock* xv. (1883) 83 No sooner did the..note of the discharge of its [bottle of claret's] tompion reach his ear [etc.].

**4.** In the organ: see quots.

**1864** WEBSTER, *Tampion*,..a plug used to stop closely the upper end of an organ-pipe. **1865** *Chambers' Encycl.* VII. 111/2 (*Organ*) A mouth-pipe may be stopped at the upper end by a plug called a *tompion*, the effect of which is to lower the pitch an octave.

†**5.** (See quot.) *Obs. rare*[−1].

**1611** COTGR., *Pivot*,..the Piuot, or (as some call it) the Tampin of a gate, or great doore.

**6.** = TAMPON 2.

**1877** KNIGHT *Dict. Mech., Tompion*..2 (Lithography) the inking pad of the lithographic printer; *Tompon.* [Hence in mod. Dicts.]

Hence **Ta·mpion, tompion** *v. trans.*, to insert in the manner of a tampion or plug.

**1897** *Daily News* 3 Feb. 5/3 London..is not without its trophy lamp-posts, for..in front of the house once occupied by Admiral Boscawen, are two which are tompioned into old cannon captured from the French in a naval fight.

**Tampkin,** obs. variant of TAMPION.

**Tampon** (tæ·mpǫn), *sb.* Also **tompon.** [ad. F. *tampon*: etymologically a doublet of TAMPION, introduced anew from mod. French.]

**1.** *Surg.* A plug or tent inserted tightly into a wound, orifice, etc., to arrest hæmorrhage, or used as a pessary. Also *attrib.* **tampon-screw**, an instrument used for inserting or withdrawing this.

**1860** MAYNE *Expos. Lex.*, *Tampon*.. *Obstet.*, a less inelegant term for the plug, whether made up of portions of rag, sponge, or a silk handkerchief..in cases of hemorrhage. **1872** T. G. THOMAS *Dis. Women* (ed. 3) 61 [To] keep the displaced and congested uterus out of the cavity of the pelvis by a tampon of medicated cotton. **1884** KNIGHT *Dict. Mech.* Suppl., Tampon-screw. **1888** *Scott. Leader* 14 June 4/1 The new species of cannula employed..is provided with a tampon, and is constructed [so] as to prevent hæmorrhage. **1896** *Allbutt's Syst. Med.* I. 438 Tampons are pear-shaped with the thread attached to the lower end.

**2.** The dabber or inking ball used in lithography and copperplate printing. (So also in French.)

**1877** KNIGHT *Dict. Mech.*, *Tompon*, the inking-pad of the lithographic printer. **1882** G. REID in *Encycl. Brit.* XIV. 701/1 (*Lithography*) An engraved stone is printed by using a small wooden tapper or tampon, either round at the sides, flat below, with handle at top, or square, with the corners rounded off.

**Ta·mpon,** *v. Surg.* [f. prec. sb.: cf. F. *tamponner* (15th c. in Hatz.-Darm.).] *trans.* To fill or stop (a wound, cavity, etc.) with a tampon; to plug.

**1860** J. M. CARNOCHAN *Operat. Surg.* 279 (Cent. Dict.) The hemorrhage was stopped by tamponing the bony aperture [gunshot wound in head]. **1898** *Syd. Soc. Lex.*, *Tamponing*, in Surgery the operation of plugging a wound or natural orifice with a tampon or tampons.

So **Tampona·de, Ta·mponage, Ta·mponment**

[F. *tamponnement*], the employment or application of a tampon.

**1890** BILLINGS *Nat. Med. Dict.*, *Tamponade*, the application of tampons. **1900** *Lancet* 27 Oct. 1191/1 He suggested free opening and curetting with patient and prolonged flushing and subsequent gauze tamponade. **1902** *Cassell's Encycl. Dict.*, *Suppl.*, Tamponment.

**Tampon, -pond, -poon,** obs. var. TAMPION.

†**Tampoy.** *Obs. rare.* [? Malay.] (See quots.)

**1656** BLOUNT *Glossogr.*, *Tampoy*, a curious sort of drink in the Moluccaes and Philippines made of a kind of Gilliflowers. **1823** CRABB *Technol. Dict.*, *Tampoy*, a sort of drink made of gilliflowers. **1909** *Daily Chron.* 23 Aug. 4/7 The mention of British wines..has set an octogenarian sighing for a beverage called 'tampoy', which was highly esteemed in Early Victorian days.

**Tampyne, -pyon,** obs. ff. TAMPION. **Tamquam**: see TANQUAM. **Tamricke, -riske,** obs. ff. TAMARISK. **Tam-tam,** var. TOM-TOM.

**Tamul, -ulian, -ulic**: see TAMIL.

**Tamy,** obs. form of TAMMY *sb.*[1]

**Tan** (tæn), *sb.*[1] (*a.*) Also 7 tann(e. [prob. a. F. *tan* (13th c. in Littré, also in Cotgr. 1611 '*tan*, the barke of a young Oake, wherewith, being small beaten, leather is tanned') = med.L. *tannum*, app. of Celtic origin: cf. Breton *tann* masc., oak, Cornish *glas-tannen* evergreen oak, ilex (Thurneysen). Thence the vbs., med.L. *tannāre*, OF. *tanner* to tan; cf. also Du. *taan*, late MDu. *tāne* tan, *tānen* to tan.]

**I. 1.** The crushed bark of the oak or of other trees, an infusion of which is used in converting hides into leather.

[**1604**: implied in *tan-mill*; **1611** in *tan-pit*: see C.] **1674** JEAKE *Arith.* (1696) 69 Tann, 1 Load must be 60 yards long, 1 yard high, 3 Rinds thick. **1706** PHILLIPS (ed. 6), *Tan*, the Bark of a young Oak, beaten small and us'd..for the tanning..of Leather. **1727–41** CHAMBERS *Cycl.* s.v., Not only the bark, but every part of the oak-tree..makes good Tan. **1840** *Encycl. Brit.* (ed. 7) XXI. 73/2 The word tan is sometimes, though improperly, used for the bark itself, which is the chief ingredient in the tanning of leather. **1852** MORFIT *Tanning & Currying* (1853) 38 The name *tan* is applied to coarsely-powdered bark containing a principle which is the active agent in the tanning of hides.

**b.** Spent bark from the tan-pits, used by gardeners, and for riding-courses, etc.

**1739** MILLER *Gard. Dict.* II. s.v., The best Sort of Tan for Hotbeds, is, that which is ground of a midling Size, neither too small nor too large. **1766** *Ann. Reg.* 108 A melon raised ..in Southwark upon tan was sold in Covent-garden Market. **1812** *New Botanic Gard.* I. 54 A thin covering of tan or some other substance. **1849** LONGF. *Kavanagh* xix. 101 Circus,—with its tan and tinsel. **1887** *Morn. Post* 8 July (Sport. Notes), After the usual canter [she] galloped him a mile and a quarter on the tan.

**2.** The astringent principle contained in oak-bark, etc.; tannin; also the solution of this, tan-liquor, 'ooze'.

**1800** HENRY *Epit. Chem.* (1808) 289 Until very lately, tan had been known only as a production of nature. **1810** — *Elem. Chem.* (1826) II. 284 Tan exists abundantly in the bark of the oak, the willow, &c., and in the gall-nut. **1866** ROGERS *Agric. & Prices* I. xxiv. 612 To preserve them, the nets were soaked in tan.

**II. 3.** The brown colour of tan; tawny.

**1888** *Daily News* 17 July 5/8 Simplicity is the word of command as regards outlines, and tan is the special colour of this season. **1888** *Lady* 25 Oct. 378/1 [Gloves] in the beautiful shades of brown, chocolate, oak, tans, and black.

**b.** *esp.* The bronzed tint imparted to the skin by exposure to the sun or the weather.

**1827** CLARE *Sheph. Cal.* 48 And scare the tan from summer cheek. **1851** HAWTHORNE *Ho. Sev. Gables* v, The clear shade of tan, and the half-a-dozen freckles. **1885** *L'pool Daily Post* 7 May 5/3 With the tan of a southern sun upon his face.

**4.** *pl.* [ellipt. use of the adj.] Articles of dress, etc., of a tan colour; *esp.* tan shoes or boots.

**1902** *Daily Chron.* 17 Sept. 5/2 Please say..where these boots can be bought. I always buy my tans in the cheapest market. **1904** *Ibid.* 2 July 8/5 Tans are in far greater demand than has been known for years.

**B.** *adj.* Of the colour of tan or of tanned leather; of a yellowish or reddish brown; tawny.

**1665** WOOD *Life* 6 May (O.H.S.) II. 35 A pair of tan leather gloves. **1845** DISRAELI *Sybil* IV. vii, Beautiful black and tan spaniels. **1887** W. S. GILBERT *Ruddigore*, I kept guinea pigs..and a small black and tan [dog]. **1896** *Monthly Packet* Christm. No. 61 The daintiest of tan shoes. **1896** EDITH THOMPSON *ibid.* 98 Too well-fitting tan boots..only adapted to mountain excursions of the picnic order. **1908** *Betw. Trent & Ancholme* 218 The white or tan sails pass by.

**C.** *attrib.* and *Comb.*

**1.** from the sb. (in senses 1, 1 b) [some perhaps partly from the verb-stem: cf. TAN-HOUSE], as *tan-colour*, *-liquor*, *-mill*; *tan-burning*, *-strewn*, *-trodden* adjs.; **tan-ball**: see quot.; **tan-bark**, = sense 1; **tan-bath**, a bath containing an infusion of oak-bark in water (*Cent. Dict.* 1891); **tan-bay**, the loblolly bay, *Gordonia Lasianthus* (ibid.); **tan-bed**, a hot-bed made of spent tan; a bark-bed; **tan-extractor**, a device for extracting the tannic acid and astringent principles from bark (Knight *Dict. Mech.* 1877); **tan-fat**, = TAN-VAT; **tan-fork**, a gardener's hand-fork for lifting tan; **tan-gallop**, = *tan-ride*; **tan-loft**, the loft of a tan-house; **tan-ooze, -pickle**, the liquor of a tan-vat: = OOZE *sb.*[1] 2; **tan-pit**, (*a*) = TAN-VAT; (*b*) in gardening, a tan-bed; **tan-press**, a machine for expressing moisture from the spent tan (*Cent. Dict.*); **tan-ride**, a riding-track covered with tan; cf. RIDE *sb.*[1] 2 a; **tan-spud**, a curved chisel for peeling the bark from oak or other trees; a peeler; **tan-stove**, a bark-stove; also, a hot-house with a bark-bed; †**tan-tub**, = TAN-VAT; **tan-turf**, spent tan pressed into bricks for fuel; = *tanners' turf* (TANNER[1] b); **tan-work, -yard**, a place where tanning is carried on; a tannery.

**1882** OGILVIE (Annandale), **Tan-balls*, the spent bark of the tanner's yard pressed into balls or lumps, which harden on drying and serve for fuel. **1799** W. TOOKE *View Russian Emp.* I. I. ii. 34 The *tanbark-tree..and many others. **1891** *Cent. Dict.*, Tan-bark. **1903** *Smart Set* I. 140/1 She had ridden her first horse over the tanbark of Durland's. **1739** MILLER *Gard. Dict.* II. s.v., There are some Persons who make their *Tan-beds much wider than what is here mentioned. **1812** *New Botanic Gard.* I. 81 The pots should be plunged into a tan-bed. **1882** PATON in *Encycl. Brit.* XIV. 382/2 'Spent tan', usually to be burned in a special form of *tan-burning furnace for raising steam. **1811** *Self Instructor* 539 Dark browns, minims, and *tan-colours. **1859** THOMPSON *Gard. Assist.* 124 *Tan-fork. **1856** 'STONEHENGE' *Brit. Sports* II. I. x. § 2. 357/2 A *tan-gallop..made permanently on a course three-quarters of a mile in circumference. **1882** PATON in *Encycl. Brit.* XIV. 382/2 One of the commonest plans for ascertaining the strength of the *tan liquor technically called ooze, or wooze, is by means of a kind of hydrometer called a barkometer. **1852** HANNA *Chalmers* IV. xxi. 404 Dr. Chalmers opened the *tan-loft for public worship. **1604** E. G[RIMSTONE] *D'Acosta's Hist. Indies* IV. xii. 243 Instruments, which beat this stone like vnto *tanne milles. **1839** URE *Dict. Arts* 1195 (*Sugar*) The first machines employed to squeeze the canes, were mills ..somewhat like tan-mills. **1901** F. ADAMS in *N. & Q.* 9th Ser. VII. 412/1 '*Tan ouse', tanner's ouse, or oak bark, an infusion of which is employed for tanning hides. **1820** T. MITCHELL *Aristoph.* I. 259 On him fell *tan-pickle, and nectar on you. *a* **1859** MACAULAY *Hist. Eng.* (1861) V. 181 The drink tasted like tanpickle. **1611** COTGR., *Coudroir*, a Tanfat, or *Tanpit. **1707** MORTIMER *Husb.* I. 123 What improves it to that Value is the emptying of the Town Tanpits on it. **1810** BOSWELL *Edinburgh* Poet. Wks. (1871) 48 Neighbouring tan-pits scent the passing gales. **1858** GLENNY *Gard. Every-day Bk.* 34/1 Although a tan-pit is not absolutely necessary to make a hot-house, it is necessary to have bottom-heat at command. **1863** LAWRENCE *Border & Bast.* iv. 70 In the centre is a large fountain of white marble, round which is a broad *tan-ride. **1884** YATES *Recoll.* II. ii. 81 A tan-ride furnished with various obstacles for leaping experiments. **1828** WEBSTER, **Tan-spud*, .. **Tan-stove*. **1904** *Blackw. Mag.* June 796 Chilcote glanced over the *tan-strewn ride. **1887** J. ASHBY STERRY *Lazy Minstrel* (1892) 42 What studies of man and of woman and horse Here pass up and down on the *tan-trodden course! **1586** J. DAVIS *Voy.* (Hakl. Soc.) 17 They found bags of trayne oyle,..seale skinnes in *tan tubs, with many other such trifles. **1799** *Hull Advertiser* 2 Mar. 2/1 Tan-yard, bark-mill,..tan-tubs, vats and materials. **1851** MAYHEW *Lond. Labour* II. 87/2 *Tan-turf is oak bark made into turf after its virtues have been exhausted in the tan-pits. **1822** J. FLINT *Lett. Amer.* 125 An iron foundery..a *tan-work, a glass-house. **1711** *Customs Notice* in *Lond. Gaz.* No. 4862/4 Any Tan-house, *Tan-yard, Work-house. **1777** J. ADAMS in *Fam. Lett.* (1876) 241 A mill to grind bark for the tanyard.

**2.** adjs. from A. 3, or B, chiefly parasynthetic, as *tan-coloured*, *-faced*, *-sailed*, *-skinned*, *-tinted*.

**1630** J. TAYLOR (Water P.) *Proclamation* Wks. II. 252/2 The Sunburnt tanskind Indians. **1685** *Lond. Gaz.* No. 2037/4 A black-brown Gelding..Tan mouth'd. **1861** L. L. NOBLE *Icebergs* 63 Scudding under their tan-colored canvas. **1869** *Routledge's Ev. Boy's Ann.* 454 A tan-faced digger. **1888** *Dict. Nat. Biog.* XIII. 142/2 The tan-sailed barges sailing through the flats. **1892** *Daily News* 29 Mar. 2/4 An Eton jacket of the tan-tinted cloth, with sleeves to match.

**Tan,** *sb.*[2] Short for FAN-TAN, a Chinese gambling game.

**1883** STEVENSON *Silverado Sq.* 189 Where he might..lose his little earnings at the game of tan.

**Tan** (tæn), *v.* Also 5–6 tanne, 6–7 tann. Pa. t. and pple. tanned (tænd). [Late OE. *tannian*, evidenced *c* 1000 in pa. pple. *getanned*, and agent-n. *tannere*, prob. f. med.L. *tannāre* (*tanare* in Erfurt Gl. *a* 900) to tan (whence pa. pple. *tannātus*, in Du Cange), f. *tannum* TAN *sb.* Cf. also OF. *tanner*, *taner* (13th c. in Littré), whence app. the ME. and modern vb. Cf. also Du. *tānen* to tan, generally held to be from Fr.]

**1.** *trans.* To convert (skin or hide) into leather by steeping in an infusion of an astringent bark, as that of the oak, or by a similarly effective process.

*c* **1000** [see TANNED 1]. [**1321–2** *Rolls of Parlt.* I. 415/2 Et xiiii li. pur quirs tannés de faire Barhides, & Sakes as draps.] *c* **1350** [see TANNED 1]. **14..** *Rule Syon Monast.* ix. in Aungier *Syon Monast.* (1840) 272 Withe hosen and schone tanned. *c* **1440** *Promp. Parv.* 486/2 Tannyn, or barkyn, *frunio*. **1481** CAXTON *Godeffroy* clxviii. 249 There was seint peter herberowed in a tanners hows, that tanned leder. **1503–4** *Act 19 Hen. VII*, c. 19 *Preamble*, No corryour.. [shall] cory any hyde of Leyther but such as afore be sufficiantly tanned. **1630** *Tom Thumbe* 56 in Hazl. *E. P. P.* II. 179 His bootes and shoes a mouses skin, there tand most curiously. **1768** BOSWELL *Corsica* iii. (ed. 2) 195 In the island of St. Kilda they tan with the tormentil root. **1875** URE *Dict. Arts* III. 85 About three months is usually occupied in tanning calf-skins.

**b.** *transf.* To treat (fishing-nets, sails, etc.) with tanners' ooze or some preserving substance; also, to act upon as an astringent.

**1601** J. KEYMOR *Dutch Fishing* (1664) 7 Shee [the Herring Buss] imployeth..at Land..Tanners to Tan their Nets and Sayles. **1615** [see TAN-VAT]. **1889** J. M. DUNCAN *Clin. Lect. Dis. Wom.* xii. (ed. 4) 82 The styptic may pass into the uterine veins in the broad ligament, and produce changes there—tanning the parts. **1905** *Daily News* 26 July 6 'Drink less tea', says he, 'but, above everything, mind the infusing'..The British interior will continue to be tanned until the sun of Albion shall set.

**c.** In the manufacture of artificial marble, to steep (the composition) in a hardening and preservative preparation: cf. TANNAGE 1.

**1891** in *Cent. Dict.*

**2.** To make brown (the face or skin), esp. by exposure to the sun or weather; to embrown, sunburn; hence, to make dark or tawny in colour.

**1530** PALSGR. 752/2, I tanne in the sonne, or am sonne brente...You shall tanne your selfe more upon the see than upon lande. **1590** SPENSER *F. Q.* I. vi. 35 His..face all tand with scorching sunny ray. **1601** HOLLAND *Pliny* I. 127 The neerer they approch to the riuer Indus, the deeper coloured they are and tanned with the Sun. **1660** F. BROOKE tr. *Le Blanc's Trav.* 102 The people are..of a good stature, but a little tann'd. **1746–7** HERVEY *Medit.* (1767) I. 262 Heat, whose burning Influence..tans into Soot the Ethiopian's Complexion. **1812** BYRON *Ch. Har.* II. lxix, In war well season'd, and with labours tann'd. **1853** MRS. GASKELL *Cranford* xv, His face was deep brown, as if tanned and re-tanned by the sun.

*fig.* *c* **1645** HOWELL *Lett.* (1650) II. 17 All Egypt and Barbary, with Lybia and the Negro's Country, are tainted and tand with this black Religion.

**b.** *intr.* (for *refl.*) To become sunburnt or darkened by exposure.

**1530** [see 2]. **1884** *Illustr. Lond. News* 26 Jan. 91/2 One advantage you swarthy people have over us—you don't tan. **1889** *Nature* 24 Oct. 633/2 The capacity to tan, or become darker by exposure, varies much.

**3.** *trans.* *To tan* (a person's) *hide*, also simply *to tan* (a person): to thrash soundly. *slang* or *colloq.* (Cf. HIDE *v.*[2] 2.)

*c* **1670** *Expost. Let. Men Buckhm.* 2/2 Let not your Worships thick skin be too sensible that we thus Tan your Hide. **1731** COFFEY *Devil to Pay* iv. (1733) 13 Come, and spin, you lazy Drab, or I'll tan your Hide for you. **1835–40** HALIBURTON *Clockm.* (1862) 120 I'll tan your hide for you, you may depend. **1890** J. CURTIN tr. *Sienkiewicz' With Fire & Sword* xli. 475 To-day you tan people, to-morrow they tan you. **1903** *Spectator* 14 Feb. 245 Midshipmen, who are boys, are 'tanned', but not Lieutenants of twenty-five.

**Tan** = *to han*, to have: see T'[1] and HAVE.

*c* **1407** [see TAME *v.*[2] 2].

**Tan,** obs. inf. and pa. pple. of TAKE *v.*; obs. phonetic var. of *þan* THEN.

**Tan.,** *Math.* abbreviation of TANGENT B. 1.

‖ **Tana**[1] (tā·nä). *E. Indies.* Also tanna(h, tha(n)na(h. [Hindī *thāna*, *thānā*.] A police station in India; formerly, a military station or fortified post.

**1803** WELLINGTON in Gurw. *Desp.* (1837) II. 251, I give you notice, that you may have your tannahs prepared in your villages and desire them to defend them. **1834** A. PRINCEP *Baboo* II. xi. 202 (Stanf.) The Burkundazes at last came up from the Thana. **1879** Low *Jrnl. Gen. Abbott* iii. 214 Thannahs (posts) for the protection of the Cabul were re-established. **1895** MRS. B. M. CROKER *Village Tales* (1896) 212 They were found..near the police thana on the Futupore Road.

Hence ‖ **Tanadar** (tānădā·ɹ) [Hindī *thānadār*], the head officer of a police station in India; formerly the commander of a military post.

**1802** C. JAMES *Milit. Dict.* (1816), *Tannadar*, a commander of a small fort. **1834** A. PRINCEP *Baboo* I. xviii. 326 (Stanf.) Thou must be a Thanadar at least. **1897** L. J. TROTTER *J. Nicholson* xvii. (1908) 233 He suspended a thanadar whom he caught in an act of oppression.

**Tana**[2], *Zool.*: see TUPAIA.

†**Tanacles,** *sb. pl. Obs. rare*⁻⁰. Also 6 -akles, 7 -ackels. [app. var. TENACLE, ad. L. *tenāculum*, modified after It. *tanaglie* pl. pincers, tongs:—L. *tenācula*.] (See quots.) Hence †**Tanacle** *v. Obs. rare*⁻⁰.

**1598** FLORIO, *Tanaglie*, toongs, pincers, tanakles, mullets. *Tanagliare*, to torture, to pinch, to tanakle with toongs, pincers or tanakles. **1623** COCKERAM, *Tanackels*, Pincers for tortures. **1656** BLOUNT *Glossogr.*, *Tanacles*. **1721** BAILEY, *Tanacles*,..Instruments of Torture like Pincers.

**Tanager** (tæ·nădʒəɹ). *Ornith.* Also 7– tangara. [ad. mod.L. *Tanagra* (Linnæus 1758), for Tupi *tangara* (used by Brisson 1760).] A bird of the genus *Tanagra* or family *Tanagridæ* of passerine birds, of Central and South America.

There are numerous species, named from their colour, as *black-headed*, *green-headed*, *red*, *scarlet*, *spotted*, *variegated*, *yellow tanager*; from other characteristics, as *crested*, *grand hooded*, *silent t.*; from their native locality, as *Brazilian*, *Mississippi t.*; from resemblance to other birds, as *bullfinch*, *oriole t.*; from their discoverer, as *Cooper's t.*, etc.

**1614** PURCHAS *Pilgrimage* IX. iv. 843 The Tangara which haue the falling-sicknes, the rest dancing about that which is fallen, with a noise, from which they will not be skarred till they haue done. [**1648** MARCGRAVE *Hist. Nat. Brasil.* 214 *Tangara* Brasiliensibus; (reperiuntur ejus aliquot species colore variantes).] **1688** R. HOLME *Armoury* II. 243/1 The Brisilian Tangara [hath] Legs and Feet cinereous, inclining to dusky. **1825** WATERTON *Wand. S. Amer.* (1882) 26 A numerous species of bird called Tangara. **1844** *Zoologist* II. 444 The occurrence of the Red-breasted Tanager near Cheltenham. **1857** MAYNE REID *War Trail* xlv, The sweet warbling voices of the silvias, finches, tanagers, that.. adorn the American woods with their gorgeous colours. **1863**

THOREAU *Excursions* 31 The tanager flies through the green foliage as if it would ignite the leaves. **1893** W. H. HUDSON *Idle Days Patagonia* x. 156 It is impossible to say of many species which are finches and which tanagers. **1896** NEWTON *Dict. Birds* 943 *Tanager*..adapted from the quasi-Latin *Tanagra* of Linnæus,..an adaptation, perhaps with a classical allusion, of *Tangara*, used by Brisson and Buffon.

Hence **Ta·nagrine** *a.*, of or pertaining to tanagers; belonging to the family *Tanagridæ*, or subfamily *Tanagrinæ* (*Cassell's Encycl. Dict.* 1887); **Ta·nagroid** (tangaroid) *a.*, resembling the tanagers; akin in structure to the tanager family.

**1879** E. P. WRIGHT *Anim. Life* 254 The Tangaroid Perchers.

**Tanaid** (tæ·nā,id), *a.* and *sb. Zool.* [f. mod.L. *Tanaidæ*, f. generic name *Tanais*.] **a.** *adj.* Of or pertaining to the *Tanaidæ*, a family of cheliferous isopod crustaceans, typified by the genus *Tanais*. **b.** *sb.* A member of this family.

**1893** STEBBING *Crustacea* xxi. 327 The marital Tanaid frequently sacrifices his mouth-organs to the enormous development of his chelipeds.

**Tanaist, Tanakin**, obs. ff. TANIST, TANNAKIN.

**Tanakaha**: see TANEKAHA.

**Tand**, obs. f. *tanned*, pa. pple. of TAN *v.*

**Tandem** (tæ·ndem), *sb.*[1] and *adv.* Also 8–9 *erron.* tandum. [app. L. *tandem* at length (of time) used punningly.]

**A.** *sb.* **1.** A two-wheeled vehicle drawn by two horses (or other beasts of draught) harnessed one before the other.

**1785** GROSE *Dict. Vulg. T.*, *Tandem*, a two wheeled chaise, buggy, or noddy, drawn by two horses, one before the other, that is *at length*. **1789** *Loiterer* No. 42. 12, I have not the smallest desire to ride in Mr. Whirligig's Tandem. **1807** BYRON *Let. to Miss Pigot* 11 Aug., We shall..proceed in a tandem..to Inverary. **1821** A. HODGSON *Lett. fr. N. Amer.* (1824) II. 110 Painted sleighs..are dashing along [Broadway, New York] in all directions,..some with two horses abreast; some harnessed as tandems, and others with four in hand. **1850** *N. & Q.* 1st Ser. I. 382/1 We have a practical pun now naturalized in our language in the word 'tandem'. **1861** HUGHES *Tom Brown at Oxf.* i, They drove tandems in all directions, scattering their ample allowances..about roadside inns.

**b.** *transf.* A pair of carriage-horses harnessed one before the other. Also *fig.*

**1795** W. FELTON *Carriages* (1801) II. 120 A Tandum..is ..two horses in a team, or one before the other, to draw a two-wheeled chaise. *a* **1805** A. CARLYLE *Autobiog.* (1860) [449 In the end of summer [of 1764] I went again with Mrs. Carlyle to Harrogate,.. I got an open chaise with two horses—one before the other, and the servant on the first. *Ibid.*] 458 Blackett's horse was very heavy, and my tandem far outran them. **1859** CORNWALLIS *New World* I. 104, I..equipped a dog-cart and tandem, for a drive to the diggings. **1885** *Pall Mall G.* 14 Jan. 3/2 The old political tandem, in which the poor man with talent and the rich man without it pulled together, is no longer possible.

**2.** Short for *tandem bicycle* (*tricycle*), *canoe*, *engine*: see C.

**1884** *Daily News* 19 Sept. 3/3 Cycling on a 'tandem' in Norway...When our tandem..was placed upon the pier, we were surrounded by an eager crowd. **1888** *Encycl. Brit.* XXIII. 560/1 For nearly every make of single tricycle there is a corresponding tandem. **1900** *Engineering Mag.* XIX. 778/1 Triple-expansion engines,..having 1 high, 1 intermediate and 2 low pressure cylinders arranged as twin vertical tandems.

**B.** *adv.* One behind the other, in single file; originally of a team of two horses. Also *fig.*

**1795** W. FELTON *Carriages* (1801) II. Gloss., *Tandum*, the manner of driving two horses in a team. **1818** T. L. PEACOCK *Nightmare Abbey* i, His fellow-students..drove tandem and random in great perfection. **1837** *Chron.* in *Ann. Reg.* 1 Jan. 1/2 The letters are conveyed daily from Canterbury to Dover on sledges drawn by three and four horses, tandem. **1893** *Atlantic Monthly* Feb. 196/1 Three logs chained tandem constituted the load, and we vaulted upon the last log for a ride to the boom. **1897** *Outing* (U.S.) XXX. 135/1 The patient mules, driven tandem, were dragging a heavy barge down the canal.

**C.** *attrib.* and *Comb.*, as *tandem-curricle*, *-drag* (DRAG *sb.* 1 *d*), *-driving*, *-horse*, *-sleigh*, *-team*, *-whip*; *tandem-wise* adv.; **tandem bicycle** (**tricycle**), **canoe**, a bicycle (tricycle) or canoe for two persons, one seated behind the other; **tandem engine**, a steam engine with two cylinders one in front of the other, the two pistons working on a common piston-rod; **tandem-play**: see quot.

**1899** *Daily News* 11 Jan. 2/4 In the Soudan they used a small dynamo driven by means of a *tandem bicycle. **1815** *Reviewers Reviewed* 18 Even Doctor Solomon..is ready with his *tandem curricle to invite him to Gilead Hall. **1817** J. PALMER *Jrnl. Trav. in U.S.* etc. (1818) 217 [At Montreal] I have seen a *tandem dog cart, the dogs harnessed and belled the same as horses. **1825** C. M. WESTMACOTT *Eng. Spy* I. 86 Since she put down her *tandem drag. **1850** THACKERAY *Pendennis* xix, Riding and *tandem-driving were the fashions of the ingenuous youth. **1878** *Engineer* XLVI. 23 (Paris Exhibition), 60 Horse Power Compound *Tandem Engine. [Cf. **1901** *Feilden's Mag.* IV. 413/1 The fan engines, which were tandem-compound, were afterwards fitted with low-pressure relief-valves, in addition to those fitted in the high-pressure cylinders.] **1830** LYTTON *P. Clifford* xxxi, A light cart drawn by two swift horses in a *tandem fashion awaited the fugitives. **1890** W. J. GORDON *Foundry* 73 They are being built with the high-pressure above the low-pressure, tandem fashion, with a piston-rod common to both. **1801** FELTON *Carriages* II. App. 6 When loaded, a leading or *Tandum horse, is mostly applied. **1895** *Baily's Mag.* May 353/2 A useful house-of-call, at which you could pop on a *tandem leader. **1895** *Funk's Stand. Dict.*, *Tandem-play (Football), a play in which the man running with the ball is preceded or followed, or both preceded and followed, by other men of his own side..to assist him in breaking through the opposing line. **1863** 'OUIDA' *Held in Bondage* (1870) 31 Dashing on with his *tandem-team too quickly for identification. **1835** WILLIS *Pencillings* I. xxxiii. 230 It might have been touched from the deck with a *tandem whip. **1860** *All Year Round* 496 The two horses which he has..had harnessed to it *tandem-wise.

Hence **Ta·ndem**, **Ta·ndemize** *vbs.*, *intr.* to drive a tandem; *trans.* to harness or drive (a horse, etc.) tandem fashion; **Ta·ndemer, Ta·ndemist**, one who rides a tandem bicycle or tricycle.

**1828** *Sporting Mag.* XXII. 132 We *tandem'd on to Melton for a finishing treat. **1898** *Speaker* 16 July 87 They tandemed the donkey to drag their impedimenta up the slope of 1,200 feet. **1894** *Daily News* 3 May 8/6 At 5 miles the *tandemers had cut the record by a good deal over 2 min. **1885** *Cyclist* 5 Aug. 1026/2 The silken fetters of matrimony convert a happy bicyclist into..an equally happy *tandemist. **1824** *Blackw. Mag.* XV. 115 Reginald ..drinks—games—hunts—*tandemizes. **1840** *New Monthly Mag.* LIX. 492 Tandemizing, cricketizing, boatizing,..is not to be carried on without a considerable expenditure.

† **Tandem**, *sb.*[2] *Obs.* [Origin unascertained: perh. from a place-name.] Name of some kind of linen, in 18th c. classed among Silesia linens. *U.S.*

**1747** *Boston* (U. S.) *Even. Post* 18 May 2/2 To be sold cheap..Lloyd's Garlets, Tandems, Cambricks, Taffatees. **1754** *Boston Gaz.* 31 Dec. 3/2 Just Imported from London, And Sold By Samuel Abbot,..3-4th and yard wide garlix's, tandems, hollands, cambricks. **1755** *Boston Even. Post* 26 May 4/2 Ten Pieces yard wide Tandems,..three Pieces Osnabrigs. **1783** *Circular from Hamburg* in *Pennsylv. Gaz.* 26 Nov. 3/1 German cloth of every quality and colour ..Silesia linens..Rough dowlas, Quadruple tandems, Brown Silesias.

**Tandle, tanle** (ta·nd'l, tā·n'l). *Sc.* and *north. dial.* Also 8–9 taanle, tawnle, 9 taunle, tannel. [perh. an altered form of ON. *tandr*, *tandri* fire = OHG. *zantaro*, *zantro*, MHG. *zanter*, *zander*: but the history is incomplete.] A large fire in the open air, a bonfire; esp. one made at certain seasons in the year, as on May Day, Midsummer Eve, or the first of November.

**1788** PICKEN *Now-a-days* Poems 62 Thae flirds o' silk..Had I our doghter's at a candle, They'd mak' a been an' rowsan tandle. **1793** *Statist. Acc. Scotl.* VII. 622 An antient practise..of kindling a large fire, or tawnle as it is usually termed, of wood. **1802** SIBBALD *Scot. Poetry* Gloss. s. v., The custom of kindling large fires or Taanles, at Midsummer, was formerly common in Scotland. **1845** *New Statist. Acc. Scotl.* V. 223 The custom of the baal-fire or Tannel is still observed on the last day of July, St. Margaret's Day. **1887** J. SERVICE *Dr. Duguid* iv. 28 Bigging great taunles on the holms o' the Garnock.

‖ **Tandour** (tæ·ndūᵊɹ). Also 7 tenur, tenner, 8–9 tendour, 9 tan-, tendoor. [= F. *tandour*, a. *tandūr*, Turkish pronunc. of Pers. and Arab. تنور *tannūr* oven, portable furnace, a. Aramaic תנורא *tannūrā*, Heb. תנור *tannūr*, Assyrian *tinūru* furnace, oven.] A heating apparatus consisting of a square table with a brazier under it, round which persons sit for warmth in cold weather in Persia, Turkey, and adjacent countries.

**1662** J. DAVIES tr. *Olearius' Voy. Ambass.* 294 They [Persians] call this kind of Stoves *Tenner*. *Ibid.* 303 In Winter they have their *Tenurs* against the Cold. **1718** LADY M. W. MONTAGU *Let. to Mrs. Thistlethwayte* 4 Jan., Warming themselves..neither by chimney nor stoves, but a certain machine called a *tendour*, the height of two feet, in the form of a table, covered with a fine carpet or embroidery. This is made only of wood, and they put into it a small quantity of hot ashes, and sit with their legs under the carpet. **1802** *Edin. Rev.* I. 51 The tandour supplies the want of grates and chimnies. **1840** FRASER *Trav. Koordistan*, etc. I. vi. 150 A sort of oven called a *tendour*. *Ibid.* II. ix. 200 *Tendoor*.

**Tandrec**, variant of TANREC.

‖ **Tandstickor** (tæ·nd,sti:kəɹ). [a. Swed. *tändstickor* matches, pl. of *tändsticka*, f. *tända* to light, kindle + *sticka* splinter, spill. The Eng. popular use was taken from the word 'Tändstickor', i.e. 'matches', on boxes of matches made in Sweden.] More fully, *tandstickor match*, a cheap kind of lucifer match imported from Sweden.

**1884** *Pall Mall G.* 19 July 20/1 Who ever sees the Tändstickors nowadays except in Continental hotels? **1889** RIDER HAGGARD *Allan's Wife*, etc. 313 It was a 'tandstickor' match, and burnt slowly and dimly. **1898** *Westm. Gaz.* 3 June 4/3 The public which purchases the ordinary or tandstickor match.

† **Tandy**, ? obs. form of TAWNY.

**1496** *Fysshynge with an Angle* (1883) 34 The tandy flye at saynt Wyllyams daye, the body of tandy wull & the wynges..of the whitest mayle of þe wylde drake.

**Tane**, obs. pa. pple. of TAKE *v.*; Sc. and north. dial. f. TONE, in *the tone* = the one.

‖ **Tanekaha** (tānekā·hā). Also tana-. [Native Maori name.] A New Zealand conifer, the Celery-topped Pine, *Phyllocladus trichomanoides*

**1875** T. LASLETT *Timber Trees* xxxviii. 306 The Tanakaha Tree..is found scattered over a large portion of the northern island of New Zealand. **1883** J. HECTOR *Handbk. N. Zealand* (1886) 101 Tanekaha, Celery-leaved Pine. A slender, handsome tree, 60 ft. high.

**Tang** (tæŋ), *sb.*[1] Forms: *α.* 4–7 **tange**, 7–8 **tangue**, 8–9 *dial.* **taing**, 5– **tang**. *β.* 5–6 **tong(g)e**. [Known in literature from 14th c., but prob. in much earlier use in northern Eng.: a. ON. *tange* point, spit of land, tang of a knife, etc., Norw., Da. *tange*, Sw. *tång(e*, Færoese *tangi*.]

**I. 1.** A projecting pointed part or instrument. **a.** The tongue of a serpent, formerly thought to be the stinging organ; the sting of an insect. (Now *dial.*)

*a* **1350** *St. Matthew* 58 in Horstm. *Altengl. Leg.* (1881) 132 Men þat þai [serpents] bifore had biten And with þaire tanges ful sare smetyn. *c* **1440** *Promp. Parv.* 496/2 Tongge, of a bee, *aculeus*. *c* **1440** STAUNTON *St. Patrick's Purg.* (1900) 61 þei maden to me an hudious noyse..with blaryng owt of here brennyng tanges. **1483** *Cath. Angl.* 378/1 A Tange of A nedyr, *aculeus, acus, pugio*. **1530** PALSGR. 281/2 Tonge of a bee, *esguillon*. **1787** GROSE *Provinc. Gloss.*, *Tang*,..a sting. **1876** *Whitby Gloss.*, *Tang*, a sting or point. **1877** *N. W. Linc. Gloss.*, *Tang*,..the tongue of a snake, with which people believe it has the power of stinging. ..The sting of an insect.

**b.** *fig.* A 'sting', a pang.

**1724** RAMSAY *Health* 156 The flagg'd embrace, and mercenary squeeze, The tangs of guilt, and terrors of disease. **1868** LANIER *Jacquerie* I. 73 Oh, sharper tangs pierced through this perfumed May.

**c.** *dial.* A sharp point or spike; the pin of a buckle; one of the prongs or tines of a fork; a prong or tine of a stag's horn.

The sense 'leg of a pair of tongs' in R. Holme may have been derived from the tang of a fork.

**1688** R. HOLME *Armoury* II. 132/2 [Of a horn] The lower Tang [is] the Brow-Antlier. [*Ibid.* III. xiv. (Roxb.) 7/1 He beare[th] Sable, a paire of Tonges closed in ye tanges Argent.] **1781** J. HUTTON *Tour to Caves* (ed. 2) Gloss., *Tang*, a pike. **1828** *Craven Gloss.*, *Tang*, *Teng*,..the prong of a fork. 'A fork wi three tangs'. **1843** *Civil Eng. & Arch. Jrnl.* VI. 147/1 On the lower edge [of the excavator or shovel] are four tangs or points, which serve to penetrate and loosen the soil. **1868** ATKINSON *Cleveland Gloss.*, *Tang*, the tongue of a buckle, the prong of a fork. **1877** E. PEACOCK *N. W. Linc. Gloss.*, *Tang*, the tongue of a buckle.

**d.** † The barb of a hook (*obs.*); the tongue of a Jew's-harp (also *fig.*).

**1688** R. HOLME *Armoury* III. xvi. (Roxb.) 80/1 The tongue of the hooke is that little tang or slip on the inside of it, which..hinders the hooke from comeing out. Some call it the barbe. **1887** *Suppl. to Jamieson*, *Tang o' the trump*,.. the tongue of the Scottish trump or Jew's harp;..the chief or most important person in a company.

**e.** (See quot.) *dial.* (So in Old Norse.)

**1822** HIBBERT *Shetl. Isles* 518 A narrow stripe of land stretches out that is named the Taing of Torness. The word Taing expresses the character of the low projecting cape. [Cf. p. 479 Ting of Torness.]

**2.** An extension of a metal tool or instrument, as a chisel, file, knife, ax, coulter, pike, scythe, sword, etc., by which it is secured to its handle or stock.

Originally a spike or rod to thrust into the stock; hence extended to a piece of any shape or form having the same function: see quots. Now the chief literal sense.

*c* **1440** *Promp. Parv.* 496/2 Tongge of a knyle, *pirasmus*. **14..** *Nom.* in Wr.-Wülcker 735/19, 20 *Hoc tenaculum*, *Hic spirasmus*, a tang. **1483** *Cath. Angl.* 378/1 A Tange of A knyfe, *parasinus*. **1649** BLITHE *Eng. Improv. Impr.* (1653) 67 The Stayl must be plated with Iron,..through which, as also the Wood, the tange of the Coulter must come. **1688** R. HOLME *Armoury* III. 321/2 The Cheeks, or Plates, or Tangs [of a hammer are] the Irons which hold the Head on. *Ibid.* xxii. (Roxb.) 284/1 The handle is neere a yard long, with an Hoop at the end for the Tang of the Trowell to be fastned in. **1831** J. HOLLAND *Manuf. Metal* I. 281 The tang, or part by which it [a penknife blade] is to be held during grinding, and ultimately to be fixed in the haft. **1837** WHITTOCK *Bk. Trades* (1842) 226 In forming the tangs of most files, it is necessary to make the shoulders perfectly square and sharp. **1864** R. F. BURTON *Dahome* 44 African battle-axes with..the tangs set in the hafts. **1884** W. H. RIDEING in *Harper's Mag.* June 78/2 The blade..is welded, in the case of a dinner-knife, to a piece of iron, which forms the 'tang' or the part that is inserted in the handle. **1904** BUDGE *Guide 3rd & 4th Egypt. Rooms Brit. Mus.* 7 Two bronze ribbed spear-heads, with tangs.

**b.** A root or fang of a tooth; a root or branch of a tree. Now chiefly *dial.*

**1715** MOLYNEUX in *Phil. Trans.* XXIX. 372 Strong Tangs or Roots,..by which the Tooth receives its Sense and Nourishment. **1886** HOLLAND *Chester Gloss.*, *Tangs*, (2) the principal roots or branches of a tree.

**3.** One of various fishes having spines: see quots.

**1734** MORTIMER in *Phil. Trans.* XXXVIII. 317 *Turdus rhomboïdalis*. The *Tang*. This Fish hath on each side the Tail a sharp pointed Bone, which it can erect in its own Defence. **1902** WEBSTER Suppl., *Tang*,..any West Indian species of surgeon fish, as the common tang (*Teuthis hepatus*), the blue tang (*T. cæruleus*), and the ocean tang (*T. Bahianus*).

**4.** *Stereotyping.* **a.** The piece of superfluous metal formed at the end of the plate; the pour-piece. **b.** That part of the papier-maché flong or mould which overlaps the tail end of the matrix so as to prevent the metal from flowing under the end of the mould in the casting-box; the tail-piece.

**a. 1880** F. J. F. WILSON *Stereo- & Electrotyping* 43 When the casting is sufficiently cool the superfluous metal at the head, called the 'tang', or 'pour-piece', may be removed by the circular saw or sharp-pointed hook. *Ibid.* 65 The 'pour-piece', or tang, is removed from the top end of the plate, and the bevel formed at the same time. **b. 1891** in *Cent. Dict.* **1910** H. HART *Let. to Editor*, Occasionally the tang is lengthened, for use in a large casting-box, by pasting on to it a piece of thick paper or thin cardboard.

**II. 5.** A penetrating taste or flavour; usually (but not always) an after-taste, or a disagreeable or alien taste from contact with something else.

**c 1440** *Promp. Parv.* 496/2 Tongge, or sharpnesse of lycure yn tastynge, *acumen*. **1582** BRETON *Floorish vpon Fancie* (Grosart) 41/2 At first, me thought the tast was reasonable good: But..it left (alas) a bitter tang behinde. **1598** FLORIO, *Piccante*, a tartenes vpon the toong, a tang left vpon the toong. **1624** A. WOTTON *Runne from Rome* 3 (As new vessels doe) keeping a tang of the first liquor wherewith I was seasoned. **1660** FULLER *Mixt Contempl.* (1841) 225 The best oil is said to have no taste, that is, no tang. **1736** BAILEY *Househ. Dict.* 100 Brandy either French or English, that has no burnt tang or other ill taste. **1806–7** J. BERESFORD *Miseries Hum. Life* (1826) IX. xv, A strong tang of tallow or onion in your bread and butter. **a 1825** FORBY *Voc. E. Anglia*, *Tang*, a strong flavour; generally, but not always, an unpleasant one. **1883** MRS. E. H. ROLLINS *New Eng. Bygones* 180 Apples..picked freshly fallen from the earth had a keen spicy tang.

*fig.* **1612** T. TAYLOR *Comm. Titus* i. 15 The sweetest sinnes would carry a bitter tang, if we would but remember what sweete comfort of the creatures we haue forfeited for them.

**b.** A pungent odour, a penetrating scent.

**1858** GEN. P. THOMPSON *Audi Alt.* I. xxx. 117 All places smell of hangman, it is everywhere the same tang; we might as well be hooped up with the body of a deceased felon on a gibbet of the olden style. **1883** STEVENSON *Silverado Sq.* 163 Like the smell of a washing-house, but with a shrewd tang of the sea salt. **1899** CROCKETT *Kit Kennedy* xxxvii. 262 The tang of the cottage peat reek hangs like the peculiar incense of home. **1903** *Sat. Rev.* 14 Nov. 607 The air has a tang of its own, recognisable even in the closest lanes.

**c.** ? A pungent or stinging effect; 'something that leaves a sting or pain behind it' (J.).

But the meaning here is disputed: cf. TANG *sb.*[2] Shakspere may in this use have associated the two words.

**1610** SHAKS. *Temp.* II. ii. 52 But none of vs car'd for Kate. For she had a tongue with a tang, Would cry to a Sailor, goe hang!

**6.** *fig.* A slight 'smack' *of* some quality, opinion, habit, form of speech, etc.; a 'suspicion', a suggestion; a trace, a touch *of* something.

**1593** HARVEY *New Letter* Wks. (Grosart) I. 285, I cannot but..conceiue as it were a tang of pleasure in mine owne displeasure. **a 1625** FLETCHER *Hum. Lieut.* I. i, Before I thought ye To have a little breeding—some little tang of Gentry. **1645** PAGITT *Heresiogr.* (1662) 137 The teachers have a strong tange of Pelagius. **1651** *Life Father Sarpi* (1676) 37 He had always kept a tang of the Neapolitan Dialect. **1657** AUSTEN *Fruit Trees* II. 153 Although the graft changes the sap of the wild stock into its owne nature, yet..a tang of the wild nature remains. **1751** GRAY *Wks.* (1825) II. 162 The language has a tang of Shakespear that suits an old fashioned fable very well. **1854** H. ROGERS *Ess.* II. i. 74 A still more serious fault in Locke is what we may venture to call a tang, if not of materialism, of something that displays a latent tendency towards it.

**b.** Distinctive or characteristic flavour or quality.

**1868** ALEX. SMITH *Last Leaves* 242 You cannot touch the tang of any literary coterie. **1900** H. HARLAND *Cardinal's Snuff-box* xv. 122 His speaking-voice..was sweet, but with a kind of trenchant edge upon it, a genial asperity, that gave it character, tang. **1903** *Daily Chron.* 8 Oct., Such a phrase as 'Food-taxers' has not the requisite tang.

**Tang** (tæŋ), *sb.*[2] A word sometimes app. purely echoic, denoting the strong ringing note produced when a large bell or any sonorous body is suddenly struck with force, or a tense string is sharply plucked; but often denoting a sound of a particular tone, esp. (? under the influence of TANG *sb.*[1]) one of an unpleasant kind; a twang.

(Some place here Shakspere's 'tongue with a tang' (see TANG *sb.*[1] 5 c), which has prob. influenced some of the later uses here quoted.)

**1669** HOLDER *Elem. Speech* 78 There is a pretty affectation in the Allemain, which gives their Speech a different Tang from ours. **1686** BUNYAN *Country Rhymes* xxix. 37 Nor is there anything gives such a tang When by these Ropes these Ringers ring them well. **1866** LOWELL *Study Wind.* 120 But he had hoped for a certain tang in the down-come of the bell. **1871** P. H. WADDELL *Ps. in Scotch* Pref. 2 Mony a tang o' his [David's] harp had its ain sugh eftirhen' in Gethsemane. **1880** [see TANKARD 3]. **1883** *Century Mag.* XXVI. 888 A sort of fever which lent a petulant tang to her speech. **1892** *Star* 9 Aug. 1/7 The organist has..a hard task in eradicating the awful Cambridgeshire tang from the voices of his raw material. **1897** MISS BROUGHTON *Dear Faustina* xiv, Faustina is still fondly smiling, but in her tone there is the slight tang of displeasure. **1899** CROCKETT *Kit Kennedy* iii. 20 A..voice..with the snell Scottish scolding 'tang' in it, which is ever more humorous than alarming to those whom it addresses.

**b.** quasi-*adv.* As an imitation of the sound of a vibrating string.

**1812** H. & J. SMITH *Rej. Addr.*, *Theatre* 25 Tang goes the harpsichord, too-too the flute.

**Tang** (tæŋ), *sb.*[3] *dial.* [Of Norse origin; = Norw., Da., Færoese *tang*, Sw. *tång* seaweed, Icel. *þáng* fucus. The Norns of Orkney and Shetland had also, like Norwegian, *tang*.] A collective name for large coarse seaweeds, esp. species of *Fucus*; tangle, sea-wrack; also called *sea-tang*.

**Black tang**, the bladder-wrack, *Fucus vesiculosus*. **Prickly tang**, *F. aculeatus*. **Yellow tang**, *F. nodosus*.

**1547** SALESBURY *Welsh Dict.*, *Dylysc*, Tang. **1655** Br. J. RICHARDSON *Observ. O. T.* 11 The likeliest reason is from the Hebrew appellation, calling it the sea of weeds, or sedge, *mare algosum*, of flag, or rush, or tange. **a 1733** *Shetland Acts* 33 in *Proc. Soc. Ant. Scot.* (1892) XXVI. 201 That none take bait nor cast tang in another man's ebb. **1769** PENNANT *Zool.* III. 169 Lying under the stones among the tang on the rocky coasts of Anglesea. **1796** *Statist. Acc. Scot.* XVII. 233* The sea-oak (*Fucus vesiculosus*, Lin.), which we denominate black tang. **1809** EDMONDSTON *View Zetland Isl.* II. viii. 6 Before 1808, the yellow tang and the black tang were the only species used in the manufacture of kelp. **1810** *Edin. Rev.* XVII. 146 The prickly tang..often grows intermixed with the bladder-wrack. **1859** H. KINGSLEY *G. Hamlyn* xxxiv, Wet-footed and happy, dragging a yard or so of sea-tang behind her.

**b.** *Comb.*, as *tang-covered* adj.; **tang-fish**, the seal; **tang-sparrow**, the rock pipit (*Anthus obscurus*); **tang-whaup**, the whimbrel (*Numenius phæopus*).

**1888** JESSIE M. E. SAXBY *Lads of Lunda* 122 The *tang-covered crown of the Skerry. **1809** EDMONDSTON *Zetland* II. 292 Seals are seen..[on] the coast of Zetland, and are vulgarly known by the name of *tang-fish. **1822** HIBBERT *Shetl. Isl.* 586 The smaller seals, or Tang-fish, so named from being supposed to live among the Tang. **1880** JAMIESON, *Tang-sparrow*. **1885** SWAINSON *Provinc. Names Birds* 46 Rock pipit..called from being exclusively confined to the sea shore..also..Tang sparrow (Shetland Isles). **1808–18** JAMIESON, *Tang-whaup*, the whimbrel, Orkn. **1833** *Montagu's Ornith. Dict.* 534 Whimbrel...*Provincial.* Curlew knot...Tang-whaup.

**Tang** (tæŋ), *sb.*[4] Also **tangue.** [f. native name.] = TANREC. **1891** in *Cent. Dict.*

**Tang** (tæŋ), *v.*[1] Also 5 taang, 7–9 *dial.* teng. [f. TANG *sb.*[1]]

**1.** *trans.* †To pierce; to prick (*obs.*); to sting as a serpent or an insect. Also *absol.* (Now *dial.*)

**a 1400–50** *Alexander* 4798 At oþir time of oure tulkis was tangid to dede And slayn with þa serpents a sowme out of noimbre. **c 1400** MAUNDEV. (Roxb.) xxxi. 141 Þai had within þam nedders, þat taanged þe husbands. **c 1440** *Alph. Tales* 473 A serpent..tanged hym hugelie. **1684** MERITON *Praise Ale* 149 Hee [an ox]'s teng'd, hee'l dee; Let's stick him. **1788** W. MARSHALL *Yorksh.* II. Gloss., *Teng*, to sting, as the bee or the adder. **1888** *Sheffield Gloss.* s. v., That bee has tanged me.

†**b.** *fig.* To pierce with grief or compunction.

**a 1400–50** *Alexander* 3637 Þan was he tangid with tene & turbled vnfaire.

**2.** To furnish with a tang, spike, flange, etc.

**1566** in *Invent. R. Wardr.* (1815) 169 Item sex pair of brasin calmes tangit with irne serving for battertis, moyanis, falconis. **1608** SYLVESTER *Du Bartas* II. iv. III. *Schisme* 122 But I will have your carrion shoulders goar'd With scourges tang'd with rowels [orig. *garnez de cloux*]. **1839** BYWATER *Sheffield Dial.* 33 He mood'st blade...Then he tangs it. **1879** *Cassell's Techn. Educ.* IV. 298/1 The end of the tube is bent and hammered over..and is afterwards 'dubbed' or 'tanged'.

†**b.** *fig.* To give point or effective force to. *Obs.*

**a 1518** SKELTON *Magnyf.* 2234 Tushe! these maters that ye moue are but soppys in ale; Your trymynge and tramynge by me must be tangyd.

**3.** To affect with a tang or (unpleasant) taste.

**1686** F. SPENCE tr. *Varillas' Ho. Medicis* 330 They tang'd the good and added to the bad. **1742** *Lond. & Country Brew.* I. (ed. 4) 36 The Liquor suffers, and will be tanged with a noxious Taste.

**Tang** (tæŋ), *v.*[2] [Mainly echoic, like TANG *sb.*[2] (cf. TING *v.*, TONG *v.*); but in some instances affected by TANG *sb.*[1]]

**1.** *trans.* To strike (a bell or the like) so as to cause it to emit a sharp loud ringing note.

**1556** OLDE *Antichrist* 10 Is it ynough for him to tang the watchebell? **1841** C. H. HARTSHORNE *Salop. Antiq.* Gloss. 590 *Tang*, to make a harsh discordant noise by striking against a piece of metal: chiefly used in reference to the swarming of bees. Ex. 'Tang the fryingpan'. **1842** AKERMAN *Wilts. Gloss.* s. v., 'To tang the bell' is to pull it.

**2.** To utter with a tang or ringing tone.

**1601** SHAKS. *Twel. N.* II. v. 163 Let thy tongue tang arguments of state; put thy selfe into the tricke of singularitie. **1863** COWDEN CLARKE *Shaks. Char.* ii. 54 Touchstone..can tang out a sarcasm with any professor of cynicism.

**b.** To impart a tang or twang to. *nonce-use.*

**a 1849** H. COLERIDGE *Young & Contemp.* Poems (1851) II. 328 So long shall Gray, and all he said and sung, Tang the shrill accents of the school-girl's tongue.

**3.** *intr.* To emit a sharp and loud ringing or clanging sound; to ring, clang.

[**1601** SHAKS. *Twel. N.* III. iv. 78 Let thy tongue langer [**1767** CAPELL tang] with arguments of state.] **1686** BUNYAN *Country Rhymes* xxix. 36 When ringers handle them with Art and Skill, They then the Ears of the bservers fill, With such brave Notes they ting and tang so well As to out strip all with their ding, dong, Bell. **1842** AKERMAN *Wilts. Gloss.*, *Tang*, to make a noise with a key and shovel at the time of swarming of a hive. **a 1845** HOOD *Tale of Trumpet* xxxvi, The smallest urchin whose tongue could tang, Shock'd the Dame with a volley of slang.

**4.** *trans. dial.* To affect (swarming bees) with a clanging noise, so as to make them settle: = TING *v.*

**1881** MISS JACKSON *Shropsh. Word-bk.* s. v., Mak' 'aste an' fatch the warmin'-pon an' the kay o' the 'ouse to tang the bees.

**5.** *intr.* To move *on* with a tang.

**1906** *Daily Chron.* 7 June 4/7 The car 'tanged' on.

‖**Tanga** (tæŋgă, ‖ tɒŋgă). *East Ind.* Forms: 6– tanga; 6–7 tango, 7 tang, tanghe, 8 tange, 9 tungah, tanja, tanka. [app. a. Pg. *tanga*, ad. *ṭaṅka* in various Indian vernaculars:—Skr. *ṭaṅka*, a weight = 4 māshās (beans), a coin; also, *ṭaṅkaka*, a stamped coin: see Note below.] A name (originally of a weight) given in India, Persia, and Turkestan to various coins (or moneys of account), the value of which varied greatly at different times and places; it is still applied in certain places to a copper, in others to a silver coin. **a.** in Goa, and on the Malabar coast: see quots.

**1598** W. PHILLIP *Linschoten* xxxv. 69/1 There is also a kinde of reckoning of money which is called Tangas, not that there is any such coined, but are so named onely in telling, fiue Tangas is one Pardaw,..foure Tangas good money are as much as fiue Tangas bad money. *Ibid.* xcii. 161/2 Foure Tangoes. **1615–16** R. STEELE in Purchas *Pilgrimes* (1625) I. IV. xiii. 523 Their moneyes in Persia..are ..of Copper, like the Tangas and Pisos of India. **1662** J. DAVIES tr. *Mandelslo's Trav.* 107 Five *Tanghes* make a Serafin of silver, which..is set at 300. Reis, and six *Tanghes* make a *Pardai.* **1698** FRYER *Acc. E. India & P.* 207 [Coins in Goa], 60 Rees make a Tango. **1700** S. L. tr. *Fryke's Voy. E. Ind.* xii. 180 Some Chests of Tanges and Larines, (which is a certain Money of that Country). **1766** GROSE *Voy. E. Ind.* (1772) I. 283 (Y.) Throughout Malabar and Goa, they use tangas, vintins, and pardoo xeraphin. **1858** SIMMONDS *Dict. Trade*, *Tanga*, *Tanja*, a money of Goa on the Malabar coast, worth about 7½*d.* [**1886** YULE *Hobson-Jobson* 682 The name still survives at Goa as that of a copper coin equivalent to 60 reis or about 2*d.*]

**b.** in Turkestan, Persia, Tibet, etc.

**1740** THOMPSON & HOGG in Hanway *Trav.* (1762) I. IV. lii. 242 Their coin [at Khiva] is ducats of gold,..also tongas, a small piece of copper, of which one thousand five hundred are equal to a ducat. *Ibid.* 244 Their money [at Bokhara] is ducats of gold,..also a piece of copper, which they call *tongas*, that pass at fifty to eighty to a ducat, according to their size. **1815** MALCOLM *Hist. Persia* II. xx. 250 One tungah..a coin about the value of five pence. **1904** *Times* 19 Sept. 12/6 (*Tibet*) The official rate of exchange is three tankas to a rupee.

[*Note.* Under the Mogul sovereigns, the silver ṭaṅka was the chief silver coin, the same as the silver dinar or later rupee; mention is also made in 14th c. of a ṭaṅka or dinar of gold, worth 10 silver dinars. About 1500 there were black or copper ṭaṅkas, of which 20 went to the old silver ṭaṅka. In the end of the 16th century, the *tanga* was a money of account, and afterwards a copper coin, at Goa, where it is still in use: see quot. 1886. The name also survives, in derived forms, in most of the Indian vernaculars, as that of a copper coin, and in Urdū, in its Sanskrit form and sense, as that of a weight. The identity of the Turkī *tanga*, *tonga* with the Sanskrit word has been disputed, and the word attributed to a Chagatai Turkī origin.]

**Tanga**, var. of TONGA, an Indian cart.

‖**Tangalung** (tæŋgălʊŋ). Also tangga-. [Malay *tanggălung*.] The civet cat of Sumatra and Java, *Viverra tangalunga*; the Sumatran civet.

**1820** SIR S. RAFFLES in *Trans. Linn. Soc.* (1822) XIII. 251–2. **1824** T. HORSFIELD *Zool. Researches Java*, etc. s. v. *Viverra Rasse*, A very perfect specimen of the Viverra Zibetha, the Tanggalung of the Malays, forwarded from Sumatra by Sir Stamford Raffles...The Tanggalung is two feet six inches long; the head measures six inches and three-fourths, and the tail eleven inches. **1843** *Penny Cycl.* XXVI. 406/2.

**Tangara, Tangaroid**: see TANAGER.

**Tange**, obs. form of TANG, TANGA, TONG.

**Tanged** (tæŋd), *a.* [f. TANG *sb.*[1] and *v.*[1] + -ED.] Having a tang; furnished with a tang to fix in a handle; barbed; forked.

**1888** *Sheffield Gloss.*, *Tanged*, forked. **1891** R. DAY in *Proc. Soc. Antiq.* 22 Jan. 226 A small tanged chisel. **1896** KIPLING *Seven Seas* 125, I left my views of Art, barbed and tangled below the heart Of a mammothistic etcher at Grenelle. **1899** R. MUNRO *Prehist. Scotl.* v. 167 Arrow points may be divided into tanged and untanged. **1904** BUDGE *Guide 3rd & 4th Egypt. Rooms Brit. Mus.* 8 Iron javelin-head, tanged...Barbed and tanged arrow-heads of iron.

**Tangena**: see TANGHIN.

**Tangence** (tæ·ndʒĕns). *rare.* [a. F. *tangence* (1835 in Dict. Acad.), f. *tangent* adj.: see -ENCE] The act or fact of touching, touch; point of contact.

**1840** *Blackw. Mag.* XLVIII. 275 They [Correggio's paintings] stand betwixt passion—the tangence of mentality and materiality, and the distinctly intellectual and moral.

**Tangency** (tæ·ndʒĕnsi). [f. L. type **tangentia*, f. *tangent-em* TANGENT: see -ENCY.] The quality or condition of being tangent; state of contact.

*Problem of tangencies*, in old *Geom.*, a problem in which it is required to describe a circle passing through given points, and touching straight lines or circles the position of which is given, the data being limited to three.

**1819** *Pantologia* s. v., Problem of Tangencies. *Ibid.*, The treatise of tangencies was restored by Vieta. **1867** F. H. LUDLOW *Little Brother* 34 The wildest point of tangency which Man's railroads make with Weaver's woods. **1895** H. P. STOKES in *Athenæum* 16 Nov. 690/1 Points of tangency between certain Elizabethan celebrities.

**Tangent** (tæ·ndʒĕnt), *a.* and *sb.* [ad. L. *tangens*, *tangent-em*, pr. pple. of *tang-ĕre* to touch; used by Th. Fincke, 1583, as sb. in sense = L. *linea tangens* tangent or touching line. In F. *tangent*, *-e* adj., *tangente* sb. (Geom.), Ger. *tangente* sb.] **A.** *adj.*

**1.** *Geom.* Of a line or surface in relation to another (curved) line or surface: Touching, i. e. meeting at a point and (ordinarily) not intersecting; in contact.

A surface may also be tangent to another surface along a *line* (e.g. a plane in contact with a cylinder). In quot. 1869, Taking place along a tangent. Cf. B. 1 b.

**1594** BLUNDEVIL *Exerc.* II. (1597) 48 b, Our moderne Geometricians haue of late inuented two other right lines belonging to a Circle, called lines Tangent, and lines Secant. **1644** DIGBY *Nat. Bodies* xiii. § 8. 114 The reflexion must follow the nature of tangent surfaces. **1713** BERKELEY *Guard.* No. 126 ⁋ 2 Hence..the earth,..without flying off in a tangent line, constantly rolls about the sun. **1866** PROCTOR

*Handbk. Stars* 33 The cone, instead of being a tangent-cone, is supposed to be a secant-cone, intersecting the sphere. **1869** TYNDALL in *Fortn. Rev.* 1 Feb. 245 All the vibrations tangent to the little circle..are reflected perfectly polarized. **1876** *Catal. Sci. App. S. Kens. Mus.* § 102 Model exhibiting the simultaneous transformation..of the tangent paraboloid of the conoïd into the tangent plane of the cylinder.

†**b.** *Cryst.* Applied to a plane replacing an edge or solid angle of a crystal (which is more properly a *secant* plane). *Obs.*

**1823** H. J. BROOKE *Introd. Crystallogr.* 109 Edges replaced by tangent planes. **1851** RICHARDSON *Geol.* v. 88 Crystals often present the appearance of having lost their edges and solid angles, which are then said to be replaced by tangent planes.

**c.** *transf.* Said of the wheel of a bicycle or tricycle having the spokes tangent to the hub.

**1885** *Bicycling News* 6 Aug. 664/1 Laced tangent wheels, hollow rims, Hancock's tyres.

**2.** *fig.* 'Flying off at a tangent' (see B. 1 c); divergent, erratic.

**1787** BURNS *Let. to Moore* 23 Apr., If once this tangent flight of mine were over, and I were returned to my wonted leisurely motion in my old circle. **1799** E. DU BOIS *Piece Family Biog.* I. 152 The voluble loquacity and tangent style of reasoning of their new companion.

**3.** In general sense. **a.** Touching, contiguous.

**1846** ELLIS *Elgin Marb.* I. 107 Beaten together till the tangent surfaces were fitted to each other.

**b.** Of or pertaining to touch; *tangent sense*, sense of touch. *nonce-use.*

**1802** E. DARWIN *Orig. Soc.* III. 424 Say, did these fine volitions first commence From clear ideas of the tangent sense?

**B.** *sb.*

**1.** *Math.* (ellipt. for *tangent line.*) [= Fr., Ger. *tangente.*] **a.** *Trigonometry.* One of the three fundamental trigonometrical functions (cf. SECANT, SINE), originally considered as functions of a circular arc, now usually of an angle (viz. that subtended by such arc at its centre): *orig.* The length of a straight line perpendicular to the radius touching one end of the arc and terminated by the *secant* drawn from the centre through the other end; in mod. use, the ratio of this line to the radius, or (equivalently, as a function of the angle) the ratio of the side of a right-angled triangle opposite the given angle (if acute) to that of the side opposite the other acute angle (the tangent of an obtuse angle being numerically equal to that of its supplement, but of opposite sign). Abbrev. *tan.*

Tables of tangents and cotangents were constructed and used by the Arab mathematicians of the 9th and 10th c. (see Nallino *Al Battani, Opus astronomicum*, Milan 1903, I. 182); but began to be constructed in Christendom late in the 15th c. The names *tangens* and *secans*, introduced by Thos. Fincke (Finkius) in 1583, had no connexion with the names used by the Arabs.

[**1583** FINCKE *Geometriæ Rotundi* v. 64 De semicirculi sinibus, tangentibus, secantibus. *Ibid.* 73 Recta sinibus connexa est tangens peripheriæ aut eam secans.] **1594** BLUNDEVIL *Exerc.* II. (1597) 57 b Of which Arke the line A D is the Tangent, and the line C D is the Secant thereof. **1635** [see COTANGENT]. **1658** PHILLIPS, *Tangent*,.. a Mathematical Term used chiefly in Astronomy,..signifies, a right line perpendicular to the Diameter drawn by the one extream of the given Arch, and terminated by the Secant. **1690** LEYBOURN *Curs. Math.* 397 Which Scales of Tangents..let be extended to 75 deg. at least. **1728** PEMBERTON *Newton's Philos.* 366 The refracting powers.. will be in the duplicate proportion of the tangents of the least angles, which the refracted light can make with the surfaces of the refracting bodies. **1828** HUTTON *Course Math.* II. 3 As the arc increases from 0, the sines, tangents, and secants, all proceed increasing, till the arc becomes a whole quadrant.., and then the sine is the greatest it can be..; and both the tangent and secant are infinite.

**b.** *Geom.* A straight line which touches a curve (or curved surface), i. e. meets it at a point and being produced does not (ordinarily) intersect it at that point.

In Higher Geometry a tangent is regarded as the limiting position of a line intersecting a curve when the two (or more) points of intersection coincide, and is hence defined as a straight line passing through two (or more) consecutive points of the curve. If the curve be conceived as traced by a moving particle, the tangent at any point of it represents the direction of motion at that point; hence a body moving in a curve, when the restraining force is withdrawn, flies off *at a tangent*, i. e. along the tangent (cf. the *fig.* use in c). At a point of inflexion, where the curvature (i. e. deviation from the straight line) changes its direction, the tangent intersects as well as touches the curve.

**1655** T. GIBSON *Syntaxis Math.* xiii. 142 To draw a tangent [cf. 1551 RECORDE *Pathway*, touche line] to any point assigned in any section, or from any point without the section. **1704** J. HARRIS *Lex. Techn.* I, *Tangent*, of a Parabola, (or other Conick Section, or Geometrical Curve) is a Right Line Drawn, cutting the Ax Produced, and touching the Section in one Point without cutting it. **1706** W. JONES *Syn. Palmar. Matheseos* 221 A Tangent to any point of the Circumference [of a circle] is Perpendicular to the Radius drawn to that Point. **1832** *Nat. Philos.* II. *Introd. Mech.* p. xvi. (Usef. Knowl. Soc.), If a stone, whirled round in a sling, gets loose at the point A.., it flies off in the direction AB: this line is called a tangent.

**c.** In general use, chiefly *fig.* from b, esp. in phrases (*off*) *at, in, upon a tangent*, i. e. off or away with sudden divergence, from the course or direction previously followed; abruptly from one course of action, subject, thought, etc., to another.

**1771** SMOLLETT *Humph. Cl.* (1815) 219 After having twelve times described this circle, he lately flew off at a tangent to visit some trees at his country-house in England. **1815** *Paris Chit-Chat* (1816) II. 92 The passengers on the roof, being at the highest point of projection flew off in a tangent, and were precipitated..into a field of new-mown hay. **1825** BENTHAM *Ration. Reward* 393 That manner which they have..of flying off in tangents when they are pressed. **1865** LECKY *Ration.* (1878) I. 284 *note*, Flying off at a tangent from his main subject. **1875** WHITNEY *Life Lang.* viii. 150 To abandon the established habits of speech and go off upon a tangent. **1879** MISS BRADDON *Clov. Foot* x, Smoking his cigar, and letting his thoughts wander away at a tangent every now and then.

**2.** The upright pin or wedge fixed at the back of each of the keys of a clavichord, which on the depression of the key pressed up against the string and caused it to sound, acting also as a bridge to determine the pitch of the note. [= Ger. *tangent.*]

[**1614** PRÆTORIUS *Syntagma Musicum* III. 68 Es hat aber ein solch Geigenwerk an statt der Tangenten [etc.].] **1878** A. J. HIPKINS in Grove *Dict. Mus.* I. 367 The tangents..not only produced the tones but served..to measure off the vibrating lengths required for the pitch of the notes. **1896** C. W. NAYLOR *Shaks. & Music* 68 *note*, The German clavichord had 'tangents' of brass at the ends of the key levers.

**3.** Short for *tangent scale, tangent galvanometer*: see C.

**1861** W. H. RUSSELL in *Times* 14 May, His guns were without screws, scales, or tangents. **1905** PREECE & SIVEWRIGHT *Telegraphy* 404 Perhaps the most useful galvanometer for general testing purposes is the Tangent.

**4.** A straight section of railway track. *U. S. colloq.* **1895** in *Funk's Stand. Dict.*

**C.** Combinations and special collocations.

(Some of these are examples of the adj. qualifying a sb.)

**Tangent backsight**, = *tangent scale* (*a*); **tangent balance**, a balance in which the weight is shown on a graduated arc by a pointer attached to the beam; the bent-lever balance, common as a letter-balance; **tangent compass** = next; **tangent galvanometer**, a galvanometer in which the tangent of the angle of deflection of the needle is proportional to the strength of the current passing through the coil; **tangent scale**, (*a*) in *Gunnery*, a kind of breech-sight in which the heights of the steps or notches correspond to the tangents of the angle of elevation; (*b*) a graduated scale indicating the tangents of angles (see quot. 1902); **tangent screw**, a screw working tangentially upon a toothed circle or arc so as to give it a slow motion for delicate measurements or adjustments; **tangent sight**, = *tangent scale* (*a*).

For *tangent cone, line, plane, surface*, etc., see A. 1.

**1862** *Catal. Internat. Exhib.* II. XI. 23 The 'Tangent back-sight' is elevated by a rack and pinion, the latter having a micrometer wheel for finer readings than the divisions on the tangent stem allow. **1873** MAXWELL *Electr. & Magn.* (1881) II. 325 The current is..proportional to the tangent of the deviation, and the instrument is therefore called a 'Tangent Galvanometer.' **1876** PREECE & SIVEWRIGHT *Telegraphy* 267 The insulation resistance is the only test which is taken by means of the tangent-galvanometer. **1859** F. A. GRIFFITHS *Artil. Man.* (1862) 51 A *Tangent scale is affixed to the breech of Guns, and Howitzers, by means of which the requisite elevation may be given. **1902** SLOANE *Stand. Electr. Dict., Tangent scale*, an arc of a circle in which the number of graduations in any arc starting from zero are proportional to the tangent of the angle subtended by such arc. The system is for use with tangent galvanometers. **1862** *Catal. Internat. Exhib.* II. XIII. 5 Circumferenter or miner's dial, with *tangent screw adjustment. **1877** KNIGHT *Dict. Mech., Tangent-screw*, an endless screw tangentially attached to the index-arm of an instrument of precision, enabling a delicate motion to be given to the arm after it has been clamped to the limb, and permitting angular measurements to be made with greater exactness than could be done were the movement entirely effected by hand. **1908** *Treat. Serv. Ordn. Roy. Artill.* 513 The *tangent sights consist of triangular nickel-plated steel bars graduated on the rear face.

**Tangental** (tændʒe·ntăl), *a.* [f. TANGENT *sb.* + -AL.] Of, pertaining to, or of the nature of a tangent; = next, 1. Hence **Tange·ntally** *adv.*

**1849** H. MILLER *Footpr. Creat.* x. 109 Nor are the openings of the medullary rays frequent in the tangental section. **1856** DOVE *Logic Chr. Faith* I. ii. II. § 1. 91 These motions..are the result of two somethings, one of which is tangental, the other centripetal. **1867** J. HOGG *Microsc.* I. iii. 207 They are sometimes called the horizontal, vertical and tangental. **1891** *Cent. Dict.*, Tangentally.

**Tangential** (tændʒe·nʃăl), *a.* (*sb.*) [f. L. type **tangentia* (see TANGENCY) + -AL.] Of or pertaining to tangency or a tangent.

**1.** Of, pertaining to, or of the nature of a tangent; identical with, or drawn at, a tangent to a curve or curved surface.

**1630** R. DELAMAINE *Grammalogia* App. 62 If the Declination be above 38. gr. 3. m. you may move the Tangent of 45. softly alonge by the Tangentiall degrees of Declination in the fixed, untill 45. gr. in the moveable be opposite to 45. gr. in the fixed. **1763** *Phil. Trans.* LIII. 68 The proposed demonstration of this tangential property. **1828** J. M. SPEARMAN *Brit. Gunner* 265 The apparent level is a straight line tangential to the surface of the earth, or true level. **1881** TAIT in *Nature* XXV. 128 The glass is extended in a radial and compressed in a tangential direction.

**b.** Of motion or force: Acting along a tangent to a curved line or surface.

**1709** STEELE *Tatler* No. 43 ⁋ 7 The Tangential and Centripetal Forces, by their Counter-struggle, make the Celestial Bodies describe an exact Ellipsis. **1768** TUCKER *Lt. Nat.* (1834) I. 413 He might give the heavy planets their tangential motion by one strong and exactly poised stroke. **1880** BESSEY *Botany* 129 The tangential growth of the surrounding cells. **1883** *Science* I. 523/1 The tangential tension of the bark increases with the growth of the stem.

**c.** Of a thing: That lies in a tangent to a curved surface.

**1854** J. SCOFFERN in *Orr's Circ. Sc., Chem.* 388 One part [of a globular box] is furnished with a tangential jet. **1899** *Allbutt's Syst. Med.* VIII. 331 The tangential fibres of the cortex. **1901** A. J. EVANS in *Oxf. Univ. Gaz.* 12 Feb. 339/2 A small vase with incised returning spirals and tangential leaves. **1905** BOND *Goth. Archit.* 164 The ambulatory with tangential chapels.

**d.** *spec.* (*a*) Of the spokes of a wheel (as in a bicycle): Arranged as tangents to the hub. (*b*) Of a fabric (as a tire-cover): Having layers of thread lying diagonally from edge to edge, so as to distribute the strain.

**1898** *Cycling* 63 The best results are obtained from a fabric which..consists of layers of independent threads running diagonally from edge to edge of the cover and not interwoven. This is called a 'tangential' fabric because the pull travels lengthwise along the threads (as in a tangent spoke) and not across them.

**2.** *fig.* Going off suddenly 'at a tangent'; erratic; divergent; digressive.

**1867** F. H. LUDLOW *Genre Pict., Little Briggs & I*, 199 A remedy to this day sovereign..for all tangential aberrations from the back of a colt or the laws of society. **1876** T. HARDY *Ethelberta* (1890) 297 Those devious impulses and tangential flights which spoil the works of every would-be schemer who instead of being wholly machine is half heart. **1903** *Spectator* 31 Jan. 184/2 A collection of mixed and tangential information.

**b.** That merely touches a subject or matter.

**1825** HAZLITT *Spirit of Age, Coleridge* (1886) 46 Our author's mind is (as he himself might express it) tangential. There is no subject on which he has not touched, none on which he has rested. **1885** O. W. HOLMES *Emerson* 165 Emerson had only tangential relations with the experiment.

**B.** *sb. Geom. Tangential of a point* (in a curve of the third or higher order), the point at which a tangent at the given point meets the curve again.

**1858** CAYLEY *Coll. Math. Papers* II. 558 A derivative which may be termed the 'tangential' of a cubic, viz. the tangent at the point $(x, y, z)$ of the cubic curve $(*)(x, y, z)^3 = 0$ meets the curve in a point $(\xi, \eta, \zeta)$, which is the tangential of the first-mentioned point. **1859** *Ibid.* IV. 188. **1879** G. SALMON *Higher Plane Curves* v. (ed. 3) 130.

Hence **Tangentiality** (-ʃi,æ·liti), the quality or condition of being tangential.

**1889** *Philos. Mag.* Apr. 335 The perpendicularity of E and the tangentiality of H to the surface.

**Tangentially** (tændʒe·nʃăli), *adv.* [f. prec. + -LY [2].] In a tangential way; in the manner, position, or direction of a tangent; at a tangent.

**1839** URE *Dict. Arts* 479 The fusees are fixed obliquely and not tangentially to their peripheries. **1854** J. SCOFFERN in *Orr's Circ. Sc., Chem.* 269 A force acting..tangentially to the circle. **1884** BOWER & SCOTT *De Bary's Phaner.* 620 They are connected one with another in their longitudinal course by numerous anastomoses both radially and tangentially. **1903** *19th Cent.* July 82 The rapidly moving fragment flies away tangentially.

**Ta·ngently**, *adv. rare.* [f. TANGENT *a.* + -LY [2].] At a tangent.

**1903** *Times* 6 Feb. 9/6 Some of them were occasionally thrown off tangently.

**Tangerine** (tændʒĕrī·n), *a.* and *sb.* Also 8 -een, 9 -ene. [f. *Tanger, Tangier* + -INE [1].] **A.** *adj.* Of or pertaining to, or native of Tangier, a seaport in Morocco, on the Strait of Gibraltar. *Tangerine orange*, a small flattened deep-coloured variety of orange from Tangier, *Citrus nobilis* var. *Tangeriana.*

**1710** ADDISON *Tatler* No. 250 ⁋ 3 An old Tangereen Captain with a Wooden Leg. **1841** TILLERY in *Gard. Chron.* 781 The Tangerine Orange.—I beg to draw attention to the cultivation of this as a fruit for the dessert. **1882** *Garden* 18 Feb. 122/2 Two dishes of Tangerine Oranges.

**B.** *sb.* **1.** A native of Tangier.

**1860** *All Year Round* No. 71. 491 Winterfield was sold to a Tangarene.

**2.** A Tangerine orange: see A.

**1842** *Gard. Chron.* 6 The Tangerine I suspect to be only a variety of it [the Mandarin Orange]. **1891** *Daily News* 26 Dec. 5/4 There is an unusually good supply of tangerines. **1908** R. W. CHAMBERS *Firing Line* vi, Please get me a few tangerines—those blood-tangerines up there.

**b.** A deep orange colour; also *attrib.*

**1899** *Daily News* 16 Sept. 7/3 Ruddy pink and tender amethyst, tangerine, orange, mist-grey [etc.]. **1904** *Ibid.* 6 Oct. 8/4 Taking as the colour key-note, the fashionable tangerine shade.

**Tanges**, obs. form of TONGS.

**Tanggalung**: see TANGALUNG.

**Tanggyl**, var. of TANGYL *a. Obs.*

‖**Tanghan, tangun** (tā·ŋhăn, tæ·ŋgʊn), **tānyan** (tā·nyăn). *East Ind.* [Hindi *ṭāṅghan*, f. Tibetan *rTañan*, f. *rTa* horse (Yule).] The native horse of Tibet and Bhutān, a strong and sure-footed little pony. Also *tanghan horse, pony.*

**1774** in Aitchison *Treaties*, etc. (1876) I. 155 That.. the Deb Rajah shall pay an annual tribute of five Tangun horses to the Honorable Company. *c* **1774** BOGLE *Narr.* in

Markham *Tibet* (1876) 17 We were provided with two tangun ponies of a mean appearance. **1793** HODGES *Trav. India* 31 These horses are called tanyans, and are mostly pye-bald. **1840** *Penny Cycl.* XVI. 143/2 The small horses, the *Tanguns*, are noted for their hardihood and activity, but they are not natives, but introduced from Tibet, and.. they degenerate on the south of the Himalaya Mountains.

**Tanghe**, obs. form of TANGA.

**Tanghicin**: see after next.

‖ **Tanghin** (tæ·ŋgin). Also 8 **tanguin**, 9 **tanquen, tangkin, tangena, -gina.** [a. F. *tanghin*, ad. Malagasy *tangena, tangen'.*]

**1.** A poison obtained from the kernels of *Tanghinia venenifera*, N.O. *Apocynaceæ*, a shrub of Madagascar, the fruit of which is a large purplish drupe. The kernels were formerly used by the natives to test the guilt of a suspected person. Also *attrib.*, as *tanghin poison*; *tanghin camphor* = *tanghinin* (see below).

**1788** tr. *Sonnerat's Voy.* III. 44 The tanguin is one of the most terrible poisons in the vegetable world. **1842** *Penny Cycl.* XXIV. 31/1 This name [*Tanghinia*] was given by Aubert du Petit Thouars to the plant which produces the celebrated Tanghin poison of Madagascar. *Ibid.*, He..insisted that the Tanghin should be administered to himself. **1860** R. F. BURTON *Centr. Afr.* II. 357 The Tangina poison of the Malagash. **1880** J. SIBREE *Gt. African Isl.* xiv. 282 The chief use of the tangena ordeal was for the detection of witchcraft, by which the African races understand the use of poisonous drugs for evil purposes.

**2.** The shrub itself: more properly *tange·na* or *tangi·na*. Also *attrib.*

**1866** *Treas. Bot.* 1123/1 Tanghin or Tanquen is the only plant belonging to a genus which botanists have named Tanghinia. **1880** J. SIBREE *Gt. African Isl.* xiv. 281 The tangena is a small and handsome tree growing in the warmer parts of the island, and the poison is procured from the nut of its fruit. **1889** AGNES MARION *Tangena Tree* xiii, Horror-stricken, she flung the Tangena-fruit away.

Hence † **Ta·nghicin**, † **Ta·nghin**, **Ta·nghinin**, the poisonous principle of tanghin, tanghin camphor.

**1838** T. THOMSON *Chem. Org. Bodies* 926 A peculiar crystallized matter is extracted, to which they have given the name *tanghicin*. **1868** WATTS *Dict. Chem.* V. 658 The kernels.. contain..a crystallisable substance called tanghin-camphor or tanghinin...Tanghinin is very poisonous.

‖ **Tangi** (tæ·ŋi). *N. Zealand.* [Maori, = lament, dirge.] A formal lamentation; a dirge, a coronach.

**1845** E. J. WAKEFIELD *Adv. N. Zealand* I. vii. 194 They ..bore it [a corpse]..to the village, where the usual *tangi* took place. **1883** RENWICK *Betrayed* 41 'Tis the tangi floats on the sea-borne breeze, In its echoing notes of wild despair. **1901** *Scotsman* 9 Apr. 6/5 The..Agent-General for New Zealand recently received from the Maori inhabitants of his colony a 'tangi' or 'lament' on the death of Queen Victoria.

**Tangibility** (tændʒibi·lĭti). [f. as TANGIBLE: see -ILITY.] The state or quality of being tangible; perceptibility to the touch; tangibleness.

**1665** NEEDHAM *Med. Medicinæ* 99 As if they did touch after the gross manner of tangibilitie. **1678** CUDWORTH *Intell. Syst.* I. v. 770 Tangibility and impenetrability, were elsewhere made by him the very essence of body. **1823** COLERIDGE *Table-t.* 3 Jan., Define a vulgar ghost...It is visibility without tangibility.

**b.** With *a* and *pl.*: A tangible thing or matter.

**1849** H. MILLER *Footpr. Creat.* xiv. 255 Cut off..from all the tangibilities of the real waking-day world.

**Tangible** (tæ·ndʒĭb'l), *a.* [ad. L. *tangibilis* that may be touched, f. *tangĕre* to touch: see -BLE. So F. *tangible* (16th c. in Littré).]

**1.** Capable of being touched; affecting the sense of touch; touchable.

**1589** PUTTENHAM *Eng. Poesie* II. i. (Arb.) 78 Of the things that haue conueniencie by relation, as the visible by light colour and shadow: the audible by stirres, times and accents:..the tangible by his obiectes in this or that regard. **1678** CUDWORTH *Intell. Syst.* I. v. 769 That body, or that which is tangible and divisible, is the only substantial thing. **1825** MACAULAY *Ess., Milton* (1887) 11 The.. desire of having some visible and tangible object of adoration. **1886** MYERS *Phantasms of Living* I. Introd. 59 These sounds, these movements, these tangible apparitions.

**b.** Hence, Material, externally real, objective.

**1620** T. GRANGER *Div. Logike* 56 Whereof externall, and tangible workes are produced. **1827** HARE *Guesses* Ser. I. (1873) 3 The threatenings of Christianity are material and tangible. **1874** L. STEPHEN *Hours in Library* (1892) I. iii. 117 He would not have had much chance of winning tangible rewards. **1875** FORTNUM *Maiolica* i. 1 From a very early period of human existence, known to us only by the tangible memorials of primitive inhabitants.

**2.** That may be discerned or discriminated by the sense of touch; as *a tangible property* or *form*.

**1664** JER. TAYLOR *Dissuas. Popery* i. 5 This method..is the best, the most certain, visible and tangible. **1684** J. P. tr. *Frambresarius' Art Physic* i. 14 [They have] so many real Agreements of Tangible Qualities. **1709** BERKELEY *Th. Vision* § 45 Certain ideas perceivable by touch—as distance, tangible figure, and solidity. **1814** CHALMERS *Evid. Chr. Revel.* viii. 211 The only way to learn its tangible properties is to touch it.

**3.** *fig.* That can be laid hold of or grasped by the mind, or dealt with as a fact; that can be realized or shown to have substance; palpable.

**1709** BERKELEY *Th. Vision* § 96 Tangible ideas. *a* **1763** BYROM *Crit. Rem. Horace* Poems 1773 I. 310 That none of you touch a most tangible Blunder. **1839** JAMES *Louis XIV*, II. 284 These proposals assumed a more tangible form..after the arrival of Turenne. **1852** GROTE *Greece* II. lxxiii. (1862) VI. 415 Without any tangible ground of complaint.

**4.** Capable of being touched or affected emotionally.

**1813** L. HUNT in *Examiner* 11 Jan. 22/2 He..is like the ..Executioner,..tangible neither by groan nor by indignation.

Hence **Ta·ngibleness**, the quality or state of being tangible; **Ta·ngibly** *adv.*, in a tangible manner.

**1727** BAILEY vol. II, **Tangibleness*, capableness of being touched or felt by the Touch. **1843** MILL *Logic* I. ii. § 4 When only one attribute..is designated by the name; as visibleness; tangibleness; equality; squareness; milkwhiteness; then the name can hardly be considered general. **1893** C. A. WINGERTER in Barrows *Parl. Relig.* II. 1410 We have not appreciated it [duty to the poor] fully unless we recognize its tangibleness. **1847** WEBSTER, *Tangibly. **1858** MACDONALD *Phantastes* v. (1878) 73 The human forms appeared..more tangibly visible.

**Tangina, tangkin**: see TANGHIN.

**Tangis**, obs. Sc. form of TONGS.

**Tangle** (tæ·ŋg'l), *sb.*[1] [= Norw. *taangel, tongul*, Færoese *tongul*, ON. and Icel. *þöngull* (:— *þangulr*) 'the stalk of *Laminaria digitata*', app. deriv. of *þang* bladder-wrack, TANG *sb.*[3]

The etymological history is not clear; *tangle* cannot have come down from ON., because ON. *þ* remains in Sc. and Eng. as *th*: cf. *Thurso, Thorpe, Thwaite, Thoresby*, etc.; it must therefore either have spread south from Orkney and Shetland, where ON. *þ* had become *t*, or be a later adoption from Norwegian or other lang. having *t* for ON. *þ*. (The name 'tangle' is not mentioned among the Algæ in Lightfoot's *Flora Scotica*, 1778.)]

**1.** A general term for the larger seaweeds, species of *Fucus* and allied genera; = TANG *sb.*[3] Often *sea-tangle*. (Prob. orig. an inaccurate use; cf. 2.)

**1536** BELLENDEN *Cosmogr.* xiv. in *Cron. Scot.* (1821) I. p. xlix, Maister Alexander Galloway..liftet up ane seetangle, hingand full of mussill schellis fra the rute to the branchis. **1596** DALRYMPLE tr. *Leslie's Hist. Scot.* (S.T.S.) I. 62 He saw bred of a sey tangle, mussilis. **1603** HOLLAND *Plutarch's Mor.* 676 It hath gotten about the keele a deale of mosse, reits, kilpe, and tangle. **1664** *Phil. Trans.* I. 13 Upon which..Rock-weed or Sea-tangle did grow a hand long. **1744** PRESTON *ibid.* XLIII. 61 There are Plenty of Sea-weeds, called Tangle, growing on the Rocks, of which might be made Kelp. **1895** CROCKETT *Men of Moss-Hags* lii, Certain..persons were carrying away sea-tangle from his foreshore.

**2.** *spec.* Either of two species of seaweed, *Laminaria* (*Fucus* L.) *digitata* and *L. saccharina*, having long leathery fronds, the young stalk and fronds of which are sometimes eaten. (This is the Norse sense, and prob. the proper one.)

**1724** RAMSAY *Tea-t. Misc.* (1733) I. 91 Scrapt haddocks, wilks, dulse and tangle. **1807** THOMPSON *Cat. Plants Berwick-on-Tweed* 112 *Fucus digitatus*, Fingered Fucus; Tangle. **1820** SCOTT *Monast.* Answ. Introd. Epist., I never saw it cast ashore any thing but dulse and tangle. **1845** EDMONSTON *Flora of Shetland* 54 *Laminaria digitata* is by them [the Orcadian peasantry] termed Tangle. **1846** LINDLEY *Veg. Kingd.* 21 The young stalks of Laminaria digitata and saccharina are eaten under the name of 'tangle'. **1875** J. H. BALFOUR in *Encycl. Brit.* I. 508/2 Dulse and tangle was formerly a common cry in the streets of Edinburgh.

**3.** *Comb.*, as *tangle-strewn, -tasselled* adjs.; **tangle-fish**, a popular name of the needle-fish or pipe-fish, *Syngnathus acus*; **tangle-picker**, a bird, the Turnstone (*Strepsilas interpres*); **tangle-tent**, in surgery, a tent or pledget of seaweed; **tangle-weed, tangle-wrack**, = sense 1.

**1838** PARNELL in *Mem. Werner. Soc.* VII. 394 *Syngnathus acus*, *Tangle-Fish, Scotland, [so called] by the fishermen, in consequence of its being found under seaweed, which they call tangle. **1882** YARRELL *Hist. Birds* (ed. 4) III. 290 Searching among sea-weed for its food: whence its appropriate Norfolk name of '*Tangle-picker'. **1882** *Good Cheer* 41 Cool sea scented breezes came up from the *tangle-strewn sands. **1812** W. TENNANT *Anster Fair* I. xxvi, Up-propp'd from sea, a *tangle-tassell'd shape. **1889** J. M. DUNCAN *Clin. Lect. Dis. Women* v. (ed. 4) 17 The cervix [uteri] was dilated by a *tangle-tent. **1834** M. SCOTT *Cruise Midge* (1863) 20 Far down amongst the *tangleweed and coral branches at the bottom of the deep green sea. **1890** W. PATER *Wks.* (1901) VIII. 23 All around the gulf there is but an expanse of *tanglework. **1721** RAMSAY *Prospect of Plenty* 228 Wild shores.. Plenish'd with nought but shells and *tangle-wreck.

**Tangle** (tæ·ŋg'l), *sb.*[2] [f. TANGLE *v.*[1]]

**1.** A tangled condition, or *concr.* a tangled mass; a complication of threads, hairs, fibres, branches, boughs, or the like, confusedly intertwined or interlaced, or of a single long thread, line, or rope, involved in coils, loops, and knots; a snarl, ravel, or complicated loose knot. Also *transf.* of streams, paths, etc. similarly intertwisted or confused.

**1615** W. LAWSON *Country Housew. Gard.* (1626) 20 That it [the soil] may run among the small tangles [of the roots] without straining or bruising. **1637** MILTON *Lycidas* 69 To sport with Amaryllis in the shade, Or with the tangles of Neæra's hair. **1667** — *P. L.* IX. 632 Hee [the serpent] leading swiftly rowld In tangles, and made intricate seem strait, To mischief swift. *a* **1774** TUCKER *Lt. Nat.* (1834) II. 35 If upon combing his head he meets with a tangle that tears off two or three hairs. **1842** DARWIN in *Life & Lett.* (1887) I. 321 This bow became covered with a tangle of creepers. **1856** KANE *Arct. Expl.* I. xxix. 378 The rise and fall of the tides always breaks up the ice..in a tangle of irregular, half-floating masses. **1861** D. COOK *P. Foster's D.* vii, One of a small tangle of courts between Long Acre and New Street, Covent Garden. **1873** HALE *In His Name* v. 26 In a tangle of low, scrubby oaks. **1879** M. D. CONWAY *Demonol.* I. III. ix. 386 The Gorgon's head ..with its fearful tangle of serpent tresses. *Mod.* This string is all in a tangle.

**b.** *spec.* A dredger for sweeping the sea-bed, consisting of a bar to which are attached a number of hempen 'mops', in the fibres of which the more delicate marine specimens are entangled.

**1883** LESLIE tr. *Nordenskiöld's Voy. Vega* 97 The hempen tangles were used, and brought up a very abundant yield of large, beautiful animal forms. **1884** *Science* IV. 227/2 The true province of the tangles is a very rocky bottom, where neither the dredge nor trawl can be safely used.

**2.** *fig.* A complicated and confused assemblage; a muddle, jumble, complication, medley, puzzle; a confused network of opinions, facts, etc.; also, a perplexed state.

**1757** DYER *Fleece* II. Poet. Wks. (1761) 110 And silent, in the tangles soft involv'd Of death-like sleep. **1800** COLERIDGE *Death Wallenst.* 183 Where's he that will unravel This tangle, ever tangling more and more? **1858** SEARS *Athan.* III. x. 330 The tangles of metaphysics in which they sought to involve the great Apostle. **1866** J. H. NEWMAN *Gerontius* v. 42 Methinks I know To disengage the tangle of thy words. **1873** MORLEY *Rousseau* II. 126 The complex tangle of the history of social growths. **1883** SIR T. MARTIN *Ld. Lyndhurst* xi. 285 The skill with which he reduced into method and compass the enormous tangle of facts and figures.

**3.** *Comb.* = in a tangle, tangled, as *tangle-twine, -twist, -wood*; *tangle-haired, -headed, -tailed* adjs.; also **tangle-swab**, one of the mops of a tangle for dredging (sense 1 b).

**1861** L. L. NOBLE *Icebergs* 68 They were a russet, *tangle-haired and shaggy-bearded set. **1908** *Westm. Gaz.* 15 Aug. 15/3 A gipsy woman, with *tangle-headed children, carrying faggots on their backs. **1884** *Science* IV. 148/1 Several *tangle-swabs were generally attached to the hinder end of the bag. *Ibid.* 227/2 The use of hempen tangle-swabs attached to the dredge was introduced by the English exploring-steamer Porcupine in 1868 or 1869. **1883** W. G. COLLINGWOOD *Philos. Ornament* v. 121 The builders of early Italian cathedrals..now run wild with the northern *tangle-tailed mysteries. **1878** BROWNING *La Saisiaz* 94 The wreaths, *Tangle-twine of leaf and bloom. **1889** *Chicago Advance* 6 June, 'Twould take ten miles o' this here *tangletwist to make one. **1894** *Ibid.* 26 Apr., He scuttled off in a wild panic through the thick *tanglewood.

**Ta·ngle**, *sb.*[3] *Sc.* and *north. dial.* [Of uncertain origin: perh. belonging to TANGLE *sb.*[1] or [2], or due to a vague combination of the two notions, or to some association with *dangle*.]

**1.** A pendent icicle *Sc.*

**1673** *Wedderburn's Voc.* 34 (Jam.) *Stiria*, a tangle of yce. **1813** E. PICKEN *Misc. Poems* I. 77 (E.D.D.) Frae ilk buss, the tangles gay, Hang skinklin' in the mornin' ray. **1888** BARRIE *Auld Licht Idylls* i, The waterspout that suspends its 'tangles' of ice over a gaping tank.

**2.** A tall and limp or flaccid person. *Sc.*

**1789** ROSS *Helenore* (ed. 3) 21 She's but a tangle, tho' shot out she be.

**3.** Anything long and dangling, as a tress of hair, a long root-fibre, a torn loosely-pendent strip of cloth, etc.

**1864** S. BAMFORD *Homely Rhymes*, etc. 148 Her bonny tangles Were hung wi star-spangles. **1892** M. C. F. MORRIS *Yorksh. Folk-talk* 386 When t' tang'ls is brokken they [potatoes] can't taatie. **1904** *Eng. Dial. Dict.* s. v. (W. Yks.), Her gown was all rives and tangles.

**4.** Applied to plants having long, winding, and often tangled stalks, as the species of *Myriophyllum* (Water Milfoil) and *Potamogeton* (Pondweed); and to plants of tangled growth, as *Blue Tangle(s* (U.S.), *Red Tangle*: see quots.

**1857** DUNGLISON *Med. Lex.*, Tangles, Blue, *Gaylussacia dumosa*. **1866** *Treas. Bot.*, *Blue Tangle*, an American name for *Gaylussacia frondosa*. **1886** BRITTEN & HOLL. *Eng. Plant-n.*, Tangle, Red, *Cuscuta Epithymum*.

**b.** *Comb.* **tangle-berry** = *Blue Tangles* (see 4), DANGLE-BERRY.

**Ta·ngle**, *a. Sc.* [f. TANGLE *sb.*[3]] Long and limp; tall and loose-jointed. Also in comb., as *tangle-backed*.

*c* **1817** HOGG *Tales & Sk.* I. 291 She was perfectly weak and tangle, her limbs being scarcely able to bear her weight. **1825** JAMIESON, *Tangle*, tall and feeble, not well knit..as, 'a lang tangle lad'. **1896** L. KEITH *Ind. Uncle* x. 172 Yin o' the tangle-backit kind.

**Tangle** (tæ·ŋg'l), *v.*[1] Also 4–5 **tangil, -yl**, 4–6 **-el(e**, 6 **-ell.** [Known first in later 14th and early 15th c. MSS. of Hampole's *Psalter* (*a* 1340), as a variant reading for *tagil, -yl*, the form in the earliest MSS., used also in other works attributed to Hampole: see TAGLE *v.*, of which *tangle* was app. a nasalized variant.

The vb. thus appears a century and a half earlier than TANGLE *sb.*[1] seaweed, from which some have suggested its derivation. It is however possible that the later senses 4 and 5 may have been associated with and influenced by that sb. TANGLE *sb.*[2] was a direct derivative of the vb.]

† **1.** *trans.* To involve or engage (a person) in affairs which encumber and hamper or embarrass, and from which it is difficult to get free; = ENTANGLE *v.* 2. Chiefly *refl.* and *pass.*; also, to embarrass, confuse (the brain, mind, conscience, etc.).

*a* **1340** HAMPOLE *Psalter* xxxix. 16 (MS. U.) Na man may wit how many vices ere þat men ere tangild with. [*So* 8 *MSS.*: tangild, -gyld, -glyd, -glid, -gled, -geled; 2 *earliest MSS.* tagild.] — *Ibid.*, *Abacuc* 31 [see TAGLE *v.*]. **1526** *Pilgr. Perf.* (W. de W. 1531) 63 b, With the whiche he wyll tangle theyr myndes and trouble theyr conscyences. **1526** TINDALE *1 Tim.* vi. 10 Coveteousnes.., which whill some lusted after, they..tanglyd them selves with many sorowes. **1530** PALSGR. 752/2, I am tangled in busynesse, and can nat tel howe to wynde me out. **1561** NORTON & SACKV. *Gorboduc* IV. ii, O happie wight, that suffres not the snare Of murderous minde to tangle him in bloode. **1577–87** HOLINSHED *Chron.* III. 1133/2 The queene tangling hir selfe contrarie to promise in hir husbands quarrell. **1671** MILTON *Samson* 1665 Not willingly, but tangl'd in the fold Of dire necessity.

**2.** To involve in material things that surround or wind about, so as to hamper and obstruct; also, to cover or wreathe with intertwined growth or with something that obstructs. Also *fig.*

**1506–11** SIR R. GUYLFORDE *Pylgr.* (Camden) 60 We were soo tangled in among the sayde deserte yles that we coude not gette oute frome amonges them. **1593** DRAYTON *Eclogues* vi. 167 See where yon little..Lambe of mine It selfe hath tangled in a crawling Breere. **1727** DE FOE *Hist. Appar.* iv. (1840) 44 But hang..upon the mere thread, and choose to hamper and tangle themselves. **1829** SIR W. NAPIER *Penins. War* II. 265 He could not, alone, force his way to Lisbon,..through a country tangled with rivers. **1853** G. JOHNSTON *Nat. Hist. E. Bord.* I. 144 The sloes and brushwood that tangle the brae. **1856** KANE *Arct. Expl.* I. xx. 250 His journal-entry referring to the 23ᵈ, while tangled in the ice. **1867** LADY HERBERT *Cradle L.* x. 280 Beautiful gardens..tangled over with ipomeas and other bright creepers. **1885** R. BUCHANAN *Annan Water* v, The hedges were tangled with wild rose bushes.

**3.** To catch and hold fast in or as in a net or snare; to entrap. Chiefly, in early use always, *fig.*

**1526** TINDALE *Matt.* xxii. 15 The farises..toke counsell howe they myght tangle him in his wordes. — *1 Cor.* vii. 35 This speake I..not to tangle you in a snare: but for that which is honest and comly vnto you. **1540–1** ELYOT *Image of Gov.* 20 They woorke theyr nette so finely,..that in one meishe or other he shall be tangled. **1592** SHAKS. *Ven. & Ad.* 67 Looke how a bird lyes tangled in a net. **1593** — *2 Hen. VI*, II. iv. 55 [They] Haue all lym'd Bushes to betray thy Wings, And flye thou how thou canst, they'le tangle thee. **1635** BARRIFFE *Mil. Discip.* i. (1643) 5 They doe but tangle themselves in their owne snares. **1806** J. GRAHAME *Birds Scotl.* 43 May never fowler's snare Tangle thy struggling foot.

**4.** To intertwist (threads, branches, or the like) complicatedly or confusedly together; to intertwist the threads or parts of (a thing) in this way; to put or get (a long thread or a number of threads, etc.) into a tangle. Also *fig.*

**1530** PALSGR. 752/2, I tangell thynges so togyther that they can nat well be parted a sonder...You have tangled this threde so that it is marred. **1577** B. GOOGE *Heresbach's Husb.* II. (1586) 54 They come vp as it weere to one roote, and tangled together. **1665** *Phil. Trans.* I. 35 Those insects..tangled together by their long tailes. **1671** GREW *Anat. Plants* iii. App. § 9 As we are wont to tangle the Twigs of Trees together to make an Arbour Artificial. **1850** SCORESBY *Cheever's Whalem. Adv.* ix. (1858) 117 As the different coils run from the tub, they sometimes, when not well laid down, get 'foul' or tangled. **1855** MACAULAY *Hist. Eng.* xxii. IV. 798 He had cut the knot which the Congress had only twisted and tangled.

**5.** *intr.* for *refl.* To be or become tangled or confusedly intertwined. In quot. 1908, to have a tangled course, to twist about confusedly.

**1575** TURBERV. *Falconrie* 175 The falcon bating this way and that way, she shall never twinde nor tangle bicause the ring followeth hir still. **1623** WEBSTER *Duchess Malfi* III. ii, My hair tangles. **1657** W. COLES *Adam in Eden* cci, It [dodder] tangleth about it like a net. **1713** J. PETIVER in *Phil. Trans.* XXVIII. 204 The whole Plant is clammy, and its branches tangle much. **1902** *Westm. Gaz.* 3 Sept. 3/1 Above them [graves] tall grass grows and tangles, as if it were holding them together. **1908** *Sat. Rev.* 26 Sept. 392/1 She wandered..Down lanes that tangled through the countryside.

† **b.** *fig.* To become involved in contention. *Obs.*

**1535** *St. Papers Hen. VIII*, II. 249 Perceyving that thErle of Ossorie soo stedfastely and ernestly tanglid against the same traictors. **1536** *Ibid.* 330 OConor his he that now moste begynneth newly to tangle ageinst the army.

**6.** *Comb.* of the verb-stem with an object, as **tangle-leg(s**, that which tangles the legs: a popular name of an American shrub, the Hobble-bush, *Viburnum lantanoides*; also for strong beer or spirits; cf. TANGLEFOOT b; **tangle-toad**, a name for the creeping buttercup, *Ranunculus repens* (*Eng. Dial. Dict.*).

**1860** BARTLETT *Dict. Amer.* s. v. *Hobble Bush*, A straggling shrub, also called Tangle-Legs and Wayfaring. **1880** R. JEFFERIES *Gt. Estate* iv. 68 Some more 'tangle-legs'—for thus they called the strong beer. **1882** SALA *Amer. Revisit.* (1885) 285 The particular kind of whiskey known as 'tangle-leg'.

† **Ta·ngle**, *v.*² *Obs.* [freq. of TANG *v.*²: see -LE 3.] *intr.* To give out a quick succession of ringing sounds. Cf. TWANGLE, TINKLE. Hence † **Ta·ngling** *vbl. sb.*

*c* **1580** JEFFERIE *Bugbears* Epil., Song ii. in *Archiv Stud. Neu. Spr.* (1897), With janglynges, with banglynges, with tanglynges, A sprityng go we! *a* **1652** BROME *Queene's Exchange* II. ii, The great Bells of our Town, they tingle they tangle, They jingle they jangle, the Tenner of them goes merrily.

**Tangled** (tæ·ŋg'ld), *ppl. a.* [f. TANGLE *v.*¹ + -ED¹.] Interlaced or intertwined in a complicated and confused manner; matted, mixed up confusedly; *fig.* complicated, intricate.

**1590** SHAKS. *Mids. N.* v. i. 125 His speech was like a tangled chaine: nothing impaired, but all disordered. **1634** MILTON *Comus* 181 The blind mazes of this tangl'd Wood. *a* **1717** PARNELL *Health* 45, I lead where Stags thro' tangled Thickets tread. **1750** SHENSTONE *Rural Elegance* 204 The tangled vetch's purple bloom. **1808** SCOTT *Marm.* VI. xvii, Oh what a tangled web we weave When first we practise to deceive! **1874** M. CREIGHTON *Hist. Ess.* i. (1902) 20 The tangled thread of Italian politics.

**Tanglefoot** (tæ·ŋg'lfut), *a.* and *sb.* [f. TANGLE *v.*¹ + FOOT *sb.*] **a.** *adj.* That tangles or entangles the foot. **b.** *sb.* That which tangles or entraps the foot; *spec. U. S. slang*, an intoxicating beverage, esp. whisky. Also *attrib.* So **Ta·ngle-footed** *a.*, having tangled feet, stumbling.

**1860** BARTLETT *Dict. Amer.*, *Tangle-foot*, one of the Western figurative terms for whiskey. **1871** *Hartford Courant* 17 Mar. (Farmer *Slang*), He proceeded..toward a neighboring saloon in quest of tangle-foot. **1881** 'MARK TWAIN' *Innoc. at Home* ii, He could..hold more tanglefoot whisky without spilling it than any man in seventeen counties. **1888** *Voice* (N. Y.) 27 Dec., [Stories] of this tanglefooted variety, which trip up and throw themselves by their absurdity and self-contradiction. **1893** *Chicago Advance* 28 Sept., The tangle-foot complications in which it was sure to involve its defenders. **1900** *Daily News* 11 Apr. 3/2 The poisonous 'Cape Smoke', or 'tanglefoot', which they [soldiers] get in too great abundance out here. **1908** W. R. HEARST in *Westm. Gaz.* 2 Oct. 5/1 The deeper he sinks into the tangle-foot of corruption and contradiction.

**Tangle-leg(s**: see TANGLE *v.*¹ 6.

**Tanglement** (tæ·ŋg'lmĕnt). [f. TANGLE *v.*¹ + -MENT.] The fact or condition of being tangled; an instance of this; a tangle.

**1831** J. WILSON *Unimore* ii. 199 All matted thick with briery tanglement Like Indian Jungle. **1879** J. MORISON in *Expositor* IX. 122 A little tanglement of phraseology. **1892** *Chambers's Jrnl.* 6 Aug. 508/2 We lay utterly helpless amidst this tanglement of weeds.

**Tangler** (tæ·ŋglər). [f. TANGLE *v.*¹ + -ER¹.] One who or that which tangles.

*c* **1520** M. NISBET *N. Test. in Scots*, *Jas.* ii. 21 *margin*, Abraham was nocht a wayne tangler of faith.

**Ta·nglesome**, *a.* [f. TANGLE *sb.*² or *v.*¹ + -SOME.] Full of tanglement, tangled, confused. Also *dial.* (see quot. 1823).

**1823** E. MOOR *Suffolk Words & Phr.*, *Tanglesome*, discontented—obstinate—fretful—not essentially different from *Tankersome*. **1888** *Engineer* LXV. 317 Things are in such a tanglesome condition.

**Ta·ngling**, *vbl. sb.*¹ [f. TANGLE *v.*¹ + -ING¹.] The action of TANGLE *v.*¹; complicated or confused intertwining; complication; † contention.

[*c* **1340**: see TAGLE *v.*] **1535** *St. Papers Hen. VIII*, II. 272 Which had bene wele forwardes by this tyme, yf this wilful tangeling with OConour had not bene. **1538** in *Lett. Suppress. Monasteries* (Camden) 169 Many leasses grauntede oute by the olde prior,..with muche tangullyng and besines. *a* **1633** AUSTIN *Medit.* (1635) 282 When wee thus let slip these heavenly Thred Lines..wee fall to tangling, tying, and knitting. **1868** *Rep. U. S. Commissioner Agric.* (1869) 289 The silk skeins are tied to prevent tangling.

**b.** *concr. pl.* Things that tangle or entangle.

**1575** TURBERV. *Venerie* 138 Me thinkes I see the Toyle, the tanglings and the stall Which are prepared and set full sure, to compasse me withall. **1591** PERCIVAL *Sp. Dict.*, *Cazcarias*, tanglings about chickins feete. **1904** *Daily News* 26 Nov. 6/8 Clinging tanglings of the thorny briar.

**Tangling**, *vbl. sb.*²: see TANGLE *v.*²

**Ta·ngling**, *ppl. a.* [f. TANGLE *v.*¹ + -ING².] That tangles, in various senses of the verb.

*a* **1586** SIDNEY *Ps.* XXV. x, This Lord..will set free My feet from tangling net. **1667** MILTON *P. L.* IV. 176 The undergrowth Of shrubs and tangling bushes. **1756** H. JONES *Earl of Essex* 17 Amidst thy tangling snares involv'd. **1801** BLOOMFIELD *Rural T.*, *Walter & Jane* 115 When to these tangling thoughts I've been resigned.

Hence **Ta·nglingly** *adv.*, in a tangling manner. **1847** in WEBSTER.

**Tangly** (tæ·ŋgli), *a.*¹ [f. TANGLE *sb.*¹ + -Y.] Strewn with, full of, or consisting of tangle.

**1762–9** FALCONER *Shipwr.* III. 777 Helpless, on the tangly beach he lay. *a* **1851** MOIR *Old Seaport* iii, Far beneath the surf upheaved The sea-weed's tangly arms.

**Ta·ngly**, *a.*² [f. TANGLE *sb.*² + -Y.] Abounding in tangles; tangled.

**1813** J. C. HOBHOUSE *Journey* (ed. 2) 655 A tangly flat, overrun with low shrubs. **1887** C. L. PIRKIS *Dateless Bargain* I. ii. 44 More limp and tangly than a skein of silk. **1899** *Westm. Gaz.* 12 June 1/3 Plunge in the jungle's tangly growth.

**Ta·ngly**, *a.*³ *Sc.* and *north. dial.* [f. TANGLE *sb.*³ + -Y.] Long and limp, or flaccid; feeble, flabby; = TANGLE *a.*

**1812** P. FORBES *Poems* 57 (E.D.D.) Tanglie taperin' tails. **1855** ROBINSON *Whitby Gloss.*, *Tangling* or *Tangly*, untidy in dress, ragged or hanging in shreds. 'A lang tangly lass', having the well-known meaning of 'long and lazy'. **1904** *E. Dial. Dict.* s. v., (N. Yks.) He's a great tangly lad.

**Tango**, var. TANGA, East Indian coin.

**Tangram** (tæ·ngræm). [Origin obscure: second element app. -GRAM.] The name given to a Chinese geometrical puzzle consisting of a square dissected into five triangles, a square, and a rhomboid, which can be combined so as to make two equal squares, and also so as to form several hundred figures, having a rude resemblance to houses, boats, bottles, glasses, urns, birds, beasts, men, etc.

(The Chinese name is *Ch'i ch'iao t'u* 'seven ingenious plan'. The name *tangram* seems to have been given in England, or perhaps in U.S. but some have conjectured for the first element Chinese *t'an* 'to extend', or *t'ang* commonly used in Canton for 'Chinese'. Others have conjectured *Tan* to be the name of the inventor; but no such person is known to Chinese scholars.)

**1864** WEBSTER, *Tangram*, a Chinese toy made by cutting a square of thin wood, or [the like] into seven pieces. **1874** [see PUZZLE *sb.* 3 b]. **1908** H. E. DUDENEY *Tales with Tangrams* in *Strand Mag.* Nov. 581 It is probable that Tangrams were originally designed not as a pastime, but as a means of instruction...Professor Max Müller said that 'the science of Tangrams gave evidence of a higher state of civilization than now exists in China'.

**Tangs**, northern and Sc. form of TONGS. **Tangue**, obs. f. TANG *sb.*¹ and ⁴. **Tanguin**: see TANGHIN. **Tangun**, var. TANGHAN, Tibetan horse.

† **Tangyl**, *a. Obs.* (See quot.)

*c* **1440** *Promp. Parv.* (E.E.T.S.) 473 Tangyl [*v.r.* tanggyl], or froward and angry, *bilosus..*, *ffelleus*.

**Tan-house.** [f. TAN *v.* and *sb.*¹ + HOUSE.]

**1.** A building in which tanning is carried on.

**14..** *Voc.* in Wr.-Wülcker 585/7 *Frunitorium*, a tanhous. **1529** *Act* 21 *Hen. VIII*, c. 13 § 32 Be it enacted..That no Spiritual Person..have..any Manner of Tan-house. **1626** *Knaresb. Wills* (Surtees) 102 All the barke in the tann house..all the tubbes and seasterans in the tanhouse. **1791–1823** D'ISRAELI *Cur. Lit.*, *Bibliomania*, I [Bruyere] as little..care to visit the tan-house, which he calls his library.

**2.** [f. TAN *sb.*¹] A building for storing tan-bark.

**1858** SIMMONDS *Dict. Trade*, *Tan-house*, a deposit place for tanners' bark.

‖ **Tania, tanier, tannier** (ta·nyă, tæ·nyəɹ). [a. Tupi *taña, taya*, Carib *taya*.] A species of *Caladium* or *Xanthosoma* (*X. sagittifolium*), N.O. *Araceæ*, cultivated in Brazil, the West Indies, and tropical Africa, for its farinaceous tuberous root; it is closely allied to the EDDOES.

[**1625** PURCHAS *Pilgrims* IV. 1310 There are certaine Taiaobas, that are like Cabiges.] **1756** P. BROWNE *Jamaica* 332 The purple Cocco and Tannier. **1766** J. BARTRAM *Jrnl.* 10 Feb., in W. Stork *Acc. E. Florida* (1790) 32 Breakfasted on a mess of tanniers, a species of eddo. **1792** MAR. RIDDELL *Voy. Madeira* 84 The *arum virginiana*, or *tannier*, and the *arum esculentum*, or *eddoe*, are two excellent farinaceous vegetables. **1871** KINGSLEY *At Last* vi, His patch of provision-ground..gives him..yam, tania, cassava, and fruit too. **1898** L. CROOKALL *Brit. Guiana* vi. 83 Then there are white yams and buck yams,..tannias and eddoes.

**Tanin**, obs. form of TANNIN.

**Tanist** (tæ·nist). *Anc. Irish* and *Gaelic Law.* Also 6 **taniste, tanistih, tanest, taynist**, 9 **tanaist**; cf. TANISTER. [ad. Irish and Gael. *tánaiste*, OIr. *tanaise, -aiste*, anything parallel or second to another; the next heir to an estate.] The successor apparent to a Celtic chief, usually the most vigorous adult of his kin, elected during the lifetime of the chief: see TANISTRY.

**1538** *St. Papers Hen. VIII*, III. 56 Murghe Obreene, the said Obrenes broder, being the tanest, or successour to Obreene. **1543** *Ibid.* 481 He have restored this berer, his eldist brother, to the office or rombe of Taniste. **1596** SPENSER *State Irel.* Wks. (Globe) 612/1 The Tanistih hath also a share of the countrey allotted unto him. **1646** SIR J. TEMPLE *Irish Rebell.* 9 *note*, In every Irish country there was a Lord or Chieftain, and a Tanist, who was his successor apparent...He that was most active, of greatest power, and had most followers, alwayes caused himself to be chosen Tanist. **1761–2** HUME *Hist. Eng.* (1806) III. xlvi. 690 The chieftains and the tanists, though drawn from the principal families, were not hereditary, but were established by election, or, more properly speaking, by force and violence. **1813** SCOTT *Rokeby* IV. vi, The Tanist he to great O'Neale. **1861** PEARSON *Early & Mid. Ages Eng.* XXX. 373 Any one of the reigning family might succeed the chief. The heir-apparent was nominated by election among the tribe in the chief's lifetime, and called 'tanist'.

**b.** *Comb.*, as **tanist-abbot** (see quot.); **tanist-stone**, a name given to some large monoliths, popularly supposed to mark the spot where tanists were formerly elected.

*a* **1627** C. MAGEOGHEGAN tr. *Ann. Clonmacnois* 147 He was called in Irish tanaise abbaid, tanist [*lit.* second] of the abbot, or seenab [= secundus abbas], in anglo-irish, tanist-abbot. **1851** D. WILSON *Preh. Ann.* (1863) I. v. 140 The Tanist-Stones, where the new chief or king was elected. **1885** *Blackw. Mag.* July 116/1 In Scotland, Tanist stones..have been frequently found.

Hence **Ta·nistship**, the office or dignity of a tanist. So **Tani·stic** *a.*, of, pertaining to, or proceeding by the system of tanistry.

**1585** in Hardiman *O'Flaherty's Iar-Connaught* (1846) 313 That the..titles of captayneships, taynistships..be utterlie abollyshed. **1590** SIR J. PERROT in *Carew MSS.* (1869) 28 The captainries and tanistships. **1881** *Athenæum* 29 Jan. 157/3 The ancient earldoms were not partible, and the succession was tanistic.

† **Ta·nister.** *Obs. rare*⁻¹. [ad. Irish and Gael. *tanaistear*, f. *tanaiste* (see prec.) + *fhear* man.] = prec.

**1612** DAVIES *Why Ireland*, etc. (1787) 182 For every theft under fourteen pence, a fine of five marks should be paid; forty-six shillings and eight pence to the Captain, and twenty shillings to the Tanister.

**Tanistry** (tæ·nistri). *Anc. Irish* and *Gaelic Law.* Also 6 **-istrye**, 7 **-estry**, 7–8 **thanistry.** [f. TANIST + -RY.] A system of life-tenure among the ancient Irish and Gaels, whereby the succession to an estate or dignity was conferred by election upon the 'eldest and worthiest' among the surviving kinsmen of the deceased lord.

1596 SPENSER *State Irel.* Wks. (Globe) 611/2 All the Irish doe hold theyr landes by Tanistrye. *a* 1604 HANMER *Chron. Irel.* (1633) 17 The two sonnes were put beside, and the eldest of the sept (after the Irish Tanistrie) tooke place. 1617 MORYSON *Itin.* II. 6 The Irish Law of Tanistry (by which a man is preferred to a boy, and the Vncle to that Nephew whose Grandfather ouerliues the Father, and commonly the most actiue Knaue, not the next Heire, is chosen). 1663 SIR R. GORDON *Govt. Scotl.* in *Macfarlane's Geogr. Collect.* (S.H.S.) II. 391 The law of Tanistrie wes that a Prince dying and leaving behind him children in minority..the neerest male of the blood royall..tooke the government upon him. 1778 *Phil. Surv. S. Irel.* 396 Him they called Thanist, and the Custom Thanistry. 1827 HALLAM *Const. Hist.* (1876) III. xviii. 344 The law of tanistry, of which the principle is defined to be that the demesne lands and dignity of chieftainship descended to the eldest and most worthy of the same blood. 1904 *Times, Lit. Supp.* 22 July 229/1 Despite tanistry..Scotland managed to have real Monarchs when Ireland had none.

**b.** The office of a tanist (= Gael. *tanaisteachd*).

1813 SCOTT *Rokeby* IV. vi, Against St. George's cross blazed high The banners of his Tanistry.

**Tanja**, var. TANGA, East Indian coin.

**Tanjib**: see TANZIB.

**Tank** (tæŋk), *sb.*[1] Forms: 7 tanke, tanque, tancke, tanck, 7– tank. [In sense 1, perh. immediately from an Indian vernacular: cf. Guz. *tānkh* an underground reservoir for water (Shakespear), *ṭānki* a reservoir of water, a small well (Wilson); Marāthi *ṭānken*, *tāken*, a reservoir of water, a tank (Wilson); *tānkā* a cistern of stone inside a house, etc., a reservoir for rain-water: words which some would connect with Skr. *taḍāga* pond, lake, pool; others think that they are all derived from Pg. *tanque* pond = Sp. *estanque*, F. *étang*:—L. *stagnum* pond, pool, with which at least the Indian words were identified by the Portuguese, who even in the *Roteiro de Vasco da Gama* and through the 16th c. applied *tanque* to the Indian reservoirs, called also in Fr. *estang* (Pyrard de Laval *c* 1610). The 17th c. Eng. forms *tanque* and *tanke* appear to be taken from the Pg.; *tanck*, *tank*, on the other hand, with It. *tancho* (Varthema 1510), may have been from Guz. *tānkh*. As to the Eng. use in senses 1 b and 2, it is not clear whether this came from Anglo-Indian usage, or was immediately related to Pg. *tanque*. It could scarcely arise out of earlier Eng. or Sc. *stank* 'pond, fish-pond, stagnant pool, ditch', since this never in sense approached that of *tank*.]

**1.** In India, A pool or lake, or an artificial reservoir or cistern, used for purposes of irrigation, and as a storage-place for drinking-water.

*c* 1616 TERRY *Voy. E. Ind.* (1655) 105 Besides their Rivers, ..they have many Ponds, which they call Tanques,..fill'd with water when that abundance of Rain fals. 1634 SIR T. HERBERT *Trav.* 51 Tancks or couered ponds of water, fild by the beneficiall raines, for the vse and drink of Trauellers. 1638 W. BRUTON in Hakluyt *Voy.* (1807) V. 50 (Y.) A very faire Tanke,..a square pit paved with gray marble. 1698 FRYER *Acc. E. India & P.* 159 Oblong stone Tank...In this all of both Sexes Wash (this Solemnity being called the *Jatry*, or Washing). 1799 SIR T. MUNRO in G. R. Gleig *Life* (1830) I. iv. 241 One crop under a tank, in Mysore or the Carnatic, yields more than three here. *c* 1813 MRS. SHERWOOD *Stories Ch. Catech.* xxiv. (1873) 258 Near to the mosque were many trees, and a stone tank, full of clear water. 1877 G. CHESNEY in *19th Cent.* Nov. 610 The greater part of the irrigation in southern India is effected by means of tanks...These tanks in fact resemble the reservoirs for water-works now to be found in most parts of England... Artificial lakes..they more properly deserve to be called. 1886 *Daily Tel.* 16 Jan. (Cassell), The tank covers seventy-two acres, and is one of the largest in India.

**b.** A natural pool or pond; a 'stank'. *dial.* and *U.S.* (Quot. 1678 perh. belongs to 1.)

1678 PHILLIPS (ed. 4), *Tank*, (old word) a little Pool or Pond. 1825 BROCKETT *N. C. Words*, *Tank*, a piece of deep water, natural as well as artificial. 1867 LADY HERBERT *Cradle L.* vii. 169 They took a walk..to the 'Pool of David', a square tank at the bottom of the valley full of rain water. 1890 *Amer. Antiquarian* July 201 Here and there great hollows filled with rain-water. These places are called 'tanks' by the ranchmen. 1896 *Dialect Notes* (Amer.) I. 426 (E.D.D.) Drive your horse into the tank.

**2.** An artificial receptacle, usually rectangular or cylindrical and often of plate-iron, used for storing water, oil, or other liquids in large quantities.

1690 DRYDEN *Don Sebast.* II. ii, Here's plentiful provision for you, Rascal, sallating in the Garden, and water in the tanck. 1706 PHILLIPS, *Tank*,..a Cistern to keep Water in. 1835 SIR J. ROSS *Narr. 2nd Voy.* xxiv. 234 The ice in the tanks was this day reduced. 1837 GORING & PRITCHARD *Microgr.* 197 The stop-cocks..being opened, the water from the tank will flow freely into the vessels O and H. 1869 E. A. PARKES *Pract. Hygiene* (ed. 3) 12 Tanks to hold rain-water require constant inspection. 1871 *YoungGentleman's Ann.* Dec. 28 Other engines..carry their water in a tank (called a saddle-tank) which rests on the top of the boiler. 1881 RAYMOND *MiningGloss.*, *Tank*, a subterranean reservoir into which a pump delivers water for another pump to raise. 1891 *New York Tribune* 17 Oct. 12/3 (Funk) The gas tank was fifty feet in diameter.

**3.** Short for *tank-engine*, *-steamer*, etc.

1891 *Daily News* 23 Sept. 3/3 They were picked up in a very exhausted condition by a German oil tank from New York to Rotterdam. 1903 *Westm. Gaz.* 31 Dec. 3/2 Trains hauled..by a mammoth tank.

**4.** *attrib.* and *Comb.*, as *tank-head*, *-maker*, *-room*, *-sinker*, *-storage*, *-top*, *-work*; *tank-like* adj.; *spec.* in sense 1, as *tank-cultivation*, *-sill*, *-system*, *-water*; *tank-watered* adj.; in sense 2, constructed as or fitted with a tank for conveying liquids, etc., esp. mineral oils in bulk, as *tank-barge*, *-boat*, *-car*, *-steamer*, *-train*, *-truck*, *-van*, *-vessel*, *-wagon*; **tank-engine**, a railway engine which carries the fuel and water receptacles on its own framing and not in a separate tender; **tank-furnace**, a glass-making furnace furnished with a tank (*Cent. Dict.* 1891); **tank-iron**, plate-iron of a thickness suitable for making tanks; **tank-locomotive** (*U. S.*) = *tank-engine*; **tank-man**, **tank-pipe**: see quots.; **tank-plate** = *tank-iron*; **tank-runner**, the pheasant-tailed Jacana, or Water-pheasant, *Hydrophasianus chirurgus*, of India and Ceylon, so called from its ability to run over floating lotus-leaves, etc.; **tank-station**, a station or place where a tank or tanks are provided, e. g. on a railway for supplying water to the engines or for storing oil, in a mine for storing water; **tank-valve**: see quot.; **tank-waste**, the insoluble sediment from the dissolving tanks in alkali works; **tank-worm**, a nematoid worm inhabiting the mud of Indian tanks, and believed to be the young of the guinea worm.

1894 *Labour Commission* Gloss., **Tank-barges*,.. used specially for conveying tar and oil in bulk in large tanks fitted or built in the barges. 1889 *Daily News* 2 Jan. 2/4 The..recent explosion of a *tank-boat near Calais. 1874 KNIGHT *Dict. Mech.* 457/2 *Tank-car. 1877 *Ibid.*, *Tank-car*, a large tank mounted on a platform-truck for carrying petroleum or other liquid. 1904 *Daily Chron.* 23 Mar. 7/3 The railway provides tank cars and tank stations along its route for Russian oil only. 1875 *Madras Revenue Board Rep.*, The *tank cultivation suffered most. 1850 *Pract. Mech. Jrnl.* III. 33 The centre of the boiler..is 3½ inches lower in the *tank engine. 1864 WEBSTER, Tank engine. 1902 *Westm. Gaz.* 4 July 12/1 A tank-engine of absolutely novel type and colossal dimensions. 1895 *Funk's Standard Dict.*, **Tank-head*, the head or end of a metal tank. 1864 WEBSTER, *Tank-iron. 1897 *Daily News* 18 June 8/4 Round in shape, but flat and *tank-like on the top. 1905 *Westm. Gaz.* 21 May 1/3 It consisted of three terraces and a tank-like pond on the basement floor. 1877 KNIGHT *Dict. Mech.*, **Tank-locomotive*,..one having a tank or tanks enabling it to carry a supply of water sufficient for its own consumption without a tender. 1858 SIMMONDS *Dict. Trade*, **Tank-maker*, a manufacturer of iron cisterns for ships, or of slate, or well-secured plank cisterns on shore. 1909 *Westm. Gaz.* 21 May 4/1 The tank-makers in Germany cannot buy their raw material from abroad. 1891 *Labour Commission* Gloss., **Tank-men*, men employed in large steamers to look after the water tanks. 1894 *Ibid.* s.v. *Pipes*, **Tank pipes*, pipes used for filling or emptying the water ballast or fresh water tanks. 1892 *Daily News* 4 July 9/7 *Tank-plates are quoted £6 10s, and rods £7. 1901 *Scotsman* 2 Mar. 9/1 The circulation of sea-water in the *tank-room [of the zoological station]. 1905 A. ANDREW *Ind. Problems* ii. 51 In most places *tank silt can be got. This is a valuable manure. 1900 H. LAWSON *On Track* 37 Bush-fencers, *tank-sinkers, rough carpenters, &c.—were finishing the third and last culvert of their contract. 1889 *Daily News* 2 Jan. 2/4 The *tank steamer Oka..represents the advance so far made towards perfection in the building of ships designed for the carriage of [petroleum]. 1902 S. SMITH *Life-Work* xxii. 214 In Southern India the *tank system prevails. 1900 *Engineering Mag.* XIX. 678 The margin plates of the *tank top are put on, and the tank-top plating itself. 1901 *Munsey's Mag.* XXV. 749/1 Racks for the loading of *tank trains. 1904 *Blackw. Mag.* May 609/1 A crowd of Wadaruma women..rushed out to fill their gourds from the *tank-truck behind the engine. 1877 KNIGHT *Dict. Mech.*, **Tank-valve*, (Railway Engineering) a form of valve used in locomotive water-supply tanks, for admitting water to the discharge-pipe. 1887 *Daily News* 27 July 6/3 The commoner fish brought in *tank vans was sold by the consignees from the vans. 1877 KNIGHT *Dict. Mech.*, *Tank-vessel. *c* 1890 *Nature*, Disasters during the discharge of cargoes from tank-vessels. 1886 *Pall Mall G.* 10 June 14/1 [He] has invented a system of delivering oil in bulk by means of a street *tank-waggon. 1889 *Ibid.* 3 Aug. 7/1 A new process for the manufacture of soda..recovers the sulphur of the *tank waste. 1905 A. ANDREW *Ind. Problems* ii. 53 Cultivator of *tank-watered land. 1898 *Engineering Mag.* XVI. 133/1 A Notable Piece of Lead *Tank Work. 1883 *Chambers's Encycl.* s. v., There is extreme probability that these *tank-worms are the origin of the guinea-worm.

† **Tank**, *sb.*[2] *Herb. Obs.* [ME. *tanke*; origin obscure.] The Wild Carrot; according to Gerarde, the Wild Parsnip.

*a* 1400–50 *Stockh. Med. MS.* 181 Bryddys neste or tanke: *daucus asininus.* *Ibid.* 182 Þe lesse tank: *daucus creticus.* 14.. *MS. Arundel* 272, lf. 46 (Halliw.) Brydswete or tank. Hit hath leves like to hemlok, and a quite flower. 1597 GERARDE *Herbal* App., Tanke is wild Parsnep.

† **Tank**, *sb.*[3] *Obs.* Erroneously shortened from *copped tank*: see COPINTANK.

1688 R. HOLME *Armoury* II. 55/2 Like long Hatters Blocks, or capped tanks, *i.e.* Hats with Brims. *Ibid.* III. 271/1 A Womans Head couped..on her Head a Capped Tank Embowed, and Tied under her Chin. *Ibid.* 395/2 Mens heads are..covered with..Caps, Cowles, Tankes, Morions, Insulas, Hats and Hoods.

**Tank**, *sb.*[4] *rare*—°. = TANG *sb.*[1]

1858 SIMMONDS *Dict. Trade*, *Tank*,..the end of a file, etc. inserted in a socket.

‖ **Tank**, *sb.*[5] [Cf. TANGA.] (See quots.)

1698 FRYER *Acc. E. India & P.* 206 (jewel weights) 1 *Miscall* is 1 *Tank.* 1858 SIMMONDS *Dict. Trade*, *Tank* ..a small Indian dry-measure, averaging 240 grains in weight; a Bombay weight for pearls, of 72 grains.

**Tank**, *sb.*[6] *dial.* In 7 tanck. [Echoic.] 'A blow, a knock' (E.D.D.).

1686 PLOT *Staffordsh.* 30 The Operators in Iron..are all awakened with a little blow (or tanck) upon a pair of their tongues (which is the common means they use for that purpose). [1904 in *Eng. Dial. Dict.* from Yorksh. to Northampton and Worcestersh.]

**Tank**, *v.* [f. TANK *sb.*[1]]

**1.** *trans.* To lift or measure in a tank.

1886 *Sci. Amer. Suppl.* 9130 If this [water] can be tanked or weighed, no material error should occur. 1890 *Colliery Advert.*, The water pumped or tanked out.

**2.** To store or preserve in a tank.

1900 *Lancet* 22 Sept. 873/2 Sailors..who have had to drink tanked and often impure water.

**3.** To treat in a tank or tanks.

1891 *Cent. Dict.*, *Tanking*, the operation or method of treating in tanks, as fish for the extraction of oil, by boiling, settling, etc.

**4.** To immerse in a tank; to duck. *dial.*

1863 READE *Hard Cash* xxxviii. III. 68 They tanked her cruel,they did; and kept her under water till she was nigh gone.

‖ **Tanka** (tæ·ŋkă). Also tankia, tanchia. [f. Chinese *tan*, lit. 'egg', + Cantonese *ka*, in South Mandarin *kia*, North Mandarin *chia*, family, people.] The boat-population of Canton, who live entirely on the boats by which they earn their living: they are descendants of some aboriginal tribe of which *Tan* was apparently the name. *Tanka boat*, a boat of the kind in which these people live.

1839 *Chinese Repository* VII. 506 The small boats of Tanka women are never without this appendage. 1848 S. W. WILLIAMS *Middle Kingd.* I. vii. 321 The *tankia*, or boat-people, at Canton form a class in some respects beneath the other portions of the community. *Ibid.* II. xiii. 23 A large part of the boats at Canton are *tankia* boats, about 25 feet long, containing only one room, and covered with movable mats, so contrived as to cover the whole vessel; they are usually rowed by women. 1909 *Westm. Gaz.* 23 Mar. 5/2 The Tankas, numbering perhaps 50,000 in all, gain their livelihood by ferrying people to and fro on the broad river with its creeks.

**Tanka**, var. TANGA, East Indian coin.

**Ta·nkage** (-édʒ). [f. TANK *sb.*[1] or *v.* + -AGE.]

**1.** Tanks collectively; a provision or system of storage-tanks, sometimes with special reference to its capacity. Also *attrib.*

1866 J. E. H. SKINNER *After the Storm* I. xvii. 226 There was more fencing in and a greater show of tankage about the wells at Pithole Run...Huge tanks, like brewers' vats surrounded '54'. 1883 *Century Mag.* XXVI. 332 A tankage capacity of over thirty millions of barrels. 1892 *Daily News* 21 July 2/3 The Baltimore Electric Refining Company..has already contracted to double its tankage. 1893 *Westm. Gaz.* 27 Mar. 6/1 The Russian firms have an extensive tankage system in England. 1904 *Daily Chron.* 2 June 7/5 A depôt..will be secured..for the purpose of erecting several big tankages, warehouses, and the necessary plant for the unloading of the company's own tank steamers.

**2.** The act or process of storing liquid in tanks; the price charged for this. 1891 in *Cent. Dict.*

**3.** The residue from tanks in which fat, etc. has been rendered, used as a coarse food, and as manure.

1886 *Sci. Amer.* LV. 149 A new drier adapted for drying ..tankage, sewage, clay, fertilizers, etc. 1887 F. H. STORER *Agric.* (1892) I. xiv. 388 Under the name of tankage, a kind of flesh-meal is prepared in this country [U.S.] from the refuse meat, entrails, and other offal that accumulate in slaughter-houses. 1898 *Engineering Mag.* XVI. 128/1 The receiving tanks,..each receiving the cooked garbage, called tankage, from four digesters.

**Tankard** (tæ·ŋkəɹd). Also 4–5 (8) tancard, 5–7 -kerd, 6 -(c)karde, -ckerd, *Sc.* -kert, 7 (9 *Sc.*) tanker. [= MDu., Du. *tanckaert* = *kitte*, L. *obba*, *cantharus* (= sense 2 below), (Kilian); also F. *tanquart*, pl. *tanquars* (Rabelais). Ulterior history unknown: ? transposition of **kantar*(*d*, *cantharus*.]

†**1.** A large open tub-like vessel, usually of wood hooped with iron, etc. (sometimes of leather); *spec.* such a vessel used for carrying water, etc.; often used to render L. *amphora*. *Obs.*

1310 *Acc. Exors. T. Bp. of Exeter* (Camden) 10 De iijs. de xij tancardis ferro ligatis debilibus. 1341–2 *Ely Sacr. Rolls* (1907) II. 118 In ligatura unius tankard cum ferro. 1352 *Acc. Excheq. Q. R.* (Bundle 20 No. 27 Publ. Rec. Office), Pro quadam [*sic*] magno vase..vocato 'tankard'. 1382 WYCLIF *Zech.* v. 6 This is an amfer [*gloss* or a vessel that sum men clepen a tankard] goynge out. *c* 1440 *Promp. Parv.* 486/2 Tankard, *amphora.* *c* 1475 *Pict. Voc.* in Wr.-Wülcker 771/31 *Hec amphora*, a tancard. 1551–2 *Act* 5 & 6 *Edw. VI*, c. 15 § 2 Such as make Males,..Leather Pottes, Tanckardes, Barehides or any other Wares of Leather. 1573–80 BARET *Alv.* T 56 A Tankerd of nine gallons, *amphora*. 1688 R. HOLME *Armoury* III. xxi. (Roxb.) 253/2 He beareth Vert, a Dary womans Tankerds, or Milk Tankerds, or two Tankerds of Milk.

**2.** A drinking-vessel, formerly made of wooden staves and hooped; now *esp.* a tall one-handled jug or mug, usually of pewter, sometimes with a lid: used chiefly for drinking beer.

1485 *Naval Acc. Hen. VII* (1896) 51 Drynkyng bolles of tree..xx, Tankerdes..viij. 1495 *Ibid.* 260 Tankardes of a galon apece. 1513 DOUGLAS *Æneis* III. viii. 30 A mekle tankert [L. *magnum cratera*] with wyne fillit to the throt. 1515 BARCLAY *Egloges* iv. (1570) C vj/1 Talke he of tankarde, or of his boxe of tarre. 1530 PALSGR. 279/1 Tankard a vessell, *brocq*, *pot*, *broc*. **1566** *Eng. Ch. Furniture* (Peacock) 91 A penny tanckerd of wood. **1601** F. Tate *Househ. Ord. Edw. II*, § 47 (1876) 29 Thei shal wash the tankers, cups, and al manner of vessel which thei have custody of. **1710** Hearne *Collect.* (O. H. S.) III. 99 Charlett then order'd a Tankard of Ale to be fetch'd. **1819** Wordsw. *Waggoner* ii. 58 What tankards foaming from the tap. What store of cakes in every lap. **1873** 'Ouida' *Pascarèl* I. 53, I have seen a good many of our people with their noses buried in the tankards.

b. *transf.* in Cool tankard, q. v.

3. Applied to a sheep-bell, from its shape. *dial.*

**1880** R. Jefferies *Gt. Estate* vi. 123 'It's Johnson's flock; I know the tang of his tankards'. The flat-shaped bells hung on a sheep's neck are called tankards.

4. *attrib.* and *Comb.*, as *tankard-cup*, *-lid*; *tankard-shaped* adj.; **tankard-turnip**, a variety of turnip with a long tuber; † **tankard-woman**, a female tankard-bearer; † **tankard-yeoman** = Tankard-bearer.

**1729** Swift *Direct. Servants, Butler*, When any one calls for ale..fill the largest *tancard cup topfull. **1642** Milton *Apol. Smect.* Wks. 1851 III. 263 No marvell, if he brought us home nothing but a meer *tankard drollery. **1852** Wiggins *Embanking* 85 Such sluices..have what are called *tankard-lid doors, working on a bar with rounded ends in a cheek, attached to each side of the sea end of the 'gutter', as it is there called. **1796** W. Marshall *Midland Counties* II. Gloss., **Tankard-turnep*, the pudding, or longrooted turnep. **1828–32** Webster, *Tankard-turnep*, a sort of turnep that stands high above the ground. *a* **1667** Cowley *Ess. in Verse & Pr.*, *Of Obscurity*, He had taken great pleasure in hearing of a *Tanker-woman [*aquam ferens muliercula*, Cicero *Tusc.* 5. 36. 105] say as he past, This is that Demosthenes. **1553** Becon *Reliques of Rome* (1563) 52 That theyr Patrone was some good *tankerd yeoman.

**Ta·nkard-bea·rer.** One who bears a tankard; *spec.* †a. One employed in drawing and carrying water from the public pumps and conduits (*obs.*); b. A cup-bearer.

*c* **1515** *Cocke Lorell's B.* 10 Tankarde berers, bouge men, and spere planers. **1532** More *Confut. Barnes* viii. Wks. 738/2 King or subiect, carter or cardinal, butcher or bishop, tanckerdberer or kennel raker. **1538** Elyot, *Amphorarius*, he that beareth the potte, a tankarde bearer. **1598** B. Jonson *Ev. Man in Hum.* i. ii, Like a tankard-bearer at a conduit. **1601** *Ibid.* (Qo.) iii. iii, What? a tankard-bearer, a thread-bare rascall, a begger. **1675** Brooks *Gold. Key* Wks. 1867 V. 164 He begs water of a poor tankard-bearer to refresh himself in his weariness and thirst: John xix. 28.

So **Ta·nkard-bea·ring** *a.*

**16..** Marvell *Tom May's Death*, For a tankard-bearing Muse must we, As for the basket, Guelphs and Ghibelines be.

**Tanker** (tæ·ŋkəɹ). *colloq.* [f. Tank *sb.*[1] + -er [1].] A tank-steamer.

**1905** *Daily News* 20 Mar. 7 A tanker stood ready in the bay to take the English residents to a place of safety.

**Tanker**, obs. form of Tankard.

**Tankful** (tæ·ŋkful). [f. Tank *sb.*[1] + -ful.] As much as a tank will contain.

**1887** J. Ashby Sterry *Lazy Minstrel* (1892) 19 Anemone-hunters roam over the rocks, All hoping to fish up a tankfull. **1890** *Mission Herald* (Boston) June 237 The teacher had his tankful [of water] stored up.

**Tankia**, variant of Tanka.

**Ta·nkle**, *sb.* The second element in the reduplicated Tinkle-tankle, sometimes used by itself to express a less acute sound than Tinkle. So **Ta·nkle** *v.*, **Ta·nkling** *vbl. sb.*

**1864** Webster, *Tankling*, a ringing noise; a tinkling. **1894** Wister in *Harper's Mag.* Sept. 514 The flat can-like tankle of the square bell. *Ibid.* 518 The bell..tankled.

**Tankless** (tæ·ŋklès), *a.* [f. Tank *sb.*[1] + -less.] Without a tank.

**1894** H. D. Lloyd *Wealth agst. Commw.* 237 The donors might drive the churches, which have no tank-cars, out of the business, as they have done the tankless refiners [of oil].

**Ta·nling.** *rare.* [f. Tan *a.* + -ling [1].] One tanned by the sun's rays; a person of dark skin.

**1611** Shaks. *Cymb.* iv. iv. 29 To be still hot Summers Tanlings, and The shrinking Slaues of Winter. **1830** Tennyson *Dualisms* Poems 146 Mid May's darling golden-locked Summer's tanling diamond-eyed. **1877** Blackie *Wise Men* 41 Behind the march Of some barbarian tanling, cradled now Behind the Oscan hills.

† **Tanmerack.** *Sc. Obs. rare.* [Corruption of Ir. *tarmanach*, var. of *tarmachan*.] = Ptarmigan.

**1792** *Trans. Antiq. Soc. Scotl.* II. 70 Here also is the Tanmerack, a fowl of the size of a dove, which always inhabits the tops of the highest mountains.

**Tannable** (tæ·năb'l), *a.* [f. Tan *v.* + -able.] Capable of being tanned. **1879** in Webster *Suppl.*

**Tanna(h, Tannadar**, var. Tana, Tanadar.

**Tannage** (tæ·nèdʒ). [f. Tan *v.* + -age; or perh. a. F. *tannage* (14th c. in Hatz.-Darm.).]

1. The art or process of tanning; also *concr.* the produce of tanning. (With quot. 18.. cf. Tan *v.* 1 c.)

**1662** J. Davies tr. *Olearius' Voy. Ambass.* 42 They are as yet unacquainted with Tannage. **1778** *Phil. Trans.* LXVIII. 128 The leather..is of a superior quality to that of the old tannage. **18..** *Marble-Worker* § 129 (Cent. D.) The most important operation in the composition of artificial Marbles is that of tannage, without which it would be impossible for the cabinet maker to scrape and polish the material. **1893** *Times* 13 Dec. 3/5 Up-country tannages had a fair market throughout... Bombay tannages were in fair request at about last sales prices. **1901** *Daily Chron.* 18 Nov. 3/7 The sterling quality of English sole leather—good, honest, oak-bark tannage—has passed into a proverb. *attrib.* **1732** Tannage bill [see Tannery 2].

b. *transf.* The tanning or sunburning of the skin.

**1845** Browning *Flight of Duchess* iii, They should have got his cheek fresh tannage.

2. A tannery. *Sc.*

**1799–1812** [A tannery known as 'the Tannage' existed in Hawick in the lane still called *Tannage Close*]. **1867** D. Black *Hist. Brechin* 185 A piece of ground formerly occupied as a cornyard and tannage was purchased.

† **Ta·nnakin.** *Obs.* Also 6 tannikin, 7 tanakin. A diminutive pet-form of the name Ann or Anna (cf. *Tann* = *St. Ann*, *Ted* = Edward); *spec.* used for a German or Dutch girl.

**1557** P. Hoby *Let. to Cecil* in Burgon *Gresham* (1839) I. 227, I praie ye, desire my Lady to come, and to bringe Tannikin [Cecil's daughter Anne] with her. **1596** Nashe *Saffron Walden* 130 Like a Germane, that neuer goes to the warres without his Tannakin. **1605** Marston *Dutch Courtezan* i. i, A pretty nimble eyd Dutch Tanakin. **1608** Armin *Nest Ninn.* (1880) 47 Like a Dutch Tannakin, sliding to market on the ise.

**Tannate** (tæ·nĕ't). *Chem.* [a. F. *tannate* (Proust 1798), f. Tann-ic + -ate [4].] A salt of tannic acid.

**1802** *Nicholson's Jrnl.* II. 72 The small quantity of tanin dissolved in this water would combine with the lime..and would form a tanate of lime. *Ibid.* 198 The tannate of tin. **1808** Henry *Epit. Chem.* 240 The gallate and tannate of iron are..essential constituents of inks. **1882** *Encycl. Brit.* XIV. 385/1 [It] gives up its dissolved gelatin to the tan of the stronger solution outside to form tannate of gelatin.

**Tanné, -ee**, obs. forms of Tawny.

**Tanned** (tænd), *ppl. a.* [f. Tan *v.* + -ed [1].]

1. Converted into leather; preserved by tanning.

*c* **1000** Ælfric *Gloss.* in Wr.-Wülcker 118/7 ȝetannede hyd. *c* **1350** *Usages Winchester* in *Eng. Gilds* (1870) 358 Eueryche cart þt bereþ y-tanned leþer to selle. **1497** *Naval Acc. Hen. VII* (1896) 102 Tanned hides. *a* **1548** Hall *Chron.*, *Hen. VII* 4 b, Their brest plates..were made of tanned lether. **1666** Wood *Life* Jan. (O. H. S.) II. 98 For a tan'd paire of gloves, 1s. **1837** M. Donovan *Dom. Econ.* II. 54 Herodotus says the tanned human skin excels all others in whiteness and brilliancy.

b. *slang.* Beaten, thrashed.

**1905** *Dundee Advertiser* 8 July 6 Away back in boyhood's happy days..'a tanned hide' had a significance all its own.

2. That has been rendered brown or tawny, esp. by exposure to the sun; sunburnt.

**1564–78** Bulleyn *Dial. agst. Pest.* (1888) 29 A Lackey clothed in Orenge Taunie and White, with a paire of bare tanned legges. *c* **1600** Shaks. *Sonn.* lxii, Beated and chopt with tand antiquitie. **1632** Milton *L'Allegro* 90 If the earlier season lead To the tann'd Haycock in the Mead. **1709** O. Dykes *Eng. Prov. & Refl.* (ed. 2) 190 As diligent as any toiling tann'd Hay-maker in the Field upon a Sunshiny Day. **1859** Jephson *Brittany* ix. 137 The healthy tanned complexions which mark a seafaring population.

b. Of a reddish brown or tawny colour.

**1575** Turberv. *Venerie* 10 Such [deer] as be dunne on the backe hauing their foure quarters redde or tanned, and the legs of the same coloure, as it were the colour of a hares legs. **1616** Surfl. & Markh. *Country Farme* 675 The white hound, the fallow or taund hound, the grey-hound, and the blacke hound. **1719** London & Wise *Compl. Gard.* vii. vi. 166 A certain tann'd and red Colour which covers all the Rind. **1863** W. C. Baldwin *Afr. Hunting* iii. 76 [The inyala] is of the bush buck species,..with spiral horns, tanned legs, very long hair on his breast and quarters.

3. Spread or covered with tan.

**1870** *Daily News* 6 June, The thoroughbreds were led round the well-tanned enclosure. **1891** *Ibid.* 6 Mar. 3/5 A thick ring of spectators surrounded the tanned enclosure.

4. *humorous nonce-use.* Made or governed by Kett the tanner.

**1549** Cheke *Hurt Sedit.* 8 The other rable of Norfolke rebelles, ye pretend a common welth...A marueylous tanned common welth.

**Tanner** [1] (tæ·nəɹ). Also ? 1 tannere, 2–3 tanur, 4 tannere, 4–5 -our, 5 -ar(e, 6 -ar, tanyer. [The form corresponds with a rare OE. *tannere* from *tannian* to tan, and with OF. *tanere* (1226 in Godef. *Compl.*), nom. case of *taneör*, *tanour*:—L. *tannātor*, *tannātōr-em*, but perh. actually represents the French word. The form *tanyer* appears to be assimilated to words like *sawyer*, *hosier*, *farrier*; but cf. OF. *tanière* (1280 in Godef.).]

One whose occupation is to tan hides or to convert them into leather by tanning.

*a* **975** *Grant by K. Eadgar* in Kemble *Cod. Dipl.* II. 411 Be eastan ea and tannera hole [*lit.* tanners' hole]. ? *a* **1189** in *Rep. Hist. MSS. Comm., Var. Coll.* IV. 50 Deorlingno tanur, Iordano cordwaner. **1226** in J. T. Gilbert *Hist. & Munic. Doc. Irel.* (Rolls) 83 Willelmus, filius Iohannis tanur. *c* **1350** *Usages Winchester* in *Eng. Gilds* (1870) 359 Eueryche tannere þt halt bord in þe heyestret of Wynchestre. **1393** Langl. *P. Pl.* C. i. 223 Taylours and tanners and tyliers of erthe. **1415** *Ordo paginarum* in *York Myst.* Introd. 19 Tannours. [*In heading of Play* (c 1435) *called* The Barkers.] **14..** *Customs of Malton* in *Surtees Misc.* (1888) 63 A tannar schall not use nor ocupy schomakar crafte. **1526** Tindale *Acts* ix. 43 He taryed many days in Joppa with one Simon a tanner. **1565** *Old Order Bk. in the Tower* 39 Also we present, all the Tanyers that wash their skins within the Tower Ditch. **1739** Miller *Gard. Dict.* II. s. v. *Tan*, I find there are several Degrees of Fineness, to which the Tanners do grind their Bark. **1868** Freeman *Norm. Conq.* II. viii. 177 In every form which the story has taken.., the mother of the Conqueror appears as the daughter of a tanner at Falaise.

b. *Comb.* **Tanner eagle**, a rendering of Gr. βυρσαίετος (*lit.* hide-eagle), as a designation of Cleon, who was a tanner. Also compounds of *tanner's*, *tanners'*, as *tanner's* or *tanners' bark*, *hair*, *mill*, *ooze*, *waste*, *water*; **tanners' sumac**, the tree *Rhus Coriaria*, the dried and chopped leaves and shoots of which are used in tanning; **tanners' tree**, *Coriaria myrtifolia*, a low deciduous shrub of Southern Europe used in tanning; also = *tanners' sumac*; **tanners' turf**, tan-turf.

**1820** T. Mitchell *Aristoph.* I. 179 Your snake—and snake, so runs the prophecy, Shall beat the *tanner-eagle. **1837** Wheelwright tr. *Aristoph.* I. 304 This Paphlagonian is the tanner-eagle. **1731** Miller *Gard. Dict.* s.v. *Acacia*, The third, sixth, and seventh Sorts..should have a Hot-bed of *Tanner's Bark. **1707** Mortimer *Husb.* (1721) II. 254 A stock of Clay well mix'd with Horse-dung to prevent its freezing, and with *Tanner's Hair to prevent its cracking. **1611** Cotgr. s.v. *Tan*, *Moulin à tan*, a *Tanners mill. **1587–1725** *Tanners owze, etc. [see Ooze *sb.*[1] 2 *a*, *b*]. **1858** Hogg *Veg. Kingd.* 222 *Tanners' sumach. **1884** Miller *Plant-n.*, *Sumach*, Tanner's, *Rhus Coriaria*. *Ibid.*, *Tanner's tree, *Coriaria myrtifolia* and other species. **1688** R. Holme *Armoury* iii 86/2 *Tanners [*Turfe*]..the Bark cast out of the Tan-Pits,..wrought into Turfes, which dried is good fire Fuel. **1815** J. Smith *Panorama Sc. & Art* II. 608 The bark of oak, or *tanners' waste, when completely putrefied..greatly improves cold, stiff heavy soils. **1552** Huloet, *Tanners water, *nautea*, *æ*.

**Tanner** [2] (tæ·nəɹ). *slang.* [Origin uncertain: see hearsay account in B. Hooper *Leather Manufact.* (1891) 65.] A sixpence. Also *attrib.*

**1811** *Lex. Balatr.*, *Tanner*, a sixpence. **1812** J. H. Vaux *Flash Dict.*, *Tanner*, a sixpence. Three and a tanner. **1844** Dickens *Mart. Chuz.* xxxvii, 'How much a-piece?' The man in the monument replied, 'a Tanner'. It seemed a low expression, compared with the monument. **1908** *Daily Express* 3 Feb. 1/1 Seventeen tannercabs [sixpenny cabs] made their appearance in the streets on Saturday, and were in great demand.

**Tannery** (tæ·nəri). [f. Tanner [1] + -y: see -ery. Cf. F. *tannerie* (13th c. in Hatz.-Darm.).]

1. A place where tanning is carried on.

[**1396–1401** *Rolls of Parlt.* I. 228/2 Coreum, cortices et utensilia in tanneria sua.] **1736** J. M'Ure *View Glasgow* 285 There is a stately Brewarie..adjacent to the above great Tannarie. **1839** *Penny Cycl.* XIV. 437/1 The tanneries of Marocco. **1856** Stanley *Sinai & Pal* vi. 269 A tradition..describes the premises to have been long employed as a tannery. *attrib.* **1852** Hanna *Chalmers* IV. xxi. 401 Never was the true work of school and church done better than in that old tannery-loft.

2. The process or trade of tanning; tannage.

**14..** *Beryn* 3237 And I shall tech hym, as I can,..Tyll it be abill of prentyse to crafft of tan[e]ry. **1732** *Rec. Convent. Roy. Burghs* V. 529 A propper clause in the tannage bill for saving the rights of the cordiners of..royal burghs as to their priviledge of tannery. **1837** Carlyle *Fr. Rev.* III. v. vii, Gun-boring, Altar-burning, Saltpetre-digging, and miraculous improvements in Tannery!

*attrib.* **1887** *Pall Mall G.* 12 Sept. 8/2 A great fire broke out..in the extensive tannery works.

**Tannic** (tæ·nik), *a.* *Chem.* [f. Tann-in + -ic.] In *tannic acid*, a name introduced in 1834 by Pelouze instead of Tannin, in recognition of its acid character and reactions; originally applied to the tannin principle obtained from oak-galls, a white amorphous strongly astringent substance, $C_{14}H_{10}O_9$, now more particularly distinguished from other forms of tannin as Gallotannic *acid*. Now chiefly used in a general sense to include a great number of allied substances, which differ in the proportion of their elements.

These are distinguished by compound names indicating their source, as *quercitannic acid*, that obtained from oak-bark, $C_{15}H_{12}O_9$; also *caffetannic* ($C_{15}H_{18}O_8$), *catechutannic* ($C_{17}H_{17}O_9$), *cincho-* or *quinotannic* ($C_{14}H_{16}O_9$), *fraxitannic*, *kinotannic*, *ratanhiatannic acids*, obtained from coffee, catechu, cinchona, ash-leaves, kino, and ratanhia respectively.

[**1834** (Feb. 17) Pelouze in *Ann. de Chimie* LIV. 337 La place du tannin, qu'il serait plus convenable d'appeler *acide tannique*, est marqué à côté de l'acide gallique lui-même.] **1836** Brande *Chem.* (ed. 4) 925 A peculiar proximate principle, designated *tannin*... It has been obtained in a distinct form by Pelouze, and its characters are such that it may be appropriately termed *tannic acid*. **1869** Roscoe *Elem. Chem.* (1871) 405 Tannin, or Tannic Acid,..is contained widely diffused in certain parts of plants. **1874** Garrod & Baxter *Mat. Med.* (1880) 281 The cincho-tannic and red cinchonic acids are powerfully astringent—like tannic and gallic acids.

**Tannier**, variant of Tania.

**Tanniferous** (tæni·fĕrəs), *a.* [f. Tanni(n + -ferous.] Yielding or abounding in tannin.

**1878** Ure *Dict. Arts* IV. 897 The most advantageous tanniferous substance is an extract of the chestnut, costing about 3*d.* per lb.

**Tannigen** (tæ·nidʒen). *Pharm.* [f. Tanni(n + -gen.] A compound of tannin and acetyl, used as an intestinal astringent; acetyl-tannin.

**1898** in *Syd. Soc. Lex.* **1905** H. D. Rolleston *Dis. Liver* 297 If this [diarrhœa] is troublesome, bismuth, aromatic chalk and opium mixture, dilute sulphuric acid, tannigen..should be given.

**Tannikin**, variant of Tannakin.

**Tannin** (tæ·nin). *Chem.* [a. F. *tanin*, 'le principe tannant' (1798 Proust in *Ann. de Chimie* XXV. 225), f. *tan* Tan *sb.*[1] + -in [1].] Any member of a group of astringent vegetable substances, the *tannins*, which possess the property of combining with animal hide and converting it into leather.

The first member of this group isolated and so named was the tannin of gall-nuts, subsequently also called Tannic *acid*; and to this the names *tannin* and *tannic acid* are still often specifically applied. But the discovery that the astringent principles of other vegetable substances were not chemically identical with that of gall-nuts made it needful to distinguish the various tannins. The original or 'ordinary tannin' became distinctively GALLOTANNIN, other members of the group being named *caffetannin*, *catechu-tannin*, *kinotannin*, *quercitannin*, etc. (cf. TANNIC), or particularized as *oak-bark tannin*, *alder*, *beech*, *hop*, *horse-chestnut*, *larch*, *rhatany tannin*, according to their source.

**1802** *Nicholson's Jrnl.* II. 198 Abridgment of a Memoir of Mr. Proust on Tanin and its Species. **1804** *Phil. Trans.* XCIV. 210 The effects which it produced on gelatin, also demonstrate the presence of tannin. **1836** BRANDE *Chem.* (ed. 4) 928 *note*, The tannin of catechu is said to contain less oxygen than that of galls. **1838** T. THOMSON *Chem. Org. Bodies* 109 Pure tannin is colourless. **1867** BAKER *Nile Tribut.* viii. (1872) 123 It is rich in a hard gum, which appears to be almost pure tannin. **1895** MUIR & MORLEY *Watts' Dict. Chem.* V. 632/1 The origin of tannin in plants has given rise to much debate.

**b.** *attrib.* and *Comb.*, as *tannin drop*, *pill*, *treatment*; *tannin-like* adj.; **tannin-glycerol**, glycerin of tannic acid; **tannin-sac**, a vessel in plants which secretes tannin.

**1874** GARROD & BAXTER *Mat. Med.* (1880) 357 Tannin Lozenges. **1875** BENNETT & DYER *Sachs' Bot.* 628 Tannin-like compounds are formed in particular cells. **1879** *St. George's Hosp. Rep.* IX. 800 It soon passed off again with rest and the opium and digitalis and tannin pills. **1884** BOWER & SCOTT *De Bary's Phaner.* 153 We may here introduce these organs as Tannin-sacs. They occur as elongated sacs, especially near to the vascular bundles, in the parenchyma of the stem and petiole of many Ferns (Marsilia, Polypodiaceæ, Cyatheaceæ, Marattiaceæ, &c.). **1898** P. MANSON *Trop. Diseases* vi. 121 The tannin treatment.. might also be tried.

Hence **Ta·nnined** (-ind) *a.*, charged or impregnated with tannin; **Tanninge·nic** *a.*, in *tanningenic acid*, a synonym of CATECHUIC *acid* and CATECHIN.

**1898** E. F. SPENCE in *Westm. Gaz.* 6 Sept. 3/3 For breakfast we had undrinkable coffee, which we exchanged for tannined tea. **1852** MORFIT *Tanning & Currying* (1853) 69 Catechuine or tanningenic acid.

**Tanning** (tæ·niŋ), *vbl. sb.* [f. TAN *v.* + -ING [1].] The action of the verb TAN; an instance of this.

**1481** in *Eng. Gilds* (1870) 332 As in tannyng, coryyng, cuttyng, or sowyng. *c* **1515** *Cocke Lorell's B.* 2 A tanner for euyll tannyng of lether. **1598** FLORIO, *Adustione*,..a tanning in the sunne. **1794** *Rigging & Seamanship* I. 85 The tanning of sails in the royal navy has been tried. **1863** SIR G. G. SCOTT *Glean. Westm. Abb.* (ed. 2) 65 Witnessing the 'tanning' of the rascal's 'hide'. *attrib.* **1727-41** CHAMBERS *Cycl.*, *Tan*, the bark of the oak, chopped, and ground, by a tanning-mill, into a coarse powder.

**Ta·nning**, *ppl. a.* [-ING [2].] That tans.

*a* **1717** PARNELL *Health* 35 Her hardy face repels the tanning wind. **1828** P. CUNNINGHAM *N. S. Wales* II. 75 If our..tanning barks, and bark extracts, do not continue to pay. **1857** MILLER *Elem. Chem.* III. xi. 672 Sewing up the hide, filling it with the tanning infusion.

**Tanno-.** *Chem.* Combining base of *tann-ic*, *tann-in*, used in forming names of tannin compounds, etc., and also in compound substantives, e.g. *tannometer* for *tannin-meter*. **Tanno-caffe·ic** *acid*, = CAFFETANNIC *acid*. **Ta·nnoform**, $C_{29}H_{20}O_{18}$, a product of gallotannic acid and formaldehyde; a reddish white, light powder, insoluble in water, but soluble in alkaline solutions. **Tannoga·llate**, **Tannoga·llic** *a.* = GALLOTANNATE, -TANNIC. **Tannoge·latin**, a mixture of gelatin with a solution of tannin.

*c* **1865** in *Circ. Sc.* I. 351/1 *Tanno-caffeic acid, when roasted, develops the agreeable smell of coffee. **1899** *Allbutt's Syst. Med.* VIII. 726 Powders of *tannoform, salicylic acid, talc, bismuth, or lycopodium may be employed. **1819** BRANDE *Chem.* 394 The *tannogallate of iron is of the utmost importance, as forming the basis of writing ink, and of black dyes. **1836** — *Chem.* (ed. 4) 928 Tannin forms a white precipitate in solution of gelatin (*tannogelatin), which, when carefully dried, becomes hard and tough. **1877** KNIGHT *Dict. Mech.*, **Tannometer*, a hydrometer for determining the proportion of tannin in tanning liquor.

**Tannoid** (tæ·noid), *a. Chem.* [f. TANN-IN + -OID.] Of the nature of, or akin to, tannin.

**1898** *Naturalist* 186 The choking influence exerted by the tannoid compounds.

**Tanny(e**: see TAWNY. **Tan-pit**: see TAN *sb.*[1] C.

‖**Tanquam** (tæ·nkwæm). *Obs.* Also (in sense 3) tam quam. [L. *tam quam*, *tanquam* so much as, as much as, as if, as it were.]

**1.** Something that has only an apparent existence; a mere seeming; an 'as it were'.

**1654** WHITLOCK *Zootomia* 537 He sheweth the Visibles, or Things of this World to be but *tanquams*, only *as it weres*.

**2.** In the University of Cambridge [from L. *tanquam socius*, 'as if a fellow']: see quots.

*a* **1661** FULLER *Worthies* (1662) II. 207 Thomas Dove D.D. was born in this City,..bred a Tanquam (which is a Fellowes Fellow) in Pembroke-Hall in Cambridge. **1706** PHILLIPS (ed. 6), *Tanquam*.. In the Universities.. is taken for a Person of Worth and Learning, that is fit Company for the Fellows of Colleges, &c.

**3.** *Law.* = QUI TAM: see quot. 1907. (From the words *tam ... quam ...*, beginning the two clauses.)

*c* **1570** *Pride & Lowl.* (1841) 47 For I declare (quod he) in the *Tam quam* How so the matter goe, they gette no cost [i.e. because costs are not given against the Crown]. **1592** GREENE *Upst. Courtier* Wks. (Grosart) XI. 258 Suppose some be so stuborne as to stand to the triall, yet can this cunning knaue declare a *Tamquam* against them, so that though they be cleered, yet can they haue no recompence at all, for that he doth it in the courts behalfe. **1809** in TOMLINS *Law Dict.* [**1907** *Encycl. Laws of Engl.* VII. 239 s.v. *Informer*, Actions by common informers are termed *qui tam* actions, or popular actions, when the informer recovers the statutory penalty (*tam pro domino rege quam pro se ipso*).]

‖**Tanrec, tenrec** (tæ·n-, te·nrĕk). Also 8 tondruck, tendrac. [= F. *tanrec*, ad. Malagasy *tàndraka*, dial. form of *tràndraka*, the native name.] An insectivorous mammal, *Centetes ecaudatus*, allied to the hedgehog, and covered with spiny bristles intermixed with silky hairs; the Madagascar hedgehog. Also any species of the genus *Centetes* or family *Centetidæ*.

**1729** R. DRURY *Madagascar* (1890) 81 A creature which I call a ground-hog, and which in their language is called 'tondruck'. **1785** SMELLIE tr. *Buffon's Nat. Hist.* (1791) VII. 86 The Tanrecs or Tendracs are small East Indian animals, which have some resemblance to our hedgehog. **1835** KIRBY *Hab. & Inst. Anim.* II. xxiv. 514 The hedgehog and tenrec present.. something more than an analogy to the porcupines and some of the rats. **1852** TH. ROSS *Humboldt's Trav.* II. xvii. 134 The tanrecs, or Madagascar hedgehogs,.. pass three months of the year in lethargy. **1879** E. P. WRIGHT *Anim. Life* 69 The Spiny Tanrec (*Ericulus spinosus*) is considerably smaller than the previously-mentioned species [*Centetes ecaudatus*]. **1900** *Westm. Gaz.* 8 Sept. 8/2 Two curious little creatures,..called Tenrecs.., have just been added to the Zoo.

**Tansy** (tæ·nzi). Forms: 5 tanesey, 5-8 tansie, 5-9 tansey, 6 -sye, -say, taunsey, 7-8 tanzy, -zey, 5- tansy. [a. OF. *tanesie* (13th c.), *tanoisie*, *tenasie*, mod.F. *tanaisie*, aphetic form of *athanasie* 'the hearbe Tansie' (Cotgr.), ad. med.L. *athanasia* tansy, a. Gr. ἀθανασία immortality. Cf. also It. *atanàsi* 'Tansie or siluerwort' (Florio 1611), *atanàsia* the herb tansy (Baretti 1824), Pg. *atanasia* or *athanasia*, the herb tansy. Hatz.-Darm. mention also a med.L. *tanasia*, but without reference. But apart from this it seems clear that OF. *tanesie* was aphetic for *atanesie*, the name prob. referring to the long persistence of the flowers: cf. quot. 1597; also EVERLASTING and F. *immortelle*.

Med.L. had also the name *Tanacētum* (now the botanical generic name) with the variants *tanesetum*, *tansetum*, *tanicetum*. *Tanezatum* and *athanacetum* (*c* 1250) are also cited by Burgess. These seem to show that *athanacetum* and *tanesetum* were latinized formations from OF. *tanesie*, although the force of the suffix is not clear.]

**1.** An erect herbaceous plant, *Tanacetum vulgare*, N.O. *Compositæ*, tribe *Corymbiferæ*, growing about two feet high, with deeply cut and divided leaves, and terminal corymbs of yellow rayless button-like flowers; all parts of the plant have a strong aromatic scent and bitter taste.

Formerly much used in medicine as a stomachic, and in cookery. *Curled tansy*, a variety with curled leaves, is used, like parsley, for garnishing dishes.

[*c* **1265** *Names of Plants* in Wr.-Wülcker 556/17 *Tanesetum*, [AFr.] *tanesie*, [Eng.] helde.] *c* **1420** *Liber Cocorum* (1862) 50 Þen grynde tansy þo iuse owte wrynge, To blynde with þo egges with owte lesynge. *c* **1425** tr. *Arderne's Surgery* (E.E.T.S.) 74 Porcelane, bursa pastoris, rede rose, tanesey, wormode, horsmynt. **14..** *Nom.* in Wr.-Wülcker 712/33 *Hoc tansetum*, tansaye. *c* **1450** *Alphita* 16/1 *Atanasia*.. tanacetum idem. Hanc utuntur Salerniani et Hispanni similiter, tansie. **1538** TURNER *Libellus*, *Athanasia* que grece tagetes, latine tanacetum, anglice dicitur Tansey. **1549** *Compl. Scot.* vi. 67, I sau tansay, that is gude to purge the neiris. **1597** GERARDE *Herbal* II. cxcix. 526 Tansie.. in Latine *Tanacetum* and *Athanasia*, as though it were immortall; because the floures do not speedily wither. **1599** A. M. tr. *Gabelhouer's Bk. Physicke* 124/1 Take the herbe Tansy. **1688** HOLME *Armoury* II. 89/1 Curled Tansy, the leaves are..somewhat crumpled together. **1743** *Lond. & Country Brew.* II. (ed. 2) 101 Tanzy..or any other bitter Herbs. **1770** *Phil. Trans.* LX. 10, I observed quantities of juniper and tanzey. **1785** MARTYN *Rousseau's Bot.* xxvi. (1794) 385 Of the first section, with discoid flowers, you have the Tansy. **1838** T. THOMSON *Chem. Org. Bodies* 478 Oil of tansey ..is extracted from the leaves and flowers of the *tanacetum vulgare*, or common tansey... It has the peculiar flavour of tansey. **1885** RUSKIN *Præterita* I. iii. 103, I passed my days much as the thistles and tansy did.

**2.** Applied to other plants, esp. the Silverweed or Goose-grass, *Potentilla anserina*, often distinguished as *Wild tansy* and *Dog's* or *Goose Tansy*; also locally to Yarrow, *Achillea Millefolium*, and Ragwort, *Senecio Jacobæa* (Britten and Holl.).

[*c* **1440** *Promp. Parv.* 486/2 Tanze, herbe (*K.*, *P.* tansy), *tanasetum domesticum*, *quia tanazetum silvestre dicitur* gosys gresse, *vel* cameroche.] *c* **1530** *Pol.*, *Rel. & L. Poems* (1866) 36 Take wylde tansey, and grynde yt, and make yt neshe, & ley it therto, and it wyl bryng it owght. **1605** TIMME *Quersit.* III. 181 Infused in water of silverweed, called wilde tansey. **1671** SALMON *Syn. Med.* III. xxii. 391 Argentina, 'Αθανασία ὑλόεσσα, wilde-Tansie, stops all Fluxes whatsoever. **1707** MORTIMER *Husb.* (1721) I. 312 Goose-grass or Wild-tansie is a Weed that strong Clays are very subject to. **1860** MAYNE *Expos. Lex.*, *Tansy, Wild*, a common name for the *Potentilla anserina*, or silver-weed.

**b.** With distinctive additions: **Cape Tansy**, *Athanasia capitata* var. *glabrata*; **Maudlin T.**, *Achillea Ageratum*; **Shrubby T.**, *Tanacetum suffruticosum*; **White T.**, (in Lyte) *Achillea nobilis* of Southern Europe; erroneously applied to other plants.

*c* **1711** PETIVER *Gazophyl.* ix. Tab. 81 Box-leaved *Cape Tansey... Leaves pale green, and thick set round the Stalk. **1668** WILKINS *Real Char.* II. iv. 84 *Ageratum*. *Maudlin Tansy. **1855** DUNGLISON *Dict. Med.* (ed. 12), M[audlin] Tansey, *Achillea ageratum*. **1578** LYTE *Dodoens* I. x. 17 There be two sortes of Tansie. The one great and yellow, the other small and white.. *Tanacetum minus*, *White Tansie.. The second groweth in some places of Italie; in this countrey ye shall not finde it but in the gardens of certayne Herboristes. **1688** R. HOLME *Armoury* II. 72/1 The White Tansie, or Agrimony..is a short shrub of no height.

**3.** A pudding, omelet, or the like, flavoured with juice of tansy: see also 5. *arch.* or *dial.*

Said to have been eaten at Easter in memory of the 'bitter herbs' of the Passover.

*c* **1450** *Two Cookery-bks.* 86 Tansey. Take faire Tansey, and grinde it in a morter; And take eyren, yolkes and white, And drawe hem thorgh a streynour, and streyne also þe Iuse of þe Tansey..; and medle the egges and the Iuse togidre [etc.]. **1513** *Bk. Keruynge* A vj b, A tansye fryed, & other bake metes. *c* **1530** *Caroll in Anglia* XII. 588 At Easter commeth alleluya With butter cheese and a tansay. **1561** HOLLYBUSH *Hom. Apoth.* 18 Let him take Neppe that cattes delite in..and make a taunsey thereof. *a* **1601** ? MARSTON *Pasquil & Kath.* I. 154 There's but two Lambs,..three tartes, and foure tansies, for supper. **1621** FLETCHER *Pilgrim* III. vi, They [eggs] shall be all addle, And make an admirable tanzey for the devil. **1634-5** BRERETON *Trav.* (Chetham Soc.) 69 A dainty tansy of gooseberries. **1652** CULPEPPER *Eng. Physic.* 17 A Tansie or Caudle made with eggs and the juyce thereof while it is young, putting to it some Sugar and Rose-water. **1666** PEPYS *Diary* 20 Apr., And there spent an houre or two with pleasure with her, and eat a tansy. **1748** MRS. SARAH HARRISON *Housekpr.'s Pocket-Bk.* iii. (ed. 4) 11 Trotters, To be served up as a Tanzey. **1754-6** *Connoisseur* No. 48 (1767) II. 95 Mince-pie..is as essential to Christmas, as..tansy to Easter. **1787** BEST *Angling* (ed. 2) 60 If you can catch enough of them they make an excellent tansy, their heads and tails being cut off; and fried in eggs. **1837** DISRAELI *Venetia* I. iv, A Florentine tourte, or tansy.

**b.** A merrymaking or festive gathering; a village feast held on Shrove Tuesday. *dial.* See *Eng. Dial. Dict.*

†**4.** Phrase. *Like a tansy*: properly, fittingly, perfectly; perfect. *Obs.* [Origin unascertained.]

**1611** BEAUM. & FL. *King & No K.* v. i, To have a Leg broken, or a Shoulder out, with being turn'd o' th' Stones like a Tansie. **1694** MOTTEUX *Rabelais* IV. xxii, That's well said,..now this is something like a Tanzy [orig. *C'est bien dit et advisé*]. **1738** SWIFT *Pol. Conversat.* i. 89 *Miss*. Look, Lady Answerall, is it not well mended? *Lady Ans.* Ay, this is something like a tanzy. **1759** STERNE *Tr. Shandy* II. vi, I would work..like a horse, and make fortifications for you something like a tansy.

**5.** *attrib.* and *Comb.*, as *tansy flower*, *leaf*, *tea*; *tansy-leaved* adj.; **tansy-cake**, **tansy-pudding**, culinary preparations appropriate to Easter; **tansy-faced** *a.*, having a yellow complexion; **tansy mustard**: see quot.; **tansy oil**, the essential oil of tansy.

*c* **1420** *Liber Cocorum* (1862) 50 For a *tansy cake. Breke egges in bassyn..þen grynde tansy [etc.]. **1725** BOURNE *Antiq. Vulg.* xxiv. 198 Recreations and Diversions on Easter Holy Days,.. playing at Hand-Ball for a Tanzy-Cake. **1777** BRAND *Pop. Antiq.* 253 The winning a Tanzy Cake at the Game of Hand-Ball, depends chiefly upon Swiftness of Foot. **1894** O. HESLOP *Northumb. Gloss.*, *Tansy-cake*, a girdle-cake flavoured with tansy. **1624** MIDDLETON *Game at Chess* v. iii, A sun-burnt, *tansy-fac'd belov'd. **1905** *Daily Chron.* 18 Oct. 4/5 A pond, lying deep among *tansy flowers. **1822** *Hortus Anglicus* II. 181 *S[isymbrium] Tanacetifolium*, *Tansey-leaved Wild Rocket. **1882** *Garden* 12 Aug. 145/3 The Tansy-leaved Thorn. **1856** A. GRAY *Man. Bot.* (1860) 36 *S[isymbrium] canescens*,..*Tansy Mustard. **1894** MUIR & MORLEY *Watts' Dict. Chem.* IV. 638/1 *Tansy Oil, the essential oil obtained by distillation of the tansy contains 1 p.c. of a terpene $C_{10}H_{16}$, 26 p.c. of an alcohol $C_{10}H_{18}O$, and 70 p.c. of tanacetyl hydride $C_{10}H_{16}O$. **1769** MRS. RAFFALD *Eng. Housekpr.* (1778) 177 A *Tansey Pudding of ground Rice. **1771** H. WALPOLE *Let.* 5 Aug., There are three or four very high hills,..exactly in the shape of a tansy pudding. **1908** *Daily Chron.* 18 Apr. 7/5 Chester still clings to its Tansy pudding, symbolical of the bitter herb commanded at the paschal feast.

**Tant**, var. TAINT *sb.* (C. 3); obs. f. TAUNT.

**Tanta·dlin, tanto·blin.** *slang* or *dial.* Also 7 tantaublin, 7-9 -ablin, 9 -ablet; -adling.

**1.** A tart or round piece of pastry. Now *dial.*

**1630** J. TAYLOR (Water P.) *Gt. Eater Kent* Wks. I. 146/1 Pancake, or Fritter,..Mackeroone, Kickshaw, or Tantablin. *a* **1825** FORBY *Voc. E. Anglia*, *Tantablet*, a sort of tart, in which the fruit is not covered by a crust, but fancifully tricked and flourished, with slender shreds of pastry. **1876** T. M. BOUND *Hereford. & Shropsh. Provinc.* (E.D.D.), *Tantadlin*, an apple dumpling made in circular form.

†**2.** A lump of excrement, a turd. *Obs.*

**1654** GAYTON *Pleas. Notes* III. ii, But our Don could not distinguish a Tantoblin from a Pancake. *Ibid.* IV. iv. 191 Such odour breath'd, and such strong airs were hobling, As use to ascend from a new laid Tantaublin. **1785** GROSE *Dict. Vulg. T.*, *Tantadlin tart*, a sirreverence, human excrement.

**3.** *attrib.* or *adj.* (?)

**1871** COWDEN CLARKE in *Gentl. Mag.* Aug. 336 Horace Walpole (who, by the way, seems to have been a tantaddling old eaves-dropper) has recorded that he [Addison] died drunk with brandy.

**Tantalate** (tæ·ntălĕt). *Chem.* [f. TANTAL(UM + -ATE [4].] A salt of tantalic acid.

**1849** D. CAMPBELL *Inorg. Chem.* 275 Tantalates of the alkalies, obtained when a solution is evaporated, or by boiling, are acid insoluble salts. **1873** WATTS *Fownes' Chem.* (ed. 11) 495 In all these minerals tantalum exists as a tantalate of iron and manganese.

**Tantalean** (tæntī·liăn), *a.* Also -ian. [f. L. *tantale-us* (f. TANTALUS) + -AN.] Of or pertaining to Tantalus; like that of Tantalus; tantalizing.

*a* **1618** DAVIES *Wittes Pilgr.* Wks. (Grosart) II. 24 Men ouertoild in Common-Wealth affaires Gett much Tantalian wealth by wealthie paines. **1671** H. M. tr. *Erasm. Colloq.* 540 The Lord will take away the Tantalean stone [orig. *Dominus tollet saxum Tantaleum*, i.e. the rock that threatened to fall on Tantalus; hence, the impending punishment for sin]. **1866** J. B. ROSE tr. *Ovid's Met.* 157 Niobe With tongue Tantalian reprobate and free.

**Tantalic** (tæntæ·lik), *a.*[1] *Chem.* [f. TANTAL-UM + -IC.] Of or derived from tantalum; in names of chemical compounds in which tantalum is pentavalent, as *tantalic chloride, fluoride*; *tantalic oxide, anhydride*, $Ta_2O_5$; *tantalic acid, hydrated tantalic oxide*, $H_2O \,.\, Ta_2O_5$.

**1842** PARNELL *Chem. Anal.* (1845) 70 After having been heated to redness, alone, tantalic acid is insoluble in all liquids. **1849** D. CAMPBELL *Inorg. Chem.* 273 A compound of this metal [tantalum] with oxygen—namely, tantalic acid—is found in the minerals *tantalite* and *columbite* of Bavaria and North America. **1877** WATTS *Fownes' Chem.* I. 466 Tantalum, in its principal compounds, is quinquivalent, the formula of tantalic chloride being $TaCl_5$..and that of tantalic oxide (which, in combination with bases forms the tantalates), $Ta_2O_5$.

**Tantalic** (tæntæ·lik), *a.*[2] [f. TANTALUS + -IC.] = TANTALEAN; tantalizing.

**1882** H. C. MERIVALE *Faucit of B.* I. I. vi. 96 One of those Oxonian breakfasts which..haunt like Tantalic phantoms the egg and bacon of later years. *Ibid.* III. II. xx. 187 He..sketched Tantalic pictures of wealthy homes.

**Tantaline** (tæ·ntăləin), *a. Ornith.* [f. TANTAL-US 3 + -INE[1].] Of or pertaining to the *Tantalinæ* or wood storks, a sub-family of the *Ciconiidæ* or stork family, typified by the genus TANTALUS.

† **Tantalism** (tæ·ntăliz'm). *Obs. rare.* [f. TANTAL-US + -ISM.] Punishment or torment like that of Tantalus; tantalization.

*c* **1614** FLETCHER, etc. *Wit sev. Weapons* II. ii, Think on my vengeance, choak up his desires, Then let his banquetings be tantalisme. **1711** ADDISON *Spect.* No. 90 ¶ 6 A Person lying under the Torments of such a kind of Tantalism, or Platonick Hell. **18..** JOS. QUINCY (Webster, 1828), Is not such a provision like tantalism to this people?

**Tantalite** (tæ·ntăləit). *Min.* [ad. Ger. and Sw. *tantalit* (named 1802 by Ekeberg), f. TANTALUM (of which it is a source): see -ITE[1].] Native tantalate of iron or ferrous tantalate, found in black lustrous crystals.

**1805** NISBET *Dict. Chem.*, Tantalium..constitutes a component part of tantalite and yttrotantalite. **1809** WOLLASTON in *Phil. Trans.* XCIX. 246. **1868** WATTS *Dict. Chem.* V. 666 Ferrous Tantalate, $FeO \,.\, Ta_2O_5$.. occurs native as tantalite..rarely however quite pure, the iron being generally more or less replaced by manganese, and the tantalum by niobium, tin, and zirconium.

† **Tantalium** (tæntēi·liŏm). *Chem. Obs.* An early variant of the name TANTALUM (after other names of metals in -IUM).

**1805** NISBET *Dict. Chem.*, *Tantalium* is a new metal, which has lately been discovered by Mr. Ekeberg, a Swedish chemist. **1812** SIR H. DAVY *Chem. Philos.* 50. **1839** URE *Dict. Arts* 309 It is also called Tantalium.

**Tantalization** (tæntăləizēi·ʃən). [f. next + -ATION.] The action of tantalizing or fact of being tantalized.

**1654** GAYTON *Pleas. Notes* IV. xv. 253 Poor Rosinant.. whose paines and Tantalizations..were more irksome to the beast, than all his other out-ridings. **1821** *Blackw. Mag.* X. 729 The delay and tantalization is horrific.

**Tantalize** (tæ·ntăləiz), *v.* [f. TANTAL-US + -IZE. So mod.F. *tantaliser* (Littré *Suppl.*).]

**1.** *trans.* To subject to torment like that inflicted on Tantalus; to torment by the sight, show, or promise of a desired thing which is kept out of reach, or removed or withheld when on the point of being grasped. Also *absol.*

**1597** TOFTE *Laura* III. xii, Ah doo not still my soule thus Tantalize, But once (through grace) the same imparadize. **1646** TRAPP *Comm. John* vi. 55 Our Richard II. was starved at Pomfret Castle by being tantalized. **1784** KING *Cook's Voy. Pacific Ocean* VI. ix. III. 432, I should otherwise have felt exceedingly tantalized with living under the walls of so great a city, full of objects of novelty, without being able to enter it. **1803** WELLINGTON in Gurw. *Desp.* (1837) II. 461, I was tantalized all the morning with the sight of the enemy's camp, pitched at the distance of twenty miles. **1860** TYNDALL *Glac.* I. iv. 36 The mirage..which so tantalized the French soldiers in Egypt.

**b.** *fig.* To tease or torture into an artificial form.

**1807** CRABBE *Parish Reg.* III. 217 Where those dark shrubs that now grow wild at will, Were clipt in form and tantaliz'd with skill. **1897** *Westm. Gaz.* 25 Mar. 3/2 Chiffon tantalised into a hundred tucks bristling all over the brim and the crown.

† **2.** *intr.* To act Tantalus, to suffer like Tantalus.

**1640** FULLER *Joseph's Coat, Comm.* 1 *Cor.* xi. 20 The poor people in Corinth did see, and smell, what the rich men tasted; Tantalizing all the while, and having their penury doubled by the 'antiperistasis' of other's plenty. **1648** E. SPARKE *Pref. to Shute's Sarah & Hagar* b j b, But, not to tell you of a Banquet, and make you Tantalize. **1673** *Ess. Educ. Gentlewom.* 25 Men are very cruel..; to make any thus to tantalize is a great torment.

Hence **Ta·ntalized** *ppl. a.*, **Ta·ntalizing** *vbl. sb.*

**1640** NABBES *Bride* IV. iii, To have seen this wench and not to enjoy her is such a tantalizing to me. **1659** *Gentl. Calling* v. (1696) 64 A sort of Tantalized creatures, not peculiar only to this latter age. **1694** MOTTEUX *Rabelais* v. xvi. (1737) 72 Without any long..Tantalizing in the Case.

**Tantalizer** (tæ·ntăləizəɹ). [f. prec. + -ER[1].] One who or that which tantalizes.

**1792** G. WAKEFIELD *Mem.* (1804) I. i. 16 Alas! this episcopal tantalizer was only gratifying his facetious propensity at the expence of an unsuspecting child of simplicity and innocence. **1844** WARDLAW *Lect. Prov.* (1869) I. 50 The blessed God is no tantalizer. **1889** *Pall Mall G.* 11 July 6/1, I have received a puzzle of the 'Pigs in Clover' kind. ..'Penning the Lambs' is the name by which the latest variation of the original tantalizer has been christened.

**Ta·ntalizing,** *ppl. a.* [f. as prec. + -ING[2].] That tantalizes; tormenting by exciting desires which cannot be satisfied.

**1657–83** EVELYN *Hist. Relig.* (1850) I. 206 Tantalizing and horrible torments. **1754** MRS. DELANY in *Life & Corr.* (1861) III. 271 It was a tantalizing sort of entertainment to those who love dancing or eating. **1873** HOLLAND *A. Bonnic.* iii, Answering all inquiries concerning it, with the tantalizing statement that it was 'a secret'.

Hence **Ta·ntalizingly** *adv.*; **Ta·ntalizingness.**

**1847** WEBSTER, *Tantalizingly*. **1864** *Q. Rev.* CXVI. 151 There are few things in history more tantalisingly obscure. **1889** *Scribner's Mag.* Nov. 555/2 Imagine the tantalizingness of this.

**Tantall,** obs. anglicized form of TANTALUS.

**Tantalous** (tæ·ntăləs), *a. Chem.* [f. TANTAL-UM + -OUS.] Applied to compounds containing a greater proportion of tantalum than those called *tantalic*, as *tantalous oxide*, tantalum dioxide, $TaO_2$.

**1868** WATTS *Dict. Chem.* V. 665 Dioxide of Tantalum, or Tantalous Oxide.. is a dark-grey mass, which scratches glass, and acquires metallic lustre by burnishing.

**Tantalum** (tæ·ntălŏm). *Chem.* Also TANTALIUM. [f. TANTAL-US, with the ending *-um* (more usually *-ium*), appropriate to metallic elements: cf. *aluminum* and *aluminium*; see quot. 1802.] One of the rare metals, occurring in combination in various rare minerals, and in certain metallic ores; discovered in 1802 by Ekeberg in two minerals, one from Finland and the other from Sweden, which he named tantalite and yttrotantalite. It has been isolated as a solid of greyish-white colour and metallic lustre, and is used (since 1906) for the incandescent filament in electric lamps. Atomic weight 182; symbol Ta. Also *attrib.*, as *tantalum lamp*, etc.

[Cf. **1802** EKEBERG in *Kongl. Vetenskaps Acad. Handl.* XXIII. 80 (tr.) This new recruit among the metals I call TANTALUM, partly following the custom which favours names from Mythology, partly in allusion to its incapacity, when immersed in acid, to absorb any and be saturated.]

**1809** WOLLASTON in *Phil. Trans.* XCIX. 246 The Swedish metal has retained the name of Tantalum given to it by M. Ekeberg. **1810** HENRY *Elem. Chem.* (1826) II. 69 The oxide of tantalum, ignited with charcoal, melts and agglutinates. **1906** *Price Sheet*, Siemens Tantalum Lamps for continuous current...The Tantalum Lamp differs from the ordinary glow lamp in having a filament of the rare metal Tantalum instead of carbon. **1907** *Outlook* 23 Mar. 378/1 Tantalum..is so hard and brittle that no ordinary metallurgical process was able to turn it into wire.

**Tantalus** (tæ·ntălŏs). Also anglicized 4 **Tantale, Tantaly,** 7 **Tantall.** [L., a. Gr. Τάνταλος.]

**1.** Name of a mythical king of Phrygia, son of Zeus and the nymph Pluto, condemned, for revealing the secrets of the gods, to stand in Tartarus up to his chin in water, which constantly receded as he stooped to drink, and with branches of fruit hanging above him which ever fled his grasp; a rock is also said to have hung over him threatening to fall. Hence *allusively*.

*c* **1369** CHAUCER *Dethe Blaunche* 709, I haue more sorowe than Tantale. **1390** GOWER *Conf.* II. 139 Ther is a peine.. Benethe in helle, which men calle The wofull peine of Tantaly. **1580** LYLY *Euphues* (Arb.) 396 As the Apples that hang at Tantalus nose. **1599** HAKLUYT *Voy.* (1809) 642 He gathereth fruits as they say, out of Tantalus his garden. **1738** GRAY *Propertius* III. 89 The long thirst of Tantalus allay. **1767** B. THORNTON tr. *Plautus, Miser* v. vi, The masters of our age..I call them Gripe-alls, Harpies, Tantalusses. **1835** SIR J. ROSS *Narr. 2nd Voy.* xlvii. 610 It was now long since it had been but the water of Tantalus. **1853** KANE *Grinnell Exp.* xliii. (1856) 397 It seems like our cup of Tantalus: we are never to reach it. **1897** *Westm. Gaz.* 21 July 7/2 It serves as a veritable tantalus to the market.

**2.** A stand containing usually three cut-glass decanters which, though apparently free, cannot be withdrawn until the grooved bar which engages the stoppers is raised.

**1898** *To-Day* 5 Nov. 1/2 He crossed to a recess, and touched the spring of a tantalus. It flew back with a harsh click. **1904** *Strand Mag.* Mar. 246/2 A tantalus containing brandy and whiskey. **1904** *Daily News* 30 Aug. 8 The winner of the sack race received a two-bottle tantalus.

**3.** *Ornith.* A genus of storks, including *T. ibis* (formerly erroneously identified with *Ibis religiosa* of Egypt); the wood stork or wood ibis.

**1824** STEPHENS in Shaw *Gen. Zool.* XII. 1 The Tantali in many respects resemble the Storks. *Ibid.* 2 The White-headed or Ceylonese Tantalus, is the largest of the genus. **1827** R. JAMESON tr. *Cuvier's The. Earth* 313 M. Macé also sent us a tantalus. *Ibid.*, The Tantalus ibis of naturalists. **1896** *List Animals Zool. Soc.* 423 American Tantalus. *Ibid.* 424 African Tantalus..Indian Tantalus.

**4.** *attrib.* and *Comb.*, as *tantalus-draught*; *tantalus-like* adj.; **tantalus-case, -stand** = sense 2; **tantalus-cup**: see quot. 1842; also *fig.*

**1601** YARINGTON *Two Lament. Trag.* v. ii. in Bullen *O. Pl.* IV, Yet Tantall-like, he shall but glut his eye Nor feede his body with salubrious fruite. **1842** BRANDE *Dict. Sc.*, etc., *Tantalus's cup*, a philosophical toy which amusingly exhibits the principle of the siphon...The legs of the siphon are concealed by the hollow figure of a man whose chin is on a level with the bend of the siphon; so that the figure stands like Tantalus in the fable,—up to the chin in water, but unable to quench his thirst. *a* **1850** MARG. F. OSSOLI *Life Without & Within* (1860) 30 Tantalus-like, he makes this world a Tartarus. **1884** RIDER HAGGARD *Dawn* vii, No misadventure came to mock them, dashing the Tantalus cup of joy to earth before their eyes. **1899** DOYLE *Duet* viii. (1909) 46/2 The Tantalus spirit-stand stood upon the walnut sideboard. **1905** *Daily Chron.* 11 July 7/1 Presents, including..a tantalus case, a diamond pin, and other trifles. **1908** *Edin. Rev.* July 101 The Tantalus-draught escaped his thirsty lips.

† **Ta·ntamount,** *sb. Obs.* Also 7 **tant amount, tantamont,** 8 **tant'amount.** [app. from TANTAMOUNT *v.*; perh. influenced by *amount* sb. beside *amount* vb.] That which amounts to as much, or comes to the same thing; something equivalent (*to*); an equivalent.

**1637** HEYLIN *Brief Answ.* 26 You come very neare it, to a tantamont. **1641** PRYNNE *Disc. Prel. Tyr.* II. 216 He pronounced no particular sentence..but he did tant amount or more. **1642** W. PRICE *Serm.* 40 Anger, and rancored envy, which..are a Tantamount to murder. **1646** BP. MAXWELL *Burd. Issach.* 41 Letters of caption (that is..the tant'amount of the Writ *De Excommunicato capiendo*).

**Tantamount** (tæ·ntămaunt), *a.* Also 7 **tant a mount, tanta-mount, tantamont,** 7–8 **tant'-amount.** [app. from the sb. The earlier quots. under a. are scarcely distinguishable from quot. 1641 in the sb. Perh. influenced by *paramount.*] As much; that amounts to as much, that comes to the same thing; of the same amount; equivalent.

† **a.** In predicate without construction. *Obs.*

**1641** O. ST. JOHN *Argument of Law*, etc. 24 If a man take the broad Seale from one Pattent, and put it to another, here he is counterfeiting, it's tantamount, and therefore Treason. **1686** GOAD *Celest. Bodies* I. xv. 80 Conjunction, Opposition, and Quadrate go for Tant-amount in the Meteorological Part. **1769** BURKE *Corr.* (1844) I. 169 Provided instructions (or thanks, which are tantamount but more respectful,) should be the mode proposed. **1826** SOUTHEY *Vind. Eccl. Angl.* 224 You..avoid the word, and speak of the Real Presence, as if the terms were tantamount.

† **b.** Const. *as*, *with*. *Obs.*

**1644** BP. MAXWELL *Prerog. Chr. Kings* 10 Howsoever their tenets by deductions and consequences are tant'amount as theirs. **1664** J. GOODWIN *Innoc. & Truth Triumph.* (1645) 11, I utterly renounce the consequence, conceiving it to be tantamont with an absolute mistake. **1684** T. BURNET *Th. Earth* I. 256 For this is tantamount with the former. *a* **1692** POLLEXFEN *Disc. Trade* (1697) 57 Tant a mount, as if carried from us in Money.

**c.** Const. *to*. The current use.

**1652** HEYLIN *Cosmogr.* Introd. 7 That saying of Berosus will prove tantamount to a Text of Scripture. **1659** — *Certamen Epist.* 389 They are tantamount to a plain acknowledgement. *a* **1692** POLLEXFEN *Disc. Trade* (1697) 93 They ..laid such Impositions on our Woolen Goods, as was tant a mount to a Prohibition. **1777** J. LOVELL in Sparks *Corr. Amer. Rev.* (1853) I. 411 Is not this..tantamount to a disavowal of the first treaty? **1874** CARPENTER *Ment. Phys.* I. i. § 18 Is not this tantamount to saying that they go on by a force of their own?

**d.** attributively. *rare.*

**1692** BP. PATRICK *Answ. Touchstone* 17 Giving us express Words, and not words Tantamount. **1798** WASHINGTON *Let.* Writ. 1893 XIV. 29 The President; to whom I have expressed tantamount sentiments in more concise terms. **1868** ROGERS *Pol. Econ.* i. (1876) 3 A tantamount service should be given in exchange for them.

† **Ta·ntamount,** *v. Obs.* Also 7 **tant amount, tant-amount, tant'amount.** [a. AF. *tant amunter*, or perh. (in 17th c.) ad. It. *tanto montare* to amount to as much.

Cf. **1292** *Year-bk. Trin.* 20 *Edw. I* (Rolls) 31 Tant amunte qe Adam neyt pas plus procheyn heyr. **1303** *Year-bk. Mich.* 31 *Edw. I* 335 Herle dist..qe tant amunte qil ne entra pas dans soun baroun.]

**1.** *intr.* To amount to as much, to come to the same thing; to be or become equivalent. Const. *to* or *unto* (something).

**1628** COKE *On Litt.* I. i. § 1. 10 They doe tant amount to a feoffment or grant. *Ibid.* 391 It ought to be pardoned specially, or by words which tant amount. **1642** JER. TAYLOR *Episc.* ix. (1647) 36 Yet this will not tant'-amount to an immediate Divine institution for Deacons. **1659** FULLER *App. Inj. Innoc.* III. 7 His not denying tant-amounteth to the affirming of the matter. **1699** SALMON *Bate's Dispens.* (1713) a vij, Those Things..which may tantamount to more than an hundred times its Value. **1716** M. DAVIES *Athen. Brit.* II. 211 Tant-amounting, in a more reform'd Perfection, to the different Religious Orders.

**2.** *trans.* To amount or come up to (something); to equal.

**1659** T. PECKE *Parnassi Puerp.* 132 Account Hercules Labours; they Twelve tantamount. **1683** *Vind. Case relating to Green-Wax-Fines* 65 Your peaceable Subjects.. whose indearment in that Case will tant-amount the Profits falling short.

Hence † **Ta·ntamounting** *ppl. a.* (*obs. rare*—[0]); whence † **Ta·ntamou·ntingly** *adv.*, 'equivalently, in effect' (Davies).

**1655** FULLER *Ch. Hist.* II. ii. § 28 Did it not deserve the Stab of Excommunication, for any dissenting from her practice, tantamountingly to give her the Lie?

**Tan-tan** (tæ·ntæn). [In quot. 1653 a. obs. F. *tantan* 'the bell that hangs about the necke of a cow' (Cotgr.): in earlier F. also *tentan, tenten, -tent*; in quot. 1893 purely echoic.] Name for a bell; also applied to the sound of a kettle-drum.

**1653** URQUHART *Rabelais* I. xvii, They would serve very well for tingling Tantans and ringing Campanels. **1893** J. HOWLAND in *Mission. Herald* (Boston) Aug. 341 The droning sound of..a rude kind of flute, and the monotonous tan-tan of a drum.

**Tantany**, obs. form of TANTONY.

**Tantara** (tæntǎrǎ, tæntā·rǎ), *int.* and *sb.* Also extended **tantara·ra, ta·ntara-ra·ra, ta·ntarata·ra.** (Cf. TARATANTARA.) [Echoic.]

**A.** *int.* Imitative of the sound of a flourish blown on a trumpet, or sometimes of a drum.

*c* **1537** W. GRAY '*Hunt is up*' iv. in W. Chappell *Popular Music* I. 60 The woddes rejoyce at the mery noise Of hey tantara tee ree! **1580** H. GIFFORD *Gilloflowers* (Grosart) 60 Tantara, tantara, the trumpets sound, Which makes our hearte with joy abound. **1589** *Love & Fortune* C iij b, Then, tantara tara, we shall haue good play. **1590** NASHE *Pasquil's Apol.* I. B iv, Tantara, tantara, is he fled indeede? let me sende a Sakar after him. *a* **1600** *Winning of Cales* Chorus, in Percy *Reliques* (1765) II. 224 Dub a dub, dub a dub, thus strike their drums, Tantara, tantara, the Englishman comes. **1644** Z. BOYD *Gard. Zion* in *Zion's Flowers* (1855) App. 12/1 The trump of war doth still Tantara blow. **1680** OTWAY *Caius Marius* III. ii, Tantarara go the Trumpets. **1846** A. BECKETT *Comic Nursery Tales* 35.

**B.** *sb.* A fanfare, or flourish of trumpets; hence, any similar sound.

**1584** *Reg. Stationers' Co.* 19 July (Arb.) II. 434 [License to print a ballad entitled] The saylers newe tantara. **1605** SYLVESTER *Du Bartas* II. iii. III. *Law* 1009 A Heav'nly Trump, a shrill Tantara blowes. **1641** EARL MONM. tr. *Biondi's Civil Warres* III. 118 There should want instruments to outdoe the Tantaraes of the enemies contemptible Campe. **1750–51** MRS. DELANY in *Life & Corr.* (1861) Ser. I. III. 17, I heard a tantararara at the door, and in walked my Mrs. Hamilton. **1843** LEVER *J. Hinton* lv, Amid a cheer.. and a tantarara from the trumpets.

*attrib.* **1800** WORDSWORTH *Andrew Jones* i, I wish the press-gang or the drum With its tantara sound would come And sweep him from the village!

**Tantarum**, var. TANTRUM. **Tantaublin**: see TANTADLIN. **Tante**: see TAUNT, ATAUNT I. **Tanten**: see TANTON.

† **Tanterueale.** The name of some bird.

**1575** E. HAKE *Newes Powles Churchyarde* D ij b, Stent, Stockard, Stampine, Tanterueale, and Wigeon of the best.

‖ **Tanti** (tæ·ntəi). [L. *tanti* 'of so much (value)', gen. of *tantum*, neut. of *tantus* so much.] Of so much value, worth so much; worth while. Formerly also as an exclamation of contempt or depreciation: So much *for*...!

**1590** MARLOWE *Edw. II*, I. i, *Tanti*; I'll fawn first on the wind That glanceth at my lips, and flieth away. **1633** J. FISHER *Fuimus Troes* III. vii. F iij, No kingly menace or censorious frowne Doe I regard. Tanti for all your power! **1639** T. LECHFORD *Note-Bk.* (1885) 89 If the State & the Elders thinke that the matters I treate on are not tanti or that they are just occasion of Disturbance. *a* **1640** DAY *Parl. Bees* Prol., That slights your errant or his art that penn'd it, Cry *Tanti*: bid him kisse his Muse and mend it. **1757** WARBURTON *Let. to Garrick* 25 Jan., in *Garrick's Corr.* (1831) I. 78 Is it *tanti* to kill yourself, in order to leave a vast deal of money to your heirs? **1888** *Athenæum* 29 Sept. 415/2 Was it quite *tanti* to write a fresh small monograph so soon after Mr. Froude's 'Bunyan'.

† **Tantilla·tion.** *Obs. nonce-wd.* [f. L. *tantillum* a trifle, dim. f. *tantus* so great + -ATION (here irregularly used).] A trifling space (of time).

**1651** BIGGS *New Disp.* ℙ 237 As if in such a tantillation or moment of time.

† **Tan-tin.** *Obs. nonce-wd.* Imitation of the sound of a bell: in quot. advb.

**1721** AMHERST *Terræ Fil.* No. 41 (1754) 217, I scarce had slept: at six, tan tin The bell goes: servitor comes in.

**Tantiny**, obs. form of TANTONY.

**Tantipartite** (tæntipā·rtəit), *a. Math.* [f. L. *tantus, -um* as much + *partītus* divided.] Homogeneous and of the first degree in each of a number of sets severally, and so of total degree equal to the number of the sets.

**1858** CAYLEY *Math. Papers* II. 517 Such covariants may be termed *tantipartite* covariants. **1860** *Ibid.* IV. 604 A function which is linear in respect to several distinct sets of variables separately is said to be tantipartite... Thus a determinant is a tantipartite function of the lines or of the columns.

**Ta·ntity,** *nonce-wd.*, a rendering of mod. L. *tantitās*, 'the fact of being or having so much', f. L. *tāntus* so much.

[Attributed in some recent dictionaries (from Annandale's Ogilvie, 1882, onward) to James Mill, who used only the Latin (*Elem. Human Mind*, 1829, II. xiv. § 2, 50) '*Quantitas*, if it was kept to its original meaning, would still connote *tantitas*; just as *paternity* connotes *filiality*'.]

**Tantivy** (tæ·ntivi, tænti·vi), *adv.*, *sb.*, *a.*, *int.* Now *rare* or *arch.* Also 7 **tantivie, -vey, -ve,** 8 **-vee, -vi, tantwivy.** [Origin obscure: ? echoic, representing the sound of a horse's feet.]

† **A.** *adv.* At full gallop: swiftly; headlong.

**1641** BROME *Jov. Crew* IV. i, Up at five a' Clock in the morning..And Tantivy all the country over, where Hunting, Hawking, or any Sport is to be made. **1648** *Fraction in the Assembly* 7 Till her Tongue travel'd tantivie, and more then a Canterbury pace. **1690** *Pagan Prince* xxi. 58 (*heading*) How he rode Tantivy to Papimania. **1705** HICKERINGILL *Priest-Cr.* II. A ij b, (Like so many Asses) to let Hypocrisy bestride them,..and ride them—Tantivee. **1785** GROSE *Dict. Vulg. Tongue* s. v., Away they went tantwivy, away they went full speed. **1823** SCOTT *Peveril* xxxiii, There are those amongst us who ride tantivy to Rome, and have already made out half the journey.

**B.** *sb.* **1.** (from the adverb.) A rapid gallop; a ride at this pace. Also *transf.* and *fig.*

*a* **1658** CLEVELAND *Reply Parlt.-Officer* Wks. (1687) 93, I expected to hear from you in the Language of..the Prodigal Son, and not in such a Tantivy of Language. **1680** V. ALSOP *Mischief Imposit.* xi. 94 Jogging on their own pace, neither the high-trot nor the Tantivey. **1721** CIBBER *Refusal* IV, Ah! poor Soul! piteous bad! All upon the Tantivy again! **1854** THOREAU *Walden* iv. 125 The Tantivy of wild pigeons, flying by twos and threes athwart my view..gives a voice to the air.

**2.** A nickname given to the post-Restoration High-Churchmen and Tories, esp. in the reigns of Charles II and James II.

This arose 1680–81, when a caricature was published in which a number of High Church clergymen were represented as mounted upon the Church of England and 'riding tantivy' to Rome, behind the Duke of York. Cf. **1681** *Trial of S. Colledge* 25 *Dugdale*. And there is one Picture that I have not shewed yet...*Jefferies*. There are some Church-men; what are they a doing? *Dugdale*. They are a parcel of Tantivy men riding to Rome, and here's the Duke of York, half Man, half Devil, trumpeting before them. *Ibid.* 59 *Mr. Charlett*. It was the pictures of the Tantivies and the Towzer [Roger L'Estrange], and he told me they were made by Colledge, he was a very ingenious man. *a* **1734** NORTH *Exam.* I. ii. § 130 About Half a Dozen of the Tantivies were mounted upon the Church of England, booted and spurred, riding it, like an old Hack, Tantivy to Rome.

**1680–81** G. HICKES *Spirit of Popery* 23 The Clergy..called them Priests, and Bishops, which in these days would pass for Episcopal tantivies. **1681** LUTTRELL *Brief Rel.* (1857) I. 124 The former are called by the latter, tories, tantivies, Yorkists, high flown church men, &c. **1706** PHILLIPS (ed. 6), *Tantivy*...Also a Nick-name given by the Dissenters to a Worldly-minded Church-man, that bestirs himself for Preferment. **1707** HEARNE *Collect.* 24 Feb. (O. H. S.) I. 336 Hei! day! What is the High-Rope! a high-Flyer and a Tantivi! **1730** SWIFT *Vind. Ld. Carteret* 27 Favouring none but High-Church, High-flyers,..Tip-top-gallon-men, Jacobites, Tantivyes, Anti-Hanoverians [etc.]. **1841** MACAULAY *Ess.*, *Comic Dramatists* (1887) 613 Collier..was a Tory of the highest sort, such as in the cant of his age was called a Tantivy. **1849** — *Hist. Eng.* ii. I. 256.

**3.** *erron.* applied to a blast or flourish on a horn.

**1785** GROSE *Dict. Vulg. Tongue* s. v., Tantwivy was the sound of the hunting horn in full cry, or that of a post horn. **1834** MEDWIN *Angler in Wales* II. 97 A schoolboy put an end to all the Childe Harolding by a tantivy on a bugle.

**C.** *adj.* ? orig., in *tantivy men* and the like, attrib. use of B. 1; afterwards often of B. 2.

**1681** T. FLATMAN *Heraclitus Ridens* No. 7 (1713) I. 42 In favour of the Tory and Tantivy Party. **1682** MRS. BEHN *City Heiress* 30 Perverted with Ill Customs, Tantivie-Opinions, and Court-Notions. **1682** *New News fr. Bedlam* 26 Whereas you say it was a high Presbyterian Trot, I rather believe it was a Tantivy Gallop. **1691** *Andros Tracts* II. 246 Had King Rehoboam kept his Tantivy Doctrine of Passive Obedience and Non Resistance to himself,..the poor People had been his Servants for ever. **1715** *State Quacks* 21 High Tantivee Scaramouches make Choice of a vast Heap of Epithets as unintelligible..as impertinent. **1826** SCOTT *Woodst.* xx, Master Wildrake is one of the old school—one of the tantivy boys. **1884** *Q. Rev.* July 32 Birmingham itself ..to become as great a stronghold of 'tantivy' politics as it was in the days when it rabbled Priestley.

**D.** *int.* An imitation of the sound of galloping or scudding feet; later (*erron.*) of the sound of a horn.

**1697** VANBRUGH *Æsop* II. i, *Æsop*..But (like some of our friends) they found 'Twas safer much to scour. *Rog.* Tantive! Tantive! Tantive! **1719** D'URFEY *Pills* (1872) II. 188 Tantivee, tivee, tivee, tivee, High and Low. Hark, hark how the merry merry Horn does blow. **1821** *Sporting Mag.* VIII. 156 Tantivy! tantivy! the hunting-horn blew.

† **Tantivy,** *v. Obs. rare.* [f. prec.]

**1.** *intr.* To ride full tilt; to hurry away.

**1681** T. FLATMAN *Heraclitus Ridens* No. 29 (1713) I. 186 You will Tantivy then out of Town. **1796** MME. D'ARBLAY *Camilla* III. viii, Pray where are they gone, tantivying?

**2.** *trans.* ? To call 'tantivy'; to 'give it him' for calling one 'tantivy'.

**1681** T. FLATMAN *Heraclitus Ridens* No. 34 (1713) I. 218 Never a word said to them for Torying, Tantivying and Masquerading his Majesty's most loyal and dutiful Subjects. **1711** SWIFT *Jrnl. to Stella* 10 Oct., I'll 'tantivy' him with a vengeance.

† **Tantivyism.** *Obs.* [f. as prec. + -ISM.] The practice or principles of tantivies: see TANTIVY *sb.* 2.

*c* **1680** HICKERINGILL *Hist. Whiggism* II. Wks. 1716 I. 100 He was afterwards made Bishop of Chichester, and then Bishop of Norwich, just as Mr. Mountague leapt, and perhaps upon the same rise and advantage of the ground, Tantiviisme. **1681** T. FLATMAN *Heraclitus Ridens* No. 7 (1713) I. 40 A Church of England Man maintaining the necessity of the words *As by Law now Establish'd*, which you know is Tantivyism and Toryism in the highest degree. *Ibid.* No. 20 I. 135 To profess sincere Loyalty to his Majesty's Person and Government, to give him humble Thanks for his Gracious Promises in his Declaration..is now become perfect Toryism, Tantivyism, and *tantum non* Abhorrism.

[**Tantling,** in Johnson (whence in subsequent dictionaries), a suggested alteration of TANLING in Shaks. *Cymb.* IV. iv. 29.]

‖ **Tant ne quant,** *adv. phr. Obs. rare.* Also 4 **taunt ne caunt.** [OF. (*ne*) *tant ne quant.*] In no wise, not at all.

**13..** *S. Eng. Leg.* (MS. Bodl. 779) in Herrig's *Archiv* LXXXII. 341/256 He ne tornyd one his þouȝt noþer taunt ne caunt. **1390** GOWER *Conf.* I. 241 Mi goode Sone, as of Supplant Thee thar noght drede tant ne quant.

† **Ta·nto,** *sb. Obs. rare.* [app. erroneous form and use of Sp. *tanteo* computation, calculation, number of counters for marking a game: perh. *tantoes* is mispr. for *tanteos*.] A counter used in gaming.

**1646** EARL MONM. tr. *Biondi's Civil Warres* IX. 196 Honours are the Alchimy of Princes, which like Gamesters Tantoes, are worth as much, as they are made to be worth.

‖ **Tanto** (ta·nto), *adv. Mus.* [It.:—L. *tantum* so much.] So, so much: as *allegro non tanto*, fast, but not too much so.

**1876** STAINER & BARRETT *Dict. Mus. Terms.*

**Tantoblin**: see TANTADLIN.

† **Tanton.** *Obs.* [Short for *Saint Anthon*: cf. T 7, and next.] In *Tanton man*: an inmate of a hospital, or the like, dedicated to Saint Anthony.

**1515** *Test. Ebor.* (Surtees) V. 65 To every Tanten man ther dwellyng iiij d., to pray for my sowll.

**Tantony** (tæ·ntəni), *sb.* Also 7 **-any,** 8 **-iny.** [f. T 7 + ANTHONY.] A shortened form of *St. Anthony*, chiefly used *attrib.* in reference to the attributes with which the saint was represented (cf. Mrs. Jamieson *Sacred & Legendary Art* (1848) II. 367–379), as *tantony crutch, tantony pouch*. *spec.* **b.** (more fully *tantony bell*) a hand-bell; a small church bell: see quots. **c.** (more fully *tantony pig*) [St. Anthony being the patron of swine-herds, and represented as accompanied by a pig], the smallest pig of a litter; also *fig.* said of one who very closely or obsequiously follows another: cf. context of quot. 1598, and quot. 1662 s.v. ANTHONY.

**a.** **1594** LYLY *Moth. Bomb.* II. i, The dudgen dagger, by which hanges his tantonie pouch.

**b.** **1567** *Gude & Godlie B.* (S.T.S.) 175 The Paip He had to sell the Tantonie bell And Pardonis thairin was. **1854** MISS BAKER *Northampt. Gloss.*, *Tantony*, the small bell over the church-porch, or between the chancel and the nave: the term is also applied to any small hand-bell. 'Ring the tantony' is evidently a corruption of St. Anthony, the emblem of that saint being a bell at his tau-staff, or round the neck of his accompanying pig. **1872** ELLACOMBE *Ch. Bells Devon*, etc. ix. 497. **1904** in *Eng. Dial. Dict.* (Hunts.), *Tantony*, the name given to a bell which is rung at the entrance gate of the grounds at Kimbolton Castle to give notice of the arrival of visitors. [See *N. & Q.* 8 Feb. 1851, 105/1; 14 June 484/1.]

**c.** [**1598** STOW *Surv. Lond.* (1603) 185 Whereupon was raysed a prouerbe, such a one will follow such a one, and whine as it were an Anthonie pig.] **1659** GAUDEN *Tears of Ch.* 595 Some are such Cossets and Tantanies that they congratulate their Oppressors and flatter their Destroyers. **1738** SWIFT *Pol. Conversat.* 76 She made me follow her last Week through all the Shops like a Tantiny Pig. **1765** BICKERSTAFFE *Love in Village* I. ix, To see you dangling after me every where, like a tantony pig. **1891** BESANT *St. Katherine's by the Tower* I. 148 They run the same way—like Tantony pigs.

Hence † **Ta·ntony, ta·ntany** *v.*, to follow constantly or closely like a tantony pig.

**1675** CROWNE *Country Wit* v, Do not follow and tantany us, Mr. Ramble, for, I declare positively, thou shalt never have my daughter.

‖ **Ta·ntra.** [Skr. *tantra* loom, warp, hence groundwork, principle, system, doctrine, f. *tan* to stretch, extend.] One of a class of Hindu religious works in Sanskrit, of comparatively recent date, chiefly of magical and mystical nature; also, of a class of Buddhist works of similar character.

**1799** *Asiatic Researches* V. 53 The Tantras form a branch of literature highly esteemed. though at present much neglected. *Ibid.* 62, I am informed, that the Tantras collectively are noticed in very ancient compositions. **1901** *Mission. Rec. U. F. Ch. Scotl.* Sept. 411/2 The Tantras, the sacred books of the Shakti worshippers.

Hence **Ta·ntric** *a.*, of or pertaining to the Tantras; **Ta·ntrism,** the doctrine or principles of the Tantras; **Ta·ntrist,** an adherent of tantrism.

**1882** OGILVIE (Annandale), Tantrism. **1891** tr. *De La Saussaye's Hist. Sc. Relig.* lxxv. 622 Tantrism..is common to Buddhist and Hindu communities. **1891** *Cent. Dict.* Tantrist. **1905** *Q. Rev.* July 201 The Buddhist worship of these deities is undoubtedly due to Tantric influence.

**Tantrum** (tæ·ntrŏm). *colloq.* Also 8–9 **tantarum.** [Origin unascertained.

(In Wallis's *Room for the Cobbler of Gloucester* (1668) 4 *tantrum* appears as a Welshman's mispronunciation of *anthem*, but apparently has no connexion with this word.)]

An outburst or display of petulance or ill-temper; a fit of passion. Mostly in *pl.*

**1748** FOOTE *Knights* II. Wks. 1799 I. 84 None of your fleers!..Your tantrums!—You are grown too headstrong and robust for me. **1754** SHEBBEARE *Matrimony* (1766) I. 122 Where did the Wench get these Tantarums into her Head? **1776** MRS. DELANY in *Life & Corr.* Ser. II. (1862) II. 206 Treating him with some contempt when he is in his tantrums. **1824** W. IRVING *T. Trav.* I. 217 An author, who was always in a tantrum if interrupted. **1837** DISRAELI *Venetia* I. vi, He goes into his tantarums at the abbey. **1884** *Times* 12 Mar. 3 The defendant told him not to get into a tantrum.

† **Ta·ntuple,** *a. Obs.* [f. L. *tantus* so great,

after QUADRUPLE, etc.] That is so many times another quantity; equimultiple.

**1656** HOBBES *Six Lessons* iii. Wks. 1845 VII. 240 The antecedents are of their consequents totuple or tantuple, that is, equimultiple.

**Tan-vat** (tæ·nvæt). Also 6–8 -fat. [f. TAN *v.* or *sb.* + VAT.] The receptacle, a tub, cistern, pit, or the like, containing the 'ooze' in which the hides are laid in tanning.

**1592** GREENE *Upst. Courtier* Wks. (Grosart) XI. 261 Howe comes this to passe? by your tanne-fats for sooth. **1615** E. S. *Britain's Buss* in Arb. *Garner* III. 630 Every net must be tanned in a tan-fat. **1655** FULLER *Ch. Hist.* VI. ii. § 1. **1779** E. BEATTY in J. L. Hardenbergh *Jrnl.* (1879) 65 There was a tanfat farm with several Hides at a tannery which the soldiers got. **1828** WEBSTER, Tan-vat. **1895** S. R. HOLE *Little Tour Amer.* 86 Grant tried that [tanning], but found no gold in the tan-vat.

**Tany, Tanya,** var. TAWNY, TANIA.

**Tanyan,** var. TANGHAN, Tibetan horse.

† **Ta·nystome.** *Ent. Obs.* [a. F. *tanystome*, f. Gr. τανύ-ειν to stretch + στόμα mouth.] A fly of Latreille's second family of Diptera, *Tanystomata*, including the gad-flies and their allies. Hence † **Tany·stomate,** † **Tany·stomine,** † **Tany·stomous** *adjs. Obs.*

**1860** MAYNE *Expos. Lex.*, *Tanystomus*..long-mouthed; applied to a Family..of the *Diptera*: tanystomous.

**Tanzey, tanzie, tanzy,** variants of TANSY.

‖ **Tanzib** (tanzī·b). Also 8 tanjeeb, 9 tanjib. [Persian, f. تن *tan* body + زیب *zib* adornment.] A fine kind of Indian muslin made chiefly in Oudh.

**1727–41** CHAMBERS *Cycl.* s.v. *Muslin*, There are various kinds of muslins brought from the East-Indies; chiefly Bengall; betelles, tarnatans,..tanjeebs. **1854** J. S. BUCKLE *Manuf. Compend.* p. xi, 49 inches wide Tanjib, 38 yards long 14×10—i.e., 14 picks or threads in ¼ inch of the warp, and 10 picks or threads in ¼ inch of the weft. **1880** BIRDWOOD *Ind. Arts* II. 85 A tanzib or tanjib muslin.

**Taoism** (tā·o‚iz'm). Also taou-, tau-, tavism. [f. Chinese *tao* way, path, right way (of life), reason + -ISM.] A system of religion, founded upon the doctrine of the ancient Chinese philosopher Laotsze (or Lao-tzŭ), born 604 B.C., set forth in the work *Tao tê king*, 'Book of reason and virtue', attributed to him. It ranks with Confucianism and Buddhism as one of the three religions of China.

**1839** *Chinese Repository* VII. 511 We have all this time been working through the mazes of Taouism..merely to give a better explanation of the notions of this sect. **1858** MAX MÜLLER *Chips* (1880) I. ii. 51 The religious system of Laotse, or the Tao-ism of China. **1903** *Rev. Missions* Mar. 539 Taoism, an older religion than Buddhism—dating indeed from before the teachings of Confucius—was so purely beautiful as delivered by Lao-tsze, its great teacher.

**Taoist** (tā·o‚ist), *sb.* (*a.*) Also taou-. [f. as prec. + -IST.] An adherent of Taoism.

**1839** *Chinese Repository* VII. 520 The Taouists are by no means behind in referring to an abode of lasting bliss, which does however still exist on earth. **1863** ALCOCK *Capital Tycoon* I. 392 [To] feel, or affect, great contempt for any creed but that of Taouists. **1885** *Athenæum* 17 Oct. 500/3 It [the 'Taou-tih-king'] may be considered, therefore, as the Bible of the Taouists.

**b.** *attrib.* or as *adj.* Of or belonging to the Taoists or to Taoism.

**1839** MALCOLM *Trav.* II. III. v. 184 Great officers, and even the emperor himself, build and endow Boodhist and Taouist temples. **1882** *Athenæum* 16 Sept. 361/2 With the exception of Laou-tsze, the early Taouist philosophers have found no place in English literature...Though professing to be followers of Laou-tsze, they never perfectly understood him, and perverted his doctrines into childish babblings.

Hence **Taoi·stic** *a.*

**1856** MEADOWS *Chinese* 440 Representatives of a Buddhistic or Taouistic element that is struggling with the Confucian element to assert for itself a place in the new religion. **1884** *Brit. & For. Evangelical Rev.* Apr. 367 The Taoistic, or Rationalistic system is about as old as Confucianism.

**Tap** (tæp), *sb.*[1] Forms: 1 tæppa, 4 teppe, 5–7 tappe, 7 tapp, 5– tap. [Com. Teutonic: OE. *tæppa* (wk. masc.) = OLG. *tappo (MDu., MLG., LG. *tappe*, EFris. *tappe*, *tap*, Du. *tap*, NFris. *tâp*), OHG. *zapfo* (MHG. *zapfe*, Ger. *zapfen*), ON. *tappi* (Sw. *tapp*, Da. *tap*):—OTeut. *tappon-, orig. a tapering cylindrical stick or peg (cf. *tap-root*).]

**1.** A cylindrical stick, long peg, or stopper, for closing and opening a hole bored in a vessel; hence, a hollow or tubular plug through which liquid may be drawn, having some device for shutting off or governing the flow; used especially in drawing liquor from a cask, or water from a pipe, and for regulating the flow of gas, steam, etc.; a cock, a faucet.

*c* **1050** in *Techmer's Int. Zeitschr. für allg. Sprachwissensch.* II. 120 Ðonne þu win habban wille, þonne do þu mid þinum twam fingrum, swilce þu tæppan of tunnan onteon wille. *Ibid.*, Tæppan teon. **1340** *Ayenb.* 27 Vor hit behoueþ þet zuich wyn yerne by þe teppe ase þer is ine þe tonne. *c* **1440** *Promp. Parv.* 486/2 Tappe, of a vessel, *ductillus, clipsidra*. **1530** PALSGR. 279/1 Tappe or spygote to drawe drinke at, *chantepleure*. **1588** *Marprel. Epist.* (Arb.) 38 Sir Ieffry..tooke such vnkindenes at the alehouse, that he sware he would neuer goe againe into it..the tap had great quietnes and ease therby. **1688** R. HOLME *Armoury* III. xx. (Roxb.) 231 The Cock or Tapp, letting out the hot water. **1768** COOK *Voy. round World* I. ii. (1773) 17 It was impossible..to draw out any of its contents by a tap. **1874** MICKLETHWAITE *Mod. Par. Churches* 185 A few taps only are turned, and all is ready for lighting.

**b.** *fig.*

*c* **1386** CHAUCER *Reeve's Prol.* 36 As many a yeer as it is ..Syn that my tappe [*v. r.* tap] of lif began to renne. **1599** *Broughton's Let.* xi. 37 This whole tractate of yours,..is but the droppings of other mens taps. **1658** GURNALL *Chr. in Arm.* II. verse 16. viii. (1669) 203/2 Labour to take the advantage of thy present relenting frame,..now the Ordinance hath thawed the Tap. **1907** *Daily Chron.* 18 Apr. 5/6 There was certainly a 'tap on', as the vulgar phrase is, in the market yesterday, and much scrip was thrown out at ½ to ⅛ premium.

**c.** *On* (*in*) *tap*, on draught, ready for immediate consumption or use (*lit.* and *fig.*). † *To sell by tap* (*Sc. Obs.*), to sell in small quantities, to retail.

**1483** *Seill of Caus, Edin.* 2 May (Jam.), That no common cremaris of the toune wse to sell be tap ony hammermans work. **1862** LOWELL *Biglow P.* Ser. II. 54 Who is he that.. has eloquence always on tap? **1891** T. HARDY *Tess* i, There's a pretty brew in tap at the Pure Drop.

**2. a.** A tap-room or tap-house. *colloq.*

**1725** *New Cant. Dict.* s.v. *Tape*, The Renters of the Tap ..in Newgate. **1771** SMOLLETT *Humph. Cl.* II. 11 June, Rabbit him! the tap will be ruined. **1837** J. D. LANG *N. S. Wales* II. 102 He had been drinking in the Tap over-night. **1857** HUGHES *Tom Brown* I. iv, Guard emerges from the tap, where he prefers breakfasting.

**b.** A pit in which tan-liquor is mixed; = LEACH *sb.*[2] 2. ? *Obs.*

**1797** *Encycl. Brit.* (ed. 3) XVIII. 307/1 Strong liquor called ooze or wooze prepared in pits called letches or taps kept for the purpose, by infusing ground bark in water.

**3. a.** The liquor drawn from a particular tap; a particular species or quality of drink. Also *fig.* a particular strain or kind of anything. *colloq.*

**1623** tr. *Favine's Theat. Hon.* I. i. 1 Such a one was called a Gentleman of the first Tappe. **1832** L. HUNT *Redi Bacchus in Tuscany* 75 Those Norwegians and those Laps Have extraordinary taps. **1848** THACKERAY *Van. Fair* xxxiv, I wish my aunt would send down some of this to the governor; it's a precious good tap. **1872** O. W. HOLMES *Poet Breakf.-t.* vi. (1885) 139 Sentiment wasn't his tap. **1902** A. BIRRELL *W. Hazlitt* iv. 55 His [Hazlitt's] 'tap' was too bitter, his stride too long.

**b.** Short for *Tap-cinder*: see 6.

**1878** URE *Dict. Arts* IV. 493 Using such purple ore in the ordinary way, as fettling in conjunction with 'tap', pottery mine, etc.

**4.** *Mech.* A tool used for cutting the thread of an internal screw, consisting of a male screw of hardened steel, grooved lengthways to form cutting edges, and having a square head so that it may be turned by a wrench.

**1677** MOXON *Mech. Exerc.* ii. 31 Turn about the tap in the hole, and make grooves and threds in the Nut. **1816** [see *screw nut*: SCREW *sb.*[1] 22]. **1875** *Carpentry & Join.* 81 A tap ..to cut the requisite thread inside the nut. **1884** F. J. BRITTEN *Watch & Clockm.* 232 Taps for watch makers' use are made by running a piece of steel through a screw plate.

**5.** An object having the shape of a slender tapering cylinder, as an icicle; *esp.* a tap-root.

**1658** PHILLIPS, *Isicle*,..a tappe of ice, a drop of water frozen. **1796** C. MARSHALL *Garden.* xix. (1813) 318 The tap of the oak will make its way downward, in a direct line, through the hardest soils. **1857** H. MILLER *Test. Rocks* xi. 497 The central axes of the trees do not elongate downwards into a tap but throw out horizontally on every side a thick net-work of roots.

**6.** *attrib.* and *Comb.*, as, in sense 1, *tap-dropping* (also *taps-droppings*), *-maker*, *-spirits*; in sense 2, *tap-boy*, *-man*; also **tap-auger**, an auger for boring tap-holes; **tap-bar**, a testing bar placed in a cementation furnace and withdrawn for inspection during the process (*Cent. Dict.* 1891); **tap-bolt**, a threaded bolt which is screwed into a part, as distinguished from one that penetrates it and receives a nut; **tap-borer**, a tapering instrument for boring bung-holes or tap-holes; **tap-cinder**, the slag or refuse produced in a puddling furnace; **tap-dressing**, decoration of wells at Whitsuntide, a Derbyshire custom; † **tap-lead**, = *tap-trough*; **tap-plate**, a steel plate having holes, wormed and notched, for cutting external threads; a screw-plate (Knight *Dict. Mech.* 1877); **tap-rivet, tap-screw**, = *tap-bolt* (hence **tap-rivet** *v. trans.*, to secure by tap-rivets; **tap-riveting**, the use of tap-rivets); † **tap-shackled** *a.*, 'fettered' by drink, drunk; † **tap-staff**, a staff used to stop the tap-hole of a mash-tub; † **tap-stone**, (?); **tap-tool**, = sense 4; † **tap-tree**, = *tap-staff*; † **tap-trough**, a leaden trough used in brewing; **tap-water**, water drawn through a tap; *spec.* water supplied by a system of pipes and taps for household use; † **tap-whips, tap-whisk**, dialect variants of TAP-HOSE; † **tap-wort**, the dregs of ale or beer; **tap-wrench**, a wrench for turning a tap-tool. See also TAP-HOLE, TAP-HOSE, etc.

**1688** R. HOLME *Armoury* III. 317/2 (Coopers' Instruments) *Tap Auger. **1864** WEBSTER, **Tap-bolt*. **1877** KNIGHT *Dict. Mech.*, **Tap-borer*. **1801** G. HANGER *Life* II. 97 A *tap-boy at a public-house. **1861** *Lond. Rev.* 16 Feb. 167 In the process of making malleable iron, which is called 'puddling', there is a large quantity of refuse, known as '*tap-cinder'. **1894** *Daily News* 23 Apr. 8/4 Some time ago it was discovered that this tap-cinder contained an amount of phosphorus which rendered it of sufficient service for basic steel-making as to justify the cost of its transmission for that purpose to the continent. **1851** in *N. & Q.* 2nd Ser. IX. 431/1 A great deal of taste and fancy is exhibited in the..'*tap-dressing'. **1860** *Ibid.* 430/2 [He] was collecting [flowers] for the Pilsley 'Well' or 'Tap' dressing. **1892** *Daily News* 22 Sept. 3/1 The Rev. G. S. Tyack's account of the curious custom of well-dressing, or 'tap-dressing', as it is called. **1608** MIDDLETON *Fam. Love* IV. iii, How rank the knave smells of grease and *taps-droppings! **1678** *Quack's Academy* 4 Vials filled with Tap-droppings. **1429** in Rogers *Agric. & Pr.* III. 550/1 *Vas plumbeum* called *tapled. **1892** *Pall Mall G.* 23 Mar. 6/3 One of his former friends,.. a *tap-maker. **1907** *Month* July 7 Not but what priests doctor their stuff and give short measure like any *tap-man. **1869** SIR E. J. REED *Shipbuilding* ii. 43 They are each composed of two angle-irons, *tap-riveted or screwed (and not through riveted) to the bottom plating. **1874** THEARLE *Naval Archit.* 79 It is connected to the stem, either by angle-irons on each side, through riveted, and tap riveted to the stem. *Ibid.* 129 In riveting the angle-irons of bilge keels to the bottom plating *tap rivets are used. *Ibid.*, *Tap riveting is employed in securing plates to forgings. **1891** *Cent. Dict.*, **Tap-screw*. **1604** J. MORRIS *Commpl.-bk.* (Brit. Mus. Roy. MS. 12 B v) lf. 6 b, A scholler of Cambridge being somewhat *tap-shackled walking in the streete met a blacke bull. *c* **1608** HEALEY *Disc. New World* 82 [He] being truely tapp-shackled, mistooke the window for the dore. **14..** *Voc.* in Wr.-Wülcker 572/13 *Ceruida*, a *tapstaf. **1688** R. HOLME *Armoury* III. 319/2 The Brewers Thorn with the Tap Staff through the middle of it. **1703** J. MORE *Engl. Interest* (ed. 2) 66 After this, you must lift up your Tap-staffe, and let out about a Gallon [from the mash-vat]..and put it up again, stopping your Tap-hole. **1522** *Wills & Inv. N. C.* (Surtees 1835) 106 Also I bequeth to my son John Trollop.. the brewehouse..a brewelede with a mashefatt and a *tapstone with a boltong arke and the bras pottes called Thornley Pottes. **1874** THEARLE *Naval Archit.* 127 Screwing the rivet into a screw hole previously prepared for it by means of a '*tap tool'. **1483** *Cath. Angl.* 378/1 A *Tap tre, *ceruida, clipsidra*. **1743** R. MAXWELL *Sel. Tr. Soc. Improv. Agric. Scot.* 284 Take out your Cork, or Tap-tree, and have a Tub below to receive the Lee that comes off. **1335** in Riley *Lond. Mem.* (1868) 194, 1 *tappetroghe [of lead]. **1881** TYNDALL *Float. Matter Air* 81 Ice-water, distilled water and *tap-water..deprived of their powers of infection. **1898** P. MANSON *Trop. Diseases* i. 32 Wash in tap water and then in distilled water, dry and mount in zylol balsam. **1743** *Lond. & Country Brew.* IV. (ed. 2) 267 In [a Mash-Tub] fix a Brass Cock of three Quarters of an Inch Bore in a *Tapwhips, or do it by Plug and Basket. **1854** MISS BAKER *Northampt. Gloss.*, *Tap-whisk. **1881** *Leicester. Gloss.*, *Tap-whisk*,..the wicker strainer placed at the back of the tap inside a mash-vat, &c. **1582** BRETON *Toyes Idle Head* Wks. (Grosart) 26/2 A cuppe of small *Tap worte. **1815** J. SMITH *Panorama Sc. & Art* I. 40 The *tap-wrench is simply a lever, with a hole..to admit the rectangular head of the tap, for the purpose of turning it round.

**Tap** (tæp), *sb.*[2] Forms: 4 tap(p)e, 5 tapp, 6– tap. [f. TAP *v.*[2] So OFris. *tap*; cf. F. *tape* slap.]

**1.** A single act of tapping; a light but audible blow or rap; the sound made by such a blow.

**13..** *Gaw. & Gr. Knt.* 406 Ȝif I þe telle trwly, quen I þe tape haue. *Ibid.* 2357 At þe þrid þou fayled þore, & þerfor þat tappe ta þe. *a* **1466** CHAS. DK. ORLEANS *Poems* (Roxb.) 7 As strokis grete not tippe, nor tapp, do way The rewdisshe child so best lo shall he wynne. *a* **1577** GASCOIGNE *Adv. F. I.* Wks. (Roxb.) I. 463 Much greater is the wrong that rewardeth euill for good, than that which requireth tip for tap. **1597** SHAKS. 2 *Hen. IV*, II. i. 206 This is the right Fencing grace (my Lord) tap for tap and so part faire. *c* **1614** FLETCHER, etc. *Wit at Sev. Weapons* III. i, But when a man's sore beaten o' both sides already, Then the least tap in jest goes to the guts on him. **1720** JENYNS *Art Dancing* II. Poems (1761) 21 Let them a while their nimble feet restrain, And with soft taps beat time to ev'ry strain. **1794** MRS. RADCLIFFE *Myst. Udolpho* vii, A gentle tap at the chamber-door roused her. **1862** SALA *Seven Sons* II. vii. 194 The convicts were called off by the tap of a drum. **1877** *Encycl. Brit.* VII. 609/2 Rolling croquet..is made by trailing the mallet after the balls as soon as the stroke or tap is made.

**b.** **Tap-tap**, a repeated tap; a series of taps; also *adv.*

**1837** THACKERAY *Ravenswing* ii, Mr. Tressle's man.. ceased his tap-tap upon the coffin. **1840** MARRYAT *Poor Jack* xxiii, The water went tap, tap, tap against the bends. **1905** E. CHANDLER *Unveiling of Lhasa* xii. 212 The tap-tap of the Maxim, like a distant woodpecker, in the valley.

**2.** Pl. **Taps** (*U.S. Milit.*): a signal sounded on the drum or trumpet, fifteen minutes after the tattoo, at which all lights in the soldiers' quarters are to be extinguished. Sounded also, like *last post* (POST *sb.*[3]) over the grave of a soldier.

**1862** *Index* (U.S.) 25 Sept., I well remember how 'at taps' we were wont to huddle together in our narrow quarters, each man's knapsack serving for his pillow. **1869** T. W. HIGGINSON *Army Life* (1870) 34 The mystic curfew which we call 'taps'. **1891** *Cambridge* (Mass.) *Tribune* 10 Jan. 8/5 The customary volleys were fired over the grave, and Bugler Fitzgerald sounded 'taps', the soldier's last sad farewell. **1904** J. A. RIIS *Roosevelt* viii. 199 Taps had been sounded long since.

**3.** A piece of leather with which the worn-down heel or sole of a boot is made up and repaired or 'tapped' (*U.S.*); a plate or piece of iron with which the heel is shielded; also, the sole of a shoe (*Eng. dial.*). (Cf. TAP *v.*[2] 3.)

*On one's taps*, on one's feet; on the move; busy.

**1688–c 1850** [see HEEL-TAP *sb.* 1]. **1844** W. BARNES *Poems Rural Life* Gloss., *Tap*, the sole of a shoe. **1855** HALIBURTON *Nat. & Hum. Nat.* II. 332 They have to be on their taps most all the time. **1864** WEBSTER, *Tap*..the piece of leather fastened upon the bottom of a boot or shoe in tapping it, or in repairing or renewing the sole or heel. **1882** JAGO

*Cornw. Gloss.*, *Tap*, the sole of a boot or shoe. Also the iron..'scute' of the heel, 'heel tap'.

**4.** *Comb.* **Tap-piece** = 3; hence **Tap-piece** *v.*, to repair with a tap-piece.

1903 R. Watson *Closeburn* xiv. 235 Mony a day I hae tappieced and heeled your auld shoon.

**Tap,** *sb.*3 [app. short for Tapnet; cf. also Top *sb.*3] A rush-basket (usually containing *c* 28 lbs.) in which figs of an inferior quality are imported. *Comb.* **tap-figs** (colloq. shortened to *taps*), figs of the quality imported in taps.

*c* 1860 [Recollected in use]. 1909 *Wholesale Grocer's Price-list*, Figs..Layers 40/-..50/- per cwt. Taps, 19/-..Naturals 25/6. 1910 *Produce Mark. Rev.* 19 Feb. 155 Figs..Layer Figs..Pulled figs..Naturals..Comadra, Taps.

‖ **Tap** (tæp), *sb.*4 *East Ind.* [a. Pers. *tap* fever, heat; = Skr. *tapa* heat, *tāpa* heat, pain, torment.] Malarial fever.

1882 F. M. Crawford *Mr. Isaacs* xii, Unless I feared the *tap*, the bad kind of fever which infests all the country at the base of the hills.

**Tap** (tæp), *v.*1 Forms: 1 tæppian, 5–6 tappe, 6 tape, 7–8 tapp, 5– tap; also *Sc.* (in sense 4, 4 b) 5–7 top(pe, 6 talp, 6–7 tope, 7 taip, (topt). [Com. Teutonic: OE. *tæppian*, from *tæppa* Tap *sb.*1 = MLG., MDu., LG., and Du. *tappen*, MHG., Ger. *zapfen*, ON., Sw. *tappa*, Da. *tappe*, all from the cognate sbs. Cf. F. *taper*, to plug, from OLG.]

**I.** To open (a cask, reservoir).

**1.** *trans.* To furnish (a cask, etc.) with a tap or spout, in order to draw the liquor from it.

*c* 1050 in *Techmer's Int. Zeitschr. für allg. Sprachwissensch.* (1885) II. 125 ȝyf þe ȝedryptes wines lyste, þonne do ðu mid þinum swyþran scytefingre on þine wynstran hand, swylce þu tæppian wille, and wænd þinne scytefinger adune. 1483 *Cath. Angl.* 378/1 To Tappe, *ceruidare*. 1570 Levins *Manip.* 27/22 To Tappe, *fistulum addere*. 1696 Phillips (ed. 5), To *Tapp a Vessel*, to fix a Tapp in the Bung-hole.. thereby to draw out the Liquor. 1832 Lytton *Eugene A.* III. iii, I will tap a barrel on purpose for you. 1880 *Act* 43 & 44 *Vict.* c. 24 § 90 The rectifier must not..tap, open, alter, or change any cask..containing any such spirits.

**2.** To pierce (a vessel, tree, etc.) so as to draw off its liquid contents; to broach; to draw liquid from (any reservoir); *slang*, to draw blood from the nose.

e. g. To bore into (a tree) so that sap may exude; to allow the molten metal to run from (a furnace); to pierce the wall of (a reservoir), to drain (a marsh).

1694 Westmacott *Script. Herb.* 12 It [the Quicken] will yield a liquor, if tapt as we do birch in the spring. 1792 Belknap *Hist. New Hampsh.* III. 114 The season for tapping the [maple] trees is in March. 1809 *Nat. Hist.* in *Ann. Reg.* 843/1 The maple tree..the oftener it is tapped the better. 1832 Ht. Martineau *Hill & Vall.* iv. 60 He was just going to tap the furnace, i. e. to let out the fused iron. 1840 Dickens *Barn. Rudge* li, Perhaps, sir, he kicked a county member, perhaps sir he tapped a lord.. blood flowed from noses, and perhaps he tapped a lord. *c* 1865 J. Wylde in *Circ. Sc.* I. 419/2 The tree is 'tapped'; that is, a hole is cut into it.., and the resin exudes. 1868 Carlyle *Fredk. Gt.* (1872) X. App. 199 What bogs he has tapped and dried, what canals he has dug. 1878 Huxley *Physiogr.* 27 The natural reservoir being thus tapped, a spring of water flows out. 1900 G. C. Brodrick *Mem. & Impr.* 315 The Braemar air..coming across treeless granite mountains which tap the rain-clouds as they sweep over.

**b.** *spec.* in *Surg.* To pierce the body-wall of (a person) so as to draw off accumulated liquid; to drain (a cavity) of accumulated liquid.

1655 [see Tapping *vbl. sb.*1]. 1709 Steele *Tatler* No. 62 ⁋ 11, I have ever since my Cure been..dropsical; therefore I presume it would be much better to tap me. 1778 Latham in *Phil. Trans.* LXIX. 56, I tapped her once in a fortnight. 1807–26 S. Cooper *First Lines Surg.* (ed. 5) 527 If any of the viscera protruded..he used to reduce them, and then tap the hydrocele in the common manner. 1869 G. Lawson *Dis. Eye* (1874) 71 Tapping the anterior chamber with a fine needle, and letting off the aqueous, will often do good. 1898 *Allbutt's Syst. Med.* V. 788 The peritoneal cavity and pleura become repeatedly full of fluid and have to be tapped again and again.

**c.** *To tap an electric wire* or *cable*: to divert part of the current, esp. so as to intercept a telegraphic communication.

1879 Prescott *Sp. Telephone* 108 The telephone presents facilities for the dangerous practice of tapping the wire. 1892 *N. Y. Tribune* 15 Jan. 7/5 (Funk) By tapping the wire for a message from Guttenburg the operator could interrupt communication with all three. 1897 *Westm. Gaz.* 3 Apr. 9/3 It would be an unheard of thing for any casual merchant steamer to 'tap' a company's cable out at sea in order to gratify a private whim for news. 1897 *Daily News* 14 July 3/4 Extraordinary allegations of 'tapping' telegraph wires were made yesterday in a case heard at the Liverpool County Court.

**3.** *fig.* To open up (anything) so as to liberate or extract something from it; to open, penetrate, break into, begin to use.

e. g. To open up (a country, district, trade, mineral vein, etc.); to extract money or elicit information from (a person); to rob (a till or house), pick (a pocket); to break (money) (Break *v.* 2 e); to broach (a subject).

1575 *Gamm. Gurton* II. iii, Ye see..that one end tapt of this my short devise, Now must we broche t'other to, before the smoke arise. 1750 H. Walpole *Lett.* (1846) II. 358 How does *cet homme là*..dare to tap the chapter of birth? 1768 — *Hist. Doubts* 43 Dr. Shaw no doubt tapped the matter to the people. 1781 — *Let. to W. Mason* 22 May, After tapping many topics, to which I made as dry answers as an unbribed oracle, he vented his errand. 1828 *Craven Gloss.* s. v., To tap a note or sovereign, to get it changed. 1840 Dickens *Old C. Shop* lxiii, Here I am—full of evidence —Tap me! 1864 *Home News* 19 Dec. 19/2 So well had the interior of India been tapped by new roads. 1872 Raymond *Statist. Mines & Mining* 268 It is the intention of the owner to tap the vein by a tunnel. 1878 W. J. Thoms in *Folk Lore Rec.* I. Pref. 16 Mr. Gomme has 'tapped'—(I thank thee, Horace Walpole, for teaching me that word)—has tapped a subject which is, I believe, new in this country. 1901 *Essex Weekly News* 29 Mar. 5/1 The first gentleman who was tapped for a subscription generously promised £30. 1903 F. W. H. Myers *Human Personality* I. 315 While he was entranced, we endeavoured to 'tap' Mr. Browne.

**II.** To draw off (liquid, etc.).

**4.** To draw (liquor) from a tap; to draw and sell in small quantities. Also *fig.*

1401 *Pol. Poems* (Rolls) II. 95 Me thynkith ȝe ben tapsteres in alle that ȝe don: ȝe tappe ȝour absoluciones that ȝe bye at Rome. 1589 Nashe *Anat. Absurd.* 20 These Bussards thinke knowledge a burthen, tapping it before they haue halfe tunde it. 1621 *Sc. Acts Jas. VI* (1816) IV. 669/2 Four pundis..of ilk Tune of wyne To be toppit, ventit, and sauld in smallis within the said burgh. 1665 *Phil. Trans.* I. 46 The boyled liquor..is tapp'd out of the said Kettles, through holes beneath. 1677 *Act* 29 *Chas. II*, c. 2 § 1 Any..person or persons who doe or shall sell or tap out Beere or Ale publiquely or privately. 1737 (*title*) An Act for laying a Duty of Two Penies Scots upon every Scots Pint of Ale and Beer brewed for Sale, brought into, vended, tapped, or sold within the Town of Aberbrothock. 1743 *Lond. & Country Brew.* III. (ed. 2) 236 The Beer or Ale in a Week after should be tapt. 1871 B. Taylor *Faust* I. ii. (1875) II. 13 The City Council too must tap their liquor. 1872 Yeats *Techn. Hist. Comm.* 126 On festive occasions, these lords alone possessed the privilege of tapping wine.

†**b.** *transf.* To retail (any commodity). *Sc. Obs.*

1478–9 *Burgh Rec. Edinb.* (1869) I. 37 That na regratour by nor tap any vittale to regrate agane vnder the payne of pvnissing be the baillies after the tenour of the first act. *Ibid.*, Top [see Tapper1 1 b]. 1538 *Aberdeen Regr.* XVI. (Jam.), For the spilling of the merkat in bying of wittail in gryt, & topping tharof befor none. 1573–4 *Burgh Rec. Glasgow* (1876) I. 450 To pas to Dunbertane to arreist schippis for talping of greit salt. 1605 in Gross *Gild Merch.* (1890) I. 222 To tapp tar, oil, butter, or to tapp eggs. 1615 *Stirling Council Rec.* in *Trans. Nat. Hist. & Archæol. Soc. Stirling* (1902) 61 Na craftsman [sal] buy, top, nor sell any merchand wairis.

**c.** *absol.* To draw liquor; to act as tapster.

*a* 1597 Peele *Jests* Wks. (Rtldg.) 619/1 Those bomborts that live by tapping, between the age of fifty and three-score. 1598 Shaks. *Merry W.* I. iii. 11, I will entertaine Bardolfe: he shall draw; he shall tap. 1625 Massinger *New Way* IV. ii, For which gross fault I here do damn thy license, Forbidding thee ever to tap or draw.

**5.** To draw off (liquid) from any source.

1597 [see Tapping *vbl. sb.*1]. 1825 J. Nicholson *Operat. Mechanic* 357 When the fluid lead is tapped, or drawn off. 1853 'C. Bede' *Verdant Green* I. xi, He told Verdant, that his claret had been repeatedly tapped. 1873 Tristram *Moab* xviii. 361 Little rills tapped from the springs. 1894 Bowker in *Harper's Mag.* Jan. 417 [It] floats on the top, and is easily tapped off.

†**b.** *intr. fig.* To 'turn on the tap' of gifts; to open the purse or pocket; to spend or 'bleed' freely. *slang. Obs.*

1712 Addison *Spect.* No. 550 ⁋ 1 A certain Country Gentleman begun to tapp upon the first Information he received of Sir Roger's Death. 1713 Steele *Guard.* No. 58 ⁋ 6, I design to stand for our borough the next election, on purpose to make the squire on t'other side tap lustily for the good of our town.

**III.** Technical uses.

**6.** *Mech.* **a.** To furnish (a hole) with an internal screw-thread, or (any part) with a threaded hole.

1808 Henry in *Phil. Trans.* XCVIII. 287 The lower orifice..is tapped internally, for the purpose of receiving a small screw. 1825 J. Nicholson *Operat. Mechanic* 131 A screw..is cut on the gudgeon..and a piece of iron..is tapped to fit it. 1833 Holland *Manuf. Metal* II. 105 The [gun] barrel having been tapped at the stouter end, and being fitted with the breech screw. 1902 Marshall *Metal Tools* 32 Holes of varying sizes..are drilled and tapped.

**b.** To furnish with an external screw-thread; to convert (a bolt or rod) into a screw.

1815 J. Smith *Panorama Sc. & Art* I. 40 The bolt or pin intended to be tapped, either with a screw-plate or stocks, is tapered in a small degree at the extremity. 1837 *Civil Eng. & Arch. Jrnl.* I. 48 The lower part of the king-bolt is tapped with a screw and nut. 1888 Rutley *Rock-Forming Min.* 23 Each rod is tapped with a [screw-]thread.

**c.** To cause to pass through or in by screwing.

1869 Sir E. J. Reed *Shipbuild.* ii. 44 The angle-irons..are secured to the plating by 1 inch screws tapped through it. 1885 C. G. W. Lock *Workshop Receipts* Ser. IV. 341/2 The hook should be 'tapped' in very tight.

**7.** To deprive (a plant) of its tap-root.

1792 *Trans. Soc. Arts* X. 6 Young Oaks..are for the most part tapped at the time of removal.

Hence **Tapped** (tæpt), *ppl. a.*

1670 W. Simpson *Hydrol. Ess.* 111, I caused a tap'd vessel to be filled. 1839 Ure *Dict. Arts*, etc. 158 Two tapped holes in the bar. 1874 Thearle *Naval Archit.* 79 Four of the rivets..are through, and four are tapped. 1880 C. R. Markham *Peruv. Bark* 459 Regularly tapped trees do not exceed 60 feet in height. 1881 W. E. Dickson *Organ-Build.* viii. 95 Tapped Wires..are pieces of wire about 3½ inches in length..and cut with a screw-thread upon about half their length. 1902 Marshall *Metal Tools* 63 The thread should be tried into a nut or tapped hole of the right size from time to time until a proper fit is arrived at.

**Tap** (tæp), *v.*2 Forms: 3 tep, 5 tappe, 9 tapp, 5– tap. [ME. *tapp-en*, of echoic origin, either immediately in Eng. (cf. Rap *v.*), or through F. *taper* in same sense (12th c. in Godef.).]

**1.** *trans.* To strike lightly, but clearly and audibly; rarely applied by meiosis to a sharp knock or rap. *To tap up*, to rouse, cause to get up by tapping at the door.

*a* 1225 *Ancr. R.* 296 Ne ȝif him neuer inȝong, auh tep him oðe schulle, uor he is eruh. *c* 1440 *Promp. Parv.* 487/1 Taspyn, *palpo*.. Taspynge (*K.*, *P.* tappynge), *palpacio*, *palpitacio*. 1603 Knolles *Hist. Turks* (1621) 971 Tapt the said Resuan once or twice about the pate. 1761 Sterne *Tr. Shandy* IV. Introd., This faithful slave..has carried me.., continued he, tapping the mule's back, above six hundred leagues. 1777 Cook *Voy. Pacific* II. xi. (1784) I. 409 The person who is to pay obeisance, squats down before the Chief, and bows the head to the sole of his foot;..having tapped, or touched it with the under and upper side of the fingers of both hands, he rises up, and retires. 18.. Moore *Song, The Woodpecker*, Every leaf was at rest, and I heard not a sound, But the woodpecker tapping the hollow beech tree. 1839 Ure *Dict. Arts* 517 s. v. *Founding*, Before lifting off the frame, we must tap the pattern slightly, otherwise the sand enclosing it would stick to it. 1840 Marryat *Poor Jack* xxiv, I went to bed, was tapped up..by Bessy. 1848 Thackeray *Van. Fair* xxvi, He sate there tapping his boot with his cane. 1888 Burgon *Lives 12 Gd. Men* I. i. 71 He tapped my fingers in the way which was customary with him. 1904 W. E. Norris in *Longm. Mag.* Dec. 168 A parchment-visaged priest..taps his insistent gong.

**b.** To strike (the foot, hand, etc.) lightly upon something.

*a* 1500 *Ragman Roll* 131 in Hazl. *E. P. P.* I. 75 And your foot ye tappyn, and ye daunce. 1820 W. Irving *Sketch Bk.*, *Rip Van Winkle*, The bystanders began now to..tap their fingers against their foreheads. 1847 Tennyson *Princ.* Prol. 149 Upon the sward She tapt her tiny silken-sandal'd foot.

**2.** *intr.* and *absol.* To strike a light but distinct blow; to make a sound by so striking, e. g. on a drum; *esp.* to knock lightly *on* or *at* a door, etc. in order to attract attention.

*c* 1425 *Cast. Persev.* 2111 in *Macro Plays* 140 Putte Mankynde fro þi castel clere, or I schal tappyn at þi tyre. 1791 Mrs. Radcliffe *Rom. Forest* x, She tapped gently at the door. 1831 Poe *Raven* iv, So faintly you came tapping. 1873 Black *Pr. Thule* xix, He tapped with his stick on one of the panes. 1888 F. Hume *Mme. Midas* I. ii, Tapping with his wooden leg on the floor. 1891 T. Hardy *Tess* xliv, They heard her footsteps tap along the hard road as she stepped out to her full pace.

†**b.** *spec.* of a hare or rabbit: To make a drumming noise with the feet in rutting-time. *Obs.*

1575 Turberv. *Venerie* 238 A hare and a conie beateth or tappeth. 1650 [see Tapping *ppl. a.* below]. 1706 Phillips (ed. 6) s. v., Among Hunters, a Hare is said to Tap or Beat, i. e. to make a Noise. 1711 Puckle *Club* (1817) 90 And told us..a goat rats, a boar freams, a hare tapps.

**c.** To walk with sharp light steps.

1749 Fielding *Tom Jones* XI. ii, Old England for ever!.. my brave lad! I am going to tap away directly.

**3.** *trans. dial.* and *U.S.* To add a thickness of leather to the sole or heel of (a shoe) in repairing; cf. Tap *sb.*2 3.

1818 J. Kitto in Eadie *Life* ii. (1861) 44 Set to tapping leather shoes to-day. 1846 Worcester *Dict.*, *Tap*, to add a new sole or heel to a shoe. 1847–78 Halliw., *Tap*, to sole shoes. 1880 *W. Cornw. Gloss.* s. v., The tap of your shoe is wearing; it wants tapping.

Hence **Tapping** *ppl. a.*

1650 Fuller *Pisgah* III. ix. 338 Here..the beating Hares [are said] to forme, the tapping Conies to sit. 1816 *Sporting Mag.* XLVII. 177 The Oilman is a tapping and inoffensive hitter. 1890 'R. Boldrewood' *Col. Reformer* (1891) 240 Far and faint..whips resound..like a tapping-bird or the snapping of dried sticks.

**Tap**, Sc. dial. form of Top.

‖ **Tapa** (ta·pā). Also **tappa**. [Com. Polynesian *tapa* (in dialects which substitute *k* for *t*, *kapa*).] A kind of unwoven cloth made by the natives of Polynesia from the bark of the Paper Mulberry (*Broussonetia papyrifera*).

1823 Byron *Island* II. ii, In summer garments be our limb array'd; Around our waists the Tappa's white display'd. 1845 J. Coulter *Adv. Pacific* xvii. 268 The beating out of the tappa or native cloth. 1898 F. T. Bullen *Cruise Cachalot* 296 All..were furnished only with a 'maro' of 'tapa', scanty in its proportions, but still enough to wrap round their loins.

**b.** *attrib.* and *Comb.*, *as tapa-cloth*, *-kilt*, *-mallet*, *-mat*; *tapa-shrouded* adj.

1853 *Househ. Words* VII. 135/2 This tappa cloth is made by beating a part of the bark..with a sort of wooden mall. 1866 *Treas. Bot.* 172/2 An exceedingly tough cloth, called tapa or kapa cloth. 1870 Meade *N. Zealand* 305 The unpleasant sound of the tappa mallet. 1891 Stevenson *Vailima Lett.* iv. (1895) 47 With blacked faces, turbans, tapa kilts, and guns, they looked very manly. 1899 *Blackw. Mag.* Nov. 671/2 The tapa-shrouded, slumbering forms of the few native passengers. 1906 *Macm. Mag.* Apr. 479 Sitting cross-legged on the tappa-mats.

‖ **Tapaculo** (tapăkū·lo). Also **tapacolo**. [Sp., f. *tapa* cover + *culo* backside.] A South American passerine bird, *Pteroptochus albicollis* (*megapodius*), which carries its tail inclined towards its head, also called in Chili *tualo*; the Chilian rock-wren.

1839 Darwin *Voy. Nat.* xiv. 329 It is called Tapacolo, or 'cover your posterior'. *Ibid.* 330 The tapacolo is very crafty..It is also an active bird. 1896 Newton *Dict. Birds* 947 The true Tapaculo, *P. albicollis*,.. rarely flies, hops actively..with its tail erect or turned towards its head.

‖ **Tapadero** (tapădē·ro). Also -dera, tapi-. [Sp. *tapadero* cover, lid, stopper, f. *tapar* to stop up, cover.] A heavy leather housing for the front of the stirrup, used in California to protect the foot against thorny undergrowth and keep it from slipping forward.

**1891** *Cent. Dict.*, Tapadera. **1897** *Westm. Gaz.* 8 Oct. 2/1 Tapideros, or leather coverings for the stirrups, avoid the danger of the foot going right through the stirrup.

**Tapalpite** (tăpæ·lpəit). *Min.* [Named 1869 from Sierra de Tapalpa (Mexico): see -ITE $^1$.] Sulphotelluride of bismuth and silver, found in grey metallic masses (Chester).

‖**Tapayaxin** (tæpăyæ·ksin). [Native Mexican.] The orbicular horned lizard, *Phrynosoma orbiculare*, incorrectly called the *horned frog* or *toad*.

[**1615** F. HERNANDEZ *Cuatro Libr. Naturaleza* 188 Del animal que llaman tapayaxin y los Españoles camaleon. **1693** RAY *Syn. Quad.* 263.] **1753** CHAMBERS *Cycl. Suppl.*, *Tapayaxin*,..a very remarkable species of lizard, called by Hernandez the *lacertus orbicularis*. **1858** BAIRD *Cycl. Nat. Sci.* s. v. *Agamidæ*, The Tapayaxin, *Agama orbicularis*.

**Tapcery**, var. TAPISSERY *Obs.*, tapestry.

**Tape** (tē$^i$p), *sb.*$^1$ Forms: 1 tæppe, (5 tappe, 6 tapp); 4- tape. [OE. *tæppe* or *tæppa* (nom. not found); origin unascertained. The lengthening of the vowel from ME. *tappe* to *tāpe* is unexplained.]

**1.** A narrow woven strip of stout linen, cotton, silk, or other textile, used as a string for tying garments, and for other purposes for which flat strings are suited, also for measuring lines, etc.

*c* **1000** *Ælfric's Voc.* in Wr.-Wülcker 107/33 *Tenia*, tæppan (pl.), *uel* dolsmeltas. *c* **1386** CHAUCER *Miller's T.* 55 The tapes of hir white voluper Were of the same suyte of hir coler. *c* **1425** *Voc.* in Wr.-Wülcker 655/15 *Hec tenea*, tappe. **1519** *Churchw. Acc. St. Giles, Reading* 5 For tapis for iij$^o$ Amys i$^d$ ob. **1573–80** BARET *Alv.* T 60 A Tape, to knit the apron about with. **1690** *Lond. Gaz.* No. 2529/4 Lost.., a black Box..tied about with a white Tape. **1805** *Trans. Soc. Arts*, etc. XXIII. 119 A measuring tape..having inches on one side. **1833** HOLLAND *Manuf. Metal* II. 225 When the rollers revolve, the motion of the tapes carry the sheet of paper with them, and deliver it over another roller, ..where it is taken up by two sets of endless tapes. **1879** JAS. GRANT in *Cassell's Techn. Educ.* IV. 270/1 A partner in the manufactory of inkles and tapes.

**b.** Without article, as name of the material or substance. Also *fig.*: see RED-TAPE.

**1537–8** *Rec. St. Mary at Hill* 378 Paid for silke tape iij*s* iiij*d*. **1546** in W. H. Turner *Select. Rec. Oxford* (1880) 184 For viij yardes and a half of tape. **1653** WALTON *Angler* vii. 158 A convenient quantitie of tape or filiting. **1714** GAY *Sheph. Week* Monday 37 This pouch, that's ty'd with tape of reddest hue. **1856** READE *Never too late to mend* xxv, Twenty years gone in tape and circumlocution. **1898** J. BERWICK *Philos. Romance* iv. 46 Reams of blue paper tied with pink tape.

**c.** A piece of tape suspended across the course at the finishing point in a race, or (formerly) between the goal-posts in Association football.

**1867** *Routledge's Handbk. Football* 54 Football Association Rules...A goal shall be won when the ball passes between the goal-posts under the tape. **1868** H. F. WILKINSON *Mod. Athletics* 17–18 The Goal..should consist of a piece of stout white tape tied to the post at one side..and held loosely by the judge across the course, so that when the winner passes the post he may carry the tape away. **1880** *Times* 12 Nov. 4/5 The ball is shot under the tape or over the bar, and the call of time immediately afterwards proclaims the game at an end.

**2.** A long, narrow, thin and flexible strip of metal or the like; *esp.* such a strip of steel used as a measuring line in surveying.

**1884** *Health Exhib. Catal.* 77/2 Solid Copper Tape Lightning Conductor. **1884** *Edin. Rev.* July 48 The main stem of the conductor shall consist of a copper rod or tape. **1900** H. M. WILSON *Topogr. Surv.* xxi. 500 The steel tape is capable of giving a precision indicated by a *probable error* of one 2,000,000th part of a measured line. *Ibid.*, Base measurement with steel tapes.

**b.** The paper strip or ribbon on which messages are printed in the receiving instrument of a recording telegraph system.

**1884** *Pall Mall G.* 27 Dec. 5/2 This 'tape' is supplied by a telegraphic company, and automatically records in dozens of different offices in the City the variation of prices from hour to hour inside the House. **1888** BESANT 50 *Years Ago* 213 Now we watch the tape, day by day, and hour by hour. **1905** PREECE & SIVEWRIGHT *Telegraphy* 171 Punching and feeding the tape forward is performed by an electromagnet. *Ibid.* 172 To produce a type-printed page from the record perforated on the tape.

**3.** *slang.* Spirituous liquor, esp. gin (*white tape*); *red tape*, brandy. Cf. RIBBON *sb.* 4 c.

**1725** *New Cant. Dict.*, *Tape*, *Red* or *White*, Geneva, Aniseed, Clove-Water, &c. so called by Canters and Villains, and the Renters of the Tap..in Newgate, and other Prisons. **1755** *Connoisseur* No. 53 ⁋ 4 Every night-cellar [will] furnish you with Holland Tape, three yards a penny. **1830** LYTTON *P. Clifford* x. (1854) 80 Red tape those as likes it may drain. **1837** THACKERAY *Ravenswing* vi, Gin.., under the name of 'tape', used to be measured out pretty liberally in what was..his Majesty's prison of the Fleet.

**4.** *attrib.* and *Comb.*, as, in sense 1, *tape-length*, *-maker*, *-making*, *-moulding*, *-purl* (PURL *sb.*$^1$ 2), *-ribbon*, *-seller*, *-string*, *-stripe*, *-weaver*, *-work*; *tape-like*, *-slashing* adjs.; in sense 2 b, 'of, or recorded by, the telegraphic tape', *tape-price*, *-report*, *-system*; *tape-printing* adj. Also **tape-bound** *a.*, bound with tape; = *tape-tied*; **tape-carrier**, a frame in which a tape sprinkled with powdered corundum is mounted as a cutting or filing instrument; **tape-fish**, an eel-like fish having a flat elongated body, a ribbon-fish; **tape-fuse**, a ribbon-like fuse, very rapid in action; **tape-grass**, an aquatic herb, *Vallisneria spiralis*, with narrow grass-like leaves; **tape-line**, a line of tape; *spec.* a strip of linen or steel marked with subdivisions of the foot or metre, sometimes coiling in a cylindrical case with a winch or spring; **tape-machine**, (*a*) the receiving instrument of a recording telegraph system, in which the message is printed on a paper tape; (*b*) = *tape-sizing machine* (*Cent. Dict.*, *Supp.* 1909); **tape-man**, in Surveying, each of the two men who measure with the tape-line; **tape-measure**, a measuring line of prepared tape, marked with feet and inches, etc., esp. one of five or six feet long used by tailors, dressmakers, etc.; **tape-needle**, an eyed bodkin for inserting tape; **tape-primer**, an obsolete primer for fire-arms, consisting of a flexible paper or other band containing small fulminating charges at equal distances; **tape-sizer**, a man in charge of the machine (*tape-sizing machine* or *tape-machine*) for sizing the cotton warp threads to be used in weaving; = TAPER *sb.*$^3$; **tape-stretcher**, a contrivance to maintain a uniform tension of the measuring line in surveying; **tape-ticker** = *tape-machine*; **tape-tied** *a.*, tied with tape; also *fig.* bound by 'red-tape', restricted by officialism; so **tape-tying** *a.*

**1900** *Westm. Gaz.* 5 July 5/2 Should the *tape-bound authorities in Pall Mall blankly refuse to equip..the 320 extra men. **1885** C. F. HOLDER *Marvels Anim. Life* 101 The band or *tape-fishes, from their snake-like appearance, are first worthy of notice. **1857** GRAY *First Lessons Bot.* (1866) 167 This may be..seen..in the leaves of the Fresh-water *Tape-Grass (*Vallisneria*), under a good microscope. **1900** H. M. WILSON *Topogr. Surv.* xxiii. 533 Both tapemen keep a record of the number of *tape-lengths between stations. **1880** BARWELL *Aneurism* 6 Broad, *tape-like ligatures were used. **1897** *Allbutt's Syst. Med.* III. 838 The passage of pipe-like or tape-like motions is..due merely to the action of the sphincter. **1847** WEBSTER, *Tapeline. **1858** in SIMMONDS *Dict. Trade*. **1893** SELOUS *Trav. S. E. Africa* 91 A few measurements..taken on the spot with a tape-line. **1891** *Daily News* 9 Apr. 7/1 Some twenty or thirty men, who were crowding round a '*tape machine'.. waiting for the result of the second race of the day to come through. **1900** H. M. WILSON *Topogr. Surv.* xxiv. 532 The *tapemen measure the distance with the steel tape, which is stretched by a twenty-pound tension on the front end by the fore tapeman with a spring-balance. **1877** KNIGHT *Dict. Mech.*, *Tape-measure. **1907** *Westm. Gaz.* 20 Mar. 10/1 As tested by the tape-measure..the..giantess might make an excellent claim to be the 'greatest' woman who has ever lived. **1863** *Archæol. Cantiana* V. 14 A portion of the old *tape moulding or parallel band. **1852** MRS. STOWE *Uncle Tom's C.* xv, I'll look your box over.—Thimble, wax,.. scissors, knife, *tape-needle; all right. **1880** *Plain Hints Needlework* 68 Tape-needle is generally used in the North of England instead of this word [bodkin]—and..would be better if more generally used, to describe what it really is, a needle to run a piece of tape into a hem, or caseing. **1895** *Daily News* 14 June 5/2 The machines set up in the offices record the prices on the familiar strips of paper from which the name of '*tape prices' is taken. **1903** *Q. Rev.* Jan. 106 Tape-prices do not represent actual transactions. **1877** KNIGHT *Dict. Mech.* 2495/2 The *tape-primer required a peculiar lock, having a recess for containing the tape and mechanism for advancing each primer successively to the nipple. **1903** *Westm. Gaz.* 25 Aug. 2/3 The fee charged for maintaining and superintending the *tape-printing telegraph machine which supplies the Peers with news in the Prince's Chamber. *a* **1652** BROME *Queen & Concub.* IV. i, *Lol.* Can you handle the Bobbins well, good Woman? Make statute-Lace? you shall have my Daughter. *Pogg.* And mine, to make *Tape-Purles. **1901** *Westm. Gaz.* 20 June 6/3 The '*tape' report ..said there was no opposition to the Charing Cross, Euston, and Hampstead Railway scheme. **1647** CLARENDON *Hist. Reb.* VIII. § 128 He commanded every Man to tye a white *tape Ribban, or Handkerchief above the Elbow of their right Arme. **1835** WILLIS *Pencillings* I. ii. 20 The Marseilles *tapeseller. **1897** S. WEBB *Indust. Democ.* I. iv. iv. 105–6; II. II. x. 478 *Tape-sizers. **1891** *Labour Commission* Gloss., The machine used by the taper is called the *tape-sizing machine. **1882** *Standard* 7 Sept. 2/3 The enormous *tape-slashing machines,..followed. **1900** H. M. WILSON *Topogr. Surv.* xxi. 501 *Tape-stretchers. **1871** *Figure Training* 57 The ladies..prohibit all restriction of the waist except by the aid of a broad band and *tape-strings. **1865** CARLYLE *Fredk. Gt.* xx. v. (1873) IX. 78 These long lanes, or *tape-stripes of the Torgau Forest. **1904** *Daily News* 6 July 7 Mr. Francis E. Macmahon, inventor of the *tape ticker, died very suddenly at Newmarket yesterday morning. **1732** POPE *Ep. Bathurst* 301 A flock-bed.. With *tape-ty'd curtains, never meant to draw. **1748** THOMSON *Cast. Indol.* I. 502 Whose desk and table make a solemn show, With tape-tied trash. **1900** *Daily News* 1 Aug. 3/1 Good scouts..of more importance to an army in the field than all the tape-tied intelligence officers out of Hades. **1832** *Fraser's Mag.* Oct. 382 The *tape-tying crew who had wriggled themselves into office. **1725** *Lond. Gaz.* No. 6380/12 Robert Johnson, ..*Tape-weaver. **1890** W. J. GORDON *Foundry* 208 The paper supports itself all through the machine, and the *tapework is reduced to a minimum.

**Tape** (tē$^i$p), *sb.*$^2$ *dial.* [var. of TALPE, *taupe*: cf. *chafe* from Fr. *chauffer*.] The mole.

**1847–78** HALLIW., *Tape*, a mole. *South*. **1881** *Isle of Wight Gloss.*, *Tape*, or *Teype*, a mole, or want. *Tape-taker*, a mole-catcher.

**Tape** (tē$^i$p), *v.* [f. TAPE *sb.*$^1$]

**1.** *trans.* To attach a tape or tapes to; to supply with a tape; to fit with tapes; to tie *up*, fasten, bind, or wind with tape (also *fig.*); *spec.* in *Bookbinding*, to join the sections of (a book) with tape.

**1609** T. COCKS *Diary* (1901) 85 Given nursse for tapinge & starchinge my cuffes ij*d*. **1854** H. MILLER *Sch. & Schm.* xv. (1857) 347 Of that accessible store-house in which the memories of past events lie arranged and taped up. **1854** E. MAYHEW *Dogs* (1861) 241 [He] first, by way of precaution, tapes the animal; that is, he forms a temporary muzzle, by binding a piece of tape thrice firmly round the creature's mouth. **1859** THACKERAY *Virgin.* lxxxiv, Every scrap of paper which we ever wrote, our thrifty parent..taped and docketed and put away. **1894** BOTTONE *Electr. Instr. Making* (ed. 6) 115 The armature must also be most carefully taped and varnished. No part of the iron, where the wire has to be wound, should be left uncovered.

**2.** *trans.* To measure with a tape-line.

**1886** [implied in TAPING *ppl. a.* below].

**3.** *intr.* To appear (of such a size) on measurement with a tape; to measure (so much).

**1895** J. G. MILLAIS *Breath fr. Veldt* (1899) 237 *note*, A good Mashonaland head seldom tapes more than 12 inches.

**4.** *trans. Sc.* To measure *out* in tape-lengths; to deal out slowly or sparingly; to use sparingly.

**1721** RAMSAY *To R. H. B.* vii, Then let us grip our Bliss mair sicker, And tape our Heal and sprightly Liquor. **1818** SCOTT *Hrt. Midl.* xii, Ye sall hae a' my skill and knowledge to gar the siller gang far—I'll tape it out weel.

Hence **Taped**, **Ta·ping** *ppl. adjs.*, **Taping** *vbl. sb.*

**1892** *Daily News* 13 Oct. 7/2 Two large taped frames in the centre. **1886** *Blackw. Mag.* Sept. 337 Temporary taping-boys [employed on Ordnance Survey].

**Tape**, obs. form of TAP.

**Tapecer, -ere, -ery**, var. TAPISSER, -ERY *Obs.*

**Tapeinocephalic**, etc.: see TAPINO-.

**Tapeism, Tapeist**: see TAPISM, -IST.

**Tapeless** (tē$^i$·plės), *a.* [f. TAPE *sb.* + -LESS.] Without tape, without the use of tapes.

*Mod.* A tapeless printing machine; a machine giving a tapeless delivery of printed sheets.

**Tapen** (tē$^i$·pən), *a. rare.* [f. TAPE *sb.*$^1$ + -EN$^4$: cf. *oaken*, *silken*.] Composed of tape. In quot. *fig.*

**1856** READE *Never too Late* xxv, His heart broke.. its tapen bonds, and the man of office came quickly to the man of God.

†**Ta·pener.** *Obs. rare.* [Derivation obscure.] A kind of clothworker; ? a weaver of burel.

*a* **1400** *Usages of Winchester* in *Eng. Gilds* (1870) 350 Þe Tapeners þat worcheþ þe burelles..shullen take for þe cloth xviij d. *Ibid.* 352 Þe chaloun of foure ellen and o quarter of langnesse, shal habbe tweye ellen and an halfe to-fore þe tapener in þe werke.

**Taper** (tē$^i$·pəɹ), *sb.*$^1$ Also 1 tapor, -ur; 3–5 tapere, 4–5 tapre, -ur, -ir, 5 -yr, 5–7 tapper, 6 tapar, -ire, 7 tapor, -our. [OE. *tapur*, *-or*, *-er*: not in the cognate langs. According to Kluge, *Engl. Stud.* XX. 335, a dissimilated form of **papur*, ad. L. *papyrus*, which in glossaries (*a* 1100) is rendered 'taper', and in some Romanic forms has the sense 'wick of a candle', for which the pith of the papyrus was used. See Körting No. 6852.]

**1.** Originally, A wax candle, in early times used chiefly for devotional or penitential purposes; now *spec.* a long wick coated with wax for temporary use as a spill, etc. *To hold a taper to the devil*: cf. CANDLE *sb.* 5 b.

*c* **897** K. ÆLFRED *Gregory's Past. C.* xxxvi. 258 He hiene onælð mid ðæm tapore [*Hatton MS.* tapure] ðæs godcundan lieʒʒes. *c* **1000** *Sax. Leechd.* III. 202 Wex oððe taperas, ʒesihð blisse hit ʒetacnat. *a* **1100** *Voc.* in Wr.-Wülcker 267/12 *Lampas*, leohtfæt. *Candela*, candel. *Papirus*, taper. *c* **1200** *Trin. Coll. Hom.* 47 On ure honde beren candele berninde, taper oðer candele. *c* **1290** *S. Eng. Leg.* I. 19/12 Seint Dunstones moder taper a fuyre werth a-non. **1377** LANGL. *P. Pl.* B. XVII. 203 To a torche or a tapre þe trinitee is lykned. *c* **1460** *Brut* 508 She was enioyned to open penaunce, forto go thrugh Chepe, bering a tapere in hir hand. *a* **1512** FABYAN *Will* in *Chron.* (1811) Pref. 4 That they doo purvay for .iiii. tapers of iii lb. evry pece, to brenne aboute the corps and herse for the forsaid .ii. seasons. **1530** PALSGR. 279/1 Tapar of waxe, *cierge*. **1601** SHAKS. *Jul. C.* IV. iii. 275 How ill this Taper burnes. **1635** A. STAFFORD *Fem. Glory* 153 Very many Tapours were burning in the Church. **1653** GATAKER *Vind. Annot. Jer.* 36 To stoop so low, as to hold a taper before the Divel. **1696** PHILLIPS (ed. 5), *Taper*, a long and large siz'd Light made in form of a Pyramid made of Wax, and made use of in Churches for the most part. **1742** YOUNG *Nt. Th.* v. 720 Our birth is nothing but our death begun; As tapers waste, that instant they take fire. **1869** TOZER *Highl. Turkey* II. 115 The number of tapers, which,..on festivals, were lighted in all parts of it [a church]. **1878** HUXLEY *Physiogr.* 79 A glowing taper bursts into flame when plunged into oxygen.

**b.** *fig.* Something that gives light or is figured as burning; in modern use esp. a thing that gives a feeble light.

*a* **1000** *Phœnix* 114 in *Codex Exon.*, Sweʒles tapur. **1588** SHAKS. *L. L. L.* v. ii. 267 Tapers they are, with your sweete breathes puft out. **1635** A. STAFFORD *Fem. Glory* 8 The Apostles, those holy Tapours of the primitive Church. **1646** J. HALL *Horæ Vac.* 8 The Tapour of Devotion burnes but dimly. **1646** JENKYN *Remora* 22 God may suffer the taper of the opportunity to burn out. **1699** POMFRET *Poems* (ed. 11) 44 The twinkling Tapers of the Night. **1770** GOLDSM. *Des. Vill.* 87 To husband out life's taper at the close. **1808** SKURRAY *Bidcombe Hill* 23 Whilst from the sky, the new-born moon display'd Her feeble taper, twinkling thro' the gloom. **1821** SHELLEY *Adonais* v, And happier they..Whose tapers yet burn through that night of time In which suns perished.

**2.** *attrib.* and *Comb.*, as *taper-flame, -fly, -light, -spark, -stand, -stick; taper-bearer, -holder, -maker; taper-lighted* adj.; † **ta·perwort**, the Great Torch Mullein (*Verbascum Thapsus*).

c 1450 in Aungier *Syon* (1840) 342 They schal reuerently holde them styl in ther handes, ȝe also the *tapereberers as moche as they may,..in to tyme they haue offred hem at autyr to the preste. 1818 Keats *Endymion* iii. 116 Like *taper-flame..He rose in silence. 1616 Drumm. of Hawth. *Song* Poems (1656) 60 Like a *Taper-fly there burne thy Wings. 1907 *Daily Chron.* 11 Apr. 3/7 A little pierced *taper-holder, with gadrooned edge, dated 1764. 1577 tr. *Bullinger's Decades* (1592) 103 Let..no man sette pearchers or *taper light before the Gods. 1595 Shaks. *John* iv. ii. 14 With Taper-light To seeke the beauteous eye of heauen to garnish, Is wastefull, and ridiculous excesse. 1814 Scott *Ld. of Isles* iii. viii, A taper light gleams on the floor. 1850 Allingham *Poems, Light[house]* ii, Our fire and *taper-lighted room. 1396–7 *Abingdon Acc.* (Camden) 66 Johannes *Tapermaker ' pro Rectore de Appleton '. 1877 Allingham *Songs, Ball. & Stories, Pilot Boat* ii. A cottage by the strand With its feeble *taper-spark. 1837 Lockhart *Scott* vi. (1839) I. 253 His first fee..was expended on a silver *taper-stand for his mother. 1546 in Hardiman *O'Flaherty's Iar Connaught* (1846) 230 Two candell or *tapire styckes of Shylver. 1601 Holland *Pliny* II. 274 The great Mullen or *Taperwort. [Cf. 1578 Lyte *Dodoens* 118 The whole top with his pleasant yellow floures sheweth like to a waxe candell or taper cunningly wrought.]

**Taper** (tēi·pəɹ), *sb.*$^2$ [In sense 1, app. f. Taper *sb.*$^1$; in other senses, app. from the vb. or adj.]

I. 1. A spire or slender pyramid; a figure which tapers up to a point.

1589 Puttenham *Eng. Poesie* ii. xi. (Arb.) 108 Of the Spire or Taper called Pyramis. The Taper is the longest and sharpest triangle that is, and while he mounts vpward he waxeth continually more slender, taking both his figure and name of the fire, whose flame..is alwaies pointed.

II. 2. Gradual diminution in width or thickness in an elongated object; continuous decrease in one direction; *fig.* gradual decrease of action, power, capacity, etc.

1793 Smeaton *Edystone L.* § 81 From thence its taper diminishing more slow, its sides by degrees come into a perpendicular. *Ibid.* § 303 Iron plugs..upon a very gentle taper. 1840 J. Buel *Farmer's Comp.* 145 They should be square, with a gradual taper to the point. 1875 R. F. Martin tr. *Havrez' Winding Mach.* 22 To try and manufacture steel ropes with a continuous taper.

3. Anything that gradually diminishes in size towards one extremity, as a tapered tube.

1882 *Worc. Exhib. Catal.* iii. 16 Sanitary tubes, bends, junctions, tapers, sluice valves.

4. *Comb.*, as **taper-vice**, a vice adapted to hold objects which have not parallel sides.

1877 Knight *Dict. Mech.* 2495 Taper-vise.

**Taper** (tēi·pəɹ), *sb.*$^3$ *Cotton-weaving.* [f. Tape *v.* + -er$^1$.] (See quot. 1891.) Also *tape-sizer.*

1891 *Labour Commission* Gloss., *Tapers*, those in the cotton mills who take a number of 'beams' or bobbins as they come from the warper,..and run them through the 'size' upon another beam (called the weaver's beam). When this process is complete the produce is called a 'warp'. 1904 *Dundee Advert.* 5 July 10 The late Mr. Eli Higham, originally a taper at a cotton mill at Sabden.

**Taper**, *sb.*$^4$: see Tadpole$^2$.

**Taper** (tēi·pəɹ), *a.* Also 5 tapre. [f. Taper *sb.*$^1$: perh. through the earlier Taperwise: cf. quot. 1496.] Diminishing gradually in breadth or thickness towards one extremity (originally, upward); becoming continuously narrower or more slender in one direction; tapering.

1496 *Bk. St. Albans, Fishing* h j b, Thenne shaue your staffe & make hym tapre wexe [*a* 1450 *Fysshynge wyth an Angle*, 'tapur wyys waxing']. *a* 1625 *Nomenclator Navalis* (Harl. MS. 2301), *Taper bore*, is when a Peece is wider at the Mouth than towards the Breech. 1649 Blithe *Eng. Improv. Impr.* v. (1653) 24 Make thy Drain, or Trench, somewhat Taper (*viz.*) Narrower and Narrower downwards. 1678 Moxon *Mech. Exerc.* vi. 113 All sorts of Stuff or work that are smaller at one end than at the other, and diminish gradually from the biggest end, is said to be *Taper*. 1688 R. Holme *Armoury* iii. 318/1 The lower part [of a drawing iron is] Taper, ending in a point. 1697 Dryden *Virg. Past.* vii. 54 Fair Galatea,..Tall as a Poplar, taper as the Bole. 1706 Phillips (ed. 6), *Taper* or *Tapering*,..like a Cone, or Pyramid. 1758 *Vacation* in Dodsley *Collect. Poems* VI. 151 If Marian chance to shew Her taper leg and stocking blue. 1770 *Chron.* in *Ann. Reg.* 152/1 The body runs taper to the tail. 1821 Combe *Wife* iii. (Chandos ed.) 330 To the fine taper fingers' ends. 1888 Hasluck *Model Engin. Handybk.* (1900) 38 The piston-head has a taper hole through it, into which the tapered end of piston-rod is forced.

b. *fig.* Of resources: Diminishing, becoming more and more 'slender'. *colloq.* or *slang.*

1851 Mayhew *Lond. Labour* I. 224/1 Just in the critical time for us, as things was growing very taper. *Ibid.* (1861) II. 237/1 That sort of thing soon makes money show taper.

c. *Comb.*, chiefly parasynthetic in -ed$^2$, as *taper-bored, -headed, -limbed, -moulded, -pointed* (but in some of these *taper* may be sb.); also with a participle, as *taper-grown.*

1626 Capt. Smith *Accid. Yng. Seamen* 32 To know whether she be equally bored, camber, taper, or belbored. 1634–5 Brereton *Trav.* (Chetham) 165 They are called drakes. They are taper-bored in the chamber. 1664 Power *Exp. Philos.* i. 13 Bristles or prickles like whin-pricks perfectly taper-grown. 1678 Phillips (ed. 4), *Taper-board*, in Gunnery, is when a piece is wider at the mouth than towards the breech. 1725 Philips *To Miss Carteret* 41 Then the taper-moulded waist With a span of ribbon brac'd. 1828 J. E. Smith *Eng. Flora* II. 12 Leaves broad, taper-pointed, angular rather than toothed. c 1843 Carlyle *Hist. Sk.* (1898) 270 The taper-limbed Apollo figure.

**Taper** (tēi·pəɹ), *v.* [f. Taper *sb.*$^1$: cf. also Taper *sb.*$^2$ 1, of same date.]

1. *intr.* To rise or shoot up like a flame, spire, or pyramid (*obs.*); *fig.* to rise or mount up continuously in honour, dignity, rank, etc. *Obs.*

1589 Puttenham *Eng. Poesie* ii. xi. (Arb.) 109 Like as this faire figure Of tall comely stature By his kindly nature Endeuors soft and faire To Taper in the ayre. c 1645 Howell *Lett.* I. i. ii, Sir George Villiers..tapers up apace, and grows strong at Court. 1697 *Wars Eng. & Fr.* in *Harl. Misc.* (1810) X. 298 The Black Prince, having now won his spurs, and being tapered up to his full growth. 1887 *Pall Mall G.* 7 Mar. 2/1 Might it interest him..to watch the workings of Synods all over Prussia, tapering up (if I may use the term) by a process of elimination into a General Synod and its standing committee?

†b. (?) *nonce-use.* ? To talk loftily. *Obs.*

1683 E. Hooker *Pref. Pordage's Mystic Div.* 103 How magnificously soever wee bragg and vapor and taper of our Reason, or Faith, Intellect, intelligibl Ideas and æternal Verities.

2. *intr.* To narrow or diminish gradually in breadth or thickness towards one end; to grow smaller by degrees in one direction. Const. *away, off*, etc.

1610 [see Tapering *vbl. sb.*]. 1687 A. Lovell tr. *Thevenot's Trav.* ii. 27 The Castle,..situated on a little hill of an oval figure, that tapers from the bottom to the top. 1797 S. James *Narr. Voy.* 164 A beautiful river, which tapers away..into a pleasant rivulet. 1815 Elphinstone *Acc. Caubul* (1842) I. 127 Peaks of great height and magnitude, which do not taper to a point. 1884 Bower & Scott *De Bary's Phaner.* 420 The bundles taper off gradually and terminate below the apex of the leaf. 1886 *Law Rep.* 32 Chanc. Div. 72 A strip [of land] tapering from a width of twelve inches to a point.

b. *fig. To taper off* (*away*): To become gradually less in intensity, etc.; also *colloq.* to leave off a process or habit by degrees, *esp.* to diminish gradually the quantity or potency of one's drink.

1848 Webster *Let.* 18 Sept., in *Corr.* (1857) II. 285 My catarrh has been..severe. I hope it will soon begin to taper off. 1860 Russell *Diary India* II. xii. 218 We saw him tapering away till he appeared a mere speck, as he went down the mountain-side, and finally disappeared altogether. 1871 Napheys *Prev. & Cure Dis.* i. iii. 109 He makes..an unavailing effort to 'taper off' [from the use of ardent spirits]. 1898 *Allbutt's Syst. Med.* V. 947 If [the murmur] begin with the diastole of the heart and taper off during the pause, it is an easy sign to interpret. 1903 *Smart Set* IX. 12/2, I had been drinking hard for six months, and there was no such thing as clipping it short all at once. I had an idea of tapering off.

3. *trans.* To reduce gradually and regularly in breadth or thickness in one direction; to make tapering.

1675 Hobbes *Odyssey* 106 They smooth'd and taper'd it, as I would have it. 1771 Luckombe *Hist. Print.* 315 This Bar..is tapered away. 1802 Beddoes *Hygëia* vii. 42 As if the narrow chest had been lengthened or tapered out into neck. 1860 *All Year Round* No. 57. 159, I taper the point of my pencil. 1875 R. F. Martin tr. *Havrez' Winding Mach.* 26 A specimen of this sort of rope..was tapered in a length of 25 metres from ·30 metre at one end down to ·18 at the other.

b. *fig.* To reduce gradually in quantity; to diminish by degrees: esp. with *off.*

1899 *Allbutt's Syst. Med.* VIII. 419 The best method..would be to 'taper off' the daily amount of drink.

**Tapered** (tēi·pəɹd), *a.* [f. Taper *sb.*$^1$ + -ed$^2$.] Lighted by, or accompanied by the use of, tapers.

1745 Warton *Pleas. Melanch.* 196 The taper'd choir, at the late hour of pray'r. 1792 S. Rogers *Pleas. Mem.* ii. 325 The chanted hymn, the tapered rite. 18.. Campbell *On Poland* 49 The taper'd pomp—the hallelujah's swell.

**Tapered** (tēi·pəɹd), *ppl. a.* [f. Taper *v.* + -ed$^1$.] Made to taper; diminished in breadth or thickness by degrees; tapering, taper.

1669 Sturmy *Mariner's Mag.* v. xii. 63 If you will make for tapered bore Guns, your Forms must be accordingly tapered. 1783 Justamond tr. *Raynal's Hist. Indies* I. 141 Ten or twelve pinnated leaves, tapered towards the top, very broad at their bases. 1839–40 W. Irving *Wolfert's R.* (1855) 49 A lady's glove, of delicate size and shape, with beautifully tapered fingers. 1882 Nares *Seamanship* (ed. 6) 75 The fore and main tacks are tapered ropes.

**Taperer** (tēi·pərəɹ). [f. Taper *sb.*$^1$ + -er$^1$.] The bearer of a taper in a religious ceremony.

c 1450 in Aungier *Syon* (1840) 276 The taperers schal holde the tapers, turnyng westwarde, whilst the seyd herse is in sensyng. *Ibid.* 307 The ij taperers..schal take the two torches, and folowe the banerer al thre in surplys. 1901 W. H. St. J. Hope in *Archæol. Jrnl.* Mar. 6 The cross-bearer and taperers, followed by the censer-bearer. 1905 *Daily News* 24 Apr. 2 Behind him comes the cross, with its attendant taperers, next the banners.

†**Ta·per-fashion**, *a.* and *adv. Obs.* [f. Taper *sb.*$^1$ + Fashion *sb.*] Of or in the fashion or form of a taper; taper-like in shape; tapering, tapered.

1545 Ascham *Toxoph.* (Arb.) 126 Those [stales, i. e. stems of arrows] that be lytle brested and big toward the hede called by theyr lykenesse taperfashion, reshe growne. 1551 Recorde *Cast. Knowl.* (1556) 147 Then doth the shadow [in an eclipse] growe lesser and lesser in spyre forme, or taper fashion.

†**Ta·pering**, *sb. Obs. nonce-wd.* [f. Taper *sb.*$^1$ + -ing$^1$.] The using of tapers.

1599 Sandys *Europæ Spec.* (1632) 140 Willing by his Testament to bee buried in the night without their attending, tapering, censing or singing.

**Ta·pering**, *vbl. sb.* [f. Taper *v.* + -ing$^1$.] The action of the verb Taper in various senses. Also *concr.* a thing or part that tapers.

1610 W. Folkingham *Art of Survey* i. iii. 6 The boaling, spreading,..and tapering of trees. 1677 Moxon *Mech. Exerc.* ii. 30 The Screw-plate will, after it gets a little below the tapering, go no further, but work and wear off the thred again it made about the tapering. 1884 Bower & Scott *De Bary's Phaner.* 485 Those [cells]..must further show a conical tapering. 1890 L. C. D'Oyle *Notches* 186 It will take you months of steady tapering down.

**Ta·pering**, *ppl. a.* [-ing$^2$.] That tapers; taper.

*a* 1625 *Nomenclator Navalis* (Harl. MS. 2301) s. v., I have seene in Flemings the Top saile Tapering. 1665 *Phil. Trans.* I. 35 Insects with large Heads and small tapering Bodies. 1787 A. Clarke in *Life* iv. (1863) 33 After the tapering thread of life is spun out. 1807 Hutton *Course Math.* II. 267 A piece of tapering timber. 1893 Liddon, etc. *Life Pusey* I. i. 5 Long hands and tapering fingers.

Hence **Ta·peringly** *adv.*, in a tapering manner.

1878 H. S. Wilson *Alp. Ascents* iii. 92 As a champagne bottle has to be taperingly elongated. 1883 C. Robson in *Science Gossip* May 106 The posterior portion of the abdomen beyond the cornua prolonged taperingly considerably.

**Ta·perly**, *adv. rare.* [f. Taper *a.* + -ly$^2$.] In a tapering manner, taperingly, slenderly.

1802 *Sporting Mag.* XX. 292 A small dog, taperly and elegantly formed.

**Taperness** (tēi·pəɹnės). [f. Taper *a.* + -ness.] The condition of being taper; tapering shape.

1741 *Compl. Family-Piece* ii. ii. (ed. 3) 330 Fine Sprouts..that will answer for Taperness to one another. 1818 Keats *Endymion* i. 783 Fold A rose-leaf round thy finger's taperness, And soothe thy lips. 1871 *Figure Training* 76 A waist of remarkable taperness.

**Taperwise** (tēi·pəɹwəiz), *adv.* [f. Taper *sb.*$^1$ + -wise: cf. Taper-fashion.] In the manner of a taper; with gradual diminution of thickness towards one end.

*a* 1450 *Fysshynge wyth an Angle* (1883) 8 Then shaue the stafe and make hyt tapur wyys waxing [1496 *Bk. St. Albans* tapre wexe]. 1575 Laneham *Lett.* (1871) 6 Eache with hiz syluery Trumpet of a fiue foot long, foormed Taperwyse. 1601 Holland *Pliny* I. 392 The scape or stalk..not aboue 10 cubits in height, growing taper-wise, small and sharp in the top. 1609 C. Butler *Fem. Mon.* v. (1623) M j, A handfull..of Boughes with hearbs, bound taper-wise together. 1727 *Bradley's Fam. Dict.* s. v. *Dog*, His tail or stern strong set on, waxing Taper-wise towards the top.

**Taperwort**: see Taper *sb.*$^1$

†**Ta·pery.** *Obs. nonce-wd.* [f. Tape *sb.*$^1$ + -ery, after *napery, drapery.*] Tape and the like.

1657 Howell *Londinop.* 90 Weavers of divers sorts, to wit, of Drapery or Tapery, and Nappery.

**Tapes, Tapes(ch)er**: see Tapis *v.*$^3$, Tapisser.

‖**Tapesium** (tăpi·siŏm). *Bot.* [mod.Lat. for med.L. *tapecium, tapetium*, ad. Gr. ταπήτιον, dim. of τάπης carpet.] A carpet or layer of mycelium on which the receptacle is seated in discomycetous fungi (Phillips *Brit. Discomycetes*, Gloss.).

1887 W. Phillips *Brit. Discomycetes* 42 Seated on a distinct tapesium. *Ibid.* 279 Cups 200 to 300μ broad, seated on a dark radiating tapesium.

**Tapessarie, -erie**, var. Tapissery *Obs.*

†**Tapester, -ister.** *Obs. rare.* Also 5 tapster. [Corruption of *tapeser* Tapisser, prob. by association with trade names in *-ster*; cf. Tapestry.] = Tapisser. Also *attrib.*, as *tapester-work.*

1472–3 *Rolls of Parlt.* VI. 37/2, xii Quyssions of Tapsterwork. 1594 R. Ashley tr. *Loys le Roy* 29 b, Smithes, glasiers, tapisters, painters. 1609 Bible (Douay) *Exod.* xxxv. 35 To make the workes of a carpenter, a tapester, an embroderer of hyacinth and purple. [1859 Parker *Turner's Dom. Archit.* III. iii. 62 The most lucrative trade of the fifteenth century was that of a 'tapister'.]

**Tapester**, obs. form of Tapster.

**Tapestry** (tæ·pėstri), *sb.* Forms: 5 **tapstery**, 5–6 **tapestrye**, 5–8 **tapistry**, 6 **tapstry, -ye, tappistre**, 6–7 **tapes-, tapis-, tapstrie**, 6– **tapestry.** [Corruption of *tapesry, tapesserie, tapisry*, or other form of Tapissery. The *t* may have developed phonetically between *s* and *r*, or may have been aided by words in *-istry*: cf. Tapester. (In Milton and Dryden a disyllable.)]

1. A textile fabric decorated with designs of ornament or pictorial subjects, painted, embroidered, or woven in colours, used for wall hangings, curtains, covers for seats, to hang from windows or balconies on festive occasions, etc.; especially, such a decorated fabric, in which a weft containing ornamental designs in coloured wool or silk, gold or silver thread, etc., is worked with bobbins or broaches, and pressed close with a comb, on a warp of hemp or flax stretched in a frame. Often loosely applied to imitative textile fabrics.

1434 [implied in Tapestry-work]. 1467 *Mann. & Househ. Exp.* (Roxb.) 387 My mastyr bowte of Skukborow of Cornelle, xij. peces of curse tapstery. 1500–20 Dunbar *Poems* lxxvii. 49 The streittis war all hung with tapestrie. 1513 Douglas *Æneis* ix. vi. 120 Prowd tapystry, and mekle precius ware. 1545 *Rates of Custom* C vij, Tapistry wyth sylke the ell xx d. 1570 Levins *Manip.* 106/13 Tapstrye, *tapētum*. 1573–80 Baret *Alv.* T 62 Tapestrie, or hangings, in which are wrought pictures of diuerse colours. 1590 Shaks. *Com. Err.* iv. i. 104 In the Deske That's couer'd o're with Turkish Tapistrie. 1633 G. Herbert *Temple, Church Porch* xlv, I care not though the cloth of state should be Not of rich arras, but mean tapestrie. **1649** MILTON *Eikon.* xxvii. Wks. 1851 III. 513 To be struck as mute and motionless as a Parlament of Tapstrie in the Hangings. **1700** DRYDEN *Pal. & Arc.* III. 104 Rich tapestry spread the streets, and flowers the posts adorn. **1777** WATSON *Philip II* (1839) 47 Arras was famous for tapestries, which still retain the name of that place. **1835** *Penny Cycl.* IV. 68/1 *Bayeux Tapestry*, a web or roll of linen cloth or canvass, preserved at Bayeux in Normandy, upon which a continuous representation of the events connected with the invasion and conquest of England..is worked in woollen thread of different colours. **1842** BRANDE *Dict. Sc.* etc. s. v., In Painting, *tapestry* is applied to a representation of a subject in wool or silk..worked on a woven ground of hemp or flax. **1858** HAWTHORNE *Fr. & It. Note-Bks.* I. 162 Gobelin tapestry.. brilliant as pictures.

**b.** *transf.* and *fig.*

**1581** SIDNEY *Apol. Poetrie* (Arb.) 25 Nature neuer set forth the earth in so rich tapistry, as diuers Poets haue done. *c* **1630** RISDON *Surv. Devon* § 175 (1810) 184 A bridge, whose chiefest tapestry is Ivy. **1693** EVELYN *De la Quint. Compl. Gard.* II. 179 Squares covered with Green Herbs, compleat the tapestry, that adorns the Ground. **1831** CARLYLE *Sart. Res.* I. x. (1858) 38 Looking at the fair tapestry of human Life. **1845** STOCQUELER *Handbk. Brit. India* (1854) 215 The rich tapestry of the jungles. **1875** LOWELL *Under Old Elm* II. iii, Present and Past..inseparably wrought Into the seamless tapestry of thought.

**2.** Short for *tapestry-carpet*: see 3.

**1879** *Cassell's Techn. Educ.* IV. 390/1 In the Brussels the coloured wools make up the bulk of the carpet, while in the 'tapestry' the wool..is..all on the surface.

**3.** *attrib.* and *Comb.*, as *tapestry artist, covering, hall, -hanging, -maker, -making, -man, room, table-cover*; *tapestry-covered, -like*, adjs.; **tapestry beetle**, a dermestid beetle, *Attagenus piceus*, the larva of which is destructive to tapestry, woollens, etc.; **tapestry-carpet**, a carpet resembling Brussels, but in which the warp-yarn forming the pile is coloured so as to produce the pattern when woven; **tapestry-cloth**, a piece of tapestry; *spec.* a corded linen prepared for 'tapestry-painting' (*Cent. Dict.*); **tapestry-moth**, a species of clothes-moth, as *Tinea tapetzella*; cf. *carpet-moth*; **tapestry-painting**, painting on linen in imitation of tapestry; material thus prepared; **tapestry-stitch**, properly = GOBELIN *stitch*; also applied to the cross- and tent-stitch work on fine canvas (*tapisserie au petit point*); **tapestry-weaver**, one who weaves tapestry; also, a species of spider; **tapestry-weaving**, the weaving of tapestry; the method of weaving by bobbin and comb, used in making tapestry, as distinct from weaving in a loom with a shuttle. See also TAPESTRY-WORK.

**1908** *Times, Lit. Suppl.* 3 Sept. 286/3 Designs prepared by a *tapestry artist from bird's-eye views specially drawn by William Van de Velde the Elder. **1858** SIMMONDS *Dict. Trade*, **Tapestry-carpets*, the name generally given to a.. two-ply or ingrain carpet, the warp or weft being printed before weaving, so as to produce the figure in the cloth. **1579** TOMSON *Calvin's Serm. Tim.* 656/2 Long and large *tapistrie clothes. **1552** HULOET, *Tapestry coueryinge, *instratum*. **1634** MILTON *Comus* 324 Honest-offer'd courtesie Which oft is sooner found in lowly sheds With smoaky rafters, than in *tapstry Halls And Courts of Princes. **1552** HULOET, *Tapestrye hangynges for noble mens houses. **1700** CONGREVE *Way of World* II. vi, Like Solomon at the dividing of the Child in an old Tapestry Hanging. **1884** J. TAIT *Mind in Matter* (1892) 95 *Tapestry-like designs. **1611** COTGR., *Tapissier*, a *Tapistrie-maker. **1876** ROCK *Text. Fabr.* 95 The art of *tapestry-making. **1727-41** CHAMBERS *Cycl.* s. v., The design, or painting the *Tapestry-man is to follow, is placed underneath the warp. **1815** KIRBY & SP. *Entomol.* viii. (1818) I. 233 *T[inea] tapetzella*, or the *tapestry moth, not uncommon in our houses, is most injurious to the lining of carriages. **1859** W. COLLINS *Q. of Hearts* (1875) 23 A rugged *tapestry table-cover. **1796** MORSE *Amer. Geog.* II. 345 The Flemings formerly engrossed *tapestry-weaving to themselves. **1889** ALAN S. COLE *Cantor Lect., Egyptian Tapestry* I. 8 The process [anciently] employed is the same as that which was used by the great Flemish weavers..for making their splendid war tapestries, and is now commonly known as the tapestry weaving or Gobelins process.

**Tapestry** (tæ·pėstri), *v.* [f. prec. sb. See also TAPISTER.]

**1.** *trans.* To cover, hang, or adorn with, or as with, tapestry. (Chiefly in *pass.*)

*c* **1630** RISDON *Surv. Devon* § 192 (1810) 206 The ruins..is ..tapestried with ivy. **1798** CHARLOTTE SMITH *Yng. Philos.* II. 102 The hardiest plant that tapestries the rude bosom of the North. *Ibid.* 165 My walls..were tapestried with the rock lichen. **1881** MRS. C. PRAED *Policy & P.* II. 14 The grape-leaves with which the verandah was tapestried.

**2.** To work or depict in tapestry.

**1814** SCOTT *Wav.* lxiii, Remnants of tapestried hangings. **1876** T. HARDY *Ethelberta* II. xl, Where Elizabethan mothers and daughters..had tapestried the love-scenes of Isaac and Jacob.

Hence **Ta·pestried** *ppl. a.*, adorned with tapestry; woven in the manner of tapestry.

**1769** SIR W. JONES *Pal. Fortune* 24 Some tap'stried hall, or gilded bower. **1794** SOUTHEY *Retrospect* 104 Still with pleasure I recall The tapestried school, the bright brown-boarded hall. **1814** [see 2]. **1848** THACKERAY *Bk. Snobs* xlii, Making covers of..net-work for these tapestried cushions.

**Ta·pestry-work.** = TAPESTRY *sb.* 1.

**1434** *N. C. Wills* (Surtees 1908) 43 Lectum meum de tapstriwerke cum leonibus et pelicano. **1459** in *Paston Lett.* I. 479 Item, j testyr of blewe tapistry warke. **1587** FLEMING *Contn. Holinshed* III. 1332/1 The feast was excellentlie well furnished of all things, & speciallie of tapistrie worke & other deuises of sugar. **1601** HOLLAND *Pliny* VIII. xlviii. 227 The course rough wool..hath been of auncient time highly commended and accounted of in tapestrie worke. **1812** MAR. EDGEWORTH *Vivian* viii, Miss Strictland [followed] bearing her ladyship's tapestry work.

*Comb.* *c* **1515** *Cocke Lorell's B.* 9 Borlers, tapstry worke, makers, and dyers.

So **Ta·pestry-worked** *a.*, tapestried; **Ta·pestry-worker**, one who works or makes tapestry.

**1727** (*title*) The Practice of Perspective..a work highly necessary for Painters, Embroiderers, Jewellers, Tapestry Workers. **1883** LD. R. GOWER *Rec. & Remin.* xxi. II. 60 Two large tapestry-worked screens.

†**Tapet**, *sb. Obs.* (exc. *Hist.*). Forms: 1 tęped, tæpped, tæppet; 3-4 (9) tapit, 4-5 tapyt, 4-6 tapite, -yte, -ete (also 9), 5 tapytt, -e, (tepit), 5-6 tapett, -e, tappet, 6 -ett, -e, *Sc.* tapeit, taphet, 4- tapet. [The OE. *tęped* was WGer. ad. late L. *tapētum*: cf. OHG. *tęppid, tęppith* (more usually *tęppih*, Ger. *teppich*). The later OE. *tæpped, -et* (cf. also MLG. *teppet*) may have been re-influenced by Latin. ME. *tapet, tapit*, etc. perh. came down from OE.; but the word may have been introduced anew in 13th c. from L., or from Prov. *tapit* or other Romanic form: cf. MDu. *tapijt*, and see TAPIS.] A piece of figured cloth used as a hanging, table-cover, carpet, or the like.

*a* **900** *Kentish Glosses* in Wr.-Wülcker 61/1 *Tapetibus pictis*, ȝemetum tepedum. *c* **1000** ÆLFRIC *Voc.* in Wr.-Wülcker 152/1 *Sipla*, an healfhruh tæppet. *c* **1050** in Thorpe *Charters* (1865) 429, VII ofbrædelsas and II tæppedu.

*a* **1300** *Cursor M.* 11240 Was þar na pride o couerled [*v. r.* couerlite] Chamber curtin ne tapit [*v. rr.* -ite, -yte]. **13..** *Gaw. & Gr. Knt.* 858 Tapytez tyȝt to þe woȝe, of tuly & tars, & vnder fete, on þe flet, of folȝande sute. **1382** WYCLIF 2 *Sam.* xvii. 28 Coueryinge clothis, and tapetis [**1388** tapitis]. **1398** TREVISA *Barth. De P. R.* v. lxii. (Bodl. MS.), The flesche þat lieþ in þe vtter parties of bones..is as it were a nedeful tapet and esement. **1425** *Rolls of Parlt.* IV. 298/1 Þere was on a nyght [a man] taken by hynd a tapet in ye said Chambre. *c* **1477** CAXTON *Jason* 97 b, Medea.. brought him into the chambre where they satte vpon a moche riche tapyte. **1513** DOUGLAS *Æneis* I. xi. 8 Amang prowde tapeitis and miche riche apparale Hir place sche tuik. *a* **1562** G. CAVENDISH *Wolsey* (1893) 227 Leanyng ayenst the tappett or hangyng of the chamber. **1585** T. WASHINGTON tr. *Nicholay's Voy.* II. v. 35, 4. tapites floured, of pinsed satten. **1591** SPENSER *Muiopotmos* 276 Each doth chuse What storie she will for her tapet take. [**1859** PARKER *Turner's Dom. Archit.* III. iv. 104 The bed..consisted of a selour, a testor, a counterpoint, six tapits of arras [etc.]. **1875** POLLEN *Anc. & Mod. Furn.* 31 Carpets, *tapete*, blankets, or other woollen coverlids for sofas or beds, were made at Corinth.]

**b.** In figurative and allusive uses: cf. CARPET *sb.* 2 b and 3.

*c* **1380** WYCLIF *Wks.* (1880) 246 Summe ladies ben menys to haue a daunsere, a trippere on tapitis, or huntere or haukere. *c* **1430** LYDG. *Compl. Bl. Knt.* 51 The soyle was ..oversprad with tapites that Nature Had made her selfe. *c* **1470** HARDING *Chron.* CXV. vii. (MS. Ashm. 34) lf. 90 God sette neuer Kynge to be a Ryotoure To trippe on tapites and leue in Idilnesse. **1563** *Mirr. Mag.* Induct. i, The gladsom groves that nowe laye overthrowen The tapets torn, and every blome down blowen.

**c.** *attrib.* †**Tapet-hook**, a hook for hanging 'tapets' or tapestry-hangings to the wall.

**1480** *Wardr. Acc. Edw. IV* (1830) 121 Crochetts and tapethooks for the hangyng of the same verdours.

†**Ta·pet**, *v. Obs.* [f. prec. sb.] *trans.* To hang with 'tapets' or tapestry; to adorn with tapestry. Also *fig.*

*c* **1369** CHAUCER *Dethe Blaunche* 260 Hys hallys I wol do peynte with pure golde And tapite hem ful many folde. *c* **1407** LYDG. *Reson & Sens.* 2766 The launde rounde aboute ..Tapited al the large pleyn Of herbys and of fressh[e] flours. **1412-20** — *Chron. Troy* I. 1659 [Medea] koude..in wynter with flowris fresche of hewe, Araye þe erþe and tapite hym in grene.

**Tapet, -ette**: see TAPPET.

**Tapetal** (tăpī·tăl), *a. Bot.* [f. TAPET(UM + -AL.] Of or pertaining to the TAPETUM (2).

**1882** VINES *Sachs' Bot.* 480 These divisions produce a tapetal layer at an early stage which surrounds each group of spore-mother-cells. **1882** — in *Nature* 19 Oct. 595/2 The surrounding protoplasm which is derived from the disorganised tapetal cells.

‖**Tapeti** (tæ·pėti). Also 7 tapati. [Tupi.] The Brazilian rabbit, *Lepus brasiliensis.*

**1613** PURCHAS *Pilgrimage* (1614) 842 The Tapati also barke like Dogges. **1774** GOLDSM. *Nat. Hist.* (1776) IV. 54 The Tapeti, or the Brasilian rabbit, is in shape like our English ones, but is much less.

‖**Tapetum** (tăpī·tŏm). [Late and med.L. *tapētum* (pl. *tapēta* in Probus), for L. *tapēte* carpet.]

**1.** *Comp. Anat.* An irregular sector of the choroid membrane in the eyes of certain animals (e.g. the cat), which shines owing to the absence of the black pigment; also *tapetum lucidum* or *t. choroideæ.*

**1713** DERHAM *Phys. Theol.* IV. ii. 102 This Illumination he speaks of, is from the Tapetum in the bottom of the Eye. **1799** *Monthly Rev.* XXX. 146 The posterior half of a cat's eye..was immersed in a bason of water, and examined. The tapetum appeared very bright, the retina not having acquired sufficient opacity to become visible. **1869** H. USSHER in *Eng. Mech.* 3 Dec. 270/3 A..shining appearance at the bottom of the eye, called the 'tapetum' or 'carpet'.

**2.** *Bot.* The layer of epithelial cells which lines the inner wall of the sporangium in ferns, etc., or of the pollen-sac in flowering-plants.

**1882** VINES *Sachs' Bot.* 437 The inner cell again forms four tabular segments which are parallel to the outer parietal cells and which constitute the tapetum. **1885** GOODALE *Physiol. Bot.* (1892) 171 *note*, The epithelium which lines the pollen-sac has been termed the *Tapetum*.

**Tapeworm** (tēi·pˌwɒ̄ɹm). [f. TAPE *sb.*[1] + WORM; from its flat ribbon-like form.] A cestoid worm (e.g. *Tænia solium*), which when adult infests the alimentary canal of vertebrates; = TÆNIA 5.

**1752** J. HILL *Hist. Anim.* 15 The flat Tænia. The Tape-worm..is found in the human intestines, and in those of many other animals. **1799** *Med. Jrnl.* I. 277 Successful experiments, not only to discover that unwelcome visitor the tape worm, but likewise to destroy and expel it. **1860** G. H. KINGSLEY in *Vac. Tour.* 163 The trout in some of the lakes have been infested with tapeworm.

**b.** *fig.* A parasite.

**1824** W. IRVING *T. Trav.* II. x. (1849) 246 They were absolute tape-worms to my little theatre; the more it took the poorer it grew. **1860** EMERSON *Cond. Life, Culture* Wks. (Bohn) II. 369 Can we never extract this tape-worm of Europe from the brain of our countrymen?

**c.** *attrib.* and *Comb.*, as *tapeworm infection*; *tapeworm-shaped* adj.; **tapeworm-plant**, an Abyssinian tree, *Brayera anthelmintica* (N. O. *Rosaceæ*), the pistillate inflorescence of which is used as a vermifuge (*Cent. Dict.* 1891).

**1839** G. ROBERTS *Dict. Geol.*, *Tænianus*, .. tape worm shaped. **1897** *Allbutt's Syst. Med.* II. 1019 In many instances of tape-worm infection, the parasite appears to give rise to no inconvenience whatever.

**Tapheit, -eta, -ettye, -ite**, obs. ff. TAFFETA.

**Taphiser**, variant of TAPISSER *Obs.*

**Tap-hole** (tæ·pˌhōᵘl). [f. TAP *sb.*[1] + HOLE *sb.*]

**1.** The hole in a cask, vat, or the like, in which the tap is inserted.

**1594** PLAT *Jewell-ho.* III. 10 These halfe tubs hauing tap-holes within. **1707** MORTIMER *Husb.* (1721) II. 322 Put it back again, stopping your Tap-hole.

**2.** A small opening in a furnace, through which the metal, or slag, or both, may be run out; also, a hole in a cementation furnace in which tap-bars (see TAP *sb.*[1] 6) are inserted.

**1825** J. NICHOLSON *Operat. Mechanic* 341 Each pot has also small openings in its end, through which the ends of two or three of the bars are left projecting in such a manner, that by only removing one loose brick from the external building, the bars can be drawn out..; these are called the tap-holes. **1839** URE *Dict. Arts* 320 In the melting furnaces, the metal is run out by a tap-hole in the side. **1861** FAIRBAIRN *Iron* 101 The fluid iron, as it flows from the tap-hole, is fully white hot, and perfectly limpid.

**Tap-hose** (tæ·pˌhōᵘz). Now *dial.* Also 7 tapwaze, 8 -owze, 9 -ooze, -wees. [f. TAP *sb.*[1]

The precise sense in which *hose* is used in the second element is not clear; in later use it has been associated with other words, esp. OOZE, WASE, bundle of straw.]

A strainer placed over the tap-hole in a mash-tub or the like, to prevent any solid matter from passing into or through the tap.

**14..** *Voc.* in Wr.-Wülcker 606/28 *Quaxillum*, a tappehose. **1480** *Maldon, Essex, Court Rolls* (Bundle 51, No. 3 b), i vatte, I taphose, I rother. **1609** C. BUTLER *Fem. Mon.* (1634) 157 But first provide..a Tub or Kive, with a Tap, and Tapwaze. **1707** MORTIMER *Husb.* (1721) II. 322 Till it [wort] runs clear, which it will not do at first tho' your Tap-hose be never so well adjusted. **1736** BAILEY *Househ. Dict.* 232 Having an open headed cask with a tap, and tap-owze. **1854** MISS BAKER *Northampt. Gloss.*, *Tap-ooze*, *Tap-whisk*, the wicker strainer placed over the mouth of the tap in a mash-vat when brewing, to allow the wort to ooze through, and to prevent the grains passing. [See also TAP *sb.*[1] 6.]

**Ta·p-house.** [f. TAP *sb.*[1] + HOUSE *sb.*[1]] A house where beer drawn from the tap is sold in small quantities; an ale-house; sometimes in connexion with a brewery. Also, the tap-room of an inn. Also *fig.*

**1500-1** in Swayne *Sarum Churchw. Acc.* 55 In emendando hostium de le Taphouse, iiij*d.* **1591** NASHE *Prognostication* Wks. (Grosart) II. 153 That their Hoffes and tappe houses shall be more frequented, then the Parishe Churches. **1603** SHAKS. *Meas. for M.* II. i. 219. **1642** MILTON *Apol. Smect.* vi. Wks. 1738 I. 120 To creep into every blind Tap-house that fears a Constable more than a Satyr. **1764** *Low Life* 35 Some Gentlemens Coachmen at the Tap-Houses of the Inns. **1896** *Daily News* 20 May 5/6 'Tap-houses' of breweries; licences to enable distilleries to sell two gallons of spirit, more, but not less, for home consumption.

*attrib.* *c* **1639** R. DAVENPORT *Surv. Sciences* Poems (1890) 328 That Tap-house trick of fidling. **1883** S. C. HALL *Retrospect* I. 120 He got drunk like a tap-house sot.

‖**Taphrenchyma** (tæfre·ŋkimă). *Bot.* [mod. L. (Morren), f. Gr. τάφρος pit + ἔγχυμα infusion.] Pitted tissue; = BOTHRENCHYMA.

**1876** J. H. BALFOUR in *Encycl. Brit.* IV. 87/1 The names of *bothrenchyma* and *taphrenchyma* have been given to a tissue composed of such cells.

‖**Tapia** (tā·piă). [Sp. *tapia* mud-wall: see Diez.] Clay or mud puddled, rammed, and dried: used for walls. Also *attrib.*

**1748** *Earthquake of Peru* iii. 268 The Walls are of Clay ramm'd between two Planks, which they call Tapias. **1834-47** J. S. MACAULAY *Field Fortif.* (1851) 146 Loop-holes, when they can be given a regular form, as in mud or tapia walls. **1878** HOOKER & BALL *Marocco* 322 The remains of massive walls of tapia. **1883** *Sunday Mag.* 689 Strengthened by an unbroken ring of solid walls built of tapia or concrete.

**Tapice, Tapicer**, var. TAPIS *v.*[1], TAPISSER.

†**Tapinage.** *Obs.* Also 4 tapy-, tapnage. [a. OF. *tapinage* place of concealment, f. *tapin* a

concealed or disguised person, f. *tapir*: see TAPIS *v.*[1]] Hiding, concealment, secrecy.

13.. *K. Alis.* 7116 (Bodl. MS.), Whiles þe kyng in his Tapynage [*Weber* tapnage] Sent after Antioche þe Ostage. **1390** GOWER *Conf.* II. 187 This newe tapinage of lollardie. *c* **1400** *Rom. Rose* 7363 That they wolde gone in tapinage, As it were in a pilgrimage. [**1616** BULLOKAR *Eng. Expos.*, *Tapinage*, secrecie, slilinesse. **1656** BLOUNT *Glossogr.*, *Tapinage*, secrecy, a lurking, or lying close.]

**Taping**: see TAPE *v.*; also, the occupation or work of a tape-sizer: see TAPE *sb.*[1] 4 and TAPER *sb.*[3]

**Tapinocephalic, tapeino-** (tăpəi:nŏ,sǐfæ·lik), *a. Anthrop.* [f. Gr. ταπεινός low + κεφαλή head + -IC: see CEPHALIC.] Of the nature of, or having, a low flattened skull. So **Tapi:noce·phalism, Tapi:noce·phaly,** the condition of being tapinocephalic.

**1878** BARTLEY tr. *Topinard's Anthrop.* I. v. 176 Tapinocephalic. *Ibid.* Index, Tapinocephaly. **1886** *Jrnl. Anthrop. Inst.* XVI. 150 The skulls thus agree with the ordinary Bushman skull in most respects being microseme, platyrhine, tapeinocephalic. **1897** *Ibid.* XXVII. 281 The former inclining to tapeinocephalism. **1898** A. C. HADDON *Study of Man* ii. 47 The East Anglians have a form of skull slightly different to that of the South Saxons. It is rather broader, less tapeinocephalic (i. e. less low in the crown).

† **Tapinophoby.** *Obs. nonce-wd.* [f. Gr. ταπεινός low, base + *-phoby*: see -PHOBIA.] (See quot.)

**1772** R. GRAVES *Spir. Quixote* I. vi. (1783) I. 18 Such readers as are possessed with the modern tapino-phoby, or dread of every thing that is low..in writing.

† **Tapino·sis.** *Rhet. Obs.* [ad. Gr. ταπείνωσις lowness (of style).] (See quots., and cf. DIMINUTION 2 b.) Hence † **Tapino·tically** *adv.*, by way of tapinosis.

**1589** PUTTENHAM *Eng. Poesie* III. xvii. (Arb.) 195 If ye abase your thing or matter by ignorance or errour in the choise of your word, then is it by vicious maner of speach called *Tapinosis*. *c* **1600** *Timon* II. iv. (1842) 35 *Pseud*... They did obscure the sunne beames with wette clothis. *Demeas.* A *tapinosis* or diminution. **1652** URQUHART *Jewel* Wks. (1834) 292 Words diminishing the worth of a thing, tapinotically. **1657** J. SMITH *Myst. Rhet.* 57 In Meiosis, the speaker ought to take care that he fall not into that fault of speech, called *Tapinosis*, humility, that is when the dignity or majesty of a high matter is much defaced by the basenesse of a word; as to call the Ocean a stream, or the Thames a brook.

**Tapioca** (tæpi,ōu·kă). Forms: 8–9 **tipioca**, 9 (**tapiaca**), **tapioca.** [a. Pg., Sp., F. *tapioca*, a. Tupi-Guarani *tipioca*; f. *tipi* residue, dregs + *og*, *ók* to squeeze out. (Cavalcante in Skeat.)] A starch used for food, the prepared flour of the roots of the CASSAVA plant. Also *attrib.*

[**1612** CAPT. SMITH *Map Virginia* 13 The chiefe roote they haue for foode is called *Tockawhoughe*... Raw it is no better then poison, and being roasted except it be tender..it will prickle and torment the throat extreamly. **1648** MARCGRAVE *Hist. Nat. Brasil.* 67 Fecula albissima, quam indigenæ vocant Tipioja, Tipiaca & Tipiabica.] **1707** SLOANE *Voy. Jamaica* I. 131 The juice evaporated over the fire gives the Tipioca meal. **1753** CHAMBERS *Cycl. Supp.*, *Tipioca*, a name given..to a sort of cream or flower made from the yucca or manihot-root..after expressing the juice. **1792** *Encycl. Brit.* (ed. 3) IX. 79/2 Starch, which the Brasilians export in little lumps under the name of *tapioca*. **1812** J. SMYTH *Pract. of Customs* (1821) 253 Tapioca is the farina, obtained by subsidence in a very fine state, after washing the pulp of the root of the Cassava, which grows in South America. **1869** R. F. BURTON *Highl. Brazil* II. 39 The sediment of the juice that comes from the mass is called tipioca (our tapioca) and the liquor is thrown away. **1891** KIPLING *Life's Handicap* vii. 169 Smoked tapioca pudding.

b. In generalized application.

**1856** *Farmer's Mag.* Nov. 409 Properly granulated and dried, potato meal forms an excellent tapioca.

**Tapiolite** (tæ·piŏləit). *Min.* [ad. Sw. *tapiolit* (A. E. Nordenskiöld 1863); named after *Tapio*, a Finnish deity: see -LITE.] 'Columbo-tantalate of iron, resembling tantalite, but containing no manganese' (Chester).

**1868** DANA *Min.* (ed. 5) 518 Tapiolite..occurs near the Kulmala farm, in the village of Sukula, in the parish of Tammela, Finland.

**Tapir** (tē̆i·pəɹ). Also 8 **tapyr.** [ad. Tupi *tapira* or *tapyra*, now usually called *tapyra-ete* 'true' or 'real tapir', and *tapir-ussu* 'great tapir', to distinguish it from European cattle, to which the name *tapira* was also given by the aborigines.] An ungulate mammal of tropical America of the genus *Tapirus* or family *Tapiridæ*, somewhat resembling the swine (but more nearly related to the rhinoceros), having a short flexible proboscis.

Originally applied to the species *Tapirus americanus* of Brazil; thence extended to the two Central American species, *T. Dowii* and *T. Bairdi* (also *Elasmognathus*), and the Malay Tapir, *T.* (or *Rhinochœrus*) *indicus*.

[**1568** tr. *Thevet's New Found Worlde* 78 (*heading*) Tapihire, a beaste. **1580** DE LERY *Voyage au Brésil* 312 Tapiroussou, une beste qu'ils nomment ainsi. **1648** MARCGRAVE *Hist. Nat. Brasiliae* VI. vi. 229 Tapiierete Brasiliensibus, Lusitanis Anta. **1693** RAY *Syn. Quad.* 126 Tapiierete. **1753** CHAMBERS *Cycl. Supp.*, *Tapijerete*..the name of an animal found in some parts of America, and called by the Portuguese *anta*.] **1774** GOLDSM. *Nat. Hist.* (1776) IV. 331 The tapir may be considered as the hippopotamos of the New Continent. **1796** STEDMAN *Surinam* II. xxiii. 176 The flesh of the tapira is delicate, being accounted superior to the best ox-beef. *Ibid.* (*Plate*), Tapir. **1834** *Nat. Philos.* III. *Phys. Geog.* 55/2 (Usef. Knowl. Soc.) In America, the only representative of these large pachydermatous animals is the tapir. **1865** TYLOR *Early Hist. Man.* xi. 305 The snout of the tapir..protrudes a little more than that of our pigs.

b. *attrib.* and *Comb.* **Tapir mouth**: see quot.

**1891** *Syd. Soc. Lex.* s. v. *Mouth*, *Tapir mouth*, Landouzy's term for the peculiar tapir-like expression of mouth produced by wasting of the muscles of the face in myopathic atrophy. **1902** P. FOUNTAIN *Mts. S. America* iii. 87 Tapir-beef is the best meat to be obtained in South America.

So **Tapiri·dian,** *a.* belonging to the family *Tapiridæ*; *sb.* an animal of this family; **Ta·pirine** *a.*, of or pertaining to the tapirs; **Tapi·rodont** *a.* [Gr. ὀδούς, ὀδοντ- tooth], marking a dentition similar to that of the tapirs (*Cent. Dict.* 1891); **Ta·piroid** *a.*, allied to or resembling the tapirs.

**1880** *Libr. Univ. Knowl.* (N. Y.) VII. 474 The herbivora will contain the suborders proboscidians,..*tapiridians, having long noses but not prehensile or only very slightly so, as the rhinoceros and tapir. **1891** C. F. HOLDER *Darwin* 206 Animals without the peculiar *tapirine teeth. **1849–52** *Todd's Cycl. Anat.* IV. 926/1 In the transverse divisions of the crown we perceive the affinity to the *Tapiroid type. **1880** DAWKINS *Early Man* ii. 30 In France [the tapir] is associated with two tapiroid genera.

**Tapis** (tæ·pis, ‖ tà·pi), *sb.* Forms: 5 **tappes,** 6 *Sc.* **tapeis,** 7– **tapis.** [a. F. *tapis*, OF. *tapiz* (12th c.) = Sp., Pg. *tapiz* (pl. *tapices*):—pop. L. type **tappētium*, for late L. *tapētium* (-*ēcium*), ad. Gr. ταπήτιον, dim. of τάπης (acc. τάπητα) cloth wrought with figures in various colours, tapestry.

Late L. *tapētium* might also be inferred from *tapētia*, pl. of cl. L. *tapēte*, neuter; L. had also *tapēta* pl., as from **tapētum*, and *tapētæ* pl., as from **tapēta*; also (immed. from Gr.) acc. sing. masc. *tapēta*, pl. *tapētas*, as from **tapēs* masc. In later and med.L., Isidore has pl. *tapēta*; later forms cited by Du Cange are *tapēcius*, *tapēsium* (from *tapētium*), and *tapētiæ* pl. Beside the forms mentioned above, It. has *tappeto*, Sp. and Pg. *tapete*, Pr. *tapit*. From late L. and Rom. came also OE. *tęped*, *tæpped*, -*et*, and the cognate forms mentioned under TAPET.]

† **a.** A cloth worked with artistic designs in colours, used as a curtain, table-cloth, carpet, or the like.

**1494** FABYAN *Chron.* VI. cxli. 129 Beholde now this house, where are now the ryche tappes & clothis of golde. **1539** *Inv. R. Wardrobe* (1815) 50 Item four grete pece of tapis of Turque, off the quhilkis ane is of silk. Item fiftene litle tapis of Turque. *a* **1600** in Pinkerton *Anc. Scott. Poems* (1786) I. 257 Thy beddis soft, and tapeis fair. **1800** J. HURDIS *Fav. Village* 134 What loom e'er furnish'd for imperial floor Tapis more rich, or grateful to the foot.

**b.** Phrase. *On* (*upon*) *the tapis* [from F. *sur le tapis*], on the table-cloth, under discussion or consideration. Cf. CARPET *sb.* 1 b.

**1690** CLARENDON *Diary* 2 May, Lord Churchill and Lord Godolphin went away, and gave no votes in the matter which was upon the tapis. **1782** *Europ. Mag.* I. 248 Several marriages are adjusted, and many others are on the tapis. **1809** HAN. MORE *Cœlebs* II. xxxiv. 128, I had..been trying to bring Lucilla on the tapis. **1865** *York Herald* 18 Mar., The question of the legitimate claimant has for a long time been upon the *tapis*. **1880** *Manch. Guardian* 23 Nov., This view was held by Mr. Stansfield when his successor's bill was on the *tapis*.

**Tapis, tapish** (tæ·pis, -iʃ), *v.*[1] *Obs.* or *arch.* Forms: 4–7 **tapis** (4 **tapise, -ice**), 6–7 **tappas,** 6–8 **tapish,** 7 **tappish, tappes,** 7–9 **tappis,** 9 **tappice.** [f. OF. (*se*) *tapir*, *tapiss-* (12th c. in Hatz.-Darm.); ulterior origin uncertain: see -ISH[2].] *intr.* To lie close to the ground, lie low so as to be hid; to lurk, skulk, lie hid. (The *pa. pple.* is commonly used in intransitive sense: cf. *fallen*, *risen*.)

*c* **1330** R. BRUNNE *Chron.* (1810) 3 With joy alle at ons þei went tille Snawdone On Inor & Ini, þat tapised by þat side, To purueie þam a skulkyng, on þe Englis eft to ride. *c* **1330** — *Chron. Wace* (Rolls) 11529 Þou schal nought tapice a night to slepe. **1592** WARNER *Alb. Eng.* VII. xxxvi. (1612) 175 Now tappas closely, silly Heart,..The Huntsmans-selfe is blind. **1599** A. HUME *Hymns, Day Estivall* 126 The hart, the hynd, and fallow deare, Are tapisht at their rest. **1611** MARKHAM *Countr. Content.* I. iv. (1668) 25 Hee will tappish oft, that is, he will ever and anon be lying down and lurking in dark holes and corners. **1613** DRUMM. OF HAWTH. *Cypress Grove* Wks. (1711) 119 The spider; that pitcheth toyls, and is tapist, to prey on the smaller creatures. **1659** *Lady Alimony* II. vi. in Hazl. *Dodsley* XIV. 322 Sir Reuben..like a ranger may tappis where he likes. **1688** SHADWELL *Sqr. Alsatia* v. i, You'll find him tappes'd in some Ale-house. **1823** SCOTT *Peveril* xxxiii, Your father ..is only tappiced in some corner. *a* **1825** FORBY *Voc. E. Anglia*, *Tappis*, to lie close to the ground. A sportsman's phrase..'It is so wet the birds cannot tappis'.

**b.** *trans.* (and *refl.*) To hide, conceal. *arch.*

*a* **1660** *Contemp. Hist. Irel.* (Ir. Archæol. Soc.) II. 127 If you yett insiste to see the disposition of man to the quicke discouered, and take of the veile wherwith [it is] tapissied. **1831** SCOTT *Cast. Dang.* xi, Having tappiced herself behind the little bed.

Hence † **Ta·pised** (**tapist, tapiced**) *ppl. a.*, hidden, concealed; † **Ta·pissing** *vbl. sb.*, in quot. *concr.* a hiding-place.

*a* **1340** HAMPOLE *Psalter* xvii. 13 He sett myrknesis his tapissynge [L. *latibulum*]. **1621** LADY M. WROTH *Urania* 35 Wee..made them as fearefully rush vp, as a tapist Buck will doe, when he finds his enemies so neere.

**Tapis, tapish** (tæ·pis, -iʃ), *v.*[2] Now *dial.* Forms: 4 **tapis,** 8–9 **tapish,** 9 **tappish.** [perh. for **tabish*, f. L. *tābēscere* to waste away, decline.] *intr.* (*a*) To languish, pine away; (*b*) to be mortally sick or diseased. (Often in *pa. pple.* in intrans. sense.)

*c* **1375** *St. Aug.* 499 in Horstm. *Altengl. Leg.* (1878) 70, I ..þat sum tyme was a bitter berkere..Aȝeynes lettres goode and mete..And I tapissed [L. *tabescebam*] vndur such lettring. **1747** HOOSON *Miner's Dict.* V j, When Miners are troubled in the Mines by Damps,..yet..are preserved by being timely helped, and escape with Life; such a one we say, is Tapish'd, more or less. **1865** SLEIGH *Derbysh. Gloss.* s.v., Hur tappish'd yest' morn. **1875** *Manch. Guard.* 1 Mar. (E.D.D.), His brother said he thought he was 'tappished' with a decline. *Ibid.* 29 Mar., 'This arm's tappished',..'This wood's tappished'. **1891** *Sheffield Gloss.* Suppl. 58 *Tapish*, to waste or pine away...'He tapished and died'.

† **Tapis,** *v.*[3] *Obs.* Forms: 6 **tappes,** 6–7 **tapes,** 7 **tapis.** [a. F. *tapisse-r* (15th c. in Hatz.-Darm.), in OF. *tapissier*, f. *tapis*: see TAPIS *sb.*] *trans.* To hang, cover, or adorn with tapestry; also, to adorn with figures, as tapestry.

**1528** LYNDESAY *Dreme* 325 That myrke Mansioun is tapessit with stynk. **1562** LEIGH *Armorie* (1597) 122 Chamber, richly arrayed and tappesed with Arras. **1601** HOLLAND *Pliny* XIX. iv, The windowes beautified with green quishins, wrought and tapissed with floures of all colours. **1602** CAREW *Cornwall* 111 b, Onely there remaine the Iuie-tapissed wals of the keepe.

**Tapism** (tē̆i·piz'm). [f. TAPE *sb.*[1] + -ISM.] Official formality or routine; = RED-TAPISM.

**1852** *Q. Rev.* Mar. 418 There affection bursts the cold priggery of tapeism—she vents her sorrows at his departure.

† **Tapisser.** *Obs.* exc. *Hist.* Forms: 4–5 **tapycer, tapecer, -e, tapicer, tapesere, taphiser,** 5 **tapiser, tapser,** 5–6 **tapisser,** *Sc.* **tapescher.** [a. AF. *tapicer* = OF. *tapicier* (13th c.), mod.F. *tapissier*, f. OF. *tapiz*, F. *tapis*, figured cloth: see TAPIS *sb.* and -ER[2].] A maker or weaver of figured cloth or tapestry.

*c* **1386** CHAUCER *Prol.* 362 A Webbe, a Dyere, and a Tapycer [*v.rr.* taphiser, tapecer(e)]. **1388** WYCLIF *Exod.* xxxviii. 23 A tapesere and a broderere of iacynt, purpur, vermyloun and bijs. **1439** in *Ancestor* July (1904) 17 A coverlit and a testre of tapicers werk. **1541** *Acc. Ld. High Treas. Scotl.* VIII. 42 Given to the tapescher for his warkmanschip. **1591** SPARRY tr. *Cattan's Geomancie* 225 He shall be a tapisser or spinner of cloth of golde. **1883** M. E. HAWEIS in *Contemp. Rev.* Sept. 426 Chaucer describes the fat dyer and tapiser in his prologue. **1892** BESANT *London* 194 When certain tapicers were charged with selling false blankets.

Hence †**Tapisser-work** *Obs.*, tapestry-work.

**1459** *Test. Ebor.* (Surtees) II. 227 Hengyng for ye halle and parlor of tapisserwerk.

† **Ta·pissery.** *Obs.* Also 5 **tapecery(e, tapcery, tapisery, -yssere,** 5–6 **-ery(e (tapserye),** 6 **tapyceryе, -esserie, -essarie** (*Sc.*), **tappyssery, tapissary, -arie, tapisry, -issrie,** 7 **-issry.** [a. F. *tapisserie* (14th c. in Hatz.-Darm.), f. *tapissier* a tapestry-worker, or *tapisser* to cover with carpet, f. *tapis* carpet, table-cloth: see TAPIS *sb.* and -ERY.] The early form of the word TAPESTRY. Also *attrib.*

**1426** *E. E. Wills* (1882) 76 A blewe bedde of Tapecery. *c* **1430** LYDG. *Min. Poems* (Percy Soc.) 6 Clothis of gold, silk, and tapcery. *c* **1430** *Brut* 460 Alle the stretes..were hanged with clopes of arras and with clothes of tapissery werk. **1497** *Caxton's Chron. Eng.* VII. (W. de W.) S vj b/1 The stretes were couerył ouer his heed wyth sylk of tapisery. **1525** LD. BERNERS *Froiss.* II. li. 181 Chambres hanged with tapyceryes and curteynes. **1530** PALSGR. 279/1 Tappyssery werke, *tapisserie*. *a* **1548** HALL *Chron.*, *Hen. VI* 115 b, Riche clothes of Arras and Tapissrie. **1555** W. WATREMAN *Fardle Facions* II. xi. 260 The grounde couered and garnisshed with natures Tapesserie. **1578** T. N. tr. *Conq. W. India* 183 Rich Mantels, Tapissary Targats, tuffes of feathers. **1683** EVELYN *Diary* 4 Oct., The new fabriq of French tapissry. **1697** — *Numismata* viii. 285 Clemens Alexandrinus in the Tenth Book of his Tapisseries.

**Tapist** (tē̆i·pist). [f. TAPE *sb.*[1] + -IST.] = RED-TAPIST.

**1852** JERDAN *Autobiog.* II. 41, I do not think he could leave the amount of a tapist's quarter's salary behind him.

† **Ta·pister, -tre,** *v. Obs.* [f. *tapister*, TAPESTER *sb.*] = TAPESTRY *v.*

**1587** HARMAR tr. *Beza's Serm.* 263 Flowers with which the earth is tapistred. **1592** GREENE *Upst. Courtier* B j, A vale all tapistred with sweet and choice flowers. **1644** EVELYN *Diary* 7 Nov., The room..is tapisstred with crimson damasq embrodred with gold.

**Tapister,** var. TAPESTER *Obs.*, tapestry-worker.

† **Ta·piter.** *Obs. rare.* [f. *tapit*, TAPET *sb.* + -ER[1].] = TAPISSER. Also *attrib.*

*c* **1440** *York Myst.* xxx. 270 (*title*) The Tapiteres and Couchers. **1485** *York Council Bk.* II. IV. 74 ibid. Introd. 27 *note*, It was determyned that the Tapiters Cardemakers and lynwevers of this Citie be togeder annexid to the bringing furth of the padgeantes of the Tapiter craft and Cardmaker.

**Tap-lash** (tæ·p,læʃ). Now *dial.* Also 7 **-lush.** [f. TAP *sb.*[1] + LASH *v.*[1]]

**1.** The 'lashings' or washings of casks or glasses; dregs or refuse of liquor; very weak or stale beer.

**1623** J. TAYLOR (Water P.) *Disc. by Sea* B vij, To murder men with drinking, with such a deale of complementall oratory, As, off with your Cup, winde vp your bottome, vp with your taplash, and many more eloquent phrases. **1681** W. ROBERTSON *Phraseol. Gen.* (1693) 597 Very taplash; dead drink. **1813** *Sporting Mag.* XLII. 118 Liquors of all denominations from champagne to humble tap-lash. **1828** *Craven Gloss.*, *Tap-lash*, thick small beer; poor, vapid liquor of any kind.

*fig.* **1672** MARVELL *Reh. Transp.* I. 227 This the Tap-lash of what he said. **1769** COLMAN *Prose Sev. Occas.* (1787) III. 157 Thou..draw'st the taplash of another's brains.

**b.** *attrib.* or *adj.*

1642 in J. B. Williams *Eng. Journalism* (1908) 36 They have filled the City..with the fruits of their taplush inventions. 1673 Bp. S. Parker *Repr. Reh. Transp.* 197 Bandied up and down by the School-men in their taplash disputes. 1682 Hickeringill *Mushroom* Wks. 1716 II. 366 Stale Taplash droppings, old and sowr.

†2. Applied contemptuously to a publican. *Obs.*

c 1648 *Eng. Ballad, 'No Money, No Friend'* (Farmer), Each Taplach..would cringe and bow, and swear to be My Servant to Eternity. 1719 D'Urfey *Pills* (1872) IV. 320 Thus is it not evident Tap-lashes don't thrive?

†**Ta·plin, tapling.** *Obs.* (See quots.)

1748 Brownrigg *Making Salt* ii. ii. § 1. 54 The pan .. is placed over the furnace, being supported at the four corners by brick work; but along the middle, and at the sides and ends, by round pillars of cast iron called taplins, which are placed at three feet distance from each other, being about eight inches high, and at the top, where smallest, four inches in diameter. 1753 Chambers *Cycl. Supp., Taplings*, in the English salt-works, the name given to certain bars of iron which support the bottom of the pan in which the brine is boiled. 1797 *Encycl. Brit.* (ed. 3) XVI. 626/2 [as in quot. 1748].

**Ta·plings,** *sb. pl.* 'The strong double leathers made fast to the ends of each piece of a flail'; the middle-band. (Halliwell 1847–78.)

**Tapnage**: see Tapinage.

**Ta·pnet, †topnet.** [In 16th c. *topnet*, app. altered from Toppet (*tappet*) q.v. Cf. Tap *sb.*3] A basket made of rushes, in which figs (formerly also raisins, etc.) are imported; also a conventional measure of quantity; = Frail *sb.*1

α. 1524 in Rogers *Agric. & Prices* III. 535/4 [Figs] Topnets. 1537 in J. H. Blunt *Myrr. oure Ladye* Introd. 31 Dyuerse sortes of Spices and fruyttes..Nutmygges..Corans..Gynger..Isonglas..Figge doodes v Topnettes ij lb.—xj s. ix d. c 1550 *Customs Duties* (B. M. Add. MS. 25097), Figgs dodes, the topnet, xx d. 1882 Rogers *Agric. & Prices* IV. 671 Between 1516 and 1540 the price of figs by the toppet or topnet is a little over 2s. 3d. .. Such a price .. suggests..that the toppet contained about 30 lbs., and that it corresponds to the earlier frail...In 1533 figs are bought by the topnet at Cambridge and by the frail at Stonor, at the same price, 2s. 6d.

β. 1553 W. Cholmeley *Request & Suite true-hearted Eng.* in *Camden Misc.* II. 17 Fyggis at xxd the tapnet. 1556 W. Towrson in Hakluyt *Voy.* (1589) 99 Three Tapnets of figges, two pots of oyle. 1682 *Privil. Citizens Lond.* 71 For Tapnets and Frails of Figs per Ton..xx d. 1812 J. Smyth *Pract. of Customs* (1821) 88 Frails, or Tapnets, are baskets made of rushes. 1858 in Simmonds *Dict. Trade.* 1910 *Grocer, Diary* 47/1 *Figs*, Faro, tapnets, 28 lbs.

*attrib.* 1578 Lyte *Dodoens* v. lxxxi. 652 Currantes or Raysens of Corinthe, do not much differ in vertue, from tapnet or frayle Raysens.

†**Ta·pon.** *Sc. Obs.* Also 6 tappone, tawpon, talpoun, 7 tapoun. [a. F. *tapon* (1382 in Hatz.-Darm.), earlier form of *tampon* plug, etc., f. *taper* to plug (of OLG. origin: see Tap *v.*1).] A word having the general sense 'plug, peg, pin', in various applications.

**1.** A peg in a drinking-vessel, a pin; = Peg *sb.*1 2 b, Pin *sb.*1 1 f.

1543 *Burgh Rec. Edinb.* (1871) II. 112 That all nichtboures..sendand for wyne..haif thair pynts of just mesure merkett with the townis merk, and that the samyn haif ane talpoun as vse is in vther pairts. 1543-4 *Ibid.* 115 Stowppis of mesour with tawponis in the hals, merket with the townis merk. 1551 *Ibid.* 161 That the samyn haue ane tappone as vs is in vther pairtis.

**2.** A peg acting as a tappet (Tappet 1).

1640 A. Melville in *Extracts fr. Comm.-pl.* (1899) 29 The said quheill hath of taponis that liftis ye hamer 8.

**3.** A main branch or ramification of the root of a tree or plant; a subsidiary root.

1641 R. Baillie *Lett., to Mrs. Baillie* 6 Feb. (1841) I. 298 We trust God will putt them [the Bishops] doun, bot the difficultie to gett all the tapouns of their roots pulled up are yet insuperable by the arme of man.

**4.** *Tapon staff*, ?the stave containing the vent-peg.

1661 *Sc. Acts Chas. II* (1820) VII. 230/2 That no barrell be sooner made and bloune, but the Coupers birne be set theron, on the tapon staff thairof.

**Tap-ooze, -owze,** etc.: see Tap-hose.

**Tapotement** (tăpō·tmĕnt). *Med.* [a. F. *tapotement*, f. *tapoter* to tap: see -ment.] Percussion, esp. as a part of the treatment in massage.

1889 *Lancet* 2 Mar. 423/1 Best attained by certain manipulations which include circular movements, kneading, and *tapotement*. 1896 *Allbutt's Syst. Med.* I. 374 Tapotement is the application of rapid blows delivered with the ulnar edge of the hand.

**Tapp,** obs. f. Tap. **Tappa,** variant of Tapa.

**Ta·ppable,** *a.* [f. Tap *v.*1 + -able.] Capable of being tapped or pierced for juice; fit for tapping.

1910 *Westm. Gaz.* 13 Apr. 10/1 [The estate] already possesses no fewer than 40,780 [rubber] trees, with 14,700 at a tappable age. 1910 *Morning Post* 22 Apr. 1/3 [The] C. Rubber Company.. having over 100,000 tappable trees between four and 10 years old.

‖**Tappal, -aul** (tăpǭ·l). *Anglo-Ind.* [Of obscure and uncertain origin: see Yule.] The transmission of letters, etc. by relays of runners; the organization by which this is carried on; the postal matter or conveyance, the mail; one who carries the post; an arrival or dispatch of letters.

1791 Jas. Anderson *Corr.* 64 A letter by the Tappal or Dawk. 1799 Wellington in Gurw. *Suppl. Desp.* (1858) I. 303, I have sent orders to the postmaster at Seringapatam to run a tappall from thence to Nuggur. 1809 Ld. Valentia *Voy.* I. vii. 385, I might go by tappaul the whole way to Seringapatam. 1889 *Blackw. Mag.* Feb. 199 Farewell to telegrams and tappals for a fortnight.

Hence ‖**Tappal-wallah** [cf. *competition-wallah*], a runner who carries the post in S. India.

1865 *Daily Tel.* 12 Dec. 7/2 The tappal-wallah does not turn up with the letters at the proper time.

**Tappas,** var. Tapis *v.*1 to lie hid.

**Tappe,** obs. form of Tap, Tape.

‖**Tappen** (tæ·pĕn). [Sw. and Norw. *tapp-en* the plug.] The plug by which the rectum of a bear is closed during hibernation.

[1830 L. L. Lloyd *Field Sports N. Europe* I. v. 89 His bowels and stomach become quite empty, and..the extremity of them is closed by an indurated substance, which in Swedish is called *tappen*. 1835 *Penny Cycl.* IV. 85/1 *note*, The plug (in Norway termed the *Tappen*), found in the rectum of fat hybernating bears.] 1865 Wood *Illustr. Nat. Hist.* I. 393 The 'tappen' is almost entirely composed of pine-leaves, and the various substances which the Bear scratches out of the ants' nests.

**Tapper**1 (tæ·pəɹ). Forms: 1 tæppere, 2 -are, 6– tapper, *Sc.* tappar, topper. [OE. *tæppere*, f. *tæppa*, Tap *sb.*1, *tæppian*, Tap *v.*1: see -er 1.]

†**1.** One who taps casks or draws liquor; a tavern-keeper; = Tapster 2. *Obs.*

*a* 1000 *Ags. Gloss.* in Wr.-Wülcker 202/14 *Caupus, i. tabernarius qui uinum uendit*, tæppere. *a* 1050 *Liber Scintill.*, etc. (1889) 226 Na byþ ȝerihtwisud tæppere [L. *caupo*] fram synnum welera. c 1537 *Thersites* in *Four O. Pl.* (1848) 82 The tapper of Tauystocke & the tapsters potte. 1618 D. Belchier *Hans Beer-pot* B j b, Ioaske Flutterkin, a Tapper.

†**b.** A retailer; cf. Tap *v.*1 4 b. *Sc. Obs.*

1478-9 *Burgh Rec. Edinb.* (1869) I. 37 The provest and counsale of the towne ordanis the meilmen topperis fremen of the towne and [to] top his meill daylie. 1580 *Burgh Rec. Glasgow* (1876) I. 82 That na topparis of small salt..by ony salt in greit..quhill ix houris of the daye. 1605 in Macgregor *Hist. Glasgow* xviii. (1887) 157 Tappers of woollen and linen cloth.

**2.** One who or that which taps, in various senses; e.g. one who taps trees for the sap or juice; a machine for milking cows.

1884 C. G. W. Lock *Workshop Receipts* Ser. iii. 309/1 The tapper then goes round provided with the bark scraper. 1884 J. Scott *Barn Implements* xvii. 157 Tube-milkers, or tappers; Sucking-machines; and Mechanical hand-milkers, or squeezers and strippers. 1908 *Westm. Gaz.* 2 Mar. 5/2 The ruthless destruction of date palms by 'tappers' is said to be most evident in Madras.

**3.** One who works a screw-cutting tap for threading holes or orifices: cf. Tap *v.*1 6.

1909 in *Cent. Dict. Suppl.*

**Tapper**2 (tæ·pəɹ). [f. Tap *v.*2 + -er 1.]

**1.** One who taps or lightly strikes: e.g. one who taps at a door, etc.; one who taps the wheels of railway carriages, to test their soundness; a shoemaker who rivets on soles and heels; a dialect name of the lesser spotted woodpecker.

1810 *Splendid Follies* III. 89 If the young gentleman did not immediately return to town, and satisfy their urgent demands, a tapper would..make his appearance at Mistley. 1837 Dickens *Pickw.* xxxii, A low tap was heard at the room door. Mr. Bob Sawyer..bade the tapper come in. 1883 *Macm. Mag.* Feb. 269 The honest tapper of every wheel [of a railway train]. 1885 Swainson *Provinc. Names Birds* 99 Lesser Spotted Woodpecker (*Dendrocopus minor*). Also called..Wood tapper...Tapperer,..or Tapper. 1903 *Daily Chron.* 11 Sept. 8/4 Boot Trade, repairs.—Smart tapper to finish on machines.

**2.** That which taps or lightly strikes, as a hammer for striking a bell; *spec.* a key in an electric telegraph which is depressed (with a tapping sound) to complete the circuit, a telegraph key; in wireless telegraphy, a device for restoring the filings to their original condition; also *tapper-back*.

1876 Preece & Sivewright *Telegraphy* 43 There are two forms of the single needle instrument in general use, viz. the drop-handle and the pedal or tapper form. *Ibid.* 47 The sending portion of the 'pedal' or 'tapper' form of single needle. 1898 *Edin. Rev.* Oct. 306 The restoration to the coherer of its defective efficacy is brought about by the automatic action of a 'tapper'. 1903 *Sci. Amer.* 26 Dec. 483/2 In 1894 he [Sir O. Lodge] exhibited at Oxford his first 'tapper-back', or automatic system of decohering the iron filings after each impulse.

**Tapper, Tappes,** obs. ff. Taper, Tapis.

**Tappet** (tæ·pėt). Also 8–9 tapit, 9 tapet, tappit, tabbot. [app. f. Tap *v.*2 + -et; but the use of the suffix is abnormal. Cf. mod.F. *tapette* a flat piece of wood for driving in corks.]

A projecting arm or part in a machine, which by the movement of the latter comes intermittently into contact with another part, so as to give or receive motion.

1745 *Specif. Kay & Stell's Patent* No. 612 There are likewise fixed in the sliding beam or hollow rowler, at proper distances, sundry tapits. 1824 R. Stuart *Hist. Steam Engine* 114 The pins or tappets [are] fixed on the plug-frame (or tappet rod)..: at the ascent or descent of these pins, they strike on the ends of the levers or spanners.. connected with the valves,..and open or shut them. 1831 J. Holland *Manuf. Metal* I. 241 As the wheel shaft revolves, the tappits successively strike the hammer tail. 1839 Ure *Dict. Arts*, etc. 1287 *T* is the shaft of the eccentric tappets, cams, or wipers, which press the treddle levers alternately up and down. 1870 J. M. Nutter in *Eng. Mech.* 4 Mar. 610/2 Much depends upon the description of loom and make of tabbots in treading motion. 1907 *Westm. Gaz.* 28 Nov. 4/1 The inclined valves and new valve tappets ..mark it [a motor car engine] with a distinctiveness all its own.

**b.** *attrib.* and *Comb.*; appositive, 'that is a tappet', as *tappet-arm, -lever, -pin, -plate*; 'of a tappet or tappets', as *tappet action, -bevel, -bowl, motion*; 'having or worked by a tappet or tappets', as *tappet-port, -rod, -valve, -wheel.*

1824 Tappet rod [see above]. 1837 H. Stansfeld in *Civil Eng. & Arch. Jrnl.* I. 54/2 Certain Machinery of a Tappet and Lever Action. 1839 Ure *Dict. Arts*, etc. 1287 Heddle leaves, actuated by the tappet wheels upon the axis Q. 1895 *Model Steam Engine* 46 Simply altering the position of the tappet lever by means of two screws. 1908 *Westm. Gaz.* 28 Apr. 4/2 The valve-stems may be lengthened or the tappet-ports enlarged.

**Tappet,** 16th c. var. Toppet, basket.

**Tappet, -ett, -ette,** variants of Tapet.

†**Tappette.** *Obs. rare.* [? dim. of Tap *sb.*1: see -ette.] A catkin.

1561 Hollybush *Hom. Apoth.* 34 b, Take the tappettes or flouringe of Walnuttes and Filberts when they florishe, new gathered after that they be fallen from yᵉ trees.

**Tappice,** var. Tapis *v.*1 to lie hid.

**Tappil, tapple, Tappit,** var. (chiefly *Sc.*) of Topple, Topped. **Tappin,** Sc. f. Topping.

**Tapping** (tæ·piŋ), *vbl. sb.*1 [f. Tap *v.*1 + -ing 1.] The action of Tap *v.*1 in various senses.

1597 A. M. tr. *Guillemeau's Fr. Chirurg.* 20 b/2 In the drawing or tappinge of the water. 1655 Culpepper *Riverius* vii. v. 164 The Opening or Tapping for the Dropsie. 1713 Cheselden *Anat.* iii. x. (1726) 228 This kind of dropsie is sometimes cured by tapping. c 1865 J. Wylde in *Circ. Sc.* I. 410/2 They are..obtained from the tree.., by the process of 'tapping'. 1905 H. D. Rolleston *Dis. Liver* 171 A woman..eventually died after her sixtieth tapping. 1909 *Installation News* II. 172/1 Alternating current..is carried into one side of the transformer giving 50 volts on the secondary at one tapping for lighting purposes, and three other tappings at 7, 12½ and 20 volts for cooking and heating.

**b.** *concr.* That which is drawn by tapping, or runs from a tap; a means of tapping.

1597 A. M. tr. *Guillemeau's Fr. Chirurg.* 53 b/1 His drinck, harshe and noughtye tappinges of wyne. 1686 Plot *Staffordsh.* 17 It smelt just like the soure tappings of dead beer in a Cellar. 1862 Dana *Man. Geol.* 648 All wells and springs are tappings of these subterranean waters.

**c.** *attrib.* and *Comb.*, as *tapping-apparatus* (Knight *Dict. Mech.* 1877); **tapping-bar**, a sharp-pointed crowbar used in opening the tap-hole of a furnace; **tapping-clay**, plastic clay used to close a tapping-hole; **tapping-cock**, a cock having a taper stem, which allows it to be driven firmly into an opening; **tapping-drill**, a drill for boring holes in water-pipes; **tapping-gouge**, a gouge used in tapping the sugar-maple; **tapping-hole**, (*a*) a tap-hole in a furnace; (*b*) a hole drilled in metal to be tapped or furnished with an internal screw-thread; **tapping-iron** = *tapping-gouge*; **tapping-machine**, (*a*) a machine for cutting internal screw-threads; (*b*) a machine for tapping water- or gas-mains, a tapping-drill; **tapping-pot**, a pot to receive liquid metal from the tap-hole; **tapping-tool**, (*a*) = Tap *sb.*1 4; (*b*) any implement for tapping the sugar-maple.

1861 Fairbairn *Iron* 133 The fire is to be carefully raked out at the *tapping hole, which is again to be made good with loam. 1894 Bowker in *Harper's Mag.* Jan. 418 A channel known as the tapping-hole, taps the metal from the crucible. 1840 Gosse *Canadian Nat.* vi. 68 A semicircular incision is made [in the tree] with a large iron gouge, called a *tapping iron.

**Ta·pping,** *vbl. sb.*2 [f. Tap *v.*2 + -ing 1.] The action of Tap *v.*2; the sound made by this action; † in *Etching*: see quot. 1688 (*obs.*). Also reduplicated, tap-tapping, repeated or continued tapping.

c 1440 [see Tap *v.*2 1]. 1688 R. Holme *Armoury* iii. 151/1 *Tapping*, is wip[ing] or sliding ones hand upon the Varnish to make it smooth and even on the Plate. 1786 Mme. D'Arblay *Diary* 6 Nov., I heard a tapping from a window upstairs. 1860 Russell *Diary in India* II. xvii. 321, I was informed that the tents were going to be struck immediately, and the tap-tapping of the kelassees confirmed the fact. 1872 Black *Adv. Phaeton* xxxi, Here a tapping all round the table greeted the orator.

**b.** The soling or heeling of boots and shoes. *dial.* and *U.S.*

1857 Eadie *J. Kitto* ii. (1861) 44 Revelations about list and leather, tapping and closing.

**c.** *attrib.* and *Comb.*, as *tapping test*; **tapping-room**, a room in which tapping or boot-soling, etc. is done.

1895 *Westm. Gaz.* 17 Apr. 2/3 So the tapping test for railway carriage axles is a fraud. 1905 *Ibid.* 21 Sept. 7/1 An adjoining factory used..as a tapping room.

**Tappis, tappish,** variant of Tapis *v.*1, 2.

**Tappit** (tæ·pit), *ppl. a. Sc.* = Topped *ppl. a.*; *esp.* crested, tufted; chiefly in the collocation **tappit hen, a.** a hen having a crest or topknot; **b.** a drinking-vessel having a lid with a knob; *spec.* one containing a Scotch quart.

1721 Ramsay *Ode to the Ph—* iii, That mutchkin stoup it hauds but dribs, Then let's get in the tappit hen. 1794 Burns *Lines on Tumbler* ii. 1814 Scott *Wav.* xi, A huge pewter measuring-pot, containing at least three English quarts, familiarly denominated *a tappit hen.* 1821 Galt

*Ann. Parish* ii, His head powdered and frizzled up like a tappit-hen. **1906** *Athenæum* 30 June 803/3 Of genuine old pewter..here are..flagons, tappit-hens, toddy-ladles.

**Tapple up tail**: see TOPPLE *v.*

† **Tappy**, *v. Obs. rare*—⁰. = TAPIS *v.*[1]

**1706** PHILLIPS (ed. 6), To *Tappy*, (among Hunters) to lie hid as a Deer does.

**Ta·p-room.** [f. TAP *sb.*[1] + ROOM *sb.*[1]] A room in a tavern, etc., in which liquors are kept on tap.

**1807** *Sporting Mag.* XXIX. 78 Gore was in the doorway between the tap room and the bed room. **1838** DICKENS *O. Twist* viii, [He] turned into a small public-house, and led the way to a tap-room. **1855** MACAULAY *Hist. Eng.* xii. III. 184 The ambassador was put one night into a miserable taproom full of soldiers smoking.

**Tap-root** (tæ·pıriūt), *sb.* [f. TAP *sb.*[1] + ROOT.] A straight root, of circular section, thick at the top, and tapering to a point, growing directly downwards from the stem and forming the centre from which subsidiary rootlets spring.

**1601** HOLLAND *Pliny* XVI. xxxi. 477 The Fir and Larch have one tap root and no more; for upon that one maine maister-root they rest and are founded. **1733** TULL *Horse-Hoeing Husb.* i. 1 The Tap-Root commonly runs down Single and Perpendicular, reaching sometimes many Fathoms below. **1815** J. SMITH *Panorama Sc. & Art* II. 597 Such plants have no tap-roots, but strike their fibres horizontally in the richest part of the soil. **1851** GLENNY *Handbk. Fl.-Gard.* 160 It has a tap-root like a carrot, but small. *fig.* **1825** COLERIDGE *Aids Refl.* (1836) 349 Its fibres are to be traced to the tap-root of humanity. **1887** LOWELL *Democr.* 36 This sentiment, which is the very tap-root of civilization and progress. *attrib.* **1890** *Eng. Illustr. Mag.* Christm. No. 158 That's a tap-root idea, Fraser.

Hence **Ta·p-root** *v. intr.*, of a plant, to send down a tap-root (whence **Ta·p-rooting** *ppl. a.*); **Ta·p-rooted** *a.*, having a tap-root.

**1725** *Bradley's Fam. Dict.* s.v. *Ilex*, These, like our English Oak, are tap-rooted, and therefore delight in deep Soil. **1769** L. EDWARD in *Hist. Linc.* (1834) I. 20 The oak roots stand upon the sand, and tap-root into the clay. **1805** R. W. DICKSON *Pract. Agric.* I. 12 In loosening the ground for carrots, or other tap-rooted plants. **1897** WILLIS *Flower. Pl.* I. 185 Tap-rooting plants..would not be able to cling to their supports in time to prevent falling off.

† **Ta·psail, -seil.** *Obs. rare.* Some kind of East Indian cotton material.

**1725** *Lond. Gaz.* No. 6388/2 The following Goods, viz... Negannepants, Tapseils,.. Arrangoes. **1851** in HILPERT *Eng.-Germ. Dict.* **18..** in FLÜGEL.

**Tapsal-, tapsie-teerie**, *Sc.*: see TOPSY-TURVY.

† **Ta·psebarbe.** *Obs. rare*—[1]. [? obs. F., ad. med.L. *T(h)apsus barbatus*, former name of *Verbascum Thapsus*.] The Great Torch Mullein.

[*c* **1450** *Alphita* (Anecd. Oxon.) 182/1 *Tapsus barbatus maior masculus*,..g[allice] molayne, an[glice] catesteyl, *uel* feldwrt.] **1526** *Grete Herball* ccccvii. (1529) Y ij b, Tapsebarbe is a maner of herbe called moleyne, wherof is made a maner of torches whan it is greased.

**Tapser, -erye**, var. TAPISSER, -ERY *Obs.*

**Tapsia**, obs. form of THAPSIA.

† **Ta·psimel.** *Obs. Old Med.* [med.L. *tapsi mel*, lit. honey of THAPSUS or Mullein (*Verbascum Thapsus*).] A plaster made of mullein and other herbs with honey.

*c* **1425** tr. *Arderne's Surgery* (E.E.T.S.) 31 Þat confeccion ..þat receyueþ Smalache, wormode, moleyne, sparge, &c., wiþ clarified hony soþen togidre at þe fire and kept by itself in a vessell is called 'Tapsimel'. *Ibid.* 35 Þat he take þe ȝolke of an ey to whiche be added þe half parte of tapsimell. *Ibid.* 73 Þis oyntment is called tapsimel, of tapsibarbati. **1658** ROWLAND tr. *Moufet's Theat. Ins.* 912, I might here set down the..Tapsimel of Arden, and all syrups that were anciently made of honey.

† **Tapskin.** *Obs. nonce-wd.* [f. TAP *v.*[2] + SKIN *sb.*] A drumstick.

**1605** *Play Stucley* in Simpson *Sch. Shaks.* (1878) I. 196 Drum [= Drummer], thump thy tapskins hard about the pate [*Stage direct.* Drum sounds] And make the ram-heads hear that are within.

**Tapster** (tæ·pstəɹ). Forms: 1 **tæppestre**, 4 **tappester**, 4–6 **tapester**, 5 **tap(p)estere**, **tapstere**, 5–6 **tappyster**, *Sc.* and *n. dial.* **tapstare**, 6 **-ar**, 5– **tapster**. [OE. *tæppestre*, fem. of *tæppere*, TAPPER[1]: see -STER.]

† **1.** *orig.* A woman who tapped or drew ale or other liquor for sale in an inn; a hostess. *Obs.*

*c* **1000** ÆLFRIC *Gram.* ix. (Z.) 36 *Caupona*, tæppestre. *c* **1385** CHAUCER *Prol.* 241 He knew..euerich Hostiler and Tappestere. *c* **1440** *Promp. Parv.* 486/2 Tapstare, *ducillaria, propinaria, clipsidraria.* **1474** CAXTON *Chesse* III. vi. h vj b, That I haue sayd of the seruauntes beyng men, the same I say of the women as chaumberers and tapsters. *c* **1485** *Digby Myst.* III. 495 With sum praty tasppysster wold I fayne rown. *a* **1518** SKELTON *Magnyf.* 420 A tappyster lyke a lady bryght. **1568** *Satir. Poems Reform.* xlviii. 100 Thre lassis..That tyme that thay wer tapstaris.

**2.** A man who draws the beer, etc. for the customers in a public house; the keeper of a tavern.

The word in the first three quots. may be feminine.

*c* **1400** *Destr. Troy* 1594 Tauerners, tapsters, all the toune ouer. *c* **1450** *Mankind* 267 in *Macro Plays* 11, I haue be sethen with ȝe comyn tapster of Bury. **1530** PALSGR. 279/1 Tapster, *boutelier, boutiliere.* **1570** LEVINS *Manip.* 77/4 A Tapster, *promus.* **1598** SHAKS. *Merry W.* I. iii. 17 An old Cloake, makes a new Ierkin: a wither'd Seruingman, a fresh Tapster. **1612** W. PARKES *Curtaine-Dr.* (1876) 26 Ther's Tom the Tapster peerelesse for renowne, That drank three hundred drunken Dutch-men downe. **1676** *Lond. Gaz.* No. 1103/4 John Bowman,..late Tapster at the Bear Inn in Bath. **1720** SWIFT *Stella's Birthday* 9 Though the treach'rous tapster Thomas Hangs a new angel two doors from us. **1871** SMILES *Charac.* i. (1876) 14 The decayed serving-men and tapsters who filled the Commonwealth's army.

† **3.** One who sells by retail or in small quantities.

**1402** *Pol. Poems* (Rolls) II. 95 Me thynkith ȝe ben tapsteres, in alle that ȝe don; ȝe tappe ȝour absoluciones that ȝe bye at Rome. *c* **1450** *Godstow Reg.* 101 The abbesse graunted that her men of Wycombe shold be tempters or tapsters of brede and ale in the fee of the same abbesse.

**4.** *Comb.*, as *tapster-like* adj.

**1607** R. C[AREW] tr. *Estienne's World of Wonders* A iv b, Leauing inkhorne phrases and tapsterlike termes for the tauerne. **1842** F. HOWES *Horace's Sat.* I. 2 This tapsterlike retailer of the laws.

Hence **Ta·pstering** *ppl. a.*, acting as a tapster; **Ta·psterly** *a.*, characteristic of or befitting a tapster; **Ta·pstership**, the office of a tapster; † **Ta·pstry**, a tap-room.

**1861** SALA *Dutch Pict.* xii. 187 Is he going to scour the country with his marauding, *tapstering butchers? **1589** NASHE *Pref. Greene's Menaphon* (Arb.) 9 In anie *tapsterlie tearmes whatsoeuer. **1598** BARRET *Theor. Warres* I. i. 5 Honest and valiant men, not tapsterly praters. **1597** *1st Pt. Return fr. Parnass.* v. ii. 1538 As for youre *tapstershipp in hell, it were a good office in soe whott a place. **14..** *Beryn* 299 The Pardoner..Stalkid in to the *tapstry.

**Tapstery, -strie, -stry, -e**, obs. ff. TAPESTRY.

**Ta·pstress.** [f. TAPSTER + -ESS; formed after *tapster* had ceased to be feminine: cf. *seamstress, songstress*.] A female tapster.

**1631** HEYWOOD *1st Pt. Maid of West* I. Wks. 1874 II. 269 You are some tapstresse. **1667** SIR C. LYTTELTON in *Hatton Corr.* (Camden) 52 Hee has married a dirty tapstresse. **1839** H. AINSWORTH *J. Shepherd* III. xiii, The tapstress was full of curiosity.

**Tap-tap, Tap-tapping**: see TAP *sb.*, TAPPING *vbl. sb.* **Taptoo, taptow**, obs. ff. TATTOO *sb.*[1]

**Tapu**: see TABOO.

† **Tapul.** *Obs.* [Of uncertain origin: perhaps orig. an error.] A name applied by Hall (*a* 1548) to some part of the body-armour; thence, by modern antiquaries taken as a name for the vertical central ridge of the breastplate.

*a* **1548** HALL *Chron., Hen. IV* 12 One company had the plackard,..the tasses, the lamboys, the backpece, the tapull, and the border of the curace all gylte. [MEYRICK *Anc. Armour* (1824) II. 258 commenting says 'Perhaps the projecting edge perpendicularly along the cuirass, from the French *taper*, to strike'. Hence the following:] **1834** PLANCHÉ *Brit. Costume* 243 The breast-plate was still [reign of Hen. VIII] globose, but towards the end of this reign rose to an edge down the centre called the tapul—a revival of an old fashion. **1869** BOUTELL *Arms & Arm.* ix. (1874) 155 A ridge (in England called the *tapul*) which divides the breast-plate and cuirass into two compartments, and is carried out to a point..over the middle of the body. **1870** C. C. BLACK tr. *Demmin's Weapons of War* 226. **1896** E. J. BRETT *Anc. Arms & Armour* Plate I. **1909** ASHDOWN *Arms & Armour* 283.

**Tap-waze**, etc.: see TAP-HOSE.

† **Tapyn**, obs. f. TAPON, TAMPION plug.

**14..** *Voc.* in Wr.-Wülcker 569/40 *Calopodium*, a tapyn.

**Taqua-nut**, (erron.) var. of TAGUA-*nut*.

*a* **1864** S. F. BAIRD in WEBSTER. Hence in mod. Dicts.

**Tar** (tāɹ), *sb.* Forms: *α.* 1 **teru, teoru** (-o), (-**tearo**); 3–5 (6– *Sc.*) **ter**, 4 (*Sc.* 4–) **terr**, 4–6 **terre**, 4–5 **teer**, (5 **tere**). *β.* 4–7 **tarre**, 4–8 **tarr**, 5 **taar**, 6– **tar**. *γ.* 1 **tyrwe**, 2 **tirwe.** [OE. *teru* (gen. *terw-es*), *teoru* (-o):—**terwo-* neut. = MLG. *ter, tere*, LG. and (thence) mod.Ger. *teer*, Du. *teer*; also ON. *tjara* fem. (Norw. *tjøra*, Sw. *tjära*, Da. *tjære*). OE. had also the deriv. form **tierwe, tyrwe*:—**terwjōn*. Generally considered to be a deriv. of OTeut. **trewo-*, Goth. *triu*, OE. *treow* tree (Indo-Eur. *derw-*: *dorw-*: *dru-*): cf. Lith. *darvà* pine-wood, Lett. *darwa* tar, ON. *tyr-viðr* pine-wood. Thus *terwo* may have meant orig. 'the product (pitch) of certain kinds of trees'.]

**1.** A thick, viscid, black or dark-coloured, inflammable liquid, obtained by the destructive distillation of wood (esp. pine, fir, or larch), coal, or other organic substance; chemically, a mixture of hydrocarbons with resins, alcohols, and other compounds, having a heavy resinous or bituminous odour, and powerful antiseptic properties; it is much used for coating and preserving timber, cordage, etc. See also COAL-TAR.

In some early quots. used for BITUMEN: cf. 2.

*α.* *a* **700** *Epinal Gloss.* 677 (Sweet *O.E.T.*) *Napta*, blaecteru. *Ibid.* 858 *Resina*, teru. *c* **725** *Corpus Gloss.* 1360 *Napta*, blaec-teoru. *Ibid.* 1716 *Resina*, teoru. *c* **1000** *Sax. Leechd.* II. 76 Meng wiþ sote, sealt, teoro, hunig, eald sape, smire mid. *c* **1050** *Voc.* in Wr.-Wülcker 412/6 *Gluten*, lim, oððe tero. *c* **1250** *Gen. & Ex.* 662 To maken a tur, wel heȝ & strong, Of tiȝel and ter, for water-gong. *a* **1300** *Cursor M.* 11899 Þai..drund him in pike and terr. **1436** *Libel Eng. Policy* in *Pol. Poems* (Rolls) II. 171 Peltre-ware, and grey pych, terre, borde and flex. **1483** *Cath. Angl.* 380/2 Ter, *bitumen.* **1508** KENNEDIE *Flyting w. Dunbar* 335 Thou salbe brynt, With pik, fyre, ter, gun puldre, or lint. **1522** MORE *De Quat. Noviss.* Wks. 74/1 Thei had leuer eate terre than tryacle. **1720** in *Jrnl. Derbysh. Archæol. Soc.* (1905) XXVII. 215 Ter and oile.

*β.* **1355–6** *Abingdon Rolls* (Camden) 9 In tarr et rubea petra xx d. *c* **1440** *Pallad. on Husb.* XII. 239 Rubrike and taar [L. *pix liquida*] wormys & auntis sleth. ? *a* **1500** *Chester Pl.* vii. 33 Heare is tarr in a pot. **1555** PHILPOT in Foxe *A. & M.* (1583) 1835/1 He that toucheth tarre, can not but be defiled therby. **1610** SHAKS. *Temp.* II. ii. 54 She lou'd not the sauour of Tar nor of Pitch. **1681** *Patent Specif.* (1856) No. 214. 1 A new way of makeing pitch and tarre out of pit coal. **1813** DAVY *Agric. Chem.* iii. (1814) 98 Tar and pitch principally consist of resin in a partially decomposed state. **1872** OLIVER *Elem. Bot.* II. 247 Tar is distilled from faggots of Pine, chiefly Scotch Fir, in the North of Europe.

*γ.* *c* **1000** ÆLFRIC *Hom.* I. 20 ȝeclæm ealle þa seamas mid tyrwan. *a* **1175** *Cott. Hom.* 225 Iclem hall þe seames mid tirwan.

**b.** Proverb. *To lose the sheep* (dial. *ship*) *for a ha'p'orth of tar*: see HALFPENNYWORTH b.

**c.** *fig.* in reference to extraction from a negro or dark-coloured ancestry: cf. TAR-BRUSH b.

**1897** ANNE PAGE *Afternoon Ride* 68 There was a touch of tar in this buxom dame.

**2.** Applied, with distinctive epithets, to natural substances resembling tar, as petroleum or bitumen: see quots. 1796, 1875, and MINERAL *a.* 5.

**1747** WESLEY *Prim. Physick* (1762) 37 Half a teaspoonful of Barbadoes Tar. **1796** MORSE *Amer. Geog.* I. 558 A spring, on the top of which floats an oil, similar to that called Barbadoes tar. **1875** *Ure's Dict. Arts* III. 397 In a great number of places..a more or less fluid inflammable matter exudes. It is known as Persian naphtha, Petroleum, Rock-oil, Rangoon tar, Burmese naphtha, &c.

**3.** A familiar appellation for a sailor: perh. abbreviation of TARPAULIN. Cf. JACK-TAR.

**1676** WYCHERLEY *Pl. Dealer* II. i, *Nov.* Dear tar, thy humble servant. **1695** CONGREVE *Love for L.* IV. xiv, You would have seen the Resolution of a Lover,—Honest Tarr and I are parted. **1706** SWIFT *To Peterborough* xi, Fierce in war, A land-commander, and a tar. **1709** STEELE *Tatler* No. 31 ⁋ 2 A Boatswain of an East-India Man..like a true Tar of Honour. **1820** SCORESBY *Acc. Arctic Reg.* I. 514 The chief mate..a resolute and noble tar. **1862** BARING-GOULD *Iceland* (1863) 179 The jolly tars seize the horses and ride them helter skelter up hill and down dale.

**4.** *attrib.* and *Comb.* **a.** *attrib.* Made of, from, or with tar; consisting of, containing, or derived from tar: as *tar-baby, -ball, -bath, -creosote, derivative, -dye, -lotion, -mark, -oil, -ointment, -pill, -plaster, product, -salve, -soap, -spring, -tincture, -vapour, -varnish, -wash*; covered or impregnated with tar, as *tar-bandage, -cloth, -cord, -neckcloth, -paper, -paving*; used for holding, or in making, tar, as *tar-boiler*, † *-boist* (= TAR-BOX 1), *-bucket, -can, -copper, -funnel, -horn, -kettle, -pit*, † *-pough*, † *-stoup, -trough, -tub* (in quot. *fig.*). **b.** objective, instrumental, etc., as *tar-burning*; *tar-bind, -brand, -paint* vbs., *tar-bedaubed, -clotted, -laid, -painted, -paved, -roofed, -scented, -soaked* adjs., *tar-spraying, -sprinkling*; *tar-like* adj. **c.** Special Combs.: **tar acne**, *Path.*, an inflammatory disease of the skin produced by rubbing with tar, etc.; **tar-beer**, a mixture of tar and beer, used medicinally (cf. TAR-WATER 1); **tar-board**, see quot.; 'a building-paper saturated with tar' (*Cent. Dict.*); † **tar-breech** *a.*, wearing tarry breeches: epithet for a sailor (cf. *tarry-breeks*); **tar-kiln**, a covered heap of wood or coal from which tar is obtained by burning; **tar-lamp**, a lamp in which tar is used as the illuminant (Knight *Dict. Mech.* 1877); **tar-lubber**, contemptuous name for a sailor (cf. 3); **tar-marl, -marline** (*dial.*), tarred twine used in thatching; † **tar-pitch** (*terpiche*) = sense 1; **tar-pot**, (*a*) a pot containing tar; (*b*) humorously applied to a sailor (cf. 3); **tar-putty**, a viscid substance made by mixing tar and lamp-black; **tar-weed**, *U.S.*, name for plants of the genera *Madia, Hemizonia*, and *Grindelia*, from their viscidity and heavy scent; **tar-well**, a receptacle in gas-works for collecting the tarry liquid which separates from the gas; **tar-wood**, resinous wood from which tar is obtained; **tar-work, -s**, a place for making tar; **tar-worker**, a workman employed in making tar; **tar-yard**, a yard in which tar is made. See also TAR-BARREL, -BOX, -BRUSH, etc.

**1899** *Allbutt's Syst. Med.* VIII. 918 A form of eruption very similar to this occurs in workers in creasote and tar—'tar acne'. **1881** J. C. HARRIS *Uncle Remus* ii. 20 Brer Fox ..got 'im some tar, en mix it wid some turkentime, en fix up a contrapshun what he call a *Tar-Baby. **1735** BRACKEN in Burdon *Pocket Farriery* 39 *note*, There is a Ball under the name of *Tar Ball. **1891** *Cent. Dict.*, *Tar bandage*, an antiseptic bandage made by saturating a roller bandage, after application, with a mixture of 1 part of olive oil and 20 parts of tar. **1899** *Allbutt's Syst. Med.* VIII. 605 A *tar bath..has not only an anti-pruritic but also a curative action. **1906** *Daily Chron.* 31 Aug. 3/2 In his patched and very much *tar-bedaubed punt. **1857** DUNGLISON *Med. Lex.* s.v. *Pinus sylvestris*, Tar water..is employed chiefly in pulmonary affections...A wine or beer of tar, *Tarbeer, Jews' beer, has been employed in Philadelphia in similar cases. **1909** *Westm. Gaz.* 30 Aug. 2/1 There are two distinct methods of *tar-binding the surface of our roads. **1877** KNIGHT *Dict. Mech.*, *Tar-board*, a strong quality of millboard made from junk and old tarred rope. ? *a* **1500** *Chester Pl.* vii. 78 With *Tarboyst most bene all tamed, Penigras, and butter for fat sheepe. **1890** 'R. BOLDREWOOD' *Col. Reformer* (1891) 120 Flock..to be counted, or drafted, or shifted, or *tar-branded. **1582** STANYHURST *Æneis* IV. (Arb.) 108 A runnagat hedgebrat, A *tarbreeche quystroune dyd I take. **1864** CARLYLE *Fredk. Gt.* XV. i. (1873) V. 270 Mankind.. took to..*tar-burning and *te-deum*-ing on an extensive scale.

1888 J. Shallow *Templars' Trials* xi. 24 He approached..as cautiously as a boy with a *tar can does a wasp's nest. 1899 T. Hardy in *Academy* 18 Nov. 599/1 Great guns were gleaming there—Cloaked in their *tar-cloths. 1900 H. G. Graham *Soc. Life Scotl. 18th C.* xv. (1901) 513 Thin, short *tar-clotted fleeces of the sheep. 1768 *Chron.* in *Ann. Reg.* 113/2 A fire broke out in a tar-yard..by the *tar-copper boiling over. 1879 Jefferies *Wild Life in S. C.* 47 A couple of flakes fastened together with *tar-cord. 1868 *Q. Rev.* Apr. 346 A very singular product called *tar-creosote or carbolic acid. 1896 *Allbutt's Syst. Med.* V. 45 Among the *tar derivatives [may be specially mentioned] creosote and guaiacol. 1894 *Westm. Gaz.* 8 Mar. 3/3 The stockings.. are dyed with *tar-dyes, which are perfectly harmless. 1573 Tusser *Husb.* (1878) 38 A sheepe marke, a *tar kettle. 1755 *Gentl. Mag.* XXV. 551/1 A sufficient crop of these old knots (which are full of rosin) for the *tar-kilns. 1856 Kane *Arct. Expl.* II. i. 26 We have been using up our *tar-laid hemp hawsers. 1683 Robinson in *Ray's Corr.* (1848) 137, I have observed the inhabitants of Languedoc get a *tar-like substance out of the Juniperus. 1899 *Allbutt's Syst. Med.* VIII. 521 The use of tar soaps, followed by *tar lotions, is sometimes more efficacious. 1610 Healey *St. Aug. Citie of God* 707 Another *Tarre-lubber bragges that hee is a souldiour. 1844 Stephens *Bk. Farm* III. 1282 The letter P..on the rump to shew the *tar-mark of the farm on which..it had been bred. 1863 *Stamford Mercury* 27 Sept., He got some *tar-marline and tied the horse's mouth. 1713 Steele *Englishman* No. 47. 303, I stood by just now, when a Fellow came in here with a *Tar Neckcloth. 1891 *Cent. Dict.*, **Tar-oil*, a volatile oil obtained by distilling tar. 1895 *Outing* (U.S.) XXVI. 365/1 The little black bottle of tar-oil. 1906 *Westm. Gaz.* 13 Sept. 10/2 The cost of *tar-painting a road eight yards wide averages about £60 a mile. 1907 *Putnam's Monthly* July 482/1 A whole house covered with *tar paper and studded with brass tacks sat complacently upon a hay wagon. 1883 *Proc. Assoc. Munic. Engin.* X. 53 The tar macadam roadways and *tar paved footways.. I found in good.. order. 1808 *Med. Jrnl.* XIX. 225 *Tar pills made up with magnesia were also administered. 1839 Ure *Dict. Arts* 963 A considerable quantity is distilled over into the *tar-pit. a 1387 *Sinon. Barthol.* (Anecd. Oxon.) 34 *Pix liquida*,..*terpiche. 1899 *Allbutt's Syst. Med.* VIII. 582 A *tar plaster is better than one of chrysarobin. 1573 Tusser *Husb.* (1878) 30 With tar in a *tarpot. 1641 Best *Farm. Bks.* (Surtees) 23 One of the girles is to keepe fire under the tarr-potte. 1903 F. T. Bullen in *Daily Chron.* 8 June 3/3 Like many other old tar-pots, I have been intensely annoyed and disgusted by the so-called 'real' sea-books put forward. c 1394 *P. Pl. Crede* 618 Þei may trussen her part in a *terre powȝe! 1903 *Westm. Gaz.* 16 Sept. 2/1 The value of the annual output of *tar products is over ten millions. 1888 *Engineer* LXVI. 521 '*Tar-putty'..a viscous mixture of tar and well calcined lampblack. 1896 Howells *Impressions & Exp.* 282 A *tar-roofed shanty. 1844 Stephens *Bk. Farm* III. 1118 Applying *tar-salve to sheep. 1892 *Pall Mall G.* 22 Sept. 14/2 The *tar-soaked logs burn with a peculiar brilliance. 1899 *Allbutt's Syst. Med.* VIII. 584 To take frequent baths with *tar soap. 1909 *Westm. Gaz.* 30 Aug. 2/1 Roads..treated by the cheaper method of *tar-spraying them on the surface. 1775 R. Chandler *Trav. Greece* (1825) II. 367 The *tar-springs of Zante are a natural curiosity deserving notice. 1899 *Allbutt's Syst. Med.* VIII. 605 To paint the skin with a strong *tar tincture. 1534 *Acc. Ld. High Treas. Scotl.* VI. 235 For the lane of ane *tar troch, viij d. 1697 tr. *C'tess D'Aunoy's Wks.* (1715) 375 He ran to his nasty *Tar-tub of a Mistress. 1805 Dickson *Pract. Agric.* I. 48 The outside.. properly payed over with pitch or *tar-varnish. 1898 J. Hutchinson in *Arch. Surg.* IX. No. 36. 373, I prescribed a *tar wash and it suited admirably. 1884 Miller *Plant-n.*, *Tar-weed, Californian, the genera *Madia* and *Hemizonia*. 1909 *Daily Chron.* 8 Mar. 4/6 The unjustly named 'tar-weed'..scattered over great tracts of wild country..California smells of it, and smells very pleasantly. 1857 Miller *Elem. Chem.* III. 558 The tar, as it accumulates..flows over into the *tar wells. 1856 Emerson *Eng. Traits* iv. 65 King Hake..sets fire to some *tar-wood. 1791 *Trans. Soc. Arts* IX. 132 The iron-masters furnish the *Tar-works with coal. 1906 *Westm. Gaz.* 10 Aug. 10/2 The average life of *tar-workers is eighty-six. 1768 *Tar-yard [see *tar-copper* above].

**Tar** (tāɹ), *v.*[1] Pa. t. and pple. **tarred** (tāɹd). Forms: 1 **tierwian, tyrwian**; 3–5 **terren**, 4 **tere**; 5–7 **tarre**, 6–8 **tarr**, 6– **tar**. [f. OE. *teoru, teorw-*, Tar *sb.*]

*trans.* To smear or cover with tar. Also *absol.*

[a 1000 *Beowulf* 295 Niw tyrwydne [=new-tarred] nacan on sande arum healdan.] c 1250 *Gen. & Ex.* 2596 In an fetles of riȝesses wroȝt, Terred ðat water dered it noȝt, Ðis child wunden ȝhe wulde don. c 1300 *Havelok* 707 Hise ship..He dede it tere, an ful wel pike. c 1440 *Promp. Parv.* 489/2 Terryn, wythe terre, *colofoniso*. 1495 *Naval Acc. Hen. VII* (1896) 214 Hawsers olde & ffeble Tarred—iij; New Hawsers nott tarred—j. 1600 Shaks. *A. Y. L.* iii. ii. 63 Our hands..are often tarr'd ouer, with the surgery of our sheepe. 1689 *Lond. Gaz.* No. 2483/3 They had Tarr'd the Bridge, and laid Combustible Stuff in order to burn it. 1783 M. Cutler in *Life*, etc. (1888) I. 94 Tarred apple-trees to keep the millers from going up. 1840 Longf. in *Life* (1891) I. 361 The canker-worms have begun their journey up the trees, and to-morrow I shall tar. 1884 *Act* 47 & 48 *Vict.* c. 76 § 5 A person shall not, without due authority,.. paint or tar any post office,..telegraph post, or other property.

**b.** To smear (a person's body) over with tar; esp. in phr. *to tar and feather*, to smear with tar and then cover with feathers: a punishment sometimes inflicted by a mob (esp. in U.S.) on an unpopular or scandalous character.

(The practice was imposed by an ordinance of Richard I in 1189 as a punishment in the navy for theft: see Rymer *Foedera* (1704) I. 65/2, Hakluyt *Voy.* (1599) II. 21, Holinshed *Chron.* (1807) II. 213; in Howell's *Fam. Lett.* (1650, I. iii. xxvii. 81) it is said to have been applied in 1623 by a bishop of Halverstade to a party of incontinent friars and nuns; but in neither case is the specific term used.)

1774 J. Adams in *Fam. Lett.* (1876) 12 Pote..railed away at Boston mobs, drowning tea, and tarring Malcom. 1774 T. Hutchinson *Diary* 1 July, K[ing George III].—I see they threatened to pitch and feather you. H[utchinson].—Tarr and feather, may it please your Majesty. 1774 Burke *Amer. Tax.* Wks. II. 374 You must send the ministers tarred and feathered to America. 1774 *Chron.* in *Ann. Reg.* 127/2 Mr. John Malcomb, an officer of the customs at Boston, who was tarred and feathered, and led to the gallows with a rope about his neck. 1784 Dk. Rutland *Corr. w. Pitt* (1890) 37 Persons are daily marked out for the operation of tarring and feathering. 1846 Hare *Mission Comf.* ii. (1876) 61 [We] tar and feather our feelings with the dust and dirt of earth. 1850 N. Hawthorne in Bridge *Pers. Recoll.* (1893) 114 If I escape from town without being tarred and feathered, I shall consider it good-luck.

**c.** *fig.* To dirty or defile as with tar; esp. in phr. *tarred with the same stick* (or *brush*), stained with the same or similar faults or obnoxious qualities. (In quot. a 1612, ?to darken, obscure; in quot. 1622 in allusion to the protective and curative use of tar by shepherds, etc.)

a 1612 Harington *Epigr.* (1633) i. lxviii, To purge the vapours that our cleare sight tarres. 1622 Fletcher & Massinger *Span. Curate* iii. ii, I have nointed ye, and tarr'd ye with my doctrine, And yet the murren sticks to ye. 1818 Scott *Rob Roy* xxvi, They are a' tarr'd wi' the same stick—rank Jacobites and Papists. 1823 Cobbett *Rural Rides* (1885) I. 283 'You are all tarred with the same brush', said the sensible people of Maidstone. 1860 Reade *Cloister & H.* xl, Now this Gerard is tarred with the same stick. 1881 W. E. Forster in Reid *Life* (1888) II. viii. 368 My replacement by some one not tarred by the coercion brush.

**Tar**, † **tarre**, *v.*[2] *Obs.* or *arch.* Forms: α. 1 tyrw(i)an, 5 terw-yn; 4–5 terre(n, 4 ter, 4– Sc. terr. β. 4–7 tarre, 5– tar. [ME. *terren*, app. representing OE. *tęrw(i)an (*tięrw-, tyrw-), collateral form of *tęrgan* (*tięrg-, tyrg-*) to vex, irritate, provoke. For the phonology cf. Tar *v.*[1] See also Tary *v.*

OE. *tęrgan* (WSax. *tięrg-, *tyrgan*), *tęrw(i)an (*tięrw-, *tyrw(i)an*) = OLG. **tęrgan*, MLG. *tergen, targen*, LG. and EFris. *targen*, Da. *tærge*, MDu., Du. *tergen*, to provoke, irritate, exasperate, vex, tease (Kilian, '*terghen* irritare, lacessere, infestare, vexare, provocare ad iram, exacerbare'), mod. Ger. *zergen*; pointing to an OTeut. **targjan*. The phonology of the OE. by-form *tęrw(i)an* has not been satisfactorily explained. Relationship to Russian *dergat'* 'to pluck, pull, tweak' has been suggested.]

**1.** *trans.* To irritate, vex, provoke. Now only in *tar on* (Shaks. *tarre on*), to incite, hound on.

α. *Guthlac* 259 (288) Beoð þa ȝebolȝne þa þec breodwiað, tredað þec and terȝað and hyra torn wrecað. a 900 *Kentish Gl.* 508 Tirhþ, *inridet*. 10.. *Lambeth Ps.* lxxiii. 10 Usque quo deus improperabit inimicus: *gl.* hu longe tyrweþ fynd. *Ibid.* lxxvii. 8 Generatio praua et exasperans: *gl.* þweor mæȝþ & tyrwiende *vel* þurhbitter. *Ibid.* 40 Quotiens exacerbaverunt eum: *gl.* hu ȝelome hiȝ tyrwedon hine. *Ibid.* 41 Hiȝ tyrwadon *vel* gremedon. *Ibid.* 55 Hiȝ costnadon & tyrwodan god þane healican.

c 1380 Wyclif *Serm.* Sel. Wks. II. 44 To terre [*v.r.* ter] men for to fiȝte. 1382 — *Deut.* iv. 25 That ȝe terren [*v.r.* *MSS.* a 1400 tarre] hym to wraþþe. — *Eph.* vi. 4 ȝe fadris, nyle ȝe terre ȝoure sones to wraþþe. 1387 Trevisa *Higden* (Rolls) V. 355 Þe kynges..sone..gan to tarry [*v. r.* terre] and to angre [*probrosis verbis lacessivit*] þe Longobardes. 1395 Purvey *Remonstr.* (1851) 18 Thei blasfemen God and terren him to wraththe.

β. a 1400 Tarre [see quot. 1382 above]. 1561 in *Three 15th Cent. Chron.* (Camden) 119 They came unto me rounde aboute my chamber,..stearde me, and tarde me, and so vexed me as I was never in all my lyffe so soore troubled. 1595 Shaks. *John* iv. i. 117 And, like a dogge,..Snatch at his Master that doth tarre him on. 1602 — *Ham.* ii. ii. 370 The Nation holds it no sinne, to tarre them to Controuersie. 1606 — *Tr. & Cr.* i. iii. 392 Pride alone Must tarre the Mastiffes on, as 'twere their bone. 1837 Carlyle *Fr. Rev.* I. ii. ii, The cries, the squealings of children,..and other assistants, tarring them on, as the rabble does when dogs fight. 1859 Kingsley *Misc.* II. v. 225 The selfishness of the memorialists led them to tar on the rival selfishness of the water companies.

† **2.** To weary, fatigue. *Obs. rare.*

[Known only in form *terw-yn*. The sense in *Promp. Parv.* corresponds rather to the trans. use of OE. *téorian* to tire, but was possibly an offshoot from that of 'vex, harass'. The same sense-development appears also in the cognate Tary *v.* 2.]

c 1440 *Promp. Parv.* 489/2 Terwyn, or make wery or weryyn, *lasso, fatigo*. Terwyd, *lassatus, fatigatus*. Terwynge, *lassitudo, fatigacio*. *Ibid.* 522/2 Weryyn, or make wery or terwyn, *fatigo, lasso*.

† **3.** *intr.* *Tar and tig, tig and tar*, to act forcefully or wantonly; to use force and violence. *Sc.*

c 1470 Henryson *Mor. Fab.* v. (*Parl. Beasts*) i, [The fox] That luifit weill with pultrie to tig and tar [*Bann. MS.* tere]. a 1568 Balnaves in *Bannatyne Poems* (Hunter. Cl.) 391 To tar and tig, syne grace to thig, That is ane petouss preiss. *Ibid.* 392 To tig and tar, syne get the war, It is evill merchandyiss.

Hence † **Tarring** (**terring**) *vbl. sb.*, provocation.

1382 Wyclif 2 *Kings* xxiii. 26 The Lord is not turned aweye fro the wrath of his grete woodnes..for the terryngis in the whiche Manasses hadde terred hym. — *Ps.* xciv. 9 As in the terring [1388 the terryng to wroþþe], after the day of tempting in desert.

**Tar**, obs. f. *tare, tore*, pa. t. of Tear *v.*[1]

‖ **Tara** (tā·rä), *sb.* [? Native name in Tasmania.] The edible fern of Tasmania and New Zealand, a variety of the common brake, *Pteris aquilina* var. *esculenta*. Also *tara fern*.

1834 Ross *Van Diemen's Land Ann.* 129 (Morris *Austral Eng.*) The most extensively diffused eatable roots..are those of the tara fern..[which] greatly resembles *Pteris aquilina*, the common fern, brake,..or brackin, of England, ..it is known among the aborigines by the name of tara.

**Tara**, *int.* An exclamation. (Cf. F. *tarare*; also Taratantara.)

In quot., it occurs in a passage burlesquing a scene in Dryden's *Tyrannic Love* iv. i.

1672 Villiers (Dk. Buckhm.) *Rehearsal* v. i. (Arb.) 113, 1 *King*. Tara, tara, tara, full East and by South. 2 *King*. We sail with Thunder in our mouth.

**Taradiddle, tarradiddle** (tæ:rădi·d'l; *main stress shifting*), *sb. slang* or *colloq.* Also 9 **tarri-, tally-**. [cf. Diddle *v.*[3] 2, *sb.*[2]: the first element is obscure: cf. prec.] A trifling falsehood, a petty lie; a colloquial euphemism for a lie; a 'fib'.

1796 Grose *Dict. Vulg. Tongue* (ed. 3), *Taradiddle*, a fib, or falsity. 1844 J. T. Hewlett *Parsons & W.* xliv, Telling a tarradiddle or two. 1865 Mrs. Gaskell *Wives & Dau.* xlvii, Oh, don't call them lies, sister; it's such a strong, ugly word. Please call them tallydiddles, for I don't believe she meant any harm. 1882 J. Payn *Thicker than Water* i, Our widow paid..the compliment of telling a 'tarradiddle' or white lie. 1885 Huxley *Let.* 23 Feb. in *Life* (1900) II. 97 Everybody told us it would be very cold, and, as usual, everybody told taradiddles.

**Ta·radi·ddle, tarradiddle**, *v. slang* or *colloq.* [f. prec.] **a.** *intr.* To tell taradiddles or fibs. **b.** *trans.* To impose upon, or bring into some condition, by telling fibs. Hence **Ta·radi·ddler**, one who taradiddles, a petty liar.

1828 *Examiner* 658/1 His enemies..squibbed, and paragraphed, and taradiddled him to death. 1847–78 Halliwell, *Tarra-diddled*, imposed upon, generally by lies. 1880 *Society* 29 Oct., Perhaps there is not a more facile..taradiddler than the London correspondent of the provincial newspaper. 1909 *Athenæum* 6 Mar. 281/1 A barefaced tarradiddler or a prophet.

† **Ta·rage**, *sb.*[1] *Obs.* Also 5 **tarrage**: see also the collateral form Tallage *sb.*[2] [app. of F. origin; etymology unascertained.] Taste, flavour; quality, character; esp. as derived or communicated.

c 1407 Lydg. *Reson & Sens.* 3943 Swich is the tarage of the roote, Somtyme as any sugre soote And bitter sodeynly as galle. 1429 *Pol. Poems* (Rolls) II. 141 Of all these thy grene tender age,..Of manly prowesse shal taken tarage. c 1430 Lydg. *Min. Poems* (Percy Soc.) 180 Ner the vyne his holsome fressh tarage, Whiche yeveth comforte to al maner age. *Ibid.* 192 Thus every thing,..As frute and trees, and folke of every degré, Fro whens they come thei take a tarage. c 1450 Lydg. & Burgh *Secrees* 1886 Watrys that renne be many diuers londys,..Which tarage haue of foreyn dyvers sondys. 14.. *Epiphanye* in *Tundale's Vis.* 119 Thys day he turned water into wyne..of tarage [*MS. Soc. Antiq.* 134 lf. 26 talage] inly gud and fyne.

† **Tarage**, *sb.*[2] *Obs.* [app. variant form of Terrage.] ? A ground in artistic representation.

1439 in *Archæologia* XXI. 37 An Image of Seynt George beyng upon a grene tarage, wᵗ a damasell knelyng. c 1468 *Ibid.* XXXI. 336 On every tarage a tree of gold.

† **Ta·rage**, *v. Obs.* [f. Tarage *sb.*[1]] To have a character or quality *of* some kind, to 'taste of', 'smell of' (*intr.* and *trans.*). So † **Ta·raged** *a.*, having a (specified) quality or character.

c 1407 Lydg. *Reson & Sens.* 3378 Hyr tayl ys werray serpentyne, And hir bely eke Capryne,..whan she is hoot, Rammysh taraged as a goot. c 1430 — *Min. Poems* (Percy Soc.) 217 Frut fet fro fer tarageth of the tre. 1430–40 — *Bochas* iv. xv. (MS. Bodl. 263) lf. 243/2 How man and beeste & euery creature Tarageth the stok of his natynite. *Ibid.* viii. xxiv. lf. 402/1 Eche werm sume parti taragethe of his brood.

† **Taragmite** (tăræ·gməit). *a. Geol. Obs. rare.* [f. Gr. τάραγμα disturbance, f. ταράσσειν to disturb + -ite[1].] (See quots., and cf. Phanerite.)

a 1857 J. Fleming *Lithol. Edinb.* v. (1859) 50 The first or Taragmite series, have been formed subsequently to the dressings, and, where present, repose upon them. 1859 Page *Geol. Terms*, *Taragmite Series*..a term employed by Dr. Fleming in his 'Lithology of Edinburgh' to embrace the Boulder Clay, or lowest stage of the modern epoch, as 'having been formed when violent aqueous movements were taking place, and probably at a period when the state of our island was widely different from the present'.

**Taragon**, var. of Tarragon.

‖ **Tarairi** (tărai·ri). Also **taraire**. [Maori name.] A timber tree of New Zealand, *Beilschmiedia Tarairi*, N.O. *Lauraceæ*: see quots.

1873 *Catal. Vienna Exhib.* (Morris), Tarairi. Used for most of the purposes for which sycamore is applied in Europe. 1883 J. Hector *Handbk. N. Zealand* (1886) 106 Tarairi. A lofty forest tree, 60 ft. to 80 ft. high, with stout branches. Wood white, splits freely, but not much valued.

‖ **Taran** (tā·răn). *Sc.* [Gael. *taran*.] The ghost of an unbaptized child.

1775 L. Shaw *Hist. Moray* vi. iv. 307 It was likewise believed..that Children dying unbaptized (called *Tarans*) wandered in woods and solitudes, lamenting their hard fate, and were often seen. 1776 Pennant *Tour Scotl. in 1772* II. Addit. 13. 1813 Ellis *Brand's Pop. Antiq.* (1849) II. 73.

† **Ta·rand, tara·ndre.** *Obs.* Also **tarandule**, and in L. forms **tarandus, -andrus**. [a. F. *tarande*, obs. *tarandre*, ad. med.L. *tarand-us*, L. *tarandr-us* (Pliny), name of a northern beast, supposed to be the reindeer.] A name given to some northern quadruped, at length identified with the reindeer.

1572 Bossewell *Armorie* ii. 57 The fielde is of the Topaze, a Tarandre tripping, Rubye, unguled Diamonde. Tarandrus is a beaste in bodye like a great Oxe, hauing an head like to an harte, and hornes full of branches. *Ibid.* iii. 22 b, The Tarandule is a beaste commonly called a Buffe, which is like an Oxe, but that he hath a bearde like a Goate. 1613 Purchas *Pilgrimage* (1614) 559 The Tarandus is a Beast somewhat resembling an Oxe. in quantitie, a Hart in shape. 1753 CHAMBERS *Cycl. Supp.*, *Tarandus*, in zoology, a name given by Agricola and some other authors, to the rein-deer.

**b.** Said to have, like the chameleon, the power to 'change himselfe into the thing he toucheth or leaneth vnto' (Florio); so Rabelais IV. ii. Also *fig.*

It is not certain that *tarand* (applied scurrilously to Christ) in quot. *c* 1440, is the same word.

*c* 1440 *York Myst.* xxxiii. 381 (*iii Miles*) All þin vntrew techyngis þus taste I, þou tarand. 1642 R. CARPENTER *Experience* II. xi. 218 Like the Tarrand, which walking in a Garden, represents the colour of every flower on his skin. 1694 MOTTEUX *Rabelais* IV. ii. 1. 1702 *Eng. Theophrast.* 363 As the tarand changes its colour with every plant that it approaches so the wise man adapts himself to the several humours and inclinations of those he converses with.

**Ta·rantant.** *rare.* [See -ANT.] = TARANTATO.

1883 *Chamb. Jrnl.* 1 Dec. 761/1 When the tarantant had by this means recovered, he or she remained free from the disease until the approach of the warm weather in the next year.

**Tarantara**: see TARATANTARA.

‖ **Tarantass** (tarantɑ·s). Also **-as.** [ad. Russ. тарантасъ, *tarantas*ʺ.] A four-wheeled Russian travelling-carriage without springs, on a long flexible wooden chassis.

1850 (*title*) The Tarantas, travelling impressions of Young Russia, by Count Sollogub. 1876 BURNABY *Khiva* xxxvi. 342 The tarantass..resembled a hansom cab without the wheels, ..fastened in a brewer's dray. 1882 H. LANDELL *Through Siberia* I. 135 A roofless, seatless, springless, semi-cylindrical tumbril, mounted on poles which connect two wooden axle-trees..called by the general name of *tarantass*.

‖ **Tarantato** (tarantā·to). *rare.* Pl. **-ati** (-ā·ti). Also fem. **taranta·ta**, *pl.* **-ate.** [It. *taranta·to* 'bitten with a tarantula' (Florio), affected with tarantism, f. *Taranto* name of the town: see -ISM.] One who has been bitten by a tarantula; one suffering from tarantism.

1685 BOYLE *Effects of Mot.* vi. 76 Narratives of the effects of Music upon the *Tarantati*. 1717 BERKELEY *Tour Italy* Wks. 1871 IV. 544 The tarantato that we saw dancing in a circle paced round the room. *Ibid.* 545 None danced but the tarantata. Her father certainly [was] persuaded that she had her disorder from the tarantula.

‖ **Tarantella** (tærănte·lă). Also 9 **tarent-**, and from F., **tarent-, tarantelle.** [It. *tarantella* (in F. *tarentelle*, Sp. *tarantela*), dim. formation from *Taranto* the town of *Tarentum* in southern Italy. Popularly associated with *tarantola, tarantula* the spider, also a deriv. of *Taranto*. (Etymologically, *tarantella* might be a further dim. of *tarantula*: cf. L. *fabula, tabula, fabella, tabella*.)] A rapid whirling South Italian dance popular with the peasantry since the fifteenth century, when it was supposed to be the sovereign remedy for tarantism.

1782 *Char.* in *Ann. Reg.* II. 11/2 The Tarantella is a low dance, consisting of turns on the heel, much footing and snapping of the fingers. 1844 DISRAELI *Coningsby* IV. xi, He could dance a Tarantalla like a Lazaroni. 1866 ENGEL *Nat. Mus.* vii. 259 According to popular belief, a person bitten by the venomous spider Tarantula can be recovered from the state of nervous disorder which the poison produces, only by dancing the Tarantella until complete exhaustion compels him to desist from the vehement exercise. 1894 *Times* 3 Mar. 11/2 While the plaintiff was dancing a tarantella with a tambourine her foot slipped, owing, as she alleged, to the negligent stretching of the carpet, or 'stage cloth'.

**b.** The music for such a dance, or composed in its rhythm, formerly quadruple, but now always in 6–8 time, with whirling triplets, and abrupt transitions from the major to the minor.

1833-5 BABINGTON tr. *Hecker's Epidemics* (1859) 113 The Italians..have retained the Tarantella, as a particular species of music employed for quick lively dancing. 1884 C. F. WOOLSON in *Harper's Mag.* Jan. 216/1 A gay Tarantella, which set all the house-maids dancing.

**Tarantism** (tæ·răntiz'm). Also 9 **tarent-**, and (in L. form) **tarant-, tarentismus.** [ad. mod.L. *tarantismus* = It. *tarantismo*, F. *tarentisme*, from It. *Taranto* name of the town (see prec.); but popularly associated with *tarantola* the tarantula spider, whence sometimes called *tarantulism*.] A hysterical malady, characterized by an extreme impulse to dance, which prevailed as an epidemic in Apulia and adjacent parts of Italy from the 15th to the 17th century, popularly attributed to the bite or 'sting' of the tarantula.

The dancing was sometimes held to be a symptom or consequence of the malady, sometimes practised as a sovereign cure for it.

1638-56 COWLEY *Davideis* I. Notes § 32 We should hardly be convinced of this Physick, unless it be in the particular cure of the Tarantism, the experiments of which are too notorious to be denyed or eluded. 1770 *Phil. Trans.* LX. 237 People ..get a little money, by dancing when they say the tarantism begins. *Ibid.*, In Sicily, where the summer is still warmer ..the Tarantula is never dangerous, and music is never employed for the cure of the pretended tarantism. 1822-34 *Good's Study Med.* (ed. 4) III. 338 This form of the disease appears to be a near relation to the tarantismus of Sauvages. 1833-5 BABINGTON tr. *Hecker's Epidemics* ii. (1859) 106 The origin of tarantism itself is referrible..to a period between the middle and the end of this century, and is consequently contemporaneous with that of the St. Vitus's dance (1374). 1883 *Chambers' Encycl.* IX. 296/2 *Tarantism* may be defined a leaping or dancing mania, originating in, or supposed to originate in, an animal poison... The gesticulations, contortions, and cries somewhat resembled those in St. Vitus's Dance, and other epidemic nervous diseases of the middle ages. 1883 *Chamb. Jrnl.* 1 Dec. 760/2 The earliest mention of *tarantismus* is found in the works of Nicolas Perotti, who died in 1480.

**Tarantula** (tăræ·ntiŭlă). Also 6 **tarentula,** 7 **-entola, tarantule.** [a. med.L. *tarantula* (*Onomast. Lat. Græc.*), It. *tarantola*, f. *Taranto* a town in modern Apulia, :—L. *Tarentum*, ad. Gr. Τάρας (Τάραντα). Cf. F. *tarentule* (16th c. in Littré; in OF. only *tarente*).]

**1.** A large wolf-spider of Southern Europe, *Lycosa tarantula* (formerly *Tarantula Apuliæ*), named from the town in the region where it is commonly found, whose bite is slightly poisonous, and was fabled to cause TARANTISM.

1561 T. HOBY tr. *Castiglione's Courtyer* I. (1577) C v b, Them that are bitten with a Tarrantula. [*margin*] A kind of spiders, which being diuers of nature cause diuers effectes, some after their biting fal a singing, some laugh [etc.]. 1584 LYLY *Sappho* IV. iii, I was stung with the flye Tarantula. 1592 GREENE *Philom.* (1615) G iij b, Such as are stung by the Tarentula, are best cured by Musicke. 1601 R. JOHNSON *Kingd. & Commw.* (1603) 113 In this countrey is bred the Tarantola, whose venom is expelled with the fire and musick. 1630 J. TAYLOR (Water P.) *Bawd* Wks. I ij/1 Saint Vitus or Vitellus,..an excellent patron or proctor to cure those that are bitten of a Spider called Tarrantulla, or Phallanx. 1658 J. ROWLAND *Moufet's Theat. Ins.* 1061 All those that are stung with the Tarantula, dance so well, as if they were taught to dance, and sing as well as if they were musically bred. 1711 *Let. to Sacheverel* 20 Such a Frenzy ran thro the Nation, as if they had been all bitten with Tarantulas. 1771 D. CIRILLO in *Ann. Reg.* 85/1 Several experiments have been tried with the Tarantula; and neither men nor animals, after the bite, have had any other complaint, but a very trifling inflammation upon the part. 1861 HULME tr. *Moquin-Tandon* II. v. ii. 263 The Common Tarantula..is about an inch in length... A number of fabulous tales, all of them equally absurd, have been related of the Tarantula.

**b.** Popularly applied to other noxious spiders, esp. to the great hairy spiders of the genus *Mygale*, natives of the warmer parts of America.

1794 MORSE *Amer. Geog.* 597 Scorpions and tarantulas are found here [Dutch Guiana] of a large size and great venom. 1834 PRINGLE *Afr. Sk.* ii. 142 The terror of snakes, scorpions, tarantulas, and other noxious creatures of the African clime. 1871 KINGSLEY *At Last* xvii, The chief engineer exhibited a live 'Tarantula', or bird-catching spider. 1893 KATE SANBORN *Truthf. Wom. S. California* 107 Tarantulas never come out at night...Mr. Wakely, who has caught more of these spiders than any living man, does not seem to dread the job in the least.

† **c.** By confusion, mistaken for or applied to some (supposed) venomous reptile: see quots. *Obs.*

[1598 FLORIO, *Tarantola*, a serpent called an eft or an euet, some take it to be a flye whose sting is..deadly, and nothing but diuers sounds of musicke can cure the patient. Also a fish so called.] 1615 G. SANDYS *Trav.* 249 Hereabout ..are great store of Tarantulas: a serpent peculiar to this countrey. 1616 BULLOKAR *Eng. Expos.*, *Tarantula*, a little beast like a Lizard, hauing spots in his necke like starres. 1753 CHAMBERS *Cycl. Supp.*, *Tarantula*, in zoology, a name given by the Italians to a peculiar species of lizard. [1896 *List Anim. Zool. Soc.* 577 *Tarentola mauritanica*.. Moorish Gecko.]

**2.** Contextually, The bite of the tarantula; hence, erroneously, = TARANTISM.

*a* 1586 SIDNEY *Arcadia* I. ix. (1590) 38 b, This word, Louer, did not lesse pearce poore Pyrocles, then the right tune of musicke toucheth him that is sick of the Tarantula. 1633 G. HERBERT *Temple, Dooms-day* ii, Peculiar notes and strains Cure Tarantulaes raging pains. 1651-3 JER. TAYLOR *Serm. for Year* I. xix. 250 He dies with a Tarantula, dancing and singing till he bowes his neck, and kisses his bosome with the fatall noddings and declensions of death. *fig.* 1828 *Lights & Shades* II. 278 My wife's tarantula is never cured, her fingers are never out of her harpsichord.

**3.** *fig.* from 1 and 2.

1608 MIDDLETON *Trick to Catch Old One* I. i, Hence, courtesan, round-webb'd tarantula. 1652 URQUHART *Jewel* Wks. (1834) 280 Stung with the tarantula of a preposterous ambition. 1666 R. WILDE *Poems* (1870) 103 May he resume King David's harp, and play The tarantule of discontent away. 1685 *Answ. Dk. Buckhm. on Lib. Consc.* 4 Stung with the Tarantula of his Paper, which may make me dance and caper. 1721 PRIOR *Dial. Dead* (1907) 268 You find others bit with the same Tarantula. 1837 CARLYLE *French Revolution* II. I. vi. (*Je le jure*), Saw the sun ever such a swearing people? Have they been bit by a swearing tarantula?

¶ **4.** Erroneously for TARANTELLA, the dance.

1698 FRYER *Acc. E. India & P.* 111 They labour as much as a Lancashire Man does at Roger of Coverly, or the Tarantula of their Hornpipe. 1865 *Daily Tel.* 14 Dec. 7/3 All the dances of the civilised world, from the tarantula to the *trois temps*.

**5.** *attrib.* and *Comb.*, as *tarantula bite, dance, dancer, spider, sting*, etc.; *tarantula-stung* adj.; **tarantula-hawk, -killer,** names in Texas for a kind of wasp, *Pepsis formosa.*

1647 HARINGTON in *Nugæ Ant.* (1779) II. 92 We grasp but airy blisses, and thus, tarantula-stung, dye amidst laughing fits. 1688 R. HOLME *Armoury* II. 215/2 The Tarantula Spider ..of Apulia..hath only six legs, and a stretched out tail. 1833-5 BABINGTON tr. *Hecker's Epidemics* ii. (1859) 110 The excitement which the Tarantula dancers felt at the sight of anything with metallic lustre. 1899 D. SHARP in *Camb. Nat. Hist.* VI. iii. 105 *P[epsis] formosus*, Say, is called in Texas the tarantula-killer; according to Buckley, its mode of attack on the huge spider is different from that made use of by its European ally. 1902 *Westm. Gaz.* 12 Aug. 10/1 In Orsuna [Spain]..there is a 'Guild of Tarantula-players'..who earn considerable fees by skipping round their members to heal the sufferers from the tarantula bite.

Hence **Tara·ntular, Tara·ntulary, Tara·ntulous** *adjs.*, of or pertaining to the tarantula (in quots. *fig.*); **Tara·ntulate** [cf. It. *tarantolato*], † **Tara·ntulize** *vbs.*, *trans.* to affect with tarantism; **Tara·ntulism** = TARANTISM.

1857 *Chamb. Jrnl.* VIII. 227/1 Seized with the *tarentular phrensy. 1781 E. POULTER *Peripatetics* 14 In Bath..Perpetual Dancing's our disorder here. Gronovius proves them, to the plainest sense, Under *Tarantulary influence. 1737 M. GREEN *Spleen* 146 Motions unwill'd its powers have shown *Tarantulated by a tune. 1774 'JOEL COLLIER' (Bicknell) *Mus. Trav.* 14, I drove away the evil spirit, and cured her of her *tarantulism that night. 1652 BENLOWES *Theoph.* III. lix. 44 In Saul, disguis'd When Satan oft *Tarantuliz'd, The Psalming Harp was 'bove thy swaying Scepter priz'd. 1895 *Lit. World* 23 Aug. 141/1 The reputation.. will survive the *tarantulous bites of envious detractors.

**Tarapin(e,** obs. form of TERRAPIN.

**Taras, -asse,** obs. forms of TERRACE.

‖ **Tarata** (tā·răta). [Maori.] Native name in New Zealand of a small evergreen tree (*Pittosporum eugenioides*), also called *lemon-wood*.

1876 W. N. BLAIR in *Trans. N. Zeal. Inst.* IX. 143. 1879 J. B. ARMSTRONG *ibid.* XII. 329 (Morris) The tarata or Lemon-wood, a most beautiful tree, also used for hedges.

**Taratantara** (tărătæ·ntără, -tæntā·ră). Also 6 **taratauntara,** 7 **taratantarra, tarratantara, tara-tantaro** (**taratamara**); also, 6–7 **taratantar,** 7–9 **tarantara,** 9 **tarantarratara.** Cf. TANTARA. [Echoic: cf. L. *tarata·ntara* (Ennius) sound of the trumpet (so It. *taratanta·ra* in Florio), and med.L. *taratantarum* a sieve or winnowing machine (*Cath. Angl.*, s. v. *Tempse*); It. *taratanta·ro* a mill-clack (Florio).]

**1.** A word imitating, and hence denoting, the sound of a trumpet or bugle (in quot. 1620, of a drum). Also *attrib.*

1553 T. WILSON *Rhet.* 92 b, Or when one is lustye to saye Taratauntara, declaringe therby that he is as lustye, as a Trumpette is delitefull, and styrringe. 1557 GRIMALD *Death Zoroas* in *Tottell's Misc.* (Arb.) 120 Now clattering arms.. Gan passe the noyes of taratantars clang. 1620 T. GRANGER *Div. Logike* 66 The Drum soundeth taratantara. 1621 BURTON *Anat. Mel.* II. iii. VII. (1652) 354 Let drums beat on, trumpets sound Taratantarra, let them sack cities. 1638 RANDOLPH *Hey for Honesty* I. ii, I would have blown a Trumpet Tarantara. 1660 Z. CROFTON *Fastening St. Peter's Fetters* 72 The Tarratantara murmur of the Lincoln-shire and York-shire men in their rebellious holy pilgrimage. 1667 DENHAM *Direct. Paint.* II. vii, To raise it, we must have a Naval War, As if 'were nothing but Tara-Tan-Tar. 1698 VANBRUGH *Æsop* II, *Æsop.* To boot and saddle again they sound. *Rog.* Ta ra! tan tan ta ra! ra ra tan ta ra! 1873 'OUIDA' *Pascarèl* I. 121 Their Tirolean postilions roused the echoes..with a tarantarratara upon their tassellated bugles.

† **2.** *fig.* High-flown, loud, extravagant, or pretentious talk. Also *attrib.* *Obs.*

1599 *Broughton's Let.* ii. 11 To coyne an epistle..with such Taratantara fictions and applauses. 1670 EACHARD *Cont. Clergy* 43 Making a high rant about a shittle-cock, and talking tara-tantaro about a feather. 1674 R. GODFREY *Inj. & Ab. Physic* 29 [To] please himself in talking Tara-tan-tara about the Philosophers stone and Horizontal Gold.

Hence **Tarata·ntar, Tarata·ntarize** [= med.L. *taratantarizāre*] *vbs.*, *intr.* to sound, or imitate the sound of, a trumpet; *trans.* to sound with a loud noise like the blare of a trumpet.

1656 BLOUNT *Glossogr.*, *Tarantarize*,..to sound a trumpet, to sing or sound *taratantara*. 1840 G. RAYMOND in *New Monthly Mag.* LIX. 244 She taratantared a dozen bells.

**Taraxacin** (tăræ·ksăsin). *Chem.* [f. next + -IN [1].] A bitter crystalline substance obtained from the juice of dandelion-root. So **Taraxa·cerin,** resin of taraxacum.

1858 HOGG *Veg. Kingd.* 462 A peculiar crystallizable principle was discovered in the juice by M. Polex, which he called *taraxacin*. 1868 WATTS *Dict. Chem.* V. 671 The bitter substance of the root [of the dandelion], the so-called taraxacin, and the resin, have been examined by Polex (Arch. Pharm. xix. 50). 1890 THORPE *Dict. Applied Chem.* I. 646/1 From that part of the coagulum left undissolved by the water alcohol extracts *taraxacerin* $C_8H_{16}O$ (Kromayer).

‖ **Taraxacum** (tăræ·ksăkŏm). [med.L. from Arabic, ultimately Persian. The *Synonymia Arabo-Latina* of Gerard of Cremona (died 1189) has '*Tarasacon*, species cichorei'. This appears to have been a corruption or misreading of the Arabic name طرخشقوق *ṭarakhshaqōq* or *ṭarkhshaqōq*, itself according to the Burhan-i-Kāti (native Persian lexicon), originally an arabicized form of the Persian تلخ چکوک *talkh chakōk* 'bitter herb'.

Many corrupt forms of the name (due chiefly to misreading of unpointed similar consonants in a foreign word) are given by Ibn Baithar. 'The reading *ṭarakhshaqōn*, with ن for ق, appears in the glossary of Ibn al Hashsha on the work of Razi' (Devic in Littré *Supp.*), and appears to be the source of Gerarde's *tarasacon*.]

**a.** *Bot.* Name of the genus of Composite plants (by Linnæus included in *Leontodon*) including the dandelion (*T. Dens-leonis*, *T. officinale*, or *Leon-*

*todon Taraxacum*). b. *Pharm.* A drug prepared from the root of the dandelion, used as a tonic and in liver complaints.

1706 PHILLIPS (ed. 6), *Taraxacum* or *Taraxacon*, (Gr.) the Herb Dandelion, or Sow-Thistle. 1845 BUDD *Dis. Liver* 36 Some principles of rhubarb and taraxacum might pass off in it likewise. 1857 G. BIRD *Urin. Deposits* (ed. 5) 436 Taraxacum, a popular cholagogue, owes its diuretic action..to a similar cause. 1875 H. C. WOOD *Therap.* (1879) 425 Diuretic properties have also been ascribed to taraxacum.

**Tar-barrel** (tā·ɹ,bærĕl). A barrel containing or that has contained tar: esp. as used for making a bonfire; formerly also in the carrying out of capital punishment by burning.

*c* 1450 *B. M. Add. MS.* 10036 (Destr. Jerus. by Vespasian) lf. 24 With bowes schot and with arblast, With tarbarelle and with wilde fyre. 1580 *Vestry Bks.* (Surtees) 120 Item paid for a tarbarrell at cronation day, vj d. 1685 *Lond. Gaz.* No. 2080/3 A large Bonfire or high Piramid of Tar-barrels, being erected in the said Market place. 1725 RAMSAY *Gentle Sheph.* v. i, Till in a fat tar-barrel Mause [a witch] be burnt. 1850 CARLYLE *Latter-d. Pamph.* i. 2 The European populations everywhere hailed the omen; with shouting and rejoicing, leading-articles and tar-barrels.

† b. Applied opprobriously to a person. Cf. TAR-BOX b. *Obs.*

1695 CONGREVE *Love for L.* III. vii, If I were a man, you durst not talk at this rate,..you stinking tar-barrel.

**Tarbet** (tā·ɹbĕt). *Sc. local.* Also **tarburt.** [ad. Gael. *tairbeart* peninsula, isthmus.] A neck of land, an isthmus; hence, a portage between two lochs or navigable channels. (Also, a proper name of villages, etc. so situated.)

1843 *Statist. Acc. Scotl.* VII. 136 A narrow isthmus or tarburt over which boats were drawn. 1875 W. MCILWRAITH *Guide Wigtownshire* 64 Advantage was taken of the conformation of the land to form a tarbet.

**Tarboggin, -bogin,** var. TOBOGGAN.

‖ **Tarboosh** (taɹbū·ʃ). Also 8 tarpous, 9 tarboush, -bouch, -bush. [a. Arabic طربوش *ṭarbūsh*; so called in Egypt (Freytag); in F. *tarbouch.*] A cap of cloth or felt (almost always red) with a tassel (usually of blue silk) attached at the top, worn by Mohammedans either by itself or as part of the turban; the *fez* is the Turkish form.

1702 W. J. tr. *Bruyn's Voy. Levant* xx. 91 This Tarpous, which serves the Women as a sort of a Head-dress, is a large Cap of Six or eight Quarters, made of Cloth of Gold. 1839 LANE *Arab. Nts.* (1859) I. iv. 256 He took the turban with its tarboosh,..and kept them himself. *Ibid.* 288 *note*, The Tarboosh is a woollen skull-cap, of a deep blood-red colour, having a tassel of dark blue silk attached to the crown. It is worn by most Arabs of the higher and middle classes. 1884 J. COLBORNE *Hicks Pasha* 105 The tarboosh, or fez—as it is called in Turkey—..is adopted by Mussulmans, as it allows for the fulfilment of the Mahommedan observance in prayer of touching the earth with the forehead. 1885 LADY BRASSEY *Trades* 291 Turks Islands derive their name from a beautiful scarlet cactus, in shape like a fez or tarbouch.

Hence **Tarbooshed, tarbushed** (-bū·ʃt) *a.* [-ED [2]], wearing a tarboosh.

1873 LELAND *Egypt. Sketch-Bk.* viii. 106 Through them tarbushed or turbaned and dark men peered curiously at the strangers.

**Tar-box** (tā·ɹ,bǫks). A box formerly used by shepherds to hold tar as a salve for sheep.

*c* 1420 ? LYDG. *Assembly of Gods* 326 The rewde god Pan.. Clad in russet frese, & breched lyke a bere, With a gret tar box hangyng by hys syde. 1523 FITZHERB. *Husb.* § 41 And a shepeherde shoulde not go without his dogge, his shepe hoke, a payre of sheres, and his terre boxe. 1602 *2nd Pt. Return fr. Parnass.* v. ii. 2088 A shepards hooke, a tarbox, and a scrippe. 1658 OSBORN *Jas. I*, Wks. (1673) 514 (Spight of his Tarbox) he died of the Scab.

† b. Applied contemptuously to a person: = 'stinking fellow'. *Obs.*

*a* 1592 GREENE *Jas. IV*, III. i, Such as rub horses do good service in the commonweal, ergo, tarbox, master courtier, a horse-keeper is a gentleman. 1687 SETTLE *Refl. Dryden* 12 Tarbox Muly Lahas is not the Fool this bout.

**Tar-brush** (tā·ɹ,brɒʃ). A brush used for smearing anything with tar. *Knight of the tar-brush*, allusively applied to a sailor: cf. TAR *sb.* 3.

1711 W. SUTHERLAND *Shipbuild. Assist.* 135 Tarr Brushes—2. 1865 KINGSLEY *Herew.* vi, Do any of you knights of the tar brush know whether we are going to be drowned in Christian waters?

b. *fig.*, esp. in such phrases as *a dash* or *touch of the tar-brush*, i.e. of negro or Indian blood, showing itself in the complexion. (In first quot. applied to a negro.)

In quot. 1895 *touched with the same tar-brush* = 'tarred with the same brush': see TAR *v.*[1] c.

1835–40 HALIBURTON *Clockm.* (1862) 179, I great opinion of you, Pompey; I make a man of you, you dam old tar brush. 1859 LANG *Wand. India* 50 The mother must have been very fair, if she were a native, the boy is so very slightly touched with the tar-brush. 1864 TREVELYAN *Compet. Wallah* (1866) 198 Brunette! I should rather think she is! There's a strong touch of the tar-brush in that quarter. 1895 *Month* Aug. 547 On this occasion all alike were touched with the same tar-brush.

So **Ta·r-bru:sher,** one who uses a tar-brush; *fig.* one who 'blackens' a reputation, a defamer.

1884 *Pall Mall G.* 5 June 5/1 Mr. Brewer was neither a whitewasher nor a tar-brusher; he had very few fads.

**Tarcat,** obs. Sc. form of TARGET.

† **Tarcay·s.** *Obs. rare*[−1]. [a. OF. *tarquais* (13th–16th c.) = It. *turcasso*, med.L. *turcasia*, med.Gr. ταρκάσιον, a. Pers. ترکش *tarkash* quiver: see Devic in Littré Suppl. s. v. *Carquois.*] A quiver.

1490 CAXTON *Eneydos* xv. 54 She hadde a fayr tarcays, couered wyth fyne cloth of damaske, alle fulle of arowes.

**Tarcel,** obs. f. TARSEL, TERCEL. **Tarcelet,** obs. f. TERCELET. **Tarche, Tarchon,** obs. ff. TARGE *sb.*[1], TARRAGON. **Tard,** obs. f. TARRED.

† **Ta·rdance.** *Obs.* [a. obs. F. *tardance* (1307 in Godef.), f. *tarder* TARDE *v.*: see -ANCE.] Delaying, delay. Also † **Ta·rdancy** (-ency).

1595 *Q. Eliz. & Levant Co.* (1904) 53 Whose [ambassador] playnly excuseth the tardance thereof by reason thatt his maysters treasury..is exhausted. 1635 J. HAYWARD tr. *Biondi's Banish'd Virg.* 227 If any tardancy of mine bee the occasion of your Highnesse sufferings. 1654 COKAINE *Dianea* IV. 340 Dorcone arrived just upon that time there, when tardency could not but be perilous.

† **Tarda·tion.** *Obs.* [ad. late L. *tardātiōn-em*, n. of action f. *tardāre* to delay. Cf. OF. *tardation* (14th c. in Godef.).] The action of delaying, delay; slackening of speed, retardation. (In quot. 1601, want of motion, or stagnation.)

1500–20 DUNBAR *Poems* lxxi. 35 Thy tardatioun caussis ws to think lang. 1601 DOLMAN *La Primaud. Fr. Acad.* III. lix. 271 Raine-water..doth putrifie through tardation and slownes. 1674 PETTY *Disc. Dupl. Proportion* 113 The degrees of Tardation, which Bullets make in..their way. 1727 BAILEY vol. II, *Tardation*, a Loitering, Lingering.

† **Ta·rdative,** *a. Obs.* [f. L. *tardāt-*, ppl. stem of *tardāre* to delay, tarry + -IVE.] Tending to slacken speed, retarding.

1665–6 *Phil. Trans.* I. 274 Whatever effect (accelerative or tardative).

† **Tarde,** *a.* (*adv.*) *Obs.* [ad. L. *tard-us* slow.]

1. Slow: = TARDY *a.* 1 a.

1547 BOORDE *Brev. Health* § 321 If naturally a mans memory is tarde of wyt and knowlege. 1624 HEYWOOD *Gunaik.* VII. 334 They neither speed, Nor doth their pace seeme tarde.

b. Late: = TARDY *a.* 1 b. *rare*[−0].

1613 R. CAWDREY *Table Alph.* (ed. 3), *Tarde*, late.

2. *To take tarde*, to overtake, surprise; = 'to take tardy' (TARDY *a.* 2).

1547 SALESBURY *Welsh Dict.*, *Dala ar y gamfa*, take tarde. 1578 TIMME *Caluine on Gen.* iii. 11. 102 But God shall alwayes take vs tarde in the sinne of Adam. 1584 R. SCOT *Discov. Witchcr.* xv. xxiii. (1886) 369 They were convicted, and..almost taken tarde with the deed doing.

B. *adv.* a. Late. b. Slowly. [F. *tard* adv.]

1557 in *Rep. Hist. MSS. Comm., Var. Collect.* IV. 223 Forasmoche as Mr. John Hooper [and 5 others]..came into this house tarde, after nyne of the clocke this day, therefore they..are amerced in 12*d.* a peece. 1597 A. M. tr. *Guillemeau's Fr. Chirurg.* 11/1 The winter, when as the corruptione goeth somwhat tarder or sloer forwarde.

† **Tarde,** *v. Obs. rare.* [a. F. *tarde-r* (12th c. in Godef.):—L. *tardāre.*] *trans.* To retard, delay.

1524 *St. Papers Hen. VIII*, VI. 364 The said Duke and his armye was so tarded and retracted, that [etc.].

**Tardency,** erron. f. TARDANCY *Obs.*

† **Tardida·tion.** *Obs. rare*[−1]. [irreg. ? for *tardation* or *tarditation.*] = TARDATION.

1647 HERRICK *Noble Numb.*, *Salutation* 49 Avoid all snares Of tardidation in the Lords Affaires.

**Tardie, tardife,** obs. forms of TARDY.

**Tardigrade** (tā·ɹdigrēɪd), *a.* (*sb.*) [a. F. *tardigrade* (*a* 1615 in Godef. *Compl.*), or ad. L. *tardigrad-us* walking slowly, f. L. *tardus* slow + *-gradus* stepping, going.]

1. Walking or going slowly; slow-paced.

1623 COCKERAM, *Tardigrade*, a slow goer. 1656 BLOUNT *Glossogr.*, *Tardigrade*, that goeth slow, or hath a slow pace. 1852 MUNDY *Our Antipodes* (1857) 185 The *Deborah* proved a marine hackney-coach of the most tardigrade order. 1875 W. HOUGHTON *Sk. Brit. Insects* 145 The Meloë..a bloated, tardigrade, wingless beetle upon the meadow.

b. *fig.* Sluggish in thought or action, unprogressive, 'slow-going'.

1883 *Pall Mall G.* 28 Dec. 4/2 Even in our tardigrade West Country the farmer has begun to discover,..that he, too, is an economical power.

2. *Zool.* a. Belonging to the sub-order (*Tardigrada*) or family (*Bradypodidæ*) of edentate mammals, comprising the sloths.

1799 CARLISLE in *Phil. Trans.* XC. 101 The habits of life among the tardigrade animals, give occasion for the long continued contraction of some muscles in their limbs. 1892 W. H. HUDSON *Natur. La Plata* xxii. 350 Tardigrade mammals of arboreal habits.

b. Belonging to the group *Tardigrada* of Arachnids, comprising the minute aquatic animals called water-bears or bear-animalcules.

1847–9 *Todd's Cycl. Anat.* IV. 415/1 Doyere states that he has found zoospores in the tardigrade Infusoria. 1891 *Cent. Dict.* s. v., *Tardigrade rotifers* [obs.], the *Tardigrada Arctisca*; bear-animalcules.

B. *sb.* a. An edentate mammal of the sub-order *Tardigrada*; a sloth.

1827 GRIFFITH tr. *Cuvier's Anim. K.* III. 251 The tardigrades will form the first class [of the Edentata]...Their name is derived from their excessive slowness. 1835 KIRBY *Hab. & Inst. Anim.* II. xvii. 208 The last family..in the present Order [Edentates] is very well distinguished by the name of *Tardigrades.*

b. An arachnid of the group *Tardigrada*; a water-bear.

1860 *All Year Round* No. 43. 387 The tardigrades dwell in the same localities as the rotifers. 1872 DARWIN in *Life & Lett.* III. 169 On this view, a Rotifer or Tardigrade is adapted to its humble conditions of life by a happy accident; and this I cannot believe.

**Tardigradous** (taɹdi·grădəs), *a.* [f. L. *tardigradus* + -OUS: see prec.] = TARDIGRADE *a.*

1658 SIR T. BROWNE *Pseud. Ep.* III. xxviii. (ed. 3) 227 [The tiger] is but a slow and tardigradous animal. 1848 JOHNSTON in *Proc. Berw. Nat. Club* II. No. 6. 310 Mite about a line in length,..tardigradous. 1866 *Pall Mall G.* 17 Sept. 4 Meanwhile Dissent does not wait for the tardigradous action of superior authorities.

† **Tardi·loquent,** *a. Obs. rare*[−0]. [f. L. *tard-us* slow + *loquent-em*, pr. pple. of *loqui* to speak: cf. L. *tardiloquus.*] Speaking slowly, slow-speaking. So † **Tardi·loquy** *Obs. rare*[−0].

1623 COCKERAM, *Tardiloquie*, slow speech. 1656 BLOUNT *Glossogr.*, *Tardiloquent*, that speaks slowly, or draws his speech out at length.

**Tardily** (tā·ɹdĭli), *adv.* [f. TARDY *a.* + -LY [2].] In a tardy manner. a. Slowly; with slow movement or progress.

1597 SHAKS. *2 Hen. IV*, II. iii. 26 For those that could speake low, and tardily, Would turne their owne Perfection, to Abuse. 1791 COWPER *Retired Cat* 67 The night rolled tardily away. 1793 SMEATON *Edystone L.* § 219 *note*, I found it [cement] to set very tardily. 1872 MORLEY *Voltaire* (1886) 10 The great tides of circumstance swell so tardily, that whole generations wait in vain for the full flood on which the race is borne to new shores.

b. After the proper or expected time; after delay; late, lately. c. Sometimes implying 'not readily, reluctantly'.

1821 JOANNA BAILLIE *Met. Leg.*, *Columbus* xlviii, Four small vessels..yet granted tardily For such high service. 1839 JAMES *Louis XIV*, IV. 198 Those motives were somewhat tardily felt, and were..soon forgotten. 1855 MACAULAY *Hist. Eng.* xxii. IV. 744 Harcourt..had with difficulty reconciled his conscience to the oaths, and had tardily and unwillingly signed the Association.

**Tardiness** (tā·ɹdinĕs). [f. as prec. + -NESS.] The quality of being tardy. a. Slowness of movement or action.

1605 SHAKS. *Lear* I. i. 238 A tardinesse in nature, Which often leaues the history vnspoke That it intends to do. 1751 JOHNSON *Rambler* No. 111 ⁋ 4 Something of the tardiness and frigidity of age. 1802 PALEY *Nat. Theol.* xvi. (1817) 138 The tardiness of his pace seems to have reference to the capacity of his organs. 1863 KINGLAKE *Crimea* II. 247 They..conformed with great care to the tardiness of our advance.

b. Delay in time; lateness.

1752 JOHNSON *Rambler* No. 200 ⁋ 6 The tardiness of his return, gave me reason to suspect that time was taken to deliberate. 1781 COWPER *Retirement* 475 He chides the tardiness of every post, Pants to be told of battles won or lost. 1825 J. NEAL *Bro. Jonathan* II. 201 Hence the tardiness of our information.

† **Ta·rdious,** *a. Obs. rare*[−1]. [irreg. f. TARDY *a.* + -OUS.] = TARDY *a.*

? *c* 1580 T. HACKET *Treas. Amadis de Gaule* 159, I never shewed my selfe to be tardious nor slouthfull.

**Ta·rditude.** *rare*[−1]. [ad. L. *tarditūdo*, f. *tardus* slow: see -TUDE.] = next; in quot. 'slowness' or unwillingness *to do* something.

1794 COLERIDGE *Lett.*, *to Southey* (1895) 85 My inconsistencies have given me a tarditude and reluctance to think ill of any one.

**Tardity** (tā·ɹdĭti). Now *rare.* Also 5 -ee, 6–7 -ie. [a. OF. *tardité* (1420 in Godef.), earlier *tardeté*, ad. L. *tarditās*, f. *tard-us* slow: see -ITY.]

1. Slowness of movement or action: = TARDINESS a. In later use, a technical term of *Physics*, opp. to *velocity*.

[*c* 1386 CHAUCER *Pars. T.* ⁋ 644 The synne that men clepen Tarditas, as whan a man is to laterede or tariyng er he wole turne to god.] *c* 1450 *Mirour Saluacioun* 4410 Wightlayke delyvrenesse with out ony tarditee. 1586 B. YOUNG *Guazzo's Civ. Conv.* IV. 178 b, For his rude simplicitie and tarditie. 1603 SIR C. HEYDON *Jud. Astrol.* xxiii. 514 [He] confesseth velocitie, and tarditie, in the Moone. 1656 S. HOLLAND *Zara* (1719) 2 The Champion began to tax himself of tardity. 1714 DERHAM *Astro-Theol.* VII. v. (1769) 180 The tardity of the periodic motion in their respective orbits. 1852 DE MORGAN in Graves *Life Sir W. R. Hamilton* (1889) III. 353 In every semicircle, the intension of the breadth [ordinate] begins from the utmost degree of velocity, and terminates at the utmost degree of tardity in the middle of the arc.

2. The fact of being late; lateness.

1599 NASHE *Lenten Stuffe* 33 [They] furrowe vp the rugged brine and sweepe through his tumultuous oous [ooze] ..rather then in tendring their alleagance they should be benighted with tardity. 1601 BP. W. BARLOW *Defence* 41 For tarditie and suspence of the assent, may arise by some obstacle not remooued. 1638 WOTTON *Let.* in *Reliq.* (1651) 486, I beseech you..not to conceive by the tarditie of my Answer unto you, any faintnesse in the acknowledgment of your favors.

**Tardive** (tā·ɹdiv), *a.* [mod. a. F. *tardif, -ive*: see TARDY.] Characterized by lateness, or tending to appear late; of late appearance or development. So † **Tardi·vity** [F. *tardiveté*], lateness of development or maturity. *Obs. rare.*

1725 *Bradley's Fam. Dict.*, *Tardivity*, a Term, says Monsieur Chomel, which may and ought to be made use of, tho' at present obsolete, when such a Fruit is mention'd on the account of its becoming late ripe. 1905 H. D. ROLLESTON

*Dis. Liver* 320 A case of tardive hereditary syphilis with stricture of the hepatic duct.

**Tardle** (tā·ɹd'l). *dial.* A tangled mass, a tangle. Cf. *tardle* vb. to entangle (Dorset) in Eng. Dial. Dict.

**1898** T. Hardy *Wessex Poems* 204 While her great gallied eyes, through her hair hanging loose Sheened as stars through a tardle of trees.

**Tardy** (tā·ɹdi), *a.* (*adv.*) Forms: α. 5 tardyve, 6 tardife. β. 6 tardye, -dee, 6–7 tardie, (7 tar'de), 6– tardy. [a. F. *tardif, -ive* (12th c. in Littré) = Sp. *tardio*, It. *tardivo*:—pop.L. type **tardīvus*, f. *tardus* slow: see -ive. In the β forms the ending *-ive* is reduced to *-ie, -ye, -y*: see -ive, par. 3.]

**1.** Slow: in various senses. **a.** Slow in motion, action, or occurrence; making little progress in a comparatively long time; of slow nature, sluggish.

α. **1483** Caxton *Gold. Leg.* 23 b/2 We ought to gyue thankynges to the dyuyne dyspensacion, for the tardyue creaunce of holy faders to us necessarye. ? *c* **1580** T. Hacket *Treas. Amadis de Gaule* 155 Trusting that..ye wil not be tardife in so good a worke. **1600** F. Walker tr. *Sp. Mandeville* 59 The chollerick man is commonly hasty and heedelesse..and the flegmatick more slowe and tardife.

β. **1590** Shaks. *Com. Err.* ii. i. 44 Say, is your tardie master now at hand? **1594** — *Rich. III*, ii. i. 89 Some tardie Cripple bare the Countermand. **1713** Young *Last Day* iii. 176, I faint, my tardy blood forgets to flow. **1751** Johnson *Rambler* No. 169 ¶ 1 Thus the firmest timber is of tardy growth. **1866** G. Macdonald *Ann. Q. Neighb.* xxviii, To watch the gradual and tardy awakening of the intellect.

**b.** Not acting, coming, or happening until after the proper, expected, or desired time; late, behindhand; delaying, or delayed; dilatory; sometimes, delaying through unwillingness, reluctant, 'slow' (*to* some action, or *to do* something).

**1667** Milton *P. L.* x. 853 On the ground Outstretcht he lay,..oft Curs'd his Creation, Death as oft accus'd Of tardie execution. **1742** West *Let.* in *Gray's Poems* (1775) 147 O join with mine thy tuneful lay, And invocate the tardy May. **1749** Johnson *Van. Hum. Wishes* 160 See nations slowly wise, and meanly just, To buried merit raise the tardy bust. *a* **1822** Shelley *Chas. I*, ii. 355 Oh be our feet still tardy to shed blood. **1849** Macaulay *Hist. Eng.* ii. I. 191 Then, at length, tardy justice was done to the memory of Oliver. **1908** *Betw. Trent & Ancholme* 47 When a girl used to think her admirer rather tardy in asking for the wedding-day.

†**2.** Phr. *To take* (also rarely *catch, find*) a person *tardy*: to overtake (? orig. on account of slowness of advance); to surprise; to come upon unprepared or unawares; hence, to detect, 'catch' in a crime, fault, error, etc.: often merely synonymous with Take *v.* 8. *Obs.*

**1530** Palsgr. 554/1 s.v. *Forage*, As we went a foragynge the laste daye, we were almoste taken tardy of a bande of horse men. **1542** Udall *Erasm. Apoph.* 253 He tooke her tardie with a plaine lye. **1579** Fulke *Refut. Rastel* 725, I haue taken him tardye alreadie in falsifying the scripture. **1594** Shaks. *Rich. III*, iv. i. 52 Be not ta'ne tardie by vnwise delay. **1601** Dent *Pathw. Heaven* 355 So shall the comming of the sonne of man to iudgement, take the world tardy and unprepared. **1620** Rowlands *Night Raven* 16 A Drunkard, (whom the cup did tardy catch). **1640** Brathwait *Boulster Lect.* 94 Who, being found tardy, said he was troubled with a Spirit. **1677** *Conn. Col. Rec.* (1852) II. 499 Pawbequenuck ..being found tardy of inticeing the surrenderers to depart from the English .. was sent to prison. **1690** C. Nesse *O. & N. Test.* I. 306 To sing morning hymns..from which exercise this angel must not be taken tardy, much less be absent.

†**b.** *ellipt.* for 'taken tardy': Detected in a fault, caught tripping. *Obs.*

**1591** R. Turnbull *Exp. Jas.* 150 b, Adulterie, a grieuous euill, .. yet David (the man of God) was tardie therein. *a* **1643** J. Shute *Judgement & Mercy* (1645) 118 Montanus, in whose heresie Tertullian (though else a good man) was tardie. **1705** tr. *Bosman's Guinea* 358 A Negroe, who had been tardy with one of the King's Wives. **1706** Phillips (ed. 6), *Tardy*,..also guilty, found tripping, or in a Fault.

**3.** quasi-*adv.* Behind time, late. Phr. *to come tardy off*, to fall short, to be done or carried out inadequately (*obs.* or *arch.*: cf. Come *v.* 61 i).

**1586** Warner *Alb. Eng.* ii. xiii. (1589) 54 When Troy was ouer stoute,..and tardie lookt aboute. **1592** Shaks. *Rom. & Jul.* ii. vi. 15 Too swift arriues as tardie as too slow. **1718** Hickes & Nelson *J. Kettlewell* i. vi. 23 He never .. incurred the least Censure, as by Neglect of.. Prayers, or coming Tardy to them. *a* **1836** Leverett *Lexicon Lat.-Eng.* Pref., In such a case, the work is better overdone than come tardy off.

**4.** *Comb.*, as *tardy-gaited, -moving, -rising* adjs.

**1599** Shaks. *Hen. V*, iv. Prol. 20 The confident and ouerlustie French, Doe..chide the creepple-tardy-gated Night, who..doth limpe So tediously away. **1719** Young *Busiris* 63 How like the dyal's tardy moving Shade! **1757** Dyer *Fleece* i. Poems (1761) 82 Thither crowds Each greedy wretch for tardy-rising wealth, Which comes too late.

† **Tardy,** *v. Obs.* [f. prec. adj.] *trans.* To make tardy; to delay, retard, keep back.

**1611** Shaks. *Wint. T.* iii. ii. 163 Which had been done, But that the good mind of Camillo tardied My swift command. **1623** tr. *Favine's Theat. Hon.* vi. ix. 153 So much tardied and neglected by the miserable estate and condition of France.

**Tare** (tēəɹ), *sb.*[1] Forms: 4– tare, *pl.* 4 taren, 4–5 taris, 5– tares; also 5 thare, 6 taar(e, terre, ter(e, 9 *dial.* tar, tor. [A word of obscure origin and history: known first *c* 1330 in sense 1, also *c* 1400 in *wiilde tare*, a vetch of some kind, and in the later Wycliffite N. Test., 1388, used to render Gr. L. *zīzania*. For the form Kluge compares ODu. **taruwe*, MDu. *terwe, tarwe*, a name of wheat, cogn. with Lith. *dirva* a wheat-field. But no satisfactory explanation has been offered of the transference of sense.]

**1.** The seed of a vetch: usually in reference to its small size. (Probably familiar in early times, as too frequently present in seed-corn.)

*c* **1330** *Arth. & Merl.* (Kölbing) 7354 Þei our folk tohewen waren To smale morsels, so beþ taren. **1530** Palsgr. 279/1 Taare a corne lyke a pease, *lupins.* **1555** Eden *Decades* 9 Many of them [grains of gold] .. were as bygge as tares or fytchis. **1576** Baker *Jewell of Health* 185 Take of this masse vnto the quantity of three Tares. **1657** R. Ligon *Barbadoes* 65 This vermine will get..under the nayl of your Toes, and there make a habitation..as bigge as a small Tare. **1808** *Med. Jrnl.* XIX. 287 A globule, about the size of a small tare, being thrown on paper moistened. **1876** Bristowe *The. & Pract. Med.* (1878) 669 The follicles enlarge to the size of a tare or pea.

†**b.** Taken as a type of a very small particle; a whit, a jot, an atom. *Obs.*

*c* **1386** Chaucer *Reeve's T.* 80 But ther of sette the Millere nat a tare.

**2.** A name given to some species of vetch: **a.** in early times, esp. to those occurring as weeds in corn-fields. (Lyte, 1578, uses it only of these, applying 'vetch' or 'fitch' to *Vicia sativa* (sense b); with Gerarde, Ray, and later writers, 'tare' and 'vetch' become synonymous.)

Still entering into the names of the 'Hairy or Rough-podded Tare', *Vicia hirsuta* (*Ervum hirsutum*), and 'Smooth Tare', *V. tetrasperma* (*E. tetraspermum*), cornfield weeds: see also Strangle-*tare*, Tine-*tare*. In quots. 1573–78, applied (after Dodoens) to *Lathyrus Aphaca*, now a rare 'colonist' in English corn-fields, but perhaps then more common, being imported with dirty seed-wheat. Formerly also applied vaguely to other plants of these and allied genera, or to weeds resembling them in their habit.

*c* **1400** *Lanfranc's Cirurg.* 88 Orabum þat is wiilde tare. *c* **1450** *Alphita* (Anecd. Oxon.) 131 Orobus, *gall.* uesche, *anglice* thare uel mousepese. *Ibid.* 186 *Trifolium acutum*, wildetare *uel* tintare **1523** Fitzherb. *Husb.* § 20 There be diuers maner of wedes, as thistyls, kedlokes, dockes,..dogfenell, mathes, ter, and dyuers other small wedes. *Ibid.*, Terre is the worste wede,..and groweth mooste in rye, and it groweth lyke fytches, but it is moche smaller, and it wyll growe as hyghe as the corne, and with the weyght therof, it pulleth the corne flatte to the erth, and freteth the eares away. **1573–80** Baret *Alv.* T 63 Tares which commonlie growe amongst corne, are temperate in heat, *aphaca.* **1578** Lyte *Dodoens* iv. xxviii. 485 The Tare groweth in feeldes, & is found growing in this Countrie, in fertil groundes amongst wheat & Rye. **1598** Sylvester *Du Bartas* ii. i. iii. *Furies* 166 Cockle, wilde Oats, rough Burs, Corn-cumbring Tares.

**b.** Now, in general agricultural use, applied to the cultivated vetch, *Vicia sativa*, grown (often with oats, etc.) as fodder. In a collective sense, or as name of a crop, used in *plural* form (cf *oats*, in like use).

**1482** *Cely Papers* (Camden) 109 Yowre yonge horsse.. wull ete noo mete yett but grasse and grene tarys. **1530** Palsgr. 278/2 Taars a kynd of corn, *dragee.* [See Dredge.] **1552** Huloet, Tares or vetches, a kinde of pulse or grayne, *eruila, eruum, orobum, i.* **1577** Harrison *England* ii. vi. (1877) i. 153 Horssecorne, I meane, beanes, peasen, otes, tares, and lintels. **1697** Dryden *Virg. Georg.* i. 110 Where Vetches, Pulse, and Tares have stood. **1760** R. Brown *Compl. Farmer* ii. 87 Tares are of as great advantage to land as other pulses are. **1801** Mason *Suppl. to Johnson, Tare*, a name frequently given to the common vetch. **1846** J. Baxter *Libr. Pract. Agric.* (ed. 4) II. 312 Tares will do well on any rich or good soil. **1887** Bowen *Virg. Eclogue* iii. 100 Lean my bull, though he feeds on the richest tares.

**3.** *pl.* Used in the later Wycliffite (or Purvey) version of the N.T. (*Matt.* xiii. 25), also in some MSS. of the earlier text, and thence in Tindale's and subsequent 16–17th c. versions, to render L. *zizania* (Vulg.), Gr. ζιζάνια, as name of an injurious weed among corn, which in the first Wyclif version had been rendered 'dernel or cokil', the latter going back in translations and quotations to Old English, the former to Early ME.: see Darnel, Cockle. *Obs.* exc. as a biblical use, and as in b.

Evidently Purvey and his co-revisers adopted *tares* as in their opinion more intelligible than the earlier 'dernel' or 'cokil'. Probably they thought of *Vicia hirsuta* the Strangle-tare, or other species of wild vetch, as familiar noxious weeds in English cornfields.

**1388** Wyclif *Matt.* xiii. 25 Whanne men slepten, his enemy cam, and sewe aboue taris [1382 dernel; *gloss* or cokil] in the myddil of whete. **1526** Tindale *ibid.*, Whyll men slepte ther cam his foo and sowed tares amonge the wheate. **1594** Hooker *Eccl. Pol.* iii. i. § 9 His Church he compareth unto a field, where tares manifestly known and seen by all men do grow intermingled with good corn. **1611** Bible *Matt.* xiii. 36 Declare vnto vs the parable of the tares [1388 Wyclif taris, Tindale tares] of the field. *a* **1674** Clarendon *Surv. Leviathan* (1676) 307 These are the men who..watched the tares..and pulled them up.

**b.** Hence in allusive and fig. uses.

*a* **1711** Ken *Direct. Prayers* Wks. (1838) 354 The tares of sedition have been industriously sown among you. **1806** Jefferson *Writ.* (1830) IV. 64 They will not suffer friend or foe to sow tares among us. **1816** Southey *Lay Laureate* lxvii, The heart of man is rich in all good seeds; Neglected, it is choak'd with tares and noxious weeds. **1818** Byron *Ch. Har.* iv. cxx, Weeds of dark luxuriance, tares of haste, Rank at the core, though tempting to the eyes. **1878** Stubbs *Const. Hist.* III. xxi. 615 In the new world, as in the old, the tares are mingled with the wheat.

**4.** *attrib.* and *Comb.*, as *tare hay, seed, verdage*; **tare-grass** (*dial.* **tar-grass**), some species of wild tare or vetch (' *Vicia hirsuta* or perh. *V. Cracca*', Britten & Holland); **tare-thistle**, ? the sow-thistle (*Sonchus arvensis*), a prickly plant growing as a weed in corn; **tare-sown** *a.*, sown with tares (sense 3); **tare-vetch** (**-fitch, tarvetch, -fitch**), name for *Vicia hirsuta* and other wild or weedy species of vetch and allied plants.

**1686** Plot *Staffordsh.* 204 The wild Vetch, here call'd *Tar-grass. **1694** W. Westmacott *Script. Herb.* 192 These wild sorts [of Tares] are called by some Tar-grass. **1763** *Museum Rust.* (ed. 2) I. 225, I had last summer a crop of *tare-hay that was astonishing. **1578** Lyte *Dodoens* iv. xxviii. 486 The *Tare seede is of a restringent vertue like yͤ Lentil. **1797** T. Park *Sonn.* 110 The *tare-sown plains of age we feebly reap. **1753** Chambers *Cycl. Supp.* s. v. *Rabbit*, The general cure is the keeping them low, and giving them the prickly herb, called *tare-thistle, to eat. **1778** [W. Marshall] *Minutes Agric., Digest* 44 Horses require very little corn when they are on a *tare-verdage. **1530** Palsgr. 279/1 *Tarefytche a corne, *lupyn.* **1813** T. Davis *Agric. Wilts* Gloss., *Tare-vetch*, withwind, the red and white striped convolvulus, these two plants are the plague of a weak wheat-crop in the sand-lands. **1886** Britten & Holland *Eng. Plant-n.*, Tar-fitch, .. *Vicia hirsuta.—Salop.* Blue Tar-fitch, *Vicia Cracca.—Cheshire.* Yellow Tar-fitch, *Lathyrus pratensis.—Chesh..* Tar Vetch (or Tar-Vatch), *Vicia hirsuta.—Dorset.*

**Tare** (tēəɹ), *sb.*[2] [a. F. *tare* (15th c. in Hatz.-Darm.) waste or deterioration in goods, deficiency, imperfection, also as in Eng., = med.L., It., Pr., Sp., Pg. *tara*, OSp. *atara* (Littré), ad. Arab. طرحة *ṭarḥah* that which is thrown away, f. طرح *ṭaraḥa* to reject.]

The weight of the wrapping, receptacle, or conveyance containing goods, which is deducted from the gross in order to ascertain the net weight; hence, a deduction made from the gross weight to allow for this; also, the weight of a motor vehicle without its fuel and other equipment.

**1486** *Naval Acc. Hen. VII* (1896) 13, ij barrelles Gonnepowdre conteyning in weight besides the tare D iij lbs. *Ibid.* 14 A barrell of gonnepoudre weying the tare abated cc lb. **1598** Florio, *Tara*, the tare, waste or garbish of any marchandise or ware. **1599** Hakluyt *Voy.* II. 274 Note yᵗ in Ormuz they abate tare of all sorts of commodities. **1617** Sir D. Carleton in *Buccleuch MSS.* (Hist. MSS. Comm.) I. 190 The reducing the matter of Tare to the same terms as it was. **1670** Blount *Law Dict.*, *Tare* and *Tret*, the first is the weight of Box, Straw, Cloaths, &c. wherein Goods are packed. The other is [etc.]. **1674** Jeake *Arith.* (1696) 639 If 132 lb. abate 12 lb. for Tare, then 1 C. shall be but 120 lb. **1812** J. Smyth *Pract. of Customs* (1821) 11 The Tares on several sorts of Goods were ascertained by the Farmers of his Majesty's Customs, in the year 1667, a Table whereof was then published by their order. **1882** *Mechanical World* 4 Mar. 137/1 The method of weighing is to ascertain the weight of load and truck combined, and then deduct the tare of the latter from the total. **1892** *Labour Commission* Gloss., The *tare* of the tub is the weight of the empty tub or hutch used in conveying the coals. **1903** *Motor. Ann.* 64 A steam lorry, which will carry any weight up to seven tons, and has a tare of scarcely three tons.

*attrib.* **1900** *Engineering Mag.* XIX. 738 Dependent.. upon the total useful load it is possible to carry on a vehicle of a given tare weight. **1901** *Westm. Gaz.* 16 Nov. 2/1 It is difficult to see why in the case of motors there should be a tare-limit of three tons.

**b.** *Chem.* The weight of a vessel in which a substance is weighed, or of another vessel equal to it, deducted in ascertaining the weight of the substance.

**1888** *Amer. Chem. Jrnl.* X. 319 The difference between the weights of the crucibles plus the oxide and those of their tares was then determined.

**c.** *fig.* (Cf. F. *tare* defect, vice, blemish.)

**1630** Lennard tr. *Charron's Wisd.* i. xiv. § 17 The Spirit hath its maladies, defects, tares or refuse. **1896** Vern. Lee in *Contemp. Rev.* June 822 Is there not in this case a tare—a diminution of aesthetic value to our detriment?

**d.** *Tare and tret*: the two ordinary deductions in calculating the net weight of goods to be sold by retail: see Tret; also, the rule in arithmetic by which these are calculated.

**1670** [see above]. **1692** Coles, *Tare and tret*, (allowance for) the weight of box, bag, &c. and waste on emptying, &c. **1709** Steele *Tatler* No. 46 ¶ 1 He gave diurnal Audiences concerning Commerce, Politicks, Tare and Tret, Usury. **1844** Dickens *Mart. Chuz.* xix, We learnt Tare and Tret together, at school.

*fig.* *c* **1838** De Quincey *Pope* Wks. 1863 XV. 121 The allowance for tare and tret as a discount in favour of Pope.

**e.** *Comb.* †**tare-master** = Tarer. *Obs.*

**1625** *Laws Stannaries* xi. (1808) 21 The poiser, the tare-master and their deputies, ought to be sworn in the stannary-court.

**Tare** (tēəɹ), *v.* [f. Tare *sb.*[2]] *trans.* To ascertain, allow for, or indicate the tare of.

**1812** J. Smyth *Pract. of Customs* (1821) 168 Two Jars tared three pounds each. *Ibid.* 247 It is the practice at the West India Docks to make a memorandum of the packages which are tared, on the back of the blue book. **1880** Lomas *Alkali Trade* 246 It is usual not to tare the casks at all, but to invoice the gross weight as soda. **1890** *Pall Mall G.* 29 Sept. 8/2 The Custom House authorities have given notice that on and after October 1 their officers will have instructions to weigh and tare packages of tea to the half-pound instead of to the pound, as heretofore.

Hence **Tared** *ppl. a.*, of which the tare or weight when empty has been ascertained.

1854 J. Scoffern in *Orr's Circ. Sc., Chem.* 333 Being collected on a tared filter, its weight may be estimated. 18.. *U. S. Dispensatory* 575 (Cent. Dict.) The neck of a bottle..marked for the quantity of liquid to be percolated, ..or of a tared bottle, if the percolate is to be weighed.

**Tare**, obs., arch., and dial. f. and pa. t. of Tear *v.*1; var. Tear *sb.* fine flax: var. Tehr, Himalayan goat; obs. f. There: see T 8.

**Taree**: see Toddy.

**Tarentine** (tæ·rĕntəin), *a.* (*sb.*) [ad. L. *Tarentīn-us* of Tarentum.] Of or pertaining to Tarentum. † **Tarentine spider**, the Tarantula. † **b.** *sb.* Name of some herb.

c1440 *Pallad. on Husb.* ii. 372 And yf thou wolt ha nuttis Tarentyne. 1668 *Phil. Trans.* III. 660 The structure of the body of this Tarentin Spider. 1698 Fryer *Acc. E. India & P.* 119 Herbs for Salading are Purslain, Sorrel, Lettice, Parsley, Tarentine, Mint, and Sog, a sort of Spinach.

**Tarentism**, variant of Tarantism.

‖ **Tarentola** (tăre·ntǝlă). [It.: see Tarantula.] A harmless lizard, *Tarentola* (*Platydactylus*) *mauritanica*, the Moorish Gecko, found in southern Europe and northern Africa. Also the genus to which this belongs. So **Tarente**.

[1838 *Penny Cycl.* XI. 104/2 Those lizards which the Italians called *Tarentola*.] 1883 in *List Anim. Zool. Soc.* (1896) 577.

**Tarentola, -tula**, obs. ff. Tarantula.

† **Ta·rer.** *Obs.* [f. Tare *sb.*2 + -er 1.] An assay-officer of the stannaries, who ascertained the amount of dross or foreign matter in the tin.

1625 *Laws Stannaries* ix. (1808) 20 If the tin be not found faulty to the value assessed by the tarer [etc.]. *Ibid.* x, If any man..hide worse matter than tin within his..blocks of tin, which the tarer by his outward essay with his chizel cannot come at.

† **Tare·tte.** *Obs. rare.* Also 4 ta·rrit. [a. OF. *tarete, = *taride* (13th c. in Godef.), = med.L. *tarīda*, *tarēta* 'navis onerariæ species, eadem quæ Tartana vocitata, ut quidam volunt' (Du Cange), a. Arab. طريدة *tarīdah* 'actuaria navis'; cf. med. Gr. ταρίδος = δρόμων (ibid.).] A kind of ship of burden or merchant vessel of the Middle Ages. Cf. Tartan *sb.*2

a1352 Minot *Poems* iii. 80 Eight and forty galays and mo, And with tham als war tarettes two. [1354 in Rymer *Fœdera* (1825) III. i. 274/1 Sciatis quod suscepimus in protectionem..tres taritas, diversis bonis & mercimoniis carcatas, quæ juxta insulas nostras..jacent ancoratæ.] 1362 *Ibid.* (1830) III. ii. 641 Quædam magna navis, vocata Tarrit, et tres aliæ grossæ naves.

† **Tarf**, *sb. Obs.* [A deriv. of Tirve *v.* to turn: cf. Turf *sb.*2] The turn or facing of a cap.

1545 *Rates of Customs* A viij, Cappes with syngle tarfs the dossen xiii. s. iiii d. 1555 Watreman *Fardle of Facions* ii. xi. 245 Then aftrewarde are thei [Janizarie] chosen into souldie, and haue giuen them..a white cappe, with a tarfe tourned vpwarde.

Hence †**Ta·rfed** *a.*, having a tarf. See also Turfed.

1545 *Rates of Customs* A viij, Cappes double tarfed & necked, and all other of frenche makyng.

‖ **Tarfa** (ta·rfā). Also tarfah. [a. Arab. طرفا *ṭarfā*.] The tamarisk, *Tamarix gallica*, which exudes a gum called manna. Also *attrib.*

1858 Bonar *Hymns Faith & Hope* 216 Creeping through the wiry boughs Of these tarfas. 1859 Martin tr. *Kurtz's Hist. Old Covt.* III. 31 The manna produced on the tarfah shrub is caused by the prick of an insect. 1870 Jas. Hamilton *Moses* xiii. 216 Jehovah did not ignore the few drops which already trickled from the tarfah-trees.

**Targat(e, -gatt**, obs. forms of Target.

**Targe** (tāɹdʒ), *sb.*1 Now *arch.* and *poet.* Forms: 3– targe; also 4 tarche, 5 taarge, 6 terge, *Sc.* 6– tairge. [In late OE. *targe* fem., *targa* masc., ME. *targe*, = OF. *targe* (11th c. in *Roland*) = It. *targa*, Pr. *targua*, ad. ON. *targa* fem. (c950 in Vigf.), shield, cogn. with OHG. *zarga* fem., 'edging, border'. OE. *targe* fem., *targa* masc. were prob. from ON.; ME. *targe* from OF.; the Pr. and Sp. *tarja*, MHG. *tartsche*, early mod.Du. *tartsche*, *targie*, also from French. (The OCat. *darga*, Sp. and Pg. *adarga*, appear to be from Arab. الدرقة *al-darqah* the shield of leather and wood.)]

**1.** A shield; *spec.* a light shield or buckler, borne instead of the heavy shield, esp. by footmen and archers.

[c997 *Charter of Ædderic* in Kemble *Cod. Dipl.* III. 304 Twa targan and twegen francan. c1015 *Charter of Æðelstan Æðeling* ibid. 363 Ic ȝeann Ælmere minen discðene..mines taregan.] 1297 R. Glouc. (Rolls) 7462 Wiþ stronge targes hom biuore þat archers ne dude hom noȝt. 13.. *Sir Beues* (A.) 4214 Þo Beues seȝ is strokes large, He kepte his strokes wiþ is targe. c1386 Chaucer *Prol.* 471 On hir heed an hat As brood as is a bokeler or a targe [*rime* large]. c1470 Henry *Wallace* viii. 799 Feill Inglismen..With schot was slayn, for all thar targis strang. 1549 *Compl. Scot.* vi. 42 Tua handit sourdis and tairgis. 1569 Stocker tr. *Diod. Sic.* i. xiii. 22 His footemen which carried the terges and scaling ladders. 1667 Milton *P. L.* ix. 1111 Those Leaves They [Adam & Eve] gatherd, broad as Amazonian Targe,..To gird thir waste. 1715–20 Pope *Iliad* xiii. 513 The spacious targe (a blazing round, Thick with bull-hides and brazen orbits bound). 1810 Scott *Lady of L.* v. xv, Ill fared it then with Roderick Dhu, That on the field his targe he threw. 1894 Gladstone *Odes Horace* ii. vii, Philippi's headlong rout we shared, I parted from my targe, not well.

**b.** *fig.*

a1300 *Cursor M.* 9972 (Cott.) Maria maiden, mild o mode ..standes vs for sceild and targe [*Laud* tarche]. 1536 Bellenden *Cron. Scot.* (1821) II. 181 Knawing weill that devine helpe is the only targe and sicker munition of kingis and realmes. a1578 Lindesay *Chron. Scot.* (S.T.S.) I. 127 Ane faithfull subiect and sicker tairge to the commone weill. 1599 Jas. I Βασιλ. Δωρον (1682) To Rdr., To which hydra of diverslie enclined spectators, I have no targe to oppone.

† **2.** A name applied in the reigns of the first three Edwards to the King's private or privy seal (perh. bearing a shield as its device). *Obs.*

[1309 *Rolls of Parlt.* I. 444/2 Quant as Brefs de la targe, le Roy voet, qe l'Ordenance soit gardee, qe en fust fait en temps le Roy son pere, laquele est en Chancellerie. a1315 *Lib. de Antiq. Leg.* (Camden) App. 252 Ces lettres desuz son prive seal de la targe. 1315 *Rolls of Parlt.* I. 339/1 Par Bref de la targe. 1347 *Ibid.* II. 193/1 Briefs soutz le grant Seal, & Lettres soutz la targe.] c1492 *Gest Robyn Hode* ccclxxxv. in Child *Ballads* III. 75/1 He toke out the brode targe [*v.r.* seale], And sone he lete hym se.

† **b.** (See quot.) *Obs. rare.*

c1440 *Promp. Parv.* 487/1 Targe, or chartyr, *carta*.

**3.** *attrib.* and *Comb*: targeman, a man armed with a targe.

?17.. *Battle of Sheriff-Muir* (Cent. Dict.), He stoutly encounter'd the targemen. 1895 *Daily News* 29 Oct. 6/5 The twin targe brooch that clasps her robe.

† **Targe**, *sb.*2 *Obs.* [f. Targe *v.*1] Tarrying, delay.

13.. *Coer de L.* 2790 Whenne that ilke man hadde hys charge, Home they wolden, withouten targe.

**Targe**, *sb.*3 *Sc.* [f. Targe *v.*3] = Targer.

1887 Service *Dr. Duguid* ix. 67 Bessie Graham was a terr'ble tairge, and had a tinkler tongue in the heid of her. 1896 J. Horne *Canny Countryside* iv. 40 Fat wud ye do wi' a targe lek her?

† **Targe**, *v.*1 *Obs.* [a. OF. *targier*, *targer* (11th c. in Godef.) to tarry:—pop.L. type *tardicāre, deriv. of L. *tardāre* to be late, to tarry, f. *tardus* slow. (For Fr. form cf. *juger*:—L. *jūdicāre*.) See also Tarry *v.*] *intr.* To delay; = Tarry *v.* Hence † **Targing** *vbl. sb.*

c1250 *O. Kentish Serm.* in *O. E. Misc.* 36 Ne solde no man targi for to wende to godalmichti ne him to serui. c1290 *S. Eng. Leg.* I. 350/177 Þo he [Askebert] targede a luyte þis luþere dede to done. 1297 R. Glouc. (Rolls) 2363 War-to [= why] targe [*MSS.* 1400– tarie, tarye] we so long to quelle him atten ende? a1330 *Otuel* 833 Þo wenten þei forþ wiþouten targing. c1400 *Laud Troy Bk.* 7588 So weri thei ben and ouer-charged, Here socour foule fro hem targed. c1440 *Pallad. on Husb.* iii. 1075 Fructifying wodes.. Wherof sum fruit wol targe & sum wol hie.

† **Targe**, *v.*2 *Obs. rare.* [f. Targe *sb.*1, or a. OF. *targier*, *targer* (13th c. in Godef.) to protect, defend (cf. mod.F. *targuer*, a. It. *targar(si)*), f. *targe*: see Targe *sb.*1] *trans.* To protect or defend as with a targe or shield; to shield.

c1430 *Pilgr. Lyf Manhode* i. cxxviii. (1869) 68 This targe targede him as longe as he bar it with him. 1489 Caxton *Faytes of A.* i. i. 2 Couenable to couure & targe the body of man agaynst the strokes of dartes.

**Targe**, *v.*3 *Sc.* Also tairge, terge. [Origin and, hence also, the sense development uncertain. Jamieson and E. D. D. start with the sense 'to beat, strike, thrash', but quote no instances before 1833. (L. *tergere* to rub, wipe, cleanse, correct, has been suggested.) The 'soft' *g* (dʒ) suggests Romanic origin.]

**1.** *trans.* To question closely, cross-examine.

1786 Burns *Inventory* 41, I on the questions tairge them tightly. 1819 W. Tennant *Papistry Storm'd* (1827) 213 Tairge them about it now..O' sic ane styk untill this day We never heard a cheep! 1869 Trollope *Phineas Finn.* (ed. Tauchn.) II. iii, He..had on this occasion targed two or three commissariat officers very tightly with questions respecting cabbages and potatoes.

**2.** To keep in strict order, look after strictly.

1814 Scott *Wav.* xlii, Callum Beg..discharging the obligation, by mounting guard over the hereditary tailor of Sliochd nan Ivor; and, as he expressed himself, 'targed him tightly' till the finishing of the job. 1858 Trollope *Linda Tressel* i. 13 Linda..was..targed more strictly in the reading of godly books.

**3.** To reprimand, scold loudly; to beat, thrash.

1825 Jamieson, To *Targe*, *Tairge*, to beat, to strike, *Perths.* 1833 J. S. Sands *Poems* Ser. i. 105 (E.D.D.) Targed him tightly till he fell. 1861 R. Quin *Heather Lintie* (1866) 165 Targe him tichtly wha debases Frail human nature.

**Targer** (tā·ɹdʒəɹ). *Sc.* Also tairger, terjer. [f. Targe *v.*3 + -er 1.] One who targes; a termagant; a scold.

1822 Carlyle *Early Lett.* (1886) II. 104 Where is the targer? 1886 Murdoch *Sc. Readings* Ser. ii. 59 Happily rid o' his awfu' terjer o' a mither-in-law. 1899 Crockett *Kit Kennedy* xxix, O, she's a tairger.

**Target** (tā·ɹgĕt), *sb.*1 Forms: α. 5 tergett, 5–7 targett, 4– target; β. 5–6 targat, 6 -gatt, tergat(e, -guette, *Sc.* tergatt, tarcat, 6–7 targuet. [dim. of Targe *sb.*1: cf. F. *targete*, *-ette*, also 15–16th c. *targuet(t)e*, It. *targhetta*.

The actual history is uncertain, chiefly from the ambiguity of the spelling *target*. The current pronunciation with 'hard *g*' (g) is carried back to 15th c. by the spelling *targat* (so in 16th c. *-guet*), but the early spelling *target* might be (tā·ɹdʒet), which would have been the natural English diminutive of Targe. In French also, the ordinary form was *targete*, *targette* (-ʒe·t); but, alongside of this, *targuete* (-ge·t), is cited of 1494, and *-guette* in 16th c. (possibly after Pr. *targuetta* or It. *targhetta*). It is possible that Eng. *target* had at first 'soft g' (dʒ) after *targe* and OF. *target(t)e*, but that this was at an early date changed to the present pronunciation with 'hard g', after F. *targuet(t)e*, and the Prov. and Italian forms.]

**1.** A light round shield or buckler; a small targe. Also *fig.* Now chiefly *Hist.*

α. c1400 Maundev. (Roxb.) xxi. 97 Þai bere a grete target, with whilk þai couer all þaire body. a1400–50 *Alexander* 2622 Taches in-to targetis tamed þaire brenys. c1440 *Promp. Parv.* 487/1 Ta(r)get, or defence,..*scutum*, *ancile*. 1483 *Cath. Angl.* 380/1 A Tergett, *pelta*. a1548 Hall *Chron., Hen. VIII* 2 The kynges banner and courser, his coate of armes, his sworde, his target, and his helme. 1633 T. Stafford *Pac. Hib.* i. iv. (1821) 55 At whom hee discharged his Pistoll, which lighted upon his Targett. 1724 De Foe *Mem. Cavalier* (1840) 147 [The highlanders] carried great wooden targets, large enough to cover the upper part of their bodies. 1791 Boswell *Johnson* 17 Oct. an. 1773, He strutted about the room with a broad sword and target. 1869 Boutell *Arms & Arm.* ix. (1874) 164 The Scots auxiliary troops, who took a part with the French forces at the battle of Fontenoy, appeared with shields or targets.

β. 14.. *Voc.* in Wr.-Wülcker 615/27 *Targia*, a targat, or a pavys. 1507 *Acc. Ld. High Treas. Scot.* III. 394 To Simon Glasfurd buklarmakar, for hornyng of foure tergatis, ..iij li. 1508 *Ibid.* IV. 121 Item, payit..for ane sicht of ane tarcat, thre lokkis to basnetis, xij bukkilles. 1513 Douglas *Æneis* viii. vii. 146 The horrible tergate, bustuus Egida, Quhilk is the grevit Pallas grysly scheild. 1542 Udall *Erasm. Apoph.* 314 The image of the same Quintus made with his terguette. 1556 *Chron. Gr. Friars* (Camden) 93 Havyng their targattes on their sholderes.

† **2.** A shield-shaped ornament or plaque of precious metal, often jewelled, worn esp. as a decoration in the head-dress. *Sc. Obs.*

1507 *Acc. Ld. High Treas. Scot.* IV. 15 Tua targetis for bonetis hornyt with gold for bonetis. 1542 *Inv. Roy. Wardrobe* (1815) 68 Item ane bonet of blak velvott with ane tergat of the marmadin, hir taill of dyamonttis. 1556 Lauder *Tractate* 439 Nocht haueand respect..To Tergats, Chenis, nor goldin Ryngis. a1578 Lindesay (Pitscottie) *Chron. Scot.* (S.T.S.) I. 368 He gaif hir great giftis of cheinzeis targattis and tablattis and ringis. ?a1600 *Johnie Armstrong*, Ther hang nine Targats at Johnys Hat, And ilk an worth Three hundred Pound.

† **b.** A piece of money: app. a scudo, an écu.

[Cf. med.L. *scutum*, *scutatum* a coin of the early French kings (Du Cange).] 1671 H. M. tr. *Erasm. Colloq.* 79 What price dost thou set upon thyself? At ten targets [orig. *Decem scutatis*].

**3.** Orig., A shield-like structure, marked with concentric circles, set up to be aimed at in shooting practice; hence, any object used for the purpose.

1757 E. Perronet *Mitre* i. cxxxix, The Target of the Muse. [*Note.* This word is here used in the military sense, and signifies a But or mark to be shot at.] 1801 Strutt *Sports & Past.* ii. i. § 17, I have seen the gentlemen who practise archery in the vicinity of London, repeatedly shoot from end to end, and not touch the target with an arrow. 1802–16 C. James *Milit. Dict.*, *Target*,..a mark for the artillery, &c. to fire at in their practice. 1859 *Musketry Instr.* iv. 51 The targets are to be six feet in height and two in breadth, constructed of iron of sufficient thickness to be rifle-bullet proof. 1871 Tyndall *Fragm. Sc.* (1879) I. xvi. 423 In firing a ball against a target the projectile, after collision, is often found hot.

*fig.* 1900 Ld. Roberts in *Daily News* 27 July 5/3 The enemy were strongly entrenched, fought stubbornly, and gave no target.

**b.** *fig.* Something aimed at or to be aimed at; *esp.* a person who is the object of general abuse, scorn, derision, or the like; = Butt *sb.*4 5.

1757 [see 3]. 1842 Tennyson *Locksley Hall* 146 They to whom my foolish passion were a target for their scorn. 1889 *Tablet* 14 Dec. 947 A target for the abuse of the prejudiced, the ignorant and the profane. 1906 *Times* 24 July 8/5 A target for popular ridicule.

**c.** A shooting match; the score made at such a match.

1825 *Sporting Mag.* XVI. 426 A grand target of the Reedwood Foresters took place the middle of August at Blithfield. 1858 Greener *Gunnery* 313 A comparison between the largest 'target' of to-day, and the best that Colonel Hawker ever made with his crack Joe Manton, will show a progressive improvement of nearly 100 per cent., not only in closeness of shooting, but also in penetration. 1884 *Pall Mall G.* 26 July 8/2 The Artists' team have made a magnificent target, and are scarcely likely to be beaten.

**4.** Applied to various objects resembling a target or shield. † **a.** A cymbal. *Obs.*

1696 tr. *Du Mont's Voy. Levant* xxi. 275 They have a kind of Violin, with three Strings,..and several little Brazen Targets, which..they knock against one another.

**b.** *Cookery.* The neck and breast of lamb as a joint; the fore-quarter without the shoulder.

1756 Gray *Let. to W. Mason* 19 Dec., Lord Surrey loved buttered lyng and targets of mutton for breakfast. 1872 Mary Jewry *Every-day Cookery* 72/2 Roast Target of Lamb. *Ibid.*, Target is only the breast and neck joints not separated.

**c.** The sliding sight on a levelling staff; a vane.

**d.** A disk-shaped signal on a railway switch, etc., indicating its position. *U. S.*

1877 Knight *Dict. Mech.*, *Target*,..the sight, sliding on a leveling-staff. Also called a vane. 1884 *Ibid.* Suppl. 810/1 Two targets, generally a round and an oblong one, and generally painted red and white respectively, are set at right angles to each other on a revolving shaft. *Ibid.*, A common form of ordinary switches is an upright pivoted lever with target on top. **1900** H. M. WILSON *Topogr. Surveying* xv. 311 Leveling rods are of two general types: 1 Target rods; and 2 Speaking or self-reading rods. *Ibid.* 313 The Boston [leveling] rod has a fixed target, and all readings upon it are obtained by extending the rod.

**5.** *attrib.* and *Comb.*, as *target-firing, -practice, -range, -shooting, -shot*; *target-like, -proof, -shaped* adjs.; **target-card**: see quot.; † **target-fence**, a protective fence or covering formed by targets or shields; a testudo; **target-lamp, -lantern**, *U. S.*, a lamp or lantern attached to a signal-target (see sense 4 d), the function of which it discharges at night; **target-man**, † (*a*) a man armed with a target (*obs.*); (*b*) *U. S.* a signal-man who works signalling targets: see sense 4 d; **target-rifle**, a rifle adapted to target shooting; † **target-roof**, a testudo (= *target-fence*); **target-ship**, a condemned ship used as a target.

**1875** *Encycl. Brit.* II. 378 (*Archery*) *Target-card, a card coloured in the same manner as the target, containing the names of the shooters, and used for scoring their respective hits. **1598** GRENEWEY *Tacitus, Ann.* XIII. ix. (1622) 191 Hauing deuided his armie into foure parts, he [Corbulo] lead some close and thicke ranked together, for a *target fence to vndermine and beate downe the rampire. **1653** H. COGAN tr. *Pinto's Trav.* lxix. (1663) 280 The Elephants withall setting their Trunks to the target fences.. tore them down in such sort, as not one of them remained entire. **1832** G. DOWNES *Lett. Cont. Countries* I. 138 A shooting-establishment, where *target-firing is practised. **1555** EDEN *Decades* 55 He browght furth al his *target men for feare of theyr venemous arrowes. **1884** KNIGHT *Dict. Mech.* Suppl. s. v. *Signaling Target*, Turned by the targetman by means of a hand-lever. **1844** *Regul. & Ord. Army* 288 The Surgeon, or Assistant-Surgeon, is to attend all Field Days, and invariably at *Target-practice. **1902** *Bible Student* Oct. 198 They may safely tolerate attacks as the target practice of children. **1895** *Outing* (U.S.) XXVI. 79/1 The State owns two large *target ranges which are also used as camp grounds. **1901** *Westm. Gaz.* 23 Dec. 4/3 As a *target-rifle the Lee-Metford is by no means in the front rank. **1601** HOLLAND *Pliny* I. 189 The vse..of the pauois, mantelets, *targuet-roofs, for the assault of cities. **1610** — *Camden's Brit.* I. 36 The Romans with a Testudo, or targuet-roofe..tooke the place. **1837** P. KEITH *Bot. Lex.* 200 The pedicle..supports a *target-shaped substance. **1901** *Pall Mall G.* 23 July 1 A *target ship, on board of which every new type of armour was tested. **1905** *Blackw. Mag.* May 646/2 It is foolish for an indifferent *target-shot to go lion-hunting.

**Ta·rget**, *sb.*[2] *Sc.* [Etym. uncertain; Jamieson compares Sw. *targa* to tear.] A tatter, a shred.

**1773** R. FERGUSSON *Compl. Plainstanes* 86 The weight o' ilka codroch chiel, That does my skin to targets peel. **1789** D. DAVIDSON *Th. Seasons* 120 Until her apron was sae stent, The strings in targets, flew.

**b** *Targets of skate*, 'long slices of this fish dried' (Jam.).

**Ta·rget**, *v.* [f. TARGET *sb.*[1]]

† **1.** *trans.* To protect with or as with a target; to shield. *Obs.*

**1611** G. H. *Anti-Coton* 18 [He] targets himselfe with the authoritie of Siluester. **1686** F. SPENCE tr. *Varillas' Ho. Medicis* 337 The garrison of Florence..was not sufficient to ward and target it from insult.

**2.** To use (a person) as a target. Also *fig.*

**1837** *Fraser's Mag.* XVI. 244 If you doubt my word, load and target me again. **1844** W. H. MAXWELL *Sports & Adv. Scott.* iii. (1855) 49 To be targetted through..the..newspapers and executed afterwards in effigy.

**3.** *U. S.* To signal the position of (a railway switch, etc.) by means of a target (TARGET *sb.*[1] 4 d).

**1893** *Columbus* (Ohio) *Dispatch* 17 Nov., The crews of both trains claim to have had the crossing targeted.

**Targeted** (tā·ɹgėtėd), *a.* [f. TARGET *sb.*[1] + -ED[2].] Furnished with a target or shield, or with something resembling one.

**1653** GAUDEN *Hierasp.* 527 Not rough and targetted as the Rhinoceroes, but soft and gently clothed as the sheep. **1848** CLOUGH *Bothie* Poems (1892) 202 The Marquis's targeted gillies.

**Targeteer** (tāɹgėtīᵊ·ɹ). *Obs.* exc. *Hist.* Also 6–7 targe(t)tier, 7 targatier, -tyer, targuattier, targue(t)tier, targueteere. [prob. ad. It. *targhettiere* (Florio), f. *targhetta* target: see -EER.] A foot-soldier armed with a target; a peltast.

**1586–8** in Hakluyt *Voy.* (1600) III. 812 Our General himselfe with certaine shot and some targettiers went ouer into the maine. **1590** MARLOWE *Edw. II*, III. ii, A band of bow-men and of pikes, Brown bills and targeteers, four hundred strong. **1600** HOLLAND *Livy* XXVIII. v. 670 A thousand targuattiers called Peltati. **1601** R. JOHNSON *Kingd. & Commw.* (1603) 18 He [Chas. VII of France]..adioined to them Targatiers, Harbengers, Mustermasters. **1676** HOBBES *Iliad* 53 He found him out With many targetiers environed. **1824** MACAULAY *Misc. Writ.* (1860) I. 176 The targeteers of Iphicrates. **1881** JOWETT *Thucyd.* I. 147 The Chalcidian hoplites..were assisted by a few targeteers.

† **Targeter.** *Obs.* In 4 tergeter. [f. TARGET *sb.* + -ER[1].] A shield-maker, or a shield-bearer.

**1382** WYCLIF *2 Chron.* xii. 10 The golden tergetis..for the whiche the kyng made brasen, and toke hem to the princis of the tergeteris [1388 scheeld makeris; Vulg. *scutariorum*]. *Ibid.* 11 Whanne the kyng schulde goone in to the house of the Lord, the tergeters [Vulg. *scutarii*] camen, and token hem.

† **Ta·rgeting.** *Sc. Obs. rare.* [f. TARGET *sb.*[1] 2 + -ING[1] 1 f.] Work consisting of targets; target-like trimmings of women's dresses.

**1563** KNOX *Hist. Ref.* IV. Wks. 1848 II. 389 The seally sowll..can neather cary with it gold, garnassing, targatting, pearle, nor pretious stanes. *a* **1651** CALDERWOOD *Hist. Kirk* (1843) II. 216 The preachers spake freelie against the targetting of weomen's tailes, and the rest of their vanitie.

**Tar-grass**: see TARE *sb.*[1] 4.

**Targum** (tā·ɹgǫm, ‖ taɹgū·m), *sb.* Also 6–7 thargum. [a. Chaldee תרגום *targūm* interpretation, f. תרגם *targēm* to interpret: see DRAGOMAN.] Each of several Aramaic translations, interpretations, or paraphrases of the various divisions of the Old Testament, made after the Babylonian captivity, at first preserved by oral transmission, and committed to writing from about A.D. 100 onwards.

The extant Targums together comprise all the books except Ezra, Nehemiah, and Daniel.

**1587** GOLDING *De Mornay* xxvii. (1592) 427 The Thargum of Hierusalem and the Onkelos which are bookes of cheefe authoritie among the Iewes. **1613** PURCHAS *Pilgrimage* (1614) 174 This the Hebrewes call *Targum*, that is, the Translation, which hath with them no lesse credit then the Text it selfe. **1646** SIR T. BROWNE *Pseud. Ep.* v. x. 249 Jonathan who compiled the Thargum, conceives the colours of these banners to answer the pretious stones in the breastplate, and upon which the names of the Tribes were engraven. **1706** A. BEDFORD *Temple Mus.* viii. 159 We find the Targum of Onkelos to be mark't with the Accents. **1776** BURNEY *Hist. Mus.* I. 228 *note*, The Targum, or Chaldee Paraphrase, mentions an instrument not to be found in the original, or in any of the translations. **1864** *Reader* 16 Jan. 74/1 The Targums are versions of the Old Testament in what has been called Chaldee, but which is, in fact, the language of Aram or Syria.

Hence **Targum** *v. trans.*, to interpret or paraphrase (Scripture) in the manner of the Targums (also *absol.*); **Targumic** (taɹgū·mik), **Targu·mical**, *adjs.*, of or pertaining to the Targums; **Targu·mically** *adv.*, in the manner of the Targums.

*a* **1873** DEUTSCH *Rem.* (1874) 361 The authenticity of the Targumic Texts. **1883** F. DELITZSCH in *Athenæum* 26 May 668/3 A considerable number of Targumic and Talmudic words..occur in the Assyrian and Babylonian language. **1883** EDERSHEIM *Life & Times Jesus* I. II. viii. 206 At that time each one Targumed for himself...The New Testament writers..when it seemed necessary, literally or Targumically rendered a verse. *Ibid.* II. v. xiv. 574 S. Matthew, Targuming this prophecy in form as in its spirit.

**Targumist** (tā·ɹgǫmist, taɹgū·mist). [f. TARGUM *sb.* + -IST.] **a.** One of the translators and commentators who compiled the Targums. **b.** 'One versed in the language and literature of the Targums' (Ogilvie).

**1642** MILTON *Apol. Smect.* i. Wks. 1851 III. 282 Then we must conclude that Jonathan, or Onkelos the Targumists were of cleaner language then he that made the tongue. **1695** J. EDWARDS *Perfect. Script.* 482 It can't be expected that these Targumists should render the Hebrew word for word. **1851** M. A. DENHAM *Slogans N. Eng.* p. ix, The Targumists state that the banners were distinguished by their colours. **1891** T. K. CHEYNE *Orig. Ps.* viii. 444 Is the Targumist altogether wrong in his general view?

Hence **Targumi·stic** *a.*, of or pertaining to the Targumists.

**1890** *Andover* (U. S.) *Rev.* VII. 101 (Cent. Dict.) Showing the prevalence of the Targumistic exegesis.

**Ta·rgumize**, *v.* [f. TARGUM *sb.* + -IZE.] *trans.* To make a Targum of or upon.

**1671** LIGHTFOOT *Horæ Hebr., John* viii. 59 The Book of Job..Targumised; (that is, renderd into the Chaldee Tongue). *a* **1873** DEUTSCH *Rem.* (1874) 399 The Book of Esther..has been targumised many times.

**Tarheel** (tā·ɹ,hīl). *U. S. colloq.* [f. TAR *sb.* + HEEL *sb.*] A nickname for a native or inhabitant of North Carolina, in allusion to tar as a principal product of that State. Also *attrib.*

**1888** *American Humorist* 2 June (Farmer *Americanisms*), A little volume of North Carolina sketches, written by a talented young friend of mine, in the genuine tarheel dialect. **1889** *Jrnl. Amer. Folk-Lore* II. 95 The mountain 'tarheel' gradually drifted into a condition of dreary indifference to all things sublunary but hog and hominy.

**Ta·rhood.** *nonce-wd.* [f. TAR *sb.* 3 + -HOOD.] The general body of sailors; sailors collectively.

**1749** H. WALPOLE *Lett.* (1846) II. 264 This circumstance.. has been so ridiculed by the whole tar-hood, that the romantic part has been forced to be cancelled.

**Tarie**, obs. f. TARRY *sb.* and *v.*, var. TARY *v.*

**Tarier**, obs. form of TARRIER, TERRIER[2].

**Tariff** (tæ·rif), *sb.* Forms: 6–8 tariffa, 7 terrif, 8 terif, 8–9 tarif, 7– tariff. [a. It. *tariffa* 'arithmetike or casting of accounts' (Florio), 'a book of rates for duties' (Baretti), = Sp., Pg. *tarifa*, ad. Arab. تعريف *taʿrīf* notification, explanation, definition, article, f. عرف *ʿarafa* in 1st conj. to notify, make known. So F. *tarif.*

The word came into general use as a technical term (sense 2), and this character it long retained in English use, being hardly found, except as applied to the Customs 'tariff'; its more general application (sense 3), found earlier on the Continent and in U. S., has become more common in Great Britain only since *c* 1890.]

† **1.** An arithmetical table or statement; a table of multiplication, a ready reckoner, or the like.

**1591** *Garrard's Art Warre* 224 So that helping your memorie with certain *Tablei* or *Tariffas* made of purpose to know the numbers of the souldiers that are to enter into ranke. **1704** J. HARRIS *Lex. Techn.* I, *Tarif*, (in *Arithmetick*) is either a small Table..to expedite Multiplication; or else a Proportional Table contrived for the expediting a Question in the Rule of Fellowship. **1726** COLSON in *Phil. Trans.* XXXIV. 170 Reduce the Dividend and Divisor to small Figures, and form a Tariffa or Table of all the Multiples of the Divisor as far as 5. **1727** BAILEY vol. II, *Tariff* (with Arithmeticians) a proportional Table contrived for the speedy resolving Questions in the Rule of Fellowship;.. Also a Table framed to shew..any Multiple or Divisor, taken any Number of Times under ten. **1770** *Monthly Rev.* 507 That a tariff or table may be established of these proportions.

**2.** An official list or schedule setting forth the several customs duties to be imposed on imports and exports; a table or book of rates; any item of such a list, the impost (on any article); also the whole body or system of such duties as established in any country.

**1592** WOTTON *Lett., to Ld. Zouche* 3 Oct. (1907) I. 288 The book that I put to be copied for your Honour is not yet ended, nor the *tariffa* of all the towns in the Grand Duke's territories, in my hands. *a* **1700** B. E. *Dict. Cant. Crew, Tariff*, a Book of Rates or Customs. **1713** *Treaty Utrecht* in Magens *Insurances* (1755) II. 495 The general Tariff made in France the 18th Day of September in the Year 1664, shall take place again. *a* **1719** ADDISON (J.), A tariff, or declaration of the duties of import and export. **1725** *Lond. Gaz.* No. 6414/2 The putting..into Execution the new Tarif or Book of Rates. **1816** (Feb. 12) SEC. DALLAS in *Ann. Congress* (1854) 1674 A statement of the general principles for reforming the tariff of the United States. **1845** McCULLOCH *Taxation* II. v. (1852) 238 The duties in this tariff mostly vary from 40 to 5 per cent. *ad valorem.* **1868** M. E. G. DUFF *Pol. Surv.* 25 The kingdom's wealth might be economized by the adoption of a free-trade tariff. **1879** ROGERS in *Cassell's Techn. Educ.* IV. 128/2 A tariff..of a highly protective character, in the interest of employers or manufacturers.

**3.** A classified list or scale of charges made in any private or public business; as, a hotel tariff, a railroad tariff (*U. S.*).

*a* **1751** BOLINGBROKE *Fragments* xxx. Wks. 1754 V. 246 Even in times less antient, the church of Rome found it necessary to publish a tariff, or book of rates, which I have seen in print, wherein the price is set over against every sin, lest purchasers should be imposed upon. **1837–9** HALLAM *Hist. Lit.* I. iii. § 147 The university of Paris proceeded to establish a tariff, according to which every edition was to be sold. **1838** *Murray's Hand-bk. N. Germ.* 428 Tariff per post of 2 German miles. **1867** HOWELLS *Ital. Journ.* 204 Show me the tariff of fares. **1881** *Chicago Times* 12 Mar., The following is the present railroad tariff on flour, grain, and boxed meats from Chicago to the eastern points named.

**4.** *attrib.* and *Comb.*; **a.** attrib., as *tariff-act, -bill, -duty, -legislation, -monger, -movement, -office, -party, -preference, -question, -treaty*; **b.** instrumental, as *tariff-born, -bound, -fed, -protected, -raised, -ridden* adjs.; **c.** objective and obj. gen., as *tariff-maker*; *tariff-mongering, -raising, -regulating, -tinkering* adjs. See also TARIFF-REFORM.

**1816** *Ann. Congress* (1854) 1137 The provisions of the proposed new tariff duties. **1821** J. Q. ADAMS *Mem.* (1875) V. 309 The revival at the next session of Congress of Mr. Baldwin's tariff bills. **1824** *Ibid.* VI. 282 There had been sharp words in the tariff debate this day in the House. **1831** *Ibid.* (1876) VIII. 438 The Free-Trade and Tariff Conventions. **1832** PRES. JACKSON *Message Congr. U. S.*, A mistaken view of the considerations which led to the adoption of the tariff system. *c* **1843** GLADSTONE in Morley *Life* (1903) I. II. viii. 267 Endeavouring to make tariff treaties with foreign countries. **1862** *Macm. Mag.* Sept. 413 Stories about tariff grievances. **1884** S. E. DAWSON *Handbk. Dom. Canada* 288 As promoters of private legislation, or as tariff-doctors, or as volunteer advisers, interested or disinterested. **1891** *Century Dict.*, *Tariff-ridden*, burdened with a tariff or tariffs; carrying an excessive burden of indirect taxation. **1897** *Daily News* 21 Sept. 2/3 American tariff-tinkering. **1898** *Ibid.* 8 Aug. 8/2 A little tariff-card [of a hotel] enclosed showed that the sum stated was liable to some little expansion. **1900** *Jrnl. Sch. Geog.* (U. S.) Apr. 147 There have been twenty-five tariff acts prescribing, modifying or regulating tariff duties, the first being the Calhoun Act, 1816. **1904** *Daily News* 3 Mar. 8 A warning against tariff-mongers, tariff-meddlers, and tariff-muddlers of all denominations. **1904** JUDGE PARKER (U. S.) in *Daily Chron.* 11 Nov. 5/5 To prevent the tariff-fed Trusts and illegal combinations from absorbing the nation's wealth.

Hence (chiefly *nonce-wds.*) **Ta·riffable** *a.*, that can be subjected to a tariff; **Tariffa·de** [after *crusade*], an agitation in favour of a tariff; **Ta·riffica·tion**, (*a*) the fixing of a tariff; (*b*) conversion to a pro-tariff party; **Ta·riffism**, the principle or system of imposing a tariff, advocacy of a (high or low) tariff; **Ta·riffist**, an advocate of a tariff; **Ta·riffite**, = prec.; also *attrib.*; **Ta·riffize** *v.*, *trans.* to subject to a tariff or system of tariffs (in quot. in sense 3); **Ta·riffless** *a.*, without a tariff.

**1895** *Funk's Stand. Dict.*, *Tariffable, subjectable to a tariff. **1904** P. GEDDES in *Ideals Sc. & Faith* 201 To play his patriotic part in the approaching, ever-victorious *Tariffades by which the megalopolitan wealth and imperial greatness are to be assured. **1892** *19th Cent.* Dec. 940 Sir B. Samuelson's proposal to make compulsory the method of *tariffication..which has been optional with railway companies for forty years past. **1908** *Westm. Gaz.* 29 May 2/3 The complete tariffication of the Unionist Party. **1903** *Daily Chron.* 25 Sept. 4/5 The chief apostle of high *tariffism. **1901** *Westm. Gaz.* 3 Apr. 2/3 Taking the two bodies together the Low *Tariffists are in a majority of one. **1905** *Daily Chron.* 8 Sept. 4/4 The tariffists and purblind economists see the chief reason of Germany's industrial prosperity in its protective system. **1906** *Ibid.* 12 Jan. 5/2 This has excited great indignation on the part of the *Tariffite candidate. **1848** *Tait's Mag.* XV. 319 This would *tariffize the world. **1891** MISS DOWIE *Girl in Karp.* 271 A total stranger condescended to..make a *tariffless hotel of their house.

**Ta·riff**, *v.* [f. prec. sb. So F. *tarifer.*]

† **1.** *intr.* To have to do with a tariff. *nonce-use.*

**1756** Mrs. Calderwood *Jrnl.* (1884) 292 A tariff of fixed duties [was] to have been settled at the treaty of Utrecht, but .. was referred to commissaries; of this number was Blair's uncle, John Drummond, who tariffed all his days... Andrew Mitchell..who tariffed at Bruxells for some years.

**2.** *trans.* To subject to a tariff-duty; to fix the price of (something) according to a tariff; in quot. *a* 1868, to rate (a person) according to a tariff.

**1828** Webster, *Tarif* v. t., to make a list of duties on goods. **1864** Trevelyan *Compet. Wallah* (1866) 169 If the Sidonians ..had paid five per cent. on Madapollams tariffed at ninepence. *a* **1868** M. J. Higgins *Ess.* (1875) 158 A slow sulky conductor he silently endures, and tariffs him accurately on reaching the end of the stage. **1870** *Daily News* 6 Oct., If the siege lasts long enough, dogs, rats, and cats will be tariffed. **1887** *Westm. Rev.* June 362 In 1583 the best Gascony wine was tariffed in London..at £13 the tun. **1904** Mrs. Dauncey *Englishw. Philippines* vi. (1906) 49 For these schools and..schoolmasters this pastoral country [the Philippines] is taxed and tariffed to breaking point.

**3.** To make into a pro-tariff party. *nonce-use.*

**1909** *Westm. Gaz.* 2 Mar. 2/2 The way in which the Tory Party has been tariffed.

Hence **Tariffed** (tæ·rift) *ppl. a.*, priced by or subjected to a tariff.

**1874** Symonds *Sk. Italy & Greece* (1898) I. xiv. 299 The pay is reduced to its tariffed medium. **1903** *Westm. Gaz.* 17 Aug. 2/1 The ingenious device of buying highly tariffed foreign coffee and sending it to Cape Colony, whence it was re-shipped as preferred East Indian coffee.

**Ta·riff-refo·rm.** *gen.* The reform of a tariff, or of existing tariff conditions; *spec.* in recent U. S. politics, 'a reform favouring a general reduction of import duties, and in general a movement away from Protection' (*Cent. Dict.* 1891); in British politics since *c* 1903 (usually with capitals, *Tariff Reform*), the extension of the tariff on imports, as opposed to 'Free Trade'. Also *attrib.*, as *Tariff Reform League*, *movement*, *party*, *policy*, etc.

**1891** in *Cent. Dict.* **1895** *Funk's Stand. Dict.*, *Tariff-reform*, ..applied in the United States to a movement away from the policy of protection. **1903** Morley *Gladstone* I. II. viii. 264 It was by the principles of free trade that Peel and his lieutenant justified tariff-reform. **1903** J. Chamberlain *Sp.* Introd. 8 They [speeches] have .. been .. supplemented by statistics and details..which it is the function of the Tariff Reform League and the Imperial Tariff Committee to supply in their publications. **1908** E. E. Williams in *Westm. Gaz.* 20 Feb. 2/3 [Formed May 14, 1903 as the Protection League] A fortnight later it changed the name to the Tariff League, and again a fortnight later to that of the Imperial Tariff League..[after] some six or seven weeks it was formally amalgamated with an inchoate body (comprising chiefly members of Parliament in sympathy with the new movement) under the title of the Tariff Reform League. **1903** *Westm. Gaz.* 24 Aug. 2/2 If [Mr. Bryan's] declaration means anything, it is a notable advance in what Americans call 'Tariff Reform'—i. e., a change of the Tariff in the direction of Free Trade.

Hence **Tariff-reformer**, an advocate or supporter of tariff-reform; in British politics from 1903, an advocate of an extended tariff on imports.

**1903** J. Chamberlain *Sp.* Introd. 9 The Tariff Reformers ..believe that..by re-arming ourselves with the weapon of a moderate tariff, we may still defend our home market against unfair competition.

**Tariment**: see Tarryment.

**Taring** (tē°·riŋ). [f. Tare *sb.*[2] and *v.* + -ing [1].] The calculation and abatement of the tare on goods; † abatement for defective goods (*obs.*).

**1622** Misselden *Free Trade* ii. 51 To haue drawne the Taring [*margin*, That is, abating for the faults thereof] of Cloth into Holland, where the Buyers are in some sort, Iudges and Parties. **1882** Bithell *Counting-ho. Dict.*, *Taring*, is the process of calculating and making the Tare. **1883** *Times* 2 Apr. 4 The planter..can..put a stop to..the taring of the chest of tea by the Customs.

**Taris**, obs. form of Terrace.

**Ta·rish**, *a. rare.* [f. Tare *sb.*[1] + -ish [1].] Having the nature or character of tares (in allusion to the parable of the tares: see Tare *sb.*[1] 3).

**1601** Bp. W. Barlow *Defence* Pref. 6 Pregnant natures, are like lustie groundes, .. neglected and vntilled, [prove] tarish and weedy. **1610** J. Robinson *Justif. Separat.* iii. § 6 Wks. 1851 II. 125 A singular spirit of..discerning, by which they do discover..this tarish disposition under the veil of holiness.

**Tarisum**: see Tarrysome.

**Tarlatan** (tā·ɹlătăn). Also 8 **tarnatan**, 9 **tarlatane**, **tarleton**. [a. F. *tarlatane*, dissimilated from *tarnatane* (1723 in Hatz.-Darm.: cf. quot. 1727-41); prob. of Indian origin.] A kind of thin open muslin, used esp. for ball-dresses.

**1727-41** Chambers *Cycl.* s. v. *Muslin*, There are various kinds of muslins brought from the East-Indies; chiefly Bengal; betelles, tarnatans, mulmuls [etc.]. **1853** Lowell *Lett.* (1894) I. iii. 219 The cheapening of a tarlatan muslin. **1858** Simmonds *Dict. Trade*, *Tarlatan*, a kind of book-muslin principally made in Scotland. **1873** Miss Woolsey *What Katy Did at Sch.* x. 166 Cecy has got some beautiful new dresses,—a white muslin, a tarlatan, and a pink silk. **1903** *Daily Chron.* 3 Oct. 8/4 Tarlatan is another old-world material now being resuscitated for evening dresses.

† **Ta·rlea:ther** [1]. *Sc. Obs.* Also 6 **-ledder**, 7 **-ladder**. [app. a. Gael. *tarr-leathar* belly-leather, f. *tarr* belly + *leathar*, ad. Eng. Leather.] 'A strip of raw sheep-skin (cut from the belly of the skin when it was newly flayed), salted and dried, and cut up into thongs for ties or mid-couples of flails' (*Suppl.* to Jamieson, 1887).

**1566** *Burgh Rec. Edinb.* (1875) III. 226 The saidis flescheouris.. cuttis ane tarledder of the skyn thairwith, diminisching thairby bayth the skynnis and the woll in lenth and breid. *Ibid.*, Nor yit to diminische the samyn be cutting of ony sic pairt as thai call the tarledder. *a* **1585** Polwart *Flyting w. Montgomerie* 571 His shaven shoulders shawes the marks, no dout, Of teugh tarladders, tyres, and other tawes.

Hence † **Tarleathered** (-letherit, etc.) *ppl. a.*, *Sc. Obs.*, applied to a sheep-skin from which a tarleather has been cut.

**1570** *Rec. Convent. Roy. Burghs* I. 21 [To] be presentitt ..with the skyn and byrn vn tarletheritt, and plukkitt or powitt. **1585** *Burgh Rec. Edinb.* (1882) IV. 407 That na merchants tak vpoun hand to by any skynns quhilk ar plukket and tarletherit as said is, vnder the pain foresaid.

† **Tarleather** [2]. *Obs. rare*[—1]. A term of opprobrium applied to a woman.

**1575** *Gamm. Gurton* III. iii. C iij b, Comst behynd me thou withered witch; & I get once on foote, Thouse pay for all, y^u old tarlether.

† **Ta·rltonize**, *v. Obs. nonce-wd.* *intr.* To act or speak like Tarlton, a celebrated comic actor of the latter part of the 16th century.

**1592** G. Harvey *Four Lett.* Wks. (Grosart) I. 168 His vaine-glorious and Thrasonicall brauinge: his piperly Extemporizing, and Tarletonizing. *Ibid.* 202 The very Timpanye of his Tarltonizing wit.

**Ta·r maca·dam.** [f. Tar *sb.* + Macadam *sb.*] A mixed material for making roads, consisting of some kind of broken stone or ironstone slag in a matrix of tar alone, or of tar with some mixture of pitch or creosote.

**1882** (June 17) *Proc. Assoc. Municipal Engineers* VIII. 91 In Barnsley we have tarred macadam, and the cost of it was 1*s.* 2*d.* *Ibid.* 92, I should have liked to have heard more about the cost of the tar-macadam roads. **1883** (Sept. 28) *Ibid.* X. 53 Tar macadam for roadways was first introduced in Sheffield. **1909** J. W. Smith *Dustless Roads* i. 10 The macadamised road construction of the future is to be found in the use of tar: that is to say, in what is termed tar macadam.

Hence **Ta·rmac**, the registered trade-mark of a kind of tar macadam consisting of iron slag impregnated with tar and creosote. Also *attrib.*

**1903** *Trades Mark Jrnl.* 1 July, Class 17. Tarmac. **1904** *Westm. Gaz.* 13 Dec. 4/2 Mr. Montagu suggested .. the making of all roads..by the Tarmac process. **1905** *Times* 1 Aug. 14/2 He suggests that the club..should entirely remake some..stretch of road near London with Tarmac.

**Tarmachan, -michen**, obs. ff. Ptarmigan.

**Tarmagon, tarmegant**, obs. ff. Termagant.

**Tarmaret, -rick**, obs. erron. ff. Turmeric.

**Tarn** (tāɹn). Forms: 4-5 **terne**, 5-6 **tarne**, 7 **tearn**, (8 *Sc.* **tairn**), 7- **tarn.** [ME. *terne*, a. ON. **tarnu*, *tjorn*, *tjǫrn*; = Swed. dial. *tjärn*, *tärn*, Norw. *tjörn*, Da. *tjern.*]

A small mountain lake, having no significant tributaries. (Originally local northern English, now generally used by geologists and geographers.)

[**1256** *Assize Roll* 979 m. 10 d (Westmorland), Agnes .. appellat..Edelinam filiam Ricardi de Blaterne [= Blea-tarn] quod ipsa dederat ei potum mortiferum bibere.] **13..** *E. E. Allit. P.* B. 1041 Þer ar tres by þat terne of traytoures. *c* **1420** *Avow. Arth.* x, Gauan, with any more, To the tarne con he fore, To wake hit to day. **14..** (*heading*) The Awntyrs off Arthure at the Terne Wathelyne. **1587** Harrison *England* I. xv. in Holinshed I. 95/1 The Air or Arre riseth out of a lake or tarne south of Darnbrooke. **1674** Ray *N. C. Words*, *A Tarn*, a Lake or Meer-pool, a usual word in the North. **1797** Coleridge *Christabel* I. Concl. 28 By tairn and rill, The night-birds all that hour were still. **1810** Wordsw. *Scenery Lakes* i. (1823) 24 Tarns are found in some of the vales, and are numerous upon the mountains. **1813** Scott *Trierm.* I. x, Though never sunbeam could discern The surface of that sable tarn, In whose black mirror you may spy The stars, while noon-tide lights the sky. **1880** Haughton *Phys. Geog.* v. 235 The largest river in the world takes its most remote origin among the Andean Highlands, in a little inky tarn.

**b.** *attrib.* and *Comb.*

**1873** M. Collins *Miranda* II. 83 Miranda, whose aureate hair and tarn-brown eyes had something unique about them. **1884** Swinburne *W. Collins* Misc. (1886) 59 A picture of upland fell and tarnside copse in the curving hollow of a moor. **1885** Burton *Arab. Nts.* (abr. ed.) I. 72 The sorceress took in hand some of the tarn-water. **1903** *Smart Set* IX. 133/2 Hers is one of those clear, tarnlike natures which one gauges quickly.

**Tarn**, obs. and dial. form of Tern, the sea-bird.

**Tarnal** (tā·ɹnăl), *a.* (*adv.*) *slang*, chiefly *U. S.* Aphetic dial. pronunciation of *eternal*, vulgarly used as an expression of execration, passing into a mere intensive: cf. Eternal *a.* 7. Hence **Ta·rnally** *adv.*

**1790** R. Tyler *Contrast* II. ii. (1887) 39 The snarl-headed curs fell a-kicking and cursing of me at such a tarnal rate, that..I was glad to take to my heels. *Ibid.* 90 Laugh by rule! Well, I should like that tarnally. *a* **1821** [J. W. Masters] *Dick & Sal* lxii. (E. D. D.), Dare was a tarnal sight of meat. **1828** *Craven Gloss.*, *Tarnal*, eternal. **1848** Lowell *Biglow P.* II. 72, I darsn't skeer the tarnal thing fer fear he'd run away with 't.

**Tarnatan**, variant of Tarlatan.

**Tarnation** (taɹnē^i·ʃən), *sb.*, *a.*, *adv. slang*, chiefly *U. S.* A variant of *darnation*, Damnation *sb.* 3; app. associated with Tarnal.

**A.** as *sb. rare.*

**1801** Col. G. Hanger *Life* II. 151 The Americans say, Tarnation seize me, or swamp me, if I don't do this or that. **1832** *New England Mag.* (Boston) III. 380 We have 'Tarnation' and 'darnation' for damnation.

**B.** as *adj.* Damned, damnable, execrable.

**1784** W. Wilson in *Mem.* (1896) 47 They only came to look at the 'tarnation Tories' from Canada. **1835-40** Haliburton *Clockm.* (1862) 54 Now, says he, I'm in a tarnation hurry. **1857** Mrs. Carlyle *Lett.* (1883) II. 329 After having been all but asphyxiated with tarnation folly.

**C.** as *adv.* Damnably, desperately, execrably.

**1790** R. Tyler *Contrast* v. i. (1887) 88 What the rattle makes you look so tarnation glum? **1830** Galt *Lawrie T.* II. i, Which is tarnation bad. **1890** Gunter *Miss Nobody* vi, People..don't call me '*my good* man', for they know I'm a tarnation *bad* one when I'm riled, sonny!

**Ta·rn-cap.** *rare.* [ad. Ger. *tarnkappe.*] A magic cap, securing the invisibility of the wearer.

**1856** R. A. Vaughan *Mystics* (1860) I. 3 Rings of Gyges, coats of darkness, tarn-caps, and other means of invisibility.

**Tarne**, var. Therne, *Obs.*, girl.

**Tarnish** (tā·ɹniʃ), *sb.* [f. Tarnish *v.*] The fact of tarnishing or condition of being tarnished; loss of brightness, discoloration; stain, blemish; also *concr.* the substance of such discoloration; the tarnished coating. Also *fig.*

**1713** *Gentl. Instr.* II. ix. (ed. 5) 182 Care is taken to wash over the Foulness of the Subject with a pleasing Tarnish. **1738** *Gentl. Mag.* VIII. 580/2 The same Thing again is to be said of Tarnish, Discolouring, &c. from Time, the Air, &c. **1865** Dickens *Mut. Fr.* II. xiii, Effacing the old rust and tarnish on the money. **1877** Dana *Text-bk. Min.* II. (1891) 190 A surface possesses the steel tarnish, when it presents the superficial blue color of tempered steel. **1878** Huxley *Physiogr.* 75 There are many metals, such as gold, which never exhibit rust or tarnish.

**Tarnish** (tā·ɹniʃ), *v.* [ad. F. *terniss-*, extended stem of *ternir*, *ternissant* (15th c. in Godef.) (see -ish [2]), f. *terne* adj. dull, dark; of doubtful origin.

Referred by Diez and others to OHG. *tarnan*, MHG. *ternen* (= OS. *dernjan*, OE. *diernan*) to conceal, hide, f. OHG. *tarni* (OS. *derni*, OE. *dierne*, *derne*) hidden, secret, obscure. But there are difficulties, arising from the late appearance of the Fr. word, as well as from the form and sense. The change from *tern-* to *tarn-* appears to have taken place in English; but no example of *ternish* has been found.]

**1.** *trans.* To dull or dim the lustre of, to discolour (as a metallic surface by oxidation, etc.); to cause to fade; to spoil, wither.

**1598** Florio, *Ternire*, to tarnish, to darken any glasse with breathing vpon it [**1611** to tarnish or darken and mist-ouer, as burnished plate or glasse will be being breathed vpon]. **1709-10** Addison *Tatler* No. 121 ¶ 1 Her Clothes were very rich, but tarnished. **1726** *Adv. Capt. R. Boyle* (1768) 103 The Sun's tarnishing my Complexion. **1858** Lardner *Hand-bk. Nat. Philos.*, etc. 367 Whatever tarnishes or roughens the surface of metal, increases its radiation.

**b.** *fig.* To take away from the purity of, cast a stain upon; to sully, taint; to bring disgrace upon.

**1697** Collier *Ess.* II. *Value of Life* (1698) 31 Nothing that may..tarnish the Glory, and weaken the Example of the Suffering. **1786** W. Thomson *Watson's Philip III* (1839) 355 Unwilling that his reputation should be tarnished. **1884** L. J. Jennings *Croker Papers* I. ii. 44 The naval glory of England was tarnished by the successes of the American naval force.

**2.** *intr.* To grow dull, dim, or discoloured; to fade, wither; *esp.* of metals, to lose external brightness or lustre.

**1678** Phillips (ed. 4) s. v., Any thing that is Gilded, is said to Tarnish, when it begins to lose its Luster [**1706** to grow dull, to lose its Gloss, Lustre, or Brightness]. **1696** Tate & Brady *Ps.* cii. 27 And, like a Garment often worn Shall tarnish and decay. **1758** Johnson *Idler* No. 35 ¶ 9 The brass and pewter..are only laid up to tarnish again. **1878** Huxley *Physiogr.* 75 Many metals rapidly rust or tarnish when exposed to even the driest air.

**b.** *fig.* To become dull, dim, or sullied.

**1681** Dryden *Abs. & Achit.* 249 Till thy fresh glories, which now shine so bright, Grow stale, and tarnish with our daily sight. **1789** Mrs. Piozzi *Journ. France* II. 102 Travellers who seek for images that never tarnish, and for truths that never can decay. **1810** *Splendid Follies* II. 95 The frailties of your nature predominated the glare of your riches,..from that hour they tarnished.

Hence **Ta·rnishing** *vbl. sb.* and *ppl. a.*; also **Ta·rnishable** *a.*, that may tarnish or be tarnished; **Ta·rnisher**, one who or that which tarnishes.

**1858** Simmonds *Dict. Trade*, *Tarnishing*, a process of giving gold or silver a pale or dim cast, without either polish or burnish. **1864** Webster, *Tarnisher.* **1885** *Proc. Roy. Soc.* 7 May 340 A means of rendering tarnishable metals and alloys less tarnishable. **1894** Du Maurier *Trilby* II. 22 A tarnishing breath had swept over the reminiscent mirror of his mind.

**Tarnished** (tā·ɹniʃt), *ppl. a.* [f. prec. + -ed [1].] Having lost purity or lustre, faded; also *fig.* sullied, dishonoured.

**1716** Lady M. W. Montagu *Let. to C'tess Bristol* 22 Aug., Like a poor town lady of pleasure..with tarnished silver-laced shoes. **1726-46** Thomson *Winter* 182 The..forest.. sheds What of its tarnished honours yet remain. **1855** Macaulay *Hist. Eng.* xxii. IV. 765 He had ceased to be called by the tarnished name of Monmouth.

**Tarnowitzite** (tā·ɹnovitsəit). *Min.* [a. G. *tarnowitzit* (Breithaupt 1841): see def.] A variety of Aragonite containing about 4 per cent. of carbonate of lead, found at Tarnowitz in Silesia.

**1866** Brande & Cox *Dict. Sci.*, etc. II. 532/2. **1867** *Ibid.* III. 703/2. **1868** Dana *Min.* (ed. 5) 696 Tarnovicite.

**Taro** (tā·ro, tæ·ro). Also 8 **tarrow**, 9 **tara**, **tarro**. [Native Polynesian name, found by Cook in the Sandwich Islands.] A food-plant, *Colocasia antiquorum*, N.O. *Araceæ*, cultivated in many varieties (*C. esculenta*, *macrorhiza*, etc.) in most tropical countries for its starchy root-stocks, or its succulent leaves or stems, which in a raw state are acrid, but lose their acridity by boiling.

1779 COOK *Voy. Pacific* (1784) III. v. iv. 79 Each man carrying..bread-fruit, *taro*, and plantains in his hand. *Ibid.* vi. 106 These plantations consist of the tarrow or eddy root, and the sweet potatoe [etc.]. 1802 *Brookes' Gazetteer* (ed. 12) s.v. *Ranai*, It produces very few plantains and bread-fruit trees, but abounds in yams, sweet potatoes, and taro. 1894 *Dublin Rev.* Oct. 460 Yams and taros are cultivated.

**b.** *attrib.*, as *taro patch*, *-plain*, *-plant*, *-plantation*, *-root*, *-swamp*.

1814 W. BROWN *Hist. Propag. Chr. among Heathen* II. 400 A large piece of ground stocked with breadfruit, cocoa nuts, and tarro roots. 1846 LUNDIE *Mission. Life Samoa* xxii. 141 All are busy building houses and clearing for taro-patches. 1847 WHITTIER *Dan. Wheeler* 79 Amidst Owyhee's hills of blue And taro-plains of Tooboonai. 1894 *Daily News* 11 Sept. 6/1 Streams of water..fertilising thousands of taro plantations. 1894 B. THOMSON *S. Sea Yarns* 111 The taro swamp was hard and fissured.

**Taroc** (tæ·rǫk). Also 7–9 **tarok**, **tarock**. [ad. It. **tarocco*, in pl. *tarocchi*, of unknown origin. Also Ger. *tarock*, F. *tarot*: see TAROT.]

**a.** = TAROT a. **b.** (also in *pl.*) = TAROT b.

**a.** 1611 FLORIO, *Tarocchi*, a kind of playing cardes called Tarocks or Terestriall triumphs.

**b.** 1739 GRAY *Let. to R. West* in Mason *Mem.* (1807) I. 211 Play at Ombre and Taroc, a game with 72 cards all painted with suns, and moons, devils and monks. [1816 SINGER *Hist. Cards* 236 The pack of cards with which *Tarocco* is played, consists of two parts; the first is fifty-six cards of the usual Italian suits, *Spade*, *Coppe*, *Bastoni*, and *Denari*...The other part consists of twenty-two cards,..twenty-one of these are called *Tarocchi*, and the twenty-second *Il Matto*, or the fool.] 1887 BEATTY-KINGSTON *Music & Manners* II. 318 Skilful players of écarté and tarok.

‖ **Tarot** (tàro). [F. *tarot* (also 16th c. *tarault*, *tarau*), ad. It. **tarocco* (pl. *tarocchi*): see prec.] **a.** One of a set of playing-cards, first used in Italy in the 14th c. (Also used in fortune-telling.) Also *attrib.* **b.** *pl.* The game played with these.

The tarots, strictly speaking, are a series of 22 figured cards (21 of which are numbered), all being trumps, which are added to a set of 56 (in four suits), forming a pack of 78.

1598 G. DE LA MOTHE *French Alph.* (1639) 148 Will you play at Tables, at Dyce, at Tarots, and Chesse? 1872 W. SKEEN *Early Typogr.* 55 A single pack of 'tarots', admirably painted about 1415 by Marziano,..cost the enormous sum of 1500 golden crowns (about £625). 1888 *Chambers' Encycl.* II. 763/1 No Spanish *tarots* are known to exist. 1899 *Fortn. Rev.* Oct. 611 Piot..was..the first to collect 'Tarots', those valuable playing cards, which now fetch such a high price. 1900 *Pall Mall G.* 18 Aug. 2 (Cassell *Suppl.*) As fall the Tarot cards, so fell Each rose-page of the Oracle.

**Tarow**, obs. f. TARROW *v. Sc.*, to tarry.

‖ **Ta·rpan.** *Zool.* [According to Pallas, *Zoogr. Rosso-Asiatica* 1831, called Tarpàn by the Kirghiz Tatars. (So F. *tarpan*, Littré 1874.)] The wild horse of Tartary: see quots.

1841 C. HAMILTON SMITH *Nat. Hist. Horses* 160 The Tahtar or even the Cossack nations..assert that they can distinguish a feral breed from the wild by many tokens; and..denominate the real wild horse *Tarpan* and *Tarpani*. *Ibid.* 163 Real Tarpans are not larger than ordinary mules, their colour invariably tan, Isabella, or mouse. *Ibid.* 164 There is always a certain number of expelled Tarpan stallions among them [feral herds]. 1905 W. RIDGEWAY *Origin of Thoroughbred Horse* 34 It would appear that Prejvalsky's horse is nothing more than the Tarpan of the older writers. 1910 DR. P. CHALMERS MITCHELL *Let. to Editor*, I think it is clear that the name Tarpan belongs to a genuine wild horse, a true species, but that it has been subsequently applied to the progeny of escaped domestic horses.

† **Tarpaulian**, *sb.* and *a.* *Obs.* Forms: 7 **tarpailian**, **-paulian**, **-pollian**, 8 **-polian**, **-pawlian**. [from next, after adjs. and sbs. in *-ian*.] **a.** *sb.* = next, 2. **b.** *adj.* = next, 3 b.

*a* 1656 USSHER *Ann.* vi. (1658) 124 The number of horse-boyes, and foot-boyes, and of hangers-on, and the tarpailians in the corn-ships,..he thinks to be greater..than that of the souldiers came unto. *c* 1660 W. G. *Ode to Gresham College* in Weld *Hist. Roy. Soc.* (1848) I. 80 Every Tarpaulian shall then with ease Saile any ship to the Antipodes. 1673 HICKERINGILL *Greg. F. Greyb.* 140 Shall not your pilot, holla, whoop? And rowze Tarpollians that lye sleeping. 1719 D'URFEY *Pills* II. 60 Hear the noise of the Tarpawlian Boys; Port, Port, Port.

**Tarpaulin** (taɹpǭ·lin), *sb.* Forms: 7 **tarpaulling**, **tarr pawlin**, **tarrpawling**, **tarpolin**, **-palling**, **-palin**, (**-pallion**), 7–8 **-pawlin**, 7–9 **-pawling**, **-pauling**, 7– **tarpaulin**. [Generally thought to be f. TAR *sb.* + PALL *sb.*[1] + -ING[1] 1 f, g (as in *netting*, *grating*, and cf. AWNING).

The blackness of tarred canvas may have suggested its likeness to a funeral pall; though, in the absence of any instance of *tar-pall*, this origin must remain conjectural.]

**1.** A covering or sheet of canvas coated or impregnated with tar so as to make it waterproof, used to spread over anything to protect it from wet. Also, without *a* or *pl.*, canvas so tarred; sometimes applied to other kinds of waterproof cloth.

1605 B. JONSON *Volpone* IV. i, On the one [wall] I strain me a fair tarpauling, and in that I stick my onions, cut in halves. *a* 1625 MANWAYRING *Nomencl. Naval.* (Harl. MS. 2301), *Tarpawling*, is a peece of Canvas that is tar'd all over to Lash upon a Decke or Grating to keepe the Raine from Soaking through. 1626 CAPT. SMITH *Accid. Yng. Seamen* 30 A trar-pawling [*sic*] or yawning. 1652 ASHMOLE *Theat. Chem. Brit.* Prol. 12 To Hang a Presence Chamber with Tarpalin, instead of Tapestry. 1719 DE FOE *Crusoe* I. 68, I made me a large Tent,..and cover'd the uppermost with a large Tarpaulin which I had sav'd among the Sails. 1800 COLQUHOUN *Comm. Thames* 639 Each Lighter is furnished with a Tarpaulin to protect the Cargo from damage. 1890 W. J. GORDON *Foundry* 150 In the days when the London and Birmingham Railway considered it so beneath their dignity to carry coals to London that they introduced tarpaulins for the purpose of hiding the vulgar freight of which they were ashamed.

**b.** A sailor's hat made of tarpaulin.

1841 in TOTTEN *Naval Text-Bk.* (Webster). 1845 S. JUDD *Margaret* II. xi, A burly fellow in a tarpauling and blue jacket. 1858 in SIMMONDS *Dict. Trade*.

**2.** *transf.* A nickname for a mariner or sailor, esp. a common sailor. Now *rare* or *arch.* (Cf. TARPAULIAN, TAR *sb.* 3.)

1647 CLEVELAND *Char. Diurnal-maker* Wks. (1687) 82 He is a perfect Sea-man, a kind of Tarpawlin. 1660 HOWELL *Parly Beasts* 12 To be a Mariner, or Tarpaling, is one of the most servile and slavish condition of life that can be. 1687 SETTLE *Refl. Dryden* 21 He was too blame for making his Hametalhaz a Courtier and no Tarpolin. 1722 DE FOE *Col. Jack* i, Every tarpawling, if he gets but to be lieutenant of a press smack, is called captain. 1849 DICKENS *Dav. Copp.* xxi, What does this here blessed tarpaulin go and do? 1893 STEVENSON *Catriona* xxx. 366 The seamen pursued us... They were but bandy-legged tarpaulins after all.

**b.** Formerly applied to a sea-bred superior officer (captain, etc.) as contrasted with the military officers often appointed to command men-of-war. (Cf. 3 b.) In quot. 1909 erron. taken as = 'ranker'.

*c* 1690 R. GIBSON (B. M. Add. MS. 11602, lf. 40), Upon the Different Conduct between Seamen and Gentlemen Commanders in ye Navy (not bredd Tarr Pawlins) since 1652. 1855 MACAULAY *Hist. Eng.* xvi. III. 716 There was an end of privilege if an Earl was to be doomed to death by tarpaulins seated round a table in the cabin of a ship. 1894 C. N. ROBINSON *Brit. Fleet* 347 Drake and his brother tarpaulins. 1909 *Naval Warrant Officers' Jrnl.* Dec. 138/2 It would have been deeply interesting had Mr. Hannay *en passant* designated those Admirals and Captains who were called 'Tarpaulins' because of their ranker origin. *Ibid.*, Captain James Cook, the explorer, Captain C. Askew, and Captain J. Coglan are three of many names of 'Tarpaulins' which might be cited.

**3.** *attrib.* **a.** in sense 1: Made of tarpaulin.

1627 CAPT. SMITH *Seaman's Gram.* xiii. 61 A plug lapped in Okum, and well tarred in a tarpawling clout. 1688 in *Danielt's Catal. Autograph Lett.* (1904) July 30/2 Yesterday my Ld. Chancellour was taken at Wapping in a tarpalin habitt. 1832 C. M. GOODRIDGE *Voy. South Seas* 25 Carefully secured from the damp in a tarpawling bag. 1833 MARRYAT *P. Simple* xliii, There's many a clear head under a tarpaulin hat.

**b.** in sense 2 or 2 b: Of, belonging to, or that is, a mariner or sailor: sea-bred. Now *rare*.

1647 WARD *Simp. Cobler* 16 A shamefull sliding into other such tarpauling tenets. 1654 WHITLOCK *Zootomia* 221 A learned vote that any Tarpawlin Marriner might have nulled. *c* 1690 R. GIBSON (B. M. Add. MS. 11602, lf. 47), I finde many Accidents to have happened for want of Tarrpawling Commanders or Gentlemen throughly acquainted with Maritime Affaires. 1692 LUTTRELL *Brief Rel.* (1857) II. 354 Divers tarpawlin masters of ships recommended by the Trinity house, have passed examination in order to be received into the King's service. 1696 in *Ab. De la Pryme's Diary* (Surtees) 278 Chattam, a small tarpaulin town, joyning to Rochester. 1836 W. IRVING *Astoria* III. 222 John Young, the tarpawling governor of Owyhee. 1889 DOYLE *Micah Clarke* 23 He was one of the old tarpaulin breed, who had fought..against Frenchman, Don, Dutchman, and Moor.

**4.** *Comb.*, as *tarpaulin-maker*, *-covered* adj.

1858 SIMMONDS *Dict. Trade*, *Tarpaulin-manufacturer*, one who oils or tars canvas for covers. 1897 *Outing* (U. S.) XXX. 261/2 A tarpaulin-covered box of tackle belonging to Harry. 1907 *Daily Chron.* 25 Oct. 7/2 A young tarpaulin-maker of nineteen.

Hence **Tarpau·lin** *v.*, *trans.* to cover with a tarpaulin; *intr.* to shelter oneself under a tarpaulin; **Tarpau·lined** *a.*, covered with a tarpaulin.

1882 'F. ANSTEY' *Vice Versâ* xvi, Some tarpaulined cattle-vans. 1891 CONST. MACEWEN 3 *Women in 1 Boat* 85 We discussed whether we would 'tarpaulin' there for the night. 1894 *Outing* (U. S.) XXIV. 376/2 We had another boat, but it was housed and tarpaulined on deck.

**Tarpeian** (taɹpī·ăn), *a.* [f. L. *Tarpei-us*, or ad. L. *Tarpeiān-us* adj., f. proper name *Tarpeius* or *Tarpeia*.] Denoting a rock-face on the Capitoline Hill at Rome over which persons convicted of treason to the state were thrown headlong.

1607 SHAKS. *Cor.* III. i. 213 Beare him toth' Rock Tarpeian, and from thence Into destruction cast him. *Ibid.* III. iii. 88 Let them pronounce the steepe Tarpeian death. 1671 MILTON *P. R.* IV. 49. 1746 FRANCIS tr. *Hor. Sat.* I. vi. 51 From the Tarpeian rock's tremendous height, Or to the hangman Cadmus give their fate. 1843 MACAULAY *Horatius* xvi, Now, from the rock Tarpeian, Could the wan burghers spy The line of blazing villages.

**Tarpon** (tā·ɹpǫn). Forms: 7 **tarpom**, 8 **-oen**, 9 **-um**, 9 **tarpon**. [So Du. *tarpoen*: origin not ascertained.] The Jew-fish, *Megalops atlanticus*, a giant representative of the herring tribe found in the warmer waters of the western Atlantic: see JEW-FISH and ELOPS. Sometimes extended to the E. Indian species *M. cyprinoides* (*M. thrissoides*).

1685 L. WAFER *Voy.* (1729) 321 Of these they make nets for fishing, but only for great fish, as Tarpoms, or the like. 1699 DAMPIER *Voy.* II. II. 12 The Tarpom is a large scaly Fish, shaped much like a Salmon, but somewhat flatter ..with Scales as big as a Half Crown. 1796 STEDMAN *Surinam* II. 229 A large fish..called tarpoen..which is white, about 2 feet 6 inches. 1888 GOODE *Amer. Fishes* 406 The sailors' name for this fish,..is 'Tarpum' or 'Tarpon'. 1901 *Scotsman* 4 Oct. 5/1 The largest tarpon ever captured ..weighed 205 lb., and measured 8 ft. and 2 in. in length.

**b.** *attrib.* and *Comb.*

1887 *Sporting Life* 22 June 2/6 Tarpon fishing is not half so exciting as catching man-eating sharks with a hand-line. 1888 GOODE *Amer. Fishes* 412 Tugging at a tarpum-line in the Gulf of Mexico. 1895 *Blackw. Mag.* Aug. 281 He has made a special study of tarpon-tackle during his annual visits to the best tarpon-waters.

**Tarrace**, obs. form of TARRAS, TERRACE.

**Tarradiddle, Tarrage**: see TARA-.

**Tarragon** (tæ·răgən). Also (6–8 **tarchon**), 6–9 **taragon**. [Given in 1538–48 as the English for med.L. *tragonia* and *tarchon*: cf. 16th c. F. *targon* (Rabelais, Cotgr. 1611), It. *taracone*, *tarcone* (Florio 1598, 1611), Sp. *taragontia*, *-goncia* (Matthioli 16th c., Percival, Minsheu). *Tarchon* appears in the Latin version of Symeon Sethus *De Cibariis* (Basle 1538), repr. Byzantine Gr. ταρχών. Sethus compiled from Arab sources, and his ταρχών represented Arab. طرخون *ṭarkhōn* (in Ibn Beithar, Avicenna, Razi), *altarcon* in Gerard of Cremona, *a* 1187; according to Arabic lexicographers a foreign word: some think ad. Gr. δράκων (Devic), by an early association, similar to what is found in the 16th c., with the Gr. δρακόντιον, -οντία (Hippocr., Diosc.), the name of *Arum Dracunculus*.

The two plants were included by Matthioli, 1565, under Δρακοντία, *Dracunculus*, the Tarragon being distinguished as *Hortensis Dracunculus*; he also gives, as including both, It. *dragontéa*, Sp. *taragontia*, F. *serpentine*, all originally names of *Arum Dracunculus*. This association is commemorated in the botanical names *Artemisia Dracunculus* and *Arum Dracunculus* (now *Dracunculus vulgaris*), as well as in 16–17th c. applications of the name DRAGON, DRAGONS. The 16th c. herbalists' L. *Tragonia*, and the Sp. *estragon*, Pg. *estragão*, F. *estragon*, are all derived from *tragon*, *targon*, *tarchon*; the 16th c. Sp. *taragoncia* and mod. Sp. *taragona* show the nearest relationship to the Eng. name.]

**1.** A plant, *Artemisia Dracunculus*, N.O. *Compositæ*, of the wormwood genus, a native of Southern Russia and Eastern Europe, the aromatic leaves of which are used to flavour salads, soups, etc.

1538 ELYOT, *Tragonia*, an herbe nowe callid Taragon, late sene in this realme, whiche hath a tast like gynger. 1548 TURNER *Names of Herbs*, *Tarchon*..is called wyth vs Tarragon. 1579 LANGHAM *Gard. Health* (1633) 630 Tarragon is good in Sallads with Lettuse as Rocket is. 1693 EVELYN *De la Quint. Compl. Gard.* II. 202 Tarragon is one of the perfuming or Spicy Furnitures of our Sallets. 1706 PHILLIPS (ed. 6), *Tarchon*, Taracon, or Garden-Dragon, an Herb. 1767 ABERCROMBIE *Ev. Man his own Gard.* (1803) 668/1 Tarragon: fine flavoured aromatic plant, to improve the flavour of soups and sallads. 1882 *Garden* 21 Jan. 50/1 Keep up good supplies of Tarragon and small salads.

†**2.** Sometimes applied (by confusion of names) to the Garden Dragon, *Dracunculus vulgaris*, N.O. *Araceæ*, or the Green Dragon, *Arisæma Dracontium*, N.O. *Orontiaceæ*: see DRAGONS. *Obs.*

1591 PERCIVALL *Sp. Dict.*, *Taragontia*, taragon, *Draguntea*. 1598 FLORIO, *Taracone*,..the hearbe Taragon or garden Dragon.

**3.** *attrib.*, as *tarragon leaf*; **tarragon vinegar**, vinegar flavoured with the leaves or oil of tarragon.

1855 DELAMER *Kitch. Gard.* (1861) 138 Tarragon vinegar, pickled tarragon leaves, and sometimes the fresh green leaves in salad, are..powerful agents in the hands of a skilful and judicious cook. 1883 W. WILLIAMS in *Knowledge* 20 July 35/2 Stock broth, tarragon vinegar, ketchup, &c.

**Tarrapin, Tarrar**, varr. TERRAPIN, TERRIER[1].

**Tarras** (tæ·răs), *sb.* ? *Obs.* Also 6–8 **tarrace**, 7–8 **tarris**, 8 **terrace**, 8–9 **terras**, 9 **tarrass**. See also TRASS. [ad. early mod.Du. *tara·sse*, *terra·s*, *tira·s* (Kilian), Du. *tras* neut., Ger. *trasz* masc. (17th c., Kluge), also *tarrasz* (Sanders 1865); of Romanic origin: cf. OF. *terrace* (12th c.), *-asse*, *tierasse*, *-aisse* fem., 'torchis, terre à foulon, trass' (Godef.), It. *terraccia*, *-azza* fem., 'rubble or rubbish' (Florio 1611):—late L. **terrācea* earthy, earthen: cf. TERRACE.]

A kind of rock, allied in composition to pozzolana, consisting largely of comminuted pumice or other volcanic substance; it is found along the Rhine between Cologne and Mainz, and was formerly imported from Holland for making a mortar or hydraulic cement. Hence, the mortar or cement made of this, used for pargeting, lining cisterns, etc.; also applied to other similar cements.

1612 STURTEVANT *Metallica* xiii. 95 Part or appurtenance in buildings,..made either of Bricke, Tile, Lead, Wood, Tarras, or Free-stone. 1662 *Stat. Irel.* (1765) II. 416 Tarras, the barrel 6s. 8d. 1698 LISTER *Journ. Paris* (1699) 52 Which I make no doubt are set in Cement or Tarras, that is, the *Pulvis Puteolanus*. 1735 J. PRICE *Stone-Br. Thames* 5 All the Joints set in Tarris. 1765 *Museum Rust.* IV. lviii. 244 To make it almost as hard as terras. 1775 SMALL in *Phil.*

*Trans.* LXVI. 444 By laying the ground-floor with terrace. **1786** *Projects* in *Ann. Reg.* 96/1 Dutch terras is a *tufa* stone, found on the rocky banks of the Rhine. **1800** *Hull Advertiser* 5 Apr. 1/3 Mortar..mixed..with a due proportion of Terrace or other Water Cement. **1813** Sir H. Davy *Agric. Chem.* (1814) 327 Tarras, which was formerly imported in considerable quantities from Holland, is a mere decomposed basalt. **1822** G. Young *Geol. Surv. Yorks. Coast* (1828) 139 The manufacture of terras, or Roman cement. **1838** *Civil Eng. & Arch. Jrnl.* I. 412/2 Tarras, or trass, is a bluish black cellular trap or lava, quarried at Andernach on the Rhine into mill-stones. *Ibid.*, Of late years, these stones [*septaria*], burnt and reduced to powder, ..have entirely superseded the employment of puzzolana and of Dutch tarras. **1842–76** Gwilt *Archit.* Gloss., *Tarras*, a strong cement, useful formerly in water-works.

**b.** *attrib.* and *Comb.*, as *tarras mortar, work*; *tarras-layer*.

**1596** Lodge *Wits Miserie* (Hunter. Cl.) 33 His nose sticks in the midst like an embosment in Tarrace worke. **1741** Sympson in *Phil. Trans.* XLI. 856 Strong Cement composed of Lime, Sand, Brick-dust, &c. which the Masons of that Country [Lincoln] call Terrace-mortar. **1819** W. S. Rose *Lett.* I. 54 Many Venetian tarrass-layers have set out, upon invitation, to Russia. **1838** *Civil Eng. & Arch. Jrnl.* I. 413/2 Tarras mortar, made of white lime and tarras, requires long and repeated beating to bring it to perfection.

**Tarras,** *v.* ? *Obs.* Forms: see prec.; also 5 terys, 8 terass. [In later use app. f. Tarras *sb.*; but in earlier use prob. f. F. *terracer, terrasser* in some of its senses: see Terrace *v.*] *trans.* To cover, coat, or lay with plaster; in later use, with tarras. Hence **Tarrassed** *ppl. a.*

**1485** *Churchw. Acc. St. Mary at Hill* (Nichols 1797) 94 Paid the Dawber for terysing of floris per day 8d. **1611** Florio, *Pauimentare*, to paue, to terrace. **1615** tr. *De Monfart's Surv. E. Indies* 7 The houses..are lowe enough, vaulted under, and tarassed on the top. **1705** *Lond. Gaz.* No. 4163/1 His Royal Highness has ordered the Towers of the old Castle..to be vaulted and terrassed, to prevent the Effect of the Bombs. **1764** Harmer *Observ.* I. iii. 89 An upper-story, which is flat on the top and either terraced with hard plaister, or paved with stone. **1789** *Trans. Soc. Arts* (ed. 2) II. 235 The plants were..put in a stone cistern, well terassed. **1795** *Statist. Acc. Scot.* XVI. 4 [The] space under the tarrass'd floor was filled with earth. **1796** Morse *Amer. Geog.* II. 492 [Great Wall of China] being terrassed and cased with bricks. **1819** W. S. Rose *Lett.* I. 117 Collecting the rain on tarrassed roofs, as at Malta.

**Tarras, tarrass(e,** obs. ff. Terrace.

**Tarred** (tāɹd), *ppl. a.* Also 7 tard. [f. Tar *v.*[1] + -ed[1].] Smeared or covered with tar. (In quot. 1688, marked or formed with tar.)

**1615** Markham *Eng. Housew.* II. v. (1649) 167 With a pair of sheeres..she shall cut away all the course locks, pitch, brands, tar'd locks, and other feltrings. **1688** *Lond. Gaz.* No. 2377/4 A Tarr'd P. on her Rump. **1828** J. M. Spearman *Brit. Gunner* (ed. 2) 147 Tarred cordage is chiefly useful for cables and ground tackle, which are constantly soaked in water. **1887** *Pall Mall G.* 29 Sept. 6/1 The erection and re-erection of tarred barricades.

**Tarrer** (tā·rəɹ). [f. Tar *v.*[1] + -er[1].] One who tars. (In quot. in reference to tarring and feathering: see Tar *v.*[1] b.)

**1894** *Columbus* (Ohio) *Dispatch* 8 Aug., The cases of the tarrers have not been passed upon yet.

**Tarrer(e, Tarres,** obs. ff. Tarrier [2], Terrace.

†**Ta·rriage.** *Obs. rare*[−1]. In 5 taryage. [f. Tarry *v.* + -age.] Tarrying, delay: = next, 1.

*c* **1470** Henry *Wallace* x. 416 Than for to fle he tuk no taryage.

**Tarriance** (tæ·riǎns). *arch.* Also 5 tary-, 5–7 tari-, 6–7 tarry-; 5–6 -ans, 5–7 -aunce, 6–7 -ence. [f. Tarry *v.* + -ance.]

**1.** The action of tarrying; delay, procrastination.

**1460** *Paston Lett.* I. 527 Besechyng your maistership not to be dysplesed with my long taryans. **1542** Udall *Erasm. Apoph.* 295 b, To make no ferther delaie ne taryaunce. **1563** Golding *Cæsar* v. (1565) 137 Fabius..making no long tarience in hys iorney, met hym with hys Legion. **1576** Fulwel *Ars Adulandi* vii. (1579) G iij, Better is a litle tariance then a raw dinner. **1591** Shaks. *Two Gent.* II. vii. 90, I am impatient of my tarriance. **1694** S. Sewall *Diary* 6 Apr. (1878) I. 390 Sawing and fitting this board made some inconvenient Tarriance. **1808** Southey *Chron. Cid* 173 The tarriance that had been made. **1898** T. Hardy *Wessex Poems* 90 Worn with tarriance I care for life no more.

**2.** Temporary residence or continuance in a place; sojourn, abiding.

**1530** Palsgr. 279/2 Taryaunce, abyding, *demourance*. **1681** R. Knox *Hist. Ceylon* II. vi. 56 Making these Tents stronger or slighter, according to the time of their tarriance. **1721** Strype *Eccl. Mem.* III. vi. 66 After a year or two's tarriance in London. **1885** T. Hodgkin *Italy & Inv.* III. IV. viii. 307 It may have been during this tarriance at Rome that Theodoric commenced..draining the Pontine Marshes.

†**3.** Abiding in expectation; awaiting, waiting.

**1561** T. Norton *Calvin's Inst.* II. 105 To confirme them in loking for him, that they should not waxe faint with long tarriance. **1599** ? Shaks. *Pass. Pilgr.* vi, Cytherea .. A longing tariance for Adonis made. **1646** Trapp *Comm. John* xx. 6 The good ground brings forth fruit with patience or tarriance.

†**4.** The causing of delay; hindrance. *Obs.*

**1598** R. Bernard tr. *Terence, Andria* v. v, Neither is there any let or tarriance, but that I may marry her out of hand.

**Tarriar,** obs. form of Terrier.

**Tarrididdle,** variant of Taradiddle.

**Tarrier** [1] (tæ·riəɹ). *arch.* Also 4 tariere, 4–6 tarier, 5 teryar, -iar, 6 tar(r)yer, -iar. [f. Tarry *v.* + -er[1].]

**1.** One who tarries or delays; a lingerer, procrastinator; one who stays or remains.

**1382** Wyclif *Jer.* Prol., God is redi to ȝyue good, to punshen a tariere. *c* **1440** *Promp. Parv.* 489/2 Teryar, or longe lytare (*P.* teriar or longe bidar). **1530** Palsgr. 317/2 Longe taryer. **1531** Elyot *Gov.* I. xxiv, Called of them *Fabius cunctator*, that is to saye the tariar or delayer. **1577** Northbrooke *Dicing* (1843) 95 Saint Paule admonisheth women..to be byders and tariers at home. **1581** J. Bell *Haddon's Answ. Osor.* 496 There be behind yet many tarryers, I will not say Traytors to the Common weale. **1665** Brathwait *Comment Two Tales* (Chaucer Soc.) 29 This Chanterer was a notable Tarrier. **1845** Browning *Glove* 91 Sound the trumpet, no true knight's a tarrier!

†**2.** One who (or that which) delays some one; a hinderer, obstructor; an obstruction. *Obs.*

**1614** B. Jonson *Barth. Fair* I. v, Why doe you stop, am I your Tarriars? **1622** J. Rawlins *Fam. Recovery Ship of Bristol* E j b, To catch the soules of mortall men, and entangle frailty in the tarriers of horrible abuses, and imposturing deceit.

**Tarrier** [2] (tæ·riəɹ). Forms: 5 tarrer(e, 6 tarryour, 7–8 terrier, 9 tarrier. [In 15th c. *tarrer(e*, a. OF. *tarere* (*c* 1200 in Godef.), mod.F. *tarière*:—late L. *taratrum* (Isidore XIX. xix. 15, '*taratrum* quasi *teratrum*'): cf. Gr. τέρετρον borer, gimlet.] A boring instrument, an auger; now, an instrument for extracting a bung from a barrel.

*c* **1460** J. Russell *Bk. Nurture* 65 Looke þow haue tarrers two a more & lasse for wyne. *Ibid.* 71 So when þow settyst a pipe abroche...With tarrere or gymlet perce ye vpward þe pipe ashore. **1513** *Bk. Keruynge* in *Babees Bk.* (1868) 266 Than loke ye haue two tarryours, a more & a lesse. **1611** Cotgr., *Terriere*, a Terrier, or Augar. **1706** Phillips (ed. Kersey), *Terrier*..a sort of Awger to bore with. **1904** *Daily Chron.* 19 Feb. 3/2 A London cellarman asks for his 'tarrier' to take out a bung from the barrel.

† **Tarrier** [3], **tarriour.** *Obs.* [f. **tarry* vb. in *tarrying-iron* + -er[1], -our.] A pair of tiring-irons.

**1601** Deacon & Walker *Answ. to Darel* To Rdr. 4 The very frame itselfe..resembleth fitlie a paire of tarriours, or tyring yrons.

**Tarrier,** obs. or vulgar form of Terrier [2] (dog).

**Tarriness:** see Tarry *a.*

**Tarring** (tā·riŋ), *vbl. sb.* [f. Tar *v.*[1] + -ing[1].] The action of coating or smearing with tar.

**1473–4** in Swayne *Sarum Churchw. Acc.* (1896) 15 For the tarryng of the hempon cabul. **1542** *Acc. Ld. High Treas. Scotl.* VIII. 132 Mending and tirring of lxx ald somes. **1589** *Pappe w. Hatchet* E j b, I thinke them woorth neither the tarring, nor the telling. **1669** J. Owen in *State Papers, Dom.* 576 We spend 2 [lasts of tar] at a tarring. **1861** *Illustr. Lond. News* 17 Aug. 152/1 The tarring and feathering of defenceless individual Northerners.

*attrib.* **1851–4** Tomlinson *Cycl. Arts* (1867) VI. 468/1 The tarring-house is separated from the other buildings by a second partition.

**Tarris,** obs. form of Tarras, Terrace.

**Tarrish** (tā·riʃ), *a. rare.* [f. Tar *sb.* + -ish[1].] Resembling tar; having a taste or consistency like that of tar. **b.** [f. Tar *sb.* 3.] Of or belonging to sailors; nautical.

**1681** R. Knox *Hist. Ceylon* I. vi. 25 They are small like a Fly, and black,..their honey somewhat tarrish. **1841** *Fraser's Mag.* XXIV. 307, I saw there were swabs opposite me. (This is the tarrish tongue for officer or epaulette.)

**Tarro,** variant of Taro, the plant.

**Tarrock** (tæ·rǫk). [Of uncertain origin; the ending *-ock* is app. diminutive, as in *puttock*, etc.] A name applied locally to various sea-birds: in the Shetland Islands, to the Arctic Tern; elsewhere to the Kittiwake, to the young of the Common Gull, and to the Common Guillemot.

**1674** Ray *Collect. Words, Water Fowl* 94 The Tarrock: Cornub: *Larus cinereus Bellonii.* **1678** — *Willughby's Ornith.* 346 Bellonius his ash-coloured Gull, called in Cornwal, Tarrock. **1768** Pennant *Zool.* II. 424 Linnæus.. makes this species [winter mew] synonymous with the *Larus tridactylus* or *Tarrock.* **1771** — *Tour Scot. in 1769*, 36 Kittiwakes, or Tarrocks. **1774** Goldsm. *Nat. Hist.* (1776) VI. 79 It is..the tarrock, and the terne, that venture to these dreadful retreats, and claim an undisturbed possession. **1833** *G. Montagu's Ornith. Dict.* 505 *Tarrock*, a name for the Gull in its immature plumage. *Ibid.* 508 Common Tern, *Sterna hirundo. Provincial.*..Tarrock, or Tarret. **1880** J. Skelton *Crookit Meg* iv. 48, I promised to get a tarrock's wing for Eppie.

**Tarrow** (tæ·rou), *v. Sc.* [app. a parallel form to Tarry *v.* (sense 3): cf. *harrow* and *harry*, *worow* and *worry*.] *intr.* To delay, hesitate, show reluctance. (Nearly = Tarry *v.* 3.)

*c* **1375** *Sc. Leg. Saints* xxxiii. (*George*) 133, & gyf þu tarowis it to do..we sal bryne þe & al þine. *c* **1470** Henryson *Mor. Fab.* XIII. (*Frog & Mouse*) xxii, And it to cun perqueir se thow not tarrow. *a* **1568** in *Bannatyne Poems* (Hunter. Cl.) 268 On twenty schilling now he tarrowis To ryd the he gait by the plewis. **1637** Rutherford *Lett.* (1862) I. 295, I am sure it is sin to tarrow at Christ's good meat, and not to eat when he saith, 'Eat, O well beloved'. **1666** J. Livingstone in *Sel. Biog.* (Wodrow Soc.) I. 282 Tarrow not of this my dealing. **1725** Ramsay *Gentle Sheph.* I. ii, Like dawted wean that tarrows at its meat. **1786** Burns *Dream* xv, I hae seen their coggie fou, That yet hae tarrow't at it. **1899** Spence *Shetland Folk-Lore* 216 The mair he tarrows the less he gets.

Hence **Ta·rrowing** *vbl. sb.* and *ppl. a.*; **Ta·rrowingly** *adv.*, reluctantly.

*c* **1375** *Sc. Leg. Saints* xxxix. (*Cosme & Damyane*) 60 He It tuk tarowandly. *c* **1598** D. Ferguson *Sc. Prov.* § 42 (1785) 4 A tarrowing bairn was never fat. **1632** Rutherford *Lett.* (1862) I. 91 Let your soul, like a tarrowing and mislearned child, take the dorts. **1832** A. Henderson *Sc. Prov.* 131 Lang tarrowing taks a' the thanks awa.

**Tarrow,** variant of Taro.

**Tarry** (tæ·ri), *sb.* Also 4–6 tary, 6 tarie, *Sc.* tairrie. [f. Tarry *v.*]

†**1.** The act of tarrying; spending or loss of time; delay, procrastination. *Obs.*

*c* **1375** *Sc. Leg. Saints* xxvii. (*Machor*) 485 Þane machore ..reprowyt þe mastir man of his tary & his slawnes. **1451** Capgrave *Life St. Gilbert* (E.E.T.S.) 113 He, with-oute ony tary, mad calle all þe court of Rome. *c* **1510** Barclay *Mirr. Gd. Manners* (1570) E v, In tary is no trust, but ieopardy mortall. **1562** Sir R. Maitland *Poems* (1830) 17 To cheis and tak ane husband without tarie. *a* **1578** Lindesay (Pitscottie) *Chron. Scot.* (S.T.S.) I. 142 The king determinat to compell them that was within the house, be lang tairrie to rander and gif it ower. **1745** Wright in *N. Eng. Hist. & Gen. Reg.* (1848) II. 207 We made no tarry but set forward for Fort Dummer.

**2.** Temporary residence, sojourn; a 'stay'. Now chiefly *U. S.*

*c* **1375** *Sc. Leg. Saints* xviii. (*Egipciane*) 1272 Vith hym na langer tary scho vald ma. **1516** Allen in Lodge *Illustr. Brit. Hist.* (1791) I. 11 He sayth his tarry is but short her. **1589** *Reg. Privy Council Scot.* IV. 425 In cais our tary sal happin..to be langair. **1786** M. Cutler in *Life*, etc. (1888) II. 273 To..make provisions for a much longer tarry. **1817** *London Courier* 7 July, The Duke of Wellington was on his arrival received by a guard of honour, and the band of the 88th continued to play during his Grace's tarry. **1866** Whittier *Marg. Smith's Jrnl.* Pr. Wks. 1889 I. 89 He is to make some little tarry in this town.

**Tarry** (tā·ri), *a.* [f. Tar *sb.* + -y.]

**1.** Consisting or composed of tar; of the nature of tar.

**1552** Huloet, Tarrye, or of tarre, *piceus.* **1782** J. Trumbull *M'Fingal* 65 From nose and chin's remotest end, The tarry icicles depend. **1841** *Civil Eng. & Arch. Jrnl.* IV. 12/1 Its change from..a solid to that of a tarry, viscous, semifluid. **1899** *Allbutt's Syst. Med.* VIII. 517 All tarry and resinous substances absorb oxygen rapidly or slowly.

**b.** Resembling tar; having the consistence, colour, or flavour of tar.

**1880** M. Mackenzie *Dis. Throat & Nose* I. 154 The blood [of the heart] is [in certain cases of diphtheria] fluid and tarry. **1896** C. E. Ryan *With Ambulance thro' Franco-German War* v. 63 A small patch of blood-stained earth beside him —not red, but tarry-black. **1904** *Daily News* 27 Dec. 10 The Souchong teas..have a special flavour..which the trade describe as 'tarry'.

**2.** Covered, smeared, soiled, or impregnated with tar; tarred; black as if smeared with tar.

*a* **1585** Polwart *Flyting w. Montgomerie* 745 Tary tade [= toad], thous defate. **1641** Best *Farm. Bks.* (Surtees) 23 Such [locks of wool] as are hairy and tarry. **1686** *Lond. Gaz.* No. 2201/4 [He] had..an old black Tarrey Hat on his head. **1753** *N. Jersey Archives* XIX. 283 A Pair of tarry Duck Trowsers. **1824** McCulloch *Highl., etc. Scot.* I. 382 In contact with her tarry sides. **1840** Dickens *Old C. Shop* v, Two or three tarry boys.

**b.** *fig.* Thievish. (Cf. *tarry-fingered* in 4.)

**1822** Galt *Sir A. Wylie* II. xvii. 158 The gipsies hae tarry fingers, and ye would need an ee in your neck to watch them.

**3.** *fig.* ? Foul, unclean; ? rude, uncultured.

**1579** W. Wilkinson *Confut. Familye of Loue* 57 b, Poysoned speaches, and tarrye Rhetorick. **1779** J. Adams *Diary* 11 May, Wks. 1851 III. 200 Dr. W. told me of Tucker's rough, tarry speech about me, at the navy board.

**4.** *Comb.*: **tarry-breeks** (orig. *Sc.*), **-jacket, -John,** humorous nicknames for a sailor (cf. Tar *sb.* 3); **tarry-fingered, -fisted** *adjs.*, having the fingers or hands smeared with tar; *fig.* thievish.

**1786** Burns *Dream* xiii, Young royal *Tarry Breeks [Prince William], I learn, Ye've lately come athwart her. **1855** Kingsley *Westw. Ho* xxx, No old tarry-breeks of a sea-dog. **1825** Jamieson, **Tarry-fingered, Tarry-handit*, dishonest, disposed to carry off by stealth. **1906** *Daily Chron.* 4 Aug. 8/4 All the gold that has ever been gathered by *tarry-fisted gentry of the Bragwell and Rudge order. **1822** Scott *Nigel* iv, My husband must be the slave of every *tarry jacket that wants but a pound of oakum. **1888** Stevenson *Black Arrow* IV. vi, Long-headed *tarry-Johns, that fear not fire nor water.

Hence **Ta·rriness,** tarry condition or quality.

**1892** Walsh *Tea* (Philad.) 193 This smokiness and 'tarriness' does not develop until after the teas have left China.

**Tarry** (tæ·ri), *v.* Now chiefly *literary* in Gt. Brit., still *colloq.* in U.S. Forms: 4–6 tarye, 4–7 tarie, tary, (5 tery, tare), 6 tarrye, 6–7 tarrie, 5– tarry. [Of obscure origin: some would identify it with Tary *v.* to irritate, or with Tar *v.*[2], *tarre*, OE. *tergan* to vex; to both of which the sense is an obstacle. See *Note* below.]

†**1.** *trans.* To delay, retard, defer, put off (a thing, an action); to protract, prolong. *Obs.*

*c* **1320** R. Brunne *Medit.* 597 Thos howndes were lothe hys deþ for to tarye. *c* **1386** Chaucer *Reeve's Prol.* 51 Sey forth thy tale, and tarie nat the tyme. **1388** Wyclif *Ecclus.* iv. 3 Tarie thou not [Vulg. *non protrahas*] the ȝifte to a man that is set in angwisch. **1398** Trevisa *Barth. De P. R.* XI. vii. (Bodl. MS.) lf. 109/2 ȝif rayn is yuel and distemporat ..it..tarieth and letteþ repinges of corne and of fruyte. **1494** Fabyan *Chron.* VII. ccxxviii. 278 That he shulde for no mede tary rightfull sentence. **1583** Stocker *Civ. Warres Lowe C.* IV. 52 b, Whiche Citie not meanyng to tarrie the siege, rendred to the saied Count.

†**2.** To detain, delay, retard, keep back (a person or agent) for a time; to keep waiting; to hold in check, impede, hinder. *Obs.*

**1340** HAMPOLE *Pr. Consc.* 3921 Þat he may..In purgatory qwyte alle þe dett, Þat hym fra blis may tary or lett. *c* **1386** CHAUCER *Sqr.'s T.* 65, I wol nat taryen yow for it is pryme. **1387** TREVISA *Higden* (Rolls) VII. 235 Duke William and his men were longe y-taried in Seynt Valerik his haven. **1470-85** MALORY *Arthur* XVIII. vii. 735 Sir kyng, he sayd, tary me noo lenger for I may not tary. **1571** GOLDING *Calvin on Ps.* xxix. 7 So many stops tary us and stay us back. **1609** SKENE *Reg. Maj.* I. 114 b, But gif..the parties wald set them to tary the court, with exceptions frivolous.

**3.** *intr.* To delay or be tardy in beginning or doing anything, esp. in coming or going; to wait before doing something; to linger, loiter.

*c* **1350** *Will. Palerne* 3128, I coniure þe..þatou titli me telle & tarie nouȝ no lenger. **1382** WYCLIF *Ecclus.* xiv. 12 Be thou myndeful for deth shal not tarien [Vulg. *mors non tardat*]. *c* **1400** *Rule St. Benet* 60/445 Bot chaistese þam & tery noght. *c* **1440** *Promp. Parv.* 489/2 Teryyn [*MS. S.* tarryyn] or longe a-bydyn, *moror, pigritor*. **1489** CAXTON *Faytes of A.* III. xii. 193 Yf he had taried to the morn after. *a* **1586** SIDNEY *Arcadia* III. (1622) 238 Not daring to tary long about it. **1611** BIBLE *Judg.* v. 28 Why tarie the wheeles of his charets? **1693** CONGREVE *Old Bach.* IV. i, Nothing can be done here till I go, so that I'll tarry, d'ye see? **1756** C. LUCAS *Ess. Waters* I. 32 The waters cannot tarry long in their passage, but..run towards the..level grounds. **1849** MACAULAY *Hist. Eng.* v. I. 610 He saw that if he tarried the royal cavalry would soon be in his rear. **1892** *Nation* (N. Y.) 27 Oct. 318/2 The good monks..were ..going to attend high mass.., so we had no time to tarry.

**b.** To linger in expectation of a person or occurrence, or until something is done or happens; to wait. Const. *till, for,* Sc. *on, upon* (with *indirect passive*).

**1390** GOWER *Conf.* I. 187 This false knyht..Hath taried til thei were aslepe. **1515** BARCLAY *Egloges* iv. (1570) Dj b/2 What, tary man a while till better fortune come. **1526** TINDALE *John* xxi. 23 Yf I will have hym to tary [WYCLIF dwelle, **1611** tarry] tyll I come what is that to the? **1535** COVERDALE *Tobit* v. 7, I praye the, tary for me, tyll I haue tolde my father. **1560** DAUS tr. *Sleidane's Comm.* 274, I.. would tary to se the ende. **1580** LYLY *Euphues* (Arb.) 427 Euphues knowing the tyde would tarrye for no man. **1609** SKENE *Reg. Maj.* I. 124* He quha is challenged sall be taried vpon, vntill he returne hayme. **1765** M. CUTLER in *Life*, etc. (1888) I. 9 Then the sacrament was administered (which I did not tarry to see). **1816** SCOTT *Antiq.* i, Time and tide tarry for no man. **1870** E. PEACOCK *Ralf Skirl.* I. 167 They had not long to tarry for the coming of their host.

†**4.** *intr.* To remain, stay, abide, continue (in some state or condition). *Obs.*

*c* **1450** LOVELICH *Merlin* 4521 Thus it Taryede jn-to pentecost feste. **1480** *Robt. Devyll* 25 in Hazl. *E. P. P.* I. 219 Wyueles longe, said the duke, haue I taryed. **1551** T. WILSON *Logike* (1580) 38 If the generall woorde be taken awaie, the kinde tarieth not. **1597** A. M. tr. *Guillemeau's Fr. Chirurg.* 17 b/2 Els the ioyncte might be criple, and tarrye lame. **1637-50** ROW *Hist. Kirk* (Wodrow Soc.) 488 Pardoned by the King, provyding they tarie well in tyme comeing. **1776** R. KING in *Life & Corr.* (1894) I. 24 Few of the men now with Genl. will tarry longer than the expiration of their enlistments. **1814** SCOTT *Wav.* xii, Declining the Baron's invitation to tarry till after dinner [etc.].

**b.** To abide temporarily, to sojourn; to stay, remain, lodge (in a place). *arch.* exc. in *U. S.*

**13..** *E. E. Allit. P.* C. 87, I schal tee in-to Tarce, & tary þere a whyle. **1432-50** tr. *Higden* (Rolls) VI. 127 The Danes taryenge in wynter at Repyndoun. **1538** ELYOT, *Pernocto*.., to tarye all the nyghte. **1599** MASSINGER, etc. *Old Law* IV. i, As long as she tarried with her husband, she was Ellen. **1611** BIBLE *Ps.* lxviii. 12 She that taried at home, diuided the spoile. **1741** RICHARDSON *Pamela* (1824) I. cii. 499 Miss Cope came..and tarried with me three days. **1765** J. INGERSOLL *Lett. Stamp-Act* 62, I tarried that Night at Mr. Bishop's. **1820** W. IRVING *Sketch Bk., Leg. Sleepy Hollow*, Ichabod Crane..sojourned, or, as he expressed it, 'tarried', in Sleepy Hollow, for the purpose of instructing the children of the vicinity. **1850** HAWTHORNE *Scarlet L.* viii, I must tarry at home, and keep watch over my little Pearl. **1871** R. ELLIS *Catullus* lxv. 2 Ortalus, I no more tarry the Muses among. **1877** FREEMAN *Norm. Conq.* (ed. 3) II. x. 469 There they were to tarry [*earlier edd.* remain] through Lent.

**5.** *trans.* To wait for, wait in expectation of; to await, expect; † to stay for (a meal). † *Tarry out*, to stay till the end of. *To tarry* a person's *leisure*: see LEISURE 3 c. *arch.*

**1432-50** tr. *Higden* (Rolls) VI. 23 Messias whom þe Iues taryede. **1579** G. HARVEY *Let. to Spenser* Wks. (Grosart) I. 20 The Tyde tarryeth no manne, but manye a good manne is fayne to tarry the Tyde. **1654** EVELYN *Diary* 10 July, On Monday, I went again to the schools,..and..tarried out the whole Act in St. Mary's. *a* **1662** HEYLIN *Laud* (1668) 176 He caused me to tarry Dinner with him. **1829** LYTTON *Devereux* I. viii, I pressed him..to tarry your coming. **1868** MILMAN *St. Paul's* xi. 283 The Lord Mayor tarried the sermon, which lasted into the night.

†**b.** To outstay, stay over (a given time). *Obs.*

?*a* **1500** *Symmye & Bruder* 66 in *Bannatyne Poems* (Hunter. Cl.) 416 Bot or thay twynd him and his dudis, The tyme of none wes tareit; Wa worth this wedding, for be thir widis, The meit is al miskareit.

[*Note.* It cannot be disputed that the ME. forms of this verb are identical with those of TARY 'to provoke, irritate, harass, vex, excite', both being in ME. *tery-, tary-* (the spelling *tarry* being rare before 1500). Original identity with *tary*, and thus derivation from OE. *tergan*, would also account for the apparent identity of *tarry* and TARROW, since both could go back to the OE. variant types *tergan* (*tærgan*), *terw(i)an* (*tærw(i)an*), with phonetic development according to the position of the *g* and *w* in different inflected forms: cf. HARROW and HARRY, *worow* and WORRY. The consequent identification with OF. *tarier* might also help to explain the existence of the derivatives *tarriage, tarriance, tarryment*, with French suffixes (although it is to be noted that these appear as derivatives of *tarry* and not of *tary*). But no sense in the least approaching 'tarry' occurs in OE. *tergan, terw(i)an*, or in OF. *tarier*, and the difficulty of deriving this sense from that of 'provoke, vex, harass' seems almost insurmountable. Some have suggested an influence upon *tarry* of the synonymous TARGE *v.*[1], OF. *targier*; but this seems impossible. Others, seeing that ME. *terwen, terre,* TAR *v.*[2] and TARY had both a (rare) sense (2) 'to weary, fatigue, tire' (as if influenced by OE. *téorian*, ME *tiere, tere,* TIRE) have thought that this sense provided a connecting link between the notions of 'vex' and 'delay, retard'; but there is nothing in the quotations to confirm this view, and the actual history of *tarry* in its existing sense remains unascertained.]

**Tarryer**, obs. form of TARRIER[1], TERRIER[2].

**Tarrying** (tæ·riɪŋ), *vbl. sb.* [-ING[1].]

**1.** The action of the verb TARRY, q. v.; delaying, delay, waiting, loitering, etc.

**1340-70** *Alex. & Dind.* 818 Wiþ-oute tariynge tid þis tiþingus come. *c* **1350** in *Eng. Gilds* (1870) 357 Þey sholde, at here aȝe-comynge, ȝelde trewe a-counte.. by-þowte taryȝynge. *c* **1440** *Promp. Parv.* 489/2 Teryynge, or longe a-bydynge, *mora, pigricia*. *a* **1450** MYRC *Festial* 18 This þe taryng of Thomas byleue broght vs yn full byleue. **1535** COVERDALE *Ps.* xxxix. 17 Make no longe tarienge, o my God. **1596** DALRYMPLE tr. *Leslie's Hist. Scot.* x. (S. T. S.) 395 Tha wald tyne waichtie materis,.. throuch thair Absense, or lang tarieng. **1865** W. G. PALGRAVE *Arabia* I. 86 We determined to march on without further tarrying.

**2.** Abiding, sojourning: see TARRY *v.* 4 b.

**1445** in *Anglia* XXVIII. 271 In the she had a restyng place or tarying ony while. **1577-87** HOLINSHED *Chron.* III. 826/2 If he of his noble courage would giue him tarieng and abode. **1607** R. JOHNSON *Pleas. Conceites Old Hobson* (Percy Soc.) 14 During the time of his taring there.

†**3.** (See quots., and cf. BUNDLE *v.* 5.) *U. S.*

**1775** A. BURNABY *Trav.* 83 A very extraordinary method of courtship, which is sometimes practised amongst the lower people of this province, and is called Tarrying. **1778** ANBUREY *Trav. Amer.* xlix. (1791) II. 87 That custom [bundling]..is in some measure abolished; but they still retain one something similar, which is termed *tarrying*.

**Ta·rrying,** *ppl. a.* [f. as prec. + -ING[2].] That tarries: **a.** Delaying, lingering, tardy; **b.** Remaining, abiding.

*c* **1386** CHAUCER *Pars. T.* ¶ 644 The synne that men clepen Tarditas, as whan a man is to laterede or tariynge er he wole turne to god. **1422** tr. *Secreta Secret., Priv. Priv.* 223 Tarynge of speche, the voyce ful and stronge. **1483** *Cath. Angl.* 378/1 Taryinge, *morosus* (A.). **1654** Z. COKE *Logick* 38 Action is either Immanent and tarrying [or] Transient and passing.

Hence **Ta·rryingly** *adv.*, lingeringly, tardily.

**1450-1530** *Myrr. our Ladye* 26 The systers fulfyll the offyce of theyr seruyce somwhat more tareyngly.

**Tarrying-iron**: see TIRING-IRON.

†**Ta·rryment.** *Obs. rare*—[1]. In 6 tariment. [f. TARRY *v.* + -MENT.] Delay, tarrying.

**1560** ROLLAND *Crt. Venus* I. 804 Withouttin tariment It salbe done.

**Tarryour**, obs. form of TARRIER[2].

†**Ta·rrysome,** *a. Sc. Obs. rare.* In 6 tari(e)sum. [f. TARRY *sb.* or *v.* + -SOME.] Characterized by tarrying; slow, lingering; wearisome.

**1513** DOUGLAS *Æneis* IV. xii. 100 Haffand rieuth,..Off hir lang sorow and tarisum deid. **1535** STEWART *Cron. Scot.* (Rolls) II. 6 It war ouir lang and tariesum to tell.

†**Tars, tarse.** *Obs.* Also 5 tarsse. [a. OF. *tarse* (1345 in Godef.); in med.L. *pannus Tarsicus*; formerly held to be the same word as *Tarse*, Tarsus in Cilicia (either because fabricated at or imported by way of Tarsus); but probably referring to Tarsia or Tharsia, described in Maundeville (xxiv, Roxb. xxvii) as 'the kingdom of Tarse', upon which the land of Cathay 'marcheth toward the west', app. Turkestan; hence prob. the same as TARTAR *sb.*[3], and TARTARIN[1] 2, q.v.] A rich and costly stuff of Oriental origin, used in the West in the 14th and 15th c. Also *cloth of Tars*.

[**1295** *Visitatio Thesaur. S. Pauli Londin.* (Du Cange), Casula de panno Tarsico, Indici coloris.] **13..** *Gaw. & Gr. Knt.* 571 Dubbed in a dublet of a dere tars. **1377** LANGL. *P. Pl.* B. xv. 163 As gladde of a goune of a graye russet As of a tunicle of tarse or of trye scarlet. ?*a* **1400** *Morte Arth.* 3190 In toges of tarsse fulle richelye attyrde. *c* **1400** MAUNDEV. (Roxb.) vi. 20 Cledd in clathe of gold or tars, or in chamelet. *a* **1400-50** *Alexander* 1515 [He] arais all þe cite, Braidis ouire with bawdkyns all þe brade stretis, With tars & with tafeta þar he trede sulde. *Ibid.* 4673 Doubeletis of damaske & sum of dere tars. [**1834** PLANCHÉ *Brit. Costume* 105 The rich stuff called 'cloth of tars' is mentioned in this reign [Edw. I]. It was latinized *tarsicus* and *tartarinus*. **1880** BIRDWOOD *Indian Arts* II. 74 Cloth of Tars is from Tarsus, or perhaps from Tabriz.]

**Tarsal** (tā·ɹsăl), *a.* (*sb.*) [ad. mod.L. *tarsāl-is*, f. L. *tars-us*: see TARSUS and -AL.]

**1.** Of or pertaining to the tarsus of the ankle or foot, in its various senses.

**1817** KIRBY & SP. *Entomol.* (1818) II. xxiii. 328 The grasshoppers with setaceous antennæ..have four tarsal joints. **1826** *Ibid.* III. xxxv. 670 The tibia or shank is the fourth joint of the leg, which..is the analogue..of the tarsus or tarsal bones of vertebrate animals. **1840** G. V. ELLIS *Anat.* 712 The tarsal artery..gives branches to the extensor, to the bones of the tarsus and their articulations. **1851** RICHARDSON *Geol.* viii. (1855) 314 The foot, like the hand, [consisting] of three ranges of bones, tarsal, metatarsal, and phalanges. **1875** C. C. BLAKE *Zool.* 94 The number of tarsal scales is a specific test in most birds. **1875** CAMBRIDGE in *Encycl. Brit.* II. 295/2 The third, or inferior tarsal claw [of spiders]. **1883** THOMPSON tr. *Müller's Fertil. Fl.* 51 The carrying-power of the tarsal brushes is increased.

**2.** Of or pertaining to the tarsi of the eyelids.

**1839** T. BEALE *Nat. Hist. Sperm Whale* 119 The eyelids are without cilia and tarsal cartilages. **1889** G. A. BERRY *Dis. Eye* i. 2 An oily secretion is formed in the tarsal, or Meibomian glands. **1890** WEBSTER, *Tarsal tetter*,.. an eruptive disease of the edges of the eyelids.

**B.** *sb.* Short for *tarsal bone, joint*, etc.

**1881** MIVART *Cat* 341 The tarsals each ossify from one centre, as do the carpals. **1888** *Athenæum* 17 Mar. 344/3 A paper..'On the Carpus and Tarsus of the Anura.'..In the hind foot they recorded the discovery of a fourth tarsal. **1889** E. D. COPE in *Amer. Naturalist* Oct. 863 Carpals and tarsals not distinct in form from metapodials.

**Tarsalgia**: see TARSO-.

**Tarsall**, obs. form of TERCEL, hawk.

†**Tarse**[1]. *Obs.* Also 6 terse. [OE. *teors* = OHG., MHG. *zërs*, MDu. *teers, teres*.] The penis.

*c* **1000** *Sax. Leechd.* I. 358 Wið hærþena sare & teorses bares brægen meng wið huniȝ. *c* **1000** *Voc.* in Wr.-Wülcker 265/33 *Calamus*, teors, þæt wæpen *uel* lim. **1382** WYCLIF 1 *Sam.* xviii. 25 No sposeils, but oonli an hundrid tersis [1388 prepucies] of Philisteis. **14..** *MS. Porkington* x (Halliw.) Now ȝe speke of a tarse. **1500-20** DUNBAR 7 *Deidly Synnis* 88 Tersis. **1530** PALSGR. 279/2 Tarse of a man or beest, *vit*. **1730-6** in BAILEY (folio).

**Tarse**[2] (tāɹs). *rare*—[0]. [a. F. *tarse*, ad. L. TARSUS.] = TARSUS 1.

**1842** in BRANDE *Dict. Sc.*, etc. Hence in later Dicts.

**Tarse**, variant of TARS *Obs.*

**Tarsectomy, -ectopia**: see TARSO-.

†**Tarsel, tarcel.** *Obs.* Also 5-6 -ell; 6 tersele. Apparently a corrupt variant of TASSEL.

**1459** *Paston Lett.* I. 487 Item, j. prikkyng hat, covered withe blake felwet. Item, ij. tarcellys on hym be hynde. **1558** in Feuillerat *Revels Q. Eliz.* (1908) 92, v dd. of tarsells by him made of ye same sylver. **1570** LEVINS *Manip.* 57/11 A Tarsel, *appendix*. **1578** *Richmond Wills* (Surtees) 278, j grose of statut lace v[s]. viij[d]. iiij gernesh tersele xij[d].

Hence † **Tarcelled** *a.* = TASSELLED.

**1558** in Feuillerat *Revels Q. Eliz.* (1908) 39 Clothe of sylver tarcelled with cullen sylver.

**Tarsel, -ell, -elet,** obs. ff. TERCEL, -ELET.

‖ **Tarsia** (tā·ɹsiă). Also 7 **tersia**. [a. It. *tarsia* 'marquetry or small inlaid workes of diuers colours of bone, horne, wood or Iuorie' (Florio).] A kind of mosaic inlaid work in wood of various colours and shades. Also *attrib.* as *tarsia-work*.

**1665** SIR T. HERBERT *Trav.* (1677) 138 But if Mosaick be in wood 'tis called *Tersia*: the several pieces of which are boil'd and dyed into what colour the workman fancies. **1875** POLLEN *Anc. & Mod. Furn.* 28 The wood veneered or inlaid with marquetry or tarsia work of ivory, ebony, box, palm. **1883** FR. M. PEARD *Contrad.* I. 228 Cortina.. with its great schools of filigree and tarsia work. **1901** *J. Black's Carp. & Build., Home Handicr.* 61 Tarsia..was a species of wood inlay or mosaic of which the Italians of the late Mediæval period were the great exponents.

**Tarsier** (tā·ɹsiəɹ). *Zool.* [a. F. *tarsier*, f. *tarse* TARSUS. So named by Buffon from the structure of the foot: see quots.] A small lemuroid quadruped, *Tarsius spectrum*, of Sumatra, Borneo, Celebes, and the Philippines, called also malmag or spectre, related to the aye-aye of Madagascar.

**1774** GOLDSM. *Nat. Hist.* (1776) IV. 248 The last animal of this class is called, by Mr. Buffon, the Tarsier...The bones of..the Tarsus, are..so very long, that from thence the animal has received its name. **1785** SMELLIE *Buffon's Nat. Hist.* (1791) VII. 171 The Tarsier, or Woolly Jerboa..is remarkable for the excessive length of its hind legs. The bones of the feet, and particularly those which compose the upper part of the tarsus, are prodigiously long. **1882** A. R. WALLACE in *Contemp. Rev.* Mar. 427 The Tarsier, or spectre-lemur, of the Malay islands.

**Tarsiped** (tā·ɹsiped), *sb.* (*a.*) *Zool.* [ad. Zool. L. generic name *Tarsipēs, -ped-em*, f. L. TARSUS + *pēs, ped-* foot.] A small marsupial mammal, *Tarsipes rostratus*, the *tait* of West Australia. **b.** *adj.* Of or belonging to the family *Tarsipedidæ*, of which this animal is the type. So **Tarsi·pedid, -ine, -oid** *adjs.*, belonging to the family *Tarsipedidæ*.

‖ **Tarsitis** (taɹsəi·tis). *Path.* [mod.L., f. Gr. ταρσός the rim of the eyelid + -ITIS.] Inflammation of the tarsus of the eyelid.

**1890** in BILLINGS *Nat. Med. Dict.*

†**Ta·rso.** *Obs.* [a. It. *tarso*.] A white siliceous stone found in Italy, formerly used in glass-making.

**1662** MERRETT tr. *Neri's Art of Glass* viii, Tarso..makes ..fairer glass than any sand that is in Tuscany. **1712** tr. *Pomet's Hist. Drugs* I. 105 Beat..finely and searse your Tarso, Crystal, &c. **1799** G. SMITH *Laboratory* I. 171 The fluxes used in the other are salts, or arsenic, and the body consists of tarso, white river pebbles, and such stones.

**Tarso-** (tā·ɹso), before a vowel **tars-**, comb. form of Gr. ταρσός, TARSUS, a formative of technical terms of anatomy, pathology, and surgery.

‖ **Tarsa·lgia** [Gr. -αλγια, ἄλγος, pain], (*a*) a general term for pain in the tarsus; (*b*) see quot. **Tarse·ctomy** [Gr. ἐκτομή excision], excision of one or more of the tarsal bones. ‖ **Tarsecto·pia** [ECTOPIA], displacement of the tarsus. ‖ **Tarso·-clasis** [Gr. κλάσις fracture], (*a*) rupture of the tarsal cartilages (*Syd. Soc. Lex.* 1899); (*b*) rupture of the fibrous tissue forming the basis of the eyelids (Cassell *Suppl.* 1902). ‖ **Tarsomalacia** (-ē̆l·ʃiă) [Gr. μαλακία softness], a softening of the palpebral cartilages (*Syd. Soc. Lex.* 1899). **Tar-**

**sophala·ngeal** *a.*, pertaining to or connecting the tarsus and the phalanges. ‖ **Tarsophy·ma** [Gr. φῦμα tumour], a swelling or tumour of the tarsus (Dunglison, 1857). **Ta·rsoplasty** [-PLASTY], plastic surgery of the eyelid (*Syd. Soc. Lex.*). **Tarso·rrhaphy** [Gr. ῥαφή seam], plastic suture of the eyelid. **Tarsota·rsal** *a.*, = *medio-tarsal* (see MEDIO-). **Tarsoti·bial** *a.*, = TIBIOTARSAL. **Tarso·tomy** [Gr. τομή cutting]: see quot. 1857.

**1890** BILLINGS *Nat. Med. Dict.*, **Tarsalgia*, .. peculiar neuralgic affection of the foot, often with some flattening of the arch and contraction of the plantar muscles; observed in policemen, soldiers, etc. *Ibid.*, **Tarsectomy*. **1891** *Lancet* 28 Feb. 491/1 A case in which Syme's amputation had been performed on one foot and tarsectomy on the other for severe talipes. **1860** MAYNE *Expos. Lex.*, **Tarsectopia*. **1890** in BILLINGS *Nat. Med. Dict.* **1871** HUXLEY *Anat. Vertebr. Anim.* viii. 333 The *tarsophalangeal synostosis above described is freely movable on the astragalus. **1846** BRITTAN tr. *Malgaigne's Man. Oper. Surg.* 277 In the second case are employed excision of the conjunctiva, excision of the tarsal cartilage, V shaped excision of the lid, 'tarsoraphy. **1898** P. MANSON *Trop. Diseases* xxvi. 421 Tarsorraphy for ectropion of the lower lid..may sometimes have to be performed. **1857** DUNGLISON *Dict. Med. Sc.*, **Tarsotomy*,.. the section or removal of the tarsal cartilages. **1893** *Brit. Med. Jrnl.* 18 Feb. 341/2 Tarsotomy..is of service where the varus is the chief defect.

**Tarso-metatarsal** (tā·ɹso͵metătā·ɹsăl), *a.* and *sb. Comp. Anat.* **a.** *adj.* (*a*) Of or pertaining to the tarsus and the metatarsus, as 'the tarso-metatarsal ligaments'; (*b*) Of or pertaining to a tarso-metatarsus. **b.** *sb.* Short for *tarso-metatarsal bone* or *ligament*.

**1835-6** *Todd's Cycl. Anat.* I. 288/1 In the Grallatores.. the tarso-metatarsal bone is remarkably elongated. **1851** MANTELL *Petrifact.* ii. § 1. 79 There are also tarsometatarsals of a remarkable extinct genus named *Aptornis*. *Ibid.* § 3. 116 The longest tarso-metatarsal bones I have seen are eighteen inches and a half in length. **1872** HUMPHRY *Myology* 28 Near the insertion of the middle portions of the tarso-metatarsals. **1875** SIR W. TURNER in *Encycl. Brit.* I. 841/2 The configuration of its tarso-metatarsal joint and the attachment of the transverse metatarsal ligament prevent the great toe from being thrown across the surface of the sole as the thumb is thrown across the palm.

‖ **Tarso-metatarsus** (tā·ɹso͵metătā·ɹsǒs). *Comp. Anat.* Also in Fr.-Eng. form **ta·rso-me·tatarse**. The bone formed by ankylosis of the tarsus and the metatarsus in birds and early reptilian types.

**1854** OWEN *Skel. & Teeth* in *Orr's Circ. Sc.* I. *Org. Nat.* 224 The period at which these several constituents of the 'tarso-metatarse' coalesce is shorter in the birds that can fly than in [the others]. **1870** ROLLESTON *Anim. Life* 18 The fibula never articulates with the tarso-metatarsus.

**Tarsse**, variant of TARS *Obs.*

‖ **Tarsus** (tā·ɹsǒs). *Anat.* Pl. **-i**. [mod.L., a. Gr. ταρσός the flat of the foot between the toes and the heel; also the rim of the eyelid; in F. *tarse.*]

**1.** The first or posterior part of the foot: a collective name for the seven small bones of the human ankle, arranged in two transverse series, the proximal or tibial, consisting of the astragalus and os calcis (or calcaneum), and the distal, or metatarsal, consisting of the naviculare (centrale, or scaphoides), the cuboides, and the three ossa cuneiformia; also, the corresponding part in mammalia generally, and in some reptiles and amphibia.

**1676** WISEMAN *Chirurg. Treat.* VII. ii. 479 The Conjunction is called *Synarthrosis*; as in the joyning..the Tarsus to the Metatarsus. **1693** tr. *Blancard's Phys. Dict.* (ed. 2), *Tarsus*..also eight backward Bones of the Foot, ordered like Grates. **1704** J. HARRIS *Lex. Techn.* I, *Tarsus*, is the Space between the lower end of the two Focils, and the beginning of the Five long Bones which sustain, and are articulated with the Toes. **1872** NICHOLSON *Palæont.* 305 The small bones of the ankle, known as the tarsus. **1875** HUXLEY & MARTIN *Elem. Biol.* (1883) 225.

**b.** In birds, the third segment of the leg, the shank (which is rarely fleshy or feathered), corresponding to the mammalian tarsus and metatarsus conjoined: = TARSO-METATARSUS.

**1828** STARK *Elem. Nat. Hist.* I. 253 (Birds, *Bucco*) Tarsus shorter than the exterior toe; the anterior toes united to the second joint. **1874** COUES *Birds N. W.* 321 Tarsi nearly naked, the feathers extending but a little way below the heel-joint. **1880** A. R. WALLACE in *19th Cent.* XXXV. 100.

**c.** In insects and other *Arthropoda*, a series of small articulations forming the true foot; in spiders, the last joint, forming, with the preceding joint or metatarsus, the foot.

**1826** KIRBY & SP. *Entomol.* III. xxviii. 48 [In insects] the foot or Tarsus, is almost universally monodactyle. **1828** STARK *Elem. Nat. Hist.* II. 155 (Crustacea, *Cryptopoda*) None of the tarsi are fin-shaped. **1834** MCMURTRIE *Cuvier's Anim. Kingd.* 311 (Arachnides, *Clotho*) The tarsi, only, are furnished with spines. **1867** J. HOGG *Microscope* II. iv. 587 The tarsus, or foot of the Fly consists of a deeply bifid, membranous structure.

**2.** The thin plate of condensed connective tissue found in each eyelid. Now *rare* or *Obs.*

**1691** RAY *Creation* II. (1692) 119 The side of the Triangle, which is toward the little Corner of the Eye, and is moveable, was reinforced with a Border, which supplies the place of the Tarsus. **1727-41** CHAMBERS *Cycl.*, *Tarsus* is also a name given by some anatomists to the cartilages which terminate the palpebræ, or eyelids.

**Tart** (tāɹt), *sb.* Also 4-6 tarte, 5 taarte, tartt, 6 tairte, 9 *Sc.* tairt, teart. [a. F. *tarte* (13th c.), an open tart, in our sense 1 b (*a*), = med. L. *tarta* (1103 in Du Cange); of uncertain origin.

F. *tarte* was held by Diez to be altered from OF. *torte*, F. *tourte*, a disk-shaped cake or loaf, also a pasty, a pie, late L. *torta panis*, a kind of loaf or bread (Vulg.); and the two words certainly sometimes run together in use: cf. It. (Florio) *torta*, *tortara* 'a tart' (Baretti), *torta* 'a pasty'; Sp. (Minsheu) *torta*, *tarta* 'a tart', mod. Sp. *torta* a covered pasty, *tarta* a tart; but there are phonetic difficulties in the identification, which is rejected by Hatz.-Darm. Du. *taart*, tart, is from Fr. The Welsh *torth*, Breton *tors* round loaf, are from L. *torta* or OF. *torte*.]

**1.** Name for various dishes consisting of a crust of baked pastry enclosing different ingredients; †**a.** formerly with meat, fish, cheese, fruit, etc.: the same or nearly the same as a *pie*. **b.** In current use restricted to (*a*) a flat, usually small, piece of pastry, with no crust on the top (so distinguished from a pie), filled with fruit preserve or other sweet confection; (*b*) a covered fruit pie: = PIE *sb.*[2] 1 (*c*): in this application formerly chiefly *dial.* or *local*, now in polite or fashionable use.

**a.** ? *a* **1400** *Morte Arth.* 186 Tartes of Turky, taste whane þeme lykys. *c* **1400** *Rom. Rose* 7041 With tendre gees, & with capons, With tartes, or with chesis [*MS.* cheffis] fat, With deynte flawnes, brode & flat. **14..** *Voc.* in Wr.-Wülcker 565/44 *Artocrea*, *an*^ce^ a tart. *c* **1430** *Two Cookery-bks.* (E.E.T.S.) 47 Tartes de chare... Tartes of Fyssche. *c* **1440** *Promp. Parv.* 487/1 Taarte, bake mete.., *tarta*. **1523** SKELTON *Garl. Laurel* 1245 The Balade also of the Mustarde Tarte; Suche problemis to paynt it longyth to his arte. **1552** HULOET, Tarte or march pane, *chanona*. **1598** *Epulario* H iij, To make Tarts..of Creuisses. *Ibid.* H iij b, To make Tarts of Eeles. **1771** MRS. HAYWOOD *New Present* 192 A Tart [made of veal suet, seasoning, bread, eggs, veal sweetbreads,..etc. made in a dish].

**b.** *c* **1430** *Two Cookery-bks.* (E.E.T.S.) 48 Tartes of Frute in lente. **1562** TURNER *Herbal* II. 119 b, The tartes made onlye of Heppes serue well to be eaten of them that vomit to much. **1580** in *Hist. MSS. Comm.*, *Var. Collect.* (1903) 444 b, Dinner. To my Master...A boild meat of mutton [etc.]. Second course. Rabytes roste. Chickins roste [etc.]. ..Arttigoges, and strobarye tairte. **1584** COGAN *Haven Health* cvii. (1636) 108 Boyle them [fruit]..till they be soft, then to draw them, as yee doe a tart. **1668-9** PEPYS *Diary* 24 Feb., A mighty neat dish of custards and tarts. **1696** PHILLIPS (ed. 5), *Tart*, a sort of Baked Dish, consisting of Summer Fruits bak'd in Paste. *c* **1710** CELIA FIENNES *Diary* (1888) 218 One of ye West Country tarts..its an apple pye with a Custard all on the top. **1725** *Bradley's Fam. Dict.* s. v., When the Tart is made, you must cover it at top with some Bands of Paste, and having sugar'd it, bake it in the Oven. **1737** *Gentl. Mag.* VII. 307/2 Need I the currant sing, or goosberry praise, Prepar'd in tarts which artful females raise? **1769** MRS. RAFFALD *Eng. Housekpr.* (1778) 215 To preserve Currants for Tarts. **1899** W. H. MALLOCK *Individualist* xix. 187 Her rejection of a nice little jam tart ..'she never touched *patisserie*'.

**2.** *fig.* Applied (orig. endearingly) to a girl or woman (often one of immoral character). *slang*.

**1887** *Morn. Post* 25 Jan., The paragraph..referred to the young ladies in the chorus at the Avenue and spoke of them as 'tarts'. It was suggested on the part of the prosecution that the word 'tart' really meant a person of immoral character. **1894** *Daily News* 5 Feb. 2/7 Some of the women described themselves as 'Tarts'..and said that they got their living in the best way they could. **1898** in M. Davitt *Life & Progr. Austral.* xxxv. 192 And his lady love's his 'donah', Or his 'dinah', or his 'tart'. **1903** FARMER *Slang*, *Tart* (common). Primarily a girl, chaste or not; now (unless loosely used) a wanton, mistress, 'good-one'.

**3.** *attrib.* and *Comb.*, as *tart-dish*, *-maker*, *-seller*; †**tart-stuff**, a confection of fruit for making tarts (*obs.*); **tart-woman**, a woman who sells tarts.

**1782** WITHERING in *Phil. Trans.* LXXII. 329 Vessels.. made like a common *tart-dish, with a spreading border. **1886** *Pall Mall G.* 15 May 3/2 Verses, eulogizing the *tart-maker and her handiwork. **1851** MAYHEW *Lond. Labour* I. 199/1 I've been a cake and a *tart-seller in the streets for seven or eight years. **1623** *Althorp MS.* in Simpkinson *Washingtons* (1860) p. xlvii, Lumpe sugar for *tarte stuffe. **1848** THACKERAY *Van. Fair* l, When he was rich he would buy Leader's pencil-case, and pay the *tart-woman. **1851** — *Eng. Hum.* iii. (1863) 126 This boy went invariably into debt with the tart-woman.

**Tart**, *a.* Forms: 1 teart, 6-7 tarte, 4, 6- tart. [OE. *teart*; ulterior derivation obscure: by some referred to root of *ter-an* to TEAR.

The sense-history is also deficient. *Teart* appears in OE. only in reference to punishment, pain, or suffering, which use of *tart*, after many centuries, reappears late in 16th c. In the ME. period, the word is known only by a single instance in Chaucer (if this is the adj.), continued after 1500, in sense 'of a sharp, pungent, or sour taste'. In 1500 it is also applied to a sharp or pungent weapon; and about 1600 to sharp, bitter, caustic, or stinging words. It is difficult from these data to infer the sense-development; and the order here followed is provisional.]

†**1.** Of pain, punishment, suffering, discipline, law: Sharp, severe, painful, grievous. *Obs.*

In OE.; not known in ME.; in mod.Eng. possibly newly developed from sense 2.

*c* **1000** in Napier *O. E. Glosses* 52/1946 *Acerrimo*, *i. asperrimo*, on þære teartestan. *Ibid.* 168/218 *Acra*, i. tearte. *c* **1000** ÆLFRIC *Hom.* II. 344 Ac beo hem ȝesæd, ær he ȝewite, ða teartan witu, þæt his heorte mid ðære biternysse beo ȝehrepod.

**1577** HANMER *Anc. Eccl. Hist.* v. xvi. 89 Themison..tasted not of the tarte conyzance of confession, before the tyrant. **1579** GOSSON *To Gentlew. Cit. Lond.* in *Sch. Abuse* (Arb.) 61 My Schoole is tarte, but my counsell is plesaunt. **1602** FULBECKE *Pandectes* xi. 81 And Iustinian his Law is tarte: *Si quis..auserit, capitali pœna feriatur.* **1605** SHAKS. *Lear* IV. ii. 87 Another way The Newes is not so tart.

**2.** Sharp to the sense of taste; † biting, pungent (*obs.*); now *esp.* sour, acid, or acidulous.

(The sense in the Chaucer quot. is not quite clear.)

*c* **1386** CHAUCER *Prol.* 381 To boille the chiknes with the Marybones And poudre Marchant tart and galyngale. *a* **1529** SKELTON *El. Rummyng* 435 Myghty stronge meate For the deuyll to eate; It was tart and punyete. **1601** HOLLAND *Pliny* II. 219 The Patient is to eat tart and sharp meats and poignant sauces [*margin* As Radish roots and oxymell]. **1626** DEAN *Spadacrene Angl.* Title-p., A Brief Treatise of the Acid Tart Fountain in the Forest of Knaresborough.

**1530** PALSGR. 327/1 Tarte, sharpe in taste as vinagre is, *aigre*, *poignant*. **1552** HULOET, Tarte, *acidus*. *Ibid.*, Tarte or somewhat eyger, *subacidus*. **1652** CULPEPPER *Eng. Physic.* (1809) 356 If you love tart things, add ten drops of oil of vitriol to your pint. **1772-84** COOK *Voy.* (1790) I. 139 Cherries..the juice of which was agreeably tart. **1850** SIR T. D. ACLAND in *Jrnl. Roy. Agric. Soc.* 755 There is a great deal of grass land on the borders of the lias hills, which scours cattle. It is said to be 'teart'; that is tart or sour.

† **b.** Of the sense of taste: Keen. *Obs. rare*^—1^.

**1605** B. JONSON *Volpone* II. i, Would you be ever fair and young? Stout of teeth, and strong of tongue? Tart of palat? quick of ear?

†**3.** Sharp, keen (as an edge, point, or weapon).

*c* **1500** MEDWALL *Nature* (Brandl) 777, I bought thys dagger at the marte, A sharp poynt and a tarte. **1600** MARLOWE & CHAPMAN tr. *Hero & Leander* v. K iij b, Thin like an iron wedge, so sharpe and tart, As t'were of purpose made to cleaue Loues heart.

**4.** *fig.* Of words, speech, a speaker: Sharp in tone or tendency, biting, cutting, acrimonious, caustic.

**1601** BP. W. BARLOW *Serm. Paules Crosse* Pref. 10 Here I renounce all tart and soure speach. **1615** BRATHWAIT *Strappado* (1878) 35 Where wilt thou begin With thy tart phrase, to stinge and nettle him? **1669** GALE *Crt. Gentiles* I. III. x. 106 The Cynics..were very tart and satyric in their Declamations against this..kind of Oratorie. **1691** HARTCLIFFE *Virtues* 185 Sometimes a tart Irony goes for Wit. **1710** ADDISON *Tatler* No. 157 ¶ 6 Entertaining the Company with tart ill-natured Observations. **1822** W. IRVING *Braceb. Hall* xxix, Her mind was made up, and she grew tart on the least contradiction. **1855** MACAULAY *Hist. Eng.* xxii. IV. 719 Ill humour..might sometimes impel him to give a tart answer.

**5.** *Comb.*, as *tart-tongued*.

**1602** FULBECKE *2nd Pt. Parall.* 26 b, Being a tart-tounged detractor.

**Tart**, *v. rare.* ? *Obs.* [f. prec. adj.: cf. *to sour*.]

**1.** *trans.* To make tart, to sour; † to make pungent, give pungency to (*obs.*).

**1616** T. SCOTT *Christ's Politician* 32 One sponefull of vineger will soone tart a great deale of sweete milke. *a* **1634** RANDOLPH *Poems* (1668) 28 To walk on our own ground.. The best of sawce to tart our meats.

**2.** *intr.* To become tart or sour.

**1629** GAULE *Holy Madn.* 244 An ill Liquor that being kept too long, hath tarted and tainted the Caske.

**Tartan** (tā·ɹtăn), *sb.*[1] orig. *Sc.* Also 6–7 tartane, tertane, (6 teartane). [Of uncertain origin: in use early in 16th c.

It has been conjectured to be a. F. *tiretaine* (1247 in Godef. *Compl.*) 'a kind of cloth, half wool, half linen or cotton', for which a variant *tertaine* is quoted by Godefroy of date 1487: cf. the 16th c. Sc. spelling *tertane*. Another conjecture would identify the cloth with that called *tartar* or *tartarin* (q. v.), of which the 15th c. forms *tartarne*, *tarterne*, somewhat approach *tartane*. But the quots. for TARTAR and TARTARIN point to a richer and more costly stuff.]

**1.** A kind of woollen cloth woven in stripes of various colours crossing at right angles so as to form a regular pattern; worn chiefly by the Scottish Highlanders, each clan having generally its distinctive pattern. Also, the pattern or design of such cloth. Also applied to silk and other fabrics having a similar pattern. *Shepherds' tartan*, shepherds' plaid: see quot. 1882. In quot. 1810 *pl.* tartan garments.

? *a* **1500** *Symmye & Bruder* 22 in Sibbald *Chron. Sc. Poetry* (1802) I. 360 Syne schupe thame up, to lowp owr leiss, Twa tabartis of the tartane. **1533** *Acc. Ld. High Treas. Scotl.* VI. 79 For fresing of ane tartane galcot. *Ibid.* 80 Ane uthir tartane galcoit gevin to the King be the Maister Forbes. **1538** *Ibid.* 436 Item, for iij elnis of heland tertane to be hois to the Kingis grace, price of the elne iiijs. iiijd. **1546** *Aberdeen Regr.* (1844) I. 236 Item, ane vob of tartane, contenand x ellis, the price of ell iiijs. *Ibid.*, Ane blankat of tartane. **1548-51** *Ibid.* XX. (Jam.), Ane gelcoit of quhit tertane. **1630** J. TAYLOR (Water P.) *Pennilesse Pilgr.* Wks. I. 135/1 Stockings (which they call short hose) made of a warme stuffe of diuers colours, which they call Tartane. **1806** *Gazetteer Scotl.* (ed. 2) 395 Of late the greater part of the tartan for the army has been manufactured in this parish [St. Ninians]. **1810** SCOTT *Lady of L.* III. xxvii, Their feathers dance, their tartans float,.. A wild and warlike groupe they stand. **1855** MACAULAY *Hist. Eng.* xiii. III. 354 Men wearing the same tartan, and attached to the same lord, were arrayed against each other. **1862** 'SHIRLEY' *Nugæ Crit.* vi. 239 Dressed in a bodice and kirtle of shepherd tartan. **1882** OGILVIE (Annandale), *Shepherd's..tartan*, a kind of small check pattern in cloth, woven with black and white warp and weft; (b) a kind of cloth..woven in this pattern—generally made into shepherd's plaids. **1891** *Cent. Dict.* s.v., *Silk tartan*, a silk material for women's dresses and men's waistcoats, woven in the style of the Scottish clan tartans. **1905** *Times* 7 Sept. 5/4 Considerable success has followed the bringing out of quite a variety of tartans for next spring. **1906** *Athenæum* 2 June 671/2 The whole question of the date of clan tartans is difficult.

**b.** *transf.* Applied to one who wears tartan; a Highlander; collectively, those who wear tartan;

the body of Highlanders; the men of a Highland regiment.

**1817** CANNING in Hanna *Mem. Chalmers* (1849) II. v. 102 The tartan [so runs the speech attributed to him, i.e. Canning, regarding Dr. C.] beats us all. **1859** COLIN CAMPBELL in A. Forbes *Life* v. 127 [Then Sir Colin called to Colonel Ewart,] 'Ewart! Bring on the tartan!'..[and the seven companies of the Ninety-Third dashed from behind the bank].

**2.** *Angling.* Name of an artificial salmon-fly.

**1867** F. FRANCIS *Angling* x. 315 The Tartan is a strange looking fly. [Description follows.]

**3.** Short for *tartan-purry*: see 4 b. *Sc.*

**1893** HENDERSON *Old World Scotl.* 80 Of oatmeal we have tartan—a pudding made chiefly of chopped kale and oatmeal.

**4.** *attrib.* **a.** Made of tartan; having a chequered pattern like that of tartan.

**1533** [see 1]. **1549** *Fragm. Ayr Burgh Rec.* (Gen. Reg. Ho., Edinb.), Item for teartane claith, aucht lib. **1721** RAMSAY *Tartana* 78 Who 'midst the snows the best of limbs can fold In Tartan Plaids, and smile at chilling cold. *c* **1750** in Ritson *Sc. Songs* (1794) II. 107 O! to see his tartan trouze, Bonnet blue, and laigh-heel'd shoes! **1853** 'C. BEDE' *Verdant Green* I. vii, A gentleman clad in tartan-plaid. **1869** E. A. PARKES *Pract. Hygiene* (ed. 3) 403 One pair of tartan trousers in rifle regiments.

**b. Tartan-purry** (*Sc. local*): see quots.

*c* **1746** FORBES *Dominie* II. (1785) 35 Tartan-purry, meal and bree, Or butt'ry brose. **1790** SHIRREFS *Poems* Gloss., *Tartan purry*, a sort of pudding made of red colewort chipped small, and mixed with oatmeal. **1819** W. TENNANT *Papistry Storm'd* (1827) 52 Some ran to parritch, some to kail;..And some to tartan-purry. **1866** T. EDMONDSTON *Gloss. Shetl. & Orkn.*, *Tart-and-purrie*, porridge made with the water in which cabbage has been boiled.

**Tartan, tartane** (tā·ɹtăn, ‖ tarta·n), *sb.*[2] Also 7 **tartain**. [a. Fr. *tartane* (1632 in Hatz.-Darm.), a. It., = Sp., Pg. *tartana*, supposed by Diez to be derived from Arab. *tarīdah*: see TARETTE. But connecting evidence is wanting.] A small one-masted vessel with a large lateen sail and a foresail, used in the Mediterranean; = TARTANA[1].

**1621** *Admiralty Crt. Exam.* No. 43. 24 Aug., A small vessel called a tartain flotinge and driveinge to and fro in the sea. **1666** *Lond. Gaz.* No. 77/2 A small Tartane arrived here two daies since from Provence. **1697** DAMPIER *Voy. round World* (1699) 30 Captain Wright..had taken a Spanish Tartan, wherein were 30 men, all well armed. **1756–7** tr. *Keysler's Trav.* (1760) IV. 119 A Turkish tartane, with red colours, emblazoned with three crescents, &c. was performing quarantine. **1805** WILKES in *Mem.* II. 171, I could not go in a small tartan without some one friend. **1896** VIZETELLY *Zola's Rome* 295 The few tartanes which brought wine from Sicily, never came higher than the Aventine.

**Tartan**, *sb.*[3] *rare*—[0]. = TARTANA[3].

**1858** SIMMONDS *Dict. Trade*, *Tartan*,..a long covered carriage.

‖ **Tartan**, *sb.*[4] [Assyrian. See 2 Kings xviii. 17, Isa. xx. 1.] The ancient Assyrian commander-in-chief.

**1880** CHEYNE *Isaiah* (1884) I. 16 No Satraps nor Tartans are necessary. **1893** SAYCE *Higher Crit.* (1894) 427 The 'tartan' of Sargon entered Jerusalem and forced Hezekiah to become his tributary. **1899** T. NICOLL *Rec. Archæol. & Bible* vii. 255 The Tartan fought against Ashdod and took it.

**Ta·rtan**, *v.* [f. TARTAN *sb.*[1]] *trans.* To clothe or array in tartan; also *fig.* So **Tartaned** (tā·ɹtănd) *a.*, clothed in tartan, wearing tartans.

**1813** HOGG *Queen's Wake* 283 Tartaned chiefs in raptures hear The strains, the words, to them so dear. **1875** A. SMITH *Aberdeenshire* I. 656 The crested chief led on his tartaned band. **1881** J. F. CAMPBELL in Ld. A. Campbell *Rec. Argyll* (1885) 441, I was first tartaned, more than fifty years ago.

‖ **Tartana**[1] (tartā·na). [It. *tartana*: see TARTAN *sb.*[2]] = TARTAN *sb.*[2]

**1588** *Ancaster MSS.* in *Hist. MSS. Comm.* (1907) XLV. 113 They have almost two hundred Tartanars, which are a kind of fish boats they use in the Straits. **1617** LD. CAREW *Lett.* (Camden) 92 They have allso 200 tartenas, which are a kind of flat-bottomde boates. **1773** *Phil. Trans.* LXV. 1, I hired a fishing vessel, called a *tartana*, with eighteen men in her. **1884** W. SIME *To & Fro* 17 Here are tartanas waiting the voyager.

† **Tartana**[2] (taɹtā·nă). *Obs. rare.* [Pseudo-latinized form of TARTAN[1].] = TARTAN *sb.*[1] 1.

**1721** RAMSAY *Tartana* 82 Bright Tartana's waving in the wind. *Ibid.* 315 A bright Tartana veiled the lovely fair.

‖ **Tartana**[3]. [Sp. *tartana*.] A covered vehicle used in Spain, esp. in Valencia.

**1829** W. IRVING in *Life & Lett.* (1864) II. 408 We made our journey..in a kind of covered cart called a Tartana, drawn by a mule. **1845** FORD *Handbk. Spain* I. 438 A *Tartana*, the common Valencian vehicle...It may be compared to a Venetian gondola on wheels. **1882** *Harper's Mag.* Sept. 564 In summer it is covered with tartanas, bouncing little covered waggons lined with crimson curtains.

**Tartane**: see TARTAN *sb.*[1] and [2], TERTIAN.

**Tartar** (tā·ɹtăɹ), *sb.*[1] Also 4 **tartre**, 5 **tarter**, **-are**, (6 **tartarum**, 7–8 **tartarus**). [a. F. *tartre* = Sp., Pg., It. *tartaro*, med.L. *tartarum* (*tartharum*), med.Gr. τάρταρον; perh. of Arabic origin: Simon of Genoa (fl. 1292), *Synonima* (ed. 1473), has '*Tartar* arabice, tartarum quod ex uino in lateribus uegetis generatur'.

But there is some doubt as to this, the usual Arabic term being *durdī*, from Pers. *durd* sediment, dregs; *tartīr*, found in mod.Arabic lexicons from 1639, is held by Dozy to be borrowed from European langs. The med.L. *tartarum* appears in the *Dictionarius* of Joh. de Garlandia, *c* 1225.]

**1.** *Chem.* Bitartrate of potash (acid potassium tartrate), present in grape juice, deposited in a crude form in the process of fermentation, and adhering to the sides of wine-casks in the form of a hard crust, also called *argal* or ARGOL, which in the crude state varies from pale pink to dark red, but when purified forms white crystals, which are *cream of tartar*.

(† In quot. *c* 1425 applied to the dregs of malt liquor.)

*c* **1386** CHAUCER *Can. Yeom. Prol. & T.* 260 Of Tartre, Alum glas, berme, wort and argoille. **1398** TREVISA *Barth. De P. R.* XVI. xcix. (Tollem. MS.), Tartar is wyn drastes [*tartarum est vini fæculentia*], and like to a softe ston cleuynge harde to þe sides of þe tonnes. *c* **1425** tr. *Arderne's Surgery* (E. E. T. S.) 49 Ffirst I made hym ane emplastre of tartare of ale, i.[e]. dreggez. *c* **1550** LLOYD *Treas. Health* B vij, Wyne Lyes called Tartarum..menglid in oyle and Veniger is verye good. **1679** V. ALSOP *Melius Inquir.* Introd. 32 Like Tartar, [it] is so baked and crusted to the sides of the Vessel, that till you knock off the Hoops and take the frame in pieces, no Art of Man will free the Cask from a tang at least of the old mustiness. **1732** ARBUTHNOT *Rules of Diet* in *Aliments*, etc. 259 Small Wines with little Oil and much Tartar. **1797** *Encycl. Brit.* (ed. 3) IV. 495/2 The tartar of the white wines is of a greyish white colour, called white tartar; and that of red wine has a red colour, and is called red tartar. **1883** *Hardwich's Photogr. Chem.* (ed. Taylor) 96 Tartaric Acid..is derived from a substance called Tartar, deposited from the juice of the Grape during fermentation. This Tartar is an Acid Tartrate of Potash.

**b.** Hence, 'A generic name for salts of tartaric acid' (Watts).

**c.** Commercially, applied not to the argol or original deposit, but to a product that has undergone partial purification: see quot.

**1893** THORPE *Dict. Applied Chem.* III. 783 The crust is known as 'argol', and when recrystallised produces 'tartar', which by further crystallisation is converted into 'cream of tartar', technically known as 'cream'.

**d.** *fig.*

**1590** MARLOWE *2nd Pt. Tamburl.* IV. i, A soul Created of the massy dregs of earth, The scum and tartar of the elements. *a* **1631** DONNE *Serm.* (1649) II. xix. 153 Impatience in affliction..a leaven so kneaded into the nature of man, so innate a tartar, so inherent a sting. **1683** BURNET tr. *More's Utopia* Pref. (1684) 4 Our Language has, like a rich Wine, wrought out its Tartar. **1824** LANDOR *Imag. Conv.*, *Ld. Brooke & Sir P. Sidney*, Desire of lucre...It is the tartar that encrusts economy.

**2.** *transf.* Any calcareous or other incrustation deposited from a liquid upon bodies in contact with it. (With quot. 1605 cf. TARTARER, TARTAROUS 2.)

**1605** TIMME *Quersit.* III. 161 Of the congelations of these salts comes goutes..and diuers kinds of obstructions, according to the diuersitie of tartars and of salts which are ingendred and procreate to nature in our bodie. **1756–7** tr. *Keysler's Trav.* (1760) III. 151 This water is impregnated with tartar, so that the bottom and pillars..are incrusted with it. **1789** MRS. PIOZZI *Journ. France* I. 427 [It] incrusted a stick with its tartar in two minutes.

**b.** *spec.* A deposit of calcium phosphate from the saliva, which tends to harden and concrete upon the teeth. (So F. *tartre*; cf. Ger. *weinstein*.)

**1806** *Med. Jrnl.* XV. 30 We find that this coagulum has the greatest similarity with the tartar adhering to the teeth. **1822–34** *Good's Study Med.* (ed. 4) I. 65 The teeth are always subject to be covered over with layers of an earthy material secreted as a constituent part of the saliva, and denominated tartar. **1897** *Allbutt's Syst. Med.* IV. 743 The concretions of tartar that gather round the teeth.

**3.** Phrasal combinations:

**a. Cream of tartar**: see 1 and CREAM *sb.* 4; † **magistery of tartar** = *vitriolated tartar*: see b; † **oil of tartar**, old name for a saturated solution of potassium carbonate; † **salt of tartar**, an old name of potassium carbonate; **spirit of tartar**, the liquid obtained by dry distillation of tartar; it contains pyrotartaric acid and other substances.

**1584** R. SCOT *Discov. Witchcr.* XIV. i. (1886) 295 These things are of necessitie to be used; namelie..claie made with horsse doong, mans haire, *oile of tartre, allum, glasse, woort, yest, argoll. **1660** BOYLE *New Exp. Phys. Mech.* xxiv. 189 As strong a solution of Salt of Tartar in fair Water as could be made (we having no Oyl of Tartar *per deliquium* at hand). **1706** PHILLIPS, *Oil of Tartar per Deliquium*, the fixt Salt of Tartar dissolved by being expos'd to the Air in a Cellar, or other cool moist place. **1707** *Curios. in Husb. & Gard.* 67 Spirit of Vitriol and Oil of Tartar..mingled together, are surprizingly hot. **1646** SIR T. BROWNE *Pseud. Ep.* 87 A pint of *salt of tartar exposed unto a moist aire untill it dissolve, will make far more liquor, or as some tearm it oyle, then the former measure will contain. **1794** SULLIVAN *View Nat.* I. 339 Moisture drawn from it [the air] by dry salt of tartar, in such quantity, as to make the salt become intirely fluid. **1832** G. R. PORTER *Porcelain & Gl.* 83 Precipitating with salt of tartar (sub-carbonate of potass). **1860** MAYNE *Expos. Lex.*, *Spirit of Tartar*, a name for pyrotartaric acid. [**1868** WATTS *Dict. Chem.* V. 402.]

**b.** † **Chalybeate tartar, tartar chalybeated**, potassio-ferric tartrate, $C_4H_4K(FeO)O_6$; † **regenerated tartar**, acetate of potassium, $C_4H_6O_3 . K_2O$; † **soluble tartar**, neutral potassium tartrate, $C_4H_4K_2O_6$; also applied to ammonium potassium tartrate, $C_8H_4(NH_4)KO_6$; † **vitriolated tartar, tartar vitriolate**, sulphate of potassium, $K_2SO_4$.

**1727–41** CHAMBERS *Cycl.* s.v. *Crystal*, Crystal of *tartar chalybeated, is when it is impregnated with the most dissoluble parts of iron. **1860** MAYNE *Expos. Lex.* s.v. *Tartar*, *Chalybeate Tartar..., a name for the *Potassio-tartras ferri.* **1753** CHAMBERS *Cycl. Supp.* s.v., The good effects of *regenerated tartar in the cure of obstructions of the bowels. **1860** MAYNE *Expos. Lex.*, *Regenerated Tartar*, term for the *Acetas potassæ.* **1704** J. HARRIS *Lex. Techn.* I, **Soluble Tartar*, is made by boiling in 3 Pints of Water, 8 Ounces of Cream of Tartar, and 4 Ounces of the Fix'd Salt of Tartar. **1860** MAYNE *Expos. Lex.*, *Soluble Tartar*, a term for the *Tartras potassæ.* **1704** J. HARRIS *Lex. Techn.* I, **Tartar Vitriolate*, is made by pouring Spirit of Vitriol on Oil of Tartar *per Deliquium*, by little and little. **1727–41** CHAMBERS *Cycl.* s.v., *Vitriolated Tartar, which some call Magistery of Tartar, is oil of Tartar mixed with rectified spirit of vitriol. **1820** T. THOMSON *Syst. Chem.* II. 435 Known by the name of *vitriolated tartar*, till the French chemists called it *sulphate of potash*..in 1787.

**c. Ta·rtar-eme·tic**, † *emetic tartar*, common name in pharmacy of potassio-antimonious tartrate, $C_4H_4K(Sb.O)O_6 + \frac{1}{2}H_2O$, a poisonous substance, used in medicine to excite vomiting. Hence **Ta·rtar-eme·ticize** *v.* (*nonce-wd.*), *trans.* to dose with tartar-emetic.

**1704** J. HARRIS *Lex. Techn.* I, *Tartar Emetick.* See *Emetick Tartar.* *Ibid.*, *Emetick Tartar*, is only Cream or Crystal of Tartar poudred and mixt with a quarter part of *Crocus Metallorum*, and..the Mixture..boil'd in an earthen Pan in a sufficient quantity of Water, for about 8 or 9 Hours. **1758** J. S. tr. *Le Dran's Observ. Surg.* (1771) 334 A Dose of Tartar Emetic. **1795** GAITSKELL in *Memoirs Med.* IV. 79 (heading) Observations and Experiments on the external absorption of Emetic Tartar and Arsenic. **1846** MRS. CARLYLE *Lett.* (1883) I. 383 Dosing me with tartar-emetic and opium. **1844** J. T. HEWLETT *Parsons & W.* vi, Tartar-emeticising the establishment at breakfast.

**Tartar** (tā·ɹtăɹ), *sb.*[2] (*a.*), **Tatar** (tā·tăɹ). Also 6 *pl.* **Tartaries**, 7, 9 **Tâtar, Tahtar.** [a. F. *Tartare* (OF. also *Tartaire*, 13th c.), or ad. med.L. *Tartarus*, pl. *Tartari*, ethnic name; in Sp., Pg., It. *Tartaro*; Du. *Tartaar*, *Tarter*, Ger., Da. *Tartar*, Sw. *Tartar*, *Tartarer*; Polish *Tatar*, Turk., Pers. *Tātār*. In OF. more usually *Tartarin*, med. L. *Tartarīnus*, TARTARIN; cf. Russ. *Tatarin*ᵘ.

The original name (by which the people in question either called themselves or were designated by their neighbours) is generally held to have been, as in Persian, etc., *Tātār*, as to the language and meaning of which various conjectures have been put forth; but in Western Europe, they appear from the first as *Tartari*, *Tartares*, or *Tartars*, their name being apparently associated with *Tartarus*, hell. See the saying attributed by many historians to St. Louis of France *a* 1270, in Littré, s.v. *Tartare*, and a translation in quot. 1842 below. The form *Tâtar* and its derivatives are now often used in ethnological works in sense 1, but the long-established *Tartar* is always used in the derived senses, and is also held by some to have been the original name: see quot. 1885, and its context.]

**1.** A native inhabitant of the region of Central Asia extending eastward from the Caspian Sea, and formerly known as Independent and Chinese Tartary. First known in the West as applied to the mingled host of Mongols, Tartars, Turks, etc., which under the leadership of Jenghiz Khan (1202–1227) overran and devastated much of Asia and Eastern Europe; hence vaguely applied to the descendants of these now dwelling in Asia or Europe; more strictly and ethnologically, to any member of the Tâtar or Turkic branch of the Ural-Altaic or Turanian family, embracing the Turks, Cossacks, and Kirghiz Tartars. (In all these uses, but esp. the last, now often written *Tatar*, *Tâtar*.)

*c* **1386** CHAUCER *Sqr.'s T.* 20 This noble kyng this Tartre, Cambynskan. *Ibid.* 258 This Tartre kyng. **1474** CAXTON *Chesse* IV. iii. (1883) 170 Therfore the tartaris haue their wyues in to the felde with hem. **1525** LD. BERNERS *Froiss.* II. ccxxiii. 363 The dealyng of the turkes and tartaries with yᵉ portes and passages of the kynges, soudans and miscreantes. **1585** T. WASHINGTON tr. *Nicholay's Voy.* III. x. 86 Moores, Indians, or Tartares. **1588** PARKE tr. *Mendoza's Hist. China* 18 It [the great wall] was for his defence against the Tartaries, with whome he had warres. **1590** SHAKS. *Mids. N.* III. ii. 101 Looke how I goe, Swifter then arrow from the Tartars bowe. **1600** HAKLUYT *Voy.* (1810) III. 55 They be like to Tartars, with long blacke haire, broad faces, and flatte noses. **1612** BREREWOOD *Lang. & Relig.* (1614) 94 It is alleaged that the word *Tatari*, or *Totari*, (for so indeed they are rightly called, as learned men obserue, and not *Tartari*) signifieth in the Syriaque and Hebrew tongues, a Residue or Remainder such as these Tartars are supposed to bee of the Ten Tribes. **1745** P. THOMAS *Jrnl. Anson's Voy.* 241 Since the Tartars have been Emperors of China, the Lamas have succeeded the Chinese Bonzes in the Direction of Religious Affairs. **1837** CARLYLE *Fr. Rev.* III. I. i, Into the body of the poor Tatars execrative Roman History intercalated an alphabetic letter; and so they continue Tartars, of fell Tartarean nature, to this day. **1842** *Penny Cycl.* XXIV. 73 The name of Tatar is still given to the Turkish inhabitants of southern and eastern Russia...The Tatars call themselves Turks, and feel highly offended by being called Tatars, a name which in their idiom signifies 'robbers'. **1842** tr. *Let. S. Louis* (*a* 1270) ibid., In the present danger of the Tartars either we shall push them back into the Tartarus whence they are come, or they will bring us all into heaven. **1885** E. PEARS *Fall Constantinople* 15 *note*, I write Tartar instead of Tatar because I agree with Dr. Koelle that the first is the form which the Tartars themselves used until they came into contact with foreigners, like the Chinese and Russians, who had changed the form of the word.

**2.** Transferred uses. **a.** A military valet. [So in F.]

**1747** *Gentl. Mag.* Dec. 570/2, 13,421 Convents of monks.. which may be called the Field regiments, and, together with the brother servitors, invalids, tartars and scullions, may amount to 160,000. **1839** tr. *Lamartine's Trav.* 168/1 Our moukres, Tatars, and horsemen, bivouacked in the orchards.

† **b.** An old cant name for a strolling vagabond,

a thief, a beggar. Cf. BOHEMIAN *sb.*, GIPSY *sb.*, TARTARIAN *sb.* b. *Obs.*

**1598** SHAKS. *Merry W.* IV. v. 21 Here 's a Bohemian-Tartar taries the comming down of thy fat-woman: Let her descend. **1697** VANBRUGH *Relapse* IV. vi, Here, pursue this Tartar, bring him back.

c. As an opprobrious appellation.

**1590** SHAKS. *Mids. N.* III. ii. 263 Thy loue? out tawny Tartar, out. **1828** *Craven Gloss.*, *Tartar*, a covetous, griping person.

**3.** *fig.* A savage; a person supposed to resemble a Tartar in disposition; a rough and violent or irritable and intractable person: when applied to a female, a vixen, a shrew, a termagant.

**1663** DRYDEN *Wild Gallant* II. i, I never knew your grandmother was a Scotchwoman: Is she not a Tartar too? **1771** SMOLLETT *Humph. Cl.* (1815) 146 He is generally a tartar at bottom; a sharper, a spy, or a lunatic. **1778** JOHNSON in *Mme. D'Arblay's Diary* 23 Aug., They will little think what a tartar you carry to them. **1818** BYRON *Juan* I. clxxxiv, His blood was up: though young, he was a Tartar. *a* **1845** HOOD *Tale of Temper* i, However, cooks are generally Tartars. **1865** DICKENS *Mut. Fr.* I. viii, The old man was a awful Tartar. **1891** *Athenæum* 11 Apr. 469/2 When provoked he proved a tartar.

b. *slang.* One hard to beat or surpass in skill, an adept, a 'champion'. (Cf. slang use of 'bully'.)

**1785** GROSE *Dict. Vulg. T.* s.v., He is quite a tartar at cricket, or billiards.

**4.** Phrase: *To catch a Tartar*: to get hold of one who can neither be controlled nor got quit of; to tackle one who unexpectedly proves to be too formidable. Also in allusive expressions.

**1663** BUTLER *Hud.* I. III. 865 Now thou hast got me for a Tartar, To make me 'gainst my will take quarter. **1678** DRYDEN *Kind Keeper* v. i, What a Tartar have I caught! **1690** J. MACKENZIE *Siege London-Derry* 39/2 As it happily fell out, they Catcht a Tartar. **1700** S. L. tr. *Fryke's Voy. E. Ind.* 96, I rather hug'd my self that I had let my Tartar go. **1720** DE FOE *Capt. Singleton* xvi. (1906) 260 Tell him, if he should try, he may catch a Tartar. **1725** *New Cant. Dict.* s. v., *To catch a Tartar*, is said, among the Canting Varlets, when a Rogue attacks one that he thinks a Passenger, but proves to be of this Class.., who, in his Turn,..robs,..and binds him. **1850** SCORESBY *Cheever's Whalem. Adv.* vi. (1858) 80 Many an old whaler..has been compelled to give in as beaten when fast to one of these 'North-west Tartars' [whales]. **1897** FLOR. MARRYAT *Blood Vampire* xiv, You must give up flirting, my boy, or if I mistake not, you'll find you've caught a Tartar.

**5.** (*absol.* use of B.) The language of the Tartars.

**1884** G. SMITH *Short Hist. Chr. Missions* ix. 109 He [Monte Corvino, 1305] translated the New Testament and Psalter into Tartar.

**B.** *adj.* **1.** Of or pertaining to the people referred to in 1 above, or their country. Also noting animals, plants, etc., belonging to Tartary. **Tartar bread**: see TARTARIAN *a.*[1] b.

**1731** *Hist. Litteraria* III. 250 He settles wherever he comes, and like a Tartar-Hord, never quits the Ground while there is a bit of green Herbage left. **1811** PINKERTON *Mod. Geog.* (ed. 3) 346 A beautiful Tatar girl astride on a cow. **1815** ELPHINSTONE *Acc. Caubul* (1842) II. 202 Their features..refer them at once to the Tartar stock. **1842** J. B. FRASER *Mesopot. & Assyria* xv. 369 There were also the shore-lark..and the Tartar lark (*A*[*lauda*] *tartarica* of Pallas). **1866** *Treas. Bot.* 168/2 *Tartar Bread*, the fleshy root of *Crambe tatarica*. **1858** *St. Paul's Mag.* July 485 Scratch an amateur actor as you would a Russian, and the Tartar vanity will come through. **1883** MORFILL *Slavonic Lit.* i. 6 The Russian language is hemmed in on..the east by Finnish and Tatar dialects.

**2.** *fig.* Tartar-like; rough and violent, savage.

**1809** MALKIN *Gil Blas* II. vii. ⁋ 22 Little do you fathom my character, to be deceived..by my Tartar contour! **1880** J. NICOL *Poems & Songs* 23 The winter came with all its Tartar rigour.

**C.** *Comb.*, as *Tartar-like* adj.; **Tartar-nosed** *a.*, snub-nosed like a Tartar.

**1827** T. L. MCKENNEY *Tour Lakes* 380 [The Chippeway Indians] Their tents and belts are all Tartar-like. **1837** *Boston Advert.* 17 Jan. 4/4 Miss Stevens was a tartar-like looking lady, very long and unbending. **1897** MRS. RAYNER *Type-writer Girl* xiv, He..called you a Tartar-nosed imp.

Hence † **Tartare·sque** *a.* Tartar (language) (*obs. rare*); **Ta·rtarism,** a Tartar state or condition.

**1693** P. GORDON *Geog. Gram.* II. vii. (1725) 184 The language of the Crim-Tartars is the Scythian or pure Tartaresque, which hath such a Resemblance to the Turkish as the Spanish to the Italian. **1892** *Harper's Mag.* July 255/1 A line which divides the Tartarism of Russia from the civilization of Europe.

† **Ta·rtar,** *sb.*[3] *Obs.* Also 5 **tarter, -yr, -or,** 5–6 **-ir,** (6 **tarterus, tartarium).** [= OF. *tartare, tartaire* (*c* 1300 in Godef.), med.L. *tartarium, tartareus* (*pannus*) 'cloth of Tartary'. Cf. TARS, TARTARIN[1] 2, and quot. 1880.] A rich kind of cloth, probably silk, used in 15th and 16th centuries; the same as TARTARIN[1] 2.

**1473** *Acc. Ld. High Treas. Scotl.* I. 16 Item, for v. elne of tartar to lyne a gowne of clath of gold to the King. **1488** *Ibid.* 85 Item, a couering of variand purpir tartar, browdin with thrissillis and a vnicorne. **1494** *Ibid.* 224, j ell of tartor to lyne the hud. **1496** *Ibid.* 298 Item, for viij elne of tartyr, to the Kingis jakat of clath of gold,..vij*li.* iiij*s.* *a* **1500** *Flower & Leaf* 212 On every trumpe hanging a brood banere Of fyn tartarium, were ful richly bete. **1501** *Acc. Ld. High Treas. Scotl.* II. 28 Item, for half an elne tartir to the tothir scarlet hos to bordour thaim with. **1502** ARNOLDE *Chron.* 73 Item of carde, bokram, fustian, clothes of gold and of silke, veluet, damask, sateyn, taffata, tarterus, couerchis,..the same broker shall haue for the valur of euery xx. s. iij. d'. **1602** SEGAR *Hon. Mil. & Civ.* II. xi. 71 One Knight shall giue him his shirt, another his hose, the third his dublet, another shall apparell him in a kertle of red Tartar. [**1880** BIRDWOOD *Ind. Arts* II. 73 Tartariums, Colonel Yule believes, were so called 'not because they were made in Tartary, but because they were brought from China through the Tartar dominions'.]

b. Comb. *Tartar-satin.*

**1483–4** in Swayne *Sarum Churchw. Acc.* (1896) 35 Pro tribus le nailes de tartersaten' pro emendacione vestamenti.

† **Ta·rtar,** *sb.*[4] *Obs.* Also 6 **Tartare.** [a. F. *tartare*, or ad. L. *Tartarus*, a. Gr. Τάρταρος.] = TARTARUS; the infernal regions; hell. Also *attrib.*

**1500–20** DUNBAR *Poems* lxxxvi. 20 Tryumphand tempill of the Trinite, That turned us fra Tartar eternall. **1590** SHAKS. *Com. Err.* IV. ii. 32. **1591** SPENSER *M. Hubberd* 1294 His snakie wand, With which the damned ghosts he governeth, And furies rules, and Tartare tempereth. **1601** SHAKS. *Twel. N.* II. v. 225 If you wil see it follow me. *To.* To the gates of Tartar, thou most excellent diuell of wit.

† **Ta·rtar,** *v. Obs. rare*[−1]. [f. TARTAR *sb.*[1]] *trans.* To treat with tartar-emetic.

(In quot. with play on TARTAR *sb.*[4], Tartarus.)

**1647** WARD *Simp. Cobler* (1843) 19 When I want physick for my body, I would not have my soule tartared, nor my Animal Spirits purged.

**Tartaræ·an,** *a. rare*[−1]. [Cf. Gr. Ταρτάρειος.] = TARTAREAN[1].

**1872** K. H. DIGBY *Ouranogaia* xii. I. 264 The monster.. Whom Tartaræan sisters even hate.

**Ta·rtarated,** *a. Chem.* [f. TARTAR *sb.*[1] + -ATE + -ED.] Combined with tartar; as in *tartarated antimony, iron, soda.*

**1863** W. AITKEN *Sc. & Pract. Med.* (1866) II. 67 Tartarated iron (*Ferrum tartaratum*) is also a useful remedy. **1868** GARROD *Mat. Med.* (ed. 3) 139 Tartarated Soda. Tartrate of Soda and Potash. **1876** HARLEY *Mat. Med.* (ed. 6) 164 Tartarated Soda was discovered in 1672. **1899** *Allbutt's Syst. Med.* VIII. 578 Tartarated antimony has been praised..in the acute stages of the disease [psoriasis].

† **Tarta·real,** *a. rare.* [f. as next + -AL.] = next.

**1602** F. HERING tr. *Oberndorf's Anat.* 6 Trying their Tartareall conclusions, by more then Tragicall Deaths.

**Tartarean** (tāɹtēə·riăn), *a.*[1] [f. L. *Tartareus* of or pertaining to TARTARUS + -AN.] Of or belonging to the Tartarus of the ancients; hence, pertaining to hell or to purgatory; infernal.

**1623** COCKERAM, *Tartarean*, belonging to hell. **1667** MILTON *P. L.* II. 69 Mixt with Tartarean Sulphur, and strange fire. **1702** POPE *Thebais* 435 Drives the dead to dark Tartarean coasts. **1759** W. WILKIE *Epigon.* IV. 110 Many still, who yet enjoy the day, Must follow down the dark Tartarean way. **1870** LOWELL *Among my Bks.* Ser. I. (1873) 125 The tartarean impostor and his companions at once vanished.

b. *fig.* (cf. *infernal*).

**1806–7** J. BERESFORD *Miseries Hum. Life* (1826) IV. xxxii, Your ear is..engaged by the Tartarean yell of its driver. **1851** CARLYLE *Sterling* I. iii. (1872) 14 At a safe distance.. lie the tartarean copper forges of Swansea.

† **Tartarean,** *a.*[2] *Obs.* = TARTARIAN *a.*[1]

**1759** GOLDSM. *Bee* No. 6. 11, The other offered himself up as a sacrifice to the Tartarean enemy. **1804** C. B. BROWN tr. *Volney's View Soil U. S.* (Philad. ed.) 364 A distinct race, with no Tartarean features.

**Tartaren, -ene,** variants of TARTARIN[1].

**Tartareous** (tāɹtēə·rĭəs), *a.*[1] [f. mod.L. *tartare-us* (f. *tartarum* TARTAR *sb.*[1]) + -OUS.]

† **1.** *Path.* Of the nature of a tartar, or calcareous or earthy deposit; characterized by such deposits. (Cf. TARTAROUS 2.) *Obs.*

**1625** HART *Anat. Ur.* II. x. 119 From whence do they [Paracelsists] inferre a great number of such tartareous diseases, as they call them? *Ibid.*, Abundance of a tartareous or terrestrious substance. **1658** A. FOX *Würtz' Surg.* III. xi. 249 This moisture..doth join with the gluten of the joint, and groweth tartareous. **1677** PLOT *Oxfordsh.* 211 A Tartareous humor got together in the veins under the tongue.

† **2.** Like tartar in consistence or formation; of the nature of a concretion or crust; gritty. *Obs.*

**1669** W. SIMPSON *Hydrol. Chym.* 131 Every tartareous recrement fastened to the sides of the said vessels. **1671** J. WEBSTER *Metallogr.* xvi. 238 Mingled with other metals, as lime and tartareous stones, in which black floats and slats do break. **1677** GREW *Anat. Seeds* i. § 1 The Tartareous Stone of a Plum. **1683** A. SNAPE *Anat. Horse* v. i. (1686) 195 A Bone is said to be..made of the most earthy and tartareous part of the Seed in the Womb.

† **3.** *Chem.* Having the quality of tartar or argol; containing or derived from tartar; *tartareous acid*, early name of tartaric acid. (Cf. TARTAROUS.) *Obs.*

† *Tartareous acidulum* (F. *acidule tartareux*), an old name of tartar.

**1663** BOYLE *Usef. Exp. Nat. Philos.* II. v. xix. 283 Meats that are Salt and Tartareous. *c* **1790** tr. *De Morveau's*, etc. *Table Chem. Nom.* (*Encycl. Brit.* ed. 3 IV. 598 a), Radical principle of the tartareous acid. **1800** tr. *Lagrange's Chem.* II. 198 When exposed to heat in contact with the air, the tartareous acidulum is decomposed, fuses, swells up. **1822** IMISON *Sc. & Art* II. 183 The tartareous acid dissolves the oxide of tin.

**4.** *Bot.* Of a crust-like structure like tartar: descriptive of certain lichens.

**1845** LINDLEY *Sch. Bot.* ix. (1858) 155 Thallus thick, granular and tartareous, greyish-white. **1861** H. MACMILLAN *Footn. fr. Page Nat.* 75 We have no data from which to ascertain the age of tartareous species, which adhere almost inseparably to stones.

† **Tarta·reous,** *a.*[2] *Obs.* [f. L. *tartare-us* (f. TARTARUS) + -OUS.] Of or pertaining to Tartarus; Tartarean, infernal, hellish, very wicked.

**1619** BAINBRIDGE *Descr. Late Comet* 37 Never was there more need of circumspection, then in this fæculent and tartareous age. [Here perh. a fig. use of prec.] **1667** MILTON *P. L.* VII. 238 The Spirit of God..downward purg'd The black tartareous cold infernal dregs Adverse to life.

† **Ta·rtarer.** *Obs. rare*[−1]. [f. TARTAR *sb.*[1] + -ER[1].] One who attributed diseases to the presence of tartar.

**1662** J. CHANDLER *Van Helmont's Oriat.* 230 What things I have read out of many Books, which Paracelsus writeth concerning Tartarers, I will contract into a brief tract.

**Tartaret** (tā·ɹtărĕt). [a. obs. F. *tartaret*, also *tartarot* (16th c. in Godef.), f. TARTAR *sb.*[2]: app. because supposed to come from Tartary.] In full **tartaret falcon**: the Barbary Falcon, *Falco barbarus.*

**1575** TURBERV. *Falconrie* 26 That falcon which is called the Tartaret or Barbary Falcon, whome they doe chiefly vse in Barbary. **1860** H. AINSWORTH *Ovingdean Grange* 61 Gallant to behold was the Barbary or tartaret falcon. **1867** 'OUIDA' *C. Castlemaine* (1879) 11 She would stroke, half sadly, the smooth feathers of her tartaret falcon Gabrielle.

**Tartarian** (tāɹtēə·riăn), *sb.* and *a.*[1] Also 5–6 **Tartarien,** 9 **Tatarian.** [*c* 1400 (see A) a. OF. *Tartarien* (13th c. in Godef.); later f. med.L. *Tartaria* TARTARY + -AN.]

**A.** *sb.* = TARTAR *sb.*[2] 1.

*c* **1400** MAUNDEV. (1839) xxiii. 247 Of the lawe & the customs of the Tartarienes, duellynge in Chatay. *Ibid.* 252 Alle the Tartarienes [*Roxb.* xxvi. 124 Tartarenes] han smale eyen. **1538** Tartarien [see RUSSIAN *sb.*[1]]. **1599** THYNNE *Animadv.* (1875) 54 The Tartarians obteyned the kingdome of Syria in the yere 1240. **1708** E. COOK *Sot-weed Factor* (1900) 10 My Friend suppos'd Tartarians wild, Or Chinese from their Home exiled. **1835** K. H. DIGBY *Mores Catholici* VI. ii. (1846) II. 27/2 Fitter for those hords of Tartarians than for a commonwealth of Christians.

b. 'A cant word for a thief' (Nares).

**1608** *Merry Devil Edmonton* in Hazl. *Dodsley* X. 212 There's not a Tartarian nor a carrier shall breathe upon your geldings. **1640** *Wandering Jew* 3 (Nares) If any thieving Tartarian shall break in upon you, I will, with both hands nimbly lend a cast of my office to him.

**B.** *adj.* Of or pertaining to Tartary or its people; = TARTAR *a.*

**1590** WEBBE *Trav.* (Arb.) 18 The Tartarian Souldiers had wonderfull greate and rich spoyles. **1603** KNOLLES *Hist. Turks* (1638) 196 Tamerlane the great Tartarian prince,..in a great battell at mount Stella, abated the Othoman pride. **1634** W. WOOD *New Eng. Prosp.* (1865) 30 As swift as arrow from Tartarian Bow. *a* **1725** LD. WHITWORTH *Acc. Russia in 1710* (1758) 9 Casan and Astracan were Tartarian kingdoms. **1839** *For. Q. Rev.* XXII. 109 Interesting to the readers of Tartarian tales. **1845** *Proc. Philol. Soc.* II. 171 The Tartarian class of languages..furnishes a valuable confirmation of this theory.

b. In names of things of actual or supposed Tartar origin; as **Tartarian bread** (see quot. 1829); **Tartarian lamb,** the 'Scythian' or 'vegetable lamb', a polypodiaceous fern, *Cibotium Barometz*, from the resemblance which its woolly root-stock, inverted, bears to a lamb: see BAROMETZ, and cf. Maundeville (1839), ch. xxvi (Roxb. xxix). Also *Tartarian cherry, honeysuckle, maple, motherwort, oat,* etc., for which see the sbs.

**1805** DICKSON *Pract. Agric.* I. 578 In the Siberian or Tartarian oat the grains are thin and small. **1811** PINKERTON *Mod. Geogr.* (ed. 3) 346 The..Tatarian honey-suckle, Tatarian mulberry, and the Daourian rose, form thickets of exquisite beauty. **1817** SHELLEY *Rev. Islam* VI. xix, A black Tartarian horse of giant frame Comes trampling o'er the dead. **1823** CRABB *Technol. Dict.*, Tartarian lamb. **1829** LOUDON *Encycl. Plants* 557 [Crambe] tatarica is called by the Hungarians *Tatar-Kenyer* or Tartarian bread, and its root stripped of the bark and sliced is eaten with oil, vinegar, and salt. **1836** *Penny Cycl.* VI. 431/2 The Tartarian cherries of the English gardens. **1866** *Treas. Bot.* 280/2 *C*[*ibotium*] *Barometz*, sometimes called *C. glaucescens*, is believed to be the Baranetz, *Agnus Scythicus*, or Tartarian Lamb, about which travellers have told so wondrous a tale. **1882** *Garden* 13 May 322/2 The ordinary white-flowered form of the Tartarian Honeysuckle [*Lonicera tatarica*].

**Tarta·rian,** *a.*[2] *rare.* [f. L. TARTAR-US + -IAN.] Pertaining to Tartarus; infernal; = TARTAREAN *a.*[1]

**1864** KINGSLEY *Rom. & Teut.* xi. 297 (tr. *Ep. to Pepin* an. 755) Lest your bodies and souls be torn and tormented for ever, in inextinguishable and Tartarian fire with the devil and his pestiferous angels. **1875** JOWETT *Plato* (ed. 2) III. 33 Cocytus and Styx,..and the rest of their Tartarian nomenclature.

**Tartaric** (tāɹtæ·rik), *a.*[1] *Chem.* [f. TARTAR *sb.*[1] + -IC; in mod.L. *tartaric-us*, F. *tartarique.*] Of the nature of, related to, or derived from tartar or argol. *Tartaric acid* (formerly *tartareous* or *tartarous acid*), an organic acid, $C_4H_6O_6 = C_4H_2O_2 + (OH)_4$, or $CO_2H{\cdot}(CHOH)_2{\cdot}CO_2H$, of which there are five isomeric forms, differing in their optical properties, viz. *dextrotartaric* acid (dextrorotary), *lævotartaric* acid (lævorotary), *paratartaric* acid (distinctively called RACEMIC acid), *mesotartaric* acid (optically inactive), and *metatartaric* acid; specifically, the first of these, a colourless crystalline compound, occurring largely in the vegetable kingdom, esp. in unripe grapes, and as a potassium salt in argol or tartar of wine, from which it is commercially prepared. So *tartaric amide, anhydride, ether,* an amide, anhydride, or ether of tartaric acid.

1790 KERR *Lavoisier's Elem. Chem.* 190 Tables of the combinations of Oxygen with the compound radicals. Name of radical: Tartaric. Name of resulting acid (new nomencl.): Tartarous acid. Unknown till lately. 1794 G. PEARSON tr. De Morveau, etc. *Table Chem. Nomencl.* 28 The radical Tartaric yields only the tartareous Acid in which the basis is conceived to predominate. 1810 HENRY *Elem. Chem.* (1826) II. 227 The tartaric acid is generally obtained from the bi-tartrate of potassa (purified cream of tartar). 1813 SIR H. DAVY *Agric. Chem.* (1814) 107 The tartaric acid may be obtained from the juice of mulberries and grapes. 1827 FARADAY *Chem. Manip.* vi. 189 Tartaric acid or tartrates have an extraordinary power in rendering many metallic oxides soluble. 1876 HARLEY *Mat. Med.* (ed. 6) 729 Tartaric acid—the acid of tartar—was discovered by Scheele in 1770.

1868 WATTS *Dict. Chem.* V. 690 Tartaric Amides. *Ibid.* 691 Insoluble Tartaric Anhydride, $C_4H_4O_5$. *Ibid.* 692 The acid tartaric ethers are formed by the direct action of tartaric acid on the alcohols. *Ibid.*, Ethylic Tartrate, or Tartaric Ether, $C_8H_{14}O_6$ .. is decomposed by sodium, with evolution of hydrogen.

**Tartaric** (tāɹtæ·rik), *a.*[2] Also **Tataric.** [f. TARTAR *sb.*[2] + -IC.] Of, pertaining to, or connected with the Tartars or Tartary.

1811 PINKERTON *Mod. Geog.* (ed. 3) 335 Europe can in future have little to apprehend from the Tataric swarms. 1834 *Penny Cycl.* II. 478/1 The Tartaric region, as it is next the Siberian, so it resembles it in most respects. 1855 MAX MÜLLER *Lang. Seat of War* 96 Tataric has become the name of that class of Turanian languages of which the Turkish is the most prominent member.

† **Ta·rtarin, -ine,** *sb.*[1] *Obs.* Forms: 4 **tarterine,** 5 **-yn(e, -en, -on**; 4–5 **tartaryn(e,** 5 **-en(e, -on(e, (-yan), tarturyn, (tatterine), tarturne**; 6 **tartarne, -erne, -orn(e, tartron,** 6–7 **tartern,** 7 **tartarin, -ine.** [a. OF. *Tartarin* = med.L. *Tartarīn-us*, f. *Tartar-us*, TARTAR *sb.*[2] and [3], with suffix -INE[1], as in *Tarentine*, etc. (med.L. pl. *Tartarīnī* also embodying the notion 'people of Tartarus'); in OF. also in sense 2.]

**1.** = TARTAR *sb.*[2] 1; in *pl.* = med.L. *Tartarīnī*.

*a* 1400–50 *Alexander* 5484 Of terands of þir tartaryns twa & twenti kyngs. *c* 1400 MAUNDEV. (1839) xxi. 224 Tartarynes [*Roxb.* xxiv, folk of Tartre] & þei þat duelle in the grete Asye, þei camen of Cham. *c* 1400 *Three Kings Cologne* 148 Þe wich pepil cleped hem-self Tartaryns.

**2.** A rich stuff, apparently of silk, imported from the East, prob. from China through Tartary; = TARTAR *sb.*[3] Cf. SARSENET. [OF. *tartarin*, earlier *drap tartarin* (1295 in Godef.).]

1343 *Enrolled Acc.* (W. & H.) 3 m. 38 b, ij vlnis panni serici ix peciis Tartaryn et j pecia Samitell. 1345–9 *Wardr. Acc. Edw. III* in *Archæologia* XXXI. 72/2, j. frontale de tartaryn. *Ibid.* 85/2, vj. vln. de Tartaryn. *c* 1400 MAUNDEV. (1839) xxiii. 255 Cloþes of gold, & of Camakaas, & tartarynes [*Roxb.* xxvi. 125 tartarene, *F. text* tartaires]. 1407 *Nottingham Rec.* II. 50 Pro dimidia virga de viridi tarteren, xviijd. 1411 in *Somerset Medieval Wills* (1901) 50 [One hanging of black and white] 'Wyrsted' 'cum penna de Tatterine'. 14.. *Epiph.* in *Tundale's Vis.*, etc. (1843) 114 Wer ther of gold any clothes fownde Of sylke damaske or of tartryn. 1444 *Test. Ebor.* (Surtees) II. 110 Myn aulterclothe of reed tarteryn with ye corteyns. 1455 *Coventry Leet Bk.* 283 To make a newe pensell in Tarturne xvj d. 1459 in *Somerset Medieval Wills* (1901) 191 Curteynes of tarteron. 1512 *Acc.* 4 *Hen. VIII*, c. 6 *Preamble*, Saten, sarsenet, tartron, chamblet, and every other Cloth of Silke. *c* 1530 LD. BERNERS *Arth. Lyt. Bryt.* (1814) 381 Florence layd her downe in her bedde in a lyghte kyrtell of chaungeable vyolet tartorne. 1538 in *Lett. Suppress. Monasteries* (Camden) 268, ij. copes of redd tartarne. *a* 1548 HALL *Chron., Hen. VII* 1 b, Ye third [standard] was of yelowe tarterne, in the which was peinted a donne kowe. 1661 MORGAN *Sph. Gentry* IV. i. 5 Having Mantles of silk over a Kirtle of red Tartarin. 1683 R. HOLME *Armoury* III. 55/2 Another puts on him a Kirtle of red Silk or Tartarine.

*fig. c* 1430 LYDG. *Min. Poems* (Percy Soc.) 30 Thi chekes hangen, thyn eyene wax read as wyne, And wel belyned with good read tartaryne.

*attrib. a* 1400–50 *Alexander* 1547 (MS. D) Tyrett alle in tonacles of tartaren webbys. [1861 *Our Eng. Home* 92 The rich taffeta, the velvets, and Tartaren silks, were often worn without a shred of underclothing.]

† **Ta·rtarin,** *sb.*[2] *Obs.* [f. TARTAR *sb.*[1] + -IN[1].]

**1.** A name given by Kirwan to potash.

1796 KIRWAN *Elem. Min.* (ed. 2) II. 5 Vegetable Alkali (which I call Tartarin). 1799 — *Geol. Ess.* v. 150 The tartarin lately discovered in clays and many stones.

**2.** 'Native sulphate of potassium, also called Arkanite and Glaserite' (Watts *Dict. Chem.* V. 696).

Hence **Ta·rtarinated** *a.*, combined with tartarin.

1796 KIRWAN *Elem. Min.* (ed. 2) II. 311 The Acido Tartarinated Calx is fusible *per se*.

**Tartarin,** *sb.*[3] (tā·ɹtărin, ‖ tartareṅ). Name of a bombastic character, 'Tartarin of Tarascon', created by A. Daudet; hence, used allusively as sb. or adj.

1903 *T. P.'s Weekly* 11 Sept. 459/3 In his vivid red sash he carried two enormous pistols—tartarin pistols, ..that not alone did not, but could not fire a shot. 1905 *Blackw. Mag.* May 643/1 There are too many loquacious Tartarins abroad without the engaging ways of the man of Tarascon. 1906 *Academy* 17 Nov. 492/1 Its Gasconing is in the Tartarin vein.

† **Ta·rtarine,** *sb. Obs.* [a. F. *tartarin.*] (See quot.)

1607 TOPSELL *Four-f. Beasts* (1658) 10 There was at Paris another beast called a Tartarine, and in some places a Magot (much like a Baboun), ..being as great as a Gray-hound.

**Tartarine,** variant of TARTARIN *sb.*[1]

† **Ta·rtarine,** *a.*[1] *Obs.* [f. TARTAR *sb.*[1] + -INE[1].] = TARTAROUS *a.*

1731 S. HALES *Stat. Ess.* I. 198 The like tartarine concretions are also frequently formed in some fruits. 1775 SIR E. BARRY *Obs. Wines* 193 These concretions from spring water are of a Tartarine kind.

† **Ta·rtarine,** *a.*[2] *Obs. rare*—[0]. = TARTAREAN *a.*[1]

1656 BLOUNT *Glossogr.*, *Tartarine*, *Tartarean*, ..of hell, hellish, terrible.

**Tartarish** (tā·ɹtăriʃ), *a.*[1] *rare.* [f. TARTAR *sb.*[1] + -ISH[1].] **a.** Of wine: Inclined to deposit tartar. **b.** Of the eyes: Inclined to form concretions (cf. TARTAROUS 2).

1757 A. COOPER *Distiller* II. ii. (1760) 118 Without the peculiar Taste and Flavour of the Plant, but generally somewhat tartarish and limpid. 1807 SOUTHEY *Lett.* (1856) II. 4 My son is rather ailing just now..His eyes are as Tartarish as his sister's.

† **Ta·rtarish,** *a.*[2] *Obs. rare*—[1]. [f. TARTAR *sb.*[2] + -ISH[1]: cf. *Turkish.*] = TARTAR *a.* 1.

1670 *Lond. Gaz.* No. 431/2 The Tartarish Envoye in this Court, presented the Count de Montecuculi with an excellent Tartarian Horse.

**Tartarite,** variant of TARTRITE.

**Tartarium**: see TARTAR *sb.*[3]

† **Ta·rtarizated,** *ppl. a. Chem. Obs.* [f. mod. L. *tartarizāt-us* tartarized + -ED[1].] Tartarized.

1651 FRENCH *Distill.* vi. 187 Pour upon them rectified Spirit of Wine tartarizated. *Ibid.* 196 Adde the tartarizated quintessence. 1794 G. PEARSON tr. De Morveau, etc. *Table Chem. Nom.* § 14 Tartarisated Bases.

**Tartariza·tion**[1]. *Chem.* [f. TARTARIZE *v.*[1] + -ATION.] The action or process of tartarizing.

1720 S. PARKER *Biblioth. Bibl.* I. 438 By Sublimation, and Precipitation or Tartarisation.

**Tartarization**[2, 3]: see TARTARIZE[2, 3].

**Tartarize** (tā·ɹtărəiz), *v.*[1] *Chem.* [f. TARTAR *sb.*[1] + -IZE.] *trans.* To treat or impregnate with tartar; to rectify by means of the salt of tartar.

(Usually in *pa. pple.*: see TARTARIZED *pa. pple.*[1])

1706 PHILLIPS (ed. 6), To *Tartarize*, (in Chymistry) to refine, or purify by the means of Salt of Tartar. 1727–41 CHAMBERS *Cycl.*, *Tartarizing*, a term used by some writers, for the act of refining or purifying, by means of salt of Tartar. 1755 JOHNSON, *Tartarize*, to impregnate with tartar.

**Ta·rtarize,** *v.*[2] Also **Tatarize.** [f. TARTAR *sb.*[2] + -IZE.] *trans.* To convert or transform into a Tartar. Hence **Ta·rtarized** *ppl. a.*; also **Tartariza·tion**[2], the process of Tartarizing, the condition of being Tartarized.

1877 D. M. WALLACE *Russia* xxii. 347 The Khans never for a moment dreamed of attempting to Tartarize their Russian subjects. 1878 H. A. WEBSTER in *Encycl. Brit.* VIII. 702/2 The Tchuvashes are a Tatarized branch of the Finns of the Volga. 1889 J. ABERCROMBIE *East. Caucasus* 210 To the west of Derbend I found Tāts who .. are in process of becoming wholly Tatarized.

**Ta·rtarize,** *v.*[3] *rare.* [f. L. TARTAR-US + -IZE. (Representing Gr. ταρταροῦν, 2 *Pet.* ii. 4.)] *trans.* To consign to Tartarus; to condemn to punishment in hell. Hence **Tartariza·tion**[3].

1675 R. BURTHOGGE *Causa Dei* 32 So..doth Peter speak, when..he saith God did Tartarize the Angels in Chains of Darkness, or put them in Chains of Darkness in Tartarus. 1819 G. S. FABER *Dispensations* (1823) I. I. vii. 422 We may collect that the precipitation of the messengers into Tartarus bore a strong resemblance to the overthrow of Sodom and Gomorrah..though the very agent employed in their tartarization might be used also as an instrument in God's hand of bringing on the deluge.

**Tartarized** (tā·ɹtărəizd), *ppl. a.*[1] [f. TARTARIZE *v.*[1] + -ED[1]; cf. F. *tartarisé*, mod.L. *tartarizatus.*]

**1.** Rectified by treatment with cream of tartar.

*a* 1648 DIGBY *Chym. Secr.* (1683) 70 Tartarised S[piritus] V[ini]. 1694 SALMON *Bate's Dispens.* I. ii. (1713) 60/2 This Tartaris'd volatile Spirit, is highly deobstructive. 1758 REID tr. *Macquer's Chym.* I. 115 Ardent spirits may be freed from much of their phlegm by means of these salts thoroughly dried... When rectified in this manner it is called Tartarised Spirit of Wine. 1844 J. T. HEWLETT *Parsons & W.* xxv, Fiery, tartarized, brandied products of Spain.

**2.** Mixed or impregnated with tartar; holding tartar in solution.

1694 SALMON *Bate's Dispens.* II. vi. (1713) 593/1 A Tartarised Julep. 1710 T. FULLER *Pharm. Extemp.* 83 Elixir Proprietatis Tartarised 4 scruples. 1784 M. UNDERWOOD *Dis. Childr.* (1799) I. 27 The tartarised wine of antimony is a very proper [emetic]. 1802–3 tr. *Pallas's Trav.* (1812) I. 353 The tartarised spirit of sal ammoniac rendered the water white as milk.

**3.** Combined with tartaric acid, so as to form a tartrate: = TARTRATED.

1732 *Hist. Litteraria* IV. 27 A tedious way of preparing Tartarised Tartar. 1758 REID tr. *Macquer's Chym.* I. 126 Soluble Tartar. It is also called the Vegetable Salt, as being obtained from vegetables only; and again Tartarized Tartar, because it consists of the acid and the alkali of Tartar combined together. 1788 WALKER in *Phil. Trans.* LXXVIII. 398 Tartarized natron (Rochelle salt). 1796 KIRWAN *Elem. Min.* (ed. 2) II. 470 Tartarised Iron being more soluble than Tartarised Uranite. 1857 MILLER *Elem. Chem.* III. 330 A solution of tartarized antimony acts as a violent emetic and cathartic poison.

**Tartarized,** *ppl. a.*[2]: see TARTARIZE *v.*[2]

**Tartarly** (tā·ɹtăɹli), *a. nonce-wd.* [f. TARTAR *sb.*[2] + -LY[1].] Tartar-like; rough and fierce.

1821 BYRON *John Keats* i, Who kill'd John Keats? 'I', says the Quarterly, So savage and Tartarly, ''Twas one of my feats'. 1894 A. BIRRELL *Ess.* v. 49 It was enough to sting Scott to fury, and make him fall upon the old man in a manner somewhat too savage and tartarly.

**Tartarne, -taron(e,** variants of TARTARIN[1].

**Tartaro·logy.** [f. Gr. Τάρταρο-ς TARTARUS + -LOGY.] A doctrine as to Tartarus; hence, a doctrine of hell and future punishment.

1867 KINGSLEY *Water of Life*, etc. vi. 93 The Middle Ages, when men really believed in that same Tartarology, with the same intensity with which they now believe in the conclusions of astronomy or of chemistry. 1868 *Contemp. Rev.* VII. 158 The ordinary Tartarology flows far more directly from the sixth book of the Æneid than from anything in Holy Scripture.

† **Tartarous** (tā·ɹtărəs), *a. Obs.* [f. TARTAR *sb.*[1] + -OUS; = F. *tartareux.*]

**1.** Of the nature of, consisting of, or containing tartar or argol.

1655–87 H. MORE *App. Antid.* (1712) 215 The tartarous parts of Wine, that are driven outward to the sides of the vessel. 1658 R. WHITE tr. *Digby's Powd. Symp.* (1660) 81 Tartarous lees, which fall to the bottom. 1710 T. FULLER *Pharm. Extemp.* 214 By reason of a delicate Tartarous Acidity. 1768 *Woman of Honor* II. 196 A jollitry, raised by a wretched tartarous wine.

**2.** *Path.* Said of indurations, inspissated fluids, phlegms, etc., attributed to the presence of tartar in the body. (Much employed in 17th and early 18th centuries by the followers of Paracelsus.)

1605 TIMME *Quersit.* I. xiii. 64 The oile of pepper doth attenuat .. and cut tartarus matters in the body. 1657 *Physical Dict.*, *Tartarous matter*, congealed hard substances of an acrimonious sharp nature .., being coagulated in the joynts, it's the principal cause of the gout. 1718 QUINCY *Compl. Disp.* 123 In Tubercles and Tartarous Indurations of the Lungs. 1744 BERKELEY *Siris* § 86 The asperity of tartarous salts, and the fiery acrimony of alkaline salts irritating and wounding the nerves, produce nascent passions and anxieties in the soul.

**3.** *fig.* Having elements of acerbity, unrefined, rough. *rare.* (? with play on TARTAR *sb.*[2])

1601 B. JONSON *Poetaster* v. i, I iudge him of a rectified spirit, ..refin'd From all the tartarous moodes of common men.

**4.** In early Chemistry: **a.** Of the appearance, consistency, or supposed character of tartar or argol.

1707 *Curios. in Husb. & Gard.* 66 Air..contains some.. tartarous and metallick Parts. *Ibid.* 327 When the Fern was burnt, it was between dry and wet: thus the Salt was as it were Tartarous and Substantial.

**b.** Of the nature of or derived from tartar; *tartarous acid*, an earlier name of TARTARIC *acid.*

1790 Tartarous acid [see TARTRITE]. 1794 G. ADAMS *Nat. & Exp. Philos.* I. xii. 502 Obtained by distillation..from tartar, from all tartarous salts. 1812 SIR H. DAVY *Chem. Philos.* 121 The tartarous acid is entirely separated from lime, and the oxalic acid from oxide of lead, by quantities of sulphuric acid, merely sufficient to saturate the two bases.

Hence † **Ta·rtarousness,** tartarous quality, acerbity. *Obs.*

1657 R. LIGON *Barbadoes* Index 84 a, The salt and tartarousnesse of this Temper, causes it to turn, as Milk does, when any soure or sharp liquor is put into it.

‖ **Ta·rtarum, ta·rtarus** [mod.L.], early synonyms of TARTAR[1].

‖ **Tartarus** (tā·ɹtărŏs), *sb.* [L. *Tartarus*, a. Gr. Τάρταρος.] The infernal regions of ancient Greek and Roman mythology, or the lowest part of them; hence sometimes used for hell.

[1508 KENNEDIE *Flyting w. Dunbar* 552 Spynk, sink with stynk ad Tertara Termagorum.] 1586 SIR E. HOBY tr. *Cognet's Pol. Disc. Truth* xxxi. 146 The strange kinde of punishmentes .. prepared for the wicked in the gayle of vengeance, which he calleth *Tartarus*, a place of darkenesse and torments. 1651 HOBBES *Leviath.* III. xxxviii. (1839) 445 For example, that they [the damned] are in Inferno, in Tartarus, or in the bottomless pit. 1658 SIR T. BROWNE *Hydriot.* iv. 60 Condemned unto the Tartara's of Hell. *a* 1774 TUCKER *Lt. Nat.* (1834) II. 321 The enjoyments of Elysium and punishments of Tartarus. 1895 SALMOND *Chr. Doctr. Immort.* I. vii. 146 The incurably corrupt are hurled into Tartarus.

**b.** A place likened to Tartarus, in situation or character.

1821 DE QUINCEY *Confess.* I. (1822) 42 She never emerged from the dismal Tartarus of the kitchens, &c. to the upper air. 1853 KANE *Grinnell Exp.* xxxi. 271 The temperature and foulness of air in the between-deck Tartarus can not be amended. 1887–8 tr. *Hugo's Notre-Dame* VIII. ii, This Tartarus was called simply The Question Chamber.

Hence **Ta·rtarus** *v. nonce-wd.*, *trans.* to consign to Tartarus (repr. Gr. ταρταροῦν, 2 *Pet.* ii. 4).

1856 S. R. MAITLAND *False Worship* 31 The apostle's statement respecting the sinning Angels is, that, having been tartarus'd, ..they have been reserved unto Judgment.

**Tartary** (tā·ɹtări). [a. F. *Tartarie*, ad. med.L. *Tartaria*, land of the Tartars: associated with TARTARUS: hence sense 2.]

**1.** The country of the Tartars: see TARTAR *sb.*[2]

*c* 1369 CHAUCER *Dethe Blaunche* 1025 Ne sende men..into Tartarye..ne in-to Turkye. 1500–20 DUNBAR *Poems* xxxiii. 5 Me thocht a Turk of Tartary Come throw the boundis of Barbary. 1719 DE FOE *Crusoe* (1858) 575 A part of the Great Karakathy, or Grand Tartary. 1886 KINGTON OLIPHANT *New English* I. 536 From Tartary came *hordas.*

† **b.** = TARTAR *sb.*[3]

*c* 1400 MAUNDEV. (1839) xxiii. 247 Þei ben cloþed with precious cloþes of Tartarye & of cloþes of gold.

† **2.** Tartarus, as a region. *Obs.*

*c* 1588 SPENSER *Virg. Gnat* 543 Lastly the squalid lakes of Tartarie, And griesly Feends of hell him terrifie. 1591 *Troub. Raigne K. John* (1611) 59 Let the blacke tormentors of deep Tartary Vpbraide them with this damned enterprise. *c* 1620 T. ROBINSON *Mary Magd.* 735 Amonge ye blacker sonnes of Tartary, Seu'n hideous fiery sprights shee euocates.

**Tartaryn(e**, variant of TARTARIN[1] *Obs.*

**Tarten** (tā·rt'n), *v. rare*$^{-1}$. [f. TART *a.* + -EN[5].] *trans.* To make tart or sharp; = TART *v.*

1882 BLACKMORE *Christowell* III. iii. 49 There was no such apple on the place, to bring out and tarten up the flavour of the gentle ones in cider.

**Tarter**, obs. f. TARTAR. **Tarteran, -terine, -tern(e, -teyn, -tian**, etc., var. TARTARIN[1] *Obs.*

**Tarterus**: see TARTAR *sb.*[3]

**Tartillo**, obs. f. (or ?mispr. for) TORTILLA.

‖ **Tartine** (tartīn). [F. *tartine* (Oudin, 1642) little tart, bread and jam, bread and butter (also fig. as in b), f. *tarte*, TART *sb.*] 'A slice of bread spread with butter or preserve' (Stanf.).

1826 [H. BEST] *Four Years France* 237 The tea equipage, with its usual accompaniments of tartines and toast. 1842 THACKERAY *Fitz-Boodle Papers* ii, She placidly handed out this decoction, which we took with cakes and tartines. 1885 WARREN & CLEVERLY *Wand. Beetle* 15 Bread and butter was better than nothing, so we got her to cut us some enormous tartines.

b. *fig.* A big article of commonplace character.

1907 *Athenæum* 13 July 48/2 In a first glance through the galleries you stop before the huge 'tartines', the more ..sensational pictures which aim at attracting the crowd.

**Tartir**, variant of TARTAR *sb.*[3]

**Tartish** (tā·ɹtiʃ), *a.* [f. TART *a.* + -ISH[1].] Somewhat tart, slightly pungent or acid; also *fig.*

1712 E. COOKE *Voy. S. Sea* 338 Another Sort like a Curan.. eats tartish. 1747 *Gentl. Mag.* Oct. 488/2 Let spirit of vitriol be mixed therewith..in such quantity as to give the tartish taste. 1828 J. WILSON in *Blackw. Mag.* XXIV. 511 The Monthly [Magazine] so smartish—the Westminster, so tartish. 1890 STANLEY *Darkest Afr.* I. ix. 212 The tartish, crimson, and oblong fruit of the amoma.

Hence **Ta·rtishly** *adv.*, somewhat tartly.

1823 J. WILSON *Trials Marg. Lyndsay* xxxii, Snuffy-nosed maiden aunts..sourishly and tartishly disposed.

**Tartlet** (tā·ɹtlėt). Forms: 5 **tartlote, tartlett, tartelat,** 8– **tartlet.** [a. F. *tartelette* (14th c. in Littré), dim. of *tarte*, TART *sb.*; in 18th c. perh. formed anew on TART *sb.*] A small tart.

c1420 *Liber Cocorum* (1862) 41 Tartlotes. Take porke sothun, and grynde hit wele...Kover hit with lyddes, and pynche hit fayre,..And bake hit forthe. c1460 J. RUSSELL *Bk. Nurture* 521 Iusselle, tartlett, cabages, & nombles of vennure. c1475 *Pict. Voc.* in Wr.-Wülcker 789/6 *Hec artocria*, a tartelat. 1788 V. KNOX *Winter Even.* (1790) II. xxix. 194 The puffs and tartlets of the pastry-cook. 1836–9 DICKENS *Sk. Boz, Mistaken Milliner*, Plum-pudding and apple-pie and tartlets without number. 1837 T. HOOK *Jack Brag* xiv, Three raspberry tartlets.

**Tartly** (tā·ɹtli), *adv.* [OE. *teartlīce*: see TART *a.* and -LY[2].] In a tart manner; sharply; with acidity; usually *fig.* with asperity of tone. In quot. 1599, 'with sourness of aspect' (J.).

c1000 in Napier *O. E. Glosses* 81/3011 *Acriter*, teartlice. *Ibid.* 122/4730 *Acrius*, teartlicor. 1599 SHAKS. *Much Ado* II. i. 3 How tartly that Gentleman lookes, I neuer can see him, but I am heart-burn'd an howre after. a1661 FULLER *Worthies* (1662) III. *Worc.* 169 One jeeringly saluted him, 'Good morrow, Bishop quondam', to whom Bonner as tartly returned, 'Good morrow, Knave semper'. 1791 BOSWELL *Johnson* 19 Apr. an. 1773, Johnson, offended,..answered tartly, 'No, Sir; do you read books through?' 1876 MISS BRADDON *J. Haggard's Dau.* II. 163 'You may as well wait till tea's finished', exclaimed Judith tartly.

**Tartness** (tā·ɹtnės). [OE. *teartnysse*: see TART *a.* and -NESS.] The quality of being tart.

†1. Severity; painfulness. *Obs.* (In later quots. fig. from 2.)

c1000 in Napier *O. E. Glosses* 85/3158 *Acerbitatem*, teartnesse. a1602 W. PERKINS *Cases Consc.* (1619) 61 The sweetnesse of comfort..if it bee alaied with some tartnesse of the Law. 1647 TRAPP *Comm. Matt.* x. 24 Sweeten me the tartness of all our sufferings with this sentence, as with so much sugar.

2. Sharpness of taste; †pungency (*obs.*); acidity.

1530 RASTELL *Bk. Purgat.* III. vii. F iij b, That eyer wyll ..vapour out the tartnes and sowernes of that humour. 1538 ELYOT, *Acrimonia*, tartnes, which biteth the tunge, and perceth the heed, as in the taste of garlyke, oynions, and other lyke thynges. 1562 TURNER *Herbal* II. 58 b, Vnrype mulberries besyde theyr tartnes they haue also a sournes. 1634 T. JOHNSON *Parey's Chirurg.* XXVI. vii. (1678) 632 Acidity or tartness is also in verjuice. 1770 COOK *Voy. round World* III. i. (1773) 501 The juice had an agreeable tartness, though but little flavour.

3. *fig.* Sharpness of disposition, language, etc.; biting or caustic manner or character; acerbity, pungency, acrimony, asperity of tone.

1548 UDALL, etc. *Erasm. Par. Mark* ix. 67 Which with the tartenesse of truth byteth awaye. 1579 GOSSON *Sch. Abuse* (Arb.) 31 The bitternesse of rebukes, and..the tartenesse of euery taunt. 1607 SHAKS. *Cor.* v. iv. 18 The tartnesse of his face, sowres ripe Grapes. 1709 HEARNE *Diary* in *Remains* (O.H.S.) II. 196 The Plowman's Tale...If it were Chaucer's, it was left perhaps out of his Canterbury Tales, for y$^e$ Tartness against the Popish Clergy. 1748 SMOLLETT *Rod. Rand.* xliv, I told him with some tartness, ..he might have chosen a more convenient opportunity. 1866 *Lond. Rev.* 3 Mar. 242/1 Lord Russell with a good deal of tartness declared that before February was out the Bill should be before the house.

**Tartor**, variant of TARTAR *sb.*[3]

†**Ta·rtora, ta·rtorary.** *Obs.* [? corruptions of It. *tartaro* TARTAR[1].] ? = TARTAR *sb.*[1]

1545 *Rates of Customs* C vij b, Tartorary the pounde xij.d. 1586 *Ibid.* E viij, Tartora the pound xii.d.

**Tartorne**, variant of TARTARIN[1] *Obs.*

**Tartralic** (taɹtræ·lik), *a. Chem.* [ad. F. *tartralique* (Frémy 1838), arbitrarily formed on *tartr-ique* (f. *tartre* TARTAR[1] + *-ique*), to indicate derivation from tartaric acid: cf. TARTRELIC. (*Annales de Chimie* LXVIII. (1838).)] In *tartralic acid* (also called *ditartaric* or *isotartaric acid*), $C_8H_{10}O_{11} = 2C_4H_6O_6—H_2O$, an amorphous deliquescent substance obtained by heating tartaric acid. Its salts are **Tartralates.**

1857 MILLER *Elem. Chem.* III. 332 If tartaric acid be heated to 374°, it fuses; two equivalents of the acid lose one equivalent of water, and thus become converted into a new acid, termed by Fremy the *tartralic*. If tartaric acid be kept longer in fusion half its basic water is expelled, and tartrelic acid is formed. *Ibid.*, A soluble tartralate of this base is formed. 1868 WATTS *Dict. Chem.* V. 691 *Ditartaric Acid*,..called *Tartralic acid* by Frémy, *Isotartaric acid* by Laurent and Gerhardt.

**Tartramic** (taɹtræ·mik), *a. Chem.* [f. TARTR(O- + AM(MONIUM) + -IC.] In *tartramic acid*, $C_4H_7NO_5$, an amidated derivative of tartaric acid. Its salts are **Ta·rtramates.** Also *tartramic ether*, a name of *ethylic tartramate*, obtained by the action of alcoholic ammonia on tartaric ether; also called **Tartrame·thane.**

1857 MILLER *Elem. Chem.* III. 318 It is they [the dibasic acids] only that can furnish the amidated acids, such as the oxamic, tartramic, and lactamic acids. 1868 WATTS *Dict. Chem.* V. 697 Tartramate of calcium..is very soluble in water..and forms large tetrahedral crystals.

**Ta·rtrami·de.** *Chem.* [f. TARTR(O- + AMIDE.] The amide of tartaric acid, $C_4H_4(NH_2)_2O_4$, a crystalline body produced by passing dry ammonia gas into an alcoholic solution of tartaric ether.

1868 WATTS *Dict. Chem.* V. 697.

**Ta·rtranil.** *Chem.* [f. TARTR(O- + ANIL 3.] A granular compound, $C_{10}H_9NO_4$, = *phenyltartrimide*, produced by dehydration of acid tartrate of aniline by expulsion of $2H_2O$. Hence **Tartra·nilate,** a salt of tartranilic acid; **Tartrani·lic** *acid*, $C_{10}H_{11}NO_5$, obtained by boiling tartranil with aqueous ammonia; **Tartra·nilide,** $C_{16}H_{16}N_2O_4$, a substance produced by the action of heat on neutral tartrate of aniline, by expulsion of $2H_2O$.

1868 WATTS *Dict. Chem.* V. 698 Tartranil..separates, on cooling from hot solutions, as a white granular powder, or in nacreous laminæ. *Ibid.*, Tartranilide crystallises in colourless, nacreous, slender, interlaced needles. *Ibid.* 697 The tartranilic acid separates in light red warty masses and shining laminæ. *Ibid.*, *Tartranilate of Barium*.. crystallises in shining spangles.

**Tartrate** (tā·ɹtrět). *Chem.* [a. F. *tartrate*, f. *tartre*, TARTAR *sb.*[1]: see -ATE[1].] A salt of tartaric acid ($CO_2H.(CHOH)_2.CO_2H$) formed by substituting a metal or radical for the hydrogen of the carbonyl groups ($CO_2H$).

These salts are very numerous, and are *acid* or *neutral*, according as one or both of the hydrogen atoms are replaced; thus, *acid potassium tartrate* is $CO_2H.(CHOH)_2.CO_2K$; *neutral potassium tartrate*, $CO_2K.(CHOH)_2.CO_2K$. The H atoms can also be replaced by two different metals or radicals, forming double salts, as *sodium potassium tartrate*, $CO_2.Na.(CHOH)_2.CO_2K$, *potassium antimonyl tartrate*, $CO_2K.(CHOH)_2.CO_2SbO$.

1794 G. ADAMS *Nat. & Exp. Philos.* I. App. 547 Tartrats—the earthy insoluble in water, the alkaline soluble. 1815 J. SMITH *Panorama Sc. & Art* II. 436 Tartaric acid..unites with the alkalies, and most of the earths. The salts formed with it are called tartrates. 1869 ROSCOE *Elem. Chem.* (1871) 200 Potassium Carbonate can be obtained perfectly pure by heating pure potassium tartrate to redness.

**Ta·rtrated,** *ppl. a. Chem.* [f. prec. + -ED.] Made into a tartrate; tartarated.

1879 *St. George's Hosp. Rep.* IX. 162 Treatment with a calomel purge and an emetic of tartrated antimony and ipecacuanha. 1899 CAGNEY tr. *Jaksch's Clin. Diagn.* vii. (ed. 4) 318 An alkaline solution of tartrated soda.

**Tartrazine, Tartre**: see TARTRO-, TARTAR[1].

**Tartrelic** (taɹtre·lik), *a. Chem.* [ad. F. *tartrélique* (Frémy 1838), arbitrarily formed, along with TARTRALIC, q.v., to indicate derivation from tartaric acid by further heating; the *a* and *e* indicating the order of production of these modifications. (*Annales de Chimie* LXVIII. (1838).)] In *tartrelic acid*, soluble tartaric anhydride, $C_4H_4O_5 = C_4H_6O_6 - H_2O$, obtained as a yellowish deliquescent mass by quickly heating small quantities of tartaric acid. Its salts are **Ta·rtrelates.** See TARTRALIC.

1838 R. D. THOMSON in *Brit. Ann.* 319 Tartrelic acid. 1857 MILLER *Elem. Chem.* III. 332 [see TARTRALIC]. 1868 WATTS *Dict. Chem.* V. 691 Chloride or acetate of calcium added to the solution [of tartrelic acid] throws down tartrelate of calcium.

**Tartrethylic**, etc.: see TARTRO-.

†**Ta·rtrite.** *Chem. Obs.* Also **tartarite.** [a. F. *tartrite* (1787), f. F. *tartre*, TARTAR[1] (whence the earlier *tartarite*): see -ITE[1].] A salt of tartarous or tartareous acid. (As this is now *tartaric* acid, the tartrites are now called *tartrates*.)

1790 KERR tr. *Lavoisier's Elem. Chem.* 255 As the acid from tartar is not fully saturated with oxygen, we call it tartarous acid, and the neutral salts formed by its combinations with salifiable bases tartarites. *Ibid.*, Cream of tartar ..in our new nomenclature is named acidulous tartarite of potash. 1794 G. PEARSON in *Phil. Trans.* LXXXIV. 396 From the precipitation of tartrite of pot-ash..this acid might be supposed to be the tartareous.

**Tartro-**, before a vowel **tartr-** [f. F. *tartre*, TARTAR[1]], in names of chemical compounds containing or derived from tartaric acid; as **Ta·rtrazine** [AZO- + -INE[5]], a fast and brilliant dye-stuff of rich orange yellow; **Tartrethy·lic** *acid* [ETHYLIC] = *ethyltartaric acid*, $C_6H_{10}O_6$: see quot. 1868; its salts are **Tartre·thylates; Tartromethy·lic** *acid* [METHYLIC] = *methyltartaric acid*, $C_5H_8O_6$: its salts are **Tartrome·thylates; Tartrovi·nic** *acid* = *tartrethylic acid*. So *tartrocarbhydric*, *tartroglyceric*, etc.

1894 *Times* 15 Aug. 12/1 *Tartrazin, a colour noteworthy not only for its fastness to light, but also because of its brilliancy and purity. 1857 MILLER *Elem. Chem.* III. 318 Vinic or ethylic acids, such as sulphethylic, oxalethylic, and *tartrethylic. 1868 WATTS *Dict. Chem.* V. 694 *Tartrethylic* or *Tartrovinic acid*..crystallises in elongated prisms, with oblique bases; it is colourless, inodorous, tastes both sweet and sour. 1837 R. D. THOMSON in *Brit. Ann.* 342 When tartaric and racemic acids are treated..with pyroxylic spirit..similar acids are formed which may be termed *tartro carbydric and racemo carbydric acids. 1838 T. THOMSON *Chem. Org. Bodies* 182 *Tartromethylate of potash may be obtained in the same way as tartrovinate of potash. *Ibid.* 180 *Tartromethylic acid..was also discovered by M. Guerin-Varry. 1837 R. D. THOMSON in *Brit. Ann.* 340 **Tartrovinic acid*, M. Guerin Varry.. obtained it by boiling tartaric acid with absolute alcohol for a considerable time [etc.]. 1838 T. THOMSON *Chem. Org. Bodies* 174 A dilute solution..left exposed to an atmosphere of 77°, lets fall some..crystals of tartrovinic acid.

**Tartron**, variant of TARTARIN[1] *Obs.*

**Tartronic** (taɹtrǫ·nik), *a. Chem.* [ad. F. *tartronique* (Dessaignes 1854), arbitrarily f. *tartrique* (perh. with *ni-* of *nitro-*). (*Comptes Rendus* XXXVIII. 44.)] In *tartronic acid*, a dibasic acid, $C_3H_4O_5$, produced by the spontaneous decomposition of nitro-tartaric acid, crystallizing in large prisms. Its salts are **Ta·rtronates.**

1866 ODLING *Anim. Chem.* 133 Mesoxalic acid is convertible by deoxidation or hydrogenation into tartronic acid. 1868 WATTS *Dict. Chem.* V. 698 The tartronates of the alkali-metals are soluble in water. 1873 RALFE *Phys. Chem.* p. xxix, Uric acid..is often represented as consisting of one radical of tartronic acid and two of urea.

**Ta·rtrous,** *a.* [ad. F. *tartreux*, f. *tartre* TARTAR *sb.*[1] + -OUS.] Encrusted with (dental) tartar.

1904 *Brit. Med. Jrnl.* 20 Aug. 369 Tongue heavily coated, teeth tartrous.

**Ta·rtryl.** *Chem.* [f. TARTR(O- or F. *tartre* + -YL.] The radical $C_4H_2O_2$ of tartaric acid. Hence **Tartry·lic** *a.*, a synonym of *tartaric*.

1868 WATTS *Dict. Chem.* V. 698.

**Tartryn, -yne**, variants of TARTARIN[1] *Obs.*

‖ **Tartuffe, Tartufe** (tartu·f, -tu·f). Also 7–8 **tartuff.** [F. *Tartufe*, *Tartuffe*, name of the principal character (a religious hypocrite) in a comedy by Molière (1664): app. = OF. *tartuffe*, It. *tartuffo* truffle, as a concealed production.

Littré cites It. *Tartufo*, name of a character in the Malmantile of Lippi, as app. Molière's source.]

A hypocritical pretender to religion, or, by extension, to excellence of any kind.

1688 *Pulpit Popery, True Popery* 72 Well, let Schoolmen and Cardinals..be call'd in, they are but Tartuffs; for Exposition and Representation are now the Standard of Romish Doctrine. 1738 WARBURTON *Div. Legat.* I. Ded. 24 Tartufes without Religion. 1765 STERNE *Tr. Shandy* VIII. ii, The arrantest *Tartuffe* in science, in politics,—or in religion. 1878 J. PAYN *By Proxy* I. xii. 138 A touch of the Tartuffe or the Joseph Surface.

Hence **Tartu·fferie, -ery** [F. *tartuferie*], **Tartuf(f)ism,** the character or conduct of a Tartuffe, hypocrisy; **Tartu·ffian, Tartu·f(f)ish** *adjs.*, pertaining to or characteristic of a Tartuffe, hypocritical, pretentious; hence **Tartu·ffishly** *adv.*

1851 *Fraser's Mag.* XLIII. 151 Her national *Tartuffery augmented and became more offensive. 1906 *Sat. Rev.* 13 Oct. 450/1 That incorrigible 'Tartufferie' which marks all our conquests. 1872 *Routledge's Ev. Boy's Ann.* 672 In such a very *Tartuffian way. 1768 STERNE *Sent. Journ.* (1778) I. 66 God help her!..she has some mother-in-law, or *tartufish aunt..to consult upon the occasion. 1824 *Examiner* 594/1 That Alliance so *tartuffishly termed 'holy'. 1688 *Pulpit Popery, True Popery* 72 The *Tartuffism of Deposition of Princes, and Adoration of Images, and the rest of the once old and new Pulpit-Popery. 1891 *Sat. Rev.* 10 Oct. 403/1 The victim of Tartufism of the most disgusting kind.

**Tarturne, Tartyr**, variants of TARTARIN[1], TARTAR *sb.*[3] **Tar-vetch**: see TARE *sb.*[1] 4.

**Tarve** (tāɹv). [app. the same as TARF.] A turn; a bend, a curve.

1848 F. COOPER *Bee-hunter* ii, I can't say much for your axe, stranger, for this helve has no tarve to 't.

**Ta·r-wa:ter.** [f. TAR *sb.* + WATER *sb.*]

1. An infusion of tar in cold water, formerly in repute as a medicine.

1740–1 BERKELEY *Let. T. Prior* 8 Feb., I believe tar-water might be useful to prevent..such an evil [a felon]. 1744 — (*title*) Philosophical Reflexions and Inquiries concerning the Virtues of Tar-Water [*ed.* 2 Siris, a Chain of Philosophical [etc.]]. 1744 GRAY *Let. to Wharton* 26 Apr., Mr. Trollope and I are in a course of Tar-Water. 1756 H. WALPOLE *Let. to Mann* 8 Dec., He [Sir H. Mann's brother] has been drinking tar-water since the middle of November. 1840 E. FITZGERALD *Letters* (1889) I. 60, I have also just concocted two gallons of Tar water under the directions of Bishop Berkeley. **1891** SYDNEY *Eng. in 18th C.* I. 311 No remedy was more popular during the second half of the eighteenth century than tar-water.

**2.** 'The ammoniacal water of gas-works' (Simmonds *Dict. Trade*, 1858).

‖ **Tarwhine** (tā·ɹ₁hwəin). Also **tarwine.** [? Native name.] An Australian fish, *Chrysophrys sarba*, used for food.

**1880** INGLIS *Austral. Cousins* 298 In the brackish waters near Lake Macquarie, are most plentiful supplies of black bream, tarwine, flathead, whiting, river gar-fish and others. **1883** E. P. RAMSAY *Food Fishes N. S. Wales* 12 (Fish. Exhib. Publ.) The black bream (*Chrysophrys australis*) and the tarwhine (*Ch. hasta*) are both valuable food-fish,..they attain a weight of 4 to 5 lbs.

† **Tary,** *sb. Obs.* Also 6 **tarie, -ye.** [f. TARY *v.*] Vexation, trouble, annoyance.

**1528** LYNDESAY *Dreme* 277 For to rehers thare lyffis vitious, It wer bot tarye to the auditouris. **1533** GAU *Richt Vay* (S.T.S.) 66 We haiff mekil tarie of it [our body] heir in ye wardil. *c* **1576** MAITLAND *Poems* (1830) 40 And tak ane wyf to bring him selffe in tarye, For fresche Maii and cauld Januarij Agreeis nocht upone ane sang in tune.

† **Ta·ry,** *v. Obs.* Forms: 4–5 **tarien,** 5 **teryyn,** (**tarry**), 5–6 **tarie, -ye,** (**tarrie**), **tary.** [ME. *tery-yn, tari-en* appears to represent in form and sense both OE. *tęrgan, *tærg(e)an, tyrian, *tęrian*, to provoke, and OF. *tarier* to provoke, excite, in F. dial. to vex, irritate, torment, tease (of doubtful origin). In so far as *tary* was of OE. origin, it was a doublet of TAR *v.*[2] See Note.]

**1.** *trans.* To provoke, vex, worry, harass.

*a* **1300** *E. E. Psalter* cv[i]. 8 [7] Þai taried [*irritaverunt*] vpsteyand in se, Rede se. *a* **1325** *Prose Psalter* ibid., Tariden. **13..** *Cursor M.* 28153, I womman haue vn-buxum bene And tarid myn husband to tene. **1340** HAMPOLE *Pr. Consc.* 1189 Þa þat wille him folow, he..scornes and taries in his nedes. **1387** (MS. *c* **1410**) TREVISA tr. *Higden* (Rolls) V. 355 Þe kynges..sone..gan to tarry [*v.r.* terre; orig. *lacessivit*] and to angre þe Longobardes wiþ despitous wordes. *c* **1400** *Destr. Troy* 7287 He was tarriet with the Troiens, & tenit full euyll. *c* **1440** *Promp. Parv.* 489/2 Teryyn, or ertyn. [Ertyn, *irrito*.] *c* **1440** *Psalmi Penit.* (1894) 38 Yn this world ys no scharpur arwe, Than the turment [*MS.* turnement] that me gan tarie [*rime* marie]. **1567** *Gude & Godlie B.* (S.T.S.) 176 Kingis to marie, and sum to tarie, Sic is his power and mycht.

**2.** To weary, tire, fatigue. (Cf. TAR *v.*[2] 2.)

*c* **1375** in T. Wright *Rel. Antiq.* I. 9 *Fatigatus*, y-taried.

Hence † **Tarying, teryynge** *vbl. sb.*, provoking; † **Taryer, teryare,** a provoker, vexer; † **Taryingness,** provocation.

*a* **1300** *E. E. Psalter* xciv. 9 [xcv. 8] Als aftre dai in taryingesse Ofe fandinge in wildernesse. *a* **1400** HYLTON *Scala Perf.* (W. de W. 1494) II. xxii, Of tarienges & temptacions that Soules fele bi her ghostly enmyes. *c* **1440** *Promp. Parv.* 489/2 Teryare, or ertare, *irritator*. .. Teryynge, or ertynge, *irritacio*.

[*Note.* The form *teryyn* (= *tery-en, teri-en*) in Promp. Parv., with its derivatives *teryare, teryynge*, points to OE. *tęrgan*, with the palatal *g* reduced to *y* consonant or *i*, as in the actually recorded late OE. form *tyrian* (imper. *tyrie*, pa. t. *tyrgde, tyrigde, tyride*), giving a ME. *teri-en* (*tery-yn*), with a variant *tary-en, tari-en*, perh. from an Anglian **tærg(e)an*, as in *weryen, warien*, from OE. *węrgean, wærgean, wiergan, wyrgean, wyrian*, WARRY, to curse. The coincidence of *tarien* in form and meaning with OF. *tarier* would tend to reinforce it as the leading form. It is noteworthy that ME. examples of *tary-* are not known before *c* 1300, and that *tery-* is cited only from *Promp. Parv.* As to possible connexion with TARRY see Note to that vb.]

**Tary, Taryance, -ans,** etc., obs. ff. TARRY, TARRIANCE. **Taryar, -er,** obs. ff. TERRIER[2].

**Tas,** obs. f. TASS. **Tas** = *takes*: see TAKE *v.* A.

‖ **Tasajo** (tasā·χo). Also 8 **tassajo,** 9 **tassago.** [Sp. *tasajo* a slice of dried meat, in Pg. *tasalho*; cf. Cat. *tasco*. Of uncertain origin: see Diez 490.] Buffalo meat cut into strips and dried in the sun.

[**1760–72** tr. *Juan & Ulloa's Voy.* (ed. 3) II. 244 The flesh after having been cut into thin slices, is salted, and this is what they call Tassagear.] **1783** JUSTAMOND tr. *Raynal's Hist. Indies* V. 365 The inhabitants [of Trinidad] shoot them [wild cattle], and cut their flesh into slips..which they dry...This provision, which is called Tassajo, is sold in the French settlements. **1851** MAYNE REID *Scalp Hunt.* xxvi, Those who remain cut the [buffalo] meat into long thin strips, and hang it over the lines already prepared for this purpose. It is thus left to be baked by the sun into '*tasajo*'. **1858** SIMMONDS *Dict. Trade, Tasajo*, a name in New Granada for dried meat; hung beef. **1891** *Cent. Dict.*, Tassago.

**Tasar,** var. TUSSER, TUSSORE, an Indian silk.

† **Tascal.** *Sc. Obs.* exc. *Hist.* [a. Gael. *taisgeal* the finding of anything that was lost, f. *taisg* a treasure, *taisg* to deposit, hoard, bury.] In *tascal money*, a reward formerly paid in the Scottish Highlands for information regarding stolen cattle.

*c* **1730** BURT *Lett.* (1754) II. xxiv. 243 Sending Persons into the Country suspected, and by them offering a Reward (which they call Tascal Money) to any one who should discover the Cattle, and those who stole them. **1827** J. ANDERSON *St. Soc. & Knowl. Highl.* 70 He who..received tascal money as informer, met scorn, perhaps death. **1907** A. LANG *Hist. Scot.* IV. xv. 368 Tascal money used to be paid to traitors among the robbers.

† **Ta·sco, ta·scony.** *Obs. rare*⁻⁰. [ad. It. *tasconio* 'a kind of white clay or marble, whereof goldsmiths pots ... were made' (Florio 1598), ad. L. *tasconium* (Pliny).] (See quots.)

**1726** BAILEY, *Tasco*, a sort of Clay, for making Melting-Pots. **1730** — (folio), *Tascony*, a sort of white Earth like Chalk, and is the only Earth that endures the Blast of the Bellows and Heat of the Fire and running Metal. **1823** CRABB *Techn. Dict.*, Tasco.

**Tase,** obs. form of *takes*, inflexion of TAKE *v.*

**Tase,** var. TEISE *v.*, *Obs.*, to stretch, bend (a bow).

**Tasel, -ell(e,** obs. ff. TEASEL.

**Taseometer** (tæsĭ₁ǫ·mĭtəɹ). [f. Gr. τασε-, stem of τάσις tension + -METER.] (See quot.)

**1880** *Telegraphic Jrnl.* VI. 126. **1884** KNIGHT *Dict. Mech.* Suppl., *Taseometer*, invented by Steiner, of Vienna, for measuring the strains of structures. It depends upon the tone given out by a wire or strip when stretched. The wire being attached the variation in length of the bar causes a change in the tone.

**Tases,** obs. f. *tasses* thigh-armour: see TASSE *sb.*[1] **Tash,** *dial.*, blemish, **Tashed,** tarnished: see TACHE *sb.*[1] and *v.*[1]

‖ **Tashlik, tashlich** (taʃlī·k). [Heb. תשליך *taʃlī·k* 'thou shalt cast', future Hiphil of שלך *ʃālak* to cast.] A symbolical custom, popularly in vogue among Jews, of repairing, on New Year's Day, to a stream of running water, and repeating certain biblical verses indicative of sin and forgiveness, specially Micah vii. 19, 'Thou wilt cast all their sins into the depths of the sea'.

**1880** *Jewish World* 30 Sept., Tashlich..a simple fad of mediæval rabbinism, of late date and origin, and wholly unknown to our ancient sages. **1902** *Daily Chron.* 2 Oct. 7/1 They have imported with them from their native ghettos the singular practice known as 'Tashlikh', which is performed by the side of a stream of running water or on the seashore...A favourite resort for the purpose of 'Tashlikh' is the Custom House Quay, and the front walk of the Tower.

**Tasil(l,** obs. ff. TEASEL.

**Tasimeter** (tăsi·mĭtəɹ). [f. Gr. τάσι-ς tension + -METER.] An electrical apparatus for measuring minute variations of temperature, length, moisture, etc. by means of changes in the electrical conductivity of carbon resulting from alterations of pressure caused by these variations.

**1878** *Nature* 25 July 329/2 An account..of Edison's Tasimeter. **1879** H. W. WARREN *Recr. Astron.* iv. 62 If the temperature of a summer morning rises ten or twenty degrees we scarcely notice it; but the magnetic tasimeter measures 1/50000 of a degree. **1881** *Nature* 25 Aug. 390/2 No satisfactory results have been obtained in the attempt to measure the heat of the stars with the tasimeter. **1893** *Review of Rev.* Dec. 606 A little machine called the tasimeter, which measures degrees of heat, of moisture..of odours and sound.

Hence **Tasime·tric** *a.*, of or pertaining to the tasimeter or to tasimetry (*Cassell's Encycl. Dict.* 1888); **Tasi·metry,** the measurement of pressures (*Funk's Standard Dict.* 1895).

**Task** (tɑsk), *sb.* Also 4–7 **taske,** 5–7 **tasque.** [a. ONF. *tasque* (13th c. in Godef.) = OF. *tasche*, F. *tâche*; or ad. med.L. *tasca* (*taschia*) (*c* 800 in Du Cange), according to Diez, by metathesis for *taxa*, f. L. *taxāre* to rate, estimate, value, in med.L. to impose or assess a tax.]

**I.** † **1.** A fixed payment to a king, lord, or feudal superior; an impost, tax; tribute. *Obs.*

[**1114–18** *Laws Hen. I*, c. 78 § 5 Persoluantur uel in taschis uel huiusmodi suggerendis, sicut de b[a]st[ar]dis est institutum.] *c* **1400** *Laud Troy Bk.* 17918 This is the somme that Gregays aske, That thei wole haue vnto her taske: Ten hundrid thousand pound of golde. **14..** in *Wars Eng. in France* (1864) II. 525 Tasques, taylles, inposicione of the comyns. *c* **1440** *Promp. Parv.* 487/1 Taske, or talyage, *taliagium, taxa*. *c* **1475** *Harl. Contin. Higden* (Rolls) VIII. 454 Grete exaccions and taskes. **1530** PALSGR. 279/2 Taske that a prince gadereth, *taulx*. **1624** *Maldon, Essex, Borough Deeds* (Bundle 108 lf. 12), xxd. payd the collectors of the taske for twoe fifteenes and tenths. *a* **1625** SIR H. FINCH *Law* (1636) 298 High Collectors of any Taske, Subsedie, or lone. **1766** BLACKSTONE *Comm.* II. v. 75 By statute 25 Edw. I. c. 5 & 6..it was enacted, that the king should take no aids or tasks but by the common assent of the realm.

**2.** A piece of work imposed, exacted, or undertaken as a duty or the like; originally, a fixed or specified quantity of labour or work imposed on or exacted from a person; later, the work appointed or assigned to one as a definite duty.

*a* **1300** *Cursor M.* 5872 And taron sett he men at ask Of ilk dai to yeild þair task [*v.r.* taske]. **13..** *Ibid.* 29000 Has he [Christ] sett vs certain task Quilk ar þai bones for to ask. *c* **1400** *St. Alexius* (Laud 622) 675 Nouȝth as a Man of task. **1530** TINDALE *Exod.* v. 14 Wherfore haue ye not fulfilled youre taske in makinge brycke? **1549** COVERDALE, etc. *Erasm. Par. Rom.* 8 The Iewes..whiche hauyng..become christian men, & worke no longer now, as it wer by tasque, but vnfainedly & purely put theyr trust in him. **1573–80** BARET *Alv.* T 79 The Taske, or worke that one is appointed to do. **1645** MILTON *Tetrach.* Wks. 1851 IV. 237 A task we know is a proportion of work, not doing the same thing absolutely every day, but so much. **1699** BURNET 39 *Art.* xxv. (1700) 283 Prayers gone through as a Task can be of no value. **1711** ADDISON *Spect.* No. 111 ¶ 6 The silk-worm, after having spun her task, lays her eggs and dies. **1758** JOHNSON *Idler* No. 13 ¶ 6 She..appoints them a task of needle-work. **1856** OLMSTED *Slave States* 435 In getting fuel from the woods..one cord is the task for a day. **1892** WESTCOTT *Gospel of Life* 272 Each age has its own task, and we can dimly see our own.

**b.** *spec.* A portion of study imposed by a teacher; a lesson to be learned or prepared. Now *arch.*

**1742** SHENSTONE *Schoolmistress* 155 Eftsoons the urchins to their tasks repair, Their books of stature small they take in hand. **1760** FRANKLIN *Ess.* Wks. 1840 II. 126 These lessons might be given every night as tasks. **1811** BYRON *Hints fr. Hor.* 231 Fines, tutors, tasks, conventions threat in vain. **1901** *Northern Whig* 8 May (E.D.D.), An Ulster lad, when at school, gets his 'tasks'.

**3.** In more general sense: Any piece of work that has to be done; something that one has to do (usually involving labour or difficulty); a matter of difficulty, a 'piece of work'. Cf. JOB *sb.*[2] 4.

**1593** SHAKS. *Rich. II*, II. ii. 145 Alas poore Duke, the taske he vndertakes Is numbring sands, and drinking Oceans drie. **1637** T. MORTON *New Eng. Canaan* (1883) 182 My taske..is to intreat of the naturall indowments of the Country. **1641** BROME *Jov. Crew* II. Wks. 1873 III. 384 Alass poor Knave! How hard a tasque it is to alter Custome! **1754** *Connoisseur* No. 42 ¶ 7 To rescue our Native Language ..is a task worthy those who are accounted Ornaments of our Seats of Learning. **1841** W. SPALDING *Italy & It. Isl.* III. 101 Never had sovereigns been called upon to perform a task more difficult than that which lay before the restored princes of Italy. **1858** FROUDE *Hist. Eng.* III. xvii. 525 He had taken upon himself a task beyond the ordinary strength of man.

**II.** Phrases. † **4. a.** *At task*: (*a*) at so much for a specified amount or piece of work, by the piece; (*b*) ? taken to task, blamed (a doubtful sense, the reading being uncertain). **b.** *By task, to task*, by the piece. **c.** *Under task*, under the command of a taskmaster; by compulsion. *Obs.*

**a. 1477–8** in Swayne *Sarum Churchw. Acc.* (1896) 364 Helyng and poyntyng in dyvers places atte Taske. **1605** SHAKS. *Lear* I. iv. 366 (Fol. 1) Yet vnder pardon You are much more at task [*Qo.* 1 attaskt] for want of wisedome, Then prai'sd for harmefull mildnesse. **b. 1601–2** in Willis & Clark *Cambridge* (1886) II. 628 Item for caruing the eight beastes by taske. **1803** *Naval Chron.* XV. 58 A job note..an actual statement of the work performed by job and task. **1476–7** in Swayne *Sarum Churchw. Acc.* (1896) 363 Swaryng of timber to carpenters to taske viijd. **c. 1671** MILTON *Samson* 35 To grind in Brazen Fetters under task With this Heav'n-gifted strength.

**5.** *To take to task*: † (*a*) to undertake as one's task or special piece of work; † (*b*) to challenge (a person) to a task; † (*c*) to take (a person or thing) in hand, to deal with; (*d*) *esp.* (in current use), to deal with or tackle in the way of fault-finding or censure, to call to account about a matter: cf. TASK *v.* 5, TAX *v.* 6.

**1546** *Accts. Osney & St. Frideswyde's* (MS. Wood, D. 2, p. 585), To a laborer pulling downe stone at Osney church, for yᵉ masons yᵗ took yᵉ walle to taske at frideswides. **1570** J. DEE *Math. Pref.* a iv b, Geographie did principally take the Element of the Earthes description .. to taske. **1589** PUTTENHAM *Eng. Poesie* III. xix. (Arb.) 253 He..would take any common souldier to taske at wrastling, or weapon, or in any other actiuitie..of armes. **1649** BP. HALL *Cases Consc.* (1650) 265 Apollos..knew nothing but the Baptisme of John: till Aquila and Priscilla took him to task, and more perfectly expounded to him the way of God. **1682** WOOD *Life* 31 May (O.H.S.) III. 19 George Royse..took his principles to taske and exposed them very smartly. **1740** tr. *De Mouhy's Fort. Country-Maid* (1741) I. 84 What is the Matter, my pretty Girl?..has any one been taking you to Task? **1760–72** H. BROOKE *Fool of Qual.* (1792) I. 81 [He] shut the door, and called him to task. **1822** *Examiner* 365/1 The *Quarterly* is taken to task for neglecting its duty. **1890** DOYLE *Capt. 'Polestar'*, etc. 205 My employer took me severely to task.

**III. 6.** *attrib.* and *Comb.*, as, † (in sense 1) *task-book, -cope, -gatherer, -money, -roll* (obs.); (in senses 2 and 3), *task-book, -house, -labour, -labourer, -lord, -officer, -reading, -verse*; *task-like* adj.; **taskman,** an officer who sets a task, a taskmaster; **task-note,** a memorandum of work done by the piece, a job-note: see quot. 1803 in 4 b; **task-system,** the system of working by the piece. See also TASKMASTER, etc.

**1624** *Maldon, Essex, Borough Deeds* (Bundle 108 lf. 8), xs. payd to Samwell Chese for new writing of the *taske booke (in parchment) this yere. **1882** J. PARKER *Apost. Life* I. 17 Some men hardly can open the Bible..because they remember that in early days it was the task-book. **1463** in *Bury Wills* (Camden) 21 To aquyte the said Seynt Marie preest of the *taske Abbot's cope and alle manner charges generally at ony [time] askyd by ony manner of mene. **1552** HULOET, *Taske gatherer, *exactor*. **1847** LD. LINDSAY *Hist. Chr. Art* I. Introd. 168 There was my place of prayer, there the *task-house of my most wretched flesh. **1812** *Gen. Hist.* in *Ann. Reg.* 161/2 The working of mines, and other *task labour. **1838–9** FR. A. KEMBLE *Resid. in Georgia* (1863) 28 In the part of Georgia where this estate is situated, the custom of task labour is universal. **1897** A. DRUCKER tr. *Ihering's Evol. Aryan* 116 The Egyptians knew no mercy for their *task-labourers. **1830** FR. A. KEMBLE *Let.* in *Rec. Girlhood* (1878) II. iv. 115 With what *task-like feeling I set about most of my work. **1605** SYLVESTER *Du Bartas* II. iii. III. *Law* 137 They labour hard, eat little, sleeping lesse, No sooner layd, but thus their *Task-Lords presse. **1856** OLMSTED *Slave States* 435 One cord is the task for a day. ..The *taskman selecting the trees..that he judges will split easiest, one hundred a day. **1593** *Jack Straw* I. in Hazl. *Dodsley* V. 379 Thou hast thy *task-money for all that be here. **1803** *Naval Chron.* XV. 58 Is there any particular form of job or *task note? **1865** J. H. INGRAHAM *Pillar of Fire* (1872) 135 Enrolling them under *task-officers. **1577** in *10th Rep. Hist. MSS. Comm.* App. IV. 439 A *taske rowle made for the manor of Romseley. **1863** P. BARRY *Dockyard Econ.* 57 Examined as to the operation of what is known as the *task and job system. **1875** LOWELL *Wks.* (1890) IV. 360 At school Wordsworth wrote some *task-verses on subjects imposed by the master.

**Task** (tɑsk), *v.* [f. Task *sb.* Cf. *to fine*, etc.]

**I.** †**1.** *trans.* To impose a tax upon; to tax; to exact tribute from. *Obs.*

**1483** Caxton *Gold. Leg.* 64 b/2 He shal taske and dyme your corn and sheues. *a* **1500** in *Arnolde's Chron.* (1811) p. xix, This yere lost the Kinge Normandy and Angeoy, and euery plough land [was] tasked at iij. s. for to gete it ageyne. **1530** [see 2]. **1596** Shaks. 1 *Hen. IV*, iv. iii. 92 Hee..in the neck of that, task't the whole State. **1598** W. Phillip *Linschoten* i. xcii. 152/1 All the townes men [were] tasked euery one at a certaine summe of mony. **1642** Rogers *Naaman* 424 He taskes thee not to the cost of Jewish worship, or Popish wast.

**2.** To force, put, or set (a person) to a task; to impose a task on; to assign a definite amount of work to.

**1530** Palsgr. 753/1, I taske, I put or sette one to his taske what laboure he shall do or what he shall paye, *je tauxe*. **1588** Shaks. *L. L. L.* ii. i. 20 But now to taske the tasker. **1667** Woodhead *St. Teresa* ii. xi. 93 Let her task, and employ them in..Exercises. **1784** Cowper *Task* ii. 23 Thus man devotes his brother, and destroys;..Chains him, and tasks him, and exacts his sweat With stripes. **1828** *Life Planter Jamaica* 154 The negroes complained more of the [fact] of being tasked, than..of the additional labour.

**b.** Const. *to*, with *sb.* or *inf.* Often *fig.*

*c* **1590** Greene *Fr. Bacon* xiv. 53 To task yourself to such a tedious life As die a maid. **1596** Shaks. 1 *Hen. IV*, iv. i. 9 Nay, taske me to my word; approue me Lord. *c* **1600** — *Sonn.* lxxii, O least the world should taske you to recite, What merit liu'd in me that you should loue. **1607** — *Cor.* i. iii. 39 A Haruest man, that ['s] task'd to mowe Or all, or loose his hyre. **1726** Pope *Odyss.* xx. 134 Twelve female slaves..Task'd for the royal board to bolt the bran From the pure flour. **1809** W. Irving *Knickerb.* v. iv, Man alone.. tasks creation to assist him in murdering his brother worm!

**3.** *transf.* and *fig.* To occupy or engage fully or burdensomely; to subject to severe burden, labour, or trial; to put a strain upon; to put in a condition of stress or difficulty; to put to the proof; = Tax *v.* 4.

**1598** Shaks. *Merry W.* iv. vi. 30 Doctor Caius.. Shall shuffle her away, While other sports are tasking of their mindes. **1599** — *Hen. V*, i. ii. 6 Some things of weight, That taske our thoughts. **1647–8** Cotterell *Davila's Hist. Fr.* (1678) 28 At length he resolved to task the King's inclinations. **1742** Richardson *Pamela* IV. 61 You must not task me too high. **1850** W. Irving *Goldsmith* i. 22 He tasked his slender means to the utmost in educating him. **1872** Yeats *Growth Comm.* 115 It tasked his diplomatic skill to effect his departure in safety.

**b.** *spec.* To test the soundness of (a ship's timbers, a plank, etc.).

**1803** *Naval Chron.* X. 259 That..frigate is..to be, what is called in the language of the dock yard, tasked, to see if her timbers are sound. **1867** Smyth *Sailor's Word-bk.*, *Tasking*, examining a vessel to see whether her timbers are sound.

**4.** To give or portion *out* (work) as a task.

*a* **1641** Bp. Mountagu *Acts & Mon.* vii. (1642) 438 They have their work for the day tasked out unto them. **1812** [see Tasker 3 b].

**II.** †**5.** To take to task; to censure, reprove, chide, reprehend; = Tax *v.* 6. *Obs.*

**1580** G. Harvey *Let. to Spenser* Wks. (Grosart) I. 87 If it lyke you in the meane while..to see howe I taske a young Brother of myne. **1608** Topsell *Serpents* (1658) 721 There is another pretty fable in Esop, tasking discontented persons under the name of Frogs. **1614** J. Cooke *Tu Quoque* F j, I call thee vp, and taske thee for thy slownesse. **1632** Massinger & Field *Fatal Dowry* i. ii, To say 'the late dead Marshal, The father of this young lord here, my client, Hath done his country great and faithful service' Might task me of impertinence.

Hence **Tasked** (tɑskt) *ppl. a.*; **Ta·sking** *vbl. sb.* and *ppl. a.*

**1543** *Harding's Chron.* cxvi. viii. P vj b, Saint Edmundes landes he hurt by great taskyng [*Bodl. MSS.* taxinge] And tallage. **1812** Tasked work [see Tasker 3 b]. **1848** Lowell *Vision Sir Launfal* i. Prelude 28 Bubbles we buy with a whole soul's tasking. **1852** D. G. Mitchell *Dream Life* 199 The fruits..hanging heavily from the tasked trees. **1856** Olmsted *Slave States* 435 It is the driver's duty to make the tasked hands do their work well. **1872** J. S. Blackie *Ascent Cruachan* v. in *Lays Highl.* 103 We have done our tasking bravely, With the thews of Scottish men.

**Ta·skage.** *nonce-wd.* [f. Task *sb.* or *v.* + -age.] Tasking; imposed labour; tasks collectively.

**1830** W. Taylor *Hist. Surv. Germ. Poetry* II. 73 Sisyphus also I saw, with unwelcomest taskage tormented.

**Tasker** (tɑ·skəɹ). [f. Task *v.* (or *sb.*) + -er [1].]

†**1.** One who assesses or regulates a rate or price (e. g. of lodgings, things brought to market, etc.).

**1538** Elyot, *Agoranomus*, he that setteth the pryce of vyttayle, a tasker. **1577** Harrison *England* ii. iii. (1877) i. 82 Vicechancelors are changed euerie yeare, as are also the proctors, taskers, maisters of the streates and other officers. **1614** Purchas *Pilgrimage* ii. ii. (ed. 2) 113 They had ten Aediles, Taskers or Iudges of the Market. [Cf. Taxer 1 b.]

**2.** One who imposes or sets a task; a taskmaster.

**1588** Shaks. *L. L. L.* ii. i. 20 But now to taske the tasker. **1654** Whitlock *Zootomia* 297 This Avaricious Plenty is its own Tasker, its owne Pharaoh. **1678** Dryden & Lee *Œdipus* iii. i, Hear, ye sullen powers below: Hear, ye taskers of the dead. **1827** W. Kennedy *Poems* 63 It may not be, My taskers call me to the sea.

**3.** One who works or is paid by the task or piece, as distinct from a day-labourer, etc. (*dial.*).

**1621** Burton *Anat. Mel.* Democr. to Rdr. 12 If our greedy Patrons hold vs to such hard conditions..they will make some of vs at last turne Taskers, Costermongers, sell Ale..or worse. **1623** R. Carpenter *Conscionable Christian* 3 A due Tasker and Day-labourer for the appointed wages and gaine. **1794** T. Davis *Agric. Wilts.* 90 In cutting the lent corn, few 'taskers' are employed, the resident labourers being generally sufficient.

**b.** *spec.* One who threshes corn with a flail, as Task-work or piece-work: see quot. 1792.

[**1375** (MS. 1487) Barbour *Bruce* v. 318 (Cambr. MS.) He suld..haf..A flaill, as he a taskar [*Edinb. MS.* (an. 1489), thresscher] ware.] **14..** *Nom.* in Wr.-Wülcker 697/19 *Hic triturator*, a tasker. *c* **1575** *Balfour's Practicks* (1754) 377 He that is tasker in ony man's barn. **1744–50** W. Ellis *Mod. Husb.* IV. iv. 125 (E.D.S.) A tasker who threshes out his quota of grain. *Ibid.* 131 Tasker-servant. **1792** *Statist. Acc. Scotl.* II. 353 The taskers are those, who are employed in threshing out the corn; and they receive..the twenty-fifth part for their labour; and this has been their fixed and stated wages, as far back as can be remembered. **1812** Sir J. Sinclair *Syst. Husb. Scot.* i. 82 The tasker, (or thresher who worked by tasked work), had to take it from the heap,.. to lay it on the floor, to shake it well, and then to thresh it.

**Ta·skma:ster.** [f. Task *sb.* + Master *sb.*[1]] One whose office is to allot tasks and see to their performance; an overseer; a middleman; *spec.* in plastering (see quot. 1892); also *fig.* one who allots a duty, or imposes a heavy burden or labour.

**1530** Tindale *Exod.* i. 11 And he [Pharao] sette taske-masters ouer them. *Ibid.* 14 And the officers of the children of Israel which Pharaos taskmasters had sett ouer them, were beaten. **1631** Milton *Sonn.*, '*How soon hath Time*', All is, if I have grace to use it so, As ever in my great task Masters eye. **1797** Godwin *Enquirer* i. viii. 67 There is no equality between me and my Task-master. **1869** W. P. Mackay *Grace & Truth* (1875) 212 The task-master's whip held over his head. **1892** *Labour Commission* Gloss., *Taskmaster*, one who takes work from the original contractor in the plastering industry, and sets a given quantity of work to be done in a certain time.

Hence **Ta·skma:stership**, the office or position of a taskmaster.

**1815** *Zeluca* I. 70 All the arts, and all the sciences..all conned in submission to taskmastership. **1898** *Daily News* 12 Nov. 3/6 Having..passed through both the terrible ordeal of a lower boy's life at Eton and..having enjoyed the delights of cruel taskmastership.

**Ta·skmi:stress.** [f. as prec. + Mistress *sb.*] A woman (or something personified as female) who assigns tasks, or apportions labour.

**1603** H. Crosse *Vertues Commw.* (1878) 150 His taske-mistresse Iuno was faine to crie out, *Defessa sum iubendo.* **1741** Richardson *Pamela* (1824) I. ix. 245 You will consider yourself as the task-mistress, and the..female servants as so many negroes. **1817** Shelley *Rev. Islam* xi. xvii, For which, O willing slaves to Custom old, Severe taskmistress, ye your hearts have sold. **1899** Crockett *Kit Kennedy* 212 Kit knew that his task-mistress was listening.

**Ta·sk-work.** [f. Task *sb.* + Work *sb.*]

**1.** Work performed as a task; forced labour; hence, oppressive or burdensome work.

**1582** Stanyhurst *Æneis* i. (Arb.) 34 Shee frams firmlye statuts, and task wurcks equalye parteth. **1814** Jefferson *Writ.* (1830) IV. 241 It was the heaviest task-work I ever went through. **1827** Scott *Jrnl.* 14 Jan., I feel a dislike to order and to task-work of all kinds. **1849** Grote *Greece* ii. xxxviii. V. 28 The canal-cutting..was..distributed under their measurement as task-work among the contingents of the various nations. **1885** Bible (R. V.) *Prov.* xii. 24.

**2.** Work done by the piece; piece-work.

**1486–7** in E. B. Jupp *Carpenters' Co.* (1887) 349 That no persone of the said crafte hereafter make any foreign carpenter his fellows..in any taske werke takyng. **1581** in Feuillerat *Revels Q. Eliz.* (1908) 344 a, Tasque work viz. to John Rose for a Mount. **1721** Perry *Daggenh. Breach* 77 They work'd two or three Times as much by Task-work as by the Day, or by the Tide. **1855** J. R. Leifchild *Cornwall Mines* 142 In Cornish mines, the sinking of shafts and the driving of levels is paid by tut-work or task-work, at so much per fathom.

**Tasle, Tasler**, obs. ff. Teasel, Teaseler.

**Taslet** (tæ·slėt). *Sc. arch.* Usually in pl. **taslets, in 6 teslottis, teslettis, tasletis.** [A deriv. of Tasse *sb.*[1] (or its French original), with dim. suffix -let; perhaps from Tasset with suffix-change. Cf. also OF. (Picard) *tasselet*, dim. of *tassel* plastron or frontlet of a lady's dress (1507 in Godef.), Rouchi *tasselet* 'petite plaque de plomb'.] *pl.* Tasses, tassets: see Tasse *sb.*[1], Tasset.

**1507** *Acc. Ld. High Treas. Scotl.* III. 391 For vj quartaris rede to covir the Kingis tasletis,..xx *s.* **1541** *Ibid.* VIII. 33 Deliverit..to lyne the teslottis of harnes maid to his Grace, vij quarteris blak sating..lvj s. **1542** *Ibid.* 54 Ane lycht harnes with doubill teslettis..to the Kingis grace. **1819** Scott *Leg. Montrose* ii, Thigh-pieces of steel, then termed taslets, met the tops of his huge jack-boots. **1870** *Athenæum* 22 Jan. 126 Over his trunk-hose are steel thigh-pieces or taslets.

**Tasmanian** (tæzmēⁱ·niăn, tæs-), *a.* Of or pertaining to Tasmania in Australasia. In names of animals, plants, etc., native to Tasmania, as *Tasmanian devil* (see Devil 7), *T. wolf* (see Wolf). Also *Tasmanian cranberry, currant, honeysuckle, ironwood*, etc.: see the sbs.

**Tasmanite** (tæ·zmănəit). *Min.* [f. *Tasmania* + -ite [1].] A resinous hydrocarbon containing sulphur, occurring in reddish-brown scales on the Mersey river, Tasmania.

**1864** A. H. Church in *Phil. Mag.* XXVIII. 465 On Tasmanite, a new Mineral of Organic Origin. *Ibid.* 467 When Tasmanite is heated in the air, it burns readily with a very smoky flame and offensive odour.

**Tasol, Tasque**, obs. ff. Teasel, Task.

**Tasp, Tasping**: see Tap *v.*[2] 1, quot. *c* 1440.

**Tass** [1] (tɑs). Now only *dial.* Also **4 tas, 4–5 tasse, 5 (7) taas.** [a. OF. *tas* masc. (Wace, 12th c.), also *tasse* fem. (13th c. in Godef.), = Pr. *tatz*; generally held to be of Low German origin: cf. Du. *tas*, MDu. also *tass* heap (not known elsewhere in Teut.): see Franck.] A heap, pile, stack.

*c* **1330** *Arth. & Merl.* 6719 Thei lay of paiens mani tasse, Wide and side more and lasse. *c* **1386** Chaucer *Knt.'s T.* 147 To ransake in the taas of the bodyes dede. **1412–20** Lydg. *Chron. Troy* iv. 2397 Worþi knyȝtes..In þe feld on ouþer part y-lorn, Which in þe taas ful besely þei souȝt. *c* **1440** *Promp. Parv.* 487/1 Tasse, of corne, or oþer lyke, *tassis.* **1577** B. Googe *Heresbach's Husb.* (1586) 42 Bestowe your Corne in severall tasses and moowes. **1616** Bullokar *Eng. Expos.*, *Taas*, an heape. **1735–6** Pegge *Kenticisms* (E.D.S.), *Tass-cutter*, that utensil or implement with which they cut hay in the stack. *Ibid.*, An hay-tass is an hay-mow. **1887** *Kentish Gloss.*, *Tas*, or *tarse*, a mow of corn.

**Tass** [2] (tæs). Now chiefly *Sc.* Forms: 5–9 **tasse, 6 tais, tas, 6– tass.** [a. OF. *tasse* goblet (1380 in Godef.), in mod.F. cup = Pr., Cat., med. L. *tassa* (1337 in Du Cange), Sp. *taza*, Pg. *taça*, It. *tazza*, app. a. Arab. طسّ, طسّة, *ṭass, ṭassah* basin, usually held to be ad. Pers. تست *tast* cup, goblet.] A cup or small goblet, esp. one of silver or the like; the contents of this; a small draught of liquor.

*c* **1483** Caxton *Dialogues* 21 Pawteners, tasses [Fr. *Aloyeres, tasses*], Coffyns and penners. **1513** Douglas *Æneis* xiii. ix. 25 The cowpis greit and drynkyn tassis fyne. **1549** *Compl. Scot.* xvii. 145 To drynk vattir..in ane glas, or in ane tasse of siluyr. **1583** *Leg. Bp. St. Androis* Pref. 136 We toome a tass of wyne. **1653** Urquhart *Rabelais* i. li, Great antick vessels, huge pots,..big tasses. **1725** Ramsay *Gentle Sheph.* iii. ii, Elspa, haste ye,...And fill him up a tass o' usquebæ. **1818** Scott *Rob Roy* xviii, A tass of brandy or aquavitæ, or sic-like creature comfort. *a* **1825** Forby *Voc. E. Anglia*, *Tass*, a dish or a dram; as a tass of tea, or a tass of brandy. **1859** Thackeray *Virgin.* liv, A little tass of Cherry-brandy! **1899** Crockett *Kit Kennedy* 321 Scottish stone-ale, 'virulent as a tass of raw brandy'.

**Tass**, obs. form of Tache *v.*[1], to stain.

**Tassago, tassajo**, var. Tasajo, dried meat.

**Tassal**, variant of Tassel *sb.*[2]

**Tassar**, var. Tusser, tussore, an Indian silk.

**Tasse** (tæs), *sb.*[1] *Obs.* exc. *Hist.* Only in pl. **tasses** (tæ·sėz), in 6 **taisses, 6–7 tases, taces, 7 taishes.** [In form the same word as OF. *tasse* purse, holster; in sense = F. *tassette*, obs. *tassete*, a small pocket or pouch, a steel plate intended to guard the thigh, dim. of *tasse*.

The connexion of sense is not clear; but cf. It. *scarsella* a pocket; *scarselloni* bases or tasses for a horseman (Florio 1611); Sp. *escarcela*, 'escarcelle, gibier, bourse; aussi la tassette' (Oudin 1660); *escarcela*, a satchel, pouch, or bag; the armour from the waist to the thighs (Stevens 1706).]

*pl.* A series of articulated splints or plates depending from the corslet, placed so that each slightly overlapped the one below it, forming a sort of kilt of armour to protect the thighs and the lower part of the trunk.

*a* **1548** Hall *Chron.*, *Hen. IV* 12 One company had..the tasses, the lamboys, the backpece, the tapull and the border of the curace all gylte. **1579–80** North *Plutarch* (1676) 212 Their legs were armed with Greaves, and their thighs with Tases. **1581** Styward *Mart. Discipl.* ii. 165 To haue good curates for their bodies, taces for their thighes. **1596** Warner *Alb. Eng.* xii. lxix. (1612) 291 The Taishes, Cushies, and the Graues, staffe, Pensell, baises. **1598** Barret *Theor. Warres* Gloss. 253 Taisses, a French word, and is the arming of the thighes, annexed vnto the forepart of the Corslet. **1688** R. Holme *Armoury* iii. xix. (Roxb.) 166/1 Armour for the thighes, of the French called Cuissets, and Taces or Tasses, because they are tached or tacked on with straps of leather to the corslett. **1869** Boutell *Arms & Arm.* x. (1874) 203 Below the waist, and there connected with the bottom of the breastplate, the body was protected by a series of narrow overlapping plates..denominated taces. **1888** F. Cowper *Capt. of Wight* (1889) 337 The taces of his armour had saved his thigh.

†**Tasse**, *sb.*[2] *Obs. rare*⁻¹. app. the same as Tassel *sb.*[1]: perh. an erroneous form.

**1570** Levins *Manip.* 34/33 Ye Tasse of a purse, *appendix.*

†**Tasse**, *v.* *Obs. rare*⁻¹. [a. OF. *tasser* (12th c. in Godef. *Compl.*), going with *tas, tasse* heap, Tass [1].] *trans.* To heap, pile.

*a* **1400** *Octouian* 695, I woll vpon thy body tasse [*rimes* masse, passe] Well many a dent.

**Tasse**, variant of Tass [2], a cup.

**Tassel** (tæ·s'l), *sb.*[1] Also 5 **tasshel, tasselle, 6–9 tassell, 7 tastle, tossell, 8 tossel** (also 9 *dial.*), **-il**, *Sc.* **taisel.** See also Tarsel. [a. OF. *tasel, tassel* clasp (*c* 1150 in Godef.): cf. It. *tassello* the collar of a cloak, a label; med.L. *tassellus, tacellus*: see Du Cange. Referred by Diez to L. *taxillus* small die (cf. next): but this is doubtful. The sense-development in Italian, French, and English has not been clearly made out: see Diez, Godefroy, Du Cange. The variant *tossel* (now *dial.*) suggests some association with Toss *v.*]

†**1.** A clasp or fibula by which the two sides of a cloak or the like are held together. *Obs.*

*a* **1300** *Cursor M.* 4389 He drou, sco held, þe tassel brak, Þe mantel left, he gafe þe bak. **13..** *Guy Warw.* (A.) 5736 Gij bi his mantel drouȝ so, Þat þe tassels brosten ato. *c* **1420** *Anturs of Arth.* xxviii. (Irel. MS.), Monli in his mantille he sate,..The tassellus were of topeus. [**1876** Planché *Cycl. Costume* I. 503 *Taselle, tasseau*, Fr...Also used for the clasp or fibula through which the cords passed which secured the mantle on the shoulder.]

**2.** A pendent ornament consisting of a bunch or thick fringe of threads or small cords hanging in a somewhat conical shape from a solid rounded knob or mould, or from a knot formed by their junction with a cord. Frequently attached to a curtain, cushion, walking-cane, umbrella, etc., or forming the pull of a blind-cord or bell-cord.

**13..** *Gaw. & Gr. Knt.* 219 A lace..Wyth tryed tasselez þerto tacched in-noghe. *c* **1440** *Promp. Parv.* 487/1 Tassel, *tassellus.* **1480** *Wardr. Acc. Edw. IV* (1830) 125 For the makyng of xvj laces and xvj tasshels for the garnyssh-ing of divers of the Kinges bookes. **1530** PALSGR. 279/2 Tassell that hangeth at a thyng of sylke or golde, *houppe doree.* **1590** SPENSER *F. Q.* I. viii. 3 An horne of bugle small, Which hong adowne his side in twisted gold And tasselles gay. **1624** CAPT. SMITH *Virginia* II. 35 All their tailes meete in the toppe of their head like a great Tassell. *a* **1625** FLETCHER *Nice Valour* II. i, And smile, and wave a chair with comely grace too, Play with our tastle gently. **1706** PHILLIPS (ed. 6), *Tassels of a Coach*, certain Silk-cords fasten'd on each Side the Doors, which serve for a Stay to those that ride in it. **1718** *Free-thinker* No. 44 ¶ 10 A young Damsel..tied a Gold Cord with two large Tossels of Gold to his Sword. **1755** *Connoisseur* No. 97 ¶ 1 The fellow-commoners, noblemen, and other rich students, whom ..the courtesy of the University [of Cambridge] has honoured with a cap adorned with a gold tossel. **1792** in *Hist. Broughton Place Ch. Edin.* (1872) 20 A' their taisels, vain an' gay To mak us stare. *a* **1815** in G. Rose *Diaries* (1860) II. 438 He put out his hand to pull the bell, but could not catch the tassel. **1849** LAYARD *Nineveh & Rem.* I. iii. 49 A knotted girdle, ending in tassels, encircled the loins. **1886** RUSKIN *Præterita* I. vii. 233 A cushion of crimson velvet.. with gold tassels at the corners.

†**b.** *Univ. slang.* One who wears a cap with a tassel; an undergraduate. Cf. TUFT. *Obs.*

**1828** *Sporting Mag.* XXI. 428 A capital front rank of 'tassells'..all eager for a 'slap at a snob'.

**3.** Anything resembling or suggesting a tassel: **a.** In a tree or plant, a pendent catkin, blossom, flower, or bud; *spec.* the staminate (terminal) inflorescence of the maize-plant (*U.S.*): see also *tassel-hyacinth* in 5.

**1646** WINTHROP *New-Eng.* (1826) II. 267 Great harm was done in corn..by a caterpillar...They eat up first the blades of the stalk, then..the tassels, whereupon the ear withered. **1755** *Gentl. Mag.* Sept. 408/2, I found a fine stalk of Indian corn..; I cut off the male tossil as soon as it appeared, and there was produced a large ear, but no good grains upon it. **1824** MISS MITFORD *Village* Ser. I. (1863) 61 In early spring, when the fragrant palms were on the willow, and the yellow tassels on the hazel. *a* **1835** MRS. HEMANS *Voice of Spring* iii, The larch has hung all his tassels forth. **1863** KINGSLEY *Water-Bab.* i. 15 The bird-cherry with its tassels of snow. **1894** E. EGGLESTON in *Century Mag.* Apr. 850 Our country people, when speaking of the male flower of the maize, preserve the broad vowel of their ancestors: 'tossell' it will remain in spite of the schoolmaster.

†**b.** A tuft; a fringe. *Obs.*

**1609** C. BUTLER *Fem. Mon.* i. (1623) B iij, Besides their Soueraigne, the Bees haue also subordinate Gouernours... For difference from the rest they beare for their crest a tuft or tossell, in some coloured yellow, in some murrey, in manner of a plume. **1672** JOSSELYN *New Eng. Rarities* 35 The other is nothing but Bones with Tassels hanging from their Jaws, with which they [whales] suck in their prey.

¶**4.** In med. (Anglo-) Latin, *tassellus* is given by Du Cange as used = *fimbria*, fringe of a cope or chasuble. Dr. Rock, *Church of our Fathers* (II. 32–), explains Du Cange's quots. otherwise, and holds that *tassellus* had the following uses: **a.** The large thin sheet of gold or silver hanging behind on the cope; **b.** Any piece of gold or silver plate fastened to a vestment (copes and chasubles having 'their *tasselli* sparkling with gems, hung all about them'); **c.** The ornaments on the back of episcopal gloves, when not done in embroidery, but made of silver or gold plate. By Dr. Rock himself, and some writers after him, the English word *tassel* has been used in senses b and c.

[*c* **1188** GERV. CANT. in Dugdale *Monast. Angl.* (1655) I. 21 Duas capas de pallio cum tassellis auro paratis. *c* **1250** MATT. PARIS *Vitæ Abb. S. Albani* (1639) 55 Capam unam purpuream, morsu et tassellis charissimis redimitam. *a* **1252** *Visit. Churches St. Paul's* 14 in *Camden Misc.* (1895) IX, Item capa chori crocea cum duobus tassellis brusdatis Majestate et Maria.] **1849** ROCK *Ch. our Fathers* II. 161 *note*, These tassels, as we said before, were thin plates of beaten gold or silver. **1887** *Archæologia* L. II. 448 Upon the 'tassels' of the cope of Richard Ruffus were depicted the martyrdoms of St. Stephen and St. Thomas.

**5.** *attrib.* and *Comb.*, as *tassel-board, -drop, -maker, -making*; *tassel-hung* adj.; **tassel-cock**, a game-cock which has a tuft of feathers in place of the comb; **tassel-corn**, (*U.S.*) the grain of maize borne abnormally on the 'tassel' (see 3 a); **tassel-fish**, an Australian fish, *Polynemus quadridactylus*, the pectoral fins of which terminate in a number of long threads; **tassel-flower**, (*a*) a tassel-like flower; *spec.* the orange, scarlet, or yellowish blossom of *Emilia sagittata* (*Cacalia coccinea*), N.O. *Compositæ*, or the plant itself; (*b*) a shrub or tree of the genus *Inga* (*Cent. Dict.* 1891); **tassel-grass**, (*a*) a grass or (?) sedge with pendent spicules; (*b*) *Ruppia maritima*, an aquatic herb of which the seed-vessels are borne on clusters of lengthened pedicels; **tassel-hyacinth**, *Muscari comosum*, the stalk and flower of which resemble a tassel; also called *purse-tassel*, *purple tassels* (Miller *Plant-n.* 1884); **tassel-pondweed** = *tassel-grass* (*b*) (ibid.); **tassel-stitch**, an embroidery stitch used in forming a fringe, loops of thread being left, which are afterwards cut; **tassel-tree** = TASSEL-BUSH (*Cent. Dict.* 1891); **tassel-worm**, a grub which feeds on the tassel of the maize-plant.

*a* **1639** SPOTTISWOOD *Hist. Ch. Scot.* VI. (1677) 407 Every Chair had a *Tassel-boord covered with fine Velvet. **1898** *Pall Mall G.* 3 Feb. 9/1 'Henny' cocks .. have won more battles..than any other birds, except it be the '*tassel' cock. **1883** E. L. STURTEVANT in *Science* I. 234/1 (Variability of Maize) *Tassel-corn,—some of the kernels heavily, others slightly husked. **1852** R. S. SURTEES *Sponge's Sp. Tour* (1893) 150 A chased and figured fine gold brooch, with two pendent *tassel-drops. **1898** MORRIS *Austral Eng.*, **Tassel-fish*, a thread-fish of Queensland, of the genus *Polynemus.* **1902** J. T. CRITCHELL in *Encycl. Brit.* XXXII. 110/2 Several species of the tassel fish (*Polynemus macrochoir*), from which isinglass is procured, have been taken by fishermen. **1885** G. ALLEN *Babylon* vi, Do you know the *tassel-flower? **1810** SOUTHEY *Kehama* XIII. xi, *Tassel-grass, whose silvery feathers play O'ertopping the young trees. **1861** MISS PRATT *Flower. Pl.* V. 336 Sea Ruppia or Tassel-grass..has slender, much-branched stems ..and long slender bristly leaves with sheaths. **1850** TENNYSON *In Mem.* cii, The low love-language of the bird In native hazels *tassel-hung. **1902** *Daily Chron.* 9 Sept. 3/6 A number of the *tassel-makers were independently interviewed in their own homes while at work...*Tassel-making is one of the three worst paid of the various home industries open to sweating. **1882** CAULFEILD & SAWARD *Dict. Needle-work* 194/2 **Tassel Stitch*, a stitch used to make a looped fringe as an edging to Embroideries.

**Tassel, torsel** (tæ·s'l, tǭ·s'l, tǭ·ɹs'l), *sb.*[2] *Arch.* Also 7–9 **tossel**, 9 **tassal**. [a. OF. *tassel*, mod.F. *tasseau*, = It. *tassello* a bit of stone or wood to stop a hole, :—L. *taxillus* a small die. The form *torsel* app. arises from workmen's lengthening of the vowel in *tossel.*] A short board or 'templet' placed under the end of a beam or other timber where it rests on brickwork or stonework.

**1632** in E. B. Jupp *Carpenters' Co.* (1887) 301 The making of all mantletrees tassels and footepaces of timber. **1654** *Ibid.* 316 That no Timber..be laid in Chimneys except the mantle trees Tassells and Discharges. **1667** PRIMATT *City & C. Build.* 82 Allow six foot of Timber for every Chimney, for Mantle-trees and Torsels. **1703** MOXON *Mech. Exerc.* 264 When you lay any Timber on Brick-work, as Torsels for Mantle-Trees to lye on. **1823** P. NICHOLSON *Pract. Build.* 595 *Torsel*, a piece of wood laid into a wall for the end of a timber or beam to rest on. **1842–76** GWILT *Archit.* Gloss., *Tassal*, *Tassel*, *Torsel*, or *Tossel*, the plate of timber for the end of a beam or of a joist to rest on.

**Tassel** (tæ·s'l), *v.* Also 4 **tassil**, 5 **tacel**, 8 **tassel**. [f. TASSEL *sb.*[1]]

**1.** *trans.* To furnish or adorn with or as with a tassel or tassels.

In *pa. pple.* in *Her.* indicating that the tassel or tassels are of a tincture different from that of the rest of the bearing.

? *a* **1366** CHAUCER *Rom. Rose* 1079 A robe..With orfrays leyd was everydel,.. And with a bend of gold tasseled. *c* **1386** — *Miller's T.* 65 By hir girdel heeng a purs of lether Tasseled with grene and perled with latoun. **14..** *Sir Beues* (MS. N.) 3777+7 Tacellid wiþ rosys off syluyr bry3t. **1572** BOSSEWELL *Armorie* II. 92 He beareth Argente, a pursse gules, doble tasseled d'azure. **1724** *Lond. Gaz.* No. 6290/2 A Velvet..Cushion edged and tasselled with Gold. **1894** *Blackw. Mag.* Sept. 317/2 The blond sallow tasselled itself with gold.

**2.** *intr.* Of maize and sugar-cane: To form 'tassels', to flower, bloom. Chiefly *U. S.*

**1785** WASHINGTON *Writ.* (1891) XII. 227 It [Indian corn] should be kept clean and well worked..till it shoots and tassels at least. **1881** NICHOLSON *Fr. Sword to Share* xxii. 153 Cane grew..almost everywhere..at altitudes up to 3,000 feet above sea-level, at half that height it ceased to blossom or tassel.

Hence **Ta·sselling, ta·sseling** *vbl. sb.* (also *concr.* work composed of tassels) and *ppl. a.*

**1829** *Anniversary, Beatrice* 232 She couches in the pleached bower Which tasselling honeysuckles deck. **1881** NICHOLSON *Fr. Sword to Share* xxix. 222 In November the cane tops will throw out a feathery, dove-coloured blossom, called tasselling. **1902** *Westm. Gaz.* 12 July 7/3 The sides of the stairs..are..finished off with gold tasselling.

**Tassel**, obs. form of TEASEL, TERCEL.

**Ta·sselated**, *ppl. a. rare*[−1]. [f. assumed vb. **tasselate* (f. TASSEL *sb.*[1] + -ATE[3]) + -ED[1]: cf. *tessellated, castellated, foliated*, etc.] = TASSELLED.

*c* **1860** B. HARTE *My Otherself* in *Fiddletown*, etc. (1873) 127 There was no rustle of the tasselated corn.

**Tassel-bush** (tæ·s'lbuʃ). [f. TASSEL *sb.*[1] + BUSH *sb.*[1]] The common name in America of an evergreen shrub, *Garrya elliptica*, a native of California, Mexico, Cuba, and Jamaica: so called from its elegant long drooping catkins.

**1891** in *Cent. Dict.* **1900** *Field* 22 Dec. 972/1 The Tassel Bush..is an evergreen bush from California, the tip of every young growth being now laden with clusters, or bunches of soft-grey tassels or catkins, that give to it a very distinct and ornate appearance.

**Tasselet** (tæ·sělět, -ět). [f. TASSEL *sb.*[1] + -ET.] A diminutive tassel.

**1577** HARRISON *England* II. v. (1877) I. 121 Two mantels.. with laces, tasselets, and knops of blue silk.

**Tassel-gentle, tassel-hawk**: see TERCEL.

**Tassell**, obs. form of TEASEL, TERCEL.

**Tasselled, -eled** (tæ·s'ld), *ppl. a.* [f. TASSEL *sb.*[1] or *v.* + -ED.] **a.** Furnished or adorned with or as with a tassel or tassels; of a person, wearing a tassel or tassels. **b.** Formed into, or resembling in some way, a tassel or tassels; of a fern, having divisions like tassels at the apex of each frond.

**a.** **1611** COTGR., *Houpé*..tufted, or tasselled. *c* **1633** MILTON *Arcades* 57 Ere the..tasselld horn Shakes the high thicket, haste I all about. **1784** COWPER *Task* II. 749 The tasseled cap and the spruce band. **1808** SKURRAY *Bidcombe Hill* 49 Not long ago, on Cherwell's banks we rov'd, Link'd arm in arm, like other tassell'd youths. **1841–4** EMERSON *Ess.* Ser. I. xi. (1876) 263 You shall still see..the tasselled grass, or the corn-flags.

**b.** **1882** *Garden* 29 Apr. 301/3 A very elegant Hare's-foot Fern, having the long graceful fronds tasselled at the tips.

**Tasseller, -eler** (tæ·sĕləɹ, tæ·s'ləɹ). [f. TASSEL *v.* + -ER[1]; cf. OF. *taseleor.*]

†**1.** One who makes tassels. *Obs. rare.*

**1301** *Rolls of Parlt.* I. 248/2 Matilda la Taselere. *Ibid.* 255/2 Gilbert le Tanselere.

**2.** One who wears a cap with a tassel; †*gold tasseller*, a nobleman who is a member of a university, distinguished by his academic cap having a tassel of gold thread: cf. TASSEL *sb.*[1] 2, quot. 1755.

**1846** LANDOR *Citation Shaks.* Wks. II. 285/2 The worst question to any gold tasseller is, 'How do you do?'

**Ta·sselly, -ely**, *a.* [f. TASSEL *sb.*[1] + -Y.] Characterized by or abounding in tassels.

**1611** COTGR., *Houpelu*..lockie, tassellie, tufted. **1901** *Elizabeth & Germ. Gard.* 164 Four little podgy, buttony, tasselly red chairs.

**Tasset.** *Archæol.* Only in pl. **tassets** (tæ·sěts). [ad. F. *tassette*, in OF. *tassete*: see TASSE *sb.*[1]]

In *pl.* = *tasses*: see TASSE *sb.*[1] (App. only in recent archæological or romantic use.)

**1834** PLANCHÉ *Brit. Costume* 241 Tassets and cuishes, composed of several plates instead of one, are seen upon the thigh. **1872** LONGF. *Wayside Inn* III. *Charlemagne* 49 His greaves And tassets were of iron. **1876** H. AINSWORTH *Leaguer of Lathom* (1878) 32 Both were accoutred in steel breastplates and tassets.

‖ **Tassette** (tæse·t). [Fr. dim. of *tasse*, TASS[2]: see -ET.] A small pointed infusible earthenware cone, used in sets of three to support objects in a kiln or muffle, in place of a stilt or triangle.

**1891** in *Cent. Dict.*

**Tasshel**, obs. form of TASSEL *sb.*[1]

**Tassie** (tæ·si). *Sc.* [dim. of TASS[2]: see -IE.] A small cup or 'tass'.

**17..** *Homely Ballad* (in *Burns' Poems* (1834) II. 229 *note*), Ye'll bring me here a pint of wine, A server and a silver tassie. **1788** BURNS *My Bonie Mary* i. *a* **1810** in Cromek *Rem. Nithsdale Song* 94 But here's my Jean's health i' the siller-lipped-tassie!

**Tassil, -ill**, obs. forms of TEASEL, TERCEL.

**Tastable**: see TASTEABLE.

**Taste** (tēɪst), *sb.*[1] Forms: 4–8 **tast**, 4–5 **taast**, 4–6 (*Sc.* –7) **taist**, (6 *Sc.* **test**), 5– **taste**. [a. OF. *tast* touching, touch, = It. *tasto* a feeling, a touch, a trial, a taste (Florio); f. OF. *taster* (mod. F. *tâter*), It. *tastare*: see TASTE *v.* Cf. also OF. *taste*, It. *tasta*, a surgical probe.]

**I.** †**1.** The sense of touch, feeling (with the hands, etc.); the act of touching, touch. *Obs.*

[**1292** BRITTON III. ii. § 13 Et puis soynt chargez qe eles.. enquergent de la femme qe se fet enceynte par tast de soen ventre et de ses mameles.] **13..** *Cursor M.* 542 (Cott.) Þis vnder wynd him gis his aand, þe erth þe tast, to fele and faand. **1422** tr. *Secreta Secret.*, *Priv. Priv.* 208 The taste is a commyn witte, Spraden throgh the body, but hit Shewyth hym most by the handys..; by that witte we knowen hote, colde, dry, moyste, and other Suche thynges. *c* **1430** *Pilgr. Lyf Manhode* I. lxxii. (1869) 42 At the taast, and at the sighte, at the smellinge, and at the sauouringe, bred and wyn it may seeme.

†**2.** A trying, testing; a trial, test, examination.

**1377** LANGL. *P. Pl.* B. XII. 131 Kynde witte cometh of alkynnes si3tes,..of tastes of treuthe, and of deceytes. **1586–7** Q. ELIZ. in *Four C. Eng. Lett.* (1880) 30 To make tast of the greatest witz amongs my owne, and then of French and last of you. **1605** SHAKS. *Lear* I. ii. 47, I hope for my Brothers iustification, hee wrote this but as an essay, or taste of my Vertue. **1663** *Flagellum, or O. Cromwell* (1672) 155 To appoint a Tast or Recognition of the Government.

†**b.** A trial, an attempt. *Obs. rare*[−1].

*c* **1330** R. BRUNNE *Chron. Wace* (Rolls) 5400 He wende haue taken þe toun in hast, Bot he failled of his tast.

**II.** †**3.** The act of tasting, or perceiving the flavour of a thing with the organ of taste (sense 4); the fact of being tasted. *Obs.*

**13..** *Coer de L.* 3075 When he has a good tast, And eeten weel a good repast. **1340–70** *Alex. & Dind.* 357 Þere-of we taken a tast what time þat vs nedeþ. **1393** LANGL. *P. Pl.* C. I. 228 Tauerners 'a tast for nouht' tolden þe same. **1579** LYLY *Euphues* (Arb.) 176 For before the tast of the Gospel I was worse then a beast. **1592** SHAKS. *Rom. & Jul.* II. vi. 13 The sweetest honey Is loathsome in his owne deliciousnesse, And in the taste confoundes the appetite. **1667** MILTON *P. L.* I. 2 The Fruit Of that Forbidden Tree, whose mortal tast Brought Death into the World, and all our woe. **1766** ENTICK *London* IV. 367 They obtained a grant of..the taste and assize of bread.

**b.** *transf.* The means of tasting; hence, such a small quantity as admits of being tasted; a very small quantity (esp. of alcoholic drink), a sip.

**1530** in W. H. Turner *Select. Rec. Oxford* (1880) 91 He sent for the tast of wyne..dew to him of every hoggshed.

15.. *Aberdeen Reg.* (Jam.), And send one taist of the wyne to the yerll of Rothes. 1723 S. Sewall *Diary* 4 Apr., My wife sent them a Taste of her Dinner. 1888 'R. Boldrewood' *Robbery under Arms* xxxviii, Bring me a taste of grog, will ye? 1904 in *Eng. Dial. Dict.* [from Scotl., Irel., N. Engl.].

**c.** *fig.* A slight experience, received or given; a slight show or sample *of* any condition or quality.

1390 Gower *Conf.* II. 373 Whanne I beclippe hire on the wast, Yit ate leste I stele a tast. 1526 *Pilgr. Perf.* (W. de W. 1531) 234 That is none other thynge but a taste how swete our lord Jesu is. 1586 Day *Eng. Secretary* I. (1625) A ij b, Socrates in his cradle had no taste of his after-wisedome. c1595 Capt. Wyatt *R. Dudley's Voy. W. Ind.* (Hakl. Soc.) 40 Most of them havinge some little tast of the Spanish tounge. 1669 Penn *No Cross* xxi. § 39 A soul Mortified to the World, and quickned to some Tasts of a Supernatural Life. 1825 Lamb *Elia* Ser. II. *Superannuated Man*, Where was..the promised rest? Before I had a taste of it, it was banished. 1897 A. Morrison *Dorrington Deed-box* i, My first taste of grouse-shooting was a complete success.

**d.** *A taste* (advb.): *colloq.* to a small but perceptible degree; slightly; a little. Cf. Bit *sb.*[2] 5.

1894 Hall Caine *Manxman* I. v, Aisy! Your legs a taste higher, sir, just to keep the pickle off your trousers. *Ibid.* III. xii, 'Nancy will tidy the room a taste', she said coaxingly.

**4.** The faculty or sense by which that particular quality of a thing described in 5 is discerned, the organs of which are situated chiefly in the mouth; one of the five bodily senses.

c1380 Wyclif *Serm.* Sel. Wks. I. 87 Whan þer tast is freishe, for to juge þe goodnesse, and after whan þei ben drunken and þer taist failiþ, þanne he puttiþ wers wyn. c1394 *P. Pl. Crede* 537 Þanne haue y tynt all my tast touche and assaie! 1398 Trevisa *Barth. De P. R.* III. xx. (1495) d vj b/2, The taast is a wytte of knowynge sauours. 1587 Mascall *Govt. Cattle, Horses* (1627) 111 Sometimes a horse will loose his tast, which commeth of sorrow. 1600 Shaks. *A. Y. L.* II. vii. 166 Second childishnesse, and meere obliuion, Sans teeth, sans eyes, sans taste, sans euery thing. 1680 Morden *Geog. Rect., Germany* (1685) 119 Fruits more pleasant to the sight or tast. 1861 Hulme tr. *Moquin-Tandon* II. I. 49 Taste is a species of touch of still more delicate character. 1884 *Cornh. Mag.* Dec. 620 Taste..is not equally distributed over the whole surface of the tongue alike.

**b.** *Out of taste*, not able to distinguish flavours.

a1541 Wyatt *Sonnets* xviii, And if I have, after such bitterness, One drop of sweet, my mouth is out of taste. 1646 Jenkyn *Remora* 20 The palat..is put out of taste. 1729 Swift *Direct. Servants, Footman* ¶ 28 Your mistress will confess that her mouth is out of taste.

**5.** That quality or property of a body or substance which is perceived when it is brought into contact with certain organs of the mouth, etc., esp. the tongue; savour, sapidity; the particular sensation excited by anything in this manner.

1382 Wyclif *Jer.* xlviii. 11 Therfore abod stille his tast in hym, and his smel is not chaungid. c1400 Maundev. (1839) xxvii. 273 Full gode fissch..of right goode tast. c1430 Lydg. *Min. Poems* (Percy Soc.) 15 Damysyns wiche withe her taste delyte. 1535 Coverdale *Wisd.* xvi. 2 A new & straunge taist. 1594 Plat *Jewell-ho.* II. 11 A far more liuely & penetratiue tast. 1605 Timme *Quersit.* I. v. 19 Diuers kindes of saltes..haue diuers tastes. 1702 J. Purcell *Cholick* (1714) 87 The acid Taste of this Recrement, and its coagulating of Milk, are undoubted. 1800 tr. *Lagrange's Chem.* II. 74 Iron..has a styptic taste, very sensible. 1857 Miller *Elem. Chem.* (1862) III. 161 Sometimes a wine acquires a peculiar flavour known as the 'taste of the cask'.

*fig.* 14.. Hoccleve *Compl. Virgin* 213 Ther-in fynde I a bittir taast; For now the taast I feele & the streynynge Of deeth. 1579 Lyly *Euphues* (Arb.) 176 How comfortable is the feeling and tast of grace. 1605 Shaks. *Macb.* V. v. 9, I haue almost forgot the taste of Feares. 1720 Mrs. Manley *Power of Love* (1741) III. 187 All the Favours upon Earth, from the greatest Beauties could have no Taste for Roderigo. 1904 *Daily News* 14 Dec. 5 The poems leave a nasty taste in the mouth; the taste of a snarl and a sneer.

**†b.** Odour, scent, smell. *Obs.*

c1400 *Destr. Troy* 1668 Þat smelt is & smethe, smellis full swete, With taste for to touche the tabull aboute. ?c1475 *Sqr. lowe Degre* 850 Frankensence and olibanum That whan ye slepe the taste may come.

**III. †6.** Mental perception of quality; judgement, discriminative faculty. *Obs.* exc. as in 8.

13.. *Cursor M.* 11327 (Cott.) Þis symeon þat had his tast Toched o þe hali gast. a1425 *Ibid.* 18889 (Trin.) Þe salmes seiþ bi good taast His wonynge shulde be wilde & waast. 1502 Atkynson tr. *De Imitatione* I. xxii. 171 Thou hast no spirituall tast. 1692 Dryden *St. Euremont's Ess.* 350 If so be they demand of me..more than discretion in Commerce, and a taste in Confidence.

**7.** The fact or condition of liking or preferring something; inclination, liking *for*; † appreciation.

c1477 Caxton *Jason* 72 Therfore wille thou..employ thy corage after the taste of our desires. 1552 *Godly Prayers* in *Liturg. Serv. Q. Eliz.* (1847) 253 That we..may have some taste and feeling for it in our hearts. ?c1580 T. Hacket *Treas. Amadis* 236 She hath somewhat a regarde to things that are agaynst my owne taste. 1635 N. R. *Camden's Hist. Eliz.* II. 153 From the time that I had any tast of Religion. 1711 Addison *Spect.* No. 93 ¶ 13 A Man that has a Taste of Musick, Painting, or Architecture. 1727 Pope, etc. *Art of Sinking* 73 The taste of the bathos is implanted by nature itself in the soul of man. 1728 Swift *Intelligencer* No. 3 ¶ 3 Whoever hath a taste for true humour. 1791 Mrs. Inchbald *Simp. Story* III. v. 70 She had acquired a taste for those amusements. 1838 Lytton *Alice* I. ix, The other girl is more amusing, more to my taste. 1880 L. Stephen *Pope* iv. 86 Every opportunity for the indulgence of his favourite tastes.

**† b.** Enjoyment, pleasure, 'relish'. Const. *in*, *of*.

1604 E. G[rimstone] *D'Acosta's Hist. Indies* III. ix. 150 He found not in himselfe any disposition to goe to any other place, nor to take any taste in any thing. a1716 Blackall *Wks.* (1723) I. 15 The Happiness of a Man's life consists not in the Abundance of the things that he possesses..But in the taste and relish that he has of them.

**c.** *transf.* The object of one's liking or preference.

1739 G. Stone in *Buccleuch MSS.* (Hist. MSS. Comm.) I. 392 White beauties..are the taste of the Irish nation.

**8.** The sense of what is appropriate, harmonious, or beautiful; *esp.* discernment and appreciation of the beautiful in nature or art; *spec.* the faculty of perceiving and enjoying what is excellent in art, literature, and the like.

1671 Milton *P. R.* IV. 347 Sion's songs, to all true tasts excelling Where God is prais'd aright. 1694 Congreve *Double Dealer* I. ii, No, no, hang him, he has no Taste. 1712 Addison *Spect.* No. 409 ¶ 1 Rules..how we may acquire that fine Taste of Writing, which is so much talked of among the Polite World. 1768 W. Gilpin *Ess. Prints* 160 There is a fine taste in his landskips. 1776 Sir J. Reynolds *Disc. Art* (1778) 311, I have mentioned taste in dress, which is certainly one of the lowest subjects to which this word is applied. 1784 J. Barry in *Lect. Paint.* ii. (1848) 108 The word Taste, as applied to objects of vision,..means..that quick discerning faculty or power of the mind by which we accurately distinguish the good, bad, or indifferent. a1834 Coleridge *Treat. Method* i. (1849) 16 A fine Musical taste is soon dissatisfied with the Harmonica, or any similar instrument of glass or steel. 1835 Ure *Philos. Manuf.* 254 Taste is displayed both in the forms and grouping of the figures, and the disposition of the colours. 1850 W. Irving *Goldsmith* xxvii. 268 The latter part of the year 1768 had been made memorable in the world of taste by the institution of the Royal Academy of Arts. 1872 Minto *Eng. Prose Lit.* Introd. 29 The word *taste*..in its wider sense is equivalent to artistic sensibility,..in its narrower sense it may be expressed as artistic judgment.

**b.** Style or manner exhibiting æsthetic discernment; good or bad æsthetic quality; the style or manner favoured in any age or country.

1739 Labelye *Short Acc. Piers Westm. Br.* 44 The People who design'd and executed London-Bridge, and other Bridges in the same Taste. 1755 *Compl. Lett.-writer* (1759) 227 Her own old-fashioned breast-plate in the taste of the last century. 1819 Scott *Ivanhoe* xxviii, A rich habit, which partook more of the Eastern taste than that of Europe. 1826 Disraeli *Viv. Grey* II. xii, Nothing could be more moderate, or, as Miss Gusset said, 'in better taste'. 1843 Borrow *Bible in Spain* xxxvi. (Pelh. Libr.) 256 It was..built something in the Moorish taste.

**IV. 9.** *attrib.* and *Comb.*, as *taste-area*, *-centre*, *-fibre*, *-meter*; *taste-pleasing* adj.; **taste-beaker, -bud, -bulb, -goblet,** one of the flask-shaped bodies in the epithelium of the tongue, believed to be organs of taste; **taste-cell**: see quot.; **taste-corpuscle** = *taste-cell*; **taste-cup, -pit,** one of the minute pits found on the epipharynx of an insect, having in the centre a peg, the termination of a nerve; **taste-hair,** one of the setæ or bristles, near the mouth of an insect or other arthropod, supposed to be organs of taste; **† taste-paper,** in the (old) Greats examination at Oxford, the paper in which passages were set from the classical authors for critical and exegetical treatment.

1901 E. B. Titchener *Exper. Psychol.* I. iv. 64 Each papilla carries a number of *taste-beakers, clusters of taste-cells and supporting cells, which constitute the specific end-organs of taste. 1883 *Science* I. 232/2 The *taste-bulbs, numbering 700 or more, lying in the papillary wall of the valla. 1888 J. G. M'Kendrick in *Encycl. Brit.* XXIII. 79/2 The terminal organs of taste consist of peculiar bodies named taste-bulbs or taste-goblets. 1890 Billings *Nat. Med. Dict.* s.v. *Taste*, **Taste-cells*, spindle-shaped or staff-shaped cells in the interior of the taste-bulbs. 1891 *Cent. Dict.*, **Taste-center*, the gustatory nervous center, located by Ferrier in the gyrus uncinatus of the brain. 1898 Packard *Text-bk. Entomol.* 45 The structure and armature of the epipharyngeal surface even besides the *taste-pits, *taste-cups, and rods, is very varied. 1899 *Allbutt's Syst. Med.* VI. 793 Whether the *taste-fibres pass by the second or third divisions of the nerve. 1905 *Jrnl. R. Micros. Soc.* Apr. 180 *Taste-hairs, homologous with Kræpelin's taste-hairs in Muscidæ, are found in various orders of insects. 1814 Coleridge in Cottle *Remin.* (1837) II. 211 This *taste-meter to the fashionable world, gives a ludicrous portrait of an African belle. 1860 Hughes *Tom Brown at Oxf.* xxiv, In the *taste paper.., as they compare notes, he seems to have almost struck the bull's eye in his answers. 1898 *Taste-pit [see *taste-cup*]. a1586 Sidney *Arcadia* I. (1622) 8 A place cunningly set with trees of the most *tast-pleasing fruits.

**Taste** (tēist), *sb.*[2] *U. S. local.* [Origin unascertained.] A kind of narrow thin silk ribbon used for edge-binding: now commonly called taffeta-binding. See also Wire-*taste*.

1847 in Webster. a1889 F. A. P. Barnard in *New Haven* (Conn.) *Palladium* 18 Apr., If..Mrs. S. has any taste she will oblige me by sending me half a yard, no matter of what color, so it be not black.

**Taste** (tēist), *v.* Forms: 3–5 **tasten,** (3 **tasti,** 4 **tasty, taaste,** 4–6 **taast,** 4–8 **tast,** 4–7 **taist,** 6 *Sc.* **test,** 7 **teast),** 4– **taste.** [ME. *tasten*, a. OF. *tast-er* to touch, feel (12th c.), in 13–14th c. also to taste, mod.F. *tâter* to feel, touch, try, taste, = Pr., OSp. *tastar*, It. *tastare* to feel, handle, touch, grope for, try (Florio):—Com. Romanic or late pop.L. **tastare*, app. from **taxtāre* :—**taxitāre*, freq. of *taxāre* to touch, feel, handle (Gellius, etc.): see Tax *v.*]

**I.** Of touch, feeling, or experience generally.

**† 1.** *trans.* To try, examine, or explore by touch; to feel; to handle. *Obs.*

c1290 *St. Michael* 312 in *S. Eng. Leg.* I. 308 With þat finguer he wole hit tasti ȝif it is a-riȝt i-wrouȝt. c1330 R. Brunne *Chron. Wace* (Rolls) 9011 He tasted his pous,..He seide he knew his medycyn. c1330 *Amis & Amil.* 1401 Leches..That gun to tasty his wounde. 1390 Gower *Conf.* III. 315 This noble clerk, with alle haste Began the veines forto taste. 1480 Caxton *Ovid's Met.* x. vii, She toke hardynes for the derknes, and tasted the waye on the ryght side & lyft. 1525 Ld. Berners *Froiss.* II. xxxviii. 115 The men of armes entre into the dykes,..and tasted the dyke with their speares, and passed ouer to the fote of the wall. 1648 Crashaw *Delights Muses, Music's Duel* 112 With a quiv'ring coynesse tasts the strings.

**† b.** *intr.* To feel, touch; to grope. *Obs.*

1377 Langl. *P. Pl.* B. xvii. 147 Þe fyngres..Bitokneth sothly þe sone..Þat toched and tasted atte techynge of þe paume. c1450 *Merlin* xxxiii. 681 She be-gan to taste softly till he fill on slepe. 1481 Caxton *Reynard* xii. (Arb.) 27 Isegrym..crope a lityl in, and tasted here and there, and at laste he sayde..what I seche I fynde not. 1483 — *G. de la Tour* F ij b, He tasted aboute & founde well that the dede was trewe.

**† c.** *trans.* To come into contact with, to touch.

1634 Sir T. Herbert *Trav.* 18 Such as haue the Scuruy..so soone as they taste the shore..eat three-leafed-grasse.

**† 2.** *trans.* To put to the proof; to try, test. *Obs.*

13.. *Cursor M.* 12934 (Gött.) Þe warlou wili..wold him tast wid sin, To witt if he had part him in. c1450 Lovelich *Grail* lii. 603 He lyht Adown..and tasted his harneis In that stede, þat it scholde not faille whanne he hadd nede. 1585–6 Sir T. Sherley in *Leycester Corr.* (Camden) 174, I thowght to tast her affectyon unto your lordship. 1615 Chapman *Odyss.* xxi. 211 And he now began To taste the bow. 1670 Cotton *Espernon* II. v. 206 Him he first tasted by Lafin, the same who had made himself a Mediator betwixt the Duke of Espernon and l'Esdiguieres in Provence.

**b.** *spec.*: see quots.

1711 W. Sutherland *Shipbuild. Assist.* 164 *Tasting of Plank or Timber*, chipping of it with an Addice to try the Defects. c1850 *Rudim. Navig.* (Weale) 155 *Tasting of plank or timber*, chipping it with an adze, or boring it with a small augur, for the purpose of ascertaining its quality.

**† c.** To attempt, try *to do* something. *Obs. rare.*

c1330 R. Brunne *Chron. Wace* (Rolls) 13834 On many manere ilk oþer tasted Ilk oþer to slo, ilk oþer to wounde. c1450 *Merlin* xxxii. 649 He caste a-wey his clubbe and tasted to chacche the kynge in his armes.

**3.** *fig.* To have experience or knowledge of; to experience, feel; to have a slight experience of.

Often (in later use perh. always) *fig.* from 4.

a1300 *Cursor M.* 18940 Als gaf to þaim þe haligast Alkin wiit to tuche and tast. c1380 Wyclif *Serm.* Sel. Wks. I. 126 He shal not taaste þe longe deþ. 1576 Fleming *Panopl. Epist.* 35 In ciuil commotions all thinges are miserable:..this our present age also hath oftentimes tasted. 1630 *R. Johnson's Kingd. & Commw.* 138 [The Gaules] who from Caesars time till then, had not tasted the force of a forren power. 1693 *Humours Town* A ij b, You have tasted the Pleasures of the Town. 1717 Ockley in *Lett. Lit. Men* (Camden) 353, I enjoy more repose here than I have tasted these many years. 1864 Burton *Scot Abr.* I. iv. 207 John Knox, who was just returned from tasting the tender mercies of France as a galley-slave.

**† b.** To have carnal knowledge of. *Obs.*

1611 Shaks. *Cymb.* II. iv. 57 If you can mak't apparant That you have tasted her in Bed; my hand, And Ring is yours. a1639 T. Carew *Poems* (1651) 32 So shalt thou be despis'd, fair Maid, When by the sated lover tasted. 1752 Young *Brothers* IV. i, What, see, talk, touch, nay taste her!

**II.** Of the special sense that resides in the tongue and palate.

**4.** *trans.* To perceive by the sense of taste; to perceive or experience the taste or flavour of.

1340–70 *Alex. & Dind.* 952 In menskinge of mouþ mirþe we hauen, In tendere touchinge of þing, & tastinge of swete. c1375 *Cursor M.* 23456 (Fairf.) In þis werlde has men liking..squete spiceri to tast [*Cott.* fell] & smelle. c1430 Lydg. *Min. Poems* 14 Wellys most holsom of savour, For to be tasted of every governour. c1440 *Promp. Parv.* 487/1 Taastyn, *gusto*. 1535 Coverdale 2 *Sam.* xix. 35 This daye am I foure score yeare olde. How shulde I..taist what I eate or drynke? 1592 Shaks. *Rom. & Jul.* I. iii. 30 When it did tast the Worme-wood. 1774 Goldsm. *Nat. Hist.* (1776) VI. 242 When once it has tasted human flesh, it never desists from haunting those places where it expects the return of its prey. 1909 *Daily Chron.* 17 Nov. 8/4 She said the smells were so bad that they could be tasted as well as smelt.

**† b.** *fig.* To perceive or recognize as by the sense of taste. *Obs.*

1583 Babington *Commandm.* i. 10 Euen a world it is to see how all, as dead, doo tast no sinne in it. 1591 Harington *Orl. Fur.* Pref. ¶ viij b, Three syllabled wordes..which who mislike, may tast lamp oyle with their eares. 1616 B. Jonson *Devil an Ass* I. vi, Nay, then I taste a Trick in 't.

**c.** *absol.* or *intr.* To experience or distinguish flavours; to have or exercise the sense of taste.

1387 Trevisa *Higden* (Rolls) II. 181 Þey..mowe noþer see ne hire, ne taste, ne smelle. c1560 A. Scott *Poems* (S. T. S.) xxxi. 18 No wit salbe degest, To heir, se, smell, nor test. 1601 Shaks. *Twel. N.* I. v. 98 O, you are sicke of selfe-loue, Maluolio, and taste with a distemper'd appetite. *Mod.* I have got a very bad cold, and can neither taste nor smell.

**5.** *transf.* (*trans.*) To perceive by some other sense, esp. smell. Now only *poet.* or *dial.*

1656 Earl Monm. *Advt. fr. Parnass.* 380 Would you have men taste the odoriferousness of those Aromaticks which you ..have brought from the Indies? 1674 Ray *N. C. Words*, To *Tast*; i. e. to smell in the North. 1796 Pegge *Derbicisms* (E.D.S.), *Taste*, to smell, in the North. See Ray. You commonly ask a person to *taste* your snuff. 1819 Keats *Isabella* ix, I must taste the blossoms that unfold In its ripe warmth this gracious morning time. 1844 Kinglake *Eothen* ii. (1878) 25 To taste the cold breath of the earliest morn.

**6.** To try the flavour or quality of by the sense of taste; to put a small quantity of (something) into the mouth in order to ascertain the flavour, etc.; *spec.* to test the quality of by tasting, for trade purposes. Also *absol.*

*a* **1300** *Cursor M.* 13403 (Cott.) Þai fild a cupp þan son in hast, And gaf it þe architricline to tast. *Ibid.* 16773 (Gött.) Þat bitter drinc..He tasted it, bot noght he dranc. **1388** WYCLIF *Rom.* xi. 16 If a litil part of that that is tastid be hooli, the hool gobet is hooli. **1535** COVERDALE *Job* xxxiv. 3 For like as the mouth tasteth [1382 WYCLIF bi tast demeth] the meates, so the eare proueth & discerneth the wordes. **1552** HULOET, Taste afore or fyrste, *prolibo.* **1604** in *Eng. Gilds* (1870) 435 The ale teaster to teast the ale before they sell it. **1769** COOK *Voy. round World* I. iii. (1773) 44 Having tasted the liquor, they returned it, with strong expressions of disgust. **1837** WHITTOCK, etc. *Bk. Trades* (1842) 441 This system of tasting constitutes the acme of the great Teaman's trade.

**b.** *intr.* with *of*: see 12 a.

**c.** *spec.* (*trans.*) To test or certify the wholesomeness of (food provided) by tasting it; also *absol.* to act as taster *to* a person. Also *fig.*

**1595** SHAKS. *John* v. vi. 28 How did he take it [poison]? Who did taste to him? **1600** J. PORY tr. *Leo's Africa* Introd. 32 He [the emperor] is tasted vnto, not before, but after he hath eaten and drunke. **1678** DRYDEN *All for Love* I. i. 15 Thou and I, Like Time and Death, marching before our Troops, May taste fate to e'm; Mowe e'm out a passage. **1682** SOUTHERNE *Loyal Brother* I. i, True, I make bold To taste their letters to 'em, as they pass Through my Employment.

**d.** *fig.* To make trial of as by the sense of taste; to try the quality of. Also with *obj. cl.*, and *absol.* or *intr.* Cf. sense 2.

**1382** WYCLIF *Ps.* xxxiii. 9 [xxxiv. 8] Tastith, and seeth, for sweete is the Lord. **1390** GOWER *Conf.* II. 395 Mi fader, nay; bot I have tasted In many a place as I have go, And yit love I nevere on of tho. **1597** MORLEY *Introd. Musicke* Annot., Who hath tasted the firste elements of musicke. **1601** B. JONSON *Poetaster* v. iii, Then come home, And taste a piece of Terence. **1819** KEATS *Isabella* xlix, O turn thee to the very tale, And taste the music of that vision pale. **1896** MRS. CAFFYN *Quaker Grandmother* 294 She waited breathlessly to taste the quality of her mercy.

**7.** To have or take a taste of (food or drink); to take only as much as is sufficient to try or perceive the taste of, to eat or drink a little; but often by meiosis, simply for 'eat' or 'drink'. Negatively, *not to taste* = not even to taste, not to eat or drink at all. Also *fig.* to get a 'taste' of.

*a* **1300** *Cursor M.* 12559 (Cott.) Noþer durst þai drinc ne ete, Ne brek þair brede, ne tast þair mes Til he war cummen til þair des. **1382** WYCLIF *Luke* xiv. 24, I seie to ȝou, for noone of tho men that ben clepid, schal taaste my souper. **1596** DALRYMPLE tr. *Leslie's Hist. Scot.* (S. T. S.) I. 69 Of mony things we sal taist a few as we may. **1624** QUARLES *Job* xi. Medit. 35 Wisdom digests, what knowledge did but tast. **1653** WALTON *Angler* i. 2, I often..taste a cup of Ale there. **1700** ASTRY tr. *Saavedra-Faxardo* I. 31 It will suffice therefore for a Prince to tast the Arts and Sciences. **1754** GRAY *Pleasure* 60 She eyes the clear crystalline well [of Pleasure], And tastes it as it goes. **1853** KINGSLEY *Hypatia* x, He had tasted no food since noon the day before.

**b.** *absol.* or *intr.* ellipt. for 'taste wine or alcoholic drink'; to take a little drink. *Sc.*

**1823** GALT *R. Gilhaize* v. (E.D.D.), He pressed my grandfather to taste. **1901** S. MACNAUGHTON *Fortune of Chr. M'Nab* ii, 'Thank you', said Christina, 'I do not taste'. *Mod. Sc.* Will you not taste? Do you never taste?

**8.** To like the taste of (usually *fig.*); to relish, approve of, enjoy, like, take pleasure in; in earlier use sometimes in neutral sense: to appreciate. Now *arch.* or *dial.*

**1605** EARL OF SALISBURY in *Buccleuch MSS.* (Hist. MSS. Comm.) 81 This [proposal] was at first but little tasted by them. *a* **1617** BAYNE *On Eph. i.* (1634) 244 Many.. taste their pottage, like Esau, better than their birthright. **1624** BEDELL *Lett.* iv. 81 A more sensible proofe how the Pope tastes these Titles. **1751** CHATHAM *Lett. Nephew* ii. 6, I hope you love and taste those authors [Homer and Vergil] particularly. **1768** EARL HARDWICKE *Let.* 17 May, The king seemed to taste the Duke of Grafton, and commended his parts. **1791** BOSWELL *Johnson* 2 Apr. an. 1775, If I wondered at Johnson not tasting the works of Mason and Gray, still more have I wondered at their not tasting his works. **1805** MRS. R. TRENCH in *Rem.* (1862) 170 Mad. de Sévigné, whom for the first time I really taste and admire. **1879** GEO. ELIOT *Theo. Such* i. 10 The work..I am told is much tasted in a Cherokee translation. **1896** 'IAN MACLAREN' *Kate Carnegie* 33 The story was much tasted by our guard's admirers.

**9.** *intr.* Of a substance: To have a taste of a specified or implied kind; to produce a certain taste in the mouth; to have a taste or flavour *of.*

**1552** HULOET, Tastynge or castynge an yll taste or sauoure, *virosus.* **1615** G. SANDYS *Trav.* 66 Blacke as soote and tasting not much unlike it. **1653** WALTON *Angler* iii. 73 It looks well, and tastes well. **1655** FULLER *Ch. Hist.* I. ii. § 11 This new Wine, put into old Vessels, did in after-Ages taste of the Caske. **1681** CHETHAM *Angler's Vade-m.* xxxix. § 1 (1689) 253 It will make him to tast very sour. **1729** SWIFT *Direct. Servants, Cook* ⁋ 26 If your butter tastes of brass, it is your master's fault. **1871** CALVERLEY *Proverb. Philos.* in *Verses & Transl.* (ed. 4) 95 Let him drink deeply.., nor grumble if it tasteth of the cork. *Mod.* The milk has begun to turn; it tastes rather sour.

**b.** *fig.* To produce a particular effect upon the mind or feelings; to partake of the nature, character, or quality *of*; to savour *of.*

**1559** W. CUNNINGHAM *Cosmogr. Glasse* 5 All other artes (whiche taste of the Mathematicalles). *c* **1575** J. HOOKER *Life Sir P. Carew* (1857) 19 His behaviour tasting after the French manner. **1613** SHAKS. *Hen. VIII*, II. iii. 89 How tasts it? Is it bitter? **1621** SANDERSON *Serm.* I. 179 This ungodly king Ahab; see how all that come of him, taste of him. **1840** CLOUGH *Dipsychus* Poems (1892) 109 The place, the air Tastes of the nearer north.

†**c.** *trans.* To savour of. *Sc. Obs.*

**1596** DALRYMPLE tr. *Leslie's Hist. Scot.* x. 417 Ony thing ..of him said that taisted not Ill talk, haitred, and Invie.

†**10.** To cause a pleasant taste in (the mouth); to affect (the palate) agreeably; hence *fig.* to please, suit, be agreeable to. (Orig. *intr.* with dative obj.; in quot. 1672 with *to.*) *Obs.*

*a* **1586** SIDNEY *Arcadia* III. (1622) 352 Bitter griefs tastes mee best, pain is my ease. **1624** HEYWOOD *Gunaik.* VIII. 383 When wholesome foode would not tast their mouths, they devised sweet meates to realish their pallats. **1631** — *Maid of West* III. Wks. 1874 II. 299 Call for what wine best tasts you. **1672** MARVELL *Reh. Transp.* I. 184 Nothing less will taste to your palate.

**11.** To impart a taste or flavour to; to flavour; also *fig.* Now *rare.*

*a* **1577** GASCOIGNE *Flowers* Wks. (1587) 40 A salad or a sauce, to tast your cates withall. **1598** B. JONSON *Ev. Man in Hum.* I. iv, We will have a bunch of radish and salt to taste our wine. **1904** J. WELLS *J. H. Wilson* xxi. 293 All his teachings were coloured and tasted by the channel through which they ran.

**12. Taste of,** a construction used in several senses, sometimes simply = taste, sometimes = take a taste of, eat or drink a little of. So *taste on* (now *dial.*), † *taste to* (obs.).

In some cases, as in quots. 1526 in b and c, perhaps a literalism of translation (not found in the Vulgate, Wyclif, or Rhemish N. T.); but see OF 29 a, and cf. *take a taste of.*

**a.** To make trial of by tasting, to try the taste of; = 6. Also *fig. arch.*

*a* **1400–50** *Alexander* 2074 Þan pullis him vp þe proude kyng & on þe pepire tastis. *c* **1491** *Chast. Goddes Chyld.* 11 The bee goth and tasteth of many fair floures. *c* **1550** CHEKE *Matt.* xxvii. 34 When he had tasted on it [TINDALE therof], he wold not drink. **1604–63** *Inscr. on Ch. Bells* in North *Ch. Bells Linc.* (1882), I sweetly toling men do call to taste on meats that feeds the soule. **1807** SOUTHEY *Espriella's Lett.* II. 196 We tasted of this bread: it was dry, but not unpleasant. **1848** J. H. NEWMAN *Loss & Gain* 154, I taste of every thing, I depend on nothing.

**b.** To eat or drink only a little of; with negative, not to eat or drink at all; = 7. Also *fig.*

**13..** *K. Alis.* 5070 (Bodl. MS.) The kyng..forbed..Þat non ne shulde..Of þe water drynk ne taste. *c* **1400** *Destr. Troy* 6427 The tydis not to taste of þis triet meite. **1526** TINDALE *Luke* xiv. 24 None of those men which were bidden shall tast of my supper [μου τοῦ δείπνου]. **1591** SHAKS. 1 *Hen. VI*, II. iii. 79, I craue..that we may Taste of your Wine. **1607** TOPSELL *Four-f. Beasts* (1658) 19 Asses are subject to madness when they have tasted to certain herbs growing neer Potnias. **1667** MILTON *P. L.* IX. 651 Of this Tree we may not taste nor touch. **1699** DRYDEN *Epist. to J. Dryden* 61 For age but tastes of pleasures, youth devours. **1765** T. HUTCHINSON *Hist. Mass.* I. ii. 232 They had but tasted of the words..of the gentlemen.

**c.** To have experience or knowledge of; to feel, experience; = 3.

**1526** TINDALE *Matt.* xvi. 28 Some there be a monge them that here stonde, whych shall nott taste of deeth [οὐ μὴ γεύσωνται θανάτου], tyll they shall [etc.]. **1552** LATIMER *Serm. 4th Sund. Epiph.* (1584) 315 b, He himself hath tasted of al trouble. *a* **1562** G. CAVENDISH *Metr. Vis., Earl of Essex* vi, I ame tastyng on the payn. **1599** MASSINGER, etc. *Old Law* II. ii, So contentedly, You cannot think unless you tasted on't. **1667** MILTON *P. L.* IX. 476 Hope here to taste Of pleasure. **1742** GRAY *Adversity* 6 The Proud are taught to taste of pain. **1832** HT. MARTINEAU *Ireland* v. 75 Wherever the population had tasted of oppression.

†**d.** = 3 b. *Obs.*

**1607** TOURNEUR *Rev. Trag.* II. ii, I do embrace this season for the fittest To tast of that yong Lady.

**e.** See 9, 9 b.

**Tasteable, tastable** (tēⁱ·stăb'l), *a.* Also 6 **tastible.** [In ME. a. OF. *tastable* having the capacity of feeling, f. *taster* to feel, touch; in mod. Eng. f. TASTE *v.* + -ABLE.]

**I.** †**1.** Capable of feeling or perceiving by the sense of touch. *Obs. rare*⁻¹.

*c* **1400** tr. *Secreta Secret., Gov. Lordsh.* 98 Þe wyttys þat er yn þe hondes ys in a touchable & tastable stryngh [F. *li sens qi est en la main est en force touchable e tastable*; L. *palpatiua*].

**II. 2.** Capable of being tasted. Also *fig.*

**1572** J. JONES *Bathes of Bath* II. 18 The fittest instrument, the truest touchestone, of all properties, trying both toucheable and tasteable qualities. **1589** PUTTENHAM *Eng. Poesie* II. i. (Arb.) 78 Things that haue conueniencie by relation, as the visible by light..: the tastible by sauours to the rate: the tangible by his objectes in this or that regard. **1627–77** FELTHAM *Resolves* II. xliv. 245 Pleasures are not truly tasteable, but in the solid tracts of Temperance. **1755** MILLER in *Phil. Trans.* XLIX. 163 This juice has no other tasteable quality but that of heating without turning sour. **1829** JAS. MILL *Hum. Mind* (1869) I. 13 We should have no idea of objects as seeable, as hearable, as touchable, or tasteable.

†**3.** Pleasant to the taste; savoury, 'tasty'. *Obs.*

*a* **1641** BP. MOUNTAGU *Acts & Mon.* vii. (1642) 443 Esseni are those that live the life of Monks, eating no pleasant or tasteable meat at all. **1791** *Gentl. Mag.* Feb. 127/1 The fruit was tasteable.

**Tasted** (tēⁱ·stĕd), *ppl. a.* and *adj.* [f. TASTE *v.* and *sb.*¹ + -ED.]

**A.** *ppl. a.* [f. TASTE *v.*] Perceived by the taste, etc.: see the verb.

*c* **1403** ? LYDG. *Crt. Sapience* Proeme vii, As tasted bytternesse All swete thynge maketh be more precyous.

**B.** *adj.* [f. TASTE *sb.*]

**1.** Having a specified taste (with adj. or adv.).

**1604** JAS. I *Counterbl.* in *Ess. Poesie*, etc. (Arb.) 107 The miraculous omnipotencie of our strong tasted Tobacco. **1607** TOPSELL *Four-f. Beasts* (1658) 208 They are much fatter and better tasted. **1682** WHELER *Journ. Greece* IV. 295 The white..is very well tasted. **1684** BUNYAN *Pilgr.* II. 133 They were very good tasted Fruit. **1707** MORTIMER *Husb.* (1721) II. 297 A pleasant tasted Perry. **1725** DE FOE *Voy. round World* (1840) 328 The water..was very sweet, wholesome, and good tasted. **1812** SOUTHEY in *Q. Rev.* VII. 69 *note*, The milk..is ill tasted. **1836** W. IRVING *Astoria* (1849) 409 Mountain mutton..extremely well tasted.

**2.** Having taste or critical discernment (of a specified kind).

**1802** H. C. ANDREWS *Bot. Rep.* I. 255 The late elegantly tasted Mrs. North.

**Tasteful** (tēⁱ·stfŭl), *a.* Also 7–8 **tastful.** [f. TASTE *sb.*¹ + -FUL.]

†**1.** Having the capacity of tasting or trying.

**1647** CRASHAW *Poems, Flaming Heart* 50 What is't your tasteful spirits do prove In that rare life of her and love?

**2.** Having an agreeable taste; palatable, toothsome, tasty. Now *rare.*

**1611** COTGR., *Savoureux*, sauorie, tastfull, tart, well smacking. **1621** BP. MOUNTAGU *Diatribæ* 358 Stolne waters are sweet,..no Bread so tastefull, as that of the Sanctuarie. **1707** *Curios. in Husb. & Gard.* 217 The tasteful Cider. **1747** *Gentl. Mag.* May 243/2 With Temp'rance came, delightful guest! Health,—tasteful food, and balmy rest. **1887** HISSEY *Holiday on Road* 177 Sheep that live upon such a pasturage should yield a tasteful dish.

†**b.** *fig.* Mentally pleasant or agreeable. *Obs.*

*a* **1659** OSBORN *Ess.* iii. Wks. (1673) 562 Since nothing is more tasteful to Humanity, than Understanding. *a* **1701** MAUNDRELL *Let. to Sir C. Hedges* in *Journ. Jerus.* (1732) Pref., An Affectation, which however tastful it may be to the Persons who use it [etc.].

**c.** Full of taste; highly-flavoured. *rare.*

**1881** SALA in *Illustr. Lond. News* 14 May 467/3 Punch is too strong and tasteful with turtle soup.

**3.** Having or showing good taste, as a person; displaying good taste, as a work of art, etc.

**1756** *Connoisseur* No. 120 ⁋ 6 These are the poets who favour us with..tasteful compositions. **1816** SINGER *Hist. Cards* 213 They were drawn on the blocks by the tasteful pencil of Stothard. **1849** *N. & Q.* I. 28/2 The tasteful publisher of the 'Aldine Poets'. **1863** LYELL *Antiq. Man* ii. 10 The pottery..is of a more ornamental and tasteful style.

**b.** Of or pertaining to taste; æsthetic.

**1851** J. HAMILTON *Royal Preacher* x. (1858) 134 Conceding ..the same right to exert his tasteful and intellectual faculties when listening to a sermon as when perusing a..book.

Hence **Ta·stefully** *adv.*, in a tasteful manner, with good taste; **Ta·stefulness,** the quality or state of being tasteful (in various senses).

**1611** COTGR., *Savoureusement*, sauorily, *tastfully, tastingly, with a good stomacke. **1808** MRS. KEMBLE *Day after Wedding* 3 A Lady's Dressing-room tastefully furnished. **1900** *Westm. Gaz.* 22 Oct. 4/2 The tastefully-arranged gardens which are to be found at many stations on that railway. **1727** BAILEY vol. II, **Tastefulness*, Relishableness, Palatableness. **1844** DICKENS *Mart. Chuz.* ix, Mr. Pecksniff's delight in the tastefulness of the house.

**Tasteless** (tēⁱ·stlĕs), *a.* Also 7–8 **tastless.** [f. TASTE *sb.*¹ + -LESS.]

**1.** Destitute of the sense of taste; unable to taste. Also *fig.* Now *rare.*

**1591** SYLVESTER *Du Bartas* I. iv. 148 When wilfully his taste-less Taste delights In things unsavory to sound appetites. *a* **1631** DONNE *Funeral Elegy* Poems (1654) 219 As aged men are glad Being tastlesse grown, to joy in joyes they had. **1704** CIBBER *Careless Husb.* v. (1705) 60 Won't you think me tastless to the Joy you've given me? **1713** ROWE *Jane Shore* v. i, My tasteless Tongue cleaves to the clammy Roof. **1820** C. R. MATURIN *Melmoth* (1892) III. xxvii. 104 Every thing that could tempt the tasteless palate of age.

**2.** Without taste or flavour; exciting no sensation of taste; insipid.

**1611** FLORIO, *Insaporito*, vnsauorie, tastelesse. **1661–79** BOYLE *Scept. Chem.* IV. Wks. 1772 I. 533 He never was able to make them [chymical oils] tasteless. **1748** *Anson's Voy.* II. xii. 267 Very dry and tasteless food. **1831** J. DAVIES *Manual Mat. Med.* 329 A powder of an orange yellow colour, inodorous, and tasteless.

**3.** *fig.* Exciting no interest; dull, insipid, uninteresting.

**1603** FLORIO *Montaigne* (1634) 143 Enterludes and commedies rejoyce and make us merry, but to players they are tedious and tastelesse. **1781** COWPER *Conversat.* 715 The song of Sion is a tasteless thing, Unless when rising on a joyful wing. **1814** WORDSW. *Excurs.* I. 612 A while on trivial things we held discourse, To me soon tasteless. **1822** LAMB *Elia* Ser. I. *Distant Corr.*, If it [sentiment] have time to cool, it is the most tasteless of all cold meats.

**4.** Devoid of good taste; of persons, lacking in discrimination, or in critical discernment and appreciation; of things, showing want of good taste.

**1676** ETHEREDGE *Man of Mode* III. ii, Nature..puts sophisticate dulness often on the tasteless multitude for true wit and good-humour. **1709** SWIFT in *Lett. Lit. Men* (Camden) 342 Your Lordship is universally admired by this tastless People. **1791** GILPIN *Forest Scenery* II. 75 It not only shews the hand of art; but of the most tastless art. **1843** PRESCOTT *Mexico* I. ii. (1864) 17 As different from their ancestors as are the modern Egyptians from those who built,—I will not say, the tasteless pyramids. **1853** KINGSLEY *Hypatia* vii, The tasteless fashion of an artificial and decaying civilization.

Hence **Ta·stelessly** *adv.*, in a tasteless manner; without taste.

**1854** *Tait's Mag.* XXI. 386 Even that comes tastelessly

on the ear of the player on the world's stage, unless it is accompanied with a bouquet. **1880** *Daily News* 30 Nov. 3/1 Their houses..are solidly if tastelessly furnished.

**Tastelessness** (tēⁱ·stlĕsnės). [f. prec. + -NESS.]

**1.** Lack of the sense of taste; *fig.* lack of relish or appreciation. Now *rare*.

**1626** DONNE *Serm.* iv. (1640) 38 Our palate dead in a tastlesnesse. **1713** BERKELEY *Guard.* No. 49 ¶ 9 A secret indignation at the tastelessness of mortal men, who, in their race through life, overlook the real enjoyments of it. *a* **1774** TUCKER *Lt. Nat.* (1834) II. 404 Such austerities and labours of devotion, such a tastelessness of all innocent enjoyments.

**2.** Absence of taste or flavour; insipidity. Also *fig.*

**1600** SURFLET *Countrie Farme* III. lxi. 567 Their sharpnes, sowrenes, tartnes, harshnes, eagernes, sweetenes, and tastlesnes. **1875** H. C. WOOD *Therap.* (1879) 468 On account of its tastelessness, this preparation..is sometimes employed as a purgative for children.

**3.** Absence or want of æsthetic discernment.

**1778** MALONE *Note on Tit. A.* in *Shaks.'s Wks.* VIII. 561 One of their own fraternity, (who cannot well be suspected of asinine tastelessness, or Gothic prepossessions). **1825** *Blackw. Mag.* XVIII. 240 Others assign it to the nonchalance and tastelessness of managers. **1855** DORAN *Hanov. Queens* II. i. 30 Garrick, considering he was a man of taste, displayed great tastelessness on this occasion.

† **Ta·sten**, *v. Obs. rare*⁻¹. [f. TASTE *sb.*[1] + -EN [5].] *trans.* To produce a sensation of taste in.

**1579** LODGE *Def. Poetry* 15 The receipt is bitter, therfore I would wysh you first to tasten your mouth with the Sugar of perseuerance.

**Taster**[1] (tēⁱ·stəɹ). Forms: 4–6 tastour, 5 -ar, taastowre, 6– taster. [a. AF. *tastour* = OF. *tasteur*, f. OF. *taster*: see TASTE *v.* Later treated as agent-n. of the Eng. vb.: see -ER [1].]

**1.** One who tastes, or tries the quality of a thing by tasting; *spec.* one whose office, business, or employment is to test the quality of victuals sold to the public, as ale, wine, tea, etc. by taste; hence in comb. ALE-TASTER, TEA-TASTER, q. v. Also *fig.* In quot. 1596, the mouth.

*c* **1440** *Promp. Parv.* 487/1 Taastowre, *gustator, ambro.* *c* **1450** in *Surtees Misc.* (1888) 62 Two ale tastars, yᵉ qwhyche two tastars..schall taste the ale of all common brewers every weke. **1526** *Pilgr. Perf.* (W. de W. 1531) 274 b, To be vynteners, discerners, and tasters of the same. **1596** HARINGTON *Metam. Ajax* (1814) 36 Riding on a great sow and holding before her taster a dirty pudding. **1633** G. HERBERT *Temple, Odour* i, As Amber-greese leaves a rich sent Unto the taster. **1756** C. LUCAS *Ess. Waters* I. 79 Judicious tasters dilute hot liquors. **1854** LOWELL *Jrnl. in Italy* Pr. Wks. 1890 I. 115, I reckon myself a good taster of dialects. **1866** CARLYLE *Remin., E. Irving* (1881) 314, I.. demanded back my poor MS. from Murray, received with it some apologetic palaver (enclosing an opinion from his taster..), and much hope [etc.]. **1905** *Sat. Rev.* 17 June 816/1 On the whole the first literary 'taster' of the MS. was, we think, justified in rejecting Coryat.

**b.** *transf.* A device which tests as by tasting.

**1837** WHEWELL *Hist. Induct. Sc.* (1857) III. 24 Which thus acted as a sort of electric taster.

**2.** A domestic officer whose duty it is to taste food and drink about to be served to his master, in order to ascertain their quality, or to detect poison.

**1387** TREVISA *Higden* (Rolls) VIII. 197 A monk..made a drink of venym,..and drank to þe kyng as it were his tastour. **1580** HOLLYBAND *Treas. Fr. Tong* s. v. *Eschanson*, A taster of meates to kinges or other. **1602** T. FITZHERBERT *Apol.* 31 The Emperour Claudius, poysoned by his taster. **1662** HIBBERT *Body Div.* I. 206 Princes have their tasters before they eat, lest there should be poison in the dish. **1738** SWIFT *Pol. Conversat.* i. 13 What, Miss, Will you be my Taster [of a dish of tea]? **1895** *Westm. Gaz.* 30 Oct. 3/2 Not a morsel or a drop ever passes the Sultan's lips, they say, until he has tried it first on a taster. *fig.* **1640** REYNOLDS *Passions* xvii. 179 Knowledge is Appetites Taster.

**3.** An implement by which a small portion of anything is taken for tasting.

**a.** A small shallow cup of silver, often with an embossed or corrugated bottom which reflects the light through the liquor, for tasting wines.

**1420** *E. E. Wills* (1882) 46 A tastour of seluer with myn owne merke ymade in þe bottom. **1530** PALSGR. 279/2 Tastour a lytell cuppe to tast wyne, *tasse a gouster le uin.* **1681** *Lond. Gaz.* No. 1665/4 One Silver Brandy Taster, marked with R. H. A. **1704** *Ibid.* No. 4055/4 Two long footed Silver Cups, one Taster. **1858** [see b].

**b.** An instrument by which a small portion is taken from the interior of a cheese; a skewer for testing the condition of hams.

**1784** TWAMLEY *Dairying* 79, I told her Cheese of that countenance always was sweet. I put my taster into one and gave it her to taste. **1811** [see *cheese-taster*, CHEESE *sb.*[1] 7]. **1858** SIMMONDS *Dict. Trade, Taster*,..a scoop for tasting cheese; a skewer for trying hams; a dram cup.

**4.** A small portion of food, etc., or of anything, for a sample; a taste.

**1826** SYD. SMITH *Granby* Wks. 1867 II. 90 It shall be the taster of the cheese, and we are convinced it will sell the whole article. **1891** *Daily News* 28 July 7/2 He went to the defendant's [an ice-cream vendor] stall in London-wall and asked him for a 'taster'. **1899** *Westm. Gaz.* 20 May 2/1 The 'taster', a free gift bestowed of yore in order to retain the..goodwill of regular but temporarily impecunious customers.

‖ **Taster**[2] (ta·stəɹ). *Zool.* [G. *taster* feeler, antenna, f. *tasten* to feel, touch.] In certain Hydrozoa, A modified zooid situated on the polypstem, and somewhat resembling the polypites, but having no mouth; a hydrocyst or feeler.

**1884** *Stand. Nat. Hist.* I. 100 Alternating with the polypites at intervals along the polypstem are found very curious bodies called tasters, which have a close likeness to the flask-shaped zoöids. [**1888** ROLLESTON & JACKSON *Anim. Life* 770 *Siphonophora*...The various parts..(1) The polypite or gastrozooid...(2) Hydrocysts or feelers (= Taster of German writers)...These structures are polypites in which the distal or oral extremity is imperforate and usually armed with cnidoblasts. The pedicle is absent or short.]

† **Ta·stesome**, *a. Obs. rare.* [f. TASTE *sb.*[1] + -SOME.] Pleasant to the taste; 'tasty', toothsome.

**1598** FLORIO, *Gusteuole*, smacking, tastesome, tasting well.

**Tastily** (tēⁱ·stĭli), *adv.* [f. TASTY *a.* + -LY [2].] In a tasty manner; tastefully.

**1799** R. WARNER *Walk* (1800) 80 The slope..is tastily managed and appropriately ornamented. **1809** PINKNEY *Trav. France* 24 The fruits were in plates very tastily painted in landscape. **1845** M. J. HIGGINS *Ess.* (1875) 216 Tastily but inexpensively dressed.

**Tastiness** (tēⁱ·stinės). [f. as prec. + -NESS.] The quality or state of being tasty.

**1882** HOWELLS in *Longm. Mag.* I. 44 Lexington has escaped the ravages alike of 'tastiness' and of enterprise. **1902** MARY E. MANN *Fields Dulditch* iii. 39 He ain't to comparison in tastiness to th' gage.

**Tasting** (tēⁱ·stiŋ), *vbl. sb.* [-ING [1].]

**1.** The action of the verb TASTE. **a.** In a general sense, trying, testing; † esp., in early use, touching, feeling; also the sense of touch (*obs.*).

**13..** *K. Alis.* 4031 (Bodl. MS.) It is ywrite þat euery þing Hym self sheweþ in þe tastyng. *c* **1375** *Sc. Leg. Saints* vi. (*Thomas*) 407 Wittis four,..sycht, herynge, gustyne, tastyne. *c* **1430** *Pilgr. Lyf Manhode* I. cxxi. (1869) 63 Alle tastinges generalliche is vnderstonde bi the hondes. **1711**, **1850** [see TASTE *v.* 2 b].

**b.** Now, the action of TASTE *v.* II; † also formerly, the faculty or sense, and the quality of a substance so apprehended: = TASTE *sb.*[1] 4, 5 (*obs.*).

**1390** GOWER *Conf.* III. 33, I take of love my fiedinge Withoute tastinge or fielinge. **1426** AUDELAY *Poems* 7 Thi heryng, thi seyng, as I the schewe, Thi syȝt, thi smellyng, here be iij. Thi touchyng, thi tastyng, here v. ther be. *c* **1460** J. RUSSELL *Bk. Nurture* 1199 Credence is vsed, and tastynge, for drede of poysenynge. **1530** PALSGR. 279/2 Tastyng with the mouthe, *govster.* **1774** GOLDSM. *Nat. Hist.* (1776) II. 183 The sense most nearly allied to smelling is that of tasting. **1841–4** EMERSON *Ess., Exper.* Wks. (Bohn) I. 178 Intellectual tasting of life will not supersede muscular activity. **1898** 'IAN MACLAREN' in *Woman at Home* Oct. 56/1 If Thomas takes to tasting [i. e. tippling, drinking] ..it's all over with him.

**2.** quasi-*concr.* A small portion taken to try the taste; a taste (esp. of spirituous liquor). Also *fig.*

**1526** *Pilgr. Perf.* (1531) 49 For they be but tastynges, shadowes, or tokens of the gloryous fruytes to come. **1830** CUNNINGHAM *Brit. Paint.* II. 69 He gave them a tasting of his spirit in two or three sarcastic sentences. **1893** J. SKINNER *Autobiog. Metaphysician* vii. 48 He got a glass from Mr. Reed and another tasting from another neighbour.

**3.** *attrib.* and *Comb.*, as *tasting power*; **tasting-bone**, a bone put into the broth to give it a taste or flavour; **tasting-knife**, a cheese-taster (see TASTER 3 b); **tasting-order**, an order to visit stores of wine, etc., and to taste or sample them.

**1850** MRS. CARLYLE *Let. to Carlyle* 8 Sept., It [Kingsley's *Alton Locke*] seems to me..a mere..broth of *Morning-chronicle-ism*, in which you play the part of the *tasting-bone of Poverty Row. **1757** H. WALPOLE tr. *Hentzner's Trav.* 52 At last came an unmarried Lady..and along with her a married one, bearing a *tasting-knife. **1859** SALA *Gas-light & D.* xiv, Quite gone in liquor and overcome with the *tasting-orders of years. **1599** DAVIES *Immort. Soul* ccxv, Therefore the Soule doth vse the *tasting power.

**Ta·sting**, *ppl. a.* [-ING [2].] That tastes.

**1598** [implied in next]. **1907** *Contemp. Rev.* Oct. Lit. Suppl. 2 The tasting sense is soon ruined.

**Ta·stingly**, *adv.* [f. prec. + -LY [2].] In a tasting manner.

**1598** FLORIO, *Saporitamente*, sauourly, smackingly, tastingly, hungerly. **1894** BARING-GOULD *Kitty Alone* II. 150 The fire..sending the tips of its flames tastingly towards him.

† **Ta·stive**, *a. Obs. rare*⁻¹. [f. TASTE *sb.*[1] or *v.*: see -IVE.] Having the quality of taste; sapid.

**1644** DIGBY *Nat. Bodies* xxvii. § 6. 246 The same thinges that yield also tastiue particles.

**Tastle**, obs. form of TASSEL.

**Tasty** (tēⁱ·sti), *a.* Now *colloq.* and *dial.* [f. TASTE *sb.*[1] + -Y.]

**1.** Pleasing to the taste; appetizing, savoury.

**1617** HIERON *Wks.* II. 203 Sowre herbs, with which that tastie meat, the paschall lambe..was to be eaten. **1795** in *Spirit Pub. Jrnls.* IV. 220 A tasty bird, that pheasant. **1849** CURZON *Visits Monast.* 144 A famous pie, or pilau, with rice and a tasty sauce. *a* **1862** BUCKLE *Misc. Wks.* (1872) I. 381 The arts of compounding a pleasant pudding or combining a tasty pie.

**b.** *fig.* Pleasant, agreeable, attractive.

**1796** MRS. M. ROBINSON *Angelina* III. 179 'Here you are, my tasty ones!' exclaimed Sir Edward. 'Why, you played us a trick'. **1821** CLARE *Vill. Minstr.* I. 201 Pausing o'er each tasty flower.

**2.** Characterized by or displaying good taste; tasteful, elegant. Now *rare*.

**1762** GOLDSM. *Cit. World* lxxvii, [The silk] is at once rich, tasty, and quite the thing. **1784** *New Spectator* No. 16. 5 [Ranelagh] This region of taste was visited on Friday evening, by a great number of tasty people indeed. **1813** J. C. HOBHOUSE *Journey* (ed. 2) 501 The head-dress of the younger girls is tasty; their hair falls down their backs in profusion. **1821** COLERIDGE in *Blackw. Mag.* X. 254, I wish I could find a more familiar word than *aesthetic*...To be sure, there is *tasty*; but that has been long ago emasculated for all unworthy uses by milliners, tailors, and..dandies. **1862** THACKERAY *Philip* xxiv, My..waistcoat..is a much more tasty thing than these gaudy ready-made articles.

**3.** *Comb.*, as *tasty-looking*.

**1867** F. FRANCIS *Angling* x. (1880) 375 This is a very tasty-looking fly. **1888** F. COWPER *Capt. of Wight* (1889) 50 Some tasty-looking rolls, fresh butter, and cheese.

**Tasul, tasyl, -yll, -ylle**, obs. ff. TEASEL.

**Tat** (tæt), *sb.*[1] *slang.* Also **tatt.** [Origin unascertained.] *pl.* **Tats**: Dice; *esp.* false or loaded dice. **b.** *Comb.* as **tat-box**, a dice-box; **tat-monger**, a sharper who uses false dice. See also TATSMAN.

**1688** SHADWELL *Sqr. Alsatia* I, *H*...Pox o' the Tatts for me! I believe they put the Doctor upon me. *B.* Tatts and Doctor! what's that? *S.* The tools of Sharpers, false dice. *Ibid.*, He was but a Sharper, a tat-monger. *a* **1700** B. E. *Dict. Cant. Crew, Tatts*, false Dice. *a* **1809** J. PALMER *Like Master* (1811) I. xv. 215 He ransacks every house in St. James's parish, where the tats are at work, to punish those for what he, himself, practised. **1812** J. H. VAUX *Flash Dict., Tatt-box*, a dice-box. **1887** HENLEY *Villon's Straight Tip* ii, Rattle the tats, or mark the spot.

**Tāt** (tāt), *sb.*[2] *East Ind.* Also **taut.** [Hindī *ṭāṭ* a strip of very thick hemp-canvas, about 10 inches wide, of which several are sewn together to make a mat or screen.] Coarse canvas made from various fibres, esp. jute, and used as sacking.

**1820** *Trans. Lit. Soc. Bombay* III. 244 (Y.) Made into coarse cloth taut, by the Brinjaries and people who use pack bullocks, for making bags (gonies) for holding grain, &c. **1858** SIMMONDS *Dict. Trade, Tat*, a name in India for cloth made from the fibre of the *Corchorus olitorius*. Hence **1864** in WEBSTER; and in later Dicts.

**Tat, tatt**, *sb.*[3] *Anglo-Ind.* Short for TATTY *sb.*

**1812** MARIA GRAHAM *Jrnl. Resid. India* 125 (Y.) During the hot winds tats (a kind of mat), made of the root of the koosa grass,..are placed against the doors and windows. **1837** *Lett. fr. Madras* (1843) 77, I have a tatt, or thick mat, at my window, which excludes the sun, and men sit outside pouring water on it all day, so that the wind..blows always cooled through the water.

**Tat, tatt**, *sb.*[4] *Anglo-Ind.* Short for TATTOO *sb.*[3], a native pony of India.

*c* **1840** in Parker *Bole Ponjis* (1851) II. 215 With its bright brass patent axles, and its little hog maned tatts. **1845** STOCQUELER *Handbk. Brit. India* (1854) 109 The pony (familiarly called *tat*—corruption of the native name for the small animal, *tattoo*). **1891** *Blackw. Mag.* May 684 Cantering his tat up to the door.

**Tat**, *sb.*[5] *slang.* [Origin uncertain: cf. OE. *tættec* a rag, and TATTY *a.*] A rag.

**1851** MAYHEW *Lond. Labour* I. 424/2 I'll tell you about the tat (rag) gatherers; buying rags they call it.

**Tat**, *sb.*[6] *Sc.* Also (*erron.*) **taut, tawt.** [Origin obscure: cf. TATTY *a.*] (See quot.)

**1887** JAMIESON *Suppl., Tat, taut, tawt*, a tangle, matted tuft or lock of wool or hair.

**Tat**, *sb.*[7], in phr. *tit for tat*: see TIT.

**Tat**, *v.*[1] [Origin uncertain: ? echoic; cf. *tap, pat.*] *trans.* **a.** To touch lightly, pat, tap. *dial.* † **b.** A euphemism for To flog. *Obs. slang.*

**1607** DEKKER & WEBSTER *Northw. Ho* II. i, Come tit me, come tat me, come throw a kiss at me. **1812** J. H. VAUX *Flash Dict., Tat*, to flog, or scourge. **1847–78** HALLIWELL, *Tat*...(3) To touch gently. *Hants.*

**Tat**, *v.*[2] Also **tatt.** [Origin unknown: cf. TATTING.] **a.** *intr.* To do tatting. **b.** *trans.* To make by tatting.

[**1842**: see TATTING.] **1882** MRS. ALEXANDER in *Belgravia* July 104 Winnie produced her tatting, and applied herself to it...At the mention of his mother Laura involuntarily clasped her hands, and Winnie ceased to tatt. **1905** MRS. E. GLYN *Viciss. Evangeline* 123 They knitted ties and crocheted comforters, and one even tatted.

**Tat**, *v.*[3] *slang.* [f. TAT *sb.*[5]] *intr.* To gather rags.

**1851** MAYHEW *Lond. Labour* I. 417/1 He goes tatting and billy-hunting in the country (gathering rags and buying old metal). **1910** *Nottingham Guardian* 2 June, The prisoner ..told the police that he came in possession of the lead when he went round 'tatting'.

**Tat**, *v.*[4] *Sc.* and *north. dial.* [Goes with TAT *sb.*[6]] *trans.* and *intr.* To tangle, or make tangled or matted: see TAUT *v.*

**1829** BROCKETT *N. C. Gloss.* (ed. 2), *Tat*, to mat, to entangle. **1887** in JAMIESON *Suppl.* **1894** *Northumb. Gloss.*, *Tat*, to mat together.

**Ta-ta** (tā tā·), *int.* A nursery expression for 'Good-bye'; also used playfully by adults.

**1837** DICKENS *Pickw.* xxvii, 'Tar, tar, Sammy', replied his father. **1878** F. C. BURNAND *Strapmore* i. 15 Ta-ta, little one *très cher*! Bye-bye. **1891** MRS. WALFORD *Mischief of Monica* III. 171 'Ta-ta'; and the speaker slipped behind backs and vanished.

**Tataow**, obs. f. TATTOO *v.*[2] **Tatar**: see TARTAR [2]. **Tatarwagge**: see TATTER *sb.*[1] 3. **Tatch, tatche**: see TACHE. **Tatchy**, dial. f. TETCHY.

**Tate** (tēt, tiət), *sb.*[1] *Sc.* and *north. dial.* Forms: 7–9 tait, 8 teat, tet, tett, 6– tate. [Origin obscure; prob. Norse: cf. Icel. *tæta* to tear to shreds, to tease, *tæta* a shred; also, fluff of wool, etc., a particle of anything.]

**1.** A small tuft or lock of hair, wool, or other fibrous material, consisting of only a few fibres; a small handful of grass, hay, or corn.

**1513** DOUGLAS *Æneis* VI. v. 11 Apon his chin feill cannos haris gray, Lyart feltat tatis. **1570** LEVINS *Manip.* 39/14 A Tate, *fibra.* **1618** *Trial Marg. Barclay*, etc. in Scott

*Demonol.* ix. (1831) 318 He was found.. strangled and hanged [in his cell].. with a *tait* of hemp, or a string supposed to have been his garter. *a* **1774** FERGUSSON *Iron Kirk Bell* Poems (1845) 43 Auld Reekie's childer now Maun staup their lugs wi' teats o' tow Thy sound to bang. **1782** BURNS *Death of Mailie* 34 Wi' teats o' hay an' ripps o' corn. **1818** SCOTT *Hrt. Midl.* xxii, There's a chield can spin a muckle pirn out of a wee tait of tow! **1856** R. SIMPSON *Covenanters of South* 332 The wool.. was to be found here and there in handfuls, or in tates, as they are called, lying on the heath. [In *Eng. Dial. Dict.* Northumb., to N. Lanc. and Yorks.]

**2.** *gen.* A small piece; a particle or morsel (of anything); in quot. 1722 *advb.* = 'a bit', a little.

With *tate* of meal, etc., cf. the common Sc. *a hair* of meal, of salt, etc. in same sense.

**1722** RAMSAY *Three Bonnets* I. 143 Observing Jouk a wee tate tipsy. **1805** G. M'INDOE *Poems, Million of Potatoes*, But to disperse them a' in taits, Through different hands, at different rates,.. I ne'er could wi' be troubled. **1891** H. HALIBURTON *Ochil Idylls* 68 O' winter snaw there's but a tate remainin'. *Mod. Sc.* No a tate o' meit was left.

† **Tate, tath,** *sb.*[2] *Obs.* Also 7 **tathe.** [In Irish *taite*; but held to be a borrowed word: cf. Joyce *Ir. Names of Places* I. 246. Some think it derived from prec.] A measure of land formerly used in Ireland, equal to 60 Irish acres.

**1607** DAVIES *Lett. Earl Salisb.* i. Tracts (1787) 229 Every ballybetagh.. containeth sixteen taths; every tath containeth three-score English acres or thereabouts. *a* **1660** *Contemp. Hist. Irel.* (Ir. Archæol. Soc.) I. 339 Every ballyboe, quarter, pole, or tathe of land. *Ibid.* 349 Twoe tates of the three tates of Ballagh. **1842** S. C. HALL *Ireland* II. 354 The lesser divisions were known by the various appellations of quarters, half quarters, ballyboes, gneeves, tates, &c. **1861** REEVES in *Proc. Roy. Ir. Acad.* VII. 484.

† **Tate,** *a. Sc. Obs. rare*⁻¹. ? variant of TAIT *a.* in sense 'wanton, brisk, untamed'.

*c* **1375** *Sc. Leg. Saints* iv. (*Jacobus*) 328 For scho had bulis wilde and tate, þat scho nocht trewit mycht ȝokkit be In carte, na wane, be ony degre.

**Tate,** obs. form of TEAT. **Tater,** dial. and vulgar corruption of POTATO; obs. form of TATTER.

**Tath** (taþ), **tathe** (tēⁱð), *sb. Sc.* and *dial.* Also 5 **taitht,** 9 **taith, teath.** [a. ON. *tað* dung, manure, whence *taða* fem. the manured home-field, hay from this field, *teðja* to dung, manure. In Norw. and Sw. dial. *tad* dung.]

**1.** The dung of cattle, sheep, etc. left for manure on land on which they have been pastured.

**1492** *Act. Dom. Conc.* (1839) 289/2 þe saidis personis sall content & pay.. for þe wanting of þe taitht & fulȝe of þe said nolt & scheip. **1545** *Acct.* in *Paston Lett.* VIII. (B.M.), Itm. for the tathe of ccvj Shepe at Beekham, due att Myddesomer.. lxvj s. vj d. **1611** SPEED *Theat. Gt. Brit.* xviii. (1614) 35/1 These heaths by the compasture of the sheepe (which we call Tathe) are made so rich [etc.]. **1854** *Jrnl. R. Agric. Soc.* XV. I. 100 To mix the teath with the soil. **1867** *Ibid.* III. II. 534 [Geese] eat far cleaner than sheep, and, in fact, leave nothing but their 'taith', which answers admirably as a preparation for the next wheat-crop.

**b.** (See quot. 1701.)

*a* **1641** SPELMAN *Icenia* in *Posth. Wks.* (1698) 162 Stercorationem *Tath*.. appellant. **1701** *Cowell's Interpr.*, *Tath*, in Norfolk and Suffolk the Lord of each Mannor had the Privilege of having their Tenants Flocks of Sheep brought at Night upon their own Demesne Ground, there to be foulded for the benefit of their Dung, which liberty of so improving their Land is called *Tath*.

**2.** *transf.* Rich or rank grass growing where the land has been manured in this way, or, by extension, where it has been flooded (*water-tath*). ? *Obs.*

**1807** *Ess. Highl. Soc.* III. 468 All grasses which are remarkably rank and luxuriant, are called *tath*, by the stock farmers, who distinguish two kinds of it; *water tath*, proceeding from excess of moisture, and *nolt tath*, the produce of dung.

**3.** *Sea-tath*: a sea-bottom covered with sediment.

**1796** *Statist. Acc. Scotl.* XVII. 70 Oysters are found on a strong clay bottom, on rocks and stones, and sometimes, though but thinly, in what is called by the fishers *sea tathe*. These last are of a very inferior quality.

**4.** *attrib.* and *Comb.*, as **tath-field, -fold,** a field or fold in which cattle or sheep are confined in order to manure it.

**1752** MACCOLL in *Scots Mag.* (1753) Aug. 394/1 They were harrowing the tath-field. **1795** *Statist. Acc. Scotl.* XIV. 143 The spots thus manured are called tath-fields. **1825** JAMIESON, *Tath-fauld, tath-faud*, a fold in which cattle are shut up during night, to manure the ground with their dung.

**Tath,** obs. f. *taketh*: see TAKE *v.* A. 3 b *β*.

**Tath, tathe,** variants of TATE *sb.*[2]

**Tathe, tath,** *v. Sc.* and *dial.* Also 5 **taþin,** 8 **taith,** 8–9 **teath.** [f. TATH *sb.*: cf. ON. *teðja* to manure.]

**1.** *trans.* To manure (land) by turning sheep or cattle upon it (usually said of the cattle); also, by extension, by flooding it (*to water-tathe*).

*c* **1440** *Promp. Parv.* 487/2 Tayin [*v.r.* tathyn] londe wythe schepys donge,.. *rudero*,.. *stercoro*. **1628** COKE *On Litt.* 57 As if I lend to one my Sheepe, to tathe his land. **1743** MAXWELL *Sel. Trans. Soc. Improv. Agric. Scot.* 38 It has.. been in Pasture these twelve Years... It is well tathed. **1799** J. ROBERTSON *Agric. Perth* 64 The outfields lying farthest from the townships, were taithed or dunged by confining the cattle in folds, over night, during summer and autumn, upon that particular portion.. which was to be ploughed next spring. **1808** J. WALKER *Econ. Hist. Hebr. & Highl. Scot.* (1812) I. 167 There is yet another way in which the sediment of water may be applied as a manure,.. this is, by.. Water-tathing. *Ibid.* 168 When a field has been water-tathed.. but for one winter, the growth of grass upon it is more early. **1843** *Jrnl. R. Agric. Soc.* IV. I. 122 Teathing the barley-stubble which is intended for turnips will cause the anbury.

**2.** *intr.* Of cattle, etc.: To drop dung *upon* land so as to manure it.

**1743** MAXWELL *Sel. Trans. Soc. Improv. Agric. Scot.* 123 The Dung of Horses is not proper for sandy Grounds, being too hot, as may be observed from the Grounds they tathe upon in Summer.

Hence **Ta·thing** *vbl. sb.* (also *concr.*).

*c* **1440** *Promp. Parv.* 487/2 Taynge [*v.r.* tathing] of lond, *ruderacio*. **1529** *Anc. Deed* A. 13557 (P.R.O.) To fynd the tenauntz.. tathyng to ther londes. **1792** *Statist. Acc. Scot.* II. 404 A priest.. who had a right to every seventh acre of Ladifron, and to the tathing (dung as left on the ground) every seventh night. **1793** *Ibid.* VI. 268.

**Tatianist** (tēⁱ·ʃiănist). [f. *Tatian* (name of a Christian apologist of the 2nd century, who afterwards became a Gnostic) + -IST.] A follower of Tatian; a member of the ascetic sect of Encratites; also incorrectly **Tatian** in same sense. So **Tatianic** (tēⁱʃiˌæ·nik) *a.*, of or pertaining to Tatian, or to his DIATESSARON or harmony of the Gospels.

**1585–7** T. ROGERS 39 *Art.* vi. (1628) 32 Some accepted onely the Acts of the Apostles, as the Tatians. **1635** PAGITT *Christianogr.* III. (1636) 60 Heretiques as the Tatians,.. teaching against Marriage. **1754–8** BP. NEWTON *Obs. Dan.* xiii. 200 The mystery of iniquity continued to work very strongly in.. the Tatianists. **1862** G. H. TOUNSEND *Man. of Dates* s.v. *Encratites*, Tatian flourished about A. D. 173. His followers were called in addition to Encratites, Tatianists, Apotactites, and Hydroparastates. **1907** MOFFAT in *Expositor* July 62 The Tatianic arrangement reflects the original order [of the N. T. books].

**Tatie, 'tato,** dial. and vulgar corruptions of POTATO: see *Eng. Dial. Dict.*

**Tato, tatoo,** obs. forms of TATTOO.

‖**Tatou, tatu** (ta·tu). Also 6 **tattou,** 8 **tattu,** 9 **tatoo, tattoo.** [Native name in Tupi. So F. *tatou*, Sp. *tato*, Pg. *tatu*.] An armadillo.

**1568** tr. *Thevet's New Found Worlde* 84 There are founde great number of Tattous, that are beasts armed. **1613** PURCHAS *Pilgrimage* (1614) 842 The Tatu or Armadilla, which digs as much as many men with mattocks. **1766** E. BANCROFT *Guiana* ii. (1769) 145 The Tattu, or Armadillo, of Guiana, is the largest of that species of animals. **1805** T. LINDLEY *Voy. Brazil* 134 He was waiting for tatoos, or armadilloes, which seldom appear before dusk. **1894** *Outing* (U.S.) XXIV. 176/2 In Brazil, where he is called the 'tattoo', his flesh is much prized.

**b.** In combination with defining words, applied (in Tupi and Guarani) to various species, as **ta·touay·** (**tatou-áiba**), the wounded armadillo; **tatouete** (**tatuete**), [-*ete* true] *Tatusia verdadeira*; **ta·touhou·, ta·tou-pe·ba,** = PEBA; **ta·tou-po·you,** = POYOU: see quots.

[**1648** MARCGRAVE *Hist. Nat. Brasil.* VI. viii. 231 Tatv & Tatv-peba Brasiliensibus, Armadillo Hispanis, Encuberto Lusitanis. *Ibid.*, *Tatv-ete* Brasiliensibus,.. priori est minor. **1693** RAY *Quadrupeds* 233 *Tatuete* Brasiliensibus, Armadilli secunda species.] **1753** CHAMBERS *Cycl. Supp.*, *Tatuete*,.. a species of tatu, or armadillo, smaller than the common one. **1774** GOLDSM. *Nat. Hist.* IV. iv. 132 The third [kind of Armadillo] is the Tatuette, furnished with eight bands. **1834** *Penny Cycl.* II. 352/1 The peba (*D[asypus] peba*), called by the Guaranis *tatouhou*, or *black tatu*, is extremely common in Paraguay. *Ibid.* 352/2 The peba, or, as it is commonly called in Brazil, tatu-peba, has thirty-two teeth. *Ibid.* 353/2 The *poyou*.. or yellow-footed armadillo (for thus Azara interprets the name)... The *tatu-poyou* is easily distinguished.. by the unusual flatness and broadness of its body. *Ibid.* 354/2 The *Tatouay* (*D. Tatouay*, Desmarest), or wounded armadillo, is so called by the Indians in allusion to its tail, which is naked, or as it were rudely deprived of the crust or bony tube which covers this organ in all the other species.

**Tatsman** (tæ·tsmæ̆n). *slang.* [f. *tats* dice, pl. of TAT *sb.*[1] + MAN *sb.*[1]] A dice-player, or a sharper who cheats with dice.

**1825** C. M. WESTMACOTT *Eng. Spy* (1907) I. 211 *note*, A *tats man*, a proficient with the bones, one who knows every chance upon the dice.

**Tatt:** see TAT. **Tattaow,** obs. f. TATTOO *v.*[2]

**Tat-tat** (tæ·tˌtæ·t). [Echoic: cf. TAT *v.*[1]] = RAT-TAT.

**1786** MME. D'ARBLAY *Diary* 17 July, A tat-tat at my door followed, and a lady entered.

**Tattee,** variant of TATTY *sb.*

**Tatter** (tæ·təɹ), *sb.*[1] Also 5–6 **tater,** (5 **tatar**), 7 **tattar** (**totter**), 8 *Sc.* **tetter.** [Known only from *c* 1400, but evidenced in earlier use by TATTERED *a.* Of Scandinavian origin: cf. ON. **taturr* (later Icel. *tǫturr, tötturr*), pl. *tötrar* tatters, rags, in Norw. dial. *totra*, pl. *totror*. In OF. an instance of *tatereles* rags, tatters ('a ces vies tatereles vestues') occurs in *Aucassin et Nicolette* vi.

(Notwithstanding similarity of sense, the Norse and Eng. word has no known etymological or phonetic connexion with MLG. and LG. *talter*, pl. *talteren, taltern*, tatters, rags (Brem. Wbch.), whence app. Norw. dial. *taltra*, pl. *taltrar*.)]

**1.** An irregularly torn piece, strip, shred, or scrap of cloth or similar substance, hanging loose from the main body, esp. of a garment; more rarely applied to the separate pieces into which a thing is torn; a rag. In *pl.* often = tattered or ragged clothing; rags.

In early quots. applied in contempt to the 'dags' or projecting pieces of a slashed garment; in quot. 1470–85 to the sharp points or jags in a dragon's tail.

**1402** *Pol. Poems* (Rolls) II. 69 Of suche wide clothing, tateris and tagges, It hirtith myn hert hevyly. **1470–85** MALORY *Arthur* v. iv. 165 A dredeful dragon.. his hede.. enameled with asure.., his taylle ful of tatters. **1520** *Treat. Galaunt* 137 in *Ballads fr. MSS.* I. 450 With longe taters downe to the ars behynde. **1612** ROWLANDS *Knaue of Harts* 23 A suite of ragges and tatters on my backe. **1621** T. WILLIAMSON tr. *Goulart's Wise Vieillard* 172 To goe woolward, in sackcloth, and haire cloth, in totters and ragges. **1686** tr. *Chardin's Trav. Persia* 97 They go Barefoot, and all in Tattars. **1791** MRS. RADCLIFFE *Rom. Forest* ii, The remains of tapestry hung in tatters upon the walls. **1840** R. H. DANA *Bef. Mast* xxv. 82 Furl the sail before it blows to tatters. **1873** 'OUIDA' *Pascarèl* I. 25 What does a tatter or two in the dress signify? **1884** BOWER & SCOTT *De Bary's Phaner.* 216 Thin very obscure tatters of the ruptured tissue clothe the walls of the mature passage.

**b.** *fig.* or in fig. context.

**1576** FLEMING *Panopl. Epist.* 81 Torne to tatters with a thousand tempests of troubles. **1602** SHAKS. *Ham.* III. ii. 11 To see a robustious Pery-wig-pated Fellow, teare a Passion to tatters, to verie ragges. **1607** *Barley-Breake* (1877) 5 Then Hate, and Enuie, all to totters went. **1792** COWPER *Let. to W. Hayley* 4 June, Returned from my walk, blown to tatters. **1875** JOWETT *Plato* (ed. 2) I. 189 Philosophers,.. who tear arguments to tatters.

†**2.** *transf.* A person wearing tattered or ragged clothes; a tatterdemalion. *Obs.*

*c* **1600** DAY *Begg. Bednall Gr.* v. (1881) 110 How, mary with a Beggar? mix the blood of Strowds with a tatter? *a* **1635** RANDOLPH *Hey for Hon.* III. i, Well spoke, my noble English tatter, Lead up the vanguard. **1637** HEYWOOD *Roy. King* II. viii, What Tatter's that that walkes there?

**3.** *attrib.* and *Comb.*, as †*tatter-rag*; *tatter-fudded* (Sc.: see FUD), *tatter-tailed* adjs.; † **tatter-wag** (**tatar-wagge**), **tatter-wallop** (*Sc.* and *n. dial.*), a fluttering tatter or rag; also, a person in ragged clothes.

**1880** J. NICOL *Poems & Songs* 29 The dirty *tatter-fudded Poor stowaway. **1570** LEVINS *Manip.* 10/36 *Tatterraggs, *panniculi*. *c* **1600** RUGGLE *Club Law* (1907) III. ii, This is some *tattertaild Athenian. *c* **1400** *Rom. Rose* 7257 And grey clothis not full clene But fretted full of *tatarwagges. *c* **1400** *Laud Troy Bk.* 9247 He hewys his mayles res by res, He hewys hem alle In taterwagges, His hauberk heng alle In ragges. **1808** JAMIESON, **Tatter-wallops*, tatters, rags in a fluttering state. **1819** W. TENNANT *Papistry Storm'd* (1827) 204 Hood.. cowl and clout, In tatter-wallops flew about. **1828** *Craven Gloss.*, *Tatter-wallops*, a woman with ragged clothes. **1910** *Chambers's Jrnl.* Jan. 30/1 Ye're aye tearin' yer clothes, ye wee tatter-wallops!

**Tatter,** *sb.*[2] *rare.* [f. TAT *v.*[2] + -ER[1].] In *Needlework*: One who tats or does tatting.

**1881** *Faith & Unfaith* I. iv. 54 Miss Peyton.. confronts this eminent tatter.

**Tatter,** *a. dial.* [?] Cross, peevish, testy.

**1579** TWYNE *Phisicke agst. Fort.* I. xv. 17 b, His two wiues, most tatter and testie olde women. *Ibid.* cx. 139 When a man maketh hym selfe seruiceable and subiect to a tatter olde foole. **1736** LEWIS *Isle of Thanet* Gloss., *Tatter*, ragged, cross, peevish, 'he is a very tatter man'. **1887** *Kentish Gloss.* s.v., The old 'ooman's middlin' tatter to-day, I can tell ye.

**Ta·tter,** *v.*[1] Also 4 **tater.** [app. a back-formation from TATTERED.] *trans.* To tear or reduce to tatters; to make ragged; to tear in pieces, mangle. Also *fig. To tatter a kip* (slang): see KIP *sb.*[3] I.

(The ppl. adj. *tattered* and vbl. sb. *tattering* are known before the simple vb.)

[*c* **1380**: see *tattering* vbl. sb. below.] *c* **1440** *York Myst.* xlvi. 44 (Of Christ scourged and crowned with thorns) Ilk tag of þat turtill so tatterid and torne es.] **1608** SYLVESTER *Du Bartas* II. iv. v. *Decay* 342 A Lion, that hath tatterd heer A goodly Heifer, there a lusty Steer. **1652** *Persuasive to Compliance* 6 A Nation so exhausted and tattered by divisions. **1766** GOLDSM. *Vic. W.* xx, To assist at tattering a kip, as the phrase was, when we had a mind for a frolic. **1837** C. LOFFT *Self-formation* I. 34, I tattered some good poetry to rags, expressly for her gratification. *a* **1845** HOOD *Forge* II. xvi, Shrieking for flesh to tear and tatter.

**b.** *intr.* To be or become tattered. *rare.*

**1595** [see *tattering* ppl. adj. below].

Hence **Ta·ttering** *vbl. sb.*[1] (in quot. *c* 1380, slashing of garments) and *ppl. a.*[1]

*c* **1380** WYCLIF *Sel. Wks.* III. 124 Men deformen hor body by hor foule atyre.. and tatering of clothes. *c* **1580** JEFFERIE *Bugbears* Epil., Song ii. in *Archiv Stud. Neu. Spr.* (1897), With battrynges, with plattrynges, with tattrynges. **1595** SHAKS. *John* v. v. 7 After such bloody toile, we bid good night, And woon'd our tott'ring colours clearly vp, Last in the field, and almost Lords of it.

**Ta·tter,** *v.*[2] *Obs.* exc. *dial.* In 4–5 **tater.** [Appears before 1400: = MDu. and Du. *tateren* to stammer, MFl., Fl., to speak imperfectly or inarticulately, MLG., LG., and EFris. *tateren, tatern, tattern* to babble, speak nonsense; to chatter. From the same (prob. echoic) stem as TATTLE.] *intr.* **a.** To talk idly, chatter, prate, tattle. **b.** 'To scold; to chide; to be furious or cross' (E.D.D.). Hence **Ta·ttering** *vbl. sb.*[2] and *ppl. a.*[2]

*c* **1380** WYCLIF *Wks.* (1880) 192 Oure fleschly peple haþ more lykynge in here bodely eris in sich knackynge & taterynge þan in herynge of goddis lawe. *c* **1440** *Promp. Parv.* 487/1 Tateryn, or iaueryn, or speke wythe owte resone (*K.* or iangelyn,.. *P.* iaberyn). *Ibid.*, Taterynge, or iauerynge (*S.* iaperynge, *P.* iaberinge), *garritus*. **1888** ELWORTHY *W. Somerset Gloss.* s.v., Come now, there's to much tatterin' by half, let's have less noise and more work!

**Ta·tter,** *v.*[3] *dial.* [Origin obscure: the form

is frequentative; cf. *patter.*] *intr.* To move or bestir oneself actively; to go or run at a great rate.

*a* **1825** FORBY *Voc. E. Anglia, Tatter, v.* to stir actively and laboriously...'He is a very pains-taking man; always *towing* and *tattering* after his business'. **1828** T. C. CROKER *Fairy Leg.* II. 127 Away they went tattering along the road making the fire fly out of the stones at no rate. **1842** S. LOVER *Handy Andy* xiv, The bell rang violently. 'There, do you hear him tattering?' **1897** CROCKETT *Lochinvar* v. 68 Running fleet-foot .. as though the devil himself had been tattering at his tail.

**Tatter**, erron. variant of TOTTER.

**Tatterdemalion, -demallion** (tæːtədɪ̆mēɪ·liən, -mæ·liən). Forms: *α.* 7–9 **tatterdemallion**, (7 **tatter-, totter-de-mallion, -timallion**). *β.* 7–9 **tatterdemalion**, (7 **tatter-, totter-demalian, -dimalian, -demalean**, 8 **-demelon**). [f. TATTER *sb.*[1], or more prob. TATTERED *a.*, with a factitious element suggesting an ethnic or descriptive derivative. The earlier pronunciation rimes with *battalion, Italian, stallion*, as shown by the frequent doubling of *l.*]

A person in tattered clothing; a ragged or beggarly fellow; a ragamuffin.

*α.* **1611** B. JONSON *Introd. Verses* in *Coryat's Crudities*, This Horse pictur'd showes that our Tatter-de-mallian Did ride the French Hackneyes and lye with th' Italian. *a* **1626** MIDDLETON *Mayor of Queenb.* v. i, He's not so wise as he ought to be, to let such tatterdemallions get the upper hand of him. **1630** CAPT. SMITH *Trav. & Adv.* xvi. 30 Yet those tattertimallions [Tartars] will have two or three horses, some foure, or five. **1642** HOWELL *For. Trav.* (Arb.) 37 Great numbers of poore French tatterdimallians, being as it were the Scumme of the Countrey. **1693** *Oxford-Act* 2 Loyal Oxford..Soon form'd in Squadrons and Battalions To Swinge the Duke's Tatterdemallions. *a* **1700** B. E. *Dict. Cant. Crew, Tatter-de-mallion*, a ragged, tatter'd Begger,..having better Cloths at Home. **1879** *Scribner's Mag.* XIX. 296/1 It is rare to see a tatterdemallion in Paris.

*β.* **1608** DEKKER *Belman Lond.* (1640) 3 Rector Chory (the Captain of the Tatterdemalions). **1622** DEKKER *Virg. Mart.* III. i, Among so many millions of people, should thou and I onely be miserable totterdemalions? **1637** HEYWOOD *Roy. King* II. vii, A Tatterdemalean, that stayes to sit at the Ordinary to day. **1650** HOWELL *Giraffi's Rev. Naples* I. 7 A few poore Tatterdimalians had made all that noise. **1771** SMOLLETT *Humph. Cl.* 24 May, Mrs. Bramble..said, she had never seen such a filthy tatterdemalion. **1858** O. W. HOLMES *Aut. Breakf.-t.* xi. 108 A group of young tatterdemalions playing pitch-and-toss.

**b.** *attrib.* or as *adj.*

**1614** J. COOKE *Greene's Tu Quoque* K j b, Puh, the Italian fashion? the tatterd-de-malian fashion hee meanes. **1651** BIGGS *New Disp.* § 53 That Tatterdemalion Linostema of Peripatetical and Galenical predicaments. **1837** CARLYLE *Fr. Rev.* I. IV. iii, Saint-Antoine..reinforced by the unknown Tatterdemalion Figures, with their enthusiast complexion and large sticks. **1855** CHAMIER *My Travels* II. vi. 85 The most beggarly remnants of tatterdemalion garments. **1893** *Spectator* 25 Nov. 738/1 These tatterdemalion scraps and fragments of political discontent.

Hence (*nonce-wds.*) **Tatterdema·lionism**, the style or practice of a tatterdemalion; **Ta·tterdema·lionry**, the body of tatterdemalions.

**1840** *Blackw. Mag.* XLVIII. 491 Hungarian, Croatian, and Wallachian tatterdemalionry. **1884** *Dumbarton, Vale of Leven*, etc. 27 The tatterdemalionism with which we usually associate the abodes of such. **1887** *Blackw. Mag.* CXLI. 821 His coat was out at both elbows...It was..a kind of defiant tatterdemalionism that the Colonel liked to hug.

**Tattered** (tæ·təɹd), *a.*, *ppl. a.* Forms: *α.* 4 **tatered, tatrid, tatird,** 5 **tatyrd, tatterid,** 5–7 **tatterd,** 6– **tattered, -r'd.** *β.* See TOTTERED. [app. orig. f. TATTER *sb.*[1] + -ED[2]: cf. RAGGED *a.*; subseq. treated as pa. pple. implying a vb.: see TATTER *v.*[1]]

†**1.** Having 'tatters', jags, or long pointed projections; denticulated, jagged; slashed or laciniated, as a garment. *Obs.*

*c* **1394** *P. Pl. Crede* 753 His syre a soutere.., His teeþ wiþ toylinge of leþer tatered as a sawe. **1470–85** MALORY *Arthur* v. iv. 165 His [a dragon's] taylle whiche is al to tatterd sygnefyeth the noble knyghtes of the round table. **1501** DOUGLAS *Pal. Hon.* I. xxv, Dragouns,..With mouthis gapand, forkit taillis tatterit.

**2.** Torn or rent so as to hang in tatters; ragged. (See also TOTTERED *ppl. a.* 1.)

**1596** SPENSER *F. Q.* v. xii. 28 Their garments yet, Being all rag'd and tatter'd. **1600** HOLLAND *Livy* II. xxiii. 58 His apparrell was all to tattered, foule and loathsome. **1709** ADDISON *Tatler* No. 100 ¶ 3 Crowds of People in tattered Garments. **1791** COWPER *Odyss.* IX. 80 Our tatter'd sail-cloth crackled in the wind. **1905** R. GARNETT *Shaks.* 26 The last year's tattered foliage That long ago has rustled to the earth.

**3.** *transf.* †**a.** Clad in jagged or slashed garments (*obs.*). **b.** Having tattered or ragged garments.

**1340** HAMPOLE *Pr. Consc.* 1537 Som has þair clethyng hyngand als stoles Som gas tatird als tatird foles. *c* **1380** WYCLIF *Wks.* (1880) 148 In here gaye pellure & precious cloþis & wast festis & tatrid squeyeres & oþere meyne. **1596** [see TOTTERED *ppl. a.* 1]. **1623** MASSINGER *Dk. Milan* III. i, To see the tatter'd'st rascals of my troop Drag them out of their closets. ? *a* **1750** *Nursery Rime, House that Jack Built* viii, This is the man all tattered and torn. **1883** *Century Mag.* July 419/2 An aged and tattered negro was the mule's ring-master.

†**4.** Having unkempt dishevelled hair, of irregular length; shaggy. Cf. TATTY *a. Obs.*

**1340** [see 3]. *c* **1460** *Towneley Myst.* I. 137 Now ar we waxen blak as any coylle, And vgly, tatyrd as a foylle. **1709** STEELE & SWIFT *Tatler* No. 70 ¶ 10 A..French Mongrel, that was..in a tatter'd Condition, but has now got new Hair.

†**5.** Of a ship, building, or other solid structure: Dilapidated, battered, shattered. *Obs.* (See also TOTTERED *ppl. a.* 2.)

**1599** NASHE *Lenten Stuffe* Wks. (Grosart) V. 277 Nothing of that Castle saue tattered ragged walles nowe remaines. **1666** DRYDEN *Ann. Mirab.* cxxxiv, [He] warns his tattered fleet to follow home. **1700** S. L. tr. *Fryke's Voy. E. Ind.* 30 To mend our tattered ships. **1797–8** JANE AUSTEN *Sense & Sens.* xviii, I do not like ruined, tattered cottages.

†**b.** Of troops: Routed and broken up, shattered, disintegrated. *Obs.*

**1675** OTWAY *Alcibiades* III. i, Their tatter'd troops are scatter'd o'er the plain. **1728** MORGAN *Algiers* I. iii. 40 Where he continued till he had recruited his tattered army.

Hence **Ta·tteredly** *adv.*

**1673** E. BROWN *Trav. Germ.*, etc. (1677) 126 The Windows ..being of Glass, looked not so tatterdly as the ragged Paper Windows of Florence.

**Tattering**, *vbl. sb.* and *ppl. a.*: see TATTER *v.*[1], [2].

†**Ta·tterly**, *a. Obs. rare.* [f. TATTER *sb.*[1] + -LY[1].] Of the nature of tatters; tattered.

**1739** MACHIN in Rigaud *Corr. Sci. Men* (1841) I. 354 Impudently sending them in such tatterly rags a begging to your worship.

**Tattertimallion**, obs. f. TATTERDEMALION.

**Tattery** (tæ·təri), *a.* [f. TATTER *sb.*[1] + -Y.] Full of tatters; tattered, ragged.

*c* **1843** CARLYLE *Hist. Sk.* (1898) 242 Deluges of tangled tattery hair. **1867** — *Remin.* (1881) II. 21 Books in tattery, ill-bound or unbound condition.

**Tattie**, Sc. dial. or vulgar corr. of POTATO.

**Tattie**, var. TATTY *sb.*; obs. f. TATTY *a.*

**Tatting** (tæ·tiŋ). [Origin unknown: perh. an arbitrary formation. It has the form of a verbal sb. from TAT *v.*[2]; but that verb is of more recent appearance, as if merely a back-formation from *tatting.*] **a.** *sb.* A kind of knotted lace, netted with a small flat shuttle-shaped instrument from stout sewing-thread; used for edging or trimming, and sometimes for doyleys, parasol covers, etc. (called in F. *frivolité*, Ger. *frivolitäten*). **b.** *vbl. sb.* The action or process of making this. Also *attrib.* as *tatting-cotton, -edging, -net, -shuttle, -stitch, -work.* (Tatting-shuttles exist which are said to have been used before 1820.)

**1842** MRS. GAUGAIN *Lady's Assist. Knitting*, etc. II. 411 Common Tatting Edging. *Ibid.* 412 If the Tatting has not been properly worked, this scollop will not draw. All Tatting stitches must be formed with the loop round the fingers. **1864** *Sat. Rev.* 22 May, It retires to talk scandal over her tatting with any fashionable old maid with whom the party may be tormented. **1865** *Reader* 28 Oct. 479/3 In 1851 the Census showed a return of 902 pupils in the various arts of crochet laces, point lace.., pillow lace,..plain sewing, knitting and tatting. **1877** KNIGHT *Dict. Mech., Tatting-shuttle*, a small shuttle used in tatting. **1895** *Times* 2 Jan. 13/2 Orders for cotton embroidery edgings, trimmings, and tattings have been disappointing. **1901** CLARA MORRIS *Life on Stage* 46 The 'tatting' craze was sweeping over the country [U.S.A.] then [*c* 1863]; everybody wore tatting, and almost everybody made it.

**Tattle** (tæ·t'l), *sb.* Also 6 **tatle**: see also TITTLE-TATTLE. [f. next. Cf. LG. *tätel* in same sense.] The action of tattling; idle or frivolous talk; chatter, gossip.

*a* **1529** Tyttel tattyll [see TITTLE-TATTLE]. **1589** GREENE *Menaphon* (Arb.) 40 Amidst other tattle, they prattled of the beautie of Samela. **1654** WHITLOCK *Zootomia* 57 At Gossipings, Funeralls, at Church before Sermons, and the like opportunities of tattle. **1713** SWIFT *Cadenus & Van.* 320 They..told the tattle of the day. **1869** DIXON *Tower* I. xviii. 215 All this tattle was repeated..to the Queen. **1895** C. GORE *Dissert.* I. vi. 60 The reserve of the canonical and the vulgar tattle of the apocryphal Gospels.

**b.** with *a* and *pl.* A fit of tattling; a 'gossip'. Now *rare.*

**1583** BABINGTON *Commandm.* vii. (1590) 309 The dalying tatles of these courting dayes,..and the wanton greetings in euery place now vsed. **1612** tr. *Benvenuto's Passenger* II. i. § 16 Like olde wiues tales, or tattles. **1783** *Priv. Lett. Ld. Malmesbury* (1870) I. 485, I understand there have been some little tattles going between us. *c* **1824** PRAED *Pol. & Occ. Poems, Coronat. Chas. X*, Three dukes were very nearly slain, Which would have made a tattle For many a day.

**c.** *attrib.* and *Comb.*, as *tattle-basket* (cf. *chatter-box*), *-monger.*

**1736** AINSWORTH *Lat. Dict.* II, *Lingulaca*,..(2) A prating gossip, a tattle-basket. **1848** THACKERAY *Bk. Snobs* iv, She knew..how all the tattle-mongers..watched the movements of the Snobkys with interest. **1874** LISLE CARR *Jud. Gwynne* I. ix. 272 A prosaic friendship, that has nothing in it at which the tattlemongers of this place may chatter.

**Tattle** (tæ·t'l), *v.* Also 8 **tattel**; *pr. pple.* and *gerund* 5–6 **tatelyng**(e, 5–7 **tatling.** [Appears in Caxton's 'Reynard the Fox', 1481, where it reproduces MFlem. *tatelen*, a parallel form to the more usual MFlem., MDu., MLG., also Flem., Du., EFris. *tateren* (see TATTER *v.*[2]), with exchange of frequentative suffixes *-er, -el.* LG. has also *tateln, täteln* to gabble, cackle (whence *tatelgos* gabbling goose), Brem. Wbch. Cf. also TITTLE *v.*, and TITTLE-TATTLE, in LG. *titeltateln.* Ultimately onomatopœic.]

†**1.** *intr.* To speak hesitatingly, falter, stammer; *esp.* to prattle as a young child; to utter baby-talk.

**1481** [see TATTLING *vbl. sb.* 1]. **1579** LYLY *Euphues* (Arb.) 129 When the babe shall now begin to tattle and call hir Mamma. **1586** DAY *Eng. Secretary* I. (1625) 68 A childe.. whose infancy tatling with a pleasant lisping sound, shall become an incredible delight to the Parents hearing. *a* **1719** ADDISON tr. *Ovid, Birth Bacchus* 40 In her trembling gate she [Juno] totters on, And learns to tattle in the Nurse's tone.

**2.** To utter small talk; to talk idly or lightly; to chatter, babble, prate; to chat, gossip.

**1547** [see TATTLING *vbl. sb.* 2]. [**1550**: see TATTLER 1.] *a* **1568** *Bannatyne Poems* (Hunter. Cl.) 1082 Louers must be tatling; Go to, good sir, you ar ane foole, yow dull me with your pratling. **1581** J. BELL *Haddon's Answ. Osorius* 490 To tattle and clatter without Judgement of matters of Divinitie. **1668** DRYDEN *Evening's Love* III. i, I must tell you, sir, you have tattled long enough. **1751** JOHNSON *Rambler* No. 153 ¶ 14, I was tattling with my former freedom. **1838** LYTTON *Alice* III. vii, She tattled on, first to one,..then to all.

**b.** *transf.* and *fig.*

**1576–1881** [see TATTLING *ppl. a.* b]. **1600** J. LANE *Tom Tel-troth* 37, I seeme to heare resounding Ecchoes tatling, Of misdemeanors raigning heere and there. *a* **1603** T. CARTWRIGHT *Confut. Rhem. N. T.* (1618) 581 The merite of this reliefe, whereof your by-note in the margent tatleth.

**3.** To talk without reticence so as to reveal secrets or private affairs; to blab, 'tell tales'. (Now usually with mixture of sense 2.)

**1581** [see TATTLING *ppl. a.*]. **1639** S. DU VERGER tr. *Camus' Admir. Events* 211 To have exposed her to the tatling of tongues, was a thing he feared like death. **1652** J. WRIGHT tr. *Camus' Nat. Paradox* v. 93 People of that Nature have never a greater itch to bee Tatling, than when they are commanded to be Silent, and the greater the danger is, the more are they tempted to reveal it. **1710** PALMER *Proverbs* 197 When one of the gang tattles, confesses, and accuses the rest. **1876** HOLLAND *Sev. Oaks* xx, She had always been one whom they could have in their families..she never tattled.

**4.** *trans.* To utter, say, or tell over in tattling. Now *rare.*

**1588** SHAKS. *Tit. A.* IV. ii. 168 Then let the Ladies tattle what they please. **1593** *Tell-troth's N. Y. Gift* (1876) 11 They will tatle tales. **1649** MILTON *Eikon.* xvii. 159 This intricate stuffe tattl'd here of Timothy and Titus and I know not whom thir Successors. **1729** T. COOKE *Tales, Proposals*, etc. 57 What from the Frankness of your Soul you say, The Fool may tattel, and the Knave betray.

**5.** With advb. extension: To get or bring into some condition by tattling.

**1751** JOHNSON *Rambler* No. 108 ¶ 10 Lest the hours.. should be tattled away without regard to literature. **1838** LYTTON *Alice* III. vii, She tattled on..till she had tattled herself out of breath.

Hence **Ta·ttlement**, tattling, chatter.

**1837** CARLYLE *Misc.* (1872) VI. 225 Poor little Lilias Baillie; tottering about there, with her foolish glad tattlement.

**Tattler** (tæ·tləɹ). Also 6 **tatyllar**, 6–9 **tatler.** [Agent-n. f. TATTLE *v.* + -ER[1]. So LG. *täteler.*]

**1.** One who tattles; an idle talker, a chatterer; a gossip; a talebearer, telltale.

**1550** CROWLEY *Last Trump.* 1609 Vaine tatyllars, That do vse false rumoures to sowe. **1611** BIBLE 1 *Tim.* v. 13 Not onely idle, but tatlers also, and busibodies, speaking things which they ought not. **1682** BUNYAN *Holy War* xi. (Cassell) 249 Mr. Prywell..a sober and judicious man, a man that is no tattler, nor raiser of false reports. **1781** COWPER *Friendship* xvii, Whoever keeps an open ear For tattlers, will be sure to hear The trumpet of contention. **1847** L. HUNT *Men, Women, & Bks.* II. x. 252 As great and scandalous a tattler as anybody.

**2.** *slang.* A striking watch, a repeater; a watch in general.

**1688** SHADWELL *Sqr. Alsatia* II. Wks. 1726 IV. 47 Here's a Tatler, gold, all gold, you rogue. *a* **1700** B. E. *Dict. Cant. Crew, Tattler*, an Alarm, or Striking Watch, or (indeed) any. **1844** W. H. MAXWELL *Sports & Adv. Scot.* viii. (1855) 85 He carries his 'tatler' in the waistband of his unmentionables.

**3.** *Ornith.* Any of the sandpipers of the genus *Totanus* or subfamily *Totaninæ*; so called from their vociferous cry.

**1831** RICHARDSON & SWAINSON *Faun. Bor.-Amer.* II. 388 *Totanus semipalmatus* (Temm.), Semipalmated Tatler. **1872** COUES *N. Amer. Birds* 250 The *Terekia cinerea*..stands between the godwits and tattlers. **1892** A. E. LEE *Hist. Columbus* (Ohio) I. 17 *note*, Yellow-legged snipe, or tattler, ..common in autumn on western rivers.

So **Ta·ttlery** (*rare*—°), 'idle talk or chat' (Webster 1847).

**Tattling** (tæ·tliŋ), *vbl. sb.* [f. TATTLE *v.* + -ING[1].] The action of the verb TATTLE.

†**1.** Faltering, stammering; prattling; baby-talk.

**1481** CAXTON *Reynard* xxvii. (Arb.) 65 But who can gyue to his lesynge a conclusion, and prononce it without tatelyng [*orig.* ende seit sine woerden sonder tatelen]. **1749** FIELDING *Tom Jones* XVIII. xiv, He declares the tattling of his little grand-daughter, who is above a year and a half old, is sweeter music than the finest cry of dogs in England.

**2.** Idle talking; chattering, prating; gossiping; blabbing, tale-telling.

**1547** in Strype *Eccl. Mem.* (1721) II. iv. 24 [Barlow, bishop of S. Davids..preached at court..urging..a redress of several abuses in religion...The Bishop of Winchester..was mightily disturbed at it, calling it] his tattling. **1598** SHAKS. *Merry W.* IV. i. 26 Peace, your tatlings. **1673** *Lady's Call.* I. i. § 12 When 'tis remembred that St. Paul makes tatling the effect of idleness. *a* **1693** *Urquhart's Rabelais* III. xiii. 106 The.. tatling of Jackdaws,..kekling of Hens. *a* **1720** SEWEL *Hist. Quakers* (1795) I. IV. 364 We do it in private to keep you from tattling. **1825** T. HOOK *Sayings* Ser. II. *Man of Many Fr.*, So that no discovery..might be made by any tattling amongst the servants.

**Ta·ttling**, *ppl. a.* [f. as prec. + -ING[2].] That tattles; chattering, gossiping; tale-telling.

**1581** J. Bell *Haddon's Answ. Osor.* 28 Blowen abroad.. amongest tattlyng women, foolishe children. **1664** Butler *Hud.* II. I. 77 This tattling Gossip knew too well What mischief Hudibras befell. **1712** Arbuthnot *John Bull* III. v, Tattling people that carried tales. **1841** Hood *Tale Trumpet* 92 In the prattling, tattling village of Tringham.

**b.** *transf.* and *fig.*: cf. *babbling*; sometimes = 'tell-tale'.

**1576** Gascoigne *Philomene* 35 The tatling Awbe doth please some fancie wel, And some like best, the byrde as Black as cole. **1652** Benlowes *Theoph.* IV. lxviii, When keen breath'd winds..glaze tatling stream. **1731** Swift *Cassinus & Peter* Wks. 1755 IV. I. 165 Nor whisper to the tattling reeds The blackest of all female deeds. **1881** E. Arnold *Ind. Poetry* 91 Let him hear the tattling ripple Of the bangles round thy feet.

Hence **Ta·ttlingly** *adv.* **1847** in Webster.

**Tatto**, Sc. dial. or vulgar corr. of Potato.

**Tattoo** (tætū·), *sb.*[1] Forms: *α.* 7 **tap-too, tap too, tapp too,** 7–8 **taptow,** 7–9 **taptoo.** *β.* 7 **tat too, tato,** 8 **tatoo,** 9 **tattoe,** 7– **tattoo.** [In 17th c. *tap-too*, a. Du. *taptoe* in same sense; f. *tap* the tap (of a cask), + *toe* = *doe toe* 'shut'. So Sw. *tapto*, Sp. (1706) *tatu.* Cf. Ger. *zapfenstreich*, LG. *tappenslag*, Da. *tappenstreg*, with the first element the same, and second element meaning 'stroke, beat'.

Although Du. *tap toe* was in military use in our sense 1 in the 17th c., there is reason to doubt if this was its original use. *Tap toe* = *doe den tap toe* 'put the tap to', 'close or turn off the tap', was app. already in colloquial use for 'shut up! stop! cease!'; Dr. Kluyver points out, in a play of 1639 from Emden, *Doch hier de tap van toe* = 'but here we shut up', or 'say no more'.]

**1.** *Mil.* A signal made, by beat of drum or bugle-call, in the evening, for soldiers to repair to their quarters in garrison or tents in camp.

*α.* **1644** *Col. Hutchinson's Orders* in T. C. Hine *Nottingham*, etc. (1876) App. § 8 If anyone shall bee found tiplinge or drinkinge in any Taverne, Inne, or Alehouse after the houre of nyne of the clock at night, when the Tap-too beates, hee shall pay 2*s.* 6*d.* *Ibid.* § 10 After the houre of nyne of the clock at night, after the taptoo hath beaten, untill the Revelly hath beaten the next morninge. **1645** N. Drake *Siege Pontefr.* (Surtees) 65 Not to stay there any longer but till tapp too beate, which was about 10 a clock. **1675** *Lond. Gaz.* No. 1014/4 The third night, after .. the Taptow had beaten, we made a very good Retreat, without the loss of a Man. **1706** Phillips (ed. 6), *Tat-too* or *Taptoo*, the beat of Drum at Night for all Soldiers to repair to their Tents. **1736** Ainsworth *Lat. Dict.*, Taptow, tattoo. **1803** Collins *Gen. & Garrison Orders* (1879) 30 After the beating of the taptoo. **1833** Sir C. J. Napier *Colonies* 190 The soldiers are just able to hear the 'taptoo' beat.

*β.* **1688** R. Holme *Armoury* III. xix. (Roxb.) 153/2 The drumer is to beat all maner of beats, as a Call, a Troope, a March,..a Retreit, a Tato, and a Revally. **1698** Fryer *Acc. E. India & P.* 74 None but Christians lodge within the City [Bacein], the Banyans repairing to the Suburbs upon Tattoo. **1767** in R. Rogers *Jrnls.* (1883) 238 *note*, Your memorialist must further inform you that Rum was let out of the Fort after tatoo. **1814** Scott *Wav.* lxvii, I question if the red-coats hae beat the tattoo yet, and we're not safe till then. **1844** *Regul. & Ord. Army* 259 The Tattoo is to beat at Eight o'clock in the Winter, and at Nine o'clock in the Summer Season. **1884** Grove *Dict. Mus.* IV. 63/2 The Tattoo concludes by the 'Second Post' or 'Last Post'.

**b.** A military entertainment consisting of an elaboration of the tattoo by extra music and performance of exercises by troops, generally at night and by torch or other artificial light. (So G. *zapfenstreich.*)

**1742** H. Walpole *Lett.* (1903) I. 216 You know one loves a review and a tattoo. **1904** *Daily News* 8 Aug. 7 The Sherwood Foresters..carried out the tattoo under the direction of Lieut. Parkinson. **1907** *Standard* 19 Jan. 6/7 After dark there was a torchlight tattoo, in which 800 men took part.

**c.** A drum-beat in general, as a means of raising an alarm, attracting attention, etc.

**1688** in Boys *Sandwich* (1792) 760 The news..caused us.. to keep a strong watch, and the tattoo was sent about. **1709** Steele *Tatler* No. 109 ⁋ 3 A young Lady cannot be married, but all the Impertinents in Town must be beating the Tattoo from one Quarter of the Town to the other, to show they know what passes. **1717** Prior *Alma* I. 454 All those, whose hearts are loose and low Start if they hear but the tattoo. **1872** C. Gibbon *For the King* i, The drum beat a reckless tattoe.

*fig.* **1579** Dilworth *Pope* 87 Every such advertisement is a tattoo for all the mercenary scribblers in a nation.

**2.** *transf.* A beating or pulsation as of a drum; the action of beating, thumping, or rapping continuously upon something.

**1755** H. Walpole *Lett.* (1846) III. 136 Can I help feeling a tattoo at my heart, when the Duke of Newcastle makes as great a figure in history as Burleigh or Godolphin? **1820** *Sporting Mag.* VI. 178 He..played such a tattoo upon his antagonist's head, as rendered him almost senseless. **1840** Thackeray *Bedford-Row Conspir.* iii, Beginning to play a rapid tattoo with her feet. **1878** *Masque Poets* 97 The hail begins to beat outside A tattoo for the storm.

**b.** *Devil's tattoo*: the action of idly tapping or drumming with the fingers, etc. upon a table or other object, in an irritating manner, or as a sign of vexation, impatience, or the like.

**1803** Mar. Edgeworth *Belinda* xvii, Mrs. Freke beat the devil's-tattoo for some moments. **1826** Disraeli *Viv. Grey* II. ii, The Peer sat in a musing mood, playing the Devil's tattoo on the library table. **1855** H. Spencer *Princ. Psychol.* (1872) II. VIII. iv. 544 Beating the 'devil's tattoo' with the fingers on the table, is a recognized mark of impatience.

**Tattoo** (tætū·), *sb.*[2] Forms: 8 **tat(t)aow,** 8–9 **tattow, tatoo,** 9 **tatto, tatu,** 8– **tattoo.** [In 18th c. *tattaow, tattow* (tatau·), a. Polynesian (Tahitian, Samoan, Tongan, etc.) *ta·tau* (in Marquesan *ta·tu*) sb. denoting the markings. (For the vb. the expression is *ta ta·tau* to strike or stamp tattoo.)

The word is recorded from Tahiti as *tataou* in Bougainville's *Voyage autour du Monde* 1766–9 (Paris 1771), and as *tattow* in Capt. Cook's *First Voyage* July 1769. The current Eng. *tattoo* and F. *tatou* are perversions of the native name.]

The act or practice of tattooing the skin (see Tattoo *v.*[2]); the mark or design made by tattooing.

[**1769** Cook *Jrnl. 1st Voy.* July (1893) 93 Both sexes paint their Bodys, *Tattow*, as it is called in their Language. This is done by inlaying the Colour of Black under their skins, in such a manner as to be indelible.] **1777** G. Forster *Voy. round World* I. 390 The punctuation which the natives call tattow. **1803** J. Burney *Discov. S. Sea* I. ii. 61 They [natives of the Philippines] had the custom of marking their bodies in the manner, which, to use a word lately adopted from the language of a people more recently discovered, we call tattow. **1863** R. F. Burton *Abeokuta* I. iii. 104 There was a vast variety of tattoos and ornamentation. **1906** *Athenæum* 17 Mar. 334/2 The Kenyahs and Sea-Dayaks also appear to have borrowed the practice of tatu very largely from the Kenyans; but most of the Indonesian tribes have all had..a distinctive tatu.

**b.** *attrib.* and *Comb.*

**1845** J. Coulter *Adv. in Pacific* xiv. 209 Then entered the tatoo-men. **1899** Werner *Capt. of Locusts* 9 His teeth are not filed, and he has strange tattoo-marks on his face.

**Ta·ttoo,** *sb.*[3] *East Ind.* Also 8 **tatoo,** 9 **tatto, tattu, (tut-hoo).** [a. Hindī *ṭaṭṭū.*] A native-bred Indian pony. Also *attrib.* as *tattoo horse, mare.* Abbreviated Tat (*sb.*[4]).

**1784** in Seton-Karr *Select. fr. Calcutta Gaz.* (1864) I. 15 On their arrival at the Choultry they found a miserable dooley and 15 tattoo horses. **1800** *Misc. Tr.* in *Asiat. Ann. Reg.* 171/2 A man mounted on a tattoo came forward to tell us, that [etc.]. **1809** Broughton *Lett. Mahratta Camp* xiv. (1892) 117 These tut,hoos are a breed of small ponies, and are the most useful and hardy little animals in India. **1814** Southey in *Q. Rev.* XII. 200 A Mahratta wife..frequently rides astride..upon a bullock, an ass, or a little *tattoo* horse. **1886** *Blackw. Mag.* Sept. 365/1 Drawn by tattoos and bullocks.

**Tattoo·,** *v.*[1] [f. Tattoo *sb.*[1]]

**1.** *trans.* To beat (a drum, etc.); to strike (something) with a succession of blows, to thump.

**1780** S. J. Pratt *Emma Corbett* (ed. 4) II. 51 A little drum tattoo'd by the timber instrument that served him for an arm. **1863** Cowden Clarke *Shaks. Char.* xvi. 402 Then let us hope he may not have his head tattooed.

**2.** *intr.* To beat as upon a drum; to thump, tap, or rap upon something with a succession of blows.

**1806** Wolcott (P. Pindar) *Tristia* Wks. 1812 V. 235 There Folly rushes with his dirty boots, Tattoos, and nearly thunders down the dwelling. **1832** Ht. Martineau *Ireland* iii. 39 Her father..tattooing with his brogues upon the threshold. **1883** Dutton Cook *P. Foster's D.* iv, Don't tattoo with your fingers, it fidgets me.

**b.** *trans.* To cause (something) to rap in this way (*upon* something else).

**1810** *Splendid Follies* I. 57 Miss Betty..sat tattooing one of her shoe-heels upon the hearth.

Hence **Tattoo·ing** *vbl. sb.* (also *attrib.*).

**1871** B. Harte *2nd Review Grand Army* ii, The wandering night-winds seemed to bear The sounds of a far tattooing. **1884** Allbutt *Visceral Neuroses* i. 23 Some little blinking, twitching, or tattooing trick which quickens as thoughts and words come faster.

**Tattoo·,** *v.*[2] Forms: see Tattoo *sb.*[2] [f. Tattoo *sb.*[2]; already used as a vb. by Capt. Cook.]

**1.** *trans.* To form permanent marks or designs upon the skin by puncturing it and inserting a pigment or pigments: practised by various tribes of low civilization, and by individuals in civilized communities. **a.** with the person or part as obj.

**1769** Cook *Jrnl. 1st Voy.* July (1893) 93 This method of Tattowing I shall now describe...As this is a painful operation, especially the Tattowing their Buttocks, it is performed but once in their Life times. *Ibid.* 27 Nov. 164 Few of these people were Tattow'd or marked in the face,..several had their Backsides Tattow'd. **1774** Mme. D'Arblay *Early Diary* (1889) I. 325 His hands are very much tattooed. **1774** *Charac.* in *Ann. Reg.* 61/2 His hands are tattaowed, according to the mode in his native country. **1835** Sir J. Ross *Narr. 2nd Voy.* xvi. 251 All were tattooed to a greater or less extent. **1846** Brittan tr. *Malgaigne's Man. Oper. Surg.* 88 We know that soldiers tattoo their arms and breasts, and impress and trace on them words and figures that neither lotions nor even blisters can efface. **1847** Grote *Greece* II. xxv. IV. 5 They [Illyrians] shared with the remote Thracian tribes the custom of tattowing their bodies. **1852** Mundy *Our Antipodes* x. (1855) 247 [The Maori women] tattoo the under-lip a deep blue. **1887** W. S. Gilbert *Ruddigore* I, Look at his arms—tattooed to the shoulder.

**b.** with the mark or design as object.

**1809** A. Henry *Trav.* 248 The women..usually tatoo two lines, reaching from the lip to the chin. **1857** Hughes *Tom Brown* II. ii, His long skinny arms all covered with anchors and arrows and letters, tattooed in with gunpowder like a sailor-boy's. **1877** W. H. Dall *Tribes N. W.* 89 The.. practice of tattooing perpendicular lines on the chin of women. **1902** *Man* II. 99 That a totem should be tatued on a body is a widespread practice.

**2.** *transf.* and *fig.* To mark, spot, or stain, esp. in a permanent way; to affect or characterize permanently as if by marking; to defame, vilify, 'blacken' (quot. 1884).

**1774** *Westm. Mag.* II. 145 Well I remember when tataow'd you stood, In all the dignity of H——'s blood. **1806–7** J. Beresford *Miseries Hum. Life* (1826) VI. *Miseries Stage C.* xi, A Harridan with a face tattooed with wrinkles. **1847** Longf. in *Life* (1891) II. 86 Proof-sheets of Evangeline all tattooed with Folsom's marks. **1884** *Tribune* (N.Y.) June, Mr. Blaine is tattooed...So was Abraham Lincoln...As soon as any man gains public confidence, malignant and envious creatures are found to revile him. **1886** Ruskin *Præterita* I. vi. 177 The pleasure of tattooing myself with tar among the ropes.

Hence **Tattooed** (-ū·d) *ppl. a.*, **Tattoo·ing** *vbl. sb.* (also *concr.*; also *attrib.*, as *tattooing-needle*); also **Tattoo·age** (*nonce-wd.*), a tattooed design [= F. *tatouage*]; **Tattoo·er,** one who practises tattooing; **Tattoo·ist,** a professional tattooer; **Tattoo·ment,** the action or process of tattooing.

**1846** Thackeray *Cornhill to Cairo* xiii, Above his *tattooage of the five crosses, the fellow had a picture of two hearts united. **1789** Mrs. Piozzi *Journ. France* II. 17 The accounts given us in Cook's Voyages of *tattowed Indians. **1791** Gilpin *Forest Scenery* II. 261 The Indian..doting on her black teeth, and tattooed cheeks. **1846** Keightley *Notes Virg., Georg.* III. 25 The wild-looking tattooed Britons. **1897** P. Warung *Tales Old Regime* 168 Tattooed anchor on right forearm. **1906** *Athenæum* 17 Mar. 334/2 To classify the tatued peoples of Borneo. **1837** *Fraser's Mag.* XVI. 641 The azure dye of the *tattooer is lastingly imprinted in the face of an Otaheitan. **1883** *Daily News* 26 Oct. 5/2 The great tattooers among European peoples are French soldiers and French criminals. **1773** *Charac.* in *Ann. Reg.* 3/2 They have a custom of staining their bodies ..which they call *Tattowing. **1830** Marryat *King's Own* iii, The practice of tattooing is very common in the navy. **1859** Jephson *Brittany* xii. 211 Scored..to resemble the tattooing of a New-Zealander. **1877** Knight *Dict. Mech.*, *Tattooing-needle* (Surgical), an instrument for inserting a pigment beneath the epidermis. Used..for coloring white spots on the cornea. **1894** *Pall Mall G.* 5 Dec. 2/1 *Tattooists vied with each other in their efforts to invent new designs. **1885** J. H. Dell *Dawning Grey, Mind* 35 At best But rude *tattooment of embellishment.

**Tattoo, tattou,** variants of Tatou, armadillo.

**Tattu,** variant of Tatou, Tattoo *sb.*[3]

‖**Tatty** (tæ·ti), *sb. East Ind.* Also **tattie, tattee, tatti.** [a. Hindī *ṭaṭṭī.*] A screen or mat, usually made of the roots of the fragrant cuscus grass, which is placed in a frame so as to fill up the opening of a door or window, and kept wet, in order to cool and freshen the air of a room. Abbreviated Tat (*sb.*[3]).

**1792** Williams in *Phil. Trans.* LXXXIII. 131 Tatties.. are affixed to the door or window frames, and kept constantly sprinkled with water. **1809** Broughton *Lett. Mahratta Camp* x. (1892) 83 The hot winds have set in, and we are obliged to make use of *tattees*, a kind of screens made of the roots of a coarse grass called Kus. **1811** H. Martyn in *Mem.* III. (1825) 342, I got a tattie made of the branches of the date tree, and a Persian peasant to water it. **1901** *Indian Standard* 16 Mar. 1/1 Those who..have neither Khas Tatties nor thermantidotes will pant..for want of fresh air.

*attrib.* **1848** tr. *Hoffmeister's Trav. Ceylon*, etc. vii. 277 [Rooms with] but one external entrance, and that closed up by means of a tatty-frame.

Hence **Tattied** (tæ·tid) *a.*, furnished with a tatty or tatties.

**1894** *Blackw. Mag.* Sept. 387/2 The Anglo-Indian is a close prisoner within the kus-kus tattied walls.

**Tatty** (ta·ti), *a. Sc.* Also 6 **taty, tawty, tattie,** 9 **tawtie, tautie.** [app. related in form and sense to OE. *tættec* a rag, a tatter; cf. also Tat *sb.*[4], which is not evidenced so early, and may be a back-formation.] Of hair, tangled, matted; of an animal or skin, shaggy with matted hair.

**1513** Douglas *Æneis* VII. xii. 63 A felloun bustuus and gret lyoun skyn, Terrible and rouch, wyth taty lokyrand haris. **1533** Bellenden *Livy* II. xi. (S. T. S.) I. 166 The hare of his berde was lang and taty [*v.r.* tawty]. **1818** Scott *Rob Roy* xxxiv, Wha wad hae thought there had been as muckle sense in his tatty pow. **1834** Carlyle in Froude *Life* (1882) II. xviii. 428 Old pollarded..lime trees standing there like giants in tawtie wigs (for the new boughs are still young).

**Tatu:** see Tatou, Tattoo *sb.*[2]

**Tatuete** (erron. **-ette**): see Tatou.

†**Tatuite,** = *t' atwite*, to twit, taunt: see T'[1] and Atwite *v.*

*c* **1315** Shoreham *Poems* i. 1132 For fo:-ȝetene sennes, þat oure foman aredy haueþ..Tatuite.

**Tatusiid** (tătū·siˌid), *a.* and *sb. Zool.* [ad. mod.L. *Tatusiidæ*, pl., f. *Tatusia*, f. Tupi *tatu*: see Tatou and -id[3].] **a.** *adj.* Belonging to the family *Tatusiidæ* of armadillos, typified by the genus *Tatusia*. **b.** *sb.* An armadillo of this family.

**Taty, Tatyllar,** obs. ff. Tatty *a.*, Tattler.

**Tau** (tǭ, tau). Also 4, 6 **taue,** 4 **tav,** 4–8 **taw,** 5 **tayu, tayewe.** [a. Gr. ταῦ, name of the letter T in the Greek alphabet, as in the Semitic whence the Greek was derived: see T, the letter.]

**1.** The name of the letter T in the Greek, Hebrew, and ancient Semitic alphabets. Often in the sense 'last letter', as *tau* was orig. in Greek, and continued to be in Hebrew, etc.

*a* **1300** *Cursor M.* 12199–12204 Þe letters fra alpha to taw [*Gött.* tau, *F.* taw, *Tr.* tayu], Wit sundri sight man mai þam knau [*Tr.* sew]. Quat es taw, sai first to me, And i sal vndo alpha to þe; For he þat alpha can noght se, Hu sal he wijt quat tav mai be? **1838** Jackson tr. *Krummacher's Elisha* ix. 199 Set a mark upon them..a Tau, the last letter of the Hebrew alphabet, upon their foreheads. **1883** I. Taylor *Alphabet* I. 239 The letters *he, lamed*, and *tau* are almost the same in the Siloam inscription as on the Moabite stone, which is older by a century and a half. *Ibid.* II. 106 The persistency in the shape of *tau*, which varies less than any other letter, our modern capital T hardly differing from the [Phœnician] Baal Lebanon form.

**2.** A mark of the shape of the letter T, a St. Anthony's cross; a figure of this as a sacred symbol (also in *Heraldry*). Also formerly applied to the sign of the cross as made with the hand.

**a 1300** *Cursor M.* 6078 (Cott.) On aiþer post þer hus to smer, A takin o tav on þair derner [*Gott.* On ilk derner, A sine of tau T [*Trin.* thayu] make ȝe þer]. *Ibid.* 21711-6 Þe signe o tav in ald laies Bitakens cros nu in vr daies...Tau and cros bath er als an, Bot tav has yerd a-bouen nan. **c 1446** Lydg. *Nightingale Poems* ii. 318 This banner is most myghti of vertu,..Most noble signe and token of Tau. **1700** Astry tr. *Saavedra-Faxardo* II. 316 It is by the Tau they are stampt with, that they are assured of their real Value. **1704** J. Harris *Lex. Techn.* I, *Taw*, the Heralds have an Ordinary which they reckon among the Crosses, called by this Name, and of this Figure. **1895** *Q. Rev.* July 213 Tradition may conceive that the Tau was the mark of Cain. **1908** *Ibid.* July 142 Little images of bad silver, with the Saint's bell, his 'Tau' and the notorious pig.

**b.** Applied to the *crux ansata* of ancient Egyptian symbolism, the *ankhu* ☥.

**1857** Wilkinson *Egypt. Time Pharaohs* 133 The gods hold in one hand the sacred Tau, or sign of life. **1877** A. B. Edwards *Up Nile* ix. 238. **1886** C. R. Conder *Syrian Stone Lore* 253 *note*, The emblems of the..phœnix, the tau, the labarum, and the fylfot occur, but not the cross.

**3.** A T-shaped pastoral staff.

**1855** tr. *Labarte's Arts Mid. Ages* xiii. 381 Pastoral staff called..a Tau. **1875** Maskell *Ivories* 84 The Tau..is but a form of the pastoral staff, adopted in more than one country of Western Europe early in the middle ages.

**4.** A name, or part of the name, of various animals having markings resembling the letter T. **a.** The toad-fish (*Batrachus tau*) of the Atlantic coast of N. America. **b.** A kind of moth: see quot. 1832; also, a kind of beetle, and of fly.

**1832** J. Rennie *Conspect. Butterfl. & Moths* 36 *Bombycidæ* (Stephens)...The Tau Emperor [Moth] (*Aglaia Tau*, Ochsenheimer). Said to be British on doubtful authority.

**5.** *attrib.* and *Comb.*, as **tau-shaped** adj. (= T-shaped); **tau-bone**, a T-shaped bone, as the Interclavicle; **tau-cross**, a T-shaped cross (= sense 2); so **tau-crucifix**; **tau-ring**, ? a ring inscribed with the letter T; **tau-staff**, a T-shaped staff (= sense 3).

**1474** *Will Ld. Mountioye* (Somerset Ho.), A *Tayewe crosse. **1562** Leigh *Armorie* 60 b, Ouer all a crosse Taue. **1885** *Blackw. Mag.* July 129/2 The tau cross, crux ansata, St. Anthony's cross,..is the commonest of all primitive symbols. **1888** F. G. Lee in *Archæologia* LI. 356 There are..no less than five heads of tau-crosses preserved in the South Kensington Museum. **1877** W. Jones *Finger-ring* 155 A very interesting collection of so-called *Tau (T) rings were exhibited. **1888** F. G. Lee in *Archæologia* LI. 356 A figure of a bishop or abbot..bearing a *tau-shaped staff. **1905** *Athenæum* 10 June 727/2 A tau-shaped central chamber. **1885** M'Crie *Sk. & Stud.* 37 The other carries a cross-headed or *tau-staff. **1888** F. G. Lee in *Archæologia* LI. 356 Head of a tau-staff of the eleventh century.

**Tau, Taubator**, obs. ff. Taw *sb.*$^2$, Taberdar.

**Taubron, -er**, var. Taborn, -er, *Obs.*

**Tauch, -e, taugh**, obs. or arch. Sc. ff. Tallow.

**Taucht**, obs. f. *taught*, pa.t. and pple. of Teach *v.*

**Taudr(e)y**, obs. ff. Tawdry.

**Taught** (tǭt), *ppl. a.* [pa. pple. of Teach *v*, which see for earlier Forms.]

**1.** Of a person: Instructed, trained; † learned (*obs.*). Now usually *absol.*, 'the taught', or in comb. with adverbs, as *ill-taught*, *well-taught*.

**1382** Wyclif *Eccl.* ii. 16 The taȝt man dieth also and the vntaȝt. **?a 1400** *Morte Arth.* 178 Alle with taghte mene and towne in togers fulle ryche. **1483** *Cath. Angl.* 377/1 Tawght, *doctus, instructus*. **1552** Huloet, Taught or newlye instructed, *catechizatus*. **1831-3** E. Burton *Eccl. Hist.* iv. (1845) 72 The mere necessity of instruction would give to the teachers a superiority over the taught. **1860** Pusey *Min. Proph.* 283 Truth of knowledge is the same in the Teacher and the taught.

**2.** Of a subject, art, etc.: Conveyed by instruction: see Teach *v.* 5.

**1909** *Westm. Gaz.* 4 May 5/1 This, we are assured, was not a taught trick, but a perfectly natural demonstration.

Hence † **Tau·ghtly** *adv.*, learnedly, skilfully.

**1382** Wyclif *Wisd.* xiii. 11 If any crafti man..hewe of the wode an euene tree, and of this taȝtli [1388 perfitli; Vulg. *docte*] pare awei al the rinde.

**Taught**, pa. t. and pple. of Teach *v.*; var. Taut *a.* **Tauism**, var. Taoism. **Tauk, taulke**, obs. ff. Talk. **Taulch**, obs. Sc. f. Tallow.

**Tauld(e**, Sc. f. *told*: see Tell *v.*

**Taum** (tǭm). *Sc.* and *north. dial.* Also **tawm, towm, toum, tome, tom, tam,** etc. [a. ON. *taumr* a cord, rein, line, etc., in Norw. *taum* string, line, e.g. on a fishing-rod (Aasen), in Færoese *teymur* (*ey* = ON. *au*) a short string at the end of a fishing line to which the hook is secured. Cognate with OE. *téam* line, team, OHG. *zoum*, Ger. *zaum*, OS. *tôm*, Du. *toom* rein, bridle: see Team *sb.*] A fishing-line, usually one of horse-hair twisted. Locally, also, a string of other kinds (*E. D. D.*).

**a 1733** *Shetland Acts* 11 in *Proc. Soc. Antiq. Scot.* (1892) XXVI. 198 All lines and tomes made of horse-hair. **1802** Sibbald *Chron. Scot. Poetry* Gloss., Towm. **1818** Hogg *Brownie of Bodsb.* etc. I. ix. 158 [He] cleekit a hantle o' geds and perches [out of the loch] with his toum. **1825** Brockett *N. C. Words*, *Tawm, Tam*, a fishing line. 'A lang twine tam'. **1828** *Craven Gloss.*, *Taum*, a fishing line. **1851** *Cumbld. Gloss.*, *Tome*, a hair line for fishing. **1855** Robinson *Whitby Gloss.*, *A Tawm*, a fishing line and rod. 'A fishing tawm'. **1904** *Daily Chron.* 19 Feb. 3/2 When a Scotch fisherman speaks of his line as a 'taum', he makes rather a fine use of the Old Norse word for 'bridle'.

**Taum(e**, obs. and dial. ff. Talm *v.*, to faint.

**Taune**, variant of Tawne *v.*$^1$ *Obs.*

**Taunt** (tǭnt), *sb.*$^1$ Forms: 6 **taunte, tawnte,** 6-7 **tant,** 6- **taunt.** [*Taunt* sb.$^1$ and vb.$^1$ are not found before 1500; origin obscure.

The most likely suggestion is that the sb. arose from the Fr. phrase *tant pour tant*, 'one for another, tit for tat', lit. 'as much for so much', englished in 16th c. as *taunt pour taunt* and *taunt for taunt*; hence, as primary sense, 'a return thrust, an effective rejoinder'. But the chronology of the sb. and vb. makes this doubtful.

Other suggestions, for vb. or sb., are OF. *tanter*, variant of *tenter* to try, prove, tempt; MHG. *tant* empty talk; and Du. *tanden* 'impetere, invadere aliquem' (Kilian), none of which seem adequate.]

†**1.** In phrase *taunt for* (*pour*) *taunt*, like for like, tit for tat, in reply or rejoinder. *Obs.*

**1542** Udall *Erasm. Apoph.* 311 Cicero for that he had separated & deuided hymself from Piso, who had marryed his doughter, gaue Pompeius again taunte pour taunte, for ye same kept warre against his owne father in lawe. **1548** — *Erasm. Par. Luke* iii. 48 b, Answer taunt pour taunt the one contrarie to the other. **c 1550** Croke *XIII Ps.* (Percy Soc.) 13 When they rebuked me so sore, I wold not render taunt for taunt. **1620** T. Granger *Div. Logike* 124 Regestion is commonly termed like for like, pin driuing out a pin, tint for taunt.

†**2.** A smart or clever rejoinder, a jesting quip or witty gibe; banter. *Obs.*

**1571** *Damon & Pithias* in Hazl. *Dodsley* IV. 24 Ready to answer, quick in taunts, pleasant to jest. **1579** Lyly *Euphues* (Arb.) 33 Fine phrases, smooth quippes, merry tauntes. **a 1625** Fletcher *Hum. Lieutenant* iv. i, She's as wanton as a Kid to th' out side, As full of Mocks and Taunts.

**3.** An insulting or provoking gibe or sarcasm; a mocking or scornful reproach or challenge; a casting of something in any one's teeth.

**a 1529** Skelton *Bowge of Courte* 70 Her chyef gentylwoman..Gaue me a taunte, and sayde I was to blame. **1548** Udall *Erasm. Par. Luke* ii. 25 b, There was in hym no malapertenesse of cockyng or geuyng tauntes. **1552** Huloet, Tawnte, *morsus,..pipulum*. **a 1572** Knox *Hist. Ref.* Wks. 1846 I. 12 Many tantis war gevin thame in thair teith. **1591** Shaks. *1 Hen. VI*, i. iv. 39. **1598** — *Merry W.* v. v. 151 Haue I liu'd to stand at the taunt of one that makes Fritters of English? **1603** Holland *Plutarch's Mor.* 354 True it is that a man of government may otherwhiles give a taunt and nipping scoffe, he may cast out also a merrie jest to moove laughter. **1680** C. Nesse *Church Hist.* 146 Many a taunt was cast on the old king. **1725** Pope *Odyss.* iii. 179 With ireful taunts each other they oppose. **1871** B. Taylor *Faust* (1875) I. xix. 168 With sneers and stinging taunts disgrace me.

† **b.** *transf.* An object of insulting or scornful gibes. *Obs. rare.*

**1611** Bible *Jer.* xxiv. 9, I will deliuer them..to be a reproch and a prouerbe, a taunt and a curse.

† **Taunt**, *sb.*$^2$ *Obs. rare.* [Origin unascertained.] A branch, a twig.

**1567** Golding *Ovid's Met.* vii. 91 And all the Pismeres creeping still upon his tawnts and sprigs [*Lat.* totidemque animalia ramis Ferre].

**Taunt** (tǭnt), *a.* (*adv.*) Also **tant.** [Origin and history obscure: perhaps two words; sense 2 evidently goes with Taunt *v.*$^2$ and Ataunt *adv.* 2.]

**1.** (?) Haughty; 'high and mighty'; 'stuck-up'. In *mod. dial.* saucy, pert.

**c 1500** Medwall *Nature* (Brandl) 823 Thys boy ys passyng taunte [*rime* avant]. **a 1550** *Image Ipocr.* ii. 198 in *Skelton's Wks.* (1843) II. 425/1 He is so hault and taunt That he dare hyme avaunt, All erthly men to daunt. **1880** *W. Cornw. Gloss.*, *Taunt*, pert. 'A taunt piece of goods.' **1882** Jago *Gloss. Cornw. Dial.*, *Taunt*, pert, 'high and mighty', saucy.

**2.** *Naut.* Of masts: Excessively tall or lofty.

[**c 1579**: implied in Taunt *v.*$^2$] **1622** R. Hawkins *Voy. S. Sea* lix. 138 Neither can the ship be so strong with a decke and a halfe..: nor carry her Mastes so taunt: nor spread so great a clue. **a 1625** *Nomenclator Navalis* (Harl. MS. 2301), *Taunt* is when a mast is very high for the proportion of the shipp, wee saie it is a Taunt-mast. **1627** Capt. Smith *Seaman's Gram.* iii. 15 For a man of warre, a well ordered Taunt-mast is best. *Ibid.* 17 If your Masts be taunt, your yards must be the shorter. **a 1700** B. E. *Dict. Cant. Crew*, *Tant, Tantest*, Mast of a Ship or Man, Tall, Tallest. **1736** Lewis *Hist. Thanet* Gloss., *Taant*, tall, or too high for its breadth or bigness, 'a taant mast, house'. **1831** *Examiner* 740/2 With a deep keel and sharp run, taunt sticks and spanking sails. **1851** Kipping *Sailmaking* (ed. 2) 189 *Taunt*, an epithet, at sea, signifying high or tall. It is particularly expressed of the masts, when they are of extraordinary length. **1863** Robson *Bards Tyne* 397 Tant ships, that come with rampant rig, Against its sides are rested. **1898** F. T. Bullen *Cruise Cachalot* 370 The 'crow's nests' are dismantled, taunt topgallant-masts sent up, and royal yards crossed.

† **b.** Phr. *With taunt sail(s)*, also *bearing a taunt sail*, with all sail set: cf. Ataunt 2. *Obs.*

**1622** R. Hawkins *Voy. S. Sea* liii. 124 With much winde, and a chapping Sea, bearing a taunt-sayle. **1632** Lithgow *Trav.* v. 177 Shippes were wont to passe vnder with taunt sayles. *Ibid.* x. 502 A gallant ship, puft with taunt saile.

**c.** *Comb.*, as *taunt-masted, -rigged.*

**1627** Capt. Smith *Seaman's Gram.* iii. 15 Taunt-masted. **1704** J. Harris *Lex. Techn.* I, *Taunt*, when the Masts of a Ship are too tall for her, they say she is *Taunt-masted*, or that her Masts are very *Taunt*. **1825** H. B. Gascoigne *Nav. Fame* 70 Taunt rigg'd she seems, and like a Privateer.

† **B.** *adv.* (?) To the full, thoroughly: cf. Ataunt 1. *Obs.*

**a 1550** *Hye Way to Spyttel Ho.* 542 in Hazl. *E. P. P.* IV. 49 And there they prate, and make theyr auaunt Of theyr deceytes, and drynk adew taunt.

**Taunt** (tǭnt), *v.*$^1$ Also 6-7 **tant.** [See Taunt *sb.*$^1$]

† **1.** *intr.* To make a smart or effective rejoinder; to answer back in equivalent terms; to exchange banter. *Obs.*

**1513** More *Rich. III* in Hall *Chron.* (1548) 16 b, [Jane Shore] had a proper wytte..somtyme tantyng without displeasure, and not without disporte. **a 1529** Skelton *Agst. Garnesche* ii. 37 To turney or to tante with me ye ar to fare to seke. **1548** Thomas *Ital. Dict.* (1567), *Motteggiare*, to taunt pretely, or to cutte another mans woordes wittily or finely.

† **2.** *trans.* To answer (a person) with a bantering or mocking rejoinder; to 'chaff', banter. *Obs.*

**1515** Barclay *Egloges* ii. (1570) B iv/1 If thou call for ought by worde, signe or becke, Then Jacke with the bushe shall taunt thee with a chek. **1568** Grafton *Chron.* II. 58 The king receyued him..taunting him iestingly and merily, as though one Realme were not able to holde them both. **1596** Dalrymple tr. *Leslie's Hist. Scot.* vii. (S.T.S.) 8 This man tane in the feild the Bruse mirrilie tantis, and sayis, Welcome father, says he.

**b.** *dial.* (See quot.)

**a 1825** Forby *Voc. E. Anglia*, *Taunt, v.* to teize, to pester with silly questions, importunate entreaties, or any mode of minute vexation.

**3.** To reproach (a person) *with* something in a sarcastic, scornful, or insulting way.

**1560** Daus tr. *Sleidane's Comm.* 363 b, Than waxed he also more angry, and..taunted them with sore rebukes. **1565** Cooper *Thesaurus*, *Increpare probris*, to taunte with reprochful woordes. **1601** Holland *Pliny* II. 571 Mamurra, whom the Poet Catullus..so tanted and reuiled in his verses. **1722** De Foe *Plague* (1840) 66 Taunting him with want of courage to leap into the great pit. **1802** Mar. Edgeworth *Moral T.* (1816) I. xiii. 103 It ill became a person..who did not dress nearly as well as themselves, to taunt his betters with poverty. **1879** Froude *Cæsar* xxii. 386 They taunted him with cowardice.

**b.** *intr.* To utter taunts or stinging reproaches.

**1560** Daus tr. *Sleidane's Comm.* 306, I am not so cleane without experience, but I could taunte againe. **1577** Fulke *Conf. Purg.* 370 You taunt at the author of that booke. **a 1688** Bunyan *Israel's Hope Encouraged* Wks. (ed. Offor) I. 613 Those very men that are pleased to taunt at this kind of inference. **1802** Marian Moore *Lascelles* II. 21 Mr. Richards was taunting at the disappointed Miss le Gros. **1833** Mrs. Browning *Prometh. Bound* i. 91 Here, now, taunt on!

**c.** *trans.* with *obj. cl.* To say tauntingly. *rare.*

**1873** Browning *Red Cott. Nt.-cap* ii. 462 Folk may taunt That half your rock-built wall is rubble-heap! **1878** — *La Saisiaz* 299 Taunt not 'Human work ape work divine?'

**4.** *trans.* To drive or get by taunting; to provoke.

**1813** Byron *Bride Abydos* ii. xviii, Proscribed at home, And taunted to a wish to roam. **1837** W. Irving *Capt. Bonneville* III. xlix. 253 But the Blackfeet were not to be taunted out of their safe shelter. **1888** *Pall Mall G.* 31 July 11/2 Viscount Wolmer probably repented of having helped to taunt it out of Mr. Morley.

Hence **Ta·unted** *ppl. a.*

**1818** Scott *Battle Sempach* xii, 'Shalt see then how the game will fare', The taunted knight replied. **1882** *Sat. Rev.* 6 May 567/1 When the taunted victim..has drunk deep enough of the bitterness of death.

† **Taunt**, *v.*$^2$ *Naut. Obs. rare*$^{-1}$. [app. f. Taunt *a.* 2.] *trans.* To hoist, raise, elevate.

**c 1579** Montgomerie *Misc. Poems* xlviii. 93 Vp uent our saillis, tauntit to the huins [= hunes], The trumpits soundit tuentie mirrie tuins.

**Taunter** (tǭ·ntəɹ). [f. Taunt *v.*$^1$ + -er$^1$.] One who taunts: see the verb.

**1552** Huloet, Tawnter, *nasutus*. **1558** *Cranmer's Confut. Vnwritten Verities* Pref. B viij, Taunters & fault finders with others, rather then menders of themselfes. **1579-80** North *Plutarch* (1676) 291 Socrates..was a plain simple man to them that knew him but outwardly, or else a pleasant Taunter or Mocker. **1822** *Examiner* 688/1 Cold-blooded taunter of the suffering people.

† **Tau·ntful**, *a. Obs. rare*$^{-1}$. [f. Taunt *sb.*$^1$ + -ful.] Full of taunts; reproachful.

**1715** Tickell *Iliad* i. 15 Be all thy Rage in tauntful Words exprest.

**Taunting** (tǭ·ntiŋ), *vbl. sb.* [f. Taunt *v.*$^1$ + -ing$^1$.] The action of Taunt *v.*$^1$

**1563** Winȝet *Four Scoir Thre Quest.* Wks. (S.T.S.) I. 57 The erroneous assault me be [= by] tanting and mockrie. **1563** *Homilies* ii. *Matrimony* (1859) 502 How few matrimonies there be without chidings, brawlings, tauntings, repentings. **1791** Cowper *Odyss.* xvii. 476 A tongue accustom'd much to tauntings. **1809-11** Combe *Syntax* xxvi. 356 'Tis thus I..foil their tauntings with a joke.

**Tau·nting**, *ppl. a.* [f. as prec. + -ing$^2$.] That taunts, or reproaches provokingly.

**a 1548** Hall *Chron., Hen. IV* 19 Railyng rimes, malicious meters and tauntyng verses. **1649** Roberts *Clavis Bibl.* 491 Their taunting Proverb against God is propounded. **1796** Burke *Regic. Peace* i. Wks. VIII. 106 They accompanied their notice..with every kind of insolent and taunting reflection. **1844** Thirlwall *Greece* VIII. lxii. 155 Cleomenes insulted his disappointment by a taunting letter.

**Tau·ntingly**, *adv.* [f. prec. + -ly$^2$.] In a taunting manner; with derisive or insulting reproach.

**1549** Coverdale, etc. *Erasm. Par.* 1 *Peter* 10 Not disdeynfully, nor tauntynglye as though you were offended at them. **1607** SHAKS. *Cor.* I. i. 114 (Fol. 2) The belly..tantingly replyed To'th'discontented Members. **1646** J. WHITAKER *Uzziah* 13 [It] was tauntingly spoke of Christ, He saved others, himself he cannot save. **1876** MOZLEY *Univ. Serm.* v. (1877) 116 The question has often been asked tauntingly—Why has not Christianity done away with war?

So **Tau·ntingness.** *rare*—⁰.

**1727** BAILEY vol. II, *Tauntingness*, a sharp, haughty, biting Reproachfulness. **1731** *Ibid.*, *Tauntingness*, Raillery.

**Taunt ne caunt**: see TANT NE QUANT.

**Taunton** (tǭ·ntən, *locally* tā·ntən). Name of a town in Somersetshire; hence short for *Taunton cloth*, a woollen cloth formerly made there.

**1499** in *Somerset Medieval Wills* (1901) 379 To William Busshop halfe a packe of Tauntons. **1607** *Act 4 Jas. I*, c. 2 § 7 Every Broade Cloth..called Tauntons, Bridgwaters, and Dunsters made in the Westerne partes of Somersetsheire.

**Tau·ntress.** *rare.* [f. TAUNTER + -ESS.] A female taunter, a taunting woman.

**1557** *Agst. Vnstedfast Woman* in *Tottell's Misc.* (Arb.) 177 O temerous tauntres, that delightes in toyes..Ianglyng iestres, depraueres of swete ioyes.

**Tauny**, obs. f. TAWNY. **Tauorsay**: see TAV-.

**Taupie**, variant of TAWPIE.

†**Taur.** *Obs.* [ad. L. *taur-us* or OF. *tor, taur, thaur*, bull.] A bull; the constellation Taurus.

*c* **1386** CHAUCER *Wife's Prol.* 613 Myn Ascendent was Taur and Mars ther-Inne. *c* **1425** WYNTOUN *Chron.* II. 1269 A taur, þat is a buyl..Scho saw ner by hir on þe greyn.

†**Taure.** *Obs. rare*—¹. Corruption of TOUR, a fringe of hair worn on the forehead, by association with *taurus* bull: cf. BULL-HEAD 3, quot. 1688.

**1688** R. HOLME *Armoury* II. 464/2 Women wear Hair.. in Taures when the hair on the forehead is curled and standeth out. *Ibid.*, Bull-heads, when the said curled forehead is much larger than the Taure.

**Taurean** (tǭrī·ăn), *a. rare.* [f. L. *taure-us* adj. (f. *taurus* bull) + -AN.] Of or belonging to a bull.

**1656** BLOUNT *Glossogr.*, *Taurean*, *Taurine*, of or belonging to a bull. **1900** LEWIS & SHORT *Lat.-Eng. Dict.*, *Taureus*, of a bull or ox,..[*taurea*] *vincla*, i.e. taurean bands (a poet. expression to denote glue), Lucr. 6, 1071.

**Tauri-**, combining form of L. *taurus* bull, in TAURICIDE, etc.; see TAURUS, and cf. TAURO-.

**Tau·rian**, *a. rare*—¹. [irreg. f. L. *taur-us* bull + -IAN.] = TAUREAN, TAURINE *a.*

**1882** *Harper's Mag.* Sept. 563/1 Three days of bull-fighting..with eight taurian victims each day.

**Tauric** (tǭ·rik), *a.* [f. Gr. ταῦρος or L. *taurus* bull + -IC.] Pertaining or relating to, or of the nature of, a bull; taurine.

**1816** G. S. FABER *Orig. Pagan Idol.* I. 406 The tauric Jupiter was the parent of the Cretan Minos. **1818** — *Horæ Mosaicæ* I. 314 He set up at Bethel two calves of gold in apparent imitation of the tauric Cherubim of the temple. **1882** R. BROWN *Law Kosmic Order* 43 In the tauric and bovine form.

**Tauricide** (tǭ·risəid). *rare.* [f. L. *taur-us* bull: see TAURI- and -CIDE.] **a.** A bull-slayer; a matador. **b.** The slaughter of a bull.

**1845** E. WARBURTON *Crescent & Cross* I. ix. 169 Cambyses, the tauricide,..and the desert..have left little trouble to the tourist. **1852** *Fraser's Mag.* XLV. 536 The great tauricide still hesitated. **1882** *Pall Mall G.* 11 Sept. 2 If you kill him you are guilty of felony or tauricide.

†**Taurico·rnous**, *a. Obs. rare*—¹. [f. as prec. + L. *cornu* horn + -OUS.] Having horns like those of a bull.

**1646** SIR T. BROWNE *Pseud. Ep.* v. ix. 247 Their descriptions must be relative, or the Tauricornous picture of the one, perhaps the same with the other. **1656** BLOUNT *Glossogr.*, *Tauricornous*, horned like a Bul.

**Taurid** (tǭ·rid). *Astron.* [f. TAUR-US, after LEONID, PERSEID. In F. *taurides* pl. (Littré 1877).] In *pl.* A system of meteors which appear to radiate from a point in the constellation Taurus, about the 20th of November.

**1888** *Cassell's Encycl. Dict.*, Taurides.

**Tauridor**, obs. form of TOREADOR.

†**Tauri·ferous**, *a. Obs. rare*—⁰. [f. L. *taurifer* (f. *taurus* bull) + -OUS: see TAURI- and -FEROUS.]

**1656** BLOUNT *Glossogr.*, *Tauriferous*, which beareth or nourisheth Buls or neat. **1721** in BAILEY.

**Tauriform** (tǭ·rifǭɹm), *a.* [ad. L. *tauriform-is*, f. *taurus* bull: see TAURI- and -FORM.] Having the form of a bull.

**1721** BAILEY, *Tauriform*,..in the Shape of a Bull. **1803** G. S. FABER *Cabiri* I. 347 Bud-Arc, the tauriform god of the Arc. **1809** E. DAVIES *Mythol. Druids* 170 The usual residence of the tauriform god. **1877** A. W. WARD in *Encycl. Brit.* VII. 403/2 The tauriform sun-god whom his worshippers adored with loud cries.

**Taurine** (tǭ·rəin), *sb.*¹ *Chem.* Also -in. [f. *tauro-* in *taurocholic* + -INE⁵.] A neutral crystallizable substance, $C_2H_7NSO_3$, *amido-ethyl-sulphonic acid*, obtained in 1826 by L. Gmelin from ox-bile, and contained in the bile of most other animals, resulting from the transformation of taurocholic acid under the influence of acids and alkalies.

**1845** G. E. DAY tr. *Simon's Anim. Chem.* I. 47 Taurin forms colourless regular six-sided prisms, terminated by four- or six-sided pyramids. **1868** WATTS *Dict. Chem.* V. 701 Taurocholic acid..when boiled with water, or with alkalis,..is resolved into taurine and cholic acid. **1869** ROSCOE *Elem. Chem.* (1871) 438 A peculiar substance termed taurin is obtained by the action of acids on bile.

**Taurine** (tǭ·rəin), *a.* (*sb.*²). [ad. L. *taurīn-us*, f. *taurus* bull: see -INE¹.] Of, pertaining to, of the nature of, or resembling a bull; bovine.

**1613** HEYWOOD *Brazen Age* I. Wks. 1874 III. 176 Hadst thou not stoopt thy horrid Taurine shape I would haue peece-meale rent..thy tough hide. **1809** E. DAVIES *Mythol. Druids* 173 The wounding of this bull, who represented the taurine god. **1818** R. P. KNIGHT *Symbolic Lang.* (1876) 79 The taurine figures of Bacchus and the Rivers have more or less of the original bull. **1876** M. COLLINS *Fr. Midnight to M.* III. v. 57 Immovable as a taurine statue of Nineveh.

**B.** *sb.* A taurine beast, a bull. *nonce-use.*

**1888** *Harper's Mag.* Apr. 783 Sturdy and stocky as a Jersey bull, and with not a little of that taurine's pugnacity.

**Tauriscite** (tǭ·risəit). *Min.* [ad. G. *tauriszit* (Volger 1855), from the Latin name of its locality, *Pagus Tauriscorum* (Canton Uri, Switzerland): see -ITE¹.] Native ferrous sulphate, like copperas, but occurring in acicular crystals.

**1868** DANA *Min.* 644. **1896** CHESTER *Dict. Names Min.* 266.

†**Tauri·ze**, *v. Obs. nonce-wd.* [f. L. *taur-us* bull + -IZE.] *intr.* To play the bull, to take the form of a bull.

**1727** SOMERVILLE *Wife* 12 What form great Jove would next devise, And when his godship would again Taurise?

**Tauro-**, repr. Gr. ταυρο-, combining form of ταῦρος (= L. *taurus*) bull, occurring in a few words derived from Greek and modern chemical terms, and in rare nonce-formations. **Tauro·latry** [-LATRY], worship of a bull (in quot. with allusion to 'John Bull'). **Tauromo·rphous** *a.* [Gr. ταυρόμορφος, f. μορφή form], having the form of a bull. **Tauro-se·rpentine** *a.*, relating to a bull and a serpent. See also below.

**1901** *Speaker* 8 June 278/2 Is not *Taurolatry the religion of Englishmen? **1891** *Cent. Dict.*, *Tauromorphous. **1855** BAILEY *Mystic* 58 As told in mysteries *tauro-serpentine.

**Tauroboly** (tǭrǫ·bǒli). *Gr. Antiq.* [ad. L. taurobolium (also in Eng. use), f. Gr. ταυροβόλος striking or slaughtering bulls, f. ταῦρος bull + stem of βολή cast, stroke, wound. So F. *taurobole.*] The slaughter of a bull or bulls; *spec.* a pagan sacrifice of a bull in honour of Cybele, with its attendant rites, including a bath in bulls' blood; also, the representation of such a slaughter or sacrifice in sculpture, etc.

**1700** tr. *Danet's Dict. Grk. & Rom. Antiq.*, *Tauropolium*, or *Tauropolion* [sic], Sacrifices of Bulls, which were offered to Cybele,..to render Thanks..for her teaching Men the Art to tame those Animals. **1879** FARRAR *St. Paul* (1884) I. xviii. 187 *note*, Such were the taurobolies and kriobolies—hideous blood baths. **1882** [see KRIOBOLY]. **1889** FARRAR *Lives Fathers* I. ix. 562 He [Julian] washed away the lustral waters of baptism in the reeking horrors of a Tauroboly. **1891** *Smith's Dict. Grk. & Rom. Antiq.* II. 762/2 A temple of the Magna Mater where these rites of *taurobolium* were celebrated stood on the Vatican.

**Taurochenocholic** (tǭ:roˌkīnokǫ·lik), *a. Chem.* [f. next, by insertion of *-cheno-* from Gr. χήν goose.] In *taurochenocholic acid*, a sulphuretted acid ($C_{29}H_{49}NSO_3$) found in goose-bile.

**1868** WATTS *Dict. Chem.* V. 700.

**Taurocholic** (tǭrokǫ·lik), *a. Chem.* [f. TAURO- + Gr. χολή gall, bile + -IC: cf. CHOLIC.] In *taurocholic acid*, an acid ($C_{26}H_{45}NSO_7$) found in the bile of the ox and of most other animals, mostly together with glycocholic acid. Hence **Taurocholate** (tǭrǫ·kolět), a salt of taurocholic acid.

**1857** MILLER *Elem. Chem.* III. xii. § 2. 702 Both of these resinous acids (the *glycocholic* and the *taurocholic*) contain nitrogen. The taurocholic acid also contains sulphur. *Ibid.* 706 The taurocholates of the alkalies are very soluble in water and in alcohol. **1872** THUDICHUM *Chem. Phys.* 17. **1872** HUXLEY *Phys.* v. 122 The taurocholate and glycocholate of soda, or bile salts, as they are sometimes called.

**Tau·rocol**(l. *rare.* Also in L. form **-colla.** [ad. Gr. ταυρόκολλα, f. ταῦρος bull + κόλλα glue.] Glue made from bulls' hides.

**1678** PHILLIPS, *Taurocolla*, a glutinous substance made out of Bulls Hides, and therefore so called, though oft times it is made of the Ears and Feet of fourfooted Creatures. **1753** CHAMBERS *Cycl. Supp.*, *Taurocolla*, bull-glue, a sort of glue much used among the antients in works that required strength. **1847** WEBSTER, *Taurocol.* **1882** OGILVIE (Annandale), *Taurocoll*, *Taurocolla*.

**Tauromachy** (tǭrǫ·măki). [ad. Gr. ταυρομαχία, f. ταῦρος bull + μάχη fighting (see -MACHY): so F. *tauromachie.*] The practice or custom of bull-fighting; also (with *a* and *pl.*) a bull-fight.

**1846** THACKERAY *Cornhill to Cairo* ii, It was not a real Spanish tauromachy—only a theatrical combat. **1846** *Times* 17 June 5/6 The art of tauromachy has just sustained an irreparable loss by the death of Montes, the Spanish matador. **1892** *Cornh. Mag.* Sept. 292 In the interests of civilisation and progress, it declares against the tauromachies. **1902** *Munsey's Mag.* XXVI. 524/2 Under the Bourbons, it [bull-fighting] went out of royal fashion, though it was still practised, and it was restored by Ferdinand VII, who established a college of tauromachy.

So **Tauromachian** (-mē·kiăn), **Tauromachic** (-mæ·kik) [F. *tauromachique*] *adjs.*, of or pertaining to tauromachy.

**1845** FORD *Handbk. Spain* I. 146 A tendency to gitanesque and tauro-machian slang. **1846** — *Gatherings fr. Spain* (1906) 233 The beloved monarch shut up the lecture rooms forthwith, opening..by way of compensation, a tauromachian university. **1887** *Daily Tel.* 17 June (Cassell), The matador is forbidden by the laws of tauromachic etiquette to attack the bull. **1894** *Westm. Gaz.* 13 June 2/1 There are about fifteen special tauromachic newspapers..in France.

‖ **Taurus** (tǭ·rǒs). [L. *taurus* bull.]

**1.** *Astron.* **a.** The second of the zodiacal constellations, the Bull, in which are included the groups of the Pleiades and Hyades. **b.** Also, the second of the divisions or signs of the Zodiac, into which the sun enters on or near the 21st of April: originally identical with the constellation (cf. CANCER 2). Symbol ♉.

*c* **1391** CHAUCER *Astrol.* I. § 21 As aries hath [respect to] thin heued, & taurus thy nekke & thy throte, gemyni thyn armholes & thin armes. **1398** TREVISA *Barth. De P. R.* VIII. x. (Bodl. MS.), Taurus..is an erþy signe..And he is þe hous of substaunce and of ryches and possessioun of fonging & of ȝeuynge. **1588** SHAKS. *Tit. A.* IV. iii. 69 See, see, thou hast shot off one of Taurus hornes. **1664** BUTLER *Hud.* II. III. 904 Some say the Zodiack-Constellations Have long since chang'd their antique Stations Above a Sign, and prove the same In Taurus now, once in the Ram. **1667** MILTON *P. L.* I. 769 As Bees In spring time, when the Sun with Taurus rides. **1868** LOCKYER *Elem. Astron.* § 94. 36 In 1861 it was found that a small nebula, discovered in 1856 in Taurus..had disappeared.

†**2.** *Zool.* An obsolete genus including the common ox (now *Bos taurus*).

**Taurylic** (tǭri·lik), *a. Chem.* [f. L. *taur-us* bull + -YL + -IC.] In *taurylic acid*, a colourless oil ($C_7H_8O$) obtained together with phenol from human urine and that of cows and horses.

**1868** WATTS *Dict. Chem.* V. 701 Taurylic acid..isomeric with anisol, benzylic alcohol, and cresol—perhaps identical with the latter. **1873** RALFE *Phys. Chem.* 56 Taurylic acid is a colourless, oily liquid, fluid at 18°.

**Tau-staff**: see TAU.

**Taut, taught** (tǭt), *a.* Forms: *α.* 3–4 toȝt, -e, 4 toght, touht, towt, -e, (tout); 5 towght, 5–7 (9 *dial.*) tought (7 toft). *β.* 5–9 taught. *γ.* 7–9 tort. *δ.* 8– taut. [The history of this word is in many points obscure. Though the form *taught* (now spelt *taut*) is known to us only after 1600, there is little doubt that it is the same word as the ME. *toȝt, toght, tought*, used also by Capt. Smith 1612 (and in Forby). The etymology of *toȝt, toght*, is doubtful; but it is generally held to be related in some way to the ablaut-grade *tog-, toȝ-* of OE. **tēohan, tēon*, TEE *v.*¹, Goth. *tiuhan* to draw. See Note below.]

†**1.** Tense, as a surface; tight, distended, full to distention. *Obs.*

*α.* *c* **1325** *Poem Times Edw. II* 160 in *Pol. Songs* (Camden) 331 He maketh his mawe touht off the beste. *Ibid.* 238 ibid. 334 The best he piketh up himself, and maketh his mawe touht. *c* **1380** *Sir Ferumb.* 4390 Þat ech of hem ne drof forþ on, With pakkes y-charged euerechon, Wyþ harneys y-fillid toȝte. *c* **1386** CHAUCER *Sompn. T.* 559 Than shul this cherl with bely stif and toght As any Tabour, hither ben ybrought. *c* **1450** *Songs, Carols*, etc. (E. E. T. S.) 118/24 Your brest is so towght, Tyll ye haue well cowght. **1612** CAPT. SMITH *Map Virginia* 28 They haue a great deepe platter of wood. They couer the mouth thereof with a skin, at each corner they tie a walnut,..with a small rope they twitch them togither till it be so tought and stiffe, that they may beat vpon it as vpon a drumme.

*δ.* **1878** H. M. STANLEY *Dark Cont.* I. xvii. 456 Their rounded bodies were as taut as a drumhead.

†**b.** *fig.* (?) Firm, firmly fixed or settled, clinched. (See also TOUGHT *a.*)

**13..** *E. E. Allit. P.* A. 521 Gos in-to my vyne, dotz þat ȝe conne. So sayde the lorde & made hit toȝt.

**2.** Tightly drawn, as by longitudinal tension; stiff, tense, not slack. Chiefly in nautical use.

*α.* **1604** *Peele's Tale Troy* 256 Away they fly, their tackling toft [*ed.* 1589 teft] and tight. *a* **1825** FORBY *Voc. E. Anglia*, *Taught, tought*, tight.

*β.* *a* **1625** *Nomenclator Navalis* (Harl. MS. 2301), We saie sett taught ye shrowdes yᵉ staies or anie other Roape when it is to slack. **1627** CAPT. SMITH *Seaman's Gram.* ix. 42 Cast of that Boling.., and hale vp taught the other. **1669** STURMY *Mariner's Mag.* I. ii. 18 Hawl them taught and belaye them. **1793** SMEATON *Edystone L.* § 259 We..fixed our great tackle to it..and hove all taught. **1816** SCOTT *Antiq.* viii, Haul taught and belay! *c* **1820** G. BEATTIE *John o' Arnha'* 55 (Jam.) Ilk tendon, taght like thairm, was lac'd. **1828** WEBSTER, *Taught* [pron.] *taut*, stretched; not slack. **1833** MARRYAT *P. Simple* xxx. II. 174 The yards carefully squared, and the ropes hauled taught.

*γ.* *a* **1687** PETTY *Treat. Naval Philos.* I. ii, Setting of the Shrowds loose or tort as the Condition of Sailing of the Vessel requires. **1806** W. TAYLOR in *Ann. Rev.* IV. 773 Tort and smooth threads of flax and hemp. **1847** EMERSON *Poems* (1857) 99 Yet holds he them with tortest rein.

*δ.* **1727–41** CHAMBERS *Cycl.*, *Taught*, or *Tau't*,..in the sea language, is the same as stiff, or fast. **1796** NELSON in Southey *Life* (1813) II. vi. 1 My complaint is as if a girth were buckled taut over my breast. **1840** R. H. DANA *Bef. Mast* xxvii, The land-breeze set in, which brought us upon a taut bowline. **1883** STEVENSON *Treas. Isl.* v. xxiii, The hawser was as taut as a bowstring.

*transf.* **1748** SMOLLETT *Rod. Rand.* xxiv. (1760) I. 191 Many a taught gale of wind has honest Tom Bowling and I weathered together.

**b.** Tightly or trimly done up; put into good order. Of a person: Neat in appearance.

**1870** *Daily News* 1 Dec., Shops ran up shutters, everything was made taut. **1871** WHITTIER *Sisters* xii, In the tautest schooner that ever swam He rides at anchor in Annisquam. **1880** CLARK RUSSELL *Sailor's Sweetheart* vii, By breakfast-time the ship was clean and taut fore and aft. 1881 *Scribner's Mag.* XXI. 271/1 [She appeared] in Miss B——'s shop, taut and trim. 1887 Besant *The World went* i, A fair wind, and the ship taut and trim.

c. *fig.* Of a person: Strict or severe as to duty.
1833 Marryat *P. Simple* xii, He was considered to be the taughtest (that is, the most active and severe) boatswain in the service. 1851 Kingston *Pirate Medit.* (1860) 4 What sort of a chap is our skipper? He looks like a taut hand.

[*Note.* For the interchange of *taught, tought*, cf. *aught, ought*; *naught, nought* (where however *au* is the earlier), and the falling together in sound in mod. Eng. of *bought, sought, wrought, brought, thought* (OE. *bohte, sōhte, worhte, brōhte, þōhte*) with *caught, distraught, raught, taught* (ME. *cahte, distraught*, OE. *rǣhte, tǣhte, tāhte*), where the two sounds remain distinct in Sc. (*bocht, thocht, cauwcht, tauwcht*) and northern Eng. *Toȝt, toght*, has been suggested to be:—an OTeut. *tohto² (from ablaut-grade *tog-*), which is improbable, since no trace of such a form appears in OE. or any of the cognate languages; also, to be a syncopated form of ME. *toȝed*, now *towed* (see Tow *v.*²); this seems impossible. With more probability it has been viewed as an altered form of ME. *tiȝt*, Tight, under the influence of *toȝed*, or more prob. of *toȝen* 'drawn', pa. pple. of Tee *v.*¹ It is noticeable that *toȝt, touȝt, tought*, occur also in ME. and Sc. as variants of Tough *a.*]

**Taut** (tat, tāt), *v. Sc.* Also **tawt, tat.** [Origin obscure: cf. Tatty *a.*; also Tatter *sb.*¹] **a.** *trans.* To tangle or mat together (hair or wool). **b.** *intr.* To become tangled or matted, as hair or wool. Hence **Tau·ted** (tautit) *ppl. a.*, tangled, matted; having the hair tangled.
1782 Burns *Poor Mailie's Elegy* vi, She was nae get o' moorland tips, Wi' tawted ket, an' hairy hips. 1786 — *Twa Dogs* 20 Nae tawted tyke, tho' e'er sae duddie. 1853 J. Crawford in *Whistle-Binkie* (1890) II. 224 While frae the bairnie's tautit hair The frozen crystals hung. 1882 Jamieson Supp. s.v. *Tat*, Dinna taut your hair sa. 1893 Stevenson *Catriona* xx, God's truth, it's the tautit laddie!

**Taut,** var. f. Tat *sb.*², a coarse Indian cloth.

**Taut, taute,** obs. ff. *taught*: see Teach.

**Tautaug,** variant of Tautog.

**Tautegorical** (tǭtĕgǫ·rikăl), *a. nonce-wd.* [f. Taut(o-, after Allegorical.] (See quot. 1825.) So **Tautegory** (tǭ·tĕgŏri) [after Allegory].
1825 Coleridge *Aids Refl.* 199 The base of Symbols and symbolical expressions; the nature of which as always tautegorical (i.e. expressing the same subject but with a difference) in contra-distinction from metaphors and similitudes, that are always allegorical (i.e. expressing a different subject but with a resemblance). 1825 — in *Rem.* (1836) II. 352 This part of the *mythus* in which symbol fades away into allegory but..never ceases wholly to be a symbol or tautegory. 1846 Jowett in *Life & Lett.* (1897) I. v. 146 In one word he [Coleridge] had comprised a whole essay, saying that mythology was not allegorical but tautegorical. 1862 Stanley *Jew. Ch.* (1863) I. vi. 136 The wilderness, as it intervenes between Egypt and the Land of Promise..is, as Coleridge would have said, not allegorical, but tautegorical, of the events which..we designate by those figures.

**Tauten** (tǭ·t'n), *v.* Also 9 **taughten.** [f. Taut *a.* + -en⁵.]
**1.** *trans.* To make taut, to or cause to become taut; to tighten.
*a* 1814 C. Dibdin *Song, Sailor's Jrnl.*, While taught'ning the forestay, I saw her faint. 1880 Clark Russell *Sailor's Sweetheart* III. ii. 57 The warp sang out as we tautened the bight of it. 1886 Sheldon tr. *Flaubert's Salammbo* xiii. 310 [Catapults] were tautened with levers, pulleys, capstans, or drums. 1903 L. Becke in *Pall Mall G.* 28 Mar. 2/2 In another moment or two your line is tautened out.
**2.** *intr.* To become taut, as a rope under tension.
1849 *Blackw. Mag.* LXVI. 732 The dip of the hawser scarce tautening at each strain. 1879 Beerbohm *Patagonia* v. 66 The shock, as the lasso tautened, threw his horse on its haunches. 1896 *Strand Mag.* XII. 350/2 The life-line tautened, and I was soon lifted from my feet.
Hence **Tau·tened** *ppl. a.*, **Tau·tening** *vbl. sb.*
1840 R. H. Dana *Bef. Mast* xxiii, Our ship being very good upon a tautened bowline. 1879 *Man. Artill. Exerc.* 633 Wedges, oak, small..20 Tautening lashings. 1906 E. K. Robinson *Relig. Nat.* 28 The sudden tautening of the muscles.

**Tauthrie,** obs. f. Tawdry. **Tautie,** var. Tatty.

**Tautly** (tǭ·tli), *adv.* [f. Taut *a.* + -ly ².] In a taut manner; with tautness.
1882 Nares *Seamanship* (ed. 6) 182 The bunt..will not allow the parrel to be passed tautly. 1882 O'Donovan *Merv Oasis* I. i. 20 A very thick cable..is drawn as tautly as possible across the stream.

**Tautness** (tǭ·tnės). [f. as prec. + -ness.] The state or quality of being taut.
1861 E. S. Kennedy in *Peaks, Passes & Gl.* Ser. ii. I. 166 The taughtness of the rope unavoidably makes it difficult to retain a foothold. 1889 J. M. Duncan *Clin. Lect. Dis. Wom.* xxix. (ed. 4) 233 There being only a little tautness left on one side.

**Tauto-** (tǭto), before a vowel properly **taut-**, repr. Gr. ταὐτο-, combining form of ταὐτό, contraction of τὸ αὐτό, the same (cf. Auto-); occurring in Tautology, Tautomerism, and their derivatives; also the following technical words, mostly of rare occurrence. **Tau·toba:ryd,** *Math.* [irreg. f. Gr. βαρύς heavy], that curve upon which the pressure of a heavy particle moving under gravity is the same at every point (cf. Tautochrone). **Tautogra·phical** *a.* [Gr. γραφικός descriptive], presenting the same geographical features throughout, monotonous in form. **Tautohe·dral** *a., Cryst.* [Gr. ἕδρα base], having the same face or side in common: see quot. **Tautome·tric, Tautome·trical** *adjs., Pros.* [late Gr. ταὐτόμετρος, f. μέτρον measure], of the same metre; having the same arrangement of syllables in the verse, or occupying the same position metrically. **Tautomo·rphous** *a., Cryst.* [Gr. μορφή form], applied to a symmetrical form such that corresponding points or faces of it can be brought into congruence by revolution about an axis. **Tau·tonym,** *Nat. Hist.* [Gr. ταὐτώνυμ-ος *a.*, f. ὄνυμα, ὄνομα name], a scientific name in which the same word is used for genus and species; so **Tautony·mic** *a.*, pertaining to or constituting a tautonym; **Tauto·nymy,** the use of tautonyms. **Tauto₁ou·sian** (tautou·sian), **-ious** *adjs., Theol.* [f. eccl. Gr. ταὐτοούσιος (Epiphanius), f. οὐσία essence], having absolutely the same essence. † **Tauto·pathy** [Gr. ταὐτοπάθεια, f. πάθος suffering], suffering caused by the same thing as was habitually used previously. **Tauto·phony** [med. Gr. ταὐτοφωνία (Eustathius), f. φωνή voice], repetition of the same (vocal) sound; so **Tautopho·nic, -ical** *adjs.*, repeating the same sound. **Tauto·pody,** *Pros.* [Gr. ταὐτοποδία, f. πούς, ποδ- foot], repetition of the same metrical foot; a double foot or dipody consisting of the same foot repeated twice; so **Tautopo·dic** *a.*, belonging to or constituting a tautopody. **Tautozo·nal** *a., Cryst.*, belonging to or situated in the same zone; hence **Tautozona·lity,** the quality of being tautozonal.
1891 *Cent. Dict.*, *Tautobaryd. 1860 *Temple Bar Mag.* I. 121 Syria is the most wearying, sun-baked, *tautographical place in the world,..blinding limestone ridges, limestone mule-paths, limestone valleys, limestone everything and everywhere. 1895 Story-Maskelyne *Crystallogr.* iii. § 36 When two zones have a face in common, that is to say when their zone-circles intersect in a pole, they will be spoken of as *tautohedral in that face or pole. 1894 Fennell in *Class. Rev.* Feb. 49/1 *Tautometric responsion of single words is as a rule without significance and may sometimes be due to chance. 1892 *Athenæum* 16 July 92/1 Mr. Bury has either failed to detect, or neglected to notice, ..κείνου σὺν ἀνδρός, v. 9, *tautometrical with ἀνδρὸς φιλοξεῖν-, v. 20. 1895 Story-Maskelyne *Crystallogr.* vi. § 150 It is not difficult to determine whether in any particular case correlative mero-symmetrical forms are enantiomorphous or *tautomorphous; i.e. cannot be brought into congruence, or can be so brought by revolution round one or more zone-lines. 1901 *Ibis* Oct. 722 We cannot agree with Señor Berg that everyone ought to call..the Night-Heron *Nycticorax nycticorax*, for we do not ourselves recognise the obligations of the new system of *tautonyms. 1896 *Ibid.* July 364 This repeating of the specific name seems specially awkward in the cases of the unavoidable *tautonymic names. 1908 *Athenæum* 18 Mar. 342/1 He concluded with a proposal to get rid of *tautonymy—as in *Trutta trutta, Apus (Apus) apus*, or other comical arrangements—by a plan distinguishing what was legal in the past from what is to be legal in the future. [1678 Cudworth *Intell. Syst.* i. iv. § 36. 611 That the ancient orthodox fathers, who used the word *Homoousios* against Arius, intended not therein to assert the Son to have one and the same singular or individual essence with the Father, appeareth plainly from their disclaiming and disowning those two words, Ταυτοούσιον and Μονοούσιον. Concerning the former of which, Epiphanius thus;..'We affirm not the Son to be *Tautousion*, (one and the same substance with the Father) lest this should be taken in any way of compliance with Sabellius'.] *Ibid.*, Athanasius..disclaimeth a monoousian Trinity, as Epiphanius did before a *tautousian; both of them a Trinity of meer names..they alike distinguishing them from the homoousian Trinity, as a Trinity of real Hypostases or Persons. 1846 Worcester, *Tautoöusian*, **Tautoöusious*, having the same identical essence. 1882 Ogilvie, *Tautoöusian*, same as *Tautousian*...*Tautousian, Tautousious*, in *theol.* having absolutely the same essence. 1652 N. Culverwell *Treat.* i. xvii. (1661) 152 Anacreon..by a most emphatical *Tautopathy, was choak'd with the husk..of a Grape. 1847 Webster, **Tautophonical*..**Tautophony*. 1881 G. W. Moon *Revisers' Eng.* xxiv. (1882) 64 They say 'That ye may be sons of your Father which is in heaven: for he maketh his sun to rise'..tautophony, suggestive of a pun. 1898 F. Harrison in *19th Cent.* June 942 If your ear does not hear the false note, the tautophony or the cacophony in the written sentence as you read it. 1891 *Cent. Dict.*, **Tautopodic*..**Tautopody*. 1878 Gurney *Crystallogr.* 21 They are also said to be *tautozonal, by which is meant that they all lie in one and the same zone. 1895 Story-Maskelyne *Crystallogr.* iii. § 36 Two or more poles (or their faces) are said to be tautozonal or heterozonal with a third, according as they lie in the same or different zone-circles (or zones) with it. 1880 L. Fletcher in *Philos. Mag.* Feb. 84 The property of *tautozonality is a permanent one.

**Tautochrone** (tǭ·tŏkroun). *Math.* [f. Tauto- + Gr. χρόνος time: cf. F. *tautochrone* (Dict. Trévoux 1771).] That curve upon which a particle moving under the action of gravity (or any given force) will reach the lowest (or some fixed) point in the same time, from whatever point it starts. So **Tautochronism** (tǭtǫ·krŏniz'm), the property of a tautochrone; **Tauto·chronous** *a.*, having the character of a tautochrone; occupying the same time, isochronous.
*a* 1774 Goldsm. *Surv. Exp. Philos.* (1776) II. 142 The time spent in determining the figure of a tautochrone might have been more usefully employed in this research. 1842 Brande *Dict. Sc.*, etc. s.v., Newton and Hermann also determined the tautochrone in a vacuum, when gravity is supposed to be directed towards a given centre. Newton likewise showed that the cycloid is also the tautochrone in a resisting medium, when the resistance is proportional to the velocity. 1842 *Exam. Papers* 47 (*Dubl. Univ. Cal.* 1843), Prove that the cycloid is the only plane curve possessing the property of tautochronism. 1846 Smart Suppl., *Tautochronous*, arriving at the same time; having the property of the tautochrone.

**Tautoclin** (tǭ·toklin). *Min.* [ad. Ger. *tautoklin* (Breithaupt 1830), f. Gr. ταὐτό (Tauto-) + κλίνειν to bend, incline; so called 'because it has the same rhombohedral angle as dolomite' (Chester).] A greyish-white variety of Ankerite.
1868 Dana *Min.* (ed. 5) 685.

**Tautog** (tǭtǫ·g). Also **tautaug, tetaug.** [ad. Narragansett *taut-auog*, pl. of *taut* name of the fish: see quot. 1643.] A labroid fish, *Tautoga americana* (*T. onitis*), also called *black-fish* or *oyster-fish*, abundant on the Atlantic coast of N. America, and esteemed for food.
1643 Roger Williams *Key to Lang. of America* xix. 115 Of Fish and Fishing. *Taut-aūog*. Sheeps-heads. 1828–32 Webster, *Tetaug*, the name of a fish on the coast of New England; called also black fish. 1848 Bartlett *Dict. Amer.*, *Tautaug*. 1851 Hawthorne *Ho. Sev. Gables* xviii, Real turtle, we understand, and salmon, tautog, canvass-backs, pig, English mutton. 1888 G. B. Goode *Amer. Fishes* 288 'Tautog' would consequently seem to be a word from the dialect of the Narragansett Indians.

**Tautographical, -hedral:** see Tauto-.

† **Tau·tolite.** *Min. Obs.* [ad. Ger. *tautolit* (Breithaupt 1826); 'adapted from [Gr.] ταὐτόμετρος of the same measure, referring to a supposed axial relation, and λίθος' (Chester); see Tauto- and -lite.] An obsolete synonym of Allanite.
1828 *Philos. Mag.* May 398 The tautolite seems to be related to the chrysolite, as the ceylanite to the spinelle. 1868 Dana *Min.* (ed. 5) 286 *Bucklandite* is anhydrous allanite in small black crystals...*Tautolite*..is probably the same species.

**Tautologic** (tǭtolǫ·dʒik), *a. rare.* [f. Gr. ταὐτολόγ-ία Tautology + -ic: cf. the adv. ταὐτολογικῶς in Eustathius *c* 1160.] = next, 1.
1828 *Blackw. Mag.* XXIV. 906 Dr. Johnson..he charges ..with a plethoric and tautologic tympany of sentence. 1858 Carlyle *Fredk. Gt.* vii. v. (1872) II. 287 No end of florid inflated tautologic ornamental balderdash.

**Tautological** (tǭtolǫ·dʒikăl), *a.* [f. as prec. + -al: see -ical.]
**1.** Pertaining to, characterized by, involving, or using tautology; repeating the same word, or the same notion in different words.
1620 T. Granger *Div. Logike* 387 Lest thy discourse be tedious, Tautologicall, erroneous. 1670 Blount *Law Dict.* s.v. *Alnager*, Measurer, and Alneger, which last, though it be a Tautological expression (Aulnage and Measure, being the same thing denoted in two Languages) yet long usage and custom have brought them to distinct Offices. 1800 in *Four C. Eng. Lett.* (1880) 355 Now and then, in the career of declamation, he becomes tautological and ineffective. 1869 Ingleby *Introd. Metaph.* ii. ii. 176 One writer..desperately declares that the Laws of Motion are mere truisms, or tautological judgments.
**2.** Of an echo: Repeating the same sound several times. ? *Obs.*
1677 Plot *Oxfordsh.* 7 These return syllables and words, the same oftentimes repeated, and may therefore be stiled Tautological Echo's. 1807 Joyce *Sci. Dial.* xiii. (1846) 232 Called tautological or babbling echoes.
† **3.** *loosely.* Of the nature of a repetition, identical (*with*). *Obs. rare*⁻¹.
1689 G. Harvey *Curing Dis. by Expect.* xvi. 125 Compound Waters..tautological the one with the other.

**Tautologically** (tǭtolǫ·dʒikăli), *adv.* [f. prec. + -ly ².] In a tautological manner, with tautology.
1620 T. Granger *Div. Logike* 292 Handle the same matter (homogeneously, not tautologically). 1820 Coleridge *Let. C. A. Tulk* 17 July (in *Pearson's Catal.* (1894) 14) At once superfluous and defective, tautologically superfluous in the point of co-equality, and dangerously defective in that of the subordination. 1840 Hood *Up Rhine* 61, I join with Dr. Watts' sluggard in wishing tautologically, for 'a little more sleep and a little more slumber'.
So **Tautolo·gicalness** (Bailey 1727 vol. II).

**Tautologism** (tǭtǫ·lŏdʒiz'm). *rare.* [f. Tautologize: see -ism.] The use or practice of tautology; an instance of this. Used by Farrar *spec.* for the combination of two synonymous words or syllables for the sake of precise expression of the meaning, as in Chinese.
1815 *Sporting Mag.* XLVI. 117 Hard and callous, form a tautologism. 1816 Bentham *Chrestom.* 293 The reproach of tautologism,—incurred..by the observation. 1869 Farrar *Fam. Speech* iv. (1873) 122 This chaos [of homonyms in Chinese]..is reduced to order and meaning..partly by what may be called tautologism, i.e. by using a *second* synonym to define the word which is vague; in point of fact, by making two vague words into one definite word.

**Tautologist** (tǭtǫ·lŏdʒist). [f. as prec. + -ist.] One who practises tautology.
1702 Steele *Funeral* i. 14 Oh! that Damn'd Tautologist too—That [Mr.] Puzzle and his Irrevocable Deed! 1727 Bailey vol. II, *Tautologist*, one who says the same Things over and over. 1805 W. Taylor in *Ann. Rev.* III. 649 All such literary tautologists are proper objects of epitomization.

**Tautologize** (tǭtǫ·lŏdʒəiz), *v.* [f. Tautology + -ize. (The Gr. equivalent was ταὐτολογεῖν.)

Cf. APOLOGIZE.] *intr.* To repeat the same thing in the same or different words; to use tautology. Also with *it* (quot. 1656).

1607 TOPSELL *Serpents* (1658) 761 To take occasion to tautologize, or to speak one thing twice. 1615 JACKSON *Creed* IV. iv. § 1 Even the most acute amongst the schoolmen whiles they seek to clear this doubt do but falter and tautologize. 1656 S. H. *Gold. Law* 1 We are constrained ..to Tautologize it in repetitions, even to a wearying of our selves and the world with words. ? 16.. *Plutarch's Mor.* IV. 220 (L.) The tautologizing babler, if he be a physitian, certainly is more troublesome than the disease.

Hence **Tauto·logizer**, one who tautologizes; a tautologist.

1657 J. WATTS *Vind. Ch. Eng.* 241 A vain babler, a tautologizer and a vain repeater.

**Tautologous** (tǫtǫ·lŏgəs), *a.* [f. Gr. ταὐτο-λόγ-ος repeating what has been said (f. ταὐτό the same + -λογος saying, f. λέγειν to say) + -OUS.] = TAUTOLOGICAL 1.

1714 J. FORTESCUE-ALAND *Pref. Fortescue's Abs. & Lim. Mon.* 67 The County of Devon, in the old way of Speaking.. called the County of Devonshire, which is the constant Expression in old Deeds, and signifies the same thing tho' it be tautologous. 1786 H. TOOKE *Purley* I. ix. 406, I have been purposely tautologous, that by my indifferent application of the two words *of* and *for*..the smallest..opposition between these prepositions might be done away. 1853 *Fraser's Mag.* XLVII. 358 The circuitous jargon—the tautologous gabble..of special pleading. 1884 SIR W. B. BRETT in *Law Times Rep.* 10 May 315/2, I have come to the conclusion..that the Legislature intended in this case to be verbose and tautologous, and to say the same thing twice over.

Hence **Tauto·logously** *adv.* = TAUTOLOGICALLY.

1865 J. P. COLLIER *Bibl. Catal.* I. 109 It begins thus tautologously: 'The present plagues that now we fele'. 1904 *Westm. Gaz.* 22 Oct. 3/2 'Fraud-pilfered'—the indictment is tautologously complete.

**Tautology** (tǫtǫ·lŏdʒi). [ad. late L. *tautologia* (*c* 350 in Mar. Plotin. Sacerd.), a. Gr. ταὐτολογία, f. ταὐτολόγος: see TAUTOLOGOUS; in F. *tautologie.*] **a.** A repetition of the same statement. **b.** The repetition (esp. in the immediate context) of the same word or phrase, or of the same idea or statement in other words: usually as a fault of style.

1587 FLEMING *Contn. Holinshed* III. 1553/1 This ambassage is reported in the historie of Scotland, wherevnto (for the auoiding of tautologie) we refer the reader. *a* 1653 GOUGE *Comm. Heb.* (1655) 99 To shew that there is no tautology, no vain repetition of one and the same thing therein. 1686 GOAD *Celest. Bodies* I. xii. 56 The Taedium of Tautology is odious to every Pen and Ear. *a* 1748 WATTS *Improv. Mind* II. ii. § 4 By securing you from an appearance of tautology, or repeating the same words too often. 1790 WESLEY *Wks.* (1872) IV. 487 That villanous tautology of lawyers, which is the scandal of our nation. 1869 FARRAR *Fam. Speech* iv. (1873) 134 One leading syllable thrusting itself with the most obtrusive tautology through a whole sentence.

**c.** With *a* and *pl.* An instance of this; a tautological phrase or expression; †a repetition *of* something already said (quot. 1599).

1579 FULKE *Confut. Sanders* 644 It is a foolish tautologie, for you sayed the same immediatly before. 1599 *Broughton's Let.* ix. 32 Euery later paperwork of yours is but a Tautology of the former. 1698 WANLEY in *Lett. Lit. Men* (Camden) 258, I called the library a venerable place; the Books sacred reliques of Antiquity, &c.; with half a dozen tautologies. 1844 LD. BROUGHAM *Brit. Const.* xix. § 1 (1862) 309 Repetitions and tautologies are used.

**d.** Applied to the repetition of a statement as its own reason, or to the identification of cause and effect.

1659 PEARSON *Creed* ii. (1839) 157 To assign any thing as the cause or reason of itself, is a great absurdity, and the expression of it a vain tautology. 1662 H. MORE *Philos. Writ.* Pref. Gen. (1712) 15 The resolution of such Phaenomena as we experience in ourselves..into this vital oneness,..is no vain Tautology, or the mere saying a thing is so because it is so. 1836–7 SIR W. HAMILTON *Metaph.* (1859) II. xxxix. 377 There is thus conceived an absolute tautology between the effect and its causes. We think the causes to contain all that is contained in the effect; the effect to contain nothing which was not contained in the causes.

**e.** *transf.* A mere repetition of acts, incidents, or experiences; in quot. 1650, used for the sending of a thing to its place of origin.

1650 FULLER *Pisgah* II. v. 128 Some wil object it was a real tautology to bring purples to Tyre, seeing the best of the world were made in that place. 1657 W. DILLINGHAM *Contn. Siege of Ostend* in *Sir. F. Vere's Comm.*, It was so thick stuck with bullets, that the Ordnance could scarcely shoot without a tautologie, and hitting its former bullets. 1687 NORRIS *Coll. Misc.* (1699) 324 Our whole Life is but a nauseous Tautology. 1863 COWDEN CLARKE *Shaks. Char.* i. 14 The poet has avoided a dramatic tautology (if I may so use the term) in bringing about the death of two worthy men immediately upon the heels of each other.

**Tautomerism** (tǫtǫ·mĕriz'm). *Chem.* [f. Gr. ταὐτο-, TAUTO- + μέρος part, after ISOMERISM; rendering Ger. *tautomerie* (Laar 1885).] The property exhibited by certain organic compounds of behaving in different reactions as if they possessed two (or more) different constitutions, that is, as if the atoms of the same compound or group were arranged in two (or more) different ways, expressible by different structural formulæ (e. g. the group —CH:C(OH)—, or —$CH_2$.CO—, in ethyl aceto-acetate). So **Tautomer** (tǭ·tǒməɪ), any one of the forms of a tautomeric compound in relation to another; **Tautomeric** (tǭtome·rik) *a.*, pertaining to or exhibiting tautomerism; **Tautomery** (tǭtǫ·mĕri) [ad. Ger. *tautomerie*], = tautomerism.

1885 CONRAD LAAR in *Ber. Dtsch. Chem. Ges.* XVIII. 652 Um die gegenseitige Beziehung gleichberechtigter Formeln ..kurz bezeichnen zu können, schlage ich hierfür den Ausdruck 'Tautomerie' vor.] 1886 tr. *Richter's Organic Chem.* (1899) I. 55 Laar..assumes that such compounds consist of a mixture of structural isomerides, in that an easily mobile hydrogen atom oscillates between two positions in equilibrio, and thereby the entire complex becomes mobile. He designates the phenomenon as *tautomery.* 1890 GOLDSCHMIDT & MEISSLER in *Jrnl. Chem. Soc.* LVIII. 499 Assuming that in the reactions of tautomeric compounds which take place under the influence of electrolytes, the intramolecular change is brought about by the free ions. 1890 NEF *ibid.* 983 A discussion of the alleged cases of tautomerism in ethyl succinosuccinate and analogous compounds. 1901 DIXON *ibid.* LXXIX. 543 Hitherto no isomerism (or tautomerism) has been established amongst mineral derivatives analogous to that subsisting between the normal and *iso*thiocyanates of organic radicles. 1903 *Amer. Chem. Jrnl.* May XXIX. 406 It [thio-urea] may react with the metal [silver] to form a sulphide, or its tautomer may form an insoluble silver compound. 1904 *Ibid.* Dec. 606 There are ten possible tautomeric formulas for this phenylacetylurazole, and four possible positions for the acetyl group. 1905 WALKER *Chem. Soc. Annual Rep.* 9 It is suggested that an absorption band appears wherever there is tautomeric change within the molecule.

**Tautometric** to **Tautozonal**: see TAUTO-.

**Tavarn**, obs. form of TAVERN.

† **Tava·sco.** *Obs.* Variant of TABASCO.

1652 WADSWORTH *Chocolate* 14 Some doe put into it [chocolate] black Pepper, and also Tauasco.

**Tave** (tēiv), *v.* Now *dial.* Also 7 tauve, 8–9 taave, 9 teave. [app. of Norse origin: cf. Norw. dial. *tava* to toil or struggle without much effect, to fumble, be exhausted.] *intr.* To move the limbs ineffectually, to sprawl; to strike out at random with the arms or legs; to throw oneself about, as a person in a passion, in a fever, etc.; to act violently in any way; to strive, toil, labour, or struggle in work, difficult walking, etc.

*c* 1350 *St. Mary Magd.* 401 in Horstm. *Altengl. Leg.* (1881) 85 Sethin it [the child] swelid and turned & tauyd. 14.. *Beryn* 2061 Sith yee of hym be sesid, howe evir so yee [?hee] taue, Let hym nevir pas. 1566 DRANT *Horace* A iv, Where now and then (O just rewarde) in raginge surge sum taves. 1674 RAY *N. C. Words* 47 To *Tave*; Lincoln. to rage. 1691 *Ibid.* 73 Sick People are said to *tave* with the Hands when they catch at any thing. 1681 HICKERINGILL *Black Non-Conf.* Postscr., Wks. 1716 II. 168 Him that bespoke a Picture of a Horse lying (tauveing) upon his Back. 1790 MRS. WHEELER *Westmld. Dial.* (1821) 40, I wur sae teerd wie maanderin up an dawn an teaavin ith ling, I laaid me dawn on a breaad Scar, an sean fel asleep. 1825 BROCKETT *N. C. Words*, *Taving*, irregular motion; picking the bed-clothes in febrile delirium. 1828 *Craven Gloss.*, *Tave*, to kick with the feet like a distracted person. 1855 ROBINSON *Whitby Gloss.*, To *Teeave*, to paw and sprawl with the arms and legs. 1891 T. HARDY *Tess* xii, See how I've got to teave and slave, and your poor weak father with his heart clogged like a dripping-pan.

**Tave** = *to have*: see T[1] and HAVE *v.*

† **Tavel**, *sb. Obs.* Forms: 1 tæfl, tæfel, 3 tævel, tavel. [OE. *tæfel* fem., = WGer. **tabal*, ON. *tafl*, OHG. *zabal*, ad. late L. or Com. Romanic *tav(o)la*:—L. *tabula* table, board, esp. board to play on, in which sense it was taken app. bef. 400 into WGer. See TABLE.] A die for playing with; also, a game of chance, or the board on which it is played. Also *attrib.* Hence (in OE.) **tæfl-stán**, a piece or 'man' for playing with, a die; (ME.) **tævelbred** = TABLE-BOARD 1, ON. *taflborð*; (OE.) **tæflere**, a player at tavel or with dice.

*a* 800 *Erfurt Gloss.* 6 *Alea*, tefil. *c* 1000 ÆLFRIC *Voc.* in Wr.-Wülcker 150/21–5 *Alea*, tæfel. *Aleæ*, tæfelstanas. *Aleator*, tæflere. *Pirgus*, cyningstan on tæfle. *Tessere, uel lepusculæ*, feðerscite tæfel. *c* 1000 in Thorpe *Codex Exon.* 331/19 Dryhten.. dæleð sumum tæfle cræft, bleo-bordes ȝebreȝd. *Ibid.* 345/2 Hy tweȝen sceolon tæfle ymb sittan ..habban him ȝomen on borde. *c* 1205 LAY. 8133 Summen pleoden on tæuelbrede. *c* 1275 *Ibid.*, Somme pleoide mid tauel.

† **Ta·vel**, *v. Obs.* [OE. *tæflian*, f. *tæfel*, TAVEL *sb.*] *intr.* To play at dice.

*a* 1100 *Voc.* in Wr.-Wülcker 267/8 *Cotizo*, ic tæfle. *a* 1250 *Owl & Night.* 1666 Riȝt swa me gred þe manne a schame, Þat tauelep & forleost þat gome.

**Tavel**, early var. of TEVEL *v. Obs.* or *dial.*

**Tavelett**, obs. form of TALLET.

† **Ta·velin.** *Obs.* Also 5–6 tavelyn, 6 -yng, -ing, tavalyn. [app. ad. It. *tavolino* 'any little boord, table, tablet' (or some cognate word), dim. from *tavola* 'a table, planke, or flat boorde' (Florio).] Formerly, with furriers, (in *pl.*) app. the boards between which small packages of skins were imported; hence, a small package of skins or certain portions of fur (usually or always four), put up between two boards. (Cf. TIMBER, applied to a package of forty skins between two stout boards of timber (Skene).)

1439 *Inv. T. Burgh* (Comm. Crt., Lond., Prowet 22), xxx lose tavelyns xv d. 1503 *Privy Purse Exp. Eliz. of York* (1830) 89, iiij tavelyns of shankes for the coler and fent of the said gowne, ijs. 1505 *Acc. Ld. High Treas. Scot.* III. 42 Item, for xiiij tavalyns of ermyng to the samyn goun, brocht be the Quenis maister of wardrob; ilk pece ij s. iiij d, summa..vi li. xs. 1545 *Rates of Customs* C vij b, Tauelynges the hundreth vj s. viij d. 1586 *Ibid.* E viij, Taueling the c, xiij s. iiij d.

† **Ta·vell.** *Silk-weaving. Obs.* exc. as Fr. **tavelle** (tave·l). Also 6 **tavel, tavyll, tavil.** [a. F. *tavelle* (in sense 2), app. ad. L. *tabella* tablet.]

†**1.** The bobbin on which silk is wound for use in the shuttle. *Obs.*

1523 SKELTON *Garl. Laurel* 791 To weue in the stoule sume were full preste, With slaiis, with tauellis, with hedellis well drest. *a* 1529 — *Agst. Comely Coystrowne* 34 Wele sped in spyndels and turnyng of tauellys. 1530 PALSGR. 279/2 Tavell an instrument for a sylke woman to worke with. 1538 ELYOT, *Liciatorium*, a weauers shyttel, or a sylke womans tauell, wheron sylke or threde beinge wounden, is shot through the web or lome. 1620 THOMAS *Lat. Dict.* s. v. *Liciatorium.*

‖**2.** (mod. Fr. **tavelle.**) A large drum or bobbin on which the silk is wound off the cocoons.

1868 *Rep. U. S. Commissioner Agric.* (1869) 286 These [machines] consisted of, 1st, a series of tavelles to wind, clean, and equalize the threads during their automatic winding off [etc.].

**Taver** (tēi·vəɪ), *sb. Sc.* Also 9 **taiver.** [app. of Norse origin: cf. Norw. *tave* clout, rag, any torn piece of stuff, Da. *tave* fibre, filament of tow, wool, etc.] A mere shred or filament; a 'rag' (of meat).

1808 JAMIESON, *Taivers*, s. pl. tatters; as, boiled to taivers, Fife. 1819 TENNANT *Papistry Storm'd* (1827) 15 Sorrow gin Paip was boil'd to taivers, And I'd a platefu' o' the bree! 1822 GALT *Steam-boat* xii. 288 They don't know how to cook yonder..they boil the meat to tavers.

**Taver** (tēi·vəɪ), *v. Sc.* Also 9 **taiver.** [freq. of TAVE *v.*] *intr.* To wander vaguely or aimlessly; to wander mentally, to talk incoherently as one delirious; to talk idly and foolishly. Hence **Ta·vering** *vbl. sb.* and *ppl. a.*, wandering, etc.; **Ta·vert** *ppl. a.*, fatigued or exhausted with wandering, or with toil or struggle; incoherent, confused, stupefied, stupid; also **Ta·versome** *a.*, fatiguing, exhausting.

1535 STEWART *Cron. Scot.* (Rolls) III. 420 Fra hill to hill rynnand as tha war hyrit, In mure and mos so tavert war and tyrit. *a* 1598 ROLLOCK *Serm.* Wks. 1849 I. 435 He callis our warkis tavering, going out of the way. *Ibid.* 436 His actiounis ar taverings, all wandring out of the way. [*So ed.* 1599; *ed.* 1616 wauering, wauerings.] 1808–18 JAMIESON, *Taiver*, to wander;..to rave as mad...*Taiversum*, tiresome, fatiguing. *Taivert.* 1822 GALT *Sir A. Wylie* xxx, Ye wouldna hae me..to sit till I'm taver't?..I fin' the wine rinnin in my head already. 1823 — *Entail* xviii, I would na trust the hair o' a dog to the judgment o' that tavert bodie, Gibby Omit. 1887 J. SERVICE *Dr. Duguid* xxii, The taivert tenets of the Antiburgher Kirk.

**Tavern** (tæ·vəɹn), *sb.* Forms: 3–7 taverne, (4 tavarn, 5 tawern, 6 taverin, *Sc.* taveroun), 7– tavern. [a. OF. *taverne* (1256 in Littré):—L. *taberna* a shed constructed of boards, a hut, booth, stall, shop, workshop, also a tavern or inn (so in earliest French and Eng. examples). Cf. TABERN.]

**1.** In early use, A public house or tap-room where wine was retailed; a dram-shop; in current use = PUBLIC HOUSE 2 b.

See also humorous use (word-play on name *New Inn Hall*) in quot. 1904.

[1286 *Memoranda K. R.* 14 & 15 *Edw. I* 3 b, Tauernes ke sunt en meimes la Meisun ke est assise par entre la Meison Thomas le Vineter vers le Su.] 1297 R. GLOUC. (Rolls) 4024 Hor ydelnesse hom ssal bringe to sunne of lecherye, To tauerne & to sleuþe, & to hasardrie. 1303 R. BRUNNE *Handl. Synne* 1025 Tauerne ys þe deuylys knyfe Hyt sleþ þe, oþer soule or lyfe. 1340 *Ayenb.* 56 Þe tauerne ys þe scole of þe dyeule huere his deciples studieþ. *c* 1440 *Jacob's Well* 147 Þe tauerne is welle of glotonye, for it may be clepyd þe develys scolehous. 1570 B. GOOGE *Pop. Kingd.* IV. 53 This done, they to the Taverne go, or in the fields they dine. 1593 SHAKS. *Rich. II*, v. iii. 5 Can no man tell of my vnthriftie Sonne?.. Enquire at London, 'mongst the Tauernes there. 1611 COTGR., *Tavernier*,.. a Victualler, of whom (as in our Tauernes of London) one may haue meat, and drink for his money. 1693 *Humours Town* 108 The Taverns are the Nurseries of Profaneness and Treason. 1710 SWIFT *Lett.* (1767) III. 14, I dined to-day at a tavern with Stratford. 1785 TRUSLER *Mod. Times* III. 76 When we reached London.. we put up at one of those taverns called hotels. 1809 KENDALL *Trav.* III. lxxii. 128 The doctor keeps a public house, or, as the term is, a tavern. 1840 DICKENS *Barn. Rudge* ii, This tavern would seem to be a house of call for all the gaping idlers of the neighbourhood. 1904 *Westm. Gaz.* 11 May 1/2 Richard Shute—the only first-class man ever produced by the defunct 'Tavern', as New Inn Hall [Oxford] used to be called.

†**2.** A shop or workshop attached to or under a dwelling-house; often under ground, a cellar. Cf. CELLAR 2, WINE-CELLAR. *dial. Obs.*

1521 in *Test. Ebor.* (Surtees) VI. 4 Al my tymber and bordes in the Taverne, except a kilnehouse of x postes that lieth in the laithe and in the gaitehouse. 1566 in S. O. Addy *Evolution Eng. House* (1905) 96 William Tomson for his taverne stare, iiij d. 1575 *Ibid.* 95 Payd to ij dykers for casting earth furth of the taverne iiij daies, ij s. viij d. 1583 *Will Myles Fox* (Somerset Ho.), My Shop with two undershops or Taverins. 1703 THORESBY *Let. to Ray* (W. Yorksh. Words), *Tavern*, a cellar. 1905 ADDY (as above) 94–5 In England shops in front of town houses were sometimes known as 'taverns',..and were below the surface of the streets, like cellars...These 'taverns' were entered by stairs.

**3.** As a rendering of L. *taberna*: see the etymology.

**1382** WYCLIF *Acts* xxviii. 15 Whanne bretheren hadden herd, thei runnen to vs til to the cheping of Appius, and to a place that is clepid Thre tauernes [*Vulg.* tres Tabernas]. **1611** BIBLE ibid., They came to meet vs as farre as Appii forum, and the three Tauernes.

**4.** *attrib.* and *Comb.* **a.** Attributive, as *tavern-bill, -boy, -bully, -bush* (BUSH *sb.*$^1$ 5), *-chair, -discourse, -door, -drawer* (DRAWER *sb.*$^1$ 2), *-fellow, -house, -lady, -lantern, -man, -music, -quarrel, -reckoning, -score, -supper, -talk, -wine,* etc. **b.** Objective and obj. gen., as *tavern-frequenter,* †*-ganger, -goer, -haunter, -hunter, -hunting, -keeper, -tracer.* **c.** Instrumental, locative, etc., as *tavern-gotten, -tainted* adjs. **d.** Special combs.: †**tavern-fox**, in phr. *to hunt a tavern-fox*, to get drunk: see FOX *sb.* 1 d and *v.* 2; **tavern-token**, a token given in change by a tavern-keeper, which he will again accept in payment; † *to swallow a tavern-token*, to get drunk (*obs.*).

**1611** SHAKS. *Cymb.* v. iv. 161 You shall..fear no more *Tauerne Bils. **1796** H. HUNTER tr. *St.-Pierre's Stud. Nat* (1799) III. 286 The appellation of 'good man', so frankly bestowed on him by the *tavern-boy. **1852** THACKERAY *Esmond* II. i, A *Tavern-bully beaten. **1570** FOXE *A. & M.* (ed. 2) 1206/1 Seeing good wyne nedeth no *tauerne bushe to vtter it. *a* **1668** DAVENANT *News fr. Plymouth* Wks. (1673) 2 In the Metropolis,..Where still your Taverne Bush is green and flourishing. **1787** SIR J. HAWKINS *Johnson* 87, I have heard him assert, that a *tavern-chair was the throne of human felicity. **1660** R. COKE *Justice Vind.* Pref. 12 The subject of all *tavern-discourses. **1474** *Coventry Leet Bk.* (E. E. T. S.) 400 Yf he sell any feetiff wyn his *Tauerne durre to be sealed Inne, and he to make a fyne at the kynges wyll. *a* **1704** T. BROWN *Lond. & Lacedem. Oracles* Introd., Wks. 1709 III. III. 124 The Oyster-wench in her lawful Occupation at the Tavern-door. **1721** CIBBER *Rival Fools* I. i, Can't you practise..upon a *Tavern-Drawer, or a Box-keeper at the Play-House? **1899** *Month* June 613 The roystering joviality of Prince Harry's *tavern-fellow. **1635** J. TAYLOR (Water P.) *Old Parr* C ij b, Nor did hee ever hunt a *Taverne Fox. **1483** *Cath. Angl.* 378/2 A *Tawern ganger, *attabernio*. **1797** T. PARK *Sonn.* 82 Meeting with some *tavern-goer. **1538** ELYOT, *Circumcelliones*, *tauerne haunters, or raylers aboute. **1583** GOLDING *Calvin on Deut.* li. 305 These Tauernhaunters or Alehouse Knightes which counterfeit the preachers. **13..** *Cursor M.* 28462 (Cott.) Til *tauerne huse my-seluen was wont, And draun men þer-til vmstont. **1553** BECON *Reliques of Rome* (1563) 28 The aforesayd pope made..a decree, that priestes should be no *tauern-hunters. **1641** MILTON *Animadv.* xiii. Pr. Wks. (1847) 69/2 Their laziness, their *tavern-hunting, their neglect of all sound literature. **1611** COTGR., *Tavernier*,..a *Tauerne-keeper. **1779** *Mirror* No. 46 ⁋ 23 Familiar..to the very tavern-keepers of this city. **1763** MRS. F. SHERIDAN *Discovery* II. i, I don't doubt but he is going to some of his *tavern-ladies. **1664** ETHEREDGE *Love in Tub* IV. ii, Go with a *Tavern-Lanthorn before me at Noon-day. **1755** JOHNSON, **Tavernman*, one who keeps a tavern. **1643** SIR T. BROWNE *Relig. Med.* II. § 9 That vulgar and *Taverne-Musick. **1820** HAZLITT *Lect. Dram. Lit.* 30 Marlow was stabbed in a *tavern quarrel. **1714** MANDEVILLE *Fab. Bees* (1724) I. 19 Those, that remain'd,..when they paid their *Tavern Score, Resolv'd to enter it no more. *a* **1680** BUTLER *Rem., Charac.* (1759) II. 439 He is the Whores Jackal,..and at Night has his Share in a *Tavern-Supper. **1760** *Cautions to Officers Army* 124 Tavern-Suppers are generally expensive. **1609** *Ev. Woman in Hum.* III. i. in Bullen *O. Pl.* IV, Urge no more, 'tis *Taverne talke. **1638** FORD *Lady's Trial* II. ii, You are grown a tavern-talk, Matters for fiddlers' songs. **1598** B. JONSON *Ev. Man in Hum.* I. iii, Drunk sir?..perhaps he swallow'd a *tauerne token, or some such deuise sir. **1604** *Meeting Gallants* 17 Indeed he had swallowed downe many Tauerne-tokens, and was infected with the plague of drunkennes. **1604** DEKKER *Hon. Wh.* I. iv, If he have but..a spleene not so big as a taverne token.

Hence (mostly *nonce-wds.*), **Ta·vernize** *v. intr.*, to frequent taverns; **Ta·vernless** *a.*, devoid of taverns or inns; **Ta·vernly** *a.*, smacking of the tavern; **Ta·vernous** *a.* [after *cavernous*], tavern-like; **Ta·vernry**, tavern-expenses; **Ta·vernwards** *adv.*, towards a tavern.

**1851** *Fraser's Mag.* XLIV. 425 The frequent *tavernising, if we may coin a word, is another peculiarity. Pepys was a giant in this way, and sang and roystered..in the public houses of the day. **1897** 'MARK TWAIN' *More Tramps Abroad* lxxi, The Bishop..was once making a business-progress through the *tavernless velt. **1612** SHELTON *Quix.* (1746) I. III. ii. 119 So returning him Thanks with *Tavernly Phraze for his large Offers. **1866** LD. HOUGHTON *Sp.* in *Life* (1890) I. ii. 75 The low..ill-lit, cavernous, *tavernous gallery. *a* **1670** SPALDING *Troub. Chas. I* (1851) II. 102 Thay comptit and reknit for thair *tavernrie with ther mistressis. **1892** *Daily News* 10 Mar. 2/4 Thirty young fellows..were promptly on the 'double' *tavernwards.

**Ta·vern,** *v.* Now *rare* or *Obs.* [f. prec. sb., as a rendering of med.L. *tabernāre*, f. *taberna* (common in 14–15th c.).]

†**1.** *trans.* Of a leaseholder or copyholder: To subdivide his tenement; ? *orig.* to erect a cottage (*taberna*) on his holding, and apportion a piece of land to it. *north. Obs.*

[**1365** *Durham Acc. Rolls* (Surtees) I. 38 Idem Johannes illud [tenementum] tabernavit sine licencia. *Ibid.* 42 De Johanne Anderson pro licencia tabernandi unum cotagium. **1402** *Charta* (Du Cange), Ne scolaribus detur occasio mercandi seu Tabernandi.] **1534** *Augm. Off., Convent. Leases, Yorks.* No. 888 That the said Thomas and Roger his sonne..shall not taverne the said fermhold nor no parcell therof bot to dwell and remane of the said fermhold apon payn [etc.]. **1551** *Richmond Wills* (Surtees) 72 If it happ my wife to latt or taverne any parte of said fermehold, (not beyng of habilitie to occupie the same) then I will that Roland my eldest sonne have it. **1575** [see TAVERNING 1]. **1577** *Eccl. Proc. Bp. Barnes* (Surtees) 18 And doe not let out, lease out, or taverne out, their livings.

**2.** *intr.* To frequent taverns; also *to tavern it.*

**1580**, etc. [see TAVERNING 2]. **1610** *Histrio-m.* VI. 209 Each..taverns it with drunken suppers still.

†**b.** *trans.* with *out*: To spend in 'taverning'.

**1628** FELTHAM *Resolves* II. [I.] lvii. 164 When, like Nero, thou should'st Taverne out thy time with Wantons.

**Taverner** (tæ·vəɪnəɪ). Also 4 tavernyer, tavarnere, 5 tawerner, -yrner, tavernere, 6 -ar, *Sc.* -eir, 7 -o(u)r; (5 taberner). [a. AF. *taverner* = OF. *tavernier* used in senses 1 and 2 below (*c* 1200 in Godef. *Compl.*), f. *taverne*, TAVERN, or :—post-cl. L. *tabernārius* shopkeeper.]

**1.** One who keeps a tavern; a tavern-keeper. *arch.*

**13..** *Sir Beues* (A.) 4357 He askede at þe tauarnere, þat armede folk, what it were. **1340** *Ayenb.* 44 And zelleþ ontreweliche, ase doþ þise tavernyers þet uelleþ þe mesure myd scome. **1382** WYCLIF *Ecclus.* xxvi. 28 The tauerner shal not be iustified fro synnes of lippis. **14..** *Nom.* in Wr.-Wülcker 688/19 *Hic tabernarius*, taberner. **14..** *Lytyll Thanke* 19 in Ritson *Anc. Songs* (1792) 78 They callyd the tawyrner to ffyll þe quarte, And lette note for the coste. **1500–20** DUNBAR *Poems* xxxiv. 46 (R. MS.) 'Be Godis bluid', quod the taverneir, 'Thair is sic wyne in my selleir As neuir come in this cuntrie'. **1530** PALSGR. 279/2 Tavernar a wyne sellar, *tauernier.* **1603** HOLLAND *Plutarch's Mor.* 46 Are you become indeed a Tavernour, Whose father was a woorthy governour? **1720** STRYPE *Stow's Surv.* II. 194/1 This Company anciently consisted of..The Vinteners, who were the Merchants that imported Wine.., and the Taverners, who kept Taverns for them, and sold it out by Retayl. **1760** J. ADAMS *Diary* Wks. 1850 II. 85 [He] may..multiply taverns and dram shops, and thereby secure the votes of taverner and retailer. **1868** E. EDWARDS *Ralegh* I. iv. 66 Under the powers of the assigned patent, [he] considerably increased the number of licensed taverners.

†**2.** One who frequents a tavern or taverns; a tippler. *Obs.*

**1340** *Ayenb.* 51 Vor alþeruerst he becomþ tauernyer, þanne he playþ ate des. **1579** TWYNE *Phisicke agst. Fort.* II. xc. 278 b, There is..nothyng more vayne then typplers and Tauerners. **1612** T. TAYLOR *Comm. Titus* i. 7 (1619) 129 So should I be a swearer? a taverner? a drunkard?

**Ta·verning,** *vbl. sb.* Now *rare* or *Obs.* [f. TAVERN *v.* + -ING$^1$.] The action of the verb TAVERN.

†**1.** See TAVERN *v.* 1. *Obs.*

**1575** SIR J. FORSTER in *St. Papers Eliz., Borders* XIX. 81 (P.R.O.) When anye Inhabitant here hath..a Tenement ..scant sufficient for the meinteignaunce of one person, yf he chaunce to dye havinge two sonnes, he devydeth the said Tenement betwixt them bothe, and thus the taverninge of the Queynes lande ys hinderance for kepinge of hors and armor.

**2.** The action or practice of frequenting taverns.

**1580** in *Liturg. Serv. Q. Eliz.* (Parker Soc.) 574 The Sabboth days..is spent full heathenishly, in taverning, tippling, gaming, playing and beholding of Bear-baiting and Stage plays. **1597–8** BP. HALL *Sat.* II. i, Or wicked Rablais dronken revellings, To grace the mis-rule of our tavernings. **1654** WHITLOCK *Zootomia* 503 Another cries out on the ones Taverning (where he would not spend a six pence, he never knew any come to good that did). *attrib.* **1837** *New Monthly Mag.* LI. 41 No wonder that, with these taverning habits, Jonson lived poor and died no richer.

**3.** The keeping of a tavern.

**1774** J. WENTWORTH in F. Chase *Hist. Dartmouth Coll.* (1891) I. 264 Inquiring into the reasons of granting license to Mr. Payne for taverning and retailing.

**Tavert,** *ppl. a.*: see TAVER *v.*

**Tavism,** variant of TAOISM.

† **Ta·vistock.** *Obs.* In 6 Tave-. A woollen cloth formerly made at the town of Tavistock.

**1535–6** *Act 27 Hen. VIII*, c. 12 § 3 Any clothes called Tavestockes, Westerne doseyns, Friseys, Kendalles, Cottons, and all manner of course clothes made for lynynges. **1545** *Rates of Customs* d iij b, vj. Tauestockes for a clothe. [**1551–2** *Act 5 & 6 Edw. VI*, c. 6 § 29 Any Clothe or Clothes made in the Towne of Tavestoke in the Countie of Deuon..commenlye called Tavestoke Clothes.]

**Tavistockite** (tæ·vistǫkəit). *Min.* [Named by Dana, 1868, from *Tavistock*, a town in Devonshire, where found: see -ITE$^1$.] 'Hydrous phosphate of aluminum and calcium, found in microscopic acicular crystals' (Chester *Names Min.*).

[**1865** A. H. CHURCH in *Jrnl. Chem. Soc.* 264 Our present mineral is from Tavistock, Devonshire.] **1868** DANA *Min.* 582 Tavistockite.

† **Tavorsay.** *Old Cookery. Obs.* [?] A dish of spiced cod's head and liver.

*c* **1450** *Two Cookery-bks.* 114 *Tauorsay.* Nym ye hed of ye codlyng & ye liuere, & pike out ye bones, cast therto goud poudre of piper & gyngiuer, and gif forth.

† **Taw,** *sb.*$^1$ *Obs. rare.* [f. TAW *v.*$^1$]

**1.** Tawed leather; white leather.

*c* **1562** in J. T. Gilbert *Calr. Anc. Rec. Dublin* (1891) II. 23 Gloves, purses, whit tawe and suche like wurke apperteyninge to thoccupacion of glover.

**2.** A thong, whip, lash.

Perh. a different word; app. the sing. of TAWS, TAWSE (which is evidenced much earlier).

**1787** GROSE *Provinc. Gloss., Taw*, a whip. N. **1853** W. WATSON *Poems* 28 (E.D.D.) The nippy taw Comes whiskin' whiles athort us a'. [**1864** WEBSTER, *Taw*,..(*pl.*). A whip or instrument of punishment used by a schoolmaster.]

**Taw** (tǭ), *sb.*$^2$ Also 8 tau, 9 tor. [Origin unascertained, and order of senses uncertain: perh., like *alley*, ALLY *sb.*$^2$, an abbreviation.]

A large choice or fancy marble, often streaked or variegated, being that with which the player shoots.

**1709** STEELE *Tatler* No. 30 ⁋ 1 He is hiding or hoarding his Taws and Marbles. *a* **1761** CAWTHORN *Wit & Learn.* Poems (1771) 48 He minded but his top, or taw. **1807, 1833** [see ALLY *sb.*$^2$]. **1837** DICKENS *Pickw.* xxxiv, After enquiring, whether he had won any alley tors or commoneys lately. **1843** THACKERAY *Irish Sk. Bk.* xxiv, Large agate marbles or 'taws'. *a* **1845** HOOD *Clapham Acad.* xiv, Five who stoop The marble taw to speed. **1857** HUGHES *Tom Brown* I. iii, His small private box was full of peg-tops, white marbles (called 'alley-taws' in the Vale), [etc.]. **1876** GRANT *Burgh Sch. Scotl.* II. v. 179 A still greater favourite is shooting a 'taw', which requires no small dexterity.

**b.** *transf.* A game played with such marbles.

**1709** STEELE *Tatler* No. 112 ⁋ 3 A Game of Marbles, not unlike our modern Taw. **1784** COWPER *Tiroc.* 307 To kneel and draw The chalky ring, and knuckle down at taw. **1798** *Sporting Mag.* XII. 169 At cricket, taw, and prison-bars, He bore away the bell. **1840** THACKERAY *Paris Sk.-bk.* (1869) 45, I would lay a wager that..their school learning carried them..only to the game of taw.

**c.** The line from which the players shoot in playing the game. Hence in phrases: see quots.

**1740** DYCHE & PARDON s.v. *Knuckle*, They frequently say, *Knuckle down to your taw*, or fit your hand exactly in the place where your marble lies. **1854** MISS BAKER *Northampt. Gloss.* s.v., 'Shoot from taw'. 'You don't stand at taw'..' If you don't do so and so I'll bring you to taw'. **1881** *Leicesters. Gloss.* s.v., A ring is scratched on the ground, and at some distance from it a straight line called taw. *Ibid.*, We thus get the phrases..'come up to scratch' and 'come up to taw'.

† **Taw,** *sb.*$^3$ *Obs. rare.* [Derivation unascertained.] A rootlet, a fibre of a root.

**1615** W. LAWSON *Country Housew. Gard.* (1626) 16 Though they get some hold in the earth with some lesser taw, or tawes, which giue some nourishment to the body of the tree. *Ibid.* 24 To dresse the roots of trees, to take away the tawes, and tangles, that lap and fret and grow superfluosly. **1670** CAPT. J. SMITH *Eng. Improv. Reviv'd* 58 A Plant by its Roots and Tawes, or Fibres, sucks in the Juice of the Earth. **1765** *Museum Rust.* V. 117 Its root..is round, and thick set with taws.

**Taw** (tǭ), *v.*$^1$ Forms: 1 tawian, 3 (*Orm.*) tawwenn, 3–4 tauwen, 4–6 tawe, 6– taw. [OE. *tawian* = MLG., MDu., Du. *touwen*, LG. *tauen*, *töwwen* to prepare (leather), to tan, to curry, OHG. *zawjan, zowjan* (MHG. *zouwen, zöuwen*) to prepare, make, Goth. *taujan* to do, make :—OTeut. **tawōjan* and **tawjan*; from a stem *taw-, tōw-*, not certainly found in pre-Germanic.]

**1.** *trans.* To make ready, prepare, or dress (some raw material) for use, or for further manipulation; e. g. to soften (hides) by beating, to heckle (hemp), etc.; † in early use, to till (land).

*a* **900** tr. *Bæda's Hist.* IV. xxix. (1890) 366 Þa bæd se Godes man þæt him man isern ȝeloman mid hwæte ðyder brohte þæt land mid to tawienne. *c* **1200** ORMIN 15903 All swa summ þe nowwt i ploh þe turrnenn erþe & tawwenn. **1545** *Rates of Customs* C v, Sylke tawe[d] and died the pounde viii s. **1555** W. WATREMAN *Fardle Facions* II. ix. 193 He.. taweth the skinne betwixte his handes, vntill it become very souple and soft. **1628** *Robin Goodfellow* II. (1841) 28 And whilst that they did nimbly spin, The hempe he needs must taw. **1651** BIGGS *New Disp.* Pref. 7 Being tawed open by wedge after wedge. **1861** *Jrnl. Brit. Archæol. Assoc.* Mar. 20 A slick-stone for tawing or softening hides by friction.

**2.** *spec.* To make (skins) into leather by steeping them, after suitable preparation, in a solution of alum and salt; the product is white and pliant, and is known as *alum, white,* or *Hungarian leather.*

(In early quots. not separable from sense 1.)

*a* **1225** *Ancr. R.* 418 Þet heo [ower cloðes] beon unorne & warme, & wel i-wrouhte—uelles wel i-tauwed. *a* **1300** *Sat. People Kildare* ix. in *E. E. P.* (1862) 154 Daþeit þe sotter þat tawiþ ȝure leþir. *c* **1410** *Master of Game* (MS. Digby 182) vi, þe furrure..is not feyre; and also it stynketh euer, but if hit be wele ytawede. **1474** *Coventry Leet Bk.* (E.E.T.S.) 401 The sise of a whittawer is that he make nor tawe no maner of lether but Shepes lether, Gettes lethir, deris ledur, horse-lethir, or houndes-lether. **1560** *Let.* in Hakluyt *Voy.* (1598) I. 307 If you send 100 of them [seal skins] tawed with the haire on, they will bee solde, or else not. **1607** TOPSELL *Four-f. Beasts* (1658) 45 The hides..being tawed and wrought artificially they make garments of them. **1613** FLETCHER, etc. *Captain* III. iii, Yes if they taw him as they do whit-leather Upon an iron. **1711** *Lond. Gaz.* No. 4862/4 Mills..where they shall Tan, Taw or Dress..any such Hides. **1877** KNIGHT *Dict. Mech., Tawing*, a process of tanning in which mineral agents are substituted for vegetable extracts. **1879** *Cassell's Techn. Educ.* IV. 88/1 Carefully-prepared goat-skin, tanned, tawed, dyed, and grained.

†**3.** *fig.* To treat (a person) abusively or with contumely; to vex, torment; to harass, afflict; to abuse, outrage, profane. *Obs.*

*c* **893** K. ÆLFRED *Oros.* IV. i. § 1 Þa þe þær ȝefongne wæron, hie tawedan mid þære mæstan unieðnesse. *c* **1000** ÆLFRIC *Saints' Lives* (1890) II. 102 Forðan ðe he godes templ tawode to bysmore. *c* **1000** — *Hom.* II. 486 And se deofol eow tawode þurh his drymen. *a* **1023** WULFSTAN *Hom.* xxxiii. (Napier) 162 [Hi] scendað and tawjað to bysmore þæs þeȝnes cwenan and hwilum his dohtor. **13..** *Minor Poems fr. Vernon MS.* liv. 76 To a piler I was I-piht, Togget and tauwed al þe niht. **1549** CHALONER *Erasm. on Folly* G ij, To be briefe, they are not tawed nor plucked asunder with a thousand thousand cares.

**b.** To whip, flog, thrash. *Obs.* exc. *dial.*

**1600** HOLLAND *Livy* VIII. xxviii. 301 He caused him to be stripped naked, and whipping cheare to be presented unto him. The poore stripling thus pitteously tawed and torn, ran forth into the open street. **1614** B. Jonson *Barth. Fair* iv. iv, You know where you were taw'd lately, both lash'd, and slash'd you were in Bridewell. **1682** D'Urfey *Butler's Ghost* 43 Truss'd on her Knee she'd briskly taw him, And, like Virago, clapperclaw him. **1863** Sala *Capt. Dangerous* viii, I grew sick of being tawed for offences I had never committed. **1883** Cleland *Inchbracken* xvi. 126, I would have her tawed through the town at the cart's tail.

**Taw** (tǭ), *v.*[2] Chiefly *dial.* [f. Taw *sb.*[2]] *intr.* To shoot or aim with a taw or marble.

**1863** Mrs. Toogood *Yorks. Dial.*, You don't taw fairly. **1883** *Almondbury & Huddersf. Gloss.* s.v. *Hundreds*, When . . the one who is on for his pizings manages to taw into the hole, the game is concluded. **1898** [see Tawer [2]].

**Taw,** obs. form of Tau, Tow.

‖ **Tawa** (tā·wă, *colloq.* tau·ă). [The Maori name.] A tall and handsome forest tree of New Zealand, *Beilschmiedia* (*Nesodaphne*) *Tawa*, N.O. *Lauraceæ*, with damson-like fruit; allied to the Taraire, but inferior as timber.

**1866** *Treas. Bot.* 786/1 Called Tawa by the natives. **1883** J. Hector *Handbk. N. Zealand* (1886) 106 *Tawa*, a lofty forest tree 60 ft. to 70 ft. high, with slender branches. The wood is light, and soft, and is used for making butter-kegs.

† **Tawak,** = to awake: see T'[1].

*c* **1315** Shoreham *Poems* i. 1412 Ta-wak Hy þet slepeþ ine senne slep.

**Tawbern, -bron, -burn,** Sc. var. Taborn *Obs.*

**Tawche, tawcht,** obs. Sc. forms of Tallow.

**Tawcht,** obs. Sc. f. *taught*: see Teach *v.*

**Tawd,** obs. Sc. f. *told*, pa. t. and pple. of Tell *v.*

† **Tawder,** *v. Obs. nonce-wd.* [f. Tawdry *a.*] *trans.* To deck *out* in tawdry garments.

**1716** Lady M. W. Montagu *Let. to C'tess of Bristol* 22 Aug., A sort of shabby finery, a number of dirty people of quality tawdered out.

**Tawdrily** (tǭ·drĭli), *adv.* [f. Tawdry *a.* + -ly [2].] In a tawdry manner; with cheap finery.

**1736** Pulteney *Let. to Swift* 21 Dec., A rabble of people . . seeing her very oddly and tawdrily dressed, took her for a foreigner. **1816** *Sporting Mag.* XLVIII. 189 A lady observing her neighbour in a public room, dressed very tawdrily. **1879** Froude *Short Stud.* (1883) IV. v. 351 The two figures . . are tawdrily coloured in white and red and gold.

**Tawdriness** (tǭ·drinės). [f. as prec. + -ness.] The quality of being tawdry.

**1670** *Moral State Eng.* 161 There was a kind of tawdriness in their Habits. **1753** Hogarth *Anal. Beauty* vi. 35 That tawdriness may not destroy the proper effect of variety. **1841** Gallenga *Italy* (1848) I. 139 The tinsel and tawdriness of an imitative dauber.

† **Taw·drum.** *Obs. nonce-wd.* [f. Tawdry, with L. ending: cf. *nostrum*.] A tawdry decoration.

**1680** Betterton *Revenge* v. iv. 65 No matter for Lace and Tawdrums.

**Tawdry** (tǭ·dri), *sb.* and *a.* Also 6 tauthrie, tawdrie (see next); 7 taudrey, tawdery, 7–8 taudry. [As sb. short for Tawdry lace, q. v.; hence referring to the showy but cheap quality of these in the 17th century.]

**A.** *sb.* † **1.** Short for Tawdry lace. *Obs.*

**1612** Drayton *Poly-olb.* ii. 46 Of which the Naïdes, and the blew Nereïdes make Them Taudries for their necks. *Ibid.* iv. 50 Not the smallest Beck But with white Pebles makes her Taudries for her neck.

**2.** Cheap and pretentious finery.

*a* **1680** Butler *Rem.* (1759) I. 223 Applaud th' outsides of Words, but never mind, With what fantastic tawdery th'are lin'd. **1747** Richardson *Clarissa* (1811) II. xx. 139 Only for the sake of having a little more tawdry upon his housings. **1831** *Examiner* 390/1 A dress circle! . . look at the tawdry and the ennui! **1867** Smiles *Huguenots Eng.* (1880) 349 A poor bedizened creature, clad in tawdry.

**B.** *adj.* **1.** Of the nature of cheap finery; showy or gaudy without real value.

**1676** Etheredge *Man of Mode* ii. ii, A Woman that Can doat on a senseless Caper, a Tawdry French Riband, and a Formal Cravat. **1686** Burnet *Lett.* (1708) 288 A Tawdry Imbroidery of Gold and Silver. **1711** Steele *Spect.* No. 80 ⁋ 3 A gay West Indian, who appeared in all the Colours which can affect an Eye that could not distinguish between being fine and taudry. **1805** Repton *Landscape Gard.* 160 The lavish profusion of tawdry embellishment. **1859** Jephson *Brittany* ii. 14 The high altar is wretchedly tawdry.

† **b.** Untidy; slovenly; ungraceful. *Obs. rare.*

**1671** Grew *Anat. Plants* v. § 3 A Flower without its Empalement, would hang as uncouth and taudry, as a Lady without her Bodies. *c* **1820** Joanna Baillie *Summer's Day* 83 His awkward . . lad, Who trails his tawdry armful [of hay] o'er the field.

**2.** *transf.* Of persons or their condition: Tawdrily dressed or decked out; cheaply adorned.

**1676** Wycherley *Pl. Dealer* v. i, Taudry affected Rogues, well drest. **1706** Phillips (ed. 6), *Taudry* or *Tawdry*, . . tricked up with such tinsel Stuff, or Lace as is usually sold at Audery-Fair in Cambridge-shire. **1851** Helps *Comp. Solit.* vii. (1874) 133 Like one of those tawdry girls who pass by me. **1862** Miss Braddon *Lady Audley* xxvii, An aspect of genteel desolation and tawdry misery not easily to be parallelled in wretchedness.

**3.** *fig.* esp. of style, diction, etc.; hence of a speaker or writer: Trumpery.

**1696** R. L'Estrange *Seneca's Mor.* (ed. 6) Afterth. 12 Without forcing the Design of the Author, or intermixing any Tawdry Flowrishes by the By. *a* **1718** Penn *Maxims* § 126. Wks. 1726 I. 850 'Tis but Taudry Talk, and next to very Trash. **1764** Goldsm. *Traveller* Ded., Him they dignify with the name of poet: his tawdry lampoons are called satires. **1808** Scott *Let. to Lady L. Stuart* 19 Jan. in *Lockhart*, His language is too flowery and even tawdry.

† **Tawdry lace.** *Obs.* [See T (the letter) 7.] In the earliest quotation *St. Audrey's lace*, i. e. lace of St. Audrey, Etheldrida, or Æþelðryþ (daughter of Anna king of East Anglia, and patron saint of Ely): A silk 'lace' or necktie, much worn by women in the 16th and early 17th c.; sometimes taken as a type of female adornments.

[As to the origin of the name, it is told, originally by Bæda (*Eccl. Hist.* iv. ix.), and after him by Ælfric in the Life of St. Æþelðryth, Virgin (*Ælfric's Lives of Saints*, ed. Skeat, 1885, xx. ll. 49–60), that St. Audrey died of a tumour in her throat, which she considered to be a just retribution, because in her youth she had for vain show adorned her neck with manifold splendid necklaces, 'forðan þe ic on iuᵹoðe frætwede mine swuran mid mæniᵹfealdum swurbeaᵹum'. In the 16th century, N. Harpsfield, Archdeacon of Canterbury under Philip and Mary (died 1588), after relating the story in his (Latin) *Historia Anglicana Ecclesiastica* (Douay 1622), adds 'Our women of England are wont to wear about the neck a certain necklace [*torquem quendam*], formed of thin and fine silk, perchance in memory of what we have told'. See also, more particularly, quot. 1674 below. Skinner in his *Etymologicon* (licensed 1668), explains *Tawdry lace* as 'Ties, fringes, or bands, bought at the fair held at the fane of St. Etheldreda, as rightly points out Doctor Th. Henshaw'. There is no discrepancy between the two statements. 'St. Audrey's laces' would naturally be largely offered for sale at her fair, and though this did not give the article its name, it doubtless made it more widely known, and led to the production of cheap and showy forms for the 'country wenches' (see Nares s. v.), which at length gave to *tawdry* its later connotation.]

[**1530** Palsgr. (ed. 1) 63/2 Seynt Audries lace, *cordon*.] **1548** Patten *Exped. Scotl.* Pref. civ b, Pardon Beades, Tanthonie belles, Tauthrie laces, Rosaries, Collets. **1579** Spenser *Sheph. Cal.* Apr. 135 Binde your fillets faste, And gird in your waste, For more finesse, with a tawdrie lace. **1593** *Jack Straw* iii. D iv, *Queen*. . . I will speake for thee. *T. M.* Will you in faith, and I will giue you a tawdrie lace. **1610** Fletcher *Faithf. Sheph.* iv. i, The Prim-Rose Chaplet, taudry-lace and Ring, Thou gavest her for her singing. **1611** Shaks. *Wint. T.* iv. iv. 253 Come you promis'd me a tawdry-lace, and a paire of sweet Gloues. **1674** Blount *Glossogr.*, *Taudrey Lace*, so called from St. Audrey (Etheldreda) who thought her self punished for wearing rich Necklaces of Jewels; and therefore women after that wore Necklaces of fine silk, called Taudrey Laces. *c* **1750** Shenstone *Elegies* xi. 18 To deck my native fleece with tawdry lace!

† **Taw·dryne.** *Obs. nonce-wd.* [App. an arbitrary formation on *tawdry*.] = prec.

**1586** W. Webbe *Eng. Poetrie* (Arb.) 84 See ye not your selues doo demeane too rudely: Bynd the fillets: and to be fine the waste gyrt Fast with a tawdryne [Webbe's rendering in sapphics of Spenser's stanzas: see quot. 1579 in prec.].

**Tawed** (tǭd), *ppl. a.* [f. Taw *v.*[1] + -ed [1].] Made, as white leather, by the process of tawing. Also *transf.* (cf. *tanned*).

**1545** *Rates of Customs* b iv, Graye tawed, the tymber vi. s. viii. d. **1563** *Mirr. Mag.*, *Induct.* xxxix, With tawed handes, and hard ytanned skyn. **1642** T. Lechford *Plain Dealing* (1867) 115 For the Winter they have boots, or a kind of laced tawed-leather stockins. **1711** *Lond. Gaz.* No. 4862/4 Hides and Skins, Tanned, Tawed or Dress'd. **1852** Morfit *Tanning & Currying* (1853) 412 The tawed leather is the raw skin combined with subchloride of aluminium. **1879** *Cassell's Techn. Educ.* I. 150/2.

**Tawer** [1] (tǭ·əɹ). Forms: 4–5 tawier(e, 4–7 tawyer, (5 toyar, 6 tawhear, 8 tawar), 5– tawer. [f. Taw *v.*[1]: see -er [1]. With the earlier *tawyer*, cf. *lawyer*, *sawyer*.] One who taws; one who prepares white leather; = White-tawer.

[**1311** *Letter Bk. D. Lond.* lf. 127 Walterus le Whitawyer. **1346** *Ibid. F.* lf. 126 b, Les bones gentz Megucers appellez Whittawyers.] **1382** Wyclif *Acts* ix. 43 Many dayes he dwellide in Joppe, at Symound, sum coriour [*gloss* or tawier, *v. rr.* tawer, tawiere]. **1480** [see Tawing 1]. **1481–90** *Howard Househ. Bks.* (Roxb.) 505 Payd to the toyar for iiij. boke skynnys. **1559** Machyn *Diary* (Camden) 208 A tawhear of skynnes. **1570** Levins *Manip.* 74/44 A Tawer, *alutarius*. **1607** Topsell *Four-f. Beasts* (1658) 169 The skins of this Beast are dressed by Tawyers, with the fat of fishes and Alum. **1658** R. Franck *North. Mem.* (1821) 280 There live the tanners, tawyers, fell-mongers, parchment, and vellum-dressers. **1795** *Statist. Acc. Scotl.* XIV. 552 There are 17 tanners, 18 curriers, and 13 tawers. **1883** *Century Mag.* XXVII. 75 In this part of Paris live all tanners and tawers and their kindred.

**Taw·er** [2]. [f. Taw *v.*[2]] One who aims a taw.

**1898** Alice B. Gomme *Games* II. 113 If one player knocks out a marble, he is entitled to 'taw' at the rest in the ring until he misses; and if a sure 'tawer' not one of the others may have the chance to taw.

**Tawern,** obs. form of Tavern.

**Tawery** (tǭ·əri). *rare.* [f. Tawer [1] or Taw *v.*[1]: see -ery.] An establishment where skins are tawed.

**1830** Maunder *Dict. Eng. Lang.*, *Tawery*, a manufactory in which skins are dyed with alum. **1885** C. T. Davis *Manuf. Leather* 656 (Cent. Dict.) In Parisian taweries calves' brains, intimately mixed with wheat flour, are used as a substitute for yelk of egg.

**Tawes,** obs. form of Taws.

**Tawght, tawhte,** obs. ff. *taught*: see Teach *v.*

‖ **Tawhai** (tā·hwai). Also tawai. [Maori.] The native name in New Zealand of several species of beech, called by the settlers *birches*.

**1873** *Catal. Vienna Exhib.*, *Tawhai*, large and durable timber, used for sleepers. **1883** J. Hector *Handbk. N. Zealand* (1886) 102 *Tawhai*, Red-birch (from the colour of the bark). A handsome tree, 80 ft. to 100 ft. high.

‖ **Tawhiri** (taˌhwī·ri). Also tawiri. [Maori.] Native name of the New Zealand tree *Pittosporum tenuifolium*, noted for its fragrant white blossoms.

**1872** A. Domett *Ranolf* vi. i. 108 Its floor . . with faint tawhiri-leaves besprent. **1884** T. Bracken *Lays Maori* 21 The early breeze that . . stole the rich Tawhiri's sweet perfume.

**Tawie** (tǭ·i), *a. Sc. dial.* [? f. Taw *v.*[1] + -y, in sense 'easy to taw': cf. *wieldy*.] Tractable, docile, easy to manage.

**1786** Burns *To Auld Mare* v, Ye ne'er was donsie; But hamely, tawie, quiet, an' cannie, An' unco sonsie.

**Tawing** (tǭ·iŋ), *vbl. sb.* [f. Taw *v.*[1] + -ing [1].]

**1.** The action or process of preparing white leather: see Taw *v.*[1] 2.

**1408** *Litt. Red Bk. Bristol* (1900) II. 99 Qe nulle homme . . ne vse ascun manere tawing de ascuns pealx en lez ditz schopes. **1480** *Wardr. Acc. Edw. IV* (1830) 121 And to John Massy tawyer for tawing of a ymbre of hole sables iiij s. **1517–18** in Swayne *Sarum Churchw. Acc.* (1896) 59 For Tawynge of Buckys skynnys to couer ij Mase Bokys, xij d. **1711** *Lond. Gaz.* No. 4862/4 Their Places of tanning, tawing, or dressing of such Hides. **1884** Knight *Dict. Mech.*, *Tawing*, tanning a lamb-skin with the wool on it.

*attrib.* **1588** L. M. tr. *Bk. Dyeing* 49 Take your tawing stocke, and taw it [black leather] well therewith. **1882** Paton in *Encycl. Brit.* XIV. 389/2 They receive . . a second treatment with the tawing mixture.

**b.** (*pl.*) *concr.* (See quot.)

**1611** Cotgr., *Megis*, tawings; the offals, or peeces cut from skinnes in tawing.

† **2.** The action of flogging or punishing. *Obs.*

**1620** Shelton *Quix.* (1746) IV. vii. 54 Fearing least the Whipping-task and Tawing might light upon him. **1622** Mabbe tr. *Aleman's Guzman d'Alf.* i. 240 He would willingly haue the tawing of mee. **1642** Rogers *Naaman* 30 The Lords own tawing of him [Job] . . to wring this speech from him.

**Tawk(e, tawlke,** obs. forms of Talk.

**Tawlche,** obs. Sc. f. Tallow. **Tawld,** obs. Sc. f. *told*: see Tell *v.* **Tawle,** obs. f. Tall.

**Tawm,** dial. f. Talm *v.*, to faint.

† **Tawn,** *v. Obs. rare*[−1]. [app. an alteration of Tan *v.* under the influence of Tawny *a.*] *trans.* To make tawny; to bronze, 'tan'. So † **Tawn** *sb.*, the bronzing of the skin produced by exposure.

**1721** Ramsay *Tartana* 94 While scorching Titan tawns the shepherd's brow. *a* **1734** North *Lives* (1826) III. 96 It was a considerable time before this upper lip having been long shaded . . took the same tawn as the rest of his face.

† **Tawne, taune,** *v.*[1] *Obs.* [Early ME. *tawne(n*, *taun-e(n*, aphetic form of **at-awne(n*, *at-aune(n*, f. At- *pref.*[1] + *awne(n*, in Ormin *awwnenn*, Awn(e *v.*[2], to show, exhibit. OE. **awnian* has not been found, but ME. *t-awnen* is parallel to MLG., MDu., LG. *t-ōnen*, Du. *t-oonen*, MHG. *z-ounen* to show. These point to an OTeut. **at-awnôjan*, as a by-form of Goth. *at-augjan* (OS. *t-ogian*, OE. *æt-eowan*, *æt-iewan*) to bring before the eyes, to show, f. OTeut. **augon-*, *augn-*, *awn-*, stems of *augon-* eye. See Feist *Got. Etymol.*, s.v. *Augō*, Brugmann ed. 2, § 165, § 681, Schade s.v. *zougan*, Franck s.v. *toon*, *toonen*.]

*trans.* To show, manifest, exhibit.

*c* **1220** *Bestiary* 767 Ful wel he [Christ] taunede his luue to man. *c* **1250** *Gen. & Ex.* 636 God . . Taunede him in ðe walkene a-buuen Rein-bowe. *Ibid.* 1022 Ðis time oðer ȝer Sal ic me to ðe taunen her. *Ibid.* 2034 To tawnen ðe ðe soðe her-bi. *Ibid.* 3444 On oðer daiȝes morȝen quile, God tauned moysi quat he wile.

† **Tawne,** *v.*[2] *Sc. Obs. rare*[−1]. [? Deriv. of Taw *v.*[1]; ? for *taw-en*.] *trans.* To tame, subdue, soften.

**1606** Birnie *Kirk-Buriall* xv. D iv, The sore sight of that saint his syres death, did so tawne the truculent turke.

**Tawniness** (tǭ·ninės). [f. Tawny *a.* + -ness.] The quality or condition of being tawny.

*c* **1550** Lloyd *Treas. Health* F viij, Coluer dounge ground in vyneger and smeared ouer thy face putteth away al morphewe & tawnines. **1623** Middleton *More Dissemblers Besides Wom.* v. ii, She's the sun's masterpiece for tawniness. **1727** Bailey vol. II, *Tawniness*, . . the Being of the Colour of tanned Leather. **1875** Browning *Aristoph. Apol.*, *Herakles* 406 He spread The tawniness behind—his yellow head Enmuffled by the brute's.

† **Taw·nish,** *a. Obs. rare.* [f. Tawn(y *a.* + -ish [1].] Somewhat tawny; tanned.

**1675** *Lond. Gaz.* No. 1020/4 Having black strait hair, a tawnish complexion. **1684** *Ibid.* No. 1972/4 A tall slender Man, . . of a Tawnish Complexion.

**Tawnt(e,** obs. forms of Taunt.

**Tawny** (tǭ·ni), *a.* and *sb.* Forms: *α.* 4–7 tauny, 5– tawny; also 4 tawne, (4–5 taunde), (6 tawneye, 6–7 -ie, 6–9 -ey). *β.* (chiefly *north.* and *Sc.*) 5 tannye, tannee, 5–6 tanne, tany, 5–7 tanny; see also Tenne. [ME. *tauny*, *tawne*, a. AF. *taune*, OF. *tané* (12–13th c. in Godef. *Compl.*), later *tanné*, 'foncé comme le tan', f. *tan*, Tan *sb.*[1] The *au*, *aw* appears to have arisen from the OF. pronunciation, in which the *a* before *n* was nasalized, *tâne* (taṅne): cf. *pawn*, *aunt*, † *demaund*, † *Fraunce*.]

Name of a composite colour, consisting of brown with a preponderance of yellow or orange; but formerly applied also to other shades of brown.

**A.** as *adj.* Having, or being of, this colour.

*α.* **1377** Langl. *P. Pl.* B. v. 196 Þanne cam coueytise . . in a tauny tabarde of twelue wynter age. **1395** *E. E. Wills* (1882) 5, I deuyse to . . my doughter a tawne bed of silk. **1487** in *Surrey Archæol. Soc. Collect.* (1865) III. 163, I bequeathe my tawny velvet gowne to be made a chesible thereof. **1538** *Test. Ebor.* (Surtees) VI. 85 My tawney chamlett dublett. **1578** LYTE *Dodoens* I. xxi. 32 Peruincle.. The floure most commonly is blew, & sometimes white, & tawnie, but very seldome. **1599** DAVIES *Immort. Soul* clxxxviii, As the World's Sun..Makes the Moor black, the European white; Th' American tawny. **1601** B. JONSON *Poetaster* III. iv, We must haue you turne fiddler againe,.. get a base violin at your backe, and marche in a tawnie coate. **1632** LITHGOW *Trav.* IV. 162 The other Turkes which are borne in Asia major and Ægypt..are of a greater stature, tauny. **1706** PHILLIPS (ed. 6), *Tawny*, that is of a tanned, or yellowish, or dusky Colour. **1791** COWPER *Iliad* X. 211 A lion's tawny skin Around him wrapp'd. **1844** DICKENS *Mart. Chuz.* xii, That port, being a light and tawny wine. **1856** DELAMER *Fl. Gard.* (1861) 60 *Hemerocallis flava.*—Day Lily; a plant with yellow or tawny flowers. **1904** *Blackw. Mag.* July 2 The patched old tawny sails.

β. *c* **1425** tr. *Arderne's Surgery* (E.E.T.S.) 27 Puluer of gallez and psidie and puluer tanny. **1564** *Reg. Privy Council Scot.* I. 308 Sex pece of broun and tanne clayth. *a* **1585** POLWART *Flyting w. Montgomerie* 736 Tanny cheeks, I think thou speiks with thy breeks. **1638** JUNIUS *Paint. Ancients* 270 They resemble the similitude of a tanie or a white man. **1652** J. WRIGHT tr. *Camus' Nat. Paradox* 362 Her complexion (which is somewhat tanny by beeing much exposed to the Sun).

**B.** as *sb.* **1.** Tawny colour. In *Her.* = TENNE.

*a* **1400–50** *Alexander* 4335 Nouthire to toly ne to taunde transmitte we na vebbis, To vermylion ne violett ne variant littis. *c* **1410** *Master of Game* (MS. Digby 182) xiii, þe best hue of rennynge houndes whiche be goode, is cleped broune tanne. **1493** *Mem. Ripon* (Surtees) III. 164 Pro xij virgis panni coloris de tawne pro vestura choristarum. **1601** HOLLAND *Pliny* XXIV. iv. 178 Without forth of a light tawnie or yellowish red. **1610** GUILLIM *Heraldry* I. iii. (1660) 20 Tawny (saith Leigh) is a Colour of Worship, and of some Heralds it is called Bruske. **1641** G. SANDYS *Paraphr. Song Sol.* I. i, This Tawney from the Sun I took. **1756** C. LUCAS *Ess. Waters* I. 103 The bright red is reduced to somewhat of a tawny. **1848** THACKERAY *Van. Fair* xxiv, I ain't particular about a shade or so of tawny.

†**2.** Cloth of a tawny colour. [Cf. OF. *tanné.*]

α. **1416** in *Somerset Med. Wills* (1901) 75, j joup de Taune furr[ata] cum nigro. **1462** *Mann. & Househ. Exp.* (Roxb.) 149 Ffor a ȝerd and di. off tawny, vj.s. vj.d. **1566** in Hakluyt *Voy.* (1598) I. 358 Some blacks for womens garments, with some Orenge colours and tawneis. **1572** in Feuillerat *Revels Q. Eliz.* (1908) 187 Of Satten Tawnie twelve yardes. **1587** FLEMING *Contn. Holinshed* III. 1333/1 Clothed in white, yellow, & orange tawnie.

β. **1462** *Paston Lett.* II. 103 Your son wolle haue to hys jakets murry and tany. **1494, 1502** Rowane tanne [see ROWAN[3]]. **1497** *Acc. Ld. High Treas. Scot.* I. 343 For iij elne and ane half of Rowane tannee. **1501** *Ibid.* II. 49, iiij elne Franch tanne.

†**b.** *pl.* Garments made of this cloth. *Obs.*

*c* **1800** R. CUMBERLAND *John de Lancaster* (1809) III. 116 The..livery-men brushing up their orange tawnies.

**3.** A brown-skinned person; = TAWNY-MOOR. *arch.*

**1660** F. BROOKE tr. *Le Blanc's Trav.* 347 There are Tawnies amongst them, they weare in their eares rings of gold and silver. **1681** *Lond. Gaz.* No. 1672/4 Run away.. a Tall slender Indian Tawney. **1751** FRANKLIN *Observ.* Wks. 1887 II. 234 In America, where we have so fair an opportunity, by excluding all blacks and tawnys, of increasing the lovely white and red. **1850** SMEDLEY *Frank Fairlegh* xxx, Rajah somebody or other..on his elephant, attended by a train of tawnies.

†**4.** A sweet beverage, so called from its colour.

β. *c* **1430** *Two Cookery-bks.* 26 Take almaunde Mylke, & Sugre, an powdere Gyngere, & of Galyngale, & of Canelle, and Rede Wine, & boyl y-fere: & þat is gode tannye.

**5.** A local name for the common bullfinch, from the colouring of the female.

**1847–78** HALLIWELL, *Tawny*, a bullfinch. Somerset. **1885** SWAINSON *Provinc. Names Birds* 67 The same parts in the female are reddish-brown; hence Tawny (Somerset).

**C.** Combinations and special collocations. **a.** Parasynthetic, etc., as *tawny-coloured, -faced, -haired, -skinned, -tanned, -visaged, -whiskered.*

**1572** in Hakluyt *Voy.* (1600) III. 465 The people of the countrey are of a good stature, tawny coloured, broad faced, flat nosed. *a* **1618** SYLVESTER *Spectacles* x, When the Leaves in Autumn wither With a tawny-tanned Face. **1687** *Lond. Gaz.* No. 2298/3 A tawny visaged Man. **1740** PINEDA *Span. Dict.* s.v. *Denostar*, A tawny fac'd Woman dress'd up, reviles the fair one. **1839** BAILEY *Festus* v. (1852) 65 Red, black or white, olive, or tawny-skinned. **1859** GEO. ELIOT *A. Bede* v, Some tawny-whiskered, brown-locked, clear-complexioned young Englishman. **1862** BURTON *Bk.-Hunter* I. 18 He was not a black-letter man..or a tawny-moroccoite [collector of books bound in tawny morocco].

**b.** With other names of colour, expressing a modification by tawny, as *tawny-brown*, etc.

**1502** *Privy Purse Exp. Eliz. of York* (1830) 9, iiij yerdes ..of sarcenet of tawny grene. **1725** DE FOE *Voy. round World* (1840) 121 The people were black, or rather of a tawny dark brown. **1751** *Affect. Narr. of Wager* 97 Their Colour a Tawney Olive. **1812** SIR H. DAVY *Chem. Philos.* 280 It..becomes of a tawney yellow colour. **1839** URE *Dict. Arts* 619 For..tawny-gray,..the stuff must receive a previous blue ground by dipping it in the indigo vat. **1905** *Westm. Gaz.* 4 Mar. 2/3, I looked across the desert, tawny-gold beneath the pitiless sun.

**c.** In special collocations, esp. in names of particular species of animals of a tawny colour, or plants with tawny flowers, as *tawny bunting, monkey, owl, thrush, vulture*; *tawny day-lily, sedge*; also in collectors' names of moths, as *tawny pinion, tawny wave*, etc.; **tawny emperor**, collectors' name for *Apatura herse*, a large butterfly (cf. EMPEROR 4); also †**tawny-coat**, an ecclesiastical apparitor, from the colour of his livery.

**1766** PENNANT *Zool.* I. 112 *Tawny Bunting. **1591** SHAKS. *1 Hen. VI*, I. iii. 56 Out *Tawney-Coates, out Scarlet Hypocrite. **1634** HEYWOOD *Mayden-head Lost* I. Wks. 1874 IV. 114 Though I was neuer Tawny-coate, I haue playd the summoners part. **1768** PENNANT *Zool.* I. 158 The *Tawny Owl...The color of this kind is sufficient to distinguish it from every other. **1859** MISS PRATT *Brit. Grasses* 35 C[arex] fulva (*Tawny Sedge). **1783** LATHAM *Synopsis* III. 28 **Tawny Thrush*, Arct. Zool...Head, back, and wing coverts tawny. **1891** *Cent. Dict.* s.v., *Tawny thrush*, the veery, or Wilson's thrush, *Turdus fuscescens*, one of the four song-thrushes which are common in eastern parts of North America. **1781** LATHAM *Synopsis Birds* I. 19 *Tawny Vulture...Inhabits Falkland Islands.

Hence † **Taw·ny** *v. trans.*, to make tawny; to tan. *Obs. rare.*

**1602** BRETON *Mother's Blessing* (Grosart) 9/1 The Sunne so soone, the painted face will tawny. **1613** HEYWOOD *Brazen Age* II. ii, He smels all smoake, and with his nasty sweate Tawnies my skinne.

†**Taw·ny-moor.** *Obs.* [f. TAWNY + MOOR *sb.*[2]: cf. BLACKAMOOR.] A name given to the tawny or brown-skinned natives of foreign lands; prob. originally to natives of northern Africa.

**1603** OWEN *Pembrokeshire* v. (1892) 42 They seeme more like tawney Moores, then people of this lande. **1650** R. STAPYLTON *Strada's Low C. Warres* I. 22 Military Revells: wherein the Emperour himself ran a tilt, habited like a Tauny-moor. **1686** J. DUNTON *Lett. fr. New-Eng.* (1867) 27 Tho' he was a Tawney-more Indian, yet he was a Converted one. **1717** MRS. CENTLIVRE *Bold Stroke for Wife* I. i. (1749) 14 There's a Black, a Tawnymoor, and a Frenchman. [**1849** A tawny Moor: see MOOR *sb.*[2] 1.]

**Tawpie, tawpy** (tǭ·pi), *sb.* and *a. Sc.* Also 9 taupy, taupie, tawpee. [Prob. from Norse: cf. Norw. *taap* 'half-witted person, chiefly of women' (Ross), Da. *taabe* fool, simpleton, Sw. *tåp* simpleton, *tåpig* foolish, weak-minded.]

**A.** *sb.* A foolish, senseless, or thoughtless girl or woman; *idle tawpie*, a slattern.

**1728** RAMSAY *Monk & Miller's Wife* 135 'Pottage', quoth Hab, 'ye senseless tawpie!' **1787** BURNS *Verses at Selkirk* iv, Gawkies, tawpies, gowks, and fools, Frae colleges and boarding-schools. **1824** MISS FERRIER *Inher.* xl, That light-headed tawpee [a servant] is off to a sick mother. **1834** *Tait's Mag.* I. 610/2 Many of his female friends were very accomplished, whom he thought useless tawpies for all that. **1902** *Ardrossan & Saltcoats Herald* 5 June 2 The word *taupie* meaning a foolish petted person.

**B.** *adj.* Foolish, senseless, empty-headed. (Said in reference to a girl or woman.) Now *rare.*

**1814** *Saxon & Gael* I. 46 (Jam.) Comin' to his table wi' my tawpy dochter in her auld gown. **1823** GALT *Entail* xvi, The tawpy taunts of her pridefu' customers. **1826** J. WILSON *Noct. Ambr.* Wks. 1855 I. 174 Great langlegged, tawdry and tawpy limmers standin at closes. *a* **1836** AFFLECK *Poet. Wks.* 80 (E.D.D.) Taupie Meg is just as bad, A common limmer.

**Tawridore**, obs. form of TOREADOR.

**Taws, tawse** (tǭz), *sb.* Chiefly *Sc.* Forms: 6 tawis, -es, 8 tawz, taz, 8– tawse, 9– taws. [app. plural of TAW *sb.*[1] 2 (but evidenced much earlier); sometimes treated as a singular.]

**1.** A whip for driving a spinning top; esp. one made of a thong: see quot. 1892. (In quot. 1513 prob. *pl.* as in 2.)

**1513** DOUGLAS *Æneis* VII. vii. 91 As..the round top of tre [wooden top] Hit with the twynit quhyp, dois quherle, we see..smyttin wyth the tawis dois rebound, And rynnis about, about, in cirkill round. **1892** *Ballymena* (Antrim) *Observer* (E.D.D.), *Tawse*, a few strips of leather tied to a shaft, used by boys in spinning tops.

**2.** *spec.* An instrument of family or school discipline, used in Scotch and many English schools, consisting of a leathern strap or thong, divided at the end into narrow strips. Also *transf.* and *fig.*

In Sc. const. as plural, and in phrase *a pair of taws.*

*a* **1585** POLWART *Flyting w. Montgomerie* 57 In thy teeth bring mee the tawes, With beckes my bidding to abide. *Ibid.* 571. **1719** RAMSAY *2nd Answ. to Hamilton* vi, I've kiss'd the tawz, like a good bairn. **1721** — *Lucky Spence* ix, Vild hangy's taz ye'r riggings fast Makes black and blae. **1725** — *Gentle Sheph.* v. iii. Prol., The tawz Was handled by revengefu' Madge. **1825** BROCKETT *N. C. Words, Taws*, a *pair of taws*, a leather strap used by schoolmasters for chastising children. **1825** CARLYLE *Early Lett.* (1886) II. 329 A pedagogue called Fate; he is an excellent teacher, but his fees are very high, and his tawse are rather heavy. **1834** M. SCOTT *Cruise Midge* (1863) 207, I took out the Tawse, and laid them on the closed Bible as a terror to evil doers. **1865** R. CHAMBERS *Ess.* Ser. II. 79 He carried a pair of short but impressive taws. **1892** *Schoolmaster* 31 Dec. 1165/2 Nottingham School Board. The Board authorises assistants to administer corporal punishment to the extent of a light stroke with a cane or tawse. *Mod. Sc.* Behave yoursel', or you'll get the taws.

*Comb.* **1865** G. MACDONALD *A. Forbes* 49 The smile, which, in spite of pain, had illuminated his tawse-waled cheeks. **1885** 'S. MUCKLEBACKIT' *Rural Rhymes* 142 The ancient tawse-swasher pled weariness.

Hence **Tawse** *v. trans.*, to chastise with the taws.

**1790** SHIRREFS *Poems* Gloss., *Taz*, to whip, scourge, belabour. **1883** *Mem. A. Maclean* 240 He was tawsed for his obstinacy.

**Tawt**, var. TAUT *v.* **Tawte, tawth**, obs. ff. *taught*: see TEACH *v.* **Tawyer**, obs. var. TAWER. **Tawz**, obs. f. TAWS.

**Tax** (tæks), *sb.*[1] Also 4–7 **taxe**, *Sc.* 5–7 **taxt** (6 taxte). [app. f. TAX *v.* Appears earlier than F. *taxe* (1405 in Godef. *Compl.*; rare bef. 16th c.), f. *taxer* vb.; also earlier than med.L. *taxa* in Du Cange. In ME., *taxe* and *taske*, TASK *sb.*, were at first almost synonymous; but in their sense-development they were differentiated, *tax* following that of the corresponding verb, as an assessed *money* payment.]

**1.** A compulsory contribution to the support of government, levied on persons, property, income, commodities, transactions, etc., now at fixed rates, mostly proportional to the amount on which the contribution is levied.

'Tax' is the most inclusive term for these contributions, esp. when spoken of as the matter of *taxation*, and in such phrases as *direct* and *indirect tax* (see DIRECT *a.* 6 e, INDIRECT 2 c), including also similar levies for the support of the work of such local or specific bodies as county or municipal, councils, poor law or school boards, etc. But in British practice few of the individual imposts are called by the name, the most notable being the INCOME TAX, LAND TAX, and PROPERTY *tax* (also *dog-tax, match-tax, window-tax*), the rest being mostly styled 'duties', as *excise, import, export, estate, house, stamp, death duties*, etc. The 'taxes' levied by local bodies are usually called 'rates', e.g. *borough, county, poor, school, water rate*, etc. In U.S. 'tax' is more generally applied in ordinary language to every federal, state, or local exaction of this kind: cf. the combs in 7.

† *To pay double taxes* (quot. 1759), i.e. to have two residences on which the assessed taxes were paid.

*a* **1327** *Pol. Songs* (Camden) 151 Mo then ten sithen told y my tax. *c* **1330** R. BRUNNE *Chron.* (1810) 247 þe lerid & þe lay granted þat þei said, & assigned a day, þat taxe to be laid. *c* **1380** WYCLIF *Sel. Wks.* III. 298 Oure clergie schal paie no subsidie ne taxe. *c* **1420** *Brut* 382 þere was grawnted vnto þe King, to maynetayne his warres, bothe of spiritualte & temporalte, an hole taxe and a dyme. *c* **1430** *Syr Gener.* (Roxb.) 5537 Taxe geteth he noon of Perse lond. **1480** CAXTON *Chron. England* cxlix, Kyng Iohan..let arere an huge taxe thurgh oute all englond, that is to say xxxv. M. marc. **1483** *Cath. Angl.* 378/2 A Taxe, *tallagium.* **1533** *Acc. Ld. High Treas. Scot.* VI. 129 Lettrez to Dunde, Perth [etc.] to inbring thair taxtis for furnesing of wageouris. **1535** COVERDALE *1 Kings* ix. 15 The summe of the taxe, that kynge Salomonraysed to the buyldinge of the house of the Lorde. **1552** HULOET, Taxe or subsidye graunted. **1607** COWELL *Interpr.*, *Task*, alias *Taxe*,..is such a kinde of tribute, as being certainly rated vpon euery towne, was wont to be yearely paide...Now is it not paide, but by consent giuen in Parlament, as the Subsidie is. **1651** HOBBES *Leviath.* II. xx. 106 Men ought to pay such taxes as are by Kings imposed. **1752** HUME *Ess. & Treat.* (1777) I. 344 A tax on German linen encourages home manufactures. **1759** DILWORTH *Pope* 116 Pope..was able to pay double taxes, and lived like a man in a genteel independance. **1765** BLACKSTONE *Comm.* I. viii. 308 The land tax, in it's modern shape, has superseded all the former methods of rating either property, or persons in respect of their property. **1776** ADAM SMITH *W. N.* v. ii. (*heading*) Part II, Of Taxes. *Ibid.* (1869) II. 461 A direct tax upon the wages of labour,..though the labourer might perhaps pay it out of his hand, could not properly be said to be even advanced by him. **1801** HAMILTON *Wks.* (1886) VII. 192 There is, perhaps, no item in the catalogue of our taxes which has been more unpopular than that which is called the direct tax. **1840** MCCULLOCH in *Encycl. Brit.* (ed. 7) XXI. 95 A tax may be either *direct* or *indirect*. It is said to be *direct* when it is immediately taken from income or capital; and *indirect* when it is taken from them by making their owners pay for liberty to use certain articles, or to exercise certain privileges. **1846** (*title*) The Local Taxes of the United Kingdom. **1878** JEVONS *Prim. Pol. Econ.* xvi. § 97. 129 In England the taxes amount to something like ten per cent., or one pound in every ten pounds.

†**b.** The rate at which anything is charged.

**1455** *Rolls of Parlt.* V. 308/2 Eny Dismes or Subsidies.. aftir the taxe or quantite of an hole Disme.

**c.** *The taxes*, the tax-collector. *colloq.*

**1874** W. S. GILBERT *Charity* III, Nobody calls on him except the taxes. **1888** STEVENSON *Popular Authors* II, Even the Rates and Taxes..have actually read your tales.

**2.** *fig.* Something compared to a tax in its incidence, obligation, or burdensomeness; an oppressive or burdensome charge, obligation, or duty; a burden, strain, heavy demand.

*a* **1628** F. GREVIL *Let. to Hon. Lady* iv. Wks. 1870 IV. 267 When Nature..foresaw this distresse or taxe, like to fall vpon her freedome. **1691–8** NORRIS *Pract. Disc.* (1711) III. 65 Sleep, that great Tax and Custom of Nature upon the life of man. **1713** STEELE *Guard.* No. 85 ⁋ 1 To suffer scandal..is the tax which every person of merit pays to the publick. **1727** DE FOE *Eng. Tradesman* xix. (ed. 2) 258 A young beginner has such a tax upon him before he begins, that he must sink perhaps..half..his stock in painting and gilding, wainscoting and glazing, before he..can open his shop. **1826** DISRAELI *Viv. Grey* II. xiv, You great men must pay a tax for your dignity. I am going to disturb you. **1862** H. SPENCER *First Princ.* I. i. § 8 The greatness of the question..justifies even a heavier tax on the reader's attention.

†**3.** = TASK *sb.* 2, 2 b. *Obs. rare.*

**1390** GOWER *Conf.* I. 94, 'I bidde nevere a betre taxe' Quod sche, 'bot ferst, er thou be sped, Thou schalt me leve such a wedd, That [etc.]'. **1559** *Mirr. Mag.* (1563) O j, A certayne taxe assygnd they have To shyne, and tymes divyde. **1564** *Advertmts.* in Cardwell *Doc. Ann.* (1839) I. 294 The archedeacon shall appoynte the curates to certaine taxes of the Newe Testamente to bee conde without booke. And at theire nexte synode to exact a rehearsall of them.

†**4.** The action or an act of taxing or charging a person with some offence; a charge, accusation; censure. *Obs.*

**1611** BEAUM. & FL. *Knt. Burn. Pestle* Induct., Flie far from hence All private taxes, immodest phrases, What e'r may but shew like vicious. **1621** VENNER *Tobacco* in *Via Recta*, etc. (1637) 354 They shall not passe without my tax. **1634** JACKSON *Creed* VII. xiv. § 6 It was not a prophecy but a sharp reproof or tax. **1642** *Declar. Lords & Com.* 7 Nov. 4 After many high taxes of Us and Our Government.

†**5.** A price-list, tariff. [So F. *taxe.* *Obs. rare*[−1].

1625 D. GORDON (*title*) Pharmaco-Pinax, or a Table and Taxe of all the Pryces of all usuall Medicaments.

†**6.** Phr. *To have in tax*, to have laid upon one, to have in hand. *To take in tax*, to take to task.

1635 *Voy. Foxe & James to N. W.* (Hakl. Soc.) 422 They being pertinent to the purpose I have in taxe. 1667 PEPYS *Diary* 16 May, Sir Edward Savage did take the said Moyer in tax about it.

**7.** *attrib.* and *Comb.* **a.** General: attributive, as *tax-claim, -law, -levy, -master, -mistress, -money, -paper, -rate, -return, -revenue, -system*; objective and obj. gen., as *tax-assessor, -collector, -controller, -dodger, -dodging, -extortioner, -farmer, -farming, -layer, -levying* adj., *-receiver*; instrumental, etc., as *tax-born, -bought, -burdened, -free, -laden* adjs. **b.** Special combs.: **tax-bond** (*U.S.*), a state bond receivable as taxes (*Funk's Stand. Dict.* 1895); **tax-book**, a list of property subject to taxation, with the amount of the taxes; **tax-certificate** (*U.S.*), a certificate given to a purchaser at a tax-sale by the authorized official, entitling the holder to a tax-deed at a certain date (*Funk*); **tax-deed** (*U.S.*), a conveyance made and delivered by the authorized official to a purchaser of land at a tax-sale (*Cent. Dict.* 1891); **tax-duplicate** (*U.S.*), a duplicate record of all tax-assessments, furnished to a tax-collector (*Funk*); **tax-eater**, one who is supported from the public revenue; so **tax-eating** *sb.* and *a.*; **tax-lien** (*U.S.*), the lien held by the state on property subject to taxation, which has priority over all other claims (*Funk*); **tax-list, tax-roll** = *tax-book*; **taxman**, a tax-collector; **tax-sale** (*U.S.*), a sale of the property of a delinquent tax-payer, made in order to defray the taxes due by him (*Cent. Dict.*); **tax-title** (*U.S.*), the title conveyed to the purchaser of property sold for taxes (*Funk*). See also TAX-CART, TAX-GATHERER, TAX-PAYER, etc.

1892 *Daily News* 20 Feb. 6/7 Any one who has had dealings with *tax assessors will not easily be convinced that they are men to be hoodwinked in this simple way. *c* 1630 RISDON *Surv. Devon* § 76 (1810) 78 So I find it in the *tax-book of England. 1846 M^cCULLOCH *Acc. Brit. Empire* (1854) II. 211 A certificate..that this portion was entered in the public tax-books, for an amount of land-tax entitling the possessor to a vote. 1823 BYRON *Juan* XI. xli, If he found not this spawn of *tax-born riches. 1831 E. ELLIOTT *Corn-Law Rhymes, Caged Rats* i, But ye are fat,..And fill'd with *tax-bought wine. 1904 *Q. Rev.* July 182 Plunging his *tax-burdened people into the horrors of a sanguinary and needless war. 1899 *Daily News* 24 Nov. 4/7 Dr. Robert refused as Mayor to sign the *tax-claims. 1862 MISS BRADDON *Lady Audley* xxi, Does she still take me for a *tax collector? 1876 *Nation* (N. Y.) 30 Mar. 202 The *tax-dodger is one who, finding that the rate of taxation in Boston is too high for his means, flies..to some rural town. 1895 *Westm. Gaz.* 4 Sept. 2/3 What the Tax-Dodger thinks he is doing is to defraud Sir William Harcourt's successor at the Exchequer of the gains of a tyrannical impost. *Ibid.*, [Those] who practise the gentle art of *tax-dodging in this respect are in the long run defrauding their own order. 1818 COBBETT *Pol. Register* XXXIII. 350 If you were to see one of my sons now becoming a *tax-eater, as a commissioned officer in the army. 1817 — *Wks.* XXXII. 25 Who look upon the poor as rivals in the work of *tax-eating. 1822 — *Rur. Rides* (1885) I. 151 Some one of the tax-eating crew had..called me an 'incendiary'. 1903 D. M'LEAN *Stud. Apost.* x. 141 Palestine..fell under this *tax-farming system. 1704 ADDISON *Italy* (1733) 126 The Fowl and Gibbier are *tax free. 1842 MIALL in *Nonconf.* II. 201 The *tax layers and the tax payers. 1892 GRIFFITH tr. *Fouard's St. Peter* 45 To exempt them from the *tax-levies every seventh year. 1902 *Westm. Gaz.* 5 June 4/2 Representation in the law-making and *tax-levying assembly. 1898 ANTROBUS tr. *Pastor's Hist. Popes* VI. 91 The *tax-list..has been preserved, and is interesting. 1830 MRS. BRAY *Talba* x. 83 The griping *taxman, and the conquered and taxed Moor. 1891 R. DOWLING *Isle Surrey* 21 The taxman and the gasman and the waterman. 1796 MORSE *Amer. Geog.* II. 549 Plundered by collectors and *tax-masters. 1738 *Gentl. Mag.* VIII. 193/1 [Fashion] keeps them perpetually busy in doing and undoing; and Folly is her Prime Confident and *Taxmistress. 1610 *Histrio-m.* VI. 205 Soft, sirs, I must talk with you for *tax-money, To relieve the poor. 1658 J. HARRINGTON *Oceana* 77 The Parishes having Levied the Tax money,..shall return it unto the Officers of the Hundreds. 1858 E. B. RAMSAY *Remin.* v. (1870) 102 The provost sends me a *tax paper. 1876 BANCROFT *Hist. U. S.* VI. xxxix. 207 In proportion to the general *tax-rates. 1886 W. J. TUCKER *E. Europe* 57 As long as..he is able to keep pace with his tax-rates, which..are daily becoming more exorbitant. 1830 COBBETT *Rur. Rides* (1885) II. 343 Your petitioners are the bees, and..the *tax-receivers are the drones. 1888 BRYCE *Amer. Commw.* II. xliii. (1889) I. 498 Apt to turn their property into these exempted forms just before they make their *tax returns. 1891 GRIFFITH tr. *Fouard's Christ* I. 225 Engaged in farming out the *tax-revenue of the provinces. 1545 *Reg. Privy Council Scot.* I. 21 To bring in with him the *taxt roll. 1841 SPALDING *Italy & It. Isl.* I. 399 In Campania..Honorius was compelled in the year 395 to expunge from the tax-roll, as become utterly waste, more than three hundred thousand acres of land.

†**Tax**, *sb.*² *Obs.* Also in 6 **taxe**. [ad. L. *tax-us* yew.] The yew-tree (also *tax-tree*); *transf.* a bow made of the wood of the yew.

1541 *Act* 33 *Hen. VIII*, c. 9 § 6 No bowyer shall sell..any bowe of ewe of the taxe called elke, aboue the price of iii. s. iiii. d. 1618 BOLTON *Florus* IV. xii. (1636) 331 Poyson ..is commonly there scruzed out of tax-trees. 1651 G. HILL *On Cartwright's Incomparable Poems* in *C.'s Poems*, Their unbridled Muse [can] securely run Undaunted through the rage of Tax or Gun.

**Tax** (tæks), *v.* Also 4–7 **taxe**. [app. a. OF. *taxe-r* (13th c. in Littré), ad. L. *taxāre* to censure, charge, tax with a fault; to rate, value, reckon, compute (at so much), make a valuation of; in med.L. also to impose a tax. The inherited form was OF. *tausser, taucer* (later, by assimilation, *tauxer*), It. *tassare*, Sp. *tasar*, Pg. *taxar*. Senses 1, 3, 6 are all in French.]

**I. 1.** To estimate or determine the amount of (a tallage, fine, penalty, damages, etc.); to assess; rarely, to impose, levy (a tax); also, to settle the price or value of. *Obs.* exc. in *Law*, to assess (costs). Const. † *to* (the amount).

[680 K. CÆDUALLA *Grant* in Earle *Land-Charters* 281 Hanc libertatem sub estimatione LXX tributariorum taxauimus.] *c* 1290 *Beket* 397 in *S. Eng. Leg.* I. 118 A taillage þov taxt fram ȝer to ȝer þoruȝ-out al þi londe. [1314–15 *Rolls of Parlt.* I. 290/2 La partie serra atteynt du trespas ..& les damages taxes a la volunte son adversair.] 13.. *Cursor M.* 27321 (Cott.) [To] knau þe circumstances o þe plight, for to tax þe penance right. 1387 TREVISA *Higden* (Rolls) VIII. 271 Þe chirches of Engelond were i-taxed to þe verray value [orig. *secundum valorem taxatæ sunt*]. 1424 *Paston Lett.* I. 13 The damages..were taxed to cxx li. 1530–1 *Act* 22 *Hen. VIII*, c. 15 Fines and amerciamentes affiered, taxed, sette, extreted, or judged. 1551 in W. H. Turner *Select. Rec. Oxford* (1880) 207 Taxable..to suche taxe and tallenge as shall be uppon hym taxed and sessyd. 1552 HULOET, Taxe damages in sute, *æstimare litem*. 1592 *Acts Court Requests* 97 The costs to be taxed to the vttermost charge approved due. 1768 BLACKSTONE *Comm.* III. xxiv. 400 These costs on both sides are taxed and moderated by the..proper officer of the court. 1885 *Daily Tel.* 24 Dec. (Cassell), A returning officer, whose bill of costs has been taxed on the application of the candidates.

†**2.** To impose, ordain, prescribe (a thing) *to* a person; also, to order (a person) *to* or *to do* something. *Obs.*

*c* 1350 *Will. Palerne* 5124 Loke..þat neuer þe pore porayle be piled for þi sake, ne taxed to taliage. 1390 GOWER *Conf.* I. 147 To the knyht this lawe he taxeth, That he shall gon and come ayein [etc.]. *Ibid.* 287 Such a Statut thanne he sette, And in this wise his lawe taxeth. *c* 1450 *Songs, Carols*, etc. (E.E.T.S.) 79/249 [Fortune] as her-self liste ordre & devise, Doth euery man his parte devide & taxe. *c* 1500 *Melusine* 210 We taxe you to pay to this noble pucelle all such dommages that she hath had at your cause. 1814 SCOTT *Diary* 6 Aug. in *Lockhart*, The islanders retort, that a man can do no more than he can; that they are not used to be taxed to their work so severely.

†**b.** To settle, fix, determine the extent of. *Obs.*

1390 GOWER *Conf.* III. 223 Whan Salomon his bone hath taxed, The god of that which he hath axed Was riht wel paid.

**3.** To impose a tax upon; to subject to taxation. Also *fig.*

*c* 1330 R. BRUNNE *Chron.* (1810) 247 Þe dettes þat men þam auht, þer stedes & þer wonyng, Wer taxed & bitauht to þe eschete of þe kyng. *c* 1380 WYCLIF *Sel. Wks.* III. 342 For oon mai seie þat..he [the Pope] haþ power singuler to taxe gracis, as him likiþ. 1453 *Rolls of Parlt.* V. 233/1 Rightfully charged or taxed to the Dismes. 1560 DAUS tr. *Sleidane's Comm.* 360 It shalbe lawfull for euery Magistrate to taxe y^e people for y^e same cause. 1598 HAKLUYT *Voy.* I. 486 The people of the countrie..being taxed and pilled so often as he thinketh good. 1627 SIR E. COKE in Rushw. *Hist. Coll.* (1659) I. 501 The King cannot tax any by way of Loans. 1657 in Picton *L'pool Munic. Rec.* (1883) I. 214 The same Ley..being unduly taxed. 1776 ADAM SMITH *W. N.* v. ii. (1869) II. 420 In the Venetian territory all the arable lands which are given in lease to farmers are taxed at a tenth of the rent. 1857 BUCKLE *Civiliz.* I. vii. 351 It was in the same reign that there was settled the right of the people to be taxed entirely by their representatives.

**b.** *To tax into* or *out of* some state.

1891 SCRIVENER *Fields & Cities* 70 Proposals have been made..to tax the landlords out of existence.

**4.** *fig.* To burden; to make serious demands upon; to put a strain on.

1672 MARVELL *Rehearsal Transp.* I. 51 Some Critical People, who will..tax up an old-wife's fable to the punctuality of History. 1697 DRYDEN *Æneid* Ded., Ess. (ed. Ker) II. 232 What had become of me, if Virgil had taxed me with another book. 1772 MACKENZIE *Man World* II. v, I have no right to tax you with my sorrows. 1832 LYTTON *Eugene A.* I. x, We will not tax the patience of the reader. 1853 KANE *Grinnell Exp.* xxxvi, My ingenuity was often taxed for expedients. 1876 GEO. ELIOT *Dan. Der.* III. xxvi, Most men are afraid of being bored or taxed by a wife's family.

**5.** *U.S.* (esp. *New Engl.*) *colloq.* To price (a thing *at* so much); to charge (a person so much *for* a thing).

1846–7 MRS. WHITCHER *Widow Bedott Papers* 218 (Bartl.) In trading with the clergy [he] only taxed his goods at half price. 1860 BARTLETT *Dict. Amer.* s. v., 'What will you tax me a yard for this cloth?' 1888 FARMER *Americanisms* s. v., An everyday colloquialism is 'What will you tax me?'

**II. 6.** To censure; to reprove, blame (a person, his action, etc.); to accuse, charge; to take to task, call to account.

1569 LD. CECIL *Let.* in Strype *Ann. Ref.* (1709) I. liii. 532 To think of us as our evil willers are disposed..to tax us. 1589 PUTTENHAM *Eng. Poesie* I. xi. (Arb.) 41 Another kind of Poet, who intended to taxe the common abuses and vice of the people in rough and bitter speaches. *a* 1619 FLETCHER, etc. *Knt. Malta* I. iii, If any therefore can finde manners tax..Let 'em speak now. 1692 DRYDEN *Cleomenes* II. ii, I have been to blame; And you have justly taxed my long neglect. 1709 POPE *Ess. Crit.* 589 Fear most to tax an Honourable Fool Whose right it is, uncensur'd to be dull. 1768 H. WALPOLE *Hist. Doubts* 12 *note*, That Chronicle.. which seems to tax the envy and rapaciousness of Clarence as the Causes of the dissention. *a* 1806 BP. HORSLEY *Serm.* (1816) II. xvi. 39 Eve..taxes the serpent as her seducer. 1873 TRISTRAM *Moab* v. 96, I was next taxed, and replied that [etc.].

**b.** Const. †*for*, *of* (now rare), *with* (now usual); †also inf. and obj. clause (*obs.*).

1548 PATTEN *Exped. Scot.* E viij, Apertly to tax their gouernour w^t y^e note of dissimulacion. 1603 KNOLLES *Hist. Turks* (1621) 1375 All the world would taxe him to have violated the law of nations. 1615 BRATHWAIT *Strappado* (1878) 82 Thy lippes..so modest as nere taxt of sinne. 1624 CAPT. SMITH *Virginia* IV. 159, I know I shall bee taxed for writing so much of my selfe. 1651 *Life Father Sarpi* (1676) 11 Taxing him to be an Usurper and an unjust Tyrant. 1665 DRYDEN *Ind. Emperor* III. ii, None shall tax me with base Perjury. 1697 DRYDEN *Virg. Past.* Pref. (1721) I. 86 A celebrated French Writer taxes him for permitting Æneas to do nothing without the assistance of some God. 1703 *Rules Civility* 262 A Magistrate..has been taxed, that instead of Administring Justice fairly, he sells it to the highest Bidder. 1726 POPE *Odyss.* XX. 437 Tax not..Of rage, or folly, my prophetic mind. 1777 [see sense 7]. 1833 HT. MARTINEAU *Berkeley* I. iii, I do not mean to tax Rhoda with falsehood. 1871 R. ELLIS *Catullus* lxiv. 322 Chants which an after-time shall tax of vanity never.

†**c.** *absol.* To censure, find fault. *Obs.*

1589 PUTTENHAM *Eng. Poesie* I. xv. (Arb.) 48 In those days when the Poets first taxed by Satyre and Comedy, there was [etc.]. 1621 BURTON *Anat. Mel.* Democr. to Rdr. 4, I did sometime laugh and scoffe with Lucian, and Satyrically taxe with Menippus.

†**7.** To call in question; to challenge, dispute (a statement, etc.). *Obs.*

1614 SIR R. DUDLEY in *Fortesc. Papers* (Camden) 8 In all wherin my honour nor honestye may not be taxed. 1642 ROGERS *Naaman* 24 Prone to taxe Gods wisedom, and call him to our barre. 1777 PRIESTLEY *Matt. & Spir.* (1782) I. xvi. 191 If..any person will tax my opinion..I shall tax him with great stupidity.

**III.** †**8.** Used to render Gr. ἀπογράφειν, to enter in a list, to register, enroll, enter in a list or statement of property. *Obs. rare.*

1526 TINDALE *Luke* ii. 3 And every man went in to his awne shyre toune there to be taxed. *Ibid.* 5 And Joseph also ascended from Galile..in to a cite of David, which is called bethleem..to be taxed. 1534 (ed. 2) *Ibid.* ii. 1 Ther went oute a commaundment from Auguste the Emperour, that all the woorlde shuld be taxed [1526 shulde be valued; *Vulg.* describeretur; WYCLIF schuld be discryued; *Geneva*, 1611 taxed; *Rheims*, 1881 (R.V.) enrolled].

**Taxable** (tæ·ksăb'l), *a.* (*sb.*) [a. AF. *taxable* (13th c. in Godef.), f. *taxer* to tax + -ABLE.]

†**1.** Liable to be assessed (*to* a tax, impost, or charge); assessable. *Obs.*

1474 *Rolls of Parlt.* VI. 115/2 Which to the Dismes with the Possessions of the Clergie be not taxed nor taxable. 1551 in W. H. Turner *Select. Rec. Oxford* (O.H.S.) 207 The same to be taxable..to suche taxe and tallenge as shall be uppon hym taxed and sessyd. 1569 ABP. PARKER *Let. to Sir W. Cecil* 18 May, Benefices of xxx *li.* and upward taxable to the provision of armour.

**2.** Liable to be taxed; subject to a tax or duty. In quot. 1685, liable to the *taille* in France, from which nobles were exempt.

1583 GOLDING *Calvin on Deut.* xcv. 587 Whereas there are some persons which are still taxable (as they terme it).. whether it be in their goods or in their persons. 1647 *Virginia Stat.* (1823) I. 341 A just and exact list of all taxable goods, land and tithable persons. 1683 *Apol. Prot. France* iii. 2 They ruine all the Protestants that are Taxable in France. 1685 COTTON tr. *Montaigne* (1711) I. xv. 68 Both himself and his Posterity [were] declared ignoble, taxable, and for ever incapable of bearing arms. 1762 tr. *Busching's Syst. Geog.* VI. 319 This structure is reckoned a taxable house. 1817–18 COBBETT *Resid. U. S.* (1822) 84 To learn..the taxable capacities of their farms. 1870 *Sat. Rev.* 2 Apr. 432 The consumers of taxable commodities had no reason to complain of Mr. Lowe's Budget. 1908 *Daily Chron.* 11 Jan. 4/3 He forgot that if taxation has increased, so also has what the politicians call 'taxable capacity'.

†**3.** Liable to a charge or accusation; chargeable (*with* some fault); censurable, blamable, reprehensible. *Obs.*

1610 HEALEY *St. Augustine's Citie of God*, To affect soueraignty..is taxable of indecency. 1617 HIERON *Wks.* II. 402 Men..worthily taxeable with this doctrine. 1654 H. L'ESTRANGE *Chas. I* (1655) 266 Not taxable with any vice. 1690 NORRIS *Beatitudes* (1692) 10 Taxable for a too earthly and downward disposition of soul. 1792 W. ROBERTS *Looker-on* No. 2 (1794) I. 20 The Old Bachelar was thought too taxable a shape to appear in.

**4.** *Law.* Of legal costs or fees: Liable to be taxed or reduced by the taxing-master.

1828–32 WEBSTER, *Taxable*..2. That may be legally charged by a court against the plaintif or defendant in a suit; as, taxable costs. 1885 *Law Times* 14 Feb. 286/2 The fees of a manor steward as such, though a solicitor, are not taxable.

**B.** *sb.* One who or that which is subject to taxation; *esp.* in *pl.* persons or things liable to a tax. Orig. *U.S.*

1662 in *Mag. Amer. Hist.* Jan. (1884) 39 (Act of Assembly, Maryland) That every householder and freeman..should take up ten shillings per poll..for every taxable under their charge and custody. 1701 *Maryland Laws* v. (1723) 17 To levy such Tax by the Poll on the Taxables of such Parishes. 1825 JEFFERSON *Autobiog.* Wks. 1859 I. 32 He..was for their voting..according to the number of taxables. 1861 J. G. SHEPPARD *Fall Rome* x. 565 Thus, the population was divided in the language into horsemen and taxables.

Hence **Taxabi·lity, Ta·xableness**, the quality or condition of being taxable; liability to taxation;

**Ta·xably** *adv.*, in a taxable manner; in quot. 1906, in relation to taxability.

**1804** W. TAYLOR in *Ann. Rev.* II. 351 When one considers the easy taxability of the rent derived from all this shipping, and of that yielded by our lands, houses, [and] machines. **1847** WEBSTER, Taxableness, Taxably. **1865** MERIVALE *Rom. Emp.* VIII. lxvii. 289 The citizenship with its attendant taxability was bestowed on many. **1906** *Contemp. Rev.* Jan. 94 Its Lowland-Scots virtues of thrift and adhesiveness, which made the province taxably so capable.

**Taxaceous** (tæksēⁱ·ʃəs), *a. Bot.* [f. mod.L. *Taxace-æ* (f. *taxus* yew) + -OUS: see -ACEOUS.] Belonging to the N.O. *Taxaceæ* (often made a suborder of *Coniferæ*), including the yew. So **Ta·xad** (tæ·ksăd) [cf. ARAD], Lindley's name for a tree or shrub belonging to the *Taxaceæ*.

**1846** LINDLEY *Veg. Kingd.* 230 Mr. Bennett..is of opinion that Taxads should not form a distinct Natural Order, but ought to be associated with Conifers. **1904** *Jrnl. R. Microsc. Soc.* Feb. 78 *Taxoxylon Philpii*..represents the first taxaceous fossil wood from Queensland.

† **Ta·xage.** *Obs. rare.* [f. TAX *v.* + -AGE: cf. med.L. *taxāgium* (1216 in Du Cange).] Taxation.

**1483** *Cath. Angl.* 378/2 A Taxage, *taxacio*.

**Taxameter, -metric**: see TAXIMETER, -RIC.

**Taxaspidean** (tæksæ̆spi·diăn), *a. Ornith.* [f. mod.L. *Taxaspidea*, neut. pl. (f. Gr. τάξις arrangement + ἀσπίς shield) + -AN.] Belonging to the division *Taxaspidea* of passerine birds, having the metatarsus regularly scutellated behind.

**1899** A. H. EVANS in *Cambr. Nat. Hist.* IX. 488 The taxaspidean metatarsus is moderate or short in the Thamnophilinæ, and remarkably long in the Grallariinæ.

**Taxation** (tæksēⁱ·ʃən). Forms: 4 **taxacioun**, 5–7 **-acion**, 6 **-atioun** (*Sc.* **taxtatioun**, 7 **taxtion**, **taction**), 6- **taxation**. [a. AF. *taxacioun* = OF. *taxation* (13th c. in Godef. *Compl.*), ad. L. *taxātiōn-em*, n. of action f. *taxāre* to TAX.]

**1.** The fixing of the sum of an impost, damages, price, etc.; assessment, valuation. *Obs.* exc. *Hist.*

[**1297** *Rolls of Parlt.* I. 239/2 E la taxacioun des Biens de ceaus des villes seit fete par autres loiaux gentz.] *c* **1325** *Poem Times Edw. II* 301 in *Pol. Songs* (Camden) 337 If the king in his lond maketh a taxacioun. **1387** TREVISA *Higden* (Rolls) VIII. 271 þe chirches of Engelond were i-taxed to the verray value, and seþþe voyded þe taxacioun of Norþwiche [L. *taxatio Norwycensis*] þat was made by þe fourþe Innocencius. **1543–4** *Act* 35 *Hen. VIII*, c. 10 Suche somes as..shal be taxed..for satisfaccion of any suche breakyng and defacyng..shal be paide..wᵗin ten dayes next after the saide Taxacion. **1592** WEST *1st Pt. Symbol.* § 24 Buying and selling is perfected, by the certein appointing of the thing to be sold, and the taxation of the price thereof, with the mutuall consent of the buyer and seller. **1601** SHAKS. *Twel. N.* I. v. 225, I bring no ouerture of warre, no taxation of homage; I hold the Olyffe in my hand. **1622** BACON *Hen. VII* 67 When the Commissioners entred into the Taxation of the subsidie in Yorkeshire,..the people vpon a sudaine grew into great mutinie. **1859** EYTON *Antiq. Shropshire* IX. 28 The Taxation of 1291 values the Church..at £10 per annum. **1895** RASHDALL *Univ. of Middle Ages* II. 399 The taxation of Halls by a joint board of burgesses and Masters is a custom which was established from the earliest times in all medieval Studia.

**b.** *Taxation of costs*, the allowing or disallowing, by certain officials of courts of law, of the charges made by solicitors or other persons (e.g. arbitrators) subject to the jurisdiction of the court.

**1552** HULOET, Taxacion, or assessment of a taxe or subsidye, or of costes in iudgement, *taxacio*. **1760** FOOTE *Minor* I. Wks. 1799 I. 235 He is generous, and will discharge your bill without taxation. **1883** *Wharton's Law Lex.* s. v., As between party and party a taxation of costs is always had.

**2.** The imposition or levying of taxes (formerly including local rates); the action of taxing or the fact of being taxed; also *transf.* the revenue raised by taxes. With *a* and *pl.*, an instance of this.

**1447–8** *Shillingford Lett.* (Camden) 79 Al other taxacions taliages and charges..to the Kyng owre soverayne lord graunted. *a* **1578** LINDESAY (Pitscottie) *Chron. Scot.* (S.T.S.) II. 260 Thair was gret taxtatiounis layd on thame befoir. **1593** SHAKS. *Rich. II*, II. i. 260 He hath not monie for these Irish warres: (His burthenous taxations notwithstanding). **1647** in Picton *L'pool Munic. Rec.* (1883) I. 143 Agreed that a Ley or Taxacion of xiiˡ be imposed upon the Towne. **1776** ADAM SMITH *W. N.* v. ii. (1869) II. 442 There are..two circumstances which render the interest of money a much less proper subject of direct taxation than the rent of land. **1781** GIBBON *Decl. & F.* xvii. II. 61 The policy of Constantine and his successors preferred a simple and direct mode of taxation, more congenial to the spirit of an arbitrary government. **1827** WHATELY *Logic* (1837) 318 Taxation—the revenue levied from the subject in return for the protection afforded by the Sovereign. **1838** THIRLWALL *Greece* V. xlii. 205 A new valuation of all private property had been made with a view to a more equable system of taxation. **1863** FAWCETT *Pol. Econ.* IV. i. (1876) 518 Taxation implies that the right to levy a tax is given by law.

*attrib.* **1886** CHAMBERLAIN in *Pall Mall G.* 22 Apr. 11/1 It is to deal with three-fourths of the taxation revenue of Ireland. **1905** *Daily Chron.* 26 Apr. 5/2 The railways..are not merely a transport agency, but are utilised as a machine for taxation purposes.

† **3.** A charging with a fault or offence; accusation; censure, reproof, blame. *Obs.*

**1591** SYLVESTER *Du Bartas* I. iii. 6 Sharpe taxation Of Bribes, Ambition, Treason, Avarice. **1600** SHAKS. *A. Y. L.* I. ii. 91 You'l be whipt for taxation one of these daies. **1631** BP. WEBBE *Quietn.* (1657) 147 Some..there are who deserve this sharp taxation. *a* **1653** GOUGE *Comm. Heb.* (1655) 474 The Apostles taxation of the Hebrews non-proficiency.

† **4.** Enrolment, registration, census. Cf. TAX *v.* 8. *Obs. rare*⁻¹.

**1686** PLOT *Staffordsh.* 324 The last taxation, numbering, or review of the Provinces, taken under the Cæsars Vespasians Father and Son, both Emperors and Censors.

Hence **Taxa·tional** *a.*, of or pertaining to taxation.

**1879** R. H. ELLIOT *Written on Foreheads* I. 205 You will have no taxational draft on your capital till you have coffee to meet it.

**Taxative** (tæ·ksătiv), *a. rare.* [ad. med. or mod.L. *taxātīvus* (Alciatus *c* 1530), f. ppl. stem of *taxāre* to TAX: see -ATIVE. (Cf. F. *taxative-ment*, Littré *Suppl.*)]

† **1.** Of limiting or defining nature. *rare.*

**1676** FOUNTAINHALL in M. P. Brown *Suppl. Decis.* (1826) III. 67 Where it allows them to work in such and such work, which fell not naturally and properly under the subject-matter of their own occupation, the same is so far from being taxative, that it is demonstrative and in their favours. **1726** [implied in TAXATIVELY].

**2.** Having the function of taxing; of or pertaining to taxation.

**1862** R. H. PATTERSON *Ess. Hist. & Art* 174 A taxative system which..had been in operation for two thousand years. **1870** STUBBS *Sel. Charters* Introd. 50 This completed the taxative powers of parliament. **1902** *Cambr. Mod. Hist.* I. 301 Upholding the representative legislative and taxative body by frequent sessions of Parliament.

Hence **Ta·xatively** *adv.*, in a taxative manner.

**1726** AYLIFFE *Parergon* 339 If these Ornaments or Furniture had been put Taxatively and by Way of Limitation, such a Thing bequeath'd as a Legacy shall not be paid, if it wants Ornaments or Furniture.

**Taxator** (tæksēⁱ·tǫɹ). Also 5–6 **-our**. [ad. med.L. *taxātor*, agent-n. from *taxāre* to TAX. So F. *taxateur* (16th c. in Hatz.-Darm.).]

**1.** One who assesses a subsidy, impost, or tax; an assessor; one who levies a tax. Now *Hist.*

**1424** *Sc. Acts Jas. I* (1814) II. 5 Þat ilk bischop in ilk denry of his diocise gar his officiall and his dene summonde all þe tenandis and frehaldaris befor him, and cheiss taxatouris. **1585–6** *Reg. Privy Council Scot.* IV. 47 Allegeing that the saidis taxatouris hes stentit thame..abone thair habilitie. **1848** *Fraser's Mag.* XXXVIII. 129 The loan is under the *surveillance* of the Woods and Forests, and pinched by the long-clawed taxators.

**2.** In the mediæval universities: = TAXER 1 b. (In contemporary use as a Latin word.)

**1831** SIR W. HAMILTON *Discuss.* (1852) 412 In the same year [1231] Taxators are established in both Universities. **1897** A. GORDON in *Dict. Nat. Biog.* LII. 182/2 In 1608 he [R. Sibbes] was appointed taxator [Camb.].

† **Tax-cart.** *Obs.* = *Taxed cart*: see next, 2 a.

**1806–7** J. BERESFORD *Miseries Hum. Life* xx. *Poet. Epist.* 29 While each tax-cart and shay To the Fair jolts away. **1837** HOWITT *Rur. Life* VI. x. (1862) 503 Away they go, in gigs and tax-carts, or on scampering horses. **1858** SIMMONDS *Dict. Trade, Tax-cart*, a spring-cart paying a low rate of duty. **1884** DOWELL *Taxation* III. III. iii. 231 Vehicles not over the value of 21 l., formerly termed 'taxed carts', and since their exemption from tax, usually called, in the provinces, tax carts.

**Taxed** (tækst), *ppl. a.* [f. TAX *v.* + -ED¹.]

**1.** † **a.** Assessed, determined by authority. *Obs.*
**b.** Subjected to a tax.

**1483** *Cath. Angl.* 378/2 Taxed, *taxatus*. **1552** HULOET, Taxed, *census*. *Ibid.*, Taxed by the pole,..*capite census*. **1689** BURNET *Tracts* I. 5 To buy of it at a taxed price. **1773** Taxed duty [see 2 c]. **1776** ADAM SMITH *W. N.* v. ii. (1828) III. 446 The rise in the price of the taxed commodities. **1842** W. C. TAYLOR *Anc. Hist.* xvii. § 8 (ed. 3) 544 His payment of the tax, by buying the taxed article, seems to be voluntary.

**2.** In special collocations. **a. Taxed cart**, a two-wheeled (orig. springless) open cart drawn by one horse, and used mainly for agricultural or trade purposes, on which was charged only a reduced duty (afterwards taken off entirely).

**1795** *Act* 35 *Geo. III*, c. 109 § 2 For and upon every Carriage with less than four Wheels,..which shall have the Words 'A taxed Cart', and also the Owner's Name and Place of Abode, there shall be charged and paid the yearly Sum of ten Shillings. **1801** W. FELTON *Carriages* Suppl. vi. 115 Taxed Carts. **1837** GEN. P. THOMPSON *Exerc.* (1842) IV. 279 The remission of taxation upon what by an odd perversion is called a taxed cart. **1859** GEO. ELIOT *A. Bede* xxxviii, The inn-keeper..offered to take him back to Oakbourne in his own 'taxed cart'.

**b. Taxed costs**: see quot.

**1858** SIMMONDS *Dict. Trade, Taxed-costs*, the allowed charges of a solicitor, which have been legally examined and assessed before a taxing-master.

**c. Taxed ward**, formerly, in Scottish land tenure, a wardship in which a fixed annual sum was paid to the superior in lieu of the whole profits.

**1603** *Reg. Privy Council Scot.* Ser. I. VI. 545 To grant the warde landis in taxt warde. **1710** FOUNTAINHALL in M. P. Brown *Suppl. Decis.* (1826) IV. 788 Part of the lands holding black or simple-ward, and part taxed-ward. **1773** ERSKINE *Instit.* II. v. § 5 If the ward was taxed, the minor retained the possession, and the superior had nothing to demand but the yearly taxed duty.

**Taxeopodous** (tæksiˌǫ·pŏdəs), *a. Zool.* [irreg. f. Gr. τάξις (gen. τάξεως) arrangement + -ποδος -footed (f. πούς foot) + -OUS.] Having each one of the carpal or tarsal bones of one row articulated with one of the other row; opposed to *diplarthrous*. So **Ta·xeopod**, *a.* = *taxeopodous*; *sb.* a member of the division *Taxeopoda* of ungulate mammals (comprising the *Proboscidea* and the extinct *Condylarthra*), having this arrangement of the tarsal bones; **Taxeo·pody**, taxeopodous condition.

**1887** E. D. COPE in *Amer. Nat.* XXI. 987 All ungulates in passing from the taxeopodous to the diplarthrous stages, traversed the amblyopodous. **1890** *Ibid.* May 471 In the equine line, after the development of diplarthry in the posterior foot, a tendency to revert to taxeopody appears. **1891** *Cent. Dict.*, Taxeopod, *a.* and *sb.* **1897** COPE in *Amer. Nat.* June 485 In this order of Ungulates the carpus is taxeopodous.

**Taxer, taxor** (tæ·ksəɹ, -ǫɹ). Forms: 4 **taxour(e**, 6–9 **taxor**, 6- **taxer**. [a. AF. *taxour*, agent-n. from *taxer* to TAX; with suffix subseq. reduced: see -ER² 3.]

† **1.** One who determines the amount of a tax, fine, price, etc.; an assessor. *Obs.*

[**1297** *Rolls of Parlt.* I. 239 Qe en chescun Counte seient deus Chivaliers, Taxours e Quilleurs, ou un Chevalier & un Serjaunt.] **1377** LANGL. *P. Pl.* B. VI. 40 Þowgh ȝe mowe amercy hem, late mercy be taxoure. **1552** HULOET, Taxer of prises, *agoranomus*. **1611** COTGR., *Tauxeur*, a rater, taxer, assessor, prisor, praisor. **1695** KENNETT *Par. Antiq.* ix. 312 In every Deanery new Taxers were commission'd.

**b.** *spec.* In the ancient universities, An officer (one of two) who fixed the rents of students' lodgings. At Cambridge, where the 'Taxors' also regulated the prices of commodities, kept the standard of weights and measures, and punished those who offended in these matters, the office and title (*taxor*) continued into the 19th c. Now *Hist.*

**1532–3** *Act* 24 *Hen. VIII*, c. 1 § 10 This Acte..shall not..bee prejudiciall..to the Chancellers Vychancellers Proctours Taxers & Scholers..of the Vnyversities. **1563** ABP. SANDYS in Strype *Ann. Ref.* (1709) I. xxxv. 359, I was scrutitor, I was taxer, I was proctor, and I was vicechancellor. *c* **1618** MORYSON *Itin.* IV. IV. i. (1903) 315 The vniversityes of Germany, haue no Taxers (or Clarkes of the Markett) for the price of vittles (as our vniversityes haue). *Ibid.* 429 [At Bologna] two Taxers are chosen to taxe the Students lodgings, and see that they pay not more then in former yeares. **1797** *Cambr. Univ. Calendar* 141 The taxatores, taxers or taxors in this university,..were first appointed to regulate the price of the lodgings of the students. **1841** G. PEACOCK *Stat. Cambr.* 25 The two taxors were regents appointed by the house of regents, who were empowered, in conjunction with two burgesses, to tax or fix the rent of hostels and houses occupied by students, in conformity with the letters patent of Henry III (1231). They also assisted the proctors in making the assize of bread and beer, and in other affairs relating to the regulation of the markets. **1895** RASHDALL *Universities in Middle Ages* II. 361 It is worthy of notice that the office of Taxor, which has only recently been abolished in the University of Cambridge, was the earliest University office at Oxford [*c* 1209].

**2.** One who levies a tax or taxes.

**1603–4** BACON *Sp. touching Purveyors*, Instead of takers, they become taxers; instead of taking provision for your Majesty's service, they tax your people *ad redimendam vexationem*. **1820** LAMB *Elia* Ser. I. *Two Races Men*, He [the borrower] is the true taxer who 'calleth all the world up to be taxed'. **1884** DOWELL *Taxation* I. v. i. 96 The taxors and collectors and their clerks..were accused of acting in an arbitrary..manner.

† **3.** One who finds fault or censures. *Obs.*

**1601** W. PARRY *Trav. Sir A. Sherley* 8 The Turks (our Taxers) told us. **1611** SPEED *Hist. Gt. Brit.* IX. viii. (1623) 559 [They] were also..his most bitter Taxers.

**Ta·x-ga·therer.** *arch.* A collector of taxes.

[**1552** HULOET, Taske gatherer, *exactor*.] **1693** DRYDEN *Disc. Orig. & Progr. Satire* in *Ess.* (ed. Ker) II. 77 Casaubon..says that Horace, being the son of a tax-gatherer..smells everywhere of the meanness of his birth. **1771** GOLDSM. *Hist. Eng.* (1789) IV. 271 The oppressions of the tax-gatherers..were considered as so severe, that the army once more rose to vindicate their freedom. **1826** SYD. SMITH *Let. on Cath. Quest.* Wks. 1859 II. 232/1 The tax-gatherer is the most indulgent and liberal of human beings;..and is candidly and impartially oppressive to every description of the Christian world. **1904** *Expositor* Mar. 213 Christ..certainly had a taxgatherer for one of his chief disciples.

**Taxi** (tæ·ksi). Also **taxy**. Colloquial abbreviation of TAXIMETER; also of TAXI-CAB.

**1907** *Daily Chron.* 26 Mar. 6/7 Every journalist..has his idea of what the vehicle should be called. It has been described as the (1) taxi, (2) motor-cab, (3) taxi-cab, (4) taximo,..(7) taximeter-cab. **1908** *Ibid.* 4 Feb. 4/7 Within the past few months the 'taxi' has been the name given to the motor-cab. **1908** *Daily News* 30 Apr. 2 Many ladies..now take a 'taxy' regularly for the morning's shopping. There are about 350 horsed 'taxies' on the road. **1908** E. V. LUCAS *Over Bemertons* iv, He went away in a taxi.

*attrib.* and *Comb.* **1907** *Daily Chron.* 27 Aug. 4/7 'Take me to the New Theatre', said the fare. 'Which one, sir?' respectfully asked the 'taxy' driver. **1909** *Daily News* 3 Mar. 6 You can safely leave the rest to the taximen. **1909** *Westm. Gaz.* 20 Sept. 5/4 To qualify for the taxi-driving 'profession'.

**Taxiarch** (tæ·ksiˌaɹk). *Anc. Gr. Hist.* [ad. Gr. ταξίαρχ-os, f. τάξι-s, TAXIS + ἀρχός, f. ἄρχειν to rule.] The commander of a taxis: see TAXIS 3.

**1808** MITFORD *Hist. Greece* I. v. iv. 287 The rank of the [Athenian] Taxiarch..was nearly that of our colonel. **1837** WHEELWRIGHT tr. *Aristophanes* II. 269 A taxiarch or general, to receive some share of honour. **1846** GROTE *Greece* II. viii. II. 607 The tribe appears to have been the only military classification known to Athens, and the taxiarch the only tribe-officer for infantry, as the phylarch was for cavalry, under the general-in-chief. **1875** JOWETT *Plato* (ed. 2) V. 83 The generals thus elected shall propose the taxiarchs or brigadiers.

**Taxi-cab, taxicab** (tæ·ksiˌkæb). [Short for TAXIMETER *cab*, and itself shortened to TAXI.] A cab for public hire, fitted with a taximeter; *esp.* an automobile or motor-cab so furnished.

**1907** *Daily Chron.* 28 Mar. 2/5 The 'taxicab', as the new taximeter motor-cab is called, is fast becoming a familiar feature in the streets of London. **1907** *Ibid.* 3 May 8/3 London has taken kindly to the Taxicab. **1908** *Westm. Gaz.* 7 May 4/2 How much the taxi-cab has done..to educate the non-motoring public to the utility of the motor-car.

*attrib.* and *Comb.* **1907** *Daily Chron.* 3 May 8/3 Any taxicab driver who demands payment for an extra passenger is breaking the law. **1909** *Ibid.* 12 Jan. 1/4 She made quickly for her taxicab door, which was held open by police.

**Taxicorn** (tæ·ksikǫ̈ɪn), *a.* and *sb. Entom.* [a. mod.L. *Taxicornes* pl. (Latreille, 1817), app. f. Gr. τάξις order, arrangement, a row or series + L. *cornu* horn: perh. after Gr. ταξίφυλλος with leaves set in rows.] **a.** *adj.* Having perfoliate antennæ, as the beetles of the obsolete family *Taxicornes* (now mostly referred to *Tenebrionidæ*). **b.** *sb.* A beetle of this family. Also **Taxico·rnate, Taxico·rnous** *adjs.*

**1842** BRANDE *Dict. Sc.*, etc., *Taxicorns*, [L.] *Taxicornes*. ..The name of a family of Coleopterous insects, including those in which the antennæ gradually augment in size as they extend from the head, or terminate in an enlargement. **1860** MAYNE *Expos. Lex.*, Taxicornate.

**Taxidermal** (tæksidǝ̄·ɹmăl), *a.* [f. TAXIDERM-Y + -AL.] = next.

**1877** COUES & ALLEN *N. Amer. Rod.* 20 At first, we thought this was a taxidermal or other accident, but all the specimens show the same thing. *Ibid.* 67. **1898** *Naturalist* 171 The material More turned out from his taxidermal or herbarial laboratories.

**Taxidermic** (tæksidǝ̄·ɹmik), *a.* [f. as prec. + -IC.] Of or pertaining to taxidermy.

**1847** in WEBSTER. **1860** in MAYNE *Expos. Lex.*

**Taxidermist** (tæ·ksidǝ̄ɹmist). [f. TAXIDERMY + -IST.] One skilled in taxidermy; a professional stuffer of animals for preservation. Also *attrib.*

**1828** in WEBSTER. **1849** LONGF. *Kavanagh* xv, The taxidermist..was not there. **1851** MANTELL *Petrifact.* ii. § 3. 108 *note*, The eminent taxidermist..to whom I entrusted the skins of Notornis, Apteryx, &c. to be stuffed and mounted. **1869** *Eng. Mech.* 31 Dec. 381/1 The glass eyes used by taxidermists are generally too spherical.

**Taxidermize** (tæ·ksidǝ̄ːɹməiz), *v.* [f. as prec. + -IZE.] **a.** *trans.* To treat by taxidermy; to prepare, preserve, and set up (a skin, etc.). **b.** *absol.* or *intr.* To practise taxidermy (*Funk's Stand. Dict.* 1895). Hence **Ta·xide·rmized** *ppl. a.*, prepared by taxidermy.

**1889** *Pop. Sci. Monthly* Apr. 779 His [the buffalo's] head taxidermized..fetches as much as the robe or even more. **1890** LEFFINGWELL *Shooting* 307 Game pictures, taxidermised specimens, wood-paintings of birds.

**Taxidermy** (tæ·ksidǝ̄ːɹmi). [mod. f. Gr. τάξι-ς arranging, arrangement + δέρμα skin: cf. Gr. παχυδερμία thickness of skin.] The art of preparing and preserving the skins of animals, and stuffing and mounting them so as to present the appearance, attitude, etc. of the living animal.

**1820** (*title*) Taxidermy: or the Art of Collecting, Preparing, and Mounting Objects of Natural History. For the Use of Museums and Travellers. **1842** BRANDE *Dict. Sc.*, etc. s.v., The most popular treatise on taxidermy is Mr. Swainson's volume in Lardner's Cyclopedia. **1854** BADHAM *Halieut.* 112 The inhabitants of the sea cannot be preserved except as mummies; they are the opprobrium of taxidermy.

**Taxildar**, variant of TAHSILDAR.

**Taximeter** (tæksi·mitəɹ). Also 9 **taxameter.** [ad. F. *taximètre*, f. *taxe* tariff + *-mètre* = -METER. The form *taxameter*, used a few years earlier, was from German: cf. med.L. *taxa* tax. (An earlier German name from *c* 1875 was *taxanom*.)]

An automatic contrivance fitted on a cab or other vehicle to indicate to the passenger at any point the distance traversed and the fare due.

The earliest forms of this indicator were simply distance-recorders, but it was soon made to comprise an automatic fare-reckoner and index.

α. [**1890** *German Patent Spec.* 56310 Taxameter-Fabrik Westendorp & Pieper in Hamburg.] **1894** *Times* 2 June 19/1, I have severally interviewed the proprietors of the 'taxameter', owners of cabs at Hamburg, and several of their *employés*. **1898** *Daily Chron.* 21 Mar., An illustration and description of the taxameter has been sent us. **1898** *Westm. Gaz.* 30 Apr. 7/3 Each vehicle will be provided with a taxameter—the little instrument for registering distance which has found such favour in Paris and Berlin.

β. **1898** *Daily News* 14 Apr. 7/2 One of the new Berlin taximeters, attached to a London hansom cab, on which it has been in operation for the past six months in an experimental way, was shown [etc.]. **1907** *Ibid.* 4 Feb. 7/5 The Committee's report..declared strongly in favour of the taximeter as a means of regulating fares. **1908** *Whitaker's Almanack* 434/1 The fare payable for the hiring of a Motor Hackney Carriage fitted with a Taximeter shall be..(a) Not exceeding one mile, or..ten minutes..8d. **1909** *Westm. Gaz.* 22 June 7/3 A taxi-meter was tried on horse-cabs in London over half-a-century ago.

**b.** *attrib.* and *Comb.*, as *taximeter cab, -driver, hansom, -maker, scale, system, vehicle.*

α. **1899** *Westm. Gaz.* 23 Mar. 8/1 A report..from our Consul-General at Berlin on the subject of taxameter cabs in that city, and its nature should bid our Taxameter Syndicate, Limited, be of good cheer despite recent rebuffs. **1903** *Daily Chron.* 16 Nov. 4/5 Some years ago there was an attempt to introduce the taxameter system, which is the rule in all big German towns. The London cabman would have none of it. **1906** *Ibid.* 20 Feb. 4/1 A few minutes later a taxameter motor brougham drove up with the bride.

β. **1907** *Daily News* 18 Mar. 9 By the end of this week London may expect that about sixty taximeter motor cabs will be plying for hire in the streets. **1907** *Daily Chron.* 23 Sept. 3/4 A horse cab driver..was charged with assaulting [a] taximeter cab driver.

Hence **Taxi·metered** *a.* (also **Taxime·tric** *a.*), provided with a taximeter.

**1907** *Daily Chron.* 18 Mar. 4/7 The competition of the *taximetered motor-cab will entitle the poor old four-wheeler no more than ever to the name of 'growler'. **1908** *Even. Standard* 1 Feb. 1/3 Seventeen taximetered hansoms took the London streets to-day. **1906** *Westm. Gaz.* 15 Mar. 2/3, I have just returned from Paris, where most cabs are now '*taxametric'.

**Taxin** (tæ·ksin). *Chem.* [f. L. *tax-us* yew + -IN [1].] 'A resinous substance obtained from the leaves of the yew-tree' (Watts *Dict. Chem.* (1868) V. 702). So **Ta·xine** (-əin) *sb.*, a poisonous alkaloid found in these leaves (*Syd. Soc. Lex.* 1899).

**1907** *Daily News* 21 Dec. 9 A post-mortem examination showed that he had eaten a quantity of yew leaves, which ..contained taxine, a very active poison.

**Taxine** (tæ·ksəin), *a. Bot.* [f. as prec. + -INE [1].] Pertaining to, connected with, or resembling the genus *Taxus*; yew-like.

**1888** DAWSON *Geol. Hist. Plants* 22 The débris of fossil taxine woods, mineralised after long maceration in water.

**Ta·xing,** *vbl. sb.* [f. TAX *v.* + -ING [1].] The action of the verb TAX in various senses.

**1413** *Pilgr. Sowle* (Caxton 1483) IV. xxxiv. 83 To these shyrreues belongeth to punysshe mysdoers by taxyng of money. **1526** TINDALE *Luke* ii. 2 This taxynge [WYCLIF discryuyng, *Rheims* enrolling, *R.V.* enrolment] was fyrst executed when Syrenus was leftenaunt in Siria. **1535** COVERDALE 1 *Esdras* ii. 19 They shal not only refuse to geue trybutes and taxinges, but also rebell vtterly agaynst the kynge. **1676** DRYDEN *Aurengzebe* II. i, Impose; but use your power of Taxing well. **1737** WHISTON *Josephus, Antiq.* XVIII. ii. (1812) III. 60 The taxings were come to a conclusion. **1841** MYERS *Cath. Th.* iii. § 35. 128 This is an undue taxing of any man's faith. *a* **1859** MACAULAY *Hist. Eng.* xxiii. (1861) V. 56 The only power which..Washington and Franklin denied to the Imperial legislature was the power of taxing.

**b.** *attrib.* and *Comb.* **Taxing district** (U. S.): see quot.; **taxing-master,** an officer in a court of law who examines and allows or disallows items in a solicitor's bill of costs when disputed.

**1890** *Cent. Dict.* s.v. *District*, *Taxing district, in the United States, the territory or region into which (for the purpose of assessment merely) a State, county, town, or other political district is divided. *H. H. Emmons.* **1848** WHARTON *Law Lex.*, **Taxing masters*, officers of the courts, who examine and allow costs. **1882** H. C. MERIVALE *Faucit of B.* II. I. xvii. 22 That exquisite and rational product of British law, the taxing-master.

**Ta·xing,** *ppl. a.* [f. TAX *v.* + -ING [2].] That taxes, in various senses of the verb.

**1798** *Anti-Jacobin* xix. (1852) 84 Again the taxing-man [Pitt] appear'd—No deadlier foe could be. **1813** SCOTT *Let. to Joanna Baillie* 10 Dec. in *Lockhart*, As to the taxing men, I must battle them as I can: they are worse than the great Emathian conqueror. **1859** DICKENS *T. Two Cities* II. ix, All the taxing authorities were armed.

**Taxinomy** (tæksi·nŏmi), a more etymological form of TAXONOMY. So **Taxino·mic** *a.* = TAXONOMIC; **Taxi·nomist** = TAXONOMIST.

**1865** BENDYSHE tr. *Blumenbach's Anthropol. Treat.* Pref. 11 Truths whose importance no one can dispute in anthropological taxinomy. **1866** *Reader* 15 Dec. 1066 Those sciences of life which modern teaching has, with inexact taxinomy, and worse Greek, termed Biology. **1899** *Nature* 21 Sept. 489/2 The position that all taxinomy (which form he prefers, on etymological grounds, to the more usual 'taxonomy') must conform to logical requirements. *Ibid.*, Labours of scientific taxinomists. *Ibid.* 490/1 All who engage in taxinomic work.

‖ **Taxis** (tæ·ksis). [a. Gr. τάξις arrangement, order, n. of action from τάσσειν to arrange.]

**1.** *Surg.* A manipulative operation employed for replacing parts which have quitted their natural situation, reducing hernia, etc.

**1758** J. S. *Le Dran's Observ. Surg.* (1771) 198 The Reduction was attempted in vain, by the Operation called the *Taxis*. **1800** *Med. Jrnl.* IV. 38 In about an hour after, the reduction was compleated, by again having recourse to the inverted position and the taxis. **1887** D. MAGUIRE *Massage* iii. (ed. 4) 43 The taxis which surgeons use on ruptures, is but..a methodical pressure used by the hand on a ruptured tumour for reducing it.

†**2.** *Arch.* Structural adaptation of elements; the adaptation of parts to the end for which a building is erected; ordonnance. *Obs.*

**1727-41** CHAMBERS *Cycl.*, *Taxis*.., in the ancient architecture, signifies the same with Ordonnance in the new, and is described by Vitruvius to be that which gives every part of a building its just dimensions, with regard to its use.

**3.** *Anc. Gr. Hist.* A company of soldiers, esp. foot-soldiers; a division of troops varying in size in different military organizations, and accordingly answering to a modern company, battalion, regiment, or brigade; in Athens, the quota of foot-soldiers supplied by each of the ten local tribes or Phylæ.

**1850** GROTE *Greece* II. lvi. VII. 108 Each taxis or company,..had its own taxiarch. **1856** *Ibid.* II. xcii. XII. 80 The Macedonian Phalanx...The largest division of it which we find mentioned..is called a Taxis. How many of these Taxeis there were in all, we do not know.

**4.** *Philol.* Order or arrangement of words.

**1885** *Amer. Jrnl. Philol.* VI. 361 The double taxis (grammatical and logical) of the Latin.

**5.** *Nat. Hist.* Classification, taxonomy.

**1891** in *Cent. Dict.*

**6.** *Biol.* The reaction of a free organism to external stimulus by movement in a particular direction.

**1904** *Science* 14 Oct. 487 The mechanical interpretations of the tropisms and taxes as held by Loeb, Bethe and Uexkull. **1908** DRIESCH *Sc. & Philos. Organism* II. 9 In the simple free directive movement or 'taxis' it is the typical relation between the direction of the stimulus and the direction of the effect, with regard to the main axis or the plane of symmetry of the organism, which separates this type of motion from others. *Ibid.* 13 'Taxis' signifies the specific orientation of a specific axis of the organism with regard to the direction of any directed agent of the medium.

**Taxless** (tæ·kslės), *a.* [f. TAX *sb.*[1] + -LESS.] Free from taxes or taxation; untaxed.

**1615** SYLVESTER *Job Triumphant* III. 555 If Tithe-lesse, Taxe-lesse, Wage-lesse, Right-lesse, I Have eat the Crop, or caused the Owners dye. **1845** LD. CAMPBELL *Chancellors* (1857) IV. lxxviii. 61 They depicted..the happy tranquil, taxless times which the more aged might still remember. **1909** *Daily Chron.* 3 Sept. 4/4 Compelled to fly the Channel, and seek some taxless shore.

Hence **Ta·xlessly** *adv.*, without taxation.

**1894** J. S. MORTON in *Forum* (U. S.) June 389 The most efficacious remedy..is, to give the farmers of the United States the right to taxlessly buy in the markets of all the civilized world wherein they are compelled to sell.

**Taxman,** obs. f. TACKSMAN; see also TAX *sb.*[1] 7.

† **Taxment.** *Obs. rare*⁻¹. [f. TAX *v.* + -MENT: perh. a. AF. *taxement* (13–15th c. in Godef.), med. L. *taxāmentum*.] Assessment of a tax.

**1612** in W. M. Williams *Ann. Founders' Co.* (1867) 226 Pd...to the Chamberlain of the Cytie of London for the laste payment of £35. for the taxments for Ireland..£7. 10. 0.

**Taxo-,** irreg. used as combining form of Gr. τάξις arrangement (of which the comb. form in Greek is ταξι-, *taxi-*): see TAXOLOGY, -ONOMY, etc.

**Taxocrinid** (tæksǫkri·nid). *Palæont.* [f. mod. L. *Taxocrinidæ*, f. *Taxocrinus*, name of the typical genus, f. Gr. τάξος yew + κρίνον lily: see -ID [3].] A member of the extinct family *Taxocrinidæ* of articulate crinoids. So **Taxocrinoid** (-kri·noid) *a.*, belonging to this family; *sb.* = taxocrinid.

‖ **Taxodium** (tæksǭu·diŏm). *Bot.* [mod.L., f. Gr. τάξος, L. *taxus* yew: see -ODE.] An American genus of coniferous trees, comprising the bald cypress, *T. distichum*, of the United States, and the Mexican cypress, *T. mucronatum*.

**1836** J. MITFORD *Lett. & Remin.* (1891) 82 You will outlive all the Ba-o-babs and taxodiums in the world.

**Taxodont** (tæ·ksǒdǫnt), *a. Zool.* [f. Gr. τάξις arrangement + ὀδούς, ὀδοντ-, tooth.] Of a bivalve shell: Having the hinge formed by a long series of similar teeth and sockets, as in the group *Taxodonta*, containing the ark-shells and the genus *Leda*. Said also of the hinge, and of the arrangement.

**1896** *Science* 27 Nov. 771 A series of vertical crenulations or taxodont denticles.

**Taxology** (tæksǫ·lŏdʒi). *rare*⁻⁰. [f. TAXO- + -LOGY.] The science of classification; the study of taxonomy.

**1860** MAYNE *Expos. Lex.*, *Taxologia*,..applied by Devereux to all that relates to classification: taxology.

**Taxonomy** (tæksǫ·nŏmi). [ad. F. *taxonomie* (De Candolle 1813), irreg. f. Gr. τάξις arrangement, order (see TAXIS) + -νομία distribution: see TAXO- and -NOMY. See also TAXINOMY.] Classification, esp. in relation to its general laws or principles; that department of science, or of a particular science or subject, which consists in or relates to classification.

[**1813** DE CANDOLLE *Theor. Elem. de la Botanique.*] **1828** in WEBSTER. **1832** *Encycl. Brit.* (ed. 7) V. 70/2 Taxonomy is that branch of botany which has for its object the combination of all our observations on plants, so as to form a system or classification. **1839** G. ROBERTS *Dict. Geol.*, *Taxonomy*, the classification or putting things in their proper order. **1852** DANA *Crust.* I. 59 The long posterior legs of certain Maioid species have been allowed to have the same value in Taxonomy. **1872** COUES *N. Amer. Birds* 49.

So **Taxo·nomer,** a scientific classifier; **Taxono·mic, -ical** *adjs.*, pertaining or relating to taxonomy, classificatory (hence **Taxono·mically** *adv.*); **Taxo·nomist** = *taxonomer*. (See also *taxinomic, taxinomist*, s. v. TAXINOMY.)

**1885** *Athenæum* 1 Aug. 146/2 It is now generally admitted by *taxonomers that their affinities are..close. **1897** *Naturalist* 94 One instance wherein the author differs from most recent taxonomers. **1852** DANA *Crust.* I. 10 We deem it of so little *taxonomic importance. **1894** NEWTON *Dict. Birds* 820 The taxonomic position of the *Palamedeidæ*.. has been much debated. **1875** C. C. BLAKE *Zool.* Pref., A sub-class which vindicates the value of its *taxonomical character by its numerical superiority. **1880** HUXLEY in *Times* 25 Dec. 4/1 The palæontological facts which have come to light..have completely broken down existing taxonomical conceptions. **1899** *Nature* 14 Sept. 460/1 To successfully handle *taxonomically groups so dissimilarly ordained as the Bony Fishes and Echinoderms. **1877** HUXLEY *Anat. Inv. Anim.* xii. 656 The views of *Taxonomists

..are undergoing..incessant modifications. **1904** *Athenæum* 6 Aug. 175/3 Then the pendulum swung in the opposite direction:..field botanists were placed on a level with postage-stamp collectors, taxonomists were looked on as laborious triflers.

**Taxor, -our(e**: see TAXER.

**Ta·xpay·er, tax-payer.** One who pays a tax or the taxes generally; one who is liable to taxation; in U.S. including local rate-payers.

**1816** J. KENNEDY in A. McKay *Hist. Kilmarnock* (1880) 229 Only 2,700 have a right of voting for members of Parliament;..197,300, although tax-payers, directly or indirectly, having no more right of voting than if they were an importation of slaves from Africa. **1853** *Inaug. Address Mayor of Boston (U.S.)*, [Of] interest to every water taker and tax payer in the City. **1855** MACAULAY *Hist. Eng.* xix. IV. 324 Some part..might, with advantage to the proprietor, to the taxpayer and to the State, be attracted into the Treasury. **1878** JEVONS *Prim. Pol. Econ.* xvi. 130 To demand a tax when the taxpayer is likely to be able to pay it.

So **Ta·xpay·ing** *sb.*, the payment of taxes; *a.*, that pays taxes (or rates); subject to taxation.

**1851** *Inaug. Address Mayor of Boston (U.S.)*, The sale would cause discontent..to a very large number of tax-paying citizens. **1882** T. HUGHES in *Macm. Mag.* XLV. 281 Doing his share of fighting, taxpaying, keeping the peace. **1894** *Pop. Sci. Monthly* XLV. 719 Formerly they were checked by the rage of the taxpaying classes.

**Taxt**, obs. Sc. f. TAX *sb.*[1]; var. of TAXED.

**Ta·x-ta·ker.** One who takes or collects taxes; a levier or receiver of taxes.

**1610** HEALEY *St. Aug. Citie of God* II. xix. 85 Even the very soldiers and taxe-takers themselves would heare and regard well. **1656** EARL MONM. tr. *Boccalini's Advts. fr. Parnass.* II. lxxxii. (1674) 234 Their grievances were encreased by the greedy Tax-takers. **1832** HT. MARTINEAU *Each & All* iii. 43 We must reach the extreme..of having our whole produce in the hands of land-owners and tax-takers. **1860** DICKENS *Lett.* (1880) II. 117 The tax-taker was the authority for the wretched creature's impoverishment.

**Taxt ward**: see TAXED 2 c.

‖ **Ta·xus.** *Obs.* Mediæval Latin name of the badger: formerly sometimes used in English.

**1535** COVERDALE *Ezek.* xvi. 10, I made the shues of Taxus lether. **1567** MAPLET *Gr. Forest* 104 b, Of Taxus or the Badger. **1577** tr. *Bullinger's Decades* III. v. (1592) 340 Three coueringes more, the vppermost whereof was of Taxus leather, wel able in raine to keepe water out. **1753** CHAMBERS *Cycl. Supp.*, *Taxus*, in zoology, the name of the badger.

**Taxwax** (tæ·ksˌwæks). Now *dial.* Also 9 **taxy waxy.** [Var. of PAXWAX.] The tendon of the neck: = PAXWAX.

**1709** BLAIR in *Phil. Trans.* XXVII. 78 From above this Tax-Wax in the Neck, do arise two Muscles. **1713** DERHAM *Phys.-Theol.* VI. iii. 362 That strong tendinous and insensible Aponeurosis, or Ligament—Called the Whitleather, Packwax, Taxwax, and Fixfax. **1829** J. HUNTER *Hallamsh. Gloss.*, *Tax-wax*, the tendon of the neck. **1879** MISS JACKSON *Shropsh. Word-bk.* s.v., Gie the baby that piece o' taxy waxy, it's better than india-rubber.

**Taxy**: see TAXI.

**-taxy**, comb. element, ad. Gr. -ταξία, f. τάξις arrangement, order; as in ATAXY, PHYLLOTAXY.

†**Tay, tey.** *Obs.* Also 5 **teye**, 6 **taie**, 6–7 **taye**. [In 5 *teye*, a. obs. F. *teie*, in Palsgr. *taye* (in senses 2, 3):—L. *t(h)ēca*:—Gr. θήκη case, covering, sheath.]

**1.** A case, sheath, outer covering.

*c* **1440** *Promp. Parv.* 487/2 Teye, of a cofyr or forcer, *teca, thecarium*.

**2.** A web or cataract in the eye.

**1547** RECORDE *Judic. Ur.* 59 b, It healeth creythys, and also the webbe and the tey in the eye. **1597** LOWE *Chirurg.* (1634) 31 Some cataract or taye which covereth the prunall called the windowe of the eye. *Ibid.* 166 The Cataract or tey.

**3.** The outer membrane of the brain. [Cf. F. *teie dure* = *dura mater*.] Also taken as 'skull', and 'brain'.

*a* **1568** '*My wofull Hairt*', etc. 44 in *Bannatyne Poems* (Hunter. Cl.) 83 Vpoun my heid thay thrang a croun of thorn,..The thorne pykis thay to my tay dang doun. *c* **1580** JEFFERIE *Bugbears* I. i. in *Archiv Stud. Neu. Spr.* (1897) XCVIII. 306 In stide of taies, he hathe bugbeares in his head.

**Tay**, obs. or dial. f. TEA, THEE, TIE, TOE; obs. form of THEY after a dental.

**Tay, taye**, variants of TAEL.

‖ **Tayassu, tayaçu** (tāˌyăsū·). Also **tajacu, tajassu.** [Tupi *tayaçu·* (Diaz *Dicc. Ling. Tupy* 1858), = tania-eater, f. *taña, taja*, TANIA + *çu* to eat.] The common or collared peccary, *Dicotyles torquatus* (*D. tajacu*).

[**1580** DE LERY *Voy. Brésil* 312 Taiasou, sanglier du pays. **1648** MARCGRAVE *Hist. Nat. Brasil.* VI. vii. 229 Tajaçu Brasiliensibus, porcus est silvestris.] **1698** TYSON in *Phil. Trans.* XX. 137 The Tajacu, or the Mexico Musk Hog. **1774** GOLDSM. *Nat. Hist.* III. 183 That animal which..most resembles an hog,..is called the Peccary, or Tajacu.

**Taych**, variant of TACHE *sb.*[3], sugar-pan.

**Tayel, Tayewe**, obs. ff. TAEL, TAU.

**Tayke**, obs. form of TAKE *v.* and *sb.*

**Tayl(e, tayll(e**, obs. ff. TAEL, TALE, TAIL, TEAL.

**Taylage, tayllage**, obs. ff. TALLAGE *sb.*[1]

**Taylagier**: see TALLAGER.

**Tayler, -or, -ur**, etc., obs. ff. TAILOR.

**Taylorism** (tēi·ləriz'm). [f. the name of N. W. Taylor, of New Haven, Connecticut (1786–1858): see -ISM.] The theological system of N. W. Taylor, a modified form of Calvinism.

**1882–3** *Schaff's Encycl. Relig. Knowl.* III. 2306 It was popularly termed 'The New Haven Theology'. Sometimes it was called 'Taylorism'. **1885** C. A. BRIGGS in *Encycl. Brit.* XIX. 700/1 Puritan theology had developed in New England into Edwardism and then into Hopkinsianism, Emmonsism, and Taylorism.

**Taym(e**, obs. or dial. f. TAME, TIME. **Tayn(e**, obs. var. *tane, ta'en*, pa. pple. of TAKE. **Taynt(e, Taynter**, obs. ff. TAINT, TENT, TENTER.

†**Tayout**, obs. form of TALLY-HO.

**1808** SCOTT in *Strutt's Queenhoo Hall* iv, Gregory..followed, encouraging the hounds with a loud tayout.

‖ **Tayra** (tai·rä). Also **taira.** [Tupi *taira*.] Native name in Brazil of a mammal of the weasel family, *Galera* (or *Galictis*) *barbara*.

**1854** *Zoologist* XII. 4283 The Tayra is another American form, whose marten-like agility renders it always conspicuous. **1896** *List of Animals Zool. Soc.* 85 Galictis barbara (Linn.). Tayra..South America.

†**Tays, teys.** *Obs.* ? Some material or accessory used for vestments.

**1350–1** *Durham Acc. Rolls* (Surtees) 381 In ture, orfrays, teyses, frenges, filo. **1380–81** *Ibid.* 389 In ij peciis de tays empt. pro vestimentis, ij s. **1395–6** *Ibid.* 392 In freyns, tays, carde, et aliis diversis necessariis, xxx s. j. d. **1404** *Ibid.* 395 Item iiij pecie de tayses de cerico pro vestimentis.

**Tayse**, var. TEISE *sb.* and *v. Obs.* **Tayt**, var. TAIT *a. Obs.*, cheerful. **Tayte**, north. dial. f. TOTE *Obs.*, hill. **Taythe, Tayu**, obs. ff. TITHE, TAU. **Taz, Tazel(l, -ill, tazle**, obs. ff. TAWSE, TEASEL.

‖ **Tazza** (ta·ttsa). Pl. **tazze** (ta·ttse). [It. *tazza*: see TASS[2].] A shallow ornamental bowl or vase; properly, one supported on a foot.

**1841** *Civil Eng. & Arch. Jrnl.* IV. 141/1 The symmetrical forms of the many elegant vases and tazzas. **1877** *Times* 17 Feb. (Stanf.), Silver vases and tazze. **1877** MAR. M. GRANT *Sun-maid* viii, Beautiful tazzas of jasper, lapis-lazuli, and malachite.

*attrib.* and *Comb.* **1871** E. J. WORBOISE *Nobly Born* 404, I saw her take up her large tazza-glass, and dispose of its contents. **1878** NESBITT *Catal. Glass Vessels S. Kens. Mus.* 118 Tazza Bowl. Plain glass. **1895** *Daily News* 24 May 6/6 A fine green jade tazza-shaped dish.

**T-bandage, -bar, -beard**, etc.: see T 2, 3.

**Tch-**, occas. used for CH- (tʃ), esp. in foreign words.

**Tcha, tchah** (tʃa, tʃā), *int.* An exclamation of impatience or contempt; = PSHAW.

**1844** DICKENS *Mart. Chuz.* xxxvii, 'Tcha, Mr. Pinch!' cried Charity, with sharp impatience. **1887** FENN *Dick o' Fens* (1888) 22 Tchah! who cares? I don't.

†**Tcheir, tchyre**, obs. Sc. forms of CHAIR.

**1535** LYNDESAY *Satyre* 1941 Heir sall the Carle clim vp and sit in the Kings tchyre. *Ibid.* 1953, I sall sit heir, into this tcheir.

‖ **Tchetvert** (tʃe·tvert). Also **chetvert.** [Russian *tchetvert'* quarter, f. *tchetvero* four.] A Russian measure of capacity, = ·68 of an imperial quarter.

**1855** *Englishwoman in Russia* 184 The landowners in Russia..sent millions of tchetvas of corn out of the country, and left their own people in a state of absolute starvation. **1890** *Daily News* 5 Nov. 5/6 Of rye,..there were yielded 113 million tchetverts, the Russian quarter, as against 112, the average for the last five years.

**Tchibouk**, variant spelling of CHIBOUK.

**Tchick** (tʃik), *sb.* Also **chick, tchek.** A representation of the click made by pressing some part of the tongue against the palate and withdrawing it with suction. Properly, the unilateral palatal click, used to urge on a horse; in quot. 1849, the dental click used to express vexation (in this case also spelt '*ts*, or *tut*). So **Tchick** *v. intr.*, to utter this exclamation, or to make a sound resembling it.

**1823** SCOTT *Quentin D.* xiv, Summing up the whole with a provoking wink and such an interjectional *tchick* as men quicken a dull horse with. **1824** — *Redgauntlet* Let. vii, We heard Benjie gee-hupping, tchek-tcheking, and above all flogging, in great style. **1849** MRS. CARLYLE in *Lett.* (1883) II. 55 The young lady tchick-tchicked, and looked deprecatingly. **1887** *Harper's Mag.* Dec. 32/2 'That that's moughty good string',..Sterling could not refrain from observing, as the stout twine 'tchicked' in several pieces under a garden knife.

‖ **Tchin** (tʃɪn). [Russian ЧИНЪ rank.] Rank; person or persons of quality.

**1885** *Contemp. Rev.* Jan. 105 The name of the father is also the same: the tchin (rank) likewise! **1904** *Daily Chron.* 29 July 4/4 M. Plehve..well knew that the Tsar, the amiable youngster,..was a tool in the hands of the omnipotent tchin.

*Comb.* **1904** *Contemp. Rev.* Aug. 165 The dismal tchin-ridden Russian villages.

‖ **Tchincou** (tʃi·ŋkū). [Javanese.] A black-crested monkey of Java, *Semnopithecus melalophus*.

**1891** in *Cent. Dict.*

**Tchu, tchuh** (tʃʊ), *int.* An exclamation expressing impatience, dissent, or the like.

**1859** GEO. ELIOT *A. Bede* ii, 'Tchu!' said Ben,..'what's folks's kin got to do wi't? Not a chip'. **1861** — *Silas M.* vii, 'Tchuh!', said the farrier. And then he asked,..'How much money might there be in the bags, Master Marner?'

**Tchyre**, obs. Sc. f. CHAIR: see TCHEIR.

**Tck**, *int.* [Palatal click formed by suction.] An exclamation of surprise or vexation: cf. TCHICK.

**1893** KIPLING *Many Invent.* 199 Tck! Tck! And thou art in charge.

**Te**, var. TEE *v.*[1] *Obs.*; obs. f. TO *prep.*

**Te**, ME. assimilated form of THE, THEE, after dentals, etc.: see T 8.

**Te-**, obs. or dial. variant of TO- *pref.*

**Tea** (tī), *sb.* Forms: 7 (9) **tay, tey, 7 té, thé, the**, 7–8 **tee, thea**, 7– **tea.** See also CHA, CHIA. [= F. *thé*, Sp. *te*, It. *tè*, Du. and Ger. *thee*, Da., Sw. *te*, mod.L. *thea*; ad. (perh. through Malay *te, teh*) Chinese, Amoy dialect *t'e*, in Fuchau *tiä* = Mandarin *ch'a* (in ancient Chinese prob. *kia*); whence Pg. and obs. Sp. *cha*, obs. It. *cià*, Russian *chaĭ*, Pers., Urdu چا *chā* (10th c.), Arab. شاي *shāy*, Turkish چاي *chāy*. The Portuguese brought the form *cha* (which is Cantonese as well as Mandarin) from Macao. This form also passed overland into Russia. The form *te* (*thé*) was brought into Europe by the Dutch, prob. from the Malay at Bantam (if not from Formosa, where the Fuhkien or Amoy form was used). The original English pronunciation (tē), sometimes indicated by spelling *tay*, is found in rimes down to 1762, and remains in many dialects; but the current (tī) is found already in the 17th c., shown in rimes and by the spelling *tee*.]

**1.** The leaves of the tea-plant (see 3), usually in a dried and prepared state for making the drink (see 2); first imported into Europe in the 17th century, and now extensively used in various parts of the world.

According to Meyer, *Konversations-Lexikon*, the first mention of it in Europe is due to the Portuguese in 1559 (under the name *cha*); *chia* is mentioned in Maffei's *Historia Indica* in 1588. Under the name *te, thee*, it was imported by the Dutch from Bantam (where brought by Chinese merchants from Amoy) *c* 1610; first known in Paris 1635, in Russia (by way of Tartary) 1638, in England about 1650–55.

[**1598** W. PHILLIP tr. *Linschoten* I. xxvi. 46/1 The aforesaid warme water is made with the powder of a certaine hearbe called Chaa.] **1655** tr. *Semedo's Hist. China* I. iii. 19 *Chà* is a leafe of a tree, about the bignesse of Mirtle; [*marg. note*] its called also Tay. *c* **1660** [T. GARWAY] (*title*) An Exact Description of the Growth, Quality, and Vertues of the Leaf Tee, alias Tay. *c* **1665** *Ibid.*, These are to give notice that the said Thomas Garway hath Tea to sell from sixteen to fifty shillings the pound. **1667** *Lond. Gaz.* No. 206/3 The most considerable Wares being Cinamon, Ebony, Thea, and Camphire. **1667–8** *E. Ind. Co.'s Let.* 24 Jan. (Letter Bks. IV. 137), Wee desire you to procure and send us by these ships 100[lb]. weight of the best Tey that you can gett. **1676** BEAL in *Phil. Trans.* XI. 586 The tops of red Sage in blossom,..dried in the shade,..did excel the famous Thea, the Chinois themselves being Judges. **1680** *Lond. Gaz.* No. 1573/4 A small parcel of most excellent tea..to be sold,..the lowest price is 30s. a pound. **1728** MRS. DELANY in *Life & Corr.* Ser. I. (1861) I. 172 The man at the Poultry has tea of all prices,—Bohea from thirteen to twenty shillings, and green from twelve to thirty. **1832** *Veg. Subst. Food* 375 Tea..first imported into Europe by the Dutch East-India Company, in the..seventeenth century. **1838** T. THOMSON *Chem. Org. Bodies* 858 Tea..is composed of the dried leaves of the *thea bohea* and *thea viridis*.

**b.** With qualifying words, denoting various kinds, chiefly distinguished by the mode of preparation (also applied to the beverages made from these: see 2): the main classes being **black tea**, which is exposed to the air for some time, so as to produce fermentation, before roasting; and **green tea**, which is roasted almost immediately after gathering, and often also artificially coloured.

Black teas include BOHEA, CONGOU, OOLONG, PEKOE, SOUCHONG; green teas, GUNPOWDER (or PEARL), HYSON, etc. See also *brick-tea* (BRICK *sb.*[1] 10), †*cowslip tea* (COWSLIP 3).

**1704** *Lond. Gaz.* No. 4059/4 Green and Bohee Tea. **1712** ADDISON *Spect.* No. 328 Green, Imperial, Peco, and Bohea-Tea. **1785** *Rolliad* 53 What tongue can tell the various kinds of Tea? Of Blacks and Greens, of Hyson and Bohea; With Singlo, Congou, Pekoe and Souchong, Cowslip the fragrant, Gun-powder the Strong. **1795** ANDERSON *Brit. Embassy China* 186 The Imperial and gunpowder teas:..the former..collected from the first, and the other from the successive blossoms of that plant. **1832** *Veg. Subst. Food* 379 There are three kinds of green tea..one called hyson, hayssuen, is composed of leaves..carefully picked. **1888** J. PATON *Tea* in *Encycl. Brit.* XXIII. 97/2 Black and green tea are made indifferently from the leaves of the same plant.

**2.** A drink made by infusing these leaves in hot water, having a somewhat bitter and aromatic flavour, and acting as a moderate stimulant; largely used as a beverage.

[**1601–1625**: see CHIA. **1631** BONTIUS *Hist. Nat. et Med. Indiæ Orient.* I. vi. (1658) 12 *Dur.* Memineras de Chinensium *Thee* vocato Potu, quid tu de eo sentis? *Bont.* Herbula unde hoc The conficitur [etc.].] **1658** *Mercurius Politicus* 23 Sept. 887 *Advt.*, That excellent..drink called by the Chineans Tcha, by other Nations Tay alias Tee. **1660** PEPYS *Diary* 25 Sept., I did send for a cup of tee (a China drink) of which I never had drunk before. **1663** DRYDEN *Wild Gallant* I. ii, I sent for three dishes of tea. **1679** LOCKE in Ld. King *Life* (ed. Bohn) 135 Foreign drinks to be found in England are..coffé, thé and chocolate at coffee houses. **1694** CONGREVE *Double Dealer* I. i, They are at the end of the gallery, retired to their tea and scandal..after dinner. **1711** ADDISON *Spect.* No. 10 ℙ 2 All well-regulated Families, that set apart an Hour in every Morning for Tea and Bread and Butter. **1711** POPE *Rape of Lock* III. 8 Here, thou, great Anna! whom three realms obey, Dost sometimes counsel take—and sometimes Tea. *c* **1720** PRIOR *To Yng. Gentl. in Love* 58 He thank'd her on his bended knee; Then drank a quart of milk and tea. **1762** *Gentl. Mag.* Apr. 187/2 No crowding sycophants from day to day, Came to admire the babe—but more the tea. **1834** Lang in *Tait's Mag.* I. 414/1 In the bush, or uncultivated country in New South Wales, tea is the universal beverage. **1858** Lytton *What will he do* I. vi, Your tea will get quite cold.

**3.** The plant from which tea is obtained, a shrub of the genus *Thea* (now often included in *Camellia*), N.O. *Ternstrœmiaceæ*, with white flowers, and oval pointed slightly toothed evergreen leaves; cultivated from ancient times in China, Japan, India, and adjacent countries. (Now chiefly in comb., as *tea-leaf*, *-plant*, etc.)

The plants yielding the tea of commerce are comprised in the species *T. chinensis* or *C. theifera* (including two varieties *T. Bohea* and *T. viridis*, sometimes reckoned as different species), of China and Japan, and *T.* (or *C.*) *assamica*, of Assam and India; the latter is found wild in Upper Assam, and is by some supposed to be the original type.

**1663** Boyle *Usef. Exp. Nat. Philos.* II. ii. 104 That Herb, which the French and we call *Thé*, or *Té*, which is much magnified here. **1685** J. Chamberlayne *Coffee, Tea & Choc.* 38 The most excellent leaves of Cha, or Tea, are found in the provinces of Kiangnon. **1745** P. Thomas *Jrnl. Anson's Voy.* 193 Because warm Water is unpalatable.., they [the Chinese] bethought themselves of putting some Leaves of a Tree into it, to give it a better Taste. Those of Tea seemed to be the best.

**4.** A meal or social entertainment at which tea is served; *esp.* an ordinary afternoon or evening meal, at which the usual beverage is tea (but sometimes cocoa, chocolate, coffee, or other substitute).

*High tea*, *meat tea*: see High *a.* 21, Meat *sb.* 6. *Tea and turn-out*: see Turn-out.

**1738** Swift *Pol. Conversat.* Introd. 2 Whether they meet.. at Meals, Tea, or Visits. **1778** Miss Burney *Evelina* (1791) I. xxvi. 144, I was relieved by a summons to tea. **1789** Wesley *Wks.* (1872) IV. 453 At breakfast and at tea, on these two days, I met all the Society. **1833** Ht. Martineau *Loom & Lugger* I. iii, She asked Rebecca if she would come to tea at their house. **1882** Fr. A. Kemble *Later Life* II. 187 My first introduction to 'afternoon tea' took place during this visit to Belvoir [in 1842]. I do not believe that the now universally-honoured institution of 'five o'clock tea' dates further back than this. **1897** Miss Harraden *H. Strafford, Remitt. Man* iii, A rattling good tea—hot rolls, fried potatoes, and quail. **1901** Clark Russell *Ship's Adv.* iv, Mrs. Brierly spread a liberal tea upon the table.

**b.** *To take tea with* (colonial slang): to have dealings with, associate with; *esp.* to deal with in a hostile manner, engage with, encounter.

**1888** 'R. Boldrewood' *Robbery under Arms* xxxvii, 'Maybe we'll take tay with the rest of 'em now'. They didn't know the man they were after, or they'd have just as soon have gone to 'take tea', as they called it, with a tiger. **1896** Kipling *Seven Seas, Lost Legion* ii, Take tea with the giddy Masai. **1905** *Daily Chron.* 2 June 3/3 In polite circles genealogies are tabooed, the slightest trace of hybridity barring 'taking tea', as the local phrase has it.

**5.** Used as a general name for infusions made in the same way as tea (sense 2), usually from the leaves, blossoms, or other parts of plants; mostly used medicinally, sometimes as ordinary drinks.

Commonly with defining words, as *alehoof*, *balm*, *beef*, *camomile*, *camphor*, *coffee*, *cowslip*, *hartshorn*, *laurel*, *lemon*, *lemon-grass*, *poppy*, *rosemary*, *sage*, *saloop*, *sassafras*, *senna*, *tilleul*, *valerian*, *willow* (etc.) *tea*: see these words. So humorously *limestone tea* (quot. 1723).

**1665-6** *Phil. Trans.* I. 250 They dry..Sage-leaves..and prepare them like The, and..get for one pound of it, four times as much The. **1699** Evelyn *Acetaria* § 27. 27 Some of them [flowers] are Pickl'd, and divers of them make also very pleasant and wholsome Theas, as do likewise the Wild Time, Bugloss, Mint, &c. **1723** Stukeley *Let.* 22 July, in *Mem.* (Surtees) III. 249, I am just drinking your health in a swinger of limestone thea [Bath water]. **1724** Watts *Logic* I. iv. § 4 Tea, which was the proper name of one sort of Indian leaf, is now-a-days become a common name for many infusions of herbs, or plants, in water: as sage-tea, alehoof-tea, limon-tea, etc. **1727** A. Hamilton *New Acc. E. Ind.* II. l. 222 He treated me with Tartarian Tea, which I took to be Beans boyled in Milk, with some salt. **1731** *Gentl. Mag.* I. 314 Of some of these Ingredients [Marsh Mallow, &c.] so dried, make Tea, as you do common Tea, with boiling hot Water. **1778** R. James *Diss. Fevers* 135 Any syrup, jelly of currants, barley-water, gruel, or any sort of tea. **1783** S. Chapman in *Med. Commun.* I. 305 He was advised to leave off drinking foreign tea, and to drink valerian, or rosemary, tea. **1795** tr. *Thunberg's Trav.* I. 128 Of the leaves of the *barbonia cordata* the country people made tea. **1863** Bates *Nat. Amazon* iv. (1864) 92 The men had made a fire in the galley, to make tea of an acid herb called 'erva cidreira'. **1866** *Treas. Bot.* 1127 *Lemon-grass Tea*, an infusion of the leaves of *Andropogon Schœnanthus*, substituted for tea in many of the interior districts of India. *Ibid.*, *Tea..of heaven*, a Japanese name for the leaves of *Hydrangea Thunbergii*. **1881** *Trans. Obstet. Soc. Lond.* XXII. 32 The word 'tea' is by the natives of this island [Jamaica] applied to any infusion made from leaves of plants either fresh or dry. 'Cotton leaf tea' is made from the green leaves of one of the shrubs that produces the cotton of commerce. **1893** Baring-Gould *Cheap Jack Z.* II. xvi. 41 It is given poppy tea, and that sends it to sleep.

**6.** With defining words, applied to various plants whose leaves, flowers, etc. are used in the same way as tea, either for beverages, or medicinally (also to the leaves, etc. themselves, or the drink infused from them). (See also Tea-plant, Tea-tree.)

**Abyssinian tea** = *Arabian tea*, (*a*). **Algerian tea,** species of *Paronychia*, from whose flowers a medicinal tea is made. **Appalachian tea,** (*a*) *Viburnum cassinoides*; (*b*) *Ilex Cassine*, *I. vomitoria*, or *Prinos glaber*. **Arabian tea,** (*a*) *Catha edulis*, whose leaves furnish a stimulating beverage used in Arabia; (*b*) = *Algerian tea*. **Australian tea,** (*a*) 'several species of *Leptospermum* and *Melaleuca*' (*Treas. Bot.* 1866): see Tea-tree 2; (*b*) = *Botany Bay tea* (Morris *Austral Eng.* 1898). **Barbary tea,** the box-thorn or Duke of Argyll's tea-tree, *Lycium barbarum*. **Bencoolen tea,** *Glaphyria nitida* (*Leptospermum nitidum*), of the Malayan islands. **Blue Mountain** or **Golden Rod tea,** *Solidago odora* of North America, from whose leaves and flowers a beverage is made. **Botany Bay tea,** an Australian species of sarsaparilla, *Smilax glycyphylla*, also called *sweet tea*. **Bourbon tea** = *Faham tea*. **Brazil** or **Brazilian tea,** *Stachytarpha jamaicensis*. **Bush tea,** *Cyclopia genistoides* of S. Africa. **Canada tea** = Tea-berry: see Canada. **Canary tea,** *Sida canariensis* (*S. rhombifolia*). **Carolina tea,** *Ilex vomitoria*: = *Appalachian tea*, (*b*). **†Ceylon tea,** *Elæodendron glaucum*: see Tea-tree 3 (*obs.*). **Faham tea,** a tropical orchid, *Angræcum fragrans*. **†False tea** = *Paraguay tea*. **Hottentot's tea,** *Helichrysum serpyllifolium* (see Hottentot 3). **Jesuits' tea,** (*a*) *Psoralea glandulosa* (see Jesuit *sb.* 4 c); (*b*) = *Paraguay tea* (Cent. Dict.). **Kaffir tea,** *Helichrysum nudifolium* (see Kaffir 4). **Labrador tea,** *Ledum latifolium* and *L. palustre* (see Labrador). **Malay tea,** (*a*) = *Bencoolen tea*; (*b*) *Eugenia variabilis*. **Marsh tea,** *Ledum palustre* (Cent. Dict.). **Mexican tea,** (*a*) *Ambrina* (*Chenopodium*) *ambrosioides*; (*b*) = *Jesuits' tea*, (*a*): see Mexican A. b. **Mountain tea** = Tea-berry: see Mountain 9 d. **New Jersey tea,** *Ceanothus americanus* (see quot. 1858). **New Zealand tea,** *Leptospermum scoparium*: see Tea-tree 2. **Oswego tea,** a N. American aromatic labiate, *Monarda didyma*, used as a tonic and stomachic. **Paraguay tea,** *Ilex paraguayensis*, extensively used in S. America as a substitute for tea: see Paraguay 1. **St. Bartholomew's tea** = *Paraguay tea* (Cent. Dict.). **St. Helena tea,** *Beatsonia* (*Frankenia*) *portulacifolia*. **Soldiers' tea** = Matico. **South Sea tea** = *Paraguay tea*; also an erroneous name for Carolina tea. **Surinam tea,** 'various species of *Lantana*' (Miller *Plant-n.*). **Sweet tea** = *Botany Bay tea*. **Teamster's tea,** a N. American plant, *Ephedra antisyphilitica*, used as a remedy for venereal affections. **Theezan tea,** *Sageretia theezans*, a thorny rhamnaceous shrub of S. China, whose leaves are said to be used for tea by the poorer classes. **West Indian tea,** *Capraria biflora*, also called *goat-weed*. **Wild tea,** a N. American leguminous shrub, *Amorpha canescens*, also called *lead-plant*.

**1727-41** Chambers *Cycl.*, South-Sea tea [see Paraguay 1]. **1760** J. Lee *Introd. Bot.* App. 321 Osweego Thea, *Monarda* [*didyma*]. *Ibid.* 329 False Tea, *Ilex*. *Ibid.*, New Jersey Tea, *Ceanothus*. *Ibid.*, Paraguay Tea, *Ilex*. *Ibid.*, South-sea Tea, *Ilex*. **1764** *Museum Rust.* II. xxxviii. 117 The South-Sea tea, which is thought to be the same plant as the Paraguay tea; but whether it is the same as the tea brought from China, is yet undetermined. **1788** D. Considen *Let. to Banks* in *Hist. Rec. N. S. Wales* (1892) I. II. 220, I have sent you some of the sweet tea of this country, ..it is a good anti-scorbutic. **1790** J. White *Voy. N. S. Wales* 195 The sweet-tea is a creeping kind of vine.. the taste is sweet, exactly like the liquorice root of the shops. **1814** Roxburgh *Hort. Bengal.* 18 *Elæodendrum glaucum*, Ceylon Tea. **1857** Henfrey *Elem. Bot.* § 508. 336 [The leaves] of *Ilex Paraguayensis*, called Maté or Paraguay Tea, resemble Tea in property. **1858** Hogg *Veg. Kingd.* lxvi. 237 The leaves of *Ceanothus americanus* were used during the revolutionary war as a substitute for tea, and hence it is called New Jersey Tea. *Ibid.* cxv. 482 The leaves [of *Gaultheria procumbens*]..make an excellent substitute for tea...and the plant is..called Tea-berry and Mountain Tea. *Ibid.* cxix. 489 *Ilex vomitoria* has been erroneously called South Sea Tea, from the supposition that it was the same plant as *I. paraguensis*. **1866** *Treas. Bot.* 49 *Ambrina ambrosioides*, or Mexican Tea,..long naturalised in the south of Europe, is used medicinally. *Ibid.* 369 The leaflets of [*Cyclopia genistoides*] are used at the Cape in infusion or decoction for promoting expectoration... It is called Bush Tea. [*Ibid.* 1005 *S*[*ageretia*] *theezans*, the Tia of the Chinese, is a thorny shrub, with..finely-toothed egg-shaped leaves..somewhat resembling those of the tea-shrub.] *Ibid.* 1090 [The] leaves [of *Stachytarpha jamaicensis*] are sometimes used to adulterate tea, and in Austria they are sold under the name of Brazilian tea. *Ibid.* 1127 Tea, Abyssinian, .. Appalachian [etc.], .. Arabian, .. Australian [etc.]. **1904** *Dunglison's Dict. Med.* (ed. 23), *Matico*... the leaves of Piper angustifolium or soldiers' tea or herb.

**7.** *slang.* **a.** Spirituous or intoxicating liquor. **†b.** Urine (*obs.*).

**1693** *Remonstr. Batchelors* in *Harl. Misc.* (ed. Park) IV. 505 Since their sex has been so familiar with brandy (blasphemed by the name of cold tea). **1716** Gay *Trivia* II. 176 The thoughtless Wits.. Who 'gainst the Centry's Box discharge their Tea. **1887** Hissey *Holiday on Road* 370 Tea or coffee were always at our command, Scotch tea also (i. e. whisky). **1902** *Times* 29 Oct. 5/6 It was all owing to the 'tea'. ..He understood that this was a slang term for drink.

**8.** Florists' abbreviation of Tea-rose.

**1889** *Pall Mall G.* 6 July 3/2 At Cheshunt about 200,000 standard rose seedlings and 40,000 'teas' are sown every year. **1901** *Eliza. & German Gard.* 17, I wish now I had put teas there. 18, I made my teas face a northern winter.

**9.** *attrib.* and *Comb.* **a.** *attrib.* Of, pertaining or relating to, dealing or connected with tea as a commodity, as *tea act*, *bill*, *-broker*, *-dealer*, *-duty*, *-hong* (see Hong), *industry*, *merchant*, *-shop*, *-tax*, *trade*, *warehouse*; or as a beverage, as *tea-breakfast*, *-dinner*, *-dregs*, *junketing*, *picnic*, *soirée*, *-supper*, *-visit*; containing or intended to contain tea, as *tea-bowl*, *-hamper*, *-jar*, *-pail*; of or pertaining to the tea-plant or its cultivation, as *tea crop*, *cultivation*, *culture*, *district*, *estate*, *-farming*, *-field*, *-hill*, *nursery*, *plantation*, *-seed*, *-tract*. **b.** Objective and obj. gen., as *tea-blender*, *-grower*, *-packer*, *-producer*, *-sipper*, *-spiller*; *tea-blending*, *-growing*, *-loving*, *-packing*, *-picking* sbs. and adjs.; instrumental and parasynthetic, as *tea-coloured*, *-covered*, *-inspired*, *-sodden* adjs.

**1746** Lockman *To 1st Promoter Cambrick & Tea Bills* 13 *note*, Since the *Tea-Act pass'd last session, the revenue is increased 85,000*l.* per annum. **1904** *Westm. Gaz.* 15 Aug. 6/2 The big *tea-blenders naturally took advantage of this cheapness to push and extend their business. **1901** *Daily Chron.* 6 May 9/3 Man wanted for *tea blending warehouse. **1865** G. Meredith *Rhoda Fleming* xxxii, The squire.. drank, defying ladies and the new-fangled subserviency to those flustering *tea-bodies. **1886** *Guide Galleries Brit. Mus.* 209 On the upper shelves are examples of..*tea-bowls. **1825** Hone *Every-day Bk.* I. 951, I..got up to a hot *tea-breakfast. **1770** *Chron.* in *Ann. Reg.* 154/2 A *tea-broker, charged with forging a warrant for the delivery of three chests of tea. **1902** *Westm. Gaz.* 31 Dec. 9/3 The *Tea Clearing House has succumbed to the attack of tea producers, importers, dealers, and brokers. **1829** W. H. Maxwell *Stories Waterloo* I. 194 Short tights of *tea-coloured leather. **1897** J. A. Graham *Threshold Three Closed Lands* ii. 30 As our eye follows up one of the *tea-covered spurs it lights on the houses of Darjeeling. **1906** *Month* Feb. 177 Sides green with sprouting *tea crops. **1842** *Penny Cycl.* XXIV. 286/2 Papers respecting *tea cultivation in India. *Ibid.* 286/1 The *tea-culture in Assam. **1758** *Chron.* in *Ann. Reg.* I. 111/1 Four *tea dealers were tried before the commissioners of excise. **1886** C. E. Pascoe *London of To-day* xxii. (ed. 3) 216 The premises of one of the oldest firms in London—those of the Messrs. Twining, tea-dealers and bankers. **1862** R. C. Mayne *Brit. Columbia* 121 We lunched with him, returning to the fort for a *tea-dinner. **1896** *Allbutt's Syst. Med.* I. 402 That customary but very unwholesome combination the tea-dinner is to be avoided. **1842** *Penny Cycl.* XXIV. 286/1 There are green tea and black *tea districts. *Ibid.* 291/1 The tariff of 1842 has made no alteration in the *tea-duty. **1886** *Pall Mall G.* 19 May 6/1 The new industry of *tea-farming..promises to become a new source of wealth to Ceylon. **1895** Clive Holland *Jap. Wife* 110 The cemeteries and *tea-fields stretched below us. **1888** J. Paton in *Encycl. Brit.* XXIII. 98/1 Comparatively few regions are suited for practical *tea-growing. *Ibid.* 99/1 The capacities of Assam as a tea-growing country. **1854** *Zoologist* XII. 4206 The *tea-hills in the province of Chekiang. **1885** *Cornh. Mag.* Mar. 281 [The tea-leaves are] fired under their own supervision in the great *tea-hongs. **1888** J. Paton in *Encycl. Brit.* XXIII. 102/1 Next to the United Kingdom, the greatest *tea-importing nation is the United States. *Ibid.* 99/1 The *tea industry has developed in Ceylon with marvellous rapidity. **1891** B. E. Martin *Footpr. Chas. Lamb* iii. 65 Hazlitt, with..his *tea-inspired turgidity. **1820** W. Irving *Sketch Bk.* xxvi. (1859) 189 Little humdrum *tea junketings. **1883** *Cassell's Fam. Mag.* Aug. 529/1 The *tea-loving English public. **1888** J. Paton in *Encycl. Brit.* XXIII. 99/1 It is these tender shoots.. which alone are gathered for *tea manufacture. **1842** *Penny Cycl.* XXIV. 291/2 The number of *tea merchants who resort to Canton. *Ibid.* 286/2 When the *tea nurseries were established in Assam. **1904** *Daily News* 13 Oct. 12 The dispute between the *tea-packers and the management of the Co-operative Wholesale Society. **1898** *Daily Chron.* 24 Sept. 10/6 Boy wanted..in *tea-packing warehouse. **1906** *Macm. Mag.* Apr. 457 Their .. method is to stalk the Chinese of either sex when they are engaged in *tea-picking. **1842** *Penny Cycl.* XXIV. 286/2 The *tea plantations established in the Kumaon and Gurhwal districts. **1894** *Westm. Gaz.* 5 Jan. 6/3 The British have become..the greatest *tea-producers..in the world. **1888** J. Paton in *Encycl. Brit.* XXIII. 98/2 Till well into the 19th century .. China and Japan were the only two *tea-producing countries. **1786** M. Cutler in *Life*, etc. (1888) I. 190, I have no doubt the *tea seed..may be obtained from the East Indies in a vegetative state. *a* **1745** Swift (J.), The mistress of the *tea shop. **1860** J. R. Edkins *Chinese Scenes* (1863) 153, I shall try to give you a little picture of the tea-shop. **1756** Hanway *Ess. Tea* viii. 245 Were they the sons of *tea-sippers, who won the fields of Cressy and Agincourt? **1849** Thackeray *Pendennis* xliv, A brilliant **tea soirée*. **1877** G. W. Balfour in *Encycl. Brit.* VII. 482/1 *Tea-sots are well known to be affected with palpitation and irregularity of the heart. **1837** W. Phillips in C. Martyn *Life* (1890) 96 Certainly we sons of the *tea-spillers are a marvellously patient generation! [Cf. Tea-party 2 a.] **1892** Zangwill *Childr. Ghetto* I. 198 The story-book which Moses read out after *tea-supper. **1888** J. Paton in *Encycl. Brit.* XXIII. 101/1 Dependent on China for its *tea supply. **1907** *Edin. Rev.* July 97 The *tea-tax strikes tea-drinkers only. **1842** *Penny Cycl.* XXIV. 286/2 At first only a few [indigenous] *tea-tracts were discovered [in Assam]. **1756** Hanway *Ess. Tea* xii. 258 The *tea trade employs six hundred seamen..together with six ships, which we annually send to Canton. **1888** J. Paton in *Encycl. Brit.* XXIII. 102/2 The only other considerable *tea-using nation is Russia. **1765** J. Brown *Chr. Jrnl.* (1814) 331 Yonder professors come from a *tea-visit. **1807-8** W. Irving *Salmag.* i. (1824) 7 When ladies paid tea-visits at three in the afternoon. **1888** *Pall Mall G.* 9 May 10/1 Certain *tea warehousemen of the City of London.

**c.** Special Combs.: **tea-basket,** a basket containing the requisites for afternoon tea in a railway train or the like; **tea-bell,** a bell rung to summon a household or company to tea; **tea-billy** (Billy[2] 1 c), a tin can used by Australian bushmen as a tea-kettle or tea-pot; **tea-boiler,** a vessel used for boiling tea; **tea-box,** a box for containing tea; in quot. = Tea-chest 2; **tea-boy,** a man-servant (Ireland); **tea-bread,** a kind of light bread eaten at tea; **tea-broom,** New Zealand name for *Leptospermum scoparium* and *L. ericoides* (= Manuka a, b, Tea-tree 2); **tea-bug,** a destructive insect which infests tea-plants; **tea-bush** = *tea-shrub*; **tea-caddy,** a small box with divisions for holding tea (= Caddy[1] 1); **tea-cake,** a light kind of flat cake to be eaten at tea; in quot. 1892 *attrib.* resembling a tea-cake; **tea-canister** = *tea-caddy*; also, *slang* for 'brandy-flask' (cf. 7 a); **tea-case,** a case for holding a set of small articles, as spoons, etc. used at tea (*Cent. Dict.*); **tea-china,** china tea-cups and saucers, etc.; **tea-circle,** a group or society of persons who meet and take tea together; **tea-clam**, a name in U.S. for a very small clam (CLAM *sb.*[2] 1 d: see quot.); **tea-clipper**, a clipper or fast-sailing vessel formerly employed in the tea trade; **tea-cloth**, a cloth used for wiping tea-things after washing them; (*b*) *afternoon t.*, a small table-cloth used at afternoon tea; **tea-coat**, a garment worn by women at the tea-table (cf. COAT *sb.* 2 b, and *tea-jacket*); † **tea-conversation** (see CONVERSATION 9, quot. 1787); **tea-cooper**, a workman at a dock who unloads tea and does any necessary repairs to the packing, etc.: cf. COOPER *sb.*[1] 1; **tea-cosy**, a covering for a tea-pot to keep it hot (see COSY B. 2); † **tea-dish**, old name for a tea-cup (cf. DISH *sb.* 1 b); **tea-drunkard**, one who habitually drinks tea to such excess as to suffer from its toxic effects; † **tea-equipage** = *tea-service, tea-things*; † **tea-faced** *a.*, ? having a sallow or effeminate countenance like one addicted to tea-drinking; **tea-fight**, *colloq.* or *slang*, humorous name for a tea-party or tea-meeting; **tea-frock**, **tea-gown**, names for special fashions of garments worn by girls and women at tea; † **tea-grouter** (see quot.); **tea-hour**, the hour at which tea is taken, or the time occupied by it; **tea-house**, a refreshment-house where tea is served (esp. in China or Japan); **tea-jacket**, a garment worn by women at tea (cf. *tea-coat*); **tea-lead**, an alloy used for lining tea-chests (see quot.); **tea-maker**, (*a*) a person who dries the leaves and prepares the tea of commerce; (*b*) one who makes or infuses tea; (*c*) a vessel or apparatus for infusing tea; so **tea-making** *sb.* and *a.*; **tea-meeting**, a public social meeting (usually in connexion with a religious organization) at which tea is taken; **tea-night**, an evening on which guests are entertained at tea; **tea oil**, (*a*) an oil resembling olive-oil, obtained from the seeds of species of *Camellia* (allied to the tea-plant), and used for various purposes in China and Japan; (*b*) a narcotic essential oil obtained from tea-leaves; **tea-punch**, punch containing tea as an ingredient; **tea-roller**, a machine for rolling or curling tea-leaves for the market; so **tea-rolling**; **tea-room**, a room in which tea is served in a refreshment-house, etc.; notably, that of the British House of Commons, the scene of numerous informal meetings of members; **tea-root**, the root of a tea-plant; **tea-sage**, a species or variety of sage used for making sage-tea; † **tea-saucer**, a saucer for supporting a tea-cup; **tea-scent**, 'a European fern, *Nephrodium montanum*' (*Cent. Dict.*); **tea-scented** *a.*, having a scent like that of tea: applied to a variety of rose (see TEA-ROSE); **tea-scrub**, a scrub or thicket of 'tea-trees' (in Australia, etc.): see TEA-TREE; **tea-service**, **tea-set**, a set of articles used in serving tea at table; a set of tea-things; † **tea-shine**, *colloq.* a tea-party (cf. *tea-fight*); **tea-ship**, (*a*) a ship engaged in the tea-trade; (*b*) a tea-stand with two or more shelves or 'decks'; **tea-shrub**, the common tea-plant (see 3); **tea-sifter**, (*a*) a person engaged in sifting tea; (*b*) an apparatus for sifting tea; **tea-stall**, **tea-stand**, a stand on which cups, saucers, plates, etc. are placed for use at tea; **tea-stick**, a stick cut from the Australian tea-tree; **tea-stone**: see quots.; **tea-things** *sb. pl.*, the articles used for serving tea at table, as tea-pot, milk-jug, sugar-basin, cups, saucers, plates, etc., together forming a *tea-set* or *tea-service*; **tea-time**, the time at which the meal called tea is taken (see sense 4); † **tea-tongs**, a former name for sugar-tongs; **tea-urn**, an urn with a tap, placed upon a tea-table, to hold hot water for making tea; **tea-ware**, vessels, etc. for serving tea, tea-things; **tea-water**, (*a*) water for making tea; (*b*) *Sc.* the beverage tea (= sense 2); **tea-wine**, a fermented liquor made from tea (see quot.). See also TEA-BERRY, -BOARD, -CHEST, etc.

**1901** *Wide World Mag.* VIII. 135/1 There is a lump of sugar in the *tea-basket. **1867** AUG. J. E. WILSON *Vashti* i, The sound of the *tea-bell terminated her reverie, and she walked to the dining-room. **1894** H. NISBET *Bush Girl's Rom.* 133 A number of *tea-billies were ranged on the clay hobs, some with tea already brewed, and some with water only. **1825** J. NICHOLSON *Operat. Mechanic* 632 The lead which lines the Chinese *tea-boxes is reduced to a thinness which our plumbers cannot, it is said, approach. **1848** THACKERAY *Van. Fair* xxvii, Major O'Dowd..was..as obedient to his wife as if he had been her *tay-boy. **1831** JANE PORTER *Sir E. Seaward's Narr.* I. 22 Some johnny cakes, a West Indian sort of *tea-bread. **1872** A. DOMETT *Ranolf* Notes 505 Mánuka...The settlers often call it '*tea-broom'. **1893** *Athenæum* 16 Dec. 853/3 Mr. Waterhouse..exhibited male and female specimens of a Helopeltis (the *tea-bug),..and stated that it had occurred only in Assam. **1908** *Dollar Mag.* Mar. 32 The *tea bushes were miserably poor just there. **1837** HOWITT *Rur. Life* VI. ix. (1862) 500 *Tea-caddies, workboxes of rosewood and pearl. **1866** R. M. BALLANTYNE *Shift. Winds* xvii, [She] went to a cupboard..and took therefrom a tea-caddy, which she set on the table. **1892** *Daily News* 31 Dec. 2/1 The bonnet of the moment is set well back on the head, forming a sort of garland above the '*teacake' coiffure. **1897** R. HICHENS *Londoners* ix. 156 Mr. Bush..was closely engaged with a tea-cake. **1800** HELENA WELLS *Constantia Neville* (ed. 2) III. 121 The *tea-cannister contained only Congou of no very superior quality. **1859** F. FRANCIS *Newton Dogvane* (1888) 184 Pass us the tea-canister. **1830** MISS MITFORD *Village* Ser. IV. 332 The dresser was..adorned with the remains of a long preserved set of *tea-china, of a light rambling pattern. **1831** CARLYLE *Sart. Res.* III. ix, Thou..perhaps in many a literary *Tea-circle wilt open thy kind lips. **1883** G. B. GOODE *Fish. Indust. U. S. A.* 47 Some are taken so small that 2,000 are required to fill a barrel; these, when about one inch in diameter, are called '*tea-clams'. **1895** *Mem. Jas. Anderson* ii. 8 Mr. and Mrs. Anderson set sail from London in a *tea-clipper. **1888** *Cassell's Encycl. Dict.*, **Tea-cloth*, a cloth used in washing up tea-things. **1891** *Cent. Dict.*, *Tea-cloth*, a cloth for a tea-table or a tea-tray. **1899** *Westm. Gaz.* 12 Aug. 2/1 She came into the room..in a black-and-blue sort of *tea-coat. **1887** *Pall Mall G.* 19 Sept. 2 Years ago the *tea-coopers, who are skilled workmen, had a union. **1871** 'M. LEGRAND' *Camb. Freshm.* 18 The elaborate worsted-work teapot cover—technically termed, I believe, a *tea-cosey. **1886** [see COSY B. 2]. **1711** EUSDEN *Spect.* No. 87 ℙ 8, I saw a gentleman turn as pale as ashes, because an idol turned the sugar in a *tea-dish for his rival. **1716** LADY M. W. MONTAGU *Lett.* 10 Oct. (1887) I. 129 They showed me..a cup, about the size of a tea-dish, of one entire emerald. **1709** MRS. MANLEY *Secret Mem.* (1720) II. 290 He cleans his *Tea-Equipage with his own Hands. **1833** T. HOOK *Parson's Dau.* I. ii, The tea equipage was on the table. **1728** RAMSAY *Archers diverting themselves* 26 When av'rice, luxury, and ease, A *tea-fac'd generation please. **1849** ALB. SMITH *Pottleton Leg.* xxxv, Their various small parties—'*tea-fights' as young Grant called them. **1901** *Scotsman* 5 Mar. 7/5 The good people..organise a splendid weekly tea-fight and concert for our behoof. **1903** *Westm. Gaz.* 27 Aug. 4/1 The *tea-frock—the form of the tea-gown nice for the younger folks. **1878** *The World* in *Royal Exchange* 9 Nov., Ladies, who a few years ago would have considered the idea appalling, calmly array themselves in the glorified dressing robe known as a '*tea gown'. **1891** *Woman* 15 Jan. 4/1 The factor which has revolutionised the novelistic attire of to-day is the evolution of the tea-gown. *a* **1833** J. T. SMITH *Bk. for Rainy Day* (1905) 76 A prognostication announced to my dear mother by an old star-gazer and *tea-grouter. *Note.* A fortune-teller by tea-leaves, the leaves being 'grouted', or turned over in the cup. **1884** G. ALLEN *Philistia* I. 109 Monopolised the..visitor himself for almost the entire *tea-hour. **1689** *Lond. Gaz.* No. 2481/4 Catalogues are given at..Mr. Mainwaring's *Tea-house. **1909** *Daily Chron.* 7 June 4/6 This revolution..practically commenced when in 1657 Garraway opened his famous tea-house in Exchange-alley. **1896** *Daily News* 5 Dec. 6/4 The increasing neatness of the tea-gown is perhaps partly owing to the smartness of cut of its rival, the *tea jacket. **1815** J. SMITH *Panorama Sc. & Art* I. 52 The metal with which tea-chests are lined, familiarly called *tea-lead, is an alloy principally composed of lead and tin. **1842** *Penny Cycl.* XXIV. 286/1 The process..as practised in Assam and Java by the Chinese *tea-makers. **1868** HOLME LEE *B. Godfrey* ii, The parson asked the tea-maker for another cup. **1900** *Daily News* 18 Sept. 6/3 It is put into a perforated receiver, suspended in the 'tea-maker', and boiling water poured over it. **1826** (*title*) Tsiology; a discourse on Tea. Being an account of that exotic,..*Tea-making... By a Tea Dealer. **1833** T. HOOK *Parson's Dau.* I. xii, The operation, which, at Cambridge, is not called by so gentle a term as tea-making. **1888** *Encycl. Brit.* XXIII. 100/1 In Chinese tea-making that juice is squeezed out of the leaves. **1894** MRS. DYAN *All in a Man's K.* (1899) 207 Without a falter she performed the dainty little service of tea-making. **1897** *St. James's Gaz.* 18 Feb. 11/1 The posting of bills for soirees and *tea-meetings. **1824** SCOTT *St. Ronan's* xxxiv, To secure the necessary degree of crowd upon her *tea-nights, Lady Penelope was obliged to employ some coaxing. **1837** R. D. THOMSON in *Brit. Ann.* 358 *Tea oil. **1838** T. THOMSON *Chem. Org. Bodies* 439 Tea oil is expressed from the seeds of the Camellia oleifera. **1728** CHAMBERS *Cycl.* s. v. *Punch*, Punch Royal. Milk-Punch. *Tea-Punch. **1890** *Pall Mall G.* 1 Oct. 2/3 The *tea-rolling machine represented in our view..is the first *tea-roller which has been used on English soil. **1796** MME. D'ARBLAY *Camilla* I. 167 They were proceeding to the *tea-room. **1884** *Pall Mall G.* 26 Sept. 2/2 Even a tea-room compromise [between political parties] would be welcome at the present moment. **1690** EVELYN *Diary* 11 Mar., I much admired the contortions of the *Thea root, which was so perplexed, large, and intricate. **1727–41** CHAMBERS *Cycl.* s. v. *Sage*, Kinds..used and cultivated by us are the *Tea-Sage, or Sage of Virtue [etc.]. **1761** DUNN in *Phil. Trans.* LII. 185 An artificial horizon of sweet oil in a *tea-saucer. **1845** *Florist's Jrnl.* 207 Coupe de Hebe (*tea-scented). **1849** *Florist* 318 Tea-scented Roses cannot be cultivated with success as border Roses, unless in the extreme south and west of England. **1852** MUNDY *Our Antipodes* (1857) 13 Shady paths,..winding among the '*tea-scrub', or skirting the rocky shores [at Sydney]. **1858** SIMMONDS *Dict. Trade*, *Tea-service, Tea-things. **1869** TROLLOPE *He knew he was right* i, He gave silver cups when the girls were born, and now bestows tea-services as they get married. **1849** LYTTON *Caxtons* I. iv, I would rather the best *tea-set were broken. **1838** MRS. CARLYLE *Lett.* (1883) I. 98 Two *tea-shines went off with *éclat*. **1876** BANCROFT *Hist. U. S.* IV. l. 273 The Boston *tea-ships had sailed. **1905** *Westm. Gaz.* 11 Nov. 3/1 The servant went out, and, returning with a three-decker tea-ship, asked whether anything else was required. **1704** PETIVER *Gazophyl.* III. xxi, The 'Thea Shrub is here Figured. **1798** *Monthly Mag.* July 30/1 The Arabs, to whom we stand indebted for the first accounts of the tea-shrub. **1871** *Windsor & Eton Express* 4 Nov., Two silver *tea-sifters having the Royal crest engraved upon them. **1902** *Westm. Gaz.* 31 Jan. 2/1 The wheeled *tea-stall which appears at about four o'clock in all large stations. **1697** in *14th Rep. Hist. MSS. Comm.* App. II. (1894) 592 Your Lord who broke the *tea-stand. **1865** H. KINGSLEY *Hillyars & Burtons* lxii, You should have a *tea-stick, and take them [dogs] by the tail,..and lay on like old gooseberry. **1848** S. W. WILLIAMS *Middle Kingd.* xiii. II. 116 Spectacles are cut..from..a variety of rose quartz resembling the cairngorm stone, which the Chinese call *cha-tsing*, or *tea-stone, from its color. **1860** J. SCARTH *Twelve Yrs. China* 5 Shaded ..by a huge pair of tea-stone spectacles. **1747** H. WALPOLE *Lett.* (1846) II. 192 You will think I have removed my philosophy from Windsor with my *tea-things hither. **1869** TROLLOPE *He knew he was Right* xxxi, Dorothy was seated behind the urn and tea-things at a large table. **1756** *Pol. Ballads* (1860) II. 332 And now being *tea-time..we put on the kettle. **1782** MISS BURNEY *Cecilia* VI. iii, Sometimes he appeared again at tea-time. **1889** 'J. S. WINTER' *Mrs. Bob* (1891) 46, I shall be back before tea-time. **1738** SWIFT *Pol. Conversat.* iii. 200 Lady Smart mistakes the *Tea-tongs for the Spoon. **1797** *Nicholson's Jrnl. Nat. Philos.* I. 63 Bended up in the figure of a pair of tea-tongs. **1786** COWPER *Let. to Lady Hesketh* 24 Dec., You may purchase..a *tea-urn. **1808** T. MACGILL *Trav.* I. xviii. 231 The Russian tea-urns..are made of brass..in place of an iron heater, they have long tubes, into which live charcoal is put. **1825** J. NICHOLSON *Operat. Mechanic* 483 The insides of *tea-ware are well washed with a liquid which forms, when fired, a thin coating of glass. **1693** SOUTHERNE *Maid's last Prayer* III. iii, Betty, set on the *Tea-water. **1818** SCOTT *Hrt. Midl.* xxvi, Breakfast wi' us yoursell—ye ken how to manage thae porringers of tea-water. **1892** WALSH *Tea* (Philad.) 203 A pleasing drink is also prepared by treating the ordinary infusion with a little yeast and sugar, a *tea-wine being produced from it.

Hence (*nonce-wds.*) **Tea·ey** *a.*, having the characteristic properties of tea; **Tea·ish** *a.*, resembling or relating to tea; **Tea·ism**, addiction to tea.

**1890** *Spectator* 3 May, We believe Indian tea has conquered because it is the most *tea-ey of teas. **1836** *Tait's Mag.* III. 572 The *teaish propensities of her inamorato. **1904** E. NESBIT *Phœnix & Carpet* vii. 134 The meal..was not exactly tea. Let us call it a tea-ish meal. **1904** G. S. HALL *Adolescence* ix. II. 14 Excessive teaism, coffeeism, etc.,..to the prejudice of appetite for plain, wholesome nutritives,..jeopard the highest maturation of powers.

**Tea**, *v. colloq.* [f. prec. sb.]

**1.** *trans.* To supply or regale with tea; to entertain at tea; to give a tea to.

**1812** SIR R. WILSON *Diary* (1861) I. 250 General Tormanssow fed us, and the duke tea'd; so the day passed well. **1844** J. T. HEWLETT *Parsons & W.* xxxvi, I breakfast, tea, and sup my lodgers. **1888** FREEMAN in Stephens *Life & Lett.* (1895) II. 386 We *tea* the local body on Wednesday.

**2.** *intr.* To drink tea; *esp.* to take the meal called tea, to have one's tea.

**1823** in *Spirit Pub. Jrnls.* 551 'Twas moved to proceed To the hall of debate, where my Lady had 'tea'd!' **1863–5** J. THOMSON *Sunday at Hampstead* IV. i, Eight of us promised to meet here And tea together at five. **1892** FURNIVALL *Hoccleve's Minor P.* Introd. 47 We dined on the bank opposite Hampton Court and teaed on Tatham's island.

Hence **Tea·ing** *vbl. sb.* and *ppl. a.*; also **Tea·er**, one who takes tea, or attends a tea-meeting.

**1852** R. S. SURTEES *Sponge's Sp. Tour* xx. (1893) 94 Staying guests have the advantage over mere dining or teaing ones, inasmuch as they cannot well be talked over..as those who go away are. **1874** ALDRICH *Prud. Palfrey* xi, Picnics up the river..and innumerable teaings on shore. **1892** *Sat. Rev.* 30 July 141/2 But 270 Congregational teaers would surely require more than eight quarts of milk?

**Tea-act, -basket**, etc.: see TEA *sb.* 9.

**Tea·-be:rry.** The American wintergreen, *Gaultheria procumbens*: see quot.; also called *Canada tea* or *mountain tea*. Also, the fruit of this.

**1858** HOGG *Veg. Kingd.* cxv. 482 The leaves [of *Gaultheria procumbens*]..when..dried..make an excellent substitute for tea,..and the plant is on that account called Tea-berry and Mountain Tea. **1884** *Cassell's Fam. Mag.* Mar. 239/1 Here [in Houston, Texas]..the tea-berry tree, and huge orange trees..made me forget for a moment that I was expecting something very different. **1895** *Outing* (U.S.) XXVII. 18/1 Tiny white capillaire tea-berries, with a flavor like some rare perfume.

**Tea·-board.** Now *local.* A tea-tray, esp. a wooden one.

**1748** SMOLLETT *Rod. Rand.* lvii. (1760) II. 202 The coming of a servant with the tea-board prevented my presumption. **1771** MRS. HAYWOOD *New Present* 256 Tea-boards are cleaned by rubbing them well with an oily flannel. **1780** *Newgate Cal.* V. 270 They doubled a silver tea-board together..and carried it away. **1868** HOLME LEE *B. Godfrey* vi, The teaboard at the top of the table.

Hence **Tea·boardy** *a. nonce-wd.*, like a tea-board.

**1890** *Athenæum* 1 Mar. 283/1 The hardness, smoothness, and laboured polish of the surface, almost fit to be called 'teaboardy'.

**Tea-boiler** to **-case**: see TEA *sb.* 9.

**Teach** (*tītʃ*), *v.* Pa. t. and pa. pple. **taught** (*tǭt*). Forms: see below. [OE. *tǽcan, tǽcean*, pa. t. *tǽhte*, pa. pple. *(*ge*)*tǽht* :—OTeut. **taikjan*, cognate with OE. *tácn*, Goth. *taikns*, OS. *têkan*, OHG. *zeihhan*, TOKEN, from an ablaut series *teik-, taik-, tik-* to show, pre-Teut. *dig-, deig-*, also *deik-*, in Skr. *diç-*, Gr. δεικ-νύναι, δεῖγμα. Not found elsewhere in Teutonic; Ger. *zeigen*, OHG. *zeigôn* to show, has the same root. The vowel of the OE. pa. t. and pple. *tǽht(e* was apparently shortened before the two consonants, giving the Early ME. *tahte, taȝte*, whence the later *taught*, which appears already *c* 1300 dialectally as *taut(e*. But in the pa. t. a form with the long vowel survived to *c* 1300 as *tǽhte, têhte, teihte, taihte, teite, taite*. A normalized form *teached* (cf. *reached*) has been in partial use since the 14th c., but is not now accepted in educated speech.]

A. Illustration of Forms.

1. *Infin.* 1 **tǽc(e)an, 2–3 tachen, 3 teachen, (*Orm.*) tæchenn, 3–4 tache, (theche), 3–5 techen, 3–6 teche, 4–6 tech, teiche (4–5 teyche, 5 techyn, 6 teich, teache, teatch), 6– teach.**

*c* **888** K. ÆLFRED *Boeth.* xxxviii. § 3 Ic þe mæg ʒiet tæcan oðer þing. **971** *Blickl. Hom.* 109 Him tæcean lifes weȝ. *c* **1200** ORMIN 3468 To tæchenn hemm. *c* **1200** *Trin. Coll. Hom.* 17 Ic wile..tachen hit ew. *c* **1205** LAY. 2419 He..sculde..tuhlen him teachen. *c* **1325** *Spec. Gy Warw.* 141 Tweie þinges it wole þe teche. *c* **1330** R. BRUNNE *Chron.* (1810) 115 Of þe bisshop Thurston haf I comandment, þe clerkes forto tech. *c* **1375** *Cursor M.* 18710 (Fairf.) Þe traub to teiche [*other MSS.* teche]. *Ibid.* 27391 Þen agh þe leche Calde medicine þar to teyche. *c* **1375** Theching [see TEACHING *vbl. sb.* 2]. **1535** COVERDALE 2 *Sam.* i. 18 To teach the children of Iuda the bow. **1536** WRIOTHESLEY *Chron.* (Camden) I. 55 The curates should..teatch their parishiones the 'Pater noster'. **1538** STARKEY *England* I. iv. 132 Schold prech..and tech the pepul. **1596** DALRYMPLE tr. *Leslie's Hist. Scot.* I. (S. T. S.) 125 Our prædecessours .. appoyntet sik magistratis..to teiche thame..to the people.

2. *Imper.* 1 **tǽce, tǽc, 3 teke, 3–5 teche, tech, 4 teyche, 6 teache, 6– teach.**

?*a* **1000** [see B. 6 c]. *c* **1000** ÆLFRIC *Hom.* I. 258 Leof, tæce us hu we maȝon us ʒebiddan. *a* **1240** *Ureisun* in *Cott. Hom.* 183 Ihesu teke þet tu art se softe and se swote. *a* **1272** *Luue Ron* 198 in *O. E. Misc.* 99 Tech hit oþer maydenes wel. **13..** *Cursor M.* 20795 (Cott.) Teche til him þat all might. *c* **1400** *Cato's Morals* 188 in *Cursor M.* p. 1671 Teyche þou þe vnwise. **1564–78** BULLEYN *Dial. agst. Pest.* (1888) 53 Teache me a Pomeander. **1573** TUSSER *Husb.* (1878) 137 Troth twise to thee teached, teach twentie times ten.

3. *Pres. Indic.* a. *1st pers. sing.* 1 **tǽce, 3–5 teche, 6 teache, 6– teach.**

*c* **1000** ÆLFRIC *Gram.* xxviii. (Z.) 173 Ic tæce sumum men his weȝ. *a* **1272** *Luue Ron* 83 in *O. E. Misc.* 95 Ich teche þe enne treowe king.

b. *2nd pers. sing.* 1 **tǽcst, 4 teches, teychis, 4–5 techest, 6– teachest.**

*c* **1000** ÆLFRIC *Exod.* xix. 12 Þu tæcst Israhela folce ʒemæro. **13..** *Cursor M.* 12189 (Cott.) Þat þou teches [*F.* teychis; *Tr.* techest] til oþer men.

c. *3rd pers. sing.* 1 **tǽcþ, tǽhð, 2 tecð, 2–5 techeþ, 3 tekeðe, 4 tekþ, teychis, 4–6 techeth (5 -ith, 6 -yth), 6– teacheth (now *arch.*), teaches.**

*c* **1000** ÆLFRIC *Gen.* Pref. 4 Se þe tæcþ of Ledene on Englisc. *c* **1000** — *Hom.* I. 322 Se Halȝa Gast ðe tæhð rihtwisnysse. *a* **1225** *Ancr. R.* 50 Þe blake cloð also tekeðe bitocnunge. *c* **1230** *Hali Meid.* 13, & techeð her on eorðe.. þe liflade of heouene. **1340** *Ayenb.* 54 To huam þe holy gost tekþ to hyealde ordre. *Ibid.* 56 Alle uelþe he tekþ þer. *c* **1375** *Cursor M.* 12250 (Fairf.) Sum angel .. teychis him alle atte he melis. **1377** LANGL. *P. Pl.* B. I. 13 As his worde techeth [*v. r.* thecheth]. **1388** WYCLIF *Prov.* xii. 24 He that loueth him, techith bisili. **1538** STARKEY *England* I. ii. 38 Vertue hyt ys that techyth vs al.

d. *pl.* 1 **tǽcað, 3–5 techen, 3–6 teche, 5–6 *Sc.* techis, 6 teache, (-en), *Sc.* teiche, 6– teach.**

*c* **1400** *Rom. Rose* 5159 As ye me teche. *a* **1425** *Cursor M.* 12192 (Trin.) What þei teche her feres. **1456** SIR G. HAYE *Law Arms* (S. T. S.) 16 Quhilkis..techis othir symple folk ..errouris. *c* **1460** *Pol. Rel. & L. Poems* (1866) 198 Whanne þei þee techen. **1563** *Homilies* II. *Peril Idolatry* III. (1859) 242 As the Scriptures teachen. **1580** J. HAY *Demands* § 40 in *Cath. Tractates* (S.T.S.) 44 As ye teiche.

4. *Past tense.* a. 1–3 **tǽhte (1 ʒe-), 1 *north.* táhte, 2–4 tahte, tachte, (2 tahhte, tochte), 3–5 taȝte, tauhte, taute, 4 tawhte, tawghte, (taghtte), 4–5 taghte, tauȝte, taughte; 4–5 taȝt, tauht, taght, tauȝt, tawht, tawȝt, tawght, *Sc.* tacht, 5 taut, tawt, 5–6 *Sc.* taucht, tawcht, 5– taught; (5 toght, towght, 6 tought).**

*a* **900** tr. *Bæda's Hist.* III. viii. [x.] (1890) 180 Him mon setl tæhte. *c* **950** *Lindisf. Gosp.* Mark xii. 38 And tahte *vel* lærde ðæm *vel* him [*et docebat eis*]. [So **975** *Rushw. Gosp.*] *c* **1000** ÆLFRIC *Hom.* I. 68 Symle ðu tæhtest mildheortnysse. *c* **1050** *Byrhtferth's Handboc* in *Anglia* (1885) VIII. 304 An snotor wita me ʒetæhte þisne cræft. *a* **1200** *Vices & Virtues* 27 Ðis ne tahte ðe non eorðlic mann. *a* **1200** *Moral Ode* 268 Al þet þe laþe gast hechte to and tachte. *c* **1200** ORMIN 1071 Hiss boc himm tahhte. *c* **1205** LAY. 804 Brutus heom taute [*c* 1275 tehte]. *a* **1225** *Juliana* 62 Þat te engel to þe tahten. *c* **1250** *Gen. & Ex.* 3392 God taȝte hem weie. *c* **1330** R. BRUNNE *Chron.* (1810) 196 God þat þam it tauht. **13..** *Cursor M.* 741 (Cott.) Graitli taght [*v. rr.* taȝt, tauȝte] he him þe gin. *Ibid.* 17074 (Fairf.) Ther tawghtyst [*T.* tauȝtest] þou vs the way. **1375** BARBOUR *Bruce* II. 130 He taucht him siluer to dispend. *c* **1386** CHAUCER *Pard. T.* 36 As thilke hooly lew oure eldres taughte [*v. rr.* taghte, tauȝt, tauȝte, tauht]. **1390** GOWER *Conf.* I. 285 Nature..tawht hem so. *c* **1400** *Apol. Loll.* 42 Þus He tawt hem to do. *c* **1400** *Emare* 973 Emare thawȝte her sone ȝynge. **1447** BOKENHAM *Seyntys* (Roxb.) 12 And tawth hyr the feyth of Crist Jesu. **1451** CAPGRAVE *Life St. Gilbert* 87 He taute hem ferþermor oþir vertues. ?*a* **1500** *Kyng & Hermyt* 324 in Hazl. *E. P. P.* I. 25 And taugȝt hym priuely to a sted, To feche the hors corne and bred. **1568** GRAFTON *Chron.* I. 15 Those also he taught his invention.

β. 2–3 **tête; 3 teihte, taihte, taite, 3–4 teiȝte, teite.**

*c* **1175** *Lamb. Hom.* 107 He us tehte. *c* **1200** *Trin. Coll. Hom.* 83 Þe tehte..alle wise witeȝe here wisdom. *c* **1200** *Moral Ode* 272 *ibid.* 228 Al þet þe loðe gost hem tihte to and taihte. *a* **1225** *Ancr. R.* 158 He teihte us openliche. *a* **1275** *Prov. Ælfred* 634 in *O. E. Misc.* 136 Wel worþe þe wid, Þad þe first taite. *c* **1290** *Christopher* 173 in *S. Eng. Leg.* I. 276 Cristofre heom teiȝte þe riȝte bi-leue. *c* **1300** *Harrow. Hell* 233 (Digby MS.) Þou teitest me þene riȝte wey.

γ. 4–5 **teched, -id, 5–6 *Sc.* techit, 6 *Sc.* teichit, -et, -ed, 6–7 (–9 *dial.*) teached.**

**13..** *Cursor M.* 12180 (Cott.) Maister leui, þat ald man, Teched [*Gött.* Techid] him a letter þan. **1456** SIR G. HAYE *Law Arms* (S. T. S.) 38 [He] techit the folk of that contree to mak housis. **1596** DALRYMPLE tr. *Leslie's Hist. Scot.* IV. (S.T.S.) 232 Godlie men..quha..teiched the Scotis. *Ibid.* 242 Sigenie, a Scotis Preist..teichet his peiple. **1608** WILLET *Hexapla Exod.* 714 They were taught, and teached not. **1890** W. A. WALLACE *Only a Sister* x. 75 Old Mary Morley teached me that when I was growed up.

5. *Past pple.* a. 1 ***ʒetǽht, 2–4 taht, (tahht), 3–4 (i)taȝt, 4 itawt, 4–5 taght, tauht, taut, tauwȝt, (i)tauȝt, (y)tawȝt, itaught, tawht, tauwȝt, (y-tawȝtte), *Sc.* tawcht, 5–6 *Sc.* taucht, 5– taught; (5 toght, towght, 6 tought).**

*c* **1200** ORMIN 18741 He þuss haffde uss tahht. *a* **1300** *Floriz & Bl.* 404 Floris hath iwroȝt As daris him haþ itaȝt [*v. r.* itawt]. **13..** *Cursor M.* 24243 (Edin.) Ik haf him taht [*v. rr.* tagh, taȝt, taght] to þi seruis. **1340–70** *Alex. & Dind.* 217 We weren tauht Of oure doctourus dere. **1362** LANGL. *P. Pl.* A. XI. 169, I grette .. his wyf .. And tolde hire þe tokenes þat me I-tauȝt were. **1377** *Ibid.* B. XX. 185 Euelytawȝte elde. *c* **1375** *Sc. Leg. Saints* ii. (*Paulus*) 201 To thre knychttis þane wes he tawcht. *c* **1380** WYCLIF *Wks.* (1880) 157 No man schulde here goddis lawe tauwȝt. *c* **1386** CHAUCER *Melib.* ¶ 300 Whiche of hem han..taught yow best conseil. **1390** GOWER *Conf.* I. 118 The king hath..His brother tawht. *c* **1400** *Destr. Troy* 881 The tokyn hym taght. *Ibid.* 9232 When he hade..toght hym to go. **14..** *Six Ballads* (Percy Soc. No. 50) 14, I wyll nowyse be towght. **14..** in *Babees Bk.* (1868) 357 The wyse man hath hys sone y-tawȝtte. **1570** B. GOOGE *Pop. Kingd.* 6 That Christ himselfe had tought. **1573** *Satir. Poems Reform.* xlii. 20 His toung weill taucht. **1746** FRANCIS tr. *Hor., Sat.* II. vii. 125 But should not you with heavier Stripes be taught?

β. 4 **techid, 4–5 -ed, 6 *Sc.* techit, teichit, 6–7 (–9 *dial.*) teached.**

**13..** *Cursor M.* 18760 (Cott.) Quen iesus had..teched þam al þat he wild. *Ibid.* 6450 (Gött.) Grete chargis..þat fell to gastlines, Suld techid be thoru moyses. **1544** *Suppl. to Hen. VIII* in *Four Supplic.* (1871) 34 He hathe enstructe and teached the people. **1560** ROLLAND *Seven Sages* 31 Is this ȝour sone..[That] hes bene teichit? **1560–78** *Bk. Discipl. Ch. Scot.* (1621) 38 Experience hath teached us what pestilence hath been ingendered in the Kirk.

B. Signification.

I. To show, etc. [OE. or early ME. (exc. 3 b).]

†1. *trans.* To show, present or offer to view.

*a* **900** tr. *Bæda's Hist.* IV. i. § 2 (MS. T) Tæhte þa þam biscope..sumne ʒedefne munuc, þæs noma wæs Andreas.

†2. To show or point out (a thing, the way, a place, etc.) to a person. *Obs.*

*a* **900** tr. *Bæda's Hist.* III. viii. [x.], Him mon setl tæhte, and he sæt mid him æt þæm symble. *Ibid.* v. xvii. [xix.] § 4. **971** *Blickl. Hom.* 109 Þa men þe bearn habban .. him tæcean lifes weȝ. *c* **1000** ÆLFRIC *Gram.* xxviii. (Z.) 173 Ic tæce sumum men his weȝ. *c* **1250** *Gen. & Ex.* 3392 God taȝte hem weie, wis and pert. *c* **1400** *Destr. Troy* 7836 He..went with þo worthy, & þe way taght.

†3. To show (a person) the way; to direct, conduct, convoy, guide (*to, from* a place); to send away; also, to direct or refer (*to* something). *Obs.*

Orig. with dative of person and prep. (*to, into, over, from*), as if elliptical for *teach him (the way) to a place*.

*c* **893** K. ÆLFRED *Oros.* III. iii. § 1 Ic ʒehwam wille þærto [= to þinum bocum] tæcan þe hiene his lyst ma to witanne. **925–35** *Laws of Athelstan* II. c. 22 Non mon ne tæce his ʒetihtledan mon from him. *c* **961** ÆTHELWOLD *Rule St. Benet* lviii. (1885) 97 Tæce him mon siððan to niȝcumenra manna huse. *a* **1000** *Cædmon's Gen.* 2900 (Gr.) On þære stowe þe him se stranga to, wærfest metod wordum tæhte. **13..** *K. Alis.* 5204 (Bodl. MS.) He shulde hem teche to sum Ryuere. *Ibid.* 5206 Hem tauȝtte ouer a wode. *c* **1386** CHAUCER *Nun's Pr. T.* 129, I shal my self to herbes techen yow That shul been for youre hele. *c* **1425** *Cast. Persev.* 553 in *Macro Plays* 93 Þou art a nobyl knawe to techyn men fyrst fro goode! *a* **1440** *Sir Degrev.* 914 Damesel..Teche me to that ylke place. *c* **1450** *Merlin* XX. 316 Oo hym taught in-to a chamber wher thei were. ?*a* **1500** *Kyng & Hermit* 136 in Hazl. *E. P. P.* I. 18 Late thy knave go, To teche me a myle or two.

b. *Ship-building.* (*absol.*) Of a line: To point in a particular direction.

*c* **1850** *Rudim. Navig.* (Weale) 155 We say, 'let the line or mould *teach fair* to such a spot'. **1867** SMYTH *Sailor's Word-bk.*, To *Teach*, in marine architecture, is applied to the direction which any line or curve seems to point out.

†4. To show what is to be observed or done; to direct, appoint, prescribe, decree, enjoin. Const. as in II. *Obs.* or absorbed in II.

*c* **897** K. ÆLFRED *Gregory's Past. C.* xxi. 161 Eft he him tæhte to fultome ðæt he him ʒename ane iserne hearstepannan. *c* **1000** ÆLFRIC *Exod.* xix. 12 Þu tæcst Israhela folce ʒemæro abutan þone munt. *a* **1023** WULFSTAN *Hom.* xxxiii. 165 Þæt hy betan heora misdæda, swa swa bec tæcan. *c* **1175** *Lamb. Hom.* 107 Uten don elmessen swa he us tehte, gode to luue. *c* **1250** *Long Life* 23 in *O. E. Misc.* 156 Do ase he [Solomon] þe tahte [*v. r.* tauhte]. **1362** LANGL. *P. Pl.* A. II. 7, I lokede on þe luft half as þe ladi me tauhte. *c* **1380** WYCLIF *Sel. Wks.* III. 431 Cerimonyes of þe olde lawe..ben tauht to be left. *c* **1420** *Chron. Vilod.* 3838 Þe whyche tauȝt hym euer to don amys. **1567** *Gude & Godlie B.* (S.T.S.) 45 Syne he did his Apostillis teiche Throw all the warld for to pas.

II. To show by way of information or instruction. (Now the leading sense.)

In this group the original construction had an accusative of the thing imparted, with dative of the person or recipient when expressed. The loss of the dative inflexion, or, as in the pronouns, its identification with the accusative, was sometimes replaced by the preposition *to*, but oftener left two objects, of which the indirect, denoting the recipient, became more and more viewed as the direct object, and as such was made the subject of the passive voice, not only when the original direct object was an infinitive, as *he was taught to dance*, but even when it was a sb., as *he was taught Latin*, in preference to *Latin was taught him*.

5. *To teach a thing*: To impart or convey the knowledge of; to give instruction or lessons in (a subject); † to make known, deliver (a message). With simple obj. or obj. clause.

**971** *Blickl. Hom.* 43 Þa mæsse-preostas..sceolan heora scrift-bec mid rihte tæcan and læran. ?*a* **1000** *K. Ælfred's Boeth.* xxxiv. § 9 (MS. B.) Þæt þu..ne forȝite þæt þæt ic ær tæhte. *c* **1000** ÆLFRIC *Hom.* I. 322 Se Halȝa Gast ðe tæhð rihtwisnysse. *a* **1175** *Cott. Hom.* 229 [Christ] tochte richwisnesse and soðfestnesse. **13..** *Gaw. & Gr. Knt.* 1485 Þou hatz for-ȝeten ȝederly þat ȝisterday I taȝtte. **1340–70** *Alex. & Dind.* 1077 Þis kariede sonde Þat þus tiþinge tolde & tauhte þis wordes. *c* **1380** WYCLIF *Wks.* (1880) 235 Crist & his apostlis tauten neuere..siche profession. **1451** CAPGRAVE *Life St. Aug.* 12 He cam first hom..and þer taute he gramer. **1560** DAUS tr. *Sleidane's Comm.* 42 The Preachers shall teache the Gospell. **1563** WINȜET *Four Scoir Thre Quest.* xix. Wks. (S.T.S.) I. 85 Quhy tech ȝe that thai are all indifferentlie of ane efficacitie? **1653** WALTON *Angler* To Rdr. 4 To teach the Art of Fencing. **1790** PALEY *Horæ Paul.* xvi, He was convinced of the truth of what he taught. *Mod.* What subjects does he teach in the school?

6. *To teach a person a thing, a thing to a person* (or *agent*): To communicate something to a person, by way of instruction; † to inform.

*c* **888** K. ÆLFRED *Boeth.* xxxviii. § 3 Ic þe mæg ʒiet tæcan oðer þing. *a* **1050** in *Sax. Leechd.* III. 256 Eac ʒewisse dæʒmæl us swa tæcað. *c* **1200** *Trin. Coll. Hom.* 99 Ure helende sat ofte and tahte wisdom þan þe him folȝeden. **1297** R. GLOUC. (Rolls) 4827 Ȝif ȝe nolle englissemen godes lawes teche. *a* **1300** *Cursor M.* 24306 (Edin.) To techen þaim quat tai sul don. **1426** LYDG. *De Guil. Pilgr.* 36 Thynges that I shal teche the. **1564–78** BULLEYN *Dial. agst. Pest.* (1888) 53, I praie you teache me one or twoo kinde of Pilles. **1715–20** POPE *Iliad* VI. 108 Thou Hector to the town retire, And teach our mother what the gods require. **1741–2** GRAY *Agrippina* 135 Wrinkled beldams Teach it their grandchildren. **1820** SCOTT *Monast.* xxxv, I see it is ill done to teach the cat the way to the kirn. **1857** BUCKLE *Civiliz.* I. xii. 667 It was English literature which taught the lessons of political liberty, first to France, and through France to the rest of Europe. **1874** GREEN *Short Hist.* vii. § 1. 352 The sufferings of the Protestants had failed to teach them the worth of religious liberty.

b. The subject of the passive voice was originally the thing taught; it is now usually the person or indirect object.

*a* **1300** *Cursor M.* 16324 Qui askes þou? it es þe forthwit taght. **1390** GOWER *Conf.* II. 363 Upon the pointz, as we ben taught, Stant sacrilege. **1573** TUSSER *Husb.* (1878) 30 As huswiues are teached, in stead of a clock, How winter nights passeth, by crowing of cock. **1637** (*title*) Romvlvs and Tarqvin. First Written in Italian by the Marques Virgilio Malvezzi: And now taught [= translated into] English, by H. C[arey]. **1745** BUTLER *Serm.* Wks. 1874 II. 276 It is true..children may be taught superstition, under the notion of religion. **1825** R. H. FROUDE *Rem.* (1838) I. 190, I am being taught French.

c. With the thing taught expressed by an infinitive (or sb. clause): To show or make known to a person (how to do something, etc.).

**971** *Blickl. Hom.* 43 Þa lareowas sceolan synnfullum mannum eadmodlice tæcan and læran þæt, hie [etc.]. ?*a* **1000** *K. Ælfred's Boethius* Final Prayer (MS. B.), Tæc me þinne willan to wyrcenne. *c* **1250** *O. Kentish Serm.* in *O. E. Misc.* 35 Ne apostle ne prechur..ne hem tachte hu [h]i solde [etc.]. *a* **1300** *Cursor M.* 15373, I sal yow teche him for to knau. *a* **1352** MINOT *Poems* (ed. Hall) ix. 3 Þe north end of Ingland teched him to daunce. **1470–85** MALORY *Arthur* VII. xvii. 238 His [the red knight's] wyly fyghtyng taughte syr Beaumayns to be wyse. **1542** UDALL *Erasm. Apoph.* II. 342 b, For which we saie in Englyshe to teache our dame to spynne. **1616** *Withal's Dict.* 575 You teach your good Maister: teach your grandam to grope her duck. **1750** GRAY *Elegy* 84 Many a holy text .. that teach the rustic moralist to die. **1868** RUSKIN *Arrows of Chace* (1880) II. 178 Education .. means teaching children to be clean, active, honest, and useful.

*fig.* *c* **1400** *Rom. Rose* 3319 He tought it [my heart] so hym for to obey. **1625** BACON *Ess.*, *Of Delayes* (Arb.) 525 To teach dangers to come on, by ouer early Buckling towards them, is another Extreme. **1633** P. FLETCHER *Purple Isl.* XI. iv, Thou..taught'st his heart to frame his Canto's best. **1715–20** POPE *Iliad* IX. 723 Is it for him these tears are taught to flow? **1825** T. HOOK *Sayings* Ser. II. *Sutherl.* (Colburn) 35 James's lank hair..was taught to curl gracefully *à la Brutus*.

d. Used by way of threat: To let one know the cost or penalty of something.

**1575** *Gamm. Gurton* III. iii. Ciij b, And I get once on foote ..ile teach the what longs to it. *a* **1619** FLETCHER *Mad Lover* III. ii, I'll teach you to be treacherous! **1697** DRYDEN *Virg. Past.* III. 76 I'll teach you how to brag another time. **1778** MISS BURNEY *Evelina* (1791) I. xxxvi. 191 She will.. teach you to know who she is. **1889** A. LANG *Pr. Prigio* ii. 10 I'll teach you to be too clever, my lad.

7. *To teach a person* or *agent* (with personal object only): To impart knowledge to, give instruction to; to inform, instruct, educate, train, school. *To teach (a) school*: see SCHOOL *sb.*[1] 1 d.

*c* **1000** *Eccl. Instit.* 20 in Thorpe *Ags. Laws* II. 414 Hiȝ sceolon swiðe lustlice his onfon, and him estlice tæcan. *c* **1250** *Hymn Virg.* 34 in *Trin. Coll. Hom.* 256 Maide dreiȝ & wel itaucht. *a* **1275** *Prov. Ælfred* 142 in *O. E. Misc.* 129 He sal banne þat wiȝt Þat him first taȝte. *c* **1325** *Spec. Gy Warw.* 570 Houre swete lord..Hise deciples began to teche. **1393** LANGL. *P. Pl.* C. I. 120 Ȝe sholde be here fadres and techen hem betere. **1484** CAXTON *Fables of Auian* iii, He whiche wil teche and lerne some other, ought first to corryge & examyne hym self. **1558** *Peebles Burgh Rec.* (1872) 244 The haill inqueist ordanis Walter Haldane to teche thair Grammare Scoill. **1596** DALRYMPLE tr. *Leslie's Hist. Scot.* VIII. (S.T.S.) 110 A wyfe..weil taucht and brocht vp. **1667** MILTON *P. L.* XII. 446 All Nations they shall teach. **1722** in Picton *L'pool Munic. Rec.* (1886) II. 75 A charity school

..for teaching and instructing poor children in. **1877–9** RUSKIN *St. Mark's Rest* ii. § 18 There is nothing like a little work with the fingers for teaching the eyes. **1908** [MISS FOWLER] *Betw. Trent & Ancholme* 21 Master Teanby ..taught him and others.

**b.** With prepositional extensions (*to teach of*, etc.). † *To teach to*: to train to, to accustom to the use or practice of (*obs.*).

**1297** R. GLOUC. (Rolls) 2197 Men bet iteiȝt to ssofle & to spade. **1382** WYCLIF *Matt.* xxi. 17 There he dwelte, and tauȝte hem of the kyngdam of God. *c* **1450** *St. Cuthbert* (Surtees) 6659 A clerke..þat couthe teche his men to faythe. *a* **1553** UDALL *Royster D.* I. iii. (Arb.) 24, I haue not bene taught to kissing and licking. **1660** F. BROOKE tr. *Le Blanc's Trav.* 166 These Lions..are taught to it, when they are young.

**8.** *absol.* or *intr.* To communicate knowledge; to act as a teacher; to give instruction.

*c* **1000** ÆLFRIC *Hom.* I. 242 ȝif se lareow wel tæce..doð swa swa he tæcð. **1340–70** *Alex. & Dind.* 237 Folk þat fain is to teche. **1382** WYCLIF *Matt.* xi. 1 Jhesus.. passide fro thennes for to preche and teche in the citees of hem. *c* **1440** *Gesta Rom.* xlv 178 (Harl. MS.) The whiche prophesied and tawte aȝenst synne. **1552** HULOET, Teache in a schole, *didascolo*. **1651** HOBBES *Leviath.* II xxvii. 158 One that teacheth by publique Authority. **1674** (Mar. 15) *Warrant for appreh. Bunyan*, One John Bunnyon..Tynker hath divers times within one month last past..preached or teached at a Conventicle meeteing or assembly. **1878** R. W. DALE *Lect. Preach.* viii. 226 He must learn how to teach.

**III.** †**9.** To deliver, hand over, give; to give in trust, commit, entrust, commend to the keeping of some one. *Obs.*

In OE. usually expressed by *betǽcan*, BETEACH; even quot. *c* 1000 below is difficult to separate from sense 4.

*c* **1000** ÆLFRIC *Hom.* I. 46 Ða ȝesetnysse ðe us Moyses tæhte [*Vulg.* tradidit nobis Moyses]. *c* **1205** LAY. 22599 Ich tache þe mine leofen sunen. *a* **1300** *Cursor M.* 15349 His bodi suld be taght His fas þat war felun. *Ibid.* 15411 In handes yur i sal him teche. *c* **1300** *Havelok* 2214 Hauelok his sone he him tauhte, And hise two douhtres, and al his auhte. *c* **1375** *Sc. Leg. Saints* xxii. (*Laurentius*) 84 To sancte Syxt þane tacht [he] It. **1375** BARBOUR *Bruce* x. 43 To the gud lorde of Douglas,..He taucht the archaris euirilkane. *c* **1420** *Anturs of Arth.* 605 Swylke a touche at þat tyme he taughte hym in tene. *c* **1475** *Rauf Coilȝear* 772 Ane Chalmer with Armour the King gart richt than Be taucht to ane Squyar.

†**b.** To commend or commit (a person) to God; to bid adieu to; to wish (good day) to: cf. BETEACH *v.* 4, 4 b. *Obs. rare.*

*c* **1400** *Rowland & O.* 1268 Charlles.. Taughte hym to godde. *a* **1425** *Cursor M.* 8068 (Trin.) Þe kyng..tauȝte hem god & good day.

**Teachable** (tīˑtʃăb'l), *a.* [f. TEACH *v.* + -ABLE.]

†**1.** Able or apt to teach. *Obs.*

**1483** *Cath. Angl.* 378/2 Techeabylle, *docibilis, qui faciliter docet alios; docilis, qui faciliter docetur.* **1641, 1695** [implied in TEACHABLENESS 2].

**2.** Capable of being taught (as a person); apt to receive instruction; docile; tractable.

**1483** [see in 1]. **1583** GOLDING *Calvin on Deut.* ii. 7 And let such knowledge make us teachable. **1684** J. SCOTT *Chr. Life* (ed. 3) 160 To keep our Minds in a teachable temper. **1725** BERKELEY *Proposal*, etc. Wks. 1871 III. 226 They are ..less conceited, and more teachable. **1855** KINGSLEY *Heroes* Pref. (1868) 12 These old Greeks were teachable, and learnt from all the nations round.

**3.** Capable of being taught (as a subject); that may be communicated or imparted by instruction.

**1669** GALE *Crt. Gentiles* I. III. v. 63 He brings in Socrates refuting that opinion of the Stoics, That virtue was..teachable. **1816** BENTHAM *Chrestom.* 17 The subject,—in so far as teachable by exhibition of figure, colour, and other sensible qualities,—will be taught. **1860** RUSKIN *Mod. Paint.* V. VIII. ii. § 12. 174 To teach you..everything that is teachable.

Hence **Teachabiˑlity** = next 1, 3.

**1876** *Daily News* 4 Dec. 3/1 It requires an unusual modesty and teachability of disposition. **1882** *Pop. Sc. Monthly* XXI. 436 Carnivores..exhibit only moderate teachability. **1887** ST. G. STOCK *Plato's Meno* 26 The same diversity of opinion..with regard to the teachability of virtue.

**Teaˑchableness.** [f. TEACHABLE + -NESS.] The quality or state of being teachable.

**1.** Aptness or capacity for being taught; readiness to receive instruction, docility.

**1571** GOLDING *Calvin on Ps.* xxv. 9 This teachablenesse will nowhere bee founde, as long as the mynde [is] lifted up with pryde. **1651** BAXTER *Inf. Bapt.* 105 Not only Docible, but Exemplary, for their Teachableness. **1726** SWIFT *Gulliver* IV. iii, My teachableness, civility, and cleanliness, astonished him. **1863** HOLLAND *Lett. Joneses* xii. 172 The prominent characteristic of all really great men is teachableness. **1897** BP. CREIGHTON in *Life & Lett.* (1904) II. vii. 255 Humble submission and teachableness to a higher law.

†**2.** Capacity of teaching; instructiveness. *Obs.*

**1641** MILTON *Animadv.* v. Wks. 1851 III. 224 Wherefore wee should not attribute a right Method to the teachablenesse of Scripture, there can bee no reason given. **1695** TRYON *Dreams & Vis.* iv. 57 There would be much teachableness in Dreams, as they are derived from, and demonstrate [etc.].

**3.** The quality of being communicable by instruction.

**1871** JOWETT *Plato* I. 109 Protagoras began by asserting ..the teachableness of virtue.

**Teaˑchably,** *adv.* [f. as prec. + -LY [2].] In a teachable manner; with docility.

**1804** EUGENIA DE ACTON *Tale without Title* I. 143 If these superficial gentry would..be teachably humble. **1849** MACAULAY *Hist. Eng.* i. I. 47 The child who teachably and undoubtingly listens to the instructions of his elders.

**Teache,** variant of TACHE *sb.*[3]

**Teached** (tītʃt), *ppl. a. Obs.* or *dial.* = TAUGHT.

**1639** LD. DIGBY, etc. *Lett. conc. Relig.* (1651) 96 By the frequent misapprehension of the teached,..either let slip or supplanted. **1644** G. PLATTES in *Hartlib's Legacy* (1655) 176 The Teachers and the Teached were nothing else but the blind leading of the blind.

**Teacher** (tīˑtʃəɹ), *sb.* Forms: see TEACH *v.*; also 4 *Sc.* -ure, 5–6 -ar, *Sc.* -our. [f. TEACH *v.* + -ER [1].]

†**1.** That which shows or points out; an indicator; the index-finger. *Obs. rare.*

*c* **1290** *S. Eng. Leg.* I. 308/314 The feorþe finguer hatte 'techere', for þere-with men techez i-wis.

**2.** One who or that which teaches or instructs; an instructor; also *fig.*; *spec.* one whose function is to give instruction, esp. in a school.

**13..** *K. Alis.* 17 (Bodl. MS.) For Caton seiþ, þe gode techer, Oþere mannes liif is oure shewer. *c* **1375** *Sc. Leg. Saints* xl. (*Ninian*) 98 Scorne it ware gret to se þe thechure suld vnkennand be. **1382** WYCLIF *Matt.* xxii. 35 Oon of hem, a techer of the lawe, axede Jhesus, temptynge hym. **1439** *Coventry Leet Bk.* 190 To sette hys chylde to skole to what techer off Gramer that he likyth. **1456** SIR G. HAYE *Law Arms* (S. T. S.) 16 Fals prechouris and techouris of errouris. **1538** STARKEY *England* I. iv. 136 For lake of gud techarys and instructarys. **1662** PLAYFORD *Skill Mus.* I. xi. (1674) 48 Experience is the Teacher of all things. **1799** *Med. Jrnl.* I. 302 The retirement of Dr. Matthew Baillie, as a teacher of anatomy. **1807** WORDSW. *Song Feast Brougham Castle* 162 His daily teachers had been woods and rills,..The sleep that is among the lonely hills. **1870** *Act* 33 & 34 *Vict.* c. 75 § 3 The term 'teacher' includes.. every person who forms part of the educational staff of a school. **1884** H. COXWELL in *Contemp. Rev.* Oct. 533 The French are our acknowledged teachers in ballooning.

**b.** Formerly, in New England Congregational churches, One of several officers appointed to teach.

**1834** BARNES *On Romans* xii. 7 The churches in New England had, at first, a class of men who were called teachers..distinct from the pastor.

**c.** *Teacher's node* (Path.), name given to a chronic inflammation of the vocal chords, characterized by minute whitish nodules on the upper surface of the chords. (Cf. NODE *sb.* 3 a.)

**1897** *Allbutt's Syst. Med.* IV. 832 *Chorditis tuberosa*, or 'singer's nodule', or 'teacher's node', is a clinical variety of pachydermia.

**3.** *attrib.* and *Comb.*, as *teacher-habit, -student, -training*; *teacher-ridden* adj.; **teacher edition**, an edition of a work prepared especially for the use of teachers.

*a* **1704** T. BROWN *Two Oxford Scholars* Wks. 1730 I. 11 They have been Teacher-ridden for many Years. **1865** DICKENS *Mut. Fr.* II. i, Perhaps it scarcely required the teacher-habit to perceive that [etc.]. **1894** *Westm. Gaz.* 28 Mar. 2/2 Our only example of the teacher-training institution. *Ibid.* A certain number of teacher-students. **1900** STODDARD *Evol. Eng. Novel* 63 A picture of the soul-life of the struggling teacher-governess of Haworth.

Hence † **Teaˑcher** *v. Obs. rare, trans.*, to tutor, prompt, 'coach'; **Teaˑcherdom**, the community of teachers; **Teaˑcheress**, a female teacher.

**1619** VISCT. DONCASTER in *Eng. & Germ.* (Camden) 164 Finding him as I thinke..*teachered by some higher directions (whether it be of Rome or Spayne or both in one). **1908** *Times, Lit. Supp.* 6 Aug. 252/1 She ruled her staff and spread her unconscious influence throughout *teacherdom. **1382** WYCLIF *Wisd.* viii. 4 Forsothe the *techeresse [Vulg. *doctrix*] it [wisdom] is of the discipline of God. **1657** J. SERGEANT *Schism Dispach't* 630 The word Mistress may signify..a Teacheress (as I may say) or one which instructs, and so is coincident with Magistra.

**Teachership** (tīˑtʃəɹʃip). [f. TEACHER + -SHIP.] The office, function, or position of a teacher.

**1846** THORPE *Ælfric's Hom.* II. 35 Stephen..is first in martyrdom, and first in teachership. **1868** M. PATTISON *Academ. Org.* vi. 253 The teacherships are filled by men of real knowledge. **1870** *Athenæum* 14 May 643 The most pressing wants of the University, in which they included.. a Demonstratorship of Chemistry and Teachership of Palæontology and Modern Languages. **1885** *Harper's Mag.* LXX. 210 If she had succeeded in getting the little town school teachership.

**Teaˑ-chest.** [f. TEA *sb.* + CHEST *sb.*[1]]

†**1.** = *Tea-caddy*: see TEA *sb.* 9 c. *Obs.*

**1740** MRS. DELANY in *Life & Corr.* (1861) II. 97, I have got a very neat tea-chest for Mrs. Yate, which shall be filled with tea, and delivered to her. **1775** ASH, *Teachest*, a small kind of cabinet in which tea is brought to table. **1780** MME. D'ARBLAY *Diary* Apr., I was putting away the tea-chest. *c* **1850** [Remembered in use at Cambridge].

**2.** A large box or chest of cubical form, lined with sheet-lead, in which tea is packed for transport: cf. CHEST *sb.*[1] 6. Also *attrib.*

**1801** HULME in *Phil. Trans.* XCI. 403 Flat lead, such as lines Chinese tea-chests. **1893** F. F. MOORE *I Forbid Banns* (1899) 100 The furniture had not the appearance of being made out of flour barrels and tea-chests. There was not much of the tea-chest look about the old oak dresser.

**Teachie, Teachily,** obs. ff. TETCHY, TETCHILY.

**Teaˑching,** *vbl. sb.* Forms: see the verb. [f. TEACH *v.* + -ING [1].] The action of the verb TEACH.

†**1.** Showing the way; direction, guidance. *Obs.*

**13..** *Cursor M.* 11656 (Gött.) Forth þai went þar wai fra þan Widvten teching of ani man.

**2.** The imparting of instruction or knowledge; the occupation or function of a teacher.

*c* **1175** *Lamb. Hom.* 93 Alle þeo..him ihersummede efter godes tecunge. *c* **1275** *Passion* 255 in *O. E. Misc.* 44 He hym axede of his techinge And of his disciples. *c* **1375** *Sc. Leg. Saints* xxvii. (*Machor*) 372 Thru theching of þe haly gast. **1456** SIR G. HAYE *Law Arms* (S. T. S.) 68 The barnis..wald nouther tak teching na chastisement of the fader. **1530** PALSGR. 279/2 Teching, lerning, *enseignement*. **1617** HIERON *Wks.* II. 189 It may bee for teaching-sake parted into two portions. **1656** tr. *Hobbes's Elem. Philos.* (1839) 80 Teaching is nothing but leading the mind of him we teach, to the knowledge of our inventions, in that track by which we attained the same. **1715** DE FOE *Fam. Instruct.* I. i. (1841) I. 8, I can say that without teaching. **1862** HELPS *Organization* 50 In teaching, he has not to display knowledge, but to impart it.

**b.** That which is taught; a thing taught, doctrine, instruction, precept.

*a* **1300** *Cursor M.* 2655 And if þou halds mi techeyng; O þe sal com bath prince and king. **1377** LANGL. *P. Pl.* B. VII. 74 *Cui des, videto* is catounes techynge. **1482** *Monk of Evesham* (Arb.) 42 Whyche may be to alle the worlde a nobylle document and techyng. **1542–3** *Act* 34 & 35 *Hen. VIII*, c. 1 Suche bookes, writinges..teachinges and instructions, as be pestiferous, and noysome. **1853** J. H. NEWMAN *Hist. Sk.* (1873) II. I. iii. 139 In the middle of the fourteenth century, the teaching of Wickliffe gained ground in England. **1856** STANLEY *Sinai & Pal.* xiii. 426 A character and teaching, human Hebrew, Syrian, in its outward form and colour, but in its inward spirit..Divine.

† **3.** Delivering, handing over. *Obs. rare.*

*c* **1300** *Cursor M.* 15416 (Cott.) In handes yur i [Judas] sal him teche;..And godder-hail þan sal þou se, For luue o þis techeing.

**4.** *attrib.* and *Comb.*

**1617** HIERON *Wks.* II. 169 God hath put this teaching-businesse into their hands. *Ibid.* 283 Vnable to performe this teaching-seruice. **1849** ROCK *Ch. of Fathers* I. iv. 300 The Church is the teaching-house of holiness. **1879** P. BROOKS *Influence of Jesus* i. 25 Jesus is coming home from one of his teaching-tours in Galilee. **1881** *Nature* 17 Feb. 379/2 Preserving the soft tissues..as teaching-specimens.

**Teaˑching,** *ppl. a.* [f. as prec. + -ING [2].] That teaches, or has the quality or function of teaching.

**1853** J. CUMMING *Foreshadows* vii. (1854) 188 The great typical and teaching disease. **1899** *Allbutt's Syst. Med.* VIII. 217 Differences of opinion between the teaching and the medical professions. **1899** *Daily News* 19 Apr. 3/5 What was needed was teaching sermons. *Mod.* To change the University of London from a merely examining into a teaching university.

Hence **Teaˑchingly** *adv. rare*, in a way that teaches, instructively.

**1870** SPURGEON *Treas. David* Ps. xxx. 7 How touchingly and teachingly God corrected his servant's mistake.

**Teachless** (tīˑtʃlės), *a. rare.* [f. TEACH *v.* + -LESS.] Without teaching, untaught.

**1819** SHELLEY *Julian & Maddalo* 164 The religions and old saws..Which break a teachless nature to the yoke.

† **Teaˑchment.** *Sc. Obs.* [f. TEACH *v.* + -MENT.] Teaching, instruction.

**1562** WINȜET *Cert. Tractates* i. Wks. (S. T. S.) I. 5 Hes not mony throw inlak of techement in mad ignorance mysknawin thair deuty? **1563** DAVIDSON *Confut. Kennedy* in *Wodrow Soc. Misc.* (1844) 200 Without teachement and instructione of uthers. *a* **1578** LINDESAY (Pitscottie) *Chron. Scot.* (S. T. S.) I. 147 To abolische and put away the rude maner of teichment.

**Teachy,** obs. form of TETCHY.

**Tea-circle** to **-crop**: see TEA *sb.* 9.

**Teaˑ-cup.** A cup from which tea is drunk: usually of small or moderate size, with a handle.

**1700** CONGREVE *Way of World* IV. xi, Let Mahometan Fools..be damned over Tea-Cups and Coffee. **1714** ADDISON *Lover* No. 10 ℙ4 The fashion of the teacup..has run through a wonderful variety of colour, shape, and size. **1770** GOLDSM. *Des. Vill.* 235 While broken tea-cups.. Ranged o'er the chimney, glistened in a row. **1884** H. P. SPOFFORD in *Harper's Mag.* Nov. 889/1 In a sort of Oriental divination they always turned their tea-cups,..after the tea-drinking which they loved. *Mod.* The subject has been mentioned 'over the tea-cups' [*i.e.* unofficially; speaking of the establishment of a public institution].

**b.** As much as a tea-cup contains, a teacupful.

**1757** PULTNEY in *Phil. Trans.* L. 81 She took something more than a tea-cup of the infusion.

**c.** Phr. *A storm in a tea-cup*: a great commotion in a circumscribed circle, or about a matter of small or only local importance: see STORM.

**1872** BLACK *Adv. Phaeton* xix, She has raised a storm in a tea-cup by her..unwarranted assault. **1884** *Pall Mall G.* 19 Sept. 4/1 M. Renan's visit..to his birthplace in Brittany has raised a storm in the clerical teacup. **1900** G. C. BRODRICK *Mem. & Impr.* 360 Here the storm in the Oxford teacup raged as furiously as in the open sea.

**d.** *attrib. Tea-cup-and-saucer comedy*, comedy of a mild and 'proper' character.

**1830** TENNYSON *Talking Oak* xvi, Beauties, that were born In teacup-times of hood and hoop, Or while the patch was worn. **1895** *Athenæum* 8 June 748/2 'Tea-cup-and-saucer comedy'..was the invention of Thomas Purnell. **1898** *Westm. Gaz.* 30 Mar. 2/3 A little too much like..the tea-cup business of Alice in Wonderland. **1902** *Daily Chron.* 23 Sept. 3/3 Young girls..find a gentle interest in her mild heroics of tea-cup-and-saucer comedy.

Hence **Teaˑcupful**, as much as a tea-cup will contain. (Pl. *teacupfuls*; erron. *tea-cups full*.)

**1705** *Phil. Trans.* XXV. 1790 [I] took about a Tea-cupful. **1789** PILKINGTON *View Derby.* I. viii. 355 The dose 2 tea-cups full or more. **1838** *Q. Jrnl. Agric.* IX. 290 A salt-spoonful of salt and a tea-cupful of warm water.

**Tead, teade,** var. TEDE *Obs.*, torch.

**Tea-dealer** to **-dregs**: see TEA *sb.* 9.

**Teaˑ-driˑnker.** One who drinks tea, *esp.* one who drinks it habitually or in large quantities.

**1756** HANWAY *Ess. Tea* v. 225 The pernicious effects of tea.. as it is used by the bulk of tea-drinkers. **1888** J. PATON in *Encycl. Brit.* XXIII. 101/1 The quantity of theine consumed by even the most hardened tea-drinker is exceedingly minute.

So **Tea·dri·nking,** *a. vbl. sb.* the drinking of tea; † also, a social gathering at which tea is provided (*obs.*); also *attrib.*; **b.** *ppl. a.* that drinks tea.

**1756** HANWAY *Ess. Tea* viii. 243 (*heading*) The Prevalency of Example in Tea-drinking. **1799** MAR. EDGEWORTH *Lottery* i, She learned to love gossiping and tea-drinkings. **1813–14** T. SOMERVILLE *Life & Times* (1861) 280 The individuals who met at a tea-drinking party one afternoon. **1675** WYCHERLEY *Country Wife* II. i, Every raw, peevish, out-of-humoured, affected, dull, *tea-drinking, arithmetical fop, sets up for a wit. **1845** AGNES STRICKLAND *Queens Eng.* VIII. 310 Catherine of Braganza was certainly the first tea-drinking queen of England.

**Tea-drunkard** to **-frock**: see TEA *sb.* 9.

**Teaer, Teaey**: see after TEA *v.*, *sb.*

**Tea·-ga·rden.**

**1.** A garden or open-air enclosure, connected with a house of entertainment, where tea and other refreshments are served.

**1802** *Picture of London* 370 Shepherd and Shepherdess Tea Gardens, &c., City Road...Much frequented in the summer time by tea parties, &c. **1829** DE VEGA *Jrnl. Tour* ix. (1847) 81 A charge of three-pence is demanded on entering the delightful 'Tea Gardens'. **1900** *Daily News* 12 Nov. 6/3 Tea garden resorts..have entirely vanished.

**2.** A plantation in which tea-plants are grown. (Cf. *hop-garden*.)

**1882** SPONS *Encycl. Manuf.* v. 1994 There is scarcely a tea-garden but what is mainly filled with hybrids..between these two species [*Thea chinensis* and *T. assamica*]. **1888** J. PATON in *Encycl. Brit.* XXIII. 98/2 Undulating well-watered tracts..are the most valuable for tea gardens.

Hence **Tea·-ga·rdened** *a.*, having a tea-garden; **Tea·-ga·rdener**, the keeper of, or a worker in, a tea-garden; **Tea·-ga·rdeny** *a.*, *colloq.* resembling, or having the style of, a tea-garden (sense 1).

**1843** THACKERAY *Irish Sk.-Bk.* vii, What a prim,..green-railinged, tea-gardened, gravel-walked place would it have been. **1862** G. H. KINGSLEY *Sport & Trav.* (1900) 368 The public gardens, small and insignificant enough, indeed a little tea-gardeny. **1879** *Dickens's Dict. Thames* (1880) 120/2 There is little..of the ancient abbey to be found among the present tea-gardeny ruins. **1903** *Daily Chron.* 16 Sept. 6/7 Miura, a [Japanese] tea gardener, assures his young and pretty wife Ohana that she is unsightly.

**Teagle** (tī·g'l), *sb.* [A dial. var., chiefly northern, of TACKLE; cf. the forms *taikle, teakle, -kil,* s. v.] A hoisting apparatus: = TACKLE *sb.* 3; *esp.* one used for moving goods from floor to floor of a warehouse, etc. Also *attrib.*

**1828** *Craven Gloss.*, *Teagle*, a crane. **1835** URE *Philos. Manuf.* 45 This apparatus is called a hoist or teagle. **1887** *Manchester Courier* 21 May 7/2 The teagle did not hang over the street, but was in a recess. He saw no one guiding the teagle rope. **1901** *Act* 1 *Edw. VII*, c. 22 § 10 Every hoist or teagle and every fly wheel.

**b.** *transf.* (See quot.)

**1908** *Times, Lit. Supp.* 4 June 180/3 A detestable method of bird-catching .. specially-manufactured fish-hooks are baited and fastened to a string, known as a 'teagle', which is laid down in a place which the birds are likely to frequent. **1909** *Spectator* 21 Aug. 269/1 A law was passed making it illegal to catch any bird by means of the teagle.

Hence **Tea·gle** *v. trans.*, (*a*) to hoist or raise with or as with a teagle; = TACKLE *v.* 2; (*b*) to catch birds with a teagle (see b above). *dial.*

**1841** R. W. HAMILTON *Nugæ Lit.* 355 To *Teagle* is to raise any thing by pulley or wheel. **1892** M. C. F. MORRIS *Yorksh. Folk-Talk* 386 Wa mun start ti teeagle 'em up wi' t'hosses. **1910** *Sat. Rev.* 4 June 712/1 Sympathy with 'teagling', a barbarous but popular practice.

**Tea-gown** to **-growing**: see TEA *sb.* 9.

**Teague** (tēg, tīg). *colloq. Obs.* or *arch.* Also 7 teg, 8 teigue. [Anglicized spelling of the Irish name *Tadhg*, variously pronounced (tēg, tīg, taig), fancifully identified with *Thaddeus* and its familiar form *Thady*.] A nickname for an Irishman.

[**1583** in Dillwyn *Contrib. Hist. Swansea* (1840) 18 William Tege and Daniell John, Irishmen, made suet to be admytted Fremen.] **1661** *Merry Drollery* II. 143 Let not poor Teg and Shone Vender from der houses. **1682** *New News fr. Bedlam* 3 Those Sham Intrigues, From French, from English, and from Irish Teagues. **1689** in *Harl. Misc.* (1746) VIII. 603/1 Irish Frize..to rig a whole Regiment of his new-raised Teagues. *c* **1720** PRIOR *On Person who wrote ill*, His case appears to me like honest Teague's, When he was run away with, by his legs. **1727** SWIFT *Market-hill Thorn* Wks. 1755 IV. I. 90 Pigs and fanaticks, cows and teagues.. To tear thy hedges join in leagues. **1865** LOWELL *Pr. Wks.* (1890) II. 20 If we took warning by the example of Teague and Taffy. **1899** H. C. HART in *Phil. Soc. Trans.* 8 *Jeremiah* has Irish equivalent *Diarmid* or *Darby*;..*Theophilus, Teddy*; *Thaddeus, Thady*...The last two are from Irish *Tadhg* or *Teig* or *Thady*, a poet, which gives rise also to *Teague*, a name not now in use, but formerly a sobriquet (like the modern Paddy) for an Irishman. **1900** S. J. WEYMAN *Sophia* i, A raw-boned, uncouth Teague.

Hence † **Tea·guism**, the characteristics of a Teague or Irishman; † **Tea·gueland**, Ireland; † **Tea·guelander**, an Irishman. *Obs.*

**1689** *Answ. Lords & Commoners Sp.* 27 Not to mention those Teague Land Sparks put over them. *Ibid.* 28 The Teague-Landers and others like them. *a* **1700** B. E. *Dict. Cant. Crew*, *Teague-land*, Ireland. *Teague-landers*, Irishmen. **1710–11** SWIFT *Jrnl. to Stella* 30 Mar., Sir Thomas Mansel..saw Patrick, and swore he was a Teaguelander. **1732** SIR C. WOGAN *Let. to Swift* 27 Feb., The English writers take the hints from them [Irish]..and delight in gratifying the flattest nonsense..upon teigueism.

**Tea-hamper** to **-junketing**: see TEA *sb.* 9.

**Teaish, Teaism**: see after TEA *sb.*

**Teak** (tīk). Forms: 7–8 teke, 8 teek, tecka, 8–9 teck, 9 tick, tæk, teake, 8– teak. [ad. Pg. *teca* (1602–1644 in Yule), ad. Malayāl. *tēkka*; in Tamil *tēkku*, Telugu *tēku*, Tulu *tekki*, Canarese *tēgu, tēga, tēṅgu*.]

**1.** A large East Indian tree (*Tectona grandis*, N.O. *Verbenaceæ*), with opposite egg-shaped leaves and panicles of white flowers; more usually, its timber, a dark, heavy, oily wood of great strength and durability, used largely in the construction of ships and railway carriages, and in India also for building houses, and for sleepers, furniture, etc.; distinctively called *Indian Teak.*

**1698** FRYER *Acc. E. India & P.* 142 The Sheds here were round, thatch'd, and lined with broad Leaves of Teke (the Timber Ships are built with). *Ibid.* 178 Teke..is the firmest Wood they have for Building. **1757** J. H. GROSE *Voy. E. Indies* 174 As to the wood, it is a sort, called teak, to the full as durable as oak. **1783** JUSTAMOND tr. *Raynal's Hist. Indies* II. 244 Their ships..of a very strong wood called Teck. **1793** HODGES *Trav. India* 87, I found the teek, a timber remarkable for its hardness and size. **1808** A. PARSONS *Trav.* x. 215 This timber and plank are peculiar to India only;..it is called tick. **1811** *Niebuhr's Trav. Arab.* cliv, That excellent wood called Tæk. **1853** WAYLAND *Mem. Judson* I. xi. 413 Large forests of teak have been discovered in the interior [of Burma]. **1883** *Chambers's Encycl.* IX. 325/1 Indian Teak (*Tectona grandis*).

**2.** Applied, usually with defining words, to other trees which produce strong or durable timber, or otherwise resemble the Indian teak; as **African Teak**, *Oldfieldia africana* (N.O. *Euphorbiaceæ*), or its wood, which is too heavy to be exclusively used in shipbuilding. **Bastard Teak**, an East Indian tree, *Pterocarpus Marsupium*, from which kino is obtained; yielding hard and durable timber. **Ben Teak**, *Lagerstrœmia microcarpa*, of tropical Asia; also, a poor quality of teak. **Teak of New South Wales**, a small tree, *Endiandra glauca*, N.O. *Leguminosæ*, the wood of which is fine-grained and dense (Miller *Plant-n.* 1884). **Teak of New Zealand**, the PURIRI, *Vitex littoralis*. **White Teak**, of Queensland, a species of *Flindersia*, N.O. *Meliaceæ*. In Australia also applied to *Dissilaria baloghioides*, N.O. *Euphorbiaceæ* (Morris *Austral Eng.*).

**1842** BRANDE *Dict. Sc.*, etc. 1217/1 A species of timber called African teak is pretty largely imported..from the west coast of Africa...It is not teak. **1858** HOGG *Veg. Kingd.* 663 African Teak, or Oak, is the wood of *Oldfieldia africana*. **1866** *Treas. Bot.* 1128 Ben Teak, the wood of *Lagerströmia microcarpa*; also applied to inferior Teak. New South Wales Teak, *Endiandra glauca*. **1878** H. M. STANLEY *Dark Cont.* II. vi. 156 Many a village stood..embowered in the thick shade of tamarind and bombax, teak. **1883** *Chambers's Encycl.* IX. 325/1 The leaves of many different trees have been brought to botanists as those of the African teak. **1884** MILLER *Plant-n.*, *Vitex littoralis*, New Zealand Teak or Puriri-tree.

**3.** *attrib.* and *Comb.*, as *teak forest, ship, timber, -tree, -wood*; *teak-built* (in quot. fig.), *-lined, -producing* adjs.; **teak-oak**, the teak (sense 1).

**1727** A. HAMILTON *New Acc. E. Ind.* I. xv. 177 Gundavee .., where good Quantities of Teak Timber are cut. **1783** J. PRICE *Tracts* I. 191 (Y.) Ships..built in India of tekewood, and bound with iron spikes and bolts. **1783** RENNELL *Mem. Map Hindoostan* vi. 89 *note*, Teek ships of 40 years old and upwards, are no uncommon objects. **1800** *Misc. Tr.* in *Asiat. Ann. Reg.* 187 During the two last days I had occasionally observed the teak-tree. **1848** DICKENS *Dombey* xxxii, That teak-built and trim ballad. **1869** SIR E. J. REED *Iron-Clad Ships* ii. 26 In the 'Bellerophon', the armour-plating is 6 inches, and the teak backing 10 inches thick. **1884** MILLER *Eng. Plant-n.*, African Teak-tree, *Oldfieldia africana*. **1896** *Daily News* 30 Dec. 6/3 The library at Groote Schuur is a cosy, teak-lined room.

**Tea·-ke·ttle.** A kettle in which water is boiled for making tea.

**1705** *Lond. Gaz.* No. 4063/4 A Tea Kettle, a gilt Tea-Pot. *a* **1774** TUCKER *Lt. Nat.* (1834) II. 397 He that snatches up the copper handle of a tea kettle, and burns his fingers. **1865** *Times* 23 Aug., Wiesbaden..is as close and hot in the summer as a steaming tea-kettle.

*transf.* **1857** DUFFERIN *Lett. High Lat.* iv. (ed. 3) 18 There was a great demand in Australia for small river steamers. ..The difficulty, however, was to get such fragile tea-kettles across the ocean.

*attrib.* **1746** MILES in *Phil. Trans.* XLIV. 55 The Spirits were such as we use for the Tea-kettle Lamp. **1837** DICKENS *Pickw.* vi, Crimson silk tea-kettle holders. **1896** *Peterson Mag.* Jan. 63/2 Martha dropped the tea-kettle cover with a bang.

**Teakil, -kle,** obs. forms of TACKLE.

**Teal** (tīl). Forms: 4–6 tele, 5 teill, 5–6 teele, 6–7 teyle, teale, 7 teil, tayle, 8 teall, 7– teal. [ME. *tele*, exemplified early in 14th c., but pointing to an unrecorded OE. *tæle, tēle*:—WGer. **taili*. Du. has a deriv. form *taling, teling* masc., in Kilian *teelingh*, MDu. *tēling, teiling*, MLG. *tēlink* masc., teal. (Connexion with Du. *teling* fem., generation, LG. *teling* fem., brood, from Du. and LG. *tēlen* to breed, is improbable.)]

**1.** A small fresh-water fowl, *Querquedula* or *Anas crecca*, or other species of the genus, the smallest of the ducks, widely distributed in Europe, Asia, and America; also locally applied to other genera of the *Anatidæ*. Also as collective pl.

**1314** in *Wardrobe Acc. Edw. II* 21, 2 teles 3[d]. *c* **1325** *Gloss. W. de Bibbesw.* in Wright *Voc.* 151 Turbe de cercels [*gl.* teles]. **14..** *Voc.* in Wr.-Wülcker 563/45 *Anacius*, a tele. *c* **1440** *Promp. Parv.* 487/2 Tele, bryd, *turcella, turbella.* **1486** *Bk. St. Albans* d j, I haue seen them made sum to sle the pie sum to sle the Tele vppon the Reuer. **1530** PALSGR. 279/2 Teele a byrde, *plignon*. *c* **1532** DU WES *Introd. Fr.* ibid. 912 The teyle, *le cercelle*. **1538** ELYOT, *Querquedula*, a waterfowle callyd a teale. **1575** TURBERV. *Falconrie* 191 Some water plashet or pitte where wylde fowle lye, as Teales or suche lyke. **1614** MARKHAM *Cheap Husb.* VII. xviii. (1668) 123 So you may nourish Teils, Widgens, Sheldrakes or green Plovers. **1661** LOVELL *Hist. Anim. & Min.* 183 Teales and Widgins...Commonly they are very fat and sweet of taste. **1773** G. WHITE *Selborne* xxxix. 99, I saw young teals taken alive in the ponds of Wolmer Forest. **1873** G. C. DAVIES *Mountain & Mere* ix. 70 A couple of teal came within shot. **1876** SMILES *Sc. Natur.* xiii. (ed. 4) 259 The Teal..and the Eider duck visit the loch occasionally in winter.

**b.** The flesh of this bird as food.

? *c* **1475** *Sqr. lowe Degre* 320 With deynty meates that were dere,.. The tele, the ducke and the drake. **1620** VENNER *Via Recta* iii. 65 Teale..excelleth all other water-fowle. **1735** SHERIDAN in Swift *Let. to Mrs. Whiteway* 8 Nov., His teal was spoiled in the roasting.

**2.** With distinctive prefixes, applied to various species of *Querquedula* and allied genera: as **American** or **Green-winged Teal**, *Q. carolinensis*; **Baikal** or **Japanese Teal**, *Q.* (*Eunetta*) *formosa*; **Blue-winged Teal** of N. and S. America, *Q. discors* or *cyanoptera*; **Brazilian Teal**, *Q. brasiliensis*; **Chilian Teal**, *Q. flavirostris*; **Cinnamon** or **Redbreasted Teal**, *Q. cyanoptera*; **Falcated Teal**, *Q. falcata*, of China; **Summer, Cricket** (see CRICKET *sb.*[1] 3), or **Garganey Teal**, the GARGANEY, *Q. circia*; also **Chinese Teal**, the mandarin duck, *Aix galericulata*; **Goose Teal**: see GOOSE *sb.* 8; **Salt-water** or **Brown Diving Teal**, the RUDDER-*duck* (G. Trumbull *Game Birds* 1888).

**1678** RAY *Willughby's Ornith.* 378 Of the Summer-Teal, called by Gesner Ana circia. **1754** CATESBY *Carol.* I. 99 The Blue-Wing Teal. **1785** PENNANT *Arct. Zool.* II. 569 American Teal. **1785** LATHAM *Gen. Syn.* VI. 557 Baikal Teal. **1824** STEPHENS in *Shaw's Gen. Zool.* XII. II. 143 Garganey Teal. *Ibid.* 153 Mexican Teal. **1837** *Penny Cycl.* IX. 181/2 The beautiful *Anas* (*Boschas*) *formosa*, Sw., or Baikal Teal of methodists. *Ibid.* 182/1 Such a species is actually the blue-winged Teal of North America. **1896** *List Anim. Zool. Soc.* 447 [Seven species named]. **1896** NEWTON *Dict. Birds* 949 In ordinary talk 'Teal' stands for any Duck-like bird of small size. *Ibid.*, In the same loose sense the word is often applied to the two most beautiful of the Family *Anatidæ*, belonging to the genus *Æx*..—the Carolina or Wood-Duck of North America, *Æ. sponsa*.., and the Mandarin-Duck of China, *Æ. galericulata*.

**3.** *attrib.* and *Comb.*, as *teal-catcher, -duck, -flapper* (FLAPPER *sb.* 3), *-shooting, -springing*; **teal-house** = *tealery* (see below).

**1668** WILKINS *Real Char.* II. v. § 4. 156 To the Teal-kind should be reduced that other fowl..called Garganey. **1845** *Statist. Acc. Scot.* XIV. 122 Teal-duck..are found here. **1874** J. W. LONG *Amer. Wild-fowl* xv. 193 In no other branch of wild-fowling is a breech-loader of more advantage than in teal-shooting. **1888** 'R. BOLDREWOOD' *Robbery under Arms* iii. (1890) 16, I was off the old pony and into the water like a teal-flapper. **1902** T. W. WEBBER *Forests Upper India* xviii. 247 A..canoe..which belongs to the teal-catchers. *Ibid.*, Most bungalows in Gorakhpur have a teal house..where teal are fattened.

Hence **Tea·lery**, a place in which teal are kept and fattened.

**1890** *Cornh. Mag.* July 17 Here are..the cow-house, and the tealery, and the quailery. **1894** E. BRADDON in *Blackw. Mag.* Sept. 387/2 The teal..kept and fattened in a tealery.

**Teal, Tealer**: see TELE, TIL, TILL, TILLER.

**Tealde,** obs. f. *told*: see TELL *v.*

**Teale,** dial. form of TALE.

**Tea·-leaf.** The leaf of the tea-plant; *esp.* in *pl.* the leaves after being infused to make the beverage.

**1756** HANWAY *Ess. Tea* vi. 237 You have also heard that your maids dry your tea-leaves, and sell them. **1798** *Monthly Mag.* July 30/1 Texeira, a Spaniard who visited the East Indies about the year 1600, saw the dried tea-leaves first in Malacca. **1851** MAYHEW *Lond. Labour* II. 133/1 An extensive trade..is carried on in tea-leaves..after their having been subjected, in the usual way, to decoction. *Ibid.* 133/2 The tea-leaves are often reserved..to be thrown on the carpets when swept, as a means of allaying the dust. *c* **1865** *Circ. Sc.* I. 351/2 The tea-leaves have..to be infused with boiling-water.

So **Tea-leaved** (tī·līvd) *a.*, having leaves like those of the tea-plant: specifically applied to a species of willow (*Salix phylicifolia*).

**1806** GALPINE *Brit. Bot.* § 409. **1861** MISS PRATT *Flower. Pl.* V. 106.

**Tealess** (tī·lės), *a.* [f. TEA *sb.* + -LESS.] Without or destitute of tea; not having had one's tea.

**1821** *Blackw. Mag.* X. 562 Day pass'd, defrauded of its moistest meals, Breakfastless, milkless, tealess, soupless. **1849** THACKERAY *Pendennis* lxiv, He..sat..rapt in wonder, tealess, and bread-and-butterless. **1858** TROLLOPE *Dr. Thorne* xxx, There she waited till ten o'clock, tealess.

† **Tealt,** *a. Obs.* [OE. *tealt* adj. (whence *tealtian, tealtrian*, to be unsteady, shake, totter): app. not represented in the cognate languages] Unsteady, insecure, shaky; *fig.* unreliable, precarious, uncertain. Hence † **Tealte** *adv.*, insecurely.

*a* **1000** *Runic Poem* xxi. (Gr.), ȝif hi sculun neðan on nacan tealtum, and hi sæyða swiðe bregað. *a* **1023** WULFSTAN *Hom.* xxx. (N.) 149 Swa tealte syndon eorðan welan. *Ibid.* l. 273 Hu læne and hu lyðre þis lif is,..hu tealt. *c* **1315** SHOREHAM i. 231 For ȝef þat water his kende lest, þat cristning stant te tealte.

**Team** (tīm), *sb.* Forms: 1–4 **team, tem,** (2–7 **theam, theme**), 3–6 **teme,** 4 **teom(e, tyme,** (3–7 **them**), 4–7 **teeme, teem** (9 *dial.*), 6 **teyme,** 6–7 **teame,** 7 **taime,** *Sc.* **thame,** 7– **team.** [OE. *téam* = OFris. *tám*, WFris. *team*, bridle, also progeny, family, line of descendants; OS. *tôm*, MDu., Du. *toom* bridle, rein, Du. dial. *toom* brood, NFris. *toom* rope, LG. *toom* draught with the net; OHG., MHG. *zoum*, Ger. *zaum* bridle, rein, ON. *taumr* rein, bridle, rope, cord:—OTeut. **taumo*z, prob. from **taugmo*z the action of drawing, draught, from ablaut series *teuh-*, *tauh-*, *tuh-*, *tug-*, to draw, L. *dūcĕre* to lead: cf. TEE *v.*[1] The original literal sense is not found in OE., but perh. appears later in sense 9; our sense 1 is known also in OFris., and in Dutch dialects. The developed branches II and III are only in Eng. German has, in senses 1, 2, 8, 9, the cognate *zucht*:—OTeut. **tuhti*z.]

**I.** †**1.** The bringing forth of children; child-bearing. *Obs.* [Cf. MHG. *kint ziehen* to bring forth children, Ger. *viehzucht* cattle breeding.]

*c* **1000** ÆLFRIC *Hom.* in Assmann *Ags. Hom.* (1889) 20/159 Þæt eald wif sceole ceorles brucan, þonne heo forwerod byð and teames ætealdod. *Ibid.* 38/339 His wif..wearð mid.. Esau and Iacob, and heo ȝeswac ða teames. *c* **1200** *Trin. Coll. Hom.* 133 God ches two lif holi men him [Seint iohan baptiste] to fader and to moder, þe weren boðe teames ateald.

**b.** A family or brood of young animals; now *dial.* applied to a litter of pigs, a brood of ducks. In quot. *a* 1225 *fig.*

*c* **1000** ÆLFRIC *Hom.* II. 10 Beon: hi tymað heora team mid clænnysse. *a* **1225** *Ancr. R.* 336 Drauh togedere al þene team [cf sins] under þe moder. **14..** *Voc.* in Wr.-Wülcker 579/39 *Educamen*, a teme of checonn. **1511** *MS. Acc. St. John's Hosp., Canterb.*, For a teme off ix pygys iiijs iijd. **1767** G. WHITE *Selborne* xi, We have a few teams of ducks, bred in the moors. **1887** *Kentish Gloss.*, *Team*, a litter of pigs or a brood of ducks.

†**2.** Offspring, progeny, issue, family, line of descendants; race, stock; cf. BAIRN-TEAM. *Obs.*

**902** in Thorpe *Charters* (1865) 152 Ðreo witeþeowe men ..ða me salde bisceop & þa hiwan to ryhtre æhta & hire team. *c* **950** *Lindisf. Gosp.* Mark xii. 21 Ðe æfterra onfeng ða ilca & dead wæs & ne ðes forleort sed *vel* team [Vulg. *semen*]. *c* **1000** ÆLFRIC *Saints' Lives* (1885) I. 432 Eall his team wearð ȝewurðod þurh god. *c* **1000** — *Gen.* v. 31 *Rubric*, Hu he Noe bearh and his wife and his teame æt þam miclan flode. *a* **1225** *Juliana* 60 Weox swa his team þat ne mahte hit namon tellen. **1297** R. GLOUC. (Rolls) 5241 Is foure gode sones woxe uaste ynou, Adelbold & adelbriȝt, adelred & alfred, Þis was a stalwarde tem [*v.rr.* teme, tyme]. *c* **1330** R. BRUNNE *Chron. Wace* (Rolls) 4794 Cassibolan was Androcheus eem, Luddes broþer of þat teem. *c* **1330** — *Chron.* (1810) 20 Ethelbert..Adelwolfes broþer, of Egbrihtes team. *c* **1435** *Torr. Portugal* 2022 This child is come of gentille teme.

**II. 3.** A set of draught animals; two or more oxen, horses, dogs, or other animals harnessed to draw together. (Plural, after a numeral, *team.*)

[*c* **825** *Vesp. Hymns* v. 34 Mid feoðurtemum [L. *cum quadrigis*].] *c* **1000** ÆLFRIC *Voc.* in Wr.-Wülcker 120/32–3 *Inus*, oxa on þam forman teame. *Binus*, on þam æfteran teame. *a* **1250** *Owl & Night.* 776 An hors..drahþ bi sweore [*v.r.* biuore] grete temes. *c* **1290** *St. Lucy* 129 in *E. E. Poems* (1862) I. 105 Stronge temes he let fecche: of Oxen menie on. **1362** LANGL. *P. Pl.* A. VII. 127 Bote Treuþe schal techen ow his Teome for to dryue. **1377** *Ibid.* B. IX. 257 Grace gaue Piers a teme [C. XXII. 262 teome] foure gret oxen. **1486** *Nottingham Rec.* III. 249 Drawyng þerof..with a teme of oxen. **1590** SPENSER *F. Q.* III. iv. 33 A teme of Dolphins raunged in aray Drew the smooth charett of sad Cymoent. **1621** G. SANDYS *Ovid's Met.* xii, A log he tooke Which scarce two teeme could draw. **1633** G. HERBERT *Temple, Praise* III. iii, Not all the teams of Albion in a row Can hale or draw it out of doore. **1688** *Andros Tracts* III. 89 Greatly disappointed by this loss [of a horse] which was all the Teame he had. **1805** W. TAYLOR in *Ann. Rev.* III. 258 The cannons are..dragged about with a team of eight horses. **1835** SIR J. ROSS *Narr. 2nd Voy.* xix. 292 Drawn by a team of six good dogs. **1840** THIRLWALL *Greece* VII. lviii. 298 A thousand team of cattle conveyed the timber to the coast. **1870** MORRIS *Earthly Par.* II. III. 283 With jingling bit and trace Came the grey team from field.

**b.** *transf.* The stock or 'lot' of horses (or other beasts) belonging to one owner or stable. *dial.*

**1655** tr. *Com. Hist. Francion* VII. 6, I would have laid Pyebald against the best Mare in my Brother-in-Laws teem. **1876** *Surrey Gloss.* s.v., 'A good team of cows' is the general expression for a nice lot of cows.

**4. a.** *fig.* Applied to persons drawing together.

**1614** B. JONSON *Barth. Fair* II. v, 'Twere like falling into a whole Shire of butter: they had need be a teeme of Dutchmen, should draw him out. **1668** BP. HOPKINS *Serm.*, *Vanity* (1685) 123 They are so enslaved to the work of the devil, that he puts them into his team, makes them draw and strain for their iniquities. **1748** RICHARDSON *Clarissa* (1811) VII. x. 61, I will add a string of bells to it, to complete thee for the fore-horse of the idiot team. **1837** CARLYLE *Fr. Rev.* I. III. vi, When a team of Twenty-five Millions begins rearing, what is Loménie's whip?

**b.** *transf.* A number of persons associated in some joint action; now *esp.* a definite number of persons forming a side in a match, e.g. in a football match or a 'tug-of-war'; in *Shoe-making*, etc., a company of workmen each of whom performs one operation in completing a process.

*a* **1529** ? SKELTON *Vox Populi* 204 All theise men goo to wracke, That are the body and the staye Of your graces realme allwaye... Thei must be.. Your streinghe and your teme, For to defende your realme. **1622** MASSINGER & DEKKER *Virg. Martyr* IV. ii, Hear me, my little team of villains, hear me. **1644–7** CLEVELAND *Char. Lond. Diurn.* 6 Beleeve him [Cromwell] as he whistles to his Cambridge Teeme of Committee-men. **1859** DICKENS *T. Two Cities* I. ii, The team had capitulated and returned to their duty. **1885** *Manch. Exam.* 10 July 5/1 The Northern [cricket] team, batting first, were disposed of for 192. **1888** *Daily News* 20 July 7/3 'A team' [in boot-making] here would consist of three men, while in America there would be six in 'a team'. **1902** *Westm. Gaz.* 28 Apr. 5/2 They were beaten by a [football] team superior to themselves. *Ibid.*, The two teams took up their positions.

**5.** Two or more beasts, or a single beast, along with the vehicle which they draw; a horse and cart, or wagon with two horses (now *dial.*); also, *U.S. local*, a cart, wagon, or other vehicle of burden for one horse (*single team*) or two horses (*double team*).

**1641** *Boston* (U. S.) *Town Records* 27 Sept., The Richer ..Inhabitants shall afford three dayes' worke of one man, except such as have Teames. **1675** *3 Inhumane Murthers* 2 He being out with his Father-in-Law's Teame..to fetch Coals. **1688** R. HOLME *Armoury* III. 339/2 A Waine, or Oxe Taime, when drawn by Oxen, and hath a Waine Cop. **1787** (Mar. 1) *Massachusetts Statute* (Bridge-toll), Toll..for each team drawn by more than one beast, nine pence. **1806** (Mar. 4) *Ibid.*, Toll..for each cart, sled, sleigh, or other team of burthen, drawn by one beast, sixteen cents. **1798** *Sporting Mag.* XI. 48 He was returning from Cowley with a loaded team. **1898** *Boston Even. Transcript* 23 Feb. 16/3 To make the hill less perilous to the poor horses obliged to drag teams up or down it.

†**b.** A team-load. *Obs. rare.*

**1789** *Trans. Soc. Arts* VII. 36 The quantity of manure was two teams of dung to each pit, value three pence per team.

**6.** A flock of wild ducks or other birds flying in a line or string.

**1688** R. HOLME *Armoury* II. xiii. 311/1 Team of ducks. **1697** DRYDEN *Æneid* VII. 965 Like a long team of snowy swans on high, Which clap their wings, and cleave the liquid sky. **1726** POPE *Odyss.* XIX. 627 A team of twenty geese (a snow-white train!). **1720** *Humourist* Ded. 5 [He] took a trip to your Dominions upon a Team of wild Geese. **1848** H. W. HERBERT *Field Sports* II. App. B. 334. **1871** 'STONEHENGE' *Brit. Sports* I. ix. § 1 Wild-fowl Nomencl...A 'team' of ducks (when in the air).

**7.** Phrases. **a.** *Naval*: see quots.

**1829** MARRYAT *F. Mildmay* viii, Nothing can be more dull and monotonous than a blockading cruize 'in the team', as we call it; that is, the ships of the line stationed to watch an enemy. **1867** SMYTH *Sailor's Word-bk.* s.v., Ships blockading a port, being generally formed in a line, are said to be 'in the team'.

†**b.** *To lay in team*: to couple, join together.

**13..** *E. E. Allit. P.* C. 37, I schall me poruay pacyence, & play me with boþe; For in þe tyxte, þere þyse two arn in teme layde, Hit arne fettled in on forme, þe forme and þe laste.

**III.** In Anglo-Saxon Law.

(In this sense recorded only in Eng.; but in MHG. the cognate vb. *ziehen* was used to express the bringing of an action, and the action is expressed by *zug* in *Gewährzug*.)

**8.** In a suit for the recovery of goods alleged to have been stolen, the action or procedure by which the holder transferred or referred it back to a third person (generally the party from whom he received the goods) to defend the title to them; vouching to warranty. *Obs.* exc. *Hist.*

In med. (Anglo) L. *advocatio ad warantum*; in Anglo-Fr. *revoche garaunt*; called by Liebermann *Gewährzug*, by Schmid *Gewährschaftszug* (*Gesetze* Glossar s. v.).

*a* **800** *Laws Hlothhære & Eadric* (*c* 685) c. 16 Þonne tæme he to wic to cyninges sele to þam mæn þe him sealde, ȝif he þane wite and æt þam teame ȝebrengen mæȝe. **901–924** *Laws Eadweard* I. c. I § I And ȝif hwa butan porte ceapiȝe, ðonne sy he cyninges oferhyrnesse scyldiȝ; and gange se team þeah forð, oð þæt man wite, hwær he oðstande. **946–***c* **961** *Laws Edgar* I. c. 4 Buton þara oðer hæbbe, nele him mon nænne team [*Lat. text* cenningam] ȝeþafian. **960–975** in Earle *Land Charters* 201 Ða tymde Wulfstan hine to Æðelstane æt Sunnanbyrȝ. Ða cende he tem, let ðone forberstan, forbeh ðone andaȝen. ? **997** *Laws Æthelred* III. c. 6 Ælc team and ælc ordal beo on þæs kyninges byriȝ. **1027–34** *Laws Cnut* II. c. 24 § 1 And ȝyf..he þyllice ȝewitnesse næbbe, ne beo þær nan team, ac aȝyfe man þam aȝenfriȝan his aȝen. **1130–35** *Laws Edw. Conf.* c. 22 § 3 Team [*v. rr.* Theam, Them]: quod, si aliquis aliquid interciebatur [*v.r.* intertietur] super aliquem, et ipse non poterit warantum suum habere, erit foresfactura et iusticia; similiter de calumpniatore, si deficiebat. **12..** *Leges Burgorum* c. 12 in *Scot. Stat.* (1844) I. 335 Per legem burgi se defendet nisi sit de prodicione vel de them [*c* **1400** *transl.* thruch lauch of burgh he sall were hym bot gif it be of tresoun or of theme]. **1387** TREVISA *Higden* (Rolls) II. 95 [see also in c] *Theam*, Frensche, *reuoche garant* [**1432–50** tr. *Higden* ibid., *Thean*, that is, to lawde the auctor, in Frenche, *reuouche g[a]raunte*; orig. *Theam* [*v.r. them*], id est, laudare auctorem; Gallice, *reuoucher garaunt*]. **1628** COKE [see c]. **1900** A. LANG *Hist. Scotl.* I. vi. 148.

**b.** The right or prerogative of jurisdiction in a suit of *téam*, together with the fees and profits thence accruing; from the 11th c. usually included in charters granting land (in which it regularly followed *toll*, esp. in the formula *with sac and soc, toll and team, infangthief*, etc.).

*Saca and socne* (without *toll and team*) is first found in a charter of 1020 or later (see INFANGTHIEF); *toll and team* (alone) is known first in a charter *a* 1023; the formula combining them appears just after the accession of Edward the Confessor, 1042, and occurs in numerous charters ascribed to him, mostly existing only in later copies. It occurs also in the Laws of Wm. I and Henry I. The meaning of *team* was still known when the 'Laws of Edw. the Confessor' were compiled *c* 1130–35 (see above). After the 12th c. it was an obsolete term, the meaning of which was largely a matter of conjecture, and was generally mistaken: see c.

**1066** *Charter Edw. Conf.* in Thorpe *Charters* (1865) 405 Donavi..abbati Eadwino..consuetudinem quæ dicitur teames. *a* **1400** in *Scot. Stat.* (1844) I. 742 De Curia de theme. **1664** SPELMAN *Gloss.* 533 s. v. *Team* al. *Theam*, *Theam* significare videtur jurisdictionem cognoscendi in Curiâ suâ de advocationibus, sive intertiatis; hoc est..*de vocatis ad Warrantiam*. **1895** POLLOCK & MAITLAND *Hist. Eng. Law* II. 157 *note*, The team of the Anglo-Norman charters seems to be the right to hold a court into which foreigners, i. e. persons not resident within the jurisdiction, may be vouched.

**1017–23** *Charter of Ælfweard Abbot* (Earle *Land Charters* 236), And toll and team sy aȝifen into þam mynstre. **1046–60** *Charter of Ealdred Bishop* (Kemble No. 805), Ut habeant et possideant iure aecclesiastico perpetua haereditate, cum saca et socne, tolle et teame, reditibus et campis [etc.]. **1046–60** *Charter Edw. Conf.* (Kemble No. 829, later copy), And icc an heom eft alswa ðat hi habben ðarto sacc and socne, toll and team, infangeneðef and flemenesfermð [etc.]. *a* **1066** *Charter* (Kemble No. 843) [see INFANGTHIEF]. **1090–1135** *Laws of Wm. I*, c. 2 § 3 E cil francs hom ki ad e sache e soche e toll e tem e infangentheof, se il est enplaidé [etc.]. **1114–18** *Laws Hen. I*, c. 20 § 2 Archiepiscopi, episcopi, comites..sacam et socnam habent, tol et theam et infangentheaf. **12..** *Reg. Maj.* I. ii. in *Scot. Stat.* (1844) I. App. i. 234 Qui habent et tenent terras suas cum soko et sako furca et fossa toll et them et infangandthefe et vtfangandthefe. [SKENE *tr.* Judges..quha hes power to hald their courts, with sock, sack, gallous, and pit, toll, and thame, infang-thief, and outfang-thief.] **1657** SIR W. MURE *Hist. Rowallane* Wks. (S. T. S.) II. 241 The Mures..being free Barones yrof, holding in cheife of the crowne, infeft cum furca et fossa, sock et sack, thole et theam, infang theif et outfang theif. **1871** FREEMAN *Norm. Conq.* IV. xviii. 208 One among them, whether by seniority or by hereditary right, further enjoyed the profitable privileges of toll and team.

¶ **c.** By the end of the 12th c., the process of *téam* being obsolete, the meaning of the word was to a great extent forgotten. Legal writers erroneously explained it from sense 2, as 'the property of the lord in the *team* or offspring and posterity of his serfs'.

This appears in a 12–13th c. Latin version of a charter of Edward the Confessor, whence it was regularly repeated by later writers, some of whom, as Higden, Rastall, Skene, and Coke, offer both explanations.

**1200–25** *Latin version of Charter of Edw. Conf.* (Kemble No. 843) [..saca and socna, toll and team] cum priuilegio habendi totam suorum seruorum propaginem. *c* **1250** *Expositio Vocab.* in *Placita de Quo Warranto* (1818) 275/2 *Them*, aver progeny de vos humes. *c* **1290** FLETA I. xlvii. § 9 *Them*, acquietantiam amerciamentorum sequelæ propriorum suorum. **1387** TREVISA *Higden* (Rolls) II. 95 [see also in a] Somtyme *Theam* is i-cleped þe sewte of bonde men [orig. *Them*..quandoque dicitur sequela nativorum]. **1579** *Expos. Terms Law* 177 b, *Them*, that is that you shall haue all ye generations of your Villaines wyth ther suites & cattel wheresoeuer they shall bee found in England. **1597** SKENE *De Verb. Sign.*, *Theme*, is power to haue servandes and slaues, quhilk ar called *nativi, bondi, villani*, and all Barronnes infeft with Theme, hes the same power: For vnto them all their bond-men, their bairnes, gudes, and geare properly perteinis, swa that they may dispone thereupon at their pleasure. **1628** COKE *On Litt.* II. xi. § 172. 116 *Theme* (sometime written Theame corruptly) is an old Saxon word, and signifieth *Potestatem habendi in nativos sive villanos cum eorum sequelis, terris, bonis & catallis.* But *Teame*, sometime corruptly written *Theam*,..is also an old Saxon word and signifieth where a man cannot produce his Warrant of that which he bought according to his Voucher. **1895** POLLOCK & MAITLAND *Hist. Eng. Law* I. 566 Then [13th c.] *team* is taken to mean the brood, the offspring, the 'sequela' of one's villeins; but this we may be sure is a mistake.

¶ **d.** At other times *team* was app. taken as a mere complement to *toll*, and was evidently thought to be some kind of impost.

**1456** SIR G. HAYE *Law Arms* (S.T.S.) 238 Pilgrymes..suld nouthir pay toll na teme, aucht na custume, na payage, quhill thai ar on thair voyage.

**IV.** Later senses related to II.

(But sense 9 may represent an Anglicizing of ON. *taumr*. In that sense also, apparently sometimes associated with L. *tēmo* a beam, pole, tongue of a plough, carriage, cart, etc.)

**9.** Part of the gear by which oxen or horses were harnessed to a plough, harrow, or wain. In mod. dialect use, 'a chain to which oxen are yoked in lieu of a pole' (*Eng. Dial. Dict.*); 'in plough equipment, the main or leading chain, by which the whole of the oxen or horses drag the implement' (F. T. Elworthy). *Foot-team*, the foot-chain of a plough.

*c* **1350** *Nominale Gall.-Angl.* 858 *Trecters et temons*, Plowestryngges and tem. *c* **1425** *Voc.* in Wr.-Wülcker 665/20 Nomina pertinencia ad carectariam... *Hoc plaustrum*, wayne. *Hec tema*, teme. *Hec torques*, wythe. **1483** *Cath. Angl.* 379/2 A Teme, *temo*. **1523** FITZHERB. *Husb.* § 4 Yf he wyll haue his plough to go a narowe forowe..he setteth his foteteame in the nycke nexte to the ploughe-beame. *Ibid.* § 15 An oxe-harowe..the formes[t] slote must be bygger than the other, bycause the fote-teame shall be fastened to the same with a shakyll, or a withe to drawe by. **1530** PALSGR. 279/2 Teme of a plough or oxen, *atellee*. *c* **1540** *Inv. Monast. Lylleshull* in *Archæologia* XLIII. 209, iij waynes with themes and other thyngys necessary. **1570** LEVINS *Manip.* 208/17 A Teame, cheane, *temo, onis*. **1575** *Richmond Wills* (Surtees) 255, ij yooks furnysshed viijd, ij teymes, j horse draught, j buck shackill, j plewghryng, ij paire toggwethes, ij axill nayles iijs. iiijd. **1605–6** in *N. Riding Rec.* (1884) I. 27 Duos torques ferreos, Angl. Iron horseteames. **1616** SURFL. & MARKH. *Country Farme* 533 When they draw two and two together in the bearegeares,..then there is needfull the plow-cleuise, and teame [etc.]. **1788**

W. MARSHALL *Yorksh.* Gloss., *Team*, an ox-chain, passing from yoke to yoke. **1889** *N. W. Linc. Gloss.*, *Team*,..(2) harness for a draught of horses or oxen.

**10.** *dial.* A chain (generally).

**1828** *Craven Gloss.*, *Team*, a strong iron chain. **1840** SPURDENS *Suppl. to Forby's Voc. E. Anglia* s. v., A string or chain of sausages is called 'a team of links'. **1904** *Eng. Dial. Dict.*, *Team*..an iron chain usually with a ring at one end and hook at the other. Used for putting round stones to fasten the crane chain to when lifting. (W. Yorksh.)

**V. 11.** *attrib.* and *Comb.*, as, in sense 3, *team-beast*, *-driving*, *-horse*, *-labour*, *-length*, *-master*, *-plough*; in sense 4 b, *team-game*, *-match*, *-play*, *-race*, *-system*, *-training*; also **team-band**, a fastening for securing the drawing-gear to the plough, etc.; **team-boat**, a boat drawn or propelled by horse-power; †**team-land**, = PLOUGH-LAND; **team-man** (also **teamsman**), a teamster; **team-railway**, a railway system worked by horse-power (Ogilvie 1882); **team-shovel**: see quot.; †**team-ware**, (*a*) a team of horses, etc.; (*b*) = *team-land*; **team-work**, (*a*) work done with a team of beasts; (*b*) the combined action of a team of players, etc.; (*c*) work done by a team of operatives.

**1808** VANCOUVER *Agric. Devon* 115 A swing-plough with a beam..at the end of this beam is occasionally fastened a graduated iron to which the *team-band is affixed. **1847–78** HALLIWELL, *Team-bands*, the same as *Start-chains*. **1573–80** BARET *Alv.* T 96 A *Teame beast, euerie beast that draweth or beareth burdens. **1818** *Pict. New York* 222 A *team or horse boat sails..to Brooklyn every quarter of an hour. **1820** *Boston* (U.S.) *Daily Advert.* 26 Apr. 2/4 A team-boat propelled by twenty-five horses. **1867** SMYTH *Sailor's Word-bk.*, *Team-boat*, a ferry-boat worked with horses by paddle-wheel propulsion. **1895** *Forum* (N. Y.) May 378 The 'team-boat', or ferry-boat propelled by horse power, ..ran for some time in competition with steam ferries. **1893** *Westm. Gaz.* 3 Feb. 10/3 As recently as last week he was..able to give lessons in *team-driving. **1907** *Daily Chron.* 18 Jan. 9/5 The very essence of all *team games is unity of action. **1698** FRYER *Acc. E. India & P.* 58 Such Trappings as our finest *Team-Horses in England wear. **1778** [W. MARSHALL] *Minutes Agric., Digest* 18 Sheep are profitable..because they save, considerably, the expence of *team-labour. **1387** TREVISA *Higden* (Rolls) VIII. 177 Iohn..toke anon tribute of everiche *teme lond [orig. *hyda, id est carucata*] in Engelond þre schelynges. **1627** SPEED *England* xxviii. § 3 In the Booke of Domesday *Caruca*—the Teame-land—was in quantitie of Acres proportioned to the qualitie of Soile. **1904** *N. & Q.* 10th Ser. I. 354/2 The extent of the plough or teamland. **1387** TREVISA *Higden* (Rolls) VII. 225 I-leide þre *teme lengþe from þe stok. **1867** MORLEY *Burke* vi. 56 He would talk of..the turnips, and the hay, with the *team-men and the farm-bailiff. **1909** *Daily News* 1 Mar. 12 Their demands are for an increase of wages of *teamsmen to 28*s.* **1894** *Westm. Gaz.* 13 Dec. 7/2 The Manhattan Chess Club has sent by mail to the British Chess Club a challenge for a *team match of five boards, to occupy one sitting, the moves being cabled. **1895** *Outing* (U. S.) XXVII. 247 Our game [Canadian football]..abounding in combined skill and *team play unknown to English experts. **1805** DICKSON *Pract. Agric.* I. 346 The breast-spade or common *team-plough..will be found preferable. **1877** KNIGHT *Dict. Mech.*, **Team-shovel*, an earth-scraper. A scoop drawn by horses or oxen. **1895** *Daily News* 15 Apr. 2/3 The '*team system' [in boot-making] is also strongly resisted, as tantamount to a decline in the remuneration. **1567** GOLDING *Ovid's Met.* v. (1593) 125 His sacred *teeme-ware through the aire to drive abroad agen. **1577** HARRISON *England* I. viii. in *Holinshed* I. 12/2, 600 families which are all one with Hidelandes, Plowghlandes, Carrucates, or Temewares. **1828** WEBSTER, **Team-work*, work done by a team, as distinguished from personal labor. *New England.* **1886** *S. W. Linc. Gloss.*, *Team-work*, work done with wagon and horses; a regular item in a way-warden's Account Book. **1887** MRS. H. CAMPBELL *Prisoners of Poverty* ii. 26 (Funk) What is known as 'team work', flaps [of shirts] being done by one, bosoms by another, and so on. *Mod. U. S.* The team-work of the [base-ball] nine is excellent.

**Team** (tīm), *v.* Also 6 teem. [f. TEAM *sb.* II.: cf. *to yoke*, *to harness*, etc. A late formation, the original derivative verb being TEEM *v.*[1]]

**1.** *trans.* To harness (beasts) in a team; to yoke. Also *fig.*

**1552** HULOET, Teame horses togyther, *dextero, as.* *Ibid.*, Teame oxen togither, *iugo, as.* **1597** MIDDLETON *Wisdom Solomon* xiv. 1 The shipman cannot team dame Tethys waves. **1733** TULL *Horse-Hoeing Husb.* xxiii. 172 Every Workman knows how to team the Limbers. **1875** *Encycl. Brit.* II. 663/1 The horses [in a horse-artillery battery] are teamed in pairs,—lead, centre, and wheel.

**2.** To convey or transport by means of a team. **b.** *absol.* or *intr.* To drive a team, to do teamster's work. *U.S.* Cf. TEAMING.

**1841** EMERSON *Ess.* Ser. I. ii. (1876) 66 A sturdy lad.., who teams it, farms it, peddles. **1852** WIGGINS *Embanking* 114 A portion was teamed 1½ mile. **1856** WHITTIER *Ranger* 126, I..can hear him teaming Down the locust-shaded way. **1888** L. OLIPHANT *Sci. Relig.* iii. 60, I..teamed as a common teamster through the rigours of a Canadian winter.

**3.** *trans.* To get (work) done by a team or teams of workmen; to let (work) to a contractor who employs teams of workmen. *U.S.*

**1877** [see TEAMING]. **1891** in *Cent. Dict.*

Hence **Teamed** *ppl. a.*, harnessed in a team.

**1591** SPENSER *Virgil's Gnat* 314 By this the Night forth from the darksome bowre Of Herebus her teemed steedes gan call.

**Tea-maker**, etc.: see TEA *sb.* 9 c.

**Teaman, tea-man** (tī·mæ̆n).

**1.** A merchant who deals in tea; a tea-dealer.

**1837** WHITTOCK, etc. *Bk. Trades* 441 Teaman. Such is the simple title assumed for their trade by many distinguished dealers in London—indeed, the most distinguished. They are generally those who deal in tea only. *Ibid.*, This system of tasting is what constitutes the acme of the great Teaman's trade. **1891** *Daily News* 16 May 5/4 The Chinese tea-men are reported to maintain a sort of incredulous non-chalance..in the face of that almost complete capture of the English market by the Indian and Ceylon teas.

**2.** *Prison slang.* (See quot.)

**1877** 5 *Years' Penal Servitude* ii. 85 'Tea men'..have the privilege..of having one pint of tea every evening instead of gruel.

**Teamer** (tī·məɹ). [f. TEAM *sb.* or *v.* + -ER[1].] One who drives a team; a teamster.

**1840** *Civil Eng. & Arch. Jrnl.* III. 391/2 These latter..discharging their contents, and leaving none to be shovelled out by the teamers. **1879** *Daily News* 8 Apr. 3/7 A horse was instantaneously killed by a flying brickbat, but the teamer, who stood near,..escaped uninjured. **1895** *Ibid.* 4 Dec. 3/7, I let my ten acres of glebe to an industrious fellow—once a 'teamer' or team man on a farm near by.

**Tea·ming**, *vbl. sb.* [f. TEAM *v.* + -ING[1].] The action of the verb TEAM. Also *attrib.*

**1733** W. ELLIS *Chiltern & Vale Farm.* 317 A Teaming-pin of about eleven Inches long. **1829** *Glover's Hist. Derby* I. 182 The breeding of heavy, or teaming horses. **1852** WIGGINS *Embanking* 115 Cutting and filling 5*d.* per yard. Teaming ⅞ths of a mile 0½*d.* per yard. **1877** KNIGHT *Dict. Mech.*, *Teaming*..2. The operation of transporting earth from the cutting to the embankment. 3. A certain mode of manufacturing work, which is given out to a boss, who hires a gang or team to do it, and is responsible to the owner of the stock. **1883** *Harper's Mag.* Aug. 390/2 All the teaming is done with one-horse carts.

**Tea·mless**, *a. rare.* [f. TEAM *sb.* + -LESS.] Without a team: cf. TEAM *sb.* 5.

**1894** *Columbus* (Ohio) *Dispatch* 5 Sept., The majority of the pioneers brought with them no personalty..save their teams,..some came even teamless.

**Teamster** (tī·mstəɹ). [f. TEAM *sb.* + -STER.] The driver or owner of a team; a teamer.

**1779** *Boston* (*Mass.*) *Town Records* 19 Feb. *Ibid.* 17 Aug., Thomas Chase..had agreed with a Number of Teamsters for the Publick service at the rate of eighteen Shillings a Mile. **1824** W. IRVING *T. Trav.* I. 219 Drovers and teamsters who travel that road. **1840** J. BUEL *Farmer's Comp.* 144 In using the harrow, the teamster should understand the object, and take care to accomplish it. **1901** *Census Schedule Instructions*, Agricultural labourers should be entered according to the particular work on which they are usually engaged, such as..Teamster on farm.

**Teanel** (tī·nĕl). Now *n.w. dial.* Forms: 1 tænil, -el, tenil; 5 tenel; 9 teanal(e, teanel, tennil. [OE. *tǽnil*, *-el* = MHG. *zeinel*, deriv. of OTeut. **tainjā*, in Goth. *tainjô* wicker basket, OHG. *zeinnâ*, *zeinâ*, MHG. *zeine* weak fem., ON. **teina*, pl. *teinur* basket, creel; deriv. of **taino*ᶻ, ON. *teinn* (:—*teinr*), OE. *tán*, OHG. *zein* twig, osier-wand.] A basket.

*a* **700** *Epinal Gloss.* (O.E.T.) 403 *Fiscilla*, taenil. *a* **800** *Erfurt Gloss.* 403 *Fiscella*, tenil. *c* **1000** ÆLFRIC *Saints' Lives* (1890) II. 44 Him on hand ȝenam ænne lytelne tænel mid caricum ȝefylledne. *a* **1100** *Ags. Voc.* in Wr.-Wülcker 336/9 *Sportella*, tænel. *c* **1440** *Promp. Parv.* 489/1 Tenel, or crele, *cartallus*. *Ibid.*, Tenel, vessel, *tenella*. **1869** *Lonsdale Gloss.*, *Teanel*, an osier fish-basket. **1882** *Lancs. Gloss.*, *Tennil*, a large basket.

**Tea-night** to **Tea-pail**: see TEA *sb.* 9.

**Teany**, var. TENNÉ, the heraldic tincture.

**Tea·-party.**

**1.** A party assembled to take tea together; a social entertainment at which tea is taken.

**1778** MISS BURNEY *Evelina* (1791) I. xvi. 61 The arched recesses that are appropriated for tea-parties [at Ranelagh]. **1843** THACKERAY *Men's Wives, Mr. & Mrs. Berry* ii, The Reverend Lemuel Whey is a tea-party man. **1851** D. JERROLD *St. Giles* xix. 196 As comfortable as any dowager at a tea-party.

**2.** *transf.* (*colloq.* or *slang.*) **a.** *Boston tea-party*, a humorous name for the revolutionary proceeding in 1773, when the tea was thrown overboard from the ships in Boston harbour as a protest against the taxation of the American colonies by the British Government. **b.** A lively proceeding, a disturbance.

**1864** WEBSTER *App.*, *Names Fiction*, Boston Tea-party. **1874** O. W. HOLMES *Ballad of Boston Tea-party* 28 The storm broke loose, but first of all The Boston teapot bubbled! **1903** *Westm. Gaz.* 20 Jan. 9/2 An electrician's 'tea-party' is brought about by a short circuit...In particularly bad cases..explosions of the circuit breakers occur, and showers of molten copper, which often start fires, render the 'tea-party' of the liveliest description.

**Tea·-plant.**

**1.** The plant from which tea is obtained, the tea-shrub: = TEA *sb.* 3.

**1727–41** CHAMBERS *Cycl.* s.v. *Tea*, The Tea plant affects valleys, and the feet of mountains, and a stony soil. **1770** ELLIS in *Phil. Trans.* LX. 525 One of the first tea-plants that has been produced from seed in this kingdom. **1888** J. PATON in *Encycl. Brit.* XXIII. 97/2 The tea-plant is cultivated in China as an evergreen shrub.

**2.** Applied to various other plants: see TEA *sb.* 6.

**1798** *Monthly Mag.* Mar. 211 The tea plant of St. Domingo; *Capraria biflora*,..the leaves of which are employed..for the same purpose as the tea of China and Japan. **1864** *Athenæum* 10 Dec. 788/2 Leptospermum, the tea-plant of Australia. **1866** *Treas. Bot.* 701 *L*[*ycium*] *barbarum*..is commonly known as the Tea plant. **1884** [see TEA-TREE 3]. **1903** A. C. P. HAGGARD *Sporting Yarns* 136 (*Canada*) The long grass and Labrador tea-plants on the banks.

**Tea·-planter.** One who makes it his business to cultivate tea-plants. So **Tea·-planting.**

**1888** J. PATON in *Encycl. Brit.* XXIII. 99/1 Tea-planting has also been successfully established in Natal. **1897** *Daily News* 19 June 2/2 Japan must..abandon her primitive methods of tea-planting in small patches. **1897** *Allbutt's Syst. Med.* III. 736 A case that I saw some years ago in a tea-planter. *Mod.* He is now a tea-planter in Assam.

**Tea·-pot.** A pot with a lid, spout, and handle, in which tea is made or brought to table.

[**1616** COCKS *Diary* (Hakl. Soc.) I. 215, I sent..a silver *chaw* pot..to Capt. China wife. **1662** J. DAVIES tr. *Mandelslo's Trav.* II. (1669) 156 There have been Tsia-pots, which had cost between six and seven thousand pound sterling.] **1705** *Lond. Gaz.* No. 4063/4 A Tea Kettle, a gilt Tea-Pot. **1784** COWPER *Task* IV. 776 There the pitcher stands A fragment, and the spoutless tea-pot there. **1867** TROLLOPE *Chron. Barset* II. lxix. 261 She sat behind her old teapot, with her hands clasped. **1874** [see TEA-PARTY 2].

**b.** Phr. *Tea-pot tempest*, *tempest in a tea-pot* (U. S.): = *storm in a tea-cup* (see TEA-CUP 4).

**1854** ANDREWS *Lat. Dict.* s.v. *Simpulum*, *Excitare fluctus in simpulo*,..to raise a tempest in a teapot. Cic. Leg. 3. 16, 36. **1891** *Cent. Dict.* s. v. *Tempest*, *A tempest in a tea-pot*, a great disturbance over a small matter. **1896** *Peterson Mag.* Jan. 104/1 What a ridiculous tea-pot tempest!

Hence **Tea-pot** *v. nonce-wd.*, to present with a tea-pot; **Tea·potful**, as much as a tea-pot contains.

**1854** 'C. BEDE' *Verdant Green* II. v, Gentlemen who get upon their legs to return thanks for having been 'tea-potted'. **1895** W. WRIGHT *Palmyra & Zenobia* xxii. 255 The teapotful of dirty water.

‖ **Teapoy** (tī·poi). *Anglo-Ind.* Also tepoy. [f. Hindī *tīn*, in comb. *tir-* three + Pers. *pāē*, *pāī* foot. The legitimate Persian name is *sihpāya* or *sipāī*; the Hindī *tirpad* or *tripad* (Yule).]

A small three-legged table or stand, or any tripod; (by erron. association with *tea*), such a table with a receptacle for tea or a tea-caddy.

**1828** MRS. SHERWOOD *Lady of Manor* VI. xxix. 246 A low *teapoy* of *sessoo* wood. **1844** [? SIR J. KAYE] *Peregrine Pultuney* I. v. 112 A tepoy or tinpoy is a thing with three feet, used in India to denote a little table. **1887** YAN PHOU LEE *When I was a Boy in China* 25 [The tables] were flanked by two rows of chairs..with tea-poys between that served to hold the cups of guests.

**1858** SIMMONDS *Dict. Trade*, *Tea-poy*, an ornamental pedestal table, with lifting top, enclosing caddies for holding tea. **1886** YULE & BURNELL *Hobson-Jobson*, *Teapoy*,..often in England imagined to have some connexion with *tea*, and hence, in London shops for japanned ware and the like, a *teapoy* means a tea-chest fixed on legs. But this is quite erroneous.

**Tear** (tīəɹ), *sb.*[1] Forms: see below. [OE. *téar* = OFris. *târ*, ON. *tár* (Sw. *tår*, Da. *taar*, *taare*), contr. from earlier OE. **teahr*, **teagr*, *teagor*, ONorthumb. *tehr* = OHG. *zahar*, *zahhar* (MHG. *zaher*, *zâr*, Ger. *zähre*), Goth. *tagr*; cogn. with Gr. δάκρ-υ, OL. *dacrima* (L. *lacrima*, *-uma*), OPr. *dacr*, *dēr*, Welsh *dagr* tear. The medial *h* or *ȝ*, already lost in OE., is found as *ch* in 16th c. Sc.]

**A.** Illustration of Forms.

**α.** OE. **teaȝor**, ONorthumb. **teher, tæher, tehher, tehr**; 5–6 *Sc.* **techyr** (*pl.* **techrys**), **tichwr, teicher.**

*Guthlac* (E. E. T. S.) 1340 Teaȝor yðum weol hate hleordropan. *a* **950** *Rituale Eccl. Dunelm.* (Surtees) 40 Folces tehhero eft bisih (*gloss on* populi lacrimas respice). *Ibid.* 192 Pund saltes, of ðon sindon salto tehero. *c* **950** *Lindisf. Gosp.* Mark ix. 24 Mið teherum he ȝecuæð ic ȝelefo. — Luke vii. 38 Mið tæherum *vel* tearum. *Ibid.* 44 Mið tearum *vel* tehrum. **1513** DOUGLAS *Æneis* IV. xii. 5 With cheikis freklit, and all of tichwris [*ed.* 1553 teris] bysprent. *Ibid.* XIII. Prol. 26 At euery pilis point and cornis croppis The techrys [*ed.* **1553** teicheris] stude, as lemand beriall droppis.

**β.** 1–3 **téar** (**teor**), 1–6 **ter**, 2 **tiar**, 3 **ti**(**e**)**r**, **tær**, 4 **tyar**, 4–5 **teer**, 4–6 **tere**, 5 **terre**, 5–6 **teere**, **tyer**, 5–8 *Sc.* **teir**, 6–7 **teare**, 6– **tear.**

*c* **888** K. ÆLFRED *Boeth.* x, Fulneah dead for tearum & for unrotnesse. *a* **900** tr. *Bæda's Eccl. Hist.* IV. xxix. [xxviii.] § 2 Mæniȝe þara broðra..tearas guton. *c* **975** *Rushw. Gosp.* Mark ix. 24 Mið teorum [*Lindisf.* teherum] he ȝicwæð ic ȝilefo. *c* **1000** *Sax. Leechd.* III. 292 Wiþ mist & wiþ ter. *a* **1175** *Cotton Hom.* 217 Al swa an huni tiar felle upe ȝiure hierte. *c* **1200** *Vices & Virt.* 57 Mid bitere teares. *c* **1200** ORMIN 13849 Þurrh beȝȝske & sallte tæress. *a* **1300** *K. Horn* 654 Wiþ tieres al birunne. *Ibid.* 960 Spak wiþ bidere tires. **13..** *Cursor M.* 25551 Wit tere [*Gött.* ter] of ei. **1340** *Ayenb.* 173 Y-kuegt..be tyares of ssrifte. *c* **1380** WYCLIF *Serm.* Sel. Wks. II. 205 She þis haþ waished my feet wiþ teeris. **1422** tr. *Secreta Secret.*, *Priv. Priv.* 199, I haue..Seyn thy terris. *c* **1440** *Promp. Parv.* 489/1 Teere, of wepynge, *lacrima.* *c* **1489** CAXTON *Blanchardyn* xxxiii. 123 He fonde him the terres at the eyes of hym. **1500–20** DUNBAR *Poems* ix. 15 With teiris of sorrow. **1563** WINȜET *Four Scoir Thre Quest.* § 46 Wks. (S. T. S.) I. 107 Mourning and teris. **1584** POWEL *Lloyd's Cambria* 199 The women check their tears. **1593** SHAKS. 3 *Hen. VI*, II. v. 76 Weepe wretched man: Ile ayde thee Teare for Teare. *a* **1600** MONTGOMERIE *Sonn.* iv. 5 With bendit brou, and tuinkling teirs, I trou. **1661** LOVELL *Hist. Anim. & Min.* 72 The teares found dry in the corners of the eyes.

**B.** Signification.

**1.** A drop of the limpid fluid secreted by the lachrymal gland appearing in or flowing from the eye; chiefly as the result of emotion, esp. grief, but also of physical irritation or nervous stimulus: usually in *pl.*

*Beowulf* 1872 Hruron him tearas blondenfeaxum. **971** *Blickl. Hom.* 189 Þa wæron his eaȝan ȝefyllede mid tearum.

*c* **1175** *Lamb. Hom.* 159 þe ter þat Mon schet. *c* **1300** *Havelok* 285 For hire was mani a ter igroten. **1377** LANGL. *P. Pl.* B. XIII. 45 But if þei synge for þo soules and wepe salt teres. **1422, 1593,** *a* **1600** [see A. β]. **1737** [S. BERINGTON] *G. di Lucca's Mem.* (1738) 62, I saw his [Eyes] swimming in Tears. **1782** COWPER *Let. to W. Unwin* 4 Nov., You tell me that John Gilpin made you laugh tears. **1808** SCOTT *Marm.* I. Introd. 186 Drop upon Fox's grave the tear, 'Twill trickle to his rival's bier. **1855** BAIN *Senses & Int.* II. iv. § 22 (1864) 297 There are also tears of joy. **1866** HUXLEY *Phys.* (1869) ix. § 25 Under certain circumstances..the secretion of the lachrymal gland exceeds the drainage power of the lachrymal duct, and the fluid, accumulating,..overflows in the form of tears.

**b.** As the visible feature of weeping: hence, put for this, or as the expression of grief or sorrow. *In tears*, weeping, in sorrow or commiseration.

*a* **1340** HAMPOLE *Psalter* cxxv. 6 Þa þat dos goed werkis in terys of penaunce. **1388** WYCLIF *Ps.* cxxv[i]. 5 Thei that sowen in teeris; schulen repe in ful out ioiyng. **1435** MISYN *Fire of Love* 18 Is not þis þe vayle of teris & tribulacion? **1560** DAUS tr. *Sleidane's Comm.* 18 The people..are all in teares and mournyng. **1637** MILTON *Lycidas* 14 He must not flote upon his watry bear..Without the meed of som melodious tear. **1719** DE FOE *Crusoe* (1840) II. i. 7, I was happy in listening to her tears. **1750** GRAY *Elegy, Epitaph* ii, He gave to Mis'ry all he had, a tear. **1814** WORDSW. *Laodamia* 164 Yet tears to human suffering are due.

**2.** *transf.* and *fig.* A drop of any liquid; *spec.* a drop or bead of liquid spontaneously exuding.

(Sometimes with allusion to grief or lamentation: cf. 1 b.)

*a* **900** CYNEWULF *Crist* 1174 Ða wearð beam moniȝ blodiȝum tearum birunnen. *c* **1000** *Sax. Leechd.* II. 28 ȝenim cileþonian..& huniȝes teares. *a* **1175** [see A. β]. *a* **1240** *Ureisun* in *Cott. Hom.* 200 Swete iesu..min huni ter. **1594** SHAKS. *Rich. III*, v. iii. 284, I would these dewy teares were from the ground. **1616** SURFL. & MARKH. *Country Farme* 609 The vine sometimes poureth forth great store of teares, whereupon..it looseth his force altogether. *a* **1626** BACON *New Atl.* (1650) 29 The Teares or Woundings of Trees. **1697** DRYDEN *Virg. Georg.* III. 505 The pearly tears Of Morning Dews. **1820** L. HUNT *Indicator* No. 20 I. 156 The tears of the sky at least were dried up. **18..** B. TAYLOR *Manuela* Poems (1866) 316 With the tears of amber dropping. **1865** DICKENS *Mut. Fr.* I. xiv, Hawse-holes long discoloured with the iron's rusty tears. **1883** *Century Mag.* Oct. 873/1 Carrying large candles, which drip their waxen tears along the road [at a funeral].

†**b.** *pl.* The Italian sweet wine known as LACHRYMA CHRISTI. *Obs. rare*⁻¹.

**1526** *Pilgr. Perf.* (1531) 53 b, There groweth the myghty swete wynes, as malueseys, tyeres & muscadels.

**3.** *spec.* Applied to various gums that exude from plants in tear-shaped or globular beads, which then become solid or resinous.

*a* **1000** ÆLFRIC *Voc.* in Wr.-Wülcker 139/28 *Opobalsamum*, balsames tear. *a* **1400–50** *Alexander* 4974 Þar trekild doun of þa teres of iemmes, Boyland out of þe barke bawme & mirre. **1578** LYTE *Dodoens* III. xvi. 308 Euphorbium is the gumme or teare of a certayne strange plante growing in Lybia. **1585** T. WASHINGTON tr. *Nicholay's Voy.* II. vi. 36 The Mastic is the teare or droppings of the Lentiscus. **1604** E. G[RIMSTONE] *D'Acosta's Hist. Indies* IV. xxviii. 286 One kinde..which they call Opobalsamum, which be the very teares that distil. **1686** W. HARRIS tr. *Lemery's Course Chym.* (ed. 2) 467 Opium is a Tear which distils of itself, or by Incision of the heads of Poppies. **1715** tr. *Pancirollus' Rerum Mem.* I. I. xii. 29 Myrrh, is a Drop or Tear, distill'd from a Tree in Arabia Felix. **1825** J. NICHOLSON *Operat. Mechanic* 753, ½ oz. mastic in tears. **1838** T. THOMSON *Chem. Org. Bodies* 671 Gum arabic..is in small rounded drops or tears. **1895** *Daily News* 25 Nov. 7/1 Fine tears of frankincense, the gum resin produced by an Indian tree.

**4.** Anything resembling or suggesting a tear: see quots.; e.g. (*a*) a defect in glass caused by a small particle of vitrified clay: see quot. 1832; (*b*) a detonating bulb, or Prince Rupert's drop.

**1832** G. R. PORTER *Porcelain & Gl.* xi. 249 Tears are, perhaps, the greatest defect that can be found in glass. *Ibid.*, Wherever these tears exist, the material is brittle in a very high degree, so as frequently to crack, without any apparent cause. **1837** *Penny Cycl.* VII. 15/1 The smaller and rounder the eyes, the better the cheese is reckoned. They should contain a clear salt liquor, which is called the tears. **1839** URE *Dict. Arts* 746 It [Plomb-gomme] has been found only at Huelgoet, near Poullaouen, in Brittany, covering with its tears or small concretions the ores of white lead and galena. *Ibid.* 1250 The block of metal is heated till it becomes brittle, when..it is broken to pieces, and presents an agglomeration of elongated grains or tears; whence it is called grain tin. **1857** LIVINGSTONE *Trav.* xxxi. 650 It [iron] occurs generally in tears or rounded lumps. **1858** O. W. HOLMES *Aut. Breakf.-t.* ii, A Prince-Rupert's-drop..is a tear of unannealed glass. **1877** KNIGHT *Dict. Mech.*, *Tears*, the vitreous drops from the melting of the walls of a furnace.

**5.** With defining words, in special senses: as *glass tear* [F. *larme de verre*], (*a*) a detonating bulb (see DETONATING *ppl. a.*); (*b*) a pear-shaped glass-drop used for ornament (*Cent. Dict.* 1891); *St. Lawrence's tears*, a popular name for the Perseids, the meteors occurring about St. Lawrence's day, Aug. 10; *tears of St. Peter*, a West Indian plant, *Anthacanthus microphyllus* (*Treas. Bot.*); *tears of strong wine*, drops of liquid forming on the inner sides of a glass partly filled with strong wine. Also CROCODILE *tears*, JOB'S *tears*, JUNO'S *tears*.

**1899** R. H. ALLEN *Star Names* 335 In the later Middle Ages they were known as the *Larmes de Saint Laurent*, Saint Laurence's Tears, his martyrdom upon the red-hot gridiron having taken place on the 10th of August, 258.

**6.** *attrib.* and *Comb.*: **a.** attributive, as *tear bath*, *-drop*, *-flood*, *-fount*, *-spring*; **b.** objective and obj. gen., as *tear-compeller*; *tear-compelling*, *-creative*, *-distilling*, *-falling* (FALL *v.* 49), *-shedding*, *-wiping* adjs.; **c.** instrumental, as *tear-baptized*, *-bedabbled*, *-bedewed*, *-besprinkled*, *-blinded*, *-commixed*, *-composed*, *-dewed*, *-dimmed*, *-distained*, *-dropped*, *-drowned*, *-filled*, *-fraught*, *-freshened*, *-glistening*, *-shot* (cf. *bloodshot*), *-stained*, *-stubbed*, *-swollen*, *-washed*, *-wet*, *-worn*, *-wrung* adjs.; *tear-nourish* vb.; **d.** of other kinds, as *tear-bright*, *tear-like*, *tear-shaped*, *tear-thirsty* (cf. *bloodthirsty*) adjs.

**1624** QUARLES *Sion's Sonn.* Div. Poems (1717) 359 My *tears-baptized Love. *a* **1600** in Farr *S. P. Eliz.* (1845) II. 444 Thou let'st me wash thy feete in my *teare-bath. *a* **1644** QUARLES *Sol. Recant.* ch. xii. 5 (1645) 58 To meet Thy *tear-bedabled fun'rals in the Street. *c* **1610** *God Heares*, etc. in Farr *S. P. Jas. I* (1848) 110 Thy *teares-bedewed praiers, And thy repentant sighes, shall haue accesse Before the throne of heaven. **1906** *United Free Ch. Mag.* Mar. 28/1 Crowds with tear-bedewed cheeks thronged the streets. **1809** MALKIN *Gil Blas* IX. iv. (Rtldg.) 314 My *tear-besprinkled visage. **1813** SCOTT *Rokeby* v. xvi, *Tear-blinded to the Castle-hall Came as to bear her funeral pall. **1874** M. COLLINS *Frances* II. 191 Her hazel eyes *tear-bright with glee. **1868** — *Sweet Anne Page* I. 210 That *tear-compelling tragedy. *a* **1618** SYLVESTER *Panthea* Author's Invoc. 5 In this *teare-composed terrene Globe. *a* **1600** J. BRYAN in Farr *S. P. Eliz.* (1845) II. 333 Heare, heare with acceptation The *teare-dew'd words I speake. **1811** W. BRISTOW *Little Wanderer* ii, She cannot see my *tear-dim'd eye. **1593** SHAKS. *Lucrece* 1586 About her *teare-distained eye Blew circles stream'd. **1799** H. GURNEY *Cupid & Psyche* 10 (Jod.) No *tear-drop fills his frozen eye. **1830** TENNYSON *Talking Oak* xli, A teardrop trembled from its source, And down my surface crept. **1776** MICKLE tr. *Camoens' Lusiad* VII. 298 The *tear-dropt bough hangs weeping in the vale. **1598** SYLVESTER *Du Bartas* II. i. II. *Imposture* 406 His *tear-drown'd eyes, a night of Clouds bedims. **1594** SHAKS. *Rich. III*, IV. ii. 66 *Teare-falling Pittie dwells not in this Eye. *a* **1631** DONNE *Valediction* ii, No *teare-floods, nor sigh-tempests move. *a* **1600** J. BRYAN in Farr *S. P. Eliz.* (1845) II. 334 My long *teare-fraught eies Haue seene thy plagues redoble Vpon mine enemies. **1842** FABER *Styrian Lake*, etc. 261 White flowers, *tear-freshened, for pale sorrow's brow. **1811** W. BRISTOW *Stanzas written in —— church-yd.* iii, At widow'd Love's *tear-glistning shrine. **1567** MAPLET *Gr. Forest* 32 This Tree..by and by droppeth and distilleth a certaine humor, in a manner *tearlike. **1873** E. BRENNAN *Witch of Nemi*, etc. 70 For she *Tear-nourishes the bud her true love bare Unto her lord. **1632** LITHGOW *Trav.* I. 5 *Teare-rent Sophyre, Synon-like betrayd What voltall oathes, loues sterne fort, ne'er bewrayd. **1893** HODGES *Elem. Photogr.* (1907) 88 *Tear-shaped markings may be produced. **1598** DRAYTON *Heroic. Ep., Matilda to K. John*, If all remorcelesse, no *teare-shedding eie, My selfe will moane my selfe. **1840** BROWNING *Sordello* III. 744 Lashless eyes Inveterately *tear-shot. **1593** SHAKS. 2 *Hen. VI*, II. iv. 16 Ile prepare My *teare-stayn'd eyes, to see her Miseries. **1858** ADAH I. MENKEN *Infelicia* (1883) 120 Take my cold, tear-stained face up to yours. **1593** NASHE *Christ's T.* Wks. (Grosart) IV. 12 That which my *Teare-stubbed penne..hath attempted. **1768** C. SHAW *Monody* i, These *tear-swoln eyes beheld her fall. **1579** GOSSON *Sch. Abuse* (Arb.) 49 Calling [Mars] the bloody God, the angry God,..πολυδακρυς the *tearethirsty God. **1755** J. SHEBBEARE *Lydia* (1769) II. 431 The *tear-washed eye surveyed the severe trials. *c* **1630** DRUMM. OF HAWTH. *Poems* Wks. (1711) 33 Her *tear-wet locks hang'd o'er her face. **1605** SYLVESTER *Du Bartas* II. iii. I. *Vocation* 151 O contrite heart's restorer! *Tears-wiping tame-griefe! **1786** BURNS *Lament* viii, My toil-beat nerves, and *tear-worn eye. **1823** BYRON *Age of Bronze* xiv, They voted..*tear-wrung millions—why? for rent!

**e.** Special Combs.: **tear-bag**, (*a*) = *tear-pit*; (*b*) = *tear-gland*; **tear-duct**, (*a*) the lachrymal or nasal duct, which carries off tears from the eye to the nose; (*b*) the lachrymal canal, which supplies tears to the eyes; **tear-gland**, the lachrymal gland; **tear-passage**, = *tear-duct*; **tear-pit**, the lachrymal or sub-orbital sinus found in many species of deer, a fold or cavity beneath the inner corner of the eye, containing a thin waxy secretion; = LARMIER 2; **tear-pump** (*slang*) [cf. PUMP *sb.*¹ d, *v.* 6], the source of tears shed effusively or in feigned emotion; **tear-punctum**: see PUNCTUM 4 b; **tear-sac**, = *tear-pit*. See also TEAR-BOTTLE.

**1893** LYDEKKER *Horns & Hoofs* 64 The lachrymal fossa—in which rests the gland termed the crumen, larmier, or '*tear-bag'. **1892** *Pall Mall G.* 30 Mar. 4/3 The treatment of obstructions of the *tear passages. **1834** *Penny Cycl.* II. 69/1 The possession of lachrymal sinuses, or, as they are vernacularly called with reference to the stag and fallow-deer, *tear-pits,..distinguishes the greater number of the antelopes. **1903** FARMER *Slang Dict.* s.v., *To work the *tear-pump*,..to weep. **1878** T. BRYANT *Pract. Surg.* I. 348 The *tear puncta..lie in contact with the ocular conjunctiva.

**Tear** (tēᵊɹ), *sb.*² [f. TEAR *v.*¹]

**1.** An act of tearing or rending; the action of tearing; hence, damage caused by tearing (or similar violent action); usually in phr. *tear and wear*, *wear and tear*, including damage due both to accident and to ordinary wear: see WEAR; also used *fig.* in reference to body or mind.

**1666** PEPYS *Diary* 29 Sept., The wages, victuals, wear and tear..will come to above £3,000,000. **1705** R. CROMWELL *Let.* in *Eng. Hist. Rev.* (1898) XIII. 123 A third for wages tare and ware, and upholding the stock. **1765** FOOTE *Commissary* I. Wks. 1799 II. 12 At that time of life, men can bustle and stir..; it is the only tear and wear season. **1767** A. YOUNG *Farmer's Lett. to People* 282 With ease to the horses, and not half the tear of irons, &c. **1874** BLACKIE *Self-Cult.* 65 Plated work will never stand the tear and wear of life. **1901** *Scotsman* 6 Mar. 9/7 The tear and wear of the campaign is telling severely on the..Yeomanry.

**2.** *concr.* A torn part or place; a rent or fissure.

**1611** COTGR., *Deschirure*, a teare, a rent. **1755** JOHNSON, *Tear*,..a rent, a fissure. **1824** MRS. CAMERON *Pink Tippet* II. 21 Mother has darned up the tears. **1891** *Amiel's Jrnl.* 195 Each darn and tear has its story. **190.** *Bookseller's Catal.*, This copy has the title cut round and mounted, a few slight tears in margins, in one case the tear extends to text.

**b.** The line along which a piece of cloth or the like naturally tears.

**1857** H. MILLER *Test. Rocks* vi. 232 What a draper would term the *tear* of the one layer or fold.

**3.** An act of tearing, in senses 8 and 9 of the verb. **a.** A rushing gallop or pace; esp. in advb. phrase *full tear*, full tilt, headlong. **b.** A spree (*U. S. slang*). **c.** A rage or passion; a violent flurry. **d.** Here may belong the Irish interjectional phr. *tear and ages* (?*aches*), *wounds*, expressing astonishment.

**a. 1838** DICKENS *O. Twist* xxxiii, He could have..galloped away, full tear, to the next stage. **1892** *Sat. Rev.* 2 Jan. 16/1 The rattling tear across country.

**b.** *c* **1869** B. HARTE *How Santa Claus*, etc. Wks. (1872) 363 May be ye'd all like to come over to my house to-night and have a sort of tear round. **1895** *Outing* (U. S.) XXVII. 189/2 Then I should go on a tear—a regular one you know—and not come home for three whole days. **1896** *Harper's Mag.* XCII. 775/2 Got me off on a tear somehow, and by the time I was sober again the money was 'most all gone.

**c. 1880** *W. Cornwall Gloss.* s.v. *Taer*, 'She got into a pretty taer'. **1890** *Anthony's Photogr. Bull.* III. 128 If you keep quiet you may see a way out of the difficulty that you most certainly would not if you got in a 'tare'.

**d. 1841** LEVER *C. O'Malley* lxvii, Tear and ages! how sore my back is. **1842** S. LOVER *Handy Andy* iii, 'Tare an' ouns!' roared Murphy, 'how Andy runs'. **1893** BARING-GOULD *Cheap Jack Z.* I. i. 13 'Tear and ages!' sez I; 'that's a wonder of the world'.

**Tear** (tēᵊɹ), *a.* and *sb.*³ Now *techn.* Forms: 5 ter, 5–6 tere, 5–7 teer(e, 6 teir, teyre, 7 teare, 7–8 tare, 7– tear. [Known *c* 1400; app. from Du. or LG.: cf. MDu., MFl., MLG., LG. *teer*, *têr*, contracted from *teeder*, *têder* fine, thin, delicate, tender: cf. OE. *tiedre*, *týdre*, *tydder* tender.]

†**A.** *adj.* Fine, delicate; of the best quality. (Said esp. of flour and hemp.) *Obs.*

*c* **1400** *Trevisa's Higden* (Rolls) III. 9 Salomon his mete was euery day þritty corues of clene [*v.rr.* teer, tere, ter] floure and foure score corues of mele. **1501** DOUGLAS *Pal. Hon.* I. 542 Damisflure, tere pyle, quhairon thair lyis Peirle, Orphany quhilk euerie stait renewis. **1532** *Test. Ebor.* (Surtees) VI. 34, ij pare of harden shettes, ij pare of hempe tere, and ij pare of lynan shettes. **1544** *Ibid.* 214 A pare of newe hempe tere shetes. **1541–2** in *Lanc. Wills* (1857) 80 A xj payre of teir hempen shetis.

**B.** *sb.* (The adj. used absol.) Something of the finest or best quality: †**a.** The finest wheaten flour. *Obs.* **b.** The finest fibre of flax or hemp.

**a.** *c* **1440** *Promp. Parv.* 489/1 Teere, of flowre, *amolum.* **1521** WHITINTON *Gram.* B vj, *Pollis vel pollen..est idem in tritico quod flos in siligine*, the tere of floure. **1521** *Coventry Leet Bk.* 669 But on haly-cake, and that they put no more theryn but the Teyre of thre stryke of whete.

**b. 1541–2** in *Lanc. Wills* (1857) 81, xxv teir of hempe slippingis. **1601** HOLLAND *Pliny* XIX. i, As for the good Flax indeed, which is the teere or marrow as it were within of the Line. **1657** W. COLES *Adam in Eden* cclxxxi, The Summer Hemp affordeth most Teere as they call it. **1706** PHILLIPS (ed. 6), *Tare of Flax*, the finest dress'd part of it made ready for the Spinner. **1805** *Usef. Proj.* in *Ann. Reg.* 851/2 A machine for discharging a woolcomb or combs, by separating the tears from the noiles. **1837** WHITTOCK, etc. *Bk. Trades* (1842) 238 (Flax Dresser) The strike is to pass through a fine hackle, and the hurds coming from thence saved for middling cloth, and the tear itself for the best linen.

**Tear** (tēᵊɹ), *v.*¹ Pa. t. **tore** (tōᵊɹ), *arch.* and *dial.* **tare** (tēᵊɹ). Pa. pple. **torn** (tōᵊɹn). Forms: see below. [OE. *ter-an*, pa. t. *tær*, pl. *tǽron*, pa. pple. *toren*, = OLG. **teran* (MD., MLG. *teren*, Du. *teren*, OHG. *zeran* (MHG. *zeren*, *zern*, Ger. *zehren*) to destroy, consume, Goth. *gatairan* to destroy. OTeut. **teran* (*tar*, *tǣ·ron*, *to·ran-*) was cognate with Gr. δέρειν to flay, OSlav. *derg* to tear asunder, Skr. *dar-* to burst. The OE. pa. t. *tær* (:–*tar*) survived as *tare* to 17th c., when it gave place in standard Eng. to *tore*, with *o* from pa. pple. *toren*, *torn*: cf. *bore*, *swore*. A weak pa. t. and pple. *terede*, *tered*, found in 15th c., are still dialectal, along with a mixed form *tored*, *tord*.]

**A.** Illustration of Forms.

**1.** *Infin.* and *Pres. Stem.* 1 **teran** (**teoran**, **tearan**) (3 *pers. sing.* **tirð**, **tyrþ**), 2–5 **teren**, 3 **teoren**, 3–6 **tere**, 4 **teere**, 5 **teer**, 6– *Sc.* **teir**, 6–7 **teare**, 6– **tear.** *dial.* 7– **tare**, 9 **teer**, **teear** (tīr, tīᵊɹ).

*a* **850** *Lorica Gloss.* in *O. E. T.* 172/2 *Lacerandum*, to teorenne. *c* **888** K. ÆLFRED *Boeth.* xxii. § 1 He þe tirð on ða þrotan. *c* **950** *Lindisf. Gosp.* Mark ix. 26 Suiðe ȝetearende hine. *c* **975** *Rushw. Gosp.* ibid., Moniȝe teorende hine. *a* **1000** *Riddles* xxii. 14 (Gr.) Fæst and forðweard fealleþ on sidan ðæt ic [a plough] toþum tere. *a* **1050** *Liber Scintill.* 105 Hit tyrþ ealswa snaca. *a* **1200** Tereð [see B. 2]. [*a* **1225** *Juliana* 12 Ichulle leoten deor to teoren ant to luken þe.] **1382** WYCLIF *Gen.* xl. 19 Fowlis shulen teere thi fleish. *c* **1430** *Hymns Virg.* 49 To teer him from þe top to þe toon. **1552** HULOET, Teare in pieces, *delacero. Ibid.*, Tear, *lacero.* **1567** *Satir. Poems Reform.* xi. 58 With glowing gunne that me to teir. **1662** *Rump Songs* (1874) I. 192 To tare the Rochet to such rags as these.

**2.** *Past Tense.* α. 1–2 **tær**, 3–5 **tar**, 4–5 **taar**, 4–7 **tare**; 6 *Sc.* (9 *dial.*) **tor**, 7– **tore** (9 *dial.* **tar**,

Sc. **tuir** (tȫr)). *Pl.* 1–2 **téeron**, 3 **tiere**, 3–4 **tere(n**, 4 **tare(n**, 4–5 **ter**, 5 **terre**; 5– same as sing.

*a.* c **1000** ÆLFRIC *Gen.* xxxvii. 29 Ða tær he his claðas [L. *scissis vestibus*]. c **1000** in Cockayne *Narrat.* (1861) 15 Hie mid þæm þa men wundodon and tæron. c **1275** LAY. 25850 [Ȝeo] tar hire bi þan ere. *Ibid.* 24843 Hii..tiere ȝam bi þan heere. **13..** *K. Alis.* 4642 Alisaunder his cloþes taar. *Ibid.* 6876 Heore heir heo taren. c **1330** Tar [see B. 4]. c **1400** MAUNDEV. (1839) ix. 81 And there weren Marie Cleophee and Marie Magdaleyne, and teren here heer. **14..** HOCCLEVE *Compl. Virgin* 239 A modir þat so soone hir cote taar Or rente. [**1513** DOUGLAS *Æneis* XII. x. 129 Hyr rosy chekis to-tor and scartis sche.] c **1530** *Hickscorner* A ij b, The knottes the skyn tare. **1611** BIBLE 2 *Sam.* xiii. 31 The king arose, and tare his garments. **1653–4** WHITELOCKE *Jrnl. Swed. Emb.* (1772) I. 378 Three Dutch men of war.., whom she tore, and killed many of their men. **1828** *Craven Gloss.* s. v. *Tar*, He tar his breeks to tatters.

*β.* 5 **terede, terid**, 6 **teared, tearde, teard.**

[a **1450** *Alexander* 4148 All þaire tents it to-terid.] **1578** BOWES *Let. to Burghley* in Tytler *Hist. Scot.* (1864) IV. 317 The king..teared his hairs. **1593** *Pass. Morrice* (1876) 78 Now tearde she her haire. **1599** M[OUFET] *Silkwormes* 73 Whilst herbage greene with vnseene teeth they teard.

**3.** *Pa. pple.* *a.* 1–7 **toren**, 5–8 **torne**, 5 **toryn**, 6– **torn.** *β.* 4 **i-tore**, 4–9 (now *dial.*) **tore.** *γ.* 5 **teryd**, 6 **teard**, 6–7 (9 *dial.*) **teared**, 9 *dial.* **tored.**

*a.* [a **1000** *Aldhelm Gloss.* 5386 in Napier *O. E. Glosses* 135/2 *Lacerari*, totoren.] c **1325** *Deus Caritas* 25 in *E. E. P.* (1862) 127 Crist was toren vche a lym. c **1489** CAXTON *Sonnes of Aymon* ii. 62 Many heres pulled and many gownes toren. **1499** *Promp. Parv.* 522/2 (Pynson) Weryd or worne or torne. **1619** S. ATKINSON *Gold Mynes Scotl.* (Bann. Cl.) 15 Forced and torn from his bedd. a **1631** DONNE *Hymn to Christ* 1 In what torne shipp soever I embark. **1658** WOOD *Life* May (O. H. S.) I. 253 Toren downe.

*β.* **1387** TREVISA *Higden* (Rolls) IV. 331 Whan þey were i-tore. a **1400** *Leg. Rood* (1871) 143 Til trie fruit weore tore and toyled. c **1422** HOCCLEVE *Min. Poems* (1892) 227 Hir clothes hath shee al to-rent & tore. **1730** A. GORDON *Maffei's Amphith.* 103 They were tore to pieces. **1777** *Horæ Subsecivæ* 427 (E. D. D.) Joan's pitcher is tore.

*γ.* c **1440** *Promp. Parv.* 522/2 Weryd, or teryd, or torvon. a **1529** SKELTON *Col. Cloute* 1203 To be teared thus and torne. **1558** PHAER *Æneid* II. D j b, By Grekes shall Troy not now be teard. a **1649** DRUMM. OF HAWTH. *Poems* Wks. (1711) 37/1 Kingdoms got by wrongs, by wrongs are tear'd. **1879** MISS JACKSON *Shropsh. Word-bk.* 432 I've tard my throck. **1897** E. PHILLPOTTS *Lying Proph.* I. vi, Just a rag tored off a petticoat.

**B.** Signification.

**I. 1.** *trans.* To pull asunder by force (a body or substance, now esp. one of thin and flexible consistence, as cloth or paper), usually so as to leave ragged or irregular edges; to rend. (Expressing either partial or complete separation of parts; in the latter case usually with adv. or advb. phr., as *to tear up, to tear in* (or *to*) *pieces*, etc.)

c **1000** [see A. 2]. **13..** *Seuyn Sag.* (W.) 782 The grehound wolde nowt sessed be, Til that adder ware toren of thre. c **1386** CHAUCER *Shipman's T.* 136 Though men me wolde al in to pieces tere. a **1440** *Sir Degrev.* 1688 Leve syre, where have ȝe bene, ȝoure clothus to tere. **1530** PALSGR. 754/2 He hath torne my gowne a foote and more. **1592** SHAKS. *Rom. & Jul.* v. iii. 35 By heauen I will teare thee ioynt by ioynt. **1649** BP. REYNOLDS *Serm. Hosea* i. 32 The Serpent can sting, but he cannot teare in pieces. **1709** M. PIERREPOINT *Let. to Mrs. Wortley* in *Lady M. W. Montagu's Lett.* lxiii. 104 She will..tear the letter, and never answer it. **1777** COOK *Voy. Pacific* II. vii. (1784) I. 291 They are always careful to join the small pieces lengthwise, which makes it impossible to tear the cloth in any direction but one. **1841** W. SPALDING *Italy & It. Isl.* III. 96 The unpopular minister of finance was torn in pieces by the mob. **1857** HUGHES *Tom Brown* I. vii, Engaged in tearing up old newspapers..into small pieces. **1902** BUCHAN *Watcher by Threshold* 268 The boy had torn his clothes.

**b.** *transf.* To make (a hole, etc.) by tearing.

**1593** SHAKS. *Rich. II*, v. v. 20 How these vaine weake nailes May teare a passage through the Flinty ribbes Of this hard world. *Mod.* You've torn a hole in my coat.

**c.** To break (a hard solid body) by force or violent impact; to shatter, split, rive. Now *dial.*

**1582** N. LICHEFIELD tr. *Castanheda's Conq. E. Ind.* I. lxxi. 145 b, Their Fregates..were torne in pieces and sunke. **1588** SIR W. WYNTER *Let. to J. Hawkyns* 28 Feb. (P.R.O.), This winters weather..hath..torn many of our blocks, pulleis and sheevers. a **1600** HOOKER *Answ. to Travers* § 25 As water spilt or poured into a torn dish. c **1626** *Dick of Devon.* I. ii. in Bullen *O. Pl.* (1883) II. 16 From the armed winds an hoast brake forth which tare their shipps and sav'd ours. **1746** FRANCIS tr. *Horace, Art of Poetry* 642 Like a baited Bear, If he hath Strength enough his Den to tear. **1828** *Wheeler's Mag.* Nov. 481 In this county [Hampshire] break is used for tear, and tear for break, as, I have torn my best decanter, or china dish; I have broke my cambric apron. **1888** ELWORTHY *W. Somerset Word-bk.* s.v., Mind you don't tear the pitcher. Who've a-bin an' a-tord the winder?

†**d.** Phr. *To tear a* (*the*) *cat*: to play the part of a roistering hero; to rant and bluster: cf. *tear-cat* in TEAR- 2. *Obs.*

**1590** SHAKS. *Mids. N.* I. ii. 31, I could play Ercles rarely, or a part to teare a Cat in, to make all split. **1610** *Histrio-m.* 8 Sirrha is this you, would rend and teare the cat upon a stage?

**2.** To wound or injure by rending; to lacerate.

a **1000** *Ecgbert's Confessional* § 40 (Thorpe *Laws* II. 164) ȝif hy[swin] deade men terað [*laceraverint*]. a **1050** *Liber Scintill.* 78 Terende weleras his he ȝefremð yfel. a **1200** *Moral Ode* 274 (Lamb.) Þeor beð naddren and snaken..Þa tereð and freteð þe uuele speken. **13..** *K. Alis.* 5969 (Bodl. MS.) Hij ne shulle hem wiþ tooþ tere. c **1440** *Pallad. on Husb.* VIII. 91 To tere her skynnes bothe. **1526** TINDALE *Mark* ix. 20 As sone as the sprete sawe him, he tare him. **1573–80** BARET *Alv.* T 297 All his bodie is rent, or torne.. *laceratus est toto corpore.* **1697** DRYDEN *Virg. Georg.* III. 678 Their defenceless Limbs the Brambles tear. **1743** FRANCIS tr. *Hor., Epod.* iv. 3 Thou Wretch, whose Back with flagrant Whips is torn. **1813** J. THOMSON *Lect. Inflam.* 207 In wounds, in which the divided surfaces are much torn or bruised. **1875** SIR T. SEATON *Fret Cutting* 96 To avoid tearing the wood when cutting against the grain.

*absol.* c **1000** ÆLFRIC *Hom.* II. 532 Ne sceal he teran ne bitan swa swa wulf. **1545** BRINKLOW *Compl.* 46 b, To teare lyke bearys, and to byte lyke cruel woluys.

**3.** In various *fig.* applications; *esp.*, in later use, to split into parties or factions.

c **1000** *St. Basil's Admonitio* v. (1849) 46 Ne ðu hine ne tæl ne ne ter mid wordum. **1560** DAUS tr. *Sleidane's Comm.* 122 The members of the churche tore a sondre. **1593** SHAKS. *Rich. II*, III. iii. 83 Though you thinke, that all, as you haue done, Haue torne their Soules. **1602** — *Ham.* III. ii. 11 To see a robustious Pery-wig-pated Fellow, tear a Passion to tatters. **1609** *Ev. Woman in Hum.* D iij, A Rogue..so tearing the sence, I neuer met with. **1697** DRYDEN *Virg. Georg.* II. 707 Nor, when contending Kindred tear the Crown, Will set up one, or pull another down. **1779** *Mirror* No. 21 ¶ 2 My sneezing..which, she said, tore her poor nerves in pieces. **1845** S. AUSTIN *Ranke's Hist. Ref.* III. 113 Christendom itself was torn with divisions. **1908** *Daily News* 24 Mar. 6 He, too, tears his finish, while he still has his old fault.

†**b.** *To tear* (*the name of*) *God, the body of Christ*, etc.: to blaspheme; *esp.* to swear profanely by Christ's limbs, etc. *Obs.*

c **1325** *Song of Mercy* 150 in *E. E. P.* (1862) 123 We stunt noþer for schame ne drede To teren vr god from top to to. [c **1386** CHAUCER *Pard. T.* 146 It is grisly for to heere hem swere Oure blissed lordes body they to-tere.] **1539** [see TEARING *vbl. sb.*[1] 1]. **1557** F. SEAGER *Sch. Vertue* xi. C vij, What better art thou for this thy swearyng Blasfamouslye, the name of god tearyng? a **1624** BP. M. SMITH *Serm.* (1632) 126 Did not the Spaniards sweare, and curse, and teare God?

**c.** Used of the effect of sounds, esp. loud or 'piercing' noises, on the air, etc.: = REND *v.* 4 b.

**1592** SHAKS. *Rom. & Jul.* II. ii. 162 Else would I teare the Caue where Eccho lies,..With repetition of my Romeo. **1607** — *Cor.* v. iii. 151 To teare with Thunder the wide Cheekes a' th' Ayre. **1671** MILTON *Samson* 1472 What noise or shout was that? it tore the Skie. **1697** DRYDEN *Virg. Georg.* IV. 665 All her fellow Nymphs the Mountains tear With loud Laments. **1822** LAMB *Elia* Ser. I. *Praise Chimneysweepers*, A shout that tore the concave.

**d.** To harrow, wound, 'rend' (the heart, soul, feelings, etc.).

**1666** BUNYAN *Grace Ab.* § 46 Now was I tore and rent in heavy case for many days together. **1718** POPE *Iliad* XXII. 526 Grief tears his heart. **1859** HELPS *Friends in C.* Ser. II. I. 28 That man torn by domestic affliction. **1872** BLACK *Adv. Phaeton* xi, The young man is torn asunder with doubts and fears.

**4.** *To tear* (*out*) *the hair* in a frenzy of grief or anger: now a hyperbolical expression.

c **1000** *Judith* 281 He þa..onȝan his feax teran hreoh on mode & his hrægl somod. c **1330** *K. Tars* 100 He tar the her of hed and berd. c **1489** CAXTON *Sonnes of Aymon* i. 34 He..wrange his handes and pulled his berde and tare alle his heres. **1580** LYLY *Euphues* (Arb.) 374 He tare his haire, rent his clothes. **1700** DRYDEN *Pal. & Arc.* I. 523 He roared, he beat his breast, he tore his hair. **1848** THACKERAY *Van. Fair* li, She might tear her long hair and cry her great eyes out. **1855** — *Rose & Ring* ix, Bulbo began to cry bitterly, and tore quantities of hair out of his head.

**5.** To pull, wrench, or drag by main force from its attachment or fixed place. (With various advbs. or preps. according to sense.)

**1297** R. GLOUC. (Rolls) App. XX. 188 Hare fon come þere, Adoun of his hors henri hi tere Mid yrene crokes. c **1400** *Rom. Rose* 7315 That men ne may in no manere Teren the wolf out of his hide. c **1400** *Destr. Troy* 1966, I shuld tere out þi tunge and þi tethe euyn. a **1425** *Cursor M.* 9072 (Trin.) My kingis robe of me ȝe tere. a **1533** LD. BERNERS *Huon* lv. 188 He..tare of helmes & strake out braynes. **1590** SPENSER *F. Q.* II. x. 36 The noble braunch from th' antique stock was torne Through discord. **1614** RALEIGH *Hist. World* II. (1634) 481 A great Earth-quake, which did teare downe halfe an Hill. **1667** WOOD *Life* (O.H.S.) II. 121, I find many leaves..toren out. **1699** DAMPIER *Voy.* II. III. vi. 67 By tearing up the Trees by the Roots. **1704** SWIFT *Batt. Bks.* Misc. (1711) 239 Who had tore off his Title-Page. **1705** ADDISON *Italy* 7 (tr. Lucan I.) Ships from their Anchors torn. **1821** SCOTT *Kenilw.* xl, I could tear out mine eyes for their blindness! **1849** MACAULAY *Hist. Eng.* iii. I. 387 The porters..tore down the placards in which the scheme was announced. **1899** *Allbutt's Syst. Med.* VIII. 872 They [molluscan tumours] may be easily torn out of the skin when mature.

**b.** *fig.* To take away or remove by force or violence; to force; *refl.* to force oneself away.

**1574** HELLOWES *Gueuara's Fam. Ep.* (1577) 310 Despiteful wordes that..breake her hart, & teare yͤ teares out of her eyes. **1590** SHAKS. *Mids. N.* III. ii. 287 What, will you teare Impatient answers from my gentle tongue? **1647** MAY *Hist. Parl.* I. vii. 77 If a King will suffer men to be torne from him, he shall never have any good service done him. **1797** MRS. RADCLIFFE *Italian* i, At length he tore himself away. **1829** LYTTON *Devereux* III. ii, I think I see her now, as she stood the moment after I had torn myself from her embrace. **1888** J. PAYN *Myst. Mirbridge* (ed. Tauchn.) II. ii. 27 Before the gentlemen come in and tear you away from me.

**6.** *intr.* To perform the act of tearing; to make a tear or rent. *To tear at*, to continue to pull at in order to rend or lacerate.

**1526** *Pilgr. Perf.* (W. de W. 1531) 258 b, Ye, and many moo sorowes dyd teare & thryll thorowe her herte. **1848** W. E. BURTON *Waggeries*, etc. 25 (Farmer) They..kept on tearin at each other like a pack o' wolves. **1867** AUG. J. E. WILSON *Vashti* xxxi, His hands, partially confined, were tearing at the inflamed flesh.

**7.** *intr.* (for *refl.* and *pass.*) To become torn or rent; *dial.* to burst asunder, split, snap, break.

**1526** *Pilgr. Perf.* (W. de W. 1531) 260 b, His handes & fete dyd rent & teare for the weyght of his blessed body. **1703** MOXON *Mech. Exerc.* 149 The Boards will Tear or Shake, which is in vulgar English, Split or Crack. **1710** J. CLARKE *Rohault's Nat. Phil.* (1729) I. 229 Cloths and other Stuffs of this Colour must tear and wear sooner than those of any other Colour. **1776** WITHERING *Brit. Plants* (1796) III. 352 Veil before the capsule swells, 4-sided; afterwards it tears into 2, 3, or 4 segments. **1838** DRUMMOND in *Mag. Zool. & Bot.* II. 156 If attempted to be restored without ..being first damped, the specimen tears through the middle. **1865** KINGSLEY *Herew.* vi, All of a sudden..the clouds rose, tore up into ribands, and..blew clean away.

**II. 8.** *intr.* † To rant and bluster as a roisterer (*obs.*); † to vociferate (*obs.*); to 'go on' violently, to rave in anger or excitement, to rage (*dial.*).

**1601** B. JONSON *Poetaster* III. iv, Hee will teach thee to teare and rand, Rascall, to him. **1672** DRYDEN *Marriage à-la-Mode* III. i, Three tailors..who were tearing out as loud as ever they could sing. **1690** *Andros Tracts* I. 207 Towns..which Rant and Tear at a great rate, because of a small Rate. **1736** AINSWORTH *Lat. Dict.* (1783) s.v. *Tear*, To rant, or tear along, *tumultuor, debacchor, vociferationibus vias incessu implere.* **1853** THACKERAY *Eng. Hum.* i. (1858) 33 He goes through life, tearing, like a man possessed with a devil. **1897** G. BARTRAM *People of Clopton* v. 132 She stamped and foamed, and swore and tore.

**9.** *intr.* To move with violence or impetuosity; to rush or 'burst' impetuously or violently. *colloq.*

Sometimes with the notion of a force that would tear its way through obstacles.

**1599** MASSINGER, etc. *Old Law* v. i, The nimble fencer this, that made me tear And traverse 'bout the chamber? **1637** SUCKLING *Aglaura* v. i, (Stage direct.) Enter, tearing in, Pasithas. **1779** MME. D'ARBLAY *Diary* Nov., I cannot bear to see Othello tearing about in that violent manner. **1786** tr. *Beckford's Vathek* 56, I thought I heard ..the shrieks of a thousand bats, tearing from their crannies. **1842** THACKERAY *Miss Tickletoby's Lect.* ix, Edward came tearing down to the borders on the news. **1877** A. B. EDWARDS *Up Nile* vi. 142 The boat tears on before the wind. **1894** FENN *In Alpine Valley* I. 43 This river tore down the narrow valley with headlong violence. **1901** H. FURNISS *Confess. Caricaturist* I. iii. 79 The animals snorted ..and..tore off..at a tremendous rate.

**Tear** (tīᵊɹ), *v.*[2] Now *rare.* [f. TEAR *sb.*[1]]

†**1.** *intr.* To shed tears, to weep. *Obs.* or *dial.*

c **950** *Lindisf. Gosp.* John xi. 35 Tæherende [*Rushw.* teherende] uæs se hælend. c **1430** *Pilgr. Lyf Manhode* II. li. (1869) 95, I bigan to tere and to weepe and to sigh. **1599** T. M[OUFET] *Silkwormes* 9 Its mother..Who absent bleard and tear'd as much for him. a **1660** *Contemp. Hist. Irel.* (Ir. Archæol. Soc.) II. 60 Eneas himselfe..too often teared for the losse of Troye. **1719** HAMILTON in *Christ. Instructor* (1832) 694 Some of them were so affected that they teared also. **1806** COCK *Simple Strains* (1810) I. 103 (E.D.D.), I fell in wi' Geordy Brown, And he, poor saul, was tearin'.

†**b.** *trans.* To pass (time) in weeping. *Obs.*

**1575** GASCOIGNE *Fruite of Fetters* iii, I teare my time (ay me) in prison pent.

**c.** Of the eyes: To shed or emit tears.

c **1000, 1527** [see *tearing* ppl. a. below]. **1650** in Ritchie *Ch. St. Baldred* (1880) 86 Putting sneishen in his eyes to mak them tear. **1879** [see *tearing* vbl. sb. below].

**2.** *trans.* To fill or sprinkle with or as with tears.

c **1620** Z. BOYD *Zion's Flowers* (1855) 112 Feare teares your eyes. **18..** *Century Mag.* XXXVII. 545 (Cent. Dict.) The lorn lily teared with dew.

Hence **Tea·ring** *vbl. sb.* and *ppl. a.*

c **1000** *Sax. Leechd.* I. 72 Wið tyrende eaȝan, ȝenim þa ylcan wyrte betonican. **1527** ANDREW *Brunswyke's Distyll. Waters* C iv b, The same is good put in the iyen agaynst tering iyen. a **1660** *Contemp. Hist. Irel.* (Ir. Archæol. Soc.) II. 135 The tearinge and fatherlie intercession of the saide religious persons. **1879** *St. George's Hosp. Rep.* IX. 778 A white spot formed on the cornea, along with much 'tearing' and 'fear of light'.

**Tear,** obs. form of TEER *v.*, to plaster, smear.

**Tear-,** the stem of TEAR *v.*[1] in comb.

**1.** With adv., forming sbs. or adjs., as **tear-away**, *adj.*, characterized by impetuous speed, tearing (cf. TEAR *v.*[1] 9); *sb.*, one who or that which 'tears' or rushes away, or acts with great impetuosity; **tear-off**, *adj.*, adapted to be torn off; *sb.*, a sheet or slip of paper so attached as to be easily torn off; **tear-up** *sb.*, an uprooting; a violent removal (*Cent. Dict.* 1891).

**1833** T. HOOK *Parson's Dau.* III. vii, To mount a great *tear-away chestnut horse. **1891** N. GOULD *Double Event* 67 The tearaway [a horse] of that morning..had suddenly developed into a mild, affectionate creature. **1901** S. F. BULLOCK *Irish Past.* iv. 100 Now that lassie's a tear-away. **1903** *Windsor Mag.* Sept. 394/2 The substitutes also were tear-away bowlers, but they were not so fast as the first pair. **1889** *Pall Mall G.* 21 Dec. 3/1 Blotting pads, with a *tear-off engagement-sheet at the side.

**2.** With sb. in objective relation, forming sbs. or adjs., as †**tea·r-brain**: see quot.; **tear-brass** *a.*, rowdy, prodigal; **tear-bridge** *a.*, that tears or destroys bridges: used as epithet of a river; **tear-cat**, *adj.*, swaggering, ranting, bombastic (see TEAR *v.*[1] 1 d); *sb.*, a bully, swaggerer, 'fire-eater'; †**tear-mouth**, an epithet applied to a ranting actor; †**tear-placket**, ? a cutpurse; †**tear-**

**rogue,** ? a roistering disreputable fellow; †**tear-throat,** *adj.*, that 'tears' or irritates the throat; *sb.*, a ranting actor; **tear-thumb,** two species of *Polygonum* native to North America (and Asia), the halberd-leaved tear-thumb, *P. arifolium*, and the arrow-leaved, *P. sagittatum*; so called from the hooked prickles on the petioles and angles of the stems.

**1796** G. M. WOODWARD *Eccentric Excurs.* 80 Another curious liquor called *tear-brain, composed entirely of Rum and Brandy. **1880** T. HARDY *Trumpet-Major* ix, To.. provide goods for his breaking, and house-room and drink for his *tear-brass set. **1598** SYLVESTER *Du Bartas* II. ii. III. *Colonies* 429 The di'pry verges Of *tear-bridge Tygris. **1606** DAY *Ile of Guls* Prol. (1881) 6, I had rather heare two good baudie iests then a whole play of such *teare-cat thunderclaps. **1611** MIDDLETON & DEKKER *Roaring Girl* D.'s Wks. 1873 III. 215 *D.* What's thy name fellow souldier? *T.* I am cal'd by those who haue seen my valour, Tear-Cat. **1821** SCOTT *Kenilw.* xii, A man of mettle—one of those ruffling tear-cats, who maintain their master's quarrel with sword and buckler. **1601** B. JONSON *Poetaster* III. iv, You grow rich, doe you? and purchase, you two-penny *teare-mouth? **1819** SCOTT *Let. to Southey* 4 Apr., in *Lockhart*, A copper-laced, twopenny tearmouth. *c* **1600** DAY *Begg. Bednall Gr.* IV. i, I have spent many a gray groat of honest swaggerers and *tear-Plackets..that I never drunk for. **1685** *Depos. fr. Cast. York* (Surtees) 275 He was a Monmouth *teare-rogue, and..had raysed men..for Monmouth's service. **1630** J. TAYLOR (Water P.) *Praise Hemp-seed* Wks. III. 65 The *teare-throat cough and tisick, From which, to health men are restor'd by Physicke. **1654** GAYTON *Pleas. Notes* I. vii. 24 The Poets of the Fortune and red Bull, had alwayes a mouth-measure for their Actors (who were terrible teare throats). **1866** *Treas. Bot.*, **Tear-thumb.*

**Tearable** (tēə·răb'l), *a.* [f. TEAR *v.*[1] + -ABLE.] Capable of being torn.

**1859** [implied in UNTEARABLE]. **1895** *Daily News* 7 Jan. 3/3 Everything that was breakable was broken in fragments, and everything tearable torn in pieces.

**Tear-bottle** (tīə·ɹ,bɒ·t'l). A bottle containing tears (cf. Ps. lvi. 8 'put my tears into thy bottle'); also *transf.*; *spec.* = LACHRYMATORY B. 1, applied to small bottles or phials, such as are found in ancient tombs, supposed, with doubtful correctness, to have contained tears shed for the deceased.

**1658** [see LACHRYMATORY B. 1]. **1662** J. BARGRAVE *Pope Alex. VII* (1867) 122 Called *lachrymatorij*, or tear-bottles, because the friends and relations of the defunct were in ancient time accustomed at the funeral to carry each of them a *lachrymatorio* in his hand, to save his tears that he shed for his deceased friend, and then leave those bottles behind them with the immuralld corps. **1884** 'H. COLLINGWOOD' *Under Meteor Flag* 259 Stow away the tear-bottles, coil down all tender feeling out of sight. *attrib.* **1904** BUDGE *3rd & 4th Egypt. Rooms Brit. Mus.* 35 Glass vessels..of the well-known *lacrimarium*, or 'tear-bottle' type, and belonging to the Roman period.

**Tearce,** obs. form of TERSE, TIERCE.

**Teard, -e,** obs. pa. t. and pa. pple. of TEAR *v.*[1]

**Teare,** obs. form of TEAR, TIER.

**Tearer** (tēə·rəɹ). [f. TEAR *v.*[1] + -ER [1].]

**1.** One who or that which tears or rends.

In quot. 1828 applied to a (? canine) tooth; in quot. 1862, to a mechanical device for tearing something; in quot. 1886 to a 'tearing' cold.

**1625** MASSINGER *New Way* v. i, I know you are a tearer. But I'll have first your fangs pared off, and then Come nearer to you. **1682** *Sec. Plea Nonconf.* 4 The Tearers of the Church have made at me,..but..have hurt their Nails and Fingers. **1719** D'URFEY *Pills* II. 81 To Wearers and Tearers Of Manteau and Gown. **1828** FLEMING *Brit. Zool.* 9 In the lower jaw [of the badger], the bruiser is small, the chewer large, and there is an additional tearer. **1862** *Jrnl. Soc. Arts* X. 329/2 The doughy mass is put into an iron box, or tearer, in which an iron cylinder, with iron teeth, rapidly revolves, tearing it into shreds. **1886** C. KEENE *Let.* in *Life* xi. (1892) 359, I suppose I've been boasting of my immunity from colds, for I've just had a tearer, so hoarse that I couldn't sound a note.

†**b.** *Tearer of God*, a blasphemer or profane swearer (see TEAR *v.*[1] 3 b). *Obs.*

*a* **1550** *Hye Way to Spyttel H.* 851 in Hazl. *E.P.P.* IV. 61 These blasphemers and these God terers. **1570** FOXE *A. & M.* (ed. 2) 2303/1 Blasphemous and abominable swearers or rather tearers of God.

**2.** A person who tears or rushes along or about; a ranter, roisterer, swaggerer, bully.

**1625, 1682** [see sense 1]. **1664** COTTON *Scarron.* I. Poet Wks. (1717) 8 A huffing Jack, a plund'ring Tearer. **1693** CONGREVE *Old Bach.* IV. ix, Hist! hist! bully; dost thou see those tearers [Araminta and Belinda masked]? **1828** WEBSTER, *Tearer*,..one that rages or raves with violence. **1862** M'GILVRAY *Poems* (ed. 2) 56 (E.D.D.) For faith she is a tearer, She frights the very swine.

**Tearful** (tīə·ɹfŭl), *a.* [f. TEAR *sb.*[1] + -FUL.]

**1.** Full of tears; weeping; lachrymose.

*a* **1586** SIDNEY *Arcadia* III. (1598) 372 My Pyrocles said she (with tearefull eyes and pittifull countenance). **1597** J. PAYNE *Royal Exch.* 28 Sory and fearefull, yea penitent and teare-full. **1726** POPE *Odyss.* XXI. 233 With tear full eyes o'er all their master gaz'd. **1855** HT. MARTINEAU *Autobiog.* ii. (1877) 30 The old folks and their daughters came out to meet us, all tearful and agitated. **1884** *Mem. Pr. Alice* 16 The parting was tearful, but full of hope.

**2.** Causing tears; mournful, melancholy. ? *Obs.*

*c* **1611** CHAPMAN *Iliad* XIX. 315 Then the warre, was tearefull to our foe, But now to me.

Hence **Tea·rfully** *adv.*, in a tearful manner, with tears; **Tea·rfulness,** the state of being tearful.

**1820** L. HUNT *Indicator* No. 37 (1822) I. 296 A breathing tearfulness. **1835** LYTTON *Rienzi* I. i, Anxiously and tearfully he looked..up the steep ascent of the Aventine. **1863** MONSELL *Hymn, 'O worship the Lord'* iv, Mornings of joy..for evenings of tearfulness.

**Tearing** (tēə·riŋ), *vbl. sb.*[1] [f. TEAR *v.*[1] + -ING [1].]

**1.** The action of TEAR *v.*[1], in various senses.

**14..** *Beryn* 644 The warrok..held hym right a square, by þat othir syde, As holsom was at that tyme, for tereing of his hyde. **1539** TONSTALL *Serm. Palm Sund.* (1823) 80 The tearynge of goddis name, and particular mention of all the woundes and peynes that Christe suffered for vs. **1768** TUCKER *Lt. Nat.* (1834) I. 640 Tearings of ravenous beasts, stings of venomous serpents. **1904** BENSON *Challoners* ix, It ..cut like a blunt knife with sawing and tearing.

**2.** The result of this action: **a.** A wound made by tearing. **b.** A fragment torn off.

**1607** TOPSELL *Four-f. Beasts* (1658) 346 Their flesh also being eaten, doth quickly cure and heal the bitings or tearings of a ravenous Dog. **1891** E. ARNOLD *Lt. of World* IV. 193 Truth, Lord! but crumbs fall, and the dogs may eat The children's tearings!

**3.** *attrib.* **Tearing-machine**: see quot.

**1877** KNIGHT *Dict. Mech.*, *Tearing-machine*, a machine for disintegrating woven fabric to make fiber for reworking.

**Tea·ring,** *ppl. a.*[1] [f. TEAR *v.*[1] + -ING [2].] That tears, in various senses of the verb.

**1.** Generally (chiefly in *fig.* applications); *esp.* that wounds the feelings; severely distressing, harrowing; also, causing a sensation as of rending.

**1606** SHAKS. *Ant. & Cl.* IV. xiv. 31 She..Then in the midd'st a tearing grone did breake The name of Anthony. **1686** BURNET *Lett.* (1708) 235 The tearing Anxieties, that Want brings with it. **1736** AINSWORTH *Lat. Dict.* (1783) s.v., A tearing, or very loud, voice, *vox stentora vincens.* **1839** MRS. CARLYLE *Lett., to Mrs. Aitken* 22 Nov. (1903) I. 86 One might think one's maid's tears could do little for a tearing headache; but they do comfort a little. **1898** *Allbutt's Syst. Med.* V. 11 The cough [in bronchitis is described] as 'tearing'.

**2.** Of a wind or storm: So violent as to tear things up or in pieces; raging.

**1633** T. JAMES *Voy.* 29 We had a tearing storme at North. **1889** BARRIE *Window in Thrums* 201 A tearing gale had blown the upper part of the brae clear.

**3.** Moving with impetuous speed; rushing.

**1765** STERNE *Tr. Shandy* VII. xix, You do get on at a tearing rate. **1876** *World* V. No. 106. 18 Soon afterwards the band began to play a tearing galop—the sign of the conclusion. **1887** T. A. TROLLOPE *What I remember* II. iv. 66 Readers who are not in such a tearing hurry as the unhappy world is in these latter days. **1908** *Westm. Gaz.* 11 Aug. 10/3 To that [traffic] there has lately been added the tearing motor-'buses.

**4.** Violent or reckless in action or behaviour; full of excitement; headstrong, passionate; ranting, roistering; boisterous, rollicking, exuberant. *colloq.* or *slang.* (Now *rare.*)

**1654** GAYTON *Pleas. Notes* IV. xxi. 271 Some tearing Tragedy full of fights and skirmishes. **1667** PEPYS *Diary* 7 Oct., There was so much tearing company in the house, that we could not see the landlady. **1673** S. C. *Art of Complaisance* 65 Like the two tearing fellows which the poet had designed for the characters of gentlemen. **1790** *Bystander* 343 Half a dozen young tearing rascals. **1823** SCOTT *Peveril* xxxviii, So in stole this termagant, tearing gallant. **1869** J. R. GREEN *Lett.* III. (1901) 232, I am in such tearing spirits at the prospect of freedom.

**b.** Impressive, splendid, grand; 'ripping', 'rattling', 'stunning'. *colloq.* or *slang.* (Now *rare.*)

**1693** *Humours Town* 100 That so she may make a notable Figure, and a taring show the next Sunday in the Village-Church. **1721** AMHERST *Terræ Fil.* No. 33 (1754) 176 Persons ..who cut a tearing figure in silk-gowns, and bosh it about town in lace ruffles, and flaxon tye-wigs. **1850** CUMMING *Hunter's Life S. Afr.* (1902) 29/1 A large bright comet, having a tearing, fiery tail. **1897** *Outing* (U.S.) XXX. 270/2 A mighty fine woman and a tearing beauty besides.

**5.** quasi-*adv.* Furiously. (Cf. *raving mad.*)

**1692** R. L'ESTRANGE *Fables* ccxlv. 213 This Bull..that ran Tearing Mad for the Pinching of a Mouse.

**Tearing,** *vbl. sb.*[2] and *ppl. a.*[2]: see TEAR *v.*[2]

**Tearless** (tīə·ɹlės), *a.* [f. TEAR *sb.*[1] + -LESS.] Void of tears; shedding no tears, not weeping.

**1603** NORTH *Plutarch* (1612) 1123 This dayes iourney was called for them the tearelesse battell. **1591** SYLVESTER *Du Bartas* I. ii. 879 Canst thou tear-lesse gaze..on that prodigious blaze, That hairy Comet? **1743** SHENSTONE *Elegies* xix, Ye saw with tearless eye When your fleet perish'd on the Punic wave. **1868** LYNCH *Rivulet* CXXXII. v, A star, that..Shines..to point thy way On to the tearless country bright.

Hence **Tea·rlessly** *adv.*, in a tearless manner, without weeping; **Tea·rlessness,** the quality or condition of being tearless.

**1853** C. BRONTE *Villette* xxx, He watched tearlessly. **1894** *Westm. Gaz.* 1 Mar. 3/1 What could be more..tearlessly pathetic?

**Tearlet** (tīə·ɹlėt). [f. TEAR *sb.*[1] + -LET.] A little or tiny tear.

**1858** BAILEY *The Age* 201 The sun's bright tearlets.

**Tearm, Tearn,** obs. ff. TERM, TARN.

**Tea-roller,** etc.: see TEA *sb.* 9 c.

**Tea·-ro·se, tea rose.** A variety (or group of varieties) of cultivated rose, derived from the species *Rosa indica*, var. *odorata*, having flowers of a pale yellow colour, with a delicate scent supposed to resemble that of tea. Originally, *tea-scented rose.*

**1850** *Florist* Aug. 191 The delicate and odorous Tea Rose fated to be admired and to languish in the drawing-room. **1882** *Garden* 11 Mar., Tea Roses may be pruned in April.

**b.** The colour of this rose. Also *attrib.*

**1884** *Chr. World Fam. Circle* 4 Nov. 260/4 Amongst the favourite colours are imperial yellow, Nile blue, tea rose and cardinal. **1900** *St. James' Gaz.* 21 Sept. 6/2 A bolero of tea-rose silk.

**Tearse,** obs. f. TIERCE. **Teart,** obs. and dial. f. TART. **Teartane,** obs. f. TARTAN *sb.*[1]

**Teary** (tīə·ri), *a.* [f. TEAR *sb.*[1] + -Y.]

**1.** Full of or suffused with tears; tearful. Now *colloq.*

*c* **1374** CHAUCER *Troylus* IV. 793 (821) She gan for sorwe anon Hire tery face atwixe hire armes hyde. *a* **1541** WYATT *How Lover perisheth in his delight*, With my teary eyn, swolne, and vnstable. **1848** LOWELL *Biglow Pap.* Ser. I. *Courtin'* xxi, All kin' o' smily roun' the lips An' teary roun' the lashes. **1863** W. MILLAR in *Whistle Binkie* (1890) I. 473 My e'e grew dim and tearie. **1890** *Pall Mall G.* 18 Dec. 2/1 As we drop down the grey Thames we are a teary and a melancholy company.

**2.** Of the nature of or consisting of tears. *rare.*

*c* **1420** LYDG. *Story of Thebes* III. Chaucer's Wks. (1560) 372/2 Whan the stormes, and the teary shoure Of her weping, was somwhat ouergon. **1594** CONSTABLE *Sonn.* v. viii, And on the shoare of that salt tearie sea. *a* **1600** MONTGOMERIE *Misc. Poems* xxxvii. 4 A tearie fluid does blind thir ees of myne. **1830** *Fraser's Mag.* I. 503 Did the God of Hell..weep..the iron sleet of teary shower?

**Teasable** (tī·zăb'l), *a.* [f. TEASE *v.*[1] + -ABLE.] Capable of being teased.

**1865** G. MACDONALD *A. Forbes* viii, Children..are ready to tease any child who simply looks teasable.

**Tea-sage** to **Tea-scrub**: see TEA *sb.* 9 c.

**Tease,** *sb.* Also 7–9 teaze. [f. TEASE *v.*[1]]

**1.** The action of teasing. †*Upon the tease*, uneasy from trifling irritation (*obs.*). *rare.*

**1693** C. MATHER *Wond. Invis. World* (1862) 162 After she had undergone a deal of Teaze from the Annoyance of the Spectre. **1706** MRS. CENTLIVRE *Basset-Table* III. 34 There's One upon the Teaze already. **1707** — *Platonick Lady* v. 61, I left her upon the Teaze. **1878–9** LANIER *Poems, Individuality* 10 No pitiless tease of risk or bottomry.

**2.** A person addicted to teasing; one who irritates another in a trifling or sportive way. *colloq.*

**1852** DICKENS *Bleak Ho.* xxx, What a teaze you are. **1899** MISS HARRADEN *Fowler* II. v. 190, I am a tease by nature.

**Tease** (tīz), *v.*[1] Forms: 1 tǽsan, 4–5 tese, 5 teese, 7 teise, 7–9 teize, teaze, 8 teez, teaz, 6– tease. [OE. *tǽsan* to tear or pull to pieces, tease (wool, etc.), wk. vb. = OLG. **tēsan* (MLG., LG. *tēsen*, MDu. *tēzen*, Du. *teezen* to draw, pull, scratch, NFris. *tiese*), OHG. *zeisan* str. vb., MHG. *zeisen* wk. vb., Ger. dial. (Bav.) *zaisen*, *zeisen* (Schade) to tease, pick wool:—OTeut. **taisjan* and **taisan*: cf. also TOASE *v.*]

**1.** *trans.* To separate or pull asunder the fibres of; to comb or card (wool, flax, etc.) in preparation for spinning; to open *out* by pulling asunder; to shred.

*c* **1000** *Sax. Leechd.* III. 112 Nim þanne wulle & tæs hy. ?*c* **1390** *Forme of Cury* in Warner *Antiq. Culin.* (1791) 17 Take the brawn, and tese it smal. **14..** *Noble Bk. Cookry* (Napier 1882) 102 Then teese the braun of capon or henn small. **1591** PERCIVALL *Sp. Dict.*, *Carmenar*, to picke wooll, to tease wooll, *carminare.* **1612** WOODALL *Surg. Mate* Wks. (1653) 344 Take Saffron..then tease it, I mean, pull the parts thereof asunder. **1634** MILTON *Comus* 751 To ply The sampler, and to teize the huswifes wooll. **1683** MOXON *Mech. Exerc.*, *Printing* xxiv. ⁋ 19 [He] Teizes his Wooll, by opening all the..matted knots he finds in it. **1828** P. CUNNINGHAM *N.S. Wales* (ed. 3) II. 151 While teasing out the tobacco-leaf to charge his pipe. **1851** *Art Jrnl. Illustr. Catal.* p. iv**/2 The quick moving cards teaze out the fibres, and gradually, very gradually, disentangle them. **1875** HUXLEY & MARTIN *Elem. Biol.* xi. (1876) 122 Tease out a bit of the liver in water, and examine with ⅙ obj. **1893** A. N. PALMER *Hist. Wrexham* IV. 10 The flax dressers prepared the flax for the linen spinners and weavers by 'teasing' it.

**b.** To comb the surface of cloth, after weaving, with teasels, which draw all the free hairs or fibres in one direction, so as to form a nap.

**1755** JOHNSON, *Tease*,..to scratch cloth in order to level the nap. **1829** J. L. KNAPP *Jrnl. Nat.* 48 Many of these [teasel] heads are fixed in a frame; and with this the surface of the cloth is teased, or brushed, until all the ends are drawn out. **1861** MISS PRATT *Flower. Pl.* III. 172 Blankets were made of goats'-wool, teased into a satiny surface by little Teazel-like brushes of bamboo.

†**c.** To tear in pieces. *Obs.*

*a* **1550** *Hye Way to Spyttel H.* 888 in Hazl. *E. P. P.* IV. 63 Lyke as wolues the shepe dooth take and tease.

**2.** To worry or irritate by persistent action which vexes or annoys; now *esp.* in lighter sense, to disturb by persistent petty annoyance, out of mere mischief or sport; to bother or plague in a petty way.

**1627** [see TEASED 2]. **1679** C. HATTON in *H. Corr.* (Camden) 210 After he had thus teised them for 2 or 3 houres he left them. **1686** tr. *Chardin's Trav. Persia* 162 Teizing me for two Hours together with a Thousand Impertinencies. **1710** SWIFT *Lett.* (1767) III. 23 Lord Halifax is always teazing me to go down to his country house, which will cost me a guinea to his servants, and twelve shillings coach hire. **1774** PENNANT *Tour Scot. in* 1772, 283 The violent squalls of wind..teized us for an hour. **1774** GOLDSM. *Nat. Hist.* IV. 74 To avoid teizing the reader with a minute description. **1782** MME. D'ARBLAY *Diary* 8 Dec., [They] resisted reading the book till they were teased into it. **1827** D. JOHNSON *Ind. Field Sports* 208 A boy..was teizing the animal to make it bite him. **1881** BESANT & RICE *Chapl. of Fleet* I. 14 Harry ceased to tease and torment them with little tricks and devices of mischief.

*fig.* **1774** GOLDSM. *Nat. Hist.* I. 54 The earth..constantly teized more to furnish..luxuries..than..necessities. **1856**

Mrs. Browning *Aur. Leigh* I. 1050, I..teased The patient needle till it split the thread. **1893** *Westm. Gaz.* 17 Feb. 3/1 It is all done with that flowing brush.., and there is nothing teased or overworked in the whole of it.

**b.** *absol.* or *intr.* (With first quot., cf. Touse *v.*)
**1619** Fletcher *M. Thomas* v. vii. What a coyle has this fellow kept i' th' Nunnery,..Pray Heavens he be not teasing. **1693** Dryden *Juvenal* vi. 377 Conscious of Crimes her self, she teizes first. **1751** Johnson *Rambler* No. 144 ⁋ 6 To teize with feeble blows and impotent disturbance. *a* **1861** Mrs. Browning *Little Mattie* vii, Love both ways, kiss and tease.

**3.** *slang.* To flog. ? *Obs.*
**1812** J. H. Vaux *Flash Dict.*, *Teaze*, to flog or whip. **1865** [see Teasing *vbl. sb.*[1] 3].

**Tease,** *v.*[2] *local.* Also teaze. [ad. mod.F. *tiser* (technical) 'to introduce fuel into a melting-furnace' (Littré); to fire a furnace; app. aphetic for *attiser* = It. *attizzare*, Sp., Prov. *atizar* to stir (the fire), f. *à*:—L. *ad* to + It. *tizzo*, Sp. *tizo*, L. *titio*, burning brand, fire-brand.] *trans.* To feed (a furnace fire) with fuel; to attend to (a fire or furnace).
**1818** J. Adley *Coal Trade* (Northumb. Gloss.), You must have furnacemen to teaze and rouse the fire. **1894** [see Teasing *vbl. sb.*[2]].

**Teased** (tīzd), *ppl. a.* [f. Tease *v.*[1] + -ed [1].]
**1.** Having the fibres pulled asunder: see Tease *v.*[1] 1. In quot. 1620 *fig.* Also *teased out*.
*c* **1430** *Two Cookery-bks.* 22 Caste þer-to tesyd brawn. **1620** Brinsley tr. *Virgil* 58 To sing a teased verse..a pastorall song.., drawne out small like wooll in spinning. **1851** *Art Jrnl. Illustr. Catal.* p. iv**/1 This cylinder is cleaned of the teazed cotton by means of brushes. **1875** Huxley & Martin *Elem. Biol.* (1877) 258 Treat a fresh bit of teased-out nerve with chloroform.

**2.** Irritated or annoyed in a petty way.
**1627** May *Lucan* iii. 527 Vntill the townesmens teased valour broke..The fence. **1852–5** M. Arnold *Faded Leaves, River* v, This teased o'erlabour'd heart.

**Tea·se-hole.** [f. Tease *v.*[2] + Hole *sb.*]
**1858** Simmonds *Dict. Trade*, *Teaze-hole*, the opening in the furnace of a glass-work, through which coals are put in.

**Teasel, teazle** (tī·z'l), *sb.* Forms: *α.* 1 tǽsl, tǽsel, 3–5 tesel, 5 tesell, -yl(l, tesle, 5–7 tessel, 6 tesill, teasell, teassell, teysyll, 6–7 tessele, teazell, tezel, -ill, 7–8 teasil, 7– teasel, teasle, teazel, teazle, 8 testle. *β.* 4–6 tasel, 4–7 -il, 5 -yl, -ylle, -ul, -elle, taysill, 5–7 tazel, 6 tasill, -yll, tassyll, 6–7 tasell, tasle, tazell, tassill, 7 tassel, tazill, tazle, 8 tassell. [OE. *tǽsel*, *tǽsl* = OHG. *zeisala*, *-ila*, str. fem., MHG. *zeisel*:—OTeut. **taisilā*, f. **taisan*, OE. *tǽsan* to tease, with instr. suffix *-lā*. Hence AF. *teizel*.]
**1.** A plant of the genus *Dipsacus*, comprising herbs with prickly leaves and flower-heads; *esp.* **Fullers' Teasel**, *D. fullonum*, the heads of which have hooked prickles between the flowers, and are used for teasing cloth (see 2); and **Wild Teasel**, *D. sylvestris*, held by some to be the original type, but having straight instead of hooked prickles.
[*c* **1000** *Sax. Leechd.* I. 282 Ðeos wyrt þe man camelleon alba & oþrum naman wulfes tæsl [*MS. B.* tæsel] nemneþ.] *c* **1265** *Voc. Names Plants* in Wr.-Wülcker 559/7 *Uirga pastoris*, wilde tesel. **1326** *Lett.-bk. Lond. E.* lf. 168 in Riley *Memorials* (1868) 150 [The thistles that in English are called] taseles. **1382** Wyclif *Isa.* xxxiv. 13 Ther shul springe in his houses thornes and netles, and tasil in the strengthis of it. *a* **1387** *Sinon. Barthol.* (Anecd. Oxon.) 43/1 *Virga pastoris*, i. carduus agrestis, herba est quæ multum assimulatur carduo fullonum, an. wilde tasel. *c* **1440** *Pallad. on Husb.* iv. 128 The tasul now in donged lond is sowe. **14..** *Voc.* in Wr.-Wülcker 570/41 *Cardo*, a thystell, or a tesell. *c* **1450** *Godstow Reg.* 648 All tethe of tesyls that longyn to the office of fullers. **1598** Stow *Surv.* xviii. (1603) 167 There were Tasels planted for the use of Cloth workers. **1601** Holland *Pliny* II. 280 The Tazill, called in Greeke Dipsacos, hath leaues much resembling Lectuce. **1626** A. Speed *Adam out of Ed.* ix. (1659) 62 Tassels for Cloath-workers..will thrive..in England. **1630** Drayton *Muses' Elysium* Nymph. iii. lv, By stinging Nettles, pricking Teasels Raysing blisters like the measels. **1725** *R. Bradley's Fam. Dict.* s.v., They sow their Lands in some Parts of Essex with Teasils, to dress their Bays and Cloth with. **1872** Oliver *Elem. Bot.* ii. 193 The connate leaves of Common Teasel..collect the rain and dew that trickle down the stem.

**2.** The dried prickly flower-head or bur of the fullers' teasel (see 1), used for teasing or dressing cloth so as to raise a nap on the surface.
**1377** Langl. *P. Pl.* B. xv. 446 Cloth..is nouȝt comly to were, Tyl it is fulled.., Wasshen wel with water, and with taseles [*v.rr.* taselles, taslis] cracched. **1463–4** *Rolls of Parlt.* V. 502/2 That every Fuller..use Tazels, and noo Cardes, in disseyvably hurtyng the same Cloth. **1545** *Rates of Customs* c vij, Tasels the kyue conteining v.c. viij.d. *Ibid.* c vij b, Tasels the pipe xl.s. Tasels the thousande iij.s. iiij.d. **1564** Hawkins *Voy.* (Hakl. Soc.) 27 A kinde of corne called Maise,..the eare whereof is much like to a teasell. **1565–73** Cooper *Thesaurus*, *Gnaphos*, a tesill that tuckers vse to dresse cloth. **1611** Cotgr. s.v. *Applanisseur*, The Cloathworker..with his cards of tazle. **1658** Gurnall *Chr. in Arm.* verse 14. iii. iii. § 5 (1669) 80/2 Afflictions Bernard compares to the Tezel, which though it be sharp and scratching, is to make the cloth more pure and fine. **1829** J. L. Knapp *Jrnl. Nat.* 47 The use of the teazle is to draw out the ends of the wool from the manufactured cloth, so as to bring a regular pile or nap upon the surface. **1835** Teasels [see Teasel *v.*]. **1870** Yeats *Nat. Hist. Comm.* 252 The best clothiers still prefer the teazel for finishing their cloth.

**b.** As a heraldic bearing.
**1660** *Guillim's Heraldry* iv. vii. 289 Sable, a Cheuron Ermine, between two Habicks in chief, and a Tessell in base, proper. This is the bearing of the worshipfull Company of the Cloath-workers. **1864** Boutell *Her. Hist. & Pop.* xxi. § 11 (ed. 3) 369 A tezel slipped in base or.

**c.** *fig.*
**1630** J. Taylor (Water P.) *Water Cormorant's Compl.* Wks. iii. 14/1 Though from terme to terme it be worne long, 'Tis drest still with the teazle of the tongue. **1863** Cowden Clarke *Shaks. Char.* viii. 200 She is never content except when plying the teazle upon one hapless pate or other.

**3.** *transf.* A mechanical substitute for the natural teasel in cloth-working.
**1835** Ure *Philos. Manuf.* 193 Many contrivances have..been made for substituting metallic teasels..mounted in self-acting machines, for the thistle balls.

†**4.** Cf. Teasel *v.* b. *Obs. rare.*
**1688** R. Holme *Armoury* iii. 334/1 In good Tessel, [is] ground in good order for Plowing and Sowing.

**5.** *attrib.* and *Comb.*, as *teasel crop*, *seed*; *teasel-like* adj.; **teasel-bur, teasel-head, teasel-top,** the dried flower-head of the teasel: (= sense 2); **teasel-frame,** a frame in which teasel-heads are fixed for dressing cloth (so **teasel-board, teasel-cylinder, teasel-rod**); **teaselwort,** in *pl.*, Lindley's name for plants of the N.O. *Dipsacaceæ*.
**1835** Ure *Philos. Manuf.* 195 Springs that shall support the *teasel-boards when mounted on the barrel. **1821** Clare *Vill. Minstr.* II. 135 Lone spots..Where wildness rears her lings and *teazle-burs. **1877** Knight *Dict. Mech.* s.v. *Teaseling-machine*, The teasel-burs..press..upon the whole width of the cloth which passes beneath them. **1766** *Museum Rust.* VI. 4 This crop is no injury to the *teasel crop the first year. **1835** Ure *Philos. Manuf.* 196 Conduct the cloth over the *teasel-cylinder, and keep it smoothly distended. *Ibid.* 193 Two men,..seizing the *teasel-frame by the handles, scrubbed the face of the cloth. **1764** *Museum Rust.* III. 242 After cutting off the *teasel heads, and tying them in bunches. **1844** G. Dodd *Textile Manuf.* iii. 105 The use of teazle-heads is a remarkable feature in the process; for no combination of wires has yet been found that will effect the required object so efficiently as the little elastic prickles on the surface of these teazles. **1835** Ure *Philos. Manuf.* 202 Cleaning the *teasel-rods and handles. **1721** Mortimer *Husb.* (ed. 5) II. 202 The latter end of February or the beginning of March they sow the *Tesil-seed. **1902** Cornish *Naturalist Thames* 91 The forest of tall *teazle-tops. **1846** Lindley *Veg. Kingd.* 699 Dipsacaceæ. *Teazelworts. **1866** *Treas. Bot.* 249.

**Tea·sel, tea·zle,** *v.* [f. prec. sb.] *trans.* To raise a smooth nap on (cloth) with or as with teasels; to tease. Also *transf.* Hence **Tea·seling** (teasling) *vbl. sb.* (also *attrib.*).
[**1464** *Act 4 Edw. IV*, c. 1 Qe chescun fullour..en sa arte & occupacion de fuller & scalpier ou tezeiler de drap excercise & use teizels & nulls cardes.] **1543** *transl.* That euery fuller..in his crafte & occupacyon of fullynge rowynge or taseylynge of clothe, shall exercise tasels and no cardes. **1603** Florio *Montaigne* (1634) 393 He..led him in a fullers or clothworkers shoppe, where with Cardes and Teazels..he made him to be carded, scraped, and teazled so long, untill he died of it. **1607** Markham *Caval.* vi. (1617) 55 Dride sinewes of an Oxe, well tasled and mixt with well tempered glewe. **1733** P. Lindsay *Interest Scot.* 109 We understand the picking of Cloth..but we are not so adroit at the tasselling it. **1835** Ure *Philos. Manuf.* 192 The object..is to raise up the loose fibres of the woollen yarn into a nap..by scratching it either with thistle-heads called teasels, or with teasling-cards or brushes, made of wires. *Ibid.* 193 Moisture also softens their points and impairs their teasling powers. **1877** Knight *Dict. Mech.*, *Teaseling-machine*,..in which woolen cloth is teaseled to raise a nap upon it.

†**b.** *transf.* ? To dress or improve the surface of (land). Cf. Teasel *sb.* 4. *Obs. rare.*
**1610** W. Folkingham *Art of Survey* i. x. 28 They teasil their perring wild sand with stall dung.

**Teaseler** (tī·z'lər). Also 5 tesel(l)er, 7 tasler, 8 teazeller. [f. Teasel *sb.* + -er [1]. AF. *teizeler*.]
**1.** One whose occupation is to teasel cloth.
**14..** *Voc.* in Wr.-Wülcker 570/42 *Cardinarius*, a teselere. **1485** in *10th Rep. Hist. MSS. Comm.* App. v. 318 Frizers and tesellers dwellyng..within the citie. **1779** Kelham *Dict. Norm. Lang.*, *Teizeler de draps*, a teazeller of cloth.
**2.** An implement for teaseling; in quot., a comb for thinning out a horse's mane, etc.
**1607** Markham *Caval.* v. (1617) 28 If your horses mayne be too thicke..you may with a tasler made of yron with three or foure teeth make it..as thinne as you please.

**Teasement** (tī·zmĕnt). [f. Tease *v.*[1] + -ment.] The action of teasing; petty annoyance.
**1888** Kipling *Wee Willie Winkie*, *Baa Baa, Black Sheep* ii, Beyond reach of..Harry and his teasements.

**Teaser** [1] (tī·zəɪ). Forms: 4 tezir, 5 teser, 6 teasor, 7 teyser, 7–9 teazer, 8 teizer, 8– teaser. [f. Tease *v.*[1] + -er [1].] One who or that which teases, in various senses.
**1. a.** One who teases wool, cotton, or the like.
**1483** *Cath. Angl.* 380/2 A Teser, *carponarius*. **1591** Percivall *Sp. Dict.*, *Carmenador*, a teasor, *carminator*. **1611** Cotgr., *Tireur de laine*, a Teyser of wooll. **1824** Galt *Rothelan* II. iv. i. 99 The teasers and carders had started in alarm from their tasks. **1864** Jane Cameron *Mem. Convict* I. 119 Among the female convicts there were oakum-pickers and teazers,..hair and cotton teazers.
**b.** An instrument or machine for teasing wool, etc.
**1395** *Cartular. Abb. de Whiteby* (Surtees) 614 Item pro viii swewyls, viii.d. Item pro iiii tezirs, xiiii.d. **1876** *Daily News* 17 June, The fire is thought to have originated with the 'teazer', a machine used for 'teazing' the wool in its rough state. **1879** *Cassell's Techn. Educ.* IV. 289/1 The teaser [for gutta-percha]..a drum containing a rotating cylinder armed with teeth.
*Comb.* **1882** W. Gibson *Remin. Dollar* 152 The teazer-house with all its contents was burnt down.

**2.** One who teases or annoys: see Tease *v.*[1] 2.
**1659** *Commonwealth Ballads* (Percy Soc.) 200 Old Oliver was a teazer. **1712** Steele *Spect.* No. 288 ⁋ 3 One who would lessen the Number of Teazers of the Muses. **1844** Dickens *Mart. Chuz.* xi, She's a regular teazer.
**b.** Local name of several birds which chase gulls and force them to disgorge their prey, as the skua. (Cf. *dung-teaser*, Dung 5 c, *gull-teaser*, Gull [1] c.)
**1833** *G. Montagu's Ornith. Dict.* 143 Teaser.. A prov. name for Buffon's Skua, *Lestris Buffonii*. **1885** Swainson *Provinc. Names Birds* 210 Richardson's Skua. Gulls..when engaged in fishing, are pursued and harassed by these birds till they disgorge their prey...Hence the name Teaser.
**c.** An inferior stallion or ram used to excite mares or ewes.
**1823** Bee *Dict. Turf* s.v. **1888** Elworthy *W. Somerset Word-bk.*, *Teaser*, a young ram which is allowed to run with the ewes, but is artificially prevented from copulation.
†**d.** A hound used in hunting: see Teiser. *Obs.*
**e.** In elephant-hunting: see quot.
**1888** *Pall Mall G.* 30 May 6/1 When we find them, the teasers, who are the most courageous of the hunters, begin to tease the leaders of the herd. The bulls soon become angry and excited and give chase to the teasers.

**3.** Something that teases, or causes annoyance; something difficult to deal with, a 'poser'. *colloq.* In *Pugilistic slang*, an opponent difficult to tackle or overcome.
**1759** Franklin *Ess.* Wks. 1840 III. 380 He plyed them with another teaser. **1812** *Sporting Mag.* XL. 66 The writer cannot encourage the beaten man with hopes of ever being a teazer in the gymnastic line. **1844** Dickens *Mart. Chuz.* l, It was a teaser to read. **1883** E. Pennell-Elmhirst *Cream Leicestersh.* 75 The next [fence] is indeed a teaser, where the best horse..might crack under the saddle.
**b.** *slang.* A flogging. ? *Obs.*
**1832** *Examiner* 188/1 What they had done was 'not big enough for transportation, nor for a teaser' (a whipping).

**Tea·ser** [2]. *local.* Also 8 tisor. [ad. mod.F. *tiseur* a fireman; cf. Tease *v.*[2]] **a.** One who 'teases' or attends to a fire or furnace; a stoker, fireman.
**1797** P. Wakefield *Mental Improv.* (1801) I. 148 The tisors, or persons employed in heating the large furnaces. **1835** Sir J. Ross *Narr. 2nd Voy.* xxvi. 377 Two mates, and one of the fire teasers. **1858** Simmonds *Dict. Trade*, *Teazer*, the stoker or fireman in a glass-work who attends the furnace. **1894** [see Teasing *vbl. sb.*[2]].
**b.** An instrument for 'teasing' a fire; a poker.
**1839** Ure *Dict. Arts* 63 The furnace and implements used for assaying in the Royal Mint and the Goldsmiths' Hall... Fig. 66, the teaser for cleaning the grate. Fig. 67, a larger teaser, which is introduced at the top of the furnace, for keeping a complete supply of charcoal around the muffle.

**Tea-service,** etc.: see Tea *sb.* 9.

† **Tea·sicke,** obs. illit. f. Phthisic, consumption.
*a* **1585** Montgomerie *Flyting* 321 The teasicke, the toothaike, the tittes and the tirles.

**Teasing** (tī·ziŋ), *vbl. sb.*[1] [f. Tease *v.*[1] + -ing [1].] The action of Tease *v.*[1]
**1.** The pulling asunder of the fibres of wool, hair, animal tissue, etc.: see Tease *v.*[1] 1. Also *attrib.*, as *teasing-needle*.
**1591** Percivall *Sp. Dict.*, *Carmenadura*, teasing, *carminatio*. **1851** *Art Jrnl. Illustr. Catal.* p. iv**/1 The web of cleaned cotton..is passed through a lapping machine, and..undergoes a further teazing. **1873** T. H. Green *Introd. Pathol.* (ed. 2) 118 The cells have been separated by teasing. **1891** *Cent. Dict.*, *Teasing-needle*, a needle for teasing, or tearing into minute shreds, a specimen for microscopic examination.
**2.** Petty irritation: see Tease *v.*[1] 2.
**1678** Butler *Hud.* iii. ii. 452 Not by the force of Carnal Reason, But indefatigable Teazing. **1731** Swift *On Pulteney* 1 Sir Robert weary'd by Will Pulteney's teazings. **1858** Doran *Crt. Fools* 212 He was compelled to endure the teazing of the domestics.
**3.** *slang.* A flogging: see Tease *v.*[1] 3. ? *Obs.*
**1865** *Daily Tel.* 27 Oct. 5/2 'When I've had another teasing,' said a boy thief..alluding to the hangman and his cat, 'I shall be as good as Tommy So-and-So'.

**Tea·sing,** *vbl. sb.*[2] *local.* [f. Tease *v.*[2] + -ing [1].] The keeping up of the fire in a furnace. In quot. *attrib.*
**1894** *Northumbld. Gloss.* s.v. *Teaser*, The glass-house teasers wore broad-brimmed felt hats..to protect them from the scorching fires. They also wore 'hand-hats' of thick felt, to enable them to hold the long iron teasing pokers.

**Tea·sing,** *ppl. a.* [f. Tease *v.*[1] + -ing [2].] That teases; pettily irritating, annoying, or vexatious.
**1694** Addison *Ovid's Met.* ii. *Coronis* 19 And by a thousand teizing questions drew The important secret from him. **1800** *Med. Jrnl.* IV. 311 She complains of a teazing cough. **1847** Helps *Friends in C.* I. iii. 34 This is better than to be the sport of a teasing hope without reason.
Hence **Tea·singly** *adv.*, in a teasing manner.
**1754** Richardson *Grandison* (1781) IV. xxviii. 206 You are disposed to be teazingly facetious. **1906** *Athenæum* 17 Mar. 321/3 He never becomes teasingly minute.

**Teasle, teassell,** obs. variants of Teasel.

**Tea-sodden,** etc.: see Tea *sb.* 9.

**Tea·-spoon.** A small spoon, usually of silver or silvered metal, of a size suitable for stirring tea or other beverage in a cup.
**1686** *Lond. Gaz.* No. 2203/4 Three small gilt Tea Spoons.

1704 *Ibid.* No. 4055/4, 4 Spoons, and 5 Tea-Spoons. 1825 T. HOOK *Sayings* Ser. II. *Passion & Princ.* i, Mr. Welsted ..in his agitation knocked the tea-spoon out of his glass of negus. 1849 DICKENS *Dav. Copp.* lix, We have something in the shape of tea-spoons.. But they're Britannia metal.

Hence **Tea·spoonful.**, as much as a tea-spoon will hold; in medical prescriptions taken as equal to 1 fluid-drachm.

1731 MORTIMER in *Phil. Trans.* XXXVII. 170 Not above a Tea Spoonful of Water. 1825 J. NEAL *Bro. Jonathan* II. 53 A tea-spoonful of the ashes. 1844 EMERSON *Lect., Yng. American* Wks. (Bohn) II. 301 Agricultural chemistry ..offering by means of a tea-spoonful of artificial guano, to turn a sandbank into corn. 1847 J. F. SOUTH *Housh. Surg.* (1880) 27 Adding a teaspoonful of laudanum. 1904 MARIE CORELLI *God's Gd. Man* viii, Two..teaspoonfuls of cream.

**Teast**, obs. or dial. f. TASTE *v.* **Teast, Teaster, Teasty**, etc., obs. ff. TEST, TESTER, TESTY, etc.

**Teasy** (tī·zi), *a. colloq. rare.* [f. TEASE *v.*[1] + -Y.] Teasing, irritating.

1908 *19th Cent.* Jan. 188 It's a teasy job.

**Teat** (tīt). Forms: *α.* 1 tit, titt, 3 titte, 3–5 tytte, 9 *dial.* tit (*dim.* tittie). *β.* 3–6 tete, 4–5 teet(e, 4–7 teate, 6– teat. *γ.* 4–6 tette, 4–8 tet, 8 tett. *δ.* 4 tute. [OE. *tit(t* masc., cognate with MLG., MDu. *titte*, LG. *tit(t, titte* (Du. dial. *tet*), late MHG. *zitze* fem., Ger. *zitz* masc. str., *zitze* masc. and fem. wk. *Tit* (*tittie*) is now dialectal. The *γ*-form *tette, tett, tet*, and perh. also the *β*-form *tête, teet(e, teate*, whence the current *teat*, appear to represent F. *tette*, in OF. *tete* (12–13th c.), *tette, taite*; but the form-history is not clear, and in ME. there was probably mixture of the OE. and OF. forms. The OF. as well as Sp. *teta*, It. *tetta* (and *zizza*) are themselves generally held to be of German origin, and point to an OLG. *titte* fem. Ulterior etymology unknown. (The ordinary OHG. word *tutta, tuta* fem., *tutto, tuto* masc., MHG. *tutte, tute* fem., was app. unconnected.)]

**1.** The small protuberance at the tip of each breast or udder in female mammalia (except monotremes), upon which the ducts of the mammary gland open, and from which the milk is sucked by the young; the nipple. Formerly also applied to the whole breast or udder. (In early use, and still *dial.*, of women; now usually of quadrupeds.)

*α.* c 950 *Lindisf. Gosp.* Luke xi. 27 Eadiȝ womb *vel* hrif seðe ðec ȝebær & ða titto *vel* ða breosto ða ðu ȝediides [c 975 *Rushw.* ða tito *vel* ða breost ða ðu deðedes]. c 1000 *Sax. Leechd.* I. 112 Wið titta sar wifa þe beoð melce. c 1205 LAY. 5025 Þu eært mi bærn deore. Loka her þa tittes þet þu suke mid þine lippes. *Ibid.* 11936 Ich heom wullen alle for-don & bi þan titten [c 1275 tyttes] an-hon. 1387 TREVISA *Higden* (Rolls) III. 43 A wolfesse..fedde..þe children, and made hem ofte souke of here owne tetes [*v.r.* tyttes]. a 1825 FORBY *Voc. E. Anglia*, *Titties*, *Tits*, s. pl. teats.

*β.* c 1290 *S. Eng. Leg.* I. 473/376 Þanne may mi luytel sone to hire tete take. 1382 WYCLIF *Luke* xi. 27 Blessid be the teetis whiche thou hast sokun. c 1386 CHAUCER *Miller's T.* 518, I moorne as dooth a lamb after the tete. 1450–1530 *Myrr. our Ladye* 233 Blysse we..the grete lorde, souckynge the maydenly teates of the moste meke vyrgyn. 1578 BANISTER *Hist. Man* I. 9 The fashion of Tetes in a Cowes vdder. 1662 GURNALL *Chr. in Arm.* verse 17. I. v. § 1 (1669) 255/2 Here his soul sweetly sleeps, as the Child, with the Teat in its mouth. 1774 GOLDSM. *Nat. Hist.* (1776) II. 103 The teats of some, as in the ape and the elephant, are like those of men, being but two. 1844 STEPHENS *Bk. Farm* II. 700 Sometimes there are more pigs littered than the sow has teats to give to each.

*γ.* a 1325 Tettes [see b]. 13.. *S. E. Leg.* (MS. Bodl. 779) in Herrig *Archiv* LXXXII. 342/322 Þis me lykeþ bet þan me dede in my ȝouþe mylk of any tet. 1565–73 COOPER *Thesaurus* s. v. *Admitto*, *Admittere pastum ad vbera*, to receiue to the tette. 1669 WORLIDGE *Syst. Agric.* (1681) 323 The Cows Dug by some is called the Tet. 1709 PRIOR *Callimachus' 1st Hymn to Jupiter* 55 Kind Amalthea reach'd her Tett, distent With Milk.

*δ.* c 1400 *R. Glouc.'s Chron.* (Rolls) App. G. 196 Þeos tutes [*v.r.* tetys] þou soke ylome.

†**b.** In allusive expressions, as *at the teat*, (a suckling) at the breast; *from the teat(s*, from infancy.

a 1325 *Prose Psalter* xxi[i]. 8 Þou art myn hope from þe tettes of my moder. c 1440 CAPGRAVE *St. Kath.* I. 242 Mercy from þe tetys grew wyth hyr. 1588 SHAKS. *Tit. A.* II. iii. 145 Euen at thy Teat thou had'st thy Tyranny. 1602 *2nd Pt. Return fr. Parnass.* III. v. 1454 Vs our kinde Colledge from the teate did teare. a 1635 NAUNTON *Fragm. Reg.* (Arb.) 26 He left a plentiful Estate, and such a Son, who, as the vulgar speaks it, could live without the teat.

†**c.** *fig.* A source of nourishment or supply. *Obs.*

c 1440 *Jacob's Well* 232 Putte fro þe þe tetys of ydylnes, þat þou souke no more þer-of for no delyȝt! 1569 *Irish Act* 11 *Eliz.* Stat. III. c. 1 *Preamb.*, That..most detestable coyne and liverie, which was the very nurse and teat that gave suck and nutriment to all disobediences. a 1631 DONNE *Lett.* (1651) 102 The channels of God's mercies run through both fields, and they are sister teats of his graces. 1675 HOBBES *Odyssey* VII. (1686) 88 His Riches was a never-dying Teat.

**2.** *transf.* A structure, natural or artificial, resembling a teat; a nipple: see quots.

1587 MASCALL *Govt. Cattle, Oxen* (1627) 12 Such superfluous flesh on the tongue of cattel wil hinder the beast oftentimes in eating his meate, being called of some husbandes the Barbes, Teates. 1774 GOLDSM. *Nat. Hist.* (1776) VII. 253 Nature has supplied this animal [spider] with..five dugs or teats for spinning it into thread. 1835 KIRBY *Hab. & Inst. Anim.* xix. II. 284 These teats are connected with internal reservoirs, which yield the fluid matter forming the thread or web. 1864 WEBSTER, *Teat*..2. (*Mach.*) A small nozzle resembling a teat. 1877 KNIGHT *Dict. Mech.*, *Teat*, a small, rounded, perforated projection, otherwise called a *nipple*, as that of a gun. 1890 [see *teat drill* in 3].

**3.** *attrib.* and *Comb.*, as *teat-like* adj.; teat-cup, **teat drill** (see quots.); **teat-fish** (*Australia*), a sea-slug of the genus *Holothuria*, esp. *H. mammifera*, so called from its papillæ; †**teat-head**, the nipple; **teat-stud**, one of the metal studs, commonly called 'buttons', with which the front of a page's jacket is ornamented; **teat-worm**, the common thread-worm (*Oxyuris vermicularis*).

1862 *Morn. Star* 19 June, The cow-milker..consisting of two diaphragm pumps..to which four *teat-cups are attached for receiving the teats of the cow. 1895 *Westm. Gaz.* 8 Oct. 8/2 A glass lid..enables the attendant to see when a cow is finished, and then by simply turning a stop-cock the teat-cups fall off. 1890 *Cent. Dict.* s.v. *Drill*, **Teat drill*, a square-faced cylindrical drill with a sharp, pyramidal projection or teat issuing from the center of the cutting face. 1894 B. THOMSON *S. Sea Yarns* 256 The reef swarmed with *teat-fish. 1601 HOLLAND *Pliny* I. 347 Such beasts as be very fruitful..haue many nipples or *teat heads all along their belly. 1826 KIRBY & SP. *Entomol.* III. xxx. 149 A great number of Lepidopterous larvæ..have between the under-lip and fore-legs a slender transverse opening, containing a *teat-like protuberance. 1910 J. PLATT Jun. *Let. to Editor*, **Teat-stud*, technical term, used by tailors for the tiny plated or gilt buttons which are sewn as closely together as possible down the front of a page's jacket. The teat-stud or tit-stud is quite unique in shape. 1899 CAGNEY *Jaksch's Clin. Diagn.* vi. (ed. 4) 226 Oxyuris vermicularis (common thread-worm or *teat worm).

**Teat**, obs. form of TATE, tuft, etc.

**Tea·-ta·ble.** [f. TEA *sb.* 4 + TABLE *sb.* 6.]

**1.** A table at which tea is taken, or on which tea-things are placed for a meal.

**a.** As a special piece of furniture, usually small and of a light and elegant make.

In quot. 1804, a table for the sale of tea and refreshments.

1703 *Lond. Gaz.* No. 3891/3 Lackered Tea-Tables. 1740 LADY HARTFORD *Corr.* (1806) II. 12 The Duchess of Dorset was presented with..a tea-table with a gold tea-canister, kettle and lamp. 1804 *Naval Chron.* XII. 307, I fell foul of a..woman's tea-table, at the corner of a street, and had like to have thrown the..tea-things all about. 1898 G. B. SHAW *Plays* II. *You never can tell* 274 The bamboo tea table, with folding shelves.

**b.** A table spread for tea, or as the place of a social gathering for tea and conversation.

1688 SHADWELL *Sqr. Alsatia* Epil. 37 Here no Chit chat, here no Tea Tables are. 1700 CONGREVE *Way of World* IV. v, To the Dominion of the Tea-table I submit..but..I banish all Auxiliaries to the Tea-table, as Orange-brandy, all Aniseed [etc.]. 1792 A. MURPHY *Ess. Johnson* 88 During the whole time he presided at his tea-table. 1854 MRS. GASKELL *North & S.* x, She stood by the tea-table..as if she was not attending to the conversation, but solely busy with the tea-cups.

**2.** *transf.* The company assembled at tea.

1712 ADDISON *Spect.* No. 536 ¶ 1 The..publication of it would..oblige..a whole tea-table of my friends. 1856 KANE *Arct. Expl.* II. i. 19 Explaining to the tea-table this evening's outfit.

**3.** *attrib.* (chiefly in reference to social gatherings: see 1 b).

1700 CONGREVE *Way of World* IV. v, Restrain yourself to ..simple Tea-table Drinks, as Tea, Chocolate, and Coffee. As likewise to genuine and authorised Tea-table Talk—Such as mending of Fashions, spoiling Reputations, railing at absent Friends. 1724 RAMSAY (*title*) The Tea-table Miscellany. 1779 (*title*) Tea-Table Dialogues, between a Governess and Miss Sensible. 1852 H. SPENCER *Use & Beauty* in *Ess.* (1858) 387 While ghost-stories..enliven tea-table conversation.

Hence (*humorous nonce-wds.*) †**Teatabe·lically** *adv.*, at the tea-table, in familiar conversation at tea; **Tea-ta·bular** *a.*, pertaining to the tea-table.

1768 TUCKER *Lt. Nat.* (1834) I. 475 The vast Pacific Ocean, commonly, yea, vulgarly, not to say, news-paperically, nor yet, teatabellically,..called..the South-sea. 1855 BAGEHOT *Lit. Stud.* (1895) I. 125 Torpid, indoor, tea-tabular felicity.

**Tea-taster** (tī·tē¹stəɹ). One whose business is to test the quality of samples of tea by tasting them; a tea-expert. So **Tea·-ta·sting**, the occupation or business of a tea-taster.

1858 in SIMMONDS *Dict. Trade.* 1859 *All Year Round* No. 2. 38 The tea-tasters and clerks of the different English and American houses. 1888 J. PATON in *Encycl. Brit.* XXIII. 100/2 The qualities of a sample of tea and its commercial value can only with accuracy be determined by actual infusion and trial by a skilled tea-taster. 1907 *Gentl. Mag.* May 494 Tea-tasters use the weight of a new sixpence to three and a half ounces of water.

**Teated** (tī·tėd), *a.* [f. TEAT + -ED[2].] Furnished with or having teats. Also in comb.

1661 LOVELL *Hist. Anim. & Min.* 90 The Lionesse is smooth and teated. 1769 *Aclome Inclos. Act* 2 A customary ..payment of three half-pence for every new teated cow. 1891 T. HARDY *Tess* xvii, The milkers formed quite a little battalion of men and maids, the men operating on the hard-teated animals.

**Teater**, obs. f. TETTER. **Teath**, var. TATH(E; obs. f. TITHE. **Teather**, obs. f. TETHER. **Teathy**, var. TEETHY.

**Tea-things, -time**, etc.: see TEA *sb.* 9.

**Teatish, Teaty**: see TETTISH, TEETY.

†**Tea·tling.** *Obs. rare*⁻¹. [f. TEAT + -LING.] A young animal at the teat; a suckling.

1631 *Celestina* II. 130 The teatling lambe which suckes both her damm's teat, and that of another Ewe.

**Tea-total**, etc.: see TEETOTAL.

**Tea·-tray.** A tray on which tea-things are placed.

1773 *H. Clay's Pat.* in *Sixth Rep. Dep. Kpr.* App. II. 161 Of an invention of making, in paper..Screens, Chimney Pieces, Tables, Tea Trays, and Waiters. 1831 WILLIAMS *Life & Corr. Sir T. Lawrence* I. 75 Painting sign-boards or tea-trays. 1862 MRS. H. WOOD *Mrs. Hallib.* I. i, Two candles..stood on the table behind the tea-tray.

**Teatre**, obs. form of THEATRE.

**Tea·-tree.** **1.** *properly*, The shrub or low tree, the dried leaves of which form the tea of commerce; = TEA *sb.* 3.

1760 J. LEE *Introd. Bot.* App. 329 Tea-tree, *Thea.* 1771 *Chron.* in *Ann. Reg.* 151/2 The Duke of Northumberland has at this time a tea-tree in full flower. It is the first that ever flowered in Europe. 1832 *Veg. Subst. Food* 377 The flowers of the tea-tree are white, and resemble the wild rose. 1888 J. PATON in *Encycl. Brit.* XXIII. 97/2 An indigenous tea-tree..is found in Assam.

**2.** *transf.* Applied in Australia, Tasmania, and New Zealand to various shrubs or trees of the myrtle family, chiefly of the genera *Leptospermum* and *Melaleuca*, of which the leaves have been used as a substitute for tea.

(Often spelt *ti-tree*, occasionally *ti-tri*, as if a native name.) Also with qualifying words denoting different species.

1790 J. WHITE *Voy. N. S. Wales* 229 Tea Tree of New South Wales. *Melaleuca? Trinervia.* 1802 BARRINGTON *Hist. N. S. Wales* ix. 331 The roof was bark, resembling that of the Tea-tree at Port Jackson. 1858 HOGG *Veg. Kingd.* xc. 350 *Leptospermum scoparium*, or New Zealand Tea-tree...The leaves of this species were used by Captain Cook's crew as a substitute for tea. 1866 *Treas. Bot.* 674 *L[eptospermum] lanigerum*,..commonly called Tea tree on account of its leaves having been used by the early settlers ..as a substitute for tea. 1885 MRS. PRAED *Australian Life* 112 The bottle-brush flowers of the ti-trees. 1891 *Coo-ee* (ed. Mrs. P. Martin) 282 The brown twisted branches of the ti-trees..shook their scented bottle-brush blossoms in our faces. 1891 *Cent. Dict.* s.v., *Broad-leaved tea-tree*, a myrtaceous shrub or tree, *Callistemon salignus*, of Australia and Tasmania...*Prickly tea-tree*, same as *naambarr* [*Melaleuca styphelioides*, of N. S. Wales]. *Red Scrub tea-tree*, the Australian *Rhodamnia trinervia*, a myrtaceous shrub or tree. 1909 *Westm. Gaz.* 16 Aug. 4/1 A Winter Scene in Australia...Down by the sea the tea-tree is commencing to weave its veil of flowers.

**b.** *attrib.*, as *tea-tree bark, bush, marsh, scrub.*

1820 C. JEFFREYS *Van Dieman's Land* iii. 133 For tea they [the Bush Rangers] drink a decoction of the sassafras and other shrubs, particularly one which they call the tea-tree bush. 1828 P. CUNNINGHAM *N. S. Wales* (ed. 3) II. 13 Building comfortable huts of tea-tree bark. 1835 J. BATMAN in Cornwallis *New World* (1859) I. 406 A dense tea-tree scrub, which we knew to be the surest indication of good water in its neighbourhood. 1883 C. HARPUR *Poems* 78 Why roar the bull-frogs in the tea-tree marsh?

**3.** Applied to various other trees: see TEA *sb.* 6; in Great Britain esp. to the flowering shrub *Lycium barbarum* or *chinense* (N.O. *Solanaceæ*), a native of China, also called *Duke of Argyll's tea-tree* (see quot. 1838). **African tea-tree**, *Lycium afrum*; **Ceylon tea-tree**, etc.: see quots.

1777 G. FORSTER *Voy. round World* I. 130 The spruce and the tea-trees. 1812 *New Bot. Gard.* I. 113 Ceanothus Americanus, New Jersey Tea-tree. 1838 LOUDON *Trees & Shrubs Gt. Brit.* III. 1269 One species, *L[ycium] barbarum*, is commonly called the Duke of Argyll's tea tree from the circumstance of a tea plant, (*Thea viridis*), having been sent to the Duke of Argyll at the same time as this plant, and the labels having been accidentally changed. 1858 HOGG *Veg. Kingd.* lxiv. 231 *Elæodendron glaucum*, a native of Ceylon and Coromandel, has been introduced [into S. Africa] under the name of Ceylon Tea Tree. 1884 MILLER *Plant-n.*, Tea-plant, or Tea-tree,..African, *Lycium afrum*...—, Blue Mountain, or Golden-rod, *Solidago odora*...—, St. Helena, *Beatsonia portulacæfolia*...—, Surinam, various species of *Lantana*. 1909 *Westm. Gaz.* 24 Feb. 5/1 The plant commonly known as the Duke of Argyll's tea tree, belonging to the same natural order (*Solanaceæ*) as the potato and tomato.

**Tea-urn** to **Tea-wine**: see TEA *sb.* 9.

**Teave**, var. TAVE. **Teaw, -e**, obs. forms of TEW.

**Teaz**, app. earlier form of TEE *sb.*[2], *v.*[3] (*Golf.*)

**Teaze, Teazel**: see TEASE, TEASEL.

**Teaze-tenon** (tī·z,tenən). *Carp.* ? *Obs.* Also teazle-tenon. (See quotations.)

1703 T. N. *City & C. Purchaser* 30 If it be a Timber Building, the Teazle Tennons of the Posts are Framed. Teazle Tennons are made at right Angles to those..on the Posts. 1823 P. NICHOLSON *Pract. Build.* Gloss., *Teaze-tenon.* 1842–76 GWILT *Archit.* Gloss., *Teaze Tenon*, a tenon on the top of a post, with a double shoulder and tenon from each for supporting two level pieces of timber at right angles to each other.

**Teazle**, variant form of TEASEL.

**Tec** (tek), *sb. slang.* Abbreviation for DETECTIVE.

1888 *Pall Mall G.* 11 Oct. 2/1 'Tecs and inspectors examine the place, make notes, and go away. 1888 *Daily News* 27 Dec. 7/2 Witness seized Wright and said 'I am a police officer'. Wright replied 'You are no 'tec; give me a chance', struggled violently, and got away.

Hence **Tec** *v. trans.*, to watch as a detective.

1900 G. SWIFT *Somerley* 57 Let's watch the 'head'; he might be a kleptomaniac, or whatever they call it...I'd like to 'tec the 'head'.

**Tecal, Tecat**: see TICAL, TICKET.

‖ **Tecbir** (te·kbiəɹ). Also **tekbir.** [Arab. تكبير *tekbīr* 'to magnify, proclaim the greatness of'; inf. of 2nd form of كبر *kabura* to be great.] See quot. 1708.

**1708** OCKLEY *Saracens* 111 The poor Christians, assoon as ever they heard the *Tecbîr*, (so the Arabs call the crying out *Allâh Acbar* ['God is greater']) were sensible that the City was lost. **1823** MRS. HEMANS *Siege Valencia* vi, The Moor is on his way! With the tambour-peal and the tecbir-shout. **1904** J. PARKINSON *Lays Love & War* 44 Shout the tekbir loud and long: On! swords of Islam.

**Tecch(e, techch(e,** obs. ff. TACHE *sb.*[1] **Tecchy,** obs. f. TETCHY. **Tech,** var. TETCH, TACHE *Obs.* **Teche,** obs. f. TEACH; obs. f. *techy*: see TETCHY. **Techie, Techily,** etc., obs. ff. TETCHY, etc.

**Technic** (te·knik), *a.* and *sb.* [ad. L. *technic-us* (Quint.), a. Gr. τεχνικ-ός of or pertaining to art, f. τέχνη art, craft: see -IC. So F. *technique* (1721 in Hatz.-Darm.).]

A. *adj.* **1.** Pertaining to art, or to an art: = TECHNICAL. Now *rare.*

**1612** STURTEVANT *Metallica* iii. 49 Define the Technick part. **1714** MANDEVILLE *Fab. Bees* (1729) II. vi. 347 All technick Words..and Terms of Art, belong to the respective Artists and Dealers, that primarily and literally make use of them in their Business. **1760** *Phil. Trans.* LI. 756 Terms..used in the strict technic sense. **1845** R. W. HAMILTON *Pop. Educ.* (ed. 2) viii. 187 The inhabitant of a manufacturing town has frequent proof of the intellectual difference between the rural, and the technic labourer. **1905** *Contemp. Rev.* Mar. 425 Our practical problem is now a technic and constructive one.

**2.** Skilfully made or constructed. [After Gr. τεχνικός (Hippocrates).] *rare*−¹.

**1877** BLACKIE *Wise Men* 245 What a wealth of sounds Wends through the technic chambers of the ear.

B. *sb.* **1.** A technical term, expression, point, or detail; a technicality. Chiefly *U.S. rare.*

**1826** T. FLINT *Recoll. Valley Mississippi* 86 A process, which, in the technics of the [Mississippi] boatmen is called *bush-whacking*. **1872** T. L. CUYLER *Heart Th.* 8 A right estimate of sin..is a vital point in the soul's salvation: it is more than a technic of theology. **1875** EMERSON *Lett. & Soc. Aims, Greatness* Wks. (Bohn) III. 272, I find it easy to translate all his [Napoleon's] technics into all of mine.

**2.** Technical details or methods collectively; the technical department of a subject; *esp.* the formal or mechanical part of an art (now more commonly TECHNIQUE, q.v.).

[**1798** WILLICH *Adelung's Elem. Crit. Philos.* 181 Technic 1, in a proper sense, means art, causality according to ideas, purposes.] **1855** LEWES *Goethe* I. I. v. 49 His impatient susceptibility which..prevented his ever thoroughly mastering the technic of any one subject. **1867** M. ARNOLD *Celtic Lit.* 142 Icelandic poetry..shows a powerful and developed technic. **1887** LOWELL *Old Eng. Dram.* (1892) 56 In the technic of this art, perfection can be reached only by long training.

**b.** Collective pl. **Technics** in same sense: also construed as a singular.

**1850** LEITCH tr. *C. O. Müller's Anc. Art* § 257 Antique vases..also, very grandly and beautifully designed, of the more perfect style of technics. **1871** MORLEY *Crit. Misc.* Ser. I. 256 Conformity to the accepted rules that constitute the technics of poetry. **1909** *Contemp. Rev.* Aug. 204 Literary technics, especially that of the novel, depends on reproducing experiments from life.

**3.** The science or study of art or arts, esp. of the mechanical or industrial arts: = TECHNOLOGY 1. Usually in pl. **Technics.**

**1864** in WEBSTER. **1855** S. H. HODGSON *Time & Space* II. ix. § 68 Technic and Teleologic are the two branches of practical knowledge .. and are both together, as Ethic, opposed to Theoretic. **1874** R. TYRWHITT *Sketch. Club* 87 You must study history, literature, and technics.

‖ **Technica** (te·knikă). [Latinized form of Gr. τεχνικά neuter pl. = technical matters, and of τεχνική fem. sing.] = TECHNIC B. 2, TECHNIQUE.

**1796** BURNEY *Mem. Metastasio* III. 359 Definitions of the technica of ancient music. **1855** tr. *Labarte's Arts Mid. Ages* 2 Christian art, unable so immediately to create for itself a new technica, adopted the style of antiquity in its then degenerate state.

**Technical** (te·knikăl), *a.* (*sb.*) [f. Gr. τεχνικ-ός (see TECHNIC) + -AL.]

**1.** Of a person: Skilled in or practically conversant with some particular art or subject. *rare.*

**1617** HALES *Serm. 2 Pet.* iii. 16. 19 Not to think themselues sufficiently provided vpon their acquaintance with some *Notitia*, or systeme of some technicall divine. **1817** JAS. MILL *Brit. India* III. ii. 81 The managers .. not being technical men.

†**2.** Of a thing: Skilfully done or made: cf. TECHNIC *a.* 2. *Obs. rare*−⁰.

**1656** BLOUNT *Glossogr.*, *Technical* (*technicus*), artificial, cunning, done like a workman. [Perhaps never in Eng.]

**3.** Belonging or relating to an art or arts; appropriate or peculiar to, or characteristic of, a particular art, science, profession, or occupation; also, of or pertaining to the mechanical arts and applied sciences generally, as in *technical education*, or *technical school.*

*Technical difficulty*, a difficulty arising in connexion with the method of procedure (esp. legal). †*Technical verse*, a verse intended to assist in memorizing something connected with a particular subject: cf. MEMORIA TECHNICA (*obs.*).

**1727–41** CHAMBERS *Cycl.* s. v., Technical verses are commonly composed in Latin: they are generally wretched ones, and often barbarous; but..utility is all that is aimed at. **1739** *Works Learned* I. 139 He makes use of some Technical Lines or Verses. **1755** JOHNSON *Dict.* Pref., Of the terms of art I have received such as could be found either in books of science or technical dictionaries. **1855** MACAULAY *Hist. Eng.* xv. III. 714 Torrington had..been sent to the Tower...A technical difficulty had arisen about the mode of bringing him to trial. **1868** ROGERS *Pol. Econ.* xx. (1876) 265 Technical education, that is, the acquisition of scientific method and a knowledge of the principles and practice of the applied sciences. **1909** *Kelly's Directory of Oxf.* 128/2 The City of Oxford Municipal Technical Schools..are secondary and technical schools under the regulation of the Board of Education...They consist of chemical and physical laboratories and lecture rooms, workshops, art rooms, and class rooms.

**b.** *spec.* said of words, terms, phrases, etc., or of their senses or acceptations; as, the *technical terms* of logic; the *technical sense* of 'subject' in logic.

[**1634** JACKSON *Creed* VII. xxviii. § 3 'The mercy of the Lord' or of 'the word of God' is τι τεχνικὸν, that is a word or term whose full importance cannot be had from any ordinary lexicon, unless it be such as is proper unto divinity.] *a* **1652** [implied in TECHNICALLY *adv.*]. **1704** J. HARRIS *Lex. Techn.* I. s. v., The Terms of Art are commonly called *Technical Words.* **1739** LABELYE *Short Acc. Piers Westm. Bridge* p. iv, Avoiding as much as possible all technical Terms. **1778** JEFFERSON *Autobiog.* App., Wks. 1859 I. 146 Preserving .. the very words of the established law, wherever their meaning had been..rendered technical by usage. **1809** SYD. SMITH *Charac. Fox* Wks. 1859 I. 153/1 In a science like law there must be technical phrases, known only to professional men. **1875** JOWETT *Plato* (ed. 2) IV. 420 No former philosopher had ever carried the use of technical terms to the same extent as Hegel.

**c.** *transf.* Of an author, a treatise, etc.: Using technical terms; treating a subject technically.

**1779** *Mirror* No. 48 ¶ 1, I have since been endeavouring to make it a little less technical, in order to fit it more for general perusal. *a* **1832** MACKINTOSH *Rev. of* 1688 Wks. 1846 II. 295 The Crown lawyers...Powis was feebly technical, and Williams was offensively violent. **1896** *N. & Q.* 8th Ser. IX. 160/2 [The book] is somewhat too technical for any one who is not a botanist.

**d.** Technically so called or regarded; that is such from the technical point of view.

**1860** MOTLEY *Netherl.* (1868) I. i. 20 Permission for soldiers to retreat with technical honour. **1868** [cf. TECHNICALLY].

B. *sb.* In *pl.* Technical terms or points; technicalities.

**1790** *Bystander* 352 Prone to..scold in technicals which they know not how to apply. **1825** *Eng. Life* II. 254 The cramped and barbarous technicals of law. **1863** D. G. MITCHELL *My Farm of Edgewood* 236 The latter has a wall about him of self-confidence, ignorance of technicals.

Hence **Te·chnicalism,** technical style, method, or treatment; addiction to technicalities; **Te·chnicalist,** one versed in or addicted to technicalities; **Te·chnicalize** *v. trans.*, to make technical, give a technical meaning to; **Te·chnicalness,** the quality of being technical, technicality.

**1808** BENTHAM *Sc. Reform* 80 Such ingenuity is not wanting to English-bred *technicalism. **1857** TOULMIN SMITH *Parish* Pref. 111 Not frozen-up in dry technicalism, but dealing with the human reality attaching to an important Institution of free men. **1802–12** BENTHAM *Ration. Judic. Evid.* (1827) II. 415 Not altogether a secret to the *technicalists. **1884** *Times* 9 Feb., Every technicalist takes too narrow a view. **1852** LEWIS *Methods Obs. & Reason. Politics* I. 78 Words current in the language of ordinary life..were (if we may be allowed the expression) *technicalized. **1828–32** WEBSTER, **Technicalness.*

**Technicality** (teknikæ·liti). [f. prec. + -ITY.]

**1.** Technical quality or character; the use of technical terms or methods.

**1828–32** WEBSTER, *Technicalness, Technicality*, the quality or state of being technical or peculiar to the arts. *Forster.* **1857** TOULMIN SMITH *Parish* 266 The case is a very simple one, when divested of technicality. **1863** COWDEN CLARKE *Shaks. Char.* iii. 88 He dilates upon the weapons..with an accurate and professor-like technicality.

**2.** A technical point, detail, term, or expression; something peculiar or specially belonging to the art or subject referred to. Usually in *pl.*

**1814** SCOTT *Wav.* lii, A sort of martinet attention to the minutiæ and technicalities of discipline. **1859** GULLICK & TIMBS *Paint.* 190 Various other technicalities and artistic appliances may also be explained. **1874** L. STEPHEN *Hours in Library* (1892) I. vii. 261 To translate the technicalities of Kant into plain English. **1885** S. COX *Expositions* I. xxxii. 372 This phrase, 'the Saviour of the world', has come to be little more than a technicality, which we use without much thought or emotion.

**Technically** (te·knikăli), *adv.* [f. as prec. + -LY [2].] In a technical manner; in relation to the arts and applied sciences, or to a particular art or subject; according to technical methods; in technical phraseology; in a technical sense.

*a* **1652** J. SMITH *Sel. Disc.* vi. 247 That part of divine inspiration, which was more technically and properly by the Jews called prophecy. **1774** WARTON *Hist. Eng. Poetry* lxii. (1840) III. 404 The first professed English satirist, to speak technically, is bishop Joseph Hall. **1834–5** J. PHILLIPS *Geol.* in *Encycl. Metrop.* VI. 535/1 Confined to what is technically called the Crust of the Earth. **1868** FREEMAN *Norm. Conq.* II. viii. 223 A family which, though perhaps not technically noble, was..eminent and honourable.

**Technician** (tekni·ʃăn). [f. TECHNIC + -IAN.] **a.** A person conversant with the technicalities of a particular subject. **b.** One skilled in the technique or mechanical part of an art, as music or painting.

**1833** SARAH AUSTIN *Charac. Goethe* I. 216 Grammarians and technicians are bound..to acknowledge these his efforts. **1895** H. A. KENNEDY in *19th Cent.* Aug. 331 The mere technician can never interest; the literary man, even if inexpert in stage *technique*, may do so in a high degree. **1905** *Times* 20 May 8/3 The modern violinist is not necessarily a mere technician. **1909** *Athenæum* 7 Aug. 158/3 The book..not being sufficiently detailed for the technician.

**Technicism** (te·knisiz'm). [f. as prec. + -ISM: cf. mod.L. *technicismus*, Kant 1790.] A technical term or expression, a technicality.

**1799** ANNA SEWARD *Lett.* (1821) V. 263 Bewildered in a maze of scholastic technicisms.

**Technicist** (te·knisist). [f. as prec. + -IST.] = TECHNICIAN; one who has technical knowledge.

**1881** T. HARDY *Laodicean* III. xi, Somerset himself [an architect] as chief technicist working out his designs on the spot. **1906** *Academy* 20 June 617/1 Turner's greatest admirers are the painters, and Mr. Wyllie..enjoys it [T.'s work] with the exquisite pleasure of the technicist.

**Technico-,** combining element from Gr. τεχνικός (see TECHNIC). **Technico·logy,** = TECHNOLOGY (senses 1 and 2). **Technico·philist,** *nonce-wd.* [Gr. -φιλος -loving], a lover of technicalities.

**1849** SEARS *Regeneration* III. xii. (1859) 242 The barren *technicologies of schools and sects. **1880** W. SENIOR *Trav. & Trout in Antipodes* 80 Reading out the botanical technicology. **1884** *Manch. Exam.* 17 May 4/8 Schools and museums of technicology scattered over the Continent. **1861** *Zoologist* Ser. I. XIX. 7299 This word .. has the.. merit, always prized by *technicophilists, of being more difficult to pronounce.

**Technics**: see TECHNIC B.

**Technique** (teknī·k). [a. F. (*la*) *technique*, subst. use of *technique* adj., TECHNIC. Cf. Ger. *die technik.*] Manner of artistic execution or performance in relation to formal or practical details (as distinct from general effect, expression, sentiment, etc.); the mechanical or formal part of an art, esp. of any of the fine arts; also, skill or ability in this department of one's art; mechanical skill in artistic work. (Used most commonly in reference to painting or musical performance.)

**1817** COLERIDGE *Biog. Lit.* I. iv. 83 Illogical phrases.. which hold so distinguished a place in the *technique* of ordinary poetry. **1875** FORTNUM *Maiolica* xii. 122 Mr. Robinson speaks of this specimen as 'being of the most perfect technique of the master'. **1876** STEDMAN *Victorian Poets* 289 Their [poetic] work, however curious in technique, fails to permanently impress even the refined reader. **1884** GROVE *Dict. Mus.* IV. 66 A player may be perfect in technique, and yet have neither soul nor intelligence. **1885** *Spectator* 30 May 704/2 [Victor Hugo's] improvement of the technique of versification. **1886** *Mag. Art* Dec. 42/1 (Stanf.) His technique is somewhat sketchy,..and his colours extremely light. **1900** *Jrnl. Sch. Geog.* (U.S.) June 213 The technique of raising cotton, or celery, or Indian corn.

**Technism** (te·kniz'm). *rare*−⁰. [f. Gr. τέχνη art, or Eng. TECHN-IC + -ISM; cf. *mechanism.*] 'Technicality' (Webster 1864). So **Te·chnist,** one who deals with a subject technically.

**1885** *Nature* 5 Feb. 314/2 The light of that comet was of the kind familiarly known among technists as 'the candle-spectrum'.

**Techno-** (tekno), repr. Gr. τεχνο-, combining form of τέχνη art, occurring in TECHNOLOGY, etc.; also in the following rare terms: **Technography** (-ǫ·grăfi) [-GRAPHY], the description of the arts, forming the preliminary stage of technology (TECHNOLOGY 1); hence **Techno·grapher,** one versed in technography; **Technographic** (-græ·fik) *a.* **Te·chno-mecha·nic** *a.* (*nonce-wd.*), pertaining to mechanical art (in quot. absol. as *sb.*). **Technonomy** (-ǫ·nŏmi) [-NOMY], the practical application of the principles of the arts, forming the final stage of technology; hence **Technonomic** (-nǫ·mik) *a.* (*Cent. Dict.* 1891).

**1833** SARAH AUSTIN *Charac. Goethe* I. 187 Persuaded of the co-operation of the Techno-mechanic with the Dynamo-ideal, [I] had Seebeck's cross embroidered like damask, and could now see it in whatever light I chose, clear or dim, on an uniform surface. **1881** MASON in *Smithsonian Rep.* 501 Observing and descriptive stage...Technography. Inductive and classifying stage...Technology. Deductive and predictive stage...Technonomy. **1895** *Funk's Stand. Dict.*, *Technographic.* **1900** *Amer. Anthropologist* Jan.–Mar. 164 There are two ways of looking at human inventions, the one ethnographic, the other technographic. *Ibid.*, The technographer pursues a single art over time and place until he knows it thoroughly.

**Technologic** (teknolǫ·dʒik), *a. rare*−⁰. [f. as TECHNOLOGY + -IC. Cf. mod.L. *terminus technologicus* (Alsted *Encycl.* 1630); F. *technologique* (1812 in Hatz.-Darm.).] = next. **1864** in WEBSTER.

**Technological** (teknolǫ·dʒikăl), *a.* [f. as prec. + -ICAL.] Pertaining or relating to technology.

**1.** Belonging to technical phraseology or methods: esp. of terms, words, senses; = TECHNICAL 3 b. Now *rare.*

**1627** in Capt. Smith *Seaman's Gram.* a iij, Each Science termes of Art hath wherewithall To expresse themselues, calld Technologicall. **1704** NORRIS *Ideal World* II. Pref. 20 The word λογος.. being a technological term well known among the Jews (probably from the writings of Philo). **1854** J. SCOFFERN in *Orr's Circ. Sc., Chem.* 432 This material, considered in a technological sense, may be described as an alkaline silicate.

**2.** Relating to or dealing with the study of the arts, esp. the industrial arts.

**1800** *Monthly Mag.* June 468/2 A new work .. consecrated entirely to the arts and manufactures, in the way of annals or technological memoirs. **1864** DASENT *Jest & Earnest* (1873) II. 34 The dreary columns of a technological dictionary. **1868** *Rep. U. S. Commissioner Agric.* (1869) 59 The exposition of the industrial and the technological value of the mineral wealth of the country.

**Technologist** (teknǫ·lŏdʒist). [f. next + -IST.] One versed in technology; one who studies or treats of arts and manufactures.

**1859** R. F. BURTON *Centr. Afr.* in *Jrnl. Geog. Soc.* XXIX. 437 European technologists have..vainly proposed theoretical methods for the..operation. **1884** P. HIGGS *Magn. Dynamo-Electr. Mach.* vi. 140 In a book such as this, intended for the use of technologists, it will be necessary to discuss those theoretical principles.

**Technology** (teknǫ·lŏdʒi). [ad. Gr. τεχνολογία systematic treatment (of grammar, etc.), f. τέχνη art, craft: see -LOGY. So F. *technologie* (1812 in Hatz.-Darm.).]

**1.** A discourse or treatise on an art or arts; the scientific study of the practical or industrial arts.

**1615** BUCK *Third Univ. Eng.* xlviii, An apt close of this general Technologie. **1628** VENNER *Baths of Bathe* 9 Heere I cannot but lay open Baths Technologie. **1706** PHILLIPS (ed. Kersey), *Technology*, a Description of Arts, especially the Mechanical. **1802–12** BENTHAM *Ration. Judic. Evid.* (1827) I. 19 Questions in technology in all its branches. **1881** P. GEDDES in *Nature* 29 Sept. 524/2 Of economic physics, geology, botany, and zoology, of technology and the fine arts. **1882** *Mechanical World* 4 Mar. 130/1 The Department of Applied Science and Technology.

**b.** *transf.* Practical arts collectively.

**1859** R. F. BURTON *Centr. Afr.* in *Jrnl. Geog. Soc.* XXIX. 437 Little valued in European technology it [the chakazi, or 'jackass' copal] is exported to Bombay, where it is converted into an inferior varnish. **1864** — *Dahome* II. 202 His technology consists of weaving, cutting canoes, making rude weapons, and in some places practising a rude metallurgy.

**2.** The terminology of a particular art or subject; technical nomenclature.

**1658** SIR T. BROWNE *Gard. Cyrus* v. 70 The mother of Life and Fountain of souls in Cabalisticall Technology is called Binah. **1793** W. TAYLOR in *Monthly Rev.* XI. 563 The port-customs, the technology, and the maritime laws, all wear marks of this original character. **1802–12** BENTHAM *Ration. Judic. Evid.* (1827) IV. 252 An engine, called, in the technology of that day, *fork*. **1862** *Morn. Star* 21 May, Aluminium, and its alloy with copper—which the manufacturers, with a slight laxity of technology, denominate bronze.

† **3.** = Gr. τεχνολογία: see etym. *Obs. rare*⁻¹.

**1683** TWELLS *Exam. Gram.* Pref. 17 There were not any further Essays made in Technology, for above Fourscore years; but all men acquiesced in the Common Grammar.

† **Techomahac**, obs. form of TACAMAHAC.

**1693** *Phil. Trans.* XVII. 622 The Techomahac-Tree from Mexico.

**Techy**, obs. and arch. variant of TETCHY.

**Teck**, obs. form of TEAK.

† **Te·ckelite.** *Obs.* [f. name of Count Teckely, a Hungarian Protestant leader who rose against the persecuting Austrian government, and allied himself with the Turks, whom he joined in the siege of Vienna in 1683.] In *Eng. Hist.*, A nickname given in 1683 to the Whigs, alleged to sympathize with Count Teckely in waging war against a Roman Catholic government.

**1683** R. L'ESTRANGE *Observator* 29 Aug., Why where hast thou been Bury'd of late, that thou know'st Nothing of the Teckelites? There's Another Design afoot, for the Reconciling of the True-Protestants, and the Mahometans. **1684** DRYDEN *Epil. Constantine Gt.* 22 Besides all these, there were a sort of wights, (I think my author calls them Teckelites,) Such hearty rogues against the king and laws, They favoured even a foreign rebel's cause. **1688** *Lond. Gaz.* No. 2348/1 (*Addr. fr. Carlisle*) We likewise thank Your Majesty for Your Royal Army, which really is both the Honour and Safety of the Nation; Let the Teckelites think and say what they will.

**Teckle**, obs. Sc. form of TACKLE: cf. *taikle.*

**Tecno-** (also **tekno-**), repr. Gr. τεκνο-, combining form of τέκνον child (as in τεκνογόνος bearing children, etc.); used in Eng. in a few rare technical words. ‖**Tecnocto·nia** [Gr. -κτόνος murderer], child-murder, infanticide. ‖ **Tecnogo·nia** [Gr. γονή generation], † (*a*) the age of a father at his eldest child's birth; (*b*) child-bearing, pregnancy. **Tecnology** (teknǫ·lŏdʒi) [-LOGY], the scientific study of children; pædology. **Tecnonymy, tek-** (teknǫ·nĭmi) [Gr. ὄνομα, ὄνυμα name], the practice among certain peoples of naming a parent from his or her child; so **Tecno·nymous** (tek-) *a.*, practising tecnonymy.

**1857** DUNGLISON *Med. Lex.*, *Tecnoctonia. *a* **1677** HALE *Prim. Orig. Man.* 178 Partly by adding 100 Years to that *Technogonia of the Patriarchs before Abraham, have made the Period larger by 884 Years. **1860** MAYNE *Expos. Lex.*, Tecnogonia. **1857** DUNGLISON *Med. Lex.*, **Tecnology*.., a treatise on children. **1899** *Syd. Soc. Lex.*, *Tecnology*, the study or scientific knowledge of childhood. **1888** E. B. TYLOR in *Jrnl. Anthrop. Inst.* (1889) Feb. 248 Another custom..is the practice of naming the parent from the child. ..There are above thirty peoples spread over the earth who thus name the father, and, though less often, the mother. They may be called, coining a name for them, **teknonymous* peoples. When beginning to notice the wide distribution of this custom of **teknonymy* [etc.]. **1888** *Athenæum* 1 Dec. 740/1 Another custom, here called teknonymy [by Dr. E. B. Tylor]..; as an example was mentioned the name of Ra-Mary, or Father of Mary, by which Moffat was generally known in Africa.

‖ **Tecoma** (tĭkōu·mă). *Bot.* [mod.L. (Jussieu 1789), from Aztec *tecomaxochitl*, mistakenly supposed by Jussieu to be the name of a species of the genus to which he gave this name (but really the native name of *Solandra guttata*, N.O. *Solanaceæ*).

The Aztec name is a compound of *tecomatl* + *xochitl* 'rose, flower'; the plant being named from the resemblance of its flower to that of the *tecomatl* or Calabash-tree (*Crescentia Cujete*, N.O. *Bignoniaceæ*), lit. 'pot-tree', f. *tecomatl* earthen vessel, pot.]

A large genus of *Bignoniaceæ*, mostly natives of warm climates, consisting chiefly of shrubs (erect, climbing, or twining), with leaves usually pinnate, and showy trumpet-shaped flowers of various colours (chiefly different shades of yellow and red), whence the name *trumpet-flower*; many are cultivated in greenhouses, etc. for their beauty.

Some shrubby species have sometimes been reckoned in separate genera *Tecomaria*, *Stenolobium*, *Campsis* (or *Campsidium*), and *Pandorea*; others (of which some are tall trees used for timber and in medicine) formerly included in *Tecoma*, but with digitate leaves, are now separated as *Tabebuia*. Several species are also often called *Bignonia*.

**1846** *Penny Cycl.* Suppl. II. 614/1 Several..species of Tecoma have reputed medicinal virtues. **1884** *Mag. Art* Mar. 181/2 In the foreground the brilliant tecoma climbs a tall ailanthus tree. **1888** MRS. M'CANN *Poet. Wks.* 197 Its nest the lyre bird weaves with tecomas twining o'er it.

† **Tecon.** *Obs. rare*⁻¹. A fish mentioned by Walton as a kind of salmon: see quots.

**1653** WALTON *Angler* vi. 141 There is more then one sort of them [salmon], as namely, a Tecon, and another called in some places a Samlet, or by some, a Skegger: but these.. may be fish of another kind. **1760** HAWKINS *Note*, There is another small fish,..called the Gravel Last-Spring, found only in the rivers Wye and Severn... Perhaps this is what Walton calls the Tecon. **1853** 'EPHEMERA' *Note* ibid., All the fish named, except the gravel-last-spring, are salmon-fry of different ages, from three or four months to twelve. Walton's 'tecon' may be the parr.

† **Tect**, *sb. Obs. rare*⁻¹. [ad. L. *tect-um* roof, prop. neut. of *tectus*, pa. pple. 'covered': see next.] A roof. In comb. **te·ct-demo·lished** *a.*, having the roof demolished, disroofed.

**1632** LITHGOW *Trav.* x. 432 Tect-demolished Churches, vnpassable Bridges.

† **Tect**, *ppl. a. Obs. rare.* [ad. L. *tect-us*, pa. pple. of *tegĕre* to cover.] Covered, hidden. (Const. as pa. pple. See also TECTLY.) So † **Te·cted.**

*c* **1440** *Pallad. on Husb.* vi. 180 With chaf or fern this boordis do be tecte. *Ibid.* viii. 79 The tuppe is chosun fair of altitude, Ywombed side, and tecte in whitest wolle. *c* **1557** ABP. PARKER *Ps.* cxv. 332 Why els no doubt, the Heathen sect, Would say where is their God so tect? **1657** TOMLINSON *Renou's Disp.* 459 The shells wherewith they are tected.

‖ **Tec-tec.** [? from its note.] A species of whinchat (*Pratincola sybilla*) found in some of the islands off the E. coast of Africa.

**1886** H. A. WEBSTER in *Encycl. Brit.* XX. 492/2 (*Réunion*) Among the more familiar birds are the 'oiseau de la vierge' (*Muscipeta borbonica*), the tec-tec (*Pratincola sybilla*).

**Tectibranch** (te·ktibræŋk), *a.* and *sb. Zool.* [f. L. *tect-us* covered + *branchiæ* (Gr. βράγχια) gills.] **a.** *adj.* Belonging to the order or suborder *Tectibranchiata* of gastropod molluscs, comprising marine forms having the gills covered by the mantle, and small shells often concealed by the mantle. **b.** *sb.* A gastropod belonging to this division. So **Tectibra·nchian, Tectibra·nchiate** *adjs.* and *sbs.* in same senses.

**1836–9** *Todd's Cycl. Anat.* II. 381/1 The internal or dermic shells are formed in many of the..tectibranchiate orders. **1839** *Penny Cycl.* XIV. 322/1 Gastropods are divided into the following orders..:—1. Nudibranchians... 2. Inferobranchians...3. Tectibranchians [etc.]. **1851** WOODWARD *Mollusca* I. 34 The respiratory organs form tufts..protected by a fold of the mantle, as in the Inferobranchs and Tectibranchs of Cuvier. **1894** *Proc. Zool. Soc.* 20 Nov. 666 The posterior pallial lobes of various genera of Bulloid Tectibranchs.

**Tectiform** (te·ktifǭɹm), *a. Zool.* [ad. mod.L. *tectiform-is*, f. *tect-um* roof: see -FORM.] **a.** Roof-shaped; sloping downwards on each side from a central ridge. **b.** Serving as a covering or lid.

**1834** McMURTRIE *Cuvier's Anim. Kingd.* 414 Phryganea... The wings are..strongly tectiform. **1880** WATSON in *Jrnl. Linn. Soc.* XV. 95 Shell,—high, conical, tectiform. **1884** tr. *Claus' Zool.* I. x. 582 Of slender build and with large wings, which in repose are tectiform. **1895** *Funk's Stand. Dict.*, *Tectiform*, having the form of a roof; serving as a cover or lid: as, tectiform maxillaries.

† **Te·ctly,** *adv. Obs. rare.* [f. TECT *ppl. a.* + -LY².] In a concealed manner, covertly.

**1587** HOLINSHED *Chron. Irel.* II. 176/2 He laid verie close & tectlie a companie of his men in an old house fast by the castell. **1687** *Catholic Balance* 29 Opposing these Doctoral Principles either tectly or openly.

**Tectocephalic** (tektosĭfæ·lik), *a. Path.* [f. L. *tect-um* roof + Gr. κεφαλή head + -IC: cf. CEPHALIC.] = SCAPHOCEPHALIC. So **Tectocephaly** (-se·fāli) = SCAPHOCEPHALY.

**1888** CLEVINGER in *Amer. Nat.* July 614 The Esquimaux are tectocephalic (rafter-headed), with flat pyramidal, or lozenge-shaped faces, due to excessive zygoma projection, and narrow foreheads.

**Tectology** (tektǫ·lŏdʒi). *Biol.* [ad. Ger. *tektologie* (Haeckel), for **tektonologie*, f. Gr. τέκτων carpenter, builder (cf. ARCHITECT): see -LOGY.] (See quot., and cf. PROMORPHOLOGY.) So **Tecto·lo·gical** *a.*, pertaining to tectology.

**1883** P. GEDDES in *Encycl. Brit.* XVI. 842/1 In 1866 appeared the *Generelle Morphologie* of Haeckel. Here pure morphology is distinguished into two sub-sciences,—the first purely structural, *tectology*, which regards the organism as composed of organic individuals of different orders; the second essentially stereometric, *promorphology*.

**Tectonic** (tektǫ·nik), *a.* [ad. late L. *tectonicus*, a. Gr. τεκτονικός pertaining to building, f. τέκτων, -ον-, carpenter, builder.]

**1.** Of or pertaining to building, or construction in general; constructional, constructive: used esp. in reference to architecture and kindred arts.

**1656** BLOUNT *Glossogr.*, *Tectonick* (*tectonicus*), of or belonging to a builder. **1864** *Daily Tel.* 1 Aug., That law of necessity and of demand which is at the foundation of all tectonic art. **1903** G. B. BROWN *Arts in Early Eng.* II. 178 A form produced..by the exigencies of construction—or, to use a convenient term familiar in Germany, a tectonic form.

**2.** *Geol.* Belonging to the actual structure of the earth's crust, or to general changes affecting it.

**1894** BOYD-DAWKINS in *Geol. Mag.* Oct. 459 The relation existing between the tectonic anticlines and synclines in the districts of South Wales, Gloucester, and the West of England. **1902** LD. AVEBURY *Scenery Eng.* 213 The primary configuration of the country's surface is no doubt due to tectonic causes. **1905** *Athenæum* 1 Apr. 404/3 Whilst the most powerful and destructive disturbances are of this tectonic character, many other earthquakes are no doubt connected with volcanic phenomena.

So **Tecto·nics** [= Ger. *tektonik*], term for the constructive arts in general; † **Te·ctonist** (*obs. nonce-wd.*), a constructor, a builder.

**1634** W. WOOD *New Eng. Prosp.* II. xx. (1865) 106 As is their husbands occasion these poor tectonists [the squaws] are often troubled like snailes, to carrie their houses on their backs. **1850** LEITCH tr. *C. O. Müller's Anc. Art* § 22 A series of arts which form and perfect vessels, implements, dwellings, and places of assembly...We call this class of artistic activities tectonics.

**Tectorial** (tektōᵊ·riăl), *a. Anat.* [f. L. *tectōrium* covering, a cover (f. *tectōrius*: see next) + -AL.] Covering like a roof: applied to a membrane in the internal ear (see quot.).

**1890** BILLINGS *Nat. Med. Dict.*, *Tectorial membrane*, a gelatinous structure covering [the] organ of Corti, stretching from upper part of the limbus spiralis over the outer hair-cells.

† **Tecto·rian**, *a. Obs. rare*⁻⁰. [f. L. *tectōrius* serving for covering walls, from *tegĕre* to cover.]

**1656** BLOUNT *Glossogr.*, *Tectorian* (*tectorius*), of or belonging to covering, pargetting, washing or whitelyming.

‖ **Tectrix** (te·ktriks). *Ornith.* Usually in pl. **tectrices** (tektrəi·sīz). [mod.L. *tectrix* (fem. of L. *tector*), f. *tect-*, ppl. stem of *tegĕre* to cover: see -TRIX. So F. *tectrice.*] Each of the feathers that cover the base of the quill-feathers of the wing and tail in birds: = COVERT *sb.* 5.

[**1768** PENNANT *Zool.* I. *111 Lesser coverts of the wings. Tectrices primæ... Greater coverts. Tectrices secundæ. **1842** BRANDE *Dict. Sc.*, etc., *Tectrices*, *Coverts*, the name of the feathers which cover the quill feathers and other parts of the wing.] **1874** COUES *Birds N. W.* 693 Under parts, including the inferior alar tectrices, pure white. **1896** NEWTON *Dict. Birds* 950 Each tectrix being placed on the proximal side of its corresponding remex.

Hence **Tectricial** (tektri·ʃăl) *a.*, pertaining to the tectrices. **1891** in *Cent. Dict.*

† **Te·cture.** *Obs.* [ad. L. *tectūra* a covering.] A covering (*lit.* or *fig.*); a canopy, a roof.

**1624** F. WHITE *Repl. Fisher* 579 Your..Blandishments are but Maskes and Tectures of latent perfidiousnesse. **1632** LITHGOW *Trav.* x. 443 This palatiat cloyster is quadrangled foure stories high, the vppermost whereof, is window-set in the blew tecture. **1651** *Raleigh's Ghost* Pref., He may seem to shadow..his blasphemy under the tecture of some weak and feeble reasons. **1657** TOMLINSON *Renou's Disp.* 471* Caves were their houses, the tectures of wood their cottages.

Hence † **Te·ctured** *a.*, canopied, roofed; formed with or as a roof.

**1632** LITHGOW *Trav.* VIII. 366 The streetes being couered aboue,..haue large Lights cut through the tectur'd tops.

**Tecul**, obs. form of TICAL.

**Ted** (ted), *v.*¹ Forms: 5–6 tedd, 5–7 tedde, 6 teede, 7 tede, 6– ted. [Known from 15th c.; app. representing an OE. **tęddan*, cognate with Icel. *tęðja*, pa. t. *tadda*, in special sense, to dung, manure, prob. to spread (manure) or spread (the ground) with manure: see TATHE. The more general sense appears in OHG., MHG., and mod. HG. dial. *zętten* to spread out, scatter:—**zatjan*:—OTeut. **tadjan*. The non-appearance of this vb. in OE. and ME., and in LG. and Du., is notable.]

**1.** *trans.* To spread out, scatter, or strew abroad (new-mown grass) for drying. Also *absol.*

Sometimes including the turning of the grass when dried on one side: see quot. 1669; but *tedding* and *turning* are properly distinct processes: cf. quots. 1577, 1616, 1746.

**14..** [implied in TEDDER]. **1481–90** [see TEDDING]. **1523**

FITZHERB. *Husb.* § 25 Whan thy medowes be mowed, they wolde be well tedded and layde euen vppon the grounde. **1530** PALSGR. 753/2, I teede hey, I tourne it afore it is made in cockes, *je fene.* **1577** B. GOOGE *Heresbach's Husb.* I. (1586) 45 b, The Grasse being cutte, must be well tedded and turned in the Sommer. **1616** SURFL. & MARKH. *Country Farme* 500 After you haue mowed it, and tedded it, you shall turne it twice or thrice ere you cocke it. **1669** WORLIDGE *Syst. Agric.* (1681) 333 To *Ted*, to turn or spread new mown Grass. **1746** *Poor Robin* (Nares), Tedding, turning, cocking, raking, And such bus'ness in hay making. **1815** J. SMITH *Panorama Sc. & Art* II. 624 In Middlesex, ..all the grass mown on the first day, before nine o'clock in the morning, is tedded, that is, uniformly strewn over the field. *c* **1830** *Glouc. Farm Rep.* 14 in *Libr. Usef. Knowl., Husb.* III, The hay-making machine is put to work in the field to ted or shake out every day's work.

**2.** *transf.* and *fig.* To scatter; to dissipate.

*c* **1560** A. SCOTT *Poems* (S.T.S.) xxi. 23 Thow held hir curage he on loft, And ted my tendir hairt lyk toft. **1580** LYLY *Euphues* (Arb.) 228 Then fall they to al disorder that may be, tedding that with a forke in one yeare, which was not gathered together with a rake, in twentie. **1589** *Pappe w. Hatchet* Lyly's Wks. 1902 III. 412 What foole more couetous than he, that seekes to tedd abroad the Churches goods with a forke, and scratch it to himselfe with a rake. **1788** E. PICKEN *Poems* Gloss. 246 *Ted*, to scatter, to spread. **1813** — *Misc. Poems* I. 120 (E.D.D.) Megg tedd the saut upo' the stool. **1870** J. HAMILTON *Moses* xi. 188 A day-dreamer gets hold of a beautiful..thought, and teases and teds it, and tosses it out into a cloud fine and filmy.

**3.** *dial.* **a.** To spread out (cut corn or flax) on the ground to dry. **b.** To dress (flax). **c.** To arrange, tidy (the hair, a room, etc.).

**1796** *Monthly Mag.* Apr. 223/2 When the mowers went afield The yellow corn to ted. **1811** WILLAN *W. Riding Gloss.* (E. D. S. B. 7), *Tedding*,..applied..also to the dressing of hair and flax. **1832** J. BREE *St. Herbert's Isle* 13 To mark the vale-hind ted the ripened shock. **1847–78** HALLIWELL, *Ted*,..to turn flax when it has been laid on the ground to dry. *West.* **1858** R. S. SURTEES *Ask Mamma* lxviii. 306 Producing a black..pocket-book, and tedding up a lot of characters, bills, etc. **1887** *Jamieson's Sc. Dict., Supp.* s. v., Ted your hair, and tedd up the house: West of Sc.

**Ted,** *v.*[2] *local techn.* [app. local var. of ME. *teth*, TEETHE.] *trans.* To give a finely-toothed or serrated edge to (a reaping-hook or sickle). Hence **Te·dded** *ppl a.*, **Te·dder, Te·dding** *vbl. sb.*

**1833** J. HOLLAND *Manuf. Metal* II. 55 The next operation [in making sickles] is cutting or toothing, or *tedding* as it is technically called. *Ibid.* 56 There is..a peculiarity in the handling of his hammer and chisel by a sickle tedder, which it requires considerable practice to attain. **1888** *Sheffield Gloss., Tedded*, serrated, indented. Sickles are tedded in order to make them cut better. [Cf. *c* **1440** *Promp. Parv.* 498/2 Tothyd, or tod wythe teethe, *dentatus.* **1781** HUTTON *Tour Caves* Gloss., *Tod*, to tooth sickles.]

**Teddar, -er, -ir,** obs. forms of TETHER.

**Tedded** (te·dèd), *ppl. a.*[1] [f. TED *v.*[1] + -ED [1].] Spread out for drying, as grass.

**1667** MILTON *P. L.* IX. 450 The smell of Grain, or tedded Grass, or Kine. **1844** STEPHENS *Bk. Farm* III. 970 The hay-rake..is employed to rake the tedded grass into a windrow.

**Tedded,** *ppl.a.*[2]: see TED *v.*[2]

**Tedder** [1] (te·dəɹ). [f. TED *v.*[1] + -ER[1].] One who teds new-mown grass; also, a machine for doing this; a tedding-machine.

**14..** *Voc.* in Wr.-Wülcker 578/44 *Disgerbigator*, .. a Teddere. *Ibid.* 587/48 *Herbarius*,..a teddere. **1800** HURDIS *Fav. Village* 22 Thick swarms the field with tedders. **1877** KNIGHT *Dict. Mech., Tedder*,..a machine for stirring and spreading hay, to expedite its being dried. **1886** P. S. ROBINSON *Valley Teet. Trees* 141 The mowers and tedders, sitting in the shade with their bread and cheese.

**Tedder** [2]: see TED *v.*[2]

**Tedding** (te·diŋ), *vbl. sb.*[1] [f. TED *v.*[1] + -ING [1].] The action of spreading out or scattering (new-mown grass) to be dried by the sun and wind.

**1481–90** *Howard Househ. Bks.* (Roxb.) 226 Item, to Baker for iiij. dayes teddynge of gresse iiij. d. **1523** FITZHERBERT *Husb.* § 25 Good teddynge is the chiefe poynte to make good hey. **1688** R. HOLME *Armoury* III. 72/2 Tedding is with a Pitchfork or Pikill throwing it abroad out of those rows in which the Sithe left it on the ground. **1844** STEPHENS *Bk. Farm* III. 966 The process for putting it into cocks after the tedding.

**b.** *attrib.*, as *tedding-machine.*

[**1826–44** LOUDON *Encycl. Agric.* 420 The hay-tedding machine, invented about 1800, by Salmon of Woburn.] **1843** *Jrnl. Roy. Agric. Soc.* IV. II. 482 Mr. Wedlake..produced a spreading or tedding machine. **1847–78** HALLIWELL, *Tedding-pole*, the long stick used for turning or tedding flax. *West.* **1906** *Times* 25 June 14/3 The old custom of tedding either by hand or by tedding machine is avoided.

**Tedding,** *vbl. sb.*[2]: see TED *v.*[2]

**Teddy,** pet-form of certain Christian names, as *Edward, Edmund, Theodore. attrib.* in **Teddy bear** (te·di,bēəɹ), a stuffed figure of a bear, made of rough plush, used as a toy or as a kind of mascot.

The 'teddy bear' came into vogue about 1907, and was so called in humorous allusion to Theodore Roosevelt (President of U. S. 1901–1909).

**1907** *Daily Chron.* 13 Sept. 4/7 While Europe is sending aloft the..'diabolo', America is playing with bears...The sudden delight in these mere things of the toy-shop..is due to their name—'Teddy-bears'. **1907** *Motor Boat* 19 Sept. 190/1 The boat with a Teddy bear or golliwog on the bow. **1908** *Daily Chron.* 5 Nov. 7/1 The Teddy bear, popularly so-called because the retiring President of the United States has a reputation as a bear hunter.

† **Tede,** *sb. Obs.* Also tead(-e. [ad. L. *tæda, tēda* pine-torch.] A resinous piece of pine used as a torch; a wood-torch.

**1562** TURNER *Herbal* II. 89 A tede is a fat and roseny pece of a pyne or pich tre, which hewen of, serueth for torches. **1591** SPENSER *Muiopotmos* 293 A burning Teade about his head did move. **1624** DARCIE *Birth of Heresies* xv. 61 A Lamp or high Taper, which ordinarily was of Tede or Pine. **1637** WHITING *Albino & Bellama* 27 Bellama's bridall tede is lighted now.

† **Tede,** *a. Obs. rare*[−1]. ? Tied, joined together.

**13..** *E. E. Allit. P.* B. 1634 Fyrst telle me þe tyxte of þe tede lettres, & syþen þe mater of þe mode, mene me þer-after.

**Tede, Teder,** obs. forms of TED *v.*, TETHER.

‖ **Tedesco** (tede·sko), *a.* (*sb.*) Pl. **tedeschi** (-ki). Also **tedesque** (-e·sk). [It. *tedesco* German; ad. med.L. *theodisc-us*: cf. Goth. *þiudisk*, OE. *þéodisc*, OHG. *diutisc*, MHG. *tiutsch, diutsch*, Ger. *deutsch*: see DUTCH.] The Italian word for German; esp. used to express Teutonic influence as shown in some spheres of Italian art.

**1814** BYRON *Jrnl.* 20 Feb. in Moore *Life* (1830) I. 501 The Tedeschi dramatists. **1845** FORD *Handbk. Spain* I. 551/2 The *Coro Alto* was carved in a quaint tedesque style. **1874** T. G. APPLETON in *Longfellow's Life* (1891) III. 232 Achille denounced the *Tedesco* with the traditionary hatred of the Austrian. **1883** C. C. PERKINS *Ital. Sculpture* I. iv. 51 *note*, Minute works in the 'semi-tedesco' style, then in fashion.

‖ **Te Deum** (tī· dī·ŏm). [From the opening words of the Latin original, *Te Deum laudamus*, 'Thee, God, we praise'.] An ancient Latin hymn of praise in the form of a psalm, sung as a thanksgiving on special occasions, as after a victory or deliverance; also regularly at Matins in the R. C. Ch., and (in an English translation) at Morning Prayer in the Church of England.

*c* **961** ÆTHELWOLD *Rule St. Benet* xi. (1885) 35 Æfter þæm glorian þæs feorþan repses beginne se abbod þæne lofsang Te deum laudamus. [So in *c* 1200 *Winteney Rule St. Benet* xi. 47.] *c* **1386** CHAUCER *Sompn. T.* 158 Te deum was oure song and no thyng elles. *c* **1485** *Digby Myst.* III. 2140 Te Deum lavdamus lett vs syng. **1547–8** *Rec. St. Mary at Hill* 387 Item, for iiij songe bokes of te deum in Englisshe.. viij d. **1613** SHAKS. *Hen. VIII*, IV. i. 92 The Quire With all the choysest Musicke of the Kingdome Together sung Te Deum. **1822** BYRON *Werner* v. i. 94 'Te Deum' peal'd from nations. **1896** C. K. PAUL tr. *Huysman's En Route* viii. 107 Standing, he intoned the 'Te Deum'.

**b.** With *a* and in *pl.* **Te Deums**, in reference to a recital of this, or (allusively) to any public utterance of praise to God; also, a service of (public) thanksgiving marked by the singing of this hymn.

**1679** SHADWELL *True Widow* I. 3 At home they are alwayes roaring out Te Deums for Stealing of some Town or other. **1711** *Lond. Gaz.* No. 4794/3 Letters from France begin to own that their *Te Deum* cost them extreamly dear. **1903** MORLEY *Gladstone* I. IV. x. 615 The archbishop ordered a *Te Deum.* Neither te-deums nor prayers melted the heart of the British cabinet.

**c.** A musical setting of this hymn.

**1864** [Jackson's *Te Deum* regularly used in church services.] **1880** W. H. HUSK in *Grove's Dict. Mus.* I. 625/1 In addition to the before-named compositions, Greene produced a Te Deum in D major, with orchestral accompaniments.

**d.** *attrib.* and *Comb.*

**1874** RUSKIN *Fors Clav.* xlv. (1896) II. 419 Te-Deum-singing Princes. **1896** *Daily News* 4 Aug. 3/7 A Te Deum mass in celebration of the birthday of the Empress Dowager of Russia took place yesterday at the Orthodox Church in the Rue Daru in Paris.

Hence **Te-De·uming** (*nonce-wd.*), the singing of a Te Deum or Te Deums.

**1862** CARLYLE *Fredk. Gt.* XIII. vii. (1873) V. 82 With much processioning, blaring and *te-deum*-ing. **1864** *Ibid.* xv. i. V. 270 *Te-deum*-ing on an extensive scale.

**Tedge** (tedʒ). *rare*[−0]. [Etymology unknown.] = INGATE *sb.*[2]: see quots.

**1858** SIMMONDS *Dict. Trade, Ingate*, an aperture in a mould for pouring in metal; technically called the tedge. **1877** KNIGHT *Dict. Mech., Tedge*, the ingate or aperture in a mold through which the molten metal is poured.

† **Tedia·tion.** *Obs. rare*[−1]. [n. of action f. late L. *tædiāre* to feel loathing: see -ATION. Perh. aphetic for *ated(y)acyon* (also in Caxton), a. OF.: see ATTEDIATION.] The action of wearying or condition of being wearied.

**1485** CAXTON *Chas. Gt.* 112 Ye shall do Iustyce wyth lasse tedyacyon.

† **Tedi·ferous,** *a. Obs. rare*[−0]. [f. L. *tædifer* (f. *tæda* torch + *-fer* bearing) + -OUS: see -FEROUS.] Bearing a torch.

**1656** BLOUNT *Glossogr., Tediferous* (*tedifer*), that beareth a torch or taper. **1658** in PHILLIPS. **1721** in BAILEY.

† **Te·dify,** *v. nonce-wd.* [irreg. f. L. *tædium*, TEDIUM + -FY, after *edify.*] *trans.* To affect with tedium; to weary, bore. So † **Tedifica·tion.**

**1613** T. ADAMS *Sinner's Passing-bell* Wks. 1861 I. 348 An odious, tedious, endless inculcation of things doth often tire those with whom a soft and short reproof would find good impression. Such, whiles they would intend to edify, do in event tedify. **1616** — *Divine Herbal* ibid. II. 442 Too often, till edification turn to tedification. **1633** — *Exp. 2 Peter* iii. 4 To be all utterance, no materials, and so not to edify but tedify their hearers.

**Teding-penny,** obs. f. TITHING-PENNY.

**Tedious** (tī·diəs), *a.* Forms: 5 ted(e)us, tedi-, tidiose, 5–7 tedy-, 6 tede-, tide-, tydy-, tyde-, *Sc.* tidi-, 6–7 teydi-, 7–8 teadi-, 8 tædi-, 5– tedious. (Also 6 tedy-, tiddius, *Sc.* tideus, -ews, 6–7 tedius.) [ad. late L. *tædiōs-us* irksome, f. *tædium*, TEDIUM: see -OUS; perh. partly ad. OF. *tedieus, -eux* (1387 in Godef.).]

**1.** 'Wearisome by continuance' (J.); long and tiresome: said of anything occupying time, as a task, or a journey; *esp.* of a speech or narrative, hence of a speaker or writer: prolix, so as to cause weariness.

**1412–20** LYDG. *Chron. Troy* IV. xxxiii, Me liste no more of hir woo to endite Leste vn to ȝow that it were tedious. *c* **1475** *Babees Bk.* 75 Many wordes ben rihte Tedious. **1526** TINDALE *Acts* xxiv. 4 Lest I be tedeous vnto the. **1549** *Compl. Scot.* vi. 62, I pray the to decist fra that tideus melancolic orison. **1552** LYNDESAY *Monarche* 4065 Bot tiddius it wer to tell. **1552** HULOET, Tedious speaker, or patterer, *battologus.* **1592** SHAKS. *Rom. & Jul.* v. iii. 230, I will be briefe, for my short date of breath Is not so long as is a tedious tale. **1603** — *Meas. for M.* II. i. 119 Come: you are a tedious foole: to the purpose. **1675** T. TULLY *Let. Baxter* 27 The tediousest taske I ever yet undertooke. **1709** STEELE & ADDISON *Tatler* No. 75 ⁋ 8, I would not be tedious in this Discourse. **1756** C. LUCAS *Ess. Waters* I. Pref., A series of tedious and laborious experiments. **1819** SCOTT *Let. to Ld. Montagu* 4 Mar., in *Lockhart*, Tedious hours occur on board of ship. **1875** JOWETT *Plato* (ed. 2) V. 36 If I am to discuss all these matters, I cannot avoid being tedious.

† **b.** *humorously.* Long (in time or extent). *Obs.*

**1601** SHAKS. *All's Well* II. iii. 33 Nay 'tis strange, 'tis very straunge, that is the breefe and the tedious of it. **1630** *R. Johnson's Kingd. & Commw.* 56 An old sheep-biter, with a nose too tedious for his face.

**2.** Wearisome in general; annoying, irksome, troublesome, disagreeable, painful. *Obs.* exc. *dial.*

**1454** *Paston Lett.* I. 279 To arere a power to resyst the sayd riotts, which to hem on that holy tyme was tediose and heynous. **1526** TINDALE *Rom.* xii. 11 Let not that busynes which ye have in honde be tedious to you. *c* **1689** J. WHICKER in Arb. *Garner* VII. 375 A sort of flies..drew blisters and bladders in our skin..which were very tedious for our bodies too. *a* **1694** TILLOTSON *Serm.* (1742) III. 181, I may be tedious, but I will not be long. *c* **1845** in *J. Mitford's Lett. & Rem.* 143 Johnstone ain't a drinking man nor a wife-beater, but he makes her a tedious husband. **1868** ATKINSON *Cleveland Gloss., Tedious*,..fidgetty, uneasy, requiring constant attention; of an infant or young child when teething, or poorly. **1871** R. ELLIS *Catullus* l. 17 Did I, a poem Write, my tedious anguish all revealing.

† **3.** Tired, wearied, exhausted; also, disgusted or annoyed, esp. by iteration or excess; bored.

**1430–40** LYDG. *Bochas* VIII. viii. (MS. Bodl. 263) lf. 375 Galerius..Throuh at [*sic*] thorient wex victorious Til he for age, gan wexen tedious. **1509** BARCLAY *Shyp of Folys* (1874) II. 148 So whan the Father is tedyous and old. **1540–1** ELYOT *Image Gov.* (1544) Bij, Being also tedious of his abhominations. *Ibid.* xxviii. Qiij b, Beinge tediouse of that beastely lycence.

**4.** Late, tardy, dilatory, slow. *Obs.* exc. *dial.*

*c* **1485** *Digby Myst.* IV. 1079, I was to tidiose, That holy sight to see. **1605** BACON *Adv. Learn.* I. ii. § 7 The most active or busy man..hath..many vacant times of leisure.. except he be..tedious and of no dispatch. **1698** CONGREVE *Semele* II. i, Though thou hadst on lightning rode, Still thou tedious art, and slow. **1728** MORGAN *Algiers* II. iii. 249 Barbarossa was not..very tedious in gratifying their curiosity. **1833** T. HOOK *Parson's Dau.* II. i, 'I expect Lord Weybridge; we are not ready for dinner till his lordship comes.' 'What can make him so tedious?' said Maria-Jane. **1898** [see *Eng. Dial. Dict.*].

So **Te·disome, Tediousome** *a.* (*Sc.*), tedious; † **Tedio·sity,** † **Tediouste** [= OF. *tedieusete*, 15th c.], tediousness.

? *a* **1412** LYDG. *Two Merch.* 900 Lest tediouste your erys did assayl. **1612** *Two Noble K.* III. v, What tediosity and disensanity Is here among ye! **1824** SCOTT *St. Ronan's* xxii, It was an unco pleasant show,..only it was a pity it was sae tediousome.

**Tediously** (tī·diəsli), *adv.* [f. prec. + -LY [2].] In a tedious manner; at great and wearisome length; tiresomely; slowly, tardily.

*a* **1557** MRS. M. BASSET *More's Treat. Passion* M.'s Wks. 1376/1 Oftentimes tediousely without any nede thei were faine to repete twise euery worde they said in their praiour. **1583** HOLLYBAND *Campo di Fior* 323 Thou hast made me to forget it interrupting me so tediously. **1599** SHAKS. *Hen. V*, IV. Chorus 22 The creeple-tardy-gated Night, Who like a foule and ougly Witch doth limpe So tediously away. **1653** WALTON *Angler* To Rdr. 2 Not to read dull, and tediously. **1779–81** JOHNSON *L. P., Milton* Wks. II. 154 [Comus] a drama in the epick style, inelegantly splendid, and tediously instructive. **1837** HALLAM *Hist. Lit.* III. ii. § 72 Hall.. dilates upon it sometimes more tediously, but more appositely.

**Tediousness** (tī·diəsnės). [f. as prec. + -NESS.] The quality or condition of being tedious.

**1.** Wearisomeness on account of long continuance; tiresome lengthiness, prolixity; also, wearisomeness in general; irksomeness, troublesomeness; trouble, annoyance (*obs.* or *dial.*).

**1432–50** tr. *Higden* (Rolls) II. 229 Tubal exercisede firste musike to alleuiate the tediosenes pastoralle. *Ibid.* IV. 255 The vthe age of the worlde..afflicte with moche tediousenesse [*orig.* crebris malis quassata]. **1553** T. WILSON *Rhet.* (1580) 139 Euen in this our tyme, some offende much in tediousnesse. **1599** DAVIES *Immort. Soul* cccix, She distastes them all, within a while; And in the sweetest, finds a tediousness. **1658** ROWLAND *Moufet's Theat. Ins.* 936 The bloud of beasts, which with great tediousnesse and pain he [the bee-fly] sucks out. **1798** S. & HT. LEE *Canterb. T., Yng. Lady's T.* II. 434 He..resolved rather to endure the tediousness of a passage by sea. **1881** *Times* 9 Apr. 11/3 Ecclesiastical litigation abuses the common legal privilege of tediousness.

† **2.** Weariness, ennui; disgust, distaste. *Obs.*

**1482** *Monk of Evesham* (Arb.) 25 Vnto the tedusnes of

some stondyng by, he thankyd owr lord and redemer..for innumerabulle benefetis. *c* **1561** VERON *Free-will* 46 To engender in them a hatred and tediousnesse of vyce. **1576** FLEMING tr. *Caius' Eng. Dogs* (1880) 5 These Dogges..applying to their pursuit, agilitie and nimblenesse, without tediousnesse. **1684** *Contempl. St. Man* II. v. (1699) 171 All there know God without Error...Love him without Tediousness.

**3.** Slowness, tardiness; dilatoriness. *Obs.* exc. *dial.*

**1691** T. H[ALE] *Acc. New Invent.* 6 Its tediousness in bringing on and off. **1742** H. WALPOLE *Lett. to Mann* (1834) I. xlviii. 189 By the tediousness of the post and distance of place I am still receiving letters from you about the Secret Committee. **1900** [see *Eng. Dial. Dict.*].

**Tedium** (tī·dium). Also 7–9 tædium. [a. L. *tædium* weariness, disgust, f. *tæd-ēre* to weary.] The state or quality of being tedious; wearisomeness, tediousness, ennui.

**1662** PETTY *Taxes* ii. § 37 Whereby the charge and tedium of travelling..may be greatly lessened. **1663** J. SPENCER *Prodigies* (1665) 16 Stories of Prodigies may..deceive the tædium of a winter night. **1779** J. MOORE *View Soc. Fr.* (1789) I. xviii. 141 A more infallible specific against tedium and fatigue. **1814** SCOTT *Wav.* xxv, When he remembered the tædium of his quarters. **1874** GREEN *Short Hist.* v. § 1. 216 In some of the stories..there is the tedium of the old romance.

*Comb.* **1827** CARLYLE *Germ. Lit.* Misc. Ess. 1872 I. 28 One or two sleek clerical tutors, with here and there a tedium-stricken 'squire.

**Tedure, -yr(e**, obs. forms of TETHER.

**Tee** (tī), *sb.*[1] [The origin of senses 2 and 3 is obscure: possibly they do not belong here.]

**I. 1.** The name of the letter T; also applied to objects having the form of this (T or ⊢). See also T (the letter) 2.

**1610** GUILLIM *Heraldry* IV. v. (1611) 199 He beareth Argent, a cheveron betweene three Text Tees, sable. **1877** KNIGHT *Dict. Mech.*, *Tee*, a T-shaped pipe-coupling. **1882** *Worc. Exhib. Catal.* iii. 5 Connections, elbows, tees, syphons. **1891** *Times* 28 Sept. 3/6 The demand for angles and tees is quiet, but bridge and roofing makers are taking fair lots.

**II. 2.** *Sc.* (See quot. 1882.)

**1494–5** *Acc. Ld. High Treas. Scot.* I. 228 To mak knoppis and fassis to the harnysing of briddillis and teis, xxxij pirnis of gold. **1505** *Ibid.* III. 160 For ane courpale and tee..xs. **1675** CUNNINGHAM *Diary* 27 July (1887) 56 Sent to Glasgow for a new Curpell and Tee. **1776** R. FERGUSON in Whitelaw *Bk. Scot. Song* (1875) 100 With..hat, and a feather, And housing at curpen and tee. **1882** *Jamieson's Dict.*, *Tee*. Pl. *tees*, *teis*, iron holdfasts, in shape like the letter T, suspended from a horse's collar for attachment to the shafts of a vehicle, or for connecting the bit and bridle; also, the ropes by which a sailyard is suspended.

**3.** *Mining.* (See quot. 1851.)

**1653** MANLOVE *Lead Mines* 266 Fell, Bous, and Knockbarke, Forstid-oar, and Tees. **1747** HOOSON *Miner's Dict.* S ij, After crossing of Pees, Tees, Braks, Jumbles, or what other disorder may happen that the Vein cannot be easily made out. **1851** TAPPING *Gloss. Lead-mining Terms*, *Tee*, or *Tye*, is where a cross vein approaches another vein at nearly right angles, whose side it joins without intersecting or breaking through it.

**III. 4.** *attrib.* Shaped like a T, having a cross-piece at the top or end, as *tee-frame*, *-iron*, *-joint*, *-piece*, *-square*; also in other combs., as *tee-headed*, *-shaped* adjs. See also T (the letter) 3.

**1819** PECKSTON *Gas-Lighting* 300 Wrought-iron tee-pieces for branching off from the principal service-pipe in two directions. **1822** IMISON *Sc. & Art* II. 344 Tee-squares are rulers made in the form of the letter T. **1877** KNIGHT *Dict. Mech.*, *Tee-iron*, a rod with a cross-bar at the end, for withdrawing the lower valve-box of a pump. **1884** *Health Exhib. Catal.* p. liii/2 Fire and Thief-resisting Safes..solid tee frame, and solid flange lock case. **1887** D. A. LOW *Machine Draw.* (1892) 18 At (*c*) is shown a tee-headed bolt. **1904** *Daily Chron.* 4 May 3/2 Tee-shaped and substantially built, the new pier..has a frontage of 650 ft.

**Tee** (tī), *sb.*[2] *Golf.* Orig. *Sc.* [app. a curtailed form of *teaz*, used in 17th c., the origin of which is not ascertained. For the formation cf. *pease*, *pea*.] The starting-place, usually a little heap of earth or sand, from which the ball is driven in commencing to play each hole.

**1673** *Wedderburn's Vocab.* 37, 38 (Jam.) *Baculus*, *Pila clavaria*, a goulfe-ball. *Statumen*, the Teaz. **1721** RAMSAY *Ode to Ph—* ii, Driving their baws frae whins or tee. **1875** W. A. SMITH *Lewsiana* 147 Each [shell] is seated on a sandy 'tee', formed by the wind sweeping away the sand around it. **1879** *Encycl. Brit.* X. 765/1 In starting from the hole, the ball may be teed (i.e. placed where the player chooses, with a little pinch of sand under it called a tee). **1905** *Daily News* 7 Jan. 12 At two o'clock,..the golfing party were at the first tee.

*attrib.* **1901** *Daily Chron.* 7 June 8/3 Vardon was beaten in the tee shots.

**Tee** (tī), *sb.*[3] *Curling*, etc. Orig. *Sc.* [Origin uncertain: perh. orig. the same word as TEE *sb.*[1], from the use of such a mark to define an exact spot. (A suggested derivation from ON. *tjá* to show, mark, note, is untenable.)]

The mark, a cross made on the ice and surrounded by circles, at which the stones are aimed; applied also to the 'jack' at bowls, and the 'hob' at quoits.

**1789** D. DAVIDSON *Th. Seasons, Winter* 167 Clim o' the Cleugh..A slow shot drew, wi' muckle care, Which settled on the tee. **1812** *Sporting Mag.* XL. 51 A mark is made at each end [of the rink] called a *tee*, *toesee*, or *witter*. **1820** *Blackw. Mag.* VI. 572 Each player endeavouring to possess himself of a birth near the *Tee*. **1885** *New Bk. Sports* 100 (Curling) The players who open the game begin by playing short of the tee. **1888** W. BLACK *In Far Lochaber* ii. I. 66 A trimly kept bowling-green, in which the club-members practise the gentle art of reaching the tee.

**b.** *attrib.* and *Comb.*, as *tee-shot*; *tee-drawn* adj.

**1850** J. STRUTHERS *Winter Day* II. ix, Tee-drawn shots the smooth-lead fill, Or ports are wick'd with hair-breadth skill. **1853** W. WATSON *Poems* 64 (E.D.D.) [He] Sen's up a tee-shot to a hair.

‖ **Tee** (tī), *sb.*[4] Also htee. [Burmese *h'ti* umbrella.] A metallic decoration, in the shape of an umbrella, usually gilded and hung with bells, surmounting the topes and pagodas of Burma and adjacent countries.

**1800** M. SYMES *Embassy Ava* v. 188 The whole [building] is crowned by a *Tee*, or umbrella, of open iron-work, from which rises a rod with a gilded pennant. The tee or umbrella is to be seen on every sacred building that is of a spiral form. **1858** H. YULE *Mission to Ava* ii. 42 [The Gauda-palen Temple at Pagan] is cruciform in plan..crowned by a spire and *htee*. **1882** *Edin. Rev.* Oct. 360 On the summit of the tope was a square construction known among archæologists as the 'tee'.

† **Tee**, *v.*[1] *Obs.* Forms: see below. [OE. *téon* (contr. from *téohan*), pa. t. *téah*, *tugon*, pa. pple. *togen*, a Com. Teutonic str. vb., cogn. with OSax. *tiohan*, *tôh*, *tugun*, *gitogan* (MLG. *tien*, *ten*, MDu. *tijen*, *tijghen*, LG. *teën*, EFris. *tien*, *tējen*, *tēen*), OFris. *tia* (WFris. *tjean*, Saterl. *tejen*, NFris. *tjin*), OHG. *ziohan*, *zôh*, *zugun*, *gizogan* (Ger. *ziehen*, *zog*, *gezogen*), ON. pa. pple. *toginn*, Goth. *tiuhan*, *táuh*, *tauhum*, *tauhans*, to draw, lead; = L. *dūc-ĕre* to lead, draw. A primitive Aryan vb., still important in German, but lost in Eng. by 1500. Derivatives of the same root survive in *taut*, *team*, *tie*, *tight*, *tough*, *tow*, *tug*.]

**A.** Illustration of Forms.

**1.** *Present stem.* **a.** *Inf.* 1 téon, 2–4 teon, 3–4 tuen, 3–5 teen, ten, teo, tee, te; 5 tegh.

**971** *Blickl. Hom.* 241 ȝif eow swa licize..hine teon þurh þisse ceastre lanan. *c* **1205** LAY. 791 Ich wille teo [*c* 1275 go] to-foren. *c* **1250** *Gen. & Ex.* 1344 To bersabe he gunne teen. *Ibid.* 1953 To-warde egipte he gunne ten. *c* **1290** *St. Eustace* 165 in Horstm. *Altengl. Leg.* (1881) 214 To londe he moste te. *c* **1300** *Harrow. Hell* 234 Alle..þat mine buen shule to blisse wiþ me tuen. *c* **1320** *Cast. Love* 821 Þorw on of þeos bayles he mot teon. *Ibid.* 877 Þorw þe faste ȝat he con in teo. *c* **1400** *Destr. Troy* 2541 Let hym tegh to þe tempull. *c* **1425** *Cast. Persev.* 1564 in *Macro Plays* 123 Þedyr rapely wyl I tee. *c* **1450** LOVELICH *Grail* xiii. 56 Owt of the castel of Come þat he wolde te.

**b.** *Pres. Indic.*, *Imper.* 1 teoh, teo, tio, 3–4 tee, te; 2 (*Subj.*) tye; *pl.* 1 teon, 3–4 teen, ten. *Imper.* 1 teoh, 3 tih.

*c* **897** [see B. 1 b]. *c* **1000** ÆLFRIC *Gram.* xxviii. (Z.) 176 *Traho*, ic teo,..*pertraho*, ic teo swyðe. *c* **1000** *Ags. Gosp.* John vi. 44 Buton se fæder..hyne teo [*c* **1160** *Hatton G.* hyne tye]. *Ibid.* Luke v. 4 Teoh hit on dypan. **1027–34** *Secular Laws Cnut* c. 70 Ne teo se hlaford na mare on his æhta. *c* **1205** LAY. 17416 Vther, tih þe aȝan. *c* **1220** *Bestiary* 353 Ðe hertes..If he fer fecchen fode, and he ouer water ten. **13..** *E. E. Allit. P.* B. 9 Thay teen vnto his temmple. *Ibid.* 1262 Er he to þe tempple tee. **13..** *Guy Warw.* (A.) 2018 Er þe sonne doun te.

**c.** *Pres. Indic.*, *2nd pers. sing.* 1 tiehst, tyhst, *3rd. pers. sing.* 1 tiehþ, tyhþ, tihþ, 2 tið, 3 tiȝth, tihth, teð, teoð, 4 teȝt.

*c* **897** K. ÆLFRED *Gregory's Past. C.* xxxv. 241 He tiehð his heafod in to him. *c* **1000** *Sax. Leechd.* II. 256 Læcedom se þæt yfel ut tihð of þam milte. *Ibid.* 262 Þonne þu..tyhst blod. *c* **1175** *Lamb. Hom.* 27 Hit hine tið to þan bittre deðe. *c* **1200** *Trin. Coll. Hom.* 37 Iefned to þe deore [h]wuas geres he forðteoð. *c* **1220** *Bestiary* 64 Up he teð, Til ðat he ðe heuene seð. *a* **1250** *Owl & Night.* 1435 An sum sot man hit tyhþ [*v.r.* tihþ] þar to. *c* **1315** SHOREHAM iii. 236 As he teȝt atte font-stone.

**2.** *Pa. t.* 1 téah, 2 teah, 2–3 teh, teih, tæh, tah, 3–4 teȝ, teiȝ, tey, teye, teiȝe, 4 tyh, 5 teȝe, tegh. *Pl.* 1 tuȝon, 3 tuȝen, tuhen, tuwen, 5 tyen.

*a* **900** CYNEWULF *Judith* 99 [Heo] ȝenam ða þone hæðenan mannan fæste be feaxe sinum, teah hyne. *c* **1175** *Lamb. Hom.* 129 Þurh hwam ure drihtan teh to him al moncun. *c* **1205** LAY. 640 He tah hine aȝein. *Ibid.* 805 He him seolf teih [*c* 1275 eode] bi-foren. *Ibid.* 1641 Tæh [see B. 1 b]. *Ibid.* 21616 Touwarde þæ hulle [he] tæh. *c* **1250** *Gen. & Ex.* 1135 Wið hise two dowtres ut he teȝ. *a* **1300** *Vox & Wolf* 279 in *Rel. Ant.* II. 278 The frere mid al his maine tey So longe, that [etc.]. *a* **1375** *Joseph Arim.* 57 Ioseph teiȝ to non hous bote euene to þe temple. **1390** GOWER *Conf.* II. 318 Unto his contre hom he tyh. *c* **1400** *Destr. Troy* 12907 He light into hauyn,..Tegh vnto Tuskan, & turnyt to londe. *c* **1000** *Ags. Gosp.* Luke v. 11 And hiȝ tuȝon heora scypu to lande. *c* **1205** LAY. 1834 Heo tuȝen [*c* 1275 drowen] alle to gadere. *Ibid.* 2619 Him tuwen hired men to. *a* **1225** *St. Marher.* 22 Ant tuhen alle to hire bodi. *c* **1400** *Sege Jerus.* 843 His burnes Tyen to her tentis myd tene þat þey hadde.

**3.** *Pa. pple.* 1 ȝe)toȝen, 3 i-toȝen, i-tohen, i-towen, -un, toȝen, 4–5 towen.

**971** *Blickl. Hom.* 241 Se eadiȝa Andreas wæs toȝen. *c* **1205** LAY. 10099 Luces wes wel itoȝen. *a* **1225** *Ancr. R.* 108 Heo is a grucchild, & ful itowen [*v. r.* itohen]. *Ibid.* 204 Þe nome one muhte hurten alle wel itowune earen. *c* **1250** *Gen. & Ex.* 3647 Ðis folc is after softe toȝen. **13..** *Gaw. & Gr. Knt.* 1093 For ȝe haf trauayled, towen fro ferre.

**B.** Signification.

**1.** *trans.* To draw, pull, drag, tug.

*a* **900** tr. *Bæda's Hist.* v. xiii. [xii.] (1890) 428 Tuȝon heo ða wergan gastas. *c* **1122** *O. E. Chron.* an. 1052, Godwine eorl ..teah þa up his seȝl. *a* **1225** *Juliana* 8 Ant tuhen him ȝont te tun, from strete to strete. *a* **1225** *Ancr. R.* 324 Hwo is þet durste slepen þeo hwule þet his deadlich fo heolde on itowen sweord ouer his heaued? *c* **1275** LAY. 4995 Þane hem ȝeo vp teh [*c* **1205** i-tæh] to hire cneon wel neh. **13..** *K. Alis.* 7070 To shipp he may hem beren & teen. **1375** BARBOUR *Bruce* XV. 282 He gert men..Salys to the toppis te. *c* **1400** *Destr. Troy* 10382 To tegh as a traytor, and traile vpon þe erthe. **1446** LYDG. *Nightingale Poems* ii. 166 The Iewes my flessh asonder dide tee.

**b.** To draw to oneself, to take to or upon oneself.

*c* **897** K. ÆLFRED *Gregory's Past. C.* xvi. 99 Ðæt he tio [*v.r.* teo] on hine selfne oðerra monna scylda. **925–35** *Laws Athelstan* II. c. 9 Þæt he hit on folcryht him to teo. *c* **1205** LAY. 1641 He..tæh hit to his aȝre hond. *c* **1315** SHOREHAM iii. 285 For al hys þefte þat man teȝt. *c* **1400** *St. Alexius* (Trin.) 449 Þat writ he drouȝ & ȝerne teiȝ. *a* **1500** *Sir Beues* (S.) 2319 His ryng he gan to him tee.

**c.** To lead, bring (an army, etc.). Only OE.

*a* **900** tr. *Bæda's Hist.* III. xiv. [xviii.] (1890) 208 Penda Mercna cyning teah here and fyrd wið Eastengle.

**2.** *fig.* To draw, lead, entice, allure; to bring into some condition. Const. *to*.

*c* **888** K. ÆLFRED *Boeth.* xxvi. § 1 Sio ȝecynd eow tihð to ðæm andȝite. [**971** *Blickl. Hom.* 37 Seo oferfyll þæs lichoman ȝetyhþ þone mon to synnum.] *c* **1200** *Trin. Coll. Hom.* 139 And teh folc to him to heren his wise word. *a* **1250** [see A. 1 c].

**3.** To bring up, train, discipline, educate, teach.

*c* **1000** ÆLFRIC *Gram.* (Z.) 166 *Imbuo*, ic ty [*v.r.* ic teo] oððe ic lære; *imbui*, ic teah. *c* **1205**, *a* **1225** [see A. 3]. *a* **1250** *Owl & Night.* 1725 Heo wes itowen [*v.r.* itoȝen] among mankunne. *c* **1250** *Gen. & Ex.* 1913 He wulde ðat he sulde hem ten Ðat he wel-ðewed sulde ben.

**4.** To bring forth, produce. Only OE. (Cf. TEAM *sb.*, TEEM *v.*[1])

*c* **1000** ÆLFRIC *Gen.* i. 20 Teon nu þa wæteru forð swimmende cynn. *Ibid.* 21 Eall libbende fisccinn..þe þa wæteru tuȝon forð on heora hiwum.

**5.** To draw out, protract, prolong.

*c* **1200** *Trin. Coll. Hom.* 149 Wumme..þat min biwist is teȝed here swo longe.

**6. a.** *refl.* To betake oneself; to withdraw. (Cf. DRAW *v.* 67.)

*c* **1205** LAY. 640 He tah hine aȝein ane þrowe. *c* **1275** *Ibid.* 20086 Þis i-seh Arthur..and teh hine [*c* 1205 thehte hine] a bacward.

**b.** *intr.* To proceed, go: = DRAW *v.* 68. (Cf. Ger. *ziehen*. The most usual sense in ME.)

*c* **888** K. ÆLFRED *Boeth.* xxxv. § 7 He..teah to wuda. *c* **1122** *O. E. Chron.* an. 1096, Fela..ham tuȝon. *c* **1205** LAY. 18274 Þat folc ut of wude teh. **1297** R. GLOUC. (Rolls) 4370 So gret folc of romeins..þat sone wolleþ out te [*v. r.* teo]. *c* **1300** *Harrow. Hell* 8 Þat alle mosten to helle te. **13..** *Sir Beues* (A.) 501 Forþ þe kniȝtes gonne te, Til þat hii come to þe se. **13..** *E. E. Allit. P.* C. 87, I schal tee in-to Tarce, & tary þere a whyle. *c* **1450** LOVELICH *Grail* lii. 568 Aȝens that knyht ȝe scholen not Te. *c* **1450** *Cov. Myst.* iii. (1841) 33 As to my fadyr, lete us now tee.

† **Tee**, *v.*[2] *Obs. rare.* [OE. *tīon*, *tēon*, contr. from **tīhan*, = OS. *tīhan* in *aftīhan* to refuse, OHG. *zīhan*, MHG. *zīhen* to accuse, show to be guilty, inform against, ON. *tjá* from **tīha* to show, tell, relate, report, Goth. *ga-teihan* to show, make known. Orig. a strong vb. **tīhan* (*táh*, *tigon*, *tigen*), of ablaut series *tīh-*, *taih-*, *tih-*, cognate with Gr. δεικ-νύναι to show, L. *dīc-ĕre* to tell, Skr. *dīç-* to show, point out. But already in OE. confused in inflexion with *téon* from **téohan* to draw, TEE *v.*[1], in consequence of the falling together of the contracted pres. stems *tīo-*, *tēo-*. Rare in ME. In quot. *c* 1440 *tyxste* app. = *tyhst*.] *trans.* To accuse. (In quot. *a* 1300, ? to show, make known; or ? to tell, relate.)

**871–901** *Laws of Ælfred* c. 33 Gif hwa oðerne..tion [*v.r.* teon] wille, þæt he hwelcne ne ȝelæste þara ðe he him ȝesealde [etc.]. *Ibid.* c. 36 § 1 Gif hine mon tio [*v.r.* teo] ȝewealdes on ðære dæde, ȝetriowe hine be þam wite. *c* **1000** ÆLFRIC *Gen.* xxxi. 31 Nu þu me stale tyhst. *Ibid.* xliv. 7 Hwi tihþ ure hlaford us swa micles falses? *a* **1300** *Beket* 1180 Holi churche he aboute dure [*v. r.* a-bouȝte deore] that me tiȝth on wide [*v. r.* tellez of wel wide]. *c* **1440** *York Myst.* xxxii. 287 *Kaiph.*..Fye on the, traytoure attaynte, at þis tyde; Of treasoune þou tyxste hym, þat triste þe for trewe.

**Tee** (tī), *v.*[3] *Golf.* [f. TEE *sb.*[2], and like it app. a clipt form of the 17th c. *teaz*.]

**a.** *trans.* To place (a ball) on the tee. **b.** *intr.* with *off*: To play a ball from the tee.

**1673** *Wedderburn's Vocab.* 37, 38 (Jam.) *Statumina pilam arena*, Teaz your ball on the sand. **1737** [see *teed* below]. **1828** SCOTT *Jrnl.* 14 May, I can only tee the ball; he must strike the blow with the golf club himself. **1862** *Chambers' Encycl.* IV. 823/2 An attendant, called a caddy, who carries his clubs and 'tees' his balls. **1895** LINSKILL *Golf* ii. (ed. 3) 10 To tee a ball for driving, it is usual to place it on some small eminence on the surface of the turf...A ball is sometimes teed on a few short blades of stiff grass. **1895** *Westm. Gaz.* 19 June 7/2 Will any golfer send a shilling to open the subscription? Or, preferably, will the Royal and Ancient tee off? **1906** *Macm. Mag.* Aug. 773 The golfer proceeds to the tee-ing off spot, tees up his ball, mentally imagines that he is standing on a species of gridiron, and places his feet in the position [etc.].

Hence **Teed** (tīd) *ppl. a.*, placed on or played from a tee; **Teeing** (tī·iŋ) *vbl. sb.*; also *attrib.* as **teeing-ground**, a small patch of ground from which the ball is teed off.

**1737** RAMSAY *Scot. Prov.* xxxiii. (1750) 89 That's a tee'd ba'. **1824** SCOTT *Redgauntlet* Let. xiii, All that is managed for ye like a tee'd ball. **1890** *John Bull* 5 Apr. 226/2 Two hundred yards..distance from the teeing-ground. **1893** STEVENSON *Catriona* xviii, They had taken a word from the golfing green, and called me the 'Tee'd Ball'. **1903** *Westm.*

*Gaz.* 11 Sept. 4/2 Far better to recognise that placing is virtually teeing, and have done with it.

**Tee,** *v.*[4] [f. TEE *sb.*[1]] *trans.* To connect or branch off by a tee-piece. (In quot. *absol.*)

**1908** *Installation News* II. 83/1 Bring a ½-in. tube..to the light in the hall, teeing off to the switch on the wall and from thence to the living room lights.

**Tee,** obs. f. TEA; obs. and dial. f. TIE.

**Teeder,** obs. form of TETHER.

**Teedle** (tī·d'l), *v. Sc.* [? Echoic. Cf. *deedle* in *Eng. Dial. Dict.*; also *doodle, toodle, tootle.*] *trans.* To sing (a tune) without words; to hum.

?*a* **1800** *Sc. Song, Had awa frae me Donald* (Jam.), But rock your weeane in a scull And teedle Heelan sing, Matam. **1824** MACTAGGART *Gallovid. Encycl.* (1876) 444 *Teedling*, singing a tune without accompanying it with the words. **1827** SCOTT *Chron. Canongate* v, My little Highland landlady.. stood at the door 'teedling' to herself a Highland song as she shook a table-napkin over the fore-stair.

**Teehee,** variant of TEHEE.

**Tee-hole** (tī·hōul). *dial.* The hole forming the entrance to a bee-hive.

**1669** WORLIDGE *Syst. Agric.* ix. § 3. 160 At the bottom of your little [bee-hive] doors..make an open square place just against the Tee-hole. **1891** DOYLE *White Comp.* vi. I. 110 As thick as bees at a tee-hole.

**Teek,** obs. f. TEAK. **Teel,** dial. var. TILL *v.*

**Teel, teel-oil, teel-seed**: see TIL, sesame.

**Teeld(e,** obs. pa. t. and pple. of TELL *v.*; var. TELD *sb.* and *v. Obs.*, tent. **Teele,** obs. f. TEAL.

**Teem** (tīm), *v.*[1] Forms: 1 tíeman, týman, tíman, tǽman, 1–2 teman, 3 timen, tæmenn (*Orm.*), teamen, tumen(*ü*), 3–5 temen, 3–6 teme, (4 tem, 5 temyn), 6–7 tyeme, 7–8 team, 6– teem. [OE. *tíeman*, etc.:—**taumjan*, f. OE. *téam*:—**taum*: see TEAM *sb.*]

**I.** Belonging to TEAM *sb.* I.

**1.** *trans.* To bring forth, produce, give birth to, bear (offspring). Also *fig. Obs.* or *arch.*

*c* **1000** ÆLFRIC *Hom.* I. 238 Hit bið þonne..þæt 'Nan wer ne wifað, ne wif ne ceorlað, ne team ne bið ʒetymed'. *Ibid.* II. 212 Þæt folc tymde micelne team on ðam westene. *c* **1200** ORMIN 2415 Wurrþenn swa wiþþ childe & tæmenn hire tæm wiþþ himm Alls oþre wimmenn tæmenn? *a* **1225** *Ancr. R.* 220 Two tentacions..þet temeþ alle þe oðre. *c* **1230** *Hali Meid.* 33, & cleopeð ham wunne & weolefulle þat teamen hare teames. **1599** SHAKS. *Hen. V*, v. ii. 51 The euen Meade..Conceiues by idlenesse, and nothing teemes But hatefull Docks, rough Thistles, Keksyes, Burres. **1607** — *Timon* IV. iii. 179 Common Mother, thou Whose wombe vnmeasureable, and infinite brest Teemes and feeds all. **1654** GAYTON *Pleas. Notes* III. viii. 126 My Mother,..whose very picture I am, when she teem'd me under the Line. **1667** MILTON *P. L.* VII. 454 The Earth obey'd, and..teem'd at a Birth Innumerous living Creatures. **1675** PLUME *Life Hacket* (1865) 8 It was but a small lustre..that the place where any man was teemed could cast upon him. **1786** tr. *Swedenborg's True Chr. Relig.* x. § 585 The earth.. being their common mother..brings them forth, that is, teems them from her womb into the open day.

†**2.** *intr.* To bring forth young, bear or produce offspring; to be or become pregnant. *Obs.*

*c* **1000** ÆLFRIC *Gen.* vi. 4 Godes bearn tymdon wið manna dohtra and hiʒ cendon. *c* **1000** — *Hom.* I. 250 Fuʒelas ne tymað swa swa oðre nytenu. *Ibid.* II. 10 Sindon þeah-hwæðere sume ʒesceafta þe tymað buton hæmede..; þæt sind beon. *a* **1023** WULFSTAN *Hom.* xiii. 81 Wa ðam wifum þe þonne tymað. *c* **1200** ORMIN 130 Forr ȝho wass swa bifundenn wif þatt ȝho ne mihhte tæmenn. *a* **1225** *Ancr. R.* 308 Fares & Zaram ne temeð heo neuer. *c* **1250** *Gen. & Ex.* 982 An angel..seide ȝhe sulde sunen wel And timen, and clepen it Ismael. **1532** MORE *Confut. Tindale* Wks. 644/2 Lest it should feble hys fleshe..and hyndre hys harlot of teming. **1591** *Troub. Raigne K. John* (1611) 15 Thou saist she teemde sixe weekes before her time. **1604** SHAKS. *Oth.* IV. i. 256 If that the Earth could teeme with womans teares, Each drop she falls, would proue a Crocodile. **1607** — *Timon* IV. iii. 190. **1636** JAMES *Felix's Octavius* 91 Except Jupiter be waxed old and Juno hath left off teeming.

**3.** *intr.* To be full, as if ready to give birth; to be prolific or fertile; to abound, swarm. Usually const. *with.*

**1593** [see TEEMING *ppl. a.*[1] 2]. *a* **1719** ADDISON (J.), A nation where there is scarce a single head that does not teem with politicks. **1746** SMOLLETT *Reproof* 28 Hallowed be the mouth That teems with moral zeal and dauntless truth! **1748** GRAY *Alliance* 6 The soil, tho' fertile, will not teem in vain. **1802** PALEY *Nat. Theol.* xxvi. (1819) 404 The air, the earth, the water, teem with delighted existence. **1838–9** HALLAM *Hist. Lit.* II. II. v. § 80. 234 Every canto of this book teems with the choicest beauties of imagination. **1840** DICKENS *Barn. Rudge* lxxvii, The house-tops teemed with people. **1868** E. EDWARDS *Ralegh* I. Introd. 33 A mind which ..was still teeming with projects for a good time to come.

**II.** Belonging to TEAM *sb.* III.

†**4.** *trans.* In Anglo-Saxon law: To refer or trace (property), for evidence of ownership, *to* a third person representing the party from whom it was acquired; to vouch to warranty. Only OE.

*a* **700** *Laws Ine* c. 47 Gif mon forstolenne ceap befehð, ne mot hine mon tieman [*v. r.* tyman] to ðeowum men. *Ibid.* c. 75. *a* **800**, **960–975** [see TEAM *sb.* 7].

†**5.** *intr.* To refer or appeal *to* for confirmation or testimony. *To God I teme*, I call God to witness. Also *trans.* To cite or call to witness (quot. *c* 1200).

*c* **1000** ÆLFRIC *Saints' Lives* (1881) I. 58 Benedictus..tymde to þam reʒole þe Basilius ʒesette. *c* **1000** *St. Basil's Admonitio* Prol. (1849) 32 Benedictus..tymde swa ðeah to Basilies tæcinge for his trumnysse. *c* **1200** *Moral Ode* 108 (Trin. MS.) His oȝen werc and his þanc to witnesse he sal temen. *a* **1300** *Cursor M.* 5070 (Cott.) And al was for i tald a drem Þat cummen es now, to godd i tem. *Ibid.* 12797. *Ibid.* 14791 Þe bok is wittnes for to tem.

†**6.** *intr.* To attach oneself (*to* any one) in fealty, dependence, trust, or love; to turn or draw *to. Obs.*

*c* **1205** LAY. 1265 He bi-heihte hire biheste & he hit wel laste þat to hire he wolde teman [*c* 1275 hire wolde he louie] & wrchen hire ane temple. *Ibid.* 16800 Al hit trukeð us an hond þæt we to temden. *Ibid.* 24816 Ȝif þu i þissen twælf wiken temest to þan rihten and þu wult of Rome þolien æi dome. **1303** R. BRUNNE *Handl. Synne* 9546 Al þat euer to Cryst wyl teme, Behoueþ be baptysed yn watyr and creme. **13..** *St. Erkenwolde* 15 in Horstm. *Altengl. Leg.* (1881) 266 He turnyd temples þat tyme þat temyd to þe deuelle. **13..** *E. E. Allit. P.* C. 316 Ȝet surely I hope, Efte to trede on þy temple & teme to þy seluen. *c* **1400** *Destr. Troy* 3306 Tho truly þat are takon and temyn to you, Shalbe plesit with plenty at þere playne wille.

†**7.** *trans.* To acclaim (as lord); to offer or dedicate (to God); to bring into a position or condition.

*c* **1205** LAY. 1956 He wes ihaten Brutus..þa Troinisce men þa temden hine to hærre [*c* 1275 makede hine louerd]. **13..** *Cursor M.* 6170 (Cott.) Þe forbirth o þair barnitem Fra þan þai suld to drightin tem. *c* **1384** CHAUCER *H. Fame* III. 654 But myghten temen vs opon bere.

†**8.** *intr.* or *refl.* To betake oneself, to repair, go, proceed *to*; *trans.* to repair to (q. *c* 1330). *Obs.*

*c* **1205** LAY. 1245 Albion hatte þat lond..Þer to þu scalt teman [*c* 1275 wende] & ane neowe Troye þar makian. *Ibid.* 7174 He hehte Tenancius to Cornwale temen [*c* 1275 wende]. *Ibid.* 27919 Arður ȝæf him þene tun and he þer to tumde [*v. r.* tumbde]. *c* **1320** *Sir Tristr.* 431 For drede þai wald him slo, He temed him to þe king. *c* **1330** R. BRUNNE *Chron. Wace* (Rolls) 11177 Fot-folk þat come to & fro, Innes for to teme & take.

†**b.** *intr.* To lead *to* (an issue). *Obs.*

*c* **1205** LAY. 9135 Ic wolde iwite æt þe..to whan þis tocne wule ten, to wulche þinge temen.

**Teem** (tīm), *v.*[2] Now *dial.* and *techn.* Forms: 4–6 teme, 5 *Sc.* teym, 6 *Sc.* teim, 7 teame, teeme, 7–9 team, 8 tem, 7– teem. [ME. *tēme-n*, a. ON. *tœma* (Sw. *tömma*, Da. *tömme*) to empty:—**tōmjan*, f. *tómr* empty, TOOM.]

**1.** *trans.* **a.** To empty (a vessel, etc.); to discharge or remove the contents of; to empty (a wagon, etc.).

*a* **1300** *Cursor M.* 12020 Bath he ditted þe water lade, And temed lakes þat he made. *a* **1340** HAMPOLE *Psalter* lxvii. 27 Fayre saules, þat has temyd þaire fleyss, and driyd it of þe humor of syn. *c* **1375** *Sc. Leg. Saints* xxv. (*Julian*) 544 Scho..temyt þe poyttis thre. *c* **1440** *Promp. Parv.* 488/1 Temyn or maken empty.., *vacuo, evacuo.* *c* **1470** HENRY *Wallace* VIII. 213 Saidlys thai teym off hors bot maistris thar. **1500–20** DUNBAR *Poems* xxxviii. 36 The fetteris lowsit and the dungeoun temit. **1596** DALRYMPLE tr. *Leslie's Hist. Scot.* IV. (S. T. S.) 204 Quhen he had teimed the hartes of mony of the foul puddil of errour and vice. **1650** H. MORE *Observ.* in *Enthus. Tri.*, etc. (1656) 92 Magicus will not stick to teem Urinals on your heads. **1789** BRAND *Hist. Newcastle* II. 684 *note*, Above ground..two banksmen..take off the corves at top, and empty, or, as the workmen call it, 'teem' them. **1854** MISS BAKER *Northampt. Gloss., Teem*, to empty, to pour out. 'Teem the tub.'

**b.** To discharge (something out of or from a vessel, a cart, etc.); to empty out, pour out.

**1482** *Burgh Rec. Edinb.* (1869) I. 45 Gudis ventit or temyt in the rade havin or toun of Leith. **1562** TURNER *Baths* 5 They teme or emptye out euel humores. **1648** HERRICK *Hesper., To Primroses*, Just as the modest morne Teem'd her refreshing dew. **1729** SWIFT *Direct. Servants, Butler*, You immediately teem out the remainder of the ale into the tankard. **1812** J. J. HENRY *Camp. agst. Quebec* 96 The contents were teemed into a large bason. **1863** MRS. GASKELL *Sylvia's L.* II. xv. 13 Better help her t' teem t' milk. **1863** MRS. TOOGOOD *Yorks. Dial.*, Team the water out of the kettle. **1889** *Q. Rev.* July 138 Blister steel is..poured or 'teemed' into suitable ingot moulds.

**c.** *absol.*

**1641** BEST *Farm. Bks.* (Surtees) 36 Wee have allwayes one man.. whose office is to helpe to teame, that the waines be not hindered. **1855** J. R. LEIFCHILD *Cornwall Mines* 38 Six men were teaming from the bottom into the pump. **1896** *Warwickshire Gloss.*, This teapot don't teem well.

**2.** *intr.* Of water, etc.: To pour, flow in a stream, flow copiously; of rain: to pour.

**1828** *Craven Gloss.* s.v., It rains and teems. *a* **1846** G. DARLEY *Song*, '*Sweet in her green dell*' ii, Down from the high cliffs the rivulet is teeming. *a* **1880** *Jack & William* ii. in Child *Eng. & Sc. Pop. Ball.* (1884) I. 444/2 The blood was teeming down. **1880** *Leeds Mercury* 13 Sept. 8 The water then came teeming down the shafts.

Hence **Teem** *sb. dial.*, a 'pour', a downpour of rain: see *Eng. Dial. Dict.*

†**Teem,** *v.*[3] *Obs. rare*[−1]. [app. either the simple root-verb of BETEEM *v.*[1], or perh. more prob. shortened from that vb.] *intr.* To think fit, vouchsafe.

**1593** GIFFORD *Dial. Witches* B j b, Alas man, I could teeme it to goe, and some counsell me to goe to the man at T. B. and some to the woman at R. H.

**Teem,** *a. dial.*, empty: see TOOM. **Teem, -e,** obs. or dial. ff. TEAM. **Teeme,** obs. f. THEME.

**Teemer**[1] (tī·məɹ). *rare.* [f. TEEM *v.*[1] + -ER[1].] One who or that which teems or gives birth.

**1646** H. P. *Medit. Seige* 69 But such hastie teemers many times bring forth blind whelpes.

**Teemer**[2] (tī·məɹ). Now *dial.* and *techn.* Also *erron.* teamer. [f. TEEM *v.*[2] + -ER[1].] One who teems, empties, or unloads.

**1667**? MARVELL in *Roxb. Ball.* (1883) IV. 546 Weeping to see their sons degenerate: His Romans taking up the teemer's trade, The Britons jigging it in masquerade. **1866** J. E. BROGDEN *Provinc. Words Lincolnsh.* 204 *Teamer*, the man who empties the grain from a laden cart to the stack. **1891** *Labour Commission Gloss., Teemers*, men employed at the top of the coal-shoots by means of which coal is tipped into the hold of the vessel. **1894** *Northumbld. Gloss., Teemer*, the man at a coal shipping staith who lets the coal out of the waggons.

**Teemful** (tī·mfŭl), *a.*[1] [app. f. TEEM *v.*[1] + -FUL: cf. *forgetful*. OE. had *téamfull*, f. TEAM *sb.*, in the same sense.] Prolific, productive, fruitful, teeming. Hence **Tee·mfulness,** prolificness.

[*a* **1000** *Gloss.* in Wr.-Wülcker 238/3 *Fetose*, tudderfulle, teamfulle, *uel* tuddre. *c* **1000** *Lambeth Ps.* cxliii. 13 Sceap heora teamfulle & berende.] **1755** JOHNSON, *Teemful*, pregnant, prolifick. **1855** SINGLETON *Virgil* I. 34 As standing corn To teemful tilths,—so thou all grace to thine. *Ibid.* 47 But do thou, if teemfulness Our flock shall have recruited, be of gold. **1863** G. H. CALVERT *Gentlem.* vi. 79 Exhilarated by hope,—which is the teemful mother of the ideal.

**Teem-full, teemful** (tī·mfu·l), *a.*[2] *dial.* Also team-. [f. TEEM *v.*[2] + FULL *a.*] See quots.

**1674** RAY *N. C. Words* 47 *Teamful*, Brim-ful, having as much as can be teemed in. **1727** BAILEY vol. II, *Teemful*, full up to the Top. **1787** in GROSE *Provinc. Gloss.* **1876** *Whitby Gloss., Teeam-full*, brim-full; requiring to be poured out. *c* **1900** in most northern glossaries: see E. D. D.

**Teeming** (tī·miŋ), *vbl. sb.*[1] [f. TEEM *v.*[1] + -ING[1].] The action of TEEM *v.*[1]

†**1.** The production or bringing forth of offspring; breeding; child-bearing. Also *fig. Obs.*

*c* **1430** *Hymns Virg.* 4 Heil þat alle wommen on doon calle in temynge, whanne þei ben hard bistadde! **1540** HYRDE tr. *Vives' Instr. Chr. Wom.* II. ix. (1557) 104 To haue enui at other for their beautie, & their welfare, or plentous teming. **1549** COVERDALE, etc. *Erasm. Par. Rom.* 10 Thoughe hymself was feble, and his wyfe lykewyse passed temyng. **1607** MARKHAM *Caval.* I. (1617) 50 The onely time of danger is at the first conception, and at the time of teeming. **1672** MARVELL *Reh. Transp.* I. 148 Mr. Bayes in the Preface of his Defence to excuse his long teeming before it were brought forth. **1705** HICKERINGILL *Priest-cr.* III. Wks. 1716 III. 160 They were Twins..and if old Eve had miscarried of them at her first Teeming, I think it had been no great loss.

†**b.** *concr.* Offspring, produce, progeny. *Obs.*

**1654** WHITLOCK *Zootomia* 429 The Suns..that shined with gladding Influences, on worthy Teemings of a fruitfull Brain.

**2.** Abundant productiveness, fecundity, fertility, fruitfulness.

**1856** DOVE *Logic Chr. Faith* v. i. § 2. 279 The prolific teeming of the everbearing World. **1879** *Times* 6 Sept., The rushing of water from the..rills keeps pace with the teeming of the earth and with the ripening of its fruits.

**3.** *attrib.* and *Comb.*: †**teeming-date, teeming-time,** breeding-time, reproductive period.

**1593** SHAKS. *Rich. II*, v. ii. 91 Is not my teeming date drunke vp with time? *a* **1700** *Roxb. Ball.* (1890) VII. 117 And Teeming-time we are loath to lose, and why should not Damsels go? **1737** FIELDING *Tumble-down Dick* Wks. (1766) 251/1 What shall I do to get another son, For now, alas! my teeming-time is done?

**Tee·ming,** *vbl. sb.*[2] Now *dial.* and *techn.* Also *erron.* teaming. [f. TEEM *v.*[2] + -ING[1].] The action of emptying, pouring out, or unloading; *spec.* the pouring of the molten steel into the ingot-moulds in steel-manufacture. Also *attrib.*

**1641** BEST *Farm. Bks.* (Surtees) 36 Wee usually leade to one place till such time as it beginne to bee troublesome teaminge, and then goe wee to another. **1840** *Civil Eng. & Arch. Jrnl.* III. 391/2 The wagons when teamed retaining a third of their contents plastered to the sides and bottom, and so requiring double the time for teaming. **1875** KNIGHT *Dict. Mech.* 1183/2 The operation of pouring the metal is called teaming. **1877** *Ibid.*, *Teeming-punch*, one for starting or driving a bolt out of a hole. A drift.

**Tee·ming,** *ppl. a.*[1] [f. TEEM *v.*[1] + -ING[2].]

**1.** That bears or breeds offspring; pregnant, gravid, 'breeding'. *arch.* and *dial.*

**1535** *Goodly Primer, Litany*, That teeming women may have joyful speed in their labour. **1593** DRAYTON *Eclogues* x. 46 Their teeming Eawes to helpe when they did yeane. **1676** GREW *Anat. Flowers* II. i. § 3 As Teeming Women, gradually slaken their Laces. *a* **1719** ADDISON tr. *Ovid, Calisto* 99 A lovely boy the teeming rival bore. **1822** SCOTT *Pirate* iv, Mrs. Yellowley had a remarkable dream, as is the usual practice of teeming mothers previous to the birth of an illustrious offspring.

†**b.** Fructifying; germinating, sprouting. *Obs.*

**1704** POPE *Windsor For.* 53 Kind seasons swell'd the teeming grain. **1835** URE *Phil. Manuf.* 231 The teeming seed is now covered with a sheet of paper pierced with holes.

**2.** Abundantly productive; fertile, prolific.

**1593** SHAKS. *Rich. II*, II. i. 51 This blessed plot, this earth, this Realme, this England, This Nurse, this teeming wombe of Royall Kings. *c* **1600** — *Sonn.* xcvii, The teeming Autumne big with ritch increase. **1768** BEATTIE *Minstr.* II. l, Where Nature loads the teeming plain With the full pomp of vegetable store. **1840** DICKENS *Barn. Rudge* xl, The plan..which had suggested itself to the teeming brain of his..commander.

**b.** *transf.* Abounding; swarming; crowded.

**1715** *Pattern True Love* in Halliw. *Yorks. Anthol.* (1851) 13 Odd tales which heretofore Did so amuse the teeming throng. **1725** POPE *Odyss.* IV. 240 With teeming plenty to reward their toil. **1838** PRESCOTT *Ferd. & Is.* (1846) II. ix. 464 The teeming treasures of the Indies. **1869** TOZER *Highl. Turkey* II. 202 The teeming multitudes which must have crowded the cities. *a* **1873** DEUTSCH *Rem.* (1874) 136 It shews us the teeming streets of Jerusalem.

Hence **Tee·mingly** *adv.*, productively; **Tee·mingness,** productiveness, fecundity.

**1674** N. FAIRFAX *Bulk & Selv.* 120 The hand giving a

kind of teemingness to the spring. **1895** *Clarion* 2 Nov. 1/4 Our cause spreads teemingly.

**Tee·ming,** *ppl. a.*[2] Now *dial.* [f. TEEM *v.*[2] + -ING [2].] That 'teems' or pours, pouring.

**1695** LD. PRESTON *Boeth.* I. 2 The weeping Muse..whose teeming Eyes Keep time with her's. **1880** A. B. TODD *Poet. Wks.* (1907) 222 The streams, swoln by the teeming rain.

**Tee·mless,** *a. rare.* [f. TEEM *v.*[1] + -LESS.] Not bringing forth young or fruit; barren.

**1687** DRYDEN *Hind & P.* I. 228 Such fiery tracks of dearth Their zeal has left, and such a teemless earth.

**Teen** (tīn), *sb.*[1] *arch.* Forms: 1–3 téona, (1 téon, teane), 1–5 teone, (3 tuone, toune, tone), 4 (*Ayenb.*) tyene, 3–6 tene, (4 tean), 4–5 ten, 4–5 (6 *Sc.*) teyn(e, 4–7 teene, (5 tyune, tuene), 6 *Sc.* teine, 6–9 *Sc.* tein, 6– teen. [OE. *téona* masc. hurt, trouble = OFris. *tiona, tiuna* injury, OS. *tiono* wrong, injury; also OE. *téon* neut. = ON. *tjón* neut. and fem. damage, loss. Cf. OFris. *tiona, tiuna* vb. to injure: see TEEN *v.*[1]]

†**1.** Harm inflicted or suffered; injury, hurt, mischief; damage. *Obs.*

**971** *Blickl. Hom.* 51 Æt þæm ytmestan dæge eal hit him wyrþ to teonan. *c* **975** *Rushw. Gosp.* Matt. xx. 13 Freond, ne do ic ðe teane. *c* **1000** *Ags. Gosp.* ibid., Eala þu freond, ne do ic þe nænne teonan. *c* **1175** *Lamb. Hom.* 15 Ne do he þe neure swa muchelne teone. *c* **1205** LAY. 6013 While he dude us tuone [*c* **1275** teone]. *a* **1300** *Cursor M.* 7980 (Cott.) His fas philistiens, Þat had don him mani tenis [*v. r.* -es]. *c* **1400** *Rule St. Benet* 978 It be-houes folk of religioun Suffer tenes & tribulacioun. **1590** SPENSER *F. Q.* I. xii. 18 Gainst that proud Paynim king that works her teene. **1609** HOLLAND *Amm. Marcell.* xxxi. i. 399 Working much teene and losse.

**2.** Irritation, vexation, annoyance; anger, wrath, rage; spite, ill-will, malice. *Obs.* exc. *Sc.*

*c* **1200** ORMIN 19606, & forrþi let he takenn himm To wrekenn hise tene. **1340** *Ayenb.* 66 Þe dyeuel beginþ þet uer of tyene and euel wyl uor to becleppe. **1362** LANGL. *P. Pl.* A. VIII. 100 Pers for puire teone pollede hit a-sonder. *c* **1386** CHAUCER *Knt.'s T.* 2248 Neuere was ther no word hem bitwene Of Ialousie or any oother tene. *c* **1400** *Destr. Troy* 1978 Lest the tyrand in his tene hade turnyt hym to sle. *c* **1500** *Lancelot* 3237 So hard o knycht he strykith in his ten. **1613–16** W. BROWNE *Brit. Past.* II. iv, Before a tempest's rough regardlesse teene. **1690** W. WALKER *Idiomat. Anglo-Lat.* 534, I will wreak my teen on them. **1719** RAMSAY *2nd Answ. to Hamilton* xi, Pegh, fry, and girn, wi' spite and teen. **1819** W. TENNANT *Papistry Storm'd* (1827) 37 He waxed wud wi' vera teen.

†**b.** *transf.* Something vexatious, a cause of annoyance; a trouble. *Obs.*

**971** *Blickl. Hom.* 47 Þis weorc biþ deoflum se mæsta teona. *c* **1275** LAY. 10087 Ac he ne lifuede noht longe; þat was mochel teone [*c* **1205** Þat wes his leodene hærm]. **13..** *Gaw. & Gr. Knt.* 1008 For to telle þerof hit me tene were. **1496** *Dives & Paup.* (W. de W.) IV. ix. 172 The fooll child is wrathe & tene of his fader, and sorowe of his moder.

**3.** Affliction, trouble, suffering, grief, woe. *arch.*

*c* **1290** *Beket* 1533 in *S. Eng. Leg.* I. 150 Ȝwane a man is In mest soruwe and teone, Þanne is ore louerdes grace next. *a* **1300** *Cursor M.* 10472 Vp sco ras and yod a-wai, And went hir þeþen in tene and trei. **13..** in *Pol. Rel. & L. Poems* (1866) 224 Teone and trauail shal beo my lif. **1387–8** T. USK *Test. Love* I. i. (Skeat) l. 13 Mirth is chaunged in to tene. **1393** LANGL. *P. Pl.* C. XIV. 7 Abraam for al hus good hadde muche teene, In gret pouerte he was yput. *c* **1460** *Towneley Myst.* iii. 533 With tray and with teyn and dreed mekill wogh. **1556** LAUDER *Tractate* 488 Syne turne ȝour myrth and Ioye in teine. **1594** SHAKS. *Rich. III*, IV. i. 97 Each howres ioy wrackt with a weeke of teene. *c* **1620** *Verses Death R. W.* in Farr *S. P. Jas. I* (1848) 103 Such is the verse compos'd in mournefull teene. **1719** D'URFEY *Pills* (1872) IV. 268 And bloody Knife did end the Smart, Which she sustained in woful Teen. **1801** WORDSW. *Cuckoo & Night.* xxxviii, The God of Love afflict thee with all teen. **1885–94** R. BRIDGES *Eros & Psyche* Aug. xxi, The wan face spent with tears and teen.

**b.** Trouble or pains taken about something. *arch.*

**1377** LANGL. *P. Pl.* B. VI. 135 Ȝe wasten þat men wynnen with trauaille and with tene. **1435** MISYN *Fire of Love* II. i. 70 Contemplacion in greet tynn & with greet labour is gettyn. **1600** TOURNEUR *Transf. Metamorph.* lxxvi, Much teen they bide in search for such an one. **1880** *Contemp. Rev.* Mar. 428 Art's high toil and teen.

† **c.** Pain, physical suffering. *Obs.*

*c* **1400** *Song Roland* 632 He shall tell in the town, who the tale heris, That it is correct, for tean of his eyres. *c* **1430** LYDG. *Min. Poems* (Percy Soc.) 133 For hunger I [Chichevache] feele so grete teene. ? *a* **1500** *Chester Pl.* (Shaks. Soc.) I. 224 Lazarre..Lyeth sicke..And suffereth moche teene.

†**4.** Name of a disease of hawks. *Obs.*

**1486** *Bk. St. Albans* B vj b, A medicine for an hawke that hath the teyne. An hawke that hath the teyne..will paute more for oon batyng then an other for iiii. **1678** PHILLIPS (ed. 4), *Teine*, a disease in Hawks that makes them pant,.. growing heavy, and losing her breath when she flies.

†**5.** Phr. *To take teen*, ? to take heed.

Perhaps a different word. (But not an error for *tent.*)

? *a* **1500** *Chester Pl.* vi. 734 Her hand roted, as you have seene, Wherby you may take good teene, That unbeleefe is a foule synne.

**Teen** (tīn), *sb.*[2] Usually in pl. **teens** (tīnz). [The element -TEEN in numerals treated as a separate word, usually in plural.]

**1.** *pl.* The years of the life of any person (*rarely*, of the age of anything) of which the numbers end in *-teen*, i.e. from thirteen to nineteen; chiefly in phrases *in, out of one's teens.*

**1673** WYCHERLEY *Gentl. Dancing Master* IV. i, Your poor young things, when they are once in the teens, think they shall never be married. **1693** *Humours Town* 98 A young Girl in the Teens. **1709** E. W. *Life Donna Rosina* 10 Her Daughter, who was by this time come into the Teens. **1763** CHURCHILL *Proph. Famine* 3 The stripling raw, just enter'd in his teens. **1809** MALKIN *Gil Blas* I. i. ⁋ 1 A chamber-maid who was not exactly in her teens. **1818** KEATS *Let* Wks. 1889 III. 101 Your friendship for me is now getting into its teens. **1883** *Fortn. Rev.* Feb. 296 The Republic, in the art of government..is still in its teens.

*β. sing.* **1834** T. HAWKINS *Mem. Ichthyosauri* 30, I was too young..and as inquisitive as a boy in his first 'teen' could possibly be. *attrib.* **1886** RUSKIN *Præterita* I. viii. 252 It must have been about the beginning of the teen period.

**b.** *transf. pl.* Young persons in their teens.

**1820** I. TAYLOR (*title*) Advice to the Teens; or, Practical Helps to the Formation of Character.

**2.** The numbers of which the names end in *-teen.*

**1885** *Blackw. Mag.* Apr. 548/1 We are to change the small hours of our afternoons into teens and twenties.

Hence **Tee·ner**, one in his or her teens; **Tee·nhood**, the state of being in one's teens; **Tee·ning** *a.*, in one's teens; **Tee·nish** *a.*, characteristic of persons in their teens, youthful.

**1894** BLACKMORE *Perlycross* 242 This rigid man was wound round the finger of a female '*teener'—as the Americans beautifully express it. **1893** *Scott. Leader* 14 Aug. 2 Whilst in her *teenhood she was placed with Mr. and Mrs. Charles Kean. **1818** *Religio Clerici* 169 *Teening misses, for a day-school prize, Transpose the types, and mar the prophecies. **1811** *Morn. Post* 20 Dec., Their *teenish tricks, at fifty-six, all wise folks should forego. **1818** *Blackw. Mag.* IV. 256 She's just of age! shall teenish frailties wrong her?

†**Teen,** *a.* Chiefly *north. Eng.* and *Sc. Obs.* Forms: 4–5 teyn(e, 4–6 tene, 6 teene, 7 teen. [app. f. TEEN *sb.*[1]]

**1.** Angry, vexed, enraged.

**13..** *E. E. Allit. P.* B. 1808 Entyses hym to be tene, telles [*MS.* telled] vp his wrake; Ande clannes is his comfort, and coyntyse he louyes. *c* **1375** *Sc. Leg. Saints* xxviii. (*Margaret*) 542 Þane wes þe tyrand vondir tene Quhene he hard þis of þe maydine clene. *c* **1400** *Melayne* 710 Kyng Charls..At the byschoppe was so tene. **1536** BELLENDEN *Cron. Scot.* (1821) I. 202 He wox sa tene, that he gart drown this woman. **1570** *Satir. Poems Reform.* xxi. 53 It suld ȝow mufe all to be tene. **1674** RAY *N. C. Words* 47 *Teen*, angry. **1828** *Craven Gloss.*, *Teen*, angry.

**2.** Vexatious; troublesome, distressing.

*c* **1470** *Golagros & Gaw.* 33 With outin beilding of blis, of bern or of byre; Bot torris and tene wais, teirfull quha tellis.

¶ **3.** ? Corruption of *keen. rare.*

**1579** LYLY *Euphues* (Arb.) 34 The freshest colours soonest fade, the teenest Rasor soonest tourneth his edge. **1580** *Ibid.* 249 Setting a teene edge, wher thou desirest to haue a sharp poynt. [*So edd.* 1580–1587; *edd.* 1595– keenest, keen.]

†**Teen,** *v.*[1] *Obs.* or *dial.* Forms: *a.* 1 téonian, 3–4 teone(n, 3–6 tene, 4 tyeny, 4–6 teyn (*pa. t.* and *pple.* teind, teynt), 4–7 teene, (5 tuene, 6 *pa. t.* teynd, 7 *pa. pple.* teend). *β.* 1 *tíenan, týnan, 4 (*Ayenb.*) tyenen. [*a.* OE. *téonian*, f. *téon*:—**tiun-*, TEEN *sb.*[1] = OS. (*ge*)*tiuneian*:—**tiunôjan.* *β.* OE. **tíenan, týnan*:—**tiunjan* = ON. *týna*, ODa., Sw. dial. *tyne* to injure, destroy, lose; see TINE; thence in 14th c. Kentish, *tyeny.*]

**1.** *trans.* **a.** To vex, irritate, annoy, anger, enrage.

*a. c* **1000** *Lambeth Ps.* cv. 16 Et irritaverunt *gl.* And hy teonedon *uel* hiȝ gremedon. *a* **1225** *Ancr. R.* 118 Pellican is..so wreðful þet hit sleað ofte uor grome his owune briddes, hwon heo teoneð him. **1362** LANGL. *P. Pl.* A. XI. 136 Bote Teologye haþ teoned [B. x. 180 tened; C. XII. 129 teened] me ten score tymes; For þe more I muse þeron þe mistiloker hit semeþ. *c* **1440** *Promp. Parv.* 489/1 Tenyn, or wrethyn, or ertyn.., *irrito.* **1496** *Dives & Paup.* (W. de W.) VII. iv. 279 Ne tene, ne angre thou not the poore in his myscheue. **1522** *World & Child* in Hazl. *Dodsley* I. 251 There is no emperor so keen, That dare me lightly tene. *a* **1825** FORBY *Voc. E. Anglia*, *Teen*, *v.* to trouble; to vex.

*β.* **971** *Blickl. Hom.* 47 Ne ablinnan we..þæt we Gode cwemon, & deofol tynan, dæges & nihtes. *c* **1000** *St. Basil's Admon.* iv. (1849) 44 Se wellwillenda man wyle..forberan ȝif hine man ahwær tynð. *c* **1000** *Laws of Ethelred* VI. c. 48 And þæt hy ælþeodiȝe men..ne tyrian ne ne tynan.

**b.** To inflict suffering upon; to afflict, harass; to injure, harm.

*c* **1275** *Orison of our Lord* 22 in *O. E. Misc.* 139 Wunderliche þurh wacche and fast þi swete lychome þu teonedest. **13..** *E. E. Allit. P.* B. 759 If þat twenty be trwe I tene hem no more. **1362** LANGL. *P. Pl.* A. VII. 40 Loke þou teone [**1377** B. VI. 39 tene; **1393** C. IX. 36 tene, *v. r.* tuene] no tenaunt bote treuþe wol assente. *c* **1400** *Destr. Troy* 8228 Then the grekes..turnit to the Troiens, tenit hom full euill. *c* **1430** *Hymns Virg.* 62 Quod wraþþe, 'loke þou bere þee bolde; What man þee teene, His heed þou breest'.

**c.** To cause (physical) pain or injury to; to hurt.

**1399** LANGL. *Rich. Redeles* III. 79 Þey bablid with her billis how þei bete were And tenyd with twiggis two and twenty ȝeris. *c* **1460** J. RUSSELL *Bk. Nurture* 319 Hold alwey thy knyfe sure, þy self not to tene. *a* **1550** *Christis Kirke Gr.* x, That torment so him teynd. **1607** WALKINGTON *Opt. Glass* xi. 121 The body is teend and accloid with divers.. maladies.

**2.** To cause grief or sorrow to; to grieve, distress: in various const. **a.** *trans.*; also *absol.*

*a* **1300** *Cursor M.* 10470 Þan was soruful son dame anna, Quen vtaine hir had tened [*v. r.* greuid] sua. *Ibid.* 15694 To wacken þam ne wald he noght, þat teind war wit trai. **1340** *Ayenb.* 142 Alle wordes him tyeneþ and greueþ, bote yef hi ne by to god, oþer of god, oþer uor god. *Ibid.* 161 And þus beginþ þis wordle to tyeny..þe more þet tyeneþ þis lif, þe more me wylneþ þet oþer. *c* **1430** *Pilgr. Lyf Manhode* II. cxxix. (1869) 125 Ootheres ioye teeneth me; ootheres sorwe is my mete.

**b.** *impersonal* = grieves.

*a* **1300** *Cursor M.* 19119 (Cott.) At þair talking þam tenid sare [*Trin.* Hem tened sore]. **14..** *Tundale's Vis.* (Wagner) 2288 Fulle sore hym tened at hymself than.

**c.** *refl.* To be vexed, to be angry; to distress oneself, grieve, be grieved.

*a* **1300** *Cursor M.* 10462 (Cott.) Vtaine hir can wit þis to tene. **1340** *Ayenb.* 73 Nou loke eftzone a lyte, and ne tyene þe naȝt, to þise þri þinges. *Ibid.* 99 Þet non ne ssolde him tyeny hit uorto zigge. **1362** LANGL. *P. Pl.* A. II. 83 Þen teonede him Teologye whon he þis tale herde. *c* **1400** *Destr. Troy* 4600 If ye tary ouer tyme þai tene hom þereat.

**d.** *intr.* (for *refl.*) = c.

**13..** *Cursor M.* 10462 (Gött.) Vtayne wid þis word gan tene. *a* **1400–50** *Alexander* 2193 Þen tened þe Thebees folke. *c* **1460** *Towneley Myst.* iii. 210 We women may wary all ill husbandis; I haue oone, bi mary!..If he teyn I must tary how so euer it standis. **1566** DRANT *Horace* A vij, [He] teenes if that his neyghbours goate a bygger bagge doth beare Then his. **1611** COTGR. s. v. *Dueil*, They tiple now as much as erst they teend.

Hence †**Tee·ning** *vbl. sb.*, injuring, wrong-doing; affliction; sorrowing, grief.

*a* **1200** *Moral Ode* 253 Þe luueden tening and stale. *a* **1300** *Cursor M.* 24439 (Cott.), I sagh him dei, i sorud ai,..Mi tening es sa togh.

**Teen,** *v.*[2] dial. form (chiefly Kentish) of TINE (OE. *týnan*) to fence, hedge in, make a hedge with raddles: see TINE. Hence **Tee·nage, Tee·net, -it**, brushwood for fences and hedges; **Tee·ner**, a man who teens or keeps in order a raddle fence; **Teen-hedge**, a pleached or raddle hedge.

*c* **1700** KENNETT *MS. Lansd. 1033*, lf. 389 To **Teen* (Lanc. to *Tine*), to hedge or to enclose a field, in Kent the longer wood cut for the use of hedghing is calld **Teenage*. **1706** PHILLIPS (ed. Kersey), *Teenage*, (Country-word) Brush-wood for Hedges or Fences. **1902** *Kentish Express* 29 Mar. 10/2 (*N. & Q.* 10th Ser. XI. 57/2) For sale, stakes, binders, *tenet, peasticks, good cheap, to clear. **1616** *MS. Acc. St. John's Hosp., Canterb.*, For bread and drink for the *teners and wood-makers. **1638** *Ibid.*, Payd.. for brishinge of the *teene-hedge downe *js. vjd.*

**Teen,** obs. or dial. f. *tend*, TIND *v.* to kindle, TINE *v.* to lose; dial. f. TEIND.

**-teen** (tīn), combining element. [OE. *-*tiene*, *-týne, -téne*, ME. *-tēne* = OFris. *-tēna, -tīne*, OS. *-tein* (*-tian*), LG. *-tein*, Du. *-tien*, OHG. *-zehan* (*-zeheni*), Ger. *-zehn.*] An inflected form of TEN, added to the simple numerals from *three* to *nine*, to form the names of those from *thirteen* to *nineteen.*

Hence **-teenth** (-tīnþ), forming ordinal numerals from the cardinals in *-teen*, from *thirteenth* to *nineteenth*. In ME. this took the place of earlier *-teþe*, OE. *téoþe*: cf. TENTH and -TH.

In early OE., as in the cognate langs., the simple numerals, from four upwards, had an inflected and an uninflected form, the latter commonly used before a sb., *seofon dagas*, the former in other positions, e.g. *swa ealle seofone*. The inflected forms were sbs. of the *-i* declension, with nominative pl. in *-e* (neut. *-u, -o*). Subsequently these forms were levelled, the numerals up to *twelve* retaining the uninflected form, those from thirteen to nineteen the inflected, as *teon, ten, fiftēne, fifteen.* In ME. the final *-e* of *-tēne, -teene* became mute; in mod. Eng. *-teen* it is no longer written, but the stem vowel remains long.

These compounds had originally the stress on the first element (þɜ·ɹtīn), as in *drei·zehn, tre·decim, tre·dici*, δώδεκα, etc. In modern Eng. this is retained in counting: 'twelve, thi·rteen, fou·rteen, fi·fteen', etc., also before *hundred*, as 'ei·ghteen hu·ndred and ni·nety'; but before a sb. there is a secondary stress on *-teen*, as 'ei·ghtee·n me·n'. Otherwise the two elements have usually equal stress, *thi·rtee·n, se·ventee·n, ei·ghtee·n*, which in the pause may become:—· (not —·), as 'at the age of thi·rtee·n', 'sweet se·ventee·n'. This stressing may have arisen to distinguish them clearly from the numerals in *-ty*: 'not se·ventee·n but se·venty'; 'the fo·rty days have been reduced to fou·rtee·n'. The stressing of the ordinals in *-teenth* follows the same lines.

**Teenage**: see TEEN *v.*[2]

**Teend,** obs. f. TEIND, tithe, *tend* TIND *v.* to kindle. **Teener**: see TEEN *sb.*[2], TEEN *v.*[2]

†**Tee·nful,** *a. Obs.* or *dial.* Forms: see TEEN *sb.*[1] [OE. *téonful*, ME. *teneful*, f. TEEN *sb.*[1] + -FUL.] Full of 'teen': see TEEN *sb.*[1]

**1.** Causing trouble or sorrow; vexatious, troublesome, painful, grievous, distressing.

*c* **1000** *Ags. Ps.* (Spelman) lxxvii. 10 Mægþ teonful, *generatio exasperans.* *a* **1023** WULFSTAN *Hom.* I. (1883) 273 Hu læne and hu lyðre þis lif is, hu sarlic and hu sorhful and hu ȝeswincful and hu teonful. *a* **1300** *E. E. Psalter* lxxviii. 8 Þat þai ne be als þar fadres fals, Getynge wik and tene-fulle als. **1340–70** *Alisaunder* 282 Hee made a uery uow auenged too beene Of þat teenefull tach þat hee tooke þere. *c* **1350** *Will. Palerne* 2666 Ȝe grettli aren a-greued..For þise tenful trauayles. *c* **1425** *Cast. Persev.* 1755 in *Macro Plays* 129 Teneful talys I may þee sey. *a* **1825** FORBY *Voc. E. Anglia*, *Teenful*, troublesome; vexatious.

**b.** Harmful, injurious.

(In first quot. perh. Lamentable, deplorable: cf. 1.)

**1340–70** *Alex. & Dind.* 566 Many men vp-on molde made hue by slithe To haunte hure in hordom..Of hure tenful tach ȝe taken ensample. *a* **1400–50** *Alexander* 3907 Wild berys..With ilka tenefull tothe as tyndis of harowis.

**2.** Angry, wrathful; malicious, spiteful.

*c* **1205** LAY. 4585 Þer þreo & fifti scipen..In þa teonfulle sæ torneden sæiles. *c* **1400** *Destr. Troy* 12252 Þen Thelamon was tenfull, & turnyt into yre. **1570** *Sat. P. Ref.* xiii. 89 O Teinfull tratouris! **1572** *Ibid.* xxxii. 97 O tenefull Tyrane!

**b.** Feeling sorrow; sorrowful, grieved, sad.

**1387–8** T. USK *Test. Love* II. v. (Skeat) l. 49 O bad and straite been thilke, that at their departyng, maketh men teneful and sorie. 14.. *Siege Jerus.* 213 Ac without tribute or trewes tenfulle wyes, þe knyȝtes with þe kerchef comen ful blyue.

Hence † **Tee·nfully** *adv. Obs.*, sorrowfully, sadly, lamentably, grievously; harmfully, injuriously; angrily, wrathfully.

13.. *E. E. Allit. P.* B. 160 Greuing, and gretyng, and gryspyng harde Of teþe tenfully to geder. ? *a* 1400 *Morte Arth.* 272 He askyde me tyrauntly tribute of Rome, That tenefully tynt was in tyme of myne elders. *c* 1400 *Destr. Troy* 12233 Than Thelamon..tenfully spake..all in grym yre. *c* 1460 *Towneley Myst.* xvi. 56 Free men ar his thrall full teynfully torne.

**Teenhood, Teening, Teenish**: see TEEN *sb.*2

† **Tee·nous,** *a. Sc. Obs. rare*—0. [f. TEEN *sb.*1 + -OUS.] = TEENFUL. Hence † **Tee·nously** *adv.* = TEENFULLY.

*a* 1600 *Flodden F.* 88 in Furniv. *Percy Folio* I. 321 Our prince was moued theratt..& returned him right teenouslye.

**-teenth**: see -TEEN.

**Tee·nty,** *a. U.S. colloq.* [From TEENY *a.*2] Very tiny, delicately small, 'wee'.

1894 C. F. WOOLSON in *Harper's Mag.* Feb. 429 You were six months old—a little teenty baby. 1896 *Chicago Advance* 20 Feb. 260/2 Saving our teenty, dainty roses.

**Teeny** (tī·ni), *a.*1 *Obs.* exc. *dial.* [f. TEEN *sb.*1] Characterized by 'teen'; malicious; peevish.

1594 CAREW *Tasso* (1881) 102 [He] growes so teasty, that by teeny spight, Past reasons bounds he is transported quite. 1825 J. NEAL *Bro. Jonathan* I. 342 A..teeny, mischievous, good for nothin'. 1847–78 HALLIWELL, *Teeny*.. (2) Fretful; peevish; fractious. *Lanc.*

**Tee·ny,** *a.*2 *dial.* and *colloq.* An emphasized form of TINY; esp. in childish use. Also in comb. **teeny-tiny, teeny-weeny**.

1847–78 HALLIWELL, *Teeny.* (1) Tiny; very small. *North.* 1867 *New Comical Nursery Rhymes* 157 With a teeny-tiny thump It broke her teeny nose. 1888 'R. BOLDREWOOD' *Robbery under Arms* li, All the small, teeny bits of a man's life. 1889 'LEWIS CARROLL' *Sylvie & Bruno* xvii, Such delicious *tiny* music! Such teeny-tiny music! 1894 BARING-GOULD *Queen of L.* I. 32, I am a teeny-weeny mite. 1905 ELINOR GLYN *Viciss. Evangeline* 85 He did look such a teeny shrimp, climbing after me!

**Teepe, teepee,** var. TEPEE, N. Amer. Indian hut.

**Teer** (tīəɹ), *v.* Now *dial.* and *techn.* Also 5 tere, 7–9 tear, 8 tire, 9 teere. [ME. *teren, teeren*, app. a. OF. *terer, terrer* to cover or spread with earth, to plaster, to daub, f. *terre* earth.]

**1.** *trans.* To spread or cover with earth; to daub with clay, to construct (a wall, etc.) with clay or cob; to coat with plaster or the like, to plaster.

1382 WYCLIF *Amos* vii. 7 Loo! the Lord stondynge on a wall teerid [*v.rr.* plastrid, pargeted; *Vulg.* stans super murum litum], or morterd, and in the hond of hym a truel of masoun. [Cf. *Ezek.* xiii. 10 thei dawbeden, *gloss* or pargeden, it [a wall] with fen with outen chaffis: *Vulg.* liniebant eum luto absque paleis: *French Bible*, 1543, ilz le terroient de mortier sans paille.] 14.. *Voc.* in Wr.-Wülcker 616/11 *Terro*, i. *terram alicui supponere*, to tere or daube. 1426–7 *Rec. St. Mary at Hill* 66 Also for ij lode lomb for teringe of þe chambre...Also for a lode lyme. *c* 1440 *Promp. Parv.* 489/2 Teryn, or hylle wythe erþe, *terriculo.* 1632 in *Fraser's Mag.* Oct. (1864) 518 Pd for tearing of the house & chimney, 8. o. 1742 in Graham *Soc. Life Scott. in 18th C.* (1901) I. viii. 55 *note*, For colouring and tearing the church doors and lettering them and colouring and tearing the wall opposite to your burial-place and lettering the same, 8 sh. 1847–78 HALLIWELL, *Teer*, (3) to daub with clay. Hence a clay wall is sometimes called a *teer-wall. Teere*, to plaster between rafters. *Lanc.*

**b.** To plaster or spread thickly (butter, etc.).

*c* 1850 *Northampt. Dial.*, You teer the butter all over the bread just as if it cost nothing. 1881 *Leicester Gloss.*, *Teer*, to smear; daub; spread...'Teer the treacle', *i. e.* spread it on bread.

**2.** *Calico-printing.* (See quot. 1839.)

1839 URE *Dict. Arts* 226 The colour is teared [*ed.* 1875 teered].., or spread even, with a wooden scraper as broad as the canvass. 1899 WALLACE *Schoolmaster* ix. 354 *Teerer*, a boy or girl employed to teer..the colour-sieve stretched.. on a frame at printworks.

Hence **Tee·ring** *vbl. sb.* (from sense 1), daubing or plastering with clay or cob; also, plastering or daubing generally; **Tee·ring** *ppl. a.* that 'teers'; esp. in **teering-boy** (also **teer-boy, tire-boy**), in calico-printing, a boy whose work was to spread a fresh surface of colour on the printer's 'pad' each time he used it; also **Tee·rer** (see quots.); **Tee·ry** *a. dial.*, sticky, smeary.

1426–7, 1632 Teering [see sense 1]. 1780 A. YOUNG *Tour Irel.* II. 36 Twelve printers. Twelve tire boys. Three print cutters. 1839 URE *Dict. Arts* 226 The instant before the printer daubs the block upon the canvass, the tearer [*ed.* 1875 teerer], boy or girl, runs the scraper across it to renew its surface. 1847–78 HALLIWELL, *Tiring-boy*, one who stirs the colour about in printing cloth, &c. *Lanc.* 1848 A. B. EVANS *Leicester Words* 96 *Teary*, pron. *Teery*, sticky. 'Handling the sugar will make your hands teary'...'The ground's so very "teary" after the frost', i. e. heavy and clogging. 1895 *Oracle Encycl.* I. 585/2 For each [calico-] printer an attendant or 'teerer' was required —a boy whose duty was to spread evenly the colour on a prepared smooth cloth surface, on to which the printer dipped his block. 1904 in *Eng. Dial. Dict.* s. v., Tear-boys were very common in Lancashire.

**Teer,** obs. f. TAR, TEAR, TIER *sb.*1 **Teercel, Teerd, Teerme, Teers,** obs. ff. TERCEL, TIRED, TERM, TIERCE. **Teery-leery,** etc.: see TIRRA-LIRRA. **Teese,** obs. f. TEASE; var. TEISE *v.*2 *Obs.*

‖ **Teesoo** (tī·sū). *E. Ind.* Also tesu, tesoo, teeso, tisso. [Hindī, etc. *tēsū.*] The brilliant orange-red flowers of the DHAK or PALAS of India (*Butea frondosa* and *B. superba*), or the yellow dye obtained from these. Also *attrib.*, as *teesoo-flower.*

1823 PLAYFAIR tr. *Tale of Shereef* 333 Tesoo. 1835 ROYLE *Bot. of Himalayas* 195 Teesoo, Keesoo. 1848 IRVINE *Mat. Medica Patna* 475 Tesu. 1855 J. F. ROYLE *Fibrous Plants India* 297 Useful from its large flowers, called *teesoo* and *keesoo*, yielding a beautiful dye. 1858 SIMMONDS *Dict. Trade*, *Teeso-flowers, Keeso-flowers*, the large flowers of *Butea frondosa.* 1862 BALFOUR *Timber Trees* 61 Tesu. 1871 — in *Cycl. India* s. v. *Butea frondosa*, Tesu, Kisu [names of the flowers in Deccan].

**Tee-square**: see TEE *sb.*1 4, and T (the letter) 3.

**Teest** (tīst). [Origin unascertained.] A small anvil which is set in a socket on the ordinary anvil or bench.

1877 KNIGHT *Dict. Mech.*, *Teest*, a stake or small anvil used by sheet-iron workers.

**Teest, Teester, Teestif,** obs. ff. TEST, TESTER, TESTY; **Teet, -e,** obs. forms of TEAT.

‖ **Teetee**1 (tī·tī). Also **titi.** [Native name in Tupi.] A name for Brazilian monkeys of the genus *Callithrix*; a sagoin.

1832 MACGILLIVRAY *Humboldt's Trav.* xvii. (1836) 230 The titi or Simia sciurea seems to have been a special favourite with Humboldt. 1879 E. P. WRIGHT *Anim. Life* 49 The Collared Teetee .. is of a dark reddish-brown... It inhabits Brazil. 1883 *Athenæum* 28 Apr. 545 The Secretary..called special attention..to an American teetee monkey of the genus *Callithrix.* 1896 *List Anim. Zool. Soc.* 40 Genus *Callithrix*... Moloch Teetee.. Black-fronted Teetee..Brown Teetee..Grey Teetee..Black-handed Teetee.

**Teetee**2 (tī·tī). Also **ti-ti.** [Maori name.] A name in New Zealand for the Diving Petrel (*Pelecanoides* or *Halodroma urinatrix*), and for allied species.

1882 OGILVIE (Annandale), Tee-tee. 1891 *Australasian* 14 Nov. 963/1 (Morris) The petrels—there are nine kinds,.. the short-billed ti-ti, the long-billed ti-ti [etc.]. 1898 MORRIS *Austral Eng.*, *Ti-ti*, a Maori name for the sea-bird *Pelecanoides urinatrix.*

**Teeter** (tī·təɹ), *sb. dial.* and *U. S.* Also **teater, teter.** [f. TEETER *v.*]

**1.** A see-saw; a see-sawing or swaying motion; the game of see-saw; also *fig.* hesitation between two alternatives, vacillation. Also *attrib.*, *teeter-board.*

1867 LOWELL *Biglow P.* Ser. II. iii, I tell you you've gut to larn thet War ain't one long teeter Betwixt I wan' to an 'T wunt du. 1883 *U.S. Patent* No. 292254, In a teeter, the stands A, having inclined posts *a*, that are connected on top by the socketed pivot-castings *b*, substantially as and for the purpose set forth. 1887 HAVERGAL *Hereford Gloss.* 34 'All on the teater'. 1895 *N. Brit. Daily Mail* 15 Oct. 5 The 'teter' or undulating motion..in the present cars is entirely got rid of. 1897 *Chicago Advance* 30 Sept. 437/2 We [in the U.S.] are not on a teeter-board and have no need to be incessantly concerned about the balance of power.

**2.** See quot.

1848 BARTLETT *Dict. Amer.*, *Peet-weet*.. the spotted Sandpiper.., better known..by the name of..Teeter and Tilt-up or Tip-up, from its often repeated grotesque jerking motions.

**Teeter** (tī·təɹ), *v. dial.* and *U. S.* Also **teter.** [var. of TITTER *v.* to totter, move unsteadily.]

**1.** *intr.* **a.** To see-saw.

1846 WORCESTER, *Teeter*.., to seesaw on a balanced plank, as children, for amusement. (U.S.) 1847 WEBSTER, *Teeter*, *v.* (prov. Eng. *titter*, to tremble, to seesaw..), to seesaw. (U.S.)

**b.** To move like a see-saw; to sway from side to side; to move unsteadily; *esp.* of a person or animal, to walk with a swaying motion; to balance oneself unsteadily on alternate feet. So **teeter-totter, teter-totter.**

*c* 1850 E. G. PAIGE *Serm.* I. 184 You tip and teeter about, thinking that you excite the admiration of all. 1854 THOREAU *Walden* ix. (1886) 184 The peetweets..'teter' along its stony shores all summer. 1888 J. W. RILEY in *Voice* (N.Y.) 21 June, Turn to the lane where we used to 'teeter-totter', Printing little foot-palms in the mellow mold. 1904 WINSTON CHURCHILL *Crossing* II. xiv. 422, I felt the ground teetering under my feet. 1904 in *Eng. Dial. Dict.* (Essex), A watch-maker said of a wheel of which the pivot was bent, 'It teeters'.

**2.** *trans.* To move (anything) with a see-saw motion; to tip up and down, to tilt.

1874 COUES *Birds N. W.* 30 All the while 'teetering' its body, and performing odd, nervous antics. 1906 *Daily Chron.* 14 Feb. 3/3 The author escaped the charge of a rhinoceros by the animal stepping on the same log on which Mr. Whitney was standing, and thus 'teetering' him aside. 1907 *Black Cat* June 36 As he teetered the fretting baby on his knee.

**3.** *Comb.* **Teeter-tail**, the American sandpiper: = TEETER *sb.* 2.

Hence **Tee·tering** *vbl. sb.* and *ppl. a.*

1878 MRS. STOWE *Poganuc P.* xxxv, Settled herself..on the back seat of the creaking, tetering old stage on the way to Poganuc. 1884 *Century Mag.* Jan. 359/1 The steady rolling and teetering of the ship.

**Teeth,** plural of TOOTH, q. v. for phrases, etc.

**Teeth, teethe,** obs. ff. TITHE.

**Teethe** (tīð), *v.* Forms: 5 teth, 8–9 teeth, 9 teethe. [f. *teeth*, pl. of TOOTH: there might also have been an OE. **téðan* from **tanþjan*; cf. BLEED, FEED.]

**1.** *intr.* To develop or 'cut' teeth. (Now only in pr. pple. and vbl. sb.: see TEETHING.)

*c* 1410 *Master of Game* (MS. Digby 182) vi. lf. 17 b, þei teth twyse in þe yere whan þei be wolfes [*v. r.* whelpes]. 1732 [see TEETHING *vbl. sb.* 1]. 1755 JOHNSON, *Teeth v. n.*, to breed teeth; to be at the time of dentition. 1865 PRINCESS ALICE *Mem.* 11 Mar. (1884) 90 Victoria is teething, which makes her pale and poorly.

**2.** *trans.* To furnish with teeth, to set teeth in. Chiefly *dial.*

1775 in ASH. 1794 BURNS *Song*, O merry hae I been teethin' a heckle, And merry hae I been shapin' a spoon. 1832 W. A. FOSTER in *Minstrelsy Merse* (1893) 153 Out through the mark the arrows flew, They teethed it like a harrow. 1865 E. BURRITT *Walk Land's End* 424 The cliffs that teeth the rift look as if they would shut into each other.

**3.** To 'point' (a wall, etc.) with lime or mortar.

1794 *St. Acc. Scot.* XI. 482 Stone walls teethed with lime.

Hence **Tee·thing** *ppl. a.* (in sense 1).

1832 MARRYAT *N. Forster* xxiv, The teething infant. 1897 *Allbutt's Syst. Med.* III. 761 Looseness of the bowels ..common in teething infants.

**Teethed** (tīþt), *a.* Chiefly *Sc.* and *dial.* [f. *teeth*, pl. of TOOTH *sb.* + -ED 2.] Furnished with or having teeth; toothed.

1775 ASH, *Teethed*, furnished with teeth. 1825 J. NICHOLSON *Operat. Mechanic* 659 Some persons imagine .. that teethed wheels and rackwork would be necessary where the railway was not perfectly level. 1879 J. WHITE *Jottings* 49 (E.D.D.) The instrument used for reaping in our young days was the teethed sickle.

**b.** In parasynthetic compounds, as *pearly-teethed.*

1844 W. CROSS *Disruption* xxiii. (E.D.D.), A lang-teethed heckle.

**Teethful** (tī·þful), *a.* [f. *teeth*, pl. of TOOTH *sb.* + -FUL.] Full of teeth: = TOOTHFUL *a.* 1.

1729 SAVAGE *Wanderer* v. 632 Fishers..With teethful tridents strike the scaly train.

† **Teething** (tī·þiŋ), *sb. Obs. rare*—1. [f. *teeth*, pl. of TOOTH *sb.* + -ING 1.] Material on which to exercise the teeth; provisions, food.

1673 F. KIRKMAN *Unlucky Citizen* 210 By such time as he and his are fitted with Clothing, Teething and Tooling, his money is gone.

**Teething** (tī·ðiŋ), *vbl. sb.* [f. TEETHE *v.* + -ING 1.]

**1.** The action of the verb TEETHE; the process of developing teeth, dentition; usually applied to the cutting of the milk-teeth.

1732 ARBUTHNOT *Rules of Diet* iv. in *Aliments*, etc. (1736) 414 When the Symptoms of Teething appear, the Gums ought to be relax'd by softening Ointment. 1872 L. P. MEREDITH *Teeth* (1878) 31 Fatal diseases incident to early childhood..not caused by the irritation of teething.

**2.** The pointing of the interstices between stones in a wall, or slates on a roof, with lime or mortar.

1844 STEPHENS *Bk. Farm* I. 198 The putting them [slates] on, including dressing, holing, pins for the slates, and nails for the laths, cost only 15s., and with moss for bedding 1s., ..and lime for teething 3s., 22s. the rood.

**3.** *attrib.* and *Comb.*, as *teething fever, period, rash*; **teething bannock, teething plaster**, an oatmeal cake given in Scotland to a child beginning to cut its teeth; **teething powder**, a medicinal powder given to children when teething.

1861 W. F. COLLIER *Hist. Eng. Lit.* 400 A severe teething fever deprived him of the use of his right leg. 1866 W. GREGOR *Dial. Banffshire*, Teething-bannock. 1881 — *Folk-lore* 9 The teethin bannock..was baked of oatmeal and butter or cream. 1899 *Allbutt's Syst. Med.* VIII. 586 'Red gum', 'teething rash', usually regarded as a sweat rash.

**Teethy** (tī·þi), *a.*1 Now *Sc.* and *north. dial.* Forms: 5 tethee, 6 tethy(e, 9 teathy, teethy. [Etymology obscure: app. another form of TEETY, TETTY.] Touchy, testy, peevish, crabbed.

*c* 1460 *Towneley Myst.* iii. 186 She is full tethee, ffor litill oft angre, If any thyng wrang be, Soyne is she wroth. 1566 DRANT *Horace* v. H iv b, The testie, tethye, waspishe churle, with pratlynge is offended. 1825 BROCKETT *N. C. Words*, *Teethy*, cross, fretful, peevish; generally spoken of children. 1825 JAMIESON s. v., 'A teethy answer', a tart reply. 1828 *Craven Gloss.*, *Teathy*, peevish, cross. 1892 BOYD 25 *Yrs. St. Andrews* II. 96 Nor did he fail to condemn wrong doing in a fashion which Scotch folk call teethy.

Hence **Tee·thily** *adv.*, testily.

1879 P. R. DRUMMOND *Perthshire in Bygone Days* xiv. 81 The Colonel pointed to a letter lying open on the table and said teethily [etc.].

**Teethy** (tī·þi), *a.*2 [f. *teeth*, pl. of TOOTH *sb.* + -Y.] Well supplied with teeth.

1805 A. SCOTT *Poems* (1808) 160 (E.D.D.) At his expense our teethy faes are fed. 1835 D. WEBSTER *Scot. Rhymes* 136 (E.D.D.) With hero's heart and teethy jaw, Nane like him could badger draw. 1887 *Jamieson's Dict.*, *Suppl.*, *Teethy, Toothy*, having many or large teeth.

**Teetotal** (tītōu·tăl), *a.* (*sb.*) Also erron. tea-. [A kind of emphasizing reduplication or extension of the word TOTAL: see Note below.]

**1.** Of or pertaining to total abstinence from alcoholic drinks; pledged to, or devoted to the furtherance of, total abstinence.

1834 *Preston Temperance Advocate* Apr. 29/2 (Letter signed) A Lover of Sociality, and a 'Tee-Total' Abstainer. *Ibid.* 30/2 He..is now a tee-total abstinence member, and is an ornament to the Society. *Ibid.* May 38/2 The same man has since..signed the tee-total pledge. *Ibid.* Sept. 65/2 The tee-total system is a saving of time, a saving of money. 1837 *Ibid.* Apr. 29/1 A request, that a return should be made from all the tee-total societies in the kingdom. **1837** BARHAM *Let.* in *Life* (1871), And surely the captain Won't think of adapting His taste to these tee-total fancies. **1840** DR. W. PATTON in *Jrnl. Amer. Temp. Union* June 87 Total abstinence from all intoxicating drinks is a principle of English manufacture...So they adopted what they call the *teetotal* pledge (though I don't like the name); and they sent that back to us. **1885** RUNCIMAN *Skippers & Sh.* 14 You've made me be teetotal for three months. **1899** *Allbutt's Syst. Med.* VIII. 234 Much stress has been laid by teetotal advocates on the paramount influence of parental intemperance on the procreation of a mentally deficient progeny.

**2.** *dial.* Absolute, complete, perfect, entire. (More emphatic than *total.*) Cf. TEETOTALLY.

**1840** MARRYAT *Olla Podr., S.W. and by W. ¾ W.*, A man in Bedlam is a very useless member of society, and a tee-total non-productive. **1849** J. O'CONNELL *Parl. Recoll.* II. 136 The Corn Law Abolitionists—the Teetotal men..of course saw through Sir Robert Peel's speech at once. **1884** *Lays & Leg. N. Irel.* 69 The Divil well knowin'..his teetotal want av contrition.

**B.** *sb.* (The adj. used *absol.*; now *rare* or *dial.*) **a.** The total abstinence principle or pledge; teetotalism; a society for the promotion of total abstinence. **b.** A total abstainer; a teetotaller. *rare.*

**1834** *Preston Temp. Adv.* May 38/1 The number of members is about 196: the tee-totals about 30. *Ibid.* Nov. 85/1 Every system that does not go on the basis of tee-total is quackery. *Ibid.* Oct. 77/2 Mr. H. Snell.. then came forward and signed the tee-total. *Ibid.* Nov. 83/2 There is no remedy for the sufferings of the working classes except joining the tee-total. **1845** DISRAELI *Sybil* II. x, Glass of water for the Secretary of the Mowbray Temperance and Teetotal. **1855** O. W. HOLMES *Poems* 200 Statesmen grow merry, lean attorneys laugh, And weak teetotals warm to half and half. **1857** J. STEWART *Sk. Scot. Charac.*, etc. 149 (E.D.D.), I maun join the Teetotal.

Hence **Teeto·tal** *v., intr.* to practise or advocate total abstinence; whence **Teeto·talling** *ppl. a.*

**1839** *Brit. Critic* No. 50. 267 The case of Timothy..is..made a text for 'tee-totalling' discourses. **1843** *Fraser's Mag.* XXVII. 408 The regular..religious and teetotalling artisan. **1883** *Cambridge Staircase* iii. 37 We all indulge in intoxicants..except Westbury, who teetotals.

[*Note.* The most specific account of this word is that it was first used (in sense 1) by a working-man, Richard Turner of Preston, about September, 1833, in a speech advocating total abstinence from intoxicating liquors, in preference to abstinence from ardent spirits only, as practised by some early temperance reformers. Among those present on the occasion was Mr. Joseph Livesey, one of the 'Seven men of Preston', who there formed the first Total Abstinence Society on 22 March 1832, and in whose *Autobiography* (1867–8), included in his *Life & Labours* by John Pearce (1885), particulars will be found. The *Preston Temperance Advocate*, a monthly magazine started by Mr. Livesey in Jan. 1834, shows the rapid advance of 'Dicky Turner's word' from a humorous or allusive to a fully adopted term (see quots. above). The issue for April 1836 has a full-page portrait of 'Dicky Turner, now celebrated as being the author of the word Tee-total'. This statement is also made on his tomb-stone at Preston, where he died 27 Oct. 1846. It has been suggested that Turner only used a word colloquially current in Lancashire in the general sense 2. But to this the whole tenor of contemporary evidence is opposed: and the examples of *tee-total* in sense 2 in the *Eng. Dialect Dictionary* are all of much later date. But there is proof that the adverb *tee-totally*, as an emphasized form of *totally*, was used in U.S. in 1832, and it has also been said to have been common in Ireland from a much earlier date. *Totally* is much more frequent in colloquial use than *total*, and it is quite possible that it was strengthened to *tee-totally* much earlier, and that *tee-total* in the specific sense arose independently, and without any knowledge of the adverb. It has also been asserted that, in the total abstinence sense, the word arose at Lansing, New York, in Jan. 1827, from the use on pledge cards of T. to indicate 'total', and the consequent collocation 'T.-total'. This is particularly stated in the *Century Dictionary* 1891, on the authority of the Rev. Joel Jewell, but without any contemporary evidence; while the correspondence in the *Life of Livesey* above mentioned (Pt. I. cviii–cxv) shows that the total abstinence movement in U.S., and with it the use of *teetotal*, followed and was greatly influenced by the Preston movement. By Worcester, 1846, *teetotal* is called 'a modern cant word', the letter T standing for *temperance*: 'that is *temperance-totalism*'; for it reference is made only to British periodicals. So to Webster 1847 *Tee-totaler* was 'a cant word formed in England'. Cf. 1840 in sense 1.]

**Teeto·talish,** *a.* [f. prec. + -ISH[1].] Inclined or tending to teetotalism.

**1838** W. E. FORSTER in T. W. Reid *Life* (1888) I. iii. 96, I was teetotalish for my stomach's sake, before I left Norwich. **1847** B. BARTON *Select.* (1849) 32 A song of which the chorus was certainly not teetotalish.

**Teeto·talism.** [See -ISM.] The principle or practice of total abstinence from alcoholic liquors.

**1834** *Preston Temp. Adv.* Aug. 62/2 The flame of real tee-totalism was communicated at this meeting. **1839** W. JAY in *Autobiog.* x. (1854) 104 The subject of Teetotallism I have examined physically, morally and Christianly. **1863** J. PAGET *Paradoxes & Puzzles, Ess. Art* iii. (1874) 456 Mr. Cruikshank has embraced the doctrines of teetotalism with the zeal natural to his genius. **1897** W. H. G. TEMPLE in *Chicago Advance* 18 Nov. 712/2 [On the] question of drink, there is but one safe, one reasonable stand—that of absolute teetotalism.

**Teeto·talist.** Now *rare.* [f. as prec. + -IST.] = TEETOTALLER.

**1840** *Fraser's Mag.* XXI. 154 It joins the Teetotalists, and avoids a thimbleful of alcohol. **1865** *Pall Mall G.* 25 Nov. 9 Is Mr. Wood the builder not a teetotalist, but a firm and sensible man?

So **Teeto·talize** *v. trans.*, to convert to teetotalism; hence Teeto·talized *ppl. a.*

**1847–8** H. MILLER *First Impr.* v. (1857) 69 Alas for even teetotalized human nature, when placed in trying circumstances!

**Teeto·taller, -aler.** [f. as prec. + -ER[1].] One who abstains (*esp.* one who pledges himself to abstain) from the use of any intoxicating liquor; a total abstainer.

**1834** *Preston Temp. Adv.* Aug. 57/2 What is the whole matter in dispute betwixt the moderates and the tee-totallers? **1835** (Jan. 23) E. C. DELAVAN *Let.* in *Life of J. Livesey* I. p. cxii, We [in U.S.] begin to feel the influence of your noble example. Our people by thousands are becoming *tee-totallers.* **1836** (*title*) Brief Sketch of the Life of Charles Watson, a Tee-Totaller in Liverpool. **1839** MARRYAT *Diary Amer.* Ser. I. III. 182 Massachusetts is now divided into two very strange political parties, to wit, the *topers* and the *tee-totallers.* **1869** E. A. PARKES *Pract. Hygiene* (ed. 3) 268 The 84th Regiment..numbered many teetotallers.

Hence **Teeto·talleress** *nonce-wd.*, a female teetotaller.

**1854** THACKERAY *J. Leech's Pict. Life & Char.* Wks. 1900 XIII. 484 And there was George [Cruikshank]..handing some teetotaleresses over a plank to the table where the pledge was being administered.

**Tee·to·tally,** *adv. dial.* and *U.S.* [Reduplicated form of TOTALLY.] Totally, entirely, wholly.

**1832** JUDGE JAS. HALL *Legends of W. Philadelphia* 38 [Kentucky backwoodsman says] These Mingoes..ought to be essentially, and particularly, and tee-totally obflisticated off of the face of the whole yearth. **1836** HALIBURTON *Clockm.* xix. (1837) 195, I hope I may be tee-totally ruinated, if I'd take eight hundred dollars for him. **1839** DE QUINCEY *Casuistry Rom. Meals* Wks. 1854 III. 277 An ugly little parenthesis between two still uglier clauses of a teetotally ugly sentence. **1888** DR. TANNER *Sp. Ho. Com.* 20 July, The division, if it were taken now, would be taken entirely and tee-totally—(great laughter)—upon party lines. **1890** 'R. BOLDREWOOD' *Col. Reformer* (1891) 232 They weren't tee-totally lost.

**b.** With allusion to TEETOTAL 1.

**1841** HOOD *Tale Trumpet* xxxviii, The man teetotally wean'd from liquor. **1850** *Tait's Mag.* XVII. 548/1 [Drink] a thing accursed, to be tee-totally abhorred and abandoned.

**Teetotum** (tītō·tʊm), *sb.*[1] Forms: 8 T totum, 8–9 te(-)totum, tee(-)totum, 9 (erron.) te-to-tum, tee-to-tum; see also TOTUM. [Orig. *T totum*, formed by prefixing to L. *tōtum* 'all, the whole', its initial T, which stood for it on one of the four sides of the toy (itself in earlier use called simply a TOTUM, as in 17th c. French *totum*, now *toton*).]

**1.** A small four-sided disk or die having an initial letter inscribed on each of its sides, and a spindle passing down through it by which it could be twirled or spun with the fingers like a small top, the letter which lay uppermost, when it fell, deciding the fortune of the player; now, any light top (sometimes a circular disk pierced by a short peg), spun with the fingers, used as a toy.

The letters were originally the initials of Latin words, viz. T *totum*, A *aufer*, D *depone*, N *nihil*. Subsequently they were the initials of English words, T being interpreted as *take-all*: see quot. 1801. On the French *totum* or *toton*, the letters are T, A, D, R, meaning, according to Littré, *Totum*, tout, *Accipe*, prends, *Da*, donne, *Rien* (nothing).

**1720** DE FOE *Life D. Campbell* (1841) 50 A very fine ivory T totum, as children call it. **1778** MISS BURNEY *Evelina* (1791) II. xxxvii. 245 And turn round like a tetotum. **1800** *Sporting Mag.* XV. 48 A man was lately convicted..for selling a teetotum. **1801** STRUTT *Sports & Past.* IV. iv. 341 When I was a boy the te-totum had only four sides, each of them marked with a letter; a T for take all; an H for half, that is, of the stake; an N for nothing; and a P for put down, that is, a stake equal to that you put down at first. **1818** MOORE *Fudge Fam. Paris* v. 23 Though, like a tee-totum, I'm all in a twirl, Yet even (as you wittily say) a tee-totum Between all its twirls gives a letter to note 'em. **1893** W. S. GILBERT *Utopia* II, She'll waltz away like a teetotum.

**b.** *fig.* (*a*) *Sc.* A very little person. (*b*) Something very unsteady.

**1822** GALT *Sir A. Wylie* III. xxvi. 221, I didna think Miss Mary would ever tak sic a tee totum. **1860** THACKERAY *Round. Papers, Week's Holiday* 223 Who knows how long that dear teetotum happiness can be made to spin without toppling over?

**2.** A game of chance played with this device.

**1753** SMOLLETT *Ct. Fathom* (1784) 65/1 Continue to divert ourselves at all fours, brag, cribbidge, tetotum, &c. **1842** S. LOVER *Handy Andy* xiv, O'Grady gruffly broke in with 'You'd better ask him, does he love teetotum'.

**3.** *attrib.* and *Comb.*, whirling like the top.

**1819** *Metropolis* II. 97 Mrs. S—m—r's tetotum-like turn, not without grace or activity, but with a sportive kind of oddity. **1863** COWDEN CLARKE *Shaks. Char.* x. 258 His own teetotum brain is upset.

Hence **Teeto·tum, Teeto·tumize** *vbs., intr.* to spin like a teetotum, to gyrate; **Teeto·tumism** (*nonce-wd.*), the condition of being 'in a whirl' like a teetotum; **Teeto·tumwise** *adv.*, in the manner of a teetotum.

**1831** MOORE *Summer Fête* 556 No blither nymph *tetotumed round To Collinet's immortal strain. **1897** MARY KINGSLEY *W. Africa* 199 If that wretch, the current..did not grab hold of the nose of my canoe, and we teetotummed. **1841** T. NOEL *Rymes & Roundelays* 212 Brother bards ..Ye, who..Set your brains *tetotum-izing. **1813** W. BULL in *Mem.* xvi. (1864) 350 The whirligigism of your situation,—I might have said the *teetotumism, for I think your brain must very much resemble a teetotum. **1881** *Daily News* 1 Feb. 5/4 The *Mevliveeyeh*, profanely called Dancing Dervishes, still revolve *teetotum-wise.

**Teeto·tum,** *sb.*[2] [A whimsical formation from TEETOTAL, app. after prec.] A teetotal or temperance restaurant.

**1891** *Independent* 10 Apr. 233/3 There is little to distinguish 'the Teetotum' from the ordinary Coffee Tavern or Temperance Club except the peculiarity of being 'a tied house'. **1892** *Daily News* 24 June 2/8 His Royal Highness..expressed satisfaction..at the starting of 'tee-to-tums', or temperance restaurants. **1895** *Westm. Gaz.* 7 Jan. 7/1 A kind of cross between the Gothenburg system and the Tee-to-tum scheme.

**Teety, tetty,** *a.* Now *dial.* Also 9 teaty, (tedy). [Of obscure origin: cf. TEETHY *a.*[1]] (See quots.)

**1621** BURTON *Anat. Mel.* I. ii. III. xiii. (1651) 119 They are so cholerick and tetty that no man may speak with them. **1787** GROSE *Provinc. Gloss.*, *Teety*, fretful, fractious. **1809** T. DONALDSON *Poems* 170 I'd be as tedy as a child. **1855** ROBINSON *Whitby Gloss.*, *Teaty* or *Tutty*, easily offended, testy or touchy.

**Teewit,** etc., var. TEWIT *dial.*, peewit, lapwing.

**Teez,** obs. form of TEASE.

‖**Teff** (tef). Also tef, taff, *erron.* **thaff, theff.** [a. Amharic *ṭēf*, *ṭiēf*, Tigré *ṭāf*, native names in Abyssinia.] The principal cereal of Abyssinia, *Poa* (*Eragrostis*) *abyssinica*, producing minute red or white grains from which bread is made; introduced elsewhere as a fodder plant. Also *attrib.*

**1790** J. BRUCE *Trav. Source Nile* V. 77 Teff is used by all sorts of people from the king downwards, and there are kinds of it which are esteemed fully as much as wheat. **1797** *Encycl. Brit.* (ed. 3) XVIII. 333/2 There are three kinds of meal made from teff, of which the best..is as white as flour, ..the second is of a browner colour; and the last..is nearly black. **1858** HOGG *Veg. Kingd.* 823. **1887** *Kew Bulletin* Jan. 2–6. **1894** *Ibid.* Nov. 378 A slender annual grass, known in Abyssinia as 'Taff', 'Ttheff', or 'Thaff'..cultivated for the sake of its grain all over Abyssinia... According to Richard there are green, white, red, and purple Teffs.

**Teffites,** obs. Sc. form of TAFFETA.

[**Teft** *a.*, in Peele *Tale of Troy* ed. 1589, apparently mispr. for *toft* = *toght*, TAUT, as in ed. 1604.]

**Teg** (teg), **tag** (tæg). Forms: *a.* 6 tegge, 6–9 tegg, 7– teg; *β.* 6–7 tagge, 9 tag. [Of uncertain origin; perh. Scandinavian: cf. Sw. *tacka* a ewe.]

**1.** A sheep in its second year, or from the time it is weaned till its first shearing; a yearling sheep; = HOG *sb.*[1] 4, HOGGET 2. Formerly restricted to the female; now applied to both sexes (*ewe* and *wether tegs*). Also *attrib.* as *teg sheep, wool* (see b).

**1537** in *Priory of Hexham* (Surtees) I. App. 130 One Stringor, that brought a tegg from Wresill. **1607** TOPSELL *Four-f. Beasts* (1658) 495 The first year, we call it..a Lamb, ..the second year a Hog, Lam-hog, or Teg if it be a female. **1674** RAY *S. & E. C. Words* 77 *Tagge*, a sheep of the first year. *Suss.* **1688** *Lond. Gaz.* No. 2346/4, 20 Sheep.. whereof 15 were Wethers, and 5 Tegs. **1733** TULL *Horse-Hoeing Husb.* x. 104 Lambs of three Weeks old..are called Tegs. **1789** *Trans. Soc. Arts* I. 141, I turned in my Tegs (or one year old sheep). **1844** STEPHENS *Bk. Farm* II. 39 In England..sheep bear the name of *lamb* until 8 months old, after which they are called *ewe* and *wether teggs* until once clipped. **1866** [see HOG *sb.*[1] 4 b].

*attrib.* *a* **1722** LISLE *Husbandry* (1757) 388, I had a few teg or hog-sheep. **1889** *Daily News* 16 Dec. 3/5 With regard to teg sheep, weaned within a fortnight of each other.

**b.** *Teg wool*, also ellipt. *teg.* (Cf. HOG *sb.*[1] 4 c.)

**1854** MISS BAKER *Northampt. Gloss.* II. 223 The fleeces of the first shearing, amongst wool-dealers, are called indiscriminately *Tegs* or *Hogs*. *Ibid.* 331 Teg wool is the wool of the first shearing when the sheep is little more than a year old. **1879** *Cassell's Techn. Educ.* IV. 259. **1886** ELWORTHY *W. Somerset Word-bk.*, *Teg*..is not so often applied to the sheep as 'hog', but more frequently to the wool.

†**2.** A doe or female deer in its second year. *Obs.*

**1530** PALSGR. 279/2 Tegge or pricket, *saillant.* **1568** *Hist. Jacob & Esau* I. i. A ij, If we haue lucke thys day to kill Hare, Teg, or Doe. **1636** *Althorp MS.* in Simpkinson *Washingtons* (1860) App. 78 A journey to Wormleighton with a bucke and a tegg. **1774** GOLDSM. *Nat. Hist.* (1862) I. II. v. 329 The female is called a *doe*; the first year, a *fawn*; and the second, a *tegg*.

†**3.** Applied contemptuously to a woman. *Obs.*

*a* **1529** SKELTON *El. Rummyng* 151 Full vntydy tegges, Lyke rotten egges. — *Agst. Garnesche* I. 31 Your wynde schakyn shankkes, your longe lothy legges,..Bryngges yow out of fauyr with alle femall teggys.

**Teg,** obs. var. TEAGUE, an Irishman.

**Tegh**: see TEE *v.*[1], TIE *v.* **Teght, teȝt,** pa. t. of TIGHT *v.* **Tegir,** obs. f. TIGER.

‖**Tegmen** (te·gmen). Pl. **te·gmina.** [L. *tegmen* (*tegimen, tegumen*) covering, f. *teg-ĕre* to cover; so F. *tegmen.*] A cover, covering, coating, integument. (Only in scientific use.) **a.** *gen.*

**1807** HEADRICK *Arran* 61 The pitchstone assumes a greyish tegmen, or crust, by exposure to the air.

**b.** *Entom.* (*pl.*) The wing-covers, i.e. the fore wings when modified so as to serve as coverings for the hind wings; esp. those of orthopterous insects (corresponding to the *elytra* of beetles).

**1817** KIRBY & SP. *Entomol.* xxiii. (1818) II. 350 Probably in the next order (*Orthoptera*), the *Tegmina*, or wing-covers ..assist them in flying. **1826** *Ibid.* xlvii. IV. 371 The horizontal portion of one tegmen lies longitudinally over that of the other. **1877** HUXLEY *Anat. Inv. Anim.* vii. 400 The female [cockroach] has moveable tegmina.

**c.** *Bot.* The thin inner coat of a seed, immediately enveloping the nucleus; the *endopleura.*

[1832 LINDLEY *Introd. Bot.* 183 The internal integument, ..*endopleura* of De Candolle, *hilofère* and *tegmen* of Mirbel.] 1857 HENFREY *Bot.* § 296 The inner integument, the tegmen or endopleura, is not generally distinguishable.

d. Anat. *Tegmen tympani*, a plate of bone forming the root of the tympanum of the ear, being a part of the temporal bone.

1890 in BILLINGS *Nat. Med. Dict.*

e. *Ornith.* (*pl.*) = *Tectrices*: see TECTRIX.

1891 in *Cent. Dict.*

**Tegment** (te·gměnt). *rare.* [ad. L. *tegmentum*: see below.] A covering, integument. †a. *gen. Obs. rare*—°. b. = TEGMENTUM (1 and 2).

1656 BLOUNT *Glossogr.*, *Tegment* (*tegmentum*), a covering, a garment or cloathing. 1888 *Cassell's Encycl. Dict.*, *Tegment*...1. *Anat.*: The upper part of the *crura cerebri*...2. *Bot.* (*Pl.*): The scales of a bud. 1899 *Allbutt's Syst. Med.* VI. 769 Cells, whose axis-cylinder processes pass as root fibres vertically through the tegment and pyramids.

Hence **Tegmented** (te·gmĕntĕd) *ppl. a.*, covered as with a roof, roofed over.

1891 *Cent. Dict.* s. v. *Teiidæ*, A family of..lacertilians,.. having supratemporal fossæ not tegmented or roofed over.

**Tegmental** (tegme·ntăl), *a.* [f. as prec. + -AL.] Of or pertaining to the tegmentum.

1890 in BILLINGS *Nat. Med. Dict.* 1899 *Allbutt's Syst. Med.* VII. 351 Lesions of the tegmental region are specially apt to affect the fifth, sixth, seventh, and eighth nerves.

‖**Tegmentum** (tegme·ntǒm). Pl. -a. [L. collateral form of *tegumentum* TEGUMENT.]

1. *Bot.* Each of the scales forming the covering of a leaf-bud; a bud-scale.

1832 LINDLEY *Introd. Bot.* 51 Thus, in the Beech, the tegmenta are thin, smooth, and dry. 1842 BRANDE *Dict. Sc.* 1861 BENTLEY *Man. Bot.* (1870) 94 These external modified leaves,..termed scales,..have also received the name of tegmenta.

2. *Anat.* The upper and hinder portion of each of the *crura cerebri*.

1879 *St. George's Hosp. Rep.* IX. 670 Those on the opposite surface of the crus, which form the tegmentum. 1893 SIR W. R. GOWERS *Dis. Nerv. Syst.* II. 438 There may be hemianæsthesia from softening of the tegmentum of the crus.

**Tegminal** (te·gminăl), *a. rare*—°. [f. L. *tegmen*, *tegmin-*, TEGMEN + -AL.] Of the nature of a *tegmen*; covering, protecting. 1891 in *Cent. Dict.*

**Tegre**, obs. form of TIGER.

‖**Teguexin** (tegwe·ksin). *Zool.* [ad. Aztec *tecoixin*, *tecouixin* (tekwi·ʃin) a lizard.] A large South American lizard of the genus *Teius*, esp. *T. teguexin*.

[1540 SAGAHUN *Historia de Nueva España* XI. iv. (1829) 202 Hay lagartos en esta tierra, y llamanlos *tecouixin*.] 1879 E. P. WRIGHT *Anim. Life* 376 The Teguexin (*Teius teguexin*) is not uncommon in Surinam and the Brazils. It attains a length of from three to four feet. 1892 W. H. HUDSON *Natur. La Plata* 74 The large teguexin lizard of the pampas, called iguana by the country people, is a notable snake-killer.

‖**Tegula** (te·giŭlă). *Entom.* Pl. -æ. [L., a tile, f. *teg-ĕre* to cover.] a. A small scale-like structure covering the base of the fore-wing in hymenopterous and other insects. b. Each of a pair of membranous scales (PREHALTERES) in front of the halteres in dipterous insects.

1826 KIRBY & SP. *Entomol.* xxxiii. III. 377 *Tegulæ*.., small corneous concavo-convex scales, which in many Orders, particularly *Hymenoptera*, cover and defend the base of the Upper-Wings. *Ibid.* xlvii. IV. 381 The tegulæ, or base-covers..cover and defend the base of their wings.

**Tegular** (te·giŭlăɹ), *a.* [f. as prec. + -AR; cf. F. *tégulaire*.] a. Pertaining to or of the nature of a tile; composed of or arranged like tiles. b. *Entom.* Pertaining to or of the nature of a *tegula* (*Cent. Dict.* 1891). Hence **Te·gularly** *adv.*, in the manner of tiles; so as to overlap like tiles. So **Te·gulated** *a.*, (of armour) composed of overlapping plates.

1796 KIRWAN *Elem. Min.* (ed. 2) II. 162 In flat hexahædral masses tegularly accumulated or implicated. 1828 WEBSTER, *Tegular*, pertaining to a tile; resembling a tile; consisting of tiles. 1834 PLANCHÉ *Brit. Costume* 72 A suit of..tegulated armour..composed of small square plates of steel, lapping over each other like tiles. 1842 *Blackw. Mag.* LII. 171 In rastred, or ringed, or tegulated armour.

‖**Te·gumen.** *rare*—°. [L., var. form of *tegimen*, TEGMEN.] = TEGMEN.

1882 OGILVIE, Tegmen, Tegumen.

**Tegument** (te·giŭmĕnt). [ad. L. *tegument-um* covering, f. *teg-ĕre* to cover: see -MENT. So OF. *tegument* (13th c. in Godef.).] Something that serves to cover; a covering, coating, envelope, investment, integument. a. *gen.* (natural or artificial).

*c* 1440 *Pallad. on Husb.* IV. 70 Ffor sunne and wynde hem make a tegument, Lest they in this be shake, in that to brent. 1658 SIR T. BROWNE *Hydriot.* iii. 32 Whatever was the solid Tegument, we finde the immediate covering to be a purple peece of silk. 1674 *Phil. Trans.* IX. 205 They have only a few teguments to cover themselves with in the night. 1713 DERHAM *Phys.-Theol.* III. i. 64 Beds.. lying under that upper Stratum, or Tegument of the Earth. *c* 1830 HOR. SMITH *Addr. Mummy* xiii, Why should this worthless tegument endure If its undying guest be lost for ever? 1888 A. S. WILSON *Lyric Hopeless Love* CVIII. 315 Beneath the tegument of clay.

b. *Nat. Hist.* and *Anat.* The natural covering of the body, or of some part or organ, of an animal or plant; a skin, coat, shell, husk, or the like; *spec.* = TEGMEN b (Brande *Dict. Sci.*, 1842). Now *rare* or *Obs.*; mostly replaced by INTEGUMENT.

1646 SIR T. BROWNE *Pseud. Ep.* II. vi. 97 A harder tegument or shell [in the nutmeg], which lyeth under the Mace. 1760 J. LEE *Introd. Bot.* I. ix. (1765) 19 Corolla and Calyx, are the Teguments or Covers of the Stamina and Pistillum. 1822 IMISON *Sc. & Art* I. 250 It [the eye] is composed of three coats, or teguments, one covering the other. 1864 MAX MÜLLER *Sc. Lang.* Ser. II. ii. (1868) 74 If we never find skins except as the teguments of animals.

**Tegumental** (tegiŭme·ntăl), *a.* [f. prec. + -AL.] Of, pertaining to, or of the nature of a tegument; integumental: = next.

1822–34 *Good's Study Med.* (ed. 4) IV. 463 The order of the tegumental laminæ. 1888 HUXLEY & MARTIN *Elem. Biol.* IV. 276 Visual and tegumental sense organs.

**Tegumentary** (tegiŭme·ntări), *a.* [f. as prec. + -ARY[1]; cf. F. *tégumentaire*.] Constituting, or serving as, a tegument; pertaining to or occurring in the tegument; integumentary.

1828–32 WEBSTER, *Tegumentary*, pertaining to teguments, or consisting of teguments. 1831 R. KNOX *Cloquet's Anat.* 235 They communicate with the vessels of the tegumentary membranes. 1848 LINDLEY *Introd. Bot.* (ed. 4) II. 227 The nucleus has only one tegumentary membrane. 1853 H. WALTON *Dis. Eye* (1875) 138 Tegumentary mole is a congenital tumour, often spoken of as nævus.

†**Tegu·ryon.** *Obs. rare*—¹. [ad. L. *tegurium*, also *tigurium*, *tugurium*, a hut, cottage, f. *teg-ĕre* to cover; in med.L. also *tegorium* a shrine (Du Cange).] A shrine, a canopy over a tomb.

1483 CAXTON *Gold. Leg.* 190/1 The bows of saynt denys.. the teguryon of marble whyche is vpon hym.

**Tehee** (tī·hī·), *int.* and *sb.* Forms: 4–8 ti-, 4–9 te-, 6–7 ty-, 6–9 tee-, 7 teh-, tih-, tigh-, 9 tie-; 4–9 -he, -hee, 6 -heegh, -hei, -hy, 7 -hi, 7–9 -hie: as one word, or as two, or hyphened.

A. *int.* A representation of the sound of a light laugh, usually derisive. In quots. usually in female use. Cf. HE *int.*[2]

*c* 1386 CHAUCER *Miller's T.* 554 Tehee [*v.rr.* Te hee; *Cambr.* Te he; *Corpus* Tehe; *Petw.* Ti he], quod she, and clapte the wyndow to. 1500–20 DUNBAR *Poems* lxxv. 22 'Tehe!' quod scho, and gaif ane gaufe. *c* 1550 *Peblis to the Play* xxi, Than all the wenschis Te he thai playit. 1588 N. YONGE *Mus. Transalpina* xli. Fj b, When I lament my case thou cryest..ty hy, and no no no. 1654 GAYTON *Pleas. Notes* To Rdr., Monsters where be yee? I'm Hercules, club too, Ti-hee, wi-hee. 1773 MASON *Heroic Ep. to Sir W. Chambers* 134 And all the Maids of Honour cry Te! He!

B. *sb.* A laugh of this kind; a titter, a giggle.

1593 G. HARVEY *Pierce's Super.* Wks. (Grosart) II. 273 The *Tutt* of Gentlemen, the *Tee-heegh* of Gentlewomen. 1600 E. BLOUNT *Hosp. Incur. Fooles* 116 As manie tighhees as euer came out of god Liber or Bacchus his mouth. 1753 A. MURPHY *Gray's-Inn Jrnl.* No. 58 (1756) II. 36 Tehees and Titters in the Women..totally destroy their Beauty. *a* 1754 FIELDING *Charac. Men* Wks. 1784 IX. 411 The various laughs, titters, tehes, &c. of the fair sex. 1837 CARLYLE *Fr. Rev.* I. II. v, Our poor young Prince gets his Opera plaudits changed into mocking tehees. 1858 — *Fredk. Gt.* VI. vi. (1872) II. 199 Astonishment, *flebile ludibrium*, tragical tehee from gods and men, will come of the Duel!

Hence **Tehee·** *v.*, *intr.* to utter *tehee* in laughing; to laugh affectedly or derisively; to titter, giggle. Hence **Tehee·ing** *vbl. sb.* and *ppl. a.*

?*a* 1300 *Proverb. Verses* in *Rel. Ant.* II. 14 Liþer lok and tuinkling Tihing and tikeling. 1580 HARVEY *Lett. betw. Spenser & H.* Wks. (Grosart) I. 61 The Gentlewoomen ..tyhying betweene them selues. 1598 B. JONSON *Ev. Man in Hum.* I. iii, And the wenches they doe so geere, and ti-he at him. 1603 HOLLAND *Plutarch's Mor.* 96 They fell to teighing, and now they laugh you to skorne. 1622 MABBE tr. *Aleman's Guzman d'Alf.* I. 158 My money..began to laugh and tighie in my purse. 1721 D'URFEY *Ariadne* II. i, Oh! how she would Teehee, and simper, and sneer. 1886 STEVENSON *Kidnapped* xiv, What frightened me most of all, the new man tee-hee'd with laughter as he..looked at me.

‖**Tehr, tahr** (tēəɹ). Also tare, tahir, (thar). [Name in the Western Himalayas. (Sometimes confused with *thar*, the Nepālī name of the *gural* or *gooral*, a goat-antelope of Nepāl.)] See quots.

1835 B. H. HODGSON in *Proc. Zool. Soc. Lond.* 492 The Western type of the Himalayan wild goat, called Tehr at Simla and Musuri. 1867 A. L. ADAMS *Wand. Nat. India* 214 Herds of Tare (*Capra jemlaica*, Smith) were often observed during my excursion. The short triangular horns of this species of goat distinguish it from any of its allies. 1867 JERDON *Mammals India* (1874) 286 Tehr. 1885 *Cycl. India* (ed. 3) III. 840/1 *Tehr*, the Himalayan wild goat *Hemitragus Jemlaicus*, Jerdon, pronounced *Tare*, also *Tahir*. It is the Jharal of Nepāl. 1893 LYDEKKER *Horns & Hoofs* 123 The Tahr is found in forest regions.

**Tehsildar**: see TAHSILDAR.

**Tei, Teiche**, obs. Sc. forms of TIE *sb.*, TACHE *sb.*[1]

**Teicher**, Sc. and north. f. TEAR *sb.*[1] and *v.*[2]

‖**Teichopsia** (təikǫ·psiă). *Path.* [f. Gr. τεῖχος wall + ὄψις sight + -IA[1].] Temporary blindness sometimes accompanying ophthalmic headache.

1872 *Nature* 21 Mar. 416/1 On Teichopsia, a form of transient half-blindness. 1899 *Allbutt's Syst. Med.* VIII. 223 The so-called Teichopsia, the appearance as of ebullition in objects, and other curious optical illusions, are familiar precursors of migraine.

**Teicho·scopy.** [ad. Gr. τειχοσκοπία, f. τεῖχος wall + -σκοπια, from -σκοπος -looking.] A looking from the walls; a descriptive title of the third book of Homer's Iliad.

1875 *Contemp. Rev.* XXVI. 263 He [Ulysses] is by far the most prominent person in this portrait gallery of the Teichoscopy.

**Teie**, obs. f. TIE *v.* **Teigh, teiȝ-e**, pa. t. of TEE *v.*[1] *Obs.*; obs. f. TIE *v.* **Teighing**: see TEHEE *v.*

‖**Te igitur** (tī·i·dʒitǒɹ). [L., = 'thee therefore', the opening words of the prayer.] The first prayer in the canon of the Mass in the Roman and some other Latin liturgies; hence extended to the liturgical book itself.

1819 SCOTT *Ivanhoe* xliii, Bring forward the crucifix and the *Te igitur* [*Gloss.* The service book on which oaths were sworn]. 1877 J. D. CHAMBERS *Div. Worship* IV. v. 349 The subsequent petitions are taken..from the 'Te Igitur' or first part of the Canon.

**Teigue, -ism**, obs. f. TEAGUE, Irishman, etc.

**Teil** (tīl). Now *rare* or *Obs.* Forms: 6 tilie, 6–7 teyle, 7 teile, tiel, 7–8 tile, teyl, 9 til, 7– teil. [Partly ad. L. *tilia* linden-tree; partly a. OF. *til* (12–14th c. in Godef.), *teil* (13–17th c., and mod.dial., Berry), masc. forms collateral with *tille*, *teille*, ad. L. *tilia*; cf. It. *tiglio*, †*tilio*, beside †*tilia* (Florio), Sp. *tilo*, *tila*, Pg. *til*, *tilia*. (Mod. F. has *tilleul*:—L. **tiliolus*, dim. of **tilius*.)] The lime or linden tree, *Tilia europæa*. Usually *teil-tree*.

[1398 TREVISA *Barth. De P. R.* XVII. cxcii. (MS. Bodl.) lf. 238 b/2 Þe tre tilia..bene haunteþ þe floures þerof and gadreþ þerof swetnes of hony.] 1589 FLEMING *Virg. Georg.* I. 7 The light wood of the Tilie tree is cut downe for a yoke. 1613 PURCHAS *Pilgrimage* (1614) 395 Some of them practise diuination with the leaues of the Teil-tree which they fold and vnfold in their hands. 1617 MORYSON *Itin.* I. 26 A faire meadow,..wherein is a faire Lynden or teyle tree. 1646 J. HALL *Horæ Vac.* 87 Like the shade of a Tile tree, very pleasant though the tree be unfruitfull. 1658 ROWLAND *Moufet's Theat. Ins.* 1032 They live on softer leaves, especially on the Tiel-tree. 1694 ADDISON *Virg. Georg.* IV. 233 From purple violets and the teile they [bees] bring Their gather'd sweets, and rifle all the spring. 1721 *New Gen. Atlas* 120 There are stately Walks of Tile-trees on its North Bank. 1837 WHEELWRIGHT tr. *Aristoph.* I. 270 *note*, Boards of the teil or linden. 1866 *Treas. Bot.*, Til-tree, *Tilia europæa*.

*attrib.* 1731 J. MONCRIEFF in Graham *Soc. Life Scotl. in 18th C.* (1901) I. vii. 52 A little tile-tree water.

b. In the Bibles of 1568 and 1611, used in one place to render Heb. אֵלָה *ēlāh* (elsewhere rendered 'oak' and once 'elm').

1568 BIBLE (Bishops') *Isa.* vi. 13 As a Teyle tree [so 1611; Vulg. *terebinthus*, WYCLIF terebynt, COVERD. terebyntes, CRANM. terebintes, *Geneva* elme, *Douay* and *R. V.* (1885) terebinth] and the Oke in the fall of their leaues haue yet the sappe remayning in them. 1647 TRAPP *Comm. Phil.* iv. 10 It had..withered, as an Oak in winter..and as a Teyl tree whose sap is in the root.

**Teil(l**, obs. form of TAIL, TEAL, TILL *v.*

**Teild**, var. TELD *v. Obs.*, to pitch a tent.

**Teim, Tein**, obs. Sc. ff. TEEM *v.*[2], TEEN.

**Teind** (tīnd), (*a.*) *sb. Sc.* and *north.* Forms: 3–5 tende, tend, 4–6 teynde, 4–7 teinde, (5 tyende, teend), 5–7 teynd, (6 teand, 8–9 tiend), 4– teind. (Also 5 tene, 6 teine, 9 teen, tein.) [Early ME. *tende*, adj. and sb., collateral form of TENTH, q. v.: cf. also TITHE.]

A. *adj.* See TENTH A. 1 γ, and 3.

B. *sb.* †1. The tenth part (of anything); a tenth.

*a* 1300 *Cursor M.* 968 (Cott.) O þi winning giue me þe tend [*v.r.* tende]; Of alkin fruit haf þou þe nine, For I wil þat þe tend [*Fairf.* teynde, *Trin.* tenþe] be mine. 13.. *Ibid.* 16968 (Gött.) All þe tunges of þis werld cuth noght tell þe tend [*Cott.* teind]. *c* 1330 R. BRUNNE *Chron.* (1810) 145 Þat burgh no Citez of taliage suld non telle, Þe tende suld be nouht, no þe tuende non make. *c* 1375 BARBOUR *Troy-bk.* I. 475 That mene lest nocht þe teynde to here. *c* 1375 *Sc. Leg. Saints* xii. (*Mathias*) 265 Of thre hundir þe teynd leyly, þat cumys be raknyne to thretty. *c* 1475 *Rauf Coilȝear* 474 The teind of his iewellis to tell war full teir. *c* 1475 *Golagros & Gaw.* 1083 For ony trety may tyde, I tell the the teynd [*rimes*, schend, freynde, wende].

2. *spec.* A tenth part of the produce of land or labour paid (voluntarily, or by legal enactment) for the support of religion: = TITHE *sb* 1; now, in Scotland, that portion of the estates of the laity which is liable to be assessed for the stipend of the clergy of the established church. Now chiefly in pl.

[*c* 1200 ORMIN 2715 To ȝifenn Godd te tende del Off all þin aȝhenn ahhte. — 6125 Off all þatt god te birrþ þin Godd þe tende dale brinngenn.] *a* 1300 *Cursor M.* 1062 (Cott.) Rightwis he was, and godds freind, And leli gaf he him his tend [*v.r.* tende]. 13.. *Ibid.* 27249 Quar he tas til his teindis tent. *a* 1340 HAMPOLE *Psalter* lxxviii. 1 Þai gedire þaire tendis and offrandis, And reckis noght of þe saules þat þai sould kepe. *c* 1425 WYNTOUN *Cron.* V. ix. 1810 Teyndis or monay That wes gevin in offerand. *c* 1440 *Alphabet of Tales* 168 Go byd þe preste feche þis ton of wyne for his tend. *c* 1450 *St. Cuthbert* (Surtees) 5438 Þare was a monke þe teend ast. 1535 STEWART *Cron. Scot.* (Rolls) III. 94 For to the kirk no teyndis tha wald pa. 1588 *Wills & Inv. N. C.* (Surtees) II. 256 *note*, I geue vnto my wyff the holle teand of Foulburye. 1596 DALRYMPLE tr. *Leslie's Hist. Scot.* IV. (S. T. S.) 226 This escheit suld first, of the first ȝeirlie teines, be payet to the Preistes. 1637–50 ROW *Hist. Kirk* (Wodrow Soc.) 28 The teinds are the Kirk's patrimonie, whereby the ministrie and the poore ought to be intertained. 1799 J. ROBERTSON *Agric. Perth* 78 The livings of the ministers..are fixed by the supreme court of this country, acting as a court of teinds or tithes. 1844 W. CROSS *Disruption* xiii. (E. D. D.), Raizin a plea against the laird for sumthing they call the teens. 1889 *Chambers' Encycl.* III. 528/1 The Court or Commission of Teinds, in which questions relating to the law of teinds or church tithes were decided.

**b.** *transf.* The payment, institution or system of teinds.

*c* **1817** Hogg *Tales & Sk.* II. 150 A wearisome debate on the rights of teind. **1905** *Sat. Rev.* 4 Feb. 14/2 Dr. Brown considers that teind was felt as an 'iniquitous oppression'.

**c.** *The teind to hell* (*Folk-lore*), in reference to the reputed obligation of the fairies to furnish a victim to Satan every seventh year: see Scott *Minstrelsy* Introd. to *Young Tamlane.*

**17..** *Young Tamlane* xxxvii. in Scott *Minstr. Scot. Border* (1869) 478 For aye, at every seven years, They pay the teind to hell. **1852** *Alice Learmont* ix. 124 There cam up that black road the Evil Ane,..He took back nae mortal, but an elf, as the teind to hell.

**3.** *attrib.* and *Comb.* **a.** *attrib.* Of or pertaining to teinds or tithes, as *teind-barn, court, day, -lathe* (= tithe-barn), *law, -master, office*; paid as tithe, as *teind calf, coal, corn, fish, grice, hay, lamb, sheaf, silver, skate, wheat.* **b.** objective, etc., as *teind-payer*; *teind-free* adj.

In some of these, *teind* may have been at first merely the adj. = tenth, as *teind sheaf* tenth sheaf or tithe sheaf.

**1885** W. Ross *Aberdour & Inchcolme* v. 145 Conveying the teind-sheaves..to the *teind-barns at Aberdour. *a* **1555** Lyndesay *Tragedy* 300 3e wyll not want teind cheif nor offrandis, Teinde woll, teind lambe, *teind calf, teind gryce and guse. **1475** in *Finchale Priory* (Surtees) 37 For *tende cole in Le wood. *Ibid.* 39 An accion..in the Consistory..for tyende cole of our coal minez. **1463** *Burgh Rec. Edin.* (1869) I. 21 The said fermoraris, sall gif..the *tene corne of all cornes of the said mylne. **1842** J. Aiton *Domest. Econ.* (1857) 54 Another proof that the *Teind Court are set upon paring down the income of the clergy to a mere existence. **1825** Scott *Jrnl.* 7 Dec., *Teind day;—at home of course. **1547** *Reg. Privy Council Scot.* I. 69 As to the *teynd fische of the Kirk of Kynfawnyes. **1621** *Sc. Acts Jas. VI* (1816) IV. 612/2 Act declairing summes Grasse..to be *teyndfrie. **1507–8** *Acc. Ld. High Treas. Scot.* IV. 103 For tua 3eris *teynd hay of ane medow that the Kingis hors eit. **1547** *Test. Ebor.* (Surtees) VI. 265 The teynde haye of the hall banke. **1586** *Reg. Privy Council Scot.* IV. 73 Ressaving his *teynd lambis. **1828** *Craven Gloss.*, **Teen lathe*, tithe-barn. **1801** *Farmer's Mag.* Aug. 283 Our Scots *teind laws are founded upon this principle. **1710** *Dict. Feudal Law*, **Teind-masters*, are these who have Right to Teinds. **1890** *Oliver & Boyd's Edin. Almanac* 91 The tables have been prepared from official documents in the *Teind Office. **1685** Renwick *Serm.*, etc. (1776) 151 Then shall *teind-payers be paid home. **1446** *Rental Bk. Cupar-Angus* (1879) I. 125 Our landis..and the *teinde schef of the sayd landis. **1876** A. Laing *Lindores Abbey* xiv. 133 Patrick Leslie granted a tack of the teind sheaves of the parish of Dudhope to James Scrymgeour. **1505** *Acc. Ld. High Treas. Scot.* III. 171 Payit..the *teynd silvir of the Kingis staggis in tua 3eris..xvj *d.* **1819** W. Tennant *Papistry Storm'd* (1827) 13 He'd sooner fling them back i' the sea Than gie ae *teind-skate to the bishop. **1837** Lockhart *Scott* an. 1806 II. iii. 103 There is also another blank day every other week,—the *Teind Wednesday, as it is called, when the Judges are assembled for the hearing of tithe questions.

**Teind** (tīnd), *v.* *Sc.* and *north.* ?*Obs.* Forms: see Teind *sb.* [f. Teind *sb.*: cf. *to tithe.*]

**1.** *intr.* To pay teinds or tithes.

*c* **1375** *Creation* 490 in Horstm. *Altengl. Leg.* (1878) 130 Þerfore wel to tenden buþ lef [= be glad]. **13..** *Cursor M.* 29324 (Cott. Galba) Þam..þat witandly with-haldes tendes Or falsly tendes. *c* **1460** *Towneley Myst.* ii. 294 If thou tend right thou gettis thi mede;..if thou teynd fals, thou bese alowed ther after als.

**2.** *trans.* To assess or take the tenth or tithe of.

**1483** *Cath. Angl.* 379/2 To Tende, *decimare.* **1566** *Reg. Privy Council Scot.* I. 480 To pas and teynd the cornis of the saidis toun. **1567** *Gude & Godlie B.* (S. T. S.) 188 The hirdis teindit all the corne. **1641** Best *Farm. Bks.* (Surtees) 26 As for the wooll, it may be teended and wayed that wee may knowe what is of it. *a* **1722** Fountainhall *Decis.* (1761) 391 Herrings taken on the coast of Fife, though teinded there, yet if brought to Dunbar, pay again.

Hence **Tei·nder**, one who pays or takes teind or tithe; **Tei·nding** *vbl. sb.*, tithing.

**13..** *Cursor M.* 27267 [In scrift þe preist sal frain] Anentes til-men of enuie And o þair tending [*v.r.* teinding] namli. *c* **1440** *Gesta Rom.* vi. 17 (Harl. MS.) Þe lewde men most holde vp..men of holy chirch, thoro3 almesse offryngys, and tendingys. **1627** in A. Allan *Hist. Channelkirk* (1900) 147 Quhen the ground is punishit, the heritour and teinder must nott be frie. **1655** *Records Baron Crt. Stitchill* (S.H.S.) 2 Until the first day of the teynding be past. **1884** J. Tait in *United Presbyt. Mag.* Apr. 156 The arrangement of thirders and teinders described by Arthur Young. **1905** C. B. Gunn *Baron Crt. Stitchill* Introd. 15 The minister might delay teinding until the weather was breaking.

**Teind**, obs. Sc. f. Tend, Tind *v.*

**Teine**, Sc. f. Teen, Tine, *sb.*[1]; var. Teyne *Obs.*

**Teing**, obs. f. *tying*: see Tie *v.*

**Teinland**, erron. f. *thegenland*, Thaneland.

**Teinoscope** (təi·nǒskōup). [f. Gr. τείνειν to stretch, extend + -scope.] An optical instrument in which prisms are so arranged and combined as to increase or diminish the apparent linear dimensions of objects, while the chromatic aberration of the light is corrected.

**1822** Brewster in *Edin. Phil. Jrnl.* Apr. 334 (*heading*) Description of a Teinoscope for altering the Lineal Proportions of Objects, with Observations on Professor Amici's Memoir on Telescopes without Lenses...The Instrument which I propose to describe..was invented and constructed in its simplest form about the beginning of the year 1812. **1832** *Nat. Philos.* II. *Optic. Instr.* xvi. § 110. 55 (Usef. Knowl. Soc.) Amici's teinoscope consists of four right angular prisms, having their refractive angles different and connected by pairs.

**Teint, -e**, obs. ff. Taint, Tent, Tint.

**Teinter**, obs. f. Tenter. **Teir**, obs. Sc. f. Tear; Sc. f. Tere *Obs.*, difficult. **Teirce, teirs, -e**, obs. ff. Tierce. **Teis**, obs. Sc. pl. of Tie *sb.*

† **Teise, taise,** *sb. Obs.* Also 5 teis, teys, tayse, tese. [ME. a. OF. *teise* (11th c. in Godef. *Compl.*), mod.F. *toise*, = It. *tesa*:—late L. *tensa* (sc. *brachia*) the outstretched arms.]

**1.** A lineal measure of six feet, a fathom; = Toise.

**13..** *Sir Beues* (A.) 1417 In me prisoun þow schelt abide Vnder þerþe twenti teise [*v.rr.* paise, pase]. *c* **1330** *Florice & Bl.* (1857) 241 A thousan[d] taisen be his heihe..And an hundre[d] taises he is wid And imaked with mochel prid.

**2.** A superficial measure, a square toise.

**1426–7** *Rec. St. Mary at Hill* 66 A pavier and his man to paue..v teys ij s xid. **1477–9** *Ibid.* 89, For pavyng xj teis of pament for euery teis vij d—vj s vd. **1486** *Nottingham Rec.* III. 259 To þe pauer for workyng of vj. tayses in þe same gate..he takyng for a tayse vj d: summa iij s. **1492–3** *Rec. St. Mary at Hill* 190 Item, for pavyng of þe pamentt ..for viij tese, pris þe tese, vij d.

† **Teise, taise,** *v.*[1] *Obs.* Also 4 teyse, tese, 4–6 tayse, 5 tase, 6 tais. [a. OF. *teser*, 3rd sing. pres. *teise, toise* (13th c. in Godef.):—late L. type **tēsāre*:—*tensāre* to stretch, bend (a bow), f. *tens-us* stretched, bent.] *trans.* To stretch, to bend (a bow); hence, to fit (an arrow or quarrel in a bow or arbalest) in order to shoot; to aim or direct (a shaft, etc.); to poise (a weapon) in taking aim. Also *absol.* or *intr.*

**13..** *Seuyn Sag.* (W.) 1978 And in his hond an arblast heldand, And therinne a quarel taisand. *c* **1330** R. Brunne *Chron. Wace* (Rolls) 13699 He teysed his dint, Bokkes to smyte. **1375** Barbour *Bruce* v. 623 He tasit the vyre and leit it fle, And hit the fader in the E. **13..** *Minor Poems fr. Vernon MS.* xliv. 43 So doþ þe fisschere wiþ his hok: Hou he teseþ on þe Banke A brodly breyd I þe Brok. **1382** Wyclif *Wisd.* v. 22 As at the teising the bowe of cloudis bent. *c* **1400** *Laud Troy Bk.* 6938 Paris at him euel taysed. *c* **1412** Hoccleve *De Reg. Princ.* 5262 Sore in þe bowe of treccherye he teisyth. *c* **1450** *Merlin* 590 Kynge Ban..spronge that wey with his swerde vp teysed to hym that hadde his knyght slayn. **1513** Douglas *Æneis* x. viii. 102 A bustuus lance..That lang quhile taysit he in proper tene, Leit gird at Pallas. *Ibid.* vi. 106.

† **Teise,** *v.*[2] *Obs.* Also 4 tayse, 5 teyse (6 teese), 7 tease, teaze. [Origin unascertained. The forms agree with those of Teise *v.*[1], with which however the sense does not seem compatible. Both forms and sense separate it from Tease *v.*, although in late use it may have been sometimes associated with the latter in its modern sense, and hence confounded in spelling with it.] *trans.* app. To drive (esp. a hunted beast); to chase; to urge on.

**13..** *Gaw. & Gr. Knt.* 1169 Bi þay [the deer] were tened at þe hy3e, & taysed to þe wattrez. *c* **1410** *Master of Game* (MS. Digby 182) xxxv, Who so be teysoures to þe kynge.. as ofte as any hert cometh oute, he shulde..blowe a moot and rechate and late renne after to teyse it forth. *c* **1475** *Partenay* 1295 Into see thay went, the sayl vp gan reise, To cipresse contre ther shippes gan teise. **1559** *Mirr. Mag.* (1562) B b ij, A shyppe vpon the stormy seas, Which..From shore to shore the wynde and tide do teese. **1615** Wither *Sheph. Hunt.* iii. in *Juvenilia* (1633) 407 My eager Dogs.. Then I began with quicker speed to follow And teaz'd them on with a more cheerful hallow. **1819** Keats *Isabella* xxviii, They..did tease Their horses homeward, with convulsed spur. [Cf. **1888** Elworthy *W. Som. Words, Tease* (tēz), to drive; to harass. The only way to get rid o' they rabbits is to keep on *tazin'* o'm.]

**Teise**, obs. bad spelling of Tease.

† **Teiser.** *Obs.* Forms: 5 teysoure, 6 teiser, 6–7 teaser, teazer, 7 teizer. [Agent-n. from Teise *v.*[2]] One who rouses the game; *spec.* one of the first brace or leash of deerhounds let slip. (In later use confused in spelling with Teaser.)

*c* **1410** *Master of Game* (MS. Digby 182) xxxv, Þe firste teysoure and þe resceyuour that draweth hym doune, shull parte þe skynne. *Ibid.* [see Teise *v.*[2]]. **1575** Turberv. *Venerie* 266 By this worde teasers is ment, the first greyhoundes or brase or lease of greyhoundes which is let slip. *c* **1590** Greene *Fr. Bacon* i. 5 The loftie frolicke bucks, That scudded fore the teisers like the wind. **1616** Surfl. & Markh. *Country Farme* 686 As neere the couert as you can conueniently, you shall place your Teasers, that is, the first brace of greyhounds for the course, which should be the lightest, nimblest, and swiftest dogges you haue. **1688** R. Holme *Armoury* iii. 189/1.

*fig.* **1642** Fuller *Holy & Prof. St.* ii. v. 66 But these Teazers, rather to rouze then pinch the Game, onely made Whitaker find his spirits. **1647** Clarendon *Hist. Reb.* v. § 339 The Lord Paget likewise, who..had been one of their Teizers, to broach those bold, high Overtures. **1796** *Campaigns 1793–4* II. v. 21 Francis himself, the great Carmagnol teizer.

**Teistie** (təi·sti, tī·sti). *local.* Also 8 taisté, 9 tysté, -ty, -tie, -tey, teisty, testie, tiestie. [Of Norse origin: cf. Norw. *teist*(*e*, OIcel. *þeist, þeisti.*] The Black Guillemot.

**1774** Low *Fauna Orcad.* (1813) 106 The taisté build in holes of the earth: lay but one egg. **1837** R. Dunn *Ornith. Orkney & Shetl.* 102 Uria Grylle...Tystie. Black Guillemot. Greenland Dove. **1847** *Zoologist* V. 1909 The black guillemot..or the testie. **1876** D. Gorrie *Summers & Wint. Orkneys* v. 153 Bevies of teisties were disporting themselves in front and rear. **1892** G. Stewart *Shetland Fireside T.* iv. (ed. 2) 27 He turned as fat as a tiestie. **1893** Cozens-Hardy *Broad Norfolk* 50 Sometimes there is quite a family of similar names..of the same origin. Thus the Black Guillemot is..the *tyste, taiste, toyst*, and *tysty.*

**Teisty, Teize**, obs. ff. Testy, Tease.

**Tek, Tekat**, obs. forms of Tick *sb.*, Ticket.

**Tekbir**: see Tecbir.

† **Teke, teken,** *adv.* and *prep. Obs.* Forms: 1 to éacan, 1–4 to eke(n, 3 teken (tekenn), teke. [OE. *tó éacan*, f. *tó* to, for + *éaca* addition, Eke.] **a.** *adv.* In addition, besides, moreover, eke. **b.** *prep.* In addition to, besides.

*c* 888–1200 [see Eke *sb.*[1] 4]. *c* **975** *Rushw. Gosp.* Matt. xxv. 20 Oþre fife ic to-eke 3estrionde. *c* **1200** Ormin 2886, & tekenn þatt he wass rihhtwis He was ædmod & milde. *a* **1225** *Ancr. R.* 78 Teke þet, he seið,..þet ine silence & ine hope schal beon vre strencðe. *Ibid.* 170 Let ter teken þet 3e beon swifte ase þe sunne gleam. *c* **1230** *Hali Meid.* 25 Teke þe murhðe & te menske in heuene. **13..** *Guy Warw.* (A.) 1855 To eken þat þou art mi lordes neuou.

**Teke**, obs. form of Teak, Tick.

† **Te·kelite.** *Obs. slang.* [? f. '*Tekel*: weighed in the balances, and found wanting' (Dan. v. 27) + -ite[1].] (In the cant of the Debtors' Prison, Whitecross Street, London) A defaulter, a defaulting debtor.

**1834** *New Monthly Mag.* XL. 328 This, though expressly denominated 'the defaulter's table', the only one to which the poor 'tekelite' has right of access, is invariably appropriated by the free and unexcepted knights to the washing of cups and platters.

**Teket**, obs. Sc. f. Ticket. **Tekno-**: see Tecno-.

**Tekoretin** (tīkǫrī·tin). *Chem.* Also **tec-**. [Named 1839 by Forchhammer, app. 'f. Gr. τήκειν to melt, dissolve + ῥητίνη resin, because separated by solution in hot alcohol' (Chester).] A resin similar to or identical with Fichtelite.

**1858** T. E. Clark in *Amer. Jrnl. Sc.* Ser. ii. XXV. 167 Tekoretin, being less soluble than phylloretin, crystallized first. **1868** Dana *Min.* 736 Tecoretin was obtained from pine trees [*Pinus sylvestris*] in marshes near Holtegard in Denmark. The resin from the wood..was found to contain two substances...The tecoretin was the least soluble.

† **Tel.** *Obs.* [Shortened from OE. *getæl, getel*, early ME. *itel*: cf. Tale *sb.*] Number.

*c* **1000** Ælfric *Hom.* I. 536 Heora tel bið swa meni3feald, þæt [etc.]. *a* **1225** *Ancr. R.* 372 Hundred is ful tel, & noteð perfectiun.

**Tel**: see Tele *sb.*, Tell, Till.

**Telacoustic**: see Tele-.

‖ **Telæsthesia** (teles-, telĭspī·siă). *Psychics.* [mod. L. (Myers, 1882), f. Gr. τῆλε far off (see Tele-) + αἴσθησις perception + -ia[1].] 'Perception at a distance; direct sensation or perception of objects or conditions independently of the recognized channels of sense' (Myers *Human Personality*, Gloss.).

**1882** Myers in *Proc. Soc. Psychical Research* I. ii. 147 We venture to introduce the words *Telæsthesia* and *Telepathy* to cover all cases of impression received at a distance without the normal operation of the recognised sense organs. **1903** — *Human Personality* I. 136. **1908** *Nation* 26 Sept. 907/1 Telepathy, telaesthesia and the subliminal part of man's mental being play a vast part in all these curious psychical phenomena.

**Telæsthetic** (telesþe·tik, -ĭsþe·tik), *a.* [f. as prec. + Æsthetic.]

**1.** Having physical perception of things at a distance.

**1890** C. Ll. Morgan *Anim. Life & Intell.* (1891) 249 This temperature-sense, unlike the sense of touch, may make us aware of distant bodies. It is what we may term a *telæsthetic* sense in contradistinction to a contact sense... Sight like hearing is a telæsthetic sense. Through it we become aware of certain vibratory states of more or less distant objects.

**2.** *Psychics.* Of or belonging to telæsthesia.

**1903** Myers *Human Personality* I. p. xlv, This may be done through..telæsthetic dreams or visions. **1903** *Athenæum* 28 Feb. 277/1 Examples of apparently clairvoyant, or telepathic, or telæsthetic cases.

‖ **Telamon** (te·lămǫn). *Arch.* Pl. **Telamones** (telămōu·nīz). [In pl. a. L. *telamōnes*, = Gr. τελαμῶνες, pl. of Τελαμών name of a hero in mythology.] A figure of a man used as a column to support an entablature or other structure: = Atlas *sb.*[1] 1 b.

**1706** Phillips (ed. Kersey), *Telamones*,..the Images of Men that seem'd to bear up the Out-jettings of Cornishes in the Roman Buildings, which among the Greeks were call'd Atlantes. **1797** Holcroft *Stolberg's Trav.* (ed. 2) III. lxiv. 12 Male statues of this kind were called..*Telamones.* **1882** Fennell tr. *Michaelis' Anc. Marb. Gt. Brit.* 594 A kneeling youth..serves as a *Telamon* or *Atlas*, bearing on his head and his fore-arms a large, low cup, which forms the top of the whole candelabrum.

**Telanemograph**: see Tele-.

‖ **Telangiectasis** (tĭlændʒiˌe·ktăsis). *Path.* Pl. **-ses** (-sīz). [mod.L., f. Gr. τέλος end + ἀγγεῖον vessel + ἔκτασις extension, dilatation.] Dilatation of the small blood-vessels, producing small red or purple tumours in the skin; one of such tumours. Also **Telangie·ctasy** [ad. mod.L. *telangiectasia*]. Hence **Telangiectatic** (-tæ·tik) *a.*, pertaining to or resulting from telangiectasis.

**1831** J. F. South *Otto's Path. Anat.* ii. 342 In telangiectasy, there is a peculiar degeneration of the blood-vessels connected also with widening of the smaller veins. **1868** T. G. Thomas *Dis. Women* (1872) 486 Tumors thus affected have been styled telangiectatic tumors. **1873** T. H.

Green *Introd. Pathol.* (ed. 2) 178 The various forms of nævi, and telangiectasis. **1899** *Allbutt's Syst. Med.* VIII. 833 Telangiectatic warts. *Ibid.*, The telangiectases range themselves in little groups.

**Telapoi, telapoon**: see Talapoin.

**Telar** (tī·lăɪ), *a. rare*⁻⁰. [f. L. *tēla* web + -ar [1].] Pertaining to or of the nature of a web. Hence **Te·larly** *adv.*, in the manner of a web. So **Telarian** (tĭlēə·riăn) *a.*, that spins a web, as a spider; *sb.* a spider that spins a web; † **Te·lary** *a.* = *telar, telarian* adj.

**1646** Sir T. Browne *Pseud. Ep.* v. xix. 262 We will not dispute the pictures of Telary Spiders, and their position in the web. **1658** — *Gard. Cyrus* iii. 58 Conformable to the Spiders web, and the Radii in like manner telarely interwoven. **1853** G. Johnston *Nat. Hist. E. Bord.* I. 126 Slender spokes..'telarly interwoven' somewhat after the fashion of the spider's web. **1891** *Cent. Dict.*, Telarian.

**Telar, -are**, obs. forms of Tiller.

**Telau·togram.** [f. next: after *telegram*.] A record produced by a telautograph.

**1895** in *Funk's Stand. Dict.*

**Telautograph** (telǭ·tŏgraf). Also (less correctly) **teleautograph.** [f. Gr. τῆλε far off (see Tele-) + Autograph, after *telegraph*.] A telegraphic apparatus by which writing or drawing done with a pen or pencil at the transmitting end is reproduced in facsimile at the receiving end, by means of an electric current conveyed along a wire, and (in the usual forms of the instrument) communicating movements to the receiving pen corresponding to those made with the transmitting pen or pencil. Hence **Telautogra·phic** *a.*, pertaining to the telautograph; **Telauto·graphy**, the use of the telautograph.

**1884** Knight *Dict. Mech.* Supp., *Telautograph*, an electrical device for transmitting autographs, or copying designs. ..The possibility of deception and the impossibility of automatic unquestionable record..are removed, it is said, by the employment of telautography. **1887** *Tribune* (Chicago) 25 June, Prof. Elisha Gray..is perfecting an invention with wonderful possibilities...The 'Telautograph' is the name by which the instrument will be known. **1888** *Daily News* 9 Aug. 5/7 What is known as the telautographic system, invented by Professor Elisha Gray. **1894** *Westm. Gaz.* 20 Dec. 7/1 The electricians..were shown numerous slips of paper covered with autograph writing traced by the telautograph receiver in Paris, in obedience to a person writing in London with the telautograph transmitter. **1905** *Daily Chron.* 10 Jan. 5/6 Some very successful experiments in telautography were made yesterday between the Paris Central Telephone Office and the Rouen Bourse Exchange.

**Telbent**, obs. form of Turban.

† **Teld**, *sb. Obs.* Forms: 1–5 **teld**, 1, 4–5 **telde**, (3 **tȝeld**), 4 **tield, teeld**, 4–5 **tilde**, 5 **tild, tyld, -e, telte.** [OE. *teld, geteld* = OLG. **teld* (MDu. *telde, telte*, Kilian), MLG. *telt, telde*, LG. *telt*; OHG. *zelt* (mostly *gizelt*), MHG. *zelt* (usually *gezelt*), Ger. *zelt*; ON. *tjald* (:—**teld*), pl. *tjǫld*, Norw. *tjeld*, Sw. *tält*, dial. *tjäll*, Da. *telt*, tent, pavilion, app. a deriv. of *teld-an* str. vb. to cover (cf. OE. *beteldan, oferteldan*). The late form *telte* may have been influenced by continental forms: see also Tilt.] A tent, pavilion, covering; hence, a tabernacle, dwelling.

*a* **900** tr. *Bæda's Hist.* iii. ix. [xi.] § 2 (Camb. MS.) Mon teld [*v.r.* ȝeteld] þærofer abrædde. *c* **1000** Ælfric *Gen.* xviii. 9 On þam telde heo ys. **1037** in Thorpe *Charters* (1865) 566/32 And Alfric biscop I biqueðe mine teld and min bedreaf. *c* **1205** Lay. 17491 Niȝe þusend teldes. *Ibid.* 24436 Þer weore on uelden moni þusend telden. *c* **1330** R. Brunne *Chron. Wace* (Rolls) 12598 Þey come to þe Emperours telde. When þey were at his pauyloun..þey lyghte alle doun. **13..** *Childh. Jesus* 44 in Herrig's *Archiv* LXXIV. 327 That owtelawe tuke hire to his tilde [*rimes* wilde, childe, mylde]. **1387** Trevisa *Higden* (Rolls) I. 127 Þese men.. woneþ in tabernacles and in teeldis. *a* **1400–50** *Alexander* 4581 How suld ȝe telle withouten toles or any tild rere? *c* **1400** *Laud Troy Bk.* 4656 Thei reysed vp bothe halle and tylde. *c* **1440** *Promp. Parv.* 488/1 Telte, or tente, *tentorium.* ? *a* **1500** *Chester Pl.* vii. 6 From stif stormes my sheepe to sheild..Under Tildes them to hyde.

**b.** The tilt or awning of a boat or vessel: cf. **Tilt.**

**1307–8** *Acc. Exch. K. R.* Bd. 14 No. 14 (P.R.O.), Tieldes emptis..pro dicta Bargia. **1495** *Wills Doctors' Commons* (Camden) 3 The barge with bailles, tilde, and ores belonging to the same.

**c.** A cage for carrying hawks.

**1391** *Earl Derby's Exp.* (Camden) 88 Pro tieldes per ipsum emptis ibidem ad cariandum les haukes, xiiij scot.

**d.** *Comb.*, as **teld-stede**, dwelling-place, 'tabernacle'; **teldwyrhta** (OE.), tent-wright, tentmaker.

*c* **1000** Ælfric *Hom.* I. 392 Paulus..seðe wæs on woruldcræfte teld-wyrhta. *a* **1300** *E. E. Psalter* cxix. [cxx.] 5 Wa to me, for mi telde-stede swa Forth-ferred es me fra [1388 Wyclif *ibid.*, My dwelling in an alien lond is maad long].

† **Teld, tild,** *v. Obs.* Forms: *Inf.* 1 ***teld-ian,** 2–3 **teld-en, tild-en,** 3–5 **teld(e, tild,** 5 **tield.** *Pa. t.* α. 1 **teldede, -ode,** 4–5 **tilded(e, teildid.** β. (3 **tȝelt**), 4 **tilde, teilde,** 4–5 **teld, telt, tilld (tillede), tulde, tilte,** 4–6 **telde,** 5–6 **tild.** *Pa. pple.* α. 1 *(**ȝe)telded,** 3 **i-tælded,** 3–4 **i-telded,** 4 **telded,** 4–5 **-id, -it,** 5 **i-teldyde,** 6 *Sc.* **tyldit, -et.** β. 4 **y-telde, y-tielde,** 4–5 **ytelt (i-tilled), teld, -e,** 4 **teeld, -e,** 5 **y-teld, y-tilde, tild.** [OE. *teldian* wk. vb., f. Teld *sb.*; = ON. *tjalda*. In ME. the *d* of the stem was often merged in that of the pa. t. and pa. pple. This brought the vb. into contact with Till *v.*, pa. t. *tilde*.]

**1.** *trans.* To 'spread', set up, pitch (a tent); hence, to erect (a building of any kind), to build, raise. Also *fig.*

*c* **725** *Corpus Gloss.* (O.E.T.) 591 *Con[n]ectit*, teldat. *c* **1205** Lay. 17489 Weoren a þan walde teldes itælded. **13..** *K. Alis.* 3434 (Bodl. MS.) Pauylouns were alle wiþinne Strongelich ytelt [*Linc. Inn MS.* y-tielde] by gynne. *Ibid.* 3464 Þe kyng þer telt [*v. r.* teildid] his pauylouns. *Ibid.* 5885 There biside his pauylouns, Weren y-telde by dales and dovnes. **13..** *Gaw. & Gr. Knt.* 795 Towre telded bytwene trochet ful þik. **1362** Langl. *P. Pl.* A. ii. 44 Ten þousend of Tentes I-tilled [*v.rr.* I-teldyde, teldit, teled] be-sydes. **1388** Wyclif 2 *Sam.* xvi. 22 Therfor thei tildeden Absolon a tabernacle in the soler. *c* **1400** *Destr. Troy* 11664 Here he tild vp a temple of a trew godde. *a* **1400–50** *Alexander* 1159 A hiȝe tilde as a toure teldid on schippis. *Ibid.* 2174 (Dubl. MS.) To tergarontes he tiȝt þar telde was a mynster. *c* **1460** *Launfal* 263 A pavyloun yteld he sygh. **1515** *Scot. Field* 38 in *Chetham Misc.* (1856) II, Beside the towne of Tirwin, our tentes downe we telden.

**2.** *intr.* To pitch one's tent; to encamp; to take one's station or residence; in *pa. pple.* encamped, lodged, stationed.

*c* **1250** *Gen. & Ex.* 1840 Iacob fro ðeðen wente, ic wot, tȝelt on a stede, and cald it sochot. *c* **1330** R. Brunne *Chron. Wace* (Rolls) 12588 [On] þat playne..were þe Romayns telded. *c* **1330** — *Chron.* (1810) 242 Biside a more a mod quayntly was he teld. **1393** Langl. *P. Pl.* C. xv. 150 Ryȝt as traianus, þe trewe knyght, tulde [*v.rr.* tillede, telde; B. xii. 210 tilde, tilte, dwelte] nat deep in helle. *a* **1400** *Pistill of Susan* 56 Þeos perlous prestes..turned fro his teching, þat teeld [*v.rr.* teelde, told] is in trone. *c* **1440** *York Myst.* x. 14 Wher I was telde vnder a tree.

**3.** *trans. Sc.* To cover with an awning or curtain.

**1501** Douglas *Pal. Hon.* i. 432 Reparrellit was that godlike plesand wone Tyldit abone, and to the eirth adoun. **1825** Jamieson s.v. *Tyld*, A window is said to be *tyldit*, when it is covered in the inside with a cloth or curtain.

**4.** To spread (a net), set (a trap or snare). (See also Till *v.*)

*c* **1000** *Ags. Ps.* (Thorpe) xxxiv. 8 Hi teldedon gryne and ða ȝehyddon. *c* **1175** *Lamb. Hom.* 53 Þenne þe mon wule tilden his musestoch he bindeð uppon þa swike chese. *c* **1200** *Trin. Coll. Hom.* 211 At pleȝe [þe deuel] teldeð þe grune of idelnesse. *a* **1225** *Ancr. R.* (Corpus MS.: Camden 334), Triste is þer me sit mid te greahunz forte kepe þe heare, oðer tildeð [so *Cleop.*, *Caius*; *Titus* tildes; *Nero* tillen; *Vern.* tilleþ] þe nettes aȝein him. **1413** *Pilgr. Sowle* (Caxton 1483) i. xviii. 14 Teldyng nettes, arrayng trappys and other engynes. *c* **1440** *Pallad. on Husb.* iv. 164 A green another hath for hem ytilde.

Hence † **Telding** (tildunge) *vbl. sb.*, laying of snares.

*a* **1225** *Ancr. R.* 278 Seint Antonie þet iseih al þene world ful of þes deofles tildunge.

**Teld, -e, -en**, obs. inflexions of Tell *v.*

† **Tele, tel,** *sb. Obs.* Forms: 1 **tǽl,** 4 **tél, teyl,** 5 **tele.** [OE. *tǽl* fem. (also *tál*: see Tole) = OHG. *zâla* danger, snare, trap, ON. *tál* bait, allurement. OTeut. **tǽlâ* str. fem., had app. some such general sense as 'hostile or malevolent attack, persecution', whence the specialized senses in the various langs. See also Tele *v.*]

**1.** Evil speaking, detraction, calumny, blame.

*c* **897** K. Ælfred *Gregory's Past. C.* xxxiii. 222 Ælc ðweora, & ælc ierre..& tæl sie anumen fram eow. *a* **1000** *Gloss.* in Wr.-Wülcker 196/16 *Blasphemia, uituperatio*, tæl. *Ibid.* 220/23. **1303** R. Brunne *Handl. Synne* 2042 But þogh a man sey neuer so weyl Vnto hys sawys men fynden teyl.

**2.** Deceit; enticement, allurement.

*c* **1300** *Havelok* 191 Þat he sholde yemen hire wel Withuten lac, with-uten tel Til þat she were tuelf winter hold. *a* **1450** Myrc *Par. Pr.* 368 So with cha[r]mes & wyth tele, He ys I-broȝte aȝeyn to hele.

† **Tele,** *v. Obs.* Forms: 1 **tǽlan (télan),** 2–3 **tælen** (3 *Orm.*) **tælenn,** 3–5 **tellen),** 2–4 **telen,** 3–4 **tele.** [OE. (WSax.) *tǽlan* (Angl. *télan*) = ON. *tǽla* to deceive, betray, entice:—OTeut. **tǽljan*, f. *tǽlâ*: see Tele *sb.* Cf. OHG. *zâlôn* (:—*tǽlôjan*) to rob, pillage.]

**1.** *trans.* To speak evil of, or to; to revile, calumniate; to mock, scorn, deride.

*c* **888** K. Ælfred *Boeth.* xxxviii. § 3 Ic wolde unðeawas tælan & goode herian. *c* **890** *Laws K. Ælfred* c. 37 Ne tæl ðu ðinne Dryhten. *a* **900** *Kentish Gloss.* in Wr.-Wülcker 55/19 *Et detraxerunt*, and his teldan. *Ibid.* 75/13 *Deridet*, teld. *Ibid.* 76/31 *Detrahent*, telað. *c* **950** *Lindisf. Gosp.* John xii. 48 Seðe mec teles [*c* **975** *Rushw.* teleð]. **10..** *Glosses* (Cott. Cleop.) in Wr.-Wülcker 373/26 *Carpere*, telan. *c* **1160** *Hatton Gosp.* Luke xiv. 29 Ealle þe hit ȝe-seoð aginned hine tælen [*Ags. Gosp.* tælan]. *c* **1200** Ormin 2039–40 Ȝiff þatt tu willt tælenn me þe birrþ ec hire tælenn. *a* **1250** *Prov. Ælfred* 237 in *O. E. Misc.* 116 Byfore he þe meneþ, by-hynde he þe teleþ. *c* **1490** *Promp. Parv.* 488/1 (MS. K.) Tellynge, or grochynge, *murmuracio.*

**2.** To deceive, entrap [cf. ON. *tǽla* to betray].

*c* **1325** *Metr. Hom.* (1862) 12 His [Christ's] godhed in fleis was felid Als hok in bait, quare thoru he telid The fend, that telid our fadir Adam. *Ibid.* 152 That he no haf miht us to tele With gastly dranc and wit darnele. **13..** *Metr. Hom.* (Vernon MS.) in Herrig's *Archiv* LVII. 276 But faste he fondeþ mon to tele. Vre lord vs schilde from his teolyng.

Hence † **Teling** *vbl. sb.* (also 3 **teolunge,** 4 **-yng, teliinge,** 4–5 **telyng, teeling**), deception, sorcery, witchcraft.

*a* **1225** *Ancr. R.* 208 Sigaldren, & false teolunges, leuunge on ore & of swefnes & alle wichchecreftes. *c* **1315** Shoreham iii. 178 By-lef þou in no wychecraft, Ne ine none teliinge. **13..** [see Tele *v.* 2]. **1387** Trevisa *Higden* (Rolls) III. 343 He triste on his endynge [*v.r.* endityngе] and tellynges [*v.rr.* teelingis, telyngs, tellyngys] as olde wifes useþ. *a* **1450** Myrc *Par. Pr.* 360 Wychecrafte and telynge. *c* **1450** [see Tele *v.* 1].

**Tele**, obs. f. Teal, Tell *v.*, Tile *sb.*, Till *v.*

**Tele-** (te·lĭ) (before a vowel properly **tel-**, but more often in the full form), repr. Gr. τηλε-, combining form of τῆλε afar, far off; used in numerous (chiefly recent) scientific and technical terms, mostly denoting or connected with special appliances or methods for operating over long distances; also in several terms connected with psychical research, denoting actions or impressions produced at a distance from the exciting cause, independently of the normal means of communication. (The second element is properly and usually from Greek, exceptionally from Latin or English.) The earlier and more important of these words will be found in their alphabetical places; others follow here.

**Telacou·stic** *a.*, *Psychics* [Acoustic], pertaining to or involving the perception of a sound beyond or apart from the possibility of ordinary hearing (cf. *teloptic* below). **Te·le₁ane·mograph,** 'an anemograph that records at a distance by means of electricity' (*Cent. Dict.* 1891). **Teleba·rograph,** 'a barograph that records at a distance by means of electricity' (*ibid.*). **Te·lebaro·meter,** 'a barometer that registers its indications at a distance by means of electric apparatus' (*ibid.*). **Telece·ntric** *a.*, *Optics*, applied to a lens system of which the aperture or stop is at the principal focus. **Telechi·rograph** [Gr. χείρ hand], a form of Telautograph [cf. definition of Telautograph]. **Telecry·ptograph,** a form of printing telegraph adopted for secret or private communication. **Tele·ctrograph, Tele·ctroscope:** see *telelectro-*. **Telehydrobaro·meter** [Gr. ὕδωρ water: see Barometer], an instrument for recording electrically at a distance the pressure of a head of water or other liquid. **Te·le₁ico·nograph** [Gr. εἰκών image: see -graph], an apparatus consisting of a telescope combined with a camera lucida, by which images of distant objects may be cast upon paper and traced. **Te·lekin** [mod., f. Gr. κιν-εῖν to move], a device for the electric control of machinery from a distance. ‖ **Telekine·sis,** *Psychics* [mod.L., f. Gr. κίνησις motion], movement of or in a body alleged to occur at a distance from, and without material connexion with, the motive cause or agent; hence **Telekine·tic** *a.*, belonging to telekinesis. **Telele·ctric** *a.*, producing mechanical motions or effects at a distance by electrical means. **Telele·ctrograph,** shortened **tele·ctrograph**: cf. Electrograph, an apparatus for producing at the receiving end a copy of a photograph or print at the transmitting end, by means of electric telegraphy. **Telele·ctroscope,** shortened **tele·ctroscope** [cf. prec. and -scope], an apparatus for reproducing at a distance a visual image, as that in a camera obscura, by means of electric telegraphy. **Te·lemano·meter,** a manometer which registers at a distance by means of electricity. **Telemecha·nics,** the art of transmitting power to a distance, esp. by etherial vibrations as in wireless telegraphy; **Teleme·chanism. Te·lemetaca·rpal** *a.*, *Comp. Anat.*, having vestiges only of the distal portion of the first and fifth metarcarpals, as in one group of the *Cervidæ*. **Teleme·teorograph,** a meteorograph which records electrically at a distance; a combination of telethermograph, telebarograph, and teleanemograph; hence **Teleme·teorogra·phic** *a.*, **Teleme·teoro·graphy. Telemi·croscope,** an optical instrument combining the functions of a telescope and a microscope; e. g. in enlarging a telescopic image or in projecting a microscopic image to a distance (e. g. upon a screen). **Te·lemo·tor,** an apparatus for transmitting motive power to a distance; *esp.* a device for steering a ship from some part distant from the tiller, by means of hydraulic or pneumatic pressure, etc. **Tele-ne·gative** *a.* in *telenegative lens*, the negative element in a telephotographic lens: cf. Telephotographic *a.*[2], quot. 1892 [3]. **Telengyscope** (-e·ndʒiskōᵘp), incorrectly **-engi-** [see Engyscope], an optical instrument combining the powers of a telescope and microscope (*Cent. Dict.* 1891). **Te·le-obje·ctive** *a.*, having an object-glass adapted to photographing distant objects; as a *tele-objective camera*; *sb.* (see quot.). **Telepla·stic** *a.*, *Psychics* [Plastic; after *telepathy*, etc.]: see quot. 1890. **Te·lepola·riscope,** an optical instrument consisting of a telescope combined with a polariscope. **Tele-po·sitive** *a.*, *Optics*: see quot. **Tele₁ra·dio-phone,** a radiophone producing sounds at a distance by means of an electric current as in telegraphy. **Te·lergy,** *Psychics* [after *energy*], the supposed force operating in telepathy, regarded as correlated with the various forms of physical energy, or as directly affecting the brain or organism of the percipient; so **Tele·rgically** *adv.*, by means of telergy. **Teleseism** (te·lǐsəiz'm) [Seism], a distant or remote earth-tremor as recorded on a seismograph. **Te·leseme** (-sīm) [Gr. σῆμα sign], an electric signalling apparatus used in hotels, etc., fitted with an indicator which shows the article or service required. **Te·lesoma·tic** *a.*, *Psychics* [Gr. σῶμα body]: see *teleplastic*, quot. 1890. **Telespe·ctroscope,** a combination of a telescope and a spectroscope, for spectroscopic observations of the heavenly bodies. **Teleste·reo-scope,** an instrument with two pairs of mirrors so arranged that distant objects viewed by means of it appear to stand out in relief, as in a stereoscope. **Telethe·rmograph,** a thermograph which records electrically at a distance; a self-registering telethermometer; hence **Telethe·rmogram. Te·lether-mo·meter,** a thermometer furnished with an apparatus which electrically exhibits its indications at a distance; hence **Telethermo·metry,** the use of a telethermometer. **Te·letopo·meter** [Gr. τόπος place: see -meter], name for a special form of telemeter (Telemeter 1). **Te·letype,** a type-printing telegraph; hence **Telety·pic** *a.*; **Telety·pograph,** a form of machine telegraph which records its message by perforating a tape that sets in motion a type-setting machine. **Televi·sion,** vision of a distant object or scene by means of an apparatus (not yet perfected) which electrically reproduces an image of it at the receiving end: cf. Telephote. **Telewriter** (telǐrəi·təɹ), an instrument which electrically reproduces in facsimile a written message; a form of Telautograph; hence **Te·lewrite** *v.* (*nonce-wd.*), to send a message by a telewriter. **Telo·ptic** *a.*, *Psychics* [Optic], pertaining to or involving the perception as if by sight of an object beyond or apart from the possibility of ordinary vision (cf. *telacoustic* above); so **Telo·smic** *a.* [Gr. ὀσμή smell], involving the perception of a smell in a similar way.

1893 *Telacoustic [see *teleplastic*]. 1903 *Electr. Wld. & Engineer* 20 June 1055 *Telechirograph. 1904 *Athenæum* 5 Nov. 628/3 The device for secret telegraphy or *telecryptograph of Messrs. Siemens and Halske also deserves notice. 1909 *Daily Mirror* 13 Aug. 14/2 The pictures were wired from Manchester to London last night in six minutes by the Thorne-Baker *telectrograph. 1884 Knight *Dict. Mech.* Supp., **Telectroscope*, an apparatus for reproducing by telegraph the images obtained in the camera obscura..based on the property possessed by selenium of offering a variable and very sensitive electrical resistance according to the different gradations of light. 1891 *Cent. Dict.*, *Telehydrobarometer. 1877 Knight *Dict. Mech.*, *Teleiconograph. 1905 *Sci. Amer., Suppl.* 6 May 24539 The inventor distinguishes between a simple *telekin, wherein only a single motion is considered, and a multiple telekin, which permits of a complexity of motions. 1890 Myers in *Proc. Soc. Psych. Research* Dec. 668 *Extramediumistic* operations, as thought-transference, telepathy, *telekinesis (*Fernwirkung*), or movements of objects without contact. *Ibid.* 669 For the alleged movements without contact..M. Aksakof's new word '*telekinetic' seems to me the best attainable. 1905 *Sat. Rev.* 19 Aug. 250 Of the other phenomena.. that of telekinesis, or movement of objects without material contact. 1909 *Cent. Dict., Suppl.* s.v., An organ with a *telelectric attachment. 1898 *Daily News* 10 Mar. 6/3 It is called the '*Telelectroscope', because it renders objects visible in their natural colours at a distant place by means of electricity. *Ibid.*, If we had had the 'Telelectroscope' in operation some time ago, we might have gone into a theatre in London and witnessed the eclipse of the sun in India for ourselves. 1891 *Cent. Dict.*, *Telemanometer. 1909 *Athenæum* 6 Mar. 293/1 The researches now being made..into what is called *tele-mechanics, or the art of transmitting power to a distance by waves in the ether and without wires. 1907 *Ibid.* 29 June 798/3 The phenomena..of *tele-mechanism, or the operation of machines at a distance. 1878 *Proc. Zool. Soc. Lond.* 887 Plesiometacarpal and *telemetacarpal limb—characters..closely corresponding with the distribution of the Cervidæ. 1881 *Nature* 14 Apr. 564/2 On March 26..There were repeated at the Brussels Observatory experiments with Van Rysselberghes' *telemeteorograph, which prove that the registration of the meteorological elements..may be made automatically at very great distances. *Ibid.*, The author explained to the Minister a plan of International *Telemeteorography. 1883 *Science* I. 88 The establishment of an international *telemeteorographic system. 1860 Mayne *Expos. Lex.*, *Teleomicroscopium*,..an instrument for enlarging or increasing the forms of more remote or indistinct objects: a *teleomicroscope [*sic*]. 1895 *Arena* (Boston) App. 13 Prof. D. S. Holman, the celebrated microscopist...His lectures..are illustrated by the tele-microscope, which projects upon a screen nearly all conceivable experiments. 1897 *Tit-Bits* 11 Dec. 207/3 A 10 in. telescope can, by means of the new telemicroscope be made to magnify 25000 diameters. 1890 *Nature* 3 Apr. 516/2 The steering motor is placed directly on the quadrant of the tiller, and is actuated from the bridge by means of what the author describes as a *telemotor. 1897 *Daily News* 20 Sept. 3/1 A new steam steering engine has been added, having a telemotor on Messrs. Brown Bros.' system. 1905 *Tele-negative [see *tele-positive*]. 1902 Mann, etc. tr. *P. Drude's The. Optics* I. v. 94 A..*teleobjective, which consists of a combination of a convergent and a divergent system placed at a distance apart. 1890 Myers in *Proc. Soc. Psych. Research* Dec. 669 M. Aksakof uses the term 'telesomatic' for the phenomena of so-called 'materialisation'...It would be better, I think, to give the name **tele-plastic* to all this class of alleged phenomena. 1893 *Chicago Advance* 31 Aug., Certain teleplastic, telacoustic, teloptic, and telosmic occurrences. 1878 Lockyer *Stargazing* 441 The *Telepolariscope. 1905 *Sci. Amer., Suppl.* 30 Sept. 24861 This lens, called *tele-negative*, need not be connected permanently with the ordinary objective (which is called **tele-positive*), a loose connection by means of a removable short tube being quite sufficient. 1881 *Nature* 13 Oct. 576/2 Multiple inverse electric *teleradiophone, by M. Mercadier. 1908 Sir O. Lodge in *Hibbert Jrnl.* Apr. 575 A foreign intelligence, acting either telepathically through the mind or *telergically by a more direct process straight on the brain. 1884 Gurney & Myers in *19th Cent.* May 814 Unless some such relation [of telepathy to space and to matter] can be demonstrated we cannot reasonably speak of a psychical *telergy—an action of mind on mind at a distance—as correlated with any energy which we have learnt to measure. 1903 Myers *Hum. Personality* I. Gloss., Telergy. 1891 *Cent. Dict.*, *Teleseme. 1899 *Westm. Gaz.* 8 June 10/2 The bedrooms are fitted with a model kind of call, the Teleseme—a dumb waiter. 1901 F. Harrison in *19th Cent.* June 916 Life in the States is one perpetual whirl of telephones, telesemes, phonographs, electric bells, etc. 1890 *Telesomatic [see *teleplastic* above]. 1871 tr. *Schellen's Spectr. Anal.* liii. 247 Young's *telespectroscope. 1882 Young *Sun* iii. 77 The combined instrument is then often called a tele-spectroscope. 1864 Webster, **Telestereoscope*, a stereoscope adapted to view distant natural objects or landscapes; a telescopic stereoscope. 1887 *Encycl. Brit.* XXII. 541/1 Von Helmholtz invented the Telestereoscope, an instrument which places as it were the point of view of both eyes wide apart. 1891 *Cent. Dict.*, *Telethermograph..*Telethermometer.. *Telethermometry. *Ibid.*, **Teletopometer*, a telemeter in which two telescopes are used. 1905 *Daily Chron.* 9 Feb. 3/6 To the instrument, known as the teletopometer, a telescope is fixed, in which appear two pictures of the distant object. One picture is stationary, while the other moves and is brought to cover the first. A scale attached..indicates at once the distance of the object. 1909 *Athenæum* 25 Sept. 367/3 The efforts made by Prof. Rukmer of Berlin to realize '*television'. 1908 *Times* 5 Dec. 16/3 An apparatus called a '*telewriter' for electrically reproducing at a distance handwriting, drawings [etc.]. 1908 *Daily Chron.* 21 Dec., The Lord Mayor, '*telewriting' to the Lord Mayor of Manchester, tendered his cordial greetings to him and his fellow-citizens from the City of London and himself. 1909 *Ibid.* 13 Jan. 6/1 Telewriters with telephones attached will be put in in the case of a limited number of original subscribers without any rental charges or other initial expenses. 1893 *Teloptic, *Telosmic [see *teleplastic* above].

**Telearch** (te·lĭ₁ɑ̄ɹk). *Gr. Hist.* [ad. Gr. τελέαρχος, f. τέλος office: see -arch.] The title of a magistrate in ancient Thebes.

1797 W. Johnstone tr. *Beckmann's Invent.* II. 23 At Thebes the streets were under the inspection of the telearchs.

**Teleautograph**: see Telautograph.

**Telebarograph to Telectroscope**: see Tele-.

‖ **Teledu** (te·ledu). [Native name in Javanese.] A carnivorous animal of Java and Sumatra (*Mydaus meliceps*), allied to the skunk and of similar habits; also called *stinking badger* or *stinkard*.

1824 Horsfield *Zool. Res. Java*, *Tĕlĕdu*, in the language of Java, East of Cheribon. *Ibid.*, The covering of the Tĕlĕdu is adapted to the elevated and cold regions which it inhabits. *Ibid.*, The entire neighbourhood of a village is infected by the odour of an irritated Tĕlĕdu.

**Teledynamic**: see Telodynamic.

‖ **Telega** (telē·gä). Also 6 **telego**, 9 **telaga, telegga, teljèga**, (**telegue**). [a. Russ. телѣга, *teljéga*; whence also F. *télègue*.] A four-wheeled Russian cart, of rough construction, without springs.

1558 in Hakluyt *Voy.* (1599) 315 With these Telegoes they caried our stuffe from Vologhda vnto the Mosco. 1807 Sir R. Wilson *Jrnl.* 7 Sept., in *Life* (1862) II. viii. 365, I mounted my telaga and drove to Lord Gower's. 1833 R. Pinkerton *Russia* 21 Government couriers travel in telegas, or four-wheeled simply-constructed carts. 1877 Mar. M. Grant *Sun-Maid* x, We travelled for weeks in a telèga, a sort of queer snow carriage. 1903 *19th Cent.* Mar. 421 A party of poor telega-drivers.

**Telegony** (tǐle·gŏni). *Biol.* [f. Gr. τῆλε, Tele- + -γονια begetting; cf. Gr. τηλέγονος 'born far from one's fatherland'.] The (hypothetical) influence of a previous sire seen in the progeny of a subsequent sire from the same mother.

1893 W. N. Parker tr. *Weismann's Germ-Plasm* xii. 383 The phenomenon generally known as 'infection of the germ', —which, in case it really exists, I should prefer to speak of as *telegony*. 1899 *Daily News* 20 June 8/5 'The Penycuik Experiments',..undertaken to try and throw some light upon reversion and the difficult problem of telegony. 1900 *Brit. Med. Jrnl.* No. 2046. 638 Telegony might prevail in the case of hereditary predisposition.

Hence **Telego·nic** *a.*, of or pertaining to telegony; **Tele·gonous** *a.*, 'of, pertaining to, or produced by telegony' (*Funk's Stand. Dict.* 1895).

1893 F. Finn in *Nat. Science* Dec. 436 Cases which seem difficult of explanation on any other than the Telegonic theory. 1897 *Ibid.* Feb. 80 Telegonic influence of the zebra will be looked for.

**Telegram** (te·lǐgræm). [f. Gr. τῆλε, Tele- + -gram; so F. *télégramme* (1867 in Littré), Ger. *telegramm* (1865 in Sanders).] A message sent by telegraph; a telegraphic dispatch or communication. (This term encountered at first much opposition from scholars, as not being formed on Greek analogies, which give, as in mod.Gr., τηλεγράφημα, Telegrapheme; but its practical convenience led in a few years to its general adoption. In the *Panmure Papers* it takes the place of 'telegraphic despatch' from 11 Oct. 1855. Cf. also Telegraph 3.)

1852 *Albany Even. Jrnl.* 6 Apr. (Bartlett), A friend desires us to give notice that he will ask leave..to introduce a new word...It is *telegram*, instead of *telegraphic dispatch*, or *telegraphic communication*. 1855 Ld. Clarendon 31 May in *Panmure Papers* (1908) I. 218 A message should go forth with by telegram. 1857 Lady Canning *Let. fr. Calcutta* 16 Jan. in A. Hare *Two Noble Lives* (1893) II. 140 'A telegram'—a new Yankee word for a telegraphic despatch. 1857 [see Telegrapheme]. 1857 Maj. Birch *Let.* 21 Apr. in *Morn. Chron.* 23 Oct. 4/5 A telegram to the following effect has this day been transmitted to you [etc.]. 1858 *Chamb. Jrnl.* IX. 75/2 The Longmans have promised to include the word *telegram* in their forthcoming dictionary. 1859 Lytton *What will he do* xii. xi, I sent a telegram (oh that I should live to see such a word introduced into the English language!). 1860 Lytton ('O. Meredith') *Lucile* ii. iv. § 5 *note*, Ere a cable went under the hoary Atlantic, Or the word *telegram* drove grammarians frantic. 1873 F. Hall *Mod. Eng.* 158 *note*, There is, as against the exact, but surfeiting, *telegrapheme*, our lawless *telegram*.

*attrib.* and *Comb.* 1875 G. Ager (*title*) The Telegram Code, for the Use of Bankers, Merchants, and Shipowners. 1881 *Blackw. Mag.* Apr. 470 The general telegram-sender. 1895 *Daily News* 3 Dec. 5/3 For some years past the Parisians have had the benefit of a system of 'telegram postcards' which are sent by pneumatic tubes.

Hence **Te·legram** *v.* (*rare*, ? *Obs.*), *intr.* to send a telegram, to telegraph; *trans.* to telegraph to; **Te·legrame·se** (*nonce-wd.*) = Telegraphese 1; **Te·legramma·tic, Telegra·mmic** *adjs.*, of or pertaining to telegrams; concise or condensed like a telegram. All *rare*.

1864 Sala in *Daily Tel.* 27 July, Every patriotic man is bound to resent..any insult offered to the flag of his country ..without being told or *telegrammed to shoot anybody. 1876 E. FitzGerald *Let.* 2 Aug., I ought to have telegramed back to you. 1894 *Pall Mall Mag.* Mar. 733 It [the telegram] was not written in *telegramese, and it cost more money than it ought. 1866 Visct. Strangford *Selection* (1869) II. 14 The *telegrammatic battle is no longer a simple duel between Athens and Constantinople. 1864 Webster, **Telegrammic*,..in the nature of a telegram; hence, laconic; concise; brief; succinct. 1866 *London Rev.* 25 Aug. 216/1 People insist that thought should be expressed with telegrammic brevity. 1891 G. Meredith *One of our Conq.* II. ix. 237 The letter was telegramic on the essential point.

**Telegraph** (te·lǐgraf), *sb.* [a. F. *télégraphe* (Chappe 1792), f. Gr. τῆλε afar + -γραφ-ος that writes, writer: see Tele- and -graph; so Ger. *telegraph*.

Miot de Mélito states in his *Mémoires* I. 38, that Chappe the inventor proposed to call his invention a *tachygraphe*, but was told by Miot that the name was bad, and ought to be *télégraphe*, which he at once adopted. (See Littré.)]

**1.** An apparatus for transmitting messages to a distance, usually by signs of some kind. Devices for this purpose have been in use from ancient times, but the name was first applied to that invented by Chappe in France in 1792, consisting of an upright post with movable arms, the signals being made by various positions of the arms according to a pre-arranged code. Hence applied to various other devices subsequently used, operating by movable disks, shutters, etc., flashes of light, movements in a column of liquid, sounds of bells, horns, etc., or other means. (Now *rare* in this sense, such contrivances being usually called *semaphores* or *signalling apparatus*.)

[1794 *Europ. Mag.* Sept. 166/2 It was announced to them by the Telegraphe from Lisle.] 1794 *Hist.* in *Ann. Reg.* 394 The invention of the telegraph...A number of posts are erected at convenient distances; and on each..is fixed a transverse beam with two moveable arms, the beam itself being also moveable. The different forms which the machine is capable of assuming is 16, and these represent the telegraphic alphabet. 1795 *Times* 30 Dec., in Ashton *Old Times* (1885) 127 A chain of Telegraphs is erected from Shuter's Hill to Dover. 1798 *Hull Advertiser* 14 Apr. 2/4 Orders were..transmitted by the telegraph and by express to Portsmouth. 1805 in A. Duncan *Nelson* (1806) 297 Lord Nelson conveyed the following sentence by telegraph, to the fleet—'England expects every man will do his duty'. 1813 J. W. Croker in *Cr. Papers* (1884) I. ii. 53 The Plymouth telegraph announces another complete victory of Lord W. over Soult on the 30th. 18.. Moore *Fragm. Character* v, Scarcely a telegraph could wag Its wooden finger, but Ned knew it. 1823 Pasley (*title*) Description of the Universal Telegraph for Day and Night Signals. 1834-47 J. S. Macaulay *Field Fortif.* (1851) 256 A soldier makes an excellent telegraph..varying the gestures to meet the various circumstances. 1863 W. Ladd in *Rep. British Assoc.* 19 On an Acoustic Telegraph.

**b.** Applied retrospectively to ancient devices.

1794 *Times* 20 Sept., in Ashton *Old Times* (1885) 125 The invention of the Telegraphe is now traced back to 1655, and particularly mentioned in a little book..by the Marquis of Worcester...He there gives it the name of Visual Correspondence, and calls it his own invention. 1808 J. Macdonald *Telegraphic Commun.* 37 Julius Africanus minutely details a mode of spelling words by a Telegraph. It appears, that fires of various substances, were the means made use of. 1842 *Penny Cycl.* XXIV. 145/2 Bishop Wilkins, ..after describing this telegraph of Polybius, mentions another which requires only three lights or torches.

**c.** *fig.*

1795 O'Keefe *Irish Mimick* I. i, Love is a monstrous telegraph. 1817 Coleridge '*Blessed are ye*' 103 When princely capitals are often but the Telegraphs of distant calamity.

**2.** In full, *electric* (or *magnetic*) *telegraph*: An apparatus consisting of a transmitting instrument (*transmitter*), a receiving instrument (*receiver*), and a line or wire of any length connecting these, along which an electric current from a battery or other source passes, the circuit being made and broken by working the transmitter, so as to produce movements, as of a needle or pointer, in the receiver, which indicate letters, etc., either according to a code of signs, or by pointing to characters upon a dial; in some forms the receiver works so as to print or trace the message upon a prepared strip of paper.

Also, an apparatus for wireless telegraphy: see WIRELESS.

**1797** *Monthly Mag.* Feb. 148 Dr. Don Francisco Salva had read, at the Royal Academy of Sciences, at Barcelona, a Memoir on the Application of Electricity to the Telegraph, and presented..an Electrical Telegraph of his own invention. **1823** RONALDS (*title*) Descriptions of an Electrical Telegraph. **1834** BREWSTER in *Encycl. Brit.* (ed. 7) VIII. 582/1 Mr. F. Ronalds..erected at Hammersmith an electrical telegraph, on which the inflections of the wire composed one continuous length of more than eight miles. *Ibid.* 662/2 Some German and American authors have proposed to construct galvanic telegraphs by the decomposition of water. **1842** *Penny Cycl.* XXIV. 154/1 It is to the joint labours of Messrs. W. F. Cooke and Professor Wheatstone that electric telegraphs owe their practical application. *Ibid.* 155/1 The electro-magnetic telegraph...The longest continuous line yet completed is that from Paddington to West Drayton. *Ibid.*, It is reported (July, 1842) that an electric telegraph is about to be laid down along the South-Western Railway, from London to Gosport. **1845** COL. HAWKER *Diary* (1893) II. 264, I saw the magnetic telegraph at the railway station. **1854** G. B. RICHARDSON *Univ. Code* v. 7420 Have you received any communication by electric telegraph? **1858** LONGFELLOW in *Life* (1891) II. 361 Presently the clerk says, 'The Atlantic Telegraph is laid!' **1878** G. B. PRESCOTT *Sp. Telephone* (1879) 1 More than one hundred years ago Lesage established a telegraph in Geneva by the use of frictional electricity. **1881** W. M. SPRINGER in *N. Amer. Rev.* CXXXII. 369 In..thirty years the telegraphs of the world have grown to nearly half a million miles of line, and more than a million miles of wire. *fig.* **1864** LOWELL *Fireside Trav.* 123 The magnetic telegraph of human sympathy flashes swift news from brain to brain.

†**3.** A message sent by telegraph; a telegram. *Obs.*

**1850** D. WEBSTER *Lett.* (1902) 392, I received your Telegraph last eve. **1857** LADY CANNING *Let. fr. Calcutta* 12 May in Hare *Two Noble Lives* (1893) II. 161 A telegraph had come telling of a violent outbreak of the 3rd cavalry at Meerut. ?**1861** CLOUGH *Poems* (1869) II. 423 He..found a telegraph that bade him come Straight to the country. **1862** MISS YONGE *Stokesley Secret* x. 149 Suppose a telegraph should come!

**4.** In *Cricket*, A board upon which the numbers of runs obtained and wickets taken are exhibited during a match in large figures so as to be visible at a distance; a scoring-board. Also a similar device used in other athletic sports (see *telegraph-board*, quot. 1868, in 8).

**1859** *All Year Round* No. 13. 305 There was a proper telegraph to show the 'runs got' and the 'wickets down'.

**5.** *slang.* A scout or spy.

**1825** C. M. WESTMACOTT *Eng. Spy* I. 162 Dick's a trump and no telegraph. **1888** 'R. BOLDREWOOD' *Robbery under Arms* xxiii, Warrigal [was sent out] to meet one of our telegraphs..and to bring us any information he could pick up. **1890** — *Miner's Right* xviii, These 'bush telegraphs', as the modern robber slang has dubbed them, are of all avocations and both sexes.

†**6.** A fancy name for some kind of carriage. *Obs.*

**1810** S. GREEN *Reformist* II. 130 The whimsical vehicle which conveys the man of high *ton*, be it either dog-cart, telegraph, or *barouchette*.

**7.** Used as individual name of a newspaper, a variety of plant, etc.

**1794** COLERIDGE *Lett.* I. 122, I will accept of the reporter's place to the 'Telegraph' and live upon a guinea a week. **1882** *Garden* 14 Jan. 31/1 A few seeds of Telegraph [cucumbers] may now be sown in small pots.

**8.** *attrib.* and *Comb.*, as *telegraph boy, cable* (CABLE *sb.* 3), *clerk, dial, house, instrument, line* (LINE *sb.*[2] 1 e), *message, office, service, wire*; **telegraph-block**, *Naut.* a number of small brass sheaves in a long narrow shell, with which several flags may be hoisted at the same time: used in making signals; **telegraph-board** = sense 4; **telegraph-carriage** (see quot.); **telegraph-clock**, a clock connected with another in a different room or building by means of a telegraph-wire conveying an electric current, so that the movements of the one are controlled by those of the other, and thus both indicate the same time; **telegraph-cock**, 'a compression-cock operated by a pivoted lever like the key of a telegraphic transmitter' (*Funk's Stand. Dict.*); **telegraph form**, a paper printed with spaces in which the words of a telegram are to be written for dispatch (FORM 12 b); **telegraph-key**, a small lever or other device in a telegraphic transmitter, worked by the hand, for making and breaking the circuit (KEY *sb.*[1] 12 a); **telegraph-plant**, an East Indian leguminous plant, *Desmodium gyrans*, remarkable for the spontaneous movements of its leaflets, suggesting signalling; also called *moving plant*; **telegraph-pole, -post**, one of a series of poles upon which a telegraph wire or wires are carried above the ground; **telegraph-reel**, a reel on which is wound the strip of paper on which the messages are traced in a recording telegraph; **telegraph-register**, a telegraphic receiver, or part of one, which gives a permanent record of the messages received.

**1868** H. F. WILKINSON *Mod. Athletics* 17 *Telegraph Board...Before each race or heat, the numbers of the starters..should be posted on the board. **1897** 'TIVOLI' (H. W. Bleakley) *Short Innings* iii. 48 The hundred appeared on the telegraph board. Still the batsmen hit. **1860** *Illustr. Lond. News* 25 Feb. 187/1 The servant girl, and even the *telegraph boy stand staring. **1855** *Lardner's Museum Sci. & Art* III. IV. Index, *Telegraph-cables, durability of. **1877** KNIGHT *Dict. Mech.* 2507/1 The essential features of a submarine telegraph-cable are a wire or wires for conducting and a protecting compound. *Ibid.*, **Telegraph-carriage*, a vehicle provided with the apparatus necessary for opening temporary communication with a permanent line..used .. where no line of telegraph is immediately at hand. **1858** SIMMONDS *Dict. Trade*, **Telegraph-clerk*, a subordinate officer in a telegraph-office. **1879** *Daily News* 1 Aug. (Ho. Comm.), Lord J. Manners..stated that.. the name of telegraph clerks had been changed to that of telegraphists. **1877** KNIGHT *Dict. Mech.*, *Telegraph-clock. *Ibid.*, *Telegraph-dial. **1895** *Telegraph form [see FORM *sb.* 12 b]. **1823** in Cobbett *Rur. Rides* (1885) I. 268 For what reason this pretty name [Semaphore] is given to a sort of *Telegraph house..I must leave the reader to guess. **1877** KNIGHT *Dict. Mech.*, *Telegraph-instrument. **1897** FLANDRAU *Harvard Episodes* 111 [It] sounded like the clicking of a telegraph instrument. **1877** KNIGHT *Dict. Mech.*, *Telegraph-key. **1858** SIMMONDS *Dict. Trade*, *Telegraph-line. **1860** TROLLOPE *Framley P.* xxxii, A *telegraph message makes such a fuss in the country, frightening people's wives. **1886** C. E. PASCOE *London of To-day* xxvi. (ed. 3) 242 Post-offices and railway stations opened for the receipt and dispatch of telegraph messages. **1858** J. B. NORTON *Topics* 69 On the night of the 24th, the *telegraph-office was burnt down. **1884** MILLER *Plant-n.*, *Telegraph-plant, *Desmodium gyrans*. **1869** *Daily News* 20 Dec., She is now 83 years old, and erect as a *telegraph pole. **1884** J. TAIT *Mind in Matter* (1892) 71 As callous as a telegraph pole. **1858** SIMMONDS *Dict. Trade*, *Telegraph-post. **1877** KNIGHT *Dict. Mech.*, *Telegraph-reel. *Ibid.*, *Telegraph-register. **1817** *Salisbury & Winchester Jrnl.* 29 Sept., The church of Fromelles..was reduced to ashes by lightning...An individual..in the belfry, on the *telegraph service, perished in the flames. **1875** URE *Dict. Arts*, etc. II. 242 *Telegraph wires are suspended to poles by insulators of earthenware, glass, or porcelain.

**Te·legraph,** *v.* [f. prec. sb.; cf. F. *télégraphier*.]

**1. a.** *intr.* To signal or communicate by telegraph; to send a telegram.

**1815** J. CAMPBELL *Trav. S. Afr.* xlii. 508 On the succeeding morning..the Carmarthen Indiaman, after hailing us, and finding we had no news, telegraphed, as follows: 'Peace with France!! Buonaparte dethroned!!!' **1831** TRELAWNY *Adv. Younger Son* I. 253 We saw the frigate hoist the recal signal..., and telegraph to her companion. **1858** DICKENS *Lett.* (1880) II. 79 We have telegraphed to know. **1870** MISS BRIDGMAN *Rob. Lynne* II. ix. 181, I should like Charles telegraphed for.

**b.** *trans.* To send, transmit, or announce (a message, news, etc.) by telegraph (with *simple obj.* or *obj. cl.*). In *Cricket*, etc., to exhibit (the score, etc.) on the telegraph-board (see prec. 4).

**1805** CAPT. CRUMBY in *19th Cent.* Nov. (1899) 720 Seeing the Admiral telegraph to Captain Blackwood..'I rely on your keeping sight of the enemy through the night'. **1832** MARRYAT *N. Forster* xli, The reconnoitring ships telegraphing 'a French squadron'. **1842** DICKENS *Amer. Notes* ii. (1850) 15/2 Soon afterwards the Britannia steam-packet, from Liverpool, eighteen days out, was telegraphed at Boston. **1895** *Westm. Gaz.* 9 May 5/3 The play was again spirited, and in less than ten minutes 200 was telegraphed. *fig.* **1885** RANNEY in *Harper's Mag.* Mar. 636/2 The eye.. telegraphs the outline..to the cells in the cortex.

**c.** To send a message to (a person, etc.) by telegraph; to summon by a telegram.

**1810** CAPT. MAURICE in *Naval Chron.* XXV. 218 The.. gun-brig was telegraphed to send a boat. **1828** *Sporting Mag.* XXII. 130 The pointers were telegraphed, and so were his attending boys. **1891** F. W. ROBINSON *Her Love & His Life* VII. v, Felix has been telegraphed to town.

**2.** *fig.* **a.** *intr.* To make signs, signal (*to* a person). **b.** *trans.* To make (a signal); to convey or announce by signs. **c.** To signal to (a person). Now *rare*.

**1825** [see *telegraphing* below]. **1825** C. M. WESTMACOTT *Eng. Spy* I. 167 Never telegraph'd the big wigs. **1842** S. LOVER *Handy Andy* viii, Tom Durfy..began telegraphing Biddy, who..had shoved herself well before the door. **1844** ALB. SMITH *Adv. Mr. Ledbury* xiii, Emma telegraphed a nod of assent. **1848** THACKERAY *Bk. Snobs* l, They telegraphed each other with wondering eyes. **1888** BURGON *Lives 12 Gd. Men* II. v. 63 He telegraphed to me (I was in the area) to come up to him.

Hence **Te·legraphed** (-graft) *ppl. a.*, **Te·legraphing** *vbl. sb.* and *ppl. a.*; also **Te:legraphee·**, the person to whom a telegram is sent.

**1825** T. HOOK *Sayings* Ser. II. *Sutherl.* (Colburn) 15 Nor was this telegraphing wholly unnoticed by George. *a* **1837** WARREN *Diary Late Physic.* (1838) III. 275 A kind of telegraphing courtship was carried on between them daily. **1875** KINGLAKE *Crimea* V. vi. 91 *note*, Telegraphed signals. **1894** H. DRUMMOND *Ascent Man* 234 More perfect forms of human intercourse than telegraphed or telephoned words. **1895** *Westm. Gaz.* 4 Nov. 2/3 A decision of Lord Coleridge's that there was no property in a special telegram, though it may have cost the telegraphee a thousand pounds to procure.

†**Te:legraphe·me.** [ad. Gr. type τηλεγράφημα, f. *τηλεγραφεῖν to TELEGRAPH. (Both used in mod. Gr.)] A word suggested instead of TELEGRAM, as being more correctly formed; but never generally adopted.

**1857** R. SHILLETO in *Times* 15 Oct. 7/5 May I suggest to such as are not contented with 'Telegraphic Despatch' the rightly constructed word 'telegrapheme'? I do not want it, but..I protest against such a barbarism as 'telegram'. **1867** *Routledge's Ev. Boy's Ann.* Jan. 53 The word telegram superseded telegrapheme. **1873** [see TELEGRAM]. **1896** *Westm. Gaz.* 22 Feb. 8/2 The public..absolutely revolted against telegrapheme, and insisted on telegram, though.. the famous Cambridge scholar Shilleto always talked about 'sending a telegrapheme'—never a telegram.

**Telegrapher** (te·lĭgrafəɪ). [f. TELEGRAPH *sb.* or *v.* + -ER[1].]

**1.** One who works a telegraph. (Now *rare*: the technical term being *telegraphist*.) In first two quots., one who signals by means of a semaphore or other mechanical means (TELEGRAPH *sb.* 1).

**1795** EDGEWORTH in *Trans. R. Irish Acad.* (1797) VI. 95 Flushed with victory the young telegrapher forgot his signal. **1842** *Penny Cycl.* XXIV. 151/2 Standing..with both discs held down and turned edgewise to the observer, the telegrapher indicated 'attention'. *c* **1865** J. WYLDE in *Circ. Sc.* I. 262/1 Another..source of annoyance to telegraphers.

**b.** *Telegrapher's cramp* or *palsy*: = telegraphist's cramp: see TELEGRAPHIST b.

**1890** BILLINGS *Nat. Med. Dict.*, *Telegraphers' cramp*, neurosis analogous to writers' cramp, affecting muscles of forearm of telegraph-operators.

**2.** One who telegraphs a message or news; the sender of a telegram.

**1865** *Morn. Star* 2 Feb., The telegraphers take the liberty to assert [etc.]. **1890** *Spectator* 19 Apr., If he had been flustered by the noisy memorialists and telegraphers who did their best to disturb his judgment. **1901** *Westm. Gaz.* 17 Dec. 2/3 He has not succeeded enough to induce the telegrapher to desert the wiring mode for the wireless.

**Telegraphese** (te:lĭgrafī·z). *colloq.* or *humorous.* [f. TELEGRAPH *sb.* + -ESE.]

**1.** The concise and elliptical style in which telegrams are worded.

**1885** *Pall Mall G.* 26 Sept. 2/2 We shall gradually give up English in favour of Telegraphese, and Electric Telegraphese is as short and spare as Daily Telegraphese is longwinded and redundant. **1905** *Athenæum* 7 Oct. 469/2 We rather relish the leisurely semicolons and sentences of the eighteenth century after..the 'telegraphese' of many a modern stylist.

**2.** An elaborate or inflated style, such as was attributed to leading articles in the (London) *Daily Telegraph* newspaper.

**1885** [see 1]. **1889** *Universal Rev.* Oct. 215 The man who writes for the *Telegraph* must write Telegraphese. **1892** *Leisure Hour* May 455/2 The elaborate, rounded, allusive style which has gone down to fame as Telegraphese. **1895** *Westm. Gaz.* 9 Dec. 3/1 Sala was not only the patentee of *Telegraphese*. He was also the first, and in some ways the best.

**Telegraphic** (telĭgræ·fik), *a.* [f. as prec. + -IC. Cf. F. *télégraphique*.]

**1.** Of, pertaining to, of the nature of, or connected with a telegraph; made, sent, or transmitted by telegraph. **a.** In reference to the earlier 'telegraphs' or signalling devices. Now *rare*.

**1794** [see TELEGRAPH *sb.* 1]. **1794** *Gentl. Mag.* LXIV. II. 815/2 The new-invented telegraphic language of signals. **1794** *European Mag.* Sept. 166 By a new Telegraphic Machine, invented by Citizen Chapelle the news..has been received ..in one hour. **1805** CAPT. CRUMBY in *19th Cent.* Nov. (1899) 722 Lord Nelson made the telegraphic signal, 'England expects that every man will do his duty'. **1808** J. MACDONALD *Telegraphic Commun.* 36 Homer is the first who mentions the Telegraphic art. **1829** MARRYAT *F. Mildmay* vi, Looking for the telegraphic signal-box. **1842** ALISON *Hist. Europe* (1850) XIII. lxxii. § 85. 569 On the morning of the 3d March, a telegraphic despatch from the prefect of Toulon announced the landing of Napoleon.

**b.** In reference to the electric telegraph.

[**1823** RONALDS *Descr. Electr. Tel.* 8 By the use of a telegraphic dictionary a word, or even a whole sentence could be conveyed by..three discharges.] **1840** [see TELEPHONIC]. **1841** *Encycl. Brit.* (ed. 7) XXI. 689/2 Wheatstone's Electro-magnetic Telegraph..We are convinced..will not be confined to long telegraphic lines, but will also be extensively employed in public and private establishments. **1854** B'NESS BUNSEN in Hare *Life* (1879) II. iv. 168 We received yesterday the telegraphic announcement [etc.]. **1854** GILFILLAN *Life R. Blair* B.'s Wks. 128 As if on telegraphic wires. **1857** LADY CANNING in Hare *Two Noble Lives* (1893) II. 199 The wording of telegraphic messages requires the utmost care. **1877** W. THOMSON *Voy. Challenger* I. i. 1 The wonderful project of establishing a telegraphic communication between the old world and the new.

**2.** *fig.* †**a.** Large and conspicuous, like the letters exhibited by some early forms of telegraph. *Obs.* **b.** Making signals (as by glance or gesture); conveyed by a sign or signal: cf. TELEGRAPH *v.* 2. ? *Obs.* **c.** Resembling an (electric) telegraph; conveying impulses or intelligence as by electricity. **d.** Abbreviated or concise like a telegram.

**1809** SIMEON *Let.* in Carus *Life* xi. (1847) 276 His attacks on me were frequent, with my name in telegraphic characters. **18..** T. MOORE *Country Dance & Quad.* xxix, Watchful chaperons,..Who intercept all signal tones, And read all telegraphic faces. **1838** BUCKSTONE *Shocking Events* (French's ed.) 9 Sir..I cannot allow any telegraphic dispatches with my female domestic—no winking here.

**1871** TYNDALL *Fragm. Sci.* (1879) I. iii. 95 Who .. put the soul into this telegraphic body? **1896** 'CURTIS YORKE' *Those Children* vi, [His] words .. were few, and his speech as telegraphic as though each word were paid for.

Hence **Telegra·phical** *a.* (*rare*), telegraphic; **Telegra·phically** *adv.* [see -ICALLY], by means of a telegraph, by telegraph or telegram; in relation to a telegraph.

**1808** J. MACDONALD *Telegraphic Commun.* Pref. 34 Whenever a word is to be spelt, Telegraphically. **1846** WORCESTER, Telegraphic, Telegraphical. **1847** DE QUINCEY in *Tait's Mag.* XIV. 668 Brought down telegraphically from some altitude inaccessible to himself. **1883** *Standard* 14 Feb. 5/4 He was summoned telegraphically. **1905** *Daily News* 17 Mar. 7 Queenstown is cut off telegraphically, all the poles having been blown down.

**Telegraphist** (tǐ-, tele·grăfist, te·lǐgrăfist). [f. as prec. + -IST. Cf. F. *télégraphiste.*] A person employed, or skilled, in working a telegraph; a telegraph-operator.

**1854** *Lardner's Museum Sci. & Art* IV. 60 Different telegraphists have very different powers as to celerity. *c* **1865** J. WYLDE in *Circ. Sc.* I. 261/1 No one suddenly became an expert telegraphist. **1876** PREECE & SIVEWRIGHT *Telegraphy* 113 The amount of work .. will not justify the employment of a trained telegraphist. **1879** [see TELEGRAPH *clerk*]. **1908** *Daily Chron.* 3 June 1/4 A wireless telegraphist had a terrifying experience during a terrific thunderstorm .., where the wireless station was struck by lightning.

**b.** *Telegraphist's cramp*: a paralytic affection of the muscles of the fore-arm, to which telegraph-operators are liable: cf. CRAMP *sb.*[1]

**1899** *Allbutt's Syst. Med.* VI. 539 The so-called 'Professional hyperkineses' (writer's cramp, histrionic spasm, pianist's cramp, telegraphist's cramp, &c.) admit of a similar explanation. **1908** *Daily Chron.* 26 Nov. 6/2 The supplementary report .. recommended that telegraphists' cramp should be added to the compensation list.

**Telegraphone** (tǐ-, tele·grăfōun). [Short for *telegraphophone*, f. TELE- + GRAPHOPHONE, after *telephone.*] A form of telephone in which the spoken message is recorded at the receiving end magnetically on an iron ribbon, so as to be capable of reproduction; invented by Poulsen of Copenhagen about 1900. (See also TELEPHONOGRAPH.)

[**1890**: see next.] **1900** *Engineering Mag.* XIX. 757/1 The telegraphon, or magneto-telephonograph, an invention of the Danish engineer, Valdemar Poulsen, makes use of the fact of permanent magnetism to record .. sounds .. so that they can be reproduced whenever .. desired. **1902** *Harper's Mag.* Feb. 496 This apparatus .. has been variously designated as the 'telegraphone', the 'microphonograph', and the 'magnetophonograph' in Europe.

So **Telegraphophone** (telǐgræ·fofōun): see quot.

**1890** *Voice* (N. Y.) 13 Feb., A new instrument called the telegraphone.] **1891** *Cent. Dict.*, *Telegraphophone*, an apparatus for reproducing at a distance the sounds which produced a graphophonic record; also, an apparatus for producing a graphophonic record at a distance by means of a telephonic circuit.

**Telegraphy** (tǐ-, tele·grăfi, te·lǐgrăfi). [f. TELE- + -GRAPHY. Cf. Ger. *telegraphie* (Böckmann 1794), F. *télégraphie* (Mozin *Dict. franç.-allem.* 1812).] The art or science of constructing or using telegraphs; the working of a telegraph or telegraphs.

*Wireless telegraphy*: see WIRELESS.

**1795** EDGEWORTH in *Trans. R. Irish Acad.* (1797) VI. 96 Tamerlane's telegraphy was not very refined... Whenever he laid siege to any town he used to employ three signals—the first day he set up a white flag [etc.]. *Ibid.* 111 The advantages which by means of Telegraphy would result to commerce must .. be extensive. **1847** in WEBSTER. **1858** *Times* 28 Aug. 10/6 The cause of telegraphy has too many demands upon the labours of .. these practised cable layers, to permit them to be idle here. **1861** W. FAIRBAIRN *Addr. to Brit. Assoc.*, In land telegraphy the chief difficulties have been surmounted, but in submarine telegraphy much remains to be accomplished. **1878** HUXLEY *Physiogr.* 101 In these days of electric telegraphy every one is familiar with the .. galvanic or voltaic battery. **1901** *Westm. Gaz.* 7 Oct. 10/1 It was on July 25, 1837, that the first practical trial of telegraphy was made between Euston and Camden, on the London and North-Western Railway, by Cooke and Wheatstone. *fig.* **1864** *Daily Tel.* 26 May, That kind of social telegraphy which seems to convey intelligence with a mystery and rapidity quite as wonderful as the electric wire. **1891** 'MARK TWAIN' in *Harper's Mag.* Christm. No., (*title*) Mental Telegraphy.

**Telehydrobarometer, -iconograph**: see TELE-.

**Teleianthous** (telǝiˌæ·nþǝs), *a.* *Bot. rare*—°. [f. Gr. τέλειος perfect + ἄνθος flower + -OUS.]

**1860** MAYNE *Expos. Lex.*, *Teleianthus*, .. applied by Wachsendorff to plants provided with stamens and pistils: teleianthous.

‖ **Teleiosis** (telǝiˌōu·sis). *rare*—[1]. [a. Gr. τελείωσις, f. τελειοῦν to perfect, to complete.] Perfection, completion, consummation. So † **Teleio·tical** *a. Obs. rare*—[1], making perfect, perfective.

**1601** BP. W. BARLOW *Defence* 92 The teleioticall or finall cause eternall life. **1898** GLADSTONE in *Times* 5 Jan., Truth and beauty, truth the first, and beauty the handmaid or teleiosis of truth, are the divinely appointed sustenance of the human soul.

**Telekinesis** to **Telelectroscope**: see TELE-.

**Telelograph**: see TELLOGRAPH.

**Te·lelogue** (-lǫg). [f. TELE- + Gr. λόγος word.] A message transmitted by telephone, a telephonic message; = TELEPHEME.

**1881** I. W. BATTEN in *Times* 10 Nov. 8/3 The United Telephone Co... would .. supply London with a penny Telelogue in .. addition to the .. sixpenny Telegram. **1884** *Pall Mall G.* 25 Apr. 5/2 They resolutely refuse to allow the United Telephone Company to give the public a penny telelogue. **1898** (*Heading of a book of forms for Mercantile use*) Confirmation of Telelogue.

**Teleman**, obs. Sc. form of TILLMAN.

**Telemanometer**, etc.: see TELE-.

**Telemeter** (tǐ-, tele·mǐtǝɪ). Also **telometer.** [f. TELE-, TELO-[2] + -METER. Cf. F. *télémètre*, 1852 in *Cosmos* II. 222.]

**1.** An instrument for ascertaining the distances of objects: applied to instruments of various kinds used in surveying, and in military operations.

*Acoustic telemeter*, one in which the distance is ascertained by observing the time occupied by sound in traversing it.

**1860** G. RICHARDSON *Patent Specif.* No. 2102 This improved instrument (which in commerce I intend to call a telometer). **1869** *Pall Mall G.* 31 Aug. 4 Of two batteries coming into action, the one with and the other without a telemeter, a difference of about a minute in opening fire would make the difference between accurate shooting and shooting by guesswork. **1888** A. W. WHITE in *Encycl. Brit.* XXIII. 126/1 Telemeter, or Rangefinder... Telemeters have been made on three distinct principles, and classified as acoustic, optical, and trigonometrical respectively. *Ibid.* 126/2 The Nolan range finder .. was the first telemeter used by the British artillery. **1900** H. M. WILSON *Topogr. Surv.* xiii. 274 The gradienter is used as a telemeter in measuring horizontal distances in two ways.

*attrib.* **1900** H. M. WILSON *Topogr. Surv.* 236 The stadia, telemeter, or subtend system [of measuring distances].

**2.** An apparatus for recording the readings of any physical instrument at a distance by means of an electric current; a general term including the *teleanemograph, telebarometer, telethermometer*, etc. (see TELE-). **1891** in *Cent. Dict.*

Hence **Telemetric** (telǐme·trik), **Teleme·trical** *adjs.*, pertaining to, connected with, or serving as a telemeter; also **Teleme·trograph**, an instrument for measuring and drawing plans of distant objects or areas (*Sci. Amer.* Supp., 1 Aug. 1885, 7975).

**1877** KNIGHT *Dict. Mech.* 2513 Another form of telemetric marine-glass... The telemetrical telescope of Captain Gautier. **1900** H. M. WILSON *Topogr. Surv.* xiii. 282 The range-finder furnishes a .. rough telemetric method of obtaining a fairly accurate measure of inaccessible distances.

**Telemicroscope**, etc.: see TELE-.

**Teleo-**[1] (te·liˌo), before a vowel **tele-**, repr. Gr. τελεο- (τελειο-), combining form of τέλεος, τέλειος perfect, complete, f. τέλος end: employed in Eng. in some scientific terms. **Teleobranchiate** (-bræ·ŋkiĕt), *Zool.* [Gr. βράγχια gills], *a.* belonging to the division *Teleobranchia* of gastropod molluscs, having the respiratory organs specially developed; *sb.* a gastropod of this division. **Teleocephalous** (-se·fălǝs) *a.*, *Ichth.* [Gr. κεφαλή head], belonging to the order *Teleocephali* of teleostean fishes, having the full number of bones in the skull; so **Teleoce·phal**, a teleocephalous fish. **Teleodesmacean** (-desmēɪ·ʃiăn), *Zool.* [Gr. δεσμός band], *a.* belonging to the group *Teleodesmacea* (*Amer. Jrnl. Sc.* Dec. 1889) of bivalve molluscs, having a specially developed hinge to the shell; *sb.* a mollusc of this group. **Te·leodont** (-odǫnt) *a.*, *Entom.* [Gr. ὀδούς, ὀδοντ- tooth], applied to that form of the mandibles in stag-beetles in which the projections or 'teeth' are most highly developed. **Te·leophyte** (-fǝit), *Biol.* [Gr. φυτόν plant], a plant of perfect or complete organization; one of the higher plants. **Teleoptile** (-ǫ·ptil, -ǝil), *Ornith.* [Gr. πτίλον down-feather], one of the later or mature feathers of a bird: opp. to NEOSSOPTILE. **Te·leosaur** (-sǭɪ), *Palæont.* [Gr. σαῦρος lizard], a crocodile of the extinct genus *Teleosaurus* or family *Teleosauridæ*; so **Teleosau·rian** *a.*, belonging to this genus or family; *sb.* = *teleosaur.* **Teleote·mporal**, *Anat.* and *Zool.* [TEMPORAL *a.*[2]], *a.* and *sb.*, a name for the bone called POSTCLAVICLE. ‖ **Teleozoon** (-zōu·ǫn), *Biol.* (pl. **-zoa**) [Gr. ζῷον animal], an animal of perfect or complete organization; one of the higher animals; hence **Teleozoic** (-zōu·ik) *a.*, pertaining to the teleozoa. See also TELEOSTEAN, etc.

**1890** *Amer. Nat.* May 481 *Tæniosomi.* *Teleocephals with the scapular arch subnormal, posttemporal undivided and closely applied to the back of the cranium. **1883** LEUTHNER in *Trans. Zool. Soc. Lond.* (1885) XI. 400 The gap between the mesodont and *tel[e]odont forms long remained unbridged. **1899** D. SHARP in *Camb. Nat. Hist.* VI. 193 The largest developments being called teleodont, the smallest priodont. **1863** H. SPENCER *Biol.* (1864) I. II. i. § 43. 109 A tree is an assemblage of numerous united shoots. One of these great *teleophytes is thus an aggregate of aggregates of aggregates of units, which severally resemble protophytes in their sizes and structures. **1893** GADOW in Newton *Dict. Birds* 243 The first clothing of the newly-hatched bird consists of .. soft feathers .. possessing .. characters which make it advisable to distinguish them, by the name of 'Neossoptiles' (νεοσσός, a chick), from those feathers which subsequently appear, and may be called '*Teleoptiles' (τέλεος, mature). [**1839** G. ROBERTS *Dict. Geol.*, **Teleosaurus*, perfect or complete lizard; a new genus of fossil saurian or lizard, established by M. Geoffroy St. Hilaire.] **1841** OWEN in *Rep. Brit. Assoc.* X. 76 The atlas in the Teleosaur corresponds essentially with that of the Crocodiles. *Ibid.* 70 They are longer in proportion to their breadth than most of the *Teleosaurian scutes. **1896** H. WOODWARD *Guide Fossil Reptiles Brit. Mus.* 6 Long and slender-jawed Teleosaurs and Steneosaurs. **1869** HUXLEY in *Q. Jrnl. Geol. Soc.* XXVI. 47 The ilium of a Teleosaurian. **1865** H. SPENCER *Biol.* (1867) II. IV. iv. § 169. 77 Among the *Protozoa* .. and from the minute anatomy of all creatures above these, up to the **Teleozoa.*

**Teleo-**[2], before a vowel **tele-**, combining form repr. Gr. τέλος end (stem τελε-: cf. TELEARCH), as in TELEOLOGY and its derivatives, q. v.: also in ‖ **Teleopho·bia** [mod.L.: see -PHOBIA], an aversion or unwillingness to admit the existence of design or final causes in nature; **Teleorga·nic** *a.*, serving the purposes of an organism; necessary to organic life (*Cent. Dict.*, 1891). (See also TELO-[1].)

**Teleologic** (teliˌǫlǫ·dʒik), *a.* and *sb.* [f. TELEOLOGY + -IC.] **A.** *adj.* = next.

**1842** DE QUINCEY in *Blackw. Mag.* LII. 730/2 The peculiar beauty of a kitchen-garden, or of a machine, which must be derived from their tendency to certain ends or uses, is called teleologic beauty. **1848** MILL *Pol. Econ.* III. i. § 2 (1876) 264 Value in use, or as Mr. De Quincey calls it, teleologic value, is the extreme limit of value in exchange.

**B.** *sb.* The science of final causes; that branch of knowledge which deals with ends or purposes.

**1865** S. H. HODGSON *Time & Space* II. ix. § 68. 566 Technic and Teleologic are the two branches of practical knowledge, founded respectively on conation and feeling.

**Teleological** (teliˌǒlǫ·dʒikăl), *a.* [f. as prec. + -ICAL.] Of, pertaining to, or involving teleology; relating to ends or final causes; dealing with design or purpose, esp. in natural phenomena.

**1809–10** COLERIDGE *Friend* (1818) III. 180 A teleological ground in physics and physiology. **1847** BUCH tr. *Hagenbach's Hist. Doctr.* I. 96 What is commonly called the physico-theological, or teleological proof—i.e. they infer the existence of a Creator from the works of creation. **1875** SIR W. TURNER in *Encycl. Brit.* I. 799/1 The special anatomy of an animal may be studied .. (*c*) with reference to the function, use, or purpose performed by a part or structure .., termed Teleological or Physiological Anatomy. **1907** J. R. ILLINGWORTH *Doctr. Trin.* xii. 248 The great teleological question .. what is the end of man? what is the true purpose of life's voyage?

Hence **Teleolo·gically** *adv.*, in a teleological manner; in relation to teleology.

**1842** DE QUINCEY in *Blackw. Mag.* LII. 730/2 Teleologically, that is, considered as means to an end—diamonds have as undeniably a value in use as any other article. **1907** J. R. ILLINGWORTH *Doctr. Trin.* ix. 176 The context of a rational and teleologically ordered world.

**Teleologist** (teliˌǫ·lŏdʒist). [f. as prec. + -IST.] A believer in or maintainer of the doctrine of teleology; one versed in this.

**1864** H. SPENCER *Princ. Biol.* I. II. vii. § 79. 234 The explanation of the teleologist is untrue, .. things are not arranged thus or thus for the securing of special ends. **1881** G. J. ROMANES in *Nature* XXIV. 2 The burden of proof lies with the teleologists to show that any special cases .. are to be regarded as inexplicable.

So **Teleo·logism**, teleological theory or doctrine.

**1889** *Pop. Sci. Monthly* June 278/1 In the course of his transition from strict teleologism to the full acceptance of the theory of evolution.

**Teleology** (teliˌǫ·lŏdʒi). [ad. mod.L. *teleologia* (Chr. Wolf, 1728); f. Gr. τέλος end (see TELEO-[2]) + -λογια (see -LOGY), whence also Ger. *teleologie*, F. *téléologie.*]

The doctrine or study of ends or final causes, esp. as related to the evidences of design or purpose in nature; also *transf.* such design as exhibited in natural objects or phenomena.

[**1728** WOLF *Logica* § 85 Datur .. præter eas alia adhuc philosophiæ naturalis pars, quæ fines rerum explicat, nomine adhuc destituta, etsi amplissima sit et utilissima. Dici posset *Teleologia.*] **1740** ZOLLMAN (tr. fr. French) in *Phil. Trans.* XLI. 299 Teleology is one of those Parts of Philosophy, in which there has been but little Progress made. **1807** *Edin. Rev.* X. 151 The subject of Teleology, or the doctrine of final causes, was one which occupied the thoughts of Le Sage. **1868** F. BUCKLAND in Bompas *Life* x. (1885) 224 This is the doctrine of Teleology: i.e. the doctrine that every organ is adapted to a special use. **1881** G. J. ROMANES in *Nature* 27 Oct. 604/2 Teleology in this larger sense, or the doctrine that behind all the facts open to scientific enquiry .. there is 'Mind and Will' as the ultimate cause of all things—does not fall within the scope of scientific method. **1893** H. DRUMMOND in Barrows *Parl. Relig.* II. 1322 Darwin has not written a chapter that is not full of teleology.

**Teleometer**, erron. form for TELEMETER.

**1891** in *Cent. Dict.*

**Teleophobia** to **Teleosaurian**: see TELEO-[1], [2].

**Teleostean** (teliˌǫ·stiăn), *a.* and *sb.* *Ichth.* [f. mod.L. *teleosteus* (f. Gr. τέλεος, -ειος finished, complete, TELEO-[1] + ὀστέ-ον bone) + -AN.] **a.** *adj.* Belonging to or characteristic of the order *Teleostei* (Joh. Müller 1844) or osseous fishes, having the skeleton (usually) completely ossified. **b.** *sb.* A fish of this order.

**1859** DARWIN *Orig. Species* ix. 305 Some palæontologists believe that certain much older fishes .. are really teleostean. **1872** *Ibid.* x. (ed. 6) 285 If the teleosteans had really appeared suddenly .. at the commencement of the chalk formation. **1888** ROLLESTON & JACKSON *Anim. Life* 90 The Perch... Its skeleton is typically Teleostean. *Ibid.* 429.

So **Te·leost** *sb.* and *a.*, also teliost (= F. *téléoste*), **Teleo·steous** *a.* = TELEOSTEAN.

1862 DANA *Man. Geol.* iii. 278 *note*, The skeleton is bony, as the name Teliost..implies. 1880 GÜNTHER *Fishes* i. 22 The organisation of the Teleosteous fishes. 1891 *Cent. Dict.* 6216 (figure) Skull of Pike (*Esox lucius*), a teleost fish.

**Teleostome** (te·li,ǒstoum). *Ichth.* [ad. mod.L. *teleostom-us*, f. TELEO-[1] + Gr. στόμα mouth.] A fish of the division *Teleostomi* (Th. Gill 1872), including the teleosts and ganoids (i. e. all the higher fishes), characterized by well-developed maxillary, dentary, and membrane bones. So **Teleo·stomate**, **Te:leostomatous** (-stǫ·mătəs), **Teleo·stomous** *adjs.*, belonging to or having the characters of the *Teleostomi*.

1896 H. WOODWARD *Guide Fossil Reptiles Brit. Mus.* 109 A break in the series of Teleostomatous fishes. 1900 *Nature* 20 Sept. 505/2 The Crossopterygii are a group of Teleostomous fishes. 1901 *Ibid.* 14 Nov. 38/1 The difference between the typically meroblastic egg of the shark and the holoblastic egg of such a teleostome as the sturgeon.

Teleotemporal to Teleozoon: see TELEO-[1].

**Telepathy** (tǐ-, tele·păþi, te·lǐpæþi). *Psychics.* [f. TELE- + Gr. -πάθεια feeling, perception: see -PATHY.] 'The communication of impressions of any kind from one mind to another, independently of the recognised channels of sense' (Myers *Human Personality*, Gloss.).

1882 MYERS in *Proc. Soc. Psychical Research* I. II. 147 [see TELÆSTHESIA]. 1888 *Athenæum* 18 Aug. 213/3 In.. after-dinner experiments..telepathy, thought-reading, and hypnotism are trifled with as amusements. 1894 H. DRUMMOND *Ascent Man* 234 Telepathy is theoretically the next stage in the Evolution of Language.

So **Telepath** (te·lǐpæþ) *sb.*, **Tele·pathist**, an adept in, subject of, or believer in telepathy; **Te·lepath** *v.*, (*a*) *trans.* to convey or transmit by means of telepathy; (*b*) *intr.* to practise telepathy; **Telepathe·tic** (*nonce-wd.*), **Telepa·thic** *adjs.*, pertaining to, of the nature of, or effected by telepathy; **Telepa·thically** *adv.*, in a telepathic manner, by means of telepathy; **Te·lepathi:ze** *v.*, (*a*) *trans.* to communicate with or affect (a person) by telepathy; (*b*) *intr.* to practise telepathy.

1907 *Westm. Gaz.* 9 Feb. 3/2 There is a pleasant mystery about the origin of the 9-in. shell which startled Selsey the other day...It looks as though the *telepaths would have to be called in to account for its origin. 1886 *Sat. Rev.* 4 Dec. 751/1 Whether spooks are *telepathed about..by promiscuous persons, or whether the Thibetan Adepts go spooking astrally through the world. 1891 *Review of Rev.* 15 Oct. 347/2 As soon as a man begins to speculate as to how he telepaths, he loses the power of telepathing. 1895 *Edin. Rev.* Jan. 93 It may be that these communications have really been 'telepathed' from some living mind. 1892 *Sat. Rev.* 6 Aug. 157/1 Was there, then, some 'communication' of a '*telepathetic' sort? 1884 GURNEY & MYERS in *19th Century* May 800 We hope to show that the lowest *telepathic manifestations may be used to explain and corroborate the highest. 1903 MYERS *Human Personality* II. p. xv, Telepathic intercourse, if carried far enough, corresponds to possession or to ecstasy. 1884 — in *Proc. Soc. Psychical Research* VII. 219 Drawing a picture which he feels to be *telepathically presented to his mind's eye. 1886 GURNEY, etc. *Phantasms of Living* I. 111 His aspect..is telepathically perceived. 1894 *Westm. Gaz.* 12 Sept. 3/3 Knowing myself now to be a *telepathist,..I look with regret to the many opportunities I have missed. 1900 *Pall Mall G.* 31 Oct. 3 Mr. Andrew Lang discourses..of three female professors of telepathy, concluding that Joan of Arc was a true telepathist.

**Telepheme** (te·lǐfīm). [f. TELE- + Gr. φήμη voice, report, message, etc.] Name for a message sent by telephone; a telephonic communication.

1882 W. BALESTIER in *Rochester* (N. Y.) *Post-Express* 5 Aug. (Cent.), We shall ask a dispensation to permit us to introduce a new word..telepheme. The use of such phrases as 'telephonic communication', 'telephonic message', 'news by telephone', and the like seems a little clumsy. 1898 R. O. HESLOP *Let. to Editor*, Telepheme: a telephonic message. The term is occasionally met with in commercial correspondence.

Telepherage: see TELPHERAGE.

**Telephone** (te·lǐfōun), *sb.* [f. Gr. τῆλε afar, TELE- + φωνή voice, sound, -φων-ος -voiced, -sounding (as in εὔφωνος sweet-voiced).]

**1.** An instrument, apparatus, or device for conveying sound to a distance. Now chiefly Obs.

†**a.** Name for a system of signalling by musical notes, devised by Sudré in 1828. †**b.** An instrument like a fog-horn, used on ships, railway trains, etc., for signalling by loud sounds or notes. †**c.** A tube or other device for conveying the sound of the voice to a distance, as a speaking-tube. **d.** *Lovers'* or *String Telephone*, a toy consisting of two stretched membranes or metal disks connected by a tense cord which mechanically transmits sound-waves from the one to the other.

(The name has also been applied by writers to an apparatus invented by Wheatstone, called by him 'the Enchanted Lyre', consisting of a rod connected with a sound-board, by which sounds (e. g. of a musical instrument) were conveyed from one room to another.)

1835 *Musical Libr.* [implied in TELEPHONIC q. v.]. 1844 *Times* 19 July 6/5 Yesterday week was a levee day at the Admiralty, and amongst the numerous models..was Captain J. N. Tayler's telephone instrument...The chief object of this powerful wind instrument is to convey signals during foggy weather. 1844 *Illustr. Lond. News* 24 Aug. 118/1 The Telephone; a Telegraphic Alarum. Amongst the many valuable inventions..that of the 'Telephone, or Marine Alarum and Signal Trumpet', by Captain J. N. Taylor, R. N. 1849 *Chambers' Jrnl.* 30 June 408 Mr. Whishaw's inventions: among these are speaking-tubes,..we are, it seems, to be able to speak to a distance without any connecting tube at all: across the inner quadrangle of a building, for instance, by means of large concave gutta-percha reflectors..the portable telephone would be available where the telegraph..does not admit of application. 1851 *Catal. Exhibition* I. 442 [F. Whishaw's] Gutta percha telephone. 1860 WHEATSTONE *Patent Specif.* No. 2462 Telephones in which musical pipes or free tongues are acted upon by wind. Compressed air or gas is admitted to the pipe by means of a valve acted upon by the magnetized needle of an electro-magnet. The alternation of long and short sounds may be grouped in a similar manner to the long and short lines in the alphabet of a Morse's telegraph. 1877 KNIGHT *Dict. Mech.*, *Telephone*, an instrument for conveying signals by sound...The term, until lately, has been particularly applied to a signal adapted for nautical or railroad use, in which a body of compressed air is released from a narrow orifice and divided upon a sharp edge, in the manner of a steam-whistle. 1879 tr. *Du Moncel, The Telephone* 2 One step more led to the membrane employed in string telephones.

**2.** An apparatus for reproducing sound, esp. that of the voice, at a great distance, by means of electricity; consisting, like the electric telegraph, of transmitting and receiving instruments connected by a line or wire which conveys the electric current.

**a.** Applied to an instrument devised by P. Reis in Dec. 1861, and called by him (in German) *Telephon*.

In this the sounds were received on thin vibrating membranes, whose motion was transmitted electrically to an electromagnetic receiver. This was never perfected as a practical means of communication.

1866 R. M. FERGUSON *Electricity* 257 The Telephone. 158. This is an instrument for telegraphing notes of the same pitch. Reis's Telephone (invented 1861) accomplishes this in the following way. 1883 S. P. THOMPSON *P. Reis* 49 We have now shown that Philipp Reis was the undisputed inventor [1861] of an instrument which he called the Telephone. 1889 PREECE & MAIER *Telephone* 3 Philipp Reis, of Friedrichsdorf, wrote [in German] in 1868:—I succeeded in inventing an apparatus..in which also one can produce tones of all kinds at any desired distance by means of the galvanic current, I named the instrument 'Telephon'.

**b.** Applied to the 'Electrical Speaking Telephone' of Alex. Graham Bell, introduced in 1876, and to its various modifications by Elisha Gray, Edison, Hunnings, etc.

In this the sounds of speech or music are received on and reproduced by thin vibrating disks or diaphragms. *On the telephone*, connected with a system of telephonic intercommunication.

1876 (May 10) A. G. BELL in *Proc. Amer. Acad. Arts & Sc.*, I placed the membrane of the telephone near my mouth. 1876 (Dec. 9) — *Patent Specif.* No. 4765. 8 The telephones being illustrated separately in figs. 19 and 20. 1878 EDISON in *N. Amer. Rev.* CXXVI. 534 The phonograph will perfect the telephone, and revolutionize present systems of telegraphy. 1879 *Cassell's Techn. Educ.* IV. 154/2 The telephone and microphone have far distanced any previous attempts to convey sounds from one place to another. 1879 tr. *Du Moncel, The Telephone* 8 Mr. Elisha Gray..arranged in fact about the 15th Jan. 1876, a system of speaking telephones. 1884 C. G. W. LOCK *Workshop Receipts* Ser. III. 189/2 The telephone proper differs from other instruments of a like class, in that it reproduces instead of merely conveying vibrations. 1905 F. YOUNG *Sands of Pleasure* II. iv, The hotel in the Rue de Calais was not on the telephone. 1906 *Westm. Gaz.* 29 Aug. 10/1 'It is the wonder of wonders' exclaimed Sir William Thomson (now Lord Kelvin) after he had tested the first telephone shown to the public at the Centennial Exhibition in Philadelphia in 1876.

**c.** *transf.* and *fig.*

1878 MRQ. SALISBURY *Sp. Newsp. Press Fund* 19 May, He will see the telephone [i.e. the reporters] by which these arguments and facts are conveyed to persons still open to conviction. 1898 J. ARCH *Story of Life* xvi. 396 Now the agricultural labourer has his political telephone of his vote, his Board Schools, his County Council, his Parish Council.

**3.** *attrib.* and *Comb.*, as *telephone bell*, *drum* (sense 1 b), *instrument*, *message*, *-receiver*, *-stud*, *trumpet*, *-user*; **telephone exchange**, the office or central station of a local telephone system, where the various lines are brought to a central switchboard, and communication between subscribers is effected; sometimes applied to the switchboard itself, as in an 'automatic exchange'; **telephone girl**, a girl employed at the switch-board to connect the wires so as to put two persons into communication.

1844 *Times* 19 July 6/5 [see sense 1]. 1844 *Illustr. Lond. News* 24 Aug. 118/1 The Indicator..to be placed on the Telephone Drum, to denote the signals made...The Telephone gamut notes are arranged for numbers either by the public or private key. 1855 (May 10) *Bill, Polytechnic Inst.*, Lecture by J. H. Pepper, Esq., on Professor Wheatstone's experiments.., illustrated by a Telephone concert, in which sounds of various instruments pass inaudible through an intermediate hall, and are reproduced in the lecture room. 1878 EDISON in *N. Amer. Rev.* CXXVI. 535 Were..our telephone-conversation automatically recorded. 1879 *Print. Trades Jrnl.* XXVIII. 6 On Saturday the Telephone Exchange commenced operations. 1889 PREECE & MAIER *Telephone* 111 The object of the Button Telephone is to replace the press button of an ordinary electric bell by a telephone-stud, which permits not only to ring up a person but to converse with him. 1906 *Blackw. Mag.* June 832/2 The tired clerk at the telephone-receiver rebuffed our advances. 1906 *Daily Chron.* 27 June 2/3 An installation which was going to do away with the telephone girl. 1907 H. WYNDHAM *Flare Footlights* xxviii, The warning tinkle of the telephone bell on the office wall.

**Te·lephone**, *v.* [f. prec. sb.]

**1. a.** *intr.* To convey sound to a distance by or as by a telephone; *esp.* to send a message or communicate by speaking through a telephone.

1880 *Times* 22 Sept. 7/6 Mr. Bell..has succeeded in telegraphing, or rather 'telephoning', along a beam of light. 1881 *Chicago Times* 4 June, Mr. Smith..telephoned immediately to headquarters about the matter. 1899 *Westm. Gaz.* 25 July 4/2 Instruments by which telephoning without wires can be successfully accomplished.

**b.** *trans.* To convey or announce by telephone (in quot. 1879 by sound generally).

1879 CALDERWOOD *Mind & Br.* 139 He will interpret such signs as whistling, calling,..and..proceed to the execution of the fresh orders so 'telegraphed', perhaps I should say 'telephoned'. 1882 *Daily News* 25 Aug. 3/1 You may safely defer setting out..until No. 2 has been telephoned. 1888 *Encycl. Brit.* XXIII. 127/1 This [Wheatstone's 'magic lyre'] only answers for telephoning musical sounds to short distances. 1888 *Montreal Weekly Witness* 13 June 1/4 The news was at once telephoned to Mrs. Cleveland.

**c.** To speak to or summon by telephone.

1889 WESTGARTH *Austral. Progress* 153 As he might be there, they would 'telephone' him. 1894 HOWELLS in *Harper's Mag.* Feb. 378 She telephoned you on the impulse of the moment.

**2.** To furnish with telephones; to establish a system of telephones in (a place).

1901 *Speaker* 14 Dec. 296/1 The London County Council prepared..estimates for telephoning London in 1898. 1904 *Daily News* 19 Apr. 2 If the United Kingdom were 'telephoned' in the same proportion there would be nearly 800,000 instruments on its various exchange systems, instead of some 250,000 only.

Hence **Te·lephoned** *ppl. a.*; **Te·lephoning** *vbl. sb.*; also **Te·lephoner**, one who telephones.

1884 *Whitaker's Almanack* 385/1 Remarkable trials of long distance telephoning. 1891 *Cent. Dict.*, Telephoner. 1894 Telephoned words [see TELEGRAPHED]. 1902 *Westm. Gaz.* 26 Aug. 1/3 When one has had actual experience of a thoroughly telephoned town.

**Te·lephone·tics**, *sb. pl. nonce-wd.* [f. TELEPHONE *sb.*, after *phonetics*; or f. TELE- + PHONETICS.] The practice of using a telephone; also (quot. 1893) signalling by sounds.

1877 *Daily News* 30 Nov. 5/1 The general public .. must apparently be content for the present to indulge in telephonetics only between..10 p.m. and 10 a.m. 1893 *Church Q. Rev.* Oct. 242 There was also what may be almost styled a code of telephonetics among the Benedictines, who understood what the Abbot meant when he jingled his spoons.

**Telephonic** (telǐfǫ·nik), *a.* [In earlier use, f. Gr. τῆλε (TELE-) + φωνή voice + -IC: in later use, f. TELEPHONE *sb.* + -IC.] Transmitting, or relating to the transmission of, sound to a distance. †**a.** Applied to a system of signalling by musical sounds: cf. TELEPHONY 1. *Obs.* **b.** Of, pertaining to, of the nature of, or conveyed by a telephone.

1834 WILSON *New Dict. Mus.* 259 *Telephonic Sounds*, a musical language invented by M. Sudré..for the purposes of conversation,..the communication of military or naval orders [etc.] to any distance. 1835 *Musical Library* Aug. *Suppl.* 78 This Telephonic system is one of the most ingenious contrivances we ever witnessed. 1840 WHEATSTONE *Let.* in Cooke *Electr. Telegraph* (1857) I. 114 The most efficient.. means of establishing a telegraphic (or rather a telephonic) communication between two remote points. 1877 *Daily News* 30 Nov. 5/1 We do not exactly anticipate that telephonic offices will have to be superadded by the Post Office to its existing arrangements. 1878 G. B. PRESCOTT *Sp. Telephone* (1879) 17 In the summer of 1876 Professor A. G. Bell..exhibited a telephonic apparatus. *Ibid.* 39 Mr. Edison has recently invented a telephonic repeater, which is designed to be used..for increasing the distance over which [the telephone] may be made available. 1892 *Montreal Weekly Gaz.* 21 July 8/7 The Public may now obtain telephonic communication over its long distance metallic circuit lines. *fig.* 1884 J. TAIT *Mind in Matter* (1892) 99 Mind segregates itself..from the matter..on whose telephonic powers it depends for intercourse with the world.

Hence **Telepho·nically** *adv.*, in the manner of or by means of a telephone.

1879 S. P. THOMPSON in *Nature* XXI. 180 Sounds transmitted telephonically. 1882 *Pall Mall G.* 1 May 4 It is connected telephonically with the hotel at Dalmally.

**Telephonist** (tǐ-, tele·fǒnist, te·lǐfōnist). [f. TELEPHONE *sb.* + -IST.]

**a.** A person employed in transmitting messages by telephone; one who works a telephone. **b.** One versed in telephony (*rare*—[0]).

1882 OGILVIE, *Telephonist*, a person versed in telephony, or who operates on the telephone. 1884 *Pall Mall G.* 9 May 4/2 The female voice is always clearer, and..a clear voice..is one of the chief requirements of a telephonist. 1898 *Daily News* 13 Sept. 6/5 Employed as season telephonist at the observatory on the summit of Ben Nevis.

**Telephonograph** (telǐfōu·nǒgraf). [f. TELE- + PHONOGRAPH, or f. TELEPHONE + -GRAPH.] An instrument consisting of a combination of telephone and phonograph, by which telephone messages can be recorded and subsequently reproduced. Also applied (in U. S.) to Poulsen's TELEGRAPHONE. Hence **Te·lephonogra·phic** *a.*, pertaining to or of the nature of a telephonograph; **Te·lephono·graphy**, the working or use of a telephonograph.

1878 G. B. PRESCOTT *Sp. Telephone* (1879) 549 The phonograph and telephone, when combined, form an instrument known as the telephonograph. 1889 *Telegr. Jrnl. & Electr. Rev.* 10 May 523/2 Mr. J. Hanmer, the originator of the recent telephonographic experiments between New York and Philadelphia. **1889** *Ibid.* 17 May 558/2 After the recent improvements made in the phonograph..the problem of telephonography has naturally cropped up. **1902** *Harper's Mag.* Feb. 496 The Poulsen telephonograph in its ordinary form does not speak louder than an ordinary Bell telephone.

**Telephony** (tǐ-, tele·fǒni, te·lĭfǒ͞uni). [f. Gr. τῆλε afar, TELE- + -φωνία -sounding, forming abstr. sbs. from adjs. in -φωνος, -voiced, -sounding. So mod.Ger. *telephonie*, F. *téléphonie*.]

†**1.** Name for a system of signalling by means of musical sounds, and for the practice of other early forms of telephone. *Obs.*

**1835** *Athenæum* July 531 M. Sudré, whose new system of telegraphic communication, or telephony (as he calls it) we mentioned some weeks ago. **1835** *Mech. Mag.* XXIII. 269 (*heading*) The Telephony, or Musical Telegraph.

**2.** The art or science of constructing telephones; the working of a telephone or telephones.

[**1861** (Dec.) P. REIS in *Jahres-Bericht, Frankfurt. Physik. Verein* (*title*) Ueber Telephonie durch den galvanischen Strom.] **1876** A. GRAHAM BELL in *Proc. Amer. Acad. Arts & Sc.* 10 May (*Title of Lecture*) Researches in Telephony. **1876** — in *Boston Advertiser* .. Oct., Telephony. Audible speech conveyed two miles by telegraph. Prof. A. Graham Bell's Discovery. **1878** G. B. PRESCOTT *Sp. Telephone* (1879) 53 When I commenced my researches in electric telephony. **1884** *St. James's Gaz.* 23 Oct. 5/1 The Belgians..have just started a system of public telephony. **1885** *Pall Mall G.* 18 Sept. 6/2 The solution of the problem of long distance telephony and along with it the much more important question of submarine telephony is said to be within sight. **1900** *Westm. Gaz.* 20 June 10/2 Some interesting experiments in wireless telephony are being conducted by the Post Office between the..Skerries Island and Anglesey.

**Telephotal** (-fǒ͞u·tăl), *a.* [f. as TELEPHOTE + -AL.] = TELEPHOTOGRAPHIC *a.*[2]

**1905** *Westm. Gaz.* 29 Aug. 5/1 Several..observers will be taking photographs [of the sun at an eclipse] with small cameras—some with telephotal lenses.

**Telephote** (te·lĭfǒ͞ut), *sb.* Also **telephot**. [f. Gr. τῆλε afar, at a distance, TELE- + φῶς, φωτ-, light.] A name employed or proposed for various devices or apparatus used or projected: **a.** A means of transmitting signals or messages from a distance by means of light, (*a*) by flashing beams of light by a mirror (cf. HELIOGRAPH); (*b*) by letting out flashes from a brilliant lamp by means of a moving shutter; (*c*) by using flashed beams to work a sensitive photo-electric receiving apparatus (cf. PHOTOPHONE). **b.** A device for the electric transmission of pictures, so that they are reproduced as pictures at a distance: cf. TELEPHOTOGRAPH[1], *telelectrograph* in TELE-. **c.** A projected or suggested device for the electrical transmission to a distance of visual images of things, persons, or actual scenes (cf. *telelectroscope* in TELE-): not yet practically realized. **d.** An apparatus for photographing at a great distance; a telephotographic lens or camera: see TELEPHOTOGRAPH[2].

**1880** [implied in TELEPHOTE *v.*]. **1884** KNIGHT *Dict. Mech.* Supp., *Telephote*, an instrument or apparatus for conveying messages or images by transmission of light. **1889** *Scott. Leader* 26 July 7 M. Courtonne..has deposited under seal his description of a new apparatus called a telephote, which enables one to see at a distance as the telephone enables one to hear at a distance. **1896** *Current Hist.* (Buffalo, N. Y.) VI. 950 A 'telephot'..invented by Dr. Robert d'Unger, of Chicago, Ill. [for picture telegraphy]. **1903** *Sci. American* 27 June 486/1 (*heading*) The 'Telephot', a novel apparatus for photographing at great distances. *Ibid.* 486/2 The 'Téléphot' may, moreover, be, at a moment's notice, converted into a terrestrial or astronomical telescope.

Hence **Te·lephote** *v.*, to transmit an optical image to a distance by means of electricity. **Telephotic** (-fǫ·tik) *a.*, of or pertaining to a telephote (actual or conceived), or to TELEPHOTY.

**1880** *Engineering* 7 May 361/2 Visual Telegraphy...An image of the object to be 'telephoted' is focussed on the mirror by means of a lens, and the resulting current started in each [selenium] square of the mirror by the portion of the image falling on it is transmitted by the corresponding wire to the distant station. **1889** tr. *Jules Verne* in *Tablet* 16 Feb. 249/1 Each reporter..has in front of him a set of commutators which enable him to communicate with any desired telephotic line. **1896** FLAMMARION in *N. Amer. Rev.* May 557 We need to be able to enter into telephotic communication with them [inhabitants of Mars].

**Telephoto** [cf. PHOTO 2], abbrev. of TELEPHOTOGRAPHIC *a.*[2]

**1898** *Westm. Gaz.* 26 Jan. 5/3 By means of a tele-photo lens..Mr. Lodge has secured many photographic records of great value to the ornithologist. **1900** H. M. WILSON *Topographic Surv.* xli. 869 An attachment called a *telephoto combination*, which consists in the addition of a negative or magnifying element in the rear of the combination proper. This produces larger images of distant objects.

**Telephotograph,** *sb.*[1] (tel\`ĭfǒ͞u·tǒgraf). [f. as TELEPHOTE *sb.* b, c + -GRAPH.] A picture or image electrically reproduced at a distance, a *telectrograph*; also, an apparatus for doing this. So **Telephotographic** (te:lĭfǒ͞utǒgræ·fik) *a.*[1], applied to an apparatus (*telephotographic instrument*) for producing photographs at a distance by means of an electric current. **Telephotography**[1] (te:lĭfǫtǫ·grăfi), the reproduction of pictures or scenes at a distance by means of the electric current as in the telegraph and telephone; = TELEPHOTY, *phototelegraphy*.

(This application of *telephotograph* and its derivatives had priority of date over that of TELEPHOTOGRAPH[2], by which it has been almost superseded in current use.)

**1881** S. BIDWELL in *Nature* 10 Feb. 344/1 (*heading*) Telephotography. *Ibid.* 345/1, I made a pair of 'tele-photographic' instruments...They produced a 'tele-photograph' of a gas-flame. *Ibid.* 563 Mr. Shelford Bidwell's telephotographic machine. **1881** *Standard* 30 Dec. 5/3 Mr. Shelford Bidwell's Telephotograph has gone far to prove that..the actual handwriting of the sender of a message, as well as drawings..may be transmitted by telegraph and reproduced at the other end. **1891** G. M. MINCHIN in *Philos. Mag.* Mar. 235 The second problem..is the electrical transmission of an image to any distance; in other words the construction of a telephotograph. **1895** *Current Hist.* (Buffalo, N. Y.) V. 962 The Telephotograph. This Swedish invention will reproduce to the eye pictures transmitted from a distance.

**Telepho·tograph,** *sb.*[2] [f. Gr. τῆλε (see TELE-) + PHOTOGRAPH; a back formation from TELEPHOTOGRAPHIC[2], the first-formed word of this group: see note there.] A photograph of a distant object taken with a telephotographic lens.

**1900** *Army & Navy Jrnl.* 14 July 1097 Good telephotographs have been obtained at a distance of over forty miles, and those taken beyond artillery range (ten miles) are on a sufficiently large scale to be of practical use. **1904** *Times, Lit. Supp.* 8 Apr. 109/2 We must give the palm to the striking telephotograph, facing page 184. **1909** MARRIAGE *Sculptures Chartres Cathedral* Pref. 8 Those..illustrations, generally speaking, in which the detail is on the largest scale are telephotographs.

Hence **Telepho·tograph** *v.*, *trans.* to photograph with a telephotographic lens or apparatus; **Te:lepho·tographer**, one who takes a telephotograph. So **Te:lephoto·graphy**[2], the art or practice of taking photographs of distant objects by a camera with a telephotographic lens.

**1900** *Westm. Gaz.* 27 Jan. 4/3 Owing to haze it was impossible to *telephotograph the Boers. **1899** *Pall Mall G.* 21 Dec. 3 The would-be *telephotographer was turned back. **1899** DALLMEYER (*title*) *Telephotography, an Elementary Treatise on the Construction and Application of the Telephotographic Lens. **1899** *Pall Mall G.* 21 Dec. 3 It is difficult to understand why the War Office has not taken advantage of telephotography.

**Telephotographic** (te:lĭ₁fǒ͞utǒ₁græ·fik), *a.*[2] [f. Gr. τῆλε afar off + PHOTOGRAPHIC *a.*

This word is properly formed and clearly expresses its meaning; its use and that of its derived group (see prec.), has practically superseded that of TELEPHOTOGRAPH[1] and its derivatives coinciding in form with these, which were differently composed, and of quite different application.]

Of, pertaining to, or used in the photographing of distant objects, within the field of sight but beyond the limits of distinct vision, esp. in *telephotographic lens*, a lens or combination of lenses for this purpose. (Invented by Dallmeyer 1891.)

**1892** T. R. DALLMEYER *Paper read to Camera Club* 10 Mar., A compound Telephotographic Lens. **1892** *Daily News* 26 Sept. 2/6 A remarkable view of Mont Blanc taken at a distance of 56 miles, with Dallmeyer's *tele-photographic lens. **1892** *Nature* 15 Dec. 161/2 In the simple telephotographic lens the anterior element, which is of large aperture and short focus, is a positive lens, while the posterior is negative, and of a fractional part of the focal length of the former lens. **1904** *Archæol. Surv. Ceylon, Epigr. Zeylanica* I. p. iv, The new telephotographic apparatus should be used for inscriptions on which an ordinary camera cannot be brought to bear. **1906** *Athenæum* 3 Mar. 268/2 Khan Tengri from the south, the telephotographic view of the same peak from the north.

**Telephoty** (te·lĭfǒuti). [f. as TELEPHOTE + -Y.] The art or practice of reproducing pictures or views at a distance by means of the electric current; the theory and practice of the telephote; = TELEPHOTOGRAPHY[1].

**1908** *Westm. Gaz.* 30 Apr. 5/2 The problem of 'seeing electrically' really resolves itself into the problem of electrical reproduction, and many men have been more or less successful in solving it. The system of 'telephoty', which is gaining some attention just now, was well known amongst specialists twenty-five years or more ago, but hitherto all the men who have experimented with it have given up sooner or later.

**Teleplastic** to **Telergy**: see TELE-.

†**Te·ler.** *Obs. rare*⁻¹. [app. a. AF. **teler* = OF. *telier*, *teilier*, F. *toilier*, = Pr. *telier*, Cat. *teler* :—late L. *tēlārius* (Du Cange), f. *tēla* web, cloth.] A maker or seller of cloth; a cloth-merchant.

*c* **1400** *Destr. Troy* 1586 Taliours, Telers, Turners of vesselles.

**Teler**, obs. form of TILER, TILLER.

**Telescope** (te·lĭskǒ͞up), *sb.* Also 7 **tellescope**. [ad. It. *telescopio* or mod.L. *telescopium*, the former used by Galilei, 1611, the latter by Porta in Italy and by Kepler, 1613, f. Gr. τηλεσκόπ-ος far-seeing, f. τῆλε afar off, at a distance + σκοπ-εῖν to look, -σκοπ-ος looker: see -SCOPE. The earliest English examples are in the L. and It. forms.

*Telescopio* is frequent in letters of Galilei from 1 Sept. 1611, but does not appear to have been invented by him; J. B. Porta, member of the Roman Academy of the Lincei (to which Galilei also belonged), in a letter assigned to 1613, appears to attribute the name to Prince Cesi, founder and head of the Academy: 'Telescopium multis ostendi (lubet hoc uti nomine a meo principe reperto)' (*Galilei Opere* (1901) XI. 611). Galilei had previously, in 1610–11, used *perspicillum*, Kepler in 1610 ***perspicillum, conspicillum, specillum, penicillium***.]

**1.** An optical instrument for making distant objects appear nearer and larger, consisting of one or more tubes with an arrangement of lenses, or of one or more mirrors and lenses, by which the rays of light are collected and brought to a focus and the resulting image magnified.

Telescopes are of two kinds: *refracting*, in which the image is produced by a lens (the object-glass), and *reflecting*, in which it is produced by a mirror or *speculum*; being magnified in each case by a lens or combination of lenses (the EYE-PIECE, q.v.). Large telescopes of both these kinds are used by astronomers. The smaller hand-telescopes are always refracting, and consist of two or more tubes made to slide one within another for convenience of packing into a narrow compass and for adjusting the lenses as required for focusing the image; cf. TELESCOPE *v.* 1.

[**1619** BAINBRIDGE *Descr. Late Comet* 19 For the more perspicuous distinction whereof I vsed the *Telescopium* or Trunke-spectacle.] **1648** BOYLE *Seraph. Love* xi. (1663) 59 Galileo's optick Glasses,.. one of which Telescopioes, that I remember I saw at Florence. **1657** W. RAND tr. *Gassendi's Life Peiresc* I. 143 Galilæus, by his newly invented Telescope had discovered certain great and wonderfull sights, concerning the Stars. *Ibid.*, The cause of the effects of the Telescope, or Perspective-Glasse. **1671** MILTON *P. R.* IV. 42 By what strange Parallax or Optic skill Of vision multiplyed through air, or glass Of Telescope. **1774** MACKENZIE *Maritime Surv.* I. iv. 27 Turn the Theodolite till, through the Telescope, you see the Pole A at the vertical Wire. **1837** DICKENS *Pickw.* ii, Mr. Pickwick..with his telescope in his great-coat pocket. **1842** *Penny Cycl.* XXIV. 163/2 It is ..manifest that reflecting telescopes, or optical instruments containing combinations of mirrors and lenses, were known in England before the end of the sixteenth century. **1855** BREWSTER *Newton* I. iii. 59 Sir William Herschel..completed in 1789 his gigantic telescope, forty feet in focal length, with a speculum forty-seven and a half inches in diameter! **1865** 'L. CARROLL' *Alice in Wonderland* i, Oh, how I wish I could shut up like a telescope! **1870** EMERSON *Soc. & Solit., Art* Wks. (Bohn) III. 16 Dollond formed his achromatic telescope on the model of the human eye. **1875** R. ADAMSON in *Encycl. Brit.* III. 221/2 He [Roger Bacon] certainly describes a method of constructing a telescope.

**b.** *fig.* and *allusively*.

**1656** OWEN *Mortification Sin* Wks. 1851 VI. 65 We see through a glass darkly...It is not a telescope that helps us to see things afar off. **1666** J. FRASER *Polichron.* (S.H.S.) 18 It [History] is indeed that telescope by which we see into distant ages. **1751** JOHNSON *Rambler* No. 176. ⁋ 11 Others are furnished by criticism with a telescope. **1885** J. K. JEROME *On the Stage* p. v, Now that..duty no longer demands that memory should use a telescope.

**c.** *Astron.* (Also in mod.L. form **Telescopium.**) Name (introduced by Lacaille in 1752) of a constellation south of Sagittarius.

**2.** *attrib.* and *Comb.*, as *telescope-maker*, *-stand*, *-tube*; *telescope-shaped* adj.; also applied to various things consisting of or having parts which fit or slide one within another like the tubes of a hand-telescope (cf. TELESCOPIC 4), as *telescope-bag*, *-chimney* (on a steamboat), *-joint*, *-rod*, *-table*; also **telescope-carp**, a monstrous variety of gold-fish, having protruding eyes; also called *scarlet-fish*; **telescope-driver**, a clockwork apparatus for driving an astronomical telescope so as to follow the apparent movements of the heavenly bodies and thus keep the same object continually in the field of view; so *telescope-driving* adj.; **telescope-eye**, an eye which can be protruded and retracted like a telescope-tube, as in gastropod molluscs; **telescope-fish** = *telescope-carp*; **telescope-fly**, a fly of the genus *Diopsis*, having the eyes on long stalks; **telescope-shell**, the long conical shell with numerous whorls of an Indian gastropod (*Telescopium fuscum*); **telescope-sight**, a small telescope mounted as a sight upon a fire-arm or surveying instrument, a telescopic sight.

**1804** SHAW *Gen. Zool.* V. 211 *Telescope Carp...Scarlet-Carp, with protuberant eyes, all the fins half white. **1874** SIR E. BECKETT *Clocks & Watches* 213 The following plan for a *telescope-driving clock...A still simpler *telescope-driver. **1875** *Zoologist* X. 4501 The so-called '*telescope fishes' are common gold-fishes with double tails and projecting eyes. **1882** OGILVIE, **Telescope-fly*, a dipterous insect of the genus *Diopsis*. **1858** SIMMONDS *Dict. Trade*, *Telescope-maker, Telescope-stand. **1891** CONST. MACEWEN 3 *Women in Boat* 73 We began to fish. We had three little common Japanese *telescope-rods. **1867** LATHAM *Black & White* 76 In the *telescope-shaped jacketed guns. **1753** CHAMBERS *Cycl. Supp.* App., **Telescope-shell*, the English name of a species of *turbo*, of a conic figure, with plane, striated, and very numerous spires. **1715** tr. *Gregory's Astron.* (1726) I. 284 Instruments..furnished with *Telescope Sights. **1881** YOUNG *Ev. Man his own Mechanic* § 763 A *telescope-table must be studied in all its parts and movements before any attempt can be made to mend or make one.

**Te·lescope,** *v.* [f. prec. sb.]

**1. a.** *trans.* To force or drive one into another (or into something else) after the manner of the sliding tubes of a hand-telescope: usually said in reference to railway carriages in a collision.

**1872** *Amer. R. R. Jrnl.* 20 Apr. 493 Telescoping..car raised up and sent through the advancing car, after the manner of a closing telescope. **1876** *World* V. No. 112. 14 No one has ever yet been killed in a Pullman, in which, says its inventor, you can never be 'telescoped'. **1879** *Times* 11 Oct. 5/6 A Pacific express train..ran into a locomotive, completely telescoping the baggage wagons of the express. **1890** CLARK RUSSELL *Ocean Trag.* II. xviii. 101 He closed the glass with a ringing of the tubes as he telescoped them.

*fig.* 1894 *Cornh. Mag.* Mar. 289 The stages which occupy the broom for the whole of its lifetime are telescoped, as it were, in the gorse into the first three weeks. 1909 *Expositor* July 57 It would then be just possible that St. John had to this slight extent 'telescoped' the two accounts together.

**b.** *intr.* To slide, run, or be driven one into another (or into something else); to have its parts made to slide in this manner (see quot. 1882, s.v. *telescoping* below); to collapse so that its parts fall into one another (quot. 1905).

1877 KNIGHT *Dict. Mech.* 2524/2 Two screws.., one working within the other, and both sinking or telescoping within the base. 1877 O. W. HOLMES *How not to settle it* 92 They telescoped like cars in railroad smashes. 1881 *Metal World* No. 19. 295 The proposals to stop a train by applying the power on the locomotive, which..would cause the carriages to 'telescope'. 1905 BOND *Gothic Archit.* 594 Chichester central tower telescoped within the memory of man.

**2.** *trans.* To make into or use as a telescope.

1861 [see *telescoped* below]. 1889 *Macm. Mag.* Apr. 419/1 Telescoping my hand, [I] sent a long searching look into the length of the dingy shadow.

Hence **Te·lescoped** (-skoupt) *ppl. a.*; **Te·lescoping** *vbl. sb.* and *ppl. a.*

1861 THORNBURY *Turner* (1862) II. 170 *note*, Looking through his telescoped hand. 1882 *Standard* 2 Aug. 3/5 [He] had a telescoping rod in his hand. 1890 *Nature* 11 Sept. 473/1 The telescoping of the limbs and other organs within the body of an insect larva. *Ibid.*, What may be termed the telescoping of ancestral stages one within another. 1898 *Westm. Gaz.* 3 June 3/2 The telescoped carriages and the injured men and women lying about.

**Telescopic** (teliskǫ·pik), *a.* (*sb.*) [f. TELESCOPE *sb.* + -IC.]

**1.** Of or pertaining to a telescope; of the nature of or consisting of a telescope, as *telescopic sight* = telescope-sight (TELESCOPE *sb.* 2); done by means of a telescope, as *telescopic observations*.

1705 J. HODGSON in *Phil. Trans.* XXV. 1630 The Brass Quadrant .. with Tellescopick Sights. 1855 BREWSTER *Newton* I. iii. 66 The limits of telescopic vision have not been reached. 1907 J. R. ILLINGWORTH *Doctr. Trin.* vii. 138 Like the telescopic discovery of a star which mathematical calculations have already prophesied.

**2.** Seen by means of a telescope; *spec.* of a heavenly body, visible only through a telescope (cf. MICROSCOPIC 3). Ellipt. as *sb.* a telescopic star.

1714 DERHAM *Astro-Theol.* Pref. (1726) A vj b, It is not very easy to distinguish which are Satellites, and which are Telescopick Stars. 1784 HERSCHEL in *Phil. Trans.* LXXV. 83 About 1 degree n. of..the six telescopics. 1831 BREWSTER *Nat. Magic* vi. (1833) 143 The general telescopic appearance of the coast. 1893 SIR R. BALL *Sun* 18 These asteroids.. are..entirely telescopic.

**3.** Having the property of a telescope; having the power of distant vision, far-seeing; contemplating something distant. (*lit.* and *fig.*) In quot. 1886, admitting of distant vision.

1781 COWPER *Truth* 98 Turn eastward now, and fancy shall apply To your weak sight her telescopic eye. 1856 EMERSON *Eng. Traits, Ability*, These Saxons..have..the telescopic appreciation of distant gain. 1886 BURROUGHS *Signs & Seasons, Sharp Lookout* 6 When the atmosphere is telescopic, and distant objects stand out unusually clear and sharp, a storm is near.

**4.** Consisting of parts made to slide one within another like the tubes of a hand-telescope, so as to be capable of being lengthened or shortened.

1846 *Penny Cycl.* 1st Suppl. II. 665/2 The commissioners express a very decided opinion against the safety of *telescopic axles*..by which the wheels..might be shifted at pleasure to suit different gauges. 1864 WEBSTER s.v., Constructed of concentric tubes, either stationary, as in the telescopic boiler, or movable, as in the telescopic chimney of a war-vessel. 1871 B. STEWART *Heat* § 83 Water or gas pipes are fitted to each other by telescopic joints.

**Telesco·pical**, *a.* Now *rare.* [f. as prec.: see -ICAL.] **1.** = prec. 1.

1672 *Phil. Trans.* VII. 4004 Telescopical Tubes may be considerably shortned without prejudice to their magnifying effect. 1722 WOLLASTON *Relig. Nat.* v. 81 Surveyed.. by the help of..telescopical glasses. 1793 SIR G. SHUCKBURGH in *Phil. Trans.* LXXXIII. 103 For telescopical observations of the planets. 1864–90 WEBSTER, *Telescopically*, in a telescopical manner.

**2.** = prec. 2.

1665–6 *Phil. Trans.* I. 150 By Telescopical Stars are understood such as are not seen, but by the help of a Telescope. 17.. BOLINGBROKE *Ess. Human Knowl.* iii, There are microscopical corpuscles in bodies, as there are telescopical stars in the heavens.

**Telesco·pically**, *adv.* [f. TELESCOPIC, -AL: see -ICALLY.] In a telescopic manner.

**1.** By or as by means of a telescope; as, or as if, seen through a telescope.

1846 WORCESTER, *Telescopically*, by use of a telescope. 1867–77 G. CHAMBERS *Astron.* I. i. 7 When telescopically examined. 1879 NEWCOMB & HOLDEN *Astron.* 373 Telescopically..we might classify them with Mercury and Venus.

**2.** In the manner of the tubes of a hand-telescope; by the sliding of one part within another.

1894 BARING-GOULD *Queen of L.* I. vi. 67 It appeared as though the pole were collapsing telescopically. 1898 SEDGWICK *Text-bk. Zool.* I. viii. 299 The foot or pseudopodium [in *Rotifera*] may be jointed, and the joints are often telescopically retractile.

**Telescopiform** (teliskǫ·pifǫːm), *a.* *Entom.* [f. TELESCOPE + -[I]FORM.] Having the form of a telescope; consisting of a series of joints or tubes retractile one within another.

1826 KIRBY & SP. *Entomol.* IV. xlvi. 352 Ovipositor.. Telescopiform. 1848 *Jrnl. R. Agric. Soc.* IX. I. 190 With her telescopiform oviduct she..pierces the cuticle.

**Telescopist** (tĭ-, tele·skǫ̆pist, te·lĭskopist). [f. TELESCOPE + -IST.] One skilled in using a telescope; one who makes telescopic observations.

1870 PROCTOR *Other Worlds* Pref. 6 One of the most surprising phenomena ever witnessed by the telescopist. 1878 NEWCOMB *Pop. Astron.* III. iii. 291 The earlier telescopists..scrutinized the planets very carefully.

**Telescopy** (tĭ-, tele·skopi, te·lĭskopi). *rare*—°. [f. as TELESCOPE + -Y, after Gr. words in -σκοπία. Cf. MICROSCOPY.] The art or practice of using the telescope, or of making telescopes.

1861 in COOLEY *Dict.* 1879 in WEBSTER *Supp.*

**Teleseme**: see TELE-.

†**Tele·sia**, *sb. pl.* *Obs.* [mod.L., a. Gr. τελέσια, pl. neuter of τελέσι-ος finishing, completing, perfecting. In Fr. *télésie* (Haüy 1796).] A name for the precious stones composed of crystallized alumina, as the sapphire and its class.

1812 SIR H. DAVY *Chem. Philos.* 357 Alumina..in its crystallized form coloured by small quantities of iron,.. constitutes a beautiful class of gems, distinguished by the name Telesia, including the ruby, the sapphire, the oriental topaz. 1819 *Pantologia, Telesia*,..a name given by Hauy to the sapphire.

‖**Telesis** (te·lėsis). [mod.L., a. Gr. type *τέλεσις (f. τελεῖν to finish, complete, f. τέλος end) implied in compounds, as τελεσίδρομος completing the course.] The intelligent direction of effort toward the achievement of an end.

1898 L. F. WARD *Outl. Sociology* 181, 186–190. 1905 DEALEY & WARD *Text-bk. Sociology* IV. xvi. § 280. 237 If we regard all the forces of nature..as so many means to the ends of man and society, telesis becomes the adjustment of means to ends, and all human effort is expended upon the means.

†**Telesiu·rgic**, *a.* (*sb.*) *Obs.* [ad. late Gr. τελεσιουργικός, f. τελεσιουργεῖν in its later sense (Pollux *c* 176 A.D.) 'to perform mystic or magical rites'.] Relating to the performance of mystic or magical rites; = TELESTIC. **b.** as *sb. pl.* **Telesiu·rgics**, telesiurgic matters or subjects.

1678 CUDWORTH *Intell. Syst.* I. iv. § 16. 293 Julian a Chaldean and Theurgist..(who wrote concerning Dæmons and Telesiurgicks).

†**Telesm** (te·lėz'm). *Obs.* Also 7 **telesme**, **-isme**. Also in Gr. form **telesma**, *pl.* **-mata**. [ad. late Gr. τέλεσμα completion, performance, religious rite (*a* 200 Clem. Alex.); later, a consecrated object endowed with a magic virtue to avert evil; f. τελεῖν to complete, fulfil, perform (rites), officiate (in the mysteries), consecrate; f. τέλος end, etc.] = TALISMAN [2] 1; *esp.* in Byzantine Greece, and in Asia, a statue set up, or an object buried under a pillar or the like to preserve the community, house, etc. from danger.

1646 J. GREGORY *Notes & Obs.* (1650) 33 The Claudi and the Cæci..were no other than those..Statuary Telesmes so much celebrated of old, which unless they kept the City, the watchman laboured but in vaine. *Ibid.* 38 Apollonius fetching a deep sigh, refused to make any further Telesmes against the Earthquakes. 1660 H. MORE *Myst. Godl.* VIII. xv. 432 Gaffarel tells us a very reverend story of a Telesme against Fire found under a bridge at Paris. 1693 W. FREKE *Sel. Ess.* iv. 32 Thus Telesmes, or Talismans also,—are a spawn of Astrology.

**Telesma·tic**, *a.* *rare.* [as next + -IC.] = next.

1877 SYMONDS *Renaiss. Italy* iii. 143 Telesmatic virtues were attributed to figures carved on temple-fronts and friezes.

†**Telesma·tical**, *a.* *Obs.* [f. Gr. τελέσματ-, stem of τέλεσμα, TELESM + -ICAL.] Of or pertaining to a telesm; talismanic; magical.

1646 J. GREGORY *Notes & Obs.* (1650) 41, I undertake not that the golden Mice were so ceremoniously consecrated, yet that they had a Telesmaticall way of preparation. 1658 ROBINSON *Endoxa* x. 52 The Rain bow hath a Telesmatical signification, for the preservation of the Universe from Inundation. 1693 J. EDWARDS *Author. O. & N. Test.* 145 The telesmatical figure of a stork.

Hence **Telesma·tically** *adv.*, magically.

1646 J. GREGORY *Notes & Obs.* (1650) 32 The Part of Fortune..was mysteriously included in a Statue of Brasse, Telesmatically prepared,..the Statue was called The Fortune of the City. *Ibid.* 33 Silver statues..Telesmatically consecrated..against the incursions of the Barbarians.

**Telesomatic**, etc.: see TELE-.

†**Tele·stic**, *a.* *Obs.* [ad. Gr. τελεστικός, f. τελεστής hierophant in the mysteries, f. τελεῖν: see TELESM.] Of or pertaining to the mysteries, or to a hierophant; mystical.

1678 CUDWORTH *Intell. Syst.* 293 Julian, in the time of Marcus Antoninus .. wrote the Theurgick and Telestick Oracles in Verse. *Ibid.* 792. 1788 T. TAYLOR *Proclus* I. 19 By the highest and most mystical step, he ascended to the greatest and most consummate or telestic virtues. 1822 — *Apuleius* XI. 276 *note*, As the telestic art, through certain symbols and arcane signatures, assimilates statues to the Gods.

**Telestich** (tĭ-, tele·stik, te·lėstik). [irreg. f. Gr. τέλος, τελε- end + στίχος a row, line of verse, after ACROSTIC.] A short poem (or other composition) in which the final letters of the lines, taken in order, spell a word or words. (Cf. ACROSTIC.)

*a* 1637 B. JONSON *Underwoods* lxi. 39 Had I pump'd for.. Acrostichs, and telestichs. 1673 *S' too him Bayes* 44 The arrantest dunce that ever made acrostick, telestick, or anagram. 1862 H. B. WHEATLEY *Anagrams* 46 A very ingenious form of the double acrostic, called the Telestich, has been invented. 1883 H. KENNEDY tr. *Ten Brink's E. Eng. Lit.* 36 A predilection for other metrical diversions, especially the acrostic and telestich.

**Telethermograph**, etc.: see TELE-.

**Teleutospore** (tĭ-, teliū·tǫspoəɹ). *Bot.* [f. Gr. τελευτή completion, end (f. τέλος end) + SPORE.] A special form of spore, usually produced at the end of the period of fructification, in parasitic fungi of the family *Uredineæ*. Hence **Teleutosporic** (-spǫ·rik) *a.*, of or pertaining to a teleutospore. So **Teleu·to-fo:rm**, that form or stage of the fungus which produces teleutospores.

1874 COOKE *Fungi* 202 These spores..may conveniently be called resting spores, or as De Bary calls them, teleutospores, being the last which are produced. 1882 VINES *Sachs' Bot.* 331. 1884 *Athenæum* 18 Oct. 499/3 The probability that the teleutospore of *Puccinia* is also analogous to an egg, the uredospore being 'probably a pupa state'. 1891 *Ibid.* 23 May 671/1 The extraordinary abundance..of the teleutosporic stage as compared with the comparative scarcity of the æcidial stage. 1898 tr. *Strasburger's Bot.* 367 The genus *Cronartium*, with uredo- and teleuto-forms on *Vincetoxicum* and *Ribes*.

**Television, Telewriter**: see TELE-.

**Telford** (te·lfəɹd). Surname of a celebrated civil engineer, Thomas Telford (1757–1834), used to designate the kind of road constructed by him.

1896 J. O'DONNELL in *Voice* (N.Y.) 2 Jan. 3/1 This gutter track takes care of the water perfectly. It cost less than a macadam or telford road.

**Telic** (te·lik), *a.* [ad. Gr. τελικ-ός final, f. τέλος end.]

**1.** *Gram.* Of a conjunction or clause: Expressing end or purpose.

1846 in WORCESTER (citing Prof. Stuart). 1856 ALFORD *Grk. Test.* III. 90 *note*/2 [In Eph. ii. 9 ἵνα μή τις καυχήσηται] ἵνα has in matter of fact its strictest telic sense. With God, results are all purposed. 1882 FARRAR *Early Chr.* II. 507 *note*, St. John's use of ἵνα is far wider than that of classical writers. It often loses its telic sense ('in order that') and becomes simply ekbatic or explanatory, as in Luke i. 43, John xv. 13. 1904 *Sat. Rev.* 9 Apr. 460/1 It expresses a purpose or intention. and i therefore telic.

**2** Directed or tending to a definite end; purposive.

1889 MIVAR *Truth* xxv. 438 The telic series of cyclical changes which are characteristic of all duly organized living bodies. 1903 L. F. WARD *Pure Sociology* II. v. 94 All causes are either efficient, conative, or telic. *Ibid.* II. vi. 97 The telic or final cause is not a force,..but it utilizes efficient causes in a manner wholly its own, and thus produces effects. 1906 DEALEY & WARD *Text-bk. Sociology* § 280 Civilisation chiefly consists in the exercise of the telic faculty.

**Teliferous** (tĭli·fėrəs), *a.* [f. L. **tēlifer* dart-bearing, f. *tēlum* dart: see -FEROUS.]

†**1.** Bearing darts or missiles. *Obs. rare.*

1656 BLOUNT *Glossogr.*, *Teliferous*,..which beareth darts, arrows or weapons. 1658 in PHILLIPS.

**2.** *Zool.* Armed with nematocysts or stinging cells, as the *Telifera*, a division of the Cœlenterata comprising all except the Sponges (*Porifera*).

1860 GOSSE *Hist. Brit. Sea-Anemones* Introd. 22 Teliferous System...The Actinaria are furnished with a system of armature of most extraordinary character...Their tissues contain excessively minute bodies, in the form of oblong or oval transparent vesicles, which have the power of shooting out a long thread of extensive tenuity.

**Teligraph**, variant of TELLIGRAPH.

**Teling**, *vbl. sb.*: see TELE *v.*

**Telinga** (tėli·ŋgă) *sb.* and *a.* Also 8–9 **Tellinga**, 8 **-ger**, **-gy**, **Telingee**, **Talinga**. [Of uncertain origin: supposed by some to be the original form of the word *Telugu*, and held to be itself derived from Skr. *Trilinga* meaning 'the three lingams', according to an alleged tradition that the god Śiva descended in the form of a lingam upon three mountains said to mark the boundaries of the Telugu country. But Dravidian scholars are inclined to view this as a mere etymological figment, and even doubt whether Telugu and Telinga have any original connexion. It is certain however that 17th c. English writers called the language *Telinga*, and that in Hindūstānī a Telugu is called *Tilanga* and the Telugu country *Tilangāna*: cf. *Rājpūtāna*.]

**1.** The TELUGU language. (As *sb.* or *a.*)

1698 FRYER *Acc. E. India & P.* 33 Their Language they call generally *Gentu*...The peculiar Name of their Speech is *Telinga*. 1800 *Asiatic Ann. Reg.* 186/2, I had now entered on that part of India which bears the name of Tellingana, whose inhabitants are called Tellingies, who speak what is denominated the Tellingy language.

**2.** One of the Telugu people.

1800 [see 1]. 1840 MALCOM *Trav.* 19/1 This people, whose name is often written *Telinga*, or *Kalinga*, are generally called, by European writers, *Gentoos*.

†**b.** *spec.* A native Indian soldier disciplined and dressed in quasi-European fashion; a sepoy. *Obs.*

1760 in J. LONG *Select. Unpubl. Records* (1869) 235 (Y.), 300 Telingees are run away, and entered into the Beerboom Rajah's service. 1761 *Ibid.* 258 Tellingers. 1766 GROSE *Voy. E. Ind.* (1772) I. Gloss. (Y.), Sepoys, sometimes called Tellingas. 1789 *Seir Mutaqherin* II. 92 (Y.) Hindu soldiers, armed and accoutred and disciplined in the European manner of fighting; I mean those soldiers that are become so famous under the name of Talingas. 1827 SCOTT *Surgeon's*

*Dau.* xiii, I have been a Telinga..in the Company's service, and have eaten their salt. **1883** *Sat. Rev.* 27 Jan. 120/1 The Oriental portions of Clive's army were known to the Bengalis of Nuddea as Telingas, because they came, or were supposed to have accompanied him, from Telingana or Madras.

**3.** (See quot.)

**1858** SIMMONDS *Dict. Trade, Tellinga*, a dhoney or native coasting-vessel on the coast of Coromandel.

**4.** *attrib.* **Telinga potato**, *Amorphophallus campanulatus*: see POTATO 4.

**Teliost**, variant of TELEOST.

**Telisman**, Sc. var. TILLSMAN *Obs.*

**Tell** (tel), *sb.*[1] Now *dial.* [f. TELL *v.*]

**1.** What one tells or has to tell; a tale, a statement, an account.

**1742** H. WALPOLE *Lett. to Mann* 29 July, I am at the end of my tell. **1827** F. COOPER *Prairie* I. ii. 32 From his tell, it must be a considerable stream. **1899** WESTCOTT *David Harum* xxx, As near 's I c'n make out f'm Dave's tell, he must 'a' ben red-headed.

**2.** A talk, conversation, gossip.

**1864** MRS. LLOYD *Ladies Polc.* 101, I made so bould as to come to see if you'd plase to have a bit of a tell with me afore I goes. **1901** 'ZACK' *Tales Dunstable Weir* 99 Having a tongue she dearly liked a tell.

‖**Tell** (tel), *sb.*[2] Also **tel.** [a. Arab. تل *tall* a hillock.] The Arab name for an artificial hillock or mound, usually one covering the ruins of an ancient city.

**1864** W. F. AINSWORTH *Comm. Xenophon's Anabasis* 285 The hill..appears to have been one of the numerous artificial mounds, topes, or tells, sometimes sepulchral, sometimes heaps of ruin, which abound on the plain of Babylonia. **1878** CONDER *Tentwork Pal.* (1879) II. 46 We may next notice the most remarkable of its antiquities, namely the Tellûl or Tells there found. **1878** MACLEAR *Bk. Joshua* xv. (1880) 149 The tell is very strong and it rises about 200 feet high. **1882** F. S. DE HASS *Buried Cities* III. v. 380 (Funk) Tells or conical hills.., many of them the craters of extinct volcanoes.

**Tell** (tel), *v.* Pa. t. and pple. **told** (tōuld). Forms: see below. [OE. *tęllan*, pa. t. *tealde*, pa. pple. (*ge*)*teald*, cognate with OFris. *talja*, *tella*, OS. *tęlljan* (*talda*, *gitald*), senses as in OE.; MLG., MDu., LG., Du. *tellen* to count, reckon, etc., OHG. **zęlljan*, *zęllen* (*zalta*, *gizalt*), senses as in OE. (MHG. *zęln*, Ger. *zählen* to reckon, count), ON. *tęlja* to tell, relate, say, count, speak, Sw. *tälja*, Da. *tælle* to count, number, reckon; all:—OTeut. **taljan*, f. **talā*, OE. *talu*, TALE *sb.* OE. had also a pa. pple. *getęled* (in poetry, Beda, Orosius, Lindisf. and Rushw. Gl.); Anglian had pres. t. *tęlest*, *tęleð*, and pa. t. and pple. *talde*, *getald* (Vesp. Ps.), whence ME. *tāld*, and *tōld*. *Tealde* remained in Early ME. in southern dialects. The later dial. *telld*, *tell'd*, *telt* is a new formation from *tell*: cf. the forms of SELL *v.*]

**A.** Illustration of Inflexional Forms.

**1.** Present stem. *Inf.* OE. **tellan**, ME. **telle(n, tel** (4–7), Mod.E. **tell.**

*c* **888** K. ÆLFRED *Boeth.* vii. § 3 Ute nu tellan. *Ibid.* xviii. § 3 Tele nu þa lengu. *c* **1000** *Ags. Gosp.* Matt. xi. 16 Hwam telle ic. *a* **1090**, *c* **1175** Telle [see B. 2, 1]. *c* **1200** ORMIN 9500 Crist..wrohhte wundre miccle ma Þann icc ȝuw maȝȝ nu tellenn. *c* **1250** *Kentish Serm.* in *O. E. Misc.* 27 Þet us telþ þet holi godespel. **13..** *Cursor M.* 96 Inogh to tell. *Ibid.* 10913 (Cott.) Wat þou quat for soth i tell [*Gött.* talle]? *Ibid.* 11477 Cums again and tels me. *c* **1375** *Sc. Leg. Saints* x. (*Mathou*) 30, I thinke to tel here why [etc.]. *c* **1386**, *c* **1440** Telle [see B. 1]. **1513** DOUGLAS *Æneis* VIII. viii. *heading*, Evander telland Eneas thingis seir. *a* **1592** GREENE *Vision* Wks. (Grosart) XII. 200 Thus to tellen all the truth, He infected Romes youth. **1632** Tel [see B. 3 (*b*)].

**2.** *Pa. t.* **α. 1–4 tealde** (**1 telede**), **3 tælde, 4 teelde.**

*c* **888**, *c* **1000** Tealde [see B. 1]. *a* **1000** *Andreas* 1105 (Gr.) Hi..hluton..teledon. *c* **1205** LAY. 13181 Þet heo nane manne ne tælden. *c* **1315** Tealde [see B. 4].

**β. 1, 3–5 talde, 4–6 tald, 5–9** *Sc.* **tauld.**

*a* **900** CYNEWULF *Elene* 909 Þone ic ær on firenum fæstne talde. *c* **1205** LAY. 1350 A steores-man ham talde. *Ibid.* 26884 Al heo talden [*c* 1275 tolde] þene wæi. **13..** *Cursor M.* 511 Als i tald [*Fairf.* talde] ar. **1375** BARBOUR *Bruce* I. 563 The Cwmyn raid to the king..& tald all this cass. **1567** Tauld [see B. 17]. **1816** SCOTT *Old Mort.* xxiv, Only he tauld me about it.

**γ. 3–6 tolde, 4– told.** (Also **5 toold, tolled, tolded, 6 tould(e, 8** *dial.* **towd.**)

*c* **1250** *Gen. & Ex.* 3449 Moyses tolde ðis israel. *c* **1340** He told [see B. 2]. *c* **1340** HAMPOLE *Medit. Passion* Wks. 1895 I. 93 Þou toldist it him biforen. **1418** ABP. CHICHELE in Ellis *Orig. Lett.* Ser. I. I. 5, I..toold him owre comun avis. *c* **1449** PECOCK *Repr.* 353 Which appering Constantyn toold in greet secretnes to the same Eusebi. *c* **1450** LOVELICH *Grail* xliii. 225 ȝit tolded thow it Neuere to non Man. **1540** HYRDE tr. *Vives' Instr. Chr. Wom.* (1592) F viij, What hurt should come, Cato tolde before. **1582** N. LICHEFIELD tr. *Castanheda's Conq. E. Ind.* I. vi. 15 b, All which things the Generall tolde him. **1601** Told [see B. 5]. **1790** MRS. WHEELER *Westmld. Dial.* 90 He towd Sammy he wor baun et wed wie his Cusin Ann.

**δ. 4 tellde, 4–5 telde, 4–6 teld, 5 tellid, 5–6 -yd, 5–6** (**9** *dial.*) **telled, 9** *dial.* **tell'd, 6–9** *dial.* **telt.**

*c* **1330** R. BRUNNE *Chron.* (1810) 82 Þer men him teld, who was his aduersere. **13..** *Cursor M.* 871 (Gött.), I teld [*Cott.* tald] þe. *c* **1380** WYCLIF *Serm.* Sel. Wks. I. 166 If God tellde him specialy. **1399** LANGL. *Rich. Redeles* II. 151 Trouthe..telde somme her sothes. **1453** AGNES PASTON in *P. Lett.* I. 255 Gurney tellyd hym he had byn at London. **1537** LATIMER *Let. to Cromwell* 14 Oct. in *Rem.* (Parker Soc.) 384, I telled him plainly my mind therein. **1554** *Cal. Anc. Rec. Dublin* (1889) 436 The sam telt to the wywes. **1596** SPENSER *F. Q.* VI. i. 44 Sir Calidore upcheard, and to her teld All this accord. **1790** MRS. WHEELER *Westmld. Dial.* 34, I telt Bet I wad drive tea it. **1825** BROCKETT *N. C. Words* s.v., Aw tell'd him on't. **1826** J. WILSON *Noct. Ambr.* Wks. 1856 I. 144 Mr. Scroope telt Sir Walter.

**3.** *Pa. pple.* **α. 1–2** (**ȝe**)**teald, 3 teald, 3–4 i-teld, 4 teeld.**

*c* **1000** *Leg. Rood* (1871) 5 Ða þis þam mæran kasere constantine ȝeteald wæs. *c* **1200** *Trin. Coll. Hom.* 215 Swo ich iteld habbe. *c* **1380** WYCLIF *Serm.* Sel. Wks. I. 169 Crist haþ teeld þat þis hiȝe charite techiþ a man to putte his lyf for love of hise frendis.

**β. 3 i-tald, 4 y-tald, taald, 4–8 tald(e, 5** *Sc.* **tallde, 5–9** *Sc.* **tauld, 6 tawld.**

*c* **1205** LAY. 12092 Nes hit neowhær itald. *Ibid.* 22999 Þar nas na cniht wel itald [*c* 1275 itold]. **13..** *Cursor M.* 3330 Til he þam had his errand tald. *Ibid.* 8765 Þis tre i haf of forwit taald. **1340** Y-tald [see B. 1]. **1488** *Acc. Ld. High Treas. Scot.* I. 79 Tauld in presence of the Chancellare. **1588** A. KING tr. *Canisius' Catech.* 185 As I haue tauld in tymes past. **1725** RAMSAY *Gentle Sheph.* III. ii, Do you get them tald you in your sleep? **1816** SCOTT *Old Mort.* xxxviii, I wadna hae tauld ye.

**γ. 3–5 i-told (-e), 3– told.** (Also **3–7 tolde, 4–5 toold** (**5 y-tolte**), **6 tould, towld, (tollyd).**)

*c* **1220** *Bestiary* 758 in *O. E. Misc.* 24 Ilk der..foleȝen him [the panther]..For ðe swetnesse ðe ic ȝu haue told. **1297** R. GLOUC. (Rolls) 1634 King aruirag of wan we abbeþ itold. *Ibid* 7569 As me aþ er ytold. **1303** Tolde [see B. 1]. **1382** WYCLIF *2 Sam.* iii. 23 So it is toold to Joab of tellers. **1387** TREVISA *Higden* (Rolls) VIII. 149 Rehersed how it was i-told. *c* **1400** *Destr. Troy* 12816 Tithinges hor tolde were. *c* **1420** *Chron. Vilod.* 1830 Hit was..To seynt Dunston ysende & by tokon to hym y-tolte. *c* **1430** *Hymns Virg.* 37/69 Theise .iij. þat y haue of toold. **1538** STARKEY *England* I. i. 22 A tale tollyd among deffe men. **1584** in *Cath. Rec. Soc. Publ.* V. 64 Yt was towld him by his cosine. **1586** HUNSDON in *Border Papers* (1894) I. 367, I toulde him of sondrie cawses.

**δ. 4 telld, 4–6 teld, 5–6** (**8–9** *dial.*) **telled, 6–9 telt, 8–9** *dial.* **tell'd,** *Sc.* **tell't.**

**13..** *Cursor M.* 4640 (Gött.) Nou has he Teld me. *Ibid.* 6752 (Cott.) It sal be slaghter telld o man. *c* **1489** CAXTON *Sonnes of Aymon* 174 Nowe haue I telled you that that ye haue asked me. **1560** PILKINGTON *Expos. Aggeus* (1562) 13 The thinge is true which is telled. **1596** SPENSER *F. Q.* VII. vi. 27 Witnesse, ye Heavens, the truth of all that I have teld. *a* **1818** in Scott *Hrt. Midl.* Introd., In a' thae wee bits o' ways I ha'e tell't ye. **1824** SCOTT *St. Ronan's* ii, I hae been tell'd by ane that suld ken. **1900** Telled [see B. 8 b].

**B.** Signification.

I. To mention in order, narrate, relate, make known, declare. II. To enumerate, number, count, reckon. III. To reckon, estimate, esteem, account (qualitatively).

**I.** To mention in order, narrate, make known.

* *trans. To tell things or a thing.*

†**1.** To mention or name (a series of things) one after another in order; to recount, enumerate; to give a list of. *Obs.*

*c* **888** K. ÆLFRED *Boeth.* xxxvii. § 2 Do ðæs lean to ðæm forsprecenan goodum þe ic þe ær tealde on þære þriddan bec. *c* **1000** ÆLFRIC *Hom.* (Th.) II. 428 Se sunder-halȝa..He..tealde his godan dæda. *c* **1175** *Lamb. Hom.* 9 Feole oðre..werke þe nu were long eou to telle. *c* **1200** *Trin. Coll. Hom.* 71 Þere we shule tellen alle ure gultes. *c* **1250** *Gen. & Ex.* 497 Ic wile riȝt tellen, if ic can, Adam, Seth, Enos, Caynan, Malaleel, Iareth, Enoch. **1303** R. BRUNNE *Handl. Synne* 12624 Ȝow to withholde Fro þe synnes þat byfore are tolde. **1340** *Ayenb.* 24 Alle þise guodes of kende þet ich habbe ssortliche y-tald. *c* **1386** CHAUCER *Can. Yeom. Prol. & T.* 246 Arsenyk sal Armonyak and Brymstoon And herbes koude I telle eek many oon. *c* **1440** *Jacob's Well* 152 Out of euyll tunge springeth x. braunchys. Þe v. I telde ȝou þe oþer day, þe oþere v. I schal telle ȝow now.

**2.** To give an account or narrative of (facts, actions, or events); to narrate, relate. (With simple obj. or obj. clause; sometimes with indirect obj. as in 3.) Also *to tell over.*

*c* **1000** *Leg. Rood* (1871) 5 Hi..tealdon him þa þrowunga þe ure hælend on þære rode ðrowode. *a* **1090** *O. E. Chron.* an. 1085, Þeah ic hit lengre telle. *a* **1154** *Ibid.* an. 1137, I ne can ne i ne mai tellen alle þe wunder. *a* **1225** *Juliana* 40 Þah ich þe talde al dei ne mahte ich þe tellen þe wundres. **1297** R. GLOUC. (Rolls) 7198 Þo gan he to tellen þis [vision]. *a* **1300** *Cursor M.* 141 Þar neist sal be sythen tald How þat ioseph was boght and sald. *c* **1340** *Ibid.* 1330 (Gött.) He..told him all þat he had sene. *c* **1380** WYCLIF *Sel. Wks.* II. 105 Þis gospel telliþ furþere how þes Jewis pursueden Crist. **1470–85** MALORY *Arthur* II. xiii. 91 It telleth after in the sangraylle that syre Percyualis syster halpe that lady with her blood wherof she was dede. **1526** TINDALE *Acts* xv. 12 Barnabas and Paul..tolde what signes and wondres God had shewed. **1671** MILTON *P. R.* II. 306 Others of some note, As story tells, have trod this Wilderness. **1746** FRANCIS tr. *Hor. Sat.* II. vi. 163 A country mouse, as authors tell, Of old invited to his cell A city mouse. **1779** *Mirror* No. 23 ¶ 5 These [actions] were told to his honour. **1821** SCOTT *Kenilw.* xvi, Thou art..a tattling knave to tell over again his fooleries. **1833** CRUSE *Eusebius* VII. xi. 289 After these ..he proceeds to tell what happened to him. *c* **1850** *Arab. Nts.* (Rtldg.) 552 She then went on with her narrative, and told him in what manner she had obtained an audience. *Mod.* What happened to him there has often been told.

**b.** With the narrative as obj. Now only with *tale* or *story*: see 17.

**1576** GASCOIGNE *Philomene* (Arb.) 92 She by whom I meane To tell this woful Tragedie Was called Phylomene.

**c.** *intr.* for *pass.* To be related with a particular effect; to sound (well, etc.) when told.

**1584** HUDSON *Du Bartas' Judith* in *Sylvester* (1621) 696 Then, fathers, choose your warres; for better tels To lose like Jewes, then winne like infidels. **1782** MISS BURNEY *Cecilia* VI. ii, I had as lieve the things were false as not, for they tell as well the one way as the other.

**3.** To make known by speech or writing; to communicate (information, facts, ideas, news, etc.); to state, announce, report, intimate. Usually const. with indirect obj. (*dat.*) or *to.*

(*a*) With the direct object a *sb.* or *pron.*

Examples of the direct passive are included here; for the indirect passive with the person as subj., see 8 b.

*c* **1122** [see (*b*)]. *c* **1200** *Trin. Coll. Hom.* 31 Gode tiðinge..us telleð..seinte lucas on þe holie godspelle. *c* **1290** *Beket* 1188 in *S. Eng. Leg.* I. 140 He..tolde hire al is þouȝt. **13..** *Cursor M.* 4624, I wat þou tells [*v.rr.* tellis, tellest] it me for noght. **1340–70** *Alex. & Dind.* 207 Tel me þe soþe. *c* **1380** WYCLIF *Wks.* (1880) 300 Poul telliþ here a rewele þat cristen men shulden holde. **1390** GOWER *Conf.* III. 368 Ech his oghne avis Hath told, on that, an other this. *c* **1400** *Brut* lxii. 57 Telle me þe enchesone wherefore I ame to ȝow brouȝt. **1474** CAXTON *Chesse* II. iv. (1883) 47 And they told hym the trouthe. **1513** DOUGLAS *Æneis* VIII. iv. *heading*, Evander tellis till Enee but baid, The verray caus. **1526** TINDALE *Luke* i. 45 Thoose thinges.. which were tolde the from the lorde. — *Acts* xxvii. 25, I beleve God that so it shalbe even as it was tolde me. **1611** BIBLE *Gen.* xxiv. 33, I will not eate, vntill I haue tolde mine errand. **1606** SHAKS. *Tr. & Cr.* I. iii. 284 This shall be told our Louers. **1673** *S'too him Bayes* 23 I'le tell you one piece of my mind. **1746** FRANCIS *Hor. Epist.* I. vi. 74 Let's buy a Slave to tell each Voter's Name. **1759** JOHNSON *Idler* No. 63 ¶ 6 The studious and ambitious contend..who shall tell their thoughts in the most pleasing manner. **1821** SCOTT *Kenilw.* xv, Tell us your mystery of multiplying. **1856** J. H. NEWMAN *Serm. Var. Occas.* (1881) i. 12 Nor, even though it be told to her, can she enter into it. **1896** *Standard* 15 Jan. 7/2 He said much, but told little, at to-day's meeting. *Mod.* Who told you that?

(*b*) With direct obj. a *clause*, with or without *that.*

In the direct passive the clause usually follows the vb., its place before the vb. being supplied by *it* (*It was told him that*, etc.). For the indirect passive, see 8 b.

*c* **1122** *O. E. Chron.* an. 1046, Þa..Swegen..tealde þæt his sciperes woldon wændon fram him buton he þe raðor come. **1297** R. GLOUC. (Rolls) 5357 Þou ssalt þi wille abide as ich þe abbe ytold here. *a* **1300** *Cursor M.* 4843 Tells me quat kin man yur fader be. *c* **1380** [see A. 3 *a*]. *c* **1440** *Jacob's Well* 203, I teld ȝou þat a schouyl hath iij. partys: a scho, an heued, & an handyl. **1535** LYNDESAY *Satyre* 1506 Now I will rin, but rest, And tell that all is ready. **1535** COVERDALE *1 Sam.* xxiii. 7 Then was it tolde Saul that Dauid was come to Cegila. **1560** DAUS tr. *Sleidane's Comm.* 90 b, He tolde to the other playnely that..he would take from him the wardshyp of his nephewe. **1611** BIBLE *Acts* xxiii. 30 When it was tolde me, how that the Iewes laid waite for the man. **1632** SANDERSON *Serm.* 6 Yet Salomon tels us, the poore mans wisdome is despised. **1681–6** J. SCOTT *Chr. Life* (1747) III. 523 Our Saviour himself tells us, that the Father judgeth no Man. **1790** BURNS *Tam O'Shanter* 19 She tauld thee weel thou was a skellum. **1833** T. HOOK *Parson's Dau.* I. v, And I say, Charles, tell her we are coming to coffee forthwith. **1838** LONGFELLOW *Ps. Life*, Tell me not, in mournful numbers, Life is but an empty dream! **1908** R. BAGOT *A. Cuthbert* xxviii. 367 There had always been something mysterious about Anthony Cuthbert, the doctor told himself. *Mod.* It was told me that you had been inquiring about me.

**b.** To declare, state formally or publicly; to announce, proclaim, publish. Also *fig.*

*Tell it not in Gath* (from 2 *Sam.* i. 20), publish it not to the enemy, or to the Philistine, or to the world.

*a* **1300** *E. E. Psalter* xviii. [xix.] 1 Heuens telles goddis blisse. *a* **1325** *Prose Psalter* xlix. 7 [l. 6] Þe heuens shul tellen his riȝtfulnes. *Ibid.* l. 16 [li. 15] My mouþe shall tellen þyn heryyng. **1382** WYCLIF *2 Sam.* i. 20 Woleth ȝe not telle in Geth, ne telle ȝe in..Aschalon. **1382** — *Acts* xvii. 18 He [Paul] telde to hem Jhesu and aȝen rysing. **1535** COVERDALE *Ps.* xcv[i]. 10 Tell it out amonge the Heithen, that the Lorde is kynge. **1602** SHAKS. *Ham.* I. ii. 126 No iocond health that Denmarke drinkes to day But the great Cannon to the Clowds shall tell. **1656** EARL MONM. tr. *Boccalini's Advts. fr. Parnass.* II. xxxviii. (1674) 190 The Master of the Colledge, told in the name of the whole Senate, That [etc.]. *c* **1795** COWPER *Needless Alarm* 34 Ere yet with ruthless joy the happy hound Told hill and dale that Reynard's track was found. **1819** KEATS *Isabella* x. xix, Many a chapel bell the hour is telling. **1904** MARIE CORELLI *God's Gd. Man* xx, The fact is—but tell it not in Gath—I was happier without him!

**c.** *fig.* To make known or indicate as if by language; to bespeak.

**1809** HEBER *Poems, Europe* 29 May those bleak summits tell The field of Anger where the mighty fell. **1827** CLARE *Sheph. Cal.* 148, I care not what this foolish trifling tells.

**4.** To utter (words); to say over, recite (a passage, composition, etc.); to say. Now *dial.*

*c* **1315** SHOREHAM iii. 120 Many man..hym ne douteþ of no breche Of godes hestes healde [= old]; Ac he not nefer wat hy beeþ, Ne neuer hy ne tealde. **1382** WYCLIF *Ps.* cxviii. [cxix.] 171 My lippis shuln tellen out an impne. **1390** GOWER *Conf.* I. 107 It semeth that a belle Lik to the wordes that men telle Answerth riht. **1567** *Gude & Godlie B.* (S. T. S.) 201 His [the Pope's] numerat Aueis, and Psalmes tauld. **1573–80** BARET *Alv.* T 105 To tell by heart, *recito*. *a* **1653** BINNING *Serm.* (1845) 445 You use to tell over some words in your prayers. **1841** HELPS *Ess.*, *Self-Discipline* (1875) 21 To think that a man can find nothing better to do, in the presence of his Creator, than telling off so many words! **1880** *Cornwall Gloss.* s. v., Can you tell your lessons? **1884** AUGUSTA J. E. WILSON *Vashti* vii. (*U. S.*), 'Did Ulpian tell you good-bye?' 'No, I have not seen him.'

**b.** To utter, speak, say (things).

**1377** LANGL. *P. Pl.* B. v. 408 Ȝif I bidde any bedes..Þat I telle with my tonge is two myle fro myne herte. **1535** COVERDALE *Ecclus.* xxi. 25 The lippes of the vnwyse wylbe tellynge foolish thinges. **1628** HOBBES *Thucyd.* (1822) 79 Many prophecies were told and many sung by the priests of the oracles. **1715–20** POPE *Iliad* IX. 412 Who dares think one thing, and another tell, My heart detests him as the gates of hell. **1787** BURNS *Birthday Ode* 47 Till all the frighted echoes tell The blood-notes of the chase! **1888** ELWORTHY *W. Som. Gloss.* s. v., Don't tell up such stuff.

**c.** To express in words (thoughts, things known).

*c* **1200** *Moral Ode* 285 Ne mai non heorte it þenche, ne no tunge ne can telle. *c* **1250** *Death* 57 in *O. E. Misc.* 172 Ne miȝte no tunge tellen þat euer wes iboren þe stronge pine of helle. *a* **1300** *Cursor M.* 96 (Cott.) Qua sa will of hyr faynres spell, Find he sal inogh to tell. *c* **1430** *Freemasonry* 664 The vertu therof no mon telle may. **1650** CROMWELL *Let.* 12 Sept., in *Carlyle*, Which speaking the instructed, the edified and comforted can best tell the energy and effect of. **1875** JOWETT *Plato* (ed. 2) I. 82 Let me tell you the pleasure which I feel in hearing of your fame.

**d.** *To tell out, away* (*dial.*): to drive away (pain, etc.) by uttering incantations.

**1822** HIBBERT *Shetl. Isl.* (1891) 272 (E.D.D.) The religious charmer of Shetland would mutter some words over water, ..and limbs were washed with it, for the purpose of telling out pains. **1869** REID *Art Rambles in Shetl.* 25 Papa Stourians believed that the beadle of the kirk had the power of 'telling' the sparrows away so as never to return. **1879** Low *Tour Ork. & Shetl.* 203 When she was a child..she has heard from others that a pain or a stitch has been *telled out* in that manner.

**5.** To disclose or reveal (something secret or private); to divulge. *To tell tales*: see TALE *sb.* 3 c.

*a* **1400** *Pistill of Susan* 141 We schal telle trewely We toke þe wiþ a-voutri. **1445** tr. *Claudian* in *Anglia* XXVIII. 277 Thise goddis the telle þin enemyes sleightes, and lede to þe couchis of fraude. **1601** SHAKS. *Twel. N.* II. iv. 113 She neuer told her loue. **1615** G. SANDYS *Trav.* 72 Many there are that undertake to tell fortunes. **1819** KEATS *Isabella* v, I may not speak, And yet I will, and tell my love all plain. **1848** THACKERAY *Van. Fair* xviii, She told no more of her thoughts now than she had before.

†**b.** To reveal (something future); to foretell, predict.

**1340–70** *Alex. & Dind.* 776 Tokne of þat turment tolde ȝoure eldren. **13..** *Cursor M.* 9265 (Fairf.) Crist was talde wiþ prophecy. *c* **1380** WYCLIF *Serm.* Sel. Wks. II. 2 Þis Gospel of Mark bigynneþ how Crist was teld in þe olde lawe. *a* **1400–50** *Alexander* 200 Alle þe sawis of þaire Syre as Siraphis tald þare gan þai graithly þam graue. [**1884** tr. *Lotze's Logic* 303 No perception can tell us the future with the present.]

†**6.** To pray for, beg, ask. *Obs. rare.*

**1393** LANGL. *P. Pl.* C. VIII. 298 Ich praye ȝow, peers, paraunter yf ȝe meteþ Treuthe, telleþ to hym þat ich be excused. **14..** *Trentalle St. Gregorii* in *Tundale's Vis.* (1843) 79 God moder my dere dame..Of Gode to tell mercy thou gine. **14..** *Lybeaus Disc.* 1755 To the castell he rod,.. To Jhesu bad and tolde, To sende hym tydynge glad.

**7.** To discern so as to be able to say with knowledge or certainty; hence, to distinguish, recognize, decide, determine.

**1687** A. LOVELL tr. *Thevenot's Trav.* II. 142 It is hard to tell whether it be a Horse or an Elephant. **1746** FRANCIS tr. *Hor. Sat.* II. iv. 58 None before me so sapient to engage To tell the various nature, or the age Of fish and fowl. **1840** R. H. DANA *Bef. Mast* xiii. 29 They can be told by their complexions, dress, manner, and also by their speech. **1883** GILMOUR *Mongols* xvi. 195 An ordinary man of common intelligence can tell a wall raised by..a competent builder from the attempted imitation of a bungling amateur. **1899** A. BIRRELL in *Daily News* 4 Nov. 3/2 Is it possible to tell a good book from a bad one?

**b.** Preceded by *can*: To be able to state; to know; to discern, perceive, make out, understand. Usually in negative or interrogative sentences, as *Nobody can tell, Who can tell?* Cf. SAY *v.*[1] 6 b.

? **1370** *Robt. Cicyle* 244 Wher such cloþ was to selle, Ne ho hit made, couþe noman telle. *a* **1400–50** *Alexander* 248 Þai can swyth of a sweuyn all þe swepe tell. *c* **1449** PECOCK *Repr.* III. xii. 353 No man can telle who wroot it. **1526** TINDALE *John* xvi. 18 We cannot tell what he saith [*Gr.* οὐκ οἴδαμεν τί λαλεῖ: *R. V.* 1881 We know not what he saith]. **1553** T. WILSON *Rhet.* (1580) 160 Neither can he otherwise chuse but stumble: that gropyng in the darcke can not tell where he is. **1783** JOHNSON *Let. to Mrs. Thrale* 23 July, Whether this short rustication has done me any good I cannot tell. **1838** ARNOLD *Hist. Rome* (1848) I. 99 Nor can any one tell at what time they attained to their present shape. **1873** MRS. OLIPHANT *Innocent* II. 231 It was..a dog-cart..he could tell as much by the sound. **1888** 'J. S. WINTER' *Bootle's Childr.* vi, Jane doesn't seem to like it—I can't tell why.

** *trans. To tell a person* (the originally indirect or dative personal object becoming the direct).

Some uses, as 9, hover between * and **.

**8.** To inform (a person) of something; to make aware, apprise, acquaint; to instruct. Also *colloq.* and *dial.* To direct the attention of (a person) to a fault or the like by way of admonition. Const. *of, about*; also *so* (representing *that*, or an object clause, and thus coming very near 3 a (*a, b*).

*c* **1205** LAY. 12946 Ic þe wulle tællen Of uncuðe spællen. **1297** R. GLOUC. (Rolls) 322 Of þe maumet hii tolde brut þat hii fonde þere. *Ibid.* 3510 Me tolde him of a gret duc þat het theldryk. *a* **1300** *Cursor M.* 11393 (Cott.) Vs telles alsua iohn..Of a folk ferr and first vncuth. *c* **1440** *Jacob's Well* 152 The oþer day, I told ȝow of þe wose of glotonye. *c* **1470** HENRY *Wallace* I. 263 He tald his modyr of his sodane cas. **1573–80** BARET *Alv.* T 108 He shewed me, or tolde me of my fault. **1713** BERKELEY *Hylas & Phil.* iii, Moses tells us of a creation. *Mod.* Sit down and tell us about it.

*c* **1412** HOCCLEVE *De Reg. Princ.* 717, I tolde hym so; & euer he seyde nay. **1609** B. JONSON *Sil. Wom.* IV. ii, I told you so, sir, and you would not beleeue me. *Mod.* They told us so at the station.

**b.** The passive is not only used with the const. *of, about*, but is often substituted for that of sense 3 (*a*), as in *he was told the truth, we were not told the reason*; and now usually for that of 3 (*b*), as *I was told that you were coming.*

**1600** SHAKS. *A. Y. L.* III. ii. 361, I haue bin told so of many. **1607** — *Timon* IV. iii. 214 Thou wast told thus. **1611** — *Wint. T.* II. ii. 31 He must be told on't, and he shall. **1781** COWPER *Expost.* 66 Pleasure is deaf when told of future pain. **1821** SCOTT *Kenilw.* xxxvi, Wherefore was I not told of all this? **1898** MRS. H. WARD *Helbeck* I. v. 101 He's that masterful he woan't be towd. **1900** H. SUTCLIFFE *Shameless Wayne* xiii. 170 He's getten a peffing cough.., but he willun't be telled. *Mod.* Has any one been told about it?

**1599** SHAKS. *Hen. V*, III. vii. 113, I was told that, by one that knowes him. **1599** — *Much Ado* v. iv. 96, I was told, you were in a consumption. **1863** KINGSLEY *Lett.* (1878) II. 149 When I am told that the Lancashire system is perfect. **1895** KAY in *Law Times Rep.* LXXIII. 623/1 He asked if his wife was there, and being told she was not, he..left the lodge.

**9.** To assert positively to; to assure (a person). Often *parenthetically* in expressions of emphasis.

*c* **1440** *York Myst.* xxx. 452 This touches no tresoune, I telle you. **1526** TINDALE *Luke* xii. 59, I tell the thou departest not thence, tyll thou have made goode the vtmose farthynge. *a* **1596** *Sir T. More* I. i. 110 And he is in a good forwardnesse, I telle ye, if all hit right. **1712** STEELE *Spect.* No. 480 ¶ 3 Give me leave to tell you, Sir, this is the reason. **1732** BERKELEY *Alciphr.* IV. § 2 Let me tell you I am not to be persuaded by metaphysical arguments. **1817** T. L. PEACOCK *Melincourt* vii, Very orthodox old wine in the cellar, I can tell you. **1905** F. YOUNG *Sands Pleas.* I. iii, I tell you, it got on my nerves.

**10.** To order or direct (a person) *to do* something; to bid, to request authoritatively.

**1599** B. JONSON *Cynthia's Rev.* II. i, Place your mirror in your hat, as I told you. [In *passive*, as you were told.] **1693** R. LYDE *Retaking Ship called Friend's Adventure* 10, I told him to knock down that Man at the Helm. **1879** T. L. CUYLER *Pointed Papers* 19 Christ nowhere tells sinners to wait for revivals. **1891** MISS DOWIE *Girl in Karp.* 19, I told the man to go on. [In *passive*, The man was told to go on.] **1899** KIPLING *Stalky* i. 15 Tell the Sergeant to keep his eye open.

†**11.** To direct (a person) to a place: cf. TEACH *v.* 3. *Obs. rare.*

**1470–85** MALORY *Arthur* XVI. x. 678 Canst thow telle me vnto somme chappel where that I may burye this body?

*** *Intransitive uses.*

**12.** To give an account, description, or report. Const. *of, about.* (*intr.* of 1 and 2.)

*a* **1300** *Cursor M.* 2139 Begine we now to tell at sem And siþen of his bern-tem. *Ibid.* 4238 Leue we now iacob in þis care To tell of ioseph and his fare. *c* **1440** *Alphabet of Tales* 164 Seneca tellis of a philosophur þat hight Picta-goricus. **1590** SPENSER *F. Q.* I. v. 26 What art thou, that telst of Nephews kilt? **1738** GRAY *Propertius* III. 59 Sailors to tell of Winds and Seas delight. **1812** CRABBE *Tales* II. 510 He told of bloody fights. **1830** SCOTT *Hrt. Midl.* vi. *note*, A near relation of the Author's used to tell of having been stopped by the rioters, and escorted home in the manner described.

†**13.** To make a statement, communication, or announcement; to speak, discourse. *Obs.* (*intr.* of 3.)

*c* **888** K. ÆLFRED *Boeth.* vii. § 3 Ute nu tellan beforan swilcum deman swilce þu wille. **13..** *Seuyn Sag.* (W.) 1228 'Sei on dame!' and sche bigan To tellen als a fals wimman. **1382** WYCLIF *Isa.* vii. 2 And thei tolden to the hous of Dauid, seiende, Siria rested vp on Effraym. *c* **1450** *Merlin* i. 21, I pray the..tellith to Blase my moders confessour. **1535** LYNDESAY *Satyre* 2154 Tell on. Ar ȝe content? **1558** PHAER *Æneid.* II. C iij b, They..fixt with eies ententiue did behold, Whan Lord Æneas..from his bench thus he told.

**14.** *fig.* To give evidence, be an indication *of.* (*intr.* of 3 c.)

**1798** COLERIDGE *Anc. Mar.* VII. x, All was still, save that the hill Was telling of the sound. **1833** HT. MARTINEAU *Briery Creek* v, There was so little that told of delusion in the calm simplicity of the doctor's countenance. **1853** KINGSLEY *Hypatia* i, His hard hands and sinewy sunburnt limbs told of labour and endurance. **1873** TRISTRAM *Moab* vi. 111 Blocks of basalt..telling of a still more ancient Moabite city.

**15.** To speak, talk, converse, gossip. Cf. TALE *v.* 6. Now *dial.* (*intr.* of 4.)

*a* **1652** BROME *Damoiselle* I. i. Wks. 1873 I. 385 At his Inne in Holborne Telling a little with the Host. **1888** ELWORTHY *W. Somerset Gloss.* s. v., I zeed 'em tellin' together..the night avore. **1892** SARAH HEWETT *Peasant Sp. Devon* 21 'E's behind telling tu Mr. Baker.

**16.** To disclose something wished to be kept secret; to play the informer, inform, tell tales, blab. Const. *on, of* (a person). (*intr.* of 5.)

**1539** BIBLE (Great) 1 *Sam.* xxvii. 11 Dauid saued nether man nor woman alyue..for feare (sayeth he) leste they shuld telle on vs. **1818** SCOTT *Rob Roy* xi, I ask no questions—no man bound to tell on himsell. **1835** MARRYAT *Jac. Faithf.* xxxiii, I had resolved to tell, and did so, narrating distinctly the circumstances by which the money had been obtained. **1860** GEO. ELIOT *Mill on Fl.* I. v, He didn't want to 'tell' of Maggie. **1897** 'TIVOLI' (H. W. Bleakley) *Short Innings* xiv, Oh, I'll not tell if you don't want me to. **1897** C. M. CAMPBELL *Deilie Jock* i. 16 Bobe..used to get mair than his fair share o' the tawse as it was, without my tellin' on him.

**** *Phrases and locutions.*

**17.** *To tell a tale*, to relate a story or narrative; *to tell one's tale*, to relate one's story; also, to say what one has to tell, to deliver one's message: see TALE *sb.* 3.

*c* **1275** *Passion* 1 in *O. E. Misc.* 37 One lutele tale, þat ich eu wille telle. *c* **1386** CHAUCER *Prol.* 792 That ech of yow to shorte with oure weye In this viage shal telle tales tweye. *c* **1450** tr. *De Imitatione* I. xvii. 19 Þou art called to suffre & to labore, not to be idel & telle tales. *a* **1548** HALL *Chron., Edw. IV* 199 b, The erle had not halfe tolde his tale. **1549** *Compl. Scot.* vi. 63, I thynk it best that euyrie ane of vs tel ane gude tayl or fabil, to pas the tyme quhil euyn...Than the eldest scheiphird began, and al the laif follouit, ane be ane in ther auen place. **1567** *Satir. Poems Reform.* vii. 4 Eich of thame his taill in ordoure tauld. **1596** SHAKS. *Merch. V.* IV. i. 276 When the tale is told, bid her be iudge. **1601** WEEVER *Mirr. Mart.* iv, One tale is good, untill another's told. **1613** PURCHAS *Pilgrimage* (1614) 208 A great part of the day after they sit at Cardes, or telling of Tales. **1875** JOWETT *Plato* (ed. 2) V. 366 My tale is one which many a man would be afraid to tell.

In the passage **1632** MILTON *L'Allegro* 67 'And every Shepherd tells his tale Under the Hawthorn in the dale', *tells his tale* probably belongs here, though some modern editors refer it to sense 21, taking it as 'counts his number or sum (i. e. of sheep)'; but no instance has been found before the 19th c., of 'tell his (or a) tale' in a numerical sense: while the expression in its ordinary sense has been common since the 13th century. Cf. also quot. 1549 for the telling of tales by each shepherd in turn, and see the whole passage, also the context of quot. 1613 in sense 21, where 'underneath a hawthorn' appears as the place of the shepherds' recreation.

**b.** *To tell tales*: see TALE *sb.* 3 c.

**c.** So *to tell a story*: see STORY.

*a* **1225** *Ancr. R.* 154 Me schal..tellen ou þeos storie, uor hit were to long to writen ham here. **1590** SHAKS. *Com. Err.* I. i. 121 To tell sad stories of my owne mishaps. **1681** DRYDEN *Span. Friar* IV. ii, Before I tell my fatal story out. **1798** FERRIAR *Illustr. Sterne* ii. 45 Another of his speakers tells the following story. **1840** W. H. MILL *Observ.*, etc. I. 114 The experience and history of mankind tells, uniformly, a different story from this. **1841** LANE *Arab. Nts.* I. 97 This is not a time for telling stories, when I am in this prison.

**18.** *To tell* (*the*) *truth* († *sooth*), to make a true statement; to state or report the fact or circumstance as it really is. Also used parenthetically (*to tell the truth, truth to tell*, etc.) to emphasize a statement: cf. SAY *v.*[1] B. 7. So *to tell a lie* (*a falsehood, an untruth*), to make a wilfully false statement or report. (See also the sbs. SOOTH, TRUTH, LIE, etc.)

*c* **1350** *Will. Palerne* 34 Soþ forto telle, al his cler colour comsed forto fade. *Ibid.* 160 But trewþe for to telle whan time come of daye [etc.]. *c* **1400** *Destr. Troy* 2338, I shall telle you the trewthe how me tyde euyn. **1536** CHEKE *Rem. Sedition* B ij, All thynges telle truthe but man. **1596** SHAKS. 1 *Hen. IV*, III. i. 58 Tell truth, and shame the Deuill. **1596–** [see LIE *sb.*[1] 1]. **1764** GRAY *J. Twitcher* 27 The prophet of Bethel, we read, told a lie. **1848** THACKERAY *Van. Fair* lii, It was not the habit of this dear creature to tell falsehoods, except when necessity compelled. **1855** H. ROGERS *Ess.* II. vii. 323 Sooth to tell, the narrative of the achievements..draws largely on our faith.

**19.** *To hear tell* († *told*); usually const. *of*: see HEAR *v.* 3 c. Now chiefly *dial.* and *colloq.*

*c* **1220** Herd told, **1297** Hurde tell [see HEAR *v.* 3 c]. *c* **1330** R. BRUNNE *Chron.* (1810) 101, I haf herd told of þis duke Roberd. **1375** BARBOUR *Bruce* II. 46 That Ik herd neuir in Romanys tell. *c* **1400** *Melayne* 47 That Charls was thare he herde telle. **1545** ASCHAM *Toxoph.* I. (Arb.) 100 Was never sene nor hard tel on yet. **1589, 1603, 1861, 1892** [see HEAR *v.* 3 c]. **1886** STEVENSON *Kidnapped* ii. 9, I asked him if he had ever heard tell of a house they called the house of Shaws.

**20.** In various colloquial expressions:

*Never tell me, don't tell me*, expressing incredulity or impatience. *Do tell!* (U. S., New Engl.), an exclamation of surprise, = 'is it possible?', 'you don't say so!' *I'll tell you what* = 'I'll tell you what it is', or 'I'll tell you something'. *To tell any one his own*: to tell him frankly of his faults.

**1604** SHAKS. *Oth.* I. i. 1 Neuer tell me, I take it much vnkindly. **1764** FOOTE *Patron* III. Wks. 1799 I. 356 Not to be spoke with! Don't tell me, Sir; he must, he shall. **1848** J. H. NEWMAN *Loss & Gain* III. ix. (1904) 323 Error of judgment! don't tell me. I know how these things happen quite well. **1860** BARTLETT *Dict. Amer.* s. v. *Do*, The dairy-maid after hearing the story through, exclaimed, *Do tell!* **1596** SHAKS. 2 *Hen. IV*, I. i. 51 My Lord: Ile tell you what, If my yong Lord your Sonne, haue not the day [etc.]. **1877** TENNYSON *Harold* I. ii, I'll tell thee what, my child; Thou hast misread this merry dream of thine. **1897** VIOLET HUNT *Unkist, Unkind* ii, I tell you what, Janet, we must have a man down who doesn't shoot—to amuse us! **1519** HORMAN *Vulg.* 61, I shall tell hym his owne, in a lytell byll of myne owne hande. **1865** R. HUNT *Pop. Rom. W. Eng.* Ser. II. 182 Every one is humorously 'told their own', without offence being taken.

**II.** To mention numerically, to count, reckon.

**21.** *trans.* To mention or name (the single members of a series or group) one by one, specifying them as *one, two, three*, etc.; hence, to ascertain from the number of the last how many there are in the whole series; to enumerate, reckon in; to reckon up, count, number. Also *absol.* Now *arch.* or *dial.*

*c* **1000** ÆLFRIC (*Heptat.*) *Gen.* xv. 5 Telle þas steorran. — *Num.* iii. 15, 16 Telle ælcne wepnedman..Moises þa tealde. *c* **1175** *Lamb. Hom.* 87 Fram þan halie hester dei boð italde fifti daȝa to þisse deie. *c* **1200** ORMIN 4550, & whase wile tellenn hemm Bi tale he findeþþ ehhte. *c* **1205** LAY. 24377 To tellen þat folc of Kairliun Ne mihte hit na mon idon. *a* **1300** *Cursor M.* 13302 (Cott.) Tuelue þai war to tell in tale. **1398** TREVISA *Barth. De P. R.* VIII. xxi. (Bodl. MS.), He knowithe how many þei bene þat nombreþ and telleþ þe sterres. **1483** CAXTON *Gold. Leg.* 143/2 He tolde atte table syttyng xiii poure pylgryms. **1523** FITZHERB. *Husb.* § 30 Let hym goo to the ende of his lande, and begynne and tell .ix. sheues, and let hym caste out the .x. shefe in the name of god. **1535** COVERDALE 1 *Sam.* xiv. 17 Tell and se which of vs is gone awaye. And whan they nombred, beholde, Ionathas & his wapen bearer was not there. **1613** W. BROWNE *Sheph. Pipe* v. i, Morne had got the start of night..When the shepheards from the fold All their bleating charges told. 1657 J. WATTS *Vind. Ch. Eng.* 43 Every countreyman can tell his Geese, and reckon right. 1719 DE FOE *Crusoe* (1850) 236 He could not tell twenty in English, but he numbered them, by laying so many stones in a row, and pointing to me to tell them over. 1748 J. MASON *Elocut.* 24 A Comma stops the Voice while we may privately tell one, a Semi-colon two; a Colon three: and a Period four. 1821 CLARE *Vill. Minstr.* II. 31 The shepherd had told all his sheep. 1869 [see TELLING *vbl. sb.* 3].

**b.** *spec.* To count (voters or votes). Also *absol.* *To tell noses*, to count heads: see NOSE *sb.* 6 d.

1511 in W. H. Turner *Select. Rec. Oxford* (1880) 4 Foster desyred off the mayre..to tell the fremen..for thalecc'on off a alderman;..they were men truly told. 1657, *a* 1734 [see NOSE *sb.* 6 d]. 1669 MARVELL *Corr.* Wks. (Grosart) II. 289 The tellers for the ayes chanced to be very ill reckoners, so that they were forced to tell severall times over. 1731 SWIFT *To Gay* 60 Nor think yourself secure in doing wrong By telling noses with a party strong. 1870 *Daily News* 7 May 2/1 After the division Mr. Dodson brought to the knowledge of the Committee the circumstance that he had appointed Sir H. B. a teller, but that that hon. baronet had refused to tell. 1899 *Jrnls. Ho. Comm.* 18 May, The House was told by Mr. Speaker, and, 24 members only being present, Mr. Speaker retired from the Chair until four of the clock, when the House was again told.

**c.** Phrases. (*a*) *To tell one's beads* (*rosary*): see BEAD *sb.* 2 b; so *to tell one's prayers.* †Also allusively *to tell tears*, to weep (quot. 1588).

1588 T. L. *To Ch. Rome* (1651) 18 Thow..canst not goe downe and sit, and tell tears with him. 1641, 1759 [see BEAD *sb.* 2 b]. 1789 MRS. PIOZZI *Journ. France* I. 265, I.. see nothing..but people telling their beads. 1819 SCOTT *Ivanhoe* xl, Richard..beheld the jovial Friar on his knees, telling his rosary. 1852 ROCK *Ch. of Fathers* III. ix. 326 That noble Anglo-Saxon lady Godiva told her prayers on gems threaded together for that purpose. 1857 EMERSON *Hermione* i, On a mound an Arab lay,..And told his amulets. 1871 L. STEPHEN *Playgr. Eur.* x. (1894) 250 The women.. kneel reverently..whilst they diligently tell their beads.

†(*b*) *To tell the clock*, to count the hours as shown by a clock; hence, to pass one's time idly; cf. *tell-clock* in TELL-. *Obs.*

1678 BUTLER *Hud.* III. III. 577 An old dull Sot, who'd told the Clock For many years at Bridewel-dock. 1738 tr. *Guazzo's Art Conversation* 14 They are fit for nothing, unless it be to tell the Clock [*ed.* 1586 count the clock], which they always think goes too slowly.

(*c*) *To tell* (so many) *years*: to have lived (so many) years; to be aged (so much). Cf. NUMBER *v.* 6. *Obs.* or *arch.*

1810 S. GREEN *Reformist* I. 103 The little girl had not quite told five years. 1818 LAMB *Elia* Ser. II. *Wedding*, [She at] nineteen was [married] by her..cousin..who told some few years older. 1835 LYTTON *Rienzi* I. iv, Thou hadst told but thy tenth year.

(*d*) *All told*: when all are counted; in all.

1850 SCORESBY *Cheever's Whalem. Adv.* ii. (1858) 24 They are four hundred all told. 1858 J. S. MANSFIELD in *Merc. Marine Mag.* V. 19 The hands numbered 19 all told. 1885 LD. WOLSELEY in *Times* 22 Jan. 5/4 Stewart's force was about 1,500 all told.

**22.** To count out (pieces of money) in payment; hence, to pay (money); now chiefly *to tell down, out, into one's hand*, etc. *arch.* or *dial.*

*c* 1250 *Gen. & Ex.* 1993 So michel fe ðor is hem told, He hauen him [Joseph] boȝt, he hauen sold. *a* 1300 *Cursor M.* 4835 We..haue.. Al redi penijs for to tell If we moght find her oght to sel. *c* 1375 *Sc. Leg. Saints* xii. (*Mathias*) 270 He [h]is master to þame said, For thretty pennys to hym talde. 1515 *Scot. Field* 40 They paid him tribute trulie: many told thousands, that the[y] might liue in their land. 1565–73 COOPER *Thesaurus* s.v. *Dinumero, Dinumerare pecuniam, pro Dissoluere, sæpissime accipitur*, to pay or tell out money. 1621 T. WILLIAMSON tr. *Goulart's Wise Vieillard* 84 His promise should passe for ready pay, and for money told on the nayle. 1645 RUTHERFORD *Tryal & Tri. Faith* (1845) 34 Should any buy a field of land, and refuse to tell down the money. 1723 DE FOE *Col. Jack* (1840) 37 He told the money into my hand. 1739 *Joe Miller's Jests* No. 200 The money'd Man fell to telling out the Sum in Shillings. 1819 SCOTT *Ivanhoe* xxxiii, Tell down with all speed an hundred crowns. 1893 W. RAYMOND *Gentl. Upcott* ii, Biddlecombe drew a bag from his pocket and told the money out in gold.

*fig.* 1637 SHIRLEY *Gamester* IV. ii, Let her tell down Her virgin tears on Delamore's cold marble.

**b.** To reckon up or calculate the total amount or value of (money or other things); to count. Also *to tell out, over. arch.*

*c* 1000 *Ags. Gosp.* Luke xiv. 28 Hu ne sytt he ærest & teleð [*Lindisf. G.* ȝetelles] þa andfengas þe him behefe synt. 1340–70 *Alex. & Dind.* 323 We mowe tellen our time whan þe time fallus. *c* 1380 WYCLIF *Wks.* (1880) 46 þei wolen tell gold and money. 1475 *Bk. Noblesse* (Roxb.) 85 Forto numbre and telle the quantite and porcion of everie manis part that they broughte. 1526 *Pilgr. Perf.* (W. de W. 1531) 160 b, Yf I sholde tell money or carue, wryte, or sowe ony subtyll worke, whiche requireth synglar or specyall study. 1594 GREENE & LODGE *Looking Gl.* Wks. (Rtldg.) 121/2 Come, sir, will you dispatch, and tell your money? 1653 MARVELL *Corr.* Wks. (Grosart) II. 4 Those who weigh and tell over money. 1723 DE FOE *Col. Jack* (1840) 78 What his cargo amounted to I knew not, for I never told it. 1827–35 WILLIS *Wife's Appeal* 99 As a miser tells his gold.

**c.** *intr.* with refl. or passive sense: To be counted; also *to tell for*, (*up*) *to*: to count as, count for, amount to. Now *rare.*

1362 LANGL. *P. Pl.* A. v. 128 Putte hem in a pressour and pinnede hem þer-Inne Til ten ȝerdes oþer twelue tolden out þrettene. 1774 BURKE *Corr.* (1844) I. 488 Lord Verney.. has told in parliament, including himself, for four members.

*c* 1794 SUSANNA BLAMIRE *Poems, Meeting* ii, Our butter tells to fourteen pun'. 1825 ESTHER HEWLETT *Cottage Comforts* vi. 45 Put it in the savings' bank, and it will tell up to something.

**d.** *To be telling*: to be worth or as good as (so much) to; to be to the advantage or credit of (a person). *Sc.* and *north. dial.*

1629 *Orkney Witch Trial* in *County Folk-lore* (1903) III. 79 Haid [she] lettin yow abid with your brother it haid bene telling hir xl.£. 1822 *Corspatrick of Raymondsholm* II. 8 (Jam.) It wad hae been telling some that are now safe frae skaith gin it had never been blither. 1875 P. PONDER *Kirkcumdoon* 85 (E.D.D.) It wud be tellin' the pairish an' himsel' gin Josey gaed less aboot the Wallace Arms. 1889 H. JOHNSTON *Chron. Glenbuckie* vii. 80 It would have been telling me a ten-pound note [if I had taken your advice]. *Mod. Sc.* It would be telling some people if they took a leaf out of his book.

**23.** With adverbs: **a.** *Tell out*: to separate or exclude by counting; to count out. *arch.* or *dial.*

1535 COVERDALE 2 *Chron.* ii. 2 Salomon..tolde out thre score and ten thousande men to beare burthens. 1812 *Sporting Mag.* XXXIX. 138 Burn..had been long told out of the London list as a cur.

**b.** *Tell off*: to count off from the whole number or company; to separate, detach, esp. so many men for a particular duty; hence *gen.* to appoint to a particular task, object, position, or the like.

1827 SCOTT *Jrnl.* 29 Jan., How could the castes be distinguished or told off in a populous nation? 1837 MARRYAT *Dog-Fiend* I, The troops were told-off into the boats. 1858 FROUDE *Hist. Eng.* III. xiii. 173 Ten knights were then told off, and ten followers for every knight, to ride down to Doncaster. 1890 *Guardian* 23 July 1159/3 A constable had been told off to watch the defendant. 1893 FORBES-MITCHELL *Remin. Gt. Mutiny* 84 The sentries were posted on the ramparts and regular reliefs told off.

**c.** *Tell off* (*intr.* for *refl.*). *Mil.* Of a rank or troop of men: To number themselves in succession.

1833 *Regul. Instr. Cavalry* I. 86 The men are to be instructed to tell off by files and by threes.

**III.** To account, or estimate, qualitatively.

†**24.** To account, consider, reckon, estimate, esteem as being (something). With *compl.* or *for*. *Obs.*

*c* 897 K. ÆLFRED *Gregory's Past. C.* iii. 35 He fleah ðæt rice, & tealde hine selfne his suiðe unwierðne. *c* 1000 *Ags. Gosp.* Matt. xi. 16 Hwam telle ic þas cneorysse ȝelice? *c* 1230 *Hali Meid.* 43 Sone so þu telles te betere þen an oðer. *c* 1330 R. BRUNNE *Chron. Wace* (Rolls) 2789 Ȝyf men dide hem any wo, Hit was teld for felonye. *Ibid.* 10555 He [a knight] was told of non honour Bot he had ben wyþ kyng Arthour. *c* 1374 CHAUCER *Troylus* III. 765 (814) Wordly selynesse Which clerkes tellyn fals felicite. 1411 *Rolls of Parlt.* III. 651/1 They schall tellen hem well payed with favour and grace. *c* 1425 *Eng. Conq. Irel.* 1 Leynyster, that is I-told þe fifte parte of Irland. *c* 1430 *Syr Gener.* (Roxb.) 4132 Doo way, quod the king.., I tel hir myne.

†**b.** *To tell scorn*: to count it scorn, to scorn (*to do* something). *Obs.*

1477 *Paston Lett.* III. 185 The fawcon Which is alofte, tellith scorne to loke a down.

†**25.** *intr.*, or *trans.* with cognate *obj.* (*to tell tale*): To make account *of*; to have a specified estimate or opinion *of*; to think (much or little) *of*; to set (much or little) store *by* (*to*). *To tell* (*more*, etc.) *price*: see PRICE *sb.* 8. *Obs.*

*c* 1175 *Lamb. Hom.* 147 An oðer is þet he telle swa lutel tale þerof. *a* 1225 *Leg. Kath.* 89 To..beon icleopet lefdi, þet feole telleð wel to. *a* 1250 *Owl & Night.* 793 Telstu bi me þe wrs for þan þat ic bute enne craft ne kan? *c* 1380 WYCLIF *Wks.* (1880) 468 Whanne þey tellen more bi a cronycle of foly..þan þey tellen bi cristis lawe. *c* 1400 *Rom. Rose* 5053 For litel sholde a man telle Of hir, that wolle hir body selle. *c* 1400 *Laud Troy Bk.* 2178 Thei tolde right nauȝt of thyn awe. *c* 1450 LOVELICH *Grail* xlv. 38 This peple, he seide ful Schortly, Nis non thing Forto tellen by. *c* 1475 *Partenay* 3029 Thys Geaunt noght told of hym in no degre.

**26.** *intr.* To count (for something); to be of account or weight; to have its effect, be effective, act or operate with effect; to make an impression.

Perh. orig. a pugilistic expression.

1797 *Monthly Mag.* III. 546 Every blow that they receive upon their projecting surface, tells. 1811 LAMB *Genius & Char. Hogarth* Wks. (1895) 277 Everything in the print, to use a vulgar expression, tells. 1812 *Sporting Mag.* XXXIX. 102 Several blows of consequence told. 1833 L. RITCHIE *Wand. by Loire* 24 These peculiarities make the place tell well in an outside view. 1865 KINGSLEY *Herew.* iii, Martin Lightfoot saw that his appeal to the antipathies of race had told. 1887 SIR R. H. ROBERTS *In the Shires* ii. 32 Going.. at a pace..that began to tell upon the horses.

**b.** To have weight or influence *in favour of* or *against*.

1799 DUNDAS in Owen *Wellesley's Desp.* (1877) 637 It is a transaction which tells in our favour. 1870 FREEMAN *Norm. Conq.* I. App. 648 It tells somewhat against his interpretation.

**Tell-**, the stem of TELL *v.* in combination with a sb. (in objective or attributive relation), used as *sb.* or *adj.*: **Tell-box, tell-card**, contrivances used by card-sharpers, to enable them to turn up a particular card; †**tell-cause**, *Rhet.*: see quot.; †**tell-clock**, one who 'tells the clock': see TELL *v.* 21 c (*b*); an idler who merely marks time; **tell-fare** = TELL-TALE 2 f; †**tell-love**: see quot.; **tell-pie, tell-piet**, a tale-bearer: cf. *tale-piet*, TALE *sb.* 10. See also TELL-TALE, TELL-TRUTH.

1865 *Athenæum* No. 1941. 13/1 This simple *tell-a-story style. 1894 MASKELYNE *Sharps & Flats* viii. 194 The contrivances..are known as '*tell-boxes'. *Ibid.*, Any card which lies immediately upon the smooth face of a '*tell-card' will slip easily. 1589 PUTTENHAM *Eng. Poesie* III. xix. (Arb.) 236 This assignation of cause the Greekes called *Etiologia*, which if we might without scorne of a new inuented terme call *Tell cause it were right according to the Greeke originall. 1609 ELLESMERE *Sp. on Post-nati* 17 They are called thither by the Kings Writ, not to sit as *Tell-clockes, or idle hearers. 1618 S. WARD *Jethro's Justice* (1627) 65 Is there no meane betweene busiebodies and tell-clocks, between factotum and fay't neant? 1865 GASKELL (*title*) Patent Cab Indicator, or *Tell-Fare. 1640 *Erotomania* 176 Poppy..Theocritus cals this hearb τηλέφιλον ..as if we should say, *Tel-loue. 1828 *Craven Gloss.*, **Tell-pye*, a tell-tale. 1897 SARAH GRAND *Beth Bk.* xii, If you tell secrets, you know, you're a tell-pie. *Ibid.* xv, Don't you be put upon by tell-pie-tits. 1855 ROBINSON *Whitby Gloss.*, **Tell-pyet* or *Telly-pie*, a tale-bearer, a tell-tale.

**Tell, telle,** obs. ff. TILL *v.*, *prep.*, and *conj.*

**Tellable** (te·lăb'l), *a.* [f. TELL *v.* + -ABLE.] Capable of being told or narrated; fit to be told; worth telling.

1483 *Cath. Angl.* 379/1 Tellabylle, *vbi* spekabylle. 1818 MOORE *Mem.* (1853) II. 196 Practical jokes, not easily tellable. 1830 GREVILLE in *Mem.* (1875) I. vii. 272 The details of his life are not tellable.

**Tellar**, var. TILLER *sb.*[3], a young tree.

**Tell-box**, etc.: see TELL-.

**Tellen** (te·lĕn). [ad. L. *tellīna*, a. Gr. τελλίνη a kind of shell-fish. So F. *telline*, It. *tellina*.] A bivalve of the genus *Tellina* or family *Tellinidæ*.

*c* 1711 PETIVER *Gazophyl.* Dec. vii–viii. Tab. 78 Rib-welted Limington Tellen. 1833 *Penny Cycl.* I. 466/2 They are supposed to have long syphons, like the Tellens. 1854 WOODWARD *Mollusca* II. 310 The Tellens are found in all seas, chiefly in the littoral and laminarian zones.

*Comb.* 1839 *Penny Cycl.* XIV. 319/1 Tellen-like Nymphidæ.

**Teller** (te·lər). Also 4 -ere, 6 -or. [f. TELL *v.* + -ER[1].] One who or that which tells, in various senses.

**I. 1.** One who relates, makes known, or announces.

13.. *K. Alis.* 1577 Teller of jeste is ofte myslike. 1382 WYCLIF *Acts* xvii. 18 He is seyn for to be a tellere of newe deuelis. 1547–64 BAULDWIN *Mor. Philos.* (Palfr.) 125 There is no difference betweene a great teller of tydings and a lyer. 1548 UDALL, etc. *Erasm. Par. Mark* xii. 76 We knowe ryght well that thou arte a teller of trouthe, and feareste no man. 1552 HULOET, Teller of fortune, *ominator, uel trix.* 1606 SHAKS. *Ant. & Cl.* I. ii. 99 The Nature of bad newes infects the Teller. 1825 LAMB *Elia* Ser. II. *Stage Illusion*, The teller of a mirthful tale has latitude allowed him. 1874 L. STEPHEN *Hours in Library* (1892) I. iv. 145 He had been a teller of stories before he was well in breeches.

**b.** A thing that makes known or announces.

1761 BLISS in *Phil. Trans.* LII. 176 Mr. Phelps lost the final contact, by mistaking the teller of the clock. 1877 *N. & Q.* 5th Ser. VII. 164/1 At Frisby and elsewhere these tolls [for the dead] are called 'tellers'. 1898 TYACK *Bk. about Bells* i. 8 The use of bells as tellers of the passing time. 1909 DEEDES & WALTERS *Ch. Bells Essex* 149 We now come to the uses of the tellers, for which the normal custom is 3 × 3 strokes for a man, 3 × 2 for a woman, including children, usually both beginning and end of tolling.

**II. 2.** One who counts or keeps tally; now *esp.* one who counts money; *spec.* an officer in a bank who receives or pays money over the counter.

1480 *Howard Househ. Bks.* (Roxb.) 9 John Fytzherberd, one of the tellers of the money. 1535 *Act 27 Hen. VIII*, c. 14 § 2 Euery porte..where no tellers nor packers at this present time be. 1576 GASCOIGNE *Steele Gl.* (Arb.) 80 When Siluer sticks not on the Tellers fingers. 1601 J. KEYMER *Obs. Dutch Fish.* (1664) 7 Shee [the Herring-Buss] imployeth..at Land..Packers, Tellers, Dressers. 1632 BROME *Court Begg.* I. i, To put you to some Tellers Clearke to teach you Ambo-dexterity in telling money. 1766 ENTICK *London* IV. 342 [At the mint] A weigher and teller,.. blanchers, moniers, &c. 1843 *Civil Eng. & Arch. Jrnl.* VI. 278/2 The inconveniences to which the 'tellers' were subjected in weighing gold for the public. 1887 *Times* 26 Aug. 8/4 The bank, in which there were only the teller and a clerk.

**b.** One of four officers of the Exchequer formerly charged with the receipt and payment of moneys.

The office was abolished in 1834, the duties being now performed by the Comptroller of the Exchequer.

1488 *Naval Acc. Hen. VII* (1896) 34 William Page oon o. the Tellers of the Kyngs said Receipt. 1583 in Feuillerat *Revels Q. Eliz.* (1908) 360–1 Table iii, One of the Tellors of the saide receipte. 1702 *Lond. Gaz.* No. 3782/3 One of the Four Tellers of His Majesty's Exchequer. 1812 WHITBREAD *Sp. Ho. Comm.* 7 May, The..emolument drawn by the late first Lord of the Admiralty as Teller of Exchequer. 1884 T. WALDEN in *Harper's Mag.* Aug. 424/2 At the entrance of the Hall..you passed the Exchequer. You may yet see over the doorway the grotesque effigies of the teller.

**c.** In a deliberative assembly (esp. the House of Commons), A person (usually one of two or more) who counts the votes on a division.

1669 [see TELL *v.* 21 b]. 1682 N. O. *Boileau's Lutrin* IV. 146 Let faithful tellers take the Poll, and note The Ay's and Noe's. 1775 BURKE *Corr.* (1844) II. 8 Rose Fuller was..one of the tellers on the division. 1857 TOULMIN SMITH *Parish* 62 The tellers must then give in to the Chairman the number found on each side, as agreed on between them. 1888 *Times* (weekly ed.) 29 June 10/1, 644 members, including the Speaker and tellers.

**III. 3.** *Pugil. slang.* A telling blow.

1814 *Sporting Mag.* XLIII. 70 He sometimes put in some good tellers on his opponent's body. 1834 H. AINSWORTH *Rookwood* IV. ii, A teller vos planted..upon his smeller.

**Teller**, dial. variant of TILLER, sapling.

**Tellership** (te·ləɹʃip). [f. prec. + -SHIP.] The office or position of a teller.

1788 W. EDEN in G. Rose *Diaries* (1860) I. 77 Ought I to seek for my son the second reversion of a Tellership? 1807

W. TAYLOR in *Ann. Rev.* V. 565 Abolishing tellerships and auditorships of the exchequer. **1875** *Contemp. Rev.* XXVI. 454 The interesting history of the Exchequer, its sinecure tellerships,..its clerkships of the pells.

**Tell-fare**: see TELL-.

**Te·llicherry bark.** [f. *Tellicherry*, a town on the Malabar coast, north of Calicut.] The bark of *Wrightia dysenterica*; also called CONESSINE bark.

**1822–34** *Good's Study of Med.* (ed. 4) I. 626.

**Te·lligraph.** *Hist.* [ad. med. (Anglo-) L. *telligraphum, -ium*, irreg. f. L. *tellus* land: see -GRAPH.] A description of the boundaries of land; a charter of lands in which the bounds are described: = TERRIER [1].

[**816** in Haddan & Stubbs *Councils* (1871) III. 582 Tamen serventur libros primordiales cum aliis telligraffis, ne inposterum aliquod scrupulum contraditionis innitere conantur. **1783** REEVES *Hist. Eng. Law* I. i. 8 An Anglo-Saxon charter of land has also been called *Telligraphum*,..but this appellation has been given to them most likely since the Conquest, as a translation of the word *Landboc*.] **1882** W. BEAMONT *Domesday Bk.* (ed. 2) Introd. 6 The witnesses would probably produce the telligraphs by which they held their lands. **1903** G. F. BROWNE *St. Aldhelm* 249 These land-books were sometimes called telligraphs, a word which sounds curiously modern.

†**Tellinet.** *Obs.* [f. L. *tellīna* TELLEN + -ET.] A small shell of the genus *Tellina*.

**1708** *Phil. Trans.* XXVI. 79 *Tellinites*, the Tellinet, or Lesser Muscle-shell.

**Telling** (te·liŋ), *vbl. sb.* [f. TELL *v.* + -ING [1].] The action of the verb TELL.

**1.** The action of relating, making known, or saying; relation; communication, conversation (now *dial.*).

**13..** *Cursor M.* 29163 (Cott. Galba) If þe prest..Be vnwise in his gifing, Or els þe synful in his telling. **1382** WYCLIF 2 *Macc.* ii. 25 The tellyngis of stories. **1390** GOWER *Conf.* I. 296 So wolde I my wordes plie, That mihten Wraththe and Cheste avale With tellinge of my softe tale. **1546** J. HEYWOOD *Prov.* (1867) 67 A good tale yll tolde, in the tellyng is marde. **1700** DRYDEN *Pref. Fables* Wks. (Globe) 496 The form which he has given to the telling makes the tale his own. **1789** MRS. PIOZZI *Journ. France* I. 117 The theatres here are beautiful beyond all telling. **1906** *Athenæum* 13 Oct. 434 The narrative loses nothing in the telling.

**b.** An account, description. Now *dial.* or *arch.*

**1382** WYCLIF 1 *John* i. 5 This is the tellyng, that we herden of him, and tellen to ȝou. **1904** *Blackw. Mag.* Dec. 811/2 The father was a terrible man by all tellings.

**c.** Phrase *that's telling(s*, that would be to divulge something secret. *colloq.*

**1837** MARRYAT *Dog-Fiend* xiv, 'Where is this cargo to be seen, and when?'..'That's tellings', replied the man. **1878** E. JENKINS *Haverholme* 178 'How do you get your information?' 'That's tellings', said the Monsignor.

**2.** The action of counting or numbering.

**1387–8** T. USK *Test. Love* II. i. (Skeat) l. 114, I can not passen the tellinge of thre as yet. *c* **1440** *Promp. Parv.* 488/1 Tellynge, or nowmerynge, *numeracio*. **1589** [? LYLY] *Pappe w. Hatchet* E j b, I thinke them [sheep] woorth neither the tarring, nor the telling. **1594** PLAT *Jewell-ho.* III. 89 There must bee no time lost in the telling [of the money]. **1689** *Answ. Lords & Commoner's Sp.* 12 Notwithstanding the often telling of Noses. **1847** *Infantry Man.* (1854) 60 The telling off by threes. **1901** *Scotsman* 13 Mar. 9/4 This mixed telling did not mean mixed voting, for the division closely followed party lines.

†**b.** *transf.* Value, amount, force. *Obs. rare*⁻¹.

**1636** RUTHERFORD *Lett.* (1862) I. 188 There is much telling in Christ's Kindness!

**3.** *Comb.*, as †*telling-board, -house*: see quots.

**1552** HULOET, *Tellinge bourde or table for exchaunge to tell money. **1597** *Catal. Anc. Deeds* (1906) V. 485 In the *Telling howse usuallie appointed for receiptes and paimentes. **1869** BLACKMORE *Lorna D.* ii. *note*, The 'telling-houses' on the moor are rude cots where the shepherds meet, to tell their sheep at the end of the pasturing season.

**Te·lling**, *ppl. a.* [f. TELL *v.* + -ING [2].] That tells; effective, forcible, striking.

**1852** J. A. ROEBUCK *Hist. Whig Ministry* II. i. 129 This observation..was..what is called in debating language, a *telling* reply. **1859** DE QUINCEY *Wks.* XI. Pref. 18 Into this great *chef-d'œuvre* of Milton, it was no doubt Johnson's secret determination to send a telling shot at parting. **1870** STANHOPE *Hist. Reign Anne* (1872) I. i. 28 It was drawn up with telling force. **1903** *Times, Lit. Supp.* 8 May 143/1 He is master of a singularly lucid, nervous, and telling style.

Hence **Te·llingly** *adv.*, effectively.

**1860** THACKERAY *Round. Papers, Notes Week's Holiday*, How tellingly the cool lights and warm shadows are made to contrast. **1875** WHITNEY *Life Lang.* xiv. 299 A curious fact, and one tellingly illustrative.

**Tellinite** (te·linəit). *Palæont.* [ad. mod.L. *tellīnītēs*, f. *tellīna*: see TELLEN and -ITE [1].] A fossil shell of, or resembling, the genus *Tellina*; a fossil tellen.

**1799** R. KIRWAN *Geol. Essays* 252 A number of shells, mostly tellinites, filled with striated shining hornblende. **1802–3** tr. *Pallas's Trav.* (1812) I. 515 Hard layers..interspersed throughout with pectinites, tellinites, and oolites.

**Tellograph** (te·lǫgraf). [Short for **telelogograph*, f. Gr. τῆλε (TELE-) + λόγος word + -GRAPH.] A form of 'telegraph' or signalling apparatus invented by R. L. Edgeworth, consisting of a number of posts, each carrying a pointer in the form of an isosceles triangle which could be turned into various positions so as to express different numbers, the combinations of which denoted letters or words according to a pre-arranged code.

**1795** EDGEWORTH in *Trans. R. Irish Acad.* (1797) VI. 126 I shall, with a slight alteration, adopt it [the name telegraph] for the apparatus which I am going to describe. *Telegraph* is a proper name for a machine which describes at a distance. *Telelograph*, or contractedly *Tellograph*, is a proper name for a machine that describes *words* at a distance. **1796** *Let.* 17 Nov. in *13th Rep. Hist. MSS. Comm.* App. VIII. 288 Your plan for establishing a communication of intelligence between Cork and Dublin and between Dublin and Belfast..by means of a tellograph of your invention.

Hence **Tellogra·phic** *a.*

**1797** EDGEWORTH in *Trans. R. Irish Acad.* VI. 138 The means of Tellographic communication which I have invented.

**Tellor**, obs. form of TELLER.

**Tell-tale** (te·lˌtēˡl), *sb.* (*a.*)

**1.** One who tells tales (TALE *sb.* 3 c); one who idly or maliciously discloses private or secret matters; a tale-bearer, a tattler. So, in nursery phrase, *tell-tale-tit*.

*a* **1548** HALL *Chron., Hen. IV* 2 b, He..was very glad (as tell tales and scicophantes bee..) to declare to the kyng what he had heard. **1597** MIDDLETON *Wisd. Solomon* xvii. 18 Babbling Echo, tell-tale of each sound. *a* **1639** W. WHATELEY *Prototypes* III. xxxix. (1640) 4 Most men will hate such as complaine of them, and call them tel-tales. **1731** SWIFT *Strephon & Chloe* Wks. 1755 IV. I. 158 A tell-tale out of school Is of all wits the greatest fool. **1841** HOOD *Tale of Trumpet* iii, Falsehood, or folly, or tell-tale-tit. **1877** BLACK *Green Past.* xxxi, Peace, you chatterer, you tell-tale. **1906** *Times* 10 Oct. 5/1 Booksellers..who had failed to receive the library orders..played tell-tale-tit to the Publishers' Association.

**b.** *transf.* A thing that reveals or discloses something not intended to be made known.

**1778** (*title*) The Fashionable Tell-Tale; containing a Great Variety of Curious and Interesting Anecdotes of Kings [etc.]. **1829** SCOTT *Anne of G.* xv, This gown may be a tell-tale..help me to pull off my upper garment. **1849** M. ARNOLD *Memory Picture* 42 Paint those eyes, so blue, so kind, Eager tell-tales of her mind.

**c.** A name of species of Sandpiper (*spec.* in *U.S.*), from their loud cry: see quots.

**1824** STEPHENS in Shaw *Gen. Zool.* XII. 154 Tell-Tale Sandpiper (*Totanus melanoleucus*). It is a noisy and clamorous species..; it is much dreaded by sportsmen..upon the appearance of any one it immediately sounds the alarm, and totally frustrates his intentions. [**1876** BLACK *Madcap V.* xxii, That abominable wretch the curlew, for he is a screaming tell-tale.] **1882** in OGILVIE. **1896** NEWTON *Dict. Birds*, *Tell-tale*, the name long used in North America for *Totanus melanoleucus* and *T. flavipes*..from 'their faithful vigilance in alarming the ducks'.

**2.** *Mech.* A device for mechanically indicating or recording some fact or condition not otherwise apparent; an indicator, a gauge.

*spec.* **a.** A pointer or the like attached to an organ to show the state of the wind-supply. **b.** *Naut.* An indicator near the wheel which shows the position of the tiller; an automatic or patent log; a tell-tale compass: see 3 c. **c.** A turnstile which registers the number of persons who pass through it. **d.** A gauge which indicates the pressure of wind, or of steam or gas in a cylinder or the like; also, an apparatus attached to the meter at a gasworks which registers any irregularity in the production of gas. **e.** A row of cords or straps suspended over a tramway or railway in such a position as to give warning of one's approach to a bridge or other overhead obstruction (*Cent. Dict.* 1891). **f.** An indicator of distance travelled or fare due in a cab, etc.; also called *tell-fare*; a TAXIMETER. **g.** = *tell-tale clock*; see 3 c.

**1832** *Examiner* 801/2 A contrivance called the tell-tale, which denotes any error in the working of the machinery. **1881** *Chicago Times* 4 June, An ingenious machine, called the 'tell-tale', has been introduced recently on the Erie railroad. It registers the speed of trains, when and where they stop, and how long. **1884** C. G. W. LOCK *Workshop Receipts* Ser. III. 68/2 Electrical apparatus is eminently adapted for alarms, tell-tales, and time signals. **a. 1801** BUSBY *Dict. Mus.*, *Tell-Tale*, a moveable piece of ivory or lead, suspended in the front of a chamber organ on one side of the keys, by a string, one end of which being attached to the bellows within, rises as they sink, and apprises the performer, in what degree the wind is exhausted. **b. 1815** BURNEY *Falconer's Dict. Marine*, *Tell-tale* (*axiometre*, Fr.), a small piece of wood, traversing in a groove across the front of the poop-deck, which, by communicating with a small barrel on the axis of the steering-wheel, indicates the situation of the helm. **1358** H. BURRIDGE in *Merc. Marine Mag.* V. 53 The steering-compass at the wheel, and a tell-tale in the Master's berth. **c. 1824** *Examiner* 552/1 He paid the toll, and went through the piece of machinery called a tell-tale. **d. 1877** KNIGHT *Dict. Mech.*, *Telltale*,..4. Gas-making. A device attached to a station-meter to point out any irregularity in the production of gas. **f. 1863** GASKELL *Patent Specif.* No. 2989 Improvements in Telltales or Indicators for Cabs, &c. **g. 1832** BABBAGE *Econ. Manuf.* viii. (ed. 3) 55 The instrument, aptly called a *tell-tale*, informs the owner whether the man had missed any, and what hours during the night.

**3.** *attrib.* or as *adj.* **a.** That tells tales, that is a tell-tale. Now *rare* or *Obs.* in *lit.* sense.

**1594** SHAKS. *Rich. III*, IV. iv. 149 Let not the Heauens heare these Tell-tale women Raile. **1678** DRYDEN & LEE *Œdipus* III. i, This tell-tale ghost Perhaps will clear 'em both. **1824** [see 1 c.].

**b.** Applied to a thing: That reveals or betrays something meant to be kept secret.

*a* **1577** GASCOIGNE *Adv. F. I.* Wks. (Roxb.) I. 416 This teltale paper. **1579** G. HARVEY *Letter-bk.* (Camden) 75 This wofull letter with the telltale obligation. **1628** E. SPENCER *Brittain's Ida* II. iii, The thicke-lockt bowes shut out the tell-tale Sunne. **1743** R. BLAIR *Grave* 508 The tell-tale echo, and the babbling stream. **1821** SCOTT *Kenilw.* xxxvi, These tell-tale articles must not remain here. **1862** MRS. H. WOOD *Mrs. Hallib. Troub.* I. iii, He might have accomplished it better, but for his tell-tale face.

**c.** That gives notice or warning of something.

*Tell-tale clock*, a clock with an attachment of some kind requiring attention at certain intervals, by which the vigilance of a watchman may be checked; *tell-tale compass*: see quot. 1877; *tell-tale pipe*, a pipe from a tank or cistern which overflows when the contents reach the level at which it is fixed.

**1867** SMYTH *Sailor's Word-bk.*, *Tell-tale shake*, the shake [i.e. shaking] of a rope from aloft to denote that it wants letting go. **1877** KNIGHT *Dict. Mech.*, *Tell-tale compass* (*Nautical*). A compass is suspended overhead in the cabin. The face of the card is downward, so that it is visible from below, and enables the captain to detect any error or irregularity in steering. **1879** *Nature* 12 June 145/2 A small 'tell-tale' pipe from the cistern.., designed to show when the cistern had been filled. **1890** *Times* 21 Jan. 9/3 There should be tell-tale clocks to afford evidence of the punctual discharge of their duties.

**Te·ll-truth.** ? *Obs.* Also 6 -troath, 7–8 -troth.

**1.** One who or that which tells the truth; a veracious or candid person or writing.

**1558** *Cranmer's Confut. Unwritten Verities* Pref. B iv b, Which sermon & al other tel truthes, openinge the abuses and tirannye of the bishop of Rome, are now put to silence. **1580** H. GIFFORD *Gilloflowers* (1875) 147 Is not Tom teltroath euerywhere, A busie cockcombe deem[d]e? **1600** J. LANE *Tom Tel-troth* 5 That, like a tell-troth, it may boldly blaze. **1618** *Barnevelt's Apology* C, Are you, with whome lying is familiar and ordinary, a telle-truth? **1692** WASHINGTON tr. *Milton's Def. Pop.* v. M.'s Wks. 1851 VII. 139 But hear what follows, my honest Tell-troth. **1700** ASTRY tr. *Saavedra-Faxardo* I. 345 Would these Tell-truths be guided by Prudence..a Prince would more value Truth. **1809–10** COLERIDGE *Friend* vi. (1865) 27 Tell-truths in the service of falsehood we find everywhere.

**2.** The telling of the truth; candour. *rare.*

*a* **1734** NORTH *Lives* (1826) II. 419 He was very seldom guilty of offence to any except in the way of tell-truth, which he could scarce ever forbear.

**Te·llur-, tellu·ri-,** *Chem.*, used as combining forms of TELLURIUM in certain names of compounds; as **Tellure·thyl**, ethyl telluride, $(C_2H_5)_2Te$, also called *tellurhydric* or *hydrotelluric ether*; **Tellurhy·dric** *acid*, a synonym of hydrogen telluride; † **Tellu·ri-salt**, a salt of telluric or tellurous acid.

**1857** MILLER *Elem. Chem.* III. 215 *Tellurethyl. **1864** WATTS *Dict. Chem.* II. 550 Tellurethyl is a deep yellowish-red liquid heavier than water...It appears to be very poisonous. **1873** — *Fownes' Chem.* (ed. 11) 215 *Tellurhydric acid is a gas, resembling sulphuretted and selenietted hydrogen. **1877** *Ibid.* (ed. 12) I. 228 Hydrogen telluride, $H_2Te$, Tellurhydric acid, Hydrotelluric acid, or Telluretted hydrogen. **1860** MAYNE *Expos. Lex.*, *Tellurisal*..term applied to a Class..resulting from the combination of tellurides with tellururets..: a *tellurisalt.

**Tellural** (telĭū°răl, te·lĭŭrăl), *a.* [f. L. *tellūr-em* the earth + -AL.] Of or pertaining to the earth; terrestrial. **1847** in WEBSTER; and in later Dicts.

†**Te·llurane.** *Chem. Obs.* [f. TELLUR-IUM + -ANE 2 a.] Davy's name for tellurium chloride.

**1812** SIR H. DAVY *Chem. Philos.* 410 When tellurium is burnt in chlorine an easily fusible substance is formed, which rises in vapour at a strong heat, and crystallizes...It appears this compound, or tellurane, consists of 2 in weight of metal to 1.83 of chlorine.

**Tellurate** (te·lĭŭrėⁱt). *Chem.* [f. TELLUR- + -ATE [1] I c.] A salt of telluric acid.

**1826** HENRY *Chem.* II. 112 It not only unites as a base with acids, but also itself possesses the character of an acid, and forms a class of salts, which may be called tellurates. **1868** WATTS *Dict. Chem.* V. 716 *Tellurates.*—Telluric acid forms with the alkali-metals, neutral, acid, and hyperacid salts, represented by the formulæ, $M_2TeO_4$, $MHTeO_4$, and $MHTeO_4.H_2TeO_4$, respectively.

**Telluret** (te·lĭŭret). Also † **tellu·ruret.** *Chem.* Now *rare.* [f. TELLURIUM: see -URET.] A compound of tellurium with hydrogen or a metal, as *telluret of sodium*, $TeNa_2$: now usually TELLURIDE.

**1842** PARNELL *Chem. Anal.* (1845) 259 Tellurets. **1854** J. SCOFFERN in *Orr's Circ. Sc., Chem.* 476 Metallic bismuth is liberated, and sulphuret and telluret of sodium formed. **1860** MAYNE *Expos. Lex.* s. v. *Tellururetum*, Berzelius reserves this name for a combination of tellurium with an electro-positive metal, in which the atomic relations are the same as in the bases: a tellururet.

**Telluretted** (te·lĭŭreted), *a. Chem.* Now *rare.* [f. as prec. + -ED.] Combined with tellurium, as in *tellure(t)ted hydrogen*, a gaseous compound of hydrogen and tellurium, $TeH_2$, formerly also called *hydrotelluric* or *tellurhydric acid*, and now *hydrogen telluride*.

**1819** CHILDREN *Chem. Anal.* 49 Telluretted Hydrogen Gas. **1826** HENRY *Chem.* II. 502 Tellureted hydrogen is absorbed by liquid potassa, but not by acetate of lead. **1869** ROSCOE *Elem. Chem.* (1871) 146 With hydrogen tellurium forms a colourless gas, telluretted hydrogen, which cannot be distinguished by its smell from sulphuretted hydrogen.

**Tellurian** (telĭū°riăn), *a.* and *sb.* [f. L. *tellūr-em* the earth + -IAN.] **A.** *adj.* Of or pertaining to the earth; earthly, terrestrial.

**1846** DE QUINCEY *Syst. Heavens* Wks. 1854 III. 172 They absolutely hear the tellurian lungs wheezing, panting, crying. **1862** *Parthenon* 26 July 405 The stratified cemetery of the 'tellurian' crust. **1887** A. LANG *Myth, Ritual, & Relig.* II. 120 There were..solar, lunar...[and] tellurian..methods of accounting for a myth.

**B.** *sb.* An inhabitant of the earth.

**1847** DE QUINCEY *Joan of Arc* Wks. 1854 III. 237 If any distant worlds..are so far ahead of us Tellurians in optical resources. *c* **1851** — *Ess. Finlay's Greece* Posth. Wks. 1893 II. 75 Our own case, the case of poor mediocre Tellurians.

**Telluric** (tel<sup></sup>iū°·rik), *a.*[1] *Chem.* and *Min.* [f. TELLURIUM + -IC.] Derived from or containing tellurium. Applied to compounds in which tellurium is present in a smaller proportion than in tellurous compounds, as *telluric acid*, $H_2TeO_4$; *telluric oxide* = *tellurium trioxide*, $TeO_3$, etc. Also in *telluric gold, silver, bismuth*, the tellurides of these metals occurring as native alloys: see TELLURIDE. *Telluric ochre* = TELLURITE 1.

1800 HENRY *Epit. Chem.* (1808) 253 Carbonated and pure alkalies precipitate the telluric oxide. 1842 BRANDE *Dict. Sc.*, etc. s. v. *Tellurium*, It forms a protoxide and a peroxide, often called tellurous and telluric acids. 1864 WEBSTER s. v., *Telluric silver*, a mineral consisting of tellurium and silver in combination. 1868 DANA *Min.* (ed. 5) 30 Telluric Bismuth. *Ibid.* 50 Telluric Silver. 1873 WATTS *Fownes' Chem.* (ed. 11) 214 Crystallised telluric acid is freely, although slowly, soluble in water. 1882 *Rep. to Ho. Repr. Prec. Met. U.S.* 607, I have only found, as yet, telluric gold in two mines in Nevada County.

**Telluric** (teliū°·rik), *a.*[2] [f. L. *tellūr-em* the earth + -IC.] Of or belonging to the earth, terrestrial; pertaining to the earth as a planet; also, of or arising from the earth or soil.

1836 I. TAYLOR *Phys. The. Another Life* ii. 24 The equal periods that are marked for us by the celestial and telluric revolutions. 1842 *United Service Mag.* I. 289 The great problem of telluric magnetism. 1849 SIR J. STEPHEN *Eccl. Biog.* (1850) II. 433 If my ideas had still obeyed those laws of association to which, in my telluric state, they had been subject. 1861 T. J. GRAHAM *Pract. Med.* 666 Epidemic influences..dependent in a great measure upon obscure atmospheric or telluric conditions. 1883 *St. James' Gaz.* 21 Dec. 5/1 The spectrum..exhibits great breadth in the telluric or atmospheric lines,..due to aqueous vapours..in.. the atmosphere. 1884 *19th Cent.* Feb. 320 A 'telluric poison' is generated in it [the Campagna] by the energy of the soil.

**Telluride** (te·liŭrəid). *Chem.* [f. TELLUR-IUM + -IDE.] A combination of tellurium with an electro-positive element (e.g. hydrogen or a metal), or with a radical; as *telluride of hydrogen, hydrogen telluride*, the same as *telluretted hydrogen*, $H_2Te$; *organic tellurides*, those of organic radicals, as *ethyl telluride*.

*Telluride of bismuth*, telluric bismuth, tetradymite, or bornite, perh. an isomorphous mixture of tellurium and bismuth, sometimes $Bi_2Te_3$. *Telluride of gold and silver* = SYLVANITE. *Telluride of lead*, black telluride, PbTe, found native as NAGYAGITE. *Telluride of silver*, bitelluret of silver, $Ag_2Te$, found native as HESSITE and PETZITE.

1849 D. CAMPBELL *Inorg. Chem.* 307 Telluride of hydrogen ..is colourless, and in odour resembles sulphide of hydrogen gas...It forms with metals tellurides, analogous to the sulphides. 1868 WATTS *Dict. Chem.* V. 707 The tellurides belong to the class of metallic alloys: those of bismuth, gold, lead, and silver are found native. *Ibid.* 708 Organic tellurides: Tellurides of amyl, ethyl, methyl. 1877 — *Fownes' Chem.* (ed. 12) II. 141 *Ethyl Telluride*, Telluric Ethide, or Tellurethyl, $Te(C_2H_5)_2$..is a heavy, oily, yellowish-red liquid . having a most intolerable odour. 1897 *Daily News* 30 Apr. 2/7 The vein contains telluride of gold, good quality.

*attrib.* 1877 RAYMOND *Statist. Mines & Mining* 305 The prominent mines of the telluride belt. *Ibid.* 311 Small seams of the usual telluride ore.

**Tellurion** (teliū°·riǫn). Also **tellurium.** [f. L. *tellūs, tellūr-em* the earth.] An apparatus illustrating the effect of the earth's diurnal rotation and annual revolution and obliquity of axis in causing the alternations of day and night and the succession of the seasons; a simple kind of orrery.

1831 *Mechanics' Mag.* XIV. 370/2 When the tellurion [*pr.* -ian] is to be used, the sign Cancer must be set toward the north. 1842 FRANCIS *Dict Arts, Tellurion*, an instrument for showing the effect of the earth's motions and the obliquity of her axis. 1891 *Cath. News* 24 Jan. 4/4 Irreverent persons echoed the inquisitive auditor's query as to the uses of a tellurion.

**Tellurious,** *a.*: see TELLUROUS.

**Tellurism** (te·liŭriz'm). [f. L. *tellūr-em* the earth + -ISM: in sense 1 = Ger. *tellurismus*, in sense 2 = F. *tellurisme*.]

1. A magnetic influence or principle supposed by some to pervade all nature and to produce the phenomena of animal magnetism; also the theory of animal magnetism based on this, propounded in 1822 by Kieser in Germany.

1843 HARTSHORN tr. *Deleuze's Anim. Magn.* x. 209 There are in magnetism two different actions. One which depends upon a vital principle spread throughout nature, and circulating in all bodies;..the first sort of magnetism, which he calls tellurism or siderism. 1849 S. R. MAITLAND *Illustr. Mesmerism* 63 They [the Ancients] did not write systems of Animal Magnetism, or Tellurism, or Geisterkunde.

2. Influence of the soil in producing disease.

1890 in BILLINGS *Nat. Med. Dict.* 1899 in *Syd. Soc. Lex.*

**Tellurite** (te·liŭrəit). [f. TELLUR-IUM + -ITE[1] 2 b, 4 b.]

1. *Min.* Native oxide of tellurium, found in minute whitish or yellow crystals; telluric ochre.

1799 *Monthly Rev.* XXX. 349 Among the metals, are overlooked the Tellurite, the Chromite, and Titanite. 1849 NICOL *Min.* 429. 1868 DANA *Min.* (ed. 5) 188.

2. *Chem.* A salt of tellurous acid.

1847 in WEBSTER. 1868 WATTS *Dict. Chem.* V. 714 *Tellurites.* Tellurous acid forms, with the alkali-metals, neutral and acid salts analogous to the sulphites and selenites. *Ibid.*, Tellurites are mostly fusible. 1869 ROSCOE *Elem. Chem.* (1871) 146 When tellurium or a tellurite is fused with nitre, potassium tellurate is formed.

**Tellurium** (teliū°·riŏm). *Chem.* [mod. L., f. L. *tellūs, tellūr-em* the earth + *-ium*, suffix of names of metals. So called by Klaproth, 1798, prob. in contrast to *uranium* (Gr. οὐρανός heaven), a metal which he had discovered in 1789.

Cf. Klaproth in Crell's *Chem. Annalen* 1798, pt. I. 100, 'welchem ich hiermit den von der alten Muttererde entlehnten Namen Tellurium beylege'.]

One of the rarer elements, a tin-white shining brittle substance, formerly from its outward characters classed among the metals, but in its chemical properties and relations belonging to the same series as sulphur and selenium. It occurs native in rhombohedral crystals, isomorphous with those of antimony, arsenic, and bismuth. Symbol Te; atomic weight 128.

1800 tr. *Lagrange's Chem.* I. 447 With sulphur this metal forms a grey sulphuret of tellurium, of a radiated structure. 1801 HATCHETT in *Phil. Trans.* XCII. 63 Other metals lately discovered, such as uranium, titanium, and tellurium. 1816 P. CLEAVELAND *Min.* 565 Native Tellurium is never perfectly pure. It always contains a greater or less quantity of gold, and sometimes embraces iron, silver, lead, copper, and sulphur. 1862 MILLER *Elem. Chem.* (ed. 2) III. 52. 1881 LUBBOCK in *Nature* 1 Sept. 409/2 In Aldebaran..we may infer the presence of hydrogen, sodium, magnesium, iron, calcium, tellurium, antimony, bismuth, and mercury; some of which are not yet known to occur in the sun. 1882 ROSCOE *Elem. Chem.* 121 Oxygen, sulphur, selenium, and tellurium form a natural group of elements, each uniting with two atoms of hydrogen to produce a series of bodies possessing analogous properties.

b. With qualifying words, applied to minerals or ores containing a preponderance of tellurium, as *bismuthic tellurium*; *black tellurium, foliated tellurium*, synonyms of NAGYAGITE; *graphic tellurium, yellow* or *white tellurium*, synonyms of SYLVANITE. (Dana *Min.* 1864.)

1849 D. CAMPBELL *Inorg. Chem.* 304 The [ore] named bismuthic tellurium is that from which it is most easily obtained. 1864 [see c.].

c. *attrib.* and *Comb.* (*a*) *attrib.* = 'of tellurium', in names of chemical compounds, as *tellurium bromide, chloride, dioxide, salts, nitrate, sulphate*, etc.; in other uses, as *tellurium acids, alloys, minerals, ores*; (*b*) in obj. relation, as *tellurium-bearing* adj.; (*c*) **tellurium glance** *Min.*, nagyagite, or black telluride of lead.

1834 PROUT *Chem.*, etc. I. ix. § 3 (1855) 113 Sulphur acids, selenium acids, and tellurium acids. 1853 URE *Dict. Arts* II. 200 They are celebrated for their tellurium ore. 1864 DANA (Webster), *Tellurium glance*, a blackish or lead-gray sectile mineral, of a splendent luster, consisting chiefly of tellurium, sulphur, lead, and gold;—called also *black tellurium*. 1869 ROSCOE *Elem. Chem.* (1882) 121 When heated in the air it [tellurium] burns with a bluish-green flame, forming white fumes of tellurium dioxide, $TeO_2$. 1874 RAYMOND *Statist. Mines & Mining* 298 The belt of tellurium-bearing veins is found to extend from the Gray Eagle lode.., in a southerly direction. 1877 *Ibid.* 304 In all, the characteristic tellurium minerals have been found. 1877 WATTS *Fownes' Chem.* (ed. 12) I. 227 Tellurium salts—sulphate, nitrate, oxalate, chloride. *Ibid.* 228 Tellurium sulphides..chlorides.

**Tellurous** (te·liŭrəs), *a. Chem.* Also 9 †**tellurious.** [f. TELLUR-IUM + -OUS; substituted for the more regularly-formed *tellurious*.] Characterized by or of the nature of tellurium; said of compounds containing a greater proportion of tellurium than those called *telluric*; as *tellurous acid*, $H_2TeO_3$; also formerly applied to *tellurous oxide* (= tellurium dioxide), $TeO_2$.

1842 [see TELLURIC *a.*[1]]. 1849 D. CAMPBELL *Inorg. Chem.* 307 It deposits anhydrous tellurous acid in octohedral crystals. Tellurous acid hydrated precipitates in white flocks, of a bitter metallic taste. 1854 J. SCOFFERN in *Orr's Circ. Sc., Chem.* 476 Two oxides of tellurium are known, tellurious acid $Te O_2$, and telluric acid $Te O_3$. 1869 ROSCOE *Elem. Chem.* (1871) 146 With water the dioxide forms tellurous acid.

**Tellururet**: see TELLURET.

‖ **Tellus** (te·lŏs). [L. *tellūs*.] In Roman mythology, the goddess of the earth; hence, the earth personified; the planet Earth, the terrestrial globe.

*c* 1430 LYDG. *Min. Poems* (Percy Soc.) 24 Tellus and Ymo be dullid of theire chere. 1602 SHAKS. *Ham.* III. ii. 166 Neptunes salt Wash and Tellus Orbed ground. 1608 — *Per.* IV. i. 14, I will rob Tellus of her weede. 1681 COTTON *Wond. Peake* (ed. 4) 28 The Spring swell'd by some smoaking Shower, That teeming Clouds on Tellus surface poure. 1738 *Gentl. Mag.* VIII. 544/2 Reason, like Sol to Tellus kind, Ripens the products of the mind. 1818 KEATS *Endymion* III. 71 Tellus feels her forehead's cumbrous load.

**Telmatology** (telmătǫ·lŏdʒi). [f. Gr. τέλμα, τελματ- a bog + -OLOGY.] That department of physiography which deals with peat-bogs.

1903 OLSSON-SEFFER in *Amer. Nat.* XXXVII. 784 A name of a more international character, telmatology,..has been used by some authors (Klinge, J., for example, nearly twenty years ago), and seems acceptable.

**Telo-**[1] (telo), combining form repr. Gr. τέλος, τελε-ος end, occurring in a few scientific (biological, etc.) terms: see also TELEO-[2]. **Te·loblast** [Gr. βλαστός germ], each of a number of proliferating cells at one end of the embryo in segmented animals, as insects and annelids. **Telolecithal** (-le·siþăl) *a.* [Gr. λέκιθος yolk], applied to an ovum having food-yolk collected at or near one end (opp. to *alecithal* and *centrolecithal*). **Te·lophase** (-fēɪz) [PHASE], term for the final stage of mitosis or cell-division in an ovum. **Te·lopore** [PORE *sb.*[1]], an opening at one end of an embryo, formed by invagination of the *teloblasts*. **Telosto·miate** *a.* [f. Gr. στόμι-ον dim. of στόμα mouth], having the mouth at one end of the main axis of the body.

1890 PATTEN in *Q. Jrnl. Microsc. Sc.* Aug. 369 A forward continuation of the anterior wall of the terminal pore or *telopore. *Ibid.*, Three longitudinal sections, showing successive stages in the formation of a telopore by the invagination of *teloblasts. 1880 BALFOUR *Comp. Embryol.* I. iii. 90 The ova in which the yolk is especially concentrated at one pole I should propose to call *telolecithal. 1888 E. R. LANKESTER in *Nature* 29 Mar. 507/1 The classification of animal eggs proposed by Balfour is adopted, viz. alecithal, telolecithal, and centrolecithal. 1900 G. C. BOURNE *Comp. Anat.* iii. 115 The last stages of mitosis are known as the *Telophase. *Ibid.* 116 The centrosomata..divide very precociously during the telophase. 1890 *Telopore [see *teloblast*]. 1877 E. R. LANKESTER in *Q. Jrnl. Microsc. Sc.* Oct. 422 Radial and bilateral symmetry and *telostomiate and prostomiate conditions. *Ibid.* 423 A specialisation of the ciliated ectoderm at a time when the organism was telostomiate.

**Telo-**[2], repr. Gr. τηλο-, combining form of τῆλε or τηλοῦ far off, occurring exceptionally instead of τηλε- (TELE-), as in τηλοπέτης far-flying. Rarely used in Eng. compounds, as in TELODYNAMIC, *telometer* (see TELEMETER), TELOTYPE.

**Telodynamic** (te:lodinæ·mik, -dəi-), *a.* Also (more regularly) **teledynamic.** [f. TELO-[2] + DYNAMIC.] Term applied to a cable used for transmitting mechanical power to a distance.

1870 J. ANDERSON in *Eng. Mech.* 14 Jan. 427/1 A given pressure on the piston.., like the telodynamic cord, will transmit mechanical work in proportion. 1877 KNIGHT *Dict. Mech., Telodynamic Cable*, a means for transmitting power,..in which high speed is employed to give the momentive effect of great mass. 1889 E. MATHESON *Aid Bk. Engineer. Enterpr.* II. 466 The teledynamic cables—as the endless, transmitting ropes are called—are of comparatively recent introduction.

**Telometer**: see TELEMETER. **Teloogoo**: see TELUGU. **Teloptic, Telosmic**: see TELE-.

‖ **Telos** (te·lǫs). [a. Gr. τέλος end.] End, purpose, ultimate object or aim.

1904 *Daily Chron.* 5 Aug. 3/2 The triple aim which had formed the telos of every development. 1905 F. HARRISON *Herbert Spencer Lecture*, The Telos of Philosophy is a constructive reorganization of all human knowledge in a synthesis, or correlation of parts. The Telos of human life is the practical and continuous amelioration of the material, social, and moral conditions of the Human Organism—the unity of the Brotherhood of Man on this planet.

**Telotroch** (te·lǫtrǫk). *Zool.* [f. Gr. τέλος end (TELO-[1]) + τροχός wheel. Cf. mod.L. *Telotrocha* neut. pl., as name for larvæ having this structure.] A zone of cilia circling either, or each, end of the preoral (and perianal) segments of a free-swimming polychætous annelid larva. b. A larva of this kind. Hence **Telo·trochal, Telo·trochous** *adjs.*, possessing a telotroch or telotrochs; of the nature of a telotroch.

1877 E. R. LANKESTER in *Q. Jrnl. Microsc. Sc.* Oct. 426 The telotroch appears to be a metameric repetition of the architroch, or of its branchiotrochal moiety. 1877 HUXLEY *Anat. Inv. Anim.* 186 This larva exactly resembles those forms of polychætous Annelidan larvæ which are called Telotrocha. *Ibid.* 192 The free Rotifers present marked resemblances to the telotrochous larvæ of Annelids. 1878 BELL *Gegenbaur's Comp. Anat.* 137 By these the larvæ of the Chætopoda are divided into mesotrochal, telotrochal, and polytrochal forms.

**Telotype** (te·lǫtəip). [f. TELO-[2] + TYPE.] An electric telegraph that automatically prints the messages as received; also, a telegram so printed.

1858 SIMMONDS *Dict. Trade Products, Telotype*, the name given to a printing electric telegraph. 1877 KNIGHT *Dict. Mech., Telotype*, a printed telegram.

**Telpher** (te·lfəɪ), *a.* and *sb.* [Syncopated from *telepher* or *telephore* (see quot. 1884 in TELPHERAGE), f. Gr. τῆλε, TELE- + -φορος bearing.] a. *adj.* or *attrib. sb.* Of or relating to a system of telpherage; *telpher line, railway*, a light overhead line on which the haulage is worked by electric power; so *telpher train*. b. *sb.* Any travelling unit on a telpher line; also, the plant and rolling stock of a system of telpherage. c. *Comb.*, as *telpherman*.

1884 (May 14) F. JENKIN in *Jrnl. Soc. Arts* XXXII. 648/2 Telpher lines are adapted for the conveyance of minerals and other goods at a slow pace, and at a cheap rate. *Ibid.* 655/2 We are enabled to start or stop any number of telpher trains without disturbing the running of others. 1884 *Sat. Rev.* 31 May 712/2 In hilly country, where roads are difficult to construct, the telpher line might be eminently useful. 1888 W. E. AYRTON in *Times* 10 Sept. 11/3 The first track on which electric trams were run in series was the experimental 'Telpher line' erected in Glynde in 1883.. for the automatic electric transport of goods. 1901 *Munsey's Mag.* XXV. 363/1 The traveling unit is called a 'telpher'. The fixed cable serves as a rail.., and above it, in the same vertical plane, is a feed wire from which the telpher takes current. 1904 *Jrnl. Franklin Inst.* Oct. 266 With a machine and an assistant, a telpherman can convey 250 tons per day over a distance of 1,000 feet.

Hence **Te·lpher** *v. trans.*, to transport (goods, etc.) by means of telpherage.

1885 F. JENKIN in *Gd. Words* 132 We may possibly hereafter speak of telphering goods as we now speak of telegraphing messages. **1890** W. E. AYRTON in *Spectator* 19 Apr., To electrically propel may be aptly named to 'telepher', or, say 'telpher' as an abbreviation.

**Telpherage** (te·lfĕrédʒ). [f. as TELPHER + -AGE.] Transport effected automatically by the aid of electricity; *spec.* a system adapted to the conveyance of minerals and other goods in vessels suspended from a cable, and moved by means of an electric motor supplied with current from an adjacent conductor. Also *attrib.*

**1883** *Engineering* 23 Nov. 481/2 The transmission of vehicles to a distance by electricity, independently of any control exercised from the vehicle, is called 'Telpherage' by Professor Fleeming Jenkin. **1884** F. JENKIN in *Jrnl. Soc. Arts* XXXII. 648/2 The word [telpherage] is intended to designate all modes of transport effected automatically with the aid of electricity. According to strict rules of derivation, the word would be 'telephorage'; but in order to avoid confusion with 'telephone'..I have ventured..to substitute ..'telpher' for 'telephore'. **1888** W. H. PREECE in *Times* 7 Sept. 5/3 Goods, minerals, and fuel can be transmitted by telpherage.

**Telson** (te·lsən). *Zool.* [a. Gr. τέλσον a limit.] The last segment of the abdomen or its median axis in certain crustaceans and arachnidans, as the middle flipper of a lobster's tail-fin, the long sharp spine of the king-crab, or the sting of the scorpion.

**1855** C. SPENCE BATE in *Brit. Assoc. Rep.* 28 The last [appendage of the abdomen], which for convenience we shall designate by the name of Telson,..is a rudimentary appendage, modified upon the type of the preceding three. **1872** NICHOLSON *Palæont.* 144 The last segment of the abdomen is known as the 'telson', and it is variously regarded as a somite without appendages, or as an unpaired appendage placed in the middle line of the body. **1880** HUXLEY *Crayfish* i. 19 The abdomen [has] a terminal flap which is called the *telson*.

**Telthe**, obs. form of TILTH.

‖ **Telugu, Teloogoo** (te·lugū), *sb.*, *a.* Also 8 Telougou, 9 Telug. [Native name of the language, and of a man of the race. Origin and derivation uncertain. The language is also called *Tenugu*, which native pundits treat as the original form, and explain as 'mellifluous', from *tēne* honey. The relationship of either of these names to TELINGA, formerly applied to the same language and people, is disputed. The Tamil name for the language is *Vaḍugu* or 'the Northern'; thence the old Portuguese name *Badages*, and the old German *Waruga*.]

**1.** The name of a Dravidian language, spoken on the Coromandel coast of India, north of Madras.

[**1731** T. S. BAYER *Let. to La Croze*, Hinc natione Tamulis, Tamulica; Warugis, Warrugica. **1748** J. F. FRITZ *Orient. u. Occident. Sprachm.* 87 Alphabethum Telugicum sive Warugicum.] **1813** *Q. Rev.* Oct. 257 Languages and Dialects...Sanscrit..Telug. **1850** S. HISLOP in G. Smith *Life* iii. (1889) 82 The Telugu began to be spoken even at that village. **1856** BP. CALDWELL *Dravid. Gram.* Introd. 5 The Telugu is spoken all along the eastern coast of the Peninsula, from the neighbourhood of Pulicat, where it supersedes the Tamil, to Chicacole, where it begins to yield to the Uriya; and inland it prevails as far as the eastern boundary of the Maratha country and Mysore. **1886** YULE & BURNELL *Hobson-Jobson*, *Teloogoo*, the first in point of diffusion, and the second in culture and copiousness, of the Dravidian languages of the Indian Peninsula. *Ibid.*, *Telugu* is the name given to the language by the people themselves, as the language of Telingāna. **1893** *Madras Manual of Administr.* III. s. v., Teloogoo is the softest of all Eastern languages..but Teloogoo is a very poor language in everything except outward appearance.

**2.** One of the Dravidian people or race who speak this language. (See also GENTOO.)

**1789** *Seir Mutaqherin* II. 93 *note* (Y.), The first Sipahees that came in Bengal..were all Talingas or Telougous born. **1893** *Madras Manual of Administr.* III. s. v., The pronunciation of Sanscrit among the Teloogoos corresponds with the purest pronunciation used at Benares. **1903** J. TORRANCE *Story Maratha Missions* viii. 65 A Telugu applied for baptism.

**3.** *attrib.* or *adj.* Of or pertaining to this language, people, or country.

**1888** G. SMITH *S. Hislop* iii. (1889) 83 The Hislops marched slowly south to Nellore, the Telugu station of his Church.

**4.** *Comb.* as *Telugu-speaking* adj.

**1903** *United Free Ch. Scot. Mission. Record* Aug. 352/2 There are always in them Telugu-speaking girls.

† **Telwe**, *v.* *Obs. rare.* [a. ON. *telgja* to cut to shape, cut with a knife: prob. introduced into late OE. as **telgian*, or into Early ME. as **telȝen*: cf. OE. *folgian*, ME. *folȝen*, *folwen*, to FOLLOW.] *trans.* To thwite, to whittle (a stick).

*c* **1440** *Promp. Parv.* 488/1 Telwyn, or thwytyn (*H.* twhytyn, *S.*, *P.* twytyn), *abseco*, *reseco*. *Ibid.*, Telwynge, or twhytynge (*K.* telwhynge or whytynge), *scissulatus*.

**Telyevie, telȝevie**, var. TAILYEVEY *Sc. Obs.*

**Tem**, phonetic var. of *þem*, THEM, after a dental.

**Temantale**: see TENMANTALE.

**Tembre**, obs. form of TIMBER.

† **Teme**, *v.* *Obs.* Forms: 1 tęmman, tęmian, tymian, 2–3 temien, 3 temie, 3–4 teme, 4 tyme. [OE. *tęmman*, *tęmian*, = OLG. **temmjan* (MLG., MDu. *temmen*, *temen*, Du., LG. *tämen*), OHG. **zammjan*, *zęmman* (MHG. *zem(m)en*, Ger. *zähmen*), ON., Norw. *tęmja* (Sw. *tämja*, Da. *tæmme*), Goth. *tamjan*, f. OTeut. **tamo*[z], TAME *a.* The OE. regular form *tęmman* was superseded by *tęmian* (Sievers *Ags. Gram.* § 400 Anm. 2), whence ME. *temien*, *teme*, which was displaced in 15th c. by *tamen*, TAME *v.*, conformed to TAME *a.* (The forms *tymian*, *tymen*, are irregular.) The cognate langs. have preserved the umlauted form.]

**1.** *trans.* To bring (a wild animal, etc.) under the control of man; to reclaim from the wild state, to domesticate; = TAME *v.* 1.

*c* **1000** ÆLFRIC *Gram.* xxiv. (Z.) 138 Ic temiȝe, *domo*. *c* **1000** *Sax. Leechd.* III. 184 Nytenu tymian. *Ibid.* 200 Wilde deor temian. *c* **1290** *S. Eng. Leg.* I. 39/173 Þe Bollokes wilde were..For huy ne scholden heom temie nouȝt. **1387** TREVISA *Higden* (Rolls) II. 357 Hercules..temede þe world.

**2.** To bring (a person, passions, etc.) under control; to subdue, subjugate, curb; = TAME *v.* 2.

*c* **897** K. ÆLFRED *Gregory's Past. C.* lvi. 433 Mon temeþ nis unaliefde lustas mid ðæm wordum ðære halȝan lare. *c* **950** *Lindisf. Gosp.* Mark v. 4 Næniȝ monn mæhte hine temma. [So *c* **975** *Rushw. Gosp.*] *c* **1200** *Trin. Coll. Hom.* 63 To temien þe lichames orguil. **1306** *Pol. Songs* (Camden) 214 So hue [bishops and barons] were temed tho. *a* **1340** HAMPOLE *Psalter* lxvii. 27 Fayre saules, þat has temyd þaire fleyss. *c* **1394** *P. Pl. Crede* 742 Y miȝt tymen þo troiflardes to toilen wiþ þe erþe.

**Teme**, obs. f. TEAM, TEEM, THEME.

‖ **Temenos** (te·menǫs). *Gr. Antiq.* [a. Gr. τέμενος, f. τεμ-, stem of τέμνειν to cut off, sever.] A piece of ground surrounding or adjacent to a temple; a sacred enclosure or precinct.

**1820** T. S. HUGHES *Trav. Sicily* I. iv. 108 Tradition says, that this square formed in very early ages the temenos of a temple. **1885** *Times* 3 Jan. 12 Pious sons had set up..a dedicatory inscription in a temenos, or sacred enclosure. *attrib.* **1891** A. B. EDWARDS *Pharaohs, Fellahs & Expl.* 29 Close outside the temenos-wall of one of these temples.

† **Te·mera·re**, *a.* *Sc. Obs.* Also 6 temerar, -air. [a. F. *temeraire* (1461 in Godef. *Compl.*), ad. L. *temerārius*: cf. next and TEMERARY.] = next, 1.

**1549** *Compl. Scot.* (1873) 6, I..hes tane ane temerare consait to present to ȝour nobil grace ane tracteit of the fyrst laubir of my pen. *Ibid.* xvii. 153 Kyng cresus vas temerair in his question. **1581** *Sat. Poems Reform.* xliv. 333 Of haly Kirk ȝour temerar dispysing.

**Temerarious** (temĕrēə·riəs), *a.* Now only *literary.* [f. L. *temerāri-us* fortuitous, rash (f. *temere* blindly, rashly (see TEMEROUS) + *-āri-us*; cf. *contr-ārius*, *extr-ārius*, *necess-ārius*) + -OUS.]

**1.** Characterized by temerity; unreasonably adventurous; reckless, heedless, rash.

**1532** MORE *Confut. Tindale* Wks. 620/2 He is somwhat ouer temerarious & bold. *a* **1533** FRITH *Answ. More* (1548) E vj b, Because they shall not of temeraryous presumpcion reiect this olde father. **1611** SPEED *Hist. Gt. Brit.* IX. xvi. § 37 The King was one of the first that entred [the breach], choosing rather to be thought temerarious than timorous. **1645** HAMMOND *View Infallib.* 38 Your resolves are temerarious and presumptuous. **1781** JOHNSON in *Boswell* (1887) IV. 130 Does it not suppose, that the former judgment was temerarious or negligent? **1890** J. R. LUNN in *Ch. Times* 21 Feb. 196/4, I do not think any one will be temerarious enough to maintain that.

† **2.** Acting or happening at random; fortuitous, casual, haphazard. *Obs.*

**1660** STANLEY *Hist. Philos.* IX. (1701) 386/1 Now in heaven nothing is produced casually, nothing temerarious. **1682** NORRIS *Hierocles* 53 But we should ascribe nothing..to a fortuitous and temerarious cause. **1775** HARRIS *Philos. Arrangem.* iii, These two principles are not merely casual and temerarious.

Hence **Temera·riousness.**

**1711** in *10th Rep. Hist. MSS. Comm.* App. v. 133 He was overruled by the temerariousness of Orange. **1775** ASH, *Temerariousness*, rashness, temerity.

**Temera·riously**, *adv.* [f. prec. + -LY [2].]

**1.** With temerity; rashly.

**1535** JOYE *Apol. Tindale* (Arb.) 24 Thus temerariously and abominably to write. **1638** SIR T. HERBERT *Trav.* (ed. 2) 310 They account them happiest, who out of a frantick zeale, temerariously throw their naked bodies in the way. *a* **1745** SWIFT *Disc. Antiq. Eng. Tongue* ad fin., I have ventured (perhaps too temerariously) to contribute my mite to the learned world. **1863** LYTTON *Caxtoniana* I. 50 To be..corrected in any subsequent edition of the work in which such descriptions had been temerariously adventured.

† **2.** At random; fortuitously. *Obs.*

**1669** *Address yng. Gentry Eng.* 86 As temerariously and blindly they [Gamesters] cast round about them these firebrands. **1678** CUDWORTH *Intell. Syst.* I. iv. § 7. 198 The Atheists make the Universe..to be devoid of Counsel, and therefore..to be carried on Temerariously and Fortuitously.

† **Temera·rity.** *Sc. Law. Obs.* [f. L. *temerāri-us*: see next and -ITY.] Reprehensible or culpable heedlessness or negligence.

**1475** *Sc. Acts Jas. III* (1814) II. 112/1 Gif it be fundin þ[t] þe first assise acqwite þe trespassour be temerarite,..sa mony as beis conuict of þ[t] temerarite to be punist eftir þe forme of þe auld law. **1499** *Reg. Privy Seal Scotl.* I. 62 Schir William Dowy..of wilfull temerarite perseverand in his said baratry.

† **Te·merary**, *a.* *Obs.* [ad. L. *temerārius* fortuitous, rash, f. *temere*: see TEMEROUS and -ARY [1]. Cf. TEMERARE.] Rash, reckless; = TEMERARIOUS 1.

*c* **1410** LOVE *Bonavent. Mirr.* xv. (1908) 93 A presumptuouse and temerarie demere of othere men. *c* **1425** tr. *Arderne's Surgery* (E. E. T. S.) 4 That he be noȝt y-founden temerarie or bosteful in his seyingis or in his dedes. *c* **1450** tr. *De Imitatione* I. Contents 1 Of eschuying of temerary iuggement. **1650** GENTILIS *Cons.* 176, I should be reputed rash and temerary.

**b.** *Civ.* and *Eccl. Law.* Reprehensibly heedless or careless; culpably negligent: cf. TEMERARITY.

**1681** CONSETT *Pract. Spir. Crts.* I. iii. 1. § 2 If it..appear there was..Administration granted by any other Judge.. and that it is evident touching their temerary Administring. *Ibid.* VI. i. 1. § 18 In a Matrimonial Cause..a Testamentary Cause, a Cause of Temerary Administration.

Hence † **Te·merarily** *adv.*, rashly.

*c* **1450** tr. *De Imitatione* III. xxix. 98 Of oþir mennes dedes or seienges deme no þinge temerarily.

† **Te·merat**, *a.* *Sc. Obs. rare*[—1]. [In form, ad. L. *temerāt-us*, pa. pple. of *temerāre*: see next.] Adventurous, headstrong, forward.

*c* **1560** A. SCOTT *Poems* (S.T.S.) xxx. 37 Thocht wemen self be temerat, Thay luve no man effeminat.

† **Te·merate**, *v.* *Obs.* [f. L. *temerāt-*, ppl. stem of *temerāre*, f. *temere* rashly; as if to treat presumptuously or irreverently.] *trans.* To violate or break (a promise, bond, etc.); to profane.

**1635** SIR S. D'EWES *Autobiog.* (1845) II. 131 They have temerated the oath they had taken. **1637** BASTWICK *Litany* II. 23 To say nothing of my owne experience, as I am a Physitian,..because I will not in any thing temerate our function. **1654** H. L'ESTRANGE *Chas. I* (1655) 57 The French King returned answer that the Rochellers had first temerated and slighted their Faith with him.

† **Temera·tion.** *Obs. rare.* [n. of action from prec.: see -ATION; cf. post-cl. L. *temerātio* a forging.] Violation, profanation.

**1641** SIR S. D'EWES in Rushw. *Hist. Coll.* (1692) III. I. 314 After the reiterated temeration of his Faith and Promises. **16..** JER. TAYLOR *2nd Serm. Ministers' Duty* ¶ 6 Those Cryptick ways of institution by which the Ancients did hide a light, and keep it..from the temeration of ruder handlings.

**Temeritous** (tĭme·ritəs), *a.* [f. TEMERIT-Y + -OUS; cf. *iniquitous*.] Full of temerity; rash.

**1892** *Daily Chron.* 18 Feb. 3/2 And his book is dedicated to Professor Dowden. O temeritous Mr. Shorter! **1900** *Academy* 21 July 51/1 The attempt to define is, we know, foolishly temeritous.

† **Teme·ritude.** *Obs. rare*[—0]. [ad. L. *temeritūdo*.] = next.

**1623** COCKERAM II, Rashnesse..*Temeritude*.

**Temerity** (tĭme·rĭti). Forms: 5 -yte, 6 -ite, -atie, 6–7 -itie, 6– -ity, (6–7 timeritie, 7 -ity). [ad. L. *temeritās*, *-tātem*, rashness, f. *temere* adv. by chance, blindly: see -ITY. So F. *témérité* (15th c. in Godef. *Compl.*).]

**1.** Excessive boldness; rashness; foolhardiness, recklessness.

**1432–50** tr. *Higden* (Rolls) III. 467 Infancy ioyethe in simplicite, yowthe in temeryte [*temeritate* [*gaudet*] *juventus*], age in debilite. **1551** BP. GARDINER *Explic. True Cath. Faith* 20 b, To auoyde the temerite of deniyng (as neuer) or affirmyng (as euer) which be extremities. **1598** BARCKLEY *Felic. Man* VI. (1603) 595 Fortitude referred to any other thing, then to godliness, falleth into temeritie or rashness. **1656** STANLEY *Hist. Philos.* VIII. (1701) 336/2 Affirming, that they have done wickedly, is not to be attributed to their timerity, but to Fate. **1750** JOHNSON *Rambler* No. 19 ¶ 9 Marlborough might have been made to repent his temerity at Blenheim. **1803** REPTON *Landscape Gard.* (1805) 33 There is..no more temerity in marking trees to be taken down than those to be planted. **1884** F. J. BRITTEN *Watch & Clockm.* 80 Mr. Denison's temerity was justified by his success.

**b.** with *a* and *pl.* An act or instance of rashness.

*a* **1677** BARROW *Serm. Titus iii.* 2 Wks. 1687 I. 237 Among all temerities this is one of the most noxious. **1847** LEWES *Hist. Philos.* Introd (1857) 33 The unhesitating temerities of Plato and Plotinus.

† **2.** Chance, fortuity: cf. TEMERARIOUS 2. *Obs.*

**1678** CUDWORTH *Intell. Syst.* I. iii. § 23. 168 Although there be not the least appearance of fortuitousness or temerity in it. *Ibid.* iv. § 24. 415 Of all things..most opposite to Chance, Fortune, and Temerity.

**Temerity, -itie**, var. TIMERITY *Obs.*, timidity.

**Temerosity**, obs. f. TIMOROSITY, timidity.

**Temerous** (te·mĕrəs), *a.* Now *rare.* [f. L. type **temerōsus* rash, f. *temere* adv., by chance, blindly, heedlessly: see -OUS.

(*Temere* is generally held to be the loc. sing. of a sb. **temos* = Skr. *tămas* darkness, hence in darkness, blindly.)]

Rash, foolhardy; = TEMERARIOUS 1.

**1461** [implied in TEMEROUSLY]. **1535** *Act 27 Hen. VIII*, c. 20 § 1 Diuers..dispise the..decrees of the ecclesiastical courtes..in more temerous and large maner than before this time hath ben sene. *a* **1562** G. CAVENDISH *Wolsey* Prol. (1893) 2 Thus may all men of wisdom and discretion understand the temerous madness of the rude commonalty. **1622** MISSELDEN *Free Trade* 88 Temerous, rash, and litigious suites of law. **1678** COLEMAN *Two Lett.* i. 3 Our Parliament..by the temerous Counsels of our Ministers, who then Governed, could never be useful. **1888** *Atlantic Monthly* Feb. 281, I have not the temerous intention of disputing.. the correctness of the modern Latin pronunciation.

Hence **Te·merously** *adv.*, with temerity; rashly, presumptuously; **Te·merousness**, rashness, temerity.

**1461** *Rolls of Parlt.* V. 463/2 Henry..temerously ayenst rightwisnes..rered were at Flynte in Wales. **1550** COVERDALE *Spir. Perle* xiii. (1588) 140 [They] attempt not any thing temerously and rashly. **1562** WINȜET *Last Blast* Wks. (S.T.S.) I. 40 Osias, quha temeruslie in his arrogance ingerit him self to make sacrifice at the altare of God. **1597** A. M. tr. *Guillemeau's Fr. Chirurg.* 42 b/1 Or els throughe temerousnes & timorousnes of the Chyrurgian. **1727** BAILEY Vol. II, *Temerousness*, Rashness, Unadvisedness.

**Temerous**, obs. form of TIMOROUS.

‖ **Temia** (tīˑmiă). *Ornith.* [The native Javanese name of the bird.] (See quots.)

1809 SHAW *Gen. Zool.* VII. 372 Temia Crow. *Corvus Temia.* ..Size of a Thrush, but longer bodied: bill and legs black. 1890 *Cent. Dict.* s. v. *Crypsirhina*, The temia or so-called variable crow of Java.

**Temir**, obs. Sc. var. *timmer*, TIMBER.

**Temize, Temmes**, obs. ff. TEMSE, THAMES.

**Temnospondylous** (temnospǫˑndiləs), *a.* *Comp. Anat.* [f. Gr. τέμν-ειν to cut + σπόνδυλ-ος vertebra + -OUS.] Having vertebræ composed of separately ossified parts.

1901 GADOW in *Camb. Nat. Hist.* VIII. viii. 286 The vertebræ are typically temnospondylous, consisting each of three pairs of separately ossified pieces.

**Temp**, Sc. form of TEMPT.

**Tempe** (teˑmpi). [a. L. *Tempē*, a. Gr. Τέμπη.] The proper name of a charming valley in Thessaly, watered by the Peneus, between Mounts Olympus and Ossa; used (already by the Roman writers) as a general name for a beautiful valley; hence for any delightful rural spot.

1594 NASHE *Terrors of Night* Wks. (Grosart) III. 264 Farre vnworthie am I to spend the least breath of commendation in the extolling so delightfull and pleasant a Tempe. 1612 DRAYTON *Poly-olb.* To Rdr., Refusing to walke forth into the *Tempe* and Feelds of the Muses. 1616 SURFL. & MARKH. *Country Farme* To Rdr., Seeing that the whole earth was once a Tempe, an Eden (that is, a place of all pleasures and delights). 1770 H. WALPOLE *Let. to G. Montagu* 17 July, The gay solitude of my own little Tempe.

Hence **Tempean** (tempīˑăn) *a.*, of or pertaining to Tempe; resembling Tempe in natural beauty.

1864 in WEBSTER; hence in mod. Dicts.

**Temper** (teˑmpəɹ), *sb.* Forms: 4–6 **tempre**, 5 **tempere, -yr, -our, -ure, tymper,** 6– **temper.** [f. TEMPER *v.* Cf. rare OF. *tempre* proportion, etc. (12th c. in Godef. *Compl.*), later and mod.F. *trempe* (15th c.) tempering, temper of steel, physical constitution of man.]

**I. †1.** The due or proportionate mixture or combination of elements or qualities; the condition or state resulting from such combination; proper or fit condition; *in temper, out of temper*, in, out of proper condition, etc. Now *rare* or *Obs.*

1387 TREVISA *Higden* (Rolls) I. 75 Þere is helþe, for þe aier is in tempre, noþer to hote noþer to colde. 1422 tr. *Secreta Secret., Priv. Priv.* 246 Als longe as the natural hette duryth in ryght tempure by euenesse of the foure humores. 1548 UDALL *Erasm. Par. Luke* ix. 86 b, The delectable swetenesse of the glorie should be brought to a tempre with the mencion of death. 1573 *Treas. Hid. Secrets* (1633) xviii, Keepe your water in a temper; and, when it is very hot, let it out, and put it in cold water. 1579 LYLY *Euphues* (Arb.) 138 For the curing and keeping in temper of the body. 1607 HIERON *Wks.* I. 191 It shall be wisedome for vs..to sing of mercy and iudgment too; both together will make an excellent temper. 1622 *Rel. Eng. Plant. in Plymouth N. Eng.* in Arber *Pilgr. Fathers* (1897) 448 To make our pieces and furniture ready, which by the moisture and rain were out of temper. 1651 T. STANLEY *Poems* 106 As soon as the cup was brought tempered with water, they call on Jupiter..the author of temper and commixtion. 1655 MOUFET & BENNET *Health's Impr.* (1746) 389 Health itself is but a kind of Temper gotten and preserved by a convenient Mixture of Contrarieties. 1734 tr. *Rollin's Anc. Hist.* (1827) I. 82 To keep their limbs pliable and in a right temper. 1743 *Lond. & Country Brew.* II. (ed. 2) 120 The London Brewer ..lets in a parcel of cold Water directly and thereby brings all his Liquor into a Temper at once. [1879 GEO. ELIOT *Theo. Such* 117 What is temper? Its primary meaning, 'the proportion and mode in which qualities are mingled', is much neglected in popular speech.]

**2.** Proportionate arrangement of parts; regulation, adjustment; hence, mean or medium, a middle course; a compromise; a settlement. *arch.*

1523 FITZHERB. *Husb.* § 4 Their most speciall temper is at the bolster, where as the plough beame lyeth. [Cf. TEMPER *v.* 17.] 1597 HOOKER *Eccl. Pol.* v. lxxvi. § 5 A moderate, indifferent temper, betweene fulnesse of bread, and emptinesse. 1647 JER. TAYLOR *Lib. Proph.* Ep. Ded. 24 Therefore they made Decrees of Toleration, and appointed tempers and expedients. 1692 BURNET *Past. Care* viii. 95 So strongly does the World love Extreams, and avoid a Temper. 1757 BURKE *Abridgm. Eng. Hist.* III. iv, The king..compiled a new body of laws, in order to find a temper between both. 1855 MACAULAY *Hist. Eng.* xiii. III. 260 He would probably have preferred a temper between the two rival systems, a hierarchy in which the chief spiritual functionaries should have been something more than moderators and something less than prelates.

**3.** Mental balance or composure, esp. under provocation of any kind; moderation in or command over the emotions, esp. anger; calmness, equanimity: now usually in the phrases *to keep* or *lose* (*one's*) *temper, to be out of temper.*

1603 SHAKS. *Meas. for M.* II. ii. 185 Neuer could the Strumpet..Once stir my temper. 1611 B. JONSON *Catiline* IV. ii, Restore your selves unto your temper, fathers, And, without perturbation, hear me speak. 1659 HAMMOND *On Ps.* civ. 9. Paraphr. 511 It observes..a temper in its madness. 1694 CONGREVE *Double Dealer* v. iv, Let your wild fury have a vent; and when you have temper, tell me. 1697 COLLIER *Immor. Stage* iii. (1698) 120 Creon keeps himself within Temper, and gives no ill Language. 1703 ROWE *Ulyss.* Ded., The Temper which you have reserv'd to our Councils. 1711 STEELE *Spect.* No. 140 ⁋ 11, I keep my Temper, and win their Money. 1743 J. MORRIS *Serm.* vii. 191 The good man was out of temper. 1782 V. KNOX *Ess.* (1819) II. lxxxvi. 148 Public affairs are seldom treated with temper either in writing or conversation. 1838 THIRLWALL *Greece* V. xxxvii. 20 Teleutias entirely lost his temper. 1840 DICKENS *Barn. Rudge* xxxii, It would put me out of temper, which is a state of mind I can't endure. 1871 SMILES *Charac.* i. (1876) 9 A weakness..was his want of temper; his genius was sacrificed to his irritability. 1878 S. WALPOLE *Hist. Eng.* II. 458 Sir Joseph Yorke told him that he would lose his place if he did not keep his temper.

**II. †4.** The constitution, character, or quality of a substance or body (orig. supposed to depend upon the 'temper' or combination of the elements); = TEMPERAMENT 3. *Obs.*

*c* 1400 *Lanfranc's Cirurgie* 332 Coold mater..ne schal not be putt awei wiþ repercussiuis, but wiþ medicyns þat ben hoot and drie in tempere. 1483 *Cath. Angl.* 379/2 A Tempyr ..*temperacio rerum.* 1604 E. G[RIMSTONE] *D'Acosta's Hist. Indies* IV. iii. 209 In the highest mountains and inaccessible rockes of a rough temper. 1625 N. CARPENTER *Geog. Del.* I. iii. (1635) 45 [He] found the causes of most magneticall motions hid in the magneticall temper and constitution of the Earth. 1703 MOXON *Mech. Exerc.* 67 Examine the Temper of your Stuff, by easy Trials, how the Plane will work upon it. 1707 MORTIMER *Husb.* (1721) I. 60 In sowing of Land great regard ought to be had to the Weather, and the Temper of the Land you design to sow. 1759 J. MILLS *Duhamel's Husb.* I. ix. (1762) 52, I come now to your lands of a light temper.

**† b.** Of things immaterial: Character, quality.

1598 B. YOUNG tr. *Montemayor's Diana* 109 His strength and courage was not of such a temper, that mortall wounds could daunt his minde. 1602 *Life T. Cromwell* II. i. 86 Now, sir, your heart is fram'd of milder temper. 1635 PAGITT *Christianogr.* I. iii. (1636) 125 The Georgians have ..a peculiar language of a middle temper, which well agreeth with the position of their country, betweene the Tartarians and the Armenians. 1651 BACON *Disc. Govt. Eng.* II. lxii. 194 Treason was anciently used only as a crime of breach of trust or fealty..; now it grows into a sadder temper, and is made all one with that of *Laesa Majestas.*

**5.** The particular degree of hardness and elasticity or resiliency imparted to steel by tempering: see TEMPER *v.* 14.

*c* 1470 HENRY *Wallace* II. 189 O wareide suerd, of tempyr neuir trew. 1590 SIR J. SMYTH *Disc. Weapons* 4 Rapier blades..made of a verie hard temper to fight in priuat fraies. 1591 SHAKS. 1 *Hen. VI*, II. iv. 13 Between two blades, which beares the better temper. 1611 CORYAT *Crudities* 340 Milanese Cutlers..are accounted very excellent workmen for making of kniues, targets, and swordes of a singular temper. 1703 MOXON *Mech. Exerc.* 61 The blew Colour gives the Temper to Springs in general. 1881 *Metal World* 8 Oct. 338 The temper of steel is due to the chemical union of the iron with the carbon.

*fig.* 1601 B. JONSON *Ev. Man in Hum.* (Qo.) II. ii. 73 Not caring how the temper of your spirits [*Fol.* metal of your minds] Is eaten with the rust of idlenesse. 1784 COWPER *Task* v. 664 Harden'd his heart's temper in the forge Of lust, and on the anvil of despair. 1866 J. MARTINEAU *Ess.* I. 41 Intellectual implements of more ethereal temper.

**† 6.** The condition of the atmosphere with regard to heat and cold, dryness and humidity; the prevailing condition of the weather at a place; = CLIMATE *sb.* 3, TEMPERAMENT 4. *Obs.*

1483 *Cath. Angl.* 379/2 A Tempyr,..*temperies Aeris est.* 1525 LD. BERNERS *Froiss.* II. clxvi. [clxvii.] 500 The wether was fayre and clere, and the ayre in good temper. 1604 E. G[RIMSTONE] *D'Acosta's Hist. Indies* I. ix. 33 It is a land of an excellent temper, being in the midst of two extremes. 1622 *Rel. Eng. Plant. in Plymouth N. Eng.* in Arber *Pilgr. Fathers* (1897) 490 For the temper of the air here, it agreeth well with that in England. 1697 DRYDEN *Virg. Georg.* I. 565 With the changeful Temper of the Skies, As Rains condense, and Sunshine rarifies. 1705 ADDISON *Italy* 208 The Temper of their Climate..relaxes the Fibers of their Bodies.

**†7.** The relative condition of a body in respect of warmth or coldness; = TEMPERATURE 7. *Obs.*

1562 TURNER *Baths* 16 Let therefore your both meat and drinke be in such temper, that they be not cold but warme. 1626 BACON *Sylva* § 326 This will be performed partly by the Temper of the Fire. 1657 R. LIGON *Barbadoes* 27 The other foure months it is not so hot, but is neer the temper of the aire in England. 1677 YARRANTON *Eng. Improv.* 109 The Cloth is always kept in a constant heat and temper. 1693 E. HALLEY in *Phil. Trans.* XVII. 655 The Thermometers..in use are of Two sorts; the one shewing the differing Temper of Heat and Cold by the Expansion of Spirit of Wine, the other by the Air. 1733 MILLER *Gard. Dict.* s. v. *Tan*, The Bark will begin to heat, and when it is found of a due Temper, the Plants may be removed into it. 1884 F. J. BRITTEN *Watch & Clockm.* 75 Sufficient heat will pass along the wire to lower the temper of the hole.

**† 8.** Bodily habit, constitution, or condition. *Obs.*

Sometimes attributed to the various proportions in which the four humours are combined; sometimes to the combination of physical qualities: see TEMPERAMENT 3, 6.

1599 B. JONSON *Cynthia's Rev.* II. i, A creature of a most perfect and divine temper: one, in whom the humours and elements are peaceably met..he is neither too..melancholy, too..phlegmatic [etc.]. 1615 CROOKE *Body of Man* 272 The Temper of the whole body is to be esteemed according to the Temper of the principall parts, especially of the heart and the Liuer. 1634 W. WOOD *New Eng. Prosp.* I. ii, Agreeing well with the temper of our English bodies. 1650 [see EXQUISITENESS d]. 1653 H. MORE *Antid. Ath.* II. x. § 7 (1712) 71 The Hare, whose temper and frame of body are plainly fitted on purpose for her Condition. 1661 LOVELL *Hist. Anim. & Min.* Introd., As for their [serpents'] temper, some are cold, and others hot. 1707 FLOYER *Physic. Pulse-Watch* 300 All the Climates above 45 towards the Æquator have exceeding Pulses, and Choleric thin Tempers and Habits.

**9.** Mental constitution; habitual disposition; = TEMPERAMENT 7.

1595 SHAKS. *John* v. ii. 40 A noble temper dost thou shew in this. 1611 — *Wint. T.* IV. iv. 478 You know my Fathers temper: at this time He will allow no speech. 1669 STILLINGFL. *Serm. Whitsunday* ⁋ 14 Did the beginning Christians alter their natural temper? 1720 HEARNE *Collect.* (O.H.S.) VII. 111 A Lady of a sweet Temper, strict Virtue. 1754 EDWARDS *Freed. Will* I. ii. 10 The particular Temper which the Mind has by Nature, or that has been introduced and established by Education, Example, Custom or some other Means. 1777 H. BLAIR *Serm.* (1780) II. 70 Temper is the disposition which remains after these emotions are past; and which forms the habitual propensity of the soul. 1842 BORROW *Bible in Spain* xlviii, He..had been educated for the Church, which, not suiting his temper, he had abandoned. 1874 GREEN *Short Hist.* viii. § 2. 466 The temper of the Puritan was eminently a temper of law.

**10.** Actual state or attitude of the mind or feelings; frame of mind; inclination, humour.

*a* 1628 PRESTON *New Covt.* (1634) 118 If thy heart continue in that temper, it is impossible. 1680 BURNET *Rochester* (1692) 62 Thereby to nourish a devout temper in us. 1719 DE FOE *Crusoe* I. 320 He brought me an Account of the Temper he found them in. 1777 BURKE *Let. Sheriffs Bristol* Wks. III. 162 A conciliatory temper must precede and prepare every plan of reconciliation. 1838 LYTTON *Leila* IV. vii, The excitement, the wrath of the troops, produced the temper most fit for action. 1855 MACAULAY *Hist. Eng.* xv. III. 501 The Commons were in no temper to listen to such excuses. 1875 JOWETT *Plato* (ed. 2) IV. 317, I would recommend you..not to encourage yourself in this polemical and controversial temper.

**b.** In *good-temper, ill-temper, bad temper* (the latter leading to sense 11).

1768 [implied in GOOD-TEMPERED]. 1792 A. YOUNG *Trav. France* 69 A feature of that good temper which appears to me so visible every where in France. 1793 BURKE *Cond. Minority* Wks. VII. 267 He would not be able to get the better of the ill temper, and the ill doctrines, he has been the means of exciting. 1828 WEBSTER s. v., Disposition of mind; the constitution of the mind, particularly with regard to the passions and affections; as, a calm temper; a hasty temper; a fretful temper. This is applicable to beasts as well as to man. *a* 1832 BENTHAM *Deontology* (1834) I. 26 *note*, The tranquillity and good temper of a disputant. 1855 Bad temper [see BAD *a.* 6]. 1884 J. HALL *Chr. Home* 159 Servants..sometimes suffer from the ill-temper of their employers.

**11.** = *Ill-temper*: Heat of mind or passion, showing itself by outbursts of irritation or anger upon slight provocation; explosive ill-humour.

1828 WEBSTER, *Temper*..5. Heat of mind or passion; irritation. The boy showed a great deal of temper when I reproved him. So we say, a man of violent temper, when we speak of his irritability. (This use of the word is common, though a deviation from its original and genuine meaning.) 1836 SMART, *Temper*,..from the original sense, calmness, moderation; by a special application of the latter derivative senses, heat, irritation. *a* 1846 J. W. CROKER (Worc.), Johnson, when the first ebullition of temper had subsided, felt that he had been unreasonably violent. 1880 CHURCH *Cathedral & Univ. Serm.* (1892) 197 What we all understand when we speak of a man 'showing temper'. 1900 ELEANOR GLYN *Visits Elizabeth* (1906) 21, I can't tell you, Mamma, what a temper I was in.

**III. 12.** Concrete senses, in technical use.

**† a.** Applied to mortar or plaster. *Obs. rare*$^{-1}$.

1594 PLAT *Jewell-ho.* I. 18 An olde wall whose temper was made of Lime and Sand.

**b.** *Sugar-making.* A solution containing lime or some other alkaline substance serving to neutralize the acid in the raw cane-juice and clarify it.

1657 R. LIGON *Barbadoes* 90 A liquor made of water and Withs which they call Temper. 1797 *Encycl. Brit.* (ed. 3) XVIII. 59/1 When the clarifier is filled, a fire is lighted, and a quantity of Bristol quicklime in powder..called temper, is poured into the vessel. 1839 URE *Dict. Arts* 1202 If an excess of temper be used, the gluten is taken up again by the strong affinity which..exist[s] between sugar and lime.

**c.** An alloy of tin and copper.

1875 KNIGHT *Dict. Mech.*, *Pewterer's Temper*, an alloy of 2 parts tin and 1 copper. 1885 *Encycl. Brit.* XVIII. 725/1 The finest pewter (sometimes called 'tin and temper') is simply tin hardened by the addition of a trifle of copper.

**IV. 13.** *attrib.* and *Comb.*, as *temper-flaw*; *temper-spoiling, -trying* adjs.

1788 COWPER *Poet's N.-Y. Gift* ii, To wish thee fairer is no need,..Or more ingenious, or more freed From temper-flaws unsightly. 1893 *Outing* (U.S.) XXII. 121/2 Fly-fishing is pretty, but it is a futile and temper-spoiling art on a narrow, crooked, bush-grown brook. 1895 KIPLING in *Daily Chron.* 3 July 3/7 The mass of profitless, temper-wearing detail that attaches itself to any extended market-work.

**14.** Special Comb. (perh. from stem of TEMPER *v.*): **temper-pot**: see quots.; **temper-screw**, a set-screw for adjustment; *esp.* in boring, a screw-connexion for automatically adjusting the drill as the boring proceeds. See also TEMPER-PIN.

1875 URE *Dict. Arts* III. 67 When..the ladle becomes chilled, it is dipped into a small vessel containing lead of a higher temperature than that which is being worked, and known by the name of a *temper-pot. 1884 C. G. W. LOCK *Workshop Receipts* Ser. III. 361/2 The temper-pots hold about a ton of metal each. *a* 1864 GESNER *Coal, Petrol.*, etc. (1865) 28 The *Temper Screw is attached to a rope which connects with the end of the walking-beam, and serves to regulate the descent of the drill, without the inconvenience of lengthening the rope at short intervals. 1877 KNIGHT *Dict. Mech.*, *Temper-screw*,..one which brings its point against a bearing or an object. 1883 *Century Mag.* July 330/1 Then there is the 'temper-screw' which lowers the drilling apparatus inch by inch as it goes down.

**Temper** (teˑmpəɹ), *v.* Forms: 1 **temprian**, 3 **temprien**, (*Orm.*) **temmprenn**, 3–4 **tempren**, 3–6 **tempre**, (4–5 **tempire**, 4–6 **-ere, -ir, -or,** 5 **-yr, -ore,** 5–6 **-ier**), 4– **temper.** See also TAMPER *v.*[1] [OE. *temprian* (so also in OS. *temperon*), ad. L.

*temperāre* to divide or proportion duly, to mingle in due proportion, to combine properly; to qualify, temper; to arrange or keep in due measure or proportion, to keep within limits, to regulate, rule. Thence OF. *temprer* (12th c.), later (*tremprer*) *tremper*, 13th c. in Godef. (whence TRAMP *v.*[2] to soak); also *tempérer* (learned form after L.) to moderate by some mixture. The sense-development of the Eng. verb was prob. influenced by the French. A differentiated form is TAMPER *v.*[1]

L. *temperāre* is generally held to be a deriv. of *tempus*, *tempor-* a time or season, the proper time or season; but the sense history of both words is prehistoric and obscure: see Walde *Lat. Etymol.*]

**I. 1.** *trans.* To bring (anything) to a proper or suitable condition, state, or quality, by mingling with something else; to qualify, alloy, or dilute by such mixture or combination. Also *fig.* *arch.*

*a* **1000** *Blickl. Glosses* Ps. ci. 10 Potum meum cum fletu temperabam, *glossed* ic temprede. **13..** *K. Alis.* 7850 Venym he tok, and tempred hit with wyn. **1382** WYCLIF *1 Cor.* xii. 24 But god tempride the bodi [Vulg. *Deus temperavit corpus*], ȝyuynge more worschipe to it, to whom it failide. *c* **1425** tr. *Arderne's Surgery* (E.E.T.S.) 72 Þe ȝolk of a raw ey tempered with bole armoniac to sich þikknes þat it may by a clistery be ȝette into þe lure. **1486** *Bk. St. Albans* b vj b, Take Oyle of spayne and tempere it with clere wyne. **1544** PHAER *Pestilence* (1553) Mv, In a hote season it is good to temper yᵉ said wine with a litle rose-water. *a* **1591** H. SMITH *Serm.* (1637) 134 As wine is tempered with water, so let discretion temper zeale. **1660** BURNEY *Κέρδ. Δῶρον* (1661) 110 To compound an absolute one (*Temperamentum ad pondus*) of the other 3 forms of Government [Spartan, Athenian, Roman], as the ingredients, and .. tampering with Monarchy. **1711** ADDISON *Spect.* No. 106 ¶ 3 The good old Knight..tempered the Inquiries after his own Affairs with several kind Questions relating to themselves. **1756** NUGENT *Montesquieu's Spir. Laws* (1758) I. IV. viii. 55 There was a necessity for tempering them with others that might soften their manners.

**2.** To modify (some unsuitable or excessive state or quality, or some thing or person in respect of such), esp. by admixture of some other quality, etc.; to reduce to the suitable or desirable (middle) degree or condition free from excess in either direction; to moderate, mitigate, assuage, tone down.

*c* **1000** ÆLFRIC *Hom.* II. 46 And eft ȝetemprie seo bilewitnys þæt fyr, þæt hit to reðe ne sy. *a* **1050** *Liber Scintill.* x. 52 Bryne lichamena mid ceaIdrum estum to temprigenne ys [L. *temperandus est*]. *c* **1200** ORMIN 2893 Forr aȝȝ birrþ rihhtwisnesse ben þurrh mildheorrtnesse temmpredd. *a* **1340** HAMPOLE *Psalter* cvi. 29 Þe persecuciouns he tempird and made þaim suffrabil. **1552** HULOET, Temper sorow with mirth. **1596** SPENSER *State Irel.* Pref. 2 We may wish that in some passages it had bin tempered with more moderation. **1596** BACON *Max. & Use Com. Law* Ep. Ded. (1636) 3 Kings which..do temper their magnanimity with justice. **1768** STERNE *Sent. Journ.* (1778) II. 176 (*Maria*) God tempers the wind, said Maria, to the shorn lamb. **1781** J. MOORE *View Soc. It.* (1790) I. xxxix. 420 Our admiration of the Romans is tempered with horror. **1834** MRS. SOMERVILLE *Connex. Phys. Sc.* xxvi. (1849) 291 The cold currents from the poles tempering the intense heat of the equatorial regions. **1871** MACDUFF *Mem. Patmos* x. 132 He..who tempers judgment with mercy. **1878** HUXLEY *Physiogr.* 80 In tempering the activity of the oxygen with which it is associated.

**b.** *intr.* (for *pass.*)

**1860** DICKENS *Uncomm. Trav.* ix, A flavour of damaged oranges, which, a little further down towards the river, tempered into herrings, and gradually toned into a cosmopolitan blast of fish.

**3.** To mix, mingle, blend (ingredients) *together*, or (one ingredient) *with* another, in proper proportions. Also *fig.* *arch.*

*c* **1386** CHAUCER *Can. Yeom. Prol. & T.* 348 Er þat the pot be on the fir ydo Of metals with a certeyn quantitee My lord hem tempreth and no man but he. *c* **1440** *Promp. Parv.* 488/1 Temperyn, or menge to-gedur, *commisceo*, *misceo*. **1530** PALSGR. 754/1 Whan metalles be well tempered togyther they wyll be all as one. **1671** J. WEBSTER *Metallogr.* v. 88 They are said to grow of sulphur and argent vive mixt and tempered together. **1759** J. MILLS *Duhamel's Husb.* I. viii. (1762) 21 To fling and temper amongst it ashes or chalk. **1876** BLACKIE *Songs Relig. & Life* 195 If wisely you temper, and skilfully blend The hard-headed Scot with the quick-witted Grecian.

**4.** To prepare by mingling; to make by due mixture or combination; to concoct, compound, compose, make up, devise. *lit.* and *fig.* *Obs.* or *arch.*

**1390** GOWER *Conf.* III. 10 In cold I brenne and frese in hete: And thanne I drinke a biter swete With dreie lippe and yhen wete. Lo, thus I tempre mi diete. **1542** UDALL *Erasm. Apoph.* 195 He wrote..to Pausanias his physician that he should..tempre drynkes and medecines for hym. *a* **1569** KINGESMYLL *Man's Est.* ix. (1580) 44 But there is a strong medicine a temperyng. **1600** HOLLAND *Livy* VIII. xviii. 294 That certain dames of Rome..boiled and tempered ranke poisons (to kill their husbands). **1650** BULWER *Anthropomet.* 155 Sometimes they will temper a certain Colour, with Hens dung and Saffron.

†**5.** To restore the proper 'temper' or 'temperament' to; to bring into a good or desirable state of body or health; to cure, heal, refresh.

*c* **1000** ÆLFRIC *Hom.* I. 474 Se ðe wile mid soðum læcecræfte his lichaman ȝetemprian, swa swa dyde se witeȝa Isaias. *c* **1430** LYDG. *Min. Poems* (Percy Soc.) 196 Ayer of nature yevith inspiracioun..To tempre the spiritis by vertu vegetatiff. **1486** *Bk. St. Albans* b ij b, Bot it tempur yowre hawke, that is to say ensayme yowre hawke with in .iiij. days, I meruell. **1561** HOLLYBUSH *Hom. Apoth.* 44 b, He may drinke a litle wyne vpon it, to tempere hys mouth of the bitternesse. **1613** PURCHAS *Pilgrimage* III. xvii. 284 Gallus, a riuer..the waters whereof, temperatly drunken, did exceedingly temper the braine, and take away madnes.

**6.** To bring into a suitable or desirable frame of mind; to dispose favourably, to persuade; also, to appease, mollify, pacify. *Obs.* or *arch.*

**1525** LD. BERNERS *Froiss.* II. xci. [lxxxvii.] 271 If he be nat reasonable, the duke of Berrey and the duke of Burgoyne wyll so temper hym, that ye shal be frendes and cosyn to the kynge. **1546** *St. Papers Hen. VIII*, XI. 44 How moch the Emperour hath doone soo to tempre the French King, it appered in his last bargayn with Fraunce. **1588** SHAKS. *Tit. A.* IV. iv. 109 Now will I to that old Andronicus, And temper him with all the Art I haue, To plucke proud Lucius from the warlike Gothes. **1678** TEMPLE *Let. to Sir L. Jenkins* Wks. 1731 II. 470, I found both the King and the Duke growing so angry upon it, that I thought it my part to temper them as far as I could. **1710** STEELE *Tatler* No. 194 ¶ 7 The Lady so well tempered and reconciled them both, that she forced them to join Hands. **1874** BUSHNELL *Forgiven. & Law* 59 Is it true that God must be gained or tempered transactionally..in order to the letting forth of grace upon his enemies?

**II. 7.** To keep, conduct, or manage in just measure; to regulate; to control, direct, guide, rule, govern, overrule. *Obs.* exc. *dial.*

*c* **1000** *Sax. Leechd.* III. 250 Ac heo [seo sunne] temprað ða eorðlican wæstmas æȝðer ȝe on wæstme ȝe on ripunge. **13..** *Coer de L.* 659 Kyng Rychard the fyre bet, Thomas to the spytte hym set, Fouk Doyly tempryd the wood. *a* **1340** HAMPOLE *Pr. Consc.* 7616 Þai [the heavens] tempre þe streng[t]he of alle þe elementes. *c* **1400** GOWER *Praise of Peace* 160 Though thou the werres darst wel undirtake, Aftir reson yit tempre thi corage. *c* **1440** *Promp. Parv.* 488/1 Temporyn, or sette yn mesure, *tempero*. **1528** TINDALE *Obed. Chr. Man* 148 b, All the Apostles chose two.. and cast lottes desyringe God to temper them that the lotte myght fall on the most ablest. **1576** GOSSON *Spec. Hum.* vi. in *Sch. Abuse* (Arb.) 77 Thou God..that..turnes the spheares, and tempers all on hie. **1591** SPENSER *M. Hubberd* 1294 His snakie wand, With which the damned ghosts he governeth, And furies rules and Tartare tempereth. **1659** LEAK *Waterwks.* 32 There is a Pipe with a Cock..which serves to temper the course of the Water. **1725** POPE *Odyss.* IV. 326 Supremest Jove Tempers the fates of human race above. **1835** D. WEBSTER *Orig. Scot. Rhymes* 152 (E.D.D.) This birkie bodie can wi' speed Temper yer ilka thrum and thread.

**8.** To restrain within due limits, or within the bounds of moderation; in later use often simply, to restrain, check, curb.

*a* **1050** *Liber Scintill.* xxviii. (1889) 107 Forþi hi na tempredon [L. *non temperauerunt*] ȝefernysse hætan. **1297** R. GLOUC. (Rolls) 1624 He dude hom ssame ynou & temprede hom vol wel & made hom sone milde ynou þo hii were rebel. **13..** *E. E. Allit. P.* B. 775 Ȝif þou tynez þat toun, tempre þyn yre. *c* **1394** *P. Pl. Crede* 743 To toilen wiþ þe erþe, Tylen & trewliche lyven & her flech tempren. *c* **1400** *Brut* 31 Lud his sone..gouernede wel þe lande, and miche honourede gode folc, and temprede and amendit wickede folc. **1538** STARKEY *England* I. iv. 120 Yf we coude fynd a way to tempur and refrayne thayr malyce. **1599** *Warn. Faire Wom.* II. 737 Learne to temper your excessive griefe. **1777** ROBERTSON *Hist. Amer.* II. v. 81 Cortes..was more solicitous to temper than to inflame their ardour. **1821** BYRON *Sardan.* I. ii. 347 Since they are tumultuous, Let them be temper'd, yet not roughly.

†**b.** *refl.* To control or restrain oneself. *Obs.*

*c* **1000** ÆLFRIC *Hom.* I. 360 An is, þæt ȝehwa hine sylfne ȝetempriȝe mid ȝemete on æte and on wæte. **13..** *Cursor M.* 17244 (Cott.) For-sak þi serc o silk and line, And temper þe wit[h] alle and wine. **1531** ELYOT *Gov.* III. xxiv. (1883) 379 He coulde nat tempre him selfe in redyng Greke bokes whyles the Senate was sittyng. **1600** HOLLAND *Livy* v. xlv. 209 So as they could scarcely temper themselves and forbeare, but presently set upon them. **1651** HOBBES *Govt. & Soc.* vii. § 4. 114, I wish that not onely Kings, but all other Persons.. would so temper themselves as to commit no wrong.

†**c.** *refl.* To restrain oneself or refrain *from* († *of*).

**1560** DAUS tr. *Sleidane's Comm.* 100 b, Warnyng men to tempre themselues from entryng in to wycked warres. **1561** T. NORTON *Calvin's Inst.* I. 42 If the readers will temper them of curiositie, and not more gredily than mete is, seke for combersome and entangled disputations. **1658** W. BURTON *Itin. Anton.* 180, I could not temper my self..from causing his discourse to be transcribed hither.

**9.** To regulate suitably to need or requirement; to fit, adapt, conform, accommodate, make suitable. Const. *to*. Now *rare* or *Obs.*

**1450–1530** *Myrr. our Ladye* 86 The sufferaunce of god, whyche temperyth all thynges to hys seruauntes, as they may bere to theyr mooste profyt. **1573–80** BARET *Alv.* T 113 To Temper his talke to the fantasie and pleasure. **1649** MILTON *Eikon.* i. 5 They were indeed not temper'd to his temper. **1662** STILLINGFL. *Orig. Sacr.* II. v. § 8 God tempered the Ceremoniall Law much according to the condition and capacity of the persons it was prescribed to. **1665** MANLEY *Grotius' Low C. Warres* 243 If the one King..had tempered himself and his Laws, according to the strength and prevalence of parties.

**III.** Various technical uses.

**10.** To bring (clay, mortar, etc.) to a proper consistence for use by mixing and working it up *with* water, etc. Also *fig.*

**13..** *Cursor M.* 22940 (Fairf.) Þe potter..al new he tempris his clay. **1387** TREVISA *Higden* (Rolls) I. 271 Whan þat stoon is i-tempred wiþ water and torned to playstre. *c* **1400** *Brut* 57 Wille ȝe slee me for my blode forto temper wiþ ȝoure morter? **1535** COVERDALE *Ecclus.* xxxviii. 30 He fashioneth the claye with his arme, and with his fete he tempereth it. **1617** MORYSON *Itin.* I. 32 Lime tempered, not with water, but with wine, incredibly durable. **1719** YOUNG *Busiris* v. i, Yes, I will..temper all my cement with their blood. **1884** C. T. DAVIS *Manuf. Bricks*, etc. v. (1889) 130 The object of tempering the clay is to thoroughly mix it, and prepare the material for the use of the moulder.

†**11.** To moisten (a substance, usually medicinal or culinary ingredients in a comminuted state) so as to form a paste or mixture; to mix to a paste.

*c* **1400** MAUNDEV. (Roxb.) xxi. 94 Take þe lefes..and stampe þam and tempre þam with water and drink it. *c* **1400** *Rom. Rose* 4180 A plastre dolorous..Which is not tempred with vynegre, But with poverte & indigence. *c* **1440** *Anc. Cookery* in *Househ. Ord.* (1790) 426 Take soden porke and grynde hit smal, and tempur hit with rawe yolkes of eyren. **1563** T. GALE *Antidot.* II. 15 The herbes must be mixed and tempered with Axungia. **1668** CULPEPPER & COLE *Barthol. Anat.* I. ix. 22 Some moisture to temper the meat and make it liquid. **1674** RAY *Collect. Words, Smelting Silver* 115 With water tempered into a past to a due quality.

**b.** *spec.* in *Painting*: To prepare (colours) for use by mixing them with oil, etc.

**1531** ELYOT *Gov.* III. xix. (1883) 318 In temperynge his colours, he lacked good size, wherwith they shulde have ben bounden, and made to endure. **1691** RAY *Creation* I. (1692) 97 The most skilful Painter cannot so mingle and temper his Colours. **1837** SIR F. PALGRAVE *Merch. & Friar* (1844) 9 The metallic or body colours are to be tempered or mixed with oil. **1859** SALA *Gaslight & D.* ii. 25 Colours.. ground in water, and subsequently tempered with size.

†**12.** To steep or dissolve (a substance) in a liquid (cf. TRAMP *v.*[2]); *fig.* to drench, suffuse. *Obs.*

*c* **1489** CAXTON *Blanchardyn* 147 Wyth eyen all tempred wyth teerys. **1530** PALSGR. 754/1, I temper, I laye breed or other thynges in stepe...You muste temper your breed in vynayger. **1600** HOLLAND *Livy* XXX. xv. 750 Which [poison] hee commaunded him to temper in a goblet of wine, and to carie it to Sophonisba. **1669** STURMY *Mariner's Mag.* VII. xxxiv. 50 Take blew Smalts, temper it in Water, and rub the Picture with it.

†**13.** *trans.* To soften (iron, wax, etc.) by heating; to melt. Also *intr.* for *pass.* *Obs.*

**1535** COVERDALE *Isa.* xliv. 12 The smyth taketh yron, and tempreth it with hote coles, and fashioneth it with hammers. **1590** SIR J. SMYTH *Disc. Weapons* 19 b, The Archers did vse to temper with fire a conuenient quantitie of waxe, rosen, and fine tallowe together. **1597** SHAKS. *2 Hen. IV*, IV. iii. 140, I haue him alreadie tempering betweene my finger and my thombe, and shortly will I seale with him.

**14.** To bring (steel) to a suitable degree of hardness and elasticity or resiliency by heating it to the required temperature and immersing it, while hot, in some liquid, usually cold water; applied also to the hardening of copper, etc. Also *fig.*

*c* **1381** CHAUCER *Parl. Foules* 214, I say Cupide .. hise arwis forge & file..And wel his doughtyr temperede al this whyle The heuedis in the welle. **14..** *Tundale's Vis.* 1059 As men shulde temper irne or stele. **1530** PALSGR. 754/1 They have a great advauntage in Spayne, to temper their blades well, bycause of the nature of their ryvers. **1603** HOLLAND *Plutarch's Mor.* 115 We must doe as the Smithes who temper yron: For when they have given it a fire, and made it by that meanes soft, loose and pliable, they drench and dip it in cold water, whereby it becommeth compact and hard, taking thereby the due temperature of stiffe steele. **1758** REID tr. *Macquer's Chym.* I. 64 The hardness of Steel may be considerably augmented by tempering it; that is, by making it red-hot, and suddenly quenching it in some cold liquor. **1881** *Metal World* No. 8. 121 This they converted into the purest steel, and tempered to the hardest and yet the most elastic pitch.

**b.** *intr.* (for *pass.*).

**1881** RAYMOND *Mining Gloss.* s. v., A metallic compound in which these qualities [hardness and elasticity] can thus be produced is said to temper, or to take temper. **1884** W. H. GREENWOOD *Steel & Iron* xvii. § 669 Mild steel containing from 0·05 to 0·20 per cent. of carbon will weld, but does not temper.

†**15.** To tune, adjust the pitch of (a musical instrument). *Obs.* exc. as in b.

*c* **1300** *Prov. Hending* x. in *Salomon & Sat.*, etc. (1848) 272 He nul no gle bygynne er he haue tempred is pype. **1390** GOWER *Conf.* III. 301 He takth the Harpe and in his wise He tempreth, and of such assise Singende he harpeth forth withal. **1575** LANEHAM *Let.* (1871) 41 For fyling his napkin, temperd a string or too with his wreast. **1593** *Bacchus Bountie* in *Harl. Misc.* (Malh.) II. 274 Whereupon M. Barlycap tempered up his fiddle, and began.

**b.** *spec.* To tune (a note or instrument) according to some temperament: see TEMPERAMENT 10. See also TEMPERED 1 e.

**1727–41** CHAMBERS *Cycl.* s.v. *Temperament*, To mend these imperfect concords, the musicians have bethought themselves to temper, i. e. give them part of the agreeableness of perfect ones... All such divisions of the octave are called tempered, or temperative systems. **1788** CAVALLO in *Phil. Trans.* LXXVIII. 250 All the fifths, all the thirds, and in short all the chords of the same denomination, are equally tempered throughout. **1875** A. J. ELLIS tr. *Helmholtz' Sensat. Tone* III. xvi. 509 It is clearly not necessary to temper the instruments to which the singer practises.

**16.** To bring into harmony, attune. Const. *to*. *Obs.* or *arch.*

*c* **1374** CHAUCER *Boeth.* III. met. xii. 84 (Camb. MS.) And there he [Orpheus] temprede hise blaundysshynge soonges by resownynge strenges. **1637** MILTON *Lycidas* 33 Mean while the Rural ditties were not mute, Temper'd to th' Oaten Flute. **1754** GRAY *Progr. Poesy* 26 Thee the voice, the dance, obey, Temper'd to thy warbled lay. **1860** WARTER *Sea-board* II. 367 If we make melody in our hearts, and if our souls are tempered to harmony, then is the Divinity enlarged within us.

**17.** To set or adjust the share and other parts of (a plough) in the proper position for making the furrow of the required depth and width. ? *Obs.*

**1523** FITZHERB. *Husb.* § 4 It is necessarye for an housbande to knowe howe these plowes shulde be tempered, to plowe and turne clene, and to make no reste balkes. *Ibid.*, All these maner of plowes shulde haue all lyke one maner of temperyng in the yrens. **1844** STEPHENS *Bk. Farm* I. 33 The ploughman will be able to afford him ocular proof how he places (*tempers*) all the irons of the plough in relation to the state of the land. *Ibid.* 404 To 'temper a plough' is the great aim of the good ploughman.

†**18.** To regulate (a clock). *Sc. Obs.*

**1538** *Aberdeen Regr.* (1844) I. 157 For his gud seruice to be done in keiping and temporing of thair knok within the tolbutht, for his fee. **1592–3** in *Spottiswoode Misc.* (1845) II. 269 Wnderstanding the great pains and travels of Archibald Stedman in tempering the knock.

**Temper**, obs. var. TAMPER *v.*; obs. f. TEMPTER; var. TEMPRE *a. Obs.*

‖**Tempera** (te·mpera). Also 9 **tempra**. [It. *tempera*, in phr. *pingere a tempera* to paint in distemper.] The method of painting in distemper: see DISTEMPER *sb.*[2] 1.

**1832** GELL *Pompeiana* I. viii. 148 A beautiful Venus painted in tempra. **1888** *Encycl. Brit.* XXIII. 157/2 Tempera is called in Italy 'fresco a secco' as distinguished from 'fresco buono', or true fresco, painted on freshly laid patches of stucco. *a* **1890** W. B. SCOTT *Autobiogr. Notes* I. 168 The best preserved early pictures there [Italy] are tempera, not fresco.

**b.** *Comb.*, as *tempera-painting*, *-picture*.

**1862** THORNBURY *Turner* I. 142 Passages of transparent colour, either upon white grounds, or introduced to enrich tempera pictures. **1898** HUEFFER in *Contemp. Rev.* Aug. 185 In the same year, he again attempted tempera-painting.

**Temperable** (te·mpərăb'l), *a.* Now *rare.* [prob. ad. med.L. *temperābil-is*; but perh. f. TEMPER *sb.* and *v.* + -ABLE: cf. *agreeable*, *customable*, *peaceable*.] †**a.** Of weather or climate: = TEMPERATE *a.* 3. †**b.** Of a person: = TEMPERATE *a.* 1.

*c* **1400** *Lanfranc's Cirurg.* 16 In somer he muste haue temperable eir. *c* **1450** LOVELICH *Grail* xxxvi. 496 That he myhte beste herberwed to be, Into Most temperable place Abowtes þe see. **1570** LEVINS *Manip.* 4/18 Temperable, *temperabilis*. **1618** BOLTON *Florus* I. viii. 30 That the fierce people might bee made temperable, through the feare of the Gods. **1629** MAXWELL tr. *Herodian* (1635) 31 Yet for a while, was the Prince more temperable, out of respect to his Fathers memory, and his Counsellours gravitie.

**c.** That may be tempered or made plastic.

**1841** EMERSON *Ess.*, *Hist.* P 44 The fusible, hard, and temperable texture of metals.

Hence **Temperabi·lity** (*Funk's Stand. Dict.* 1895).

†**Tempera·de.** *Obs.* (See quot.)

*a* **1700** B. E. *Dict. Cant. Crew*, *Temperade*, an East-Indian-dish, now in use in England, being a Fowl Fricasied, with high Sauce, Blancht Almonds and Rice.

**Te·mperal**, *a. nonce-wd.* [f. TEMPER *sb.* + -AL.] Of, pertaining to, or resulting from tempering.

**1816** ACCUM *Chem. Tests* (1818) 106 Other articles of steel ..either bend or lose their shape in the hardening..or resist the tool, when wrought in the temperal state.

**Temperal(l, -alite, -alte**, obs. ff. TEMPORAL, -ALITY, -ALTY.

†**Temperality.** *Obs.* Humorously misused for TEMPER or TEMPERATURE.

**1597** SHAKS. *2 Hen. IV*, II. iv. 25 Me thinkes now you are in an excellent good temperalitie.

**Temperament** (te·mpĕrăměnt), *sb.* Also 5 **temperment**. [ad. L. *temperāmentum* due mixture, f. *temperāre* to TEMPER: see -MENT. So Fr. *tempérament* (16th c. in Godef. *Compl.*).]

**I.** †**1.** A moderate and proportionable mixture of elements in a compound; the condition in which elements are combined in their due proportions.

? *a* **1412** LYDG. *Two Merch.* 303 Yiff..heete or blood passe his temperament, In to a fevere anoon a man it leedith. **1576** NEWTON *Lemnie's Complex.* (1633) 50 Crasis or Temperament..is an agreement, and conveniency of the first qualities and Elements among themselves: Or, an equall mixture or proportion of the qualities of the Elements, wherein no excesse blame-worthy or faulty is to be found. **1658** PHILLIPS, *Temperament*, a moderate and proportionable mixture of any thing, but more peculiarly of the four humours of the body. **1684** tr. *Bonet's Merc. Compit.* IV. 124 The cure of a wasting Flux..consists in the restitution of the temperament. **1684** J. P. tr. *Frambresar. Art Physick* i. 18 A Temperament is a proportion of the four chief Elementary Qualities proper for the true exercise of the Natural Functions.

†**2.** State or condition with respect to the proportion of ingredients or manner of mixing; consistence, composition; mixture. *Obs.*

**1471** RIPLEY *Comp. Alch.* IV. xiv. in Ashm. *Theat. Chem. Brit.* (1652) 147 A temperament not so thyk as the Body ys, Nother so thyn as Water. **1610** BARROUGH *Meth. Physick* VIII. (1639) 469 Boyle it again until it come to the temperament of an ointment. **1641** MILTON *Reform.* II. Wks. 1851 III. 57 The best founded Commonwealths..have aym'd at a certaine mixture and temperament, partaking the severall vertues of each other State. **1660** N. INGELO *Bentiv. & Ur.* II. (1682) 203 That the Soul is not a Temperament of Corporeal Humours is manifest. *a* **1673** J. CARYL in Spurgeon *Treas. Dav.* Ps. lxvi. 12 A due temperament of heat and cold, of dryness and moistness.

**II.** †**3.** In the natural philosophy of the Middle Ages: The combination of supposed qualities (*hot* or *cold*, *moist* or *dry*) in a certain proportion, determining the nature of a plant or other body (= COMPLEXION *sb.* 1); characteristic nature; known *spec.* as *universal temperament* (cf. 6). *Obs.*

**1471** RIPLEY *Comp. Alch.* I. xviii. in Ashm. *Theat. Chem. Brit.* (1652) 133 For soe to temperment ys brought our Stone, And Natures contraryose, fower be made one. **1578** LYTE *Dodoens* I. lxvi. 97 Some men write of this herbe [Water Plantayne], that it is of temperament colde and dry. **1612** WOODALL *Surg. Mate* Wks. (1653) 209 Let no man attribute to all salts one temperament. **1665** G. HAVERS *P. della Valle's Trav. E. India* 70 Of temperament, 'tis held to be hot, and good to promote digestion. *a* **1677** HALE *Prim. Orig. Man.* II. iv. 153 The experience of various temperaments and operations of those Herbs.

**4.** The condition of the weather or climate as resulting from the different combinations of the qualities, heat or cold, dryness or humidity; climate. *Obs.* or *arch.*

**1610** BARROUGH *Meth. Physick* IV. xiii. (1639) 245 Of all temperaments of the aire, the worst is that which is hot and moist. **1684** R. WALLER *Nat. Exper.* 10 Not onely from the season of the Year, and temperament of the Air, but from the Nature of the Soils and Countries themselves. **1713** DERHAM *Phys.-Theol.* I. ii. 17 The Cause assigned to malignant, epidemical Diseases;—and that is, an hot and moist Temperament of the Air. **1822–34** *Good's Study Med.* (ed. 4) I. 459 Change of air..where the difference of temperament, or even of temperature, can be rendered very considerable. **1875** JOWETT *Plato* (ed. 2) I. 492 The temperament of their seasons is such that they have no disease.

†**5.** Condition with regard to warmth or coldness; = TEMPERATURE 7. *Obs.*

**1658** A. FOX *Würtz' Surg.* IV. i. 304 Wound Unguents and wound Plaisters should alwaies stand in one temperament. *a* **1704** LOCKE *Elem. Nat. Phil.* xi. (1754) 51 Bodies are denominated hot and cold in proportion to the present temperament of that part of our body to which they are applied. **1741** *Compl. Fam.-Piece* II. iii. 352 To keep up your Heat to the same Temperament. **1799** *Phil. Mag.* III. 419 A given quantity of cold water, or water of any given temperament.

**6.** In mediæval physiology: The combination of the four cardinal humours (see HUMOUR *sb.* 2 b) of the body, by the relative proportion of which the physical and mental constitution were held to be determined; known *spec.* as *animal temperament*; also, The bodily habit attributed to this, as *a sanguine*, *choleric*, *phlegmatic*, or *melancholic temperament* (see the adjs.). See TEMPER *sb.* 8.

In modern use the term *temperament* and the names of the four temperaments continue, without any theory of combination of humours.

**1628** FELTHAM *Resolves* II. [I.] xxx. 95 Though the soule be not caused by the body; yet in the generall it followes the temperament of it. **1652** BP. HALL *Invisible World* II. § 1 Galen was not a better Physician than an ill Divine, while he determines the soul to be the complexion and temperament of the prime qualities. **1657** TOMLINSON *Renou's Disp.* 10 That [Medicament]..which..doth work a manifest mutation on our bodies,..either in temperament, in matter or form. **1676** DRYDEN *Aurengzebe* Ded., Our Minds are perpetually wrought on by the Temperaments of our Bodies. **1727–41** CHAMBERS *Cycl.* s.v., The ancient physicians brought these animal temperaments to correspond with the universal temperament..: the sanguine temperament was supposed to coincide with hot and moist, the phlegmatic with cold and moist [etc.]. **1818** T. L. PEACOCK *Nightmare Abb.* i, This gentleman was naturally of an atrabilarious temperament. **1836** A. WALKER *Beauty in Wom.* 202 The ancients classed individuals in one or other of four temperaments, founded on the hypothesis of four humours,..the red part [of the blood], phlegm, yellow, and black bile...Hence were derived the names of the sanguine, the phlegmatic, the choleric, and the melancholic temperaments. **1843** R. J. GRAVES *Syst. Clin. Med.* xxxi. 421 Edward Fitzgerald, labourer,..temperament sanguineous.

**7.** Constitution or habit of mind, esp. as depending upon or connected with physical constitution; natural disposition; = TEMPER *sb.* 9.

**1821** BYRON *Juan* III. liii, He was a man of a strange temperament. **1842** MRS. BROWNING *Grk. Chr. Poets* 135 The poetic temperament. **1843** LYTTON *Last Bar.* III. v, Despite this general smoothness of mien, his temperament was naturally irritable [and] quick. **1856** EMERSON *Eng. Traits*, *Truth* Wks. (Bohn) II. 55 A slow temperament makes them less rapid and ready than other countrymen. **1868** MISS BRADDON *Dead Sea Fr.* III. v. 64 Visions..such ..as the man of sanguine temperament can always evolve. **1873** HAMERTON *Intell. Life* I. iv. (1875) 25 The active temperament likes physical action for its own sake. **1891** *Speaker* 2 May 534/1 The unbiassed temperament which is essential to the true historian. **1894** W. B. CARPENTER *Son of Man amg. Sons of Men* v, Temperament is a convenient phrase to describe those qualities and dispositions which belong to him from birth.

**III.** The action or fact of tempering.

**8.** Moderating, moderation; lightening, alleviation, mitigation; due regulation. *Obs.* or *arch.*

**1475** *Rolls of Parlt.* VI. 144/2 That a dewe moderation and temperament be observed. **1576** NEWTON *Lemnie's Complex.* (1633) 2 Unlesse he have the knowledge of his owne body, and be ripe and skilfull in the temperament thereof. **1697** BP. PATRICK *Comm. Exod.* xxii. 11 But there were some Temperaments of this Law; for every Man was not admitted to purge himself by an Oath. **1861** *Temple Bar Mag.* IV. 54 That a certain temperament of speed was ensured.

**9.** The action of duly combining or adjusting different principles, claims, etc.; adjustment, compromise. *Obs.* or *arch.*

**1660** *Trial Regic.* 12 There is that excellent Temperament in our laws, that..the King cannot rule, but by His Laws. **1678** SIR G. MACKENZIE *Crim. Laws Scot.* II. xxiv. § 6 (1699) 261 By this just Temperament, the Interest of the Commonwealth, and the Imbecility of Minors are both salved. **1686** F. SPENCE tr. *Varillas' Ho. Medicis* 52 The friends of Piero ..propounded a temperament which equally fitted the king of Naples and duke of Milan's turn. **1790** BURKE *Fr. Rev.* 86 These admit no temperament and no compromise. **1794** — *Corr.* (1844) IV. 253 There is no medium,—there is no temperament, there is no compromise with Jacobinism. **1818** HALLAM *Mid. Ages* (1872) II. iv. 43 As a fortunate temperament of law and justice with the royal authority.

**b.** A middle course or state between extremes of any kind; a medium, mean. *Obs.* or *arch.*

**1604** R. CAWDREY *Table Alph.*, *Temperament*, temperatenesse, meane, or due proportion. **1656** BLOUNT *Glossogr.*, *Temperament*,..a moderation, mean or measure. **1697** tr. *C'tess D'Aunoy's Trav.* (1706) 45 Wearied and tired, roasted by the heat of the Sun, or frozen by the Snows (for there is seldom any Temperament between these Two Extreams). **1741** MIDDLETON *Cicero* II. xi. 476 Rewards and punishments; in which..as in every thing else, a certain medium and temperament is to be observed. **1823** BENTHAM *Not Paul* 249 The causes..of this temperament—this *mezzo termino*—this middle course. **1827** HALLAM *Const. Hist.* (1876) I. ii. § 4. 88 A judicious temperament, which the reformers would have done well to adopt in some other points.

**10.** *Mus.* The adjustment of the intervals of the scale (in the tuning of instruments of fixed intonation, as keyboard instruments), so as to adapt them to the purposes of practical harmony: consisting in slight variations of the pitch of the notes from true or 'just' intonation in order to make them available in different keys; a particular system of doing this. (Sometimes extended to any system of tuning, including that of just intonation.)

The chief temperaments that have been practically used are *mean-tone temperament* (see MEAN TONE); and *equal temperament* (now almost universal), in which the octave is divided into twelve (theoretically) equal semitones, so that the variations of pitch are evenly distributed throughout all keys.

**1727–41** CHAMBERS *Cycl.*, *Temperament*,..in music, denotes a rectifying or mending the false or imperfect concords, by transferring to them part of the beauty of the perfect ones. **1788** CAVALLO in *Phil. Trans.* LXXVIII. 242 This alteration of the just lengths of strings, necessary for adapting them to several key-notes, is called the temperament. **1881** BROADHOUSE *Mus. Acoustics* 354 Mean tone temperament was perfected by Salinas, A.D. 1577. *Ibid.* 356 The principle usually adopted at the present day for all keyed instruments is that called 'Equal Temperament', which professes to divide the octave into twelve exactly equal parts, though it does not actually so divide it. **1898** STAINER & BARRETT *Dict. Mus. Terms* 437/1 The question of melodic progressions, as affecting the excellence of temperaments, is too extensive for our limits.

**Te·mperament**, *v. rare.* [f. prec. sb.] *trans.* To endow with a temperament; in **Te·mperamented**, **Te·mperamenting** *ppl. adjs.*

**1855** EMERSON *Woman* Misc. (1884) 349 Men are not to the same degree temperamented. **1870** — *Soc. & Solit.*, *Work & Days* Wks. (Bohn) III. 70 The earth with its foods; the intellectual temperamenting air;..are given immeasurably to all.

**Temperamental** (tempĕrăme·ntăl), *a.* [f. TEMPERAMENT *sb.* + -AL.] Of or relating to the temperament (chiefly in sense 7); constitutional.

**1646** SIR T. BROWNE *Pseud. Ep.* 18 By a temperamentall inactivity we are unready to put in execution the suggestions or dictates of reason. **1650** CHARLETON *Paradoxes* 139 The constitution or temperamentall disposition of the organ. **1812** COLERIDGE in *Lit. Rem.* (1836) I. 381 These temperamental *pro*-virtues will too often fail. **1824** *New Monthly Mag.* XI. 321 In spite of her temperamental gaiety..she had moments of intense melancholy. **1907** H. WALES *The Yoke* i, People there are who appear to have been given a special temperamental adaptation for an ascetic and abstinent life.

**Temperame·ntally**, *adv.* [f. prec. + -LY [2].] By temperament; constitutionally.

**1861** *Romance Dull Life* xxviii. 204 They were both temperamentally incapacitated for catching a prevalent emotion. **1908** *Times, Lit. Supp.* 17 Dec. 479/1 Persons who are temperamentally faddists.

**Temperance** (te·mpĕrăns). Also 4–5 **temperans**, 4–6 **-aunce**, 6 **-anse**; (5–6 **temporaunce**, 7 **-ance**). [a. AF. *temperaunce* (R. Grosseteste *a* 1250), ad. L. *temperāntia* moderation, f. *temperānt-em*, pr. pple. of *temperāre* to TEMPER. As to previous history, see Note below.]

**I. 1.** The practice or habit of restraining oneself in provocation, passion, desire, etc.; rational self-restraint. (One of the four cardinal virtues.)

**a.** Self-restraint and moderation in action of any kind, in the expression of opinion, etc.; suppression of any tendency to passionate action; in early use, esp. self-control, restraint, or forbearance, when provoked to anger or impatience.

[*a* **1250** R. GROSSETESTE (in Godef. *Compl.*), C'est force et temperaunce.]

*a* **1340** HAMPOLE *Psalter* xxxiii. 2 Debonere men þat has temperaunce in all thynge. **1382** WYCLIF *Col.* iii. 12 Therfore clothe ȝou..[with] the entrailis of mercy, benygnite, and mekenesse, temperaunce [Gr. πραότητα, L. *modestiam*, TINDALE to *R.V.* meekness], and pacience. *c* **1386** CHAUCER *Frankl. T.* 57 On euery wrong a man may nat be wreken, After the tyme moste be temperaunce. **14..** in *Tundale's Vis.* (1843) 135 Hys hart dawnt so by temperance To voyde rancour and plante in sufferaunce. **14..** in *Wars Eng. in France* (1864) II. 521 The iiij. cardinalle vertuse, named Justice, Prudence, Force, and Temperaunce. **1511** COLET *Serm. Conf. & Ref.* B vij b, The lawes that commaunde sobernes ..and temperance in adournynge of the body. **1552** HULOET, Temperaunce..is a moderate gouernaunce of reason, and also as one of the car[di]nall vertues. **1590** SPENSER *F. Q.* I. viii. 34 He..calmd his wrath with goodly temperance. **1654** WHITELOCKE *Jrnl. Swed. Emb.* (1772) II. 421 Yett it pleased God to give me much patience and temperance to beare this..ingratitude. **1781** GIBBON *Decl. & F.* xxvii. III. 9 The choice of a venerable old man.. announced to the court of Constantinople the gravity and temperance of the British usurper. **1851** HUSSEY *Papal Power* iii. 162 The moral force of the testimony..is weakened by the manifest defects of the case, and some want of temperance in the mode of conducting it.

**b.** Self-restraint in the indulgence of any natural affection or appetency; moderation in the pursuit of a gratification, in the exercise of a feeling, or in the use of anything; in early use often = chastity.

**1340** *Ayenb.* 124 Temperance [lokeþ þane man] þet he ne by be none kuede loue amerd. **1526** TINDALE *Acts* xxiv. 25 As he preached of Iustice, temperaunce [*Vulg.* castitate, WYCLIF, COVERD. chastite, *Rhem.* chastitie], and Iudgement to come, Felix trembled. **1535** COVERDALE *Gal.* v. 23 The frute of the sprete is loue, ioye, peace,..goodnesse, faithfulnes, mekenesse, temperaunce. **1576** FLEMING *Panopl. Epist.* 270 She forgetteth temperance, and waxeth incontinent. **1603** HOLLAND *Plutarch's Mor.* 65 When it ruleth and ordereth our lust or concupiscense, limiting out a certaine measure, and lawfull proportion of time unto pleasures, it is called Temperance. **1656** STANLEY *Hist. Philos.* v. (1701) 164 Temperance, the Principle of subduing Desires, and yielding to no Pleasures, but living Moderately. **1846** TRENCH *Mirac.* i. (1862) 112 The secret of temperance lies not in the scanty supply, but in the strong self-restraint. **1875** MANNING *Mission H. Ghost* x. 266 Temperance is the excellence of the will in controlling the passion for pleasure.

**2.** *spec.* The avoidance of excess in eating and drinking; *esp.*, in later use, moderation in regard to intoxicants, sobriety. Now often applied to the practice or principle of total abstinence from alcoholic drink; teetotalism.

[**1509** FISHER *Funeral Serm. C'tess of Richmond* Wks. (1876) 293 Her sobre temperaunce in metes & drynkes was knowen to al them that were conuersaunt with her.] **1542** BOORDE *Dyetary* ix. (1870) 251 Surfetes do kyll many men, and temporaunce doth prolonge the lyfe. **1697** DAMPIER *Voy.* (1729) I. 69 Having..agreed upon some particular Rules, especially of Temperance and Sobriety. *a* **1718** PENN *Tracts* Wks. 1726 I. 909 Temperance,..Properly and strictly speaking it refers to Diet. **1727** BAILEY vol. II, *Temperance*..the two Species of it are *Sobriety*, which moderates our eating and drinking, and *Chastity*. **1727–46** THOMSON *Summer* 1609 Sound Temperance, Healthful in heart and look. **1775** ASH, *Temperance*, Moderation, the opposite to gluttony and drunkenness. **1826** (*title*) American Society for the Promotion of Temperance. **1849** COBDEN in Morley *Life* xviii. (1902) 69/1 With a delicate frame..I have been enabled, by temperance, to do the work of a strong man. **1887** MISS BRADDON *Like & Unlike* i, Where I can enjoy a stiff glass of grog with my feet on the hobs, and with nobody to preach temperance. **1890** BESANT *Demoniac* i, Not the least breath of suspicion had ever rested upon him in the matter of temperance.

**b.** *attrib.* usually, Pertaining to, practising, or advocating total abstinence, as *temperance association, drink, lecture, man, meeting, movement, reformation, society, work*; temperance hotel, inn, one where no intoxicants are sold or provided.

**1836** J. HUME *Sp. Ho. Com.* 24 Mar., There were perhaps many present, who were advocates of Temperance Societies. **1837** DICKENS *Pickw.* xxxiii, The Brick Lane Branch of the United Grand Junction Ebenezer Temperance Association. **1850** E. ELLIOTT *More Verse & Prose, Beware Dogmas* 9 James..keeps, abjuring rum and gin, A Temperance inn. **1855** *Zoologist* XIII. 4681 Assisting Father Mathew in the temperance-movement. **1886** C. E. PASCOE *London of To-day* iii. (ed. 3) 55 One of the best 'temperance' dining-places in London. **1890** BESANT *Demoniac* v, Captain and crew must be all temperance men: there is not to be one single drop of drink..put on board. **1890** DAWSON BURNS (*title*) Temperance History.

**II.** †**3. a.** The action or fact of tempering; mingling or combining in due proportion, adjusting, moderating, modification, toning down, bringing into a temperate or moderate state (see TEMPER *v.* 1–5): = TEMPERAMENT 8, 9.

**1398** TREVISA *Barth. De P. R.* v. xli. (Bodl. MS.), For temperans and keling of þe lifte side. *c* **1440** *Alphabet of Tales* 280 Be temperans of a mervalos evynhed, ather of þaim loste ane ee. **1530** PALSGR. 279/2 Temperaunce, *atrempance, attemperance.* **1531** ELYOT *Gov.* III. xxiv, By the whiche mutuall coniunction and iust temperaunce of those two studyes he attayned to suche a fourme in all his gouernaunce. **1552** HULOET, Temperaunce or temperynge, or moderation of mynglyng thynges togither, *temperatura.* **1596** DALRYMPLE tr. *Leslie's Hist. Scot.* I. (S.T.S.) 111 A forme of commoune weil, quhair the people haue the hail authoritie,..bot wᵗ sik temperance, that cheif vpon thair king, and counsel..the Repub. does depend.

†**b.** A tempered or properly proportioned consistence, constitution, or state; temperate condition, moderateness: = TEMPERAMENT 1, 2. *Obs.*

**1471** RIPLEY *Comp. Alch.* IV. iv. in Ashm. *Theat. Chem. Brit.* (1652) 145 And so promotyd unto most perfyt temperance. **1533** ELYOT *Cast. Helthe* (1539) 1 b, Fyre..is the clarifier of other elementes, if they be vyciate or out of their naturall temperaunce. *Ibid.* 17 They be in the highest degree of heate and drithe, aboue the iuste temperaunce of mannes body. **1595** SPENSER *Col. Clout* 553 Through the myld temperance of her goodly raies. **1607** TOPSELL *Four-f. Beasts* (1658) 345 Boiled until they come unto a soft temperance. **1638** COWLEY *Love's Riddle* III. i, But were all Men of my Temperance, and Wisdom too, You should woo us.

†**c.** The keeping of time in music. *Obs.*

**1549** *Compl. Scotl.* vi. 39 Ther syndry soundis hed nothir temperance nor tune.

†**4.** Moderate temperature; freedom from the extremes of heat and cold; mildness of weather or climate; temperateness; cf. TEMPERAMENT 4, 5, TEMPERATURE 6, 7. *Obs.*

**1432–50** tr. *Higden* (Rolls) I. 75 Hit ioyethe in temperaunce, felenge neither coldenesse ne heete. *c* **1440** *Alphabet of Tales* 96 Whar þer was temperans of þe ayr & sownd of watir rynyng, & syngyng of burdis, and gude smell of flowris. **1542** BOORDE *Dyetary* viii. (1870) 247 In your beed lye not to hote nor to colde, but in a temporaunce. **1596** DALRYMPLE tr. *Leslie's Hist. Scot.* (S.T.S.) I. 5 Sa grett clemencie and temperance of the wathir. **1610** SHAKS. *Temp.* II. i. 42 It [the island] must needs be of subtle, tender, and delicate temperance.

[*Note.* L. *temperantia* (whence F. and Eng. *temperance*) was used by Cicero to render Plato's σωφροσύνη 'soundmindedness, prudence, moderation, sobriety, self-control', in Plato and in the Stoics, one of the original four (cardinal) virtues, φρόνησις, δικαιοσύνη, ἀνδρεία, σωφροσύνη, rendered in L. by Jerome and Augustine *prudentia, iustitia, fortitudo, temperantia*; also in Albertus Magnus, Aquinas, and the mediæval writers generally, and in the med.L. version of Aristotle's Nicom. Ethics. Thence the use of *temperaunce* by Grosseteste, and the earlier Eng. use. But *temperantia* was not orig. a Christian word: it occurs nowhere in the Vulgate or the Antiqua; it is not one of the 'fruits of the Spirit', even in the expanded list in the Vulgate, in Galat. v. 23. By Wyclif, however, *temperaunce* was used to render L. *modestia* 'moderation', in the Rhemish, *modestie*. In the Eng. versions from Tindale onward, *temperance* or *temperancie*, renders Gr. ἐγκράτεια 'self-mastery or restraint, esp. of certain sensual impulses', in L. commonly *continentia*. In Acts xxiv. 25 Tindale, Cranmer, Geneva, 1611, and Revised have *temperance*, where Vulgate has *castitate*, Wyclif, Coverdale, Rhemish *chastite, -tie*. In 2 Peter i. 6 (bis) T. and Cov. have *temperancy*, Cr., Gen. etc., *temperaunce, -ance*; V. *abstinentia*, W. and Rhem. *absty-, abstinence*. In Gal. v. 22, T., Cr., Gen., have *temperancye, -ie*, Cov., 1611, Rev., *tempera(u)nce*; Vulg. (which interpolates 3 additional 'fruits of the spirit'), *continentia*, Wycl. and Rhem., *contynaunce, continencie*. Of the Engl. senses above, 1 a. corresponds to the L. *temperantia*, Gr. σωφροσύνη; 1 b. in general to Gr. ἐγκράτεια, of which sense 2 may be considered a specialized use.]

†**Temperancy.** *Obs.* Also 6 -ie. [ad. L. *temperantia*: see prec. and -ANCY.] = prec., as a quality or state, in senses 1, 2, 3 b; *esp.* moderation. Common in 16th c.; rare after 1630.

As to use in N.T. translations, see note to prec.

**1526** TINDALE *Gal.* v. 23 The frute off the sprete is love, ioye, peace, longe sufferynge,..meknes, temperancy [so CRANMER]. — *2 Pet.* i. 6 In vertue knowledge, and in knowledge temperancy [so COVERDALE], and in temperancy pacience. **1545** RAYNOLD *Byrth Mankynde* IV. iii. (1634) 190 If the matrix be distempered..then must ye reduce it againe to temperancie, by such remedies. **1577** tr. *Bullinger's Decades* (1592) 237 Some..will haue temperancie to extend farther than continencie. **1594** T. B. *La Primaud. Fr. Acad.* II. 232 According to the temperancie or intemperancie that is in vs, the affections of the soule also will be more moderate or immoderate. **1620** VENNER *Via Recta* ix. (1650) 263 Variety..of meats may offend with immoderation, never with temperancy. **1635** A. STAFFORD *Fem. Glory* (1869) 21 She knew Temperancy to be Gods, and Natures Favorite.

†**Temperant,** *a.* (*sb.*) *Obs.* Also 5 -aunt(e. [ad. L. *temperānt-em*, pr. pple. of *temperāre* to observe moderation: see TEMPER *v.* So F. *tempérant* (16th c. in Godef. *Compl.*).]

**1.** Of persons: Observing temperance or moderation; sober, temperate.

**1382** WYCLIF *1 Tim.* iii. 3 Not ȝouun moche to wyn, not smyter, but temperaunt [*v. r.* and 1388 temperat]. **1382** — *Tit.* iii. 2 Amoneste hem..for to be not litygious but temperaunt [*gloss* or pacient; *v. r.* and 1388 temperat] schewinge al myldenesse to alle men. *a* **1400** HYLTON *Scala Perf.* (W. de W. 1494) II. xxxix, Sleeth lustes of glotenye & makyth the soule sobre & temperaunte. **1594** T. B. *La Primaud. Fr. Acad.* II. 235 If the body be not temperant, hardly wil the soule be; and if the soule be intemperate, the body desireth not to be temperant.

**2.** Of climate: Temperate, mild, equable.

*c* **1440** *Pallad. on Husb.* I. 121 Northwarde in places hote, in places colde Southwarde, and temporaunt in Est and West.

**B.** *sb.* (*pl.*) Medicines that correct sharp humours; palliatives: = med.L. *temperantia*.

**1661** LOVELL *Hist. Anim. & Min.* 418 The catarrhe, cough, and difficulty of respiration..are..cured by temperants and impedients.

**Temperate** (te·mpĕrĕt), *a.* Forms: 4–7 temperat, (4–6 -orat(e), 6–7 temprate, 5– temperate. [ad. L. *temperāt-us* tempered, regulated, restrained, pa. pple. of *temperāre* to TEMPER.]

**1.** Of persons, their conduct, practices, etc.: Keeping due measure, self-restrained, moderate.

**a.** in earlier use *esp.* = L. *modestus*, Gr. ἐπιεικής, Not swayed by passion, gentle, mild, forbearing; in later use *esp.* not extreme, violent, or strongly partisan; moderate, dispassionate.

*c* **1380** WYCLIF *Wks.* (1880) 305 Clene religioun..is chast, pesible, temperat, tretable. **1382–8** [see TEMPERANT 1]. **1538** ELYOT, *Moderatus*, moderate, temperate. *Modestus*, temperate, well aduised. **1546** J. HEYWOOD *Prov.* (1867) 61 Without any temprate protestacion, Thus he began. **1560** DAUS tr. *Sleidane's Comm.* 378 He waxed hote..and rayled moste bitterly on them both, being a Germain,..both the Spaniardes and Italians were a great deale more temperate. **1595** SHAKS. *John* II. i. 195 Peace Lady, pause, or be more temperate. **1797** MRS. RADCLIFFE *Italian* xvii, Their conduct was more temperate. **1840** MILL *Diss. & Disc.* (1875) I. 407 This is a temperate statement. **1849** MACAULAY *Hist. Eng.* iv. I. 490 He belonged to the mildest and most temperate section of the Puritan body. **1888** BRYCE *Amer. Commw.* (1889) II. lxxxv. 337 A majority is tyrannical when it..suppresses fair and temperate criticism.

(*b*) Of a horse: Not over-excitable or impetuous.

**1890** 'R. BOLDREWOOD' *Col. Reformer* (1891) 150 The filly..proving after trial high-couraged and temperate.

**b.** Moderate and self-controlled as regards the indulgence of appetites or desires; abstemious, sober; continent; in late use *spec.* moderate or abstemious in the use of alcoholic drinks.

*c* **1430** LYDG. *Min. Poems* (Percy Soc.) 66 Temperat dyete, temperat travaile. **1531** ELYOT *Gov.* III. xx, He that is temperate fleeth pleasures voluptuous, and with the absence of them is nat discontented. **1573–80** BARET *Alv.* T 116 A moderate and temperate supper. **1598** BARCKLEY *Felic. Man* (1631) 503 A temperate man that is contented with little. **1678** tr. *Lessius*, etc. (title) The Temperate Man, or the right way of Preserving Life and Health. **1799** S. & HT. LEE *Canterb. T., Old Wom.* (ed. 2) I. 367 [His] temperate habits made him look on luxury with disgust. **1836** J. HUME *Sp. Ho. Com.* 24 Mar., I would wish to bring the people round to temperate habits by giving them cheaper wines. **1875** JOWETT *Plato* (ed. 2) V. 76 The temperate life has gentle pains and pleasures. **1890** BESANT *Demoniac* ii, That a young man of strictly temperate habits should thus suddenly become a drunkard.

**2.** Of things, actions, qualities, conditions, etc.: Tempered, not excessive in degree; moderate.

**1398** TREVISA *Barth. De P. R.* v. xxiii. (Bodl. MS.), He makeþ þe voice smeþe & euen & temperatte. *Ibid.* x. viii. (1495) 379 By temperate blaste of wynde sparkles ben kyndlyd, and quenchyd by stronge blaste. **1471** RIPLEY *Comp. Alch.* v. xviii. in *Ashm.* (1652) 152 Make thy fyre so temperat. *Ibid.* x. xi [see QUINARITY]. **1551** TURNER *Herbal* I. F ij, Thys herbe semeth to be of a temporate warmnes. **1610** HOLLAND *Camden's Brit.* (1637) 689 Yorkeshire..is thought to be in a temperate measure fruitfull. **1625** BACON *Ess., Plantations* (Arb.) 533 Let not the Gouernment..depend vpon too many Counsellours,..but vpon a temperate Number. **1687** A. LOVELL tr. *Thevenot's Trav.* I. 144 They put their Eggs in Ovens, which they heat with so temperate a warmth,..that chickens are..hatched in them. **1844** H. H. WILSON *Brit. India* I. I. viii. 561 With respect to extending Christianity..it must proceed from temperate and gradual proceedings. **1855** PRESCOTT *Philip II*, I. I. iv. 51 At the temperate hour of nine, the bridal festivities closed.

**3.** *spec.* Of the weather, season, climate, etc.: Moderate in respect of warmth: neither too hot nor too cold; of mild and equable temperature.

**1432–50** tr. *Higden* (Rolls) II. 239 That tyme was as the temperate tyme of yer. **1484** CAXTON *Fables of Æsop* v. viii, This yere shalle be the most temperate and the moost fertyle that euer thou sawest. **1587** *Mirr. Mag., Albanact* xliv, So cleare the ayre, so temperate the clime. **1625** N. CARPENTER *Geog. Del.* II. ii. (1635) 22 Who findes not by experience one Countrey hot, another cold, a third temperate? **1698** FRYER *Acc. E. India & P.* 186 It enjoys a Temperater Air than would be allowed by the Poet under the Fifth Zone. **1781** GIBBON *Decl. & F.* xvii. (1869) I. 437 The climate was healthy and temperate. **1830** LYELL *Princ. Geol.* I. 107 Mild winters and less temperate summers.

**b.** *Temperate zone*: Each of the two zones or belts of the earth's surface lying between the torrid and frigid zones; i. e. the *north temperate zone* between the tropic of Cancer and the arctic circle, and the *south temperate zone* between the tropic of Capricorn and the antarctic circle.

**1551** RECORDE *Cast. Knowl.* (1556) 64 Betweene those Frozen zones, and the Burning zone, they appointed two Temperat zones. **1625** N. CARPENTER *Geog. Del.* I. ix. (1635) 206 The Temperate Zone is the space contained betwixt the Tropicke and the Polar circle. **1880** HAUGHTON *Phys. Geog.* iii. 125 The temperate zones owe very little of their heat to the latent heat of vapour formed in the torrid zone.

**4.** Of monarchy or sovereignty, hence also of the sovereign: Restricted in extent of authority; not absolute; limited; constitutional. *Obs.* or *arch.*

**1560** DAUS tr. *Sleidane's Comm.* 307 Themperour hath done herein the duty of a temperate Prince. **1604** E. G[RIMSTONE] *D'Acosta's Hist. Indies* VII. x. 525 These Barbarians, of temperate Kings became tyrants. **1621** BURTON *Anat. Mel.* II. iii. III. (1651) 325 Whether Monarchies should be mixt, temperate, or absolute. **1852** TENNYSON *Ode on Wellington* vii, That sober freedom out of which there springs Our loyal passion for our temperate Kings.

†**5.** Of clay or earth: = TEMPERED 1 d. *Obs.*

**1574** HYLL *Planting* 85 Close it with good temperate earth about the graffe.

**6.** *Music.* = TEMPERED 1 e.

**1876** tr. *Blaserna's Sound* vii. 137 The fruit of these manifold attempts..is the temperate scale, which reached its full development in the middle of the last century, especially by means of the works of Sebastian Bach.

†**7.** = *Tempered*, pa. pple. of TEMPER *v.* *Obs.*

**1398** TREVISA *Barth. De P. R.* III. xix. (1495) d vj b/1 By the drawynge of the ayre the brayne is temperat & comforted. **1634** HOLLAND *Pliny* xx. xiv. II. 61 [Nep] mixed with a third part of bread, and so temperat [*ed.* 1601 tempered] and incorporat with vinegre to the form of a liniment.

†**Te·mperate,** *v.* *Obs.* [f. ppl. stem of L. *temperāre* to TEMPER. (Occurs earlier as pa. pple. = L. *temperātus*: see prec. 7: cf. -ATE[3] 3–5.)] = TEMPER *v.*

**1.** *trans.* To mix suitably; to moderate, qualify, mitigate, allay; = TEMPER *v.* 1, 2; to bring into a proper state or condition; = TEMPER *v.* 5.

*a* **1540** BARNES *Wks.* (1573) 217/1 For mollifying, and temperatyng of those thinges, that seemed to bee somewhat hardly spoken. **1549** *Compl. Scot.* vi. 53 The verteous heyt of it [the sun] temperatis al the sternis of the firmament. **1597** A. M. tr. *Guillemeau's Fr. Chirurg.* *iv, I endevoured to temperate the rigoure of the first Chyrurgians. **1607** TOPSELL *Four-f. Beasts* (1658) 431 The same..doth temperate and confirm the brains of any man. **1615** G. SANDYS *Trav.* 228 A clime..exceeding hote;..yet sometimes temperated by the comfortable winds. **1698** CROWNE *Caligula* IV. Dram. Wks. 1874 IV. 407 If I were wise I'd temp'rate love with art. **1750** JOHNSON *Rambler* 17 ¶ 10 Nor is fear..less to be temperated by this universal medicine of the mind.

**2.** To rule; to curb, restrain; = TEMPER *v.* 7, 8.

*a* **1568** ASCHAM *Scholem.* (Arb.) 112 This fulnes as it is not to be misliked in a yong man, so in farder aige..it is to be tempered, or else discretion and iudgement shall seeme to be wanting in him. **1642** H. MORE *Song of Soul* II. i. II. xliii, She temperates Her starrie orb, makes her bright forms to wend Even as she list. **1648** LIGHTFOOT *Horæ Hebraicæ* (1684) II. 572 Let him..learn from you to temperate his passions.

Hence **Te·mperated** *ppl. a.*, tempered, moderated; **Te·mperating** *vbl. sb.* and *ppl. a.*

*a* **1540** Temperatyng [see sense 1]. **1643** PRYNNE *Sov. Power Parl.* App. 77 Placing the power in such sort in the King, that the temperating of it should be in the middle Iudge. **1737** BOYSE *The Olive* xviii, Hence the mild Sweets of temperated Sway. **1753** N. TORRIANO *Gangr. Sore Throat* 22 Broths mixt with Juice of aperitive and temperating Herbs. **1788** *Misc.* in *Ann. Reg.* 134/2 The moon was darting her temperated rays through the shade. **1831** J. DAVIES *Manual Mat. Med.* 5 Acids, when weak or diluted, act..as refrigerant and temperating medicines.

**Temperately** (te·mpĕrĕli), *adv.* [f. TEMPERATE *a.* + -LY [2].]

In a temperate manner or degree; moderately; in or with moderation, without excess.

**1398** TREVISA *Barth. De P. R.* v. xxv. (Bodl. MS.), If þe heed is temperatlich greete and þe nolle of þe nekke sommedele greet. **1528** PAYNELL *Salerne's Regim.* a iv b, Blud ..is temperatlye hotte and moyste. **1542** BOORDE *Dyetary* xi. (1870) 262 Breade .must be temporatly salted. **1594** BLUNDEVIL *Exerc.* IV. xix. (1636) 474 Venus is temperatly cold and moyst. **1670** EACHARD *Cont. Clergy* 91 Oh, how prettily and temperately may half a score children be maintained with almost twenty pounds per annum! **1870** J. BRUCE *Life Gideon* xvii. 316 The Lord's own quiet and kindly admonition would excite temperately the fears of Gideon.

**b.** With self-restraint; without violence or passion; dispassionately; chastely.

**1525** LD. BERNERS *Froiss.* II. xli. 127 [He] determyned in hymselfe to answere temporatly. **1556** J. HEYWOOD *Spider & F.* v. 31, I temprately must temper mine inuension, To pleade my right in reason not in rage. **1613** FLETCHER, etc. *Hon. Man's Fort.* I. iii, When our affections had their liberty, Our kisses met as temperatelie as The hands of sisters, or of brothers. **1796** BURKE *Regic. Peace* iv. Wks. IX. 32 It must be pardoned by those, who are very regularly and temperately in the wrong. **1818** A. THOMSON in Landreth *Life & Min.* iv. (1869) 168, I and other dissenting ministers firmly but temperately remonstrated against this. **1869** H. AINSWORTH *Hilary St. Ives* II. xxiii, When you speak more temperately,..I will answer you.

**c.** With moderation in eating and drinking; soberly, abstemiously.

*c* **1400** MAUNDEV. (Roxb.) xxxii. 144 Þai liffe so temperately and so soberly in meet and drink. **1617** MORYSON *Itin.* III. 87 He could not..use it temperately, but either would allow us no wine at all, or at one meale drunke off a whole great bottell. **1741** MIDDLETON *Cicero* I. vi. 449 The more temperately they would use it. *Mod.* A hot climate is not dangerous to those who live temperately.

**Te·mperateness.** [f. as prec. + -NESS.] The quality of being temperate.

**1.** Moderateness, moderation; freedom from excess; temperance.

**1398** TREVISA *Barth. De P. R.* v. xxvii. (Bodl. MS.), Þe spirites þat comeþ fro þe senewes and veynes ben isaued by temperatnes and ynorsched. *Ibid.* VIII. iii, It was nede þat þere were wateres to bringe þat heuenlich heete to temperattnes. **1592** WYRLEY *Armorie, Ld. Chandos* 56, I.. would not spare But liberall be, fraught with temperatenesse. **1651** *Life of Bucer* in *Fuller's Abel Rediv.* (1867) I. 186 He was much admired..for his temperateness in his diet. **1746** R. JAMES *Health's Impr.* Introd. 56 All Heat beyond Temperateness..must necessarily be pernicious in all Distempers, where there is a Tendency to an alcaline Putrefaction.

**b.** Self-restraint; freedom from passion or mental heat; mildness, calmness.

**1595** DANIEL *Civ. Wars* (1609) I. xxv, Langley; whose mild temperatness Did tend unto a calmer quietnesse. **1865** *Sat. Rev.* 18 Feb. 184/2 The peculiar temperateness of assertion,..for which extremely young men are so notorious. **1871** *Athenæum* 15 July 84 The same temperateness and fairness is displayed; while the author maintains what is commonly called orthodoxy.

**2.** *spec.* Of climatic conditions: Freedom from extremes of heat and cold or atmospheric disturbance; equability and mildness of climate.

**1525** LD. BERNERS *Froiss.* II. clxxi. [clxvii.] 506 By reason of this hayle the ayre was brought into a good temperatenesse. **1563** GOLDING *Cæsar* Pref. (1565) 7 The fertility of the soile, the temperatenesse of the aire. **1603** KNOLLES *Hist. Turks* (1638) 265 Where the temperatenesse of the aire, and liuely springs, with the fruitfulnesse of the soile, doth euery where yeeld plenty. **1610** HOLLAND *Camden's Brit.* I. 2 The temperatenesse..of this Iland. **1828** WEBSTER s.v., The temperateness of the weather or of a climate.

† **Tempera·tion.** *Obs. rare*[−1]. [ad. L. *temperātiōn-em*, n. of action from *temperāre* to TEMPER.] The action of tempering; qualification.

**1615** CROOKE *Body of Man* 408 The end also is the same, to wit, nutrition, temperation or qualification, and expurgation.

**Temperative,** *a.* Now *rare* or *Obs.* [ad. late L. *temperātīv-us*, f. *temperāre*: see TEMPER *v.* and -IVE.] Having the quality of tempering; alleviative, mitigating; tending to temperateness.

*c* **1430** LYDG. *Min. Poems* (Percy Soc.) 196 Ayer of nature yevith inspiracioun, To mannys herte thyng moost temperatiff. **1621** T. GRANGER *On Eccles.* 15 The ayr drawne in, and sent forth by the breath, which is temperatiue of the hearts heate. **1825** J. WEDDELL *Voy.* 95 This climate appears to be in general much more temperative now than it was forty years ago.

**b.** *Mus.* Having the purpose of tempering or producing temperament: see TEMPERAMENT 10.

**1727–41** [see TEMPER *v.* 15 b].

† **Te·mperator.** *Obs. rare.* In 6 -our. [ad. L. *temperātor*.] One who tempers, rules, or directs.

**1591** SPARRY tr. *Cattan's Geomancie* 25 They called ♄ [Saturn] the Father of the gods, and temperatour of times.

**Temperature** (te·mpĕrătiŭɹ). [ad. L. *temperātūra* the process or result of tempering, due measure and proportion, f. ppl. stem of *temperāre*: see -URE. Cf. F. *température* (1539 in Godef.).]

† **1.** The action or process of tempering, in various senses of the verb; mixing or combination (of elements). *Obs.*

**1550** LATIMER *Serm. at Stamford* Serm. (1562) 100 We should learne *viam dei*, Goddes waye, and that truly, withoute mixture, temperature, blaunching, powderyng. **1569** J. SANFORD tr. *Agrippa's Van. Artes* 159 Plinie declareth that, in the time of Tiberius..the temperature of glasse was invented. **1600** HOLLAND *Livy* IX. xlvi. 350 Upon this good temperature of degrees, he purchased the surname of Maximus. **16..** HOLLAND (Webster, 1864), Made a temperature of brass and iron together. **1677** *Cleveland's Poems* Life, He was Judge Advocate..and, by an excellent temperature of both, was a just and prudent Judge for the King, and a faithful Advocate for the Countrey.

† **b.** *concr.* That which tempers. *Obs. rare.*

**1609** BIBLE (Douay) *Ezek.* xiii. *Comm.*, A wal of clay or morter without straw or other temperature, is washed away with rayne.

† **2.** The fact or state of being tempered or mixed, mixture; also, the condition resulting from the mixture or combination in various proportions of ingredients or elements; the composition, consistence, or complexion, so produced. *Obs.*

**1533** ELYOT *Cast. Helthe* (1541) 8 By the increase or diminution of any of them [the four humours] in quantitie or qualytie, ouer or vnder their natural assignement, inequall temperature commeth into the body. **1538** — *Dict.* Addit., *Crasis*, a greke worde, sygnyfieth complexion, temperature, or myxture of naturall humours. **1562** TURNER *Herbal* II. 28 b, There is in it a small temperature of the principales of the ayer and fyre. **1601** HOLLAND *Pliny* XXIV. ix. II. 505 The last temperature is that, which in Latine they call Ollaria, as one would say, the pot-brasse, for it taketh the name of that vessell whereto it is most emploied; and this is by tempering with every hundred pound weight of brasse, three or four pound weight of argentine lead or tin. **1602** *How Man may Chuse Gd. Wife* IV. iii, Hath he not..Upon that crimson temperature of your cheeks, Laid a lead colour with his boist'rous blows? **1605** TIMME *Quersit.* I. ix. 36 Ashes have not exactly one temperature. **1675** *Art Contentm.* IV. xii, In all the concerns [of human life]..there is such a temperature and mixture, that the good do's more than equal the ill. *a* **1768** SECKER *Serm.* (1770) III. i. 6 The first of these, and the Foundation of all the rest, is a proper Temperature of Fear and Love. **1786–7** BONNYCASTLE *Astron.* xxi. 374 It is not credible that beings of our make and temperature could live upon them. **1826** R. HALL *Wks.* (1832) VI. 53 Such a temperature of light and shade as that which distinguishes all his discoveries of himself.

† **3.** Due measure and proportion in action, speech, thought, etc.; freedom from excess or violence; moderation. *Obs.*

**1536** CROMWELL in Merriman *Life & Lett.* (1902) II. 3 To haue the same vsed and setfurthe in suche a temperature, as by your wisedome ye shall thinke may conduce to thadvauncement of his affayres there. **1539** *Ibid.* 172 Vsing ..in the proposicion therof & answers to be geven that sobernes and temperature as he may perceive is to be vsed. **1609** HOLLAND *Amm. Marcell.* XXVI. ii. 286 As I hope, Fortune..will give the same unto me, seeking diligently.. after a temperature and moderation. **1659** C. NOBLE *Mod. Answ. Immod. Queries* 14 If he would but say and do with that moderation and temperature as the late Protector.. has said and done.

† **b.** A middle condition or position, a mean between opposites; a middle course, a compromise.

**1594** *Mirr. Policie* (1599) D iij, A vertuous temperature betweene two vicious extremities. **1601** HOLLAND *Pliny* (1634) I. 37 In the midst of the earth there is an wholesome mixture from both sides:..the habit of mens bodies of a mean and indifferent constitution, the colour also shewing a great temperature. **1652** NEEDHAM tr. *Selden's Mare Cl.* 37 To finde..some kinde of temperature, whereby the Republick might receive the Rights belonging thereunto from the Austrian subjects sailing those Seas. **1712**? HUGHES *Spect.* No. 467 ¶ 9 His Constitution is a just Temperature between Indolence on one hand and Violence on the other.

† **4.** The character or nature of a substance as supposed to be determined by the proportions of the four qualities (*hot* or *cold*, and *dry* or *moist*); = TEMPERAMENT 3. *Obs.*

**1533** ELYOT *Cast. Helthe* (1539) 17 Of the temperature of meates to be receyued. *Ibid.* 34 b, Drythe..happeneth in the substance of the body, either by to moche labour, or by the proper temperature of age. **1578** LYTE *Dodoens* lxiv. 95 Hartes Horne is colde and dry in temperature much like Plantayne. **1601** HOLLAND *Pliny* XVII. xxii. I. 529 If the ground be of a middle temperature, there ought to bee a space of fiue foot distance betweene every vine. **1610** GUILLIM *Heraldry* III. xii. (1611) 120 The general received opinion is that the life of all things doth consist in calido and humido which is the temperature of blood. **1616** SURFL. & MARKH. *Country Farme* 589 As concerning the temperature of beere there is no doubt but that it is hot. [**1771** LUCKOMBE *Hist. Print.* 366 An unproper temperature of the Tympan..is, when it is dry in one place and moist in another.]

† **5.** The combination of 'humours' in the body; also, the bodily habit or constitution attributed to this; = TEMPERAMENT 6. *Obs.*

**1561** HOLLYBUSH *Hom. Apoth.* 15 b, To know by what complexion or temperatur yᵉ diseases are caused. *a* **1577** SIR T. SMITH *Commw. Eng.* (1609) 5 In a mans body foure complexions or temperatures, as cholericke, sanguine, flegmatique & melancholique. **1600** HAKLUYT *Voy.* (1810) III. 340 The victuall of the countrey..might have been thought to have altered our temperatures. *a* **1618** RALEIGH *Rem.* (1644) 134 It is evident also, that men differ very much in the temperature of their bodies. **1750** JOHNSON *Rambler* No. 43 ¶ 1 There is no temperature so exactly regulated but that some humour is fatally predominant. **1837** T. JONES *Chr. Warrior* IV. vi. 97 He [Satan] observes the temperature and complexion of such a man. If he be sanguine .. he tempts him to incontinency.

† **b.** Constitutional bent of mind; disposition; = TEMPERAMENT 7. *Obs.*

**1594** SPENSER *Amoretti* xiii, In that proud port..Most goodly temperature ye may descry; Myld humblesse, mixt with awfull majesty. **1605** BACON *Adv. Learn.* I. iii. § 4 As touching the manners of learned men..no doubt there be amongst them, as in other professions, of all temperatures. **1610** BARROUGH *Meth. Physick* I. xxviii. (1639) 45 It..is chiefly engendred of melancholy occupying the mind, and changing the temperature of it. **1768** STERNE *Sent. Journ.* (1778) I. 167 Any one may do a casual act of good-nature, but a continuation of them shews it is a part of the temperature.

† **6.** A tempered or temperate condition of the weather or climate; also, a (qualified or specified) condition of these. *Obs.*

**1531** ELYOT *Gov.* III. xxvi, The temperature or distemperature of the regions. **1578** T. N. tr. *Conq. W. India* 217 Desiring of Him by Prayers to give raine and temperature, that the Earth may bring foorth Corne, Fruite, Hearbes,..and all other necessaries. **1585** T. WASHINGTON tr. *Nicholay's Voy.* IV. xxiv. 139 Thracia..[is] of an yll temperature, the ayre being vnwholesome, & not healthfull. **1624** CAPT. SMITH *Virginia* II. 21 The temperature of this Country doth agree well with English constitutions. **1697** DAMPIER *Voy.* I. xix. 529, I look upon this latitude [the Cape of Good Hope] to be one of the mildest and sweetest for its temperature, of any whatsoever. **1727** SWIFT *State Irel.* ¶ 35 A country so favoured by nature..both in fruitfulness of soil, and temperature of climate.

**7.** The state of a substance or body with regard to sensible warmth or coldness, referred to some standard of comparison; *spec.* that quality or condition of a body which in degree varies directly with the amount of heat contained in the body, and inversely with its heat-capacity; commonly manifested by its imparting heat to, or receiving it from, contiguous bodies, and usually measured by means of a thermometer or similar instrument. (Now the ordinary sense.)

**1670** BOYLE (*title*) Of the Temperature of the Submarine Regions as to Heat and Cold. *Ibid.* iii, This person I diligently examined..as to the temperature of the lower parts of the sea (the knowledge of which is that alone that concerns us in this place); he several times complained to me of the coldness of the deep water. **1710** STEELE *Tatler* No. 179 ¶ 7 A moderate Expence of Fire,..serves to keep this large Room in a due Temperature. *a* **1743** G. MARTINE *Ess. & Obs. Thermometers* (1772) 46 There is a Thermometer in frequent use in England, wherein they conceive the middle temperature of the air as neither hot nor cold, which..they mark Gr. o, and number both above and below. **1791** tr. *Pictet's Ess. Fire* 11 The thermometer will show, by the degree observed on its scale, the temperature of the liquid. **1815** J. SMITH *Panorama Sc. & Art* II. 47 The cause of them is, the difference in temperature between the air over the land and that over the water. **1820** W. SCORESBY *Acc. Arctic Reg.* I. 48, I have determined the mean temperature of the month of May. **1860** TYNDALL *Glac.* I. xvi. 113 To record the lowest winter temperatures at the summit of the mountain. **1876** BRISTOWE *The. & Pract. Med.* (1878) 99 The normal temperature of the body has been variously estimated; but, on the average, seems, in the adult, to range between 98·4° and 99·5°. **1878** HUXLEY *Physiogr.* 72 A comparison of the temperatures shown by the two thermometers. **1888** MISS BRADDON *Fatal Three* I. v, I took their temperatures this morning before I went to church.

*fig.* **1862** STANLEY *Jew. Ch.* (1877) I. xiv. 272 The temperature of the zeal of the different portions of the nation.

**b.** (*colloq.*) *To have a temperature*, i. e. one higher than the normal, as in fever.

**1898** P. WHITE *Millionaire's Dau.* (ed. Tauchn.) 88 Do you think I have a temperature? **1904** E. F. BENSON *Challoners* (ed. Tauchn.) 318 He has..had a temperature for nearly a week.

† **8.** The temper of steel; = TEMPER *sb.* 5. *Obs.*

**1580** FRAMPTON *Iron & Steele* in *Joyf. Newes* (1596) 145 Iron so harde..that being wrought, it serueth for Steele, chiefly with a temperature that is giuen to it. **1601** HOLLAND *Pliny* XXXIV. xiv. II. 514 All our steele is of a more soft and gentle temperature than that of the Levant. **1603** [see TEMPER *v.* 14]. **1630** *R. Johnson's Kingd. & Commw.* 249 Giving them the Iron Mines of Biskay .. with the temperature of Baion, Bilbo, Toledo, and Calataiut.

† **9.** *Music.* = TEMPERAMENT *sb.* 10. *Obs. rare*[−1].

**1592** LYLY *Gallathea* III. iii, An Organist to tune your temperatures.

**10.** *attrib.* and *Comb.*, as *temperature-compensator, correction, log, sense*; **temperature-alarm**: see quot. 1877; **temperature-chart**, (*a*) a chart or card containing a *temperature-curve* or its equivalent; (*b*) a chart of a region indicating temperatures at different points, as by isotherms; **temperature-curve**, a curve showing variations of temperature, usually in relation to equal periods of time, *esp.* in clinical use.

**1871** W. SQUIRE (*title*) Temperature Variations in the Diseases of Children. **1877** KNIGHT *Dict. Mech.*, *Temperature alarm*, a device which automatically makes a signal when the temperature of the place where it is exceeds or falls below a determinate point. **1888** H. MORTEN *Hospital Life* 29, I admire her neat temperature chart, and then pass on to Nurse Lorna. **1893** A. S. ECCLES *Sciatica* 59 It appears to be possible, by close attention to the distribution of hyperæsthesia, temperature-sense for heat, and loss of cutaneous temperature, to localize in a measure the extent to which the nerve-trunk or its branches is involved. **1899** *Allbutt's Syst. Med.* VII. 639 A high temperature, marked fluctuations in the temperature curve, a rapid pulse. **1901** *Daily News* 12 Jan. 6/2 All the levers,.. connecting rods, carriers, supporting rods, bell cranks, temperature compensators.

Hence **Te·mperatured** *a.*, in comb., having temperature of a stated kind.

**1892** *Temple Bar Mag.* Nov. 444 The inner door shuts her ..into this pleasant-temperatured privacy.

**Tempere**, var. TEMPRE *a. Obs.*

**Tempered** (te·mpəɹd), *a.* [f. TEMPER *v.* and *sb.* + -ED.]

† **1.** Brought to or having a proper or desired temper, quality, or consistence (usually by mixture of elements or mingling of qualities); hence, of an intermediate or moderate quality free from either extreme; temperate. *Obs.* except as below.

*c* **1375** *Sc. Leg. Saints* xliv. (*Lucy*) 288 Þat [pyk & brynstan] grewit hyre nomare Na It a tempryt bath ware. **1422** tr. *Secreta Secret., Priv. Priv.* 222 The fryste tokyn of good complexcion Is temperid flesshe betwene nesshe and harde, and namely be-twen lene and fatte. *a* **1450** *Knt. de la Tour* (1906) 9 It is good to serue God..and lyue tempered and moderat lyff. **1577** HANMER *Anc. Eccl. Hist.* (1619) 422 Leaving in the midst a court, open to the tempered aire.

**b.** with adverbial qualification.

**1638** JUNIUS *Paint. Ancients* 284 To worke in us the impression of an excellently tempered complexion. **1726** LEONI *Alberti's Archit.* I. 101/2 Wine..kept in a dry cool place, always equally tempered. **1875** JOWETT *Plato* (ed. 2) III. 692 In the heaven above an excellently tempered climate.

**c.** That has been brought to the required degree of hardness and elasticity, as steel; also said vaguely or poetically of other metals.

**1655** MRQ. WORCESTER *Cent. Inv.* § 85 Such..bolts..being made of tempered Steel. **1697** DRYDEN *Æneid* VIII. 699 The temper'd metals clash, and yield a silver sound. **1727** GAY *Fables* xii. 6 Some..head the darts with tempered gold. **1789** R. HOLE *Arthur* v, No temper'd mail resists Fiacha's might. **1884** C. G. W. LOCK *Workshop Receipts* Ser. III. 271/1 The word 'tempered' (as applied to steel) should properly apply to all degrees of hardness denotable by colour in the colour test.

**d.** Mixed or compounded in due proportion; worked up to a suitable consistency.

**1697** DRYDEN *Virg. Georg.* I. 259 Delve of convenient Depth your thrashing Floor; With temper'd Clay then fill and face it o'er. **1707** MORTIMER *Husb.* (1721) II. 255 Cover the Head of the Stock with temper'd Clay, or with soft Wax. **1778** BP. LOWTH *Transl. Isaiah* Notes 158 Bricks, made with tempered clay and chopped straw.

**e.** *Mus.* That has been tuned or adjusted in pitch according to some TEMPERAMENT (sense 10).

**1727-41** [see TEMPER *v.* 15 b]. **1788** CAVALLO in *Phil. Trans.* LXXVIII. 250 One may easily perceive, how small is the difference between the perfect fifths of the latter, and the tempered ones of the former. **1829-32** GEN. P. THOMPSON *Exerc.* (1842) II. 139 Nobody denies that the different keys on tempered instruments have different qualities. **1875** ELLIS tr. *Helmholtz' Sensat. Tone* III. xvi. 510 We cannot.. fail to recognise the influence of tempered intonation upon the style of composition. **1879** C. H. H. PARRY in Grove *Dict. Mus.* II. 11/2 The larger intervals contained in the tempered octave are all to a certain extent out of tune.

**2.** Constituted or endowed with a specified temper or disposition (in various senses of *temper*).

**a.** Qualified by an adv.

**1390** GOWER *Conf.* I. 266 For his corage is tempred so, That thogh he mihte himself relieve, Yit wolde he noght an other grieve. **1456** SIR G. HAYE *Law Arms* (S.T.S.) 119 He that is vertuous in the vertu of that force, is ay temperit that he excedis nocht. **1529** MORE *Dyaloge* I. Wks. 162/2 It is so meruaylously tempered that a mouse may wade therin, and an Olyphaunt be drowned therin. **1615** BRATHWAIT *Strappado* (1878) 143 Perseus (one better tempered, Then to behold a Virgine slaughtered, Without assayd reuenge). *a* **1628** F. GREVIL *Sidney* (1907) 13 A quiet and equally tempered people. **1760-72** H. BROOKE *Fool of Qual.* (1809) III. 119 Children, sweetly tempered like their mother. **1839** THIRLWALL *Greece* VI. xlv. 15 Indications that its form of government was not unhappily tempered.

**b.** Qualified by an adj., so as to become a parasynthetic deriv. of TEMPER *sb.*: Having a temper of such a kind (*mild-tempered* = of mild temper).

(The 18th c. quots. show the gradual change from a.)

**1680** MOXON *Mech. Exerc.* x. 178 Heavy unequal tempered Stuff. **1747** tr. *Astruc's Fevers* 169 A cold mild-tempered easy patient. **1747** RICHARDSON *Clarissa* I. ii. 11 She aimed to be worse-tempered than ordinary. **1768** [see GOOD-TEMPERED]. **1788** MRS. HUGHES *Henry & Isabella* I. 80 Lamented that so mild a tempered, pretty kind of woman, should be subject to his tyranny. **1796** CHARLOTTE SMITH *Marchmont* III. 146 So unhappy a tempered woman. **1868** FARRAR *Seekers* III. i. (1875) 267 Controlled, modest, faithful, and even-tempered. **1901** *Wide World Mag.* VIII. 149/2 Hard at bargaining..and cross-tempered withal.

**3.** Modified by the admixture or influence of some other element; seasoned; moderated, mitigated, allayed, toned-down; limited.

**1654** JER. TAYLOR *Real Pres.* 298 In a moderated proportion..wine is mingled with water, as the Spirit with a man. And he receivs in the Feast..tempered wine unto faith. **1763** J. BROWN *Poetry & Mus.* v. 85 Sophocles appeared next; of a more sedate and tempered Majesty. **1791** BURKE *App. Whigs* Wks. VI. 135 No man can be a friend to a tempered monarchy who bears a decided hatred to monarchy itself. **1794** MRS. RADCLIFFE *Myst. Udolpho* xliv, They proceeded to a third room with a more tempered step. **1828** D'ISRAELI *Chas. I*, I. vi. 157 At this crisis, the tempered wisdom of the Queen saved the nation. **1893** *Westm. Gaz.* 23 Mar. 2/3 He..listened to his tempered speech—it was a much milder note than on Tuesday.

**Temperel**, obs. form of TEMPORAL.

**Temperer** (te·mpərəɹ). [f. TEMPER *v.* + -ER [1].] One who or that which tempers.

**1.** † One who mixes (*obs.*); one who prepares (clay, mortar, etc.); one who tempers (steel).

*a* **1617** HIERON *Wks.* II. 2 Still there will be..some temperers of leaven with the sweet lumpe of Gods sacred truth. *a* **1619** FOTHERBY *Atheom.* (1622) Pref. 6 Temperers of Lyme and Mortar. **1629** in Cochran-Patrick *Rec. Coinage Scotl.* (1876) II. 19 The Wardane Counterwardane Sinker and Temperer of the yrnes. **1839** URE *Dict. Arts* 883 The needles are now ready for the tempering..they..are carried in boxes to the temperer. **1896** *Chambers's Jrnl.* XIII. 22/2 The temperer requires a supply of water for the sufficient moistening of the clay.

† **2.** One who or that which allays or mitigates.

**1630** *R. Johnson's Kingd. & Commw.* 6 Whereas cold can without doors receive no temperer; heat on the contrarie is capable of very many. **1638** RIDER *Hor. Odes* I. (1644) 32 O thou my labour's sweetest temperer [L. *lenimen*].

**3.** One who uses or advocates temperament in music: see TEMPERAMENT 10.

**1829-32** GEN. P. THOMPSON *Exerc.* (1842) II. 140 Do the temperers maintain..that it is possible to mend this passage by any alteration in the intonation?

† **4.** = CRATER 1, mixing vessel. *Obs.*

**1675** HOBBES *Odyssey* 32 Then Nestor bids one fill the temperer With wine that aged was eleven year. **1676** — *Iliad* I. 452 Filled with sweet wine the Temp'rers stood.

**Tempering** (te·mpəriŋ), *vbl. sb.* [f. TEMPER *v.* + -ING [1].] The action of the verb TEMPER, in various senses; an instance of this.

**1382** WYCLIF *Prov.* xii. 11 Who is sweete, liueth in tempringis [1388 temperauncis]. — *Ezek.* xiii. 14 [see TEMPERURE 1]. *c* **1440** *Promp. Parv.* 488/2 Temperynge, or mesurynge of sundry thyngys to-gedyr. **1486** *Nottingham Rec.* III. 241 To a warkman for temperyng of morter. **1523** FITZHERB. *Husb.* § 4 The temperynge [of the plough] to go brode and narowe is in the settyng of the culture. **1538** [see TEMPER *v.* 18]. **1592** SHAKS. *Ven. & Ad.* 565 What waxe so frozen but dissolues with tempering? **1600** HOLLAND *Livy* XLI. xxv. 1113 Proxenus..dranke a cup of poison of his wives tempering, whereof he died. **1655** MOUFET & BENNET *Health's Improv.* (1746) 90 Concerning the tempering of the Air in our Houses. **1661** BOYLE *Unsucceeding Exper.* Wks. 1772 I. 341 The tempering of steel. **1726** LEONI tr. *Alberti's Archit.* I. 42/1 The Workman's..Manner of Building depends partly upon..his Stone, and partly upon the tempering of his Mortar. **1839** [see TEMPERER 1]. **1848** R. I. WILBERFORCE *Doctr. Incarnation* xiv. (1852) 409 Through the happy tempering of His natural qualities. **1875** OUSELEY *Harmony* v. 67 This interval..in tuning a keyed instrument, will require a much greater alteration, or tempering.

**b.** *attrib.* and *Comb.*, as *tempering-bar*, *-bath*, *-furnace*, *-machine*, *-screw*, *-wheel*: see quots.

**1823** J. BADCOCK *Dom. Amusem.* 138 The fusion is to be raised to the tempering height. **1825** J. NICHOLSON *Operat. Mechanic* 668 The tempering screw..is..added to keep the waggon in its proper situation, in whatever way the spring of the weighing machine may be acted upon by the friction. **1864** WEBSTER, *Tempering color*, the shade of color that indicates the degree of temper in tempering steel. **1877** KNIGHT *Dict. Mech.*, *Tempering-furnace*,..one specially contrived for imparting an equal heat to the articles to be tempered. *Ibid.*, *Tempering-machine*, one for handling heavy steel plates during the operations in tempering. *Ibid.*, *Tempering-wheel*, a device for..tempering clay for making brick, etc. **1891** *Cent. Dict.*, *Tempering-oven*, in glass-manuf., an annealing-oven used after the melting-oven.

**Te·mpering**, *ppl. a.* [f. as prec. + -ING [2].] That tempers; softening, mitigating.

**1612** SELDEN *Drayton's Poly-olb.* vi. Notes 97 Those that sing the tempering and mollifying Pæans to Apollo. **1817** BYRON *Lam. of Tasso* viii, Like steel in tempering fire. **1846** MCCULLOCH *Acc. Brit. Emp.* (1854) I. 91 The tempering influence of the ocean.

**Te·mperless**, *a. rare.* [f. TEMPER *sb.* + -LESS.] Having no moderation of temper.

*a* **1618** SYLVESTER *Panaretus* 1374 So swelling proud; so surly-browd the while; So temper-lesse.

**Temperment**: see TEMPERAMENT 3, quot. 1471.

**Temperour**, variant of TEMPERURE *Obs.*

**Temper-pin.** *Sc.* [f. TEMPER *sb.* + PIN *sb.*]

**1.** The wooden screw used in regulating the tightness of the band of a spinning-wheel; *fig.* temper, disposition.

**17..** in Ritson *Sc. Songs* (1794) I. 175 My spinning-wheel is auld and stiff,..To keep the temper pin in tiff, Employs aft my hand, sir. *a* **1796** BURNS *There was a Lass* i, Ay she shook the temper-pin. **1864** LATTO *Tam. Bodkin* iii, A hole in her chackit apron claught haud o' the temper pin, whan doon gaed Bessie an' the wheel. *Ibid.* x, Mr. G.'s temper pin was nae wise improved by the..catastrophe.

† **2.** A tuning-screw or peg of a violin, etc. *Obs.*

**1786** BURNS *Ep. Maj. Logan* iv, Heaven send your heart-strings aye in tune, And screw your temper-pins aboon. **1788** SHIRREFS *Poems* (1790) 339 Gin the temper-pin ye'll screw, And gi'es a sang.

**Temper-pot, -screw**: see TEMPER *sb.* 14.

† **Temperure.** *Obs.* Also 4-5 temprure, temperour(e. [a. OF. *tempreüre* (12th c. in Godef.) :—L. *temperātūra*: see TEMPERATURE.]

**1.** Tempering; *concr.* tempering liquid, etc.

**1388** WYCLIF *Ezek.* xiii. 14, Y schal distrie the wal, which ȝe pargetiden with out temperure [1382 temperynge; *Vulg.* absque temperamento]. *c* **1400** *Rom. Rose* 4177 The temprure of the mortere Was maad of licour wonder dere. **1426** LYDG. *De Guil. Pilgr.* 23524 Of their morter the temprure, Founded vppoun charyte, Of concord and fraternyte.

**2.** Adjustment of pitch, tuning; tunefulness.

**1390** GOWER *Conf.* I. 39 Arion, Which hadde an harpe of such temprure, And therto of so good mesure [etc.]. *Ibid.* III. 303 Of hire Harpe the temprure He tawhte hire ek.

**3.** Condition of the weather or climate; *esp.* temperate or good condition; = TEMPERATURE 6.

**1387** TREVISA *Higden* (Rolls) I. 179 Good corn contray, where þere is good temperure of heuene and of wedir [*coeli temperies*]. *Ibid.* II. 291 Þe temperure þat comeþ of hiȝnesse and lownesse of sterres and planetes, comeþ aȝen to temperure at þe fiftiþe ȝere. *a* **1485** FORTESCUE *Wks.* (1869) 477 Temperour of the ayre, clerenes of the sea.

**4.** = TEMPER *sb.* 5 (of steel, etc.), TEMPERATURE 8.

*c* **1407** LYDG. *Reson & Sens.* 1191 A bryght helme..of swych temprure, That pollex swerde ne noon armure May do therto no violence. *c* **1440** *Partonope* 1943 Hawbrek.. of goode mesure Mighty and strong and of good temperure.

**5.** Temperance, self-control, moderation.

*c* **1380** WYCLIF *Sel. Wks.* II. 256 Þe þridde vertue..is temperoure in oure dede. *c* **1440** *Jacob's Well* 142 Glotonye is, whan þou hast a talent, wyth-outyn temperure & mesure, to mete or drynke.

**Tempest** (te·mpėst), *sb.* Forms: 3- tempest; also 3-6 tempeste, 4-5 tempast, -e. [a. OF. *tempeste*, fem. (11th c. in *Roland*) = It., Prov. *tempesta*:—pop.L. **tempesta-m*, for cl. L. *tempestās*, *-ātem* season, weather, storm, f. *tempus* a time, a season; also a. OF. *tempest* masc. (13th c. in Godef.) = Prov. *tempest*:—L. **tempestum*. OF. had also **tempeste*, acc. sing. *tempesté*, pl. *tempestez* (12th c.) = Sp. *tempestád*, Pg. *tempestade*, It. *-ate*, *-ade*, :—L. *tempe·stās*, *tempestā-t-em*.]

**1.** A violent storm of wind, usually accompanied by a downfall of rain, hail, or snow, or by thunder.

*c* **1250** *Old Kentish Serm.* in *O. E. Misc.* 32 So hi were in þo ssipe so a-ros a great tempeste of winde. **1297** R. GLOUC. (Rolls) 1151 Hor folc hii lore in þe se þoru tempest [*v.r.* tempeste] moni on. *a* **1300** *Cursor M.* 6027 (Cott.) Israel for þis tempest [*Gött.* tempast] Was noþer harmed, man ne beist. **13..** *K. Alis.* 5810 (Bodl. MS.) Þe wederes stronge and tempestes þat hem duden grete molestes. *c* **1386** CHAUCER *Manciple's T.* 197 Euere crie agayn tempest and rayn. **1390** GOWER *Conf.* III. 203 A cruel king lich the tempeste, The whom no Pite myhte areste. *c* **1400** *Destr. Troy* 12467 Trees thurgh tempestes, tynde hade þere leues. **1535** COVERDALE 2 *Kings* ii. 1 Whan the Lorde was mynded to take vp Elias in the tempest. **1665** SIR T. HERBERT *Trav.* (1677) 389 Seven whole dayes and nights this tempest lasted. **1697** DRYDEN *Virg. Georg.* IV. 608 A Station safe for Ships, when Tempests roar. **1815** J. SMITH *Panorama Sc. & Art* II. 46 In some places the time of change is attended with calms, in others..with violent tempests. **1856** STANLEY *Sinai & Pal.* i. § 3. 68 The whole air filled..with a tempest of sand driving in your face like sleet.

**b.** A thunder-storm. *dial.*

*c* **1532** DU WES *Introd. Fr.* in *Palsgr.* 946/1 To be killed with tempest, *fouldroier*. **1712** HEARNE *Collect.* 30 June (O.H.S.) III. 408 We were forc'd by a tempest to stop at Yarnton. **1839** G. BIRD *Nat. Phil.* 212 Several instances have occurred of the fatal effects of a tempest..at a considerable distance from the spot..where the violence of the lightning appeared to have been chiefly exerted. *c* **1860** *Northamp. Dial.*, It's very still and black. I think we shall have a tempest to-night. **1883** *Hampsh. Gloss.*, *Tempest*, a thunder-storm.

**2.** *transf.* and *fig.* A violent commotion or disturbance; a tumult, rush; agitation, perturbation. *Tempest in a tea-pot*: see TEA-POT.

*c* **1315** SHOREHAM vii. 642 Þat best..þat hyt hedde ine hym y-nome Soche a tempeste. **13..** *Guy Warw.* (A.) 273 Now is Gij in gret tempest, Sorwe he makeþ wiþ þe mest. **1472** *Coventry Leet Bk.* 373 The gret tempestes diuisions & troubles that in late daies haue be in this our Reaume. **1588** SHAKS. *Tit. A.* I. i. 458 Cheere the heart, That dies in tempest of thy angry frowne. **1606** S. GARDINER *Bk. Angling* 12 Waues of tribulation, tempests of tentations. **1770** BURKE *Corr.* (1844) I. 243 In the midst of all this tempest the ministers..seem much at their ease. **1894** H. NISBET *Bush Girl's Rom.* 61 Helen Craven was very pale and very silent during this parental tempest. **1909** *Daily Chron.* 3 Dec. 1/2 This fine passage..drew a tempest of cheering.

† **b.** Calamity, misfortune, trouble. *Obs.*

*c* **1330** R. BRUNNE *Chron. Wace* (Rolls) 16541 Moryne & hunger..had reft..al þe folk wyþ tempest vnkynde. *c* **1470** HENRY *Wallace* VII. 394 For sleuth nor sleip sall nayne remayne in me, Off this tempest till I a wengeance se.

**3.** A confused or tumultuous throng; † a crowded assembly: cf. HURRICANE 2 b (*obs.*); a rushing or tearing crowd.

**1746** SMOLLETT *Advice* 30 *note*, Not unaptly styled a drum, from the noise and emptiness of the entertainment. There are also drum-major, rout, tempest, and hurricane, differing only in degrees of multitude and uproar. **1755** J. SHEBBEARE *Lydia* (1769) II. 309 How to spend their hours in London more agreeably than in routs, drums, hurricanes, and tempests. **1866** CARLYLE in *Morning Star* 5 Apr. 5/5 It turned out to be a tempest of wild horses, managed by young lads who had a turn for hunting with their grooms.

**b.** A person of stormy temper.

**1852** MRS. STOWE *Uncle Tom's C.* xxiii, Henrique is a regular little tempest—his mother and I have given him up long ago.

† **4.** A time; a period, an occasion. (A verbalism of translation.) *Obs.*

**1382** WYCLIF 2 *Chron.* xxviii. 9 In that tempest [Vulg. *ea tempestate*] was ther a prophete of the Lord. **1387** TREVISA *Higden* (Rolls) II. 337 In þat tempest [*sub ea tempestate*] went out þat man þat heet Liber pater.

**5.** *attrib.* and *Comb.* **a.** simple attrib., as *tempest-anger*, *-cloud*, *-pitch*, *-rack* (RACK *sb.*[1] 3), *-shock*,

*-speed, -spirit, -time*; **b.** instrumental, etc., as *tempest-beaten, -blown, -born, -driven, -flung, -harrowed, -rent, -rocked, -swept, -torn, -troubled, -winged, -worn* adjs.; also TEMPEST-TOSSED; **c.** objective, etc., as *tempest-bearing, -clear, -loving, -proof, -scoffing, -walking* adjs.; also *tempest-raiser.*

**1898** W. WATSON *Poems, Tomb of Burns*, Byron's *tempest-anger, tempest-mirth. **1747** DUNKIN in *Francis's* tr. *Horace, Ep.* II. ii. 307 Nor yet expos'd to *Tempest-bearing Strife. **1591** SYLVESTER *Du Bartas* I. v. 433 The *tempest-beaten Vessel's stern. **1759** JOHNSON *Rasselas* xxi, I rejoiced like a tempest-beaten sailor at his entrance into the harbour. **1865** BARING-GOULD *Werewolves* x. 177 To leave the summer cirrus and turn to the *tempest-born rain-cloud. **1868** M. COLLINS *Sweet Anne Page* I. 149 Always the white sky should be *tempest-clear. **1849** tr. *De la Motte Fouqué's Sir Elidoc* 166 His *tempest-driven heart. **1776** MICKLE tr. *Camoens' Lusiad* 80 On many a *tempest-harrowed ocean tost. **1727–46** THOMSON *Summer* 1123 The *tempest-loving raven scarce Dares wing the dubious dusk. **1660** BOND *Scut. Reg.* 403 Like one Ship..*tempest-proof upon a troubled Sea. **1844** LOWELL *Legend of Brittany* II. xi, Before its eyes the sullen *tempest-rack Would fade. **1877** tr. *Lacroix's Sc. & Lit. Mid. Ages* (1878) 225 A special class of sorcerers called *tempest-raisers. **1822** T. MITCHELL *Aristoph.* I. 186 Must I be thus *tempest-rent? *c* **1820** S. ROGERS *Italy, Camp. Florence* 176 Now *tempest-rocked, now whirling round and round. **1837** *Spirit of the Woods* 84 Mid sorrow's *tempest-shock. **1854** J. S. C. ABBOTT *Napoleon* (1855) II. iv. 79 Struggling along the drifted and *tempest-swept defile. **1633** FORD *Broken H.* IV. ii, Like *tempest-threaten'd trees unfirmly rooted. **1598** DRAYTON *Heroic Ep., Brandon to Q. Mary* 77 After long trauaile, *tempest-torne and wrack'd. **1825** RICHARDSON *Sonnets* 141, I marked the *tempest-troubled wave. **1727–46** THOMSON *Summer* 344 Till, *tempest-wing'd, Fierce Winter sweeps them from the face of day.

**Tempest** (te·mpėst, † tempe·st), *v.* [ad. OF. *tempeste-r* (12th c.), f. *tempeste*: see prec.]

**1.** *trans.* To affect by or as by a tempest; to throw into violent commotion, to agitate violently.

**1390** GOWER *Conf.* II. 167 And whan hir list the Sky tempeste, The reinbowe is hir Messager. *c* **1430** *Pilgr. Lyf Manhode* IV. i. (1869) 174 Tempested it was gretliche, of gret tempestes and of wyind. **1480** CAXTON *Ovid's Met.* XI. xix, The wyndes..renne so radely, that nothing may lette them to tempeste alle the see. **1638** *Penit. Conf.* (1657) 346 Rooted most when most tempested. **1667** MILTON *P. L.* VII. 412 Fish..part huge of bulk Wallowing unweildie, enormous in thir Gate, Tempest the Ocean. **1715–20** POPE *Iliad* XXI. 30 The huge dolphin tempesting the main. **1830** H. N. COLERIDGE *Grk. Poets* (1834) 129 As when two winds—the north and west..suddenly tempest the sea. **1857** H. MILLER *Test. Rocks* iii. 137 Its wonderful whales..of the reptilian class..must have tempested the deep.

**2.** *fig.* To disturb violently (a person, the mind).

*c* **1374** CHAUCER *Boeth.* II. pr. iv. 28 (Camb. MS.), I haue som what conforted the so þat thow tempest the nat thus with al thi fortune. *a* **1415** LYDGATE *Temple of Glas* 1157 For no turment, þat þe fallen shal, Tempest þe not. **1521** FISHER *Serm. Luther* Wks. (1876) 312 Ioannes wiccliff with other moo which were sore tempested the chyrche. **1621** T. WILLIAMSON tr. *Goulart's Wise Vieillard* 25 Tempested with disordered thoughts and vnruly passions. **1762** GOLDSM. *Cit. W.* xlvii, A mind..tempested up by a thousand various passions. **1819** CAMPBELL *Spec. Brit. Poets* I. 164 A man..has hardly tied the fatal knot when his house is tempested by female eloquence.

**3.** *intr.* Of the wind, weather, etc., and *impers.*: To be tempestuous, to blow tempestuously; to rage, storm. Also *fig.* ? *Obs.*

*c* **1477** CAXTON *Jason* 56 Sone after the winde began to rise and tempest horrible and impetuouse. **1530** PALSGR. 754/1 Herde you nat howe it tempested to nyght? **1601** B. JONSON *Poetaster* v. i, Other Princes..Thunder, and tempest, on those learned heads, Whom Caesar with such honour doth aduance. **1615** G. SANDYS *Trav.* 207 (tr. *Ovid's Met.* XI. 521) Blind night in darkness tempests.

Hence **Te·mpested** *ppl. a.*, tossed or afflicted by a tempest; **Te·mpesting** *vbl. sb.*

*a* **1631** DONNE *Serm.* xxxvii. (1640) 366 No repentance [can] stay his tempested and weather-beaten conscience. **1811** SHELLEY *St. Irvyne* ix. Pr. Wks. 1888 I. 196 And the moon dimly gleam'd through the tempested air. **1846** TRENCH *Miracles* iv, The Church of Christ has evermore resembled this tempested bark. **1882** MYERS *Renewal of Youth* 288 Rocked by strange blast and stormy tempestings.

† **Tempesta·rian.** *Obs. rare*⁻¹. In 8 (erron.) **tempestrian.** [f. med.L. *tempestāri-us* (8th c. in Du Cange) + -AN.] (See quot.)

**1708–22** BINGHAM *Antiq.* XVI. v. § 6 (1840) VI. 68 The capitulars of Charles the Great, where decrees were made against calculators, enchanters, and 'tempestrians', as they are called, that is raisers of storms and tempests.

† **Tempestative,** *a. Obs. rare*⁻¹. [a. obs. F. *tempestatif, -ive* (15th c. in Godef.): see TEMPEST *sb.* and -ATIVE.] That raises a tempest.

**1694** MOTTEUX *Rabelais* IV. xx, If I come near thee..and chastise thee like any Tempestative Devil.

**Tempesteous, -ious**: see TEMPESTUOUS.

**Tempestive** (tempe·stiv), *a. arch.* [ad. L. *tempestīvus* timely: see TEMPEST and -IVE.]

**1.** Timely, seasonable.

**1611** SPEED *Hist. Gt. Brit.* IX. ix. § 60 That prouidence which the King of Scotland..vsed, was, as more tempestiue, so more commendable. **1620** VENNER *Via Recta* vii. 107 The moderate and tempestiue vse of them may be very good and profitable. **1635** HEYWOOD *Hierarch.* VIII. Comm. 532 The chearefull and tempestiue showres. **1852** *Fraser's Mag.* XLV. 172 After the tempestive banquet at two o'clock.

¶ **2.** *erron.* = TEMPESTUOUS 2.

**1848** *Tait's Mag.* XV. 118 Every reader will..point out living examples amid brawling and tempestive politicians.

**Tempe·stively,** *adv. arch.* [f. prec. + -LY ².] Seasonably, opportunely.

**1621** BURTON *Anat. Mel.* III. ii. III. iv. (1676) 305/2 Dancing is a pleasant recreation of body and mind..if tempestively used. **1654** H. L'ESTRANGE *Chas. I* (1655) 131 The severall processes..will more tempestively occurre in the ensuing series of this narration. **1702** BAYNARD in Sir J. Floyer *Hot & Cold Bath.* II. (1706) 367 Hot and Cold Baths..tempestively, cautiously, and wisely prescrib'd.

† **Tempesti·vious,** *a. Obs. rare*⁻¹. [Erron. for **tempestivous*, f. as prec. + -OUS.] Seasonable; = TEMPESTIVE I.

**1574** NEWTON *Health Mag.* 6 Exercise fittest to be vsed.. in seasonable and tempestiuious times of the yeare.

† **Tempesti·vity.** *Obs.* [ad. L. *tempestīvitās*, f. *tempestīv-us* TEMPESTIVE: see -ITY.]

**1.** Seasonableness, timeliness.

**1576** NEWTON *Lemnie's Complex.* (1633) 124 Appointing to each function his proper turne, and tempestiuity. **1646** SIR T. BROWNE *Pseud. Ep.* 287 Since their [Jews'] dispersion and habitation in Countries, whose constitutions admit not such tempestivity of harvests. **1656** BLOUNT *Glossogr.*, *Tempestivity*,..fitnesse of time, seasonablenesse.

**2.** A season, a time of a particular character.

**1569** NEWTON *Cicero's Olde Age* 21 b, To euery part of a mans life and age, are geeuen hys conuenyente tymes and propre tempestiuytyes. **1642** S. ASHE *Best Refuge* 19 Times. The word signifies the tempestivity, the season of time. The Septuagint renders it right, Ἐν εὐκατρίαις. **1683** E. HOOKER *Pref. Pordage's M. Div.* 20 In these last Daies there wil hang over us..periculous tempestivities, hard seasons.

† **Te·mpestous,** *a. Obs.* [a. AF. *tempestous*, OF. *-eus*, ad. L. type **tempestōs-us*, for L. *tempestuōs-us*; in It. *tempestoso*, Prov. *tempestos* and *tempestuos* (Littré).] = TEMPESTUOUS 1, 2.

*c* **1374** CHAUCER *Troylus* II. Proem 5 This see clepe I þe tempestous matere Of desper þat Troylus was Inne. *c* **1500** *Three Kings Sons* 131 If bifore dyner he were hote and tempestous, now is he colde and sobre. **1508** FISHER 7 *Penit. Ps.* xxxviii. I. Wks. (1876) 69 The tempestous trybulacyons wherwith the herte of synners is troubled & vexed.

**Tempestrian**: see TEMPESTARIAN.

**Te·mpest-to:ssed, -to:st** (-tǫst, *poet.* tǫ·sėd), *a.* Tossed by or as by a tempest. Hence **Te·mpest-to:ss** *v. trans.* and *intr.*, to toss or pitch about as a tempest or a tempestuous sea; to agitate or be agitated violently; **Te·mpest-to:ssing**, violent agitation by or as by a tempest, etc.

**1592** SHAKS. *Rom. & Jul.* III. v. 138 The windes thy sighes ..will ouer set Thy tempest tossed body. **1605** — *Macb.* I. iii. 25 Though his Barke cannot be lost, Yet it shall be Tempest-tost. **1681** *Roxb. Ball.* (1886) VI. 77 Where peevish coyness and disdain Do tempest-toss the mind. **1747** FRANCIS tr. *Horace, Ep.* I. xi. 19 Though by strong Winds your Bark were Tempest-tost. **1867** H. MACMILLAN *Bible Teach.* xii. (1870) 233 Those very afflictions and tempest-tossings which the Church bewails.

† **Tempe·stuate,** *v. Obs. rare*⁻¹. [f. L. *tempestu-*, stem of next: see -ATE ³ 7.] = TEMPEST *v.*

**1702** C. MATHER *Magn. Chr.* VII. vi. (1852) 577 Those parts of New England..were thus tempestuated by a terrible war.

**Tempestuous** (tempe·stiuəs), *a.* Forms: *α.* 5 **tempesteuous** (? = **-evous**), 6 **-eous, -yous,** 6–8 **-ious**; *β.* 6 **-uouse, -uus,** 6– **tempestuous.** [In the *β* form, ad. L. *tempestuōs-us*: cf. *tempestu-s*, collateral form of *tempestās* TEMPEST; so obs. F. *tempestueus, -uos* (14th c.), mod.F. *tempêtueux* = Pr. *tempestuos*, Sp., Pg. *tempestuoso*. The *α* forms appear to be analogical, after other adjs. in *-eous, -ious*, of various etymology.]

**1.** Of, pertaining to, involving, or resembling a tempest; subject to or characterized by tempests; stormy, very rough or violent.

*α.* **1509** HAWES *Past. Pleas.* xxxvii. (Percy Soc.) 194 It thondred loude wyth clappes tempestious. *a* **1548** HALL *Chron., Hen. IV* 18 b, A great tempesteous rage and furious storme. **1592** MORYSON *Let.* in *Itin.* I. (1617) 37 The weather was very tempestious, and not likely to change.

*β.* **1538** STARKEY *England* I. ii. 61 The trowblus and tempestuus see. **1538** ELYOT, *Tempestuosum*, tempestuous or stormy. **1610** HOLLAND *Camden's Brit.* (1637) 501 A turbulent and tempestuous storme arose. **1639–40** LAUD *Diary* 25 Jan., A very blustering and a tempestuous day. **1799** HT. LEE *Canterb. T., Old Wom.* (ed. 2) I. 348 The weather grew lowering and tempestuous. **1878** BOSWORTH SMITH *Carthage* 121 The dangerous storms to which the south of Sicily was exposed after the rising of the tempestuous Orion.

**2.** *transf.* and *fig.* Characterized by violent agitation or commotion; turbulent, tumultuous; impetuous, passionate; agitated as by a tempest.

*α.* **1447** [implied in *tempesteuously*: see next]. **1509** HAWES *Past. Pleas.* xxvii. (Percy Soc.) 120 O Mars! me succoure in tyme tempestyous. *Ibid.* xxxiv. 177 So shall you swage the tempesteous floode Of their stormy myndes. *a* **1586** SIDNEY *Ps.* XXXI. xi, In that tempestious hast, I said, that I from out thy sight was cast. **1710** *Brit. Apollo* III. No. 25. 3/1 Tempestious Ills, in wild Confusion hurl'd.

*β.* **1509** HAWES *Past. Pleas.* xxxiii. (Percy Soc.) 169 To the last ende of my matter troublous, With waves enclosed so tempestuous. **1648** HERRICK *Hesper., Delight in Disorder*, A winning wave (deserving note) In the tempestuous petticote. **1653** R. SANDERS *Physiogn., Moles* 21 The tempestuous persecutions of her own kindred. **1663** DAVENANT *Siege of Rhodes* Wks. (1672) 2 The Shriller Trumpet and Tempestuous Drum. **1782** MISS BURNEY *Cecilia* VIII. iv, Cecilia was still in this tempestuous state. **1865** SWINBURNE *Atalanta* 1016 Fill the dance up with tempestuous feet.

**Tempe·stuously,** *adv.* [f. prec. + -LY ².] In a tempestuous manner.

**1447** BOKENHAM *Seyntys* (Roxb.) 73 Trowblyd in hym selph tempesteuously. **1596** WARNER *Alb. Eng.* XI. lxiii. (1612) 272 Tempestiously Arzinaas Rhode receiued Sir Hugh at last. **1642** MILTON *Apol. Smect.* Pref., Wks. 1851 III. 276 Signe, that he meant ere long to be most tempestuously bold, and shamelesse? **1721** R. KEITH tr. *T. à Kempis' Solil. Soul* xvi. 230 The Air may of a sudden be tempestuously stirred. **1876** F. HARRISON *Choice Bks.* (1886) 138 The evils of which you tempestuously complain.

**Tempe·stuousness.** [f. as prec. + -NESS.] The state or quality of being tempestuous or stormy; storminess, turbulence.

**1648** HEXHAM *Dutch Dict.* II, *De stuerigheyt der Zee*, the tempestuousnesse, or the storminesse of the Sea. *a* **1652** J. SMITH *Sel. Disc.* x. iv. (1673) 461 That impetuous violence and tempestuousness with which men are acted in pretensions of Religion. **1798** *Hist.* in *Ann. Reg.* 154/2 The tempestuousness of the times appeared favourable to such an attempt. **1877** DOWDEN *Shaks. Prim.* vi. 117 There is no tempestuousness of passion and no artistic mystery.

**Tempir(e,** obs. forms of TEMPER *v.*

**Templar** (te·mplăɹ), *sb.* Forms: 3–7 **templer,** 4–5 **-ere,** (5 **templeer**), 5– **templar.** [a. AF. *templer*, OF. *templier* (*c* 1200 in Godef.), = med.L. *templārius* (Du Cange), f. *templum*, TEMPLE *sb.*¹: see -ER ² 2; also *templārēs*, pl. of cl. L. *templāris*, in papal document of 1157 in Muratori *Antiq., Diss.* XI. (1774) II. 329. For later spelling see -AR ².]

**1.** A member of a military and religious order, consisting of knights (*Knights Templars, Knights* or *Poor Soldiers of the Temple*), chaplains, and men-at-arms, founded *c* 1118, chiefly for the protection of the Holy Sepulchre and of Christian pilgrims visiting the Holy Land: so called from their occupation of a building on or contiguous to the site of the Temple of Solomon at Jerusalem. They were suppressed in 1312.

*c* **1290** *Beket* 2264 in *S. Eng. Leg.* I. 171 He [K. Hen. II, as part of his penance] scholde finde to hundret knyȝtes to fiȝte Al ane ȝer with þe templers for holi churche riȝte. **13..** *Coer de L.* 3920 Hys..Templeres and hys Hospytalers. *c* **1330** R. BRUNNE *Chron.* (1810) 305 A templer of pris, Sir Brian þe geay, Maister templere he was on þis half þe se. **1387** TREVISA *Higden* (Rolls) VIII. 293 Þe fifte Clement was pope..he dampned þe ordre of Frere Templers. **14..** *Nom.* in Wr.-Wülcker 681/23 *Hic templarius*, a templer. **1598** HAKLUYT *Voy.* I. 146 The Templars which were therein returned home out of Fraunce. **1603** KNOLLES *Hist. Turks* (1638) 29 Hugh Paganus first Master of the Templers.. returned with a great number of zealous Christians, ready to lay down their liues for defence of the Christian faith and religion. **1610** HOLLAND *Camden's Brit.* (1637) 427 A church for Knights Templars, which they had newly built according to the forme of the Temple neere unto the Sepulchre of Our Lord at Hierusalem. **1700** TYRRELL *Hist. Eng.* II. 745 One Durand a Knight-Templar. **1839** KEIGHTLEY *Hist. Eng.* I. 266 It was in the reign of Edward II that the potent and wealthy order of Knights Templars was suppressed throughout Europe. **1910** C. PERKINS in *Eng. Hist. Rev.* Apr. 224 There do not appear to have been over fifteen or twenty knights in the total of 144 Templars in the British Isles.

**b.** Phrase.

**1653** URQUHART *Rabelais* I. v. 26, I drink no more then a spunge, I drink like a Templer Knight [*orig.* je boy comme ung Templier]. **1819** SCOTT *Ivanhoe* xxxv, Now, to drink like a Templar is the boast of each jolly boon companion!

**2.** A barrister or other person who occupies chambers in the Inner or Middle Temple (see TEMPLE *sb.*¹ 5).

**1588** *Marprel. Epist.* (Arb.) 26 Let the Templars haue M. Trauers their preacher restored againe vnto them. **1628** in *Crt. & Times Chas. I* (1848) I. 311 On Saturday last, the Templars chose one Mr. Palmes..their lord of misrule. **1683** TRYON *Way to Health* 481 But very few Inns of Court Gentlemen or Templers. **1687** MONTAGUE & PRIOR *Hind & P. Transv.* 22 Many a young Templer will save his shilling by this Stratagem of my Mice. *a* **1760** H. BROWNE *Pipe Tobacco, Imit.* v, Blest leaf! whose aromatic gales dispense To Templars modesty, to Parsons sense. **1815** LAMB *Let. to Southey* 6 May, I am a Christian, Englishman, Londoner, Templar. **1818** SCOTT *Hrt. Midl.* i, The part which is common to the higher classes of the law at Edinburgh, and which nearly resembles that of the young Templars in the days of Steele and Addison. **1902** J. HUTCHINSON (*title*) A Catalogue of Notable Middle Templars.

**3. a.** A member of an order of Freemasons calling themselves Knights Templars, extensively established in the United States.

**1859** (*title*) A Service for the Encampments of Knights Templars together with a Sketch of the History of the Order. *Ibid.* 30 [see TEMPLARY *sb.* 3]. **1878** [see ENCAMPMENT 3]. **1904** *Westm. Gaz.* 2 Aug. 2/3 The Royal Arch degree, the possession of which in these later times has been held essential to a Knight Templar.

**b.** Short for GOOD TEMPLAR, q. v.

**1874–** [see GOOD TEMPLAR]. **1885** *Daily Chron.* 3 Sept. (Cassell) He had often feared lest any of..their juvenile templars should be decoyed away on their journey to or from the meetings. **1905** *Daily News* 30 Oct. 8 The Baron ..being by no means a templar according to the jargon of today—'templar' or 'teetotaler', whatever the phrase may be.

**4.** An official of the Jewish temple. *nonce-use.*

**1884** H. W. BEECHER in *Chr. World Pulpit* XXV. 11/3 It was this [the raising of Lazarus]..that brought..the determination of the templars that He should perish.

**5.** *attrib.*, as *Templar Knight, order*, etc.

*c* **1440** *Alphabet of Tales* 233 Cesarius tellis how some tyme þer was a preste of þe Templer ordur. **1537** *Orig. & Sprynge Sectes* 15 Templare Lordes. *Ibid.* 16 Templare Knyghtes. **1819** SCOTT *Ivanhoe* xxxviii, A huge volume, which contained the proceedings of the Templar Knights.

Hence **Te·mplardom**, the community or body of Templars; † **Templa·rian** *a. Obs.*, of or pertaining to the Templars; **Te·mplarism**, the principles of Templars (in any of the senses, e.g. = *Good Templarism*); **Te·mplarlike** *adv.*, like a Templar.
1877 G. H. KINGSLEY *Sport & Trav.* (1900) 345 The most temperate races of the world are apt to burst out..to the utter confusion of all 'Good *Templardom'. 1600 W. WATSON *Decacordon* (1602) 19 Seditious *Templarian Iesuiticall sectaries. 1612 T. JAMES *Jesuits' Downf.* 48 For as they liue iust Templarlike in all things, so there will be a right Templarian downefall. 1888 J. SHALLOW *Templars Trials* 69 M. Loiseleur dilates..on the difference between Gnosticism and *Templarism. 1893 *Voice* (N. Y.) 15 June, He spoke of the drink question as affecting native races, and the spread of Templarism in India, Africa and Australasia.

**Templar** (te·mplăr), *a.* [ad. late L. *templār-is*, f. *templum*, TEMPLE *sb.*[1]: see -AR [1].] Of, pertaining to, or characteristic of a (or the Jewish) temple.
1728 R. MORRIS *Ess. Anc. Archit.* 3 The Example of.. Solomon in Templar and Domal Architecture. 1812-29 COLERIDGE in *Lit. Rem.* (1838) III. 112 It would be better to regard solitary, family, and templar devotion as distinctions in sort, rather than differences in degree. 1840 MILMAN *Hist. Chr.* II. 415 In the East, where the churches retained probably more of the templar form. 1845 J. MARTINEAU *Misc.* (1852) 118 They have no templar and sacerdotal duties, can offer no sacrifice, absolve from no sin.

**Templary** (te·mplări), *sb.* Also 5 *pl.* -arijs. [ad. med.L. *templāri-us*, TEMPLAR *sb.*: see -ARY [1].]
† 1. = TEMPLAR *sb.* 1. *Obs.*
1432-50 tr. *Higden* (Rolls) VIII. 293 Þis pope..dampned the ordre of Templaryes [*ordinem Templariorum*]. 1460 CAPGRAVE *Chron.* (Rolls) 177 He procured the distruccion of Templaries. c1460 tr. *Oseney Regr.* 108 Þe templarijs. 1599 HAKLUYT *Voy.* II. I. 35 (an. 1249) The [holy] land.. might soone be woon to Christendome, were it not for rebellious Templaries, with the Hospitalaries, and their followers. 1616 BULLOKAR *Eng. Expos.*, *Templaries*, certaine Christian souldiours dwelling about the Temple at Hierusalem, whose office was to entertain Christian strangers that came hither for deuotion. 1656 BLOUNT *Glossogr.*, *Templaries*, Knights of the Temple.
† 2. An estate or benefice belonging to the Knights Templars. *Obs. rare*—[1].
1592 *Sc. Acts Jas. VI* (1814) III. 564/1 Þe rentaillis of all bischoiprikis, abbacies, priorijs, provestries,..chaiplanries, templaries, and vtheris benefices.
3. Templars collectively; *Hist.* the system or organization of the Templars; in 19th c., the Masonic and Temperance societies so called.
a1661 FULLER *Worthies, Oxford.* (1662) II. 329 The Holy Land, where thorough the Treachery of Templary, cowardize of the Greeks, diversity of the Climate, distance of the place, and differences betwixt Christian Princes, much time was spent,..many lives lost,..but little profit produced. 1859 *Service for Encampments of Knights Templars* 30 Any attempt..to make Masonry perfect without Templary, or on the other hand, to perpetuate an order of Templars independent of Freemasonry must only shew ignorance of the real history of both Societies. 1874, 1897 [see GOOD TEMPLAR]. 1904 *Westm. Gaz.* 2 Aug. 2/3 At Louisville [in 1901]..a colossal pageant descriptive of the history of Knight Templary from the time of the Crusades.

† **Te·mplary**, *a. Obs. rare.* [ad. late L. *templāris* pertaining to a temple: see -ARY [2].]
1. Of or pertaining to a temple: = TEMPLAR *a.*
1607 *Schol. Disc. agst. Antichr.* I. i. 55 We scorne papistes that pretende a ciuill worshippe in templarie bowing.
2. Of, pertaining to, or named from the Temple at Jerusalem; *Templary Knights* = Knights Templars: see TEMPLAR *sb.* 1.
1617 MORYSON *Itin.* I. 84 In the Priory of St. Iohn, belonging of old to the Templary Knights, and now to the Knights of Rhodes or Malta. *Ibid.* 190 (*Paris*) On the left hand as you come in, is the house of the Templary Knights.

**Template**, variant of TEMPLET [1].

**Temple** (te·mp'l), *sb.*[1] Forms: 1–2 **templ, tempel**, (3 *Orm.* **temmple**), 3– **temple.** Also 4 **tempel, -ele, -ile, -ille, (templee)**, 4–6 **tempil(l, -yll**, 5 **-yl(e, -ul**, 5–6 **-ull(e**, 6 **-ell.** [OE. *templ, tempel*, ad. L. *templum*; reinforced in ME. by F. *temple* (10th c. in Godef. *Compl.*) = Pr. *temple*, Sp., Pg. *templo*, It. *tempio*:—L. *templum.*]
I. 1. An edifice or place regarded primarily as the dwelling-place or 'house' of a deity or deities; hence, an edifice devoted to divine worship.
a. In a general sense. (Often, as in quot. c825, going back to a specific use.)
*Cave-* or *cavern-temple*, a natural cave used as a temple.
c825 *Vesp. Psalter* xlvii. 10 We onfengun god mildheortnisse ðine in midle temples ðines. *Ibid.* lxxviii. 1 Tempel halig ðin. 13.. *E. E. Allit. P.* A. 1061 Chapel ne temple þat euer watz set. 14.. *Voc.* in Wr.-Wülcker 626/2 Tempulle, *templum.* 1526 TINDALE *Acts* vii. 48 But he that is hyest of all dweleth not in temples made with hondes. 1529 MORE *Dyaloge* I, God is as myghtye in the stable as in the temple. 1610 SHAKS. *Temp.* IV. i. 153 The Clowd-capt Towres, the gorgeous Pallaces, the solemn Temples, the great Globe it selfe..shall dissolue. 1642 FULLER *Holy & Prof. St.* III. xxiv. 219 Take Temple for a covered standing structure, and the Jews had none till the time of Solomon. 1832 DISRAELI *Cont. Flem.* v. iv, There is not a more beautiful and solemn temple in the world, than the great Cathedral of Seville. 1837 PRICHARD *Phys. Hist. Man.* (ed. 3) II. 243 The great cavern-temple of Tulzis. a1845 SYD. SMITH in Lady Holland *Mem.* (1855) I. iii. 55 The true Christian.. loves the good, under whatever temple, at whatever altar he may find them. 1850 LEITCH tr. *C. O. Müller's Anc. Art* § 52. 26 The simplest temples (σηκοί) of the primitive ages were merely hollow trees in which images were placed.

b. Historically applied to the sacred buildings of the Egyptians, Greeks, Romans, and other ancient nations; now, to those of Hinduism, Buddhism, Confucianism, Taoism, Shintoism, and the ethnic religions generally.
971 *Blickl. Hom.* 221 He maniȝ templ & deofolgyld ȝebræc & ȝefylde. c1000 ÆLFRIC *Hom.* II. 574 [Hi] ðam fela templa arærdon. c1205 LAY. 10178 Alle þa templen [c1275 temples] þe þa heðene hafden itimbrid. 1297 R. GLOUC. (Rolls) 318 A temple hii vovnde vair inou & a maumet amidde. c1375 *Sc. Leg. Saints* v. (Johannes) 293 Þe tempil of dyane. c1400 *Destr. Troy* 1358 All tight to þe tempull of þere tore goddes. 1596 DALRYMPLE tr. *Leslie's Hist. Scot.* II. (S.T.S.) 135 *margin*, Tempilis & places of sacrifice to prophane Godis. 1634 SIR T. HERBERT *Trav.* 205 The Citie [Meaco in Japan] has seuenty Temples, in one of which are set three thousand three hundred thirty three gilded Idols. 1667 MILTON *P. L.* I. 402 The wisest heart Of Solomon he [Moloch] led by fraud to build His Temple right against the Temple of God. 1756-7 tr. *Keysler's Trav.* (1760) II. 441 The temple of the Sibylla Tiburtina spoken of by Lactantius. 1860 GARDNER *Faiths World* II. 588/2 Pagoda..In Hindustan, Burmah, and China..implies a temple in which idols are worshipped. *Ibid.* 894/1 Their [Taoists] priests live in the temples, and are supported by the produce of the grounds attached to the establishment.
c. *spec.* The sacred edifice (or any one of the successive edifices) at Jerusalem, the 'House of the Lord', and seat of the Jewish worship of Jehovah.
c897 K. ÆLFRED *Gregory's Past. C.* xxxvi. 252 Þa stanas on ðæm mæran temple Salomonnes wæron ær swæ wel ȝefeȝede. 971 *Blickl. Hom.* 27 He hine asette ofer þæs temples scylf. c1000 *Ags. Gosp.* Matt. iv. 5 Ða ȝebrohte se deofol hine..and asette hine ofer þæs temples heahnesse. c1200 ORMIN 11880 Te deofell brohhte Crist Uppo þatt hallȝhe temmple. c1325 *Metr. Hom.* 75 In the temple fand thai than Seynt Symeon. 1382 WYCLIF *Matt.* xxi. 12 Jhesus entride in to the temple of God. a1425 *Cursor M.* 10946 (Laud) Zakarie to tempille yede. *Ibid.* 13745 (Trin.) Ihesu .. say noon in þe tempul leued. 1533 GAU *Richt Vay* (S. T. S.) 23 The rewlers of the tempil and the cheif prestis. 1611 BIBLE *John* viii. 2 Earely in the morning hee came againe into the Temple. 1877 C. GEIKIE *Christ* lvii. (1879) 692 The Temple was built of white stones of great size, the length of each about 37½ ft., some even 45 ft.
d. *transf.* and *fig.*
c1607 DONNE *Lett.*, *to Sir H. Goodere* 14 Aug. (1651) 116 That time [for the outward service] to me towards you is Tuesday, and my Temple, the Rose in Smith-field. 1771 *Junius Lett.* lix. (1820) 311 The temple of fame is the shortest passage to riches and preferment. 1860 TYNDALL *Glac.* I. ii. 19 A temple of science now in ruins. 1877 C. GEIKIE *Christ* xxxi. (1879) 370 The true worship has its temple in the inmost soul. 1879 STAINER *Music of Bible* 5 Whose temple of worship was the canopy of heaven.
2. *transf.* A building dedicated to public Christian worship; a church: esp. applied to a large or grand edifice.
1399 LANGL. *Rich. Redeles* Prol. 3 A temple of þe trinite [in Bristol]..That cristis chirche is cleped. 1538 STARKEY *England* II. i. 176 Magnyfycal and gudly housys, fayr tempullys and churchys. 1560 DAUS tr. *Sleidane's Comm.* 367 Whan the last of them are come to the church, the Souldiours by and by discharge their pieces: and..about the Temple kepe warde till the counsell breake vp. 1849 MACAULAY *Hist. Eng.* iv. I. 471 The king determined to hear mass with the same pomp with which his predecessors had been surrounded when they repaired to the temples of the established religion. 1867 D. DUNCAN *Disc.* 120 By some classes of professing Christians, their places of worship are called temples..and are reverenced as sacred or holy. 1876 *Haydn's Dict. Dates* 706/2 The 'City Temple', a dissenters' chapel..was opened 19 May, 1874.
b. *spec.* In France and some French-speaking countries, a Protestant as distinguished from a Roman Catholic place of worship (the term 'church' (*église*) being usually confined to the latter).
1566 CLOUGH in Burgon *Life Gresham* (1839) II. 154 *note*, They have laid and begun the foundation of four new tempells [in Antwerp], besides the great barne at St. Mychell's, which ys very handsomely trymmed for a preaching place. [1843 *Murray's France* 465/2 There are 12,000 Protestants at Nismes, who have 2 churches (*temples*).] 1879 STEVENSON *Trav. Cevennes* (1886) 150 One of the first things I encountered in Pont de Montvert was..the Protestant temple.
c. The central place of worship of the Mormons.
1858 *Encycl. Brit.* (ed. 8) XV. 591/1 This great undertaking of Nauvoo was the building of the Mormon temple. 1874 J. H. BLUNT *Dict. Sects* 347/2 A revelation of great length..gave directions for the building of a splendid temple, the first stone of which was laid with great pomp on April 6th, 1841. *Ibid.* 354/1 The tithes are supposed to be devoted to the building of the temple.
3. *fig.* Any place regarded as occupied by the divine presence; *spec.* the person or body of a Christian.
c975 *Rushw. Gosp.* John ii. 19 Un-duað ðone tempel ðis & on ðrim dagum ic awecco ðæt. *Ibid.* 21 He wutudlice ȝicwæð of temple lichoma his. c1000 ÆLFRIC *Hom.* II. 580 Nyte ȝe þæt eowere lima syndon þæs Halgan Gastes tempel, seðe on eow is? c1200 ORMIN 15843 Crisstene follc iss Cristes hus & Cristess hallȝhe temmple. c1290 *St. Kath.* 21 in *S. Eng. Leg.* I. 92 Ȝwy ne bi-holde ȝe þe heiȝe temple ..Of þe heie heuene þat geth a-boute a-bouen eov niȝt and dai. 1388 WYCLIF 1 *Cor.* iii. 16 Witen ȝe not, that ȝe ben the temple of God, and the spirit of God dwellith in ȝou? c1400 *Destr. Troy* 11781 Couetous men comynly are cald aftur right, A temple to the tyrand, þat tises to syn. c1450 *Godstow Reg.* 5 Iff we make clene oure tempil with-ynne. a1515 DUNBAR *Poems* lxxvi. 19 Tryumphand tempill of the Trinite ..Princes of peiss..O mater Jhesu, salue Maria! 1605 SHAKS. *Macb.* II. iii. 73 Most sacrilegious Murther hath broke ope The Lords anoynted Temple, and stole thence The Life o'th'Building. 1681-6 J. SCOTT *Chr. Life* (1747) III. 55 How could his Spirit's dwelling in us constitute us Temples of God, unless he himself were God? a1700 DRYDEN tr. *Hymn, Veni, Creator Spiritus* 6 From sin and sorrow set us free, And make thy temples worthy thee. 1839-52 BAILEY *Festus* (ed. 5) 464 My favoured temple is an humble heart. 1875 MANNING *Mission H. Ghost* i. 21 Yet they have been made temples of the Holy Ghost.
II. † 4. The head-quarters of the Knights Templars, on or contiguous to the site of the temple at Jerusalem; hence, the order or organization of the Templars. *Obs.*
a1131 *O. E. Chron.* an. 1128 Ðes ilces ȝeares com fram Ierusalem Hugo of þe temple. c1400 MAUNDEV. (1839) x. 88 Towardes the south right nygh, is the temple of Salomon... And in þat temple duellen the knyghtes of the temple, that weren wont to be clept Templeres, & þat was the fundacioun of here ordre. c1400 *Brut* 148 Amonge þe castelles he made an house of þe temple. 1656 BLOUNT *Glossogr.*, *Templaries*, or Knights of the Temple.
5. *spec.* Name of two of the Inns of Court (see INN *sb.* 5 c) in London, known as the *Inner* and the *Middle Temple* (see quot. 1727–41), which stand on the site of the buildings once occupied by the Templars (of which the church alone remains).
c1386 CHAUCER *C. T.* Prol. 567 A gentil Maunciple was ther of a temple. 1462 J. PASTON in *P. Lett.* II. 92 To myn ryth reverent..fader, John Paston, beyng in the Inder Temple. 1556 *Chron. Gr. Friars* (Camden) 97 The xviij day of August [1556] the mayer dynned at the rederes denner at the Tempulle. 1591 SHAKS. 1 *Hen. VI*, II. v. 19 We sent vnto the Temple, vnto his Chamber. 1656 BLOUNT *Glossogr.* s. v. *Templaries*, These Templars first founded and built the Temples or Templars Inne in Fleetstreet. 1709 STEELE *Tatler* No. 60 ¶ 1 A Student of the Inner Temple. 1727-41 CHAMBERS *Cycl.*, *Temples*,..two inns of court, thus called, because anciently the dwelling-house of the knights-templars..They are called the inner and middle temple, in relation to Essex-house, which was also a part of the house of the templars, and called the outer temple, because situate without Temple-Bar. 1905 C. T. MARTIN (*title*) Minutes of Parliament of the Middle Temple.
b. Name of the place in Paris which formed the head-quarters of the Templars in Europe.
1617 MORYSON *Itin.* I. 190 (Paris) The second gate towards the East, is the gate of the Temple. 1735 [see *temple diamond* in 6]. 1888 T. A. ARCHER in *Encycl. Brit.* XXIII. 160/2 Louis VII..gave them a piece of marsh land outside Paris, which in later times became known as the Temple, and was the headquarters of the order in Europe.
III. 6. *attrib.* and *Comb.* a. Simple attrib., in senses 1–3, as *temple-book, -building, -captain, -chamber, -chief, -companion, -court, -door, -end, -fellow, -festival, -fronton, -gate, -gift, -guard, -hill, -hospital, -land, -master, -ministrant, -mount, -music, -musician, -pavement, -pediment, -porch, -priest, -priesthood, -prophet, -revenue, -roof, -ruin, -sanctuary, -sculpture, -service, -shrine, -singer, -staff, -stair, -stead, -system, -tax, -treasury, -union, -veil, -vision, -wall, -warden, -wardenship, -worship, -yard*; in sense 5, as *temple-exchange, -garden, -hall*, etc.; appositive, as *temple-house, -palace, -pyramid, -tomb, -tower.* b. Obj. and obj. gen., as *temple-keeper, -robber, -sweeper, -visiting*; *temple-haunting* adj.; instrumental, similative, etc., as *temple-crowned, -like, -sacred, -treated* adjs. c. Special combs.: **temple children**, girl children enslaved to the service of heathen temples in India; **Temple church**: see 5; † **temple diamond** (see quot.); **temple-foundling**, ? a foundling deposited at the Temple (sense 5); **Temple parliament**, = PARLIAMENT *sb.*[1] 5 b; † **temple-pickling** (*obs. slang*): see quot.; **temple-ring** (see quot.); **temple-title**, the name under which a deceased Chinese emperor is worshipped; **temple-trotter** (see quot.). Also TEMPLE-BAR.
1448-9 METHAM *Amoryus & Cleopes* 28 Ther othe thei toke, Sweryng vpon the *tempyl-boke. 1857 J. HAMILTON *Lessons fr. Gt. Biog.* (1859) 219 The occupants of these *temple-chambers. 1727-41 CHAMBERS *Cycl.* s.v., The chief officer was the master of the temple...And from him the chief minister of the *temple-church is still called the master of the temple. 1846 GROTE *Greece* I. xi. 263 Pindar,..Euripidês and Apollodôrus, name Erichthonius..as the being who was thus adopted and made the *temple-companion of Athênê. 1884 R. BRIDGES *Prometheus* 758 The *temple-crowned heights. 1735 *Dict. Polygraph.* I. S vij, The factitious diamonds..call'd *temple Diamonds, because the best of them are made in the temple at Paris, are vastly short of the genuine ones. 1760 FOOTE *Minor* I. Wks. 1799 I. 239 He sits..every evening, from five till eight, under the clock, at the *Temple-exchange. 1614 SELDEN *Titles Hon.* Pref. Cj, Honor and deseruing Vertue .. were *Temple-fellowes in old Rome. 1905 *Athenæum* 29 July 146/1 The last of the *Temple foundlings, Mary Ann Littlefield, survived as late as 1865, and was supposed to have been the original of Miss Flite in Dickens's 'Bleak House'. 1591 SHAKS. 1 *Hen. VI*, II. iv. 125 This brawle to day, Growne to this faction in the *Temple Garden, Shall send betweene the Red-Rose and the White, A thousand Soules to Death and deadly Night. 1595 SPENSER *Epithal.* xii, Open the temple gates unto my love, Open them wide that she may enter in. 1605 SHAKS. *Macb.* I. vi. 4 This Guest of Summer, The *Temple-haunting Martlet. ?13.. *All Saints* 41 in Herrig's *Archiv* LXXIX. 435 Thus was ordeynd þis *temple-hous [the Pantheon] Off all deuyllus, to haue þer cours. a1670 SPALDING *Troub. Chas. I* (1829) 63 He gave them the superiorities of the haill *temple-lands within their burrow. 1663 GERBIER *Counsel* e iij, Representing

Solomons *Temple-like Foundations of a State. **1860** Pusey *Min. Proph.* 398 Habakkuk must have been entitled to take part in the *temple-music, and so must have been a Levite. **1891** Cheyne *Psalter* ii. 69 It [Ps. 37] is evidently the work of a *temple-musician. **1851** *Buried City East Nineveh* vii. 105 The architecture of the Assyrians, as illustrated in its only relics, the great *Temple-palaces. **1641** W. Mountagu in *Buccleuch MSS.* (Hist. MSS. Comm.) I. 285 Friday is the day of *Temple parliament. **1905** *Daily News* 15 July 4 The transactions of the Middle Temple 'Parliaments', beginning from the year 1501. *a* **1700** B. E. *Dict. Cant. Crew*, **Temple-pickling*, the Pumping of Bailives, Bumms, Setters, Pick-pockets, &c. *a* **1711** Ken *Hymnotheo* Poet. Wks. 1721 III. 77 The *Temple-Porch two arched Cloysters flank'd. **1711** Hickes *Two Treat. Chr. Priesth.* (1847) II. 251 A dissolution of the *temple-priesthood. **1905** D. Smith *Days His Flesh* vii. 59 Every adult Israelite..had to pay an annual tax of half a shekel to the *Temple-revenue. **1877** W. Jones *Finger-ring* 298 Another betrothal ring..called '*temple' or 'tower', from the figure of the sacred temple placed on their summit. **1637** Nabbes *Microcosm.* in Dodsley *O. Pl.* IX. 163 The *temple-robber..to the altar flies. *a* **1661** Holyday *Juvenal* (1673) 249 Temple-robbers..stealing away plates of gold from the statues of the gods. **1857** J. Hamilton *Lessons fr. Gt. Biog.* (1859) 86 He heard from the *temple-roof a whisper in his ear. **1860** Pusey *Min. Proph.* 24 The condition..in which there should be none of the special *Temple-service. *a* **1711** Ken *Hymnotheo* Poet. Wks. 1721 III. 78 Hymnotheo..Kiss'd the Saints' feet, who trod the *Temple-Stairs. **1870** Morris *Earthly Par.* III. 299 Now fain I would unto the *temple-stead. **1904** R. J. Farrer *Garden Asia* 118 The great *temple-tomb is in high festival for the Birthday of the Saviour [Buddha]. **1863** *W. Smith's Dict. Bible* 158/2 s.v. *Babel*, An ancient Babylonian *temple-tower. **1873** Browning *Red Cott. Nt.-cap* 680 A quaint device, Pillared and *temple-treated Belvedere. **1861** *Sat. Rev.* 30 Nov. 560 An extremely low lawyer's clerk, of the genus which in old professional slang was called '*Temple-trotter'. *c* **1340** *Cursor M.* 16762+85 (Cott.) Þe *temple vayl clef in twoo. **1609** Bible (Douay) *Zeph.* i. 4 The names of the *templewardens with the priests. **1904** W. M. Ramsay *Lett. to Seven Ch.* xvii. 232 The fourth *Temple-Wardenship seems to be of Artemis. **1680** Allen *Peace & Unity* 102 The corrupt estate of the Jewish church..both in *Temple-worship and in Synagogue-worship. **1714** R. Fiddes *Pract. Disc.* II. 138 The ceremonial ordinances which chiefly gave directions about the temple-worship.

Hence **Te·mpleful**, as many or as much as fills a temple; **Te·mpleward** *adv.*, towards the temple.

**1868** Whittier *Meeting* 21 Nor ritual-bound nor templeward Walks the free spirit of the Lord! **1909** *Expositor* Oct. 316 A whole templeful of men whose consciences kept them from casting a stone.

**Temple** (te·mp'l), *sb.*² Also 4-5 **tempil**, 5 **-elle, -ylle**, 6 *Sc.* **tympille**. [a. OF. *temple* fem. (11th c. in *Roland*), = Prov. *templa*, It. *tempia*:—pop.L. type **tempula*, **templa*, app. for cl. L. *tempora*, pl. of *tempus* 'temple of the head' (taken later as fem. sing.: cf. Bible). OF. *temple* (still in Dict. Acad. 1694-1740) is represented in mod.F. by *tempe* (already in Palsgr., 1530).]

1. The flattened region on each side of the (human) forehead. (Chiefly in *pl.*)

*c* **1310** *St. Margaret* 219 in Horstm. *Altengl. Leg.* (1881) 231 Sche toke him bi þe temples [*earlier version* bi þe toppe]; about sche him swong. *a* **1340** Hampole *Psalter* cxxxi. 5 Þe tempils of þi heued waxis heuy. *a* **1400** *Poem on Blood-letting* in *Rel. Ant.* I. 189 Two [places] at the templys thay mot blede. **14..** *Voc.* in Wr.-Wülcker 631/2 Tempelle, *tempora*. **1535** Coverdale *Judg.* iv. 21 Then Iael..smote the nale in thorow the temples of his heade, so yt he sancke to ye earth. **1643** Sir T. Browne *Relig. Med.* II. § 12 Let no dreames my head infest, But such as Jacobs temples blest. **1703** Pope *Vertumnus* 34 And wreaths of hay his sun-burnt temples shade. **1813** Scott *Rokeby* I. viii, A scorching clime, And toil, had..Roughened the brow, the temples bared. **1814** Cary *Dante, Paradise* xxv. 11, I..shall claim the wreath Due to the poet's temples.

**b.** *transf.* A corresponding part in lower animals.

**1769** E. Bancroft *Guiana* 181 The temples, rump and belly are of a violet colour. **1826** Kirby & Sp. *Entomol.* III. 365 External anatomy of insects...*Tempora* (the Temples). Those parts which lie on the outside of the posterior half of the eyes. **1850** R. G. Cumming *Hunter's Life S. Afr.* (1902) 87/1 My dinner consisted of a piece of flesh from the temple of the elephant. **1860** Mayne *Expos. Lex.*, *Temple*,.. *Ornithol.*, *Zool.* Applied to the lateral region of the head comprised between the eyes and ears.

† **2.** *pl.* Ornaments of jewellery or needlework formerly worn by ladies on the sides of the forehead. *Obs.*

*c* **1430** Lydg. *Min. Poems* (Percy Soc.) 56 A fowle visage with gay temples of atyre. **1439** *E. E. Wills* (1882) 116 (C'tess Warwick) That my grete templys with the Baleys be sold to the vtmest pryse. [**1656** Dugdale *Antiq. Warwick.* 330/1 [marg. note on quot. 1439] Jewels hanging on womens foreheads by Bodkins thrust into their hair.]

**3.** Each of the side-members or limbs of a pair of spectacles, which clasp the sides of the head of the wearer. *U.S.*

**1877** Knight *Dict. Mech.*, *Temple*..one of the bars on the outer ends of the spectacle bows [i.e. rims of the lenses] by which the spectacles are made to clasp the head of the wearer. [Hence in later Dicts.]

**4.** *attrib.* and *Comb.*, as *temple-bone*, *-pulse*, *-shot*; **temple-spectacles**, spectacles having jointed side-limbs that grasp the temples.

**1615** Crooke *Body of Man* 583 Where it yssueth out of the *Temple-bone it is broader and thicker. **1793** Holcroft *Lavater's Physiogn.* xiv. 75 The temple-bones..are slow in coming to perfection. **1891** *Daily News* 28 Oct. 7/2 The witness was feeling the *temple pulse while administering. **1899** F. V. Kirby *Sport E. C. Africa* xxi. 232, I ran in and killed him with a *temple shot from my Metford. **1762** Goldsm. *Cit. W.* lv, He had more powder in his hair,..a pair of *temple spectacles, and his hat under his arm.

**Temple** (te·mp'l), *sb.*³ [a. F. *temple* fem. (also *templet*, *temploir*, *templu*), Littré: perh. orig. the same word as *temple*, *tempe*, Temple *sb.*²]

**1.** A contrivance for keeping cloth stretched to its proper width in the loom during the process of weaving. Usually *pl.*

In the hand-loom, a pair of flat rods, having toothed ends which caught the selvedge on each side; in the power-loom, various rotary devices are used.

**1483** *Cath. Angl.* 379/2 A Tempylle of a wefere, *virgula*. **1688** R. Holme *Armoury* III. viii. 348/1 *Temples*, two Staves with broad ends set with sharp Pins,..by the pins putting into the selvage of the Cloth it is kept open while it is in Weaving. **1733** P. Lindsay *Interest Scotl.* 169 The Sum that is now given for the Encouragement of that Branch [Weaving], exclusive of the Reeds, Harness, Shuttles, and Temples. **1863** J. Watson *Art Weaving* 150 The Breast Beam is the rail in front of the loom...It is on this rail that the self acting temples are fixed. **1888** Elworthy *West Somerset Word-bk.*, *Temples*, a wooden stretcher of adjustable length, having points at either end, used by weavers to keep the cloth as woven of the proper width in the loom. Often called a 'pair o' temples'. **1898** *Leeds Mercury Suppl.* 10 Dec. (E. D. D.), The temples on looms to-day ..consist of wheels on either side of the woven piece, having projecting pins all round their circumferences.

**2.** = Templet¹ 2. Also *attrib.*

**1688** R. Holme *Armoury* III. ix. 394/2 Temple Moulds.. are Boards cut in that for[m] as the Stone is to be cut. **1847-78** Halliwell, *Temple-mold*, a pattern, or mould used by masons in fashioning their work.

**Temple** (te·mp'l), *v.* [f. Temple *sb.*¹]

**1.** *trans.* To enclose in or as in a temple, to enshrine; to honour with a temple or temples, to build a temple to or for. Also *fig.*

**1593** Southwell *St. Peters Compl.* 27 Christ, as my God, was templed in my thought. **1628** Feltham *Resolves* II. [I.] lxxxiv. 242 The Heathen (in many places) Templed and adored this drunken god. **1838** S. Bellamy *Betrayal* 57 Templed, and taught, and rited as thou art. **1839** Bailey *Festus* xxxi. (1852) 514 Immured.. In..her holy home, With many a lovely handmaiden around In starry palace templed.

**2.** To make or fashion into a temple.

**1839-49** [implied in Templed *ppl. a.* 2].

† **3.** *intr.* To reside or dwell as in a temple. *Obs.*

*a* **1711** Ken *Hymns Evang.* Poet. Wks. 1721 I. 62 Bless'd Jesu! deign to Temple in my Mind. — *Sion* ibid. IV. 412 O Jesu,..I feel thee templing in my Heart.

Hence **Te·mpling** *vbl. sb.*

*a* **1638** Mede *Wks.* (1672) 641 The Deifying and invocating of Saints and Angels,..the adoring and templing of Reliques. **1677** Gale *Crt. Gentiles* II. III. 105 In the Demon-worship they had many other rites, as worshipping of Columnes, Templing of Reliques.

**Te:mple-ba·r.** [f. Temple *sb.*¹ 5 (because of its position close to the Temple buildings) + Bar *sb.*¹ 13.] The name of the barrier or gateway closing the entrance into the City of London from the Strand; removed in 1878.

[**1314-15** *Rolls of Parlt.* I. 302/2 Le pavement du chemyn par entre la Barre du Novel Temple de Lundres.] **1354** *Ibid.* II. 262/1 Qe l'Estaple de Westmr. comence sa bounde a Temple-barre. *c* **1400** *Brut* 238 Seynt Clementis cherche wiþout Temple-Barr. **1467-8** *Rolls of Parlt.* V. 579/2 A Tenement withoute the Temple Barres of London. **1598** Stow *Surv.* (1908) I. 193 The Queenes Maiestie..entered the citie by Temple Barre, through Fleetstreete, Cheape [etc.]. **1727-41** [see Temple *sb.*¹ 5]. **1773** Johnson 30 Apr. in Boswell *Life* (1887) II. 238 When we got to Temple-bar he [Goldsmith] stopped me, pointed to the [rebels'] heads upon it, and slily whispered me 'Forsitan et nostrum nomen miscebitur istis'. **1851** *London as it is To-day* i. (1855) 9 At [the] extremity [of Fleet St], separating the cities of London and Westminster, stands Temple Bar, the only one of the city boundaries now remaining. **1864** *Chambers' Bk. Days* II. 233/2 The heads of these two [Jacobites executed in 1746] were..stuck over Temple Bar, where they remained till 1772.

**Templed** (te·mp'ld), *ppl. a.* [f. Temple *v.* or *sb.* + -ed.]

**1.** Enshrined in a temple.

**1610** G. Fletcher *Christ's Vict.* I. xx, Gods of wood, Of stocks, and stones, with crowns of laurell stood Templed. **1854** S. Dobell *Balder* iii. 15 The seat of templed Power.

**2.** Made into or like a temple.

**1839** Bailey *Festus* i. (1852) 3 O'er which ye rise in templed majesty. **1849** Quinton *Heaven's Antid. Curse Labour* 42 Canticles of praise will resound through the templed cottage.

**3.** Furnished or adorned with a temple or temples.

**1852** *Meanderings of Mem.* I. 114 We..Rambled such river sides and templed lands. **1878** H. Rice *Sel. Poems* 35 Go tread the templed hills of Orient clime.

**Templeless** (te·mp'l,lès), *a.* [f. Temple *sb.*¹ + -less.] Having no temple, destitute of a temple.

*c* **1460** *Towneley Myst.* xxiii. 493 He shuld make vs tempylles, And gar it cleyn downe fall. **1642** Fuller *Holy & Prof. St.* III. xxiv. 221 And yet that the Persians were wholly Temple-lesse will hardly be believed. **1848** Lytton *Caxtons* IV. ii, Druidism, passing from its earliest templeless belief into the later corruptions.

**Templer, -ere**, obs. forms of Templar.

**Templet**¹ (te·mplėt). Also 9 **template.** [Of uncertain origin.

L. *templum* 'temple' had also the sense 'rafter'; *templet* in sense 1 here (but hardly in sense 2) might possibly be a dim. from this. F. *templet* is given by Littré only as a synonym and presumably a derivative of *temple* fem., a weaver's stretcher, Temple *sb.*³ The spelling *template* is evidently pseudo-etymological, after *plate*.]

**1.** *Building.* A horizontal piece of timber in a wall, or spanning a window or doorway, to take and distribute the pressure of a girder, or of joists or rafters; a plate.

**1677** Moxon *Mech. Exerc.* (ed. 2) 26 When you lay any timber on brickwork, as lintels over windows, or templets under girders, lay them in loom. **1802** *Trans. Soc. Arts* XX. 216 The templets or wall-plates on which the Girder rests. **1819** P. Nicholson *Archit. Dict.*, *Templet*. **1855** *Act* 18 & 19 *Vict.* c. 122 § 15 Every bressummer bearing upon any party wall must be borne by a templet, or corbel of stone or iron, tailed through at least half the thickness of such wall, and of the full breadth of the bressummer. **1879** *Cassell's Techn. Educ.* III. 195 The purpose of templates is similar to that of wall-plates. **1901** *J. Black's Carp. & Build., Scaffolding* 53 The templets must..be bedded in good strong portland cement mortar before being wedged up tightly.

**b.** *Shipbuilding.* One of the wedges for a block under the keel. **1877** in Knight *Dict. Mech.*

**2.** An instrument used as a gauge or guide in bringing any piece of work to the desired shape; usually a flat piece of wood or metal having one edge shaped to correspond to the outline of the finished work; also used as a tool in moulding, and as a guide in forming moulds for castings or pottery, in an automatic lathe, etc.

**1819** P. Nicholson *Archit. Dict.*, *Templet*, a mould used in masonry and brickwork for the purpose of cutting or setting the work. **1823** — *Pract. Build.* 359 It will be necessary to have one templet made convex, to try the faces of bricks to. **1825** J. Nicholson *Operat. Mechanic* 586 Form a templet or cradle to the surface intended. **1844** *Civil Engin. & Arch. Jrnl.* VII. 187/1 The propeller was of cast iron, and was moulded in loam without a model, by means of iron templates cut to the required curve. **1863** Smiles *Indust. Biog.* 271 His [R. Roberts's] system of templets and gauges, by means of which every part of an engine or tender corresponded with that of every other engine or tender of the same class. **1879** *Cassell's Techn. Educ.* I. 3/2.

**b.** A flat plate or strip perforated with holes used as a guide in marking out holes for riveting or drilling. Also *attrib.*

Also, a wooden frame corresponding to the base of any piece of machinery that requires to be fixed by bolts, having holes by means of which the permanent holding-down bolts can be previously fixed in concrete in the exact position to pass through the bolt-holes in the base in question.

**1874** Thearle *Naval Archit.* 98 Templates are used for taking account of the rivet holes in the inside strakes corresponding to those in the frames, when the plates are too heavy to be held in place, and there marked. **1877** Knight *Dict. Mech.* 2529/2 Perforated templets are used by boiler-makers and others to lay out the holes for punching. **1895** A. J. Evans in *Jrnl. Hellenic Stud.* XIV. 320 The symbol might have been a simple kind of stencilling plate known as a 'template', such as is still in use among decorators. *Ibid.* 323 The template symbol.

**Templet**², **-ette.** [In sense 1, a. F. *templette*, dim. of *temple* fem. (in mod.F. *tempe*), Temple *sb.*² Sense 2 may be a different word.]

† **1.** An ornament worn by women on the head; = Temple *sb.*² 2. *Obs.*

**1530** Palsgr. 279/2 Templet a thynge made of latyn, *templete*. *c* **1532** Du Wes *Introd. Fr.* in *Palsgr.* 907 (Names of womens rementes) The templettes, *les templettes*.

**2.** Each of the four-sided facets which surround and 'support' the table of a brilliant.

**1889** *Cent. Dict.*, *Bezel*..2, the oblique side or face of a gem; *spec.* one of four similarly situated four-sided facets on the top or crown of a brilliant, which are sometimes called templets.

**Templet**³. *Weaving.* [dim. of Temple *sb.*³: as mod.F. *templet* (which may be the source).] = Temple *sb.*³ 1.

**1831** G. R. Porter *Silk Manuf.* 223 The woven silk is kept at its proper degree of extension by small hooks, called templets. **1877** Knight *Dict. Mech.* 2529/2 The templet of the horsehair-loom is a pair of jaws for each selvedge.

**Templet**⁴ (te·mplėt). Also **-ette.** [f. Temple *sb.*¹ + -et.] A small or miniature temple.

*a* **1843** in Southey *Comm.-pl. Bk.* III. 657/1 *Fagutal*, a beechen temple or templet under Jupiter Fagutalis. **1848** J. G. Wilkinson *Dalmatia*, etc. I. 183 A little round templet, or open lantern on columns, in style and name worthy of a tea-garden. **1892** *Harper's Mag.* Aug. 355/1 This temple —it is so small that they might call it a templette.

**Te·mplify**, *v. rare.* [f. L. *templ-um*, Temple *sb.*¹ + -fy.] *trans.* To make into a temple.

**1615** Bp. Andrewes *Serm.*, *John* ii. 19 (1841) II. 361 If we can take order that while we be here, before we go hence, our bodies, we get them templified as I may say. **1690** C. Nesse *O. & N. Test.* I. 101 The body must be a stately structure which is thus templify'd by the Holy Ghost.

**Te·mplin-oi:l.** [= Ger. *Templinöl*, Pharmaceut. L. *oleum templinum*, said by Flückiger (*Mittheil. naturf. Gesellsch. Bern*, 1855, 139) to have been used by Haller, 1755: origin unascertained.] (See quots.)

[**1860** Mayne *Expos. Lex.*, *Templinum oleum*,..oil obtained from the cones or nuts of the pine-tree. Germ. syn. *Tannenzapfenöl*.] **1868** Watts *Dict. Chem.* V. 719 *Templin-oil*, *oil of Pine-cones*..isomeric with, and very similar to, oil of turpentine, obtained by distillation of the cones of *Pinus Pumilio*.., and in some parts of Switzerland from the cones of the silver-fir (*Abies Picea*).

† **Te·mplize**, *v. Obs. nonce-wd.* [f. Temple *sb.*¹ + -ize.] *intr.* To assume the form or character of a temple.

**1650** Fuller *Pisgah* IV. iv. 72 The Rabbins conceive that during the abode thereof at Shiloh, the Tabernacle began to templize, getting walls..round about it, chiefly because about that time it is thrice termed a Temple.

‖ **Tempo** (te·mpo). Pl. tempi (te·mpi). [It., :—L. *tempus* time.]

**1.** *Mus.* Relative speed or rate of movement; pace; time; *spec.* the proper or characteristic speed and rhythm of a dance or other tune (in phr. *tempo di gavotta, tempo di marcia, tempo di minuetto*, etc.).

*Tempo primo*, first or former time; a direction to resume the original speed after an alteration of it. *Tempo rubato*, 'robbed or stolen time; time occasionally slackened or hastened for the purposes of expression' (Stainer & Barrett).

**1724** *Short Explic. For. Wds. in Mus. Bks., Tempo*, Time. Thus, *Tempo Di Gavotta*, is Gavot Time, or the Time or Movement observed in playing a Gavot. *Tempo Di Minuetto,..Tempo Di Sarabanda.* **1839** LONGF. *Hyperion* IV. iv, In his hurry he got the *tempo* about twice too slow. **1866** ENGEL *Nat. Mus.* ii. 63 They sing in a more subdued tone; the *tempo* is slower. **1884** F. TAYLOR in Grove *Dict. Mus.* IV. 82 Verbal directions as to tempo are generally written in Italian. **1888** *Athenæum* 17 Mar. 349/1 The composer has reconsidered the *tempi* of some portions..; he also indulged ..in the *tempo rubato.*

†**2.** A term in fencing: see quot. *Obs. rare.*

**1688** R. HOLME *Armoury* III. xix. (Roxb.) 159/2 A Tempo, is to take heed neuer to make a thrust or blow at aduersarie, without thou hast a faire opportunity to hit, or within measure, that he be within thy reach.

**Tempor, -e**, obs. forms of TEMPER *v.*

**Temporad** (te·mpŏræd), *adv. Physiol.* [f. TEMPOR-AL *a.*[2] + *-ad*, as in DEXTRAD, etc.] Towards the temples.

**1808** BARCLAY *Muscular Motions* 470 Rotatory motions Mesiad, and Temporad. *Ibid.* 471 In such motions the *coronal rectus* is made to turn the pupil coronad;..the *temporal*, temporad.

**Temporal** (te·mpŏrăl), *a.*[1] and *sb.*[1] Also 4-7 -er-; 4-5 -el, -ell(e, -ale, 4-6 -alle, 4-7 -all. [ad. L. *temporāl-is*, f. *tempus, tempor-*, a space or point of time, time; in B. 2, ad. eccl. L. *temporāle.*]

**A.** *adj.* **1.** Lasting or existing only for a time; passing, temporary. Now *rare* or merged in 2.

**1382** WYCLIF *Matt.* xiii. 21 He hath nat roote in hym self, but it is temporal; that is, it lastith bot a litil tyme. **1382** — 2 *Cor.* iv. 18 Sothli tho thingis that ben seyn, ben temperal, or duryng by short tyme. **1598** SYLVESTER *Du Bartas* II. ii. I. *Ark* 500 [Rainbow] A temporall beauty of the lampfull skies. **1762** tr. *Busching's Syst. Geog.* I. 49 Others begin to run in spring,..and cease again towards autumn, and are called temporal Springs. **1879** STEVENSON *Trav. Cevennes* (1886) 127 What seems a kind of temporal death to people choked between walls..is only a.. living slumber to the man who sleeps a-field.

**2.** Of or pertaining to time as the sphere of human life; terrestrial as opposed to heavenly; of man's present life as distinguished from a future existence; concerning or involving merely the material interests of this world; worldly, earthly. (Opp. to *eternal* or *spiritual.*)

*c* **1375** *Sc. Leg. Saints* vi. (*Thomas*) 315 þat þai..ȝarnis til hafe na temporale gud, outane anerly clath & fud. *c* **1380** WYCLIF *Wks.* (1880) 5 Temperal almes. *c* **1400** *Rom. Rose* 7066 So that the tour were stuffed wel With alle richesse temporel. *c* **1532** DU WES *Introd. Fr.* in *Palsgr.* 1036 The lytell goodes temporals that it hath pleased to God to sende me. **1685** BAXTER *Paraphr. N. T.* Mark ii. 15 He would not set up a temporal Kingdom. **1772** PRIESTLEY *Inst. Relig.* (1782) I. 306 The Jews..expected..a temporal prince. **1832** HT. MARTINEAU *Life in Wilds* vii. 91 Fear for the temporal prosperity of the whole race.

**3.** Secular as opposed to sacred; lay as distinguished from clerical. Of law: civil or common as distinguished from canon. Of rule, authority, or government: civil as distinguished from ecclesiastical. *Lords Temporal*: see LORD *sb.* 9. (Opp. to *spiritual.*)

*c* **1340** HAMPOLE *Prose Tr.* 24 Itt longith to som temporalle men the which han soueraynte. *c* **1400** MAUNDEV. (1839) v. 43 He was Lord Spirituelle & Temporelle. *c* **1440** *Brut* 468 þe King..borowed a somme of gold þurghout þe Reame, of temporall peple, þat amounted a c. M[l] marc of money, to sende his peple ouer the see. **1451** CAPGRAVE *Life St. Aug.* 27 Ambrose had..mad neuly many ympnys, for all þe temperal ympnys ar ny of his making, as primo dierum omnium, & þoo þat folow. **1578** *Knaresborough Wills* (Surtees) I. 130 And after come to practice as a temporall Lawyer. **1596** SHAKS. *Merch. V.* IV. i. 190 His Scepter shewes the force of temporall power, The attribute to awe and Maiestie. **1672** PETTY *Pol. Anat.* (1691) 36 The Government of Ireland is by the King, 21 Bishops..and the Temporal Peers. **1774** PENNANT *Tour Scot. in 1772* 149 A charter erecting the lands belonging to the abbacy into a temporal lordship. **1898** C. H. BOWDEN *Dict. Cath., Temporal Power of the Pope.*—1. His right to possess and govern the Patrimony of St. Peter and other States of the Church; 2. His rights as Vicar of Christ in relation to other sovereigns and states.

†**4.** Applied to 'artificial hours', i. e. twelfths of an 'artificial day': see ARTIFICIAL 5. *Obs. rare.*

**1594** BLUNDEVIL *Exerc.* III. I. lii. (1636) 370 Note also that the unequall houres are called sometime artificiall, and sometime temporall houres.

**5. a.** *Gram.* and *Pros.* Relating to or depending on the quantity of syllables (i. e. the time taken in pronouncing them). *Temporal augment* (Gr. Gram.): see AUGMENT *sb.* 2.

**1678** PHILLIPS (ed. 4), *Temporal Augment*, an Augmentation which is made in a Greek Verb, by increasing in several Tenses, the quantity of the first Vowel or Dipthong, as ἄγω ἦγον. **1860** MARSH *Lect. Eng. Lang.* 540 The ancient temporal metres were inexhaustible, because the permutations and combinations of the prosodical feet were infinite. **1867** tr. *Curtius's Gr. Gram.* (ed. 2) § 235 The Temporal Augment is used in all verbs which begin with a vowel.

**b.** *Gram.* Of or pertaining to the tenses of a verb; of tense; also, expressing or denoting time, as an adverb, a clause, etc.

**1786** H. TOOKE *Purley* II. viii. (1798) 650 Our language has made but small progress, compared either with the Greek or with the Latin..even in this Modal and Temporal abbreviation. **1886** W. G. HALE in *Amer. Jrnl. Philol.* VII. 459 The tenseless phrase *in order to*, used alike for present and past purposes in English, fails to convey the temporal ideas conveyed by the Latin present and imperfect subjunctive. **1889** *Ibid.* X. 334 In Latin all the uses of the ablative absolute sprang from the temporal use of the ablative.

**6.** In general sense: Of, pertaining, or relating to time, the present time, or a particular time.

**1877** MALLOCK *New Republic* II. III. ii. 15 Merely temporal people, who are just as narrow-minded and dull as.. merely local people—the natives of a neighbourhood. **1886** A. WEIR *Hist. Basis Mod. Europe* (1889) 481 A vast quantity of temporal and spatial experience. **1906** D. W. FORREST *Authority Christ* VI. i. 309 In speaking of the last day we are using a temporal expression for an unspeakable and timeless reality.

**B.** *sb.* **1. a.** That which is temporal: esp. in *pl.* Temporal things or matters.

**1390** GOWER *Conf.* I. 32 Noght only of the temporal But of the spirital also. *Ibid.* 276 To day is venym schad In holi cherche of temporal, Which medleth with the spirital. **1471** FORTESCUE *Wks.* (1869) 534 In his persone and his kingdome, which bothe be temporales onely. **1625** BURGES *Pers. Tithes* 16 Hee that partakes of Gods blessing in Temporals. **1755** YOUNG *Centaur* iv, Joy from temporals, is a terrestrial joy, And, like all things terrestrial, has a dreg in it. **1897** H. DRUMMOND *Ideal Life* 140 Trying by some other way than through these homely temporals, to learn the spiritual life.

**b.** Temporal power, possession, or estate; TEMPORALITY; chiefly in *pl.* = temporalities.

*c* **1450** HOLLAND *Howlat* 277 That sen it nechit Natur, thar alleris mastriss, Thai couth nocht trete but entent of the Temperale. **1545** BRINKLOW *Compl.* xxii. (1874) 51 Of their temporals, let .viij. or .x. pound and not aboue of euery hundreth be granted to the Kyng. **1594** R. ASHLEY tr. *Loys le Roy* 54 b, The Pope commaundeth ouer the temporall of the Church called S. Peters patrimonie, as King. **1795** ABBE BARRUEL *Hist. Clergy during Fr. Rev.* 99 They did not reject the new French constitution, or the laws concerning temporals. **1863** BLYTH *Hist. Fincham* 39 The temporals were such lands or other property as may have accrued to the church by gift or purchase, and belonged chiefly to the regular or monastic clergy. **1880** BROWNING *Dram. Idylls* Ser. II. *Pietro* 362 I'll to Rome, before Rome's feet the temporal-supreme lay prostrate!

**2.** (Also in L. form **Temporale** (temporē·li, -āle).) That part of the breviary and missal which contains the daily offices in the order of the ecclesiastical year, as distinct from those proper for Saints' days: cf. SANCTORALE.

**14..** *Table Lessons*, etc. in *Wyclif's Bible* IV. 690 Here endith the Temperal, and here bigynneth the Propre Sanctorum. *c* **1475** *Pict. Voc.* in Wr.-Wülcker 755/21 *Hoc temperalium*, a temperal. **1483** CAXTON *Gold. Leg.* 63/2 This is the Rewle of the temporal thurgh the yere. **1517** in *Archæologia* LXI. 83 Item a legend hoole of the temporall...Item a legend hoole of the Sanctorum. **1872** Temporale [see SANCTORALE].

**Temporal** (te·mpŏrăl), *a.*[2] and *sb.*[2] *Anat.* Also 6 tymporall. [ad. L. *temporāl-is*, f. *tempora* the temples: see TEMPLE *sb.*[2]] Of, belonging to, or situated in the temples: esp. in names of structures, as *temporal artery, bone, muscle, vein*, etc.

*Temporal canals*, small passages for vessels and nerves through the malar bone to the temporal surface; *temporal lobe*, the lowest lobe of the brain lying below the Sylvian fissure; *temporal fossa*, that in which the temporal muscle originates.

**1597** A. M. tr. *Guillemeau's Fr. Chirurg.* 11/2 We should not hurte the temporalle muscle. *Ibid.* 29 b/1 The thirde is called the temporall, or vayne of the temples, which in divers branches ascendeth in the temples of the heade. **1732** ARBUTHNOT *Rules of Diet* in *Aliments*, etc. 327 Copious Bleeding by opening the temporal Arteries. **1842** E. WILSON *Anat. Vade M.* (ed. 2) 23 The Temporal Bone is..divisible into a squamous, mastoid, and petrous portion. **1854** H. SPENCER *Personal Beauty* Ess. 1891 II. 390 The chief agents in closing the jaws are the temporal muscles.

**B.** *sb.* Elliptical for *temporal artery, bone, muscle*, etc.

**1541** R. COPLAND *Guydon's Quest. Chirurg.* F j, Those [muscles] are called tymporalles, and are ryght noble and very sensyble, & therfore theyr hurt is very peryllous. **1758** J. S. *Le Dran's Observ. Surg.* 8 The Temporal became ossified. **1899** *Allbutt's Syst. Med.* VII. 228 The muscles of mastication—the masseters, temporals, and pterygoids. **1900** J. HUTCHINSON in *Arch. Surg.* XI. No. 41. 23 The old woman's temporals were scarcely, if at all, enlarged.

‖ **Temporale**: see TEMPORAL *sb.*[1] 2.

**Temporalism** (te·mpŏrăliz'm). [f. TEMPORAL *a.*[1] + -ISM.]

**1.** The spirit of 'the world' (as opposed to a religious spirit); secularism; addiction to temporal or mundane interests.

**1872** *Dublin Rev.* Jan. 10 Exhibition of the evil spirit which we have called 'temporalism', in that hatred of restraint and subordination. **1897** *N. York Voice* 16 Sept. 3/1 He..takes leave of animalism, temporalism, provincialism, and becomes consciously a son of God.

**2.** The principle of the temporal power of the Pope.

**1899** *Spectator* 7 Jan. 15 This war, which is not the warfare, nor in the interest, of the Roman Catholic Church, but of temporalism, is carried into every field where intolerant Catholicism has any power.

So **Te·mporalist**, one who maintains or supports the temporal power of the Pope.

**1901** *Mission. Record U. F. Ch. Scot.* June 272/1 The next Pope will be a strong Temporalist.

**Temporality** (tempŏræ·lĭti). Also 5 -er-; 4-6 -ite, 5 -yte, -itee, -ytee, 5-6 -itie, (6 temporallytie). [ad. late L. *temporālitās* (Tertullian), f. *temporāl-is*, TEMPORAL: see -ITY. Substituted in 14-15th c. for *temperalté*, TEMPORALTY, q.v.]

†**1.** Temporal power, jurisdiction, affairs, property, etc.: *esp.* the temporal property of the clergy; = TEMPORALTY 1. *Obs.*

**1393** LANGL. *P. Pl.* C. XXIII. 128 Prelates thei maden, To holde with Antecrist here temporalite to saue. **1497** *Acc. Ld. High Treas. Scot.* I. 314 Resauit fra Maister Johne Fresel, elect of Ros, for the compositioun of his admissioune to the temporalitee of Ros. **1501** *Reg. Privy Seal Scotl.* I. 93/1 A Precept of Admission made to Jane Forman, Prioress of Eklis, to the temporalite of al landis, rentis, and possessionis of the sammyn. **1613** SHERLEY *Trav. Persia* 3 The lesser Princes of Italy being not likely to endure the Churches so great encrease of Temporality. **1818** SCOTT *Hrt. Midl.* xlii[i], That the said incumbent might lawfully enjoy the spirituality and temporality of the cure of souls at Knocktarlitie.

**b.** *pl.* Temporal or material possessions (esp. of the church or clergy).

*c* **1475** *Harl. Contn. Higden* (Rolls) VIII. 546 The comons putte up a bylle in the parlement to the kynge as for the temporalytees beynge in the handes of the spirituelte. *a* **1552** LELAND *Itin.* VI. 1 The Kynge had reteynid the Temporallyties of the Byshoprike for a tyme. **1593** in Row *Hist. Kirk* (Wodrow Soc.) 150 To considder what great prejudice the Kirk sustains by the erecting of the tithes of diverss prelacies into temporalities, so that these kirks cannot be planted. **1660** R. COKE *Power & Subj.* 204 The Pope..gave to the said Nicholas the said Abby, with all the said Spiritualities, and Temporalities. **1726** AYLIFFE *Parergon* 129 After all which, the Bishop is introduced into the King's Presence to do his Homage for his Temporalities or Barony. **1854** H. MILLER *Sch. & Schm.* xxv. (1857) 546 The Church..might, I believed, have to forfeit the temporalities, if her decision differed from that of the law courts.

**2.** The body or class of temporal persons; = TEMPORALTY 2.

**1456** SIR G. HAYE *Law Arms* (S.T.S.) 24 The Emperour ..to be lord and juge..of the temporalitee. *c* **1470** HENRY *Wallace* X. 1002 The byschoprykis inclynyt till his croune, Bathe temperalite and all the religioune. **1543** HEN. VIII *Sp. Parl.* 24 Dec., in *Coll. Poems* 165 You of the Temporality be not clean and unspotted of Malice and Envy. **1679** BURNET *Hist. Ref.* I. 582 Here both the temporality and spirituality gave great subsidies to the king.

**3.** The quality or condition of being temporal or temporary; temporariness; relation to time.

**1634** RAINBOW *Labour* (1635) 11 Though in the act of our labours..we place temporality, yet ought we alwayes before our intentions to set æternity. **1659** H. L'ESTRANGE *Alliance Div. Off.* v. 158 As the Western Church observed this very day [All Saints day], so did also the Eastern, or at least some other, in temporality and point of time very near it. **1678** T. JONES *Heart & its Right Sov.* 587 What can any mortal excellency, that has..perishing temporality stamp'd upon it signifie to Christians, who are not of this world? **1909** *Westm. Gaz.* 15 May 4/1 Gaining thereby the attributes of eternity, without losing its own qualities of temporality.

**Te·mporalize**, *v. rare.* [f. TEMPORAL *a.*[1] + -IZE.] *trans.* To make temporal in character. **a.** To secularize; **b.** to limit in time.

**1828** PUSEY *Hist. Enq.* I. 146 They led to the ultimate temporalizing and annihilation of everything peculiarly Christian in the system. **1890** *Spectator* 5 July, Many who turned from a worship which seemed to localise and temporalise the Divine.

**Te·mporally**, *adv.* [f. as prec. + -LY [2].]

**1.** For a time, temporarily. *rare.*

**1450-1530** *Myrr. our Ladye* 185 The maker of all thynges rested temperally in the,..thow vyrgyn.

**2.** In regard to temporal matters; in, or with respect to, this world; in the present life.

*c* **1380** *Antecrist* in Todd 3 *Treat. Wyclif* 119 Antecrist havyng glorie of þe world temporally. **1456** SIR G. HAYE *Law Arms* (S.T.S.) 20 As evill bitter wateris gerris mony folk dee temporaly, sa dois..heresy and lollardry the saule dee spiritualy. **1552** ABP. HAMILTON *Catech.* (1884) 39 Punitions quhilk God sendis to synnaris temporallie. **1679** WHITEBREAD in *Speeches Jesuits* 2, I pray God bless His Majesty both Temporally and Eternally. *a* **1716** SOUTH *Serm.* (J.), Sinners who are in such a temporally happy condition, owe it not to their sins, but wholly to their luck.

**Te·mporalness.** *rare.* [f. as prec. + -NESS.] The quality of being temporal.

**1611** COTGR., *Secularité*,..worldlinesse, temporallnesse.

**Temporalty** (te·mpŏrălti). *Obs.* or *arch.* Also 4-6 temper-; 4-5 -el-; 4-6 -te, -tee, 4-7 -tie, 5-6 -tye, (6 temporalltie). [app. a. AF. *temporelté = F. temporalité (13th c.), f. OF. *temporel*, TEMPORAL: see -TY. Cf. *commonalty, cruelty, loyalty*, etc. In 14-15th c. assimilated to the L. form, as *temper-, temporalité*; now TEMPORALITY.]

**1.** Temporal or secular things, affairs, business; temporal authority. ? *Obs.*

**1396-7** in *Eng. Hist. Rev.* (1907) XXII. 299 Temporelte

and spirituelte ben to partys of holi chirche. *c* **1400** MAUNDEV. (Roxb.) iii. 10 He es þare lorde bathe of tempe-raltee and of spiritualtee. *c* **1483** CAXTON *Dialogues* 45 *Cest grand folye De donner le eternalite Pour le tempo-ralite*, it is grete folye For to gyve the eternalite For the temporalte. *c* **1511** *1st Eng. Bk. Amer.* (Arb.) Introd. 30/2 In ye temperalte haue they one Emperour. **1621** BURTON *Anat. Mel.* III. i. I. ii. (1651) 415 The mutability of all temporalties. **1651** *Life Father Sarpi* (1676) 47 Lands that in the temporalty are subject to the state of Venice, and in the spirituality are under the Arch-Bishop of Milan. **1700** ASTRY tr. *Saavedra-Faxardo* I. 183 The Spiritualty and Temporalty are two distinct Jurisdictions.

**b.** Chiefly *pl.* Temporal possessions; esp. those of an ecclesiastical person or body: = TEMPOR-ALITY 1 b. ? *Obs.*

[1306 *Rolls of Parlt.* I. 220/1 Ont donez terres, tenementz, & avoesons, & tieles autres temporautez, as Prelatz de seinte Eglise.] **1377** LANGL. *P. Pl.* B. xx. 127 Prelates þei hem maden, To holden with antecryste her temperaltes to saue. *c* **1380** WYCLIF *Wks.* (1880) 103 Subsidies & dymes for here temperalties. **1449** *Rolls of Parlt.* V. 157/2 Prouffitez of the temperaltees of Bisshuprichez. **1570-6** LAMBARDE *Peramb. Kent* (1826) 229 A stately Monasterie (the temporalties whereof did amount to a hundreth fiftie and five poundes). **1607** COWELL *Interpr.*, *Temporalties of Bishops* (*Tempo-ralia Episcoporum*) be such reuenewes, lands, and tenements, as Bishops haue had laid to their Sees by the Kings and other great personages of this land from time to time. *a* **1715** BURNET *Own Time* I. IV. (1724) 760 The Cardinal was chosen by the Chapter Vicar, or Guardian of the temporalties.

**2.** The body of temporal persons or laymen, the laity; the temporal estate or estates of the realm, i.e. the temporal peers and the commons.

**1387** TREVISA *Higden* (Rolls) VII. 335 Kyng William was sterne..and rulede boþe temperalte and spiritualte at his owne wille. **1480** CAXTON *Chron. Eng.* ccxliv. 301 Ther was graunted vnto the kyng..bothe of spirituelte and of temporalte an hole taxe and a disme. *a* **1529** SKELTON *Col. Cloute* 61 For the temporalte Accuseth the spiritualte. **1621** ELSING *Debates Ho. Lords* (Camden) App. 129 The subsidies of the Temporalty and the Clergie brought into the House from the King. *a* **1715** BURNET *Own Time* an. 1663 (1823) I. II. 340 The convocation gave..four sub-sidies, which proved as heavy on them, as they were light on the temporalty. **1874** S. WILBERFORCE *Ess.* II. 191 The old compact between the spirituality and the temporalty.

† **b.** The condition or estate of a layman. *Obs.*

*c* **1440** *Bone Flor.* 1032 Ther was lefte no man in that town..That was of temporalte. **1482** *Monk of Evesham* (Arb.) 38 Sothely some flowryd in prosperite in the spyrytu-alte. Some in the temporalte and some in relygyon.

**Te·mporalwa·rd,** *adv. rare.* [f. TEMPORAL *a.*[2] + -WARD.] Towards the temples or temporal region; = TEMPORAD.

**1904** TITCHENER tr. *Wundt's Physiol. Psychol.* I. 236 Retinal points that lie temporalward.

**Temporance,** obs. form of TEMPERANCE.

† **Tempora·neal,** *a. Obs. rare*$^{-1}$. [f. as next + -AL.] = next (in quot. in sense 2).

**1625** JACKSON *Creed* v. xviii. § 2 As if the temporaneal coexistence of these two effects had sufficiently argued the one's causal dependence upon the other.

**Temporaneous** (tempŏrēⁱ·niəs), *a.* Now *rare* or *Obs.* [f. L. *temporāne-us* timely, opportune (f. *tempus, tempor-* time) + -OUS.]

† **1.** Lasting only for a time, temporary. *Obs.*

**1656** [see 2]. **1681** HALLYWELL *Melampr.* 68 (T.) Those things may cause a temporaneous disunion. **1782** A. MONRO *Compar. Anat.* 120 The temporaneous grinders are placed ..upon the internal set. **1806** W. TAYLOR in *Ann. Rev.* IV. 244 This book is so driftless, so useless, so temporaneous. **1818** [implied in *temporaneously, -ness*: see below].

**2.** Pertaining or relating to time, temporal.

**1656** BLOUNT *Glossogr.*, *Temporaneous*, done suddenly, at a certaine time, pertaining to time; variable for the time. **1694** *Phil. Trans.* XVIII. 67 A Temporaneous progressive motion of the parts of the Air at the rate of 276 Paces in a second Minute of time. **1878** F. FERGUSON *Pop. Life Christ* x. 40 He uses only the connective particle 'and' and not the temporaneous 'then'.

Hence **Tempora·neously** *adv.*, for the time; **Tempora·neousness,** temporary character.

**1727** BAILEY vol. II, Temporaneousness. **1818** G. S. FABER *Horæ Mosaicæ* I. 328 His title to the perpetually entailed, though temporaneously alienated, inheritance of his fore-fathers. *Ibid.* II. 208 The testimony which it bears respect-ing its own temporaneousness.

**Temporarily** (te·mpŏrărili), *adv.* [f. TEM-PORARY *a.* + -LY [2].] In a temporary manner.

**1.** For a time (only); during a limited time.

*c* **1694** in Somers *Tracts* (1748) I. 193 Derogatory to the King's Prerogative, relative to Parliaments, and temporarily changing the very Constitution thereof. **1803** GODWIN *Life Chaucer* III. 189 (Jod.) An oligarchical council temporarily administering the affairs of the nation. **1873** *Act* 36 & 37 *Vict.* c. 88 § 7 The vacancy shall be temporarily filled.

**2.** In relation to time, temporally. *rare.*

**1877** E. CAIRD *Philos. Kant* II. xi. 447 All spatially or temporarily determined phenomena.

**Temporariness** (te·mpŏrărinės). [f. next + -NESS.] The quality or state of being temporary.

**1695** J. SAGE *Article*, etc. Wks. 1844 I. 197 The perpetuity or temporariness of it doth not affect its nature. **1876** W. BATHGATE *Deep Things of God* ii. 36 The..suddenness and temporariness of the physical process of breathing.

**Temporary** (te·mpŏrări), *a.* (*sb.*) [ad. L. *temporāri-us*, f. *tempus, tempor-* time: see -ARY.]

**1.** Lasting for a limited time; existing or valid for a time (only); not permanent; transient; made to supply a passing need.

**1547-64** BAULDWIN *Mor. Philos.* (Palfr.) 60 The authority of princes & gouernors..is truely to be called temporarie, that is, but for a time. *a* **1628** PRESTON *New Covt.* (1634) 45 The creature is temporary, whereas the soul is immortall. **1651** HOBBES *Leviath.* II. xix. 99 For their perpetuall, and not temporary security. **1777** COOK *Voy. Pacific* II. vii. (1784) I. 292 A large space had been cleared, before the temporary hut of this Chief. **1817** JAS. MILL *Brit. India* II. IV. ix. 293 The adaptation of temporary expedients to temporary exi-gencies. **1858** J. H. NEWMAN *Hist. Sk.* (1873) III. v. i. 434 Inconveniences which they felt to be only temporary.

**b.** *Temporary star* (*Astron.*), a star which appears suddenly, shines for a time, and then almost or entirely disappears; *temporary tooth*, a deciduous tooth, milk-tooth.

**1802** *Med. Jrnl.* VIII. 559 The first teeth, or those of childhood, the author calls temporary, the set which suc-ceeds them he terms permanent. **1833** HERSCHEL *Astron.* xii. 383 The phænomena we allude to are those of temporary stars. **1842** E. WILSON *Anat. Vade M.* (ed. 2) 51 The Temporary teeth are 20 in number, 8 incisors, 4 canine, and 8 molars.

† **c.** Belonging or relating to the particular time; of the period; hence, of passing interest, ephe-meral. ? *Obs.* (or merged in 1).

**1777** BURKE *Corr.* (1844) II. 164, I send you a trifling temporary production, made for the occasion of the day, and to perish with it. **1778** MUSGRAVE 25 Apr., in Boswell *Johnson*, A temporary poem always entertains us. **1805** W. COOKE *S. Foote* I. 152 Though it ['Devil upon Two Sticks'] admits of some temporary strokes, such as the ridicule on the college of physicians,..&c., [it] exhibits them worked up in so brilliant and general a manner, as to be always new.

† **2.** Belonging to the present life or this world: = TEMPORAL *a.*[1] 2. *Obs.*

(In quot. 1603, of a person: 'not a meddler with temporal or secular affairs'.)

**1603** SHAKS. *Meas. for M.* v. i. 145 *Duke.* Know you that Frier Lodowick that she speakes of? *Peter.* I know him for a man diuine and holy, Not scuruy, nor a temporary medler, As he's reported by this Gentleman. **1668** HOWE *Bless. Righteous* (1825) 63 In our temporary state, while we are under the measure of time. **1674** OWEN *Holy Spirit* (1693) 207 Spiritual and Eternal things are more excellent than things Carnal and Temporary. **1751** JOHNSON *Rambler* No. 153 ⁋ 13 The wise use of temporary riches.

† **3.** *Metaph.* Occurring or existing in time (not from eternity). *Obs.* (Cf. TEMPORAL *a.*[1] 6.)

*a* **1677** HALE *Prim. Orig. Man.* I. ii. 69 Collectively they make up a good moral evidence touching a temporary in-ception of the humane Nature. **1678** CUDWORTH *Intell. Syst.* I. i. § 31. 39 They who conceived the World to have had a Temporary Beginning or Creation, held the Coevity of all Souls with it. **1701** NORRIS *Ideal World* 327 These truths are temporary, because those relations could not be-gin to exist before those created beings were produced.

† **4.** = TEMPORAL *a.*[1] 4. *Obs. rare.*

*a* **1656** USSHER *Ann.* To Rdr. ⁋ 10 That from the evening ushering in the first day of the World, to that midnight which began the first day of the Christian æra, there was 4003 years, seventy dayes, and six temporarie howers.

**B.** *sb.*

† **1.** *pl.* Things belonging to this life, temporal goods. Cf. TEMPORALITY 1 b. *Obs.*

**1596** H. CLAPHAM *Briefe Bible* II. 218 Wee haue taken Bread and other temporaries without begging them at thy hands. **1665** SIR T. HERBERT *Trav.* (1677) 172 A large Castle, which now by age or war (the canker-worms of all temporaries) is moth-eaten.

† **2.** A person whose religious life or devotion endures only for a time. (In allusion to Matt. xiii. 21, etc.) *Obs.* (In quot. 1903 used (? by misunder-standing) for: A time-server, temporizer.)

**1619** W. SCLATER *Exp. 1 Thess.* (1630) 59 Our Tempora-ries, or rather Temporizers..are carried full saile to the pro-fession of Faith; whom yet the least note of reproach.. makes ready to deny and abiure the Truth. **1647** TRAPP *Comm. 2 Cor.* xiii. 8 A temporary may so fall away as to persecute the truth that he once professed. [**1903** A. SMELLIE *Men of Covt.* xxiii. (1904) 253 A Temporary,—one who tries year in and year out to 'carry his dish level', and adjusts his sails to catch the changing winds.]

† **3.** A contemporary. *Obs.*

**1649** *Alcoran* 6 We left this punishment, as an advertise-ment to their temporaries and posteritie.

**4.** A person employed or holding a post tem-porarily; a 'casual'.

**1848** DICKENS *Dombey* iii, Being only a permanency I couldn't be expected to show it like a temporary. **1892** *Pall Mall G.* 7 Oct. 7/1 The 'permanent temporaries' are liable to dismissal at any time, but are practically fixed, some having been in the service from eight to ten years. **1907** *Westm. Gaz.* 1 July 7/2 Servants who are merely casuals (i.e., temporaries) in purely private families.

**Temporat(e, -aunce**: see TEMPERATE, -ANCE.

**Temporicide** (te·mpŏrisəid). *nonce-wd.* [f. L. *tempus, tempor-* time + -CIDE.]

**1.** The 'killing' of time.

**1851** *Chambers' Papers for People* IX. No. 72. 9 Short romantic stories, adaptable for purposes of temporicide. **1856** GRINDON *Life* xxiv. (1875) 305 Pleasure..such as will outweigh whole nights of the mere temporicide popularly esteemed the *beau idéal* of pastime.

**2.** One who 'kills' time.

*a* **1876** M. COLLINS *Th. in Gard.* (1880) II. 208 D., who would catch the tide, G., with his notions wide, Each is temporicide—Time's reckless murderer.

† **Te·mporist.** *Obs.* [f. as prec. + -IST: cf. TEMPORIZE *v.*] A temporizer, a time-server.

**1596** NASHE *Saffron-Walden* Wks. (Grosart) III. 123 Heilding Dicke..is a temporist that hath faith inough for all Religions. **1607** MARSTON *What you will* II. i, Why, turne a temporist, row with the tide, Pursew the cut, the fashion of the age. **1650-66** WHARTON *Poems* Wks. (1683) 333 Touch me not, Traytor!..I am no Temporist.

**Temporization** (tempŏrəizēⁱ·ʃən). [f. next + -ATION.] The action of temporizing.

**1.** Time-serving, 'trimming'; compromise.

**1763** JOHNSON *Misc. Lives, Ascham* Wks. IV. 631 Charges of temporization and compliance had somewhat sullied his reputation. **1839** *Fraser's Mag.* XX. 97 Her policy is one of temporisation. **1851** *Ibid.* XLIII. 139 A union..was con-sequently thought of, as the best means of temporization.

**2.** Procrastination, delay; gaining of time.

**1888** *Times* 19 Oct. 5/1 The inevitable reaction against the policy of adjournment and temporization.

**Temporize** (te·mpŏrəiz), *v.* [a. F. *temporiser* (14–15th c. in Hatz.-Darm.) to pass one's time, wait one's time, = med.L. *temporizāre* = *tempor-āre* to put off the time, delay (Du Cange), It. *temporeggiare* to observe, obey, or follow times (Florio), f. L. *tempus, tempor-* time: see -IZE.]

**1.** *intr.* To adopt some course for the time or occasion; hence, to adapt oneself or conform to the time and circumstances; to 'trim'.

[1555-63: cf. TEMPORIZER 1.] **1579** G. HARVEY *Letter-bk.* (Camden) 69, I pray the spare the world And give men leave to temporize. **1617** MORYSON *Itin.* II. 51 Most part of the rest temporised with the State, openly professing obedience..but secretly relieuing the rebels. **1752** FIELDING *Amelia* IX. ix, How do you expect to rise in the church, if you cannot temporise, and give in to the opinion of your supporters? **1849** MACAULAY *Hist. Eng.* viii. II. 298 Penn, therefore, exhorted the fellows..to submit, or at least to tem-porise. **1877** FROUDE *Short Stud.* (1883) IV. I. iii. 38 The pope..had privately advised Becket to avoid a quarrel with the king and to temporise.

† **b.** *trans. Obs. rare.*

**1600** [see TEMPORIZED below].

† **2.** *intr.* To let time pass, spend time, 'mark time'; to procrastinate; to delay or wait for a more favourable moment. Also with *it*. *Obs.* exc. as in 3.

**1579-80** NORTH *Plutarch* (1676) 358 Charging them they should not stir, and only to temporize and forbear, untill the Enemies came within a stones cast of them. **1600** HOLLAND *Livy* XXIV. xiii. 517 So Anniball contrariwise temporised, being not so readie now to credite the Nolanes. **1633** T. STAFFORD *Pac. Hib.* I. xiii. (1821) 147 Having temporized all this while. **1694** MOTTEUX *Rabelais* v. xviii. (1737) 76 We lay by and run adrift, that is, in a Landlopers Phrase, we temporis'd it. **1696** PHILLIPS (ed. 5), *Temporize*..also, to delay, to take time to consider.

**3.** *intr.* To act, negotiate, parley, treat, deal (*with* a person, etc.), so as to gain time.

**1586** J. HOOKER *Hist. Irel.* in *Holinshed* II. 118/1 They did yet so temporise with them, as they gained time, till further order might be taken. **1586** DAY *Eng. Secretary* I. (1625) A iij b, My prouision is too small to perfect on a sudden so spacious a ground-worke, I will temporize with those duties which..by time may be in me supported. **1871** FREEMAN *Norm. Conq.* IV. xviii. 133 William was still temporizing with Stigand; the time for his degradation was not yet come.

**4.** To negotiate, to discuss terms; to arrange or make terms, to effect a compromise (*with* a per-son, etc., *between* persons or parties).

**1579** FENTON *Guicciard.* I. (1599) 4 Knowing discreetely howe to temporise betweene Princes confederate. **1586** J. HOOKER *Hist. Irel.* in *Holinshed* II. 142/1 His lord-ship granted hir request, and temporised with the earle. **1636** E. DACRES tr. *Machiavel's Disc. Livy* I. 137 The safer course is, to temporise with it, then strive forthwith to ex-tinguish it. **1823** SCOTT *Peveril* xxxvi, I have behaved like a fool..; I ought to have temporised with this singular being, learned the motives of its interference, and availed myself of its succour. **1863** KINGLAKE *Crimea* I. iii. 48 This calm Mahometan..strove to temporise as well as he could betwixt the angry Churches.

† **b.** *trans.* ? To negotiate, manage, accomplish (a result). *Obs. rare.*

**1596** WARNER *Alb. Eng.* x. lvii. (1612) 251 Of ancient Peeres, of valiant Men, great Lords, and Wise men all, By forced Warre, or fraudfull peace to temporize the fall.

¶ **5.** *trans.* To provide for the time, improvise, extemporize. (*Erroneous use.*)

**1880** J. NICOL *Poems & Songs* 41 No fire nor firing, goblet, pan, nor pot Nor wherewithal to temporize a bed.

Hence **Te·mporized** *ppl. a.*; † **Te·mporizement** (*obs. nonce-wd.*), = TEMPORIZATION 1.

**1600** W. WATSON *Decacordon* (1602) 20 Whether then all religious zeale, being turned into temporized platformes, to cast *omnia pro tempore, nihil pro veritate*. *Ibid.* 33 [The Jesuits] were vnworthy the name of temporized statists ..if they should not denie all and change their opinions, agreeing to time, person and place. **1647** M. HUDSON *Div. Right Govt.* Ep. Ded. 5, I hope..[to] vindicate the inno-cency of my thoughts from all such unworthy Sycophancy and Temporizement.

**Temporizer** (te·mpŏrəizəɹ). Also 6 -our, *Sc.* -ar, 7 -or. [Agent-noun f. prec.: cf. F. *tempori-seur* (*a* 1600 in Littré).] One who temporizes.

**1.** One who complies for the time, or yields to the time; a time-server, a 'trimmer'.

**1555** R. P[OWNOLL] tr. *Musculus* (title) The Temporisour (that is to say, the Obseruer of Tyme) translated into Inglishe. **1563** WINȜET *Four Scoir Thre Quest.* To Rdr., Wks. (S.T.S.) I. 53 Werray finȝeit hypocritis, and temperizaris with the tyme contrare thair conscience. **1563-87** FOXE *A. & M.* (1596) 1885/1 One by iudgement reformed, is more worth then a thousand transformed temporizers. **1611** SHAKS. *Wint. T.* I. ii. 302 A mindlesse Slaue, Or else a houering Temporizer. **1617** MORYSON *Itin.* II. 290 They would neuer be dissembling temporisors. **1710** NORRIS *Chr. Prud.* ii. 101

The Policy of Temporizers, men that steer their course by the compass of Worldly Interests. **1812** SHELLEY *Address* Prose Wks. 1888 I. 258 The dangers which lie beneath the footsteps of the hypocrite or temporizer.

**2.** One who seeks to gain time; a procrastinator, delayer; one who waits for a favourable time.

**1609** HOLLAND *Amm. Marcell.* 370 Like unto that auncient and warie temporizer [Q. Fabius Maximus]. **1636** FEATLY *Clavis Myst.* xxix. 383 Doth Satan play the temporizer and time all his suggestions? **1736** *Gentl. Mag.* VI. 469/1 The famous Advice..which ought to be observed by all Temporizers; viz. Time was; Time is: but take Care to lay hold on the Opportunity before the Time is past.

**Temporizing** (te·mpŏrəizin), *vbl. sb.* [f. as prec. + -ING [1].] The action of the verb TEMPORIZE.

**1.** Temporary compliance, etc.; time-serving, 'trimming'; parleying: see TEMPORIZE 1.

**1590** J. SMYTHE in *Lett. Lit. Men* (Camden) 64 By your Majesties bearinge and temporizinge with the woonderfull disorders and abuses. *c* **1618** MORYSON *Itin.* (1903) 287 Our Ministers could not safely liue [in Ireland] without some temporising, and applying himselfe to thaire humours. **1707** NORRIS *Treat. Humility* iii. 98 By temporizing or time-serving, I mean, when a man conforms his principles or practices to the times,..so as to be ready to take up new principles,..whenever a new turn of the times..shall make it for his advantage so to do. **1757** BURKE *Abridgm. Eng. Hist.* viii, John, deserted by all, had no resource but in temporizing and submission. **1816** SCOTT *Old Mort.* xxxviii, This..is no time for temporising with our duty.

**2.** Putting off, delaying, procrastination; negotiation so as to gain time: see TEMPORIZE 2, 3.

**1586** J. HOOKER *Hist. Irel.* in *Holinshed* II. 113/2 By temporising and gaining of time all matters were pacified. **1653** H. COGAN tr. *Pinto's Trav.* xlvii. 270 Without further temporising, he passed over the very same day to the other side of the river. **1685** *Gracian's Courtiers Orac.* 49 A rational temporizing ripens secrets and resolutions.

**Te·mporizing,** *ppl. a.* [f. as prec. + -ING [2].] That temporizes: see the verb.

**1.** Time-serving, 'trimming'.

**1600** E. BLOUNT *Hosp. Incur. Fooles* a ij, Another puts on the Foxe with temporizing humilitie. **1680** C. NESSE *Church Hist.* 210 That temporizing parasitical priest. **1693** DRYDEN *Juvenal* Ded. (1697) 65 A Temporizing Poet, a Well-manner'd Court-Slave, and a Man who is often afraid of Laughing in the right place. **1796** BURKE *Regic. Peace* i. Wks. VIII. 87 They..consider a temporizing meanness as the only source of safety. **1828** J. W. CROKER *Diary* 12 July, I thought a timid or temporising course would create great dissatisfaction.

**2.** Designed to gain time.

**1800** *Misc. Tr.* in *Asiat. Ann. Reg.* 140/1 My people became so clamorous that temporizing measures were no longer to be pursued. **1843** R. J. GRAVES *Syst. Clin. Med.* xvi. 191 His treatment was purely expectant and temporising. **1903** J. GAIRDNER in *Camb. Mod. Hist.* II. xiii. 447 Henry wrote a temporising reply.

Hence **Te·mporizingly** *adv.*, in a temporizing way, in a way designed to gain time.

**1847** in WEBSTER. **1894** *Temple Bar Mag.* CII. 136 He..talked temporizingly, with suggestions of possible arrangements.

**Temporo-** (te·mpŏro), before a vowel sometimes **tempor-**, used in *Anat.* as combining form of L. *tempora* temples (of the head), forming adjectives in the sense 'pertaining to the temple or temples and (some other part)', as *temporo-alar* belonging to the temporal region and the wing: noting a muscle in birds, *-auricular*, *-facial*, *-hyoid*, *-malar*, *-mandibular*, *-mastoid*, *-maxillary*, *-occipital* (also *temporoccipital*), *-parietal*, *-sphenoid*, *-sphenoidal*, *-zygomatic*.

**1842** E. WILSON *Anat. Vade M.* (ed. 2) 400 The *Temporo-facial gives off a number of branches which are distributed over the temple and upper half of the face. **1899** *Allbutt's Syst. Med.* VIII. 168 The distribution of the *temporo-malar or any other sensory nerve. **1842** E. WILSON *Anat. Vade M.* (ed. 2) 337 The *Temporo-maxillary vein formed by the union of the temporal and internal maxillary. **1890** BILLINGS *Nat. Med. Dict.*, **Temporo-occipital artery*... **Temporo-parietal suture*, that between temporal and parietal bones. **1879** *St. George's Hosp. Rep.* IX. 341 Between the frontal and *temporo-sphenoid lobes. **1890** BILLINGS *Nat. Med. Dict.*, **Temporo-zygomatic surface*, external surface of great wing of sphenoid.

**Tempour, Tempra**, obs. ff. TEMPER, TEMPERA.

**Temprate**, obs. variant of TEMPERATE.

†**Te·mpre,** *a. Obs.* Also 4–5 **temper(e**, 5 **tempur(e.** [a. AF., OF. *tempré* (12th c. in Godef.), pa. pple. of *temprer* to TEMPER. The final *-e*, originally pronounced, became at length mute: cf. ASSIGN, COSTIVE.] Tempered; temperate.

*a* **1340** HAMPOLE *Psalter* l. 1 It is a tempre kynd of praiynge. *Ibid.* cxxxvii. 5 All tempre men, þat gouernes þair flesch in mesure. *c* **1385** CHAUCER *L. G. W.* Prol. 128 Now hadde the tempre sonne al that releuyd. *c* **1400** *Laud Troy Bk.* 130 Large of ȝiftes and ryght ffre, Wondur fair and ryght tempere. **1422** tr. *Secreta Secret., Priv. Priv.* 247 Slepe.. vpon a nessh Bedde and in a place tempure.

**Tempre, -en**, obs. forms of TEMPER *v.*

†**Temprely,** *adv. Obs.* Also 4 **temperel(l)y.** [f. TEMPRE *a.* + -LY [2].] In moderation, temperately.

*c* **1386** CHAUCER *Shipm. T.* 262 (Harl. MS.) Gouerneth ȝow also of ȝour diete Al temperelly [*v.rr.* temperally [?-atly], atemprely] and namely in his hete. **1422** tr. *Secreta Secret., Priv. Priv.* 237 Men whych kepyth reysonabill diette and lywen temprely, bene more hole of body. *Ibid.* 242 Drynke a lytill and colde temprely.

So †**Te·mpreness** (tempurnes), temperateness.

**1486** *Bk. St. Albans, Her.* a ij, That other theirde parte of the worlde which shall be calde affrica, that is to say the contre of tempurnes.

**Temprure**, variant of TEMPERURE *Obs.*

**Temps, Tempse**, obs. ff. TENSE, TEMSE.

**Tempt** (tem^p^t), *v.* Forms: 3– **tempt**, 3–7 **temt**, 4–6 (*Sc.* –9) **temp.** [a. OF. and AF. *tempte-r* (12–14th c.), learned form, beside the popular form *tenter*, *tanter*:—L. *temptāre*, *temtāre* to handle, touch, feel, try the strength of, put to the test, try, attempt: cf. Pr. *temptar*, Cat., Sp., Pg. *tentar*, It. *tentare*. The Eng. form has always followed L. *tem(p)tare*, the form *tent* being very rare (see TENT *v.*[2]); but the sb. *temptation* had from 13th c. the collateral form *tentation*, which during the 16th and 17th c. was much used by theological writers.

In inscriptions and early MSS., the Latin vb. is always *tempt-* or *temtāre*; this became in due course *tentāre* in Romanic (see above, and cf. *promptus*, *pronto*, etc.); about the 13th c. scribes began to introduce this spelling in Latin MSS., whence it came into printed books and Latin Dicts., being supported by an assumed etymology as freq. of *tendĕre*, *tentum* to stretch, strive, aim, endeavour, try (meeting at length with sense 3 below); but this is now rejected in favour of a root *tem-*, *temp-*: see Walde *Lat. Etym. Wörterbuch* s. v. *tempto*.

Sense 4, a later development in L., common in the Vulgate and Christian use, is the earliest recorded in Eng.]

**I.** To test, put to the test, try.

†**1.** To try, make trial of, put to the test or proof; to try the quality, worth, or truth of. *Obs.* exc. as in 2.

*a* **1300** *Cursor M.* 5030 Lauerd..þat..tempted abraham þi dere Of his aun sun offrand to mak. **1382** WYCLIF *Gen.* xxii. 1 Aftyr that thes thingis weren doon, God temptide [1388 assaiede] Abraham [**1535** COVERD. *ibid.*, After these actes God tempted Abraham; **1611** BIBLE *ibid.*, It came to pass after these things, that God did tempt [1885 (*R.V.*) prove] Abraham]. **1382** — *Dan.* i. 12 Tempte [*gloss* or assaie; **1535** COVERD. Proue with; 1611, 1885 Prove] vs thi seruauntis ten days, and be potage ȝouen to vs for to ete. *c* **1386** CHAUCER *Clerk's T.* 402 He hadde assayed hire ynogh bifore..what neded it Hire for to tempte and alwey moore and moore? **1390** GOWER *Conf.* III. 45 With questions echon of tho He tempteth ofte. **1483** CAXTON *Gold. Leg.* 73/1 The quene of Saba cam fro fer contreys to see hym & to tempte hym in demaundes and questyons. **1538** STARKEY *England* II. i. 176 To haue some [sick persons] to go aboute ..to proue and tempt theyr louyng charyte. **16..** SIR W. MURE *Sonn.* iii. 6 To try my treuth and temp my loyall loue. *a* **1644** QUARLES *Hieroglyph.* xiii. Wks. 1881 III. 195 Tempt not your Salt beyond her power.

†**b.** *transf.* To act upon as a 'trial' or severe test; to try with afflictions; to afflict sorely, distress. Cf. ATTEMPT *v.* 4. *Obs. rare.*

**13..** *E. E. Allit. P.* B. 283 Felle temptande tene towched his hert. **1483** CAXTON *Gold. Leg.* 152 b/2 And thise xvii first yere I was moche tempted by the brennyng of the sonne moche asprely.

**2.** To make trial of, put to the proof, or test, in a way that involves risk or peril.

**a.** *To tempt God*: to put to the test, or experiment presumptuously upon, His power, forbearance, etc.; to try how far one can go with Him; hence sometimes passing into 'to provoke, defy'. So *to tempt providence*, etc.

*a* **1340** HAMPOLE *Psalter* lxxvii. 21 Þai tempte god þat puttis þaim selfe in any perill forto fande if god will delyuer þaim. **1382** WYCLIF *Deut.* vi. 16 Thow shalt not tempte the Lord thi God, as thow hast temptid in the place of temptynge. **1390** GOWER *Conf.* III. 43 He tempteth hevene and erthe and helle. **1533** GAU *Richt Vay* (S.T.S.) 12 Thay sine alsua aganis this command that tempis god. **1552** HULOET, Tempt or prouoke, *pellitio, tento, temto, verso.* **1611** BIBLE *Acts* v. 9 How is it that yee haue agreed together, to tempt the Spirit of the Lord? **1714** SWIFT *Pres. St. Affairs* ¶ 22 Religion teacheth us, that providence ought not to be tempted. **1715–20** POPE *Iliad* v. 44 Nor tempt the wrath of Heav'ns avenging Sire.

**b.** In *to tempt fate, fortune*, etc., the sense approaches a.

**1603** KNOLLES *Hist. Turks* (1621) 119 Who thus overthrowne, resolved no more to tempt fortune. **1693** CREECH in *Dryden's Juvenal* xiii. (1697) 339 Thy Perjur'd Friend will quickly tempt his Fate. **1746** FRANCIS tr. *Hor., Epist.* I. i. 9 Wisely resolv'd to tempt his Fate no more.

**c.** *To tempt* (*the storm, flood, sea*, etc.): to adventure oneself in or upon; to risk the perils of. (Cf. ATTEMPT *v.* 2.) Chiefly *poet.* Also *to tempt the worst, tempt reprisals*, etc.

**1667** MILTON *P. L.* II. 404 Who shall tempt with wandring feet The dark unbottom'd infinite Abyss? **1697** DRYDEN *Virg. Georg.* III. 123 The first to lead the Way, to tempt the Flood. *Ibid.* 581 Nor tempt th' inclemency of Heav'n abroad. **1703** ROWE *Ulyss.* IV. i, Know'st thou what 'tis to tempt a Rage like mine? **1704** POPE *Windsor For.* 389 Tempt icy seas, where scarce the waters roll. **1797** MRS. RADCLIFFE *Italian* i, I will tempt the worst at once. **1835** J. P. KENNEDY *Horse Shoe R.* lii, [They] preferred to tempt the rigors of the mountain rather than remain in their own dwellings.

†**3.** To try, endeavour, essay: with *inf.* (*to do* something), or equiv. clause; = ATTEMPT *v.* 1.

Sometimes aphetic for ATTEMPT.

*c* **1375** *Sc. Leg. Saints* xxii. (*Laurentius*) 697 Þe feynd, þat ay wil besy be to tempt þat þame twa had Inwy. **1382** WYCLIF 2 *Macc.* ii. 24 So we temptiden, or assayeden, for to abregge in to oo boke, thingus comprehendid..in fyue bookis. — *Acts* xvi. 7 Whanne thei camen into Misye, thei temptiden [COVERD. proved, 1611 assayed] for to go into Bithinie. **1494** FABYAN *Chron.* v. cxiv. 88 Whan Chilperich had temptyd by many sondrye meanes to haue theym out of the sayde preuylege. **1538** STARKEY *England* I. i. 21 Yet in some tyme and certayn place hyt ys not to be temptyd of wyse men [to meddyl wyth materys perteynyng to the wele of hys hole cuntrey].

**b.** *with simple object.* To attempt, to try.

**1697** DRYDEN *Æneid* VI. 214 Ere leave be giv'n to tempt the nether skies. [**1730** SWIFT *Panegyrick on Dean* 324 In vain I 'tempt too high a flight.]

†**c.** To make an attempt upon, to try to obtain; to assail. (Aphetic for ATTEMPT.) *Obs.*

*a* **1721** PRIOR *Henry & Emma* 518 O wretched maid! Whose roving fancy would resolve the same With him, who next should tempt her easy fame. **1746** FRANCIS tr. *Hor., Epist.* I. xviii. 127 Be not by foolish Love betray'd To tempt your Patron's favourite Maid.

**II.** To try to attract, allure, incite, induce.

**4.** *trans.* To try to attract, to entice (a person) to do evil; to present attractions to the passions or frailties of; to allure or incite to evil with the prospect of some pleasure or advantage. Const. *to* something, *to do* something. Also *absol.* (The earliest use in Eng.)

*a* **1225** *Ancr. R.* 60 Tauh ne rouhte heo neuer þauh he þouhte toward hire, & were of hire itempted [*MS. Cott.* ifondet]. *Ibid.* 226 Strongliche was he itemted er he so ueolle. *a* **1300** *Cursor M.* 15654 (Cott.) Rises vp, and wakes wel, Ar yee tempted [*Gött.* tempid] be. *a* **1340** HAMPOLE *Psalter* lv. 1 Þe deuel, þat neuyre styntis to temp þi seruauntis. *c* **1380** WYCLIF *Sel. Wks.* III. 107 To praye þat we be nouȝt ytempted of þe fende. *c* **1440** *Alphabet of Tales* 127 Ane vnwyse confessur began to tempe hur vnto syn. *c* **1450** *Cov. Myst.* xxv. (Shaks. Soc.) 240 Thryes I tempte hym..Aftyr he fast fourty days. **1500–20** DUNBAR *Poems* xxxiv. 2 Me thocht the Devill wes tempand fast The peple. **1530** PALSGR. 754/1 He hath tempted me..to go a thevynge with hym. **1548** UDALL *Erasm. Par. Luke* iii. 48 b, Adam also was tempted, and ouercomed: Christe beeyng tempted, ouercame the temptour. **1606** SHAKS. *Tr. & Cr.* IV. iv. 93. **1665** MANLEY *Grotius' Low C. Warres* 317 Then they tempted the Fidelity of Caspar Ensem the Governour, both by Rewards and Fear, but he was resolv'd against both. **1667** MILTON *P. L.* IX. 296 For hee who tempts, though in vain, at least asperses The tempted with dishonour foul. **1706** PHILLIPS (ed. Kersey), To *Tempt*, to allure or entice, to egg on or set a-gog, to induce to Evil. **1852** MRS. STOWE *Uncle Tom's C.* xix, Only when I've been very much tempted. **1869** SPURGEON *J. Ploughm. Talk* 9 Idle men tempt the devil to tempt them.

**b.** To try to draw (a person) to contradict, confute, or commit himself. *arch.*

(In N.T. versions, repr. Vulg. *tem(p)tare*, Gr. πειράζειν.)

**1382** WYCLIF *Matt.* xxii. 35 Oon of hem, a techer of the lawe, axede Jhesus, temptynge hym, Maistre, whiche is a greet maundement in the lawe? — *John* viii. 6 Sothli thei seiden this thing temptinge him, that thei myȝten accuse him. — *Mark* xii. 15 What tempten ȝe me? brynge ȝe to me a peny, that I se. **1526** TINDALE *ibid.*, Why tempte ye me? Brynge me a peny, that I maye se yt. [So **1611** and *R. V.* **1881**.]

**5.** To attract or incite *to* some action or *to do* something; to allure, entice, invite, attract; to dispose, incline. Sometimes, contextually, To induce, persuade.

**1340–70** *Alex. & Dind.* 98 Þat i ne am temted ful tid to turne me þennus. *a* **1548** HALL *Chron., Edw. IV* 226 b, The vsing of such gentill fashions toward them,..so tempted theim that they could none otherwise do. *a* **1674** CLARENDON *Surv. Leviath.* (1676) 15 Which might temt him to undervalue. **1716** GAY *Trivia* I. 164 The rowing crew, To tempt a fare, clothe all their tilts in blue. **1742** W. COLLINS *Pers. Ecl.* IV. 31 Unhappy land! whose blessings tempt the sword. **1825** SCOTT *Betrothed* xix, He was tempted to think that he had been something hasty in listening to the arguments of the Archbishop. **1875** JOWETT *Plato* (ed. 2) V. 42 The sick are tempted by pleasant meats and drinks. *Mod.* One is tempted to think that it had been pre-arranged. The fine morning had tempted many out.

Hence **Te·mpted** *ppl. a.* (also *absol.*).

*c* **1340** HAMPOLE *Prose Tr.* 5 Sothely I haue na wondyr if þe temptid fall. **1591** SHAKS. *Two Gent.* II. vi. 8 If thou hast sin'd, Teach me (thy tempted subiect) to excuse it. **1603** [see TEMPTER 1]. *c* **1611** CHAPMAN *Iliad* x. 436 Lest from their tempted rest Some other God should stir the foe. **1667** [see 4]. **1839** BAILEY *Festus* xxix. (1852) 484 May God forbear, To judge the tempted purpose of my heart! **1844** MRS. BROWNING *Brown Rosary* xiv, The Tempted is sinning.

†**Tempt,** *sb. Obs. rare.* [app. aphetic f. ATTEMPT *sb.*] = ATTEMPT *sb.*

**1597** HOOKER *Eccl. Pol.* v. lxxvi. § 6 By the issues of all tempts they found no certaine conclusion but this. **1652** BENLOWES *Theoph.* VIII. xxxvii, Because Gods Æqual, Serpents tempts are quell'd. *a* **1668** LASSELS *Voy. Italy* (1670) I. 114 Which [Castle] staveth off all tempts of strangers.

**Temptable** (te·m^p^tăb'l), *a.* Also 9 -ible. [f. TEMPT *v.* + -ABLE.] That may be tempted; liable or open to temptation.

**1628** FELTHAM *Resolves* II. [I.] lxvi. 188 There is sometimes a selfe-constancie, that is not temptable. **1678** CUDWORTH *Intell. Syst.* I. iv. § 15. 268 Whether or no a Philosopher be temptable by it, or illaqueable into it. **1724** SWIFT *Drapier's Lett.* iv. ¶ 21 If the parliament of Ireland were as temptable as any other assembly within a mile of Christendom. **1819** COLERIDGE in *Lit. Rem.* (1836) II. 239 Macbeth's mind, rendered temptible by previous dalliance..with ambitious thoughts. **1883** J. PARKER *Apost. Life* II. 319 In all points temptable though invulnerable.

Hence **Temptabi·lity, Te·mptableness,** accessibility to temptation.

**1682** H. MORE *Annot. Glanvill's Lux O.* 78 What can this freedom of Will consist in so much as in a temptableness by other Objects that are of an inferiour nature? **1825** COLE-

RIDGE *Aids Refl.* (1848) I. 223 A soul surrounded with temptation, and having the worst temptation within itself in its own temptability.

**Temptation** (temptē̆ⁱ·ʃən). Forms: *α.* 4– tempt-, 5–7 temt- ; *β.* 3–7 (9 *arch.*) tent-. [a. OF. *temptaciun, -tation* (12th c.), *tentation* (13th c. in Godef. *Compl.*), ad. L. *tempt-, tentātiōn-em*, n. of action from *temptāre, tentāre* to TEMPT, q.v.]

**1.** The action of tempting or fact of being tempted, esp. to evil ; enticement, allurement, attraction.

(Sometimes with more or less approach to senses 2 and 3.) *The Temptation* (in *Christian Theol.* and *Art*), that of Jesus in the wilderness (Matt. iv, etc.). Also used of those of mediæval saints by evil spirits, e.g. 'The Temptation of St. Anthony'.

*α.* **1340** *Ayenb.* 158 Huanne he [the devil] comþ ine gyse of angle..þanne is þe temptacion mest strang. *Ibid.* 228 Temptaciun. **13..** *Matt.* vi. 13 in Paues *14th C. Eng. Bibl. Version*, And ne lede us not in temptacyon. *c* **1450** *Mankind* 219 in *Macro Plays* 9 The temtacyon of þe flesch, ȝe must resyst lyke a man. **1526** TINDALE *Matt.* xxvi. 41 Watche and praye that ye fall not into temptacion. **1667** MILTON *P. L.* VIII. 643 And all temptation to transgress repel. *Ibid.* IX. 364 Seek not temptation then, which to avoide Were better. **1837** DICKENS *Pickw.* ii, The temptation to take the stranger with him was equally great. **1846** TRENCH *Mirac.* i. (1862) 112 But man is to be perfected, not by exemption from temptation, but rather by victory in temptation. **1877** MOZLEY *Univ. Serm.* xvi. 271 Old-established rank has the temptation to luxurious indolence and pride. **1887** CLARA BELL tr. *Woltmann & Woermann's Hist. Paint.* II. III. II. i. 109 [Martin Schongauer's] well-known plate of the Temptation of S. Antony.

*β.* **1447** BOKENHAM *Seyntys* (Roxb.) 9 As for the cardiacle that tentacyoun Betoknyth..Of oure gostly enmye. **1534** MORE *Comf. agst. Trib.* II. Wks. 1177/2 The first might we cal tentation, the second persecucion...So is tentacion tribulacion to a good man. **1563** WINȜET *Four Scoir Thre Quest.* Wks. (S.T.S.) I. 120 The guid in the battell throw tentatioun may fall. **1650** BULWER *Anthropomet.* 58 To suffer this tentation from evil spirits. **1650** (*Scottish*) *Psalms in Metre* xcv. 8 Then harden not your hearts, as in the provocation, As in the desert, on the day of the tentation. **1678** SIR G. MACKENZIE *Crim. Laws Scot.* I. xvii. § 6 (1699) 89 He is more guilty, seing he wants the natural tentation of the Adulterer.

**b.** With *a* and *pl.* An instance of this.

*α.* *a* **1225** *Ancr. R.* 32 Þeo þet beoð ine stronge temptaciuns. *a* **1340** HAMPOLE *Psalter* xxvi. 6 If temptacyons wax ageynes me. *c* **1491** *Chast. Goddes Chyld.* 2 The more knoweng a man hathe the stronger ben his temptacyons. **1848** MAURICE *Lord's Prayer* vii. 91 We shall gain little.. by changing that word for 'trials', as if every 'trial' did not of necessity involve a temptation.

*β.* *a* **1225** *Ancr. R.* 246 Al so a muchel tentaciun, þet is þes feondes bles. *a* **1568** COVERDALE *Hope Faithf.* xvii. (1574) 136 Bodely fraile lustes and tentations. **1625** DONNE *Serm.* iii. (1640) 22 Such a measure of grace as shall make me discerne a tentation and resist a tentation. **1693** *Apol. Clergy Scot.* 43 The many Incumbrances, Tentations, Weaknesses, that we daily encounter. **1818** SCOTT *Hrt. Midl.* xliii, When ye are pressed wi' ensnaring trials and tentations and heart-plagues.

**c.** Tempting quality, enticingness. *rare.* ? *Obs.*

*c* **1430** LYDG. *Min. Poems* (Percy Soc.) 108 Lordes and laymen and spryttualle her gave chase, For her fayer beawté grette temtacyon she hase. **1760–72** H. BROOKE *Fool of Qual.* (1809) III. 5 The..trees reached forth fruits of irresistible temptation.

**d.** *transf.* A thing that tempts ; a cause or source of temptation.

**1596** SHAKS. *Merch. V.* I. ii. 106 Set a deepe glasse of Reinish-wine on the contrary Casket, for if the diuel be within, and that temptation without, I know he will choose it. **1676** DRYDEN *Aureng-z.* v. ii, Dare to be great, without a guilty crown; View it, and lay the bright temptation down. **1786** BURNS *Address to Unco Guid* vi, Ye're aiblins nae temptation. **1856** FROUDE *Hist. Eng.* (1858) I. i. 17 The command of a permanent military force was a temptation to ambition.

**2.** The action or process of testing or proving ; trial, test. *Obs.* or *arch.*

**1382** WYCLIF 1 *Macc.* ii. 52 Wher [1388 Whether] Abraham in temptation was not founden feithful. **1535** COVERDALE *Ecclus.* xxvii. 5 The ouen proueth the potters vessell, so doth tentacion of trouble trye righteous men. **1552** ABP. HAMILTON *Catech.* (1884) 21 Thair is temptatioun quhairby man temptis God. **1677** GILPIN *Demonol.* (1867) 58 Temptations are distinguished into trials merely, and seducements. **1885** BIBLE (R. V.) *Deut.* iv. 34 To..take him a nation from the midst of another nation by temptations [so all versions from Wyclif: *marg.* Or, trials; or, evidences], by signs, and by wonders.

† **3.** A severe or painful trial or experience ; an affliction, a trial. *Obs.*

*c* **1595** CAPT. WYATT *R. Dudley's Voy. W. Ind.* (Hakl. Soc.) 43 Theire victuall spent and fresh water consumed, they susteyned a great temptacion. *c* **1610** *Women Saints* 198 Troubles and tentations which I endured by being..driuen out of my contrie. **1652** CROMWELL *Let. to Ld. Wharton* 30 June in *Carlyle*, [They] may be too great a tentation to her spirit.

**4.** *Comb.*, as *temptation-proof*, adj., etc.

*a* **1631** DONNE *Serm.* lx. (1640) 603 To bring me to thinke myselfe tentation proofe, above tentation. **1691** NORRIS *Pract. Disc.* 197 The Greatness of the happiness there.. will make him Temptation-Proof against any present good or evil. **1889** C. C. R. *Up for Season* 101, I leave without reluctance your temptation-guarded fold. **1908** *Westm. Gaz.* 30 Oct. 13/3 The champion temptation-resisters.

Hence **Tempta·tional** *a.*, of the nature of temptation ; **Tempta·tionless** *a.*, without temptation, to which there is no temptation.

**1643** HAMMOND *Serm. John xviii. 40* Wks. 1683 IV. 513 An empty, profitless, temptationless sin. **1882** J. CALDWELL in *Homiletic Q. Mag.* VI. 106/2 The two verbs used here to describe the temptational agency of Lust.

**Temptatious** (temptē̆ⁱ·ʃəs), *a.* Also 8 tent-. [f. prec. : see -OUS.] Full of temptation ; tempting, seductive, alluring.

**1601** CHETTLE & MUNDAY *Death Robt. Earl of Huntingdon* II. ii. F j, I my Liege, I: O! that temptatious tongue Had no where to be plac't but in your head. **1702** C. MATHER *Magn. Chr.* III. I. iv. (1852) 329 His removal..was clogged with many temptatious difficulties. **1724** R. WELTON *Chr. Faith & Pract.* 210 Those that in this tentatious world deny their religion. **1889** *Harper's Mag.* Mar. 665/2 There was something..winning and temptatious in it.

† **Te·mptative,** *a. Obs. rare*⁻¹. [f. TEMPT *v.* + -ATIVE ; or ad. med.L. *temptātīv-us* 'seducens, fallax' (1377 in Du Cange).] = prec.

*c* **1449** PECOCK *Repr.* (Rolls) 105 The natural temptatyue wrecchidnessis which other men haue.

† **Tempta·tor.** *Obs.* [a. L. *temptātor, tentātor*, agent-n. from *temptāre* to tempt. Cf. F. *temptateur* (14th c. in Godef.), mod.F. *tentateur.*] = TEMPTER.

**1491** CAXTON *Vitas Patr.* (W. de W. 1495) I. xlvii. 85 b/2 Whanne we haue good hope, we ouercome the deuyll our temptatour. **1632** LITHGOW *Trav.* x. 438 First they be Imitators; next, Mutators; thirdly, Temptators.

**Te·mptatory,** *a. rare.* [f. ppl. stem of L. *temptāre* to tempt + -ORY ². cf. F. *tentatoire* tempting (Palsgr. 279/2).] Of tempting nature ; temptatious.

**1900** G. SWIFT *Somerley* 88 We were jolly ready to spend an hour or so with the temptatory damsel.

**Tempter** (te·mptəɹ). Also 4–6 -our. [ME. *temptour* = obs. F. *tempteur* (14th c.), *tenteur* (16th c.), OF. **tempteor*, in nom. *temptere, -teire* (13–14th c. in Godef.) :—L. *temptātōr-em*, agent-n. from *temptāre* to tempt.]

**1.** One who or that which tempts or entices to evil ; *the tempter*, (*spec.*) the devil.

*a* **1380** *St. Bernard* 717 in Horstm. *Altengl. Leg.* (1878) 53 To þe temptour softeliche He seide þeos wordus. **1382** WYCLIF *Matt.* iv. 3 And the tempter cummynge niȝ, saide to hym, ȝif thou be Goddis sone, say that these stoons be maad looues. **1533** GAU *Richt Vay* (S.T.S.) 95 We haiff iii tempers (and we ar tempit be iii vayis) quhilk is of ye body of the dewil and of ye vardil. **1548** Temptour [see TEMPT *v.* 4]. **1603** SHAKS. *Meas. for M.* II. ii. 163 The Tempter, or the Tempted, who sins most? **1673** O. WALKER *Educ.* 60 That the Temter may find no bait to cover his poyson. **1788** WESLEY *Wks.* (1872) VI. 377 Because he is continually inciting men to evil, he is emphatically called 'the Tempter'. **1907** SANDAY *Life Christ in rec. Res.* I. i. 28 There are three scenes in which the Son of God is assailed by the Tempter.

† **2.** One who tests ; a taster of ale or bread. *Obs.*

*c* **1450** *Godstow Reg.* 101 That they shold have ben tempters or tapsters of brede and ale in the said towne.

**Te·mpting,** *vbl. sb.* [f. TEMPT *v.* + -ING ¹.] The action of the verb TEMPT ; temptation ; † trying (*obs.*).

**1303** R. BRUNNE *Handl. Synne* 7506 Ihesu..sagh weyl hys grete temptyng. *c* **1450** *Mirour Saluacioun* 4054 The temptyngs of the werld ere many. **1613** SHAKS. *Hen. VIII*, I. ii. 55, I am much too venturous In tempting of your patience. **1628** WITHER *Brit. Rememb.* I. 709 He having meanes to doe His pleasure, and perhaps, strong temptings too. **1903** W. H. GRAY *Div. Sheph.* iv. 71 If others tempt us let us not yield to their temptings.

*attrib.* **1814** BYRON *Lara* I. xviii, And this same impulse would, in tempting time, Mislead his spirit equally to crime.

**Te·mpting,** *ppl. a.* [f. as prec. + -ING ².] That tempts.

**1.** That entices to evil, or with evil design.

**1546** BALE *Eng. Votaries* Pref. A iij, The more part of their temptynge spretes they haue made she deuyls. **1644** MILTON *Jdgm. Bucer* xliii. Wks. 1851 IV. 336 Let us see what our Lord answer'd to the tempting Pharisees about Divorce, and second Marriage. **1850** MRS. JAMESON *Leg. Monast. Ord.* (1863) 329 A tempting demon.

**2.** Seductive, attractive, alluring, inviting.

**1596** SHAKS. *Tam. Shr.* Induct. i. 118 With kinde embracements, tempting kisses. **1680** OTWAY *Orphan* v. i, If a tempting Fair you find That's very lovely, very kind. **1818** SIR T. LAWRENCE 23 May in Williams *Life & Corr.* (1831) II. iii. 173 'Tis such a tempting offer. **1855** MACAULAY *Hist. Eng.* xviii. IV. 135 The profits of the Indian trade were so tempting.

† **3.** Afflicting, distressing, 'trying'. *Obs.*

**13..** *E. E. Allit. P.* B. 283 Felle temptande tene towched his hert.

**4.** *Comb.*, as *tempting-looking*.

**1875** J. P. HOPPS *Princ. Relig.* xv. (1878) 47 If you are told not to eat this or that tempting-looking berry, and you disobey and get poisoned.

Hence **Te·mptingly** *adv.*, **Te·mptingness.**

**1593** NASHE *Christ's T.* 2 b, They erred most temptingly and contemptuously. **1802** BENTHAM *Mem. & Corr.* Wks. 1843 X. 396 My first act of mendicancy, and that extorted from me by the mere temptingness of the opportunity. **1877** LADY BRASSEY *Voy. Sunbeam* xiv. (1878) 246 Articles of apparel are temptingly displayed.

**Temptive** (te·mptiv), *a. rare.* [f. TEMPT *v.* + -IVE.] Tending to tempt, tempting.

**1886** J. M. LUDLOW in *Homilet. Rev.* (U.S.) Sept. 260 While..every man 'is tempted by his own lusts', we are unwise to overlook the temptive occasions.

**Temptress** (te·mptrès). [f. TEMPTER + -ESS.] A female tempter.

**1594** NASHE *Unfort. Trav.* Wks. (Grosart) V. 80 The place..was a pernicious curtizans house named Tabitha the Temptresses. **1633** FORD *Broken H.* v. ii, Be not jealous, Euphranea; I shall scarcely prove a temptress. **1826** SCOTT *Woodst.* ii, That the daughter..would, like the wicked wife of Job, become a temptress to her father in the hour of affliction. **1883** G. H. BOUGHTON in *Harper's Mag.* Jan. 179/1 St. Anthony and his undraped temptress.

**Te·mptsome,** *a. rare.* [f. TEMPT *v.* + -SOME.] Apt to tempt, tempting.

**1849** *Tait's Mag.* XVI. 629 Temptsome bargains catch her eager gaze.

**Tempur(e, -nes,** var. TEMPRE, -NESS, *Obs.*

**Temse** (tems, temz), *sb.* Now *dial.* Forms: 1 temes-, 4 temys, 5 temeze, tymze, 5–7 temze, tem(m)es, tempse (9 *dial.*), 7 temize, 7–9 tems, 5– temse ; 9 *dial.* temmis, timse, teems. [OE. **tęmes* (in *tęmes-pile, tęmesian*), app. Common WGer. ; cf. MLG. *têmes(e, temse*, LG. *têms (tams)* ; MDu. *têms(e, teems(e*, Du. *teems*; EFris. *têms(e, tàms(e*, NFris. *tems*; HG. dial. *zims*; all fem., meaning 'sieve' ; the cognate OHG. *zemisa* renders 'furfures', i.e. bran, siftings. These forms point to a Common WGer. **tamis(j)ô-*, coinciding with the Romanic stem *tamisio-* of F. *tamis*, It. *tamigio* (Florio), med.L. *tamisium* (Du Cange), by many thought to be from WGer. A Celtic source has been conjectured, but Thurneysen finds no satisfactory Celtic root.]

**1.** A sieve, esp. one used for bolting meal ; a searce, a strainer. In mod. local use *esp.* a sieve used in brewing.

[*a* **1050** *Gerefa* c. 17 in Liebermann *Gesetze* 455 Man sceal habban syfa..hriddel, hersyfe, tæmespilan (= temsing-staff), fanna.] ? **1362** *Durham Acc. Rolls* (Surtees) 566 Pro duabus temys emptis pro pistrina, ij s. *c* **1425** *Voc.* in Wr.-Wülcker 633/4 *Hoc taratantarum*, temse. *c* **1440** *Promp. Parv.* 488/2 Temze, sive (*K.*, *P.* temse, syue, *S.* temeze), *setarium.* *c* **1483** CAXTON *Dialogues* 38/22 Ghyselin the mande maker Hath sold..his temmesis to clense with [F. *a vendu..ses tammis*]. **1483** *Cath. Angl.* 379/2 A Tempse (A. *taratantorium*). **1557** in *Wills & Inv. N.C.* (Surtees) I. 159 A borde wth ij trestes & ij temeses ijs viijd. **1612** CAPT. SMITH *Map Virginia* 17 They use a small basket for their Temmes. **1616** SURFL. & MARKH. *Country Farme* 577 The boulter which is for this purpose must be a course searse or a fine temze. **1674** RAY *N. C. Words* 47 A *Temse*, a fine sierce, a small sieve..whence comes our Temse bread. **1725** [see *temms-maker* in 2]. **1904** *Eng. Dial. Dict.*, *Tems(e*, teems, temes, temis, tempse, temz, timse [in various dialects, Roxb. to Lancash., Notts., Lincoln]...3. A sieve used in brewing. W. Yks. Still common. Used when speaking of the strainer used in brewing to separate the hops, etc., from the ale.

¶ A suggested substitution of *temse* for *Thames* in 'to set the Thames on fire' has no historical basis : see THAMES.

**2.** *attrib.* and *Comb.*, as *temse-maker*, *-sieve* ; **temse-bread, -loaf,** bread or a loaf made of finely sifted flour, temsed bread.

**1600** CHETTLE & DAY *Blind Begg.* II. (1902) 24 Good Beef, Norfolk *temes bread, and Country home bred drink. **1611** COTGR., *Miche*,..the countrey people of France call so also, a loafe of boulted bread, or Tems bread. **1674** [see 1]. **1552** *Will of Leppingwell* (Comm. Crt. Lond.), A *Temes loffe. **1573** TUSSER *Husb.* (1878) 39 Temmes lofe on his table to haue for to eate. **1725** *Lond. Gaz.* No. 6432/6 Hosea Emmott, late of Bridgehouses..,*Temms-maker.

**Temse** (tems, temz), *v.* Now *dial.* Forms: see prec. [OE. *tęm(e)sian*, f. *tęmese* (see prec.) : cf. MLG. *temesen*, MDu., Du. *temsen, teemsen* to sift.] *trans.* To sift or bolt (flour, etc.) with a temse.

*c* **950** *Lindisf. Gosp.* Mark ii. 26 Huu inn-eode hus godes .. & hlafo fore-ȝeȝearwad *vel* temised ȝebréc. *c* **1440** *Promp. Parv.* 488/2 Temzyn wythe a tymze (*S.* temsyn with a tenze),..*attamino, setario.* **1483** *Cath. Angl.* 379/2 To Tempse, *taratantarizare.* **1600** SURFLET *Countrie Farme* v. xx. 714 Barley bread must be made..of that.. which hath beene temzed and cleansed from his grosse bran. **1641** BEST *Farm. Bks.* (Surtees) 103 To measure the meale ..afore it be temsed. **1809** T. DONALDSON *Poems* 73 Sifting meal..Or timsing flour. **1828** *Craven Gloss.*, *Tems*, to sift. **1904** *Eng. Dial. Dict.* s.v., Fifty years ago flour was not very common with cottagers esp., and when they wanted some they would temse some rough meal.

Hence **Temsed** *ppl. a.* ; *temsed bread* = *temse-bread* (see prec. 2) ; **Te·msing** *vbl. sb.*, chiefly in comb. as *temsing bread, -chamber, -staff, -trough.* Also **Te·mser, te·mzer** = TEMSE *sb.* 1.

**1641** BEST *Farm. Bks.* (Surtees) 104 Our own *tempsed-breade. *Ibid.*, An upheaped bushell of tempsed meale. **1777** *Horæ Subsecivæ* 428 (E.D.D.) Tems'd or temmas bread, white [bread] made of flour finely sifted. **1696–7** in Kennett *MS. Lansd.* 1033 lf. 4 **Temzer*, a range or coarse searche. *c* **1450** *Medulla* in *Promp. Parv.* 488 *note*, *Cervida*, lignum quod portat cribrum, a *temsynge staffe. [Cf. **1904** *Eng. Dial. Dict.*, *Timse-sticks*, the small frame supporting two laths or sticks on which the 'timse' slides.] **1599** *Wills & Inv. N. C.* (Surtees) II. 287 In the bowltinge house. One temsinge troughe. *a* **1800** PEGGE *Suppl. Grose*, *Temsing-chamber*, the sifting-room. **1828** *Craven Gl.*, *Temsin-breead.*

**Temulence** (te·miŭlĕns). *rare.* [f. as next : see -ENCE.] = next.

**1803** D. H. URQUHART *Comm. Class. Learn.* iv. *Euripides* 149 An eulogium on wine and temulence. **1860** MAYNE *Expos. Lex.*, *Temulentia*,..temulence.

**Temulency** (te·miŭlĕnsi). Now *rare.* [ad. post-cl. L. *tēmulentia* drunkenness, f. *tēmulent-us* : see next and -ENCY.] Drunkenness, inebriety.

**1623** COCKERAM, *Temulencie*, drunkennesse. *a* **1640** JACKSON *Creed* x. vii, Without impeachment to his sobriety, or censure of temulency. **1732** ARBUTHNOT *Rules of Diet* in *Aliments*, etc. 260 Used in great Quantities it will produce Temulency or Drunkenness. **1853** BADHAM *Halieut.* (1854) 525 The vigorous lines in which Crabbe depicts the progress of temulency amongst a club of topers.

**Temulent** (te·miŭlĕnt), *a.* Now *rare.* [ad. L.

*tēmulent-us*, from root *tēm-* in *tēmētum* intoxicating drink, after *vinolentus* from *vinum* wine.] Drunken, intoxicated; given to, characterized by, or proceeding from drunkenness; intoxicating.

**1628** JACKSON *Creed* VI. xiii. § 1 Clytus, whom he had newly slain in his temulent rage. **1668** G. C. in H. More *Div. Dial.* Pref. i. (1713) 14 Such tipsie and temulent Raptures. *a* **1770** CHATTERTON in *Europ. Mag.* (1804) XLV. 85 Sooner..Than I, to frenzy temulent, with love, False to its palpitating precepts prove. **1822–34** *Good's Study Med.* (ed. 4) III. 494 Sometimes it produces a temulent effect.

Hence **Te·mulently** *adv.*, **Te·mulentness**; also, † **Temule·ntious,** † **Temule·ntive** *adjs.*, drunken.

**1652** URQUHART *Jewel* Wks. (1834) 210 The Spaniards are proud: The French inconstant:..the Dutch *temulencious. **1628** FELTHAM *Resolves* II. [I.] lxxxiv. 241 A swimming Eye; a Face both roast and sod; a *temulentive Tongue. **1623** COCKERAM II, Drunkenly done, **temulently*. **1727** BAILEY vol. II, *Temulently*, after a drunken Manner. **Temulentness*, Drunkenness.

**Temys, Temzə,** obs. ff. TEMSE, THAMES.

**Ten** (ten), *a.*, *sb.* (*adv.*). Forms: *α. uninflected*: 1 tíen, tén, later týn, (*north.* **téa**), 2 tyen, teon, 4–6 tenn, 4–7 tenne, 6 tien; 1– ten. *β. inflected*: 1 tíene, týne, 1–5 téne. [OE. *tíen, -e*, Anglian *tén, -e*, Comm. Teut., = OLG. **tehan*, OFris. *tîan*, *tîen*, OS. *tehan* (*tian*, *tein*), (MDu., Du. *tien*, MLG. *tein*, LG. *tein*, *tien*, EFris. *tein*, *tian*, *tien*); OHG. *zehan* (MHG. *zehen*, *zên*, Ger. *zehn*); Goth. *taihun*; ON. *tiu*, *tio* (Norw. *tie*, *tio*, Sw. *tio*, Da. *ti*):—OTeut. **teχan*, beside **teχun* = pre-Teut. **de·km*, L. *decem*, Gr. δέκα, OSl. *desja(ti)*, Skr. *daça(n-*. As final *-n* regularly fell away in OTeut., the normal form for OE. would have been **teha*, *téa* (as found in ONorthumbrian); but the actual form, as in OFris., OS., and OHG., had final *-n*, app. taken from the inflected form, whence also the umlaut in *tíen*, *týn*, *tén*. The inflected form, a plural *i-* stem (:—*teχanīz*), in OE. *tíene*, etc. (neut. *-u*, *-o*, gen. *-a*, dat. *-um*), ME. *tēne*, was used when the numeral stood absolutely (sense 2); the uninflected was used with a sb., and at length, in ME., in all positions. (But see -TEEN, from *-tēne*.)]

The cardinal numeral next higher than nine; the number of the digits on both hands or feet, and hence the basis of the ordinary or decimal numeration.

Expressed by the figures 10, or symbol X, x.

**A.** *adj.* **1.** In concord with a sb. expressed.

*c* **888** K. ÆLFRED *Boeth.* xxxviii. § 1 Þa wæron hi sume ten ʒear on þam ʒewinne. *c* **897** — *Gregory's Past. C.* xvii. 124 Þa stænenan bredu þe sio æw wæs on awriten mid tien bebodum. *a* **900** tr. *Bæda's Hist.* I. xiii. [xxiii.] § 1 Þreotteno ʒer & syx monað & tyn daʒas. *c* **1050** *Charter of Eadwine* in Kemble *Cod. Dipl.* IV. 259 Ic an ðat lond..buten ten acres ic ʒiue ðer into ðere kirke. *a* **1175** *Cott. Hom.* 219 He ʒescop tyen engle werod. *a* **1300** *Cursor M.* 7015 Tene [*v.r.* ten] yeir had [Manigath] þe folk in yeme. **1382** WYCLIF *Matt.* xxv. 1 The kyngdam of heuenes shal be lic to ten virgynys. *a* **1400** *R. Glouc. Chron.* (MS. B) (1724) 430 Hys doȝter was a ten ȝer old. *a* **1400–50** *Alexander* 649 Ten ȝere of age. **1502** ARNOLDE *Chron.* (1811) 189 The rood of reynysh wyne of Dordreight is x. awames. **1513** MORE *Rich. III* (1641) 299 Which rage of water lasted tenne dayes. **1571** *Act* 13 *Eliz.* c. 8 The rate of tenne pound for the lone of one hundred pound for a yeare. **1653** HOLCROFT *Procopius, Pers. Wars* I. 4 A narrow passage, for ten Horse abreast. **1805** SCOTT *Last Minstr.* I. v, Ten squires, ten yeomen, mail-clad men, Waited the beck of the warders ten. *Mod.* I shall be with you in ten minutes.

**b.** As multiple of another higher cardinal number, as in *ten hundred*, *ten thousand*, etc.; also in the ordinals of these, as *ten thousandth*.

*c* **950** *Lindisf. Gosp.* Matt. xviii. 24 Tea ðusendo cræftas. *c* **975** *Rushw. Gosp.* ibid., Ten þusende. *c* **1000** *Ags. Gosp.* ibid., Tyn þusend punda. *c* **1160** *Hatton Gosp.* ibid., Teon þusend punde. *c* **1400** *Apol. Loll.* 107 Sunnar is þe prayor hard of o buxum man, þan tenþowzand of a dispicer. **1560** DAUS tr. *Sleidane's Comm.* 257 b, The footemen were teen thousande. **1685** BOYLE *Enq. Notion Nat.* iii. 53 The cælestial part of the universe, in comparison of which the sublunary is not perhaps the ten thousandth part. **1709** CHANDLER *Effort agst. Popery* 20 'Tis Ten Thousand Pities that a Difference in Opinion and Practice herein should cause such Distances and Withdrawings. **1782** PRIESTLEY *Corrupt. Chr.* I. I. 5 The subject [is] considered by thousands and ten thousands. **1893** GOW *Comp. Sch. Classics* xxxiii. (ed. 3) 303 The ten-thousandth part of each grain must make a proportionate part of noise. **1905** *Westm. Gaz.* 23 Mar. 2/2 The guarantee for the ten-million loan.

**c.** Used vaguely or hyperbolically, esp. in *ten times*, *tenfold*, and the like. Cf. HUNDRED, THOUSAND.

For hyperbolical use of *ten thousand* see THOUSAND.

**1388** WYCLIF *Baruch* iv. 28 ȝe..schulen seke hym ten sithis so myche. **1508** DUNBAR *Flyting* 87 Suppois thy heid war armit tymis ten. **1593** SHAKS. *Rich. II*, I. i. 180 A Iewell in a ten times barr'd vp Chest. **1883** D. C. MURRAY *Hearts* II. 162 His easy cynicism made him ten times more believable than any moral profession could have done.

† **d.** Occasionally used in the sense of the ordinal TENTH. *Obs.*

(But in 10 Jan., 10 Vict., etc., usually read *tenth*.)

**14..** in Todd *Three Treat. Wyclif* p. xxvii, Siþ þe ten part [*v.r.* tenþe part] of þe fruyt sufficide for alle þes clerkis. **1567** in *Cath. Record Soc. Publ.* I. 49 Commytyd the x. day of June 1562. **1582** L. KIRBY in Allen *Martyrd. Campion* (1908) 77 This morning, the x of Januarie, he was committed to the dongeon. **1586** W. WEBBE *Eng. Poetrie* (Arb.) 62 Make short either the two, foure, sixe, eight, tenne, twelue sillable, and it will fall out very absurdly. **1597** J. PAYNE *Royal Exch.* 24 Let vs solace our selves with these words in the tenn of the Hebr.

**e.** In special applications.

† *Ten bones*, the ten fingers: *by these ten bones* (ellipt. *these ten*), also *ten ends of flesh and blood*, an oath (*obs.*). *Ten Commandments* (also † *bebode*, *bodewords*, *hests*, etc.), the Mosaic decalogue; *slang*, the ten fingers; see also COMMANDMENT 2, 3. † *Ten groats*, formerly a lawyer's fee, or that paid to the priest for reading the marriage service (*obs.*). *Ten tribes*, the lost tribes of Israel; *humorously*, the Jews, as money-lenders.

*c* **1485** *Digby Myst.* (1882) I. 20 By thes bonys ten thei be to you vntrue. *c* **1537** *Thersites* in Hazl. *Dodsley* I. 429 By this ten bones, She served me once A touch for the nonce. **1562–3** *Jack Juggler* ibid. II. 125, I am a servant of this house, by these ten bones. **1601** CHETTLE & MUNDAY *Death Robt. Earl of Huntington* V. i. ibid. VIII. 305 By these ten ends of flesh and blood I swear. **1621** B. JONSON *Masque Gipsies* vi. Wks. (Rtldg.) 621/2, I swear by these ten, You shall have it agen.

**971** *Blickl. Hom.* 35 We sceolan þa ten bebodu healdan. *c* **1200** ORMIN 4377 Þa tene bodewordess. **1362** LANGL. *P. Pl.* A. VIII. 170 To Breke þe ten hestes. *c* **1375** *Sc. Leg. Saints* xxxiv. (*Pelagia*) 213 Þe commaundmentis tene, Þat god mad for to teche men. *c* **1540** J. HEYWOOD *Four P's* in Hazl. *Dodsley* I. 381 [That] thy wife's ten commandments may search thy five wits. **1902** SNAITH *Wayfarers* vi, She's not seen you use your ten commandments, young man.

**1601** SHAKS. *All's Well* II. ii. 22 As fit as ten groats is for the hand of an Atturney. *a* **1625** FLETCHER *Woman's Prize* I. iii, I'll take Petruchio In's shirt, with one ten groats, to pay the priest, Before the best man living.

**1889** DOYLE *Micah Clarke* 118 The ten tribes have been upon me, and I have been harried..and despoiled.

**2.** Absolutely or with ellipsis of sb. (which may usually be supplied from the context).

Often short for *ten years* of age; also for *ten shillings*, in *ten and six(pence*, or other number of pence, *ten-and-sixpenny*. In OE. and Early ME. inflected, nom. *-e*, neut. *-o*, *-u*; gen. *-a*, dat. *-um*.

*Beowulf* 2847 Ða hild-latan..tyne æt-somne. *c* **950** *Lindisf. Gosp.* Mark x. 41, & ʒe-herdon ða teno. *c* **975** *Rushw. Gosp.* ibid., & ʒiherdun ða tenu. *c* **1000** *Ags. Gosp.* ibid., Þa ʒe-bulʒon þa tyne hi. *c* **1160** *Hatton Gosp.* ibid., Þa ʒe-bulʒe þa teone hyo. *a* **1000** *Ags. Gloss.* in Wr.-Wülcker 217/21 *Decanus*,..tyna aldor. *c* **1205** LAY. 3388 Do we awai þane twenti, a tene [*c* **1275** ten] beoð inohȝe. *Ibid.* 31930 Bi sixe bi seouene, bi tene bi eolleue, bi twelue bi twenti. *a* **1300** *Cursor M.* 4848 Elleuen breþer es we liuand, An at ham, ten in þis land. *c* **1375** *Sc. Leg. Saints* xviii. (*Egipciane*) 514 Sone I fand Of ȝongmen tenne in a place stanand. **1377** LANGL. *P. Pl.* B. XIII. 270 In þe date of owre dryȝte..A þousande and thre hondreth tweis thretty & ten. ? *a* **1500** *Chester Pl.* xxii. 143 But of the Tenne the first three sone wear consumed away. **1548–9** (Mar.) *Bk. Com. Prayer*, *Catechism*, Q. Tell me how many [commandments] there bee. *A.* Tenne. **1726** DE FOE *Hist. Devil* I. x. (1840) 169 Ten of the twelve tribes. **1814** SCOTT *Wav.* xv, When I was a girl about ten, there was a skirmish fought. **1823** BYRON *Juan* x. xxxiii, Thermometers sunk down to ten, Or five, or one, or zero. **1874** T. HARDY *Far fr. Madding Crowd* xxvi, Am I any worse for breaking the third of that Terrible Ten than you for breaking the ninth? **1891** C. JAMES *Rom. Rigmarole* 25 Two girls of, perhaps, eight and ten. **1908** *Installation News* II. 30/2 Witness our first attempt of a ten-and-six-penny kettle.

**b.** *esp.* of the hour of the day: orig. *ten hours*, *ten of the clock*: see CLOCK *sb.*[1] 3.

*c* **1386** CHAUCER *Pars. Prol.* 5 Ten of the clokke it was tho as I gesse. [**1427** [see HOUR 1 b]. **1582–8** *Hist. Jas. VI* (1804) 116 At ten hor in the morning.] **1681** T. WHITE in *12th Rep. Hist. MSS. Comm.* App. v. 55 Yesterday about tenne in the morning. **1712–13** SWIFT *Jrnl. to Stella* 27 Jan., He went away at ten. **1753** HANWAY *Trav.* (1762) II. I. v. 25 There is admittance till ten, for a toll of one stiver each person. **1795** tr. *Moritz's Trav. Eng.* ii. (1886) 17 It might be about ten or eleven o'clock. **1810** SCOTT *Let. to Miss J. Baillie* 30 Jan. in *Lockhart*, The play..lasting till half-past ten. **1843** BORROW *Bible in Spain* xxxix. (Pelh. Libr.) 268 About ten at night, Maria Diaz..arrived with her son. **1897** *Daily News* 18 Nov. 8/5 'You are the ten o'clock man', meaning that he came on duty at that time.

**c.** In phrases and specific uses.

† *Ten in the hundred*, a rate of interest on loans formerly current; hence usury; also *transf.* a usurer. *Ten to one*, ten chances to one; odds of ten times the amount offered in a bet; hence, an expression of very strong probability. *The Ten*, †(*a*) the Decemvirs, (*b*) the Council of Ten: see COUNCIL *sb.* 9. *Card of ten*: see CARD *sb.*[2] 2. *Hart of ten*: see HART 1 b. *Upper ten* (= *upper ten thousand*): see UPPER *a.*

**1594** *Death of Usury* 10 He that puts forth money dare not exceede the rate of 10. in the 100. **1618** *Epitaph J. Combe* in Brathwait *Rem. after Death* (ad fin.), Ten in the hundred must lie in his graue, But a hundred to ten whether God will him haue.

**1589** *Hay any Work* 30 Ten to one [I haue bin] among some of these puritans. **1650** W. BROUGH *Sacr. Princ.* (1659) 481 Is it not ten to one odds if ever thou be called? **1782** MISS BURNEY *Cecilia* VI. vii, Ten to one but that happens to be the very thing I want. **1889** J. K. JEROME *Three Men in Boat* 248 Bet us ten to one we didn't.

**1636** E. DACRES tr. *Machiavel's Disc. Livy* I. 231 As it appear'd in the example of Manlius, and in that of the tenne. **1820** BYRON *Mar. Fal.* III. ii. 193 A sceptic of all measures which had not The sanction of 'the Ten'. **1878** VILLARI *Life & Times Machiavelli* (1898) I. IV. iv. 205 The old Magistracy of the Ten for war affairs was preserved. *Ibid.* II. iii. 41 The Ten brought swift and exemplary justice to bear.

*c* **1410** *Master of Game* (MS. Digby 182) xxii, An hynde commonlyche hathe..more openn þe clee before þenn an herte of tenn. **1486** *Bk. St. Albans* E j b, Then shall ye call hym forchyd an hert of tenne. **1637** B. JONSON *Sad Sheph.* I. ii, A hart of ten, I trow he be.

**B.** *sb.* (With plural *tens*; and (less usually) possessive *ten's*.)

**1.** The abstract number; also, a symbol or the figures representing this.

*c* **950** *Lindisf. Gosp.* Matt., Prol. (1887) 4 Oðer..tal..ðe to tenum wið fore-cyme. *c* **1000** *Sax. Leechd.* III. 228 Tele þu..oð þæt þu cume to þrittiga foh eft on þone niwan oð tyne. *c* **1200** ORMIN 4312 Þe firrste staff iss nemmnedd I, & tacneþþ tale off tene. **1398** TREVISA *Barth. De P. R.* XIX. cxxiii. (1495) 923 The nombre of ten passyth nyne by one. *c* **1440** *Promp. Parv.* 488/2 Tenne, nowmyr, *decem*. **1530** PALSGR. 367 *Dix*, tenne, x. **1594** BLUNDEVIL *Exerc.* I. (1636) 84, 12 tens, which do make 2 sixties. **1837** WHEWELL *Hist. Induct. Sc.* (1857) I. 52 Ten is a perfect number. *Mod.* Five tens are fifty.

**b.** In a number expressed in decimal notation, the digit expressing the number of tens, e. g. in 1837 the figure 3.

**1542** RECORDE *Gr. Artes* 116 b, Then come I to the articles of tennes, where in the fyrste summe I fynde 90, and in the seconde summe but only 40. **1806** HUTTON *Course Math.* I. 9 Set..the numbers under each other,..that is, units under units, tens under tens, hundreds under hundreds, &c...Add up the figures in the column or row of units, and find how many tens are contained in that sum.

**c.** A thing or person distinguished by the number ten, usually as the tenth of a series. Also *number ten*.

**1888** H. MORTEN *Sk. Hosp. Life* 70, I say, tell Ten I am so sorry for him. I wish I could go to the ward! **1907** *Cassell's Mag.* Feb. 295/1 For fourteen [days] he was put on '10 A', which is short for no grog, no tobacco. *Mod.* Number ten, it is your turn to play.

**2.** A set of ten things or persons.

*Ten of rupees*, a unit of account in Indian money.

*c* **961** ÆTHELWOLD *Rule St. Benet* xxii. (1885) 47 Tynum and twentiʒum on anum inne ætgædere restan mid heora ealdrum. **1539** BIBLE (Great) *Gen.* xviii. 32, I wil not destroye them for tens sake [**1885** BIBLE (*R. V.*) for the ten's sake]. **1611** BIBLE *Deut.* i. 15, I..made them..captaines ouer tennes. **1894** *Field* 9 June 839/1 They came forth in their tens, for thirty-eight members turned out on the occasion of the first meet. **1895** *Westm. Gaz.* 4 Sept. 5/1 The revenue was better by 74,000 tens of rupees. **1897** FLANDRAU *Harvard Episodes* 94 One never said of Wolcott, as is said of some fellows, 'He made the first ten of the Dicky'.

**3.** *Coal-mining.* A measure of coal, locally varying between 48 and 50 tons, being the unit of calculation on which the lessor's rent or royalty is based. (See quot. 1894.) *n. dial.*

**1590** *Wills & Inv. N. C.* (Surtees) II. 181 At the grannde lease pitts, ccclxxxviij tenns of coolls, the twelfth parte is xxxij tenns, and the thirde parte of a tenn, praised worthe 2[l] per tenn is 64[l] 13/- 4[d]. **1789** BRAND *Hist. Newcastle* II. 279 In the year 1622 there were vended by the society of hostmen of Newcastle 14,420 tens of coals. **1851** GREENWELL *Coal-trade Terms Northumb. & Durh.* 54 *Ten*, the measure of coals upon which the landlord's rent is paid. It usually consists of 440 bolls of 8 pecks, but varies much under different landlords, generally, however, within the range of from 418 to 440 bolls. **1894** *Northumbld. Gloss.*, *Ten*, a measure of coals upon which the lessor's rent or royalty is paid. In the seventeenth century the term meant ten score bolls, barrows, or corves of coal.

**4.** A playing-card marked with ten pips. *Catch the ten*, a card-game played in Scotland in which the ten of trumps may be taken by any honour-card, and counts ten points, the game being a hundred. *Long ten*, the ten of trumps in this game: cf. *long trump* (LONG *a.*[1] 5 b). See also quot. 1870.

**1593** SHAKS. 3 *Hen. VI*, V. i. 43 But whiles he thought to steale the single Ten, The King was slyly finger'd from the Deck. **1680** COTTON *Compl. Gamester* xv. (ed. 2) 94 The rest follow in preheminence thus; the King, the Queen, the Knave, the Ten. *Ibid.* xvi. 97 You are not to play a ten first. **1816** SCOTT *Old Mort.* xli, These were Claver'se's lads a while syne, and wad be again, maybe, if he had the lang ten in his hand. **1870** *Modern Hoyle, Cribbage* 77 The court-cards and the ten of each suit count ten, and they are all indiscriminately spoken of as 'tens' during the game. **1887** P. M'NEILL *Blawearie* 146 They are playing at 'catch the ten', the stake being a few pence a-head.

**5.** Short for (*a*) ten-oared boat; (*b*) ten-pound note.

**1875** BLAKE-HUMFREY *Eton Boating Bk.* p. ix, The first eight had a strong picked crew, whilst the ten had several 'courtesy' oars...Mr. Canning was sitter in the ten. **1894** A. ROBERTSON *Nuggets*, etc. 190 To their intense disgust they only got about £200 in notes (chiefly tens).

**6. a.** Short for *tenpenny nail* (i.e. costing 10*d.* a hundred); *double ten*, a nail costing the double of the tenpenny (i. e. 20*d.* a hundred). **b.** A tallow candle weighing ten to a pound.

**1572** in Feuillerat *Revels Q. Eliz.* (1908) 175 Nayles v[c] of single tenns—iiij s. ij d. c. Dubble tens—xviij d. **1629** *MS. Acc. St. John's Hosp., Canterb.*, Itm halfe a hundred of double tennes xd. **1665** J. WEBB *Stone-Heng* (1725) 124 An huge old Nail, in Shape somewhat like those which we call commonly double Tens, or Spikes, such as are used in Scaffolding. **1717** [see DOUBLE A. 6]. **1802** *Sporting Mag.* XX. 15 Some have gone so far as to illuminate our discussions with tens instead of long-sixes.

† **C.** *quasi*-adv. Ten times, tenfold. *Obs.*

*c* **1330** *King of Tars* (Ritson) 336 Thaugh heo weore ten so briht. *c* **1385** CHAUCER *L. G. W.* 736 (*Thisbe*) Forbede a loue & it is ten so wod. **1387** TREVISA *Higden* (Rolls) II. 177 Þe lengþe of a manis body..be..ten so moche as þe depnesse þat is from þe rugge to þe wombe. **1399** LANGL. *Rich. Redeles* III. 168 Þei ffor þe pesinge paieth pens ten duble That þe cloþe costened. *c* **1400** *Siege of Troy* 396 in *Archiv neu. Spr.* LXXII. 21 Ector is ten so strong as þou [*older version*, ten siþe streyngor þen þow]. *c* **1420** *Sir Amadas* (Weber) 746 Yette was Y ten so glad When that thou gaffe all that thou had.

D. Combinations.

**1. a.** Adjectives, formed by *ten* with a sb., meaning consisting of, containing, measuring, or costing ten of the things named (also occasionally *ellipt.* as sb.), as *ten-acre, -bell, -cell, -cent, -course, -day, -dollar, -drachm, -grain, -guinea, -horse, -hour, -inch, -league, -mile, -minute, -month, -point, -second, -shilling, -stone, -syllable, -toe, -ton,* etc.; also, phrases thus formed prefixed to a simple adjective, forming a compound adj., as *ten-mile-long, ten-inch-thick,* etc. See also 2, and TENPENNY. **b.** Parasynthetic adjs., formed on such phrases as those in a, as *ten-acred, -armed, -barrelled, -coupled, -cylindered, -fingered, -footed, -headed, -horned, -jointed, -keyed, -oared, -parted, -peaked, -rayed, -ribbed, -roomed, -spined, -stringed, -syllabled, -talented, -tongued, -toothed* (also *-teethed*), *-wheeled,* etc. **c.** Parasynthetic sbs. (see -ER[1] 1), as *ten-bedder, -knotter, -seater, -tonner, -wheeler*; see also *ten-pointer* in 2, TENPOUNDER. **d.** Compounds of *ten* sb., as *ten bed* (= bed No. 10), *ten-bore, ten-gauge, ten-team* (team of ten); also *ten-shaped* adj. (=X-shaped); *tentale* [TALE *sb.* 6], used *attrib.* in phr. *tentale rent*: see quots.

**1826** MISS MITFORD *Village* Ser. II. 55 (*Copse*) On inquiring my destination, and hearing that I was bent to the *ten-acre copse. **1871** KINGSLEY *At Last* ii, Having a considerable quantity of land in each parish allotted to ten-acre men (i. e. white yeomen). **1807** VANCOUVER *Agric. Devon* (1813) 377 A *ten-acred enclosure might be as..proper a size as any other. **1881** *Times* 15 Jan. 5/6 The short *ten-barrelled Gatling was brought to the front. **1888** H. MORTEN *Sk. Hosp. Life* 69 [He] operated on that boy in *Ten bed; but, I fear, unsuccessfully. **1899** KIPLING *Stalky* iii. 79 She's busy in the middle of King's big upper *ten-bedder. **1905** *Daily News* 24 Apr. 2 In 1817 a *ten-bell record of 12,312 changes of Grandsire Caters was rung on these bells. **1892** GREENER *Breech Loader* 127 The *10-bore duck-gun full-choked, weighing 8½ lbs. and over. **1876** PREECE & SIVEWRIGHT *Telegraphy* 28 A *ten-cell Leclanché [battery]. **1903** J. K. JEROME *Tea Table Talk* (ed. Tauchn.) 31 The *ten-course banquet. **1898** *Westm. Gaz.* 1 Nov. 10/1 The *ten-day fog of 1880, credited with such heavy mortality. **1891** H. HERMAN *His Angel* 138 Underwood took three *ten-dollar bills from his wallet. **1886** *Guide Exhib. Galleries Brit. Mus.* 145 A *ten-drachm piece of Athens. **1894** *Outing* (U. S.) XXIV. 443/1 A couple of *ten-gauge breech-loaders. **1861** *Photogr. News Alm.* in *Circ. Sc.* (1865) I. 160/2 A *ten-grain silver solution. **1752** FOOTE *Taste* I. Wks. 1799 I. 8 A poor *ten-guinea job. **1678** BUTLER *Hud.* III. II. 1117 And turn'd the Men to *Ten-Horn'd Cattel, Because they came not out to Battel. **1837** P. KEITH *Bot. Lex.* 107 It is as if there was a certain ponderable mass which the application of a *ten-horse power was utterly incapable of moving. **1905** *Westm. Gaz.* 7 Mar. 5/2 The new scale is calculated on a *ten-hour basis. **1903** *Ibid.* 18 June 5/1 The shell which was being filled was a *ten-inch shell. **1839** *Penny Cycl.* XV. 84/1 In the genus Melolontha the antennæ are *ten-jointed. **1843** BORROW *Bible in Spain* xxxi. (Pelh. Libr.) 228 After the *ten-league journey of the preceding day. **1876** 'OUIDA' *Winter City* ix, A *ten-mile stretch across the open country. **1806** LAMB *Let. to Manning* 5 Dec., They all had their *ten-minute speeches. **1711** SHAFTESB. *Charac.* (1737) III. 265 To find a plain defect in these *ten-monosyllable heroicks. **1886** C. SCOTT *Sheep-Farming* 64 *Ten months old lambs. **1800** *Hull Advertiser* 16 Aug. 1/4 A *ten-oared cutter..with twelve volunteers. **1874** GARROD & BAXTER *Mat. Med.* (1880) 297 Capsule ovoid, inflated, *ten-ribbed. **1882** MISS BRADDON *Mt. Royal* II. ix. 180 The shabby little *ten-roomed house in South Belgravia. **1898** *Westm. Gaz.* 30 Nov. 5/3 Doubt..whether the Oriten '*ten-seater' machine exhibited at the Stanley Show could be ridden. **1907** *Daily Chron.* 30 Nov. 4/6 More technically known as the 'crux decussata'—the '*ten-shaped cross', because its form is identical with that of the Latin numeral X. **1745** M. FOLKES *Eng. Gold Coins* 9 Double-crowns or *ten shilling pieces. **1900** *Daily News* 4 Dec. 6/1 A *ten-stone man, who has to ride, is of more use than a twelve-stone man. *a* **1300** *E. E. Psalter* cxliii[i]. 9 To þe sal I sing in *ten-strenged sautre. **1535** COVERDALE *ibid.*, That I maye..synge prayses vnto the vpon a tenstrynged lute. **1881** H. MORLEY *Eng. Lit. Q. Vict.* iii. (ed. Tauchn.) 89 The all pervading couplets of *ten-syllabled lines. **1883** GRESLEY *Coal Mining Gloss.*, **Tentail rent*, a rent or royalty paid by a lessee upon every ten of coals which are worked in excess of a minimum or certain rent. **1888** NICHOLSON *Coal Trade Gloss.* s. v. *Rent* (E.D.D.), A surplus or tentale rent payable for the coal worked..above the certain quantity. **1901** *Daily Chron.* 17 July 5/2 One *ten-team of one N. C. officer of any rank and nine lance-corporals or privates from any regiment, battalion, or depot. **1883** *Harper's Mag.* Aug. 442/2 Some of the rated *ten-tonners were..over twenty-two tons in displacement. **1844** STEPHENS *Bk. Farm* II. 536 The wheels..are *ten-toothed. **1904** *Westm. Gaz.* 28 Dec. 3/2 Powerful *ten-wheeled tank engines. **1904** *Ibid.* 29 Jan. 5/1 This mammoth *ten-wheeler cost £5,000.

**2.** Special combinations and collocations: **ten-finger**, a species of star-fish: cf. FIVE-FINGER 2; **ten-foot** *a.*, measuring, or having, ten feet; *ten-foot coal*, a thick seam in Yorkshire; *ten-foot rod*, a levelling-pole; **ten-hours act**, a law limiting the hours of work in factories; *spec.* the popular name of the Act 10 & 11 Vict., c. 29; so, in U. S. A., **ten-hour law** (*Cent. Dict.* 1891); **ten-o'clock**, an American name for *Ornithogalum umbellatum*, the flowers of which open late in the morning (*Cent. Dict.* 1891); also, a light meal taken at ten o'clock; **ten-pointer**, a stag having antlers with ten points; a 'hart of ten'; **ten-pound** *a.*, of or involving the amount or value of ten pounds; also, weighing ten pounds; spec. *ten-pound land* (*Sc.*), land of the annual value of ten pounds; *ten-pound householder*, = TEN-POUNDER 2 b; **ten-spot** *a.*, having ten spots, as 'ten-spot ladybird', *Coccinella decem-punctata*; *sb.* (*U.S.*), a ten-dollar 'bill'; also, a playing-card, = TEN *sb.* 4; **ten-strike**, in the game of ten-pins, a throw which bowls over all the pins; hence *fig.*; **ten-week stock**, *Matthiola annua*, said to continue ten weeks in flower; **ten-yard coal**, a very thick seam of coal near Dudley; **ten-year** *a.*, of ten years' duration or standing, as *ten-year-old*, also as *sb.*; spec. *ten-year-man*, at Cambridge University: see quot. 1903. See also TENPENNY, TEN-PINS, etc.

**1701** MOXON *Math. Instr.* 19 **Ten foot Rods*, See Station-staffs. **1793** ANNA SEWARD *Lett.* (1811) III. 322 The iambic accent, unmixed with the trochaic, especially in the ten-feet couplet. **1834–5** J. PHILLIPS *Man. Geol.* (1855) 190 The thickest coal in the district,..that called the thick or ten-foot coal in Yorkshire. **1838** HOWITT *Rur. Life* I. II. iii. 161 Betty mean-time has put up their 'luncheons' or '*ten-o'clocks'. **1883** E. L. PEEL in *Longm. Mag.* Nov. 72 We had..stalked and slain a fine *ten-pointer upon the Caenlochan marches. **1673** *S'too him Bayes* 5 You..would have lost your *ten pound wager. **1845** DISRAELI *Sybil* II. vi, It is a great thing in these ten-pound [franchise] days to win your first contest. **1855** J. R. LEIFCHILD *Cornwall Mines* 263 Send the author a ten-pound-note for his advice—good in either event! **1863** H. COX *Instit.* I. viii. 106 A new uniform qualification [to vote]..frequently designated that of the 'ten-pounds householders'. **1890** *Cent. Dict.* s. v. *Pound, Ten-pound Act*, a statute of the colony of New York (1769) giving to justices of the peace and other local magistrates jurisdiction of civil cases involving not more than the sum named. **1888** *Boston* (Mass.) *Jrnl.* 6 Nov. 2/3 The point was seen at once, and the '*ten spot' was forthcoming. *c* **1895** *Thompson St. Poker Club* 65 The Rev. Mr. Smith dealt Mr. Williams two cards,..helped himself to the last ten-spot remaining in the pack. **1850** HAWTHORNE in Bridge *Pers. Recollect.* (1893) 111, I may calculate on what bowlers call a *ten-strike. **1889** FARMER *Dict. Amer.*, *Ten-strike*, where..all the men are bowled over at one throw...Hence..a fortunate occurrence: a thoroughly well done and complete work. **1785** MARTYN *Rousseau's Bot.* xxiii. (1794) 323 The Annual or *Ten-week Stock differs in having an herbaceous stalk. **1909** *Daily Chron.* 20 Mar. 7/6 A well-grown aster or ten-week stock is a beautiful object in itself. **1834–5** J. PHILLIPS *Geol.* in *Encycl. Metrop.* VI. 594/2 The upper part of the *ten-yard coal separates from the rest of the beds. **1839** URE *Dict. Arts* 980 The very remarkable seam near the town of Dudley, known by the name of the ten-yard coal, about 7 miles long, and 4 broad. **1693** G. STEPNEY in *Dryden's Juvenal* viii. (1697) 216 Courage to sustain a *Ten Years War. **1813** *Gentl. Mag.* LXXXIII. II. 530. **1816** *Ibid.* LXXXVI. I. 200/1 A query respecting the Ten-Year-Men at Cambridge. **1838** DICKENS *Nich. Nick.* xxx, Ever since he had first played the *ten-year-old imps in the Christmas pantomimes. **1868** *Rep. U. S. Commissioner Agric.* (1869) 443 The average yield for a three-year old vine is one peck;..full grown, ten-year old vine, twenty-five bushels. **1895** *Westm. Gaz.* 17 July 8/1 What terrible tyrants these ten-year-olds are! **1900** *Ibid.* 7 Mar. 7/1 What the terms of the new war loan for thirty millions in ten-year bonds will be, or ought to be. **1903** *Daily Chron.* 4 Feb. 5/1 The Ten Year man..being over twenty-four years of age, was admitted, and after keeping his name on the boards of a college for ten years was allowed to proceed B.D. on payment of certain fees. **1906** *Ibid.* 18 Aug. 4/4 An average of 11.4 in the previous ten-year period.

†**Ten,** obs. variant of TENNÉ, *Her.*

**1677** PLOT *Oxfordsh.* To Rdr. b ij b, If ever hereafter I shall meet with any bearing Purpure, Ten, or Sanguine;.. Ten [shall be represented] with lines salter-ways, mixt of Vert and Purpure.

**Ten,** obs. form of TEE *v.*[1], TEEN *sb.*[1]

**Tenabi·lity.** [f. next: see -ITY.] = TENABLENESS.

**1845** S. WILBERFORCE in Ashwell *Life* (1879) I. viii. 303 Only to maintain in the abstract, the tenability of a certain position. **1865** MASSON *Rec. Brit. Philos.* 201 When one looked again at his own position..one could not see its superior tenability in the new conditions of the campaign. **1875** RUSKIN *Fors Clav.* li. 67 *note*, Discussing the relative tenability of insects between the fingers.

**Tenable** (te·năb'l, †tī·n-), *a.* Also 7 **teneable.** [a. F. *tenable* (12th c. in Godef.), f. *ten-ir* to hold + -ABLE: see -BLE, and cf. TENIBLE.]

**1.** Capable of being held (in various senses of HOLD *v.*); that may be kept, kept in, kept back, retained, restrained, or held in control. Now *rare.*

**1602** SHAKS. *Ham.* I. ii. 248 (Qo.) If you have hitherto concealed this sight Let it be tenable [*Fol.*[1] treble] in your silence still. **1649** HEYLIN *Relat. & Observ.* II. 1 That Party ..being..tenable by no Oaths, Principles Promises, Declarations. **1856** RUSKIN *Mod. Paint.* IV. v. xii. § 14 Others tottering and crumbling away from time to time, until the cliff had got in some degree settled into a tenable form.

**2.** Capable of being held against attack; that may be successfully defended.

**1579** FENTON *Guicciard.* xv. (1599) 693 The City being not tenable..it yeelded. **1673** *S'too him Bayes* 105 Except you ..thrust your self in at every place that is not teneable. **1793** GOUV. MORRIS in Sparks *Life & Writ.* (1832) II. 297, I do not think the position taken at Louvain is tenable. **1855** PRESCOTT *Philip II*, I. IV. iii. 421 They might retire from a post that was no longer tenable.

**b.** *fig.* Of statements, opinions, etc.: Capable of being maintained or defended against attack or objection.

**1711** ADDISON *Spect.* No. 186 ¶ 5 The Atheist has not found his Post tenable, and is therefore retired into Deism. **1796** BURKE *Regic. Peace* iv. Wks. IX. 67 The Tartarian doctrine is the most tenable opinion. **1837** WHEWELL *Hist. Induct. Sc.* (1857) I. 286 The letter of their theories is no longer tenable.

**3.** Capable of being held, occupied, possessed, or enjoyed.

**1840** THIRLWALL *Greece* VII. lvi. 142 The office was tenable for four years. **1883** *L'pool Courier* 5 Oct. 4/9 The scholarships..are tenable for three years.

**Tenable, -s,** corruption of TENEBRES.

**Tenableness** (te·năb'lnės). [f. TENABLE + -NESS.] The quality of being tenable.

**1647** SPRIGGE *Anglia Rediv.* IV. vii. (1854) 266 Distrusting their own strength, or the garrison's tenableness. **1849** J. H. NEWMAN *Disc. Mixed Congregat.* Ded., A doubt..of the tenableness of the theological theory.

**Tenace** (te·nės). *Whist.* [ad. Sp. *tenaza*, lit. 'pincers, tongs', used in card-playing as here. Cf. also F. *demeurer tenace* (*Dict. de Trevoux*, 17..) 'to have the tenace'.] A name given to the combination of two cards of any suit, consisting of the next higher and the next lower in value than the highest card held by the other side, esp. when this combination is held by the fourth player: see quot. 1746. Used esp. in phr. *to have the tenace*, formerly *tenaces*.

**1655** J. COTGRAVE *Wits Interpr.* (1662) 356 If you have Tenaces in your hand, that is two cards which, if you have the Leading, you are sure to lose one of them; if the Player lead to you, you are sure to win them both. **1710** SWIFT *Lett.* (1767) III. 17 Then in that game of spades, you blundered when you had ten-ace. **1746** HOYLE *Whist* (ed. 6) 70 Having the Tenace in any Suit supposes the having the first and third best Cards, and being the last Player, and consequently you catch the Adversary when that Suit is play'd. **1870** *Modern Hoyle* 12 Tenaces...1st major tenace—ace, queen. 2nd major tenace—king, knave. 3rd major tenace—queen, ten...1st minor tenace—four, two. 2nd minor tenace—five, three. 3rd minor tenace—six, four. *Ibid.* 19 Tenaces are always most valuable, because most certain, to the fourth player.

**Tenacious** (tĭnē·ʃəs), *a.* Also 7 -atious, -aceous. [f. L. *tenāx*, *tenāci-* holding fast (f. *ten-ēre* to hold) + -OUS: see -ACIOUS.]

**1. a.** Holding together, cohesive; tough; not easily pulled in pieces or broken.

**1607** TOPSELL *Four-f. Beasts* (1658) 152 The bones of Fishes are more tenacious. **1750** tr. *Leonardus' Mirr. Stones* 71 Amiaton is..like feathered alumn, but more tenacious. **1834** *Brit. Husb.* I. xiii. 310 It acts as manure physically, or substantially, through the effect of the clay in rendering soils tenacious. **1869** ROSCOE *Elem. Chem.* (1871) 185 Gun-metal, or bronze, is a hard and tenacious alloy.

**b.** Adhesive; viscous, glutinous; sticky.

**1641** WILKINS *Math. Magick* II. xii. (1648) 251 Provided, that this oyl..bee supposed of so close and tenacious substance, that may slowly evaporate. **1697** DRYDEN *Virg. Georg.* IV. 58 Not Birdlime, or Idean Pitch, produce A more tenacious Mass of clammy Juice. **1784** COWPER *Task* I. 216 Female feet, Too weak to struggle with tenacious clay. **1868** CARPENTER in *Sci. Opinion* 6 Jan. (1869) 174/2 The bottom consisted of a bluish-white tenacious mud.

**2.** Holding fast or inclined to hold fast; grasping hard; clinging tightly.

**1656** BLOUNT *Glossogr.*, *Tenacious*, that holds fast,..good and sure. **1681** tr. *Willis' Rem. Med. Wks.* Vocab., *Tenacious*, holding or cleaving fast. **1800–24** CAMPBELL *Poems, Chaucer & Windsor* 4 Old oaks..Whose gnarled roots, tenacious and profound. **1869** TOZER *Highl. Turkey* I. 232 The palluria..is covered all over with tenacious hooked prickles.

**3.** Keeping a firm hold, retentive of something.

*c* **1645** HOWELL *Lett.* (1650) II. ii. 2 The Badger..is said to be so tenacious of his bite, that he will not give over his hold, till hee feels his teeth meet. **1726** LEONI *Alberti's Archit.* I. 27/1 The Fir..is..very dry, and very tenacious of the Glue. **1758** R. BROWN *Compl. Farmer* II. (1760) 23 All.. are very tenacious of water on the surface.

**4.** *fig.* Strongly retaining or inclined to retain, persist in, preserve, or maintain (a principle, method, secret, etc.); holding persistently; of memory, retentive. Const. *of.*

**1640–1** LD. J. DIGBY *Sp. in Ho. Com.* 9 Feb. 13 A man tenatious of the liberty..of the subject. **1656** EARL MONM. tr. *Boccalini's Advts. fr. Parnass.*, The tenacious memory of benefits received. **1657** JER. TAYLOR *Disc. Friendship* ¶ 13 Free of his money and tenacious of a secret. **1708** ROWE *Royal Convert* I. i, Tenacious of his Purpose once resolv'd. **1800** MAVOR *Nat. Hist.* (1811) 230 The frog is remarkably tenacious of life. **1877** FROUDE *Short Stud.* (1883) IV. I. xii. 145 He had read largely, and his memory was extremely tenacious. **1898** J. T. FOWLER *Durham Cath.* 62 So tenacious are boys of traditional terms.

**5.** Persistently continuing; persistent; resolute; perseveringly firm; obstinate, stubborn, pertinacious.

**1656** BLOUNT *Glossogr.*, *Tenacious*,..also hard to be moved, stiff necked. **1661** LOVELL *Hist. Anim. & Min.* Introd., The life is more tenacious in them, than in the sanguineous. **1750** JOHNSON *Rambler* No. 14 ¶ 14 He is hot and dogmatical, quick in opposition and tenacious in defence. **1861** STANLEY *East. Ch.* vi. (1869) 193 Tenacious adherence to the ancient God of Light.

†**6.** *spec.* Unwilling to part with or spend money or the like; close-fisted, niggardly. Also *transf.*

**1676** DRYDEN *Aurengzebe* v. i. 82 True love's a Miser; so tenacious grown, He weighs to the least grain of what's his own. **1681–6** J. SCOTT *Chr. Life* (1747) III. 79 Give me a covetous, a niggardly and tenacious Man; I will return him to thee liberal.

†**7.** Persistently chary of or averse to any action. (*erroneous use.*) *Obs.*

**1766** *Compl. Farmer* s.v. *Tuberose*, Mons. Le Cour, of Leyden..for many years was so tenacious of parting with any of the roots..that he caused them to be cut in pieces, that he might have the vanity to boast of being the only person in Europe who was possessed of this flower. **1802** MARIAN MOORE *Lascelles* I. 142 Since the adventure..Mrs. Carisbrooke had been very tenacious of being late on the road. **1811** *R. Cecil's Wks.* I. 69 Mr. Cecil..was tenacious of being interrupted in his pursuits.

**Tenaciously** (tǐnēi·ʃəsli), *adv.* [f. prec. + -LY ².] In a tenacious manner; with a strong hold; persistently, stedfastly, stubbornly.

*a* **1667** JER. TAYLOR *Serm. for Year* III. i. (1841) 352/2 To resent an error deeply,..to remember it tenaciously, to repeat it frequently. *a* **1677** HALE *Prim. Orig. Man.* 250 Ocellus Lucanus..tenaciously asserted the Eternity of the World. **1777** ROBERTSON *Hist. Amer.* I. II. 111 Columbus adhered tenaciously to his original opinion. **1808** SCOTT in *Lockhart* (1837) I. i. 37 My memory..seldom failed to preserve most tenaciously a favourite passage of poetry. **1882** A. W. WARD *Dickens* i. 16 It is not surprising that..the name should have clung to him so tenaciously.

**Tenaciousness** (tǐnēi·ʃəsnės). [f. as prec. + -NESS.] The quality of being tenacious; tenacity.

**1.** = TENACITY 1.

**1658** ROWLAND *Moufet's Theat. Ins.* 1069 Clammy stuffe that drawes like Bird-lime, which loseth not its tenaciousnesse by drinesse nor by moysture. **1794** SULLIVAN *View Nat.* II. 44 The tenaciousness of their cohesion..seem[s] to prove them to consist of viscous parts.

**2.** = TENACITY 2.

**1642** ROGERS *Naaman* 128 Fourthly and lastly, the Tenaciousnesse of selfe: I meane when she is put hard to it. **1669** W. SIMPSON *Hydrol. Chym.* 122 Solidity of judgement, and tenaciousness of memory. **1786** JEFFERSON *Writ.* (1859) II. 78 What I learn of the temper of my countrymen and their tenaciousness of money. **1860** *All Year Round* No. 43. 389 Extraordinary examples of tenaciousness of life.

**Tenacity** (tǐnæ·sĭti). [ad. rare L. *tenācitās*, f. *tenāx, tenāci-* tenacious: see -ACITY. So F. *tenacité* (14th c. in Godef. *Compl.*).] The quality or property of being tenacious.

**1.** Cohesiveness, toughness; viscosity, clamminess (of a liquid); also, adhesive quality, stickiness.

**1555** EDEN *Decades* 145 A certeyne..iuise, whose substaunce is of suche tenacitie and clamminesse, that it wyll neuer weare awaye. **1660** BOYLE *New Exp. Phys. Mech.* ii. 41 Water, to which Sope has given a Tenacity. **1718** QUINCY *Compl. Disp.* 3 For the same reason..many light Substances have such strong Cohesions or Tenacities. **1805–17** R. JAMESON *Char. Min.* (ed. 3) 261 By tenacity is understood..the different degrees of cohesion of the particles of minerals. **1866** ROGERS *Agric. & Prices* I. xxi. 538 No doubt the bigness of the [plough-] shoe varied..with the lightness or tenacity of the soil.

**2.** The quality of retaining what is held, physically or mentally; firmness of hold or attachment; firmness of purpose, persistence, obstinacy.

**1526** *Pilgr. Perf.* (W. de W. 1531) 175 Some whose tenacite & hardnes is reproued in this peticyon. **1682** SIR T. BROWNE *Chr. Mor.* II. § 5 The tenacity of Prejudice and Prescription. **1794** PALEY *Evid.* I. i. (1817) 21 They clung to this hope..with more tenacity as their dangers or calamities increased. **1823** *Spirit Pub. Jrnls.* (1824) 492 They..began tugging him towards the door, he..clinging to every hold he made with astonishing tenacity. **1830** J. W. CROKER in *C. Papers* 14 May, That tenacity of life which his family have constitutionally. **1878** LECKY *Eng. in 18th C.* I. iv. 552 The tenacity of the English bull-dog.

**b.** Retentiveness (of memory).

**1814** SCOTT *Wav.* iii, A memory of uncommon tenacity. **1871** BLACKIE *Four Phases* I. 93 What animal when it has learned anything can retain the lesson with equal tenacity?

†**3.** Tendency to keep fast hold of money; miserliness, niggardliness, parsimony. *Obs.*

**1586** DAY *Eng. Secretary* I. (1625) 32 Vnbridled lust, couetous tenacitie, prodigality, or detestable excesse. **1651** HOBBES *Leviath.* II. xxix. 173 The passage of mony to the publique Treasure obstructed, by the tenacity of the people. **1656** BLOUNT *Glossogr.*, *Tenacity*, fast-keeping, sure holding, niggardlinesse, misery. **1706** in PHILLIPS.

**Tenacle** (te·năk'l). Now *rare.* [ad. L. *tenāculum* holder: see below.]

†**1.** *pl.* Forceps, pincers, nippers; cf. next, 1. *Obs.*

*c* **1400** *Lanfranc's Cirurg.* 308 Þou schalt take vp þe skyn wiþ tenaclis, and putt in þin hoot iren þoruȝ þe hole of þe tenaclis, & brenne þe skyn. **1597** A. M. tr. *Guillemeau's Fr. Chirurg.* 15 b/2 Rounde pinsers or tenacles, to take away the trepanede percelle of bone.

**2.** That by which a plant, a fruit, etc. is upheld or supported: † a stalk, peduncle, or petiole (*obs.*); in *pl.* the organs by which some climbing plants attach themselves.

*c* **1500** BOLLARD tr. *Godfredi on Pallad.* 157 The furste [kind of cherry] hath shorte tenacles v. stalkys. **1658** SIR T. BROWNE *Gard. Cyrus* iv, Ivy, divided from the root, we have observed to live some years, by the cirrous parts commonly conceived but as tenacles and holdfasts unto it. **1860** TRENCH *Serm. Westm. Abb.* xxvi. 305 We all know how the ivy..casts out innumerable little arms and tenacles by which it attaches and fastens itself.

†**3.** ? A holster or the like in which to hold the staff of a standard or flag when borne. *Obs.*

**1556** *Chron. Gr. Fr.* (Camd.) 50 A generalle processione from Powlles unto sent Peters in Cornehylle with alle the chelderne of Powlles scole, & a crosse of every parishe churche with a banner and one to ber it in a tenacle [*MS.* tenache].

**Tenacull**, obs. form of TUNICLE.

‖ **Tenaculum** (tǐnæ·kiŭlŏm). Pl. -ula. [mod. uses of L. *tenāculum* a holder, f. *ten-ēre* to hold.]

**1.** *Surg.* A species of forceps: see quots.

**1693** tr. *Blancard's Phys. Dict.* (ed. 2), *Tenaculum*, the same with *Forceps*. **1726** QUINCY *Lex. Physico-Med.*, *Tenacula*,..a chirurgical Instrument, not much differing from the Forceps. **1857** DUNGLISON *Med. Lex.*, *Tenaculum, Assalini's*,..consists of a forceps, or double tenaculum. **1899** *Syd. Soc. Lex.*, *Tenaculum*, a variety of artery forceps for arresting hæmorrhage.

**b.** See quot. 1842.

**1842** BRANDE *Dict. Sc.* etc., *Tenaculum*, a surgical instrument, consisting of a fine sharp-pointed hook, by which the mouths of bleeding arteries are drawn out, so that in operations they may be secured by ligaments. **1860** J. M. CARNOCHAN *Operat. Surg.* 62 (Cent.) These [arterial branches] are difficult to tie, even when picked up by the tenaculum.

**2.** *Entom.* The abdominal process by which the springing organ is retained in the *Poduridæ* or spring-tails.

**1878** PACKARD *Guide Stud. Insects* 622 The Collembola [are characterized] by their spring (*elater*), its holder (*tenaculum*) [etc.].

‖ **Tenaille** (tǐ-, tenēi·l). Forms: 6–8 tenaile, 7 tenal, 8–9 tenail, 7– tenaille. [F. *tenaille* (tənā^l^y) forceps (12th c. in Godef. *Compl.*), also in Fortification as in sense 2 (16th c. in Littré) = Pr. *tenalhia*, It. *tanaglia*:—L. *tenācula*, pl. of *tenāculum* holder: see prec.]

†**1.** *pl.* Pincers, forceps: cf. prec., 1. *Obs.*

**1597** LOWE *Chirurg.* (1634) 98 To doe that operation, thou shalt be meetest, and with smallest paine to be done, with Tenals incisiues. **1727** *Bradley's Fam. Dict.* s.v. *Cray-fish*, They have forked Claws, in the Form of black Tenails, or Pincers.

**2.** In *Fortification*, A small low work, consisting of one or two re-entering angles (*single* or *double tenaille*), placed before the curtain between two bastions. *Tenaille of the place*, the face of a fortress: see FACE *sb.* 17.

**1589** IVE *Fortif.* 33 The defences in so small Forts as these proceede chiefly, either of bulwarks, halfe bulwarks, and tenailes [etc.]. **1677** R. BOYLE *Treat. Art War* 81 All sort of Works by which the Camp is invironed, and shut up, as Redoubts, Bastions, Ravelins, Forts, Tennailes, Hornworks [etc.]. **1708** *Brit. Apollo* No. 63. 4/2 They will fill up the Ditch, in order to storm the Tenaile. **1886** N. L. WALFORD *Parl. Generals Grt. Civ. War* 214 A second party of forty or fifty men..attacked a tenaille which by its fire flanked one of the breaches.

‖ **Tenaillon** (tenæ·liǫn). *Fortif.* [F. *tenaillon* (tənā^l^yoṅ) in same sense, f. *tenaille* (see prec.).] A work sometimes placed before each of the faces of a ravelin, leaving the salient angle exposed.

**1842** BRANDE *Dict. Sc.* etc., *Tenaillon*...Seldom adopted. **1845** STOCQUELER *Handbk. Brit. India* (1854) 287 On the north side where Lally attacked, the bastion and demi-bastion are detached and the works near the sea covered by a tenaillon. **1859** F. A. GRIFFITHS *Artill. Man.* (1862) 262 *Lunettes* and *Tenaillons* are works (consisting of two faces) constructed on each side of ravelins.

‖ **Tena·lia**, *sb. pl. Obs. rare.* [med.L. *tenālia* forceps (Du Cange), latinized from F. *tenaille(s*, It. *tanaglia*.]

**1.** Pincers, forceps: = TENAILLE 1.

In quot. for tearing the flesh.

**1603** KNOLLES *Hist. Turks* (1621) 1119 Some they roasted, and some they put unto the Tenalia.

**2.** *Fortif.* = TENAILLE 2.

**1649** CROMWELL *Let.* 16 Sept., in *Carlyle*, Colonel Brandly did with forty or fifty of his men very gallantly storm the *Tenalia*; for which he deserves the thanks of the State. *Ibid.* 17 Sept., There was a *Tenalia* to flanker the south wall of the Town, between Duleek Gate, and the corner Tower.

**Tenancy** (te·nănsi). [f. TENANT: see -ANCY; representing med.L. *tenentia* (1116 in Muratori *Antiquitates* IX. (1776) 430), also *tenantia* (*c* 1200 in Du Cange). Cf. OF. *tenance* (12th c. in Godef.).] The state or position of being a tenant; the holding or occupation of lands, etc.; tenure.

**1.** *Law.* A holding or possession of lands or tenements, by any title of ownership.

**1590** SWINBURNE *Testaments* 72 Besides this men married lost their tenanc[i]es by the curtesie, women their dowries; finally the prince himselfe lost the profits of the landes of persons attainted. **1598** KITCHIN *Courts Leet* (1675) 484 The other pleads several Tenancy. **1614** SELDEN *Titles Hon.* 266 By the substance, I mean their being immediat Tenancies of the Crown, or as we say in chief. **1766** BLACKSTONE *Comm.* II. xii. 194 As to the incidents attending a tenancy in common. **1818** CRUISE *Digest* (ed. 2) I. 51 The practice of creating manors or tenancies in gross was effectually prevented by the statute *Quia Emptores*. *Ibid.* VI. 418 The Court at first held this to be a tenancy in common; but afterwards upon good consideration it was adjudged to be a joint tenancy, for so it was implied.

**b.** Occupancy of lands or tenements under a lease. (The ordinary current sense.) Also (contextually) the duration of a tenure; the period during which a tenement is held.

**1598** MARSTON *Sco. Villanie* I. ii, Tis all one, for life to be a beast, A slaue, as haue a short term'd tenancie. **1817** W. SELWYN *Law Nisi Prius* (ed. 4) II. 673 A notice to quit at the expiration of the current year of the tenancy. **1834** HT. MARTINEAU *Moral* II. 75 Partnership tenantcies affect the security of property by rendering one tenant answerable for the obligations of all his partners. **1858** LD. ST. LEONARDS *Handy Bk. Prop. Law* xv. 99 Such a lease..creates a tenancy from year to year, and terminable by half a year's notice. **1875** *Report* in Woodfall *Law Landl. & Ten.* (1877) 719 Some counties pay for no guano used in the last year but one of the tenancy. **1876** DIGBY *Real Prop.* v. § 1. 208 A tenancy at will is where the land is held by the tenant so long as lessor and lessee please that the tenancy should continue. *attrib.* **1906** *Westm. Gaz.* 30 July 5/2 Conspiring by false pretences to acquire several valuable tenancy agreements in various parts of London.

**2.** Occupation or enjoyment of, or residence in, any place, position, or condition.

**1597–8** BP. HALL *Sat.* IV. ii. 124 Thine heyr, thine heyres heyre, and his heire againe,..Shall climbe up to the chancell pewes on high, And rule and raigne in their rich tenancie. **1856** FROUDE *Hist. Eng.* I. v. 425 The queen was at Ampthill, ..having entered on her sad tenancy..as soon as the place had been evacuated by the gaudy hunting party. *attrib.* **1903** *Westm. Gaz.* 2 June 2/1 The district contract system was expanded into a district tenancy system, wherein the whole of the business was conducted by the contractor.

†**3.** That which is held by a tenant. **a.** A holding, a TENEMENT. **b.** A post or office; occupation, employment. *Obs. rare.*

**1579** J. STUBBES *Gaping Gulf* D iij, The greatest castelles, honors, and manors are but mesnalties or rather very messuages and tenancyes paraual. **1580–1** *Act 23 Eliz.* c. 4 Parte of the same Habytacions, Tenauncyes and Farmes have byn reduced rather to pasturing of Cattell then to the Mayntenaunce of Men of Service. *Ibid.*, What Tenauncyes and Howses of Habitacions be..ruyned and decayed. **1597–8** *Proc. Star Chamb.* in Ribton-Turner *Vagrants & Vagr.* (1887) 123 The said John Scripe had..divided a Tenement in Shordich, into, or about seventeene Tenancies or dwellings,..inhabited by divers persons. **1670** BLOUNT *Law Dict.*, *Tenancies* (23 Eliz. c. 4) are Houses for Habitation, Tenements, or places to live in, held of another.

**Tenant** (te·nănt), *sb.* Forms: *α.* 4–6 tenaunt, -aunte, -ante, *Sc.* -ente (4 *pl.* -auns), 5 ten(e)-awnte, -awunt, *pl.* -aunce, 5–6 tennaunte, 6–7 -ant, -ent(e, 7 -ent, 7–8 tenent, 4– tenant. *β.* *Sc.* and *n. dial.* 4–6 tenand(e, 5 tennend, 5–6 -and, 6 tenaind. [a. F. *tenant* sb. (12th c. in Godef.), orig. pr. pple. of *tenir*:—L. *tenēre* to hold.]

**1.** *Law.* One who holds or possesses lands or tenements by any kind of title. (In English Law implying a *lord*, of whom the tenant holds.)

[**1292** BRITTON I. i. § 13 En counteez et hundrez et en Court de chescun fraunc tenaunt.] *c* **1330** R. BRUNNE *Chron.* (1810) 19 Adelwolf of Westsex, after his fadere dede, At Chestre sette his parlement, his tenantz þerto bede. *c* **1375** *Lay Folks Mass Bk.* (MS. B.) 369 Oure frendes, tenandes, & seruandes. *c* **1380** WYCLIF *Serm.* Sel. Wks. I. 22 Oþir tenauntis of þe lord shal receyve me into þere housis. *c* **1450** HOLLAND *Howlat* 609 An ilk scheld in that place Thar tennend or man was. *c* **1460** FORTESCUE *Abs. & Lim. Mon.* x. (1885) 134 By escheittes þer mey not so muche lande fall to any man as to þe kyng, by cause þat no man hath so many tenantes as he. **1563** *Homilies* II. *Rogation Week* IV. (1859) 496 Whereby the lord's records, (which be the tenant's evidences,) be perverted..sometime to the disheriting of the right owner. **1594** SHAKS. *Rich. III*, IV. iv. 481 Where be thy Tenants, and thy followers? **1607** COWELL *Interpr.* (1672), *Tenant* or *Tenent*,..one that holds or possesses Lands or Tenements by any kind of Right, be it in Fee, for Life, Years, or at Will. **1766** BLACKSTONE *Comm.* II. v. 59 The thing holden is therefore styled a tenement, the possessors thereof tenants, and the manner of their possession a tenure. **1827** HALLAM *Const. Hist* (1876) II. IX. 129 The military tenants were frequently called upon in expeditions against Scotland, and last of all in that of 1640. **1845** POLSON *Eng. Law* in *Encycl. Metrop.* II. 828/1 He is called *tenant* [*in fee simple*] in virtue of the doctrine.. which treats the king as the universal landlord—a doctrine so far recognised by our law, that in corporeal inheritances ..the tenant in fee simple is formally styled as being seised in *his demesne as of fee*.

**b.** With qualifications indicating the species of tenure, the relation between lord and tenant, etc., as *customary, kindly, mesne, several, sole, very tenant*: see the adjs. Also JOINT-TENANT; *tenant in burgage, in capite, in chief, in common, by courtesy, in dower, paravail*, etc.: see these words, and quots. here. *Tenant through law of England* = tenant by courtesy; *tenant to the præcipe*, a tenant against whom the writ præcipe was brought, being one to whom an entailed estate had been granted by the owner in order that it might be alienated by a recovery; see RECOVERY 4. See also TENANT AT WILL.

*a* **1325** *MS. Rawl. B. 520* lf. 17 b, Þat is i-seid for women holdinde in dowere, ant tenauns þoru lawe of yngelonde. **1461** *Rolls of Parlt.* V. 485/2 The same halfendele.. enjoye to hym, for terme of his lyf, as Tenaunt by the Curtesie. **1475** *Ibid.* VI. 149/1 That the said Maude have.. actions by Writts of Dower,..ayenst all persones Tenaunt or Tenauntes of the Frehold. **1495** *Ibid.* 508/2 Discontinuances made by Tenauntes in Dower. [**1602** COKE *Reports* III. *Case of Fines* 88 Entant qu'il ne fuit tenant al Precipe.] **1607** COWELL *Interpr.* (1672), *Tenant per Statute-Merchant*, that holds Land by vertue of a Statute forfeited to him...*Tenant in Frank-marriage*.., he that holds Lands or Tenements by vertue of a Gift thereof made to him upon Marriage between him and his Wife...*Tenant by Elegit*, that holds by vertue of the Writ called an Elegit. *Tenant in Mortgage*, that holds by means of a Mortgage. *Tenant by the Verge* in ancient Demesne.., is he that is admitted by the Rod in a Court of ancient Demesne. *Tenant by Copy of Court-Roll*, is one admitted Tenant of any Lands, &c. within a Mannor, which time out of mind have been demisable, according to the Custome of the Mannor...*Tenant by Charter*, is he that holdeth by Feoffment in Writing, or other Deed...*Tenant in Chief*, that holdeth of the King in Right of his Crown...*Very Tenant*, that holds immediately of his Lord...For if there be Lord, Mesne and Tenant, the Tenant is very Tenant of the Mesne, but not to the Lord above...There are also *Joynt-tenants*, that have equal

Right in Lands..by vertue of one Title...*Tenants in Common*, that have equal Right, but hold by divers Titles... *Sole tenant*.., he that hath no other joyned with him. *Several tenant* is opposite to Joynt-tenant, or Tenants in Common. *Tenant al Præcipe* is he against whom the Writ *Præcipe* is to be brought... *Tenant in Demesne*.., is he that holdeth the Demeans of a Mannor for a Rent without Service. *Tenant in Service*.., is he that holdeth by Service... *Tenant by Execution*.., that holds Land by vertue of an Execution upon any Statute, Recognisance, &c. **1818** CRUISE *Digest* (ed. 2) V. 333 So that he could make a good tenant to the *præcipe*. **1827** JARMAN *Powell's Devises* (ed. 3) II. 113 It was held that the reversion in the settled lands passed, although the wife was tenant for life, and the daughter tenant in tail, in those lands under the settlement. **1844** SIR J. STEPHEN *Eccl. Biog.* (1850) I. 26 And held them [their crowns and mitres]..immediately, as tenants *in capite*, from the one legitimate representative of the great postle. **1863** H. COX *Instit.* I. iii. 11 The right of all tenants-in-chief of the Crown..to be summoned to a common council of the realm.

**2.** One who holds a piece of land, a house, etc., by lease for a term of years or a set time. (The ordinary current sense. Correlative of *landlord*.)

**1377** LANGL. *P. Pl.* B. xv. 305 To take of her tenauntz more þan treuth wolde. *c* **1380** WYCLIF *Sel. Wks.* III. 414 He begges not þis rent of þo lordis tenaunte. **1479–81** *Rec. St. Mary at Hill* 110 Yevyn to ther tenauntes at the Receyvyng of the Rentes, and in potacions amonge them.. xs. vd. **1523** FITZHERB. *Husb.* § 123 Than shall his farme be twyse so good in profyte to the tenaunt as it was before. **1526** TINDALE *Mark* xii. 2 When tyme was come he sentt to the tennauntes a servaunt that he myght of the tenauntes receave of the frute of the vyneyarde. **1639** HORN & ROB. *Gate Lang. Unl.* xxxii. § 386 He is a tenant, to whom house and grounds, and hired farms are, for a certain rent, let out to farm for a set time. **1770** *Junius Lett.* xxxvi. (1820) 179 Like broken tenants, who have had warning to quit the premises. **1838** DICKENS *Nich. Nick.* xvi, Of this chamber, Nicholas became the tenant; and having..paid the first week's hire in advance [etc.]. *Mod.* (*Title*) The Law of Landlord and Tenant.

**3.** *transf.* and *fig.* One who or that which inhabits or occupies any place; a denizen, inhabitant, occupant, dweller.

**1388** WYCLIF *Job* xix. 15 The tenauntis of myn hows, and myn handmaydis hadden me as a straunger. **1602** SHAKS. *Ham.* v. i. 50 That Frame [the gallows] outliues a thousand Tenants. **1728–46** THOMSON *Spring* 788 While thus the gentle tenants of the shade Indulge their purer loves. **1764** GOLDSM. *Trav.* 65 The shudd'ring tenant of the frigid zone. **1774** — *Nat. Hist.* (1824) II. 327 One of the most splendid tenants of the Mexican forests. **1799** CAMPBELL *Pleas. Hope* I. 268 The dim-eyed tenant of the dungeon gloom. **1827** SCOTT *Highl. Widow* v, As if sorrow, or even deep thought, should as short a while as possible be the tenant of the soldier's bosom. **1879** *Daily News* 27 Sept. 6/3 Tenants of our British waters. **1882** *Daily Tel.* 19 May, Mr. Bettesworth was the incoming tenant [i.e. batsman], and, after some slow play, the 50 went up.

**4.** *attrib.* and *Comb.* Simple attrib., as *tenant-holding* (HOLDING *vbl. sb.* 3), *-risk*, *-system*; appositive, as *tenant-cultivator*, *-farmer* (hence *tenant-farming* sb. and adj.), *-occupier*, *-purchaser*, *-soul*; also **tenant-sted** *a. Sc.*, occupied by a tenant. See also TENANT-RIGHT.

**1860** *All Year Round* No. 71. 485 Those down-trodden vassals, the *tenant farmers. **1887** *Edin. Rev.* Oct. 301 In Rhône..*tenant-farming is unprofitable. **1891** *Daily News* 11 Dec. 6/4 He came of a tenant farming race. **1591** in A. McKay *Hist. Kilmarnock* (1880) 359 We give and grant all the *tenant-holdings, free holdings [etc.]. **1906** *Westm. Gaz.* 7 Nov. 9/2 Entitled to be on the list as the *tenant-occupier of a dwelling-house, being part of a house, and such part being separately occupied. **1895** J. E. REDMOND in *19th Cent.* Dec. 913 The *tenant-purchasers have been remarkably punctual in their payments. **1880** A. ARNOLD *Free Land* 68 *Tenant-risk and the absence of tenant-right have contributed to drive capital away from agriculture. **1710** LD. FOUNTAINHALL *Decis.* (1761) II. 568 The rest of the rooms were lying waste, and this was only *tenant-sted. **1906** *Daily Chron.* 13 Sept. 5/7 The canteen is run on the *tenant system.

**Tenant** (te·nănt), *v.* [f. prec. sb.]

**1.** *trans.* To hold as tenant, to be the tenant of (land, a house, etc.); *esp.* to occupy, inhabit.

**1634** HABINGTON *Castara* (Arb.) 125 To the cold humble hermitage Not tenanted but by discoloured age. **1667** PRIMATT *City & C. Build.* 34 Houses..without Tenants, decay sooner than those which are Tenanted. **1711** STEELE *Spect.* No. 107 ¶ 5 The greatest Part of Sir Roger's Estate is tenanted by Persons who have served himself or his Ancestors. **1795** SOUTHEY *Vis. Maid of Orleans* I. 96 Damsel, look here! survey this house of death; O soon to tenant it. **1830** LYELL *Princ. Geol.* (1872) I. I. xiv. 300 Birds, quadrupeds, and reptiles, which tenanted the fertile region. **1855** TENNYSON *Brook* 222 We bought the farm we tenanted before.

**b.** *fig.* To occupy, fill, take up (a space, etc.).

**1670** J. NEWBURGH *Observ. Cider* in Evelyn *Pomona* 54 A Barrel newly tenanted by small Beer. **1806–7** J. BERESFORD *Miseries Hum. Life* (1826) VI. x, A pair of boundless slippers that have been tenanted by a thousand feet. **1873** MISS BROUGHTON *Nancy* II. 183 Alternate clouds and sunshine tenant the sky.

**2.** *intr.* To reside, dwell, live *in*. *rare.*

**1650** WELDON *Crt. Jas. I* 133 Surely never so many brave parts, and so base and abject a spirit tenanted together in any one earthen Cottage. **1851** S. WARREN *Lily & Bee* II. 190 A sparrow..In yonder tree he tenanteth alone.

†**3.** *trans.* To let *out* to a tenant or tenants. *rare.*

**1721** STRYPE *Eccl. Mem.* I. xvi. 123 Three acres more he converted into a highway..; and the rest he tenanted out. **1776** ADAM SMITH *W. N.* v. iii. (1869) II. 536 The lands in America and the West Indies, indeed, are in general not tenanted nor leased out to farmers.

Hence **Te·nanted** *ppl. a.*, held by a tenant or tenants, occupied; **Te·nanting** *vbl. sb.* and *ppl. a.* So **Te·nanter**, one who tenants, an occupant.

**1798** J. HUCKS *Poems* 43 The little family of hope, The young-ey'd tenanters of happiness. **1886** *Pall Mall G.* 22 Apr. 8/2 The immediate landlord of any tenanted estate. **1903** MORLEY *Gladstone* I. ii. 38 An eager pilgrimage to the newly tenanted grave of his hero.

**Tenant**, obs. form of TENENT, TENON.

**Tenantable** (te·nantăb'l), *a.* [f. TENANT *v.* and *sb.* + -ABLE.]

**1.** Capable of being tenanted or inhabited; fit for occupation. Also *fig.*

**1542** *Richmond Wills* (Surtees) 32 Ye same howse so to be mayde tenandhable. **1576** in W. H. Turner *Select. Rec. Oxford* (1880) 382 To leve yt repayred and tenaunteable. **1633** FORD *Love's Sacr.* IV. ii, A good tenantable and fertile womb. **1753** HERVEY *Theron & Asp.* (1757) I. xii. 472 It [the body] is kept in tenantable condition for the soul. **1849** DE QUINCEY *Eng. Mail Coach* Wks. 1862 IV. 292 The only room tenantable by gentlemen. **1852** BEARN in *Jrnl. R. Agric. Soc. Eng.* XIII. I. 90 He therefore cannot keep the property in tenantable repair.

**2.** [f. the sb.] Befitting a tenant. *rare.*

**1856** H. BROOME *Comm. Common Law* 15 A tenant..is bound to use a farm in a good and tenantable manner, and according to the rules of good husbandry.

Hence **Te·nantableness**, tenantable condition. **1727** in BAILEY vol. II.

**Te·nant at wi·ll.** *Law.* A tenant who holds at the will or pleasure of the lessor. Also *fig.*

*c* **1500** *Lichfield Gild Ord.* (E.E.T.S.) 14 It is ordenyd that ..no tenaind at wyll shall make a tenand. **1598** *Child-Marriages* 164 Acceptans of the said Robert Fletcher to be his tenaunte at will of the said shop. **1628** COKE *On Litt.* 55 The lessee is called Tenant at will, because hee hath no certain nor sure estate, for the lessor may put him out at what time it pleaseth him. **1746–7** HERVEY *Medit.* (1818) 27 Let us look upon ourselves only as 'tenants at will'; and hold ourselves in perpetual readiness to depart at a moment's warning. **1878** JEVONS *Prim. Pol. Econ.* x. 92 Tenants at will have no inducement to improve their farms.

**Tenantcy**, erron. form of TENANCY.

**Tenanting**: see TENANT *v.*, TENONING.

**Te·nantism.** *nonce-wd.* [f. TENANT *sb.* + -ISM, after *landlordism*.] The principles and practice of tenants; tenantry; the tenant interest collectively.

**1880** *Daily News* 3 Nov. 5/6 Exacting 'landlordism' and recalcitrant 'tenantism' seem..to have said their last word.

**Tenantless** (te·năntlės), *a.* [f. as prec. + -LESS.] Without a tenant or tenants; untenanted, unoccupied, empty. *lit.* and *fig.*

**1591** SHAKS. *Two Gent.* v. iv. 8 Leaue not the Mansion so longe Tenant-lesse, Lest growing ruinous, the building fall. **1814** CARY *Dante, Inf.* xx. 85 Plying her arts, remain'd, and lived, and left Her body tenantless. **1826** DISRAELI *Viv. Grey* II. ix, Is it true that all the houses..are tenantless? **1871** R. ELLIS *Catullus* lxiv. 181 Also a desert lies this region, a tenantless island.

**b.** Const. *of*: Untenanted by.

**1613–16** W. BROWNE *Brit. Past.* II. ii. 46 Or haue the Parcæ..Left some friends body tenantlesse of life? **1868** *Rep. U. S. Commissioner Agric.* (1869) 346 Streams heretofore tenantless of fish are now well stocked artificially.

**Te·nant-right.** [f. TENANT *sb.* + RIGHT *sb.*] In general sense, The right that a person has as a tenant (of any kind). With special applications varying in time and place, as **a.** the right of a customary tenant: see quot. 1886; **b.** the right of a tenant at will or for a term of years to compensation for unexhausted improvements: **c.** the right of a tenant at will to sell his interest and goodwill to the incoming tenant. *Ulster tenant-right*: see quot. 1878.

**1542** *Richmond Wills* (Surtees) 27 Item I gyve and bewheth mye hole tityll and tenandright off my howse and farmehold.., aftere my decesse, unto Thomas Borowe. **1596** *Calr. Border Pap.* II. 134 The said tenantes hould the seuerall landes and tenementes aforesaid by a custumary estate, which they call and claime to be, Tennant right. **1665** MANLEY *Grotius' Low C. Warres* 906 There is extant a Charter..which grants to the Earl of Holland, to possess as his own Free-hold, what before he enjoy'd but by a kind of Tenant-Right. *a* **1734** NORTH *Lives* (1826) I. 289 In Cumberland the people had joined in.., pretending a tenant-right; which, there, is a customary estate, not unlike our copyholds. **1778** *Phil. Surv. S. Irel.* 315 So it is with us, where the present occupier is supposed to have a tenant-right. **1851** SIR F. PALGRAVE *Norm. & Eng.* I. 519 The tenant right of the beneficiary or feudal vassals. **1868** T. HUGHES *Sp. Ho. Com.* in *Morn. Star* 13 Mar., Tenant right was really an immemorial custom prevailing in a great portion of Ireland, but unrecognised yet in courts of law, or statute books, under which the ordinary tenant at will has acquired the right of selling the succession to his holding. **1874** STUBBS *Const. Hist.* (1875) I. iii. 52 The practice of careful husbandry demanded for the cultivator a tenant-right in his allotment. **1878** JEVONS *Prim. Pol. Econ.* x. 93 Tenant right, which consists in giving the tenant a right to claim the value of any unexhausted improvements, which he may have made in his farm, if he be turned out of it. *Ibid.*, Tenant right..has existed for a long time in the north of Ireland, where it is called the Ulster tenant right. A new tenant there pays the old tenant a considerable sum of money for the privilege of getting a good farm with various improvements. **1880** LD. DUFFERIN in *Times* 4 Jan. (1881) 4/4 Under the Act of 1870, if the landlord buys up the tenant-right of a farmer, it is declared to be extinguished for ever. **1886** H. HALL *Soc. Eliz. Age* App. i. 154 The customary tenants enjoy [in 1583] the ancient custom called tenant-right: namely, 'To have their messuages and tenements to them during their lives, and after their deceases to the eldest issues of their bodies lawfully begotten'.

*attrib.* **1713** *Act 12 Anne* Stat. I. c. 2 § 49 Copies of Admittances to Custom-Right, or Tenant-Right Estates, not being Copyhold, which pass by Deed, Surrender, and Admittance.

Hence **Te·nant-ri·ghter** (*colloq.*), an advocate or supporter of tenant-right.

**1865** *Morn. Star* 13 Mar., Mr. Greer, you are aware, is a great tenant-righter, and in the palmy days of the League he occupied a prominent place in that body. **1886** *Pall Mall G.* 4 Oct. 8/1 Recognized as a prominent representative of his class in the North and as a strong tenant-righter.

**Tenantry** (te·năntri). Forms: 4 *Sc.* **teneindri**, 4–6 *Sc.* **ten(n)andry**, **-endry**, 5–6 **tenentry**, 5– **tenantry**. [f. TENANT *sb.* + -RY.]

**1.** The state or condition of being a tenant; occupancy as a tenant; tenancy; tenantship.

**1391** in Fraser *Lennox* (1874) II. 43 Murthow..sal indow hir in the barony of the Redehall with the apportenantis in tenandry and in demayn. **1597** SKENE *De Verb. Sign.* s. v. *Manus*, The King may be thereby prejudged in his tennendrie, dewtie and service. **1606** WARNER *Alb. Eng.* XVI. ciii. 406 To take the foyson Lords haue skill, On Tainters setting Tenentries, oft for Expences ill. **1846** J. BAXTER *Libr. Pract. Agric.* (ed. 4) I. p. xxi, It was only by the tenantry of the peaceful monks that the land was even tolerably tilled. **1889** *Cornh. Mag.* Dec. 563 The Miss Tremenheeres had almost come to an end of their tenantry at Elm Place.

**2.** Land held of a superior; land let out to tenants; also, the profits of such land.

**1385** in *3rd Rep. Hist. MSS. Comm.* 410/1 Somonde at the chef plaz of the teneindri of Tyilton. **1438** *St. Andrews Regr.* (Bann. Cl.) 430 Ovirmalgask is fundin a tenandry in yhour awyn court of þe fornemmyt lordschip. *c* **1460** *Oseney Regr.* 20 With all churchis and chapells londis rentis tenauntries and tithes possessions and other thynges to þe saide church of seynte George perteynyng. **1584** *Reg. Privy Council Scot.* III. 673 Thair saidis tennendreis salbe annext to the Kingis Majesteis propirtie as his propir rent. **1597** SKENE *De Verb. Sign.* s.v. *Recognition*, Lands..annalied, and sauld be them heritably, to be halden of themselues and their aires, ceasis to be propertie to them, and becomes tennendry immediately halden of them and their aires.

†**b.** The holding of a tenant; a piece of land, a dwelling-house, or the like, held by a tenant under the landlord. Also *transf. Obs.*

*c* **1450** *Godstow Regr.* 149 To lete to oony man the foresayde tenantry ne no perte of hit with-owte specuall licence of þe foresayde abbesse. **1465** MARG. PASTON in *P. Lett.* II. 176 Ther be dyvers of your tenantrys at Mauteby that had gret ned for to be reparyed. **1521** *MS. Acc. St. John's Hosp., Canterb.*, The wyndowes of the tenauntry in Doklane. **1528** TINDALE *Obed. Chr. Man* 50 b, Let Christen londlordes be contente with their rent and olde customes not..lettinge ij. or iij. tenauntryes vnto one man. **1547** *Act 1 Edw. VI*, c. 3 § 9 Tenauntries cotages or other convenient howses to be lodged in. **1613–14** *Tack Roll* 20 Jan. in *Glasgow Daily Herald* (1864) 24 Sept., Cruixsfie propertie and tennandrie, 100 lib.

**c.** A set of houses owned by tenants collectively.

**1905** *Westm. Gaz.* 23 Aug. 8/3 It is here sought to prove as a sound economical principle..the collective ownership of a house with individual responsibility. No one tenant owns any distinct house in any 'tenantry', but the profits that accrue from that particular 'tenantry', after the deduction of interest on the money, cost of repairs, &c., are shared amongst the tenants.

**3.** *spec.* That part of a manor or estate under common or open-field husbandry (Tusser's 'champion countrie', *Husb.* lxiii.) occupied by tenants, as distinct from the lord's demesne (as in Domesday Survey, 'terra *in dominio*' and 'terra *in villenagio*'). Hence, locally applied to the condition or system of tenancy under open-field husbandry. See also *tenantry acre*, *field*, *flock*, *land*, in 5.

**1794** T. DAVIS *Agric. Wilts.* 14 The abolition of common-field husbandry (or as it is called in Wiltshire 'Tenantry'). *Ibid.*, Modern improvements..cannot be adopted to any extent, in lands lying in a state of tenantry. *Ibid.*, Tenantry yard-lands (or customary tenements)..are still subject to the rights of common. **1844** LITTLE in *Jrnl. R. Agric. Soc. Eng.* V. I. 178 Most of these commons are now enclosed;..some still remain in pasture, and the common field husbandry, or 'tenantry', as it is called, is abolished.

**4.** The body of tenants on an estate or estates. (Now the most usual sense.)

**1628** WITHER *Brit. Rememb.* VII. 752 That they have begger'd halfe their Tenantry. **1781** COWPER *Hope* 252 Kind souls! to teach their tenantry to prize What they themselves, without remorse, despise. **1868** MILL *Eng. & Irel.* 37 Those landlords who are the least useful in Ireland, and on the worst terms with their tenantry. **1875** MRS. RANDOLPH *W. Hyacinth* I. 46, I shall introduce you to the tenantry as their future mistress.

**b.** *transf.* A set of occupants or inhabitants.

**1798** H. MELVILLE in Spurgeon *Treas. Dav.* Ps. cxix. 18 The tiny tenantry [of a drop of water] are carrying on their usual concerns. **1880** E. KIRKE *Garfield* 44 Under the sway of terrestrial laws, winds blow, waters flow, and all the tenantries of the planet live and move.

**5.** *attrib.* and *Comb.*, as, in sense 3, *tenantry acre*, *down*, *field*, *flock*, *land*, *road*; tenantry dinner, a dinner given to the tenants on an estate.

**1794** T. DAVIS *Agric. Wilts.* 61 In the common fields..the usual rule is, to allow one thousand sheep to fold what they call a *tenantry acre (about three-fourths of a statute acre) per night. **1903** *Westm. Gaz.* 9 Jan. 7/2 The *tenantry dinner. **1794** T. DAVIS *Agric. Wilts.* 58 The old custom of the *tenantry fields of Wiltshire was..to give a year's fallow previous to wheat. **1813** *Ibid.* Gloss., *Tenantry Fields and Downs*, fields and downs in a state of commonage on the ancient feudal system of copyhold tenancy. **1793** A. YOUNG *Agric. Sussex* 69 A *tenantry flock [of sheep] (the joint property of several people) belonging to the parish of Denton. **1853** W. D. Cooper *Sussex Gloss.* 65 *note*, The proportion between the tenantry and the statute acre is very uncertain. The *tenantry land was divided first into laines, of several acres in extent, with good roads..between them; at right angles with these were formed..*tenantry roads,..dividing the laines into furlongs.

**Tenantship** (te·năntˌʃip). [f. Tenant *sb.* + -ship.] The condition or position of a tenant; tenancy, occupancy.

**1883** A. Wilder in Max Müller *India* ii. 67 The tenure and law of inheritance varies with the different native races, but tenantship for a specific period seems to be the most common. **1889** T. Gift *Not for Night-time* 127 He handed me the key in token of my new tenantship. **1892** *Daily News* 25 Mar. 4/8 To aim at the extension of tenantships as well as that of peasant proprietorships.

†**Te·nanty.** *Obs.* [? erroneous form, or mispr.] = Tenancy 3 a.

**1612** Davies *Why Irel.*, etc. 168 By the Irish Custome of Gauellkinde, the inferiour Tennanties were partible amongst all the Males of the Sept. [**1875** So quoted in Maine *Hist. Inst.* vii. 185.]

**Tenar**, obs. variant of Thenar.

**Tenasm(e, -asmus**, obs. forms of Tenesmus.

†**Tena·smon.** *Obs. rare.* [a. obs. F. *tenasmon* (15th c. in Godef.), f. med.L. *tenasmus*, Tenesmus, q. v.] = Tenesmus.

*c* **1425** tr. *Arderne's Treat. Fistula*, etc. 39 He shal fele ..akyng, stirryng, and prikkyng, and tenasmon; þat is, appetite of egestion. *Ibid.* 71 Tenasmon is a sekenez within þe lure þat makeþ þe pacient for to desire purgyng of his womb byneþ-forþ.

**Tenaunt(e**, obs. form of Tenant, Tenon.

**Tenax** (te·næks, tī·næks), *a.* and *sb.* [a. L. *tenax* tough: see Tenacious.]

†**A.** *adj.* Tough, tenacious. *Obs. rare*⁻¹.

**1605** Timme *Quersit.* iii. 144 The substance of sulphur..is tenax & retentiue.

**B.** *sb.* A trade name of fine carded oakum used as a surgical dressing (Billings).

**1889** *Athenæum* 31 Aug. 283/1 She..made a pillow for the back out of a piece of pink cambric stuffed with tenax [at Ladysmith]. **1891** *Scenes Life Nurse* 20 Some tenax (a kind of oakum) was lying with some other dressings on the side table.

**Tence**, obs. form of Tense.

**Tench**[1] (tenʃ). Also 4–6 **tenche**, 5 **tenych**, 6 **teyns(h)e**. Pl. **tenches**, collect. **tench**. [a. OF. *tenche* (in Cotgr.; cf. Picard *tenke* in Godef. *Compl.*), mod.F. *tanche* (13th c. in Littré):—late L. *tinca*.]

**1.** A thick-bodied freshwater fish, *Tinca vulgaris*, allied to the carp, inhabiting still and deep waters; also, the flesh of this fish as food.

**1390** *Earl Derby's Exp.* (Camden) 73 Pro tenches et roches.., iiij scot. xij d. **1392** *Ibid.* 155 Pro xij tench et xij anguillis grossis, iij s. vj d. *c* **1425** *Voc.* in Wr.-Wülcker 614/24 *Suctus*, a tenche. *Ibid.* 615/43 *Tengiagio*, a tenche. *c* **1440** *Promp. Parv.* 488/2 Tenche, fysche, *tencha*. **1485** *Nottingham Rec.* III. 240, ij grete eles and a grete tenche. *a* **1552** Leland *Itin.* V. 73 A preati Poole wherin be good Luces and Tenchis. **1653** Walton *Angler* ix. 175–6. **1787** Best *Angling* (ed. 2) 49 The tench the fishes physician (so called because his slime is said to be very healing to wounded fishes). **1802** Bingley *Anim. Biog.* (1813) III. 80 Tench are partial to foul and weedy waters. **1867** F. Francis *Angling* iii. (1880) 86 The tench is a very curious fish in his habits.

**2.** *attrib.* and *Comb.*, as *tench-broth*, *-fishing*; **tench-weed**, a local name of pondweed.

**1598** *Epulario* I j, Halfe a pint of Pike or *Tench broth. **1888** Goode *Amer. Fishes* 419 The season for *Tench fishing in Germany is from July to October. *a* **1825** Forby *Voc. E. Anglia*, **Tench-weed*, a sort of pond-weed, having a slime or mucilage about it...It is *Potamogeton natans*.

†**Tench**[2]. *Sc. Obs. rare.* [a. Picard *tenche*, OF. *tence* dispute (12th c. in Godef.), f. *tencier*, *tencer* to contend:—pop. L. type **tentiāre*, f. *tentus*, pa. pple. of *tendĕre* to stretch, strive, etc.] (?) A taunt, reproach.

**1513** Douglas *Æneis* ix. Prol. 23 The ryall style, clepyt heroycall,..Suld be compilit but tenchis or voyd word.

**Tench**[3] (tenʃ). *slang.* Abbreviation of *detention*, *penitentiary*.

**1850** *Broad Arrow* ii. 32 (Farmer) Prisoners' barracks, sir—us calls it Tench [Hobart Town Penitentiary]. **1887** Horsley *Jottings fr. Jail* i. 12, 'I..got remanded to the Tench' (House of Detention). **1897** P. Warung *Tales Old Regime* 143 We were all sent to a place called a tench and there we were signed off to Defferent masters.

†**Tencion** (te·nʃən). *Obs.* Also -chon, -cyon. [ad. OF. *tençon*, *tenchon*, *tenson* (12th c.) a contest, a quarrel = Pr. *tenso*, It. *tenzone*, ad. L. *tensiōn-em*, f. *tend-ĕre* to stretch, strive, contend.] A contention, dispute, quarrel.

**1471** Caxton *Recuyell* (Sommer) 521 A grete strif or tenchon [F. *une tençon et debat*] that is fallen betwene them. **1474** — *Chesse* iii. vi. (1883) 129 Hit happeth ofte tymes that ther cometh of glotonye tencyons stryfs ryottes [etc.]. *c* **1477** — *Jason* 8 That the wyn had surmounted hem in wordes and tencions.

†**Te·n-city.** *Obs. rare*⁻¹. Literal translation of Gr. Δεκάπολις *Decapolis*, a district of Roman Palestine comprising ten cities.

*c* **1550** Cheke *Matt.* iv. 25 A greet nomber from galilee, yᵉ tencitee,..and places beiond Jordan.

†**Tend**, *sb. Obs. rare.* [f. Tend *v.*[1]] The action or fact of tending; aim, tendency.

**1655** Mrq. Worcester *Cent. Inv.* Ded. ii. (1663) A vij, The taking off such Taxes or Burthens..which, I dare say, is the continual Tend of all your indefatigable pains.

**Tend** (tend), *v.*[1] Also 4–7 **tende**, (5 **tenne**). Pa. t. and pple. **tended** (5 **tende**). [Aphetic form of Attend *v.*, Entend *v.*, Intend *v.*, F. *attendre*, *entendre*, which largely ran together in sense in OF. and ME.]

†**1.** To turn one's ear, give auditory attention, listen, hearken; = Attend *v.* 1. **a.** *intr. Obs.*

13.. *Cursor M.* 2542 (Gött.) Abram..all bad till him tendand [*Cott.* tentand] be. **1340–70** *Alisaunder* 7 Tend yee tytely to mee & take goode heede. *c* **1430** *Hymns Virg.* 99 To þe ten heestis y haue not tende þoruȝ slouþe, wraþþe, & glotenie. *a* **1550** *Friar & Boy* 6 in Hazl. *E. P. P.* III. 60 God..gyue them good lyfe and longe That lysteneth to my songe, Or tendeth to my tale. **1610** Shaks. *Temp.* i. i. 8 Take in the toppe-sale: Tend to th' Masters whistle. **1816** G. Muir *Clydesdale Minstr.* 61 'Tend to my plaint, ye bonny lasses.

†**b.** *trans.* To turn one's ear to, listen to. *Obs.*

**1340–70** *Alisaunder* 997 Whan þis tale was tolde & tended of all. **1340–70** *Alex. & Dind.* 365 Tale tende we non þat turneþ to harme.

**2.** To turn the mind, attention, or energies; to apply oneself. **a.** *intr.* with *to*, *unto*: to attend to, look after (a thing, business, etc.); = Attend *v.* 2, 4. *Obs.* exc. *dial.*

13.. *Cursor M.* 255 (Gött.) Sum quat to þat thing to tende [*C.* tent] þat þai þair mede may wid amende. *c* **1330** R. Brunne *Chron. Wace* (Rolls) 655 Þat scheo tende to no þynge elles. *c* **1380** *Sir Ferumb.* 5122 Þe Amyral..ne miȝt noȝt tendy þer-to. *c* **1460** *Play Sacram.* 195 Ye owe tenderli to tende me tylle. **1523–4** *Rec. St. Mary at Hill* 323 For blowyng the Orgons and tendyng to the chirch euery sonday, to haue ij d. **1901** *Cornh. Mag.* Nov. 678 Some folks..cassn't be satisfite wi' 'tendin' to their own [business]. **1901** J. Prior *Forest Folk* ii. 14 To let me tend to the commoners first.

†**b.** with *inf.* To turn one's attention, apply oneself *to do* something; = Attend *v.* 4 d, Intend *v.* 9.

*c* **1330** R. Brunne *Chron. Wace* (Rolls) 14100 Þey tenden nought hem self to fende. **1340–70** *Alex. & Dind.* 846 3e tende nauht to tulye þe erþe. **1623** Whitbourne *Newfoundland* 82 Three men may fetch a-land salt, and tend to wash fish, and dry the same. **1682** Bunyan *Greatness Soul* Wks. 1853 I. 136 He could tend to do nothing but to find out how to be clothed in purple and fine-linen. *a* **1688** — *Accept. Sacrif.* ibid. 691 There is none else that either understand or that can tend to hearken to Him...But now the broken in heart can tend it.

**c.** *trans.* To attend to, mind (a thing); = Attend *v.* 4, Intend *v.* 12. Now *rare.*

**1549** Chaloner *Erasm. on Folly* O ij, How many princes ..dooe..onely tende theyr owne pleasure. **1594** Barnfield *Affect. Sheph.* ii. lvi, Speake ill of no man, tend thine owne affaires. **1650** Jer. Taylor *Holy Living* iv. § 6 (1727) 224 We rest also that we may tend holy duties. **1741–2** Gray *Agrippina* 7 To tend Her household cares, a woman's best employment. **1847** Helps *Friends in C.* I. i. 11 Your business..will be best tended in this way. **1866** Jul. Kavanagh *Sybil's Second Love* i, Tending the fire.

**3.** *trans.* To apply oneself to the care and service of (a person); now *esp.* to watch over and wait upon, to minister to (the sick or helpless); = Attend *v.* 6, Intend *v.* 11 b.

*c* **1489** Caxton *Sonnes of Aymon* xxv. 539, I..praye you that ye tende well my children. **1697** Dampier *Voy.* I. xviii. 520 Jeoly..had been sick for 3 months: in all which time I tended him as carefully, as if he had been my Brother. **1712–14** Pope *Rape Lock* ii. 91 Our humbler province is to tend the Fair. **1722** De Foe *Plague* (1840) 84 Nurses to tend those that were sick. **1805** Scott *Last Minstr.* i. Introd. ii, That they should tend the old man well.

**b.** To have the care and oversight of; to take charge of, look after (a flock, herd, etc.); = Attend *v.* 5. Said also (now *dial.* and *U. S.*) of a shop, toll-gate, bridge, etc.

**1515** Barclay *Egloges* iv. (1570) C iv, Nedes must a Shepheard bestowe his whole labour In tending his flockes. **1593** Shaks. 3 *Hen. VI*, ii. v. 31 So many Houres, must I tend my Flocke. **1602** Rowlands *Tis Merrie* 16 My Husband's forth, our Shoppe must needes be tended. **1702** Pope *Sappho* 100 Bid Endymion nightly tend his sheep. **1843** Carlyle *Past & Pr.* iv. i, Gurth could only tend pigs. **1855** Macaulay *Hist. Eng.* xii. III. 359 The horses had been ill fed and ill tended among the Grampians. **1889** Farmer *Dict. Amer.* s. v., Shops, stores, and businesses of every description are in America *tended* and not kept.

**c.** To bestow attention upon, attend to; *esp.* to foster, cultivate (a plant, etc.); to work or mind (a pump, a machine, etc.).

**1631** Gouge *God's Arrows* iii. § 95. 367 By peace..gardens, vineyards, and other like fruitfull places [are] tended. **1667** Milton *P. L.* ix. 206 Well may we labour still to dress This Garden, still to tend Plant, Herb, and Flour. **1703** *Lond. Gaz.* No. 3915/3 The Men..not being able to tend the Pumps, she sunk. **1838** Arnold *Hist. Rome* I. xi. 203 This Lucius Quinctius let his hair grow, and tended it carefully. **1865** Kingsley *Herew.* x, He..tended the graves hewn in the living stone. **1885** S. Cox *Expositions* xxix. 386 Always seeking to multiply the seed they sow and tend.

**4.** To wait upon as attendant or servant; to attend on; to escort, follow, or accompany for the purpose of rendering service or giving assistance; = Attend *v.* 7. Now *dial.*

*a* **1400–50** *Alexander* 4534 Appollo with a quite swan is paid him to tende. *c* **1500** in *Eng. Gilds* (1870) 418 It is ordered..that the new Mayor tenne the old Mayor at his owne house and goe home with the sword before him. **1594** Shaks. *Rich. III*, iv. i. 93 Go thou to Richard, and good Angels tend thee. *a* **1625** Fletcher, etc. *Fair Maid Inn* ii. ii, By your leave, Sir, I'll tend my master, and instantly be with you. **1719** De Foe *Crusoe* (1840) II. xii. 248 The man that tended the carpenter had a great iron ladle in his hand. **1888** Elworthy *W. Somerset Word-bk.* s. v., A mason's labourer always describes his work 'I do tend masons'.

**b.** *intr.* To attend *on* or *upon*; *spec.* to wait at table; = Attend *v.* 7 b, c. Also *fig.*

**1593** Shaks. 2 *Hen. VI*, iii. ii. 304 Three-fold Vengeance tend vpon your steps. **1641** Best *Farm. Bks.* (Surtees) 117 The bridegroome and the brides brothers or freinds tende att dinner. **1642** Rogers *Naaman* 41 Not [to] expect till Elisha tend upon him. **1722** De Foe *Plague* (1840) 106, I tend on them, to fetch things for them. **1818** Mrs. Shelley *Frankenst.* i. (1865) 35, I loved to tend on her. **1859** Tennyson *Enid* 1772 And Enid tended on him there.

**5.** *trans.* To give one's presence at (a meeting, ceremony, etc.); = Attend *v.* 12. Now *dial.* and *U. S.* Also *intr.* with †*of* (*obs.*), *on* (*dial.*).

**1460** *Rolls of Parlt.* V. 375/1 So that the seid Waulter may tende daily of this youre Parlement, as his dute is to doo. **1579–80** North *Plutarch* (1676) 290 Cato said that Scipio..tended Plays, Comedies, and Wrestlings. **1801** H. Macneill *Poet. Wks.* (1856) 220 (E.D.D.) Our lads are doing little but tending the drill. **18..** *Maj. Jones's Trav.* (Bartlett), Most of the passengers..had been up to Augusta to tend the convention. **1890** *Dialect Notes* I. i. 22 *U. S.* One 'tends out on' church, 'tends out on' the public library. **1901** El. G. Hayden *Trav. Round our Vill.* x. 168, I 'tends church reg'lar!

**6.** *trans.* †To wait for, await; to look out for expectantly; = Attend *v.* 13; also, to watch, observe (*obs.*); in *dial.* use, to watch for and scare away (birds), = Tent *v.*[1] 6.

**1604** T. Wright *Passions* v. § 3. 182 Then tend thy turne, when neighbors housen burne. **1669** Sturmy *Mariner's Mag.* ii. xiv. 85 Tending the Sun until he be upon the Meridian. **1675** Bunyan *Light in Darkn.* 178 Now the Soul can tend to look about it, and thus consider with it self. **1818** Keats *Endymion* ii. 185 By all the stars That tend thy bidding. **1875** *Sussex Gloss.* s. v., He goos to work rooktending, and he comes home of nights that hoarse that you can't hardly hear him speak.

†**b.** *absol.* or *intr.* To wait in expectation or readiness; = Attend *v.* 16. *Obs.*

**1602** Shaks. *Ham.* i. iii. 83 The time inuites you, goe, your seruants tend. *Ibid.* iv. iii. 47 The Barke is readie, and the winde at helpe, Th' Associates tend.

**7.** To have it in the mind as a purpose *to do* something; = Intend *v.* 18. (Cf. Attend *v.* IV.) *Obs.* exc. *dial.* (After 1500 chiefly *Sc.*)

**1340–70** *Alex. & Dind.* 1128 Now tende we to touche more of þis tale. *c* **1500** *Melusine* 128 We tende & purpose to gyue bataylle to the Sawdan. **1525** *Sc. Acts Jas. V* (1814) II. 293/2, I neuir as ȝit did hir grace ony harme..nor neuer tendis to do. **1580** *Reg. Privy Council Scot.* III. 291 Tending..to be fugitive fra the law. *a* **1615** *Cron. Erlis of Ross* (1850) 6 The sepulture of his fathers, quhair he tendit to be buryed. **1897** R. M. Gilchrist *Peakland Faggot* 95 I'm tendin' to do well for them. **1900** N. Lloyd *Chronic Loafer* i. 13 [U. S.], I didn't 'tend to open it.

†**8.** *trans.* To understand or apprehend (a matter, a word, etc.); = Intend *v.* IV, ME. *entende*, F. *entendre*. *Obs.*

*c* **1375** *Cursor M.* 21803 (Fairf.) Qua-sim þis tale can beter tende [*Cott.* a-tend] For cristis loue he hit amende. *c* **1450** Holland *Howlat* 434 The siluer in the samyn half, trewly to tend, Is cleir corage in armes.

Hence **Te·nding** *vbl. sb.*[1] and *ppl. a.*; **tending-string**, a leading-string; **tending boy**, a boy employed to 'tend' or scare birds.

**1605** Shaks. *Macb.* i. v. 38 One of my fellowes..almost dead for breath..Giue him tending, He brings great newes. **1816** T. Chalmers in Hanna *Mem.* (1849) II. iv. 81 The shrubbery, in absence of the tending hand, had become a tangled wilderness. **1821** Clare *Vill. Minstr.* II. 73 The cowboy..Leading tam'd cattle in their tendingstrings. **1865** Dickens *Mut. Fr.* iii. viii, In its tending of the sick. **1898** *Agric. Gaz.* 7 Mar. 276/3, I am dressing the seed with tar, otherwise tending boys would be at a premium. **1909** *Lady's Realm* Feb. 466/1 The large log-house..and the tending slaves.

**Tend** (tend), *v.*[2] Forms: 6–7 **tende**, 6 *Sc.* **teind**, 4– **tend**. See also Tent *v.*[5] [In branch I, a. F. *tend-re* (11th c.):—L. *tendĕre* to stretch, stretch out, extend, also intr. for *tendere cursum*, *gressum*, *passus*, to direct one's course, one's steps, to proceed in any direction. The main sense-development took place in L. and F., and the Eng. sense-groups II and III have been taken in at different times, and not in logical order.]

**I.** To have a motion or disposition to move towards, and derived senses. [= OF. *tendre* (11th c.), L. *tendĕre* intr.]

**1.** *intr.* To direct one's course, make one's way, move or proceed towards something. **a.** *lit.* of persons or things in motion. *Obs.* or *arch.*

*c* **1350** *Will. Palerne* 1781 To me tended þei nouȝt, but tok forþ here wey wilfulli to sum wildernesse. **1426** Lydg. *De Guil. Pilgr.* 10797 Wheder that euery goode Pylgryme Tendyth in his pylgrymage. **1500–20** Dunbar *Poems* lxix. 29 Tending to ane uther place, A journay going everie day. **1667** Milton *P. L.* i. 183 Thither let us tend From off the tossing of these fiery waves. **1745** *Paraphr. Sc. Ch.* xxvii. xi, As the Rains from Heaven distil Nor thither tend again.

**b.** Of a road, course, journey, series of things.

**1574** *Calr. Scott. Papers* V. 9 Leith wes his port quhairunto his course teindit. **1703** Moxon *Mech. Exerc.* 256 Arches..whose Joints tend to the Center. **1863** Hawthorne *Our Old Home* (1879) 64 A green lane..tended towards a square, gray tower. **1873** Black *Pr. Thule* xxv, Understanding that their voyage should tend in that direction.

**c.** *intr.* To have a natural inclination to move (in some direction). (Cf. 2, 3.)
**1641** WILKINS *Math. Magick* I. ii. (1648) 12 Whereby condensed bodies do of themselves tend downwards. **1711** POPE *Temp. Fame* 429 As weighty bodies to the centre tend. **1776** ADAM SMITH *W. N.* IV. vii. (1869) II. 217 That part of the capital .. which .. tended and inclined, if I may say so, towards the East India trade. **1828** HUTTON *Course Math.* II. 140 The power or force in moving bodies, by which they continually tend from their present places. **1834** MRS. SOMERVILLE *Connex. Phys. Sc.* xxxvii. (1849) 432 Though the stars in every region of the sky tend towards a point in Hercules.

**2.** *intr. fig.* To have a disposition to advance, go on, come finally, or attain *to* (*unto, towards*) some point in time, degree, quality, state, or other non-material category; to be drawn *to* or *towards* in affection.
*c* **1374** CHAUCER *Boeth.* I. pr. vi. 17 (Camb. MS.) Remembres thow..whider þat the entensy[o]n of alle kynde tendeth? *c* **1440** *Gesta Rom.* lv. 238 (Harl. MS.) Whenne I saide þat oþer was thi childe, þou tendeist al to him, and dispisidist þat oþere. **1538** ELYOT, *Specto..*, to behold,..to tende to some conclusion. **1581** PETTIE *Guazzo's Civ. Conv.* III. (1586) 127 b, Nature alwaies tendeth to the best. **1659** PEARSON *Creed* (1839) 110 Towards the setting of the sun, when the light of the world was tending unto a night of darkness. **1776** BURKE *Corr.* (1844) II. 96 It is to this point all their speeches, writings, and intrigues of all sorts, tend. **1818** CRUISE *Digest* (ed. 2) VI. 517 The trust being expressly limited for life, the same did not tend to a perpetuity. **1893** J. A. HODGES *Elem. Photogr.* (1907) 157 Their use..certainly tends in the direction of uniformity.

**b.** *Tending to*, approaching (in quality, colour, etc.); having a tendency to.
**1600** HAKLUYT *Voy.* III. 51 A temperate aire rather tending to cold. **1615** W. LAWSON *Country Housew. Gard.* (1626) 18 A faire and broad leafe, in colour tending to a greenish yellow.

**3.** *intr.* To have a specified result, if allowed to act; to lead or conduce *to* some state or condition. Const. *to*, rarely *against*.
**1560** BIBLE (Genev.) *Prov.* x. 16 The labour of the righteous tendeth to life. **1615** G. SANDYS *Trav.* 289 The place doth not greatly tend vnto tranquillity. **1729** LAW *Serious C.* xxii. (1732) 441 [Not to] do anything to us, but what certainly tended to our benefit. **1818** CRUISE *Digest* (ed. 2) IV. 558 The register acts would tend much more to the security of purchasers and mortgagees..if it were established [etc.]. **1847** HELPS *Friends in C.* I. iii. 34 To indulge in despair as a habit..manifestly tends against nature. **1868** FARRAR *Silence & V.* ii. (1875) 35 We know that righteousness tendeth to life.

**b.** To lead or conduce to some action. (*a*) Const. *to* with noun of action.
**1565** *Reg. Privy Council Scot.* I. 36 Tending to the furthsetting of thair Majesteis autoritie. **1651** HOBBES *Leviath.* II. xxiii. 126 Other acts tending to the conservation of the Peace. **1765** BLACKSTONE *Comm.* I. xv. 422 Such declaration cannot now tend to the reformation of the parties. **1849** MACAULAY *Hist. Eng.* iv. I. 484 None of them said anything tending to his vindication. **1874** GREEN *Short Hist.* ii. § 5. 82 The King's reforms tended directly to the increase of the royal power.

(*b*) Const. *to* with *inf.*
**1604** BACON *Apol.* Wks. 1879 I. 436 A sonnet directly tending and alluding to draw on her Majesty's reconcilement to my lord. **1662** STILLINGFL. *Orig. Sacr.* III. iv. § 10 It may further tend to clear the truth of the Scriptures. **1710** *Lond. Gaz.* No. 4688/2 All the..Warlike Preparations ..tended only to amuse the King of Sweden. **1800** *Med. Jrnl.* IV. 337 If they tend in the least to diminish the sufferings of the child. **1851** CARPENTER *Man. Phys.* (ed. 2) 378 It tends to undergo a rapid and complete degeneration. **1879** M. ARNOLD *Mixed Ess., Democr.* 10 To live in a society of equals tends..to make a man's spirits expand.

**4.** *Naut.* Of a ship at anchor: To swing round with the turn of the tide or wind.
**1770** COOK *Voy. round World* III. ix. (1773) III. 651 In the mean time, as the ship tended, I weighed anchor. **1776**, **1867** [see *tending* below]. **1794** *Rigging & Seamanship* II. 299 The ship begins to tend to leeward. **1828** WEBSTER, *Tend*.. to swing round an anchor, as a ship.

**b.** *trans.* (app. a causal use of prec.; in quot. 1867, erroneously associated with TEND *v.*[1] 6).
**1794** *Rigging & Seamanship* II. 300 To tend a ship for a weather tide. The simplest way of tending a ship, is to keep each tide to leeward of her anchor. **1815** BURNEY *Falconer's Dict. Marine* 553/1 To *Tend*..is to turn or swing a ship round when at single anchor, or moored by the head in a tide-way, at the beginning of the flood or ebb. *Ibid.*, To Tend a Ship with the Wind a few points across the Tide. **1867** SMYTH *Sailor's Word-bk.*, *Tend*, to watch a vessel at anchor on the turn of a tide, and cast her by the helm, and some sail if necessary, so as to keep the cable clear of the anchor or turns out of her cables when moored.

**II.** [= F. *tendre*.]

† **5.** *trans.* To offer, proffer; *spec.* in *Law* = TENDER *v.*[1] I. *Obs.*
**1475** *Rolls of Parlt.* VI. 148/1 Uppon the same Travers tended, or title shewed. **1483–4** *Act* 1 *Rich. III*, c. 6 § 1 The seid defendaunt..may..tende an issue [F. *de tendre issue*], that the same contract..was not..made within the feire tyme. **1529** *Act* 21 *Hen. VIII*, c. 5 § 1 Suche testament beyng laufully tended or offred to them to be proved.

**b.** To furnish, provide, supply; to reach or hand (a thing) to some one. *Obs.* exc. *dial.*
**1579** LYLY *Euphues* (Arb.) 130 Dilligent in tending and prouiding all things necessary. **1882** JAGO *Cornwall Gloss.* s. v., One boy tended the stones as the other threw them at the apples.

† **6.** *intr.* To extend, stretch, or reach (*to* a point, or in a particular direction). Also *fig. Obs.*
**1604** E. G[RIMSTONE] *D'Acosta's Hist. Indies* VI. vi. 444 All the knowledge of the Chinois, tendes only to reade and write, and no farther. **1630** *R. Johnson's Kingd. & Commw.* 223 That huge tract of Land, which tendeth from Cape Aguer, to Cape Guardafu. **1725** DE FOE *Voy. round World* (1840) 145 The land tending to the west.

**III.** [Later senses from F. *tendre* and L. *tendĕre*.]

† **7.** *trans.* To stretch, make tense or taut; to set (a trap, snare, etc.). *Obs.*
**1646** H. LAWRENCE *Comm. Angells* 45 Their nets are alwayes spread; they tende their snares alwayes. **1677** PLOT *Oxfordsh.* 289 The longer, or less tended, any string is, the farther it moves. **1799**, **1834** [see TENDED *ppl. a.*[2]].

† **8.** To bend or direct (one's steps): cf. L. *tendere gressum, passus*. *Obs.*
**1611** RICH *Honest. Age* (Percy Soc.) 17 Whether will you tend your steppes. *a* **1644** QUARLES *Sol. Recant.* ch. III. xx, Both tend Their paces to the self-same Journies end.

† **9.** To relate or refer to; to concern. (*trans.*, or *intr.* with *to*.) *Obs.*
**1571** SIR R. LANE in *Buccleuch MSS.* (Hist. MSS. Comm.) I. 224, I have received your letter with a packet...The matter which they do tend indeed requireth speed. **1576** FLEMING *Panopl. Epist.* 156 My taulke tendeth to matters of such moment and weight. **1647** N. BACON *Disc. Govt. Eng.* I. lxxi. (1739) 196 The rule foregoing tended only to Freemen and their Lands. **1654** MARVELL *Corr.* Wks. (Grosart) II. 11 Which I attributed to our dispatch, and some other businesse tendinge thereto.

Hence **Te·nding** *vbl. sb.*[2]
**1587** GOLDING *De Mornay* ii. (1592) 18 The whole worlde and all things contayned therein, do by their tending vnto vs, teach vs to tend vnto one alone. **1846** D. KING *Lord's Supper* vi. 175 It is all outward in its tendings.
**b.** *Naut.* **1776** FALCONER *Dict. Marine*, *Tending*, the movement by which a ship turns or swings round her anchor in a tide-way, at the beginning of the flood or ebb. **1867** SMYTH *Sailor's Word-bk.*, *Tending*, the movement by which a ship turns or swings round when at single anchor, or moored by the head, at every change of tide or wind.

**Tend**, obs. f. TEIND *sb.* and *v.*, tithe; earlier form of TIND *v. Obs.*, to kindle.

† **Te·ndable**, *a. Obs.* [f. TEND *v.*[1] + -ABLE: cf. *suitable*.] Ready to give attention; attentive.
*c* **1450** [implied in TENDABLY]. **1509** HAWES *Joyf. Medit.* xxvii, Vnto our soueraync be meke and tendable. **1530** PALSGR. 327/1 Tendable, as one that dothe wayte well.. *ententif*. **1533** MORE *Debell. Salem* Wks. 943/2 Good sad honeste vertuous wydowes, that wolde be tendable & tender to sicke folke. **1547** BOORDE *Brev. of Health* Pref. 5 Let euery person be tendable aboute theym [physicians] and do as they shall commaunde them. **1654** GAYTON *Pleas. Notes* IV. ii. 180 Wherein shee is very tendable, and handy.

So † **Te·ndably** *adv.*, attentively, with care.
*c* **1450** in Aungier *Syon* (1840) 312 Eche of them schal enforme suche as be assygned to them..charitably and tendably.

**Tendance** (te·ndăns). Also 8–9 (*improperly*) tendence. [Aphetic form of ATTENDANCE, or sometimes f. TEND *v.*[1] + -ANCE.]

**1.** The attending to, or looking after, anything; tending, attention, care.
**1573** TUSSER *Husb.* (1878) 128 Hops dried in loft, aske tendance oft. **1667** MILTON *P. L.* VIII. 47 They at her coming sprung And toucht by her fair tendance gladlier grew. **1790** H. BOYD *Ruins of Athens*, What cautious care The propagation, tendence, nutriment Of this ethereal seminary claim. **1835** TRENCH *Justin Martyr*, etc. (1862) 17 That by careful watering And earnest tendance we might bring The bud, the blossom and the fruit. **1897** *Scotsman* 10 Nov. 8/4 The working and tendence of every machine ..should be reserved for its members.

**b.** The object of care or attention. *rare*−[1].
**1645** MILTON *Tetrach.* I. Wks. 1851 IV. 153 Whether it [loneliness] be a thing, or the want of somthing, I labour not; let it be their tendance, who have the art to be industriously idle.

**2.** The bestowal of personal attention and care; ministration to the sick or weak.
**1578** *Chr. Prayers* in *Priv. Prayers* (Parker Soc.) 544 That I may not have need of so great strength, tendance, and cunning. **1683** KENNETT tr. *Erasm. on Folly* 42 How troublesome our tendance in the cradle. **1760–72** H. BROOKE *Fool of Qual.* (1809) IV. 39 My..affectionate tendance shall..compensate for my want of address. **1876** GEO. ELIOT *Dan. Der.* lxvi, His daughter's dutiful tendance.

**b.** Attendants collectively; train or retinue.
**1607** SHAKS. *Timon* I. i. 80 All those..Follow his strides, his Lobbies fill with tendance. **1814** SCOTT *Ld. of Isles* III. vii, Now torch and menial tendance led Chieftain and knight to bower and bed. **1868** GEO. ELIOT *Sp. Gipsy* I. 113, I shall send tendance as I pass, to bear This casket to your chamber.

† **3.** Waiting in expectation. *Obs.*
**1591** SPENSER *M. Hubberd* 908 Unhappie wight..That doth his life in so long tendance spend!

**Tendance**, obs. form of TENDENCE.

† **Te·ndancy.** *Obs. rare*−[1]. In 8 (*improp.*) -ency. [f. TEND *v.*[1] + -ANCY.] Attention, care.
*a* **1774** TUCKER *Lt. Nat.* (1834) II. 86 Man..may, indeed, contrive machines that shall go a little way in performing his works;..but then they require correcting, repairing, and continual tendency.

**Te·ndant**, *a.* and *sb. arch.* Also 4 -aunt, 7 (*improp.*) -ent. [Aphetic f. ATTENDANT.]

**A.** *adj.* Attending, giving attention or service, waiting (upon).
**13..** *Cursor M.* 19034 (Gött.) Thre hundreth men and wiuis, Þat desseli bath late and are þar tendant to þe apostlis ware. **1387** TREVISA *Higden* (Rolls) III. 279 Socrates, þat was alway tendaunt to a spirit þat was i-cleped demon. **1592** WARNER *Alb. Eng.* VIII. xliii. (1612) 206 Henry the second vpon whom the Scotch-King tendant was. **1824** WIFFEN *Tasso* II. lvii, Tendant on each knight Rode many a page and armour-bearer bold.

**B.** *sb.* An attendant.
**1586** DAY *Eng. Secretary* II. (1625) 111 A farre other end and purpose, then of euery ordinary tendant is commonly required. **1614** T. ADAMS *Devil's Banquet* 24 Great men are vnmercifull to their Tenants, that they may be ouermercifull to their Tendents; that stretch them as fast as they retch the others. **1632** VICARS *Æneid* IV. 114 Her tendants saw her fal'n upon her sword.

**Tendant**, obs. f. TENDENT *a.*, tending.

**Tende**, obs. f. TEIND; var. TIND *v. Obs.*, to kindle, TINE *v.*[1], to enclose.

**Te·nded**, *ppl. a.*[1] [f. TEND *v.*[1] + -ED[1].] Attended to, looked after, cared for.
**1667** MILTON *P. L.* V. 22 Mark how spring Our tended Plants. **1866** NEALE *Sequences & Hymns* 82 Year by year, the steeple-music O'er the tended graves shall pour.

† **Te·nded**, *ppl. a.*[2] *Obs.* [f. TEND *v.*[2] 7 + -ED[1].] Stretched; taut, tense.
**1799** YOUNG in *Phil. Trans.* XC. 134 It may be proved, that every impulse is communicated along a tended chord with an uniform velocity. **1834** MRS. SOMERVILLE *Connex. Phys. Sc.* xvii. (1849) 164 A body vibrating near insulated tended strings.

**Tendence** (te·ndĕns). Now *rare* and *literary*. Also 7–8 -ance. [ad. med.L. *tendentia* (Bonaventura *a* 1274, Duns Scotus *a* 1308), f. L. *tendentem*, pr. pple. of *tendĕre*: see TEND *v.*[2] and -ENCE: cf. F. *tendance* (12th c. in Godef. *Compl.*).] = next.

**1.** = TENDENCY 1.
**1627** SANDERSON *Serm.* I. 259 There shall appear..a direct tendance to the advancement of Gods glory. **1669** GALE *Crt. Gentiles* I. I. i. 7 The scope and tendence of this Discourse is to Demonstrate, that [etc.]. **1714** R. FIDDES *Pract. Disc.* II. 219 Afflictions have..a tendence to promote our spiritual good. **1833** SARAH AUSTIN *Charac. Goethe* II. 331 A melancholy proof of the modern realistic tendence.

† **2.** = TENDENCY 1 b. Also *fig. Obs.*
**1644** DIGBY *Nat. Bodies* xi. (1658) 116 These atoms..are forced from the complete effect of their tendance, by the violence of the current. **1645** OWEN *Two Catech.* xii. Wks. 1855 I. 482 *note*, The death that Christ underwent was eternal in its own nature and tendence. **1698** TYSON in *Phil. Trans.* XX. 118 The Tendence or Direction of the Muscular Fibres of this Pair.

**b.** *attrib.*: **tendence-writing**, a writing with a purpose (Ger. *tendenz-schrift*). Cf. TENDENCY 3.
**1875** M. ARNOLD in *Contemp. Rev.* XXV. 968 Our Gospels are more or less *Tendenz-Schriften*, tendence-writings,—writings to serve an aim or bent of their several authors.

**Tendence, -ency**, obs. ff. TENDANCE, -ANCY.

**Tendencious**, variant of TENDENTIOUS.

**Tendency** (te·ndĕnsi). [f. as TENDENCE: see -ENCY.]

**1.** The fact or quality of tending to something; a constant disposition to move or act in some direction or toward some point, end, or purpose; leaning, inclination, bias, or bent toward some object, effect, or result.
**1628** T. SPENCER *Logick* 53 If any inquire how tendency.. can haue an actuall exercise vnto doing. **1671** FLAVEL *Fount. Life* vii, He did not..do an Act..but it had some Tendency to promote the great Design of our Salvation. **1679** C. NESSE *Antid. agst. Popery* Ded. 6 Gods prevalent actings, in tendency to our deliverance. *a* **1680** BUTLER *Rem.* (1759) II. 185 He seldom converses but with Men of his own Tendency. **1710** J. CLARKE *Rohault's Nat. Phil.* (1729) I. 80 A Body in Motion has always a Tendency to describe that Line, which it would describe if it were at liberty. **1778** [W. MARSHALL] *Minutes Agric.* 13 Sept. an. 1774, Placed..with their points tending forward, the line of their tendency making an angle with the horizon of about 45°. **1806** A. HUNTER *Culina* (ed. 3) 104 Where there is a gouty tendency, this dish must seldom be indulged in. **1870** JEVONS *Elem. Logic* xxxi. 267 A tendency..is a cause which may or may not be counteracted. **1870** J. H. NEWMAN *Gram. Assent* II. viii. 313 A regular polygon, inscribed [in a circle], its sides being continually diminished, tends to become that circle, as its limit; but..its tendency to be the circle, though ever nearer fulfilment, never in fact gets beyond a tendency.

† **b.** Movement or advance in the direction of something; a making toward something. *Obs.*
**1654** Z. COKE *Logick* A ij, As if the Donations of Heaven were opposed, subordinated in mans tendency to Bliss and Glory. **1661** BLOUNT *Glossogr.* (ed. 2), *Tendency*..a going forward, a making toward. **1721** BRADLEY *Philos. Acc. Wks. Nat.* 1 Which time of their Tendency to Perfection I shall..call the Time of their Growth.

**c.** Drift, trend, or aim of a discourse; in recent use, conscious or designed purpose of a story, novel, or the like. (= Ger. *tendenz*.)
**1732** BERKELEY *Alciphr.* II. § 21 Upon hearing this, and other lectures of the same tendency. **1751** JOHNSON *Rambler* No. 153 ¶ 2 My narrative has no other tendency than to illustrate and corroborate your own observations. **1791** BURKE *App. Whigs* Wks. VI. 132 Neither can they shew any thing in the general tendency and spirit of the whole work unfavourable to a rational and generous spirit of liberty. **1832** HT. MARTINEAU *Demerara* i. 12 The tendency of all he said was to prove his own merits.

† **2.** A relation *to*, or bearing upon something.
**1651** BAXTER *Inf. Bapt.* 195 They will say that all their obedience hath no other tendency to their salvation and finall Absolution, but as meer signs.

**3.** *attrib.* *Tendency drama, novel, story*, one composed with an unexpressed but definite purpose. [After Ger. *tendenz-drama*, *-roman*, etc.]

**1838** DE MORGAN *Ess. Probab.* 23 They may all be referred either to that [assertion] just made, or to a tendency argument of the same character. **1889** JACOBS *Æsop* 206 The Fable..is a Moral Tendency-Beast-Droll. **1909** *Cent. Dict.* Suppl., *Tendency theory*..the theory of the Tübingen school that the books of the New Testament..were put together for the purpose of upholding current opinions, and that they thus have a 'tendency'.

**Tendent** (te·ndĕnt), *a.* Now *rare.* Also 4–7 -ant, 6 -aunt. [a. OF. *tendant*, pr. pple. of *tendre* to stretch, to proceed: see TEND *v.*[2]] Tending, having a tendency (*to* or *towards* some end). *Obs.* before 18th c.; revived late in 19th.

*a* **1340** HAMPOLE *Psalter* iv. 9 It is tendant in til lastandnes and vnchaungeabile ioy. **1512** *Helyas* in Thoms *Prose Rom.* (1828) III. 92 Tendaunt to the ende to take and holde in his hande the said duchy. **1657** *Divine Lover* 14 Wee..shal remayne vnable as not tendant towards our foresaid end. **1900** STODDARD *Evol. Eng. Novel* 103 The historical novel is magnetized history in which every fact is quiveringly tendent toward some focal pole of unity.

**Tendent**, obs. var. TENDANT.

**Tendential** (tende·nʃăl), *a.* [f. as next + -AL.] Of the nature of, or characterized by having, a tendency; *spec.* = next.

**1889** J. M. ROBERTSON *Ess. Crit. Method* Pref. 3 A division of thinking men into tendential parties, in each of which there is a substantial agreement, resulting in different degrees from bias, prejudice, and reasoning towards consistency. **1904** *Amer. Jrnl. Relig.*, etc. May 75 (Cent. D., Supp.) Deliverance..from the power of those other tendential ideas against which he has been struggling.

**Tendentious** (tende·nʃəs), *a.* Also -cious. [as if f. med.L. *tendenti-a* TENDENCY + -OUS, after G. *tendenziös*.] Having a purposed tendency; composed or written with such a tendency or aim.

**1900** T. DAVIDSON *Hist. Educ.* I. iv. 70 Xenophon's *Cyropædia*..is a mere edifying, tendentious romance, intended to recommend to the Athenians the Spartan type of education. **1905** *Times, Lit. Suppl.* 28 July 239/2 He [Zimmer, in 'Die Keltische Kirche'] thinks that the legend of St. Patrick was tendencious, springing up to support a special ecclesiastical thesis. **1909** C. LOWE in *Contemp. Rev.* July 42 A false and tendencious account of what had taken place.

**Tender** (te·ndəɹ), *sb.*[1] Also 5 -our. [f. TEND *v.*[1] + -ER[1], or aphetic form of ATTENDER.]

**1.** † One who tends, or waits upon, another; an attendant, nurse, ministrant (*obs.*); a waiter; an assistant to a builder or other skilled workman (*dial.*).

*c* **1470** HENRYSON *Orpheus & Eur.* 20 The anseane and sad wyse men of age Wer tendouris to ȝung and Insolent, To mak þame in all vertewis excellent. **1601** R. JOHNSON *Kingd. & Commw.* 139 Two hundred horsemen in Moscouie, require three hundred packehorses, and so many tenders, who must all be fedde. **1637** BRIAN *Pisse-Proph.* iii. (1679) 25 Some nurse or tender of sick persons. **1683** TRYON *Way to Health* 285 As Waiters, Tenders or Servitors to execute and obey the Commands of the Spirit of the Lord. *a* **1825** FORBY *Voc. E. Anglia*, *Tender*, a waiter at a public table, or place of entertainment. *c* **1830** *Glouc. Farm Rep.* 11 in *Libr. Usef. Knowl., Husb.* III, On the other rick there are one or two builders, with a sufficiency of tenders to carry on the work with expedition and efficiency. **1880** *W. Cornw. Gloss.*, *Tendar*, a waiter at an inn; the guard of a train.

**2.** One who attends to, or has charge of, a machine, a business, etc., as *bar-tender* (a barman), *bridge-tender*, *machine-tender*; now esp. *U. S.*

**1825** J. NICHOLSON *Operat. Mechanic* 671 That the engine tender may not be at a loss when to throw his machinery into geer. **1856** EMERSON *Eng. Traits* vi. 107 The machines ..prove too much for their tenders. **1883** *Daily News* 16 Oct 6/2 The bar tender [in U. S.]..demanded payment. **1897** RHOSCOMYL *White Rose Arno* 94 'Show this brass then', said the bridge-tender. **1910** *Times* 18 May 10/2 Dissatisfaction among the power-loom tenders at their scale of pay. ..The wages of the tenders..were increased to 35*s*.

**3.** A ship or boat employed to attend a larger one in various capacities. **a.** Originally, A vessel commissioned to attend men-of-war, chiefly for supplying provisions and munitions of war, also for conveying intelligence, dispatches, etc. Now, in the British Royal Navy, A vessel commissioned to act (in any capacity) under the orders of another vessel, her officers and crew being borne on the ship's books of the latter (called the parent ship).

In current use the term includes torpedo-boats and torpedo-boat destroyers. All the 'destroyers' of a flotilla are technically tenders of the depôt-ship, although this exists merely in order to carry stores for them, and the necessary staff for doing their clerical work.

**1675** *Lond. Gaz.* No. 1054/2 Here are arrived five Dutch Men of War, and four Tenders. **1710** *Ibid.* No. 4677/3 Yesterday..came down hither her Majesty's Ship the Lyme, with the Star-Bomb and her Tender. **1732** LEDIARD *Sethos* II. IX. 291 The greater seem'd only to be the retinue or tenders upon the less. **1772** *Hist. Rochester* 18 A tender in the river..employed in pressing seamen. **1812** SHELLEY *Let. to Miss Hitchener* 10 Mar., A Magistrate..gave him the alternative of the tender or of military servitude. **1898** *Whitaker's Almanack* 223/1 *Cockchafer*, 2nd cl. gunboat.. tender to *Rodney* [1st cl. battle-ship, used as coastguard] Queensferry N. B. **1906** *King's Regul. & Admiralty Instr.* Art. 1802 § 2 The Officer in charge of stores in the parent ship is to be responsible, and is to account for stores supplied to the tender. **1910** *Naval & Mil. Rec.* 21 Sept., The Wear, destroyer,..recommissioned..for service in the third (Nore) Destroyer flotilla as tender to the St. George.

**b.** In general use, A small steamer used to carry passengers, luggage, mails, goods, stores, etc., to or from a larger vessel (usually a liner), esp. when not otherwise accessible from shore. Also, in U. S., a boat or ship attending on fishing or whaling ships, to carry supplies to them, and to bring the fish, oil, or whalebone, to the ports or landing-places.

**1853** KANE *Grinnell Exp.* xxi. (1856) 162 It was wisely determined by..old Sir John that he would leave the Mary, his tender of twelve tons. **1868** *Daily News* 20 July, As the tender was puffing out to us in Queenstown Harbour. **1887** J. BALL *Nat. in S. Amer.* 28 To go on board a small tender that lay alongside of a half-ruined wharf. **1910** AGNES WESTON *Life among Bluejackets* 54 We waited at the Royal Hotel, Plymouth, for the signal that the tender would shortly put off.

**c.** *fig.*

**1700** CONGREVE *Way of World* II. v, Here she comes, i' faith, full sail, with..a shoal of fools for tenders. **1865** *Even. Standard* 6 June, [A weekly newspaper] a tender to this peculating concern..conducted upon the same principle, or with the same lack of principle. **1889** *Daily News* 27 Dec. 2/3 They are jolly tars and..have a couple of smart-looking tenders [sweethearts] in tow.

**4.** A carriage specially constructed to carry fuel and water for a locomotive engine, to the rear of which it is attached.

**1825** MACLAREN *Railways* 32 *note*, A small waggon bearing water and coals follows close behind the engine, and is called the Tender, i. e. the 'Attender'. **1878** F. S. WILLIAMS *Midl. Railw.* 662 The tender will hold 2320 gallons of water, it has a coal space for 4 tons.

*attrib.* **1838** *Civil Eng. & Arch. Jrnl.* I. 134/1 The same apparatus may be attached to the tender axles. **1894** *Westm. Gaz.* 6 Feb. 7/2 In the outrush of water from the tender tank. **1897** *Daily News* 1 Sept. 2/2 He applied the vacuum brake and the fireman the tender brake, but could not stop the engine.

**5.** In specific technical uses: see quots.

**1877** KNIGHT *Dict. Mech.*, *Tender*..a small reservoir attached to a mop, scrubber, or similar utensil. **1894** *Northumbld. Gloss.*, *Tender*, in a pit, the former name for a small rapper or signal rope.

**Tender** (te·ndəɹ), *sb.*[2] Also 6 tendre, tendour. [f. TENDER *v.*[1]] An act of tendering.

**1.** *Law.* A formal offer duly made by one party to another.

*Tender of amends*, an offer of compensation by the delinquent party. *Tender of issue*, a plea which in effect invites the adverse party to join issue upon it.

**1562–3** *Act* 5 *Eliz.* c. 1 § 17 All suche persons shalbee compellable to take the Othe upon the seconde Tender or Offer of the same. **1647** HAMMOND *Power of Keys* iv. 60 This magisteriall affirmation having no tender or offer of proof annext to it. **1768** BLACKSTONE *Comm.* III. i. 15 If tender of amends is made before any action is brought. **1848** WHARTON *Law Lex.* s. v., A tender of satisfaction is allowed to be made in most actions for money demands.. and a tender to one of several joint creditors is sufficient. **1872** *Ibid.* s. v. *Amends, Tender of Amends*, is by particular statutes made a defence in an action for a wrong.

**b.** *spec.* An offer of money, or the like, in discharge of a debt or liability, *esp.* an offer which thus fulfils the terms of the law and of the liability.

*Plea of tender*, a plea advanced by a defendant that he has always been ready to pay and has tendered to the plaintiff the amount due, which he now produces in court.

**1542–3** *Act* 34 & 35 *Hen. VIII*, c. 2 § 2 The same Collectour..as shall so make tendre of all suche money. **1544** tr. *Littleton's Tenures* (1574) 70 Where suche lawefull tender of the money is made. **1817** W. SELWYN *Law Nisi Prius* (ed. 4) II. 966 The defendant pleaded non-assumpsit as to all except 3*l.*, and as to that a tender. **1863** A. J. HORWOOD *Yearbks.* 30 & 31 *Edw. I*, Pref. 26 *note*, The reason for the tender of the demy-mark in a writ of right. **1883** *Wharton's Law Lex.* s. v., By the Coinage Act, 1870.., it is provided that a tender of payment of money, if made in coins legally issued by the Mint..shall be a legal tender.

**2.** *gen.* An offer of anything for acceptance.

**1577** HARRISON *England* Pref., I dare presume to make tendour of the protection thereof vnto your Lordships hands. **1602** SHAKS. *Ham.* I. iii. 100 *O.* He hath my Lord of late made many tenders Of his affection to me. *P.*..Doe you beleeue his tenders, as you call them? **1761–2** HUME *Hist. Eng.* (1806) V. lxxi. 286 [He] made a tender of his sword and purse to the prince of Orange. **1855** MACAULAY *Hist. Eng.* xiii. III. 287 They had not yet been put into possession of the royal authority by a formal tender and a formal acceptance. **1871** R. ELLIS tr. *Catullus* l. 6 Tenders jocular o'er the merry wine-cup.

**3.** *Comm.* An offer made in writing by one party to another (usually to a public body) to execute, at an inclusive price or uniform rate, an order for the supply or purchase of goods, or for the execution of work, the details of which have been submitted, often through the public press, by the second party.

**1666** PEPYS *Diary* 14 July, The business of Captain Cocke's tender of hempe. **1691** *Lond. Gaz.* No. 2636/3 The Principal Officers and Commissioners of Their Majesties Navy,..will ..be ready to receive any Tenders.., and to Treat and Contract with the Tenderers thereof. **1851** MAYHEW *Lond. Labour* I. 291/2 The privilege..is disposed of by tender. **1868** ROGERS *Pol. Econ.* xxiii. (1876) 312 The Government.. may fix the sum and invite tenders for the lowest amount of interest at which borrowers will be willing to make the loan. **1882** *Statist* X. 485 The lowest tender was accepted.

**4.** (esp. *legal*, *lawful*, or *common tender*.) Money or other things that may be legally tendered or offered in payment; currency prescribed by law as that in which payment may be made.

In the British Isles, current bronze and silver coins are legal tender for sums not exceeding one shilling and forty shillings respectively; current gold coins are legal tender for any amount. Bank of England notes are legal tender (except by the Bank of Eng.) in England and Wales only.

**1740** W. DOUGLASS *Disc. Curr. Brit. Plant. Amer.* 20 France never made their State Bills a common Tender. **1765** T. HUTCHINSON *Hist. Mass.* I. i. 27 Indian corn..was made a tender in discharge of all debt. **1777** *Jrnls. Amer. Congress* 14 June, Recommended..to pass laws to make the bills of credit, issued by the Congress, a lawful tender, in payments of public and private debts. **1838–42** ARNOLD *Hist. Rome* II. xxvii. 73 Land and cattle became legal tender at a certain fixed rate of value. **1866** CRUMP *Banking* iv. 95 A cheque is not a legal tender, and for that reason may be objected to. **1883** GILMOUR *Mongols* xxxii. 369 In Urga, brick tea and silver are the common tenders.

**Tender** (te·ndəɹ), *a.* (*adv.*) and *sb.*[3] Forms: 3–6 tendre, 4– tender; also 4 teyndir, 4–5 tendyr, -ere, 4–6 (chiefly *Sc.*) -ir, 5 -ire, -ur(e. [a. F. *tendre* (11th c.) = Pr. *tenre*, *tendre*, Sp. *tierno*, Pg. *tenro*, It. *tenero*:—L. *tener-um* (nom. *tener*) tender, delicate.]

**A.** *adj.* **I.** Literal and physical senses.

**1.** Soft or delicate in texture or consistence; yielding easily to force or pressure; fragile; easily broken, divided, compressed, or injured; of food, easily masticated, succulent. † *Tender bread*, newly baked bread (*obs.*).

Formerly (and still *dial.*) used in wide sense as a synonym of *soft* (e. g. of stone or coal).

*a* **1225** *Ancr. R.* 114 Vor his fleschs was al cwic ase is þe tendre eien. *a* **1300** *Cursor M.* 18844 (Cott.) Forked fair þe chin he bare And tender berd wit mikel hare. **13..** *E. E. Allit. P.* B. 630 A calf..þat watz tender & not toȝe. **13..** *Coer de L.* 3413 Eet theroff..As it wer a tendyr chycke. *c* **1400** MAUNDEV. xxxiii. 150 Þe tendre erthe was removed fra his place and þare become a valay, and þe hard erthe habade still. **1422** tr. *Secreta Secret., Priv. Priv.* 247 Tendyr brede makyd of the floure of Whete. *a* **1500** *Sir Beues* 2529 (Pynson) Beuys..hyt the dragon vnder the wynge,..There was he tender wythout skale. **1596** DALRYMPLE tr. *Leslie's Hist. Scot.* (S.T.S.) I. 26 The Skout.. being sodin,..is maist tendir. **1650** BULWER *Anthropomet.* 186 Their bones being yet tender, soft, and cartilaginious. **1697** DRYDEN *Virg. Georg.* III. 501 The tender Grass, and budding Flower. **1787** BEST *Angling* (ed. 2) 39 He bites very freely, but is often lost when struck, his mouth being very tender. **1793** SMEATON *Edystone L.* § 272 Moorstone ..being a tender kind of stone in respect to the union of its component parts. **1832** LYELL *Princ. Geol.* II. 281 Many tender and fragile shells. **1881** BINNS *Guide Worc. Porcelain Wks.* (1883) 24 The ware up to this point..is most tender, and can only be handled with the greatest care.

*fig.* *c* **1386** CHAUCER *Merch. T.* 946, I haue..a soule for to kepe..and also myn honour And of my wyfhod, thilke tendre flour. **1709** STEELE & SWIFT *Tatler* No. 67 ¶ 12 There is Nothing of so tender a Nature as the Reputation and Conduct of Ladies.

**b.** Of the ground: Soft with moisture; easily giving way beneath the feet; 'rotten'. *dial.*

**1789** *Trans. Soc. Arts* VII. 68 Some of the lands are so tender, that a board or patten..is fixed to each foot of every horse. **1904** *Eng. Dial. Dict.* s. v. (Warwick), Behand Spetchley the roads was very tender.

**c.** *Tender porcelain*: soft porcelain; see quots.

**1839** URE *Dict. Arts* 1021 There are two species of porcelain..; the one is called hard, and the other tender. *Ibid.* 1022 Tender porcelain, styled also vitreous porcelain.. always consists of a vitreous frit, rendered opaque and less fusible by the addition of a calcareous and marly clay. **1884** KNIGHT *Dict. Mech.* Suppl., *Tender porcelain*, a soft body porcelain made in Europe.

† **2.** Frail, thin, fine, slender. *Obs. rare.*

**1390** GOWER *Conf.* III. 52 The happes over mannes hed Ben honged with a tendre thred. **1703** MOXON *Mech. Exerc.* 208 That..it draw not the thin and tender Blade of the Hook into it.

**II.** Transferred from I.

**3.** Of weak or delicate constitution; not strong, hardy, or robust; unable or unaccustomed to endure hardship, fatigue, or the like; delicately reared, effeminate.

*a* **1225** *Ancr. R.* 112 Godes fleschs..þet was inumen of þe tendre meidene. **1297** R. GLOUC. (Rolls) 6441 Non byleued nere, Bote is tueye ȝonge sones, þat so feble & tendre were. **1340** *Ayenb.* 31 Þou ne miȝt naȝt do þe greate penonces. Þou art to tendre. **1382** WYCLIF *Deut.* xxviii. 56 A tendre womman and a delicate. **1484** CAXTON *Fables of Æsop* v. x, I shalle not ete the, For thow sholdest hurte my tendre stomak. **1535** COVERDALE *Susanna* 31 Now Susanna was a tender person, and maruelous fayre of face. **1552** HULOET, Tender man not able to indure hardnes, *effæminatus*. *a* **1627** MIDDLETON *More Dissemblers* III. i, A tender, puling, nice, chitty-fac'd squal 'tis. **1859** TENNYSON *Enid* 395 To stoop and kiss the tender little thumb, That crost the trencher as she laid it down.

**b.** Of animals or plants: Delicate, easily injured by severe weather or unfavourable conditions; not hardy; needing protection. Cf. HARDY *a.* 4 b.

**1614** MARKHAM *Cheap Husb.* VII. xvii. (1668) 121 Turkies when they are young are very tender to bring up. **1657** AUSTEN *Fruit Trees* I. 56 The May-Cherries are tender, the Trees must be set in a warm place. **1791** E. DARWIN *Bot. Gard.* I. Note xiv. 27 The bulbs..are found in the perennial herbaceous plants which are too tender to bear the cold of the winter. **1796** C. MARSHALL *Garden.* xii. (1813) 161 Fig trees will mostly survive hard winters, when in standards,..though shoots trained to a wall are tenderer.

**c.** *dial.* In delicate health, weakly, frail.

**1645** R. BAILLIE *Let. to G. Young* 8 July, Mr. Henderson is much tenderer than he wont. **1747** WESLEY *Prim. Physic* (1762) p. xviii, Tender People should have those ..who are much about them sound and healthy. **1818** SCOTT *Hrt. Midl.* v, I had been tender a' the simmer, and scarce ower the door o' my room for twal weeks. **1864** LD.

Houghton *Let.* in *Life* (1891) II. 124 It keeps me rather 'tender' and nervous.

**4.** Having the weakness and delicacy of youth; not strengthened by age or experience; youthful, immature. Chiefly in phrases *tender age, years* (also † *tender of age*).

*c* **1330** R. Brunne *Chron.* (1810) 252 He was tendre & ȝing. **13..** *E. E. Allit. P.* A. 412, I watz ful ȝong & tender of age. **1454** *Rolls of Parlt.* V. 242/1 An Acte made in the tendre age of the Kyng. **1539** Bible (Great) *Gen.* xxxiii. 13 My Lorde, Thou knowest, that the chyldren are tendre. **1563** *Homilies* II. *Sacrament* II. (1859) 449 The true Christians in the tender time of Christ's Church called this Supper Love. **1586** *Let. Earle Leycester* 8 Infected with Poperie from her tender youth. **1610** Holland *Camden's Brit.* (1637) 250 He departed this life in his tender yeares. **1732** Berkeley *Alciphr.* I. § 5 Early instruction instilled into our tender minds. **1844** Ld. Brougham *Brit. Const.* xix. § 3 (1862) 332 The great evil of imprisoning boys and girls of a tender age.

**5.** In reference to colour or light (rarely, sound): Of fine or delicate quality or nature; soft, subdued; not deep, strong, or glaring.

**1503** Dunbar *Thistle & Rose* 50 The purpour sone, with tendir bemys reid. *c* **1694** Prior *Celia to Damon* 67 The tender accents of a woman's cry Will pass unheard. **1754** Gray *Pleasure* 8 April.. Scatters his freshest, tenderest green. **1812** J. Wilson *Isle of Palms* I. 19 A zone of dim and tender light. **1894** Fenn *In Alpine Valley* I. 42 The tender green of the young ferns.

**6.** Of things immaterial, subjects, topics, etc.: Easy to be injured by tactless treatment; needing cautious or delicate handling; delicate, ticklish.

**1625** Bacon *Ess., Cunning* (Arb.) 437 In Things, that are tender and vnpleasing, it is good to breake the Ice, by some whose Words are of lesse weight. **1647** N. Bacon *Disc. Govt. Eng.* I. vi. (1739) 14 The times were too tender to endure them to be declarative on either part. **1725** De Foe *Voy. round World* (1840) 325 They considered not..upon what tender and ticklish terms their navigation stood. **1821** Scott *Kenilw.* xi, Fearful of touching upon a topic too tender to be tampered with.

**III.** Tender toward or in regard to others.

**7.** Of an action or instrument: Not forcible or rough; gentle, soft; acting or touching gently.

**1340–70** *Alex. & Dind.* 952 In tendere touchinge of þing & tastinge of swete. **1592** Shaks. *Ven. & Ad.* 353 Her other tender hand his faire cheeke feeles: His tenderer cheeke, receiues her soft hands print. **1602** Marston *Antonio's Rev.* III. i, I presse you softly with a tender foote. *a* **1628** Preston *Breastpl. Faith* (1630) 128 The smoking Flax, he did blow with a tender breath to kindle it more, hee dealt not roughly with it. **1833** Coleridge *Table-t.* 30 Aug., The more exquisite and delicate a flower of joy, the tenderer must be the hand that plucks it.

† **b.** Easy; not 'hard' or difficult. *Obs. rare*—[1].

**13..** *Gaw. & Gr. Knt.* 2436 How tender hit is to entyse teches of fylþe.

**8.** Of persons, their feelings, or the expression of these: Characterized by, exhibiting, or expressing delicacy of feeling or susceptibility to the gentle emotions; kind, loving, gentle, mild, affectionate.

*The tender passion* or *sentiment*, sexual love.

*a* **1300** *Cursor M.* 24245 (Cott.) Mi suet moder, tender of hert. *c* **1375** *Sc. Leg. Saints* vi. (*Thomas*) 444 Synciane, þat wes vorthy, & tendir frende to mygdony. *c* **1420** *Brut* 346 He kept þat office but iiij wokis, because he was so tendir and gentill vn-to þe cetezens of London. **1534** More *Treat. Passion* Wks. 1273/1 The wily wrech perceiued..the tender mynde that the man had to hys make. **1535** Coverdale *Ps.* xxiv. [xxv.] 6 Call to remembraunce, O Lorde, thy tender mercies & thy louing kindnesses. **1576** in Feuillerat *Revels Q. Eliz.* (1908) 416 In tendre consideracion wherof may yt please your honour. **1691** T. H[ale] *Acc. New Invent.* p. cxxiii, Seamen..are entituled to a more tender Protection from the Crown than other Subjects are. **1775** Sheridan *Duenna* I. iii, I delight in the tender passions. **1848** Thackeray *Van. Fair* xxxvii, His little sisters, in whose welfare she still took the tenderest interest. **1867** *Athenæum* 20 July 77/2 The rivalry of the class-room is unfavourable to the tender sentiment.

† **b.** *transf.* That is the object of tender feeling; tenderly loved; dear, beloved, precious. *Obs.*

*c* **1450** Holland *Howlat* 439 As his tenderest and deir In his maist misteir. **1485** *Sc. Acts Jas. III* (1814) II. 171/1 His hienes has diuers tymez..maid supplicacioun..for þe promocioun of his tendir clerk & consalour. **1591** Shaks. *Two Gent.* v. iv. 37 How I loue Valentine, Whose life's as tender to me as my soule. **1611** Bible *Prov.* iv. 3 Tender and onely beloued in the sight of my mother [Coverd. tenderly beloved of my mother].

† **c.** *Sc.* Nearly related, akin; esp. in phrase *tender of blood*. *Obs.*

**1508** Dunbar *Poems* vii. 15 Welcum our tendir blude of hie parage. **1565** Q. Mary in Keith *Hist.* (1734) App. 103 Lady Margaret Countes of Lennox, being alswa sa tendir of Blude to hir Majestie. **1630–56** Sir R. Gordon *Hist. Earls Sutherland* (1813) 125 One who wes so tender of kinred and blood to him.

**9.** *Tender of* (*for, on behalf of*, etc.): Careful of the welfare of; careful to preserve from harm or injury; considerate of, thoughtful for; fond of.

*c* **1305** *St. Kenelm* 136 in *E. E. P.* (1862) 51 His norice.. Tendre was of þis child, for heo him hadde deorest iboȝt. **1340** Hampole *Pr. Consc.* 905 Whar-to þan es man..Swa tendre of his vile body? *a* **1400–50** *Alexander* 3317 Be tendire of my kniȝtis. **1551** T. Wilson *Logike* (1580) 33 Then should all Capitaines..be tender ouer their poore warriours and base Souldiours. **1605** Bacon *Adv. Learn.* I. iii. § 10 Some person, tender on the behalf of philosophy, reproved Aristippus. **1642** *Declar. Lords & Com.* in Rushw. *Hist. Coll.* (1721) V. 45 The Priviledges of Parliament, which the Contrivers..seem to be so tender of. **1709** Swift *Vind. Bickerstaff* ¶ 1, I am too tender of his reputation to publish them. **1783** Burke *Affairs India* Wks. XI. 334 Mr. Barwell ..ought to have been tender for his honour. **1868** Rogers *Pol. Econ.* xvii. (1876) 240 So tender is the legislature of his interest.

**b.** Solicitous or careful to avoid or prevent something; chary *of*; scrupulous, cautious, circumspect; reluctant, loth. Const. *of, in.*

**1651** N. Bacon *Disc. Govt. Eng.* II. xxvii. (1739) 120 He was tender of the least diminution of his Honour. **1656** Finett *For. Ambass.* 41, I was tender in taking any course without his Lordship's directions. **1667** Pepys *Diary* 28 Oct., I confess, I am sorry to find him so tender of appearing. **1729** Law *Serious C.* xxiii. (1732) 478 Very tender in censuring and condemning other people. **1840** Lady C. Bury *Hist. Flirt* xix, Her heart should be tender of ridiculing their suffering.

**IV.** Easily affected, sensitive.

**10.** Sensitive to, or easily affected by, external physical forces or impressions; *spec.* † **a.** Having a delicate or finely sensitive perception of smell.

*c* **1410**, **1700** [see *tender-nosed* in C.]. **1445** tr. *Claudian* in *Anglia* XXVIII. 277 As blode houndys with her tendir nose tel thingis or thei appiere. **1593** Shaks. *Lucr.* 695 Looke as the full-fed Hound, or gorged Hawke, Vnapt for tender smell, or speedie flight.

**b.** Sensitive in relation to bodily feeling or touch.

*c* **1600** Shaks. *Sonn.* cxli. 6, I doe not loue thee with mine eyes...Nor are mine eares with thy toungs tune delighted, Nor tender feeling to base touches prone. **1715** Desaguliers *Fires Impr.* 43 The difference between the Action of Cold Air upon animate and tender, or inanimate and insensible Bodies.

**c.** *spec.* Acutely sensitive to pain; painful when touched; easily hurt.

[**1613** Shaks. *Hen. VIII*, II. ii. 144 But Conscience, Conscience; O 'tis a tender place, and I must leaue her.] **1709** [implied in Tenderness 3]. **1799** *Med. Jrnl.* I. 159 The tumor being hard, and very tender. **1898** *Allbutt's Syst. Med.* V. 749 The skin over the pericardium was tender and sensitive.

† **d.** Of scales for weighing: Delicate, sensitive.

**1665–6** *Phil. Trans.* I. 232 If I had had..tender Scales.

**e.** Of a ship: Leaning over too easily under sail-pressure; crank, not 'stiff'.

**1722** De Foe *Col. Jack* (1840) 190 The ship..was leaky and tender. **1726** Shelvocke *Voy. round World* 5, I told them, 'if the ship was tender, it was caus'd by her being pester'd so much aloft'. **1823** Scoresby *Jrnl. Whale Fish.* 293 We found the ship so tender (yielding greatly to the influence of the wind), that we could scarcely carry sail. **1899** F. T. Bullen *Log Sea-waif* 201 We..slid gently down the coast under easy sail, the vessel being 'tender' from scanty allowance of ballast.

**f.** Of a horse: *To go tender*, to go as if lame or sore-footed and unable to put down his foot freely.

**1849** Lever *R. Cashel* II. 269, I defy any one to know whether a horse goes tender, while galloping in deep ground.

**11.** Susceptible to moral or spiritual influence; impressionable, sympathetic; sensitive to pious emotions. Now chiefly in phrase 'tender conscience'; formerly also of persons.

*c* **1586** Bryskett *Mourn. Muse Thestylis* 55 Your teares a hart of flint Might tender make. [**1613**: see sense 10 c.] **1655** Fuller *Ch. Hist.* II. vi. § 21 The sight of him made all tender Beholders Cripples by Sympathie. **1660** Chas. II *Declar. fr. Breda*, We do declare a Liberty to tender Consciences. **1672** G. Fox *Jrnl.*, The people being generally tender and open. **1685** Evelyn *Mrs. Godolphin* 46, I found her..all in feares, for never was Creature more devout and tender. **1728** P. Walker *Peden* Pref. (1827) 23 Which have made so many tender Christians to scruple and scunner to take the Food of their Souls out of their unclean Hands. **1788** Wesley *Wks.* (1872) VII. 191 One of a tender conscience is exact in observing any deviation from the word of God, whether in thought, or word, or work. **1844** Ld. Brougham *Brit. Const.* xvi. (1862) 250 The form of words used, out of regard to tender consciences.

† **b.** as *adv.* Tenderly, impressionably. *Obs.*

**1424** *Coventry Leet Bk.* 96 That causyd the people the more & tenderer to her his prechyng.

**12.** Sensitive to injury; ready to take offence; 'touchy'. *Obs.* exc. as *fig.* from 10 c.

*a* **1635** Naunton *Fragm. Reg.* (Arb.) 46 On such trespasses she was quick and tender, and would not spare any whatsoever. **1645** Fuller *Good Th. in Bad T.* (1841) 3, I am choleric by my nature and tender by my temper. **1749** Chesterf. *Lett.* (1792) II. 300 Men are in this respect tender too, and will sooner forgive an injury than an insult. **1857** Buckle *Civiliz.* I. x. 613 The nobles, however, who felt that they had been aggrieved in their most tender point, were not yet satisfied.

† **13.** *transf.* Sensitively felt; that touches sensitive feelings or emotions. *Obs.*

**1705** Stanhope *Paraphr.* I. 115 Which cannot but..make the Sense of present Sufferings more tender and afflicting. **1779** *Mirror* No. 1 (1787) I. 5 A misfortune of the tenderest kind threw me, for some time, into retirement.

**B.** *sb.* [absolute use of the adj.]

† **1.** Tender state or condition. *Obs.*

*c* **1400** *Brut* 254 þat þe Kyng, for tendre of his age, shulde be gouernede be tuelf grete Lordes of Engeland. *a* **1691** Boyle *Hist. Air* xx. (1692) 196 Not only to blast the Fruit, but the very Leaves of such Trees..just in the Tender,.. *i. e.* when they are newly expanded out of the Buds.

† **2.** Tender feeling, tenderness. (Cf. Tendre.) *Obs.*

**1668** Dryden *Evening's Love* v. i, To disengage my heart from this furious tender, which I have for him. **1710** Mrs. Centlivre *Man's Bewitched* Pref., 'Tis Natural to have a kind of a Tender for our own Productions. *Ibid.* v. *ad fin.*, I had a kind of a Tender for Dolly; but since she's dispos'd of, I'll stand as I do. **1742** Richardson *Pamela* IV. 113 Let the Musick express, as I may say, Love and the Tender, ever so much.

† **3.** Tender consideration; care, regard, concern. (Cf. Tender *v.*[2] 3.) *Obs. rare.*

**1596** Shaks. *1 Hen. IV*, v. iv. 49 Thou hast..shew'd thou mak'st some tender of my life In this faire rescue thou hast brought to mee. **1605** — *Lear* I. iv. 230 The redresses.. Which in the tender of a wholesome weale, Might in their working do you that offence.

**C.** Combinations; chiefly parasynthetic adjs., as *tender-bearded, -bladed, -bodied, -bowelled, -faced, -hoofed, -hued, -minded, -natured, -personed, -skinned, -souled, -tempered, -witted*, etc. Also, = tenderly, in *tender-domestic, -imped, -looking, -taken* adjs. Special Combs.: **tender-dying** *a.*, dying young; **tender-eared** *a.* (*fig.*), sensitive to blame or criticism; **tender-eyed** *a.*, (*a*) having tender or sore eyes; † (*b*) fond, doting, partial; **tender-floss** [Floss [3]]: see quot.; **tender-foreheaded** *a.*, modest, ready to blush; † **tender-hefted** *a.*, set in a delicate 'haft' or bodily frame; hence, womanly, gentle; **tender-mouthed** *a.*, (*a*) of a horse: having a tender mouth, answering readily to the rein; † (*b*) fastidious, dainty, choice; (*c*) gentle in speaking, not harsh; † **tender-nosed** *a.*, (*a*) keen-scented; (*b*) timid, timorous; **tender-sided** *a.* [? after *crank-sided*], = sense 10 e (*Cent. Dict.* 1891); † **tender-skull**, a variety of walnut; † **tender-tinder**, ? readily inflammable material (in quot. *fig.*). See also Tender-conscienced, Tenderfoot, etc.

**1591** Sylvester *Du Bartas* I. iii. 296 A Tree, whose *tender-bearded Root being spred In dryest sand. **1804** tr. *Ovid's Remedy of Love* I. 102 (Jod.) The *tender-bladed grain, Shot up to stalk. **1607** Shaks. *Cor.* I. iii. 6 When yet hee was but *tender-bodied. **1650** Jer. Taylor *Holy Living* (1727) 162 Be *tender-bowelled, pitiful, and gentle. **1849** Clough *Amours de Voy.* I. 116 One of those natures Which have their perfect delight in the general *tender-domestic. **1591** Shaks. *1 Hen. VI*, III. iii. 48 As lookes the Mother on her lowly Babe, When Death doth close his *tender-dying Eyes. **1529** More *Dyaloge* IV. Wks. 248/1 The bad themself be not so *tendereared, that for the only talking of their faultes they would banish the bokes that were good in other thinges besyde. **1683** Kennett tr. *Erasm. on Folly* Pref. (1709) 8 Which makes me wonder at the tender-eared humour of this age. **1535** Coverdale *Gen.* xxix. 17 Lea was *tender eyed [Wyclif, with blerid eyen]. **1591** Percivall *Sp. Dict.*, *Pitañoso*, bleare eied, tender eied. *a* **1619** Fletcher *Wit without M.* III. i, You must not think your sister, so tender eyed as not to see your follies. **1823** W. Taylor in *Mirror* 12 July, He [Thomson] was so *tender-faced..and so devilish difficult to shave. **1839** Ure *Dict. Arts* 712 If its fracture be contorted, and contains a great many empty spaces or air-cells, the metal [cast iron] takes the name of cavernous-floss, or *tender-floss. **1659** *Tender-foreheaded [see Foreheaded 1]. **1825** Coleridge *Aids Refl.* Aph. xvii. 67 What need that Christians should be so tender-foreheaded as to be put out of countenance. **1605** Shaks. *Lear* II. iv. 176 Thy *tender-hefted [Q[os] hested] Nature shall not giue Thee o're to harshnesse. **1624** Middleton *Game at Chess* III. i, Thy conscience is so *tender-hoof'd of late, Every nail pricks it. **1598** Sylvester *Du Bartas* II. Ded. 12 Observe a while our *tender-imped Lark. **1605** Shaks. *Lear* v. iii. 31 To be *tender minded Do's not become a Sword. **1620** Venner *Via Recta* iv. 72 Some (That are very *tender mouthed) deeme this fish not so pleasant in taste. **1708** *Yorkshire-Racers* 3 He's tender-mouth'd, manag'd with easy bit. **1656** Duchess Newcastle *True Relation* in *Life* (1886) 313 Also I am *tender natured, for it troubles my conscience to kill a fly. *c* **1410** *Master of Game* (MS. Digby 182) xxxiii, þe redyer and moste *tendrenosed hounde. **1700** R. Cromwell *Let.* in *Eng. Hist. Rev.* XIII. 120 The other tow tender nosed gentlemen would not come. **1819** Keats *Lamia* II. 238 The *tender-personed Lamia. **1679** Evelyn *Kal. Hort.* (ed. 5) 38 Wallnuts, the Early-nut: the *Tender-Scull, the Hard shell. **1872** Symonds *Introd. Stud. Dante* 248 Most *tender-souled of feudal heroes. *a* **1821** Keats *Last Sonnet*, Still, still to hear her *tender-taken breath, And so live ever—or else swoon to death. **1882** F. M. Crawford *Mr. Isaacs* ii, Arab stallions,..sure-footed as a mule, and *tender-tempered as a baby. **1615** Brathwait *Strappado* (1878) 94 *Tender-tinder of Affection, If I harbour thee againe, I will doe it by direction Of some graue experienc't swaine. **1560** Becon *New Catech.* Wks. I. 542 b, The children, whiche eyther are tender, or *tender witted, or fearefull, or easye to be reclaymed: the Scholemaster ought gently to entreat.

**Tender** (te·ndəɹ), *v.*[1] Also 6–8 tendre. [a. F. *tendre* to hold out, offer (11th c. in Godef. *Compl.*):—L. *tendĕre* to stretch, hold forth. (The retention of the ending of the French infinitive is unusual, but cf. Render *v.*)]

To offer or present formally for acceptance.

**1.** *trans. Law.* To offer or advance (a plea, issue, averment; evidence, etc.) in due and formal terms; *spec.* to offer (money, etc.) in discharge of a debt or liability, esp. in exact fulfilment of the requirements of the law and of the obligation.

**1542–3** *Act* 34 & 35 *Hen. VIII*, c. 2 § 2 If..the saide Collectoures..tendre paiement of all suche moneye..within the saide three monethes. **1544** tr. *Littleton's Tenures* (1574) 22 b, The Lorde maye tender a conuenient mariage wythout disparagyng of such an heire female. **1607** Cowell *Interpr.* s. v., To tender his law of *non Summons*..is to offer himselfe ready to make his law, whereby to prooue that he was not summoned. *c* **1611** Chapman *Iliad* XXII. 302 If ten or twenty times so much, as friends would rate thy price, Were tendered here. **1621** Elsing *Debates Ho. Lords* (Camden) 97 Sr John Bennett was ready to tender his apperaunce. **1730–6** Bailey (folio), To *Tender an Averment* (in Law), to offer a Proof or Evidence in Court. *a* **1774** Tucker *Lt. Nat.* (1834) II. 120

In all courts of judgment the burden of the proof lies upon him who tenders the issue. **1848** WHARTON *Law Lex.* s. v., No copper coin can be tendered when the debt is such an amount that it can be paid in silver or gold. **1885** *Law Times Rep.* LIII. 51/2 Evidence was..tendered on behalf of the appellant to prove the construction of the furnace.

†**b.** *Tender down*: to lay down (money) in payment: cf. *pay down*. Also *transf. Obs. rare.*

**1602** HEYWOOD *Wom. Kilde* Wks. 1874 II. 108 Sir I accept it [money],..Come gentlemen, and see it tendred downe. **1603** SHAKS. *Meas. for M.* II. iv. 180 Had he twentie heads to tender downe On twentie bloodie blockes, hee'ld yeeld them vp. **1607** — *Timon* I. i. 54 You see how all Conditions..tender downe Their seruices to Lord Timon.

**2.** *gen.* To present (anything) for approval and acceptance; to offer, proffer.

**1587** HARRISON *England* II. xxii. (1877) I. 340 Then doo they tender licences, and offer large dispensations vnto him. **1593** SHAKS. *Rich. II*, II. iii. 41 My gracious Lord, I tender you my seruice. **1607** DEKKER & WEBSTER *Hist. Sir T. Wyatt* Wks. 1873 III. 110 Who was it yonder, that tendered vp his life To natures death? **1635** A. STAFFORD *Fem. Glory* (1869) 149 All tendred their respects. **1713** ADDISON *Ct. Tariff* ¶ 21 As he tendered his ears. **1786** tr. *Beckford's Vathek* (1868) 45 The governor..tendered every kind of refreshment. **1849** MACAULAY *Hist. Eng.* vi. II. 101 Several Aldermen, who..loved neither Popery nor martial law, tendered their resignations. **1853** C. BRONTE *Villette* xii, She tendered not even a remonstrance. **1871** R. ELLIS *Catullus* lxv. 15 Yet mid such desolation a verse I tender. *fig.* **1588** SHAKS. *L. L. L.* II. i. 244 As Iewels in Christall ..tendring their own worth from whence they were glast.

**b.** *To tender an oath*, to offer or present an oath *to* a person, that he may take it; to put it *to* anyone to take an oath. (*Rarely* to take the oath: quot. 1838.)

**1562** *Act* 5 *Eliz.* c. 1 § 6 To tender or minister the Othe aforesayd, to every..Ecclesiasticall person. **1710** HEARNE *Collect.* (O.H.S.) II. 355 The Oaths are also order'd to be tender'd to them. **1838** PRESCOTT *Ferd. & Is.* (1846) I. v. 222 The principal grandees..soon presented themselves from all quarters, in order to tender the customary oaths of allegiance. **1871** MORLEY *Crit. Misc.* Ser. I. *J. De Maistre* (1878) 107 The authorities vainly tendered him the oath.

†**c.** To offer *to do* something. *Obs. rare*⁻¹.

*a* **1618** RALEIGH *Maxims St.* (1651) 31 Especially if it tender to take from them their commodities.

**3.** [from TENDER *sb.*² 3.] *intr.* To offer by tender *for* a proposed contract, or the like.

**1865** *Pall Mall G.* 12 Oct. 5 Cases..in which the grocery supply..is regulated by friendship [with] some particular grocer—a condition under which open tendering becomes altogether a farce. **1910** *Times* 9 Feb. 4 Seven firms tendered in competition.., the tenderers all sat at a table.

Hence **Te·ndered** (-əɹd) *ppl. a.*; **Te·ndering** *vbl. sb.*

**1613** T. GODWIN *Rom. Antiq.* (1658) 112 A certain ticket or token..at the tendring whereof..certain doles and measures of corn were given. *a* **1677** BARROW *Wks.* (1686) III. xxxvi. 404 His tendering upon so fair and easie terms an endless life in perfect joy and bliss. **1883** *Pall Mall G.* 12 May 4/1 Mdlle. Jeanne receives the tendered homage with the condescension of well-acknowledged desert.

**Tender** (te·ndəɹ), *v.*² *arch.* or *dial.* [f. TENDER *a.*: cf. OF. *tendr-ir*.]

†**1.** *intr.* To become tender; to be affected with pity; to grow soft, soften. *Obs.*

**1390** GOWER *Conf.* I. 270 The wo the children made, Wherof that al his herte tendreth. *c* **1400** *Laud Troy Bk.* 17447 The kynges herte ful sore tendres. *c* **1489** CAXTON *Sonnes of Aymon* xix. 430 Whan Reynawde herde his brother Rycharde speke so to hym, his herte tendred with all ryght sore. **1553** *Respublica* III. iv. 753, I on youe soo tendre.

**2.** *trans.* To make tender (in various senses). **a.** To render gentle, compassionate, or contrite; to soften. ? *Obs.* exc. among Quakers.

**1390** GOWER *Conf.* I. 115 Al naked bot of smok and scherte, To tendre with the kynges herte. **1483** CAXTON *Gold. Leg.* 14 b/2 He added therto wepyng..to tendre our hertis. **1678** R. BARCLAY *Apol. Quakers* v. xvi. 147 It works powerfully upon the Soul, mightily tenders it, and breaks it. **16..** PENN *To J. H.*, etc. (Cent.), I pray God forgive you, open your eyes, tender your hearts. *a* **1718** — *Life* Wks. 1726 I. 61 We were all sweetly tender'd and broken together. **1797** LAMB *To Chas. Lloyd* 15 Deal with me, Omniscient Father! as thou judgest best And in thy season tender thou my heart. **1812** MRS. FRY in Clay *Prison Chaplain* (1861) 81, I heard weeping, and I thought they [female convicts] appeared much tendered.

†**b.** To make less stringent or strict; to mitigate. *Obs. rare.*

*a* **1656** BP. HALL *Specialties Life* Rem. Wks. (1660) 10, I..besought him to tender that hard condition.

**c.** To make tender or delicate. Now *dial.*

**1725** CHEYNE *Ess. Health* vii. § 7 Much and heavy Cloaths ..tender and debilitate the Habit, and weaken the Strength. **1805** R. W. DICKSON *Pract. Agric.* II. 1042 Manure..blanching and tendering the grass plants in the spots where it remains. **1886** *S. W. Linc. Gloss.*, *Tender*, to make tender: as 'It'll tender him for the winter'.

**d.** To make (physically) tender, soft, or weak; to soften, weaken. Now *dial.* and *techn.*

**1764** *Museum Rust.* II. lxxvi. 261 The band seldom breaks there, unless it be made of too small a quantity, or of corn much tendered. **1806** A. HUNTER *Culina* (ed. 3) 182 Stew it till quite tender...When sufficiently tendered, take out the bones. **1874** W. CROOKES *Dyeing & Calico-print.* II. vii. 517 If too strongly acid or alkaline it [the mordant] will have a corrosive action, and the goods, as it is technically called, will be 'tendered'. **1880** *Antrim & Down Gloss* s. v., The fibre (of flax) tendered by excess of moisture.

**3.** To feel or act tenderly towards; to regard or treat with tenderness: with various shades of meaning. **a.** To have a tender regard for, to hold dear; to be concerned for or solicitous about; to treat with consideration; to regard, care for, value, esteem. *arch.* See also f.

**1439** *Rolls of Parlt.* V. 8/2 Þeir worshipp which þei tendre most of any ertly thing. **1469** *Paston Lett.* II. 352 Be my trowthe ther is no gentylwoman on lyve that my herte tendreth more then it dothe her. **1524** [see f.]. **1579** GOSSON *Sch. Abuse* (Arb.) 30 Dion..forbiddeth.. gentlewomen that tender their name and honor, to come to Theaters. **1633** BP. HALL *Hard Texts, N. T.* 87 It must needs be more cause of joy to all that tender the glory of God. *a* **1677** BARROW *Wks.* (1687) I. viii. 98 By our charity and benignity to those whose good he tenders. **1786** *Francis the Philanthropist* III. 72 He advised me, as I tendered my own safety, to keep aloof from his house. **1828** SOUTHEY in *Q. Rev.* XXXVIII. 569 As we tender the safety of the Royal Oak. **1857** [see f].

†**b.** To regard or receive favourably; to attend to or comply with (a request) graciously. *Obs.*

*c* **1430** *Life St. Kath.* (1884) 9 Besechynge ȝowre hyȝe excellence to tendre our desyr and to graunte vs..a graciouse answer. **1523** SKELTON *Garl. Laurel* 56 My supplycacyon to thee I arrecte, Whereof I beseche you to tender the effecte. **1593** SHAKS. *Lucr.* 534 Then for thy husband and thy childrens sake, Tender my suite.

†**c.** To regard or treat with pity; to take pity on, have mercy on; to feel or show compassion for.

**1442** HEN. VI in Ellis *Orig. Lett.* Ser. III. I. 78 That ye soo tendryng thees oure necessitees wol lene vnto vs for the socours and relief of oure seid Duchie [etc.]. **1523** LD. BERNERS *Froiss.* I. ccxxxi. 311 To knowe yf he wolde receyue you..and for pytie somwhat to tendre your nede and necessyte. **1581** T. HOWELL *Deuises* (1879) 183 The Lyon doth tender the beast that doth yeelde. **1649** ROBERTS *Clavis Bibl.* 25 Seeing he so tenders them in affliction.

**d.** To treat with affectionate care; to cherish, foster; to take care of, look after. *Obs.* or *dial.*

**1449** *Rolls of Parlt.* V. 152/2 Fadres of the Church, that shuld most specially tendir þe dere bought monnys soule. **1556** J. HEYWOOD *Spider & F.* lxvii. 15 He tenderlie tendreth his childerne and wife. **1611** SPEED *Hist. Gt. Brit.* IX. ix. (1623) 617 He rather ought to haue tendred him as a Father. *a* **1711** KEN *Hymns Festiv.* Poet. Wks. 1721 I. 386 You in their Infant-age, To tender them engage. **1844** MRS. SHERWOOD *Hist. J. Marten* xxv, [Irish lad says] I was obliged to lead him about,..and tender him, and help him, as if he had been a girl.

†**e.** To have regard or respect to as something to be dreaded and avoided. *Obs.*

**1615**, **1625** [see f]. **1633** T. STAFFORD *Pac. Hib.* I. viii. (1821) 113 Beseeching your Lordship..not to faile, as you tender the overthrow of our Action. **1672–1901** [see f].

**f.** *Phrases.* Royal Proclamations formerly ended with the phrase 'as they [you, etc.] tender our pleasure' (in sense a above), which was used as late as 1701, but in the 17th c. was largely supplanted by 'as they tender our displeasure' (see sense e), which occurs as early as 1615, and remained in use in proclamations for continuing persons in office, issued on the accession of a sovereign, down to the accession of Edward VII, after which the Demise of the Crown Act (of July 1901) rendered such proclamations unnecessary. Proclamations for general fasts or thanksgivings have from 1641 ended with the phrase 'as they tender the favour of Almighty God'.

**1490** *Warrant* in *Coventry Leet Bk.* 539 Fayle ye not herof..as ye & every of yowe tendre our singler pleasir and woll eschewe þe contrarie. **1524** HEN. VIII in *Buccleuch MSS.* (Hist. MSS. Comm.) I. 220 We..commaunde you.. to..suffre hym so to do, without any your let, chalenge, or contradiccion, as ye tender our pleasur. **1618** (July 6) *Procl.* 16 *Jas. I*, (Inhibiting all persons, etc.) as they tender Our pleasure and will avoid Our indignation and displeasure. **1619** (Nov. 10) *Procl.* 17 *Jas. I*, As they tender Our pleasure, and will avoide the contrary. **1669** (June 23) *Procl.* 21 *Chas. II.* **1701** (Mar. 9) *Procl.* 1 *Anne* (Continuing Persons in Office) as they and every of them tender Her Majesty's pleasure.

**1615** (Dec. 9) *Procl.* 13 *Jas. I* (Requiring the Residencie of Noblemen, etc.) as they tender Our indignation and displeasure. **1625** (May 26) *Procl.* 1 *Chas. I* (For reforming disorders in His Majesty's Household) as they will give account to Us thereof and tender Our high displeasure for neglect of this service. **1672** DK. NEWCASTLE in *12th Rep. Hist. MSS. Comm.* App. v. 24 His Majesty..hath required me to prohibit your further proceeding therein as you tender His Majesty's displeasure. **1688** (Feb. 19) *Procl.* 1 *Wm. & Mary* (Continuing Officers in Plantations) as they and every of them tender Our Displeasure. **1701** (Mar. 8) *Procl.* 1 *Anne* (Continuing Persons in Offices) as they and every of them tender Her Majesty's utmost displeasure. **1704** N. N. tr. *Boccalini's Advts. fr. Parnass.* III. 156 But above all things, as he tender'd his Majesty's Displeasure, he should take particular Care never to part with any of 'em. **1727** (June 16) *Procl.* 1 *Geo. II*, as they and every of them tender Our utmost Displeasure. **1901** (Jan. 23) *Procl.* 1 *Edw. VII*, [same words].

**1625** (July 3) *Procl.* 1 *Chas. I* (For a public generall and solemn Fast) as they tender their duties to Almighty God, and to their Prince and Countrey. **1641** (Jan. 8) *Procl.* 17 *Chas. I* (For a general Fast) as they tender the favour of Almighty God. **1805** (Nov. 7) *Procl.* 46 *Geo. III* (For a General Thanksgiving) [same words]. **1857** (Sept. 24) *Procl.* 21 *Vict.* (For a day of Solemn Fast) [same words].

Hence **Te·ndered** *ppl. a.*²; **Te·ndering** *vbl. sb.*, a making or becoming tender; **Te·ndering** *ppl. a.*, that produces tenderness; affecting. *arch.*

**1635** J. HAYWARD tr. *Biondi's Banish'd Virg.* 66 Parting from her deerely-*tendred girle. **1577** B. GOOGE *Heresbach's Husb.* II. (1586) 92 b, Diligent in the *tendering of the tree. **1640** BP. REYNOLDS *Passions* xxvii, Out of a tendering of its own safety. **1684** O. HEYWOOD *Diaries* (1885) IV. 104, I..poured out my soul to god for him, and now at last see some tenderings. **1762** J. WOOLMAN *Jrnl.* viii. (1840) 115 Pure gospel love was felt to the tendering of some of our hearts. *c* **1694** PENN in Janney *Life* xxvii. (1856) 388 In a *tendering and living power she broke out.., 'Let us all prepare [etc.].' **1760** J. RUTTY *Spir. Diary* (ed. 2) 154 A sweet humbling, tendering time. **1824** *Summary View of Amer.* x. 137 He kissed one, took another in his arms, and proved himself so affectionate a father, that it was a tendering sight.

**Te·nder**, *v.*³ [f. TENDER *sb.*¹] *trans.* To ship (mails, luggage, etc.) on board a tender.

**1905** *Westm. Gaz.* 4 Dec. 12/1 The work of 'tendering' and stowing the bags accomplished, the usual special train run on occasions of the kind left Plymouth Docks at 6.43 p.m...and arrived at Paddington at 10.53 p.m.—247 miles in 250 minutes.

**Tenderable** (te·ndərăb'l), *a. Comm.* [f. TENDER *v.*¹ + -ABLE.] That may be tendered; available for delivery in fulfilment of contract.

**1882** *Manch. Guard.* 29 Oct. 4 The supply of 'tenderable' American [cotton] in Liverpool, that is to say of qualities suitable to be accepted in fulfilment of contracts for future delivery. **1884** *Pall Mall G.* 13 Dec. 5/2 By the existing rules of the Petroleum Association the oil tenderable in fulfilment of a contract must be American. **1891** *Standard* 7 Feb. 6/2 The rapid rise has naturally made a large volume of tea tenderable.

†**Te·nderance.** *Obs. rare.* [f. TENDER *v.*² + -ANCE.] Tender treatment or regard.

**1454** *Rolls of Parlt.* V. 257/2 For the grete tenderaunce, trust and love, that the seid James..hade. *c* **1500** MEDWALL *Nature* (Brandl) 296 Of great tenderaunce and spyrytuall loue that god oweth to mankynde. *Ibid.* 606 To accept hym to your fauour and tendraunce.

**Tender-conscienced** (te·ndəɹ₁kǫ·nʃěnst), *a.* [Parasynthetic f. *tender conscience* (TENDER *a.* 11) + -ED².] Having a tender conscience; scrupulous.

*a* **1617** HIERON *Wks.* II. 446 As if you were so tender conscienced that you would not keepe ought from him that were his. **1710** *Let. to New Member Parlt.* in *Harl. Misc.* (1810) XI. 156 Those tender-conscienced people, our moderate dissenters. **1880** SWINBURNE *Stud. Shaks.* 169 The high-hearted and tender-conscienced Hamlet.

**Tenderee·.** [f. as next + -EE¹.] The person to whom a tender is made.

**1883** JUDGE T. MILLER in *New York Reports* XCI. 536 Where a tender is made, for the purpose of obtaining property..sold and in the hands of the tenderee claiming to own the same.

**Tenderer**¹ (te·ndərəɹ). [f. TENDER *v.*¹ + -ER¹.] One who tenders or makes a formal offer; *spec.* one who tenders for a proposed contract.

**1650** J. MUSGRAVE *Pressures & Grievances N. C.* 21 Mʳ Chambers at Allhallowes, tenderer of oath for the Lord Newcastle. **1691** [see TENDER *sb.*² 3]. **1865** *Pall Mall G.* 1 Nov. 4 We announced that the workhouse contracts must in future be given to the lowest tenderer.

**Tenderer**² (te·ndərəɹ). [f. TENDER *v.*² + -ER¹.]

**1.** One who tenders or treats with pity.

**1584** LODGE *Alarum* (Shaks. Soc.) 72 Fatherly, and prudent tenderers of gentry grown into povertie.

**2.** One who or that which makes something tender.

**1890** *Sci. Amer.* 8 Mar. 158/1 Inventions...Steak tenderer.

**Tenderfoot** (te·ndəɹfut). *U. S.* and *Colonial.* Pl. **-foots, -feet.** [f. *tender foot*: see quot. 1887¹.] A name given, originally in the ranching and mining regions of the western U. S., to a newly arrived immigrant, unused to the hardships of pioneer life; a greenhorn; hence, a raw, inexperienced person.

**1881** L. P. BROCKETT *West. Empire* I. vii. (1882) 72 (Funk) Slang expressions of this mining dialect...New-comers are 'Tender-feet'. **1887** L. SWINBURNE in *Scribner's Mag.* II. 508 'Pilgrim' and 'tenderfoot' were formerly applied almost exclusively to newly imported cattle. **1887** *Q. Rev.* July 49 British 'tenderfeet' were induced to invest a great deal of cattle in the business. **1891** *Pall Mall G.* 4 Jan. 2/1 Wailings of inexperienced men and 'tender foots'.

**b.** *attrib.* or as *adj*

**1888** *San Francisco Wkly. Bulletin* (Farmer *Dict. Amer.*), The boys were of the tenderfoot kind. **1897** *Daily News* 30 July 7/1 Most of the best claims have already been secured by tenderfoot prospectors. **1900** O. WISTER *Virginian* ii, In my tenderfoot innocence I was looking indoors for the washing arrangements.

**Te·nder-foo·ted**, *a.* [f. as prec. + -ED².] Having tender feet; hence, moving with or as with tender feet; also *fig.* cautious, timid. Hence **Te·nderfoo·tedness.**

**1682** *Lond. Gaz.* No. 1694/4 Stolen..,an Iron Grey Gelding, ..a little tender-footed on the Stones. **1690** *Ibid.* No. 2535/4 A white Stone-horse..tender-footed before. **1854** J. W. GRIMES in *N. Amer. Rev.* CXXIII. 189 My friends were tender-footed, and did not wish me to denounce the Nebraska infamy. **1891** *Cent. Dict.*, Tenderfootedness.

**Te·nderful**, *a. Obs.* or *dial.* [f. TENDER *a.* + -FUL.] Full of tenderness; affectionate, tenderly kind or attentive. Hence **Te·nderfully** *adv.*

**1640** O. SEDGWICK *Christ's Counsell* 25 Oh how cheerfully, how tenderfully, how much more fully and fruitfully is thy soule inabled after those duties rightly performed. **1901** 'ZACK' *Tales Dunstable Weir* 136 Tenderful for others.

**Te·nder-hea·rted**, *a.* [Parasynthetic f. *tender heart* + -ED².] Having a tender heart; easily moved by †fear, pity, sorrow, or love; †timid; pitiful, compassionate; loving; impressionable.

**1539** Bible (Great) *2 Chron.* xiii. 7 Whan Rehoboam was young & tender hearted. **1560** — (Genev.) *Eph.* iv. 32 Be ye courteous one to another, & tender hearted [1539 mercy-full], forgiuing one another. **1652** Kirkman *Clerio & Lozia* 69 Tenderhearted mothers bewail the loss of their dear children. **1888** 'J. S. Winter' *Bootle's Childr.* vii, Terry was very tender-hearted when women and children were concerned.

Hence **Te·nder-hea·rtedness.**

**1607** Hieron *Wks.* I. 186 Few men haue that tender-heartednesse, to account themselues..parties in the calamities of other Christians. **1798** Southey *Grandmother's T.* Poet. Wks. 1838 III. 12 She little thought This tender-heartedness would cause her death! **1876** L. Stephen *Eng. Th. in 18th C.* II. xii. vii. 444 They lay a new stress upon the advantage of tender-heartedness and sympathy.

So **Te·nder-heart,** a tender-hearted person.

**1904** *Blackw. Mag.* Oct. 513/1 Cheer up, little tender-heart.

**Te·nderish,** *a.* [f. Tender *a.* + -ish [1].] Somewhat tender, rather tender.

**1796** C. Marshall *Garden.* xix. (1813) 354 The variegated [snapdragon] (as all stripes are) is tenderish.

**Tenderize** (te·ndərəiz), *v. rare.* [f. as prec. + -ize.] *trans.* To make tender: = Tender *v.*[2] 1.

**1733** M. L. Killigrew in *Jrnl. Roy. Inst. Cornw.* (1887) Dec., At his going away, his behaviour had tenderised me. **1772** *Test Filial Duty* II. 182 This pastoral life has tenderized you prodigiously.

**Tenderling** (te·ndəɹliŋ). [See -ling [1].]

**1.** A delicate person or creature; *contemptuously,* an effeminate person. Now *rare.*

**1541** Coverdale tr. *Chr. State Matrimonye* (1543) 86 b, The more gorgiouse tenderlynges they be, the better shall they please theyr heade the deuell. **1556** Olde *Antichrist* 9 As for the talkes of some fyne fyngred tendrelinges, they are not worth the hearing. **1649** W. Sclater *Comm. Malachy* (1650) 123 Those tenderlings unused to hardship, how doth a little affright them? **1802** Beddoes *Hygëia* v. 29 Persons, accustomed to be buffetted by storms..much exceed the inactive fireside tenderling.

**2.** A person of tender years; a young child.

**1587** Holinshed *Chron.* III. 628/1 The verie tenderlings who might appeare to be toward and teachable. **1606** Warner *Alb. Eng.* xiv. lxxxiii. 348 His Highness then a Tenderling. **18..** G. Massey *Babe Christabel,* Poems (ed. 1889) 13 They [angels] snatched our little tenderling, So shyly opening into view.

†**3.** *pl.* The soft tops of a deer's horns when they are coming through. *Obs.*

**1575** Turberv. *Venerie* 129 The Noombles, handes and tenderlings, which are the soft toppes of his hornes when they are in bloude, doe pertayne to the Prime or chiefe personage. **1688** R. Holme *Armoury* iii. 189/1.

**Te·nderloin.** *U. S.* [f. Tender *a.* + Loin *sb.*]

**1.** The tenderest or most juicy part of the loin of beef, pork, etc., lying under the short ribs in the hind quarter, and consisting of the psoas muscle; the fillet or 'undercut' of a sirloin. Also *attrib.*

**1828** in Webster. **1869** T. W. Higginson *Army Life* (1870) 37 Is it customary to help to tenderloin with one's fingers? **1884** G. P. Keese in *Harper's Mag.* July 299/1 The division is made into the various pieces here named,..viz., loins, ribs, ..hams, shoulders, tenderloins, striploins, sirloins, butts, rump butts, strips, rounds, and canning beef. **1906** *Breakfast Menu, S. Y. Argonaut* 10 July, Tenderloin Beefsteaks.

**2.** *slang.* In full *tenderloin district*: applied to the police district of New York which includes the great mass of theatres, hotels, and places of amusement; thence extended to similar districts of other American cities.

Understood to have reference to the large amount of 'graft' said to be got by the police for protecting illegitimate houses in this district, which rendered it the 'juicy part' of the service.

**1895** in *Funk's Stand. Dict.* **1898** *N. York Voice* 6 Jan. 4/3 If laws generally suitable to a city do not suit some Slavic, Polish, or other quarter, or some 'tenderloin' district, the local police must pass upon those laws. **1907** *Amer. Trial* in *Daily Chron.* 9 Feb. 5/3 This loose tattle of the Tenderloin. **1908** H. Train *True Stories Crime* xi. 317 Apart from a handsome weekly stipend to his sister, Hummel's money all went into the Tenderloin or the race-track.

**Tenderly** (te·ndəɹli), *adv.* [f. Tender *a.* + -ly [2].] In a tender manner; with tenderness.

**1.** With delicacy or softness of touch, action, or treatment; softly, gently.

*c* **1385** Chaucer *L. G. W.* Prol. 171 And Zepherus and flora gentilly Yaf to the floures softe and tenderly. *c* **1440** *York Myst.* xxx. 135 Tendirly me touche. **1604** Shaks. *Oth.* i. iii. 407 The Moore..will as tenderly be led by th' Nose As Asses are. **1712** Steele *Spect.* No. 526 ⁋ 3, I should be glad to have them handled a little tenderly. **1885** *Athenæum* 23 May 669/1 *Sous Bois*..is another tenderly painted, broad, and expressive piece.

†**b.** So as to be tender or soft. †**c.** In a slight or fragile manner. *Obs.*

**1604** E. Grimstone *Hist. Siege Ostend* 220 Old shooes tenderly sodden. **1721** Bradley *Philos. Acc. Wks. Nat.* 142 The Body of the Bee is divided into three Parts, very tenderly join'd together.

**2.** With tender feeling. **a.** With affection or compassion; lovingly, dearly, kindly; pityingly, mercifully, leniently.

**13..** *Cursor M.* 17288+281 Oute-taken his moder þat loued him tenderly. **1465** *Paston Lett.* II. 200, I pray yow that ye will tenderly understond this letter. **1593** Shaks. *Rich. II,* iii. iii. 48 The which..My stooping dutie tenderly shall shew. **1663** Butler *Hud.* i. i. 226 Rather than fail, they will defy That which they love most tenderly. **1826** Penn in *Pa. Hist. Soc. Mem.* I. 204 Thy remembrance..I tenderly received. **1849** Macaulay *Hist. Eng.* v. I. 640 He will generally connive at it, or punish it very tenderly. **1891** E. Peacock *N. Brendon* I. 230 She looked at Basil tenderly. **1900** *Westm. Gaz.* 30 July 7/2 A tenderly-worded message of condolence.

†**b.** With kind or friendly consideration or attention; indulgently. (Cf. Tender *v.*[2] 3.) *Obs.*

*c* **1380** Wyclif *Wks.* (1880) 371 þerfore lordis schulden take hede fulle tendirly to þis voyce of criste. **1571** in Feuillerat *Revels Q. Eliz.* (1908) 408 All which I beseech your honour tenderly to consider. **1594** West *2nd Pt. Symbol., Chancerie* § 98 The premisses tenderly considered.

**c.** With tender emotion; with acute sensibility or sensitiveness.

*a* **1300** *Cursor M.* 14308 Tenderli he wep, and said, 'And quar haf yee his bode laid?' *c* **1400** Maundev. (Roxb.) xi. 46 Petre grette full tenderly, when he had forsaken Criste. **1609** Daniel *Civ. Wars* viii. lxxxii, The Lady Bona takes most tenderly To be so mockt. *a* **1674** Clarendon *Life* (1759) I. 163 [This] the Chancellor took very heavily, and the Lord Falkland out of his Friendship to him, more tenderly. **1796** H. Hunter tr. *St.-Pierre's Stud. Nat.* (1799) II. 320 Greece alone, you tell me, presents scenes and points of view so tenderly affecting.

**3.** With delicate nurture; softly, indulgently; effeminately; also, with the tenderness of youth.

*c* **1386** Chaucer *Man of Law's T.* 171 Sent..Fro freendes þat so tendrely hire kepte. *c* **1440** *Jacob's Well* 104 Þou hast be norysched tenderly. **1552** Huloet, Tenderlye, *molliter, muliebriter.* **1638** Junius *Paint. Ancients* 182 Polycletus made Diadumenon tenderly youthfull. **1848** Mrs. Jameson *Sacr. & Leg. Art* (1850) 369 Such works..as tenderly-nurtured women shrink from.

**4.** Timidly, charily, cautiously. (Cf. 1.)

*a* **1628** Preston *Breastpl. Love* (1631) 149 When a man hath no ground to set his foote on, he will doe it tenderly and warily. **1822** Lamb *Elia* Ser. ii. *Detached Th. on Bks.,* The poor gentry..venturing tenderly, page after page.

†**Te·nderly,** *a. Sc. Obs. rare.* [f. as prec. + -ly [1].] Of a tender sort.

**1567** *Sc. Acts Jas. VI* (1814) III. 13/2 Experience of the naturall affectioun and tenderly lufe he hes in all tymes borne.

**Tenderness** (te·ndəɹnės). [f. Tender *a.* + -ness.] The quality or state of being tender.

**1.** Physical softness or delicacy; fragility; inability to stand rough usage; weakness, frailty; † youthfulness (*obs.*); effeminacy, womanishness.

**13..** *Cursor M.* 25337 (Cott.) Thoru tendernes of vr flexs. **1387** Trevisa *Higden* (Rolls) VI. 301 Þou doost riȝtfulliche ..þat confortest þe tendernesse [= newness] of my professioun. *c* **1430** Lydg. *Min. Poems* (Percy Soc.) 220 How myght I the woo endure, In tendrenesse of wommanheede? **1596** Dalrymple tr. *Leslie's Hist. Scot.* (S.T.S.) I. 19 In tendirnes of thair flesh thay [sheep] are lyke the cattel. **1623–33** Fletcher & Shirley *Night-Walker* i. iii, Alas poor gentlewoman, Must she become a nurse now in her tenderness? **1708** J. C. *Compl. Collier* (1845) 35 According to the tenderness or hardness of the Coal. **1774** Pennant *Tour Scotl. in 1772* 258 Through the age and tenderness of the parchment, little could be read. **1856** Ruskin *Mod. Paint.* IV. v. xx. § 4 [Such a person] can hardly be said to know what tenderness in colour means at all.

**b.** quasi-*concr.* Tender substance.

**1382** Wyclif *Jer.* li. 34 He fulfilde his wombe with my tendernesse. **14..** *Metr. Voc.* in Wr.-Wülcker 627/7 Thye, *crus,* hepe, *femur,* the tendurnesse of þe thye, *famen.* **1548** Thomas *Ital. Dict.* (1567), *Lanugine,* the tendernesse or downe of a yonge bearde.

**2.** The quality of being tender in regard or treatment of others; gentleness, kindness, compassion, love; considerateness, mercy, leniency.

*a* **1300** *Cursor M.* 9994 (Cott.) Takening..O tendernes and truth stedfast. *c* **1450** *Merlin* i. 2 Grete loue he hadde to man and gret tendirnesse. **1526** *Pilgr. Perf.* (W. de W. 1531) 58 b, So longe as suche tendernes is to the no distraccion from goostlynes. **1668** Owen *Expos. Ps.* cxxx. Wks. 1851 VI. 415 What love and tenderness there is in God to receive us. **1751** Johnson *Rambler* No. 179 ⁋ 3 Deformity itself is regarded with tenderness rather than aversion. **1844** Ld. Brougham *Brit. Const.* xix. § 5 (1862) 343 Who visited their offences with tenderness.

**b.** with *a* and *pl.* An instance of this.

**1660** F. Brooke tr. *Le Blanc's Trav.* 284 Then there was amongst us such a tyde of tendernesses. **1850** Lynch *Theo. Trin.* ix. 154 Hypocritical exhibitors of prettynesses and tendernesses.

**3.** Sensitiveness to impression; impressionableness, soft-heartedness; sensibility to pain, esp. when touched; crankness (of a ship).

*c* **1440** *Partonope* 2713 Som wept for tendyrnesse of hert. **1594** Carew *Huarte's Exam. Wits* vi. (1596) 78 Memory is nothing els but a tendernesse of the braine, disposed..to receiue & preserue that which the imaginatiue apprehendeth. **1709** Stanhope *Paraphr.* IV. 176 Till the Patient be awaken'd into Tenderness and Smart, there is no Hope of a Cure. *a* **1716** South *Serm.* (J.), True tenderness of conscience is nothing else but an awful and exact sense of the rule which should direct it. **1781** Gibbon *Decl. & F.* xxix. III. 113 The disgrace of his daughter..wounded the tenderness, or, at least, the pride, of Rufinus. **1843** R. J. Graves *Syst. Clin. Med.* xviii. 210 Judging from the extreme epigastric and abdominal tenderness during life. **1854** Brewster *More Worlds* xvi. 231 Such a tenderness of retina, that he could, in a dark night, see and distinguish plainly colours of ribands. **1887** *Daily Tel.* 10 Sept. 2/5 She stood up well under her canvas. She showed no signs of tenderness.

†**Te·ndership.** *Obs. rare*−[1]. [f. as prec. + -ship.] Tenderness; tender regard or esteem.

*c* **1460** *Wisdom* 634 in *Macro Plays* 56, I serue myghty lordeschyppe, Ande am in grett tenderschyppe.

†**Te·ndful,** *a. Obs. rare*−[1]. [f. Tend *v.*[1] + -ful 1.] Assiduous in tending; attentive.

*a* **1697** Aubrey *Brief Lives* (1898) II. 209 A good woman ..who was very carefull and tendfull of him.

†**Te·ndicle.** *Obs. rare*−[0]. [ad. L. *tendicula* snare: see next.]

**1727** Bailey vol. II, *Tendicle* (*tendicula,* L.), a Gin or Snare to take Birds or Beasts, &c. **1780** in Sheridan.

†**Te·ndicule.** *Surg. Obs. rare.* [ad. L. *tendicula,* f. *tendĕre* to stretch: see -cule.] Name of an instrument for dilating an opening; a dilator.

*c* **1425** tr. *Arderne's Treat. Fistula,* etc. 24 Þan take þe tendicule and putte þe snowte of þe nedle in þe hole of þe fistule in puttyng it strongly.

**Tendinal** (te·ndinăl), *a. rare*−[1]. [ad. mod.L. type **tendināl-is,* f. mod.L. *tendo, -din-em*: see Tendon and -al.] = Tendinous. So **Tendineal** (tendi·niăl) *a. rare*−[1].

**1887** *Science* 24 June 624/2 A tendinal slip is shown cut short,..which evidently belongs to this muscle. *Ibid.* 5 Aug. 71/2 [The propatagial slip] also raises the elongated neck-feathers, while special development of its tendineal portion aids in strengthening the *tensor propatagii.*

**Tendinous** (te·ndinəs), *a.* [ad. F. *tendineux* (Paré, 16th c.), f. med. or mod.L. *tendo, tendin-em* Tendon.] Of the nature of a tendon; consisting of tendons.

**1658** Rowland *Moufet's Theat. Ins.* 931 His head is full of sinewes, his body soft, his tail tendinous. **1715** Cheyne *Philos. Princ. Relig.* i. 110 The Elasticity of Tendinous Bodies. **1822** J. Parkinson *Outl. Oryctol.* 194 A bivalve shell adherent to marine bodies..by a tendinous cord. **1875** Huxley & Martin *Elem. Biol.* (1883) 200 The pectoral region; part..only covered by tendinous tissue.

†**Tendite** = *to endite*: see T' and Indite *v.*

*c* **1384** Chaucer *H. Fame* i. 381 To longe tendyte. *c* **1385** — *L. G. W.* 1345 (*Dido*) So gret a reuthe I haue for tendite.

†**Te·ndle.** *Obs.* or ? *dial.* Also 9 tennle, tennel. [A deriv. of OE. *tend-an,* Tind *v.* to kindle, light: perh. a variant of Tandle *sb.* Cf. also Tindle.] **a.** In 15th c. Exact sense uncertain: perh. (as suggested by editors of *Destr. of Troy*) 'a splint of resinous wood used as a candle'; but perh. rather = Tandle, a beacon-fire or bonfire. **b.** In later use: see quot. 1887.

*c* **1400** *Destr. Troy* 6038 Brode firis & brem beccyn in þe ost, Torchis and tendlis the tenttes to light. *Ibid.* 7353 Tore fyres in the tenttes, tendlis olofte! **1887** Donaldson *Suppl. to Jamieson, Tendle, Tennle, Tennel,* lit. Firewood; dried twigs, furze, scrub, &c., gathered for fuel. [No authority or locality given.]

†**Te·ndment.** *Obs. rare.* [Aphetic f. Attendment. Cf. Tend *v.*[1] and OF. *tendement* intention.]

**1.** Meaning, significance. [Cf. F. *entendement.*]

**1519** Horman *Vulg.* 77 That worde may haue double tendement.

**2.** Care, attention.

**1597–8** Bp. Hall *Sat.* ii. iv. 21 Whether ill tendment, or recurelesse paine Procure his death.

‖**Tendo** (te·ndo). *Anat.* [med. or mod.L.: see next.] = Tendon: frequent in *tendo Achillis* (see next), and in comb. as **tendo-synovitis,** inflammation of the synovial membrane of a tendon.

[**1693** tr. *Blancard's Phys. Dict.* (ed. 2), *Tendo,* a Tendon, a similar nervous part annexed to Muscles and Bones.] **1874** Carpenter *Ment. Phys.* i. ii. § 30 (1879) 30 Pulling upwards the heel by means of the great Tendo Achillis. **1899** *Allbutt's Syst. Med.* VI. 528 Hence the terms 'elbow-jerk', 'wrist-jerk', 'tendo-Achillis-jerk'. *Ibid.* 598 Tendo-synovitis of the flexor tendons of this finger.

**Tendon** (te·ndən). Also *β.* 6 **tenaunt, tennon,** 7 **tenon, tendant,** 8 **tendent.** *Pl.* 6–7 (perh. Lat.) **tendones.** [ad. med.L. *tendo, tendōn-em* and *tendin-em,* app. ad. Gr. τένων, τενοντ- sinew, tendon, influenced by L. *tend-ĕre* to stretch; so F. *tendon* (16th c.), also It. *tendone, tendine,* Sp. *tendon.*

To Celsus, a.d. 50, τένων was still a Greek word. In Cælius Aurelianus, *c* 400–420, it retains Gr. inflexions, e.g. acc. pl. *tenontas*; but in Theod. Priscianus has L. abl. pl. *tenontibus.* In med.L. it became *tendon* or *tendo*: the latter in Theod. Gaza, tr. Aristotle's *Hist. Anim.,* 1476. The pl. occurs as *tendones* in the tr. of Galen by Nicolaus Calaber of Reggio *a* 1350, and there is later evidence that the *o* was long, *tendōnes.* Another pl. *tendines* (after *ordines,* etc.) was used in 16th c. and later. (I. Bywater.) The *β*-forms *tenon, tenaunt* perh. preserve traces of the Gr. forms, confused with other words.]

A band or cord of dense fibrous tissue forming the termination of a muscle, by which it is attached to a bone or other part; a sinew: usually applied to such when rounded or cord-like, broad flat tendons being called *fasciæ* and *aponeuroses.*

*Tendon of Achilles* (L. *tendo Achillis*), the tendon of the heel; the tendon by which the muscles of the calf of the leg are attached to the heel, being the principal extensor of the foot. So named from the mythological account that when the infant Achilles was dipped by his mother Thetis in the Styx, to render him invulnerable, he was held by the heel, which thereby escaped dipping and remained vulnerable.

**1543** Traheron *Vigo's Chirurg.* i b/1 Chordes or tendones. **1563** T. Gale *Enchirid.* 41 b (Stanf.) Nerues, tendons, ligamentes. **1578** Banister *Hist. Man* iii. 44 b, A tendon is the white part in the Muscle beyng hard, thicke, and shynnyng. **1610** Healey *St. Aug. Citie of God* xiv. xxiv. (1620) 498 Small sinews and *Tendones.* **1726** Gay in *Swift's Lett.* (1766) II. 59 The surgeon..told him, that his fingers were safe, that there were two nerves cut, but no tendon. **1872** Mivart *Anat.* 149 The radius,..its posterior surface is grooved for the passage of tendons.

*β.* **1541** R. Copland *Guydon's Quest. Chirurg.* F iv, The tenauntes moeuyng the heade and the necke, whiche are

.xx. in nombre. *Ibid.*, The tenaunt muscles and the strynges..that maketh the heade bowe. **1598** FLORIO, *Tendini*, as *Tendoni*, the tennons. **1607** MARKHAM *Caval.* VII. (1617) 7 There is one maine tendant or sinewe. **1630** J. TAYLOR (Water P.) *Praise Cleane Linnen* Ded., Wks. II. 166 The Legge..ennamel'd with Sinewes, interwoven with Membranes, intermixt with Tenons, embost with Ankles. **1708** *Lond. Gaz.* No. 4484/1 Convulsive Motions of the Tendents.

**b.** *Entom.* (See quot.)

**1826** KIRBY & SP. *Entomol.* III. 381 *Tendo* (the *Tendon*), a strong bristle, or bristles observable at the base underneath in the under-wings of many *Lepidoptera*, which plays in the *Hamus* of the upper-wings.

**c.** *attrib.* and *Comb.*, as *tendon cell, corpuscle* (see quot.), *jerk* (JERK *sb.*[1] 2 b), *muscle, reaction, reflex* (REFLEX *sb.* 6), *sheath, thread.*

**1890** BILLINGS *Nat. Med. Dict.*, *T[*endon*] *cells* or *corpuscles*, connective tissue cells found in tendons and ligaments, arranged in rows following the course of the fibres. **1899** *Allbutt's Syst. Med.* VII. 62 The increased activity of the *tendon-jerks is manifested by an excessive jaw-jerk. **1541** *Tenaunt muscles [see *β*. above]. **1878** *Med. Times* 2 Feb. 107 [Erb] applied to it the name '*tendon-reflex'. **1899** *Allbutt's Syst. Med.* VI. 519 The knee-jerk is sometimes spoken of as a 'tendon reflex'. **1897** *Ibid.* III. 67 Effusion into the *tendon sheaths. **1906** SIR F. TREVES in *Daily Chron.* 3 Aug. 3/4 Skins sewn together with a bone needle and a *tendon thread.

**Tendonous** (te·ndŏnəs), *a.* [f. prec. + -OUS.] = TENDINOUS. Hence **Te·ndonousness**, *rare*⁻¹ (in quot. 1597 = tendinous part).

**1597** A. M. tr. *Guillemeau's Fr. Chirurg.* 20/2 We must avoyde the synnuishe tendonousnes of the right muscle. **1660** BOYLE *New Exp. Phys. Mech., Digress.* 341 Having stabb'd himself, and pierced the Diaphragme in the thinner or tendonous part. **1753** HERVEY *Theron & Asp.* (1757) I. xii. 450 An assemblage of fine tendonous fibres. **1877** ROSENTHAL *Muscles & Nerves* xi. 199 The natural ends of the muscle-fibres while still closed with the tendonous substance.

**Tendoor, -our**, var. of TANDOUR, Persian stove.

**Te·ndotome.** *Surg.* An improper form of TENOTOME, assimilated to *tendon.*

**1882** in OGILVIE (Annandale).

**Tendour**, obs. form of TENDER *sb.*[1], [2].

**Tendrac**, variant of TANREC.

‖ **Tendre** (tāndr'). Now *rare.* [F. *tendre* sb., from *tendre*, TENDER *a.*] A tender feeling or regard; a fondness, an affection; a tenderness.

**1673** DRYDEN *Marr. à la Mode* III. i, I have such a *tendre* for the court, that I love it even from the drawing-room to the lobby. **1695** CONGREVE *Love for L.* I. xv, I will, because I have a *tendre* for your ladyship. **1748** SMOLLETT *Rod. Rand.* xlii, A pretty maid, who had a *tendre* for me. **1833** T. HOOK *Parson's Dau.* II. ii, I am quite relieved..since you tell me there had been no *tendre* between her and Mr. Harvey. **1848** THACKERAY *Van. Fair* xv, You poor friendless creatures are always having some foolish *tendre.*

† **b.** An expression of tenderness. *Obs. rare.*

**1705** VANBRUGH *Confed.* IV. i, O Pox!..I desire none of your *Tendres.*

**Tendre**, obs. form of TENDER, TINDER.

**Tendren**, obs. form of TENDRON.

‖ **Tendresse.** *Obs.* exc. as Fr. [F. *tendresse* (tāndrɛ·s), 14th c. in Godef., f. *tendre*, TENDER *a.*] = TENDERNESS.

**1390** GOWER *Conf.* I. 195 For Moderhed and for tendresse. **1399** *Rolls of Parlt.* III. 451/2 To have rewarde to tendresse of her age. *a* **1766** MRS. F. SHERIDAN *Sidney Bidulph* IV. 64 But have not you at the same time a small tendresse for her fortune? **1850** W. IRVING in *Life & Lett.* (1864) IV. 76 The fair Truffi, for whom I still cherish a certain degree of *tendresse.* **1885** *Athenæum* 17 Oct. 503/2 The..sister who conceals her *tendresse* for the hero in maidenly fashion.

**Tendril** (te·ndril), *sb.* Also 6 -yll, -elle, 6–8 -el, 7 -ell, 8 -ill. [Origin uncertain; app. from L. *tendĕre*, F. *tendre* to stretch; in its actual form and sense only in Eng. See Note below.]

**1.** A slender thread-like organ or appendage of a plant (consisting of a modified stem, branch, flower-stalk, leaf, or part of a leaf), often growing in a spiral form, which stretches out and attaches itself to or twines round some other body so as to support the plant. (Distinguished from a *twining stem* by not bearing leaves.)

**1538** ELYOT, *Capreolus*,..the tendrell of a vyne, whiche wyndeth diuers ways, called also Pampinus. **1578** LYTE *Dodoens* III. lxxxviii. 441 Litle claspers or tendrelles, wherewithal it taketh holdefast vpon hedges, trees, poles, and rayles. **1611** COTGR., *Tendron*..a tendrell, or the tender branch, or sprig of a plant. **1667** MILTON *P. L.* IV. 307 Her ..tresses..in wanton ringlets wav'd As the Vine curles her tendrils. **1768** STERNE *Sent. Journ.* (1778) II. 175 (*Maria*) A couple of vine leaves, tied round with a tendril. **1807** J. E. SMITH *Phys. Bot.* 224 *Cirrus.* Tendrils or claspers when young are usually put forth in a straight direction; but they presently become spiral. **1858** CARPENTER *Veg. Phys.* § 538 Nearly all the plants of the group are climbers, and most of them support themselves by tendrils.

**b.** *transf.* Something resembling a tendril of a plant: as, a slender branch of a vein; a curl or ringlet of hair. (Cf. also *tendril-footed* in 3 b.)

**1615** CROOKE *Body of Man* 79 Sometime also seueral tendrils are communicated vnto it from the spermatical veines. **1814** BYRON *Lara* II. xxi, The glossy tendrils of his raven hair. **1859** GEO. ELIOT *A. Bede* xliii, The dark tendrils of hair,..the rounded cheek and the pouting lips.

**c.** *fig.*, esp. in reference to a 'clinging' affection or attachment.

**1841** EMERSON *Lect., Man the Reformer* Wks. (Bohn) II. 238 Inextricable seem to be the twinings and tendrils of this evil. **1852** MRS. STOWE *Uncle Tom's C.* xxii, Her own earnest nature threw out its tendrils, and wound itself around the majestic book. **1891** T. HARDY *Tess* II. xiv, Her foolish soul sent back tendrils of yearning towards it [her father's house].

†**2.** Used to render F. *tendron* bud (see TENDRON) in fig. sense 'young girl'. *Obs.*

**1603** FLORIO *Montaigne* III. ix. (1632) 554 Continually stored with young tendrels or lasses, to keepe his old-frozen limbs warme a nights. **1639** S. DU VERGER tr. *Camus' Admir. Events* 313 Hee sends this tendrell to schoole againe.

**3.** *attrib.* and *Comb.* **a.** *attrib.* Having or bearing tendrils, as *tendril brier, hop, vine*; of or belonging to a tendril, resembling or consisting of a tendril, as *tendril-ring, -talon.* **b.** objective, instrumental, parasynthetic, etc., as *tendril-bearer, -climber*; *tendril-footed, -like* adjs.

**1872** DARWIN *Orig. Spec.* vii. (ed. 6) 196 Gradations.. between simple twiners and *tendril-bearers. *c* **1711** PETIVER *Gazophyl.* VI. Tab. lviii, Triangular *Tendril Bryar... A very odd Anomalous Plant. **1875** BENNETT & DYER *Sachs' Bot.* 197 A distinction is drawn between *Tendril-climbers (as *Vitis*) and Stem-climbers (as *Phaseolus, Humulus, Convolvulus*, &c.). **1843** CARPENTER *Anim. Phys.* 94 The class *Cirrhipoda*, or *tendril-footed animals. **1757** DYER *Fleece* I. 62 The curling growth Of *tendril hops, that flaunt upon their poles. **1836–9** *Todd's Cycl. Anat.* II. 146/2 The *tendril-like branches of the arteria profunda. **1791** E. DARWIN *Bot. Gard.* II. 150 Long horrent thorns his mossy legs surround, And *tendril-talons root him to the ground. **1743** FRANCIS tr. *Hor., Epod.* xv. 3 When round my Neck as curls the *Tendril-Vine—(Loose are its Curlings, if compar'd to thine). **1896** *Westm. Gaz.* 20 Oct. 10/2 Framed in Romanesque *tendril work.

Hence **Te·ndril** *v.* (*nonce-wd.*) *intr.* to curl like a tendril; **Te·ndrilled, -iled** (-ild) *a.*, having a tendril or tendrils (in quot. 1839 *transf.* curly); **Tendrili·ferous** *a.* [-FEROUS], bearing tendrils; **Te·ndrilly, Te·ndrilous** *adjs.*, full of tendrils; resembling a tendril.

**1894** CROCKETT *Lilac Sunbonnet* 18 Fair hair, crisping and *tendrilling over her brow. **1806** GALPINE *Brit. Bot.* § 319 Fumaria..stem climbing: petioles *tendrilled. **1822** *Hortus Angl.* II. 126 *A*[*ntirrhinum*] *Cirrhosa.* Tendriled Toad Flax. **1839** BAILEY *Festus* xx. (1852) 375 Some young thing with tiny hands, And rosy cheeks, and flossy tendrilled locks. **1900** W. WALLACE in *Ann. Bot.* Dec. 639 A *tendriliferous liane. **1863** HOLME LEE *Annie Warleigh* III. 25 A Virginian creeper twined its thousands of *tendrilly sprays up the rustic pillars. **1857** WOOD *Com. Objects Sea Shore* 58 The long, curling, *tendrilous appendages .. affix themselves to sea-weeds..and..anchor the egg firmly.

[*Note.* With *tendril*, cf. F. *tendrillon* bud, tender sprout or shoot, dim. of *tendron* in same sense, also fig. a 'bud', a young girl; also cartilage; which Hatz.-Darm. refer to *tendre* adj. tender. But Paré (16th c.) took *tendron* as synonymous with *capréole* tendril, clasper ('La vigne par ses tendrons ou capréoles tortues embrasse toutes choses'), and L. *capreolus* (rendered by Elyot 1538 'tendrell') was by R. Estienne, 1536, glossed by *tendon*, a deriv. of L. *tendĕre*, F. *tendre* to stretch. There was thus in 16th c. F. some confusion between *tendon* and *tendron*, which appears to have influenced the Eng. use of *tendril* and associated it with *tendre* to stretch rather than with *tendre* tender. See also Weekley in *Trans. Philol. Soc.* 1909.]

**Tendron** (te·ndrən). Also 5 tenderon, tendrone, 5–6 -ren, -ringe, 7 -ering, 8 -ring, 9 -erone. [a. F. *tendron* bud, young sprout or shoot; also cartilage; f. *tendre*, TENDER *a.*: but see prec.]

**1.** A young tender shoot or sprout of a plant; a bud. Now *rare.*

**14..** *Stockh. Med. MS.* I. 340 in *Anglia* XVIII. 303 Take þe lewys of þe reed docke, þe tendronys in þe mydward awey do knocke. *c* **1420** *Liber Cocorum* (1862) 34 Take tenderons of sauge..And stop one [cofyn] fulle up to þo ryng. *c* **1440** *Promp. Parv.* 488/2 Tendrone, of a vyne.., *botrio.* **1601** HOLLAND *Pliny* (1634) II. 28 So soon as new buds and tendrons appeare aboue ground from the root. *Ibid.* 196 The juice drawne and pressed out of the tendrons or yong sprouts of brambles. **1707** MORTIMER *Husb.* (1721) II. 152 Cut off all the Blossoms that are likely to bear no Fruit, also the small tendrings, the barren Branches. **1895** W. RAYMOND *Tryphena in Love* 5 The inconstant shade of leafy tendrons quivering in the wind.

† **b.** *transf.* A small branch, as of a vein. *Obs.*

**1578** BANISTER *Hist. Man* I. 7 The little Tendringes or Spriggie braunches of veines.

**2.** (*pl.*) The cartilages of the ribs (*esp.* in *Cookery*, of a deer or calf).

**1398** TREVISA *Barth. De P. R.* V. i. (1495) f vij/2 The tendrenes of the ribbes defende the lyuer. **15..** *Wyll Burke his Test.* (Halliw.) 54 Bake dowcetts and tendrens and the liver rostid. **1768** *Chron.* in *Ann. Reg.* 170/2 The bill of fare ..Venison, Tendrons, Quails. **1806** J. SIMPSON *Cookery* (1816) 43 (Stanf.) The tenderones are the gristle bone of the breast of veal cut into thin slices. **1845** BREGION & MILLER *Pract. Cook* 43 *Tendrons* (Veal), are found near the extremity of the ribs.

†**Tendry.** *Obs.* [f. TENDER *v.*[1], F. *tendre*: cf. OF. *tend(e)rie* (14th c.) the act of stretching, etc., f. *tendre* to stretch; cf. RENDRY.]

**1.** An act of tendering or offering; a tender, offer, proffer; a formal offer.

**1624** BP. MOUNTAGU *Immed. Addr.* 18, I suppose it a tendry of Kindness rather, a Gentle Inuitation, to come and Call. **1656** HEYLIN *Surv. France* 322 The Tenants made no tendry of this Champart, and so it lay amongst concealments. *a* **1667** JER. TAYLOR *Reverence due to Altar* Wks. 1849 V. 319 A tendry of our service. **1681–6** J. SCOTT *Chr. Life* II. vii. § 5 God..had as undoubted a Right to exchange them with Christ's for his Life, upon the free Tendry which he made of it.

**2.** *spec.* The tendering or delivering of something to be mentally accepted or considered; hence, a doctrine delivered or presented for acceptance, a deliverance; *pl.* articles of belief, tenets.

**1624** BP. MOUNTAGU *Immed. Addr.* 146 In Gods Precepts and Tendries of beleefe, I will subiect..my enquiring into plaine beleefe. **1636** HEYLIN *Sabbath* I. Pref. A v, You would not shut your eyes, against the tendrie of those truths. **1652–62** — *Cosmogr.* I. (1677) 209/1 Arianism: not ejurated till the year 588, when that whole Nation did submit to more Catholick tendries. *a* **1662** — *Laud* (1668) 261 The general Tendries of the Protestant, Lutheran, and Calvinian Writers beyond the Seas. **1675** V. ALSOP *Anti-Sozzo* 467 Religion must appear before the Tribunal of Reason; and if it does not acquit itself well, and give a Rational and Satisfactory account of its Tendries, it must be bored through the Tongue with a red-hot Iron for an Heretic.

[**Tendsome**: see *List of Spurious Words.* In **1847** WEBSTER and later Dicts.]

†**Tendure** = *to endure*: see T'.

**1480** CAXTON *Descr. Brit., Irel.* 27 These swyne may not be kept..for tendure in likenes of swyne ouer thre dayes.

**Tendy**, obs. inf. of TEND *v.*[1]

**Tene**, obs. f. TEEN; var. TIND *v. Obs.*, to kindle.

**Teneble, -blus**: see TENEBRES.

‖ **Tenebræ** (te·nėbrī, -brē). *R. C. Ch.* See also TENEBRES. [L. *tenebræ* darkness; in med. L. in the eccles. sense: see Du Cange.] The name given to the office of matins and lauds of the following day, usually sung in the afternoon or evening of Wednesday, Thursday, and Friday in Holy Week, at which the candles lighted at the beginning of the service are extinguished one by one after each psalm, in memory of the darkness at the time of the crucifixion. Also *attrib.*

**1651** in Morris *Troubles Cath. Foref.* I. vi. (1872) 304 We were forced to read our Office and even the Tenebræ Matins in the work chamber. **1656** BLOUNT *Glossogr.* s.v., The service or mattins used in the Roman Church..cal'd *tenebræ* (thence *tenebræ wednesday, thursday, &c.*). **1708** OZELL *Boileau's Lutrin* IV. (1730) 192 Others more sad and phlegmatick than he Guess'd it the Toning of the Tenebrae. **1753** CHALLONER *Cath. Chr. Instr.* 219 Called the Tenebræ Office. **1864** J. H. NEWMAN *Apol.* i. (1904) 21/1 We attended the Tenebræ, at the Sestine, for the sake of the Miserere.

†**Te·nebrate,** *ppl. a. Obs. rare.* [ad. L. *tenebrāt-us*, pa. pple. of *tenebrāre* to darken, f. *tenebræ* darkness.] Darkened, dark. So **Tenebra·tion**, *rare*⁻⁰ [ad. L. *tenebrātiōn-em*: see -ATION], darkening, obscuration.

**1492** RYMAN *Poems* lxxxv. 3 in *Herrig's Archiv* LXXXIX. 255 The orient Phebus And the tenebrat nyght In nature be full different. **1862** A. J. COOLEY *Dict.*, Tenebration.

†**Te·nebres.** *Obs.* Forms: *α.* 5–9 tenebres; in sing. form 5 tenebre, 6 teneber, tenabur. *β.* 5 teneblus, 5–6 tenables; in sing. 6 teneble, -byll, tenable. [a. F. *ténèbres* (11th c., in sense 1), ad. L. *tenebræ, -ās*, darkness. The *β*-forms were corruptions, confusing the word with *tenable.*]

**1.** Darkness, obscurity.

*α.* **1413** *Pilgr. Sowle* (Caxton 1483) III. iii. 51 Enuy is the doughter of the grete tenebre. **1483** CAXTON *Gold. Leg.* 420 b/1 Thou shalte deye here in tenebres or derkenesse. **1483** — *G. de la Tour* I vj b, For grete pyte..to see them goo and falle in the tenebres of helle. **1490** — *Eneydos* ii. 14 Under the tenebres and derkenes, departed Eneas. **1656** BLOUNT *Glossogr.*, *Tenebres*.., darkness, obscurity.

*β.* **1530** PALSGR. 184 *Les tenebres*..a sodayne darkenesse or tenables,..or want of lyght in the night season.

**2.** = TENEBRÆ.

**1539** *Bk. Ceremonies* in Strype *Eccl. Mem.* (1721) I. App. cix. 292 The same service is called tenebres. **1658** PHILLIPS, *Tenebres.* **1703** in *Cath. Rec. Soc. Publ.* VII. 146 Mr Nelson ..was wth him at ye Tenebres at St Tho⁸. **1801** *Lusignan* IV. 138 [He] arrived there at the hour of the tenebres.

*β. a* **1450** MYRC *Festial* 117 Hyt ys called wyth you teneblus; but holy chyrch callyþe hit tenebras, þat is to say, derkenes.

**b.** *attrib.* in sing. form tenebre, teneber (but the former may be the L. *tenebræ*), as *tenebre candle, lesson, matins, service, Tenebre Wednesday.*

**1477–9** *Rec. St. Mary at Hill* 91 Paid to Roger Middilton, wex Chaundeler, for..tapris, prickettes and tenebre candill, for euery lb, ob—xj s. ix d. **1525** in Nichols *Churchw. Acc.* (1797) 273 For makyng of the paskall, wt the tenabur candell. **1529** MORE *Dyaloge* I. xviii. Wks. 143/2 In the tenebre lessons leueth her candel burning styll. **1530** PALSGR. 811/2 On Tenebre wednysdaye, *le mercredy des Tenebres.* *a* **1548** HALL *Chron., Hen. VIII* 199 b, Which Richard..was boyled in Smythfelde the Teneber wednisday followyng.

*β.* **1530** PALSGR. 280/1 Teneble wednisday,.. *mercredy saint.* **1554** *Rec. St. Mary at Hill* 397 Lyghtes that was burned of tenebyll weddyns day. **15..** in *Brand's Pop. Antiq.* (1849) I. 48 Tenable candylls for the Judas. **1588** PARKE tr. *Mendoza's Hist. China* 151 [He] arriued at the mouth of the riuer Pagansinan vpon tenable wednesday.

**Tene·bricose,** *a. rare.* [ad. L. *tenebricōs-us*, f. *tenebric-us* dark, gloomy: see -OSE.] Full of darkness; dark, obscure; gloomy.

**1730–6** in BAILEY (folio). **1817** T. L. PEACOCK *Melincourt* xxxi, He..has taken a very opaque and tenebricose view of how much of the spheroidical perception belongs to the object.

**Tenebrific** (tenĭbri·fik), *a.* [f. (? mod.L. *tenebrific-us*, f.) L. *tenebræ* darkness: see -FIC.] Causing or producing darkness; obscuring. (In quot. 1785 loosely for 'dark, gloomy'.)

*Tenebrific stars* or *constellations*; see TENEBRIFICOUS.

1785 BURNS *Ep. to Davie* x, It lightens, it brightens, The tenebrific scene. 1825 CARLYLE *Schiller* III. (1873) 99 Its interpreters with us have been like 'tenebrific stars'. 1827 — *Misc. Ess., St. Germ. Lit.* (1840) I. 92 These are its 'tenebrific constellation', from which it 'doth ray out darkness' over the earth. 1848 LOWELL *Biglow P.* Poems 1890 II. 113 Grammar, a topic rendered only more tenebrific by the labors of his successors. 1858 CARLYLE *Fredk. Gt.* IV. i. I. 383 Books done by pedants and tenebrific persons under the name of men. 1868 BROWNING *Ring & Bk.* III. 789 Now begins The tenebrific passage of the tale.

So **Tenebri·ficate** *v. rare, trans.* to darken, obfuscate; † **Tenebri·ficous** *a. Obs.*, tenebrific.

*c* 1743 in *Mem. Eliz. Carter* (1808) II. 147 The complete science of circumlocution, and the whole art of confounding, perplexing, puzzling, and *tenebrificating a subject. 16.. W. RAMSEY (quoted in *Spectator*: see next quot.), There are *tenebrificous and dark stars, by whose influence night is brought on, and which do ray out darkness and obscurity upon the earth as the sun does light. 1714 *Spect.* No. 582 ¶ 5, I could mention several Authors who are tenebrificous Stars of the first Magnitude. 1852 K. H. DIGBY *Compitum* VI. 8.

‖ **Tenebrio** (tĕne·briǫ). Also 7 **tenebrion.** [L. *tenebrio* one who lurks in the dark, f. *tenebræ* darkness; F. *ténébrion* (Rabelais, 16th c.).]

†**1.** One who lurks in the dark; a night-prowler; also, a night-spirit, a nocturnal visitant. *Obs. rare.*

1656 BLOUNT *Glossogr.*, *Tenebrion*, one that will not be seen by day, a lurker, a night-thief; also a night-spirit, a hobgoblin. *a* 1693 *Urquhart's Rabelais* III. xxiv, The approach of the Suns radiant Beams expelleth Goblins, Bugbears,.. Night-walking Spirits, and Tenebrions. *a* 1734 NORTH *Exam.* I. i. § 7 (1740), The very rankest of [the Hackney Libellers], which .. came forth, like Nocturnal Tenebrios, from the dark and dirty Recesses of the Party.

**2.** *Entom.* The typical genus of the family *Tenebrionidæ* of heteromerous beetles, which live in dark places on decaying matter and excrement (hence known as stinking beetles). It includes the two meal-worms, *Tenebrio molitor* and *T. obscurus*, and numerous species that live in decayed trees.

1753 CHAMBERS *Cycl. Supp.* App., *Tenebrio*... Mouffet has called it the *blatta fœtida*. 1811 PINKERTON *Voy.* X. 190 The women of Arabia and Turkey make use of another tenebrio, which is found among the filth of gardens. 1833 A. CRICHTON *Hist. Arabia* II. ix. 462.

**Tenebrious** (tĕne·briəs), *a.* [app. altered form of TENEBROUS: not on L. analogies.] Of or pertaining to darkness; of dark nature; = TENEBROUS.

1594 *Selimus* A iv b, The caue tenebrious, and damned spirits holt. 1624 HEYWOOD *Gunaik.* IX. 459 A place so palpably tenebrious, into which the eyes of Heauen cannot pierce and see me. 1742 YOUNG *Nt. Th.* IX. 963 Were Moon, and Stars, for Villains only made? To guide, yet screen them, with tenebrious Light? 1820 FOSTER *Ess. Evils Pop. Ignorance* 216 All this therefore passes before him with a tenebrious glimmer, and is gone. 1907 *Speaker* 19 Jan. 471/1 Thoughts tenebrious and impassioned.

Hence **Tene·briously** *adv.*, darkly.

1861 J. THOMSON *Ladies of Death* xv, Thy lidless eyes tenebriously bright.

**Tenebrity** (tĕne·brĭti). [f. as next + -ITY.] The quality of being dark; darkness, material or mental.

1792 A. YOUNG *Trav. France* 147 With all these shades of darkness, these clouds of tenebrity, this universal mass of ignorance.

† **Te·nebrize,** *v. Obs.* [f. L. *tenebræ* darkness + -IZE.] *intr.* To pass one's time in darkness.

*a* 1657 R. LOVEDAY *Lett.* (1663) 68 So long as I tenebrize it here in this blind corner; where I almost live like a flye in winter.

**Tenebrose** (te·nĭbrōus), *a.* [ad. L. *tenebrōsus* dark, f. *tenebræ* darkness: see -OSE.] Dark.

1490 CAXTON *Eneydos* xv. 53 The sprynge of the daye.. hadde putte awaye the nyghte tenebrose. 1801 *Lusignan* IV. 215 The tenebrose gloom of the place. 1830 W. PHILLIPS *Mt. Sinai* II. 274 At night's meridian tenebrose.

**b.** *fig.* Mentally or morally dark; gloomy; obscure in meaning.

1677 GALE *Crt. Gentiles* II. III. 208 Those times were very tenebrose. 1825 *New Monthly Mag.* XIII. 450 All this was wormwood in the teeth of the tenebrose Visigoth of the middle ages. 1839 *Blackw. Mag.* XLV. 533 That most tenebrose of all poets, Fulke Greville, Lord Brooke.

**Tenebrosity** (tenĭbrǫ·sĭti). [a. F. *ténébrosité* (14th c. in Godef.), f. L. *tenebrōs-us*: see prec. and -ITY.] Darkness; obscurity.

1490 CAXTON *Eneydos* i. 13 The thicke tenebrosite of the blacke smoke. 1603 HOLLAND *Plutarch's Mor.* 1080 That tenebrosity or darknesse is directly opposite unto light and cleerenesse. 1656 in BLOUNT *Glossogr.*

**Tenebrous** (te·nĭbrəs), *a.* (*sb.*) [a. OF. *tenebrus* (11th c.), mod.F. *ténébreux*, Pr. *tenebros*, Sp., It. *tenebroso*, ad. L. *tenebrōs-us* TENEBROSE.]

**1.** Full of darkness, dark.

*c* 1420 ? LYDG. *Assembly of Gods* 1169 Tyll Cerberus Had hem beshut withyn hys gates tenebrus. *c* 1489 CAXTON *Blanchardyn* xxxii. 121 A tenebrouse & derke dongeon. *c* 1530 LD. BERNERS *Arth. Lyt. Bryt.* (1814) 204 The aduentures of the Tenebrous, or Darke Tower. 1608 R. JOHNSON *Seven Champions* II. T iv, Therewith drewe on the darke and tenebrous night. 1725 *Bradley's Fam. Dict.* s.v. *Vertigo*, The other they call Scotomia, or Tenebrous Vertigo, when the Eyes are darkned and, as it were, cover'd with a Cloud. 1847 LONGF. *Ev.* II. ii. 29 Over their heads the towering and tenebrous boughs of the cypress Met in a dusky arch.

**b.** *fig.* Obscure, gloomy.

1599 NASHE *Lenten Stuffe* Wks. (Grosart) V. 220 To.. run astray..raking out of the dust-heape or charnell house of tenebrous eld, the rottenest relique of the monuments. *a* 1693 *Urquhart's Rabelais* III. xvii. 137 Heraclitus, the grand Scotist, and tenebrous darksome Philosopher. 1823 *New Monthly Mag.* VIII. 13 The most tenebrous holes and corners of their author's obscurity. 1849 *Blackw. Mag.* LXV. 307 Even in that tenebrous philosophy which he has imported..he is very much at fault.

†**2.** as *sb.* Darkness. *Obs. rare*⁻¹.

*c* 1450 LOVELICH *Grail* lvi. 418 At ȝoure Castel there is Swich tenebrowse, that No man there Other May se.

Hence **Te·nebrousness** (*rare*⁻⁰), darkness. 1727 in BAILEY vol. II.

† **Tenedish.** *Obs.* See quot.

1688 R. HOLME *Armoury* III. 152/2 A Tenedish, which is a piece of Lead made like a Muscle shell, in which the black (called Painter) is kept moist to work withal. [? Some error: *Tin-dish* and *teint-dish* have been conjectured. See *N. & Q.* 11th Ser. II. 394.]

**Tenel,** obs. f. TEANEL, a basket.

[**Tenel, -ing,** in *E. E. Allit. P.*, etc.: see TEVEL.]

† **Tene·llous,** *a. Obs. rare*⁻¹. [f. L. *tenell-us*, dim. of *tener* tender + -OUS.] Somewhat tender.

1651 BIGGS *New Disp.* § 285 How much of more tenellous meats is swallowed in a surfet.

**Tenement** (te·nĭmĕnt). Also 5 tenne-, 6 tennand-, tena-. [a. AF., = OF. *tenement* (12th c. in Godef.), ad. med.L. *tenement-um* (1081 in Muratori *Antiquitates* IX. (1776) 660), also *teni-, tena-, teneamentum* (12th c. in Du Cange), f. L. *tenēre* to hold + *-mentum*, -MENT.]

†**1.** The fact of holding as a possession; tenure. *Free tenement* = FRANK-TENEMENT, FREEHOLD.

As by the theory of English Law all land is held immediately or ultimately of the sovereign, 'tenement' embraced all forms of proprietorship or occupation of real property.

*a* 1325 *MS. Rawl. B. 520* lf. 41 Þoru suuche dede sokage is ibore out in to fre tenement. *c* 1330 R. BRUNNE *Chron.* (1810) 34 To do doun Edwy at a parlement, & tille his broþer Edgare gyf þe tenement. *Ibid.* 83 William passid þe se, þer of he mad þe skrite, Of France to hold þat fe of oþer tenement alle quite. *Ibid.* 255 Depriued þei our kyng of alle þe tenement Of londes of Gascoyn. 1651 G. W. tr. *Cowel's Inst.* 79 Free Tenement or free-hold is, where Lands and Tenements are held only for life of the Tenant.

**2.** Land or real property which is held of another by any tenure; a holding.

*Tenement at will*, a tenement held at the will of the superior; also *fig.*

[1315 *Rolls of Parlt.* I. 349/2 Johan de Eston demaunda ces Tenementz,..come son dreit.] *c* 1330 R. BRUNNE *Chron.* (1810) 48 If he saued to his heyers oiþer lond or tenement. *c* 1460 FORTESCUE *Abs. & Lim. Mon.* iii. (1885) 114 Somme of thaim þat were wont to pay to his lorde for his tenement, wich he hiryth by the yere, a scute. *c* 1489 CAXTON *Blanchardyn* xvi. 52, I shal..make hym pryuated from all his tenementes that he holdeth of me. 1593 SHAKS. *Rich. II*, II. i. 60 This deere-deere Land,..Is now Leas'd out..Like to a Tenement or pelting Farme. 1700 TYRRELL *Hist. Eng.* II. 812 The Tenement (i. e. the Real Estate) of the Deceased. 1766 BLACKSTONE *Comm.* II. ii. 16 *Tenement* is a word of still greater extent [than land], and though in it's vulgar acceptation it is only applied to houses and other buildings, yet in it's original, proper, and legal sense, it signifies every thing that may be *holden*, provided it be of a permanent nature; whether it be of a substantial and sensible, or of an unsubstantial ideal kind. 1822 WORDSW. *Scenery of Lakes* ii. (1823) 44 The multitude of tenements (I..mean..small divisions of land, which belonged formerly each to a several proprietor, and for which separate fines are paid to the manorial lord at this day).

**b.** *pl.* 'The technical expression for freehold interests in things immovable considered as subjects of property, they being not "owned" but "holden"' (Digby *Real Property* ii. § 2); *esp.* in *lands and tenements*, i. e. lands and all other freehold interests.

In the common modern usage of English lawyers leaseholds are included, though some authorities think this incorrect, for the reason that, being (in England) *personal property*, they are not the subject of tenure in the strict sense.

[1292 BRITTON I. xix. § 4 Et ausi des terres et des tenementz alienez par felouns.] *a* 1325 *MS. Rawl. B. 520* lf. 29 b, No religious or ani oþer ani londes ore tenemens buche ne sulle..on ani maner..ware þoru thulke londes or tenemens in ani manere miȝte comen in to dede hond. 1387 TREVISA *Higden* (Rolls) VIII. 265 Kyng Edward and þe lordes made a statute aȝenst maynmort, so þat after þat tyme no man schulde ȝeve..ne by oþere title assigne londes, tenementis ne oþer rentes to men of religioun wiþouten þe kynges leve. 1494 FABYAN *Chron.* VII. 390 Statutes made to refourme suche persones as mysused the landes and tenementes, commynge to theym by reason of the dower, or landes of theyr wyues. 1529 CROMWELL *Will* in Merriman *Life & Lett.* (1902) I. 56, I will myn executours undernamed ..shall purchase londes tenementes and hereditamentes to the clere yerelye value of xxxiij[li] vj[s] viij[d]. 1530 PALSGR. 280/1 Tenementes, *reuenues*. 1542 *Richmond Wills* (Surtees) 33 The one halff off all the saide lands, tennandments, rents and all other servyces, with revertions and appertenawnces belonging ye same. 1568 GRAFTON *Chron.* II. 142 The Shirifes of London at those dayes might lawfully enter into the towne of Westminster, and all other Tenementes, that the Abbot had within Middlesex. 1580 LUPTON *Sivqila* 141 All deedes and writings of any lands, tenements, houses, woods, or such like, that are solde. 1622 CALLIS *Stat. Sewers* (1647) 108 The word *Tenements* is of larger extent then Lands; for it containeth all which the word *Lands* doth, and all things else which lyeth in Tenure. 1691 WOOD *Ath. Oxon.* I. 322 He [was] then possessed of several lands and tenements in Taunton. 1818 CRUISE *Digest* (ed. 2) VI. 219 The words lands, tenements, and hereditaments, will pass every species of property. 1848 WILLIAMS *Law Personal Property* (1870) 1 In ancient times property was divided into *lands, tenements and hereditaments* on the one hand, and *goods and chattels* on the other. 1876 DIGBY *Real Prop.* ii. § 2. 72 *note.*

**3.** *gen.* A building or house to dwell in; a dwelling-place, a habitation, residence, abode.

*c* 1425 *Brut* 367 So was he brouȝt to þe Whit-Freris yn Flet-strete; and þere was do and made a ryal & solempne tenement for hym. 1477–9 *Rec. St. Mary at Hill* 84 For ij ml tiles spent in reparacion of the tenement of William Blase and of othir tenementes, xs viij d. 1513 DOUGLAS *Æneis* XIII. x. 9 Syne Troianis foundis tenementis for thame self. 1588 *Knaresborough Wills* (Surtees) I. 159 The lease ..in the tenement where I now dwell. 1607 NORDEN *Surv. Dial.* III. 106 Whether are there within this Mannor, any new erected Tenements or Cotages, barnes, Walls. 1779 FORREST *Voy. N. Guinea* 95 The tenement contains many families, who live in cabins on each side of a wide common hall, that goes through the middle of it. 1833 HT. MARTINEAU *Briery Creek* iii, The resources which they wasted would have..turned their habitation of logs into a respectable brick tenement. 1844 WILLIAMS *Real Prop.* (1875) 13 The word *tenement* is often used in law, as in ordinary language, to signify a house. 1848 DICKENS *Dombey* vii, The dingy tenement inhabited by Miss Tox was her own.

**b.** *transf.* and *fig.* An abode; a dwelling-place, esp. applied to the body as the abode of the soul; also, the abode of any animal.

1592 G. HARVEY *Four Lett.* iii. Wks. (Grosart) I. 195 The poore tennement of his Purse..hath bene the Diuels Dauncing schoole, anie time this halfe yeare. 1604 T. WRIGHT *Passions* IV. ii. 136 Doubt not but selfe-loue and vanitie possesse the best tenement of his heart. 1635 QUARLES *Embl.* III. i. 40 My weary soul, that long hath been An inmate in this tenement of sin. *a* 1639 T. CAREW *Epit. Lady M. Villiers* 2 The purest Soule that e'er was sent Into a clayie tenement. *a* 1668 DAVENANT *Jeffereidos* II. Wks. (1673) 226 Snaile.. with all his Tenement on 's back. 1774 GOLDSM. *Nat. Hist.* (1776) III. 371 Their nest is generally the original tenement of the squirrel. 1847 C. BRONTË *J. Eyre* xxi, That spirit—now struggling to quit its material tenement.

**4.** *spec.* **a.** In England, A portion of a house, tenanted as a separate dwelling; a flat; a suite of apartments, or even a single room so let or occupied.

'In modern Eng. practice, a *tenement* is anything that can be separately held, including therefore a flat, etc.' (Sir F. Pollock).

1593 NASHE *Christ's T.* 53 b, Almes-houses..let out in Tenements. 1625 (May 2) *Procl.* 1 *Chas. I* (Concerning Buildings), That no person..within the City of London..doe diuide any dwelling House..into or for any more Tenements or dwellings, then are at this present..vsed within the same. 1817 (April) D. WEBSTER *Speech in Goodrich Case* U. S. (Cent. Dict.), The two tenements, it was true, were under the same roof; but they were not on that account the same tenements. 1898 *Daily News* 14 Nov. 5/1 The Council never have any unlet, except a few four-room tenements for which there is less demand than for those with only two or three rooms. 1905 *Ibid.* 28 Sept. 9 Mr. J. Keir Hardie, M.P., claimed as occupier of a tenement at Nevill's-court.

**b.** In Scotland, more particularly applied to a large house (i. e. edifice under one roof) constructed or adapted to be let in portions to a number of tenants, each portion so separately occupied being considered and called a 'house'. Called also *tenement of houses, land of houses* (= *tenement house* in 5).

Thus a 'house' in England may form one 'tenement', or contain a number of 'tenements' (and is then a 'tenement house': see 5); in Scotland, a 'tenement' may form one 'house', or contain a number of 'houses' or dwellings.

1693 STAIR *Inst. Law Scot.* II. vii. § 6 When divers Owners have parts of the same Tenement, it cannot be said to be a perfect division, because the Roof remaineth Roof to both, and the ground supporteth both. 1808 JAMIESON, *Tenement* ..often denoting a building which includes several separate dwellings; as *a tenement of houses*. 1825 R. CHAMBERS *Tradit. Edinb.* 172 How the great of the land could live in the fourth and fifth flats of wooden tenements, the various apartments of which, as occupied at present by humble mechanics, seem confined and inconvenient to the last degree. 1841 in Rankine *Treat. Ownership Lands Scot.* xxxiii. (1879) 509 Houses so often found in Scotland, called technically 'lands', or 'tenements of land'—terms which have been defined as applicable to 'a single or individual building, although containing several dwelling-houses, with, it may be, separate means of access, but under the same roof and enclosed by the same gables or walls'. 1910 *Scotsman* 8 Oct. 3/3 For Sale by Public Roup..(1) Six self-contained Dwelling Houses...(2) House, No. 27 St. Bernard's Crescent...(3) Tenement, No. 12 St. Bernard's Crescent.

**c.** The offset at the back of a house. (Devon and Cornw.); cf. OUTSHOT 1, quots. 1817, 1820.

**5.** *attrib.* and *Comb.*: **tenement house** (orig. U. S.), a house or edifice let out in flats or sets of apartments for separate tenants; **tenement householder**, a tenant in a tenement house; † **tenement man**, an owner of tenements, a landlord.

1879 H. GEORGE *Progr. & Pov.* IX. iii. (1881) 405 To substitute for the *tenement house, homes surrounded by gardens. 1884 *Q. Rev.* Jan. 150 Tenement-houses, *i.e.* houses let to more than one family, are placed under still stricter conditions. 1894 *Daily News* 7 June 7/3 Mr. Gibb led the way in placing all lodgers who lived in a house in which no landlord resided, on the householders' list... *Tenement householders have ever since been regarded not as lodgers but as householders. *c* 1500 *Merch. & Son* 7 in Hazl. *E. P. P.* I. 133 He was a grete *tenement man, and ryche of londe and lede.

**Teneme·ntal,** *a.* [f. med.L. *tenement-um* TENEMENT + -AL.] Of, pertaining to, or of the nature of a tenement; let out to tenants.

1766 BLACKSTONE *Comm.* II. vi. 90 The other, or tenemental, lands they distributed among their tenants. 1875 MAINE *Hist. Inst.* v. 130 The Manor with its Tenemental lands held by the free tenants of the Lord. 1887 *Edin. Rev.* Jan. 10 In the fifteenth century the land was divided into the private demesne of the lord of the manor and the tenemental land of the association.

**Tenementary,** *a.* [f. as prec. + -ARY[1]: cf. med.L. *tenementāri-us.*] **a.** Leased to tenants. **b.** Consisting of tenements or dwelling-houses. See also FRANK-TENEMENTARY.

*a* **1641** SPELMAN *Feuds & Tenures* vii, Such were the Ceorls among the Saxons; but of two sorts, one that hired the Lord's Outland or Tenementary Land (called also the Folcland) like our Farmers. **1701** *Cowell's Interpr.* s. v., The Saxon Thanes who possess'd Bocland, or Hereditary free Estates, divided them into..Inland and Outland...The Outland was granted out to Tenants under Arbitrary Rents and Services, and therefore call'd Tenementary Land, the Tenants Land, or the Tenancy. **1872** *B'ham Daily Post* 28 Feb. 7/2 Assisting her mother who was the owner of some small tenementary property at Saltley. **1905** *Daily Chron.* 31 Jan. 3/5 By doing this he [a landlord who removes from one of his tenement houses to another] converts the lodgers into tenementary occupiers and the tenementary occupiers into lodgers, the result being that all of them lose their votes ..through no fault of their own.

**Te·nemented,** *ppl. a.* [f. TENEMENT + -ED[1].] Let in tenements or separate dwellings: said of a building, house, or house property.

**1883** *Pall Mall G.* 17 Feb. 4/1 They have..crowded into tenemented property in the immediate neighbourhood. **1888** *Ibid.* 24 Nov. 5 Most of the population of Glasgow living in the rooms of tenemented buildings. **1890** *Daily News* 18 July 2/4 The Chancellor of the Exchequer..stated that tenemented houses of less than 20*l.* per annum were exempt from house duty whether they had two front doors or not, so long as they were intended to be dwelling-houses within seven and sixpence per week.

**Te·nementer.** [f. as prec. + -ER[1]. Cf. med. L. *tenementātor* (1214 in Du Cange).] The holder of a tenement; a lease-holder or tenant. *Frank-tenementer* = FREEHOLDER.

**1574** *Reg. Privy Council Scot.* II. 353 Alexander Dunbar frank tenementar of Cumknok. **1588** in *Scott. N. & Q.* Mar. (1890) 184 Robert Erskine, Elder, Frank tenementer of Dun, my grandschir. **1875** A. SMITH *Hist. Aberdeen.* II. 724 The holders of the Rawes appear to have been only tenementers.

‖ **Tenendas** (tĭne·ndæs). *Sc. Law.* [L. acc. pl. fem. of gerundive of *tenēre* to hold = '(the lands) to be held'.] See quot. 1710.

**1681** STAIR *Inst. Law Scot.* xiii. § 15. 236 In all Charters, both by King and Subjects, the Clause *Tenendas* useth to be insert. **1710** *Dict. Feudal Law, Tenendas,* is that Clause of a Charter, which expresses what way and manner the Lands are to be holden of the Superior. **1765–8** ERSKINE *Inst. Law Scot.* II. iii. § 24 The next clause in a charter is the *Tenendas,* so called from the first words, *Tenend. prædictas terras.* **1815** R. BELL *Treat. Conveyance* ii. 16 The charter, as an original right, necessarily contains the *tenendas,* by which the nature of the holding is expressed.

‖ **Tenendum** (tĭne·ndɒ̆m). *Eng. Law.* [L., = 'to be held', neut. gerundive of *tenēre* to hold.] That part of a deed which defines the tenure by which the things granted are to be held (cf. HABENDUM).

**1628** COKE *On Litt.* 6 There haue beene eight formall or orderly parts of a deede of feoffment, viz. 1. the premisses of the deed implied by Littleton. 2. the habendum...3. the tenendum...4. the Reddendum. 5. the clause of warrantie [etc.]. **1766** BLACKSTONE *Comm.* II. xx. 298 Next come the *habendum* and *tenendum*...The *tenendum* 'and to hold', is now of very little use, and is only kept in by custom. It was sometimes formerly used to signify the tenure by which the estate granted was to be holden. **1787** C. BUTLER *Coke On Litt.* 108a *note,* Those grants from the crown which in the *tenendum* are expressed to be *ut de honore et non in capite.* **1862** WASHBURN *Amer. Law Real Prop.* (1864) II. 612 (Funk) The *tenendum,* limiting and defining the tenure by which the lands are to be held, and once an important clause in the deed, is useless in this country. **1884** ELPHINSTONE *Conveyancing* 100 The tenendum was of use before the passing of the Statute of *Quia Emptores* to state whether the purchaser was to hold of the vendor or of his lord; but it is now useless.

† **Tenent,** *sb. Obs.* Also 7 tenant. [a. L. *tenent* 'they hold', 3rd pers. pl. pres. indic. of *tenēre* to hold.] = TENET.

Etymologically a *tenet* ought to be the opinion of one, what *he holds,* a *tenent* the opinion of a number, what *they hold;* but this distinction, if ever observed in using the words as English, was soon lost. *Tenent* was apparently more used in the 17th c. than *tenet,* but became obs. *c* 1725.

**1551** ABP. BROWNE (of Armagh) *Serm.* in *Phenix* (1721) I. 134 They shall be your greatest enemies, speaking against the Tenents of Rome, and yet be set on by Rome. **1618** HALES *Gold. Rem.* II. (1673) 59 Episcopius..required that it might be lawful for them to set down their own Tenents. **1621** BURTON *Anat. Mel.* II. ii. III. (1651) 254 But..to grant this their tenent of the earths motion. **1643** FULLER *Serm.* 27 Mar. 18 Being so fickle in their Tenents. **1646** SIR T. BROWNE (*title*) Pseudodoxia Epidemica, or Enquiries into very many received tenents, and commonly presumed Truths. **1722** WOLLASTON *Relig. Nat.* v. 111 People of differing religions judge and condemn each other by their own tenents.

**Tenent** (te·nĕnt), *a. rare*[−1]. [ad. L. *tenēnt-em* holding, pr. pple. of *tenēre* to hold.] Holding.

**1861** T. WEST in *Trans. Linn. Soc.* (1862) XXIII. 408 That these [hair-like appendages] are the immediate agents in holding is now admitted by almost all; it will be convenient to term them 'tenent hairs', in allusion to their office.

**Tenent, -ry,** obs. ff. TENON, TENANTRY.

**Tener,** obs. f. TEENER, TENNER, TENOR, TENURE.

**Teneral** (te·nĕrăl), *a. Entom.* [f. L. *tener* tender + -AL.] Said of the imperfect imago of a neuropterous insect, when it has just emerged from the pupa state, and is still soft. In quot. *fig.*

**1891** in *Cent. Dict.* **1902** *Sat. Rev.* 1 Mar. 256 The Liberal League has now emerged in triumph, though at present perhaps in a teneral state, not yet endowed with its full brilliancy of colour.

† **Tene·ritude.** *Obs. rare*[−1]. [ad. L. *teneritūdo,* f. *tener* tender.] Tenderness, softness. So † **Tene·rity** *Obs.* [ad. L. *teneritās*], in same sense; † **Te·nerous** *a Obs.* [f. L. *tener* + -OUS], tender.

*c* **1440** *Pallad. on Husb.* VI. 157 So wol their fatnesse and *teneritude With hem be stille. **1623** COCKERAM, **Teneritie,* softnesse, tendernesse. **1642** H. MORE *Song of Soul* II. iii. III. lviii, Faithfulnesse, heart-struck teneritie; These be the lovely playmates of pure veritie. **1706** PHILLIPS (ed. Kersey), *Tenerity,* a Philosophical Word for Tenderness; as 'The tenerity of Young Plants'. **1597** A. M. tr. *Guillemeau's Fr. Chirurg.* 34/1 Engendring a *tenerouse fleshe, which by little and little, hardeneth.

‖ **Tenesmus** (tĭne·zmɒ̆s). *Path.* Also 6–8 **tenasmus**; β. (from Fr.) 6–7 **tenasm(e,** 7 **tinesm.** [med.L. *tēnesmus, tēnasmus* (Du Cange), = L. *tēnesmos* (Pliny), a. Gr. τεινεσμός, τηνεσμός straining, f. τείνειν to stretch, strain. So F. *ténesme* (16th c.).] A continual inclination to void the contents of the bowels or bladder, accompanied by straining, but with little or no discharge.

**1527** ANDREW *Brunswyke's Distyll. Waters* D ij b, Payne of the gutte of the fondament named tenasmus, that is whan a man thynketh that he wolde go to stole, but he can do nothyng. **1578** LYTE *Dodoens* II. xxviii. 182 Good for them that haue the laske, the blouddie flixe and Tenasme. **1601** HOLLAND *Pliny* (1634) II. 443 The broth of fish..dispatcheth those sharp and fretting humors which are the cause of the Tinesm. **1732** ARBUTHNOT *Rules of Diet* in *Aliments,* etc. 423 Attended with a Tenesmus. **1748** *Anson's Voy.* I. iv. 39 Afflicted with fluxes and tenasmus's. **1754–64** SMELLIE *Midwif.* I. 120 Something like a tenesmus at the *os uteri.* **1876** BRISTOWE *The. & Pract. Med.* (1878) 684.

*fig.* **1642** MILTON *Apol. Smect.* vi. Wks. 1851 III. 294 This tetter of Pedagoguisme that bespreads him with such a tenasmus of originating. **1669** *Address Hopeful Yng. Gentry Eng.* 48 That exulcerate feebleness of reason which by an impotent tenesmus betrays the infirmities of those we almost idoliz'd to scorn and hatred.

Hence **Tene·smic** *a.*, of, pertaining to, or of the nature of tenesmus. **1891** in *Cent. Dict.*

**Tenet** (te·nĕt, †tī·nĕt). [a. L. *tenet* 'he holds', 3 sing. of *tenēre* to hold. See also TENENT *sb.*

Prob. adopted from mod. Latin writings, in which it introduced the opinion or doctrine that a person, church, or sect holds. Cf. similar use of *habitat, incipit, explicit.*]

A doctrine, dogma, principle, or opinion, in religion, philosophy, politics, or the like, held by a school, sect, party, or person.

*a* **1619** FOTHERBY *Atheom.* II. iv. § 3 (1622) 230 And this ..is not onely his owne particular opinion..; but the generall Tenet, of all the Philosophers. *a* **1641** BP. MOUNTAGU *Acts & Mon.* (1642) Summary 3/2 The Church of Englands Tenet, that no salvation, but by Christ alone. **1706** PHILLIPS (ed. Kersey), *Tenet,* or *Tenent,* a Doctrine, or Opinion. **1791** BURKE *App. Whigs* Wks. VI. 210 The practical consequences of any political tenet go a great way in deciding upon its value. **1858** BUCKLE *Civiliz.* (1869) II. i. 51 The liberality of every sect depends, not at all on its avowed tenets but on the circumstances in which it is placed.

**b.** More trivially: Any opinion held.

**1630** BRATHWAIT *Eng. Gentlem.* (1641) 288 My tenet is, 'one cannot truely love, and not be wise'. **1656** EARL MONM. tr. *Boccalini's Advts. fr. Parnass.* I. lxxvii. (1674) 102 You have infinitely verified the Tenet which all the Literati have of you. **1742** *Lond. & Country Brew.* I. (ed. 4) 42 Vouching it to be a true Tenet, that, if Hops are boiled above thirty Minutes, the Wort will have some or more of their worser Quality. *c* **1765** GRAY *Satire* 28 The Master of Benet Is of the like tenet.

**Tenetz, teneys,** obs. forms of TENNIS.

**Teneur,** obs. form of TENOR.

**Tenfold** (te·nfō̆ʊld), *a., adv.* [OE. *tienfeald.*]

**A.** *adj.* **1.** Ten times as great or as much; ten times increased or intensified; also *indefinitely,* many times as great.

*c* **1200** *Trin. Coll. Hom.* 135 His michelnesse was unhiled on ten fold wise and mo. **1557** RECORDE *Whetst.* B ij, *Decupla*..10 to 1: 20 to 2...Tennefolde. **1588** SHAKS. *Tit. A.* III. ii. 6 Thy Neece and I..cannot passionate our tenfold griefe, With foulded Armes. **1625** N. CARPENTER *Geog. Del.* II. ix. (1635) 149 The Aire..being by a Tenne-fold proportion thinner then the Water. **1849** MACAULAY *Hist. Eng.* iii. I. 412 His mind reacted with tenfold force on the spirit of the age.

**b.** As predicate, passing into substantive use; cf. HUNDREDFOLD C.

**1769** HOME *Fatal Discov.* IV, Euran! whate'er the lavish Pict has promis'd To tempt thee to betray thy master's house, Tenfold I'll give thee to preserve thy faith. **1832** SOUTHEY *Hist. Penins. War* III. xxxvii. 219 But the loss had been tenfold of what was there stated.

**2.** Ranged in ten folds, or ten deep. *nonce-use.*

**1807** J. BARLOW *Columb.* I. 316 Stretch'd o'er the broad-back'd hills, in long array, The tenfold Alleganies meet the day.

**B.** *adv.* Ten times (in amount or degree).

**1538** ELYOT, *Decuplo*..if it be an aduerbe, it sygnifyeth tenne times, or tenne fold. *Decuplum,* like wyse. **1606** SHAKS. *Ant. & Cl.* IV. vii. 15, I will reward thee Once for thy sprightly comfort, and ten-fold For thy good valour. **1667** MILTON *P. L.* II. 705 The grieslie terrour..So speaking and so threatning, grew ten fold More dreadful and deform. **1827** SYD. SMITH *Wks.* (1850) 485 Is not the Church of England tenfold more rich and more strong than when the separation took place? **1884** TENNYSON *Becket* I. iii, False to himself, but ten-fold false to me!

Hence **Te·nfoldness,** the condition or quality of being tenfold.

**1891** J. E. H. THOMSON *Books which influenced our Lord* III. i. 382 There is no explanation of the tenfoldness exhibited in the symbols.

**Te·nfold,** *v.* [f. prec.] *trans.* To increase ten times; *loosely,* to multiply indefinitely.

**1858** BUSHNELL *Nat. & Supernat.* xiii. (1864) 420 Transforming the world, tenfolding its forces and uses, and all that constitutes its value. **1858** — *Serm. New Life* viii. (1869) 102 The capacity of religion..may be fivefolded, tenfolded, indefinitely increased. **1902** KROPOTKIN *Mut. Aid* vi. (1904) 208 It tenfolded their forces.

**Tenful,** variant of TEENFUL *Obs.*

**Tengerite** (te·ŋərəit). *Min.* [Named after a Swede, C. Tenger, who examined it: see -ITE[1].] According to Svanberg and Tenger, a carbonate of yttrium, found as a whitish coating on gadolite.

**1868** DANA *Min.* (ed. 5) 710. **1889** *Nature* 19 Dec. 163/1 Many more [minerals], such as cyrtolite, molybdite, allanite, tengerite..have been found.

**Tenia, Tenioid,** var. TÆNIA, TÆNIOID.

**Tenible** (te·nĭb'l), *a. rare.* [f. L. type **tenibilis,* f. *ten-ēre* to hold: cf. *docible.*]

†**1.** Capable of being held; = TENABLE 2. *Obs.*

**1633** T. STAFFORD *Pac. Hib.* II. viii. (1821) 320 Corke was a weake towne and not tenible against a powerfull enemy.

**2.** Able to retain or hold in (i. e. in quot., the saliva). *rare.*

**1871** R. ELLIS *Catullus* xliii. 3 A nose among the larger, Feet not dainty,..Mouth scarce tenible [L. *nec ore sicco*], hands not wholly faultless.

**Tenis, tenise,** obs. forms of TENNIS.

**Tenker,** obs. form of TINKER.

**Tenmanland.** *Obs.* exc. *Hist.* A local name in East Anglia, in 12th and 13th c., for an aggregate of ten holdings; containing 120 acres, and so = CARUCATE. So, in same sense, **Tenmanlot** (-loth).

*c* **1225** *Ely Inqu.* in *MS. Claudius C. xi* lf. 193 (Vinogr.) *De militibus et libere tenentibus*...Jacobus le francels et Thomas de Northwaude tenent dimidium tenmanland, scilicet lxacras terre...*De Consuetudinariis et censuariis,* Alanus et Matheus..et eorum participes tenent unam tenmanland, scilicet sexies viginti acras terre. **1892** VINOGRADOFF *Villainage in Eng.* II. i. 255 In the Norfolk lands of Ely Minster we find tenmanlands of 120 acres in the possession of several copartitioners, *participes.* **1908** — *Eng. Soc. in 11th c.* II. § 1. ii, In the north [west] corner of Norfolk, in a fen-district bordering on Lincolnshire, we find in the local custom of the manor of Walpole, a division of the land according to tenmanlands or tenman-lots.

*c* **1200** *Inqu. of Walepole* in *MS. Cott. Tib. B. ii* lf. 167 b, Willelmus Franceis et Thomas de Nordwolde tenent dimidium tenmanloth, scilicet sexaginta acras...*De Consuetudinariis.* Galfridus de Cattestone et participes tenent unam tenmanloth, scilicet sexcies uiginti acras pro decem solidis. ? *a* **1244** *Anc. Deed A.* 7435 (P.R.O.), Confirmauimus thome filio Alani de Walepol..sextam partem vnius tinmanlot in villa de Walepol.

**Te·nmantale, tenmentale.** *Obs.* exc. *Hist.* Forms: 2 tien, tyen, **ten manna tale, tenmanne tale**; **the(n)manetale, temantale**; **tenemen-, teneman-,** 7 **te(n)men-,** 8– **te(n)-man-tale.** [OE. type **tien manna talu* 'numerum decem hominum', a number (tale, or reckoning) of ten men.]

**1.** According to the 'Laws of Edward the Confessor', the contemporary Yorkshire (or ? general Danelaw) name of the Anglo-Saxon TITHING, and also of the *friþborh* or FRANK-PLEDGE by which the members of a tithing were made sureties for each other.

(The only known ancient authority for this is the 'Laws of Edward the Confessor', compiled *c* 1130–35. The alleged addition to the *Treaty of Ælfred and Guðrum,* from which the term is quoted by Spelman and Du Cange, is found in no MS., and is apparently of later authorship.)

**1130–35** *Laws Edw. Conf.* c. 20 Alia est pax..scilicet sub fideiussionis stabilitate, quam Angli uocant fri[th]borgas, preter Eboracenses, qui uocant eam tyen [*v.rr.* ten, tien] manna tale, hoc est numerum x hominum. *a* **1200** HOVEDEN *Chron.* (Rolls) II. 228 (quoting prec.) Quod sit Frithborg, quod Eboracenses vocant tenementale, id est, sermo decem hominum. **1664** SPELMAN *Gloss.,* Temestale, *vel* Tenmentale, Sax. tienmantale, *Decuria, Tithinga.* **1872** E. W. ROBERTSON *Hist. Ess.* 118 A Tything, or Tenmantale, of the Hundred, in which a Decanus, annually chosen in the Hundred-court, presided in the petty court in the place of the Tungreve [*tun-gerefa*].

**2.** In parts of England under Danish influence, a name in 12th and 13th c. for the land tax levied on a carucate; the carucage.

In this sense the name was perh. connected with the *tenmanland* or *tenmanlot,* and *tale* may have had the sense 'sum, account, reckoning'.

*c* **1135** *Charter of Wm. Paganellus to Drax* (Charter Roll 4 Edw. II m. 4), Quam..defendemus contra omnes homines de murdre de Danegelde, de The[n]mantale. *a* **1154** *Cartular. Abb. de Rievalle* (Surtees) 142 Et ii solidi de Danegeld, id est The[n]manetale, quoquo anno eveniebant super illas ix carrucatas. **1166–76** *Calr. Charter Rolls* (1908) III. 342 Tenementa predicta [at Lessness, Kent] habeant et teneant libera et quieta ab omnibus geldis et danegeldis et scutagiis et murdro et latrocinio..et clausuris et hidagiis et scotagiis et querelis et s[c]yris et hundredis et tethingis et tenemannetale. **1194** HOVEDEN *Chron.* (Rolls) III. 242 Rex constituit sibi dari de unaquaque carucata terræ totius Angliæ duos solidos, quod ab antiquis nominatur Temantale. *a* **1200**

*Whitby Cartul.* (Surtees) I. 196 Quod Monasterium michi ..duos solidos annuatim persolvent, et Themantel, pro omnibus serviciis. **1747** CARTE *Hist. Eng.* I. 760 An impost, called by some writers Carucage, and Temantale, but in the Pipe-rolls termed Hidage.

**Tennand, -ant,** obs. ff. TENANT, TENON.

**Tennandment,** obs. corrupt f. TENEMENT.

**Tennantite** (te·nǟntəit). *Min.* [Named, 1819, in honour of Smithson Tennant: see -ITE[1].] A sulph-arsenide of copper and iron, closely related to tetrahedrite (Chester).

**1839** DE LA BECHE *Rep. Geol. Cornwall*, etc. xv. 590 From among them tennantite has been separated by Phillips. **1851** MANTELL *Petrifact.* ii. § 1. 78 In this case are specimens of .. variegated copper ore; Tennantite. **1900** L. FLETCHER in *Brit. Mus. Return* 156 A crystallographic and chemical research.., the result of which has been to establish the specific identity of Binnite and Tennantite.

**Tenné, tenny** (te·ni), *a.* and *sb. Her.* Also 7 tenney, 9 teany. [a. obs. F. *tenné* (16th c.), var. of *tanné*, TAWNY; cf. *tennet*, var. of *tannet* tawny cloth (14th c. in Godef.).] 'Tawny' as a heraldic colour: variously described as 'orange-brown' or 'bright chestnut'; in engraving represented by diagonal lines from sinister to dexter, crossed by others, according to some authors, vertically, according to others, horizontally.

**1562** LEIGH *Armorie* 19 Now to the sixth coloure, whiche we calle Tawney, and is blazed by thys woorde, Tenne. It is a worshipfull colour, and is of some Herhaughtes called Bruske,..it is made of two bright colours which is Redde and Yellowe. **1575** LANEHAM *Let.* (1871) 39 The Fess Tenny, which iz a cooler betokening dout & suspition. **1704** J. HARRIS *Lex. Techn.* I, *Tenny*, or *Tawney*,..is expressed in Engraving by thwart Strokes or Hatches. **1882** CUSSANS *Heraldry* 51 Tenné (bright chestnut).

**Tennement, Tennendrie,** obs. ff. TENEMENT, TENANTRY.

**Tennent,** obs. form of TENANT, TENON.

**Tenner** (te·nəɹ). *colloq.* [f. TEN + -ER[1].] A term applied to a number or amount of ten; *spec.* **a.** A ten-pound note; in U. S. a ten-dollar bill.

**1861** HUGHES *Tom Brown at Oxf.* xix, 'No money?' 'Not much; perhaps a tenner.' **1884** G. ALLEN *Philistia* III. 218, I had in my purse..five tenners—Bank of England ten-pound notes, you know. **1887** BLACK *Sabina Zembra* xxi. 208 You might make the fiver a tenner. **1893** SALTUS *Madam Sapphira* xvi, At the rate of eight dollars a column and a tenner for the 'beat'.

**b.** A period of ten years.

**1866** *Morn. Star* 19 Dec., I will tell the truth, or else I shall get a 'tenner' (ten years' penal servitude). **1904** *Daily News* 7 Nov. 9 [He] has been chief magistrate..for the past nine years uninterruptedly, and..the Corporation has just asked him to extend it and make a 'tenner' of it.

**Tenner,** obs. form of TENOR; var. TANDOUR.

**Tennes, -ice,** obs. ff. TENNIS. **Tennet,** dial. variant of TINNET. **Tenney,** obs. f. TENNÉ.

**Tennikill,** obs. Sc. form of TUNICLE.

**Tennil,** var. TEANEL *dial.*, basket.

**Tennis** (te·nis), *sb.* Forms: *α.* 4–5 tene·tz, 5 teneys, 6 ten(n)es; *β.* 5 tenyce, tenyys, 5–6 tenys, -yse, tennys, -yse, 6 tenice, tennysse, (tinnis), 6–7 tenis, -ise, tennise, -ice, (7 *Sc.* tinneis), 6– tennis. [Known *c* 1400 in form *tene·tz*, later *tenne·s*, *teney·s*, *-ys*, *-yce*, *teni·se*; in It. mentioned in the *Cronica di Firenze* of Donato Velluti (who died in 1370) as *tenes*, and said to have been introduced into Florence by French knights early in the year 1325. For ulterior history and etymology see Note below.]

**1.** A game in which a ball is struck with a racket and driven to and fro by two players in an enclosed oblong court, specially constructed for the purpose, and (in the developed form of the game) having an enclosed corridor on one of the long sides roofed over by a penthouse.

The game had originally a much simpler form, the ball being struck with the palm of the hand (hence F. *la paume*). It was also played in the open air, as still in some places in France, and down to about 1800 in England under the name *field-tennis*, of which *lawn-tennis* (sense 2) may be considered a greatly modified revival.

*c* **1400** GOWER *In Praise of Peace* 295 Of the Tenetz [*ed.* **1532** tennes] to winne or lese a chace, Mai no lif wite er that the bal be ronne. *c* **1440** *Promp. Parv.* 488/2 Teneys, pley, *teniludus* (P. *manupilatus*, *tenisia*). **1441** *Court Roll Pershore, Worc.* (Westminster Ch. Munim.), Nullus eorum .. frequentabit ludum qui vocatur the tenyse playng in communi via domini Regis nec in aliquo loco privato ibidem. *c* **1460** *Towneley Myst.* xiii. 736, I bryng the bot a balle: Haue and play the with alle, And go to the tenys [*rime* pennys]. **1463** *Mann. & Househ. Exp.* (Roxb.) 221 Pleyynd at the tennys. *a* **1470** TIPTOFT *Tulle on Friendsh.* (Caxton 1481) C iv, Lyke corage & disposicion to pleyeng atte tenyce. **1525** LD. BERNERS *Froiss.* II. xxvi. 74 Gascone and his brother yuan fell out toguyder, playeng at tennes. **1535** *Act 27 Hen. VIII*, c. 25 § 8 Any open..place for commen bowling, dysyng, carding, closhe, tenys, or other unlawfull games. **1540** MORYSINE *Vives' Introd. Wysd.* C j b, Oft tymes he commeth vp a pase, that can playe well at tennysse. **1550** CROWLEY *Last Trumpet* 562 To play tenise, or tosse the ball. **1565–73** COOPER *Thesaurus* s. v. *Bonus*, Good at tennice. **1601** HOLLAND *Pliny* (1634) I. 190 Pythus was the first plaier at tennise. **1602** SHAKS. *Ham.* II. i. 59. **1617** MINSHEU *Ductor*, *Tennis play*..aut à *tenez* Gal: i. *hould*, which word the Frenchmen, the onely tennis players, vse to speake when they strike the ball, at tennis. **1634** ROWLEY *Noble Souldier* II. ii, I ha been at Tennis, Madam, with the King. I gave him 15 and all his faults. **1679** C. HATTON in *H. Corr.* (Camden) 189 Last Wednesday his Ma[ty] play'd at tenis. **1789** MRS. PIOZZI *Journ. France* II. 26 He invited them to..play a great match at tennis. **1793** *Sporting Mag.* 29 Sept. 371 Field-tennis threatens ere long to bowl out cricket. **1865** MERIVALE *Rom. Emp.* VIII. lxiv. 116 Then he uses strong exercise for a considerable space at tennis. **1878** JULIAN MARSHALL (*title*) The Annals of Tennis.

*fig.* **1611** TOURNEUR *Ath. Trag.* II. iv, Drop out Mine eye-bals and let enuious Fortune pla At tennis with 'em. **1654** WHITLOCK *Zootomia* 463 In the Tennis of Fortune. **1899** S. K. HOCKING in *Daily News* 2 Sept. 6/3 He had a decided objection to 'playing tennis with the seventh commandment'.

**2.** Short for LAWN-TENNIS (q. v.), a game played with a ball and rackets on an unenclosed rectangular space on a smooth grass lawn or a floor of hard gravel, cement, asphalt, etc., called a court.

Introduced about 1874 (see LAWN-TENNIS); reduced to its present form in 1877.

**1888** *St. James' Gaz.* Aug., It is melancholy to see a word which has held its own for centuries gradually losing its connotation. Such a word is 'tennis', by which nine persons out of ten to-day would understand the game of recent invention played on an unconfined court. **1895** SCULLY *Kafir Stories* 80 The tennis-ground was overgrown with grass—his predecessor's family evidently had not cared about tennis.

**3.** *attrib.* and *Comb.* **a.** Of, belonging to, or used in playing tennis (sense 1), as *tennis coat*, *tennis game*; see also TENNIS-BALL, -PLAY, etc.

**1516** *Harl. MS.* 2284 lf. 21 Blew velwete for a *Tenes Cote for the king. **1552** HULOET, *Tennyse game, or playinge at tennyse, *sphæromachia*.

**b.** Of, pertaining to, used or worn in lawn-tennis, as *tennis-bag*, *-game*, *-ground*, *-hat*, *-jacket*, *-lawn*, *-racket*, *-suit*; **tennis-arm, -elbow, -knee**, an arm, elbow, or knee sprained in playing lawn-tennis; **tennis-ground**, a piece of ground laid or marked out for the game of lawn-tennis; a lawn-tennis court or set of courts. See also TENNIS-BALL, -COURT, -PLAYER.

**1897** *Outing* (U.S.) XXX. 466/1 Each with a flannel *tennis-bag in her hand. **1908** R. W. CHAMBERS *Younger Set* viii, Eileen..strolled houseward across the lawn, switching the shaven sod with her *tennis bat. **1883** *Pall Mall G.* 30 May 3/1 If *tennis elbow becomes anything like as usual an ailment as tennis playing is an accomplishment. **1891** 'J. S. WINTER' *Lumley* v, He was sitting on the garden seat near the *tennis-ground. **1890** *Army & Navy Stores Catal.* Mar. 1180 *Tennis Hats various colours from 1/0. **1888** BARRIE *When a Man's Single* xiv, A man in a *tennis jacket, carrying a pail. **1901** *Brit. Med. Jrnl.* No. 2097. 562 The country doctor called it a '*tennis-knee', which might mean anything. **1899** E. J. CHAPMAN *Drama Two Lives* 13 The *tennis-lawns and pathways all Are bright with beauty. **1892** F. M. CRAWFORD *Three Fates* II. iv. 95 Her first *tennis-racquet, now battered and half-unstrung. **1897** ANNE PAGE *Afternoon Ride* 7 A..girl with a tennis-racket in her hand. **1908** R. W. CHAMBERS *Younger Set* viii, Yes, I've plenty of *tennis-shoes. Help yourself. **1897** MRS. RAYNER *Type-writer Girl* i, A baronet in a *tennis suit.

Hence **Te·nnisdom**, the world or realm of tennis- (or lawn-tennis) players; **Te·nnisy** *a.*, *colloq.* addicted to lawn-tennis.

**1890** *Blackw. Mag.* Feb. 256/2 As with horsy women... *tennis-y* girls .. become intolerable nuisances to their neighbours. **1897** *Outing* (U.S.) XXX. 464/2 The reputation of the Bentley brothers had gone forth into tennisdom with a very high brand on it.

[*Note.* The introduction of some form of tennis into Florence by the French knights in 1325, and the use of the name *tenes*, appear not to be recorded elsewhere than in Velluti's *Cronica*, nor does either game or name appear to have been long retained; the name was manifestly foreign, and opposed to Italian word-formation. But its use in Florence at least 30 and perhaps 70 years before the earliest known English example, implies either that the Eng. name came from Italy, or that both had a common source. The latter is the more likely; it was French knights who introduced the game at Florence, and the Eng. *tene·tz*, *teney·s*, with their final stress, imply French origin. The difficulty is that the game has app. never borne any such name in Fr., where, from 1350 or earlier, it has been called *la paulme*, *la paume*. The only Fr. word akin in form is *tenez* (AF. *tenetz*), 2 pers. pl. pres. indic. and imper. of *tenir* 'to hold', also 'to take, receive what is offered'. Hence the suggestion made by Minsheu 1617, and favoured by Skeat, Jusserand, and others, that the name originated in the Fr. imperative *tenez* 'take, receive', called by the server to his opponent. There is of course the difficulty that no mention of this call has yet been found in French, where it must have been used if thence taken into It. and Eng. But in the Colloquies of Cordier and Erasmus, the server's call is latinized as *accipe* and *excipe*, and in the *Carmen de ludo pilæ reticulo* of R. Fressart, Paris, 1641, 'excipe', 'pilam excipe', 'mitto pilam in tectum, excipe', with other uses of *excipere* and *accipere*, occur eight times in the portion printed by Julian Marshall *Annals of Tennis* 27–29. These Latin words witness to the use of *tenez* or some equivalent call in French, and favour the conclusion that this call gave rise to the 14th c. It. and Eng. name.]

† **Te·nnis,** *v. Obs.* Also 6 -esse. [f. prec. sb.]

**1.** *trans.* To toss to and fro like a ball at tennis. Also *absol.*

**1565** W. ALLEN in Fulke *Confut. Purg.* (1577) 145 How fast they will tennesse one to an other in talke. **1596** SPENSER *State Irel.* Wks. (Globe) 652/2 These fowre garrisons issuing foorthe..will so drive him [the enemy] from one side to another, and tennis him amongest them, that he shall finde no where safe.

**2.** *intr.* To play tennis. Hence † **Te·nnising** *vbl. sb.*, tennis-playing; also † **Te·nniser**, a tennis-player.

*a* **1475** *Myrc's Par. Pr.* 11 *note*, Danseyng, cotteyng, bollyng, tenessyng, handball, fott ball, stoil ball & all manner other games. **1579** RICE *Invective agst. Vices* E iv b, Bowlyng, Dicyng, Cardyng, Tennesyng, with such like actes and deedes of the fleshe. *Ibid.* F j, Dicers, Bowlers, Carders,..Tenessers.

**Tennis-ball.** [f. TENNIS *sb.* + BALL *sb.*[1] 4.] The small ball used in tennis or lawn-tennis.

*c* **1450** *Brut* ccxliv. 374 Yn scorne & despite he [the Dauphin] sent to hym [King Henry V] a tonne fulle of teneys-ballis, be-cause he schulde haue sumwhat to play with-alle. **1561** T. NORTON *Calvin's Inst.* I. 60 As if God did to make himself pastime to tosse men like tennise balles. **1599** SHAKS. *Hen. V*, I. ii. 258. **1726** SWIFT *Gulliver* II. v, Such cruel bangs .. as if I had been pelted with tennis-balls. **1805** SCOTT *Last Minstr.* II. xxxi, Like tennis-ball by raquet tossed. *attrib.* **1786** ABERCROMBIE *Arr.* in *Gard. Assist.* p. vii, Tennis-ball cabbage lettuce.

**b.** *fig.*; *esp.* a thing or person that is tossed or bandied about like a tennis-ball.

**1589** WARNER *Alb. Eng.* VI. XXX. 151 Vulcan, Venus,.. Daphne turnd to Tree..tennis balles to euery tongue of euery Deitee. **1610** HOLLAND *Camden's Brit.* (1637) 570 The very tennise-ball, in some sort, of fortune. **1642** H. MORE *Song of Soul* II. App. lxxxviii, A cluster of them makes not half a Moon, What should such tennis-balls do in the skie? **1890** DAKYNS *Xenophon* I. p. xciv, We find this great Athenian captain playing the ignoble part of tennis-ball to rival Spartan harmosts.

**Te·nnis-court.** [f. TENNIS *sb.* + COURT *sb.* 4.]

**1.** The enclosed quadrangular area, or building, in which the game of tennis is played.

**1564** in Willis & Clark *Cambridge* (1886) I. 143 Boards to make a tennyse court £1. 0. 0. **1611** COTGR., *Blouse*, a close Tennis court, or a Tennis court in a hall, hauing a house on either side to serue on. **1630** in *Proc. Soc. Antiq. Scot.* (1896) XXX. 57 The tinneis courtis thairof and all utheris houses. **1763** *Brit. Mag.* IV. 55 It was agreed to build a new theatre, where the Tennis-court then stood, in Lincoln's-inn-fields. **1791** MACKINTOSH *Vind. Gallicæ* Wks. 1846 III. 24 They were summoned by their President to a Tennis-Court, where they were reduced to hold their assembly. **1878** JULIAN MARSHALL *Annals of Tennis* 114 One of the greatest obstacles to the spreading of the love of Tennis has always been the scarcity of Tennis-courts. [*Ibid.* 113 Their number [in England] at the present moment is twenty-one.]

*fig.* **1605** EARL STIRLING *Alexand. Trag.* v. i, I thinke the world is but a Tenis-court where Fortune doth play States, tosse men for Balls. **1738** G. LILLO *Marina* I. ii, Winds and waters, In their vast tennis-court, have, as a ball, Used me to make them sport.

*Comb.* **1597** SHAKS. *2 Hen. IV*, II. ii. 21 But that the Tennis-Court-keeper knowes better then I. *a* **1637** B. JONSON *Eng. Gram.* viii. *note*, *Sæpè tria coagmentantur nomina, ut*, a foot-ball-player, a tennis-court-keeper.

**2.** The plot of ground prepared and marked out for lawn-tennis.

**1881** 'RITA' *My Lady Coquette* i, I wanted to see the tennis-courts made.

**Te·nnis-play.** [f. as prec. + PLAY *sb.*]

**1.** The game of TENNIS; playing at tennis.

*c* **1440** *Promp. Parv.* 68/1 Chace of tenys pley, or oþyr lyke, *sistencia*. **1530** PALSGR. 280/1 Tennysplay, *jeu de la paulme*. **1594** NASHE *Christ's T.* To Rdr., Prouided it bee not a Tennice-play of Pots and Cups, like the Centaurs feast. **1651** HOBBES *Leviath.* II. xxv. (1839) 249 He that useth able seconds at tennis play, placed in their proper stations.

† **2.** = TENNIS-COURT. *Obs.*

**1507–8** *Court of Frank-pledge, Oxford*, Four men presented for keeping tenysplayes, an illegal sport. **1577–87** HOLINSHED *Chron.* III. 1223/1 In Wisbich was a garden, a tennise plaie, & a bowling allie walled about with bricke. *Comb.* **1530** in *Vicary's Anat.* (1888) App. ii. 101 Item, for Anthony Annesley, tenesplay-keper vj s viij d.

**Te·nnis-play:er.** [f. as prec.] One who plays at tennis; now, usually, at lawn-tennis.

*c* **1440** *Promp. Parv.* 488/2 Teneys pleyare, *teniludius*. **1635** STAFFORD *Fem. Glory* (1869) 106 The best Tennis-player living cannot shew his cunning. **1674** TEMPLE *Let. to Sir J. Temple* Wks. 1731 II. 297 We were both together young Travellers and Tennis Players in France. **1801** STRUTT *Sports & Past.* II. iii. (1876) 161 We have..authority to prove that Henry VII was a tennis player. **1884** *Harper's Mag.* Jan. 304/2 The champion tennis-players.

So **Te·nnis-playing**, playing at tennis.

**1441** [see TENNIS 1]. **1495** *Act 11 Hen. VII*, c. 2 § 5 Where..tenys pleiyng bowles Clossh or any other unlawfull game..shalbe used. **1583** STUBBES *Anat. Abus.* II. (1882) 33 They spend it in dicing, carding, bowling, tennise plaieng.

**Tennon, Tennor, -our, Tenny, Tennys, -yse,** obs. ff. TENON, TENOR, TENNÉ, TENNIS.

**Tennysonian** (tenisō̆u·niăn), *a.* and *sb.* [f. the name of the poet Alfred (Lord) Tennyson (1809–1892) + -IAN.]

**A.** *adj.* Of or pertaining to Tennyson, his works, or his style.

**1853** LONGF. in *Life* (1891) II. 249 [M. Arnold's poems] Very clever; with a little of the Tennysonian leaven in them. **1851** *Times* 10 Oct., His success exceeds that of his predecessors who have attempted the rendering of this Tennysonian classic [*Catullus*]. **1876** STEDMAN *Vict. Poets* vi. (1887) 227 These effects, which the Laureate employs with such variation and continuance that the resultant style is known as Tennysonian, were Dorian first of all.

**B.** *sb.* An admirer, imitator, disciple, or student of Tennyson.

**1883** *Harper's Mag.* Feb. 469/1 By all the Tennysonians of this generation it will be deeply regretted.

Hence **Tennyso·nianism, Te·nnysonism,** a

characteristic trait or mannerism of Tennyson's style; an imitation of that style.

**1843** Mrs. Browning *Let. to C. Mathews* 14 Mar. (in *Davey's Catal.* (1895) 15), I had been pleased with the poetical sense of his [Lowell's] book, which he sent me long ago,—notwithstanding the Tennysonianisms of it. *a* **1849** Poe *Channing* Wks. 1864 III. 234 The affectations—the Tennysonisms of Mr. Channing.

**Teno-**, combining element, arbitrarily formed from Gr. τένων, Tendon: cf. Tenonto-. **Tenography** (tenǫ·grăfi) [-graphy], description of tendons. **Teno·logy** [-logy], that part of anatomy which relates to the tendons. **Teno·rrhaphy** [Gr. ῥαφή a seam], suture of a tendon. **Te·nosu·ture** [L. *sūtūra* a seam], = *tenorrhaphy*. **Te·no-synovi·tis** [see Synovia and -itis], inflammation of a tendon and its sheath. See also Tenotomy.

**1890** Billings *Nat. Med. Dict.*, *Tenography, *Tenology, *Tenorrhaphy. **1899** *Syd. Soc. Lex.*, **Teno-suture*, the sewing together of the divided ends of a tendon. **1890** Billings *Nat. Med. Dict.*, *Tenosynovitis. **1896** *Allbutt's Syst. Med.* I. 379 The results [of massage] in sprains, tenosynovitis and the like, are sometimes amazing.

**Tenon** (te·nən), *sb.* Forms: α. 5 **tenown**, 5– **tenon**, (6–8 **tennon**); β. 6 **tenaunt**, **-e**, 6–7 (9 *dial.*) **tenant**, 7 **-ent**, 7–8 **tennant**, **-ent**. [a. F. *tenon* (15th c. in Godef. *Compl.*), f. *tenir* to hold + suffix *-on* (= L. *-ōnem*). The β-forms show assimilation to the word Tenant, and to L. *tenent-em* pr. pple., holding: cf. *talon*, *talent*, and see -ant [3].]

**1.** A projection fashioned on the end or side of a piece of wood or other material, to fit into a corresponding cavity or Mortise in another piece, so as to form a close and secure joint.

α. **14..** *Voc.* in Wr.-Wülcker 616/1 *Tentum*, a tenon, *quod ponitur in commissura*. *c* **1440** *Promp. Parv.* 489/1 Tenown, knyttynge of a balke or oþer lyke yn tymbyr (*S.* tenowre), ..*tenaculum*, *gumfus*. **1545** Elyot, *Cardo*..it is also the tenon, whiche is put into the mortayse. **1577** tr. *Bullinger's Decades* (1592) 339 Euery boorde had two tenons like pikes, whereby they were stucke into the sockets. *a* **1661** Fuller *Worthies* (1662) III. *Stafford.* 38 There is a fair House on London Bridge, commonly called None-such, which is reported to be made without either Nailes or Pins, with crooked Tennons fastened with wedges and other (as I may term them) circumferential devices. **1852** Wright *Celt, Rom. & Sax.* ii. 59 Each of the upright stones [at Stonehenge] had two tenons or projections on the top. **1889** *Work* 29 June 227/1 In cutting dovetails and tenons.

β. **1551** Recorde *Cast. Knowl.* (1556) 51 Then must you make lyke morteyses..to receaue those tenauntes. *a* **1677** Hale *Prim. Orig. Man.* IV. iv. 330 If Chance could make a Beam.., and..Tenents at either end,yet it is not possible to conceive that Chance could..fit the Mortises of other pieces of Timber to those Tenents. **1703** Moxon *Mech. Exerc.* 116 *Tennant*..a square end fitted into a Mortess. **1778** *Eng. Gazetteer* (ed. 2) s. v. *Yardley*, The spire..for want of tennents being pinned down, was blown off.

**b.** *Tenon and mortise* (also *mortise and tenon*: see Mortise *sb.* 1 b), the combination of these.

**1610** Holland *Camden's Brit.* 251 With a small tenents and mortescis. **1611** Speed *Hist. Gt. Brit.* VII. xii. § 3. 267 Fastned with tenons and mortaises, the one into the other. **1688** R. Holme *Armoury* III. xviii. (Roxb.) 139/1 Fastned in them with a Mortais and Tenent. **1856** Emerson *Eng. Traits, Stonehenge* Wks. (Bohn) II. 124 The good beasts must have known how to cut a well-wrought tenon and mortise.

†**c.** The lower part of a graft which is cut thin so as to be inserted into the stock. *Obs.*

**1523** Fitzherb. *Husb.* § 139 Take thy graffe and cut it in the ioynt to the myddes, & make the tenaunt therof half an inche longe or a lytell more al on the one syde. **1641** in Maidment *Bk. Scott. Pasquils* 131 Whose tennons small, if they be left in ground, Like ill weeds soon will waxe.

†**d.** *fig.* That which firmly connects or unites two things. *Obs. rare*[−1].

**1617** Hieron *Wks.* II. 145 There are then two things concurre in the producing of man...This I thinke to bee the surest tenon.

**2.** *attrib.* and *Comb.*, as *tenon-helve*, *-joint*, *piece*; **tenon-auger**, a hollow auger for forming tenons on the ends of spokes, chair-legs, etc.; **tenon-saw**, a fine saw for making tenons, etc., having a thin blade, a thick back, and small teeth very slightly 'set'.

**1881** Raymond *Mining Gloss.*, **Tenant-helve*, see *Frontal-hammer*. **1865** *Reader* No. 133. 73/3 Mortice and *tenon joints. **1901** *J. Black's Carp. & Build., Home Handicr.* 14 A pin of hard wood..driven in through the *tenon piece and the mortise. **1549** *Privy Council Acts* (1890) II. 351 *Tenant sawes, iiij. **1703** Moxon *Mech. Exerc.* 103 The Tennant-Saw, being thin, hath a Back to keep it from bending. **1823** P. Nicholson *Pract. Build.* 251 The Tenon-saw derives its name from being used for forming the shoulders of tenons.

**Tenon** (te·nən), *v.* Also 7–8 **tenant**, **tennant**, 8 **tenent**, **tenont**. [f. prec. sb.]

**1.** *trans.* To fix together with tenon and mortise.

**1649** Blithe *Eng. Improv. Impr.* (1653) 203 The beam.. runs down into the plough-head, and is there tenanted and pinned into the head. **1665** J. Webb *Stone-Heng* (1725) 91 If mortised and tenanted. **1711** W. Sutherland *Shipbuild. Assist.* 25 Tenant [in *Errata* corr. to *Tenon*] the Post into the Keel. **1769** Falconer *Dict. Marine* (1789) C iv b, The stern-post..is tenented into the keel. **1844** Stephens *Bk. Farm* II. 289 The whole of the posts are likewise tenoned into the sill.

**b.** *fig.* To join or fix firmly and securely.

**1596** Bp. Andrewes *Serm., Luke xvi. 25* (1841) II. 86 We tenon both these together, as antecedent and consequent. **1659** O. Walker *Instruct. Oratory* 18 The several pieces of Invention..must next be sowed and tenanted together. **1856** Whitman in *Scott. Rev.* (1883) 285 My foothold is tenon'd and mortis'd in granite.

**2.** To furnish or fit with a tenon.

**1771** Luckombe *Hist. Print.* 302 These two Rails are each of them tenoned at each end. **1793** Smeaton *Edystone L.* § 174 Cramping the stones together, as well as tenoning the ends. **1873** J. Richards *Wood-w. Factories* 156 For this we have the remedy of tenoning both ends at the same time.

**b.** *intr.* To engage or fit in by or as by a tenon.

**1797** *Encycl. Brit.* (ed. 3) XVII. 404/1 The two beams.. should be placed conformable to the two uprights, so that they may tenon in them. **1842** *Civil Eng. & Arch. Jrnl.* V. 361/2 They tenon between the strings *e* and *n*.

Hence **Te·noned** *ppl. a.*, furnished or made with a tenon; **Te·noner**, a machine for forming tenons.

**1771** Luckombe *Hist. Print.* 323 [He] besmears the whole tenoned ends and tenons well with soap. **1875** *Carpentry & Join.* 49 The tenoned and mortised ends of the pieces. **1891** *Cent. Dict.*, Tenoner.

**Tenon**, obs. and dial. form of Tendon.

**Tenonian** (tĕnōᵘ·niăn), *a. Anat.* [f. name of J. R. Tenon, a French anatomist (1724–1816) + -ian.] Discovered or described by Tenon; as in *Tenonian fascia* or *capsule* (*Tenon's capsule*), a delicate band of fascia with involuntary muscle fibres disposed round the eyeball (*Syd. Soc. Lex.*). So **Tenoni·tis**, inflammation of Tenon's capsule.

**1890** Billings *Nat. Med. Dict.*, Tenon's capsule. *Ibid.*, Tenonitis. **1891** *Cent. Dict.*, The Tenonian fascia or capsule. **1901** *Brit. Med. Jrnl.* No. 2097. 575 The symptoms of tenonitis.

**Te·noning**, *vbl. sb.* [f. Tenon *v.* or *sb.* + -ing [1].]

**a.** The process of jointing or joining together with tenon and mortise. **b.** Furnishing with tenons. So **Te·noning** *ppl. a.*, that tenons or furnishes with a tenon.

**1678** *Lond. Gaz.* No. 1327/4 As in Plaining,..Mortessing and Tennanting, Moldings, &c. **1769** Falconer *Dict. Marine* (1789), *Assembler*, to unite the several pieces of a ship, as by..scarfing, scoring, tenenting, &c. **1847** Smeaton *Builder's Man.* 112 Little need be said..as to morticing and tenoning, or dovetailing.

**c.** *attrib.* and *Comb.* (of the *vbl. sb.* or *ppl. a.*), as **tenoning attachment**, a mechanical fitting for converting a moulding machine into a tenon-cutter; **tenoning chisel**, a double-blade chisel which makes two cuts, leaving a middle piece which forms a tenon (Knight *Dict. Mech.*); **tenoning cutter**, **tenoning machine**, a machine for cutting timber with a tenon.

**1895** *Daily Chron.* 6 Dec. 1/5 Moulding Machine (4-cutter) with *tenoning attachment, band-saw, vertical spindle. **1870** *Eng. Mech.* 4 Feb. 498/1 For tenoning, the planing cutters..are replaced by *tenoning cutters. **1873** J. Richards *Wood-working Factories* 157 To move them backward and forward is the main labour in operating a *tenoning machine. **1881** Young *Ev. Man his own Mechanic* § 216 Tenoning and trenching machines.

**Tenonitis, Tenon's capsule**: see Tenonian.

**Tenonto-.** [f. Gr. τένων, τενοντ- tendon.] A formative of technical terms relating to the tendons; cf. Teno-. **Tenontography** (tenǫntǫ·grăfi), = Tenography. **Tenonto·logy**, = Tenology. **Tenontophyme** (tĕnǫ·ntǫfəim) [Gr. φῦμα growth], **Teno·ntophyte** [Gr. φυτόν plant], a tumour or morbid growth on a tendon. **Teno·ntostome** [*ostoma*, Osteoma], an osseous tumour in a tendon.

**1860** Mayne *Expos. Lex.*, *Tenontographia*..tenontography... *Tenontologia*..tenontology... *Tenontophyma*.. tenontophyme... *Tenontophytum*..tenontophyte...*Tenontostoma*..tenontostome. **1899** *Syd. Soc. Lex.*, Tenontophyte.

**Tenor** (te·nəɹ), *sb.*[1] (*a.*) Also 4 **tenur**, 4–6 **-oure**, 4–9 **-our**, 5 **-owre**, **-eur**, 6 **-ore**, **-er**, **tennour**, (**teanor**), 6–7 **tennor**, 7 **tenner**. β. 4–8 **tenure** (5 **teneure**). [a. OF. *tenor*, *-our*, 13th c. (also *tenoire*, *-eure*, *-ure*, 13–14th c.), mod.F. *teneur* fem., substance, import of a document, etc.:—L. *tenōr-em* course, import (of a law, etc.), f. *tenēre* to hold. The musical term was in 14–15th c. F. *tenor* masc. and fem., 'a tenor part, voice, or singer', mod.F. *ténor* masc., after It. *tenore* and med.L. *tenor*, to which also the English word in all senses has been conformed. Confusion with Tenure prevailed from 13th to 18th c.: see β.]

**I. 1.** The course of meaning which holds on or continues through something written or spoken; the general sense or meaning of a document, speech, etc.; substance, purport, import, effect, drift.

In technical legal use (as in Fr.) implying the actual wording of a document, or a transcript thereof (distinguished from *effect*): cf. b. *Proving of the tenor* (Sc. Law): see quot. 1838.

*a* **1300** *Cursor M.* 17614 Þai did þan for to write a writt, Þis þan was þe tenur of hit. **13..** *K. Alis.* 2977 Anothir lettre he sent heom tho, And of a more bitter tenour. **1387** Trevisa *Higden* (Rolls) III. 35 Þe tenor of his lawes was suche. **1413–22** Marg. of Anjou *Lett.* (Camden) 22 Youre gracieux letters of prive seal, the teneur of the which we have wel understand. **1526** Tindale *Acts* viii. 32 The tener off the scripture which he redde was this. **1535** Stewart *Cron. Scot.* (Rolls) II. 355 This was the tennour that tyme of thair band. **1603** Shaks. *Meas. for M.* IV. ii. 216 Hee..receiues letters of strange tenor. **1664** H. More *Myst. Iniq.* 112 This is the tenour of the New Covenant. **1703** *Lond. Gaz.* No. 3953/1 (Scotl.) Act for proving the Tenor in Favours of Anna Cockburn. **1825** Jefferson *Autobiog.* Wks. 1859 I. 10 The tenor of these propositions being generally known. **1838** W. Bell *Dict. Law Scot.* s.v. *Proving*, The terms of a deed which has been lost or destroyed may be proved in an action peculiar to the Court of Session, called an action of proving the tenor. **1870** L'Estrange *Miss Mitford* I. i. 20 Such was the general tenour of Mrs. Mitford's letters.

β. [**1292** Britton VI. iv. § 9 Solom la tenure del Pone (*tr.* according to the tenor of the Pone).] **13..** *K. Alis.* 1707 (Bodl. MS.), A letter par amoure Of whiche swiche was þe tenure. **1427** *Rolls of Parlt.* IV. 332/2 Ayeins the teneure and forme of the saide Statutes. **1512** *Act 4 Hen. VIII*, c. 11 Certen Indentures wherof the tenure hereafter ensuyth. **1596** Shaks. *Merch. V.* IV. i. 235 Bid me teare the bond. *Iew.* When it is paid according to the tenure. **1682** *Lond. Gaz.* No. 1733/4 According to the Tenure of his Majesties Letters Patents.

**b.** *concr.* An exact copy of a document, a transcript. (In quot. 1523, a written statement.) Now *techn.*: see prec. sense.

*c* **1450** *Godstow Reg.* 366 Even as hit apperith of submyssions of the same parties, Tenouris of the which folow bynethe. **1523** Ld. Berners *Froiss.* I. ccxii. 257 Than he shall delyuer to vs a tenour of that he ought to do. **1588** Lambarde *Eiren.* IV. xviii. 591 Sometimes they are to certifie and send vp onely a Tenor (or Transcript) as I sayd, of the Record. **1842** S. Greenleaf *Evidence* (1844) I. § 502. 575 In such cases, nothing is returned but the tenor, that is, a literal transcript of the record, under the seal of the Court.

**c.** The value of a bank note or bill as stated on it: in phr. *old tenor*, *middle tenor*, *new tenor*, referring to the successive issues of paper currency in the colonies of Massachusetts and Rhode Island in the 18th c. *Hist.*

**1740** W. Douglass *Disc. Curr. Brit. Plant. Amer.* 40 All Bills of the old Tenor when brought into their Treasury, to issue out no more. **1811** J. Adams *Wks.* (1854) IX. 638 It is worse than old tenor, continental currency, or any other paper money. **1878** F. A. Walker *Money* XV. 319 In 1741 the Assembly made 6s. 9d. of the new-tenor equal to 27 shillings of the old. *Ibid.* 320 By act of 1770, the old-tenor notes were to be exchanged at this rate.

**2.** †**a.** The action or fact of holding on or continuing; continuance, duration. *Obs.*

**1398** Trevisa *Barth. De P. R.* VI. i. (Bodl. MS.), Þe age is of a man nouȝ elles is but tenour and during of kinde vertues. **1502** *Ord. Crysten Men* V. iv. (1506) 393 The melodye of the glorye of the blessyd shall not haue tenoure yf the paynes of the dampned were not eternall. **1621** Burton *Anat. Mel.* I. i. I. v. (1651) 12 'Tis most absurd..for any mortal man to look for a perpetual tenor of happiness in his life. *a* **1694** Tillotson *Serm.* (1742) IV. 539 Let not a perpetual tenor of health and pleasure soften and dissolve your spirits.

**b.** Continuous progress, course, movement (*of* action, etc.); way of proceeding, procedure.

**1398** Trevisa *Barth. De P. R.* VIII. ii. (Tollem. MS.), Heuen with his roundnesse and cerclis forsakeþ nouȝt, noþer leueþ þe sadde tenor of his ordre. **1596** Spenser *F. Q.* IV. vii. 47 Ne ought mote make him change his wonted tenor. **1676** Hale *Contempl.* I. 400 The constant tenour of a just, virtuous, and pious life. **1750** Gray *Elegy* 76 Along the cool sequester'd vale of life They kept the noiseless tenour of their way. **1784** Johnson *Lett. to Mrs. Thrale* 26 June, Of doing good a continual tenour of distress allowed him few opportunities. **1814** Cary *Dante's Inf.* X. 133 She of thy life The future tenour will to thee unfold. **1865** Seeley *Ecce Homo* iv. (ed. 8) 29 The contrast between Christ's pretensions and the homely tenour of his life.

β. **1720** W. Gibson *Diet. Horses* xii. (1731) 185 A continued easy Motion, and constant Tenure in Feeding.

**c.** The length of time that a bill is drawn to run before presentation for payment.

**1866** Crump *Banking* v. 100 The tenor [of foreign bills].. depends upon a variety of circumstances, and may be extended to almost any period, provided the parties thereto are agreed. *Ibid.* 101 The term 'usance'..denotes the customary tenor at which bills are drawn.

**3.** Quality, character, nature; condition, state. †**a.** in physical sense; in early use *esp.* quality of tone (cf. 4). *Obs.*

**1530** Palsgr. 47 The redar shall sounde them all under one tenour, and never rest upon them nor lyft up his voice. **1595** Spenser *Epithal.* 9 Your string could soone to sadder tenor turne. **1618** Bp. Hall *Serm.* V. 103 There can be no harmony, where all the strings or voices are of one tenor. **1725** *Bradley's Fam. Dict.* s.v. *Elm*, The Tenor of the Grain makes it also fit for all Kinds of Carved-Work. **1729** Shelvocke *Artillery* II. 90 The Air in them must be of the same Tenor with the circumambient Air.

**b.** in non-physical sense: the way in which a thing continues; *esp.* habitual condition of mind. Now *rare* or merged in 2 b.

**1589** Puttenham *Eng. Poesie* III. v. (Arb.) 163 No fault or blemish, to confound the tennors of the stiles for that cause. **1697** Dryden *Æneid* XII. 305 Nor shake the steadfast tenour of my Mind. **1756** Burke *Subl. & B.* II. viii, The senses, strongly affected in some one manner, cannot quickly change their tenour. **1831** Carlyle *Misc.* (1857) II. 190 Spiritual, of calm tenour.

**II. 4.** *Mus.* **a.** The adult male voice intermediate between the bass and the counter-tenor or alto, usually ranging from the octave below middle C to the A above it; also, the part sung by such a voice, being the next above the bass in vocal part-music.

So called app. because the melody or *canto fermo* was formerly allotted to this part.

**1388** [see Counter-tenor 1 b]. *c* **1430** Lydg. *Minor Poems* (Percy Soc.) 54 Treble meene and tenor discordyng as I gesse. *c* **1460** *Wisdom* 620 in *Macro Plays* 55 *Mynde*. A tenowur to yow bothe I brynge; .. *Wyll.* And, but a trebull I owt wrynge, The deuell hym spede, þat myrthe exyled! **1530** PALSGR. 280/1 Tenour a parte in pricke songe, *teneur*. **1597** MORLEY *Introd. Mus.* II. 100 You haue your plainsong changed from parte to part, firste in the treble, next in the tenor, lastlie in the base. **1638–56** COWLEY *Davideis* I. Wks. (1669) 13 Water and Air he for the Tenor chose, Earth made the Base, the Treble Flame arose. *a* **1791** WESLEY *Wks.* (1872) VIII. 319 When they [singers] would teach a tune to the congregation, they must sing only the tenor. **1873** HALE *In His Name* vi. 49 The voice was a perfectly clear and pure tenor.

**b.** A singer with a tenor voice; one who sings the tenor part; a tenor singer.

?*c* **1475** *Sqr. lowe Degre* 782 Than shall ye go to your euensong, With tenours and trebles a mong. **1552** HULOET, Tenor, or he that singeth a tenor, *succentor*. **1616** *Cheque Bk. Chapel Royal* (Camden) 9 The next place that shall.. fall voyd by the deathe of any tenor. **1821** BYRON *Juan* IV. lxxxvii, The tenor's voice is spoilt by affectation. **1884** F. M. CRAWFORD *Rom. Singer* i, He asked me if I would not let him educate that young tenor.

**c.** = *Tenor bell*: see B. 1. *Second tenor* (quot. 1541), the next bell to the tenor. Also (quot. 1562) applied to a string of tenor pitch in an instrument, as a harp.

**1541** *Ludlow Churchw. Acc.* (Camden) 7 Payde.. for mendynge the whele of ye secounde tenor..ij d. **1562** J. HEYWOOD *Prov. & Epigr.* (1867) 186 Which string..wouldst thou..harpe on. Not the base..Nor the standyng tennor. ..Nor the counter tennor. *a* **1627** MIDDLETON *Mayor Queenb.* v. i, Let the Bells ring...'Las the Tenor's broken, ring out the Treble. **1909** *Daily Chron.* 1 Oct. 7/2 The present 'tenor', as the deepest bell of a peal is always called, was cast here in 1738.

**d.** A name for the tenor violin or VIOLA.

**1836** DUBOURG *Violin* i. (1878) 11 The tenor, or *viol da braccia*, was larger than the modern tenor, or *viola*. **1883** H. R. HAWEIS in *Gentl. Mag.* July 48 He learns the violoncello or tenor. **1884** *Girl's Own Paper* Nov. 21/2 The viola is sometimes called the tenor, but the former is the preferable name.

**B.** *attrib.* or *adj.*, and *Comb.* (in sense 4 above).

**1.** *attrib.* or *adj.* Applied to a voice, part, instrument, string, etc. of the pitch described in sense 4 above, or intermediate between bass and alto.

*Tenor bell*, the largest bell of a peal or set. *Tenor C*, the note an octave below middle C, being the lowest note of a tenor voice. *Tenor clef*, the C clef when placed upon the fourth line of the stave. *Tenor violin* (†*viol*), the viola.

**1522** *MS. Acc. St. John's Hosp., Canterb.*, For a bawdryk to the tenoure bell. **1597** MORLEY *Introd. Mus.* I. 21 In the Tenor part of the Gloria of his Masse *Aue Maris stella*. **1609** B. JONSON *Masque Queenes* Wks. (1616) 964 That most excellent tenor voyce. **1662** PLAYFORD *Skill Mus.* (1674) 99 The Tenor-Viol is an excellent inward Part. *a* **1670** HACKET *Abp. Williams* II. § 33 (1693) 30 The Bishop himself bearing the Tenour part among them often. **1806** CALLCOTT *Mus. Gram.* ii. 10 The Tenor Clef is used for the middle voices of men. **1838–9** FR. A. KEMBLE *Resid. Georgia* (1863) 127 Their voices seem oftener tenor than any other quality.

**2.** *Comb.*, as *tenor-maker* (sense 4 d), *-wheel* (4 c).

**1648–9** in Swayne *Sarum Churchw. Acc.* (1896) 219 Mending yᵉ Tenor Wheele—1 s. **1836** DUBOURG *Violin* ix. (1878) 266 Martin Hoffman and Hunger, both of Leipsic, were excellent tenor-makers.

Hence **Tenor** *v.*[1] *intr.* (with *it*), to sing tenor; **Te·norless** *a.*, having no tenor or purport.

**1893** *Scribner's Mag.* XIV. 61 A tame cornet tenored it throatily Of beer-pots and spittoons. **1810** BENTHAM *Packing* (1821) 265 The purely conjectural, tenorless, uncognoscible, and impostrous state of unwritten, alias common law.

**Tenor,** *sb.*[2] Now *dial.* Also 5 tenowre, 8–9 tenner. Corrupted form of TENON *sb.* Tenor-saw = *Tenon-saw*. Hence Tenor *v.*[2] = TENON *v.*

*a* **1485** *Promp. Parv.* MS. S. (1908) 476 Tenowre, knytting of a balk or odyre lyk tymbre, *cenaculum*. **1747** HOOSON *Miner's Dict.* Q iij, Instead of a Collar made on the Forks, we make Tenners, so that the Forks are Tennered at both ends, and the Sliders are Slotted at both Ends to receive the Forks. **1851** W. ANDERSON *Rhymes* (1867) 116 (E.D.D.) You're just as rough's a tenor saw. **1877** *N. W. Linc. Gloss.*, *Tenner*, a tenon.

**Tenor,** obs. form of TENURE.

†**Tenoral,** *a. Obs. rare.* [f. TENOR *sb.*[1] + -AL.] Of or pertaining to the tenor or ordinary course.

**1606** BIRNIE *Kirk-Buriall* xvi. (1833) E j, Buriall exemple, in all the which there is a tenorall processe so equally and vnchangeably..obserued.

**Tenorist** (te·nŏrist). [= F. *tenoriste* (15–16th c. in Godef.), It. *tenorista*, f. *tenore*, TENOR *sb.*[1] 4: see -IST.] (See quot. 1898.)

[**1724** *Short Explic. For. Wds. in Mus. Bks.*, *Tenorista*, one that has a Voice proper for a Tenor.] **1865** tr. *Spohr's Autobiog.* II. 155 We were so successful as to engage..the tenorist Cornet of Hamburg. **1898** STAINER & BARRETT *Dict. Mus. Terms*, *Tenorist*, one who sings the tenor part, or plays the tenor violin.

**Tenorite** (te·nŏrəit). *Min.* [Named, 1841, after Prof. G. Tenore, President of Naples Academy: see -ITE[1].] Black oxide of copper, found in thin iron-black scales on lava at Vesuvius: see quot.

**1865** MASKELYNE in *Athenæum* No. 1980. 472/3 Crystallised Melaconite and Tenorite. **1868** DANA *Min.* 804 As the names tenorite and melaconite were given the same year, and tenorite was made non-isometric (hexagonal) by its describer, it appears to be right that tenorite should be sustained for the above mineral, and melaconite be left for the isometric kind, if any such proves to be a native species.

**Tenoroon** (tenŏrū·n). [f. TENOR + *-oon* in *bassoon*, or short for *tenor bassoon*.] **a.** An obsolete wooden reed-instrument intermediate in pitch between the oboe and the bassoon; also called *tenor oboe* or *tenor bassoon*. Also *attrib.*, as *tenoroon oboe*. **b.** A reed-stop in an organ, resembling the oboe stop, but not extending below tenor C. Also applied to any stop not extending below tenor C; also *attrib.*, as *tenoroon diapason*.

**1849** *Chambers' Inform. People* II. 766/2 The tenoroon, a wood instrument played with a reed, is seldom employed. **1879** STAINER *Music of Bible* 79 The tenor oboe or tenoroon. **1881** C. A. EDWARDS *Organs* xxii. 155 When it ceases at tenor C this stop [double open diapason] is named the Tenoroon. **1884** W. H. STONE in Grove *Dict. Mus.* IV. 88 *Tenoroon*, a name..given to the Tenor Bassoon or Alto Fagotto in F...It has entirely gone out of use. **1898** STAINER & BARRETT *Dict. Mus. Terms*, *Tenoroon*..(2) A word affixed to an organ stop to denote that it does not proceed below tenor C, as *tenoroon hautboy*. A *tenoroon diapason* is a double diapason which does not extend below tenor C.

**Tenorrhaphy,** etc.: see TENO-.

†**Te·nory.** *Obs. rare*[−1]. [Alteration of TENOR *sb.*[1] or It. *tenore*: cf. 13th c. F. *tenoire*, as if:—L. **tenoria*.] = TENOR *sb.* 4.

*c* **1460** *Towneley Myst.* xiii. 186 *Primus pastor*. Lett me syng the tenory. *IJus pastor*. And I the tryble so hye.

**Tenotomy** (tĕnǫ·tŏmi). *Surg.* [ad. F. *ténotomie*: see TENO- and -TOMY.] Cutting or division of a tendon; also *attrib.*, as *tenotomy knife*. So **Te·notome** (te·nŏtōum), a surgeon's slender knife for (subcutaneous) division of tendons; **Teno·tomist,** a surgeon who performs tenotomy; **Teno·tomize** *v. trans.*, to perform tenotomy upon.

**1842** *Lancet* 31 Dec. 509/1 Discussions in the Académie Royale de la Médicine on the subject of Tenotomy, or the section of the muscular tendons for the relief of club-foot and other..deformities. *Ibid.*, There are two classes of tenotomists, the scientific and able.., and the empirical, or ignorant operators. **1846** BRITTAN tr. *Malgaigne's Man. Oper. Surg.* 7 Subcutaneous Incisions..may be made with the common straight bistoury, with the tenotome or tendon-knife, or any other special instrument. **1872** T. G. THOMAS *Dis. Women* (ed. 3) 123 Performed subcutaneously by an ordinary tenotomy knife. **1891** *Cent. Dict.*, Tenotomize. **1901** A. H. TUBBY in *Lancet* 12 Jan. 91/2 The tendons on the radial side were tenotomised.

**Tenoun, -own, Tenour(e, -owr(e,** obs. ff. TENON, TENOR, TENURE.

**Tenpence** (te·npĕns). [TEN *a.* + PENCE.] A sum of money equal to ten pennies; a foreign coin of about this value, a franc, a lira; sometimes used contemptuously, because the amount wants something of a shilling: cf. next.

*c* **1592** MARLOWE *Jew of Malta* IV. iv, Gentleman! he flouts me: What gentry can be in a poore Turk of tenpence? **1749** FIELDING *Tom Jones* XIV. iii, As sure as ten-pence, this is the very young gentleman. **18..** RUSKIN in *B'ham Inst. Mag.* Dec. (1896) 71, I never pass a begging friar without giving him sixpence, or the equivalent fivepence of foreign coin, extending the charity even occasionally as far as tenpence, if no fivepenny bit chance to be in my purse. **1903** FARMER & HENLEY *Slang* s. v., *Only tenpence in the shilling*, a description of weak intellect.

**Tenpenny** (te·npĕni), *a.* (*sb.*)

**1.** Valued at, costing, or amounting to ten pence; sold at tenpence the piece, dozen, hundred, pound, quart, gallon, yard, or other customary unit (see also b); also in contempt: cf. *twopenny*. *Tenpenny piece* = B. 1. *Tenpenny-worth*, the amount of anything to be bought for tenpence.

**1592** *Arden of Feversham* v. i, All the tenpenny alehouses would stand euery morning with a quart pot in their hand, saying, 'will it please your worship drinke?' **1607** DEKKER & WEBSTER *Westw. Hoe* IV. ii. Wks. 1873 II. 339 If all the great Turks Concubins were but like thee, the ten-penny-infidell should neuer neede [etc.]. *c* **1645** HOWELL *Lett.* (1650) I. v. vii. 141 Lieutenant Felton..made a thrust with a common tenpeny knife..at the Duke. *a* **1668** DAVENANT *News fr. Plymouth* Wks. (1673) 2 A cloth Of Network edg'd with a Ten-penny-Lace. **1724** SWIFT *Drapier's Lett.* i. ⁋ 36 A yard of ten-penny stuff. **1821** SCOTT *Kenilw.* ii, A tenpenny-worth of cord. **1842** S. LOVER *Handy Andy* xxi, She had given him a tenpenny-piece. **1875–7** RUSKIN *Morn. in Florence* Pref., I have done more work than you will ever know of, to make them good ten-pennyworths to you.

**b.** *Tenpenny nail*: originally, a nail sold at tenpence a hundred: see PENNY 10. Now, vaguely, a nail of large size.

**1426–8** [see PENNY 10]. **1486** *Naval Acc. Hen. VII* (1896) 16 Xpeny nailes. *c* **1555** HARPSFIELD *Divorce Hen. VIII* (Camden) 172 To make the whole matter fast and sure, as it were with a tenpenny nail. **1666** W. BOGHURST *Loimographia* (1894) 66 Stomacks like Ostriches able to digest a tenpenny nail. **1826** SCOTT *Woodst.* xii, Were his nails tenpenny nails, and his teeth as long as those of a harrow.

**B.** *sb.* **1.** A piece of money: = TENPENCE. **a.** The token of the Bank of Ireland for 10*d.*, issued in 1805, 1806, and 1813. **b.** A franc or lira.

**1824** A. THOMSON in *Life & Min.* iv. (1869) 217 A gentleman..sent me seven ten-pennies—5*s.* 10*d.* Irish. **1825** *Hist. Little Pat* in *Houlston Tracts* I. No. 11. 12 Having received a present of a tenpenny from a gentleman. **1904** *Eng. Dial. Dict.* s. v. *Ten*, (Guernsey) When I get a bad tenpenny I put it in my purse and pass it.

**2. a.** A tenpenny nail. **b.** A child's school-book (originally) costing tenpence: formerly the third book used in teaching to read. *Sc.*

**1820** J. H. REYNOLDS *Fancy* (1906) 22 We've driven a hundred tenpennies already. **1893** CROCKETT *Stickit Minister* iii. 35 They stammered like a boy new into the tenpenny.

**Ten-pins** (te·npinz), *sb. pl.* Chiefly *U. S.* A game in which ten pins (see PIN *sb.*[1] 8) or 'men' are set up to be bowled at; cf. NINEPINS; *spec.* a game so played in U. S., called in England 'American bowls'. Also, the pins with which this game is played; in sing. *tenpin*, one of these.

[**1600** ROWLANDS *Lett. Humours Blood* iv. 64 To play at loggets, nine holes, or ten pinnes.] **1807** CRABBE *Par. Reg.* III. 106 When justice winked on every jovial crew, And ten-pins tumbled in the parson's view. **1842** DICKENS *Amer. Notes* vi, Ten-Pins being a game of mingled chance and skill, invented when the legislature passed an act forbidding Nine-Pins. **1884** H. C. BUNNER in *Harper's Mag.* Jan. 298/2 Base-ball and ten-pins are in no great favor. **1893** *Nation* (N. Y.) 20 July 54/2 Even a ten-pin must be set up before it is knocked down.

**b.** *attrib.* and *Comb.*, as *ten-pin alley*, *ball*.

**1868** M. H. SMITH *Sunshine & Shadow N. York* 218 The click of the billiard ball, and the booming of the ten-pin alley, are distinctly heard. **1895** *Outing* (U. S.) XXVI. 444/1 You rush to the bottom like a ten-pin ball sent spinning down its alley.

**Ten-pounder** (te·n,pau·ndəɹ). [Parasynthetic f. *ten pound*(*s* + -ER[1].]

**1. a.** A thing (e. g. a ball, a fish) weighing ten pounds; *spec.* a fish, *Elops saurus*, about three feet long, inhabiting the warmer parts of the Pacific and Atlantic Oceans; also called Big-eyed Herring. **b.** A cannon throwing a ten-pound shot.

**1695** *Lond. Gaz.* No. 3112/3, 69 Pieces of Cannon,..viz... 9 ten Pounders. **1699** DAMPIER *Voy.* II. II. 71 Tenpounders are shaped like Mullets, but are so full of very small stiff Bones..that you can hardly eat them. **1888** GOODE *Amer. Fishes* 407 The 'Big-eyed Herring' or 'Ten-pounder', *Elops saurus*.

**2.** Something of the value of, or rated at, ten pounds. **a.** A ten-pound note. **b.** A voter in a borough who was enfranchised in virtue of occupying property of the annual value of ten pounds.

**1755** JOHNSON s. v. *Pounder*, A note or bill is called a twenty pounder or ten pounder. **1829** MARRYAT *F. Mildmay* iv, I pocketed the little donation—it was a ten-pounder. **1834** *Oxford Univ. Mag.* I. 46 No candidate would venture to present himself before a body of ten-pounders. **1880** DISRAELI *Endym.* xvii, There were several old boroughs where the freemen still outnumbered the ten-pounders.

Hence **Ten-pou·ndery** *nonce-wd.*, the body of ten-pound householders.

**1840** *Fraser's Mag.* XXI. 237 He was hanged to oblige the tenpoundery of the day.

**Tenrec:** see TANREC.

**Tense** (tens), *sb.* Also 4–6 tens, temps, 6 tence. [a. OF. *tens*, 11–13th c. (also *tans*, 11–16th c.); mod.F. *temps* from 13th c. = Pr. *temps*, Sp. *tiempo*, Pg., It. *tempo*:—L. *tempus* time.]

†**1.** Time. *Obs.* (exc. in allusion to 2).

*c* **1315** SHOREHAM *Poems* I. 1061 And foluelle þat remenaunt Ine purgatoryes tense Eft-sone. *c* **1380** WYCLIF *Serm.* Sel. Wks. I. 377 Þe Gospel of Maudelen Dai is red on Fridai in Quarter Tense in Septembre among Ferials. [*Editor's note.* 'Quatuor Tempora', or, as it is called in Ireland, Quarter Tense; for the gospel read on St. Mary Magdalen's day (July 22) is the same as that for Ember Friday in September.] *c* **1386** CHAUCER *Can. Yeom. Prol. & T.* 322 It is to seken..That future temps hath maad men dissevere, In trust ther-of, from al þat euere they hadde. **1509** HAWES *Past. Pleas.* xliv. (Percy Soc.) 214 For onely of hym it is especiall,..in finall, The future tence to knowe directly. [**1843** CARLYLE *Past & Pr.* II. v, There are three Tenses, *Tempora*, or Times; and there is one Eternity.]

**2.** *Gram.* Any one of the different forms or modifications (or word-groups) in the conjugation of a verb which indicate the different times (*past*, *present*, or *future*) at which the action or state denoted by it is viewed as happening or existing, and also (by extension) the different nature of such action or state, as continuing (*imperfect*) or completed (*perfect*); also *abstr.* that quality of a verb which depends on the expression of such differences.

**1388** WYCLIF *Prol.* xv. 57 A participl of a present tens..may be resoluid into a verbe of the same tens, and a coniunccion copulatif. **1530** PALSGR. Introd. 31 These thre accidentes, mode, tens and declination parsonall. **1571** GOLDING *Calvin on Ps.* vii. 2 The tenses or tymes of verbes are oftentymes chaunged among the Hebrewes. **1580** — in Baret *Alv.* To Rdr. viii, The Coniugation, Number, Person, Tence, And Moode of Verbes. **1580** FULKE *Martiall Confut.* iv. 169 Findeth fault with him for giuing the aoristes the signification of the present temps. **1599** MASSINGER, etc. *Old Law* IV. i, Thou præterpluperfect tense of a woman. **1643** SIR T. BROWNE *Relig. Med.* I. § 11 In Eternity there is no distinction of Tenses. **1751** HARRIS *Hermes* I. vii. Wks. (1841) 152 The tenses are used to mark present, past, and future time. **1871** ROBY *Lat. Gram.* II. xvi. § 549 [In Latin there are] Six tenses...Three, denoting incomplete action... Three, denoting completed action. **1876** MASON *Eng. Gram.* (ed. 21) § 212 The tenses of the English verb are made partly by inflection, partly by the use of auxiliary verbs.

*Comb.* **1871** ROBY *Lat. Gram.* II. xvi. § 550 All verbs in the passive have in the Indicative only three simple tense-forms. **1875** WHITNEY *Life Lang.* vii. 123 A case or two of verbal tense-making. **1886** *Amer. Jrnl. Philol.* Dec. 448 That the present subjunctives of *posse* and *videri*..can ..become tense-expressing.

**b.** *fig.* or *allusively*, in conjunction with *mood*: see MOOD *sb.*[2] 2 b.

**Tense** (tens), *a.* [ad. L. *tens-us*, pa. pple. of *tendĕre* to stretch.]

**1.** Drawn tight, stretched taut; strained to stiffness; tight, rigid: chiefly said of cords, fibres, or membranes. Opposed to *lax, flaccid*. Also *transf.* of a sensation, the breathing, the pulse.

**1670** *Phil. Trans.* V. 2059 Whether the Mercury.. be sustain'd by the external Air, or by a Tense matter within. **1676** WISEMAN *Surg.* (R.), The skin was tense, also rimpled and blistered. **1728** RUTTY in *Phil. Trans.* XXXV. 563 She complain'd.. now and then of a tense Pain and a Difficulty in Respiration. **1756** C. LUCAS *Ess. Waters* I. 75 Fiddle-strings are..much more tense in wet weather than in dry. **1802** *Med. Jrnl.* VIII. 518 A small spasmodic and very tense pulse of 120, which as the pain increased, resembled the vibration of a musical string. **1834** J. FORBES *Laennec's Dis. Chest* (ed. 4) 529 The artery remains full and tense, and resists strongly the compressing finger. **1879** TOURGEE *Fool's Err.* xxxvi. 254 With every muscle as tense as those of the tiger waiting for his leap.

**b.** *Entom.* Applied to the abdomen when not divided or transversely folded, as in spiders.

**1826** KIRBY & SP. *Entomol.* IV. 350 [Abdomen] *Tense*.. when it is not folded. Ex. Most *Araneidæ*.

**2.** *fig.* In a state of nervous or mental strain or tension; strained; highly strung; 'on the stretch'; excited, or excitable; keenly sensitive.

**1821** COLERIDGE in *Blackw. Mag.* X. 254 These distinctive faculties being in a tense and active state. **1845–6** DE QUINCEY *Notes Gilfillan's Lit. Portr.* Wks. 1859 XII. 281 This collapse of a tense excitement. **1860** HOLLAND *Miss Gilbert* ix, Her sensibilities, kept tense through the long winter,..refused to respond. **1876** GEO. ELIOT *Dan. Der.* III. xxi, Gwendolen..looked at her with tense expectancy, but was silent. **1902** R. HICHENS *Londoners* 161 The house-party were now tense with excitement.

**3.** *Comb.*, as *tense-drawn, tense-fibred*, etc.

**1761** PULTENEY in *Phil. Trans.* LII. 353 Robust and tense fibred. **1891** KIPLING *Light that Failed* vii. 134 The Americans, whose rasping voices..strain tense-drawn nerves to breaking-point. **1908** *Westm. Gaz.* 15 May 2/1 The haggard, tense-eyed men, the expensively attired, withered, yet beautiful women.

**Tense,** *v. rare.* [f. TENSE *a.*; perh. at first in pa. pple. *tensed*, repr. L. *tensus* stretched, strained.] *trans.* To make tense; to stretch tight. So **Tensed** *ppl. a.*, stretched tight, tense.

**1676** H. MORE *Remarks* 141 In his supposed tensed and rarefied bodies. *Ibid.* 156 The contraction or restitution of the tensed matter. **1884** *Mind* Jan. 109 A maximal effort of tensing the extensor instead of the flexor muscles.

**Te·nseless,** *a.* [f. TENSE *sb.* + -LESS.] Having no tenses or distinctions of tense (*loosely*, not having the ordinary function of a tense, i. e. not expressing time). Hence **Te·nselessness.**

**1886** Tenseless [see TEMPORAL *a.*[1] 5 b]. **1887** W. G. HALE in *Amer. Jrnl. Philol.* Apr. 59 A sweeping doctrine like that of the tenselessness of all dependent subjunctives. **1889** *Classical Rev.* Feb. 9 Maintaining that the tenses of the subjunctive are not tenseless.., but have each their proper temporal significance.

**Tenselle,** obs. form of TINSEL, loss.

**Tensely** (te·nsli), *adv.* [f. TENSE *a.* + -LY [2].] In a tense manner. **1.** Tightly.

**1782** A. MONRO *Compar. Anat.* (ed. 3) 16 The cellular part of the peritoneum..is tensely stretched over them. **1839** LONGF. *Beatrice* xiv, Even as a cross-bow breaks, when 'tis discharged, Too tensely drawn the bow-string and the bow. **1846** HAWTHORNE *Mosses* I. v, And girdled tensely by her virgin zone. **1860** O. W. HOLMES *Elsie V.* xxiii, To keep the thong tensely stretched between his neck and the peak of the saddle.

**2.** *fig.* With intellectual, mental, or nervous strain or tension; intensely.

**1778** [W. MARSHALL] *Minutes Agric., Digest* 2 Mathematics (..perhaps this, in preference to every other science, teaches and habituates Mankind to think systematically and tensely). **1849** *Tait's Mag.* XVI. 220 We left,..deeply moved, and with nerves more tensely strung. **1893** *Nat. Observ.* 23 Dec. 127/2 There are dozens most tensely anxious for the restitution.

**Tensen,** variant of TINSEN *Obs.*

**Tenseness** (te·nsnės). [f. TENSE *a.* + -NESS.] The state or condition of being tense (*lit.* or *fig.*).

**1707** FLOYER *Physic. Pulse-Watch* 29 The Tenseness makes the Distention less. **1776** SAUNDERS in T. Percival *Ess.* (1776) III. App. 307 According to the uniformity there is between the tenseness of the fibres of the several boards, and the tone of the different pipes. **1904** W. M. RAMSAY *Lett. to 7 Ch.* xix. 261 [Grace] strains the city like a lyre into tenseness harmonious with itself.

**Tenser, -or** (te·nsəɹ). *Obs.* exc. *Hist.* Also 5 -ur, -ure, 6 tenssar. [a. OF. **tensier* = med.L. **tensārius*, f. OF. *tense, tence* defence, protection (= med.L. **tensa*), f. OF. *tenser* = med.L. *tensāre* to defend, protect: cf. OF. *tense-, tencement*, med.L. *tensāmentum*, defence, protection, also a payment to a lord for his protection and defence; also OF. *tenserie*: see next. Ulterior etymology uncertain.] An inhabitant of a city or borough who was not a citizen or freeman, but paid a rate for permission to reside and trade; a denizen.

**1444** *Rolls of Parlt.* V. 125/2 Yef eny Burgeys or Tenser of the seid Toun [Shrewsbury] be attached for eny accion personell, or for suerte of the pees within the seid Toun. **1467** in *Eng. Gilds* (1870) 383 [Ordinances of Worcester] That no maner citezen, tensur, nor inhabitaunt wᵗyn the seid cite..put out eny wolle in hurting of the seid cite. *Ibid.* 394 That euery tensure that hath ben wᵗyn the cyte a yere or more dwellynge,..be warned to be made citezen,..and yf he refuse that, that he shalle yerly pay to the comyn cofre xl.*d.* **15..** *Early Chron. Shrewsb.* in *Trans. Shropsh. Archæol. Soc.* (1880) III. 246 This yeare [1449–50] the burgesses and tenssars in Shrewsbury dyd varye. **1519** *Corpor. Accts.* in T. Phillips *Hist. Shrewsb.* (1779) 168 Ordered that Tensors selling ale should pay 6d. quarterly. **1779** T. PHILLIPS *Hist. Shrewsb.* 161 Tensors fines, to be levied before the feast of St. Catharine. **1891** F. A. HIBBERT *Eng. Gilds* 156 There could no longer be any invidious distinction between freemen and non-freemen..gildsmen and tensers.

So † **Te·nserie** *Obs.* [corresp. to OF. *tenserie* protection, = med.L. *tenseria*, **tensāria* payment for protection, tallage (Du Cange): see above], a tallage or tax exacted by lords from their vassals or tenants, in name of a payment for protection and defence; **Tensership**, the status of a tenser, or rate paid for this privilege.

[**1151** *Concilium Londin.* i. (Du Cange), Ut ecclesiæ et possessiones ecclesiasticæ ab..exactionibus, quas vulgo tenserias sive tallagias vocant, omnino liberæ permaneant.] **1154** *O. E. Chron.* (Laud MS.) an. 1137, Hi læiden gæildes o þe tunes..& clepeden it tenserie. [**1176** *Pipe Roll 22 Hen. II* (1904) 75 Baldwinus Spinc reddit compotum de .xx.s. pro tenseria [C. R. tensaria] quam accepit de Brantona]. **1700** GOUGH *Hist. of Myddle* 128 This Richard Muckleston.. commenced a suite against the Towne of Shrewsbury for exacting an imposition upon him which they call tensorship. **1747** *Poll for Borough of Shrewsb.* 29–30 June in *Trans. Shropsh. Archæol. Soc.* III. 234 This Tensership is a ffine or acknowledgment commonly paid by persons following trade in the town that are no Burgesses.

**Tensible** (te·nsĭb'l), *a.* [ad. mod.L. **tensibil-is* that may be stretched, f. *tens-*, ppl. stem of *tendĕre* to stretch.] Capable of being stretched; = TENSILE 1. Hence **Tensibi·lity.**

**1626** BACON *Sylva* § 327 Gold..is the Closest..of Metals: And is likewise the most Flexible, and Tensible. **1861** FAIRBAIRN *Iron* 191 Direct tensible strength, compressive strength. **1676** *Phil. Trans.* XI. 707 What is the matter, structure, tenacity, tensibility,..and various use of Fibres?

**Tensify** (te·nsifəi), *v. rare.* [f. L. *tens-us*, TENSE *a.* + -[I]FY.] *trans.* To make tense.

**1869** BUSHNELL *Wom. Suffrage* iii. 50 Fibred, tensified and toned for action.

**Tensile** (te·nsil, -əil), *a.* Also 7 tensil. [ad. mod.L. *tensil-is* capable of stretching, f. *tens-*, ppl. stem of *tendĕre* to stretch: see -IL, -ILE.]

**1.** Capable of being stretched; susceptible of extension; ductile.

**1626** BACON *Sylva* § 845 All bodies ductile, and tensile, that will be drawn into wires. **1666** J. SMITH *Old Age* (1676) 173 The dry, solid, tensile, hard, and crusty parts of the body. **1794** MRS. PIOZZI *Synon.* I. 175, I have omitted *tensile* on the list,..only because 'tis out of use in talk. **1874** TAIT *Rec. Adv. Phys. Sc.* xiii. (1876) 313 It [a soap-bubble] has two tensile surfaces with a layer of water between them.

**2.** Of, of the nature of, or pertaining to tension; exercising or sustaining tension.

**1841** *Civil Engin. & Arch. Jrnl.* IV. 31/2 Cast iron..will bear a very considerable tensile strain. **1857** WHEWELL *Hist. Induct. Sci.* (ed. 3) II. 444 Wrought iron yields to compressive somewhat more easily than to tensile force. **1868** JOYNSON *Metals* 90 It possesses a tensile strength double that of good malleable iron. **1898** *Allbutt's Syst. Med.* V. 936 This tensile strain is due to the stress of the hypertrophied left ventricle.

**3.** Of a musical instrument: Producing sounds from stretched strings. *rare*—°.

In recent Dicts.

Hence **Te·nsiled** *a.* (*rare*—°), 'made tensile; rendered capable of tension' (Webster 1864); **Te·nsilely** *adv.*, in relation to tension; **Tensi·lity**, tensile condition or quality.

**1871** *Standard* 28 Jan., Small forgings are generally tensilely stronger proportionately than large ones. **1659** H. MORE *Immort. Soul* II. x. (1662) 102 The libration or reciprocation of the spirits in the tensility of the muscles. **1910** *Daily News* 14 Apr. 6 A tensility which almost doubles when the metal is wrought and drawn.

**Tension** (te·nʃən), *sb.* Also 7–8 tention. [prob. a. F. *tension* (*a* 1530 in Godef. *Compl.*), ad. late L. *tensiōn-em*, n. of action f. *tendĕre* to stretch (pa. pple. *tens-us, tent-us*). But the Eng. word may have been direct from 16th c. medical Latin.

With *tension* agree *distension, extension, pretension*; the variant *tention* agrees with *attention, contention, intention*.]

The action of stretching or condition of being stretched: in various senses.

**1.** *Physiol.* and *Path.* The condition, in any part of the body, of being stretched or strained; a sensation indicating or suggesting this; a feeling of tightness. (The earliest use in English.)

**1533** ELYOT *Cast. Helthe* (1541) 59 b, There is felt within the bulke of a man..a weyghtynesse with tension, or thrustyng outwarde. **1603** HOLLAND *Plutarch's Mor.* 656 The veines..upon the tention and commotion whereof..drunkennesse doth proceed. **1615** CROOKE *Body of Man* 739 The first is a streatching or Tention not without strife or contention. **1704** F. FULLER *Med. Gymn.* (1705) 30 What I mean by this Tension or Tone of the Parts. **1725** *Bradley's Fam. Dict.* s. v. *Vomiting*, The tention of the Hypocondria and confus'd Sight. **1756** BURKE *Subl. & B.* IV. iii, An unnatural tension of the nerves. **1855** H. SPENCER *Princ. Psychol.* II. xi. § 55. 213 A correspondingly strong sensation of muscular tension.

**b.** *Bot.* Applied to a strain or pressure in the cells or tissues of plants arising from changes taking place in the course of growth.

**1875** BENNETT & DYER *Sachs' Bot.* 708 Causes of the condition of Tension in Plants. The elasticity of the organised parts of plants results in tension chiefly from the operation of three causes. *Ibid.* 713 In a turgid cell, the cell-wall is..in a state of negative, the contents in a state of positive tension. *Ibid.* 720 It is only when the epidermis is becoming cuticularised and the walls of the bast-cells are beginning to thicken that the tensions become perceptible.

**2.** *fig.* A straining, or strained condition, of the mind, feelings, or nerves. **a.** Straining of the mental powers or faculties; severe or strenuous intellectual effort; intense application.

*a* **1763** SHENSTONE *Economy* I. 151 When fancy's vivid spark impels the soul To scorn quotidian scenes,.. what nostrum shall compose Its fatal tension? **1826** W. GIFFORD *Let.* in Smiles *Mem. J. Murray* (1891) II. xxv. 172 It is a fearful thing to break down the mind by unremitted tension. **1875** JOWETT *Plato* (ed. 2) IV. 12 The mind cannot be always in a state of intellectual tension.

**b.** Nervous or emotional strain; intense suppressed excitement; a strained condition of feeling or mutual relations which is for the time outwardly calm, but is likely to result in a sudden collapse, or in an outburst of anger or violent action of some kind.

**1847** DISRAELI *Tancred* IV. vi, The expression..of extreme tension..had disappeared. **1852** MRS. STOWE *Uncle Tom's C.* vii, As the danger decreased with the distance, the supernatural tension of the nervous system lessened. **1878** LECKY *Eng. in 18th C.* II. vii. 311 Society cannot permanently exist in a condition of extreme tension. **1885** *L'pool Daily Post* 11 Apr. 64/7 A tension of feeling which has had no parallel since the outbreak of the Crimean war.

**3.** *Physics.* A constrained condition of the particles of a body when subjected to forces acting in opposite directions away from each other (usually along the body's greatest length), thus tending to draw them apart, balanced by forces of cohesion holding them together; the force or combination of forces acting in this way, esp. as a measurable quantity. (The opposite of *compression* or *pressure*.)

**1685** BOYLE *Effects of Mot.* viii. 92 If you cut the string of a bent bow asunder, the..extreams will fly from one another suddenly and forcibly enough to manifest that they were before in a violent state of Tension. **1782** V. KNOX *Ess.* xxi. I. 101 The string which is constantly kept in a state of tension will vibrate on the slightest impulse. **1825** J. NICHOLSON *Operat. Mechanic* 570 The strain occasioned by pulling timber in the direction of its length is called *tension*. **1853** KANE *Grinnell Exp.* xxviii. (1856) 232 The tension of the great field of ice over which we passed must have been enormous. It had a sensible curvature. **1881** *Metal World* No. 18. 277 A weight being placed on a beam or girder (..resting on the support at each end..), the top is ..thrown into compression and the bottom into tension.

**b.** Inexactly used for the expansive force of a gas or vapour, properly called *pressure*.

**1678** CUDWORTH *Intell. Syst.* I. v. 851 A pressure upon the optick nerve, by reason of a tension of the intermedious air, or æther. **1826** FARADAY *Exp. Res.* xxxiii. 200 The air..has a certain degree of elasticity, or tension. **1844** *Civil Engin. & Arch. Jrnl.* VII. 155/1 The steam..is retained between the boiler and the plate until by its 'tension' or elasticity it is forced downwards and underneath the edge of the plate. **1863** TYNDALL *Heat* i. § 9 (1870) 8 He wishes to apply the force of his steam, or of the furnace which gives tension to his steam, to this particular purpose.

**c.** *transf.* A device in a sewing-machine for regulating the tightness of the stitch. Also *tension-device*.

**1877** KNIGHT *Dict. Mech.* s. v., By adjustment of the pressure at the tension device, the required tightness of stitch is obtained...There are many..kinds of tensions, in different machines. Fig. 6309 shows the..automatic tension...The automatic tension-device..is placed in the standard of the machine.

**4.** *Electr.* The stress along lines of force in a dielectric. Formerly applied also to surface density of electric charge, and until about 1882 used vaguely as a synonym for potential, electromotive force, and mechanical force exerted by electricity: still so applied, in industrial and commercial use, in *high* and *low tension*: see sense 5.

**1802** *Nicholson's Jrnl. Nat. Phil.* I. 137 (tr. Volta) In the one case, as well as in the other, the electric tension [*la tensione elettrica*] rises, during the contact, to the same point. **1833** FARADAY *Exp. Res.* (1855) I. 97 The attractions and repulsions due to the tension of ordinary electricity. **1837** BREWSTER *Magnet.* 159 The sun heating and illuminating the earth, and producing a magnetic tension. **1839** G. BIRD *Nat. Phil.* 218 On their separation they are found to possess..a certain quantity of free electricity of low tension. **1841** W. FRANCIS (tr. Ohm 1827) in *Taylor's Sci. Mem.* II. 416 (*Ohm's Law*) The force of the current in a galvanic circuit is directly as the sum of all the tensions [*die Summe aller Spannungen*], and inversely as the entire reduced length of the circuit. **1849** NOAD *Electricity* (ed. 3) 135 *Tension*, Mr. Harris applies to the actual force of a charge to break down any non-conducting or dielectric medium between two terminating electrified planes. **1866** R. M. FERGUSON *Electr.* (1870) 64 Tension is the power to polarise and effect discharge. **1871** TYNDALL *Fragm. Sc.* (1879) II. xvi. 439 Such machines deliver a large quantity of electricity of low tension. **1873** MAXWELL *Electr. & Magn.* (1881) I. 59 Finding the phrase *electric tension* used in several vague senses, I have attempted to confine it to.. the state of stress in the dielectric medium which causes motion of the electrified bodies, and leads, when continually augmented, to disruptive discharge. **1881** S. P. THOMPSON *Electr. & Magn.* 203 *note*, The word *tension*..is so often misapplied in text-books...The term would be invaluable if we might adopt it to denote only the mechanical stress across a dielectric, due to accumulated charges. **1882** *Nature* 12 Oct. 570/2 M. Gariel breaks free from servitude to the consecrated term 'tension', so often misused as a synonym for potential, electro-motive force, and we know not what. *fig.* **1859** KINGSLEY *Misc.* (1860) II. 75 Everything..has exasperated, not calmed, the electric tension of the European atmosphere.

**5. High tension**: a high degree of tension (of any kind); **a.** *esp.* in *Electr.* a term for a high degree of electromotive force or difference of potential: now chiefly used by makers of motor-cars, and of magnetic and induction coils. So **Low tension.** (See sense 4.) Chiefly *attrib.* as in *high* or *low tension system* (of electric lighting, etc.); also *h. t.* or *l. t. charge, contact, current, fuse,* etc.

**1889** *Daily News* 7 Oct. 3/1 Mr. Crompton does not say that the high tension system will not succeed. He says both will succeed; but that the low tension system is safer and cheaper. **1891** *Cent. Dict.* s.v. *Tension*, A body is said to have a high-tension charge, or a charge of high-tension electricity, and a conductor to carry a high-tension current, when the stress in the medium surrounding the body or the conductor is high. **1900** *Engineering Mag.* XIX. 715 When required for high-tension fuses, the armature of this exploder is wound with very fine wire; when for low-tension, with coarse wire. **1903** *Motor. Ann.* 221 The low tension system is one which will undoubtedly come to the fore. In this the actual current from the battery, or magneto machine, is interrupted inside the cylinder, thus causing a spark. **1906** *Westm. Gaz.* 13 Nov. 4/2 High-tension magneto, it is noted, is gaining in popularity—the low-tension system being confined almost exclusively to the very high-priced cars. **1907** *Ibid.* 5 Dec. 4/2 The low-tension make and break is made on platinum points by means of a cam, whilst the high-tension contact is made through metal contacts by a revolving carbon brush.

**b.** Of the pulse: cf. TENSE *a.* 1 (quot. 1802).

**1898** *Allbutt's Syst. Med.* V. 983 The low-tension pulse presents marked fluctuations of the base line. *Ibid.* 1024 Sir W. Broadbent considers that this modified high tension pulse is almost constant in mitral stenosis.

**6.** *attrib.* and *Comb.*, as *tension area, device* (see 3 c), *thrill*; *spec.* applied to parts of a structure subjected to tensile stress, as *tension-bar, -member, -rod*; **tension-bridge**, a bridge in which there is tensile stress between parts of the structure, as a bowstring-bridge (see BOWSTRING 3, and quot. here); **tension-fuse**, a form of electric fuse which is fired by a spark at a break in a circuit; **tension magnet** (see quot.); **tension-pulley, -roller**, a free pulley or roller over which a belt, etc. passes to keep it stretched tight; a tightening-pulley; **tension-rail**, a rail for stretching cloth during the process of printing; **tension-spicule**, in sponges (see quot.); **tension-spring**, a spring for carriages, etc. composed of inner and outer leaves, connected at the ends, but free in the middle, so as to elongate independently under strain.

**1871** TYNDALL *Fragm. Sc.* I. i. 20 At the beginning the *vis viva* was zero and the *tension area was a maximum. **1877** KNIGHT *Dict. Mech.*, **Tension-bridge*, a bridge constructed on the principle of the bow, the arch supporting the track by means of tension-rods, and the string acting as a tie. **1890** *Cent. Dict.* s.v. *Fuse*, **Tension-fuse*, an electric fuse in which the conducting circuit is not complete, the firing being accomplished by the passage of a spark. **1891** *Ibid.* s.v., An electromagnet surrounded by a coil of many turns and high electrical resistance was called by Henry a **tension magnet*. **1844** STEPHENS *Bk. Farm* II. 303 For the purpose of keeping a due degree of tension on the chain, a small movable *tension pulley is applied. **1890** W. J. GORDON *Foundry* 169 To..draw in the apparently endless plain white calico, zigzagging it over *tension rails, and running it on, giving it an extra colour at every turn. **1838** *Civil Eng. & Arch. Jrnl.* I. 126/1 Each pair of rafters is tied by means of a *tension rod. *Ibid.* 381/1 The platform, or roadway, was laid upon cast iron beams, suspended from the main chains by perpendicular iron bars or tension rods, about five feet apart. **1835** URE *Philos. Manuf.* 196 The *tension or stretching-roller has its axle mounted in the segment-racks as usual. **1886** VON LENDENFELD in *Proc. Zool. Soc.* 21 Dec. 564 Called Flesh-spicules or Microsclera (**Tension-spicules* of Bowerbank). **1877** KNIGHT *Dict. Mech.*, **Tension-spring*, a spring for wagons, railway-carriages, etc...The outer leaves..impart a tensile strain to the inner ones. **1893** T. E. BROWN *Old John*, etc. 111 To him the sorrows are the *tension-thrills Of that serene endeavour.

Hence **Te·nsion** *v. trans.*, to subject to tension, tighten, make taut (hence **Te·nsioned** *ppl. a.*, **Te·nsioning** *vbl. sb.*); **Te·nsional** *a.*, of, pertaining to, of the nature of, or affected with tension; **Te·nsionless** *a.*, without tension, unstrained.

**1872** *Daily News* 28 Feb., The whole nation was hanging in a *tensioned spasm of fear. *a* **1879** TYNDALL (Webster Supp.), A highly tensioned string. **1893** DE LONG in *Chicago Advance* 28 Sept., How tensioned are our nerves! **1898** *Cycling* 48 Upon the correct tensioning of the spokes [of a bicycle] depends the 'truth' of the wheel. **1906** *Cycl. Tour. Club Gaz.* Aug. 311 The tensioning is done by turning the three screws at the back of the saddle upwards from the right to left, so as to withdraw them. Most riders make the mistake when tensioning the saddle of turning the screws the wrong way. **1862** *Catal. Internat. Exhib.* II. x. 6 The *tensional parts of a pair of rigid trusses. **1881** *Athenæum* 2 July 16/3 The total energy of vibrations as being made up of two parts, one statical or tensional, and the other kinetic. **1905** *Dundee Advertiser* 22 Dec. 9/2 A lecture on the subject of 'The *Tensionless Drive'. The lecturer treated of the efficacy of belts as a means of transmitting power.

**Tensity** (te·nsĭti). [f. L. *tens-us* TENSE *a.* + -ITY: cf. *intensity*.] The quality or condition of being tense; a state of tension.

**a.** *lit.* (chiefly *Physiol.* and *Path.*).

**1658** PHILLIPS, *Tensity*, stiffnesse, or a being stretched out hard. **1676** COLE in *Phil. Trans.* XI. 604 There could be, in that supposition of a Continuity of fibre, tensity enough in the Intestins to carry on such a motion. **1717** J. KEILL *Anim. Oecon.* (1738) 261 That robust Tensity of the Fibres, which makes strong People the less liable to accidents.

**b.** *fig.*

**1862** CARLYLE *Fredk. Gt.* XI. vii. (1872) IV. 95 It braced him into such a tensity of spirit. **1884** W. COLLINS *I say No* I. ix, The first change of expression which relaxed the iron tensity of the housekeeper's face showed itself.

**Tensive** (te·nsiv), *a.* [a. F. *tensif, -ive* (Paré 16th c.), f. L. *tens-*, ppl. stem of *tendĕre* (see TENSE *a.* and -IVE). Cf. *intensive*.] Having the quality of stretching or straining; causing tension; in *Path.* applied to a sensation of tension or tightness in any part of the body.

**1702** J. PURCELL *Cholick* (1714) 95 After violent Exercises we always feel a Tensive Pain in the Left side. **1897** *Allbutt's Syst. Med.* IV. 149 The pain is usually dull and tensive.

**Tensome** (te·nˌsǝ̆m), *a.* (*sb.*) *Sc.* [f. TEN + -SOME.] Ten together, consisting of a company or set of ten. Also as *sb.* A set or cluster of ten.

**1563** WINȜET tr. *Vincent. Lirinensis* Wks. (S. T. S.) II. 75 Al in the haly number of that table of ten-sum at Ephesus. *a* **1584** MONTGOMERIE *Cherrie & Slae* 453 Maire honor is to vanquisch ane, Nor feicht with tensum and be tane. **1898** J. PATON *Castlebraes* ix. 284 The glee o' Tensome an' Twalsome Faimilies.

‖ **Tenson** (te·nsǝn, tãnsoṅ). Also 9 **tenzon.** [F. *tenson* = Pr. *tenso*, a poetical contest; in OF. contention, contest: see TENCION.] A contest in verse beween rival troubadours; a piece of verse or song composed for or sung in such a contest.

**1840** BROWNING *Sordello* II. 686 While, out of dream, his day's work went To tune a crazy tenzon or sirvent. **1883** A. H. WODEHOUSE in Grove *Dict. Mus.* III. 585/1 The *tensons*, or contentions, were metrical dialogues of lively repartee on some disputed point of gallantry. **1895** H. GAELYN *To Elise*, Would I could write for my Elise Trim triolets and tensons tender!

**Tensor** (te·nsǭɹ, -ǝɹ). [a. mod.L. *tensor*, agent-n. from *tendĕre* to stretch.]

**1.** *Anat.* (also *tensor muscle*): A muscle that stretches or tightens some part. Opp. to *laxator*.

In mod. use, distinguished from an *extensor* by not altering the direction of the part.

**1704** J. HARRIS *Lex. Techn.* I, *Tensors*, or *Extensors*, are those common Muscles that serve to extend the Toes, and have their Tendons inserted into all the lesser Toes. **1799** HOME in *Phil. Trans.* XC. 10 The combined action of the tensor and laxator muscles varying the degree of its [the membrana tympani] tension. **1808** BARCLAY *Muscular Motions* 384 The biceps..being a flexor and supinator of the fore-arm, and at the same time a tensor of its fascia. **1879** *St. George's Hosp. Rep.* IX. 591 The functions of the adductors and tensors are more delicate.

**2.** *Math.* In Quaternions, a quantity expressing the ratio in which the length of a vector is increased.

**1853** HAMILTON *Elem. Quaternions* II. i. (1866) 108 The former element of the complex relation..between..two lines or vectors [*viz.* their relative length], is..represented by a simple ratio.., or by a number expressing that ratio. *Note*, This number, which we shall..call the *tensor* of the quotient,..may always be equated..to a positive scalar. **1886** W. S. ALDIS *Solid Geom.* xiv. (ed. 4) 235 Since the operation denoted by a quaternion consists of two parts, one of rotating OA into the position OB and the other of extending OA into the length OB, a quaternion may be..represented as the product of two factors,..the versor..and ..the tensor of the quaternion.

**b.** *Comb.*, as *tensor-twist*, in Clifford's biquaternions, a twist multiplied by a tensor.

**Tensor, tensur, -ure**, var. ff. TENSER *Obs.*

† **Tensue** = *to ensue*: see T' and ENSUE *v.*

**1513** BRADSHAW *St. Werburge*, *2nd Balade* 16 The for tensue, that art theyr lode-sterre.

† **Te·nsure.** *Obs.* [ad. mod.L. *tensūra* stretching, f. *tendĕre* to stretch: see -URE.] Stretching, strain; = TENSION.

**1611** BARREY *Ram Alley* Epil. in Hazl. *Dodsley* X. 380 But he..Submits the tensures of his pains To those, whose wit and nimble brains Are able best to judge. **1626** BACON *Sylva* § 12 This Motion upon Pressure, and the Reciprocall thereof, which is Motion upon Tensure; we use to call (by one common Name) Motion of Liberty. **1653** R. G. tr. *Bacon's Hist. Winds* 318 As for the freeing from tensure or stretching. **1672** WALLIS in *Phil. Trans.* VII. 5165 Its Spring being of a like tensure with that of the outward Air.

**Tensyn**, variant of TINSEN *Obs.*

**Tent** (tent), *sb.*[1] Forms: 3–6 **tente**, (5 **teinte, teynte**, 5–6 **tentt(e**, 6 **tenthe**), 4– **tent.** [a. OF. *tente* (12th c. in Godef. *Compl.*):—L. *tenta*, pl. of *tentum*, pa. pple. of *tendĕre* to stretch; = med.L. *tenta, tentum* tent (in Du Cange); cf. also It., Pr. *tenda*, Sp. *tienda*, med.L. *tenda* (13th c. in Du Cange), assimilated to *tendĕre*.]

**1.** A portable shelter or dwelling of canvas (formerly of skins or cloth), supported by means of a pole or poles, and usually extended and secured by ropes fastened to pegs which are driven into the ground; used by travellers, soldiers, nomads, and others; a pavilion; also, a similar shelter erected on a travelling boat or wagon.

**1297** R. GLOUC. (Rolls) 4156 Hii come to barbesflet & piȝte þer bi syde Hor tentes & hor pauilons. *a* **1300** *Cursor M.* 7709 He sett his tentes in a dale. *Ibid.* 7714 Þai went, Vn-to þe kings aun tent. *c* **1330** R. BRUNNE *Chron.* (1810) 67 Þar loges & þare tentis vp þei gan bigge. **1387** TREVISA *Higden* (Rolls) III. 125 Antecrist schal be slawe in his owne tent in þe mount Olyuete. *c* **1400** *Destr. Troy* 10190 The troiens.. Takyn þere tenttes, turnyt hom vnder. *c* **1450** *Merlin* iii. 46 How he wolde come be nyght hym-self to his teynte. **1535** COVERDALE 1 *Kings* xii. 16 Get the to thy tentes [WYCLIF, Turne aȝen into thi tabernaclis] O Israel [*Geneva*, **1611**, To your tents, O Israel]. **1552** HULOET, Tent or bouthe in a fayre or market. *a* **1570** in Feuillerat *Revels Q. Eliz.* (1908) 407 Comptroller of her graces Revelles tenthes & pavillions. **1594** SHAKS. *Rich. III*, v. iii. 7 Vp with my Tent, heere wil I lye to night, But where to morrow? **1617** MORYSON *Itin.* II. 82 The weather grew so extreme, as it blew downe all our Tents, and tore them in pieces. **1717** LADY M. W. MONTAGU *Let. to Abbé Conti* 17 May, The Sultan is already gone to his tents, and all his Court. **1719** DE FOE *Crusoe* I. 285 Friday and I, in about two Hours Time, made a very handsome Tent, cover'd with old Sails. **1844** LONGF. *Day is done* 43 The cares, that infest the day, Shall fold their tents, like the Arabs, And as silently steal away. **1844** [see PITCH *v.*[1] 4].

† **b.** A sheet or screen of canvas or the like.

**1572** in Feuillerat *Revels Q. Eliz.* (1908) 179 Hanging up Tentes to keepe away the wynde & snow from dryving into the hall.

**2.** *transf.* Something likened to or resembling a tent; *spec.* **b.** in *Photogr.*, a curtained box serving as a portable dark-room; **c.** the silken web of a tent-caterpillar.

**1599** DAVIES *Immort. Soul* IV. xxi, Heav'ns wide-spreading Tent. **1862** B. TAYLOR *Poet's Jrnl.* III. *Myst. Summer* 52 Its little bell expands, for me, A tent of silver lily fair.

**d.** The name given to a local 'lodge' or 'habitation' of the Rechabites; also of the Zionists.

[From the tents in which the ancient Rechabites dwelt, Jer. xxxv. 7, and those in which Israel dwelt in the wilderness.]

**1886** *Rechabite Mag.* July 151 (Cassell) The sick funds in the possession of the various tents. **1897** E. REICH in *19th Cent.* Aug. 261 At the head of religious Zionism are the numerous 'Tents' of the 'Lovers of Zion'. *Ibid.* Oct. 633 The English Association, known as the Chovevi Zion..has 35 established 'Tents', spread through the length and breadth of the United Kingdom.

**e.** Applied to a hut.

*a* **1873** DEUTSCH *Rem.* (1874) 178 The people dwelling during their lifetime in tents of mud. **1887** HALL CAINE *Deemster* xxxvii. 247 A little disjointed gipsy encampment of mud-built tents pitched on the bare moor.

**3.** *fig.* An abode, residence, habitation, dwelling-place; esp. in phrases *to have, pitch one's tent(s.*

*c* **1366** CHAUCER *A. B. C.* 9 Bountee so fix hath in þin herte his tente. **1535** COVERDALE *Ps.* lxxxiii[i]. 10 To dwell in the tentes of the vngodly [**1611** tents of wickednesse]. **1624** DAVIES *Psalm xv*, Lord! who shall dwell in thy bright tent with Thee? **1700** DRYDEN *Theodore & Hon.* 59 To Chassis' pleasing plains he took his way, There pitched his tents, and there resolved to stay. **1827** *Edin. Weekly Jrnl.* 28 Feb., They..spoke of the theatre as of the tents of sin. **1887** HALL CAINE *Coleridge* iv, Roscoe invited him to pitch his tent in Liverpool.

**4.** *Sc.* A portable pulpit set up in the open air for the preacher on sacramental or other occasions when the worshippers are too numerous to be accommodated in the church.

**1678** LADY METHVEN *Let.* in *Ladies of Covt.* (1853) Introd. 34 They had their tent set up upon your ground. **1689** in *Faithful Contendings* (1780) 381 A tent being set up before, Mr. Shields continued in his lecture. **1785** BURNS *Holy Fair* xiv, But, hark! the tent has chang'd its voice. **1837** LOCKHART *Scott* May an. 1819, Every kirk in the neighbourhood being left empty when it was known he was to mount the tent at any country sacrament. **1885** EDGAR *Old Ch. Life Scot.* 177 Besides a church, every parish required a tent. This..was not a tabernacle of canvas for sheltering the worshippers, but a moveable pulpit made of wood for the preacher to stand in.

**5.** *attrib.* and *Comb.* **a.** Simple attrib. 'of, consisting of, belonging to, used in, dwelling in, a tent or tents', as *tent accommodation, -cloth, -curtain, -fashion, -fellow, -frame, -house* (also *fig.*), *-life, -mate, -pole, -post, -roof, -rope, -sail* (SAIL *sb.*[1] 7), *-school, -skirt, -staff, -table, -tomb, -wagon*; objective and obj. genitive, as *tent-holder, -keeper, -owner, -pitcher, -pitching*; instrumental, etc., as *tent-clad, -dotted, -dwelling, -like* adjs.; also, in sense 4, *tent-preaching, -reader, -sermon.*

? **1780** W. CARTER *Disbanded Subaltern* 22 Close at the bottom of this *tent-clad hill. **1552** HULOET, *Tente clothes, wherwith tentes are couered. **1836** *Uncle Philip's Convers. Whale Fishery* 13 The sinews..they use in sewing their coats and tent cloths. **1648** OWEN *Serm. Hab. iii. 1–9* Wks. 1851 VIII. 98 The *tent-dwelling Arabians. **1856** KANE *Arct. Expl.* II. xvi. 176 Their neat canvas housing rigged *tent-fashion. **1904** *Expositor* Apr. 311 Men from all parts of Greece were *tent fellows and messmates. **1905** *Daily Chron.* 22 Aug. 6/5 At a largely attended meeting of *tent-holders at Scuthend..it was pointed out that, according to legal advice, the tent-owners were in the position of trespassers. **1625** *Balcarres Proclam.* No. 1431 *Tent-keeper. **1688** R. HOLME *Armoury* III. xix. (Roxb.) 164/1 Dayly pay..Pioners each 1s. Tent Keepers each 18d. **1858** G. RHODES (*title*) Tents and *Tent-Life, from the Earliest Ages to the Present Time. **1864** TREVELYAN *Compet. Wallah* (1866) 114 Tent-life in the winter months is very enjoyable. **1840** LONGF. *Spanish Stud.* III. v, Behold, how beautiful she stands Under the *tent-like trees! **1695** tr. *Colbatch's New Lt. Chirurg. put out* 48 Seeing some of his *Tent-mates, I asked them if he was distracted? **1875** SIR T. SEATON *Fret Cutting* 77 Tell your *tent-pitcher to give me two long tent-pins and two short ones. **1706** *Lond. Gaz.* No. 4189/4 Out of the Albion Frigat,..Pictures, *Tent Poles. **1855** MILMAN *Lat. Chr.* V. 13 The Mamelukes..tied him to a *tent-post with his hands behind his back. **1825** JAMIESON s. v., Scottish Presbyterians..still feel some degree of partiality to *tent-preaching. *a* **1722** PENNECUIK *Wks.* (1815) 345 (E.D.D.) He was *tent-reader of our service book. **1424** *Mem. Ripon* (Surtees) II. 151 Pro ij wellrapis, ij *tenterapis, et j veylrape cum j corda..5*s.* **1828–40** TYTLER *Hist. Scot.* (1864) I. 152 Douglas..penetrated to the royal tent, [and] cut the tent-ropes. **1892** RIDER HAGGARD *Nada* 2 The shivering natives..took refuge on the second waggon, drawing a *tent-sail over them. **1909** *Jrnl. Educ.* Apr. 294/2 South Australia...A new plan for the education of children in remote parts of the State...The first *tent school has already been established and is to be found in the Hundred of Shannon, on Eyre Peninsula. **1805** J. RAMSAY *Scot. & Scotsm. in 18th C.* (1888) II. i. 25 *Tent-sermons were retained by general consent. **1896** 'M. FIELD' *Attila* IV. 106 At last they caught the *tent-skirt in their hands And entered one by one. **1864** BOUTELL *Her. Hist. & Pop.* xxi. § 11 (ed. 3) 369 The *tent-staff and pennon all or. **1893** *Month* Apr. 523, I live in a *tent-wagon.

**b.** Special Combs.: **tent-barge**, a barge having a tent-like canvas awning; **tent-bottom**, a board floor fitted to a tent; **tent-caterpillar**, the gregarious larva of a North American bombycid moth, *Clisiocampa*, which spins a tent-like web; **tent-fly**: see FLY *sb.*[2] 4 b; also, an exterior sheet stretched over the ridge-pole so as to cover the ordinary tent-roof with an air-space between; **tent-man**, (*a*) a tent-dweller; (*b*) one who has charge of a tent; **tent-master**: see quot.; **tent-pin** = TENT-PEG; **tent-tree**, a species of screw-pine: see quot. See also TENT-BED, TENT-DOOR, etc.

**1796** STEDMAN *Surinam* II. xix. 71 A decent *tent-barge with six oars. **1902** *Fortn. Rev.* June 988 The wooden *tent-bottoms are placed outside the tents and thoroughly scrubbed three times a week. **1884** ROE *Nat. Ser. Story* iv, A colony of jays would soon destroy all the *tent-caterpillars. **1901** *Board Agric. Leaflet* No. 69. 1 Two species of so-called 'Tent Caterpillars' are frequently found on various fruit trees. **1897** H. PORTER in *Cent. Mag.* Apr. 831 A hospital *tent-fly was stretched in front of the office tent so as to make a shaded space. **1880** L. WALLACE *Ben-Hur* 231 Drink, for this is the fear-naught of the *tentmen. **1660** HEXHAM, *Een Tenten-meester*, a *Tent-master, or a Marshall of a Campe. **1807** WILKINSON in Pike *Sources Mississ.* II. (1810) App. 24 We found..many *tent-pins made of wood. **1875** [see *tent-pitcher* in a]. **1884** MILLER *Plant-n.*, **Tent-tree*, of Lord Howe's Island, *Pandanus Forsteri*.

Hence **Te·ntful**, as many as fill a tent; **Te·ntwards** *adv.*, towards a tent; **Te·ntwise** *adv.*[1], in the manner or shape of a tent.

**1897** *Daily News* 24 May 6/5 The whole *tentful of people rose and the gentlemen reverently uncovered. **1893** *Westm. Gaz.* 7 Oct. 2/1 Four weird figures tramping *tentwards after a long day abroad. **1530** TINDALE *Exodus* Table Expound. Words, *Tabernacle*, an house made *tentwise, or as a pauelion. **1846** MRS. GORE *Sk. Eng. Char.* (1852) 39 A genteel youth..whose straight, yellow hair is combed up, tent-wise, on the top of his head.

**Tent** (tent), *sb.*[2] Now *Sc.* and *north. dial.* Also 4–5 **tente**, (5 **teynt**). [Aphetic for ATTENT and *entent*, INTENT: cf. TEND *v.*[1], of which *tent* is practically a deriv., as *attent* of *attend*, *intent* of *intend*.]

**1.** Attention, heed, care; nearly always in the phrases †*give tent*, to give heed, pay attention (*obs.*), and *take tent*, to take heed, take care; with *to*, to pay attention to, take heed to; = ATTENT *sb.* 1, 2, INTENT *sb.* 2.

*a* **1300** *Cursor M.* 661 Lok for-þi, þat ȝee tak tent þat ȝee ne brek mi commament. *Ibid.* 19464 A child hight saulus ..Tok tent to-quils to þair wede. *Ibid.* 19514 Þar þe folk wit full assent Til his wordes gaf þair tent. *c* **1325** *Song of Mercy* 8 in *E. E. P.* (1862) 118 Of whuche, to on i toke goode tent. *c* **1330** R. BRUNNE *Chron. Wace* (Rolls) 7025 Þe kyng til hym gaf no tent. **1382** WYCLIF *Ps.* lxxvii. 1 Taketh tente, my puple, to my lawe. — 1 *Tim.* iv. 1 In the laste tymes summen schulen departe fro the feith, ȝyuynge tent to spiritis of errour. **1388** — *Ps.* xxxix. [xl.] 1 He ȝaf tent to me. *c* **1400** *Laud Troy Bk.* 4333 To theire schippis hadde thei no teynt. **1533** GAU *Richt Vay* (S. T. S.) 65 Tak tent that thow sine na mair. *a* **1637** B. JONSON *Underwoods, Eupheme* I. viii, The high parliament Of Heaven; where Seraphim take tent Of ordering all. **1728** RAMSAY *Last Sp. Miser* xvii, I took good tent, That double pawns ..Lay in my hands. **1816** SCOTT *Old Mort.* xliii, 'This is the way', said the little girl; 'follow me, gin ye please, sir, but tak tent to your feet'. **1855** ROBINSON *Whitby Gloss.* s. v., Mind and tak tent on 'em.

†**2.** Intent, purpose; = INTENT *sb.* 1, ATTENT *sb.* 3. *Obs.*

*a* **1300** *Cursor M.* 14288 Bot mari was in a-noþer tent [*v. r.* entent] Wit hir lauerd to speke sco went. **1399** LANGL. *Rich. Redeles* II. 97 Trouthe haþe determyned þe tente to þe ende. **14..** *Beryn* 126 For ethir-is þouȝt & tent was, othir to begile. *c* **1450** *St. Cuthbert* (Surtees) 18 Þe autours of his tente he tellys.

**Tent** (tent), *sb.*[3] *Surg.* Also 4–7 **tente**, 6 **teynte**, 6–8 **taint**, 7 **taynt**. [a. F. *tente* (12th c. in Godef. *Compl.*), sb. f. *tenter*:—L. *temptāre*, *tentāre*; see TENT *v.*[2]: cf. It. *tenta*, Sp. *tienta* a probe.]

†**1.** A probe. Also *fig.* *Obs.*

*c* **1375** *Cursor M.* 26638 (Fairf.) A tent þe wers to hit will reche Quen hit rotis for defaute of leche. **1606** SHAKS. *Tr. & Cr.* II. ii. 16 Modest Doubt is cal'd..the tent that searches To' th' bottome of the worst. **1693** tr. *Blancard's Phys. Dict.* (ed. 2) s. v. *Tenta*, A Chyrurgeons Instrument, called Specillum, the vulgar call it *Tenta*, a Tent, from trying.

**2.** A roll or pledget, usually of soft absorbent material, often medicated, or sometimes of a medicinal substance, formerly much used to search and cleanse a wound, or to keep open or distend a wound, sore, or natural orifice.

*c* **1400** *Lanfranc's Cirurg.* 34, I heeld þe wounde open aldai wiþ a litil smal tent & a schort. *c* **1425** tr. *Arderne's Treat. Fistula* 34, I putte in tuo tentes or þre..in þe larger holes. **1547** BOORDE *Brev. Health* Pref. 4 Let them be sure in serchynge of the depnes of woundes and fystules, and accordyng to the depnes to make the tentes. **1610** MARKHAM *Masterp.* II. cxiii. 407 Hauing cleansed the soare by tying a taint of flaxe or fine linnen cloth. **1639** T. DE GRAY *Compl. Horsem.* 292 A linnen clowt rowled up in the fashion of a great taynt. **1753** CHAMBERS *Cycl. Supp.*, *Tent[s]* in surgery..are of service [1.] to convey medicines to the most inner recesses..of the wound. 2. To prevent the Lips of the wound from uniting before it is healed at the bottom...Tents whose office is to enlarge..the mouth of any wound, or ulcer..are usually called sponge-tents. **1867** HARRIS *Dict. Med. Terminol.*, *Sponge Tent*, a tent made of prepared sponge. **1872** T. G. THOMAS *Dis. Women* 78 Preparation of sea-tangle tents.

*fig.* *a* **1548** HALL *Chron.*, *Hen. V* 35 b, Now to finde a remedy for a mischief and a tent to stop a wounde, the Clergy..agreed to offre..a greate some of money. **1672** T. JORDAN *Lond. Triumphant* 15 But yet our wounds have neither tent nor balm, We freeze in Fire, drown in a Calm.

†**3.** *transf.* (from the shape or appearance.) *Obs.*

**1578** LYTE *Dodoens* VI. lvi. 730 After these tentes or catkens the leaues begin to showe.

†**4.** A paste which sets hard, used in setting precious stones: see quot. 1656. *Obs.*

[This may be a different word.]

**1594** PLAT *Jewell-ho.* III. 62 An excellent tent for a Diamond. Bvrne Iuorie in a crusible..into a blacke powder, then take a little..thereof, and mingle it with a few drops of..Oyle of Masticke, and in the setting of the stone you must haue care that it touch not the tent. **1647** R. STAPYLTON *Juvenal* Ep. Ded., Just as a pigmey should throw away a diamond bigger then himselfe, onely because the tent it stood upon was black. **1656** BLOUNT *Glossogr.* s. v., Jewellers call that Tent which they put under Table Diamonds when they set them in work, and is made of mastick and turpentine.

Hence **Tentwise** *adv.*[2], in the way of a surgical tent or plug.

**1639** T. DE GRAY *Compl. Horsem.* 272 A salve .. which must be applyed eyther plaister-wise or taint-wise.

**Tent** (tent), *sb.*[4] Forms: 6 **tynt**, **tente**, **teynt**, 7 **tint**, 7– **tent**. [ad. Sp. *tinto* dark-coloured:—L. *tinctus*, pa. pple. of *tingĕre* to dye: see TINCT, TINGE. Cf. Sp. '*vino Tinto*, a blackish wine in Spaine' (Minsheu 1599).] A Spanish wine of a deep red colour, and of low alcoholic content. Also *tent wine*. (Often used as a sacramental wine.)

**1542** BOORDE *Dyetary* x. (1870) 255 Also these hote wynes, as..caprycke, tynt. **1580** FRAMPTON *Dial. Yron & Steele* 159 Casting wine called Tente vpon burning yron. **1612** in *Halyburton's Ledger* (1867) 335 Sackes Canareis Malagas Maderais..Teynts and Allacants. *c* **1645** HOWELL *Lett.* (1650) II. lv. 74 The Vinteners make Tent (which is a Name for all Wines in Spain except white) to supply the place of it. **1748** *Anson's Voy.* II. x. 246 Spanish wines, such as tent and sherry. **1881** *Med. Temp. Jrnl.* XLVIII. 199 Tent..is the least objectionable of intoxicating wines.

**Tent,** *sb.*[5] ? *Obs.* [f. TENT *v.*[3]; or shortened from TENTER *sb.*[1]] A frame on which embroidery or tapestry is kept stretched while making; a stretching frame for various purposes.

**1548** ELYOT, *Tendicula*..a nette or snare to take byrdes or beastes in, also a teynter, and a tent that brotherers woorke on. **1688** R. HOLME *Armoury* III. xxi. (Roxb.) 251/2 A long square of wood, made after the maner of an Embrautherers tent to slip up and down. *a* **1704** *Compl. Servant-Maid* (ed. 7) 62 To wash and starch Points. Take your Points and put them into a Tent, then lay your Tent upon a Table. **1741** LADY POMFRET *Lett.* (1805) III. 113 The working of the tapestry, which is done in a different manner.., the tent being set edgewise.

† **Tent,** *a.* *Sc.* *Obs. rare.* [Aphetic f. ATTENT or INTENT *a.*] Attent, watchful; intent.

**1789** DAVIDSON *Seasons* 77 Up cam Tam Tell an' Sutor Sam..As tent upo' the aftergame, As hounds loos'd frae a kennel. *Ibid.* 90 Up started Rosy Dougan, As tent as if she had been a puss.

**Tent,** *v.*[1] Now *Sc.* and *north. dial.* [Closely related to, and app. formed from, TENT *sb.*[2]: perh. short for *take tent*; but cf. also TEND *v.*[1]]

†**1.** *intr.* To give or pay attention, to 'take tent'; to attend, give heed, take notice. Const. *to*, *unto*, *till*; = TEND *v.*[1] 1, 2. *Obs.*

*a* **1300** *Cursor M.* 16910 Armed knightes þar þai left þat to þe tumb suld tent. *Ibid.* 19034 Þai..desseli bath late and are War tentand to þe apostels lare. *c* **1330** R. BRUNNE *Chron.* (1810) 91 Þe Kyng was in affray, he might not tent þerto. *c* **1380** WYCLIF *Serm.* Sel. Wks. II. 294 Þei tenten neiþer to bodi ne to soule. *a* **1425** *Cursor M.* 3619 (Trin.) His modir tent [*Cott. & Gött.* tok tent] to ysaac And herde þo wordis þat he spac. *c* **1475** *Golagros & Gaw.* 342, I rede ye tent treuly to my teching. **1530** PALSGR. 754/2, I tente to my busynesse, I take hede to the thinges I have in hande. **1572** *Satir. Poems Reform.* xxxviii. 99 Tent to ȝourselfis.

†**b.** Const. *to* with *inf.* *Obs.*

*a* **1300** *Cursor M.* 21167 Symon zelote..His lauerd al to serue he tent. **1357** *Lay Folks Catech.* (MS. T.) 194 Noght than for to tent to tary with the world, Ne lyue in lykyng ne lust. *c* **1410** LOVE *Bonavent. Mirr.* xxxiii. (1908) 159 Onely tentinge to plese god.

**c.** *trans.* To give or pay mental attention to; to attend to, give heed to, take notice of (a person, his words, a matter); cf. TEND *v.*[1] 1 b.

*c* **1330** R. BRUNNE *Chron. Wace* (Rolls) 13630 Þey ne roughte where þey ȝede Ne nought rewarded how [*v.r.* no tentid not] þey were in drede. **13..** *E. E. Allit. P.* B. 935 Þay token hit as-tyt & tented hit lyttel. *Ibid.* C. 59 Wyl ȝe tary a lyttel tyme & tent me a whyle. *c* **1400** *Destr. Troy* 10237 He blamyt full bitturly þan his blithe qwene, Þat euer he tentit hir tale. **1724** RAMSAY *Gentle Sheph.*, *To Burchet* viii, Yet, tent a poet's zealous prayer. **1785** BURNS *Death & Dr. Hornbook* ix, Ye're maybe come to stap my breath; But tent me, billie; I red ye weel, tak care o' skaith, See, there's a gully [= big knife]!

**2.** To attend to the safety and needs of, to take or have charge and care of; to look after, see to, mind, attend to, tend (a person, flock, plant, machine, etc.). Now *dial.* esp. *Sc.*

**13..** *E. E. Allit. P.* B. 676 Þis ilke wyȝ þat wendez with oure lorde, For to tent hym with tale & teche hym þe gate. *c* **1430** *Syr Gener.* 2832 Felows he had the toure to tent Which were redie at his comaundment. *c* **1450** *Bk. Curtasye* 430 in *Babees Bk.* 312 The lordys chambur, tho wadrop to, Þo vssher of chambur schalle tent þo two. **1557** in Sharp *Cov. Myst.* (1825) 73 Payd for tyntyng the yerthequake, iiij d. **1641** BEST *Farm. Bks.* (Surtees) 120 After that [he] setteth a boy or girle to tente them. **1686** G. STUART *Joco-Ser. Disc.* 64 When Foxes preach tent weel your Geese. **1728** RAMSAY *Tea-t. Misc.*, *There's my Thumb* iii, Tenting my flocks lest they should wander. **1789** BURNS *Capt. Grose* i, If there's a hole in a' your coats, I rede you tent it. **1844** G. DODD *Textile Manuf.* iv. 125 This 'plucker' is generally attended or 'tented', to use a factory phrase, by a boy. **1859** *Autobiog. Beggar Boy* 51, I soon got engaged to tent a herd of oxen for the day.

**3.** To take (ocular) notice of, observe, watch. *Sc.*

**1721** RAMSAY *Prospect of Plenty* 3 Tent how the Calidonians, lang supine, Begin, mair wise, to open baith their een. **1875** W. WALSH *Poet. & Pr. Wks.* 1 When young you heedless tent the sky. **1888** A. REID *Sangs Heatherland* (1894) 86 Tent her when she hides her face.

**4.** To be careful, to beware (with clause). *Sc.*

**1737** RAMSAY *Scots Prov.* xxxiv. § 88 Tent wha ye take by the hand. **1789** *Sheph. Wedding* (ed. 2) 15 (E.D.D.) Tent what you say!

**5.** To take care to prevent or hinder (a person) *from* doing something. *north. dial.*

**1781** HUTTON *Tour Caves* (ed. 2) Gloss., *Tent*, to watch or guard from doing a thing. **1863** MRS. TOOGOOD *Yorks. Dial.* s. v., He was going into toon but his father tented him. **1868** *Accrington Times* 16 May (E.D.D.) Tent 'em fro' breyking aot o' th' ranks. **1874** *Sheffield Indep.* (ibid.), He thinks to come here, but I'll tent him [i. e. take care that he does not].

**6.** To watch for and scare away (birds); also, to guard (corn, seed, etc.) from birds. *north. dial.*

**1858** BAILEY *Age* 73 I'd give you the congenial occupation Of scaring crows, and 'tenting' vegetation. **1877** *N. W. Linc. Gloss.*, *Tent*...to scare birds from corn. **1889** *Ibid.* (ed. 2), Tent is used either of the things watched over, or the things guarded against. 'Oor Bill's tentin' to'nup-seäd e' th' Beckboddoms. When I was a lad I spent moäst o' my time tentin' craws an' stock-duvs.'

Hence **Te·nted** *ppl. a.*, **Te·nting** *vbl. sb.* and *ppl. a.*; **tenting-lad** *dial.*, a lad or boy employed to watch the crops and scare birds. Also combinations of the verb-stem, as **tent-boy** = *tenting-lad*.

*c* **1645** T. TULLY *Siege of Carlisle* (1840) 14 Daily skirmishes ..aboute y[e] fetching in of Cattell, or y[e] tenting y[m] in their places of pastures. **1721** RAMSAY *Prospect of Plenty* 37 The tempting bait, and tented string, Beguile the cod, the sea-cat, tusk, and ling. **1877** *N. W. Linc. Gloss.*, *Tenter*, *Tenting-lad*, a boy who scares birds from corn. **1888** L. WILSON in J. Brown *Lit. Laureat.* (1890) 63 Here seated in his rustic grace, The 'tent' boy blew his horn.

† **Tent,** *v.*[2] *Obs.* [a. F. *tent-er* = Sp. *tentar*, It. *tentare*:—L. *temptāre* to TEMPT, in med.L. (after Romanic langs.) *tentāre*.] A variant of TEMPT, occasional down to 16th c. Hence † **Tenting** *vbl. sb.*

*a* **1225** *Ancr. R.* 228 Nu an oðer elne ouh muchel urouren ou, hwon ȝe beoð itented...God..is treowe: nul he neuer þolien þet te deouel tempti us ouer þet he isihð wel þet we muwen iðolien. *Ibid.* 230 Ure Louerd, hwon he iðoleð þet we beoð itented, he plaieð mid us. *c* **1440** *York Myst.* xxviii. 243 Euelle spiritis is neghand full nere, That will ȝou tarie at þis tyme with his tentyng. *a* **1555** BP. GARDINER in Foxe *A. & M.* (1563) 738, I know your Grace only tenteth me with such reasones.

† **Tent,** *v.*[3] *Obs.* Also 5 **tente**, **teynt**. [Connected with L. *tendĕre*, *tent-um*, F. *tendre* to stretch; also with TENT *sb.*[5], TENTER *sb.*[1]; but exact history not evidenced.] Hence † **Tenting** *vbl. sb.*

**1.** *trans.* To stretch (cloth) on tenters: = TENTER *v.* 1.

**1377** LANGL. *P. Pl.* B. xv. 447 Cloth..is nouȝt comly to were Tyl it is fulled vnder fote.. Ytouked, and ytented [*v. r.* y-teynted] & vnder tailloures hande. *c* **1440** *Promp. Parv.* 489/1 Tente clothe, *extendo*, *lacinio*. **1463–4** *Rolls of Parlt.* V. 501/1 Brode clote..after almanere rakkyng streynyng or teyntyng therof.

**2.** (?) To embroider in a tent or frame.

**1507** *Acc. Ld. High Treas. Scot.* IV. 79 Payit to the broudstar for half ane hank gold threid for tenting, and gret papir for the Kingis doublat.

**Tent** (tent), *v.*[4] *arch.* [app. f. TENT *sb.*[3]; but cf. F. *tenter* in obs. sense (= *sonder*) to try the depth of, to sound; = med.L. *tentāre* to try.]

† **a.** *trans.* To probe (*obs.*). **b.** To treat by means of a tent; to apply a tent to (a wound, etc., also to a person); to distend or plug with a tent. Also *fig.* Hence **Te·nting** *vbl. sb.*

**1597** A. M. tr. *Guillemeau's Fr. Chirurg.* 51/2 Ether in tenting of the wounde, by inscisione, by cauterisation. **1612** WEBSTER *White Devil* v. ii, Search my wound deeper; tent it with the steel That made it. **1639** SHIRLEY *Maid's Rev.* III. vi, I have a sword dares tent a wound as far As any. **1685** CROWNE *Sir C. Nice* IV. Dram. Wks. 1874 III. 328 Yes, if you 'noint it presently with a good dish o' jelly-broth, and tent it with a bone o' roast beef. **1695** tr. *Col-*

*batch's New Lt. Chirurg. Put out* 32 Stitched them up.. for fear they should have been kept open by tenting. **1828** SCOTT *F. M. Perth* vii, Methinks I can tent this wound, and treat it with emollients.

† **Tent,** *v.*5 *Obs. rare.* [var. form of TEND *v.*2, perh. on analogy of TEND *v.*1 and TENT *v.*1]

**1.** *trans. Law.* To offer, proffer: = TEND *v.*2 5, TENDER *v.*1 1.

**1459** *Rolls of Parlt.* V. 371/1 An enquest takyn aforne his Eschetour..the which Offices John Fastolf Knyght, and othir, tentid to traverse, and by that meane hadd the said Manere. **1512** *Act* 4 *Hen. VIII*, c. 18 § 24 All Traverses peticions monstrance de droit..to be tentyd or sued by eny persone or persones.

**2.** *intr.* To direct itself, be directed (*to* some end); = TEND *v.*2 2.

**1551** UDALL, etc. *Erasm. Par. Mark* xii. 184 This deceiptful propheme tented [*ed.* 1548 tended] to this end, that if he had geuen sentence for the phariseis, then should he haue bene accused of the Herodians for an authour of rebellion, or insurreccion agaynst the Emperour.

**Tent** (tent), *v.*6 [f. TENT *sb.*1: a number of unconnected uses.]

**1.** *intr.* To abide or live in a tent; to encamp. Also *to tent it.*

**1856** KANE *2nd Grinnell Exp.* I. xxvii. 357 We will be gone for some days probably, tenting it in the open air. **1867** LADY HERBERT *Cradle L.* 154 Our travellers tented on a small level sward just outside the Convent-gates. **1881** MRS. HOLMAN-HUNT *Childr. Jerus.* 189 Do you think we shall ever go tenting again, mother? **1893** *Scribner's Mag.* June 703/2 The river crew is tenting out and clearing the stream.

**b.** *fig.* To dwell temporarily; to sojourn, to tabernacle; to have one's abode; of a thing: to have its seat, 'reside'.

**1607** SHAKS. *Cor.* III. ii. 116 The smiles of Knaues Tent in my cheekes, and Schoole-boyes Teares take vp The Glasses of my sight. **1751** R. SHIRRA in *Rem.* (1850) 52 He tented or tabernacled in flesh among us. **1871** MACDUFF *Mem. Patmos* xxii. 305 The Word came and dwelt (or lit. 'tented') among us. **1893** E. G. HIRSCH in Barrows *Parl. Relig.* II. 1304 Wherever man may tent, there also will curve upward the burning incense of his sacrifice.

**2.** *trans.* To cover or canopy as with a tent.

**1838** MRS. BROWNING *Seraphim* II. 604 The heavy darkness which doth tent the sky Floats backward as by a sudden wind. **1883** LD. R. GOWER *My Remin.* I. xx. 410 A garden flanked by colonnades and covered passages had been tented in.

**3.** To accommodate, put up, or lodge in tents. Also *fig.*

**1863** LD. LYTTON *Ring Amasis* II. 81 Powers we can neither summon nor dismiss, are camped upon the brain and tented in the veins of men. **1869** E. A. PARKES *Pract. Hygiene* (ed. 3) 481 The men should be tented, the tents should be well ventilated. **1882** ARMSTRONG *Garland fr. Greece, Orithyia* 8, I have tented the nymphs of the rills in pavilions of frozen spray. **1898** *Daily News* 9 Mar. 3/2 All officers are tented in the same manner as the men.

† **4.** To pitch or spread (a tent); to put up, fix up, stretch, as a tent or its canvas. *Obs.*

**1553** *Douglas's Æneis* VIII. x. 23 That from the top of the hillys hyght The army all thai mycht se at a sight With tentis tentit [*ed. Small*, stentit] strekand to the plane. **1634** W. WOOD *New Eng. Prosp.* I. ii. (1865) 7 By good fires they sleepe as well and quietly (having their mayne sayle tented at their backes, to shelter them from the winde) as if they were at home.

**Tent,** obs. and dial. form of TENTH.

**Tentability** (tentăbi·līti). *rare.* [f. Lat. type *tentābil-is, OF. *tentable* liable to be tempted (*c*1340 in Godef.), or from Eng. **tentable* for TEMPTABLE: see -BILITY.] = TEMPTABILITY.

**1844** W. H. MILL *Serm. Tempt. Christ* ii. 39 The tentability of the Incarnate Lord. **1860** ELLICOTT *Life our Lord* iii. 112 *note*, In estimating the nature of our Lord's tentability. **1863** A. BARRY in *Smith's Dict. Bible* III. 1148/2 It is this tentability of man, even in his original nature, which is represented in Scripture as giving scope to the evil action of Satan.

**Tentable** (te·ntăb'l), *a.* [f. med.L. *tentāre* for *temptāre* to try, or f. TENT *v.*4 to probe, etc. + -ABLE.] Liable to be probed, 'picked', or 'tried': cf. TENTATION 2 a.

**1862** *Catal. Internat. Exhib.* II. XXXI. 10 Locks with crypted guards, with never tentable by instrument or true key.

**Tentacle** (te·ntăk'l). [ad. mod.L. TENTACULUM.] *Zool.* A slender flexible process in animals, esp. invertebrates, serving as an organ of touch or feeling; = FEELER 3, PALP.

**1762** DU PONT in *Phil. Trans.* LIII. 58 The fingers, or tentacles, end in a deep blue. **1835** KIRBY *Hab. & Inst. Anim.* I. v. 181 An infinity of cells..from which the tentacles issue to collect their food. **1857** WOOD *Com. Obj. Seashore* v. 53 On the arms, legs, feet, or tentacles of the cuttles, are arranged rows of suckers. **1866** TATE *Brit. Mollusks* iii. 47 The head [of a snail or slug] bears two long slender tentacles or horns. **1868** OWEN *Vertebr. Anim.* I. v. 411 Tentacles depend from the rostral prolongation of the Sturgeon, and from the mandibular symphysis of the Cod.

**b.** *Bot.* Applied to a sensitive filament, as the viscous gland-tipped leaf-hairs of the Sundew.

**1875** DARWIN *Insectiv. Pl.* i. 5 A tentacle consists of a thin, straight, hair-like pedicel carrying a gland on the summit. **1879** LUBBOCK *Sci. Lect.* i. 4 In our Common Sundew..the rounded leaves are covered with glutinous glandular hairs or tentacles.

**c.** *fig.* = FEELER 2 b.

**1847** DE QUINCEY *Secret Societies* Wks. VI. 235 This plot ..stretched its horrid fangs, and threw out its foreruning feelers and *tentacles*, into many nations. **1883** H. DRUMMOND *Nat. Law in Spir. W.* viii. (ed. 2) 300 The soul.., waving its tentacles piteously in the empty air, feeling after God if so be that it may find Him. **1895** MAHAFFY *Empire Ptolemies* x, Prepared to fall easily into the tentacles of the all-devouring Republic [Rome]. **1901** *Scotsman* 7 Mar. 7/5 One of De Wet's tentacles had been stretched out to obscure the approach of Nesbitt's horse.

**d.** *attrib.* and *Comb.*, as *tentacle-like* adj.; **tentacle-sheath**, the sheath-like structure surrounding the base of the tentacles of many molluscs.

**1835–6** *Todd's Cycl. Anat.* I. 683/2 Their tentacle-like arms [i. e. of Cirripeds] resemble the antennae of lobsters.

Hence **Tentacled** (te·ntăk'ld) *a.*, furnished with or having tentacles.

**1857** GOSSE *Omphalos* 119 Every individual cell,..inhabited by its tentacled Hydra, has..budded out from a branch.

**Tentacular** (tentæ·kiŭlăı), *a.* [f. mod.L. TENTACULUM + -AR 1.] Of, pertaining to, or of the nature of a tentacle or tentacles.

**1828** STARK *Elem. Nat. Hist.* II. 117 With two conical perforated and tentacular papillæ at its upper extremity. **1870** ROLLESTON *Anim. Life* Introd. 84 The mouth is surrounded by a cartilaginous ring, carrying anteriorly tentacular outgrowths.

**Tentaculate** (tentæ·kiŭlĕt), *a.* (*sb.*) *Zool.* [f. as prec. + -ATE 2.]

**1.** Furnished with tentacles or tentaculiform appendages; rarely = TENTACULIFORM.

**1846** DANA *Zooph.* (1848) 320 Polyps obsolescently tentaculate. **1877** HUXLEY *Anat. Inv. Anim.* ii. 109 In the Acinetae, the tentaculate stage is the more permanent, the ciliated stage transitory.

**2.** Of or pertaining to the *Tentaculata*, or stalked Echinoderms. **b.** *sb.* A member of the Tentaculata; a pelmatozoan.

**Tentaculated** (tentæ·kiŭle'ted), *a. Zool.* [f. as prec. + -ED 1.] = prec. 1.

**1804** SHAW *Gen. Zool.* V. II. 359 *Tentaculated Shark*... Shark with serrated snout tentaculated on each side. **1880** BASTIAN *Brain* iii. 58 Sedentary forms of life, like the Hydra, the Sea-anemone, or some of the tentaculated worms.

**Tentacule** (te·ntăkiul). *Zool.* [a. F. *tentacule*, ad. mod.L. TENTACULUM: see -CULE.] = TENTACLE. Also in *Comb.* as *tentacule-like* adj.

**1835–6** *Todd's Cycl. Anat.* I. 37/1 Very extensile tentacule-like cirri. **1851** RICHARDSON *Geol.* viii. (1855) 216 The mouth ..is surrounded with numerous filaments or tentacules..furnished with vibratile cilia. **1870** P. M. DUNCAN *Transform. Insects* (1882) 77 It suddenly pokes out a spotted tentacule.

**Tentaculi-** (tentæ·kiŭli). Combining form of mod.L. TENTACULUM, used in zoological terms. **Tenta·culibra·nchiate** [L. *branchiæ* gills], *a.* of or pertaining to the *Tentaculibranchia*, i. e. the *Bryozoa* or *Polyzoa*, regarded (by Lankester 1877) as a class of the branch *Lipocephala* of the phylum *Mollusca*; *sb.* a member of this class. **Tenta·culicy·st** = TENTACULOCYST; hence **Tenta·culicy·stic** *a.* **Tenta·culiform** *a.*, having the form or appearance of a tentacle. **Tentaculi·gerous** *a.* [-GEROUS], = next.

**1902** *Cassell's Encycl. Dict., Suppl.*, *Tentaculibranchiate. **1891** *Cent. Dict.*, *Tentaculicyst. **1837** *Penny Cycl.* IX. 258/1 It..gives exit to*tentaculiform cirrhi. **1880** W. S. KENT *Infusoria* I. 396 A prolonged tentaculiform appendage. **1877** HUXLEY *Anat. Inv. Anim.* iii. 174, m. *tentaculigerous canal.

**Tenta·culi·ferous,** *a.* [f. mod.L. TENTACULUM + -(I)FEROUS.] Bearing tentacles: said of an animal or organ; *spec.* of or pertaining to the *Tentaculifera* or *Acinetaria*, a division of the Plegepod Protozoa; sometimes, pertaining to the *Tentaculifera* or *Glossophora*, among Mollusca.

**1830** J. E. GRAY in *Encycl. Metrop.* (1845) XXI. 592/1 Its edge divided into four or eight diverging, tentaculiferous lobes. **1835** KIRBY *Hab. & Inst Anim.* I. v. 167 The tentaculiferous mouths of the polypes. **1880** W. S. KENT (*title*) A Manual of the Infusoria: including a Description of all known Flagellate, Ciliate, and Tentaculiferous Protozoa. **1883** — in *Nature* 8 Mar. 433/1 In other tentaculiferous animals, such as a sea-anemone, tubiculous annelid, or cuttle-fish. **1885** E. R. LANKESTER in *Encycl. Brit.* XIX. 431/2 The tentaculiferous 'arms' of the Brachiopoda.

**Tentaculite** (tentæ·kiŭləit). *Palæont.* [ad. mod.L. *Tentāculītēs*: see TENTACULUM and -ITE 1 2 a.] A fossil mollusc of the genus *Tentaculites* or family *Tentaculitidæ* (thought by some to be allied to the Pteropods) of which the conical usually ringed shells abound in the Middle Devonian strata.

*Tentaculite beds*, strata of the Ilfracombe group of Middle Devonian age, characterized by the abundance of *Tentaculites scalaris*. *Tentaculite limestone*, in the New York Geological Survey, a subdivision of the Water-lime group of Upper Silurian strata, similarly characterized.

**1839** MURCHISON *Silur. Syst.* II. 628. **1863** DANA *Man. Geol.* 252.

**Tentaculocyst** (tentæ·kiŭlo,sist). *Zool.* [f. TENTACULUM + Gr. κύστ-ις bladder, CYST.] One of the vesicular or cystic tentacles of a hydrozoan, representing a reduced and modified tentacle: see quots. Also TENTACULICYST.

**1880** E. R. LANKESTER in *Nature* 4 Mar. 414/1 What I have elsewhere termed 'tentaculocysts', modified tentacles which act as auditory organs and have often eye-spots on them as well. **1881** — in *Encycl. Brit.* XII. 555/2 Combined visual and auditory organs in the form of modified tentacles (tentaculocysts).

**Tentaculoid** (tentæ·kiŭloid). *Biol.* [f. next + -OID.] A tentaculiform process in some diatoms.

**1892** T. H. BUFFHAM in *Jrnl. Quekett Micr. Club* July 28 From the extremities of the minor axis there are mammiform protuberances through which pass long processes of the same substance [investing periglœa]: these we might call *tentaculoids.*

‖ **Tentaculum** (tentæ·kiŭlŏm). Pl. **-a.** [mod. L. *tentācul-um*, f. *tentā-re* = *temptāre* to feel, try; cf. TENTACLE, TENTACULE, and see -CULE.] A feeler; = TENTACLE.

**1752** J. HILL *Hist. Anim.* 100 The upper lip is prominent beyond the rest of the mouth, and has two tentacula. **1804** SHAW *Gen. Zool.* V. II. 360 From each side springs a long and flexible tentaculum or feeler, of a flattened shape. **1880** BASTIAN *Brain* iv. 71 This ganglion receives branches from the tentacula guarding the orifice of the oral funnel. *fig.* **1867** BAGEHOT *Eng. Constit.* ix. (1882) 275 The political characteristic of the early Greeks, and of the early Romans, too, is that out of the *tentacula* of a monarchy they developed the organs of a republic. **1893** MCCARTHY *Dictator* xxiv, He had seen only too clearly which way her love was stretching its tentacula.

**Tentage** (te·ntĕdʒ). [f. TENT *sb.*1 + -AGE.] Equipment of tents, tent accommodation.

**1603** DRAYTON *Bar. Wars* II. xv, Upon the Mount the King his Tentage fixt. **1870** *Daily News* 27 July 5 Each mess was complete for all purposes of camping and tentage.

‖ **Tentamen** (tentē¹·mĕn). Pl. **tentamina** (-æ·mină). [L. *tentāmen*, f. *tentāre* = *temptāre* to try: see TEMPT.] An attempt, trial, experiment.

**1673** MARVELL *Reh. Transp.* II. 284 After this Tentamen of your veracity you tax me for saying, ''Tis demonstrable [etc.]'. **1736** CHESTERF. in *Fog's Jrnl.* No. 376 An essay or tentamen to some greater design. **1863** N. W. SENIOR *Biog. Sk.* 387 [Bacon's Essays] were intended,..as the word *essay* in its original acceptation expresses, to be *tentamina*; not finished treatises, but sketches, to be filled up by the reader.

**Tentar,** obs. form of TENTER *sb.*1

**Tentation** (tentē¹·ʃən). [ad. L. *tentātiōn-em*, late form (after Romanic) of *temptātiōn-em*, n. of action from *temptāre* (*tentāre*) to try, TEMPT.]

**1.** Obsolete form of TEMPTATION, q. v.: sometimes specially expressing experimental trial, as distinct from enticement to evil.

**2.** *techn.* A mode of working or adjusting by trial or experiment.

**a.** '(*Locksmithing.*) A mode of picking locks in which the bolt is pressed backward constantly, and the tumblers released one by one from the stud'

**b.** '(*Compass-adjusting.*) Professor Airy's mode of adjusting compasses in iron ships, in which boxes of iron chain and magnets are experimentally placed and shifted..until the disturbing influence of the iron hull is neutralized' (Knight *Dict. Mech.* 1877 s. v.).

**Tentative** (te·ntătiv), *a.* and *sb.* [ad. med.L. *tentātīvus* adj. (*tentātīva* sb. in Schol.L.), f. *tentāt-*, ppl. stem of *tentāre* for *temptāre* to try: see TEMPT *v.* and -IVE. So F. *tentative* sb. (16th c. in Godef. *Compl.*), examination, attempt; also as adj., experimental (*obs.*).]

**A.** *adj.* Of the nature of an experiment, trial, or attempt; made or done provisionally as an experiment; experimental.

**1588** [implied in TENTATIVELY]. **1626** BP. HALL *Contempl., O. T.* xx. iii, Falshood, though it be but tentative, is neither needed nor approved by the God of truth. **1768** JOHNSON *Pref. to Shaks.* Wks. IX. 240 Works tentative and experimental must be estimated by their proportion to the general and collective ability of man. **1851** D. WILSON *Preh. Ann.* (1863) II. IV. ii. 241 The interpretations must therefore be regarded as tentative. **1874** GREEN *Short Hist.* vii. § 3. 364 A policy of this limited, practical, tentative order was.. best suited to the England of her day.

**B.** *sb.* Something done as an experiment or trial; an essay, an attempt; † a hostile attempt (*obs.*).

**1632** J. HAYWARD tr. *Biondi's Eromena* 175 They had no time to get out..any tentative of theirs serving them to no purpose, for that the citie was walled round about. **1687** RYCAUT *Hist. Turks* II. 321 He was going to make a tentative upon Palotta, a place of good strength. **1692** TEMPLE *Mem.* Wks. 1731 I. 431 They tried some little Tentatives upon us, whether we would be content to leave out all Mention of his Majesty's Mediation, as well as that of the Pope's? **1898** *Pop. Sci. Monthly* Sept. 609 Tentatives were made in both directions.

**b.** Trying, experimenting; experimentation.

**1865** GROTE *Plato* I. xvii. 493 A process, more or less tedious, of tentative and groping.

**Tentatively** (te·ntătivli), *adv.* [f. TENTATIVE *a.* + -LY 2.] In a tentative manner; by way of trial or experiment; experimentally.

**1588** J. HARVEY *Disc. Probl.* 7 But to put the case, and.. to proceede tentatiuely, and discoursiuely, as the foresaid schoolemen vse to call it. **1637** JACKSON *3rd Serm. Jer. xxvi. 19* Wks. 1844 VI. 95 He said it solemnly and publicly, not tentatively or by way of trial only. **1874** GREEN *Short Hist.* iv. § 2. 170 It was only slowly and tentatively that this principle was applied.

**Te·ntativeness.** [f. as prec. + -NESS.] The quality of being tentative; experimental character.

**1861** DR. WOODHAM WEBB in *Med. Times* 18 May 526/1 In Hospital work especially, we want the steadying influence of age..as well as the impetuous tentativeness of youth. **1894** *Athenæum* 6 Jan. 11/2 It only produces an appearance of uncertainty and tentativeness.

† **Te·ntatory,** *a. Obs. rare*−1. [f. L. *tentāt-*, ppl. stem of *tentāre* = *temptāre* to try: see TEMPT *v.* and -ORY 2.] = TENTATIVE *a.*

*a* 1624 Bp. M. Smith *Serm.* (1632) 27 The question is tentatory, (will you also go away?) I haue deserued better of you.

**Te·nt-be·d.** [f. Tent *sb.*1 + Bed *sb.*] **a.** A small and low bed used in a tent; a camp bed. **b.** A bed having an arched canopy and covered sides. Hence **tent-bedstead.**

1752 H. Walpole *Lett.* (1846) II. 432 Offered her a tent-bed, for fear of bugs in the inns. 1802 Anna Seward *Lett.* (1811) VI. 9 His daughter could be constantly with him, and sleep in a tent-bed in his apartment. 1815 Scott *Guy M.* xliv, One of the bed-posts of a sort of tent-bed was broken down. 1827 Roberts *Voy. Centr. Amer.* 231 [I found him lying] in an English tent-bed. 1838 Dickens *Nich. Nick.* xi, In the other stood an old tent bed-stead.

†**Te·ntbob,** erron. form of **taint-bob*: see Taint *sb.* C. 3. *Obs.*

1696 Aubrey *Misc.* (1857) 138 The little red spider, called a tentbob (not so big as a great pins head).

**Tent-boy**: see Tent *v.*1

**Tent-door** (te·nt,dōə·ɹ). The entrance or opening of a tent.

1535 Coverdale *Gen.* xviii. 1 He sat in his tent dore in the heate of ye daie. 1725 De Foe *Voy. round World* (1840) 336 Looking out at their tent-door. 1816 Keatinge *Trav.* (1817) I. 205 [They] seat themselves cross-legged,..before the Bassa's tent-door. 1867 Lady Herbert *Cradle L.* v. 152 There are still women..preparing the fatted kid at the open tent-door.

**Tented** (te·ntėd), *a.* [f. Tent *sb.*1 and *v.*6]

**1.** Of a place: Covered with or full of tents.

1604 Shaks. *Oth.* i. iii. 85 These Armes of mine..haue vs'd Their deerest action, in the Tented Field. 1725 Pope *Odyss.* iv. 584 Fast by the deep, Along the tented shore. 1773 Wheeler in *Gentl. Mag.* XLIII. 343/1 On Poictou's tented plains by valour won. 1832 Longf. *Coplas de Manrique* lx, In tented field and bloody fray.

**2.** Formed or shaped like a tent or pavilion; made into a tent-like structure.

1747 Collins *Ode on Poet. Charac.* 26 He, who call'd with thought to birth Yon tented sky, this laughing earth. 1825 Scott *Talism.* vi, Weapons..were scattered about the tented apartment, or disposed upon the pillars which supported it. 1839 Bailey *Festus* xix. (1852) 296 High as the tented mountains of the earth.

**b.** Having the wings when at rest meeting in a ridge over the back.

1849 Helps *Friends in C.* ii. 187 The tented moth said suddenly to me with a clear crisp voice.

**3.** Of persons: Lodged in, or furnished with, a tent or tents. Also *fig.*

1811 Wordsw. *Epist. to Sir G. H. Beaumont* 100 Wastes where now the tented Arabs dwell. 1902 Sir E. Arnold *Nativity* in *Delineator* Dec. 575 Grander than stricken fields and tented armies.

**Tenter** (te·ntəɹ), *sb.*1 Forms: 4–5 **teyntur,** 5 **tayntour, tentowre,** 5–6 **tentour,** 5–7 **taynter, teynter, tenture,** 5–8 **tentor,** 6 **teynto(u)r, -tree, tentar,** 6–7 **tainter, teinter, -or,** 6– **tenter.** [The varieties of the suffix make the exact origin somewhat obscure: the forms in *-ur, -our, -or, -er, -ar,* point to an AF. or OF. **tentour*, L. **tentōr-em* stretcher, agent-n. from *tend-ĕre* to stretch, which suits the sense; but neither the OF. nor the L. word is known in the sense 'tenter'.

The rare form *tenture* is equated by Promp. Parv. with L. *tentūra*, but this ought to mean the process of stretching or its product: cf. F. *tenture* action of stretching, also tapestry hangings; which does not agree with the sense of 'stretching instrument or apparatus'. On the other hand, if the word were merely an Eng. agent-n. from Tent *v.*3, it would be difficult to account for the various forms of the ending. The forms in *teynt-, taynt-, teint-, taint-* also offer difficulty, suggesting some association with F. *teint* dye.]

**1.** A wooden framework on which cloth is stretched after being milled, so that it may set or dry evenly and without shrinking. Also †*a pair of tenters* (obs. rare) and in pl. form *tenters.*

Formerly tenters of the length of a web of cloth stood in rows in the open air in *tenter-fields* or *grounds*, and were a prominent feature in cloth-manufacturing districts; but the process of drying and stretching is now generally done much more rapidly in *tenter-houses* by *tenter-* or *tentering-machines.*

13.. *Charter Holy Ghost* (Vernon MS.) in *Hampole's Wks.* I. 361 Whon þe Iewes hedden þus nayled Criston þe cros as men doþ cloþ on a tey[n]tur [*v.rr.* streynour, rakke]. 1408 *Nottingham Rec.* II. 60 Johannes London occupat unum croftum cum taynters. 1435 *Coventry Leet Bk.* 172 No walker off the Cite of Couentre..Shall Rakke no Clothe on the Tey[n]tur that schall be solde ffor wette-clothe. *c* 1440 *Promp. Parv.* 489/1 Tenture, for clothe (*S.* tentowre), ..Ug. V. in V. *tentura* (P. *constrictorium*). 1483 *Act* 1 *Rich. III*, c. 8 § 1 Many of the seid Clothes..ben sett uppon Tayntours and drawen out in leyngth and brede. 1495 *Nottingham Rec.* III. 284 Accyon off trespas for takynge vp teynters. 1530 Palsgr. 280/1 Tentar for clothe, *tend, tende.* *a* 1535 Fisher *Wks.* i. 394 Neuer anye Parchement skynne was more strayghtlye stratched by strength vpon the tentors. 1548 *Nottingham Rec.* IV. 94 For a gardeyn and a peyre of teyntors at the Bridgende. *a* 1552 Leland *Itin.* I. 93 A great Numbre of Tainters for Wollen Clothes. 1592 Greene *Upst. Courtier* in *Harl. Misc.* (Malh.) II. 242 That he drawe his cloth and pull it passing hard when he sets it vpon the tenters. 1642 in *J. Lister's Autobiog.* (1842) 78 The cannon..beat down the barrs of a tenter. 1646 Sir J. Temple *Irish Rebell.* 95 [He] led the boy to his Fathers tentors, and there hanged him. 1657 C. Beck *Univ. Charac.* L vj, A tenture or tenter to stretch cloth in. 1727–41 Chambers *Cycl.*, *Tenter, Tryer,* or *Prover,*..in the cloth manufactory..is usually about four feet and a half high, and for length exceeds that of the longest piece of cloth. 1791 Hamilton *Berthollet's Dyeing* II. ii. ii. v. 108 It is dried on the tenters in the open air. 1849 C. Bronte *Shirley* ii, The cloth was torn from his tenters and left in shreds in the field.

*fig.* 1602 Dekker *Satirom.* Wks. 1873 I. 247 O Night..That like a cloth of cloudes dost stretch thy limbes; Vpon the windy Tenters of the Ayre. 1611 Speed *Hist. Gt. Brit.* ix. xvii. § 4 Albeit his Words intended no Treason..yet..the tenture of the Law made them his death. 1674 N. Fairfax *Bulk & Selv.* To Rdr., As the one had wrackt and limm'd my thoughts, with endless tenters and boundless retchings out.

†**2.** = Tenter-hook 1. *Obs.*

1598 Sylvester *Du Bartas* ii. i. iii. *Furies* 708 Then Avarice all-arm'd in hooking Tenters. 1678 *Massacre in Ireland* 3 Two Boys [were] wounded and hung upon Butchers Tenters. 1743 *Phil. Trans.* XLII. 425 The little Papillæ..on the Surface of the Arms assist them like so many Hooks or Tenters to hold their Worms barely by touching them. 1795 Wolcott (P. Pindar) *Liberty's last Squeak* Wks. 1812 III. 422 And hang their Hearts, like Butcher's Meat, on tenters. 1810 Crabbe *Borough* i. 130 Fences..(With tenters tipp'd) a strong repulsive bound.

*fig.* 1635 Quarles *Embl.* i. v. 17 Abused Statutes had no tenters, And men could deal secure without indentures. 1849 J. Sterling in *Fraser's Mag.* XXXIX. 416 Slight Folly's pen, not Passion's burning tenter, Tears up our roots.

†**b.** *transf.* A hooked organ or part. *Obs.*

1613–16 W. Browne *Brit. Past.* ii. i, Thornes and tangling bushes Whose tenters sticking in her garments sought..to help her. 1817 Kirby & Sp. *Entomol.* (1818) II. xxiii. 323 Palms, pattens, or soles [of flies' feet]..beset underneath with small bristles or tenters.

†**3.** *fig.* esp. in phrases: **a.** *To put, set, stretch,* etc. *on* (*the*) *tenter*(*s*, = *to set on tenter-hooks*; to rack: see Tenter-hook 2, 2 b. *Obs.*

*a* 1533 Ld. Berners *Gold. Bk. M. Aurel.* (1546) C c ij b, Ye haue strayned it on the tentours, and drawen it on the perche. *a* 1556 Cranmer *Wks.* (Parker Soc.) I. 60 But the papists have set Christ's words upon the tenters, and stretched them out so far, that they make his words to signify as pleaseth them, not as he meant. 1583 Stubbes *Anat. Abus.* ii. (1882) 33 They inhance the rents, and set their fines on tenter. 1656 *Artif. Handsom.* 133 Nor ought the conscience in these to be set upon the rack and tainter. 1742 Richardson *Pamela* III. 341, I have pity'd him many a time, when I have seen him stretched on the Tenters to keep thee in Countenance.

**b.** *To be on* (*the*) *tenter*(*s*, i.e. in a position of strain, difficulty, or uneasiness; to be in a state of anxious suspense. Now *rare* or *Obs.*, superseded by *on tenter-hooks*: see Tenter-hook 2 c.

1633 Ford *Broken H.* i. iii, My very heart-strings Are on the tenters. 1726 *Adv. Capt. R. Boyle* (1768) 27, I was upon the Tenters to know the Reason of my Confinement. 1796 Scott *Let. to Miss C. Rutherford* 5 June, Your curiosity will be upon the tenters to hear the wonderful events. 1806 Fessenden *Democr.* I. 39 Stretch'd on the tenters of anxiety By blunder, crime, or impropriety.

†**4.** A stretching implement: ? = Tent *sb.*3 *Obs.*

1607 Topsell *Four-f. Beasts* (1658) 147 Put in the Opponax, and of both together make like taynters or splints, and thrust them into the wound. *Ibid.* 808 This applied to the bitten place in a linnen cloth, and tentures twice a day, did perfectly recover her health within a month. 1681 Grew *Musæum* iv. i. 360 A Box of Anatomick Instruments; sc. Saws, Steel and Ivory Knives,..a Tenter.

**5.** *attrib.* and *Comb.*, as *tenter-stretched* adj.; **tenter-balk** (**-bauk**), **-bar**: see quots.; **tenter-field, -place,** = Tenter-ground; **tenter-frame** = sense 1; **tenter-house, -machine**: see sense 1 (note); **tenter-timber,** timber for making tenters. See also Tenter-ground, -hook, -yard.

1876 *Whitby Gloss.*, **Tenter-bauks*, the beams to which the butcher's meat-hooks are fastened. 1877 Knight *Dict. Mech.*, **Tenter-bar*, a device for stretching cloth. 1844 G. Dodd *Textile Manuf.* iii. 104 The cloth is stretched out and hung up to dry. This used to be done in the *tenter-fields. 1835 Ure *Philos. Manuf.* 192 When the fulling is finished, the cloth is stretched once more on the *tenter-frame, and left in the open air till it is dry. 1861 C. C. Robinson *Leeds Gloss.* s. v. *Tenters*, The tenter-frames are upright bars placed at a short distance from each other and connected by other horizontal ones, top and bottom, having an array of hooks at equal distances on which the cloth is fastened by the listing of both sides. 1457 in Arnolde *Chron.* (1811) 72 All thoo in the said cite or subbarbis that ocupye..*teynter placys for fullers. 1641 Sir B. Rudyard in Rushw. *Hist. Coll.* iii. (1692) I. 167 Not to press such *Tenter-stretched Arguments. 1562 *Richmond Wills* (Surtees) 152 Stees, stanggs, peatts, old *tenture tymber, xs.

**Tenter** (te·ntəɹ), *sb.*2 [f. Tent *v.*6 + -er 1.] One who lives or lodges in a tent.

1888 *Harper's Mag.* Oct. 801/1 The pretty girl of our civilization, who pushes into the canvas home of the tenters. 1907 *Daily News* 27 Nov. 3/2 Originally intended for the benefit of gipsies, the evangelism..has attracted adherents from all classes, now proud to style themselves 'tenters'.

**Tenter** (te·ntəɹ), *sb.*3 *dial.* [f. Tent *v.*1 + -er 1.]

**1.** One who minds, or has charge of, anything requiring attention, as a machine, a flock, etc.

1828 *Craven Gloss.*, *Tenters*, watchers, moor-tenters. 1863 Mrs. Toogood *Yorks. Dial.*, I will hire that boy as a tenter for my sheep. 1870 *Inquiry Yorks. Deaf & Dumb* 59 Simeon Smith, cropping-machine tenter. 1885 *Manch. Exam.* 20 Feb. 5/3 The engine tenter..found the doors of the mill unlocked.

**b.** Applied to a watch-dog.

1844 S. Bamford *Walks S. Lancs.* 47 (E.D.D.) Will he do for a tenter? will he bark at night?

**2.** An attendant on a skilled workman, who gives him unskilled help, supplies materials, etc.

1894 *Labour Commission Gloss.*, *Tenters*, assistants to the weaver, generally children, who have gone through a short process of probation.

**Tenter** (te·ntəɹ), *v.* [f. Tenter *sb.*1]

**1.** *trans.* To stretch (cloth) on a tenter or tenters.

1437 *Coventry Leet Bk.* 187 Yeff so be that hit wol-not bere the seyde lengeth than that the walker Teynter hym out to the lengethe off xv yerdes. 1473 in Arnolde *Chron.* (1811) 78 The vntrouth falshed and desept..now daily vsed in the fullyng teynteryng or settyng and sheryng of wullen cloth. 1583 Stubbes *Anat. Abus.* ii. (1882) 24 After they haue bought their cloth, they cause it to be tentered, racked, and so drawne out, as it shall be both broader and longer than it was. 1626 Bacon *Sylva* § 12 As when.. Leather or Cloth tentured spring back. 1673 O. Heywood *Diaries*, etc. (1882) I. 354 Having some land..where his cloth is tentered. 1789 Brand *Hist. Newcastle* II. 320 The ordinary of this society, called anciently walkers, ..enacted that no brother should..tentor cloth on a Sunday. 1876 Cudworth *Bradford* vii. 466 Returning home.., the cloth was 'tentered'—that is, if weather permitted.

†**b.** *transf.* To hang or stretch as on a tenter or tenters. *Obs.*

1615 Crooke *Body of Man* 244 If the heart needed any tension, it might better haue beene tentered, and with shorter stringes to the spine of the back. 1648 Bp. Hall *Easter at Higham* Rem. Wks. (1660) 194 Do the cruel tormentors tenter out his pretious limmes? *a* 1677 Barrow *Expos. Creed* Wks. 1716 I. 430 We may easily imagine what acerbity of pain must be endured in his limbs being stretched forth, racked and tentured.

†**2.** *fig.* To set on the tenter, or on tenter-hooks: see Tenter *sb.*1 3, Tenter-hook 2 b. Also, to injure or pain as by stretching; to rack, torture (the feelings, etc.). *Obs.*

1612 R. Fenton *Usury* 38 Verily if vsurie were not, men would tenter their wits, either in trading themselues or imploying others. 1622 Fletcher *Beggar's Bush* ii. iii, He does stretch, Tenter his credit so. 1652 J. Wright tr. *Camus' Nat. Paradox* iii. 49 It might be done without tentering his Conscience. *a* 1734 North *Exam.* ii. iv. § 32 (1740) 247 It is plain..that Pepys, being once tentered, should have come off *secundum artem.*

†**3.** *intr.* Of cloth: To admit of being stretched on the tenter; to bear tentering. *Obs. rare*—1.

1626 Bacon *Sylva* § 841 Parchment or leather will stretch, paper will not; woollen cloth will tenter, linen scarcely.

†**Te·nterbe:lly.** *Obs.* [f. Tenter *v.* + Belly *sb.*] One who distends his belly; a glutton.

1621 Burton *Anat. Mel.* iii. ii. vi. i. (1651) 546 Not with sweet wine..as many of those Tenterbellies do. 1630 J. Taylor (Water P.) *Gt. Eater Kent* 10 A cheating bable, in comparison of this Nicolaitan, Kentish tenterbelly.

**Tentered** (te·ntəɹd), *ppl. a.* [f. Tenter *v.* and *sb.*1 + -ed.]

**1.** Stretched on or as on a tenter; racked.

1652 Benlowes *Theoph.* vii. xxxvii, As my tenter'd Minde its Spirits still Strains forth. 1835 Ure *Philos. Manuf.* 203 In order to dry the tentered cloth within it.

**2.** Stuck or studded with tenter-hooks.

1768 Tucker *Lt. Nat.* (1834) I. 222 Another person..might still expect uneasiness in the tentered cask, nevertheless, might choose it as the lesser evil. 1795 Southey *Joan of Arc* iv. 111 How Maximin,..In such deep fury bade the tenter'd wheel Rend her life piecemeal.

†**Te·nter-ground.** *Obs.* [f. Tenter *sb.*1 + Ground *sb.*] Ground occupied by tenters for stretching cloth, etc.

1714 *Lond. Gaz.* No. 5266/8 In the Tentor Ground by the Dog house in Bunhill fields. 1769 Gray *Let. to Wharton* 18 Oct., I entered Kendal almost in the dark, and could distinguish only a shadow of the castle on a hill, and tenter-grounds spread far and wide round the town. 1887 Lecky *Eng. in 18th C.* VI. xxiii. 247 To steal woollen cloth from a tenter-ground.

**Tenter-hook** (te·ntəɹ,huk). Forms: see Tenter *sb.*1; also 5 **tayntyr-, tentyr-,** 6 **tentur-,** 7 **tentry-.** [f. Tenter *sb.*1 + Hook *sb.*]

**1.** One of the hooks or bent nails set in a close row along the upper and lower bar of a tenter, by which the edges of the cloth are firmly held; a hooked or right-angled nail or spike; *dial.* a metal hook upon which anything is hung.

1480 *Wardr. Acc. Edw. IV* (1830) 139 Tentourhokes, cc. 1492–3 *Rec. St. Mary at Hill* 186 Item, for tayntyrhokes and ffor wachyng of the sepulture, xij d. *a* 1518 Skelton *Magnyf.* 1002 Her naylys sharpe as tenter hokys! 1579 in Feuillerat *Revels Q. Eliz.* (1908) 324 Tainter Hookes at viiid the c. *a* 1683 Sidney *Disc. Govt.* iii. xxxii. (1704) 369 The King of Marocco may stab his Subjects, throw them to the Lions, or hang them upon tenterhooks. 1688 R. Holme *Armoury* iii. 348/1 The *Tentry Hook* is a Nail with a crooked Head, yet sharp pointed, that it may strike into any thing hung upon it. 1777 Howard *Prisons Eng.* (1780) 404 The partition between this and the garden..strong palisades with tenter-hooks. 1825 Waterton *Wand. S. Amer.* iii. iii. 254 On examining his teeth I found that they were all bent like tenter-hooks, pointing down his throat. 1888 *Sheffield Gloss.*, *Tenter-hooks*, the hooks upon which the valances of a bed are hung. 1889 *N. W. Linc. Gloss.* (ed. 2), *Tenter-hooks*, strong iron hooks put in ceilings and ..joists.., on which bacon and other such things are hung.

**b.** *transf.* = Tenter *sb.*1 2 b.

1665 Hooke *Microgr.* xxxv. 164 It was arm'd likewise with the like Tenterhooks or claws with those of the sheath. 1713 Derham *Phys.-Theol.* To Rdr. 6 The Beards (or Tenter-hooks [of a bee's sting] as Dr. Hook calls them) lie only on one side of each Spear, not all round them. 1816 Kirby & Sp. *Entomol.* xxiii. (1818) II. 323 These tenter-hooks in the suckers of flies..are mere fancies.

**2.** *fig.* That on which something is stretched or strained; something that causes suffering or painful suspense. Cf. Tenter *sb.*1 3.

**1532** MORE *Confut. Barnes* VIII. Wks. 797/1 The churche ..is stretched out in the stretcher or tenter hookes of the crosse, as a church well washed and cleansed. **1601** CHESTER *Love's Mart.* (1878) 138 Ract on the tenter-hookes of foule disgrace. **1823** BYRON *Juan* XIV. xcvii, [It] keeps the atrocious reader in suspense; The surest way for ladies and for books To bait their tender or their tenter-hooks.

**b.** esp. in phrases *to put, set, strain, stretch on the tenter-hooks*: to strain, distort the sense of (words) (? *obs.*); to strain (conscience, truth, authority, credit, etc.) beyond the proper, normal, or natural extent, limit, or scope; to put a strain on (a faculty, power, or capacity). Now *rare.*

**1583** STUBBES *Anat. Abus.* II. (1882) 29 He racketh it, straineth it, and as it were so setteth it on the tenter hookes. **1603** H. CROSSE *Vertues Commw.* (1878) 58 By setting the conscience on the tainter-hookes, to rise vp by his fall. **1630** *R. Johnson's Kingd. & Commw.* 134 Nor doe I here stretch my discourse on the tenter-hookes of partiality. **1700** W. KING *Transactioneer* 57 The poor People have set their Wits, as if it were on the Tenter-hooks, to make Turnep-Bread in Essex. **1841** D'ISRAELI *Amen. Lit.* (1867) 213 (*Invent. Printing*) Honest men .. sometimes strain truth on the tenter-hooks of fiction.

**c.** *To be on* (*the*) *tenter-hooks*: i. e. in a state of painful suspense or impatience: cf. TENTER *sb.*[1] 3 b.

**1748** SMOLLETT *Rod. Rand.* xlv, I left him upon the tenter-hooks of impatient uncertainty. **1812** SIR R. WILSON *Pr. Diary* (1861) I. 127 Until I reach the imperial head-quarters I shall be on tenter-hooks. **1897** *Sat. Rev.* 25 Dec. 754/1 The author keeps..the reader..on tenterhooks.

**3.** *attrib.*

**1576** FLEMING tr. *Caius' Dogs* (1880) 37 This dogge..is violent in fighting, & wheresoeuer he setteth his tenterhooke teeth, he taketh such sure & fast holde, that a man may sooner teare and rende him in sunder, then lose him and seperate his chappes. **1907** *Westm. Gaz.* 12 Sept. 2/1 What may be called 'tenterhook living' or existence on the crust of a volcano.

Hence † **Te·nter-hoo:king** *a.*, laying hold with tenter-hooks (in quot. *fig.*).

**1615** BRATHWAIT *Strappado* (1878) 197 Avoid such tenter-hooking men.

**Tentering** (te·ntəriŋ), *vbl. sb.* [f. TENTER *v.* + -ING [1].] The action of the verb TENTER; the stretching (of cloth) on tenters or by means of other mechanical devices.

**1483-4** *Act* 1 *Rich. III*, c. 8 § 7 No maner persone..set nor drawe .. any maner of Wollen Cloth .. by the meane of teynteryng or otherwise. **1597-8** *Act* 39 *Eliz.* c. 20 (*title*) An Acte aginst the deceitfull stretching and taintering of Northerne Cloth. **1677** JORDAN *Lond. Tri.* 20 The Tentering I wot Must not be forgot. **1706** A. BOYER *Ann. Q. Anne* IV. 28 The tentring or stretching of any the aforesaid draperies. **1858** SIMMONDS *Dict. Trade*, *Tentering*, a technical term for stretching woven goods to dry, after being stiffened or dyed.

**b.** *attrib.*, as *tentering-house, -machine, -room.*

**1877** KNIGHT *Dict. Mech.*, *Tentering-machine*, a machine for stretching fabrics. **1881** *Daily News* 21 Jan. 5/6 Her body was found in the ruins of the tentering house. *c* **1890** W. H. CASMEY *Ventilation* 19 These fans are supplied with warm air from the finishing and tentering rooms adjoining.

† **Te·nter-yard.** *Obs.* [f. TENTER *sb.*[1] + YARD *sb.*] A yard or enclosure with tenters for stretching cloth, etc.

**1481-90** *Howard Househ. Bks.* (Roxb.) 303 He to have his howse that he dwellyth in, and the teynter yerd. **1545** *Act* 37 *Hen. VIII*, c. 12 § 10 Any mansion house with a..tymber yarde, teyntree yarde, or gardeyne bilonginge to the same. **1598** STOW *Surv.* (1908) I. 127 The fields on either side be turned into Garden plottes, teynter yardes, Bowling Allyes, and such like.

**Tentful,** *sb.*: see TENT *sb* [1]

**Te·ntful,** *a.* Now *dial.* [f. TENT *sb.*[2] + -FUL.] Careful; full of attention.

*c* **1450** HOLLAND *Howlat* 420 And vthir signess, forsuth syndry I gess, Off metallis and colouris in tentfull atyr. **1870** LADY VERNEY *L. Lisle* vi. 77 He's a very 'tentful man.

**Tenth** (tenþ), *a.* and *sb.* Forms: see below in A. 1. [Various formations from the cardinal numeral TEN, at earlier and later stages of its history. The early forms represent Indo-Eur. *dekmtos (Gr. δέκατος, Lith. *deszim̃tas*, OSlav. *desętyĭ*) simply, or with assimilation to the form of the cardinal; the later are new formations on *ten*, with the suffix *-th, -d, -t*, ablaut forms of pre-Teut. *-tos*. Like the other ordinals, only of the weak declension: in OE. with sing. masc. *-a*, fem. and neut. *-e*, pl. *-an*. The form-groups are: α. OE. (Anglian) **teoȝoða, -ēða, -ða* (Northumb. *teiȝ(e)ða, teiða*), corresp. to OFris. *tegotha, -atho, -etha*, OS. *tegotho, -atho* (MLG. *tegede, teigede*, LG. *tegede, tegde*), going back through **teȝuþo*, to OTeut. **teȝunþo-*. Its mod. repr. is TITHE. β. The ordinary OE. (WSax.) *tēoða* (early ME. *tēþe*), app. from **teoh(e)ða*, going back through **tehuþo*, to **tehunþo-*, with *h* in place of *ȝ* under the influence of the cardinal **tehun*. This form is found only in Eng.; it survived dialectally to the 16th c. as *tēthe*. γ. Early ME. *tēnde* (later *tend, teind*), appearing in Ormin *c* 1200, but probably existing earlier, also in Kentish in the Ayenbite 1340. It corresponds in consonants to OFris. *tianda, tienda* (Du. *tiende*), OS. *tehando*, OHG. *zehanto*; Goth. *taihunda*, Norse *tionde, tiunde*. δ. Early ME. *tenðe* (*tyenðe, teonðe*), *tenþe*, now TENTH, a new formation from *ten* with suffix -TH. ε. ME. *tent*, also from *ten*, with suffix *-t*. Now *dial.*, chiefly northern and north midl. See *Note* below.]



The ordinal numeral corresponding to the cardinal number TEN; that which comes next to the ninth.

**A.** *adj.* **1.** In concord with a substantive expressed or understood.

α. 1 *Anglian.* teoȝoða (in *teoȝoðian* TITHE *v.*), teoȝeða, teoȝða; *Northumb.* (teȝða: in *teȝðigan* TITHE *v.*), teiȝða, teiða, 2–3 tiȝeðe, 3 tiȝðe, 4–5 tiþe, tyþe [4–9 tithe, tythe, etc.: see TITHE *sb.*].

*a* **900** tr. *Bæda's Hist.* v. xxii[i]. § 1 Ðy teoȝeþan [*v.r.* teoðan] dæȝe Iunius monþes. *c* **950** *O. E. Martyrol.* (1900) 80 On þone teoȝðan [*MS. C.* teoðan] dæȝ þæs monðes. *Ibid.* 116 On ðone teoȝeþan [*MS. C.* teoðan] dæȝ þæs monðes. *c* **950** *Lindisf. Gosp.* John i. 39 Tid uæs suelce ðio teiȝða [*Ags. G.* teoðe tid]. *Ibid.* Matt. *Prolog. X Canon.* Skeat 3, l. 18 In regula ða teiða. *c* **1250** Tiȝðe [see A. 3]. **1297** R. GLOUC. (Rolls) 8935 Het was ido in þe teþe [*v. rr.* teoþe, tenþe] ȝer of þe kinges kinedom, & enleue hondred & þe tiþe, þat vr louerd an-erþe com. *c* **1375** Tyþe [see A. 3].

β. 1 téoða, téða, 2 tioðe, tieðe, 3–4 teoþe, teothe, teþe.

*c* **900** tr. *Bæda's Hist.* v. xxii[i]. § 1 Þy teoðan [*Ca.* teoȝeþan] dæȝe Iunius monþes. *Ibid.* Teðan [see A. 3]. *c* **955** *O. E. Chron.* an. 955 He ricsade teoþe healf ȝear. *c* **1000** ÆLFRIC *Gen.* viii. 5 And þa wætera..wanedon oþ þæne teoþan monþ. *a* **1175** *Cott. Hom.* 219 Swa fele þe me mihte þat tioðe hape fulfellen. *c* **1200** *Trin. Coll. Hom.* 137 Þe tieðe [wise] is þat michele hereword þat ure helend him gaf. *c* **1290** *S. Eng. Leg.* I. 76/205 In þe teoþe ȝere also. *a* **1300** *Fall & Passion* 15 in *E. E. P.* (1862) 13 For þe prude of lucifer þe teþe angle fille in to helle. *c* **1315** SHOREHAM III. 329 Þe teþe hest þe for-bet Wyl tou oþer manne þynge. **1387** Teþe [see A. 2].

γ. 2–5 tende, 4 teinde, teynde, 4–5 tend, teind, 5–6 teynd [8 tiend, etc.: see TEIND].

*c* **1200** ORMIN 4518 Þe tende bodeword wass sett þurrh Godd forr þine nede. *Ibid.* 12745 Summ itt off þatt daȝȝ þe tende time wære. *c* **1250** *Gen. & Ex.* 3141 Ðe tende dai it sulde ben laȝt, And ho(l)den in ðe tende naȝt. **1340** HAMPOLE *Pr. Consc.* 3990 Þe tend [token] es of þe grete dome final. **1340** *Ayenb.* 2 Þe tende godes heste. *Ibid.* 13 Þe tende article is þellich. **13..** Teind [see ε]. **1375** BARBOUR *Bruce* IV. 460 On the tend day..the king..Arivit. *c* **1460** *Towneley Myst.* i. 144 Thou art fallen, that was the teynd, ffrom an angell to a feynd.

δ. 2 tenðe (tyenðe), 2–4 teonðe, 4 tenþe (tentþe, tennyth), 4–6 tenthe, 4–5 tienthe, 5– tenth.

*a* **1150** *MS.* (in *Anglia* XI. 370), On þan tenðen dæiȝe. *a* **1175** *Cott. Hom.* 219 Þat teonðe werod abreað. *Ibid.*, Þa wes þes tyenðes [*ed.* tyendes] hapes alder swiþe fiel isceapen. *c* **1175** *Lamb. Hom.* 117 Þe teonðe [*ed.* teouðe] unþeau is þet biscop beo ȝemeles. *c* **1380** WYCLIF *Wks.* (1880) 354 Þe tentþe [*ed.* tenteþ] propirte þat suiþ. **1382** — *John* i. 39 The our was as the tenthe. **1398** TREVISA *Barth. De P. R.* IX. xxxiii. (Bodl. MS.), In the moneþ of September .. on tenþe dai of þat moneþ. **1480** CAXTON Tienthe [see quot. 1387 in A. 2]. **1495** *Trevisa's Barth. De P. R.* IX. xxxiii. 369 The tenth daye of Septembre. **1526** TINDALE *John* i. 39 It was about the tenthe [**1539** tenth] houre. **1530** PALSGR. 372/1 *Dixiesme*, tenthe. **1599** SHAKS. *Hen. V*, I. ii. 77 King Lewes the Tenth. **1828** SCOTT *F. M. Perth* xiii, Not a man claiming in the tenth degree of kindred but must repair to the brattach of his tribe.

ε. 4– tent (*Sc.* 5–6 teynt).

**13..** *Cursor M.* 515 (Cott.) Þe tent [*v.rr.* tende, teind] ordir for to fullfill. *c* **1400** *Destr. Troy* 4480 To saile somyn vnto Troy..And the tent yere truly..Þere worship to wyn. **1513** DOUGLAS *Æneis* XI. vi. 156 The Grekis conquest..prolongit was quhill the tent ȝeir. **1562** WINȜET *Cert. Tractates* ii. Wks. (S. T. S.) I. 18 The tent day of Marche. 1561. **1657** SIR W. MURE *Hist. Rowallane* Wks. (S. T. S.) II. 251, 1415, the tent year of his governale. **1905** [*Tent* is now the local form in Scotland, most of England down to Shropsh., Worcester, Leicester, Lincolnsh., and parts of Ulster. See Wright, *Eng. Dial. Gram.* 269.]

**2.** The last of each row or series of ten; each or every tenth individual or part.

*c* **890-901** *Laws K. Ælfred* Introd. c. 38 Þine teoðan sceattas & þine frumripan..ȝif þu Gode. *a* **1000** *Cædmon's Gen.* 2122 (Gr.) Ðæs hereteames ealles teoðan sceat Abraham sealde Godes biscope. **1297** R. GLOUC. (Rolls) 6713, & tolde of hom þe teþe out, & þe nine slou. **1387** TREVISA *Higden* (Rolls) I. 395 Al þe teþe [Caxton (**1480**) tienthe] londe, þat þe kyng hadde assigned him. **1535** STEWART *Cron. Scot.* (Rolls) III. 384 Confermit wes with the paip of the new..That king Dauid the tent penny suld haif. **1551** CROWLEY *Pleas. & Pain* 343 The tenth increase by sea and lande. **1617** MORYSON *Itin.* II. 37 Disarming the souldiers and executing the tenth man. **1759** *Hist.* in *Ann. Reg.* 55 *note*, The French court have stopt the payment of..the rents created on the two sols per pound of the tenth penny. **1844** LD. BROUGHAM *Brit. Const.* xi, In 1205 a Parliament..ordered every tenth knight to be raised and mounted at the charge of the other nine.

**b.** *Tenth wave*: every tenth wave was formerly held to be larger than the nine preceding waves; hence allusively. (Cf. DECUMAN I.)

**1585** HIGINS *Junius' Nomencl.* 400/1 *Fluctus decumanus*, the tenth waue, that is a mighty, huge, violent and great waue or surge. **1628** LE GRYS tr. *Barclay's Argenis* 297 This tenth waue will either put an end to the storme or sinke my beaten barke. **1752** YOUNG *Brothers* IV. i, This, Fate, is thy tenth wave, and quite o'erwhelms me. **1884** *Harper's Mag.* Aug. 472/1 A mighty tenth wave of cheers and cries.

**3.** *Tenth part* († *deal*, † *dole*), any one of the ten equal parts into which a whole may be divided.

**854** *Charter of Æthelwolf* in Birch *Cart. Sax.* II. 80 Ða ða he teoðode ȝynd eall his cyne rice ðone teoðan dæl ealra his landa. *a* **900** tr. *Bæda's Hist.* IV. xxx. [xxix.] § 4 Ealra wæstma & æppla & hræȝla ðone teoðan [*Ca.* teðan] dæl for Gode to ælmessum ðearfum sealde. **971** *Blickl. Hom.* 35 We sceolan..syllan þone teoþan dæl ure worldspeda. *c* **1200** ORMIN 6125 Off all þatt god te birrþ þin Godd þe tende dale brinngenn. *c* **1250** *Gen. & Ex.* 895 Habram ȝaf him ðe tiȝðe del Of alle [h]is biȝete. *a* **1300** *Cursor M.* 20026 A thusand yeir moght i noght reke..Til tend [*v.rr.* tende, tenþe] part of hir louing. *c* **1350** *Will. Palerne* 4715 What wise i miȝte quite þe teþe dool of his tour ryche. *c* **1375** *E. E. Allit. P.* B. 216 Bot þer he tynt þe tyþe dool of his tour ryche. *c* **1400** MAUNDEV. (Roxb.) xix. 87 Vnnethes will any Cristen man suffer half so mykill, ne þe tende parte. *c* **1460** *Towneley Myst.* i. 257 The ten [*v. r.* teynd] parte felle downe with me. *Ibid.* xx. 277 Of the tresure that to vs fell, the tent parte euer with me went. **1606** SHAKS. *Tr. & Cr.* II. ii. 95 Discharging lesse then the tenth part of one. *Mod.* Not a tenth part of his income.

**B.** *absol.* and *sb.* [Orig. the adj. used elliptically or absolutely, and declined as adj., pl. *þa teoðan*; but from *c* 1200, treated as sb. with pl. (*tiȝeþes, tithes, tethes, tendes, tenthes*) *tenths*. In sense 1 b, form α was retained in standard Eng., and form γ in Scotland and north. Eng., giving TITHE and TEIND, q. v. for these differentiated uses.]

**1.** A tenth part (A. 3) *of* anything; any one of ten equal parts into which a whole may be divided. *Submerged tenth* (i. e. of the population): see SUBMERGED.

*a* **1300**–*c* **1475** [see TEIND]. **1600** W. WATSON *Decacordon* (1602) 139 Neither all, nor halfe, nor third, nor tenths of all shall be saued. **1692** LOCKE *Lower. Interest* 52 Money now is $^{9}/_{10}$ less worth than it was the former year. **1707** MORTIMER *Husb.* (1721) II. 97, 1 Foot 5 Inches and 2 tenths of an Inch. **1873** LELAND *Egypt. Sketch Bk.* 291 Englishmen of culture, who have not seen one-tenth of the great cathedrals of their own country. **1909** *Daily Chron.* 14 July 4/7 There are things in the world that you can get for a tenth of a penny.

**b.** *spec.* A tenth part of produce or profits, or of the estimated value of personal property, appropriated as a religious or ecclesiastical due, a royal subsidy, etc.

In the ecclesiastical use, †(*a*) *orig.* = TITHE, TEIND. (*b*) *spec.* The tenth part of the annual profit of every living in the kingdom, originally paid to the pope, but by Act 26 Hen. VIII, c. 3 (1534) transferred to the crown, and afterwards made a part of the fund known as Queen Anne's Bounty (BOUNTY 5 a). As a royal subsidy or aid formerly levied, see quot. 1765, and cf. FIFTEENTH B. 1.

[*a* **1100** *Laws of Athelstan* I. § 2 Ic ðe wille ȝesyllan mine teoþan. *Ibid.* § 3 ȝif we ure teoðan ȝesyllan nyllaþ, us ða nyȝon dælas biþ ætbrædene, & se teoþa an us biþ to laf. *c* **1200** Tiȝeþes: see TITHE B. 1. *c* **1250** Tiȝþes: see *ibid.* *a* **1300**–*c* **1450**: see TEIND.] **1474** CAXTON *Chesse* III. i. (1883) 77 That they rendre and gyue to god the tienthes of her goodes. **1496-7** [see FIFTEENTH B. 1]. **1535-6** *Act* 27 *Hen. VIII*, c. 42 The said firste frutes and tenthe. **1560** DAUS tr. *Sleidane's Comm.* 39 b, The fyrst fruictes, & the tenthes. **1587** HARRISON *England* II. i. (1877) I. 24 To returne to our tenths, a paiement first as deuised by the pope. **1587** FLEMING *Contn. Holinshed* III. 1378/1 An vniuersall taxation was made in nature of a tenth and fifteenth ouer all the countrie of Kent. **1611** SPEED *Hist. Gt. Brit.* IX. ix. (1623) 628 The Tenths of the Clergie..should haue been receyued. **1686** tr. *Chardin's Coronat. Solyman* 147 They pay both Tribute and Tenths. **1765** BLACKSTONE *Comm.* I. viii. 308 Tenths and fifteenths were temporary aids issuing out of personal property, and were formerly the real tenth or fifteenth part of all the movables belonging to the subject. Originally the amount was uncertain, but was reduced to a certainty in the eighth year of Edward III., when new taxations were made of every township, borough, and city in the kingdom, and recorded in the Exchequer. **1792** A. YOUNG *Trav. France* 537 No such thing was known in any part of France ..as a tenth: it was always a twelfth, or a thirteenth, or even a twentieth of the produce. **1855** MACAULAY *Hist. Eng.* XV. III. 557 The hereditary revenue..was derived from the rents of the royal domains,..from the first fruits and tenths of benefices [etc.].

† **2.** Every tenth number (below a hundred) in the natural series of numbers; *pl.* the multiples of ten, the 'tens'. *Obs.*

**1543** RECORDE *Ground of Artes* 136 These be all the nombers from 1 to 10, and then all the tenthes within 100. *Ibid.* 136 b, Loke how you did expresse single vnities and tenthes in the lefte hande, so must you expresse vnities and tenthes of hundredes, in the ryghte hande. *Ibid.*, So the fourme of euery tenthe in the lefte hande serueth [in the ryghte hand] to expresse lyke nomber of thousandes, so yͤ fourme of 40 standeth for 4000.

**3.** *Mus.* A note ten diatonic degrees above or below a given note (both notes being counted); the interval between, or consonance of, two notes ten diatonic degrees apart.

**1597** MORLEY *Introd. Mus.* 71 *Phi.* Which distances do make vnperfect consonants? *Ma.* A third, a sixt, and their eightes: a tenth, a thirteenth [etc.]. **1694** HOLDER *Harmony* iv. (1731) 40 A Tenth ascending is an Octave above the Third. **1869** OUSELEY *Counterp.* xvi. 122 Double counterpoint at the tenth is that in which either of the parts is transposed a tenth, the other remaining unmoved. **1880** C. H. H. PARRY in Grove *Dict. Mus.* I. 670/1 The use of tenths in this example [of 'Diaphony' of the 10th century] is remarkable, and evidently unusual, for Guido of Arezzo,.. a full century later, speaks of the 'symphonia vocum' in his Antiphonarium, and mentions only fourths, fifths, and octaves.

**C.** *Comb.*: **tenthmetre**, a metre divided by the tenth power of ten (= one ten-millionth of a millimetre); **tenth-rate** *a.*, of the tenth rate or relative quality, very inferior; so **tenth-remove** *a.*

**1876** G. F. CHAMBERS *Astron.* x. iii. 848 The wave-lengths of the principal Fraunhofer lines expressed in 'tenthmetres', a tenthmetre being the $1\text{-}10^{10}$ of a metre. **1834** *Tait's Mag.* I. 440/1 He tears himself away from the smiles of a 'tenth-rate figurante of the *Academie Royale*. **1889** *Spectator* 9 Nov. 626/2 A people seeking nothing but material prosperity of the tenth-rate kind. **1905** *Westm. Gaz.* 28 Mar. 4/1 Constable is too remote and difficult, but a *tenth-remove derivative, properly browned, will serve their turn.

[*Note.* The etymological history of some of the prec. forms (as in other numerals) presents points of which the explanations are more or less conjectural. The direct OTeut. repr. of Indo-Eur. **dekmto's* was by Verner's Law **tegundos*; with this the Gothic *taihunda*, OS. *tehando*, OHG. *zehanto*, agree, except in having *h* for *g*, apparently under the influence of the cardinal **tehun, -an*. The OTeut. **tegunþo-*, whence OS. and OFris. *tegotho, -a*, OAnglian *teo(g)þa*, implies a pre-Teut. **dekm·tos*, with shifted stress (implied also in some other ordinals). Assimilation of this form also to the cardinal would give **tehunþo-*, whence **tehúþa*, *teoh(o)ða, téoða*. The history of *tēnde* is more uncertain: the four ordinals, *sefende, eȝtende, neȝende, tēnde*, in ME., Northern and Kentish, form a group of which only the first is known in OE., repr. by *siofunda, seofonda*, in the Lindisf. and Rushw. glosses. *Siofunda*, like Goth. **sibunda*, OS. *sibundo*, OHG. *sibunto*, represents an OTeut. **sibundo-*, Indo-Eur. *sep(t)mto's*. OE. *nigenda* (*a* 1066), OS. *nigundo*, OHG. *niunto*, Goth. *niunda*, had prob. a parallel history. The ME. *ehtende* appears to have been conformed in its ending to *sefende*; and *tende*, from its late appearance, was prob. formed from *tēn* on the same model. *Ten-th* has the suffix which in OE. appears in *feorða, seofoða, eahtoða, nigoða, teoȝeða*, and which has now been extended to all the ordinals from *fourth* onward. On the other hand, *ten-t* has the form of the suffix which was regular in OE. *fifta* (OS. and OFris. *fifto, -ta*, OHG. *fimfto*, Goth. *fimfta*, OTeut. **fimfto-*), and *sixta* (OS. and OHG. *sehsto*, Goth. *saihsta*, OTeut. *sexsto-*), which in OE. was also used in *endlefta* (*ellefta*) and *twelfta*, and in North. and North-Midl. dialects has since been extended to all the ordinals from *fourt* to *hundert*.]

**Tenth,** *v. rare.* [f. TENTH *sb.*] *trans.* To decimate, to tithe.

**1598** BARRET *Theor. Warres* I. ii. 9 As did Iulius Cæsar.. *Dezimare* or tenth the ninth Legion by sound of the horne. **1647** TRAPP *Comm. Ep., Heb. vii. 6* 371 Received tithes of Abraham. Gr. Tithed or tenthed Abraham. **1878** HOOKER & BALL *Marocco* 470 At last came the holiday *l'ashora*, or the day of the Sultan's tenthing.

**Tenthe,** obs. form of TENT *sb.*[1]

**Tenthly** (te·nþli), *adv.* [f. TENTH *a.* + -LY [2].] In the tenth place.

**1623** in *Fasti Aberd.* (1854) 282 Tentlie, that [etc.]... Tuellftlie, that [etc.]. **1648** D. JENKINS *Wks.* 38 Tenthly, wee maintaine that [etc.]. **1727** BAILEY vol. II, *Tenthly*, in the tenth Place or Order.

†**Te·nt-hook.** *Obs. rare.* In 5–6 taynt-. [f. TENT *sb.*[5] + HOOK *sb.*] A tenter-hook.

**1491** *Churchw. Acc. St. Dunstan's, Canterb.*, Payde for threde and taynt hookes j d. **1533** *MS. Acc. St. John's Hosp., Canterb.*, For taynt hokys j d.

‖**Tenthredo** (tenþrī·do). *Entom.* [Latinized form of Gr. τενθρηδών, -δον-, a kind of wasp; the stem being taken erroneously as *tenthredin-*.] A saw-fly: in early use vaguely applied; in modern scientific use, after Linnæus 1748, and as restricted by Leach 1819, a genus of hymenopterous insects, typical of the family *Tenthredinidæ*, comprising the large saw-flies called hornet-flies. Hence **Tenthre·dinid,** *a.* belonging to the *Tenthredinidæ*; *sb.* a member of this family.

**1658** ROWLAND *Moufet's Theat. Ins.* 929 Now let us proceed to the Insect called Tenthredo. **1706** PHILLIPS (ed. Kersey), *Tenthredo*,..the lesser Hornet, or Bastard Hornet; an Insect. **1752** J. HILL *Hist. Anim.* 81 The black Tenthredo, with clavated antennæ. **1753** CHAMBERS *Cycl. Supp.*, *Tenthredo*, in natural history, the name of a fly of the stinging kind. [**1874** LUBBOCK *Orig. & Met. Ins.* ii. 33 Although Tenthredinidæ and Siricidæ are caterpillars, more or less closely resembling those of Lepidoptera.]

†**Te·ntible,** *a. Obs. rare.* [f. TENT *v.*[1] to attend + -IBLE.] Apt to attend, attentive.

**1603** H. CROSSE *Vertues Commw.* (1878) 29 If these see but a small moate amisse, a wrinkle awry, how tentible they be to mend it. *Ibid.* 120 The minde is nothing so tentible at a good instruction..as at a vaine and sportiue foolerie.

†**Te·nticle.** *Obs.* [f. TENT *sb.*[1] as if after a L. type **tenticula*: see -CULE.] A small tent.

**1548** PATTEN *Exped. Scotl.* K iv, These whyte ridges.. wear the tenticles or rather cabayns and couches of theyr souldiours. **1587** FLEMING *Contn. Holinshed* III. 988/2 Foure miles on this side Edenburgh, occupied in largenesse with diuerse tents and tenticles.

**Tentie,** variant of TENTY *a.*

†**Tentiginous** (tenti·dʒinəs), *a. Obs.* [f. L. *tentīgo, -in-em* (see next) + -OUS.]

1. Excited to lust; itching, lecherous.

**1616** B. JONSON *Devil an Ass* II. iii, Were you tentiginous? ha? Would you be acting of the Incubus?

2. Provocative of lust; lascivious.

**1684** tr. *Bonet's Merc. Compit.* XVI. 569 What he here orders to be given is heating and therefore tentiginous. **1704** SWIFT *Mech. Operat. Spirit* ii. Misc. (1711) 308 Nothing affects the Head so much as a tentigenous Humour, repel'd and elated to the upper Region.

‖**Tentigo** (tentəi·go). *Obs.* [L. *tentīgo* tenseness, lust.] An attack of priapism, an erection; lecherousness, lust.

*a* **1603** in Nichols *Progr. Q. Eliz.* (1823) III. 336 If any be trobled with the tentigo. **1827** D. JOHNSON *Ind. Field Sports* 228 Tentigo also attends. **1860** MAYNE *Expos. Lex.*, *Tentigo*,..old term for Priapism.

†**Te·ntik,** *a. Obs. rare*[−1]. Aphetic form of *attentik*, AUTHENTIC, duly qualified, trustworthy.

**1534** *St. Papers Hen. VIII*, IV. 666 Yat ȝe sall speyk with Master Adem Oterbowrn, or cawis sowm tentyk man to speyk with hym.

‖**Tenti·llum.** *Zool.* [mod.L., f. L. *tempt-, tent-*, stem of *temptāre, tentāre* to feel + dim. suffix: cf. *tentacle*.] One of the unbranched twigs which stud the retractile tentacles of some Siphonophora.

**1898** SEDGWICK *Text-bk. Zool.* I. iv. 140 These aggregations of thread-cells are especially found upon the tentilla, where they give rise to..the cnidosacs or batteries.

**Tentily** (te·ntīli), *adv. Sc. rare.* [As if f. TENTY *a.* + -LY [2]; but perh. a worn-down form of TENTIVELY (see -IVE), TENTY not being found until much later.] With care and attention; carefully.

?*a* **1400** *Morte Arth.* 3618 Tolowris tentyly takelle they ryghttene. **1721** RAMSAY *Cupid Thrown* v, He tentily Myrtilla sought. **1768** ROSS *Helenore* I. 9 Back with the halesome girss in haste she hy'd, An' tentyly unto the sair apply'd.

**Tenting** (te·ntiŋ). [f. TENT *v.*[6] + -ING [1].]

1. *vbl. sb.*[1] Lodging in or as in tents; encamping; sojourning. Chiefly *attrib.*

**1858** MACDUFF *Bow in Cloud* (1870) 32 Tenting-time here—resting-time yonder. **1870** *Standard* 14 Dec., They were in excellent marching trim, carryed neither knapsack nor tenting equipage. **1873** TRISTRAM *Moab* xiii. 234 A little plain.., a lovely tenting spot. **1883** 'ANNIE THOMAS' *Mod. Housewife* 81 That a house in the country, a short distance from London, was a more expensive form of tenting than an equally highly-rented one in the heart of the great metropolis.

2. *sb.* [f. TENT *sb.*[1]; cf. *bedding, sacking.*] Material for tents; in quot. *attrib.*

**1887** *Pall Mall G.* 4 June 8/2 The rain, instead of running off as it should have done on first-class tenting material, dripped through persistently, until the tents were perfectly uninhabitable.

**Tenting,** *vbl. sb.*[2–5]: see TENT *v.*[1–4].

**Te·nting,** *ppl. a.* [f. TENT *sb.*[1] + -ING [2].] Resembling a tent; converging as the sides of a tent.

**1818** KEATS *Endym.* II. 400 Coverlids..Not hiding up an Apollonian curve Of neck and shoulder, nor the tenting swerve Of knee from knee, nor ankles pointing light.

†**Tention** [1]. *Obs. rare.* Short for INTENTION.

**1587** FLEMING *Contn. Holinshed* III. 1417/1 To further our tention and honorable and iust actions at that time in such sort. **1653** SCLATER *Fun. Serm.* 25 Sept. (1654) 13 In the will, perfect fruition of the Divine glory, tention, and (for the measure of the Creature) Comprehension.

†**Tention** [2]. *Obs. rare.* Short for CONTENTION.

**1602** FULBECKE *2nd Pt. Parallel* Introd. 6 My neyghbours are full of sension and tention, and so cunninge, that they will make you beleeue, that all is gold, which glistereth.

**Tention** [3] ('tention). Short for ATTENTION (5).

**Tention,** obs. form of TENSION.

**Te·ntive,** *a. Obs.* exc. *dial.* Also 4–5 -if(e, -yf, 6 -yue. [a. OF. *tentif* (14th c. in Godef.), aphetic form of F. *atentif*; or aphetic form of INTENTIVE and (in later use) ATTENTIVE.] = ATTENTIVE.

*c* **1386** CHAUCER *Melib.* ⁋ 149 (Harl. MS.) As to warissching of ȝoure douȝter..we schullen do so tentyf [*v.r.* ententif] besynes fro day to night þat..sche schal be hool. ?*a* **1400** *Cato's Mor.* 337 in *Cursor M.* p. 1673 Loke þou be tentife, if þou haue lered alle þi life. **1570** *Satir. Poems Reform.* xxiii. 66 With tentyue eir vnto my taill attend. **1582** STANYHURST *Æneis* II. (Arb.) 43 Wyth tentiue lystning eeche wight was setled in harckning. **1791** J. LEARMONT *Poems* 329 (E.D.D.) Nouther party's tentive how to please. **1902** R. M. GILCHRIST *Natives of Milton* 97 Yo're as 'tentive an' as capable as onyone could be.

So **Te·ntively** *adv.* = ATTENTIVELY; **Te·ntiveness** = ATTENTIVENESS.

*c* **1350** *Will. Palerne* 2258 ȝif ȝe *tentifly take kepe & trewe be to-gadere. *Ibid.* 5124 But tentyfli þow help, þat al þis lond be lad in lawe as it ouȝt. **1438** *Rolls of Parlt.* V. 439/1 Thei put tentiflye their hole labours and diligences for his worship. **1876** *Whitby Gloss.*, *Tentifly*,..with attention. **1382** WYCLIF *Wisd.* xii. 20 If forsothe the enemys of thi seruauns,..with so myche *tentifnesse, thou tormentedist, and deliueredest. **1610** J. MELVILL *Diary* (Wodrow) 556 Want of skill, tentivnes, faithfulness and guid effectioune.

**Tentless** (te·ntlės), *a.*[1] *Sc.* [f. TENT *sb.*[2] + -LESS.] Heedless, careless, inattentive. Hence **Te·ntlessness.**

*a* **1584** MONTGOMERIE *Cherrie & Slae* 1290 Aftymes a tentless merchand tynes, For bying geir be gess. **1785** BURNS *To J. Smith* x, I'll wander on, wi' tentless heed How never-halting moments speed. **1836** J. STRUTHERS *Dychmont* Poet. Wks. 1850 II. 49, I With tentless step was wont to roam. **1883** D. R. SELLARS in *Mod. Scot. Poets* vi. 157 His tentlessness he rues In calmer mood.

**Tentless** (te·ntlės), *a.*[2] [f. TENT *sb.*[1] + -LESS.] Without a tent or tents; having no tent.

**1814** BYRON *Lara* II. xi, The tentless rest beneath the humid sky. **1820** MILMAN *Fall Jerus.* (1821) 39 The wind That sweeps the tentless desert. **1901** KIPLING *Kim* xiii, They lay out somewhere below him, chartless, foodless, tentless.

**Tentlet** (te·ntlėt). [f. TENT *sb.*[1] + -LET.] A miniature tent.

**1879** STEVENSON *Trav. Cevennes* 7 In case of heavy rain I proposed to make myself a little tent, or tentlet.

†**Te·ntly,** *adv. Obs.* [f. TENT *a.* + -LY [2].] Attently, attentively.

?*a* **1400** *Cato's Mor.* 303 in *Cursor M.* p. 1673 Þe mare þou art of prise, And gracious to office, Serue þou mare tentli, Þat þou ne be calde vn-wise.

**Te·nt-ma:ker.** 1. One who makes tents.

**1565** T. STAPLETON *Fortr. Faith* 107 b, He that weareth the crowne on his head, besecheth the teintmaker [St. Paul], and the fisher both dead to be his protectours. **1582** N. T. (Rhem.) *Acts* xviii. 3 They were tentmakers by their craft [TINDALE, Their crafte was to make tentes; 1388 WYCLIF, of roop-makeris crafte]. **1884** J. HALL *Chr. Home* 87 Paul was a tent-maker, and he was not ashamed of it.

2. (See quot., and cf. TENT *sb.*[1] 2 c.)

**1863** L. L. CLARKE in *Intell. Observer* IV. 1 Micro-lepidoptera. (Coleophora, or Tent-makers.)

So **Te·nt-ma:king,** the business of making tents.

**1641** 'SMECTYMNUUS' *Vind. Answ.* xii. 113 We pardon his ..comparison betweene S. Pauls Tent-making..& the State imployment of our Bishops.

**Tent-man:** see TENT *sb.*[1] 5 b.

**Tentor,** obs. form of TENTER.

**Tento·rial,** *a. Anat.* [f. L. *tentōri-um* (see below) + -AL.] Of or pertaining to the tentorium.

**1863** HUXLEY *Man's Place Nat.* iii. 149 Longitudinal and vertical sections of the skulls of a Beaver..and a Baboon.., the tentorial plane. **1881** MIVART *Cat* 69 The ossified tentorial plate. **1899** *Syd. Soc. Lex.*, *Tentorial angle*, angle formed by the intersection of the basio-cranial axis with plane of tentorium.

So †**Tento·rian** *a. Obs. rare*[−0].

**1656** BLOUNT *Glossogr.*, *Tentorian*, belonging to a tent or pavilion.

‖**Tentorium** (tentōᵊ·riŏm). [L. *tentōrium* tent, f. *tend-ĕre, tent-* to stretch: see -ORIUM.]

†1. A tent-like covering; an awning; a canopy.

**1661** EVELYN *Fumifug.* Misc. Writ. (1805) I. 230 If there were a solid tentorium, or canopy over London.

2. *Anat.* A membranous (sometimes ossified) partition between the cerebrum and cerebellum.

**1800** *Phil. Trans.* XC. 435 There is a very uncommon peculiarity in it, which is, that there is a bony falx of some breadth, but no bony tentorium. **1801** HOME *ibid.* XCII. 78 The tentorium is entirely membranous. **1854** OWEN *Skel. & Teeth* in *Orr's Circ. Sc.* I. *Org. Nat.* 232 The parts of the dura mater or outer membrane of the brain, called 'tentorium',..are ossified. **1863** HUXLEY *Man's Place Nat.* ii. 99 What is termed the *tentorium*—a sort of parchment-like shelf or partition which..is interposed between the cerebrum and cerebellum. **1878** BELL *Gegenbaur's Comp. Anat.* 512 In many Mammalia the tentorium is ossified.

†**Te·ntory.** *Obs.* [ad. L. *tentōri-um* tent: see -ORY [1].] A tent; the awning of a tent.

**1412-20** LYDG. *Chron. Troy* II. 7109 Wher þe kyng sat in his tentorie. *Ibid.* IV. 2515 For lak of socour þe Grekis wern eche in his tentorie Of Troylus slayn. **1664** EVELYN *Sylva* IV. viii. (1775) 615 The women.. who are said [2 Kings xxiii. 7] to weave hangings and curtains for the grove, were no other then makers of tentories, to spread from tree to tree.

†**Tentour.** *Obs. rare*[−1]. [In quot., rendering L. *tentōria* tents: cf. -OR 3.] A tent.

*a* **1325** *Prose Psalter, Hab.* iii. 7 Y seȝe þe tentours [Vulg. *tentoria*; LXX. σκηνώματα] of Ethiop for her wickednes, & þe skynnes [Vulg. *pelles*; LXX. σκηναί] of þe londe of Madian shul ben trubled.

**Tentour, -owre,** obs. forms of TENTER.

**Te·nt-peg.** One of the (usually wooden) pegs, with a notch at the upper end, to which when stuck in the ground the ropes of a tent are fastened. Hence **Te·nt-pe:gging,** an Indian cavalry sport, in which the player, riding at full speed, tries to transfix and carry off, on the point of his lance, a tent-peg fixed in the ground. Also *attrib.* So **Te·nt-pe:gger,** one who takes part in this exercise.

**1869** E. A. PARKES *Pract. Hygiene* (ed. 3) 326 Between the tent-pegs of every tent. **1878** *N. Amer. Rev.* CXXVII. 155 'Tent-pegging' is a very favorite amusement of the sowar. **1900** *Daily News* 26 June 3/1 The tugs-of-war, tent-peggings, V.C. races, etc., were well contested. **1901** *Daily Chron.* 31 May 6/2 'Bobs'..was himself the champion tent-pegger against all comers.

**Tentral,** erron. form of TRENTAL.

†**Tentretene** = *to entertain*: see T'.

**1481** CAXTON *Godeffroy* iii. 21 This puissaunt kynge.. assigned grete reuenues therto for tentretene it [the temple].

**Te·nt-stitch.** Also ten-. [First element uncertain. One conjecture would refer it to TENT *sb.*[5]] A kind of embroidery or worsted-work popular in the 17–18th c., in which the pattern is worked in series of parallel stitches arranged diagonally across the intersections of the threads. Also called *petit point*. Also *attrib.* So **Tent-work,** needle-work done in tent-stitch.

**1639** MAYNE *City Match* IV. i, Let me never more Be thought fit to instruct young Gentlewomen, Or deale in Tent-stitch. **1669** MRS. THORNTON *Autobiog.* (Surtees) 12 Blacke velvett, imbroidered with flowrs of silke worke in ten stich. *c* **1710** CELIA FIENNES *Diary* (1888) 296 Many fine pictures under Glasses, of tentstitch, sattin stitch,..and Strawwork. **1798** EDGEWORTH *Pract. Educ.* XX. II. 530 Our great grandmothers distinguished themselves by substantial tent work [*ed.* **1811** ten-stitch] chairs and carpets. **1800** MRS. HERVEY *Mourtray Fam.* III. 199 During the interesting scene, by the tent stitch frame. **1882** CAULFEILD & SAWARD *Dict. Needlewk.*, *Tent Stitch*, a stitch employed in Tapestry Work and in fine Embroideries,..produced by crossing over one strand of canvas in a diagonal direction, sloped from right to left, and resembles the first half taken in Cross Stitch. **1908** *Westm. Gaz.* 1 July 2/1 An oval fire-screen in tent-stitch, of quaint pattern and beautiful execution.

†**Tent-taker.** *Obs.* [TENT *sb.*[2] 1.] One who 'takes tent' or gives heed.

*c* **1430** in *Pol. Rel. & L. Poems* (1866) 187 To triflis y haue be a greet tent taker.

**Tenture** (te·ntiŭr). *rare.* [a. F. *tenture* tapestry hangings, ad. L. type **tentūra* stretching, f. *tendĕre, tent-* to stretch.] Hangings for a wall; wall-paper.

**1858** SIMMONDS *Dict. Trade.* **1877** KNIGHT *Dict. Mech.*

**Tenture,** obs. form of TENTER.

**Tentwise,** *adv.* [1], [2]: see TENT *sb.*[1], 3.

**Te·nt-work**[1]. [f. TENT *sb.*[1] + WORK *sb.*] **a.** The work of tent-making. **b.** A work of the nature or form of a tent. **c.** Work done or carried out in tents or under canvas.

1645 BP. HALL *Remedy Discontents* 92 There we find the most glorious Apostle .. stitching of skins for his Tent-work. 1866 H. COLLINS *Cistercian Order* 53 They erected a tent-work with some pieces of blanketing. 1878 CONDER *(title)* Tent-Work in Palestine.

**Tent-work** [2]: see TENT-STITCH.

**Tentwort** (te·ntwɒɹt). Also 6 teynt-. [? f. TAINT *sb.*: see quot. 1727.] An old name for a small fern, the Wall Rue, *Asplenium Ruta-muraria.*

*c* 1550 LLOYD *Treas. Health* Y ij, Agaynst the Tertian of yellowe choler..take yᵉ rotes of fennel, parcely, teynt wort, mayden heare, endyue [etc.]. 1666 MERRETT *Pinax Brit.* 2 *Adianthum album*, sive Ruta muraria, sive Salvia Vitæ, Wall rue, and Tentwort. 1727 THRELKELD *Syn. Stirpes Hibern.* A ij, Our ancestors gave it [the Ruta muraria] the name of *Tent-wort*, deeming it a sovereign remedy against the..*Taint*, doubling of the Joints, and in a more general word, Rickets. 1860 MAYNE *Expos. Lex.*, Tent-wort. 1866 *Treas. Bot.*, Tentwort.

**Tenty** (te·nti), *a. Sc.* Also **tentie**. [Later form of *tentif*, TENTIVE, with *-if* reduced to *-ie*, *-y*: see -IVE.] Watchful, attentive, observant, cautious.

*c* 1555 MAITLAND in Pinkerton *Anc. Scot. Poems* (1786) 276 Be wyse, and tentie, in thy governing. 1728 RAMSAY *Tea-t. Misc., Bonny Scot* iii, Fair winds and tenty boat-man. 1785 BURNS *Halloween* viii, Jean slips in twa wi' tentie e'e; Wha 'twas, she wadna tell. 1886 STEVENSON *Kidnapped* xii. 112 Never a gun or a sword left .. but what tenty folk have hidden in their thatch.

† **Te·nuate,** *v. Obs. rare.* [f. L. *tenuāt-*, ppl. stem of *tenuāre* to make thin, f. *tenu-is* thin.] *trans.* To make thin or slender; to attenuate.

1656 BLOUNT *Glossogr.*, *Tenuate*,..to make small, thin or slender. 1657 TOMLINSON *Renou's Disp.* 505 To tenuate and prepare humours.

‖ **Tenue** (tənü). [Fr. *tenue* deportment, sb. use of fem. pa. pple. of *tenir* to hold, keep; = Pr. *tenguda*, Sp., It. *tenuta*.] Carriage, bearing, deportment; also, costume, 'rig'.

1892 *Q. Rev.* Apr. 380 To the end that he might appear in proper tenue at any place of fashionable resort. 1901 *Ibid.* Apr. 325 The Queen had an extreme respect for *tenue* in all its forms.

**Tenues**, pl. of TENUIS.

**Tenui-** (teniu,i). Combining form of L. *tenuis* 'thin, narrow, slender', in scientific use in adjectives, as **te:nuico·state** [L. *costa* rib], having slender ribs; so **te:nuifa·sciate** [L. *fascia* band], **te:nuiflo·rous** [L. *flōs, flōrem* flower], **te:nuifo·lious** [L. *folium* leaf], having narrow or thin leaves, **te·nuipede** [L. *pēs, ped-em* foot], **te:nuistri·ate** [L. *stria* groove], having slender striæ.

1860 MAYNE *Expos. Lex.*, *Tenuicostatus*,..*tenuicostate. *Ibid.*, *Tenuiflorus*,..*tenuiflorous. 1657 *Physical Dict.*, **Tenuifolious*, thin leav'd. 1658 SIR T. BROWNE *Gard. Cyrus* iv, Why Coniferous trees are tenuifolious or narrow-leaved? 1860 MAYNE *Expos. Lex.*, *Tenuifolius*,..tenuifolious. *Ibid.*, *Tenuipes*,..having the feet small and compressed: *tenuipede. *Ibid.*, *Tenuistriatus*,..*tenuistriate.

† **Te·nuine,** *a. Obs. rare*[−1]. [f. L. *tenu-is* thin, app. after *genuine*.] Attenuated; weak; weakened.

*a* 1660 *Contemp. Hist. Irel.* (Ir. Archæol. Soc.) II. 79 To continue..in such tenuine condition as he was at present.

**Tenu·ious,** *a.* Now *rare.* [f. L. *tenui-s* thin + -OUS (cf. *lugubri-ous*).] Thin, attenuated.

**1.** = TENUOUS 1.

1495 *Trevisa's Barth. De P. R.* v. lxiv. I viij b/1 The skynne of the vysage is more tenurus [? tenuius; *orig.* alijs tenuior] & thynne. 1656 BLOUNT *Glossogr.*, *Tenuious, Tenuous*,..slender, thin [etc.]. 1659 STANLEY *Hist. Philos.* XIII. (1701) 563/1 A natural Philosopher, who conceived that all things are generated of tenuious little Bodies. 1698 KEILL *Exam. Th. Earth* (1734) 185 Not huge lumps of solid matter, but little tenuious particles or small dust.

**2.** = TENUOUS 2.

1634 T. JOHNSON *Parey's Chirurg.* XI. (1678) 274 The Aqua vitæ..is of so tenuious a substance, that it presently vanisheth into the air. 1696 WHISTON *Th. Earth* IV. (1722) 317 The Atmosphere would..become in a greater degree tenuious. 1757 WALKER in *Phil. Trans.* L. 130, I observed a tenuious blueish vapour rising. 1760–72 tr. *Juan & Ulloa's Voy.* (ed. 3) II. 73 These mists are so tenuious.

**3.** *fig.* = TENUOUS 3.

1656 STANLEY *Hist. Philos.* I. v. 148 The tenuious, loose, remisse phantasy. 1885 G. MEREDITH *Diana* xii, Emma went through a sphere of tenuious reflections in a flash.

**Tenuiroster** (te·niu,irɒ·stəɹ). *Ornith.* [ad. F. *tenuirostre*, ad. mod.L. *tenuirostris*, f. *tenui-s* thin + *rostrum* beak, bill.] A member of the *Tenuirostres*, passerine or insessorial birds with slender bills; a slender-billed bird. So **Te:nuiro·stral** *a.*, of or pertaining to the *Tenuirostres*; also = next. **Te·nuiro·strate** *a.*, slender-billed.

1837 SWAINSON *Nat. Hist. & Classif. Birds* III. iii. II. 13 This we think is the tenuirostral type of the circle. 1837 *Penny Cycl.* VIII. 146/2 According to Mr. Vigors, the Certhiadæ on one side lead the way to the Tenuirostral group. 1842 BRANDE *Dict. Sci.*, Tenuirosters. 1860 MAYNE *Expos. Lex.*, Tenuirostrate. 1874 WOOD *Nat. Hist.* 305 The large group of birds which are termed Tenuirostral, or Slender-billed.

‖ **Tenuis** (te·niu,is). *Gram.* and *Phonology.* Pl. **tenues** (te·niu,īz). [L., = thin, slender, fine: used in Craston's Latin version of Lascaris's Greek Grammar 1480, and in other early Greek grammars, to translate Gr. ψιλόν 'bare, smooth', applied by Aristotle to the consonants κ, τ, π (for which Priscian's term was *lēvis* smooth), as opposed to the *aspiratæ* or aspirates (in Gr. δασέα, pl. of δασύ rough, thick).]

One of the Greek letters κ, τ, π, or the corresponding *k, t, p* of Latin, English, and other languages; esp. the sounds represented by these; also called *surds, hard mutes*, and by Bell *breath stops.*

[1480 CRASTON *Lascaris Erotemata* a iij, Mutæ..quarum tenues quidem tres, cappa, pi, taf.] 1650 E. REEVE *Introd. Gk. Tongue* 38 The Tenuis consonant..is changed into his aspirate: as, ἀφ' ἡμῶν for ἀπὸ ἡμῶν. 1841 [see MEDIA 1]. 1842 *Proc. Philol. Soc.* I. 7 When the final letter of the verb was one of the tenues.. *t* was substituted. 1887 MAX MÜLLER in *Fortn. Rev.* May 705 The tenuis becomes aspirate in Low-German.

**Tenuity** (těniū·iti). [ad. L. *tenuitās* thinness, f. *tenuis* thin: see -ITY. So F. *ténuité* (15th c.).]

**1.** Thinness of form or size; slenderness.

1578 BANISTER *Hist. Man* IV. 47 The other [muscle].. sustayneth his sinewie tenuitie to the hard tunicle of the eye. *a* 1677 HALE *Prim. Orig. Man.* 8 If we consider..the many parts thereof, that either in respect of their tenuity or distance escape the reach of our Senses. 1777 JOHNSON 22 Sept. in *Boswell*, He is not well-shaped; for there is not the quick transition from the thickness of the forepart, to the tenuity—the thin part—behind, which a bull-dog ought to have. 1802 PALEY *Nat. Theol.* ix. (ed. 2) 150 The tenuity of these muscles [in the iris of the eye and the drum of the ear] is astonishing. 1860 TYNDALL *Glac.* I. i. 3 Mica..is sufficiently tough to furnish films of extreme tenuity. 1882 *Nature* 12 Oct. 587/1 Platinum has been rolled into sheets which..reach the surprising tenuity of less than one twenty-five-thousandth of an English inch.

**2.** Thinness of consistence; dilute or rarified condition; rarity.

1603 HOLLAND *Plutarch's Mor.* 740 By reason of this tenuitie and continuitie when oile doth froth or fome, it suffereth no winde or spirit to enter in. 1658 R. WHITE tr. *Digby's Powd. Symp.* (1660) 23 It becomes part of the aire, which in regard of its tenuity is invisible unto us. 1759 JOHNSON *Rasselas* vi, Precipices..so high as to produce great tenuity of air. 1802 PLAYFAIR *Illustr. Hutton. Th.* 415 The tenuity and fineness of the mud. 1860 MAURY *Phys. Geog. Sea* (Low) i. § 27 Air may be expanded to an indefinite degree of tenuity.

**b.** Faintness (of light); thinness (of voice).

1794 G. ADAMS *Nat. & Exp. Philos.* IV. xliv. 206 The great distance of the planet Saturn, and the tenuity of its light. 1832 L. HUNT *Sir R. Esher* 123 He ran into high tenuities of voice. 1858 HAWTHORNE *Fr. & It. Note-Bks.* II. 10 A shrill, yet sweet, tenuity of voice.

**3.** *fig.* Meagreness; slightness, slenderness, weakness, poverty.

1535–6 *Act 27 Hen. VIII*, c. 42 § 1 By reason of the tenuytie of lyvyng. 1648 *Eikon Bas.* xvii. 178 The tenuity and contempt of Clergy-men will soon let them see, what a poore carcasse they are, when parted from the influence of that Head, to whose Supremacy they have been sworn. *a* 1734 NORTH *Lives* (1826) I. Pref. 14 My tenuity of style and language. 1867 BURTON *Hist. Scot.* (1873) I. x. 343 The tenuity of the evidence. 1895 *Pop. Sci. Monthly* July 386 Any cause which makes for intellectual tenuity.

¶ **4.** 'Simplicity, or plainness. (*Obs.*)', Webster 1864: hence in later Dicts. App. an error.

**Tenuous** (te·niu,əs), *a.* [A syncopated formation from L. *tenuis* thin + -OUS; the etymologically regular form, preserving the L. stem *tenui-*, being TENUIOUS, now obs. or rare.]

**1.** Thin or slender in form; of small transverse measure or calibre; slim.

1656 [see TENUIOUS 1]. 1664 POWER *Exp. Philos.* II. 134 The uppermost surface of the Quicksilver..is dilated into a tenuous Column, or Funicle. 1666 J. SMITH *Old Age* (1752) 77 A most tenuous vestment for the humours. 1822 *Blackw. Mag.* XII. 411 The spider..touches his tenuous line.

**2.** Thin in physical consistency; sparse; rare, rarified, subtile; unsubstantial.

1597 LOWE *Chirurg.* (1634) 147 When the vaines are repleat with a tenous blood. 1635 J. SWAN *Spec. M.* v. § 2 (1643) 171 Their [wind and air] substances being too tenuous to be perceived. 1794 SULLIVAN *View Nat.* I. xvi. 192 Air..is too subtile, too tenuous a substance. 1864 SIR F. PALGRAVE *Norm. & Eng.* IV. 456 Just as a tenuous film of breath, imperceptible to our senses, prevents the globules of mercury from coalescing. 1892 *Leisure Hour* Aug. 706/1 A very tenuous medium called the ether exists everywhere. 1909 *Eng. Rev.* Apr. 70 Your dress brushed the shrubs: it was grey and tenuous.

**3.** *fig.* Slender, of slight importance or significance; meagre, weak; flimsy, vague, unsubstantial.

*a* 1817 T. DWIGHT *Theol.* (1830) I. xv. 254 A subject perhaps as tenuous, and difficult to be fastened upon. 1858 BUSHNELL *Serm. New Life* 312 The tenuous and fickle impulse. 1881 *Standard* 7 May, A more tenuous or unsatisfactory claim could hardly exist. 1903 *Speaker* 9 May 145/1 The poems of the three somewhat tenuous singers. 1905 *Athenæum* 5 Aug. 166/1 [They] are sure to live as letters apart from..the tenuous story in which they are set.

Hence **Te·nuously** *adv.*, thinly, sparsely; **Te·nuousness**, thinness, tenuity.

1892 ZANGWILL *Bow Mystery* i, When King Fog masses his molecules of carbon in serried squadrons in the City, while he scatters them tenuously in the suburbs. 1901 *Yorksh. Post* 28 Nov. 6/6 The bubble..is better pricked than left to burst of its own tenuousness.

**Tenur**, obs. form of TANDOUR, TENOR, TENURE.

**Tenure** (te·niŭɹ). Forms: α. 5– tenure, (5 tenur, 7 tenuer); β. 6 tener, ten(n)or, 6–7 tenour. [a. AF., OF. *tenure* (13th c. in Godef.):—earlier OF. *teneüre* (11–15th c.), in med.L. *tenitūra*, *tenetūra* (*c* 1200 in Du Cange), f. *tenē-re* to hold: see -URE. Med.L. had also (from OF.) *teneura*, *tenura* (11th c. in Du Cange). OF. had in same sense *tenor*, *-our*, *teneur*, app. by some confusion with TENOR *sb.*, whence the β-forms in ME., etc.

A further result of this use of *tenor* in sense of *tenure* in OF. and ME. was that *tenure* was also used for TENOR: see the latter.]

**1.** The action or fact of holding a tenement (esp. in *Eng. Law*): see TENEMENT 1.

α. [1292 BRITTON I. xix. § 7 En les queus dreitz nul ne se deit eyder par excepcioun de lounge tenure (*tr.* to aid himself by exception of long tenure).] 1442 *Surtees Misc.* (1888) 18 We..serched a tenement,..in þe tenur of John Wetelay. 1546 *Mem. Ripon* (Surtees) III. 16, xv acres of arable lande ..in tholdinge of Richard Carlell xvs. one tenemente in Northstanley in the tenure of John Hyrde vs. 1614 SELDEN *Titles Hon.* 31 Those inferior Kings are like in some proportion to those of Man, who haue had it alwayes by a tenure from their soueraigns, the Kings of England. 1614 RALEIGH *Hist. World* III. (1634) 113 Some land there was in the tenure of the Locrians. 1651 BAXTER *Inf. Bapt.* 100 Is not the Law of the Land..the cause of..every mans right in the Tenure of his Estate? 1874 STUBBS *Const. Hist.* I. ii. 34 We have not the mark system, but we have the principle of common tenure. 1878 SIMPSON *Sch. Shaks.* I. 53 Hooker wrote to Carew .. that the Barony of Odrone was in the tenure of a sect called the Cavanaghs.

β. *c* 1505 *Plumpton Corr.* (Camden) 200 A certayne land in Rybstone, of long tyme in the tennor of one John Ampleforthe. 1589 *Wills & Inv. N. C.* (Surtees) II. 166 My glebe land in Learmouth, now in the tenor of Johne Moore, for xxj yeares. 1612–13 in *N. Riding Rec.* (1884) II. 11 A parcell of meadow called the Wraie in the tenour of Rich. Michell. 1658 *Knaresb. Wills* (Surtees) II. 237 A messuage with land..now in tenor of William Wilkenson.

**b.** *gen.* and *fig.* The action or fact of holding anything material or non-material; hold upon something; maintaining a hold; occupation.

1599 B. JONSON *Cynthia's Rev.* v. iv, Lady, vouchsafe the tenure of this ensigne. 1638 ROUSE *Heav. Univ.* (1702) Pref., A Christians tenure of religion is far more excellent and assured than that of the Pagan. 1738 *Gentl. Mag.* VIII. 411/1 They were more One than either Espousals, or a Joint-Tenure of the Throne, could make them. 1810 WELLINGTON in Gurw. *Desp.* (1838) V. 497 Their existence in safety at Seville depends upon the tenure of the pass of Monasterio. 1844 LD. BROUGHAM *Brit. Const.* App. ii. (1862) 414 Their salary cannot be altered during their tenure of office. 1855 BREWSTER *Newton* II. xxvi. 378 Warned of his slight tenure of life. 1875 JOWETT *Plato* (ed. 2) V. 330 The tenure of the priesthood should always be for a year and no longer.

**2.** The condition of service, etc., under which a tenement is held of the superior; the title by which the property is held; the relations, rights, and duties of the tenant to the landlord. *Tenure at will*: cf. TENANT AT WILL.

1436 *Rolls of Parlt.* IV. 501/2 Yᵉ Five Portes and tenure of Gavelkynde. 1523 FITZHERB. *Surv.* 12 All these tenauntes maye holde their landes by dyuers tenures, customes, and seruyces: as by homage, fealtie, escuage, socage..burgage tenures, and tenure in vyllenage. *Ibid.*, Also it is to be enquered..who holdeth by charter and who nat, and who by the olde tenure. 1554 *Act 1 & 2 Phil. & Mary*, c. 8 § 54 The Donor..maye reserve to him and his heires for ever a Tenure in Franck Almoigne. 1605 CAMDEN *Rem.* (1637) 132 As he that held Land by tenure to say a certaine number of Pater nosters for the soules of the Kings of England. 1607 COWELL s.v., Tenure is the manner, whereby tenements are houlden of their Lords. 1628 COKE *On Litt.* 85 b, Tenure in Socage, is where the Tenant holdeth of his Lord the tenancie by certaine seruice for all manner of seruices, so that the seruice be not Knights seruice. 1641 CAPT. MERVIN in Rushw. *Hist. Coll.* III. (1692) I. 214 The abortive Judgment of the Tenure *in Capite*, where no Tenure was exprest. 1765 BLACKSTONE *Comm.* I. Introd. iii. 73 A very extensive comment upon a little excellent treatise of tenures, compiled by judge Littleton in the reign of Edward the fourth. *Ibid.* xiii. 398 Those, who by their military tenures were bound to perform forty days service in the field. 1774 PENNANT *Tour Scot. in 1772*, 45 The right of voting is vested by burgess tenure, in certain houses. 1818 CRUISE *Digest* (ed. 2) I. 7 The circumstance of annexing a condition of military service to a grant of lands does not imply that they are held by a feudal tenure. *Ibid.* 27 Where lands held by an allodial tenure were voluntarily converted into feuds. *Ibid.* 381 Enfranchisement, by which the tenure is changed from base to free. 1844 H. H. WILSON *Brit. India* II. xii. II. 549 Involving a complicated texture of rights and tenures, which almost defied unravelling. 1875 J. CURTIS *Hist. Eng.* 396 The statute 12 Car. II, c. 24, which abolished the military tenures, converting them into freehold. 1892 *Pall Mall G.* 17 Mar. 7/1 The new and purely tenure-at-will system gradually gaining ground. 1908 *Fenland N. & Q.* Apr. 177 Keyhold Tenure at Crowland...That house was his because he built it, and because he held the key which admitted him to it and enabled him to keep other people out of it.

β. ? 1510 PYNSON (*title*) Leteltun teners newe correcte. 1535 (ed. 1562) *Act 27 Hen. VIII*, c. 26 § 2 After the english tenour without diuision or parcion. 1633 T. STAFFORD *Pac. Hib.* I. ii. (1821) 38, I hold my Lordships and Lands..by very ancient Tenour, which Service and Tenour none may dispence withall. 1649 G. DANIEL *Trinarch.*, *Rich. II*, lxi, And some (who were in law more Conversant), Demand release of Tenors.

**b.** *transf.* Terms of holding; title; authority; hold over a person or thing; control.

1871 FREEMAN *Hist. Ess.* Ser. I. vii. 184 Few Englishmen understand the difference between the English tenure of Bourdeaux and the English tenure of Calais. *a* 1879 in

Drysdale *Philemon* Introd. 21 To understand the tenure of Philemon over Onesimus, we should keep in mind the stringency of Phrygian bondage.

c. *fig.* (Cf. 1 b.)

**1659** HAMMOND *On Ps.* xxxiv. 8 Paraphr. 181 There is no such assured tenure in or title to all the felicity in the world. **1726** SWIFT *Gulliver* III. iii, The office of a favourite hath a very uncertain tenure. **1790** BURKE *Fr. Rev.* 42 Rendering their government feeble in its operations, and precarious in its tenure. **1840** ALISON *Hist. Europe* (1847) XI. xlix. § 7. 54 The mutable tenure of popular applause. **1863** W. PHILLIPS *Sp.* iii. 53 Republics exist only on the tenure of being constantly agitated.

β. **1682** H. MORE *Annot. Glanvill's Lux O.* 117 Whether Regeneration be not a stronger tenour for enduring Happiness.

**3.** *concr.* A holding; = TENEMENT 2. Now *rare.*

**1439** *Rolls of Parlt.* V. 16/2 The saide Tennauntz dare nat abide in thaire Tenures and Places, ne no laboure there do. **1461** *Ibid.* 476/1 All Tenures within the same Lordship been Chartre land, and Free land. **1766** ENTICK *London* IV. 443 Greenwich-park..is still a royal tenure.

**4.** *attrib.* and *Comb.*, as *tenure land*, *roll.*

**1859** EYTON *Antiq. Shropshire* IX. 39 The Tenure-Roll of 1285 brings up another Ralph de Clotley. **1891** *Pall Mall G.* 22 Sept. 7/2 Property, consisting of a mansion and several miles of tenure land (twenty-one villages)..in North Jutland.

Hence † **Te·nurage,** *Obs.*, what belongs to a tenure or tenures; general conditions of tenure; † **Te·nurer,** *Obs.* = TENANT; † **Te·nurist,** *Obs.*, one who deals with or treats of tenures.

**1610** W. FOLKINGHAM *Art of Survey* III. ii. 68 Tenant in the first signification sometimes imports duety of *Tenurage: as Tenant by Knight-seruice, Socage, Tenant in Villenage, Burgage. *Ibid.* IV. Concl. 88 Inroll all the Feudataries & Suiters to the Court with their Fees, Tenurage, Rents, and Seruices. **1660** WATERHOUSE *Arms & Arm.* 106 Nor could they be chargable with what should disable the *Tenurer to do his service. **1588** FRAUNCE *Lawiers Log.* Ded. ¶ ij, It cannot bee, sayde one great *Tenurist, that a good scholler should euer prooue good Lawyer. *a* **1628** DODERIDGE *Eng. Lawyer* (1631) 53 Defiled by the Feudary Tenurist writers of the middle age.

**Tenurial** (teniū°·riăl), *a.* [f. med.L. *tenūra* TENURE + -IAL.] Of, pertaining to, or of the nature of the tenure of land. Hence **Tenu·rially** *adv.*, in respect of tenure.

**1896** F. W. MAITLAND in *Eng. Hist. Rev.* Jan. 18 The borough court is not founded on a tenurial or feudal principle. *Ibid.*, The burgesses were a tenurially heterogeneous group. **1898** — *Township & Borough* 69 The tenurial rent paid by tenant to lord becomes practically indistinguishable from the mere rent charge which implies no tenure. *Ibid.* 72 Because feudally, tenurially, the borough is patchwork. **1908** *Spectator* 20 June 978/1 All land-holding having become tenurial, the lord's consent was necessary to each alienation.

‖ **Tenuto** (tenū·to), *a.* and *adv. Mus.* [It., = held.] Held, sustained: a direction to a performer to sustain a note its full length. Usually abbreviated *ten.*

**Tenys, -yse,** obs. forms of TENNIS.

**Tenzon,** variant of TENSON.

‖ **Teocalli** (tīₒkæ·li). Also 7 **teucalli.** [Mexican *teocalli*, f. *teotl* god + *calli* house.] A structure for purposes of worship among the ancient Mexicans and Central Americans, usually consisting of a four-sided truncated pyramid built terrace-wise, and surmounted by a temple.

**1613** PURCHAS *Pilgrimage* VIII. xii. 670 Gomara saith, that this and other their Temples were called *Teucalli*, which signifieth Gods house. **1843** PRESCOTT *Mexico* II. viii. (1850) I. 304 The floor and walls of the *teocalli* were then cleansed, by command of Cortés, from their foul impurities. **1844** LONGF. *Arsenal at Springfield* v, And Aztec priests upon their teocallis [*rime* palace] Beat the wild war-drums. **1852** TH. ROSS *Humboldt's Trav.* Introd. 17 A description of the *teocalli*, or Mexican pyramids.

**Teology, Teom(e, Teon(e,** obs. ff. THEOLOGY, TEAM, TEEN, TUNE.

‖ **Te·opan.** [Shortened from Mex. *teo-*, *teupantli* temple, f. *teotl* god + *pantli* wall.] A Mexican temple, a teocalli. **1891** in *Cent. Dict.*

‖ **Teosinte** (tīₒsi·nti). [In F. *téosinté* (*Bull. Soc. d'Acclim.* 1871, 38), ad. Mex. *teocintli* 'seu spica Maizii montana' (Hernandez *Op.* 1790, II. 120), app. f. *teotl* god + *cintli*, *centli* dry ear or cob of maize. In Ramirez *Sinon. Plant. Mex.* 67 *teoxintli.*] An annual grass of Central America, *Euchlæna luxurians*, of large size, allied to maize; now widely cultivated as a valuable fodder plant, sometimes also as a cereal.

**1877** *Gardener's Chron.* 55 Teosinta. **1878** *Kew Report* 13 Téosinté. **1880** SCHOMBURGK (S. Australia) in *Kew Bulletin* (1894) 380, I have now cultivated Teosinte for three years, and it is one of the most prolific fodder plants. **1894** *Ibid.* Nov. 375 A very valuable fodder grass belonging to this group is the Teosinte (*Euchlæna luxurians*). *Ibid.* 381 The great value of Teosinte as a food plant has been established in many parts of India. **189.** *Experiment Station Recd.* IX. 346 Analyses were made of samples of corn-stover and teosinte from the inside and outside of the shocks.

**Teothe, Teothinge,** obs. ff. TITHE *v.*, TITHING.

**Tep,** early form of TAP *v.*[2], to strike.

**Tepal** (te·păl, tī·păl). *Bot. rare*⁻⁰. [app. formed by transposition from PETAL: cf. SEPAL.]

**1866** *Treas. Bot.*, *Tepal*, another name for petal. Also the pieces of a perianth, being of an ambiguous nature, between calyx and corolla.

**Tepat(e, tepet,** obs. forms of TIPPET.

**Tepee** (tī·pi, ti·pi). Also **teepee, tepie, teepe.** [Sioux or Dakota Indian *tīpī* tent, house, dwelling, abode (Rigg, *Dakota-Eng. Dict.* 1890).] A tent or wigwam of the American Indians, formed of bark, mats, skins, or canvas stretched over a frame of poles converging to and fastened together at the top. Also *attrib.*

**1872** W. F. BUTLER *Gt. Lone Land* ix. 125 One has to travel far..before the smoke of your wigwam or of your tepie blurs the evening air. **1877** BLACK *Green Past.* xlv, At length we descried..three teepees—tall, narrow, conical tents with the tips of the poles on which the canvas is stretched appearing at the top. **1899** STUTFIELD in *Blackw. Mag.* Mar. 546 That evening we dispensed with the teepee and camped in the open air. *Ibid.* 542 Now and then we saw the teepee poles of old Indian camping-grounds.

**Tepefaction** (tepĭfæ·kʃən). *rare*⁻⁰. [n. of action f. L. *tepefacĕre*: see next and -FACTION.]

**1658** PHILLIPS, *Tepefaction*,..a making lukewarm.

**Tepefy** (te·pĭfəi), *v.* Also **tepify.** [f. L. *tepefacĕre* to make tepid, f. *tepē-re* to be lukewarm: see -FY.] **a.** *trans.* To make tepid or moderately warm; to warm. **b.** *intr.* To become tepid.

**1656** BLOUNT *Glossogr.*, *Tepefie*.., to make warme. **1745** COOPER *Power Harm.* I. 17 The flood of life, Loos'd at its source by tepefying strains. **1774** GOLDSM. *Nat. Hist.* (1862) II. III. ii. 323 Except..the shallows at the edges of the stream become tepified by the..rays of the sun. **1847** WEBSTER, *Tepefy*, v.i. To become moderately warm. **1866** J. B. ROSE *Virg. Ecl. & Georg.* 129 As vital humours tepify.

‖ **Tephillim, -in** (tĭfi·lĭm, -ĭn), *sb. pl.* [Rabb. Heb. תפלים *t'phillīm*, Aramaic תפלין *t'phillīn*, heteroclite pl. of תפלה *t'phillāh* prayer.] A name for Jewish phylacteries, or (quot. 1863) for the texts inscribed on them: see PHYLACTERY I.

**1613** PURCHAS *Pilgrimage* II. xv. 162 This peece of worke they call Tephillim, to put them in mind of often prayer. **1842** BONAR & M'CHEYNE *Miss. to Jews* 1 July (1843) 237 There were about thirty in the synagogue, all wearing the *Tallith* or shawl with fringes, and the *Tephillin* or phylacteries, because this was the hour of morning prayer. **1863** *Smith's Dict. Bible* III. 1167/2 (*Scribes*) Repeating their Tephillim, the texts inscribed on their phylacteries.

**Tephrite** (te·frəit). *Min.* [f. Gr. τεφρός ash-coloured (f. τέφρα ashes) + -ITE[1]. Cf. L. *tephrītis* (Pliny) an ash-coloured precious stone.] Name given to a class of volcanic rocks related to the basalts. Hence **Tephritic** (-i·tik) *a.*, pertaining to or consisting of tephrite; **Te·phritoid,** a variety of tephrite containing no nepheline.

**1879** RUTLEY *Stud. Rocks* xiii. 253 The tephrites, or those rocks which are characterised by the presence of nepheline or leucite in conjunction with plagioclase. **1889** *Amer. Nat.* Apr. 259 According to the predominance of one or other of the constituents they are divided into basaltic, doleritic and tephritic varieties.

**Tephroite** (te·frₒəit). *Min.* [ad. Ger. *tephroit* (Breithaupt, 1823), irreg. f. Gr. τεφρός: see prec. and -ITE[1].] A silicate of manganese, occurring in crystalline masses of an ashy grey or reddish colour.

**1868** DANA *Min.* 259.

**Tephromancy** (te·frəmænsi). Also erron. **tephra-.** [f. Gr. τέφρα ashes + -MANCY.] Divination by means of ashes: see quots.

**1652** GAULE *Magastrom.* xix. 165 *Tephramancy* [*pr.* Tu-], by ashes; *Capnomancy*, by smoak. **1661** BLOUNT *Glossogr.* (ed. 2), *Tephramantie*..divination by ashes, blown or cast up in the air. *a* **1693** *Urquhart's Rabelais* III. xxv, Have you a mind..to have the truth..more fully..disclosed..by tephromancy: thou wilt see the ashes thus aloft dispersed, exhibiting thy wife in a fine posture. **1846** WORCESTER, *Tephramancy*, divination by the ashes of a sacrifice.

**Tepid** (te·pid), *a.* Also 5 **teped,** 6 **tepit.** [ad. L. *tepid-us* lukewarm, f. *tepēre* to be warm. So obs. or dial. F. *tépide* (16th c. in Godef.).] Moderately or slightly warm; lukewarm.

**a.** *lit.* (Usually in reference to liquids.)

*c* **1400** *Lanfranc's Cirurgie* 137 He worchiþ riȝtfulliche þat vsiþ teped oilis. **1626** BACON *Sylva* § 346 For as a great heat keepeth bodies from putrefaction, but a tepid heat inclineth them to putrefaction. **1664** EVELYN *Kal. Hort.* (1729) 201 Let the Water stand in the Sun till it grow tepid. **1744** BERKELEY *Siris* § 78 A blister on the spot, and plenty of tepid tar-water. **1884** F. M. CRAWFORD *Rom. Singer* ii, A cold sirocco, bringing showers of tepid rain from the south.

**b.** *fig.* = LUKEWARM 2.

**1513** DOUGLAS *Æneis* XI. Prol. 60 Gyf Crystis faithfull knychtis lyst ws be,..Than man we..Nowder be abasit, tepit, nor ȝit blunt. **1641** GAUDEN *Love of Truth* 30 A tepid and Laodicean love. **1740** CHEYNE *Regimen* 333 Of the two Evils, Infidelity and Tepidity is..the worst..in regard of the Infidels and Tepid themselves. **1873** H. SPENCER *Stud. Sociol.* viii. (1874) 179 Remind them of certain precepts..in the creed they profess, and the most you get is a tepid assent.

Hence **Te·pidly** *adv.*, in a tepid or lukewarm manner; **Te·pidness** = TEPIDITY. So † **Te·pidous** *a. Obs.*, tepid, lukewarm.

**1696** PHILLIPS (ed. 5), **Tepidly*, lukewarm. **1873** H. SPENCER *Stud. Sociol.* viii. (1874) 179 The precepts tepidly assented to. **1821** BYRON *Diary* Poet. Wks. (1846) 510/2 Some **tepid*-ness on the part of Kean, or warmth on that of the author. **1903** LD. ROSEBERY in *Westm. Gaz.* 13 Oct. 8/2 This may explain a slight tepidness on the part of Australia. **1607** J. CARPENTER *Plaine Mans Plough* 186 Those Angells..which were sometime *tepidous and backeward.

‖ **Tepidarium** (tepidē°·riŏm). Pl. **-ia.** Also 6 in anglicized form **tepidarie.** [L., f. *tepidus* TEPID: see -ARIUM.] The warm room in an ancient Roman bath, situated between the *frigidarium* and the *caldarium.*

**1585** T. WASHINGTON tr. *Nicholay's Voy.* II. xxi. 58 b, [Bathers] doe first goe in to the Tepidarie too make themselues sweate. **1818** E. BLAQUIERE tr. *Pananti* 223 He successively passes through the *frigidarium*, and *tepidarium*, until he reaches the *calidarium* of the Romans. **1834** LYTTON *Pompeii* I. vii, The more luxurious departed by another door to the *tepidarium.*

**Tepidity** (tĭpi·dĭti). [ad. late or med.L. *tepiditās* (631 in *Gallia Christiana* II. 186), f. *tepidus* TEPID. So F. *tépidité* (14th c. in Godef. *Compl.*).] The quality or condition of being tepid; moderate or slight warmth; lukewarmness. **a.** *lit.*

**1656** BLOUNT *Glossogr.*, *Tepidity*, lukewarmnesse. **1676** in *Phil. Trans.* XI. 601 Any perceptible degree of tepidity. **1750** JOHNSON *Rambler* No. 80 ¶ 3 The body, chilled with the weather, is gradually recovering its natural tepidity.

**b.** *fig.*

*a* **1631** DONNE *Select.* (1840) 220 This heat may overcome my former frigidity and coldness, and..my succeeding tepidity and lukewarmness. **1740** [see TEPID b]. **1819** *Metropolis* I. 48 The mawkish tepidity of his manner. **1884** *Fortn. Rev.* Jan. 138 Tepidity of political belief.

**Tepit,** obs. form of TAPET *sb.*, TEPID.

† **Tepor.** *Obs.* Also 7 **-our.** [a. L. *tepor*, f. *tepēre* to be lukewarm. So obs. F. *tepeur* (14th c.).] Moderate or slight warmth; tepidity. Also *fig.*

[**1608** BP. ANDREWES *Serm.*, *Mark xvi. 1–7* (1629) 404 An hower of *fervor*, more worth then a month of *tepor.*] **1657** TOMLINSON *Renou's Disp.* 389 They will not grow..unless they find tepour. *a* **1735** ARBUTHNOT (J.), The small pox..grew more favorable by the tepor and moisture in April.

So † **Te·porous** *a.* (*Obs. rare*), tepid.

**1821** SIR J. D. PAUL *Rouge et Noir* 29 The spirit must be tame, indeed, and teporous That's frightened by a scarecrow dress'd in dudds.

**Tepoy,** variant of TEAPOY.

**Ter,** obs. f. TAR, TARE, TEAR; var. TOR *a. Obs.*

**Ter-** (tɜɹ), the L. adv. *ter* 'thrice', in comb.

**1.** Prefixed to *adjs.*, in sense 'thrice, three times', as **ter-tri·nal,** consisting of three sets of three; also expressing a high degree, as **ter-sa·cred** [L. *ter sacer*], thrice sacred.

**1600** W. WATSON *Decacordon* (1602) Pref. A vj b, The tersacred Apostolicall Romane Church. *Ibid.* 7 Directing his hand to that tender tersacred and euer blessed heart. **1876** DOUSE *Grimm's L.* § 25. 53 It is certain that the symmetrical ter-trinal trinity constituted by all these three systems together cannot have existed from all time.

**b.** Prefixed to *adjs.* and *sbs.*: expressing threefold recurrence or continuance; as **ter-diu·rnal** *a.*, occurring or done thrice a day; **ter-mi·llenary** [after *tercentenary*], a three-thousandth anniversary.

**1892** LD. KELVIN *Presid. Addr. R. Soc.* 30 Nov., The largeness of the solar semi-diurnal, ter-diurnal, and quarter-diurnal constituents found by the harmonic analysis. **1864** *Realm* 15 June 6 The festivities held there by so many millions of our dusky fellow-subjects in honour of the ter-millenary of that sweet swan of Nerbudda.

**c.** See also TERCENTENARY, TERGEMINATE, etc.

**2.** *Chem.* With the names of classes of compounds, as *acetate*, *bromide*, *chloride*, *chromate*, *fluoride*, *iodate*, *nitrate*, *oxide*, *sulphate*, *tannate*, etc., expressing the presence of three atoms, molecules, or combining equivalents of the element or radical indicated by the rest of the word, as *nitrogen terchloride*, $NCl_3$, *potassium terchromate*, $K_2O \cdot 3CrO_3$, or $K_2Cr_3O_{10}$, *ternitrate of bismuth*, $Bi(NO_3)_3$, etc. Now mostly superseded by TRI-.

**1836** BRANDE *Chem.* (ed. 4) 773 Terchloride of Chromium. (Chr + O3C.) **1838** T. THOMSON *Chem. Org. Bodies* 258 It is ..a tertannate. **1849** D. CAMPBELL *Inorg. Chem.* 111 Besides this iodate of potash, there are other two, namely, a biniodate and a teriodate. **1853** W. GREGORY *Inorg. Chem.* (ed. 3) 240 Antimony...This valuable metal is chiefly found in the mineral called antimony, which is a tersulphuret, $SbS_3$. **1853** URE *Dict. Arts* I. 1058 The explosive compound, the teriodide of nitrogen. **1856** MILLER *Elem. Chem.* II. 914 Terfluoride of chromium forms deep red fumes of chromic acid. **1869** ROSCOE *Elem. Chem.* 230 A third salt, termed ter-chromate [*ed.* 1882 trichromate], $K_2Cr_3O_{10}$, crystallizes out. **1883** *Hardwich's Photogr. Chem.* (ed. Taylor) 55 There are two Chlorides of Gold—viz., the Protochloride and the Terchloride. The latter is the one used in Photography.

**b.** In other compounds, as † **ter-atomic** *a.*, of three atoms, TRIATOMIC; **ter-equi·valent, -valent** *a.* = TRIVALENT; **te·r-vale·nce** = TRIVALENCE.

**1860** FRANKLAND in *Q. Jrnl. Chem. Soc.* XIII. 192 Organo-metallic compounds are uniatomic, biatomic, teratomic, or quadratomic, according to the number of molecules requisite to complete their saturation. **1866** MACADAM *G. Wilson's Inorg. Chem.* § 1109 The Triatomic, Trihydric, or Terequivalent (Terivalent) elements. **1869** *Eng. Mech.* 12 Nov. 198/3 The elements are classified as..triatomic or tervalent, with three attractions, as nitrogen. **1903** *Athenæum* 3 Jan. 22/2 We wish that the translator had avoided the use of such hybrid words as monovalent, divalent, trivalent, tetravalent, and pentavalent when he had to hand the equally expressive and less mongrel words univalent, bivalent, tervalent, quadrivalent and quinquevalent.

**Terabracioun, Terafyn, Terage,** obs. forms of TEREBRATION, TERAPHIM, TERRAGE.

**Teraglin** (te·răglin). [Aboriginal name.] A fish of New South Wales, *Otolithus atelodus*, sometimes called Silver Jew-fish.

**1880** *Rep. Royal Comm. Fisheries N. S. Wales* 20 One of our species, the Teraglin. **1883** E. P. RAMSAY *Food-Fishes N. S. W.* 17 (Fish. Exhib. Publ.) The Teraglin..is in many respects very like the Jew-fish..but does not grow to such a large size, and the flesh is of a finer grain. **1895** *Chambers' Jrnl.* XII. 645/1 The deep waters..teem with..gurnard, flathead, whiting, trevally, teraglin, and other eatable species.

‖ **Terai** (těrai·, -rəi·). [From *Terai* (Hindī *tarāī* moist (land), f. *tar* moist, damp), name of a belt of unhealthy marshy and jungly land, lying between the lower foothills of the Himalayas and the plains, where this form of hat was first worn by hunters and travellers.] A wide-brimmed felt hat with double crown and special ventilation, worn by travellers, hunters, and white men generally in sub-tropical regions where the heat is not so intense as to necessitate the use of the *sola topee* or pith sun-helmet. More fully *terai hat*.

**1899** F. V. KIRBY *Sport E. C. Africa* xix. 207 Nothing beats a broad-brimmed terai, with double crown, well-ventilated with holes at the sides. **1899** WARNER *Capt. of Locusts* 188 Replacing on his head a 'Terai' hat. **1904** D. SLADEN *Lovers in Japan* xi, Silk puggarees folded to a hair round their broad-brimmed grey *terai* hats.

**Terand, -ane, Terandry**, obs. ff. TYRANT, -RY.

**Terap-**: see THERAP-.

**Teraphim** (te·răfim). Forms: *α. pl.* 4 theraphym, -yn, teraphyn, -fyn, 4–6 theraphim, -in, 6– teraphim (7 -in); also const. as sing., whence 7– *pl.* teraphims. *β.* 9 *sing.* teraph, *pl.* teraphs. [a. eccl. L. *theraphim* (Vulg.), Gr. θεραφίν (LXX), ad. Heb. תרפים *tᵉrāphīm*, or Aram. *-īn*.

A Heb. word of doubtful origin and meaning, plural in form, but often (as a pl. of majesty) sing. in use. Occurs 15 times (on 8 occasions) in O.T., in all of which it is retained in the Revised Version, 1885, but only 6 times (2 occasions) in that of 1611; in other places rendered *images*[5], *image*[2], *idols*[1], *idolatry*[1]. The LXX have θεραφίν[6] (τὸ[2], τά[1]), εἴδωλα[3], κενοτάφια[2], and other renderings; Vulgate *theraphim*[4], *idola*[6], also *statuam*, *simulacrum*, *-acra*, *idolatria*, *figuras idolarum*, once each. In Genesis xxxi. 30, Laban the Aramæan calls them את אלהי *eth ĕlōhāi* 'my gods'.]

A kind of idols or images, or an idol or image; app. *esp.* household gods; an object of reverence and means of divination among the ancient Hebrews and kindred peoples.

**a.** Plural or indefinite.

**1382** WYCLIF *Judg.* xvii. 5 Mychee..made a cocpe [1388 ephod], and theraphyn [1388 theraphym, *v.r.* a theraphym], *gloss* that is, the prestis clooth, and mawmettis [1388 ydols]. **1382** — *Hos.* iii. 4 The sonys of Yrael shuln sitte..with out teraphyn. **1388** *Ibid.*, With out terafyn [*gloss* that is, ymagis]. **1539** BIBLE (Great) *Judg.* xvii. 5 And the man Micah had a temple of goddes, and made an Ephod and Theraphin, (That is to saye, a garment for the prest, and Idolles). [1560 (Geneva) Teraphim.] **1641** MILTON *Prel. Episc.* ad fin., If any shall strive to set up his ephod and teraphim of antiquity against the brightness and perfection of the gospel. **1707** M. HENRY *Serm.* Wks. 1853 II. 596/1 Some think Laban's teraphim were the effigies of his ancestors. **1860** PUSEY *Min. Proph.* 563 The *teraphim* were used as instruments of divination. **1862** STANLEY *Jew. Ch.* (1877) I. iii. 52 Rachel stole the *teraphim*, the household gods of her family.

**b.** as sing. with *a*; pl. *teraphims*.

**1388** [see a]. **1624** T. GODWIN *Moses & Aaron* ix. (1641) 170 Michal tooke an Image, (a Teraphim) and laid it in the bed. *a* **1631** DONNE *Select.* (1840) 198 Without an ephod, and without a teraphim. *a* **1641** BP. MOUNTAGU *Acts & Mon.* vii. (1642) 382 Commonly they had Teraphims, Altars, Groves in high places. **1845** FORD *Handbk. Spain* II. 671/1 The silversmiths..by whom many workmen are employed in making little graven images, teraphims and lares. **1856** STANLEY *Sinai & Pal.* (1875) 396 A teraphim, and a graven image, and a priesthood of irregular creation.

**c.** sing. *teraph*; pl. *teraphs*.

**1801** SOUTHEY *Thalaba* II. ix, Khawla to the Teraph turn'd, 'Tell me where the Prophet's hand Hides our destined enemy?' **1850** KITTO *Bible Illustr.* xxxiii. § 6 (1881) 240 Michal has a teraph. **1886** FARRAR *Hist. Interpr.* vii. 366 Scripture was declared to be a sort of oracular teraph.

**d.** *Comb.*

**1848** KINGSLEY *Saint's Trag.* v. ii, My magic teraph-bust, full packed, and labelled. **1905** J. ORR *Probl. O. Test.* v. 134 Teraphim-worship, human sacrifices and the like were prominent features of the religion.

**Terapin(e**, obs. form of TERRAPIN.

**Teraplene**, obs. form of TERREPLEIN.

**Terassed**, obs. f. *terraced*: see TERRACE *v.*

‖ **Terata** (te·rătă), *sb. pl. Biol.* and *Path.* [mod.L., = Gr. τέρατα, pl. of τέρας a marvel, prodigy, monster.] Monstrous formations or births.

**1902** *Brit. Med. Jrnl.* 5 Apr. 850 The..type of double terata known as pygopagous twins. **1904** *Ibid.* 17 Dec. 1643 In describing the embryonic terata.

**Teratical** (teræ·tikăl), *a. rare.* [f. Gr. τέρας, τερατ- (see TERATA) + -IC + -AL.] Relating to marvels or prodigies. So **Teratism** (te·ratiz'm), (*a*) love of the marvellous or prodigious; (*b*) 'monstrosity' (*Cent. Dict.* Supp.).

**1722** WOLLASTON *Relig. Nat.* iii. § 16 (1738) 56 Herodotus, possibly delighting in teratical stories. **1901** *Folk-Lore* Mar. 20 That attitude of mind for which Mr. Marett has invented the term Teratism.

‖ **Teratogenesis** (te·rătoˌdʒe·nesis). *Biol.* and *Path.* [mod.L., f. Gr. τέρας, τερατ- (see TERATA) + γένεσις GENESIS.] The production of monsters or misshapen organisms. So **Teratogeny** (-ǫ·dʒĕni) in same sense; **Teratogenetic** (-dʒĭne·tik), **Teratogenic** (-dʒe·nik) *adjs.*, pertaining to teratogenesis; producing monsters.

**1857** DUNGLISON *Med. Lex.*, *Teratogeny*, the formation of monsters. **1879** tr. *De Quatrefages' Hum. Spec.* 112 Among microcephali a teratogenic cause..acted on part of the organism. **1901** *Nature* 11 Apr. 579/1 On the comparative value of saline and sugar solutions in experimental teratogenesis. **1902** *Cassell's Encycl. Dict., Supp.*, Teratogenetic. **1904** *Brit. Med. Jrnl.* 17 Dec. 1643 A very able historical account of the theories of teratogenesis.

**Teratoid** (te·rătoid), *a. Biol.* and *Path.* [f. Gr. τέρας, τερατ- (see TERATA) + -OID.] Having the appearance or character of a monster or monstrous formation; *teratoid tumour* = TERATOMA.

**1876** BRISTOWE *The. & Pract. Med.* (1878) 51 Tumours originating in proliferation, which he subdivides into histioid tumours,..organoid, and teratoid, or those comprising a combination of organs. **1890** BILLINGS *Nat. Med. Dict.*, *Teratoid tumour*, congenital tumour due to inclusion in one fœtus of portions of another.

**Teratolite** (te·rătoləit). *Min.* Also erron. terratolite (*Cent. Dict.*). [ad. Ger. *teratolith* (Glocker, 1839), f. Gr. τέρας, τερατ- marvel, prodigy + λίθος stone (see -LITE), in allusion to the earlier names *Saxonische wundererde* and *terra miraculosa Saxoniæ* (C. Richter, 1732), due to its supposed sovereign virtues.] An impure clay-like hydrous silicate of aluminium, allied to pholerite.

**1868** DANA *Min.* 473 A. Knop holds (Jahrb. Min. 1859, 546) that the teratolite is an impure lithomarge-like pholerite.

**Teratological** (te·rătolǫ·dʒikăl), *a.* [f. TERATOLOGY + -IC + -AL.] Of or pertaining to teratology; treating of monstrosities or abnormal formations in animals or plants; involving monstrosity, monstrous. Also **Teratolo·gic** *a.* (*rare*).

**1857** E. C. OTTÉ tr. *De Quatrefages' Rambles Nat.* I. 346 *note*, A normal, and not a teratological or abnormal state. **1878** *N. Amer. Rev.* CXXVII. 507 Teratological researches. **1894** *Naturalist* 56 Singular from the teratologic viewpoint. **1898** *Allbutt's Syst. Med.* V. 708 Works on Teratological Anatomy. **1909** J. W. JENKINSON *Exper. Embryol.* 155 Experiments..of the highest interest from a general teratological point of view.

**Teratologist** (terătǫ·lŏdʒist). [f. next + -IST.] **a.** One who deals in stories of marvels or prodigies. **b.** One versed in teratology (sense 2).

**1882** in OGILVIE; hence in later Dicts.

**Teratology** (terătǫ·lŏdʒi). [f. Gr. τέρας, τερατ- a marvel, prodigy, monster + -LOGY. So F. *tératologie* (Littré).]

**1.** A discourse or narrative concerning prodigies; a marvellous tale, or collection of such tales.

**1678** PHILLIPS (ed. 4), *Teratology*, a discourse of prodigies and wonders. **1727** BAILEY Vol. II, *Teratology*, is when bold Writers, fond of the sublime, intermix something great and prodigious in every Thing they write, whether there be Foundation for it in Reason or not, and this is what is call'd Bombast. [Hence **1755** JOHNSON, *Teratology*, bombast, affectation of false sublimity.] **1856** C. J. ELLICOTT in *Cambr. Ess.* 158 The aimless fables and teratologies of Thomas the Israelite or the Gospels of the Infancy. **1884** BLACKMORE *Tommy Upm.* II. 104 Big enough to exhaust even his teratology.

**2.** *Biol.* The study of monstrosities or abnormal formations in animals or plants.

**1842** in BRANDE *Dict. Sc.*, etc. **1860** MAYNE *Expos. Lex.*, *Teratology*..name given by M. J. Geoffroy de St. Hilaire, to the study or consideration of monsters, or anomalies of organization. **1869** M. T. MASTERS (*title*) Vegetable Teratology. **1904** *Brit. Med. Jrnl.* 17 Dec. 1643 Almost the whole of embryonic pathology is..included within the limits of teratology.

‖ **Teratoma** (terătōu·mă). *Path.* Pl. **teratomata** (-ǫ·mătă). [mod.L., f. Gr. τέρας, τερατ- (see TERATA), after *sarcoma*, etc.] A teratoid tumour: see quots.

**1890** BILLINGS *Nat. Med. Dict.*, *Teratoma*, a tumor composed of various tissues or systems of tissue, as bone, teeth, etc., which do not normally exist at the place where the tumor grows. **1899** *Allbutt's Syst. Med.* VI. 100 Teratoma or dermoid cyst is another variety of dermoid tumour...It is affirmed that a teratoma never originates in the lung.

Hence **Terato·matous** *a.*, of the nature of a teratoma. **1891** in *Cent. Dict.*

**Teratoscopy** (terătǫ·skŏpi). *rare.* [f. Gr. τέρας, τερατ- marvel, prodigy + -σκοπια observation.] Observation of or augury from prodigies.

**1663** J. SPENCER *Prodigies* (1665) Pref., When the Sunshine of the Gospel hath discovered the transparency of all those thin and curious Arts,..why should their contemporary, Teratoscopy, survive them all? *Ibid.* 298 Teratoscopy ..was anciently only a rational attendance to those..signs with which the Providence of Nature..was noted to preface her works of greater note.

**Terawndry, Terawnte**, obs. ff. TYRANTRY, TYRANT.

**Terbentine, -yne**, early forms of TURPENTINE.

**Terbium** (tɜ·ɹbiŏm). *Chem.* [mod.L., from the last two syllables of the name of *Ytterby* in Sweden: cf. ERBIUM.] One of the rare metallic elements found (together with yttrium and erbium) in gadolinite and other minerals. So **Te·rbia** [after ERBIA], the earth or oxide of terbium.

**1843** MOSANDER in *L., E., & D. Philos. Mag.* XXIII. 251 What chemists have hitherto considered as yttria, does not consist of one oxide only, but is..to be regarded as a mixture of at least three...If the name of yttria be reserved for the strongest of these bases, and the next in order receive the name of oxide of terbium, while the weakest be called oxide of erbium, we find [etc.]. **1907** ROSCOE & SCHORLEMMER *Chemistry* II. 783 Terbium Tb = 158 (H = 1)...The existence of the earth originally called erbia by Mosander was denied by Berlin (1860), and by Bahr and Bunsen (1866), but was confirmed by Delafontaine (1878) and by Marignac. It then received the name of terbia...Pure terbium compounds were first obtained by Urbain [1905, 1906].

**Terce** (tɜ̄ɹs). Also 5 teirs, tairs, 7 tearce. [A variant of TIERCE, now used in a special sense.]

**1.** Obsolete, archaic, or variant form of TIERCE, q. v. in various senses.

**2.** *spec.* in *Sc. Law*, A life-rent competent by law to a widow (unless she has accepted some other special provision) of the third of the heritable subjects in which her husband dies infeft, provided that the marriage has endured for a year and a day, or has produced a living child. Cf. DOWER *sb.*[2] 1.

**1473** in *Laing Charters* (1899) 43 The quhilk our teirs extendis ȝerly till viij markis. *Ibid.*, Tairs. **1476** *Acta Auditorum* 19 July, Hir brefe of terce anent ye land of Lethbert. **1568** *Reg. Privy Council Scot.* I. 619 Thair subwassellis, ladiis of terce, conjunct fearis, and lyverentaris. **1597** SKENE *De Verb. Sign.* s. v. *Breve*, The brieue of Terce. **1665** J. FRASER *Polichronicon* (S.H.S.) 197 Shee, haveing a tearce of the lordship, was well furnished..with all manner of provision. **1681** *Sc. Acts Chas. II* (1820) VIII. 247/2 (*title*) Act concerning wives Terces. **1752** J. LOUTHIAN *Form of Process* (ed. 2) 286 That Services of Relicts to their Terce pay one Half of special Services. **1868** *Act* 31 & 32 *Vict.* c. 101 § 118 All rights of courtesy and terce competent to the husband or wife of any such creditor.

**b.** *attrib.* **Terce land**, the land of which the rent is assigned to a widow's terce (usu. in *pl.*).

**1552** *Reg. Privy Council Scot.* I. 129 Spirituall menis landis, togidder with all waird landis, terce and conjunct fie landis. **1565** in J. Fraser *Polichronicon* (S.H.S.) 152 Item upon her terce lands of Lovat five oxen. **1581** *Reg. Privy Council Scot.* III. 409 Hir haill fermes of hir terce landis of Westraw.

Hence **Te·rcer** († tiercear), a widow who has terce.

*c* **1575** *Balfour's Practicks* (1754) 336 A Lady tiercear, or conjunct-fear, havand ane tierce or conjunct-fie of ward landis, or blanche landis. **1773** ERSKINE *Instit. Laws Scot.* II. ix. § 44 The widow [is hence styled] the tercer. **1808–25** JAMIESON, *Tercer, tiercer*..a term still commonly used in our courts of law.

**Terce**, var. TARSE *Obs.*; obs. f. TERSE.

**Tercel, tiercel** (tɜ̄·ɹs'l, tīə·ɹs'l). Forms: *α.* 5 tercelle, -sell(e, 5–7 -cell, -sel, 6–8 -sal (7 terssell), 4– tercel. *β.* 5–7 tarcel(l, -sell, 6 -sall, 7–8 -sel, 8 -cel. *γ.* 5–7 tassell, 6–9 tassel (7 -il(l, 6 tossell). *δ.* 6 tyercelle, 7 -cell, 7– tiercel. [a. OF. *tercel* (*a* 1200 in Godef.), beside *terçuel* (12–13th c.), also *tresuel*, *tercieul*, = Pr. *tersol*, *tresol*, Sp. *terzuelo*, It. *terz(u)olo*:—pop. L. *tertiolus* (13th c. in Du Cange), dim. from L. *tertius* third: cf. L. *fīlius*, dim. *fīliolus*, It. *figliuolo*, F. *filleul*. With the *tar-* forms, cf. *bark*, *barn*, *clerk*, etc.; the *γ*-forms confuse *tarsel* and *tassel*; the *δ*-forms are influenced by mod.F.]

The male of any kind of hawk; in Falconry esp. of the peregrine falcon (TERCEL-GENTLE) and the goshawk. *Tercel jerkin* [JERKIN[2]]: see quot. 1623.

Said by some to have been so called as being one-third smaller than the female bird, by others because a third egg in a nest was believed to be smaller and to produce a male bird: cf. quot. s. v. TERCELLENE.

*α.* *c* **1381** (MSS. 1430–) CHAUCER *Parl. Foules* 405 And therwithal the tersel [*v. rr.* tarsell, tercel, tersell] gan she calle. **14..** *Nom.* in Wr.-Wülcker 701/28 *Hic tercellus*, a tercelle. **1486** *Bk. St. Albans* A iij, If she be a Goshawke or Tercell that shall be reclaymed euer fede hym with washe meete at the drawyng. **1615** BOYLE in *Lismore Papers* (1886) I. 78, I sent a Tercell of a goshawk to my cozen. **1623** COCKERAM III. s. v. *Hawks*, A Gerfalcon, the male is called the Tercell Ierkin thereof. **1834** R. MUDIE *Brit. Birds* (1841) I. 86 The falcon always means the female, and the male is called the tercel. **1842** BROWNING *Count Gismond* xxi, And have you brought my tercel back?

†*β.* **14..** *Voc.* in Wr.-Wülcker 615/24 *Tardarius*, a tarcel. *a* **1500** *Chaucer's Parl. Foules* 415 (MS. R. 3. 19, Trin. C.C.) Thys Royall Tarcell spake and taryed nought. **1500–20** DUNBAR *Poems* xxxiii. 81 The tarsall gaif him tug for tug. *c* **1640** J. SMYTH *Lives Berkeleys* (1883) I. 303 The falcons, tarsells, and other hawkes. *c* **1704** PRIOR *Henry & Emma* 110 When Emma hawks: With her of tarsels and of lures he talks. **1774** GOLDSM. *Nat. Hist.* (1862) II. II. i. 30 The male is called by falconers a *tarcel*; that is, a tierce or third less than the other [the female].

†*γ.* **1495** *Act* 11 *Hen. VII*, c. 17 § 3 Any Hawke of the brede of Englond callid Nyesse, gossehauke, tassell,..or fawcon. **1545** *Rates of Customs* b iv, Goshaukes the pece xiii.*s.* iiii.*d.* The tassell vi.*s.* viii.*d.* **1635** SWAN *Spec. M.* (1670) 355 The Tassel of the Saker is called a Hobbie, or Mongrel Hawk. **1727** *Bradley's Fam. Dict.* s. v. *Hawk*, The Male of an Eyess, is an Eyess-Tassel,..and of a Haggard, the Haggard-Tassel.

*δ.* **1575** TURBERV. *Falconrie* 3 All these kynde of hawkes haue their Tyercelles, whiche are the male byrdes and cockes. **1658** PHILLIPS, *Tiercel*,..the same as *Tassel* [1678 adds] and *Tercel*. **1688** R. HOLME *Armoury* II. 236/1 A Tyerclet, or Tyercell of a Goshawk. **1865** *Cornh. Mag.* May 625 Tiercels are better than falcons for magpie-hawking.

as they are unquestionably quicker amongst hedgerows, and can turn in a smaller compass.

**b** *fig.* Applied to a person.

*a* **1585** MONTGOMERIE *Flyting* 90 Foule..tersell of a taide! **1611** CHAPMAN *May Day* Plays 1873 II. 355 Whose foole are you? are not you the tassell of a Gander? **1856** BOKER *Leonor de Guzman* I. ii, The ragged tercel that takes all our wealth.

**Tercelet, tiercelet** (tɜ̄·ɹslėt, tīə·ɹslėt). Forms: 4–5 **ters-**, **terce-**, **terse-**, **tarse-**, 4–6 **tarce-**, 6 **tierse-**, **-let** (**-lett**); 4– **tercelet**, 6– **tiercelet**. [a. AF. *tercelet*, = F. *tiercelet* (dim. of OF. *tercel*, TERCEL), whence later Eng.] = prec.

[**1363** *Rolls of Parlt.* II. 282/2 Quiconque persone qui troeve Faukoun, Tercelet,..ou autre Faucoun.] *c* **1381** CHAUCER *Parl. Foules* 529 Foulis of lauyne Han chosyn..The terselet of the facoun. **1580** HOLLYBAND *Treas. Fr. Tong, Vn Sacret*, the tiercelet of a Saker. **1616** SURFL. & MARKH. *Country Farme* 711 The Faulcon, as all other birds of prey, hath her Tiercelet, and they are called of the Latines *Pomiliones*. **1720** MRS. MANLEY *Power of Love* (1741) 249 He made bold to present his Lordship with a very excellent Tercelet of a Faulcon. **1813** SCOTT *Rokeby* VI. ii, Perched on his wonted eyrie high, Sleep sealed the tercelet's wearied eye. **1852** R. F. BURTON *Falconry Valley Indus* ii. 13 The tiercelet or male, is, as usual, much smaller than the female.

**Tercel-ge·ntle.** [f. TERCEL (q. v. for Forms), after FALCON-GENTLE.] The male of the falcon.

**1486** *Bk. St. Albans* D iij b, Ther is a Fawken gentill, and a Tercell gentill, and theys be for a prynce. **1546** *Will of Brinckley* (Somerset Ho.), Unto the vicar of Boston my tossell gentle. **1590** SPENSER *F. Q.* III. iv. 49 A Tassell gent, Which after her [a dove] his nimble winges doth straine. **1673** HICKERINGILL *Greg. F. Greyb.* 203 The tassil-gentle, once upon the wing..makes a stoop at a jack-daw. **1839** LONGF. *Hyperion* IV. i, Thou art not less a woman, because thou dost not sit aloft in a tower, with a tassel-gentle on thy wrist.

**b.** in *fig.* and allusive use.

**1592** SHAKS. *Rom. & Jul.* II. ii. 160 Hist Romeo hist, o for a falkners voyce, To lure this Tassel gentle back againe. **1630** J. TAYLOR (Water P.) *Wks.* II. 95/2 So She..by casting out the Lure, makes the Tassell Gentle come to her fist. *a* **1700** B. E. *Dict. Cant. Crew, Tercel-gentle*, a Knight or Gentleman of a good Estate; also any rich Man. **1820** SCOTT *Abbot* iv, Marry, out upon thee, foul kite, that would fain be a tercel gentle!

† **Tercellene.** *Obs. rare*$^{-1}$. [deriv. of TERCEL.] = TERCELET, TERCEL.

*a* **1682** SIR T. BROWNE *Tracts* v. (1683) 119 When they [hawks] lay three Eggs,..the first produceth a Female and large Hawk, the second of a midler sort, and the third a smaller Bird, Tercellene or Tassel of the Male Sex.

**Tercentenary** (tɜ̄ɹse·ntĭnări, -sentī·nări) *a.* and *sb.* [f. TER- + CENTENARY, after L. *ter centēni* three hundred each. For the special use in reference to years cf. CENTENARY.]

**A.** *adj.* Of or belonging to the number of three hundred; usually, of or pertaining to a completed period of 300 years; tercentennial.

**1844** S. R. MAITLAND *Dark Ages* xiii. 221, I mean no offence to the gentleman from whose tercentenary sermon it purports to be an extract. **1882–3** *Schaff's Encycl. Relig. Knowl.* III. 2421/1 Bishop Francis David..died in 1579,—an event which received in 1879 its tercentenary celebration in the land of his martyrdom [Transylvania].

**B.** *sb.* A duration of three hundred years; the three-hundredth anniversary of an event, or a celebration of it.

**1855** W. G. CLARK in *Cambr. Ess.* 283 The grammar-schools, which have for the most part celebrated their tercentenary. **1879** *Sat. Rev.* 4 Oct. 412/1 Duo-centenaries, tercentenaries, and quin-centenaries have all lately taken place. **1884** *Nonconf. & Indep.* 17 July 698/2 The tercentenary of the death of William of Nassau..has been celebrated this week at Delft.

Hence **Tercentena·rian** *a.*, that has lasted three centuries; three hundred years old (cf. *centenarian*); **Tercente·narize** *v. trans. nonce-wd.*, to celebrate the tercentenary of.

**1881** *Sat. Rev.* 23 July 116/2 The wholesale excommunication of a tercentenarian Established Church. **1866** *Pall Mall G.* 14 Nov. 10 How Shakspeare was lately tercentenarized everybody knows.

**Tercentennial** (tɜ̄ɹ,sente·niăl), *a.* and *sb.* [f. TER- + CENTENNIAL.] **a.** *adj.* Of or belonging to a period of three hundred years; of three hundred years' standing; of or relating to the three-hundredth anniversary. **b.** *sb.* The three-hundredth anniversary *of* an event; a tercentenary.

**1882–3** *Schaff's Encycl. Relig. Knowl.* III. 2007 The third tercentennial jubilee of the Reformation (1817) marks a return to the doctrines and principles of the Reformers. **1884** *Lit. World* (U. S.) 23 Feb. 58/2 The forthcoming celebration of the ter-centennial of the University of Edinburgh.

**Terceroon** (tɜ̄ɹsĕrū·n). *rare.* Also 8–9 **terceron**, 9 **tierceroon**. [a. Sp. *tercerон, f. *tercero* a third person, f. *tercio* third: cf. *cuarteron*, *quinteron*.] The offspring of a white person and a mulatto, being third in descent from a negro; = QUADROON 1 a: see note there. (Distinguished from QUADROON 1 b.)

**1760–72** tr. *Juan & Ulloa's Voy.* (ed. 3) I. 29 The Tercerones, produced from a White and a Mulatto, with some approximation to the former, but not so near as to obliterate their origin. **1819** W. LAWRENCE *Lect. Physiol.*, etc. 296 Europeans and Mulattos produce Tercerons (sometimes also called Quarterons, Moriscos, and Mestizos)... Europeans and Tercerons produce Quarterons or Quadroons. **1878** BARTLEY tr. *Topinard's Anthropol.* II. vii. 374 The mixed breeds of negroes and Europeans have various names... The first are called mulatoes, the second, tierceroons.

**Tercet** (tɜ̄·ɹsėt). Forms: 6–7 **terset**, 7 **tercett**, (**terzetta**), 7–9 **terzet**, 8 **-ett**, (9 **terzette**), 7–9 **tiercet**, 9 **tercet**. [ad. It. *terzetto*, dim. f. *terzo* (:–L. *tertius*) third + *-etto*, -ET. Thence also obs. F. *tiercet* (*c* 1500 in Jean Le Maire) and mod.F. *tercet* (17th c. in Boileau), whence the later Eng. forms.]

**1.** *Pros.* A set or group of three lines riming together, or bound by double or triple rime with the adjacent triplet or triplets; *spec.* **a.** each of the triplets of the Italian TERZA RIMA; **b.** each of the two triplets usually forming the last six lines of a sonnet.

**1598** FLORIO, *Terzetto*, a terset of rymes, rymes that ryme three and three. **1656** EARL MONM. tr. *Boccalini's Advts. fr. Parnass.* I. lxxvi. (1674) 93 The..Princes..were proof against every pungent Terzetta. *Ibid.* II. xiv. 154 The pleasant Tersets. **1755** JOHNSON, *Tiercet*..a triplet; three lines. **1838–9** HALLAM *Hist. Lit.* II. II. v. § 44. 208 The first lines or quartets of the sonnet excite a soft expectation, which is harmoniously fulfilled by the tercets or last six lines. **1885** A. J. BUTLER *Dante, Paradise* XIX. 257 *note*, Observe the structure of this and the following tercets.

**2.** *Mus.* **a.** A third. (? An error.) **b.** A triplet (*Cent. Dict.* 1891).

**1706** PHILLIPS (ed. Kersey), *Tercet*, a Third in Musick. [So **1721** BAILEY, **1775** ASH, and many 19th c. Dicts.]

**Tercia**: see TERTIA. **Tercian, -ane**, etc., **Terciar**, obs. ff. TERTIAN, TERTIAR.

**Tercine** (tɜ̄·ɹsin). *Bot.* [= F. *tercine* (Mirbel 1828), f. F. *tiers*, *tierce*, or L. *tertius* third: see -INE[1].] A third integument supposed by some to occur in certain ovules: cf. PRIMINE.

**1832** *Encycl. Brit.* (ed. 7) V. 52 *note*, The extensible side of the secundine, and even of the tercine or nucleus, soon ceases to increase. **1861** BENTLEY *Man. Bot.* (1870) 322 The embryo-sac is surrounded by a thin layer of cells, which has received the name of tercine.

**Tercio, tertio** (tɜ̄·ɹsio, tɜ̄·ɹʃio). Now only *Hist.* See also TERTIA. [a. Sp. *tercio* (Minsheu), obs. It. *tertio* (Florio), mod.It. *terzo*, Pg. *terço* a regiment:–L. *tertium* a third.] *orig.* A regiment of the Spanish infantry of the 16–17th c.; applied also to the Italian forces of that period; hence, A body of foot forming a main division of an army.

**1583** STOCKER *Civ. Warres Lowe C.* II. 65 Hee..sent thether Sardigne his Regiment or Tertio, with the Maister of his Campe, and three Ensignes of the Regiment or Tertio of Lombardes. **1590** SIR J. SMYTH *Disc. Weapons* 10 b, A Tercio is not to bee holden for compleate of anie smaller number than of 3000. soldiers. **1598** BARRET *Theor. Warres* 15 The Campe is deuided into sundry Tertios or Regiments. **1622** F. MARKHAM *Bk. War* V. i. 161 The Colonell of a Foot-Regiment..amongst the old Romans..commanded a Tertio or Regiment. **1904** *Edin. Rev.* July 116 The deep formation in solid squares—that of the renowned tercios—was still dominant.

**Tercyary**, obs. form of TERTIARY.

**Terdle**, obs. f. TREDDLE, dung of sheep, etc.

**Terdye**, obs. form of TARDY.

† **Tere, teir**, *a.* *Sc.* and *north. dial.* *Obs.* [Origin obscure. From the variant readings in *Wars of Alexander* 1404 and elsewhere, it would seem to have been an alteration of *tore*, TOR *a.*, in the same sense, under the influence of *tere* vb. to TIRE; or to have arisen out of *tere* vb. by change of syntax and identification of the resulting adj. with *tore*.] Difficult, tedious, tiresome, toilsome.

*a* **1400–50** *Alexander* 1404 (MS. A.) It ware tere [*MS. D.* It wald tere] any tonge to of his turnes rekyn. *Ibid.* 4918 It ware to tere me to tell þe tirement to-gedire. *a* **1400** *Anturs of Arth.* 121 To telle þe todes þerone my tonge were fulle tere [*v.r.* were to tere]. *a* **1440** *Sir Degrev.* 1409 To tell here metus was tere, That was served at here sopere. *c* **1450** HOLLAND *Howlat* 578 The order of thar armis, it war to tell teir. **1456** SIR G. HAYE *Law Arms* (S.T.S.) 27 Mony otheris that tere is to tell. **1513** DOUGLAS *Æneis* XI. Prol. 197 For sa schort renovne [thay] warryn so bald To sustene weir and panis teir ontald.

So † **Te·refull** (5 **teirfull, tyrefull**) *a.* *Sc.* *Obs.*

*c* **1450** HOLLAND *Howlat* 421 It war tyrefull to tell, dyte or address. *c* **1475** *Golagros & Gaw.* 760 It war teirfull to tell treuly the tend Of thair strife sa strang. *Ibid.* 33, 42.

**Tere**, obs. form of TAR, TEAR, TEER.

**Terebate**: see under TEREBIC.

‖ **Terebella** (terĭbe·lă). Pl. **-æ**. [mod.L., dim. of *terebra* a borer.]

**1.** *Zool.* A genus of worms, typical of the *Terebellidæ*, a family of marine tubicolous polychætous annelids; a member of this genus.

**1826** GOOD *Bk. Nat.* (1834) II. 11 Another genus of molluscous worms is the terebella. **1857** WOOD *Com. Obj. Seashore* viii. 95 Sometimes the terebella becomes ambitious, and ..affixes a stone of some size to his tube. **1874** CARPENTER *Ment. Phys.* I. ii. § 43 (1879) 43 A Terebella (a marine Worm that cases its body in a sandy tube).

† **2.** *Surg.* = TEREBELLUM 1. *Obs.*

**1860** MAYNE *Expos. Lex.*, *Terebella*..*Med.*, *Surg.* Old name of an instrument with which bones were pierced;..it was the trepan or trephine.

**3.** *Entom.* The ovipositor of a saw-fly.

**1826** KIRBY & SP. *Entomol.* III. 391 *Terebellæ*, instruments by which the insect saws or bores a passage for its eggs.

‖ **Terebellum** (terĭbe·lŏm). Pl. **-a**. [mod.L. dim. of *terebrum*, collateral f. *terebra*: see prec.]

† **1.** *Surg.* A trepan or trephine. ? *Obs.*

**1678** PHILLIPS (ed. 4), *Terebellum*, a Chyrurgions instrument. **1688** R. HOLME *Armoury* III. 420/2 The Terebellum..an Instrument to take up broken or bruised Skulls.

**2.** *Zool.* Lamarck's name for the genus Seraphs of bivalve molluscs.

**1851** WOODWARD *Mollusca* 106 The animal of *terebellum* has an operculum like *strombus*.

**Terebene** (te·rĕbīn). *Chem.* [f. TEREB(INTH) + -ENE.]

† **1.** A name given by Soubeiran and Capitaine 1839 (*Comptes Rendus* IX. 654) to a liquid obtained by decomposing artificial camphor, $C_{10}H_{16}HCl$, with lime. *Obs.* **b.** Used by Deville 1840 (*Ann. Chimie* LXXV. 38) for a liquid obtained by the action of sulphuric acid on pinene, now known to be a mixture of terpenes together with cymene: one of the drugs of the British Pharmacopœia; hence *attrib.*, terebene soap, etc.

**1898** *Brit. Pharmac.* 334 Terebenum. Terebene, a mixture of dipentene and other hydrocarbons, obtained by agitating oil of turpentine with successive quantities of sulphuric acid [etc.]. **1898** *Allbutt's Syst. Med.* V. 37 The inhalation of steam medicated with terebene. **1900** *C. S. S. A. Price List, Index*, Terebene hair-wash, lozenges, soap.

† **2.** Sometimes a synonym of TERPENE *Obs.*

**1857** MILLER *Elem. Chem.* III. vii. § 1. 437 These isomeric bodies may be subdivided into two metameric classes; in one of which the molecule is represented by $C_{20}H_{16}$; ..the members of which are termed *terebenes* or *camphogens*. **1871** ROSCOE *Elem. Chem.* 426 Oxidation products of the terebenes.

Hence **Terebe·nic** *a.*, in *terebenic acid*, synonym of TEREBIC *acid*: see quot. 1868 s. v.

**Terebenthene** (terĕbe·nþīn). *Chem.* [a. F. *térébenthène*, f. F. *térébenth-ine*, ad. L. *terebinthina* (*rēsīna*): see TEREBINTHINE, TURPENTINE; with suffix -ENE as in BENZENE.] Name given by Berthelot to the TERPENE which forms the chief constituent of French turpentine-oil, obtained from *Pinus Pinaster* (*P. maritima*).

Terebenthene is the lævorotary form of pinene, and is now usually called *lævopinene*, as distinguished from *dextropinene*, the chief constituent of American turpentine oil (that most used in England), obtained from *Pinus australis*, whence formerly called *Austroterebenthene* and *Australene*.

**1857** MILLER *Elem. Chem.* III. 439 According to Berthelot, if the ordinary Bordeaux turpentine be distilled *in vacuo*, after saturating the acids which it contains, a homogeneous hydrocarbon, *terebenthene*,..is obtained. **1873** ROSCOE *Elem. Chem.* 426 The best known natural varieties are *terebenthene* from *Pinus maritima*..possessing a left-handed rotation of −42° 3′, and *Austroterebenthene* from *Pinus australis*.

**Terebe·ntic**, *a.* *Chem.* [f. L. *ter(e)bent-inus* (see TEREBINTHINE) + -IC.] Of the nature of turpentine; in *terebentic acid*, $C_9H_{14}O_5$, a crystalline substance obtained by digesting oil of turpentine with oxide of lead.

**1894** MORLEY & MUIR *Watts' Dict. Chem.* IV. 657.

**Terebentine, -tyne**, early forms of TURPENTINE. Cf. TEREBINTHINA, TEREBINTHINE B. 2.

**Terebic** (tĕre·bik), *a.* *Chem.* [f. TEREB(INTH) + -IC.] Of, belonging to, or derived from turpentine, as in *terebic acid*, $C_7H_{10}O_4$, a dibasic acid, a product of the action of nitric acid on turpentine-oil also called *turpentinic*, *terebenic*, and *terebilic acid*. So *terebic ether*, an acid ether of terebic acid. Hence **Te·rebate**, a salt of terebic acid.

**1857** MILLER *Elem. Chem.* III. vii. § 1. 502 The compound..deposits when left to itself for some weeks small four-sided prisms with an oblique terminal face. This substance is named *terebic acid*. **1868** WATTS *Dict. Chem.* V. 723 *Terebic acid*..discovered by Bromeis.., who called it *turpentinic acid*; further examined by Rabourdin.., who designated it as *terebilic* or *terebenic acid*. *Ibid.* 724 Terebic acid is dibasic...The neutral terebates all contain water of crystallisation.

† **Terebilene** (te·rĕbilīn). *Chem.* *Obs.* [Arbitrary from TEREBENE.] Name given 1839 by Soubeiran and Capitaine (*Comptes Rendus* IX. 654) to a liquid now regarded as a mixture of terpenes.

**1857** MILLER *Elem. Chem.* III. vii. § 1. 440. **1868** WATTS *Dict. Chem.* V. 925 Terebilene is a hydrocarbon obtained by distilling the liquid monohydrochlorate of turpentine-oil with quicklime or with potassium...It smells like terebene, and is optically inactive.

Hence **Terebile·nic** *a.*, in *terebilenic acid*, $C_7H_8O_4$, crystallizing in small prisms or needles, or in trimetric forms. So **Terebi·lic** *a.*, synonym of TEREBIC: see quot. 1868 s. v.

**1894** MORLEY & MUIR *Watts' Dict. Chem.* IV. 657/2 Terebilenic Acid.

**Terebin**, obs. form of TERRAPIN.

**Terebinth** (te·rĕbinþ). Forms: 4 **theribynte**, **terebynt**, 5–6 **therebinthe**, 6 **terebynte**, **-bint**, **-binthe**, **teribinth**, 6– **terebinth**. [= OF. *therebint(e* (13th c. in Hatz.-Darm.), *-binthe*, *-bin*, *terebinte* (Godefroy *Compl.*), = Sp., It. *terebinto*; ad. L. *terebinth-us* (Pliny), a. Gr. τερέβινθος, earlier τέρβινθος and τέρμινθος, prob. a foreign word.]

**1.** A tree of moderate size, *Pistacia Terebinthus*,

N.O. *Anacardiaceæ*, a native of Southern Europe, Northern Africa, and Western Asia, the source of Chian turpentine, and a common object of veneration; also called *turpentine tree*, and *Algerine* or *Barbary mastic-tree*.

**1382** WYCLIF *Gen.* xxxv. 4 [Jacob] indeluede hem vndur an theribynte, that is bihynde the cite of Sichem. **1382** — *Ecclus.* xxiv. 22, I as terebynt streizte out my braunchis. **1535** COVERDALE *Isa.* vi. 13 As the Terebyntes and Oketrees bringe forth their frutes. **1578** BIBLE (Genev.) *Ecclus.* xxiv. 18 *margin*, Terebinth is a hard tree..wherout runneth yᵉ gumme called a pure turpentine. **1579** SPENSER *Sheph. Cal.* July 86 Here growes Melampode..And Teribinth, good for Gotes. **1601** HOLLAND *Pliny* I. 389 In Syria growes the Terebinth or Terpentine tree...This fruit of the Terebinth ripeneth with grapes. **1609** BIBLE (Douay) 1 *Kings* xiii. 14 He..found him sitting under a terebinth. **1860** TRISTRAM *Gt. Sahara* vii. 112 The terebinth is a fine oak-like tree, with a close-grained hard black wood..standing usually in solitary dignity. **1863** W. A. WRIGHT in *Smith's Dict. Bible* I. 858/1 (*Idolatry*) The terebinth at Mamre, beneath which Abraham built an altar. **1885** BIBLE (R. V.) *Isa.* vi. 13 As a terebinth, and as an oak.

**b.** Also *terebinth tree*.

**1572** BOSSEWELL *Armorie* III. 23 b, The fielde is of the Moone, a Therebinthe tree, Saturne, floured and leafed, Veneris. **1861** MISS E. A. BEAUFORT *Egypt. Sepul.*, etc. II. xvi. 36 All about Kedesh there is still a remarkable number of lofty terebinth trees.

†**2.** The resin of this tree; = TURPENTINE. *Obs.*

**1483** CAXTON *Gold. Leg.* 51 b/1 Presente to that man yeftes, a lytyl reysyns and hony..therebinthe and dates. **1585** T. WASHINGTON tr. *Nicholay's Voy.* III. xv. 99 b, To make [their hair] grow..they vse by continuall artifice Terebinthe and vernish. **1672–3** GREW *Anat. Roots* I. iii. § 21 The Root of Common Wormwood bleeds..a true Terebinth, or a Balsame with all the defining properties of a Terebinth.

Hence †**Terebi·nthen** (in 5 **terebynten**) *a.*, of terebinth; †**Terebi·nthial, -ian** *adjs.*, of or belonging to the terebinth, or to turpentine; terebinthine.

*c* **1440** *Pallad. on Husb.* III. 1018 Putte in euery hole a wegge or pyn, A birchen here, a terebynten there. **1747** *Gentl. Mag.* Mar. 146/2 The Irish prelate's Terebinthian draughts Dilute all Antitrinitarian thoughts. **1750** G. HUGHES *Barbadoes* 158 These and every other Part of this Tree have so much of a terebinthial Quality in it, that it will..burn like a candle.

**Terebinthaceous** (terebinþē¹·ʃəs), *a. Bot.* Also **-taceous**. [f. mod.L. *Terebinthāceæ*, f. L. *terebinthus*: see prec. and -ACEOUS.] Belonging to the N.O. *Terebinthaceæ*, in some classifications a synonym of *Anacardiaceæ*, or including both that and *Burseraceæ*.

**1830** LINDLEY *Nat. Syst. Bot.* 126 From Anacardiaceæ and other terebintaceous orders they [*Connaraceæ*] are at once known by the total want of resinous juice. **1852** TH. ROSS *Humboldt's Trav.* I. vi. 213 *note*, Among terebinthaceous plants, the Rhus glabrum.

‖ **Terebi·nthina.** [med.L. *terebinthina* sb., short for *terebinthina rēsina* terebinthine resin: see TEREBINTHINE B. 2.] The pharmacopœial name of turpentine.

**1693** tr. *Blancard's Phys. Dict.* (ed. 2), *Terebinthina*, is twofold, vulgar and Venetian. **1859** GULLICK & TIMBS *Paint.* 209 By Turpentine and Terebinthina is understood the generally light-coloured resinous liquid which flows from many kinds of trees. **1899** *Syd. Soc. Lex* s.v., *Terebinthina* (Ph. U. S.) is the concrete oleo-resin..; also the juice of *Pinus australis* and other species of *Pinus*.

**Terebinthinate** (terebi·nþinēt), *a.* and *sb.* [ad. med.L. *terebinthināt-us*, f. *terebinthina* turpentine: see -ATE [1], [2].]

**A.** *adj.* Impregnated with turpentine; having the nature or quality of turpentine; terebinthine.

**1680** BOYLE *Produc. Chem. Princ.* III. 123 The Terebinthinate Oyle. **1702** H. VAUGHAN in *Phil. Trans.* XXIII. 1244, I ordered him a Terebinthinate Clyster. **1821** W. P. C. BARTON *Flora N. Amer.* I. 103 Emitting a terebinthinate odour. **1874** GARROD & BAXTER *Mat. Med.* (1880) 246 Copaiva acts as a stimulant like other terebinthinate drugs.

**B.** *sb.* A terebinthine product; a medicinal preparation of turpentine.

**17..** FLOYER (J.), Salt serum may be evacuated by urine, by terebinthinates; as tops of pine in all our ale. **1822–34** *Good's Study Med.* (ed. 4) I. 248 The balsam of copaiba.. is..a terebinthinate of another kind. **1844** COPLAND *Dict. Pract. Med.* (1858) II. 130/1 The terebinthinates..are the most efficacious means of arresting the discharge.

So **Terebi·nthinate** *v. trans.*, to impregnate with turpentine; hence **Terebi·nthinated** *ppl. a.*

**1651** FRENCH *Distill.* iv. 91 Take Spirit of Wine terebinthinated ten ounces. **1898** *Allbutt's Syst. Med.* V. 88 The inhalation of an oxygenated and terebinthinated atmosphere.

**Terebinthine** (terebi·nþin), *a.* and *sb.* Also 6 **terebynthine, -bintine, -thin,** 7 **teribinthine.** [ad. L. *terebinthinus*, *ter(e)bentinus*, f. Gr. type *τερεβίνθινος, f. τερέβινθ-ος terebinth: see -INE [1]. Cf. F. *térébenthine* turpentine.]

**A.** *adj.* **1.** Of, pertaining to, of the nature of, or allied to the terebinth.

*c* **1550** LLOYD *Treas. Health* ¶ iij, Make a coife or cappe of waxe terebintine..and put it vpon the head. **1555** W. WATREMAN *Fardle Facions* II. vii. 159 The fruicte of the Terebinthine tree. **1658** PHILLIPS, *Terebinthine*,..belonging to the Terebinth, i. the Turpentine tree. **1838** JACKSON *Krummacher's Elisha* i. 2 Under the shade of the terebinthine groves of Mamre. **1846** KEIGHTLEY *Notes Virg.*, *Flora* 393 It appears that it [a tree] was of the terebinthine, and not of the coniferous family.

**2.** Of, pertaining to, or consisting of turpentine; turpentinic, turpentiny.

**1656** BLOUNT *Glossogr.*, *Terebinthine*, of or belonging to turpentine, or the tree out of which it issues. **1664** EVELYN *Sylva* 55 These knots..are well impregnated with that Terebinthine and Resinous matter, which..preserves them so long from putrifaction. **1710** T. FULLER *Pharm. Extemp.* 291 Copayba..hath a bitter, hot, Terebinthine Taste. **1796** MORSE *Amer. Geog.* I. 191 Its knots and roots being full of the terebenthine oil. **1880** *Scribner's Mag.* Feb. 505 Pine rails..spicing the air with their terebinthine perfume.

**B.** *sb.* (elliptical uses of the adj.)

†**1.** (= *Terebinthine tree*.) The terebinth. *Obs.*

[*c* **1000** *Sax. Leechd.* II. 226 Nim ða wyrt þe hatte on suþerne terebintina, swa micel swa ele berȝe.] **1513** DOUGLAS *Æneis* x. iii. 39 Mair semely..than amyd the blak terebynthine Growis by Orycia, and as the geit dois schyne.

†**2.** (= *Terebinthine resin*: cf. TEREBINTHINA.) Turpentine. *Obs.*

**1578** LYTE *Dodoens* VI. xcii. 776 The Rosen [of the larch] is called..in Douche..Termenthiin, or Terbenthiin, that is to say, Terebinthin, or Turpentyn. **1605** TIMME *Quersit.* I. xiii. 64 Out of teribinthine..a mercuriall spirit..may bee.. extracted. **1725** SLOANE *Jamaica* II. 90 Triangular berries ..smelling like terebinthine.

So **Terebi·nthinous**, †**Terebi·nthious** *adjs.*

**1718** J. CHAMBERLAYNE *Relig. Philos.* (1730) II. xxiii. § 29 The wonderful Particulars of Flowers, such as..their Store-Houses of slimy and terebinthious Matters. **1840** F. D. BENNETT *Whaling Voy.* II. 352 Every part of the tree has ..a terebinthinous odour. **1869** *Eng. Mech.* 24 Dec. 354/2 Produced by a..species of *Aphis* on a terebinthinous plant.

‖ **Terebra** (te·rĭbră). Also 7–8 **terebrum.** [L. *terebra*, *terebrum* a borer.]

†**1.** An instrument for boring; in *Surgery*, a trephine, or the boring part of it; also, a miner's drill. *Obs.*

**1611** COTGR., *Tirefond de Chirurgien*, a Surgeons Terebra, or Piercer; an Instrument which he puts vnto diuers vses. **1704** RAY *Disc.* II. v. (1713) 224 This ends at the Place which the Workmen pierce with their *Terebra*...The *Terebra* sometimes finds great Trees. **1706** PHILLIPS (ed. Kersey), *Terebra*, or *Terebrum*,..also an Instrument to engrave on Stones. **1750** *Mem. Roy. Acad. Surg. Paris* I. 162 Instruments hitherto used to raise the bones of the cranium depressed on the dura mater are..the Terebra. **1787** C. B. TRYE in *Med. Commun.* II. 149, I made several perforations in the cranium with the terebra of the trephine.

**2.** *Ent.* The modified ovipositor of certain female insects, esp. terebrant Hymenoptera, with which they puncture leaves, fruit, etc., in order to insert their eggs.

[**1691** RAY *Creation* II. (1692) 78 The hollow Instrument (*terebra* he [Malpighi] calls it, and we may English it *piercer*) wherewith many Flies are provided.] **1713** DERHAM *Phys.-Theol.* VIII. vi. 429 The..Oak-Ball Ichneumon strikes its Terebra into an Oak-Apple.

**Terebral** (te·rĭbrăl), *a.* [f. prec. + -AL.] Of or pertaining to, or of the nature of a terebra.

**1836–9** *Todd's Cycl. Anat.* II. 868/2 The serrated terebral ovipositor.

**Terebrant** (te·rĭbrănt), *a.* (*sb.*) [ad. L. *terebrānt-em*, pr. pple. of *terebrāre* to bore. So F. *térébrant*.] Boring, or having the function of boring; belonging to the division *Terebrantia* of hymenopterous insects, having a boring ovipositor.

**1826** KIRBY & SP. *Entomol.* IV. xlvii. 373 Tail of the female without a terebrant, or pungent multivalve ovipositor. **1860** in MAYNE *Expos. Lex.*

**B.** *sb.* = BORE *sb.*[2] 3. *humorous nonce-use.*

**1890** O. W. HOLMES *Over the Teacups* iv, Many a terebrant I have known who—'was great nor knew how great he was'.

**Terebrate** (te·rĭbrēt), *a. Ent.* [f. L. *terebra* borer + -ATE [2] 2.] Furnished with, or formed as, a terebra (TEREBRA 2).

**1902** in *Cassell's Encycl. Dict.* Supp.

**Terebrate** (te·rĭbreⁱt), *v.* Now *rare.* [f. ppl. stem of L. *terebrāre* to bore.] *trans.* To bore, pierce, perforate; to penetrate by boring. Also *absol.* In quot. 1774, to form by boring. In quots. 1855, 1869 *humorously* for BORE *v.*[2]

**1623** COCKERAM, *Terebrate*, to pierce with a Wimble. **1646** SIR T. BROWNE *Pseud. Ep.* II. vi. 100 If wee consider the threefold effect of Jupiters Trisulke, to burne, discusse and terebrate. **1683–4** ROBINSON in *Phil. Trans.* XXIX. 475 The Insects suck and terebrate the Tree. **1758** J. CLUBBE *Misc. Tracts* (1770) 100 An incrustated surface..too hard for my finer sort of gimblets to terebrate. **1774** G. WHITE *Selborne* 26 Feb., The bank-martin terebrates a round and regular hole in the sand or earth. **1855** O. W. HOLMES *Poems* 250 O for a world where..blunted dulness terebrates in vain! **1869** *Sat. Rev.* 14 May 582 They [women] succeed by dint of perseverance; their terebrating powers are, in the long run, irresistible.

**Terebration** (terĭbrēⁱ·ʃən). Now *rare* or *Obs.* Also 5 **terabracioun.** [ad. late L. *terebrātiōn-em*, n. of action f. *terebrāre* to bore; cf. F. *térébration* (15th c.).] The action of boring or perforating.

**a.** *Surg.* The operation of trephining.

*c* **1400** *Lanfranc's Cirurg.* 140 In almaner hurtynge of þe heed to vsen terabracioun eiþer remeuynge of þe boon wiþ handliche instrumentis. **1676** WISEMAN *Surg.* v. ix. 389, I..made a circular Incision, and raised up that part of the Hairy scalp in order to Terebration. **1767** GOOCH *Treat. Wounds* I. 261 Making terebrations to the Diploë. **1860** MAYNE *Expos. Lex.*, *Terebratio*,..old term for the operation of applying the trephine: terebration.

**b.** *gen.* The action of boring, as with an auger; perforation (esp. of fruit-trees).

**1623** COCKERAM, *Terebration*, a wimbling. **1626** BACON *Sylva* § 463 It hath been touched before, that Terebration of Trees doth make them prosper better. **1725** *Bradley's Fam. Dict.* s.v. *Juice*, Another Way of getting these Juices is by Terebration, that is by piercing the Body of the Tree with an Augar. **1745** tr. *Columella's Husb.* IV. xxix, In that which is performed by terebration you must first mark out the fruitfullest vine in the neighbourhood.

‖ **Terebratula** (terĭbræ·tiŭlă). *Zool.* and *Palæont.* Pl. **-æ**, also **-as**. Also (after F.) **terebra·tule.** [mod.L. (Lhwyd, 1699), quasi- dim. of L. *terebrātus*, fem. *-a*, pa. pple. of *terebrāre* to bore. So F. *térébratule*.] A genus of brachiopods, mostly extinct: so called from the perforated beak of the ventral valve. Formerly used more widely to include any (esp. fossil) members of the *Terebratulidæ* and related families; the lamp-shells.

**1822** J. FLINT *Lett. Amer.* 102 Limestone..is literally conglomerated with organic remains. Amongst these, the most remarkable is a species of terebratula. **1822** J. PARKINSON *Outl. Oryctol.* 250 Some of the multilocular univalves, and of the terebratulas. **1851** WOODWARD *Mollusca* I. 12 Deepest of all, the *terebratulæ* are found, commonly at fifty.. and sometimes at one hundred fathoms, even in Polar seas. **1853** TH. ROSS *Humboldt's Trav.* III. xxix. 165 Petrifactions of pecten, cardites, terebratules, and madrepores.

Hence **Terebra·tular** *a.*, of or pertaining to a terebratula; **Terebra·tuliform** *a.*, having the form of a terebratula; **Terebra·tuline** *a.*, belonging to or having the character of the *Terebratulidæ*; **Terebra·tulite**, a fossil *Terebratula* or lamp-shell; **Terebra·tuloid**, *a.* resembling or related to the genus *Terebratula*; *sb.* a species or congener of this genus.

**1822** J. PARKINSON *Outl. Oryctol.* 334 In the masses of mountain limestone..are immense accumulations of crinoideal and *terebratular remains. **1864** WEBSTER, **Terebratuliform*, having the general form of terebratula shell. **1891** *Cent. Dict.*, *Terebratuline. **1830** LYELL *Princ. Geol.* I. 127 A great calcareous formation,..in which are included corallines, productæ, *terebratulites, &c. **1853** TH. ROSS *Humboldt's Trav.* III. xxix. 166 *note*, The 'Roche à ravets' of Martinique and Hayti..is..filled with terebratulites, and other vestiges of sea-shells. **1895** F. R. C. REED *Brachiopods* (*Fossil*) in *Camb. Nat. Hist.* III. 512 The *Terebratuloids can be traced back to the primitive type *Renssoellaria*.

**Terebrum**: see TEREBRA.

**Terebynt(e**, obs. form of TEREBINTH.

‖ **Teredo** (tĕrī·do). Pl. **teredines** (tĕrī·dinīz), **teredos** (tĕrī·doz). [L. *terēdo*, ad. Gr. τερηδών a wood-gnawing worm, f. τερ-, root of τείρειν to rub hard, wear away, bore.]

**1.** *Zool.* A genus of lamellibranch boring molluscs; *esp.* the ship-worm, *T. navalis*, well known for its destruction of submerged timbers in ships, piers, sea-dikes, etc. by boring into the wood.

In accordance with the etymology, the name was formerly applied vaguely to any species of worm or larva that wears its way into wood; the ship-worm was at first supposed to be a worm, and was only in 1733 recognized as a mollusc.

**1398** TREVISA *Barth. De P. R.* XVII. xxiii. (Bodl. MS.), Cedre..is neuer destroied wiþ mowȝte noþer wiþ terredo þat is þe tree worme. *Ibid.* XVIII. cvi, Þe worme teredo is a litel worme of a tree,..and freteþ & gnaweþ moche hard treen. **1616** T. ADAMS *Soul's Sickness* Wks. 1861 I. 505 The body's infirmities..are few and scant, if compared to the soul's, which being a better piece of timber, hath the more teredines breeding in it. **1654** TRAPP *Comm. Jonah* iv, There is a worm lies couchant in every gourd to smite it, a teredo to waste it. **1707** MORTIMER *Husb.* (1721) II. 77 The Teredo..and other Worms lying between the Body and the Bark. **1791** E. DARWIN *Bot. Gard.* I. 123 Meets fell Teredo, as he mines the keel With beaked head. **1839** G. ROBERTS *Dict. Geol.* s. v., The shield of the Teredo furnished Mr. Brunel with the idea for the shield used in the Thames Tunnel. **1850** MISS PRATT *Comm. Things Sea-side* iii. 202 The teredo works with astonishing rapidity, and will completely riddle a hard and sound piece of wood, in the space of five or six weeks. **1879** A. R. WALLACE *Australas.* x. 209 The jarrah..., an almost indestructible timber, which is free from the attacks of teredo and termites. **1879** E. P. WRIGHT *Anim. Life* 562 The teredo was first recognised as a bivalve mollusc by Sellius, who wrote an elaborate treatise on the subject in 1733.

*fig.* **1823** SIR D. BREWSTER in *Home Life* (1869) viii, If some teredo of an engineer cut out a tunnel beneath. **1861** W. H. RUSSELL in *Times* 23 Sept., Others of his colleagues ..are the teredos of every plank in the Ship of State.

**2.** *transf.* 'Any disease in plants produced by the boring of insects' (*Treas. Bot.*, 1866).

**Tereen**, obs. form of TUREEN.

‖ **Terek** (te·rėk). [From the name of the river *Terek*.] A species of Sandpiper, *Terekia cinerea*, with a slightly recurved bill, found near the Caspian Sea, esp. about the mouth of the river Terek. Also called *Terek Avocet*, *T. Snipe*, *T. Godwit*.

**1785** LATHAM *Gen. Syn. Birds* V. 155 Terek Sn[ipe]. **1785** PENNANT *Arct. Zool.* II. 502 American and Terek Avoset... Terek. *Scolopax cinerea.* **1824** STEPHENS in Shaw *Gen. Zool.* XII. I. 83 Terek Godwit...This curious species is probably referable to a distinct genus, as its beak materially differs in form from that of the true Godwits.

**Terella**, obs. form of TERRELLA.

**Terene**, obs. form of TERRENE, TUREEN.

**Terenite** (te·rĭnəit). *Min.* [Named by Emmons, 1837, f. Gr. τέρην tender + -ITE [1], from its brittleness.] 'An altered scapolite, of greenish or yellowish color, near algerite' (Chester).

**1846** in WORCESTER. **1868** DANA *Min.* 323.

**Terentian** (tĕre·nʃăn), *a.* [ad. L. *Terentiān-us*, f. *Terenti-us* Terence.] Pertaining to, or in the style of, the ancient Roman dramatic poet Terence.

1599 B. JONSON *Ev. Man out of Hum.* Induct., According to the Terentian manner. 1902 BOND in *Lyly's Wks.* III. 168 A new departure, an essay in Terentian comedy.

**Terephthalic** (terefþæ·lik), *a.* *Chem.* [f. TERE-BIC + PHTHALIC.] Derived from or containing terebic and phthalic acids, as in *terephthalic acid* (also called *insolinic acid*), $C_8H_6O_4 = C_6H_4(CO_2H)_2$, a dibasic acid produced as a white tasteless crystalline powder, nearly insoluble in water, alcohol, and ether.

1857 MILLER *Elem. Chem.* III. vii. § 1. 443 The second is isomeric with phthalic acid, and is hence termed terephthalic acid. 1868 WATTS *Dict. Chem.* V. 725.

Hence **Terephtha·lamide**, an amide of terephthalic acid: see quot. 1868; **Tere·phthalate**, a salt of this acid.

1868 WATTS *Dict. Chem.* V. 726 Terephthalate of Ammonium..crystallises, by slow evaporation, in small crystals having a strong lustre. *Ibid.*, Terephthalic amides. 1. Terephthalamide, $C_8H_8N_2O_2 = N_2H_4 . (C_8H_4O_2)''$, produced by the action of ammonia on terephthalic chloride, is a white amorphous body, not dissolved by any solution.

**Terepoile**: see TERPOILE.

† **Tere·sa.** *Obs.* Also **there·se.** [prob. from the name of the Empress Maria Theresa (1717–1780).] An article of female attire in the 18th c.: see quot. 1846.

1770 FOOTE *Lame Lover* III, Throwing her Teresa aside—upon my soul she is prodigious fine. 1846 FAIRHOLT *Costume in Eng.* (1860) Gloss., *Therese*, a light gauze kerchief worn over the ladies' head-dress about 1786.

**Teresian, Theresian** (tĕrī·siăn), *sb.* and *a.* Also 9 Teresan. [f. the name of St. Teresa (a Spanish Carmelite nun, 1515–1582) + -IAN.] **a.** *sb.* A member of a reformed order of Carmelite nuns and friars founded by St. Teresa in the 16th c. **b.** *adj.* Belonging to this order.

1629 WADSWORTH *Pilgr.* vii. 73 There is..a monastery of the English poore Teresians at Antwerpe. 1767 S. PATERSON *Another Trav.* I. 352 That [sisterhood] of the Theresians is reckoned the poorest and most pitiable. 1882–3 *Schaff's Encycl. Relig. Knowl.* III. 2348 [St. Theresa] founded at Avila a convent for the Barefooted Carmelites, also called the Theresians. 1897 J. P. RUSHE (*title*) Carmel in Ireland: ..the Irish Province of Teresian, or Discalced Carmelites.

**Terester, Terestr-**: see TERR-.

**Terete** (tĕrī·t), *a.* Also 7 **teret** (9 *erron.* terate). [ad. L. *teres*, *teret-em* rounded (off).] Rounded, smooth and round; now almost always in *Nat. Hist.*, having a cylindrical or slightly tapering form, circular in cross-section, and a surface free from furrows or ridges.

*a* 1619 FOTHERBY *Atheom.* II. xi. § 6 (1622) 326 Round and teret, like a globe. [1760 J. LEE *Introd. Bot.* III. v. (1765) 184 Leaves are, *Teretes*, round like a Pillar; when they are for the most Part cylindric.] 1821 W. P. C. BARTON *Flora N. Amer.* I. 18 Stem about two feet high, terete. 1845 LINDLEY *Sch. Bot.* v. (1858) 68/*b*, Fruit terete, obovate, covered with scales or tubercles. 1877 COUES *Fur Anim.* iv. 98 Tail long, terete, uniformly bushy or very slender and close-haired, with a terminal pencil.

**b.** *Comb.*, as *terete-elliptical*, *-linear* adjs.

1847 W. E. STEELE *Field Bot.* 177 Sep[als] and pet[als] ovate-lanceolate, as long as the terate-elliptical, mucronate caps[ule]. *Ibid.* 108 Pods terate-linear.

Hence **Tere·tish** *a.*, somewhat terete. Also † **Tere·tial**, † **Te·retous** *adjs.*, terete (*obs.*).

1658 SIR T. BROWNE *Gard. Cyrus* iv. 176 Why..there are so few [plants] with teretous or long round leaves? 18.. OWEN cited in *Cent. Dict.* for *teretial*. 190. R. TUCKERMAN *N. Amer. Lichens* i. 22 (Cass. Supp.) Either narrowed and somewhat channelled, with teretish tips, or dilated.

**Tereted**: see TERRIT.

**Teretenaunt**, obs. form of TERRE-TENANT.

**Tereti-** (te·rĭti), combining form of L. *teres*, *teret-*, TERETE; used in a few scientific terms. **Te·reticau·date** *a.* [L. *cauda* tail], having a rounded tail, round-tailed (*Cent. Dict.*). **Te·retifo·lious** *a.* [L. *folium* leaf], having terete leaves. **Te·retiprona·tor**, the round pronating muscle of the forearm (*pronator radii teres*). ‖ **Te·retisca·pular** [SCAPULA], the greater round muscle (*teres major*) of the shoulder-blade.

1657 TOMLINSON *Renou's Disp.* 351 This setum..rather..than any other..teretifolious esculent. 1890 BILLINGS *Med. Dict.* cites COUES for *tereti-pronator* and *tereti-scapularis*.

† **Te·retism.** *Obs. rare*⁻¹. [ad. Gr. τερέτισμα twittering.] Twittering; *fig.* unmelodious writing.

1597–8 BP. HALL *Sat.* IV. i. 3 Rough-hewne Teretismes, writ in th' antique vain.

**Te·reto-**, irregular combining form of L. *teres* (see TERETI-). **Te·reto-seta·ceous** *a.* [L. *sēta* bristle], having smooth round bristles. **Te·reto-su·bulate** *a.* [L. *subula* awl], terete and awl-shaped.

1846 DANA *Zooph.* (1848) 593 A stony axis,..tereto-subulate and truncate. *Ibid.* 663 Branches erect, tereto-setaceous.

**Tereu** (tĭrū·). A feigned note of the nightingale. *Tēreu* vocative of Gr.-L. *Tēreus*, name in mythology of the husband of Philomela's sister Progne, and father of Itys; all, according to Ovid *Met.* VI. viii, transformed to birds; the nightingale's note being still a piteous cry to Tereus.

1576 GASCOIGNE *Compl. Philomene* in *Steele Gl.*, etc. (Arb.) 110 And for hir foremost note, Tereu Tereu doth sing. 1598 BARNFIELD *Ode* Poems (Arb.) 120 The Nightingale..(poore Bird)..sung the dolefulst Ditty, That to heare it was great Pitty. Fie, fie, fie, now would she cry Teru Teru, by and by. *a* 1627 MIDDLETON *Father Hubbard's T.* Wks. (Dyce) V. 603 Away she flew, Crying Tereu! 1657 THORNLEY tr. *Longus' Daphnis & Chloe* 124 The Nightingales began to jug and warble their Tereus and Ity's again.

**Terf**, obs. form of TURF.

**Tergal** (tɔ̄·ɹgăl), *a.* *Zool.* [f. L. *terg-um* the back + -AL.] Belonging to the tergum; dorsal.

1860 MAYNE *Expos. Lex.*, *Tergalis*..tergal. 1870 NICHOLSON *Man. Zool.* I. xxxiv. 192 The tergal elements of the thoracic rings. 1870 ROLLESTON *Anim. Life* 91 The eyes and antennae do not really belong to the tergal aspect of the ..segment. 1880 HUXLEY *Crayfish* ii. 71 When the dorsal or tergal wall of the thorax is taken away.

**Tergant** (tɔ̄·ɹgănt), **tergiant** (tɔ̄·ɹdʒiănt), *a.* *Her. rare*⁻⁰. [f. L. *tergum* the back, after *rampant*, *passant*, etc.] Showing the back; having the back turned towards the spectator: said of an animal borne as a charge. (Cf. RECURSANT.)

*c* 1828 BERRY *Encycl. Her.* I. Gloss., *Tergant*, or *Tergiant*, showing the back part..; by some termed *invertant*, or *recursant*.. *Tergiant*, *volant*, flying, showing the back part. *Tergiant*, *displayed*, an eagle, displayed, showing the back. *Tergiant*, *surgant*, or *surgiant*, as an eagle, &c. rising, with the back to sight. 1894 *Parker's Gloss. Her.*, *Tergiant*, of a Tortoise, &c., having the back turned towards the spectator.

**Tergat, Terge**, obs. forms of TARGET, TARGE.

**Tergeminate** (tɔɹ,dʒe·minĕt), *a.* *Bot.* [f. as next + -ATE[2].] (See quots.)

1793 MARTYN *Lang. Bot.*, *Tergeminum folium*, a Tergeminate or thrice-double leaf. 1832 LINDLEY *Introd. Bot.* IV. i. 391 *Tergeminate*.., when each of two secondary petioles bears towards its summit one pair of leaflets, and the common petiole bears a third pair at the origin of the two secondary petioles.

**Terge·minous**, *a.* *rare.* [f. L. *tergemin-us* (poet. for *trigeminus*, f. *tri-* three + *geminus* born together) triple: see -OUS.] (See quot. 1656.)

1656 BLOUNT *Glossogr.*, *Tergeminous*..threefold, triple; one of, or the three borne at, the same time. 1851 *Poems on Hawick Auld Brig* 4 The arch tergeminous which spanned the stream.

**Tergett, Tergiant**, var. TARGET, TERGANT.

**Tergiferous** (tɔɹdʒi·fĕrəs), *a.* *Bot. rare*⁻⁰. [f. L. *terg-um* the back: see -FEROUS.] Bearing the fructification on the back of the frond, as a fern: = DORSIFEROUS 1. Also † **Tergife·tous** *a.* [FŒTUS] in same sense.

1704 J. HARRIS *Lex. Techn.* I, *Tergefætous Plants*, such Herbs..as bear their Seeds on the backsides of their Leaves. 1847 WEBSTER s. v., Tergiferous plants.

† **Te·rgiment.** *Obs. rare*⁻⁰. [ad. med.L. *tergiment-um*, f. *tergere* to wipe, to correct.] (See quot.)

1656 BLOUNT *Glossogr.*, *Tergiment*, that which is put into the scales to make weight.

**Tergite** (tɔ̄·ɹdʒəit). *Zool.* [f. L. *terg-um* back + -ITE[1] 3.] A back-plate, formed by the fusion of a pair of serial plates of one of the somites or segments of an arthropod or other articulated animal.

1885 *Athenæum* 5 Dec. 736/2 On the opposite interior surface of the last tergite are chitinous points. 1899 G. H. CARPENTER *Insects* i. 21 The *pronotum*..is larger than the two succeeding tergites (*mesonotum* and *metanotum*).

Hence **Tergitic** (təɹdʒi·tik) *a.*, of or pertaining to a tergite. 1891 in *Cent. Dict.*

**Tergiversant** (tɔ̄·ɹdʒivɔ̄ːɹsănt), *a.* and *sb.* [ad. L. *tergiversānt-em*, pres. pple. of *tergiversārī*: see next.] **a.** *adj.* Tergiversating, shuffling, evasive, shifty. **b.** *sb.* One who tergiversates; a turncoat, renegade.

1710 *Brit. Apollo* III. No. 17. 2/1 A Future Bride, but yet under her First Courtship, and at first Opposite, Recusant and Tergiversant. 1833 MOZLEY *Let.* 4 July in *Ess.* (1878) I. Introd. 20, I expect the tergiversants will be a considerable party.

**Tergiversate** (tɔ̄·ɹdʒivəɹsēˈt, -vɔ̄ːɹseˈt), *v.* [f. L. *tergiversāt-*, ppl. stem of *tergiversārī* to turn one's back, shuffle, practise evasion, f. *terg-um* the back + *vers-*, ppl. stem of *vertĕre* to turn (cf. *versārī* to move about).]

**1.** *intr.* To practise tergiversation; to desert one's party, turn renegade, apostatize; to shift, shuffle, use subterfuge or evasion; † to refuse to obey, act the recusant. Hence **Te·rgiversated** *ppl. a.*, renegade, apostate; **Te·rgiversating** *vbl. sb.*, tergiversation, evasion; *ppl.a.*, apostatizing, renegade; † recusant; evasive, shifty.

1654 GAYTON *Pleas. Notes* II. vi. 61 That tergiversating and back-sliding Lady. 1678 CUDWORTH *Intell. Syst.* I. iv. § 36. 569 Plotinus..as if he were conscious that this *assumentum* to the Platonick Theology, were not so defensible a thing, doth himself sometime as it were tergiversate and decline it by equivocating in the word *Henades*. 1831 J. WILSON in *Blackw. Mag.* XXIX. 725, 'I am liberal in my politics', says some twenty-times tergiversated turncoat. 1852 MISS YONGE *Cameos* (1877) IV. xviii. 203 Wyatt was examined again and again, and wavered and tergiversated a good deal. 1862 WRAXALL *Hugo's Misérables* v. xvii, Tergiversation is useless, for what side of himself does a man show in tergiversating?

**2.** *lit.* To turn the back (for flight or retreat).

1875 POSTE *Gaius* IV. Comm. (ed. 2) 509 If the defendant on being summoned to appear before the magistrate tergiversates or attempts to flee.

**Tergiversation** (tɔ̄ːɹdʒivəɹsēˈ·ʃən). [ad. L. *tergiversātiōn-em*, n. of action f. *tergiversārī*: see prec. and -ATION.]

**1.** The action of 'turning one's back on', i. e. forsaking, something in which one was previously engaged, interested, or concerned; desertion or abandonment of a cause, party, etc.; apostasy, renegation. Also with *a* and *pl.*, an instance of this; an act of desertion or apostasy.

1583 STUBBES *Anat. Abus.* II. (1882) 96 Their tergiuersation and backsliding from their duties. 1618 MYNSHUL *Ess. Prison* Ep. Ded., I haue now put my name to my Book (without tergiuersation or turne coating the letters). *a* 1631 DONNE *Serm.* (ed. Alford) V. 16 No tergiversation, nor abandoning the noble work he had begun. 1721 AMHERST *Terræ Fil.* Pref. (1754) 16 It will be very unreasonable for them to..charge their own fickleness upon those, who..will not join with them in their new counsels and tergiversations. 1878 STUBBS *Const. Hist.* III. xviii. 187 If betrayal or tergiversation is to be imputed to any.

† **b.** Refusal to obey; recusance. *Obs. rare.*

1676 OWEN *Worship of God* 114 All tergiversation and backwardness in persons duly qualified and called. *a* 1740 WATERLAND *Serm. Matt. xxvi. 41* Wks. 1823 IX. 126 Jonas the Prophet discovered the like tergiversation and backwardness as to the errand he was sent upon to the Ninevites.

**2.** Turning in a dishonourable manner from straightforward action or statement; shifting, shuffling, equivocation, prevarication. Also with *a* and *pl.*, an instance of this; an evasion, a subterfuge.

1570 FOXE *A. & M.* (ed. 2) 1505/1 For all hys crafty cauteles and tergiuersations alledged out of the lawe. 1660 H. MORE *Myst. Godl.* VII. vii. 304 For the preventing of all Cavils and Tergiversations. 1760 JORTIN *Erasmus* II. 265 Here is a little tergiversation, and Erasmus seems to retract what he had advanced in many places. 1821 SCOTT *Kenilw.* xxxv, The duplicity and tergiversation of which he had been guilty. 1871 G. MEREDITH *H. Richmond* xxxviii, Applying to friends to fortify him in his shifts and tergiversations.

**3.** † **a.** The literal turning of the back. *rare.*

1660 F. BROOKE tr. *Le Blanc's Trav.* 200 He holds a stately gravity, allowing audience to none but on the knee, nor tergiversation in retiring.

**b.** The turning of the back for flight; flight, retreat (*lit.* and *fig.*). ? *Obs.*

*a* 1652 J. SMITH *Sel. Disc.* x. iii. (1856) 475 Wicked men.. seek to avoid the dreadful sentence of their own consciences by a tergiversation and flying from themselves. 1654 H. L'ESTRANGE *Chas. I* (1655) 17 The Captain Governour of the Castle viewing the tergiversation and flight of his party. 1660 BURNEY Κέρδ. Δῶρον (1661) 129 The fear of the Lord is to hate evil. Evil has a tergiversation from holy fear.

**Tergiversator** (tɔ̄·ɹdʒivəɹsēˈtəɹ). [agent-n. f. TERGIVERSATE: see -OR; cf. late L. *tergiversātor* boggler, laggard.] One who tergiversates; a renegade; a shuffler.

1716 M. DAVIES *Athen. Brit.* II. 225 The same learned Arian Tergiversator. 1829 SOUTHEY *Lett.* (1856) IV. 129 [To] deliver King and country from a set of tergiversators. 1855 J. STRANG *Glasgow & Clubs* (1856) 485 Nothing better than a political recreant and tergiversator.

So **Tergive·rsatory** *a.*, shuffling, shifty.

1891 *Sat. Rev.* 12 Sept. 295/2 The tergiversatory performances of Mr. —— and Mr. ——.

**Tergiverse** (tɔ̄·ɹdʒivɔ̄ɹs), *a.* *rare.* [f. L. *tergum* back + *versus* turned, pa. pple. of *vertĕre* to turn.] That has turned his back or practised tergiversation; renegade; shifty.

1852 ROEBUCK *Hist. Whig Min. of 1830* I. 290 *note* The tergiverse administration discovered, when too late, that they had broken the staff of their strength.

**Tergiverse** (tɔ̄·ɹdʒivɔ̄ɹs), *v.* *rare.* [ad. L. *tergiversārī* to TERGIVERSATE; so F. *tergiverser*.]

† **1.** *trans.* To turn backwards, to reverse. (In quot. in ppl. adj. **Te·rgiversed.**) *Obs.*

1600 W. WATSON *Decacordon* (1602) 23 A stay made of the planets course and heauens motion, by reason that *primum mobile*, in a tergiuersed violence of opposite race to the rest, runs a course against the haire.

**2.** *intr.* = TERGIVERSATE. Hence **Te·rgiversing** *vbl. sb.*, tergiversation.

1675 (*title*) Quakerism Canvassed: Robin Barclay..found guilty of blasphemy, treason, lying, shifting, quibling, tergiversing, &c. 1688 J. GRUBB *St. George for England* 46 The Briton never tergivers'd, But was for adverse drubbing. 1718 *Entertainer* No. 36. 243 If they don't intirely tergiverse, and become Deserters. 1896 H. REID *Cameronian Apostle* vii. 109 The arbitrary dissolution of one Assembly,..the 'tergiversing' of the Moderator and Clerk.

**Tergo-** (tɔ̄ɹgo), combining form repr. L. *tergum* the back, used instead of the regular *tergi-* in a few rare scientific terms. **Tergola·teral** *a.* *Zool.*, pertaining to the tergum and the lateral plates of the shell in cirripeds. **Tergorha·bdite**, *Entom.*, one of the pieces forming the tergum or upper surface of the abdomen in an insect, *esp.* when modified to form part of the ovi-positor (cf. RHABDITE 2).

1851 DARWIN *Cirripedia* Introd. (Palæont. Soc.) 10 In Pollicipes the margin of the Scutum adjoining the Tergum and Upper Latus, is not divided..into two distinct lines, as in Scalpellum, and is therefore called the tergo-lateral margin.

**Terguette**, obs. form of TARGET.

‖ **Tergum** (tɔ̄·ɹgŏm). Pl. **terga.** The Latin word for 'back' (synon. with DORSUM): in special scientific uses. **a.** The back, or upper surface or portion, of an arthropod or other articulated animal; more usually, the upper plate of each somite or segment of such an animal (= TERGITE): opp. to *sternum*. **b.** Each of the two upper plates of the shell in cirripeds.

**1826** KIRBY & SP. *Entomol.* III. 387 *Tergum*, the upper or supine surface of the abdomen. **1851** DARWIN *Cirripedia* Introd. (Palæont. Soc.) 2 In almost all the Lepadidæ the Terga (*i.e.* the upper or posterior lateral valves) are not characteristic. **1880** HUXLEY *Crayfish* iii. 96 Each ring [of the abdomen] consists of a dorsal, arched portion, called the *tergum* [etc.].

**Teribinth**, etc., obs. form of TEREBINTH, etc.

**Terif**, obs. form of TARIFF.

† **Te·rin.** *Obs.* [ad. OF. *tarin*, *terin* (14th c.), F. *tarin*, of unknown origin.] The siskin.

?*a* **1366** CHAUCER *Rom. Rose* 665 Thrustles, terins, and mavys.

‖ **Terjiman.** *Obs.* [ad. Arab. *tarjamān*: see DRAGOMAN, TRUCHMAN.] Interpreter, dragoman.

**1682** in Magens *Insurances* (1755) II. 691 The English Consul..at Algiers..shall be permitted to chuse his own Terjiman (Interpreter) and Broker.

**Terleis, Terlyst**, obs. Sc. form of TRELLIS, -ED.

† **Terlerie, -lery.** *Obs.* [? Related to OF. *tirelire*, a kind of rhythmical utterance or refrain in singing or dancing.] In the following combinations applied to jinking or whisking about, or performing rapid circumvolutions, with the accompaniment of rhythmical meaningless words. Cf. TIRRA-LIRRA.

[Cf. ?*c* **1500** *Cov. Corpus Christi Plays* 31 They sange terli terlow; So mereli the sheppards ther pipes can blow.] **1599** NASHE *Lenten Stuffe* 25 So many heades so many whirlegigs; and if all these haue terlery-ginckt it so friuolously of theys reckt not what, I may [etc.]. **1611** BEAUM. & FL. *Knt. Burning Pestle* v iii, With hey tricksy terlerie-whiskie, The world it runs on wheels.

† **Terlether**, obs. Sc. form of TARLEATHER [1].

*c* **1500** *Colkelbie Sow* 349 (Bann. MS.) A flekkit sowis skyn faw, With terletheris tyit hy.

**Terli terlow**: see TERLERIE.

† **Terling.** *Obs. rare.* [a. MLG. *terlink* (Schiller & Lubben), name of a pack (app. of cloth) of a definite size or quantity, dim. of *tere*, name of a pack or bale twice the size. Derivation uncertain. It is not clear whether the Du. *teerling* (Kilian *teerlinck*) 'cube, die', is connected. The quots. refer to rates at Antwerp.]

*a* **1500** in *Arnolde's Chron.* (1811) 197 Item for a grete packe, the tolle ij s. g[t]. Item for a myddel packe, the tolle xviii gret. Item for a terlyng, the tolle xij. g[t]. Item for a fardel, the tolle vi g[t]. *Ibid.*, Item for a terling in y[e] krane iiij. g[t].

**Term** (tɜ̄ɹm), *sb.* Forms: 3–7 terme, (4–5 teerme, 5 tierme), 5–7 tearme, 6–7 tearm, 4– term. [a. F. *terme* (in *Roland*, 11th c.) limit (of time or place):—*termne:—L. *terminum* limit, boundary; = Pr. *terme*, It., Sp., Pg. *termino*.]

**I.** A limit in space, duration, etc.

**1.** That which limits the extent of anything; a limit, extremity, boundary, bound (e. g. of a territory, region, or space). Usually in *pl.* Limits, bounds, borders, confines. Now *rare* or *arch.*

**13..** *E. E. Allit. P.* C. 61 Hit bitydde sum-tyme in þe termes of Iude. **1432–50** tr. *Higden* (Rolls) II. 51 That water of Seuerne..was somme tyme a terme of Englonde and of Wales. **1483** CAXTON *Gold. Leg.* 53 b/1 Fro the laste termes of egipte vnto the vtterist endes of the same. **1570** BILLINGSLEY *Euclid* I. def. iii. 2 Pointes..are..only the termes and endes of quantitie. *Ibid.* xiii. 3 A limite or terme, is the ende of euery thing. **1626** BACON *Sylva* § 328 Corruption is a Reciprocall to Generation: and they two, are as Natures two Termes or Boundaries. **1656** STANLEY *Hist. Philos.* VIII. (1701) 326/2 A Superficies is the term of a Body...A Line is the term of a Superficies...A Point is the term of a Line. **1855** BAIN *Senses & Int.* II. ii. § 12 (1864) 202 The power of movement without contact or resistance, except at the extreme terms.

**b.** Utmost or extreme limit, end; *esp.* end of duration or existence, final cessation, close, conclusion, termination. Now *rare* or *arch.*

*a* **1300** *Cursor M.* 11287 (Cott.) At þe terme of fourti dais ..þai bar þe child..vn-to þe temple. **1481** CAXTON *Myrr.* III. xxi. 182 No goodes what someuer they be shal neuer haue terme ne ende [in heaven]. **1579** SPENSER *Sheph. Cal.* Dec. 127 So now my yeare drawes to his latter terme. **1631** MILTON *On University Carrier* II. 14 Too long vacation hastned on his term. **1781** GIBBON *Decl. & F.* xxiv. (1869) I. 695 He had now reached the term of his prosperity. **1881** JOWETT *Thucyd.* I. 123 That the term of their happiness is likewise the term of their life.

**c.** That to which movement or action is directed or tends, as its object, end, or goal; (less commonly) that from which it begins or proceeds, starting-point, origin. Now *rare* or *Obs.*

*c* **1425** *Found. St. Bartholomew's* 39 We become for oure synnys to the butte and terme or marke of vniuersall kynde of man. **1551** BP. GARDINER *Explic. Cath. Faith* 108 b, Wherin eche chaunge hath his special ende and terme, (wherevnto). *a* **1628** PRESTON *New Covt.* (1634) 184 There must be a place, a terme to which you walke, some whither. *a* **1769** R. RICCALTOUN *Notes Galatians* (1772) 33 The term from which they removed, was the Gospel which Paul preached. **1800** *Hist. Ind.* in *Asiat. Ann. Reg.* 2/2 The island of Ceylon..was the usual term of their navigation. **1849** M. ARNOLD *Sonn. to Dk. Wellington* 12 Vehement actions without scope or term.

**2.** *Astrol.* A certain portion of each sign of the zodiac, assigned to a particular planet: see quots.

*c* **1386** CHAUCER *Frankl. T.* 560 He.. knew the arisyng of his moone weel, And in whos face, and terme, and euerydeel. *c* **1450** *Treat. Astrol.* (MS. Ashm. 337) lf. 7 b, Termys of planettes bene certen nombris of greis in euery signe in which degreis a planet makith gret impression. **1652** GAULE *Magastrom.* 263 There was Venus in termes, and in the house of Saturne. **1819** J. WILSON *Compl. Dict. Astrol.* 27 Essential Dignities are only five, viz. House, Exaltation, Triplicity, Term, and Face. *Ibid.* 382 Terms are certain degrees in a sign, supposed to possess the power of altering the nature of a planet to that of the planet in the term of which it is posited.

**II.** A limit in time; a space of time.

**3.** A definite point of time at which something is to be done, or which is the beginning or end of a period; a set or appointed time or date, esp. for payment of money due. *Obs.* or *arch.* exc. in specific uses.

*a* **1225** *Ancr. R.* 208 Etholden oðres hure, ouer his rihte terme, nis hit strong reflac? **1297** R. GLOUC. (Rolls) 5777 Þe welisse king..sende him þes wolues fram ȝere to ȝere, Þre þousend at certein terme. **13..** *Cursor M.* 5939 Sett vs term wen We sal for þe prai. *c* **1450** *Merlin* iii. 41 Vortiger..sowmowned his peple a-geyn the tierme that Merlyn hadde seide. **1479** *Bury Wills* (Camden) 51, x marcs at too termes of the yeer. **1597** HOOKER *Eccl. Pol.* v. lxix. § 1 They all haue..their set..termes, before which they had no being at all. **1662** STILLINGFL. *Orig. Sacr.* I. vi. § 3 There was no certainty in the ancient Græcian history, because they had no certain term..from whence to deduce their accounts. **1793** *Amer. State Papers* (1833) I. 143 State securities.. reimbursable on a given term. **1827** SCOTT *Chron. Canongate* ii, Fortune is apt to circumduce the term upon us.

**b.** *spec.* Each of the days in the year fixed for payment of rent, wages, and other dues, beginning and end of tenancy, etc.; = TERM-DAY, QUARTER-DAY. Chiefly *Sc.* (Cf. F. *terme* in same sense.)

The quarterly terms in Scotland, fixed by Acts of 1690 and 1693, were Candlemas Feb. 2, Whitsunday May 15, Lammas Aug. 1, Martinmas Nov. 11. At the change of style in 1752, Old Style was observed in most parts of Scotland for the terms, making the dates practically in use eleven days later. By an Act of 1886, the 'Removal terms', for change of houses, etc., were fixed as May 28 and Nov. 28, the dates fixed 1690–93 remaining for purposes of rent, interest, etc.

**1426** *Coldstream Chartul.* (1879) 42 Payand till ws ȝerli xl s...at thua vsuel termes of ye ȝher yat is to say Quvitsonday and Martimes. *c* **1450** *Godstow Reg.* 104, xij. d. of rente yerely..to be resceived of Raf Marchaunte and his heires at ij. termes of the yere, that is to sey, vj. d. at the fest of oure lady in Marche and vj. d. at the fest of seynt Michell. **1584** *Exch. Rolls Scot.* XXI. 600 Sa far as thay ar detbound of the said Witsounday terme. **1670** *Moral State Eng.* 30 By the next Term [he] is presented with an Execution, from his Taylor, or Landlord. **1837** LOCKHART *Scott* xxvi, The term of Martinmas, always a critical one in Scotland, had passed before this letter reached Edinburgh. **1843** MRS. MATHESON *Mem. G. Ewing* v. (1847) 219 The usual term in Scotland for entering on possession of a dwelling house.

**4.** *transf.* A portion of time having definite limits; a period, *esp.* a set or appointed period; the space of time through which something lasts or is intended to last; duration, length of time.

*a* **1300** *Floriz & Bl.* 432 Bituene þis and þe þridde day... Þulke terme him þuȝte long. **13..** *Seuyn Sag.* (W.) 64 That dar I vndertak..Within the terme of seuyn yere. **1444** *Rolls of Parlt.* V. 112/1 Departyng of Servauntz..atte ende of theire termes. **1483** CAXTON *Cato* E iv, The prophete demaunded terme and space for to answere..and the kynge gafe hym terme of thre dayes. **1579** FENTON *Guicciard.* (1618) 360 For that the tearme was expired. **1610** R. JONES *Muses Gard. Delights* XIV. ii, Full many louely tearms Did passe in merie glee. **1691** CONSETT *Pract. Eccl. Courts* (1700) 107 A Term-Probatory is said to be that time or delay, which was given to the Plaintiff, wherein he might prove what he Pleads or Sueth for. **1781** *Scot. Paraphr.* xv. i, As long as life its term extends, Hope's blest dominion never ends. **1823** BYRON *Juan* x. lxvi, Seven years (the usual term of transportation). **1868** M. E. G. DUFF *Pol. Surv.* 164 Presidents elected for a term of years.

**b.** *esp.* in phrase *for* († *to*) *term of* (*one's*) *life*: formerly often without *for* or *to*: chiefly in legal use.

**1340–70** *Alisaunder* 16 Amyntas..Maister of Macedoine, þe marches hee aught,..Trie toures, & tounes, terme of his life. *c* **1386** CHAUCER *Knt.'s T.* 171 And ther he lyueth in ioye and in honour Terme of lyue. **1544** tr. *Littleton's Tenures* (1574) 7 The husbande hath Estate in the speciall tayle, and the wife but for terme of lyfe. **1610** HOLLAND *Camden's Brit.* (1637) 725 That Henry the Sixth should enjoy the right of the Kingdome for tearme of life only. **1788** V. KNOX *Winter Even.* I. iii. 34 What men draw from their education generally sticks by them for term of life.

**5.** *spec.* Each of the periods (usually three or four in the year) appointed for the sitting of certain courts of law, or for instruction and study in a university or school. Opposed to *vacation*.

Commonly used without article, as *in term* = during the term. *To keep terms*: see KEEP *v.* 13.

**1454** *Rolls of Parlt.* V. 239/2 An action by Bille in Michell' terme last past. **1600** SHAKS. *A. Y. L.* III. ii. 350 *Orl.* Who staies it [time] stil withal? *Ros.* With Lawiers in the vacation: for they sleepe betweene Terme and Terme. **1610** HOLLAND *Camden's Brit.* (1637) 431 At certaine set times (wee call them Tearmes) yearely causes are heard and tryed. **1678** PHILLIPS (ed. 4) s. v., The first is called Hilary Term...The second is called Easter Term...The third.. Trinity Term...The fourth and last.. Michaelmas Term. **1705** HEARNE *Collect.* 4 Dec. (O.H.S.) I. 114 He might be admitted to the Degree of Master of Arts, without..keeping Terms. **1842** ARNOLD in *Life & Corr.* (1844) II. x. 323, I am obliged to give up..the hope of coming to Oxford this term. **1867** MRS. H. WOOD *Orville College* xiii, The explanation which he had deemed it well to defer until the [school] term should be over. **1883** *Wharton's Law Lex.* (ed. 7), *Terms*, the periods during which the superior courts at Westminster were open. *Ibid.* s. v. *Sittings*, By the Judicature Act, 1873, s. 26, the division of the legal year into terms is abolished, and sittings are substituted for it.

† **b.** *transf.* The session of a law-court during such a period; the court in session. *Obs.*

**1525** LD. BERNERS *Froiss.* II. cciv. 629 Than Mychelmas came, and the generall counsayle began, suche as englysshemen call the terme. *a* **1548** HALL *Chron.*, *Hen. VIII* 64 In the beginnyng of this yere, Trinite terme was begon at Oxenford, where it continued but one day, and was again adjourned to Westminster. **1591** GREENE *Disc. Coosnage* Pref. 2 The poore man, that commeth to the Terme to trie his right. **1648** D. JENKINS *Wks.* 45 At Yorke the Tearmes were kept for seven yeares, in Edward the first's time.

**6.** *Law.* An estate or interest in land, etc. for a certain period; in full, *term of* or *for years*.

*Outstanding term*, *Satisfied term*: An estate for a long term of years was given, usually to the trustees of a strict settlement, to secure to beneficiaries under the settlement the payments due to them periodically from the tenant of the settled land. If these payments were not made, the trustees could take possession of the land for the term, and sell or mortgage it, to raise the money needed to make them. When the purposes for which the estate was created were fulfilled (e. g. by the death of all the beneficiaries) it was called a *satisfied term*; but unless express provision had been made that it should then cease, or unless it was conveyed to the tenant of the freehold so that it was destroyed by merger in the freehold, it continued to exist for the period for which it was created. It was then known as an *outstanding term*, or an *attendant term*, i. e. a term accompanying the inheritance. By Act 8 & 9 Vict. c. 112 provision was made for the cessation of satisfied terms.

**1424** R. FLORE in *E. E. Wills* (1882) 58, I wul þat..my sone haue my termes þat I haf of Westminster in þe personage of Okeham. **1592** WEST *1st Pt. Symbol.* § 41. B iv b, A Particuler estate which is but onely a terme, is an estate determinable by limitation of time. **1766** BLACKSTONE *Comm.* II. ix. 143 Every estate which must expire at a period certain and prefixed,..is an estate for years. And therefore this estate is frequently called a term. **1818** CRUISE *Digest* (ed. 2) I. 502 Where a satisfied term is assigned to a trustee, upon an express trust to attend the inheritance, the owner of such inheritance acquires a right to the term, by the declaration of the parties. **1870** *Woodfall's Law Landl. & Tenant* (ed. 11) 42 A man possessed of a term of years in right of his wife..has power to grant and convey the same.

**7. a.** The completion of the period of pregnancy; the (normal) time of childbirth.

**1844** LOUISA S. COSTELLO *Bearn & Pyrenees* II. 62 The Princess of Navarre, being near her term. **1889** J. M. DUNCAN *Clin. Lect. Dis. Wom.* vi. (ed. 4) 32 The dangers attendant upon delivery of a child at or near term. **1899** *Allbutt's Syst. Med.* VII. 729 Children who..are born at full term.

† **b.** *pl.* The menstrual periods; *transf.* the menstrual discharge, catamenia, menses, courses. *Obs.*

**1545** RAYNOLD *Byrth Mankynde* (1564) 26 Termes be called in Latin *Menstrua*...In Englyshe they be named Termes, because they returne eftsoones at certayne seasons, tymes, and termes. *a* **1648** DIGBY *Chym. Secr.* II. (1682) 259 It provokes the Terms. **1714** JONTEL *Jrnl.*, etc. 143 When the Women have their Terms, they leave the Company of their Husbands.

**III.** Limiting conditions.

**8.** *pl.* Conditions or stipulations limiting what is proposed to be granted or done. Rarely in *sing.*; in quot. 1771, that which is so required or demanded, a condition or prerequisite *of* something.

*c* **1315** SHOREHAM *Poems* v. 165 Þo þat he scholde y-offred by In þe *templo domini*, Ase laȝe ȝef þe termes. *c* **1400** *Laud Troy Bk.* 79 How fele termes and trewes Were [*MS.* Where] take be-twene Troyens and Gruwes. **1599** SHAKS. *Hen. V*, v. ii. 357 Wee haue consented to all tearmes of reason. **1667** MILTON *P. L.* x. 751 Unable to performe Thy terms too hard, by which I was to hold The good I sought not. **1718** HICKES & NELSON *J. Kettlewell* III. lxvi. 353 The Church doth..prescribe her Terms of Communion. **1754** HUME *Hist. Eng.* (1761) I. ix. 200 He was obliged..to offer terms of peace. **1771** WESLEY *Wks.* (1872) V. 61 This faith is the term or condition of justification. **1861** MRS. H. WOOD *East Lynne* I. xiii, They acceded to all his terms.

**b.** Phr. 1) *In terms*: (*a*) (pred.) engaged in making or arranging conditions, in treaty, negotiating; † (*b*) (advb.) = *on terms* (*a*).—— 2) *On* or *upon terms*: (*a*) (advb.) on (such and such) conditions; also (without qualification) on certain conditions, conditionally; (*b*) (pred.) = *in terms* (*a*).—— 3) *To come to terms*: to agree upon conditions; to come to an agreement about something to be done: so *to bring to terms*.——4) *To keep terms*: to keep up negotiations, to have or continue to have dealings *with*; to deal *with* or treat in a particular way; also *fig.* to 'have to do *with*', be connected *with*. ——5) *To make terms*: to agree upon conditions, come to a settlement (= *come to terms*).——6) † *To stand on* or *upon terms*: to insist upon conditions; to stand upon one's rights or dignity.

1) **1619** DRAYTON in *Drumm. of Hawth.'s Fam. Ep.* Wks. (1711) 153, I have done twelve books more,..but it lyeth by me, for the booksellers and I are in terms. **1736** *Gentl. Mag.* VI. 730/2 No Sum of Money..is to be..given..except in the Terms prescribed by this Bill. **1748** SMOLLETT *Rod. Rand.* (1812) I. 451 He was already engaged or at least in terms with Mr. Vaudal.——2) **1611** J. MORE in *Buccleuch MSS.* (Hist. MSS. Comm.) I. 101 He hath not as yet taken a lease himself, but is upon terms to make up his four years to come 31 years. **1629** MASSINGER *Picture* III. vi, I left a letter in my chamber-window Which I would not have seen on any terms. **1647** CLARENDON *Hist. Reb.* I. § 146 A Peace was made with both, upon better terms, and condi-

tions. **1693** Dryden *Persius' Sat.* vi. 124 Well; on my Terms thou wilt not be my Heir? **1708** *Lond. Gaz.* No. 4468/1 The Fortress..had surrender'd upon Terms. **1795** T. Peake *Cases Nisi Prius* 56 *marg.*, If goods are delivered on the terms of sale or return. **1825** Carlyle *Schiller* iii. (1845) 241 The copyright..for which he was on terms with Cotta of Tübingen. **1869** J. Martineau *Ess.* II. 94 It offers initiation..on the easiest terms. **1884** *Manch. Exam.* 11 June 5/1 To..call in the help of the other Powers on their own terms.——3) *a* **1729** Congreve *Impossible Thing* Wks. 1730 III. 263 He to no Terms can bring One Twirl of that reluctant Thing. *a* **1734** North *Lives* (1826) II. 231 The creditors..rather than to contest accounts, came to terms, and agreed to take shares. **1855** Prescott *Philip II*, i. vi. (1857) 103 He had no choice but to come to terms with the enemy at once.——4) *c* **1483** in *Chron. White Rose* (1845) 231 Seeing the evil terms that the King hath kept (with) him, and cast him out of the Realm. **1748** Richardson *Clarissa* (1811) VI. i. 2 What terms wouldst thou have me to keep with such a sweet corruptress? **1806** R. Cumberland *Memoirs* (1807) I. 184 A profusion of finery, that kept no terms with simplicity. **1856** Merivale *Rom. Emp.* (1871) V. xlii. 141 The chief of the state need keep terms no longer with the popular assemblies.——5) **1856** Froude *Hist. Eng.* I. i. 58 Capital supported by force may make its own terms with labour. **1884** *Times* (weekly ed.) 17 Oct. 14/1 The Amarars have made terms with the Hadendowas, giving them a number of cattle.——6) **1586** Day *Eng. Secretary* i. (1625) 88 Before that time, I stood on some tearmes doubting the malicious dealings of the aduerse parties against me. **1611** Cotgr., *Accrester*..to strout it, or stand vpon high tearms. **1716** Atterbury *Serm., Matt. xvi. 20* (1734) I. viii. 224 One of those Great and Philosophical Minds, who stand upon their Terms with God.

**c.** *spec.* Stipulations for payment in return for goods or services; conditions with regard to price or wages; payment offered, or charges made.

**1670** R. Coke *Disc. Trade* 50 The Dutch have Pitch, Tar, Hemp..in greater quantities, and for less terms than the English can, out of Norway. **1751** Johnson *Rambler* No. 132 ⁋ 6 The terms offered were such as I should willingly have accepted. **1844** Ld. Brougham *A. Lunel* II. ii. 23, I was not very nice as to terms and agreed for my board and fifty louis a year. **1856** W. Collins *Rogue's Life* iii, To a member of the family, I suppose your terms will be moderate.

**9.** *pl.* Standing, footing, mutual relation between two persons or parties: in phrases †*in, on, upon terms*: **a.** with various qualifying words, as *on* (†*in, upon*) *equal terms, good terms, speaking terms, visiting terms, terms of intimacy*, etc.

**1543** Seymour *Let.* in Maclean *Life Sir P. Carew* (1857) 142 Fforasmuche as we doo stande in verye doubtefull tearmes with ffraunce, and yet there is no playne warre. **1605** Shaks. *Lear* i. ii. 171 Parted you in good termes? Found you no displeasure in him? **1653** H. Cogan tr. *Pinto's Trav.* xiii. 42 Though we stood in the terms of good friends with them. *a* **1660** *Cont. Hist. Irel.* (Ir. Arch. Soc.) I. 139 When they were in tearmes of greatest defiance.

**1596** Shaks. *1 Hen. IV*, v. i. 10 'Tis not well That you and I should meet vpon such tearmes, As now we meet. **1669** R. Montagu in *Buccleuch MSS.* (Hist. MSS. Comm.) I. 422, I was the willinger to put you upon good terms with her. **1670** Dryden *2nd Pt. Conq. Granada* iii. i, The Brave own Faults when good Success is giv'n; For then they come on equal Terms to Heav'n. **1748** *Anson's Voy.* i. ix. 92 At war, or at least on ill terms with their Spanish neighbours. **1758** L. Temple *Sketches* (ed. 2) 64, I could live upon good Terms even with a Deist; provided he keeps within the Bounds of Decency. **1796** *Hist.* in *Ann. Reg.* 115 Spain was..on friendly terms with France. **1877** Freeman *Norm. Conq.* (ed. 3) II. vii. 97 On the closest terms of friendship. **1881** R. Buchanan *God & Man* I. 211 There never was a time when our folk were on speaking terms with these yeomen. **1885** Sir J. Hannen in *Law Rep.* 10 P. D. 91 They had previously been on the most affectionate terms.

**b.** without qualification: *On terms*, on friendly terms, friendly, sociable; in sporting slang, on terms of equality, on an equal footing (*with*); also in reference to the score at cricket.

**1864** Trollope *Small House at Allington* xvii, The earl and Lord Porlock were not on terms. **1887** Sir R. H. Roberts *In the Shires* ii. 27 So quickly did the hounds get on terms with their fox. **1897** *Daily News* 23 July 4/5 In the end Yorkshire got on terms and ran their total to within four of the southern county.

†**10.** *pl.* Condition, state, situation, position, circumstances; (in Shaks.) vaguely or redundantly: relation, respect (rarely in *sing.*). *Obs.*

**1382** Wyclif *Matt.* vi. 16 Ypocritis..putten her facis out of kyndly termys [Vulg. *exterminant facies suas*], that thei seme fastynge to men. — *Ecclus.* xxi. 21 As an hous set out of termes, so a wisdam to a fool. **1579–80** North *Plutarch* (1676) 5 He found the Common-wealth turmoiled with seditions..and..the house of Ægeus in very ill termes also. **1596** Shaks. *Merch. V.* ii. i. 13 In tearmes of choise I am not solie led By nice direction of a maidens eies. **1602** — *Ham.* iv. vii. 26 A Sister driuen into desperate tearmes. **1604** — *Oth.* i. i. 39 Be iudge..Whether I in any iust terme am Affin'd To loue the Moore? **1642** Rogers *Naaman* Ep. Ded. 2 They liued at poore termes. **1656** Earl Monm. tr. *Boccalini's Advts. fr. Parnass.* ii. xcii. (1674) 245 [He] shewed..him in his naked tearms of devillish hypocrisie.

**IV.** Uses leading up to the sense 'expression'. See *Note* at end of article.

**11.** *Math.* (*a*) Each of the two quantities composing a ratio (antecedent and consequent), or a fraction (numerator and denominator). †Also formerly, each of two quantities multiplied together (*obs.*; now called *factors*). (*b*) Each of the quantities (of any number) forming a series or progression. (*c*) Each of (two or more) quantities connected by the signs of addition (+) or subtraction (−) in an algebraical expression or equation. *Absolute term*, that term in an equation which does not involve the variable or unknown quantity. *Lowest* (†*least*) *terms* (in phrases *to reduce to its lowest terms, in its lowest terms*): *Math.* the form of a fraction when the numerator and denominator are the least possible, i.e. have no common factor; hence *fig.* the simplest condition of anything.

**1542** Recorde *Gr. Artes* (1575) 356 You call the Numeratour and Denominatour, the Termes of the Fraction. **1570** Billingsley *Euclid* v. def. iii. 127 *marg.*, In proportions two quantities required, which are called termes. **1669** Sturmy *Mariner's Mag.* i. ii. 34 As 16 to 7: So is 8 to what? Here ..the second Term is less than the first. **1706** Phillips (ed. Kersey), *Diapente* (in *Musick*), the second of the Concords, whose Terms are as Three to Two. *Ibid.*, *Term of a Progression*,..is every Member of the Progression, whether it be Arithmetical, or Geometrical. **1806** Hutton *Course Math.* I. 13 Both the multiplier and multiplicand, are, in general, named the Terms or Factors. *Ibid.* 191 Divide both the terms of the fraction by the common measure thus found, and it will reduce it to its lowest terms. **1859** Barn. Smith *Arith. & Algebra* (ed. 6) 194 When several quantities are connected together by the signs + and −, or either of them, each of these quantities is called a Term. **1881** Burnside & Panton *The. Equations* Introd. (1886) 2 The term $p_n$, which does not contain $x$, is called the absolute term.

**b.** *In terms of*: (*Math.*) said of a series or expression stated in terms involving some particular quantity; hence *gen.*, by means of or in reference to (some particular set of symbols, ideas, etc.); in the modes of expression or thought belonging to (some particular subject or category): often associated with sense 14, as if = in the phraseology of.

**1743** Emerson *Fluxions* 38 If a Series be required to be express'd in Terms of that Quantity whose 2d, 3d Fluxion, &c. is in the Equation. **1862** H. Spencer *First Princ.* ii. v. § 58 (1875) 188 The continuity of Motion..is really known to us in terms of Force. **1866** Herschel *Fam. Lect. Sc.* 102 The nearest distance of the orbits of Venus and the earth was concluded in terms of the earth's diameter. **1890** W. James *Princ. Psychol.* xviii. II. 63 Most persons, on being asked in what sort of terms they imagine words, will say 'in terms of hearing'.

**c.** *transf.* A member or item of any series; each of the things constituting a series. Also more vaguely, an element of any complex whole.

**1841** Myers *Cath. Th.* iii. iii. 8 The Bible contains a series [of revelations] of which the earliest terms are the least. **1857** Miller *Elem. Chem.* III. i. § 2 (1862) 48 A series in which hydrogen forms the lowest term. **1863** Lyell *Antiq. Man* xxi. 419 Certain genera of plants..consist of a continuous series of varieties, between the terms of which no intermediate forms can be intercalated. **1881** Williamson in *Nature* 1 Sept. 416/1 The lower terms of the series are distinguished from one another by differences of boiling points approximately proportional to the number of atoms of carbon and hydrogen by which they differ from one another; whilst the higher terms..are distinguished..by differences of melting points.

**12.** *Logic*, etc. Each of the two things or notions which are compared, or between which some relation is apprehended or stated, in an act of thought, or (more commonly) each of the words or phrases denoting these in a verbal statement; *spec.* in relation to a proposition, each of the two elements, viz. subject and predicate, which are connected by the copula; in relation to a syllogism, the subject or predicate of any of the propositions composing it, forming one of its three elements (*major term, minor term, middle term*), each of which occurs twice (see Major *a.* 2, Minor *a.* 4, Middle *a.* 6).

**1551** T. Wilson *Logike* (1580) 25 [*Medius terminus*, called the double repeate (whiche is a word rehearsed in bothe Propositions) must not enter into the conclusion, because the other twoo partes called *Termini*, bee proued by this]. *Ibid.* 25 b, There ought not to be mo termes in an argumentation [= syllogism] then three, for otherwise there is no good argument. **1628** T. Spencer *Logick* 258 If the middle terme be both affirmed and denyed of both the extreames: then it is the second figure. **1690** Locke *Hum. Und.* iv. vi. § 16 General Propositions..are then only capable of Certainty, when the Terms used in them stand for such Ideas, whose agreement or disagreement..is capable to be discovered by us. **1725** Watts *Logic* iii. i, The matter of which a syllogism is made up, is three propositions; and these three propositions are made up of three ideas, or terms, variously joined. **1771** *Junius Lett.* liv. (1820) 282 He changes the terms of the proposition. **1827** Whately *Logic* ii. i. § 2 (ed. 2) 57 Each proposition containing two terms; of these terms, that which is spoken of is called the subject; that which is said of it, the predicate; and these two are called the terms (or extremes) because, logically, the Subject is placed first, and the Predicate last: and, in the middle, the Copula, which indicates the act of judgment. **1837–8** Sir W. Hamilton *Logic* xvi. (1866) I. 298 The word term is applied to the ultimate constituents both of propositions and of syllogisms. **1843** Mill *Logic* i. ii. § 5 (1856) I. 31 A non-connotative term is one which signifies a subject only, or an attribute only. A connotative term is one which denotes a subject, and implies an attribute. **1866** Fowler *Deductive Logic* i. i, A Term (so called from *terminus*, a boundary, because the terms are the two extremes or boundaries of the proposition) is a word or combination of words which may stand by itself as the subject or predicate of a Proposition.

**13.** A word or phrase used in a definite or precise sense in some particular subject, as a science or art; a technical expression (more fully *term of art*).

**1377** Langl. *P. Pl.* B. xii. 237 Ac of briddes and of bestes men by olde tyme Ensamples token and termes. *c* **1386** Chaucer *Prol.* 639 Than wolde he speke no word but latyn. A fewe termes hadde he, two or thre, That he had lerned out of som decree. — *Frankl. T.* 538, I ne kan no termes of Astrologye. — *Can. Yeom. Prol. & T.* 199 We semen wonder wyse, Oure termes [of alchemy] been so clergial and so queynte. — *Pard. Prol.* 25 (Harl. MS.) Sayde I wel can I not speke in terme? **1486** *Bk. St. Albans* D ij, Som folke mysuse this terme 'draw', and say that thayr hauke will draw to the Ryuer. **1590** Sir J. Smyth *Disc. Weapons* 2 b, To vse our ancient termes belonging to matters of warre. **1695** W. W. *Colbatch's New Lt. Chir. Put out* p. xi, Why he hath used so few Terms of Art, is, because he designs Plainness. **1703** Moxon *Mech. Exerc.* 109 An Explanation of Terms used among Joiners. **1748** Smollett *Rod. Rand.* (1812) I. 376 The barrister who..had recollected himself and talked in terms. **1862** Grove *Corr. Phys. Forces* (ed. 4) 96 The idea involved in the term latent heat. **1876** Tait *Rec. Adv. Phys. Sc.* i. (ed. 2) 1 Explanation of new scientific terms. **1881** Williamson in *Nature* 1 Sept. 419/1 A chain of evidence involving the use of chemical terms.

**b.** In wider application: Any word or group of words expressing a notion or conception, or denoting an object of thought; an expression (*for* something). Generally with qualifying adj. or phrase (as an abstract term, a term of reproach).

*Contradiction in terms*: see Contradiction 5 b.

*c* **1477** Caxton *Jason* 21 A trew louer vseth neuer suche termes as ye speke of. **1490** — *Eneydos* Prol. 2 Some gentylmen..desired me to vse olde and homely termes in my translacyons. **1530** Palsgr. 518/1, I disconsolate...This terme is nat yet [= no longer] comenly used. **1586** Day *Eng. Secretary* i. (1625) 2 Aptnesse of worde and sentences, consisteth in choice of good tearmes. **1605** *Play of Stucley* in Simpson *Sch. Shaks.* (1878) I. 258 Can there issue from your lips a term So base and beggarly as that of flight? **1653** Holcroft *Procopius* i. 2 The Archers in Homer's time (whose Profession grew to be a tearm of reproach). **1791** D'Israeli *Cur. Lit.* (1858) III. 70 In politics, what evils have resulted from abstract terms to which no ideas are affixed. *a* **1860** Whately *Commpl. Bk.* (1864) 265 A term of reproach is one that denotes something which is denied and thought wrong by the person to whom it is applied. **1883** H. Drummond *Nat. Law in Spir. W.* vii. (1884) 235 The apostles..accepted the term in its simple literal sense.

**14.** Only in *pl.* Words or expressions collectively or generally (usually of a specified kind); manner of expressing oneself, way of speaking, language. (Most commonly preceded by *in*.)

*c* **1386** Chaucer *Reeve's Prol.* 63 Right in his cherles termes wol I speke. *c* **1470** Henry *Wallace* ii. 92 The stwart..thocht Wallace chargyt him in termys rude. **1489** Caxton *Faytes of A.* ii. xx. 133 Thys present werke hathe spoken in general termes. **1590** Shaks. *Mids. N.* iv. i. 63 She in milde termes beg'd my patience. **1600** — *A. Y. L.* ii. vii. 16 Who laid him downe..And rail'd on Lady Fortune in good termes, In good set termes, and yet a motley foole. **1651** Hobbes *Leviath.* iii. xxxiii. 205 Which question is also propounded sometimes in other terms. **1759** Robertson *Hist. Scot.* v. Wks. 1813 I. 374 The accusation..was conceived in the strongest terms. **1849** Macaulay *Hist. Eng.* vii. II. 194 William..replied, in general terms, that he took a great interest in English affairs. **1885** *Athenæum* 23 May 660 Of the dialogue we can speak in terms of the very highest praise.

†**b.** *In terms*: in express words, expressly, plainly, 'in so many words' (also *by terms*). *Obs.*

13.. *E. E. Allit. P.* A. 1052 Alle þe apparaylmente..As Iohan þe apostel in termez tyȝte. *c* **1380** Wyclif *Wks.* (1880) 384 So oure clerkis..whan þai will speke in termis of her religion. *c* **1450** Holland *Howlat* 253 All this trety has he tald be termess in test. **1613** Purchas *Pilgrimage* iv. iv. 305 Deuouring in hope, and threatening in tearmes all those Asian Prouinces. **1667** Pepys *Diary* 29 July, He says in terms that the match..hath undone the nation.

**V. 15.** *Arch.* A statue or bust like those of the god Terminus, representing the upper part of the body, sometimes without the arms, and terminating below in a pillar or pedestal out of which it appears to spring; a terminal figure. Also the pillar or pedestal bearing such a figure. (Cf. Herm.)

**1604** Dekker *King's Entertainm.* Wks. 1873 I. 278 On either side of the Gate, stood a great French *Terme*, of stone. **1630** B. Jonson *Chloridia* Wks. (Rtldg.) 656/2 An arbour..the ornament of which were termes of satyrs. **1688** R. Holme *Armoury* iv. xiii. (Roxb.) 519/1 Their effigies ..raised higher with a Terme or Pedestall or foot..of a pillar. **1712** J. James tr. *Le Blond's Gardening* 76 Busts, Terms, Half-length Figures. **1753** Spence in *Phil. Trans.* XLVIII. 486 Another brass bust, on a term, of a youth. **1891** T. Hardy *Tess* xii, She..lifted her face to his, and remained like a marble term while he imprinted a kiss upon her cheek.

**16.** *Ship-building*. (See quot.)

*c* **1850** *Rudim. Navig.* (Weale) 155 *Terms* or *term-pieces*, pieces of carved-work placed under each end of the taffrail, upon the side stern-timber, and reaching as low down as the foot-rail of the balcony.

**VI. 17.** *attrib.* and *Comb.*, as *term-end, -keeping* (see sense 5 and Keep *v.* 13); **term-catalogue**, a catalogue of the books and other publications during a term or quarter; †**term-driver**, ? = *term-trotter* (*a*); **term-fee** (see quot.); **term-figure** = sense 15; **term-piece** = sense 16; **term-policy**, an insurance policy issued for a definite term or period; †**term-suitor**, a suitor (during term) at the law-courts; †**term-trotter**, (*a*) one who comes up to the law-courts for the term; (*b*) see quot. 1782. See also Term-day, Term-time.

*a* **1704** T. Brown *Dial. Dead, Reas. Oaths* Wks. 1711 IV. 84 One of 'em preaches against Oppression and Covetousness once a Month at least, and perhaps has appear'd in a *Term-Catalogue upon that Subject. **1906** E. Arber (*title*) The Term Catalogues 1668–1709 A.D. A Contemporary Bibliography of English Literature in the reigns of Chas. II, Jas. II, Wm. and Mary, and Anne. **1625** Massinger *New Way* ii. ii, This *term-driver, Marrall, This snip of an attorney. **1828** Webster, *Term-fee, among lawyers, a fee or certain sum charged to a suitor for each term his cause is in court. **1880** WARREN *Book-plates* iii. 23 Male and female *term-figures, busts of fairies. **1887** RUSKIN *Præterita* II. 143 Some formal *term-keeping at Oxford. **1896** *Allbutt's Syst. Med.* I. 476 *Term policies are issued for short or long periods. **1602** CAREW *Cornwall* I. 89 The *Terme-suiters may best speed their businesse. **1607** MIDDLETON *Phœnix* I. iv, I have been a *term-trotter myself any time this five and forty years. **1782** V. KNOX *Ess.* I. 336 The majority are what are called *term-trotters*, that is, persons who only keep the terms for form-sake..to qualify them for degrees.

[*Note* to branch IV. Gr. ὅρος denoted 'boundary mark' and thence 'a boundary', as in Euclid (see 1570 in sense 1). Hence in Arithmetic, applied to each of the terms in a ratio, e. g. 2 : 4; also in a proportion, and in any related series of numbers; in the statement of a mean between two numbers, as 6 : 9 : 12, 6 and 12 were the ἄκροι ὅροι 'extreme terms', and, by extension 9 was called μέσος ὅρος 'the mean term'. In Logic, ὅρος was applied to the terms in an analogy, e. g. 'as A is to B, so is C to D', where A, B, C, and D were ὅροι; also to the terms (subject and predicate) in a proposition; hence to the terms in a syllogism, the major, minor, and middle (the last being analogous to the 'mean term' in Arithmetic). By late Latin philosophical writers, ὅρος in the geometrical, arithmetical, and logical senses was rendered by *terminus* (constantly used by Boethius *a* 524). The application of ὅρος and *terminus* to the definition or limitation of a word appears in Petrus Hispanus, and led finally to the application of *terminus* to any word used in a definite or limited sense (as in sense 13 above). In Aquinas (13th c.) *terminus* is synonymous with *dictio, locutio, nomen* (see the Thomas Lexicon s. v.).]

**Term,** *v.* [In sense 1 prob. a. OF. *termer* (14th c. in Godef.) to bring to an end; to limit, fix; in sense 2, f. TERM *sb.*]

†**1.** *trans.* To bring to an end or conclusion; to terminate. *Obs.* (Cf. AF. OYER *et terminer.*)

*c* **1410** [see *terming* below]. *c* **1450** *Godstow Reg.* 89 They shold here the cause, and..terme hit with a dew ende. **1570** LEVINS *Manip.* 210/43 To Tearme, *terminare.*

**2.** To express or denote by a term or terms. †**a.** To express in particular terms, or in a specified form of words; to phrase. (Usually with *as.*) *Obs.*

*a* **1557** tr. *More's Treat. Passion* Wks. 1376/2 Now doth this man..two ways..continue his pilgrimage, that is to witte as maister Gersonne in the Latin tong termeth it,..in a naturall continuance, and in a moral continuance. **1557** RECORDE *Whetst.* N iij b, *Scholar.* This rule is very obscure in woordes. *Master.* Then will I terme it thus [etc.]. **1584** in *10th Rep. Hist. MSS. Comm.* App. v. 433 No merchant ..should transporte..any goodes that apertayned to unfreemen (as it is termed).

**b.** To give a particular or specified name to; to name, call, denominate, designate. Now only with *compl.* (for which *as* is substituted in a relative clause); formerly with other constructions.

**1560** DAUS tr. *Sleidane's Comm.* 2 Master of the holy palace (as they terme it). **1579** W. WILKINSON *Confut. Familye of Loue, Brief Descr.*, The Heresie termed, The Familie of Loue. **1632** LITHGOW *Trav.* To Rdr., Good Bookes may be tearmed wise guides. **1643** SIR T. BROWNE *Relig. Med.* I. § 36 The brain, which we tearme the seat of reason. **1726** SHELVOCKE *Voy. round World* 27 Incensing the people against..Officers, whom he term'd Blood-suckers. **1872** MIVART *Elem. Anat.* 282 Such muscles are termed rotators.

†**c.** With *obj.* and *inf.*: To state, affirm.

**1577–87** HOLINSHED *Chron.* III. 1212/1 His enimies (whome he termed to be sir Oswold Ulstrop, and maister Vaughan) were about the parke. **1590** SIR J. SMYTH *Disc. Weapons* Ded. 7 Terming those to be best soldiers that could liue without pay. **1632** LITHGOW *Trav.* III. 107 Tearming vs..to haue monstrous backes, against the execution of Iustice.

†**3.** To spend or pass (time) as in term. *Obs.*

**1654** WHITLOCK *Zootomia* 4 They Terme away their Dayes in Obsequious services of others, not allowing Themselves a Dayes vacation.

Hence **Te·rming** *vbl. sb.*; also *attrib.*

*c* **1410** *Master of Game* (MS. Digby 182) Prol., Men wote well that the grettest termynge [*Bodl. MS.* termynynge] of sekenes þat may be is swote. **1549** COVERDALE, etc. *Erasm. Par. Eph.* Prol., To seke the edification of the playne vnlearned by playne termyng of wordes. **1591** SPARRY tr. *Cattan's Geomancie* 176 The place, house, or fygure is..all one thing..yet there is some difference in the tearming. **1643** TRAPP *Comm. Gen.* xxiii. 2 We read in the Gospel of minstrels and people making a noise at the terming-house, as they call it.

**Termagant** (tə̄·ɹmăgănt), *sb.* (*a.*) Forms: α. 3 **teruagant**, 3–5 **-aunt**. β. 4–7 **termagaunt**, 6 **turmagant**, *Sc.* **tarmegant**, **termygant**, 7 **tarmagant**, **-gon**, 7–8 **termigant**, 8 **termigant**, 6– **termagant**. [In early ME. *Tervagant*, OF. *Tervagan* (in La Fontaine 17th c. *Tarvagant*), proper name in *Chanson de Roland a* 1100, as in sense 1 here. So It. *Trivigante* (Ariosto, *a* 1516). For ulterior history cf. Skeat *Etymol. Dict.* s. v.]

**1.** (with capital T.) Name of an imaginary deity held in mediæval Christendom to be worshipped by Mohammedans: in the mystery plays represented as a violent overbearing personage. (Cf. MAHOUND 1.) *Obs.* or *arch.*

In Lay. applied to gods of the Romans and heathen Saxons.

*c* **1205** LAY. 5353 For ȝif hit wulled Teruagant þe us [is] oure god of þisse lond [Rome]. *Ibid.* 16427 Þe heðene..cleopeden 'Ure godd Teruagant! whi trukest þu us an hond?' *c* **1290** *S. Eng. Leg.* I. 468/205 Ne bileuez nouȝt opon Mahun, ne on teruagaunt, [h]is fere. **1303** R. BRUNNE *Handl. Synne* 197 Þe sarysyne to hys god ȝede, And askede cunseyl...Þan answered hys termagaunt. *a* **1400** *Octouian* 910 The Sowdan, that left [= believed] yn Teruagaunt. **1570** FOXE *A. & M.* (ed. 2) 680/2 If he had made hym [Ld. Cobham] some Termagant or Mahounde out of Babilonia. **1597** BP. HALL *Sat.* I. i. 4 Nor fright the Reader with the Pagan vaunt Of mightie Mahound, and great Termagaunt. **1602** SHAKS. *Ham.* III. ii. 15, I could haue such a Fellow whipt for o're-doing Termagant: it out-Herod's Herod. **1637** HEYWOOD *Royall King* II. ii, I'le march where my Captaine leads, wer't into the Presence of the great Termagaunt. **1825** SCOTT *Talism.* iii, Down with Mahound, Termagaunt, and all their adherents.

In form **Tryvigant** (from Italian).

**1591** HARINGTON *Orl. Fur.* XII. xliv, Blaspheming Tryuigant and Mahomet [*Ariosto*: Bestemmiando Macone et Trivigante], And all the Gods adord in Turks profession.

**2.** A savage, violent, boisterous, overbearing, or quarrelsome person (or thing personified); a blusterer, bully. Now *rare* exc. as in b.

**1500–20** DUNBAR *Poems* xxvi. 115 Thae tarmegantis [Ersche-men], with tag and tatter, Ffull lowd in Ersche begowth to clatter. **1542** BALE *Yet a Course*, etc. 39 b, Thys terryble termagaunt, thys Neroth, thys Pharao. **1593** G. HARVEY *Pierce's Super.* 12 Oh, but Agrippa was an vrcheon.. Sigonius a toy, Cuiacius a bable to this Termagant. **1618** T. ADAMS *God's Bounty* ii. Wks. 1861 I. 149 Wealth may do us good service, but if it get the mastery of our trust, it will turn tyrant, termagant. **1824** SCOTT *St. Ronan's* xxi, The.. consequences that might follow from the displeasure of this Highland termagant [Captain MacTurk]. **1884** SIR S. ST. JOHN *Hayti* vii. 269 Bazin, the military termagant who led the prosecution..browbeat the witnesses, bullied the jury.

**b.** *spec.* A violent, overbearing, turbulent, brawling, quarrelsome woman; a virago, shrew, vixen. (Now the ordinary sense.)

**1659** *Lady Alimony* I. iv. B ij, And just so must all our Tavern Tarmagons be us'd. **1732** GAY *Achilles* II. Wks. (1772) 239 This girl is..such an arrant termigant, that I could as soon fall in love with a tygress. **1861** THACKERAY *Four Georges* iii, Yonder is Sarah Marlborough's palace, just as it stood when that termagant occupied it. **1896** 'IAN MACLAREN' *Kate Carnegie* v. 77 A vulgar termagant ..who would call her husband an idiot aloud before a dinner-table.

**3.** *attrib.* or *adj.* Having the character of a termagant; savage, violent, overbearing, turbulent, brawling, quarrelsome. **a.** Generally. Now *rare.*

**1596** SHAKS. *1 Hen. IV*, v. iv. 114 'Twas time to counterfet, or that hotte Termagant Scot had paid me scot and lot too. **1596** NASHE *Saffron Walden* 49 Termagant inkhorne tearmes. **1695** *Remarks some late Serm.* (ed. 2) 3 Consider the fine Knack these Gentlemen have got at Representation and Character; which you will find so luscious and termagant, as would shame even the Modesty of the Stage. **1711** 'J. DISTAFF' *Char. Don Sacheverellio* 5 A Man of great Brawn and Muscle, Large, Tall and Termagant. **1869** J. MARTINEAU *Ess.* II. 213 His dialectic assumes a termagant character.

**b.** *spec.* Of a woman (or her attributes).

**1667–8** DRYDEN & DK. NEWCASTLE *Sir Martin Mar-all* I. i, His wife, who is a termagant lady. **1678** DRYDEN *Limberham* I. i, But this Lady is so Termagant an Empress! **1761** MRS. F. SHERIDAN *Sidney Bidulph* II. 66 The most termagant spirit that ever animated a female breast. **1818** SCOTT *Hrt. Midl.* xviii, 'I tell ye', raising her termagant voice, 'I want my bairn!' **1868** FREEMAN *Norm. Conq.* II. viii. 275 The plans of his own termagant niece Queen Constance.

Hence **Termagancy** (tə̄·ɹmăgănsi) [after nouns in -ANCY from adjs. in -ANT[1]], termagant quality, violence of temper or disposition; **Te·rmagantish** *a.*, resembling, or partaking of the character of, a termagant; **Te·rmagantly** *adv.*, like a termagant, with violence of temper, outrageously.

**1709** MRS. MANLEY *Secret Mem.* (1720) III. 198 The good Emperor, mortifyed by the *Termagancy of his Mother. **1716** M. DAVIES *Athen. Brit.* II. 318 Exasperated by the sawcy Termigancy of some few insolent Dissenting Preachers. **1753** MISS COLLIER *Art Torment.* II. ii. 115 By a violent termagancy of temper, she may never suffer him to have a moment's peace. **1823** in *Spirit Pub. Jrnls.* 408 Mrs. Scarsfield had something so very *termagantish in her appearance. **1707** *Reflex. Ridicule* II. 375 To see..how *termagantly they treat their Husbands.

**Termagant,** obs. erron. form of PTARMIGAN.

**Termage** (tə̄·ɹmėdʒ). [f. TERM *sb.* + -AGE.]

†**1.** Name for the winnings in some form of gambling or cheating. *Obs. slang.*

**1591** GREENE *Conny-Catching* II. Wks. (Grosart) X. 87 In Vincents Law..He that is coosened, the Vincent. Gaines gotten, Termage.

**2.** attrib. *Termage fee* = term-fee (see quot.).

**1834** *Regula Generalis* Michaelmas, in Bingham *New Cases* I. 411 Every attorney ought to pay to the clerk of the warrants..his termage fees, being eight pence in every term.

**Termashaw,** erron. spelling of TAMASHA.

**1842** DE QUINCEY *Philos. Herodotus* Wks. 1862 VIII. 181.

**Termatic** (təɹmæ·tik), *a.* (*sb.*) *Anat.* [f. Gr. τέρμα (τερματ-) end, limit + -IC.] Belonging to the *terma* or *lamina terminalis* of the brain, a thin layer of grey matter in front of the third ventricle. Also as *sb.*, ellipt. for *termatic artery.*

**1885** WILDER in *New York Med. Jrnl.* 21 Mar. 325 The termatic artery, a small vessel arising from the junction of the precerebral arteries. **1890** BILLINGS *Nat. Med. Dict.*, *Termatic artery*, branch from anterior cerebral or anterior communicating arteries to region of lamina terminalis.

**Te·rm-day.** A day set as a term (TERM *sb.* 3); a day appointed for doing something, esp. for payment of money due. (In quot. *c* 1375, a final or concluding day; †*but terme day*, without end, for ever.) ? *Obs.* exc. as in b, c.

*a* **1300** *Cursor M.* 14040 Quen it com to þe term dai, Þai had noght quar-of for to pai. *c* **1369** CHAUCER *Dethe Blaunche* 730 He had broke his terme day To come to hir. *c* **1375** *Sc. Leg. Saints* xxxiii. (*George*) 842 To duel with hyme but terme day. **1470–85** MALORY *Arthur* IV. xxviii. 158 Whan it drewe nygh the terme day that syr gawayn syr Marhaus and syre Vwayne shold mete.

**b.** *spec.* Each of the Scottish quarter-days, esp. Whitsunday and Martinmas day, at which houses are taken, and servants engaged for the summer or winter half-year: see TERM *sb.* 3 b.

**1818** SCOTT *Hrt. Midl.* viii, On the very term-day when their ejection should have taken place. **1893** *Westm. Gaz.* 5 Apr. 6/3 The understanding..was that the bank which has now stopped might hold out till the 15th of May, which is the Scotch 'term' day. **1906** *Scot. Rev.* 1 Feb. 123/1 Candlemas Day is known to business men in Scotland as one of the quarterly term days.

**c.** Each of a series of days appointed for taking systematic scientific observations, e. g. of meteorological phenomena. In quots. *attrib.*

**1843** *Proc. Amer. Phil. Soc.* II. 247 To keep up the term-day observations. **1856** KANE *Arct. Expl.* I. xiv. 153 *note*, Who bore the brunt of the term-day observations.

†**Terment.** *Obs.* Forms: 4–6 **terement**, 5 **tyrrement**, 5–6 **tyr(e)ment**, **terment**, 6 **terrement**. [Aphetic form of INTERMENT.] Burial, funeral: = INTERMENT; also, a funeral service.

**1389** in *Eng. Gilds* (1870) 92 Þe skeueyns shullen don seyn þo messes wyhtinne vj. day after þe terement. **1402** *E. E. Wills* (1882) 11 Atte day of my terment. *c* **1440** *Promp. Parv.* 494/2 Tyrrement, or intyrrement, *funerale.* **1568** GRAFTON *Chron.* II. 578 King Henry caused a solempne obite and terrement to be kept within Paules Church of London, for Sigismond the Emperor.

**Termenteyne,** obs. corrupt f. TURPENTINE.

**Termer** (tə̄·ɹməɹ). Also 6–7 **tearmer.** [f. TERM *sb.* + -ER[1].]

**1.** One who resorted to London in term, either for business at a court of law, or for amusements, intrigues, or dishonest practices. Common *c* 1550–1675; now only *Hist.*

**1556** J. HEYWOOD *Spider & F.* xiv. 11 In westminster hall I..may be a termer all tymes and howrs. **1602** ROWLANDS *Greene's Ghost* (1860) 22 There be a band of more needy mates called Termers, who trauell all the yeere from faire to faire, and haue great doings in Westminster Hall. *Ibid.* 48 A Countrey Gentleman..walking in Poules, as tearmers are wont that wait for their lawyers. **1607** MIDDLETON *Michaelmas Term* I. i. He was here three days before the Exchequer gaped Rearage Fie, such an early termer? **1646** SUCKLING *Goblins* III. Wks. (1694) 274 Country Ladies twelve. Tearmers all. *a* **1668** DAVENANT *Epilogue* Wks. (1673) 300 To cry Plays down Is half the business Termers have in Town. **1834** MEDWIN *Angler in Wales* I. 221 Being noted 'termers', they met at the Goat and Tun. **1875** A. W. WARD *Hist. Eng. Dram. Lit.* (1899) II. vi. 516 *note*, 'Termers' was a name of opprobrium applied to persons who came up to town to make their harvest in term-time.

†**2.** *gen.* or *allusively.* One who is bound to a particular time for doing something; one who holds office only for a term or limited period. *Obs.*

**1634** R. CLERKE in Spurgeon *Treas. Dav.* Ps. cxxxvi. 1 Salvation is no termer; grace ties not itself to times. *a* **1641** BP. MOUNTAGU *Acts & Mon.* ii. (1642) 107 The High Priests being the ordinary standing Rulers of that people..and those of Iudah but Termers.

†**3.** Obs. form of TERMOR, q. v.

‖**Termes** (tə̄·ɹmīz). Pl. **termites** (tə̄·ɹmitīz). [mod.L. (Linnæus 1748), a. late L. *termes* (Isidore) a wood-worm, earlier also *tarmes*, f. root of L. *terere*, Gr. τείρ-ειν to rub, bore.] = TERMITE.

[**1706** PHILLIPS (ed. Kersey), *Termes*, (Lat.)..also a little Worm commonly call'd a Death-watch; a Maggot, or Gentle.] **1781** Termites [see TERMITE]. **1800** *Asiat. Ann. Reg.* 5/2 The *termes*, or what is called the white ant, infests this island. **1834** PRINGLE *Afr. Sk.* viii. 287 The termes of South Africa is not the destructive species.

**Termigame, -gant,** obs ff. PTARMIGAN, TERMAGANT.

**Termin,** var. TERMINE *sb. Obs.*

**Terminable** (tə̄·ɹminăb'l), *a.* (*sb.*) [f. TERMINE *v.* + -ABLE. Cf. OF. *terminable* that comes to an end, not eternal (13th c. in Godef.).]

†**1.** That may be or is to be terminated, determined, or finally decided. *Obs.*

**1424** *Acts Privy Counc.* III. 149 Alle the billes that comprehende materes terminable at the commune lawe..be remitted there to be determined. *c* **1450** *Cov. Myst.* xxv. (1841) 246 *Cayphas*...Of the lawe of Moyses I have a chef governawns, To severe ryth and wrong in me is termynable. *Ibid.* xxix. 291 My sovereyn Lord, heyest of excillens, In ȝou alle jewgement is termynabyle.

**2.** Capable of being or liable to be terminated; that may come or be brought to an end (usually, in time); limitable, finite; not lasting or perpetual.

*Terminable annuity*, an annuity which comes to an end after a definite term: see ANNUITY 3; *terminable annuitant*, one who holds a terminable annuity.

**1581** HANMER *Jesuites Banner* K iv b, Although the offence be infinite, and the satisfaction finite, or terminable. **1656** tr. *Hobbes' Elem. Philos.* (1839) 99 Space or time is said to be finite in power, or terminable, when there may be assigned a number of finite spaces or times, as of paces or hours. **1820** G. G. CAREY *Funds* 79 To find the cost..of a terminable annuity. **1858** W. M. CAMPION in *Cambr. Ess.* 199 Treated as a mere terminable annuitant. **1874** MOTLEY *Barneveld* II. xv. 185 Terminable at pleasure of any one.

†**B.** *sb.* in phr. *in terminables*: ? in definite terms, definitely (cf. *in terms*, TERM *sb.* 14 b). *Obs. rare*⁻¹.

*a* **1568** '*For Helth of Body*', etc. 70 in *Bannatyne Poems* (Hunter. Cl.) 198 Woyd all drinking with lymmaris and lechouris, And this I say in terminablis, I gess, Off dyce playeris and commoun hasardouris.

Hence **Terminabi·lity, Te·rminableness,** the quality of being terminable; **Te·rminably** *adv.*, in the way of being terminable; in quot. 1584, within definite limits of space.

1584 R. Scot *Discov. Witchcr.* (1886) 470 The holie spirit is [not] in us as a bodie placed in a place terminablie. 1846 Worcester, Terminableness. 1850 D. Thomas *Crisis Being* iii. 51 Hell, its existence or non-existence, its terminableness or eternity. 1858 Goldw. Smith in *Oxford Ess.* 279 The choice between holding the fellowship perpetually as a resident, or terminably with leave of non-residence. 1884 *Q. Rev.* Jan. 9 He relies..on the terminability of the office. 1887 Saintsbury *Hist Elizab. Lit.* ix. (1890) 344 An exception to the general rule of the terminableness of copyright.

**Terminal** (tə̄·ɹminăl), *a.* and *sb.* [ad. L. *terminăl-is*, f. *termin-us* end, boundary: see -al. Cf. F. *terminal* (16th c. in Godef.).]

**A.** *adj.* †**1.** *Her.* (See quots.) *Obs.*

1486 *Bk. St. Albans, Her.* B j b, Ther be .ix. dyuisionis of cotarmures .v. perfite & .iiii. vnperfite. The .v. perfite be theys Termynall Collaterall Abstrakte Fixall and Bastard. *Ibid.*, Termynall is calde in armys all the bretheren of right lyne hethir by fadre or by modre may bere the right heyris cotarmure with a differens calde Enbordyng. 1586 Ferne *Blaz. Gentrie* 155 All these coates were called *Terminall* because that they were terminated or limited within their embordinges, as afore sayd.

**2.** Belonging to or placed at the boundary of a region, as a landmark; in quot. 1744, presiding over boundaries (cf. Terminus 2).

1744 Paterson *Comm. on Milton's P. L.* 218 The emblem of his being the terminal god, defending the borders of that nation. 1847 Grote *Greece* ii. xvi. III. 283 A terminal pillar set up by Crœsus at Kydrara.

**b.** Applied to a statue, bust, or figure terminating in and apparently springing from a pillar or pedestal; also to the pillar or pedestal itself; and often inexactly to a pedestal which narrows towards the base. See Term *sb.* 15, Terminus 3.

1857 Birch *Anc. Pottery* (1858) II. 283 Sometimes only his bust is seen, or he appears as a terminal statue. 1858 Hawthorne *Fr. & It. Note-Bks.* I. 177 Great urns and vases, terminal figures, temples.

**3.** Situated at or forming the end or extremity of something: chiefly in scientific use; *spec.* in *Cryst.* applied to the faces, edges, or angles of a crystal at the extremities of its longest axis; in *Zool.* and *Anat.* situated at or forming the (outer) end of a part or series of parts; in *Bot.* growing at the end of a stem, branch, or other part, as a bud, flower, or inflorescence, a style, etc. (opp. to *lateral* and *axillary*). *Terminal moraine* (Geol.), a moraine at the lower end of a glacier: see Moraine.

1805–17 R. Jameson *Char. Min.* (ed. 3) 104 Terminal edges are formed by the junction of lateral and terminal planes. 1826 Kirby & Sp. *Entomol.* IV. 308 Mouth...Terminal.. When the mouth terminates the head. 1827 Steuart *Planter's G.* (1828) 448 Plantations..pruned..by the removal of Terminal Shoots, and Terminal Buds. 1833 J. Duncan *Beetles* (Nat. Libr.) 217 Terminal lobe of the maxillæ ending in a tuft of fine hair. 1847 W. E. Steele *Field Bot.* 132 The uppermost whorl terminal and capitate. 1860 Tyndall *Glac.* ii. viii. 264 The rocks and débris carried down by the glacier are finally deposited at the lower extremity, forming there a terminal moraine. 1869 Phillips *Vesuv.* x. 274 A prism with a six-sided terminal pyramid. 1876 Preece & Sivewright *Telegraphy* 160 By a terminal pole is meant not only the last pole at each end of the line to which the wires are terminated, but also any pole at which the wires form an angle approaching to 90°. 1884 Hulme *Wild Fl.* p. vi, Inflorescence terminal and axillary.

**b.** Situated at the end of a line of railway; forming, or belonging to, a railway terminus.

1878 F. S. Williams *Midl. Railw.* 68 The cost including two terminal stations and rolling stock, averaging £24,000 a mile. 1881 *Times* 13 July 6/3 In regard to terminal services the respondent [railway] company allowed a rebate. 1907 *Daily Chron.* 10 Sept. 4/6 When the Canadian Pacific Railway Company selected the spot for their western terminal port on the shores of the Pacific.

**4.** Occurring at the end of something (in time, or generally); forming the last member of a series or succession; closing, concluding, final, ultimate.

1831 *For. Q. Rev.* VII. 378 Alliterative metre is formed without .. dependence upon the aid of terminal rhyme. 1832 Babbage *Econ. Manuf.* (ed. 3) 52 Bodies, in falling through a resisting medium, after a certain time acquire a uniform velocity, which is called their terminal velocity, with which they continue to descend. 1873 H. Spencer *Stud. Sociol.* xiv. 336 The human being is at once the terminal problem of Biology and the initial factor of Sociology. 1877 Dowden *Shaks. Prim.* iv. 41 These may be found as terminal words in the blank verse of Milton and of Wordsworth. 1885 *Act* 48 & 49 *Vict.* c. 58 § 2 The sums charged ..shall..cover the costs of delivery..within..one mile of the terminal telegraphic office. 1895 *Daily News* 14 Dec. 9/4 The terminal market, though dull, has been steadier, prices marking a recovery of 3d. to 6d. on the week.

**b.** *Path.* Applied to a morbid condition forming the final stage of a fatal disease.

1891 *Cent. Dict.*, *Terminal dementia*, dementia forming the final and permanent stage of many cases of acute insanity. 1898 *Allbutt's Syst. Med.* V. 422 In the moribund a 'terminal' leucocytosis is frequently observed.

**5.** Belonging to or lasting for a term or definite period; *esp.* pertaining to a university or law term; occurring every term or at fixed terms; termly.

1827 *Q. Rev.* XXXVI. 259 Strict terminal examinations, on the topics of the college lectures, have been generally introduced. 1875 Stubbs *Const. Hist.* II. xv. 260 This council sitting in terminal courts assisted the king in hearing suits. 1885 Sir N. Lindley in *Law Rep.* 29 Ch. Div. 593 This terminal rent-charge is an incumbrance on the inheritance. 1885 *Law Times* LXXX. 5/1 A set of rooms in college..at a yearly rent payable by three terminal payments. 1885 M. Pattison *Mem.* 87 A share in the terminal examinations called 'Collections'.

**6.** *Logic.* Pertaining to a term (Term *sb.* 12).

1872 in Latham. 1891 *Cent. Dict.*, *Terminal quantity*, the quantity of a term, as universal or particular.

**B.** *sb.* †**1.** *pl.* Rendering L. *Terminālia*, name of an ancient Roman festival held annually in honour of the god Terminus: see Terminus 2, and cf. *Saturnals*, Saturnal B. 2. *Obs. rare*—°.

1656 Blount *Glossogr.*, *Terminals* (*terminalia*), feasts.. kept in February at the eighth calends of March.

**2.** A terminal part or structure, i. e. one situated at or forming the end, or an end, of something; *spec.* **a.** in *Electr.* each of the free ends of an open circuit (by connecting which the circuit is closed), or any structure forming such an end, as the carbons in an arc light, or the clamping-screws in a voltaic battery by which it is connected with the wire that completes the circuit; **b.** *Physiol.* the end or end-structure of a nerve fibre or neuron; **c.** a carving or other ornament at the end of something, as a finial.

1850 Grove *Corr. Phys. Forces* (ed. 2) 82 If the two platinum terminals of a voltaic battery be immersed in water, oxygen will be evolved at one and hydrogen at the other terminal. 1865 *Morn. Star* 27 Feb., Seats..panelled with oak, the elbow rails having carved terminals. 1869 Mrs. Somerville *Molec. Sc.* I. i. ii. 52 When the copper conducting wires are fitted with charcoal terminals and brought near to one another, the dazzling lights combine in one blaze. 1874 Carpenter *Ment. Phys.* i. ii. § 89 (1879) 99 The terminals of the sensory tract of the axial cord. 1899 *Allbutt's Syst. Med.* VIII. 325 The ultimate naked fibrils (collaterals and terminals). 1904 Windle *Rem. Prehist. Age Brit.* 100 Chapes or terminals to scabbards which may have belonged to daggers or to swords.

**3.** A final syllable, letter, or word; a termination.

1831 *Westm. Rev.* Jan. 61 The derivation of one word from another.., or rather the different states in which a root presents itself with terminals added. 1866 *Sat. Rev.* 21 Apr. 474 Madlle. Orgeni (German in spite of her patronymic terminal) comes directly from Berlin. 1904 *Athenæum* 21 May 646/2 Mr. Coleridge transposes the rhyming terminals 'healthy' and 'wealthy'.

**4.** *pl.* Charges made by a railway company for the use of a terminus or other station, and for services rendered in loading or unloading goods, etc., there: see quot. 1887.

1878 F. S. Williams *Midl. Railw.* 188 There was a sum of £5000 or £6000 for 'terminals'. 1884 *Pall Mall G.* 27 May 3/1 To charge a reasonable sum for station terminals. 1887 *Contemp. Rev.* Jan. 82 The cost of collection, loading, covering, unloading, and delivering,..are the chief items included under the denomination of 'terminals'.

**5.** A terminal station or premises on a railway, a terminus; a terminal point of a railway, a place or town at which it has a terminus. *U.S.*

1883 *Boston* (Mass.) *Jrnl.* 7 Aug. 3/2 The Canadian Pacific..company has purchased extensive dock property and terminals at Windsor, opposite Detroit. 1900 *Jrnl. Sch. Geog.* (U.S.) Apr. 135 The seaboard terminal is New York, with its three million of people. 1904 Kittredge *Old Farmer* 279 In 1801, King's Tavern, Boston, was the 'terminal' for the stages for Albany, New York, &c.

**6.** A terminal figure: = Term *sb.* 15, Terminus 3.

1876 Gwilt *Archit.* Gloss., *Term* or *Terminal. Ibid.*, *Vagina*, the lower part of a terminal in which a statue is apparently inserted.

**Terminally** (tə̄·ɹminăli), *adv.* [f. prec. adj. + -ly [2].]

†**1.** In relation to, or within, a term or limited period. *Obs.*

1657 Gaule *Sapientia Justif.* 89 That Death which reigned from Adam to Moses,..if you take the time of Deaths reigning to be betwixt them two, terminally and exclusively.

**2.** At the end or extremity.

1854 Owen *Skel. & Teeth* in *Orr's Circ. Sc.* I. *Org. Nat.* 182 The..terminally confluent parapophyses. 1875 Bennett & Dyer *Sachs' Bot.* 460 Female flowers..consisting of a naked axis..bearing the erect ovules terminally or laterally.

**3.** Every term, once a term.

1868 *Times* 26 Sept. 3/5 No house [at Oxford] can be licensed until it has been inspected by the delegates, and lodgings must be visited by them terminally. 1885 *Law Times* LXXIX. 366/2 An annual rent is paid by the undergraduate .. in some cases quarterly, triennially, or terminally. 1896 *Oxford Univ. Gaz.* 10 Nov. 110/1 The Scholarship is of the annual value of £45, payable terminally, and tenable for two years.

**Terminant** (tə̄·ɹminănt), *a.* (*sb.*) Now *rare* or *Obs.* [ad. L. *terminānt-em*, pr. pple. of *termināre* to Terminate.]

**1.** Terminating, concluding, final. Also as *sb.* A final syllable, termination, terminal.

1589 Puttenham *Eng. Poesie* ii. viii. (Arb.) 94 If one should rime to this word (*Restore*) he may not match him with (*Doore*) or (*Poore*) for neither of both are of like terminant, either by good orthography or in naturall sound. *Ibid.* 95 Gower..to make vp his rime would..write his terminant sillable with false orthographie. *Ibid.* iii. xvi. 185 Your clauses in prose should neither finish with the same nor with the like terminants.

†**2.** Determining, defining. *Obs.*

1603 Holland *Plutarch's Mor.* 1044 The terminant and defining power loveth the universall and indivisible. *a* 1610 Healey *Theophrastus* (1636) To Rdr., There being certaine properties almost in every language, which cannot, word for word, in terms terminant be expressed in another.

†**Terminary** (tə̄·ɹminări). *rare.* [ad. med. L. *termināri-us* (in Du Cange) pertaining to the end or boundary, f. *termin-us* end: see -ary. So F. *terminaire.*] A building or structure placed at the end of a walk or vista to terminate a view.

1790 W. Wrighte *Grotesque Archit.* Title-p., Hermitages, Terminaries, Chinese, Gothic, and Natural Grottos.

**Terminate** (tə̄·ɹminĕt), *ppl. a.* [ad. L. *terminăt-us*, pa. pple. of *termināre*: see next.] Terminated, in various senses: see the verb.

**1.** Limited, bounded; ended, brought to an end; having a definite limit or limits; of determinate form or magnitude. (In early quots. const. as *pa. pple.*) Now *rare* or *Obs.*

1432–50 tr. *Higden* (Rolls) I. 79 Inde is terminate from the este with the rysenge of the sonne, of the sowthe with the occean [etc.]. 1639 G. Daniel *Ecclus.* xli. 38 What if the vncertaine Date Of Mortalls in ten years be Terminate. 1645 Digby *Nat. Bodies* xxviii. § 1. 301 A terminate [*ed.* 1644 determinate] quantity or multitude of parts. 1750 tr. *Leonardus' Mirr. Stones* 35 Colour is the extremity of the perspicuous in a terminate body.

**b.** *Math.* Capable of being expressed in a finite number of terms; *esp.* of a decimal, not recurring or infinite; opp. to Interminate 1 b. *rare.*

1882 Ogilvie, *Terminate*, a., capable of coming to an end; limited; bounded; as, a *terminate* decimal.

†**2.** Determined, decided. *Obs. rare.* (as *pa. pple.*)

1432–50 tr. *Higden* (Rolls) VII. 275 The pope decrete that mater to be terminate afore the kynge of Ynglonde and bischoppes.

†**3. a.** Directed to a specified object. *Obs. rare.*

1624 F. White *Repl. Fisher* 283 Their worship is terminate in the verie Image.

†**b.** ? Directed to some point; having a definite direction in space. *Obs. rare.*

1676 H. More *Remarks* xxiii. 37, I demand, if the mobility of water upwards be not as intrinsick to it as downwards..? for where the water is rightly placed, it has no terminate motion at all.

**Terminate** (tə̄·ɹmineᵗt), *v.* [f. L. *termināt-*, ppl. stem of *termināre* to limit, end, f. *termin-us* end, boundary.] **I.** Transitive senses.

†**1.** To determine; to state definitely. *Obs. rare.*

1589 Nashe *Anat. Absurd.* 18 Who made them so priuie to the secrets of the Almightie, that they should foretell the tokens of his wrath, or terminate the time of his vengeaunce. 1706 Phillips, To *Terminate*,..to determine, or decide.

†**2.** To express in terms or words, to denominate. *Obs. rare*—[1].

1589 Nashe *Pref. Greene's Menaphon* (Arb.) 13 Which strange language of the firmament..makes vs that are not vsed to terminate heauens moueings in the accents of any voice, esteeme of their triobulare interpreter, as of some Thrasonical huffe snuffe.

**3.** To direct (an action) to something as object or end (cf. Term *sb.* 1 c). Const. *in, to, upon.* In quot. 1599, To destine to a place. ? *Obs.* (Cf. sense 8.)

1599 Nashe *Lenten Stuffe* (1871) 73 Leander .. they terminated to the unquiet, cold coast of Iceland. 1645 Rutherford *Tryal & Tri. Faith* Ded. 12 The first opening of the eye-lids of God is terminated upon the breast of Christ. 1652 Gaule *Magastrom.* 127 Idolatrous worship came..to be terminated upon other inferior creatures. 1724 R. Welton *Chr. Faith & Pract.* 188 When they terminate their thoughts upon secondary instruments. 1746–7 Hervey *Medit.* (1818) 147 The niggardly wretch whose aims are all turned inward, and meanly terminated upon himself.

†**b.** Of a thing: To be the object of (an action).

1656 Jeanes *Mixt. Schol. Div.* 81 This union..is wrought by the whole three persons, terminated unto the second person onely; that alone terminates suppositall, or personall dependance of the manhood. 1662 Stillingfl. *Orig. Sacr.* iii. i. § 3 An Idea..is nothing else but the objective being of a thing as it terminates the understanding. 1704 Norris *Ideal World* ii. iii. 108 The ideas that terminate our thoughts (and which therefore are the only true objects of them).

**4.** To bring to an end, put an end to, cause to cease; to end (an action, condition, etc.).

1615 Chapman *Odyss.* xx. 92 Her eyes Opened with teares, in care of her estate, Which now, her friends resolu'd to terminate To more delaies; and make her marry one. 1623 Cockeram, *Terminate*, to end. 1732 Arbuthnot *Rules of Diet* in *Aliments*, etc. 304 [It] will sooner terminate the cold Fit. 1796 Mme. D'Arblay *Camilla* IV. 277 She had every hope that this..would terminate every perplexity. 1855 Milman *Lat. Chr.* viii. ix, They had assisted in terminating a disastrous schism which had distracted Christendom.

**b.** To come at the end of, form the conclusion of.

1798 Sophia Lee *Canterb. T.*, *Yng. Lady's T.* II. 497 Cold thanks for her civilities..terminated the visit. 1799 *Monthly Rev.* XXX. 345 We cannot also but approve the choice of passages..which terminate this publication.

†**5.** To bring (something) to a stop, so that it extends no further; to put a limit or limits to; to restrict, confine *to* (*in*). *Obs.*

*a* 1628 Preston *New Covt.* (1634) 157 When a man will so enjoy these things that he can terminate his comfort in them. 1660 R. Coke *Power & Subj.* 80 Where it is not slavery, there the Masters power is terminated to years, moneths, weeks, daies, or houres. 1674 Hickman *Hist. Quinquart.* (ed. 2) 118 Both creation and generation are terminated to substances.

**6.** To bound or limit spatially; to form the material extremity of; to be situated at the end of.

**1634** SIR T. HERBERT *Trav.* 42 The South [of Guzerat] is terminated by the Sea. **1713** POPE *Guardian* No. 173 ¶ 5 (Odyss. VII. 168) Beds of all various herbs, for ever green, In beauteous order terminate the scene. **1746–7** HERVEY *Medit.* (1818) 103 On another side, the great deep terminates the view. **1797** *Encycl. Brit.* (ed. 3) XVII. 404/2 That which comes under the foremost beam of the gun-deck may terminate the fore part of the orlop. **1828** STARK *Elem. Nat. Hist.* II. 391 Abdomen..elongated, conical, terminated in the female by a long perforator. **1840** LARDNER *Geom.* 264 Two such semi-diameters..will be terminated at points holding corresponding positions in the elliptical quadrants.

**7.** †**a.** To give a definite border or outline to, render distinct, define (visual objects). *Obs. rare.*

**1756** FRANKLIN in *Phil. Trans.* LV. 190 Distant objects appear distinct, their figures sharply terminated. **1762** MASKELYNE *ibid.* LII. 610 M. de la Caille had a refracting telescope..which..did not terminate objects distinctly.

**b.** To finish, complete. *rare.*

**1825** CHALMERS in Hanna *Mem.* (1851) III. iv. 56 Our science is a rudimental and not a terminating one. **1857** J. S. HARFORD *Michael Angelo* I. xi. 245 During this interval of calm and prosperity, he [Michael Angelo] terminated two figures of slaves..in an incomparable style of art.

**II.** Intransitive senses (corresponding to *refl.* or *pass.* uses of those in I.).

**8.** To be directed to something as object or end.

**1699** BURNET 39 *Art.* xxii. (1700) 240 In the Presence of the King, all Respects terminate in his Person. **1856** DOVE *Logic Chr. Faith* Introd. § 6. 23 The other [says] 'My thoughts all terminate in God'. **1909** SIR O. LODGE *Ether of Space* App. III. 153 The free portion [of ether]..is not amenable to either mechanical or electric forces. They are transmitted by it, but never terminate upon it.

**9.** To come to an end (in space); *esp.* to have its end or extremity at a specified place, or of a specified form; to end *at*, *in*, or *with* something.

**1644** EVELYN *Diary* 27 Feb., A spacious gravel walke terminating in a grotto. **1675** OGILBY *Brit.* Pref. 3 Ascending till it terminate at the Top of the..Scroll. **1769** COOK *Voy. round World* 24 Apr. I. x. (1773) II. 99 These hills..continued for about three miles more, and then terminated in a large plain. **1796** MORSE *Amer. Geog.* I. 227 Their tails terminate with a hard horny spur. **1862** STANLEY *Jew. Ch.* (1877) I. v. 107 The spot where the present gulf terminates. **1868** OWEN *Vertebr. Anim.* III. 414 The left extremity of the stomach is bifid, and terminates in two round cul-de-sacs.

**b.** Of a word: To end *in* (a letter or sound).

**1824** L. MURRAY *Eng. Gram.* (ed. 5) I. iii. 84 Sometimes also, when the singular terminates in *ss*, the apostrophic *s* is not added: as, 'For goodness' sake'. **1865** *Pall Mall G.* 25 July 4/1 Greek compounds terminating in 'on' are very fashionable, and have a truly learned smack.

**10.** To come to an end, so as to extend no further; to have its end or terminus *in* something; †also, to be confined or restricted within specified limits.

**1613** JACKSON *Creed* I. xxiv. § 5 The like fearful earthquakes..fell out in Trajan's time at Antioch; but the harms [did] not terminate within her territories or the cities about her. **1646** SIR T. BROWNE *Pseud. Ep.* 130 The testimonies of ancient Writers..are but derivative, and terminate all in one Aristeus. *a* **1677** HALE *Prim. Orig. Man.* 19 My Understanding doth truly conclude that all this vicissitude of things must terminate in a first cause of things. *a* **1784** JOHNSON in *Boswell* (1816) I. 23 The rod produces an effect which terminates in itself.

**11.** To come to an end (in time); to end, cease, conclude, close.

**1815** WORDSW. *Sonn.*, '*The fairest brightest hues*' 2 The sweetest notes must terminate and die. **1849** MACAULAY *Hist. Eng.* ix. II. 519 At length the repast terminated. **1872** YEATS *Techn. Hist. Comm.* 375 The Middle Ages may be said to terminate with the invention of printing.

**b.** To issue, result (*in* something): = END *v.*[1] 5 b.

**1710** LUTTRELL *Brief Rel.* (1857) VI. 620 There has been a 2d battle in Spain, which terminated in favour of King Charles. **1775** J. BRYANT *Mythol.* II. 308 The fate of Semiramis terminated in her being turned into a pigeon. **1867** H. MACMILLAN *Bible Teach.* x. (1870) 204 A career of worldliness and sin terminates in impenitence and despair.

Hence **Te·rminating** *vbl. sb.* and *ppl. a.*

**1656** tr. *Hobbes' Elem. Philos.* (1839) 179 Within the same terminating lines there can be no more than one plane superficies. **1776** WITHERING *Brit. Plants* (1796) II. 187 Lateral and terminating fruit stalks. **1807** HUTTON *Course Math.* II. 75 At 954, the end of the first line, the o denotes its terminating in the hedge. **1837** G. PHILLIPS *Syriac Gram.* 4 The addition of a terminating consonant.

**Termination** (tə̄ɹminēⁱ·ʃən). [ad. L. *terminātiōn-em*, n. of action f. *termināre* to TERMINATE; in some senses perh. a. OF. *termination* (13–14th c.).]

**I.** The action of terminating or fact of being determined (in various senses).

†**1.** The action of determining; determination, decision. *Obs.*

*c* **1450** in Aungier *Syon* (1840) 359 The abbes..schal make al the terminacions in the chirche. **1455–6** *Cal. Anc. Rec. Dublin* (1889) 290 Wythoute eny contradiccyon aftyr the termynacyon aforesayd. *a* **1625** FLETCHER *Love's Pilgr.* II. i, You can consider The want in others of these terminations, And how unfurnish'd they appear. **1660** R. COKE *Justice Vind.* Pref. 13 If I could not ultimately resolve the dictates of my reason..into plain places of Scripture, so well as any Geometrician would any proposition of Geometry into the principles of Euclid's elements; I would be content to let them wander for ever without any termination.

†**2.** Alleged name of some operation of alchemy.

**1584** R. SCOT *Discov. Witchcr.* XIV. i, Their..amalgaming ..terminations, mollifications and indurations of bodies.

**3.** The action of ending. †**a.** Bounding, limiting, separation by spatial limits (*obs.*). **b.** Putting an end to; bringing to a close.

**1604** R. CAWDREY *Table Alph.*, *Termination*, an ending,.. finishing or bounding. **1646** SIR T. BROWNE *Pseud. Ep.* 55 The water entring the body, begets a division of parts, and a termination of Atoms united before unto continuity. **1658** PHILLIPS, *Termination*,..a limiting, ending, or bounding. **1910** *Expositor* Oct. 290 Adultery alone justifies the termination of a marriage union.

†**4.** Direction to something as an object or end; purpose: cf. END *sb.* 14. *Obs.*

?**16..** WHITE (J), It is not an idol *ratione termini*, in respect of termination; for the religious observation thereof is referred..to the honour of God and Christ.

**II.** The point or part in which anything ends.

**5.** End (in time), cessation, close, conclusion.

*c* **1500** *Melusine* xxiii. 156 Ermyne said she wold see first the termynacion of her faders syknes or she shuld procide ony ferther. **1658** SIR T. BROWNE *Hydriot.* iv. (1736) 31 Christians have handsomely glossed the Deformity of Death, by..civil Rites, which take off brutal Terminations. **1755** JOHNSON, *Termination*..3. End; conclusion. **1848** THACKERAY *Van. Fair* xliii, She abruptly put a termination to a flirtation which Lieutenant Stubble..had commenced. **1853** J. H. NEWMAN *Hist. Sk.* (1873) II. I. iv. 160 All human power has its termination sooner or later.

**b.** Outcome, issue, result: = END *sb.* 13.

**1806** V. KNOX *Serm. Isa. xxviii. 16* Wks. 1824 VI. 393 A good commencement has ever been found..auspicious to a good progress and a happy termination. **1824** SCOTT *St. Ronan's* xxix, If they do not indeed drive her to suicide, which I think the most likely termination. **1884** *Manch. Exam.* 3 May 5/1 Dissensions which could hardly have other than a hostile termination.

**6.** The ending of a word; the final syllable, letter, or group of letters; *spec.* in *Gram.* a final element affixed to a word or stem to express some relation or modification of sense; an (inflexional or derivative) ending, a suffix.

**1530** PALSGR. Introd. 27 In these syxe termynations endeth no masculyne adjectyve syngular. **1588** FRAUNCE *Lawiers Log.* I. xii. 50 b, The diuers fallinges and terminations of woords. **1614** SELDEN *Titles Hon.* Pref., Lar is but the Turkish termination plurall. *a* **1677** HALE *Prim. Orig. Man.* 165 Many times the *Literati* and *Scholares* coyn new Words, and sometimes..give Terminations and Idiotisms sutable to their Native Language, unto Words newly invented..out of other Languages. **1788** GIBBON *Decl. & F.* l. (1790) IX. 227 [Mecca] was known to the Greeks under the name of Macoraba;..the termination of the word is expressive of its greatness. **1845** STODDART in *Encycl. Metrop.* (1847) I. 108/1 The addition of an adverbial particle, like our prefix, *a*, or termination, *ly*.

**7.** A limit, bound; an end, extremity (of a material object, or of a portion of space).

**1755** JOHNSON, *Termination*..2. Bound; limit. **1828** WEBSTER s.v., The termination of a line. **1830** BOOTH *L'pool & Manch. Railw.* 42 To improve the termination of the line at the Liverpool end. **1860** TYNDALL *Glac.* I. xvii. 120 To trace the glacier to its termination. **1870** F. R. WILSON *Ch. Lindisf.* 101 At the west end is a bell-cot, with a pyramidal termination.

**b.** *pl.* Used for 'trousers' or 'breeches'.

**1863** R. F. BURTON *Wand. W. Africa* I. 32 The men are in shirts, and long terminations, or femoral a.

†**8.** ? A term, word, expression. *Obs. rare.*

**1599** SHAKS. *Much Ado* II. i. 255 Shee speakes poynyards, and euery word stabbes: if her breath were as terrible as [her] terminations, there were no liuing neere her.

**Termina·tional,** *a.* Chiefly *Gram.* [f. prec. + -AL.] Of, pertaining to, or forming a termination or terminations; closing, final (quot. 1874).

**1824** L. MURRAY *Eng. Gram.* (ed. 5) I. 347 We seem to have the three great principles of accentuation; namely, the radical, the terminational, and the distinctive. **1861** CRAIK *Hist. Eng. Lit.* I. 33 It expressed the relations of nouns and verbs..by terminational or other modifications. **1862** W. P. DICKSON tr. *Mommsen's Hist. Rome* (1875) I. 12 The richer terminational system of the Greeks. **1874** T. HARDY *Far fr. Madding Crowd* vi, His superiority was marked enough to lead several ruddy peasants..to speak to him inquiringly,..and to use 'Sir' as a terminational word.

**Terminative** (tə̄ɹminē̆tiv, -ĕtiv), *a.* [ad. L. type **terminātīvus*: see TERMINATE *v.* and -ATIVE. Cf. F. *terminatif.*] Having the function of terminating (in various senses).

**1.** Forming a boundary or limit, bounding (?*obs.*); forming the termination or extremity of something.

**1432–50** tr. *Higden* (Rolls) II. 51 The water of Thammyse ..was somme tyme as a cause terminatiue of men of Kente, of Este Saxones, West Saxones, and ofmen of the Marches. *Ibid.* 109 Mersee in Englische sowndethe as a see terminatiue [Higd. *terminans mare*], for hit disterminate[d] oon realme from an other. **1750** tr. *Leonardus' Mirr. Stones* 36 Some colour, which should be the terminative colour of the perspicuous and opaque.

†**2.** Constituting an end, final, ultimate; *esp.* constituting the ultimate object or end of some action (nearly = OBJECTIVE *a.* 1). *Obs.*

**1624** F. WHITE *Repl. Fisher* 224 Neither is the Picture or Image..the terminatiue obiect of Loue..or Worship. **1681** FLAVEL *Meth. Grace* ix. 195 No duties or ordinances (which are but the wayes or means by which we come to Christ) are or ought to be central and terminative to the soul. **1694** R. BURTHOGGE *Reason & Nat. Spirits* 244 That the Soul is but a Mediate Subject while it is in the Body, and not a Terminative. **1701** NORRIS *Ideal World* I. v. 235 There can be no act of the Divine understanding above them [the Divine Ideas], but what must of necessity suppose them as the terminative forms of it.

†**b.** Directed to something as ultimate object.

**1660** JER. TAYLOR *Duct. Dubit.* II. ii. VI. § 27 To take off this trifle of worship Relative and worship Terminative. **1679** C. NESSE *Antid. agst. Popery* 38 Their worship being not.. terminative in the creature.

**3.** Bringing or coming to an end; finishing, concluding; conclusive; in *Path.* = TERMINAL *a.* 4 b.

*a* **1680** CHARNOCK *Sinfulness & Cure Th.* Sel. Wks. (1849) 109 Thoughts are inchoative in the fancy, consummative in the understanding, terminative in all the other faculties. **1813–21** BENTHAM *Ontology* ii. § 9 Terminating or terminative motions. **1887** T. HARDY *Woodlanders* i, The interior, as seen through the window, caused him to draw up with a terminative air and watch. **1899** *Allbutt's Syst. Med.* VIII. 417 Cases of..old standing terminative dementia.

**4.** *Gram.* Denoting destination or direction towards.

**1903** *Amer. Anthropologist* Jan.–Mar. 13 Besides a general locative some of the most frequently occurring [suffixes] are inessive, superessive, introessive, ablative, and terminative.

**Te·rminatively,** *adv.* [f. prec. + -LY [2].] In a terminative manner.

**1.** So as to terminate or form the end or extremity; in the way of a boundary or limit.

**1570** DEE *Math. Pref.* *j, Though a Poynt be no Magnitude, yet Terminatiuely we recken it a thing Mathematicall..by reason it is..the end and bound of a line.

†**2.** In the way of direction to something as ultimate object; in relation to, or as, the object (nearly = OBJECTIVELY 1); ultimately. *Obs.*

**1627** BP. HALL *Best Bargaine* Wks. 515 This truth, being the thing it selfe subiectiuely, in words expressiuely, in the minde of man terminatiuely. **1661** H. D. *Disc. Liturgies* 45 Some..Pagans..might terminatively worship the Sun and Moon, as thinking those noble Creatures were the very first movers and principles. **1664** JER. TAYLOR *Dissuas. Popery* I. ii. § 11 (1686) 197 It [the worship] is terminatively to Christ or God, but relatively to the image. **1720–1** *Lett. fr. Mist's Jrnl.* (1722) II. 55 After which that eminent Person is neither terminatively, or relatively mentioned.

**3.** So as to terminate, i. e. come or bring to an end; finally; conclusively.

**1891** T. HARDY *Tess* xvii, 'O–ay, as a lad I knowed your part o' the country very well', he said terminatively.

**Terminator** (tə̄ɹminēⁱtəɹ). [a. late L. *terminātor*, agent-n. f. *termināre* to TERMINATE.]

**1.** One who or that which terminates.

**1846** WORCESTER, *Terminator*, he or that which terminates or bounds. **1890** *Illustr. Lond. News* 27 Dec. 810/2 The terminator of delights,..the desolator of abodes.

**2.** *Astron.* The line of separation between the illuminated and unilluminated parts of the disk of the moon or a planet.

**1770** HORSLEY in *Phil. Trans.* LX. 435 *note*, A great circle passing through the poles of the terminator. **1868** LOCKYER *Elem. Astron.* III. xvi. (1879) 92 The terminator—the name given to the boundary between the lit-up and shaded portions [of the Moon]. **1876** G. F. CHAMBERS *Astron.* 69 Schröter found the terminator [of Venus] slightly concave.

**Te·rminatory,** *a. rare.* [See prec. and -ORY [2].] Forming the end or extremity; terminal.

**1756** J. HILL *Hist. Plants* 156 (Jod.) The blite with spicated terminatory heads. **1775** J. JENKINSON *Descr. Brit. Pl.* Gloss. s. v., By a terminatory flower is meant the end flower. **1853** TH. ROSS *Humboldt's Trav.* III. xxx. 219 The terminatory point of the group of little mountains.

†**Termine,** *sb. Obs.* Also **termin.** [ad. L. *termin-us* boundary. Cf. OE. *termen*, OF. *termine* (12–14th c. in Godef.).] = TERM *sb.* in various senses: boundary, limit; end, extremity; limited time or period (in quot. 1609); in quot. *a* 1625 = TERM *sb.* 2.

[*c* **1000** *Sax. Leechd.* III. 228 On þam teoðan stent se termen þæt ȝemære si hwylc hit si.]

**1570** LEVINS *Manip.* 133/31 A Termin, bound, *terminus.* **1609** HEYWOOD *Brit. Troy* VI. xlix, Our great Englands Ilioue..Hath at their suite granted a termine Truce. **1616** [see TERMININE]. *a* **1625** FLETCHER *Bloody Brother* IV. ii, [The sun] hath his Termin In the degrees where she [the moon] is, and enjoys By that six dignities.

†**Te·rmine,** *v. Obs.* Also 4–5 **-yne, -yn, -ene.** [a. F. *termine-r* (in Wace, 12th c.), ad. L. *termināre* to TERMINATE.]

**1.** *trans.* To determine, decide, settle. (With simple obj. or obj. cl.; also *absol.*)

*a* **1325** *MS. Rawl. B.* 520 lf. 30 b, Þat alle þe quo warantes ben..iplaited ant itermined in Eyre of Iustises. **1382** WYCLIF 1 *Sam.* xx. 33 Jonathas vnderstood, that it was fulli termyned of his fader, that Dauyd shulde be slayn. *a* **1400–50** *Alexander* 3979 Lat vs twa termyn þe taite be-twene vs alane. **1423** *Rolls of Parlt.* IV. 256 May inquere, here, and termine all the defautes. **1496** *Dives & Paup.* (W. de W.) IV. xxvii. 194/2 They wyll entermete them of euery cause.. & termine euery cause by ther wytt. **1628** T. SPENCER *Logick* 47 By the forme the essence is termined vnto some speciall kinde. **1705** W. WALL *Hist. Inf. Bapt.* (1845) I. 464, I have not termined anything by definitive authority as if I would be the author of any dogma.

**2.** To state finally or definitely; to declare, affirm. (Const. as in 1.)

*c* **1420** LYDG. *Thebes* III. in *Chaucer's Wks.* (1561) 370/2 Thus selde is sen, the trouthe to termine That age and youth drawe by O line. **1426** — *De Guil. Pilgr.* 22599 And off my ffyle to termyne, It is I-called Dyscyplyne. **1429** *Pol. Poems* (Rolls) II. 144 Folwe discrecioun Of thy fader,..plainly to termyne, Late hym by thy myrrour and thy guyde. *c* **1475** *Harl. Contin. Higden* (Rolls) VIII. 521 The fifthe Henry, of knyȝthehode the lodesterre, Wyse and fulle manly, pleynly to termyne.

**3.** *trans.* To cause to end *in* or *at* something; *intr.* to end *in* or *at* something: = TERMINATE *v.* 3, 8.

**1634** BP. HALL *Contempl.*, *N. T.* IV. v, How absurd had these guests been, if they had termined the thanks in the servitors; and had said, 'We have it from you; whence ye had it, is no part of our care'. **1639** N. N. tr. *Du Bosq's Compl. Woman* I. 18 The other goodly qualities..all termine in Conversation, as in their Center. *Ibid.* II. 38 All their travell termines at voluptuousnesse. **1668** CULPEPPER & COLE *Barthol. Anat.* I. 26 Arising from the Cæcum, is termined in the Rectum.

**4.** *trans.* To set bounds to, bound; to define, outline; usually in *pass.* to be bounded, have its limit or end: = TERMINATE *v.* 6.

**1398** TREVISA *Barth. De P. R.* XIX. ii. (1495) 862 Clere thynge well termined [*Bodley MS.* lf. 291/1 ytermyned] is the matere of colour. **1555** EDEN *Decades* 269 Towarde the west & north it is termined with an vnknowen ende of landes & seas. **1625** N. CARPENTER *Geog. Del.* I. v. (1635) 99 An imaginary point, conceiued in a magnitude deuoyde of all quantity, yet bounding and termining all Magnitudes.

**b.** To confine or enclose within something.

**1477** NORTON *Ord. Alch.* v. in Ashm. *Theat. Chem. Brit.* (1652) 66 The shining of Gould is caused..Of pure and subtile Water termined full well. *Ibid.*, For of a Mirrour the cause none other is, But moisture termined, as all Clerks gesse. **1631** J. DONE *Polydoron* 51, I find in the most centrall and Terrestriall (that is) the Metalline bodies their life is termined, shut, imprisoned within themselues.

**5.** To bring to an end; to end, finish, conclude: = TERMINATE *v.* 4.

**1390** GOWER *Conf.* I. 168 Which to mi ladi stant enclined, And hath his love noght termined. *c* **1400** *Laud Troy Bk.* 9629 The trewes is passed and alle termened, And alle ben redy. *c* **1460** *Towneley Myst.* xxviii. 207 When he had termynd that fight he skypt outt of his wede. *c* **1500** *Melusine* xxii. 149 Before my dayes be termyned. *a* **1618** SYLVESTER *New Hierusalem* 75 For, Death is dead, Time termined, Corruption conquer'd clean.

**b.** To form the end or termination of: cf. TERMINATE *v.* 4 b.

*c* **1532** DU WES *Introd. Fr.* in *Palsgr.* 933 They [verbs] be all termined with the above sayd termination. **1552** HULOET, Poynte terminynge a sentence, *comma.*

Hence † **Te·rmining** *vbl. sb.*

*c* **1430** *Pilgr. Lyf Manhode* IV. lxiii. (1869) 206 Deth..which is þe ende of alle eerthliche thinges, and þe terminge.

**Terminer** [1], in *oyer and terminer*: see OYER.

† **Te·rminer** [2]. *Obs.* Also 5 termynour. [a. AF. *terminour* = F. *termineur* (13th c. in Godef.), agent-n. from *terminer* to TERMINE.] **a.** One who or that which terminates, ends, or limits. **b.** One who or that which determines or decides.

[*a* **1400** LANGL. *P. Pl.* C. IV. 109 [see TERMISON quot.].] **1496** *Dives & Paup.* (W. de W.) VII. xv. 301/2 Consuetude or custome in lawe posytyue..is exposytour & termynour of the lawe. **1675** WOODHEAD, etc. *Paraphr. St. Paul* 38 The terminer and bound; the scope and aim; the perfection and accomplisher.

† **Te·rminine.** *Obs. rare*[—1]. ? Error for *termining*, or extended form of TERMINE *sb.*

*c* **1590** MARLOWE *Faust.* vi. 42 One axletree, Whose terminine [*ed.* 1616 termine] is termd the worlds wide pole.

**Terminism** (tɜ·ɹminiz'm). [mod. f. L. *terminus* end, limit + -ISM. So F. *terminisme*, G. *terminismus*.] **a.** *Philos.* The doctrine that universals are mere terms or names: = NOMINALISM b. **b.** *Theol.* The doctrine (maintained by Reichenberg at Leipzig in the 17th c.) that God has appointed a definite term or limit in the life of each individual, after which the opportunity for salvation is lost. So **Te·rminist** (cf. med.L. *terminista*), one who holds or maintains terminism (in either sense); hence **Termini·stic** *a.*

**1727–41** CHAMBERS *Cycl.*, *Terminists*, *Terministæ*, a sect or party among the Calvinists. **1758** JORTIN *Erasmus* I. 335 *note*, The Terminists were Sectaries in the high Schools. ..They oppose the Thomists, the Scotists, and the Albertists: they are also called Occamists. **1764** MACLAINE tr. *Mosheim's Eccl. Hist.* XV. II. i. § 7 The Realists maintained a manifest superiority over the Nominalists, to whom they also gave the appellation of Terminists. **1860** GARDNER *Faiths of World*, *Terministic controversy*, a dispute which arose towards the end of the seventeenth century on the question, Whether God has fixed a *terminus gratiæ*, or determinate period in the life of an individual, within which he may repent.. Those who agreed with Reichenberg received the name of *Terminists*. **1882–3** *Schaff's Encycl. Relig. Knowl.* III. 2317 (heading) Terminism and the terministic controversy.

**Terminize** (tɜ·ɹminəiz), *v. rare.* [f. L. *terminus* TERM + -IZE.] *trans.* To supply with terms; to furnish a nomenclature for.

**1899** *Army & Navy Jrnl.* 19 Aug. 1221 (Cent. Supp.) The adoption [in French] of so many English words, a condition that is paralleled in the terminizing of sports, such as football and bicycling, which crossed the Channel southward.

**Terminology** (tɜːminǫ·lŏdʒi). [mod. f. L. *termin-us*, in its med.L. sense 'term' + -LOGY: used in Ger. 1786 by Prof. C. G. Schütz of Jena: see *Kant's Briefwechsel* (1900) I. 446; so *terminologisch* 1788.] Etymologically, The doctrine or scientific study of terms; in use almost always, The system of terms belonging to any science or subject; technical terms collectively; nomenclature.

**1801** *Med. Jrnl.* V. 587 Mr. Nemnich, of Hamburg, will shortly publish a complete Nosological Dictionary.. It is to consist of two parts, in the first of which the Latin terminology will be given, and in the second, the dictionary of the above languages, relating to diseases, with a Latin explanation. **1815** KIRBY & SP. *Entomol.* (1843) I. Pref. 11 In the terminology or what, to avoid the barbarism of a word compounded of Latin and Greek, they would beg to call the orismology of the science. **1837** WHEWELL *Hist. Induct. Sc.* (1857) III. 258, I designate as Terminology the system of terms employed in the description of objects of natural history. **1847** LEWES *Hist. Philos.* (1867) II. 452 Kant, who..gave old ideas a novelty by giving them a new terminology. **1854** S. THOMSON *Wild Fl.* III. (1861) 146 Some knowledge..of botanical terms—Terminology—is requisite. **1880** HUXLEY *Crayfish* 14 Every calling has its technical terminology.

Hence **Te:rminolo·gical** *a.*, pertaining to terminology (whence **Te:rminolo·gically** *adv.*); **Termino·logist**, one versed in terminology.

**1861** F. WINSLOW *Obsc. Dis. Brain & Mind* iii. (ed. 2) 36 Who can only distinguish terminologically and locally the coarser wheels of this piece of intellectual clockwork. **1894** *Pall Mall G.* 1 Nov. 3/1 A winding road ankle deep in mud..called Orchard-street. Why an orchard was so persistently associated with this God-forsaken region is a question a terminologist only can answer. **1906** W. CHURCHILL *Sp. Ho. Com.* 22 Feb., It could not..be classified as slavery ..in the extreme acceptance of the word, without some risk of terminological inexactitude. **1907** *Month* July 57 Lynx-eyed censors, keenly on the look out for the least hint of terminological inexactitude.

**Terminus** (tɜ·ɹminŏs). Pl. **termini** (-əi). [L., = end, limit, boundary; also as in sense 2.]

† **1.** *Math.* = TERM *sb.* 11. *Obs. rare.*

**1571** DIGGES *Pantom.* II. xx. Q iv, When anye proportion is geuen, there are two Numbers wherewithall it is expressed, and they are called *Termini*.

**2.** *Anc. Rom. Myth.* (With initial capital.) The deity who presided over boundaries or landmarks.

**1600** HOLLAND *Livy* I. lv. 38 The seat and house of Terminus was not stirred, and he the god alone that was not displaced and called forth of the limits to him consecrated. **1638** SIR T. HERBERT *Trav.* (ed. 2) 15 This land is the furthest part of the old knowne world, god Terminus here especially triumphing.

**3.** A statue or bust of, or resembling those of, the god Terminus; also, the pedestal of such a statue: see TERM *sb.* 15. Sometimes, a boundary post or stone.

**1645** EVELYN *Diary* 1 Mar., Statues and antiquities.. amongst which is..a Terminus that formerly stood in the Appian Way. **1754** *Phil. Trans.* XLVIII. 822 At the several angles of the square was a terminus of marble. **1758** J. KENNEDY *Curios. Wilton House* (1786) 3 Such Termini were set at their Doors without, as the Limits and Boundaries of their houses. **1842–76** GWILT *Archit.* III. i. § 2686 What is called a *terminus*, which is, in fact, nothing more than a portion of an inverted obelisk.

**4.** The point to which motion or action tends, goal, end, finishing-point; sometimes that from which it starts; starting-point. = TERM *sb.* 1 c.

*a* **1617** BAYNE *On Eph.* (1658) 42 This condition belongeth not to the chusing but to the terminus to life. **1651** tr. *Life Father Sarpi* (1676) 86 That perfection..is the very Terminus whereunto the Church, and every faithful man ought to pretend. **1668** WILKINS *Real Char.* III. iii. 310 Some of these are Absolutely determined, either to Motion, or to Rest, or the Terminus of motion. **1868** LEVER *Bramleighs of Bp.'s Folly* I. xviii. 271, I go straight to my terminus, wherever it is.

**b.** *esp.* in phr. *terminus a quo* (= 'term from which'), *terminus ad quem* (= 'term to which').

[Phrases originating in Scholastic L.: *a* 1250 in Albertus Magnus, *Phys.* 5. 2. 2; also in Aquinas Roger Bacon, Duns Scotus, etc.]

*a* **1555** CRANMER *Lord's Supper* (Parker Soc.) 272 In nutrition *terminus a quo* is the hunger and thirst of the man; and *terminus ad quem* is the feeding and satisfying of his hunger and thirst. **1618** T. ADAMS *Vict. Patience* Wks. 1861 I. 96 So there is *terminus à quo*, from whence we are freed; and *terminus ad quem*, to which we are exalted. **1905** J. R. HARRIS *Guiding Hand of God* vii. 107, I do not regard death..as a terminus, but more and more as a starting-point... It is a *terminus a quo* and not a *terminus ad quem*. **1906** *Hibbert Jrnl.* Jan. 270 The *terminus ad quem*, or the end whither the theological movement of our age tends.

**5.** A boundary, limit. *rare.*

**1673** RAY *Journ. Low C.* 122 These Sutures I found..to be the *Termini* or boundings of certain Diaphragms or partitions, which seemed to divide the Cavity of the Shell into a multitude of..Cells. **1818** HALLAM *Mid. Ages* (1872) II. vii. II. 233 The retrocession of the Roman terminus under Adrian.

**6.** The end of a line of railway; also, the station at the end; the place at which a tram-line, etc. ends. (The common current sense.)

**1836** *Mech. Mag.* XXV. 317 Perhaps it would be well to substitute the plain English *termination* for the Latin *terminus*. **1837** R. ALDERSON in *Papers Corps Engineers* II. 94 Both lines commence from the same terminus. **1841** *Penny Cycl.* XX. 272/1 A class of buildings that have sprung up of late years, namely railway termini. **1848** LONGF. in *Life* (1891) II. 137 Long walk..to the railway terminus on the sea-shore. **1878** F. S. WILLIAMS *Midl. Railw.* 226 The..competition that arises from the working of two independent routes between the same termini. **1886** C. E. PASCOE *London of To-day* xix. (ed. 3) 192 Hand-bills and time-tables to be easily had at any terminus or railway booking-office in London. *attrib.* **1908** *Westm. Gaz.* 12 Mar. 10/2 With the coming of railways..came terminus hotels, many of which were now palatial.

**b.** *transf.* or *gen.* An end, extremity; the point at which something comes to an end.

**1855** BAIN *Senses & Int.* I. ii. § 8 (1864) 30 The grey matter [of the brain] is a terminus; to it the fibrous collections tend, or from it commence. **1860** TYNDALL *Glac.* I. xxiii. 160 The..glacier pushes its huge terminus right across the valley. **1888** GOODE *Amer. Fish* 36 It is frequently found far above the terminus of the tide. **1891** *Cent. Dict.*, *Terminus*...6. The point to which a vector carries a given or assumed point. **1906** *Blackw. Mag.* May 461/2 The rugged terminus of England seems to possess a charm of its own.

† **Termison.** *Obs. rare*[—1]. In 5 -yson, -isoun. [app. an imperfect adaptation of F. *terminaison*, TERMINATION.] = TERMINATION 6.

**1393** LANGL. *P. Pl.* C. IV. 409 An adjectif Of þre trewe termysons [*MS. M.* terminours].

**Termite** (tɜ·ɹməit). [ad. L. *termes*, *termit-em*: see TERMES. So F. *termite* (Dict. Acad. 1835).

In early use always in pl. *termites*, orig. the L. plural, in 3 syllables, of *termes*, but at length treated as Eng. and Fr. pl. in 2 syllables, whence singular *termite*: cf. -ITE 2.]

A pseudoneuropterous social insect of the genus *Termes* or family *Termitidæ*, chiefly tropical, and very destructive to timber; also called *white ant.*

**1781** SMEATHMAN in *Phil. Trans.* LXXI. 160 These turret nests, built by two different species of Termites. **1815** KIRBY & SP. *Entomol.* ix. (1818) I. 261 None of them do their business so expeditiously or effectually as the Termites. **1859** R. F. BURTON *Centr. Afr.* in *Jrnl. Geog. Soc.* XXIX. 178 They [ant-hills] are generally built by the termite under some shady tree, which prevents too rapid drying. **1880** *Even. Standard* 3 Apr. 4/3 The whole village is said to be infested with the termite, which in the head resembles greatly the ant... It attacks woodwork, which it eats away.

**b.** *attrib.*, as *termite ant*; **termite-hill**, a conical mound constructed as a nest by termites.

**1849** *Sk. Nat. Hist.*, *Mammalia* IV. 208 The Great Ant-eater, or Ant-bear... The limbs are..furnished with huge hook-like claws well adapted for making forcible entrance into the solid dwellings of the termite ants. **1871** TYLOR *Prim. Cult.* II. xv. 187 Rivers, lakes, and springs,..termite-hills, trees.

Hence **Termitary** (tɜ·ɹmitări), also in mod.L. form **termita·rium** [-ARY [1] B. 2, -ARIUM], a termites' nest; **Termitic** (təɹmi·tik) *a.*, of, pertaining to, or formed by termites; **Termitid** (tɜ·ɹmitid), **Termitine** (tɜ·ɹmitəin) *a.*, belonging to the *Termitidæ*; *sb.* an insect of this family, a termite; **Termitophagous** (-ǫ·fǎgəs) *a.* [Gr. -φαγος eating], feeding upon or devouring termites; **Termitophilous** (-ǫ·filəs) *a.* [Gr. φίλος loving], inhabiting the nests of termites, as certain beetles; so **Te·rmitophile**, a termitophilous insect.

**1863** BATES *Nat. Amazon* II. i. 63 The endless ramified galleries of which a *Termitarium is composed. **1826** KIRBY & SP. *Entomol.* IV. xlix. 478 The formicary, the *termitary, the vespiary, and the bee-hive send forth their thousands. **1881** PINTO *How I crossed Africa* I. v. 121 A soil..of *termitic formation. **1898** E. P. EVANS *Evol. Ethics* vi. 211 An advanced state of termitic civilization. **1899** *Camb. Nat. Hist.* VI. 171 One member of this genus [Leptogenys] is of *Termitophagous habits. **1886** SCHWARZ in *Proc. Entom. Soc. Washington* I. 160 In North America only a few *termitophilous species have hitherto been observed.

**Termless** (tɜ·ɹmlės), *a.* [f. TERM *sb.* + -LESS.]

**1.** Having no term or limit; boundless, endless.

*c* **1586** C'TESS PEMBROKE *Ps.* LXXXIX. xii, In tearmlesse turnes, my tearmlesse truth assuring. **1596** SPENSER *Hymn Heavenly Love* 75 Ne hath their day, ne hath their blisse, an end, But there their termelesse time in pleasure spend. **1652** BENLOWES *Theoph.* IV. xl, That pen was dipt i'th Standish of thy Blood Which wrot th' Indenture of our termless Good! **1851** RUSKIN *Mod. Paint.* I. II. IV. iii. § 14 The same..laws which require perfect simplicity of mass, require infinite and termless complication of detail.

**2.** Incapable of being expressed by terms; inexpressible, indescribable. *poet.* (Cf. PHRASELESS.)

**1597** SHAKS. *Lover's Compl.* 94 His phenix downe began but to appeare Like vnshorne veluet, on that termlesse skin.

**3.** Not dependent on or limited by any terms or conditions; unconditional.

**1902** *Westm. Gaz.* 14 Oct. 1/3 Not a peace by interruption of hostilities; but the simple, unconditioned, termless peace supplied by a 'fight to the finish'.

**Termly** (tɜ·ɹmli), *a.* Now *rare.* [f. TERM *sb.* + -LY [1]; cf. *daily*, *weekly*, *monthly*.] Occurring every term or at fixed terms; periodical; *esp.* paid or due every recurrent term or at fixed terms.

**1598** LAMBARDE *Alienations* in *Bacon's Wks.* (1879) I. 595/1 The clerks are partly rewarded by that mean also [petty fees] for their..writings, besides that termly fee which they are allowed. **1695** *Sc. Acts Will. III*, c. 64 (1822) IX. 459/2 Men..who..earn their living by daily wages or by termly hire. **1829** SCOTT *Rob Roy* Introd., Chapel Errock, where the tenants of the Duke were summoned to appear with their termly rents. **1852** HANNA *Mem. Chalmers* IV. xvii. 329 Termly subscriptions for the support of the ministers..were obtained.

**Te·rmly,** *adv.* [f. as prec. + -LY [2].] Term by term; every term, or at fixed terms; periodically.

**1484** *Exch. Rolls Scotl.* IX. 284 *note*, To be pait therof yerely and termely at the termes foresaidiis. **1598** LAMBARDE *Alienations* in *Bacon's Wks.* (1879) I. 595/1 The fees, or allowances, that are termly given to these deputies, receiver, and clerks, for recompence of these their pains. **1685** *Act of Supply* (Edin.) in *Lond. Gaz.* No. 2036/3 Payable at two Terms, viz. Whitsonday and Mertimas each year, beginning at Whitsonday next..and soforth termly. **1818** SCOTT *Rob Roy* ii, I would..put it in order for you termly, or weekly, or daily.

**Termon** (tɜ·ɹmən). *Irish Hist.* [a. OIrish *termonn* (*Annals of Ulster*, 810, 830), mod.Ir. *tearmann*, 'church-territory or -liberties, privilege, sanctuary, protection', ancient adaptation of L. *terminus* 'limit, bound'; cf. the use of Ir. *crich* 'finis, terminus', in the sense 'territory', L. *fines*.]

Anciently in Ireland, Land belonging to, or forming the precinct or liberties of a religious house, which was free and exempt from all secular charges or imposts; church land. Hence **termon-land**, church land; **Te·rmoner, termon-man** (Ir. *tearmannach*), a tenant of church land.

1533 *St. Papers Hen. VIII*, II. 164 That no Inglish lorde ..make any bande or covenaunte with any Irishman to have right ought of him, or bering of men of warre, or termons, to his awne use. 1537 *Calr. Carew MSS.* 116 Termoners. 1607 Davies *1st Let. to Earl Salisbury* Tracts (1787) 233 The rest of the spiritual lands, which the Irish call *Termons*, they were granted to sundry servitors. *Ibid.* 247 Termon doth signify, in the Irish tongue, a liberty, or freedom, and ..all Church lands whatsoever are called Termon-lands by the Irish. *Ibid.* 248 Glebe-lands, the tenants.. whereof were called Termon men, and had privilege of clergy. 1764 W. Harris tr. *Ware's Antiq. Ireland* II. i. xxxv. 233 To him [the Erenach or Herenach] also and to his Family were antiently appropriated Lands called *Termon-Lands*, as being Lands freed and discharged from all Secular Impositions, but which were liable to certain Pensions and refections. payable yearly to the Bishop. 1848 O'Donovan tr. *Ann. Irel.* 1229 All the termoners of the province. 1890 J. Healy *Insula Sanct.* 275 He plundered Clonmacnoise and its termon lands three times.

**Termor** (tɜ·ɹməɹ). *Law.* Also 4 -ur, 6–7 -our, -er. [a. AF. *termer*, f. *terme*, Term: see -er [2]. In med. L. *termināriŭs* (Du C.).] One who holds lands or tenements for a term of years, or for life; one who has a term (Term *sb.* 6).

[1292 Britton ii. xxxiii. § 4 Sicum en cas ou le chief seignur engette termers.] a 1325 *MS. Rawl. B.* 520 lf. 72 Þe prou þerof were þe termurres. 1529 *Act* 13 *Hen. VIII*, c. 15 § 1 The same Leasors..have..put the same Termers from their said Terms. 1598 Kitchin *Courts Leet*, etc. (1675) 89 Glass fixt by the Termor, the Lessor cannot distrain for his Rent. a 1631 Donne *To R. Woodward* xi, Wee are but termers of our selues, yet may, If we can stocke our selues, and thriue, uplay Much, much deare treasure for the great rent day. 1818 Cruise *Digest* (ed. 2) I. 500 When terms for years became fully established, and the interest of the termor was secured against the effect of fictitious recoveries, long terms for years were frequently created.

**Te·rm-time.** The time of term.

a. The period during which the law-courts are in session; the period of study at a university or school: see Term *sb.* 5.

1426 *Rolls of Parlt.* V. 408/2 That oute of Terme tyme, nothyng be spedd in the Counsaille. 1435 *Ibid.* I. 491/1 All the high Courtes..been sette and holden..duryng all the four terme tymes of the yere. 1562–3 *Act* 5 *Eliz.* c. 23 § 2 One Writ of Capias..returneable in the same Courte, in the Terme tyme. 1600–12 Rowlands *Four Knaves* (Percy Soc.) 6 A country blew-coate serving man, In tearme-time sent to towne. 1721 Amherst *Terræ Fil.* No. 47 (1754) 251 The heads of colleges and halls..are obliged to assemble..every monday throughout the year, in vacation-time as well as in term-time. 1849 Thackeray *Pendennis* xxix, In term-time Mr. Pen showed a most praiseworthy regularity in..eating his dinners in Hall.

b. In Scotland, the time or season of either term, Whitsuntide or Martinmas.

*Mod.* The rent payable at term-time.

**Tern** (tɜɹn), *sb.*[1] Also 7 **terne**. [Of Norse origin: cf. Da. *terne*, Sw. *tärna*, Norw. and Færo. *terna*:—ON. *þerna*, the tern or sea swallow.

Some consider *tern* to be related to *stearn, stern*, which occurs in OE. as a bird-name, and, in the form *starn*, is a name in E Anglia of the Common and the Black Tern; it is mentioned by W. Turner *Avium præcipuarum historia*, 1544, as 'nostrati lingua *sterna* appellata', whence Linnæus took *Sterna* as a generic name.]

The common name of a group of sea-birds of the genus *Sterna*, or sub-family *Sterninæ*, akin to the gulls, but having generally a more slender body, long pointed wings, and a forked tail; a sea swallow.

Of the species, which are widely diffused from Arctic to extreme southern coasts, the British Museum Catalogue reckons more than 50, of which 33 are placed in the genus *Sterna*, and about 18 distributed in ten other genera. Of these, six are considered indigenous to the British coasts, and many more to those of N. America. The Common Tern of Britain and N. America is *Sterna hirundo* (or *fluviatilis*); the Sandwich T., the largest British species, now scarce, is *S. cantiaca*; the Arctic T., *S. macrura*; the Roseate T., *S. dougalli*; the Little T., *S. minuta*; the Black Tern, *Hydrochelidon* (formerly *Sterna*) *nigra*.

1678 Ray *Willughby's Ornith.* 352 This [Black Tern, *Sterna nigra*] is also the brown Tern of Mr. Johnson. *Ibid.* 353 In the Northern parts they call them Terns, whence Turner calls them in Latine, *Sternæ*. 1785 Latham *Gen. Syn.* III. ii. 356 Sandwich Tern...This species is pretty common on the coasts of Kent. 1832 Ht. Martineau *Ella of Gar.* iii, The terns and gulls screaming. 1888 Newton in *Encycl. Brit.* XXIII. 189/1 The Sandwich Tern, *S. sandvicensis* or *S. cantiaca*..is the largest of the British species.

**Tern** (tɜɹn), *a.* and *sb.*[2] [As adj., ad. L. *ternī* three each. As sb., app. a. F. *terne* (15th c.).]

† **A.** *adj. Bot.* Arranged in threes; ternate.

1760 J. Lee *Introd. Bot.* iii. xxii. (1788) 242 The Peduncle ..is said to be..*Tern*, or *three* from the same Axilla. *Ibid.* xxiii. 252 In respect to Opposition, opposite Leaves will sometimes become tern, quatern, or quine, growing by Threes, Fours, or Fives. 1828 in Webster.

**B.** *sb.* **1.** A set of three; a trio, triplet. *spec.* † **a.** *pl.* [F. *un terne*, formerly *ternes*:—L. *ternās*.] A double three in dice-playing. (In quot. *fig.*) *Obs.* **b.** In a lottery, three winning numbers drawn together; a prize gained by such a drawing. **c.** A group of three stanzas.

13.. *Coer de L.* 2009 King Richard held a tronchon true ..Ternes and quernes he gave him there. 1856 Mrs. Browning *Aur. Leigh* vii. 1247 She'd win a tern in Thursday's lottery. 1869 Browning *Ring & Bk.* xii. 158 But that he forbid The Lottery, why, Twelve were Tern Quatern! 1879 Furnivall *Chaucer's Min. P.* 419 This late Poem [*Envoy to Scogan*] composed of two Terns and an Envoy.

2. *Math.* A system of three pairs of conjugate triads of planes which together contain the twenty-seven straight lines lying in a cubic surface (i. e. one represented by an equation of the third degree).

1891 in *Cent. Dict.*

3. A three-masted schooner; a three-master. (Local, New Eng.) (*Cent. Dict.* 1891.)

† **Tern**, *v. Obs.* Also 5 **teern**. [ad. med.L. *tern-āre* ? to treble: cf. F. *terner* 'to throw a tre[y] or three' (Cotgr. 1611).] ? To throw a tern or terns in dice-playing. Hence † **Terned** *ppl. a.*, † **Te·rning** *vbl. sb.*

c 1440 *Promp. Parv.* 489/2 Ternyd, in pley or oþer thyngys (*S.* teernyt in pley or other lyk), *ternatus*. Ternyn, yn gamys pleyynge, *terno*. Ternynge, *ternatus, ternacio*.

**Tern**: see Terne *a.*[1]; obs. var. Turn *v.* and *sb.*

**Terna** (tɜ·ɹnă). [a. L. *terna* (*nomina*) three (names) at once.] In *R. C. Ch.* A list of three names submitted to the Pope or other authority to choose from.

1895 *Tablet* 28 Dec. 1030 A terna has been received at Propaganda for the appointment of a Coadjutor to the Bishop of Southwark. 1903 *Daily Chron.* 20 July 5/3 While Abbot —— is prominent on the terna, I am assured that the Bishop of ——'s name..does not appear.

**Ternado**, obs. form of Tornado.

**Ternal** (tɜ·ɹnăl), *a. rare.* [ad. med.L. *ternāl-is*, f. *tern-ī* distrib. numeral, 'three by three', f. *ter* thrice: see -al. So OF. *ternal* (15th c. in Godef.).]

1. Consisting of three; threefold, triple.

1599 A. M. tr. *Gabelhouer's Bk. Physicke* 193/1 Madefye therin a ternall reduplicated cloth [explained by 'trebled' in 'The Expositione of such wordes as are in this Booke derived of the Latines']. 1657 Tomlinson *Renou's Disp.* 652 The Oyl..by its ternal maceration..acquires more vertue. a 1680 Charnock in Spurgeon *Treas. Dav.* Ps. xcix. 3 A ternal repetition of his holiness.

2. Third (of each group of three); = Ternary 3.

1804 Southey in *Ann. Rev.* II. 526 [Of *Lybeaus Desconus*] The four ternal lines rhyming..and also the two first couplets. [The stanzas rime: aad, aad, bbd, ccd.]

**Ternar, terner** (tɜ·ɹnəɹ). *Obs.* exc. *Hist.* [ad. late L. *ternāri-us*: see Ternary.] A student of the third or lowest rank at St. Andrews, and app. in other of the Scottish Universities.

1698 (July) *Minute, St. Leonard's Coll., St. Andrews*, Many are of opinion that the distinctions of Primar, Secondar, and Ternar, ought to be taken away. 1807 Grierson *St. Andrews* 160 The Terners had gowns of an inferior sort of cloth, without trimming, and paid one guinea and a half of fees. Seconders and Terners are the only distinctions now in use. 1827 *Evid. Commissioners Scot. Univ.* (1837) III. 35 (St. Andrews) The Primars are the sons of Noblemen; the Secondars are what they call Gentlemen Commoners in England; and the Ternars are those of the common ranks of life. They pay different fees according to the rank they hold. 1907 Lang *Hist. Scot.* IV. xiii. 407 Men who could afford to pay a Secondar's fee often entered themselves as Ternars.

**Ternariant** (təɹnē°·riănt). *Math.* [f. Ternary + the ending of Invariant, etc.] (See quots.)

1882 Sylvester in *Amer. Jrnl. Math.* V. 81 *note*, I am inclined to substitute the word binariant for subinvariants, and to speak of simple, double, treble or multiple binariants. The functions similarly related to ternary forms will then be styled simple or multiple ternariants. 1890 Forsyth *ibid.* XII. 1 *note*, It has proved convenient to use the word 'ternariants' as a generic term for concomitants of ternary quantics, instead of giving it the signification which Prof. Sylvester..proposed,..viz. the leading coefficients of those concomitants.

**Ternary** (tɜ·ɹnări), *a.* and *sb.* [ad. late L. *ternārius* consisting of three, f. *tern-ī*: see Ternal and -ary [1]. Cf. F. *ternaire* (15th c.).]

**A.** *adj.* **1.** Pertaining to, consisting of, compounded of, or characterized by a set (or sets) of three; threefold, triple. *Ternary system* (of classification), one in which each division is into three parts.

c 1430 *Art Nombryng* 19 Some vsen forto distingue the nombre by threes, and ay begynne forto wirche vndre the first of the last ternary other uncomplete nombre. 1596 Bell *Surv. Popery* ii. ii. vi. 169 The ternarie number doth not determine the apparitions in themselues. 1603 Holland *Plutarch's Mor.* 1302 This ternary or threefold number. 1659 Owen *Div. Orig. Script.* Wks. 1853 XVI. 340 The Trinity..is a trinity in unity, or the ternary number of persons in the same essence. 1715 Cheyne *Philos. Princ. Relig.* ii. 129 The Profane and Ignorant may make a Jest of this Ternary Chain. 1724 Waterland *Further Vind. Christ's Div.* iv. § 10 The equality is mentioned as belonging to the ternary number, here considered as a figure of the Trinity. 1881 Westcott & Hort *Grk. N. T.* Introd. § 152 Ternary variations in which each of the three groups approximately attests a different variant. 1909 *Cent. Dict.* Suppl. s.v. *Symmetry*, If [the angle is] 120°, or the crystal repeats itself three times, the symmetry is threefold or ternary and the axis is a triad axis.

b. *Mus. Ternary measure* or *time*: triple time (? *obs.*). *Ternary form*: the form of a movement which is founded on three principal subjects (cf. *binary form*), or in which the principal subject recurs three times (= *rondo form*).

[1597 Morley *Introd. Mus.* Annot., The last of the two minimes is marked with a pricke..for perfections sake, that the ternary number may be obserued.] 1727–41 Chambers *Cycl.* s.v. *Measure*, Ternary, or triple measure, is..where two minims are played during a fall, and but one in a rise. 1898 Stainer & Barrett *Dict. Mus. Terms*, *Ternary form*, rondo form. *Ternary measure*, triple time. 1908 *Athenæum* 18 July 78/1 Another interesting instance of modification is that of binary form, which by expansion became ternary.

c. *Chem.* and *Min.* Compounded or consisting of three elements or constituents.

† By Dalton used in the sense 'Consisting of three atoms'.

1808 Henry in *Phil. Trans.* XCVIII. 283 Oxygen, hydrogen, and carbon, united in the form of a ternary compound. 1808 Dalton *Chem. Philos.* i. 213 If there are two bodies, A and B,..1 atom of A + 2 atoms of B = 1 atom of D, ternary. 1846 J. Baxter *Libr. Pract. Agric.* (ed. 4) I. 22 These ternary compounds, such as starch, gum, sugar,..are non-nitrogenized. 1851 Richardson *Geol.* 464 *Perfect granite* is a ternary compound of quartz, felspar, and di-axial mica, universally diffused. 1864 H. Spencer *Biol.* I. 11 In chemical stability these ternary compounds..are in a marked degree below the binary ones.

d. *Bot.* Arranged in threes around a common axis: usually in reference to the parts of a flower.

1830 Lindley *Nat. Syst. Bot.* 251 The ternary division of the flower of Monocotyledons is often departed from..; many Dicotyledons have also ternary floral envelopes. 1866 *Treas. Bot.*, *Ternary, ternate*, when three things are in opposition round a common axis. 1870 Hooker *Stud. Flora* 12 Berberideæ..analogy..in the 3-nary floral whorls with Monocotyledons.

e. *Math.* Constructed on the number three as a base, as *ternary logarithm, ternary scale* (of notation); involving three variables, as *ternary quantic*.

1860 Cayley *Math. Papers* IV. 604 The number of variables (the function being homogeneous) is denoted by the words *binary, ternary*, &c. 1898 *Ibid.* XIV. Index, Ternary Quadratics...Ternary Quadrics...Ternary Quantics.

f. *Astron. Ternary system*, a system of three stars which revolve under mutual attraction, or round a common centre.

† 2. *Ternary part*, one of three equal parts; a third part. *Obs. rare*—[1].

1599 A. M. tr. *Gabelhouer's Bk. Physicke* 108/2 Which poulder we must diuide into 3 æquall portions, then take therof a ternary parte.

3. Last of each successive group of three; third.

1690 Leybourn *Curs. Math.* 339 [In extracting roots] Squares..are to be marked with Points..over every Binary or second Figure. Cubes over every Ternary Figure.

4. Third in subordination, rank, or order.

1826 Kirby & Sp. *Entomol.* xlviii. IV. 443 This system ..in its ternary groups, equivalent to the Orders of Linné [etc.]. 1829 Gen. P. Thompson *Exerc.* (1842) I. 135 The only wonder is, that when they went to the secondary sense, they did not go to the ternary. 1831 Carlyle *Misc.* (1857) II. 263 In a secondary and even a ternary reflex.

**B.** *sb.* † **1.** A set or group of three; a ternion, a trio. *Obs.*

1460 Capgrave *Chron.* Ded. (Rolls) 3 Make in ȝoure soule to [= two] ternaries, on [= one] in feith anothir in love: beleve in God—Fadir, and Son, and Holy Gost: love God in al ȝoure hert, al ȝoure soule, and al ȝoure mynde. 1542 Recorde *Gr. Artes* (1575) 48 Put a pricke ouer the fourthe Figure,..ouer the vij...and so forthe, still leauing two figures betweene eche two pricks. And those two roomes betweene the prickes, are called Ternaries. 1654 Whitlock *Zootomia* 377, I conclude this Ternary of Worthies with Cato. 1686 tr. *Livy* i. i. xxiv. 15 There happened to be..three Brothers in each Army...The two Kings treated with these two ternaries of Brethren. 1779–81 Johnson *L. P.*, *Gray* ¶ 28 The second ternary of stanzas [in *The Progress of Poetry*].

† b. The Holy Trinity. [So OF. *ternaire*.] *Obs.*

1570 Dee *Math. Pref.* *j b, By the infinite goodnes of the Almighty Ternarie. 1662 Sparrow tr. *Behme's Rem. Wks.*, *1st Apol. to B. Tylcken* 79 There was Joy in Heaven *in Ternario Sancto*, in the Holy Ternary.

† 2. A number which is a multiple of three. *rare*—[1].

1557 Recorde *Whetst.* (1558) O iv b, Thei muste all waies bee ternaries, as 3. 6. 9. or 12. &c.

Hence † **Te·rnariness** *Obs. rare*, ternary condition. So † **Terna·rian**, † **Terna·rious** *adjs.*, = Ternary *a.*

1656 Blount *Glossogr.*, *Ternary, Ternarious*, of or belonging to three. 1662 J. Chandler *Van Helmont's Oriat.* 266 So the likeness of ternariness shall cease, & such an image shall badly square with the Type, whose image it is believed to be. 1715–20 Pope *Iliad* III. 214 The ternarian number.

**Ternate** (tɜ·ɹnĕt), *a.* [ad. mod.L. *ternāt-us* (in Linnæus 1750), in form pa. pple. of med.L. *ternāre* (*Promp. Parv.*) to treble or make threefold. Cf. F. *terné* (1783 in Hatz.-Darm.).] Produced or arranged in threes; *spec. Bot.* applied to a compound leaf composed of three leaflets, or to leaves arranged in whorls of three; also to leaflets borne on secondary or tertiary similarly arranged petioles (*biternate, triternate*).

1760 J. Lee *Introd. Bot.* iii. vi. (1765) 188 *Biternate*, or *Duplicato-Ternate*, when there are three Folioles on a Petiole, and each Foliole is Ternate. 1785 Martyn *Rousseau's Bot.* xvi. (1794) 177 The species is distinguished by its ternate leaves. 1812 *New Bot. Gard.* i. 28 The leaf [of *Anemone nemorosa*] is doubly ternate. 1861 Miss Pratt *Flower. Pl.* I. 4 A ternate leaf consists of three leaflets on a common stalk, as in the Clover.

So † **Te·rnated** *a. Obs. rare*—[1].

1753 Chambers *Cycl. Supp.* s.v. *Leaf*, Ternated Leaf, a compound one,..of three leaves on a common petiole.

**Ternately** (tǝ̄·ɹnėtli), *adv.* [f. TERNATE *a.* + -LY [2].] In a ternate manner; in threes.

1860 in WORCESTER citing GRAY. 1870 HOOKER *Stud. Flora* 167 Angelica...Leaves ternately 2-pinnate. 1897 A. DRUCKER tr. *Ihering's Evol. Aryan* 120 According to their duodecimal system, the Babylonians must have calculated their time for work and rest ternately: three sets or relays of working periods, each of three hours.

**Ternatisect** (tǝɹnǣ·tisekt), *a. Bot.* [f. mod. L. *ternāt-us* TERNATE + *sect-us* cut.] Cut into three lobes, the divisions extending to the midrib.

1870 HOOKER *Stud. Flora* 8 Ranunculus bulbosus..leaves 3-foliolate or ternatisect.

**Ternato-pinnate** (tǝɹnǣ·to,pi·nėt), *a. Bot.* [f. mod.L. *ternāt-us* TERNATE (after Greek combining forms in *-o*) + PINNATE.] Applied to a compound leaf having three pinnate divisions proceeding from a common petiole.

1857 HENFREY *Bot.* 60 What are called biternate and triternate compound leaves are in most cases pinnate leaves with unijugate and terminal leaflets. Such leaves should perhaps be called *ternato-pinnate* or *bi-ternato-pinnate*, &c.

**Terne**, *a.*[1] (*sb.*[1]) *Obs.* exc. as F. (tęrn). Also 6 tern. [a. F. *terne* dull, tarnished (15th c. in Godef.); of doubtful origin: see TARNISH *v.*]

†1. Gloomy; fierce. *Sc. Obs.* Also †**Terned** *a.*

1508 DUNBAR *Tua Mariit Wemen* 261 Thought ȝe as tygris be terne, be tretable in luf. *a* 1568 *O wicked Wemen*, etc. 15 in *Bannatyne Poems* (Hunter. Cl.) 769 Als terne as tygir, of tung vntollerable, O thow violent virago vennemous. 1638 R. BAILLIE *Lett. & Jrnls.* (1841) I. 160 The Moderator a most grave and wise man yet naturally somewhat terned took me up a little accurtlie.

†b. as *sb.* Gloom. *Sc. Obs. rare*⁻¹.

1500–20 DUNBAR *Poems* lxxxv. (*Ballat of Our Lady*) 7 Our tern inferne for to dispern, Helpe rialest rosyne.

‖ 2. (as Fr.) Dull, lacking brilliancy of colouring.

1901 *Daily News* 5 Feb. 6/5 In the large sketch from Tintoret's 'Adoration',..the colour is dull and terne.

**Terne** (tǝ̄ɹn), *a.*[2] and *sb.*[2] [The first element in *terne-plate* as a separate word.] **a.** *adj.* Of or pertaining to terne-plate. **b.** *sb.* = TERNE-PLATE.

1891 *Pall Mall G.* 9 Sept. 6/3 The terne mixture does not adhere to the sheets of iron, but runs off like quicksilver from certain parts of the sheet. 1904 *Daily Chron.* 15 Dec. 5/5 To the end of November he thought they would have shipped more tin, terne, and galvanised sheets than during any year in the history of Great Britain.

**Terne**, obs. f. TARN. **Terned**: see TERNE *a.*[1] 1.

**Terne-plate** (tǝ̄·ɹnplėt). Also tern-. [prob. f. TERNE *a.*[1], dull, lacking brilliancy, in reference to the dullness of terne-plate, in comparison with tin-plate.] Thin sheet-iron coated with an alloy of lead and tin; an inferior kind of tin-plate; a sheet or plate of this. Also *attrib.*

1858 SIMMONDS *Dict. Trade, Terne-plates*, thin sheet-iron coated with an amalgam of tin and lead. 1880 *Echo* 15 Oct. 2/4 Some unscrupulous packers are using terne plates instead of tin plates. 1892 *Pall Mall G.* 10 Dec. 7/1 Inferior plates, known as tern-plates and mostly used for roofing, contain a great deal of lead. 1894 [see TAGGER[1] 4]. 1907 G. E. DUCKERING *Parl. Rep. Tinning Metals* 8 No evidence of lead absorption is to be found among terne-plate workers.

**Terner**: see TERNAR.

**Ternery** (tǝ̄·ɹnǝri). *rare.* [f. TERN *sb.*[1] + -ERY.] A place where terns congregate to breed.

1891 in *Cent. Dict.*

**Ternion** (tǝ̄·ɹniǫn). [ad. L. *terniōn-em* a company of three, a triad.]

1. A set of three (things or persons); a triad.

1587 HOLINSHED *Chron.* III. 207/2 A quadrangle in geometrie compriseth in it a triangle, and a quaternion in arithmetike conteineth a ternion. 1600 HOLLAND *Livy* xxv. v. 548 The Senate..agreed that there should bee chosen two Ternions of Triumvirs. 1652 BP. HALL *Invis. World* I. § 7 Disposing them [angels] into Ternions of three general Hierarchies. *a* 1661 FULLER *Worthies, Surrey* (1662) III. 83 That happy Ternion of Brothers, whereof two eminent Prelats, the third, Lord Mayor of London. 1820 SOUTHEY *Wesley* I. 56 When I have such a Ternion to prosecute that war.

2. A quire of three sheets, each folded in two.

1609 *Skene's Reg. Maj.* H h iij b *note*, All the letters..are Ternions, or thrie sheetes in one, except *H h* in the last Alphabet. 1886 *Amer. Jrnl. Philol.* Apr. 27 They say that a given manuscript is composed of quaternions and of ternions.

**Ternity, ternyte**, obs. forms of TRINITY.

**Ternstrœmiaceous** (tǝɹnstrǣmiǣ·ʃǝs), *a. Bot.* [f. mod.L. *Ternstrœmiāceæ* (f. *Ternstrœmia*, a genus named after Ternström, a Swedish naturalist) + -OUS.] Belonging to the *Ternstrœmiaceæ*, an order of tropical trees and shrubs, with showy white (sometimes pink or red) flowers, generally borne in racemes; it includes the tea-plant and the camellia, and many plants valued as flowering shrubs.

1885 H. O. FORBES *Nat. Wand. E. Archip.* 400 Through dense forest, full of Ternstrœmiaceous trees.

†**Tero·gatores**, obs. aphetic f. *interrogatories*: see INTERROGATORY *sb.*

1511–12 *Rec. St. Mary at Hill* 279 Costes of þe spirituall courte..paid for wryting of the terogatores, iij s. iiij d.

‖ **Terp** (tǝ̄ɹp). Pl. **terpen** (also *erron.* used as sing.). [WFris. *terp* village mound, pl. *terpen*, = EFris. *terp* (Saterland), NFris. *têrp* (Sylt), *sarp* (Amrum) village:—OFris. *therp*, umlaut variant of OFris. *thorp* village: cf. THORP.] An artificial mound or hillock, the site of a prehistoric village, and still in many cases occupied by a village or church, in parts of Friesland below sea-level or liable to inundation. Also *attrib.*

These *terpen*, like the Italian *terremare* or terramares, have in modern times been excavated for the sake of the fertilizing soil which they yield, and more recently for the prehistoric remains found in them; the name has thus passed into archæological use.

[1838 *Penny Cycl.* X. 481/1 The whole land is flat..nor is there an eminence throughout it excepting some mounds, here called 'terpen', on which the antient Frisians were accustomed to take refuge in seasons of marine inundations.] 1866 *Jrnl. R. Agric. Soc. Eng.* II. I. 153 On the seaside little hillocks, 13 feet to 19½ feet high, may be observed at short distances: they are called *Terpens.* These hillocks were formed by the hand of man; and when opened, their contents prove that they belong to an ante-historical epoch. 1889 *Scott. Leader* 15 Jan. 7/1 An account of a visit to a terp mound at Aalzum in North Friesland..by Dr. Robert Munro. *Ibid.*, The general character of the antiquities found is that of the Iron Age. In the museum at Leewarden there are two rooms devoted exclusively to the antiquities from the terpen mounds. 1899 MUNRO *Prehist. Scott.* x. 401 Double-edged combs like those from the Terp-mounds in Holland. *Ibid.* xi. 436 The terpen are largely excavated on account of their rich ammoniacal deposits.

**Terpene** (tǝ̄·ɹpīn). *Chem.* [f. *terp-* in *terp-entin*, obs. f. TURPENTINE, with suffix -ENE, used in forming the names of hydrocarbons related to BENZENE. Formerly called TEREBENE.] A general name of hydrocarbons having the formula $C_{10}H_{16}$, many of which occur in the volatile oils of plants, chiefly of the coniferous and aurantiaceous orders. The commonest is PINENE, the chief constituent of turpentine-oil.

Sometimes used to include hydrocarbons of formula $C_5H_8$, and its polymers $C_{10}H_{16}$, $C_{15}H_{24}$, $C_{20}H_{32}$, etc.

[1866 KEKULÉ *Lehrb. Organ. Chemie* II. 437.] 1873 WATTS *Fownes' Chem.* (ed. 11) 778 Terpenes are volatile oils, existing in plants. 1885 REMSEN *Org. Chem.* (1888) 311 Artificial camphor..when heated alone, or with bases,..gives off hydrochloric acid, and a terpene different from the oil of turpentine is formed. 1902 POND tr. *Heusler's Chem. Terpenes* 17 Those hydrocarbons which have the empirical constitution $C_5H_8$ are termed terpenes. Four main classes are recognised: *Hemiterpenes*, $C_5H_8$, *Terpenes proper*, $C_{10}H_{16}$, *Sesquiterpenes*, $C_{15}H_{24}$, *Polyterpenes*, $(C_5H_8)x$.

Hence **Terpeny·lic** [f. TERPENE + -YL + -IC], in *terpenylic acid*, a white crystalline compound, $C_8H_{12}O_4$, obtained by oxidizing a terpene, as turpentine-oil, with chromic acid.

1881 WATTS *Dict. Chem.* VIII. 1907 Terpenylic acid..is obtained at first in the form of a syrup resembling glycerol. ..Terpenylic acid is monobasic.

**Terpentin**, early form of TURPENTINE.

**Terpiche**, i. e. *tar-pitch*: see TAR *sb.* 4.

**Terpin** (tǝ̄·ɹpin). *Chem.* Also -ine. [f. as TERPENE + -IN [1].] A derivative of pinene and other terpenes, $C_{10}H_{18}(OH)_2$, of which two modifications are known, *cisterpin*, melting at 103° C., and *transterpin*, at 156° C. **Terpin-hydrate**, a crystalline compound obtained by shaking turpentine-oil with alcohol acidified with sulphuric or nitric acid.

1848 *Chem. Gaz.* 1 Aug. 296 On the so-called Hydrate of Oil of Turpentine...Its name had consequently to be altered, and the author [Dr. C. List] adopts that of *terpine*, proposed for it by Berzelius. 1868 WATTS *Dict. Chem.* V. 923 Terpin-hydrate usually crystallises in large rhombic prisms. 1894 MORLEY & MUIR *Watts' Dict. Chem.* IV. 665/2 Terpin is best known in the form of its hydrate,..a beautifully crystalline compound which on heating to 100° loses water and leaves terpin as a vitreous mass.

Hence **Te·rpinene**, a terpene occurring in oil of cardamom; **Terpi·neol**, formerly (and still in Pharmacy) **Te·rpinol**: see quots.; **Terpi·nolene**, a terpene obtained by Wallach in 1885.

1848 *Chem. Gaz.* 1 Aug. 297 Terpinole is a colourless, very liquid oil, with the agreeable odour of hyacinths. *Ibid.* 298 When terpine is heated with concentrated hydriodic acid, it is converted into terpinole. 1857 MILLER *Elem. Chem.* III. vii. § 1. 442 Terpinol. 1894 MORLEY & MUIR *Watts' Dict. Chem.* IV. 665/1 Terpineol..is a viscous liquid, having an odour of white lilac. 1902 POND tr. *Heusler's Chem. Terpenes* 105 Terpinolene is obtained by boiling terpine hydrate, terpineol, or cineole with dilute sulphuric acid. *Ibid.* 112 Terpinene escaped the notice of the earlier investigators because they assumed that it was identical with dipentene. Wallach recognized it as a definite terpene. *Ibid.* 254 The name terpineol was formerly used to designate a substance which to-day is recognized as a mixture of isomeric alcohols, $C_{10}H_{17}OH$.

†**Terpo·dion.** *Obs.* [app. f. Gr. τέρπ-ειν to delight + ᾠδή song: cf. *melodion*, etc.] Name given to a musical instrument, invented in 1816 and improved in 1832, but never actually in use.

1834 *Mus. Libr.* Suppl., Sept. 69 A concert has been given here by Prof. Buschmann and his son, both playing on the terpodion invented by the father. 1842 *Mech. Mag.* XXXVII. 563 Nearly allied to the instrument consisting of tuning forks is the terpodion [*pr.* -ian], but the vibrating springs instead of being in the form of forks are cylindrical rods of metal. 1898 STAINER & BARRETT *Dict. Mus. Terms, Terpodion*, an instrument..resembling in appearance the pianoforte, but the tone was produced from blocks of wood struck with hammers.

†**Terpoile**, *a. Sc. Obs.* Also 6 **tere pyle.** [a. OF. *a treis poils* three-pile.] Of patterned velvet, etc.: Three-pile; pile upon pile.

1489 *Acc. Ld. High Treas. Scot.* I. 135, v elne and a half of terpoile veluus for a halff lang gowne to the King. 150[illegible] DOUGLAS *Pal. Hon.* 542 Satine figures.., Damesflure, tere pyle, quhairon thair lyis Peirle.

‖ **Terpsichore** (tǝɹpsi·kŏrĭ). [a. Gr. Τερψιχόρη 'dance-enjoying', name of the Muse of dancing and of the dramatic chorus, f. τέρπειν to delight + χορός dance, CHORUS.] The Muse of dancing; hence, a female dancer; dancing as an art.

1711 SHAFTESB. *Charac.* (1737) I. 317 The Thalia's, the Polyhymnia's, the Terpsychore's, the Euterpe's willingly join their parts. 1756–7 tr. *Keysler's Trav.* (1760) III. 427 Stranger, approach, behold this homely chair, Which e'en Terpsichore herself might chuse. 1906 *19th Cent.* Mar. 457 We should lament the death of Terpsichore.

Hence **Terpsichorean** (tǝɹpsikŏrī·ăn) *a.*, of, pertaining to, or of the nature of dancing; saltatory. So **Terpsichore·al** *a.* (*rare*) in same sense; hence **Terpsichore·ally** *adv.*, by means of dancing.

1869 *Daily News* 19 May, The loving couples..hold themselves aloof from the busy hum, or mix in it for *terpsichoreal or restorative purposes only. 1900 *Ibid.* 12 Mar. 8/4 A poem, 'Voltigia', which poem the 'Tenth Muse' condescends to interpret *terpsichoreally. 1825 T. HOOK *Sayings* Ser. II. *Sutherl.* (Colburn) 26 She had seen their *Terpsichorean evolutions. 1865 DICKENS *Mut. Fr.* I. xi, An entirely new view of the Terpsichorean art. 1899 *Allbutt's Syst. Med.* VIII. 98 Sometimes a series of coordinated gestures and movements [in hysterical persons] constitute a regular terpsichorean display.

**Terpylo·nic**, *a. Chem.* [f. as TERP-ENE + -YL + -ONE + -IC.] In *terpylonic acid*, $C_9H_{14}O_6$, a product of the oxidation of turpentine by mixture with chromic acid.

1894 MORLEY & MUIR *Watts' Dict. Chem.* IV. 672/2.

**Terr**, obs. form of TAR.

**Terr.**, abbrev. for TERRACE, TERRITORY (*U. S.*).

‖ **Terra** (te·ră). L. (and It.) *terra* earth, used, with qualifying adjectives, to form the names of medicinal and other earths, boles, and the like, as **terra alba**, pipe-clay; **terra cariosa**, tripoli or rottenstone; **terra chia**, also *chia terra*, Chian earth, an astringent and cosmetic bole formerly obtained from the island of Chios; see also quot. 1615; **terra foliata (tartari)**, = *foliated earth of tartar*, potassium acetate; **terra merita** = TURMERIC; **terra nera** [Ital. 'black earth'], see quot.; **terra nobilis**, an old name for the diamond (Ogilvie, Annandale, 1882); **terra ponderosa**, barium sulphate, heavy spar. See also TERRA FIRMA, T. JAPONICA, etc.

1871 NAPHEYS *Prev. & Cure Dis.* I. ii. 79 The insoluble white clay known in commerce as **terra alba.* 1823 CRABB *Technol. Dict.*, **Terra cariosa*..rotten stone; a species of non effervescent chalk, of a brown colour. 1615 G. SANDYS *Trav.* 12 It [Chios] hath..a certaine greene earth like the rust of brasse, which the Turkes call *Terra Chia: but not that so reputed of by the ancient Physitions. 1753 CHAMBERS *Cycl. Supp.* s. v., *Chia Terra*, in the materia medica of the antients, an earth of the marle-kind, found in the island of Chio. *Ibid.*, **Terra foliata tartari.* 1758 REID tr. *Macquer's Chym.* I. 122 This solution being evaporated to dryness leaves a matter in the form of leaves lying on each other; on which account it hath obtained the name of *Terra Foliata.* 1753 CHAMBERS *Cycl. Supp.*, **Terra merita*, ..a name given by some..to the curcuma, or turmeric-root. 1882 OGILVIE, **Terra nera*..a native, unctuous pigment, used by the ancient artists in fresco, oil, and tempera painting. 1794 SULLIVAN *View Nat.* I. 250 *Terra ponderosa.

‖ **Terra a terra.** *Obs.* Also 7 **terra terra**, (**territerr**), 8–9 **terre à terre.** [It. *terra terra* level with the ground, influenced by corresp. F. *terre à terre*, Sp. *tierra á tierra.*]

1. An artificial gait formerly taught to horses, resembling a low curvet.

[1611 COTGR., *Manege de terre à terre*, a manage more low, and more quicke then the ordinarie gallop, or curuet.] 1614 MARKHAM *Cheap Husb.* (1623) 29 In this practise you teach him [the horse] perfectly three lessons together, that is the turne Terra Terra, the Incavalare, and the Chambetta. *a* 1648 LD. HERBERT *Life* (1886) 74 The most useful *aer*, as the Frenchmen term it, is territerr. 1730 BAILEY (folio), *Terra a terra*..is a Series of low Leaps made by the Horse forward, bearing Sideways, and working upon two Treads.

2. Applied to a kind of dance. Also *fig.* and *attrib.* Without elevation of style.

(Fr. *terre à terre* 'pas de danse qui s'exécute sans sauter' Roquefort 1829.)

1727–41 CHAMBERS *Cycl.*, *Terra a terra*..applied by the French to dancers, who cut no capers, nor scarce quit the ground. And hence it is also figuratively applied to authors, whose style and diction is low and creeping. 1797 *Encycl. Brit.* (ed. 3) V. 668/1 The grander sort of dancing, and *terre à terre*, is the best adapted to such dancers. 1888 *Athenæum* 6 Oct. 443/3 His very matter-of-factness, his *terre-à-terre* fidelity to his authorities. 1898 *Daily News* 25 Oct. 2/3 It is so 'true', and yet just removed from that terre-à-terre fact which distinguishes so much portraiture.

**Terrabill, terrable**, obs. ff. TERRIBLE.

**Terrace** (te·rĕs), *sb.* Forms: α. 6 terries, 6–7 terrasse, (6 terres, 6–7 terris, 7 -ice), 7–9 terrass, -as, (8 -ase), 6– terrace. β. 6–7 tarrass(e, (tarris, -es), 6–8 tarras, -ace, 7 tarasse, (tarrase, taras), taris, tarries. [a. F. *terrace* (12th c.), also *terrasse*, *tarrasse* (15th c.), rubble, a platform, a terrace, = It. *terraccia*, *-azza* bad earth or soil, 'filthie earth' (Florio), also a terrace, later †*terraccio*, now *terrazzo*, Sp. *terrazo*, Pg. *terraço* terrace, med.L. *terrācea, -ācia* an earthen mound, a raised terrace, a flat roof, *terrācium* useless earth (Du Cange):—L. **terrācea* fem. of **terrāceus* adj., earthen, of the nature of earth, earthy, f. *terra* earth: cf. -ACEOUS. This suffix was in the Romanic langs. used to form sbs., similative, augmentative, or pejorative; hence the primary sense, useless earth, heap of earth or rubbish, whence earthen mound made for a purpose. See also TARRAS (formerly *terras, terrace*), a differentiated form of the same word in the sense 'rubbish', 'rubble', as in It. and OFr.]

**1.** A raised level place for walking, with a vertical or sloping front or sides faced with masonry, turf, or the like, and sometimes having a balustrade; *esp.* a raised walk in a garden, or a level surface formed in front of a house on naturally sloping ground, or on the bank of a river, as 'The Terrace' at the Palace of Westminster.

*a.* **1575** LANEHAM *Let.* (1871) 48 Hard all along the Castl wall iz reared a pleazaunt Terres of a ten foot hy & a twelue brode. **1611** BIBLE *2 Chron.* ix. 11 And the king made.. terrises to the house of the Lord. **1669** WORLIDGE *Syst. Agric.* (1681) 333 *Terrasse*, a walk on a Bank or Bulwark. **1693** EVELYN *De la Quint. Compl. Gard.* I. 47 It might be allow'd twelve [foot] or more, it being a Terras,..since the Terrasses adjoyning to a House can hardly ever be too broad. **1712** LADY M. W. MONTAGU *Let. to W. Montagu* 9 or 11 Dec., The terrace is my place consecrated to meditation. **1739** GRAY *Let. to West* 21 Nov., Gardens and marble terraces full of orange and cypress trees. **1786** MRS. BARBAULD in *Mem.* 70 *Y.* vi. (1883) 62 A kind of terrass..commands a most extensive view. **1814** SCOTT *Wav.* ix, The garden.. was laid out in terraces, which descended rank by rank from the western wall to a large brook. **1866** GEO. ELIOT *F. Holt* ii, The glass door open towards the terrace.

*β.* **1579–80** NORTH *Plutarch* (1595) 570 Lucullus selfe would also many times be amongst them, in those tarrasses and pleasant walkes. **1587** CHURCHYARD *Worth. Wales* (1876) 104 Like tarres trim, to take the open ayre. **1599** B. JONSON *Ev. Man out of Hum.* II. i, Stand by close under this tarras. **1632** BURTON *Anat. Mel.* II. ii. IV. (ed. 4) 269 Euery Citty ..hath his peculiar walkes, Cloysters, Tarraces. **1653** GREAVES *Seraglio* 14 Two men may walk a breast upon the Tarrase.

**b.** *transf.* and *fig.*

**1605** BACON *Adv. Learn.* I. v. § 11 A tarrasse for a wandring and variable minde, to walke vp and downe. **1655** M. CARTER *Hon. Rediv.* (1660) 193 A Gennet of gold enamelled black and red, upon a terrasse or bank of flowers. **1758** REID tr. *Macquer's Chym.* I. 399 These rows of aludels are supported from end to end by a terrass, which runs from the body of the building, wherein the furnaces are erected. **1896** *Daily News* 10 Nov. 2/2 The living terraces of cripple children..added..their shrill plaudits to the general welcome.

†**c.** *Mil.* An earthwork thrown up by a besieging force; see also quot. 1816. *Obs.*

**1579** FENTON *Guicciard.* XI. (1599) 510 Certaine of the Spanish footemen got vp to the terrasse or heape of Earth, and began to assaile the breach. **1600** HOLLAND *Livy* V. V. 182 What should I speake of the tarraces, torteises, rams, and all other engins of assault and batterie? **1816** JAMES *Milit. Dict.* (ed. 4) s. v., A terrace likewise signified..a sort of cavalier, which was carried to a great height, in order to overlook and command the walls of a town.

**2.** A natural formation of this character; **a.** a table-land; **b.** *spec.* in *Geol.*, a horizontal shelf or bench on the side of a hill, or sloping ground.

The latter is usually of soft material, formed by the action of water, and exposed by the upheaval of the sea-margin, by the deepening of a river channel, or by the diminution in volume of a lake or river.

**1674** JOSSELYN *Voy. New Eng.* 202 The white mountains, ..the highest Terrasse in New-England. **1753** HANWAY *Trav.* (1762) I. VII. xcvi. 446 Some of the steepest hills are supported by many terrasses. **1832** DE LA BECHE *Geol. Man.* 159 Captain Vetch describes six or seven terraces or lines of beach on the Isle of Jura.., which appear to have been successively raised above the present level of the ocean. **1878** HUXLEY *Physiogr.* xvii. 278 It is not uncommon to find successive terraces of gravel. **1882** GEIKIE *Text-bk. Geol.* VI. V. 901 Regular terraces, corresponding to former water-levels of the lake, run for miles along the shores at heights of 120, 150 and 200 ft.

†**c.** The ground on which anything stands. *rare.*

**1735** MAHON tr. *L'Abbat's Fencing* Pref., By turning it too much it [the foot] would have no hold of the terrace.

†**3.** A gallery, open on one or both sides; a colonnade, a portico; a balcony on the outside of a building; also, a raised platform or balcony in a theatre or the like. *Obs.* (The earliest sense in Eng.)

**1515** *Will J. Fowler* (Somerset Ho.), To be buried wt in the Terres of the church of the Monastery of Syon. **1588** in Willis & Clark *Cambridge* (1886) II. 692 For paving the Inner court and the tarris without it. **1596** BP. W. BARLOW *Three Serm.* i. 17 Wee haue dyned abroad in our Tarrises and open Galleries for the great heat. **1617** MORYSON *Itin.* I. 145 This yard is compassed with a building all of Marble, which lies open like a Cloyster (we call it a terras). *Ibid.* III. 206 This place of Iudgement is commonly in a Porch or Terras under the Senate-house, hauing one side all open towards the market place. **1690** *The Gt. Scanderberg* 131 A little Terrass, which rendred my Apartment very pleasant. **1703** T. N. *City & C. Purchaser* 258 *Tarrace*, or *Tarras*, an open Walk, or Gallary.

†**4.** The flat roof of a house, resorted to for coolness in warm climates. *Obs.*

**1572** ABP. PARKER *Let. to Ld. Burghley* 13 Dec., This shop is but little and lowe and leaded flatt,..and is made like the terris..fitt for men to stande vppon in any triumphe or shewe. **1582** N. LICHEFIELD tr. *Castanheda's Conq. E. Ind.* I. x. 27 Many faire houses of lime and stone, builded with many lofts, with their windowes and tarrisis made of Lime and earth. [**1613** PURCHAS *Pilgrimage* (1614) 268 To vnderprop the *Terratza*, or roofe.] **1687** A. LOVELL tr. *Thevenot's Trav.* I. 10 All the Houses of it are built with a terrass, or flat Roof, and one may go from one street to another upon the terrasses of the houses. **1764** HARMER *Observ.* III. iii. 93 This sleeping on the terraces of their houses is only in summer-time. **1892** E. REEVES *Homeward Bound* 203 On these roofs are 'terraces', guarded by high parapets, where the inmates sit in the cool of the evening.

**5.** A row of houses on a level above the general surface, or on the face of a rising ground; *improperly*, a row of houses of uniform style, on a site slightly, if at all, raised above the level of the roadway.

(Common in street nomenclature; *Adelphi Terrace* (formerly Royal Terrace), London, is one of the earliest examples.)

**1769** (23 June) *Lease* (in *Mortgage* 20 Aug. 1782), A parcel of Ground..[which] adjoineth towards the north on vaults situate under the houses built on The Royal Taras [Adelphi, London]. **1796** *New Plan of London* [has] 'Lambeth Terrace, behind Lambeth Palace'. **1839** *Penny Cycl.* XIV. 113/2 The terraces in the Regent's Park, Hyde Park Terrace near Bayswater, and that in St. James's Park. **1850** KINGSLEY *Alt. Locke* i, My earliest recollections are of a suburban street: of its jumble of little shops and little terraces.

**6.** A soft spot in marble, which is cleaned out and the cavity filled up with a paste. Cf. TERRACY *a.*

**1877** KNIGHT *Dict. Mech.*, *Terrases* (Masonry), hollow defects in marble or fissures filled with nodules of other substances. The hole, being cleared out, is filled with marble dust and mastic of the same color.

**7.** *attrib.* and *Comb.* Of or pertaining to, having, forming, or consisting of a terrace or terraces, as *terrace-bank, -bower, -garden, -region, -roof, -stair, -step, -walk, -wall, -work*; obj. and obj. genitive, as *terrace-keeper, -maker*; *terrace-mantling* adj.; **terrace-cultivation**, the cultivation of hill-sides in terraces; so **terrace-culture**; **terrace-epoch** (*Geol.*), see quot. 1885.

**1834** L. RITCHIE *Wand. by Seine* 94 The *terrace-banks of the Seine. **1823** *Joanna Baillie's Collect. Poems* 119 Each whisper'd sigh Of the soft night-breeze through her *terrace-bowers Bore softer tones. **1860** PUSEY *Min. Proph.* 144 The *terrace-cultivation,..clothing with fertility the mountain-sides. **1903** *Bradford Antiquary* July 346 Signs of terrace-cultivation are to be met with in different parts of the county. **1863** FAWCETT *Pol. Econ.* II. vii. (1876) 212 The establishment of *terrace culture on the hills. **1862** DANA *Man. Geol.* 554 The time when they were raised.. corresponds to the *Terrace epoch; and during the process other parallel terraces were formed. **1885** GEIKIE *Text-bk. Geol.* III. II. ii. § 3. 369 In North America, the river-terraces exist on so grand a scale that the geologists of that country have named one of the later periods of geological history, during which those deposits were formed, the Terrace Epoch. **1705** ADDISON *Italy* 59, I went to see the *Terrace-Garden of Verona, that Travellers generally mention. **1824** CAMPBELL *Theodric* 37 Clustering trees and *terrace-mantling vines. **1834** *Penny Cycl.* II. 472/2 Ten or twelve intermediate formations, constituting the *terrace-regions. **1802** GOUV. MORRIS in Sparks *Life & Writ.* (1832) III. 161, I have a *terrace roof. **1842** FRANCIS *Dict. Arts, Terrace Roof*, those which are flat like terraces. *a* **1668** DAVENANT *Man's the Master* IV. i, Pass through the gall'ry up the *tarras-stairs into my closet. **1865** J. H. INGRAHAM *Pillar of Fire* (1872) 218 We soon landed at the grand *terrace-steps of the quay. **1637** SUCKLING *Aglaura* III. i, Eleven; under the *Tarras walke; I will not faile you there. **1693** LUTTRELL *Brief Rel.* (1857) III. 174 The queens tarras walk at Whitehall, facing the Thames, is now finished. **1712** J. JAMES tr. *Le Blond's Gardening* 25 A low *Terrass-Wall, from whence you have a View of the Country round about. **1853** KANE *Grinnell Exp.* xv. (1856) 108 Its edges .. were abrupt precipices, resembling the *terrace-work of trap-rock.

Hence **Te·rracer**, one who stands or walks on a terrace: cf. TERRACING 2; **Te·rrace-wards** *adv.*, towards the terrace; **Te·rrace-wise** *adv.*, in the manner of a terrace.

**1786** MME. D'ARBLAY *Diary* 7 Aug., All the *terracers stand up against the walls, to make a clear passage for the Royal Family. **1909** *Daily Chron.* 20 July 1/1 Pilgrims who arrived on the Westminster Bridge and bent their gaze *terrace-wards. **1638** SIR T. HERBERT *Trav.* (ed. 2) 156 Each shop..archt above and..atop *tarraswise framed, and with plaister. cemented. **1898** *Daily News* 19 May 7/1 St. Pierre, Martinique,.. nestles terrace-wise against and amid a perfect paradise of greenery.

**Terrace**, obs. form of TARRAS.

**Te·rrace**, *v.* Forms: see the sb.; also 7 *pa. pple.* **terassed**. [f. TERRACE *sb.*, or a. F. *terrasser* (16th c. in Godef. *Compl.*).]

**1.** *trans.* To form into a terrace or raised bank; to fashion or arrange in terraces. Also *to terrace up.* (Chiefly in *passive* until 19th c.; cf. next.)

**1650** FULLER *Pisgah* III. ii. § 5 The ascent..was..terrased on both sides with Pillasters made of..Almuggin trees. **1682** WHELER *Journ. Greece* I. 13 The Walls also being well Terrassed. **1827** KEBLE *Chr. Y.* 3rd Sund. Advent, Mountains terrass'd high with mossy stone. **1848** MILL *Pol. Econ.* II. viii. § 3 The plots, terrassed up one above another, are often not above four feet wide. **1880** MISS BIRD *Japan* I. 85 Fields formed by terracing sloping ground. **1895** *Westm. Gaz.* 7 Oct. 2/2 The Kusi River in Bengal..brings down enormous quantities of silt,.. making fertile plains, terracing the land, changing its bed, destroying forests.

†**2.** To furnish with a 'terrace' or balcony; to provide (a house) with a loggia or terrace-roof. (Chiefly in *passive*: cf. next.) *Obs.*

**1615** G. SANDYS *Trav.* I. 31 [Minarets] tarrast aloft on the out side like the maine top of a ship. **1624** WOTTON *Archit.* in *Reliq.* (1651) 260 Which [light] we must now supply..by Tarrasing any Story which is in danger of darknesse. **1631** HEYWOOD *London's Jus Hon.* Wks. 1874 IV. 276 A faire and curious structure archt and Tarrest aboue. **1634** SIR T. HERBERT *Trav.* 49 The houses..are flat and tarrased atop.

**3.** *intr.* (*nonce-use.*) To rise in terraces (in quot., used of ranges of houses).

**1900** *Speaker* 29 Dec. 342/1 Pink and white and blue tenements..terrace recklessly above each other from the river to the sky-line.

**Terraced** (te·rĕ^i^st), *ppl. a.* [f. TERRACE *sb.* or *v.* + -ED.] Formed into or furnished with a terrace or terraces; arranged or constructed in terrace form.

In quot. 1644, Furnished with a colonnade or covered ambulatory.

**1644** EVELYN *Diary* 4 Nov., The court is square and tarrass'd. **1727–46** THOMSON *Summer* 1429 To Clermont's terrass'd height, and Esher's groves. **1797** MRS. RADCLIFFE *Ital.* i, Its terraced roofs crowded with spectators. **1869** TOZER *Highl. Turkey* I. 108 The dwellings..are..niched ..in the terraced cliffs. **1880** C. R. MARKHAM *Peruv. Bark* 365 The space between being sown with rice in terraced fields. **1904** J. T. FOWLER *Durh. Univ.* 63 The rebuilt keep conspicuous on a terraced mound.

**Terraceous** (terē^i^·ʃəs), *a. rare.* [f. L. type **terrāce-us* (see TERRACE) + -OUS: cf. -ACEOUS.] Of earthy nature or composition.

**1863** MOUAT *Adv. Andaman Island.* 151 The progress that we made through the terraceous compost was necessarily slow.

**Terraciform** (teræ·sifǭɹm), *a. rare.* [f. TERRACE *sb.* (or med.L. *terrāci-a*) + -FORM.] Having the form of a terrace.

**1890** *Smithsonian Inst. Rep.* 72 The formation is sometimes fashioned into terraces; and some of its best developments in the District of Columbia..are terraciform.

**Terracing** (te·rĕsiŋ), *vbl. sb.* [f. TERRACE *v.* or *sb.* + -ING [1].]

**1.** The formation of terraces. **b.** *concr.* A terraced structure or formation; a series or range of terraces; a platform or stand with rows of seats rising in tiers behind each other.

**1826** CHALMERS in Hanna *Mem.* (1851) III. viii. 128 [We] enjoyed..the noble terracing, and orange house. **1862** DANA *Man. Geol.* 558 The terracing of the borders of the lakes and rivers. **1864** CARLYLE *Fredk. Gt.* XVI. i. IV. 245 The diggings and terracings of the Hill-side. **1885** SIR R. BALL *Story of Heavens* iii. (1890) 67 The terracing shown in its interior [of the extinct lunar volcano Copernicus] is mainly due to the repeated alternate rise, partial congelation, and subsequent retreat of a vast sea of lava. **1902** *Daily Chron.* 8 Apr. 5/1 The terracing which collapsed with such disastrous results during the football match at Ibrox Park on Saturday.

**2.** Walking or promenading on a terrace. *rare.*

**1786** MME. D'ARBLAY *Diary* 24 July, Here we have coffee till the Terracing is over. This is about eight o'clock.

‖**Terra-cotta** (te·rä,kǫ·tă). [It., lit. baked (cooked) earth:—L. *terra cocta*. So F. *terre cuite.*]

**1.** A hard unglazed pottery of a fine quality, of which decorative tiles and bricks, architectural decorations, statuary, vases, and the like are made.

**1722** J. RICHARDSON *Statues, etc. Italy* 177 A Model in Terra Cotta as fine as ever was done. **1752** HOLLIS in *Lett. Lit. Men* (Camden) 390 Many things in glass, many in terra cotta. **1842–76** GWILT *Archit.* § 624 The west front of the church of Sta. Maria in Strada, a most elaborate work in brick and terra-cotta. **1867** W. W. SMYTH *Coal & Coal-mining* 190 The Romans have left us numerous examples in bronze and *terra cotta.*

**b.** With *a* and *pl.*: An object of art, as a statuette or figurine, made of this substance.

**1810** T. COMBE (*title*) A Description of the Collection of Ancient Terracottas in the British Museum. **1842** *Smith's Dict. Grk. & Rom. Antiq.* s. v. *Fictile*, They reckoned some of their consecrated terra-cottas .. among the safeguards of their imperial city. **1865** *Athenæum* 28 Jan. 127/3 The terra-cottas include some very remarkable coloured statuettes or *figurine* of Greek production.

**2.** The colour of this pottery, a brownish red of various shades.

**1882** *Daily News* 3 June 3/1 That colour which the uninitiated would call golden brown, but which milliners call terra-cotta. **1890** *Pall Mall G.* 25 June 2/1 The splendid terra-cottas of the rocks and the bright greens of the trees. **1900** *Westm. Gaz.* 23 Apr. 3/2 An underdress of pale blue brocade over which is arranged a tunic of terra-cotta.

**3.** *attrib.* and *Comb.* **a.** Of or pertaining to terra-cotta, as *terra-cotta works.* **b.** Made of terra-cotta, as *terra-cotta bust, figure, vase*; **c.** Of the colour of terra-cotta, as *terra-cotta feather, paper, velvet*; also *terra-cotta tinted* adj.

**1859** R. HUNT *Guide Mus. Pract. Geol.* (ed. 2) 96 Figures ..manufactured at the Mill Wall terra cotta works. **1868** *Pall Mall G.* 2 Dec. 8 Seventy-four terra cotta busts of the Roman Emperors and their families. **1877** W. S. W. VAUX *Grk. Cities Asia Minor* iv. 162 In 1853, Mr. Newton obtained many *terra-cotta* vases of a very archaic type. **1888** *Lady* 25 Oct. 378/1 Trimmings of terra-cotta faced cloth. **1891** *Truth* 10 Dec. 1242 All the doorways were draped with terra-cotta silk. **1899** *Westm. Gaz.* 19 July 3/1 Roofs.. terra-cotta tinted.

**Te·rracu·lture.** *rare*—°. [irreg. f. L. *terra* earth + CULTURE: cf. *agriculture.*] = AGRICULTURE. Hence **Terracu·ltural** *a.* = AGRICULTURAL.

**1847** in WEBSTER; whence in later Dicts.

**Terracy** (te·rĕsi), *a.* [f. TERRACE *sb.* 6 + -Y.] Of marble: Containing terraces or soft spots.

**1727–41** CHAMBERS *Cycl.* s. v. *Marble*, Terracy Marble, that with soft places in it, which must be filled up with cement, as that of Languedoc.

‖ **Te·rra damna·ta.** *Alchemy. Obs.* [L., = condemned or finally rejected earth.] = CAPUT MORTUUM 2: see quot. 1704.

**1633** B. JONSON *Tale Tub* I. iii, She's such a vessel of fæces: all dried earth, Terra damnata! **1704** J. HARRIS *Lex. Techn.* I. s.v. *Earth*, Earth, which the Chymists call *Terra Damnata* and *Caput Mortuum*, is the last of the five Chymical Principles, and is that which remains after all the other Principles are extracted by Distilation, Calcination, &c. **1710** T. FULLER *Pharm. Extemp.* 146 (Stanf.) Calcin'd Harts-horn being a meer *Terra Damnata*.

† **Te·rræfi·lial,** *a. Obs. rare.* [f. next, with *filial* from *filius*.] Earthly, worldly, sordid. So **Te·rræfi·lian** *a.*, of or pertaining to a *terræ filius*.

**1742** YOUNG *Nt. Th.* VIII. 277 Men of the world, the terræ-filial breed, Welcome the modest stranger to their sphere. **1783** BURNS *Let. to J. Murdoch* 15 Jan., Can he descend to mind the paltry concerns about which the terræfilial race fret, and fume..? **1887** SAINTSBURY *Hist. Elizab. Lit.* x. (1894) 364 His merits as well as his faults have a singular unpersonal, and, if I may so say, *terræfilian* connotation.

‖ **Terræ filius** (te·rī fi·liŏs). Pl. **terræ filii.** [L. *terræ filius*, a son of the earth, a man of unknown origin.]

**1.** A person of obscure parentage.

[*c* **1590** GREENE *Fr. Bacon* ix. 51 Those geomantic spirits, That Hermes calleth *terræ filii*.] **1621** BURTON *Anat. Mel.* II. iii. II. (1676) 199/2 Let no *terræ filius*, or upstart, insult at this which I have said, no worthy Gentleman take offence. **1622** MABBE tr. *Aleman's Guzman d'Alf.* I. III. i. 186 As if my father had beene *terræ filius*. **1679** NESSE *Antichrist* 7 This is the Terræfilius, the base-born beast that springs out of the earth. **1883** *Sat. Rev.* 2 June 688/2 Abd-el-Kader himself was very far from being *terræ filius*.

**2.** Formerly, at the University of Oxford: An orator privileged to make humorous and satirical strictures in a speech at the public 'act'. (In quot. 1882, applied to a similar orator at Dublin University.) Cf. PREVARICATOR 4.

**1651–93** WOOD *Life* [passim: see ed. Clark (1900) V. 151/2]. **1656** BLOUNT *Glossogr.*, *Terræ-filius*..the foole in the Acts at Oxford. **1674** *Ibid.* (ed. 4), *Terræ-filius*,..we may call him the *bon drol* in the Acts at Oxford, who must be a Master of Arts, to qualifie him for this Office, and is commonly chosen out of the best Wits of the University. **1669** EVELYN *Diary* 10 July, The *Terræ filius* (the Universitie Buffoone) entertain'd the auditorie with a..sarcastical rhapsodie. **1670** EACHARD *Cont. Clergy* 37 Wits..who never..were at all inspir'd from a Tripus's, Terræ-filius's, or Prævarecator's speech. **1713** STEELE *Guard.* No. 72 ¶ 2 In my time..the Terræ-filius contented himself with being bitter upon the Pope, or chastising the Turk. **1721** AMHERST *Terræ Fil.* Ded., It is very uncertain when *Terræ-Filius* will be able to regain his antient privileges in the Sheldonian theatre. *Ibid.* No. 5. 23 All men are not *Terræ-Filius's*. **1882** *Q. Rev.* Apr. 389 A scurrilous harangue..for the delivery of which, in the character of Terræ Filius, one of his [Swift's] College acquaintances narrowly escaped expulsion.

‖ **Terra firma** (te·rā fə̄·rmā). [L., = 'firm land', used in med. or mod. L. in special senses = It. *terra ferma*, F. *terre ferme*; cf. G. *festland*. In 17th c. partly a. It. *terra ferma*.]

†**1.** A mainland or continent, as distinct from portions of land partly or wholly isolated by water.

**1665** SIR T. HERBERT *Trav.* (1677) 31 He [Ptolemy] draws his *Terra firma* only to 10 degrees South from the Æquator. **1706** PHILLIPS (ed. Kersey), *Terra firma*, the Continent, or main Land; so call'd by Geographers. **1725** DE FOE *Voy. round World* (1840) 164 Our men..said that about three leagues off to the southward, there seemed to be a Terra Firma, or continent of land. **1727–41** CHAMBERS *Cycl.*, *Terra firma*..is sometimes used for a continent, in contradistinction to islands.

† **2.** *spec.* **a.** The territories on the Italian mainland which were subject to the state of Venice. *Obs.*

**1605** B. JONSON *Volpone* II. i, Gentlemen of your City; strangers of the *terra-firma*; worshipful merchants; ay, and senators too. **1645** EVELYN *Diary* June (1819) I. 192 We went to Padua...The first *terra firma* we landed at was Fusina, being onely an inn, where we changed our barge. **1832** tr. *Sismondi's Ital. Rep.* xiv. 308 The two monarchs agreed to divide between them all the *terra firma* of the Venetians.

† **b.** The northern coast-land of South America (Colombia), as distinguished from the West India Islands; also, in narrower sense, the Isthmus of Panama. *Obs.*

**1760–72** tr. *Juan & Ulloa's Voy.* (ed. 3) I. p. vii, Geographical descriptions..of the country about Carthagena,..the *Terra Firma*. **1827** ROBERTS *Voy. Centr. Amer.* 71 A race of people..more civilized than most of the other tribes, inhabiting this part of *Terra Firma*.

**3.** The land as distinguished from the sea; dry or firm land; in quot. 1785, the earth. Also *fig.*

**1693** RAY *Disc.* I. iii. 24 The whole *terra firma*, or dry Land. **1707** NORRIS *Treat. Humility* iii. 111 Here we have some *terra firma* to fix and stay our footing on. **1779** *Hist. Mod. Europe* II. I. 65 They again got footing on terra firma. **1785** BURNS *Ep. to W. Simpson* 105 While terra firma, on her axis, Diurnal turns. **1820** T. MITCHELL *Aristoph.*, *Com.* I. 72 That their feet find no resting-place on sea Or terra-firma. **1887** MISS BRADDON *Like & Unlike* xxxiv, I was not often upon *terra firma* after I left Marseilles.

† **4.** *humor.* and *colloq.* Landed estate; land.

**1698** FARQUHAR *Love & Bottle* III. ii, I have five thousand acres of as good fighting ground as any in England, good *terra firma*, sir. *a* **1700** B. E. *Dict. Cant. Crew* s.v. *Dipt*, *He has dipt his Terra firma*, he has mortgaged his dirty Acres. *Ibid.*, *Terra-firma*, an Estate in Land. **1728** FIELDING *Love in Sev. Masques* v. vi, Does your estate lie in *terra firma*, or in the stocks?

† **Te·rrage.** *Obs.* Also 5 **terage.** [a. OF. *terage* (13th c. in Godef.):—pop. L. *terrāticum* (869 in Du Cange), f. L. *terra* earth: see -AGE. Hence med.L. *terrāgium* (1030 in Du Cange).]

**1.** Land; a territory, district.

*c* **1400** *Destr. Troy* 1072 Þai comen to the cost..of the terage of Troy. *Ibid.* 13631 Þat Pirrus schuld haue þe terrage of tessayle and þe tryed corone. *c* **1440** *Promp. Parv.* 489/1 Terage, erthe, *humus, solum, terragium*.

**2.** *Old Law.* Some kind of payment or duty. (Actual meaning uncertain; see quots.)

The statements of the 17th c. law dicts. are guesses. Gross takes it as = PICKAGE. But, as some charters have *terrage* besides *stallage* and *pickage*, the meaning may be payment for the ground or 'stance' occupied at a fair or market without breaking the ground.

[**1301** *Lincoln Charter* in *Cal. Charter Rolls* III. 9. **1349** in W. Hardy *Lancaster Charters* (1845) 6 Quod..sint quieti de pavagio, passagio, paagio, lastagio, stallagio, tallagio, cariagio, pesagio, piccagio, et terragio.] **1691** BLOUNT *Law Dict.*, *Terrage* (*Terragium*) [quotes the prec. patent, and says] which seems to be an exemption *à Præcariis*, viz. Boons of Plowing, Reaping, &c. and perhaps from Money paid for digging or breaking the Earth in Fairs and Markets. **1749** in Pote *Hist. Windsor* 120 (Transl. of a Charter) That the said Custos or Canons and their tenants should for ever be free from payment of Toll, Picage, Paviage,..Terrage [etc.]. [**1890** GROSS *Gild Merchant* II. 420 *Terragium*. The same as *Picagium* (413), Duty paid by a stranger on markets and fairs to break the ground and erect a stall.]

**3.** ? A toll or duty paid for landing; landing dues.

[**1318** *Grimsby Charter* in *Cal. Charter Rolls* III. 411 [*tr.* quit of toll..hansage, anchorage, terrage, quayage, passage, and pedage].] **1664** HALE *Treat.* II. iv. in Hargrave *Coll. Tracts* (1787) I. 57 The defendants..shewed usage to have had certain customs called land-leave, terrage, &c. *Ibid.* vi. 76 *Terrage*, for the necessary unlading of goods before they come up to the common key.

‖ **Terrai·gnol.** *Obs. rare*⁻⁰. [obs. F. *terraignol* (Cotgr.), ad. It. *terrágnolo* 'drooping, downe looking, dull, heauy, as some heauy-going horses' (Florio); f. OIt. *terragno* (Dante = *terreno*):—med.L. *terrāneus* of the earth + *-olo*, L. *-olus* dim.] A heavy-going horse: see quot.

**1727** BAILEY vol. II, *Terraignol*,..is a Horse who cleaves to the Ground [etc.]..in general, one whose Motions are all short, and too near the Ground.

**Terrain** (terē̆·n), *sb.* (*a.*) Also 8–9 **terrein** (9 **terrane**, in sense 3). [a. F. *terrain* (also *terrein*), OF. *terain* (Wace 12th c.):—pop. L. **terrānum* = cl. L. *terrēnum* TERRENE.]

† **1.** (See quot. 1727.) *Obs.* **b.** Standing-ground, position.

**1727** BAILEY vol. II, *Terrain*,..is the Manage-Ground upon which the Horse makes his Pist or Tread. **1753** in CHAMBERS *Cycl. Supp.* **1816** in JAMES *Milit. Dict.* **1832** LISTER *Arlington* II. vii. 117 Viewed in the same light, and from the same *terrain* from which they view it themselves.

**2.** A tract of country considered with regard to its natural features, configuration, etc.; in military use esp. as affecting its tactical advantages, fitness for manœuvring, etc.; also, an extent of ground, region, district, territory.

**1766** W. DIGBY *Let. to G. Selwyn* 12 Apr., in Jesse *S. & Contemp.* (1843) II. 13 We rode to reconnoitre the *terrein*. **1816** JAMES *Milit. Dict.*, *Terrain*,..generally any space or extent of ground. **1879** *Cassell's Techn. Educ.* IV. 95/1 Without reference..to the physical irregularities of the terrain. **1889** BADEN-POWELL *Pigsticking* 9 Taking in at a glance the peculiarities of the terrain.

**3.** *Geol.* (Usually spelt **terrane.**) A name for a connected series, group, or system of rocks or formations; a stratigraphical subdivision.

**1823** tr. *Humboldt's Geognost. Ess.* Introd. 2 The union of several formations constitutes a geological series or a district (*terrain*); but the terms rocks, formations, and *terrains*, are used as synonymous in many works on geognosy. **1864** DANA *Man. Geol.* 81 (Cent.) Terrane..is used for any single rock or continuous series of rocks of a region, whether the formation be stratified or not. **1889** in *Q. Jrnl. Geol. Soc.* XLV. 63 The word *terrane* proposed by Prof. Gilbert to be used for a stratigraphical subdivision of any magnitude. **1895** *Pop. Sci. Monthly* Sept. 694 The slates of the Cambrian terrane.

**B.** *adj.* Of the earth, terrene, terrestrial. **a.** *Terrain tide*, a (supposed) rise and fall in the earth's crust, caused by the attraction of the sun or moon. **b.** *Terrain cure*: see quot.

**1882** MILNE in *Nature* 8 June 125/2 To determine the existence of a terrain tide, a gravitimeter might be established...If terrain tides exist, and they are sufficiently great from a geological point of view. **1897** *Allbutt's Syst. Med.* IV. 621 Regulated exercises, such as the gentle climbing, especially in mountain districts, known as the terrain cure.

‖ **Terra incognita** (te·rā inkǫ·gnitā). *Pl.* **terræ incognitæ** (*erron.* **terras incognitas**). [L., = 'unknown land'.] An unknown or unexplored region. Often *fig.*

**1616** CAPT. SMITH *Descr. New Eng.* 6 The Spaniards know ..not so much as the true circumference of *Terra Incognita*, whose large dominions may equalize the greatnesse and goodnes of America. **1630** J. TAYLOR (Water P.) *Gt. Eater Kent* Wks. I. 143/2 The place of his birth, and names of his parents are to me a meere *Terra incognita*. **1756** LADY M. W. MONTAGU *Let. to C'tess of Bute* 1 Apr., Your provinces of politics, gallantry, and literature, all [are] *terra incognita*. **1821** ANNA M. PORTER *Village of Mariendorpt* II. 121 His friend and the field-marshall were nearly terras incognitas to each other. **1901** *Scotsman* 11 Mar. 6/4 The country within a day's ride..is almost a terra incognita.

**Terraine,** obs. form of TERRENE.

‖ **Terra Japonica** (te·rā dʒæpǫ·nikă). [mod. L., = 'Japanese earth': see note s. v. CATECHU. So F. *terre du Japon*.] = CATECHU, formerly also known as *Japonic earth*.

[**1654, 1679**: [see CATECHU]. **1693** tr. *Blancard's Phys. Dict.* (ed. 2), *Catechu*, improperly called *Terra Japonica*. **1725** *Lond. Gaz.* No. 6366/1 Half a Ton of Terra Japannica. **1845** *Encycl. Metrop.* XXII. 474/1 The exports from Népál are rice, ginger, terra Japonica (*i. e.* the gum, or inspissated juice of the *Mimosa catechu*).

‖ **Terral** (tera·l). [Sp., f. L. *terra* land; so F. *terral*.] The land-breeze.

**1884** H. COLLINGWOOD *Under Meteor Flag* 299 Obliged to take to our sweeps to get across the calm belt between the terral and the trade-wind.

‖ **Terra Lemnia.** [med. or mod.L., = 'Lemnian earth', f. *Lemnos*, an island in the Ægean sea. So F. *terre de Lemnos* (Littré), It. *terra lenia* (Florio), G. *lemnische erde*.] = TERRA SIGILLATA; known also as *Lemnian earth*.

**1613** HARCOURT *Voy. Guiana* in *Harl. Misc.* (Malh.) III. 192 The earth yieldeth bole-armoniack and terra-lemnia. **1632** [see TERRA SIGILLATA 1]. **1797** *Encycl. Brit.* (ed. 3) IX. 784/2 Lemnian Earth, *Terra Lemnia*, a medicinal, astringent sort of earth, of a fatty consistence and reddish colour.

**Terralla,** erron. form of TERRELLA.

**Terramare** (terămā·ɪ, -mēə·ɪ). Pl. **-ares.** Also *β.* in It. form **terrama·ra**, pl. **terrema·re.** [a. F. *terramare* (1867 *Rev. des Deux-Mondes*, 653, in Littré), ad. dial. It. *terramara* (used in Emilia, about Bologna), for *terra-marna* (Bellini), f. *terra* earth + *marna* (dial. *mara*) MARL.

Introduced into anthropological use by Strobel and Pigarini, 1862.]

An ammoniacal earth found in the valley of the Po, in Italy, and collected as a fertilizer; it occurs in flat mounds, identified as the sites of dwellings of a people of the later neolithic period. Hence *transf.* (*pl.*) The prehistoric settlements themselves. Also *attrib.*

*a.* **1866–8** BARING-GOULD *Curious Myths Mid. Ages*, *Leg. Cross* (1877) 365 These quarries go by the name of *terramares*. They are vast accumulations of cinders, charcoal, bones, fragments of pottery. **1871** TYLOR *Prim. Cult.* I. ii. 55 Relics discovered in gravel-beds, caves, shell-mounds, terramares, lake-dwellings.

*β.* **1890** HUXLEY in *19th Cent.* Nov. 761 The pre-historic people of the terremare. **1899** R. MUNRO *Prehist. Scot.* vi. 205 Combs of bronze have been found both in the Swiss lake-dwellings and in the Terremare. *Ibid.* xi. 434 There is..in the eastern part of the Po Valley another class of ancient habitations known as *terremare*,..they may be regarded as land palafittes.

**Terrandry, -anye**: see TYRANTRY, TYRANNY.

**Terrane**: see TERRAIN.

**Terranean** (terē̆·niăn), *a.* [f. as next + -AN.] Pertaining to, or proceeding from, the earth.

**1653** W. RAMESEY *Astrol. Restored* 107 It is a terranean and earthy Angle. **18..** *Electr. Rev.* (U.S.) XVIII. 1. 9 (Cent.) The great strain on the trolley wire..would be a necessary incident of terranean supply.

**Terraneous** (terē̆·niəs), *a. rare.* [f. L. **terrāneus* (cf. *subterrāneus*), f. *terra* earth: see -OUS.] Of or pertaining to the earth; terrestrial.

*a* **1711** KEN *Edmund* Poet. Wks. 1721 II. 210 As long as this terraneous Globe endur'd. **1725** *Brice's Weekly Jrnl.* 26 Nov. 1 There may be some Sea-Shells dug at Land containing Terraneous Insects.

**b.** *Bot.* Growing upon land.

**1882** in OGILVIE (Annandale).

**Terrapin** (te·răpin). Forms: 7 (**torope**), **tarapine**, 7–9 **terrapine**, 8 **torrepine**, **terebin**, 8–9 **tarapin**, 9 **terrapene**, **terapin**, **tarrapin**, 8– **terrapin.** [Of Algonquin origin; *torope* represented the Abenaki *turepé* (also *tourepé*) in Rasles *Abenaki Dict.* rendered 'tortue', in Delaware *tulpe*. The origin of the final *-in*, *-ine* is obscure.]

A name originally given to one or more species of North American turtles; thence extended to many allied species of the turtle and tortoise family, *Testudineæ*, widely distributed over North, Central, and South America, the East Indies, China, N. Africa, and other countries. In N. America, *spec.* the Diamond-backed or Saltmarsh terrapin, *Malaclemmys palustris*, famous for its delicate flesh.

Among other well-known American species are the Red-bellied Terrapin, *Pseudemys rugosa*, the Alligator Terrapin or Snapping-turtle, *Chelydra serpentina*, and the Pine-barren Terrapin, Box-turtle, or Gopher, *Cistudo carolina*. The Catalogue of Animals in the London Zoological Gardens, 1896, contains thirty-three species of Terrapin, with distinctive appellations, as *Caspian*, *Ceylonese*, *Floridan*, *Spanish*, *Annulated*, *Black-headed*, *Ocellated*, *Painted*, *Roofed*, *Speckled*, *Wrinkled*, *Bennett's*, *Blanding's*, *Maw's*, *Oldham's*, *Spengler's Terrapin*. These are distributed in fifteen genera.

**1613** A. WHITAKER *Gd. Newes fr. Virginia* 42, I have caught with mine angle pike, carpe, eele,..creafish, and the torope or little turtle. **1672** JOSSELYN *New Eng. Rarities* 34 The Turtle that lives in Lakes and is called in Virginia a Terrapine. **1672** J. LEDERER *Discov.* 4 Every Nation gives his particular ensigne or arms, the Sasquesahanaugh a tarapine or small tortoise. **1678** PHILLIPS (ed. 4), *Terrapine*, a word used among the Virginians for that which we commonly call a Tortoise, and many call a Turtle,.. the Lake Turtle which lives in Lakes,..is that most properly called the *Terrapine*. **1714** J. LAWSON *Hist. Carolina* 133 Of terebins there are divers sorts, all which..we will comprehend under the distinction of land and water terebins. **1722** BEVERLEY *Virginia* III. iv. § 15. 151 A small kind of Turtle, or Tarapins (as we call them). *Ibid.* IV. xix. § 80. 265 Snakes, Terrapins, and such like Vermine. **1764** SMOLLETT *Trav.* xix. (1766) I. 302 The land-turtle, or terrapin, is much better known at Nice, as being a native of this country. **1844** *P. Parley's Ann.* V. 115 The growth of the terrapene is very slow. **1854** OWEN *Skel. & Teeth* in *Orr's Circ. Sc.* I. *Org. Nat.* 217 The Australian long-necked terrapene (*Hydraspis longicollis*). **1862** TROLLOPE *N. Amer.* I. 467 The terrapin is a small turtle, found on the shores of Maryland and Virginia, out of which a very rich soup is made. **1908** *Times* 22 Feb. 13/3 Three-keeled terrapin..from Guatemala.

**b.** The flesh of this animal as food.

**1867** DIXON *New Amer.* (ed. 6) II. 335 Gentlemen sitting at table sipping soup, picking terapin. **1892** F. M. CRAWFORD *Three Fates* II. 139 He had eaten terrapin and canvas back off old Saxon China.

**c.** *attrib.* and *Comb.*, as *terrapin meat*, *shell*, *soup*; terrapin-farm, a place where diamond-back terrapins are reared for the market; **terrapin paws**, a name, in Chesapeake Bay, for tongs used in capturing terrapins.

**1775** ADAIR *Amer. Ind.* 110 Torrepine-shells containing pebbles. **1845** J. COULTER *Adv. in Pacific* ix. 110, I put to it some terrapin meat. **1862** RUSSELL *Diary North & S.* (1863) 340 The Terrapin soup excellent, though not comparable..to the best turtle. **1901** H. GADOW in *Camb. Nat. Hist.* VIII. ix. 360 Enterprising men have established terrapin-farms or 'crawls' for the keeping and breeding of terrapins.

**Terraplain**, etc.: see TERREPLEIN.

**Terra·quean**, *a. rare*$^{-1}$. = next.

**1861** *Macm. Mag.* Apr. 471/2 All the places on this terraquean globe.

**Terraqueous** (terēⁱ·kwĭəs), *a.* [f. L. *terra* earth + AQUEOUS. Cf. F. *terraqué(e* (Voltaire *Memnon* 1747) from Eng.; so Sp. (*el globo*) *terrácueo*.]

**1.** Consisting of, or formed of, land and water; nearly always in *terraqueous globe*.

**1658** PHILLIPS, *Terraqueous*, composed of earth and water together. **1664** POWER *Exp. Philos.* II. 99 The halituous Effluxions and Aporrhœa's of this terraqueous Globe below. **1678** CUDWORTH *Intell. Syst.* I. iii. § 37. 171 The whole terrestrial (or terraqueous) Globe. **1742** YOUNG *Nt. Th.* I. 286 A part how small of the terraqueous globe Is tenanted by man! **1781** COWPER *Charity* 122 Providence enjoins to every soul An union with the vast terraqueous whole. **1834-5** J. PHILLIPS *Geol.* in *Encycl. Metrop.* VI. 701/1 *margin*, Relation of terraqueous agencies in ancient and modern eras. **1876** PAGE *Adv. Text-bk. Geol.* iii. 72 The maintenance of a habitable terraqueous surface.

**2.** Living in land and water, as a plant; extending over land and water, as a journey.

**1694** WESTMACOTT *Script. Herb.* 164 These Reeds belong to the terraqueous plants. **1844** JEFFREY in Ld. Cockburn *Life* (1852) II. Let. clxxiv, We drove down to the pier and resumed our terraqueous promenade.

**Terrar, terrer.** *Obs.* exc. *Hist.* Also 6 tarrer, 9 *erron.* terrarer. [ad. med.L. *terrārius* in same sense, f. *terrārius* adj., pertaining to land or lands (f. *terra* earth, land), whence also *terrāria*, *-ārium*, a piece of land, landed property, pl. *terrāria* possessions, lands, *terrārius* a tenant or holder of land, *terrārius līber*, also *terrārium*, *terrerium* a register of lands, rents, etc. (TERRIER[1]).] An officer of a religious house, who was originally bursar for the farms and manors belonging to the house, receiving rents and making disbursements on account of these; but whose office by the 16th c. at Durham was mainly connected with the entertainment of strangers.

**1401** *Rotuli Terrariorum* in *Durham Acc. Rolls* (Surtees) 299 Compotus fratris Willelmi Barry Terrarii Dunelm. **1593** *Rites of Durham* (Surtees 1903) 99 Dane Roger Watson the Terrer of yᵉ house. The Tarrers checker was as yea goe into yᵉ geste Haule...His office was to se that all yᵉ geste chambers to be cleanly keapt [etc.]..and he provyded provender for there horses [etc.]. **1864** RAINE *Priory of Hexham* I. p. cxxxiv, The Terrarer, the cellarer, the chamberlain and the bursar acted by his advice. **1901** J. T. FOWLER in *Durh. Acc. Rolls* Introd. 31 The Terrar had three copies of each roll written out. *Ibid.*, Expenses of the Terrar riding to Auckland..and other places.

**Terrar**, obs. form of TERRIER.

**Terrarium** (terē·riŏm). Pl. **-a.** [mod. f. L. *terra* earth, after *aquarium*. Also in Fr. (1873 in Littré *Suppl.*) and Ger. (Meyer *Conv. Lex.*).] A vivarium for land animals; *esp.* a glass case, or the like, in which small land animals are kept under scientific observation.

**1890** *Science* 10 Jan. 24/2 [He] describes the ways of a snake, ..which he kept in his terrarium in Zurich. **1895** *Proc. Zool. Soc. Lond.* 160 Usually after they have lived for some time in the terrarium they get dark spots, especially on the sides of the body.

**Terras, -ass(e**, obs. ff. TARRAS, TERRACE.

‖**Te·rra Sie·nna.** *Obs.* Also terra di (de) Sienna. [ad. It. *terra di Siena*, in F. *terre de Sienne*, lit. 'earth of Sienna'.] = SIENNA. Also *attrib.*

**1760** SHENSTONE *Wks. & Lett.* (1777) III. 309 A terra-sienna or very rich reddish brown. *a* **1817** T. DWIGHT *Trav. New Eng.* (1821) I. 35 A beautiful yellow earth..which yields a handsomer colour than the Terra de Sienna. It is called Terra Columbiana. **1823** P. NICHOLSON *Pract. Build.* 413 Terra di Sienna is a native ochre, and is brought from Italy, where it is generally found. **1844** J. T. HEWLETT *Parsons & W.* xxviii, That light terra sienna tint which may be seen in many of our cathedrals.

‖**Terra sigillata** (te·ră sidʒilēⁱ·tă). Also 5-6 terre sigillate, 6 terra sygyllata. [med.L., = 'sealed earth': so F. *terre seellée* (Cotgr.), *terre sigillée* (Littré), It. *terra sigillata* (Florio), G. *siegelerde*. For the reason of the name, see quot. 1802.]

**1.** An astringent bole, of fatty consistence and reddish colour, obtained from Lemnos; formerly esteemed as a medicine and antidote; sphragide; known also as †*sealed earth* (SEALED *ppl. a.* 1 d), *sigillate earth*, *Lemnian earth*, TERRA LEMNIA. Also applied to similar earths found elsewhere.

**1398** TREVISA *Barth. De P. R.* XVI. xcvii. (Bodl. MS.), A Certeyn veyne of erþe is icleped *Terra sigillata*, and is singulerliche colde and druy. *c* **1400** *Lanfranc's Cirurg.* 61 Take þe pouder of crabbis brent vj. parties, gencian .iij parties, terre sigillate oon partie, make poudre. *c* **1550** LLOYD *Treas. Health* H ij, Take one parte of Terrasygyllata, and an other of the gumme called Sarasenicum. **1632** LITHGOW *Trav.* III. 97 The soueraigne minerall against infections, called Terra Lemnia, or Sigillata. **1756** NUGENT *Gr. Tour* II. 59 Germany is famous for that sort of earth, seldom found any where else, called *Terra sigillata*. **1802** *Brookes' Gazetteer* (ed. 12) s. v. *Lemnos*, This earth [of Lemnos].. is called Terra Sigillata, being formed into small loaves sealed with the grand signior's seal, and thus dispersed over various parts of Europe.

†**2.** Red pigment; ruddle. *Obs.*

**1563** WARDE tr. *Alexis' Secr.* II. 27 b, Terrasigillata or ruddle. **1608** CAPT. SMITH *True Relat.* 35 Two Indians, each with a cudgell, and all newly painted with Terrasigillata, came circling about me as though they would have clubed me like a hare.

**Te·rrasphere.** *rare.* [f. L. *terra* earth + SPHERE: cf. *planisphere*.] = TELLURION.

**1891**– in American dictionaries.

**Terra verd, vert**, variants of TERRE-VERTE.

†**Terre**, *sb. Obs. rare*$^{-1}$. [a. F. *terre*:—L. *terra* earth.] Land; *pl.* lands, possessions.

**1526** in Dillon *Customs of Pale* (1892) 83 Also he shall forfet to the kinge all his terres and tenements.

†**Terre**, *v. Obs. rare.* [a. F. *terrer* (*a* 1200 in Godef.) f. *terre* earth.] *trans.* **a.** To cover with earth; = TEER *v.* 1. **b.** To throw on the ground.

*c* **1440** *Promp. Parv.* 489/2 Teryn, or hylle wythe erþe, *terriculo*. **1586** WARNER *Alb. Eng.* III. xvi. 72 Lo heer my gage! (he terr'd his gloue) thou knowst the victors meed.

**Terre**, obs. f. TAR, TARE, TEAR *sb.*[1]; obs. pa. t. pl. of TEAR *v.*[1]

†**Te·rreal**, *a. Obs. rare*$^{-1}$. [f. L. *terre-us* earthy, earthly + -AL.] Of or pertaining to the earth; earthly, terrestrial, mundane.

**1598** GALLOWAY *Let.* in *Napier's Mem.* (1834) 295 The knowledge of sens, as most confused and terreall, is the lowest.

†**Te·rrean**, *a. Obs. rare*$^{-1}$. [f. as prec. + -AN.] Of the earth; of earth.

**1704** HEARNE *Duct. Hist.* (1714) I. 184 Dr. Burnet supposes his Terrean Crust which had for 1500 Years held in the Waters of the Abyss was by the heat of the Sun so parch'd and crack'd, that at last it broke.

‖**Terre bleue.** *Obs. rare*$^{-1}$. [F., = blue earth.] An earthy form of the blue mineral Azurite (a hydrated basic copper carbonate); as a pigment, known as *Lambert's Blue*.

**1728** WOODWARD *Meth. Fossils* 3 *note*, Terre bleue..is.. a light, loose, friable Kind of Lapis Armenus.

**Terreer**, obs. form of TERRIER[1].

**Terrein**, obs. f. TERRAIN, TERRENE.

†**Terre·ity.** *Obs. rare.* [ad. med.L. *terreitās* (*c* 1250 in Vincent of Beauvais, *Spec. Doctr.* XII. 109): see -ITY. So obs. It. *terreità* (Florio 1598).] The essential quality of earth; earthiness.

**1610** B. JONSON *Alch.* II. v, The Aqueitie, Terreitie and Sulphureitie Shall runne together againe, and all be annull'd. **1757** tr. *Henckel's Pyritol.* 114 Such a body as returns not to its universal terreity, but is arrived to a more heightened degree of metalliety.

†**Terrell.** *Obs. rare*$^{-1}$. [Anglicized form of next.] = next, sense 1.

**1619** BAINBRIDGE *Descr. late Comet* 13 The rest intermediating in their motion, according to their distance from this little terrell, for whose vse especially those vast planetarie globes were created.

‖**Terre·lla.** *Obs.* [mod.L. dim. of *terra* earth: cf. L. *terrula*, and see -EL[2].]

**1.** A little Earth; a small orb or planet.

**1657-83** EVELYN *Hist. Relig.* (1850) I. 162 Only signifying His making greater worlds, and not these microcosm terrellas. **1682** H. MORE *Annot. Glanvill's Lux O.* 141, I should rather suspect..that the Fire will more and more decay till it turn at last to a kind of Terrella, like that observed within the Ring of Saturn. *Ibid.* 142 To let its Central Fire to incrustate it self into a Terrella.

**2.** A spherical magnet, having like the earth two magnetic poles; sometimes, for experimental purposes, marked with lines representing the earth's equator, meridians, parallels, etc.: used to illustrate the dipping of the needle, and other phenomena of terrestrial magnetism. Also, a small artificial globe having a magnet within it, which behaves in the same way, and serves the same purposes.

**1613** M. RIDLEY *Magn. Bodies* 4 The first form of the Magnet..is a large one in fashion of a round ball, boule or globe, and we do call it a *Terrella*. **1646** SIR T. BROWNE *Pseud. Ep.* 62 The Terrella or sphericall magnet geographically set out with circles of the Globe. **1773** LORIMER in *Phil. Trans.* LXV. 79 Whenever any one meets with a terrella, or spherical loadstone, the first thing he does is to find out its poles. **1822** IMISON *Sc. & Art* I. 405 A small globe, having a magnet enclosed within it, which..is called a *terrella*. **1837** BREWSTER *Magnetism* 304 Shape it..so as to give it any form.., whether of a terrella,..or any other.

†**Te·rremote.** *Obs.* [a. OF. *terremote* (12th c. in Godef.), ad. L. *terræ mōtus* earthquake. In It. and Sp. *terremoto*.] An earthquake.

**1390** GOWER *Conf.* III. 75 Wherof that al the halle quok, As it a terremote were. *c* **1450** *Mirour Saluacioun* 4681 Terremote and of graves notable apercionne.

**Terremotive** (terĭmōᵘ·tiv), *a. rare.* [f. L. *terræ mōtus* earthquake + -IVE, after *motive*.] Of or pertaining to an earthquake; seismic.

**1837** WHEWELL *Hist. Induct. Sc.* (1857) III. 459 The frequent sympathy of volcanic and terremotive action. **1840** — *Philos. Induct. Sc.* x. iii. § 4 II. 128 The greatest known paroxysms of volcanic and terremotive agency.

†**Terre·nal**, *a. Obs.* [f. L. *terrēn-us* TERRENE + -AL; cf. OF. *terrenal* (13th c. in Godef.).] Of or pertaining to the earth; terrestrial; earthly; = TERRENE *a.* 1.

*a* **1555** PHILPOT *Exam. & Writ.* (Parker Soc.) 359 They looked for a terrenal kingdom. **1581** MARBECK *Bk. Notes* 934 That the Sacrament is made of two natures, of an heauenly nature, and of a terrenall and earthly nature. **1588** PARKE tr. *Mendoza's Hist. China* 397 The riuer Ganges, one of the foure that comme foorth of paradice terrenall.

**Terrene** (tĕrī·n), *a.* Forms: *α.* 4– terrene (6-8 terene, 7 terrhene). *β.* 5 terreyn, 6 -ein, -aine. *γ.* 6-7 terren. [ult. ad. L. *terrēn-us*, f. *terra* earth; an Anglo-Fr. *terrene* occurs in Wright *Lyric Poetry* (Percy) 4. Stressed *te·rrene*, and sometimes spelt *terren*, down to *c* 1700; but *terre·ne* is instanced as early as 1635; *te·rrene* in 1797 and 1865. (The 15-16th c. spellings in *-ein*, *-eyn*, *-aine*, suggest F. origin, and may have been influenced by F. *terrain*, or *terrien*.)]

**1.** Belonging to the earth or to this world; earthly; worldly, secular, temporal, material, human (as opposed to heavenly, eternal, spiritual, divine): = TERRESTRIAL 1.

*α.* **13..** *K. Alis.* 5685 Paradys terrene is riȝth in þe Est. **1509** BARCLAY *Shyp Folys* (1570) 192 From terrene lucre that day withdrawe thy minde. **1548** UDALL *Erasm. Par. Luke* i. 17 All terrene or yearthly Kyngdomes. **1563** *Homilies* II. *Sacrament* I. (1859) 443 Not as especially regarding the terene and earthly creatures which remain. **1606** SHAKS. *Ant. & Cl.* III. xiii. 153 Alacke our Terrene Moone is now Eclipst. **1630** J. TAYLOR (Water P.) *Urania* xxxii, To keepe their Queene secure from terrene treason. **1635** QUARLES *Embl.* IV. i. (1718) 190 The common period of terrene conceit. **1638** SIR T. HERBERT *Trav.* (ed. 2) 301 They are in apparition terrhene Idolls. *a* **1711** KEN *Wks.* (1721) IV. 80 With zeal wash your own spirit clean From all concupiscence terrene. **1844** MRS. BROWNING *Catarina to Camoens* xix, Whatsoever eyes terrene Be the sweetest his have seen. **1865** SWINBURNE *Atalanta* 525 Nearer than their life of terrene days.

*β.* *a* **1450** *Knt. de la Tour* (1906) 4 And yeuithe longe lyff and stont in this terreyn and wordly thing [F. *choses mondaines et terriennes*] like as hym lust. **1546** LANGLEY *Pol. Verg. De Invent.* IV. v. 89 To declare that thei oughte to reiect terrein and yearthly substaunce. **1576** R. HILL in Farr *S. P. Eliz.* (1845) II. 305 You worldly wights, that haue your fancies fixt On slipper icy of terraine pleasures here.

*γ.* **1579** W. WILKINSON *Confut. Familye of Loue* 17 b, Our earthly and terren nature. **1620** J. WILKINSON *Of Courts Leet* 140 True faith and loialtie you shal beare of life, member, and terren honour. **1637** HEYWOOD *Dial.* v. Wks. 1874 VI. 200 Bury the thoughts of all such terren drosse.

**2.** Of the nature of earth (the substance); earthy.

**1601** HOLLAND *Pliny* II. C. I. 44 Because ouermuch of the drie terrene element is mingled in it. **1756** P. BROWNE *Jamaica* 11 Here the soil is generally terrene or earthy. **1807** VANCOUVER *Agric. Devon* (1813) 301 Combined with the finest particles of terrene matter the tidal waters could hold in suspension. **1853** J. G. MURPHY *Comm. Gen.* i. 2 The.. aerial, aqueous, and terrene materials of the preëxistent earth.

**3.** Occurring on or inhabiting the land as opposed to water: = TERRESTRIAL 5.

**1661** LOVELL *Hist. Anim. & Min.* Introd., Members common with the terrene quadrupeds. **1774** GOLDSM. *Nat. Hist.* I. 20 These [shells]..are considered as substances entirely terrene. **1854** BREWSTER *More Worlds* iv. 86 In any terrene vertebrate.

**4.** Of or pertaining to the earth (as a planet): = TERRESTRIAL 2.

**1635** SWAN *Spec. M.* (1670) 81 That the nature of the place above the Moon doth sufficiently deny the ascent of any terrene Exhalation. **1709-29** V. MANDEY *Syst. Math., Geogr.* 595 Of the Dimension of the Terrene Globe.

**5.** *absol.* or as *sb.* **a.** The earth, the world. **b.** A land or territory; also *fig.*

**1667** MILTON *P. L.* VI. 78 Many a Province wide Tenfold the length of this terrene. **1735** SOMERVILLE *Chase* IV. 16 The teeming rav'nous Brutes Might fill the scanty Space of this Terrene. **1830** W. PHILLIPS *Mt. Sinai* II. 474 The vast terrene, Hereby deep shaken to its extremest bounds. **1863** COWDEN CLARKE *Shaks. Char.* ix. 215 That rich terrene of anthology, the pages of Shakespeare. **1894** R. J. HINTON in *Voice* (N. Y.) 18 Oct. 3/5 The conservation..of our.. whole terrene—may yet be found through irrigation.

**Terrene**, var. TERRINE, early f. TUREEN.

**Terrenely** (tĕrī·nli), *adv.* [f. TERRENE + -LY [2].]

†**1.** As regards landed estate; territorially. *Obs.*

*c* **1475** *Partenay* 5014, I Hym make my proper enheritour, For yut shall he be wurthy terrenly.

**2.** In a terrene manner; mundanely.

*a* **1638** MEDE *Wks.* (1672) 290 Opposed..to an offering earthly and terrenely sanctified, as were the Typical Sacrifices of the Law by Fire and Bloud. **1747** RICHARDSON *Clarissa* (1810) I. xxxi. 213 Those confounded poets, with their terrenely celestial descriptions. **1906** *Westm. Gaz.* 9 Apr. 4/1 Let not thy plaited eyes be cast Terrenely on the pansied past.

**Terre·neness.** *rare.* Also 7 terreness. [f. as prec. + -NESS.] Terrene quality; earthiness.

**1652** FRENCH *Yorksh. Spa* xiv. 106 He saith, that all kinds of tasts arise from a kind of terreness more or less adust. **1670** W. SIMPSON *Hydrol. Ess.* 90 The vapours of the burning bitumen and adust terreness therewith. **1727** BAILEY vol. II, *Terreneness*, Earthiness.

† **Terre·nity.** *Obs.* [f. as prec. + -ITY; cf. med.L. *terrēnitās* (Du Cange).] The quality or condition of being earthy; *concr.* earthy matter.

**1627–77** FELTHAM *Resolves* 74 (L.) [It] debases all the spirits to a dull and low terrenity. **1650** CHARLETON *Paradoxes* Prol. 23 The Acid Spirit, immersed in an excessive quantity of Terrenity, becomes..languid.

‖ **Terreno** (terre·no). [= It. (*piano*) *terreno* :—L. *terrēnum* TERRENE.] A ground-floor; also, a parlour.

**1740** H. WALPOLE *Let. to H. S. Conway* 9 July, I have a terreno all to myself. **1750** — *Let. to Mann* 11 Mar., I am already planning a *terreno* for Strawberry Hill. **1787** BECKFORD *Lett. Italy* xvi. (1805) I. 156 The terreno, or ground-floor, where they live chiefly in summer, is excellent.

† **Te·rreous,** *a. Obs.* [f. L. *terre-us* earthen, earthy (f. *terra* earth) + -OUS.] Earthy, of earthy nature; pertaining to earth or ordinary soil.

**1646** SIR T. BROWNE *Pseud. Ep.* II. v. 87 There remaines a grosse and terreous portion at the bottome. **1650** *Ibid.* VII. xiii. 312 According to the temper of the terreous parts at the bottome. **1794** SULLIVAN *View Nat.* I. xxix. 421 By the concretion of terreous and other particles, which..make either adamants, pebbles, or free-stone.

**Terreplein** (tē·ɹiplēn, ‖ tęr(ə)plēn). *Fortif.* Forms: α. 6–7 terraplene, 7 -plana, -plane, teraplene, 8–9 terraplain. β. 6 terreplaine, 8–9 -plain, 9 -pleine, 8– terreplein. [In α. ad. It. *terrapieno*, in Sp. *terrapleno*, in same sense; cf. It. *terrapienare*, Sp. *terraplenar*, to fill up with earth, f. *terra* earth + *pieno* (:—L. *plēnus*) full; in β. a. corresponding French *terreplein*. Both in F. and Eng., the second element was sometimes erroneously taken as It. *piano*, F. *plain* plane, flat, level (so in Littré), whence the former spellings *-plain*, *-plane*: cf. sense 2. A form *terrapin* app. from It. *terrapieno* appears in F. in 1567 (Godefroy *Compl.*); cf. TERREPLEIN *v.* below.]

**1.** Originally, The talus or sloping bank of earth behind a wall or rampart; hence, the surface of a rampart behind the parapet; and strictly, the level space on which the guns are mounted, between the banquette and the inner talus.

α. **1598** BARRET *Theor. Warres* 130 Vpon these Terraplenes should trees be planted. *Ibid.* Gloss. 253 *Terraplene*, an Italian word,..the earth that is rampired and filled vp vnto the inside of any wall or bulwarke. **1688** R. HOLME *Armoury* III. xvi. (Roxb.) 100/1 The Terraplane or walk of the Rampire. **1689** G. WALKER *Siege of Derry* 9 The outside Wall of Stone, or Battlements above the Terra-plene is not more than two Foot in thickness. **1712** J. JAMES tr. *Le Blond's Gardening* 118 The Platform sustained by the Walls or Banks of the Terrasses..in Fortification, is call'd the Terra-plain. **1829** *Sun* 17 Sept. 1/5 The insignificance of their batteries and the smallness of their terraplains, which prevent cannon of large calibre being placed there. **1859** F. A. GRIFFITHS *Artil. Man.* (1862) 260 The Terraplein is the upper part of the rampart, which remains after having constructed the parapet.

β. **1591** *Garrard's Art Warre* 317 (Stanf.) If..you cannot make Trauerses vppon the Terreplaine, for that the Enemy doth hinder it. **1704** J. HARRIS *Lex. Techn.* I, *Terre-Plain*, in Fortification, is the Platform or Horizontal Surface of the Rampart. **1830** E. S. N. CAMPBELL *Dict. Mil. Sc.* 88 The Banquette is placed behind this parapet, and the clear space left on the rampart, called its terrepleine, has been limited to about eighteen or twenty toises, terminated towards the town by a slope of 45°. **1879** *Cassell's Techn. Educ.* IV. 138/1 Bastions are termed 'full' when the interior is level with the terre-plein of the rampart on either side of it.

*transf.* **1848** *Blackw. Mag.* July 99/2, I went out to the narrow terre-plain over the craig.

**2.** The level base (above, on, or below the natural surface of the ground) on which a battery is placed in field fortifications; sometimes, the natural surface of the ground (quots. 1669, 1756, 1853).

[This latter use is manifestly connected with the mistaken derivation from *plana*, *plaine*, plain.]

**1669** STAYNRED *Fortification* 8 The Height of the Rampire..ought to be..18 Foot above the Terra Plana. **1756** *Dict. Arts*, etc. s.v. *Foundery of Bells*, They first dig a hole of a sufficient depth to contain the mould of the bell, together with the ear or cannon under ground, and six inches lower than the terreplain where the work is done. **1828** J. M. SPEARMAN *Brit. Gunner* (ed. 2) 37 Breaching batteries..must be sunk to such a depth that the terreplein of the covered-way may coincide with the soles of the embrazures. **1853** STOCQUELER *Milit. Encycl.*, *Terre-plein*, in field fortification, the plane of site or level country around a work. **1884** *Mil. Engineering* (ed. 3) I. II. 64 Batteries may be classed as follows, viz.: 'Sunken batteries', in which the terreplein is sunk below the surface of the ground. 'Elevated batteries', in which the terreplein is on or above the natural surface of the ground.

Hence †**Te·rreplein** (corruptly **terrapin**) *v. Obs. rare*, to furnish with a terreplein.

**1672** in *Fort St. George* (Madras) *Recds.*, Whither the Curtains of the Christian Town to bee strengthened and Terrapined.

† **Terrer.** *Obs. rare.* [f. *terre*, TAR *v.*[2] + -ER [1].] A provoker, vexer: cf. *teryare* s. v. TARY *v.*

**1382** WYCLIF *Ezek.* xxiv. 3 Thou shalt saye bi prouerbe a parable to the hous, terrer to wraththe [Vulg. *ad domum irritatricem*]. **1388** *Ibid.* ii. 7–8 Thei ben terreris to wraththe [1382 wraththers]..Nyle thou be a terrere to wraththe, as the hows of Israel is a terrere to wraththe.

**Terrer**, variant of TERRAR.

**Terrer(e, Terres,** obs. ff. TERRIER, TERRACE.

**Terre sigillate,** obs. f. TERRA SIGILLATA.

[**Terresity,** mispr. in Arb. *Garner* II. 114 for *terrestritie* (see TERRESTRITY, quot. 1568), whence in dictionaries; in some assumed to be for **terrosity*.]

**Terresterity,** erron. form of TERRESTRITY.

† **Terre·stre,** *a. Obs.* Also 4–6 terestre, 4–7 -er. [a. F. *terrestre* (12th c. in Godef. *Compl.*), ad. L. *terrestr-is* earthly, f. *terra* earth.] = TERRESTRIAL; chiefly in phr. *paradise terrestre* [OF. *parais*, *paradis terrestre* (12–13th c.), mod.Fr. *paradis t.*] earthly paradise, the Garden of Eden.

**1340** *Ayenb.* 50 Ase he did to euen [= Eve] and to Adam in paradys terestre. *c* **1386** CHAUCER *Merch. T.* 88 Wyf is mannes helpe and his confort, His Paradys terrestre and his disport. *c* **1400** MAUNDEV. (1839) v. 44 The Ryvere of Gyson ..cometh out of Paradys terrestre. **1484** CAXTON *Chivalry* I In gouernynge and ordeynynge the bodyes terrestre and erthely. **1550** J. COKE *Eng. & Fr. Heralds* § 133 (1877) 97 A marvelous puissaunce and..army marytayne and terrestre. **1663** GERBIER *Counsel* a vj b, After his Building up of Terester Seats.

**Terrestreity**: see TERRESTRITY.

† **Terrestrene,** *a. Obs. rare*—[1]. [f. TERRESTRE, after TERRENE.] Terrestrial, earthly.

**1599** A. M. tr. *Gabelhouer's Bk. Physicke* 235/1 It will helpe her, if any terrestrene thing will helpe her.

**Terrestrial** (tĕre·striăl), *a.* and *sb.* Also 5 -yall(e, 5–7 -iall(e, 7 tere-. Also 5–8 terestial(l after *celestial*. [f. L. *terrestri-s* (f. *terra* earth) + -AL. Cf. obs. F. *terrestriel* (16th c. in Godef.).]

**1.** Of or pertaining to this world, or to earth as opposed to heaven; earthly; worldly; mundane.

**1432–50** tr. *Higden* (Rolls) II. 183 The hieste powere intellectiue..separate somme tyme from substaunces terrestrialle. *c* **1460** in *Pol. Rel. & L. Poems* (1866) 82 Graunt to man the blysse eternalle When he passith thys lyfe terrestryalle. *c* **1470** ASHBY *Active Policy* 592 What man is he that is terrestial But of hym thus sadly wol speke & telle? **1526** TINDALE 1 *Cor.* xv. 40 There are celestiall bodyes, and there are bodyes terrestriall. *a* **1548** HALL *Chron.*, *Hen. VI* 182 b, Depriued of his terrestrial Croune, to be recompensed with an heauenly garland. **1593** NASHE *Christ's T.* T iij b, Their eyes are dazeled with terrestiall delights. **1750** JOHNSON *Rambler* No. 67 ℙ 2 The happiest lot of terrestrial existence. **1868** LAW *Beacons of Bible* (1869) 47 The guilty have then no terrestrial refuge.

**2.** Of, pertaining, or referring to the earth; often in *terrestrial ball, globe, sphere*, the earth.

**1593** SHAKS. *Rich. II*, III. ii. 41 From vnder this Terrestriall Ball. **1638** SIR T. HERBERT *Trav.* (ed. 2) 6 Extended to the plaine of the terrestriall Horizon. **1645** EVELYN *Diary* 21 Feb., The celestial, terrestrial, and subterranean deities. **1669** STURMY *Mariner's Mag.* v. v. 19 The Sphericality of this Terrestial [*ed.* 1684 -trial] Globe. **1796** H. HUNTER tr. *St.-Pierre's Stud. Nat.* I. 563 The two terrestrial Hemispheres are not projected in the same manner. **1837** WHEWELL *Hist. Induct. Sc.* (1857) III. 38 The subject of terrestrial magnetism.

†**b.** Proceeding from, or belonging to, the solid earth or its soil; not atmospheric. *Obs.*

**1658** J. ROWLAND *Moufet's Theat. Ins.* 908 Terrestrial or earthy Honey we call that, because the dew going away, it is suckt out of the very sweat of the earth. **1660** BOYLE *New Exp. Phys.-Mech.* xviii. 139 The Terrestrial Steam may..considerably alter the gravity or pressure of the Atmosphere.

**c.** Consisting of earth or soil. (*humorous.*)

**1844** O. W. HOLMES *Lines Berksh. Jubilee* 48 No soil upon earth is so dear to our eyes As the soil we first stirred in terrestrial pies!

**d.** *spec. Terrestrial globe*, a globe with a map of the earth on its surface: see GLOBE *sb.* 3; †*terrestrial line* (obs.): see quot. 1704; *terrestrial telescope*, one used for observing terrestrial objects.

**1559** [see GLOBE *sb.* 3]. **1617** MORYSON *Itin.* I. 31 In the Clocke [of Strassburg Cathedral]..there is a terrestrial globe. **1704** J. HARRIS *Lex. Techn.* I, *Terrestrial Line*... *Line Terrestrial*, in Perspective, is a Right Line, wherein the Geometrical Plane, and that of the Picture or Draught intersect one another. **1815** J. SMITH *Panorama Sc. & Art* I. 487 The Terrestrial Telescope, or Perspective Glass. **1837** GORING & PRITCHARD *Microgr.* 153 Terrestrial telescopes will not have received their finishing touch,..until their secondary image is just as perfect as their first. **1869** TYNDALL in *Fortn. Rev.* 1 Feb. 245 The poles, equator, and parallel of latitude of an ordinary terrestrial globe.

†**3.** Of the nature or character of earth, esp. as being dry and solid or pulverulent; possessing earth-like properties or qualities; earthy. *Obs.*

**1594** PLAT *Jewell-ho.* I. 21 [Quick lime] whose moisture is altogether exhaled, so as there remaineth therein nothing else, but the terrestrial parts replenished with a fiery vertue. **1668** CULPEPPER & COLE *Barthol. Anat.* I. xviii. 49 The thick and terrestrial Excrements of the Kidneys. **1684–5** BOYLE *Min. Waters* 29 Of the division of the Cap. Mort. into saline and terrestrial and other parts not dissoluble in Water. **1756** *Phil. Trans.* XLIX. 903 Acids..do dissolve animal calculi, by acting upon their terrestrial parts.

**4.** Of, or pertaining to, the land of the world, as distinct from the waters.

**1628** HOBBES *Thucyd.* (1822) 20 We offer you a naval not a terrestrial league. **1644** EVELYN *Diary* 7 Nov., The terrestrial and naval battailes here graven. **1839** ALISON *Hist. Europe* (1849–50) VII. xlii. § 55. 136 While England was.. extending her naval dominion,..Napoleon was..advancing in his career of terrestrial empire.

**5.** *Nat. Hist.* Occurring on, or inhabiting, land: **a.** *Zool.* Living on the land as distinguished from the waters, or on the ground as distinct from the air; applied *spec.* to birds of the order *Terrestres*, and to air-breathing molluscs and crustaceans.

**1638** RAWLEY tr. *Bacon's Life & Death* (1650) 54 Fishes need lesse Refrigeration than Terrestriall Creatures. **1727–41** CHAMBERS *Cycl.* s.v. *Bird*, Birds are usually divided into terrestrial, and aquatic. **1830** LYELL *Princ. Geol.* I. 479 The subserviency of our planet to the support of terrestrial as well as aquatic species. **1859** DARWIN *Orig. Spec.* xii. (1873) 341 The distribution of terrestrial animals. **1888** ROLLESTON & JACKSON *Anim. Life* 455 A few *Gastropoda* are terrestrial and air-breathers.

**b.** *Bot.* Growing in the soil; distinguished from *aquatic*, *marine*, *parasitic*, or *epiphytic*.

**1831** J. DAVIES *Manual Mat. Med.* 424 *Fungi.* Terrestrial or parasitical plants of very variable consistence, but never of a green colour. **1849** LYELL *2nd Visit U.S.* (1850) II. 305 Land covered with a luxuriant vegetation of terrestrial plants. **1875** BENNETT & DYER *Sachs' Bot.* 660 The autumn crocus, tulip, crown imperial, terrestrial orchids.

**B.** *sb.* (The adj. used absol.) **a.** A terrestrial being; *esp.* a human being, a mortal; in quot. 1598, a man of secular estate, a layman. **b.** The terrestrial world, the earth (*rare*). **c.** *pl.* Terrestrial animals, orders, or families: see quot. 1842.

**a. 1598** SHAKS. *Merry W.* III. i. 108 (Qo. 1) Giue me thy hand, terestiall..Giue me thy hand, celestiall. **1725** POPE *Odyss.* XIX. 691 Heav'n that knows what all terrestrials need, Repose to night, and toil to day decreed. **1873** PROCTOR *Expanse Heav.* (1877) 235 Varieties of effect altogether unfamiliar to us terrestrials. **b. 1742** YOUNG *Nt. Th.* IX. 598 Thou,..Whose little heart, is moor'd within a nook Of this obscure terrestrial. **c. 1842** BRANDE & COX *Dict. Sc.*, etc., *Terrestrials*,..the name of a section of the class *Aves*, corresponding to the orders *Rasores* and *Cursores*; also of a family of Pulmonated Gastropods, and of a division of Isopodous Crustaceans.

Hence **Terre·strialism,** worldliness (as a way of life), secularity; **Terre·strialize** *v.*, *trans.* to make terrestrial or earthly.

**1856** GRINDON *Life* xxiii. (1875) 297 Falling neither into fanaticism nor terrestrialism. **1829** WILSON in *Blackw. Mag.* XXV. 389 Every breath of air we draw is terrestrialized or etherealized by imagination. **1901** *Edin. Rev.* Apr. 357 Once terrestrialised, life..is 'not a dream but may become one'.

**Terre·strially,** *adv.* [f. prec. + -LY [2].]

**1.** In a terrestrial manner; after the manner of earthly or worldly things.

**1604** DRAYTON *Moses* II. 366 These plagues seem yet but nourished beneath, And even with man terrestrially to move. **1664** H. MORE *Exp. 7 Epist.* vii. 112 [They] grosly and carnally erre touching the nature of the Resurrection-Body,..phansying it as terrestrially modify'd. **1821** *Examiner* 220/2 Our own terrestrially transient duration.

**2.** As regards the ground or soil.

**1857** T. MOORE *Handbk. Brit. Ferns* (ed. 3) 19 Indication that the locality is moist, either atmospherically or terrestrially, or both.

So **Terre·strialness** *rare* (Bailey vol. II, 1727).

† **Terre·strian,** *a. Obs. rare*—[1]. [f. L. *terrestri-s* terrestrial + -AN.] = TERRESTRIAL 5 a.

**1608** TOPSELL *Serpents* (1658) 635 The signes of such as are hurt by the Chalidonian or Chersæan Asp, and the Terrestrian are all one, or of very little difference.

**Terrestriety**: see TERRESTRITY.

† **Terre·strify,** *v. Obs. rare.* [f. as next + -FY.] *trans.* To make terrestrial.

**1646** SIR T. BROWNE *Pseud. Ep.* IV. xiii. 231 Though we should affirm..that heaven were but earth celestified, and earth but heaven terrestrified. **1656** BLOUNT *Glossogr.*, *Ter[r]estrify*, to make earthly or like earth.

† **Terre·strious,** *a. Obs.* [f. L. *terrestri-s* terrestrial + -OUS: cf. *illustrious*.]

**1.** Having the nature of earth; earthy.

**1600** SURFLET *Countrie Farme* III. xlix. 539 [The] terrestrious and earthie temperature which all sorts of peares doe much consist of. **1646** SIR T. BROWNE *Pseud. Ep.* 322 Beside the fixed and terrestrious Salt, there is in naturall bodies a *Sal niter* referring unto Sulphur. **1741** MONRO *Anat. Nerves* (ed. 3) 25 Saline and terrestrious Particles.

**2.** Of or consisting of the land surface of the earth.

**1646** SIR T. BROWNE *Pseud. Ep.* II. ii. (1650) 49 This variation proceedeth not only from terrestrious eminencies, and magnetical veins of earth laterally respecting the needle. **1862** MARSH *Lect. Eng. Lang.* 24 The geographical centre of the terrestrious portion of the globe.

**3.** Of, pertaining to, or inhabiting the land; = TERRESTRIAL 5.

**1646** SIR T. BROWNE *Pseud. Ep.* III. xxiv. 169 Some [animals] in the Sea..hold those shapes which terrestrious formes approach not. *Ibid.* 170 That nomenclature of Adam, which unto terrestrious animalls assigned a name appropriate unto their natures.

† **Terre·strity, terrestre·ity.** *Obs.* [ad. med.L. *terrestritās* (*a* 1330 in Du Cange), f. *terre-*

*stri-s* earthly: see -TY, -ITY. Hence F. *terrestrité, -eté*, Eng. *terrestrity*. In 16th c. the L. form was altered to *terrestreitās* (1533 in Du Cange), app. after words properly in *-eitās*, from adjs. in *-eus*, as *terreitās, paneitās, vineitās*, etc., and this was imitated by It. *terrestreità* (Florio), F. *terrestréité* (Roquefort), Eng. *terrestreity*. *Terrestriety* is an individual error.] The quality or condition of being earthy, or of containing earthy matter; usually *concr.* earthy matter; applied esp. to gross or residual substances.

*α.* **1568** TURNER *Of Wines* B viij, Rhennish wyne..hath fewer dregges and lesse terrestritie [mispr. in Arb. *Garner* II. 114 terresity] or grosse earthlynesse than the Clared wine hath. **1603** HOLLAND *Plutarch's Mor.* 658 Referring all to the terrestrity of the sea: for that in sea water there is mingled much earthlie substance. **1605** TIMME *Quersit.* II. ii. 107 Salt peeter pure and seperated from all terrestritie and heterogeneal..substance.

*β.* **1605** TIMME *Quersit.* III. 153 The spirit of vitriol, seperated from all terrestreitie. **1662** MERRETT tr. *Neri's Art of Glass* iii. 12 The salt yields no more terrestriety, or dregs. **1681** *Phil. Collect.* XII. 105 That all the terrestreity thereof comes to be separated. **1683** SALMON *Doron Med.* II. 392 Freed from all its terrestreity [*mispr.* -terity]. **1750** tr. *Leonardus' Mirr. Stones* 42 From their own terrest[r]eity [orig. (1533) *suæ terrestreitatis*] they will sink in water.

**Terret, -it** (te·rėt, -it). Forms: 5-8 **tyret, teret(t, tyrret, 6 tyrette, 7 tirret, terriet, 9 terret, -it.** See also TORRET. [In 15th c. *teret, tyret*, collateral form of *toret*, a. OF. *toret, touret*, dim. of OF. *tor* (12th c.), *tour* a round, circuit, circumference: see TOUR. The phonetic change from *toret, turet* to *teret, tyret* is unusual.] General sense: A round or circular loop or ring, esp. one turning on a swivel, by which a string, ribbon, or chain is attached to anything.

**a.** A ring on a dog's collar, by which a string can be attached, etc.

[**1376-7** *Durham Acc. Rolls* (Surtees) 387 In uno lese et uno pare de turetteis pro domino de Hilton. *c* **1386**: see TORRET.] **1530** PALSGR. 281/2 Tyrettes for a grayhoundes coller, *boucclettes*. **1688** R. HOLME *Armoury* II. 186/2 The Grey-hound, hath his Collar, and the Spaniel hath his Terriet.

**b.** Each of the two rings by which the leash is attached to the jesses of a hawk.

**1486** *Bk. St. Albans, Hawking* b v b, The lewnes shulde be fastened to theym [jesses] with a payre of tyrettis [*ed.* **1496** tyrrettys] wich tyrettis shuld rest vppon the lewnes, and not vppon the gesses, for hyngyng and fastynyng vppon trees when she flyeth...The terettys serue to kepe hir from wyndyng whan she backes. [**1801** STRUTT *Sports & Past.* I. ii. § 9 [from *Bk. St. Albans*] The lunes, or small thongs of leather, might be fastened to them [the jesses] with two tyrrits, or rings.]

**c.** A ring or the like by which any object can be attached to a chain; = TORRET c.

**1515** in Carte *Life of Ormonde* (1736) I. Introd. 43 A white horn of ivory, garnished at both the ends with gold and corse thereunto of white silk barred with barres of gold and a tyret of gold thereupon. **1570-80** *Fabric Rolls York Minster* (Surtees) 118 For making a tyrret and a rynge of yron to the masons well buckett, 10*d.* [**1586-7** *Ibid.* 119 For a lowpe for the mason well buckett, 4*d.*] [**1900** J. T. FOWLER *Let. to Editor*, The ring by which the chain is attached to a watch is now called the 'torret' or 'turret', but the word is going out, and they call it the 'bow'.]

**d.** In horse-harness, One of the two (brass) rings fixed upright on the pad, or saddle, and on the hames, through which the driving reins pass. Also, any ring attached elsewhere to the harness for a similar purpose, as a *head-terret*: see quot. 1794.

[**1429**: see TORRET.] **1724** BAILEY, *Tyrets*, Ornaments for Horse-Harness. **1794** FELTON *Carriages* (1801) II. 144 The Territs are what screws in the saddle, or housing, for the reins to run through...A short territ is often fixed at the top of a bridle, called a head-territ, for the leading-reins to go through. **1840** *New Monthly Mag.* LX. 173, I saw a leader's rein break halfway between the head-terret of the wheeler and the pad-terret of the leader. **1851** MAYHEW *Lond. Labour* I. 358/2, 'I..found I could make my pad territs' (the round loops of the harness pad, through which the reins are passed), 'my hooks, my buckles, my ornaments.., as well as any man.'

Hence **Te·rreted** († te·reted, tirr-, tyrr-) *a.*, provided or fitted with a terret.

**1572** BOSSEWELL *Armorie* II. 55 b, Three Greyhoundes cursante, of the Moone, with colours Rubie, studded and tereted, Solis. **1610** GUILLIM *Heraldry* IV. xi. (1611) 218 Three greyhounds collars argent edged studded and tyrretted or. **1688** R. HOLME *Armoury* III. xvi. (Roxb.) 76/2 A dog collar,..edged, studded and Tirretted.

**Terret**, obs. form of TURRET.

**Terre-tenant** (tē³·ɹ,te:nănt). *Law.* Also 5-6 **tere-, 6-7 terr-, 6-8 ter-.** [a. AF. *terre tenaunt* 'holding land', f. *terre* land + *tenaunt* TENANT.] One who has the actual possession of land; the occupant of land.

[**1308-9** *Rolls of Parlt.* I. 275/2 Les heirs, & les terres tennauntz Gregorie de Rokesleye.] **1439** *Ibid.* V. 9/1 The said Feoffes, her Heirs, Executours and Teretenauntz. **1511-12** *Act* 3 *Hen. VIII*, c. 23 *Preamble*, Processe made.. ayenst theim..their heires executours or teretenauntes. **1601-2** FULBECKE *1st Pt. Parall.* 14 All the terre tenants of the village haue caried away their corn & hay except one man onely. **1607** in COWELL *Interpr.* **1702** *Lett. fr. Soldier to Ho. Com.* 19 They chusing rather to rely on the Oaths of the Tertenants and a View of the Lands. **1766** BLACKSTONE *Comm.* II. vi. 91 These mesne or middle lords, who were the immediate superiors of the *terre-tenant*, or him who occupied the land. **1818** HALLAM *Mid. Ages* (1841) I. ii. 151 The terre tenants in villenage, who occur in our old books, were not villeins.

**Terretour**: see TERRITOIRE.

‖**Terre-verte** (tɛ̄r,vɛ̄rt). Also 7-8 **terra-vert,** 8 **terraverd.** [F. *terre verte* (De Lisle 1783), *terre verde* (Cotgr.), It. *terra verde* 'green earth'; cf. G. *grünerde*.] A soft green earth of varying composition used as a pigment; esp. that obtained from Italy (Verona), Cyprus, and France; = CELADONITE or *green earth*, a variety of glauconite.

**1658** W. SANDERSON *Graphice* 82 Earth colours are best, as all Okers..Terre-vert. **1688** R. HOLME *Armoury* II. 313/2 Terra-vert colour, a kind of a dusky green,..is an earthy Clay Painters use. **1711** *Brit. Apollo* III. No. 141. 2/2 The smallest Body'd Terravert, Lake and the Pinks. **1730** GORDON *Maffei's Amphith.* 9 Crisocolla or Terraverd. **1748** J. HILL *Fossils* 31 Blueish green indurated Clay, called by the painters Terre Verte,..one of the best and most lasting greens they have. **1884** J. C. STAPLES in *Girl's Own Mag.* 8 Mar. 354/1 Emerald green and terre vert among the greens.

**Terreyn, terrhene**, obs. ff. TERRENE.

**Terrial.** ? Error for some term in hawking; ? for TERRET b.

**1602** HEYWOOD *Wom. Killed w. Kindness* Wks. 1874 II. 99 Mine [hawk]..seisd a Fowle Within her talents; and you saw her pawes Full of the Feathers: both her petty singles [toes], And her long singles, grip'd her more then other; The Terrials of her legges were stain'd with blood. **1886** CORBETT *Fall of Asgard* II. 25 That we may strike..with claws and bill of steel, and soak our terrials with his blood.

**Terriar**, obs. form of TERRIER [2].

**Terribility** (teribi·lĭti). *rare.* Also 5 **terryblete.** [a. obs. F. *terribleté*, also later *terribilité* (15th c. in Godef.), ad. L. *terribilitās*, f. *terribilis*: see next and -ITY, -TY.] = TERRIBLENESS.

**1471** CAXTON *Recuyell* (Sommer) 41 And the terryblete of the tyrant lichaon is not to be redoubtyd whan hit bleuyth vnpunysshid. **1593** G. HARVEY *Pierce's Super.* 58 Their valour and terribility in warre. **1823** G. DARLEY in *Lond. Mag.* Dec. 648/2 The energy, passion, terribility, and sublime eloquence of the stage.

**Terrible** (te·rĭb'l), *a.* (*sb.*) Also 5-6 **terry-, 6 terra-, terre-, tirre-.** [a. F. *terrible* (12th c.), ad. L. *terribilis*, f. *terrēre* to frighten: see -BLE.]

**1.** Exciting or fitted to excite terror; such as to inspire great fear or dread; frightful, dreadful.

*c* **1430** LYDG. *Min. Poems* (Percy Soc.) 142 Ther roos up oon out of his sepulture, Terrible of face. *c* **1450** HOLLAND *Howlat* 620 That terrible felloun my spreit affrayd. **1508** DUNBAR *Tua Mariit Wemen* 266 With a terrebill tail.. stangand as edderis. **1565** in Sir J. Picton *L'pool Munic. Rec.* (1883) I. 108 The marvelloussest and terriblest storm. **1612** BRINSLEY *Lud. Lit.* xxvii. (1627) 277 In very many schooles..the whole gouernment maintained only by continuall and terrible whipping. **1721** STRYPE *Eccl. Mem.* II. I. v. 36 Punished..to the terrible example of all others. **1791** COWPER *Iliad* IV. 515 The Greeks.. With martial order terrible advanced. **1860** TYNDALL *Glac.* I. vii. 50 A foe more terrible than the avalanches. **1870** SWINBURNE *Ess. & Stud.* (1875) 311 Superb instances of terrible beauty undeformed by horrible detail.

**2.** Exciting some feeling akin to dread or awe; very violent, severe, painful, or bad; hence *colloq.* as a mere intensive: Very great, excessive. (Cf. the similar use of *tremendous, awful, frightful*, etc.)

**1596** DALRYMPLE tr. *Leslie's Hist. Scot.* (S.T.S.) I. 128 Thair constant amitie.. to thair nychtbouris the Britanis brocht a terrabill feir. **1628** EARLE *Microcosm.* (Arb.) 49 He is a terrible fastner on a piece of Beefe. **1670** MARVELL *Corr.* Wks. (Grosart) II. 315 The terrible Bill against Conventicles. **1737** L. CLARKE *Hist. Bible* IV. (1740) 227 The terriblest blow of all. **1779** *Mirror* No. 41 ¶ 6, I was told it was a great way off, and over terrible mountains. **1829** LYTTON *Devereux* I. ii, He was a terrible caviller at the holy mysteries of Catholicism. **1844** DICKENS *Mart. Chuz.* xi, She's a terrible one to laugh. **1853** KANE *Grinnell Exp.* xxxiv. (1856) 301 Even you, terrible worker as you are, could not study in the Arctic regions.

**3.** quasi-*adv.* = TERRIBLY. (Chiefly in sense 2.)

*c* **1489** CAXTON *Sonnes of Aymon* i. 42 The duke..spored hys horse terryble. **1606** S. GARDINER *Bk. Angling* 13 The world is a Sea..terrible salt thorough sin. **1634** SIR T. HERBERT *Trav.* 5 The weather being terrible hot. **1796** JANE AUSTEN *Lett.* (1884) I. 126 We were so terrible good as to take James in our carriage. **1877** FREEMAN in *Life & Lett.* (1895) II. viii. 158, I was in a terrible bad way.

**4.** *Comb.*, as *terrible-browed, -looking.*

**1876** GEO. ELIOT *Dan. Der.* liv, He seemed to her a terrible-browed angel. **1906** *Westm. Gaz.* 21 Apr. 4/1 There was only one burglar, by no means a terrible-looking fellow.

**B.** *sb.* A terrible thing or being; something that causes terror or dread. Usually in *pl.*

*a* **1619** FOTHERBY *Atheom.* I. xii. § 5 (1622) 133 Which maketh the cogitation of death, of all other terribles, to seeme the most terrible. **1682** FLAVELL *Fear* ii. 9 Job calls it the king of terrors..or the most terrible of terribles. **1850** J. STRUTHERS *Poet. Wks.* II. 149 One has, between Grecian and Gothic story, generated a new race of terribles.

**Terribleness** (te·rĭb'lnės). [f. prec. + -NESS.] The quality of being terrible; frightfulness, dreadfulness, awfulness.

*a* **1533** LD. BERNERS *Gold. Bk. M. Aurel.* (1546) T vij, The most terrible, and the laste terrible of all terriblenes. **1535** COVERDALE *Deut.* xxvi. 8 The Lorde..brought vs out of Egipte.. with greate terryblenesse thorow tokens and wonders. **1651** FULLER *Abel Rediv.* (1867) I. 257 He did not only bear the terribleness of imprisonment. **1710** ABP. SHARP *Serm. Acts xvii. 31* Wks. 1754 VI. 188 The..majesty, and terribleness of his appearance. **1887** SMILES *Life & Labour* 431 The sadness and terribleness of some of the aspects of life.

† **Te·rriblize**, *v. Obs. nonce-wd.* [f. TERRIBLE + -IZE.] *trans.* To make or render terrible.

**1605** SYLVESTER *Du Bartas* II. iii. I. *Vocation* 271 Both Camps approach, their bloudy rage doth rise, And even the face of Cowards terriblize.

**Terribly** (te·rĭbli), *adv.* [f. as prec. + -LY [2].] In a terrible manner.

**1.** So as to excite terror or dread; dreadfully.

**1526** *Pilgr. Perf.* (W. de W. 1531) 245 b, Impenitent synners..drawen downe to hell moost terribly or feerfully. **1610** SHAKS. *Temp.* II. i. 313 We heard a hollow burst of bellowing Like Buls, or rather Lyons,..It strooke mine eare most terribly. **1718** PRIOR *Solomon* I. 639 This ample azure sky, Terribly large, and wonderfully bright. *a* **1848** R. W. HAMILTON *Rew. & Punishm.* viii. (1853) 362 It is at death that the consequences of guilt are often most terribly revealed.

**2.** Very severely, painfully, or badly; passing colloquially into a general intensive: Exceedingly, extremely, excessively, very greatly.

**1604** E. G[RIMSTONE] *D'Acosta's Hist. Indies* III. xx. 184 It raines and snowes terribly. **1707** *Curios. in Husb. & Gard.* 274 Tulips are charming to the Sight, but terribly offensive to the Smell. **1774** GOLDSM. *Nat. Hist.* (1776) VI. 101 Relying on its courage, and the strength of its bill, with which it [the puffin] bites most terribly. **1867** TROLLOPE *Chron. Barset* II. lviii. 147 You must be terribly in want of your dinner. **1871** JOWETT *Plato* I. 49 Why then are they so terribly anxious to prevent you from being happy? *Mod.* I am at present terribly busy.

† **Te·rric.** *Obs. rare*[—1]. [f. L. *terr-a* earth + -IC.] (See quot.)

**1612** STURTEVANT *Metallica* II. v. 59 Terrica is an Ignick Inuention, for the cheaper making of all kinds of Burnt-earths,..wherevpon the Materialls made by this Art, are called Terricks.

**Terrice**, obs. form of TERRACE.

**Terricole** (te·rikōul), *a.* (*sb.*) [ad. L. *terricola* earth-dweller, f. *terra* earth + *col-ĕre* to inhabit.]

**1.** *Bot.* Growing on the ground, as some lichens.

**1882** J. M. CROMBIE in *Encycl. Brit.* XIV. 562/1 With respect to terricole species [of lichens], some prefer peaty soil.., others calcareous soil.

**2.** *Zool.* Living on the ground or in the earth.

**1899** *Proc. Zool. Soc.* 6 June 715 Some living specimens of the 'Harmut', *Clarias lazera*.., from Damietta.. This curious Siluroid Fish..Mr. Boulenger was not able to confirm..the account of its terricole habits.

**B.** *sb.* An animal living on the ground, or burrowing in the earth; *spec.* a member of the *Terricolæ*, a group of annelids containing the common earthworm.

**1896** *Naturalist* 78 The head-pore of aquatic species is wanting in adult terricoles.

**Terricoline** (teri·kŏlain), *a.* *Zool.* [f. as prec. + -INE [2].] = next.

**1895** in *Funk's Standard Dict.* **1902** in WEBSTER *Suppl.*

**Terricolous** (teri·kŏləs), *a.* *Zool.* [f. as prec. + -OUS.] Inhabiting the ground, not aquatic or aerial; living in the earth; *spec.* of or belonging to the *Terricolæ* or earthworms; = TERRICOLE 2.

**1835-6** *Todd's Cycl. Anat.* I. 167/1 In the terricolous annelida there are no cirri. **1860** MAYNE *Expos. Lex.*, *Terricolus*,..living on or in the earth, as the *Harpalus terricola*. Applied by Latreille and Macquart to a group ..of the *Tipularia* which deposit their eggs in the earth..: terricolous. **1877** HUXLEY *Anat. Inv. Anim.* v. 220 In the terricolous forms (Lumbricus) the vasa deferentia are continuous with the testes. **1881** DARWIN *Veg. Mould* 247 In the same manner as gallinaceous and struthious birds swallow stones to aid in the trituration of their food, so it appears to be with terricolous worms.

† **Terri·crepant**, *a. Obs. rare*[—0]. [f. L. *terri-crep-us*, f. stem of *terr-ēre* to frighten + *crep-āre* to rattle, make a noise; cf. *crepānt-em* pr.pple.]

**1656** BLOUNT *Glossogr.*, *Terricrepant*..that rebuketh terribly or bitterly.

† **Terri·culament,** *sb. Obs.* Also 7 in L. form **-mentum,** pl. **-ta.** [ad. L. *terriculāment-um* (Apuleius) a bugbear, f. *terriculum* something that excites terror, f. *terrēre* to frighten: see -MENT.] A source or object of dread, esp. of needless dread; a bugbear.

**1548** W. PATTEN *Exped. Scotl.* Pref. c iiij, His vaine terriculaments and rattelbladders. **1567-8** ABP. PARKER *Corr.* (Parker Soc.) 315 Afeared or dismayed with such vain terriculaments of the world. **1621** BURTON *Anat. Mel.* III. iv. II. vi. (1651) 720 Such terriculaments may proceed from natural causes. *a* **1661** FULLER *Worthies, Warwick* (1811) II. 404 Those who are not *Terriculamenta*, but *Terrores*, no fancy-formed Bugbears, but such as carry fear and fright to others about them. **1674** JOSSELYN *Voy. New Eng.* 182 Such like bugbears and Terriculamentaes.

Hence † **Terri·culament** *v. Obs.*, to inspire with groundless fear.

**1644** J. GOODWIN *Innoc. & Truth Triumph.* (1645) 14 The man to whom the shadowes of the mountaines seemed men, was very prudent and advised in his feare, in respect of him that is terriculamented with such apocryphall pretences of feare as these.

‖ **Terridam, terrindam.** [Native Indian name.] (See quot.)

**1727-41** CHAMBERS *Cycl.* s. v. *Muslin*, There are various kinds of muslins brought from the East-Indies; chiefly Bengall; betelles, tarnatans, mulmuls, tanjeebs, terrindams, doreas, &c. **1891** *Cent. Dict.*, Terridam.

† **Terrie, terry.** *Obs. rare*[—1]. [app. a. OF. *terry, terri* (16th c. in Godef.), dial. forms of *terris* bank, mound, trodden ground.] A trodden path,

sometimes a balk or ridge of earth separating fields or allotments.

**1563** *Homilies* II. *Rogation Week* IV. (1859) 496 They do wickedly which do turn up the ancient terries of the fields, that old men beforetime with great pains did tread out.

† **Te·rrien,** *a. Obs.* Also 5 -yen. [a. OF. *ter(r)ien* terrestrial, seigniorial (12th c. in Godef. *Compl.*) f. *terre* land + *-ien*, -IAN: corresp. to a L. type **terriānus*.] Earthly, worldly; territorial.

[**1292** BRITTON III. iv. § 21 Fey a noster Seignur le Roi..de vie et de membre, de cors et de chateaus et de terrien honour.] *c* **1450** *Merlin* xx. 334 The kynge Arthur, that is oure lorde terrien. **1484** CAXTON *Chivalry* 24 Thoffyce of a knyght is to mayntene and deffende his lord worldly or terryen. **1489** — *Faytes of A.* I. i. 5 Emperours, kynges, dukes & other lordes terryens.

**Terrier**[1] (te·riəɹ). Now in limited use. Forms: 5 terrere, 5–9 terrar, 6 tarrar, terrour, -ore, 7 terreer, 7–8 terrer, 6– terrier. [a. OF. *terrier* (13–15th c. in Godef. *Compl.*) rent-roll, subst. use of *terrier* adj. (cf. F. *registre terrier* (15th c.) = med.L. *terrārius liber*):—med.L. *terrārius*, f. *terra* land. Thence med.L. *terrērium* rent-roll (Du Cange).] A register of landed property, formerly including lists of vassals and tenants, with particulars of their holdings, services, and rents; a rent-roll; in later use, a book in which the lands of a private person, or of a corporation civil or ecclesiastical, are described by their site, boundaries, acreage, etc. Also, in extended application, an inventory of property or goods.

**1477** *Paston Lett.* III. 206 Increse the rente, and make a new terrar and rentall. **1492** *Bury Wills* (Camden) 78, I wyll that..the terrere wyth that oon partye of thys indentur be putte and kepte in the hutche of the Gyldehalle. **1527** *Luton Trin. Guild* (1906) 192 A terrore of yᵉ land yᵗ was Thomas Colemakers. **1569** *Nottingham Rec.* IV. 136 A tarrar of alle the landes and medowes..belongyng to the towne. **1584** *N. Riding Rec.* (1894) 231 An auncient and true terrour..declaringe the limits [etc.]. **1594** WEST *2nd Pt. Symbol., Chancerie* § 87 The deedes, evidences, muniments, terriers. **1655** FULLER *Ch. Hist.* III. viii. § 17 Some Diocesses in this Terreer were exactly done, and remain fairly legible at this day. **1670** BLOUNT *Law Dict.*, *Terrar* ..is a Book, Survey, or Land-Roll, wherein the several Lands..are described; containing the quantity of Acres, boundaries, Tenants names, and such like. *a* **1695** WOOD *Life* (O.H.S.) I. 398 That there was no terrier taken of the goods he had, which were bought at the college charg. **1707** E. CHAMBERLAYNE *Pres. St. Eng.* II. ix. (ed. 22) 129 The Churchwardens, whose Office is to see..that there be an exact Terrier of the Glebe-Land. **1879** *Times* 22 Sept., The dimensions of each plot by number are preserved in the official parish terrier.

b. *transf.* and *fig.*

*a* **1640** JACKSON *Creed* XI. xxii. § 5 Some..give a more particular terrar or distinct map of this heavenly life or kingdom. **1646** OWEN *Country Ess.* Wks. 1851 VIII. 55 What bounds, what terriers are to be assigned to the one or to the other. *a* **1649** R. HOLDSWORTH in Spurgeon *Treas. Dav.* Ps. cxix. 111 The holy terrier of the Celestial Canaan.

**Terrier**[2] (te·riəɹ). Forms: 5 terrere, terryare, 6 terryer, taryer, terrour, 7 terriar, terrar, tarier, tarriar, tarryer, 7–8 (9 *vulgar*) tarrier, 6– terrier. [a. F. *(chien) terrier*, also as subst. *terrier* 'a hunting-dog used to start badgers, etc., from their earth or burrow' (cf. TERRIER[3]) = med.L. *terrārius*, f. *terra* earth (see prec.).]

1. A small, active, intelligent variety of dog, which pursues its quarry (the fox, badger, etc.) into its burrow or earth; the numerous breeds are distinguished into two classes, the *short-* or *smooth-haired*, as the fox-terrier, black and tan terrier, etc., and the *long-* or *rough-haired*, as the Scotch terrier, Skye terrier, etc. (See also BULL-TERRIER, TOY *terrier*, etc.) Formerly also *terrier dog*.

*c* **1440** *Promp. Parv.* 489/1 Terrere, hownde (*v.r.* terryare), *terrarius*. **1530** PALSGR. 279/2 Taryer a dogge. *Ibid.* 280/1 Terryer a dogge, *chien terrier*. **1576** A. FLEMING tr. *Caius' Dogs* i. (1880) 4 Of the Dogge called Terrar, in Latine *Terrarius*. Another sorte..which hunteth the Foxe and the Badger or Greye onely, whom we call Terrars, because they..creepe into the grounde. **1602** *2nd Pt. Return fr. Parnass.* II. v. 871 An open table for all kinde of dogges..He hath your..Terriers, Butchers dogs, Bloud-hounds. **1644–7** CLEVELAND *Char. Lond. Diurn.* 3 Who fitter to unkennell the Fox, then the Tarryer, that is a part of him. **1648** *Hunting of Fox* 25 Like so many Tarriars we must fasten upon them with tooth and nail. **1774** GOLDSM. *Nat. Hist.* II. 166 The tarrier is a small kind of hound with rough hair. **1815** SCOTT *Guy M.* xxii, A rough terrier dog..scampered at large. **1862** HUXLEY *Lect. Wkg. Men* 110 It is a physiological peculiarity..that impels the terrier to its rat-hunting propensity. **1863** H. KINGSLEY *A. Elliot* v, Rough long-legged English fox terriers, which ran on three legs, like Scotch terriers, and held their heads on one side knowingly.

b. *fig.*

**1532** MORE *Confut. Tindale* Wks. 695/1 We shall..set in such terryers to him, that we shall..eyther course him abrode or make him euyll rest within. *c* **1622** FORD, etc. *Witch Edmonton* I. ii, Bonds and bills are but tarriers to catch fools. **1779–81** JOHNSON *L. P.*, *Otway* Wks. II. 220 Hunted..by the terriers of the law. **1818** SCOTT *Hrt. Midl.* xxxiii, The opening quest of a well-scented terrier of the law drove me from the vicinity of Edinburgh.

†2. A name given to certain beavers said to burrow instead of building. *Obs.*

**1733** MORTIMER in *Phil. Trans.* XXXVIII. 177 He [Sarrasin in *Mem. Acad. Sci.*, Paris, 1704, p. 64] says there are some Beavers called Terriers [*Castors terriers*], which burrow in the Earth. **1781** PENNANT *Hist. Quad.* II. 384 They [Beavers] are met with dispersed, or in the state of Terriers, in the wooded parts of independent Tartary. **1784** — *Arct. Zool.* I. 103.

3. A punning appellation for a territorial: see TERRITORIAL 4 b. (Cf. TERRY *sb.*[2])

**1908** *Daily Chron.* 31 Mar. 5/3 It may..be argued that 'Territorial' is not very much longer than 'Volunteer', but it is just the little that makes all the difference...[Of three suggestions, 'Terror', 'Terrier', 'Torral', it was] yesterday rather thought that 'Terrier' would carry the day. *Ibid.* 18 June 3/4 Next year, which will be the jubilee of the force now known as the 'Terriers', to distinguish them from the 'Tommies'. **1908** *Daily News* 5 Aug. 4 The admirable spirit in which his [Mr. Haldane's] 'Terriers', as the wit of London has nicknamed our Home Army, have met the [etc.].

4. *attrib.* That is a terrier; of or like a terrier. (For *terrier dog* see 1.) Also in *comb.*, as *terrier-like* adj.

**1809** SCOTT *Let. to G. Ellis* 8 July, in *Lockhart*, A terrier puppy of the old shaggy Celtic breed. **1858** LEWIS in Youatt *Dog* (N. Y.) v. 169 The imaginary beauty of a terrier crop consists in the foxy appearance of the ears. **1894** BLACKMORE *Perlycross* 292 Endowed with the terrier nose of suspicion. **1895** SCULLY *Kafir Stories* 133 He had a wiry and terrier-like appearance.

† **Terrier**[3]. *Obs.* In 5 terryer. [a. F. *terrier* (14th c. in Littré):—late L. *terrārium* mound of earth, hillock, burrow, f. *terre* earth: see prec. sbs.] The earth or burrow of a badger or fox.

**1484** CAXTON *Fables of Æsop* v. ix, The foxe..was within a terryer nyghe to the lodgys of the lyon.

**Terrier, Terriet,** obs. ff. TARRIER[2], TERRET.

**Terrif,** obs. form of TARIFF.

**Terrific** (tĕri·fik), *a.* (*sb.*) [ad. L. *terrific-us* terrifying, f. stem of *terrēre* to frighten: see -FIC. So obs. F. *terrifique* (15th c. in Godef.).]

1. Causing terror, terrifying; fitted to terrify; dreadful, terrible, frightful.

**1667** MILTON *P. L.* VII. 497 The Serpent..with brazen Eyes And hairie Main terrific. **1718** POPE *Iliad* X. 300 In arms terrific their huge limbs they dress'd. **1796** MORSE *Amer. Geog.* I. 345 Even Canonicus..the terrific Sachem of the Narragansetts, sued for peace. **1821** CRAIG *Lect. Drawing* iv. 214, I cannot..advise you to attempt any species of the terrific in painting. **1899** WARD *Hist. Dram. Lit.* (ed. 2) I. 307 A terrific woodcut depicts the most sensational situation in the story.

2. Applied intensively to anything very severe or excessive. *colloq.* (Cf. *awful*, *terrible*, *tremendous*.)

**1809** J. W. CROKER in *Croker Papers* 12 Oct., I am..up to my eyes in business, the extent of which is quite terrific. **1855** MRS. CARLYLE *Lett.* (1883) II. 262 The crowd was immense, and the applause terrific. **1899** J. HUTCHINSON in *Arch. Surg.* X. No. 38. 177 The sensation of tingling burning pain remaining the same, while the itching is 'terrific'.

B. *sb.* in *pl.* Terrific things.

**1798** ANNA SEWARD *Lett.* (1811) V. 174 To exhibit, among his mock-terrifics, some pictures that have the genuine grandeur of horror.

Hence **Terri·ficly** *adv.* = TERRIFICALLY; **Terri·ficness**, the quality of being terrific.

**1727** BAILEY vol. II, *Terrifickness*, Terribleness. **1894** *Outing* (U.S.) XXIV. 360/1 A low mountain..over which a terrificly steep path led. **1904** *Adv. Elizabeth in Ruegen* 101 Her family wept and..told her the terrificness of marrying a widower with seven children.

**Terri·fical,** *a. rare.* [f. as prec. + -AL.] = TERRIFIC.

**1831** FR. A. KEMBLE *Jrnl.* in *Recoll. Girlhood* (1878) III. 47 In the evening we had terrifical ghost stories. **1855** MISS MANNING *Old Chelsea Bun-Ho.* xvii. 286 Abundantly more terrifical.

**Terri·fically,** *adv.* [f. as prec. + -LY[2]: see -ICALLY.] In a terrific or terrifying manner; frightfully, dreadfully, shockingly.

**1814** C. CLAIRMONT in Dowden *Shelley* (1887) I. 452 *note*, A most terrifically dirty inn. **1817** J. SCOTT *Paris Revisit.* (ed. 4) 79 The reports of the distant war sound terrifically in the ear. **1846** MRS. SHERWOOD in *P. Parley's Ann.* VII. 228 Arches of rock, which hung terrifically over my head. **1904** HICHENS *Gard. Allah* Prel. vi, Terrifically greater, more overpowering than man.

b. *colloq.* in intensive use: Alarmingly, excessively, extremely. (Cf. *awfully*, *dreadfully*.)

**1859** DARWIN in *Life & Lett.* (1887) II. 160 My corrections are terrifically heavy. **1883** J. PARKER *Apost. Life* II. 188 Always be terrifically hard upon yourself. **1885** G. MEREDITH *Diana Crossways* ii, Terrifically precocious, he thought her.

**Terrification** (te:rifikē¹·ʃən). Chiefly *Sc.* [ad. L. *terrificātiōn-em*, n. of action from *terrificāre* to TERRIFY.] The action of terrifying; the fact or condition of being terrified; consternation, extreme alarm, terror, fright.

**1612** in W. James *Deeds East Lothian* (1899) 29 For ane examplar terrificatioun to all Godles harlottis to flie and abhorre the lyk. **1797** EARL MALMESBURY *Diaries & Corr.* III. 504 Now and then he tried terrification, by letting out some strong Jacobin phrases. **1833** GALT in *Fraser's Mag.* VIII. 657 He was in an awful terrification.

b. *transf.* A source of alarm or dismay; a terror.

*a* **1806** MRS. GRANT *Lett. fr. Mount.* (1806) III. 180 She was a terrification to me.

**Terrify** (te·rifəi), *v.* [ad. L. *terrificāre* to frighten, f. *terrificus* TERRIFIC: see -FY. Cf. F. *terrifier* (Littré).]

1. *trans.* To make much afraid, to fill with terror, to frighten or alarm greatly. Also *absol.*

**1578** *Chr. Prayers* in *Priv. Prayers* (Parker Soc.) 501 Thou terrifiest none but such as most horribly are afraid of thee. **1638** *Penit. Conf.* ii. (1657) 15 No Conscience to accuse, no Devil to terrifie. **1667** MILTON *P. L.* x. 338 Terrifi'd Hee fled, not hoping to escape, but shun The present. **1774** GOLDSM. *Nat. Hist.* (1776) V. 215 The fowler then discovers himself, and terrifies the quail, who..entangles himself the more in the net, and is taken. **1868** MORRIS *Earthly Par.* I. *Son of Crœsus* xxiii, Girls, sent their water-jars to fill, Would come back pale, too terrified to cry.

b. To drive *from*, *out of*, *into*, etc. by terrifying; to deter *from*; to frighten *out of*, *into*, etc.

**1575** tr. *Luther's Comm. Gal.* iii. 3. 100 b, To exhort the Galathians, and to terrifie them from a double daunger. **1690** NESSE *Hist. & Myst. O. & N. T.* I. 53 Those very angels which terrified them both from the tree. **1824** SCOTT *St. Ronan's* xxxvii, It may terrify her to death in the present weak state of her nerves. **1867** SMILES *Huguenots Eng.* iv. (1880) 55 The people who remained were at length terrified into orthodoxy.

2. To irritate, torment, worry, harass, annoy, tease. Now only *dial.*

**1641** MILTON *Ch. Govt.* II. iii, Working only by terrifying Plaisters upon the rind and orifice of the Sore. *a* **1825** FORBY *Voc. E. Anglia*, *Terrify*, to teize; irritate; annoy. A blister or a caustic is said to terrify a patient. **1876** *N. & Q.* 5th Ser. VI. 56/1 He has been terrified all night by those insects. **1898** J. A. GIBBS *Cotswold Vill.* viii. 164 'Terrify him, sir; keep on terrifying of him'. This does not mean that you are to frighten the fish; on the contrary, he is urging you to stick to him till he gets tired of being harassed.

†3. To make terrible. *Obs. rare*⁻¹.

**1643** MILTON *Divorce* II. iii, If the law, instead of aggravating and terrifying sin, shall give out licence, it foils itself.

Hence **Te·rrified** (-fəid) *ppl. a.* (whence **Te·rrifiedly** *adv.*); **Te·rrifying** *vbl. sb.* and *ppl. a.* (whence **Te·rrifyingly** *adv.*); also **Te·rrifier** (-fəi,əɹ), one who or that which terrifies.

**1821** SCOTT *Kenilw.* xxxiv, Elizabeth..hastened..along the principal alley of the Pleasance, dragging with her the *terrified Countess. **1865** DICKENS *Mut. Fr.* I. i, Her terrified expostulation stopped him. **1890** *Temple Bar Mag.* Nov. 313 She is still *terrifiedly clutching his hand. **1617** COLLINS *Def. Bp. Ely* Suppl. 548 In stead of a *terrifier, he hath brought him about now, to be a praiser. **1870** R. C. JEBB *Sophocles' Electra* (ed. 2) 72/1 The terrifier of horses. **1617** J. WOODFORD in *Buccleuch MSS.* (Hist. MSS. Comm.) I. 199 A gibbet having been set up..for the *terrifying of the people. *c* **1586** C'TESS PEMBROKE *Ps.* LXXXVIII. xi, Thou dost me fill..With *terrifying feares. **1746–7** HERVEY *Medit.* (1818) 269 At the least terrifying appearance, they start from their seats. **1849** STOVEL *Introd. Canne's Necess.* 71 Exhibitions of terrifying depravity. **1805** SURR *Winter in Lond.* (1806) I. 271 If your honour had not been so *terrifyingly flurried, I should have given you the message before.

† **Terri·genal,** *a. Obs. rare*⁻¹. [f. L. *terrigen-us* earth-born + -AL.] = TERRIGENOUS 1.

*a* **1734** NORTH *Lives* (1826) III. 347 Even his terrigenal men would be void of ambition, or knowledge of wants.

† **Terri·genist.** *Obs. rare.* [f. as prec. + -IST.] One born of the earth.

**1631** R. H. *Arraignm. Whole Creature* xiv. § 2. 248 The men of this world, those Brutigenists, or Terrigenists, as they are called, Earth-bred wormes. *Ibid.* xvi. 286.

**Terrigenous** (teri·dʒĭnəs), *a. rare.* Also *erron.* terrigeneous. [f. as prec. + -OUS.]

1. Produced or sprung from the earth; earth-born.

**1684** T. BURNET *Th. Earth* I. 189 Our terrigenous animals must have been wean'd as soon as they were born. **1830** LYELL *Princ. Geol.* I. I. iii. 31 Either these were terrigenous, or ..the animals they so exactly represent have become extinct.

†2. *Chem.* A term for those metals of which the oxides are called earths. (Cf. CALCIGENOUS.) *Obs.*

**1854** J. SCOFFERN in *Orr's Circ. Sc.*, *Chem.* 433 Silicates, either of the terrigenous or the calcigenous class. *c* **1865** J. WYLDE in *Circ. Sc.* I. 394 Tests for the terrigeneous earths.

3. *Geol.* Land-derived: applied to marine deposits derived from the neighbouring land.

**1882** GEIKIE *Text Bk. Geol.* III. II. ii. § 6. 437 Mechanical deposits of the sea..Land-derived or Terrigenous. **1884** *Nature* 22 May 84/2 Terrigenous deposits in deep water near land.

**Terrine** (tĕrī·n). [Original form of TUREEN.]

1. = TUREEN. *arch.* exc. as French.

**1706**, etc. [see TUREEN *a*]. **1888** TRAILL in *Eng. Illustr. Mag.* Apr. 508/2 A part of South America where the earth's crust seems to be so absurdly thin that you can almost see the internal contents of the telluric pie—or *terrine*, as it may perhaps be appropriately called. **1901** *Speaker* 19 Oct. 66/2 In a few moments the Republican had set before him ..a terrine of Pâté de Foie Gras.

‖ 2. *Cookery.* A French dish: see quots.

**1706** PHILLIPS (ed. Kersey), *Terrine*,..in Cookery, a Mess made of a Breast of Mutton, cut into pieces, with Quails, Pigeons, and Chickens, cover'd with slices of Bacon..and stew'd in a Pan between two gentle Fires. **1736** BAILEY *Househ. Dict.* 565 *Terrine*, is a French dish, so call'd from *Terrine*, which signifies an earthen pan; it is made of half a dozen of quails, four young pigeons and a couple of chickens, and a breast of mutton cut to pieces; bake or stew them in an earthen pan between two gentle fires [etc.].

**Terring,** provocation: see TAR, TARRE *v.*[2]

**Terris,** obs. form of TERRACE.

† **Terri·sonant,** *a. Obs. rare*⁻⁰. [f. L. *terrison-us*, f. stem of *terr-ēre* to frighten + *sonāre* to sound; cf. *sonānt-em* pr. pple.] (See quot.) So † **Terri·sonous** *a. Obs. rare*⁻⁰.

**1656** BLOUNT *Glossogr.*, *Terrisonant*, that sounds bitterly [*ed.* 1674 terribly]. **1658** PHILLIPS, *Terrisonant*, sounding terribly. **1721** BAILEY, *Terrisonous*, that soundeth terribly.

**Territ**, variant of TERRET.

†**Territoire, -tor, -tour.** *Obs.* Also terre-. [ad. F. *territoire*.] = TERRITORY 1; land.

**1456** SIR G. HAYE *Law Arms* (S.T.S.) 115 That it be nocht our [= over] hye set,..or in our harde dry territoire, or our myry erde. **1547** *Aberdeen Regr.* (1844) I. 250 The terretour of the est part of the said burgh. **1589** FLEMING *Virg. Georg.* II. 24 Cæsar Who..Doost turne away th' vnwarlike Inde from territors of Rome. **1606** HOLLAND *Sueton.* Annot. 21 The Inhabitants of it, and the territour there about.

**Territoire**, variant of TERRITORY 2.

**Territorial** (teritō°·riăl), *a.* (*sb.*) [ad. late L. *territōriāl-is*, f. *territōri-um* TERRITORY 1. Cf. F. *territorial* (18th c. in Hatz.-Darm.).]

**1.** Of, belonging or relating to territory or land, or to the territory of any state, sovereign, or ruler.

**1768** R. WOOD *Ess. Homer* (1769) 22 Three other litigated cases with regard to territorial property and dominion. **1798** WASHINGTON *Let.* Writ. 1893 XIV. 20 An actual Invasion of our territorial rights. **1845** S. AUSTIN *Ranke's Hist. Ref.* III. iv. II. 135 Freeing themselves from the territorial jurisdiction of the temporal and spiritual princes. **1875** BEDFORD *Sailor's Pocket Bk.* vi. (ed. 2) 231 'Territorial water', in its essence means any water over which, or over the entrance to which, the Power possessing the coast can throw shot. Custom has given an arbitrary range of three miles. **1906** *Daily News* 28 May 9/1 The Jewish Territorial Organization, whose aim is to secure an autonomous home for the Jews in territory under the British flag.

**b.** Of or pertaining to landed property.

**1773** *Gentl. Mag.* XLIII. 199 It will be more beneficial to the public and the East India Company, to let the territorial acquisitions remain in the possession of the Company for a limited time. **1800** *Proc. Parl.* in *Asiat. Ann. Reg.* 49/2 That the dead stock and territorial revenue of India were enlarged very much, he was ready to allow. **1844** H. H. WILSON *Brit. India* III. 492 A plan..for keeping the territorial and commercial accounts distinct in future. **1855** DELAMER *Kitch. Gard.* (1861) 1 Territorial possessions are too highly prized in England for men lightly to yield even a fraction of such property at a fair value.

**c.** Possessed of land, owning or having an estate in land; landed.

**1832** SIR F. PALGRAVE *Rise Eng. Commw.* I. i. 15 The territorial aristocracy. **1867** R. CONGREVE *Ess.* (1874) 173 The territorial and moneyed aristocracy..is being brought daily into more direct..opposition to the people which it has governed. **1884** *Manch. Exam.* 25 Mar. 5/1 The preservation of that ascendency which the territorial class now enjoys.

**2.** Of or pertaining to a particular territory, district, or locality; local.

**1625** BP. MOUNTAGU *App. Cæsar* i. 8 Each particular..Church, for speciall and particular and territoriall questions & quæres. **1772** PRIESTLEY *Inst. Relig.* (1782) II. 131 The gods..were local and territorial divinities. **1857** TOULMIN SMITH *Parish* 4 'The Parish', whether as a mere territorial division or an active Institution, is not ecclesiastical either in origin or in purpose. **1868** GLADSTONE *Juv. Mundi* iv. (1869) 111 Phthie itself is..the only territorial name [etc.].. which we find in the Greece of Homer.

**b.** *Sc. Law.* Of jurisdiction: Extending over and restricted to a defined territory: see TERRITORY 1 1 c.

**1765–8** ERSKINE *Inst. Law Scot.* I. ii. § 11 Because this kind of jurisdiction was incident to, and followed the lands or territory to which it was annexed,..it got the name of territorial. **1838** W. BELL *Dict. Law Scot.* s. v., *Territorial Jurisdiction* was at one time universal; but, becoming formidable, was repeatedly discouraged by different acts,.. and by 20 Geo. II. c. 43, all heritable jurisdictions..were abolished or annexed to the Crown, with the exception [etc.].

**c.** *Sc.* Of or pertaining to an ecclesiastical district, not a parish. *Territorial church*, one organized to serve a particular district, esp. a poor and thickly populated one, without regard to the existing parish boundaries. So *territorial minister*. Now little used. (Introduced by Dr. Chalmers.)

**1822** CHALMERS *Sp. Gen. Assembly* 24 May, Notes 52 The assignation of a territorial district to each chapel. **1863** A. H. CHARTERIS *J. Robertson* viii. 231 A territorial church furnishes the best of all means for leavening the people. **1863** W. G. BLAIKIE *Better Days for Working People* v. (1864) 119 They are the heart-breaks of the city missionary, the territorial minister and the district visitor. **1873** T. COCHRANE *Home Mission Work* vi. (1885) 144 A humble labourer in the territorial field.

**3.** Of or belonging to one of the 'territories' of the United States: see TERRITORY 1 4.

**1812** BRACKENRIDGE *Views Louisiana* (1814) 99 The territorial governor [of Missouri] acts as well in the capacity of a general agent for the United States, as in that of civil magistrate. *Ibid.* 142 In 1805, it was erected into a territorial government..by the name of the Territory of Louisiana. **1888** BRYCE *Amer. Commw.* I. I. xiii. 167 There are also eight Territorial delegates, one from each of the Territories..not yet formed into States.

**4.** *Mil.* **a.** *Territorial Regiments*, the regiments of infantry of the line of the British Army, under the scheme of Army reorganization of 1881, by which each regiment is associated in name, depot, etc., with a particular county or locality.

**1881** *Queen's Regul.* 1 Precedence of Corps...The Territorial Regiments. **1885** *Whitaker's Alm.* 158 Territorial Regiments of the Line...Arranged alphabetically by the titles directed to be used in official correspondence.

**b.** *Territorial Army* or *Force*, the British Army of Home Defence instituted (on a territorial or local basis) in 1908. Also *Territorial* as *sb.* a member of the Territorial Army.

**1907** *Outlook* 30 Nov. 706/2 There is no evident reason why any old Volunteer should hesitate about joining the Territorial Army. *Ibid.*, There is nothing to deter the ex-Volunteer from becoming a Territorial. **1908** *Westm. Gaz.* 23 Mar. 7/3 So soon as the Reserves of the Regular Army were called out, the Territorial Force, the second line, should be mobilised to go into war training. **1908** *Daily Chron.* 1 Apr. 7/4 Yesterday the existence of the Volunteers as such terminated, and to-day the Territorial Army comes into being.

**Territorialism** (teritō°·riăliz'm). [f. prec. + -ISM.] A territorial system.

**1.** A system which gives predominance to the landed class; landlordism.

**1881** PARNELL in *Philad. Record* No. 3357. 1 Appealing to the great masses of England and Scotland against the territorialism and shopocracy which dominates Parliament. **1882** KAY in *Macm. Mag.* XLVI. 150 The anomalies consequent on the various reigns of feudalism and territorialism. **1884** *Manch. Exam.* 19 June 5/1 The old flag of Tory territorialism or the new ensign of Tory democracy.

**2.** Rendering German *Territorialsystem*, applied to a theory of church government which places the supreme authority in the civil power. Cf. COLLEGIALISM.

**1882–3** *Schaff's Encycl. Relig. Knowl.* III. 1821 [Pfaff] defended the collegial system against the reigning territorialism. **1888** SCHAFF *Hist. Chr. Ch.* VI. I. viii. 25 Territorialism, whose motto is *Cujus regio, ejus religio.*

**3.** *Sc.* The organization of church work on territorial lines; the extension of the parochial system to smaller areas: see TERRITORIAL 2 c.

**1873** T. COCHRANE *Home Mission Work* vi. (1885) 133 The grand practical work of Territorialism. **1904** J. WELLS *J. H. Wilson* vi. 51 Territorialism is the parochial system in its perfection, adjusted to the needs of a great city.

**4.** The organization of the Army on a territorial or local basis: see TERRITORIAL 4.

**1903** *Sat. Rev.* 24 Oct. 503/2 Territorialism may often be good as a recruiting principle, but seldom as a limit to a regiment's definition.

**Territo·rialist.** [f. as prec. + -IST.]

**1.** A member or representative of the class of land-owners: cf. TERRITORIAL 1 c.

**1865** *Pall Mall G.* 22 July 10/2 [The candidate] has no land in the county, and very little influence over the territorialists. **1867** B. CRACROFT in Brodrick *Ess. Reform* 164 If we add 246 to 256 we get 502 as the ascertained number of the territorialists in the House of Commons. **1901** *Daily Record & Mail* 21 Dec. 4 A compulsory disposal of the land from territorialists to settlers.

**2.** A member of a Jewish organization, whose aim is to secure a separate territory for the Jews: cf. quot. 1906 s. v. TERRITORIAL 1.

**1905** *Daily Chron.* 31 July 5/3 The territorialists..were bent on forcing [the Zionist] congress to accept the Gnas Ngishu plateau as a counsel of despair. **1909** *Ibid.* 9 Sept. 3/4 The..'Territorialists'..maintain that the true aim of the Jews ought to be to obtain an autonomous settlement anywhere—Uganda, for instance, or even Argentina.

**Territoria·lity.** [f. as prec. + -ITY.] Territorial quality, condition, position, or status.

**1894** E. P. EVANS in *Pop. Sc. Monthly* XLIV. 305 The consciousness of what might be called common territoriality tends..to bind together. **1906** *Daily Chron.* 17 Nov. 4/4 Lord Rosebery urged that territoriality was of the essence of good recruiting. **1907** *Sat. Rev.* 10 Aug. 163/2 Times have changed, and ability, common-sense and general knowledge must be added to territoriality.

**Territorialize** (teritō°·riălaiz), *v.* [f. as prec. + -IZE.] *trans.* To make territorial; to place upon a territorial basis; to associate with or restrict to a particular territory or district. Hence **Territo·rializa·tion.**

**1818** COLERIDGE in *Lit. Rem.* (1836) I. 158 The Pope had recently territorialized his authority to a great extent. **1897** MAITLAND *Domesday & Beyond* 157 It is not probable that the territorializing process will stop here. *Ibid.* 165 In the territorialization of military service. **1899** *Educat. Rev.* Nov. 379 What is called by students of railway questions the 'territorialization' of railways has been wellnigh accomplished. **1901** *Scotsman* 11 Mar. 6/3 His plan..demanded the territorialisation of the army.

**Territo·rially,** *adv.* [f. as prec. + -LY 2.] In relation to or in respect of territory.

**1828** in WEBSTER citing E. EVERETT. **1885** J. FISKE in *Harper's Mag.* Feb. 408/2 The formation of the tribe, territorially regarded. **1899** F. V. KIRBY *Sport E. C. Africa* ix. 98 British Chinde was 'territorially' smaller than on my last visit. **1900** G. C. BRODRICK *Mem. & Impr.* 148 This little borough [Woodstock]..belonged politically as well as territorially to the Marlborough family.

**Territo·rian.** [f. L. *territōri-um* TERRITORY 1 + -AN.] An inhabitant of a territory.

**1887** MRS. D. DALY *Digging*, etc. *S. Austral.* Introd. 4 The magnificent harbour of which all Territorians are so proud [i. e. those of the Northern Territory of S. Australia].

**Te·rritoried,** *a. rare.* [f. next + -ED 2.] Possessing a territory. (Usually in comb.)

*a* **1654** SELDEN *Eng. Epin.* ii. Wks. 1726 III. 11 Their plurality of narrow-territoried princes.

**Territory** 1 (te·ritŏri). Also 5 teri-, tery-. [ad. L. *territōri-um* the land round a town, a domain, district, territory. Etymology unsettled: usually taken as a deriv. of *terra* earth, land (to which it was certainly referred in popular L. when altered to *terrātōrium*); but the original form has suggested derivation from *terrēre* to frighten, whence **territor* frightener, *territōrium* '? a place from which people are warned off' (Roby *Lat. Gr.* § 943). So F. *territoire* (1278 in Godef. *Compl.*): see also TERROIR.]

**1.** †**a.** The land or district lying round a city or town and under its jurisdiction. Chiefly as a rendering of L. *territōrium*. *Obs.*

**1432–50** tr. *Higden* (Rolls) V. 321 Boecius..was throtelede in the territory Mediolanense. *c* **1460** *Oseney Reg.* 99, ij. acres of Arable londe In þe territorye or grownde of Cudelynton. **1483** *Rolls of Parlt.* VI. 256/2 Persons havyng Lands and Tenements in the seid Netheracastre, and within the territory of the same. **1538** ELYOT, *Territorium*, the fyeldes or countraye lyenge within the iurisdiction and boundes of a citie, a territorie. **1598** MANWOOD *Lawes Forest* i. § 3 (1615) 19 This word [*Territorie*] is most properly a circuit of ground, contayning a libertie within it selfe, wherein diuers men hauing land within it, and yet the Territorie it selfe doth lie open and not inclosed. **1651** HOBBES *Leviath.* II. xxii. 118 As they governed the City of Rome, and Territories adjacent.

**b.** The land or country belonging to or under the dominion of a ruler or state. Often applied contextually to the land or country itself of a state, as *French territory* (= France, the land of France).

**1494** FABYAN *Chron.* VII. 304 A cytie or towne, called Menne or Meune, within the londe or territorye of y$^e$ emperour. **1548** UDALL, etc. *Erasm. Par. Acts* xxviii. 86 We came to Rhegium, a citie in ye borders of Italy situate and lyinge within the territory that belongeth to the Brutians. **1591** SHAKS. 1 *Hen. VI*, v. iii. 146 Welcome braue Earle into our Territories. *a* **1687** PETTY *Pol. Arith.* x. (1691) 114 Not being above a sixth or seventh of the whole Territory of England. **1765** BLACKSTONE *Comm.* I. Introd. iv. 93 The kingdom of England, over which our municipal laws have jurisdiction, includes not, by the common law, either Wales, Scotland, or Ireland, or any other part ..except the territory of England only. **1789** *Constitution U.S.* IV. § 3 Rules and regulations respecting the territory or other property of the United States. **1799** HT. LEE *Canterb. T., Old Wom. T.* (ed. 2) I. 359 A small port, still within the Neapolitan territories. **1835** THIRLWALL *Greece* I. i. 3 The original Hellas was included in the territory of a little tribe in the south of Thessaly. **1908** *Athenæum* 12 Dec. 754/1 The rearrangement of frontiers and territories by Napoleon.

**c.** *Sc. Law.* (See quots.)

**1765–8** ERSKINE *Inst. Law Scot.* I. ii. § 16. 27 Since no judge can pronounce sentence on persons or subjects without his territory, civil jurisdiction cannot be founded, unless the defender either, first, reside within the judge's territory, or, 2dly, be possessed of some estate or subject within it. **1838** W. BELL *Dict. Law Scot.*, *Territory of a Judge* is the district over which his jurisdiction extends in causes and in judicial acts proper to him, and beyond which he has no judicial authority.

**d.** *transf.* Each half of a football ground considered as belonging to one of the teams: so in hockey, baseball, etc.

**1896** *Field* 4 Jan. 22/2 A moment later, the visitors..invaded the home territory. Here Jones got smartly away ..and..scored a..try.

**2.** A tract of land, or district of undefined boundaries; a region.

**1610** HOLLAND *Camden's Brit.* (1637) 112 The most fertile territories of Anjou. **1834** L. RITCHIE *Wand. by Seine* 5 It was necessary to wrest a territory from the sea itself for [Havre's] foundation. **1870** YEATS *Nat. Hist. Comm.* 89 The central territory is covered with forests. **1890** 'R. BOLDREWOOD' *Col. Reformer* xvii. 201 Fascinating territories of limitless mulga-downs.

**3.** *fig.* **a.** The domain, space, or region of fact, action, meaning, etc. belonging to or included in a science, art, class, word, etc.; sphere, province.

**1640** BP. REYNOLDS *Passions* xxxviii. 485 [Going] beyond their owne bounds, into the Territories (as I may so speake) of another Science. **1852** H. ROGERS *Ecl. Faith* (1864) 271 The whole field of historic investigation seems more or less the territory of scepticism. **1867** J. MARTINEAU *Ess.* II. 2 Psychology..has been allowed its title, but not its territory. **1875** WHITNEY *Life Lang.* vii. 110 It is the customary office of a word to cover, not a point, but a territory, and a territory that is irregular, heterogeneous, and variable.

**b.** *Anat.* A tract or region of the body pertaining to a particular organ or structure.

**1897** *Allbutt's Syst. Med.* IV. 125 The supply of blood to the corresponding hepatic territory is cut off. **1899** *Ibid.* VI. 716 The symptoms may be confined to the territory of a plexus. *Ibid.* VIII. 493 A vaso-motor..disturbance, confined to the territory of the vessels concerned.

**4.** In the United States, One of certain regions in the West belonging to and under the government of the American Republic, and having some degree of self-government, but not yet admitted as a State into the Union.

**1799** J. ADAMS *Wks.* (1854) IX. 41 The organization of the government of the Mississippi territory..should perhaps be mentioned to Congress. **1806** PIKE *Sources Mississ.* (1810) 90 A certificate that he had paid the tax required by a law of the Indian territory, on all retailers of merchandize. **1862** J. E. CAIRNES *Rev. Amer.* 22 A 'territory'..is a portion of the domain of the Union which is not yet a 'state'. **1888** SCHAFF *Hist. Chr. Ch.* VI. I. xi. 84 The law of the United States is supreme in the Territories.

**5.** *attrib.* and *Comb.*

**1898** *Westm. Gaz.* 28 Oct. 7/2 There can be no compromise..about the territory rights. **1901** *Ibid.* 21 Mar. 7/2 The Powers have been territory-hunting.

†**Territory** 2, **territoire.** *Obs.* Erroneously used by Caxton to render F. *tertre*, a rising ground, hill, or eminence.

*c* **1477** CAXTON *Jason* 70 b, We shal enhabite with peple the lowe montaignes & the territoires. **1481** — *Godeffroy* xxi. 53 They..began to reassemble, and gadred them to gydre on a territorie. *Ibid.* clviii. 233 Archys is a Cyte of the lande of Fenyce, and standeth atte foote of a montayne named Lybane, in a tereitorye moche stronge.

**Territour**: see TERRITOIRE.

**Terr-oceanic** (te:rjōᵘʃiæ·nik), *a. rare*⁻¹. [f. L. *terra* earth + OCEANIC.] Of or belonging to both land and ocean: *terr-oceanic basin*, a basin or hollow consisting of a sea-basin with the surrounding land within its watershed.

*c* 1860 R. MALLET in *Q. Rev.* Apr. (1909) 495 The lines of elevation which mark and divide the great oceanic or terr-oceanic basins..of the earth's surface.

**Terro-ceme·nt.** [f. *terro-*, taken as combining form of L. *terra* earth.] Cement of earthy nature.

1838 *Civil Eng. & Arch. Jrnl.* I. 373/2 Every one is aware that mortars and terro-cement, like other earthy matters, are non-conductors of heat.

† **Terroir.** *Obs. rare.* [a. F. *terroir*, OF. *tereoir* (12th c. in Godef. *Compl.*), *terrouer* (13th c.):—med.L. *terrātōrium* (Du Cange: in Pr. *terrador*) = L. *territōrium* TERRITORY[1], q.v.]

**a.** = TERRITORY[1]. **b.** Soil.

1483 CAXTON *Gold. Leg.* 18/2 For to berye it in the terroir of the cyte of Losane. 1660 *Charac. Italy* 83 Italy is the Garden of Europe, the *Terroir* being gentle and copious.

**Terror** (te·rəɹ), *sb.* Also 4–6 -oure, 6–9 -our. [ME. *terrour*, a. F. *terreur* (14th c.):—L. *terrōr-em*, nom. *terror*, f. *terrēre* to frighten: see -OR 1.]

**1.** The state of being terrified or greatly frightened; intense fear, fright, or dread. Also, with *a* and *pl.*, an instance of this.

*c* 1375 *Sc. Leg. Saints* xxxiii. (*George*) 701 He..but rednes ore terroure Of goddis son wes confessoure. 1500–20 DUNBAR *Ballat of Passion* 137 For grit terrour of Chrystis deid, The erde did trymmil quhar I lay. 1560 BIBLE (Genev.) *Ps.* lv. 4 The terrors [COVERD. fear] of death are fallen vpon me. 1605 SHAKS. *Lear* IV. ii. 12 It is the Cowish terror of his spirit That dares not vndertake. 1615 G. SANDYS *Trav.* 20 By little and little [they] descended as their terrors forsooke them. 1657 THORNLEY tr. *Longus' Daphnis & Chloe* 46 Pan sends a Terrour upon the Methymnæans. 1711 ADDISON *Spect.* No. 7 ⁋ 3 This Remark struck a pannick Terror into several who were present. *a* 1763 SHENSTONE *Ess.* xiii. Wks. 1765 II. 51 The gloom of night..was productive of terrour. 1794 GODWIN *Cal. Williams* 236 The terrors with which I was seized..were extreme. 1837 WHEWELL *Hist. Induct. Sc.* (1857) I. 227 Showed hesitation, alarm, increasing terrour. 1871 R. ELLIS *Catullus* lxiv. 338 You shall a son see born that knows not terror, Achilles.

**2.** *transf.* The action or quality of causing dread; terrific quality, terribleness; also *concr.* a thing or person that excites terror; something terrifying.

1528 ROY *Rede me* (Arb.) 41 Threatnynge with fearfull terroure. 1560 DAUS tr. *Sleidane's Comm.* 209 He vseth hys name sometime, only for a clooke and a terrour. 1667 MILTON *P. L.* II. 704 So spake the grieslie terrour. 1712 ADDISON *Spect.* No. 333 ⁋ 22 The Messiah appears cloathed with so much Terrour and Majesty. 1788 GIBBON *Decl. & F.* l. (1846) V. 16 The ferocious Bedoweens, the terror of the desert. 1814 SCOTT *Ld. of Isles* VI. xvi, Clearing war's terrors from his eye. 1841 EMERSON *Ess., Prudence* Wks. (Bohn) I. 100 The terrors of the storm. 1864 BURTON *Scot Abr.* I. ii. 61 He became..the terror of all the well-disposed within the district. 1900 G. SWIFT *Somerley* 14 There we kept up the reputation of 'little terrors' that we had earned with Miss Graten.

**3.** *King of terrors*, Death personified.

1611 BIBLE *Job* xviii. 14 His confidence..shall bring him to the king of terrours [1560 King of feare; COVERD. very fearfulnesse shall brynge him to the kynge]. 1682 FLAVELL *Fear* 9 Job calls it the king of terrors..or the most terrible of terribles. 1794 GODWIN *Cal. Williams* xxiv, It surely is not worse to encounter the king of terrors in health,..than to encounter him already half subdued by sickness and suffering. 1827–47 HARE *Guesses* (1874) 88 It is the only voice which can triumph over Death, and turn the King of terrours into an angel of light.

**4.** *Reign of terror*, a state of things in which the general community live in dread of death or outrage; esp. in *French Hist.* the period of the First Revolution from about March 1793 to July 1794, called also *the Terror, the Red Terror*, when the ruling faction remorselessly shed the blood of persons of both sexes and of all ages and conditions whom they regarded as obnoxious.

Hence also *White Terror*, applied to the counter-revolution that followed the *Red Terror*, and to other periods of remorseless repression in various countries.

1801 HEL. M. WILLIAMS *Sk. Fr. Rep.* I. xviii. 231 This superb monument had suffered most from the reign of terror. *c* 1870 *Miniature* xi. in *The Sibyl* 1 Apr. (1893), When the Terror, with hungry throat Ravished the homes of the wide Touraine. 1877 MORLEY *Crit. Misc.* Ser. II. 132 A White Terror succeeded the Red Terror. 1883 *Fortn. Rev.* 1 Nov. 701 The red terror of the French Jacobins is insignificant by the side of the white terror of Ferdinand VII. 1891 LD. ROSEBERY *Pitt* xi. 186 On the one side there were murders, roastings, plunder of arms, and a reign of terror [in Ireland in 1797]. 1893 *Tablet* 9 Dec. 934 A little Terror reigned over the provincial commune.

**5.** *Comb.* **a.** attributive, as *terror-drop, -fit, -gleam*; **b.** objective (with pr. pples.), as *terror-breathing, -giving, -inspiring, -preaching, -stirring, -striking*, etc., adjs.; **c.** instrumental (with pa. pples.), as *terror-crazed, -fraught, -haunted, -mingled, -ridden, -riven, -shaken, -smitten, -stricken, -struck*, etc., adjs.; so *terror-strike* vb.

1598 DRAYTON *Heroic Ep., Mortimer to Q. Isabel* 114 Curses..Through the sterne throte of *terror-breathing warre. 1873 W. CARLETON *Burning of Chicago* viii, The panic-struck, *terror-crazed city. 1897 P. WARUNG *Tales Old Régime* 184 [Convicts] who sweated *terror-drops beneath their stamped blankets. 1868 LD. HOUGHTON *Select. fr. Wks.* 199 At doubt and *terror-fit he only laughed. 1868 FARRAR *Seekers* I. vii. (1875) 98 All this *terror-fraught interspace between heaven and earth. *a* 1743 SAVAGE *Public Spirit* 127 Instant we catch her *terror-giving cares. 1844 LONGFELLOW *Norman Baron* vii, The lays they chanted Reached the chamber *terror-haunted. 1854 GRACE GREENWOOD *Haps & Mishaps* 91 Enrolment in this honourable *terror-inspiring, omnipresent corps. 1799 CAMPBELL *Pleas. Hope* II. 255 Nature hears, with *terror-mingled trust, The shock that hurls her fabric in the dust. 1630 DRAYTON *Noah* 225 This good man, this *terror-preaching Noy. *c* 1611 CHAPMAN *Iliad* XXII. 320 Then all the Greekes ..admir'd his *terror-stirring lim. 1845 HIRST *Com. Mammoth* 16 Our *terror-stricken warriors quailed. 1871 MACDUFF *Mem. Patmos* iii. 35 He cowers like a terror-stricken child. 1611 BARKSTED *Hiren* (1876) 74 So her beames did *terror-strike his sight. 1598 DRAYTON *Heroic Ep., Owen Tudor to Q. Kath.* 23 His dreadfull *terror-striking name. 1799 HT. LEE *Canterb. T., Frenchm. T.* (ed. 2) I. 270 She found herself alone,..*terror-struck, bewildered. 1824 LAMB *Elia* Ser. II. *Blakesmoor in H—shire*, A sneaking curiosity, *terror-tainted.

Hence **Te·rrorful, Te·rrorsome** *adjs.*, full of or fraught with terror, terrifying.

1870 *Contemp. Rev.* XIV. 491 The points..show themselves ..with that dark jaggedness and terrorful meaning which [etc.]. 1890 *Leeds Merc.* 3 Feb. 5/1 A writer..makes it terrorsome by the following anecdote.

**Te·rror,** *v. Obs.* or *arch.* [f. prec. sb.] *trans.* To strike with terror, to terrify. Also *absol.*

1635 HEYWOOD *Hierarch.* VIII. 515 They, terror'd with these words, demand his name. 1655 FULLER *Ch. Hist.* IV. ii. Ded., A Law..as all other penal Statutes intended but to terrour. 1878 P. W. WYATT *Hardrada* 3 The terror'd heart of Tostig.

**Terrorism** (te·rŏriz'm). [a. F. *terrorisme* (1798 in *Dict. Acad., Suppl.*), f. L. *terror* dread, TERROR: see -ISM.] A system of terror.

**1.** Government by intimidation as directed and carried out by the party in power in France during the Revolution of 1789–94; the system of the 'Terror' (1793–4): see TERROR *sb.* 4.

1795 *Hist.* in *Ann. Reg.* 112/2 It would..renew the reign of terrorism. 1817 LADY MORGAN *France* VIII. (1818) II. 357 He was obliged to remain abroad during the whole reign of terrorism. 1861 GOLDW. SMITH *Irish Hist.* 85 Like..the terrorism of the Jacobins..it was a moral epidemic.

**2.** *gen.* A policy intended to strike with terror those against whom it is adopted; the employment of methods of intimidation; the fact of terrorizing or condition of being terrorized.

1798 MATHIAS *Purs. Lit.* (ed. 7) 132 The causes of rebellion, insurrection, .. terrorism, massacres, and revolutionary murders. 1847 GROTE *Greece* II. xxx. IV. 155 He could not but be sensible that this system of terrorism was full of peril to himself. 1863 FAWCETT *Pol. Econ.* II. ix. (1876) 248 If anyone should disobey the decision of the meeting, he would subject himself..to a social terrorism.

**Terrorist** (te·rŏrist). [a. F. *terroriste*, f. L. *terror* TERROR: see -IST.]

**1.** As a political term: **a.** Applied to the Jacobins and their agents and partisans in the French Revolution, esp. to those connected with the Revolutionary tribunals during the 'Reign of Terror'.

1795 *Hist.* in *Ann. Reg.* 169 The terrorists, as they were justly denominated, from the cruel and impolitic maxim of keeping the people in implicit subjection by a merciless severity. 1795 BURKE *Regic. Peace* iv. Wks. IX. 75 Thousands of those Hell-hounds called Terrorists..are let loose on the people. 1818 HERVE *Beauties of Paris* II. 296 (Jod.) He assisted La Fayette in endeavouring to defend the king from the terrorists. 1877 MORLEY *Crit. Misc.* Ser. II. 83 That pithy chapter in Machiavelli's 'Prince' which treats of cruelty and clemency..anticipates the defence of the Terrorists.

**b.** Any one who attempts to further his views by a system of coercive intimidation; *spec.* applied to members of one of the extreme revolutionary societies in Russia.

1866 FITZPATRICK *Sham Sqr.* 180 Miss G——, the daughter of a Wexford terrorist, directed many of the tortures which were so extensively practised. 1883 *Harper's Mag.* Jan. 315/2 To [Russian] Terrorists it guarantees..security on condition of a..pledge to abandon..the revolutionary party. 1905 *Westm. Gaz.* 20 Sept. 2/1 Several notables are believed to be more or less implicated in the actions of the Terrorists.

**2.** Dyslogistically: One who entertains, professes, or tries to awaken or spread a feeling of terror or alarm; an alarmist, a scaremonger.

1803 SYD. SMITH *Wks.* (1859) I. 26/1 The terrorists of this country are so extremely alarmed at the power of Bonaparte. 1805 W. TAYLOR in *Monthly Mag.* XIX. 570 Some book of the religious terrorists, which tended to infuse the alarm of foul perdition. 1861 GEN. P. THOMPSON *Audi Alt. Part.* III. clxxv. 209 What becomes of the pretended terrorists at home who affect to be alarmed for the condition of every white female in the Antilles?

**3.** *attrib.*

1801 HEL. M. WILLIAMS *Fr. Rep.* I. xi. 113 The defeat of the terrorist-party. *Ibid.* xvi. 194 Under the terrorist government of France. 1856 GOLDW. SMITH in *Oxford Ess.* 295 An advanced and slightly terrorist school of philanthropists. 1884 in *Pall Mall G.* 11 Sept. 7/2 In the struggle we are engaged in with the terrorist and autocratic Governments of Europe, and especially with that of Russia.

Hence **Terrori·stic, -i·stical** *adjs.*, characterized by or practising terrorism.

1850 *Bentley's Miscell.* XXVIII. 407 This was the Government styled 'terroristical' by the Austrians! 1875 POSTE *Gaius* I. Comm. (ed. 2) 81 This terroristic law..was not abrogated till the time of Justinian. 1884 STEPNIAK in *Contemp. Rev.* Mar. 327 The gradual progress of the terroristic tendency under the influence of Government repression. 1887 *Century Mag.* Nov. 54 The leaders of the 'terroristic' or extreme revolutionary party.

**Terrorize** (te·rŏrəiz), *v.* [f. TERROR + -IZE.]

**1.** *trans.* To fill or inspire with terror, reduce to a state of terror; *esp.* to coerce or deter by terror.

1823 *Douglas, or, Field of Otterburn* II. iii. 33 This was, alas! no crafty scheme to terrorize my mind. 1874 H. R. REYNOLDS *John Bapt.* IV. v. 260 He bade them [soldiers] to terrorize no one. 1885 CLODD *Myths & Dr.* I. ii. 18 Superstitions which yet more or less..terrorise the ignorant.

**2.** *intr.* To rule, or maintain power, by terrorism; to practise intimidation. (After *tyrannize.*)

1856 LEVER *Martins of Cro' M.* xxxvii, It is one of Kate's fancies to terrorise thus over weak minds. 1870 *Daily News* 9 Sept. 6 Count Bismarck..openly..terrorized over the Prussian Chamber by relying upon the support of the army.

Hence **Te·rrorized** *ppl. a.*; **Te·rrorizing** *vbl. sb.* and *ppl. a.*; also **Terroriza·tion**, the action of terrorizing; **Te·rrorizer**, one who terrorizes.

1889 *Columbus* (Ohio) *Dispatch* 26 Jan., The White Caps ..began their cowardly and brutal work of *terrorization in the great state of Ohio. 1903 *Contemp. Rev.* Oct. 586 The Powers can do much by terrorisation. 1865 *Sat. Rev.* 22 Apr. 470/2 The whimpering and *terrorized suppliants against High Church domination. 1892 *Ibid.* 19 Mar. 330/1 Night gangs of masked *terrorizers. 1880 MCCARTHY *Own Times* IV. liv. 153 It began to be common talk that among the trades-associations there was systematic *terrorising of the worst kind. 1865 *Sat. Rev.* 12 Aug. 194/2 A *terrorizing collection of ghastly models and pseudo-medical specimens.

**Terrorless** (te·rəɹlės), *a.* [f. TERROR + -LESS.] Devoid of terror; exciting no dread.

1813 SHELLEY *Q. Mab* VI. 61 How terrorless the triumph of the grave! 1886 RUSKIN *Præterita* I viii. 248 Like a cloudless and terrorless Arctic sea.

[**Terrosity**: see TERRESITY.]

**Terrour**, obs. form of TERRIER, TERROR.

† **Te·rrulent**, *a. Obs. rare*⁻⁰. [ad. L. *terrulentus*, f. *terra* earth: see -ULENT.] (See quots.) Hence † **Te·rrulentness.** So † **Te·rrulency** *Obs. rare*⁻⁰.

1656 BLOUNT *Glossogr.*, *Terrulent*..earthy or earthly, made of earth. 1721 BAILEY, *Terrulency*, an Earthiness, a fulness of Earth. *Ibid.*, *Terrulent*, full of Earth. 1727 — vol. II, *Terrulentness*, Earthiness, earthy Nature or Quality.

**Terry** (te·ri), *sb.*[1], *a.* [Origin uncertain: it is not clear whether the word was orig. sb. or adj.

If adj., it may have been a corruption of F. *tiré* drawn; cf. Ger. *gezogener Sammet* 'drawn velvet'.]

**A.** *sb.* **1.** The loop raised in pile-weaving (PILE *sb.*[5] 3) left uncut; also short for *terry fabric, terry-velvet*, etc., see B.

1784 J. BENNETT *Patent Specif.* No. 1437 The Prince's everlasting union pearl or terry. *Ibid.*, The silk and mohair, pearl or terry, or wove, to float as a sattin. 1853 URE *Dict. Arts* I. 380 (Carpet weaving) Inserting a tag or wire to form the rib or terry. 1861 *Abridgm. Spec. Patents, Weaving* Index 1093, Terries raised on weft. 1879 WEBSTER *Suppl.*, *Terry*, 1. A kind of heavy silk and worsted material used in upholstery. 2. Heavy red poplin for ladies' dresses. 1888 HOWELLS *Annie Kilburn* xi, The furniture was in green terry.

**2.** In rope-making, An open reel.

1877 in KNIGHT *Dict. Mech.* (Perh. not the same word.)

**B.** *adj.* Of pile-fabrics: Looped, having the loops that form the pile left uncut, as *terry pile*, *terry velvet* (in F. *velours épinglé*). Also, Of or pertaining to such a fabric.

1835 *Ladies' Cabinet* Jan. 64 The new ones [hats] are composed of..plain velvet, and Terry velvet. *Ibid.* Feb. 202 A *toque* of pink terry velvet. 1851 *Mech. Mag.* 5 Apr. 278/2 Joseph Burch...For improvements in printing terry and pile carpets [etc.]...Patent dated September 28, 1850. 1853 URE *Dict. Arts* I. 380 The fabric produced will be plain or unornamented, with a looped or terry pile. 1878 BARLOW *Hist. Weaving* 210 Both cut and terry velvets are now woven in power looms.

**C.** *Comb.*, as *terry-ribbed* adj., *terry-weaving*.

1885 *Girl's Own Paper* Jan. 202/1 The majority are made of terry-ribbed silk. 1907 *Macm. Mag.* Jan., Notes 19/2 New sections on terry weaving, the automatic supply of weft to looms, and warp stop motions, have been added.

**Terry** (te·ri), *sb.*[2] A colloquial abbreviation of TERRITORIAL, applied to members of the Territorial Army; = TERRIER[2] 3.

1907 *Daily Chron.* 31 Dec. 3/4 The 'Terries' will be made to feel that there is little or no difference between them and the Tommies. *Ibid.* 4/7 Obviously some kind of a nickname must be found for the new Territorial Army...Upon another page Mr. Charles Lowe boldly calls our soldiers of the future 'The Terries'.

**Terry,** *sb.*[3]: see TODDY.

**Terry,** var. TARY *v. Obs.*, to provoke.

**Terryare, -yer,** obs. ff. TERRIER[2], [3].

† **Te·rrye.** *Obs.* Short (or error) for TERRIER[2].

1608 SYLVESTER *Du Bartas* II. iv. *Decay* 939 The eager Dogs are cheer'd with claps and cryes,..And all the Earth rings with the Terryes yearning.

**Terryen,** var. TERRIEN *Obs.*, earthly.

† **Te·rsail.** *Sc. Obs.* In 6 tersaill. [app. ad. OF. *tercel, tiercel*, 'a measure of wine' (Godef.), deriv. of *tiers* third, TIERCE.] = TIERCE (of wine).

15.. *Aberdeen Regr.* (Jam.), Tersaill of wyne. [1825 JAMIESON, *Tersaill*,..the third part of a pipe, a tierce.]

**Tersal, Tersan,** obs. ff. TERCEL, TERTIAN.

‖ **Ter-sanctus** (tɜ̄:ɹsæ·ŋktŏs). [L. *ter* thrice + *sanctus* holy.] See quots., and SANCTUS, TRISAGION.

1832 W. PALMER *Orig. Liturg.* I. 39 After this follows the

hymn *Tersanctus*. **1842** HOOK *Ch. Dict.*, *Tersanctus*, the Latin title of the hymn in the Liturgy beginning 'With Angels and Archangels', &c...In the Liturgy of Milan it has been used from time immemorial, under the name of *Trisagium*. **1892** C. WHITAKER *Stud. Aid Prayer Bk.* 81 The Triumphal or Seraphic Hymn. This hymn is sometimes called Ter-Sanctus (Thrice holy). It is indeed a Biblical Ter-Sanctus, but it is *not* the 'Liturgical Trisagion'.

**Terse** (tɔ̄ɹs), *a.* Also 7 **terce, tearce, teirce.** [ad. L. *ters-us*, pa. pple. of *tergēre*, *-ĕre* to wipe.]

†**1.** Wiped, brushed; smoothed; clean-cut, sharp-cut; polished, burnished; neat, trim, spruce.

**1601** B. JONSON *Poetaster* III. i, I am enamour'd of this street..'tis so polite and terse. **1607** DEKKER & WEBSTER *Northw. Hoe* II. i, Ist neate, is it terse! am I hansome? ha! **1615** CROOKE *Body of Man* 20 This Man..so laboured vpon it, that he left it smooth and terce. **1623** COCKERAM, *Teirce*, fine, neat, spruce. **1640** WILKINS *New Planet* IX. (1707) 256 The concave Superficies of that Sphere [the Moon] is usually supposed to be exactly terse and smooth. **1824** MISS MITFORD *Village* Ser. I. 39 (*Mod. Antiq.*) Mrs. Frances' features..were rather terse and sharp.

†**2.** *fig.* Polite, polished, refined, cultured: esp. in reference to language. *Obs.* (passing into 3).

**1621** BURTON *Anat. Mel.* I. ii. III. xv. (1628) 132 A polite and terse Academicke. **1631** MASSINGER *Emperor East* I. ii, Your polite and terser gallants. **1695** J. EDWARDS *Perfect. Script.* 6 Castellio..hath turned the whole Bible into pure, terse, elegant Latin. **1774** WARTON *Hist. Eng. Poetry* Diss. ii. (1840) I. p. cxviii, Henry of Huntingdon..was likewise a terse and polite Latin poet of this period. *Ibid.* II. xxvii. 365 A terse conciseness of sentences.

**3.** *spec.* Freed from verbal redundancy; neatly concise; compact and pithy in style or language. (The current use.)

**1777** W. WHITEHEAD *Goat's Beard* 1 In eight terse lines has Phædrus told..A tale of goats. **1849** MACAULAY *Hist. Eng.* vi. II. 16 *note*, An eminently clear, terse, and spirited summary. **1866** FELTON *Anc. & Mod. Gr.* I. II. i. 286 The tersest simplicity and most pregnant brevity of speech. **1868** FREEMAN *Norm. Conq.* II. x. 475 *note*, The Peterborough Chronicler is almost startling in his terse brevity.

†**4.** Applied to claret; also *absol.* as *sb. Obs.*

(Perh. not the same word. Some suggest *Thiers*, name of a wine-producing place in Puy-de-Dôme.)

**1671** SHADWELL *Humourists* IV. Wks. 1720 I. 179 Must I stay 'till by the strength of terse claret you have wet yourself into courage. **1687** SEDLEY *Bellamira* II. i, I am so full I should spill terse at every jolt. *Ibid.*, He grudg'd his money for honest terse.

**Terse**, var. TARSE *Obs.*; obs. f. TIERCE.

**Tersel, -ell(e, -elet**, obs. ff. TERCEL, -CELET.

**Tersele**, variant of TARSEL *Obs.*

**Tersely** (tɔ̄ɹsli), *adv.* [f. TERSE + -LY [2].] In a terse manner or style. †**a.** In a refined or elegant manner; elegantly, politely. *Obs.*

**1599** B. JONSON *Ev. Man out of Hum.* Dram. Pers., Fastidious Brisk..swears tersely, and with variety. **1648** HERRICK *Hesper.*, *Country Life* 27 Thus thou canst tearcely live to satisfie The belly chiefly; not the eye. *a* **1661** FULLER *Worthies* (1662) II. *Lincoln.* 165 That one living in so ignorant and superstitious a generation could write so tercely.

**b.** In relation to language: Neatly, concisely.

**1874** GREEN *Short Hist.* ix. § 10. 704 The cry of the York mob..expressed tersely the creed of the English trader. **1903** *Times* 1 Apr. 9/5 The Judge has tersely summed this up.

**Terseness** (tɔ̄ɹsnės). [f. TERSE *a.* + -NESS.] The quality of being terse: †**a.** of being clean-cut; sharpness or smoothness of outline. *Obs.*

**1802** PALEY *Nat. Theol.* xv. (ed. 2) 294 The compactness of its form, arising from the terseness of its limbs. **1828** MISS MITFORD *Village* Ser. III. 183 (*Hay-carrying*) A well-made little man..with considerable terseness of feature.

**b.** Polish, elegance, or neatness of style; in mod. use, Neat and forcible conciseness.

**1782** J. WARTON *Ess. Pope* II. 314 Gay..wrote with neatness, and terseness. **1808** HAN. MORE *Cœlebs* I. ii. 21 For giving a terseness and a polish to conversation..nothing is equal to the miscellaneous society of London. **1864** *Sat. Rev.* 31 Dec. 801/2 Landor had a..terseness and force of expression, which arrested the attention and won the admiration of his immediate contemporaries.

**Terset, Tersia**, obs. ff. TERCET, TARSIA.

†**Tersion** (tɔ̄ɹʃən). *Obs. rare.* [ad. L. type **tersiōn-em*, n. of action from *tergēre* (*-ĕre*), *ters-* to wipe: see -ION.] The action of wiping.

**1676** BOYLE *Mech. Origin of Electr.* Wks. 1772 IV. 347 Another observation..about these bodies, is, that they require tersion as well as attrition;..weaker electricks require to be as well wiped as chafed. **1704** J. HARRIS *Lex. Techn.* I, *Tersion*, is Wiping or Cleansing the outside of any Body. [**1878** *Encycl. Brit.* VIII. 3/2 He [Boyle] found also that heat and *tersion* (or the cleaning or wiping of any body) increased its susceptibility of [electric] excitation.]

†**Te·rsive**, *a. Obs.* [f. L. *ters-*, ppl. stem of *tergēre*, *-ĕre* (see prec.) + -IVE.] Having power to cleanse as by wiping; detersive; detergent.

**1665–6** *Phil. Trans.* I. 359 For the Eye-waters, I conceived them more strongly tersive, and clearing the Eyes. **1677** PLOT *Oxfordsh.* 49 Such a pleasant titillation, as invites the Patient to rub on the tersive water.

**Terslet, Tertane, Tertenant**, obs. ff. TERCELET, TARTAN, TERRETENANT. **Terter**, var. TERTRE.

†**Ter-terrify**, *v. Obs. nonce-wd.* [See TER-.] *trans.* To terrify threefold; to frighten extremely.

*a* **1618** SYLVESTER *Mysterie* Wks. (Grosart) II. 317/1 Destroyeth, Buildeth,..Confounds, Confirmes; Ter-terrifies, Sweet Consolation sings.

**Te·rtia.** Now *Hist.* Also 7 **tercia.** [app. an altered form of TERCIO, TERTIO, due to obscurity of final vowel.] A division of infantry: see quot. 1870; a TERCIO; a regiment; also *transf.*

**1630** B. JONSON *New Inn* III. i, 'Twill be desired Only, the expressions were a little more Spanish;..To call them tertias—tertia of the kitchen, Tertia of the cellar, tertia of the chamber, And tertia of the stables. **1644** R. SYMONDS *Diary Civ. War* (Camden) 159 When the King's army was in Cornwall, the infantry was divided into three Tertias, and every tertia should consist of three brigades. *Ibid.* 167 Lord Astleys Tertia of foot made the approaches. **1670** DRYDEN *2nd Pt. Conq. Granada* I. i, That tertia of Italians did you guide. **1819** SCOTT *Leg. Montrose* ii. **1870** C. R. MARKHAM *Life Ld. Fairfax* vii. 61 A foot regiment was..formed in solid square battalions ten deep, called *tertias*, the pikes in the centre, and the musketeers on either flank.

**Tertial** (tɔ̄ɹʃăl), *a.* and *sb. Ornith.* [f. L. *terti-us* third + -AL.] **a.** *adj.* Of or pertaining to the third rank or row of quill- or flight-feathers in the wing of a bird. **b.** *sb.* A flight-feather of the third row; sometimes erroneously applied to secondaries on the elbow-joint. See TERTIARY B. 3.

**1836** SWAINSON *Nat. Hist. Birds* I. I. iii. 81 They [Quills]..form three divisions, distinguished as the primaries, the secondaries, and the tertials...The tertials..have their origin from the humerus. **1842** BRANDE *Dict. Sc.*, etc., *Tertials*. **1874** COUES *Birds N. W.* 665 The color of the mantle extends ..to the tips of the tertials.

**Tertian** (tɔ̄ɹʃăn), *a.* and *sb.* Forms: 4 **tertiane**, 4–6 **-cian(e, -cyan**, 6 **-cyen, -san**, (**tarcian**), 8 **tercion**, 6– **tertian.** [ME. in *fever terciane*, or *terciane*, ad. L. *febris tertiāna*, also *tertiāna* sb., f. *tertius* third: see -AN. Cf. OF. *tierçain(e* adj. (13th c. in Godef.), *tierçaine* sb. a fever (12th c.).]

**A.** *adj.* **1.** *Path.* Of a fever or ague: Characterized by the occurrence of a paroxysm every third (i. e. every alternate) day.

In early use following the sb. as in F.; cf. QUOTIDIAN.

*c* **1386** CHAUCER *Nun's Pr. T.* 139 Ye shul haue a ffeuere terciane Or an Agu. **1398** TREVISA *Barth. De P. R.* VII. xxxix. (Bodl. MS.), A Feuere Terciane..greueþ fro þe þrid daye to the þrid and namelich aboute þe þrid houre. **1625** HART *Anat. Ur.* I. v. 48 During her husbands sicknesse, being a long and tedious, first Tertian, then double Tertian feauer. **1712** tr. *Pomet's Hist. Drugs* I. 37 To cure Quotidian, Tertian and Quartan Agues. **1834** J. FORBES *Laennec's Dis. Chest* (ed. 4) 318 Sometimes it is attended at the beginning by chills, which return with the tertian, double tertian, or quotidian type.

†**2.** Third in order. *Obs.*

**1592** WYRLEY *Armorie, Capitall de Buz* 123 They made three battels and a reregard, The first had Glesquine,..The Earle of Aucer ruld the second ward, Th'archpriest did their tertian battell hold.

**3.** *Mus.* Applied to the mean-tone temperament (in which the major thirds are perfectly in tune).

**1875** A. J. ELLIS *Helmholtz's Sensat. Tone* 649 Mean-tone, Mesotonic or Tertian Temperament.

**4.** *Tertian Father*: in the Society of Jesus, a member of the order who is passing through the last of the three stages of probation, which prepares him for admission to the final vows.

**1855** [implied in TERTIANSHIP]. **1876** J. MORRIS in J. H. Pollen *Life* vii. (1896) 181 Three different communities under one Rector—the novices, scholastics, and Tertian Fathers.

**B.** *sb.* **1.** Short for *tertian ague* or *fever.*

*Double tertian*, one in which there are two sets of paroxysms, each recurring every third (i. e. alternate) day.

**1362** LANGL. *P. Pl.* A. XII. 80 Mi name is feuere, on þe ferþe day I am a-þrest euere;..men haue I tweyne, þat on is called cotidian.., Tercian þat oþer, trewe drinkeres boþe! **1460** CAPGRAVE *Chron.* (Rolls) 291 He fel in a tercian, that continued many dayes. **1565** BLUNDEVIL *Horsemanship* IV. v. (1580) 4 Manie other speciall kinds, as Quotidians, Tertians, Quartanes. **1651** WITTIE *Primrose's Pop. Err.* III. 151 Lying sick of a Tertian. **1844** LEVER *T. Burke* lxxiii, The tertian of Egypt, so fatal among the French troops, now numbered him among its victims.

†**2.** An obsolete liquid measure for wine, oil, etc., the third of a tun, i. e. 84 wine gallons (= 70 imperial gallons); also, a large cask of this capacity; a puncheon. See also quot. 1542. *Obs.*

**1423** *Rolls of Parlt.* IV. 256/1 The Terciane iiii[xx] iiii galons. **1531–2** *Act* 23 *Hen. VIII*, c. 7 Euery butt of Malmesey shuld conteyne cxxvi galons,..euery tarcian or poncheon lxxxiiii galons. **1542** RECORDE *Gr. Artes* (1575) 206 Of wine and oyle the Tertian holdeth 84 Gallons...But ..there bee other kindes of Tertians: for there be Tertians (y[t] is to saye) Thirdles of Pypes, of Hoggesheaddes, and Barrels. **1749** *Phil. Trans.* XLVI. 55 It is declared that the Tun of Wine, Oil, and Honey, should contain..252 Gallons; the Pipe or Butt 126; the Tertian 84.

**3.** In Scottish Universities (now only at Aberdeen), a student in his third year. Also *attrib.*

**1857** CLERK MAXWELL in *Life* x. (1882) 296 Where Tertian and Semi are hot in dispute And the voice of the Magistrand never is mute. **1894** W. L. LOW *D. Thomson* iv. 83 During my Tertian year we were examined by him only once. **1895** ANNA M. STODDART *J. S. Blackie* I. 228 He followed the Natural Philosophy and Moral Philosophy courses as a tertian and a magistrand.

**4.** A mixture stop on an organ, consisting of a tierce and larigot combined.

**1876** HILES *Catech. Organ* x. (1878) 77. **1898** STAINER & BARRETT *Dict. Mus. Terms*, *Tertian*, an organ stop composed of two ranks of pipes, sounding a major third and fifth of the foundation pipes, in the third octave above; a *Tierce* and *Larigot* on one slider.

**5.** *Geom.* A curve of the third order, a cubic. *rare.*

**1891** in *Cent. Dict.*

**6.** Short for *Tertian Father*: see A. 4.

Hence **Te·rtianship** (*R. C. Ch.*), the position of being a Tertian Father (see A. 4).

**1855** R. BOYLE *B. v. Wiseman* 56 After he has been associated with the Society [of Jesus] for fifteen or twenty years, he is required to retire into, what is technically called, a tertianship, or a third year's probation. **1892** J. H. POLLEN *Acts Eng. Martyrs* 358 He was Minister of the Tertianship at Ghent and then Prefect and Confessor at St. Omers.

†**Tertiar**, *v. Obs. rare.* Also 6 **terciar.** [ad. It. *tertiare* 'to thirde the pike' (Florio 1598), or ad. Sp. *terciar* (*la pica*) 'to shake or brandish a pike, to come to push of pike with the enemy' (Minsheu 1599).] (See quots.)

**1598** BARRET *Theor. Warres* 17 He ought, being a pikeman, to tertiar or charge his pike. *Ibid.* III. ii. 47 The pikes being Terciard or charged ouer hand. [*Ibid.* Gloss., *Tertiare*, a Spanish word, and is to third the pike, either to beare the same vpon his shoulder, or to charge the same ouer hand.]

**Tertiary** (tɔ̄ɹʃiări), *a.* and *sb.* Also 6 **tercyary.** [f. L. *tertiāri-us* of the third part or rank, f. *tertius* third: see -ARY [1]. So F. *tertiaire.*]

**A.** *adj.* **1.** Of, in, or belonging to the third order, rank, degree, class, or category; third.

**1656** BLOUNT *Glossogr.*, *Tertiary*,..of, or belonging to the third, or third sort, tertian. **1831** BREWSTER *Optics* ix. 84 When one prism of a different angle is thus made to correct the dispersion of another prism, a tertiary spectrum is produced. **1860** MAYNE *Expos. Lex.* s.v., A tertiary peduncle is the second degree of ramification of a compound peduncle, or a bough of the branch which gives off the peduncle. **1865** RUSKIN *Sesame* i. § 5, I venture to assume that you will admit duty as at least a secondary or tertiary motive. **1871** EARLE *Philol. Eng. Tongue* § 428 The adverb is the tertiary or third presentive word.

**b.** *Chem.* Applied to the substitution ammonias formed by the replacement of all three hydrogen atoms by an alcohol or acid radical.

**1857** MILLER *Elem. Chem.* III. 237 The tertiary amides are readily prepared from such silver salts of the secondary amides. **1862** *Ibid.* 423 *Tertiary Monamides.*—In these bodies the 3 atoms of hydrogen in ammonia are displaced by a corresponding number of radicles, one of which at least must be of an electro-negative character.

**2.** *Geol.* Forming a third series in point of origin or age. †**a.** Applied by early geologists to mountains of the most recent formation. **b.** In modern geology, Of or pertaining to the third series of stratified formations: formerly including all those above the chalk; now restricted to the strata from the Eocene to the Pliocene, both inclusive. Also called CAINOZOIC.

[G. ARDUINO *Lett.* in *Nuova Raccolta d'opusc. scient.* VI. 159 (1760) Monti..primitivi o primari..secondari..e terziari, li monti e colli del terzo ordine, che sta a ridosso del secondo e talvolta anche del primo.] **1794** SULLIVAN *View Nat.* I. x. 78 He [Pallas] maintained, that in addition to these primordial mountains, there were others of a more recent origin. These he called secondary and tertiary. [**18..** CUVIER & BRONGN. *Descr. Geol. Env. Paris* (1822) 9 Terrains tertiaires.] *a* **1812** KIRWAN (Webster 1828), Tertiary mountains are such as result from the ruins of other mountains promiscuously heaped together. **1822** CONYBEARE & PHILLIPS *Geol. Eng. & W.* I Tertiary Rocks. Comprising the Formations above the Chalk. **1824–5** D. OLMSTED *Geol. N. Carolina* (Webster), Tertiary formation, a series of horizontal strata, more recent than chalk beds...It comprehends the alluvial formation..and the diluvial formation. **1830** LYELL *Princ. Geol.* I. 49 Arduino, in his memoirs on the mountains of Padua, Vicenza, and Verona, first recognized the distinction between primary, secondary, and tertiary rocks. **1833** *Ibid.* III. p. vii, A large collection of tertiary shells. **1862** M[c]COSH *Supernatural* II. ii. § 2. 183 Nor does Man descend from the mammals which preceded him in the tertiary age. **1863** LYELL *Antiq. Man* i. 3 Previously to the year 1833,..the strata called Tertiary had been divided by geologists into Lower, Middle, and Upper.

**3.** *Painting.* Applied to a colour formed by the mixture of two secondary colours.

**1848** WORNUM in *Lect. Paint.* 211 *note*, Although there are but three primitive colours, painters have nine. These are—yellow, red, blue;..orange, purple, green, which are secondary;..russet, olive, citrine, which are tertiary, being compounds of the secondaries.

**4.** *Path.* Of or belonging to the third or last stage of syphilis.

**1875** H. C. WOOD *Therap.* (1879) 404 In *tertiary syphilis*, including in the term all cases of syphilitic bone, visceral, or nervous disease, the remedy is really of inestimable value. **1899** *Allbutt's Syst. Med.* VII. 668 It has..been considered inappropriate in this article to introduce the terms 'secondary' and 'tertiary' as applicable to the incidence of the phenomena of cerebral syphilis.

**5.** *R. C. Ch.* Of or belonging to the Third Order in certain religious fraternities: see B. 1.

A *Third Order*, of lay members not subject to the strict rule of the regulars, but retaining the secular life, was originated by St. Francis of Assisi, and is an established institution among the Franciscans, Dominicans, and others. (See *Catholic Dict.*)

**1891** R. H. BUSK in *N. & Q.* 7th Ser. XI. 289/2 The Franciscans, who loved [Dante], and in whose tertiary habit he was shrouded in the supreme hour. **1899** *Westm. Gaz.* 1 Sept. 2/3 The Tertiary Sister was discharged yesterday. **1902** *Daily Chron.* 2 Sept. 5/6 The murderer was a tertiary lay brother of the Dominican order.

**6.** *Ornith.* Applied to certain feathers of the wing: see B. 3. Cf. TERTIAL.

**1858** J. WILSON in *Encycl. Brit.* (ed. 8) XVI. 735/1 The tertials or tertiary feathers are derived from the humerus or arm-bone.

**B.** *sb.* **1.** *R. C. Ch.* A member of the Third Order of certain religious fraternities: see A. 5.
*a* 1550 *Image Ipocr.* IV. 213 in *Skelton's Wks.* (1843) II. 441/2 Some be Tercyaris, And some be of St. Marys. 1820 SOUTHEY *Wesley* II. 565 It may..deserve to be recognized as an auxiliary institution, its ministers being analogous to the regulars, and its members to the tertiaries and various confraternities of the Romish Church. 1909 *Westm. Gaz.* 15 July 3/3 The late Marquis [of Ripon], besides being a fervent Tertiary of St. Francis, was a friend in need to the Franciscan Order.

**2.** *Geol.* A stratum or formation belonging to the Tertiary system: see A. 2.
1851 WOODWARD *Mollusca* I. 45 In the miocene tertiaries of Asia Minor. 1885 *Lyell's Elem. Geol.* ix. (ed. 4) 110 The whole of the Tertiaries were at first confounded with the superficial alluviums of Europe.

**3.** *Ornith.* (*pl.*) The quill- or flight-feathers that grow upon the humerus in the wing of a bird.
1834 MUDIE *Feathered Tribes Brit. Isles* (1841) I. 10 The tertiaries or third quills of the wings. 1872 COUES *N. Amer. Birds* 36 The Tertiaries..are, properly, the remiges that grow upon the upper arm. [Cf. TERTIAL.]

**4.** *Path.* (*pl.*) Tertiary syphilitic symptoms: see A. 4.
1897 J. HUTCHINSON in *Arch. Surg.* VIII. 218 Those who remain well and never present tertiaries.

**5.** *Painting.* A tertiary colour: see A. 3.
1854 FAIRHOLT *Dict. Terms Art* s. v. *Secondary Colours*, When two secondaries are mixed together..they cannot neutralise each other, but only form half-tones or tertiaries. 1897 *Daily News* 20 May 7/4 Mr. Rhead is fortunate in handling effectively the most brilliant of positive colours as well as the quieter tertiaries.

† **Tertiate** (tǝ̄·ɹʃiˌēit), *v. Obs.* [f. ppl. stem of late L. *tertiāre*, f. *tertius* third.]
**1.** *trans.* To do (anything) for the third time: in quot. 1628, to introduce for the third time or support as third spokesman.
1623 COCKERAM, *Tertiate*, to doe a thing three times. 1628 WOTTON in *Reliq.* (1672) 559 The Personage that should first, or second or tertiate your business with the King. 1656 BLOUNT *Glossogr.*, *Tertiate*..to Till ground, or do any thing the third time [*ed.* 1674 *adds* to tri-fallow].

**2.** *Mil.* To poise (a lance or pike): cf. TERTIAR.
*a* 1691 BOYLE *Hist. Air* xix. (1692) 183 They tertiate their Lance,..that is, they poise it in their Hand.

**3.** *Mil.* To ascertain the strength of a cannon by measuring its thickness by means of caliper compasses, in three places: see quot. 1704.
1672 J. ROBERTS *Compl. Canonier* 35 To tertiate a Piece of Ordnance. 1704 J. HARRIS *Lex. Techn.* I. s.v., To Tertiate a Great Gun, is to know the thickness of the Metal at the Touch-hole, the Trunnions, and at the Muzzle. 1828 J. M. SPEARMAN *Brit. Gunner* (ed. 2) 393 To tertiate a piece of ordnance, is to examine whether it has the due thickness of metal at the vent, &c.

So † **Tertia·tion.**
1658 PHILLIPS, *Tertiation*,..a dividing into three, also a doing anything the third time.

**Tertio**, variant of TERCIO *Obs.*, a regiment, etc.

**Te·rtio-ge·niture.** *nonce-wd.* [f. *tertio-*, fr. L. *terti-us* third, after *primogeniture*.] Right of succession or inheritance belonging to the third-born.
1855 M. BRIDGES *Pop. Mod. Hist.* 420 Austria had a prospect..of ultimately succeeding to the beautiful dominions of Este, as a tertio-geniture for her family.

‖ **Tertium quid** (tǝ̄·ɹʃiǒm kwi·d). [L., app. rendering Gr. τρίτον τι, 'some third thing'.] Something (indefinite or left undefined) related in some way to two (definite or known) things, but distinct from both.
(Gr. τρίτον τι occurs in Plato *Sophist* 250. The Latin form is in Irenæus *Adv. Her.* 2. 1. 3 (*c* 196), where it doubtless represents τρίτον τι of the lost Greek original; also, in Tertullian *Adv. Praxean* 27 (*a* 220), and *tertium nescio quid* in Hilary *Synod.* 73 (*c* 358). The passage in Tertullian mentions *electrum* as an example of a body produced by the mixture of gold and silver; and app. *tertium quid* was used by the alchemists of a third substance different from its two constituents: see quot. from Bailey, and cf. next. Examples of the phrase in English context are late.)
[1613 *Theatrum Chemicum*, Index, Tertium quid. 1101, 1085.] 1724 BAILEY, *Tertium Quid*, (among Chymists) the Result of the Mixture of some two Things, which forms something very different from both. *L*[*atin*]. [1809–10 COLERIDGE *Friend* (1818) I. 157 The baleful product or *tertium Aliquid*, of this union retarded the civilization of Europe for Centuries.] 1826 *Edin. Rev.* Sept. 255 Balancing the opinions of Gall against those of Spurzheim, or compounding out of them a *tertium quid*. 1881 R. ADAMSON *Fichte* v. 110 While..we appear to assert that the two orders of facts make up all that is, we have in reality placed alongside of them..the thinking subject or mind, a *tertium quid* which certainly stands in need of some explanation. 1902 MENZIES *Demonic Possess. N. T.* vi. 187 The achievement was either devilish or divine. There was no tertium quid.

‖ **Tertium sal** (tǝ̄·ɹʃiǒm sæ·l). *Chem. Obs.* [med. L., = 'third salt'.] See quot.
1753 CHAMBERS *Cycl. Supp.*, *Tertium Sal, a third salt*, a term used in chemistry to express a salt resulting from the mixture of an acid and an alkali, which partakes so of the nature of both, as to be itself neither acid nor alkali, but neutral. 1860 in MAYNE *Expos. Lex.*

‖ **Tertius** (tǝ̄·ɹʃiǒs). [L. *tertius* third.] In some public schools, appended to a surname to designate the youngest (in age or standing) of three boys of that name. Cf. MAJOR A. 7 c, MINOR A. 7 b, PRIMUS A. 2, SECUNDUS.
1870 (At Mill Hill School this year there were) Smith Major, Minor, and Tertius. 1899 KIPLING *Stalky* vi. 175 The Head called them over, too—majors, minors, and tertiuses.

† **Tertre.** *Obs.* Also **terter.** [a. F. *tertre* a hillock (*Roland* 11th c.).] A little hill; a rising ground; an eminence. Cf. TERRITORY[2].
1480 CAXTON *Ovid's Met.* x. iv, He sat vpon a tertre in a playn felde. 1481 — *Godeffroy* cxxii. 185 The barons acorded that they wold close this litil terter and waye.

‖ **Tertulia** (tertū·liă). Also 8 **tertulla**, 8–9 **tertullia.** [Sp. *tertulia* a conference, an evening party, soirée.] An evening party in Spain.
1785 BECKFORD *Italy, Spain* [etc.] (1834) II. 305 Of goings to balls, theatres, and tertullias. 1828 W. IRVING in *Life & Lett.* (1864) II. 273, I have become one of the most dissipated men upon town; continually at *soirées* and *tertullias.* 1845 FORD *Handbk. Spain* I. ii. 161 They meet in church, on the Alameda, and at their tertulias.

**Tertu:lliana·de.** [f. as next + -ADE.] A tirade or invective after the manner of Tertullian.
1819 W. TAYLOR in *Monthly Rev.* XC. 182 A Philippic, or, rather, a Tertullianade, against theatricals.

**Tertullianism** (tǝɹtʊ·liăniz'm). *Eccl.* [f. proper name *Tertullian*, ad. L. *Tertulliān-us*.] The doctrine of Tertullian, a famous Christian writer of the late 2nd and early 3rd c., a modification of Montanism, or the rigid ascetic discipline connected with this. So **Tertu·llianist**, one of a sect who followed this doctrine and discipline.
1702 C. MATHER *Magn. Chr.* III. I. i. § 14. 19/1 He [Mr. Cotton] practically appeared in opposition to Tertullianism, by proceeding unto a Second Marriage. 1710 *Brit. Apollo* II. No. 84. 2/1 He..gave name to a Sect call'd Tertullianists about the Year 245. 1831–3 E. BURTON *Eccl. Hist.* xxii. (1845) 463 A sect of Tertullianists..continued at Carthage till the end of the fourth century.

**Teru, Teruagaunt**, obs. ff. TEREU, TERMAGANT.

‖ **Teru-tero** (te·ruˌte·ro). Also tero-tero, teru-teru. [From its noisy cry.]
The Cayenne lapwing or spur-winged plover, *Vanellus cayennensis.*
1839 DARWIN *Voy. Nat.* vi. (1873) 114 The teru-tero..is another bird, which often disturbs the stillness of the night. 1884 W. B. BARROWS in *The Auk* July 278 (Funk) Tero-tero..is the bane of all water-fowl shooting in the marshes.

**Terve**, variant of TIRVE *v. Obs.*, to turn.

**Tery, Terytory**, obs. ff. TARRY *v.*, TERRITORY.

‖ **Terza** (te·rtsă), *a.* and *sb. Mus.* Also (masc.) terzo. [It. *terza*, fem. of *terzo* third:—L. *tertia*.] **a.** *adj.* The third, as in *opera terza*, the third work; *violino terzo*, third violin. **b.** *sb.* A third; also *in terza*, in three parts; *terzo* = TRIO.
1724 *Short Explic. For. Wds. in Mus. Bks.*, *Terza*, a Third...*Opera Terza*,..*Violina Terza*. *Ibid.*, *In Terza*, ..Songs or Tunes in Three Parts, the same as *Trio* below.

**Terzain** (tǝɹzē̆ⁱ·n). *rare*[—1]. [app. ad. It. *terzina*, after *quatrain*.] A stanza or set of three lines.
1855 MILMAN *Lat. Chr.* XI. ix, The sublime terzains of Dante.

‖ **Terza rima** (te·rtsă rī·mă). [It., = 'third rime'.] An Italian form of iambic verse, consisting of sets of three lines, the middle line of each set riming with the first and last of the succeeding (*a b a*, *b c b*, *c d c*, etc.).
1819 BYRON *Proph. Dante* Pref., The measure adopted is the terza rima of Dante. 1869 TOZER *Highl. Turkey* II. 252 Italian in Dante's time rendered more manageable the intricacies of the terza rima.

**Terzet, -zetta, -zette**, variants of TERCET.

‖ **Terzetto** (tertse·tto). *Mus.* Pl. **-i** (*-i*). [It. *terzetto*: see TERCET.] A (small) trio, esp. vocal.
1724 *Short Explic. For. Wds. in Mus. Bks.*, *Terzetto*, little Airs in Three Parts. 1816 T. L. PEACOCK *Headlong Hall* xiii, Mr. Chromatic,..with the assistance of his two.. daughters, regaled the ears of the company with the following terzetto. 1833 C. MACFARLANE *Banditti & Robbers* (1837) 187 (Stanf.) At the conclusion of the duetto they begged for the grace of a terzetto.

‖ **Terzina** (tertsī·nă). [It. *terzina* a triplet.] A stanza or set of three lines; = TERCET.
1836 *Pop. Encycl.* II. 592/1 The terzina first reached its perfection in the time of Dante. 1893 *Nation* (N. Y.) 16 Feb. 129/1 Dante arranges his poem in stanzas of three lines each, and rarely overruns from *terzina* to *terzina*.

**Tescare, -caria**: see TEZKERE.

**Teschemacherite** (te·ʃĭmæːkǝrǝit). *Min.* [Named after its discoverer E. F. Teschemacher: see -ITE[1] 1 b.] Acid carbonate of ammonium, found in yellowish crystals and masses in guano.
1868 DANA *Min.* (ed. 5) 705 Teschemacherite. Bicarbonate of Ammonia.

**Teschenite** (te·ʃĕnǝit). *Geol.* Also **teschinite.** [f. *Teschen* (see def.) + -ITE[1] 1 b.] A name given to certain eruptive rocks, occurring at Teschen in Austrian Silesia and elsewhere, intercalated and intrusive in the Cretaceous formation.
Used by different geologists with very varying extension.
1866 LAWRENCE *Cotta's Rocks Class.* (1878) 140 Teschinite is the name given..to a rock whose mass is chiefly felsitic, and in which hypersthene forms long black needles. 1888 RUTLEY *Rock-Forming Min.* 115 A constant constituent of the rocks termed Teschenites.

**Tese**, obs. f. TEASE; var. TEISE *sb.* and *v.*[1] *Obs.*

† **Teseke**, obs. form of PHTHISIC.
*c* 1460 *Play Sacram.* 538 in *Non-Cycle Myst. Plays* (1909) 74 Þe poose, þe sneke, or þe teseke.

**Tesel, tesill, tesle**, obs. forms of TEASEL.

† **Tesh(e.** *Obs.* Of uncertain origin and meaning.
If the meaning is 'task', cf. F. *tâche*, OF. *tasche*.
1596 HARINGTON *Apology* Bb vij b, I haue good authorityes, for my teshe. 1596 — *Metam. Ajax* D v, I must still keep me to my tesh. 1596 — *Ulysses upon Ajax* D v b, But return we to Misacmos' teshe, I long to hear his conclusion. 1625 BRATHWAIT *Five Senses* 309 The more numerous and odious they were; when they came to the Tesh.

‖ **Tesho-, Teshu-lama**: see LAMA. **Teskari, teskere**, etc.: see TEZKERE. **Teslet, -lot**, obs. forms of TASLET. **Tesmoingnal, -monage**: see TESTIMONIAL, -MONAGE.

**Tessara-** (te·sără), also **tessera-**, a. Gr. τέσσαρα, -ερα, neuter pl. and comb. form of τέσσαρες, -ερες four, used in Greek compounds, and forming the first element in a few English words adopted from or formed on Greek. **Te:ssarade·cad** [DECAD], a group of fourteen. **Tessaradecasy·llabon** [DECASYLLABON], a line of fourteen syllables. **Te·ssaraglo:t** *a.*, in, of, or pertaining to four languages; = TETRAGLOT. **Te·ssarako:st** [ad. Gr. τεσσαρακοστή a fortieth]: see quot. **Tessara·phthong** [after DIPHTHONG], a group of four vowels. **Te:sserato·mic** *a.* [after *dichotomic*], involving division into four parts.
1855 W. H. MILL *Applic. Panth. Princ.* (1861) 152 In the text of St. Matthew, dividing the *tessarodecads at the captivity. 1874 FARRAR *Christ* 8 The symmetrical arrangement into tesseradecads. *c* 1610 BOLTON *Hypercritica* iv. § 3 Chapman's Iliads, those I mean which are translated into *Tessara-decasyllabons, or lines of fourteen Syllables. 1716 M. DAVIES *Athen. Brit.* III. 73 Whose *Tessaraglott Bible [Complutensian Polyglot] was finish'd about 1517. 1851 BORROW *Lavengro* xiv. I. 191 A tessara-glot grammar ..of the French, Italian, Low Dutch, and English tongues. 1850 GROTE *Greece* II. lxiii. VIII. 138 Receiving..three *tessarakosts (a Chian coin of unknown value) for each man among his seamen. 1887 *Sat. Rev.* 17 Dec. 818 What Mr. Gladstone would call the trichotomic, or rather the *tesseratomic, division of parties.

† **Te·ssel.** *Obs. rare.* [ad. L. or It. *tessella*. So F. *tesselle* (Littré).] = TESSELLA.
1657 TOMLINSON *Renou's Disp.* 132 Matter formed into Pils..or planed into Tessels.
So † **Te·sseled** *a.* [perh. ad. It. *tessellato*, pa. pple. of *tessellare* 'to make or worke checker-worke or inlaid worke' (Florio), f. *tessella* a small tessera: cf. F. *tessellé* (Littré)], tessellated.
1603 KNOLLES *Hist. Turks* (1621) 543 Yea all the house was paved with checker and tesseled worke.

**Tessel, -e**, obs. forms of TEASEL.

‖ **Tessella** (tese·lă). Pl. **-æ**; rarely **-as.** Also 8 **-ela.** [L., dim. of TESSERA.] A small tessera.
1693 tr. *Blancard's Phys. Dict.* (ed. 2), *Tessellæ*, the same with *Rotulæ* or *Tabellæ*. 1727–41 [see TESSELLATED 1]. 1753 CHAMBERS *Cycl. Supp.*, *Tesselæ*, a word used in pharmacy to express lozenges cut into regular figures. 1885 *Athenæum* 29 Aug. 278/3 No endeavour is made to fasten loose tessellæ into their sockets.

**Tessellar** (te·sĕlăɹ), *a.* [f. prec. + -AR.] Of the nature or form of tessellæ.
1847 in WEBSTER. 1859 *Todd's Cycl. Anat.* V. 253/2 It [Lunaria Vulgaris] consists originally of a single layer of tessellar cells.

**Tessellate** (te·sĕlĕt), *a.* (*sb.*) Also **-elate.** [ad. late L. *tessellāt-us*: see next.] = TESSELLATED.
1826 KIRBY & SP. *Entomol.* IV. xlvi. 289 *Tessellate*,.. painted in checquer-work. 1872 LONGF. *Wayside Inn* III. *Azrael* 2 King Solomon..on the pavement tesselate Was walking. 1876 J. ELLIS *Caesar in Egypt* 30 Along the floor, Chromatic, tesselate with marbles rare.

**B.** *sb.* in *Variegated tessellate*, an American butterfly, *Hesperia montivagus*, found in Florida, Mexico, and the Rocky Mountains.
1909 in *Cent. Dict., Suppl.*

**Tessellate** (te·sĕleⁱt), *v.* Also 8–9 **tesselate.** [f. ppl. stem of late or med.L. *tessellāre* (pa. pple. *tessellāt-us*: cf. also It. *tessellare* in Florio), f. L. *tessella* TESSELLA. The pa. pple. *tessellated* occurs earlier than the finite vb.: see next.]
**1.** *trans.* To make into a mosaic; to form a mosaic upon, adorn with mosaics; to construct (esp. a pavement) by combining variously coloured blocks so as to form a pattern.
1791 E. DARWIN *Bot. Gard.* I. 95 And dull Galena tessellates the floor. 1826 P. POUNDEN *France & It.* 27 The floor is tesselated with great elegance. 1862 RAWLINSON *Anc. Mon.* I. v. 125 Pieces of marble used for tesselating.
**b.** *transf.* and *fig.*
1817 COLERIDGE *Satyrane's Lett.* iii. in *Biog. Lit.*, etc. (1882) 264 The wood-work..in old houses among us..being painted red and green, it cuts and tesselates the buildings very gaily. 1858 E. FITZGERALD *Lett.* (1889) I. 269 It is most ingeniously tesselated into a sort of Epicurean Eclogue in a Persian Garden. 1869 LECKY *Europ. Mor.* I. ii. 335 The affectation of some to tesselate their conversation with antiquated and obsolete words.
**2.** To combine so as to form a mosaic; to fit into its place in a mosaic. In quots. *fig.*
1838–9 [implied in TESSELLATED 2]. 1861 J. PYCROFT *Ways & Words* 17 The sentences [of Sir J. Mackintosh] are rather tessellated than constructed; each word fitting admirably into its own place, but defying all transposition. 1879 FARRAR *St. Paul* II. 189 Many writers have maintained that this meaning is vague and general,..impossible to tesselate into any formal scheme of salvation.

**Tessellated** (te·sĕleⁱtĕd), *ppl. a.* [f. L. *tessellāt-us* or It. *tessellato* in same sense, with Eng. suffix. Used earlier than TESSELLATE *v.*, of which it subseq. became the pa. pple.]

**1.** Composed of small blocks of variously coloured material arranged to form a pattern; formed of or ornamented with mosaic work.

**1712** HEARNE *Collect.* (O.H.S.) III. 311 The tessellated Pavement at Stansfield. **1727-41** CHAMBERS *Cycl.*, *Tessellated pavement*, *pavimentum Tessellatum*, a rich pavement of mosaic work, made of curious small square marbles, bricks or tyles, called *tesselæ*, from the form of dies. **1877** C. GEIKIE *Christ* lxii. (1879) 758 The old golden seat of Archelaus, was set down in the tesselated floor of the tribunal. *fig.* **1828** MACAULAY *Misc. Writ.* (1860) I. 224 Laborious and tesselated imitations of Mason and Gray. **1864** *Sat. Rev.* 31 Dec. 789 The fall of a dovetailed and tesselated Cabinet. **1868** GLADSTONE *Juv. Mundi* xiv. § 1 (1869) 490 The several squares of that tesselated nation, each with its local patriotism and limited traditions.

**2.** Combined or arranged so as to form a mosaic.

**1838-9** HALLAM *Hist. Lit.* IV. IV. v. § 51. 253 The mind is pleased to recognise the tesselated fragments of Ovid and Tibullus. **1853** C. L. BRACE *Home Life Germany* 116 The floors are..of the most minutely tesselated marble.

**3.** *transf.* Consisting of or arranged in small cubes or squares; in *Bot.* and *Zool.* having colours or surface-divisions in regularly arranged squares or patches; chequered, reticulated.

*Tessellated cells*, cells arranged in layers. *Tessellated epithelium*, pavement epithelium (PAVEMENT *sb.* 4). *Tessellated pyrites*, iron pyrites, crystallizing in cubes.

**1695** WOODWARD *Nat. Hist. Earth* IV. (1723) 198 Crystallized Ores, and Minerals, e.g...the tessellated *Pyritæ*, or *Ludus Paracelsi.* **1777** WATSON in *Phil. Trans.* LXVIII. 866 A very pure specimen of tessellated lead ore. **1828** MISS MITFORD *Village* Ser. III. 60 (*Quiet Gentlew.*) A bit of white mosaic, a tessellated quilt. **1829** LOUDON *Encycl. Pl.* (1836) 113 Fruit..a fleshy tesselated berry. **1839** DARWIN *Voy. Nat.* v. 97 The apar [armadillo]..having only three moveable bands; the rest of its tesselated covering being nearly inflexible. **1854** *Pereira's Pol. Light* 237 What Dr. Brewster has termed tesselated or composite crystals..consist of several crystals..united so as to form a compound crystal. **1875** SIR W. TURNER in *Encycl. Brit.* I. 847/1 Tessellated..or squamous epithelium is situated on the free surface of the mucous lining of the mouth.

**Tessellation** (tesĕlēⁱ·ʃən). [n. of action f. TESSELLATE *v.*: see -ATION.]

**1.** The action or art of tessellating; tessellated condition; *concr.* a piece of tessellated work.

**1813** J. FORSYTH *Italy* 111 The work is not mosaic, for there is no tessellation. **1862** MERIVALE *Rom. Emp.* VII. lxvii. 540 Like the several pieces of a variegated tessellation. *a* **1878** SIR G. G. SCOTT *Lect. Archit.* (1879) II. 253 Wide-spreading floors, rich with marble tesselation. *fig.* **1840** H. ROGERS *Ess.* (1874) II. v. 250 Numberless passages of Jeremy Taylor..are a little better than a curious tesselation of English, Greek, and Latin. **1863** LE FANU *Ho. by Chyd.* (ed. 2) III. 307 The writings of the Apostolic Fathers are, in a great measure, a tesselation of holy writ.

**2.** An arrangement or close fitting together of minute parts or distinct colours: cf. TESSELLATED 3.

**1660** SHARROCK *Vegetables* 144 Yet they, instead of those elegant Tessellations, are beautified otherwise in their site with as great curiosity. **1822-34** *Good's Study Med.* (ed. 4) IV. 500 The whole surface of the body..having exhibited a sordid tesselation of crusts. **1905** J. ORR *Probl. O. Test.* vii. 201 The newer criticism with its multiplication of documents..and its minute tesselation of texts.

**Tessellite** (te·sĕləit). *Min.* Also tesselite. [f. TESSELLA + -ITE [1].] A variety of Apophyllite, exhibiting in polarized light a tessellated structure.

**1819** BREWSTER in *Edin. Phil. Jrnl.* June 5 The tessellated structure..is a property so singular and so distinctive, that I would propose to mark it by the name of Tesselite. **1868** DANA *Min.* (ed. 5) 416 Tesselite, from Faröe, is a cubical variety, exhibiting a tesselated structure in polarized light.

‖ **Tessera** (te·sĕră). Pl. **tesseræ**. [L., f. Ionic Gr. τέσσερες, -ρα, = Attic τέσσαρες, -ρα four.]

**1.** *Anc. Hist.* A small quadrilateral tablet of wood, bone, ivory, or the like, used for various purposes, as a token, tally, ticket, label, etc.

*Tessera of hospitality* (= L. *tessera hospitalis*), a die broken between host and guest, and kept as a means of recognition.

**1656** BLOUNT *Glossogr.*, *Tessera*, a thing in every part square as a dye; also a watchword, or signal, a note, mark or token, &c. **1846** KEIGHTLEY *Notes Virg.*, *Georg.* II. 508 In the ancient theatres..each spectator's *tessera* designated the *cuneus* and row in which he was to sit. **1850** LEITCH tr. *C. O. Müller's Anc. Art* § 412 (ed. 2) 569 One brings him a tessera of hospitality from Sisyphus. **1886** *Guide Exhib. Galleries Brit. Mus.* 186 Objects in bone and ivory, such as caskets, gladiatorial *tesseræ*, tickets for the theatre, dice.

**b.** *fig.* A distinguishing sign or token; a watchword, a password. (The earliest use in English.)

**1647** JER. TAYLOR *Lib. Proph.* i. 17 That Creed made so explicite as a tessera of a Christian. **1656** [see prec.]. **1662** OWEN *Animadv. Fiat Lux* ii. Wks. 1855 XIV. 29 Making subjection to the pope in all things the tessera and rule of all church communion. **1795** in Calderwood *Dying Testimonies* (1806) 460 Exacts it from them as a tessera of their loyalty. **1890** HATCH *Hibbert Lect.* xii. 344 It was, so to speak, a tessera or password.

**2.** *spec.* Each of the small square (usually cubical) pieces of marble, glass, tile, etc., of which a mosaic pavement or the like is composed. Usually in pl.

**1797** S. LYSONS *Rom. Antiq. Woodchester* 4 The tesseræ of which this [mosaic] pavement is composed, are, for the most part, nearly cubes of half an inch..Many are triangular, and of various other shapes. **1843** *Civil Eng. & Arch. Jrnl.* VI. 125/1 The next point to be observed with reference to the Roman tesseræ, is the want of uniformity in their size and shape. **1894** *Times* 5 Mar. 14/1 The workmen had to learn to set the tesseræ, one by one and each in its proper place, into the cement on the wall.

**b.** *transf.* Any one of the quadrilateral divisions into which a surface is divided by intersecting lines; e.g. by the lines of latitude and longitude.

**1873** MAXWELL *Electr. & Magn.* (1881) I. 198 So that the spherical surface is divided into quadrilaterals or tesseræ..bounded by meridian circles and parallels of latitude.

**c.** *Zool.* Each of the plates of which the carapace of an armadillo is composed.

**1909** in *Cent. Dict., Suppl.*

† **3.** (See quots.) *Obs.*

**1815** J. SMITH *Panorama Sc. & Art* I. 257 John's *tessera* is perhaps the best of those artificial compositions which are designed for roofing. **1842-76** GWILT *Archit.* Gloss., *Tessera*..this name was..applied to a composition used some years ago for covering flat roofs, but now..quite abandoned.

**Tessera-**: see TESSARA-.

† **Tesseraic** (tesĕrēⁱ·ik), *a. Obs. rare.* [f. TESSERA + -IC, after *mosaic*.] Of, pertaining to, or composed of tesseræ; mosaic, tessellated.

*a* **1711** SIR R. ATKYNS *Hist. Gloucester* (1712) 778/1 Stidcot ..where some of the Tesseraick Work of the Romans has lately been dug up. **1778** *Eng. Gazetteer* (ed. 2) s. v. *Woodchester*, There is a tesseraick pavement of painted beasts and flowers in its church-yard.

**Tesseral** (te·sĕrăl), *a.* [f. TESSERA + -AL.]

**1.** Of, pertaining to, or resembling a tessera or tesseræ; composed of tesseræ.

**1846** WORCESTER cites *Edinb. Rev.*

**2.** *Cryst.* = ISOMETRIC 3, CUBIC *a.* 1 c.

**1854** *Pereira's Pol. Light* 191 The cubic or octohedral system. Synonymes.—The regular, the tessular, the tesseral, or the isometric system. **1878** GURNEY *Crystallogr.* 37 Crystals possessing this highest possible degree of symmetry are said to belong to the Cubic or Tesseral System.

**3.** *Math.* Relating to the tesseræ of a spherical surface (see TESSERA 2 b), as in *tesseral harmonic*, a spherical surface harmonic which is the product of two factors depending respectively on latitude and longitude.

**1873** MAXWELL *Electr. & Magn.* (1881) I. 196 We may now write the expressions for the two tesseral harmonics. *Ibid.* 198 To find the surface integral of the square of any tesseral harmonic taken over the sphere. **1887** HOBSON in *Trans. Camb. Philos. Soc.* (1889) XIV. 211 The zonal and tesseral harmonics..are exhibited as series.

† **Tessera·rian,** *a. Obs. rare.* [f. L. *tesserārius* pertaining to tesseræ or dice + -AN.] Of or pertaining to dice or to gaming. *Tesserarian art* [L. *ars tesseraria*], the art of dice-playing. So † **Tessera·rious** *a. Obs. rare*⁻⁰, in same sense.

**1656** BLOUNT *Glossogr.*, *Tesserarious*..of, or belonging to a die, or to *tessera*. **1781** GIBBON *Decl. & F.* xxxi. III. 209 A superior degree of skill in the Tesserarian art (..the game of dice and tables). **1797** *Sporting Mag.* X. 44.

**Tesserate** (te·sĕrĕt), *a. rare*⁻¹. [f. TESSERA + -ATE [2]. Cf. obs. F. *tesseré* (Cotgr.).] = TESSELLATED. So **Te·sserated** *a. rare.* ? *Obs.*

**1717** TABOR in *Phil. Trans.* XXX. 549 A Description of the tesserated Pavement at East Bourne, near Pevensey. **1812** HOBHOUSE *Journ.* I. (1813) 969 The tesserated mosaic [in S. Sophia's] with which the concave above the windows and the dome are encrusted. **1897** F. THOMPSON *New Poems* 139 With the gold-tesserate floors of Jove.

**Tesseratomic**: see TESSARA-.

‖ **Tessitu·ra.** *Mus.* [It.] The part of the total compass of a melody or voice-part in which most of its tones lie. **1891** in *Cent. Dict.*

‖ **Tesson** (te·sən, ‖ tesoṅ). [F. *tesson* piece of broken glass or earthenware (13th c.), deriv. of OF. *test* pot.] A fragment of glass or pottery.

**1858** BIRCH *Anc. Pottery* II. 238 The tessons used for Mosaic pavements were made of marbles, glass, and of a red brick.

**Tessular** (te·siŭlăɹ), *a. Cryst.* [f. mod.L. **tessula*, irreg. dim. of TESSERA + -AR.] = TESSERAL 2.

**1796** KIRWAN *Elem. Min.* (ed. 2) I. 139 In nodules, or in half rounded masses, or tessular. **1805-17** R. JAMESON *Char. Min.* (ed. 3) 132 Where there are many crystals together, but merely simply aggregated; and these are either, 1. On one another;..[this] occurs principally in tessular crystals, as in galena or lead-glance, and calcareous-spar. **1854** *Pereira's Pol. Light* 165 The equiaxed crystals constitute one system, called the cubic, octohedral or tessular system. **1869** PHILLIPS *Vesuv.* x. 294 The crystallization is on the tessular pattern.

**Test** (test), *sb.*[1] Forms: 4-5 *pl.* **testes, -is,** 6 **teste, taest,** 7 **tast, teast,** 6- **test.** [a. OF. *test* masc., a pot (12th c.), mod. F. *têt* a cupel, etc.:—L. *testum*, *testu* neut., collateral form of *testa* a tile, earthen vessel, pot. In OF. *test* and *teste* (L. *testa*) were sometimes confused, and *teste* sometimes occurs in 15-16th c. Eng. In modern use, treated mainly as noun of action from TEST *v.*[2]]

**1.** *orig.* The cupel used in treating gold or silver alloys or ore; now *esp.* the cupel, with the iron frame or basket which contains it, forming the movable hearth of a reverberatory furnace: see CUPEL *sb.* 1.

*c* **1386** CHAUCER *Can. Yeom. Prol. & T.* 265 Of oure siluer citrinacion,..Oure yngottes testes and many mo. **1552** in P. H. Hore *Wexford* (1901) II. 237 Of 1031 lbs. weight of lead they had from the taest 14 lbs. weight of silver. **1555** EDEN *Decades W. Ind.* VI. 339 Meltynge it [gold] in a fornace in a bayne or teste of leade. **1594** PLAT *Jewell-ho.* III. 36 Get a large panne, such as they make their testes of bone ashes in. **1622** MALYNES *Anc. Law-Merch.* 281 The Copple or Teast doth drinke in some two penny weight of Siluer with the Lead. **1674** RAY *Collect. Wds.*, *Smelting Silver* (E. D. S.) 9 The test is of an oval figure, and occupies all the bottom of the furnace. **1758** REID tr. *Macquer's Chym.* I. 315 Put one half of this Lead into a test, and spread it equally thereon. **1853** URE *Dict. Arts* II. 657 The bed or bottom of the furnace, when in operation, is formed by a shallow elliptical vessel, called a test or test-bottom. **1877** KNIGHT *Dict. Mech.* 2535/2 The test is fixed as a cupeling-hearth in the reverberatory furnace.

**2.** That by which the existence, quality, or genuineness of anything is or may be determined; 'means of trial' (J.); hence, in phrases *to bring* or *put to the test*, *to bear* or *stand the test*, the testing or trial of the quality of anything; examination, trial, proof.

(Cf. **1651** FRENCH *Distill.* v. 138 Prove this tree at the test, and it yeeldeth good gold. **1661** BLOUNT *Glossogr.* (ed. 2) s. v., A broad instrument..on which Refiners do fine, refine and part gold and silver from other Mettals, or (as we use to say) *put them to the Test.*)

**1594** NASHE *Unfort. Trav.* 40 A delicate wench.. which I would faine haue had to the grand test, whether she were cunning in Alcumie or no. **1602** SHAKS. *Ham.* III. iv. 142 It is not madnesse That I haue vttered; bring me to the Test. **1610** — *Temp.* IV. i. 7 Thou Hast strangely stood the test. **1754** CHATHAM *Lett. Nephew* iv. 25 The noblest sentiment of the human breast is here brought to the test. **1813** SIR H. DAVY *Agric. Chem.* (1814) 11 Simple tests of the relative nourishing powers of the different species of food. **1820** W. IRVING *Sketch Bk.* II. 148 Invaluable maxims which have borne the test of time. **1838** JAMES *Robber* iv, I will not put them to the test. **1873** SYMONDS *Grk. Poets* iii. 89 Time, says Theognis, and experience and calamity are the true tests of friendship. **1904** NICHOLSON *Keltic Researches* Pref. 4 Even as between the Irishman and the Welshman, the language-test is not a race-test.

† **b.** A proof, sample, specimen. *Obs. rare.*

**1769** COOK *Voy. round World* II. iii. (1773) II. 328 Rather satisfied with having given a test of their courage by twice insulting a vessel so much superior to their own, than intimidated by the shot.

**c.** *Cricket.* Short for *test-match*: see 7 b.

**1908** *Westm. Gaz.* 16 Jan. 7/1 England is now a game to the bad, and there are only two more 'Tests' to play. **1909** *Ibid.* 6 Sept. 10/4 We are to play sixteen matches in all, including five Tests.

**3.** That by which beliefs or opinions, esp. in religion, are tested or tried; *spec.* the oaths or declarations prescribed by the TEST ACT of 1673; esp. in phrase *to take the test*; also, either of the test acts.

**1665** *Sp. Speaker Ho. Comm. to King* 31 Oct. in *Lords Jrnls.* XI. 700/1 We have prepared a Shiboleth a Test to distinguish amongst them, who..give Hopes of future Conformity, and who of..evil Disposition remain obdurate. **1672-3** (Mar. 12) in *Grey's Deb. Ho. Comm.* II. 97 [Mr. Harwood] Tendered a proviso for renouncing the doctrine of transubstantiation for a farther test. **1675** (May 10) *Calr. St. Papers, Dom., Chas. II* 112 The Test as now agreed on:—I, A. B., do declare [etc.]. **1682** in *Scott. Antiq.* July (1901) 4 One of the late regentis..having demurred to take the test apoynted by act of parliament. *a* **1715** BURNET *Own Time* an. 1685 IV. (1724) I. 654 The King..had declared that he would be served by none but those who would vote for the repeal of the Tests. **1789** *Constitution U. S.* Art. vi, No religious test shall ever be required as a qualification to any office. **1797** HEY *Lect. Div.* II. III. xiv. § 15. 155 A Man is deemed a Member of the Church of England, who takes the Sacrament according to the usage of the Church of England, and declares against Transubstantiation; from whence the Tests are called sacramental tests. **1889** *Pall Mall G.* 3 July 2/2 The Government promised last night to abolish tests in the case of the 'lay chairs' in the Scotch universities. **1906** H. PAUL in *19th Cent.* May 717 The belief in tests ought to be as dead as the belief in witches.

**4. a.** *Chem.* The action or process of examining a substance under known conditions in order to determine its identity or that of one of its constituents; also, a substance by means of which this may be done.

**1800** HENRY *Epit. Chem.* (1808) 322 The readiest method of judging of the contents of natural waters, is by applying what are termed tests, or re-agents. **1812** [see REAGENT 1]. **1854** J. SCOFFERN in *Orr's Circ. Sc.*, *Chem.* 479 Arseniuretted hydrogen..employed, as a means of removing and discovering arsenic, is called *Marsh's test*. **1900** BRIGGS & STEWART *Inorg. Chem.* Gen. Direct., The student is advised to learn the tests for each metal and acid. **1900** SHENSTONE *Elem. Inorg. Chem.* xxv. § 396 A solution of baryta affords us a most delicate test for carbon dioxide.

**b.** *Mechanics*, etc. The action by which the physical properties of substances, materials, machines, etc. are tested, in order to determine their ability to satisfy particular requirements.

Among these are *bending test*, *compressive t.*, *drop t.*, *tensile t.*, *transverse t.*, etc.; also with sb. in objective relation, as *boiler*, *brake*, *engine test*.

**1877** KNIGHT *Dict. Mech.* 2539 Observations are made at short intervals..until the test is closed by rapid heating.. and excessive increase of friction. **1884** *Ibid.*, *Suppl.* 888 The machine requires but little change for making tests in compression. **1894** LINEHAM *Mech. Engin.* 376 The straining cylinder, having water admitted beneath its piston for tensile, and above it for compressive tests. **1904** *Kent's Mech. Engin. Pocket Bk.* (1910) 282 In Transverse tests the strength of bars of rectangular section is found to vary directly as the breadth of the specimen tested, as the square of its depth, and inversely as its length. *Ibid.* 864 Competitive tests were made of fourteen boilers.

**5.** *Microsc.* A test object: see 7 b.

**1832** GORING in Pritchard *Microsc. Cabinet* xviii. 175 A *test* is an object which serves to render sensible both the perfection and imperfection of an instrument, as to defining and penetrating power. **1837** GORING & PRITCHARD *Microgr.* 160 A..representation of an excellent and very beautiful test, a feather from the wing of Morpho Menelaüs, (being the first object in which I observed the very remarkable property of the lines as tests).

**6.** An apparatus for determining the flash-point of hydrocarbon oils.

**1877** KNIGHT *Dict. Mech., Test*,..4. An apparatus for proving petroleum and similar hydrocarbon oils by ascertaining the temperature at which they evolve explosive vapours.

**7.** *attrib.* and *Comb.* **a.** General combs.: 'of or pertaining to a test', 'taken, done, or made as a test'; as, in sense 2, *test-bar*, *-ground*, *-log* (LOG *sb.*[1] 6), *-piece*, *-pit*, *-plaster*, *question*, *-room*, *-run*, *symptom*, *-valve*, *-work*; in sense 3, *test-formula*, *-law*, *-man*, *-monger*, *-oath*; also *test-free*, *-ridden* adjs.: in sense 4, *test-bottle*, *-liquid*, *-liquor*, *-phial*, *-solution*, *-spoon*, *-stirrer*.

**1839** URE *Dict. Arts* 71 We pour into the *test bottle 2 thousandths of the *decime* solution of silver. **1890** *Tablet* 5 July 14 A *test-ground for the historian. **1687** *Reasons to Move Protest. Dissenters* 3 You cannot say it is a Divine Law that requir'd the Parliament to make this *Test-Law... To abolish the Test-Laws therefore is Lawful. **1862** *Catal. Internat. Exhib.* II. XIII. 12 Apparatus for centigrade testing,..preparation of the *test liquors. **1904** *Electr. World & Engin.* 9 Jan. 90 (Cent. Suppl.) A typical *test-log upon a 550-hp engine. **1693** SHADWELL *Volunteers* III. i, A furious agitator and *test-man. **1687** *Reasons for Repeal of Tests* 4 In the Year 1675 the same Test was set on Foot in Parliament, by the *Test-Mongers, with design to have made it more Extensive. **1715–16** in J. O. Payne *Eng. Cath. Nonjurors of 1715* (1885) 9, I cannot take the *Test and Abjuration Oaths enjoined by Acts of Parliament. **1863** H. COX *Instit.* III. viii. 718 In consequence of his inability to take the test-oath. **1876** PREECE & SIVEWRIGHT *Telegraphy* 179 The electrical resistance of the wire..and the resistance of each *test-piece. **1909** *Service for the King* May 103 The heat is gauged by the potters.. who place in the oven test-pieces of pottery, which can be drawn out. **1896** MARY H. FOOTE in *Atlantic Monthly* May 606/2 Sinking *test-pits through layers of crusted consciousness into depths of fiery nature. **1897** *Daily News* 19 Jan. 3/6 Continued movement of the front is manifested by the cracking of *test plaster put in the fractured groining ..six months ago. **1867** FURNIV. & HALES *Percy Folio* I. 247 The *test question put to the page before the assignation is disclosed. **1889** *Pall Mall G.* 3 July 2/2 This is why.. English *test-ridden Theology lags so much behind German. **1905** *Westm. Gaz.* 20 Sept. 8/1 The methods of the *test-room are being applied..to the degree of moisture quicker methods involve. **1877** RAYMOND *Statist. Mines & Mining* 302 A *test-run made upon about three tons showed it to contain 51 ounces of silver and 41 per cent. of lead per ton. **1871** GARROD *Mat. Med.* (ed. 3) 428 The volumetric solutions of nitrate of silver and of iodine are also made use of as *test-solutions for qualitative analysis. **1910** *Westm. Gaz.* 19 Jan. 4/2 She wanted to test the gas at the purifier..but found the *test-valve choked. **1895** *Daily News* 19 Feb. 9/2 Service in relieving distress..by means of carefully-planned *test-work.

**b.** Special Combs.: **test board** (*Electr.*): see quot.; **test-boiler**, a boiler for testing fuel or steam-apparatus, or supplying steam-pressure for testing other boilers (*Cent. Dict., Suppl.* 1909); **test-bottom**, = sense 1; also, the cake of gold or silver formed in the bottom of a cupel; **test-box** (*Telegr.*), a box fitted with terminals through which the wires are led, for convenience in testing; **test case** (*Law*), a case, the decision of which is taken as determining that of a number of others in which the same question of law is involved; **test-cock**, (*a*) a valved cock for clearing a steam engine cylinder of water; (*b*) a tap through which a sample of fluid may be drawn for examination; (*c*) a tap by means of which the level of water in a boiler or the like may be ascertained; **test-frame**, the iron frame or basket in which a cupel is placed: see sense 1; **test-furnace**, a reverberatory refining furnace in which silver-bearing alloys are treated; also *fig.*; **test-glass**, a small cylindrical glass vessel for holding liquids while being tested; **test-hole**, a tap-hole in a furnace; **test-lead**, pure granulated lead used in silver assays (*C. D., Suppl.* 1909); **test letter**, (*a*) a letter sent as a test of the honesty of the messenger; (*b*) see *test-type* (*C. D., Suppl.* 1909); **test-lines**, the lines on a test-plate (*Cassell's Encycl. Dict.* 1888); **test-match** (*Cricket*), one of a series of matches played as a test which is the better of two bodies of players (e.g. of England and Australia); **test-meal**, a meal of specified quantity and composition, given as a test of digestive power; **test-meter**, (*a*) a meter for testing the consumption of gas by burners; (*b*) a meter used as a standard by which others are tried (*Funk's Stand. Dict.* 1895); **test-mixer**: see quot.; **test object**, (*a*) a minute object used as a test of the power of a microscope; (*b*) an object upon which a testing experiment is tried; **test-paper**, (*a*) a paper impregnated with a chemical solution which changes colour in contact with certain other chemicals, and thus becomes a test of the presence of the latter; (*b*) *U.S.* a document produced in court in determining a question of handwriting (Webster, 1847); (*c*) a paper set beforehand to try whether a student is fit and ready for an examination; **test-piece** = *test-specimen*; **test-plate**, (*a*) a glass plate ruled with very fine lines, used in testing the power of microscope objectives (Knight *Dict. Mech.* 1877); (*b*) a piece of pottery on which colours are tried before being used on the pieces to be decorated (*Cent. Dict.* 1891); (*c*) a slip of glass used in mixing test-solutions (Knight); **test-pump**, a force-pump used in testing pipes, cylinders, and the like; **test-ring**, (*a*) see quot.; (*b*) a ring-shaped piece of iron, etc., taken as a sample of the metal of which it is made (*Cent. Dict., Suppl.* 1909); **test-roll**, (*a*) a roll signed by those who have complied with a test or tests as prescribed by the various test acts; (*b*) the roll signed by a member of the House of Lords or Commons after having taken the oath or made the declaration required of him as such; **test specimen**, a piece of metal, etc. prepared for a mechanical test; **test-type**, letters of graduated sizes used by opticians in testing sight. Also TEST ACT, TEST-TUBE.

**1902** T. O'C. SLOANE *Stand. Electr. Dict.* App., **Test Board*, a board provided with switches or spring-jacks connected to separate lines, so that testing instruments may be readily connected to any particular line. **1853** *Test-bottom [see sense 1]. **1869** *Proc. Amer. Phil. Soc.* XI. 92 A cake or test-bottom [of silver]...Its weight was 4343 ounces Troy. **1876** PREECE & SIVEWRIGHT *Telegraphy* 273 The wire is..put to earth at the *test-box there. **1895** *Funk's Stand. Dict.*, **Test-case*. **1906** *Daily News* 25 Apr. 9/1 Important charges of street betting, which were regarded by the police as test cases. **1877** KNIGHT *Dict. Mech.*, **Test-cock* (Steam-engine), a small cock fitted to the top or bottom of a cylinder for clearing it of water. **1839** URE *Dict. Arts* 1131 In forming the cupel, several layers of a mixture of moistened bone ashes, and fern ashes,..are put into the *test-frame. **1877** KNIGHT *Dict. Mech.*, **Test-furnace*, one form of refining furnace for treating argentiferous alloy. **1896** *Godey's Mag.* Feb. 186/2, I don't believe that the immortal Sara Bernhardt could have gone through the fierce test-furnace of this rôle more superbly. **1827** FARADAY *Chem. Manip.* § 619. 285 On the top of a *test-glass. **1897** *Daily News* 14 Apr. 7/5 The prisoner [a postman] was suspected. A *test letter was sent, and it was not delivered. **1899** *Westm. Gaz.* 27 June 5/1 Not far below his big *test-match average. *Ibid.* 15 Aug. 5/3 Two test-match records were broken during the day. **1891** *Cent. Dict.*, **Test-meal*. **1897** *Allbutt's Syst. Med.* III. 409 When the contents of the stomach are examined after a test-meal, the total acidity is found to be diminished. **1877** KNIGHT *Dict. Mech.*, **Test-mixer*, a tall cylindrical bottle..graduated into..equal parts.., and..used in preparing test-alkalies, test-acids, and similar solutions. **1830** GORING *Microscopical Illustr.* 2 The difficulty of demonstrating many *test objects satisfactorily is very considerable. **1904** tr. *Hueppe's Ætiology Infectious Diseases* iii. 27 Guinea-pigs are so susceptible that we use them as the best test-object of tuberculosis. **1827** FARADAY *Chem. Manip.* § 584. 270 *Test papers are far more advantageous for use than liquids: two of them in general application..are litmus and turmeric papers. **1871** GARROD *Mat. Med.* (ed. 3) 68 The solution is neutral or slightly alkaline to test-paper. **1877** KNIGHT *Dict. Mech.* 2537/2 The angle through which the *test-piece yielded before its fracture became complete. **1881** RAYMOND *Mining Gloss.*, **Test-ring*, an oval iron frame for holding a test or movable cupelling-hearth. **1879** T. E. MAY *Parl. Practice* (ed. 8) 204 So soon as a member has been sworn, he subscribes the oath which he has taken, in a book, at the table, commonly called the '*test-roll'; and is then introduced to the Speaker by the clerk of the house. **1884** *Ninth Rep. Hist. MSS. Comm.* App. 68/2 Certificate.. Produced this day [17 Nov. 1675] on his taking the oaths and signing the Test Roll. **1894** LINEHAM *Mech. Engin.* 378 Shackles for *Test Specimens should be carefully designed. **1890** BILLINGS *Nat. Med. Dict.*, **Test types*.

**Test** (test), *sb.*[2] [ad. L. *testa* a piece of burned clay, a brick, tile, a piece of baked earthenware or pottery, an earthen pot or vessel, a potsherd, a shell of a mollusc or tortoise, a shell or covering of anything. Cf. also TEST *sb.*[1], and TESTA.]

†**1.** A piece of earthenware, an earthenware vessel; a broken piece of pottery, a potsherd. *Obs.*

**1545** JOYE *Exp. Dan.* iv. D iij, Then was y^e^ test or potsherd, the brasse, gold & sylver redacte into duste. [Cf. *Vulg.* Dan. ii. 45 testam et ferrum et æs.] **1600** SURFLET *Country Farm* I. xii. 76 It is good..to haue a dish of the plane tree or a test of earth.

**2. a.** *Zool.* The shell of certain invertebrates.

**1842** *Penny Cycl.* XXII. 371/1 This external covering or *test*, extremely delicate and fragile towards the umbones of the valves. **1854** WOODWARD *Mollusca* II. 214 The vascular processes by which, in many ascidians, the 'tunic' adheres to the 'test'. **1872** NICHOLSON *Palæont.* 60 Rhizopoda in which the body is protected by a shell or 'test'. **1888** [see TESTACEA 2].

†**b.** *Bot.* The skin of a seed: = TESTA 1. *rare.*

**1846** SMART Suppl., *Test* (or *Testa*..), the skin of a seed.

**Test** (test), *sb.*[3] *Obs.* exc. *dial.* Also 6–7 teste. [In sense 1, app. ad. L. *test-is* witness. In senses 2 and 3, perh. aphetic for *atest*, ATTEST *sb.*]

†**1.** A witness. Cf. TESTIS[1]. *Obs. rare.*

**1528** ROY *Rede me* II. (Arb.) 109 To prove it shall nede no testes. **1614** W. B. *Philosopher's Banquet* (ed. 2) 197 The faithful teste or witnesse. *a* **1626** BP. ANDREWES *Serm., Holy Ghost* (1661) 488 A Witnesse is requisite. There is no matter of weight with us, if it be sped authentically..but it is with a Teste. (Quot. 1528 may belong to TESTIS[1].)

†**2.** Evidence, witness borne. Cf. ATTEST *sb.* 1.

[*c* **1450** HOLLAND *Howlat* 253 All this trety has he tald be termess in test.] **1604** SHAKS. *Oth.* I. iii. 107 To vouch this, is no proofe, Without more wider, and more ouer Test. [Cf. **1606** — *Tr. & Cr.* V. ii. 122 That test [*Qo.* th' attest] of eyes and eares.] **1658** SIR T. BROWNE *Hydriot.* ii. (1736) 21 The lasting Tests of old Boundaries.

†**3.** = TESTE[2]. Cf. ATTEST *sb.* 2. *Obs.*

**1709** STRYPE *Ann. Ref.* I. xxvi. 277 In the term next after the test of the said writ. **1752** J. LOUTHIAN *Form of Process* (ed. 2) 174 The Court shall issue another Writ.. of the same Test, Return and Import with the former.

**4.** A will: = TESTAMENT *sb.* 1. *Sc.*

**1890** J. SERVICE *Thir Notandums* iii. 13 By ane eik to his test, he left to Peter Scartle the soom of five shillings.

**Test** (test), *v.*[1] [orig. a. OF. *tester* to bequeath, ad. L. *testārī* to bear witness, give evidence, attest, make one's will, f. *testis* witness; but in 3 app. from TESTE *sb.*[2] 2, and in 4 perh. aphetic from ATTEST.]

**I.** †**1.** *trans.* To leave by will or testament, to bequeath. *Sc. Obs. rare*[—1].

**1491** *Acta Dom. Conc.* (1839) 208/1 He allegeit It wes testit gudis, & he Intromettit þarw^t^ as executour.

**2.** *intr.* To make a will, execute a testament. (See also TESTING *vbl. sb.*[1] 1.) *Obs.* exc. *Sc.*

**1582** N. T. (Rhem.) *Heb.* ix. 17 For a testament..is yet of no value, whiles he that tested, liueth. **1681** STAIR *Inst. Law Scot.* XXX. § 18 Persons..condemned of Infamy could not test. **1822** SCOTT *Pirate* vi, I will test upon it [*Note*, i.e. leave it in my will] at my death, and keep it for a purse-penny till that day comes. **1838** W. BELL *Dict. Law Scot.* s.v. *Testament*, A wife has power to test without the consent of her husband. **1880** MUIRHEAD *Ulpian* xxiii. § 10 [In Roman Law] Soldiers are allowed to test in any way they like.

**II. 3.** *trans. Eng. Law.* To date and sign the teste of a writ, etc. (see TESTE *sb.*[2] 2).

(The pa. pple. appears in Blackstone as *teste*'d, as if formed immediately on *teste*, but it is usually written and pronounced *tested*.)

**1727** ASGILL *Metam. Man* 249 His title..is tested and dated from the Death and Resurrection of Christ, as the Cause of it. **1745** *Col. Rec. Pennsylv.* IV. 775 A Commission Tested by me under the Great Seal of the Province. **1769** BLACKSTONE *Comm.* IV. xxi. 288 A warrant from the chief, or other, justice of the court of king's bench extends all over the kingdom: and is *teste*'d, or dated, England. **1883** *Wharton's Law Lex.* s.v., All writs..were formerly tested in the name of the Lord Chancellor if issuing from the Court of Chancery, or of the Lord Chief Justice if issuing from the Queen's Bench, etc.

**4.** *Sc. Law.* To authenticate a deed or written instrument by a testing clause (TESTING *vbl. sb.*[1] 2) duly drawn up in statutory form and signed by witnesses.

**1838** W. BELL *Dict. Law Scot.* s.v. *Testament*, A testament ..must be properly tested and signed before witnesses; but if it be in the testator's own handwriting, witnesses are not required. **1911** T. HUNTER *Let. to Editor*, The Scottish law requires writings (except those *in re mercatoria*) to be either holograph or tested.

**Test** (test), *v.*[2] [f. TEST *sb.*[1]

(Before 1800 chiefly in pa. pple.; the simple vb. was considered by Southey as an Americanism.)]

**1.** *trans.* To subject (gold or silver) to a process of separation and refining in a test or cupel; to assay.

**1603** [see *Tested* below]. [**1661**: ? implied in TESTER[1].] **1828** WEBSTER, *Test*, *v.*, 3. In *Metallurgy*, To refine gold or silver by means of lead, in a test, by the destruction, vitrification or scorification of all extraneous matter. **1871** [see *Tested* below]. **1872** RAYMOND *Statist. Mines & Mining* 120 The ore tested yielded $25 per ton. *Ibid.* 335 These lodes have not been tested by the repeated and continuous milling of the ore raised from them. **1873** SYMONDS *Grk. Poets* iii. 89 You may test gold and silver, but there are no means of getting at the thoughts of men.

**2.** To subject to a test of any kind; to try, put to the proof; to ascertain the existence, genuineness, or quality of.

**1748** [see *Tested* below]. **1760–72** H. BROOKE *Fool of Qual.* (1809) I. 48 You have been sufficiently tested. *a* **1799** WASHINGTON *Address* (Webster 1828), Experience is the surest standard by which to test the real tendency of the existing constitution. **1815** JEFFERSON *Writ.* (1830) IV. 260 Materials which test the truth it contains. **1820** *Blackw. Mag.* Sept. 591/1 They have not the means of testing the statements. **1834–43** SOUTHEY *Doctor* cxlv. (1862) 397 But I will test (as an American would say..) I will test Mr. Campbell's assertion. **1837** J. H. NEWMAN *Proph. Office Ch.* 324 The Church is bound ever to test and verify her doctrine. **1838** GLADSTONE *State in Rel. Ch.* (1839) 186 This theory however has not been tested experimentally. **1888** MISS BRADDON *Fatal Three* I. v, I have tested the water in all the wells.

†**3.** To require or compel to fulfil the conditions of the Test Act as a necessary qualification for holding a public office. *Obs.*

**1687** *Reason of Toleration* 36 There is no reason they should be so cruelly Tested for Doctrines that are but either obscurely reveal'd, or not necessarily enjoyn'd. [**1687**, **1689**: see TESTING *vbl. sb.*[2], *Tested* below. **1697**: see TESTER[4].]

**4.** *Chem.* To subject to a chemical test.

**1839** URE *Dict. Arts* 71 (Assay) The testing of the normal liquor..is..less tedious than might be supposed. **1842** PARNELL *Chem. Anal.* (1845) 35 Oxide of silver is most conveniently applied, in liquid testing, in the form of nitrate of silver. **1846** G. E. DAY tr. *Simon's Anim. Chem.* II. 135 The urine..must be tested with litmus paper. **1864** in WEBSTER.

Hence **Te·sted** *ppl. a.* (in senses 1 and 2); in quot. 1689, having taken the test-oaths.

**1603** SHAKS. *Meas. for M.* II. ii. 149 Not with fond Sickles of the tested-gold, Or Stones, whose rate are either rich, or poore. **1689** *Let.* in *N. Brit. Daily Mail* 27 Dec. (1894), If we have a Convention chosen by our present tested magistrates we may expect little good from their hands. **1748** RICHARDSON *Clarissa* (1811) III. xxxi. 187 She cannot break through a well-tested modesty. **1871** TENNYSON *Last Tourn.* 284, I..heard it ring as true as tested gold.

**Test**, obs. Sc. form of TASTE.

‖ **Testa** (te·stă). [L. *testa* a tile, earthen pot, shard, shell, etc.: see TEST *sb.*[2]]

**1.** *Bot.* The skin or coating of a seed.

**1796** DE SERRA in *Phil. Trans.* LXXXVI. 500 (*Fruct. of Algæ*), Their very viscous albumen answers..all the purposes the testa accomplishes in other eggs. **1807** J. E. SMITH *Phys. Bot.* 294 *Testa*, the Skin, contains all the parts of a seed above described. **1877** HUXLEY & MARTIN *Elem. Biol.* 86 Carefully peel off the outer coat (*testa*) of the seed.

†**2.** *Zool.* The shell of certain invertebrates: = TEST *sb.*[2] 2 a. *Obs. rare.* **1847** in WEBSTER.

†**Testable** (te·stăb'l), *a.*[1] *Obs.* [ad. late L. *testābilis* that has a right to bear testimony (Gellius), f. *testārī*: see TESTATE *a.* and -ABLE; cf. obs. F. *testable* capable of making a will (1514 in Godef.) from the same source.]

**1. a.** Legally qualified to bear witness. **b.** Legally able to make a will.

**1611** COTGR., *Testable*, testable; that can make a Will; that may be deuised by Will. **1676** R. DIXON *Two Test.* 25 A Deed solemnly testified by the Testimony..of Seven Testable Persons that are..worthy to be believed. **1721** BAILEY, *Testable*.., that by the Law may bear witness.

**2.** Devisable by will.

**1693** STAIR *Inst. Law Scot.* IV. xlii. § 21 A power of legating..the Deads part of Movables, which is..most ordinarily the third of Testable Movables. **1766** BLACKSTONE *Comm.* II. xxxii. 494 Such of his goods as were testable.

**Testable** (te·stăb'l), *a.*[2] *rare.* [f. TEST *v.*[2] + -ABLE.] That may be tested or tried. (In quot. app. 'That on being put to the test prove to be'.)

**1647** TRAPP *Comm. Matt.* xii. 30 So are all testable indifferents, out of God's book of remembrance. Mal. iii. 17.

‖ **Testacea** (testē¹·ʃiă), *sb. pl.* [L., neut. pl. of *testāc-us* adj., consisting of *testæ*, i. e. tiles, shells, etc.; also, covered with a shell: see -ACEA.]

†**1.** Testaceous substances, as limestone, chalk. Cf. TESTACYE. *Obs. rare*[−1].

**1743** *Lond. & Country Brew.* III. (ed. 2) 241 Chalk and other Testacea will answer the same, but not so well.

**2.** *Zool.* A name for various groups of invertebrate animals having shells (excluding Crustacea). *spec.* †**a.** (*a*) used by Linnæus to designate his third order of *Vermes*, comprising the shell-bearing molluscs; (*b*) by Cuvier applied to the shell-bearing molluscs of his class *Acephala*. (*Obs.*) **b.** In present use, (*a*) A suborder of pteropod molluscs including all having calcareous shells, otherwise called *Thecosomata*; (*b*) an order of Protozoa having shells, with apertures through which the pseudopodia are protrusible.

**1828** STARK *Elem. Nat. Hist.* II. 4 In the last edition of his *Systema Naturæ*, Linnæus,..in the third and fourth divisions of his third order, *Testacea*, places those possessed of shells. **1830** LYELL *Princ. Geol.* I. 52 Soldani.. explained that microscopic testacea and zoophytes inhabited the depths of the Mediterranean. **1860** HARTWIG *Sea & Wond.* i. 11 Pholades and Lithodomas are marine testacea, that have the power of burying themselves in stone. **1888** ROLLESTON & JACKSON *Anim. Life* 905 The *Amœbina* may be classified as..: I. *Nuda* s. *Gymnamœbæ*: devoid of a test. ..2. *Testacea* s. *Lepamœbæ*: a test either chitinoid..or composed of chitinoid or siliceous plates cemented together.

**Testacean** (testē¹·ʃiăn), *a.* and *sb. Zool.* [f. prec.: see -ACEAN.]

**A.** *adj.* Of or pertaining to the TESTACEA; shell-bearing; chiefly applied to molluscs.

**1846** in WORCESTER, citing LYELL. **1871** LYELL *Elem. Geol.* ix. 119 Value of testacean fossils in classification.

**B.** *sb.* A member of the testacea; a shell-bearing invertebrate, *esp.* a mollusc.

**1842** BRANDE *Dict. Sc.* etc., *Testaceans.* Testacea. **1847** WEBSTER, *Testaceans* (*Zool.*), marine animals covered with shells, especially mollusks; shell-fish.

**Testacel, -elle** (te·stăsel, -e·l). *Zool.* [ad. mod.L. testacella (also in Eng. use), dim. of *testācea*, fem. of *testāc-us* adj.: see TESTACEA.] A genus of carnivorous land-slugs, typical of the family *Testacellidæ*, having a small oval shield-like shell, which covers only a small part of the back. They live upon earthworms, and inhabit Southern Europe; one species is sometimes found in England.

**1846** SMART Suppl., *Testacel*, a little shell; applied as the general name of a slug which is furnished with a diminutive shell that forms a shield to the heart. **1851** WOODWARD *Mollusca* I. 13 The testacelle..preys on the common earth-worm, following it in its burrow, and wearing a buckler, which protects it in the rear. **1910** *Daily News* 9 May 4 The slug which 'by good fortune we may catch sight of eating a worm', is testacella.

Hence **Testace·llid, Testace·llidan** *adjs.*, of or pertaining to the family *Testacellidæ*; *sbs.* a member of this family; **Testace·lloid** *a.*, resembling the *Testacella* or *Testacellidæ*.

**1895** *Funk's Stand. Dict.*, Testacellid..Testacelloid. **1895** *Cambridge Nat. Hist.* III. 440 Jaw present, radula Testacellidan, central tooth present.

**Testaceo-** (testē¹·ʃio), combining form of L. *testāceus*, used **a.** as in **Testaceo·graphy**, descriptive testaceology (Webster, 1828); **Testaceo·logy**, the zoology of the testaceous animals; hence **Testaceolo·gical** *a. rare*; **Testaceo-theology**, natural theology as illustrated by the study of testaceous animals. **b.** in sense 'of brick-red colour', as in **Testaceo-fuscous, Testaceo-piceous**, etc. *adjs.*: see the second elements.

**1803** MATON in *Trans. Linn. Soc.* VII. 119 (*heading*) An Historical Account of Testaceological Writers. *Ibid.* 121 Aristotle..seems to have been also the first writer, and the inventor of method, in Testaceology. **1755** tr. *Pontoppidan's Nat. Hist. Norway* Pref. 7 That circumstantial examination of every part which hath been undertaken and..executed by Fabricius, in his pyro- and hydro-theology,..Lesser, in his litho- and testaceo-theology.

**b. 1847** J. HARDY in *Proc. Berw. Nat. Club* II. v. 247 Legs testaceo-fuscous. *Ibid.* 256 The first joint testaceous, the rest testaceo-piceous.

**Testaceous** (testē¹·ʃəs), *a.* [f. L. *testāce-us* consisting of tiles, shells, etc.; brick-coloured; covered with a shell: see TEST *sb.*[2] and -ACEOUS.]

†**1.** Made of baked clay; pertaining to or of the nature of earthenware or a potsherd. *Obs. rare.*

**1658** SIR T. BROWNE *Hydriot.* iii. 22 In many Bricks, Tiles, Pots, and testaceous works. **1674** J. B[RIAN] *Harvest Home* ii. 6 Testaceous Vessels; obnoxious To casualties, that are most various. **1675** EVELYN *Terra* (1729) 15 Exotic Plants ..confined..to their Wooden Cases and Testaceous prisons.

**2.** Having a shell, esp. a hard, calcareous, unarticulated shell. † *Testaceous fish* = shell-fish.

**1646** SIR T. BROWNE *Pseud. Ep.* 203 All [fishes] that are testaceous, as Oysters, Cocles, Wilks, Schollops, Muscles, are excluded. **1759** STILLINGFL. tr. *Biberg's Econ. Nat.* Misc. Tracts (1762) 57 Testaceous worms..eat away the hardest rocks. **1809** W. IRVING *Knickerb.* IV. iii, The testaceous marine animal, known commonly by the vulgar name of Oyster. **1875** C. C. BLAKE *Zool.* 232 When the shell is so much enlarged that the contracted animal finds shelter beneath or within it, the animal is said to be testaceous.

**3.** Of the nature or substance of shells; shelly; consisting of a shell or shelly material.

**1668** WILKINS *Real Char.* 122 Exanguious Animals..whose bones are on their outside..testaceous; of a more hard and brittle substance. **1676** GREW *Exper. Luctation* i. § 21 Millipedes, Egg-shells, or any other testaceous Bodies of the same strength. **1794** SULLIVAN *View Nat.* I. 89 The testaceous matter of marine shells. **1881** WATSON in *Jrnl. Linn. Soc.* XV. 265 Operculum testaceous.

†**b.** *Pharmacy.* Of a medicinal powder: Prepared from the shells of animals. *Obs.*

**1710** T. FULLER *Pharm. Extemp.* 392, I think testaceous Powders exert their Virtues much easier and sooner when fine. **1789** W. BUCHAN *Dom. Med.* (1790) 549 To give the pearl-julep, chalk, crabs eyes, and other testaceous powders. **1853** DUNGLISON *Med. Lex.*, *Testaceous*,..a powder, consisting of burnt shells.

**4.** Of the colour of a tile, a flower-pot, unglazed pottery, etc.; dull red; in *Zool.* and *Bot.* applied to shades of brownish red, brownish yellow, and reddish brown.

**1688** R. HOLME *Armoury* II. 275/2 The upper part of the Body is testaceous, or potsheard colour. **1783** LATHAM *Gen. Synopsis* IV. 393 Testaceous Lark. Bill black: upper parts of the body testaceous. **1887** W. PHILLIPS *Brit. Discomycetes* 136 Cup..testaceous yellow. *Ibid.* 420 *Testaceous*, brick-coloured,..not so bright as *lateritious*.

Hence **Testa·ceousness** (*rare*[−0]).

**1727** BAILEY vol. II, *Testaceousness*, shelly Nature or Quality.

**Te·st act.** [See TEST *sb.*[1] 3.] The name given in English History to various acts directed against Roman Catholics and Protestant Nonconformists; particularly, the act of 1673 (25 Chas. II. c. 2) by which the provisions of the Corporation Act of 1661 (see CORPORATION 7) were extended to include all persons holding office under the Crown, and a declaration against transubstantiation was introduced. It was repealed 9 May, 1828.

Also sometimes applied to (*a*) an act of Elizabeth, 1563, imposing the oath of allegiance, and abjuration of the temporal authority of Rome, on all office-holders except peers; (*b*) the Corporation Act of 1661; (*c*) a Scotch act of 1681, exacting a declaration of conformity to the Episcopal Church of all holders of municipal and government offices.

**1708** *Lett. Gent. Scotl. agst. Sacr. Test* 5 This Test Act requires an End in the Receiving of the Sacrament, that must consequently prophane it. *a* **1715** BURNET *Own Time* an. 1673 (1823) II. 13 A sure law against popery, ..all that continued in office after the time lapsed, they not taking the sacrament, and not renouncing transubstantiation (which came to be called the test, and the act from it the test act) were rendered incapable of holding any office: all the acts they did in it were declared invalid and illegal, besides a fine of five hundred pounds to the discoverer. **1738** NEAL *Hist. Purit.* IV. 458 This is commonly called the *Test Act*, and was levelled against the Duke of York and the present Ministry, who were chiefly of his persuasion. **1769** BLACKSTONE *Comm.* IV. iv. 57 To secure the established church against perils from non-conformists of all denominations, infidels, turks, jews, hereticks, papists, and sectaries, there are however two bulwarks erected; called the *corporation* and *test* acts. **1874** GREEN *Short Hist.* vii. § 6. 400 But the Test Act [of 1563] placed the magistracy in Protestant hands. **1886** A. FERGUSON *Laird of Lag* iii. 36 The famous Test Act was passed by the Scots Parliament at one sitting on the 30 August 1681.

**Testacy** (te·stăsi). *Law.* [f. TESTATE *a.*, after INTESTACY.] The state of being testate; the condition of leaving a valid will at death.

**1864** in WEBSTER. **1875** POSTE *Gaius* II. Comm. (ed. 2) 229 Contra-tabular possession was sometimes equivalent to intestacy, sometimes to partial testacy. **1880** GLADSTONE *Sp. Ho. Comm.* 15 Mar., The Chancellor of the Exchequer ..has treated testacies and intestacies, as if they were something like equal. **1885** *Law Rep.* 29 Ch. D. 278 The suit settles as regards him the question of testacy or intestacy.

†**Te·stacye.** *Obs. rare*[−1]. [ad. L. *testāceum*: see TESTACEOUS.] Name for a kind of cement.

*c* **1440** *Pallad. on Husb.* VI. 192 Now yote on that scyment clept testacye Sex fynger thicke.

**Testament** (te·stăment), *sb.* Also 5 testement, 5–6 testment. [ad. L. *testāment-um* a will; also, in early Christian Latin, used to render Gr. διαθήκη covenant (see II.), f. *testārī* to be a witness, attest, make a will, etc.: see -MENT. With the form *teste-*, *testment*, cf. OF. *testement*, beside the more usual *testament*.]

**I.** In original sense of L. *testāmentum*.

This is app. later in Eng. than branch II.

**1.** *Law.* A formal declaration, usually in writing, of a person's wishes as to the disposal of his property after his death; a will. Formerly, properly applied to a disposition of personal as distinct from real property (cf. c). Now *rare* (chiefly in phrase *last will and testament*).

[**1306** *Rolls of Parlt.* I. 220/1 Les executors de tieux testaments.] *c* **1330** R. BRUNNE *Chron.* (1810) 20 Þre þousand marke he gaf with testament fulle right. **13..** *Cursor M.* 28322 Ic seketur made of testament, Ne folud noght..Þe testament for to fulfill. **1362** LANGL. *P. Pl.* A. VII. 78, I wole, ar I Wende write my Testament. **1463** *Bury Wills* (Camden) 36, I..calle vpon hym to do his part in alle thinges longyng to my testement and wille. **1464** *Rolls of Parlt.* V. 549/2 Ayenst the Testament and the last Wille of your seid noble Progenitour. **1590** SWINBURNE *Testaments* 3 A testament properly vnderstoode, is one kinde of last will, euen that wherein Executor is named. **1637** PRYNNE in *Documents agst. P.* (Camden) 99 Whom I make sole executors of this my last will and testament, revoking all former wills. **1766** BLACKSTONE *Comm.* II. i. 12 The right of disposing one's property, or a part of it, by testament. **1818** HALLAM *Mid. Ages* (1819) II. vii. 311 The ecclesiastical tribunals..took the execution of testaments into their hands, on account of the legacies to pious uses, which testators were advised to bequeath. **1880** MUIRHEAD *Ulpian* XX. § 1 A testament is the testification of our will, in the form prescribed by law, made solemnly, on purpose that it may be effectual after our death.

**b.** *transf.* and *fig.* (Cf. *legacy*.)

? *a* **1400** *Morte Arth.* 668 Take here my testament of tresoure fulle huge, As I trayste appone the, be traye thowe me never! *c* **1532** DU WES *Introd. Fr.* in *Palsgr.* 1064 The masse is the testament the which our Lorde made before his deth & passyon. **1599** SHAKS. *Hen. V*, IV. vi. 27 And so espous'd to death, with blood he seal'd A Testament of Noble-ending-loue. **1667** JER. TAYLOR *Dissuas. Popery* II. I. iii. 110 The Gospels are Christ's Testament; and the Epistles are the Codicils annex'd. **1831–3** E. BURTON *Eccl. Hist.* xix. (1845) 403 The Testaments of the Twelve Patriarchs.. professes to contain prophecies and exhortations delivered by the sons of Jacob shortly before their death.

†**c.** *transf.* Testamentary estate; personal as distinct from real property. *Obs.*

**1424** *E. E. Wills* (1882) 56, I..declare my last will.., als well of my testament as of my land þat standez in feffez handes.

**2.** *Sc. Law.* The writing by which a person nominates an executor to administer his personal or movable estate after his decease. This writing is styled, in the decree of the Court granting confirmation (i.e. probate), a **testament-testamentar** (or -ary), and the executor is an *executor-nominate*. When no executor has been nominated, an *executor-dative* is appointed by the Court, and the decree appointing him is styled a **testament-dative.** (The latter answers to Letters of Administration in English Law.)

**1526** *Sc. Acts Jas. V* (1814) II. 306/2 Quhar ony sic personis deis wᵗin age þat may noᵗ mak þar testamentis. **1564** *Acts of Sederunt* 13 Apr. (1790) 6 To the collectoris and ressaveris of the quotts, for confirmation of the testaments of the personis decessand within oure realm. **1666** *Ibid.* 28 Feb. 99 If there be no nomination or testament made by the defunct, or if the testament testamentar shall not be desired to be confirmed. *Ibid.* 101 Of all testaments, both great and small, which shall be confirmed, as well of testaments dative, as others. **1681** STAIR *Inst. Law Scot.* XXX. § 33. 170 The Nomination of Executors, is properly called a Testament. **1768–73** ERSKINE *Inst. Sc. Law* III. ix. § 7 Though nuncupative testaments are not effectual.. to support the nomination of executors, yet nuncupative or verbal legacies are valid to the extent of L. 100 Scots. *Ibid.* § 27 Where an executor named by the deceased is authorised by the Judge, it is called the confirmation of a testament-testamentary; and when the Judge confers the office of executor upon a person of his own nomination, it is styled the confirmation of a testament-dative. **1838** in W. BELL *Dict. Law Scot.*

¶ **3.** *erroneously.* = TESTIMONY; witness.

**1456** SIR G. HAYE *Law Arms* (S.T.S.) 8 The pape convertit sanct Tiburce, [and] sanct Valere be his testament. *c* **1533** *Disc. Antechrist* in Strype *Eccl. Mem.* (1721) I. App. xlv. 125 And when he shal end his testament the beast shal come from the bottomles pit..and shal slay them. **1904** in *Daily Chron.* 21 Oct. 5/7 There is first-hand testament to my statements.

II. In Christian Latin use of *testāmentum*.

Orig. a misuse of the word, arising from the fact that Gr. διαθήκη, 'disposition, arrangement', was applied both to a covenant (*pactum, fœdus*) between parties, and to a testament or will (*testamentum*). Prob. largely due to the use of διαθήκη (in the sense 'covenant') in the account of the Last Supper immediately before Christ's death, and its consequent association with the notion of a last will or testament. See also historical note s. v. COVENANT *sb.* 7.

**4.** *Script.* A covenant between God and man: = COVENANT *sb.* 7. *Obs.* or *arch.*

*a* **1300** *Cursor M.* 12718 Quen drightin gan to sprad his grace..þe testament bigan he neu. *Ibid.* 12886 þe ald testament hir-wit nu slakes, And sua þe neu begining takes. *c* **1315** SHOREHAM i. 541 Þys hys þe chalis of my blode Of testament newe. *a* **1340** HAMPOLE *Psalter* cxxxi. 12 If þi sunnys hafe kepid my testament. **1382** WYCLIF *Baruch* ii. 35 And Y shal sette to them an other testament euere durende. — *Acts* vii. 8 He ȝaf to him the testament of circumcisioun. — 1 *Cor.* xi. 25 This cuppe is the newe testament in my blood. *c* **1430** LYDG. *Letabundus* 248 in *Min. Poems*, In Reioysshyng of Crystes glad comynge; Two testamentys that day wer maad bothe Oon. **1509** HAWES *Past. Pleas.* xliv. (Percy Soc.) 216 His elect mother and arke of testament, Of holy chyrche the blessed lumynary. **1611** BIBLE 2 *Cor.* iii. 6 Able ministers of the New Testament [Gr. διακόνους καινῆς διαθήκης: WYCLIF, able mynistris of the newe testament, 1881 *R. V.* ministers of a new covenant]. *Ibid.* 14 In the reading of the old testament [*R. V.* at the reading of the old covenant].

**5.** Hence, through the application of παλαιά and καινὴ διαθήκη, in the Itala and Vulgate *vetus* and *novum testamentum*, to the Mosaic and Christian 'covenants' or 'dispensations' (cf. 2 Cor. iii. 6, 14 cited in 4), the term passed in early Christian Latin (and thence in the languages of the West) to the books or records of the old and new covenants.

(This transition of sense took place many centuries before the adoption of the word in English, where the name was simply taken over from L. or Fr. in this transferred use.)

**a.** Each of the two main divisions of the Sacred Scriptures or Bible, the *Old* and the *New Testament*, consisting of the books of the old or Mosaic and the new or Christian covenant or dispensation respectively.

*a* **1300** *Cursor M.* 120, I sal yow schew wit myn entent Brefli of aiþere testament. *a* **1340** HAMPOLE *Psalter* Prol., Þe lare of þe ald testament & of þe new. **1387** TREVISA *Higden* (Rolls) II. 293 In þe olde testament me redeþ... In þe newe testament. **1447** BOKENHAM *Seyntys* (Roxb.) Introd. 3 As the old testament beryth witnesse. **1532** ELYOT *Let. to Dk. Norfolk* in *Gov.* (1880) Life 79 Thei..doo peruse euery daye one chapitre of the New Testament. *c* **1710** CELIA FIENNES *Diary* (1888) 235 A Large window full of fine paintings—the history of the testaments. **1711** ADDISON *Spect.* No. 160 ¶ 4 In the Old Testament we find several Passages more elevated and sublime than any in Homer. **1859** DICKENS *T. Two Cities* I. ii, The coachman could..have taken his oath on the two Testaments.

**b.** The New Testament as distinct from the Old; a copy of the New Testament; a volume containing this. Common in *Greek Testament*.

**1500–20** DUNBAR *Poems* xiv. 14 So quhene the Psalme and Testament to reid Within this land was nevir hard nor sene. **1831** R. SHENNAN *Tales*, etc. 53 (E.D.D.) The Testament was his school-book. **1834** *Encycl. Brit.* (ed. 7) IX. 355 He [Erasmus] had for some time been..employed in preparing an edition of the Greek Testament. **1842** BORROW *Bible in Spain* viii. 49, I had brought with me a certain quantity of Testaments. **1869** MCLENNAN *Peas. Life* I. xvii. (E.D.D.), The Testament, and next 'the Bible', are regular class-books. **1888** MRS. WARD *R. Elsmere* 118 Her little well-worn Testament open on her knee.

**6.** *attrib.* and *Comb.*, as (sense 1) *testament-maker, -making*, (sense 4) *testament-book*; testament-man, a disciple of the New Testament.

**1573** *New Custom* III. i. in Hazl. *Dodsley* III. 50 Here, take at my hands this *Testament-book. **1533** TINDALE *Supper of Lord* B vj, Where so euer is a testament, there muste the death of the *testament maker go betwene. **1880** MUIRHEAD *Gaius* II. § 113 A female acquires the right of *testament-making on reaching twelve. **1819** W. TENNANT *Papistry Storm'd* III. (1827) 103 That mad ill-gainshon'd byke O' *Test'ment-men that doth us fyke.

Hence **Te·stament** *v.*, *intr.* to make a will; *trans.* to leave by will, bequeath; whence **Te·stamenting** *vbl. sb.*; **Te·stamented** *a. nonce-wd.*, included in the Old or New Testament Scriptures.

**1586** FERNE *Blaz. Gentrie* 117 In diuers cases in the matter of testamenting a knight is priuiledged. *a* **1878** H. AINSLIE *Pilgr. Land Burns* (1892) 198 What's cross'd the craig Can ne'er be testamented. **1907** C. GREGORY *Canon & Text N. T.* 220 He [Clement] makes short comments on all the testamented Scripture.

† **Testame·ntaire**, *a. Sc. Obs. rare*⁻¹. [a. F. *testamentaire* testamentary.] Of or belonging to a testament; *Old Testamentaire*, of or pertaining to the Old Testament or Mosaic Covenant.

*a* **1671** in R. MacWard *True Nonconf.* i. 19 The resistance of the Maccabees was Old Testamentaire, and now antiquate.

**Testamental** (testăme·ntăl), *a.* Now *rare*. [ad. late or med.L. *testāmentāl-is*, f. L. *testāmentum* TESTAMENT: see -AL.] Of, pertaining to, or of the nature of a testament.

**1606** *True & Perfect Relat.* Cc iij, And asked Garnet what interpretation hee made of this testamentall protestation. **1621** AINSWORTH *Annot. Pentat., Gen.* vi. 18 Diathekee, that is, a Testament or Disposition..may be named a testamentall covenant, or a covenanting testament. *a* **1647** HABINGTON *Surv. Worc.* in *Worc. Hist. Soc. Proc.* III. 436, I omytt the Testamentall tombestone of William Edden of Darlingscott with his..last will. **1825** J. MONTGOMERY *Hymn 'According to thy gracious word'* ii, Thy testamental cup I take, And thus remember thee.

Hence **Testame·ntally** *adv.*, in a testamental manner, by way of a testament or will; **Testame·ntalness**, testamental quality or nature.

**1774** T. WEST *Antiq. Furness* vi. 133 As well amongst the living, as testamentally. **1669** BP. PATRICK *Friendly Debate* 35 A fourth tells them there is a special Mystery in looking at the Testamentalness of Christ's Sufferings.

**Testame·ntar**, *a. Sc. Law.* [ad. F. *testamentaire* (16th c.), or L. *testamentār-ius*: see TESTAMENTARY and -AR².] = TESTAMENTARY 1, 2. *Testament-testamentar*: see TESTAMENT 2.

**1546** *Reg. Privy Council Scot.* I. 50 Tutrix testamentar to hir barnes and said umquhile Hew. **1661** *Charters rel. Glasgow* (1906) II. 41 Mary..tutrix testamentar of Esmy duke of Lennox. **1681** STAIR *Instit.* I. vi. § 5 There be three kinds of Tutors...The first is, Tutor Testamentar, or nominate.

**Testamentarily** (testăme·ntărĭli), *adv. rare.* [f. TESTAMENTARY *a.* + -LY². Cf. obs. F. *testamentairement* by will (1517 in Godef.).] In a testamentary manner, by will.

**1774** T. WEST *Antiq. Furness* ii. 35 By these presents, I will, command, and testamentarily confirm. **1880** MUIRHEAD *Gaius* Digest 601 The manumitter was entitled to deal with it testamentarily as part of his own estate.

† **Testamenta·rious**, *a. Obs. rare*⁻⁰. [f. L. *testāmentāri-us* (see next) + -OUS.]

**1656** BLOUNT *Glossogr.*, *Testamentarious*, of, or belonging to a Testament or last Will. Hence in PHILLIPS, BAILEY, ASH.

**Testamentary** (testăme·ntări), *a.* Also 6 *erron.* -ory. [ad. L. *testāmentāri-us*, f. *testāmentum* TESTAMENT; see -ARY¹. Cf. TESTAMENTAR.]

**1.** Of, pertaining to, or having relation to a testament or will; of the nature of a will.

*Testamentary capacity*, capacity to make a will. *Testamentary estate*, estate subject to disposal by will.

**1456** *Paston Lett.* I. 373 My Lord Chaunceller..is..souverain juge and ordinarie principalle under the Pope in a cause testamentarie. **1596** BACON *Max. & Use Com. Law* II. (1635) 24 Its not an estate testamentory. **1759** ROBERTSON *Hist. Scot.* II. Wks. 1813 I. 113 No matrimonial or testamentary cause could be tried but in the spiritual courts. *a* **1827** in Jarman *Powell's Devises* (ed. 3) II. 169 All the residue of his 'goods and chattels, rights, credits, personal and testamentary estate whatsoever'. **1885** *Manch. Exam.* 3 Feb. 5/1 Mrs. B. was not of testamentary capacity.

**2.** Made or done by will; appointed by will.

**1547** *Bk. Marchauntes* e j b, To haue some aniuersari foundacion, or other testamentary gift. **1659** *Gentl. Calling* v. § 24 Some testamentary charities. *a* **1794** FEARNE *Posth. Wks.* (1797) 435 In regard to testamentary dispositions of land. **1838** W. BELL *Dict. Law Scot.* 1016 A tutor-nominate or testamentary, is he whom the father..has nominated, either in a testament, or in some other writing. **1869** FREEMAN *Norm. Conq.* III. xii. 218 The groundwork of William's claim as testamentary successor to Eadward.

**b.** Expressed or contained in a will.

**1762** STERNE *Tr. Shandy* V. x, This testamentary proof he gave of his affection to his master. **1851** HAWTHORNE *Ho. Sev. Gables* xviii, In compliance with his testamentary directions. **1910** *Daily News* 20 July 4/2 It has carried out the testamentary request.

**3.** Of or pertaining to the Old or New Testament.

**1849** W. FITZGERALD tr. *Whitaker's Disput.* 28 These books..are comprised in the old and new Testaments, and are therefore styled Testamentary. **1905** J. ORR *Probl. O. T.* viii. (1906) 272 Delitzsch postulates written 'testamentary discourses' and laws of Moses.

† **Testamenta·tion.** *Obs. rare*⁻¹. [n. of action f. med.L. *testāmentāre* to give by testament, whence some dictionaries have as Eng. **Testame·ntate** *v.*] The making of a testament; the disposing of one's property by will; = TESTATION 2.

*c* **1765** BURKE *Tracts on Popery Laws* Wks. XIII. 328 By this Law the right of testamentation is taken away, which the inferiour tenures had always enjoyed.

† **Testamenti·ferous**, *a. Obs. nonce-wd.* [f. L. *testāment-um* + -FEROUS.] Bearing the covenant: applied to the Jewish 'ark of the covenant'.

**1772** NUGENT tr. *Hist. Fr. Gerund* II. 92 And whither went wandering this concave testamentiferous ark?

† **Testame·ntive**, *a. Obs. rare*⁻¹. [irreg. f. L. *testāment-um* TESTAMENT + -IVE.] Of the nature of or pertaining to a testament or will.

**1622** MABBE tr. *Aleman's d'Alf.* II. 242 Other writings, processiue,..testamentiue,..and infinite other the like.

† **Te·stamentize**, *v. Obs. rare.* [f. TESTAMENT + -IZE.] *intr.* To make one's will.

*a* **1661** FULLER *Worthies, Denbigh.* (1662) IV. 34 Whether it was..because Welsh Bishops in that age might not Testamentize without Royal assent.

‖ **Testamur** (testē̆ⁱ·mɒ̆ɹ). [From the L. word *testāmur* 'we testify', used in the document, from *testārī* to testify.] In University use: A certificate from the examiners that a candidate has satisfied them. Also, A certificate generally.

**1840** J. T. HEWLETT *P. Priggins* xvii, Balamson and Drinkwater..though it certainly was a 'shave', got their testamurs. **1860** J. BATEMAN *D. Wilson* I. vii. 115 The result was a refusal to grant the required testamur. **1863** DOWDING *Life & Corr. G. Calixtus* xxvii. 269 A formal testamur from the leading Lutherans at the Congress. **1897** ESCOTT *Soc. Transf. Vict. Age* xiv. 182 In the place of the 'Smalls' testamur..the special student was tested closely.

**Testate** (te·stĕt), *a.* and *sb.* [ad. L. *testāt-us*, pa. pple. of *testārī* (also *testāre*) to bear witness, attest, make one's will, etc.]

**A.** *adj.* **1.** That has left a valid will at death.

**1475** *Rolls of Parlt.* VI. 139/1 Persones diyng Testate and Intestate. **1589** WARNER *Alb. Eng.* v. xxvii. (1612) 136 Nor all die testate. **1726** AYLIFFE *Parergon* 132 The lawful Distribution of the Goods of Persons dying both Testate and Intestate. **1906** *Times* 27 July 3/6 He clearly desired when he died to die testate and not intestate.

**2.** *transf.* Disposed of or settled by will. *Testate duty*, succession duty on an estate passing by will.

**1792** J. BELKNAP *Hist. New Hampsh.* III. 273 All matters relative to the settlement and descent of estates, testate and intestate. **1875** POSTE *Gaius* II. Comm. (ed. 2) 229 His succession was partly intestate, partly testate. **1880** GLADSTONE *Sp. Ho. Comm.* 15 Mar., Between 1,000*l.* and 1,500*l.* the old testate duty was 30*l.*; the new..is to be 31*l.*

**B.** *sb.* †**1.** One who has given testimony; a witness; also (app.) testimony, evidence. *Obs.*

**1619** BRATHWAIT *New Spring* C ij b, When thousand Testates shall produced be, For to disclose their close hypocrisie. **1624** HEYWOOD *Captives* III. ii. in Bullen *O. Pl.* IV. 162 Is thy hart sear'd..Against just testates and apparent truthes? **1635** — *Hierarch.* VI. 357 The Stoicks Testates were to that Conviction. **1652** J. WRIGHT tr. *Camus' Nat. Paradox* a j, Reader, this Testate is just.

†**2.** The final protocol of a royal writ; = TESTE² 2.

*a* **1604** HANMER *Chron. Irel.* (1809) 345 He granted a Charter to the towne of Kilkenny..with the testate of Thomas Fitz Antony. **1641** EARL MONM. tr. *Biondi's Civil Warres* I. 3 Such gifts being of no validity without a testate of the great Seale.

**3.** One who at death has left a valid will.

**1864** in WEBSTER. **1871** *Daily News* 21 Apr. 2 To place all personal property, whether of testates or intestates, on the same scale..of a 2 per cent. duty.

**Testate** (te·steⁱt), *v. rare.* [f. ppl. stem of L. *testārī* (or -*āre*): see prec. and -ATE³ 5.]

**1.** *intr.* To bear witness, to testify, to attest.

**1624** HEYWOOD *Gunaik.* I. 2 As Epiphanius testates of him. *Ibid.* 15 In Bauron..she was likewise honoured, and as Lucan testates, in Taurus, a mountaine in Sicilie. **1908** *Westm. Gaz.* 22 July 9/4 Prisoner was also charged with ..forging the handwriting of the testating witness to the same deed.

**2.** To make one's will.

**1892** *Pall Mall G.* 21 June 2/1 As good Mdme. Dubrai remarked whilst testating, with tears in her eyes, 'He [a cat] has all his life been accustomed to his little luxuries'.

**Testation** (testē̆ⁱ·ʃən). [ad. L. *testātiōn-em*, n. of action f. *testārī* (-*āre*): see TESTATE *a.* Cf. obs. F. *testacion* (14–16th c. in Godef.).]

†**1.** Attestation, testimony. *Obs.*

**1642** H. MORE *Song of Soul* II. iii. II. xxix, A true testation Of the souls utter independency On this poor crasie Corse. *a* **1656** BP. HALL *Satan's Fiery Darts quenched* (R.), How clear a testation have the inspired prophets of God given of old to this truth? **1656** in BLOUNT *Glossogr.*

**2.** The disposal of property by will.

**1832** GEN. P. THOMPSON in *Westm. Rev.* Apr. 298 That the right of testation..is, *primâ facie*, nothing but an extension of the simple right of disposition, to the doing in a convenient way what must otherwise be done in an inconvenient one. **1861** MAINE *Anc. Law* vi. 196 It is doubtful whether a true power of testation was known to any original society except the Roman. **1876** DIGBY *Real Prop.* viii. 343.

**Testator** (testē̆ⁱ·tɔɹ). [In sense 1, a. AF. *testatour* = F. -*teur* (13th c. in Godef. *Compl.*), ad. late L. *testatōr-em*, agent-n. from *testārī* to witness, make a will. In sense 2 direct from L.]

**1.** One who makes a will; *esp.* one who has died leaving a will.

[**1306** *Rolls of Parlt.* I. 220/1 La volunte de chescun testatour.] **1447** *Ibid.* V. 129/2 Ther remayneth due to the saide Executours, for their saide Testatour,..the sum of VII or VIII m. marcs. **1535** tr. *Littleton's Nat. Brev.* 29 b, The executours..brought a wrytte of Erroure of vtlawry pronounced agaynst the testatoure in hys lyfe. **1664** *Protests Lords* (1875) I. 30 Provision made by the testator to pay honest debts. **1766** BLACKSTONE *Comm.* II. xxiii. 376 That all devises of lands and tenements shall not only be in writing, but signed by the testator. **1856** EMERSON *Eng. Traits, Cockayne* Wks. (Bohn) II. 64 A testator endows a dog or a rookery, and Europe cannot interfere with his absurdity.

†**2.** One who or that which testifies; a witness.

**1600** W. WATSON *Decacordon* (1602) 350 Come false witnes, come true testator. **1632** LITHGOW *Trav.* x. 435 To all which, and much more haue I beene an occular Testator. **1698** in *Col. Rec. Pennsylv.* I. 549, I am a perfect Testator, by report of David Evans acquittance.

Hence **Testa·torship**, the position or office of a testator; **Te·statory** *a.*, pertaining to or of the nature of evidence.

**1624** BP. ANDREWES *Serm., Heb.* xiii. 20–21 (1629) 584 Both, in His [Christ's] Pastor-ship, and in His Testatorship. **1907** *Daily News* 23 May 6 Whether anything would be gained by giving it a judicial position instead of a testatory we must be allowed to doubt.

**Testatrix** (testē̆ⁱ·triks). [a. late L. *testātrix*, fem. of *testātor*: see prec.] A female testator.

**1591** *Knaresborough Wills* (Surtees) I. 175 This testatrix and her heires. **1751** SMOLLETT *Per. Pic.* (1779) I. vii. 57 Mr. H... who was generously remembered by the testatrix. **1880** J. W. SHERER *Conjuror's Daughter*, etc. 279 The Testatrix desired to mark her high sense of [his] merits and services..by leaving the property unreservedly to him.

‖ **Testatum** (testē̆ⁱ·tɒ̆m). *Law.* [L., neut. pa. pple. of *testārī* (-*āre*) to attest, etc.]

†**1.** A writ formerly issued when a writ of capias was returned, the sheriff to whom it was first addressed testifying that the defendant was not to be found within his jurisdiction: see quots. *Obs.*

**1607** COWELL *Interpr.* s.v., If the Shyreeue return (*nihil habet in balliva mea*),..another writ shall be sent out into any other Countie..which is termed a *Testatum*, because the Shyreeue hath formerly testified, that he found nothing in his Bayliweeke to serue the turne. **1672** T. CORY *Course & Pract. Comm.-Pl.* 27 Untill..there be an Execution in the Proper County entred upon the Roll, and a *Testatum* awarded. **1848** WHARTON *Law Lex.*, *Testatum writ*, a process of execution which is issued into a different county than that in which the venue was laid in the declaration.

**2.** The witnessing-clause of a deed.

**1844** WILLIAMS *Real Prop.* (1875) 193 The *testatum*, or witnessing part, 'Now this Indenture witnesseth'.

‖**Testa·tur.** [L., 'he testifies', from *testārī* to bear witness, etc.] An attestation.

**1702** *Rouse's Heav. Univ.* Advert. 3 To which he prefixed his most solemn Vidit and Testatur.

†**Teste**[1]. *Obs. rare.* [a. OF. *teste* (11th c.), mod.F. *tête* head:—L. *testa* an earthen pot, in late L. a skull, in pop. L. head.] The head.

**13..** *K. Alis.* 7112 (Bodl. MS.) For Cades was a ferly beste þries shett teeþ weren in his teste. *c* **1450** *Two Cookery-bks.* 112 *Teste de cure*.—Nym rys..& bray hem al to doust: tempre it vp with almand mylk, cast therto poudur and safron & sugur [etc.].

**Teste**[2] (te·sti). Also 6 testey, -ty, 7 -tee. [a. L. *teste*, abl. of *testis* witness.]

**1.** The L. word *teste* in ablative absolute constr. with a pronoun (e.g. *meipso* myself) or name of a person, as used in the authenticating clause of a writ, etc.: see sense 2; hence, in same construction, in non-legal use, before the name of a person cited as witness or authority, = (So and so) being witness, on the authority or evidence of (So and so); *teste meipso, seipso*, on my or his own testimony or authority; also as *sb.* one's own evidence.

[*c* **1194**: see Note to sense 2.] **1607** COWELL *Interpr.*, *Teste*, is..so called, because the very conclusion of euery writ wherein the date is contained, beginneth with these words (*teste meipso*, etc.). **1654** GAYTON *Pleas. Notes* IV. xxiii. 277 This proofe a *Teste seipso*, is not so current as the other. **1686** SOUTH *Serm.* (1727) II. 340 Presently the Sot..vouched also by a *Teste Meipso*,..steps forth an exact Politician. **1842** BARHAM *Ingol. Leg.* Ser. II. *Blasphemer's Warn.*, Many..commanders 'Swore terribly (*teste* T. Shandy) in Flanders'. **1848** LOWELL *Biglow P.* Ser. I. ii, The Devil, *teste* Cotton Mather, is unversed in certain of the Indian dialects.

**2.** The final clause in a royal writ naming the person who authorizes the affixing of the king's seal.

Where (as in letters close and patent) the king himself authenticates the sealing, the clause has, since Rich. I, begun *teste meipso* 'witness I myself'. Where a high official authenticates (as in judicial and exchequer writs, and during the king's absence), his name and (usually) office are stated. As such a clause generally stated place and date of sealing, the term became practically = DATE *sb.*[2]

**1423** in *Letter-bk. I Lond.* (1909) 298 The teste of the which maundement ys the xx day of Feverer, the second yeer of his regne. **1467-8** *Rolls of Parlt.* V. 603/2 Oure said Letters Patentes, wherof the Teste is at Westm' the xix[th] day of Juyn. **1542-3** *Act* 34 & 35 *Hen. VIII*, c. 26 § 14 The teste of euerye bill and judiciall proces that shall passe undre the saide judiciall Seall, shalbe undre the name of suche of the saide Justices.. in lyke maner and forme as is used in the Common Place in Englande. **1577-87** HOLINSHED *Chron.* III. 1245/1 It was doone by the son in the fathers name, and vnder the teste of the son, the father yet being king in shew. **1588** LAMBARDE *Eiren.* II. ii. 106 Which..may bee in the name of the Queene, and vnder the Teste of the Iustice of the Peace, thus..Witnesse the said G. M. **1653** *Acts & Ordin. Parl.* (1658) 275 From and after the six and twentieth day of December, 1653, the Name, Style, Title and Teste of the 'Lord Protector..of the Commonwealth of England, Scotland, and Ireland, and the Dominions thereto belonging', shall be used, and no other. **1658** *Practick Part of Law* 6 This Writ may bear Teste out of the Term. **1672** CORY *Course & Pract. Comm.-Pl.* 23 Of the Teste's and Retorns of Writs in all Actions real and personal. **1765** BLACKSTONE *Comm.* I. ii. 172 No candidate shall, after the date (usually called the *teste*) of the writs..give any money or entertainment. **1792** *Act Congr.* in *Bouvier's Law Dict.* (1898) s.v., All writs and process issuing from the supreme or a circuit court shall bear teste of the chief justice of the supreme court. **1818** CRUISE *Digest* (ed. 2) V. 396 It appeared the *teste* of the warrant of attorney was after appearance.

**b.** Hence, more generally, a clause stating the name of a witness (as to a charter in writ-form).

**1611** SPEED *Hist. Gt. Brit.* VII. xliv. § 45. 380 His name is continually set downe, as a Witnesse in the testees of his fathers Charters. *c* **1617** in Hardy *Rot. Chart.* (1837) Introd. 30 There was some question about the marshalling of these testes in there due place. *Ibid.*, Whether the Duke ..should take his place in the teste as Earle of Richmond or Duke of Lenneux.

†**c.** Evidence, proof. *Obs.*

**1567** FENTON *Trag. Disc.* 214 Whyche kynde of courtyng thamarus Luchyn forgatt not too prefer as a testey of hys seruice and a furtherer of his sute. *c* **1585** *Faire Em* II. i. 100 Whose glauncing eyes..Giues testies of their Maisters amorous hart.

**Teste,** obs. form of TEST *sb.*[1], [3].

**Tested, teste'd,** *ppl. a.*: see under TEST *v.*

†**Testee·.** *Obs. rare.* [Irreg. formation from L. *testis* witness, perh. with ending -EE as in *trustee*, etc.] A witness. Cf. TESTE[2].

**1654** VILVAIN *Epit. Ess.* VI. lxxvi, No Murdrer be: Whorster: Theef: fals Testee [*rime* thee]. **1682** R. WARE *Foxes & Firebr.* II. 23 Three Testees were to wait on these Houses weekly, to take out what summs there were thrown in.

**Tester**[1] (te·stəɹ). Forms: α. 4- tester; 5 -ere, -our, -ir, -ur(e, testre, *Sc.* tyster, -yr, 5-6 teester, 6 (9) testor, 6-7 -ar, teaster (9 *dial.*), 7 taister. β. 6 test-, teasterne, testorne, 7 -arn, -ern. [prob. from OF.: cf. *testre* fem. (15th c., one example in Godef.) the vertical part of a bed behind the head; also OF. *testière*, mod.F. *têtière* a covering for the head, etc., It. *testiera*, Sp. *testera*, med.L. *testera*, *-eria* (see TESTER[2]); also med.L. *testerium*, *testrum*, *testūra*, also *testāle*, all, according to Du Cange, = 'the upper part, top, or upper covering of a bed', derivatives of L. *testa*, in late pop. L. and Comm. Romanic 'head'.

The historical relations of these words are not quite clear, but app. med.L. *testerium*, *-eria*, It. *testiera*, Sp. *testera*, OF. *testière*, and ME. *testere*, go together in form, as do med.L. *testrum*, OF. and ME. *testre*, and perh. also med.L. *testura* and ME. *testur*; though the senses are specialized in different langs. The other Eng. forms appear to have been assimilated to various endings in *-er*, *-ar*, *-or*, *-our*, and (erratically) *-ern*, *-orn*.]

**1.** A canopy over a bed, supported on the posts of the bedstead or suspended from the ceiling; formerly (esp. in phrase *tester and celure*), the vertical part at the head of the bed which ascends to and sometimes supports the canopy, or (as some think) the wooden or metal framework supporting the canopy and curtains.

α. *c* **1380** WYCLIF *Wks.* (1880) 434 In aparel of chaumbre, as in proud beddis, testeris & curteyns. **14..** *Voc.* in Wr.-Wülcker 615/17 *Tapisterium*, an[ce] a Testour. *a* **1440** *Sir Degrev.* 1474 Hur bede was off aszure, With testur and celure. *Ibid.* 1485 Ther was at hur testere The kyngus owne banere. *c* **1440** *Promp. Parv.* 489/2 Teester, or tethtere of a bed, *capitellum*. **1449** *Test. Ebor.* (Surtees) II. 156 Testur. **1454** *E. E. Wills* (1882) 133 My bed..wiþ the testour & Canape ther-to. **1530** PALSGR. 280/1 Testar for a bedde, *dossier*. **1548** in Strype *Eccl. Mem.* (1721) II. xvi. 129 A bedstead gilt, with a testor and counterpoint, with curtains belonging to the same. **1556** WITHALS *Dict.* (1568) 51/1 A teaster ouer the bedde, *canopus*. **1670** F. SANDFORD *Order Funeral Dk. Albemarle* (1722) 5 A Bed of State of black Velvet.. with black Plumes at the four Corners of the Tester. **1801** tr. *Gabrielli's Myst. Husb.* III. 4 The tester of a bed..was suspended by cords to the lofty ceiling. **1899** *Q. Rev.* Apr. 394 The tester, carved and panelled, is surrounded by a cornice, inlaid with lighter wood, from which a crimson silk valance and curtains hang.

β. **1546** in Willis & Clark *Cambridge* (1886) III. 351 A bedstok with cortins of dornix, and testerne of the same. **1565-73** COOPER *Thesaurus*, *Conopeum*..a Canapie...Some haue vsed it for a testorne to hang ouer a bed. **1599** *Nottingham Rec.* IV. 252 One olde thinne silke teasterne for a bedd. **1655** tr. *Com. Hist. Francion* IV. 11 He took a Base Violl from the testern of his Bed.

**2.** *transf.* and *fig.* Something that covers or overhangs; a shrine; a canopy carried over a dignitary; the soundboard of a pulpit, etc.

*c* **1425** WYNTOUN *Cron.* VI. x. 773 (Cott. MS.) He mad a tystyr [*v. r.* textuere] in þat qwhile, Qwhar in was cloyssit þe Ewangile, Platit oure withe siluir bricht. **1598** FLORIO, *Baldacchino*,..a testerne carried ouer Princes. **1611** COTGR., *Surciel*, the tester of a cloth of State. **1830** GALT *Lawrie T.* IV. iv, A night under the starry tester of the heavens. **1846-75** PARKER *Gloss. Archit.* s.v., The canopy over Queen Eleanor's tomb at Westminster is called a tester in old documents. **1908** *Athenæum* 1 Aug. 119/3 The remarkably fine pulpit and tester of the church of Bishop's Waltham.

**3.** *attrib.* and *Comb.*, as *tester-bed*, *-bedstead*, *-rail*; *tester-covering* adj.

**1622** DRAYTON *Poly-olb.* xxvi. 85 The rich and sumptuous Beds, with Tester-couering plumes. **1730** SOUTHALL *Bugs* 35 Oak-Bedsteds, and plain Wainscot Head-Boards, and Tester-Rails of that Wood. **1843** BORROW *Bible in Spain* xxiii. (Pelh. Libr.) 160, I was stretched on the tester bed. **1873** *Sat. Rev.* 29 Nov. 707/1 The mother of St. John the Baptist is supported by cushions in a tester bedstead.

Hence **Testered** (te·stəɹd) *a.*, having a tester.

**1790** MRS. A. M. JOHNSON *Monmouth* I. 70 The lofty testered bed..was in a ruinous state.

†**Te·ster**[2]. *Obs.* Also 5 teste·re, teestee·r, testor, ‖testiere. [a. OF. *testière* (12th c. in Godef. *Compl.*) 'any kind of head-peece, particularly a scull, sallet, or steele cap, also the crowne of a hat' (Cotgr.), mod.F. *têtière* covering of the top of the head, coif, headstall of a horse, = It. *testiera* 'head piece, a caske or helmet, testerne or head of any thing, head-stall of a bridle' (Florio), Sp. *testera* 'armour for the forehead of a horse' (Minsheu), Pg. *testeira* 'anything to cover the front', med.L. *testera*, *testeria* (Du Cange), f. *testa*, OF. *teste* head.]

A piece of armour for the head; a head-piece, a casque; also, a piece of armour for the head of a horse; a kind of mask or visor with holes for the eyes, apertures for the ears, etc.

*c* **1386** CHAUCER *Knt.'s T.* 1641 The sheeldes brighte, testeres [*v. rr.* testers, teesteers], and trappures, Gold hewen helmes, hauberkes. **1465** *Mann. & Househ. Exp. Eng.* (Roxb.) 285 The man that maketh his testor of mayle. **1484** CAXTON *Chivalry* 67 To his hors is gyuen in his hede a testiere to signefye that a knyȝt ought to do none armes without reason.

**Tester**[3] (te·stəɹ). *arch.* Forms: α. 6 testourn, teastern, 6-7 testern, -erne, -orn, -orne; β. 6-7 testor, 7 -ar, teaster, 6- tester. [app. the result of a series of corruptions or perversions of TESTON.] A name for the TESTON of Henry VIII, esp. as debased and depreciated; subsequently a colloquial or slang term for a sixpence.

α. **1546** WRIOTHESLEY *Chron.* (Camden) I. 176 Condemned for treason for counterfeiting testornes. **1560** in *Buccleuch MSS.* (Hist. MSS. Comm.) I. 223 Knowledge of the better testornes from the worse. **1579** G. HARVEY *Letter-bk.* (Camden) 72 Eloquence..were more worth then a crackd testerne in his purse. **1614** J. COOKE *Greene's Tu Quoque* D iij b, A testerne or a shilling to a seruant that brings you a glasse of beere, bindes his hands to his lippes.

β. **1567-8** in 11*th Rep. Dep. Kpr. Irel.* 180 With not more than two testors a day each. **1597** SHAKS. 2 *Hen. IV*, III. ii. 296 Hold, there is a Tester for thee. **1608** DAY *Law Trickes* III. i, Prethee giue the Fidler a testar and send him packing. **1613** TAPP *Pathw. Knowl.* 53 There is also the Tester or halfe shilling which is 6d. **1765** FOOTE *Commissary* I. Wks. 1799 II. 8, I hope you'll tip me the tester to drink. **1822** LAMB *Elia* Ser. I. *Praise Chimneysweepers*, If it be starving weather..the demand on thy humanity will surely rise to a tester. *a* **1839** PRAED *Poems* (1864) I. 94 Well! it was worth a silver tester, To see how she frowned when the Abbess blessed her.

**Tester**[4] (te·stəɹ). [Agent-n. f. TEST *v.*[2] or *sb.*[1]: see -ER[1].] One who tests or proves, or whose business is to test the quality or condition of anything; a device for testing. In quot. 1697, (?) a supporter of religious or political tests.

**1661** BOYLE *Style of Script.* (1675) 128 Those wary testers, that like not to be cheated. **1697** ISABEL WRIGHT in *Collect. Dying Test.* (1806) 42 Testers, Banders, Bloodshedders, Consenters to Blood. **1702** *Lond. Gaz.* No. 3818/4 The Queen has been pleased to appoint..Hopton Hains Esq., Weigher and Tester of the Mint. **1882** OGILVIE (Annandale), *Tester*, one who tests [etc.]; as, a good tester. **1884** KNIGHT *Dict. Mech.*, *Suppl.*, *Steam Gage Tester*, an instrument to test the accuracy of the steam gage. **1899** *Westm. Gaz.* 14 Jan. 8/1 A train..stops; a tester is going round with his hammer striking the wheels. **1910** *Ibid.* 8 Mar. 5/2 A device which commends itself to..owners of motor-cars generally is the Acer brake horse-power tester.

†**Testern,** *v. Obs. nonce-wd.* [See TESTER[3].] *trans.* To present with a tester; to 'tip'.

**1591** SHAKS. *Two Gent.* I. i. 153 To testifie your bounty, I thank you, you haue testern'd me.

**Testern(e,** obs. form of TESTER[1], [3].

**Testes,** pl. of TESTIS. **Testey,** obs. f. TESTE[2].

**Testibrachial** (te:stibrē·kiăl), *a. Anat.* [f. mod.L. *testibrachi-um* (f. *testis* TESTIS + *brachium* arm) + -AL.] Of or pertaining to the *testibrachium* or prepeduncle of the cerebellum, being the process from the cerebellum to the testis of the brain.

**1891** in *Cent. Dict.*

‖**Testicardines** (te:stikā·ɹdinīz), *sb. pl. Zool.* [mod.L., f. *testa* shell + *cardo* (*cardin-*) hinge.] A primary division of brachiopods, having hinged shells; opposed to *Ecardines*. Hence **Testica·rdine** *a. rare*, **Testica·rdinate** *a.*, having a hinged shell.

**1878** BELL *Gegenbaur's Comp. Anat.* 308 In the Testicardines it is short and largely chitinised. **1888** ROLLESTON & JACKSON *Anim. Life* 693 In the hinged Brachiopoda or *Testicardines* the dorsal valve is furnished with a projecting cardinal process to which are attached the divaricator muscles. **1895** *Cambr. Nat. Hist.* III. xvii. 467 On the inner surface of the shell of the Testicardinate Brachiopoda ..are two lateral teeth.

**Testicle** (te·stik'l). Also 5 testicule. [ad. L. *testiculus*, dim. f. *testis* TESTIS[2]: see -CULE. Cf. F. *testicule*, Sp., Pg. *testiculo*, It. *testicolo*.] Each of the two ellipsoid glandular bodies, constituting the sperm-secreting organs in male mammals, and usually enclosed in a scrotum; = TESTIS[2] 1 a.

*c* **1425** tr. *Arderne's Treat. Fistula* 14 His testicules war bolned out of mesure. **1597** A. M. tr. *Guillemeau's Fr. Chirurg.* 21 b/1 This swellinge..of the testicles. **1646** SIR T. BROWNE *Pseud. Ep.* III. iv. 112 That a Bever to escape the Hunter, bites off his testicles or stones, is a tenent very ancient. **1783** JUSTAMOND tr. *Raynal's Hist. Indies* I. 307 It is very certain, and has often been observed that the Hottentot men have but one testicle. **1876** BRISTOWE *The. & Pract. Med.* (1878) 171 (Small-pox) Inflammation of the ovary or testicle is occasionally observed.

**b.** Rarely applied to the corresponding organs in non-mammals: see TESTIS[2] 1 b.

[**1634** R. H. *Salerne's Regiment* 36 Testicles or Stones, and especially stones of fatte Cockes..be very good and great nourishers.] **1713** WARDER *True Amazons* 10 [The Drone has] a large pair of Testicles, as big as great Pins Heads. **1841-71** T. R. JONES *Anim. Kingd.* (ed. 4) 282 Both the ovary and testicle are evidently temporary organs. **1877** HUXLEY *Anat. Inv. Anim.* vii. 389 The testicle is an elongated sac which lies on the ventral aspect of the intestine.

†**c.** *transf.* The ovary in females. *Obs.*

**1545** RAYNOLD *Byrth Mankynde* I. (1634) 69 The right stone or testicle in a Woman. **1684** tr. *Bonet's Merc. Compit.* x. 364 The Womb with its Ligaments and the Testicles may hurt the Loins. **1691** RAY *Creation* II. (1692) 66 Membranes..capable of a prodigious extension, as we see in the Hydatides of the female Testicles or Ovaries.

†**d.** *pl.* An old name for an orchid, from the form of the tubers: in quot. app. applied to *Spiranthes autumnalis*. *Obs.*

**1597** GERARDE *Herbal* I. cii. 169 The first is called..in English sweete smelling Testicles or Stones.

**e.** *attrib.* and *Comb.*

1880 GÜNTHER *Fishes* 157 In the European species of Serranus a testicle-like body is attached to the lower part of the ovary. 1899 CAGNEY tr. *Jaksch's Clin. Diagn.* ix. (ed. 4) 424 Finely granular testicle-cells.

**Testicond** (te·stikǫnd), *a. Zool.* [f. L. *testis*, TESTIS [2] + *cond-ĕre* to conceal.] Having the testes contained within the body, as the *Cetacea*.

1864 DANA cited in WEBSTER.

**Testicular** (testi·kiŭlăɹ), *a.* [f. L. *testiculus* TESTICLE: see -AR [1]; cf. F. *testiculaire*.]

**1.** Of or pertaining to, containing, or having the nature or function of a testicle or testicles.

1656 BLOUNT *Glossogr.*, *Testicular*,.. belonging to the stones of man or beast. 1775 in ASH. 1841–71 T. R. JONES *Anim. Kingd.* (ed. 4) 255 The fifth segment [of the earthworm], from behind, is again testicular,..so that the first and the last segments in this region are testicular, the three intermediate ones being ovarian. 1899 CAGNEY tr. *Jaksch's Clin. Diagn.* ix, The spermatic or testicular secretion.

**2.** Resembling a testicle in form; testiculate.

1769 E. BANCROFT *Guiana* 73 Berries of a reddish yellow colour, and testicular form. 1821 W. P. C. BARTON *Flora N. Amer.* I. 53 The genus orchis..derives its name from the testicular shape of the roots in many species.

**Testiculate** (testi·kiŭlět), *a.* [ad. late L. *testiculātus*: see TESTICLE and -ATE [2].] Formed like a testicle (= prec. 2); also, applied to the twin tubers of certain species of Orchis.

1760 J. LEE *Introd. Bot.* III. xxii. (1765) 220 In Orchis, where the Species are known by the Roots being fibrose, round or testiculate. 1828 in WEBSTER.

So **Testi·culated** *a.* [-ED [1] 2] in same sense.

1725 SLOANE *Jamaica* II. 95 Berries,..two always sticking close or being join'd together, as if testiculated. 1727 BAILEY vol. II, *Testiculated Root*..consists of two Knobs, resembling a Pair of Testicles. 1751 WATSON in *Phil. Trans.* XLVII. 178 From this testiculated appearance they called these plants males. 1775 in ASH.

†**Testi·culatory**, *a. Obs. rare*—[1]. [f. as prec. + -ORY [2].] Generative.

*a* 1693 *Urquhart's Rabelais* III. xxvii. 224 Testiculatory Ability.

**Testicule**, obs. form of TESTICLE.

†**Testicu·ose**, *a. Obs. rare*—[0]. [f. L. *testicul-us* TESTICLE + -OSE [1].] So †**Testiculous** *a.*

1721 BAILEY, *Testiculous*, that hath great Cods. 1727 — vol. II, *Testiculose*,..that hath large Cods. 1775 in ASH.

**Testie**, dial. var. TEISTIE, Black Guillemot.

‖**Testiere**: see TESTER [2].

**Testif, -yf**, obs. forms of TESTY.

†**Testificate.** Chiefly *Sc. Obs.* [ad. L. *testificāt-um* (that which is) testified, subst. use of neut. pa. pple. of *testificārī* to TESTIFY.] A writing wherein a fact is attested; a certificate; *spec.* in *Sc. Law*: see quot. 1838.

1610 in Row *Hist. Kirk* (Wodrow Soc.) 277 To requyre ..a testificat of his conversation past, abilitie, and qualification for the function. 1620 SHELTON *Quix.* (1746) IV. xxxiii. 258 Which Testificate he desired. 1676 W. ROW *Contn. Blair's Autobiog.* xi. (1848) 366 Three testificates were sent over to the Committee. *a* 1722 FOUNTAINHALL *Decis.* (1761) II. 394 A testificate being returned that there was no such thing to be found in their books. 1838 W. BELL *Dict. Law Scot.*, *Testificate*, was a solemn written assertion, not on oath, used in judicial procedure...The term is now obsolete.

**b.** *fig.* Evidence, indication.

1590 GREENE *Never too late* (1600) 98 The wenches eyes are a testificate. 1637 RUTHERFORD *Lett.* (1862) I. 349 Take Christ's testificate with you out of this life—'Well done, good and faithful servant!' 1833 GALT in *Fraser's Mag.* VIII. 65 He gave a deep sigh, which was a testificate to me that the leaven of unrighteousness was still within him.

**Testification** (te:stifikē·ʃən). Now *rare.* [a. obs. F. *testificacion* (1400 in Godef.), or ad. L. *testificātiōn-em*, n. of action f. *testificārī* to TESTIFY.] The action or an act of testifying; the testimony borne; a fact or object (as a document, etc.) serving as evidence or proof.

*c* 1450 *Cov. Myst.* vii. (1841) 69 Wyttnessynge here, be trew testyficacion, That maydenys childe xal be prince of pes. 1593 ABP. BANCROFT *Daung. Posit.* I. iii. 10 A testification was made of their intentes. 1633 SANDERSON *Serm.* (1681) II. 30 Honour..is an acknowledgment or a testification of some excellency or other in the person honoured, by some reverence or observance answerable thereunto. 1640–1 *Kirkcudbr. War-Comm. Min. Bk.* (1855) 42 That he shall bring.. Margaret Sampell's testification that he is her hired servant. 1671 FLAVEL *Fount. Life* xi, Thankofferings, in Testification of Homage, Duty and Service. 1718 HICKES & NELSON *J. Kettlewell* II. xxxii. 139 For the perpetual Testification whereof there was an Instrument drawn up. 1865 G. MEREDITH *Rhoda Fleming* ix, The thin blue-and-pink paper, and the foreign postmarks—testifications to Dahlia's journey.

**Testificator** (testi·fikē:təɹ). *rare.* [Agent-n. in Latin form f. L. *testificārī* to TESTIFY: see -OR.] One who testifies or attests; a testifier.

1730 in BAILEY (folio). 1755 in JOHNSON. 1854 W. WATERWORTH *Orig. Anglicanism* 10 There has been..from the Apostolic days, an uninterrupted body of testificators.

**Testificatory** (testifikē·təri, testi·fikătəri), *a.* [See prec. and -ORY [2]; cf. OF. *testificatoire* (1387).] Of such a kind as to testify, or serve as evidence.

1593 NASHE *Christ's T.* (1613) 24 They shall haue..not one stone of thy Temple or Sanctuarie testificatory against them. 1821 CARLYLE in Froude *Life* (1882) I. xxii. 417 This morning came a decent testificatory letter from Buller. 1834 *Fraser's Mag.* IX. 169 A Fanatic..conceives the workings of his own mind..to be testificatory of the truth of opinion.

**Testified** (te·stifəid), *ppl. a.* [f. TESTIFY *v.* + -ED [1].] Attested; made known, declared.

1552 HULOET, Testified or knowen of all men, *testatus*. 1648 MILTON *Tenure Kings* (1650) 4 Justice..is the Sword of God..in whose hand soever..his testified will is to put it.

**Testifier** (te·stifəi,əɹ). [f. TESTIFY *v.* + -ER [1].] One who testifies; a witness.

1611 COTGR., *Tesmoing*, a witnesse, testis, testifier. 1659 PEARSON *Creed* i. (1662) 4 The strength and validity of every Testimony must bear proportion with the Authority of the Testifier. 1752 J. GILL *Trinity* i. 13 Though the Father, Word, and Spirit are one, yet not one person; because if so, they could not be three testifiers. 1854 E. G. HOLLAND *Mem. J. Badger* xi. 209 Testifiers to the same fact.

**Testify** (te·stifəi), *v.* Also 5–6 testy-, 5–7 teste-; 4 -fiȝe, 4–6 -fye, 4–8 -fie, 6 (*Sc.*) -fei. [ad. late or med.L. *testificāre*, cl. L. *testificārī* to bear witness, proclaim, f. *testi-s* witness + *-fic-us* making: see -FY. So obs. F. *testifier* (16th c.).]

**1.** *trans.* To bear witness to, or give proof of (a fact); to assert or affirm the truth of (a statement); to attest.

1393 LANGL. *P. Pl.* C. XIII. 172 Meny prouerbis ich myghte haue of meny holy seyntes, To testifie [*v.rr.* testefie, testefiȝe] for treuthe þe tale þat ich shewe. *c* 1420 ? LYDG. *Assembly of Gods* 452 That can Dame Nature well testyfy. 1495 *Act 11 Hen. VII*, c. 10 § 2, ij witnesses or moo that woll witnesse and testefie the seid payment. 1526 TINDALE *John* iii. 11 We speake that we knowe, and testify that we have sene. 1560 DAUS tr. *Sleidane's Comm.* 55 b, A signe wherby he maye testifie, that he careth for vs. 16.. *Rolls of Parlt.* II. 438/1 It is testified by the said Earle..that the said Arnold was taken. 1820 JEFFERSON *Writ.* (1830) IV. 325 The superlative wisdom of Socrates is testified by all antiquity.

**b.** *intr.* (usually with *of*) and *absol.*

1377 LANGL. *P. Pl.* B. XIII. 93 Þanne shal he testifye of a trinitee and take his felawe to witnesse. 1513 BRADSHAW *St. Werburge* I. 2448 That they shulde testyfy with hym in this case. 1526 TINDALE *John* ii. 25 Jesus..neded nott that eny man shulde testify off man. For he knewe what was in man. 1579 W. WILKINSON *Confut. Familye of Loue* To Rdr. *iv b, Those which take in hand to testifie of any matter whatsoever. 1746–7 HERVEY *Medit.* (1818) 192 Drop down, ye Showers, and testify as you fall, testify of His grace. 1884 J. QUINCY *Figures of Past* 228 [He] testified to me of the affection with which he was regarded by his slaves.

**2.** *transf.* of things: **a.** *trans.* To serve as evidence of; to constitute proof or testimony of. **b.** *intr.* and *absol.*

1445 in *Anglia* XXVIII. 271 Also thi writyng testifieth thi yiftes be not streyned. 1593 SHAKS. 2 *Hen. VI*, IV. ii. 158 The brickes are aliue at this day to testifie it. 1644 EVELYN *Diary* 12 Nov., Dioclesian's Bathes, whose ruines testifie the vastness of the original foundation. 1794 SULLIVAN *View Nat.* II. 132 Do not these shells testify a present, or a former communication between these contending elements of fire and water? 1849 HANNA *Mem. Chalmers* I. ii. 42 The manuscript volumes..still remain to testify his diligence. 1879 HUXLEY *Hume* vi. 116 The proposition..must mean..that the fact is testified by my present consciousness. 1596 SHAKS. *Tam. Shr.* IV. iii. 131 Why heere is the note of the fashion to testify...Reade it. 1879 M. PATTISON *Milton* iii. 37 His three Latin epigrams addressed to this lady..testify to the enthusiasm she excited in the musical soul of Milton.

**3.** *trans.* To profess and openly acknowledge (a fact, belief, object of faith or devotion, etc.); to proclaim as something that one knows or believes. Chiefly *biblical*. **b.** *intr.* To bear testimony.

1526 TINDALE *Acts* xx. 24 The ministracion which I have receaved of the lorde Jesu to testify the gospell of the grace of god. 1535 COVERDALE 2 *Esdras* ii. 36, I testifie my sauioure openly. *a* 1631 DONNE *Serm.* vii. (1640) 72 To testifie our fall in Adam, the Church appoints us to fall upon our knees. 1841 LANE *Arab. Nts.* I. ii. 112 He.. stood upon his feet,..and exclaimed, I testify that there is no deity but God. 1867 VISCT. STRANGFORD *Select.* (1869) II. 73 They testify their faith therein openly and aloud. 1784 COWPER *Task* v. 856 In vain thy creatures testify of thee, Till thou proclaim thyself. 1818 SCOTT *Hrt. Midl.* xii, Them that witnessed, and testified, and fought, and endured pit, prison-house, and transportation. 1853 KINGSLEY *Hypatia* xxx, They had no mind to be martyrs, for they had nothing for which to testify.

**4.** *intr.* and *trans.* To declare solemnly; = PROTEST *v.* 1. *Obs.* exc. in biblical use.

1526 TINDALE *John* xiii. 21 Jesus..was troubled in his sprete and testified sayinge: verely verely I saye vnto you, that won off you shall betraye me. — *Gal.* v. 3, I testifie agayne to every man..that he is bounde to kepe the whole lawe. — 2 *Tim.* iv. 1, I testifie therfore before god, and before the lorde Jesu Christ..preache the worde, be fervent, be it in season or out of season. 1535 COVERDALE 1 *Sam.* viii. 9 Testifye vnto them, and shewe them the lawe of the kynge that shall raigne ouer them. — *Ps.* xlix. 7 Let me testifie amonge you, o Israel: I am God euen thy God. 1582 N. T. (Rhem.) *Acts* xx. 21 Testifying [Gr. διαμαρτυρόμενος; Vulg. *testificans*; *earlier vv.* witnessing] to Iewes and Gentils penance toward God and faith in our Lord Iesus Christ. 1667 MILTON *P. L.* XI. 721 At length a Reverend Sire among them came,..And testifi'd against thir wayes.

**5.** *trans.* To give evidence of, display, manifest, express (desire, emotion, etc.). *Obs.* or *arch.*

1560 DAUS tr. *Sleidane's Comm.* 120 b, An oration..testifying the inward sorow, which he had conceaued. 1678 *Trans. Crt. Spain* 32 The people of Madrid testified a great desire of seeing our young Prince. 1701 W. WOTTON *Hist. Rome* vi. 107 Nothing was too much to testify the Peoples Joy. 1749 FIELDING *Tom Jones* XVIII. iv, He was the only person ..who testified any real concern. 1855 PRESCOTT *Philip II*, I. II. viii. 228 She begs her brother..to testify his own satisfaction by the most gracious letters..that he can write. 1858 CARLYLE *Fredk. Gt.* x. viii. (1872) III. 292 The grimly sympathetic Generals testified assent.

Hence **Te·stifying** *vbl. sb.* and *ppl. a.*

1575–85 ABP. SANDYS *Serm.* (Parker Soc.) 87 A testifying of our godliness towards him. 1596 NASHE *Saffron Walden* Wks. (Grosart) III. 19 For a testifying incouragement how much I wish thy encrease in those languages. 1651 BAXTER *Inf. Bapt.* 222 A seal is an engaging or obliging sign, or at least a testifying. 1818 SCOTT *Hrt. Midl.* xix, A man, exercised in the testimonies of that testifying period. 1901 C. G. MCCRIE *Ch. Scotl.* II. i. 151 It reveals no advance upon the testifyings of New Light Burghers.

†**Te·stify**, *sb. Obs. rare*—[1]. In 6 *Sc.* pl. testefeis. [f. prec.] A certificate or testimony.

1600 *Sc. Acts Jas. VI* (1816) IV. 246/2 That..they may ..produce sic testefeis of thair antiquiteis as may informe the saidis commissionaris.

**Testily** (te·stĭli), *adv.* [f. TESTY + -LY [2].] In a testy manner; irritably.

1755 in JOHNSON. 1838 DICKENS *Nich. Nick.* xxxiv, 'What does the idiot mean?' cried Ralph, testily. 1885 *Manch. Exam.* 9 Jan. 5/4 The Lord Mayor rather testily.. cut short his rhodomontade.

†**Testimonage.** *Obs. rare.* In 5 testy-, 6 tesmonage. [ad. OF. *tesmonage* (f. *tesmoigner*:—med.L. *testimōniāre* to testify), with assimilation to the L. form.] = TESTIMONY *sb.* 1.

1483 CAXTON *Gold. Leg.* 436/2 Thys same epystle may also gyue vs testymonage that our lord wyl descende [etc.]. 1490 — *Eneydos* xv. 53 She made it to couertely and close, wythoute testymonage and wythoute the knowleche of Iubyter. 1510–20 *Compl. too late Maryed* (1862) 14 Adam bereth wytnesse and Tesmonage.

†**Testimoner.** *Obs. rare*—[1]. [app. f. TESTIMON(Y *v.* + -ER [1]. Cf. OF. *tesmoigneur*.] One who or that which bears testimony; a witness.

1607 R. C[AREW] tr. *Estienne's World of Wonders* 214 Sure and certen testimoners of sinnes.

**Testimonial** (testimōu·niăl), *a.* and *sb.* Also 5 tesmoingnal; 5–6 testy-; 5 -mone-, 5–6 -mony-; 5 -ell, 5–7 -all,e. [a. OF. *tesmoignal* and *testimonial*, in phr. *lettres tes(ti)moniaulx* (13th c. in Godef. *Compl.*), ad. late L. *testimōniālis*, (*litteræ*) *testimōniālēs* credentials; f. OF. *tesmoin*, L. *testimōni-um* TESTIMONY: see -AL.]

**A.** *adj.* (now *arch.* or *technical.*) Of, pertaining to, or of the nature of testimony; serving as evidence; conducive to proof. *Testimonial proof*, proof by the testimony of a witness; parole evidence. (Quot. *c* 1430 may belong to the sb.)

*c* 1430 LYDG. *Min. Poems* (Percy Soc.) 254 To have memory upon thy passioun, Testimonial of my redempcioun. 1570 LEVINS *Manip.* 15/25 Testimoniall, *testimonialis*. 1588 J. HARVEY *Disc. Probl.* 111 Which argument how artificiall it is, being barely testimoniall, or how [etc.]. 1646 SIR T. BROWNE *Pseud. Ep.* I. vii. 25 We become enancipated from testimoniall engagements. 1680 J. C. *Vind. Oaths & Swearing* (ed. 2) 6 An Oath in matters Testimonial and pertaining to Witness-bearing is the highest proof and confirmation that can be. 1802–12 BENTHAM *Ration. Judic. Evid.* (1827) I. 69 Evidence which, though not properly testimonial, may..be called personal. 1883 *Wharton's Law Lex.*, *Testimonial proof*, parol evidence. *Civ. Law.*

†**b. Letter testimonial**, rarely **testimonial letter** (usually pl. *letters testimonial(s)*: a letter testifying to the bona fides of the bearer; credentials; = B. 3. *Obs.*

[1421 *Rolls of Parlt.* IV. 158/1 Havynge lettres testimonyalx sufficeantz of on of those degrees of the Universite.] 1425 *Ibid.* 289/2 That the same Marchant..brynge Lettres Tesmoingnals..under seel..of Maieur. 1439 *Ibid.* V. 33/2 Who so..come without Letters Testimoniall of the Chifteyn. 1597 HOOKER *Eccl. Pol.* v. lxxvii. § 10 Is it the bringing of testimoniall letters wherein so great obliquitie consisteth? 1678 W. DILLINGHAM *Serm. Funeral Lady Alston* 26 St. Paul..hath recourse unto his own Conscience for his Letters Testimonial. 1751 LAVINGTON *Enthus. Meth. & Papists* III. (1754) 134 She was furnished with Letters Testimonial to obtain Provisions on the Road.

**B.** *sb.* [Cf. obs. F. *testimoniale* sb. (Cotgr.).]

†**1.** Verbal or documentary evidence; = TESTIMONY *sb.* 1. *Obs.*

1432–50 tr. *Higden* (Rolls) III. 251 Permenides, after the testimonialle of Boice,..laborede and founde the arte of logike. 1533 BELLENDEN *Livy* II. xxii. (S.T.S.) I. 222 Als Virginius..stude in testimoniall of his meritis and loving. 1621 ELSING *Debates Ho. Lords* (Camden) 35 Fowles being brought to the barre agayne, desyred that the testimonyall of theis dyers may not be used against him. 1707 (*title*) A Cry from the Desart, or Testimonials of Several Miraculous Things lately come to pass in the Cevennes.

†**2.** Something serving as proof or evidence; a token, record, manifestation. *Obs.*

1495 in S. P. H. Statham *Dover Charters* (1902) 278 Onlesse ..ye said..purcer shew under auctentik, sufficient, or evident testimoniall yt yer is founde sufficient..surete in othir places. 1549 *Compl. Scot.* xiv. 113 Annibal send to cartage thre muis of gold ryngis..for ane testimonial of his grit victorie. *a* 1647 HABINGTON *Surv. Worc.* in *Worc. Hist. Soc. Proc.* III. 436 Without Armes or Inscription, as a testimonialle of her priveleadge. *a* 1716 SOUTH *Serm.* (1744) XI. 126 When he required a testimonial of Peter's affection. 1803 *Med. Jrnl.* IX. 182 In this second part numerous testimonials of the truth of this doctrine are given.

†**3.** A written attestation by some authorized or responsible person or persons, testifying to the truth of something; an affidavit, acknowledgement; a certificate; *spec.* an official warrant; a passport (as given to vagrants, labourers, discharged soldiers or sailors, etc.); a diploma; a credential or other authenticating document. *Obs.*

**1461** *Paston Lett.* II. 22, I send to yow a testymonyall, which is made by a greet assent of greet multitude of comons, to send to the Kyng. **1526** TINDALE *Matt.* v. 31 Hit ys sayd, whosoever put awaye his wyfe, let hym geve her a testymonyall of her devorcement. **1545** *Aberdeen Regr.* (1844) I. 223 Quhen ony strangear cumis with testimoniale, to cum and aduerteis the bailȝe that sic an strangear is at the port with testimoniale. **1560** DAUS tr. *Sleidane's Comm.* 143 b, After whan he had exhibited the testimoniall of his Ambassade, he procedeth. **1563** *Reg. Privy Council Scot.* I. 249 To direct out commissionis under the testimoniall of the greit seill. **1597–8** *Act* 39 *Eliz.* c. 17 § 2 Euery.. wandring Soldyer or Marryner..shall..haue a Testymonyall vnder the Hand of some one Justice of the Peace. **1622** MABBE tr. *Aleman's Guzman d'Alf.* II. 332 Giuing euery one of vs a Testimoniall of his sentence, wee were all chained one to another. **1698–9** *Act* 11 *Will. III*, c. 18 § 1 Such Vagabonds or Beggers .. very frequently forge or counterfeite Passes Testimonialls or Characters. **1702** W. J. *Bruyn's Voy. Levant* v. 12 Nor brought along with them Testimonials of their being in Health. **1796** JEFFERSON *Writ.* (1859) IV. 140, I will forward the testimonial of the death of Mrs. Mazzei. *a* **1806** C. J. FOX *Reign Jas. II* (1808) 119 The severity with which he had enforced the test, obtained him a testimonial from the Bishops of his affection to their Protestant Church.

† **b.** (? *erron.*) A will, testament. *Obs. rare*—¹.

**1616** R. C. *Times' Whistle* 135 To dispossesse His children of his goodes & give her all By his last dying testimoniall.

**4.** A writing testifying to one's qualifications and character, written usually by a present or former employer, or by some responsible person who is competent to judge; a letter of recommendation of a person or thing. (The current sense.)

In quots. 1571, 1727–41, = TESTIMONIUM 1.

**1571** *Act* 13 *Eliz.* c. 12 § 4 None shalbe made Mynister.. under thage of foure and twenty yeres, nor unles he fyrst bring to the Bisshop..a Testimoniall..of his honest lyfe[etc.]. **1609** *Sc. Acts Jas. VI* (1816) IV. 406/2 A sufficient testimoniall of the bischop of the dyocie..Testifeing and approveing the said pedagog to be godlie and of good religioun. **1727–41** CHAMBERS *Cycl.*, *Testimonial*, a kind of certificate .. required before holy orders are conferred. **1776** J. ADAMS in *Fam. Lett.* (1876) 144 The testimonials in his favor I shall inclose to you. **1798** M. CUTLER in *Life*, etc. (1888) II. 7 We have full testimonials that Mr. Perkins is a young man of an unblemished character. **1836** SIR H. TAYLOR *Statesman* xxix. 220 He is to make small account of testimonials and recommendations, unless subjected to severe scrutiny and supported by proved facts. **1868** M. PATTISON *Academ. Org.* v. 216 Testimonials seem in theory an unexceptionable mode of obtaining information.

**5.** A gift presented to some one by a number of persons as an expression of appreciation or acknowledgement of services or merit, or of admiration, esteem, or respect.

**1838** LD. COCKBURN *Jrnl.* I. 211 The growth of the modern things called testimonials is very curious...It has come of late to denote..a sort of homage always as a donation, and generally in a permanent form, to supposed public virtue. **1856** W. COLLINS *After Dark* ii. Prol. (1862) 148 The portrait was intended as a testimonial, 'expressive..of the eminent services of Mr. Boxsious in promoting and securing the prosperity of the town'. **1859** THACKERAY *Virgin.* xxxv, The late lamented O'Connell,..over whom a grateful country has raised such a magnificent testimonial.

**6.** *attrib.* and *Comb.*, as *testimonial craze*, *-writer*; † **testimonial-man**, a person having a testimonial (sense 3) or passport.

**1725** *Lond. Gaz.* No. 6396/4 Robert Mair, late of Liverpool, Testimonial-Man. **1895** *Pall Mall G.* 27 Sept. 1/3 The testimonial craze is becoming quite a nuisance, and is highly inconvenient to people of moderate means. **1905** *Academy* 6 May 489/1 A good many other professional and unprofessional testimonial-writers.

**Testimonialize** (testimǭu·niăləiz), *v.* [f. prec. + -IZE.] *trans.* To furnish with a letter of recommendation; also, to present with a public testimonial: see TESTIMONIAL *sb.* 4 and 5. (In quot. 1899 *Improperly*, To ask for testimonials.)

**1852** *Tait's Mag.* XIX. 344 Hanging is going out of fashion, and testimonialising is coming in. **1855** THACKERAY *Newcomes* lxiii, People were testimonialising his wife. **1886** *West. Morn. News* 27 Apr. 4/6 Sir E— H— is to be testimonialised. **1899** C. SCOTT *Drama of Yesterday* I. xii. 417, I resolved..to testimonialise the influential friends of my father.

Hence **Testimo·nialized** *ppl. a.*; **Testimo·nializing** *vbl. sb.* and *ppl. a.*; also **Testimo:nializa·tion**, celebration by means of testimonials; **Testimo·nializer**, one who furnishes, or contributes to, a testimonial.

**1898** G. B. SHAW in *Daily Chron.* 13 Oct. 4/4 The celebration and *testimonialisation of remarkable events and eminent men will always be cherished in England as a means of procuring notoriety for noisy nobodies. **1893** *Chamb. Jrnl.* 11 Mar. 145/1 A much *testimonialised medicine. **1854** *Tait's Mag.* XXI. 386 The *testimonialisers threw themselves into the business with a truly heroical enthusiasm. **1891** E. KINGLAKE *Australian at H.* 53 *Testimonialising has been rather overdone of late.

‖ **Testimonium** (testimǭu·niə̆m). [L., f. *testi-s* a witness + *-mōnium*: see -MONY.]

**1.** A letter of recommendation given to a candidate for holy orders testifying to his piety and learning; also, a certificate of proficiency given by a university, college, professor, etc.: = TESTAMUR.

**1692** SWIFT in Earl Orrery *Remarks* (1752) 11, I am still to thank you for your care in my Testimonium. **1705** HEARNE *Collect.* 21 Aug. (O.H.S.) I. 32 Dr. Mill sent to me a Testimonium to be sign'd for Cyprian & Paul Appia, Vaudois, that they may be admitted into H. Orders. **1721** AMHERST *Terræ Fil.* No. 13. (1754) 66 Punishing under-graduates, or disposing of fellowships, degrees, and testimoniums. **1799** C. WINTER in Jay *Mem. & Lett.* (1843) 49 Mr. Whitefield desired me to procure him a testimonium of myself from different places whither I had gone. **1903** *Times* 24 Oct. 10/1 In 1860, a year after he became B.A., he obtained his testimonium in the divinity school.

**2.** *Law.* That concluding part of a document, usually commencing with the words 'In witness whereof', which states the manner of its execution; also *testimonium clause.* Cf. TESTATUM, TESTE².

**1852** *Act* 15 & 16 *Vict.* c. 24 § 1 The words of the testimonium clause or of the clause of attestation. **1905** *Law Soc. Gaz.* Dec. 16 Blanks had been left in the testimonium for the day and the month.

**Testimony** (te·stimə̆ni), *sb.* [ad. L. *testimōnium*: see prec. Cf. ONF. *testimonie*, OF. *testi-*, *testemoine* (11th c. in Godef.), learned forms from Latin; the inherited OF. word being *tesmoigne*, now *témoin*, whence also *tésmoignie* and *tesmoignage*, now *témoignage*: see TESTIMONAGE.]

**1.** Personal or documentary evidence or attestation in support of a fact or statement; hence, any form of evidence or proof.

**1432–50** tr. *Higden* (Rolls) II. 423 Hit hathe somme testimony and wittenesse. *Ibid.* V. 393. **1526** TINDALE *John* viii. 17 Itt ys also written in youre lawe, that the testimony of two men ys true. **1553** EDEN *Treat. Newe Ind.* (Arb.) 9 Plinie rehearseth the testimonie of Cornelius Nepos. **1577–87** HOLINSHED *Chron.* I. 121/2 None of the cleargie.. comming from anie other place should be admitted, except he brought letters of testimonie with him. **1651** HOBBES *Leviath.* I. xiv. 70 Where a mans Testimony is not to be credited, he is not bound to give it. **1719** DE FOE *Crusoe* I. 303 He shewed all the Testimony of his Gratitude that he was able. **1805** FOSTER *Ess.* III. iii. 58 Determined by the testimony of facts. **1838** SIR W. HAMILTON *Logic* xxxiii. (1866) II. 177 Testimony, in the strictest sense of the term, therefore, is the communication of an experience or..the report of an observed phænomenon, made to those whose own experience or observation has not reached so far. **1843** R. R. MADDEN *United Irish.* Ser. II. II. xvii. 367 The Battalion of Testimony..a set of hired spies, informers, and witnesses, kept in the pay of the [Dublin] Castle.

**b.** Any object or act serving as proof or evidence.

**1597** HOOKER *Eccl. Pol.* v. lxxix. § 2 [Offerings] are Testimonies of our affection towardes God. **1601** SIR W. CORNWALLIS *Ess.* II. xxvii, To smell of sweat, the testimony of labour.

† **2.** A written certificate, a testimonial. *Obs.*

*a* **1589** *Jenkinson's Voy. & Trav.* (Hakl. Soc.) II. 375 When any man or woman dyeth..they..put a testimony in his right hand, which the priest giueth him, to testifie vnto S. Nicholas that he dyed a Christian. **1617** MORYSON *Itin.* I. 252 They that goe by land in Italy, must bring a Testimonie of Health called *Boletino*, before they can passe or conuerse. **1657** J. WATTS *Vind. Ch. Eng.* 97 The Arch-Deacon, having before examined us in private, and seen our publike Testimonies, presented us all to the Bishop.

† **3.** A sponsor. *Obs. rare.*

**1547** HOOPER *Answ. Bp. Winchester* E iij, The testimonijs of the infant to be Christeynid ar examynid in the be halfe of the chyld.

**4.** In Scriptural language (chiefly in O.T.). **a.** *sing.* The Mosaic law or decalogue as inscribed on the two tables of stone, as in *the two tables of testimony* (Ex. xxxi. 18); *ark of* (*the*) *testimony* = *ark of the covenant*, the chest containing the tables of the law and other sacred memorials; sometimes called simply *the testimony*; *tabernacle* or *tent of* (*the*) *testimony*, the tabernacle containing the ark with its contents.

[A literalism of translation, repr. Vulg. *testimonium*, LXX. τὸ μαρτύριον, rarely ἡ μαρτυρία, Heb. sing. עֵדוּת *ʿēdūth*, pl. עֵדוֹת *ʿēdwōth*.]

**1382** WYCLIF *Exod.* xxx. 6 The veyle, that hongith before the arke of testymonye. *Ibid.* xxxii. 15 Moyses..berynge in hoond two tablis of testymonye wrytun on eithir side. **1560** BIBLE (Genev.) *Exod.* xxv. 16 Thou shalt put in the Arke the Testimonie which I shal giue thee. *Ibid.* xxxii. 15 Moses..went downe from the mountaine with the Two Tables of the Testimonie [1539 wytnesse] in his hand. — *Num.* x. 11 The cloude was taken vp from the Tabernacle of the Testimonie [1539 of witnesse]. **1611** BIBLE *Num.* i. 50 Thou shalt appoint the Leuites ouer the Tabernacle of [*R.V.* the] Testimonie. *Ibid.* ix. 15 The Tabernacle, namely the Tent of the Testimony. *Ibid.* xvii. 4 Thou shalt lay them vp in the Tabernacle..before the Testimony. — *Transl. Pref.* 3 The forme [of Scripture being] Gods word, Gods testimonie, Gods oracles. **1667** MILTON *P. L.* XII. 251 Therein An Ark, and in the Ark his Testimony, The Records of his Cov'nant.

**b.** *pl.* The precepts (of God), the divine law. Rarely in *sing.*

**1535** COVERDALE *Ps.* xviii. [xix.] 7 The testimony of yᵉ Lorde is true, & geueth wisdome euen vnto babes. *Ibid.* cxviii. [cxix.] 88 So shall I kepe the testimonies of thy mouth. **1560** BIBLE (Genev.) 2 *Kings* xxiii. 3 That they shulde walke after the Lord, and kepe his commandements, and his testimonies, and his statutes. **1611** BIBLE *Deut.* vi. 17 You shall diligently keepe the Commandements of the Lord your God, and his Testimonies, and his Statutes.

**5.** Open attestation or acknowledgement; confession, profession. *Obs.* or *arch.*

*To seal one's testimony with one's blood*, to die as a martyr for one's religious profession.

**1550** (*title*) The Image of both Chvrches...Compyled by Iohn Bale an exyle also in this lyfe, for the faithfull testimony of Iesu. **1582** N. T. (Rhem.) *Rev.* i. 9, I..was in.. Patmos, for the word of God and the testimonie of Iesvs. **1597** HOOKER *Eccl. Pol.* v. lx. § 5 To seale the testimonie thereof with death. **1667** MILTON *P. L.* VI. 33 Thou..for the testimonie of Truth hast born Universal reproach. **1687** A. SHIELDS (*title*) A Hind let loose; or an Historical Representation of the Testimonies of the Church of Scotland. *a* **1720** SEWEL *Hist. Quakers* v. (1722) 226 The two first [Quakers in New England] that sealed their Testimony with their Blood were William Robinson..and Marmaduke Stevenson.

**b.** *spec.* An expression or declaration of disapproval or condemnation of error; a protestation.

**1582** N. T. (Rhem.) *Mark* vi. 11 Shake of the dust from your feete for a testimonie to them. **1818** SCOTT *Hrt. Midl.* ix, Mony an afternoon he wad sit and take up his testimony again the Paip. **1850** WHITTIER *Old Portr.*, *T. Ellwood* Wks. 1889 VI. 38 Plain, earnest men and women..having withal a strong testimony to bear against carnal wit and outside show and ornament. **1863** MRS. GASKELL *Sylvia's L.* xxxix, Alice Rose was not one to tolerate the coarse, careless talk..without uplifting her voice in many a testimony against it. **1876** C. M. DAVIES *Unorth. Lond.* 90 A 'testimony' was..circulated some years ago to the bishops and clergy of the Church of England.

† **Te·stimony**, *v. Obs.* Also 4 testimon. [ME. ad. ONF. *testimoin-er* (11th c. in Littré), *testimoni-er*, *-moi(g)ner*, *testemogner* (12th c. in Godef. *Compl.*), learned forms ad. med.L. *testimōniāre* (8th c. in Du Cange), f. *testimōnium* TESTIMONY. (The inherited popular Fr. form of the L. is *tesmoi(g)ner*, mod.F. *témoigner*). In later use f. prec. sb.]

**1.** *trans.* and *intr.* To bear witness, testify (to).

*c* **1330** R. BRUNNE *Chron.* (1810) 8 Henry of Huntyngton testimons þis title. *c* **1400** *Emare* 1029 A grette feste þer was holde..As testymonyeth þys story. *c* **1450** *Cov. Myst.* xxv. (1841) 251 To se and recorde and testymonye. **1611** TOURNEUR *Ath. Trag.* I. ii, I salute you both..and will testimonie to the integritie ——. **1642** EARL CLANRICARDE in Carte *Ormonde* (1735) III. 82 My Lord President will testimony with me in what a dangerous condition..the whole Province was in at that time.

**2.** *trans.* To test or prove by evidence.

**1603** SHAKS. *Meas. for M.* III. ii. 153 Let him be but testimonied in his owne bringings forth, and hee shall appeare to the enuious, a Scholler, a Statesman, and a Soldier.

**Testiness** (te·stinės). [f. TESTY + -NESS.] The quality or condition of being testy; petulance.

**1526** *Pilgr. Perf.* (W. de W. 1531) 93 b, Testinesse or impacyency is a frayle & hasty disposycyon, or rather accustomed & vsed vyce of angre. **1574** HELLOWES *Gueuara's Fam. Ep.* (1584) 114 Ire groweth of an occasion, and testinesse of euil condition. **1593** G. HARVEY *Pierce's Super.* 196, I haue knowen few..so contrary to frowardnesse, or testiuenesse. *a* **1641** BP. MOUNTAGU *Acts & Mon.* iv. (1642) 304 Extreame choler, wrath and testivenesse had cleane spent him. **1690** LOCKE *Hum. Underst.* II. xxii. § 10 Testiness is a Disposition or Aptness to be angry. **1838** DICKENS *Nich. Nick.* v, 'Mighty fine, certainly', said Ralph, with great testiness.

**Testing** (te·stiŋ), *vbl. sb.*¹ [f. TEST *v.*¹ + -ING ¹.] The action of TEST *v.*¹

**1.** The making of a will; the disposing of property by will.

**1681** STAIR *Inst. Law Scot.* xxx. § 37 The power of Testing is competent to all Persons, who have the use of Reason. **1788** PRIESTLEY *Lect. Hist.* v. xlviii. 362 The power of testing was first introduced by Solon. **1880** BLACKIE in *Contemp. Rev.* Jan. 44 The freedom of testing, which we derive from the law of the Twelve Tables. **1889** STEVENSON *Master of B.* 176 If I had been put to my oath, I must have declared he was incapable of testing.

**2.** *Sc. Law. Testing clause*: see quot. 1838.

(Here *testing* may be *ppl.a.*)

**1765–8** ERSKINE *Inst. Law Scot.* II. iii. § 33 That all precepts..should be ingrossed in the charter, towards the end of it; that is, immediately before the testing clause. **1838** W. BELL *Dict. Law Scot.* s.v., The testing clause is the technical name given to the clause whereby a formal written deed or instrument is authenticated. **1888** *Law Rep.* 13 App. Cas. XIII. 376 The testing clause was..'In witness whereof I and my said wife have subscribed these presents'.

**Te·sting**, *vbl. sb.*² [f. TEST *v.*² + -ING ¹.] The action of TEST *v.*²; putting to the test, trying, proving; in quot. 1687, subjecting to the Test Act.

**1687** *Good Advice* 61 The end of Testing and Persecuting. **1827** COLERIDGE in *Lit. Rem.* (1839) IV. 317 A philosophy, which has for its object the trial and testing of the weights and measures themselves. **1839**, **1842** [see TEST *v.*² 4]. **1860** *Merc. Marine Mag.* VII. 141 The application of a severe strain in testing has an injurious effect on a cable.

**b.** *attrib.* and *Comb.* Pertaining to or used for testing, as *testing-box*, *-machine*, *-office*, *station*, etc.

**1876** PREECE & SIVEWRIGHT *Telegraphy* 272 At certain stations along the line the wires are led into testing-boxes for the purpose of affording facilities for crossing, disconnecting, and putting them to earth...The testing station is always the most important station on the circuit. **1877** KNIGHT *Dict. Mech.* 2538/2 In Fairbanks's testing-machine, the crushing, breaking, or deflecting force is applied..by a cross-head. **1890** W. J. GORDON *Foundry* 111 In the same range as the roller shop is the laboratory, and further on is the testing-office. **1905** *Daily Chron.* 22 Apr. 6/4 A six-cylinder racing car with a testing body passed at a speed that was not less than forty-five miles an hour.

**Te·sting**, *ppl. a.* [f. TEST *v.*² + -ING ².] That tests or puts to the test or proof.

**1847–8** H. MILLER *First Impr.* viii. (1857) 123 His writings ..had stood their testing century but indifferently well. **1878** GLADSTONE *Glean.* (1879) I. 179, I will add another and a very testing question. **1884** *Pall Mall G.* 13 Nov. 1/1 It is a testing crisis for English democracy. **1885** BEDDOE *Races Brit.* 271 An edifice of wood and stubble, which may ..be consumed by the testing fire.

‖ **Te·stis** [1]. *Obs.* Pl. **testes** (te·stīz). The Latin word for 'witness': from its legal use (cf. TESTE [2]), occasional in English context.

In quot. *a* 1483 in Latin construction = *cum testibus* 'with the witnesses'.

*a* **1483** in *Househ. Ord.* (1790) 67 The Soveraynes here may send it with the testibus under theyre seales into the Chauncerie. **1525** LD. BERNERS *Froiss.* II. cci. [cxcvii.] 616 The charter..named in the ende many wytnesses of prelates and great lordes of Englande, who were for the more suretie testes of that dede. **1563–87** FOXE *A. & M.* (1596) 532/2 As the saide Edward Hall, your great maister and testis, was about the compiling of his storie. **1611** [see TESTIFIER].

‖ **Testis** [2] (te·stis). *Anat.* Chiefly in pl. **testes** (te·stīz). [L.: etymology uncertain.

An assumed identity with *testis* witness (quasi 'the witness or evidence of virility') is rejected by Walde, who suggests connexion with *testa*, pot, shell, etc. In 16th c. Fr., however, *tesmoing* 'witness' appears in this sense: see Godef. s. v.]

**1.** = TESTICLE. **a.** in man and mammals.

[**1693** tr. *Blancard's Phys. Dict.* (ed. 2), *Testes viriles*, Mens Testicles.] **1704** J. HARRIS *Lex. Techn.* I, *Testes*, the Testicles of a Male. *c* **1720** GIBSON *Farrier's Guide* I. ii. (1738) 16 Next to the Yard, the Testes, or Stones properly take place. **1807–26** S. COOPER *First Lines Surg.* (ed. 5) 495 The formation of such adhesions between the bowels and testis before birth, may also sometimes prevent..its descent. **1881** MIVART *Cat* 241 Two glandular structures, the testes.

**b.** in other animals.

**1841–71** T. R. JONES *Anim. Kingd.* (ed. 4) 445 In Crabs, the mass of the testis is exceedingly large. **1870** ROLLESTON *Anim. Life* Introd. 54 [In Birds] The testes are always retained within the abdomen anteriorly to the kidneys. **1877** HUXLEY *Anat. Inv. Anim.* iv. 179 The testes and vasa deferentia generally have the form of two long tubes. **1888** ROLLESTON & JACKSON *Anim. Life* 680 The testis [in Nematoda] is single; very rarely paired.

†**c.** *transf.* The ovary in females. *Obs.*

[**1693** tr. *Blancard's Phys. Dict.* (ed. 2), *Testes Muliebres*.] **1706** PHILLIPS (ed. Kersey), *Testes*,..the Organs of Seed in Men and Women. **1841** RAMSBOTHAM *Obstetr. Med.* (1855) 43 Previously to the time of Steno, who first asserted that they were analogous to true ovaria, they were called the female testes.

**2.** *transf. pl.* **a.** The posterior pair of the optic lobes or *corpora quadrigemina*, at the base of the brain in mammals.

**1681** tr. *Willis' Rem. Med. Wks.* Vocab., *Testes*, certain tubercles in the brain of a man and beasts, so called because like to the stones of a man. **1704** J. HARRIS *Lex. Techn.* I, *Testes Cerebri*, are the two lower and lesser Protuberances of the Brain. **1899** *Allbutt's Syst. Med.* VII. 345 The posterior tubercles or testes are connected by the posterior brachia with the corpora geniculata interna.

†**b.** The tonsils. *Obs.*

**1776** J. COLLIER *Mus. Trav.* 44 (Stanf.) There are other superfluities besides the *testes* and glands of the throat which obstruct the free course of the voice.

**Testive, -nesse,** obs. ff. TESTY *a.*, TESTINESS.

‖ **Testo** (te·sto). *Mus.* [It. *testo*:—L. *textu-m* TEXT.] **a.** The text or words of a song; the libretto of an opera. **b.** The text, theme, or subject of a composition.

**1724** *Short Explic. For. Wds. in Mus. Bks.*, *Testo*, the Text or Words of a Song. **1801** BUSBY *Dict. Mus.*, *Testo*,..the text, subject, or theme, of any composition...When the words are well written, the song is said to have a good *testo*. **1891** in *Cent. Dict.* **1898** in STAINER & BARRETT.

**Teston, testoon** (te·stən, testū·n). *Obs.* exc. *Hist.* Also 6 **testoune, -yon,** 6–7 **-one,** (*Sc.* **-an, -ane**), 7 **-oone.** [a. obs. F. *teston* (in Godef. *Compl.*) = obs. It. *testone*, augmentative of *testa* head: see -OON. See also TESTER [3].]

**1.** *orig.* The French name of a silver coin struck at Milan by Galeazzo Maria Sforza (1468–76), bearing a portrait or head of the duke, and called in Italian *testone*; then of the similar coin struck by Louis XII after his conquest of Milan, for currency in Italy, and by Francis I (1515–47) for use in France. Both in Italy and France, the name was soon applied to equivalent silver coins without a portrait; but always to pieces heavier than the *gros*.

**1545** *Reg. Privy Council Scot.* I. 2 All smaller peces sik as halff testanys and halff soussis be taken efter the quantite of the prices forsaidis. **1547** BOORDE *Introd. Knowl.* xxvii. (1870) 191 In syluer they [the French] haue testons, which be worth halfe a Frenche crowne; it is worth .ii. s. .iiii. d. sterlyng. **1579** J. STUBBES *Gaping Gulf* C vij, He [Monsieur] is not able to dropp halfe testons for king Phillip's pistelas. **1617** MORYSON *Itin.* I. 185, I payed [in France] two testoones and a halfe for a paire of shooes. *Ibid.* 288 Those of Solothurn..coyne a peece of mony, which the Sweitzers call *Dickenpfenning*, and the French call *Testoone*, but it is lesse worth by the tenth part then the Testoone of France. **1686** tr. *Chardin's Trav. Persia* 7 This Money of theirs [the Dutch]..chiefly consists of Crowns, Half-Crowns, Testons or Eighteen-penny pieces, and pieces of Fifteen Sous. **1901** tr. *Hugo's Notre Dame* xxvii. 275 To gain a few testons in his turn [he] was parading round the circle.

**2.** In England, A name applied first to the shilling of Henry VII, being the first English coin with a true portrait; also to those of Henry VIII, and early pieces of Edward VI. It was declared in 1543 to be equal to 12 pence, but being of debased metal it sank successively to 10*d.*, 9*d.*, and 6*d.*, and was recalled in 1548. Subsequently those still in circulation were rated even lower: see quotations 1560 and 1635.

There appear also to have been counterfeit testons, difficult to distinguish from the debased coinage of Henry VIII, and valued in 1560 at 4½*d.* and 2¼*d.* Quot. 1562 refers to the red or 'brazen' colour of the debased testons.

**1543** *Mint Indenture* (P.R.O. Exchr. Accts. Bundle 306, No. 2), Shall make sixe maner of monys of sylver That is to saye oone piece of theym called a Teston running for xij*d.* of lawfull monye of Englande and there shalbe xlviij suche pieces of theym in the pownde weight of troye. **1548** *Roy. Proclam. for calling in of Testons*, The falsyng of his highnes coyne, nowe current, specially of the peces of xii.*d.* commonly named Testons. **1549** LATIMER *3rd Serm. bef. Edw. VI* (Arb.) 85 Thy syluer is turned into, what? into testyons? *Scoriam*, into drosse. **1560** *Roy. Proclam.* in *Arch. Bodl. F.* c. 11 lf. 30 For discernyng and knowyng of the basest Testons of two pence farthing, from thother Teston of foure pence halfpeny. **1562** J. HEYWOOD *Prov. & Epigr.* (1867) 189 Of Testons. Testons be gone to Oxforde, god be their speede: To studie in Brazennose, there to proceede. Of redde Testons. These Testons looke redde:..they blushe for shame. **1577–87** HOLINSHED *Chron.* III. 1066/2 In the moneth of Iulie [1551]..he abased the peece of twelue pence, commonlie called a teston vnto nine pence. **1592** *Sc. Acts Jas. VI* (1814) III. 527/1 Ordanis the inglis testane to haue cours heireftir wtin this realme vpoun the pryce of viii s. [Scotch]. **1635** N. R. *Camden's Hist. Eliz.* I. 36 Reducing the Teston of sixpence to foure pence, another Teston to two pence farthing, for more silver there was not in them. **1752** CARTE *Hist. Eng.* III. xvi. 229 This gentleman [Sir W. Sharington, an. 1549] had coined a vast quantity of testons, of a base alloy and under standard.

†**b.** A name for the sixpenny piece; = TESTER [3].

**1577** HARRISON *England* II. xxv. (1877) I. 362 Six pence vsuallie named the testone. **1598** B. JONSON *Ev. Man in Hum.* IV. i, You cannot giue him lesse then a shilling,..for the booke..cost him a teston, at least.

†**c.** Proposed name for a suggested new coin of the value of 1*s.* 3*d.* *Obs.*

**1691** LOCKE *Lower. Interest* Wks. 1727 II. 90 The present Shilling and new Testoon, going for fifteen Pence. **1695** LOWNDES *Ess. Amend. Silver Coins* 63 One other Piece which may be called the Testoon, or Fifteen Peny Piece.

**3.** Name of a Scottish silver coin bearing a portrait of Mary Stuart, issued in 1553, and weighing about 76 grains; also applied to coins of the same weight, without the portrait, struck in 1555.

**1566** *Reg. Privy Council Scot.* I. 441 He sall..pay for his absence ane testane. **1577** *Ibid.* II. 616 His Hienes awin silver money of testanis and xxx, xx, and ten schilling pecis. **1583–4** *Burgh Rec. Edinb.* (1882) IV. 322 The payment of ane thowsand pund in Scottis fyue schilling testanes. **1621** *Compt Bk. D. Wedderburne* (S.H.S.) 171 Promisit him a mark for ilk testane he advances thairon.

**4.** The Portuguese *testão* or *tostão*, a silver coin first coined by Manoel I, *c* 1500, and weighing 122 grains; now = 100 reis, weighing 51.6 grains, and worth about 2½*d.* Also an obsolete Italian coin.

**1598** W. PHILLIP *Linschoten* (Hakl. Soc.) I. I. xxxv. 241 Pardaus Xeraphiins..which is as much as three Testones, or three hundred Reijs Portingall money. **1603** FLORIO *Montaigne* I. xlviii. (1632) 160, I saw the Prince of Sulmona at Naples ..shew all manner of horsemanship: to hold testons or reals under his knees. **1676** W. B. *Man. Goldsm.* 114 Portugal Teston. **1706** PHILLIPS (ed. Kersey) s. v., The Testoon of Portugal is worth 1*s.* 3*d.* Of Spain and Navarre 1*s.* 8*d.* Of Switzerland 1*s.* 4*d.* Of Italy 1*s.* 4*d.* **1717** BERKELEY *Tour Italy* Wks. 1871 IV. 524 The owner of the horse gave him a testoon. **1740** H. WALPOLE *Let. to R. West* 16 Apr., What the chief princes [in Italy] allow for their own eating is a testoon a day.

†**Te·stor.** *Obs. rare.* [f. TEST *v.*[1] + -OR 2 d.] One who testifies; a witness.

**1570** LEVINS *Manip.* 170/37 A Testor, *testator, -oris*. **1621** BURTON *Anat. Mel.* III. iv. II. iii, Conscience..a continual testor to give in evidence, to empanel a jury to examine us, to..cry guilty.

**Testor, -orne, -ourn,** obs. forms of TESTER [3].

†**Te·stril.** *Obs.* [A dim. alteration, or corruption of TESTER [3].] A sixpence.

**1601** SHAKS. *Twel. N.* II. iii. 34 *To.* Come on, there is sixe pence for you. Let's haue a song. *An.* There's a testrill of me too. [**1905** *Athenæum* 25 Mar. 366/3 Plenty of readers.. ready to expend their testril on such an attractive booklet.]

**Te·st-tube.** [f. TEST *sb.*[1] + TUBE.] A cylinder of thin transparent glass closed at one end, used to hold liquids under test. Also *transf.*

**1846** G. E. DAY tr. *Simon's Anim. Chem.* II. 176 The sediment must then be placed in a test-tube..and gradually raised to the boiling point. **1860** F. WINSLOW *Obscure Dis. Brain & Mind* viii. (L.), There is no possibility of the medical expert placing the diseased mental element..in a psychological crucible or test-tube. **1888** RUTLEY *Rock-Forming Min.* 6 The test-tube..is plunged into cold water.

**b.** *attrib.*, as *test-tube experiment*; **test-tube cultivation, culture,** the raising of bacteria in a nutrient medium contained in a test-tube.

**1886** H. M. BIGGS tr. *Hueppe's Bacteriol. Invest.* 142 In order to do this, test-tube cultures are employed, in which..many peculiarities of growth can be better noted. **1899** CAGNEY *Jaksch's Clin. Diagn.* vi. (ed. 4) 212 The bactericidal power of such serum has been established by numerous test-tube-experiments. *Ibid.* x. 444 It is usually expedient to make plate and test-tube..cultivations together.

**Testudinal** (testiū·dinăl), *a.* [f. as next + -AL.] Pertaining to a tortoise; shaped like a testudo; vaulted, arched.

**1823** P. NICHOLSON *Pract. Build.* 594 Testudinal Ceilings; those formed like the back of a tortoise. **1828** in WEBSTER.

**Testudinarious** (testiūdinēə·riəs), *a.* [f. L. *testūdo, testūdin-em* (see TESTUDO) + -ARIOUS.] Having the character of a tortoise; marked or coloured like tortoise-shell.

**1826** KIRBY & SP. *Entomol.* IV. xlvi. 288 *Testudinarious*.., painted with red, black, and yellow, like tortoise-shell. **1864** in WEBSTER.

**Testudinate** (testiū·dinĕt), *a.* (*sb.*) [ad. late L. *testūdināt-us*, f. as prec.: see -ATE [2] 2.]

**1.** Formed like a testudo; arched, vaulted.

**1847** in WEBSTER.

**2.** Of or pertaining to tortoises.

**1850** BRODERIP *Leaves Note-bk. Nat.* (1852) 264 The various modifications of testudinate life.

**B.** *sb.* A tortoise.

**1880** *Libr. Univ. Knowl.* (N.Y.) IV. 454 Cope..enumerates ..13 sea-saurians, 48 testudinates, and 50 sea serpents.

So **Testu·dinated** *ppl. a.* = sense 1 above.

**1727** BAILEY vol. II, *Testudinated*,..vaulted, made like the Shell of a Tortoise. **1822** MRS. E. NATHAN *Langreath* II. 267 Smoky ceiling, testudinated with cobwebs.

**Testudineal** (testiudi·niăl), *a. rare.* [f. as next + -AL.] Pertaining to or resembling a tortoise.

**1891** in *Cent. Dict.*

**Testudineous** (testiudi·niəs), *a.* [f. L. *testūdine-us*, f. TESTUDO, *testūdin-em*: see -EOUS.]

**1.** Resembling the shell of a tortoise, or a testudo.

**1656** BLOUNT *Glossogr.*, *Testudineous*,..belonging to, or bowing like the shell of a tortoise, vaulted. Also pertaining to that ancient war-engine called *Testudo*. Hence in BAILEY, JOHNSON, and later Dicts.

**2.** Slow, dilatory, like the pace of a tortoise.

*a* **1652** BROME *Love-sick Crt.* III. iii, With a countenance dejected, And testudineous pace. **1860** O. W. HOLMES *Prof. Breakf.-t.* ii, I don't think there is one of our boarders quite so testudineous as I am.

**Testudinian** (testiudi·niăn), *a.* and *sb.* *Zool.* [f. L. *testūdin-em* tortoise + -IAN.] **a.** *adj.* Of or pertaining to tortoises. **b.** *sb.* A member of the tortoise family.

**1854** OWEN *Skel. & T.* in *Orr's Circ. Sc.* I. *Org. Nat.* 213 Side-walls..are added in the..land-tortoises (testudinians).

**Testu·dinous,** *a. rare*⁻⁰. [f. as prec. + -OUS.] = TESTUDINEOUS.

**1692** COLES, *Testudinous*, belonging to or like a Testudo.

**Testudo** (testiū·do). Also 7 (in anglicized form) **testude.** [a. L. *testūdo* tortoise, etc., f. *testa* a pot, shell, etc.: see TEST *sb.*[2]]

**1.** *Path.* = TALPA 2: see quots.

*c* **1400** *Lanfranc's Cirurg.* 215 Testudines..ben engendrid of hard fleume. **1693** tr. *Blancard's Phys. Dict.* (ed. 2), *Testudo*, a soft, large Swelling, or not very hard, in the Head, broad, in form of an Arch or Tortoise. **1727–41** CHAMBERS *Cycl.*, *Testudo*. **1857** DUNGLISON *Dict. Med. Sc.*, *Testudo*,..an encysted tumour, which has been supposed to resemble the shell of a turtle..Talpa.

**2.** *Zool.* The typical genus of the tortoise family, *Testudinidæ*; a member of this genus.

*c* **1520** L. ANDREWE *Noble Lyfe* xcv, Testudo is a fysshe in a shelle & is in the se of Inde & his shelle is very great & like a muskle. **1706** PHILLIPS, *Testudo*,..the Tortoise, or Shell-crab. **1752** J. HILL *Hist. Anim.* 112 The Testudo has four legs, and its body is covered with a firm shell.

**3.** *Roman Antiq.* **a.** An engine of war used by besiegers, consisting of a screen or shelter, with a strong and usually fire-proof arched roof; it was wheeled up to the walls, which could then be attacked in safety. Also applied to similar contrivances in more recent times.

**1609** HOLLAND *Amm. Marcell.* XXIII. iv. 222 There is a mightie Testudo or frame made, strengthened with very long pieces of timber. **1622** PEACHAM *Compl. Gent.* ix. 73 All engines of warre.. Sambukes, Catapultes, Testudo's, Scorpions. **1632** J. HAYWARD tr. *Biondi's Eromena* 150 A Ram-engine..which, together with its testude, they setled on its wheels. **1644** *Lanc. Tracts* (Chetham Soc.) 187 A kind of testudo, a wooden engine running on wheeles, rooft towards the house with thick planks.

**b.** A shelter formed by a body of troops locking their shields together above their heads.

*a* **1680** BUTLER *Rem.* (1759) II. 174 He will join as many Shields together as would make a Roman testudo. **1706** PHILLIPS (ed. Kersey), *Testudo*,..a Target-Fence. **1801** RANKEN *Hist. France* I. 65 A testudo preceded the main body; and two detachments..were ready..to rush out on the enemy's wings. **1827** ROBINSON *Archæol. Græca* IV. ix. (ed. 2) 372 The military testudo,..was when the soldiers were drawn up close to each other, and the rear ranks, bowing themselves, placed their targets above their heads.

**c.** *transf.* and *fig.* (See quots.)

**1877** KNIGHT *Dict. Mech.*, *Testudo*,..is now applied to objects..employed as defenses for miners, etc. when working in ground or rock which is liable to cave in. **1903** *Daily Chron.* 30 Mar. 6/4 The stands were crowded, and a vast 'testudo' of gleaming umbrellas showed during those wild two hours how much the wretched dared.

**4.** *Anc. Music.* (See quots.)

**1702** SIR T. MOLYNEUX in *Phil. Trans.* XXIII. 1270 Who ..could compose such sweet Harmony upon the Guilded Lyre or Testudo. **1727–41** CHAMBERS *Cycl.*, *Testudo*, in antiquity, was particularly used among the poets, &c. for the ancient lyre; by reason it was originally made, by its inventor Mercury of the..shell of a..sea tortoise. **1776** BURNEY *Hist. Mus.* (1789) I. i. 294 It is disputed whether this lyre is the same as the cithara or testudo.

**5.** *Comb.*, as *testudo-shaped* adj.

**1875** POLLEN *Anc. & Mod. Furn.* 19 Occasionally they were covered in wholly with a testudo-shaped roof.

**Te·stule.** *Bot.* [ad. L. *testula*, dim. of *testa* shell.] The silicified crust or shell of a diatom: more usually called FRUSTULE. **1891** in *Cent. Dict.*

**Testy** (te·sti), *a.* Forms: α. 4–5 **testif, -yf,** 5 **teestif,** 6–7 **testive.** β. 5 **testi,** 6–7 **-ie,** 6–

testy. γ. 6–7 teastie, 6–7 (9 *dial.*) teasty (7 teisty). [a. AF. *testif, -ive* (cf. OF. *testu* heady, headstrong, obstinate, mod.F. *têtu*), f. *teste* head. For the reduction to *-ie, -y* see -IVE, par. 3.]

†1. Of headstrong courage; impetuous; precipitate, rash; in later use (passing into the next sense), Aggressive, contentious. *Obs.*

*c* 1374 CHAUCER *Troylus* V. 802 This Diomede..Was..Hardy, testyf, strong and cheualrous. *c* 1386 — *Reeve's T.* 84 Clerkes two..Testif [*v. rr.* testyf, teestif] they were and lusty for to pleye. 1412–20 LYDG. *Chron. Troy* II. 4613 Hasty, testif, to smyte rek[e]les. 1489 CAXTON *Faytes of A.* I. vii. 17 That he be not testyf, hastyf, hoot, ne angry. *c* 1510 BARCLAY *Mirr. Gd. Manners* (1570) G iij, If any testie foes ..Assayle thee. 1611 COTGR., *Testu*,..testie, headie, headstrong, wilfull, obstinate. 1658 PHILLIPS, *Testif* (old word) wild-brained, furious.

2. Prone to be irritated by small checks and annoyances; impatient of being thwarted; resentful of contradiction or opposition; irascible, short-tempered, peevish, tetchy, 'crusty'.

1526 *Pilgr. Perf.* (W. de W. 1531) 106 b, Whiche wyll suffre his pacyent though he be neuer so testy or angry. 1530 PALSGR. 327/1 Testy angrye..*ireux*..*testu*. *Ibid.* 777/2, I waxe testy, *Ie deuiens testyf*, or *testu*. 1549 CHALONER *Erasm. on Folly* K j, Some men there be so waywarde of nature, and so testiue. 1600 HOLLAND *Livy* XXXIX. v. 1025 A chollericke and testie Consull. *a* 1713 ELLWOOD *Autobiog.* (1714) 70 This made the Warden hot and testy, and put him almost out of all Patience. 1822 W. IRVING *Braceb. Hall* ii, A testy old huntsman as hot as a pepper-corn. 1887 *Spectator* 27 Aug. 1147 Folks less intractable and testy than such prejudiced disputants.

b. Of words, actions, personal qualities, etc.

1538 CROMWELL in Merriman *Life & Lett.* (1902) II. 128 How can your testie wordes..delite me? 1601 SHAKS. *Jul. C.* IV. iii. 46 Must I stand and crouch Vnder your Testie Humour? 1637 HEYWOOD *Dial.* Wks. 1874 VI. 329 We a mistresse feare, And from her teasty fingers blowes oft beare. 1806 SIR C. BELL *Anat. & Phil. Expression* (1872) 172 The testy, pettish, peevish countenance. 1858 LYTTON *What will he do* I. viii, He resumed his pipe with a prolonged and testy whiff.

†c. Of a stream, current, etc.: 'Angry'. *Obs.*

1610 HOLLAND *Camden's Brit.* I. 697 It is made more fell and teasty with a number of stones lying in his chanell. 1833 HT. MARTINEAU *Charmed Sea* i, You will not cross the testy sea to-night.

**Testy**, obs. f. TESTE[2]. **Testy-**: see TESTI-.

**Testyon**, obs. form of TESTON.

†**Tesyk(e**, obs. form of PHTHISIC.

*a* 1400–50 *Stockh. Med. MS.* 23 Tesyk. *c* 1483 CAXTON *Dialogues* 41/40 *Tesyque*..Tesyke.

**Tesyl(l**, obs. forms of TEASEL.

†**Tet** = *thee't, thee it*: see T 8 and THET. *Obs.*

*c* 1200 ORMIN 5264 Forr ȝiff þu lufesst Godd, tet birrþ Wiþþ gode dedess shæwenn. *Ibid.* 18279, & tet maȝȝ ille likenn.

**Tet**, obs. f. TEAT. **Tetan(e**: see TETANUS.

**Tetanic** (tĭtæ·nik), *a.* (*sb.*) [ad. L. *tetanic-us*, a. Gr. τετανικός.] Of, pertaining to, or of the nature of tetanus; characterized by tetanus.

1727 BAILEY vol. II, *Tetanick*, having a Crick in the Neck or Cramp in it, that holdeth it so stiff that it cannot bow. 1805 *Med. Jrnl.* XIV. 304 In the warm climates, where tetanic affections very often follow the great operations. 1822–34 *Good's Study Med.* (ed. 4) III. 495 Clonic agitation instead of a tetanic spasm. 1869 E. A. PARKES *Pract. Hygiene* (ed. 3) 102 Convulsive and tetanic symptoms.

b. as *sb.* (See quot.)

1857 DUNGLISON *Dict. Med. Sc.*, *Tetanic*,..a remedy, which acts on the nerves, and, through them, on the muscles, occasioning, in large doses, convulsions.

So † **Teta·nical** *a.*, tetanic. *Obs. rare*—°. Hence **Teta·nically** [see -ICALLY] *adv.*, by, or as by tetanus; spasmodically.

1656 BLOUNT *Glossogr.*, *Tetanical*,..that hath the crick in the neck [etc.]. 1877 ROSENTHAL *Muscles & Nerves* 36 The muscle..contracts tetanically.

**Tetaniform** (te·tănifǭɹm), *a.* [f. TETAN-US + -FORM.] = TETANOID.

1887 A. M. BROWN *Anim. Alkaloids* 153 In the common and ordinary form the dominant nervous factor is the delirium; in the cerebrospinal it is the tetaniform. 1899 *Allbutt's Syst. Med.* VII. 531 Tetaniform tonic convulsions.

**Tetanigenous** (tetăni·dʒĭnəs), *a. rare.* [f. TETAN-US + *-genous*: cf. -GEN and -OUS.] Producing tetanus. 1891 in *Cent. Dict.*

‖ **Tetanilla** (tetăni·lă). [mod.L., irreg. dim. of TETANUS.] = TETANY.

1890 BILLINGS *Nat. Med. Dict.*, *Tetanilla*,..tetany. 1899 *Allbutt's Syst. Med.* VIII. 47 Tetanilla; Remittent Tetanus.

**Tetanine** (te·tănəin). *Chem.* [f. TETANUS + -INE[5].] †a. An old name for strychnine. b. A ptomaine, $C_{13}H_{30}N_2O_4$, obtained from meat extract containing Rosenbach's microbe, the tetanus bacillus; occurring also in decaying corpses.

1857 DUNGLISON *Dict. Med. Sc.*, *Tetanine*, Strychnia. 1888 BRIEGER in *Jrnl. Chem. Soc.* LIV. 1317 Tetanine and Mytilotoxine..the hydrochlorides of these bases decompose gradually and lose their toxic properties. 1899 CAGNEY *Jaksch's Clin. Diagn.* i. (ed. 4) 55 From cultivations of the [tetanus] bacillus, Brieger has isolated several ptomaines—tetanin, tetanotoxin, and spasmotoxin.

†**Te·tanism.** *Obs. rare.* [f. TETAN-US + -ISM.] The action of tetanus.

1681 tr. *Willis' Rem. Med. Wks.* Vocab., *Tetanism*, a kind of cramp that so stretcheth forth the member, that it cannot bow or bend any way.

**Tetanizant** (te·tănəizănt). [a. F. *tétanisant*, pr. pple. of *tétaniser* to TETANIZE: see -ANT.] An agent or substance that causes tetanus.

1875 H. C. WOOD *Therap.* (1879) 357 One a tetanizant, the other a paralyzant.

**Tetanization** (tetănəizē·ʃən). [n. of action f. TETANIZE: cf. F. *tétanisation*.] The production of tetanus or tetanic contraction in a muscle.

1881 TYNDALL *Floating Matter of Air* ii. 102 He found the rapidity of putrefaction to correspond with the violence of the tetanization. 1887 G. T. LADD *Physiol. Psychol.* iii. § 4. 106 The application of rapidly repeated shocks to the nerve, such as would produce 'tetanic contraction' of the muscle, may be called the 'tetanization of a nerve'.

**Tetanize** (te·tănəiz), *v.* [f. TETAN-US + -IZE: so F. *tétaniser*.] *trans.* To produce tetanus or tetanic spasms in. Hence **Te·tanized** *ppl. a.*, **Te·tanizing** *vbl. sb.* and *ppl. a.*

1849 NOAD *Electricity* (ed. 3) 473 They then assume the tetanized condition, during which their limbs become completely stiffened. 1855 *Fraser's Mag.* LI. 544 The common crab,..finding itself a prisoner, draws in its legs rigid, as if tetanized by the touch. 1874 GARROD & BAXTER *Mat. Med.* (1880) 200 As a tetanising agent, it is inferior to strychnia and brucia. 1897 *Allbutt's Syst. Med.* IV. 819 A double electrode being applied to the posterior wall of the larynx so as to tetanise the interarytenoid.

**Tetano-** (tetănǫ), combining form of Gr. τέτανος TETANUS, as first element in some scientific terms. **Te·tano-ca·nnabine** *Chem.* [Gr. κάνναβις hemp], an alkaloid causing tetanic spasms, obtained in colourless needle-like crystals from Indian hemp, *Cannabis indica*. **Tetano·lysin** [Gr. λύσις a loosening], a toxin produced by the tetanus bacillus, to which the hæmolytic action of tetanus poison is due. **Te·tanomo·tor**: see quots. **Te·tanospa·smin** [SPASM], a poison produced by the tetanus bacillus, to which tetanic convulsions are due (*Cent. Dict. Suppl.* 1909). **Te·tanoto·xin**: see quot.

1883 HAY in *Pharm. Jrnl. & Trans.* XIII. 999 To this alkaloid I propose to give the name *tetano-cannabine, as indicative of its action. 1902 *Brit. Med. Jrnl.* 12 Apr. 920 Ehrlich and Madsen have studied *tetanolysin. 1904 *Ibid.* 10 Sept. 569 Expressed by a curve quite like the tetanolysin curve. 1860 *New Syd. Soc. Year-bk.* 35 A mechanical *Tetanomoter. 1890 BILLINGS *Nat. Med. Dict.*, *Tetanomotor*,..electro-magnetic instrument for producing muscular tetanus by repeated shocks. 1899 *Syd. Soc. Lex.*, *Tetanomotor*, Heidenhain's instrument for producing rapid direct mechanical stimulation by an ivory hammer attached to the vibrating spring of an induction machine. 1890 BILLINGS *Nat. Med. Dict.*, *Tetanotoxine*, $C_5H_{11}N$, a base obtained from beef-broth cultures of the tetanus bacillus. It produces spasm and paralysis. 1899 [see TETANINE].

**Tetanoid** (te·tănoid), *a.* (*sb.*) [f. TETAN-US + -OID.] Of the nature of, or resembling tetanus. b. *sb.* A tetanoid spasm or attack.

1856 KANE *Arct. Expl.* I. xix. 231 Obscure tetanoid symptoms..disclosed themselves. *Ibid.* xxxii. 447 If one of these tetanoids should attack them on the road.

‖ **Tetanothrum** (-ǭ·þrǒm). *Obs.* Pl. **-othra**. Also 6 **tetanother.** [L. *tetanōthrum* (Pliny), a. Gr. τετάνωθρον, f. τετανοῦν to stretch, strain, f. τετανός stretched, smooth.] A cosmetic for removing wrinkles.

1519 HORMAN *Vulg.* 169 b, They fylle vp theyr frekyllys: and stretche abrode theyr skyn with tetanother. 1755 YOUNG *Centaur* v. Wks. 1757 IV. 214, I fear they would prefer a tetanothrum to an apotheosis. 1823 CRABB *Technol. Dict.*, Tetanothra.

‖ **Tetanus** (te·tănǒs). Forms: α. 5–7 **tetane**, 7 **tetan.** β. 5 **tethanus**, 7–8 **tetanos**, **-on**, 7– **-us.** [L. *tetanus* (Pliny), a. Gr. τέτανος muscular spasm, f. τείν-ειν to stretch. Formerly anglicized *tetan(e.*]

1. A disease characterized by tonic spasm and rigidity of some or all of the voluntary muscles, usually occasioned by a wound or other injury. (Cf. LOCKJAW.)

α. *c* 1400 *Lanfranc's Cirurg.* 104 If þat a man haue a crampe or ellis a tetane þat is a sijknes þat halt þe membre lich streit on boþe sidis. *c* 1608 DONNE *Let.* in Gosse *Life* (1899) I. 195 [My sickness] hath so much of a tetane, that it withdraws and pulls the mouth. *a* 1614 — Βιαθανατος (1644) 171 In Tetans, which are rigors..in the Muscles.

β. 1398 TREVISA *Barth. De P. R.* VII. xiii. (Bodl. MS.), This..Crampe..haþ þre manere kinde..þe þrid hatte Tethanus, and is whanne þe forþer senewes and þe hinder schrinkeþ. 1576 NEWTON *Lemnie's Complex.* (1633) 24 In the Apoplexie, Palsey, Tetanus, and many diseases moe. 1753 N. TORRIANO *Non-naturals* 66 In Epilepsies and Distractions, swooning Fits, Tetanus's and Catalepsis. 1846 *J. Baxter's Libr. Pract. Agric.* (ed. 4) I. 430 Tetanus is one of the most formidable and fatal diseases to which the horse is liable. 1846 TRENCH *Mirac.* xi. (1862) 232 Paralysis with contraction of the joints..when united, as it much oftener is in the hot climates..than among us, with tetanus.

2. *Physiol.* A condition of prolonged contraction produced by rapidly repeated stimuli.

1877 ROSENTHAL *Muscles & Nerves* 34 Enduring contraction of this sort is called tetanus of the muscle to distinguish it from a series of distinct pulsations. 1877 FOSTER *Phys.* III. v. § 1 (1878) 471 The changes in which may be compared to the changes in a motor nerve during tetanus.

3. *attrib.* and *Comb.*, as *tetanus antitoxin*, *bacillus*, *culture*, *poison*; *tetanus-afflicted*, *-like* adjs.

1857 DUFFERIN *Lett. High Lat.* vii. (ed. 3) 92 Our dinner went off merrily; the tetanus-afflicted salmon proved excellent. 1896 *Allbutt's Syst. Med.* I. 237 The diphtheria and tetanus antitoxins act directly on the toxins. 1899 *Ibid.* VI. 541 In some cases..there are tetanus-like seizures. 1904 *Brit. Med. Jrnl.* No. 2280. 568 Tetanolysin, the hæmolytic substance of tetanus poison. 1908 J. RITCHIE in *Carnegie Trust Rep.* 25 The action of tetanus toxin on the central nervous system.

**Tetany** (te·tăni). [ad. F. *tétanie* intermittent tetanus, f. prec.] A tetanoid affection characterized by intermittent muscular spasms. Also *attrib.*

1890 BILLINGS *Nat. Med. Dict.*, *Tetany*,..a succession of tonic muscular spasms, mostly symmetrical, following one another at irregular intervals. 1899 *Allbutt's Syst. Med.* VIII. 47 Tetany is an affection characterised by tonic muscular spasms involving especially the distal portion of the limbs. *Ibid.* 48 The tetany spasms ceased the day after a tape-worm had been expelled.

**Tetar**, obs. form of TETTER.

**Tetarto-** (tĭtā·ɹto), combining form of Gr. τέταρτος fourth (cf. TETRA-), in scientific terms belonging chiefly to crystallography. **Teta·rtohe·dral** *a.* [Gr. ἕδρα base], having one fourth of the number of faces required by the highest or holohedral degree of symmetry belonging to its system; hence **Teta·rtohe·drally** *adv.*, in a tetartohedral manner. **Teta·rtohe·dric, -he·drical** *adjs.*, = *tetartohedral*. **Teta·rtohe·drism**, the property or quality of crystallizing in tetartohedral forms; the condition in which a crystal symmetrically develops only one fourth of the number of planes demanded by holohedral symmetry. **Teta·rtohe·dron**, a tetartohedral crystal. **Teta·rtohe·dry**, = *tetartohedrism*. **Teta·rtohexa·gonal** *a.*, having one quarter of the number of normals belonging to the hexagonal system. **Teta·rtoprisma·tic** *a.*, **Teta·rtopy·ramid**: see quots. **Teta·rtosymme·tric, -symme·trical** *adjs.*: see quot. **Teta·rtosy·mmetry**, a variety of merosymmetry, in which only one fourth of the faces of the holosymmetrical form are retained. **Teta·rtosystema·tic** *a.*, said of a form in which only one fourth of the origin-planes are extant.

1858 DANA *Min.* (ed. 4) 49 They are *tetartohedral forms, or contain only one-fourth the number of planes occurring under complete symmetry. 1864 WATTS *Dict. Chem.* II. 144 Quartz likewise exhibits other forms of tetartohedral development. 1888 RUTLEY *Rock-Forming Min.* 64 The development of certain plagihedral, or tetartohedral, faces. 1864 WEBSTER, *Tetartohedrally. 1854 *Pereira's Pol. Light* 234 Doubly oblique prismatic system..or the *tetartohedric-rhombic system. 1860 MAYNE *Expos. Lex.*, *Tetartohedrical. 1858 DANA *Min.* (ed. 4) 49 A form of this kind..is found in Titanic Iron, and is called rhombohedral *tetartohedrism. 1895 STORY-MASKELYNE *Crystallogr.* 160 The ambiguity in which the terms hemihedrism, tetartohedrism, etc. are involved. *Ibid.* 231 There can only be a single kind of *tetartohedron in the Cubic system. 1864 WATTS *Dict. Chem.* II. 144 *Tetartohedry. Quartz affords a remarkable example of a combination in which only one-fourth of the possible faces are present. 1895 STORY-MASKELYNE *Crystallogr.* 284 Six faces corresponding to three normals: *tetarto-hexagonal diplohedral forms. Three faces corresponding to three normals: tetarto-hexagonal haplohedral forms. 1847 WEBSTER, *Tetartoprismatic,..one fourth prismatic, applied to oblique rhombic prisms.—Mohs. 1851 *Richardson's Geol.* v. (1855) 98 Classification of Mohs..V. The Tetarto-Prismatic is composed of the oblique rhomboidal prism. 1891 *Cent. Dict.*, *Tetartopyramid,..a quarter-pyramid: said of the pyramidal planes of the triclinic system, which appear in sets of two (that is, one fourth the number required by a complete pyramid). 1895 STORY-MASKELYNE *Crystallogr.* 159 Mero-symmetrical forms may be hemi-symmetrical..or *tetarto-symmetrical, presenting one-quarter only of the faces of the holo-symmetrical form. *Ibid.* 160 *Tetarto-symmetry, where the form is (i) hemi-systematic and haplohedral, (ii) *tetarto-systematic and diplohedral. *Ibid.* 308 Tetarto-systematic haplohedral forms.

b. *Path.* ‖ **Tetartophy·ia** [Gr. φυή growth], a remitting quartan fever.

1857 DUNGLISON *Dict. Med. Sc.*, *Tetartophia*,..a quartan, in which the intermission is inordinately short or imperfect. 1895 *Funk's Stand. Dict.*, *Tetartophyia*.

**Tetaug**, var. TAUTOG, N. American fish.

**Tetch** (tetʃ). Now only *dial.* Also 7 **tech.** [Origin uncertain: see TETCHY.] A fit of petulance or anger; a tantrum.

1642 ROGERS *Naaman* 98, I mean not that such a tech as Naaman took here, may do it. *Ibid.* 143 An offer..which thou biddest faire for and forsookest at last in a tech. *Ibid.* 379 Meer tetches and pritches, very toyes and conceits, can alienate their love. *a* 1734 NORTH *Lives, Ld. Guilford* (1826) II. 218 But this frantic fellow took tetch at somewhat, and ran away into Ireland. 1876 J. RICHARDSON *Cummerland Talk* Ser. II. 73 Nater began to tak t' tetch wid him, an' wadden't be mead ghem on enny langer.

¶ 1623 COCKERAM, *Tetch*, thriftinesse. (App. a mistake.)

**Tetch(e**, obs. forms of TACHE *sb.*[1], 3.

**Tetchy, techy** (te·tʃi), *a.* Forms: α. 6–9 **techy**, 7 **techie**, **teachy**, **-ie**, 9 *dial.* **teachy**, **teechy**. β. 6– **tetchy**; also 7 **tetchie**, **tecchy**, **titchie**, **tichy**, 9 *dial.* **titchy**, **tertchy**. γ. *dial.* 8–9 **tatchy**, 9 **tachy**. [In form, a deriv. of TETCH, but that word being both less common and app. of later appearance, may be a back-formation from this. Derivation from TATCH *sb.*[1] (in ME. *tecche*, 16th c. *tetche*) has been suggested; but there are difficulties both of form and sense.]

1. Easily irritated or made angry; quick to take offence; short-tempered; peevish, irritable; testy.

(Cf. TOUCHY, which has been associated with this from early in the 17th c.) **a.** Of persons.

*α.* **1592** SHAKS. *Rom. & Jul.* I. iii. 32 (Qos.) Pretty foole, to see it teachie, and fall out with the Dugge. **1639** W. PERKINS in *Lismore Papers* Ser. II. (1888) IV. 55 Hee is as teachy as any wasp. **1642** ROGERS *Naaman* 99 A techie toy, that is, his prejudicate and forestalled heart. **1674** RAY *S. & E. C. Words* (1691) 117 *Techy*, i. e. *Touchy*, peevish, cross, apt to be angry. **1817** J. GILCHRIST *Intell. Patrimony* 109 This pure and honourable body was very techy and ticklish on the point of privilege. **1853** W. IRVING in *Life & Lett.* (1864) IV. 159, I was a little techy under your bantering.

*β.* **1596** HARINGTON *Ulysses upon Ajax* E vj b, For which cause you are waxt so tetchie. **1611** COTGR., *Sepiquer*, to be titchie, soone offended, quickly moued. *Ibid.* s.v. *Poincte, Chatouilleux à la poincte*..that readily answers the spurre; hence also, titchie, that will not indure to be touched. **1641** in 'Smectymnuus' *Vind. Answ.* § 2. 29 We are sullen.., tecchy and quarrelsome men. **1642** ROGERS *Naaman* 267 Jonas..was wondrous tetchy. **1733** SWIFT *Let. to D'chess Queensberry* 20 Mar., You are grown very tetchy since I lost the dear friend who was my supporter. **1851** TRENCH *St. Aug. on Serm. on Mt.* Introd. v. 69 *note*, Jerome.. whom none can deny.. to have been somewhat tetchy and prompt to take offence.

*γ.* **1746** *Exmoor Scolding* (E.D.S.) 21 Ya purting, tatchy, ..mincing Theng. **1892** HEWETT *Peas. Sp. Devon* 132, I niver zeed zich a tatchy, ill-contrived little twoad.

**b.** Of qualities, actions, etc.: Characterized by or proceeding from irritability.

**1592** *Nobody & Someb.* in Simpson *Sch. Shaks.* (1878) I. 279 Nay, now youle fall into your techy humour. **1610** GUILLIM *Heraldry* III. vii. (1660) 134 The Nettle is of so tetchie and froward a nature. **1652** *Mod. Policies* III. (1653) Colasterion, King-killing,..I know it a techy subject. **1841** LEVER *C. O'Malley* xxx, Gradually increased to a sore and techy subject. **1864–5** WOOD *Homes without H.* xxiii. (1868) 425 A mere stinging creature with a tetchy temper.

**2.** *fig.* Of land: see quots. *dial.*

**1847–78** HALLIWELL, *Tetchy*...applied to land that is difficult to work or to manage. **1904** in *Eng. Dial. Dict.*, If yer plough or roll when 'tis wet yer dew more harm nor good; that land's wonnerful tetchy, I can tell yer.

Hence **Te·tchily** *adv.*; **Te·tchiness.**

**1647** TRAPP *Comm. Ep.* 664 As any man is more industrious and ingenious, so he teacheth more *teachily and painfully. **1755** JOHNSON, *Techily*. **1862** F. W. ROBINSON *Owen* IV. vi, 'I'll not touch bit or sup to-day', she cried, tetchily; 'you can't do better than leave me to myself'. **1623** BP. HALL *Contempl., O. T.* XIX. viii, Not the unjust fury and *techiness of the patient shall cross the cure. **1793** ANNA SEWARD *Lett.* (1811) III. 246 The froward tetchiness; the unprincipled malice;..which generally darkened..the man's brain. **1905** *Times* 5 Mar. 10/3 Were it not for M. K——'s tetchiness.. I should feel inclined to..issue..a classic excuse.

‖ **Tête** (‖ tēt, tĕ̄t). *Obs.* exc. *Hist.* [F. *tête* head.] A woman's head of hair, or wig, dressed high and elaborately ornamented, in the fashion of the second half of the 18th c.

**1756** C. SMART tr. *Horace, Sat.* I. viii. (1826) II. 71 Sagana's towering tête of false hair. **1772** R. GRAVES *Spir. Quixote* (1820) I. 140, I sell as many wigs or tetes as any barber in town. **1813** *Sk. Charac.* (ed. 2) I. 81 By way of Grecian têtes, they had large cockades of hair stuck at the back of their heads. **1816** SCOTT *Antiq.* vi, This unparalleled *tête*, which her brother was wont to say was fitter for a turban for Mahound or Termagant, than a head-gear for a.. Christian gentlewoman. **1884** *Pall Mall G.* 7 May 6/1 She [a lady of time of Geo. III] wears what is called a *tête*, the monstrous head-dress that was fashionable in her time.

**b.** *Comb.*, as *tête-maker*.

**1789** WOLCOTT (P. Pindar) *Subj. for Paint.* To Rdr., Wks. 1816 II. 121 Têtemakers, perfumers,.. parliament speech-makers.

**Tete**, obs. form of TEAT.

‖ **Tête-à-tête** (tē·tātē·t, ‖ tĕ̄tatĕ̄t), *adv., sb.*, and *a.* Also 7 **tate a tate.** [F. *tête à tête* adv. and sb., lit. 'head to head' (17th c. in Molière); cf. *teste à teste* together (in single combat), 16th c. in Godef. *Compl.*]

**A.** *adv.* Together without the presence of a third person; in private (of two persons); face to face.

**1700** CONGREVE *Way of World* I. ix, Ay, tête-à-tête, but not in public. **1713** SWIFT *Hor. Sat.* II. vi. 106 My lord and he are grown so great, Always together *tête-à-tête*. **1790** SCOTT *Let. to W. Clerk* 3 Sept., I dined two days ago *tête à tete* with Lord Buchan. **1848** THACKERAY *Van. Fair* xxix, The General and I were moping together *tête-à-tête*.

**B.** *sb.* (pl. *tête-à-têtes*.)

**1.** A private conversation or interview between two persons; also *concr.* a party of two.

**1697** VANBRUGH *Relapse* IV. iii, I..have pretended Letters to write, to give my Friends a Tate a Tate. **1738** *Gentl. Mag.* VIII. 31/1 The Morning Moments, which I take to be the *Mollia Tempora*, so propitious to *Tete a Tetes*. **1768** MME. D'ARBLAY *Early Diary* 16 Nov., I had the pleasure of a delightful Tête à Tête with him. **1880** MRS. FORRESTER *Roy & V.* I. 55 Seated together on a low couch made expressly for such a tête-à-tête.

**2.** The name of some special types of sofa, settee, etc., made of such a shape as to enable two persons to converse more or less face to face.

**1864** WEBSTER, *Tête-à-tête*,.. a form of sofa for two persons, so curved that they are brought face to face while sitting on different sides of the sofa. **1877** KNIGHT *Dict. Mech.*, *Tete-a-tete*, two chairs with seats attached and facing in opposite directions, the arms and backs forming an S-shape. **1889** MISS C. F. WOOLSON *Jupiter Lights* xiii. 126 The sofa of this set was of the pattern named tête-à-tête, very hard and slippery.

**C.** *adj.* (*attrib.* use of the sb.) Of or pertaining to a *tête-à-tête*; consisting of or attended by two persons; *tête-à-tête set*, a tea-set for two.

**1728** VANBRUGH & CIB. *Prov. Husb.* II. i, A pretty cheerful *tête-à-tête* dinner. **1779** JOHNSON 26 Mar. in *Boswell*, You must not indulge your delicacy too much; or you will be a *tête-à-tête* man all your life. **1847** C. BRONTE *J. Eyre* xxiv, I was determined not to spend the whole time in a *tête-à-tête* conversation.

‖ **Tête de mouton.** *Obs.* [Fr., lit. 'sheep's head'.] A head-dress of close frizzly curls formerly worn by women.

**1737** in *Lady Suffolk's Lett.* (1824) II. 159, I beg she will not leave off her *tête de mouton* and her *pannier*. **1758** *Humble Rem.*, etc. in *Ann. Reg.* I. 374/1 It may..become a French *friseur*, to acquaint the public that he makes a *tete de mouton*, or simply a *tete*.

‖ **Tête de pont** (tĕ̄t də poṅ). Pl. **têtes de pont.** [Fr., lit. 'bridge head'.] A fortification defending the approach to a bridge; a bridge-head.

**1794** *Amer. St. Papers, Mil. Affairs* (1832) I. 89 There ought to be..close to the chain, a small *tete de pont*. **1812** *Examiner* 31 Aug. 549/2 One bridge upon the Beresina, with double *tetes-de-pont*. **1829** SCOTT *Anne of G.* ix, They were not long of discovering the *tête-du-pont* on which the drawbridge, when lowered, had formerly rested.

**Teter**: see TEETER, TETTER.

**Teterrimous** (tĭte·rimәs), *a. rare.* [f. L. *tēterrimus* most foul, superl. of *tæter* (*tēter*) foul + -OUS.] In phrase *teterrimous cause*, after L. *teterrima belli causa* 'the most foul cause of war', i. e. woman (Horace *Sat.* I. iii. 107).

[**1704** SWIFT *T. Tub* ix. **1823** BYRON *Juan* IX. lv, Oh thou 'teterrima causa' of all 'belli'. **1845** FORD *Handbk. Spain* I. iii. 362 A Christian woman now was the *teterrima causa* of the Moslem downfall.] **1864** *Daily Tel.* 24 Aug., I pronounce Orangeism the teterrimous cause of the war that has been waged for two weeks past in the heart of the town.

**Teth**, obs. form of TEETH, TEETHE.

**Tethanus**, obs. form of TETANUS.

**Tethe, Tething**, obs. ff. TITHE *v.*, TITHING.

**Tethee**, obs. form of TEETHY, testy.

**Tether** (te·ðәɹ), *sb.* Forms: *α.* 4 **tethir,** (**thether**), 6 **teyther,** 6–8 **teather,** 7 **tither, teither,** 6– **tether.** *β.* 4–5 **tedyr,** 5 **-yre,** 5–7 **teder,** 6 **teddir, tedure, teeder,** 6–8 (9 *dial.*) **tedder,** 7 **teddar** (**tedir**). [At first a northern word: app. a. ON. *tjóðr* 'tether' (Icel. and Fær. *tjóður*, Sw. *tjuder*); corresp. to 15th c. WFris. *tyader, tieder*; MLG., MDu. *tûder, tudder*, LG. *tüder, tüdder, töder, tider, tier, tir*, Du. *tuier*, all in sense 'tether'. Cf. also OHG. **ziotar, zeotar*, MHG. *zieter* (still in Bav. dial., Hess. *zetter*) in sense 'fore-pole or team'. A corresponding OE. **téoðor* has not been found.

The word points to an OTeut. **teudra-*, pre-Teut. **deutro-*, from a vb.-stem. **deu-* to fasten, with instr. suffix *-tro*.]

**1.** A rope, cord, or other fastening by which a horse, cow, or other beast is tied to a stake or the like, so as to confine it to the spot.

**1376–7** *Durham Acc. Rolls* (Surtees) 386 In duobus thethers et j feterlok pro equis. **1394–5** *Ibid.* 599 In iij Tethirs cum paribus de langalds. **1396–7** *Ibid.* 214, j tedyr. **14..** *Nominale* in Wr.-Wülcker 728/1 *Hoc ligatorium*, a tedyre. **1523** FITZHERB. *Husb.* § 148 But make thy hors to longe a tedure. **1562** *Wills & Inv. N. C.* (Surtees) I. 207, ij wayne roopes, j haire teder xijd. **1589** GREENE *Menaphon* (Arb.) 38 Who coueteth to tie the Lambe and the Lion in one tedder maketh a brawle. **1641** BEST *Farm. Bks.* (Surtees) 145 A peece of an olde broken teather. **1669** *Caldwell Papers* (Maitl. Cl.) I. 133 Ane hair tedir o. 13. 4. **1688** *Lond. Gaz.* No. 2368/4 Stolen out of the Tether.., a dark brown Gelding. **1782** BURNS *Death of Mailie* 2 As Mailie, an her lambs thegither, Were ae day nibbling on the tether. *a* **1854** H. REED *Lect. Brit. Poets* (1857) II. 70 A delicate colt at the end of each tether.

**2.** Applied to a rope used for other purposes.

† **a.** A boat's painter; a tow-rope. *Obs.*

**1503** HAWES *Examp. Virt.* II. 1 Wher was a boote tyed with a teeder. **1818** W. MUIR *Poems* 12 (E.D.D.), I saw her in a tether Draw twa sloops after ane anither.

**b.** A rope for hanging malefactors; a halter.

**1508** DUNBAR *Flyting* 176 Lyke to ane stark theif glowrand in ane tedder. *a* **1578** LINDESAY (Pitscottie) *Chron. Scot.* (S.T.S.) I. 175 They tuik ane hardin tedder and hangit him ower the brige of Lawder. **17..** *Sheriff-Muir* xvii. in *Sel. Coll. Sc. Ballads* (1790) III. 65 Then in a tether He'll swing from a ladder. **1819** W. TENNANT *Papistry Storm'd* (1827) 11 Weems cried out, 'Hang it in a tether'.

**3.** *fig.* The cause or measure of one's limitation; the radius of one's field of action; scope, limit.

**1579** TOMSON *Calvin's Serm. Tim.* 18/1 Men must not passe their tedder. **1651** N. BACON *Disc. Govt. Eng.* II. xxx. (1739) 137 A large Teather, and greater privilege than ever the Crown had. **1706** BAYNARD in Sir J. Floyer *Hot & Cold Bath.* II. (1709) 272 The length of his short Tedder of Understanding. **1734** POPE *Let. to Swift* 19 Dec., We soon find the shortness of our tether. **1865** G. MACDONALD *A. Forbes* 51 Gin his mither has been jist raither saft wi' him, and gi'en him ower lang a tether.

**b.** A bond or fetter.

**1609** F. GREVIL *Mustapha* Chorus ii, We scorne those Arts of Peace, that ciuile Tether, Which, in one bond, tie Craft and force together. **1817** BYRON *Beppo* xviii, When weary of the matrimonial tether. **1878** BROWNING *La Saisiaz* 413 Why should we expect new hindrance, novel tether?

**4.** Phrases: † *Within* (obs.), *beyond one's tether*, within, beyond the limits of one's ability, position, or reasonable action; *the end* († *extent, length*) *of one's tether*, the extreme limit of one's resources.

**1523** FITZHERB. *Husb.* § 148 As longe as thou etest within Tedure. **1549** *Latimer's 2nd Serm. bef. Edw. VI*, To Rdr. (Arb.) 51 Learne to eat within thy teather. **1627** SANDERSON *Serm.* I. 276 He shall not be able to go an inch beyond his tedder. **1690** LOCKE *Hum. Underst.* I. i. § 4 To prevail with the busy Mind..to stop, when it is at the utmost Extent of its Tether. *a* **1734** NORTH *Exam.* III. viii. § 57 (1740) 627 As to the last Order..which properly belongs to the next Reign and so beyond my Tedder. **1809** MALKIN *Gil Blas* X. ii. ¶ 8 At length she got to the end of her tether, and I began. **1860–70** STUBBS *Lect. Europ. Hist.* (1904) I. ii. 23 They had got to the length of their tether.

**5.** *attrib.* and *Comb.*, as *tether-end, -length, -rope, -string*; **tether-ball**, a ball fastened to or suspended from a pole by a string; the game played with this (Webster *Suppl.* 1902); **tether-peg, -stake, -stick, -stone**, a pin or stake of wood or iron, or a stone, fixed in the ground, to which an animal is tethered.

**1725** RAMSAY *Gentle Sheph.* I. ii, He'll look upon you as his tether-stake. **1782** BURNS *Death of Mailie* 52 Gude keep thee frae a tether string. *a* **1800** *Kempy Kaye* in Child *Ballads* I. 302/1 His teeth they were like tether-sticks. **1859** CORNWALLIS *Panorama New World* I. 144 They took my tether rope, and commenced making me fast to a tree. **1884** *Lays & Leg. N. Irel.* 13 Put a tether-stone up on the face av the hill.

**Tether** (te·ðәɹ), *v.* [f. prec. sb.]

**1.** *trans.* To make fast or confine with a tether.

**1483** *Cath. Angl.* 379/1 To Tedyr, *restringere, retentare*. **1523** FITZHERB. *Surv.* xli. (1539) 58 To tye or tedder theyr horses and mares vpon. **1577** *Nottingham Rec.* IV. 170 No man shall not teyther [his beasts] amongs the hey vnto it be gone of the ground. **1719** DE FOE *Crusoe* I. 174, I tether'd the three Kids in the best part. **1800** WORDSW. *Pet Lamb* 6 The lamb was all alone, And by a slender cord was tethered to a stone. **1882** E. O'DONOVAN *Merv Oasis* I. 396 Hundreds of horses were tethered in every direction.

**2.** To fasten, make fast generally.

**1563** WINȜET *Four Scoir Thre Quest.* § 35 Wks. (S.T.S.) I. 100 *margin*, Heir Ioh. Knox be his awin sentence aganis wtheris, is fast tedderit in the girn. **1674** GREW *Anat. Trunks* II. vi. § 4 The said Roots tethering it, as it trails along, to the ground. **1832** HT. MARTINEAU *Hill & Vall.* i, A gate,..too well tethered to be quickly opened. **1898** *Allbutt's Syst. Med.* V. 744 The heart is tethered to the bottom of the pericardium.

**3.** *fig.* To fasten or bind by conditions or circumstances; to bind so as to detain.

*c* **1470** HENRYSON *Orpheus & Eur.* 456 Suld our desyre be soucht wp in þe speris, Quhene It Is tedderit on þis warldis breris. **1624** BP. HALL *Contempl., N. T.* II. iii, He, that bounded thy power, tether'd thee shorter. **1790** BURNS *Tam O'Shanter* 67 Nae man can tether time or tide, The hour approaches Tam maun ride. **1879** H. JAMES *R. Hudson* I. 65 She would fain see me all my life tethered to the law.

Hence **Te·thered** *ppl. a.*, fastened with a tether; limited, confined, 'tied'; **Te·thering** *vbl. sb.* and *ppl. a.*, fastening with a tether or the like.

**1573** TUSSER *Husb.* (1878) 42 Get home with thy brakes, er an sommer be gon, for *teddered cattle to sit there vpon. *a* **1680** CHARNOCK *Attrib. God* (1834) I. 237 Our contracted and tethered capacities. **1845** R. W. HAMILTON *Pop. Educ.* iii. (ed. 2) 43 All this may be preferable; but it is a tethered freedom still. **1890** DOYLE *White Company* 185 A dozen tethered horses and mules grazed around the encampment. **1671** GREW *Anat. Plants* iii. App. § 9 By the Linking of their Claspers, and..by the *Tethering of their Trunk-Roots, being couched together. **1862** HISLOP *Prov. Scot.* 35 Better hands loose than in an ill tethering. **1863** WHYTE MELVILLE *Gladiators* 367 Not a vestige remained of halter or tethering ropes.

**Tethery** (te·ðәri), *a. rare.* [f. TETHER *sb.* + -Y.] Apt to become tangled or ravelled: said of long-stapled wool, the fibres of which cling together.

**1894** C. VICKERMAN *Woollen Spinning* ix. 167 It is very obvious..that a long tethery wool would be extremely difficult to divide from the lap, either by the Bolette or Martin machine.

**Tethinge(s**, var. *tithing(s*, TIDING(S.

† **Tethy**, *a. Obs. rare.* Also 5 **tithy, thethy.** Of uncertain origin and meaning.

The sense of TEETHY *a.*[1] seems unsuitable. Can it be a corruption, or rather a series of errors, for TIDY *a.*, which occurs in this poem (and elsewhere) as an epithet of approval or praise, = good, excellent, worthy, apt, brave, doughty? But such an alteration of vowel and consonant in *tidy* is unknown elsewhere, and is phonetically unwarranted.

*a* **1400–50** *Alexander* 2198 ȝe of Tebet ere tried, þe tethiest [*D.* thethiest] on erth. *Ibid.* 2784 Of our wale princes Twa of þe tethiest [*D.* tithiest] ere tint, & termynd of lyue. (Cf. *Ibid.* 2367 Ware noȝt þe tulkis out of Tire þe tidiest [*D.* triest] on erth. *Ibid.* 2371 Was noȝt þe Thebes þar-to þe th[r]ey*est [? theþeest; *D.* tithiest] of othire.)

**Tetle**, obs. f. TITLE. **Tetotum**, var. TEETOTUM.

**Tetra-** (tetră), before a vowel **tetr-**, a. Gr. τετρα-, combining form of the numeral τέτταρες, τέτταρα four, forming the first element of many words adapted from existing Greek compounds, and thence used in new analogous formations, mainly scientific and technical.

**1.** As a general etymological element.

‖ **Tetrabelodon** (-be·lŏdǫn) [Gr. βέλος a dart, ὀδούς, ὀδοντ- tooth], a genus of extinct elephantine beasts. **Tetrabla·stic** *a.*, *Biol.* [Gr. βλαστός germ], having four blastodermic membranes or germinal layers, as animals having a true cœlome or body-cavity. **Te·trabrach** (-bræk), *Anc. Pros.* (also **tetrabrachys**) [Gr. τετράβραχ-υς in same sense], a word or foot of four short syllables, as *facinora, hominibus*; as a foot usually called *proceleusmatic.* ‖ **Tetrabrachius** (-bræ·kiŏs), pl. -ii [Gr. βραχίων arm], a monster having four arms (Billings *Nat. Med. Dict.* 1890). **Tetraca·marous** *a.*, *Bot.* [Gr. καμάρα vault], having four closed carpels. **Tetraca·nthous** *a.* [Gr. ἄκανθα thorn], having four spines, as a fish, etc., or thorns in groups of four, as a plant (Mayne *Exp. L.* 1860). **Tetraca·rpellary** *a.*, *Bot.* of a compound fruit: having four carpels. **Tetracerous** (tĕtræ·sĕrəs), also † **Tetrace·ratous**, *adjs.*, *Zool.* [Gr. τετράκερως four-horned], having four 'horns' or tentacles; belonging to the *Tetracera*, a family of four-horned gastropods. ‖ **Tetrachænium** (-ăkī·niŏm), *Bot.*, pl. -ia [see ACHENE], a fruit formed of four adherent achenes. **Tetrachætous** (-kī·təs) *a.*, *Entom.* [Gr. χαίτη mane, hair], pertaining to the *Tetrachætæ*, a division of the brachycerous *Diptera*, comprising those in which the proboscis is composed of four pieces. ‖ **Tetrachirus** (-kəiə·rŏs) [L., ad. Gr. τετράχειρ], a monster with four hands (Billings 1890). **Tetrachroma·tic** *a.*, of, pertaining to, having, or distinguishing four colours. **Tetrachromic** (-krōᵘ·mik) *a.*, of four colours; capable of distinguishing (only) four colours of the spectrum. **Te·trachromist**, one who holds a theory of four colours; cf. POLYCHROMIST. **Tetrachronous** (tĕtræ·krŏnəs) *a.*, *Anc. Pros.* [Gr. τετράχρονος containing four times], = *tetrasemic*. **Te·traclone** (-klōᵘn) [Gr. κλών twig, spray], a four-rayed sponge-spicule with branched ends (*Cent. Dict. Suppl.* 1909). **Tetracoccous** (-kǫ·kəs) *a.*, *Bot.* [Gr. κόκκος berry], having four cocci or carpels; also, applied to bacteria when in four segments (Jackson *Gloss. Bot. T.* 1900). **Tetraco·ral**, one of the *Tetracoralla*, a division of corals (= *Rugosa*) in which the septa are in multiples of four; so **Tetraco·ralline** *a.*, of or pertaining to the *Tetracoralla*. **Tetracotylean** (-kǫtilī·ăn) *a.*, *Biol.* [Gr. κοτύλη cup], having four rounded pit-like suckers on the head or scolex, as a tapeworm. **Tetracrepid** (-krī·pid) *a.* [Gr. κρηπίς, κρηπιδ- boot, groundwork], a desmic sponge-spicule formed on a tetract nucleus. **Tetra·cron**, *Geom.*, pl. -a, -ons [Gr. ἄκρον summit], a solid having four vertices or solid angles, a tetrahedron; cf. POLYACRON. **Tetracy·clic** *a.*, having four cycles or circles; *spec.* in *Bot.*, having four whorls of floral organs. **Tetrade·nous** *a.*, *Bot.* [Gr. ἀδήν gland], having four glands (Mayne 1860). **Tetraë·terid**, also ‖ **-is** [Gr. τετραετηρίς, -ιδ-, f. ἔτος year], a space of four years, a quadrennium. † **Tetrafo·liate**, † **Tetrafo·lious** *adjs.*, *Bot.*, four-leaved; = *tetraphyllous*; bijugate (Mayne). **Tetragamelian** (-gămī·liăn) [Gr. γαμήλιος bridal], *a.* belonging to the *Tetragamelia*, a division of discomedusans (*Hydrozoa Acraspeda*) having four subgenital pits; *sb.* a member of this division. **Tetragamy** (tĕtræ·gămi) [Byz. Gr. τετραγαμία], a fourth marriage. **Tetragenous** (tĕtræ·dʒĭnəs) *a.*, *Bacteriol.* [-GEN[1] and -OUS], forming square groups of four, as certain micrococci. **Tetra·gnath** [Gr. τετράγναθ-ος], *a.* having four jaws; *sb.* a kind of spider with four jaws; so † **Tetragna·thian** *a.* ‖ **Tetragoni·dium**, *Bot.*, = TETRASPORE. **Tetraleioclone** (-ləi·oklōᵘn) [Gr. λεῖ-ος smooth: see *tetraclone*], a four-rayed sponge-spicule with smooth arms (*Cent. Dict. Suppl.* 1909). **Tetrale·mma**, *Logic* [cf. DILEMMA], a position presenting four alternatives. **Tetralo·phodont** *a.* [Gr. λόφ-ος ridge + ὀδούς, ὀδοντ- tooth], having molars with four transverse ridges, as the sub-genus *Tetralophodon* of mastodons. **Tetrama·sthous** *a.* [Gr. μασθός breast], having four breasts. **Tetrama·stigate** *a.* [Gr. μάστιξ, μαστιγ- whip], having four flagella (*Cent. Dict.* 1891). **Tetramyrmeclone** (-mə·ɹmĭklōᵘn) [Gr. μυρμηκιά wart: see *tetraclone*], a four-rayed sponge-spicule, the arms covered with tubercles (*Cent. Dict. Suppl.* 1909). **Tetranephric** (-ne·frik) *a.* [Gr. νεφρός kidney], having four uriniferous or Malpighian tubes. **Tetrano·mial** *a.*, *Math.* [after BINOMIAL], consisting of four (algebraic) terms; quadrinomial. **Tetraphala·ngeate** *a.*, *Comp. Anat.*, having four phalanges. ‖ **Tetrapha·rmacon** (also in L. form -pharmacum) [Gr. τετραφάρμακον], a medicine or ointment consisting of four ingredients; hence **Tetrapha·rmacal** *a.*, compounded of four ingredients. **Tetra·phony** [Gr. φωνή voice], in early mediæval music, diaphony for four voices. **Tetraphyle·tic** *a.* [Gr. φυλετικ-ός, f. φυλέτης tribesman, φυλή tribe]: see quot. **Tetraphy·llous** *a.* *Bot.* [Gr. φύλλον leaf], having or consisting of four leaves; abbreviated 4-*phyllous*. **Tetraplocau·lous** *a.*, *Bot.* [Gr. τετραπλοῦς fourfold + καυλό-ς stem]: see quot. **Tetrapneumo·nian**, *Zool.*, *a.* of or pertaining to the *Tetrapneumones*, a division of spiders with two pairs of lung-sacs (*Cent. Dict.* 1891); *sb.* a spider of this division. **Tetrapneu·monous** *a.*, *Zool.*, having four lungs or respiratory organs; applied to the *Tetrapneumones* (see prec.) and to the *Tetrapneumona*, a group of holothurians (sea-cucumbers). **Tetrapo·lar** *a.*, *Biol.*, having four (instead of only two) poles or centres of radiation: said of a karyokinetic figure. **Te·trapous** *a.* [Gr. πούς foot], four-footed. **Tetraprioni·dian** *a.* [Gr. πρίων a saw: cf. *Diprionidian*], applied to graptolites having four rows of thecæ showing four serrated edges. **Tetraprostyle** (-prǫ·stəil) *a.* [Gr. πρόστυλ-ος having pillars in front], of an ancient temple: having a portico with four pillars in front. † **Tetra·ptative**, *a. rare* [see APTATE *v.*], that combines four things. **Te·traptote**, *Gram.* [Gr. τετράπτωτ-ος], a noun with (only) four cases. **Tetra·ptych** (-ptik), *rare* [Gr. πτυχ- fold], a folding picture or the like in four compartments; cf. *triptych*. **Tetrapy·lon** [ad. Gr. τετράπυλον], a building or structure with four gates. **Tetrapy·ramid**, *Cryst.*, in the triclinic system, that form in which each of the two faces intercepts the three crystallographic axes. † **Tetrapyre·nous** *a.*, *Bot* [Gr. πυρήν fruit-stone], having four stones, as a fruit. **Tetraque·trous** *a.*, *Bot.* [mod.L. *tetraquetr-us* four-angled], having four sharp angles. **Tetrascele**: see *tetraskele*. ‖ **Tetrascelus** (tĕtræ·silŏs) [Gr. τετρασκελ-ής four-legged], a monster in which the legs are duplicated (Billings 1890). **Tetraschistic** (-ski·stik) *a.*, *Biol.* [Gr. σχιστός cloven], dividing into four by fission. **Tetrasele·nodont** *a.* [SELENODONT], having four crescentic ridges, as a molar tooth; also said of a ruminant that has such teeth. **Te·traseme**, *Pros.* [Gr. τετράσημ-ος adj.], *sb.* a foot consisting of or equal to four short syllables; *a.* = *tetrasemic*. **Tetrase·mic** *a.*, *Pros.*, equivalent to four moræ or short syllables. **Tetrase·palous** *a.*, *Bot.*, having four sepals. **Te·traskele**, also **te·trascele** (-sīl) and **tetraske·lion** [see *tetrascelus*], a figure consisting of four limbs radiating from a centre; *spec.* the FYLFOT (*C. D. Suppl.* 1909). ‖ **Tetraspa·ston** [Gr. -σπαστος, -ον, drawn]: see quot. **Tetraspe·rmous** *a.*, *Bot.* [Gr. σπέρμα seed], having four seeds, or seeds in fours; so **Tetraspe·rmal**, **Tetraspe·rmatous** *adjs.* **Tetraspheric**, **Tetraspherical** *adjs.*, *Math.*, of or pertaining to four spheres. **Tetrasy·mmetry**, *Biol.*, symmetry characterized by division into four similar parts. † **Tetrasy·ncrasy** [Gr. σύγκρασις: see CRASIS], a mixture of four elements. **Te·trateuch** *nonce-wd.*, a name for the first four books of the PENTATEUCH. **Tetrathe·cal** *a.*, *Bot.* [Gr. θήκη case, cell], four-celled, as an ovary. **Te·tratheism**, the doctrine of four persons in the Godhead. **Te·tratheite**, a believer in tetratheism. **Te·tratone**, *Mus.*, also in form **tetra·tonon** [ad. Gr. τετράτον-ον], an interval containing four whole tones; an augmented fifth. **Te·tratop** [Gr. τόπ-ος place], 'the four-dimensional angular space inclosed between four straight lines drawn from a point not in the same three-dimensional space' (*Cent. Dict.* 1891). **Tetra·xial** *a.*, having four axes, as some sponge-spicules; so **Tetra·xile** *a.* in same sense. **Tetra·xon** [Gr. ἄξων axis], *sb.* a sponge-spicule with four axes radiating from a centre; *adj.* having four axes of growth; hence **Tetraxo·nian** *a.* = *tetraxon* adj. **Tetrazo·mal** *a.* (*sb.*) *Geom.* [Gr. ζῶμα girdle], applied to a curve having an equation of the form $\sqrt{U} + \sqrt{V} + \sqrt{W} + \sqrt{T} = 0$, in relation to which the four curves $\sqrt{U} = 0$, $\sqrt{V} = 0$, etc. have properties of the nature of girdling: cf. POLYZOME. **Tetrazo·oid**, *Biol.*, any one of the four ascidiozooids developed from the germinal disk in the ascidian genus *Pyrosoma* (*Cent. Dict. Suppl.* 1909).

**1904** *Athenæum* 4 Aug. 133/3 Prof. Lankester gave a curious theory of his own as to the derivation of the elephant's trunk from the soft upper jaw and nasal area of the extinct *Tetrabelodon. **1891** *Cent. Dict.*, *Tetrablastic. [**1860** MAYNE *Expos. Lex.*, **Tetracamarus*,..applied by Mirbel to the etairium which is composed of four *camaræ*.] **1891** *Cent. Dict.*, Tetracamarous. **1900** B. D. JACKSON *Gloss. Bot. Terms*. **1860** MAYNE *Expos. Lex.*, **Tetraceratus*, ..*tetraceratous. **1891** *Cent. Dict.*, *Tetracerous. **1856** HENSLOW *Dict. Bot. Terms*, **Tetrachænium*.., a fruit formed by the separating of a single ovary into four nuts; as in the Labiatæ. **1902** BALDWIN *Dict. Philos. & Psychol.* II. 793 Ordinary vision, which is *tetrachromatic,..was called, under the dominance of the colour-triangle, trichromatic. **1902** *19th Cent.* Apr. 605 The vision of the second eye was *tetrachromic. **1903** *Nature* 19 Nov. 71/2 The second class of the colour-blind see five, four, three, two, or one colour, according to the degree of their defect, and are called pentachromic, tetrachromic, etc. **1842** WORNUM in *Smith's Dict. Grk. & Rom. Antiq.* s.v. *Painting* § 3 Ancient *tetrachromists or polychromists. **1891** *Cent. Dict.*, *Tetrachronous. *a* **1864** A. GRAY cited in WEBSTER for **Tetracoccous*. [**1888** ROLLESTON & JACKSON *Anim. Life* 743 The Palæozoic Corals are for the most part classified as *Rugosa* s. **Tetracoralla*.. The septa are arranged in four systems, which are either disposed in a bilaterally symmetrical manner..or else are regularly radiate.] **1909** *Cent. Dict. Suppl.*, *Tetracotylean. **1888** SOLLAS in *Challenger Rep.* XXV. p. lix, It ..is in some cases difficult to say, in the absence of a visible crepis, whether a desma is rhabdocrepid or *tetracrepid. *Ibid.* p. lx, Tetracrepid Desma. **1878** MACNAB *Botany* ix. (1883) 161 *Dicotyledones*... Flowers typically *tetracyclic pentamerous. **1678** PHILLIPS *New World Wds.* (ed. 4), **Tetraeterid*,..the space of four years, a word used by Astronomers, and Astrologers. *a* **1727** NEWTON *Chronol. Amended* i. (1728) 75 [The Greeks] omitted an intercalary month once in eight years, which made their Octaeteris, one half of which was their Tetraeteris. **1881** LANKESTER in *Encycl. Brit.* XII. 557/1 In the *Tetragamelian *Rhizostomæ* these pits remain distinct from one another.., but in the Monogamelian *Rhizostomæ* they unite to form one continuous sub-genital cavity. **1862** J. C. ROBERTSON *Hist. Christ. Ch.* IV. v. II. 402 *note*, He [Symeon Magister] says that the lawfulness of '*tetragamy' was believed to have been revealed to Euthymius. **1888** *Science* 15 June 283/2 The constituents of the colony turned out to be a *tetragenous microbe quite distinct from the plain atmospheric micrococcus. **1608** TOPSELL *Serpents* (1658) 771 Nicander..confesseth, that the Ash-coloured *Tetragnath, doth not by his biting infuse any venom or like hurt. *Ibid.*, If a man be wounded of the *Tetragnathian Spider, the place waxeth whitish, with an intolerable, vehement, and continual pain in it. **1835** KIRBY *Hab. & Inst. Anim.* II. xvi. 85 Those Phalangians which are denominated *Tetragnatha*, or having four jaws. **1882** VINES *Sachs' Bot.* 289 The asexual organs of reproduction are gonidia: since four are usually formed in a mother-cell, they are termed **Tetragonidia*... When the thallus consists of rows of cells, the tetragonidia are produced in the apical cell of lateral branches. **1867** ATWATER *Logic* 151 The names Trilemma, *Tetralemma, Polylemma have been sometimes given to this sort of Syllogism according to the number of members or horns. **1889** NICHOLSON & LYDEKKER *Palæont.* (ed. 3) II. 1398 In the *Tetralophodont group the number of ridges in the cheek-teeth is greater than in the former group. **1860** MAYNE *Expos. Lex.*, *Tetramasthous. **1890** BILLINGS *Nat. Med. Dict.*, *Tetramasthous*, having four breasts. **1898** A. S. PACKARD *Text-bk. Entomol.* 355 In at least one case (Melolontha), the *tetranephric is ontogenetically derived from the hexanephric condition by the suppression of one pair of tubules. **1817** H. T. COLEBROOKE *Algebra*, etc. 280 Put the binomial root for first term;..then put the trinomial, and afterwards the *tetranomial, for first radical term; until the proposed number be exhausted. **1898** *Nature* 3 Feb. 319/1 In the full-grown fœtus of a *Vespertilio* the fourth digit of the manus is *tetraphalangeate. **1657** TOMLINSON *Renou's Disp.* 143 The *Tetrapharmacal unguent, which consists..of Wax, Rosine, Pitch and Bulls fat. **1727-41** CHAMBERS *Cycl.*, **Tetrapharmacum*,..denotes any remedy consisting of four ingredients. **1842** BRANDE *Dict. Sc.*, etc., *Tetrapharmacon*, an ointment composed of four remedies; namely wax, resin, lard, and pitch. **1900** B. D. JACKSON *Gloss. Bot. Terms*, **Tetraphyletic*, applied to hybrids with four strains in their descent. **1731** BAILEY vol. II, **Tetraphyllous*. **1775** J. JENKINSON *Descr. Brit. Pl.* 158 The cup [of Charnock] is tetraphyllous and erect. **1900** B. D. JACKSON *Gloss. Bot. Terms*, **Tetraplocaulous*, having quaternary axes. **1842** BRANDE *Dict. Sc.*, etc., **Tetrapneumonians*, *Tetrapneumones*,..a section of spiders..comprehending those which have four pulmonary sacs. **1902** D. J. HAMILTON in *Encycl. Brit.* XXXI. 514/1 (Description of Plate) D. *Tetrapolar karyokinesis. E. Another form of tetrapolar division. [**1890** BILLINGS *Nat. Med. Dict.*, *Tetrapus*, having four feet.] **1899** *Syd. Soc. Lex.*, *Tetrapous. **1888** *Cassell's Encycl. Dict.*, *Tetraprionidian. **1891** *Cent. Dict.*, *Tetraprostyle. **1471** RIPLEY *Comp. Alch.* IV. viii. in Ashm. *Theat. Chem. Brit.* (1652) 146 The thyrd manner and also the last of all, Fowre Elements together whych joynyth to abyde, *Tetraptative certainely Phylosophers doth hyt call. **1656** BLOUNT *Glossogr.*, **Tetraptote*, declined in four cases. **1704** J. HARRIS *Lex. Techn.* I, *Tetraptotes*,..such defective Nouns, as have only four Cases; as *Plus*, which wants the Dative and Vocative Singular. **1904** H. C. BUTLER *Archit. & Other Arts* xii. 393 Conjectured to have been vaulted *tetrapylons at the crossing of the thoroughfares. [**1727** BAILEY vol. II, **Tetrapyrenos*, which has four Seeds or Kernels, as Agrifolium, Holly, &c.] **1882** MAW in *Jrnl. Bot.* XI. 88 The Scape..is either *tetraquetrous or triquetrous. **1885** LANKESTER in *Encycl. Brit.* XIX. 834/2 They [chlorophyll corpuscles] multiply by fission, usually *tetraschistic, independently of the general protoplasm. **1890** *Amer. Nat.* May 471 To sustain the view that the *tetraselenodont forms are the descendants of the pentaselenodont Artiodactyla. **1895** GILDERSLEEVE *Lat. Gram.* (ed. 3) 459 *Tetraseme long. **1891** *Cent. Dict.*, *Tetrasemic. **1829** LOUDON *Encycl. Pl.* (1836) 1069 A *tetrasepalous tetrapetalous flower. **1842** BRANDE *Dict. Sc.*, etc., **Tetraspaston*, in Mechanics, a machine in which four pulleys all act together. **1860** MAYNE *Expos. Lex.*, *Tetraspermatus*,..four-seeded: *tetraspermal: *tetraspermatous. **1760** J. LEE *Introd. Bot.* II. viii. (1765) 89 Monopetalous *Tetraspermous. **1889** F. A. BATHER in *Q. Jrnl. Geol. Soc.* XLV. II. 362 The structure above described for *Eugeniacrinus* is..also found..with the necessary modifications due to *tetrasymmetry, in *Tetracrinus*. **1651** BIGGS *New Disp.* § 246 If they will have the pus to be made out of a *Tetrasyncrasy or commixture of the humors. **1906** *Rev. of Theol. & Philos.* Jan. 457 An elaborate work on the Pentateuch (or rather the *Tetrateuch, since Deuteronomy is lightly passed over). **1849** BALFOUR *Man. Bot.* § 405 A quadrilocular..or *tetrathecal..anther. **1899** *Syd. Soc. Lex.*, *Tetrathecal*, *Biol.*, applied to a four-chambered ovary. **1874** J. H. BLUNT *Dict. Sects & Heresies* s.v. *Damianists*, Their theory led to the conclusion that there are four Gods, the three separate and subordinate Hypostases and the one superior Αὐτόθεος, hence they were also named *Tetratheites. **1775** ASH, **Tetratonon*, the superfluous fifth. **1801** BUSBY *Dict. Mus.* **1888** ROLLESTON & JACKSON *Anim. Life* 810 Tetractina: spicules to a great extent *tetraxile. **1886** *Proc. Zool. Soc.* 21 Dec. 581 Spicules more or less clearly *tetraxon, often branched. **1887** SOLLAS in *Encycl. Brit.* XXII. 416/2 (*Sponges*) Tetraxon Quadriradiate Type (Calthrops).—Growth from a centre in four directions inclined at about 110° to each other. **1867** CAYLEY *Math. Papers* VI. 485 On the Trizomal Curve and the *Tetrazomal Curve. *Ibid.* 486 The tetrazomals are each of them a curve of the order $4r$, and they intersect therefore in only $16r^2$ points.

**2.** In *Chemical* nomenclature, in the names of compounds and derivatives with the general sense of 'four-', 'four times'. **a.** In substantives: (*a*) Prefixed to names of binary compounds of elements or radicals, names of salts, etc., to signify four atoms, groups, or equivalents of the element or radical in question; as *tetrachloride*, a compound of four atoms of chlorine with some other element or radical; so *tetrasulphide, tetriodide,* TETROXIDE, *tetrahydroxide, tetramethide, tetracetate, tetraphosphate,* etc. (*b*) Prefixed to names of elements or radicals (or the combining forms, as *bromo-, nitro-, oxy-, phospho-, azo-*) entering into the name of a compound, to signify that four atoms or groups of the element or radical are substituted in the substance designated by the rest of the name, as *te:trabro:mobe·nzene*, $C_6H_2Br_4$, in which four of the hydrogen atoms of benzene, $C_6H_6$, are replaced by four bromine atoms; so *te:trame:thylbe·nzene*, $C_6H_2(CH_3)_4$. (*c*) In some words used irregularly, as *te:trasa·licylide*, $C_{28}H_{18}O_9$: see quot. 1875².

**1866** ODLING *Anim. Chem.* 59 C Cl₄, Carbon tetrachloride. **1869** ROSCOE *Elem. Chem.* xi. 121 Fluorine forms, with the silicon contained in the glass, a volatile compound called Silicon tetrafluoride. **1875** WATTS *Dict. Chem.* VII. 1032 When the barium salt [of pyromucic acid] mixed with soda-lime is heated, a compound called tetraphenol, $C_4H_4O$, distils over. *Ibid.* 1067 Schiff..prepares salicylide, $C_7H_4O_2$, and tetrasalicylide, $C_{28}H_{18}O_9$, by the action of phosphorous oxychloride on salicylic acid. **1880** *Athenæum* 11 Dec. 781/3 The Formation of Carbon Tetrabromide in the Manufacture of Bromine. **1880** ROSCOE & SCHORLEMMER *Treat. Chem.* II. II. 434 Rhodium tetrahydroxide $Rh(OH)_4$..this compound separates out as a green powder. **1888** MORLEY & MUIR *Watts' Dict. Chem.* I. 555 Tetrabromobenzene, $C_6H_2Br_4$; from *p*-nitro-benzoic acid and Br at 280°. **1899** SMITH *Richter's Org. Chem.* I. 187 Lead tetramethide, $Pb(CH_3)_4$, boils at 110°. **1900** *Jrnl. Soc. Dyers* XVI. 7 The solutions of the tetracetate in chloroform.

**b.** Prefixed to adjectives, in the names of acids, alcohols, aldehydes, ethers, salts, etc.; as *tetraso·dic*, containing four sodium atoms; so *tetrabo·ric*, etc.; *tetrethy·lic*, containing four ethyl groups; so *tetramy·lic*, etc.

**1868** WATTS *Dict. Chem.* V. 730 Tetraphosphamic acids..are amic acids derived from tetraphosphoric acid. **1868** *Fownes' Chem.* (ed. 10) 347 Tetrasodic Phosphate or Sodium Pyrophosphate is prepared by strongly heating common disodic orthophosphate..and re-crystallising. **1888** MORLEY & MUIR *Watts' Dict. Chem.* I. 528 Pyroboric (or tetraboric) acid, $2B_2O_3{\cdot}H_2O$ (= $H_2B_4O_7$).

**c.** In verbs and their pples. derived from sbs. as in a., as *tetrabrominated, -chlorinated, -hydrated* (containing 4 molecules of water).

**1857** MILLER *Elem. Chem.* III. 46 Tetrachlorinated Hydrochloric Ether, $C_4HCl.Cl_4$. **1873** WATTS *Fownes' Chem.* (ed. 11) 767 Propyl-benzene..forms with excess of bromine a viscid tetrabrominated compound.

**Tetrabasic** (tetrăbēⁱ·sik), *a. Chem.* [f. TETRA- + BASIC.] Of an acid: Containing four atoms of hydrogen replaceable by more electropositive elements or radicals. Of a salt: Derived from such an acid.

**1863–72** WATTS *Dict. Chem.* I. 459 Modes of distinguishing between monobasic, dibasic, tribasic, and tetrabasic acids. **1869** ROSCOE *Elem. Chem.* xv. 154 Pyrophosphoric Acid.. $H_4P_2O_7$...This acid is tetrabasic, the four atoms of hydrogen being replaceable, either all or in part, by metals.

**Tetrabelodon** to **-brachius**: see TETRA-.

**Tetrabranch** (te·trăbræŋk), *sb.* and *a. Zool.* [f. TETRA- + Gr. βράγχια gills.] **a.** *sb.* A four-gilled cephalopod: see next. **b.** *adj.* = TETRABRANCHIATE *a.* (*Cent. Dict.* 1891).

**1851** WOODWARD *Mollusca* I. 82 The Tetrabranchs could undoubtedly swim, by their respiratory jets. **1877** LE CONTE *Elem. Geol.* II. (1879) 305 If we divide all known Cephalopods into Dibranchs (two-gilled) and Tetrabranchs (four-gilled).

**Tetrabranchiate** (tetrăbræ·ŋkiĕt), *a.* and *sb. Zool.* [ad. mod.L. *tetrabranchiāt-um*: see prec. and -ATE² 2.] **a.** *adj.* Belonging to the *Tetrabranchiata*, an order of cephalopods (mostly extinct) having four branchiæ or gills. **b.** *sb.* A cephalopod belonging to this order; a tetrabranch.

**1835–6** *Todd's Cycl. Anat.* I. 557/1 The Sepia..manifests ..a near affinity to the Tetrabranchiate order. **1851** WOODWARD *Mollusca* I. 78 The shell of the tetrabranchiate cephalopods is an extremely elongated cone. **1872** NICHOLSON *Palæont.* 189 The Tetrabranchiate forms, with chambered shells, attained their maximum in the..Silurian period.

**Tetracamarous** to **-chirus**: see TETRA-.

‖ **Tetracaulodon** (-kǭ·lŏdǫn). [mod.L., f. TETRA- + Gr. καυλό-ς stem + ὀδούς, ὀδοντ- tooth.] An extinct elephantine genus having four tusks.

**1833** *Baltimore Med. & Surg. Jrnl.* Oct. (Mayne). **1839** G. ROBERTS *Dict. Geol.*, *Tetracaulodon*, a fossil extinct animal..allied to the mastodon;..having four projecting teeth. **1859** PAGE *Handbk. Geol. Terms* (1865) s. v., Professor Owen and others regard the *tetracaulodon* of Dr. Godman as the immature state of the *Mastodon Giganteus.*

**Tetrachord** (te·trăkǭɹd). [ad. Gr. τετράχορδον (*sc.* ὄργανον), a Greek musical instrument, f. τετρα-, TETRA- + χορδή string.]

**1.** An ancient musical instrument with four strings.

**1603** HOLLAND *Plutarch* Explan. Words, *Tetrachord*, an instrument in old time of foure strings. **1814** *Mann. & Cust.* in *Ann. Reg.* 490/1 Most of the Greek women sing in a pleasing manner, accompanying themselves with a tetrachord, the tones of which are an excellent support to the voice. **1849** DONALDSON *Theat. Greeks* (ed. 6) I. ii. 15 Terpander..substituted the seven-stringed cithara for the old tetrachord.

**2.** *Mus.* A scale-series of four notes, being the half of an octave. †**b.** The interval between the first and last notes of this series; a perfect fourth.

**1603** HOLLAND *Plutarch's Mor.* 1254 It was not for ignorance that in the Dorian tunes they forbare this Tetrachord. **1694** W. HOLDER *Harmony* iv. (1731) 66 (Table of Intervals), 4th, Diatessaron, Tetrachord. **1704** J. HARRIS *Lex. Techn.* I, *Tetrachord*, in Musick, is a Concord or Interval of 3 Tones. The Tetrachord of the Ancients was a rank of four Strings. **1847** GROTE *Greece* II. xvi. III. 285 Such were the three modes or scales, each including only a tetrachord, upon which the earliest Greek masters worked. **1890** *Athenæum* 4 Jan. 24/3 The tetrachord [on an Arab lute] thus comprised C, D, E flat, E, and F.

**c.** *transf.* A stanza of four lines. *rare.*

**1817** N. DRAKE *Shakspeare* I. 54 The Octant, of two tetrachords of disjunct alternate rhime. *Ibid.* 55 Three tetrachords in alternate rhime.

Hence **Tetracho·rdal** *a.*, of or pertaining to a tetrachord or tetrachords. Also ‖ **Tetrachordon** (-kǭ·ɹdǫn) [see quot.], an instrument like a cottage pianoforte in form, in which the strings are pressed against a revolving cylinder to produce the tone.

?**1850** SARAH A. GLOVER (*title*) Manual, containing a development of the *tetrachordal System. **1876** STAINER & BARRETT *Dict. Mus. Terms* s. v. *Tonic Sol-fa*, Miss Sarah A. Glover, of Norwich, about thirty years ago projected and taught..a system which she called the tetrachordal system, which was the Tonic Sol-fa notation in its original form. *Ibid.*, **Tetrachordon*..[so] called..from an idea that its sounds are similar to those produced by a string quartet.

**Tetrachotomous** (tetrăkǫ·tŏməs), *a. Zool.* and *Bot.* [f. Gr. τέτραχα in four parts + -τομος cut + -OUS.] Ramifying into four branches or divisions; doubly dichotomous. So **Tetracho·tomy**, division into four branches.

**1829** LOUDON *Encycl. Pl.* (1836) 403 *note*, Peduncles [of *Euphorbia*]..often dichotomous, trichotomous, or even tetrachotomous. **1858** C. J. ELLICOTT *Destiny Creature* Notes 172 Bull's theory is, in fact, really a 'tetrachotomy'—body, soul, spirit, and Holy Spirit.

**Tetrachromatic** to **-chronous**: see TETRA-.

**Tetraclade** (te·trăklēⁱd), *a. Zool.* [f. TETRA- + Gr. κλάδ-ος shoot, sprout.] Branching in four; having four arms or rays. So **Tetracladine** (-klēⁱ·dəin) *a.*, of or pertaining to the *Tetracladina*, a suborder of lithistid sponges having spicules branching into four or more processes; also **Tetracladose** (-klēⁱ·dōus) *a.* in same sense.

**1881** P. M. DUNCAN in *Jrnl. Linn. Soc.* XV. No. 86. 324 The quadrifid or tetraclade spicula. **1887** SOLLAS in *Encycl. Brit.* XXII. 417/1 (*Sponges*) Some or all of the rays of the primitive calthrops..may bifurcate once or twice and finally terminate by subdividing into numerous variously shaped processes; such a tetracladine desma characterizes one division of the Lithistid sponges. *Ibid.* 422/1 A distinct passage can be traced from the Tetracladose to the Rhabdocrepid group. *Ibid.*, The scleroblast..in the Tetracladine Lithistids lies in an angle between the arms.

**Tetraclone** to **Tetracron**: see TETRA-.

‖ **Tetracolon** (tetrakōu·lǫn). Pl. **-cola**. *Gr. Pros.* [a. Gr. τετράκωλον, adj. neut., having four members: see TETRA- and COLON².] A metrical period consisting of four cola or members.

**1706** PHILLIPS (ed. Kersey), *Tetracolon*,..a Stanza, or Division in Lyrick Poetry, consisting of four Verses or Lines. **1902** *Daily Chron.* 18 Dec. 3/1 The verses from the pen of Joseph and Eugenius, with their diversity and intricacy of metre (including a tetracolon heptastichon).

Hence **Tetracolic** (-kǭu·lik) *a.*, of or pertaining to a tetracolon; consisting of four cola.

**1891** in *Cent. Dict.*

**Tetract** (te·trækt), *a.* and *sb. Zool.* [f. TETRA- + Gr. ἀκτ-ίς, ἀκτῖν- ray.] **a.** *adj.* Having four rays or branches; quadriradiate. **b.** *sb.* A four-rayed sponge-spicule. So **Tetra·ctinal** *a.*, **Tetra·ctine** *a.* and *sb.*, **Tetra·ctinose** *a.*

**1886** *Proc. Zool. Soc.* 21 Dec. 581 The chief spicules are tetract. **1887** SOLLAS in *Encycl. Brit.* XXII. 416 (Fig. 12) *d.* calthrops (tetraxon tetractine). **1888** — in *Challenger Rep.* XXV. p. lix, *Tetractine.*—When all four actines of a tetraxon are present it is..a tetractine, but as the full designation of this required to distinguish it from a tetractinose triaxon is tetractine tetraxon, we shall substitute for it the equivalent 'calthrops'. **1891** *Cent. Dict.*, Tetractinal.

**Tetractinellid** (tĕ̆træktine·lid), *a.* and *sb. Zool.* [ad. mod.L. *Tetractinellidæ* (f. Gr. τετρα-, TETRA- + ἀκτίς (ἀκτῖν-) ray + L. dim. *-ella*): see -ID.] **a.** *adj.* Belonging to the *Tetractinellidæ* (also called *Tetractina*), a sub-order of siliceous sponges with four-rayed spicules. **b.** *sb.* A sponge of this order. So **Tetractine·llidan** *a.* and *sb.*, **Tetractine·lline** *a.*

**1891** *Cent. Dict.*, Tetractinellidan, Tetractinelline. **1892** *Nat. Sc.* Mar. 20 Tetractinellid spicules..occur..in the shallower regions. **1892** *Athenæum* 13 Feb. 218/2 The sponge remains..belong largely to the Monactinellidæ though tetractinellid, lithistid, and hexactinellid spicules are also present.

‖ **Tetractys** (tĕ̆træ·ktis). Also 8 **tetrachty(s**, 9 **tetraktys**. [a. Gr. τετρακτύς.] A set of four; the number four; *esp.* the Pythagorean name for the sum of the first four numbers (1 + 2 + 3 + 4 = 10) regarded as the source of all things.

**1603** HOLLAND *Plutarch's Mor.* 1317 That famous quaternarie of theirs, named Tetractys, which consisteth of foure nines, and amounteth to thirtie sixe, was their greatest oth. **1653** H. MORE *Conject. Cabbal.* Pref. (1713) 4 The Pythagoreans Oath, swearing by him that taught them the mystery of the Tetractys, or the number Four. *a* **1774** TUCKER *Lt. Nat.* (1834) II. 415 Pythagoras had his tetrachty, his mystic numbers, his symbols. **1865** GROTE *Plato* I. i. 12 *note*, The tetraktys (consecrated as the sum total of the first four numbers 1+2+3+4=10).

Hence **Tetra·ctysm**, the Pythagorean doctrine of the tetractys.

**1846** T. W. JENKYN *Baxter's Wks.* Pref. 50 Those who understand..what Tetractysm was to the Pythagoreans will ..comprehend what Triadism was to Baxter.

**Tetracyclic**: see TETRA-.

**Tetrad** (te·trăd). [ad. Gr. τετράς (τετραδ-) a group of four, the number four.]

**1.** A sum, group, or set of four; four (things, etc.) regarded as a single object of thought.

**1653** H. MORE *Conject. Cabbal.* (1713) 82 It was a solemn Oath..to swear by him that delivered to them the mystery of the Tetractys, Tetrad, or number Four. *Ibid.* [see TETRACTYS]. **1832** COLERIDGE *Table Talk* 24 Apr., The adorable tetractys, or tetrad, is the formula of God. **1895** *Athenæum* 2 Feb. 151/1 The great tetrad of senior wranglers of 1840 to 1843.

**2.** In *spec.* uses. **a.** *Chem.* An element, compound, or radical having a combining power of four units, i. e. of four atoms of hydrogen; a tetravalent element, etc.

**1865** *Reader* 1 Apr. 372/3 A tetratomic atom or tetrad. **1866** ROSCOE *Elem. Chem.* xxvii. 242 As in mineral chemistry we have radicals some of which are monads, and some dyads, triads, or tetrads. **1868** *Fownes' Chem.* (ed. 10) 259 Silicium and titanium are tetrads.

**b.** *Biol.* (*a*) A group of four cells, e. g. spores, pollen-grains. (*b*) A group of four chromosomes formed by the division of a single chromosome. (*c*) A quaternary unit of organization differentiated from a triad.

**1876** tr. *Schützenberger's Ferment.* 52 In the tetrads arranged in the form of a cross, we observe, also, two plane surfaces at right angles. **1882** VINES *Sachs' Bot.* 456 The cavity of the sporangium becomes filled with a granular plasma in which lie the mother-cells and the tetrads of spores...All the spores of the sixteen tetrads formed in the microsporangia reach maturity. **1883** [see 3]. **1895** OLIVER tr. *Kerner's Nat. Hist. Plants* II. 101 In *Rhododendron hirsutum* all the pollen-tetrads of an anther-cavity are held together by a mass of sticky viscin. *a* **1909** (in sense *b*) WILSON (cited in C. D. Suppl.) **1909** J. W. JENKINSON *Exper. Embryol.* 108 Granules of chromatin took the place of the tetrads and were unequally distributed to the spindle poles.

**c.** *Mus.* A chord of four notes (after TRIAD).

**1881** BROADHOUSE *Mus. Acoustics* 332 The great majority of major tetrads in Palestrina's Stabat Mater are in the positions 1, 10, 8, 5, 3, 2, 4, 9.

**d.** In ancient systems of arithmetical notation: A group or series of four characters corresponding to successive powers of ten.

**1883** SIR E. C. BAYLEY *Geneal. Mod. Numerals* II. 90 They [the Greeks] had however a system of 'octads' and 'tetrads' for expressing numbers of very high value.

**e.** *Math.* (See quot.)

**1889** CAYLEY *Math. Papers* XII. 590 The term 'tetrad' is used in two distinct..senses, viz. a tetrad denotes any four points; and it also denotes the four vertices of a self-conjugate tetrahedron in regard to a quadric surface...Two or more tetrads, in regard to one and the same quadric surface, are called similar tetrads.

**3.** *attrib.*, as *tetrad metal, term*; **tetrad-deme** *Biol.*, an aggregation of tetrads: see 2 b (*b*) and DEME² 2.

**1866** ODLING *Anim. Chem.* 17 The fourth or tetrad term of our series of typical hydrides. **1868** *Fownes' Chem.* (ed. 10) 445 Tin is a tetrad metal. **1883** P. GEDDES in *Encycl. Brit.* XVI. 843/2 Starting from the unit of the first order, the plastid or *monad*, and terming any undifferentiated aggregate a *deme*, we have a *monad-deme* integrating into a secondary unit or *dyad*, this rising through *dyad-demes* into a *triad*, this forming *triad-demes*, and these when differentiated becoming *tetrads*, the Botryllus-colony with which the evolution of compound individuality terminates being a *tetrad-deme*.

**Tetradactyl** (tetrădæ·ktil), *a.* and *sb.* Also -dactyle. [ad. Gr. τετραδάκτυλ-ος having four digits, f. τετρα-, TETRA- + δάκτυλος finger.] **a.** *adj.* Having four fingers or toes. **b.** *sb.* A four-toed animal (esp. a vertebrate). Hence **Tetradacty·lity, Tetrada·ctyly**, the condition of having four digits; also **Tetrada·ctylous** *a.* = a.

**1835** KIRBY *Hab. & Inst. Anim.* xvii. II. 194 The foot of birds is most commonly *tetradactyle, with one toe or thumb at the heel and the other three in front. **1847** WEBSTER, *Tetradactyl*, an animal having four toes. **1891** *Nature* 5 Feb. 329/2 If..a man has a finger amputated, his *tetradactylity is a somatogenic property. **1828** WEBSTER, *Tetradactylous. **1851** MANTELL *Petrifact.* i. § 3. 70 Narrow-toed tridactylous or tetradactylous species [of birds]. **1869** GILL-

MORE tr. *Figuier's Rept. & Birds* v. 421 The feet tetradactylous, and furnished with long and strong claws. **1904** *Amer. Nat.* XXXVIII. 3 From the ancestral canid Cynodictis of the Oligocene and lower Miocene,..to Lycaon in which structural 'tetradactyly prevails.

**Tetradarchy** (te·trădāɹki). [ad. Gr. τετραδαρχία, f. τετράς TETRAD + -αρχία rule.] = TETRARCHY.

**1839** THIRLWALL *Greece* VI. xlv. 14 Philip revived the distinction of the tetradarchies. **1842** *Smith's Dict. Grk. & Rom. Antiq.* s. v. *Tagus*, The four divisions of the country, tetrarchies or tetradarchies, which he re-established.

**Te·tradeca:ne.** *Chem.* [f. Gr. τετρα- four + δέκα ten + -ANE 2 b.] The saturated hydrocarbon or paraffin of the 14-carbon series, $C_{14}H_{30}$, = tetradecyl hydride; a waxy solid.

**1877** WATTS *Fownes' Chem.* (ed. 12) II. 50 The boiling points and specific gravities of the higher paraffins of unknown structure..are as follows:.. Tetradecane $C_{14}H_{30}$. Boiling point 236–240°.

So **Tetradecene** = *tetradecylene*. **Tetrade·cenyl**, the radical $C_{14}H_{27}$, as in *tetradecenyl alcohol*, $C_{14}H_{27}.OH$, *t. aldehyde*, etc. **Tetradeceno·ic** *a.* in *tetradecenoic acid*, $C_{14}H_{26}O_2$, a liquid boiling in vacuo at 275° to 280° C.; *t. aldehyde*, $C_{14}H_{26}O$, an oil not solid at -20° C. **Tetrade·cinene** $C_{14}H_{26} = CMe:C.C_{11}H_{23}$. **Tetradeco·ic** *a.*, in *t. acid*, $C_{14}H_{28}O_2 = C_5H_{11}.CH(C_7H_{15}).CO_2H$, a liquid (not solid at -10° C.), got by the action of moist argentic oxide, $Ag_2O$, on the aldehyde; *tetradecoic aldehyde*, $C_{14}H_{28}O$, obtained in tables very soluble in alcohol, a product of the action of sodium on an ethereal solution of œnanthol. **Tetrade·cyl** or **Tetrade·catyl**, the monatomic alcohol radical, $C_{14}H_{29}$, of this series; also *attrib.* = *tetradecylic*, as in *tetradecyl alcohol*. Hence **Tetradecy·lic** *a.*, of or pertaining to this radical; so **Tetrade·cylene**, the olefine of this series, $C_{14}H_{28} = CH_2:CH.C_{12}H_{25}$, a liquid substance; also *attrib.* as in *tetradecylene glycol*.

**1868** WATTS *Dict. Chem.* V. 728 *Tetradecyl*, or *Tetradecatyl*..also called *Myristyl*. The fourteenth term of the series of alcohol-radicles, $C_nH_{2n+1}$. *Tetradecylic hydride*, $C_{14}H_{30}$, is one of the constituents of American petroleum... *Tetradecylic* or *Myristic Alcohol*, or *Methal*, $C_{14}H_{30}O$, is one of the constituents of spermaceti.

**Tetradecapod** (tetrăde·kăpǫd), *a.* and *sb. Zool.* [ad. mod.L. *Tetradecapoda*, f. TETRA- + DECA- ten: cf. DECAPODA.] **a.** *adj.* Having fourteen feet; belonging to the *Tetradecapoda*, an order of Crustaceans. **b.** *sb.* A crustacean of this order. So (in same senses) **Tetradeca·podan** *a.* and *sb.*; **Tetradeca·podous** *a.*

**1852** DANA *Crust.* II. 1528 The two types, the Decapodan and Tetradecapodan. *Ibid.* 1576 Among the Tetradecapods there is the Chilian genus *Amphoroidea*. **1854** *Chamb. Jrnl.* I. 26/1 Attached to each of them was a small, pale, tetradecapodous animal. **1862** DANA *Man. Geol.*, *Crust.* 153 Fourteen-footed species' or Tetradecapods.

† **Tetradiapa·son.** *Mus. Obs.* [f. TETRA- + DIAPASON.] An interval of four octaves

**1704** J. HARRIS *Lex. Techn.* I, *Tetradiapason*, a Quadruple Diapason,..otherwise called a Quadruple Eighth, or Nine and Twentieth. **1801** in BUSBY *Dict. Mus.*

**Tetradic** (tĭtræ·dik), *a.* [f. TETRAD + -IC. Cf. F. *tétradique* (in Cotgr.).] Of, pertaining to, or of the nature of a tetrad.

**1788** T. TAYLOR *Proclus* (1792) I. 179 The tetradic ternary, and the triadic quaternary.

**b.** *Chem.* That is a tetrad; tetravalent.

**1868** *Fownes' Chem.* (ed. 10) 257. **1872** WATTS *Dict. Chem.* VI. 237 Carbon, which combines with 4 atoms of hydrogen, is tetratomic, tetradic, or quadrivalent. **1877** — *Fownes' Chem.* (ed. 12) I. 267 With silver..it [oxygen] forms the two oxides, $Ag_2O$ and $Ag_4O$, in the latter of which it is tetradic.

**c.** *Anc. Pros.* (*a*) Containing four different metres or rhythms. (*b*) Composed of groups of systems, each of which contains four unlike systems.

**1891** in *Cent. Dict.*

**Tetradite** (te·trădəit). *Ch. Hist.* [ad. late Gr. τετραδίτης, pl. -αι, f. τετράς, -αδ- TETRAD: see -ITE 1.] (See quots.)

**1727–41** CHAMBERS *Cycl.*, *Tetraditæ*, *Tetradites*, in antiquity, a name given to several different sects of heretics, out of some particular respect they bore to the number four. **1842** BRANDE *Dict. Sc.* etc., *Tetradites*,..the Manichees and others, who believed the Godhead to consist of four instead of three persons, bore this name. **1882–3** *Schaff's Encycl. Relig. Knowl.* I. 601 Their adversaries called them Tetradites, Τετραδῖται, because they had four gods,—the Father, the Son, the Holy Spirit, and the Divine Being—in which those three were united.

**Tetradon**: see TETRODON.

**Tetradrachm** (te·trădræm). *Gr. Antiq.* Also in L. and Gr. forms 6–9 **tetradrachma**, 7–8 **-drachmon**. [ad. Gr. τετράδραχμον: see TETRA- and DRACHM.] A silver coin of ancient Greece, of the value of four drachms: see DRACHM 1.

**1579–80** NORTH *Plutarch* (1595) 313 Foure Tetradrachmas a day. **1770** SWINTON in *Phil. Trans.* LXI. 92 A fine Punic tetradrachm. **1807** ROBINSON *Archæol. Græca* v. xxvi. 567 The less ancient tetradrachms were current during four or five centuries. **1879** H. PHILLIPS *Notes Coins* 6 The cistophori are tetradrachms bearing as their generic type a wreath and berries of ivy, surrounding a chest whence issue serpents.

Hence **Tetradrachmal** (-dræ·kmăl) *a.*, of or pertaining to a tetradrachm.

**1770** SWINTON in *Phil. Trans.* LXI. 98 The medal..is of the tetradrachmal form. **1771** RAPER *ibid.* 533 Had the first Denarius been Didrachmal or Tetradrachmal, so well-informed a writer must have known it.

**Tetradymite** (tĭtræ·diməit). *Min.* [a. Ger. *tetradymit* (W. Haidinger, 1831), f. Gr. τετράδυμ-ος fourfold + -ITE 1.] Telluride of bismuth, found in pale steel-grey laminæ with a bright metallic lustre. (The name has also been applied to WEHRLITE.)

**1850** ANSTED *Elem. Geol.* § 491 Tetradymite, Tellurium, and bismuth. **1859** PAGE *Handbk. Geol. Terms* (1865), *Tetradymite*.., sulphotelluride of bismuth..from the quadruple macles in which its crystals usually appear. **1874** *Proc. Amer. Phil. Soc.* XIV. 224 The sulphurous variety of tetradymite has been observed at several new localities.

**Tetradymous** (tĭtræ·dimǝs), *a. Bot.* [f. Gr. τετράδυμ-ος (see prec.) + -OUS.] Said of an agaric having each perfect lamella or gill separated from the next by four equal short lamellæ and three longer ones alternately placed, thus |ıllılı|; see also quots.

[**1856** HENSLOW *Dict. Bot. Terms*, *Tetradymus*, where every alternate lamella of an Agaric is shorter than the two contiguous to it, and one complete lamella terminates a set of every four pairs of short and long... Also, where four cells or cases are combined.] **1866** *Treas. Bot.*, *Tetradymous*, having four cells or cases.

‖ **Tetradynamia** (te:trădinē·miă). *Bot.* [mod.L. (Linnæus, 1735), f. Gr. τετρα-, TETRA- + δύναμ-ις power, strength + -IA 1: cf. DIDYNAMIA.] The fifteenth class in the Linnæan Sexual System, comprising plants which bear hermaphrodite flowers with six stamens in pairs, four of which are longer than the others; corresponding to the N.O. *Cruciferæ*. Hence **Tetradyna·mian** *a.*, = *Tetradynamous*; *sb.*, a plant of the class *Tetradynamia*; **Tetradyna·mious, Tetrady·namous** *adjs.*, of or pertaining to this class; having four longer and two shorter stamens.

**1760** J. LEE *Introd. Bot.* II. ii. (1765) 74 *Tetradynamia*... There are in the Flowers of this Class six Stamina, four of which are longer than the rest. **1785** MARTYN *Rousseau's Bot.* ix. (1794) 92 *Tetradynamia* is..one of your first acquaintance under the gentler appellation of cruciform flowers. **1828** WEBSTER, *Tetradynamian*. **1830** LINDLEY *Nat. Syst. Bot.* 20 The stamens are occasionally tetradynamous. **1860** MAYNE *Expos. Lex.*, Tetradynamious, or tetradynamous.

**Tetraëdral**, etc.: see TETRAHEDRAL, etc.

**Tetraëterid** to **-gnathian**: see TETRA-.

**Tetraglot** (te·trăglǫt), *a.* [ad. Gr. type *τετραγλωττ-ος, f. τετρα-, TETRA- + γλῶττα tongue: cf. POLYGLOT.] Speaking four languages; written or composed in four languages. So † **Tetraglo·ttic**, † **Tetraglo·ttical** *adjs. Obs.* in same sense.

**1580** FLEMING in *Baret's Alv.* Aaaa j, This Quadruple Dictionarie, or Lexicon tetraglottical. **1682** WHELER *Journ. Greece* I. 32 He hath printed a Dictionary Tetraglot, Ancient and Vulgar Greek, Latin, and Italian. **1721** BAILEY, *Tetraglottick*. **1881** *N. & Q.* 6th Ser. III. 456/2 A tetraglot dictionary, a century older still.

**Tetragon** (te·trăgǫn), *sb.* (*a.*). Also 7 -gone. [ad. Gr. τετράγωνον a quadrangle: see TETRA- and -GON. So late L. *tetragōn-um*, F. *tetragone* (14th c. in Godef. *Compl.*).]

**1.** *Geom.* A figure having four angles and four sides; a quadrangle considered as one of the polygons. *Regular tetragon*, a square.

**1630** LENNARD tr. *Charron's Wisd.* (1658) 22 In figures the Pentagone contains the Tetragone. **1690** LEYBOURN *Curs. Math.* 588 Half the Angle of the Tetragon or Square. **1827** HUTTON *Course Math.* I. 283 An Equilateral Triangle is also a Regular Figure of three sides, and the Square is one of four: the former being also called a Trigon, and the latter a Tetragon.

**2.** A square fort; a quadrangular building or block of buildings. Cf. QUADRANGLE *sb.* 3.

**1669** STAYNRED *Fortification* 1 A Tetragon or Square Fort. **1698** FRYER *Acc. E. India & P.* 57 The Fort is a Tetragone from Corner to Corner. **1884** *Daily News* 5 Feb. 5/7 Populations living in immense tetragons of brick and stone.

**b.** A quadrangular court surrounded by buildings or walls, e. g. a college quadrangle.

**3.** *Astrol.* The aspect of two planets when they are 90° distant from one another relatively to the earth; the square or quadrate aspect.

*a* **1626** BP. ANDREWES *Serm.* (1856) I. 185 In the horoscope of Christ's nativity...Whether a trigon or no, this tetragon I am sure there was. **1727–41** CHAMBERS *Cycl.*, *Tetragon*, ..an aspect of two planets with regard to the earth, when they are distant from each other a fourth part of a circle, or 90°... The tetragon is expressed by the character □. [**1819** J. WILSON *Compl. Dict. Astrol.*, *Tetragonus*.]

**B.** *adj.* Four-cornered, tetragonal, quadrangular.

**1794** MORSE *Amer. Geog.* 553 The remains of an ancient.. fortification: it is now a regular tetragon terrace, about four feet high, with bastions at each angle.

**Tetragonal** (tĭtræ·gŏnăl), *a.* (*sb.*) Also (in sense 4) -el. [f. prec. + -AL. So mod.F. *tétragonal*.]

**1.** Of or pertaining to a tetragon; having four angles; quadrangular.

**1571** DIGGES *Pantom.* IV. T j b, When any equiangle triangle, square, or Pentagonum is..described within a circle, ..their sides are called the trigonall, tetragonall and pentagonall Cordes of that circle. **1667** *Phil. Trans.* II. 627 Two Tetragonal Prismes of Tendons. **1874** COUES *Birds N. W.* 592 An elongated pyramid with a tetragonal base.

**2.** *Bot.* and *Zool.* Quadrangular in section, like a 'square' rod; tetraquetrous.

**1753** CHAMBERS *Cycl. Supp.* s.v. *Leaf*, A leaf that has, instead of three ribs or edges, four or five, is..called tetragonal, pentagonal, &c. **1853** ROYLE *Mat. Med.* (ed. 2) 641 Norway Spruce Fir. Leaves scattered, tetragonal. **1875** C. C. BLAKE *Zool.* 109 The bill is elongate,..tetragonal, and acuminate.

† **3.** *Astrol.* = QUARTILE *a.*, QUADRATE *a.* 2. *Obs.*

**1646** SIR T. BROWNE *Pseud. Ep.* IV. xii. 213 Reckoning on unto the seventh day, the Moone will be in a Tetragonall or Quadrate aspect, that is, 4. signes removed from that wherein the disease began.

**4.** *Her.* Represented as quadrangular: see quot.

*c* **1828** BERRY *Encycl. Her.* I. Gloss., *Tetragonel Pyramids*, piles are generally considered to represent wedges,..they are sometimes borne..square, in which latter case they may be termed square piles, or *tetragonel pyramids reversed*. **1889** ELVIN *Dict. Her.*, *Tetragonal Pyramids*.

**5.** *Cryst.* Applied to a system of crystallization in which the three axes are at right angles, the two lateral axes being equal, and the vertical of a different length.

**1868** DANA *Min.* (ed. 5) Introd. 21 Crystallography.. systems of crystallization... Having only the lateral axes equal. The Tetragonal and Hexagonal. **1878** GURNEY *Crystallogr.* 38 If four symmetral planes only intersect in the same straight line it is called an axis of tetragonal symmetry. **1879** RUTLEY *Stud. Rocks* ix. 77 Crystals belonging to the tetragonal and hexagonal systems are singly refractive when viewed in the direction of the principal crystallographic axis.

† **B.** *sb.* = TETRAGON 1. *Obs. rare*—[1].

**1684** tr. *Agrippa's Van. Arts* To Rdr., The intricate Geometrician will imprison me in his Triangles and Tetragonals.

Hence **Tetra·gonally** *adv.*, in a tetragonal manner or form; **Tetra·gonalness.**

**1727** BAILEY vol. II, *Tetragonalness*, the having four Corners, Squareness. **1888** *Cassell's Encycl. Dict.*, Tetragonally.

**Tetragonidium**: see TETRA- 1.

**Tetragonism** (tĭtræ·gŏniz'm). ? *Obs.* [ad. Gr. τετραγωνισμός squaring, quadrature; see TETRAGON and -ISM.] The squaring of the circle; the quadrature of any curve.

**1704** J. HARRIS *Lex. Techn.* I, *Tetragonism*, with some Foreign Writers is the same as the Quadrature of the Circle. **1715** tr. *Pancirollus' Rerum Mem.* II. xvii. 381 [They] affirm the Invention of the Tetragonism we are speaking of. **1727–41** in CHAMBERS *Cycl.*

So † **Tetra·gonist**, one who attempts the squaring of the circle; † **Tetragoni·stic**, † **Tetragoni·stical** *adjs.*, of or pertaining to tetragonism; *tetragonistic*(*al calculus*, the differential calculus.

**1674** BOYLE *Excell. Theol.* I. iii. 104 Such famous writers as Scaliger, Longomontanus, and other Tetragonists. **1710** J. HARRIS *Lex. Techn.* II, *Tetragonistick Calculus*, is the same with the Summatory or Differential Calculus of Leibnitz. **1727** BAILEY vol. II, *Tetragonistical Calculus*.

**Tetragonous** (tĭtræ·gŏnǝs), *a. Bot.* [f. TETRAGON or late L. *tetragōn-us* tetragonal + -OUS.] Having four angles; = TETRAGONAL *a.* 2.

**1760** J. LEE *Introd. Bot.* II. xxii. (1765) 125 Seed, a single one, oblong, often tetragonous. **1870** HOOKER *Stud. Flora* 245 Convolvulus arvensis,..peduncle..4-gonous. **1872** OLIVER *Elem. Bot.* App. 310 [Common Wheat] Inflorescence spicate,..tetragonous.

**Tetragram** (te·trăgræm). [In sense 1, ad. Gr. τὸ τετράγραμμον (Clem. Alex. 666), 'the (word) of four letters', f. τετρα- four- + γράμμα letter; in sense 2 from γραμμή stroke, line.]

**1.** A word of four letters; = next.

**1870** BREWER *Dict. Phrase & Fable* s.v. *Tetragrammaton*. The Greek *Zeus*, Latin *Jove* and *Deus*, Persian *Soru*, Assyrian *Adad*, Arabian *Alla*, Egyptian *Amon*, German *Gott*, and a host of other words significant of Deity, are tetragrams. **1882–3** *Schaff's Encycl. Relig. Knowl.* I. 27 The Jews pronounced the tetragram YHWH by giving to it the vowels of Adonai.

**2.** *Geom.* The figure composed of four straight lines in a plane and their six points of intersection: commonly called *complete quadrilateral*.

**1863** R. TOWNSEND *Mod. Geom.* I. vii. 145 Thus, for instance, in a tetrastigm or tetragram every line of connection of two points or point of intersection of two lines is said to be the opposite of that of the remaining two.

‖ **Tetragrammaton** (te:trăgræ·mătǫn). Pl. -ata. [a. Gr. (τὸ) τετραγράμματον (Philo 2. 152), 'the (word) of four letters', neut. of τετραγράμματος, adj. f. τετρα- four + γραμμα(τ- letter.] A word of four letters; *spec.* the Hebrew word written יהוה = YHWH or JHVH (vocalized as YaHWeH, JaHVeH, or JeHoVaH, q.v.); often substituted for that word (regarded as ineffable), and treated as a mysterious symbol of the name of God; sometimes used as a title of the Deity (see quot. 1689).

*a* **1400–50** *Alexander* 1592 Þe grettest of all gods names, Þis title, Tetragramaton. **1577** tr. *Bullinger's Decades* (1592) 608 Among all the names of God that is the most excellent, which they call *Tetragrammaton*, that is (if we may so say), the fower lettered name. **1606** N. BAXTER *Sir P. Sidney's Ourania* C j b, Some call him mightie Tetragrammaton Of letters fower in composition. **1649** JER. TAYLOR *Gt. Exemp.* I. Ad Sect. v. 61 The Tetragrammaton or adoreable Mystery of the Patriarchs. **1689** T. PLUNKET *Char. Gd. Commander* 44 But the tremenduos Tetragrammaton Will not, not always be a looker on. **1768** TUCKER *Lt. Nat.* (1834) I. 463 The Quaternion is the holy Tetragrammaton, the same awful name variously pronounced among the sons of men: whether Jeva, Isis, Jove, Θεος, Zeus, or Deus; or..Tien, Alla, Dios, Idio, Dieu, or Lord; for these are all Tetragrammata. **1891** T. K. CHEYNE *Orig. Ps.* vi. 300 The earliest Greek copies reproduced the Tetragrammaton.

**b.** *gen.* with *a* and *pl.* A word of four letters used as a symbol.

**1656** H. More *Enthus. Tri.* (1712) 50 In a Tetragrammaton there are five Parts, four Letters, and the Tittle Jod, from which come Nephesh, Ruach, Neschamah, Chajah, and Jachidah, five Persons of the Soul. **1665** Wither *Lord's Prayer* 17 Our English tongue as well as the Hebrew hath a Tetragrammaton, whereby God may be named; to wit, Good.

† **c.** *fig.* An emblem or symbol of something sacred. *Obs. rare.*

**1601** A. Copley *Answ. Let. Jesuit. Gent.* 79 They are so passing vain-glorious a Societie, that call ye it the verie Tetragrammaton of the Catholicke church.

† **d.** as *adj.* Consisting of four letters. *Obs.*

*a* **1610** Babington *Exp. Cath. Faith* II. (1637) 195 O name that cannot bee expressed! O name truly tetragrammaton! **1614** Selden *Titles Hon.* 50 The Tetragrammaton name of the Almightie.

Hence † **Tetragramma·tical** *a.*, consisting of four letters; pertaining to the or a tetragrammaton; **Tetragrammato·nic** *a.* [irreg. for *-atic*], of or pertaining to the tetragrammaton.

**1759** J. Yeomans *Abecedarian* (title-p.), A Discourse on the Word, or A-Tau, tetragrammatical. **1895** *Funk's Standard Dict.*, Tetragrammatonic.

‖ **Tetragynia** (tetrădʒi·niă), *a. Bot.* [mod.L., f. Tetra- + Gr. γυνή woman, female, taken in sense 'female organ, pistil'.] The name of an order or division in many of the classes of the Linnæan Sexual System of plants, comprising those having four pistils. Hence **Te·tragyn** (*rare*), a plant of this order; **Tetragy·nian, Tetragy·nious, Tetra·gynous** *adjs.*, belonging to this order of any class; having four pistils.

**1760** J. Lee *Introd. Bot.* II. viii. (1765) 92 *Tetragynia*, comprehending such Plants as have four Styles. **1828** Webster, *Tetragyn*..in botany, a plant having four pistils. *Tetragynian*, having four pistils. **1860** Mayne *Expos. Lex.*, *Tetragynius*,..tetragynious. **1899** *Syd. Soc. Lex.*, *Tetragynous*, having a gynecium of four carpels. *Mod. Ilex*, the Holly, is an example of Tetrandria, Tetragynia.

**Tetrahedral** (tetrăhī·drăl, -he·drăl), *a.* Also 8–9 tetraedral. [f. late Gr. τετράεδρος (see Tetrahedron) + -al.]

**1. a.** Having four sides (in addition to the base or ends); enclosed or contained laterally by four plane surfaces, as a *tetrahedral prism* or *pyramid*. *Tetrahedral angle, quoin*, one bounded by four planes meeting at a common apex.

**1794** G. Adams *Nat. & Exp. Philos.* II. xiv. 46 The internal cavity is found to be lined with beautiful tetrahedral prisms. **1812** Sir H. Davy *Chem. Philos.* 124 Four particles may compose a tetrahedron, five a tetraedral pyramid, six an octaedron. **1828** Stark *Elem. Nat. Hist.* II. 139 Body tetraedral, furrowed above. **1878** Gurney *Crystallogr.* 85 The tetrahedral quoins..of the rhombic dodecahedron.

**b.** Quadrilateral, quadrangular. (Also in *comb.*)

**1816** Kirby & Sp. *Entomol.* xxvii. (1818) II. 491 Cells with regular tetrahedral bottoms. *Ibid.* 494 The tetrahedral-bottomed transition cells..still preserved their usual shape of hexagonal prisms.

**2.** Of or pertaining to a tetrahedron; having the form of a tetrahedron; *spec.* in *Cryst.*, belonging to a division of the isometric system of which the regular tetrahedron is the characteristic form.

**1805–17** R. Jameson *Char. Min.* (ed. 3) 200 *Tetrahedral* (Haüy *tetraëdre*), when the crystal has the regular tetrahedron as a secondary form. Example, Tetrahedral blende. **1876** Harley *Mat. Med.* (ed. 6) 369 The spores are minute, tetrahedral granules, each presenting four facets, and are minutely ridged by a hexagonal network. **1903** A. Graham Bell in *Nat. Geog. Mag.* June 225 The Tetrahedral principle in Kite Structure. When a tetrahedral frame is provided with aero-surfaces of silk or other material..it becomes a tetrahedral kite, or kite having the form of a tetrahedron.

Hence **Tetrahe·drally** *adv.*, in a tetrahedral manner or form. So **Tetrahe·dric, Tetrahe·drical** *adjs.*, tetrahedral.

**1860** Mayne *Expos. Lex.*, *Tetrahedricus*,..tetrahedrical. **1864** Webster, *Tetrahedrally* (citing Dana). **1882** Vines *Sachs' Bot.* 13 The four spores or pollen-grains do not lie in one plane but are arranged tetrahedrally, and have moreover a somewhat tetrahedral form. *Ibid.* 438. **1890** *Smithsonian Rep.* 367 This latter [double linking] is an immediate consequence of the tetrahedric conception.

**Tetrahedrid** (tetrăhī·drid, -he·drid), *a. Cryst.* [f. as prec. + -id [2].] = Tetrahedral *a.* 2.

**1895** Story-Maskelyne *Crystallogr.* 208 Tetrahedrid merosymmetry. The second case of holo-systematic hemi-symmetry, in which every normal is represented by a single face, is that [etc.]. *Ibid.* 206, 207, 210.

**Tetrahedrite** (tetrăhī·drəit, -he·drəit). *Min.* [ad. Ger. *tetraëdrit* (W. Haidinger 1845), f. as prec. + *-it*, -ite [1] 2 b.] Native sulphide of antimony and copper, with various elements sometimes replacing one or the other of these, often occurring in tetrahedral crystals; fahlerz, fahlore.

**1868** Watts *Dict. Chem.* V. 729 Large tetrahedral crystals of tetrahedrite, having mostly a rough dull surface, are found in the Cornish mines near St. Austel. **1900** L. Fletcher in *Brit. Mus. Return* 156.

**Tetrahedroid** (tetrăhī·droid, -he·droid), *a.* and *sb.* [f. as prec. + -oid.] **a.** *adj.* Resembling or approaching the form of a tetrahedron. **b.** *sb. Geom.* The envelope of a quadric surface which touches eight given straight lines.

**1889** *Cayley's Math. Papers* I. 587 *note*, The surface here considered, the Tetrahedroid, is the general homographic transformation of the wave surface. **1899** *Geog. Jrnl.* Mar. 251 Causes, which..would go in the direction of producing tetrahedral, or tetrahedroid, deformation.

**Tetrahedron** (tetrăhī·drŏn, -he·drŏn). *Geom.* Pl. **-a** or **-ons**. Also 6–9 **tetraedron**; 6–8 **tetra(h)edrum**. [ad. late Gr. τετράεδρον sb., prop. neut. of τετράεδρος adj. four-sided, f. τετρα- four + ἕδρα base.] A solid figure contained by four plane triangular faces, a triangular pyramid; *spec.* the *regular tetrahedron*, the first of the five regular solids, contained by four equilateral triangles. Hence, any solid body, esp. a crystal, of this form.

*Orthogonal tetrahedron*, one in which the opposite edges, taken in pairs, are at right angles to one another. *Polar tetrahedron*, one of which the faces are polar to the vertices of another tetrahedron.

**1570** Billingsley *Euclid* xi. def. xxii. 319 A Tetrahedron is a solide which is contained vnder fower triangles equall and equilater. **1571** Digges *Pantom.* iv. Tij, Tetraedron.. a body Geometricall. *Ibid. margin*, Tetraedrum. **1653** H. More *Antid. Ath.* I. vii. § 5 The notion or idea of God ..is no more arbitrarious or fictitious than the notion of a cube or tetraedrum or any other of the regular bodies in Geometry. **1706** W. Jones *Syn. Palmar. Matheseos* 234 The Tetraedrum of 4 solid ∠s. **1800** tr. *Lagrange's Chem.* I. 359 Susceptible of crystallizing in tetraedra. **1875** Bennett & Dyer *Sachs' Bot.* 50 They [crystalloids] appear as cubes, tetrahedra, octohedra, rhombohedra, and in other forms. **1878** Gurney *Crystallogr.* 92 Tetrahedrons are contained by four equiangular triangles.

**Tetrahexahe·dron.** *Geom.* [f. Tetra- + Hexahedron.] A solid figure contained by twenty-four planes. † **a.** See quots. 1805–17, 1860. *Obs.* **b.** = Tetrakis-hexahedron. Hence **Tetrahexahe·dral** *a.*, pertaining to, or having the form of, a tetrahexahedron.

**1805–17** R. Jameson *Char. Min.* (ed. 3) 204 [A crystal is] tetrahexahedral..when its surface consists of..four..ranges of planes, disposed six and six above each other. **1828** Webster, *Tetrahexahedral*, in *crystalography*, exhibiting four ranges of faces, one above another, each range containing six faces. **1847** *Ibid.*, *Tetrahexahedron*, a solid bounded by twenty-four equal faces, four corresponding to each face of the cube. **1860** Mayne *Expos. Lex.*, *Tetrahexahedron*,..a figure having four ranges of bases, or faces, six in each range.

**Tetrahydric** (tetrăhəi·drik), *a. Chem.* [f. Tetra- + Hydric.] Applied to an alcohol containing four hydroxyl groups, e.g. erythrite, $C_4H_6(OH)_4$.

**1888** Morley & Muir *Watts' Dict. Chem.* I. 101 Erythrite is the only fatty tetra-hydric alcohol known.

**Tetra-icosane** (tetră,əi·kosēin). *Chem.* Also tetrak-, tetrac-. [f. Gr. τετρα- four + εἴκοσι twenty + -ane 2 b.] The saturated hydrocarbon or paraffin of the 24-carbon series, $C_{24}H_{50}$ = $CH_3(CH_2)_{22}CH_3$, a solid waxy substance.

**1894** Morley & Muir *Watts' Dict. Chem.* IV. 673/1 Tetra-icosane, $C_{24}H_{50}$. **1895** *Funk's Stand. Dict.*, Tetrakosane. **1909** *Cent. Dict. Suppl.*, Tetracosane.

So **Tetra-icoso·ic** *acid*, $C_{23}H_{47}.CO_2H$, a crystalline powder, very soluble in hot alcohol, occurring in the soap got by heating carnaüba wax with aqueous NaOH.

**1894** Morley & Muir *Watts' Chem. Dict.* IV. 673/1.

**Tetrakaidekahedron.** [f. Gr. τετρακαιδεκα- fourteen + ἕδρα base.] A fourteen-sided solid figure. Also *tessarescædecahedron* (Cent. Dict.).

**1894** *Athenæum* 17 Feb. 216/3 At the request of Lord Kelvin..Mr. J. J. Walker exhibited and described Lord Kelvin's models of his 'Tetrakaidekahedron'.

**Te·trakisa·zo-.** *Chem.* [f. Gr. τετράκις four times + Azo-.] Occurring in names of compounds containing four azo- groups.

**Te·trakisdo:decahe·dron.** *Cryst.* [f. Gr. τετράκις four times + Dodecahedron.] A solid body bounded by forty-eight triangular planes; also called Hexakisoctahedron, *octakis-hexahedron*, *tetrakonta-octahedron*, and *forty-eight scalenohedron*; esp. the variety of this described in quot.

**1895** Story-Maskelyne *Crystallogr.* 204 The complete form has the character of a pyramidion developement of the rhomb-dodecahedron, each face of the latter figure being surmounted by a rhomb-based pyramid, to which it forms a conterminous base. These therefore are the forms that may be correctly designated as *tetrakisdodecahedra* or *dodecahedrid pyramidions.*

**Te·trakis-hexahe·dron.** [f. Gr. τετράκις four times + Hexahedron.] A solid figure contained by twenty-four equal triangular planes, having the appearance of a cube with a low pyramid raised on each of its six faces. (In *Cryst.* belonging to the isometric system.) In *Geom.* the name is specially applied to the figure when the pyramids are of such a height that all the adjacent faces are equally inclined to each other, so that the figure meets the sphere circumscribing the fundamental cube at fourteen points. Also called *tetrahexahedron* (b), *cube-pyramidion*, and *fluoroid.*

**1878** Gurney *Crystallogr.* 86 A four-faced cube, or more technically a tetrakishexahedron. **1887** *Athenæum* 10 Sept. 345/2 The new crystals are sharply defined cubes, of which some have the edges replaced by faces of the rhombic dodecahedron or of a tetrakishexahedron. **1895** Story-Maskelyne *Crystallogr.* 195–6 The *tetrakis-hexahedron*.. presents the aspect of a cube each face of which is surmounted by an obtuse pyramid, and it may, on this account, be termed the cube-pyramidion...The figure is a twenty-four-faced isoscelohedron.

**Te·trakism.** *nonce-wd.* [irreg. f. Gr. τετράκις four times + -ism.] A theory or doctrine of four (persons, aspects, etc.).

**1856** Emerson *Eng. Traits* i. 18 Coleridge..went on defining, or rather refining..talked of 'trinism' and 'tetrakism', and much more.

**Tetraleioclone, -lemma**: see Tetra- 1.

† **Te·tralogue.** *Obs. rare.* [f. Gr. τετρα-, Tetra- + λόγος speech, word, etc., after *monologue, dialogue*: cf. next.] A conversation between four persons or parties; also = Tetralogy.

**1649** Roberts *Clavis Bibl.* 384 This song is also digested in forme..of a Tetralogue betwixt the Bridegroom, Christ; the Bridegrooms friends,..The Bride her selfe,..And The Churches Companions. **1822** T. Mitchell *Aristoph.* I. p. cxxvi, The works of Plato are usually divided into tetralogues.

**Tetralogy** (tĭtræ·lŏdʒi). [ad. Gr. τετραλογία, f. τετρα-, Tetra- + -λογία, -logy. Cf. F. *tétralogie.*]

**1.** *Gr. Antiq.* A series of four dramas, three tragic (the *trilogy*) and one satyric, exhibited at Athens at the festival of Dionysus.

**1656** Stanley *Hist. Philos.* v. (1701) 158/1 He made a compleat Tetralogy (four Drama's, as the manner was, when they contested, to be presented at four several Festivals). **1840** tr. *C. O. Müller's Hist. Lit. Greece* xxiv. § 2 In the several tetralogies, however, the satyrical drama must have been lost or perhaps never existed.

**b.** Hence, Any series of four related dramatic or literary compositions.

*a* **1742** [Warburton] *Ricardus Aristarchus* in *Pope's Dunciad* (1743) p. xxxi, May we not then be excused, if for the future we consider the Epics of Homer, Virgil, and Milton, together with this our poem, as a complete Tetralogy, in which the last worthily holdeth the place or station of the satyric piece? **1862** Goulburn *Pers. Relig.* iv. xii, A Tetralogy of Parables. **1883** *St. James' Gaz.* 3 Feb. 5 Wagner's 'tetralogy' of operas.

**2.** A set of four speeches. Cf. Tetralogue.

**1661** Blount *Glossogr.* (ed. 2), *Tetralogie* (Gr.), a speaking or writing in four parts. **1866** Felton *Anc. & Mod. Gr.* II. I. ix. 163 They [speeches of Antiphon] are in the form of tetralogies, each tetralogy containing a speech and a reply of the plaintiff and the defendant. **1874** Mahaffy *Soc. Life Greece* v. 127 *note*, Discussed in Antiphon's second tetralogy.

Hence **Tetralo·gic** *a.*, of or pertaining to a tetralogy.

**1889** Haigh *Attic Theatre* 27 But although the generic terms trilogy and tetralogy were of relatively late origin, it was customary at a much earlier period to give a common name to groups of plays composed on the tetralogic system.

**Tetralophodont** to **-mastigate**: see Tetra-.

**Tetramerous** (tĭtræ·mĕrəs), *a.* [f. mod.L. *tetramer-us* (ad. Gr. τετραμερής four-parted, f. τετρα-, Tetra- + μέρ-ος part) + -ous.] Having, consisting of, or characterized by four parts. *spec.* **a.** *Bot.* Having the parts of the flower-whorl in series of four. (Often written 4-*merous*.) **b.** *Entom.* Having the tarsi four-jointed, as the *Tetramera* among *Coleoptera*. **c.** Having four rays, as a starfish.

**1826** Kirby & Sp. *Entomol.* III. xxxv. 684 Tetramerous insects are those in which all the tarsi consist of four joints. **1835** Lindley *Introd. Bot.* (1848) I. 316 *Tetramerous*, if [a flower consists of organs] in fours. **1857** Henfrey *Elem. Bot.* 230 *Papaveraceæ*... Flowers regular, 2-merous or 4-merous. **1859** Darwin *Orig. Spec.* vii. (1873) 173 All the other flowers on the plant are tetramerous. **1851** Hulme tr. *Moquin-Tandon* II. III. vi. 157 A tetramerous Coleopter belonging to the family Rhyncophora.

So **Tetra·meral** *a.*, having parts in fours; also, belonging to the *Tetrameralia*, a subdivision of the *Hydrozoa Acraspeda* in Claus's classification; **Tetramera·lian** *a.* = Tetrameral; *sb.* a member of the *Tetrameralia*; **Te·tramere**, a division of the fourth order in the supporting reticular skeleton of the extinct siliceous sponges (*Cent. Dict. Suppl.* 1909); **Tetra·merism**, the condition of being tetramerous; division into four parts or into sets of four.

[**1888** Rolleston & Jackson *Anim. Life* 789 I. *Tetrameralia*: with four radial sectors...II. *Octomeralia*: with eight sectors.] **1888** *Amer. Nat.* XXII. 941 The morphological significance of the primary subdivision into four or tetramerism of the germ-bands of *Stenobothrus* and *Œcanthus*. **1899** *Syd. Soc. Lex.*, Tetramerism.

**Tetrameter** (tĭtræ·mĭtəɹ). *Pros.* [ad. L. *tetrametr-us* sb., a. Gr. τετράμετρ-ος adj., f. τετρα-, Tetra- + μέτρον measure. So F. *tétramètre.*] A verse or period consisting of four measures.

In ancient prosody, a trochaic, iambic, or anapæstic tetrameter consisted of four dipodies (= eight feet); in other rhythms a tetrameter was a tetrapody or period of four feet. The name was given specifically to the Trochaic Tetrameter Catalectic or Septenarius, as in 'Crās a͡mēt quī | nūnqu' a͡māvit ‖ quīque a͡māvit | crās a͡mēt'.

**1612** Selden *Illustr. Drayton's Poly-olb.* iv. 67 The first are couplets interchanged of xvi. & xiiii. feet, .. the second of equall tetrameters. **1693** Dryden *Juvenal* (1697) p. xli, He makes no difficulty to mingle Hexameters with Iambique Trimeters; or with Trochaique Tetrameters. **1837** Wheelwright tr. *Aristoph.* I. 93, I ask..what thou thinkest the most perfect measure, The trimeter or the tetrameter? **1869** Tozer *Highl. Turkey* II. 250 The metre..is the iambic tetrameter catalectic.

**b.** *attrib.* or as *adj.*

1770 LANGHORNE *Plutarch* V. 272 A poem, entitled Pontius Glaucus,..written by him [Cicero], when a boy, in tetrameter verse. 1811 ELMSLEY in *Edin. Rev.* Nov. 72 To introduce these refractory names into tetrameter trochaics, Aristophanes has twice used a choriambus, and once an ionic *a minore*, in the place of the regular trochaic *dipodia*. 1827 TATE *Grk. Metres* § 10.

**Tetramorph** (te·trămǭɹf). *Christian Art.* [ad. Gr. τετράμορφον, prop. neut. adj. four-shaped, f. τετρα- four- + μορφή form.] A composite figure combining the symbols of the four evangelists (derived from Rev. iv. 6–8 and Ezek. i. 5–10).

1848 MRS. JAMESON *Sacr. & Leg. Art* (1850) 80 The Evangelists, or rather the Gospels, are represented as the tetramorph, or four-faced creature. 1854 FAIRHOLT *Dict. Terms Art* 430/2 *Tetramorph*. (Gr.) In *Christian Art*, the union of the four attributes of the Evangelists in one figure, winged, standing on winged, fiery wheels; the wings being covered with eyes. 1875 R. ST. J. TYRWHITT in *Smith & Cheetham's Dict. Chr. Antiq.* I. 634/1 The most interesting 6th century representation of them [symbols of the evangelists]..is the quaintly but most grandly-conceived tetramorph of the Rabula MSS. 1898 C. BELL tr. *Huysman's Cathedral* ix. 177 With Christ enthroned..between the winged beasts of the Tetramorph.

**Tetramorphic** (tetrămǭ·ɹfik), *a.* [f. as prec. + -IC.] **a.** *Nat. Hist.* Occurring in four different forms. **b.** Of or pertaining to a tetramorph.

**a.** 1870 HOOKER *Stud. Flora* 79 Oxalis, Wood-sorrel... Tetramorphic flowers occur. 1901 A. G. BUTLER in *Proc. Zool. Soc.* 15 Jan. 25 *Limnas chrysippus* is tetramorphic both at Aden and on the White Nile.
**b.** 1901 *N. & Q.* 9th Ser. VIII. 530/1 The tetramorphic emblems..date perhaps from c. 860 A. D.

So **Tetramo·rphism**, the phenomenon of exhibiting four different forms; in *Chem.*, the property of crystallizing in four several forms.

1909 in *Cent. Dict., Suppl.*

**Tetramyrmeclone, -nephric**, etc.: see TETRA-.

‖ **Tetrandria** (tetræ·ndriă). *Bot.* [mod.L. (Linnæus, 1735), f. Gr. τετρ-, TETRA- + ἀνδρ-, stem of ἀνήρ man, male: cf. POLYANDRIA, etc.] The fourth class in the Linnæan Sexual System, comprising plants bearing hermaphrodite flowers with four equal stamens. Also an order in the classes Gynandria, Monœcia, and Diœcia, having four stamens. So **Tetra·nder**, a plant having four stamens (Webster 1828); **Tetra·ndrian** *a.*, having four stamens (*ibid.*); **Tetra·ndrious** (Mayne 1860), **Tetra·ndrous** *adjs.*, having four equal stamens; belonging to the class *Tetrandria*.

1760 J. LEE *Introd. Bot.* II. xxiii. (1765) 130 *Tetrandria*, comprehending such Plants as have four Stamina. 1806 GALPINE *Brit. Bot.* 261 Tetrandrous: spikes filiform, panicled. 1830 LINDLEY *Nat. Syst. Bot.* 72 Penæa has also tetrandrous flowers. 1872 OLIVER *Elem. Bot.* I. iv. 39 In the Nettle, then, we have..in the male flower, stamens hypogynous, tetrandrous.

**Tetrane** (te·trēⁱn). *Chem.* [f. TETRA- 2 + -ANE 2 b.] The saturated hydrocarbon or paraffin of the tetracarbon series, $C_4H_{10}$, also called *butane*, *quartane*: see TETRYL.

1893 THORPE *Dict. Applied Chem.* III. 813 Tetryl hydrides. Tetranes, butanes. I. *Normal tetrane*, *n*-butane...Occurs in crude petroleum.

**Tetrant** (te·trănt). [ad. L. *tetrans, tetrant-em* (Vitruv.), ad. Gr. τετρᾶς.] = QUADRANT *sb.*[1] 4 (*b*).

1860 WEALE *Dict. Terms* (ed. 2), *Tetrants*, the four equal parts into which the area of a circle is divided by two diameters drawn at right angles to each other.

**Tetraodon**, etc.: see TETRODON.

**Tetraonid** (tĭtrēⁱ·onid), *a.* (*sb.*) *Ornith.* [f. mod.L. *Tetraōnidæ*, f. L. *tetrao* (-*ōnem*), a. Gr. τετράων, applied by Pliny to the Black Grouse and Capercailye, perh. also to other birds: see -ID 3.] Pertaining to the family *Tetraonidæ* of gallinaceous birds, including the grouse and allied forms; also as *sb.* a member of this family. (The term has also been used more widely to include the partridges, quails, and other birds.) So **Tetra·onoid**, *a.* allied in form to the *Tetraonidæ*; *sb.* a tetraonoid bird (*Funk's Stand. Dict.* 1895); **Tetra·onine** *a.*, belonging to the *Tetraoninæ*, as a subfamily of the *Tetraonidæ*: see above and GROUSE *sb.* I.

1847 WEBSTER, *Tetraonid*, a term denoting a bird belonging to the tribe of which the *tetrao* is the type, as the grouse, partridge, quail, etc. 1862 D. WILSON *Preh. Man* I. iii. 63 The name of the English partridge..is applied to one American tetraonid (*Tetrao umbellus*), the pheasant..to another, *T. cupido*. 1868 HUXLEY in *Proc. Zool. Soc.* 14 May 299 The great series of Galline, Pavonine, Phasianine, and Tetraonine birds. 1885 NEWTON in *Encycl. Brit.* XVIII. 333/1 *note*, *Caccabis* lies 'on the Galline side of the boundary', while *Perdix* belongs to the Tetraonine group.

**Te·tra-paper.** *Chem.* [Abbrev. of the full descriptive name: see quot.] A kind of test-paper.

1899 CAGNEY *Jaksch's Clin. Diagn.* v. (ed. 4) 160 This [masking of the result] may be prevented by the use of tetra-paper (tetramethyl-paraphenyl-diamine). *Ibid.* vii. 382 Tetra-paper..immersed in the fluid will show the presence of ozone by taking a blue colour.

† **Tetrape·talose**, *a.* *Bot. Obs.* [f. as next: see -OSE [1].] = TETRAPETALOUS.

1694 *Phil. Trans.* XVIII. 278 Tetrapetalose deformed Flowers coming out of the Scales of the Leaves. *c* 1711 PETIVER *Gazophyl.* x. 96 Scarlet and blew tetrapetalose Flowers.

**Tetrapetalous** (tetrăpe·tăləs), *a.* *Bot.* [f. mod.L. *tetrapetalus* (f. Gr. τετρα- four- + πέταλον PETAL) + -OUS.] Having four petals.

1697 *Phil. Trans.* XIX. 435 A wonderful strange Heath-leaf'd Tetrapetalous..Plant. 1704 J. HARRIS *Lex. Techn.* I, *Tetrapetalous Flower*..is that which consists of but four single coloured Leaves (which the Botanists call *Petala*). 1837 KEITH *Bot. Lex.* 80 If the petals of a tetrapetalous corolla are so disposed on their receptacle as to spread out in the form of a cross, they are said to be cruciform.

**Tetraphalangeate** to **-phyllous**: see TETRA-.

† **Tetraphy·line.** *Min. Obs.* [ad. Ger. *tetraphylin* (Berzelius, 1836), f. TETRA- + Gr. φυλή tribe: see -INE [5].] An obs. name for TRIPHYLITE.

1836 *R. D. & T. Thomson's Rec. Gen. Sci.* III. 477 *Tetraphylline*. This appears to be a variety of the preceding [Triphylline]. 1896 CHESTER *Dict. Names Min.*, *Tetraphyline*...An obs. syn. of triphylite, the name given when a fourth base was discovered in it.

‖ **Tetrapla** (te·trăplă). Also 7–8 anglicized **tetraples.** [a. Gr. τετραπλᾶ, neut. pl. of τετραπλοῦς fourfold, f. τετρα-, TETRA- + -πλοος -fold. Cf. F. *tétraples* (Littré).] A text consisting of four parallel versions, esp. that of the Old Testament made by Origen. Cf. HEXAPLA, OCTAPLA.

1684 N. S. *Crit. Enq. Edit. Bible* xviii. 178 He maintains that the Tetraples and Hexaples of Origen..were call'd Tetraples, because they contain'd a fourfold Version; Hexaples because they comprehended six Versions. 1705 HICKERINGILL *Priest-cr.* IV. (1721) 242 Origen's Tetraples, Hexaples, and Octaples. 1831–3 E. BURTON *Eccl. Hist.* xxiv. (1845) 516 Origen appears at first to have published the three versions of Aquila, Theodotion, and Symmachus, together with the Septuagint: they were arranged in four parallel columns, and the work was called Tetrapla.

**Tetrapleuron** (tetrăplū·ərǫn). Pl. **-a** or **-ons.** [a. Gr. τετράπλευρον a figure with four sides, f. τετρα-, TETRA- + πλευρόν rib, side.]

**1.** A square column.

1837 *Penny Cycl.* IX. 315/1 Square pillars or tetrapleurons, with either a statue, or a caryatid figure standing before.

**2.** *Morphol.* Pl. **Tetrapleu·ra**: Organic forms with bilateral symmetry having four antimeres or corresponding opposite parts. Cf. DIPLEURA.

1883 [see DIPLEURA].

Hence **Tetrapleu·ral** *a.*, *Morphol.*, zygopleural with four antimeres. 1891 in *Cent. Dict.*

**Tetraplocaulous**, etc.: see TETRA-.

**Tetraplous** (te·trăpləs), *a.* [f. Gr. τετραπλόος, -πλοῦς fourfold + -OUS.] Fourfold, quadruple.

1899 *Proc. Zool. Soc.* 16 May 684 Down the centre of the back is a series of tetraplous bright red spots.

**Tetrapod** (te·trăpǫd), *a.* and *sb.* [ad. mod.L. *tetrapod-us*, ad. Gr. τετράπους, τετραποδ- four-footed, f. τετρα-, TETRA- + πούς (ποδ-) foot. Cf. F. *tétrapode*.] **a.** *adj.* Having four feet or four limbs; *spec.* in *Entom.*, belonging to the *Tetrapoda*, a division of butterflies having only four perfect legs, the anterior pair being unfitted for walking. **b.** *sb.* A four-footed animal; one of the *Tetrapoda*, applied by Credner to all vertebrates higher than fishes; in *Entom.*, a butterfly belonging to the *Tetrapoda*. Hence **Tetrapo·dichnite** (-i·knəit), *Geol.* [ICHNITE], the fossil footprint of a four-footed beast; **Tetrapodo·logy**, a treatise on quadrupeds; **Tetra·podous** *a.* = sense a. above.

1826 KIRBY & SP. *Entomol.* IV. xlvi. 343 *Tetrapod*,..an insect having only four perfect legs. 1835–6 *Todd's Cycl. Anat.* I. 265/2 No species of Bird ever deviates..from the tetrapodous type of formation. 1844 PAGE *Rudim. Geol.* § 215 (1851) 126 *note*, Professor Hitchcock adds a third class, *tetrapodichnites*, or the footsteps of some unknown four-footed animal. 1860 MAYNE *Expos. Lex.*, *Tetrapodologia*.., term for a treatise on quadrupeds; tetrapodology.

**Tetrapody** (tĭtræ·pŏdi). *Pros.* [ad. Gr. τετραποδία, f. τετραποδ-: see prec.] A group of four metrical feet; a verse of four feet. So **Tetrapo·dic** *a.*, consisting of four metrical feet.

1846 WORCESTER, Tetrapody. 1889 *Amer. Jrnl. Philol.* July 225 The Bactrians and Indians..appear to have found the tetrapody short enough. *Ibid.*, It seems more natural to assume the tetrapody as the primitive march-verse, and the tripody as an intentionally differentiated form for purposes of recitation. 1891 *Harper's Mag.* Mar. 570/2 Most folk-songs are constructed upon tetrapodic periods. *Ibid.* [see DIPODY]. 1895 GILDERSLEEVE *Lat. Gram.* (ed. 3) 458 Dipody..Tripody..Tetrapody.

**Tetrapolar**: see TETRA- I.

‖ **Tetrapolis** (tĭtræ·pŏlis). [a. Gr. τετράπολις of four cities; also sb.] A district of four cities; a state or political division consisting of four towns.

1846 GROTE *Greece* I. v. I. 141 The inhabitants of the insignificant tetrapolis of Doris Proper. 1884 BOSCAWEN *Lect.* in *Builder* 6 Dec., It was a tribe called the Akkadians who..founded the tetrapolis of Nimrod.

**Tetrapolitan** (tetrăpǫ·lĭtăn), *a.* [ad. mod.L. *tetrapolitān-us* of four cities, f. prec., after *metropolitan*.] Of or pertaining to four cities. *Tetrapolitan Confession*, a confession of faith drawn up by the four cities Strasburg, Memmingen, Constance, and Lindau, presented to the diet of Augsburg (1530).

1847 PRANDI tr. *Cantù's Reform. Europe* I. 103 Those who were unwilling to admit the real presence, drew up another 'tetrapolitan confession'. 1906 C. G. M'CRIE *Beza's Portr. Reformers* 82 This symbol, generally styled the Tetrapolitan from the four cities.., is also called the Strasburg Confession.

**Tetrapous** to **Tetraprionid**: see TETRA-.

**Tetrapterous** (tĭtræ·ptĕrəs), *a.* [f. mod.L. *tetrapter-us* (a. Gr. τετράπτερος four-winged, f. τετρα- four- + πτερ-όν wing) + -OUS. Cf. F. *tétraptère*.] Having four wings; *spec.* in *Entom.* applied to four-winged flies; in *Bot.* having four wing-like appendages, as certain fruits. So **Tetra·pter** (see quot. 1846); **Tetra·pteran** *a.*, tetrapterous; *sb.* a four-winged insect.

1826 KIRBY & SP. *Entomol.* III. xxix. 66 A Tetrapterous insect, the genus of which is uncertain, is said, when it is taken, to discharge its eggs like shot from a gun. *Ibid.* IV. xlvii. 376 A substance intermediate between that of the elytra of *Coleoptera* and that of the wings of the Tetrapterous Orders. 1842 BRANDE *Dict. Sc.* etc., *Tetrapterans*, *Tetraptera*,.. applied by some entomologists to the insects which have four wings, and which thus constitute an extensive primary division of the class. 1846 SMART Suppl., *Tetrapters*, insects with four wings; fossil fishes having four fins. 1860 MAYNE *Expos. Lex.*, *Tetrapterus*..*Bot.*, having four wings, as the fruit of *Tetragonia tetraptera*. 1866 *Treas. Bot.*, *Tetrapterous*, four-winged.

**Tetraptote** to **-quetrous**: see TETRA-.

**Tetrarch** (te·t-, tī·traɹk), *sb.*[1] Forms: 4 tetrarke, 5 -arche, 5– tetrarch; also 4–6 in L. form **tetrarcha.** [ad. late L. *tetrarcha* (Vulgate), cl. L. *tetrarchēs*, a. Gr. τετράρχης, f. τετρα- four- + -αρχης ruling, ruler. Cf. F. *tétrarque* (13th c.).]

**1.** *Rom. Hist.* The ruler of one of four divisions of a country or province; at a later period applied to subordinate rulers generally, esp. in Syria.

[*c* 1050 *Byrhtferth's Handboc* in *Anglia* VIII. 299 Quadrans on lyden on grecisc ys ȝecweden tetrarcha.] 1382 WYCLIF *Matt.* xiv. 1 Eroude tetrarcha [*gloss* that is, prince of the fourthe part; 1388 tetrarke], herde the fame of Jhesu. 1432–50 tr. *Higden* (Rolls) IV. 233 He and his breþer were made tetrarches, as hauenge the iiijthe parte of a realm, from proctors. 1480 CAXTON *Chron. Eng.* IV. (1520) 28/1 The Emperoure..the halfe of the Iury and Idumea gaue to Archylaus vnder name of Tetrache. 1526 TINDALE *Matt.* xiv. 1 Herod the tetrarcha. 1611 B. JONSON *Catiline* I. i, All the earth, Her kings, and tetrarchs, are their tributaries. 1718 ROWE tr. *Lucan* VII. 334 Kings and Tetrarchs proud, a purple Train. 1877 C. GEIKIE *Christ* lx. (1879) 735 The tetrarch Antipas had come up from Tiberias, to show how devoutly he honoured the law.

**2.** *transf.* and *fig.* **a.** A ruler of a fourth part, or of one of four parts, divisions, elements, etc.; also a subordinate ruler generally.

1610 *Histrio-m.* II. 19 For this aboundance pour'd at Plenties feet You shall be Tetrarchs of this petty world. 1651 DAVENANT *Gondibert* Pref. 45 The heads of the Church (where ever Christianity is preach'd) are Tetrarchs of Time; of which they command the fourth Division. 1671 MILTON *P. R.* IV. 201 If I..have propos'd What both from Men and Angels I receive, Tetrarchs of fire, air, flood, and on the earth Nations besides. 1797 BURKE *Regic. Peace* iii. Wks. VIII. 307 It is not to the Tetrarch of Sardinia..that we mean to prove [etc.].

*attrib.* 1642 FULLER *Holy & Prof. St.* III. xxi. 209 Men in whose constitutions one of the tetrarch Elements, fire, may seem to be omitted.

**b.** One of four joint rulers, directors, or heads.

*a* 1661 FULLER *Worthies, Cornw.* (1662) I. 213 This was he who was one of the first four Tetrarchs or Joint-managers in chief of Marshall matters in Cornwall. 1902 BARING in *Encycl. Brit.* XXVIII. 496/2 The Parnassian school [had] as their tetrarchs and judges Théophile Gautier, Leconte de Lisle, Baudelaire, and Banville.

**3. a.** The commander of a subdivision of an ancient Greek phalanx. (The quot. may belong here or to sense 1.)

1846 LANDOR *Imag. Conv., Scipio, Polyb., & Pan.* (1853) 351 His bringing into the front of the center, as became some showy tetrarch rather than Hannibal, his eighty elephants.

**b.** In Fourier's social organization: A ruler of the fourth (ascending) rank.

1848 *Tait's Mag.* XV. 706 There will be duarchs for four phalanx, triarchs for 12, tetrarchs for 48.

**Te·trarch,** *a.* *Bot.* [f. TETRA- + Gr. ἀρχή beginning.] Proceeding from four distinct points of origin: cf. DIARCH.

1884 BOWER & SCOTT *De Bary's Phaner.* 363 Triarch and tetrarch bundles sometimes occur in thick roots of species which are usually diarch. *Ibid.* 354 In the case of diarch and tetrarch structure of the main root. *Ibid.*, The phloem-groups of triarch and tetrarch roots of Papilionaceæ. 1895 VINES *Students' Text-bk. Bot.* 179 The stele may have—in different structures—one to many protoxylem (primitive wood) groups, and is accordingly described as monarch.. diarch..triarch..tetrarch..polyarch. 1900 W. WALLACE in *Ann. Bot.* Dec. 643 The tetrarch or triarch root [of *Actinostemma*] has no pith and..no internal phloem.

**Tetrarchate** (te·traɹkeⁱt). Also 7 -at. [f. TETRARCH *sb.*[1] + -ATE [1]: cf. *exarchate* and F. *tetrarchat*.] The office or position of a tetrarch.

1651 C. CARTWRIGHT *Cert. Relig.* I. 102 Your tetrarchate would be a gain for you to lose it. 1709 STANHOPE *Paraphr.* IV. 90 Agrippa, Herod's Successor in the Tetrarchate of Galilee. 1874 H. R. REYNOLDS *John Bapt.* i. § 5. 41 It was Herod's feverish desire to emulate the title of King..that cost him his tetrarchate.

**Tetrarchic** (tĭtrā·ɹkik), *a.* [ad. Gr. τετραρχικός of a tetrarch: see -IC.] Of or pertaining to four rulers; pertaining to a tetrarch or to a tetrarchy.

**1818** W. TAYLOR in *Monthly Rev.* LXXXV. 528 The tetrarchic government is criticized. **1898** W. M. RAMSAY in *Expositor* Aug. 132 Now began tetrarchic and then monarchic rule.

**Tetrarchical** (tĭträ·ɹkikăl), *a.* Now *rare.* [f. as prec. + -AL.] = prec.; also †of a country: Ruled by tetrarchs; divided into tetrarchies (*obs.*).

**1638** SIR T. HERBERT *Trav.* (ed. 2) 21 The whole Ile is Tetrarchicall, 4 severall Kings swaying their Ebony Scepters in each Toparchy. **1646** SIR T. BROWNE *Pseud. Ep.* v. x. (1650) 212 The Tetrarchicall or generall banners, of Judah, Ruben, Ephraim and Dan. *a* **1751** BOLINGBROKE *Ess. Author. Matters Relig.* xxxii, The patriarchs had a sort of tetrarchical, or ethnarchical authority, for I suppose it is not easy to distinguish them.

**Tetrarchy** (te·träɹki). [ad. L. *tetrarchia*, a. Gr. τετραρχία, f. τετράρχης TETRARCH *sb.*[1] Cf. F. *tétrarchie* (15th c. in Godef. *Compl.*).]

1. The district, division, or part of a country or province ruled by a tetrarch; the government or jurisdiction of a tetrarch.

**1432–50** tr. *Higden* (Rolls) IV. 291 Wherefore Octouian.. ȝafe to Archelaus the halfe parte of the Iewery, and Ydumea, in the name of a tetrarchye. **1591** G. FLETCHER *Russe Commw.* (Hakl. Soc.) 3 These shires and provinces are reduced all into foure jurisdictions, which they call chetfyrds (that is), tetrarchies, or fourth-parts. **1656** BLOUNT *Glossogr.*, *Tetrarchy*, the government of the fourth part of a countrey [1674 *adds*] or a government of the whole by four persons. **1862** MERIVALE *Rom. Emp.* VI. lix. 540 The tetrarchy of Agrippa..menaced Galilee on its eastern flank.

2. *transf.* and *fig.* A government by four persons jointly; a set of four tetrarchs or rulers; a country divided into four petty governments.

*c* **1630** RISDON *Surv. Devon* (1810) 3 The Danish tetrarchy. **1641** MILTON *Reform.* II. Wks. 1851 III. 53 Hee ought to suspect a Hierarchy..to bee as dangerous and derogatory from his Crown as a Tetrarchy or a Heptarchy. **1716** M. DAVIES *Athen. Brit.* III. *Diss. Physick* 12 The honourable Tetrarchy of Physicians, or Doctors,..Chirurgians, Apothecaries, and Chymists. **1862** RAWLINSON *Anc. Mon.* I. i. 19 In each of these districts we have a sort of tetrarchy, or special pre-eminence of four cities. **1885** *Spectator* 8 Aug. 1033/2 Mr. Chamberlain's proposal for a tetrarchy in the guise of Local Government.

**Tetrascele** to **-spherical**: see TETRA-.

‖ **Tetraspora·ngium.** *Bot.* Pl. **-ia.** [mod. L., f. TETRA- + SPORANGIUM; or f. TETRASPORE + Gr. ἀγγεῖον receptacle.] A sporangium producing or containing tetraspores. Rarely anglicized as **Te·traspora·nge** (*Cent. Dict.* 1891).

**1890** *Athenæum* 21 June 805/2 On the Development of the Tetrasporangia in *Rhabdochorton rothii.*

**Tetraspore** (te·tră₁spōᵊɹ). *Bot.* [f. TETRA- + SPORE.] A group (usually) of four asexual spores, resulting from the division of a mother cell, in the *Florideæ*, a group of *Algæ*.

**1857** BERKELEY *Cryptog. Bot.* § 88. 108 Tetraspores, mostly immersed in the fronds. **1867** BRANDE & COX *Dict. Sc.*, etc. III. 754/2 *Tetraspore* [is] one of the forms of fructification found in some sea-weeds. It consists of little clusters of spores, in most cases four in number, but very rarely eight. **1875** J. H. BALFOUR in *Encycl. Brit.* I. 508/2 Spores have a tendency to divide into four; such compound spores are called tetraspores.

Hence **Tetrasporic** (-spǫ·rik), **Tetrasporous** (tetră₁spōᵊ·rəs, tĭtræ·spŏrəs) *adjs.*, composed of or producing tetraspores.

**1857** BERKELEY *Cryptog. Bot.* § 172. 195 Distinguished by their almost constant production of tetraspores, instead of polysporic, moniliform threads. **1874** COOKE *Fungi* 26 [He] has demonstrated that they are habitually tetrasporous.

**Tetraster** (tĭtræ·stəɹ). *Biol.* [mod.L., f. TETRA- + Gr. ἀστήρ star.] A karyokinetic figure formed in the modification of a cell-nucleus by the combination of four star-like masses of chromatin united by spindles or filaments.

**1890** BILLINGS *Nat. Med. Dict.*, *Tetraster*, the figure presented when there are four centres of radiation during the indirect division of a nucleus into four daughter-nuclei. **1909** J. W. JENKINSON *Exper. Embryol.* 128 In the case where two sperm-nuclei unite with the egg-nucleus a tetraster is formed, that is four asters united by spindles in a square or rhombus.

**Tetrastich** (te·trăstik, tĭtræ·stik). *Pros.* Also 7–9 **tetra·stic(h)on**, (pl. **-a**); 7–8 **tetrastic**, **-sticke**, 7–9 **-stick**. [ad. L. *tetrastichon* a quatrain, a. Gr. τετράστιχον, neut. of τετράστιχος containing four rows, f. τετρα-, TETRA- + στίχος row, line of verse. Cf. F. *tétrastiche*, *-ique*.] A stanza of four lines.

**1580** SPENSER *Let. to Harvey* Wks. (Globe) App. ii. 709/1 Here I let you see my olde use of toying in Rymes turned into your artificial straightnesse of Verse by this Tetrasticon. **1625** USSHER *Answ. Jesuit* 325 Therefore doth Theodorus Prodromus begin his Tetrastich upon our Saviours Resurrection. **1702** *Burlesque of R. L'Estrange's Vis. Quev.* 62 What Man though always in the Pouts The following Tetrastick doubts? **1779** JOHNSON *L. P.*, *Milton* Wks. II. 92 Selvaggi praised him in a distich, and Salsilli in a tetrastick: neither of them of much value. **1824** JOHNSON *Typogr.* I. 330 The last page, on which are an Epistle and Tetrastichon in Roman. **1865** R. PALMER *Bk. Praise* 489 The two tetrastichs composing the first stanza are transposed.

Hence **Tetra·stichal**, **Tetrasti·chic** *adjs.*, of, pertaining to, or of the nature of a tetrastich, or consisting of tetrastichs; **Tetra·stichism**, the formation of tetrastichs.

**1882–3** *Schaff's Encycl. Relig. Knowl.* III. 1955 The alphabetical psalm (xxxvii)..is almost entirely tetrastichic. **1890** G. BICKELL in *Athenæum* 22 Nov. 700/3 There are hexastichic strophes throughout Prov. xxx..and tetrastichic ones in i. 7–ix. 18. **1895** *Q. Rev.* Jan. 128 A tetrastichal metre should be chosen. **1898** R. ELLIS in *Classical Rev.* XII. 120 The process which Rutherford..aptly calls tetrastichism, i. e. reduction of a larger original to a total of four verses.

**Tetrastichous** (tĭtræ·stikəs), *a. Bot.* and *Zool.* [f. mod.L. *tetrastich-us* (a. Gr. τετράστιχος: see prec.) + -OUS.] Having organs or parts in four rows.

**1866** *Treas. Bot.*, *Tetrastichous*, having a four-cornered spike.

**Tetrastigm** (te·trăstig'm). *Geom.* [f. Gr. τετρα-, TETRA- + στίγμα prick, mark, point.] The complete figure composed of four points in a plane and their six connecting straight lines; commonly called *complete quadrangle*. **1863** [see TETRAGRAM 2].

‖ **Tetrastoön** (tĭtræ·sto₁ǫn). *Arch.* Pl. **-oa.** [a. Gr. τετράστοον, neuter of τετράστοος having four porticos (f. τετρα- + στοά porch).] A court-yard having open colonnades on each of its four sides.

**1838** BRITTON *Art & Archæol. Mid. Ages*, *Tetrastoön*,.. a court-yard with porticos, or open colonnades on each of its four sides. **1908** W. M. RAMSAY in *Expositor* Nov. 411 This atrium is what Eugenius calls a tetrastoon.

**Tetrastyle** (te·trăstəil), *sb.* and *a. Arch.* [ad. L. *tetrastȳl-os* adj., *tetrastȳl-on* sb., a. Gr. τετράστυλος (neut. -ον) with four pillars, f. τετρα-, TETRA- + στῦλος pillar. Cf. F. *tétrastyle*.]

A. *sb.* A structure having four pillars or columns; a group of four pillars.

**1704** J. HARRIS *Lex. Techn.* I, *Tetrastyle*..is a Building which hath four Columns in the Faces before and behind. **1769** *De Foe's Tour Gt. Brit.* I. 369 An Organ of very good Workmanship, and supported by a Tetrastyle of beautiful Gothic Columns. **1842** FRANCIS *Dict. Art*, etc., *Tetrastyle*, a building having four columns in front.

B. *adj.* Having or consisting of four columns.

**1837** *Antiq. Athens* 42 Including the tetrastyle portico and that of the Caryatides. **1838** J. L. STEPHENS *Trav.*, *Russia* 85/1 A tetrastyle Ionic temple of the purest white marble. **1842–76** GWILT *Archit.* Gloss. s. v. *Colonnade*, If the columns are four in number, it is called tetrastyle.

So **Tetrastylic** (-sti·lik) *a.* = B.; also **Tetrasty·lous** *a. Bot.*, having four styles or pistils.

**1860** MAYNE *Expos. Lex.*, *Tetrastylus*,..having four styles ..: tetrastylous. **1895** *Funk's Stand. Dict.*, Tetrastylic.

**Tetrasyllable** (tetrăsi·lăb'l), *sb.* (*a.*) [f. TETRA- + SYLLABLE; cf. Gr. τετρασύλλαβος of four syllables.] **a.** *sb.* A word of four syllables. **b.** *adj.* Tetrasyllabic.

**1589** PUTTENHAM *Eng. Poesie* II. iii. (Arb.) 82 Euery sillable being allowed one time, either short or long, it fell out that euery tetrasillable had foure times, euery trissillable three, and the bissillable two. **1749** J. MASON *Numbers in Poet. Comp.* 17 Any two..joined together in a different Position make a different tetrasyllable Foot.

So **Tetrasylla·bic**, **Tetrasylla·bical** *adjs.*, consisting of four syllables.

**1656** BLOUNT *Glossogr.*, *Tetrasyllabical*, that hath or contains four syllables. **1775** ASH, *Tetrasyllabic*, containing four syllables. **1804** MITFORD *Inquiry* 343 *note*, Describing the antient feet, classing them as dissyllabical, trissyllabical, and tetrasyllabical.

**Tetrasymmetry** to **-theite**: see TETRA-.

**Tetrate**: see TETRIC *a.*[2]

**Tetrathionic** (tetră₁þəi₁ǫ·nik), *a. Chem.* [f. TETRA- + Gr. θεῖον sulphur + -IC: see -THIONIC.] In *tetrathionic acid*, $H_2S_4O_6$, a colourless, inodorous, very acid liquid, containing four atoms of sulphur in the molecule. Hence **Tetrathi·onate**, a salt of tetrathionic acid.

**1848** *Chem. Gaz.* 1 Jan. 13 A double salt of the pentathionate and tetrathionate of potash. *Ibid.* 15 Sept. 369 Under the name of polythionic acids the author [F. Kessner] comprises the trithionic, tetrathionic and pentathionic acids. **1852** *Fownes' Chem.* (ed. 4) 140 Tetrathionic Acid..was discovered by..Fordos and Gélis [1843]. **1854** J. SCOFFERN in *Orr's Circ. Sc.*, *Chem.* 285 Bisulphuretted hyposulphuric acid (Tetrathionic acid). **1868** WATTS *Dict. Chem.* V. 641 Tetrathionic Compounds. *Ibid.*, Tetrathionate of Barium, $Ba''S_4O_6\ 2H_2O$,..is obtained in large tabular crystals.

**Tetratomic** (tetrătǫ·mik), *a. Chem.* [f. TETR(A)- + ATOMIC.] Containing four atoms in the molecule. †**b.** = TETRAVALENT, QUADRIVALENT. *Obs.* †**c.** = TETRAHYDRIC. *Obs.*

**1862** MILLER *Elem. Chem.* (ed. 2) III. 52 Tetratomic, or Tetrabasic elements, each atom of which in combination is equivalent to $H_4$, or four atoms of hydrogen. **1865** *Reader* 1 Apr. 372/3 Carbon has been shown by Kekulé [1857 *Annalen der Chemie* 104, p. 133] to be tetratomic. **1872** WATTS *Dict. Chem.* VI. 237 Carbon, which combines with 4 atoms of hydrogen, is tetratomic, tetradic, or quadrivalent. **1880** CLEMINSHAW *Wurtz' Atom. The.* 120 Both vapours are tetratomic, or, in other words, the molecules of phosphorus and arsenic are formed of four atoms.

**Tetratone**, **-top**: see TETRA-.

**Tetratricontane** (tetra₁trəikǫ·ntēⁱn). *Chem.* [f. TETRA- + Gr. τρι(ά)κοντα thirty + -ANE.] The saturated hydrocarbon or paraffin of the 34-carbon series, $C_{34}H_{70}$.

**Tetravalent** (tĭtræ·vălĕnt, tetrăvēⁱ·lĕnt), *a. Chem.* [f. Gr. τετρα-, TETRA- + L. *valēnt-em*, pr. pple. of *valēre* to be worth.] Combining with four atoms of hydrogen or other monovalent element, or with four monovalent radicals, or capable of replacing four atoms of monovalent elements in a compound; thus the atoms of carbon and of lead are tetravalent in the compounds $CH_4$, $Pb(C_2H_5)_4$. Also called *quadrivalent*. So **Tetravalence**, the quality or fact of being tetravalent; quadrivalence.

**1868** WILLIAMSON *Chem. for Students* 124 Oxygen is.. called a divalent element. A similar reasoning shows nitrogen to be trivalent; and carbon is tetravalent. **1887** *Athenæum* 13 Aug. 217/1 Proof is thus afforded that these elements [sulphur and selenium] are at least tetravalent in function.

**Tetraxial** to **Tetraxonian**: see TETRA-.

**Tetrazole** (te·trăzōᵘl). *Chem.* [f. TETRA- + AZ(O- azote + L. *oleum* oil.] A colourless compound of carbon, nitrogen, and hydrogen, $N_4CH_2$ = N⟨CH.NH / N=N, having acidic properties, crystallizing in lustrous prisms or plates.

**1892** BLADIN in *Jrnl. Chem. Soc.* LXII. 1009 Tetrazole.. is obtained as a yellowish, crystalline mass, and is purified by crystallisation from alcohol.

**Tetrazomal**, **Tetrazooid**: see TETRA- 1.

**Te·trazone.** *Chem.* [f. TETRA- + AZ(O- + -ONE.] Name of a class of basic compounds containing four nitrogen atoms, with the formula $R_2NN:NNR_2$, in which R is any monovalent group. *Ethyl tetrazone*, $(C_2H_5)_2NN:NN(C_2H_5)_2$, is a basic liquid of alliaceous odour.

**1895** in *Funk's Standard Dict.* **1899** in *Syd. Soc. Lex.*

**Tetremimeral** (tetrĭmi·mərăl), *a. Pros.* [f. Gr. τετρα- four- + ἡμιμερ-ής half, halved (f. ἡμι- half + μέρ-ος part) + -AL; after *penthemimeral*.] Occurring at the end of four half feet.

**1906** SAINTSBURY *Hist. Eng. Pros.* I. 270 He mainly observes the tetremimeral cæsura, which is really important in rhyme-royal, very carefully.

‖ **Tetrevangelium** (tetrevændʒe·liŭm, -ge·liŭm). [After med.L. *tetrevangelia*, pl. f. Gr. τετρα- four- + εὐαγγέλιον gospel, EVANGEL.] The four gospels collected into one manuscript or book.

**1898** *N. York Independent* 27 Jan. (Cent. Suppl.) Codex Bezæ goes back not into a tetrevangelium, but into a detached collection .. in which the Lucan writings were a separate factor, unconnected with the rest. **1905** *Expositor* Aug. 123 We find it in the Tetrevangelium, a collection which was very probably made in Asia.

† **Te·tric**, *a.*[1] *Obs.* Also 6 **tetrik**, 7 **tetrick(e.** [ad. L. *tætric-us*, *tētric-us* forbidding, harsh, gloomy, f. *tæter* foul: see -IC.] = TETRICAL.

**1533** BELLENDEN *Livy* I. viii. (S.T.S.) I. 45 In þe tetrik and sorowfull science vsit amang þe sabynis. **1620** VENNER *Via Recta* iii. 23 It [wine]..correcteth the tetrick qualities which that age is subiect vnto. **1682** SIR T. BROWNE *Wks.* (1835) IV. 276 Her youthful days are over, and her face hath become wrinkled and tetrick. **1811** H. MARTYN *Diary* in *Mem.* (1825) III. 378 Amongst the others who came and sat with us, was my tetric adversary, Agra Acher.

So †**Tetri·city** [L. *tætricitās*], † **Te·tritude** [L. *tætritūdo*], the quality of being 'tetric', harshness, sourness; † **Te·tricous** *a.* = TETRIC *a.*[1]

**1623** COCKERAM, *Tetricitie*, the sourenesse of the countenance. **1656** BLOUNT *Glossogr.*, *Tetricity*, sournesse or sadnesse of countenance. *Tetritude*, idem. **1727** BAILEY Vol. II, *Tetricous*, sour in Countenance, crabbed, morose.

**Te·tric**, *a.*[2] *Chem.* [f. Gr. τετρα-, TETRA- 2 + -IC.] In *tetric acid*, a substance described by Demarçay in 1877, now believed to be $C_{10}H_{12}O_6$, or $C_5H_6O_3$. It is a colourless body crystallizing in triclinic prisms. Its salts are **Tetrates.**

**1881** WATTS *Dict. Chem.* VIII. 1918 Tetric acid and its homologues,..are formed by the successive action of bromine and alcoholic potash on the ethylic ethers of aceto-acetic acid and its homologues.

**Tetrical** (te·trikăl), *a. Obs.* or *arch.* [f. as TETRIC *a.*[1] + -AL: see -ICAL.] Austere, severe, harsh, bitter, morose.

*a* **1529** SKELTON *Replic.* Wks. 1843 I. 209 Touching the tetrycall theologisacioun of these demy diuines, and Stoicall studiantes. **1627–77** FELTHAM *Resolves* I. viii. 11 It is not good to be too tetrical and virulent. **1656** BLOUNT *Glossogr.*, *Tetrical*, rude, rough, unpleasant, sower, crabbish, hard to relish. **1772** NUGENT tr. *Hist. Fr. Gerund* II. 81 Some so tetrical, so cross-grained, and of so corrupt a taste. **1901** M. HUME *Span. People* 488 He had none of the forbidding, tetrical Spanish form of devotion.

Hence **Te·tricalness**, the quality of being tetrical.

**1653** GAUDEN *Hierasp.* 170 It requires.. diligence .. to contend with younger ignorance, and elder obstinacy, and aged tetricalness.

**Tetricity**, **-cous**, **Tetritude**: see after TETRIC[1].

[**Tetrifolie**, error in Holland (whence **tetrifoil** in Daniel) for *tre-trifoly*, i. e. *tree-trefoil.*

*Tre-trifoly* was applied by Turner to the *Cytisus* of the ancients (*Medicago arborea*). The black-wooded *Cytisus* of Pliny was the laburnum (*Cytisus Laburnum*).

**1601** HOLLAND *Pliny* XVI. xl. I. 490 Yet the Cytisus or Tetrifolie is blacker, and seemeth most to resemble the Ebene. **1606** DANIEL *Queen's Arcadia* v. i. 85 And seek out Clouer for thy little Lambes, And Tetrifoil to cheerish vp their Dammes.]

**Tetrobol** (te·trŏbǫl). Also 7–8 **tetrobolon**, **-um**, 9 **-us**. [ad. mod.L. *tetrobol-um*, a. Gr. τετρώβολον a four-obolus piece, f. τετρα- four + ὀβολός OBOLUS.] A silver coin of ancient Greece of the value of four oboli.

**1693** tr. *Blancard's Phys. Dict.* (ed. 2), *Tetrobolon*, four Drams. **1706** PHILLIPS (ed. Kersey), *Tetrobolum*, a Coin of four *Oboli*, about four Pence half-penny of our Money. **1842** *Smith's Dict. Grk. & R. Antiq.* s. v. *Drachma*, Specimens of the tetrobolus, triobolus, diobolus, three-quarter-obol, half-obol,..are still found. **1895** *Athenæum* 23 Nov. 723/1 An Æginetic hemi-drachm of about 40 grains..was equivalent to the Corinthian drachm or Attic tetrobol.

**Tetrode** (te·trǒud). *Zool.* [f. TETRA- + Gr. ὁδός way.] A sponge-spicule with four equal rays in the same plane.

‖ **Tetrodon** (te·trǒdǫn). *Ichthyol.* Also **tetraodon, tetradon.** [mod.L. (Linnæus 1766), f. Gr. τετρα- four + ὀδούς, ὀδοντ- tooth. So F. *tétrodon*.] A genus of plectognathic fishes, typical of the family *Tetrodontidæ*, in which the jaws are divided longitudinally by a groove, giving the appearance of four large teeth; a fish of this family, a globe-fish. Hence **Tetrodo·nic** *a.*, of, pertaining to, or derived from fishes of this genus; *Chem.* applied to a poisonous acid obtained from the roe of a fish of this genus (*Cent. Dict. Suppl.* 1909); **Tetrodo·nin**, a crystalline base obtained with tetrodonic acid. So **Te·trodont** (also **tetraodont**), *a.* having (apparently) four teeth; belonging to the *Tetrodontidæ*; *sb.* a tetrodon or globe-fish. Hence **Tetrodo·ntid, Tetrodo·ntoid** *adjs.* and *sbs.*

**1774** GOLDSM. *Nat. Hist.* (1776) VI. 237 These are the Sun Fish, the Tetrodon, the Lump Fish. **1822–34** *Good's Study Med.* (ed. 4) IV. 214 The genus tetradon, in one species, secretes an electric fluid. **1854** BADHAM *Halieut.* 409 The tetraodons seem as unsafe for food as the diodons. **1858** BAIRD *Cycl. Nat. Sci.* s. v. *Diodontidæ*, The true diodonts,..the tetraodonts,..and the sun-fishes. **1883** *Spectator* 19 May 639 The tetradon, a knobbly, bladder-shaped creature, used by the Chinese as a lantern, when he has been scooped.

† **Tetronymal**, *a.* *Obs. rare*—°. [f. Gr. type *τετρώνυμ-ος (f. τετρα- four + ὄνομα name) + -AL.] **1656** BLOUNT *Glossogr.*, *Tetronimal*, that hath four names.

**Tetrose** (te·trōus). *Chem.* [f. TETRA- + -OSE [2].] The name of the class of sugars containing four carbon atoms in the molecule. **1909** *Cent. D. Suppl.*

**Tetrous** (te·trəs), *a.* Now *rare.* [f. L. *tæter* (*tēter*) offensive, foul + -OUS.] Offensive, foul.

Sometimes from contiguity of form and sense confused with TETTEROUS: so in quot. 1890.

**1637** BRIAN *Pisse-proph.* (1679) 133 Your heart and head are assaulted with a tetrous vapour, so that you are melancholick and cannot take your rest. **1664** EVELYN *Sylva* (1776) 411 The Decoction [of Elder buds] is admirable to assuage inflammations and tetrous humours and especially the Scorbutis. **1890** A. W. TOURGEE in *Chicago Advance* 27 Mar., A leper whose tetrous spots threaten every soul that looks upon them.

**Tetro·xide.** *Chem.* [f. TETRA- 2 a + OXIDE.] A binary compound containing four atoms of oxygen; e. g. nitrogen tetroxide, $NO_4$.

**1866** ROSCOE *Elem. Chem.* vii. 63 The same blue body [nitric trioxide] is obtained by adding water to nitric tetroxide and drying the distillate over calcium chloride. **1872** WATTS *Dict. Chem.* VI. 239 The tetroxide..appears..to be capable of existing in the two polymeric modifications $NO_2$ and $N_2O_4$.

**Tetroxy-.** *Chem.* [f. as prec. + OXY(GEN).] In comb. equivalent to *tetrahydroxy-*, denoting the substitution of four hydroxyl groups (OH) in the compound to the name of which it is prefixed.

**Tetryl** (te·tril). *Chem.* [f. TETR(A- 2 + -YL.] The monovalent radical of the tetracarbon series, $C_4H_9$, also called BUTYL; chiefly attrib. = *tetrylic*, as in *tetryl hydride* = TETRANE, *tetryl acetate, alcohol, aldehyde, chloride, oxide, sulphide*, etc.; *tetryl compounds, group, series*, etc.

**1857** MILLER *Elem. Chem.* III. 195 Tetryl, Butyl, or Valyl ..is one of the products obtained during the electrolysis of the valerate of potash. *Ibid.* 33 Valerianic or Tetrylformic [acid]. **1862** *Ibid.* 248 Tetryl Glycol (Butyl Glycol). **1868** WATTS *Dict. Chem.* V. 732 None of the tetryl-compounds can be directly prepared from it [tetryl]. *Ibid.*, Tetryl forms compounds with other alcohol-radicles. Tetryl-ethyl, $C_6H_{14}$. ..Tetryl-amyl, $C_9H_{20}$..Tetryl-hexyl, $C_{10}H_{22}$.

Hence **Te·trylamine**, an amine or compound ammonia of tetryl, also called BUTYLAMINE; **Te·trylate**, a salt of tetrylic or butyric acid; **Te·trylene**, the olefine of the tetryl group, $C_4H_8$, also called **Tetrene** and BUTYLENE; *attrib.* as *tetrylene-diamine*; **Tetryle·nic** *a.*, pertaining to tetrylene; **Tetrylic** *a.*, of tetryl, in *tetrylic acid*, etc.

**1868** WATTS *Dict. Chem.* V. 737 With nitrate of silver, *tetrylamine forms a tawny yellow precipitate. **1857** MILLER *Elem. Chem.* III. 190 Hydrocarbons homologous with olefiant gas...4. *Tetrylene, Butylene, or Oil Gas ($C_8H_8$).. was ascertained by Faraday to be one of the products furnished by the destructive distillation of oil. **1868** WATTS *Dict. Chem.* V. 738 Tetrylene at —18° is a colourless mobile oil, having an ethereal but peculiar and penetrating odour. *Ibid.* 739 *Tetrylenic alcohol, $C_4H_{10}O_2$, *Tetryl-* or *Butyl-glycol*..a colourless, viscid, inodorous liquid, having a mild aromatic taste. *Ibid.*, Tetrylenic bromide, $C_4H_8Br_2$.. Tetrylenic chloride, $C_4H_8Cl_2$. **1857** MILLER *Elem. Chem.* III. 127 *Tetrylic alcohol is a colourless liquid of high refracting power, lighter than water.

**Tett, tette,** obs. forms of TEAT.

**Tetter** (te·təɹ), *sb.* Forms: 1 tetr, 1–6 teter, 4–5 tetre, 5 -yr, -ere, 6–7 -ar, 6–8 tettar, (7 teater, 9 *dial.* titter), 6– tetter. [OE. *teter*:— OTeut. **tetru-*, pre-Teut. **dedru-*, Skr. *dadru* a kind of cutaneous disease, f. *dṛ* to crack; cf. Lith. *dedervine* tetter. The simple word is not preserved elsewhere in Teut., but cf. OHG. *zitaroh* (:— **titruha*), MHG. *ziteroch*, Bav. dial. *zitt(e)roch, -en*, Tyrol *zittrich*; also mod.Ger. *zittermal, zitterflechte*, Swiss *zitterabel* tetter, ringworm.]

**1.** A general term for any pustular herpetiform eruption of the skin, as eczema, herpes, impetigo, ringworm, etc.

*Crusted, pustular, running tetter*, impetigo; *eating t.*, lupus; *honeycomb t.*, favus; *humid* or *moist t.*, eczema; *milky t.*, milk-blotch; *scaly t.*, psoriasis.

*a* **700** *Epinal Gloss.* (O.E.T.) 128 *Basis*, teter. *Ibid.* 502 *Inpetigo*, tetr. *Ibid.* 791 *Papula vel pustula*, spryng *vel* tetr. *c* **725** *Corpus Gloss.* (O.E.T.) 128 *Balsis*, teter. *c* **897** K. ÆLFRED *Gregory's Past. C.* xi. 71 Se ðonne hæfð teter on his lichoman se hæfð on his mode ʒitsunga. *c* **1000** *Sax. Leechd.* I. 150 Heo ofʒenimð þone scruf & þone teter. *a* **1050** *Liber Scintill.* xxv. 99 Teter witodlice hæfð on lichaman. **1387** TREVISA *Higden* (Rolls) II. 61 Þere beeþ hoote bathes, þat wascheþ of teteres, oþer sores and scabbes. *c* **1475** *Pict. Voc.* in Wr.-Wülcker 791/14 *Hec serpedo*,..a tetere. **1584** COGAN *Haven Health* xxviii. (1636) 48 For a Tettar or Ring-worme a little Mustard laid upon it within a few dayes will cure it. **1602** SHAKS. *Ham.* I. v. 71. **1622** HAKEWILL *David's Vow* viii. 284 It is good..to kill a Tetter before it spread to a Ringworme. **1712** tr. *Pomet's Hist. Drugs* I. 66 The true Oil of Cedar is admirable for curing Tetters. **1850** BLACKIE *Æschylus* I. 125 A leprous tetter with corrosive tooth [would] Creep o'er my skin, and fasten on my flesh.

*fig.* **1641** MILTON *Reform.* I. Wks. 1851 III. 19 What a universall tetter of impurity had invenom'd every part, order, and degree of the Church. **1647, 1705** [see RINGWORM 1 b]. **1693** SOUTHERNE *Maid's last Prayer* I. i, The mercenary itch in an old woman; 'tis the very tetter of that sex. **1819** W. TENNANT *Papistry Storm'd* (1827) 145 In ran the airn by chance, And lat out baith the wind and matter, That lang had lodgit in that tetter.

**2.** A cutaneous disease in animals, esp. horses.

**1552** HULOET, Tetter for horse, *herpeta.* **1575** TURBERV. *Venerie* 227 The Tettar commeth vnto many dogs naturally or by kind or by age. **1614** MARKHAM *Cheap Husb.* (1623) 119 To heale any Tetter, or drie scabbe in Goates. **1708** *Lond. Gaz.* No. 4400/4 A black Gelding..a Tetter on the off Breast. **1794** *Sporting Mag.* III. 156 A cure for warts or tetters on horses. **1819** *Pantologia*, *Tetter*, called by farriers the flying-worm, or ring-worm. It runs up and down the skin in different directions, from whence it receives its name.

† **Te·tter**, *v.* *Obs. rare.* [f. prec.] *trans.* To affect with, or as with, a tetter.

**1607** SHAKS. *Cor.* III. i. 79 So shall my Lungs Coine words ..against those Meazels Which we disdaine should Tetter vs.

**Tetter-berry** (te·təɹberi). The common Bryony, *Bryonia dioica*; also, the berry of this plant. Variously said to cure and to produce tetter.

**1597** GERARDE *Herbal* II. cccvi. 720 In English Bryonie, white Bryonie, and tetter Berrie. **1598** FLORIO, *Vitalba*, wilde vine or tetterberrie growing in hedges with red berries ..the iuice whereof will cause the skin to blister. **1640** PARKINSON *Theatr. Bot.* II. xiii. 181 Good against all fretting and running cankers, gangrænes and tetters, and therefore the berries [are] usually called of the Country people, Tetter berries. **1886** BRITTEN & H. *Plant-n.*, *Tetter-berry*.. *Hants.*, where children have an idea that the juice of the fruit will, if it touches the skin, produce tetter.

**Te·tterish**, *a.* [f. TETTER *sb.* + -ISH [1].] Of the nature of tetter: with quot. cf. 1758 in next.

**1709** *Brit. Apollo* II. No. 36. 4/2 It..heales all Tetterish Humors.

**Tetterous** (te·tərəs), *a.* [f. TETTER *sb.* + -OUS.] Of the nature of, proceeding from, or causing tetter.

In quot. 1758 perhaps an error for TETROUS, foul.

**1719** QUINCY *Lex. Physico-Med.* (1726), *Noli-me-tangere*, touch me not, is a tetterous Eruption, thus call'd, from its Soreness, or Difficulty of Cure. **1750** RUTTY in *Phil. Trans.* LI. 476 Scab, tetterous eruptions, scald head, and sore eyes. **1758** J. S. *Le Dran's Observ. Surg.* (1771) 131 A tetterous Humour..shall create an Obstruction.

**Tetter-totter**, variant of TITTER-TOTTER.

**Tetterworm** (te·təɹwɒɹm). A cutaneous affection; = TETTER; a form of ringworm.

**1622** T. SCOTT *Belg. Pismire* 28 [It] ouerspreades the face and body thereof, like a Canker or Tetter-worm. **1727** BAILEY vol. II, *Tetter-worm*, an Insect. *a* **1825** FORBY *Voc. E. Anglia*, *Titter-worm*,..a cutaneous efflorescence, a series or confluence of minute pimples,..nor is it so troublesome and obstinate an affection as the *ring-worm.* It is a miliary eruption, in form rather vermicular than annular.

**Tetterwort** (te·təɹwɒɹt). The common Celandine, *Chelidonium majus*: so called because supposed to cure tetters.

*a* **1400–50** *Stockh. Med. MS.* 175 Celydonye or teterwort, *celidonie.* **1578** LYTE *Dodoens* I. xx. 31 Called..in English Celandyne, Swallowurte, and of some Tetterwurte. **1640** PARKINSON *Theatr. Bot.* v. lxx. 618 Tetterwort..the juice often applyed to tetters..will quickly kill their sharpenesse. **1879** PRIOR *Pop. Names Plants* (ed. 3) 235 *Tetter-wort*, from its curing tetters.

b. In America, The Blood-root, or Red PUCCOON, *Sanguinaria canadensis.* **1891** in *Cent. Dict.*

† **Te·tterwose.** *Obs. rare*—°. [f. TETTER *sb.* + (?) OOZE *sb.*[3]] The Common Germander, *Teucrium Chamædrys.*

*a* **1500** *Voc.*, Wr.-Wülcker 569/47 *Camedreos*,..Teterwose.

**Te·ttery**, *a.* [f. TETTER *sb.* + -Y.] Of the nature of tetter; tetterous.

**1697** R. PEIRCE *Bath Mem.* I. iv. 72 He came for a Tettery Eruption in his Neck and Chin. **1721** *Lond. Gaz.* No. 5977/4 All Leprous, Tettery, Scabby, Scaly, Scurfy, or other.. Breakings out upon the Skin.

† **Tettish, teatish,** *a.* *Obs.* [Origin of radical part *tet* or *teat* obscure: see also TEETY *a.*] Peevish, irritable, fretful.

**1567** GOLDING *Ovid's Met.* XIII. (1575) 172 And thou the selfsame Galate art more tettish for to frame, Than Oxen of the wildernesse whom neuer wyght did tame. **1592** NASHE *P. Penilesse* (ed. 2) 16 Hee is an olde man (for those yeares are most wayward and teatish). *a* **1619** FLETCHER *Wit without M.* v. ii, This Rogue, if he had been sober, sure had beaten me, is the most tettish Knave. **1621** — *Pilgrim* I. i, Who will be troubled with a tettish girl? *a* **1625** — *Woman's Prize* v. i, Her sicknesse Has made her somewhat teatish.

‖ **Tettix** (te·tiks). [a. Gr. τέττιξ.]

**1.** The cicada or tree-cricket, a homopterous winged insect: so called by the ancient Greeks, and hence in reference to Greece, Greek poets, etc. The South European species is *Cicada orni.*

**1775** R. CHANDLER *Trav. Asia M.* (1825) I. 343 The tettix or cicada in the day-time is extremely troublesome. **1816** KIRBY & SP. *Entomol.* xxiv. (1818) II. 402 One bard entreats the shepherds to spare the innoxious Tettix, that nightingale of the Nymphs. **1871** M. COLLINS *Inn of Strange Meetings* 40 Anacreon's tettix, singing in the trees. **1900** *Daily News* 13 Dec. 5/2 The much-sung 'tettix', or cicada.

**2.** *Entom.* A genus of *Acridiidæ*, or short-horned grasshoppers, typical of the orthopterous subfamily *Tettiginæ*, having the pronotum horizontal and the antennæ thirteen- or fourteen-jointed. Two species are known in Britain and nine in U. S.

**3.** *Golden tettix* (Gr. χρυσοῦς τέττιξ), an ornament worn in the hair by Athenians before Solon's time, as an emblem of their being aboriginal.

**1874** MAHAFFY *Soc. Life Greece* v. 135 Fastened their hair with a golden tettix. **1875** BROWNING *Aristoph. Apol.* 441 Citizens Like Aristeides and like Miltiades Wore each a golden tettix in his hair.

**Tetty**, variant of TEETY, easily offended.

**Tet-work**, obs. or erron. f. TUT-WORK, piece-work. **Teucalli**, obs. form of TEOCALLI.

**Teuch, teugh,** Sc. forms of TOUGH.

**Teuchat, -it,** Sc. variants of TEWHIT, lapwing.

**Teucrin** (tiū·krin). *Chem.* [f. Bot. L. *Teucr-ium*, generic name of germander + -IN [1].]

**1881** WATTS *Dict. Chem.* 3rd Suppl., *Teucrin*,..a glucoside obtained from *Teucrium fruticans*, a Sicilian plant used as a remedy for intermittent fever.

**Teuf-teuf**: see TUFF-TUFF.

**Teuk** (tiūk). *local.* [From its note of alarm.] The name given in East Anglia, Essex, and Kent to a bird, the Redshank, *Totanus calidris.*

**1859** ATKINSON *Walks & Talks* (1892) 300 A man went with a sailor to shoot teukes. **1892** *Within an hour of Lond.* (ed. 2) 256 The redshank, pool-snipe, teuke or took. [**1910** *Westm. Gaz.* 29 Jan. 11/1 The Redshank. The clear 'teuk-teuk' will break upon the stillness that reigns around, showing your deadly presence is detected.] *Ibid.*, The 'teuk', as they call the redshank in [the Essex marshes].

**Teut** (tiūt). Colloquial abbreviation of TEUTON.

**1862** J. BROWN *Lett.* (1907) 152 That blue-eyed, soft and white-skinned Teut, polyandrous and heartless. **1876** BLACKIE *Lang. & Lit. Highl. Scotl.* i. 66 The Celts..delight in a peculiar use of the nasal organ, unknown to the Teut, whether in Saxony or in the British low countries.

**Teutenage**, obs. form of TUTENAG, zinc.

**Teuthology** (tiūþǫ·lŏdʒi). [ad. mod.L. *teuthologia*, irreg. (for **teuthidologia*) f. Gr. τευθίς (-ιδο-ς) cuttle-fish, squid + -LOGY.] That branch of zoology which deals with cephalopods. Hence **Teutho·logist.**

**1886** HOYLE in *Challenger Rep.* XVI. 61 More explicit information..would be very acceptable to teuthologists. **1891** *Cent. Dict.*, Teuthology.

**Teu·tlose.** *Chem.* [f. Gr. τεῦτλ-ον beet + -OSE [2].] **1868** WATTS *Dict. Chem.* V. 740 *Teutlose*,..a kind of sugar, resembling glucose, said to exist, under certain circumstances, in the juice of beet.

**Teuto-** (tiū·to), before a vowel **Teut-**, combining form irregularly f. TEUTON, TEUTONIC.

**1.** Combined with other ethnic sbs. or adjs. in the sense 'That is a Teuton, or Teutonic and . . .', as *Teut-Aryan, Teuto-British, -Celt, -Celtic*, etc.

**1895** *Funk's Stand. Dict.*, *Teuto-Celtic*, of mixed Teutonic and Celtic blood, as the people of northern France. **1897** *19th Cent.* May 795 The early Aryan or better Teutaryan children would seem to have used another word. **1909** *Daily Chron.* 24 Mar. 4/6 Sir Rowland Blennerhasset.. belonged to that class of international publicists represented by the Baron von Bunsen.., his Teuto-British contributions to our magazines will be much missed.

**2.** Formative of derivatives, as **Teuto·latry**, the idolizing of Teutonic or German nationality, ideas, etc.; **Teutoma·nia**, a mania for what is Teutonic or German; hence **Teutoma·niac**, one possessed with Teutomania; **Teu·tophile, -phil** *sb.*, a lover or friend of Germany and the Germans: also as *adj.*; **Teutopho·bia**, an intense dread of or aversion to Germany and the Germans; hence **Teu·tophobe**, one possessed with Teutophobia; **Teu·tophobism.**

**1893** *Chicago Advance* 17 Aug., Words of warning against the danger of '*Teutolatry' [= blind attachment to German biblical criticism]. **1848** A. HERBERT in Todd *Irish Nennius* Notes 42 That crotchet is as old as Verstegan, who says the Picts were..phichtian or fighters...This was *Teutomania. **1899** *Q. Rev.* Apr. 440 To detest the Teutomania that worked at the expense of progress and good will. **1900** *Dundee Advertiser* 16 Apr. 16/3 France, which *Teutomaniacs are wont to brand as 'Celtic'. **1904** *Jrnl. Philos. Psychol. & Sci. Meth.* 4 Feb. 58 (C. D. Suppl.) Worthy of more attention than it receives in the current *Teutophile philosophy. **1904** *Daily Chron.* 29 Mar. 4/6 The late Tsar—who, as a *Teutophobe, would never speak German. **1905** *Daily News* 9 Aug. 6 The misunderstandings..are directly attributable to the Teutophobe Press. **1903** *Sat. Rev.* 14 Mar. 330/1 A reasoned protest against English *Teutophobia. **1904** *Q. Rev.* Jan. 320 These articles, apart from their *Teutophobism, are..lucid surveys.

**Teuton** (tiū·tǫn, -t'n). [ad. L. *Teuton-ēs*, *Teuton-i* (rarely sing. *Teuton*, *-us*), ethnic name. For sense 2 see Note to TEUTONIC.]

**1.** In *pl.* (usually in L. form *Teutones*) applied to an ancient people of unknown race, said to have inhabited the Cimbric Chersonesus in Jutland *c* 320 B.C., who, in company with the Cimbri, in 113–101 B.C. devastated Gaul and threatened the Roman republic.

**1727–41** CHAMBERS *Cycl.*, *Teutonic*, belonging to the Teutons, an ancient people of Germany, inhabiting chiefly along the coasts of the German ocean. **1839** *Penny Cycl.* XIV. 420/2 The consul Manilius and the proconsul Cæpio were defeated by the Teutones and Cimbri in Gaul. **1879** FROUDE *Cæsar* v. 41 Both Teutons and Cimbri were Germans.

**2.** A German; in extended ethnic sense, any member of the races or peoples speaking a Germanic or Teutonic language; in Great Britain and its colonies, and the United States, often used like 'Saxon' in opposition to 'Celt', and in avoidance of 'German' in its modern political sense.

**1833** D. MACMILLAN in Hughes *Mem.* ii. (1883) 20, I am very glad that my mother is a Teuton. **1841** SPALDING *Italy & It. Isl.* III. 221 These isolated Teutons constituted under the Venetian government a sort of smuggling free state. **1900** A. LANG in *Blackw. Mag.* Apr. 543/2 He is a partisan of the pure Teuton.

Hence **Teu·tondom,** the land or domain of the Teutons, Germany; the German people or state; **Teutone·sque** *a.* [-ESQUE], of Teutonic character.

**1880** STALLYBRASS tr. *Grimm's Teutonic Mythol.* I. 103 Those divinities of whom there is least trace to be found in the rest of *Teutondom. **1889** R. B. ANDERSON tr. *Rydberg's Teutonic Mythol.* 22 Did they look upon themselves as aborigines or as immigrants in Teutondom? **1839** DARLEY *Beaumont & Fletcher's Wks.* I. Introd. 38 A *Teutonesque consonantal language like ours, will, however polished, want sufficient melodiousness.

**Teutonic** (tiutǫ·nik), *a.* and *sb.* Also 7 Theut-. [ad. L. *Teutonic-us*, f. *Teuton-ēs*: see Note below.]

**A.** *adj.* **1.** Of or pertaining to the Teutons; German, esp. High German.

*c* **1645** HOWELL *Lett.* (1650) II. 80 The High Dutch or Teutonic tongue is one of the prime and most spacious maternall languages of Europe. **1657** *North's Plutarch, Add. Lives* (1676) 39 He [Charlemagne] began a Vulgar Teutonick Grammar. **1719** W. OLDISWORTH *Quillet's Callipædia* IV. 746 The fam'd Teutonick Valour, priz'd in war. **1724** WATERLAND *Athan. Creed* v. 67 There is in the emperor's library at Vienna, a German, or Teutonick version of this creed. **1770** (*title*) A Compendious View of the Grounds of the Teutonic Philosophy. With considerations by way of enquiry into..the writings of J. Behmen.

**b.** Of or pertaining to the ancient Teutones.

**1618** BOLTON *Florus' Hist.* (1636) 117 The Cimbrian, Theutonicke, and Tigurin Warre. **1727–41** [see TEUTON 1].

**2.** Of or pertaining to the group of languages allied to German (including Gothic, Scandinavian, Low German, and English), forming one of the great branches of the Indo-European, Indo-Germanic, or Aryan family, and to the peoples or tribes speaking these languages: now often called *Germanic*, and sometimes *Gothic*. (See Note below.)

**1727–41** CHAMBERS *Cycl.* s.v., Teutonic language, is the ancient language of Germany, which is ranked among the mother-tongues. **1768** BLACKSTONE *Comm.* III. xxiii. 350 Stiernhook ascribes the invention of the jury, which in the Teutonic language is denominated *nembda*, to Regner, king of Sweden and Denmark. **1840** CARLYLE *Heroes* i. (1872) 22 The word *Wuotan*, which is the original form of *Odin*, a word spread..over all the Teutonic Nations everywhere. **1846** MCCULLOCH *Acc. Brit. Empire* (1854) II. 79 The Normans, as well as the Saxons, were of Teutonic extraction. **1857** MAURICE *Ep. St. John* xx. 336 He raised up the Gothic or Teutonic race. **1864** BURTON *Scot Abr.* I. i. 5 The eastern and northern parts of what now is Scotland were peopled by a race of very pure Teutonic blood and tongue. **1888** SKEAT *Etymol. Dict.* p. xviii, German, properly called High-German, to distinguish it from the other Teutonic dialects, which belong to Low-German.

**3. Teutonic Knights, Teutonic Order** (of Knights): A military order of German Knights (in med.L. *Teutonicus Ordo Militaris*, F. *l'Ordre Teutonique*, Ger. *Deutsche Ritter*, in 16th c. *Teutsche Herren*), originally enrolled *c* 1191 as the Teutonic Knights of St. Mary of Jerusalem, for service in the Holy Land.

Their first seat was at Acre; after the fall of the Latin kingdom of Jerusalem, they settled at Marienburg on the Vistula, and carried on a crusade against the neighbouring heathen nations of Prussia, Livonia, etc. Their conquests made them a great sovereign power, but from the 15th c. they rapidly declined, and were abolished in 1809. The order maintains a titular existence in Austria and Holland.

[**1586** FERNE *Blaz. Gentrie* 128 The habite and robes of a Teuch-knight was a cloake or mantell of white, with a blacke crosse vpon the same.] **1617** MORYSON *Itin.* I. 34 A house of old belonging to the Teutonike order of Knights. *Ibid.* 61 Prussen of old was subiect to the order of the Teutonicke Knights. **1645** FULLER *Gd. Th. in Bad T.* (1841) 43 Martin de Golin, master of the Teutonic order, was taken prisoner by the Prussians, and delivered bound to be beheaded. **1727** BAILEY vol. II, *Teutonick Order*, ..The Order is now little known, tho' there is still a Great Master of it kept up. **1845** S. AUSTIN *Ranke's Hist. Ref.* I. 163 On the eastern frontier, where [in 1503] the Teutonic knights were incessantly pressed upon by the Poles and Russians. *Ibid.* II. ii. I. 373 Maximilian wished to hold him in check, on the one side by the Grand Duke of Moscow, on the other by the Teutonic Order.

**4. Teutonic cross,** a cross potent, being the badge of the Teutonic Order.

**1882** OGILVIE (Annandale), *Teutonic Cross*.

**B.** *sb.* **1.** † The language of any Teutonic race, *spec.* the German language (*obs.*); now by philologists applied only to the common or primitive speech, which afterwards broke up into the languages named in A. 2; also known as *Germanic*.

**1631** WEEVER *Anc. Fun. Mon.* 684 Although the Teutonic be more mixed with other strange languages. **1668** WILKINS *Real Char.* I. i. § 3. 3 The Teutonic or German is now distinguished into Upper and Lower. **1727–41** CHAMBERS *Cycl.* s.v. *Mother tongue*, Of mother tongues, Scaliger reckons ten in Europe, viz. the Greek, Latin, Teutonic or German, Sclavonic..Irish and British. **1755** *Gentl. Mag.* XXV. 150/1 An history of our language, in which it is regularly traced from the old Gothic and Teutonic to modern English. **1864** BURTON *Scot Abr.* I. i. 14 All the way from the border to the Highland line, the people, high and low, came to speak in very pure Teutonic. **1870** HELFENSTEIN *Teutonic Gram.* 408 The perfect of the verb *haldan* must have been *ha-hald* in the primitive Teutonic.

†**2.** = TEUTON 2. *Obs.*

**1638** SIR T. HERBERT *Trav.* (ed. 2) 361 Verstegan (alias Rowley) [had not] dar'd to make us all Teutonicks. **1691** WOOD *Ath. Oxon.* II. 40 His Grandfather was by nativity a Teutonic.

†**3.** *pl.* = Teutonic Knights: see A. 3. *Obs.*

**1693** tr. *Emilianne's Hist. Monast. Orders* III. 280 The Knights of Rhodes..and the Teutonicks. **1796** MORSE *Amer. Geog.* II. 238 As grand Master of the Teutonics.

[*Note.* Late Roman writers reckoned the *Teutones* among the peoples of Germania, and *Teutonicus* became a common poetic equivalent for *Germānicus*. It is now however held by many that they were not a Germanic people. But, before 900, German writers in Latin began to follow Latin poetic precedent by using *Theutonica lingua* instead of the barbarian or non-classical *Theotisca*, to render the native *tiutisch*, *tiutsch* (OHG. *diutisc*, mod. *deutsch* = OS. *thiudisc*, OE. *þeodisc*, literally 'national, popular, vulgar') as a designation of their vulgar tongue in contrast to Latin, as if this German adj. were identical with the ancient ethnic name. In 1200 *lingua Teutonica* was similarly used, and thenceforth *Teutonicus* became a usual L. rendering of *Deutsch* or *German*. Some Early German comparative philologists (e.g. Bopp in 1820) used *Teutonisch* as the name for the family of languages including Gothic, German, Scandinavian, and English; but for this *Germanisch* is now more used in German, and *Germanic* by many in English. But in English there is an awkwardness and sometimes ambiguity in using *Germanic* beside *German* (in its ordinary political sense), which does not arise in German or French, where *germanisch* and *germanique* are entirely distinct from *deutsch* and *allemand*. To avoid this, many English scholars prefer 'Teutonic' as the term for the linguistic family, and it is commonly so used in this dictionary.]

**Teutonically** (tiutǫ·nikăli), *adv.* [f. prec.: see -ICALLY.] In the manner of a 'Teuton' or German; in German style.

**1859** J. MARTINEAU *Ess.*, etc. (1891) III. 534 The position Teutonically proved untenable to all 'thinkers of any force'. **1895** *Athenæum* 17 Aug. 232/1 Dr. Führer justly, if Teutonically, writes [etc.].

**Teutonicism** (tiutǫ·nisiz'm). [f. as prec. + -ISM.] Teutonic (i.e. German) character or practice; a Teutonic expression; a Teutonism.

**1842** SIR C. LYELL in *Life*, etc. (1881) II. 63 The terms bakery and bookbindery seem useful Teutonicisms. **1901** *Westm. Gaz.* 2 Oct. 4/3 Italian composers essaying the more classical forms are impelled to out-Herod Herod in the seriousness and Teutonicism of their productions.

**Teutonism** (tiū·tŏniz'm). [f. TEUTON + -ISM.] **1.** An idiom or mode of expression peculiar to or characteristic of the Teutonic languages, esp. of German; a Germanism.

[**1619** KEPLER *Harmonia Mundi* IV. v. in *Opera* (1864) V. 234 Idem quod vultus, facies; quod etiam noster Teutonismus habet, qui faciem solet nominare das Angesicht.] **1889** *L. E. & D. Philos. Mag.* Nov. 425 The translator has done his part of the work well, although we detect distinct Teutonisms here and there.

**2.** Teutonic or Germanic character, type, constitution, system, or spirit; German feeling and action (either in the wider ethnical or the restricted national or political sense).

**1854** MILMAN *Lat. Chr.* III. vii. (1864) II. 101 Teutonic Europe, or Europe so deeply interpenetrated with Teutonism. **1881** *Atlantic Monthly* XLVII. 230 During most of classic antiquity the centre of Teutonism seems to have been farther east than Germany. **1900** A. LANG in *Blackw. Mag.* Apr. 543/2 He regrets the Norman Conquest as an interference with unmixed Teutonism.

**Teutonist** (tiū·tŏnist). [f. as prec. + -IST.] **1.** One versed in the history, etc., of the Teutonic race or languages; one who makes much of Teutonic influence in the history of England.

**1882** *Academy* No. 511. 112 [J. R. Green's] 'Making of England'..will probably long represent the last word of the Teutonist on the nature and extent of the primitive English settlement. **1883** T. KERSLAKE in *N. & Q.* 6th Ser. VII. 301/2 A canon of the most profound English Teutonist, the late Mr. Kemble.

**2.** One whose writings have a Teutonic character or style.

**1894** G. ALLEN in *Westm. Gaz.* 25 July 3/1 You may divide our poets..into two great schools in this matter—the Classicists and the Teutonists, if I may venture so to style them...To this latter class belong Shakespeare, Keats, Coleridge, Burns, Rossetti, and the greater part of our romantic poets.

**Teuto·nity.** [f. as prec. + -ITY.] The quality or condition of being Teutonic; Teutonism.

**1877** *Athenæum* 1 Dec. 696/2 The German lieutenant has dropped some of his superfluous Teutonity. **1886** *Pall Mall G.* 24 July 3/2 If any one is inclined to think that the termination *tz* must imply Teutonity, let him remember that far from any German speech he will find such names as Retz, Batz, and Biarritz.

**Teutonize** (tiū·tŏnəiz), *v.* [f. TEUTON + -IZE.] *trans.* To make or render Teutonic or German.

**1845** *Blackw. Mag.* LVII. 478 After Teutonising the Hebrew in this manner, he next proceeds to the Egyptian. **1867** FREEMAN *Norm. Conq.* I. iii. 126 Those Celtic lands ..had been..to a great extent Teutonized. **1882** *Sat. Rev.* 17 June 768/1 Justified in treating, for all practical purposes, as Teutonic a nation so thoroughly Teutonized.

**b.** *intr.* To conform to Teutonism; to play the Teuton. **1882** in OGILVIE (Annandale).

Hence **Teu·tonizing** *vbl. sb.*; **Teutoniza·tion,** the action or process of rendering or being made Teutonic or German.

**1855** MILMAN *Lat. Chr.* IV. x. (1864) II. 435 The Franks now ..shared with the Romans the great hierarchical dignities... This Teutonising of the hierarchy [etc.]. **1872** D. H. HAIGH in *Archæol. Cantiana* VIII. 18 From Kent the Teutonization of Britain began. **1878** *Fraser's Mag.* XVIII. 571 His style underwent a process of Teutonisation.

**Teutono-,** combining form of TEUTON, as in **Teu·tonoma·nia, Teu·tonopho·be, Teu·tonopho·bia:** see TEUTO-.

**1839** DONALDSON *New Cratylus* § 97 (1850) 141 The Hellenic or Teutono-Persic language of the North. **1886** *Pall Mall G.* 18 Oct. 3/2 It was in Russia that he discovered the earthly paradise of Teutonophobia. **1897** *Current Hist.* (Buffalo, N.Y.) VII. 96 [He] is said to be neither a Teutonophobe nor a Francophil. **1905** H. PAUL in *19th Cent.* Nov. 862 Ministers..will do no good by tampering with Mr. Chamberlain's exploded Teutonomania.

**Te·vel, ta·vel,** *v. Obs.* exc. *dial.* Forms: 3–4 **tauel, teuel,** 9 *Sc.* **tevel, tevvel.** [Origin and primary meaning obscure; it is even uncertain whether there are not here two different words.

Senses 2 and 3 suggest a possible connexion with TAVE *v.* If sense 1 was orig. 'to contend (in words), we might compare Norw. *tevla*, Sw. *täfla*, 'to contend, cope, vie, rival, strive, struggle'; but these go back to ON. *tefla* to play at tables or draughts, = OE. *tæflian*, ME. TAVEL, which appears to have no connexion with this.]

†**1.** *intr.* ? To talk, converse; or perh. rather, To discuss, argue, contend in words. *Obs.*

*a* **1225** *St. Marher.* 13 Ich leote ham talkin ant tauelin of godlec ant treowliche luuien ham, wiðuten uuel wilnung. *a* **1225** *Leg. Kath.* 822 Þet he þet is nomecuðest & meast con cume cuðe þrof..& teueli [*v.r.* tauele] wið me. *Ibid.* 1254 Swa awundret of hire wittie wordes, & swa offearet & offruht, & alle hise feren, þet nefde hare nan tunge to tauelin a tint wið [*v.r.* teuelin a dint].

†**2.** To struggle, strive, contend; to labour. *Obs.*

**13..** *E. E. Allit. P.* B. 1189 Trwe tulkkes in toures teueled [*printed* teneled] wyth-inne, In bigge brutage [= brattice] of borde, bulde on þe walles. **13..** *Gaw. & Gr. Knt.* 1514 F[or] to telle of þis teuelyng of þis trwe knyȝtez, Hit is þe tytelet, token, and tyxt of her werkkez.

**3.** *intr.* To behave in a disorderly or violent manner; to rage. *Sc.*

**1828** CARLYLE *Let. to J. Carlyle* 25 Aug. in Froude *Life* (1882) II. ii. 37 Gawn up and down the country tevelling and screeching like a wild bear.

**4.** *trans.* (See quot.) *Sc.*

**1825** JAMIESON, *Tevvel*, to confuse, to put into a disorderly state, *Dumfr.*

†**Te·vell.** *Sc. Obs. rare.* [app. a. F. *tavelle* in its obs. sense 'a small edging lace, a Crowne-lace' (Cotgr. 1611): cf. TAVELL.] Lace.

**1632** in *14th Rep. Hist. MSS. Comm.* App. III. 235 Ane goun of cloth of gold, laid over with tevell of gold. *Ibid.*, Ane blak dames goun, laid over with sylver tevell.

**Tew** (tiū), *sb.*[1] *Obs.* exc. *dial.* Also 9 **tue.** [f. TEW *v.*[1]]

†**1.** The tawing of leather: see TEW *v.*[1] 1. *Obs.*

*c* **1440** *Promp. Parv.* 489/2 Tew, or tewynge of lethyr.

†**2.** The work of preparation; labour. *Obs.*

**1644** *Hartlib's Legacy* (1655) 286 Each Acre shall be worth ..at least six pound, thirteen shillings, four pence for the tew onely, and at least six pound, thirteen shillings and four pence more for the seed.

**3.** Constant work and bustling; a state of worry or excitement. *dial.* and *U.S.*

**1825** BROCKETT *N. C. Words* s.v. *Tue*, *Sare tues*, great difficulty in accomplishing any thing. **1866** E. TABOR *Rachel's Secr.* I. vii. 103 There was no end of the tew and worry in a farm-house. **1880** TENNYSON *Northern Cobbler* ix, When we coom'd into Meeätin', at fust she wur all in a tew. **1883** HOWELLS *Woman's Reason* (Tauchn.) II. 27 My wife was always in a tew about the danger.

†**Tew,** *sb.*[2] *Obs.* Also 6 **tewe,** (7 **tewgh, tiew,** 9 *dial.* **tow**). [Not known before 15th c.: app. corresp. to WFris. *túch*, late MDu., mod.Du. *tuig*, MLG., LG. *tūch*, MHG. *ziuc*, Ger. *zeug*, apparatus, gear, tools, utensils, implements, tackle: f. ablaut stem *tiug-* of *tiuhan* to draw, lead (TEE *v.*[1]).]

**1.** Fishing-tackle; nets, fishing-lines, etc.

*c* **1440** *Promp. Parv.* 490/1 Tew, of fyschynge, *piscalia*, n plurali, *retiaria* [MS. *reci*-]. **1529** *Will J. Thomson* Somerset Ho.), A mansfare of all tewe except sperlyn nett. **1619** FLETCHER *M. Thomas* I. iii, *Dor*...The fool shall now fish for himself. *Alice*. Be sure then His tewgh be tith and strong:..He'l catch no fish else. **1622** MALYNES *Anc. Law-Merch.* 246 Also that they shall be honest and true..being asked concerning the length and depth of their ropes or tewes when they are in driuing; neither shall they wittingly ..suffer their tewes to flit and run ouer one another.

*fig.* **1589** WARNER *Alb. Eng.* VI. xxix. (1612) 144 She [Queen Catharine 14..] pitched Tewe, he [Owen Tudor] masshed. **1602** *Ibid.* Epit. 391 This Cardinall, conspiring with William de la Poole,..pitched their Tew to intangle the same Protector. **1603** HARSNET *Pop. Impost.* 12 The groundes of their Art [were] layde sure and a little trying of their Tooles, whether their Tew would holde or no.

**2.** Implements, tools, materials for work generally; stuff. Also *fig.*

**1616** T. SCOTT *Philomythie* C vj b, When..all your traines and tew in order laid. *a* **1638** MEDE *Wks.* (1672) 815, I am not unwilling to communicate unto you the most of my tew, because, I perceive, you make some account of them. **1671** SKINNER, *Tew*,..Instrumentum, Materia, Arma, Armamenta. **1674** N. FAIRFAX *Bulk & Selv.* 36 Another Argument..which may happily at first blush seem to have more tiew in it than all the stands we have met with hitherto. *a* **1825** FORBY *Voc. E. Anglia*, *Tow*,..necessary tools or apparatus for any purpose (pronounced like *cow*). **1904** *Eng. Dial. Dict.*, *Tew*,..Obsol. w. Cy. Materials for work.

**Tew**, *sb.*[3] *Sc.* [Etymol. doubtful: perh. from same root as prec.] (?) The braces of a drum, or the braces and cords by which a drum is tightened.

*c* **1720** in Beveridge *Culross & Tulliallan* xix. (1885) II. 90 The council..allows the drummer to get als many new tews as will serve the drum.

**Tew** (tiū), *v.*[1] *Obs.* exc. *dial.* Forms: 4–7 **tewe**, 5 **tewhe**, **tewyn**, 6 **teawe**, 6–7 **teaw**, 7 **tiew**, **tewgh**, 8–9 **tue**, 7– **tew**. [In branch I. app. a later collateral, derivative, or altered form of TAW *v.*[1], with which it is synonymous; the form-history is obscure. Branch II. corresponds to nothing in TAW, and may be of other origin, though sense-development from branch I. is conceivable.]

**I. 1.** *trans.* To convert skin into a species of leather, by steeping, beating, and manipulation; to dress; = TAW *v.*[1] 2.

*c* **1330** R. BRUNNE *Chron. Wace* (Rolls) 12453 Fful manye kynges had he [the giant Ryton] don slo, & flow þe berdes of alle þo; Til a pane, as a furour, he did hem tewe. *c* **1440** *Promp. Parv.* 490/1 Tewyn lethyr, *frunio, corrodio.* **1530** PALSGR. 754/2, I tewe leather, *je souple.* **1601** HOLLAND *Pliny* (1634) II. 473 Certaine skinnes of leather well tewed and dressed vntill they be soft. **1681** CHETHAM *Angler's Vade-m.* xxxiv. § 3 (1689) 186 After the skin is tewed in the skinner's lime-pits. **1709** *Brit. Apollo* II. No. 49. 4/1 Were his Hide tew'd by Tanners. *fig.* **1709** *Brit. Apollo* II. No. 29. 3/2 Tew her Hide with an Oaken Plant.

**b.** *intr.* for *refl.* or *passive.*

*c* **1880** *Northants. Dial.*, Take it [the leather] out again and let it lie and tew.

**2.** To work (anything) into proper consistency by beating, etc.; to temper (mortar). Now *dial.*

**1641** BEST *Farm. Bks.* (Surtees) 138 Then doe wee water it [the earth] and tewe it well att the first, and soe leaue it for her that serveth to temper. **1688** R. HOLME *Armoury* III. 88/2 *Tew*, to Batter or draw out a peece of Iron. **1721** BAILEY, To *Tew*..to beat Mortar. To *Tew* Hemp..to beat or dress it. **1797** P. WAKEFIELD *Ment. Improv.* (1801) III. 2 Kneading and tewing the two earths together is the most laborious part of the work. **1883** *Almondbury & Huddersf. Gloss.* s. v., That lime wants better tewing.

**3.** *transf.* and *fig.* **a.** To deal with or employ.

**1489** *Churchw. Acc. Walberswick, Suffolk* (Nichols 1797) 183 Yt 1 man, or 2 men shall rec. the town doollys of heryngs and sperlings..and to tewe them to most profyte of the town.

†**b.** To prepare or bring into a proper state or condition for some purpose. *Obs.*

**1571** GOLDING *Calvin on Ps.* xxx. 9 No man can giue himselfe cheerfully vnto prayer, till he bee thoroughly teawed and well furbished by the crosse. *a* **1577** GASCOIGNE *Flowers* (1587) 1 These chattering teeth, this trembling toong Well tewed with careful cries. *a* **1619** FLETCHER *Wit without M.* III. i, So tewed him up with Sack that he lies lashing a But of Malmsie for his Mares.

†**4.** To beat, flog, thrash, belabour. Also *fig.* = TAW *v.*[1] 3, 3 b. *Obs.*

**1598** DALLINGTON *Meth. Trav.* G ij, He left them all France, tyned and tewed, as bare as a birdes bone. **1600** HOLLAND *Livy* 716 When they saw once the bodies of their Tribunes tewed with rods. **1622** FLETCHER *Begg. Bush* III. ii, Tew 'em, swinge 'em, Knock me their brains into their breeches. **1664** J. WILSON *A. Commenius* II. i, He does so tew the Pope; That man of sin, The Whore of Babylon. **1670** NARBOROUGH *Jrnl.* in *Acc. Sev. Late Voy.* I. (1694) 75 The Trees are much weather-beaten,..and the shore-sides much tewed with the surge of the Waters.

†**b.** To lay on (a rod, scourge). *Obs. rare.*

**1583** STOCKER *Civ. Warres Lowe C.* Ep. Ded. A ij b, Whiche roddes and scourges, when he hath in his great wisedome, teawed vpon them, for their amendement, he will surely..caste into the fire.

**c.** *dial.* To shake up, toss about, turn over (as hay); to tumble, rumple, crease, disarrange (dress); to pull about, pull in pieces; to discuss; to vex.

In *Eng. Dial. Dict.*, cited as in use from Northern Counties to Warw., Northamp., E. Anglia.

**II. 5.** *trans.* To fatigue or tire with hard work; *refl.* = 6. *dial.*

**1825** BROCKETT *N. C. Words* s. v. *Tue*, He tues himself. **1893** *Carlisle Patr.* 30 June 3/3 (E. D. D.), S—— went down before K——, who was sair tewed in the operation...The two giants could not be said to have tew'd themselves much. *c* **1895** 'FLIT' *Holderness Harvest* 84 I'se been tewing mysen a'most to deead all forenoon.

**6.** *intr.* To work hard, to exert oneself, to toil; to bustle *about.* Now *dial.* and *U.S.*

**1787** GROSE *Provinc. Gloss.*, To *Tew*,..also to work hard. **1825** BROCKETT *N. C. Words*, *Tue*, to labour long and patiently, to fatigue by repeated or continued exertion...*A tuing life*, a laborious life. *A tuing soul*, a hard working person. **1863** TROLLOPE *St. Olaves* II. 4 Little folks like you an' me has to tew about and fend for 'em both. **1894** BARING-GOULD *Queen of L.* xii, I tew from morning till night. **1909** *Daily News* 31 May 4 Our male folk, who after 'tewing' at the mill all the week are usually allowed to take their time at the Saturday tea table.

Hence **Tewed** (tiūd) *ppl. a.*; **Tewing** *vbl. sb.* (also *attrib.*) and *ppl. a.*

*c* **1440** *Promp. Parv.* 490/1 *Tevwyd, *frunitus.* **1488** in *Ripon Ch. Acts* (Surtees) 286, i bukskyn tewyd. **1611** COTGR., *Tracassé*, hurried, tossed tugged, tewed; spoiled, ouerworne, or misused, by much remouing. **1863** MRS. TOOGOOD *Yorks. Dial.*, *Tewed*, tired, exhausted. **1892** CARRUTH in *Kansas Univ. Mag.* I. (U. S.) (E. D. D.), I'm tewed and fretted. **1394–6** *Cartular. Abb. de Whiteby* (Surtees) 623 Item pro *tewyng xiiii pellium luporum, i. s. ix. d. *c* **1430** LYDG. *Min. Poems* (Percy Soc.) 201 Whoos tewhyng hath coost many a crowche, Hire pylche souple for to make. **1852** R. S. SURTEES *Sponge's Sp. Tour* x, Bullfrog, whom I bought him of, is very fat..and can't stand much tewing in the saddle. **1855** ROBINSON *Whitby Gloss.* s. v., 'A tewing hay time', the season wet and unfavourable for the hay,.. involving much extra labour. **1882** OGILVIE (Annandale), *Tewing-beetle*, a spade-shaped instrument for tewing or beating hemp. **1902** BARING-GOULD *Nebo the Nailer* xix, She alway was a tewin' woman.

†**Tew**, *v.*[2] *Obs.* Also 8 **tue**. [app. a derivative or altered form of TOW *v.*, of much later appearance; the phonology is obscure.] *trans.* To haul, tow (a ship, net, etc.); to drag, pull, tug; = TOW *v.*

**1600** HOLLAND *Livy* XXV. XXX. 571 Marcellus caused a great hulke, laden with armed souldiours, to be fastened by an haling rope unto a gallie.., and so in the night by strength of oares to bee tewed and drawne up after it into Acradina. **1612** DRAYTON *Poly-olb.* xii. 197 The goodly river Lee..By which the Danes had then their full-fraught navies tew'd. **1622** *Ibid.* XXV. (1748) 367 The toiling fisher here is tewing of his net. *a* **1693** *Urquhart's Rabelais* III. Prol. 7 He..tugg'd it, tew'd it, carry'd it [a tub]. **1706** BAYNARD in Sir J. Floyer *Hot & Cold Bath.* II. 386 A Sprain ..tued, hal'd and wrested by ignorant Bone-setters. **1787** GROSE *Provinc. Gloss.*, *To Tew*, to pull or tow.

**Tewch**, Sc. form of TOUGH.

**Tewel, tuel** (tiū·ĕl). Now only *dial.* Forms: 4 **tuelle**, **tuwel**, 5 **tewelle**, **touele**, **towel**, 5–7 **tewell**, 6–8 **tuell**, 7 **tuill**, **tiwill**, 4–8 **tuel**, 4– **tewel**. [a. OF. *tuel*, *tuele*, etc. (12th c. in Godef.) a tube, pipe, tuyere, mod.F. *tuyau*, = ME. TUTEL beak, Sp., Pg., Pr. *tudel* tube:—Romanic type **tūtellum*, referred to a German word repr. by MDu. *tûte*, Du. *tuit* pipe, nipple, etc., LG. *tûte*, *tüte* beak, snout, pipe, etc.: cf. also ON. *túta* teat-like prominence, Sw. *tut* pipe, Da. *tud* spout. As to ulterior etymology see Franck, s. v. *tuit.*]

†**1.** A shaft or opening for the escape of smoke, etc.; a chimney. *Obs.*

*c* **1384** CHAUCER *H. Fame* III. 559 Suche a smoke gan out wende..As dothe where that men melt lede Loo alle on high fro the tuelle. **1483** *Cath. Angl.* 380/2 A Tewelle of a chymnay, *epicausterium.* **1567** FENTON *Trag. Disc.* v. (1898) I. 236 The chamber where our Cornelio was rammed up in the tewell of a chymney.

†**b.** *transf.* The vent or opening in a pie-crust.

*c* **1420** *Liber Cocorum* (1862) 38 In myddes þo lydde an tuel þou make, Set hit in þo ovyn for to bake; ȝete take hit oute, fede hit with wyne.

†**c.** A conduit. *Obs. rare*[—1].

**1725** PEARCE *Laws & Cust. Stannaries* Introd. 13 The said Conduit, which the Tinners commonly call a *Tuell*, and may properly descend from the Latin Word *Tutela.*

**2.** The anus; the rectum, or lower bowel: now chiefly of animals, esp. horses. [Not in OFr.]

*c* **1386** CHAUCER *Sompn. T.* 440 And whan this sike man felte this frere Aboute his tuwel [*v. rr.* tuel, tewel, touele] grope there and heere. *c* **1425** tr. *Arderne's Treat. Fistula* (E.E.T.S.) 9 Þe skynne atuyx þe tewel & þe fistule. **1523** FITZHERB. *Husb.* § 85 Broken wynded is a yll dysease,.. and appereth at his nosethryll, at his flanke, and also at his tuell. **1578** LYTE *Dodoens* II. xcvii. 281 Swellings and inflammations of the tuell or fundement. **1601** HOLLAND *Pliny* XXI. xix. 106 Violets..a peculiar vertue they have.. to helpe the procidence or falling downe both of tuill and matrice. *c* **1720** W. GIBSON *Farrier's Dispens.* x. (1734) 241 Keeping the Horses tail close to his Tuel. **1895** *Gloss. E. Anglia*, *Tewel*, the vent or fundament of a horse.

**3.** (See quots., and TEW-IRON, TUYERE.)

**1677** MOXON *Mech. Exerc.* No. I. 2 In the back of the Forge..is fixed a thick Iron plate, and a taper Pipe in it.. called a Tewel, or (as some call it) a Tewl-Iron. .. Into this taper Pipe or Tewel is placed the Nose or Pipe of the Bellows. **1831** J. HOLLAND *Manuf. Metal* I. 163 A stout perforated core of..iron, called the tewel or tew-iron.

**Tewel**(**l**, **-e**, obs. forms of TOWEL.

†**Tewer.** *Obs. rare*[—0]. [f. TEW *v.*[1] + -ER [1].] One who taws leather; = TAWER.

*c* **1440** *Promp. Parv.* 490/1 Teware, *corridiator.* **1483** *Cath. Angl.* 380/2 A Tewer of skynnes,..*coriarius.*

**Tewer**, corrupt form of TUYERE.

**Tewesday, Tewet**, obs. ff. TUESDAY, TEWHIT.

**Tewfikose** (tiū·fikōus). *Chem.* [f. the name of Mohammed Tewfik Pasha (Khedive of Egypt 1879–92) + -OSE [2].] A peculiar sugar found (1890–1) in the milk of the buffalo of the East, *Bubalus Buffelus*, taking the place of the ordinary milk sugar. It yields glucose when hydrolysed.

**1891** *Daily Chron.* 18 Mar. 8/5 A sugar of a hitherto undescribed variety—'tewfikose', as it is proposed to be called in honour of the Khedive. **1902** in WEBSTER Suppl.

**Tewgh, tewhe**: see TEW *v.*[1], TOUGH.

**Tewhit, tewit** (tī·hwit, tī·wit, tiū·it; also tyū·χit, tyʊ·χit, tiū·fit). Now *local.* Forms: *α.* 5, 8–9 **tuchet**, 6 **tuechit**, 9 **teuchit**, **-at**, **tchuchet**; *β.* 7 **tuewhite**, **tequhyt**, **terwhite**, 9 **tuquheit**, **tewhit**, **teewheep**, **-whoap**; *γ.* 6 **tuwyte**, 7– **tewit** (7–9 **tewet**, 7 **teewitte**); *δ.* 8–9 **tewfet**, **tufit**, 9 **tufat**, **teufet**, **teufit**, **teafit**. [Orig. echoic: see PEWIT. The *α* and *β* forms are Sc.; the others are cited in the *Eng. Dial. Dict.* from Scotland to Yorks. and Chesh.] The common Lapwing or Pewit, *Vanellus cristatus.*

*α.* *c* **1450** HOLLAND *Howlat* 834 The Tuchet gird to the Golk, and gaif him a fall. **1549** *Compl. Scotl.* vi. 39 The tuechitis cryit theuis nek, quhen the piettis clattrit. **1746** FORBES *Dominie Deposed* III. iii, 'Tis strange what makes kirk-fouks so stupid,..Far better for them hunt the touchit. **1815** G. BEATTIE *John o'Arnha* (1826) 63 The timid teuchit slouch'd its crest. **1899** J. COLVILLE *Scot. Vernacular* 12 The teuchat..wailed out in circles round the intruder.

*β.* **1629** *Orkney Witch Trial* in Dalyell *Darker Superstit. Scotl.* (1834) 150 *note*, Get the bones of ane tequhyt, and carry thame in your clothes. **1824** MACTAGGART *Gallovid. Encycl.* s. v. *Pirr*, Eggs, somewhat like tewhit eggs in size and colour. **1835** J. M. WILSON *Tales Borders* I. 185/2 He was just in the situation o' a tewhit that had lost its mate—*te-wheet! te-wheet!* it cried.

*γ.* **1592** *Shuttleworths' Acc.* (Chetham Soc.) 76 Towe tuwytes and a snype, iijd. **1678** RAY *Willughby's Ornith.* 307 In the North of England they call it the Tewit, from its cry. **1688** J. CLAYTON in *Phil. Trans.* XVII. 997 The Tewits are smaller than the English, and have no long Toppins. **1828** *Craven Gloss.*, *Tewet*, a pewit or plover.

*δ.* **1787** GROSE *Provinc. Gloss.*, *Tewfet*, a lapwing. North. **1788** W. MARSHALL *Yorksh.* Gloss. (E. D. S.), *Tufit*,.. the peewit, or green plover. **1878** *Cumbld. Gloss.*, *Teufet.*

**Tew-iron** (tiū·əiəɹn). Also 6 **tewe ireon**, 7 **teu iyron**, 8 *dial.* **tuiron**, **tuarn**, 9 *Sc.* **tö-airn**. [Represents F. *tuyère*, through the form *tewyre*, *yre* being taken as the dial. *yre*, *ire*, IRON: see TUYERE.] See quots. 1825, 1888, and cf. TEWEL 3.

**1570** *Wills & Inv. N. C.* (Surtees) I. 329, I do gyue vnto John Dycheborne a pair of bellowis wth a tewe Ireon. *c* **1670** in Beveridge *Culross & Tulliallan* xxi. (1885) II. 166 To be discharged of their worke by stryking out of thair teu iyron, and thair other workloums. *c* **1700** KENNETT (MS. Lansd. 1033, lf. 406), Four stones or walls, that next the bellows is called the Tuarn or Tuiron wall. **1825** JAMIESON, *To-airn* (*o* pron. as Gr. *υ*), a piece of iron, with a perforation so wide as to admit the pipe of the smith's bellows, built into the wall of his forge, to preserve the pipe from being consumed by the fire. **1840** *Civil Eng. & Arch. Jrnl.* III. 42/1, 5 inches of the end nearest the tew iron were burnt completely away. **1888** ELWORTHY *W. Som. Wordbk.*, *Tew-iron* (tüe·uy·ur), the nozzle of a smith's bellows, or of a smelting furnace...Tew-irons are regular articles of ironmongery.

**Tewit**, variant of TEWHIT, lapwing.

**Te-wit, te-whit**, also 6 **teuyt**, **tueit**, imitations of the cry of some birds.

*a* **1518** SKELTON *Magnyf.* 1005 And howe styll she [hawk] dothe syt! Teuyt, teuyt! Where is my wyt? **1549** *Compl. Scotl.* vi. 39 The oxee cryit tueit. **1791** WOLCOTT (P. Pindar) *Commiss. Ep. Ld. Lonsdale* 110 Jove's bird..Turn Owl to cry Tee-whit in some old barn.

**Tewke**, var. TUKE *Obs.*, textile fabric.

**Tewly** (tiū·li), *a.* Now *dial.* Forms: 6–7 **tuly**, 7 **tuely**, 8 **tooly**, 7, 9– **tewly**. [Derivation uncertain: perh. from TEW *sb.*[1] or *v.*[1]; but the early spellings *tu-*, *too-* do not favour this.] Weak, sickly, delicate; poorly, unwell.

**1538** BALE *Temptacyon* (1870) 14 Ye are but tuly, ye are no stronge persone doughtlesse. **1619** J. DYKE *Caveat* (1620) 32 Timothy was surely weake, and but a sickely, tuely man. **1691** RAY *S. & E. C. Words*, *Tewly* or *tuly*, tender, sick: *tuly* stomached, weak stomached. **1787** GROSE *Provinc. Gloss.*, *Tooly*, tender, sickly. A tooly man or woman. *Hampsh.* **1898** *Longm. Mag.* Nov. 50 His head's wise enough, if his body be tewly.

**Tewly**, var. TULY *a. Obs.* (of silk).

**Tewne, Tewsday**, obs. ff. TUNE, TUESDAY.

†**Tewslite**, *v. Obs. nonce-wd.* [perh. intended for *to-slite*, OE. *tóslitan* to rend asunder, distract the mind of; but that vb. is not otherwise known after 1300, so that its actual survival is unlikely.]

**1590** [TARLTON] *News Purgat.* (1844) 56, I have yet left one chapter of choplodgick to tewslite you withall.

**Tew·some**, *a. dial.* [f. TEW *v.*[1], *sb.*[1] + -SOME.] Troublesome; restless, unquiet.

**1828** *Craven Gloss.*, *Teughsome*, unquiet, restless. 'For seur, this is lile teughsome barn'. **1881** *Cornhill Mag.* Oct. 392 A mother likes most the child that's most tewsome.

†**Tewtaw**, *sb. Obs.* Also 8 **tewtow**, 9 *dial.* **tewter**. [Goes with next.

If the sb. was the earlier, its derivation would prob. be from TEW *v.*[1] + TAW *sb.*[1], or TOW *sb.* = 'that which tews taw or tow'; but if the vb. was the earlier, TAW would naturally be the vb., and *tew* either TEW *sb.*[1] or some other word. The origin of the second element was app. lost before the word became *tewter*. Johnson knew only the vb., which he considered a reduplicated form of *tew.*]

An implement for breaking hemp or flax.

1649 BLITHE *Eng. Improv. Impr.* (1653) 262–3 As to the working of it, you must provide your Brakes and Tewtawes both,..the brake which bruises and toughens the harl, and the Tewtaw that cuts and divides out the coare. 1727 BAILEY vol. II, *A Tew-tow*, a Tool to break or beat Flax with. 1847–78 HALLIWELL, *Tewter*, an instrument for breaking flax, as a brake for hemp. *Chesh.* 1879 MISS JACKSON *Shropsh. Word-bk.*, *Tewter.*

† **Tewtaw,** *v. Obs.* Also 9 *dial.* tewter. [Goes with prec., q. v.] *trans.* To beat or dress (hemp or flax); = TAW *v.*[1] Hence **Tewtawing** *vbl. sb.*

1601 HOLLAND *Pliny* (1634) II. 2 Before it can be occupied, it must be watered, dried, braked, tew-tawed, and with much labor..reduced..to be as soft and tender as wooll. 1669 WORLIDGE *Syst. Agric.* (1681) 333 To *Tew-taw Hemp.* 1707 MORTIMER *Husb.* (1721) I. 155 The Method and Way of Watering, Pilling, Braking, Tew-tawing, &c. of Hemp and Flax. 1755 JOHNSON, *Te'wtaw* (formed from *tew* by reduplication), to beat, to break. 1879 MISS JACKSON *Shropsh. Word-bk.*, *Tewter*, to beat and break the hemp-stalk after it had been subjected to the action of fire.

**Tewyre,** corrupt f. TUYERE: cf. TEW-IRON.

† **Texalte** = *to exalt*: see T'[1] and EXALT.

*c* 1450 *Story Alexander* in *Wars Alexander* 281 God hath sent me..for texalte and magnifye hys lawe.

**Texan** (te·ksăn), *a.* and *sb.* [f. next + -AN.] Of or pertaining to the State of Texas. In some specific names of animals, plants, etc.: e. g. **Texan armadillo,** the PEBA; **Texan fever** = *Texas fever*; **Texan hare,** the American JACK-RABBIT; **Texan pride,** *Phlox Drummondii*, a bright-flowered annual, native in Texas; **Texan shrew-mole,** *Scalops latimanus.*

1860 BARTLETT *Dict. Amer.* 218 Jackass Rabbit..known also as Mule Rabbit, Texan Hare, and Black-tailed Hare. 1888 *Cassell's Encycl. Dict.*, Texan shrew-mole.

**Texas** (te·ksăs). The name of one of the United States, formerly a province of Mexico, then for a short time an independent republic.

**1.** *Western U. S.* The uppermost structure of a river-steamer, containing the pilot-house and officers' quarters. Also *attrib.*

1872 DE VERE *Americanisms* 128 The cabins below this [the upper deck] and above the grand saloon, where the officers of the boat are accommodated, also belong to *Texas.* 1883 'MARK TWAIN' *Life on Mississippi* iv. 43 The boiler deck, the hurricane deck, and the texas deck are fenced and ornamented with clean white railings. 1889 FARMER *Dict. Amer.*, *Texas tender*, the waiter on the Texas or upper deck of a Mississippi steamer. 1901 W. CHURCHILL *Crisis* xxi, He escorted the ladies to quarters in the texas.

**b.** 'The elevated gallery, resembling a louver or clearstory, in a grain-elevator'.

1909 in *Cent. Dict. Suppl.*

**2.** In names of native Texan plants, animals, etc.: as *Texas bead-tree, blue-grass, flax, grackle, millet, snake-root*, etc. **Texas** (cattle-) **fever,** a splenic fever, caused by the protozoan *Pyrosoma bigeminum*, localized in the Southern States, to which unacclimatized cattle are liable.

1858 SIMMONDS *Dict. Trade*, *Texas Millet*, the *Sorghum cernuum*, a prolific bread-corn cultivated in the tropics. 1902 *Westm. Gaz.* 2 June 10/2 It is officially announced that the cattle disease prevailing in Rhodesia is Texas fever which is spread by ticks.

† **Te·xed,** *ppl. a. Obs. rare*[−1]. [f. L. *tex-ĕre* to weave + -ED[1]; or perh. for *text*, ad. L. *text-us*, pa. pple. of *tex-ĕre*.] Woven.

1572 BOSSEWELL *Armorie* II. 105 Mounted on the nest texed with the slipps of the vine.

† **Texile** = *to exile*: see T'[1] and EXILE *v.*

*c* 1430 LYDG. *Min. Poems* (Percy Soc.) 14 From [us] texile alle maner hevinesse.

**Text** (tekst), *sb.*[1] Also 4 tixte, tyxt(e, 4–5 tixt, 4–6 texte, (4, 7 (9 *dial.*) tex, 6 texe, 7 texed). [a. F. *texte*, also ONF. *tixte, tiste* (12th c. in Godef.), the Scriptures, etc., ad. med.L. *textus* the Gospel, written character (Du Cange), L. *textus* (*u*-stem) style, tissue of a literary work (Quintilian), lit. that which is woven, web, texture, f. *text-*, ppl. stem of *tex-ĕre* to weave.]

**1.** The wording of anything written or printed; the structure formed by the words in their order; the very words, phrases, and sentences as written.

13.. *E. E. Allit. P.* B. 1634 Fyrst telle me þe tyxte of þe tede lettres. 13.. *Gaw. & Gr. Knt.* 1515 For to telle of þis teuelyng of þis trwe kny3tez, Hit is the tytelet, token, & tyxt of her werkkez. *c* 1500 *Melusine* xii. 45 They delyuered to Raymondyn the ground that was gyuen to hym after the texte or tenour of hys lettres. 1560 DAUS tr. *Sleidane's Comm.* 65 b, For those wordes.., this is my body, Luther vnderstode barely and symply after the texte of the letter. 1678 CUDWORTH *Intell. Syst.* I. iv. 240 The most of Plato's Followers..offering all kind of violence to his Text. 1720 SWIFT *To Stella* 138 Say, Stella, when you copy next, Will you keep strictly to the text? 1888 BRYCE *Amer. Commw.* II. liii. 326 Without venturing to propose alterations in the text of the Constitution.

† **b.** Applied vaguely to an original or authority whose words are quoted. *Obs.*

*a* 1400–50 *Alexander* 214 It be-tid on a tyme þe text me recordis, Þat þe mode kynge..farne out of toune. *c* 1400 *Destr. Troy* 4007 But truly I telle as þe text sais.

**c.** *fig.* or in allusive use.

*c* 1440 *York Myst.* xxv. 535 Hayll! texte of trewthe þe trew to taste. Hayll! kyng & sire. 1589 WARNER *Alb. Eng.* VI. xxxi. 136 Ply Sir..your busie trade, you are besides the Tex. *a* 1635 NAUNTON *Fragm. Reg.* (Arb.) 23 It is not without the text, to give a short touch on the helps, and advantages of her reign.

**d.** The wording adopted by an editor as (in his opinion) most nearly representing the author's original work; a book or edition containing this; also, with qualification, any form in which a writing exists or is current, as a *good, bad, corrupt, critical, received text.*

1841 MYERS *Cath. Th.* III. § 8. 26 Our present Received Text has been a growth—improved from many and various sources. 1845 GRAVES *Rom. Law* in *Encycl. Metrop.* II. 770/1 Hänel, the latest editor, has not inserted these seven constitutions in his text. 1870 FREEMAN *Norm. Conq.* (1877) II. App. 658 The text seems very corrupt. 1875 SCRIVENER *Lect. Text N. Test.* 7 The vast importance of preserving a pure text of the sacred writers. 1891 *Athenæum* 15 Aug. 219/1 No attempt has been made to settle the text.

**2.** *esp.* The very words and sentences as originally written: **a.** in the original language, as opposed to a translation or rendering; **b.** in the original form and order, as distinguished from a commentary, marginal or other, or from annotations. Hence, in later use, the body of any treatise, the authoritative or formal part as distinguished from notes, appendices, introduction, and other explanatory or supplementary matter.

1377 LANGL. *P. Pl.* B. XVII. 12 *Dilige deum & proximum tuum, &c.* Þis was þe tixte trewly..; þe glose was gloriously writen. *c* 1385 CHAUCER *L. G. W.* Prol. (MS. Gg) 86 The nakede tixt in englis to declare. 1388 WYCLIF *Prol.* xv. 57 This symple creature hadde myche trauaile,..to studie it [Latin Bible] of the newe, the text with the glose. *a* 1430 26 *Pol. Poems* xx. 1 The tixt of holy writ,..Hit sleeþ, but glose be among. 1532 MORE *Confut. Tindale* Wks. 406/1 Nowe cummeth Tyndale and..sheweth that the latine texte and the Greke may bee hys excuse and defence. 1576 FLEMING *Panopl. Epist.* 179 *margin*, τί τῷ λόγῳ sayth the Greeke text: *Quidnam oratione*, saith the Latine interpretation. 1700 DRYDEN *Cymon & Iphig.* 18 When his broad Comment makes the Text too plain. 1749 FIELDING *Tom Jones* III. iii, Coke upon Littleton, where the comment is of equal authority with the text. 1804 WELLINGTON in Gurw. *Desp.* (1837) III. 25 As these accompaniments, or possibly the text are seldom read. 1859 TENNYSON *Vivien* 679 And none can read the text, not even I; And none can read the comment but myself. 1875 JOWETT *Plato* (ed. 2) IV. 256 There still remains an ambiguity both in the text and in the explanation. 1908 *Athenæum* 8 Aug. 147/3 All his references are to Arabic texts.

**c.** That portion of the contents of a manuscript or printed book, or of a page, which constitutes the original matter, as distinct from the notes or other critical appendages. In first quot. *fig.*

*c* 1369 CHAUCER *Dethe Blaunche* 333 And alle the wallys with colouris fyne Were peynted, bothe text and glose. 1597 MORLEY *Introd. Mus.* Annot., I haue..thought it best to set downe in Annotations, such thinges as in the text could not so commodiouslie be handled. 1778 WARTON *Hist. Eng. Poetry* (1840) II. xxiii. 304 *note*, It is not immediately formed from the Troye-boke of Lydgate, as I have suggested in the text. 1848 MILL *Pol. Econ.* I. v. § 8 (1876) 48 *note*, Consequently, as shewn in the text, her labourers suffered. 1859 TENNYSON *Vivien* 669 Every marge enclosing in the midst A square of text that looks a little blot.

† **3.** *spec.* The very words and sentences of Holy Scripture; hence, the Scriptures themselves; also, any single book of the Scriptures. *Obs.*

13.. *E. E. Allit. P.* C. 37 For in þe tyxte, þere þyse two [Poverty and Patience] arn in teme layde. 1393 LANGL. *P. Pl.* C. III. 129 Ich theologie þe tixt knowe. *c* 1420 ? LYDG. *Assembly of Gods* 1500 Fast by Doctryne, on that oon syde, As I remembre, sate Holy Texte. 1542–3 *Act* 34 & 35 *Hen. VIII*, c. 1 § 10 It shalbe lawfull to everye noble man..to reade..any texte of the Byble..so the same be doone quietlie. 1597 SHAKS. 2 *Hen. IV*, IV. ii. 7 To heare with reuerence Your exposition on the holy Text. *a* 1668 DAVENANT *Poems* (1672) 329 Since Holy Text bids Faith to comprehend.

**b.** A copy of the Scriptures, or of a book of the Scriptures; *spec.* a volume containing the Gospels. *Obs.* exc. *Hist.* (See also TEXTUS.)

1387 TREVISA *Higden* (Rolls) I. 371 Iesus Crist apperede to Patrik, and took hym a staf, and þe text of þe gospel þat beeþ in þe contray in þe erchebisshops ward. *c* 1450 *St. Cuthbert* (Surtees) 4431 He bare a boke..Of gospelles.. with perle and stanes preciouse Þat text richely semed arayde. *Ibid.* 6800 Þe text of wangels fell in þe water. *c* 1460 *Oseney Regr.* 174 Vppon the texte whee sware, both I and my wiffe. 1536 in *Antiq. Sarisb.* (1771) 201 Textus Evangeliorum. A Text after John, gilt with gold and having precious Stones and the relicks of dyvers saints. 1849 ROCK *Ch. Fathers* I. iii. 297 The curious reader has only to look at that fine text, or book of the Gospels, bound in silver parcel-gilt, and jewelled. 1883 W. H. RICH-JONES *Reg. St. Osmund* I. 117 *note*, The 'Text', also called 'Evangelarium', was a complete copy of the four gospels.

**4.** A short passage from the Scriptures, esp. one quoted as authoritative, or illustrative of a point of belief or doctrine, as a motto, to point a moral, or esp. as the subject of an exposition or sermon.

In early practice these texts or portions of the holy text were cited in Latin from the Vulgate, connecting this use with 2.

1377 LANGL. *P. Pl.* B. III. 339 *Quod bonum est tenete*, treuthe þat texte made! *Ibid.* XIII. 125 Pieres þe ploughman..no tixte ne taketh to meyntene his cause, But *dilige deum* and *domine, quis habitabit*, &c. 1528 TINDALE *Wicked Mammon* 45 b, This texte is playner than that it neadeth to be expounded. 1579 FULKE *Heskins' Parl.* 527 The Sixtieth Chapter treateth vpon this text of S. Paule to the Hebrues: We haue an altar, &c. 1657 HEYLIN *Hist. Ref.* (1661) I. II. iv. 38 The Art of opening, or rather of undoing a Text of Scripture (as the phrase is now) was usurped by all. 1711 ADDISON *Spect.* No. 46 ⁋ 6 A meer Sermon Popgun, repeating and discharging Texts, Proofs, and Applications. 1782 PRIESTLEY *Corrupt. Chr.* II. VIII. 125 The preacher..named and opened his text. 1894 J. T. FOWLER *Adamnan* Pref. 10 A discourse for St. Columba's day on the text *Exi d terra tua.*

**b.** A short passage from some book or write considered as authoritative; a received maxim o axiom; a proverb; an adage; in later use, esp one used as a copy-book heading. Now *rare.*

*c* 1386 CHAUCER *Prol.* 177 He yaf nat of that text [*v. r* tixt, texte] a pulled hen That seith that hunters beth na hooly men. — *Manciple's T.* 132 [see TEXTUAL 1]. 158 SHAKS. *L. L. L.* IV. ii. 168 Societie (saith the text) is th happinesse of life. 1592 — *Rom. & Jul.* IV. i. 22 What mus be shall be. *Fri.* That's a certaine text. 1862 *Sat. Rev* 8 Feb. 156 'Recreation is good for mind and body', as th worn-out governess writes for a text at the top of he pupil's copy-book.

**c.** *fig.* The theme or subject on which any on speaks; the starting-point of a discussion; a state ment on which any one dilates.

1605 SHAKS. *Lear* IV. ii. 37 No more; the text is foolish 1706 E. WARD *Wooden World Diss.* (1708) 18 The granc Text they hold forth upon is the Behaviour of their Lieu tenants. 1821 SCOTT *Kenilw.* xi, Is it fit for a hereti horse-boy like thee, to handle such a text as the Catholi clergy? 1847 TENNYSON *Princess* Prol. 108 Then the Maider Aunt Took this fair day for text, and from it preach'd Ar universal culture for the crowd. 1870 J. BALDWIN BROWN *Eccl. Truth* 249 A fact is a text from another book, also o God's writing.

**5.** Short for TEXT-HAND. Also *attrib.* See also CHURCH-TEXT, GERMAN *text. Chapel-text*, an elaborated kind of church-text.

1588 SHAKS. *L. L. L.* v. ii. 42 Faire as a text B. in a Coppi booke. 1610 GUILLIM *Heraldry* IV. v. (1611) 199 He beareth Gules, three Text Esses, or. 1633 FORD *Love's Sacr.* v i, There shall be writ in text, Thy bastarding the issues of a prince. 1740 DYCHE & PARDON, *Text*,..sometimes..means a large sort of writing. 1825 J. WILSON *Noct. Ambr.* Wks 1855 I. 10 Their names are baith down in round text in the deevils doomsday beuk. 1904 *Daily Chron.* 23 June 4/ Burns wrote a fine, bold hand..as big as Cromwell's or Bismarck's—what is called in Scotland 'half-text'.

**6.** The words of a song; = TESTO.

1891 in *Cent. Dict.*

**7.** *attrib.* (see also sense 5) and *Comb.*, as *text-bill, -copy, -critic, -critical* adj., *-criticism, -monger, -mongering* vbl. sb. and ppl. adj., *-motto, -quoter, -quoting* ppl. adj., *-transmission, -verse*; **text-blindness,** word-blindness; **text-cut, -engraving, -picture,** an illustration occupying a space in the text of a book; **te·xt-divi:der,** a preacher who didactically 'splits up' his text; so **te·xt-divi·ding**; **text-ink,** ink used for the text of a manuscript or book; **text-title,** a half-title, at the beginning of the text of a book. See also TEXT-BOOK, -HAND, -LETTER, etc.

1610 *Histrio-m.* v. 62 *Capt.* Sirrah, what set you up there? *Bel.* *Text-bills for plays. 1909 *Cent. Dict. Suppl.* *Text-blindness. 1775 ASH, **Textcopy*,..a copy in text hand. 1870 MAGNUSSON tr. *Asgrimsson's Lilja* Introd. 27 Of no aid to the *text-critic of the present edition. 1905 *Expositor* July 22 [The Syriac N. T.] is quite invaluable from a *text-critical point of view. 1908 *Q. Rev.* July 70 Some centuries later *text-criticism arose. 1897 *Westm. Gaz.* 8 Mar. 2/1 The first number..contains two excellent plates and numerous *text-cuts. 1670 EACHARD *Cont. Clergy* 53 Not by every bungler and ordinary *text-divider. *Ibid.* 113 They have got..such a peculiar method of *text-dividing. 1894 *Daily News* 15 Nov. 6/2 Mr. Sheppard supplies a *text engraving of mad Margaret Nicholson. 1511 in *Rel. Ant.* I. 318 To make *texte ynke. 1883 W. S. LILLY in *Contemp. Rev.* Feb. 228 He is speaking of *textmongers. 1884 — *Anc. Relig. & Mod. Th.* 285 St. Augustine..is speaking of *textmongering. 1880 WARREN *Book-plates* xi. 122 The *text-motto occurring on Pickheimer's book-plate. 1905 *Daily Chron.* 7 July 3/3 It has nearly twenty full-page plates, and a great many *text pictures. *a* 1837 D. MCNICOLL *Wks.* 94 This *text-quoting vagabond. 1881 H. BRADSHAW in *Bibliographer* Dec. 6/2 The *text-title of Tindale's New Testament of 1534–5, as reproduced by Mr. Fry. 1908 *Q. Rev.* July 74 The common accidents of *text-transmission.

**Text,** *sb.*[2] *rare*[−1]. [ad. L. *textus* tissue: see prec.] Texture, tissue.

1854 S. DOBELL *Balder* xxviii, And, if she were..caught of morning mist, or the unseen Material of an odour, her pure text Could seem no more remote from the corrupt And seething compound of our common flesh.

**Text,** *v.* Now *rare.* [f. TEXT *sb.*[1]]

† **1.** *trans.* To inscribe, write, or print in a text-hand or in capital or large letters. Also *fig. Obs.*

1599 NASHE *Lenten Stuffe* (1871) 15 A chronographical Latin table..in a fair text hand, texting unto us, how, in the sceptredom of Edward the Confessor, the sands first began to grow into sight at low water. 1599 SHAKS. *Much Ado* v. i. 185 Yea and text vnder-neath, heere dwells Benedicke the married man. 1607 DEKKER *Wh. of Babylon* Wks. 1873 II. 265 Vowes haue I writ so deepe,..So texted them in characters capitall, I cannot race them. *c* 1616 FLETCHER & MASSINGER *Thierry & Theod.* II. i, Condemn me for A most malicious slanderer, nay, texte it Upon my forehead. 1624 HEYWOOD *Gunaik.* VII. 315 That such as ..past..might read them as perfectly and distinctly, as if they had beene texted in Capitall Letters. 1631 T. POWELL *Tom All Trades* 1 The Scriveners at Temple-barre had no imployment, but..texting of Bills for letting of Chambers in Chancery-lane. 1639 SHIRLEY *Maid's Rev.* III. i, Would ..every character [had] Been tex'd with blood!

**b.** *trans.* To write in a text-hand upon. **c.** *intr.* To write in text-hand.

1660 G. TOMLYN *Patent Specif.* No. 128 A new..way to text and flourish velumes and parchments in blacke and white. 1869 *Lonsdale Gloss.*, *Text*, to write an engrossing hand or German text. 1884 [unplied in TEXTER].

†**2. a.** *intr.* To cite texts. **b.** *trans.* To cite a text at or against (a person). *Obs.*

**1564–78** BULLEYN *Dial. agst. Pest.* (1888) 13 *M.*..And how like you this texte? *A.* Texte how they will texte, I will trust none of them all. **1615** SIR E. HOBY *Curry-combe* i. 11 When his wench told him that he kissed like a Clowter, he could text her with *Labia Sacerdotis custodiunt sapientiam.*

**Textarian** (tekstēᵊ·riăn), *a. nonce-wd.* [f. TEXT *sb.*¹, after *tractarian*, etc.] Dealing with or based upon an isolated text, or texts.

**1867** SEEBOHM *Oxford Reformers* i. § 2. 11 The scholastic divines..had fallen into a method of exposition almost exclusively textarian. *Ibid.* 15 They [Colet's lectures at Oxford 1496–7] were not textarian.

**Text-book** (te·kstˌbuk). [f. TEXT *sb.*¹]

†**1.** (See quot.) *Obs.*

**1730** BAILEY (folio), *Text-Book* (in Universities) is a Classick Author written very wide by the Students, to give Room for an Interpretation dictated by the Master, &c. to be inserted in the Interlines.

**2.** A book used as a standard work for the study of a particular subject; now usually one written specially for this purpose; a manual of instruction in any science or branch of study, esp. a work recognized as an authority (cf. TEXT-WRITER 2).

**1779** *Mirror* No. 38 The letters of the immortal Earl of Chesterfield, which I intend to use as my text-book on this occasion. **1795** SEWARD *Anecd.* I. 203 Lord Bacon's Essays ..have been the text-book of myriads of Essay-Writers. **1837** SIR F. PALGRAVE *Merch. & Friar* Ded. (1844) 9 Andrew Horne, the author of our ancient legal text-book, the Mirror of Justices. *a* **1855** MANSFIELD *Salts* Pref. (1865) 32 The current vocabulary of the chemical text-books. **1894** H. DRUMMOND *Ascent of Man* 10 In almost every department [of science] the text-books of ten years ago are obsolete to-day.

**3.** A book containing a selection of Scripture texts, arranged for daily use or easy reference.

**1861** (*title*) The Scripture Text Book and Treasury. **1877** *Bagster's Catal.* 50 The Autograph Text Book; Containing a Text of Scripture, and a Verse of Poetry..under every Day in the year.

**4.** A book containing the libretto of a musical play or opera. **1891** in *Cent. Dict.*

†**Te·xted,** *a. Obs.* [f. TEXT *sb.*¹ and *v.* + -ED.]

**1.** Skilled or learned in 'texts' or authors. *rare.*

(In this sense *texted wel* (v.r. *text wel*) appears in one group of Chaucer MSS., where another has *textuel.* The latter was prob. the original reading, but the change in some MSS. perh. implies that *texted* was known.)

**14..** *Chaucer's Manciple's T.* 131 (Harl. MS.) But for I am a man not texted wel [so *Corp.*; *Lansd.* texed, *Petw.* text; 3 *MSS.* textuel] I wil not telle of textes neuer a del. *Ibid.* 212 But as I sayd, I am nought tixted wel [*Corp.*, *Petw.*, *Lansd.* text; 3 *MSS.* textuel, -eel, tixt-].

**2.** Written in text-hand or text-letters; engrossed.

**1620** DEKKER *Dreame* 1 They beg nothing, the texted pastbord talkes all; and if nothing be giuen, nothing is spoken. **1650–66** WHARTON *Poems* Wks. (1683) 340 To write Custodes in a Texted-hand. **1693** *Lond. Gaz.* No. 3125/4 Texted Indentures for Attorneys.

**Texter** (te·kstəɹ). [-ER¹.] One skilled in writing in a text-hand (sense a); an engrosser.

**1884** *Law Times* 29 Mar. 2/2 Wanted, a re-engagement as Engrossing and General Clerk..excellent writer and texter.

**Te·xt-hand.** A fine large hand in writing. **a.** *orig.* One of the larger and more formal hands in which the text of a book was often written, as distinct from the smaller or more cursive hand appropriate to the gloss, etc. See also quot. 1688. **b.** Now usually applied to a school-hand written in lines about half an inch wide.

**1542** UDALL *Erasm. Apoph.* 224 He had taken vp..an instrumente written in greate letters of texte-hande. **1599** [see TEXT *v.* 1]. **1688** R. HOLME *Armoury* III. 414/2 These are the form of the Letters..used by the Germans; and are termed the Text Hand Letters. **1796** PEGGE *Anonym.* (1809) 475 It is called text-hand and text-letter because the text was ever wrote in a large hand and the comment in a small. As text-hand is both square and round, it means little more than a large hand of each sort. **1821** SCOTT *Kenilw.* xxxi, You seem wondrous slow in reading text hand.

†**Te·xtible,** *a. Obs. rare.* [f. L. *text-*, ppl. stem of *texĕre* to weave + -IBLE.] That may be woven; textile. **1727** in BAILEY vol. II.

**Textile** (te·kstil, -əil), *a.* and *sb.* [ad. L. *textil-is* woven, *textile* (sc. *opus*) woven fabric, f. *text-*, ppl. stem of *tex-ĕre* to weave. So F. *textile.*]

**A.** *adj.* **1.** That has been or may be woven.

**1656** BLOUNT *Glossogr.*, *Textile*,..that is weaved or wounden, embroidered. **1755** JOHNSON, *Textile*,..woven; capable of being woven. **1852** CONYBEARE & HOWSON *St. Paul* (1862) II. xx. 240 The wine and the textile fabrics of Cos. **1868** ROGERS *Pol. Econ.* viii. (1876) 74 Cotton and wool and other textile materials..from all quarters.

**b.** *Nat. Hist.* Having markings resembling a woven surface; e.g. *textile cone,* a species of cone-shell, *Conus textilis,* so marked; *textile snake.*

**1802** SHAW *Gen. Zool.* III. 462 Textile Snake. *Coluber Textilis*..Yellowish-grey Snake, freckled with black, and marked by numerous, undulated, transverse, bright-ferruginous stripes. **1891** *Cent. Dict.*, Textile cone.

**2.** Of or connected with weaving: see B. 1 b.

**B.** *sb.* **1.** A woven fabric; any kind of cloth. (Usually in *pl.*)

**1626** BACON *Sylva* § 846 In the warp and woof of textiles. **1870** ROCK *Text. Fabr.* Introd. i. 10 The word 'textile' means every kind of stuff, no matter its material, wrought in the loom. **1883** *Manch. Exam.* 5 June 5/6 Machines for the preparation of textiles. **1886** *Pall Mall G.* 3 May 4/1 The prices of textiles have fallen considerably.

**b.** *attrib.* (or as *adj.*) Of or pertaining to weaving or to woven fabrics.

**1844** G. DODD *Textile Manuf.* Introd. 6 By 'Textile manufactures' are meant those in which filaments of cotton, of flax, of silk, or of wool, are wrought into a form fitted to be used in the making of garments. **1866** ROGERS *Agric. & Prices* I. xxii. 569 The great..centre of textile industry in England was the two north-eastern counties of Norfolk and Suffolk. **1871** TYLOR *Prim. Cult.* I. i. 7 Among textile arts are to be ranged matting, netting, and several grades of making and weaving threads.

**2.** Fibrous material, as flax, cotton, silk, etc., suitable for being spun and woven into yarn, cloth, etc.

**1641** WILKINS *Math. Magick* II. xii. (1707) 141 The Materials..were not from any Herb, or Vegetable, as other Textiles, but from a Stone called Amiantus. **1883** *Nature* 8 Mar. 430/1 As to textiles, the origin of flax is somewhat complicated. **1889** *Science* 1 Feb. 81/2 The discovery of a new textile on the shores of the Caspian.

Hence **Te·xtilist,** one engaged in the textile industry; a weaver or seller of cloth.

**1855** *Ecclesiologist* XVI. 275 The handicraft of the goldsmith, stone carver, and textilist.

**Te·xtlet.** *rare.* [See -LET.] A short text.

**1831** CARLYLE *Sart. Res.* I. xi, [The] Dingy Priest..preaches forth (exoterically enough) one little textlet from the Gospel of Freedom.

†**Te·xt-le:tter.** *Obs.* [cf. TEXT-HAND.] A large or capital letter in handwriting.

**1511** in *Rel. Ant.* I. 318 Lett yt stond iij. dayes..and then thou hast good ynke for texte letter. **1600** E. BLOUNT *Hosp. Incur. Fooles* A iij, Where the renowmed folly of these men may be seene..written (as it were) in Text letters. **1605** BACON *Adv. Learn.* II. iii. § 3 To write it in such Text and Capital letters. **1657** W. MORICE *Coena quasi Κοινὴ* xx. 177 Hypocrisie would..in some Polititians be written in Court-hand, but in others in text-letters. **1706** PHILLIPS (ed. Kersey), *Text-Letters*, the Capital Letters in all sorts of Hands that are usually written.

**Text-man** (te·kstˌmæ̆n).

†**1.** One learned in scriptural texts, and apt at quoting them; also, An advocate of literal interpretation of the Bible. *Obs.*

**1619** R. HARRIS *Drunkard's Cup* 26 A very iudicious Diuine, and grounded Text-man. **1624** GODWYN *Moses & Aaron* (1641) 28 The Scribes clave to the written Word, whence they were tearmed Text-men, or Masters of the Text. **1647** TRAPP *Comm. 1 Cor.* i. 20 The Text-men, those that proceed according to the literall interpretation. **1702** C. MATHER *Magn. Chr.* IV. iii. (1852) 61 He was a notable text-man, and one who had more than forty or fifty scriptures distinctly quoted in one discourse.

**2.** The author of a text-book. *rare.*

**1900** H. G. GRAHAM *Soc. Life Scot. in 18th C.* XII. iii. (1901) 464 Bacon, Locke and Evans, Puffendorf and De Vries were welcome text-men.

**Textorial** (tekstōᵊ·riăl), *a.* [f. L. *textor, -ōrem* weaver, *textōri-us* pertaining to weaving + -AL.] Of or pertaining to weavers or weaving.

**1774** WARTON *Hist. Eng. Poetry* Diss. iii. (1840) I. p. cxciv, The cultivation of the textorial arts among the orientals. **1875** *Nat. Hist. & Antiq. Arran* 333 They will resume their textorial occupation.

So **Texto·rian** *a. rare*⁻⁰.

**1656** BLOUNT *Glossogr.*, *Textorian*,..of, or belonging to a weaver, or to weaving.

†**Te·xtour.** *Obs. rare.* [a. AF. *textour*, ad. L. *textōr-em* weaver.] A weaver.

[**1429** *Act* 8 *Hen. VI*, c. 23 Les textours..qunt ils ount overez un drap.] **1558** *Peebles Burgh Rec.* (1872) 247 The baillies.. hes nominat four werkmen textouris..to exame Gilbert Wilsone his sone..and se gif he be qualifiit to wirk on the lynning lome or nocht.

**Te·xt-pe:n.** A pen specially suitable for writing text-hand, or for engrossing.

**1589** NASHE *Pasquils Returne* Wks. (Grosart) I. 134 The Painter to bewray both his abuse of the Scriptures, and his malice against the Church, hath drawne him his worde with a Text-pen. **1593** — *Christ's T.* Ep. Ded., Your illustrate ladiship ere this (I am perswaded) hath beheld a bade florish with a Text-penne. **1594** PLAT *Jewell-ho.* III. 42 Lines drawne with a text-penne. **1858** SIMMONDS *Dict. Trade*, *Text-pen*, a metallic pen for engrossing.

†**Te·xtrine,** *a. Obs. rare.* [ad. L. *textrīn-us*, f. *textor* weaver.] Of or pertaining to weaving.

**1713** DERHAM *Phys.-Theol.* IV. xiii. 234 How so small a Creature that emits no Web, nor hath any textrine Art, can be able to convolve the stubborn leaf, and then bind it..with the Thread or Web it weaves from its own Body. *Ibid.* VIII. vi. (1752) 388 The curious structure of all parts ministring to this textrine power.

**Textual** (te·kstiuˌăl), *a.* (*sb.*) Also 4–5 -uel. [In form *textuel*, app. a. AF. (F. *textuel* only 15th c. in Godef.), ad. L. type **textuāl-is*, f. *textu-s*: see TEXT *sb.*¹ and -AL. So Sp., Pg. *textual*, It. *-ale.* The later Eng. spelling is conformed to the L. type (as in other adjs. orig. in *-el*).]

†**1.** Of a person: Well acquainted with 'texts' or authors; well-read; literally exact in giving the text. [So F. *textuel* 'qui connait les textes', 1571 in Godef. *Compl.*, also in Cotgr.] *Obs.*

*c* **1386** CHAUCER *Manciple's T.* 131 (Ellesm.) But for I am a man not textueel I wol noght telle of textes neuer a deel. *Ibid.* 212 But as I seyde I am noght textueel. — *Pars. Prol.* 57 This meditacion I putte it ay vnder correccion Of Clerkes for I am nat textueel [so *Harl.* & *Hengwrt*; 4 *MSS.* text wel. *Textuel* was prob. Chaucer's word, which being app. unknown to some scribes was altered to *text wel* and *texted wel*: cf. TEXTED 1]. **1613** R. CAWDREY *Table Alph.* (ed. 3), *Textuall*, cunning in the text.

**2.** Of, pertaining to, or contained in the (or a) text, esp. of the Scriptures.

*c* **1470** HENRYSON *Mor. Fab.* III. *Cock & Fox* xxviii. (Charteris) ȝit may ȝe find ane sentence richt agreabill, Vnder thir fenȝeit termis textuall. **1570** LEVINS *Manip.* 15/26 Textuall, *textualis.* *a* **1638** MEDE *Wks.* (1672) 347 So the Cethib or Textual reading hath it. **1731** WATERLAND *Script. Vind.* II. 125 So stands the case, upon the foot of the Textual Reading. **1859** I. TAYLOR *Logic in Theol.* vii. 309 The admitted principles of textual criticism. **1872** MINTO *Eng. Prose Lit.* II. vi. 468 His sagacity in textual emendations.

**b.** Of or belonging to the text-books.

**1863** EMERSON *Misc. Papers, Thoreau* Wks. (Bohn) III. 324 Though very studious of natural facts, he was incurious of technical and textual science.

†**3.** Recognizing only the text of Scripture as authoritative. Also as *sb.* one that does this. *Obs.*

**1613** PURCHAS *Pilgrimage* II. viii. 123 They are called *Karraim*, because they would seeme Textuall, and Scripture-men, disallowing Traditions [*ed.* **1614**, p. 143 *Karaim*, that is, Bible-men, or Textualls, and in the Roman tongue they call them Saduces].

**4.** Based on, following, or conforming to the text, esp. of the Scriptures.

**1614** BP. HALL *Recoll. Treat.* Ded. A ij b, Speculation interchanged with experience, positiue theologie with polemicall, textuall with discursorie. **1670** WALTON *Life Donne* 34 Incessant study of textual divinity. **1863** ROBINSON in *Macm. Mag.* Mar. 415 The textual system..has tended to establish a persuasion that Christian doctrines can be.. proved by detached quotations. **1908** *Sat. Rev.* 11 July 39/2 Possibly we have not got the quotation exactly textual.

**Textualism** (te·kstiuˌăliz'm). [f. prec. + -ISM.]

**1.** Strict adherence to the text, esp. of the Scriptures; the principles or method of a textualist.

**1863** M. PATTISON *Ess.* (1889) II. 286 The arbitrary textualism of the Puritan divines. **1895** *Thinker* VIII. 405 He feels unable..to burden his audience with minutiæ, subtleties, pedantries, textualisms.

**2.** That department of scholarship which deals with the text of the Bible; textual criticism.

**1888** *Church Times* 318 Reputations..acquired merely in the field of grammar and textualism, not in theology proper. **1908** *Times, Lit. Supp.* 5 Mar. 74/2 Textualism is not a popular study.

**Textualist** (te·kstiuˌălist). [f. as prec. + -IST.] **a.** One learned in the text of the Bible. **b.** One who adheres strictly to, and bases his doctrine upon, the text of the Scriptures.

**1629** LIGHTFOOT *Misc.* vi. 20 How nimble textualists and Grammarians for the tongue the Rabbins are, their Comments can witnes. But..these that are so great textualists, are not best at the text. **1834** SOUTHEY *Doctor* iii. (1848) 12 When I mention Arba, who but the practised textualist can call to mind that he was..the father of Anak, and that from him Kirjath-Arba took its name? **1885** SWINBURNE *Misc.* (1886) 181 A moderate Puritan and a textualist of the old Protestant school. **1903** J. MOFFAT in *Expositor* Dec. 470 One appealing to the textualist is Dr. R. Jansen's attempt to reconstruct the Greek text.

**Textuality** (tekstiuˌæ·lĭti). [f. as prec. + -ITY.] = TEXTUALISM 1.

**1836** *J. Martin's Discourses* Memoir 34 Textuality, he often said, appeared to him to be one of the chief excellences of a sermon. **1888** M. W. STRYKER in *Interior* (Chicago) 5 Apr., Deliverance, for those who have all their lifetimes been subject to pithiness and apothegm would come by the broadest textuality.

**Textually** (te·kstiuˌăli), *adv.* [f. as prec. + -LY². Cf. F. *textuellement.*]

**1.** In or as regards the text.

**1617** COLLINS *Def. Bp. Ely* II. ix. 351 As no lesse textually, then marginally, both waies, you blaze it. **1847** DE QUINCEY *Orthographic Mutineers* Wks. 1860 XIV. 104 In our authorized version..italics are..used..exclusively to indicate such words or auxiliary forms as, though implied and virtually present in the original, are not textually expressed.

**2.** In the actual words of the text; verbatim.

**1837** SIR F. PALGRAVE *Merch. & Friar* Ded. (1844) 10 As they only exist in manuscript, I shall place them textually before you. **1870** LOWELL *Among my Bks.* Ser. I. (1873) 205 The theory that his plays should be represented textually. **1884** *Truth* 4 Sept. 364/2 To report textually a debate from 4.30 p.m. to 2 a.m. would fill thirty columns of the *Times.*

†**Te·xtuarist.** *Obs. rare*⁻⁰. [f. next + -IST.] = TEXTUARY *sb.* 1. **1755** in JOHNSON.

**Textuary** (te·kstiuˌări), *a.* and *sb.* [ad. mod.L. type **textuāri-us*, f. *textu-s* TEXT *sb.*¹ + *-ārius* -ARY¹. So F. *textuaire* sb. (1680 in Hatz.-Darm.).]

**A.** *adj.* **1.** Of or belonging to the text; textual.

**1646** SIR T. BROWNE *Pseud. Ep.* III. xvi. 145 Pliny..hath differently translated it,..whereby he extends the exclusion unto twenty dayes, which in the textuary sense is fully accomplished in one. **1817** COLERIDGE *Lay Serm.* 411 Plucking away..from the divine organism of the Bible, textuary morsels, and fragments for the support of doctrines which they had learned beforehand. **1854** W. WATERWORTH *Eng. & Rome* 62 *note*, The textuary proofs of St. Peter's supremacy. **1882** *Sat. Rev.* LIV. 639/1 It is as genuine a result of textuary accommodation as any against which this writer protests.

†**2.** That ranks as a text-book; regarded as authoritative or as an authority. *Obs.*

**1632** LITHGOW *Trav.* IX. 395 Euclide the textuary Geometrician. **1646** SIR T. BROWNE *Pseud. Ep.* 374 He..hath left sixteen books of Opticks, of great esteem with ages past, and textuary unto our daies. **1682** — *Chr. Mor.* III. § 21 Let Pythagoras be thy Remembrancer, not thy textuary and final Instructer.

†**3.** That adheres strictly to the text of Scripture: cf. B. 2. *Obs. rare*$^{-1}$.

**1613** PURCHAS *Pilgrimage* III. x. 247 They hate the Persians,..like as the Traditionary Iew doth the Textuarie, and the Papist the Protestant.

**B.** *sb.* **1.** One learned in the text of the Bible, = TEXTUALIST a; a textual critic, scholar, or expounder; also, one well acquainted with and ready at quoting texts.

**1608** BP. J. KING *Serm.* 24 Mar. 28 Is there almost a worthier and prompter textuary in the world..in that booke of the Law? *a* **1661** FULLER *Worthies, Lincoln.* (1662) II. 167 He [Doctor Tighe] was an excellent Textuary and profound Linguist, the reason why he was imployed by King James in translating of the Bible. **1677** *Spottiswood's Hist. Ch. Scot.* App. 20 He was learned in the Hebrew, and was a great Textuary. *a* **1710** BP. BULL *Visit. Serm.* (1714) 21 If by a Textuary, we mean him who hath not only a Concordance of Scriptures in his Memory, but also a Commentary on them in his Understanding; who thinks it not enough to be ready in alledging the bare Words of Scripture, with the mention of Chapter and Verse where it is written, unless he know the Sense and Meaning of what he recites. **1720** SWIFT *Let. Yng. Poet* 1 Dec., I have made it my observation, that the greatest wits have been the best textuaries; our modern poets are all..almost as well read in the Scriptures as some of our divines. **1851** G. S. FABER *Many Mansions* 223 Mr. Scott, ..than whom there probably never was a more accomplished textuary, takes pretty much the same view of the question. **1879** *Q. Rev.* CXLVIII. 422 Having the Bible at their fingers' ends...They were not merely accomplished textuaries.

†**2.** One who adheres strictly to the letter of Scripture; = TEXTUALIST b; cf. TEXTUAL 3.

**1727–41** CHAMBERS *Cycl.*, *Textuaries*, *Textuarii*, a name given the sect of the Caraites, among the Jews. Hillel shone among the traditionaries, and Schammai among the textuaries. **1828** WEBSTER, *Textualist, Textuary*...2. One who adheres to the text.

†**3.** (See quot.) *Obs.*

**1706** PHILLIPS (ed. Kersey), *Textuary*, a Law-Book, or other Treatise, that contains only the bare Text, without any Comment or Gloss upon it. **1730–6** in BAILEY (folio).

† **Textuist.** *Obs.* [f. L. *text-us* TEXT *sb.*[1] + -IST.] A textual scholar; = TEXTUARY *sb.* 1.

**1631** R. H. *Arraignm. Whole Creature* xii. § 3. 125 Popery affording more allegorizing Origenists, than sound Textuists. **1643** MILTON *Divorce* To Parl., When I remember the little that our Saviour could prevail about this doctrine of Charity against the crabbed textuists of his time, I make no wonder. **1700** STRYPE *Lightfoot's Rem.* Pref. 3 The author designed it for some, that desired to be good textuists.

**Textularian** (tekstiulē°·riăn), *a.* and *sb. Zool.* [f. mod.L. *Textulāria*, generic name (f. L. *text-us* woven) + -AN.] **a.** *adj.* Belonging to *Textularia*, the typical genus of *Textulariidæ*, a family of perforate Foraminifera. **b.** *sb.* A member of this genus or family.

**1862** CARPENTER *Microsc. & Rev.* (ed. 3) § 317 A less aberrant modification of the Globigerine type..is presented in the two great series which may be designated..as the Textularian and the Rotalian.

**Textural** (te·kstiŭrăl), *a.* [f. L. *textūra* TEXTURE + -AL.] Of or belonging to texture.

**1835–6** *Todd's Cycl. Anat.* I. 67/1 The textural properties of the two sets of vessels. **1854** JONES & SIEVEKING *Pathol. Anat.* (1874) 23 The differences in textural quality, which fibrine often presents. **1886** T. HARDY *Mayor of Casterbridge* ii, Her skin had undergone a textural change.

**b.** *Painting*: see TEXTURE *sb.* 6.

**1859** GULLICK & TIMBS *Paint.* 229 The gem-like impasto and textural richness of the old masters. **1887** *Pall Mall G.* 8 Feb. 2/2 Never has the French master shown greater textural facility, power of expression, or frankness of colour.

Hence **Te·xturally** *adv.*, in or as regards texture.

**1866** *Reader* 19 May 500 The mare herself, with her beautiful foal, are all, to our eye, texturally perfect. **1872** COUES *N. Amer. Birds* 22 The second class of crests—those consisting of texturally modified feathers.

**Texture** (te·kstiŭı), *sb.* [ad. L. *textūra* a weaving: see TEXT *sb.*[1] and -URE. So F. *texture* (16th c. in Godef. *Compl.*).]

†**1.** The process or art of weaving. *Obs.*

**1447** BOKENHAM *Seyntys* (Roxb.) 145 Mynerve hyr self wych hath the sovereynte Of gay texture, as declayryth Ovyde. **1646** SIR T. BROWNE *Pseud. Ep.* 256 Coats of skinnes..a naturall habit..before the invention of Texture. **1656** BLOUNT *Glossogr.*, *Texture*,..a weaving. **1726** POPE *Odyss.* XX. 87 Pallas taught the texture of the loom.

†**b.** *fig.* The fabricating, machinating, or composing of schemes, conspiracies, writings, etc. *Obs.*

*a* **1641** BP. MOUNTAGU *Acts & Mon.* iv. (1642) 275 First they began their malicious texture with secret whisperings, and giving out in corners. **1656** EARL MONM. tr. *Boccalini's Advts. fr. Parnass.* II. xciv. (1674) 247 The exquisite diligence used in the texture of those his Eternal Labours.

**2.** The produce of the weaver's art; a woven fabric; a web; cloth. *arch.*

*a* **1656** BP. HALL *Rem. Wks.* (1660) 260 The invaluable sumptuousness of the Temple..;..the curious celatures, and artificial textures. **1728–46** THOMSON *Spring* 642 Others.. far in the grassy dale..their humble texture weave. **1873** BROWNING *Red Cott. Nt.-cap* 407 When the dyer dyes A texture, can the red dye prime the white?

**b.** *transf.* Any natural structure having an appearance or consistence as if woven; a tissue; a web, e. g. of a spider. Also *fig.*

**1578** BANISTER *Hist. Man* IV. 56 The notable texture of *Mesenterium*. **1615** CROOKE *Body of Man* 499 That phlegme..which distilleth out of that texture or web into the ventricles. *Ibid.* 525 That the spirits are attenuated in the textures of the small arteries, & in the strayghtes of those passages. *a* **1774** TUCKER *Lt. Nat.* (1834) II. 43 Nor the spider entangle the heedless fly in his texture. **1877** TYNDALL in *Daily News* 2 Oct. 2/4 His physical and intellectual textures have been woven for him during his passage through phases of history and forms of existence which lead the mind back to an abysmal past.

†**c.** A 'woven' or composed narrative or story.

**1611** SPEED *Hist. Gt. Brit.* VII. xxxviii. § 9. 341 A peece of ancient Saxon coine of Siluer, inscribed with his name, Anlaf Cynyng, which for the antiquity of the thing, and honor of the man we haue here imprinted, and placed, though in the texture of our English Saxon Kings.

**3.** The character of a textile fabric, as to its being fine, coarse, close, loose, plain, twilled, ribbed, diapered, etc., resulting from the way in which it is woven.

**1685** BOYLE *Salubr. Air* 79 The texture that belongs to Linen. **1791** COWPER *Odyss.* I. 556 Putting off his vest Of softest texture. **1842** in Bischoff *Woollen Manuf.* II. 176 One piece of cloth of German wool, and another piece of South Down wool..made of the same colour and texture. **1866** ROGERS *Agric. & Prices* I. xxii. 573 The linen worn by the wealthier classes differed materially in its texture.

**4.** In extended use: The constitution, structure, or substance of anything with regard to its constituents or formative elements. **a.** Of organic bodies and their parts.

**1665** BOYLE *Occas. Medit.* IV. iv, The Leaves..of a Tree.. are of a more solid Texture, and a more durable Nature than the Blossoms. **1738** WESLEY *Ps.* CXXXIX. ix, Thou know'st the Texture of my Heart, My Reins, and every vital Part. **1797** M. BAILLIE *Morb. Anat.* (1807) 212 The cartilage is smooth and thin, and very soft in its texture. **1844** STEPHENS *Bk. Farm* III. 905 Butter assumes a texture according as it has been treated. **1882** *Garden* 18 Mar. 182/3 Flavour and texture should be our watchword in raising Apples.

**b.** Of inorganic substances, as stones, soil, etc.: Physical (not chemical) constitution; the structure or minute moulding (of a surface).

**1660** BOYLE *New Exp. Phys. Mech.* xxii. 165 Air is.. endow'd with an Elastical power that probably proceeds from its Texture. **1663** — *Usef. Exp. Nat. Philos.* II. v. xiii. 242 Glass acquires a more or lesse brittle Texture, according as..it is baked. **1793** SMEATON *Edystone L.* § 106 The stone..in point of hardness and texture much like the Bath stone. **1811** PINKERTON *Petralogy* p. xxii, Mr. Kirwan has justly observed the inaccuracy of Werner and his disciples, who have confounded the texture with the fracture. **1813** SIR H. DAVY *Agric. Chem.* (1814) 5 Some lands of good apparent texture are yet sterile in a high degree. **1865** GEIKIE *Scen. & Geol. Scot.* viii. 220 Gneiss is too various in its texture and the rate of its decomposition. **1878** HUXLEY *Physiogr.* 63 The loose texture of snow.

**5.** *fig.* Of immaterial things: Constitution; nature or quality, as resulting from composition. Of the mind: Disposition, as 'woven' of various qualities; temperament, character.

**1611** SPEED *Hist. Gt. Brit.* VI. xix. § 9. 104 Albeit the very texture of this Epistle carrieth with it the true Character of Antiquity. *a* **1677** HALE *Prim. Orig. Man.* 157 Hence it is that..the texture of Zeuxes or Apelles inclines him to the invention or improving of Painting. **1692** BENTLEY *Boyle Lect.* iii. 80 An argument..of so frail and brittle a texture. **1751** SMOLLETT *Per. Pic.* (1779) III. lxxxi. 272 Had her thoughts been of a more tender texture. **1771** *Misc.* in *Ann. Reg.* 161/1 The whole texture of the fable. **1827** POLLOK *Course T.* II. 538 Creeds of wondrous texture.

**6.** In the fine arts: The representation of the structure and minute moulding of a surface (esp. of the skin), as distinct from its colour: cf. 4 b.

**1859** GULLICK & TIMBS *Paint.* 228 Impasting gives 'texture' and 'surface'. **1877** MORLEY *Crit. Misc.*, *Robespierre* Ser. II. 64 It is transparent and smooth, but there is none of that quality which the critics of painting call Texture.

**7.** *attrib.* and *Comb.*, as **texture-counter**, a thread-counter or waling-glass: see quot.

**1909** *Cent. Dict. Suppl.*, *Texture-counter*, a small magnifying-glass of low power, used in counting the number of threads, within a given space, in the texture of a fabric.

† **Te·xture,** *v. Obs.* [f. prec.] *trans.* To construct by or as by weaving; to give a texture to (anything). Usually in *pa. pple.*

**1694** R. BURTHOGGE *Reason & Nat. Spirits* 104 Now it is certain..that Matter is alter'd, figured, textur'd, and infinite ways wrought upon and moulded by means of motion. **1775** JEPHSON *Braganza* III. i. 31 This fine frame, Nerves exquisitely textur'd. **1778** [W. MARSHALL] *Minutes Agric.* 13 Sept. an. 1774, The off-horse treads that which is textured, and destroys the effect. **1835** CARLYLE *Corr.* (1883) I. vii. 65 A bright faultless vision textured out of mere sunbeams.

**Textured** (te·kstiŭıd), *a.* [f. as prec. + -ED [2].] Of a (specified) texture.

**1888** *Daily News* 1 May 5/7 One of the infinitely light-textured homespuns. **1901** *Westm. Gaz.* 3 Oct. 3/2 The addition of some very fine textured lace. **1905** *Ibid.* 20 Sept. 8/1 A close-textured, nutty-flavoured, easily-digested loaf.

**Te·xtureless,** *a.* [f. as prec. + -LESS.] Devoid of texture; exhibiting no texture.

**1851** RUSKIN *Mod. Paint.* II. III. II. v. § 14 Simple patterns upon textureless draperies. **1864** *Daily Tel.* 4 May, The whole picture [is]..disagreeably smooth and textureless. **1884** SHELDON in *West. Daily Press* 24 May 3/6 A salvy and textureless mass.

**Texturing** (te·kstiŭriŋ). [f. TEXTURE *sb.* + -ING [1].] The representation of the texture of a surface in painting or engraving.

**1882** HERKOMER in *Artist* 1 Feb. 38 To enable the engraver to render a disturbed surface by an ingenuity of lining or texturing of his own devising.

† **Te·xtury.** *Obs. rare*$^{-1}$. [f. TEXTURE *sb.* + -Y.] Weaving.

**1658** SIR T. BROWNE *Gard. Cyrus* ii, Which is beyond the common art of textury, and may still nettle Minerva, the goddess of that mystery.

‖ **Textus** (te·kstŏs). [L. *textus* TEXT.]

**1.** A manuscript or book of the Gospels; a Bible; = TEXT *sb.*[1] 3 b. *Textus-case*, a case or cover for this (*Cent. Dict.* 1891).

**1874** MICKLETHWAITE *Mod. Par. Churches* 52 The gospeller having received the textus or gospel-book from the altar. **1877** J. D. CHAMBERS *Div. Worship* 275 At Salisbury, 1222, was one great Textus. **1906** *Athenæum* 21 Apr. 478 A boss of this value was originally affixed to the centre of a Textus of the Gospels,..often the chief ornament of early altars.

**2.** *Textus Receptus*, literally, received text; *spec.* the received text of the Greek New Testament.

Strictly applied to the text of the second Elzevir edition of 1633, to which the publisher prefixed the assertion, 'Textum ergo habes nunc ab omnibus receptum' (Thou hast therefore the text now received by all); but commonly extended to any reprint of this (or of that of Stephanus 1550, on which it was founded) with or without slight revision, but without the aid of the early MSS. since discovered or published.

**1856** T. H. HORNE *Introd. Text. Crit. N. T.* 124 From this sort of boast sprang the expression 'Textus Receptus'. **1885** *Athenæum* 5 Sept. 296/1 Pascal's..'Letters'..suffered.. from..the..partiality of uncultivated admirers for an inaccurate *textus receptus*. **1901** F. G. KENYON *Handbk. Textual Crit. N. T.* 229 Some words of this re-translation ..still linger in our Textus Receptus to the present day.

**Text-writer** (te·kstˌrəi:təɹ).

†**1.** A professional writer of text-hand, before the introduction of printing; later, an engrosser of legal documents. *Obs.*

**1463** *Canterb. Corporation Acc.* (MS.), Thomas Howlet, textwriter, alias scrivener. *a* **1490** BOTONER *Itin.* (Nasmith 1778) 141 Sub custodia scriptoris text-wryter commorantis apud Seynt Mary Strond. **1491** in *York Myst.* Introd. 39 Tixt-wryters, luminers, noters, turners, and florischers.

**2.** *Law.* An author of a legal text-book.

**1845** POLSON *Law Nat.* in *Encycl. Metrop.* II. 720/1 Text-writers of authority, an authority which they obtain whenever they record the usages and practice of nations..in a spirit of impartiality. **1863** H. COX *Instit.* I. ix. 188 The language of text-writers upon the right of the Lords to reject money bills is uniform. **1902** SIR E. E. KEKEWICH in *Law Times Rep.* LXXXVI. 346/2 In dealing with a question of this kind, one is thrown back on maxims and principles, and the exposition of them by text-writers is important. **1902** JOYCE *Ibid.* 352/1 A dictum which..is copied in the text-books, and is considered by the text-writers to be law.

† **Tey,** variant of TAY *Obs.*, outer membrane of the brain, etc.

*c* **1350** *Nominale Gall.-Angl.* 6 *Toup canal et ceruel*, Toppe tey and the brayne.

**Tey,** obs. f. TEA. **Tey(e,** obs. ff. TIE *sb.* and *v.*
**Teyghte,** obs. pa. pple. of TIE *v.*
**Teyl, Teyle, Teylle,** var. TELE *Obs.*, blame, obs. ff. TEAL, TEIL, lime-tree, TILE.
**Teym,** Sc. f. TEEM *v.*[2] **Teyme,** obs. f. TEAM.
**Teyn, Teynd(e,** obs. ff. TEEN, TEIND, tithe.

† **Teyne.** *Obs. rare.* [a. ON. *tein-n* twig, rod: cf. *gull-, járn-teinn* rod of gold, of iron, MSw. *tēn* 'smal stång (af metall)', Söderwall; Sw. *ten.* Cognate with OE. *tān*, MDu. *teen* twig.] A slender rod of metal.

*c* **1386** CHAUCER *Can. Yeom. Prol. & T.* 672 He took out of his owene sleeue A teyne of siluer which þat was nat but an Ounce of weighte. *Ibid.* 676 He shoope his Ingot in lengthe and eek in breede Of this teyne. *Ibid.* 777 This preest took vp this siluer teyne anon And thanne seyde the Chanon let vs gon With thise thre teynes whiche þat we han wroght To som Goldsmyth and wite if they been ouht.

**Teyne:** see TEEN *sb.*[1], TIND *v. Obs.*, to kindle.
**Teynt(e, Teynter, -o(u)r, -ur, Teynt-wort,** obs. ff. TAINT, TENT, TENTER, TENTWORT.
**Teyre, Teyrse,** obs. ff. TEAR *a.* and *sb.*[3], TIERCE.
**Teys(e,** var. TEISE *Obs.* **Teyser,** obs. f. TEASER.
**Teysoure,** var. TEISER *Obs.*
**Teytheyng,** var. *tithing*, obs. f. TIDING.
**Tezel, tezill, Tezir,** obs. ff. TEASEL, TEASER.

‖ **Tezkere, teskere** (te·zkĕrĕ). Also 7 teskeria, -caria, 9 -caré, tischera, tezkera, teskari. [Arab. تذكرة *taδkirah*, in Turkish *tezkere*, lit. memorandum, record, note, f. ذكر *δakara*, in deriv. conj. to record, relate, remember = Heb. זכר *zākar* to remember.] A Turkish official memorandum or certificate of any kind; a receipt, order, permit, licence; *esp.* an internal passport.

**1612** CORYAT in Purchas *Pilgrims* (1625) II. x. xii. 1825 A *Teskeria* (this is a Turkish word that signifieth a Certificate written vnder his hand). **1615** G. SANDYS *Trav.* 115 We could not passe without a Tescaria from the Cadee. **1817** *By-Laws Levant Company* 26 That the Company's privilege of having tescarés or certificates..be not forfeited. **1818** BLAQUIERE tr. *Pananti* xiii. 247 No [grain] can be exported without a *tischera*, or written permit, bearing the Dey's seal. **1858** SIMMONDS *Dict. Trade*, *Tescare*, *Teskere*, a Turkish Custom-house certificate. **1890** *Daily News* 30 June 7/7 The Porte yesterday despatched a teskere to..the Armenian Patriarch, enjoining him to dissolve the Provincial Council of Van. **1904** *Daily Chron.* 13 Jan. 5/2 A tezkera or local passport costing 4*s.* **1905** *Dundee Advertiser* 29 Nov. 11/1 The teskari or passport is an essential inexorably demanded by the Turkish official.

**TH**, in words of Old English or Old Norse origin, and in words from Greek, is a consonantal digraph representing a simple sound, or rather (in Teutonic words), a pair of simple sounds, *breath* and *voice*, indicated in this dictionary by the OE. letters (þ) and (ð); the former, as in *thin*, *bath* (þin, baþ), being the breath dental spirant akin to *t*, and the latter, as in *then*, *bathe* (ðen, bēⁱð), the voiced dental spirant akin to *d*. The group t, d, þ, ð, corresponds to the group p, b, f, v. The breath spirant is identical with modern Greek *theta* (Θ, θ), and approximately with Spanish *z* (or *c* before *e*, *i*). The Greek letter, which corresponds etymologically to Sanskrit ध *dh* (and so, by Grimm's Law, to Teutonic and English D), was in early inscriptions represented by TH, and was a true aspirate; it was subsequently often written ΤΘ, τθ, and had prob. the sound (tþ); but by the second century B.C. it had sunk into a simple sound, = our (þ). The Romans, having neither the sound nor the symbol, represented the letter by TH, as in Θάψος, *Thapsus*, but app. this was pronounced, at least in late Latin (whence in all the Romanic languages), as simple *t*; cf. Greek θεωρία, L. *theōria*, It. and Sp. *teoria*; in Pg. *theoria*, F. *théorie*, spelt with *th*, pronounced with *t*; also Gr. Θωμᾶς, L. *Thōmās*, It. *Toma*, Sp. *Tomás*; Pg., F., Eng. *Thomas* all pronounced with T.

(2) In Teutonic the breath spirant (þ) was very frequent, being the regular etymological representative of Indo-Eur. *t* initially or after the stressed vowel, as in OTeut. **þrijiz*, Goth. *þreis*, OE. *þreo*, Eng. *three*, = Indo-Eur. **treies*, Skr. *trayas*, Gr. τρεῖς, L. *trēs*; OTeut. **brōþer*, Goth. *brōþar*, OE. *brōþor*, *brōðor*, Eng. *brother*, = Indo-Eur. *bhrā·tér*, Gr. φρᾱτηρ clansman, L. *frā·ter*. The voiced spirant in *brōðor*, etc., was a later development (*c* 700 in English) from the breath sound between vowels or voiced consonants, as in the parallel *v* and *z* from *f* and *s*. Initially, the same change of (þ) to (ð) took place during the Middle English period in the demonstrative group of words, *the*, *that*, and their kindred, *this*, *these*, †*tho*, *those*, *there*, *then*, *than*, *thence*, *thither*, *thus*, etc., and in the pronouns of the second person singular, *thou*, *thee*, *thine*, *thy*: these constitute the only words in English with initial (ð). In the same group of words in the cognate Teutonic languages (þ) has passed through (ð) into (d); thus Ger. *das*, Du. *dat*, Da., Sw. *det* 'that'; in High Ger., Low Ger., and Du. the same has taken place even in other original *th* words which retain (þ) in English; e.g. Ger. *dach*, *denken*, *ding*, *dick*, *donner*, *drei* = Eng. thatch, think, thing, thick, thunder, three.

(3) In the demonstrative and pronominal groups of words, change of initial *þ* to *t*, by assimilation to a preceding dental (*t*, *d*, *s*), appears in earlier English. OE. *þæt þe* became *þæt-te*, *þætte*; *þe læs þe* appears in the 11th c. as *þe læste*, whence modern *lest*. In the last section of the OE. Chronicle, from 1132, *þe* after *t* or *d* regularly becomes *te* (e.g. þat *te* king, and *te* eorles). In the Ormulum and the Cotton MS. of Cursor Mundi, this assimilation is seen in all the words of the *the-thou* group (*Orm.* þatt *tatt te* goddspell meneþþ, wrohht *tiss* boc, and *tatt te* follc all þess *te* bett; *Cursor*, ne was *tar*, here and *tare*, scho serued *taim*, als sais *te* sau). So in Ancren Riwle (and *tet* is, et *tesse* uerse, þeo þet *tus* doð, and *tes* oðer, etc.). In the course of the 14th c., this assimilation was given up, and the spirant reappeared (as ð).

(4) In the Runic alphabet (*futhorc*) the breath spirant had to itself a symbol ᚦ or þ (called *thorn*); but in the earliest known OE. writings in the Roman alphabet this was represented by *th*, the voiced spirant being often represented by *d* (ð) (sometimes by *th*). Before 700 probably, the character ð, formed by a bar across the stem of ∂, was introduced; it appears in a charter of Wihtræd, king of Kent, 700–715 (Sweet *Oldest English Texts* 428). Apparently it was first used to denote the voiced spirant: see the proper names in the Moore MS. of Bæda, *c* 737, and the *Liber Vitæ*, Cott. MS., *c* 800, and charters before 800 generally. But in the ninth century it was used for both spirants, as in the Vespasian Psalter, *c* 825 (e.g. iv. 5 ða ðe cweoðað), and in a West Saxon charter of 847 (*O. E. T.* 433). In the 8th century apparently, the thorn, þ, was adopted from the Runic futhorc, the earliest charter showing it being one of Coenwulf, king of Mercia, of 811 (O. E. T. 456); but it was not much used till late in the 9th c. A Surrey charter *a* 889 (ibid. 451) has 34 examples of ð initial, and 25 medial or final, with 49 of þ initial, and 1 medial. From the later years of the 9th c. ð and þ were used promiscuously in West Saxon works, with some preponderance of þ initially and ð finally. This continued in ME. till the 13th c. On the other hand, the Durham *Rituale* and the Lindisfarne Gospel Gloss, *c* 950, have uniformly ð in all positions (except in the compendium ꝥ for ðæt), as has also the East Anglian *Genesis & Exodus*, *c* 1250; while the Mercian portion of the Rushworth Gospel Gloss, *c* 975, and Ormin, *c* 1200, have only þ. After 1250 the ð speedily became obsolete; þ remained in use, but was gradually restricted more or less to the pronominal and demonstrative words. In later times its MS. form approached, and at times became identical with, that of *y* (the latter being sometimes distinguished by having a dot placed over it). As the continental type used by Caxton had no þ, its place in print was usually supplied by *th* for both sounds and in all positions. But in Scotland, the early printers, especially in the demonstrative and pronominal words, continued the þ as *y*, as in *y^e*, *yis*, *yat*, *you* (= thou), a practice also common in England in MS., and hardly yet extinct. Confusion with the modern *y* consonant, ME. ȝ, was avoided in Scotland, sometimes by writing the latter *yh*, but usually by continuing ME. ȝ in the form ʒ or z, so that *ye zeir* stood for *þe ȝeir*, i.e. *the year*. It is remarkable that, when OE. þ and ð were both in use, no attempt was made to differentiate them as breath and voice spirants, and app. no serious attempt even to distinguish them as initial and medio-final, as was done in Norwegian when the Roman alphabet was adopted, *c* 1200, and in Icelandic before 1300. At an earlier date (prob. *c* 800) the character ð was partially adopted from OE. in Old Saxon, and was used generally in the middle and end of words, while *th* was usual as the breath spirant initially.

(5) In a few compounds, as *anthill*, *outhouse*, *lighthouse*, *Chatham*, *Wytham*, *Yetholm*, etc., *t* and *h* come together but do not form a digraph; and in a few foreign words, chiefly East Indian, as *Thakoor*, *Thug*, *th* represents Skr. थ *th* or ठ *ṭh*, the sound being a *t* or *ṭ* followed by a slight aspiration (tʰ, ṭʰ), in Eng. commonly reduced to *t*.

In a few proper names and other words derived from or influenced by French, as *Thomas*, *Thompson*, *thyme*, *th* is pronounced as *t*; several other words were formerly so treated, and even spelt with *t*, e.g. *theatre*, *theme*, *theology*, *throne*, *authentic*, *orthography*: *t* has become fixed in *treacle*, *treasure*. The late L. and Romanic treatment of *th* as *t* often led to the spelling *th* where *t* was etymological, as in *Thames*, *Sathan*; in *amaranth*, *amianthus*, *author*, etc., the corruption has also affected the pronunciation. See the individual words. In some ME. MSS. *th* frequently appears for *t* or for *d*: e.g. *tho* to, *thyll* till, *myghth* might, *nyghth* night, *whythe* white; *thede* deed, *theer* deer, *thegree* degree, *thepartyth* departed, *tho* do, *thogh* doth, *abothe* abode, *groundeth* grounded, *iclodeth* y-clothed, *lowthe* loud, *rothe* rood, *unther* under. Early ME. scribes (prob. Norman) often confounded the English letters þ (or ð) and ȝ, writing e.g. *ȝefinge* for *þefinge*, thieving, *wiȝ*, *worȝ*, *wroȝ* for *wiþ*, *worþ*, *wroþ* (in Auchinleck MS. of *Florice and Bl.*).

(6) Etymologically, modern Eng. *th* (ð) often represents an OE. *d*, esp. before *r* or *er*, as in *father*, *mother*, *gather*, *hither*, *together*, etc.; dialectally, this sometimes extends to other words, as *bladder*, *ladder* *solder*; on the other hand some dialects retain original *d*, and extend it to other words, as *brother*, *further*, *rather*, *southern-wood*, *wether*. In *burden* and *murder*, *d* represents the earlier ð of *burthen*, *murther*.

Dialectally *th* is sometimes substituted for *f*, and vice versa: e.g. *thane*, *thetch*, *thistolow*, *thrail*, *thrae*, *throm*, *thurrow*, for *fane*, *fetch* (vetch), *fistula*, *frail* (flail), *frae*, *from*, *furrow*; also *fill*, *Fuirsday*, for THILL, THURSDAY. The Welsh name *Llewelyn* appears in Eng. as *Thlewelyn* (*Rolls of Parl.* I. 463/1, Edw. I or II), and *Fluellen* (Shaks. Hen. V). *Th* also occurs dialectally for *wh*, as in *thirl*, *thortleberry*, *thorl*, for *whirl*, *whortleberry*, *whorl*. Conversely, Sc. has *whaing*, *whang*, *white*, *whittle*, for *thwaing*, *thwang*, *thwite*, *thwittle*.

**1.** The digraph *th* and its sound.

[*c* **1400** MAUNDEV. (Roxb.) xv. 71 We hafe in oure speche in Ingland twa oþer letters þan þai [Saracens] hafe in þaire abce, þat es to say, þ and ȝ, whilk er called *þorn* and *ȝok*.] *a* **1637** B. JONSON *Eng. Gram.* Wks. (Rtldg.) 775/2 Th Hath a double and doubtful sound. *Ibid.* 776/2 Some syllabes, as *the*, *then*, *there*, *that*..are often compendiously and shortly written, as *y^e y^en y^ere y^t*. **1668** O. PRICE *Eng. Orthogr.* 24 Q. What is the sound of *th*? *A. Th* makes a hard sound in *thunder*, *through*, *thick*, *thin* [etc.]. But, *th*, makes a softer sound in *that*, *thine*, *worthy*, *father* [etc.]. **1730–6** BAILEY folio), *Th*, in English is..but one Letter, or a *Litera aspirata*. **1863** MELVILLE BELL *Princ. Speech* 180 We confound the two sounds [þ and ð] by using for both the same digraph [*th*].

**2.** Th. is an abbreviation of THORIUM, THURSDAY.

**Th-, th'** (ME. þ-), a clipped form of some unstressed monosyllables, esp. when the following word begins with a vowel or *h*.

**1.** = THE.

Still *dial.* in Lancs., etc.: cf. T' 2. See also I'TH'.

**1154** *O. E. Chron.*, Þe munekes..on cyricen byrieden þabbot hehlice. *c* **1200** ORMIN 5937 Tatt himm ummbeshorenn wass Hiss shapp o þalde wise. *c* **1330** R. BRUNNE *Chron. Wace* 5734 Þapostles holy lyf. **13..** *E. E. Allit. P.* C. 325 Þacces of anguych watz hid in my sawle. **1414–15** *Plumpton Corr.* (Camden) p. cxx, Sir Marmaduke Constable thelder, knight, ..on thone partie, & Sir Robert Plompton..on thother partie. **1485** *Naval Acc. Hen. VII* (1896) 8 To be levied by thands of Thomas Combes. **1533** MORE *Apol.* 283 More old than thage of eyght hundred yere. **1623** *Shaks.'s Lear* IV. vi. 238 Least that th'infection..take..hold on thee. — *Temp.* II. i. 120 To th'shore. *Ibid.* 131 Which end o' th'beame should bow. **1883** *Almondbury & Huddersfield Gloss.* s.v. *T*, Th' man i'th' mooin.

†**2.** = THOU. *Obs.*

*c* **1315** SHOREHAM i. 94 Þorwe þat blod þi soule his [= is] bouȝt..And þorwe þat water i-wessche þart. *c* **1330** R. BRUNNE *Chron. Wace* (Rolls) 8015 Þer wot no man of wham þart come. *c* **1500** *Debate Carp. Tools* 6 in Hazl. *E. P. P.* I. 79 Th' all neuer be thryfty man. *a* **1586** SIDNEY *Arcadia* III. *Countrie Song* 99, I rather would my sheepe Thad'st killed with a stroke. **1594** GREENE & LODGE *Looking Glasse* (Hunter. Cl.) 25 Well sirrha well, thart as thart, and so ile take thee.

†**3.** = THEY. *Obs.*

*c* **1540** in Weever *Anc. Fun. Mon.* (1631) 282 God grant hem euirlastyng lyff, To whom we hop thar gon. **1707** E. WARD *Hud. Rediv.* II. VII. 18 Th'ad put the holy Puppet on A Surplice.

**-th**, *suffix* [1], a formative of sbs. **a.** from verbs; in some words, as *bath*, *birth*, *death*, *math*, *oath*, OTeut., repr. various Indo-Eur. suffixes, as *-tos*, *-tā*, *-tis*, *-tus*, in which the *t* following the stressed syllable regularly became *þ* in Teutonic; in others, as *growth*, *tilth*, going back to ON. or OE.; in others, as *blowth*, *spilth*, *stealth*, of later analogical formation. In many words Indo-Eur. *t* remained in consequence of its position, or *þ* was subsequently changed to *t*: see -T *suffix* [3] a.

**b.** from adjs. (rarely sbs.), representing Indo-Eur. *-itā*, OTeut. *-iþō*, Goth. *-iþa*, OE. *-þu*, *-þo*, *-þ*, with prec. *i-* umlaut, forming abstract nouns of state: as *filth* (OE. *fýlþ*, OS. *fūlitha* from *fúl* foul), *health*, *length*, *mirth*, *strength*, *truth*; in ME. and also in cognate langs., *dearth*, *depth*; of later analogical formation, *breadth*, *sloth* (cf. OE. *slǽwþ*), *wealth*. In some words of this group, *þ* has, by phonetic causes, become *t*, e.g. OE. *hiehþu*, ME. *heiȝþe*, now *height*, ON. *slægð*, ME. *sleiȝþe*, now *sleight*: see -T *suffix* [3] b.

**-th**, *suffix* [2], forming ordinal numbers; in modern literary Eng. used with all simple numbers from *fourth* onward; representing OE. *-þa*, *-þe*, or *-oða*, *-oðe*, used with all ordinals except *fifta*, *sixta*, *ellefta*, *twelfta*, which had the ending *-ta*, *-te*; in Sc., north. Eng., and many midland dialects the latter, in form *-t*, is used with all simple numerals after *third* (*fourt*, *fift*, *sixt*, *sevent*, *tent*, *hundert*, etc.). In Kentish and O.Northumbrian those from *seventh* to *tenth* had formerly the ending *-da*, *-de*. All these variations, *-th*, *-t*, *-d*, represent an original Indo-Eur. *-tos* (cf. Gr. πέμπ-τος, L. *quin-tus*), understood to be identical with one of the suffixes of the superlative degree. In OE. *fifta*, *sixta*, the original *t* was retained, being protected by the preceding consonant; the *-þa* and *-da* were due to the position of the stress accent, according to Verner's Law.

The ordinals from *twentieth* to *ninetieth* have *-eth*, OE. *-oða*, *-oðe*. In compound numerals *-th* is added only to the last, as $1\frac{1}{345}$, the *one thousand three hundred and forty-fifth* part; in his *one-and-twentieth* year.

**Tha, þa, thaa, þaa**, OE. and northern forms of THO *Obs.* **Tha**, dial. form of THOU, THEE.

**Thaarm**, obs. form of THARM, intestine.

**Thaborite**, obs. f. TABORITE (Blount *Gl.* 1674).

**Thach, Thacher**, obs. ff. THATCH *v.*, -ER.

**Thack** (þæk), *sb.* Now *dial.* Forms: 1 þæc, 4 þak, þakke, 4–6 (9 *dial.*) thak, 5 thakk(e, 5–6 (9 *dial.*) thake, 5–7 thacke, 6 thecke, thaec, 6– thack (9 *Sc.* theck). [Com. Teut.: OE. *þæc* = WFris. *thek*, OLG. **þak* (MDu. *dac* (*dāke*), Du., MLG., LG. *dak*), OHG. *dach*, *dah*, *thah* (MHG., Ger. *dach*) roof, ON. *þak* roof, thatch (Sw. *tak*, Da. *tag*):—OTeut. **pako^m*, f. root *þek-* to cover, Indo-Eur. *teg-*, in L. *teg-ĕre* to cover, *tog-a* covering, gown, *tug-urium* hut, cottage, Gr. τέγ-ος, στεγ-ή roof, στέγ-ειν to cover; Lith. *stogas* roof; OIr. *teg*, Irish and Gael. *tigh* house. See THATCH *v.*]

†**1.** The roof of a house or building. *Obs.*

*a* **900** CYNEWULF *Christ* 1503 Þæt hi under eowrum þæce mosten in-ȝebuȝan. *c* **975** *Rushw. Gosp.* Matt. viii. 8 Drihten nam ic wyrðe þ ðu ga under þacu minne. *Ibid.* xxiv. 17 Seþe on þæce siæ ne stigað he niðer. *c* **1000** *Ags. Ps.* (Th.) cxxviii. 4 Þam þe on huses þæce heah aweaxeð. *c* **1330** R. BRUNNE *Chron. Wace* (Rolls) 14689 In eueses þey [sparrows] crepte, & in þe þakkes. **1489** CAXTON *Faytes of A.* II. xxxvii. 156 They ought to mounte up to the wyndowes of the houses and upon the thakkes. **1513** DOUGLAS *Æneis* IV. xii. 53 Spreding fra thak to thak, baith but and ben. **1524** LD. DACRE *Let. to Wolsey* in Ellis *Orig. Lett.* Ser. I. I. 249 Ald Howses wherof the thak and covereings ar taken awey. **1526** in T. West *Antiq. Furness* (1805) 133 The said tenant to keep his hous tennantable, upon his own charges, with thake and walle.

**2.** That with which the roof of a house or the like is covered to protect it from the weather; *spec.* the covering of straw, reeds, or the like disposed so as to carry off the rain: = THATCH *sb.* 1.

*a* **900** tr. *Bæda's Hist.* III. viii. [x.] (1890) 180 Þæs huses hrof..wæs mid ȝyrdum awunden & mid þæce beþeaht. *Ibid.* xiv. [xvi.] (1890) 202 On beamum & on ræftrum & on waȝum & on watelum & on ðeacon. *c* **1000** ÆLFRIC *Hom.* II. 136 Ða tear þæt hors þæt ðæc of ðære cytan hrofe. **14..** *Nom.* in Wr.-Wülcker 732/23 *Hectectura*, thak. **1486** *Nottingham*

*Rec.* III. 244 Thak þat the grete wynde blewe of þe house. *a* 1500 *Chaucer's Dreme* 1773 That they would ever in houses of thacke, Their lives lead. 1530 PALSGR. 280/1 Thacke of a house, *chaume*. 1578 BANISTER *Hist. Man* I. I To be well aduised..before he lay on Thack, Tile,..or Plaster. 1641 BEST *Farm. Bks.* (Surtees) 138 One to drawe thacke, and the other to serve the thatcher. 1721 RAMSAY *Ode to Mr. F*— 30 Wa's of divots, roof'd wi' thack. 1815 SCOTT *Guy M.* viii, Ye have riven the thack off seven cottar houses. 1859 GEO. ELIOT *A. Bede* x, It puts me i' mind o' the swallows as was under the thack last 'ear. *Mod. north. dial.* Wet as thack.

(In *Eng. Dial. Dict.* from Scotl. to Oxfordsh., Berksh., and from Worcester to E. Anglia.)

**b.** The covering of properly disposed straw with which the sloping top of a stack of corn or hay-rick is thatched. *Thack and rape* (*Sc.*), this thatching and the straw rope with which it is secured: often used allusively.

1786 BURNS *Brigs of Ayr* 26 An thack and rape secure the toil-won crap. 1816 SCOTT *Antiq.* xxvi, He kens.. wha feeds him, and cleeds him, and keeps a' tight, thack and rape. *Ibid.* Gloss., *Under thack and rape* means snug and comfortable. 1896 *Speaker* 3 Oct. 353/1 All is secured in the cornyard under 'thack and raip'.

**3.** *transf.* Covering (in quot. = skin).

*c* 1375 *Sc. Leg. Saints* xxxvii. (*Vincencius*) 276 Þane of þe frame he bad hym tak, Þat hale had nothi· lith na þak.

**4.** *attrib.* and *Comb.*, as *thack-roof*; **thack-board**, a wooden roofing tile, a shingle; **thack-broach** = *thack-pin, thack-prick*, BROACH *sb.* 5; **thack divot** (**dowat**) = *thack turf*; **thack-gate** (*Sc.*): see quot.; **thack house**, a thatched house; **thack-lead**, lead with which a roof is covered; **thack-nail, -peg, -pin**, a sharpened pin or peg used in fastening the thatch on a roof; **thack-prick, -prod**, a sharpened wand or stick for the securing of thatch; **thack-rape** (*Sc.* and *north. dial.*), a rope (usually of twisted straw) used in fixing the thatch on a rick or cottage roof; **thack-stone**, a thin flat stone (e.g. Stonesfield slate) used for roofing; **thack-tile** [OE. *þæctigile*; cf. G. *dachziegel*], a roofing tile; **thack turf**, a roofing turf or sod.

1354 *Mem. Ripon* (Surtees) III. 91 In ccc de *thakbord' emp. pro stauro ecclesiæ. 1375 BARBOUR *Bruce* IV. 126 (MS. E.) For fyre all cleir Soyn throu the thak [*v. r.* thik] burd can appeir. 1418 in Rogers *Agric. & Pr.* (1882) III. 402/1 Norwich, Thackboard. 1447–8 *Durham Acc. Rolls* (Surtees) 186 In repar. molendini..in Cma Thakborde. 1573 in Feuillerat *Revels Q. Eliz.* (1908) 208 Hookes & eies with *thackbroches. 1504 *Acc. Ld. H. Treas. Scot.* II. 424 For theking of divers houses with *thak dowat. 1825 JAMIESON, **Thack-gate*, the sloping edge of the gable-tops of a house, when the thatch covers them; in contradistinction from the wind-skews that are raised higher than the thatch. 1582–8 *Hist. Jas. VI* (1804) 209 He exposit.. sum of his souldiors to sum *thack housses besyd the West Port, in a windie nyght, and pat the same in fyre. 1725 RAMSAY *Gentle Sheph.* II. i, A snug thack house, before the door a green. 1894 *Northumbld. Gloss.*, 'Thack hoose'—a thatched house. 1819 W. TENNANT *Papistry Storm'd* (1827) 214 Capper and *thack-lead aff were tane. 1846 BROCKETT *N. C. Words* (ed. 3), **Thack-nail*, **Thack-peg*, **Thack-pin*, a wooden pin or stob used in fastening thatch to the roof of a building. 1828 *Craven Gloss.*, **Thack-pricks*, sharpened twigs for the securing of thatch. 1876 *Whitby Gloss.*, **Thack-reeaps*, the cords for securing the thatch. 1887 *Suppl. to Jamieson*, Thack-rape. 1442 *Calverley Charters* (1904) 253, j acre of soile..where he may gett and tak *thakstone. 1621 *Sc. Acts Jas. VI*, c. 26 (1816) IV. 627/1 To thaick þe same againe wt Sklait, or skailȝee, leade, tyild, or Thackstone. 1880 A. L. RITCHIE *Ch. St. Baldred* 37 The roof of the east end of Whitekirk Church is covered with thackstones. *c* 725 *Corpus Gloss.* (O.E.T.) 1043 *Imbricibus*, *þæctigilum. 1477 *Act 17 Edw. IV*, c. 4 Pleintile, autrement nosmer thaktile, roftile, ou crestile. 1610 W. FOLKINGHAM *Art of Survey* 4 Gallic and Thacke Tiles. *c* 1800 S. PEGGE *Anecd. Eng. Lang.* (1803) 279 In Yorkshire they call bricks wall tile, and tiles thack tile. 1576 in *Reg. Mag. Sig. Scot.* 1580. 20/1 Pro 108 oneribus focalium..et *thak turffis.

**Thack** (þæk), *v.*¹ Now *dial.* Forms: 5–6 (9 *dial.*) thak, 6 thacke, 7 thake. *Sc.* thaick, 6– **thack.** [app. partly (in form *thake*) from OE. *þacian*, f. *þæc* THACK *sb.* (so MHG., Ger. *dachen* to roof, from *dach*): cf. Sc. *mak, tak*, for *make, take*; but *thak, thack*, may also have been a later formation from the sb. See also THATCH *v.*, THEEK *v.*]

**1.** *intr.* To put thatch on houses; = THATCH *v.* 5.

*a* 1100 *Gerefa* in *Anglia* (1886) IX. 261 Me mæcg in Agusto and Septembri and Octobri ðacian, ðecgan and fald weoxian. 1486 *Nottingham Rec.* III. 247 Paid to a thakker thakkyng on þe same barne. 1523 FITZHERB. *Husb.* § 27 To mowe theyr stubble, eyther to thacke or to bren. 1523 — *Surv.* xx. (1539) 42 He shall bothe thacke and daube at his owne coste. 1641 BEST *Farm. Bks.* (Surtees) 139 Thatchers allwayes beginne att the eize [eaves], and soe thake upwards till they come to the ridge.

**2.** *trans.* To cover (a roof) or roof (a house) with thatch, formerly also with lead, tiles, etc.; = THEEK *v.* 1; *spec.* to cover the top of a rick with straw or other material so laid as to carry off the rain.

*c* 1440 *Promp. Parv.* 490/1 Thakkyn howsys, *sartatego*,.. *sarcitego*. 1474 *Coventry Leet-bk.* 389 Þat no maner man frohensfurth thak ne couer his house with strawe nor brome within this Cite. 1530 PALSGR. 754/2 Sythe I can nat tyle my house, I must be fayne to thacke it. 1552 *Inv. Ch. Goods* (Surtees No. 97) 9 The churche thacked with leade. 1611 SPEED *Hist. Gt. Brit.* v. iv. § 5. 22 Houses and cottages ..Which, as Diodorus Siculus saith were vsually thacked with reed. 1621 [see *thackstone*, prec. 4]. 1671 J. FRASER *Polichron.* (S.H.S.) 496 Tirr the Kirk to thack the quire. *a* 1825 FORBY *Voc. E. Anglia, Thack*, v. to thatch. 1863 MRS. TOOGOOD *Yorks. Dial.*, It will take two threave of strea to thack the hay-stack.

Hence **Thacked** (þækt) *ppl.a.*, thatched; **Tha·cking** *vbl. sb.*, the action of thatching; also *concr.* the material used for the purpose, thatch.

1530 PALSGR. 699/1 This is a mete man to sytte on a *thacked house to scarre away crowes. 1597 *1st Pt. Return fr. Parnass.* I. i. 134 Some thacked cottage or some cuntrie hall. 1602 *2nd Pt. Return fr. Parnass.* v. ii. 2091 True mirth we may enioy in thacked stall. 1828 *Craven Gloss.*, *Thack'd*, thatched. *c* 1440 *Promp. Parv.* 490/1 *Thakkynge, sartatectum*. 1546 *Yorks. Chantry Surv.* (Surtees) 168 The reparacion of the belles, thakkyng and other necessaries pertenyng to the sayd churche. 1613 MARKHAM *Eng. Husbandman* I. I. xvii. (1635) 103 Whole Strawe Wheate.. Husbandmen esteeme it so much for their thacking. *c* 1680 H. LEIGH in Macfarlane *Geog. Collect.* (S.H.S.) III. 252 The common and ordinary thacking is of a kind of Divet [= sod].

**Thack** (þæk), *v.*² *Obs.* exc. *dial.* [OE. *þaccian*, app. onomatopœic. Cf. THWACK.]

†**1.** *trans.* To clap with the open hand or the like; to pat, slap lightly. *Obs.*

*c* 897 K. ÆLFRED *Gregory's Past. C.* xli. 303 Swa [swa] wildu hors, ðonne we h[ie] æresð ȝefangnu habbað, we hie ðacciað & straciað mid bradre hande. *a* 900 — in Cockayne *Shrine* (1864) 185 Hine lyst bet þaccian and cyssan ðonne oðerne on bær lic. *c* 1305 *Land Cokayne* 141 To þe maid dun hi fleeþ And geþ þe wench al abute, And þakkeþ al her white toute. *c* 1386 CHAUCER *Miller's T.* 118 Whan Nicholas had doon thus euerideel And thakked [*MS. Petw.* twakked] hire aboute the lendes weel. — *Friar's T.* 261 (Harl. MS.) This carter thakketh his hors vpon the croupe.

†**b.** *intr.* To beat, to shower blows. *Obs.*

1480 CAXTON *Chron. Eng.* ccxliv. 299 Our men of armes and archyers that thakked on hem so thikke with arewes.

†**2.** *trans.* To clap (something) *on* or *in* a place.

1542 *St. Papers Hen. VIII*, IX. 42 But here he thakked on as many wordes, as he did bifore lawes in the other parte. 1589 R. ROBINSON *Gold. Mirr.* 31 The thorny thumps that Thought did thacke Within my wofull breast.

**3.** *mod. dial.* To THWACK, beat, flog.

1861 QUINN *Heather Lintie* (1863) 22 (E.D.D.) Ye weel deserve a thackin' For tellin [etc.]. 1904 in *Eng. Dial. Dict.* (Norf.), He rarely thacked th' old dicky (donkey).

**Tha·cker.** Now *dial.* [prob. representing an OE. **þæcere*, f. *þacian* to thatch.] One who covers roofs with thatch; a thatcher.

1420 *Coventry Leet-bk.* 21 Item, thakker, laborer, dawber, and palyer. 1486 [see THACK *v.*¹ 1]. 1573 TUSSER *Husb.* (1878) 86 Wheat and the rie..Such strawe some saue for thacker to haue. 1590 *Shuttleworths' Acc.* (Chetham Soc.) 62 A thacker at Tyngreve thackinge three dayes, and onne to serve him iijs vjd. 1820 *Blackw. Mag.* Oct. 14/2 Hire two-three thackers to mend the thack on the roofs.

**Thackerayan** (þæ·kəreiăn), *a.* and *sb.* [f. proper name *Thackeray* + -AN.] **a.** *adj.* Of or pertaining to, or characteristic of, William Makepeace Thackeray (1811–63) or his works. **b.** *sb.* An admirer of Thackeray or his works. So **Tha·ckeraye·sque** *a.*, **Thackeray·ian** *a.*, **Tha·ckerayite.** (All more or less nonce-wds.)

1861 W. F. COLLIER *Hist. Eng. Lit.* 491 Those queer, delightful, rambling, thoroughly Thackerayesque Roundabout Papers. 1885 *Athenæum* 17 Oct. 497/1 All interesting enough..to the professional Thackerayite. 1887 *Illustr. Lond. News* 22 Jan. 88/2 This is..almost Thackerayian, indeed. 1888 *Scott. Leader* 3 May 7 A certain cynical humour which is almost 'Thackerayan' in quality.

**Tha·ckless,** *a.* Now *dial.* = THATCHLESS.

*a* 1800 *Witch Cake* in Cromek *Rem. Nithsdale Song* (1810) 284 Some priest maun preach in a thackless kirk. 1897 LD. E. HAMILTON *Outlaws* xviii. 209 The auld Redheuch tower stands thakless and woefu' this day.

**Thackster** (þæ·kstəɪ). *Obs.* exc. *dial.* Also 5 thac-, thakstare, 6 thaxster. See also THATCHESTER. [f. THACK *v.*¹ + -STER.] = THACKER.

*c* 1440 *Promp. Parv.* 52/2 Broche for a thacstare, *firmaculum*. *Ibid.* 490/1 Thakstare, *sartitector*. 1533 in Blomefield *Hist. Norfolk* (1806) III. 206 The Reders, Thaxsters, Rede-sellers,..with their banner. 1787 W. MARSHALL *E. Norf.* Gloss. (E.D.S.), *Thackster*, a thatcher. *a* 1825 FORBY *Voc. E. Anglia, Thacker, Thackster*, a thatcher.

**Thad,** obs. form of THAT *rel. pron.*

**Thae** (ðē, ðīə), *dem. pron.* and *adj. Sc.* and *north. dial.* Forms: (1–6 þa), 6 thai, 6–7 thay, 6– *Sc.* **thae, thea,** 9 **theae,** *n. dial.* **theea, thee.** [Mod. Sc. and north. dial. repr. of OE. and northern ME. *þá, tha*, midl. and south. ME. THO. For the phonology cf. *mae, nae, sae, twae, whae*, = OE. *má, ná, swá, twá, hwá*, Eng. *mo, no, so, two, who*.]

The Sc. and north. dial. plural of THAT, = ME. *þa*, THO; mod. THOSE. **a.** *pron.*

1583 *Leg. Bp. St. Androis* 613 Gude Robert Melwene of Carnebie I should not racken in with thea. ?17.. *Auld Maitland* v. in Scott *Minstrelsy Sc. Bord.*, Thou sall hae thae, thou sall hae mae. 1780 J. MAYNE *Siller Gun* I, Her exultation was exprest In words like thae. 1790 BURNS *Tam o'Shanter* 151 Now Tam, O Tam! had thae been queans. 1873 MURRAY *Dial. S. Scot.* 182 Dynna teake theae (Don't take those).

**b.** *adj.*

*a* 1584 MONTGOMERIE *Cherrie & Slae* 85 To heir thae startling stremis cleir, Me thocht it musique to the eir. 1596 DALRYMPLE tr. *Leslie's Hist. Scot.* (S.T.S.) I. 22 Pentland it was called,..evin as this day thae mountanis declairis sa named. 1603 *Philotus* lxxviii, And send to ȝow thay claithis vnsene. 1786 BURNS *Dream* ix, Thae bonny bairntime, Heav'n has lent. 1826 J. WILSON *Noct. Ambr.* Wks. 1855 I. 186 Thae broad vine-leaves hingin in the veranda. 1837 R. NICOLL *Poems* (1843) 76 But thae hames are gane. 1904 *Eng. Dial. Dict.* (*N. Yorksh.*), Wheea's theea tweea bairns? (*Northumb.*) Thee kye; thee folk.

**Thæh, þæh,** early ME. form of THOUGH.

**Thæm, þæm,** OE. infl. of THE, THAT; f. THEM.

**Thær, þær,** obs. form of THERE, THEIR.

**Thære,** obs. infl. of THE, THAT; obs. f. THERE.

**Thæs,** obs. var. of THES, THESE.

**Thafe,** variant of THAVE *v. Obs.*

**Thaff,** obs. f. THOUGH; erron. f. TEFF.

**Thaft,** Sc. f. *thaught*, THOFT (rower's seat).

**Thag, Thagi,** var. THUG, THUGGEE.

**Thagh, thaȝ, þagh, þaih,** obs. ff. THOUGH.

**Thai,** obs. form of THEY; obs. Sc. f. THAE.

†**Thaie, thaye,** *dem. pron.* and *adj. Obs.* Forms: 1 þæȝe, ðaȝe, 3 þaie, þaye. [Late OE. *þæge*, of obscure origin and history.

Generally held to be ad. ON. *þeir*, with *r* dropped (as in Ormin's *þeȝȝ*, THEY), and with *-e* added, after plurals like *ealle, sume, swylce*. But the local distribution of the word does not favour a Norse origin.]

**1.** *dem.* (or *pers.*) *pron.* = THOSE (THEY, THEM).

*c* 1000 *Ags. Gosp.* John x. 16 Hit ȝebyrað þæt ic læde þæȝe [*Hatton G.* þa hyder] & hiȝ ȝehyrað mine stefne. *Ibid.* xiv. 12 He wyrcð maran þonne þæȝe synt [*MS. A.* þa synd]. *a* 1100 *MS. C.C.C. Camb.* No. 162 Ðæȝe wæron on fruman of Godes oroðe..ȝesceapene. *a* 1100 *Salomon & Sat.* (Kemble) 180 Saȝa me, hwæt hatton ðaȝe? *c* 1275 LAY. 18474 Þaie [*c* 1205 heo] were amorwe alle idon to deaþe. *Ibid.* 28516 Þaie he habbe nolde. *a* 1300 *Cursor M.* 20002 (Edin.) Ful mani a torfer suffrid þaie [*C., F., G.*, þai, *Trin.* þei].

**b.** as antecedent.

*c* 1275 LAY. 4240 Alle þaie [*c* 1205 þa] þat astode hii fulde to grunde. *Ibid.* 20775 Þaye þat her bi-ȝeteþ eft hii leoseþ.

**2.** *dem. adj.* = THOSE (sometimes = THE).

10.. *Ags. Gosp.* Luke xi. 5 (*Marg. note*) Ðis sceal to gangdaȝon þæȝe tweȝen daȝas. *c* 1205 LAY. 12644 He sende his sonde..æfter..alle þaie ihade gomes. *Ibid.* 19541 Alle þaie halȝen þa an hæfenne hæȝe sitteð [so 15015]. *Ibid.* 20965 Þaie ilærde men heo læiden on gleden. *c* 1275 *Ibid.* 4532 He..ferde..to-ȝeines þaie sipes. *Ibid.* 16008 Wat bi-tocneþ þaie drakes [*c* 1205 þa draken]?

†**Thail, thayl, theil,** obs. forms of TAEL.

1662 J. DAVIES tr. *Mandelslo's Trav.* I. (1669) 68 A Theil of Silver. *Ibid.* II. 106 Black Lacque, at ten Thails the Picol. *Ibid.* 147 Forty seven thousand Thayls, or crowns.

**Thaim, -e,** obs. and dial. forms of THEM.

**Thain, -e,** obs. forms of THANE, THEGN.

**Thair,** Sc. f. THAR *v. impers.*, to need; var. THIR *Obs.*, this, these; obs. Sc. f. THERE, q. v., also in Comb.: see THEREABOUT, etc.

**Thair, -e, -es,** obs. or Sc. ff. THEIR, -S. **Thairf,** var. THARF. **Thairm,** Sc. f. THARM, intestine.

**Thais(e, Thaive**: see THOSE, THEAVE.

**Thak, thakk(e,** obs. and dial. var. THACK.

†**Tha·kin,** *a.*, those kind (of): see THO and KIN 16.

13.. *Cursor M.* 27282 In þakin thinges. (Cf. THOSE II. 2 c.)

‖ **Thakur, thakoor** (tʰā·kur). *East Ind.* [a. Hindī *ṭhākur*, Skr. *ṭhā·kkura* a deity.] A word meaning Lord, used as a title and term of respect (cf. *dominus, don, seigneur*, etc.); also applied to a chief or noble, esp. of the Rajpoot race.

1800 *Misc. Tracts in Asiat. Ann. Reg.* 312/1 Burwarrah, which belongs to a Thakur named Bickermajeet. 1844 H. H. WILSON *Brit. India* II. x. II. 429 Under an active and prudent Raja the Thakurs might be subjected to control. 1862 BEVERIDGE *Hist. India* VII. vii, The leading thakoors or chiefs. 1895 MRS. CROKER *Village T.* 125 She was married to the heir of a rich thakur. 1904 *Q. Rev.* July 234 He commended the Thakors for their consistent support.

Hence **Tha·kurate,** the district or territory pertaining to a thakur.

1901 *Mission Record United Free Ch. Scot.* Aug. 363/2 Adjoining thakurates will share the boon.

**Thalam, -ame** (þæ·lăm). *rare.* [ad. L. *thalamus*: see THALAMUS.] A nuptial chamber.

1791 W. BARTRAM *Carolina* 446 A booth or pavilion.. formed of green boughs..was the secret nuptial chamber.. no one presuming to approach the sacred, mysterious thalame.

‖ **Thalamencephalon** (þæ·lămense·fălǫn). *Anat.* [f. THALAM(O- + ENCEPHALON.] That part of the brain which develops from the posterior part of the anterior cerebral vesicle, and includes the optic thalami, optic nerves, and parts about the third ventricle. Also called *diencephalon, middle brain*, etc. Also anglicized **Thalame·ncephal.**

1875 HUXLEY in *Encycl. Brit.* I. 767/1 The optic nerves are attached, as usual, to the floor of the thalamencephalon. 1875 HUXLEY & MARTIN *Elem. Biol.* (1883) 185 The fore-brain which..comprises three divisions; the thalamencephalon the cerebral hemispheres, and the olfactory lobes. 1891 *Cent. Dict.*, Thalamencephal.

Hence **Tha·lamencepha·lic** (-sĭfæ·lik), *a. Anat.* of or pertaining to the thalamencephalon.

**Thalamic** (þălæ·mik, þæ·lămik), *a.* [ad. mod.L. *thalamic-us*: see THALAMUS and -IC.] Of or pertaining to a thalamus; in *Anat.*, pertaining to the optic thalamus.

1860 MAYNE *Expos. Lex.*, *Thalamicus*, *Bot.*, applied by Lestibondois to the insertion which takes place upon the receptacle: thalamic. 1890 BILLINGS *Nat. Med. Dict.*, *Thalamic nuclei*, special collections of gray matter within the optic thalamus. 1893 W. R. GOWERS *Dis. Nerv. Syst.* (ed. 2) II. 394 Internal thalamic hæmorrhage. 1899 *Allbutt's Syst. Med.* VII. 615 Hæmorrhage in the thalamic region.

**Thalamifloral** (þæ·lămiflō°·răl), *a. Bot.* [f. mod.L. *Thalamifloræ*, De Candolle 18..(f. THALAMUS + L. *flōs, flōr-* flower) + -AL. Cf. F. *thalamiflore.*] Belonging to the sub-class *Thalamifloræ* of dicotyledons, in which the stamens are inserted on the thalamus or receptacle; hypogynous. So **Thalamiflo·rous** *a.*

1857 HENFREY *Bot.* § 454 Some Thalamiflorous Orders. *Ibid.* § 478 Parietal Thalamifloral Orders. 1872 OLIVER *Elem. Bot.* I. v. 58 Thalamifloral..as Buttercup and Wallflower. 1880 GRAY *Struct. Bot.* ix. § 2. 340 *Thalamiflorous*, petals (distinct) and stamens on the torus, i.e. free.

**Thalamite** (þæ·lămәit). *Gr. Antiq.* [ad. Gr. θαλαμίτης, f. θάλαμος inner chamber, one of the compartments of a ship.] In the ancient trireme, a rower in one of the tiers of rowers, generally supposed to be that which occupied the lowest bench; but the actual arrangement is disputed: see quots. Cf. THRANITE, ZYGITE.

1886 *Encycl. Brit.* XXI. 806/2 Behind the zygite sat the thalamite, or oarsman of the lowest bank. 1906 *Athenæum* 7 Apr. 429/2 The three orders of rowers..there seems little reason to doubt..refer to the parts into which the ship was longitudinally divided..the thalamites [being] in the bows.

‖ **Thalamium** (þălē·miŏm). *Bot.* [mod.L. dim. of THALAMUS.] (See quot. 1866.)

1861 BENTLEY *Man. Bot.* (1870) 375 The body of the apothecium constitutes the thalamium. 1866 *Treas. Bot.*, *Thalamium*, a hollow case containing spores in algals; also the disk or *lamina prolifera* of lichens, and a form of the hymenium in fungals.

**Thalamo-** (þæ·lămo), before a vowel **thalam-**, combining form of Gr. θάλαμος THALAMUS, used as a formative in some anatomical words. **Thalamocœle** (þæ·lămosī:l) [Gr. κοιλία cavity, ventricle], the cavity of the thalamencephalon; the third ventricle of the brain. **Tha·lamocru·ral** *a.*, of or pertaining to the optic thalamus and to the *crus cerebri* (CRUS 2 b). See also THALAMENCEPHALON.

1899 *Syd. Soc. Lex.*, *Thalamocœle*, cavity of thalamencephalon. The thalamic cœlia, or third ventricle. *Ibid.*, *Thalamocrural.*

‖ **Thalamus** (þæ·lămŏs). Pl. **-mi** (-mәi). Also (in sense 3) in Gr. form **thalamos.** [L. *thalamus*, a. Gr. θάλαμος an inner chamber.]

**1.** *Anat.* A part of the brain at which a nerve originates or appears to originate; *spec.* the OPTIC thalamus.

[1704 J. HARRIS *Lex. Techn.* I, *Thalami Nervorum Opticorum*, are two Prominences of the lateral Ventricles of the Cerebrum; so call'd, because the Optick Nerves rise out of them.] 1756 *Gentl. Mag.* XXVI. 517/1 The thalami here appeared very thin, and the pia mater..was overspread with blood-vessels of an unusual size. 1856 TODD & BOWMAN *Phys. Anat.* II. 38 Each tract adheres to the outer side of its corresponding thalamus for some distance. 1879 *St. George's Hosp. Rep.* IX. 513 An abscess..in the right optic thalamus, opening just behind the tænia.

**2.** *Bot.* **a.** The receptacle of a flower, on which the carpels are placed; the torus. **b.** See quot. 1842.

1753 CHAMBERS *Cycl. Supp.*, *Thalamus*, in botany, a term used to express that part of the flower..where the embryo fruits..are lodged, and where afterwards the seeds are contained. 1766 LEE *Introd. Bot.* Gloss., *Thalamus*, ..the Receptacle. 1842 *Penny Cycl.* XXIV. 274/1 Thalamus is also used in Cryptogamic botany, in common with Thallus, to express the bed of fibres from which many fungi spring up. 1861 BENTLEY *Man. Bot.* (1870) 208 The extremity of the peduncle or pedicel..is called the Thalamus, or some times, but improperly, the Receptacle.

**3.** *Archæol.* An inner or secret chamber.

1850 LEITCH tr. *C. O. Müller's Anc. Art* § 48 The thalami, secret chambers for the women. 1884 *Times* 15 Aug. 4 The same pattern as that found on the roof of the thalamos.

**Thalassal** (þălæ·săl), *a. rare.* [f. Gr. θάλασσα sea + -AL.] = THALASSIC (in quot. in sense 2).

1887 *Proc. Boston Nat. Hist. Soc.* 417 The time required for the accumulation of such a stratum in the thalassal seas is probably great.

**Thalassarctine**: see THALASSO-.

**Thalassian** (þălæ·siăn), *a.* and *sb.* [f. Gr. θαλάσσι-ος marine, f. θάλασσα sea + -AN.]

**A.** *adj.* Of or pertaining to the sea, marine; *spec.* applied to the marine tortoises and turtles.

1850 BRODERIP *Notebk. Nat.* x. (1852) 264 Nature has modified the Chelonian type into the Thalassian shape. *Comb.* 1869 BROWNING *Ring & Bk.* IX. 893 Pompilia ..Springs to her feet, and stands Thalassian-pure.

**B.** *sb.* A marine tortoise or turtle.

1850 BRODERIP *Notebk. Nat.* xi. (1852) 276 And now a few words on the natural history and capture of some of these Thalassians. 1900 F. T. BULLEN *Idylls of Sea* 164 The Thalassians or oceanic tortoises, from which alone our supplies are drawn.

† **Thala·ssiarch.** *Obs. rare*⁻⁰. [f. Gr. θαλάσσι-ος marine, maritime + -αρχος ruling, ruler.] Hence † **Thala·ssiarchy** *Obs. rare*⁻⁰. (See quots.)

1656 BLOUNT *Glossogr.*, *Thalassiarck*, an Admiral or chief Officer at sea. 1727 BAILEY vol. II, *Thalassiarchy*, the Admiralship, or the office of the Admiral.

**Thalassic** (þălæ·sik), *a.* [ad. F. *thalassique* (Brongniart 1829), f. Gr. θάλασσα sea: see -IC.]

**1.** Of or pertaining to the sea; growing or living in, or formed in or by the sea; marine. † In *Geol.* applied after Brongniart to strata supposed to be of marine formation (*obs.*).

1860 MAYNE *Expos. Lex.*, *Thalassicus, Geol.*, applied by Brongniart to the strata of superior sediment, i. e. those found from the surface of the earth to the limestone exclusively: thalassic. 1890 *Cent. Dict.* s. v. *Littoral*, Deposits ..formed in deep water, or thalassic rocks. 1897 MARY KINGSLEY *W. Africa* 423 Agnes rouses me from my thalassic couch and suggests Mass at 5.30 a. m.

**2.** Pertaining to the (smaller or inland) seas as distinct from the pelagic waters or oceans.

1883 J. R. SEELEY *Expans. Eng.* 87 [see POTAMIC]. *Ibid.*, European civilization passed from the thalassic to the oceanic state. 1884 *Q. Rev.* July 140 He [Lord Dufferin] seems to have grasped the 'oceanic' rather than the 'thalassic' nature of our Empire. 1899 *Times* 9 Jan. 6 The thalassic civilization of the Mediterranean.

So † **Thala·ssical** *a. Obs. rare*⁻⁰ (see quot.).

1656 BLOUNT *Glossogr.*, *Thalassical*, of a blew colour like the sea-waves, sea-green or blew.

**Thalassin** (þălæ·sin). *Chem.* [See -IN[1].] A poison found in the tentacles of sea-anemones.

1909 in *Cent. Dict.* Suppl.

**Thalassi·nian,** *a.* and *sb.* [f. mod.L. *Thalassina* + -IAN.] **a.** *adj.* Of or pertaining to the *Thalassinidæ*, a family of long-tailed decapod crustaceans, the scorpion-lobsters. **b.** *sb.* A crustacean of this family. So **Thala·ssinoid** *a.*

1842 *Penny Cycl.* XXIV. 274/2 Mr. Milne Edwards arranges the family of Thalassinians, or Burrowing Macrura, between the Scyllarians and the Astacians. *Ibid.*, *Cryptobranchids*,..all the Thalassinians which are without respiratory appendages suspended under the abdomen.

**Thalass(o-** (þălæ·s(o), **Thala·ssi(o-**, from Gr. θάλασσα sea, and θαλάσσι-ος marine, formative elements of learned words. **Thalassa·rctine** *a. Zool.* [Gr. ἄρκτ-ος a bear], of or pertaining to the Polar Bear, *Thalassarctos*. **Thalassico·llidan** [Gr. κόλλα glue], *a.* belonging to the *Thalassicollidæ*, a family of single-celled radiolarians; *sb.* a radiolarian of this family. **Thala·ssio-, Thala·ssophyte** [-PHYTE], a plant of the *Thalassiophyta* (see quot.); a seaweed, a marine alga; hence **Thalassio·phytous** *a.*, belonging to the *Thalassiophyta*. **Thalasso·meter** [-METER], a tide-gauge. **Thalassometri·cian** *nonce-wd.*, one who measures the sea. **Thalasso·philous** *a.* [-PHIL], fond of the sea, living in the sea. **Thalassopho·bia,** a morbid dread of the sea. **Thalassothe·rapy:** see quot. See also THALASSOCRACY, etc.

1842 *Penny Cycl.* XXIV. 277/1 **Thalassiophytes*..is the name given by Lamouroux to designate the vegetable productions of the ocean...It is equivalent to the term Hydrophytes of Lingbye, and the..Marine Algæ. 1900 B. D. JACKSON *Gloss. Bot. Terms*, Thalassophyte. 1858 SIMMONDS *Dict. Trade*, **Thalassometer*, a tide-gauge. 1652 NEEDHAM tr. *Selden's Mare Cl.* 5, I have heard of a Geometrician, or one that could measure Land; but never of a *Thalassometrician, one that could measure or lay out Bounds in the Sea. 1891 *Cent. Dict.*, *Thalassophilous. 1897 tr. *Ribot's Psychol. Emotions* II. ii. 213 Every morbid manifestation of fear is immediately fitted with a Greek designation,..and we have aïcmophobia, belenophobia, *thalassophobia, potamophobia, etc. 1899 *Syd. Soc. Lex.*, **Thalassotherapy*, treatment of disease by sea bathing, sea voyages, etc.

**Thalassocracy** (þælæ̆sǫ·krăsi). Rarely **-craty.** [ad. Gr. θαλασσοκρατία, f. θάλασσα sea + -κρατία, -CRACY.] Mastery at sea; the sovereignty of the sea.

1846 GROTE *Greece* I. xx. II. 151 The legendary thalassocraty of Minôs. 1880 B. HEAD *Guide Coins & Medals Brit. Mus.* 6 The Phocæan Thalassocracy lasted from about 602–558 B.C. 1903 *Cornh. Mag.* Feb. 258 The existence of the Phœnician thalassocracy can be proved in detail.

**Thalassocrat** (þălæ·sŏkræt). [f. after prec.: see -CRAT.] One who has the mastery of the sea.

1846 GROTE *Greece* I. xii. I. 311 An attempt on the part of the great thalassocrat to conquer Sicily. 1847 *Ibid.* II. xxxiii. IV. 327 The earliest of all Grecian thalassokrats or sea kings. 1905 G. G. A. MURRAY in *Q. Rev.* Apr. 352 At present England is the thalassocrat.

**Thalassography** (þælæ̆sǫ·grăfi). [f. THALASSO- + -GRAPHY. Cf. med.Gr. θαλασσογράφος describing the sea.] The branch of physical geography which treats of the sea, its configuration and phenomena; oceanography.

1888 A. AGASSIZ (*title*) Contribution to American Thalassography. 1888 *Times* 7 Apr. 5/2 The necessity for some such term as oceanography or thalassography is significant of the vast progress which has been made during the past 20 years in our knowledge of the ocean depths.

Hence **Thalasso·grapher,** a student or investigator of thalassography; **Thala:ssogra·phic, -ical** *adjs.*, of or pertaining to thalassography.

1881 GIGLIOLI in *Nature* 18 Aug. 358/1 The war-steamer of the Italian Royal Navy *Washington*,..left Maddalena on the 2nd inst. on her thalassographic mission. 1900 *Ibid.* 4 Jan. 228/1 Thalassographic researches in the Mediterranean. 1893 *Smithsonian Inst. Rep.* (1894) 370 *note*, Biological and thalassographical investigations.

**Thalatto-** (þălæ·to), combining form from Gr. θάλαττα, Attic for θάλασσα sea, = THALASSO-, as in **Thalattocracy** (-ǫ·krăsi), **Thalattocraty** (-ǫ·krăti) = THALASSOCRACY; **Thalatto·logy,** that branch of science which treats of the sea.

1839 T. MITCHELL *Frogs of Aristoph.* Introd. 80 The first thalattocracy which the history of the world supplies. 1874 *Proc. Physical Soc. Lond.* 7 Nov. I. 53 A sufficient theory of thalattology. 1886 *Eng. Hist. Rev.* I. 626 To reduce the Kyklades and establish a thalattokraty.

**Thale-cress** (þē·lˌkres). [f. *thale*, ad. mod.L. *thāliāna* adj. (f. *Thal* the name of a German physician, 1542–83) + CRESS.] A book-name of *Sisymbrium thalianum* (*Arabis thaliana*, Linn.), N.O. *Cruciferæ*, a small herb, bearing small white flowers. Also called *Thale Rock-cress.*

1778 LIGHTFOOT *Flora Scot.* I. 358 Thale's Cress, or coded Mouse-ear. 1835 HOOKER *Brit. Flora* (ed. 3) I. 307 *S*[*isymbrium*] *thalianum*, (common Thale-cress).

‖ **Thaler** (tā·lәr). [G. *thaler* DOLLAR.] A German silver coin; a dollar: see DOLLAR I.

1787 MATY tr. *Riesbeck's Trav. Germ.* I. xviii. 204 Making a Bailé's Dictionary..the true price of which is five guineas, sell at Vienna for 100 thalers. 1858 SIMMONDS *Dict. Trade*, *Thaler*, a German coin of 30 silver grosschen, worth about 3*s.* sterling. 1864 CARLYLE *Fredk. Gt.* XVII. v. IV. 571 'Let my ducat be a Joachimsthal one, then!'..'a *Joachimsthal-er*'; or for brevity, a '*Thal-er*'; whence *Thaler*, and at last *Dollar*.

**Thalerophagous** (þælĕrǫ·făgәs), *a. Entom.* [f. Gr. θαλερός blooming, fresh + -φάγ-ος eating + -OUS.] Feeding on fresh vegetable substances.

1819 MACLEAY *Horæ Entomol.* I. 27 Thalerophagous insects, or such as live on green or fresh vegetable food. 1826 KIRBY & SP. *Entomol.* III. xxxv. 604 The saprophagous tribes of Mr. W. S. MacLeay are commonly of a more dark and dismal aspect and colour than those which feed upon such as are living and fresh, denominated thalerophagous by the same learned author. 1840 SWAINSON & SHUCKARD *Hist. Insects* II. vi. 221 The thalerophagous groups.

‖ **Thalia** (þălәi·ă). [a. Gr. Θάλεια ('luxuriant, blooming', f. θάλλειν to bloom).]

**1.** The eighth of the Muses, presiding over comedy and idyllic poetry; also, one of the three Graces, patroness of festive meetings.

1656 in BLOUNT *Glossogr.* 1711 SHAFTESB. *Charac.* (1737) I. 317 The Thalia's, the Polyhymnia's, the Terpsychore's, the Euterpe's willingly join their parts. 1799 CAMPBELL *Pleas. Hope* II. 168 Turn to the gentler melodies that suit Thalia's harp, or Pan's Arcadian lute.

**2.** *Bot.* A genus of aquatic herbaceous plants, N.O. *Marantaceæ*, natives of tropical America.

1756 P. BROWNE *Jamaica* (1789) 112. 1878 DARWIN in *Life & Lett.* (1887) III. 287 In Thalia cross-fertilization is ensured by the wonderful movement, if bees visit several flowers.

† **3.** *Zool.* An old synonym of the genus SALPA[2].

1756 P. BROWNE *Jamaica* (1789) 384 The *Thalia*, with a square erect crest...The *Thalia*, with a rounded depressed crest. 1842 BRANDE *Dict. Sc.*, etc., *Thalidans, Thalides*.., the name of a tribe of Tunicaries, of which the genus *Salpa* or *Thalia* is the type.

**b.** A genus of coleopterous insects.

1838 F. W. HOPE *Coleopterist's Man.* II. 70.

**4.** *Astron.* The twenty-third of the Asteroids.

**Thaliacean** (þæliˌē·ʃiăn), *a.* and *sb. Zool.* [f. mod.L. *Thaliăcea* (f. *Thalia*: see prec. 3) + -AN.] **a.** *adj.* Of or pertaining to the *Thaliacea*, an order of tunicates, including the *Salpidæ*, etc. **b.** *sb.* A member of this order.

[1888 ROLLESTON & JACKSON *Anim. Life* 441 The Thaliacea are free-swimming, and more or less barrel-shaped...The test is very thin and delicate... The muscle fibres..[are] arranged in circular hoops round the barrel-shaped body.]

**Thalian** (þălәi·ăn, þē·liăn), *a.* [f. THALIA + -AN.] Of or pertaining to Thalia as the muse of pastoral and comic poetry; hence, of the nature of comedy, comic.

1864 in WEBSTER. 1882 J. WALKER *Scotch Poems* 100 My wit can wimple Thro' Thalian songs like Kate Dalrymple.

**Thalictrine** (þăli·ktrәin). *Chem.* [f. next + -INE 5.] A crystalline alkaloid contained in *Thalictrum macrocarpum*, in poisonous action resembling aconitin but less violent.

1881 DOASSANS in *Jrnl. Chem. Soc.* XL. 52.

‖ **Thali·ctrum.** *Bot.* [L. *thalictrum* (Pliny), a. Gr. θάλικτρον.] A genus of perennial herbs (N.O. *Ranunculaceæ*), bearing panicles, corymbs, or racemes of green, white, or yellow flowers, without petals or involucre. There are several species, of which three are British, *T. flavum* being the Common Meadow Rue; *T. aquilegifolium* is an Alpine species, known as the Feather Columbine.

1664 EVELYN *Kal. Hort.*, *May* (1729) 205 Flowers in Prime,..Prunella, purple Thalictrum. 1741 *Compl. Fam.-Piece* II. iii. (ed. 3) 373 Featherfew, Thalictrums of several kinds. 1883 *Century Mag.* Oct. 819/1, I saw the dainty thalictrum, with its clover-like leaves, standing in thickets there, fresh and green.

**Thalidan**: see THALIA 3, quot. 1842.

**Thallene** (þæ·līn). *Chem.* [f. Gr. θάλλ-ειν to bloom + -ENE.] (See quot. 1881.)

1872 H. MORTON in *Chem. News* 6 Dec. 272/2 The above-described body, which I may as well call thallene hereafter. 1881 WATTS *Dict. Chem.* VIII. 1918 *Thallene*, a solid hydrocarbon, isomeric with anthracene, obtained from the last products which pass over in the distillation of American petroleum. It is distinguished by a splendid green fluorescence.

**Thallic** (þæ·lik), *a. Chem.* [f. THALLI-UM + -IC.] Of, pertaining to, or derived from thallium; *spec.* applied to compounds containing thallium in smaller proportion, relatively to oxygen, than *thallious* compounds. *Thallic oxide* = Thallium trioxide, $Tl_2O_3$.

1868 WATTS *Dict. Chem.* V. 750 In solutions of thallic salts, the thallium may be estimated by reducing the thallic to thallious salts with an alkaline sulphite. **1873** — *Fownes' Chem.* (ed. 11) 411 The Trichloride or Thallic Chloride.

**Thalliferous** (þæli·fĕrəs), *a.* [f. as prec. + -FEROUS.] Bearing or containing thallium.

**1867** *Ure's Dict. Arts*, etc. III. 889 A very considerable amount of the thalliferous deposit. **1868** WATTS *Dict. Chem.* V. 742 In burning thalliferous pyrites for the purpose of manufacturing sulphuric acid.

**Thalliform** (þæ·lifǫɹm), *a. Bot.* [f. THALL-US + -FORM.] Having the form of a thallus.

**1891** in *Cent. Dict.*

**Thalline** (þæ·ləin), *sb. Pharm.* Also -in. [f. Gr. θάλλ-ειν to bloom + -INE⁵.] A trade name for a colourless compound used as an antipyretic, obtained by the reduction of the corresponding chinoline derivative.

Chemically it is tetra-hydroparamethoxyquinoline, $CH_3OC_6H_3\langle{}^{CH_2.CH_2}_{NH.CH_2}$.

**1885-8** FAGGE & PYE-SMITH *Princ. Med.* (ed. 2) I. 205 Thallin (the sulphate or tartrate of tetra-hydro-parachinanisol) is, I am disposed to think, as efficient or more so [than Antipyrin], and safer. **1898** *Allbutt's Syst. Med.* V. 234.

**b.** *attrib.* **Thalline periodide, thalline sulphate**: see quots.; **thalline urine**, urine affected by the use of thalline.

**1899** *Syd. Soc. Lex.*, *Thalline periodide*, *T. periodosulphate*. (Not official.) A combination of iodine and thalline sulphate. Black and crystalline... *Thalline sulphate*...The sulphate of a synthetically prepared base derived from chinoline...A yellowish white crystalline powder, with an odour [like] coumarin, and an aromatic bitter taste.

**Thalline** (þæ·ləin), *a. Bot.* [f. THALLUS + -INE¹.] Of or pertaining to a thallus.

*Thalline excipulum* or *exciple*, an excipulum composed of a portion of the thallus, which surrounds it and forms a bowl-like rim. (Bennett & Dyer tr. *Sachs' Bot.* (1875) 269.) **1856** W. L. LINDSAY *Pop. Hist. Brit. Lichens* 45 This thalline fringe is very conspicuous. **1871** W. A. LEIGHTON *Lichen-Flora* 179 Thalline margin entire.

**Thallious** (þæ·liəs), *a. Chem.* [f. THALLI-UM + -OUS.] Abounding in thallium; *spec.* containing thallium in greater proportion, relatively to oxygen, than *thallic* compounds. *Thallious oxide* = Thallium monoxide, $Tl_2O$.

**1868** WATTS *Dict. Chem.* V. 749 Thallic salts are easily distinguished from thallious salts by their behaviour with alkalis. *Ibid.* 750 [see THALLIC]. **1873** — *Fownes' Chem.* (ed. 11) 412 Thallious Iodide, Tl I, is formed by direct combination of its elements, or by double decomposition.

†**Tha·llite.** *Min. Obs.* [a. F. *thallite* (J. C. Delamétherie, 1792), f. Gr. θάλλ-ειν to flourish, bloom, or θαλλός young shoot (in allusion to its colour) + -ITE¹.] A rejected name for EPIDOTE occurring in yellowish-green crystals.

**1802** BOURNON in *Phil. Trans.* XCII. 291 The substance called thallite (the *epidote* of the Abbé Hauy). **1868** DANA *Min.* (ed. 5) 284 *Thallite*...was rejected because it was based on a varying character, color.

**Thallium** (þæ·liŏm). [f. Gr. θαλλ-ός a green shoot (θάλλειν to bloom), from the brilliant green line distinguishing its spectrum + -IUM.] A rare metal, bluish white in colour with leaden lustre, extremely soft and almost devoid of tenacity or elasticity; occurring in small quantities in iron and copper pyrites. Atomic weight 204; symbol Tl.

**1861** CROOKES in *Chem. News* 16 March, III. 193 On the Existence of a New Element. *Ibid.* 18 May 303, I have thought..to propose for it the provisional name of *Thallium*, from the Greek θαλλός, or Latin *thallus*, a budding twig.. which I have chosen as the green line which it communicates to the spectrum recals with peculiar vividness the fresh colour of vegetation at the present time. **1871** ROSCOE *Elem. Chem.* 262 Thallium was discovered in 1861 by Crookes, by means of spectrum analysis, in the deposit in the flue of a pyrites burner. **1874** tr. *Lommel's Light* 114 The splendid green light of Thallium is more strongly refracted than the yellow light of Sodium.

**b.** *attrib.* and *Comb.*, as *thallium alloy*, *spectrum*; **thallium glass**, a variety of glass of great density and refracting power, in the manufacture of which thallium is used instead of lead or potassium; **thallium green**, the colour of the **thallium line**, the vivid green line of the thallium spectrum.

**1863** WATTS *Dict. Chem.* V. 745 The length of the wave of the green thallium-line is 0·0005348 millimetre. *Ibid.*, Thallium-salts are highly poisonous. *Ibid.* 758 Thallium-glass.

**Thallodic** (þælǫ·dik), *a. Bot.* [f. THALLUS + -ODE + -IC.] Formed like, of the nature of, or pertaining to a thallus. So **Thallodal** (-ǒu·dăl) *a.*

**1860** MAYNE *Expos. Lex.*, Thallodic. **1871** W. A. LEIGHTON *Lichen-Flora* 179 Thallodal margin persistent.

**Thallogen** (þæ·lǒdʒen). *Bot.* [f. THALL-US + -GEN, after *exogen*, *endogen*, etc.] = THALLOPHYTE.

**1846** LINDLEY *Veg. Kingd.* 2 Those simpler plants which exist without the distinction of leaf and stem, are also destitute of flowers...Among the many names that Botanists have given such plants, that of *Thallogens* is here preferred. **1857** BERKELEY *Cryptog. Bot.* § 55. 69 Thallogens (plants in which there is a fusion of root, stems, and leaves into one general mass). **1858** CARPENTER *Veg. Phys.* § 123.

Hence **Thalloge·nic, Thallo·genous** *adjs.*, of or pertaining to the thallogens; of the nature of a thallogen.

**1854** BALFOUR in *Encycl. Brit.* (ed. 8) V. 146/1 Lichens.. belong to the Thallogenous division of Cryptogamics. **1857** H. MILLER *Test. Rocks* i. 9 The first class..in the ascending order is this humble thallogenic class.

**Thalloid** (þæ·loid), *a. Bot.* [f. THALL-US + -OID.] Of the form of a thallus. So **Thalloi·dal** *a.*

**1857** HENFREY *Bot.* § 318 A lobed, green, thalloid stem. *Ibid.* § 321 The Thalloid Hepaticæ have a broad, more or less succulent lobed leaf-like expansion in place of stem and leaf. **1875** BENNETT & DYER tr. *Sachs' Bot.* 160 In Thallophytes and thalloid Hepaticæ, dichotomy is very widely prevalent. **1900** B. D. JACKSON *Gloss. Bot. T.*, Thalloidal.

**Thallome** (þæ·lǒum). *Bot.* [ad. mod.L. *thallōma*, f. *thall-us* + *-oma*: cf. *rhizome*.] = THALLUS.

**1875** BENNETT & DYER tr. *Sachs' Bot.* 121 The thallome of Stypocaulon..shows how the apical cell of the lateral shoot grows immediately from the apical cell of the principal process as a lateral protuberance. *Ibid.* 130 It is now agreed to apply to those vegetable structures in which the morphological distinction of stem and leaves cannot be carried out..(and from which true roots are always absent), the morphological term Thallus or Thallome.

**Thallophyte** (þæ·lǒfəit). *Bot.* [f. mod.L. *Thallophyta*, pl. f. Gr. θαλλό-ς green twig + φυτόν plant.] A plant belonging to the lowest of the great groups in the vegetable kingdom, comprising those of which the vegetative body is a thallus, including Algæ, Fungi, and Lichens; a cellular cryptogam; = Lindley's THALLOGEN.

**1854** BALFOUR in *Encycl. Brit.* (ed. 8) V. 142/2 These tribes, from having no foliaceous axis but simply a cellular expansion, have been called *Thallogens* or *Thallophytes*. **1875** BENNETT & DYER tr. *Sachs' Bot.* 207 Thallophytes. Under this term are comprised Algæ and Fungi (Lichens being also included in the latter section). **1885** GOODALE *Physiol. Bot.* (1892) 164.

Hence **Thallophytic** (-fi·tik) *a. Bot.*, of or pertaining to the thallophytes. **1891** in *Cent. Dict.*

**Tha·llose**, *a. Bot.* = THALLOID.

**1900** in B. D. JACKSON *Gloss. Bot. T.*

**Thallous** (þæ·ləs), *a. Chem.* [f. THALL-IUM + -OUS: cf. *aluminous*, *tantalous*.] = THALLIOUS.

**1888** *Encycl. Brit.* XXIII. 220/1 Thallic salts are related to thallous pretty much as manganic are to manganous... Thallous chloride.

‖**Thallus** (þæ·lŏs). *Bot.* [L. *thallus*, a. Gr. θαλλός a green shoot, f. θάλλειν to bloom.] A vegetable structure without vascular tissue, in which there is no differentiation into stem and leaves, and from which true roots are absent.

**1829** LOUDON *Encycl. Pl.* (1836) 874 (*Lichenes*)..the thallus ..is either pulverulent, crustaceous, membranous, foliaceous, or branched and shrub-like. **1846** LINDLEY *Veg. Kingd.* 2 A thallus is a fusion of root, stem and leaves, into one general mass. **1854** THOREAU *Walden* xvii. (1857) 326 The lobed and imbricated thalluses of some lichens. **1875** J. H. BALFOUR in *Encycl. Brit.* I. 508/1 Algæ..consist of a brown, red, or green, flattened, cellular, leaf-like expansion, called a *thallus*.

**b.** *attrib.* and *Comb.*

**1861** BENTLEY *Man. Bot.* 67 Such are .. termed *Cormophytes* or stem-producing plants, to distinguish them from the thallus-forming plants or *Thallophytes*. **1875** BENNETT & DYER tr. *Sachs' Bot.* 160 The flat extension of the thallus or thallus-like stem. *Ibid.* 130 In contradistinction to Thallus-plants (Thallophytes), all plants in which leaves can be..distinguished might be termed Phyllophytes.

**Thalmud, -ist**, obs. forms of TALMUD, -IST.

‖**Thalweg** (tā·lveg, -vĕχ). *Geog.* [Ger. *thalweg* bottom path of a valley, f. *thal* valley (see DALE) + *weg* WAY. Also in Fr. (1815 *Traité de Paris*, Littré).] The line in the bottom of a valley in which the slopes of the two sides meet, and which forms a natural watercourse; also the line following the deepest part of the bed or channel of a river or lake.

**1862** WRAXALL *Hugo's Misérables* v. xxii, The grand sewer running along the thalweg of the valley. **1881** *Harper's Mag.* LXIV. 275 Thalweg..is a German geographical term, employed in the records of the congress of Berlin, which designates the line of lowest level formed by the two opposite slopes of a valley. **1894** (May 12) *Agreemt. betw. Gt. Brit. & Congo State* in *Parl. Papers Eng.* XCVI. 26 Thence it [the boundary] shall follow the 'thalweg' of the Nile southwards to Lake Albert. **1897** *Educat. Rev.* XIII. 89 This thalweg which forms a nearly continuous waterway from the Volga to the Amur.

**Tham**, obs. f. THEM; obs. dat. sing. and pl. of THAT, THE.

**Thamarike, Thamarind**, obs. ff. TAMARISK, TAMARIND. **Thame**, obs. f. TEAM; Sc. f. THEM.

**Thames** (temz). Forms: 1 **Temes**, 1–5 **Temese**, (4–5 Th-), 5 **Temze, Temeze (Tamise)**, 6 **Temys, Temmes(se, Themes, -ys, Themise, Thamyse**, 6–7 **Thamise**, 6– **Thames**. [OE. *Temese*:—**Tamisa*, ad. L. *Tamēsa*, *Tamēsis*, ad. Brit. *Tamēsa*: cf. Welsh *Tafwys*, F. *Tamise*.] The name of the river on which London is situated: also *attrib.* and *Comb.*, as in *Thames boat*, *Thames-side*; *Thames-built*, *-derived* adjs.

*c* **893** K. ÆLFRED *Oros.* v. xii. § 2 Neah þære ie þe mon hæt Temes [*v. r.* Temese]. **1377** LANGL. *P. Pl.* B. XII. 161 Take two stronge men and in themese caste hem. *c* **1450** *Sloane MS.* 73. lf. 214 (Halliw.) Put therto tweyne galones of clene Temese water that is taken at an ebbe. **1503** *Rolls of Parlt.* VI. 527/2 A Ryvere called the Thamyse, otherwyse called the Temmesse. **1649** LOVELACE *To Althea* ii, When flowing cups run swiftly round With no allaying Thames [i. e. water]. **1688** R. HOLME *Armoury* III. xv. (Roxb.) 26/1 He beareth Azure, a Skuller, or a Thamise boate, Or. **1712** ADDISON *Spect.* No. 383 ⁋ 5 With a good deal of the like Thames-Ribaldry. **1895** *Daily News* 28 Dec. 5/4 The Thames-derived waters show a marked improvement. **1902** CORNISH *Naturalist Thames* 169 The crowning glory of the Thames-side flats.

**b.** Phrase. *To set the Thames on fire* († *set fire to the Thames*, † *burn the Thames*), to do something marvellous, to work wonders. Usually with negative = to work no wonders, never to distinguish oneself.

A writer in *N. & Q.* of 25 Mar. 1865, p. 249, surmised that *Thames* here was orig. *temse* a sieve, which he supposed that an active fellow might set on fire by force of friction. This conjecture has no basis of fact. The phrase has also been used of the Rhine (*a* 1638) and other rivers. See *N. & Q.* 8th s. VI. 502, and Skeat *Stud. Past.* § 205-6.

**1778** FOOTE *Trip Calais* III. iii, Matt Minnikin..an honest *burgoise*,..won't set fire to the Thames, though he lives near the Bridge. **1787** [see BURN *v.* 9 c]. **1796** *Grose's Dict. Vulg. Tongue* s. v. *Thames*, He will not find out a way to set the Thames on fire; he will not make any wonderful discoveries, he is no conjurer. **18..** W. E. NORRIS (Dixon), I hardly expect him to set the Thames on fire; but I hope his mother will never have reason to be ashamed of him.

Hence **Thameser** (te·mzəɹ), one who is connected with the Thames in some way; **Thamesian** (temī·ziăn) *a.*, of or pertaining to the Thames.

**1614** T. GENTLEMAN *Way to Wealth* 43 By..the yong men of the Sea-coast Townes, euen as..amongst the Theamsers. **1859** SALA *Gaslight & D.* ix. 105 Floating on the muddy bosom of the Thamesian stream.

‖**Thamin** (þāmi·n). Also -ine, -yn, -eng. [Burmese *thămin*.] A deer (*Cervus eldi*) of Burmah and Siam, resembling the swamp deer.

**1888** *Cassell's Encycl. Dict.*, *Thamyn* .. *Rucervus eldi*, Eld's Deer, so called from Captain Eld, who discovered it in 1838. **1900** POLLOK & THOM *Sports Burma* iv. 136 In the tree-jungle beyond, I shot a thamine and hung it up. **1903** *Edin. Rev.* July 197 A peculiar looking deer is the thameng.

‖**Thammuz, Tammuz** (tæ·mŭz). Also 6 **Thamus**, 7 **Thamuz**, 7–9 **Tamuz**. [Heb. תַּמּוּז *tammūz*.] The tenth month of the Jewish civil year, and the fourth of the sacred, containing twenty-nine days, and corresponding to parts of June and July.

Also the name of a Syrian deity, identified with the Phœnician *Adōn* or Adonis, whose annual festival began with the new moon of this month.

**1535** COVERDALE *Ezek.* viii. 14 There sat women mournynge for Thamus. **1614** PURCHAS *Pilgrimage* I. xvii. 89 This is called the mourning for Thamuz, which Iunius interpreteth Osiris, whence the fourth moneth (commonly their Haruest) is called Tamuz. **1667** MILTON *P. L.* I. 446. **1827** KEBLE *Chr. Year* 17th S. after Trin. **1853** KINGSLEY *Hypatia* v. **1909** *Whitaker's Almanack* 72 Jewish Calendar: June 20 New Moon, Tamuz 1. July 6 Fast of Tamuz.

‖**Thamnium** (þæ·mniŏm). *Bot.* [mod.L. a. Gr. θαμνίον, dim. of θάμνος shrub.] (See quot.)

**1866** *Treas. Bot.*, *Thamnium*, the branched bush-like thallus of lichens.

**Than** (ðăn, ðən; as a separate word called ðæn), *conj.* Forms: α. 1–3 ð-, þonne, (1 ðone, ðon); β. 1 ðanne, þænne, 1–4 þanne, 3 þæne, 3–4 þane, 4–5 thanne; γ. 2–5 þenne, 2–3 þene, (3 þeone), 3–5 þen, (5 thenne, 7 yen), 4–8 then; δ. 1 than, 2–6 þan, 3 (*Orm.*) þann, (4 þain), 4– than (abbrev. 7–8 yⁿ, yn); ε. 5 an, 9 *dial.* 'n. [OE. *þanne*, *þonne*, *þænne*, also *þan*, *þon*; originally the same word as THEN (OE. *þanne*, *þonne*, *þænne*), the adv. of time. Its employment as the connective particle after a comparative (= L. *quam*, F. *que*) is a pre-English development, existing already in WGer.: cf. OHG. *thanne*, *danne*, MHG. *danne*, *denne*, Ger. *denn* (now largely supplanted by *als*), OS. *than*, MDu. *danne*, *dan*, Du. *dan*, all used after the comparative. (Not so in Gothic or Scandinavian.)

How the conjunctive use arose out of the adv. of time is obscure. Some would explain it directly from the demonstrative sense 'then', taking 'John is more skilful than his brother' as = 'John is more skilful; then (= after that) his brother'. Others derive it from the relative or conjunctive use of OE. *þonne* (THEN 6), = 'When, when as', thus 'When as (whereas) his brother is skilful, John is more (so)'. The analogy of L. *quam* favours a relative sense.

When interrogative or demonstrative words became conjunctive or relative they lost their stress and were liable to weakening. Already in the 8th c. OE. *þanne* appears as *ðan*, *þan*, *than*, a form exemplified in nearly every century since, though down to *c* 1500 the fuller contemporary forms of the demonstrative adv., *þanne*, *þenne*, *þane*, *þene*, etc., were also in use. When the adv. was reduced to *þen*, from the 15th c. spelt *then*, there was a strong tendency to spell the conjunction in the same way, which during the 16th c. nearly triumphed; but in the 17th c. the tide turned, and by 1700 or a little later the conjunction was differentiated from the adv. as *than*. As the latter was, and is, pronounced (ðən), it is manifest that it might be written either *then* (ðĕn) or *than* (ðăn) with equal approximation to the actual sound.]

**1.** The conjunctive particle used after a comparative adjective or adverb (and sometimes after other words: see 2–4) to introduce the second member of the comparison; the conjunction expressing the comparative of inequality (cf. As 3). In use it is always stressless, usually joined accentually to the prec. word, e.g. *more than*, *less than*, *other than* (mōə·ɹðən, le·sðən, ɒ·ðəɹðən).

The two members of the comparison are most commonly of the same grammatical form, e. g. two clauses (the latter of which may be contracted in various ways), two substantives, two pronouns, two infinitives, two adjectives, two adverbs, etc., but not invariably so: see the quots. (Two infinitives connected by *than* in mod. Eng. either both have *to* or are both without it; formerly (until *c* 1800), esp. after *had rather, had better*, the second infinitive often had *to* when the first was without it.)

Instead of *than* after a comparative, *as* (like Ger. *als*) is common in Scotland, the north of England, and in parts of Ireland and the United States; *nor* (*nar, ner*) appears to be dialectal everywhere from Shetland to Hampshire and Cornwall, as well as in Ireland and America (see E.D.D.), but seems never to have been literary except in Sc., where also *na* was formerly used. In Sc. the relation is sometimes expressed by *be* (= by) as 'this field is bigger be that' (Jamieson s. v. BE).

α. *c* 825 *Vesp. Psalter* li. 5 [lii. 3] Ðu lufedes..unrehtwisnisse mae ðon spreocan rehtwisnisse. *Ibid.* lxxxiii[i]. 11[10] Ic ʒeceas..bion in huse godes mae ðone eardian in ʒeteldum synfulra. *c* 893 K. ÆLFRED *Oros.* I. i. § 19 Seo [sæ] is bradre þonne æniʒ man ofer seon mæʒe. *c* 1000 *Ags. Gosp.* John i. 15 He wæs ær þonne ic. *a* 1175 *Cott. Hom.* 219 Þaðe hi wolde..beon betere þonne he ʒesceapen were. *c* 1205 LAY. 6515 Þe mon..þe nimeð to him seoluen Mare þonne [*c* 1275 þan] he maʒen walden.

β. 831 *Charter of Eadwald* in *O. E. Texts* 445 Nis eðelmode eniʒ meʒhond neor ðes cynnes ðanne eadwald. *a* 1000 ÆLFRIC *Colloquy* (Disc. 3) in Wr.-Wülcker 90 Leofre ys us beon beswungen for lare þænne hit ne cunnan. *a* 1175 *Cott. Hom.* 219 Wursan þanne æniʒ oðer. *c* 1205 LAY. 3030 Þe king heo louede more þanne [*c* 1275 þan] ba tueie þe oðre. *Ibid.* 8916–17 Leouere him weore þane [*c* 1275 þan] al his lond, þene al his seoluer, þæne al his gold. *c* 1220 *Bestiary* 267 More ðanne man weneð. *a* 1450 *Knt. de la Tour* (1906) 24 With fairnesse rather thanne with rudenesse.

γ. *c* 1175 *Lamb. Hom.* 17 Betere hit is þet heo beon spilled..þenne mid alle fordon. *Ibid.* 139 Þis dei is..seouensiþe brictere þene þe sunne. *c* 1205 LAY. 11954 Ma þeone [*c* 1275 þane] heo rohten. *c* 1275 *XI Pains of Hell* 121 in *O. E. Misc.* 150 Þe stude is þustrore þene þe nyht. *c* 1320 *Cast. Love* 196 And raþure he dude his wyues bode þen he heold þe heste of gode. *c* 1400 *Laud Troy Bk.* 2010 That ladi..That is gentelour, then ȝe or he. *c* 1420 *Chron. Vilod.* 3195 A nother gretter miracle ȝet þenne þis. *a* 1425 *Cursor M.* 9452 (Laud) She levyd more the fend Then god. 1470–85 MALORY *Arthur* IX. xxxv. 395, I am more heuy that I can not mete with hym, thenne for al the hurtes. 1535 COVERDALE *Ps.* xcv[i]. 4 He is more to be feared then all goddes. 1590 SHAKS. *Mids. N.* III. i. 90 A stranger Piramus, then ere plaid here. 16.. SIR W. MURE *Sonn. to Margareit* i. 13 With vertue grac'd far more yen forme of face. 1611 BIBLE *Ps.* lxxxiv. 10, I had rather be a doore keeper in the house of my God, then to dwell in the tents of wickednesse. 1667 MILTON *P. L.* II. 745, I know thee not, nor ever saw till now Sight more detestable then him and thee. 1684 EARL ROSCOM. *Ess. Transl. Verse* 48 The fault is more the Languages then theirs.

δ. 735 BÆDA *Death-song* 2 Naeniʒ uuiurthit thonc snotturra than him tharf sie. *c* 1200 ORMIN 1985 Þatt wollde bettre Drihhtin Godd..þann þatt te laffdiʒ wære shennd. *Ibid.* 15689 Þatt wass till Crist ȝet ner bitahht Þan hise possltess wærenn. 1303 R. BRUNNE *Handl. Synne* 6043 Ȝyt hyt ys wers þan ys þe lore. 13.. *Cursor M.* 23240 (Cott.) Herder þan [*Edin.* þain] es here irinn mell. 1393 LANGL. *P. Pl.* C. II. 144 And deye raþere þan to do eny dedlich synne. *c* 1440 *Jacob's Well* 302 Ȝe are more hethyne in ȝoure werkys þan we. 1474 CAXTON *Chesse* II. ii. b iv b, The chyld that so wysely contriued the lye rather than he wold discouere theyr counceyl. 1566 PAINTER *Pal. Pleas.* (1813) II. 538, I had rather dye than once to open my mouth. 1682 SIR T. BROWNE *Chr. Mor.* III. § 25 Some had rather never have lived than to tread over their days once more. 1710 ADDISON *Tatler* No. 220 ⁋ 3 Water, colder than Ice, and clearer than Christal. 1732 BERKELEY *Alciphr.* III. § 13 The generality of mankind obey rather force than reason. 1766 GOLDSM. *Vic. W.* xii, You have more circumspection than is wanted. 1774 — *Nat. Hist.* (1776) III. 30 They..rather tread their enemies to death than gore them. 1782 COWPER *Mut. Forbearance* 20 Some people are more nice than wise. 1803 JEFFERSON *Writ.* (1830) IV. 3, I had rather ask an enlargement of power from the nation..than to assume it. 1832 TENNYSON *To J. S.* ix, Great Nature is more wise than I. 1850 — *In Mem.* xxvii. 16 'Tis better to have loved and lost, Than never to have loved at all. 1848 DICKENS *Dombey* xxxii, Being a whit more venturesome than before. 1854 MRS. JAMESON *Bk. of Th.* (1877) 27 We all need more mercy than we deserve. 1875 JOWETT *Plato* (ed. 2) I. 36 Than which nothing..can be more irrational. 1908 R. BAGOT *A. Cuthbert* v. 41 She would have..accepted the results even of a *mésalliance*..rather than that Cuthbertsheugh should not pass to a son of mine. *Mod.* He likes dogs better than cats. He likes dogs better than I. That is easier said than done. He said he would sooner die than yield.

*abbrev.* 1689 *Col. Rec. Pennsylv.* I. 317 This may be sooner and safer done yn returning ne yt sum. 1705 HEARNE *Collect.* 8 July (O.H.S.) I. 2 His Latin is..better yn Salmasius's.

ε. 1463 *Somerset Medieval Wills* (1901) 197 If their title be better an myne. *c* 1900 *New Engld. dial.*, Kicked him higher 'n a kite.

**b.** With a personal or relative pronoun in the objective case instead of the nominative (as if *than* were a preposition).

This is app. the invariable construction in the case of *than whom*, which is universally accepted instead of *than who*. With the personal pronouns it is now considered incorrect.

1560 BIBLE (Genev.) *Prov.* xxvii. 3 A fooles wrath is heauier then them bothe. 1569 J. SANFORD tr. *Agrippa's Van. Artes* 165 We cannot resiste them that be stronger then vs. 1718 PRIOR *Better Answer* 27–8 For thou art a girl as much brighter than her, As he was a poet sublimer than me. 1762 GOLDSM. *Cit. W.* xxxviii, I am, not less than him, a despiser of the multitude. *a* 1774 — *Surv. Exp. Philos.* (1776) I. 163 Others, later than him, who appeal to experience as well as he, affirm the contrary. 1792 WAKEFIELD *Mem.* (1804) I. 108 He was much older than me. 1815 SCOTT *Guy M.* xvii, I..could not be expected..to be wiser than her. *c* 1825 BEDDOES *Second Brother* I. i, You are old, And many years nearer than him to death. 1861 O'CURRY *Lect. MS. Materials* 253 He is better than me, then, said the monarch. 1548 UDALL, etc. *Erasm. Par. Mark* 67 Or els forsake them, then whome..there is nothyng more deare vnto the. 1656 HEYLIN *Extraneus Vapulans* 313 An eminent Antiquary, than whom none can be fitter to give Testimony. 1667 MILTON *P. L.* II. 299 Bëëlzebub..then whom, Satan except, none higher sat. 1749 FIELDING *Tom Jones* XI. vi, Sophia, than whom none was more capable of [etc.]. 1876 GLADSTONE *Homeric Synchr.* 60 Mr. Newton, than whom no one is of greater authority, refers them [etc.].

**c.** Followed by *that*, or by *infin.* expressing a hypothetical result or consequence.

The modern idiom would often substitute *too* with the positive followed by the infinitive, for the comparative with *than*: e.g. in quot. 1611 'the bed is too short for a man to stretch himself'; in quot. 1693 'he is too modest to deny it'. Examples occur of a confusion of the two constructions, as 'too wise than that' or 'than to be'.

1528 TINDALE *Wicked Mammon* 45 b, This texte is playner than that it neadeth to be expounded. 1611 BIBLE *Isa.* xxviii. 20 The bed is shorter, then that a man can stretch himselfe on it. 1779–81 JOHNSON *L. P., Prior* Wks. III. 131 Dryden had been more accustomed to hostilities, than that such enemies should break his quiet.

1611 BEAUM. & FL. *Philaster* I. i, Your nature is more constant than to inquire after state-news. 1670 MILTON *Hist. Eng.* VI. Wks. (1847) 553/2 Of a higher spirit than to accept her. 1693 CONGREVE *Old Bach.* IV. xxii, He is more modest..than to deny it. *a* 1704–1872 [see KNOW *v.* 9 b]. 1779 *Mirror* No. 2 ⁋ 6 Mr. Creech..knew his business better than to satisfy their curiosity. 1802 JAMES *Milit. Dict.* s. v. *Rifled gun*, The bullet ought to be no larger than to be just pressed by the rifles. *Mod.* He knows better than to do that. I think more highly of him than to suppose he would do that (*or*, I think too highly of him to suppose...).

*a* 1677 BARROW *Serm. Ephes.* v. 4 Wks. 1687 I. 202 It is a good far too pretious, than to be prostituted for idle sport. 1833 I. TAYLOR *Fanat.* i. 4 Those..who..are far too wise than to be religious. *Ibid.* 14 The inquiry..is too momentous ..than that it should be diverted.

**2.** *Than* is regularly used after *other, else*, and their compounds (*another, otherwise, elsewhere*, etc.). See also OTHER, ELSE, etc.

[*c* 1200 ORMIN 9305 Nohht elless ne nohht mare þann þatt tatt ȝuw iss sett to don Ne do ȝe.] *a* 1300 *Cursor M.* 7319 Þai ask now oþer [*v.r.* anoþer] king þan me. *c* 1320 *Cast. Love* 1237 Oþer God nis non þen he. 1426 LYDG. *De Guil. Pilgr.* 9251 Ys nat my body & I al on?..Ys he a-nother than am I? 1551 RECORDE *Pathw. Knowl.* Pref., There neadeth none other proofe then Aristotle his testimony. 1573 G. HARVEY *Letter-bk.* (Camden) 1 If I do otherwise then I should do. 1587 GOLDING *De Mornay* xxiv. 408 God was not knowne and worshipped elswhere than among the people of Israell. 1666 BOYLE *Orig. Formes & Qual.* (1667) 2 The diversity..in Bodies must..arise from somewhat else then the Matter they consist of. 1799 HT. LEE *Canterb. T., Frenchm. T.* (ed. 2) I. 255 [He was] no other than the rightful lord. 1896 *Law Times* C. 410/1 The acts or defaults of any person other than himself.

**b.** Hence sometimes after adjs. or advbs. of similar meaning to 'other', as *different, diverse, opposite*, and after Latin comparatives, as *inferior, junior*: usually with clause following. (Now mostly avoided. See also DIFFERENT *a.* 1 b.)

*c* 1400 MAUNDEV. (1839) viii. 109 Þei han also dyuerse clothinge and schapp..þan oþer folk han. 1566 PAINTER *Pal. Pleas.* (1813) I. 317 If the lorde of Mendozza were inferiour in qualitie, nobility, and goods, than hee is. 1642 BAKER *Malvezzi's Disc. Tacitus* liii. 498 He was now made overseer of the building.., a much inferiour place than the other. 1754 J. HILDROP *Misc. Wks.* I. 91 They imploy their Wealth..to quite opposite Purposes than were intended. 1822 J. YATES *Let. to Parr* 19 May, in *P.'s Wks.* (1828) VIII. 250 Such a design..has a right to a far different head than mine. 1902 *Westm. Gaz.* 19 Aug. 2/3 How about the following sentence? 'Unless the London members behave differently about the Bill for London than the country members about the Bill for the country, reasons for postponement and consideration will begin to look weighty.' If 'than' is excluded, how is it to be said? [Put 'otherwise' for 'differently', and retain 'than'.]

**3.** Exceptional or peculiar uses. †**a.** With ellipsis of preceding comparative: = *rather than, more than. Obs.*

[*c* 1000 *Ags. Ps.* cxvii[i]. 8 God ys on Dryhten ʒeorne to þenceanne, þonne on mannan wese mod to treowianne. *Lat.* Bonum est confidere in Domino, quam confidere in homine.] 13.. *Minor Poems fr. Vernon MS.* xxix. 46 He was Counseyled [to] hewe of his leg: Þen longe to suffre so. *c* 1449 PECOCK *Repr.* III. v. 307 It spedith to thee that oon of thi membris perische than that al thi bodi go into helle. 1647 TRAPP *Comm. Epistles* 330 He did verily believe that Job was torne and tortured by his interpritations, then ever he had been by his botches and ulcers. *a* 1648 LD. HERBERT *Hen. VIII* 68 The apprentices being encouraged herewith,..than do nothing, brake open some prisons.

†**b.** = Nor. (? ellipsis for *any more than.*) *Obs.*

13.. *Cursor M.* 17586 (Cott.) Yeitt es he þar-wit ouer all, ..And mist noiþer in heuen þen [*v. rr.* ne, ny] here. *Ibid.* 29114 Yee wate neuer dai þen night, Yur lauerd wil cum. 1472 *Surtees Misc.* (1888) 25 That no man..bers unlawefull wepyn to the kirk then in the market. 1473 *Rolls of Parlt.* VI. 95/2 That this Acte of Resumption, then noon other Acte made or to be made..extend not neither be prejudiciall unto [etc.].

**c.** = Except, besides, but. (? ellipsis for *other than, else than, otherwise than.*) *Obs.* or *arch.*

1375 BARBOUR *Bruce* I. 501 Thar is nothir man na page,.. than thai sall be Fayn to mak thaim-selwyn fre. 1585 T. WASHINGTON tr. *Nicholay's Voy.* III. iii. 74 b, There is almost nothing left then a shadow therof. 1647 W. BROWNE *Polex.* I. v. 123 The service you had done..was such as kings could not worthily acknowledge, at least, then in giving up their crownes. 1857 RUSKIN *Pol. Econ. Art* 28 There is nothing left for him than the blood that comes.. up to the horsebridles.

¶ **d.** After *hardly, scarcely*: = When (by confusion with *no sooner than*).

1864 FROUDE *Short Stud.* (1867) I. 3 He had scarcely won for himself the place which he deserved, than his health was found shattered. 1903 F. W. MAITLAND in *Camb. Mod. Hist.* II. xvi. 584 Hardly had the Council been re-opened at Trent..than Elizabeth was allying herself with the Huguenots.

†**4.** After ERE, LESS, NIGH: see these words.

¶ **5.** Erroneously used (instead of *as*) in comparisons of equality; † *like than* = such as (*obs.*); *so .. than* = so .. as.

1592 WARNER *Alb. Eng.* VIII. xl. (1612) 195 A Warrior braue: But than his Sier, himselfe, one Sonne of his, Like Polititians seldome liude. 1595 *Trag. Sir R. Grenville* (Arb.) 64 Then which the like was neuer heard before. 1602 G. BLACKWELL in *Archpriest Controv.* (Camden) II. 226, I can blame none so much for defect of Almes then Mr. Collington and his adherents. 1677 R. BOYLE *Treat. Art of War* 12 Their substantial Diet, than which, none..have so good. 1723 MANDEVILLE *Fab. Bees* (1733) II. 201 There is nothing in which our Species so far surpasses all others, than in the Capacity [etc.].

†**Than,** *dem. pron. Obs.* [ME. repr. OE. *þam* dat. sing. of *se, séo, þæt*, THAT.] After a prep.: That; as in *for þan*, for that (reason), therefore; *for al þan*, for all that (FOR 23 b); *not* (*na*) *for than*, notwithstanding that. See also FOR-THAN.

1297 R. GLOUC. (Rolls) 1418 Ȝut for al þan..Hii broȝte oure louerd ihesu crist to deþe on þe rode. *a* 1325 *Prose Psalter, Athanasian Creed* 16 And na-for-þan þer ne ben nouȝt þre goddes. *c* 1450 LOVELICH *Grail* xlv. 365 Nevertheless not for than the water In his Eyen stille was than.

**Than, þan,** obs. and dial. form of THEN.

**Than, thana, thane,** OE. and ME. inflexions of THAT, THE.

**Thana(h, Thanadar,** more correct spellings of TANA, TANADAR.

**Thanage** (þēi·nėdʒ). *Obs.* exc. *Hist.* Also thenage. [= AF. *thaynage, thanage*, in med.L. *than-, thenagium*, f. THANE (and its variants) + OF. *-age*, med.L. *-āgium*: see -AGE.] The tenure by which lands were held by a thane; the land held by a thane, a thane-land; also the rank, office, or jurisdiction of a thane.

[1200 *Rotuli Chart.* (1837) 51/1 Sciatis nos concessisse et.. confirmasse Willelmo Bardulf et Elysabeth uxori sue et heredibus eorum totum thenagium quod..Willelmus..pater predicte Elysabeth tenuit in Hepedale et in Kokedale. 1228 in *Feodar. Priorat. Dunelm.* (Surtees) 224 Requisitus an tenementum Henrici sit drengagium, dicit quod non, sed thenagium, sed pater Henrici liberavit illud a thenagio. 1230 *Stat. Alex. II*, c. 5 in *Scot. Statutes* (1844) I. 399 Si vero in dominicis vel thanagiis domini Regis malefactor ille fuerit [14.. *transl.* ibid. 400 And gif for suth þat trespassour be in þe kingis maynis or thanagis]. ? 1305 *Rolls of Parlt.* I. 471/2 La terre approprie torcenusement a vostre Thaynage de Balhelui.]

14.. [see quot. 1230 above]. 1623 in *Thanes of Cawdor* (Spalding Cl.) 260 All and haill the lands of the thanage and barony of Calder..united into one entire and free thanage, to be called the Thanage and Barony of Calder. 1641 *Termes de la Ley* 255 The kings thanage signifieth a certain part of the kings lands, or property, whereof the rule & government appertaineth unto him, who therfore is called *Thanus*. 1807 G. CHALMERS *Caledonia* I. III. v. § 3. 366 Having no such lands [in demesne], they equally appear to have had no thanages. 1872 E. W. ROBERTSON *Hist. Ess.* 126 The Scottish Gerefa was known as the Thane or Mair, his district often as a Thanage. 1883 *Ord. Surv. Gazetteer Scot.* III. 18 It gave name to an ancient thanage.

**Thanatic** (þănæ·tik), *a. rare*—°. [ad. Gr. *θανατικ-ός*, f. *θάνατος* death: see -IC.] (See quot.)

1860 MAYNE *Expos. Lex.*, *Thanaticus*, of or belonging to death;..deadly: tha'natic. 1890 in BILLINGS *Med. Dict.*

**Thanatism** (þæ·nătiz'm). [f. Gr. *θάνατος* death + -ISM.] The belief or doctrine that at death the human soul ceases to exist. So **Tha·natist**, a believer in thanatism.

1900 *Academy* 1 Dec. 512/1 For ourselves we prefer to say that even atheism and thanatism are speculations. 1902 J. MCCABE tr. *Haeckel's Riddle Universe* xi. 67/1 We give the name of 'thanatism'..to the opinion which holds that at a man's death..his 'soul' also disappears,—that is, that sum of cerebral functions which psychic dualism regards as a peculiar entity, independent of the other vital processes in the living body. *Ibid.* 69/1. 1902 W. S. LILLY in *19th Cent.* Mar. 466, I suppose that thanatists, as it is the fashion to call them, are really not very numerous.

**Thanato-** (þæ·năto), before a vowel **thanat-**, combining form of Gr. *θάνατος* death, chiefly in scientific words. **Tha·nato-biolo·gic** *a.* (see quot.). **Thanatognomo·nic** *a.*, indicative or characteristic of death. **Thanato·graphy**, *nonce-wd.* [after *biography*], an account of a person's death. **Thanatoma·ntic** *a.* [see -MANTIC], of or pertaining to divination concerning death. **Thanato·meter** (see quots.). ‖ **Thanatopho·bia** (also **thanato·phoby**), morbid fear of death. ‖ **Thanato·psis** [Gr. *ὄψις* sight, view], a contemplation of death. **Thanatoty·phus**, malignant typhus.

1899 *Syd. Soc. Lex.*, **Thanato-biologic*, pertaining to life and death. 1862 G. W. BALFOUR tr. *Casper's Forensic Med.* § 55 II. vi. 239 The lungs in the more or less recent bodies of those drowned..present an appearance so peculiar as to be truly *thanatognomonic. 1839 THACKERAY *Catherine* vi:

The excellent 'Newgate Calendar'..contains the biographies and *thanatographies of Hayes and his wife. **1841** *Fraser's Mag.* XXV. 270 The deuteroscopic or *thanatomantic faculty of the Germans. **1860** MAYNE *Expos. Lex.*, *Thanatometrum*, ..term by Nasse [of Berlin] for a means of indicating the actual presence of death; a death-measurer: a *thanatometer. **1899** *Syd. Soc. Lex.*, *Thanatometer*, a thermometer capable of being introduced into the stomach to determine whether the depression of temperature is sufficient to be looked on as a sign of death. **1860** MAYNE *Expos. Lex.*, **Thanatophobia*, term for a dread or fear of death: *thanatophoby. **1903** *Alien. & Neurol.* May 170 Pessimism is frequently associated with morbid fear of death (thanatophobia). **1816** W. C. BRYANT (*title*) *Thanatopsis. **1860** MAYNE *Expos. Lex.*, **Thanatotyphus*. **1890** in BILLINGS *Med. Dict.*

**Thanatoid** (þæ·nătoid), *a.* *Path.* [f. Gr. θάνατος death + -OID. Cf. Gr. θανατώδης.] (See quot.)

**1857** DUNGLISON *Med. Lex.*, *Thanatoid*, resembling death; apparently dead. **1890** in BILLINGS *Nat. Med. Dict.*

**Thanatology** (þænătǫ·lŏdʒi). *rare.* [f. Gr. θάνατος death + -LOGY. Cf. F. *thanatologie*.] The scientific study of death, its causes and phenomena. So **Thanatolo·gical** *a.*, of or pertaining to thanatology; **Thanato·logist**, a student of or a person versed in thanatology; in quot. 1901 (*nonce-use*), one who studies dead animals.

**1842** DUNGLISON *Med. Lex.*, *Thanatology*, a description, or the doctrine, of death. **1862** G. W. BALFOUR tr. *Casper's Forensic Med.* II. Title-p., Thanatological division. **1881** G. R. JESSE in *Athenæum* 9 Apr. 504/1 This sums up the thanatological results of an enormous amount of cruelty in previous experiments. **1901** E. SELOUS *Bird Watching* viii. 224 We have studied animals only to kill them, or killed them in order to study them. Our 'zoologists' have been thanatologists. **1903** MITCHELL tr. *Metchnikoff's Nat. Man* xii. (1904) 298 The scientific study of old age and of death, two branches of science that may be called *gerontology* and *thanatology*.

‖**Thanatophidia** (þænătofi·diă), *sb. pl.* *Zool.* [f. *thanat-*, THANATO- + OPHIDIA.] A division of *Ophidia*, comprising the venomous snakes. Hence **Thanatophi·dian** *a.*, of or pertaining to the *Thanatophidia*; *sb.* a serpent of this division; **Thanatophidio·logist**, a student of the zoology of the *Thanatophidia*.

**1872** FAYRER (*title*) The Thanatophidia of India, being a Description of the Venomous Snakes of the Indian Peninsula. **1884** J. DONNET in *Nature* 27 Mar. 504/1, I believe it to be a generally accepted opinion among thanatophidiologists that, from what is known of the virulent properties of snake-poison, though fatal to man and other living beings, it is innoxious in its effects to serpents of like nature. **1891** *Cent. Dict.*, Thanatophidian *a.* and *sb.*

‖**Thanato·sis.** *Path.* [a. Gr. θανάτωσις a putting to death, f. θανατοῦν to put to death.]

**1860** MAYNE *Expos. Lex.*, *Thanatosis*,..term for Mortification. **1890** in BILLINGS *Nat. Med. Dict.*

**Thane**[1] (þēⁱn). *Hist.* Forms: 1 þeᵹn, þeᵹen, -in, (þeng), 1–2 þén, þeiᵹn (6–7 theigne), 2 þening, 2–3 þein (6, 9 thein), 3–4 þ-, theyn(e (6 theyn), 4 thain (8 -e), 4–6 thayn(e, 5– thane. See also THEGN. [OE. *þeᵹn*, *þeᵹen*, *þén*, = OS. *thegan*, OHG. *degan* boy, servant, warrior, hero (MHG., G. *degen*), ON. *þegn* freeman, liegeman:—OTeut. **þeᵹno*ᶻ, orig. child, boy, lad:—pre-Teut. **tek-nó-* (cf. Gr. τέκνον child), f. root *tek*: *tok* to beget.

The regular modern repr. of OE. *þeᵹn*, if the word had lived on in spoken use, would have been *thain* (cf. *fain*, *main*, *rain*), as it actually appears in some writers, chiefly northern, from 1300 to near 1600. But *thain* was in 15–16th c. Sc. written *thane* (in L. *thanus*), and this form, being used by Boece, Holinshed, and Shakspere (in Macbeth), was adopted by Selden, Spelman, and the legal antiquaries and historians of the 17th c. to represent the Anglo-Saxon *þeᵹn*, and became the usual form in Eng. history. Recent historians, as Stubbs, Freeman, and Green, in order to distinguish the Anglo-Saxon use from the Sc. in sense 4, have revived the OE. *þeᵹn* as THEGN, q. v.]

†**1.** A servant, minister, attendant; in OE. often applied to (Christ's) disciples. *Obs.*

*a* **700** *Epinal Gloss* (O.E.T.) 101 *Adsaeculam* [= *assecula*], theᵹn. *c* **725** *Corpus Gloss* 77 *Adsaeclum*, þeᵹn. *c* **888** K. ÆLFRED *Boeth.* vii. § 2, ᵹif þu þonne heora þeᵹen beon wilt. *a* **900** tr. *Bæda's Hist.* IV. xxv. [xxiv.] (1890) 346 Þa bæd he [a monk] his þeᵹn..þæt he in þæm huse him stowe ᵹeᵹearwode..Þa wundrode se þeᵹn. *c* **950** *Lindisf. Gosp.* Matt. xxiv. 45 Hwa woenes ðu is ᵹeleaf-full ðeᵹn & hoᵹa? **971** *Blickl. Hom.* 67 Iohannes, se deora þeᵹn. *Ibid.*, Lazarus þær was ana sittende mid Hælende & mid his þeᵹnum. *c* **1000** *Ags. Gosp.* Matt. xx. 26 Sy he eower þen. *Ibid.* John ii. 9 Þa þenas soðlice wiston þe þæt wæter hlodon. *a* **1175** *Cott. Hom.* 229 An þera twelf Christes þeiᵹne se þe was iudas ᵹehaten. *c* **1275** *Death* 177 in *O. E. Misc.* 179 Hwer beoþ þine þeynes þat þe leoue were? **13..** *Cursor M.* 5373 (Cott.) First he was here als our thain [*Gött.* thrall, *Trin.* þral]. **1591** LAMBARDE *Archeion* (1635) E iij, By certaine Messengers, which they tearmed Theignes; that is to say, Ministers, or Servants.

†**2.** A military attendant, follower, or retainer; a soldier. *Obs.*

*Beowulf* 400 Aras þa se rica ymb hine rinc maniᵹ þryðlic þeᵹna heap. *a* **800** CYNEWULF *Elene* 549 (Gr.) Þa cwom þeᵹna heap to þam heremeðle. *c* **893** K. ÆLFRED *Oros.* v. ii. § 3 Ueriatuses þeᵹn þæm oþrum to longe æfterfylᵹende, oþ mon his hors under him ofsceat. *c* **950** *Lindisf. Gosp.* Matt. viii. 9 Ic..hæfo under mec ðeiᵹnas [*Vulg.* milites]. *c* **1000** *Ags. Gosp.* ibid., Ic hæbbe þeᵹnas [*c* **1160** *Hatton* þeiᵹnes] under me. *c* **1000** ÆLFRIC *Voc.* in Wr.-Wülcker 119/34 *Agaso*, hors þen.

†**b.** *poet.* A warrior, a brave man. Cf. EARL 1 b.

*Beowulf* 2709 Swylc sceolde secg wesan, þeᵹn æt ðearfe. *c* **893** K. ÆLFRED *Oros.* III. vii. § 2 ᵹif ᵹe swelce þeᵹnas sint, swelce ᵹe wenað þæt ᵹe sien, þonne sceoldon ᵹe swa lustlice eowre aᵹnu brocu aræfnan. *a* **1272** *Luue Ron* 13 in *O. E. Misc.* 93 Þeos þeines þat weren bolde beoþ aglyden.

**3.** One who in Anglo-Saxon times held lands of the king or other superior by military service; originally in the fuller designation *cyninges þegn*, 'king's thane, military servant or attendant'; in later times simply *thegn*, as a term of rank, including several grades below that of an *ealdorman* or *eorl* (EARL *sb.* 2) and above that of the *ceorl* or ordinary freeman.

In this sense the name was superseded by *baron* and *knight* in the 12th c., and continued only in historical use, in which it was written *thane* in the 16th c. Recent historians have revived the OE. form as THEGN.

**805** *Charter* in *O. E. Texts* 442 Beforan wulfrede arcebiscope..& esne cyninges ðeᵹne. *a* **900** *O. E. Chron.* an. 897, Maniᵹe þara selestena cynges þena..Eadulf cynges þeᵹn..& Ecgulf cynges hors þeᵹn. **971** *Blickl. Hom.* 211 Wæs his fæder ærest cyninges þeᵹn, & ða..he wæs cininges þeᵹna aldorman. *c* **1000** ÆLFRIC *Gram.* ix. (Z.) 50 *Optimas*, ðeᵹn. *c* **1000** — *Voc.* in Wr.-Wülcker 155/20 *Primas*, heafodman, *uel* þeᵹn. *Ibid.* 155/23 *Satrapa*, þeᵹn. *c* **1029–60** *Laws Ranks* c. 1 in Liebermann *Gesetze* (1903) 456 Ælc be his mæðe, ᵹe eorl ᵹe ceorl, ᵹe þeᵹen ᵹe þeoden. *c* **1050** *Byrhtferth's Handboc* in *Anglia* (1885) VIII. 326 Þeᵹnas & ceorlas habbað landmearke. **1066** *Writ of Eadweard* in Earle *Land-Charters* 342 Eadward cyningc gret Hereman bisceop, and Harold eorl, and Godric, and ealle his þeᵹenas [L. version *barones*]. *a* **1100** *O. E. Chron.* an. 1086 (Laud MS.) Ealle þa rice men ofer eall Engla land, arce biscopas, & leodbisceopas, abbodas & eorlas, þeᵹnas & cnihtas. *a* **1175** *Cott. Hom.* 231 Mid ærlen and aldren, mid cnihten, mid þeinen. *c* **1300** *Havelok* 2260 Siþen drenges, and siþen thaynes, And siþen knithes, and siþen sweynes. *c* **1325** *Chron. Eng.* (Ritson) 583 Alle the theynes of Walschelonde He made bowe to ys honde. **1570–6** LAMBARDE *Peramb. Kent* (1826) 453 As for *twelf Pindman*, it was given to the Theyn or Gentleman, bicause his life was valued at Twelve hundreth shillings. **1598** HAKLUYT *Voy.* I. 126 If a Thein so thriued, that he serued the king, and on his message rid in his houshold, if he then had a Thein that followed him..he became an Earle.

**1577–87** HOLINSHED *Chron.* I. 190/1 Harold..slue thirtie gentlemen of honor, or thanes (as they called them). **1614** SELDEN *Titles Hon.* 267 The neerest name for Baron was that of Thane, anciently written also Thegn. *c* **1630** RISDON *Surv. Devon* § 284 (1810) 296 The thane was descended of ancient lineage, and such a one as we call gentleman. **1754** HUME *Hist. Eng.* (1761) I. App. i. 96 The nobles were called thanes; and were of two kinds, the king's thanes and lesser thanes. **1809** BAWDWEN *Domesday Bk.* 18 In *Loctvsv* (Lofthouse) two Thanes had four carucates to be taxed. **1853** Jos. STEVENSON tr. *O. E. Chron.* an. 1036, Leofric the earl, and almost all the thanes north of the Thames..chose Harold for chief of all England. **1853** — tr. *Florence of Worcester* an. 897, Ecgulf the kings horse-thane. **1875** MAINE *Hist. Inst.* v. 135 There are in the early English laws some traces of a process by which a Ceorl might become Thane. **1888** EARLE *Land-Charters* Introd. 71 These words ..eorl, gesith, thane, knight, squire, gentleman. The last two run abreast.

**4.** In *Scottish Hist.* A person, ranking with the son of an earl, holding lands of the king; the chief of a clan, who became one of the king's barons.

[**1220** *Stat. Alex. II*, c. 2, in *Scot. Statutes* (1844) I. 398 De terris episcoporum abbatum baronum militum et thanorum qui de Rege tenent.] **14..** *transl. of prec.*, Of þe landis of bischopis abbotis barounis knychtis and thaynis þe quhilkis haldis of þe Kyng. **1422** in *Thanes of Cawdor* (Spalding Club) 10 To spouse and til haf to your wife, the douchter of the saide Donald thayne of Caldor. *c* **1425** WYNTOUN *Cron.* VI. xviii. 1904 Lo, ȝonder þe thayne of Crumbaghty! *Ibid.* xix. 2318 Makduf of Fif þe thayne. *c* **1470** HENRY *Wallace* XI. 894 That Erll was cummyn off trew haill nobill blud, Fra the ald thane, quhilk in his tym was gud. **1535** STEWART *Cron. Scot.* (Rolls) II. 637 'The Thane of Glames, gude morne to him', said scho. [**1596** DALRYMPLE tr. *Leslie's Hist. Scot.* I. (S.T.S.) 112 *margin*, The first nobils in Scotland war called Thani; thay war of the clan cheif...In ald tymes Dukes war called Thani.] **1605** SHAKS. *Macb.* I. iii. 71 By Sinells death, I know I am Thane of Glamis, But how, of Cawdor? the Thane of Cawdor liues. *Ibid.* v. iii. 50 Doctor, the Thanes flye from me. **1609** SKENE *Reg. Maj.* 73 b, *Item*, the Cro of ane Earles sonne, or of ane Thane, is ane hundreth kye. *Item*, the Cro of the sonne of ane Than, is thriescore sax kye. **1759** ROBERTSON *Hist. Scot.* I. (1802) I. 229 The ancient Thanes were the equals and the rivals of their prince. **1810** A. BOSWELL *Edinburgh* 260 Hill after hill some cunning clerk shall gain, Then, in a mendicant, behold a Thane!

**b.** *transf.* to modern persons, in various senses; e. g. a Scottish lord. Often in allusion to Shaks. *Macbeth* v. iii. 50. (See above.)

**1750** SHENSTONE *Odes, Rural Elegance* 7 Ye rural thanes that o'er the mossy down Some panting, timorous hare pursue. *a* **1764** LLOYD *Poetry Prof.* Poet. Wks. 1774 I. 39 Hail to the Thane, whose patriot skill Can break all nations to his will. **1839** LD. BROUGHAM *Statesm. Geo. III*, *Dundas* I. 232 He [Pitt] held the proxies of many Scottish Peers in open opposition! Well might his colleague exclaim to the hapless Addington in such unheard-of troubles, 'Doctor, the Thanes fly from us.' **1888** BRYCE *Amer. Commw.* lxiii. II. 455 Sometimes however he is rebuffed by the powers at Washington and then his State thanes fly from him.

**5.** *Comb.* Thane-right, the legal rights and privileges of a thane; Thane-wer [OE. *þeᵹnwer*], the wer-gild of a thane (sense 3).

**1008** [see THEGNWER]. **1844** LINGARD *Anglo-Sax. Ch.* (1858) II. xii. 234 *note*, His thane-wer, and thane-right in life and in the grave means the same as his worldly goods, and Christian sepulture.

Hence **Tha·ness**, a female thane; a thane's wife.

**1827** SCOTT *Surg. Dau.* iii, All the rural thanes and thanesses attended on these occasions. **1849** J. WILSON *Christopher under Canvass* No. 5 The Thaness [Lady Macbeth] is self-stayed.

**Thane**[2], Sc. form of FANE[1].

**1496** *Acc. Ld. High Treas. Scot.* I. 286 Item, for xiij dowbill platis to be thanis to the pailȝounis. **1570** *Satir. Poems Reform.* xxii. 84 Lyke wauering thane, thy proces vane Will brew the bitter gall. **1716** in *Thanes of Cawdor* (Spalding Cl.) 417 Thanes for the horse heads [at a funeral], £80. **1782** OREM *Chanonry Aberdeen* 21 With cross thanes of iron on the top of each of them.

**Thane,** obs. f. THEN *adv.*[1]; inflexion of THE.

**Thanedom** (þēⁱ·ndəm). [f. THANE + -DOM.] The domain or jurisdiction of a Scottish thane.

*c* **1425** WYNTOUN *Cron.* VI. xviii. 1910 In his ȝouth heid Off þai thayndomes þe thayne wes maid. **1579** *Reg. Privy C. Scot.* III. 140 The lordschip and thanedome of Fettarcarne. **1776** PENNANT *Tour Scot.* II. Addit. 13 This thanedom was transferred into the house of the Campbels. **1807** G. CHALMERS *Caledonia* I. III. vii. 416 The titles of Glamis, and Cawdor, were borrowed by Boece from thanedoms of more recent origin. **1837** SKENE *Highlanders Scot.* (1902) II. v. 261 Thanedoms were certainly hereditary in Scotland.

†**Tha·nehede.** *Obs.* [f. THANE[1], in sense 1 'servant' + *-hede*, -HEAD. Essentially an earlier form of next, but unconnected with it in use, being founded on an earlier sense of OE. *þeᵹn*.] Service, servitude; bondage, thraldom.

*a* **1300** *Cursor M.* 5404 (Cott.) Land and lijth wit bodi we bede, Þat þou vs tak in þin thainhede [*v.rr.* bonde-, bundhede]; In thainhed [*Fairf.* bondehede; *Gött.* & *Trin.* þraldam, -dome] tak our landes all, For sede we mai þam sau wit-all. *Ibid.* 5791, I sal þam [Israel] bring vte of thainhede [*v.rr.* þraldome, thralhede], In-till a land, a wonsum thede. *Ibid.* 6990 In thain-hede ar þai worth to be, Þat wil noght thole, and mai be fre.

**Tha·nehood.** [f. THANE (senses 3, 4) + -HOOD. Cf. THEGNHOOD.] The condition or rank of a thane.

**1897** E. CONYBEARE *Hist. Cambs.* 89 Raised to the Thanehood by their own or their forefathers' merits.

**Tha·ne-land.** Now *Hist.* (See also THEGNLAND.) Land held by a thane, or by military tenure.

*a* **1641** SPELMAN *Feuds & Tenures* viii, For better manifestation that Thanelands were subject to no feudal Service, consider, I pray you, the Words of the Saxon passage before mention'd, where it is said that a Thane must have three Hides at least of his..own Land. **1701** *Cowell's Interpr.*, *Thane-Lands*, Lands..granted by Charters of the Saxon Kings to their Thanes. **1809** BAWDWEN *Domesday Bk.* 370 Ulnod holds one oxgang of the same land in thaneland.

**Thanen, þanen, -ene,** *adv.*: see THENNE.

**Thaneship** (þēⁱ·nʃip). [f. THANE[1] + -SHIP: cf. OE. *þeᵹnscipe*.] The office or position of a thane: esp. in the Sc. sense. (See also THEGNSHIP.)

**1766** STEEVENS *Note Shaks., Macb.* I. iii. 48 The thaneship of Glamis was the ancient inheritance of Macbeth's family. **1844** LINGARD *Anglo-Sax. Ch.* (1858) I. App. 371 These lands ceasing to support an earthly thaneship or service. **1865** KINGSLEY *Herew.* xv, He shall have..a thaneship in East Anglia. **1896** MANLY *Notes on Macbeth* 101 Since Macbeth's accession to the thaneship of Cawdor.

**Thanist, -stry,** obs. forms of TANIST, -STRY.

**Thank** (þæŋk), *sb.* Forms: *α.* 1–4 þanc, (3 ðhanc), 1–5 þank, (3 *Orm.* þannk), 4 thanc (thang), 4–5 þanke, 4–6 thanck(e, 4–7 thanke, (6 thangke), 4– thank. *β.* 1 thonc, 1–4 þonc, 2 þeonk, 2–5 þonk, (3 þong), 3–5 þonke, 4 þoncke. [OE. *þanc*, *þonc* = OFris. *thonk*, OS. **thank* (MDu. *danc*, D. *dank*), OHG., MHG. *danc* (G. *dank*), ON. *þökk* (:—*þanku* fem.), Sw. *tack*, Da. *tak*, Goth. *þagks*:—OTeut. **þanko*ᶻ, f. ablaut stem *þenk*: *þank*: *þunk*: see THINK. The primary sense was therefore *thought*.]

**I.** †**1.** = THOUGHT. *Obs.* (See also I-THANK.)

**735** BÆDA *Death-song* 2 Naeniᵹ uuiurthit thonc snotturra [*or* thoncsnotturra] than him thaarf sie. *a* **900** *Andreas* 557 (Gr.) Saᵹa þances gleaw þeᵹn, ᵹif þu cunne, hu þæt ᵹewurde be werum tweonum. *c* **1000** *Ags. Ps.* (Th.) lxxxvii[i]. 11 Ne on ðeostrum ne mæg, þances ᵹehyᵹdum, æniᵹ wislicu wundur oncnawan. *c* **1160** *Hatton Gosp.* Matt. xv. 19 Of þare heorte cumeð þa yfele þankes [*c* **1000** ᵹeþancas]. *c* **1175** *Lamb. Hom.* 3 Heo urnen on-ȝein him..mid ufele þeonke. *a* **1200** *Moral Ode* 90 He þurþsicheþ uches monnes þonc. *c* **1200** *Trin. Coll. Hom.* 9 We..folȝeð on þonke, and on speche, and on dede, þat him is iqueme. *a* **1225** *Ancr. R.* 232 He..put..a swuc[h] þonc in hire softe heorte. *c* **1300** *Prov. Hending* i. in *Sal. & Sat.*, etc. (1848) 270 Gode þonkes and monie þewes for te teche fele schrewes.

†**2.** Favourable thought or feeling, good will; graciousness, grace, favour. *Obs.*

*a* **1000** *Cædmon's Gen.* 796 (Gr.) Þis is landa betst, þæt wit þurh uncres hearran þanc habban moston. *c* **1000** *Ags. Ps.* (Th.) ci. 15 [cii. 17] Oft he þearfendra bene þance ᵹehyrde. **1340** *Ave Maria* in *Rel. Ant.* I. 42 Hayl Marie of thonke vol [Vulg. *Luke* i. 28 Ave! gratia plena]. **1609** BIBLE (Douay) *Ecclus.* xii. 1 If thou wilt doe good, know to whom thou doest it, and there shal be much thanke [*Vulg.* gratia multa] in thy good deedes.

†**b.** The genitive case *thanks*, ME. *thankes*, lit. 'of thought', 'of good will', was used adverbially in sense 'willingly, voluntarily', esp. with preceding possessive pronoun, e. g. *his thankes* = with his consent, good will, or approval: so *Godes thankes* = *Deo volente*. Cf. UNTHANKES, unwillingly. *Obs.*

*c* **888** K. ÆLFRED *Boeth.* xiii, Sæᵹe me nu hwæðer se þin wela [þines] ðances swa diore seo, þe for his aᵹenre ᵹecynde. **1008** *Charter of Bp. Theodred* in Birch *Cart. Sax.* III. 209 Mines erfes þat ic beᵹiten habbe & ᵹet biᵹete Godes þankes and hise haleȝen. 1066 *O. E. Chron.* (MS. C.), Tostiȝ ..nam of þam butse karlon sume mid him, sume þances sume unþances. 1154 *Ibid.* an. 1140 (MS. Laud), Hi of Normandi wenden alle fra þe king.., sume here þankes & sume here un þankes. *c* 1175 *Lamb. Hom.* 17 Al swa þu waldest þet me dude þe þines þonkes. *a* 1250 *Owl & Night.* 70 Ek for þe þe sulue mose Hire þonkes wolde þe totose. *c* 1386 CHAUCER *Shipman's T.* 188 Pardee, I wol nat faille yow, my thankes. *c* 1400 MAUNDEV. (Roxb.) xxxi. 140 Þis ile dare na pilgrim come in ne nere it, þaire thankes. *a* 1450 MYRC *Par. Pr.* 891 Koghe þow not þenne þy þonkes.

† **3.** Kindly thought or feeling entertained towards any one for favour or services received; grateful thought, gratitude. Rarely in *pl. Obs.*

The sense of 'gratitude, kindly or loving feeling for favour or benefit' must have been developed between that of 'good will, good feeling' generally, and that of 'the expression of gratitude'. But the feeling passes so naturally into its expression that it is not easy to separate them in the quotations, except by the accompanying verbs: *to express one's thanks*, and the archaic *to con thanks*, ought to mean to express one's *feelings of gratitude*; but *to give, offer, return* or *receive thanks*, ought to mean to give or receive *the expression of gratitude*; so *to have thanks*, but this is less clear. In many instances it is impossible to say which is meant; some of the examples given here may belong to 4.

1297 R. GLOUC. (Rolls) 9379 Muche þonc were it vs of god mid him vorto fiȝte. 13.. *Gaw. & Gr. Knt.* 1380 Haue I þryuandely þonk þurh my craft serued? *c* 1374 CHAUCER *Troylus* III. 1728 (1777) Þis encres of hardynesse and myght Com hym of loue, his ladyes thank to wynne. *c* 1400 *Destr. Troy* 12724 The lady..þonkit hym þroly with þonkis in hir hert. *c* 1420 *Brut* 343 Þanne þei..went hom ayen yn-to her owne cuntre, with grete loue & moche þanke. 1500–20 DUNBAR *Poems* xvi. 19 Or the gift deliuerit be, The thank is frustrat and expyrd. *a* 1677 BARROW *Wks.* (1687) I. viii. 94 It was a satyrical answer (that of Aristotle)..who being asked..What doth the soonest grow old? replied..Thanks.

**4.** The expression of gratitude; the grateful acknowledgement of a benefit or favour. † **a.** in sing. *Obs.*

† *Gode þank, God-thank* [= L. *Deo gratias*, F. *grâce à Dieu*], thanks (be) to God, thank God.

*Beowulf* 1779 Þæs siȝ metode þanc, ecean dryhtne, þæs ðe ic on aldre ȝe-bad. *c* 888 K. ÆLFRED *Boeth.* xxxv. § 4 Þa ȝesceafta næren nanes þonces ne nanes weorðscipes wyrðe. *c* 897 — *Gregory's Past. C.* 2 Gode almiehteȝum si ðonc ðætte we nu æniȝne on stal habbað lareowa. *a* 1000 *Cædmon's Gen.* 1116 (Gr.) Him þæs þanc sie. *c* 1375 *Sc. Leg. Saints* xxvi. (*Nycholas*) 324 Thang to al-mychtty god he ȝaulde. *c* 1440 *Promp. Parv.* 490/1 Thanke, *grates, graciarum accio, gratulamen*. 1483 CAXTON *Gold. Leg.* 195/2 Thanke and glorye to god & honoure to the vyrgyne. 1534 MORE *Treat. Passion* Introd., Wks. 1271/1 Turning to god with lawde and thanke. *a* 1553 UDALL *Royster D.* II. ii, *Doughtie*. He will thank you woman. *Madge*. I will none of his thanke. 1642 ROGERS *Naaman* 385 Is this the thanke which you returne to God?

*c* 897 K. ÆLFRED *Gregory's Past. C.* 9 Gode ðonc. *Ibid.* i. 27. *c* 1200 *Trin. Coll. Hom.* 11 Unbileue..is aiware aleid and rihte leue arered godeðonc. 1297 R. GLOUC. (Rolls) 2578 Þe King was gode þonk aboue in four batailes. *c* 1300 *Havelok* 2005 Þus wolde þe theues me haue reft, But godþank, he hauenet sure keft.

**b.** in plural. † Formerly sometimes const. as *sing.*

1340 *Ayenb.* 18 Me..him ne yeldeþ þonkes of his guodes, þet he ous heþ ydo. 1481 CAXTON *Reynard* iv. (Arb.) 8 All hath he but lytyl thanks. 1509 HAWES *Past. Pleas.* iv. (Percy Soc.) 21 At whose encreace there is great thankes rendred. 1538 ELYOT, *Grates*, thankes. 1588 SHAKS. *Tit. A.* I. i. 215 Thankes to men Of Noble mindes, is Honourable Meede. 1592 — *Rom. & Jul.* II. vi. 23 Else is his thanks too much. 1651 HOBBES *Leviath.* II. xxxi. 191 Prayers precede, and Thanks succeed the benefit. 1753 HANWAY *Trav.* (1762) I. II. xvi. 72 Our soldiers were fed luxuriously at the fisheries, for nothing more than thanks. 1805 R. FULTON in *Sinclair's Corr.* (1831) II. 64, I return it to you with my sincere thanks. 1871 R. ELLIS *Catullus* xlix. 4 Thanks superlative unto thee Catullus Renders. 1881 'RITA' *My Lady Coquette* iii, Yolande gives her a smile of thanks.

**c.** *A thank* (formerly also *a thanks*): an expression of gratitude; a thanking, a thank-you. Now *rare*.

† *To pick (get, win) a thank*: see PICK *v.*[1] 8 b. *Obs.*

13.. *Gaw. & Gr. Knt.* 1984 Vche mon þat he mette, he made hem a þonke, For his seruyse. 1474 CAXTON *Chesse* III. vii. (1883) 139 To thende that they myght haue a thanke & be preysed. 1560 DAUS tr. *Sleidane's Comm.* Pref. 5 b, Verye manye of those wryters seke to pike a thanke. *a* 1577 GASCOIGNE *Herbs*, etc. Wks. (1587) 119 While Pierce the plowman hopes to pick a thank. 1579–1627 [see PICK *v.*[1] 8 b β]. 1601 B. JONSON *Poetaster* IV. vii, Without a thankes, to be sent hence! 1678 R. L'ESTRANGE *Seneca's Mor.* I. xv. (1696) 81 He..contents himself with a bare Thank for a Requital. *a* 1810 TANNAHILL *Poet. Wks.* (1846) 67 With his lordship's thank. 1839 LONGF. *Black Kn.* 47 The children drank, Gave many a courteous thank.

**II.** Phrases and phraseological uses.

**5.** *Thanks*: a much abbreviated expression of gratitude for a favour received or recognition of a service; = *I give you my thanks, my thanks to you*, or the like. Also *many thanks, best thanks*.

1588 SHAKS. *L. L. L.* v. ii. 559 If your Ladiship would say thankes Pompey, I had done. *La.* Great thankes, great Pompey. 1605 — *Macb.* II. i. 30 *Macb.* Good repose the while! *Banq.* Thankes, Sir: the like to you! 1647 PEACHAM *Worth of a Penny* 14 He answers you with Monosyllables, ..*Yes, No, That, Thankes, True*, &c. 1803 *Forest of Hohenelbe* I. 167 Thanks, Baron, for your good wishes. 1803 PITT in *G. Rose's Diaries* (1860) II. 16 Many thanks for your letter. 1866 E. FITZGERALD *More Lett.* (1901) 82 Don't you dislike the way some People have of saying perpetually '*Thanks!*' instead of 'Thank you'?..It is like cutting Acknowledgment as short as possible...*Thanks* [is] about one of the most hideous monosyllables, even in the English Language. 1870 MISS BRIDGMAN *Rob. Lynne* II. xiv. 299 'Would you like to read the letter, Robert?' 'No, thanks'.

**6.** *Thanks to*: Thanks be given to, or are due to; hence, Owing to, as a result of, in consequence of. (Often ironical.) So *no thanks* († *thank*) *to*, no credit to, not by virtue or merit of; not because or by reason of.

1633 EARL MANCH. *Al Mondo* (1636) 115 It is no thankes to a man to pay that willingly, which he must doe of necessitie. 1633 BP. HALL *Medit. & Vows* (1851) 150 It is scarce any thank to me that he prevails. 1647 TRAPP *Comm. Rev.* iii. 4 No thank to the Pastour, who was a mercenary eye-servant. *a* 1687 PETTY *Pol. Arith.* vi. (1691) 99 No thanks to any Laws which have been made to that purpose. 1737 POPE *Hor. Epist.* II. ii. 68 But (thanks to Homer) since I live and thrive, Indebted to no Prince or Peer alive. 1813 SCOTT *Rokeby* v. vi, It is a sight but rarely spied, Thanks to man's wrath and woman's pride. 1894 *Westm. Gaz.* 21 Aug. 3/3 The passengers—thanks, I expect, to the bitter cold—behaved more quietly at night than in the morning.

† **7.** *In* (*on*) *thank, to thank*, with pleased mind, with pleasure or satisfaction; pleasantly, graciously; with thanks, gratefully. *Obs.*

*a* 1000 *Andreas* 1114 (Gr.) Hie þa lac hraðe þeȝon to þance. *a* 1000 *Cædmon's Gen.* 2442 Hie on þanc curon æðelinges est. *a* 1300 *Cursor M.* 15047 (Cott.) Þou tak to thanc þat we þe mak Sli mensking als we mai. *c* 1375 *Sc. Leg. Saints* vi. (*Thomas*) 12 Þat he in grete thank vil take, And als reward hym t[h]ankfully. *c* 1400 *Rom. Rose* 4577 He seyde, 'In thank I shal it take, And high maister eeke thee make'. *c* 1430 *Syr Gener.* (Roxb.) 9803 If I wist to thank ye wold it take, A mariage fayne wold I make. 1513 DOUGLAS *Æneis* VII. v. 153, I grant thine axing, Troiane messinger, And ȝour rewardis ressauis in thank.

**8.** *To can, con, cun* (*great, little*) *thank*(*s*, to acknowledge or express gratitude, to make known gratitude, to give thanks, to thank. *Obs.* exc. *dial.*

See CAN *v.*[1] 10, CON *v.*[1] 4.

† **9.** *To have* (or *get*) *thank*: to be thanked; also, to be thought worthy of thanks, to get the credit *for*, to have the merit or honour *of* (something); hence, contextually, *thank* = thanks due or merited, recompense, reward, credit, merit, and *ironically* discredit, blame. *Obs.*

*c* 950 *Lindisf. Gosp.* Luke xvii. 9 Ahne ðonc hafeð esne ðæm forðon dyde ða ðe him ȝehaten hæfde? *c* 1000 *Ags. Gosp.* ibid., Hæfð se þeowa æniȝne þanc forþam ðe he dyde þæt [etc.]? *c* 1020 *Rule St. Benet* v. (Logeman) 25 He for swylcere dæde æniȝne ne begitt þanc. *c* 1175 *Lamb. Hom.* 137 Þa ðe doð god for to habben ðer of aȝen in þisse liue, nabbeð heo nenne þonc on eche weorlde. 1297 R. GLOUC. (Rolls) 9915 Þe wrecche luþer giwes..a riche presant..sende þis noble kinge, ac hor þonc was lute. *a* 1300 *Cursor M.* 13841 Þar-for haf he neuer thank! *c* 1320 *Sir Tristr.* 2081 Maister, þank haue ȝe. For þou me þis bode brouȝt Mi robe ȝiue y þe. *c* 1385 CHAUCER *L. G. W.* 452 For who so yeveth a yifte or dooth a grace, Do it by tyme, his thank ys wel the more. *c* 1460 FORTESCUE *Abs. & Lim. Mon.* vii. (1885) 125 Off somme man [h]is highnes shall haue more thanke ffor money then ffor lande. 1483 *Cath. Angl.* 381/2 A Thanke, *meritum, emericio, emericium*. 1533 BELLENDEN *Livy* II. iv. (S.T.S.) I. 142 Thir twa lawis..war pronuncit allanerlie ..be auctorite of þe said valerius (þat he mycht þarethrow haue þe thank þareof). 1539 BIBLE (Great) *Luke* vi. 32 Yf ye loue them which loue you, what thanke haue ye? [so 1611, 1881; TINDALE, what thanke are ye worthy of? *Rhem.* what thanke is to you?]. 1545 ELYOT *Dict.* s.v. *Ineo*, *Gratiam inire*, to get thanke or frendes with some pleasure done vnto them. 1584 *Mirr. Mag.* 9 It is a work of more thanke to preserue health, then to cure Sicknesse. 1600 NASHE *Summers Last Will* Introd., He..must be making himselfe a publike laughing stock, & haue no thanke for his labor. 1633 BP. HALL *Hard Texts, N. T.* 4 The thanke of this is Gods, not yours. 1669 R. MONTAGU in *Buccleuch MSS.* (Hist. MSS. Comm.) I. 424 Lord Clarenden would have the thanks and credit of it.

**10.** *To give thanks* († *thank*, † *to do thank*(*s*), to express gratitude; *spec.* = 'to give thanks to God'; now esp. of saying grace at a meal. *arch.*

971 *Blickl. Hom.* 39 Don we..Drihtne þancas þe us þa wæstmas sealde. *Ibid.* 191 Þanc ic do, Crist þu ȝoda hyrde. *Ibid.* 217 He..Ælmihtiȝum Gode þære ȝife þanc sæȝde. 1477 EARL RIVERS (Caxton) *Dictes* 1 To gyue therfore synguler louynges & thankes. 1526 TINDALE *Matt.* xxvi. 26 Jesus toke breed, and gave thankes, brake it, and gave it to his disciples. 1596 SHAKS. *Tam. Shr.* IV. i. 162 Will you giue thankes, sweete Kate, or else shall I? 1765 T. HUTCHINSON *Hist. Mass.* I. 262 The general court..gave them thanks for their good services. 1808–18 JAMIESON s.v. *Grace-drink*, After the giving of thanks at the end of a meal. 1831 SCOTT *Ct. Robt.* ix, All gave me fair thanks for the knightly manner of quitting myself towards them, except one.

**11.** *To return thanks*, to render thanks in return for a benefit or favour. Now chiefly used of the formal or public expression of thanks, or of grace at a meal.

1591–1780 [see RETURN *v.* 20]. 1717 LADY M. W. MONTAGU *Let. to C'tess Mar* 18 Apr., I returned her thanks, and.. took my leave. 1827 *Edin. Weekly Jrnl.* 28 Feb., He begged leave to return thanks for the honour which had been conferred on the Patrons of this excellent Institution. 1849 C. BRONTE *Shirley* vii, 'Let us return thanks', said he; which he did forthwith, and all quitted the table.

**III. 12.** *attrib.* and *Comb.*, as *thank-receiver, thanks-prayer*; † *thank-picking, thanks-freighted* adjs.; † **thank-render**, a rendering of thanks, a thanksgiving; **thanks-day**, Thanksgiving Day (*U. S.*); **thanksdoing, thanks-living** (*nonce-wds.*, after *thanksgiving*), action or conduct indicative of a thankful spirit. See also THANK-OFFERING, THANKSGIVING, etc.

1633 FORD *Love's Sacr.* IV. i, Edged on by some *thank-picking parasite. 1786 COWPER *Let. to Lady Hesketh* 31 Jan., I will constitute you my *Thank-receiver-general for whatsoever gift I shall receive hereafter. 1548 GEST *Pr. Masse* in Dugdale *Life* (1840) App. I. 98 It is a forged worship and *thankerendre. 1696 W. BATES *Serm. Forgiveness* 123 Let our thanksgiving be joined with *thanksdoing. 1882 SPURGEON *Treas. Dav.* Ps. cxix. 65 We lose ourselves in adoring thanksgiving, and find ourselves again in careful *thanks-living. 1900 *Month* Feb. 133 Passages..which seem to have reference to this primitive *Thanksprayer.

**Thank** (þæŋk), *v.* Forms: *α.* 1–2 þancian, 2–3 þankien, 3–5 þanken, 4–6 thanken, 4–7 thanke, thanck, (4 þ-, thanc, 4–5 þanky, thange), 5– thank. *β.* 1 ðoncian, 2 þonkien, 3–5 þonke(n, (3 þonki, 4 þonkke), 4–6 thonk, (5–6 thong). [OE. *þancian, þoncian* = OS. *thankôn* (MDu., Du. *danken*), OHG. *dankôn* (MHG., G. *danken*), ON. *þakka* (Sw. *tacka*, Da. *takke*) :—OTeut. **þank-ôjan*, f. **þanko*[z] THANK *sb.*]

† **1.** *intr.* To give thanks. *Obs.* exc. as *absol.* of 3.

*c* 950 *Lindisf. Gosp.* Matt. xxvi 27, ȝenimmende calic ðoncunco dyde *vel* ðoncade & sealde him. *c* 975 *Rushw. Gosp.* ibid., ȝenom cælic þongade & salde heom. *c* 1000 *Ags. Gosp.* ibid., He ȝenam þone calic þanciende. *c* 1000 ÆLFRIC *Hom.* II. 400 Drihten ðancode ærðan ðe he ða hlafas tobræce. *c* 1290 *St. Brandan* 595 in *S. Eng. Leg.* 236 Iudas þonkede reufolliche. *c* 1500 *Melusine* xxxvi. 247 'Fayre lordes', said Geffray..that ought to be thanked for '[*indirect passive of* 'one ought to thank for that'].

† **2.** *intr.* in particular constructions. **a.** To give thanks *to* a person (orig. with simple *dative*, at length treated as *accusative*: see 3). *Obs.*

*c* 888 K. ÆLFRED *Boeth.* v. § 3 Ðonca nu Gode þæt he ðe ȝefultumade. *a* 1000 *Cædmon's Satan* 536 [Hi] þanceden þeodne, þæt hit þus ȝelomp. *c* 1000 *Ags. Gosp.* Luke xvii. 16 He..feoll to his foten & him þancode. *c* 1175 *Lamb. Hom.* 153, Iþonked wurðe him [Let it be thanked to him]. *a* 1450 *Le Morte Arth.* 1478 On knes Felle thay..And thankyd All to god. 1508 DUNBAR *Gold. Targe* 101 Syne to dame Flora..Thay saluse, and thay thank a thousand syse. 1542 UDALL *Erasm. Apoph.* 145 That persone, to whom onely..thou art bound to thanke.

† **b.** *of* (= on account of, for) a thing (orig. *genitive*): see c. *Obs.*

971 *Blickl. Hom.* 43 Ne sceal he..to lyt þancian heora ælmessan. *Ibid.* 203 Hie..þancudan þæs siȝes ðe hie ȝefered hæfdon.

† **c.** (combining a and b) to a person (*dative*), *of* a thing (orig. *genitive*), the dative (mostly a pronoun) passing into an accusative: the usual constr. in OE. and early ME.; passing into 3 b. *Obs.*

*Beowulf* 1397 Se gomela gode þancode.. þæs se man ȝespræc. *a* 1000 *Cædmon's Gen.* 257 (Gr.) He..sceolde his drihtne þancian þæs leanes. *c* 1000 ÆLFRIC *Saints' Lives* (1885) I. 104 Iulianus þa sona þæs þancode Gode. *c* 1175 *Lamb. Hom.* 39 Þet þu luuie þine drihten and him þonkien alles þinges. *c* 1200 *Vices & Virtues* 29 Þanke ðar-of ðine lauerde gode. *c* 1200 *Trin. Coll. Hom.* 197 Iob..þonkede him of þan wowe, alse dude ar of þe wele.

**3.** *trans.* To give thanks to; to express gratitude or obligation to. (Orig. *intr.* with *dat.*: see 2 a. By 1200 the *dat.* was treated as *acc.*, and might be subject of the passive voice.) Sometimes const. *that.*

*c* 1200 *Trin. Coll. Hom.* 3 Þanked be ure louerd ihesu crist. 1297 R. GLOUC. (Rolls) 1154 Vaire he þonkede is gode folc. *Ibid.* 9281 Ich þonke ȝou..Þat ȝe me so muche loue ssseweþ. *a* 1300 *Cursor M.* 3321 (Cott.) Thancand god, til erth he fell. *c* 1350 *Will. Palerne* 2794 Þat we so scaþli ar a-schaped god mowe [we] þonk. 1362 LANGL. *P. Pl.* A. XII. 48, I..þankede hure a þousand syþes. *c* 1420 *Chron. Vilod.* 461 Þey thongedone god and mournedone no more. 1537 WRIOTHESLEY *Chron.* (Camden) I. 67 The maior and aldermen riding about the cittie thancking the people. 1598 SHAKS. *Merry W.* I. i. 293, I had rather walke here (I thanke you). 1648 *Hamilton Papers* (Camden) 250 Powley is returned from London. He brings a most sleevles letter.. which signifyes nothing...Judge if I thanked him. *a* 1796 BURNS *Selkirk Grace*, We hae meat and we can eat, Sae let the Lord be thankit. 1818 SCOTT *Hrt. Midl.* xxxvii, That he has subjects in Scotland, I think he may thank God and his sword. 1841 LANE *Arab. Nts.* I. 114 The young prince kissed his hand and thanked him. 1906 *Outlook* 18 Sept. 346 He who solicits a favour by letter not infrequently concludes with the phrase, 'thanking you in anticipation', which came into vogue some ten years ago.

† **b.** Const. *of* a thing. *Obs.*

The continuation of 2 c; usual in ME.

*c* 1175 *Lamb. Hom.* 7 Ȝif we þonkiet ure drihten alles þinges þe he us sent. *c* 1230 *Hali Meid.* 19 To þonki godd of his grace & of his goddede. *a* 1300 *Cursor M.* 5304 Knele i sal befor þe king, And thank him of his grett mensking. *c* 1375 *Sc. Leg. Saints* v. (*Johannes*) 644 He..bad I suld..thange ȝou of ȝore gud vyl. *c* 1412 HOCCLEVE *De Reg. Princ.* 1062 God thanke alwey of thyne ese and of thyne smert. *a* 1533 LD. BERNERS *Huon* lxi. 212, I thanke you of your courtesye. *a* 1548 HALL *Chron., Edw. IV* 236 b, The Frenche kyng..thanked the kyng of Englande of his kynde offre.

**c.** Const. *for* a thing: now usual.

*a* 1591 H. SMITH *Serm.* (1637) 133 He is not thankfull before God, which thanks him only for his benefits. 1653 HOLCROFT *Procopius* I. 11 He thanckt the man much for his good will. 1715 DE FOE *Fam. Instruct.* I. i. (1841) I. 7 How must I thank him for it? 1764 GOLDSM. *Trav.* 72 And thanks his gods for all the good they gave. 1910 W. H. HUDSON *Introd. Study Lit.* Pref. 6, I have to thank my friend..for the invaluable assistance which..he has again rendered me.

**d.** *fig.* To make a return to a person in evidence of obligation or gratitude. (In quot. ironical.)

**1821** SCOTT *Kenilw.* xxvi, I were like to be thanked with a horse-whip.

**e.** In the future tense, used to express a request: *I will thank you to do so-and-so.*

**1843** THACKERAY *Ravenswing* vi, The page .. instantly thanked her to pay his wages. **1852** — *Esmond* III. v, I want to speak with your employer, Mr. Leach. I'll thank ye go fetch him. *Mod.* I will thank you to hand me my field-glass. I will thank you for a glass of water.

**f.** Phr. *To thank one for nothing*: esp. in (*I*) *Thank you for nothing*, an ironical expression indicating that the speaker thinks he has got or been offered nothing worth thanks.

**1703** MOXON *Mech. Exerc.* 60 But perhaps these Pretenders mean the Iron or Steel shall be as soft as Lead, when the Iron or Steel is red-hot; if so, we may thank them for nothing. **1712** ADDISON *Spect.* No. 391 ⁋ 3 Jupiter thanked him for nothing. **1754** FOOTE *Knights* I. Wks. 1799 I. 67 Part with Favourite! no, I thank you for nothing. **1848** [see THANK YOU].

**g.** Ejaculatory phrases, as *thank God* († *I thank God* (obs.), *God be thanked*, etc.), *thank goodness*, *thank heaven*. *To thank one's* (or *the*) *stars*, to congratulate oneself on one's good fortune: see STAR.

*c* **1330** R. BRUNNE *Chron.* (1810) 134 Þanked be God of heuen. **1340** *Ayenb.* 196 God be yhered and y-þonked. **1426** *Test. Ebor.* (Surtees) I. 76, I .. in gud mynd, thanket be God. *c* **1489** CAXTON *Sonnes of Aymon* xxiv. 530 Hole & sounde, thanked be god. **1530** PALSGR. 754/2, I am one of them, God be thanked! **1599** SHAKS. *Much Ado* III. v. 15 Yes I thank God, I am as honest as any man liuing, that is an old man, and no honester then I. **1796** MME. D'ARBLAY *Camilla* III. 99 Now .. I have not the gift of writing, at which, thank God, I have left off repining. **1811** L. M. HAWKINS *C'tess & Gertr.* III. 283, I was all that, thank goodness, as I always say, last grass. **1840** THACKERAY *Shabby-genteel Story* ii, I am here, thank Heaven, quite alone. **1872** [see GOODNESS 5].
**1614** B. JONSON *Barth. Fair* Induct., Yet I kept the Stage in Master Tarleton's time, I thanke my starres. **1730** FIELDING *Temple Beau* IV. iii, Sir Harry, you may thank your stars that conducted you to me. **1834** T. HAWKINS *Mem. Ichthyos. & Plesiosauri* 42 But I should .. thank the stars and the Cholera that it was no worse.

† **4.** With dative of person (indirect obj.) and accusative of thing (direct obj.): = 3 b or c. *Obs.* (Cf. TELL *v.* 3 (*a*).)

*c* **1175** *Lamb. Hom.* 5 We ahte to .. þonkien hit ure drihten þe hit us lende. *a* **1300** *Cursor M.* 16219 Herod thankes þe þi sand. **1362** LANGL. *P. Pl.* A. VII. 17 We haue no lymes to labore with; vr lord we hit þonken. *c* **1475** *Rauf Coilȝear* 271 Mair the King spak nocht, Bot thankit thame thair deid.

**b.** With the thing as sole obj.: To return thanks for, express one's gratitude for; to repay. *rare.*

*c* **1470** ASHBY *Dicta Philos.* 925 A goode man thanketh euery benefete, After the yeuers possibilite. **1818** BYRON *Mazeppa* xx, Charles forgot To thank his tale. **1819** — *Juan* I. cxii, His young lip thank'd it with a grateful kiss. **1867** MORRIS *Jason* XV. 226 And I am well aweary of it now, And of my toil, thanked with hard word and blow.

**5.** To give the thanks or credit *for* something to; to consider or hold responsible; esp. in ironical use, = to blame

**1560** DAUS tr. *Sleidane's Comm.* 189 Him that brought hym vp, and whome both he and his father may thanke for all theyr good fortune. **1667** MILTON *P. L.* X. 736 Who .. but .. will curse My Head, .. For this we may thank Adam; but his thanks Shall be the execration. **1794** MRS. RADCLIFFE *Myst. Udolpho* xxxi, She might thank herself for what happened. **1885** SIR N. LINDLEY in *Law Rep.* 14 Q.B.Div. 817 If .. any mistake was made by the sheriff, the defendant had only himself to thank for it.

**Thankee** (þæ·ŋki), vulgar colloq. for *thank ye*, THANK YOU. See 'EE.

**1824** in *Spirit Pub. Jrnls.* (1825) 302 My friends, the Yankees, For ten such plays, I guess, wouldn't give ten thankees. **1848** DICKENS *Dombey* xl, Thankee my Lady. Lord bless you, my Lady.

**Thanker** (þæ·ŋkəɹ). [f. THANK *v.* + -ER [1].] One who thanks.

*a* **1591** H. SMITH *Serm.* (1637) 132 Moe have gone away speeders, then have gone away thankers. **1800** COLERIDGE *Wallenstein* IV. ii. 111 The devil take such thankers! **1844** BROWNING *Colombe's Birthday* II, Stay, Sabyne; let me hasten to make sure Of one true thanker.

**Thankful** (þæ·ŋkfŭl), *a.* [f. THANK *sb.* + -FUL.]

**1.** Feeling or expressing thanks or gratitude; prompted by feelings of gratitude; grateful.

**971** *Blickl. Hom.* 169 Wesað þancfulle þon Hælende eoweres andleofan. **1500–20** DUNBAR *Poems* lxxvii. 72 Be thankfull to this burgh of Aberdein. **1535** COVERDALE 1 *Sam.* ii. Contents, The thankfull songe of Anna. **1592** SHAKS. *Rom. & Jul.* III. v. 149 Not proud you haue, But thankfull that you haue. **1685** DRYDEN *Thren. August.* 383 Live then, thou great encourager of arts: Live ever in our thankful hearts! **1748** BUTLER *Serm.* Wks. 1874 II. 317 The generality of mankind have cause to be thankful that their station exempts them from so great temptations. **1856** FROUDE *Hist. Eng.* I. v. 430 We have reason to be thankful that the thing, well or ill, was over.

† **b.** Satisfied, content. *Obs.*

*a* **900** tr. *Bæda's Hist.* v. xxii[i]. (1890) 478 Scottas .. wæron þoncfulle heora gemærum. *c* **1050** *Gloss.* in Wr.-Wülcker 367/18 *Contentus*, ðancful.

**c.** *fig.* Cf. GRATEFUL *a.* 2 b.

**1610** HOLLAND *Camden's Brit.* (1637) 273 The ground .. is thankefull to the husbandman, in so much as it doth affoord corne to be carried forth.

† **2.** Worthy or deserving of thanks, gratitude, or credit; pleasing, acceptable, grateful, agreeable.

*c* **1000** in *Anglia* (1890) XIII. 381 We halsiaþ .. god þæt þeow þin cync ure .. to þe .. þancfull he mæȝe becuman. *c* **1050** *Suppl. Ælfric's Voc.* in Wr.-Wülcker 191/15 *Gratiosus*, ðoncful. **1375** BARBOUR *Bruce* v. 278 He had done mony a thankfull deid. **1456** SIR G. HAYE *Law Arms* (S.T.S.) 68 Unrychtwis offerandis ar nocht acceptable na thankfull to his godhede. **1511** HEN. VIII *Let.* in Burton & Raine *Hemingbrough* 380 Wherby ye shall ministre unto us right singler and thankfull pleasore. **1552** HULOET, Thanckefull, *acceptus.* **1596** DALRYMPLE tr. *Leslie's Hist. Scot.* I. (S.T.S.) I. 130 The name of king was maist grate and thankful to thame al. **1611** TOURNEUR *Ath. Trag.* I. ii, His good successe shall be most thankeful to your trust.

† **b.** *Sc.* Of a payment: Giving satisfaction, satisfactory. *Obs.*

**1497** *Acc. Ld. High Treas. Scot.* I. 315, I resauit .. for the Erle Marschael his thankfull and reddy payment. **1527** *Caldwell Pap.* (Maitland) I. 61 Alslang and howlang ye said Johnne and his airs mak to me and my airs gud and thankful service. **1612** *Sc. Acts Jas. VI* (1816) IV. 472/1 To mak thame thankfull teynding. **1671** in *Proc. Soc. Ant. Scot.* (1892) XXVI. 194 To make tymeous and thankfull payment.

† **3.** ? Done without reward or payment; gratuitous: cf. next, 3. *Obs. rare.*

*c* **1380** WYCLIF *Serm.* Sel. Wks. I. 282 Þe fifte manere þat prestis shulden have shulde be þankful traveilinge; for ȝif þei wolen have þank of God, þei shulden here fle symonie, and neiþer sille her preching ne oþer workes þat þei done.

**Thankfully** (þæ·ŋkfŭli), *adv.* [f. prec. + -LY [2].] In a thankful manner.

**1.** With thankfulness; with thanks; gratefully.

*c* **1000** ÆLFRIC *Saints' Lives* (1890) II. 198 Þa onȝeat eustachius þæt seo fore-sæde costnung him ða æt wæs and þancfullice hi under-feng. *c* **1380** WYCLIF *Serm.* Sel. Wks. I. 130 Siþ Crist suffride þus for synne of his breþeren, þei schulden suffre þancfulli for þer own synne. **1567** *Triall Treas.* (1850) 18, I cannot but thankefully render Such commendations as is requisite to be. **1611** SHAKS. *Cymb.* I. vi. 79 Yet Heauen's bounty towards him might Be vs'd more thankfully. **1725** DE FOE *Voy. round World* (1840) 248 He accepted thankfully all my presents. **1875** JOWETT *Plato* (ed. 2) V. 365 We will desire the one to give their instructions freely, and the others to receive them thankfully.

† **b.** With satisfaction; graciously. *Obs.*

**1513** DOUGLAS *Æneis* I. ix. *heading*, How Eneas with all his rowt bedene War thankfullie ressavit of the quene. *a* **1578** LINDESAY (Pitscottie) *Chron. Scot.* (S.T.S.) I. 90 The king grantit the same verray thankfullie. **1597** A. M. tr. *Guillemeau's Fr. Chirurg.* *v, Receaue thankfully this my laboure.

† **2.** So as to gratify, please, or satisfy; acceptably, pleasingly; satisfactorily. *Obs.*

*c* **1375** *Sc. Leg. Saints* iii. (*Andreas*) 877 He liffit sa thankfully to god and mane. **1482** *Exch. Rolls Scotl.* IX. 284 *note*, That ye redily and thankfully content and pay to the said Johne .. the said yerely pensioun. **1500** *Ibid.* XI. 266 *note*, That ye cause hir to be thankfullie pait of hir said pension. **1538** ELYOT, *Placabiliter*, thankefully, contentfully. **1576** in *Maitl. Cl. Misc.* (1840) I. 16 The prices tharof salbe thankfullie allowit to ȝow in ȝour comptis.

† **3.** Gratuitously; for thanks alone. *Obs.*

**1552** HULOET, Thanckfully, or for nothynge, or without rewarde or deserte, but onelye for gramercye, *gratim.*

**Thankfulness** (þæ·ŋkfŭlnės). [f. as prec. + -NESS.] The quality or condition of being thankful.

**1.** Gratefulness, gratitude.

**1552** in *Vicary's Anat.* (1888) App. xvi. 291 Whiche thyng, with al due thanckefulnesse, thei receiued at his maiesties handes. **1611** BIBLE *Acts* xxiv. 3 Wee accept it alwayes .. with all thankfulnesse. **1741** RICHARDSON *Pamela* II. 158 O how shall I find Words to express my Thankfulness! **1856** FROUDE *Hist. Eng.* I. v. 361 Such a resolution would probably have been welcomed with passionate thankfulness.

† **b.** Contextually: Thanks. *Obs. rare.*

**1647** MAY *Hist. Parl.* I. ix. 104 The Scottish Commissioners .. returned thankfulnesse to the Parliament .. for that great sum of 300000*l.*

† **2.** Gratification, satisfaction. *Obs. rare.*

**1500** *Reg. Privy Seal Scotl.* I. 70 The hartlie lufe .. he has and beris to the said Jonet, and .. the thankfulnes done be hir oft tymes to his grace.

**Thanking** (þæ·ŋkiŋ), *vbl. sb. arch.* [f. THANK *v.* + -ING [1].] The action or an act of giving thanks; the expression of gratitude; thanks.

*c* **893** K. ÆLFRED *Oros.* I. iv. [viii.] § 2 To wundrianne þæt þa Egipti swa lytle þoncunge wiston Iosepe. *c* **950** *Lindisf. Gosp.* John vi. 23 Ðoncunge dedon Drihtne. *c* **1000** ÆLFRIC *Hom.* II. 170 He underfeng ða lac mid ðancunge. **1382** WYCLIF *Matt.* xxvi. 27 He takynge the cuppe, dede thankyngis. *c* **1420–30** *Prymer* (1895) 51 Whanne þei ben hool, þei moun ȝelde þankyngis to þee in þi chirche. **1508** BP. FISHER 7 *Penit. Ps.* cii. Wks. (1876) 190 Gyuynge thankynges vnto hym. **1611** SHAKS. *Cymb.* v. v. 407 He would haue well becom'd this place, and grac'd The thankings of a King. **1851** MRS. BROWNING *Casa Guidi W.* I. 239 We thank you that ye first unlatched the door, But will not make it inaccessible By thankings on the threshold.

**Tha·nkless,** *a.* [f. THANK *sb.* + -LESS.]

**1.** Not moved by or expressing gratitude; unthankful, ungrateful. Also *fig.* of things: Making no return, unresponsive.

**1536** LYNDESAY *Answ. Kingis Flyting* 33 Full sair I rew That euer I did Mouth thankles so persew. *c* **1560** A. SCOTT *Poems* (S.T.S.) v. 65. **1598** MARSTON *Sco. Villanie* III. ix, All as thanklesse as ungratefull Thames He slinks away, leauing but reeking steames Of dungy slime behinde. **1637** MILTON *Lycidas* 66 And strictly meditate the thankles Muse. **1792** COWPER *Stanzas Bill Mortality* 1 Thankless for favours from on high. **1865** DICKENS *Mut. Fr.* I. i, How can you be so thankless to your best friend?

**2.** Of a task, or the like: Which brings no thanks; receiving or deserving no thanks.

*a* **1547** SURREY *Æneid* II. 125 But whereunto these thanklesse tales in vaine Do I reherse? **1591** SAVILE *Tacitus' Hist.* II. lix. 88 A thancklesse office and displeasing. **1690** NORRIS *Beatitudes* (1694) I. 178 Not only a thankless, but an odious, difficult and hazardous Undertaking. **1868** MISS BRADDON *Dead-Sea Fr.* i, It is but a thankless task to catalogue such a face.

**3.** Without thanks; unthanked. *rare.*

**1638** SIR T. HERBERT *Trav.* (ed. 2) 168 The Ambassador had no patience to digest it, save by equall contempt to .. send him thanklesse back againe. **1897** *Westm. Gaz.* 22 Feb. 2/1 Prince Max comes to the Court of Ferdinand to return, thankless, a picture painted by Ferdinand.

**Tha·nklessly,** *adv.* [f. prec. + -LY [2].] In a thankless manner; without thanks; unthankfully.

**1626** BP. HALL *Contempl., O. T.* xx. ii, The will of God may be done thanklessly. **1881** in Spurgeon *Treas. Dav.* Ps. cxix. 75 Thanklessly receiving the gifts with no thought of the Giver.

**Tha·nklessness.** [f. as prec. + -NESS.] The quality or condition of being thankless; ungratefulness, unthankfulness.

**1583** GOLDING *Calvin on Deut.* vii. 41 Were it not too shamefull a thankelesnesse in vs if wee shoulde not bee [etc.]. **1628** WITHER *Brit. Rememb.* IV. 404 Thy thanklesnesse, And such like Sinnes. **1840** L. HUNT *Legend of Florence* I. ii, Friendship ends, In treachery and in thanklessness begun. **1860** PUSEY *Min. Proph.* 273 Thanklessness shuts the door to God's personal mercies to us.

† **Tha·nklewe,** *a. Obs. rare.* [f. THANK *sb.* + -LEWE.] ? Deserving of thanks, thankworthy; or ? grateful, agreeable.

**1430** in Sharpe *Lond. & Kingd.* (1895) III. 374 In perfourming at þis tyme of our prayer ye may do unto us soo notable and þanklewe service þat we wol wel considre hit in tyme comyng.

† **Tha·nkly,** *adv. Obs. rare*[−1]. [irreg. f. THANK *sb.* + -LY [2].] Thankfully.

**1591** SYLVESTER *Du Bartas* I. iii. 809 He giueth frankly what we thankly spend.

**Tha·nk-o:ffering.** [f. THANK *sb.* + OFFERING *vbl. sb.*] In the Levitical law, An offering presented as an expression of gratitude to God; hence in ordinary use, An offering or gift made by way of thanks or acknowledgement.

**1530** TINDALE *Lev.* vii. 12 Yf he offer to geue thanckes, he shall brynge vnto his thanckofferynge [**1560** (*Genev.*) for his thankes offring] swete cakes myngled with oyle. **1539** BIBLE (Great) 2 *Chron.* xxxiii. 16 He .. sacrificed theron peace offerynges, & thank offerynges. **1839** THIRLWALL *Greece* VI. xlix. 171 He dedicated the waggon in the citadel, as a thank-offering to the king of the gods. **1888** BURGON *Lives 12 Gd. Men* I. i. 45 He sent at once a thank-offering for distribution among the poor.

† **Tha·nksgive,** *v. Obs. rare*[−1]. [Back-formation from THANKSGIVING.] *trans.* To give thanks for.

*a* **1638** MEDE *Diatribe* (1642) 55 Irenæus also affirmeth, That our Saviour, by the institution of the Eucharist had confirmed oblations in the New Testament. Namely, to thanksgive or blesse a thing in way to a sacred use, he took to be an offering of it unto God.

**Tha·nksgi:ver.** [f. as next + GIVER.] One who gives thanks.

**1621** AINSWORTH *Annot. Song Sol.* i. 3 Thankesgivings, in Nehem. 12. 31 [are] for companies of thankesgivers. **1690** C. NESSE *O. & N. Test.* I. 71 The life of thanksgiving is the good life of the thanks-giver. **1818** BENTHAM *Ch. Eng.* 123 Exhausted by that same grand effort, the stock of thanksgivers is gone. **1883** J. PARKER *Tyne Chylde* 270 Thankfulness elevates and ennobles the thanksgiver.

**Thanksgiving** (þæ·ŋksˌgi·viŋ). [f. *thanks*, pl. of THANK *sb.* + GIVING *vbl. sb.*]

**1.** The giving of thanks; the expression of thankfulness or gratitude; *esp.* the act of giving thanks to God.

**1533** TINDALE *Supper of Lord* E iv b, One or other Psalme or prayer of thankes giuyng in the mother tongue. **1539** BIBLE (Great) 1 *Tim.* iv. 4 For all the creatures of God are good, and nothing to be refused, yf it be receaued with thankesgeuynge. **1562** WINȜET *Cert. Tract.* iii. Wks. (S.T.S.) I. 29 Gyf sic zeirlie memorial in blythnes and thankisgeifing wes haldin. **1588** SHAKS. *L. L. L.* II. i. 193, I cannot stay thanks-giuing. **1658** *Whole Duty Man* v. § 8 The fifth part of prayer is thanksgiving; that is, the praising and blessing God for all his mercies. **1842** MISS MITFORD in L'Estrange *Life* (1870) III. ix. 159 Think how full of thanksgiving were my prayers last night.

**b.** A public celebration, with religious services, held as a solemn acknowledgement of Divine favours; also, a day set apart for this purpose; *spec.* in *U. S.*, Thanksgiving Day (see 3 b).

**1641** *Nicholas Papers* (Camden) 10 It was resolved that there shalbe on yᵉ 7ᵗʰ of September next a publique thanksgiving for this good accord betweene yᵉ 2 nacions. **1665** MANLEY *Grotius' Low C. Warres* 217 Publick Thanksgivings were Ordered to be given to God for this Victory. **1760** J. ADAMS *Diary* 26 Nov., Night before Thanksgiving. **1869** MRS. STOWE *Oldtown Folks* xxvii, Great as the preparations were for the dinner, everything was so contrived that not a soul in the house should be kept from the morning service of Thanksgiving.

**2.** An act or expression of thanks; *esp.* a form of words, a prayer or religious service used to render thanks for Divine benefits.

*General Thanksgiving*, the first of the forms of thanksgiving in the Book of Common Prayer, that for the blessings of life in general. *Great Thanksgiving*, in early and oriental liturgies: see quot. 1708–22.

**1535** COVERDALE *Ps.* xxxix. [xl.] 3 He hath put a new songe in my mouth, euen a thankesgeuynge vnto oure God. **1552** *Bk. Com. Prayer* (*heading*), The Thankes geuing of Women after Childe birth. **1662** *Ibid.*, Prayers & Thanksgivings upon several occasions ... A General Thanksgiving. **1708–22**

J. Bingham *Chr. Antiq.* xv. iii. (1845) 770 After this the priest went on with the εὐχαριστία properly so called, that is the great thanksgiving to God for all his mercies, both of creation, providence and redemption. **1849** Macaulay *Hist. Eng.* ii. I. 185 The ministers selected from that liturgy such prayers and thanksgivings as were likely to be least offensive to the people.

**3.** *attrib.* and *Comb.*

**1641** Evelyn *Diary* Aug., The next Sunday was the thanksgiving sermons perform'd in Col. Goreing's Regiment. **1814** Southey *Carmen Triumph.* xvi, With one consent, The high thanksgiving strain to heaven is sent,..Glory to God! Deliverance for Mankind! *a* **1859** Macaulay *Hist. Eng.* xxiii. (1861) V. 17 They had still in their ears the thanksgiving sermons and thanksgiving anthems.

**b. Thanksgiving day**, a day set apart for public thanksgiving for Divine goodness; *spec.* in the United States, an annual festival religious and social, now appointed by proclamation and held on the last Thursday of November.

The first celebration was held by the Plymouth colony in 1621, in thankfulness for their first harvest in America after a year of struggle and privation, and the usage became general in New England. After the Revolution, it extended to the Middle States, and later to the West; after the Civil War gradually to the South. Its national observance has been annually recommended by the President since 1863.

**1674** Josselyn *Voy. New Eng.* 214 Towards night I returned to Boston again, the next day being Thanksgiving day, on Fryday the Tenth day we weighed Anchor. **1704** Luttrell *Brief Rel.* (1857) V. 460 Sir Christopher Wrenn is erecting a throne in St. Pauls cathedral for her majestie to sitt in on the thanksgiving day. **1714** S. Sewall *Diary* 25 Nov., Thanks-giving day; very cold. **1844** Whittier *Pumpkin* iii, Ah! on Thanksgiving day..When the gray-haired New Englander sees round his board The old broken links of affection restored. **1903** *Daily Chron.* 6 Nov. 5/1 Thanksgiving Day long remained an institution peculiar to New England, but it has been observed annually in New York State since 1817.

† **Tha·nkworth,** *a. Obs.* [f. Thank *sb.* + Worth *a.*] = next.

? **1426** *Lett. Marg. Anjou & Bp. Beckington* (Camden) 33, I quyte me soo to yow in that matere,..as were thanke worth. **1550** Coverdale *Spir. Perle* Pref. 1 b, The more daungerous be his sores and sicknes, and the more thancke worth the cure therof. **1627–47** Feltham *Resolves* 30 To trust him for an estate when we have the evidences in our iron chest, is easie; and not thankeworth.

**Tha·nkwo·rthy,** *a.* Also 6–7 **thanks-**. Worthy of thanks; deserving gratitude or credit.

**1387–8** T. Usk *Test. Love* Prol. (Skeat) l. 39 Although this booke be lytel thank worthy for the leudnesse in trauail. **1421** Sir H. Luttrell in Ellis *Orig. Lett.* Ser. ii. I. 86 Wherfore..he ys thankworthy. **1533** J. Heywood *Play Weather* (1903) 1125 Thy labour is ryght myche thankeworthy. **1534** Tindale 1 *Pet.* ii. 19 For it is thankeworthye yf a man for conscience towarde god endure grefe, sufferinge wrongfully. **1594** Carew *Huarte's Exam. Wits* xiii. (1596) 202 No lesse thanks-worthie a part of Seruice. **1672** Wilkins *Nat. Relig.* 31 It would not be thank-worthy for a man to believe that which of necessity he must believe. **1891** T. K. Cheyne *Orig. Psalter* Introd. 17 A faulty but at that time thankworthy book.

Hence **Tha·nkwo·rthily** *adv.*, in a thankworthy manner; **Tha·nkwo·rthiness,** the quality or condition of being thankworthy.

**1553** Bale *Gardiner's De vera Obed.* C vij, To exercise our selues godly and *thankeworthyly. **1874** Swinburne *Bothwell* i. i. 7 And we that do it, we do it for all men's good, For the main people's love, thankworthily. **1847** Webster, **Thank-worthiness*.

**Tha·nk you.** [Aphetic for *I thank you.*] A phrase used in courteous acknowledgement of a favour or service. *Thank you for nothing*: see Thank *v.* 3 f. So, rarely, **Thank thee.** Cf. Thankee.

**14..** *Why I can't be a Nun* 159 in *E. E. P.* (1862) 142 'Thanke yow, lady', quod I than. **1616** B. Jonson *Devil an Ass* iv. ii, *Eith.* Thanke you good Madame...Thanke thee, good Eyther-side. **1705** Vanbrugh *Confed.* i. i, Thank you kindly, Mrs. Amlet, thank you kindly. **1738** Swift *Pol. Conversat.* ii. 140 No, thank ye, Colonel. **1848** Thackeray *Van. Fair* xxiv, It's you who want to introduce beggars into my family? Thank you for nothing, Captain. **1862** Miss Yonge *C'tess Kate* ii. 24 She..said something meant for 'No, thank you'; but of which nothing was to be heard but 'q' [*i.e.* ——k you]. **1875** Jowett *Plato* (ed. 2) III. 206 [He] goes about learning of others, to whom he never even says Thank you.

**b.** as *sb.* (written with hyphen or as one word): An utterance of this phrase.

**1887** *Chr. World* 4 Aug. 589 He utters a hearty 'Thank-you!' **1894** *Westm. Gaz.* 21 Aug. 3/3 The majority of passengers retreated from the tables regardless of their running fire of 'thankyous', which were thankyous for nothing. **1900** *Ibid.* 6 Sept. 2/1 We had not said nearly enough 'thank-yous'.

**Thank-you-ma'am.** *U.S. colloq.* Also thank'ee-marm. A hollow or ridge in a road, which causes persons passing over it in a vehicle to nod the head involuntarily, as if in acknowledgement of a favour; *spec.* a ridge or hollow on a hill road serving to throw off descending rain-water.

**1849** Longf. *Kavanagh* xi, We went like the wind over the hollows in the snow;—the driver called them 'thank-you-ma'ams', because they made everybody bow. **1867** O. W. Holmes *Guard. Angel* xiv, Life's a road that's got a good many thank-you-ma'ams to go bumpin' over, says he. **1897** Howells *Landl. Lion's Head* 192 At one of the thank-you-marms in the road, the sick man stopped, like a weary horse, to breathe.

**Thanna(h,** var. Tana [1], Indian police station.

**Thanne, þanne,** obs. ff. Than, Then.

† **Tha·nnic,** *a. Chem. Obs.* [f. *Thann* (name of a town in the Vosges where Kestner the discoverer lived) + -ic.] In *thannic acid*: see quot.

**1853** *Pharmac. Jrnl.* XIII. 110 Racemic acid was..discovered by Kestner,..in the year 1820. It was called thannic acid by its discoverer.

**Thape,** dial. var. *fape*: see Feaberry, gooseberry.

‖ **Thapsia** (þæ·psiă). *Bot.* Also 4–6 **tapsia.** [L. *thapsia* (*tapsia*), a. Gr. θαψία, said to mean a plant brought from Thapsus.] A genus of umbelliferous perennials, of the tribe *Laserpitieæ*, containing four species, natives of the Mediterranean region. That formerly in medical repute is *T. garganica*, also called Deadly Carrot.

*c* **1400** *Lanfranc's Cirurgie* 195 Þe place shal be frotid in þe sunne wiþ an oynement of tapsia. *c* **1440** *Pallad. on Husb.* i. 1044 This tapsia, this wermot, and eleure, Cucumber wilde, and euery bitter kynde Of herbe is nought for hem. **1578** Lyte *Dodoens* iii. xxiv. 365 The barke of the roote of Thapsia. **1586** *Rates of Custome* E viij, Tapsia the pound xij.d. **1857** Dunglison *Med. Lex.*, *Thapsia*... The root operates violently, both upwards and downwards.

**b.** *attrib.* and *Comb.*, as *thapsia-plaster* (*Cent. Dict.* 1890), *-resin* (see quot.), *-root*.

**1890** Billings *Nat. Med. Dict.*, *Thapsia resin*, a soft extract prepared by digesting thapsia-root in hot alcohol.

‖ **Thapsus** (þæ·psŏs). *Bot.* Also 4–5 (8) **tapsus,** 8 **thapsos.** [med.L., a. Gr. θάψος a plant used for dyeing yellow (Dioscor.).] An old name of the genus *Verbascum*, esp. of *V. Thapsus*, the great mullein.

*a* **1387** *Sinon. Barthol.* 41/2 *Tapsus barbastus*, flosmus idem. **1578** Lyte *Dodoens* i. lxxxi. 119 Mulleyn is called ..in Shoppes *Tapsus Barbatus*. **1718** Rowe tr. *Lucan* ix. 1566 The Gummy Larch-Tree and the Thapsos there, Wound-wort and Maiden-weed perfume the Air.

‖ **Thar** (tʰār), *sb. Zool.* [Native name.]

**1.** The native name in Nepāl of a goat-antelope, *Nemorhædus bubalina*, belonging to the same genus as the Goral (*N. goral*).

**1833** B. H. Hodgson in *Proc. Zool. Soc.* 10 Sept. 105 As compared with the Ghōrâl, *Antilope Goral*, Hardw...the Thâr is a massive beast, twice the size, and has suborbital sinuses, and a mane along the back of the neck and shoulders. *Ibid.* 24 Sept. 111 A cavity also exists in the osseous core of the horns of the Thâr Antelope. **1834** *Ibid.* 12 Aug. 86. **1834** *Penny Cycl.* II. 89/2 The Thar (*A. thar*, Hodgson) was described for the first time in a paper by B. H. Hodgson, Esq., British resident in Nepaul...The thar inhabits the central region of Nepaul. **1885** *Cycl. India* III. 885/1 Thar, the forest goat, is the Nepal name of *Nemorhædus bubalina*, called Eimu and Ramu on the Sutlej and Kashmir, and Serow in the hills generally.

**2.** Also applied to the Tehr, or Himalayan wild goat (*Hemitragus jemlaicus*).

**1896** *List Anim. Zool. Soc.* 166 *Hemitragus jemlaicus* (Hodgs.) Thar. **1902** Webber *Forests Upper India* vi. 52 *Hemitragus jemlaicus* is a true wild goat, here called 'thar' by the natives...The thar is gregarious. **1902** Lydekker in *Encycl. Brit.* XXXIII. 939/1 The discovery of a species of thar (*Hemitragus*) in southern Arabia. **1903** *Spectator* 4 Apr. 527/2 Open and high ground..more suitable for wild sheep, such as the thar.

† **Thar,** *v. Obs.*: see Tharf.

**Thar** (ðar, þar), ME., chiefly northern, form of There. Also in compounds, as *ðar abutan*, etc.: see Thereabout and other words to Therewith.

**Thar, thare,** obs. ff. Their; var. Thir *Obs.*, these; obs. gen. and dat. sing. fem. and gen. pl. of The; 3 sing. and pl. pres. indic. of Tharf *v. Obs.*

**Tharandite** (tæ·rændəit). *Min.* [a. Ger. *tharandit* (Freiesleben, 1817), f. Tharandt in Saxony (where it occurs) + -ite [1].] A variety of dolomite occurring in greenish yellow crystals, containing a small percentage of ferrous oxide.

**1850** Ansted *Elem. Geol., Min.* etc. § 385. **1868** Dana *Min.* 682 Tharandite, from Tharand, near Dresden, is crystallized, and contains 4 p.c. of Fe.

**Tharatour,** *Sc.*: see Thereatour.

**Tharborough,** corrupt form of Thirdborough.

**Thar-, tharck-cake**: see Tharf-cake.

**Thare,** obs. f. Tare *sb.* [1]; also of There.

† **Tharf,** *sb. Obs.* Also 1 **þearf, ðærf,** 2 **þerf,** 3 (*Orm.*) **þarrfe.** [f. Tharf *v.* Cf. OS. *tharf*, OHG. *darba*, ON. *þorf.*] Need, necessity.

*Beowulf* 1798 Sele-þeᵹn..se for andrysnum ealle beweotede þeᵹnes þearfe. **735** Bæda *Death-song* 2 Thonc snotturra than him tharf sie. *c* **1000** *Sax. Leechd.* II. 84 ᵹif þearf sie, sele hwilum wyrtdrenc. *c* **1175** *Lamb. Hom.* 9 Nis hit nan þerf þet me her on þisse liue for his saule bidde pater noster. *c* **1200** Ormin 12247 Onn alle þa þatt haffdenn ned & þarrfe to þin hellpe. *c* **1330** *Arth. & Merl.* 16 And wele ysen, ʒif þai willen, Þat hem no þarf neuer spillen.

**Tharf,** *a. Obs.* or *dial.* Forms: 1 **þeorf, þearf,** (**ðorof, ðærf**), 3 (*Orm.*) **þeorrf,** 4 **þerf, -e,** 4–5 **therf,** 5 **tharf, -e.** See also Tharf-cake. [OE. *þeorf* (:—*þerf*), unleavened, unsoured; of milk, sweet; Com. Teut. = OFris. *therf, derf*, MDu. *derf* (Kilian has '*derf-brood*, panis azymus'), OHG., MHG. *derp* unleavened, Ger. *derb* solid, compact, rough, coarse, ON. *þjarfr* unleavened, insipid. With sense 2, cf. the mod. Ger. sense of *derb*; app. referring to the solid, heavy, or stiff quality of unleavened bread. Pre-Teut. etymology unknown.]

† **1.** Of bread, etc.: Not prepared with leaven, unleavened. *Obs.* exc. in Tharf-cake.

*c* **950** *Lindisf. Gosp.* Matt. xxvi. 17 Ða forma uutedlice doeᵹe ðara ðorofra [*Rushw.* ðefra *for* ðerfa] mæta. *c* **1000** Ælfric *Hom.* II. 210 Þeorfe hlafas we bringað Gode to lace. *c* **1000** — *Exod.* xii. 39 Hi..worhton þeorfe heorþbacene hlafas. *c* **1000** Ælfric *Voc.* in Wr.-Wülcker 153/32 *Azimus*, ðeorf. *c* **1200** Ormin 997 Bræd All þeorrf wiþþutenn berrme. *a* **1300** *Cursor M.* 6079 Wit therf bred and letus wild. **1382** Wyclif *Gen.* xix. 3 He made a feest, sethede therf breed, and thei eten. — *Mark* xiv. 1 Pask and the feeste of therf looues was aftir the secunde day. *c* **1400** Maundev. (Roxb.) iii. 10 Þai say we erre þat makes þe sacrement of tharf breed. *c* **1425** *Voc.* in Wr.-Wülcker 657/30 *Panis siliginius*, tharf-bred. *c* **1440** *Promp. Parv.* 490/2 Therf, wythe owte sowre dowe. **1483** *Cath. Angl.* 381/2 Tharfe, *azimus*.

**2.** *transf.* Lumpish, stiff, heavy, slow; hence *fig.* reluctant, unwilling, diffident, tardy. *dial.* Hence **Tha·rfish** *a.* in same sense; **Tha·rfly** *adv.*, in a tharf or tharfish manner.

**1747** Hooson *Miner's Dict.*, *Tharf* [is] when a Vein or Pipe alters from its own intrinsical Nature to another, that is more Hask, Barren, and Dry, and more bound up, and stiff. **1828** *Craven Gloss.*, *Tharf*, stark, stiff, metaphorically, backward, unwilling. **1876** *Mid-Yorks. Gloss.*, *Tharf*,... *Thauf*, diffident; unwilling; reluctant; tardy...Also *tharfish* adj., and *tharfly* adv. **1876** *Whitby Gloss.*, *Tharf, Tharfish*, shy, diffident. *Tharfly*, slowly. 'The rain comes nobbut tharfly'. **1894** *Northumbld. Gloss.*, *Tharf, Tharfish*, lumpish, heavy-countenanced, forbidding. Applied to substances it means 'sad', heavy, like liver in texture. *Tharfly*, slowly, reluctantly.

† **Tharf, thar,** *v. Obs.* exc. *Sc. dial.* Forms: see below. [A Com. Teutonic verb, belonging to the class of preterite-presents, in which the present tense is an original preterite (cf. Can, Dow, Dare, etc.): OE. **þurfan*, pres. *þearf—þurfon*, pa. *þorfte*, = OFris. **thurva*, *thurf*(*thorf*)—*thurvon*, OS. *thurƀan*, *tharf—thurƀun*, *thorfta*, MDu. *dorven*, *dorfte* (Du. *durven*), ON. *þurfa*, *þarf—þurfom*, *þurfta* (Sw. *tarfva*), OHG. *durfan*, *darf—durfun*, *dorfta* (MHG. *durfen*, G. *dürfen*), Goth. **þaurban*, *þarf—þaurbum*, *þaurfta*:—OTeut. **þarf-*, **þurƀ-*; corresp. to a pre-Teut. ablaut series **terp-*, **torp-*, **trp-*, which has not been certainly identified. The ME. β-forms had lost the *f* or *v*, app. first in the 2nd sing. present *þearft*, *þeart-tu*, *þer-tu*, leaving a stem *þar-*, *þer-*, *þor-*, *þur-*, which was afterwards often confused with the *dar-*, *dor-*, *dur-* of Dare *v.* [1], so that the latter had forms in *th*, while there are here forms in *d*, esp. in the 2nd and 3rd person singular of the present: see γ. This confusion of *tharf* and *dare* is also found in the cognate languages: see Dare *v.* [1]]

**A.** Inflexions.

**1.** *Pres. Indic.* **a.** 1*st sing.* 1 **þearf.**

*Beowulf* 2007 Ic þæt eall ᵹe-wræc swa..[ne] ᵹylpan þearf grendeles maᵹa. *a* **1000** *Cædmon's Gen.* 2176 (Gr.) Ne þearf ic yrfestol eaforan bytlian.

**b.** 2*nd sing.* **a.** 1 **þearft,** 2 **þerft,** (3 **þerf**).

*Beowulf* 1675 Þæt þu him on-drædan ne þearft. *c* **1000** *Sax. Leechd.* II. 180 Ne þearft þu þone wermod to don. *c* **1175** *Lamb. Hom.* 37 Soðliche ne þerft þu bidden namare. *a* **1225** *Leg. Kath.* 1160 Þu wenest ʒet þæt tu wenen ne þerf.

β. 3 **þært, þert, þer(tu),** 3–4 **þers(tou),** 4 **þertes-(tow),** 4–5 **tharst,** 5 **thar, thare.**

*c* **1205** Lay. 14482 Ne þært [*MS.* þræt] þu nauere habben kare of uncuðe leoden. *a* **1225** *Ancr. R.* 136 Ne þer tu nout dreden þe attrie neddre of helle. *c* **1300** *St. Brandan* 626 Ne therstou nothing drede. *c* **1330** R. Brunne *Chron. Wace* (Rolls) 4877 Of Kent ne þertestow fle þat cost. **1390** Gower *Conf.* II. 61 Me semeth that thou tharst noght care. *a* **1450** *Le Morte Arth.* 3285 Othure warke thou thare not wene. *c* **1460** *Towneley Myst.* ii. 293 Thar thou nowther flyte ne chyde.

γ. 3 **dert,** 4 **dars(tou, -tow).**

*c* **1205** Lay. 22923 Ne dert [*c* 1275 þert] þu nauere adrede. *c* **1320** *Cast. Love* 975 Ne darstou on erþe þenchen elles nouht. **1377** Langl. *P. Pl.* B. xiv. 55 Bi so þat þow be sobre..Darstow [*v.r.* Tharst þow, Thardestow] neuere care for corne, ne lynnen cloth ne wollen.

**c.** 3*rd sing.* **a.** 1 **ðearf, þearf** (**ðorfæð, -eð**), 2 **þerf,** 3 (*Orm.*) **þarrf,** 3–4 **þarf,** 4 **tharf.**

*c* **888** K. Ælfred *Boeth.* xxiv. § 4 Ne ðearf he nanes þinges. *c* **950** *Lindisf. Gosp.* John xiii. 10 Seðe ᵹeðuæn is ne ðorfæð [*c* **975** *Rushw.* ðorfeð] þætte aðoa hine. *c* **975** *Rushw. Gosp.* Matt. xxi. 3 Sæcgaþ þæt dryhten heora ðearf. *c* **1175** *Lamb. Hom.* 9 Nu ne þerf na mon his sunne mid wite abuggen. *a* **1250** *Prov. Ælfred* 161 in *O. E. Misc.* 113 Monymon weneþ þat he wene ne þarf longes lyues. *c* **1330** *Amis & Amil.* 935 Tharf the neuer haue of him drede.

β. 3 **þerh,** 4 (**tar**), **thars,** 4–5 **þar, thar, þare, thare, there,** 5 **tharre, tharth,** 9 *Sc. dial.* **ther.**

*a* **1300** *Cursor M.* 13554 Fra nu thar him namar be ledd. *Ibid.* 19870 (Edin.) Þat to do þare þe nochte lete. **1340** Hampole *Pr. Consc.* 2167 He þat hates þis lyfes lykyng Thar noght drede þe dedes commyng. ? **1370** *Robt. Cicyle* 325 More then thars be an c. folde. *a* **1400–50** *Alexander* 5377 Þe thare bot graunt me to geue quat guds as I craue. **1414** Brampton *Penit. Ps.* (Percy Soc.) 45 Me thar no more but aske and have. *c* **1425** *Cursor M.* 10565 (Laud) For to aske there no man Yf they were glad & ioyfull þan. *c* **1475** Tharth [see B. 2].

γ. 3 **derf,** 3–4 **darf,** 4 **darh,** 4–5 **dar, dare.**

*a* **1240** *Ureisun* in *Cott. Hom.* 187 Hwa derf beon unsauuet þe haueþ se mihti salue. **1297** R. Glouc. (Rolls) 6471 Me ne dar noʒt esse weþer he were kene þo & prout. *a* **1300** *Floriz & Bl.* 315 Ich wene ne darf me axi noʒt. *c* **1320** *Cast. Love* 733 Ne dar he seche non oþer leche. *a* **1327** *Pol. Songs* (Camden) 250 Of gode knyhtes darh him nout fail. *c* **1425** *Cursor M.* 10461 (Laud) To myrthe me dare [*early MSS.* þar] the not wene. *c* **1440** *Sir Gowther* 615 The dare not drede of thi werkys wyld.

**d.** *plural.* *a.* 1 **þurfon, ðurfan,** 1–3 **þurfe,** 3 **þurven (-uen), þorhfe, þurve, þorve.**

*c* 888 K. ÆLFRED *Boeth.* xiv. § 2 Þa ðurfon swiþe lytles, ðe maran ne willniað þonne ʒenoʒes. *Ibid.* xxiv. § 4 Hwæt þurfon [*v.r.* þurfe] we nu ma..sprecan? *c* **975** *Rushw. Gosp.* Matt. xxvi. 65 Hwæt þurfe we leng ʒewitnisse? *c* **1205** LAY. 24909 We ne þuruen [*c* **1275** þorhfe] na mare aswunden liggen here. *a* **1225** *Ancr. R.* 6. *c* **1290** *S. Eng. Leg.* I. 106/160 ȝe þorue [*Harl. MS.* þore] habbe of heom no kare.

*β.* 3 **þore,** 4 **thore,** 4–5 **thar,** 5 *Sc.* **thair.**

*c* **1290** *St. Brandan* 121 in *S. Eng. Leg.* I. 223 ȝe ne þore noþing drede. *c* **1386** CHAUCER *Melib.* ¶ 102 Yet thar ye nat accomplice thilke ordinance but yow like. *c* **1430** *Syr Gener.* (Roxb.) 6868 Ye thar not drede of hem y-wis. **1438** *Bk. Alex. Grt.* (Bann.) 9 ȝe thair nocht dreid na chaissing. *c* **1485** *Digby Myst.* III. 1437 Of þis cors we thar nat a-baffe. **1825** Thair [see B. 1].

*γ.* 4 **dorre, durre,** 5 **dar.**

**1297** R. GLOUC. (Rolls) 4 Of fon hii dorre [*v. r.* heo durre] þe lasse doute bote hit be þorȝ gyle. *c* **1477** CAXTON *Jason* 42 Ye dar not be aferd of dethe.

**2.** *Pres. Subj. sing.* 1 **ðyrfe,** 1–2 **þurfe,** 3 (*Orm.*) **þurrfe, þurve.** *pl.* 1 **ðyrfen, þurfen.**

*c* 888 K. ÆLFRED *Boeth.* xxvi. § 2 Sam hi þyrfen, sam hi na þurfon, hi willað þeah. *c* **897** — *Gregory's Past. C.* xliii. 312 Oft ðonne mon ma fæst ðonne he ðyrfe. *c* **1000** *Ags. Gosp.* John iv. 15 Syle me þæt wæter þæt..ic ne ðurfe [*c* **1160** *Hatt. G.* þurfe] her feccan. *c* **1200** ORMIN 7766 Þatt ure nan ne þurrfe Ut off þe rihhte weȝȝe gan. *c* **1275** *Woman Samaria* 26 in *O. E. Misc.* 85 Yef me þar-of to drynke Þat ich ne þurve more to þisse welle swynke.

**3.** *Past Indic. and Subj.* **a.** *sing.* *a.* 1 **ðorfte,** 2–5 **þurfte,** 3 (*Orm.*) **þurrfte,** 4–5 **thurfte.**

*a.* *c* 888 K. ÆLFRED *Boeth.* xiv. § 3 Ne þorfte he him nænne ondrædan. *Ibid.*, Ne ðorftes þu ðe nanwuht ondrædan. *Ibid.* xxvi. § 2 Ne ðorfte he no maran fultomes. *c* **1200** ORMIN 16164 Swa þatt nan mann ne þurrfte off himm. *a* **1325** *Poem Times Edw. II* 321 in *Pol. Songs* (Camden) 338 Thurfte him noht seke tresor so fer. **14..** *Sir Beues* 4219 (MS. M.) Thurfte he never after to aske leche, That sir Mylis myght ouer-reche.

*β.* 3 **þurhte, þorte,** 3–5 **þurte,** 4 **þurt, þort, þart, thourt,** 4–5 **thurt(e;** 4 **þurste,** 4–5 **þurst,** 4–5, 9 *Sc.* **thurst.**

*c* **1200** *Trin. Coll. Hom.* 35 He ne þurte naure þolen hunger ne þurst. *a* **1272** *Luue Ron* 95 in *O. E. Misc.* 96 Ne þurhte þe neuer rewe. *a* **1300** *Cursor M.* 23443 Ya forsoth thurt [*v.r.* thort] naman mare. *c* **1330** *Florice & Bl.* 259 Now thourt him neuere ful iwis Willen after more blisse. **1393** LANGL. *P. Pl.* C. x. 257 Ho so þurste hit segge. *a* **1425** *Chron. R. Glouc.* (Rolls) 6389 (MS. *β.*), He ne þurst neuer eft care of drynke ne cloþe. *c* **1460** *Towneley Myst.* xxv. 256 For no catelle thurt the craue. **1825** Thurst [see B. 1].

**b.** *plural.* *a.* 1 **þorfton, -an.** *β.* 3 **þeorte(n,** 3–4 **þurte(n,** 4–5 **thurte.**

*c* 897 K. ÆLFRED *Gregory's Past. C.* 9 Hi his sume ðorfton. *a* **1000** *Guthlac* 423 (452) No we þus swiðe swencan þorftan. *c* **1275** LAY. 18650 For ne þeorte þe cnihtes buten biwiten þat castel ȝat. *c* **1460** *Towneley Myst.* xxx. 473 Thai thurte bot aske and haue thare boyn.

**B.** Signification.

**1.** *intr.* To be under a necessity or obligation (*to do* something): = NEED *v.*[2] 6, 8.

*c* 890–901 K. ÆLFRED *Laws* Introd. c. 28 ʒif..he..ʒewitnesse hæbbe, ne þearf he þæt ʒeldan. *a* **1000** *Cædmon's Gen.* 611 (Gr.) Ic hit þe secgan ne þearf. *a* **1200** *Moral Ode* 44 Þer ne þerf he habben kare of ȝefe ne of ȝelde. *a* **1225** *Juliana* 68 Arude me þat þeos unselie ne þurue nawt seggen. *c* **1230** *Hali Meid.* 5 Ha nawiht ne þarf of oðer þing þenchen. **1825** JAMIESON s.v., 'Ye thair n' fash', you need not put yourself to the trouble. *Ibid.*, 'Ye thurstn'', ye needed not.

**2.** *impersonally.* It needs, there is need, it is needful [= L. *opus est*, Gr. δεῖ]. Const. *dat.* of person and *inf.* **a.** without subject *it.*

*c* **1200** ORMIN 12886 Ne þarrf ȝuw nohht nu follȝhenn me. *c* **1200** *Trin. Coll. Hom.* 69 Þanne ne þarf us noðer gramien ne shamien. *a* **1250** *Owl & Night.* 190 Ne þarf þerof beo no tale. *c* **1275** *Passion* 17 in *O. E. Misc.* 37 Ne þerfþ þer non adrede. *c* **1275** *Duty of Christians* 37 ibid. 142 Ne þarf vs neuer a-gryse. *c* **1320** *Sir Tristr.* 3053 Who wil lesinges layt, Þarf him no ferþer go. *c* **1330** R. BRUNNE *Chron. Wace* (Rolls) 4145 Ne neuere þurt hem haue drad no tyde. *c* **1430** *Syr Gener.* (Roxb.) 3 Ne thar him nat be idel long. *c* **1440** *Alphabet of Tales* 361 Sho said hym þurte not be seke her-for. *c* **1475** *Rauf Coilȝear* 538 Me tharth haue nane noy of myne erand.

**b.** with subject *it. rare.*

*c* **1430** *Pilgr. Lyf Manhode* I. lxxxvii. (1869) 39 It thurt not recche to write of this anoon. *c* **1460** *Towneley Myst.* iv. 117 Myn ase shalle withe vs, if it thar.

**Tharf-cake** (þā·ɹfkēk). Now *dial.* Forms: 4 **þerf, þerue cake,** 6 **therfe, tharffe,** *Sc.* **thraf, threfe cake,** 7 **tharck-cake,** 7–9 **tharcake.** [f. THARF *a.* + CAKE *sb.*] A cake of unleavened bread; now *spec.* a flat circular cake of oat-, rye-, or barley-meal, unleavened, and sometimes flavoured with butter and treacle; in the latter case = PARKIN.

**13..** *E. E. Allit. P.* B. 635 Abraham..Þrwe þryftyly þer-on þo þre þerue kakez. **1362** LANGL. *P. Pl.* A. VII. 269 A þerf Cake, And a lof of Benes and Bren I-Bake for my Children. *c* **1470** HENRYSON *Mor. Fab.* II. (*Town & C. Mouse*) xviii, Thraf caikis als, I trow, scho spairit nocht. **1560** PILKINGTON *Expos. Aggeus* (1562) 92 Elias, fleeing from Jezebel, founde a therfe cake baked in the asshes. **1634–5** BRERETON *Trav.* (Chetham Soc.) 122 The entertainment we accepted..was Tharck-cakes, two eggs, and some dried fish buttered. **1691** RAY *N. C. Words* s. v. *Bannock*, *Tharcakes*,..cakes made of oat-meal,..and fair water, without yeast, or leaven, and so baked. *c* **1746** COLLIER (Tim Bobbin) *View Lanc. Dial. Wks.* (1862) 57 'Twur os thodd'n os o Thar-Cake. **1825** BROCKETT *N. C. Wds.*, *Thauf-cake.* **1828** *Craven Gl.*, *Thar-cake*, a heavy, unleavened cake. **1888** *Sheffield Gloss.* s. v., A year or two ago I noticed that a shop-keeper..advertised tharf-cake for sale...They call it *parkin* instead of using the old word. **1893–4** *Northumbld. Gloss.*, Tharf-kyek, Thaaf-keahyk, Thaf-kyek, Tharth-kyek, Thaugh-cyek, Tharfy.

† **Tha·rfling, the·rfling.** *Obs. rare.* [OE. *ðeorfling*, f. *ðeorf* THARF *a.* + -LING.] Unleavened bread or loaf; also *attrib.* Unleavened.

*c* **1050** *Gloss.* in Wr.-Wülcker 348/28 *Azimos*, ðeorflingas. *c* **1200** ORMIN 1588 Forr þerrflinng bræd iss clene bræd, Forr þatt itt iss unnberrmedd.

**Tharl(e, -dom,** obs. ff. THRALL *sb.*[1], THRALDOM.

**Tharm** (þāɹm). Now *dial.* Forms: 1 Angl. **tharm, þarm,** WSax. **þearm, thearm;** 3 **þærm, þerm,** 3–4 **þarm,** 4 **þearm,** 5 **thaarme,** 5– **tharm;** 6–7 *dial.* **therm,** 8–9 *Sc.* **therm, thairm).** [OE. *þarm*, *þearm* = OFris. *therm* (WFris. *term*), OLG. **tharm* (MDu. *darm*, *darem*, Du. *darm*, OHG. *darm*, *daram* (MHG., MLG., Ger. *darm*), ON. *þarmr* (Sw., Da. *tarm*):—OTeut. **þarm-oz*, f. Indo-Eur. ablaut series *ter* : *tor* : *tr* to go through. Cf. Gr. τρῆμα perforation, τράμις perineum.]

**1.** An intestine; chiefly in *pl.*, bowels, viscera, entrails; in quot. *c* 1460 *transf.*

*a* **700** *Epinal Gloss.* (O. E. T.) 503 *Intestinum*, thearm. *c* **725** *Corpus Gloss.* 2140 *Viscera*, tharme, thumle. *Ibid.* 870 *Fibra*, þearm. *c* **1000** ÆLFRIC *Gram.* xiii. (Z.) 85 *Exta*, þearmas. *c* **1205** LAY. 818 Moni þusend þer flowen, þærmes heo droȝen [*c* **1275** þarmes idrowen]. **1303** R. BRUNNE *Handl. Synne* 702 Of þe chylde þat she bare..Al to-drawe were þe þarmys. *c* **1380** *Sir Ferumb.* 949 Þay stykede þorȝ guttes & þearmes, so foule with hem þei ferde. *c* **1440** *Promp. Parv.* 490/1 Thaarme (or gutte), *sumen*, *viscus.* *c* **1460** *Towneley Myst.* xiii. 391, I haue..A house full of yong tharmes,..wo is hym has many barnes. **1535** COVERDALE 2 *Macc.* ix. 5 There came vpon him an horrible payne of his bowels, & a sore grefe of the tharmes. **1721** KELLY *Scot. Prov.* 137 He that has a wide Therm, had never a long Arm. **1877** *N. W. Linc. Gloss.*, *Tharm*, the colon.

**2.** An intestine as cleansed and prepared for some purpose: see quots. Also, in *sing.*, as a substance or material; catgut for fiddle-strings, etc.

[**1545** ASCHAM *Toxoph.* II. (Arb.) 110 Eustathius..doeth tel, that in oulde tyme they made theyr bowe strynges of bullox thermes. **1631** R. H. *Arraignm. Whole Creature* xvi. 291 The strings made of Wolves will never tune right with those made of the Thermes of Sheepe.] **1671** SKINNER *Etymol. Ang.*, *Tharm*, vox agro Linc. usitatissima pro Intestinis mundatis ad Botulos seu Farcinima paranda inflatis. **1674** RAY *N. C. Wds.*, *Tharm*, guts prepared, cleansed, and blown up for to receive puddings; Lincolnsh. **1755** JOHNSON, *Tharm*, intestines twisted for several uses. **1785** BURNS *Ordination* vii, Come, screw the pegs wi' tunefu' cheep, And o'er the thairms be tryin. **1787** — *To Haggis* i, Aboon them a' ye tak your place, Painch, tripe, or thairm. **1816** J. CLELAND *Rise & Progr. Glasgow* (1820) 275 A work in which Therm was manufactured from the intestines of animals. **1824** SCOTT *Redgauntlet* Let. x, The best fiddler that ever kittled thairm with horse-hair. **1881** W. ANDERSON in *Mod. Sc. Poets* II. 238 Thairm, to mount a spinnin wheel.

**3.** *attrib.* and *Comb.*, as *tharm-band*, *-string.*

**1786** BURNS *Brigs of Ayr* 202 O had M'Lauchlan, thairm-inspiring Sage, Been there to hear this heavenly band engage. **1788** G. TURNBULL *Poet. Ess.* 185 Therm-strings for spinning Wheels and fiddles. **1825** JAMIESON, *Thairm-band*, a string or cord of catgut for..a spinning-wheel.

† **Tharn,** *v. Obs.* Forms: 3 (*Orm.*) **þarrnenn,** 4 **þarn,** 4–5 **tharn(e, (thorne).** [ad. ON. *þarna*, refl. *þarnask* to be without, lack, want, f. *þarna* (earlier **þarf-na*) sb. need, f. *þarf-*: see THARF *v.*] *trans.* To be without; to want, lack, need; to be deprived of, to lose. Hence † **Tha·rning** *vbl. sb.*, being without, lacking, want; losing, loss.

*c* **1200** ORMIN 10142 Þatt illke þing þatt tu full wel Ne mihht te sellf nohht þarrnenn. *c* **1300** *Havelok* 2835 Hise children sulde þarne Euere more þat eritage, Þat his was. **13..** *Cursor M.* 4284 (Cott.) O quat pine es herder threst, Þen tharn [*Fairf.* wante] þe thing men luues best. **1340** HAMPOLE *Pr. Consc.* 7308 Right swa þe tharnyng for ever of þat syght, Es þe mast payne in helle dyght. *c* **1375** *Sc. Leg. Saints* xvi. (*Magdalena*) 443, & scho þe lyf allane [allace?] can thorne Fra þat ilke barne wes borne. *c* **1440** *York Myst.* xliii. 12 The missing of my maistir trewe.. Makis me to morne..For tharnyng of his company. *c* **1460** *Towneley Myst.* xiv. 272 Thy waryson shalle thou not tharne.

**Tharre, Tharst, Tharth**: see THARF *v. Obs.*

**Tharst(e,** var. ff. *thrast*, obs. pa. t. of THRUST.

**Thas,** obs. form of THOSE; obs. abbrev. of *it has*; obs. infl. of THAT, THE: see THES.

**That** (ðæt), *dem. pron.*, *adj.*, and *adv.* Forms: see below. [In OE. *þæt*, nom. and acc. singular neuter of the simple demonstrative pronoun and adjective *se*, *sēo*, *þæt*, the adjectival use of which has also produced the 'definite article' THE, under which the history and obs. inflexional forms are given. *The* is the resultant form, used for all genders, numbers, and cases of the article; *that* the unweakened neuter singular, used as demonstrative pronoun and adj. for all cases of the singular. The original plural in both uses was *þá*, in ME. *þā* and THO, q. v., surviving in Sc. and north. dial. as THAE, but superseded in literary English by THOSE.

The demonstrative was also used in OE. as a relative pronoun, for which see below.]

**A.** Illustration of Forms.

**1.** In OE. inflected for gender, number, and case: see the inflexional forms under THE. Some of the inflexions remained in early ME., and in some dialects even to 1400. A few examples of these, in which the sense is demonstrative, follow here. For the plural forms see THO and THOSE.

(The masc. and fem. pronouns *se*, *sēo*, and 14th c. Kentish *ze*, *zy*, were often equivalent to 'he', 'she', and 'it'.)

*Beowulf* (Z.) 470 Se wæs betera ðonne ic. *Ibid.* 506 Eart ðu se Beowulf se ðe wið Brecan wunne? *c* **825** *Vesp. Ps.* vii. 16 Seað [he] ontynde & dalf ðone [= *eum*]. *Ibid.* cxlv. 4 In ðæm [= *illa*] deȝe. *a* **855** *O. E. Chron.* an. 597, Her ongon Ceolwulf ricsian..Se wæs Cuþaing, Cuþa Cynricing [etc.]. *c* **893** K. ÆLFRED *Oros.* I. i. § 9 Seo Ægyptus þe us near is. *Ibid.* II. iv. § 8 Seo ilce burȝ Babylonia, seo ðe mæst wæs & ærest ealra burȝa. *Ibid.* v. ix, Ic..secgan scyle,..hwa þæs [= of that] ordfruman wæron. *a* **900** tr. *Bæda's Hist.* II. vii. (1890) 118 Þæm [Mellitus] sona æfterfylȝde Iustus in biscophade. *c* **1000** *Ags. Gosp.* Matt. x. 23 Ðonne hi eow ehtaþ on þysse byriȝ, fleoþ on oþre, and ðonne hi on þære [*Hatton G.* þare] eow ehtaþ, fleoþ on þa þryddan. — John iii. 29 Se ðe bryde hæfð, se is brydguma. *a* **1175** *Cott. Hom.* 235 Si [the Law of Moses] ȝeleste sume wile. *c* **1175** *Lamb. Hom.* 37 Do þine elmesse of þon þet þu maht iforðien. *c* **1200** *Trin. Coll. Hom.* 221 Se þe her doð ani god. *c* **1200** ORMIN 17621 To þann comm icc off heffne dun. *c* **1250** *Owl & Night.* 882 Þat beoþ her wo is hom þes. *c* **1300** *Harrow. Hell* (MS. O.) 65 Þou miȝt wel witen þe bi þon [MS. E. 79 for þan] Þat ich [am] more þen ani mon. **1340** *Ayenb.* 102 Zy þet ne serueþ bote to onlepy manne. *Ibid.* 117 Ze þet ne heþ þise uondinges.

**2.** Forms of the singular neuter, and, at length, general uninflected form *that*.

1–3 **ðæt, þæt, ðet,** 1–4 **þet,** (3 **ðat, þut),** 3–6 **þat,** (3–5 **þatt,** 4 **þate,** 5 **þatte,** 5–6 **thate,** 6–7 **thatt),** 4– **that.** (Also written 4–6 **yat,** 4–8 **y**[t]**, yt.)**

*Beowulf* (Z.) 1372 Nis þæt heoru stow. **835** *Charter of Abba* (Kentish) in *O. E. Texts* 448 ʒif hiʒan ðonne oððe hlaford þæt nylle..ʒeunnan. *c* **836** *O. E. Chron.* an. 787, Þæt wæron þa ærestan scipu Deniscra monna þe Angel cynnes lond ʒesohton. *c* **1134** *Ibid.* (Laud MS.) an. 1127, Þet wes eall ðurh þone kyng Heanri of Engle land. *c* **1175** *Lamb. Hom.* 33 On cristes prisune..þet is in helle. *c* **1200** Þatt [see B. II. 1]. *c* **1205** LAY. 4542 Þet is þere quene scip. *c* **1250** *Gen. & Ex.* 59 Ðat was ðe firme morȝen tid..Wid ðat liȝt worn angles wroȝt. **1297** R. GLOUC. (Rolls) 6773 He was glad of þut cas. *c* **1330** R. BRUNNE *Chron. Wace* (Rolls) 1926 Englysche holden þate heritage. *c* **1400** Þat [see B. II. 5]. *c* **1420** *Chron. Vilod.* 840 He sayde he mervaylede muche of þatte. *c* **1460** *Towneley Myst.* i. 40 That at is dry the erth shalle be. **1533** BELLENDEN *Livy* II. i. (S.T.S.) I. 132 Tak away þat odious name tarquyne fra þe pepill. **1583** T. WATSON *Poems* (Arb.) 45 But I (alas) might curse yat dismall day. **1638** *Hamilton Papers* (Camden) 45, I had lytill hoope of uoorking of thatt by treatie.

**B.** Signification and uses.

The pronominal use goes back to the earliest OE. The adjectival demonstrative use in OE. corresponded to that of L. *is*, *ea*, *id*, or the unqualified French *ce*, *cette*, and is often indistinguishable from that of the modern definite article. But by 1200 the adjectival use of *that* began also to be more definitely demonstrative (= L. *iste*, *ille*, F. *ce . . . là*), and to be implicitly or explicitly opposed to THIS (= L. *hic*, F. *ce . . . ci*). As this appears first in Ormin, it may have been due to the influence of Norse, in which the adjectival use of *þat* as a demonstrative, opposed to *þetta* 'this', is of earlier appearance.

**I.** Demonstrative Pronoun. Pl. † THO (*obs.*), THOSE, q. v.

* *As simple demonstrative pronoun.*

**1.** Denoting a thing or person pointed out or present, or that has just been mentioned: cf. II. 1.

**a.** a thing (concrete or abstract).

Often serving instead of repetition of the name of the thing, and directing the attention back to it (thus more emphatic than *it*). Also, for emphasis, used pleonastically in apposition to the sb.; also, in mod. use, as in quot. 1880, placed (as subj.) after the predicate sb., with ellipsis of the copula. In quot. 1905, applied to a person contemptuously spoken of as a thing or creature.

*Beowulf* (Z.) 2200 Eft þæt ʒe-iode ufaran dogrum, hildehlæm-mum. *c* 888 K. ÆLFRED *Boeth.* xxxiii. § 5 Þæt eart ðu. *c* **897** — *Gregory's Past. C.* i. 28 Soðlice ða eaʒan þæt bioð ða lareowas, & se hrycg þæt sint ða hiremenn. *c* **1000** *Sax. Leechd.* I. 346 Haran cyslyb ʒeseald on wines drince, þæt wel ʒehæleþ. **1303** R. BRUNNE *Handl. Synne* 12560 Pryue synne and sacrylage, That loue y moste. **13..** in *Hampole's Wks.* (1896) I. 108 Luk nogth efter ylke a mans wile to do it, bot luk whilke es myne & do þat. **1451** CAPGRAVE *St. Augustine* 36 But þe principal cause whech Augustin supposed to spede, þat failed. **1456** SIR G. HAYE *Law Arms* (S. T. S.) 14 And with that I sall put sik thing langand warldly understanding. **1579** W. FULKE *Heskins' Parl.* 74 The errour of Vibicus. And that was this. **1665** BOYLE *Occas. Medit.* IV. v, To serve him that can give That, and much greater. **1709** *Lond. Gaz.* No. 4599/4 It had a black Ribbon tied to it, and the Key of the Watch fastened to that. **1808** ELEANOR SLEATH *Bristol Heiress* I. 63 Rank, high life, fashionable amusement—that's the go. **1842** BROWNING *Pied Piper* iv, 'Bless us', cried the Mayor, 'what's that?' **1878** T. HARDY *Ret. Native* VI. iv, 'What noise was that?' said Clym. **1880** TENNYSON *Sisters* 14 A sweet voice that—you scarce could better that. **1905** EL. GLYN *Viciss. Evangeline* 127 'Would you like to marry Malcolm?' I asked. 'Fancy being owned by that! Fancy seeing it every day!'

**b.** a person. Now noting a person actually pointed out (not one just mentioned, exc. in emphatic pleonastic use as in **a**). Chiefly as subject of the verb *to be* in stating or asking who or what *that* (person) is. (See also 6 c.)

Colloquially used in expressions of commendation, or in mod. use of anticipatory commendation by way of persuasion or encouragement (esp. to a child).

*Beowulf* (Z.) 11 þæt wæs god cyning. **1297** R. GLOUC. (Rolls) 3044 ȝif þer is Eny mon so wis þat beste red conne rede, merlin þat is. *a* **1300** *Cursor M.* 18131 Þat king o blis, quat es he, þat? **13..** *Gaw. & Gr. Knt.* 2463 Ho wayned me vpon þis wyse..Þat is ho þat is at home, þe auncian lady. **1470–85** MALORY *Arthur* I. xxv. 73 What damoysel is that? ..That is the lady of the lake. **1592** SHAKS. *Rom. & Jul.* II. iii. 47 That's my good Son. **1601** — *All's Well* III. v. 81 *Hel.* Which is the Frenchman? *Dia.* Hee, That with the plume. **1606** — *Tr. & Cr.* IV. ii. 36 Who's that at doore? **1610** — *Temp.* I. ii. 299 After two daies I will discharge thee. *Ar.* That's my noble Master. **1652** J. WRIGHT tr. *Camus' Nat. Paradox* IX. 215 By my Soul if that bee a Lady, my Husband may bee a Lady too. **1766** GOLDSM. *Vic. of W.* vii, 'Very well', cried I, 'that's a good girl'. **1841** BROWNING *Pippa Passes* III. 276 Why, there! Is not that Pippa..under the window? **1854** THACKERAY *Rose & Ring* viii, 'Who's that laughing?' It was Giglio laughing. *Mod.* Come along, that's a good boy! That's the man for me!

**c.** a fact, act, or occurrence, or a statement or question, implied or contained in the previous sentence: often used instead of repeating a clause or phrase (cf. a).

In OE. and in Sc. often referring to a following statement, where mod.Eng. commonly uses *this*. Cf. II. 1, and THIS B. I. 1 d.

*a* **855** *O. E. Chron.* an. 755, Ða on morȝenne ȝehierdun þæt þæs cyninges þeȝnas..þæt se cyning ofslæȝen wæs. *a* **900** CYNEWULF *Elene* 1168 (Gr.) Þæt is ȝedafenlic, þæt þu dryhtnes word On hyȝe healde. *c* **1000** *Ags. Gosp.* John i. 19 Þæt is Iohannes ȝewitnes. *a* **1131** *O. E. Chron.* an. 1122, On þone lenten tyde þær toforen for bearn se burch on Gleawe ceastre..Þet wes þes dæies viii id' Mr.' **1297** R. GLOUC. (Rolls) 10348 Wan þou seist, quaþ þe king, þat þat was mi þouȝt. *c* **1420** (?) LYDG. *Assembly of Gods* 2034 Goo we hens, for that hold I best. **1526** *Pilgr. Perf.* (W. de W. 1531) 3 The iewes also se almyghty god, but that was in a more excellent maner. **1602** SHAKS. *Ham.* III. i. 56 To be, or not to be, that is the Question. **1693** J. EDWARDS *Author. O. & N. Test.* 154 The Pagans would jeer the Jews for that. **1738** SWIFT *Pol. Conversat.* ii. 140, I can just carve Pudden, and that's all. **1824** SCOTT *Redgauntlet* ch. xx, I will say that for the English,..that they are a ceeveleesed people to gentlemen that are under a cloud. **1838** RUSKIN *Ess. Music & Paint.* Wks. 1903 I. 285 If others do not follow their example,—the more fools they,—that's all.

**d.** After various prepositions, referring to a precise time just mentioned, or an act or event in relation to the precise time of its occurrence: e.g. *after that* = after that time, or after that happened; *by that* = by that time, or by the time that happened; *upon that, with that* = as or immediately after that was said, done, etc. See also the prepositions.

In OE. prepositions governed other cases besides the accusative, as the dative, e.g. *æfter, ǽr, mid, onmang, tó ðǽm*, the instrumental, e.g. *for þý, mid þý*, etc. These partly survived in early ME.; e.g. *fro þan þat* (see FRO prep. 3).

**13..** *Cursor M.* 2827 (Cott.) Bi þat [*v. r.* þan] began þe light o dai. *c* **1420** *Anturs of Arth.* 565 The sone was passed, by þat, mydday and mare. *c* **1425** *Cursor M.* 14360 (Laud) Fro that forth..There folowid Ihesu folk full fele. *c* **1515** *Cocke Lorell's B.* 12 With that they cryed, and made a shoute. **1526** TINDALE *Acts* xxvii. 33 In the meane tyme, bitwixt that and daye. *a* **1715** BURNET *Own Time* (1724) I. II. 278 A proclamation was upon that issued out. **1719** DE FOE *Crusoe* (1840) II. i. 17 Some time after that.., they were ..agreeably surprised. **1802** JEFFERSON *Writ.* (1830) III. 496 Probably on the 24th, or within two or three days of that. **1833** T. HOOK *Parson's Dau.* III. i, My young mistress went to bed about eleven, and the Count went to bed before that. **1862** MISS BRADDON *Lady Audley* xl, With that the surgeon goes to fetch the envelopes.

†**e.** In apposition with a following clause introduced by *thăt* conj.; chiefly in phr. with prep., as *for thát thăt* = for that cause that, because; *in thát thăt* = in that circumstance that, inasmuch as; *to thát thăt* = to the end that, in order that. *Obs.*

Taking the place of OE. *þǽm, þám, þon*, or *þý*, in *for þám þe, on þám þe, to þám þe, for þon þe, for þý þe* or *þæt*.

**1502** *Ord. Crysten Men* I. iii. (1506) 31 To that that he be worthely dysposed to receyue the grace. **1513** MORE *Rich. III* (1883) 2 In that that manye of them were dead. **1532** — *Confut. Tindale* Wks. 659/2 The knowen catholike churche is proued to be the verye churche of Chryste, in that that from the beginning it hath..been.. kepte and contynued one. **1535** CROMWELL in Merriman *Life & Lett.* (1902) I. 417 In that that the said frensh kyng hathe.. answered at all tymes on the kinges parte. *a* **1548** HALL *Chron., Edw. IV* 222 Kynge Edward in these hys last battayles was..fortunate for that, that he at sondry..tymes ..was persecuted..of his enemyes.

**f.** *Take that!* (†*have that!*): a phrase used in delivering a blow, etc.

*a* **1425** *Cursor M.* 16290 (Trin.) Wiþ his hond a buffet He ȝaf ihesus..He seide..Take þat to teche þe lore. *c* **1425** *Cast. Persev.* 3119 in *Macro Plays*, For þi coueytyse, haue þou þat, I schal þee bunche with my bat. **1590** SHAKS. *Com. Err.* II. ii. 23 Thinkst yᵘ I iest? hold, take thou that, and that. **1833** MARRYAT *P. Simple* xii, I must do my duty, Sir,..so take that—and that—and that—(thrashing the man with his rattan). *Ibid.* xiii, Then I'll turn Protestant and damn the Pope—take that now, Father M'Grath.

**2.** Used emphatically, instead of repeating a previous word or phrase. **a.** Preceded by *and* (rarely *but*), and referring to something in the previous clause. [Cf. L. *et id, idque*, F. *et cela.*]

*c* **1000** *Sax. Leechd.* I. 278 On þam [berries] ys sæd and þæt sweart. *c* **1175** *Lamb. Hom.* 121 Crist godes sune wes ibuhsum..to þa deðe, and þet to swulche deðe swa [etc.]. *c* **1386** CHAUCER *Friar's T.* 294, I haue been syk, and that ful many a day. *c* **1485** *Digby Myst.* IV. 1067 We shall here tidinges.., And þat I trust shortlye. **1535** COVERDALE 2 *Kings* iv. 3 Borowe without of all thy neghboures emptye vessels, & that not a fewe. — *Ps.* xlvi. 5 God helpeth her, & yᵗ right early. **1581** SIDNEY *Apol. Poetrie* (Arb.) 62 Exercise indeede wee doe, but that very fore-backwardly. **1772** WESLEY *Jrnl.* 2 June, A man began to scream, and that so loud that my voice was quite drowned. **1833** L. RITCHIE *Wand. by Loire* 168 It was necessary..to act, and that promptly.

**b.** Representing a word or phrase in the previous clause or sentence: usually standing first in its own clause, with inverted construction (*that I will* = I will do that). *colloq.*

*c* **1350** *Will. Palerne* 4161 Hete hem þider wende..Þat i wol, seide william. *a* **1450** *Cov. Myst.* xxiii. (1841) 222 Hath any man condempnyd the? *Mulier.* Nay forsothe that hathe ther nought. **1598** SHAKS. *Merry W.* IV. v. 60 Was there a wise woman with thee? *Fal.* I, that there was. **1642** *Suddaine Answ. to Sud. Moderatour* 3 The Moderator is full of Rhetorick and Oratory too, that he is. **1825** T. HOOK *Sayings* Ser. II. *Man of Many Fr.* I. 196, 'I can say 'em all!' 'That you can't', said Tom. **1865** RUSKIN *Sesame* i. § 29 To feel with them, we must be like them; and none of us can become that without pains. **1872** 'L. CARROLL' *Through Looking-Glass* vi, 'They must be very curious creatures.' 'They are that', said Humpty Dumpty. **1900** F. P. DUNNE in *Westm. Gaz.* 13 June 1/3 'They'll be out here nex' week'..' They will that', Mr. Dooley replied.

**3.** In opposition to *this* (cf. II. 2): esp. in phr. *this and* (*or*) *that* = one thing and (or) another: see THIS B. I. 3. Also occas. *that.. that* = one thing..another thing.

*c* **888** K. ÆLFRED *Boeth.* xxxiii. § 2 Þonne lufað sum ðæt, sum elles hwæt. **1390–** [see THIS B. I. 3]. *c* **1450** tr. *De Imitatione* III. xvi. 84 Wheþer a good spirit or an euel stire þe to desire þat or þat. *Ibid.* lv. 130 Lete oon seke þat, a noþer þat. **1818** SCOTT *Hrt. Midl.* xvi, Lay that and that thegither! **1842** MARRYAT *Perc. Keene* xiv, Young as I was, I also could put that and that together.

**b.** *spec.* (after Latin idiom). The former: correl. to *this* = the latter: see THIS B. I. 3 b. Now *arch.* and *literary*.

*c* **1440–1868** [see THIS B. I. 3 b]. **1654** Z. COKE *Logick* (1657) A iij b, Corruption of manners, and mazing Errors... These delude and distract, that doth deboish a people.

**4.** As quasi-*sb.*, with pl. *thats*. Also (with capital T) as quasi-proper name: see THIS B. I. 3 c, d.

**1656–1895** [see THIS B. I. 3 c, d]. **1910** *Contemp. Rev.* Mar. 307 The immediacy of faith..will furnish us with the *That*, whilst we may have to look to other sources for the *What*.

**5.** Phrases, belonging to senses 1 and 2.

**a.** *That is* (more fully *that is to say*, †*to wit*, etc.): introducing (or more rarely following) an explanation of the preceding word, phrase, or statement (or a modifying correction of it).

*c* **1175** *Lamb. Hom.* 105 Þe oðer mihte is *Castitas*, þet is clenesse on englisc. *a* **1225** *Ancr. R.* 348 Efter schrifte, hit falleð to speken of Penitence, þet is, dedbote. **1340** *Ayenb.* 210 Huanne þou woldest bidde god..wisliche and diligentliche, þet is ententifliche and perseuerantliche. *a* **1440** *Relig. Pieces fr. Thornton MS.* 8 The thirde sacrement es callede penance, þat es sothefaste for-thynkyr.ge þat we hafe of oure synne. **1523** [COVERDALE] *Old God & New* (1534) B j, In all poyntes, yᵗ is to wyte bothe in his doctryne and also in his lyuynge. **1625** B. JONSON *Staple of N.* I. i, Look to me,..That is look on me, and with all thine eyes. **1802** PALEY *Nat. Theol.* xxiii. (ed. 2) 440 Every animated being has its *sensorium*, that is, a certain portion of space, within which perception and volition are exerted. **1865** RUSKIN *Sesame* i. § 21 Those who 'intrude' (thrust, that is) themselves into the fold.

**b.** *All that*: all that sort of thing; that and everything of the kind. *And all that*, and so forth, *et cetera* (see ALL A. 8 c); so, in same sense, *and that*. *Not so.. as all that*: not so..as that amounts to; not quite so..as that. *For all that*: see FOR 23 a. *Like that*, of that kind, or in that manner: see LIKE *a.* 1 ¶, *adv.* 1.

*c* **1440** *Jacob's Well* 76 3itt for all þat, manye of þe iewys hadden gret indignacyoun of hem. **1638** JUNIUS *Paint. Ancients* 36 It is for all that a greater matter to expresse in Achilles his picture the very same Art. **1702** *Mouse grown a Rat* 3 My mighty Bulk does even elevate and surprize, and all that. **1719** DE FOE *Crusoe* (1840) II. vi. 150 To talk of my repenting, alas! 'tis past all that with me...It is too late. **1742** RICHARDSON *Pamela* III. 127 If People will set up for Virtue, and all that, let 'em be uniformly virtuous. **1821** CLARE *Vill. Minstr.* II. 89 Full of chat, In passing harmless jokes 'bout beaus and that. **1848** THACKERAY *Van. Fair* lx, Dob reads Latin like English, and French and that. **1884** RUSKIN *Let. to F. Randal* Wks. 1907 XXX. Introd. 65 What do you think I would give to be your age, and able to draw like that!

**c.** *At that* (orig. U. S., *colloq.* or *slang*): estimated at that rate, at that standard, even in that capacity, in respect of that; too; 'into the bargain': 'a cant phrase..used to define more nearly or intensify something already said' (Bartlett).

Prob. extended from *dear at that, cheap at that* (*price*).

**1855** *Blackw. Mag.* Sept. 324/2 'Now then, mister', turning to the man at the bar, 'drinks round, and cobblers at that'. **1883** STEVENSON *Silverado Sq.* 167 Yet water it was, and sea-water at that. **1884** F. M. CRAWFORD *Rom. Singer* I. 226 A shoemaker, and a poor one at that. **1897** *Trans. Amer. Pediatric Soc.* IX. 73 The infant was underfed, and did not receive the correct food at that.

** *As antecedent pronoun.*

(= F. *celui*, Ger. *der, derjenige.*)

**6.** As antecedent to a relative (pron. or adv.) expressed or understood.

Here, and in 7 and 8 usually (as in II. 3) definitive rather than demonstrative, the relative clause (or dependent phrase) serving to complete the definition.

**a.** Of a thing, in general sense: *that thăt, that which* = the thing which, what; so *that whereby, wherein, wherewith, whence*, etc.

Sometimes following the relative clause, which then begins with *what*: *that* being in this case now pleonastic and emphatic.

[*a* **900** tr. *Bæda's Hist.* III. vii. [ix.] (1890) 178 Hwelc þæs cyninges ȝeleafa & modes wilsumnis in God wære, þæt æfter his deaðe..wæs ȝecyðed.] **13..** *E. E. Allit. P.* A. 535 Wyrkez and dotz þat at ȝe moun. *c* **1375** *Sc. Leg. Saints* xvi. (*Magdalena*) 605 For-þi be sikker in þat,..þat scho þe taucht. **1399** *Rolls of Parlt.* III. 452/1 Havyng consideration to that that was prayed by the comon, that thát that was evell .. shuld be..amended in this Parlement. *c* **1400** tr. *Secreta Secret., Gov. Lordsh.* 48 Þat þat semys to ȝow yn þys matere. **1526** TINDALE 1 *Cor.* xi. 23 That which I gave vnto you I receaved off the lorde. **1545** RAYNOLD *Byrth Mankynde* 127 Though the chylde reiecte and vomyte vp agayne that the whiche it receaueth. **1597** SHAKS. 2 *Hen. IV*, III. ii. 226 Hah..that thou hadst seene that, that this Knight and I haue seene. **1650** GENTILIS *Considerations* 233 Coriolanus, who could not attain to that as he wanted, should have forsaken that which he had received. **1674** GREW *Anat. Trunks* II. ii. § 3 What the Mouth is, to an Animal; that the Root is to a Plant. **1875** F. HALL in *Lippincott's Mag.* XV. 341/1 There was that about the place which filled me with a sense of utter dreariness.

**b.** Referring to a preceding sb., and equivalent to *the* with the sb.: e.g. in first quot., *that which* = 'the bread which'.

**1634** HOLLAND *Pliny* II. 141 The Sitanian bread, *i.* that which is made of three months corn. **1693** tr. *Blancard's Phys. Dict.* (ed. 2), *Rimula Laryngis*, that which is covered by the Cartilage of the Epiglottis. **1825** SCOTT *Betrothed* xv, Breaking into your apartment, [he] transported you to that where I myself received you from his arms. **1825** J. NICHOLSON *Operat. Mechanic* 68 The proportion..between the load at the maximum and that by which the wheel is stopped. **1859** RUSKIN *Two Paths* ii. § 54 Fine Art is that in which the hand, the head, and the heart..go together.

**c.** Of a person. Now only as in 1 b. In quot. 1542 *that which* = 'he who' or 'one that'.

**1542** UDALL *Erasm. Apoph.* 35 He..taunted Plato, as yᵗ whiche in rebukyng hym did committe the veraye selfe same faulte. **1591** SHAKS. *Two Gent.* IV. ii. 87 Who is that that spake? *Mod.* That was our member who spoke first at the meeting.

**7.** With ellipsis of a following relative (subj. or obj. of the relative clause): = that person or thing (*sc.* 'that' or 'which'). Now only where *that* is definitely demonstrative or emphatic, as in 1.

In earlier use the antecedent pronoun was omitted: see THAT *rel. pron.* 3. From the 16th c. onwards there are examples in which it is difficult to say whether the single *that* is the antecedent or the relative. Wherever it is emphatic it may be considered the demonstrative. Cf. also THAT *rel. pron.* 3 and 10.

[**1523** LD. BERNERS *Froiss.* I. 295 For that is myne is yours.] **1598** SHAKS. *Merry W.* III. iii. 212 May be the knaue bragg'd of that he could not compasse. **1601** — *Twel. N.* v. i. 153 Be that thou know'st thou art, and then thou art As great as that thou fear'st. **1601** — *Jul. C.* I. ii. 314 Thy Honorable Mettle may be wrought From that it is dispos'd. **1850** NEALE *Med. Hymns* 20 Here vouchsafe to all Thy servants That they supplicate to gain. **1852** M. ARNOLD *Tristram & Iseult* i. 7 Who is that stands by the dying fire? **1883** WHITTIER *Our Country* 12 The best is that we have to-day. **1894** H. GARDENER *Unoff. Patriot* 49 She was not of his fold! It was *that* she thought of.

**8.** Followed by defining words (*of* or other prep. with a sb., or a pple. or other vbl. adj.) which serve to qualify or particularize *that* in the manner of a relative clause.

**a.** Referring to something just mentioned, and equivalent to *the* with the sb., or *the one*. (Cf. 6 b.)

*c* **1400** MAUNDEV. ii. (1839) 13 ȝif alle it be so, that men seyn, that this croune is of thornes...I haue seen..many times that of Paris and that of Costantynoble:..thei were bothe..made of russches of the see. **1602** CAREW *Cornwall* 54 b, So doth their Pearch exceed that of other Countries. **1707** E. CHAMBERLAYNE *Pres. St. Eng.* III. xi. (ed. 22) 387 That at Radcliff was founded by Nicholas Gibson. **1753** CHAMBERS *Cycl. Supp.* s. v. *Rubrica*, The best in England is that from several parts of Derbyshire. **1802** MAR. EDGEWORTH *Moral T.* xii, Turning from the history of meanness to that of enthusiasm. **1825** T. HOOK *Sayings* Ser. II. *Sutherl.* I. 92 The post arrived, and brought letters...That from his sister was full of tender solicitude. *Mod.* Which house? That with a verandah. That formerly occupied by Mr. A.

**b.** In general sense = the thing that is.., what is... (Cf. 6 a.)

**1607** C. NEWPORTE in *3rd Rep. Hist. MSS. Comm.* 54/1 Not having any man to put in trust of the ship and that in her. **1844** BROWNING *Laboratory* iv, That in the mortar—you call it a gum? **1867** MORRIS *Jason* VI. 325 Careful of that stored up within our hold.

†**c.** Referring to a statement or saying cited immediately after: usually in *that of* (the author).

**1662** STILLINGFL. *Orig. Sacr.* I. v. § 2 The Ægyptians are supposed to have been best skilled as to the form of the year, according to that of Macrobius, *Anni certus modus apud solos semper Ægyptios fuit.* **1671** H. M. tr. *Erasm. Colloq.* 309 Perhaps the largess may be the greater, according to that, 'The booty which is sought for by many hands is quickly acquired'. **1679** T. PULLER *Moder. Ch. Eng.* (1843)

147 Alleging that of St. Bernard; 'Such a number of festivities is fitter for citizens, than for exiles and pilgrims'.

**II.** Demonstrative Adjective. Pl. as in I.

**1.** The simple demonstrative used (as adjective in concord with a sb.), to indicate a thing or person either as being actually pointed out or present, or as having just been mentioned and being thus mentally pointed out. (Now distinguished from the definite article THE as being *demonstrative*, i. e. pointing out, and not merely *definitive*, i. e. distinguishing or singling out.)

The use before a possessive, as in quot. 1551, is *obs.* or *arch.*, the periphrasis with *of* (see OF 44) being now substituted for the possessive.

In *Sc.* also referring to something mentioned immediately after, where mod.Eng. uses *this*. Cf. I. 1 c, and THIS B. II. 1 b.

*c* **1200** ORMIN 2490 Þe Laferrd haffde litell rum Inn all þatt miccle riche. *c* **1250** [see A. 2]. **1297** R. GLOUC. (Rolls) 205 Ich wille telle þat cas. *c* **1350** *Will. Palerne* 671 He wend to haue lauȝt þat ladi loueli in armes. *c* **1440** *Alphabet of Tales* 63 Joseph..said he sulde com agayn þat day viij dayes. **1470–85** MALORY *Arthur* II. iii. 79 That gentilwoman was causar of my faders deth. **1551** ROBINSON tr. *More's Utop.* Ep. to W. Cecylle (1895) 16 Though no commoditie of that my labour..should arise. **1661** WALTON *Angler* xix. (ed. 3) 238 [This fish] was almost a yard broad, and twice that length. **1746** P. FRANCIS tr. *Horace, Ep.* II. ii. 16 My stock is little, but that stock my own. **1794** MRS. RADCLIFFE *Myst. Udolpho* xxxiii, She hardly dared to suffer her thoughts to glance that way. **1821** BYRON *Juan* III. lxxxvi. xii, The tyrant of the Chersonese Was freedom's best and bravest friend; That tyrant was Miltiades! **1825** T. HOOK *Sayings* Ser. II. *Man of Many Fr.* I. 189 Sophy, put down that knife—Maria, that child will cut her fingers off. **1861** M. PATTISON *Ess.* (1889) I. 47 The gates were closed at nine o'clock, and on no pretext opened after that hour. **1897** *Pall Mall Mag* Feb. 188 The wife of the that time Governor.

**b.** Indicating a person or thing assumed to be known, or to be known to be such as is stated. Often (esp. before a person's name: cf. L. *iste*) implying censure, dislike, or scorn; but sometimes commendation or admiration. Freq. standing before a noun or noun-phrase in apposition with another.

*a* **1300** *Cursor M.* 11815 Þis herods..Þat caitif vn-meth and vn-meke. *a* **1400** *Stac. Rome* 405 Pope pelagius, þat holy mon. *c* **1410** LOVE *Bonavent. Mirr.* (1909) 50 The aungeles songen that ioyful songe *Gloria in excelsis*. **1526** TINDALE 2 *Tim.* i. 12 He is able to kepe that which I have committed to his kepynge agaynst that daye. **1563** *Homilies* II. *Gluttony* (1859) 301 Holofernes..had his head stricken from his shoulders by that seely woman Judith. **1591** SPENSER *Tears of Muses* 401 Thy gay Sonne, that winged God of Loue. **1611** SHAKS. *Cymb.* III. iv. 15 That Drugg-damn'd Italy. **1646** R. BAILLIE *Lett.* (1841) II. 349 Will that fool Johnstone never take any course for your books? **1713** STEELE *Guard.* No. 1 ¶ 1 Mr. Airs, that excellent penman. **1800** WORDSW. *Andrew Jones* 1, I hate that Andrew Jones; he'll breed His children up to waste and pillage. **1865** G. MACDONALD *A. Forbes* 51 He's a dour crater, that Murdoch Malison. **1866** G. MEREDITH *Vittoria* xxviii, 'Ah! in that England of yours, women marry for wealth'.

**c.** Used with a plural sb. or numeral, instead of *those*: now only with plurals treated as singulars (e. g. *means, pains*) or taken in a collective sense.

In some Sc. dialects used before plural sbs. generally.

*c* **1330** *Amis & Amil.* 2492 And in on graue thei were leyde, That hende knyghtes both two. *c* **1420** *Chron. Vilod.* 3605 He come þere þat ladyes to, And tolde hem alle. **1545** RAYNOLD *Byrth Mankynde* Hh ij, From that vaynes that be not yet affixed vnto the chorion. *Ibid.* 72 Also to wasshe that partes in water. **1575** *Reg. Privy Council Scot.* II. 473 The present troublis quhairwith that cuntreis ar inquietit. **1654–66** EARL ORRERY *Parthen.* (1676) 204, I will spare thee that pains. **1710** SWIFT *Examiner* No. 16 ¶ 7 That ill manners..I have been often guilty of. **1768** GOLDSM. *Good-n. Man* I, There's that ten guineas you were sending to the poor gentleman. **1861** TROLLOPE *Framley P.* I. xiii. 252 As to that five thousand pounds. **1865** MISS BRADDON *Only a Clod* xxiv, During that rainy six weeks. **1868** G. MACDONALD *R. Falconer* I. xx, Maybe ye wad like to luik at that anes.

**d.** *That once*, that one time: see ONCE 9 c.

**e.** = 'The same' (*obs. rare*). *That same*, † *that self*: see SAME A. 5, B. 2, 4, SELF B. 1, 2.

**1579** LYLY *Euphues* (Arb.) 190 The Rose that is eaten with the Canker is not gathered bicause it groweth on that stalke yat the sweet doth, neither was Helen made a Starre bicause shee came of that Egge with Castor.

**2.** In opposition to *this*: properly denoting the more distant of two things, but often vaguely indicating one thing as distinguished from another. Cf. I. 3 above.

13.. [see THIS B. I. 3]. **1551**– [see THIS B. II. 2].

**b.** Strengthened by *there* (also abbrev. *'ere, 'air*) immediately following: see THERE B. 3 c. Cf. *this here* (HERE *adv.* 1 d). *dial.* and *vulgar*.

**3.** In concord with a sb. which is the antecedent to a relative (expressed or understood). Cf. I. 6, 7.

Usually definitive rather than demonstrative, serving for introduction or anticipation of the relative clause, which completes the description; thus often interchangeable with *the* (cf. THE *a.* 14), but usually more emphatic. (Similarly with a noun further defined by a pple., as in quot. 1813[1].)

*c* **1470** ASHBY *Dicta Philos.* 701 That kyng that maketh his Region To be obedient to his iuste lawe. *c* **1500** *Melusine* 24 Erle Emerye and Raymondin..stode..on that syde as them semyd that the stryf was. **1532** MORE *Confut. Tindale* Wks. 450/2 A manne may saye 'the man that we spake of was here', or 'that man that we spake of was here'. **1637** HEYLIN *Brief Answ.* 75 It was ordeined, that that mans tongue should be cut out which did speake any slanderous..words. **1647–8** COTTERELL *Davila's Hist. Fr.* (1678) 21 Brought..to that issue as was intended. **1658** DRYDEN *Cromwell* xiii, Like that bold Greek who did the East subdue. **1690** LOCKE *Govt.* I. iv. § 42 By withholding that relief God requires him to afford. **1779** *Mirror* No. 50 ¶ 2 That listlessness and languor which attend a state of total inaction. **1813** EUSTACE *Italy* (1815) III. xi. 394 On that peninsulated rock called La Spilla, hanging over yonder deep cavern. **1813** SIR H. DAVY *Agric. Chem.* iii. (1814) 56 The root is that part of the vegetable which least impresses the eye.

**b.** In advb. phrases of time or place, with following relative clause (with relative usually omitted); e.g. † *by that time* (*that*).. = by the time that.. (*obs.*). (In quot. 1573 with advb. clause.) Now *rare* (replaced by *the*), unless emphatic.

*c* **1420** *Chron. Vilod.* 3160 Fulle seke he was By þat tyme þat he þedur þo come. **1523** LD. BERNERS *Froiss.* I. 240 By that tyme it was day, they came to the mountayne. **1573** L. LLOYD *Marrow of Hist.* (1653) 93 That night before they should sail in the morning, appeared unto Simonides the self-same man. **1598** GRENEWEY *Tacitus' Ann.* I. ii. (1622) 21 [They] beset the wood, that way the army should returne. **1656** S. HOLLAND *Zara* (1719) 65 By that time they were half over Styx, they espyed an aged Person. **1760** *Impostors Detected* IV. iii. II. 179 He..got me a wife by that time I had attained my fifteenth year. **1805** EMILY CLARK *Banks of Douro* I. 48 Enraptured at that time the event took place.

**4.** Indicating quality or amount: Of that kind or degree; such, so great. Const. *that* (conj.), *as* (with finite vb. or inf.), inf. (without *as*), or rel. pron. (also with ellipsis of the conj. or rel.); rarely without correlative. Now chiefly *arch.* (or *dial.*). (Cf. THAT *dem. adv.*)

*a* **1450** *Knt. de la Tour* (1906) 131 She..wepte for her synnes, þat was the loue of God and the drede that she had for her misleuinge. **1530** TINDALE *Prol. Deut.*, When I am brought in to that extremite that I must ether suffre or forsake god. **1547** BOORDE *Introd. Knowl.* iii. (1870) 133 Saynt Partryckes purgatory..is not of that effycacyte as is spoken of. **1602** SHAKS. *Ham.* I. v. 48 From me, whose loue was of that dignity, That it went hand in hand, euen with the Vow I made to her in marriage. **1648** MILTON *Tenure Kings* (1650) 57 With that cunning and dexterity as is almost imperceavable. **1678** WALTON *Life Sanderson* 53 An Error of that Magnitude, that I cannot but wonder. **1734** DUCHESS QUEENSBERRY in *Lett. C'tess Suffolk* (1824) II. 94 This enlivened us to that degree that we were mighty good company. **1821** SHELLEY in Lady S. *Mem.* (1859) 155, I hope that I have treated the question with that temper and spirit as to silence cavil. **1848** DICKENS *Dombey* xlvii, He..struck her..with that heaviness, that she tottered on the marble floor. **1865** L. OLIPHANT *Piccadilly* (1870) 241 He blushed to that degree that I felt quite shy.

**† 5.** As neuter sing. of the definite article: see THE A. 1 c. *Obs.* (exc. in *that ilk*: see ILK *a.*[1]). *That one, that other* = the one, the other: see ONE 18, OTHER B. 2; also TONE, TOTHER. *Obs.*

*c* **893** K. ÆLFRED *Orosius* I. i. § 1 Tweȝen dælas: Asia, and þæt oþer Europe. **1297** R. GLOUC. (Rolls) 7017 Þat þe on broþer..in nede helpeþ þere þat oþer. *c* **1400** *Gamelyn* 305 [He] toke him by þat on arme & threw him in a welle. **1470–85** MALORY *Arthur* x. ix. 427 Two bretheren, that one hyght Aleyn, and the other hyghte Tryan. **1509** *Sel. Cas. Crt. Star Chamber* (Selden) 194 Half of that brigge appertaigneth to the said abbot and that other half to the said Town. **1576** GASCOIGNE *Steel Gl.* (Arb.) 68 That one eye winks,..That other pries and peekes.

**III.** Demonstrative Adverb. [Closely related to the adjective use in II. 4.]

To that extent or degree; so much, so. (Qualifying an adj., adv., or pple., † rarely a vb.) Now only *dial.* and *Sc.* (exc. as in b).

*c* **1450** *St. Cuthbert* (Surtees) 6279 His sekenes þat encrest, He gert beere him..Aboute þe contre on a bere. **1616** in J. Russell *Haigs* vii. (1881) 160 If I had been that unhappy as to have such a foolish thing. *a* **1670** HACKET *Abp. Williams* II. (1693) 67 This was carried with that little noise that..the..Bishop was not awaked. **1803** BOSWELL *Change Edin.* 5 Gowd's no that scanty. **1852** DICKENS *Bleak Ho.* xxiv, I was on my guard for a blow, he was that passionate. **1870** — *E. Drood* ii. **1884** MRS. RIDDELL *Berna Boyle* vii, The rooms are that small you might reach a book off the opposite wall. **1888** 'R. BOLDREWOOD' *Robbery under Arms* xxi, He was that weak as he could hardly walk. **1902** O. WISTER *Virginian* xxxv, You were that cool! *Mod. Sc.* He's grown that big ye wad hardly ken him. He was that cunning!

**b.** With an adv. or adj. of quantity, e. g. *that far* (= as far as that), *that much, that high*: more definite than *so*, as indicating the precise amount.

**1634** RUTHERFORD *Lett.* (1862) I. 126, I repose that much in His rich grace that He will be loath to change upon me. **1805** JEFFERSON *Writ.* (1830) IV. 39 His family, which he had sent that far in the course of the day. **1856** MRS. STOWE *Dred* i. I. 5, I never liked anything that long [= six weeks]. **1870** MISS BRIDGMAN *Rob. Lynne* II. xi. 224, 'I ..recollect you that high'—holding her hand about six inches off the table.

**That** (ðæt, ðət), *relative pron.* Forms: see below. [An unstressed and phonetically weakened form of THAT *dem. pron.*, used to subordinate one predication to another.

The Common Indo-Eur. had no relative pronoun, which has been developed separately in the different linguistic families. In Latin it was evolved out of the interrogative, in Teutonic chiefly out of the demonstrative. But even within the Teutonic languages the relative is differently formed (see Wright *Gothic Grammar* § 270, *Old Eng. Grammar* § 468). In mod. English it is expressed by *thăt*, from the demonstrative pron., and by *who* (*whom*), *which*, *what* (after L. *qui, quæ, quod*, F. *qui, que, quel*) from the interrogative pronouns. In northern dialect, ME. and mod., it is commonly expressed by AT, 'AT, rel. pron. In OE. it was expressed (1) by the simple demonstrative *se, séo, þæt*; (2) by the particle *þe*; (3) by *þe* preceded by a personal pronoun or the demonstrative. For *þe*, see THE *conjunctive particle*. The use of the demonstrative as a relative appears to have come about simply by the subordination of the second of two originally consecutive sentences to the first; thus, 'he came to a river; thát (or this) was broad and deep', whence 'he came to a river thăt was broad and deep'. In OE. it is sometimes impossible to determine whether the pronoun of the second clause is still demonstrative or has become relative. Thus the words in the OE. version of *Bæda's History*, I. xii. (1890) 52 'Hi wæron Wihtgylses suna. þæs fæder wæs Witta haten. þæs fæder wæs Wihta haten. and þæs Wihta fæder wæs Woden nemned', might be read either as short consecutive sentences, 'They were sons of Wihtgyls; *his* father [lit. *that's* father] was called Witta; *his* father was called Wihta; and this Wihta's father was named Woden'; or 'They were sons of Wihtgyls *whose* father was called Witta, *whose* father was called Wihta, and *whose* (Wihta's) father was named Woden'. Bæda's Latin has *cujus* in all three places, so that the translator apparently used *þæs* as a relative. See also Wülfing *Syntax Alfreds des Grossen* I. § 275. Now, and for a long time past, the relative *that* has been stressless, and consequently with obscure vowel; but this unstressing and obscuration came gradually, and was never represented in writing, so that in the written forms there is nothing to distinguish the relative from the demonstrative.]

**A.** Examples of early inflexional forms.

(The inflexional forms were, to begin with, those of the dem. pron. and definite article (see prec. and THE); but, as relative, *that* is now invariable for gender, case, and number.)

*c* **825** *Vesp. Psalter* ix. 12 Singað dryhtne se [L. *qui*] eardað in Sion. *Ibid.* 28 Ðes [*cujus*] muð awerȝednisse & bitternisse ful is. *Ibid.* cxxxii. 3 Swe swe deaw..se astiȝeð in munt Sion. *c* **825** *Vesp. Hymns* xiii. 4 ȝehiowadas mon ðæm [*cui*] ðinre onlicnisse ondwliotan saldes ȝelicne. *c* **893** K. ÆLFRED *Oros.* I. i. § 1 Oceanus.., þone man garsecg hateð. *Ibid.* § 11 Rin þa ea, seo wilð of þæm beorȝe þe mon Alpis hætt. *Ibid.*, Donua þa ea, þære æwielme is neah Rines ofre. *Ibid.* II. vii. § 2 An burȝ in Affrica sio [*quæ*] wæs neh þæm sæ. *a* **900** tr. *Bæda's Hist.* I. xii. [xv.] (1890) 52 Wihta..þæs..fæder wæs Woden nemned. *c* **950** *Lindisf. Gosp.* Matt. xxiv. 15 Unfeȝernis slitnese ðiu [*Rushw.* þe] ȝecueden wæs from ðæm witgo. *c* **1100** *O. E. Chron.* an. 1093, Anselme..se wæs ær abbod on Bæc.

**B.** Signification.

The general relative pronoun, referring to any antecedent, and used without inflexion irrespective of gender, number, and case.

**I. 1.** Introducing a clause defining or restricting the antecedent, and thus completing its sense. (The ordinary use: referring to persons or things.)

Sometimes replaceable by *who* (of persons) or *which* (of things), but properly only in cases where no ambiguity results: cf. 2, and see WHO, WHICH, *rel.* (For ellipsis of *that*, see 10.)

*c* **825** *Vesp. Psalter* vii. 7 In bebode ðæt ðu bibude. **858** *Charter* in *O. E. Texts* 438 Ðes landes boec..ðet eðelbearht cyning wullafe sealde. *c* **888** K. ÆLFRED *Boeth.* v. § 1 Ne sece ic no her þa bec ac þæt ðæt þa bec forstent. *c* **1000** *Ags. Ps.* (Th.) lxxxviii. 41 [lxxxix. 48] Hwylc manna is þæt his aȝene.. sawle ȝenerige? *c* **1175** *Lamb. Hom.* 3 God [? goð] in þane castel þet is onȝein eou. *Ibid.* 79 Þes Mon þhet alihte from ierusalem in to ierico. *a* **1225** *Ancr. R.* 162 Þeo þet duden mid God al þet heo euer wolden. *a* **1300** *Cursor M.* 22218 All þat þe cristen finds þare. **1340** *Ayenb.* 39 Þe ualse yulemde þet vlyeþ. *c* **1374** CHAUCER *Boeth.* IV. pr. vii. 113 (Camb. MS.) Þou þat art put in the encres or in the heyhte of vertu. **1377** LANGL. *P. Pl.* B. x. 38 Þo þat feynen hem folis. **1382** WYCLIF *Matt.* iv. 16 The peple that dwelte in derknessis say grete liȝt. **1456** SIR G. HAYE *Law Arms* (S.T.S.) 244 It that was wont to be callit law. *c* **1460** FORTESCUE *Abs. & Lim. Mon.* ix. (1885) 130 The kyng off Scottis þat last dyed. **1500–20** DUNBAR *Poems* xx. 8 He rewlis weill, that weill him self can gyd. **1526** TINDALE *John* iv. 26, I thatt spake vnto the, am he. **1531** *Test. Ebor.* (Surtees) VI. 24 A distres that I take of hyr. **1596** DANETT tr. *Comines* (1614) 173 But this was not it that grieued them. **1611** BIBLE *Ps.* lxv. 2 O thou that hearest prayer. **1712** ADDISON *Spect.* No. 512 ¶ 6 A Tree that grew near an old Wall. **1798** COLERIDGE *Anc. Mar.* II. v, We were the first that ever burst Into that silent sea. **1865** SWINBURNE *Atalanta* 76 How shall I say, son, That am no sister? **1875** JOWETT *Plato* (ed. 2) I. 342 This is about all that he has to say. **1886** C. E. PASCOE *Lond. of To-day* xxx. (ed. 3) 269 The Westminster Hall that we now see.. is the building of Richard II's time.

**b.** As obj. of a preposition, which in this case stands at the end of the relative clause (in OE. and ME. sometimes immediately before the verb): e. g. *the cup that I shall drink of* = the cup of which I shall drink; ME. *these that I have of told* = these of which I have told.

(When *whom* or *which* is substituted for *that*, the prep. precedes the relative.)

*c* **1200** ORMIN 462 Þiss gode prest, Þatt we nu mælenn offe, Wass..ȝehatenn Zacaryas. *a* **1300** *Seven Sins* 44 in *E. E. P.* (1862) 19 Þe deuil is his executur of is gold and is tresure Þat he so moch trist to. *c* **1400** MAUNDEV. (1839) ii. 10 The naylles that crist was naylled with on the cros. *c* **1430** *Hymns Virg.* 37/69 Theise .iij. þat y haue of toold. **1473** *Coventry Leet-Bk.* 383 The which letter.. is in kepyng in the Tour of Sent Marie hall in the same box þat the kynges generall pardon graunted to this Citee is Ine. **1526** TINDALE *Matt.* xx. 22 Are ye able to drynke off the cuppe that y shall drinke of, and to be baptised with the baptism that y shalbe baptised with? **1611** BIBLE *Judges* xx. 48 All the cities that they came to. **1678** BUNYAN *Pilgr.* I. 49 The dangers that Mistrust and Timorus were driven back by. **1818** SCOTT *Hrt. Midl.* xxix [xxx], The ship that somebody was sailing in. **1841** S. WARREN *Ten thousand a-Year* xiv, There's nothing..that we need be afraid of. *Mod.* The play that you were talking about. The hole that the mouse ran into. The town that he came from.

**2.** Introducing a clause stating something additional about the antecedent (the sense of the principal clause being complete without the relative clause). Now only *poet.* or *rhet.*, the ordinary equivalents being *who* (obj. *whom*) of persons, and *which* of things.

But the relative clause is often merely descriptive, stating an attribute of the antecedent; or it may give the reason or a reason of the main statement, and thus be closely connected with it; the use in these cases approaches that in 1. There are thus many cases in which modern use allows either *that* or *who, which*, and in which poets prefer *that*. (*That* as in quot. *c* 1450 is now impossible.)

*c* 893 K. ÆLFRED *Oros.* I. i. § 7 On Indea londe is xliiii þeoda buton þæm iglande Taprabane, þæt hæfð on him x byrg. *a* 900 tr. *Bæda's Hist.* I. i. (1890) 24 Breoton ist garsecges ealond, ðæt wæs iu geara Albion haten. *c* 1000 *Ags. Gosp.* Matt. vi. 30 Æcyres weod, þæt ðe [*Rushw.* þæt] to dæg is & bið to morgen on ofen asend. *a* 1240 *Ureisun* in *Lamb. Hom.* 185 Ha haueþ oþer wilneþ after cunfort on eorþe, þet is fikel and fals. *a* 1300 *Cursor M.* 9406 He wroght a felau of his ban Till Adam, þat was first allan [*v. r.* his an]. *c* 1320 *Cast. Love* 8–9 God fader and Sone and Holigost, Þat alle þing on eorþe sixt and wost, Þat O God art and þrilli-hod. *c* 1386 CHAUCER *Prol.* 10 Smale foweles maken melodye, That slepen al the nyght with open eye. *c* 1450 *Godstow Reg.* 501 Yf hit happen the said priour and Covent..to faile in the payment of þe seid yerely rente (that god for-bede). *c* 1489 CAXTON *Sonnes of Aymon* xxiv. 515 Reynaude, that sawe this harde batayll, shoved himselfe among the thickest. 1548–9 (Mar.) *Bk. Com. Prayer, Litany*, O God mercyfull father, that despysest not the sighinge of a contryte hearte. 1621 BP. MOUNTAGU *Diatribæ* 16 You are a merry man..that tell me, your selfe, you are not within. 1678 *Gunpowder Treason* in *Select. Harl. Misc.* (1793) 252 Catesby..thereupon engaged Sir Everard Digby, that promised to advance fifteen hundred pounds towards it; and Mr. Francis Tresham, that gave him assurance of two thousand pounds. 1824 LAMB *Let. to W. Marten* 19 July (in *Sotheby's Catal.* 5 June (1902) 66), Pity me that have been a Gentleman these four weeks and am reduced in one day to the state of a ready writer. 1843 MACAULAY *Lays Anc. Rome, Horatius*, False Sextus That wrought the deed of shame. 1885–94 R. BRIDGES *Eros & Psyche* May 4 Lazy mists, that still Climb'd on the shadowy roots of every hill.

**3.** As subj. or obj. of the rel. clause, with ellipsis of the antecedent.

**a.** Of things: *thăt* = (the thing) that, that which, what. Very common down to 16th c.; now *arch.* and *poetic*, *what* being the prose form.

In later use the single *that* may become emphatic, and is then demonstrative with ellipsis of the relative: see THAT *dem. pron.* 7.

*c* 888 K. ÆLFRED *Boeth.* xxvi. § 1 Þonne ðu..oððe hæfdest þæt ðu noldes oððe næfdest þæt ðu woldest. *c* 1175 *Lamb. Hom.* 5 Nu scule ge understonden þet hit bi-tacnet. *c* 1250 *Gen. & Ex.* 3066 Ðat [h]ail ða bileaf sal al ben numen. *a* 1300 *Cursor M.* 3711 He ete and dranc þat was his will. *c* 1315 SHOREHAM vi. 11 Þou hast y-rygt þat was amys, Ywonne þat was y-lore. *c* 1400 *Laud Troy Bk.* 7877 Antenor did that In him was. 1477–9 *Rec. St. Mary at Hill* 91 Paid to hewe Clerk that he lackyd in his wagis. 1535 COVERDALE *Matt.* xx. 14 Take that thine is [WYCLIF that that is thine] and go thy waye. *a* 1568 ASCHAM *Scholem.* I. (Arb.) 49 Where they should neither see that was vncumlie nor heare that was vnhonest. 1600 SHAKS. *A. Y. L.* III. ii. 77, I earne that I eate: get that I weare. 1611 BIBLE *Job* xlii. 3 Therefore haue I vttered that I vnderstood not. 1887 MORRIS *Odyss.* XII. 301 In peace eat that ye have.

**b.** Of persons: *thăt* = (the person) that, he (or him) that, one that; *pl.* (persons) that, they (them), or those who. Now only after *there are* and the like: see THERE *adv.* 5 f.

*c* 1320 *Cast. Love* 1 Þat good þenkeþ good may do. ?*a* 1400 *Arthur* 1 Herkeneþ, þat loueþ honour. 1400 *26 Pol. Poems* i. 122 That taken with wrong, are goddis theues. 14.. *Why I can't be a Nun* 244 in *E. E. P.* (1862) 144 Dame chastyte..sum her loved in hert fulle dere, And there weren that dyd not so. 1560 BIBLE (Genev.) *Prov.* xi. 24 There is that scatereth, and is more increased. *c* 1585 R. BROWNE *Answ. Cartwright* 79 There were of the princes that tooke his parte. 1605 SHAKS. *Lear* I. iv. 279 Woe [*sc.* to him] that too late repents. 1611 BIBLE *Exod.* iii. 14, I am that I am. *a* 1665 DIGBY *Priv. Mem.* (1827) 272 Of her ancestors there have been that have exalted and pulled down kings.

**II.** In various special or elliptical constructions, in some of which *that* passes into a relative or conjunctive adverb. (Cf. next word.)

**4.** After *same*: sometimes strictly the rel. pron. (1); sometimes with looser construction or ellipsis: = *as*: see SAME A. 1 a, and cf. AS B. 23.

*c* 1200, etc. [see SAME A. 1 a]. *a* 1575 tr. *Pol. Verg. Eng. Hist.* (Camden No. 29) 181 William made the same awnswer that befor. 1600 SURFLET *Countrie Farme* I. xxx. 200 The mare-mule is subiect to the same diseases that the horse. 1664 H. MORE *Exp.* 7 *Epist.* viii. 124, I understand by φιλαδελφία the same that ἀγάπη, *universal Love.* 1690 W. WALKER *Idiomat. Anglo-Lat.* 387 They say Diana is the same that the Moon is. 1771 LUCKOMBE *Hist. Print.* 404 He grasps his left hand about the Foot end of the Page in the same posture that his right hand grasps the Head end. 1783 COLMAN *Prose on Sev. Occas., Notes Art Poetry* (1787) III. 97 Other criticks have taken the text..in the same sense that I have here considered it. 1819 HAZLITT *Pol. Ess.* 421 If Mr. Malthus chooses to say, that men will always be governed by the same good mechanical motives that they are at present.

**5.** Preceded by a descriptive noun or adj., in a parenthetic exclamatory clause (e.g. *fool that he is*): = AS B. 25.

*c* 1374 CHAUCER *Troylus* III. 1516 (1565) Nece, how kan ye fare? Criseyde answerede, Neuere þe bet for yow, Fox þat ye ben. *c* 1440 *York Myst.* xxx. 26 Lo! sirs, my worthely wiffe, þat sche is! 1526 TINDALE *Rom.* vii. 24 O wretched man that I am. 1591 SHAKS. *Two Gent.* v. iv. 28 O miserable, vnhappy that I am. 1605 R. R. in *Sylvester's Wks.* (1880) I. 15/1 Foole that I was, I thought in younger times [etc.]. 1855 BROWNING *Popularity* 1 Stand still, true poet that you are! I know you. 1877 E. W. GOSSE *North. Stud.*, 4 *Danish Poets* (1890) 227 A few months after Andersen—poor little forlorn adventurer that he was—left that city.

**6.** † **a.** = AS B. 13. *Obs. rare*⁻¹.

*c* 1175 *Credo* in *Lamb. Hom.* 75 Alle ge kunnen leste, þet ich wene, ower credo.

**b.** In *not that I know*, and similar expressions: = According to what, as far as. Cf. KNOW *v.* 18 c.

*c* 1460 *Towneley Myst.* xxi. 239 No word yit he spake That I wyst. 1530 PALSGR. 762/1, I never trespassed agaynst hym, that I wotte of. 1602 SHAKS. *Ham.* II. ii. 155 *Pol.* Hath there bene such a time..That I haue possitiuely said, 'tis so, When it prou'd otherwise? *King.* Not that I know. 1776 *Trial of Nundocomar* 30/1, I was not at Mongheer; nor was he there, that I know of. 1819 SHELLEY *Cenci* I. iii, Can we do nothing? *Colon.* Nothing that I see. 1840 CARLYLE *Heroes* iv. (1872) 126 But Protestantism has not died yet, that I hear of! 1864 DASENT *Jest & Earnest* (1873) II. 343 He had never seen Hall that he knew before that day. 1886 SIR N. LINDLEY in *Law Rep.* 31 Chanc. Div. 367 An injunction to restrain such proceedings has never that I know of been granted since 1851. *Mod.* He is not here, that I can learn. No one knows anything about it, that I can find.

**7.** After the word *time*, or any sb. meaning a point or space of time: At, in, or on which; when.

Usually introducing a defining clause, as in 1: sometimes an additional statement, as in 2. For ellipsis of *that*, see 10.

*Beowulf* 2646 Nu is se dæg cumen þæt ure man-dryhten mægenes be-hofað. *a* 1000 *Cædmon's Gen.* 585 (Gr.) Wæs seo hwil þæs lang, þæt ic geornlice gode þegnode. *c* 1000 ÆLFRIC *Num.* xiii. 21 Hit wæs ða se tima þæt winberian ripodon. 1303 R. BRUNNE *Handl. Synne* 862 Fro þe fryday þat he deyde, To tyme þat he ros. *c* 1386 CHAUCER *Reeve's T.* 189 Allas quod Iohn the day that I was born. 1470–85 MALORY *Arthur* VI. xvi. 209 Thyne houre is come that thou muste dye. 1525 LD. BERNERS *Froiss.* II. 53 In the meane tyme that our supper was a dressyng, this knight said to me [etc.]. 1600 SHAKS. *A. Y. L.* III. ii. 187, I was neuer so berim'd since Pythagoras time that I was an Irish Rat. 1611 BIBLE *Gen.* ii. 17 In the day that thou eatest thereof, thou shalt surely die. 1760–72 H. BROOKE *Fool of Qual.* (1809) IV. 31 You speak..like a sage..at an age that our young nobility scarcely begin to think. 1802 MAR. EDGEWORTH *Moral T.* xii, The night that he went to the play. 1879 GEO. ELIOT *Theo. Such* i. 10 One day that I had incautiously mentioned this interesting fact.

† **b.** = To the time that; till, until. *Obs.*

971 *Blickl. Hom.* 237 Nu þry dagas to lafe syndon þæt hie þe willaþ acwellan. *c* 1175 *Lamb. Hom.* 33 Þah þu liuedest of adames frumðe þet come þes dei. *c* 1205 LAY. 229 Þis lond he hire lende Þat come hir lifes ende. *c* 1320 *Cast. Love* 1412 From þe tyme þat he Adam wrougte, Þat he vp-ros and vs for-bougte.

† **c.** = From the time that; since. *Obs. rare*⁻¹.

*c* 1205 LAY. 26294 Hit is feole gere Þat heore þrættes comen here.

**8.** Connecting two clauses loosely or anacoluthically, the relative or dependent clause being imperfect (the part omitted being suggested by the principal clause); giving the effect of the ordinary rel. pron. with ellipsis of a preposition, an infinitive, etc.: cf. 7. (Now considered slipshod.)

*c* 1425 WYNTOUN *Cron.* IV. xxv. 2380 Off þe nycht next gane beforn Þat Iulyus was slayn on þe morn. *c* 1530 LD. BERNERS *Arth. Lyt. Bryt.* 494 Oftentimes people speketh of a thing that they knowe but lytle what the conclusyon shall be. 1596 SHAKS. *Merch. V.* II. vi. 9 Who riseth from a feast With that keene appetite that he sits downe? 1673 *Essex Papers* (Camden) I. 51 Who put this Citty into that disorder that I found it. 1779 *Mirror* No. 29 ⁋ 4 His fortune and his ancestry entitled him..to appear in any shape that he pleased. 1875 DASENT *Vikings* I. 146 If you will only see things..in the light that we see them.

**9.** *That* followed by a poss. pron. corresponding to the antecedent (e.g. *you that your, the man that his*, OE. *þe his*, THE particle 3 d) is an ancient mode of expressing the genitive of the relative = *whose*.

(The same idiom is used in many langs., e. g. Celtic, Semitic, etc.). Still common dialectally.

1456 *Sc. Acts Jas. II* (1814) II. 45/2 Item, it is ordanyt..at ilk man þᵗ his gudis extendis to xxᵗⁱ merckis be bodyn at þe lest wᵗ..a suerde and a buclare, a bow and a schaif of arrowis. 1470–85 MALORY *Arthur* VIII. xxxv. 327 There came a man that sire Tristram afore hand had slayne his broder. 1523 FITZHERB. *Husb.* § 148 That man that thy horse hath eten his corne or grasse wyll be greued at the. 1602 *Ld. Cromwell* I. ii, Theres legions now of beggars.. That their originall did spring from Kings. [1873 MURRAY *Dial. S. Scotl.* 196 When the Relative is used in the Possessive Case (*whose*) it is necessary to express it by..*at* (*that*) and the *possessive pronoun* belonging to the antecedent; thus 'the man ăt hys weyfe's deid'..'the wumman ăt ye ken hyr sun'.]

¶ **10.** The relative is very frequently omitted by ellipsis, esp. in senses 1, 1 b (chiefly as obj. or pred., less freq. and now only in certain connexions as subj.); also in sense 7.

This (one of the commonest idioms in colloquial English, and largely found in the literary language) prob. began with the relative *þe*, THE. Cf. also THAT *conj.* 10.

*c* 1250 *Gen. & Ex.* 297 Adam ben king and eue queen Of alle ðe ðinge in werlde ben. —751 Ilc ðing deieð ðor-inne is driuen. 13.. *Cursor M.* 4892 Yon er theues..And theif es he þam hider send. *a* 1450 *Le Morte Arth.* 72, I drede we shall discouerid be, Off the loue is vs by-twene. 1578 TIMME *Caluine on Gen.* 164 When those things should follow are set before. 1592 SHAKS. *Rom. & Jul.* I. i. 212, I do loue a woman..and shee's faire I loue. 1611 BIBLE *Gen.* iii. 5 In the day ye eate thereof, then your eyes shalbee opened. 1676 GLANVILL *Ess.* Pref. a 3 b, It shews a particular service Philosophy doth. 1690 LOCKE *Hum. Und.* II. xxi. § 32 Life it self..is a burden cannot be born under the lasting.. pressure of such an uneasiness. 1781 COWPER *Verses Alex. Selkirk* i, I am monarch of all I survey. 1850 TENNYSON *In Mem.* iv, What is it makes me beat so low? *Ibid.* v, To put in words the grief I feel. 1851 LONGF. *Golden Leg.* ii. 273 Who was it said Amen? 1855 BROWNING *Misconceptions* i, This is a spray the Bird clung to.

**That** (ðæt, ðət), *conj.* Also 1 þæt, 2–3 þet, 2–6 þat. [Uses of THAT *dem.* or *rel. pron.* in which it becomes a mere relative or conjunctive particle: cf. THE *particle*. So in the other WGer. langs. Cf. Gr. ὅτι from neuter of rel. pron. ὅστις, L. *quod* from neuter of rel. *qui*, It. *che*, Sp., Pg., Fr. *que*.]

**I. 1.** Introducing a dependent substantive-clause, as subject, object, or other element of the principal clause, or as complement of a sb. or adj., or in apposition with a sb. therein.

The dependent clause as subject is most commonly placed after the verb and introduced by a preceding *it*, e.g. 'it is certain that he was there' = 'that he was there, is certain': see IT 4 b. As object, it usually follows, e. g. 'I have heard that he was there'. (For ellipsis of *that*, see 10.)

[This use of *that* is generally held to have arisen out of the dem. pron. pointing to the clause which it introduces. Cf. (1) He once lived here: we all know *thát*; (2) *That* (now *this*) we all know: he once lived here; (3) We all know *that* (or *this*): he once lived here; (4) We all know *thăt* he once lived here; (5) We all know he once lived here. In 1, 2, 3 *that* is a demonstrative pronoun in apposition to the statement 'he once lived here'; in 4 it has sunk into a conjunctive particle, and (like the relative pronoun) has become stressless; in 5 it has disappeared, and 'he once lived here' appears as the direct object of 'we know'. After *aware, certain, conscious, suspicious, assured, informed, persuaded*, etc., *of* or some other prep. seems understood before *that*: 'I am certain of that: he once lived here'. But 'I am certain that' may have arisen as another way of saying 'I know that'; and so of the other expressions.]

*c* 888 K. ÆLFRED *Boeth.* v. § 3 Ic wat þæt ælc wuht from Gode com. *a* 900 CYNEWULF *Elene* 815 Nu ic wat þæt þu eart gecyðed and acenned allra cyninga þrym. *Ibid.* 1168 Þæt is gedafenlic, þæt þu dryhtnes word on hyge healde. *c* 1000 ÆLFRIC *Gen.* i. 4 God geseah þa, þæt hit god wæs. *c* 1175 *Lamb. Hom.* 111 Þe sixte unþeau is.. þet he for modleste ne mei his monnan don stere. *c* 1205 LAY. 13 Hit com him on mode..þet he wolde of Engle þa æðelæn tellen. *c* 1250 *O. Kent. Serm.* in *O. E. Misc.* 26 And herodes i-herde þet o king was i-bore. *a* 1300 *K. Horn* (Camb. MS.) 272 And þe sonde seide Þat sik lai þat maide. 1375 BARBOUR *Bruce* III. 481 Þen hapnyt at þat tyme..Þat þe Erle of þe Leuenax was Amang þe hillis. *c* 1380 WYCLIF *Sel. Wks.* III. 362 We ben certein þat Crist may not axe oþir obedience. *c* 1386 CHAUCER *Prol.* 500 And this figure he added eek ther to, That if gold ruste, what shal Iren doo? *c* 1440 *Generydes* 2902 What think ye best thanne..yt we shall doo? 1535 COVERDALE *Exod.* iii. 12 This shall be the token, yᵗ I haue sent the. 1567 PAINTER *Pal. Pleas.* (1813) II. 160 That I remayne in fielde it is to me greate fame. 1611 BIBLE *Prov.* xix. 2 That the soule be without knowledge, it is not good. 1726 G. ROBERTS *Four Years' Voy.* 135 Their Opinion, that it was not real, but imaginary Land we had seen. 1784 COWPER *Task* I. 156 We have borne The ruffling wind, scarce conscious that it blew. 1809 COLERIDGE *Lett.* (1895) 555 The story is as certain as that Dr. Dodd was hung. 1873 MORLEY *Rousseau* I. vii. 284 Rousseau was persuaded that Madame d'Epinay was his betrayer.

† **b.** Introducing a clause in apposition to or exemplifying the statement in the principal clause: = in that, in the fact that. *Obs.* or *arch.* (now usually expressed by *in* with gerund).

This appears to be transitional between 1 and 2.

901–24 in Birch *Cart. Sax.* II. 236 Helmstan ða undæde gedyde, ðæt he Æðeredes belt forstæl. *c* 1489 CAXTON *Sonnes of Aymon* iv. 119 We have don evyll that we have not taken surete. 1526 TINDALE *Phil.* iv. 14 Ye have wele done, that ye bare parte with me in my tribulacion. 1611 BIBLE 1 *Kings* viii. 18 Thou diddest well that it was in thine heart. — *Acts* x. 33 Thou hast well done, that thou art come [so CRANMER: WYCL. & *Rhem.* in coming: TINDALE & *Geneva*, for to come].

† **c.** Introducing a sb.-clause as obj. of a preceding preposition: = the fact that. *Obs.* and *rare*, exc. after certain prepositions with which *that* forms conjunctional phrases (*after that, before that, by that*, etc.), sometimes with special meanings, and chiefly *obs.* or *arch.*: see AFTER C. 1 b, BEFORE C. 1 a, BY *prep.* 21 c, FOR THAT 1, IN *prep.* 39, UNTO, WITH, WITHOUT. *Obs.*

*c* 1175—[see AFTER C. 1 b]. *c* 1200—[see BEFORE C. 1 a]. *a* 1300—[see BY *prep.* 21 c]. *c* 1440—[see IN *prep.* 39]. 1444 *Rolls of Parlt.* V. 121/1 To stonde and abyde for terme of her lyves, with that they dwell continuelli within the seid Toun or Fraunchise. 1484 CAXTON *Fables of Alfonce* ix, I shalle not leue the goo, withoute that thow hold to me that [etc.]. 1485 *Rolls of Parlt.* VI. 325/2 Contynued their possessions in the same; unto that Humfrey Stafford.. entred into the said mannors. 1525 LD. BERNERS *Froiss.* II. 554 The bysshoppe and the lorde de la Ryver were joyouse of that the herytaunce shulde abyde with the Vycount. *c* 1530 — *Arth. Lyt. Brit.* 493, I am angry wyth nothynge but with that Florence shold thus escape us. 1557 NORTH *Gueuara's Diall Pr.* xx. 36 This shalbe sene by that they succour the poore.

**d.** In periphrastic construction, following a clause of the form *it is* (*was*, etc.) + an adv. or advb. phr., to which emphasis is given by the periphrasis: see IT 4 d. (The sense may be less emphatically expressed by omitting *it is* (*was*, etc.) and *that*, e. g. [It was] here [that] he fell.) Cf. Onions *Advanced Eng. Syntax* § 15 a, 6.

*Beowulf* 1362 Nis þæt feor heonen mil-ȝe-mearces þæt se mere standeð. *a* 1250, etc. [see It 4 d]. 1470-85 Malory *Arthur* vi. viii. 194 Thou arte..lyke on knyȝt that I hate,..so be hit that thou be not he I wyl lyghtly accorde with the. 1672 Marvell *Reh. Transp.* i. 219 Therefore it is that they are agrieved. 1736 Mrs. Manley *Secret Mem.* II. 116 It is not always that we ought to judge by Appearances. 1780 *Mirror* No. 77 ⁋ 6 It is owing to this circumstance, that a general lover seldom forms an attachment to any particular object. 1814 Wordsw. *Yarrow Visited* 25 Where was it that the famous Flower Of Yarrow Vale lay bleeding? 1875 Croll *Climate & T.* 467 It is seldom that the geologist has an opportunity of seeing a complete section. 1877 Miss Yonge *Cameos* Ser. iii. xv. 140 It was for his own supremacy that he fought. 1890 Sir C. S. C. Bowen in *Law Times Rep.* LXIII. 735/1 It was because he failed to prove this that his case broke down.

**e.** Introducing an exclamatory clause (with or without a preceding interjection or interj. phr.) expressing some emotion, usually (now always) sorrow, indignation, or the like. (Now usually with *should.*)

Some of those with interj. or interj. phr. may be regarded as belonging to 2: cf. 'I am sorry that..', also quot. 1535 in 2.

*c* 888 K. Ælfred *Boeth.* ix, Eala þæt nanwuht nis fæste stondendes weorces. *c* 1315 Shoreham v. 223 O þat hy were blyþe, þo hye here seȝen So glorious alyue. *a* 1350 in *Hampole's Wks.* (1895) I. 345 Whan Adam sauȝ hym comen, lord, þat he was glade! *Ibid.* II. 360 Lord, þat þe was wo bigon in þat ilke tyde! *c* 1440 *Jacob's Well* 125 Allas, þat euer gadryd I monye on hepe, to trustyn þere-vpon. *c* 1460 *Towneley Myst.* iv. 195 A, Lord, that I shuld abide this day! 1470-85 Malory *Arthur* xiii. viii. 623 Allas sayd she that euer I sawe you. 1604 Shaks. *Oth.* ii. iii. 291 Oh, that men should put an Enemie in their mouthes, to steale away their Braines? 1610 — *Temp.* i. ii. 67 That a brother should Be so perfidious. 1819 Shelley *Cenci* i. ii. 54 Great God! that such a father should be mine! *Mod.* That it should ever come to this! That he should turn against us, after all his professions of friendship!

**II. 2.** Introducing a clause expressing the cause, ground, or reason of what is stated in the principal clause. (See also 1 b, e.)

In OE. often *þæs* (*þe*), gen. of *þæt*. For ellipsis of *that*, see 10.

*c* 1205 Lay. 9375 He wes glæd þat his ifon weoren dæd. 13.. *Sir Beues* (A.) 4059 Beues was glad, þat he was come. *c* 1412 Hoccleve *De Reg. Princ.* 1477 Þat þou art as thou art, god þanke and herie. 1445 in *Anglia* XXVIII. 273 Men..Merveileth þat thou so lowly art. 1533 Bellenden *Livy* ii. xi. (S.T.S.) I. 169 For þe commoun pepill reiosit þat þe wolchis war cummyn. 1535 Coverdale *Ps.* cxix. [cxx.] 5 Wo is me, yᵗ my banishment endureth so longe. 1611 Bible *Isa.* lxiii. 5, I wondered that there was none to vphold. 1810 Crabbe *Borough* xviii. 208 Men..bless their God that time has fenced their heart. 1827 Hallam *Const. Hist.* I. 697 His sincerity in this was the less suspected, that his wife..was entirely presbyterian. 1842 Macaulay in *Life & Lett.* (1876) II. 114, I should be very sorry that it were known. 1859 Geo. Eliot *A. Bede* xxxv, Mrs. Poyser was quite agreeably surprised that Hetty wished to go and see Dinah. 1866 Reade *G. Gaunt* (ed. 2) II. 14 She..thought of them all the more that she was discouraged from enlarging on them.

(*b*) Also in constructions now *obs.* or *arch.*

*a* 1000 *Andreas* 276 (Gr.) Bið þe meorð wið god, þæt þu us on lade liðe weorðe. *c* 1000 *Ags. Gosp.* Matt. xvi. 8 Hwæt þence ȝe betwux eow..þæt [*Rushw.* forþon þæt] ȝe hlafas nabbað? 13.. *Coer de L.* 831 Sche..Wrong her handes that sche was born. *c* 1555 Harpsfield *Divorce Hen. VIII* (Camden) 270 Then is there a quarrel picked against the Popes that they made such restraints. 1567 Allen *Def. Priesthood* 352 And S. Augustin excommunicated County Bonifacius that he tooke from the Churche an offender. *a* 1657 R. Loveday *Lett.* (1663) 83 Honest J. is ready to beat his wife that she forces his promise to so slothful a performance. 1790 Cowper *Let.* 27 Feb., I am crazed that I cannot ask you all together. 1829 Carlyle in *For. Rev. & Cont. Misc.* IV. 109 Neither should we censure Novalis that he dries his tears.

**b.** *Not that..* (ellipt.): = 'I do not say this because..'; or 'It is not the fact that..', 'One must not suppose that..' (sense 1): see Not *adv.* 6 a.

1601 [see Not *adv.* 6 a]. 1681 Dryden *Abs. & Achit.* 381 Such virtue's only given to guide a throne. Not that your father's mildness I contemn. 1878 T. Hardy *Ret. Native* i. ix, Where is she staying now? Not that I care. 1878 Huxley *Physiogr.* 185 Not that a particle of this substance is annihilated.

**3.** Introducing a clause expressing purpose, end, aim, or desire: with simple subjunctive (*arch.*), or with *may* (pa. t. *might*), *should*, rarely *shall*.

Formerly also preceded by *as* (As B. 21 b). See also May *v.*[1] B. 8 a. The meaning is now more fully expressed by *in order that*: see Order *sb.* 29. After *will, wish, pray, beseech*, and the like, the function of *that* seems to combine senses 1 and 3.

*a* 900 tr. *Bæda's Hist.* ii. xi. [xiv.] § 1 Þær se biscop oft.. wæs, þæt he fulwade þæt folc in Swalwan streame. *c* 1000 *Ags. Gosp.* Mark xiv. 38, ȝebiddað þæt ȝe on costnunge ne gan. *a* 1018 *O. E. Chron.* an. 1009, We ȝyt næfdon þa ȝeselða..þæt seo scipfyrd nytt wære ðisum earde. *a* 1200 *Moral Ode* 313 Ac drihte crist he ȝiue us strencþe, stonde þat we mote. 1303 R. Brunne *Handl. Synne* 3742 Ȝyf þou ȝaue euer cunsel or rede For yre, þat a man were dede. *c* 1410 Love *Bonavent. Mirr.* (1908) 106 Besy that al thing were wele and couenably done. *c* 1440 *Jacob's Well* 121 Turne þi face fro no pore man, þat god turne noȝt his face fro þe. 1683 Moxon *Mech. Exerc., Printing* x. ⁋ 8 This cutting down..is made..that the Cramp-Irons..joggle not on either side off the Ribs. 1683 *Trial Ld. Russell* in *Lady R.'s Lett.* (1807) p. xlvi, We pray for the King that the challenge may be over-ruled. 1708 *Lond. Gaz.* No. 4454/3 This is to Advertise all Persons, that they do not lend her any Mony. *a* 1774 Goldsm. *Surv. Exp. Philos.* (1776) I. 75 The bones of animals..calcined in such a manner as that all their oil should be exhausted. 1816 J. Wilson *City of Plague* i. ii. 67 Give me one look, That I may see his face so beautiful. 1874 A. J. Christie in *Ess. Rel. & Lit.* Ser. iii. 50 Christ..had prayed that Peter's faith should not fail.

†**b.** Introducing a parenthetic clause of purpose. *Obs.* (Now expressed by the inf., e. g. 'that we speak of no more' = to speak of no more.)

13.. *Pol. Rel. & L. Poems* (1866) 221 Hit beoþ þreo tymes on þo day, þat soþe to witen me mai. 1611 Bible *Transl. Pref.* 1 Synods & Church-maintenance (that we speake of no more things of this kinde) should be as safe as a Sanctuary.

**c.** In exclamations of desire or longing: with verb in subjunctive.

Now always with vb. in *past subj.* (indicating improbability of fulfilment), usually with preceding interj. (see also O *int.* 2), also (*arch.*) with *would* or *would God* (sense 1: see *would* s. v. Will *v.*). Formerly also with vb. in pres. subj. (indicating possibility of fulfilment), where *that* is now omitted. In quot. 13.. expressing a command (*that he war* = let him be).

1297 R. Glouc. (Rolls) 6189 A duc þer was..þat was traytour..þat god ȝiue him ssame. 13.. *Seuyn Sag.* 651 Goth, he seigh, to the prisone, And fechcheth forht mine sone, And quik that he war an-honge. *c* 1350 *Will. Palerne* 2795 God mowe we þonk, & oure worþi werwolf þat wel him by-tyde. 1535 [see O *int.* 2]. 1618 Corbet *Poems* (1807) 99 O that I ere might have the hap To get the bird which in the map Is called the Indian Ruck! 1790 Cowper *Rec. Mother's Picture* 1 Oh that those lips had language! 1850 Tennyson *In Mem.* xli, Deep folly! yet that this could be—That I could wing my will with might [etc.]. 1855 — *Maud* ii. iv. i, O that 'twere possible..To find the arms of my true love Round me once again!

**d.** Introducing a clause expressing a hypothetical desired result: with verb in subjunctive or its equivalent.

[1601: see 10.] 1610 Shaks. *Temp.* v. i. 150 Oh heauens, that they were liuing both in Naples The King and Queene there, that they were, I wish My selfe were mudded in that oozie bed. 1760-72 H. Brooke *Fool of Qual.* (1809) III. 114, I would give a thousand pounds that he may prove the man. 1821 Byron *Wks.* (1835) V. 216, I would gladly have given a much greater sum..that he had never been hurt. 1861 Dasent *Burnt Njal* II. 118, I would give all my goods that it had never happened.

**4.** Introducing a clause expressing the result or consequence of what is stated in the principal clause: with verb usually in indicative.

**a.** With antecedent *so* or *such*, either in the principal clause, or immediately before *that* in the dependent clause (see So, Such).

Also (*arch.*) preceded by *as*: see As B. 19 c. For ellipsis of *that*, see 10.

*c* 1000 *Ags. Gosp.* Matt. xiii. 54 He lærde hiȝ..swa þæt hiȝ wundredon. *a* 1300 *Cursor M.* 9730 Sa wel i am ya luued wit þe þat þi wisdom man clepes me. 1387 Trevisa *Higden* (Rolls) I. 419 Men lyueþ so longe in þat hurste, þat þe eldest deiȝeþ furst. *c* 1489 Caxton *Sonnes of Aymon* iv. 119 So longe they rode..that they came there as they were borne. 1564 P. Martyr *Comm. Judges* 272 To aske, not in deede so apertely that his voice should be hearde. 1667 Milton *P. L.* To Rdr., This neglect..of Rime so little is to be taken for a defect,..that it rather is to be esteem'd an example. 1705 Farquhar *Twin-Rivals* i. ii, The poor Creature is so big with her Misfortunes, that they are not to be born. 1731 *Gentl. Mag.* I. 391/1 This put Bluster into such a Passion, that he quitted the Surgery in a pet. 1849 Macaulay *Hist. Eng.* vi. II. 85 He was a man of morals so bad that his own relations shrank from him.

**b.** Simply, without antecedent: = so that. *arch.*

*c* 1175 *Lamb. Hom.* 27 Þe deofel..rixat in-nan him þet he nulle nefre forleten his sunne. *c* 1205 Lay. 1867 Forð com Corineus..þat alle hit bi-heolden. 1297 R. Glouc. (Rolls) 2690 Þun king hii bounde uaste ynou þat reulich he gan crie. 1377 Langl. *P. Pl.* B. xiv. 64 Heuene was yclosed, þat no reyne ne rone. 1470-85 Malory *Arthur* xvi. xvii. 687 Thenne were they sore affrayed that they felle bothe to the erthe. 1542 Udall *Erasm. Apoph.* 136 b, Suche as bee naught I byte, that thei smart again. 1611 Shaks. *Wint. T.* v. i. 65 Then I'ld shrieke, that euen your eares Should rift to heare me. 1719 De Foe *Crusoe* (1840) I. v. 96 The fear..made me that I never slept. 1858 G. Macdonald *Phantastes* xix, I struck one more sturdy blow..that the forest rang. 1868 Tennyson *Lucretius* 66 A fire..scorch'd me that I woke.

**c.** Introducing a clause expressing a fact (with vb. in indic.), or a supposition (with vb. in subj.), as a consequence attributed to the cause indicated by the principal clause (which is most commonly interrogative): sometimes nearly = in consequence of which; or (with indic.) = since, seeing that.

*c* 1000 Ælfric *Exod.* v. 2 Hwæt ys se drihten, þæt ic hym hiran scile and Israela folc forlætan? *c* 1205 Lay. 30280 Whæt is þe..þat þu swa wepest to-dæi? *c* 1420 *Chron. Vilod.* 2769 What desyesse is come þe to þat þou art now so sorwefulle? 1535 Coverdale *Ps.* viii. 4 Oh what is man, yᵗ thou art so myndfull of him? *Ibid.* cxiii. [cxiv.] 5 What ayled the (o thou see) that thou fleddest? 1591 Shaks. *Two Gent.* iv. ii. 40 Who is Silvia? what is she? That all our Swaines commend her? 1598 — *Merry W.* i. iv. 43, I doubt he be not well, that hee comes not home. 1611 Bible *Isa.* liii. 2 There is no beautie that we should desire him. 1787 Cowper *Stanzas Bill Mortality* 8 Did famine or did plague prevail, That so much death appears? 1842 Tennyson *Lady Clare* vi, Are ye out of your mind..that ye speak so wild? 1885 *Sat. Rev.* 21 Feb. 242/2 We are not pigeons that we should eat dry peas.

**5.** With a negative in the dependent clause (the principal clause having also a negative expressed or implied): = But that, but (= L. *quin*): see But *conj.* 12. (Now expressed by *without* with gerund: e. g. in quot. 1809, 'without her hearing'.)

Quots. *c* 1320, 1375 may belong to That *rel. pron.* 8.

*c* 1000 Ælfric *Saints' Lives* (1885) I. 378 Man ȝecwæman ne mæȝ twam hlafordum æt-somne þæt he ne forseo þone oðerne. *c* 1290 *Beket* 2128 in *S. Eng. Leg.* I. 167 For ȝwane men peyntiez an halewe, ȝe ne seoth it nouȝt bi-leued þat þere nis depeint a Roundel al-a-boute þe heued. *c* 1320 *Cast. Love* 6 Ne neuer was wrouȝt non vuel þing þat vuel þouȝt nas þe biginnyng. 1375 Barbour *Bruce* xvi. 280 Thar is no man That he ne will rew vp-on voman. *c* 1440 *Alphabet of Tales* 293 A long tyme sho mot nowder luke on þe crucifyx nor speke..of þe Passion..þatte nevur sho fell in swone as sho had bene dead. 1773 Goldsm. *Stoops to Conq.* v, I never attempted to be impudent yet, that I was not taken down. 1809 Southey *Let. to Lieut. Southey* 19 Sept., He never turned in his bed during that whole time that she did not hear. 1837 S. R. Maitland *Six Lett.*, etc. 69, I have hardly ever..turned it over for five minutes, that some gross error has not presented itself.

**6.** Added to relatives or dependent interrogatives (*who, which, what, when, where, how, why*, etc.). † Also after the demonstrative advbs. *then, there*, etc., when used as relatives. *Obs.* or *arch.*

*c* 888 K. Ælfred *Boeth.* xvi. § 2, ȝif ȝe nu ȝesawan hwelce mus þæt wære hlaford ofer oðre mys. 13.. *Cursor M.* 1247 (Cott.) Yai, sir, wist i wyderward [*v. r.* queþirward] þat [*v. r.* þere] tat vncuth contre were. *c* 1374 Chaucer *Troylus* ii. Prol. 36 Euery wyght wheche þat to rome wente. *c* 1386 — *Prol.* 41 To telle yow..in what array that they were Inne. — *Can. Yeom. Prol. & T.* 17 And in myn herte to wondren I bigan What þat he was. 14.. in *Hist. Coll. Citizen London* (Camden) 112 Faste be-syde ther that the batelle was done. 1450 *Rolls of Parlt.* V. 202/1 In whos handes that ever they were founde. *c* 1465 *Eng. Chron.* (Camden) 98 A wommanne the whiche that knewe hym. 1470-85 Malory *Arthur* xvii. xxii. 723 Wotest thou wherfor that he hath sente me? 1601 Shaks. *Jul. C.* iii. ii. 96 When that the poore haue cry'de, Cæsar hath wept. 1613 — *Hen. VIII*, iii. ii. 32 Wherein was read How that the Cardinall did intreat his Holinesse [etc.]. *a* 1814 *Spaniards* iv. i. in *New Brit. Theatre* III. 234 When that the crown..shall bind the brows Of my unnatural brother.

†**b.** *That* alone had formerly the force of 'when that', 'when', after *hardly, scarcely*, or some equivalent. So †*just that* (quot. 1648) = just when, just as. *Now that*: see Now 12 b.

13.. *Cursor M.* 8160 Vnnethes had he moned his mode, þat [*v. r.* quen] a lem fra þe wandes stode. ?*a* 1380 *St. Ambrosius* 488 in Horstm. *Altengl. Leg.* (1878) 16/1 Vnneþe Ambrose and his meyne, Weoren passed out from þat citee þat sodeynliche opened þe eorþe. 1480 Caxton *Chron. Eng.* ccvii. 189 The kyng had not yet fullych eten that ther come in to the halle another messagyer. 1530- [see Now 12 b]. 1648 Cromwell in Carlyle *Lett. & Sp.* (1871) II. 56 Until just that we came. 1780 *Mirror* No. 95 ⁋ 1 We spent our time as happily as possible, till about half a year ago, that my ill stars directed me to [etc.].

**7.** Formerly added with a conjunctive force to various words that are now commonly used conjunctionally without it; e.g. *because, if, lest, only, the* adv., *though, till, while* (see these words). *arch.* or *Obs.*

(Cf. the OE. similar use of *þe*; also prec. sense.)

*c* 1200 [see If 5]. *a* 1300 *Cursor M.* 14458 Bot al þat he wit luue þam soght, Enentis þe Iuus al was for noght. *Ibid.* 22167 Þai sal be studiand in þair thoght, Queþer þat he be crist or nai. 1505 in *Mem. Hen. VII* (Rolls) 267 The kynge ..remembrithe that mater as efectually as that hit were his aune proper cause. 1590 Spenser *F. Q.* i. i. 30 The knight.. Who faire him quited, as that courteous was. 1602 Dolman *La Primaud. Fr. Acad.* (1618) III. 736 The property thereof is to mount alwaies vpwards, vntill that it hath attained to the place destinated vnto it. 1656 A. Wright *Five Serm.* 201 The reason is, cause that Ordinances are nothing without the Lord. 1800 Coleridge *Lett.* (1895) 325 As to my schemes of residence, I am as unfixed as yourself, only that we are under the absolute necessity of fixing somewhere. 1805 tr. *Lafontaine's Hermann & Emilia* III. 97 Hermann likewise trembled, because that their early friendship was awakened in his breast.

**8.** Used (like Fr. *que*) as a substitute instead of repeating a previous conjunction, or conjunctive adverb or phrase. Now *rare* or *arch.*

*c* 1175 *Lamb. Hom.* 17 Þenne were þu wel his freond.. Gif þu hine iseȝe þet he wulle asottie to þes deofles hond..: þet þu hine lettest, and widstewest. *c* 1489 Caxton *Blanchardyn* xix. 58 When they..had seen the manere & the rewle of their enemyes, and that all wyth leyser they had seen their puyssance. *Ibid.* 59 So began he to be..all annoyed of hym self by cause he was not armed tyl his plesure, and that he myght not yssue out. *c* 1520 Barclay *Sallust* 55 Whan he had assayed many wayes, and that nothing came to purpose. 1535 Coverdale *Esther* ii. 14 She must come vnto the kynge nomore, excepte it pleased the kynge, and that he caused her to be called by name. 1569 J. Sanford tr. *Agrippa's Van. Artes* 174 b, When sleepe falleth vpon men, & that they be in bed. 1596 Shaks. *Merch. V.* iv. i. 9 Since he stands obdurate, And that no lawful meanes can carrie me Out of his enuies reach. [Also 27 other examples.] 1611 Bible *1 Chron.* xiii. 2 If it seeme good vnto you, and that it be of the Lord our God, let vs send abroad vnto our brethren. [Coverd. Yf..yf...] — *Job* xxxi. 38 If my land cry against me, or that the furrowes likewise thereof complaine. [Coverd. Yf case be that..or yᵗ...] 1655 M. Casaubon *Enthus.* (1656) 126 Because I desire not to be over-long, and that I would not glut the Reader. 1700 Tyrrell *Hist. Eng.* II. 823 So soon as the Death of King John was..known, and that the Earls..could agree where to meet. 1797 Burke *Regic. Peace* iii. Wks. VIII. 330 When one of the parties to a treaty intrenches himself.. in..ceremonies,..and that all the concessions are upon one side. 1829 Sir W. Napier *Penins. War* ix. ii. (Rtldg.) II. 16 Although the rear was attacked,..and that 50 men..were captured.

†**9.** After a comparative: = Than. (Cf. Fr. *que.*) *Obs. rare.* (See also The *part.* 1 b.)

c **1305** *St. Kenelm* 108 in *E. Eng. P.* (1862) 50 For noman nemai þan oþer bet trecherie do þat [*Laud MS.* þane] þulke þat is him next, & he trist mest to. c **1330** R. BRUNNE *Chron. Wace* (Rolls) 10602 More worschip of hym [Arthur] spoke þer was þat of any of þo þat spekes Gildas. **1422** tr. *Secreta Secret., Priv. Priv.* 175 He had Slayne by trayson two prynces bettyr that he was. c **1450** LOVELICH *Grail* xlviii. 35 And but þe holyere man he be þat I konne wit, Elles schal there non Man here syt.

¶ **10.** The conjunction *that* is very frequently omitted by ellipsis, esp. in sense 1.

(The omission prob. began with the rel. conj. *þe*, THE.)

a **1250–1650** [see IT 4 b]. a **1300** *Cursor M.* 3665 (Cott.), I dred me sare, for benison He sal me giue his malison. **1390** GOWER *Conf.* I. 263 Joab..slowh Abner, for drede he scholde be [etc.]. c **1460** *Towneley Myst.* ix. 137 Go grete hym well,..say hym I com. **1526** TINDALE *Jas.* ii. 14 Though a man saye he hath fayth. **1591** SHAKS. 1 *Hen. VI*, II. v. 37 Direct mine Armes, I may embrace his Neck. **1599** — *Hen. V*, v. i. 54 Thou dost see I eate. **1601** — *All's Well* II. iii. 66 I'de giue bay curtall, and his furniture My mouth no more were broken then these boyes. **1611** BIBLE *Luke* xx. 13 It may bee they will reuerence him. **1678** BUNYAN *Pilgr.* I. 3, I think I do. **1737** POPE *Hor. Ep.* II. ii. 266 There are who have not—and thank heav'n there are. **1805** SCOTT *Last Minstr.* VI. xxv, So bright, so red the glare, The castle seemed on flame. **1847** TENNYSON *Princess* VII. 281, I fear They will not. *Mod.* We were sorry you couldn't come.

**Thatch** (þætʃ), *sb.* Forms: 4–5 **þacche**, 5–6 **thacche, thecche, thetche**, 7– **thatch.** [A late collateral form of THACK *sb.*, conformed to THATCH *v.*, which has superseded *thack* in literary use.]

**1.** Material used in thatching; straw or similar material with which roofs are covered; particularly (**b.**) that actually forming a roof, the thatching.

*Palmetto thatch*: see PALMETTO.

**1398** TREVISA *Barth. De P. R.* XVII. clxvii[i]. (Bodl. MS.), Þe rafters beþ stronge and square..& beþ charged wtoute wt sclatte and tile oþre wt strawe and þacche [*ed.* **1495** thetche]. **1555** EDEN *Decades* 159 Theyr houses..are.. couered with reede & thetche. **1600** J. PORY tr. *Leo's Africa* Introd. 20 Their houses are built round, al of earth, flat-roofed, and couered with a kind of thatch. **17..** POPE *Imit. Spenser* iv, Hard by a Sty, beneath a roof of thatch, Dwelt Obloquy. **1850** PRESCOTT *Peru* III. viii. II. 161 The roofs of their dwellings, instead of tiles, were only of thatch. **1878** BATES *Centr. Amer.* iv. 41 Everywhere the palms yield an abundance of poles and thatch available for building purposes.

**b. 1693** EVELYN *De la Quint. Compl. Gard.* 5 The Cieling and Floor above ought to be..clad in Winter with a Thatch of Hay or Straw. **1816** in *Life W. Havergal* (1882) 13 The pretty thatch and white walls so common hereabouts. **1867** D. G. MITCHELL *Rural Stud.* 77 The roof a neat thatch of wheat straw. **1889** DOYLE *Micah Clarke* 228 They shelter the walls from the rain..by great overhanging thatches.

**c.** *transf.* A thatched dwelling.

**1693** S. HARVEY in *Dryden's Juvenal* ix. (1697) 233 The Poor Inhabitants of yonder Thatch Call'd me their Lord. a **1790** T. WARTON *Ode* viii. *Morning*, Up mounts the mower from his lowly thatch. **1793** W. HODGES *Trav. India* 67 For constant residence, these would be improved into the various thatches and huts which I have seen.

**2.** *fig.* Covering; often *humorously* the hair of the head.

a **1633** AUSTIN *Medit.* (1635) 284 The very Top and Cover, my Thatch above..growes gray. **1634** S. R. *Noble Soldier* II. i. in Bullen *O. Pl.* (1882) I. 276 Had my Barbour Perfum'd my louzy thatch here and poak'd out My Tuskes more stiffe. **1821** CLARE *Vill. Minstr.* I. 129 'Neath the hazel's leafy thatch. **1888** LOWELL *Heartsease & Rue* 193 We.. Who've paid a perruquier for mending our Thatch. **1894** MRS. DYAN *All in a Man's K.* (1899) 27 The damage he had done to his 'thatch', as he graphically styled his hair.

**3.** Name in the West Indies for several species of palms, the leaves of which are used for thatching: see quot. and *thatch-palm* in 4.

**1866** *Treas. Bot.*, Thatch, *Calyptronoma Swartzii*, and *Copernicia tectorum*. Palmetto Thatch, *Thrinax parviflora*. Silver Thatch, *Thrinax argentea*.

**4.** *attrib.* and *Comb.*, as *thatch-eave, -roof, -straw, -work* (also *attrib.*); *thatch-browed, -roofed* adjs.; **thatch-cloak**, a cloak of any thatching material; **thatch-grass**, a grass or similar plant used for thatching, as Cape T., *Restio chondropetalus*; **thatch-hook**: see quot.; † **thatch-house**, a thatched house; **thatch-palm**, name for various palms of which the leaves are used for thatching: in W. Indies, the genus *Thrinax*; in southern U. S., the genus *Sabal*, esp. *S. umbraculifera*; in Brazil, *Euterpe montana* (*Funk's Stand. Dict.* 1895); in Lord Howe's Island, *Howea forsteriana* (*Cent. Dict.* 1891); **thatch-peg, -pin, -prick**, a stick sharpened at one end to fasten down thatch; **thatch-rake**, an implement with curved teeth for straightening the thatching material as it is laid on the roof; **thatch-rod** = *thatching-rod*; **thatch-tree** (see quot. 1866); **thatch-wood**, brushwood arranged as thatch: see quot.

**1863** W. BARNES *Poems in Dorset Dial.* 61 An' by a house, where rwoses hung avore The *thatch-brow'd window, an' the open door. **1844** B. MAYER *Mexico* xxiii. 166 An Indian shepherd-boy in his long *thatch-cloak of waterflags. **1819** KEATS *Ode to Autumn* 4 The vines that round the *thatch-eaves run. **1884** MILLER *Plant-n.*, *Grass, Cape Thatch. [**1858** HOGG *Veg. Kingd.* 802 The houses at the Cape of Good Hope are commonly thatched with *Restio tectorum*,..sometimes whole huts are built with it.] **1886** *Cheshire Gloss.*, *Thatch-hooks, iron hooks, driven into the spars, to hold down the first layers of straw in thatching a house. **1521** in *10th Rep. Hist. MSS. Comm.* App. v. 399 No man shall buld, make or repayre anny straue or *tache housse, for fear of fyre and burninge.., unlesse they be covered with sklattes. **1609** *Ev. Wom. in Hum.* IV. ii. in Bullen *O. Pl.* IV, He that has not a tilde house must bee glad of a thatch house. **1866** *Treas. Bot* 1147/1 *Thrinax*.. In Jamaica these palms are commonly known by the name of *Thatch-palms. *Ibid.*, The Silver Thatch-palm is usually said to yield..Palmetto Thatch,..extensively employed for making palm-chip hats, baskets, and other fancy articles. **1897** GILCHRIST *Peakland* 62 Busily whittling *thatch pegs. **1688** R. HOLME *Armoury* III. 266/1 Thatching, is to cover..with Straw, Ferne, Rushes or Gorst, which is bound and held together by Laths, Windings, and *Thatch Pricks. **1847–94** PARKER *Gloss. Her.* s. v. *Rake*, The *thatch-rake or thatcher's rake. **1903** *Q. Rev.* July 12 They were its *thatch-rods. **1901** *Westm. Gaz.* 15 Aug. 1/3 The *thatch roof of a West-country cottage. **1847** LONGF. *Ev.* I. Prel. 9 Where is the *thatch-roofed village, the home of Acadian farmers? **1844** STEPHENS *Bk. Farm* III. 1095 To give the *thatch-straw a smoothness, it should be stroked down with a long supple rod of willow. **1756** P. BROWNE *Jamaica* 344 The *Thatch Tree. The leaves..used for thatch. **1866** *Treas. Bot.*, *Thatch-tree*, a name applied to palms generally in the West Indies. **1877** KNIGHT *Dict. Mech.*, **Thatch-wood Work*,..a mode of facing sea-walls with brushwood. Underbrush..is cut down, fagoted at its full length, and spread over the face of the banks. It is kept down by strong stakes, which have cross pins at their upper ends to rest upon the brush. **1895** WORKMAN *Algerian Mem.* xi. 113 Villages with *thatch-work houses.

**Thatch** (þætʃ), *v.* Forms: *α.* 1 **þecc(e)an**, 4 **thecche**, 4–6 **theche**, 5 **thetche**, 6–7 **thetch** (7 *dial.* **thesh**). *β.* 4 **þacchen**, 5–6 **thacche**, 5–7 **thach(e**, 6 **thatche**, 6– **thatch.** [OE. *þecc(e)an* (pa. t. *þeahte*, *þehte*, Vesp. Ps. *þæhte*, pa. pple. *geþeaht*), Common Teutonic vb.; in OFris. *bi*)-*thekk(i)a*, OS. *bi)theccian* (MDu., MLG. *decken*, Du., LG. *dekken*), OHG. *decchan* (MHG., Ger. *decken*), ON. *þekja* (Sw. *täcka*, Da. *tække*):—OTeut. **þakjan*, f. **þako*m covering, roof, THACK *sb.* The regular etymological form is *thetch*: the literary *thatch* has app. taken its vowel from THACK *sb.* Cf. also the cognate THACK *v.*[1], THEEK *v.*]

† **1.** *trans.* To cover. (Only *O.E.*)

*Beowulf* 514 Þa ʒit on sund reon þær ʒit eagor-stream earmum þehton. a **1000** *Cædmon's Gen.* 877 (Gr.) For hwon wast þu wean & wrihst sceome, ʒesyhst sorʒe & þin sylf þecest lic mid leafum. c **1000** *Ags. Ps.* (Th.) cxlvi. 8 Se þe heofen þeceð hadrum wolcnum.

**2.** *spec.* To cover or roof (a house) with straw, reeds, palm-leaves, heather, or the like, laid so as to protect from the weather; also, to cover the top of (a rick or wall) in a similar way. † Formerly also, to roof (a house) with slates, tiles, or similar roofing material.

**1398** TREVISA *Barth. De P. R.* XVII. xxxi. (Tollem. MS.), In þe norþe londe men þacchen [*ed.* **1495** thetche] here houses with reed. ? c **1500** *How Plowman lerned his Pater-Noster* 19 in Hazl. *E. P. P.* I. 210 He coude theche a hous, and daube a wall. **1555** EDEN *Decades* 101 Their houses are ..thetched with the stalkes of certayne towghe herbes. **1610** HOLLAND *Camden's Brit.* (1637) 491 Reed for to thatch their Houses. **1623–4** *Althorp MS.* in Simpkinson *Washingtons* (1860) App. 53 To Phipp one daie theshing the dove house. **1698** FRYER *Acc. E. India & P.* 66 The Houses are low, and Thatched with Oleas of the Cocoe-Trees. **1774** PENNANT *Tour Scot. in 1772* 135 Many of the churches are thatched with heath. **1865** PARKMAN *Huguenots* iv, The buildings of the fort were all thatched..with leaves of the palmetto.

**3.** *fig.* To cover as with thatch.

**1589** *Pappe w. Hatchet* C iv, If that Martin could thatch vp his Church, this mans scabship should bee an Elder. **1604** MIDDLETON *Father Hubburd's T.* Wks. (Bullen) VIII. 89 My chin was well thatched with a beard. **1614** GORGES *Lucan* v. 166 Mount Æmus now was thatch't with snow. **1662** HIBBERT *Body of Div.* II. 135 Their faces thatcht over with impudence. **1683** OWEN *Serm. Chamb. Imagery* Wks. 1855 VIII. 584 One lie must be thatched with another, or it will quickly rain through. **1816** SCOTT *Bl. Dwarf* i. *note*, His head..was thatched with no other covering than long matted red hair. **1857** EMERSON *Poems* 26 What if Trade ..thatch with towns the prairie broad. **1858** CARLYLE *Fredk. Gt.* I. v. (1872) I. 45 As if there was cloth enough..to thatch the Arctic Zone.

**4.** Of a thing: To serve as a covering or roof to; to cover, to roof.

c **1000** *Sax. Leechd.* II. 242 Sio filmen [of the milt] biþ þeccende & wreonde þa wambe & þa innofaran. **1663** GERBIER *Counsel* d v j b, Leaves of Trees do thatch their Domiciliums. **1852** MRS. STOWE *Uncle Tom's C.* ix, The shock of hair that thatched his head.

**5.** *intr.* To do thatching; to thatch houses.

**1377** LANGL. *P. Pl.* B. XIX. 232 Somme he tauʒte to tilie to dyche & to thecche. **1591** SPENSER *M. Hubberd* 264 To hedge, to ditch, to thrash, to thetch, to mowe. **1795** AIKIN & BARBAULD *Evenings at Home* vi. 105 *Gubba.* Can you thatch? There is a piece blown off the cow-house. *Alfred.* Alas! I cannot thatch.

**Thatch**, variant of THETCH *dial.*, vetch.

**Thatched, thatcht** (þætʃt), *ppl. a.* [f. THATCH *v.* (q.v. for Forms) + -ED[1].] Covered or roofed with thatch.

**1467** in *Eng. Gilds* (1870) 372 That no chimneys of tre ner thached houses be suffred wtyn the cyte. a **1548** HALL *Chron., Hen. VI* 94 The newe Constable..destroyed two or thre..litle poore thetched villages. c **1640** [SHIRLEY] *Capt. Underwit* I. in Bullen *O. Pl.* (1883) II. 327 Does this thatchd cottage head hold still in fashion? **1653** WALTON *Angler* i. 2 Sir, I know the thatcht house very well: I often make it my resting place. **1867** MISS BRADDON *Aur. Floyd* Road-side inns with brown thatched roofs.

**b.** *fig.* Covered as with thatch (in quot. 1606, with reference to its inflammability). *Thatched-head*, one who has matted hair.

**1606** *Sir G. Goosecappe* III. i. in Bullen *O. Pl.* (1884) III. 44 Such sparkes were good enough yet to set thacht dispositions a fire. **1613** BEAUMONT & FL. *Coxcomb* II. iii, Ere you go, Sirrah Thatch'd Head! wouldst not thou be whipt, and think it justice? **1889** DOYLE *Micah Clarke* 128 A pair of great thatched eyebrows.

**Thatcher** (þæ·tʃəɹ). [f. THATCH *v.* (q.v. for Forms) + -ER[1].] One who thatches; *esp.* one whose business it is to thatch houses, corn or hay ricks, etc.

c **1440** *Jacob's Well* 40 Alle men of crafte, as wryʒtes, smythes,..baxterys, thaccherys, cordewanerys..owyn to payin þe tythe. **1562–3** *Act* 5 *Eliz.* c. 4 § 30 Tharte or Occupation of a..Thatcher or Shingler. **1641** BEST *Farm. Bks.* (Surtees) 145 A thatcher hath usually two folkes to waite on, viz. one to drawe out the thatch and make it into bottles, and the other to make morter and serve him. **1879** JEFFERIES *Wild Life in S. Co.* 123 The wind never blew that was strong enough to please the thatcher.

So † **Tha·tchester** (tha·chester), in same sense.

**1583–4** *Shuttleworths' Acc.* (Chetham Soc.) 18 Vnto a thachester for thachinge..towe dayes and a halffe xijd.

**Thatching** (þæ·tʃiŋ), *vbl. sb.* [f. THATCH *v.* (q. v. for Forms) + -ING[1].] The action of THATCH *v.*

**1.** The action or process of covering a building with thatch († formerly, with any roofing material).

**1393** LANGL. *P. Pl.* C. IX. 199 Tho..peers..putte hem alle to werke,..In þresshynge, in þecchyng. **1520** *Maldon, Essex, Liber B.* lf. 95 b, Circa le thechynge unius orei apud Sabernes. c **1683** M. MACKAILE in Macfarlane *Geog. Collect.* (S.H.S.) III. 6 Gremsie affordeth only slates for thatching of houses. **1760** FOOTE *Minor* II. Wks. 1799 I. 250 Fine old hay,..damag'd a little last winter, for want of thatching. **1846** *J. Baxter's Libr. Pract. Agric.* (ed. 4) II. 316 The Somersetshire mode of thatching is preferable to all others. It consists in using unbruised straw, provincially called reed, instead of bruised straw with the ears on it.

**2.** *concr.* = THATCH *sb.* 1.

**1671** H. M. tr. *Erasm. Colloq.* 311 The very rafters themselves which bear up the thatching. **1703** T. N. *City & C. Purchaser* 260 This kind of Thatching will indure 40, 50, or 60 Years. **1844** STEPHENS *Bk. Farm* II. 405 Long straw ropes, which bound down the thatching of stacks.

**3.** *attrib.* and *Comb.*, as *thatching work*; **thatching-fork**, (*a*) a forked stick used for carrying straw to the roof for thatching; (*b*) see quot. 1882; **thatching-rod**, a long flexible rod laid on the thatch to hold it down, and tied or pinned to the framework of the roof; **thatching-spale**: see quot. 1882; **thatching-stake**, a pointed stake with which the thatch is pinned down.

**1641** BEST *Farm. Bks.* (Surtees) 139 If thatchinge worke come in hande in haytime. **1703** T. N. *City & C. Purchaser* 259 In some parts of Kent they use no Withs to bind on their Thatching-rods, but..they use Rope-yarn. **1879** JEFFERIES *Wild Life in S. Co.* 123 His small sharp billhook to split out his thatching stakes. **1882** OGILVIE, *Thatching-fork, Thatching-spale*, an implement with a forked blade and a cross handle at one end for thrusting home the tufts of straw in thatching. **1887** MOLONEY *Forestry W. Afr.* 438 The leaves..are used..for thatching purposes.

**Tha·tchless,** *a.* [f. THATCH *sb.* + -LESS.] Having the thatch of the roof missing or destroyed.

**1882** *Century Mag.* XXIII. 912 Hingeless doors and shutters, crooked and thatchless roofs.

**Tha·tchy,** *a. rare.* Abounding in thatch.

**1864** CARLYLE *Fredk. Gt.* XV. xii. (1872) VI. 88 Thatchy Trautenau, wooden too in the upper stories of it, takes greedily to the fire.

**That'n** (ðæ·t'n), *adv. dial.* Also 9 **that-en, thatn, that'ns.** [perh. for an earlier **thatkin(s* of that kind, f. THAT *dem. adj.* + KIN *sb.*[1] 6 b: cf. THISKIN, THISSEN. But no instance of *thatkin* has been cited, and the termination may have a different origin.] More fully *a that'n, -s*, in that way, in that manner, like that.

**1695** CONGREVE *Love for L.* III. iii, An you stand astern a that'n, we shall never grapple together. a **1796** PEGGE *Derbicisms*, Thatn. a **1825** FORBY *Voc. E. Anglia*, *That'ns*, ..in that manner. **1879** MISS JACKSON *Shropsh. Word-bk.*, *Athatn, athatns...Thatn,..adv.* that way.., as of the manner of doing a thing.

**Thatness** (ðæ·tnės). *Philos.* [f. THAT *dem. pron.* + -NESS.] The quality or condition of being 'that', i. e. of existing as a definite thing.

**1643** DIGBY *Observ. Relig. Med.* (1644) 86 It is evident that samenesse, thisnesse, and thatnesse, belongeth not to matter by it selfe,..but onely as it is distinguished and individuated by the forme. **1889** MIVART *Truth* 211 It apprehends what kind of a thing the object perceived may be—its 'thatness', so to speak. **1891** E. B. BAX *Outlooks fr. New Standpoint* III. 183 The phenomenon or sign of the being or of the thatness which itself ever eludes us. *Ibid.* 191 Imparting to whatness a thatness. **1904** *Athenæum* 24 Dec. 868/2 The investing of the content, which is in Bradleian language a 'what', with self-existent reality or 'that-ness'.

† **Thau**, obs. form of TAU.

**1483** CAXTON *Gold. Leg.* 317/1 A little staf that he helde whiche hadde the signe of thau. **1701** C. WOLLEY *Jrnl. New York* (1860) 31 That Rabbinical Critick the Oxford Gregory upon Cain's Thau.

**Thau, þau, þauʒ, þauh,** obs. ff. THOUGH.

**Thauel,** obs. form of THOLE *sb.*[1]

**Thaught,** variant of THOUGHT, rower's bench.

**Thaumasite** (þǭ·măsəit). *Min.* [mod. (Nordenskiöld, 1878), f. Gr. θαυμάσι-ος wonderful, marvellous + -ITE[1]: so named 'on account of its unusual composition'.] 'A white, amorphous mineral composed of silicate, carbonate and sulphate of calcium, and water' (Chester).

1921 in WATTS *Dict. Chem.* VIII. 1921.

**Thaumato-** (þǭmătọ), combining form of Gr. θαῦμα, θαυματ-, wonder, marvel. **Thaumato·genist,** a believer in or advocate of thaumatogeny. **Thaumato·geny,** [-GENY], the origination of life as a miraculous process: opposed to *nomogeny*. **Thaumato·graphy** [-GRAPHY: mod.L. *thaumatographia*], a writing concerning the wonders of nature. **Thaumato·latry** [-LATRY], excessive reverence for the miraculous or marvellous. **Thaumato·logy** [-LOGY], an account of miracles; the description or discussion of the miraculous.

1891 *Cent. Dict.*, *Thaumatogenist (citing Owen). 1868 OWEN *Vertebr. Anim.* III. 814 Nomogeny or *Thaumatogeny? 1869 MOZLEY *Ess.* (1878) II. 394 Independent of all theories of elementary formation—Evolution, Epigenesis, Nomogeny, Thaumatogeny. [1632 J. JOHNSTON (*title*) *Thaumatographia Naturalis.] 1891 *Cent. Dict.*, Thaumatography. 1827 HARE *Guesses* (1859) 98 The *thaumatolatry by which our theology has been debased. 1851 J. H. NEWMAN *Cath. Eng.* 296 In the Protestant's view..who assumes that miracles never are, our *thaumatology is one great falsehood. 1904 *Edin. Rev.* Jan. 163 In which [volume] the work of thaumatology is carried to its furthest extreme.

**Thaumatrope** (þǭ·mătrōup). [irreg. f. Gr. θαῦμα (see THAUMATO-) + -τροπος turning.] A scientific toy illustrating the persistence of visual impressions, consisting of a card or disk with two different figures drawn upon the two sides, which are apparently combined into one when the disk is rotated rapidly; also applied to a disk or cylinder bearing a series of figures which, on being rapidly rotated and viewed through a slit, produce the impression of a moving object (= PHENAKISTOSCOPE, ZOETROPE).

1827 J. A. PARIS *Philos. in Sport* III. i. 5 This toy is termed the Thaumatrope. 1839 BREWSTER *Optics* xviii. (ed. 4) 338 Thaumatrope [is] the name given by Dr. Paris to an optical toy, the principle of which depends on the persistence of vision. 1872 HUXLEY *Phys.* x. 245 The thaumatrope,..by the help of which, on looking through a hole, one sees images of jugglers throwing up and catching balls.

Hence **Thaumatro·pical** *a.*, pertaining to or having the nature or effect of a thaumatrope.

1829 *Blackw. Mag.* XXV. 82 Having read Emerson on this thaumatropical proceeding.

**Thaumaturge** (þǭ·mătɒ̄ɹdʒ). Also 8–9 -turg (-tɒ̄ɹg). [ad. med.L. *thaumatūrg-us*, ad. Gr. θαυματουργός wonder-working, a conjurer, f. θαυματ- wonder + -εργος working; in form *-urge*, conformed to F. *thaumaturge* (1663 in Hatz.-Darm.).] A worker of marvels or miracles; a wonder-worker.

1715 M. DAVIES *Athen. Brit.* I. 125 Petavius..attainted..Origen's wonder-working Scholar Gregory the Thaumaturg, with Præarianisme. 1760 WESLEY *Jrnl.* 20 Dec., You throw out a hard word,..Thaumaturg. 1826 SOUTHEY *Vind. Eccl. Angl.* 479 The Thaumaturge..knelt before the Image to intercede for them. 1860 *Sat. Rev.* X. 269/2 The half-maudlin, half-cheating thaumaturg. 1881 *Athenæum* 12 Mar. 363/2 Pious mythologists have made out that she [St. Frideswide] was a thaumaturge of the first order.

**Thaumaturgic** (þǭmătɒ̄·ɹdʒik), *a.* and *sb.* [f. as prec. + -IC.]

**A.** *adj.* **1.** That works, or has the power of working, miracles or marvels; wonder-working.

1680 *Dial. between Pope & Phanatick* 11 The Thaumatergick word of Protestant Religion have done our Cause such eminent service. 1818 G. S. FABER *Horæ Mosaicæ* I. 356 The thaumaturgic and inspired prophet Moses. 1831 CARLYLE *Sart. Res.* II. iv, The grand thaumaturgic art of Thought. 1889 PATER *G. de Latour* 65 The witchery, the thaumaturgic powers, of Virgil, or..of Shakespeare.

**2.** Of, pertaining to, or involving thaumaturgy.

1825 CARLYLE *Schiller* II. (1873) 73 Various thaumaturgic feats. 1894 STEVENSON *Let. to Miss A. Boodle* 14 July, Never expect..thaumaturgic conversions.

**B.** *sb.* †**a.** The art of constructing marvellous or apparently magical devices. *Obs.*

1570 DEE *Math. Pref.* Aj, Thaumaturgike, is that Art Mathematicall, which giueth certaine order to make straunge workes,..of men greatly to be wondred at.

**b.** *pl.* Thaumatu·rgics [see -IC 2]: feats of magic, conjuring tricks.

1730 [see THAUMATURGY, quot. 1727]. 1824 MISS MITFORD *Village* Ser. I. 290 Mr. Moon, the very pearl of all conjurors, ..with his 'wonderful..exhibition of Thaumaturgics, Tachygraphy, mathematical operations, and magical deceptions'.

**Thaumaturgical** (þǭmătɒ̄·ɹdʒikăl), *a.* [f. as prec.: see -ICAL.] = prec. adj.

1621 BURTON *Anat. Mel.* II. ii. IV. (1676) 179/1 Mills to move themselves, Archita's Dove, Albertus Brazen head, and such Thaumaturgical works. 1841 D'ISRAELI *Amen. Lit.* (1867) 642 Artful impostures..practised..by the dealers in thaumaturgical arts. 1904 R. J. CAMPBELL *Serm. Individuals* v. 74 The modern mind would..repudiate the thaumaturgical element here.

**Thaumaturgist** (þǭ·mătɒ̄ɹdʒist). [f. THAUMATURGY + -IST.] = THAUMATURGE.

1829 CARLYLE *Misc., Germ. Playw.* (1872) II. 91 No conjuror..can any longer pass for a true thaumaturgist. 1837 *Ibid. Diamond Necklace* xvi. V. 190 Cagliostro, Thaumaturgist, Prophet and Arch-Quack. 1879 FARRAR *St. Paul* I. 530 *note*, The city was visited by the thaumaturgist Apollonius. 1882 — *Early Chr.* I. 116 Rome abounded in Oriental thaumaturgists and impostors.

So **Thau·matu·rgism,** thaumaturgy (*Cent. Dict.* 1891); **Thau·maturgi·ze** *v. intr.*, to act the thaumaturge, perform wonders.

1891 *19th Cent.* Nov. 825 We find Father Anquieta thaumaturgising (if I may use the expression) on the slightest occasions.

‖ **Thaumaturgus** (þǭmătɒ̄·ɹgɒ̆s). Pl. -i. [med. L.: see THAUMATURGE.] = THAUMATURGE.

1730 BAILEY (folio), *Thaumaturgus*,..a Worker of Miracles, a Title which the Roman-Catholicks give to several of their Saints. 1849 CDL. WISEMAN *Ess., Mirac. N. Test.* (1853) I. 188 Nor is there reason to suppose, that every simple faithful was a Thaumaturgus. 1886 *Edin. Rev.* July 283 Nature, the great Thaumaturgus, has in the Vocal Memnon propounded an enigma.

**Thaumaturgy** (þǭ·mătɒ̄ɹdʒi). [ad. Gr. θαυματουργία wonder-working, conjuring, f. THAUMATO- + -εργος working: see -Y. So F. *thaumaturgie* (1878 in *Dict. Acad.*).] The working of wonders; miracle-working; magic.

1727 BAILEY vol. II, *Thaumaturgy* [1730 (folio) also *Thaumaturgicks*],..any Art that does, or seems to do Wonders, or, as it is defin'd by Dr. Dee [cf. THAUMATURGIC *sb.* a], a mathematical Science, which gives a certain Rule for the making of strange Works to be perceiv'd by the Sense, yet to be greatly wonder'd at. 1778 WARTON *Hist. Eng. Poetry* xv. (1840) II. 178 This art, with others of the experimental kind, the philosophers of those times were fond of adapting to the purposes of thaumaturgy. 1831 CARLYLE *Sart. Res.* III. viii, A World of Miracles, wherein all fabled or authentic Thaumaturgy, and feats of Magic, were outdone. 1872 MINTO *Eng. Prose Lit.* I. i. 38 Magic,—both black and white,—thaumaturgy, and necromancy.

† **Thave,** *v. Obs.* Forms: 1 þafian, þeafian, 2 þeafen, 3 þeauien, þauien, ðauen, þafe, 3–4 þaue. [OE. *þafian*: etymology unascertained; not known in the cognate langs.] *trans.* To consent to; to allow, permit; to submit to, suffer, endure; to tolerate. Cf. I-THAVE.

835 *Kentish Charter of Abba* in *O.E. Texts* 448 Ic ciolnoð mid godes ʒefe ærcebiscop ðis write and ðeafie. c 888 K. ÆLFRED *Boeth.* xxxviii. § 6 þonne þe ðincð se earmra se þæt yfel deð ðonne se þe hit þafað. c 1000 *Ags. Gosp.* Matt. vii. 4 Broþur þafa [c 1160 þafe] þæt ic ut ado þæt mot of þinum eaȝan. a 1023 WULFSTAN *Hom.* iii. (Napier) 23 Eal þæt he for us and for ure lufan þafode and ðolode. [c 1175 *Lamb. Hom.* 121 God iþeafede þet to alesendnesse alles ileffulles moncunnes.] c 1200 ORMIN 5457 Godd ne þole nohht Ne þafe laþe gastess To winnenn oferhannd off uss þurrh heore laþe wiless. c 1250 *Gen. & Ex.* 3139 Euerilc hus-folc ðe mai it ðauen On ʒer sep oðer on kide hauen. c 1300 *Havelok* 2696 Was neuere non þat mouhte þaue Hise dintes, noyþer knith ne knaue.

Hence † **Tha·ving** (in 4 þafung, etc.) *vbl. sb.*, permission, consent.

13.. *Ancr. R.* 344 (MS. Cott. Cl.) Þurch min þafunge [*MSS. Corpus, Ti.* þeafunge, *Ca.* þauunge].

**Thave,** variant of THEAVE.

**Thavel, -il, thavvle,** dial. forms of THIVEL.

**Thaw** (þǭ), *sb.* Also β. 5 thowe, 5– thow (now *north. dial.* and *Sc.*). [f. THAW *v.*: cf. ON. *þá* thawed ground; also ON. *þeyr*, ONorw. *þøyr*, Sw. *tö*, Da. *tø* thaw; also Du. *dooi* thaw.]

**1.** The melting of ice and snow after a frost; the condition of the weather caused by the rise of temperature above the freezing point.

14.. *Voc.* in Wr.-Wülcker 586/9 *Gelicidium*, thawe. a 1552 LELAND *Itin.* V. 68 The Lake of Brecnok ons frosen over, and than in a Thaue breking maketh marvelus Noise. 1568 GRAFTON *Chron.* II. 441 Vpon a sodaine thawe, the floodes agayne encreace. 1634–5 LAUD *Diary* Wks. 1853 III. 223 The Thames was frozen over,..A mighty flood at the thaw. 1686 tr. *Chardin's Trav. Persia* 349 It becomes so furious when swell'd by the Thaws of the Snow. 1726–46 THOMSON *Winter* 990 The frost resolves into a trickling thaw. 1878 HUXLEY *Physiogr.* 142 By heavy rainfall, or by rapid thaw of snow.

β. 1412–20 LYDG. *Chron. Troy* II. 5079 Newe flodis of þe sodeyn þowe Þe grene mede gan to ouerflowe. c 1440 *Promp. Parv.* 492/1 Thowe, of snowe, or yclys or yce,..*degelacio*. 1725 RAMSAY *Gentle Sheph.* I. ii, Thick-blawn wreaths of snaw, or blashy thowes. 1786 BURNS *Brigs of Ayr* 119 Arous'd by blust'ring winds an spotting thowes; In mony a torrent down his sna-broo rowes. 1876 *Whitby Gloss.*, *Thow*, thaw.

**2.** *transf.* and *fig.*

1598 SHAKS. *Merry W.* III. v. 119 A man of my Kidney..that am as subiect to heate as butter; a man of continuall dissolution, and thaw. 1684 BUNYAN *Pilgr.* II. 113 If the Sun of Righteousness will arise upon him, his frozen Heart shall feel a Thaw. 1794 BURNS *The Auld Man* ii, But my white pow, nae kindly thowe Shall melt the snaws of age. 1817 BYRON *Manfred* II. ii. 202 Now I tremble And feel a strange cold thaw upon my heart.

**b.** *spec.* A becoming less cold, formal, or reserved.

1848 DICKENS *Dombey* v, Such temporary indications of a partial thaw that had appeared with her, vanished with her. 1873 BROWNING *Red Cott. Nt.-cap* III. 326 That thaw Of rigid disapproval into dew Of sympathy.

**3.** *attrib.* and *Comb.*, as *thaw-rain, -time, -wind* (cf. G. *tauwind*); *thaw-cloven, -swamped* adjs.

a 1715 BURNET *Own Time* II. an. 1672 (1823) I. 582 In the minute in which they began to march [on the ice], a thaw wind blew very fresh. 1814 BYRON in L. Hunt *Autobiog.* (1850) II. 318, I have been snow-bound and thaw-swamped..for nearly a month. 1819 SHELLEY *Prometh. Unb.* II. iii. 34 A howl Of cataracts from their thaw-cloven ravines. 1820 — *Vision of Sea* 36 It splits like the ice when the thaw-breezes blow. 1852 DICKENS *Bleak Ho.* iii, She gave me one cold parting kiss upon my forehead, like a thaw-drop from the stone porch. 1890 STEVENSON *Let. to H. James* 29 Dec., My theories melt, and..the thaw-waters wash down my theories.

**Thaw** (þǭ), *v.* Forms: 1 þawian, (4 þewe), 5–6 thawe, 6 thau, 6– thaw. β. 4 þowe, thoue, 4–5 thowe, 5– thow (now *north. dial.* and *Sc.*). *Pa. t.* and *pa. pple.* thawed (*dial.* thowed, *pa. t.* also thew); *pa. pple.* also 8–9 thawn. [OE. *þawian*, ME. *þawen*; also ME. *thōwe*; cognate with OFris. **thâia* (:– **þawian*), whence WFris. *teije*, NFris. *tuai*; OLG. **þawian*, whence MLG. *doien*, LG. *däuen* (Dähnert), Du. *dooien*, EFris. *deien, deuen, doien*; OHG. *douwen, dewen* (cf. mod.Ger. *verdauen* to digest), ON. *þeyja* (:– **þauja*), ONorw. *þøya*, Sw. *töa*, Da. *tøe*. The late ME. and Sc. *thōwe* does not answer to OE. *þawian*, but seems to require **þówan* or **þáwan*, unrecorded. Ulterior history obscure.]

**1.** *trans.* To reduce (a frozen substance, as ice or snow) to a liquid state by raising its temperature above the freezing point; to melt (a frozen liquid). Also *thaw out* (U. S.).

c 1000 *Sax. Leechd.* III. 274 Se wind [Zephirus] towyrpð and ðawað ælcne winter. 1530 PALSGR. 755/1 Sette the potte to the fyre to thawe the water. 1596 SHAKS. *Merch. V.* II. i. 5 Where Phœbus fire scarce thawes the ysicles. 1625 N. CARPENTER *Geog. Del.* II. v. (1635) 79 Riuers..by a remission of the cold are thawed. a 1704 T. BROWN *Lond. & Lacedem. Oracles* Wks. 1709 III. III. 138 After the Snow is thawn 1790 BURKE *Fr. Rev.* 349 Mr. Bailly will sooner thaw the eternal ice of his atlantic regions, than restore the central heat to Paris. 1878 HUXLEY *Physiogr.* 64 Until the warmth of summer returns to thaw it [the snow].

β. c 1384 CHAUCER *H. Fame* III. 53 They [letters] were almost of thowed so That of the lettres oon or two Was molte away of euery name. c 1440 *Promp. Parv.* 492/1 Thowyn or meltyn, as snowe and other lyke, *resoluo*. 1596 DALRYMPLE tr. *Leslie's Hist. Scot.* (S.T.S.) I. 46 To thow the pypes and schokles of yce. 1894 A. REID *Sangs Heatherl.* 107 Storms that time had thowed.

**b.** *fig.*

1591 SHAKS. *Two Gent.* II. iv. 200 Iulia that I loue, (That I did loue, for now my loue is thaw'd..like a waxen Image 'gainst a fire..). 1615 SIR W. MURE *Misc. Poems* viii. 43 Lat beuties beames then thau away..The ycinesse of loues delay. 1725 RAMSAY *Gentle Sheph.* III. iii. Prol., To whisper out his melting flame, And thow his lassie's breast. 1785 M. CUTLER in *Life*, etc. (1888) II. 228 This cold snowy winter has considerably cooled my zeal, but when I get thawed out, in the spring, perhaps it may return. 1821 SHELLEY *Adonais* i, O, weep for Adonais! though our tears Thaw not the frost which binds so dear a head!

**2.** *intr.* Of ice, snow, or other substance: To pass from a frozen to a liquid or semi-liquid state; to melt under the influence of warmth: esp. by rise of temperature after frost. Also *thaw out* (U. S.).

c 1325 *Gloss. W. de Bibbesw.* in Wright *Voc.* 147 *Après gelé vent remoyl* [gloss] thowyng. 1387 TREVISA *Higden* (Rolls) VII. 453 Many brugges..were i-broke of þe bowynge [*v.r.* þewinge] of þe yse. 1530 PALSGR. 755/1, I thawe, as snowe or yce dothe for heate. 1552 HULOET, Thawe as yse dothe, *egelidor*. 1610 HOLLAND *Camden's Brit.* (1637) 628 As often as the Yce thereon doth thaw. 1656 M. BEN ISRAEL *Vind. Jud.* 9 The pond thawd. 1703 MAUNDRELL *Journ. Jerus.* (1732) 140 Abundance of Snow; which thawing in the heat of Summer [etc.]. 1880 HAUGHTON *Phys. Geog.* iv. 195 The water freezes in November and thaws in May. 1887 I. R. *Lady's Ranche Life Montana* 33 Before I can begin to write this letter the ink must be put down by the fire to thaw out, as it is frozen solid.

**b.** *transf.* and *fig.*

1602 SHAKS. *Ham.* I. ii. 130 Oh that this too too solid Flesh, would melt, Thaw, and resolue it selfe into a Dew. 1849 MISS MULOCK *Ogilvies* xxix, He..thawed into positive enthusiasm beneath the sunshine of her influence. 1865 SWINBURNE *Atalanta* 2104, I would that as water My life's blood had thawn. 1905 A. C. BENSON *Upton Lett.* (1906) 293 The dreariness of my heart thawed and melted into peace and calm.

**3.** *impers. It thaws*: said of the cessation of a frost, when the ice, snow, etc. begin to melt.

c 1325 *Gloss. W. de Bibbesw.* in Wright *Voc.* 160 *Ore gele*, freset; *Ore remet*, thouet. c 1425 *Voc.* in Wr.-Wülcker 665/2 *Degelat*, thowes. 1530 PALSGR. 755/1 It thaweth a pace. 1709 *Lond. Gaz.* No. 4507/3 This Morning it began to thaw. *Mod.* The frost seems to be giving way; I expect it will thaw before night.

**4.** *trans.* To free from the physical effect of frost; to unfreeze; said usually in reference to a non-liquid substance rigid with frost, also to a person or animal affected by extreme cold.

1596 SHAKS. *Tam. Shr.* IV. i. 9 My very lippes might freeze to my teeth,..ere I should come by a fire to thaw me. 1665 *Phil. Trans.* I. 48 The frozen Bodies will be harmlessly thawed. 1728 RAMSAY *Anacreontic on Love* 21, I..his handies thow'd. 1829 LYTTON *Devereux* v. ii, After I was lodged, thawed, and fed, I fell fast asleep. 1883 W. AITKEN *Lays* 98 (E.D.D.) The whusky thowed their Hielan' bluid. 1887 I. R. *Lady's Ranche Life Montana* 144 You have to thaw a bit before you can put it in a horse's mouth.

**b.** *nonce-use.* To make limp (anything stiff).

1821 SCOTT *Kenilw.* xl, Speak..at farther distance, so please you; your breath thaws our ruff.

**5.** *intr.* To become unfrozen; to become flexible or limp by rise of temperature.

1596 DALRYMPLE tr. *Leslie's Hist. Scot.* (S.T.S.) I. 46 Gif ony frosin thing be put athir in the loch or in the riuer, it thowis fra hand. 1687 A. LOVELL tr. *Thevenot's Trav.* II. 122 We found it worse when the Sun was up, and the ground began to Thaw. 1850–6 O. W. HOLMES *Spring* 25 The bog's green harper, thawing from his sleep, Twangs a hoarse note.

**6.** *fig.* **a.** *trans.* To soften to sympathy or geniality; to break down coldness and reserve.

**1582** STANYHURST *Æneis* II. (Arb.) 48 Wee thawde with weeping doo pardon francklye the villeyn. **1677** GILPIN *Demonol.* (1867) 92 An extraordinary occasion melts and thaws down the natural affections of men. **1741** RICHARDSON *Pamela* (1824) I. 102 She is a charming girl, and may be thawed by kindness. **1883** GILMOUR *Mongols* (1884) 201 Tea even fails to thaw completely their reserve. **1889** J. JEFFERSON *Autobiog.* xii. (1891) 329 A hopeless endeavor to thaw him out.

**b.** *intr.* Of a person, his feelings, manner, etc.: To become softened or 'melted' in feeling; to throw off coldness and reserve; to unbend.

**1598** BP. HALL *Sat.* IV. iv. D j b, He thaw's like Chaucers frosty Ianiuere; And sets a Months minde vpon smyling May. *a* **1631** DONNE *Valediction my Name* ix, And thou begin'st to thaw towards him for this, May my name step in. **1827** POLLOK *Course of T.* IX. 722 Pride of rank And office, thawed into paternal love. **1900** EL. GLYN *Visits Eliz.* (1906) 18 He..went on talking in the friendliest way, but I would not thaw.

**7.** The verb-stem in combination forming sbs., as *thaw-house, thaw point.*

**1892** *Pall Mall G.* 30 Aug. 7/2 Dynamite..is received at the work in a frozen state, and stored in a big magazine. From this receptacle it is taken to the thaw-house as needed. **1902** *Daily Chron.* 28 May 8/5 When 'thaw' points were needed, through which steam was forced into the hard ground, they were improvised out of rifle barrels.

Hence **Thawed** (þǭd) *ppl. a.*, warmed so as to melt (as ice), softened; *thawed out*, also, put out of work or action by a thaw; **Thaw·ing** *ppl. a.*, that thaws, melting.

**1652** CRASHAW *Mary Magd.* Wks. (1904) 259 Thawing crystall! snowy hills, Still spending, never spent! **1774** GOLDSM. *Nat. Hist.* (1776) I. 247 Clefts, from whence the thawed water trickles out. **1800** HENRY *Epit. Chem.* (1808) 37 The temperature of melting snow, or of thawing ice. **1885** *Harper's Mag.* Dec. 86/2 The now thawed-out and almost genial Miss Lisle. **1894** *Westm. Gaz.* 19 Jan. 7/2 The thawed-out skaters equalised matters by holding a carnival on wheel skates at the Wandsworth Rink last night.

**Thaw, þaw, þawe,** obs. forms of THOUGH.

**Thawer** (þǭ·əɹ). [f. prec. vb. + -ER [1].] One who or that which thaws; *spec.* in *Mining*, a device or apparatus for thawing frozen ground.

**1630** *R. Johnson's Kingd. & Commw.* 7 Even in that continuall neighbourhood of that great Thawer [i. e. the sun] have you hils perpetually covered with frost and snow. **1900** *Pop. Sci. Monthly* Feb. 461 The introduction of mining machinery, such as..thawers..has given fresh impetus.

**Thawing** (þǭ·iŋ), *vbl. sb.* [f. as prec. + -ING [1].] The action of the verb THAW (*lit.* or *fig.*). Also in *pl.* (in quot. 1886 *concr.*).

*c* **1325**, **1387** [see THAW *v.* 2]. **1586** HOLINSHED *Chron.* III. 20/2 At their dissoluing or thawing, manie bridges both of wood and stone were borne downe. **1681** FLAVEL *Meth. Grace* vii. 152 Thawings of the heart under the apprehensions of grace. **1861** THORNBURY *Turner* (1862) II. 135 The occasional thawings of natures, however frozen by habit. **1886** M. K. MACMILLAN *Dagonet* 154 The first thawings of the hard-bound road clung impedingly to our shoes.

**Thawless** (þǭ·lės), *a.* [f. THAW *sb.* or *v.* + -LESS.] That does not thaw, or that never thaws.

**1813** W. TAYLOR *Eng. Synonyms* 30 Thawless unmelting obstinacy. **1838** MARY HOWITT *Birds & Fl., Sunshine* v, Where rests the thawless snow. **1886** RUSKIN *Præterita* I. ix. 291 The winter gives them [flowers] rest under thawless serenity of snow.

**Thawrtouer,** erron. form of THWARTOVER.

**Thawt,** variant of THOUGHT [2], rower's bench.

**Thawy** (þǭ·i), *a.* [f. THAW *sb.* + -Y.] Characterized by thaw; of or pertaining to a thaw.

**1728** T. SMITH *Jrnl.* (1849) 266 There has been no thawy weather. **1809–10** COLERIDGE *Friend* (1866) 314 Thoughts brisk as beer and pathos soft and thawy. **1892** *Longm. Mag.* Dec. 206 If the day is a fine frosty one and the previous one happens to have been warm and 'thawy'.

**Thay, þay,** obs. forms of THAE, THEY, THOUGH.

**Thayffe,** obs. form of THEAVE.

**Thayl**: see THAIL, obs. f. TAEL.

**Thaym, thayme,** obs. forms of THEM.

**Thayn,** obs. form of THANE.

**Thayr, -e, -es,** obs. forms of THEIR, -S.

**The** (*bef. cons.* ðĕ, ðə; *bef. vowel* ði; *emph.* ðī), *dem. adj.* ('*def. article*') and *pron.* Forms: see below. [The reduced and flexionless stem of the OE. demonstrative *se, séo* (later *þe, þéo*), *þæt*, the neuter sing. of which has come down as the dem. pron. and adj. THAT. Com. Teut. and Indo-Eur.: = OFris. *thi, thiu, thet,* OS. (*se*), *th(i)e, thiu* (*the*), *that* (*the*), (MLG., MDu. *de* (*die*), *dat*, LG., Du. *de, dat*), OHG. *der* (*de*), *diu, daz* (mod. Ger. *der, die, das*), ON. *sá, sú, þat*, Goth. *sa, sô, þata*, also Gr. ὁ, ἡ, τό, Zend *ho, hā, tat*, Skr. *sa, sā, tat*; all the inflexional parts exc. the nom. sing. m. and f. having the stem *þa-*, Lith., Slav. *to-*, Gr. τo-, Zend, Skr. *ta-*, Indo-Eur. *to-*, found also in L. in *tam, tum, tunc, is-te, is-tud*, etc. The nom. sing. m. and f. in OTeut., as in Skr., Zend, Gr., belong to another demonst. stem *sa-*, I.-Eur. *so-*, found also in Ir., Gael., Gaulish *so* this, L. *-se* in *ip-se*. But in OHG., OS. (in most dialects), and in late OE. (10th c. in Northumbrian, and at length everywhere) the *s-* forms were superseded by forms in *þ-* (OHG. *d-*), from the same stem as the neuter *þæt* and the oblique cases, as well as the pl. *þá*, later *þō*, THO. After the middle of the 13th c. the *s-* forms are no longer found, exc. as a belated survival (*ze* m., *zy* f.) in the Kentish dial. of the Ayenbite (1340). The only surviving reprs. of the OE. forms are *the* and *that*, Du. and LG. *de, dat*; but while LG. *dat* (besides its other uses) is still the neuter article, the Eng. *that* has ceased to be any part of the article. In the following illustration of Forms all the inflexions are illustrated, but the special history of *þæt* and *þá* pl. will be found under THAT, THO.

(The nom. fem. *sío, séo* corresponds in form not to Goth. *sô*, ON. *sú*, I.-Eur. **sā*, but to OS., OHG. *siu* 'she'. Some identify it with Skt. *syā* fem. of the 'extended' demonstrative *sya, syā, tyat*; others regard it as a special WGer. formation related to Goth. *sī* 'she'.)]

**A. Illustration of Forms.**

The OE. demonstrative and definite article was thus inflected:

| SING. | MASC. | FEM. | NEUT. | PLURAL. |
|---|---|---|---|---|
| *Nom.* | se, *later* þe | sío, séo, *later* þio, þiu | þæt | þá |
| *Acc.* | þone, þæne | þá | þæt | þá |
| *Dat.* | þǽm, þám | þǽre | þǽm, þám | þǽm, þám |
| *Gen.* | þæs | þǽre | þæs | þára (þǽra) |
| *Instr.* | þý, þon | | þý, þon | |

The variants and later forms were:

**I.** Sing. **1. a.** *Nom. masc. a.* 1–3 se (1 sæ, 2 seo) [4 ze *antec. pron.*].

**805** *Charter of Cuðred* in *O. E. Texts* 442 Æðelnoð se ȝerefa to Eastoreȝe. *c* **825** *Vesp. Psalter* ix. 25 Bismerað dryhten se synfulla. *c* **950** *Lindisf. Gosp.* Mark x. 24 Sæ [*Rushw.* ðe] hælend..cuoeð. *c* **1000** *Sax. Leechd.* III. 84 Sa ruwa ȝealle byð wexenda on þan innoþe. *Ibid.*, Se blace ȝealle. *a* **1154** *O. E. Chron.* (Laud MS.) an. 1135, On þis ȝære for se king Henri ouer sæ. *a* **1175** *Cotton Hom.* 235 Þis is seo king. *c* **1250** *O. Kent. Serm.* in *O. E. Misc.* 26 Se king of gyus. [**1340** *Ayenb.* 117 Ze þet ne heþ þise uondinges.]

¶ Abnormal uses of *se* in oblique cases, and of *sa* pl., *ses* gen. sing. (In some of these, *s* may be a scribal error for *þ*.)

*c* **1121** *O. E. Chron.* (Laud MS.) an. 1114, Þæt duȝeð þæt wæs..mid se cyng. *a* **1131** *Ibid.* an. 1123, Ðis wæs eall ear ȝedon ðurh se biscop of Seresbyriȝ, & þurh se biscop of Lincolne. *Ibid.*, Hi..brohten him toforen se kyng. *Ibid.*, ȝebletsod to biscop fram se biscop of Lundene. *a* **1175** *Cott. Hom.* 235 Ures hlafordes to-cyme ses helendes ihesu cristes. **1200–25** *Peri Didaxeon* in *Sax. Leechd.* III. 94 To ðan sare þe abutan sa earan wycst. *Ibid.* 112 Wurm þanna sa handa & smyra þar mið.

*β.* 1–2 **ðe** (**ðy**), 1–4 **þe** (2–4 **te**); 2–3 **þa**, 3–5 **þo**.

The *O. E. Chron.* 1122–31 has for the nom. masc. *se*, the section 1132–54 has (exc. once, anno 1135) *þe* (and *te*).

*c* **950** *Lindisf. Gosp.* Matt. ii. 3 Herodes ðe cynig. *Ibid.* ix. 15 Cueð to him ðe hælend. *a* **1154** *O. E. Chron.* (Laud MS.) an. 1132, Was it noht suithe lang þer efter þat te king sende efter him. *Ibid.* an. 1135, Þat ilc ȝær warth þe king ded. *c* **1175** *Lamb. Hom.* 3 Hu þe helend nehlechede toward ierusalem. *c* **1205** LAY. 1327 Ne beo þa dai na swa long. *a* **1240** *Sawles Warde* in *Cott. Hom.* 267 Þe feder an te sune an te hali gast. *a* **1300** *Floriz & Bl.* 739 Þe Admiral..chaungede his chere. **13..** *Cursor M.* 6282 (Cott.) Þe lauerd o might. *Ibid.* 20185 Þan said te angel. *a* **1325** *MS. Rawl. B.* 520 lf. 31 Ȝif þat te on [Iustise] be Clerke.

**b.** *Nom. fem. a.* 1 **séo, sío, síu,** (**sa**), 1–3 **se,** 2 **sie, seo,** 3 **si,** [4 **zi, zy** *antec. pron.*].

*c* **888** K. ÆLFRED *Boeth.* xxxix. § 5 Sio godcunde ȝesceadwisnes. *c* **893** — *Oros.* II. iv. § 8 Seo ilce burȝ Babylonia, seo ðe mæst wæs..seo is nu læst. *c* **975** *Rushw. Gosp.* Matt. xii. 13 Swa siu oþeru [hond]. *c* **1000** *Ags. Gosp.* Mark xv. 40 Seo [*c* **1160** *Hatton G.*, sie] magdalenisce maria. *a* **1131** *O. E. Chron.* (Laud MS.) an. 1122, On þone lenten tyde..forbearn se burch. *c* **1160** *Hatton Gosp.* John xii. 17 Syo menio þe wæs mid him. *a* **1175** *Cott. Hom.* 233 Hwat deð si moder hire bearn? *c* **1250** *O. Kent. Serm.* in *O. E. Misc.* 28 Si Mirre signefiet uastinge. [**1340** *Ayenb.* 102 Zy þet ne serueþ bote to onlepy manne.]

*β.* 1 **ðío, ðíu,** 1–3 **ðéo, þéo,** (3 **þæ,** 2–3 **þa,** 2–4 **þo**).

*c* **950** *Lindisf. Gosp.* John ii. 1 Uæs ðiu [*Rushw.* ðio] moder and ðe hælend ðer. *Ibid.* v. 25 Cymmes ðio tid & nu is. **971** *Blickl. Hom.* 65 Þeo deaþ-berende uncyst us is eallum to onscunienne. *c* **975** *Rushw. Gosp.* John xix. 20 Neh ðær cæstre wæs ðio stow. *c* **1000** *Ags. Gosp.* ibid., Þeo stow wæs ȝehende þære ceastre. *c* **1175** *Lamb. Hom.* 15 Hit wes þa laȝe. *Ibid.* 87 Þo tid to estertide. *c* **1205** LAY. 4010 Þeo uniseli moder. *Ibid.* 9815 Þæ quene spac wið him þus. *a* **1225** *Ancr. R.* 282 Þeo heorte ne ethalt none wete of Godes grace. *a* **1250** *Owl & Night.* 26 Þo vle song hire tide.

**c.** *Nom.* and *accus. neuter.* 1 **ðæt,** 1–3 **þæt,** 2–4 **þet,** 2–5 **þat, that,** (3 **þut**): see also THAT.

*c* **893** K. ÆLFRED *Oros.* I. i. § 8 Þæt land Cilia. *Ibid.*, Irnende on þæt sond, & þonne besince eft on þæt sand. *c* **1000** ÆLFRIC *Hom.* I. 264 Þæt ðridde ȝebed is. *c* **1175** *Lamb. Hom.* 7 Þat ebreisce folc sungen heore leof-song. *c* **1205** LAY. 297 Þat child was ihaten Brutus. *Ibid.* 7843 Þæt weder heom strongliche drof. *a* **1225** *Ancr. R.* 186 Nis þet child fulitowen þet schrepeð aȝean? *a* **1250** *Owl & Night.* 1259 Þah ic hi warny al þat yer. **1297** R. GLOUC. (Rolls) 12014 Þo was þut lond in pes. *c* **1320** *Cast. Love* 139 To delen þat vuel from þe good. **1340** *Ayenb.* 2 Þet oþer heaued of þe beste of helle.

**2.** *Accus.* **a.** *masc.* 1–2 **þone,** (1 **þæne**), 2 **þana,** 2–3 **þene,** 2–4 **þane, þan, þen,** (3 **þun**), 3–4 **þon,** 4 **þanne.**

*c* **825** *Vesp. Psalter* iv. 4 ȝemiclað dryhten ðone halȝan his. *c* **1121** *O. E. Chron.* (Laud MS.) an. 1016, Eadric ealdormann ȝewende þa ðæne cyng onȝean. *a* **1131** *Ibid.* an. 1122, Þa com se fir on ufen weard þone stepel. *a* **1175** *Cott. Hom.* 223 He worhte þa þane man mid his handen. *c* **1175** *Lamb. Hom.* 7 Þurh þene halie gast. *Ibid.* 99 Crist ableow þana halȝa gast ofer þa apostlas. *c* **1200** *Trin. Coll. Hom.* 53 Ure helende..makede þen heuenliche fader sehte mid mankin. **1297** R. GLOUC. (Rolls) 2184 To rere þon stronge wal. *Ibid.* 7954 He..þen castel bisette. **1340** *Ayenb.* 187 He ne may naȝt þolye þane guode smel..namore þanne þe boterel þanne smel of þe vine. *c* **1380** *Sir Ferumb.* 2419 Ate laste þan gurdel he fond. *c* **1400** *Sowdone Bab.* 108 To Egremoure þon riche Cite.

**b.** *fem.* 1–3 **þá,** 2–3 **þeo,** 3 **þie, þo.**

*a* **900** tr. *Bæda's Hist.* III. xii. [xiv.] (1890) 196 Se biscop þa ȝeseah þa eaðmodnesse þæs cyninges. *c* **1000** *Ags. Gosp.* John xix. 17 On þa stowe. *c* **1175** *Lamb. Hom.* 9 On þa ealde laȝe. *Ibid.* 49 [Þes put] bitacneð þeo deopnesse of sunne. *c* **1200** *Trin. Coll. Hom.* 107 Þie giue god giueð ech man. *Ibid.*, Þeo giue he giueð mid þe holi husel. *c* **1205** LAY. 31 He nom þa Englisca boc þa makede seint Beda. *c* **1250** *O. Kent. Serm.* in *O. E. Misc.* 29 We mowe habbe þo blisce of heueriche.

**3.** *Dative.* **a.** *masc.* and *neut.* 1 **þǽm,** 1–2 **þám,** (2 **þa**), 2–4 **þen, þon, thon, þan, than,** (3 **þæn**), 3–4 **þo** (**ten**).

*Beowulf* 143 Se þæm feonde æt-wand. *c* **975** *Rushw. Gosp.* Matt. viii. 24 On þæm sæ. *c* **1000** ÆLFRIC *Gen.* vi. 16 Binnan þam arce. *c* **1121** *O. E. Chron.* (Laud MS.) an. 1087, Innan þam castele. **1131** *Ibid.*, On þa tun þa wæs tenn ploges. *a* **1175** *Cott. Hom.* 227 Mid þan hefonlice feder. *c* **1175** *Lamb. Hom.* 41 On þon deie. *Ibid.* 121 Ibuhsum þan heuenliche federe to þa deðe. *c* **1200** *Trin. Coll. Hom.* 25 For þo þe he us shop. *c* **1205** LAY. 8157 Þu me smiten bi þon rugge. *Ibid.* 127 On þan londe. *Ibid.* 9266 He redde al þæn kæisere. *a* **1225** *Ancr. R.* 66 Al þat lescun..of þen epple. *c* **1250** *O. Kent. Serm.* in *O. E. Misc.* 26 To-janes þo sunne risindde. *Ibid.*, Bi þo sterre. *c* **1315** SHOREHAM v. 184 Fram þan tyme he was ybore. **1340** *Ayenb.* 12 At þo daye. *c* **1386** CHAUCER *Friar's T.* 51 To..make hym grete feestes atte nale [= at ten ale].

**b.** *fem.* 1–3 **þǽre** (2 **þara**), 2–3 **þere, þer,** 2–4 **þare, þar.**

*c* **888** K. ÆLFRED *Boeth.* xli. § 3 Mid þære ilcan spræce. *c* **1000** *Ags. Gosp.* John xvii. 11 On ðære tide. *c* **1000** *Sax. Leechd.* III. 86 Byd hy to þare wunda. *a* **1175** *Cott. Hom.* 225 Binnan þara birie. *Ibid.* 235 To þar sawle. *c* **1175** *Lamb. Hom.* 3 He com to þere dune. *Ibid.* 31 Cume þenne to þer ilke chirche. *c* **1205** LAY. 1233 Mid þære sæ. *Ibid.* 4528 To þere sæ. *a* **1225** *Ancr. R.* 36 Ualleð to ðer eorðe. *a* **1250** *Owl & Night.* 31 Þe Nightegale..huhte wel ful of þare vle. *c* **1315** SHOREHAM II. 118 Þe sonne dym By-come in þare tyde.

**4.** *Genitive.* **a.** *masc.* and *neut.* 1–3 **ðæs, þæs,** 3 **þeos,** *Orm.* **þess,** 2–4 **þes, þas.** See also THES *adv.*

*c* **893** K. ÆLFRED *Oros.* I. iv. § 2 On þæs cyninges daȝum. *c* **1000** ÆLFRIC *Hom.* I. 240 For ðæs folces hreddinge. *a* **1131** *O. E. Chron.* an. 1122, Þet wes þes dæies viii idus Mr. *c* **1160** *Hatton Gosp.* Luke i. 10 Eall wered þas folkes. *c* **1200** *Trin. Coll. Hom.* 23 He sit on rihthalf þes almihtie faderes. *c* **1205** LAY. 713 To þas [*c* **1275** þis] kinges ferde. *Ibid.* 806 To telde þæs [*c* **1275** þis] kinges. *Ibid.* 7560 Þurh þeos [*c* **1275** þes] sweordes wunde. *a* **1250** *Owl & Night.* 338 Þu adunest þas monnes eren þar þu wunest.

**b.** *fem.* 1–2 **þǽre,** 2–3 **þere, þare,** 2–4 **þer.**

*c* **893** K. ÆLFRED *Oros.* I. i. § 14 On oþre healfe þære eas. *c* **1205** LAY. 331 Þere quene cun Heleine. *a* **1250** *Owl & Night.* 28 Hit wes þare vle erdingstowe. *c* **1315** SHOREHAM i. 79 Mannys blod Hys [= ys] ryȝt þer saule ȝiste.

**5.** *Instrumental*: see THE *adv.*, THON, THY *adv.*

**II.** *Plural.* **6.** *Nom.* and *acc.* 1–4 **þá,** (2–3 **ta**), (3 **þea**), 3–5 **þo** (**to**); 3 **þeo,** 4 **theo.** (See also THO *adj.*)

*a* **700** *Epinal Gl.* (O.E.T.) 439 *Funestissima*, tha deat[h]licostan. *c* **725** *Corpus Gl.* 942 Ða deadlicustan. *c* **825** *Vesp. Psalter* v. 6 Ða unrehtwisan. *a* **1200** *Moral Ode* 103 Þa swicen and ta forsworene. *c* **1200** *Trin. Coll. Hom.* 35 On þa wurhliche weden. *c* **1205** LAY. 2020 He..scæwede þea [*c* **1275** þe] leoden. *Ibid.* 2326 Þa hehste of þan hirde. *Ibid.* 5654 Þeo [*c* **1275** þe] cnihtes weoren vnwepned. **12..** *Moral Ode* (Egert. MS.) 192 He scal deme þo quike & to dede. *a* **1300** *Cursor M.* 861 Amang þa trees. *a* **1400** *K. Alis.* 4108 Theo maydenes lokyn in the glas.

**7.** *Dative.* 1 **þǽm, þám,** 2–3 **þam, þon, þan,** 3 **þen.**

*c* **893** K. ÆLFRED *Oros.* I. i. § 28 Be þæm ȝesetenum iȝlandum. *c* **1000** *Ags. Gosp.* Mark v. 2 Of þam byrȝenum. *c* **1175** *Lamb. Hom.* 27 For þan deoflan. *Ibid.* 139 To alle ðon monnen. *c* **1205** LAY. 714 To þon cnihten. *Ibid.* 747 Cuð he wes þen cnihten. *a* **1225** *Ancr. R.* 50 Þe blake cloð..deð lesse eile to þen eien.

**8.** *Genitive.* 1–2 **þára, þǽra,** 2 **þera,** 2–3 **þere,** 3 **þare, þer.**

**971** *Blickl. Hom.* 35 Ne bið þara fæstendaȝa na ma þonne syx & þritiȝ. *c* **1000** ÆLFRIC *Hom.* I. 12 Ealra þæra þinga [*a* **1175** *Cott. Hom.* 221 þara þinge]. *a* **1175** *Cott. Hom.* 229 An þera twelf Christes þeiȝne. *c* **1175** *Lamb. Hom.* 133 Þurh ðere clerkene muðe. *c* **1200** *Trin. Coll. Hom.* 121 Þer apostlene lore. *Ibid.* 129 Nan þere prophete þe ȝe wenen.

**III. 9.** General uninflected form, as definite article in all cases, genders, and numbers.

This had come to be *þe*, *the* by *c* 1150 in the East Midland dialect, and may have been so even earlier in the Northern dial., where *þe* was the nom. masc. for *se a* 950. The nom. masc. and fem. had become *þe* almost everywhere by 1300, but the neuter *þat, þet* remained longer before a vowel (see 1 c); and inflected forms of some oblique cases survived in some southern dialects till 1400 (cf. 2 a and 3 above).

2–5 **þe,** 2, 4– **the** (also written 5–8 **ye, y^e^**). (Also 2–3 **þa,** 2–4 **te** (see T 8), 3–5 **þo,** 4 **þi,** 4 **thee,** 4–5 **þeo, theo,** 5 **þey,** 6 **they,** 8–9 *dial.* **ta, te, da, de, 'ee**; *abbrev.* 2 **þ-,** 5–6 **th-,** 7–9 (now *dial.* and *poet.*) **th'**; 5–6 (8–9 *dial.*) **t'** (see T [2]), 8–9 *dial.* **d'.**

*a* **1131** *O. E. Chron.* (Laud MS.) an. 1122, Þa com se fir..and forbearnde ealle þe minstre. *Ibid.*, Se fir weax..up to þe heouene. *Ibid.* an. 1123, He com æfter þe Rome scot. *Ibid.*, In þe lenten ferde se ærcebiscop to Rome. *a* **1154** *Ibid.* an. 1132, To þe king..þe muneces..þurh þe biscop of Seresberi & te b' of Lincoln and te oþre ricemen. *Ibid.* an. 1137, Þe land was al fordon..In the hus..on þe circe..alle þe landes. *Ibid.* an. 1140, Þe kynges dohter Henries..Wyd þemperice. *Ibid.*, And te cuen of France to dælde fra þe king, and scæ com to þe iunge eorl Henri. *c* **1200** ORMIN 1485, & gaddresst swa þe clene corn All fra þe chaff togeddre. *c* **1250** *Gen. & Ex.* 2949 But if it were in ðe lond gersen, ðor-inne woren ðe ebrisse men. *Ibid.* 2962 For to bi-tournen ðe kinges ðoȝt. **13..** *Cursor M.* 6859 (Cott.) Suilk was þi lessun and þi lare [*v.r.* þe..þe]. *c* **1400** *Rule St. Benet* 12 Sua sais te prophete. *c* **1420** *Chron. Vilod.* 1910 In þe whyche water hurre to wasshe. *a* **1425** *Cursor M.* 9908 (Laud) The man that thedir-ward is fled. *Ibid.* 10005 Thee iiijᵉ turret þer e-sette. **1436** *Coventry Leet Bk.* 185 Þat þey prior be not suffered to make no more off þe Stan wall vndur þey priory. **1470–85** MALORY *Arthur* II. xiii. 91 No thyng but thold custome. **1496** *Plumpton Corr.* p. ci, The said lands..& t'ofice of the Steward. **1529** CROMWELL in Merriman *Life & Lett.* (1902) I. 58 Kept to thuse of my saide Soonne. **1529** in *Vicary's Anat.* (1888) App. II. 100 Mʳ Whittington, scolmaster to thenxmen. *a* **1533** LD. BERNERS *Huon* vi. 13 Out of temperours fauore. *Ibid.* lxxxviii. 278 His vncle themperour of Almayne. *a* **1548** HALL *Chron.*, *Rich. III* 27 b, Lo ye honorable courage of a kyng. **1603** SHAKS. *Meas. for M.* v. iii. 241 Come, come, to' th' purpose. **1632** MILTON *Penseroso* 60 Gently o're th' accustom'd Oke. **1742** YOUNG *Nt. Th.* VI. 465 Th' Almighty Fiat, and the Trumpet's Sound.

*dial.* *c* **1746** COLLIER (Tim Bobbin) *View Lanc. Dial.* Wks. (1862) p. xxxix, By th' Miss, th' owd story ogen. **1884** J. C. EGERTON *Sussex Folks & Ways* iii. 34, I can't swallow it nohows in de wurreld. **1888** ADDY *Sheffield Gloss.* 13 T' beeas has got into t' corn. **1890** BICKLEY *Surrey Hills* xxix, Let 'ee words as did vor vather do vor son. **1892** M. C. MORRIS *Yorks. Folk-talk* ii. 19 Gan inti d' hoos.

**B. Signification.**

**I.** Referring to an individual object (or objects).

* Marking an object as before mentioned or already known, or contextually particularized (e.g. 'We keep a dog. We are all fond of *the* dog').

**1.** The ordinary use.

**805–*a* 1154** [see A. I. 1 a α]. *c* **950** *Lindisf. Gosp.* Matt. ii. 9 Stearra..ȝestod ofer ðer (*vel* hwer) wæs ðe cnæht [*Rushw.* se cneht]. *c* **1000** *Ags. Gosp.* Matt. ii. 11 And gangende into þam huse hi ȝemetton þæt cild. — John ii. 7 Þæt hiȝ þa fatu mid wætere ȝefyldon. *c* **1175** *Lamb. Hom.* 133 Sum of þe sede feol an uppe þe stane..sum bi þe weie. *c* **1200** ORMIN 1082 He toc þe recless & te blod & ȝede upp to þatt allterr. **13..** *Gaw. & Gr. Knt.* 405 Quod þe gome in þe grene to Gawan þe hende. **1340** *Ayenb.* 186 Wel ssolle we habbe reuþe..þe on of þe oþre. *c* **1386** CHAUCER *Prol.* 845 (Corp.) Þe soþ is þis, þe Cut fel to þe knight. *c* **1425** *Seven Sag.* (P.) 10 The emperour and is wif Loveden the child as hare lyf. **1530** PALSGR. 45 Where they saye in frenche *le maistre*, *la dame*, we saye in our tonge *the mayster*, *the lady*; so that this word *the*, with us, counter vayleth bothe *le* and *la*. **1695** CONGREVE *Love for Love* IV. iv, What's the matter now? **1818** CRUISE *Digest* V. 494 That the recovery enured to the uses of the settlement, and therefore that the purchaser had no title. **1902** GAIRDNER *Hist. Eng. Ch. 16th Cent.* viii. (1903) 149 He re-considered the matter.

**b.** Placed before the relative pron. *which* (*whilk*) (*arch.*): see WHICH. *The one*, *the other*: see ONE, OTHER, TONE, TOTHER.

**2.** Used before a word denoting time, as *the time*, *day*, *hour*, *moment*: the time (etc.) in question, or under consideration; the time (now or then) present. *The while*: see WHILE.

[*c* **897** K. ÆLFRED *Gregory's Past. C.* xlvi. 348 Hie nanwuht godes ne maȝon ða hwile Gode brengan to ðances.] *a* **1425** *Cursor M.* 3889 (Trin.) Þe while holde lya in bedde Þenne shal þou rachel wedde. **1533** BELLENDEN *Livy* v. xxiii. (S. T. S.) II. 227 Þe said voce was contempnit and necleckit in þe tyme. **1616** J. LANE *Cont. Sqr.'s T.* viii. 213 And, iust at thinstant, all the canons plaien From towne to Campe, from Camp to towne againe. **1780** *Mirror* No. 76 ¶ 3 He comes there only as he does to the coffee-house, to enquire after the news of the day. **1848** DICKENS *Dombey* liv, At the moment, the bell rang loudly in the hall. **1864** TENNYSON *Aylmer's F.* 194 A tongue that ruled the hour. **1866** NEWMAN *Gerontius* ad fin., And I will come and wake thee on the morrow.

**b.** Used before numerals denoting years.

Now only with abbreviation, either in reference to certain historical events (see FIFTEEN A. 2, FORTY-FIVE), or in expressions denoting a particular decade of a century or of a person's life (see EIGHTY 2 b, FIFTY B. 2 b, etc.).

**1724** R. WODROW *Life J. Wodrow* (1828) 60 Elizabeth died..about the 1684 of a consumption. *a* **1776** LD. AUCHINLECK in *Scotch Acts* (1844) I. Pref. 188, I take this Manuscript to have been wrote before the 1500, and it is clear it was not wrote before the 1455. *a* **1797**, **1814** [see FIFTEEN A. 2]. **1824** SCOTT *Redgauntlet* ch. xi, Ye have heard of a year they call the Forty-five. **1862** BURTON *Bk. Hunter* III. 261 Dispersed over the Highlands to keep them in order after the '45. **1880**, **1889** [see FIFTY B. 2]. *Mod.* I think it was in the early eighties.

**c.** *The day*, *the morn*, *the night*, in *Sc.* and *north. dial.* = to-day, to-morrow, to-night.

*a* **1300** [see MORN 3 c, d]. **13..** *Cursor M.* (Cott.) 702 Þe sun was þat time..Seuen sith brighter þen þe dai [*so Fairf.*; *Gött.* to-day]. *c* **1475** *Rauf Coilȝear* 301 Cum the morne to the Court. *a* **1692** in 'J. Curate' *Sc. Presb. Eloq.* iii. 106, I have brought him to you the day. *a* **1800** in *Burns' Wks.* (1800) I. 363 For he's far aboon Dunkel the night. **1814** [see DAY *sb.* 13 b (*b*)].

**3.** Before the name of a unique object or one so considered, or of which there is only one at a time; e.g. *the sun*, *the earth*, *the sea*, *the sky*, *the air*, *the world*, *the universe*, *the Almighty*, *the Lord*, *the Messiah*, *the Saviour*, *the Gospel*, *the Bible*, *the abyss*, *the pit*, *the Devil*, *the Emperor*, *the Pope*, *the Kaiser*, *the Sultan*, *the Shah*, etc.

*c* **975** *Rushw. Gosp.* John iv. 6 Ðe hælend forðon woeriȝ wæs of gonge. *a* **1000** *Boeth. Metr.* xxvi. 6 Aulixes under hæfde þæm casere cynericu twa. *c* **1000** *Sax. Leechd.* III. 254 Seo eorðe stent on ælemiddan. *Ibid.* 268 Seo sæ and se mona ȝeþwærlæcað him betweonan. *Ibid.* 274 Seo lyft, þonne heo astyred is, byð wind. *a* **1225** *Ancr. R.* 82 Þe deouel..is leas, and leasunges feder. *a* **1240** *Ureisun* in *Cott. Hom.* 185 Iwend me from the worlde. *c* **1400** *Brut* xxxvi. 33 Þe Emperoure..he..ordeynede a stronge power. *c* **1400** *Apol. Loll.* 28 Bi lawe..of þe kirk,..ilk prest haþ þe same power to vse þe key in to ani man in þo poynt of deþ, as þe pope. **1580** in *Cath. Rec. Soc. Publ.* I. 69 To the Tuission of Thallmightie. **1590** SPENSER *F. Q.* I. i. 32 The Sunne, that measures heaven all day long. **1611** BIBLE *Ps.* xxiv. 1 The earth is the Lords, and the fulnesse thereof. **1748** CHESTERFIELD *Lett.* 31 May, Sixtus the Vth..raised himself to the Popedom by his abilities. **1842** TENNYSON *Beggar Maid* ii, As shines the moon in clouded skies.

**b.** With names of rivers, as *the Amazon*, *the Thames*; of mountains, groups of islands, or regions, in the plural, as *the Alps*, *the Azores*, *the Indies*; of places or mountains, in the sing., now only when felt to be descriptive, as *the Land's End*, *the Lizard*, *the High Street*, *the Oxford Road*, *the Jungfrau*, *the Matterhorn*, or when *the* has come down traditionally, as *the Lennox*, *the Merse*; exceptionally in *the Tyrol*. Formerly often used more widely.

*c* **893** K. ÆLFRED *Orosius* I. i. § 21 Seo Wisle is swyðe mycel ea..Seo Wisle lið ut of Weonodlande, and lið in Estmere. **1297** R. GLOUC. (Rolls) 164 Þat oþer wonder is Vpe þe hul of þe pek. *Ibid.* 4740 Wippe was king of þe march, & adelfred of humberlond. **1632** MASSINGER & FIELD *Fatal Dowry* II. i, I would they were at the Bermudas! **1653** HOLCROFT *Procopius, Goth. Wars* II. 43 When the Vesuvius casts out cynders. **1761** *Char.* in *Ann. Reg.* 52/1 The Devizes. **1784** COWPER *Task* III. 583 Th' Azores send Their jessamine. **1814** SCOTT *Wav.* xxxix, The travellers now..reached the Tor wood. **1822** — *Nigel* x, I should like to see the broad Tay once more before I die; not even the Thames can match it, in my mind. **1842** PRICHARD *Nat. Hist. Man* (ed. 2) 467 The Tupi, or native inhabitants of the Brazils. **1855** MACAULAY *Hist. Eng.* xviii. IV. 119 From the Land's End to the Straits of Dover.

**c.** With names of natural phenomena, seasons, etc., as *the spring*, *the summer*, *the autumn*, *the winter*, *the day*, *the night*; *the wind*, *the cold*, *the clouds*, etc.; of the points of the compass, as *the north*, *the east* (in OE. usually without article).

*c* **1000** *Sax. Leechd.* III. 274 Se wind hæfð mistlice naman on bocum. *a* **1300** [see EAST *sb.* 2]. **13..** *E. E. Allit. P.* B. 953 Þe rayn rueled adoun, ridlande þikke. **1382** WYCLIF *Matt.* ii. 2 We han seyn his sterre in the este. *c* **1440** *Alphabet of Tales* 106 Vppon a fayr day, whar þe wynde blew. **1697** DRYDEN *Virg. Georg.* III. 378 They That wing the liquid Air, or swim the Sea, Or haunt the Desart. **1784** COWPER *Task* I. 749 God made the country, and man made the town. **1791** — *Odyss.* IX. 194 The rosy-finger'd daughter of the dawn.

†**d.** Formerly sometimes used before abstract sbs. See also DEATH 2, 12, LIFE 7, 7 b. *Obs.*

*c* **888** K. ÆLFRED *Boeth.* iii. § 3 Þa se Wisdom þa and seo Gesceadwisnes þis leoð asungen hæfdon. *c* **897** — *Gregory's Past. C.* iii. 35 On ðære ȝesundfulnesse mon forȝiett his selfes. *Ibid.* xxxiii. 214 Ða ȝeðylde þe is modur..ealra mæȝena..[he] forlett. *c* **1450** tr. *De Imitatione* III. lxiii. 146 Þe pes stondiþ more in very mekenes þan in propre exaltacion. **14..** *Pol. Rel. & L. Poems* (1903) 257 Ase..roust on þe knife, and ase deþ to þe life. *c* **1489** CAXTON *Blanchardyn* xxi. 70 The prouost..cam sone toward the proude mayden in amours, and made to her the reuerence. *Ibid.* xxiii. 74 So cam he toward blanchardyn..And gaff hym the goode nyght. **1525** LD. BERNERS *Froiss.* II. ccxxiii. [ccxix.] 695 If Lamorabaquy wolde gyue them the heryngе. **1588** ALLEN *Admon.* 11 A verie fable to the posteritе.

**4.** With a class-name, to indicate the individual example most familiar to one, or with which one is primarily or locally concerned, e.g. *the King*, *the Emperor* (in mod. use), *the Lord Mayor*, *the Town*, *the House*, *the Court*, *the Tower*, *the Abbey*, *the River*, *the Channel*, *the Flood*, *the Reformation*, *the Revolution*; *the Gospel*, *the Epistle* (for the day).

*c* **1121** *O. E. Chron.* (Laud MS.) an. 1106, To Eastran wæs se cyng æt Baðan. *Ibid.* an. 1120, An se arcebiscop Turstein..wearð þurh þone papan wið þone cyng acordad. *a* **1154** *Ibid.* an. 1140, Sume helden mid te king and sume mid þemperice. *c* **1175** *Lamb. Hom.* 3 Seggeð þet þe lauerd haued þar-of neode. *Ibid.* 5 Ȝe iherden er on þe godspel hu ure drihten sende his .ii. apostles. *a* **1300** *Cursor M.* 20502 Þan spac þat leuedi..to þapostlis euerilkan. *a* **1568** ASCHAM *Scholem.* I. (Arb.) 68 Ye great ones in ye Court. **1621** ELSING *Debates Ho. Lords* (Camden) 16 To make his answere here at the barre. **1666** EVELYN *Diary* 13 Sept., The Queene was..in her cavalier riding habite. **1689** LUTTRELL *Brief Rel.* (1857) I. 557 The house of commons..ordered..that the then judges should attend the house. **1837** SIR F. PALGRAVE *Merch. & Friar* Ded. (1844) 1 Any bibliopolist, in or out of the Row. **1845** [see HOUSE *sb.*[1] 4 d]. **1875** TENNYSON *Q. Mary* I. i, He swears by the Rood.

**5.** Formerly with names of branches of learning, arts, crafts, games, and pursuits. Now chiefly *dial.* Also generally with gerundial vbl. sbs. (*arch.*).

*c* **1325** [see CHESS *sb.*[1] 1]. **1470–85** MALORY *Arthur* IX. xvii. 363 On a day kynge Mark played at the chesse. **1596** SHAKS. *Tam. Shr.* I. i. 37 The Mathematickes, and the Metaphysickes Fall to them. *c* **1643** LD. HERBERT *Autobiog.* (1824) 89 Any man thought worth the looking on. **1739** CHESTERF. *Lett.* (1774) I. 122 As you are now reading the Roman History. **1768** H. ST. JOHN in Jesse *Selwyn & Contemp.* (1843) II. 309, I regret the badness of our climate, and the being obliged to pass the remainder of my life in [it]. **1824** MRS. CAMERON *Pink Tippet* IV. 22 What was the use of my getting you taught the dress-making? **1887** *Wellington Weekly News* 3 Feb. (E.D.D.), Apprentices and improvers wanted to the millinery, to the dressmaking, to the currying. **1901** *Union Mag.* Apr. 150/1, I wad raither hae seen ye at the joinerin' like masel'.

**6.** With names of literary or musical compositions, as plays, poems, anthems, etc.; also of newspapers and periodicals.

*a* **1225** *Ancr. R.* 18 Þus doð..et te biginnunge of þe Venite. **1780** *Mirror* No. 99 ¶ 7 The *Orestes* of the Greek poet. **1810** SCOTT *Let.* in Smiles *Mem. J. Murray* 1891) I. 190 'Kehama'..will get it roundly in the Edinburgh Review. **1845** GOSSE *Ocean* iv. (1849) 159 Plato, in the Timæus, gives the fullest account. *Mod. The Times* has a leading article on the subject.

**7.** Formerly with names of languages; now only in consciously elliptical phrases, as *from the German* (sc. *language* or *original*).

**1593** NASHE *Four Lett. Confut.* Wks. (Grosart) II. 263 To borrowe some lesser quarry of elocution from the Latine. **1596** SHAKS. *Merch. V.* I. ii. 77 You will..sweare that I haue a poore pennie-worth in the English. **1760** *Portia, Polite Lady* xi. 28 Let not your studying the French make you neglect the English. **1795** SOUTHEY *Lett. fr. Spain* xxii. (1799) 294 Every advantage that..a complete knowledge of the Arabic could afford. *Mod.* A new translation directly from the Hebrew.

**8.** With names of diseases, ailments, etc. Now more often omitted.

*c* **1000** *Sax. Leechd.* II. 314 Wið þære ȝeolwan adle..ȝenim þæs scearpan þistles moran and betonican. *a* **1300** *Cursor M.* 11319 In his heued he has þe scall þe scab ouer-gas his bodi all. *Ibid.* 11825 Þe gutte þe potagre. **1377** LANGL. *P. Pl.* B. XIII. 325, I cacche þe crompe, þe cardiacle. *c* **1400** *Lanfranc's Cirurg.* 281 It is myn entencioun to speke of þe dropesie. *Ibid.* 293 Of þe cancre and þe mormole. **1480**, **1500–20** [see POCK *sb.* 2 a]. **1660** GAUDEN *Brownrig* 225 Sharp fits of the stone. **1671** C'TESS WARWICK *Autobiog.* (Percy Soc.) 9, I..fell..ill of the measles. **1743–1831** [see INFLUENZA]. **1787** [J. BEATTIE] *Scoticisms* 91 He has got the cold, the fever. **1809** SOUTHEY *Let. to Landor* 23 Apr., in *Life* (1850) III. 228, I instantly recognised the sound of the croup. **1839** — *Let. to Mrs. Hodson* 18 Feb. *ibid.* VI. 381 A serious attack of the influenza. *Mod.* (*familiar*) I have the toothache.

**9.** Elliptically with the names of ships, as *the* (*ship*) *Nicholas*, and of taverns, as *the Mermaid* (*tavern*), theatres, and other well-known buildings.

**1450** *Paston Lett.* I. 125 He was yn the Nicolas tyl Saturday next folwyng. **1480** WARKWORTH *Chron.* (Camden) 13 Casten in presone in the Marchalse at London. **1521** in *Essex Rev.* XIII. 221 Out of the Barbara and the Mayflower, if God send them well home. *a* **1616** BEAUMONT *To Ben Jonson*, What things have we seen Done at the Mermaid! **1710** SWIFT *Jrnl. to Stella* 15 Oct., Prior and I..sat at the Smyrna till eleven. **1779** *Mirror* No. 32 ¶ 5 Stopping at the *George* on his way home. **1905** *Daily Chron.* 24 Oct. 3/4 *heading*, Playlet at the Coliseum. *Mod. The Mauretania* has made a record passage.

**10.** Before higher titles of rank, as *the Emperor*, *King*, *Prince*, *Grand Duke*, *Marquess*, *Earl*, *Count* (but not now when followed by the name, as *King George*, *Prince Edward*, *Duke Humphrey*, *Earl Grey*, *Earl Simon*), and with the corresponding female titles *Queen*, *Duchess*, etc.; also with some courtesy titles, as *the Right Honourable*, *the Honourable*, *the Reverend*, etc. See further LORD, LADY, and the other titles.

*c* **1121** *O. E. Chron.* (Laud MS.) an. 1090, Se eorl of Normandiȝe. *Ibid.* an. 1117, Se cyng of France and se eorl of Flandra. **1340** *Ayenb.* 76 Þe leuedy fortune went hare hueȝel eche daye. **1472** SIR J. PASTON in *P. Lett.* III. 39 Robert of Racclyff weddyd the lady Dymmok. **1553** in *Rutland Papers* (Camden) 119 Therle of Oxford claymeth thoffice of great chamberlayne of England. **1603** SIR R. WILBRAHAM *Diary* (Camden) 60 The lord Thomas Howard made erle of Suffolk. **1613** SHAKS. *Hen. VIII*, II. iii. 94 The Marchionesse of Pembrooke. **1707** E. CHAMBERLAYNE *Pres. St. Eng.* II. xv. (ed. 22) 188 The Lord Chief Justice. **1794** MRS. RADCLIFFE *Myst. Udolpho* l, 'The Chevalier Valancourt!' said Emily, trembling extremely. **1827** *Edin. Weekly Jrnl.* 28 Feb., The absence of the Right Hon. the Lord Provost.

**b.** With the surnames of some Irish and Scottish chiefs of clans, as the O'Gorman Mahon, the Chisholm, the MacNab.

**1561** *Inverness Sheriff Crt. Records* II. 15 Apr. (MS.), [Secerunt] the Dollace of Cantray. **1562** *Ibid.* 7 Apr., The jugis hes consignit hir to produce the samyn and to wairne the Dollace upon ane xv dayis warning. **1847** THACKERAY *Mrs. Perkins's Ball* i. 4, I became acquainted with the Mulligan through a distinguished countryman..who..did not know the chieftain himself. **1880** A. M. SHAW *Mackintoshes* p. xxvii, Moy Hall, the residence of The Mackintosh. **1910** *Daily Chron.* 1 Feb. 4/6 Three 'Thes' have sat in the House of Commons in our time—The O'Conor Don, The O'Donoghue of the Glens, and The O'Gorman Mahon. The MacDermott, K.C.,..was an Irish law officer in Liberal Governments.

**c.** Before names and titles of men, often in ME. a corruption of F. *de*, as in *Robert the Bruce*, *Sir Simon the Montfort*, *the Mortimer*, etc. *arch.*

**1297** R. GLOUC. (Rolls) 11134 Sir Roger þe Mortimer. **1375** BARBOUR *Bruce* I. 67 That..Robert the brwys, Erle of carryk Aucht to succeid to the kynryk. *Ibid.* 435 The Clyffurd sall thaim haiff. *c* **1450** *Brut* 427 The Erle of Somersette and his brothir, and the Fytz-Watir. **1591** SHAKS. *1 Hen. VI*, III. iii. 37 *Charles.* A Parley with the Duke of Burgonie. *Burg.* Who craues a Parley with the Burgonie? **1814** SCOTT *Ld. of Isles* III. xxvii, As heroes think, so thought the Bruce.

**d.** Before the names of well-known singers, actresses, etc., in imitation of French and Italian usage.

**1786** MRS. A. M. BENNETT *Juvenile Indiscretions* V. 32 The Siddons. **1796** *Publ. Advert.* 18 Nov. in T. Campbell *Life Mrs. Siddons* II. viii. 201 Last night the Siddons and the Kemble, at Drury Lane, acted to vacancy. **1822** in *Byron's Wks.* (1846) 585/1 The Guiccioli was present. **1845** DISRAELI *Sybil* v. vii, Well, what do you think of the Dashville, Fitz?

**11.** *spec.* Used emphatically, in the sense of 'the pre-eminent', 'the typical', or 'the only.. worth mentioning'; as 'Cæsar was *the* general of Rome', i. e. the general *par excellence*; *the* being often stressed in speech (ðī), and printed in italics.

**1824** L. MURRAY *Eng. Gram.* (ed. 5) I. 257 In the history of Henry the fourth, by Father Daniel, we are surprised at not finding him *the* great man. **1829** CARLYLE *Misc., Germ. Playwr.* (1872) II. 97 Dr. Klingemann..so superlative is his vigour..we might even designate him *the* Playwright. **1863** R. B. KIMBALL *Was he Successful?* vi. (Cent.), Joel Burns was a rich man, as well as *the* man of the place. **1865** LUBBOCK *Preh. Times* 131 The axe was pre-eminently *the* implement of antiquity. **1904** S. G. TALLENTYRE *Life Voltaire* II. xxxv. 144 His Commentary remains unrivalled, and is still *the* text-book on Corneille.

**12.** With any part of the body of a person previously named or indicated, instead of the corresponding possessive pronoun; as 'he took him by the hand', i. e. *his* hand. So with *heart, soul*, used *fig.*; also with parts of personal attire.

**1154** *O. E. Chron.* an. 1137, Me henged [heom] up bi the fet..bi the þumbes, other bi the hefed. **13..** *K. Alis.* (Bodl. MS.) 2276 Fulbor he smoot vpon þe rygge. **1390** GOWER *Conf.* II. 213 That love..Ne schal noght take hem by the slieve. *c* **1460** *Towneley Myst.* xxiv. 115, I shall knap hym on the crowne That standys in my gate. **1583–93** GREENE *Mamillia* II. Wks. (Grosart) II. 220 Ruffes of a Syse, stiffe starcht to the necke. **1590** SHAKS. *Com. Err.* II. ii. 206 To put the finger in the eie and weepe. **1789** MRS. PIOZZI *Journ. France* I. 306 Heavy lace robbins ending at the elbow. **1838** DICKENS *O. Twist* lii, To be hanged by the neck, till he was dead. **1847** TENNYSON *Princess* vii. 209–12 Pale was the perfect face..And the voice trembled and the hand.

**b.** Used colloquially with names of relatives, as *the wife, the mother* = my (your) wife, mother.

**1838** J. M. WILSON *Tales Borders* No. 210 (1839) V. 9/1 What shall I say to the wife? **1853** 'C. BEDE' *Verdant Green* I. vii, 'It's a long while since the governor was here', remarked Mr. Charles Larkyns, very unfilially. **1888** The Mater [see MATER 3]. **1891** DUNCAN *Amer. Girl in Lond.* 82 The mother and sisters would like to call upon you. **1900** The pater..the mater [see PATER 3]. **1901** W. CHURCHILL *R. Carvell* xliv, [I] sent off an express to Patty and the Mother last night.

**c.** Before OWN (*a.* 2 b) and SELF (C. 1 c), q. v.

**13.** Used before names of weights and measures, in stating a rate: as (*so much*) *the pound, gallon, yard, day*, etc. Cf. A *adj.*[2] 4, PER III. 2.

**1426–7** *Rec. St. Mary at Hill* 65, iiij[c] hert latthe, pris þe hondrid, vij d..ij[ml] traunsum, þe m[l] x d. **1488–9** *Act 4 Hen. VII*, c. 22 Sold for iij li. sterling the pack. **1551–2** *Act 5 & 6 Edw. VI*, c. 6 § 1 That all colored Clothes..shall waye fourscore pounde the pece at the lest. **1596–7** S. FINCHE in *Hist. Croydon* App. (1783) 153 Bricklayers..have xv d. apeece the day. **1631** WEEVER *Anc. Fun. Mon.* 418 Appointing them xii d. the weeke to each person. **1796** SOUTHEY *Lett. fr. Spain* (1799) 118 They are very dear, ten reales the couple. **1851** MAYHEW *Lond. Labour* II. 284/2 The sherds run about 250 pieces to the bushel.

**b.** So with prepositions *by, in*, †*on*.., chiefly with reference to time, as (*so much*) *by the day* = (so much) each day.

**1477–8** *Rec. St. Mary at Hill* 79 Paid to Sir Iohn Colyns..at viij s. iiij d. by the quarter. **1530** TINDALE *Answ. More* III. i. Wks. (1572) 304/2, I finde in all ages that men..haue suffred death by the hundred thousandes in resisting their doctrine. **1533** *Acc. Ld. High Treas. Scot.* VI. 151 To Thomas Scott passing in Ingland with writtingis and credence to the King ..to him on the day iij li. **1613** SHAKS. *Hen. VIII*, v. iv. 33 What should you doe, But knock 'em downe by th' dozens? **1632** LITHGOW *Trav.* VI. 298 The Dromidory..will ride aboue 80 miles in the day. **1727** POPE, etc. *Art Sinking* xiii. 116 It may be..let out by the day. **1848** DICKENS *Dombey* xxxix, He would sit and avail himself of its accommodations..by the half-hour together. **1883** SIR J. C. DAY in *Law Rep.* 12 Q. B. Div. 206 Etymologically considered, a journeyman is one who is employed by the day.

** Marking an object not before mentioned, but now identified by a clause, phrase, or word.

**14.** Where the object is defined by a relative clause, *the* stands before the object. (The relative pronoun may be suppressed: cf. THAT *rel. pron.* 10.)

In mod. Eng. more emphatically expressed by *that*: see THAT *dem. adj.* 3. The OE. form did not distinguish these: *þæt spell* may be rendered 'that story' or 'the story'.

*a* **900** tr. *Bæda's Hist.* Pref. (1890) 2 Ic ðe sende þæt spell, þæt ic niwan awrat be Angel ðeode & Seaxum. **971** *Blickl. Hom.* 71 Seo menigo þe þær beforan ferde. *c* **975** *Rushw. Gosp.* Mark ii. 4 Þa bere in ðære þe eorð-crypel læg. *c* **1000** *Sax. Leechd.* III. 104 Þæt sindon þe teþ þe þane mete brecaþ. *c* **1200** *Trin. Coll. Hom.* 3 Þe holie tid þat me clepeð aduent. *c* **1250** *O. Kent. Serm.* in *O. E. Misc.* 26 Te dai ase ure louerd..i-bore was. *a* **1300** *Cursor M.* 14705 Þe werckes þat i werc in his nam. **1382** WYCLIF *Matt.* ii. 9 Loo! the sterre, the whiche thei sayen in este, wente bifore hem. **1472** J. PASTON in *P. Lett.* III. 75, I am not the man I was. **1596** SHAKS. *Merch. V.* v. i. 83 The man that hath no musicke in himselfe..Is fit for treasons [etc.]. **1697** T. BROWN *Dispens.* I. Wks. 1709 III. III. 67, I have known the Time, when I could go out and pick up 10 or 12 l. in a Morning. **1715–20** POPE *Iliad* XXIV. 256 Let us give To grief the wretched days we have to live. **1784** COWPER *Task* III. 141 The man, of whom His own coevals took but little note. **1805** WORDSW. *On Peele Castle*, The light that never was, on sea or land. **1850** J. H. NEWMAN *Diffic. Anglic.* I. ii. (1891) I. 48 But the passage I have quoted suggests a second observation.

**15.** Where the object is defined by a following phrase with prep. (esp. *of*, repr. an OE. genitive).

**971** *Blickl. Hom.* 55 Þeh he..ȝehyre þa word þæs halȝan godspelles. *c* **1121** *O. E. Chron.* (Laud MS.) an. 1116, On þisum ylcan ȝeare bærnde eall þæt mynstre of Burh. **1122** *Ibid.*, Se burch on Gleaweceastre. *c* **1175** *Lamb. Hom.* 53 Heo habbeð þe nome of cristene. *c* **1290** *Edmund Conf.* 387 in *S. Eng. Leg.* I. 442 In þe toun of wyricestre bi-tidde þat selue cas. **1387** TREVISA *Higden* (Rolls) II. 41 Tweie perilous places in þe see of myddel erþe. **1426–7** *Rec. St. Mary at Hill* 65 Also þe thorisday in þe Whitson weke. **1513** DOUGLAS *Æneis* IX. Prol. 7 Honeste is the way to worthynes. **1605** SHAKS. *Macb.* I. vii. 45 Like the poore Cat i' th' Addage. *a* **1734** NORTH *Exam.* I. i. § 23 (1740) 26 In the telling of this Story. **1764** GRAY *Candidate* 12 Just like the picture in Rochester's book. **1824** BENTHAM *Bk. Fallacies* Introd. vii, The Sir Charles Sedley of political morality. **1870** MORRIS *Earthly Par.*, *Jan.* 42 Midmost the time 'twixt noon and dusk. **1908** R. BRIDGES *Sel. Poems R. W. Dixon* (1909) p. xii, The Oxford of 1850 was singularly unsympathetic.

**b.** With an object defined by an infinitive phrase with *to* (where *the* may sometimes be rendered 'that..needed or proper..').

*c* **1384** CHAUCER *H. Fame* III. 966 Alle the folke that ys a lyve Ne han the kunnynge to discryve The thinges that I herde there. **1642** MILTON *Sonn.* viii. 13 The power To save th' Athenian Walls from ruine bare. **1687** A. LOVELL tr. *Thevenot's Trav.* I. 225 We had the Comfort to be pittied. **1850** J. H. NEWMAN *Diffic. Anglic.* I. iii. (1891) I. 80, I am not the person to be jealous of such facts.

**c.** With an object particularized by a pple.

**1658** PHILLIPS, *Salii*, the 12 Priests of Mars instituted by Numa Pompilius. **1876** ROGERS *Pol. Econ.* (ed. 3) ix. 81 The privileges accorded..to the merchants of the Hanse Towns. *Mod.* The book lying on your table.

**16.** *The* stands before a sb. defined by another sb. (usually a proper name) in apposition, as *the poet Virgil*.

*c* **893** K. ÆLFRED *Oros.* I. i. § 8 Se hehsta beorȝ Olimpus. *Ibid.* § 9 On westende Affrica, neh þam beorȝe Athlans. **1070** *O. E. Chron.*, Toforan þam papan Alexandre. *c* **1175** *Lamb. Hom.* 73 Of clene liflade spec þe prophete isaias. *c* **1200** ORMIN Ded. 257 Þatt..boc..Apokalypsis..Uss wrat te posstell Sannt Johan. **1297** R. GLOUC. (Rolls) 7956 Þe king..made..þe bissop ode..vorsuerie engelond. **1529** CROMWELL in Merriman *Life & Lett.* (1902) I. 325 The Jentylwoman your wyff. **1634** MILTON *Comus* 442 The huntress Dian.

**b.** More usually the proper name precedes. (Regularly so when the whole phrase becomes a recognized appellation, as *William the Conqueror*.)

*c* **950** *Lindisf. Gosp.* Matt. xii. 39 Becon iones ðæs witȝo [*Rushw.* tacen Ionas se witȝa]. *c* **1000** *Ags. Gosp.* Matt. iii. 1 On þam daȝum com iohannes se fulluhtere. *c* **1175** *Lamb. Hom.* 73 And dauid þe prophete spekeð in an salm. **13..** *Stac. Rome* (Vernon MS.) 238 Seint Ion þe Ewangelist. *c* **1400** *Brut* 299 About seint Lukes day þe euangglist. **1599** NASHE *Lenten Stuffe* (1871) 23 Their barony by William the Conqueror, conveyed over to them. **1906** *Edin. Rev.* Oct. 334 Bourdalone the physician was another favourite.

**17.** *The* is used with a sb. particularized or described by an adjective. The adj. usually precedes, but sometimes follows the sb.: in either case *the* stands first as *the good man, the church militant*.

(An adj. or pple. with a modifying addition regularly follows the sb., as 'the grass wet with dew', 'the tools needed for the work': cf. 15 c.)

A particularizing adj. often becomes a permanent epithet, as in *the Black Prince, the Lesser Bear, the Red Campion, the Great Exhibition, the Green Park, the Yellow Sea, the Count* or *County Palatine, the Prince Imperial*; the adj. and sb. may then be treated as name of a unique object, as in 3.

*c* **860** *O. E. Chron.* an. 853, Þy ilcan ȝeare sende Æþelwulf cyning Ælfred his sunu to Rome. **885** *Ibid.*, Se fore sprecena here. *c* **888** K. ÆLFRED *Boeth.* xl. § 4 Her endað sio fiorðe boc..and onginð sio fifte. **971** *Blickl. Hom.* 5 Se heofonlica cyning. **1008–11** *Laws of Æthelred* VI. c. 22 § 1 On þam halȝan dæȝe. *c* **1175** *Lamb. Hom.* 5 Þa oðre men.. stiȝen uppeon þe godes cunnes treowe. *c* **1386** CHAUCER *Knt.'s T.* 1491 Among the goddes hye it is affermed..Thou shalt [etc.]. *c* **1400** *Brut* 26 She was þe ryȝt heire of þis lande. **1413** *Pilgr. Sowle* (Caxton) v. vi. (1859) 76 The chirche militant, that laboureth here in erthe. *a* **1536** *Calisto & Melibæa* in Hazl. *Dodsley* I. 64 The mighty and perdurable God be his guide. **1575** GASCOIGNE *Making of Verse* in *Steele Gl.*, etc. (Arb.) 37 Vse your verse after thenglishe phrase. **1662** PEPYS *Diary* 20 Oct., Saw the so much desired by me picture of my Lady Castlemaine. **1710** STEELE *Tatler* No. 208 ¶ 1 They had the quite contrary Effect. **1750** GRAY *Elegy* xiv, The dark unfathom'd caves of ocean. **1819** SHELLEY *Prometh. Unb.* III. iii, The progeny immortal Of Painting, Sculpture, and rapt Poesy. **1863** H. COX *Instit.* I. xi. 262 The Long or Pensionary Parliament of Charles II. **1866** S. J. STONE *Hymn*, '*The Church's one Foundation*' iv, And the great Church victorious Shall be the Church at rest.

**b.** So with proper names of persons or places: e. g. *the judicious Hooker.* **c.** But when the adj. becomes a permanent epithet, *the* and the adj. usually follow: e. g. *Alfred the Great*; so with ordinal numerals following names of sovereigns or popes, as *Edward the Seventh*.

**b.** *c* **893** K. ÆLFRED *Oros.* I. i. § 8 Þæt land þe mon hætt seo læsse Asia. *c* **1420** ? LYDG. *Assembly of Gods* 269 Sate the good Iupyter. **1513** DOUGLAS *Æneis* X. i. 39 The fresch goldyn Venus. **1632** MILTON *L'Allegro* 86 Their savory dinner..Which the neat-handed Phillis dresses. **1743** EMERSON *Fluxions* Pref. 13 The divine Newton (whose Works will last as long as the Sun and Moon). **1906** F. THOMPSON *To Eng. Martyrs* 163 That utterance..Of the doomed Leonidas.

**c.** *c* **897** K. ÆLFRED *Gregory's Past. C.* iv. 36 Be ðæm cwæð Salomon se snottra. **971** *Blickl. Hom.* 15 Hit is Hælend se Nazarenisca. *a* **1000** *Byrhtnoth* 273 (Gr.) Þa ȝit on orde stod Eadweard se langa. **1297** R. GLOUC. (Rolls) 1861 Seint eleyne þe gode. *c* **1400** GOWER *In Praise of Peace* 1 O worthi noble kyng, Henry the ferthe. **1484** CAXTON *Curial* 5 For to them whom fortune the variable hath most hyely lyfte up. **1558** *Cal. Anc. Rec. Dublin* (1889) 475 Patrick Fitz Symon, theldor, and William Byrsall, the yonger. **1686** [ALLIX] *Dissert.* i. in W. Hopkins *Ratramnus' Body & Bl.* (1688) 8 Charles the bald chose to consult him. *Mod.* George the Fourth's Bridge in Edinburgh.

**18.** *spec.* When a sb. is particularized by a superlative, or by an ordinal number (see also 17 c), the latter is regularly preceded by *the*.

*c* **893** K. ÆLFRED *Oros.* I. i. § 22 Se man se þæt swiftoste hors hafað. **971** *Blickl. Hom.* 5 Deofol..beswac þone ærestan wifmon. *c* **1000** *Ags. Gosp.* John i. 39 Hit wæs þa seo teoðe tid [*Lindisf.* ðio teiȝða]. *c* **1000**–*a* **1225** [see FIFTH]. *a* **1225** *Ancr. R.* 60 Eien beoð..te ereste armes of lecheries pricches. *c* **1300** *Havelok* 9 He was þe wic[h]teste man at nede. **1601** SHAKS. *Jul. C.* III. ii. 187 This was the most vnkindest cut of all. **1626** C. POTTER tr. *Sarpi's Hist. Quarrels* 110 The most Potent Princes of Italy. **1748** SMOLLETT *Rod. Rand.* l, In terms the most hyperbolical. **1759** SARAH FIELDING *C'tess of Dellwyn* I. 149 Ready to take fire at every the least Provocation. **1848** MRS. GASKELL *M. Barton* ix, Th'longest lane will have a turning. **1890** LD. ESHER in *Law Times Rep.* LXIII. 692/1 The case ..is of the greatest possible weight. *Mod.* The first Consul; the hundredth time.

**b.** *The* also stands before the same adjs. when used absolutely.

*c* **1000** ÆLFRIC *Gram.* xlix. (Z.) 282 *Sextus*, se sixta. *c* **1175** *Pater Noster* in *Lamb. Hom.* 69 Þet ðridde is þes monnes wil. **1340** *Ayenb.* 33–4 Þer byeþ zix poyns [of sloth]..þe uerste is onboȝsamnesse..þe þridde is grochynge. **1470–85** MALORY *Arthur* XX. viii. 811 Amonge the thyckest of the prees. **1526** TINDALE *Matt.* xviii. 1 Who is the greatest in the kyngdom of heven? **1622** in Seton *Life Earl of Dunfermline* VI. (1882) 141 *note*, [He] took sickness the first of June 1622. **1779** *Mirror* No. 27 ¶ 1 With the best and most affectionate of husbands. **1779** WARNER in Jesse *Selwyn & Contemp.* (1844) IV. 14 Your letter of Tuesday the 19th, was brought to me on Monday. **1799** SOUTHEY *Let. to T. Southey* 5 Jan. in *Life* (1850) II. 3 These vile taxes will take twenty pounds from me, at the least. **1852** M. ARNOLD *Youth of Nat.* 71 Too deep for the most to discern. *Mod.* The third appears to be the best.

**II.** Referring to a term used generically or universally. * *With a singular sb.*

**19.** Before the name of an animal, plant, or precious stone, used generically.

Not now used with *man* or *woman*, exc. as opposed to *child, boy, girl*, or the like: cf. *the dog* is the friend of *man*, *man* has tamed *the dog*; *the child* is father of *the man*; you can see *the woman* in *the little girl*. Formerly *se man*, *séo fæmne*: cf. Ger. *der mensch*, F. *l'homme*.

*c* **888** K. ÆLFRED *Boeth.* xli. § 6 Ac se mann ana gæþ uprihte. *c* **893** — *Oros.* III. xi. § 3 Þonne seo leo bringð his hungreȝum hwelpum hwæt to etanne. *c* **1175** *Lamb. Hom.* 53 Þe tadde..ne mei itimien to eten hire fulle. *a* **1225** *Juliana* 20 Hire leofliche leor..rudi as þe rose. **13..** *K. Alis.* (Bodl. MS.) 1819 Men dreden hym..So chalf þe bere, & shep þe wolf. *c* **1440** LYDG. *Hors, Shepe, & G.* 344 The Goos may gagle, the hors may prike & praunce..A-geyn the lamb. **1553** EDEN *Treat. Newe Ind.* (Arb.) 14 The Diamande is engendred in the mynes of India, Ethiopia,..and Cyprus. *a* **1584** MONTGOMERIE *Cherrie & Slae* 21 The hart, the hynd, the dae, the rae, The fowmart, and the foxe. **1622** DRAYTON *Poly-olb.* XX. 45 The Colewort, Colifloure, and Cabidge in their season. **1727–46** THOMSON *Summer* 147 At thee the ruby lights its deepening glow. **1797** HOLCROFT *Stolberg's Trav.* (ed. 2) II. xliv. 93 They sell the heifer to the butcher. **1832** MACAULAY *Ess.*, *Burghley* (1887) 236 Burleigh..was of the willow, and not of the oak. **1854** BUSHNAN in *Circ. Sc.* I. 290/2 It purrs like the Cat.

**b.** Generally, with the name of anything used as the type of its class; e. g. with the names of musical instruments, tools, etc.

*c* **1000** *Ags. Gosp.* Matt. iii. 10 Ys seo [*Hatton* syo] æx to ðæra treowa wurtrumum asett. *c* **1300** *Havelok* 2329 Þer mouhte men here..Þe gleymen on þe tabour dinge. *c* **1450** HOLLAND *Howlat* 759 The rote, and the recordour,.. The trumpe, and the talburn. **1589** PUTTENHAM *Eng. Poesie* I. xix. (Arb.) 57 To be..song to the harpe. **1592** SHAKS. *Ven. & Ad.* 454 A red morne that..betokend, Wracke to the sea-man, tempest to the field. **1614** B. JONSON *Barth. Fair* III. ii, A notable hot Baker 'twas when hee ply'd the peele. **1711** STEELE *Spect.* No. 52 ¶ 3 The renowned British Hippocrates of the pestle and mortar. **1746** FRANCIS *Horace, Epist.* I. x. 7 You keep the Nest, I love the rural Mead, The Brook, the mossy Rock and woody Glade. **1784** COWPER *Task* II. 629 The rout is folly's circle. **1814** SCOTT *Ld. of Isles* III. xxiii, The lad can deftly touch the lute, And on the rote and viol play. **1839** LYTTON *Richelieu* II. ii. 308 The pen is mightier than the sword. **1906** *Edin. Rev.* Oct. 448 Zola has democratised the novel in another fashion.

**c.** Before *body, mind, soul*, or parts, functions, and attributes of these. (See also BODY *sb.* 1, MIND *sb.* 17.)

*c* **888** K. ÆLFRED *Boeth.* xxiv. § 3 Seo fæȝernes..þæs lichoman. *c* **1000** *Ags. Gosp.* Matt. vi. 25 Hu nys seo sawl selre þonne mete. *c* **1175** *Lamb. Hom.* 153 Ine þe eren. *a* **1225** *Ancr. R.* 4 Þe oðer riwle is al wiðuten, & riwleð þe licome. **13..** *K. Alis.* (Bodl. MS.) 6245 A folk..rouȝ as bere to þe honde. *c* **1380** WYCLIF *Serm.* Sel. Wks. I. 103 Rychesse..ryven þe soule. *c* **1400** tr. *Secreta Secret., Gov. Lordsh.* 85 His effect is properly to comforte þe brayn, þe herte, and þe stomak. **1500–20** DUNBAR *Poems* xlvii. 6 Trew luve rysis fro the splene. **1594** R. ASHLEY tr. *Loys le Roy* 24 Nothing offending, or displeasing the eare.

1692 South *Serm.* (1697) I. 361 How accidentally oftentimes does the thing..offer it self to the mind. 1736 Butler *Anal.* I. i. 30 To think the eye itself a percipient. 1841 Thackeray *Men & Pict.* 109 [They] pall on the palate.

**d.** With names of days of the week, as *on the Monday*, i.e. on Monday of any or every week, on Mondays generally.

1340 *Ayenb.* 213 Þe zonday is more holy þanne þe zeter-day. *c* 1450 Capgrave *Life St. Augustine* 16 Þat sche used to fast þe Satirday. *c* 1500–1671 [see Saturday 1]. 1854 Macaulay *Speeches* 409 On the Sunday he goes perhaps to Church. *Ibid.* 553 He returns to his labours on the Monday.

**20.** Before a word of individual meaning used as the type of a class of persons.

*c* 897 K. Ælfred *Gregory's Past. C.* xii. 74 Ðæs biscepes weorc..ðæs hierdes life. *Ibid.* xiii. (heading), Hu se lareow sceal beon clæne on his mode. *a* 900 tr. *Bæda's Hist.* Pref. ii. (1890) 6 Ðone leornere ic nu..bidde and halsige. *c* 1175 *Lamb. Hom.* 27 Ah þenne þe preost hit deð in his muþe. *a* 1225 *Ancr. R.* 84 Þe vikelare ablent þene mon. 1388 Wyclif *Ps.* xxxi[i.] 10 Many betyngis ben of the synnere. 1535 Coverdale *Isa.* xliv. 13 The carpenter (or ymage caruer) taketh me the tymbre, and spredeth forth his lyne. 1600 W. Watson *Decacordon* (1602) 334, I..craue patience of the catholike Reader. 1660 Hexham *Eng. Dutch Dict.* (title-p.), A compendious Grammar for the Instruction of the Learner. 1681 Dryden *Abs. & Achit.* 655 But where the witness failed, the prophet spoke. 1720 Watts *Mor. Songs* i, 'Tis the voice of the Sluggard. 1787 'G. Gambado' *Acad. Horsemen* (1809) 35 To ride with a lash whip; it shews the sportsman. 1843 Macaulay *Ess., Addison* (1887) 791 Steele ..was much of the rake and a little of the swindler. 1859 Tennyson *Enid* 1280 As careful robins eye the delver's toil.

**b.** esp. in phr. *To act, be, play the man, the soldier*, etc. = to sustain the character of a man, a soldier, etc.; to do that which is manly, soldier-like, etc.: see Play *v.* 34.

1426 Audelay *Poems* (Percy Soc.) 29 Thai play not the fole. *c* 1530 H. Rhodes *Bk. Nurture* in *Babees Bk.* 84 Saue thy selfe, play the man, being compelde. 1642 W. Price *Serm.* 40 Playing the drugsters or hucksters with it for gaine. 1719 De Foe *Crusoe* (1840) I. iii. 47 To act the rebel. 1748 Richardson *Clarissa* Wks. 1883 VII. 486, I will contrive to be the man. 1809–10 Coleridge *Friend* iv. (1865) 93 To act the knave is but a round-about way of playing the fool.

**21.** With an adjective used absolutely, usually denoting an abstract notion: e.g. *the beautiful*, that which is beautiful.

*c* 1420 ? Lydg. *Assembly of Gods* 882 In stede of the bettyr the worse ther they ches. 1596 Shaks. *Tam. Shr.* iv. iii. 80, I will be free, Euen to the vttermost. 1748 Smollett *Rod. Rand.* xxii, A nose inclining to the aquiline. 1756 Burke (*title*) Enquiry into the Origin of our Ideas of the Sublime and Beautiful. 1850 Tennyson *In Mem.* cvi. 8 Ring out the false, ring in the true. 1878 T. Hardy *Ret. Native* vi. iii, There is too much reason why we should do the little we can to respect it now.

* * *With a pl. sb. used universally.*

**22.** With a sb. in the plural, chiefly the name of a nation, class, or group of people, where *the* = 'those who are'; 'the . . . taken as a whole'. Also with family surnames, as 'the *Joneses* are of Welsh origin'.

*c* 1200 Ormin 188 He shall turrnenn þurrh hiss spell þe trowwþelæse leode. 1297 R. Glouc. (Rolls) 87 Þe saxons ..Seve kynges made in engelond. 1548 W. Patten *Exped. Scot.* Pref. c ij b, Neyther the Grekes [nor] the Ruthens. 1613 Purchas *Pilgrimage* (1614) 246 The bodie..was afflicted on the East by the Persians, on the West by the Gothes. 1783 Justamond tr. *Raynal's Hist. Indies* III. 380 The Rima..is not yet well known to the botanists. 1816 Crabb *Eng. Synonymes* 139/2 The Tarquins were banished from Rome. 1906 *Edin. Rev.* Oct. 429 These laws of sight the Greeks made it their business to analyse.

**23.** Before an adjective or participle having a plural application (usually of persons), as *the poor*, those who or such as are poor.

*c* 897 K. Ælfred *Gregory's Past. C.* xxiii. 175 Ða woruld-wisan..ða dysegan. *a* 1300 *Prayer* 26 in *O. E. Misc.* 193 ȝieue þe hungrie mete and te nakede iwede. 1362 Langl. *P. Pl.* A. Prol. 18 Alle maner of men þe mene and þe riche. 1426 Audelay *Poems* 7 Vysyte the seke. 1526 Tindale *John* xii. 8 The povre all wayes shall ye have with you. 1671 Milton *P. R.* iv. 157 Nothing will please the difficult and nice. 1742 Gray *Ode Spring* ii, How low, how little are the Proud, How indigent the Great! 1812 Byron *Ch. Har.* i. xxxiv, Here ceased the swift their race, here sunk the strong. 1817–18 Shelley *Rosalind & Helen* 254–5 He was a coward to the strong: He was a tyrant to the weak.

**b.** A pa. pple. so used may retain its verbal construction or complement. (In this case *those* is now more used than *the*.)

*c* 1000 *Ags. Gosp.* Matt. xxii. 3 He..clypode þa ȝelaðodan to þam gyftum. 1600 W. Watson *Decacordon* (1602) 49 Dignities which intitle the inuested with them, with a pre-heminence aboue all other persons. 1728 Chambers *Cycl.* s. v. *Jesuit*, The professed of this order renounce..all pre-ferment, and especially prelacy. 1817–18 Shelley *Rosa-lind & Helen* 474 Thou knowest what a thing is Poverty Among the fallen on evil days.

**C.** as Demonstrative (or *quasi*-personal) pronoun. In late OE. and early ME., when *þe* was substituted for the earlier masc. *se*, and subsequently became the general form of the definite article (see A. 1 a β and 9), it was also used for some time as demonstrative pronoun, = the (man), that, he, esp. as antecedent to a relative; thus early ME. *þe þe* or *þe þet* for OE. *se þe*, = that (man) that, he that. The fem. was *þéo þe* (for OE. *séo þe*) she that; the pl. *þá þe* those that, they that. (The neuter was commonly *þet þe* or *þette*.)

*c* 950 *Lindisf. Gosp.* Matt. iii. 3 Ðes is forðon ðe ðe [*Rushw.* seþe] ȝecuoeden wæs ðerh esaias. *Ibid.* xv. 24 Ðe *vel* he [L. *ipse*] soðlice onduearde. *c* 1175 *Lamb. Hom.* 95 Þe ðet bið mid þen halia gast itend. *Ibid.* 109 Þe ðe deleð elmessan for his drihtnes luuan, þe bihut his gold hord on heouene riche. *a* 1200 *Moral Ode* 217 (MS. Eg.) Þe ðe [*MS. J.* þe þat] godes milce secheð, iwis he mai is [*v.rr.* ha, hi] finde. *Ibid.* 219 Þe ðe [*v.rr.* Se þet, Þe þat] de his wille mest, he haueð wurst mede. *a* 1225 *Ancr. R.* 52 Mesire, þeo deð also þeo is betere þen ich am. *Ibid.* 86 Ase þe þe seið to þe knihte þet robbeð [etc.].

† **The,** *particle* (*conj., adv.*), *relative pron. Obs.* Forms: 1–4 ðe, þe, (2 þæ, 2–3 þa). [OE. *þe*, app. an unstressed or worn-down case or derivative formation from the stem *þa*- of That *demonst.* and *rel. pron.* Thought by some to be a worn-down locative case. Cf. Goth. *þê-ei, þei*, conj., similarly used.]

**1.** Used as a conjunction introducing clauses of various kinds: = That *conj.*

*Beowulf* 1334 Heo þa fæhðe wræc þe þu ȝystran niht grendel cwealdest. *Ibid.* 1436 He on holme wæs sundes þe sænra ðe hyne swylt for-nam. *c* 1000 *Ags. Ps.* (Th.) cxliii. 4 Hwæt is se manna, mihtiȝ Drihten, þe þu him cuðlice cyþan woldest? *a* 1250 *Owl & Night.* 941 Þe Nihtegale..wiste wel..þe wraþþe binymeþ monnes red.

**b.** *spec.* After comparatives: Than.

*c* 897 K. Ælfred *Gregory's Past. C.* xliv. 318 Ne hie selfe ðy betran ne talien þe ða oðre. 971 *Blickl. Hom.* 215 Ða he þa hæfde twæm læs þe twentiȝ wintra. *c* 1000 Ælfric *Hom.* I. 154 Þeos woruld..nis..ðe ȝeliccre ðære ecan worulde, þe is sum cweartern leohtum dæȝe. *c* 1175 *Lamb. Hom.* 151 If ȝe beoð strengre þe heo. *c* 1200 *Trin. Coll. Hom.* 119 Þe holi gost com..and alihte hem of brihtere and of festere bileue þe hie hedden er. *a* 1250 *Owl & Night.* 564 Na more þe deþ a wrecche wranne.

**c.** As correlative conjunction: '*hwæþer . . þe . .*', '*þe . . þe . .*', 'whether . . or . .'.

*c* 888 K. Ælfred *Boeth.* xxxiv. § 6 Hwæþer þincð þe þonne þæt þa þincg sien, ðe ðara soðena ȝesælða limu, þe sio ȝesælð self? 971 *Blickl. Hom.* 97 Hwyder he ȝelæded sy, þe to wite, þe to wuldre. *c* 1000 Ælfric *Hom.* II. 120 Ða Gregorius befran, hwæðer þæs landes folc cristen wære ðe hæðen. *c* 1205 Lay. 16812 Do þine iwille Whaðer swa þu wult don, Þa us slan þa us an-hon. *a* 1250 *Owl & Night.* 1064 Hweþer þu wilt wif þe meyde. *Ibid.* 1408 Sei me soþ if þu hit wost Hweþer doþ wurse fleys þe gost. 1297 R. Glouc. (Rolls) 4507 In woch half turne he nuste, þo weþer est þe west.

**2.** Relative particle. **a.** Appended to adverbs and adverbial expressions of time, place, etc., to make them relative or conjunctive. Cf. That *conj.* 6. Also in *for þan þe* because that, *ær þan þe* before that, and the like.

835 *Charter of Abba* in *O. E. Texts* 447 Ða hwile ðe hia hit mid clennisse ȝehaldan wile. *c* 1160 *Hatton Gosp.* Mark viii. 24 Þa þæ he hine be-seaȝ. *c* 1175 *Lamb. Hom.* 87 Þa þe heo comen on midden þere se. *c* 1200 *Trin. Coll. Hom.* 35 Þe fiffeald mihten þe god him gef þo þe he him shop. *a* 1240 *Ureisun* 36 in *Cott. Hom.* 193 Þer ðe neure deað ne com.

**b.** Hence as a temporal adverb (= *þá, þá þe*): When.

*c* 1205 Lay. 263 Þeos ȝunge wiman iwerd hire mid childe, þe ȝet leouede Ascanius. *Ibid.* 4150 Þe [*c* 1275 þo] Dunewale haueđe isæd, al his folc luuede þene ræd. *a* 1300 *Harrow. Hell* (MS. L.) 42 Þe [*MS. E.* þan] he com þere þo [*MS. E.* þan] seyd he asse y shal nouþe telle þe.

**3.** As relative pronoun: That, who, which.

In OE. repr. any case or number. Also with ellipsis of antecedent, = he who, that which, what, = That *rel. pron.* 3.

805–31 *Charter of Oswulf* in *O. E. Texts* 444 Ic ðe ðas ȝesettnesse sette. 847 *Charter of Æðelwulf* in *O. E. Texts* 434 Ðonon to ðæm beorȝe ðe mon hateð æt ðæm holne. *c* 888 K. Ælfred *Boeth.* xxxiv. § 3 His sio hea goodnes þe he full is. *Ibid.* xxxvi. § 4 (3) Þæt ðu mæȝe ðy bet ȝelefan ðe ic ðe..recce. *c* 893 — *Oros.* ii. i. § 4 Þy ilcan ȝeare þe Romana rice weaxan ongann. *a* 1000 *Boeth. Metr.* v. 11 Seo þe ær gladu onsiene wæs. *c* 1000 *Ags. Gosp.* Matt. vi. 9 Fæder ure þu þe eart on heofonum. — John i. 26 To-middes eow stod þe [*Lindisf.* ðone] ȝe ne cunnon. 1154 *O. E. Chron.* an. 1140, Alle þe men þe mid him heoldon. *a* 1175 *Cott. Hom.* 221 Ælra þara þinge þe on paradis beoð. *c* 1200 *Trin. Coll. Hom.* 45 Þe þre kinges þe comen of estriche. *c* 1205 Lay. 41 Wace wes ihoten þe wel couþe writen. *a* 1250 *Owl & Night.* 1386 (Cott. MS.) For heo beoþ wode, þe [*v.r.* þat] bute nest goþ to brode. *a* 1300 *Harrow. Hell* (MS. L.) 24 Moyses, þe holy wyht [*MS.* whyt], þe heuede þe lawe to ȝeme ryht. 13.. *Cursor M.* 24317 (Edin.) Wit hard thrauis þe [*other MSS.* þat] he þrow þai sau þat he to ded him drew. *c* 1350 *Will. Palerne* 4422 Sche..went Into a choys chaumber þe clerli was peinted. *c* 1460 *Oseney Regr.* 166 He Bryngeth also Anoþer charter ..the witnyssith [*orig.* Cartam..que testatur] that the Same Nicoll yafe [etc.]. *Ibid.* 170 For þe Sowle of my ffadur Robert Doylly þe þat same church foundid.

**b.** When the relative was governed by a preposition, the latter followed before the verb.

*a* 900 *O. E. Chron.* an. 885, He sende him..þære rode dæl þe Crist on þrowude. *c* 1000 *Ags. Gosp.* Mark ii. 4 Þæt bed þe se lama on læȝ.

**c.** In Old English the relative was also expressed by adding *þe* to the demonstrative pronoun *se, séo, þæt*; thus, *se-þe, séo-þe, þæt-þe* or *þætte, þæs-þe, þæm-þe*, etc.; but this combination scarcely survived after 1100.

835 *Charter of Abba* in *O. E. Texts* 448 Swælc monn se ðe to minum ærfe foe. *c* 893 K. Ælfred *Oros.* ii. iv. § 8 Seo ilce burȝ..seo ðe mæst wæs. *c* 1000 Ælfric *Gen.* vi. 2 Hiȝ ..namon him wif of eallum þam, þa þe hiȝ ȝecuron. *c* 1000 *Ags. Gosp.* Matt. iii. 3 Dys ys se þe cam ðe ȝecweden ys. *a* 1175 *Cott. Hom.* 227 Se soðe sceppende se þe ane is god. *c* 1175 *Lamb. Hom.* 5 He is iblesced þe þe her cumet on drihtenes nome.

**d.** To express the genitive case *whose, of which*, *þe* or *se ðe* was followed by a possessive pronoun: cf. That *rel. pron.* 9.

*a* 800 Cynewulf *Elene* 162 Se God..þe þis his beacen wæs. *c* 850 *O. E. Martyrol.* 118 Þære fæmnan tid þe hire noma wæs sancta Anatolia. *a* 900 *Psalm* xxxii. 11 (Thorpe) Eadiȝ byþ þæt kynn, þe swylc God byð heora God. *a* 1122 *O. E. Chron.* (Laud MS.) an. 1011, Ælmær..þe se arcb. Ælfeah ær ȝenerede his life.

**The** (ðĕ, ðə), *adv.* Also 3 þæ. [OE *þé*, originally locative or instrumental case of the demonstrative and relative pron. *se, séo, þæt.* In OE. interchanging with *þý*: see Thy *adv.*]

**1.** Preceding an adjective or adverb in the comparative degree, the two words forming an adverbial phrase modifying the predicate.

The radical meaning is 'in or by that', 'in or by so much', e.g. 'if you sow them now, they will come up the sooner'; 'he has had a holiday, and looks the better', to which the pleonastic 'for it' has been added, and the sentence at length turned into 'he looks the better for his holiday'.

*c* 897 K. Ælfred *Gregory's Past. C.* xvii. 122 Oft sio wund bið ðæs þe wierse & ðy mare. *c* 1175 *Lamb. Hom.* 87 Þa cleopede god þe ner Moyses him to. *c* 1205 Lay. 30597 Of þere brede he æt sone þer after him wes þæ bet. *c* 1290 *Beket* 1252 in *S. Eng. Leg.* I. 142 He chaungede is name, þe sikerloker forto go. *a* 1300 *Cursor M.* 3651 (Cott.) Þat he þe mai þe less mistru, Þou sal sai þou ert esau. 1398 Trevisa *Barth. De P. R.* v. xxxviii. (Bodl. MS.), He [the stomach] is rowȝe..to holde þe better þe mete þat he fongiþ. *c* 1430 *How Gd. Wife taught Dau.* 191 in *Babees Bk.* 41 Þe work is þe sonner do þat haþ many handis. 1526 Tindale *John* xix. 8 When Pilate herde that sayinge, he was the moare afrayde [1388 Wyclif, he dredde the more]. 1596 Spenser *F. Q.* vi. ii. 33 That..I may beare armes,..The rather, since that fortune hath this day Given to me the spoile of this dead knight. 1621 Fletcher *Wild Goose Chase* iv. i, 'Tis not to be help'd now. *Lil.* The more's my Miserie. 1782 Cowper *Mut. Forbearance* 24 Your fav'rite horse Will never look one hair the worse. 1838 Ruskin *Ess. Painting & Music* § 24 Wks. 1903 I. 285 And if others do not follow their example,—the more fools they. 1883 *Law Times* 27 Oct. 425/1 What student is the better for mastering these futile distinctions?

†**b.** In phrase *the less* (*the*), (= L. *quominus*), OE. *þe-læs þe*, Early ME. (*þe*) *læste*, now Lest *conj.* q. v.

[*c* 825 *Vesp. Psalter* ii. 12 Ðyles hwonne eorsie dryhten.] 971 *Blickl. Hom.* 65 Þe læs hi us besencean on helle grund. *c* 1000 *Ags. Gosp.* John v. 14 Ne synga þa, þe-læs þe þe on sumon þingon wyrs ȝetide. *a* 1100 in Napier *O. E. Glosses* i. 3675 Þe læste ȝehremde. [1175: see Lest *conj.*]

**2.** *The . . the . .*: by how much . . by so much; in what degree . . in that degree . . [= L. *quo . . eo . .*, Gr. ὅσῳ . . τοσούτῳ . .]: denoting proportional dependence between the notions expressed by two clauses, each having *the* + a comparative; one *the* being demonstrative, and the other relative. The relative clause usually comes first, e.g. 'The more one has, the more one wants'; but the order may be reversed, as 'One wants the more, the more one has'; and in either order the comparative in the relative clause is sometimes followed by *that*, e.g. 'the more that one has'. In OE. commonly *þý*; ME. *þi, þe*: see Thy *adv.*

*c* 897 K. Ælfred *Gregory's Past. C.* Pref. 5 Ðæt her ðy mara wisdom on londe wære, ðy we ma ȝeðeoda cuðon. 1297 R. Glouc. (Rolls) 7547 Þe more þat a mon can, þe more wurþe he is. 13.. *Minor Poems fr. Vernon MS.* lv. xii. 95 Þe more we trace þe Trinite, Þe more we falle in fantasye. *c* 1400 Maundev. (Roxb.) v. 14 Ay þe elder it es, þe whittere it waxes. *c* 1440 *Alphabet of Tales* 1 Yitt þai er ay þe langer þe wers. 1596 Shaks. 1 *Hen. IV*, ii. iv. 445 Though the Camomile, the more it is troden, the faster it growes; yet Youth, the more it is wasted, the sooner it weares. 1690 T. Saunders in *11th Rep. Hist. MSS. Comm.* App. vii. 111 As to our sea affairs..the lesse I say the better. 1771 in J. Watson *Jedburgh Abbey* (1894) 98 The bells must be removed, and the sooner the better. *c* 1790 Imison *Sch. Art* i. 208 The smaller a lens is, and the more its convexity, the nearer is its focus, and the more its magnifying power. 1855 Kingsley *Westw. Ho!* iv, The less said the sooner mended. 1874 Micklethwaite *Mod. Par. Churches* 26 The higher the windows are from the ground the better. *Proverbial expression.* The more, the merrier.

**The,** obs. form of Thee *pers. pron.*, Thee *v.*[1], to prosper, They, Thigh, Though.

**The, thé, thea,** obs. forms of Tea.

**Thead** (þīd). Now *dial.* Also 4 þede, 5–6 thede. [Etymology unascertained.] A brewer's strainer; = Tap-hose: see quot. *a* 1825.

13.. *E. E. Allit. P.* B. 1717 Bifore þy borde hatz þou broȝt beuerage in þede. *c* 1440 *Promp. Parv.* 490/1 Thede, bruarys instrument, *qualus*. 1530 Palsgr. 280/1 Thede a brewars instrument. *a* 1825 Forby *Voc. E. Anglia, Thead*, the tall wicker strainer placed in the mash-tub over the hole in the bottom, that the wort may run off clear. *c* 1850 *Catalogue* in *Leicester Gloss.* (1881), Spiggot and thead. 1881 *Ibid., Thead*, a 'tap-whisk'.

**Theaf(e, Theaft,** obs. ff. Theave, Theft.

**Theak,** variant of Theek *v.*, to thatch.

† **Theal, thele.** *Obs.* Forms: (1 þelu, þel, þell), 6 thele, thel, theall, 7 (9 *dial.*) theal. [In 16th c. *thele*, corresp. to OE. -*þelu* fem. occurring in comb. *bencþelu* (also neuter pl.) 'bench-floor', and *buruhþelu* 'castle-floor', agreeing in sense with *þel, þell*, neut., board, plank, floor, in one place

'(iron) plate'. These point to OTeut. forms *þelā fem., *þelo^m neuter, whence also *þeljon, *þiljōn, WGer. *þiljō, OE. *þille*, ON. *þilja* fem. deal, plank, OHG. *dilla* board, MLG. *dele*, Du. *deel* deal, plank: cf. also the Finnish borrowed word *teljo*. The long gap between the latest OE. example of *-þelu* and the Eng. *thele*, after 1500, is noteworthy; perh. the word came down within a limited district. Cf. the place-name *þelwæl* (*O.E. Chron.* an. 923), *Thelwall* in Cheshire.]

**1.** (OE.) A floor.

*a* 900 *Beowulf* 487 Eal benc-þelu blode bestymed. [Cf. *Ibid.* 1239 Benc-þelu beredon: hit ȝeond-bræded wearð beddum ond bolstrum.] *a* 1000 *Fight at Finnesburg* 30 Buruhðelu dynede.

**2.** A board, plank, deal. Cf. DEAL *sb.*³

1517 in *Market Harborough Rec.* (1890) 220, I wyll yᵗ Richard Page..shall have a lede, a mawnger, a rake and thelys, beynge at yᵉ sygne of Swanne in Harborow. 1521 *Nottingham Rec.* III. 355 Item anoyer pres borde and a thele yat ley at the kychyn dore. 1562 *Ludlow Churchw. Acc.* (Camden) 110 For thele to mende the churche dore. 1586 *Churchw. Acc. St. Martin, Leicester* in *N. & Q.* 6th Ser. VII. 249/2 Too plancke and too thels [for the library]. 1618 in *Archæologia* XLIV. 402 Item 4 greate theales of 30 foot a piece 3 foot 3 inches broad and three inches thicke. 1624 *Althorp MS.* in Simpkinson *Washingtons* App. p. lvii, Aug. 7. To Butlin 3 daies sawing theales, & 2 daies making a dore for Mʳⁱˢ Segrave's house oo o5 oo. 1847–78 HALLIWELL, *Theal*, a board; a plank; a joist. *Leic.*

**Theam, theame**, obs. ff. TEAM, THEME.

[† **Theaming**, *ppl. a.* ? Some error.
1599: see ARSEDINE.]

**Theandric** (þiˌæ·ndrik), *a.* [ad. eccl. Gr. θεανδρικός, f. θέανδρος god-man (f. θεός god + ἀνήρ man): see -IC.] Of or pertaining to both God and man; partaking of both the human and the divine.

1612 T. TAYLOR *Comm. Titus* ii. 14 It was..neither meerely diuine, nor meerely humane, but (as Diuines speake) theandrike. 1828 E. IRVING *Sermons* I. 140 + p. lxix, A class of heretics..asserting, that there was only one operation, Theandric or Godmanly. 1843 J. B. ROBERTSON tr. *Möhler's Symbolik* iii. § 11 (ed. 3) 83 So that this regeneration constitutes one theandric work.

So † **Thea·ndrical** *a. Obs.* [see -ICAL].

1656 JEANES *Fuln. Christ* 36 To performe them as God man, is appropriate to Christ..As ascribed unto him, they are, say Divines; Theandrical, that is, divinely humane. 1693 OWEN *Holy Spirit as Comforter* i. Wks. 1855 IV. 358 He who worketh them [his mediatory operations] is God, and He worketh them all as God-man; whence they are theandrical.

**Theangeline** (þiˌæ·ndʒĕləin). *rare*⁻¹. [f. Gr. θεάγγελις (-ιδ-) an intoxicating herb (Pliny) + -INE.] Name of a plant said by Pliny to grow on Libanus.

1855 BAILEY *Mystic* 33 The bruised theangeline, which gives Prophetic sense.

**Theanthropic** (þīˌǣnþrǫ·pik), *a.* [f. eccl. Gr. θεάνθρωπος, THEANTHROPOS + -IC.] Pertaining, relating to, or having the nature of both God and man; at once divine and human.

1652 BENLOWES *Theoph.* I. lxxviii, The Theanthropick Word, That Mystick Glasse of Revelations. 1864 in WEBSTER. 1868 GLADSTONE *Glean.* (1879) III. 55 The theanthropic idea, the idea of God made man without ceasing to be God, was..familiar..to the old mythology. 1879 — in *19th Cent.* Oct. 765 An anthropomorphic or theanthropic system of marvellous imaginative splendour. 1882 CAVE & BANKS tr. *Dorner's Chr. Doctr.* 197 An image of Christ..which is actually and truly human and Divine at once, that is theanthropic.

So **Theanthro·pical** *a. rare* [see -ICAL].
1846 WORCESTER cites *Bib. Rep.*

**Theanthropism** (þiˌæ·nþrŏpiz'm). [f. as prec. + -ISM.]

**1.** *Theol.* The doctrine of the union of the divine and human natures, or of the manifestation of God as man, in Christ.

1817 COLERIDGE *Biog. Lit.* xxiv. (1882) 301 Speaking theologically and impersonally, i.e. of Psilanthropism and Theanthropism as schemes of belief. 1867 WESTCOTT in *Contemp. Rev.* VI. 417 If we might venture to use a word not wholly without ancient precedent, it [Christianity] might be described as *Theanthropism*. It proclaims not a conception of God, but a manifestation of God. 1875 LIGHTFOOT *Comm. Col.* (ed. 2) 119 The monotheism of the Old Testament is supplemented by the theanthropism of the New.

**2.** *Mythol.* The attribution of human nature or character to the gods.

Cf. ANTHROPOPHUISM, which word Mr. Gladstone, writing to the Editor in July 1883, said he had given up and had 'taken refuge in theanthropism'.

1878 GLADSTONE *Prim. Homer* iii. 50 Greatly out of keeping with the anthropomorphism, or, as I would rather call it, theanthropism, of the Olympian system.

So **Thea·nthropist**, a believer in theanthropism (also *attrib.* or as *adj.*); **Theanthropo·logy** = theanthropism.

1816 COLERIDGE in *Lit. Rem.* (1836) I. 394 This is evident, that if the *theanthropist is a Christian, the psilanthropist cannot be so. 1887 *Dublin Rev.* Apr. 248 The theanthropist or Christian doctrine. 1845 F. BARHAM *A* 9 *Theanthropology, or the doctrine of God in man and the form of man.

‖ **Thea·nthropos.** *Obs.* [a. eccl. Gr. θεάνθρωπος god-man, f. θεός God + ἄνθρωπος man.] A title given to Jesus Christ as being both God and man.

1635 QUARLES *Emblems* i. *Invoc.* 33 Thou great Theanthropos, that giv'st and crown'st Thy gifts in dust. *a* 1704 T. BROWN *Dial. Dead, Friendship* Wks. 1711 IV. 54 When this great Deliverer came, they [the Jews] very fairly Murder'd him; and from this Theantropos it is that the Christians derive ..their Religion. 1730 BAILEY (folio), Thea'nthropos.

Hence **Theanthropophagy** (-ǫ·fădʒi) [-PHAGY]: see quot.; **Theanthroposophy** (-ǫ·sǒfi) [-SOPHY], a system of belief concerning the God-man; **Theanthropy** (-æ·nþrǒpi) [ad. eccl. Gr. θεανθρωπία], the fact of being God-man, the union of divine and human natures (in Christ).

1654 JER. TAYLOR *Real Pres.* xii. § 14. 281 Cardinal Perron ..says, that they deny anthropophagy, but did not deny *Theanthropophagy, saying, that they did not eat the flesh, or drink the bloud of a meer man, but of Christ who was God and man. 1817 COLERIDGE *Lett., to J. H. Green* (1895) 683 Of Schelling's Theology and *Theanthroposophy, the telescopic stars and nebulæ are too many for my 'grasp of eye'. 1658 J. ROBINSON *Endoxa* i. 19 Christ..by his *Theanthropy..knew Judas to be one [a hypocrite]. 1689 NORRIS *Refl.*, etc. (1691) 198 Here also we meet with a new Theanthropy, a strange Composition of God and Man.

**Thearchic** (þiˌā·ɹkik), *a.* [ad. eccl. Gr. θεαρχικός, f. θεαρχία: see next and -IC. In late L. *thearchicus* (Scotus Erigena, *c* 860).] Of or pertaining to thearchy.

1855 MILMAN *Lat. Chr.* XIV. ii. (1864) IX. 63 Jesus..is the Thearchic Intelligence, the super-substantial Being. 1890 HATCH *Hibbert Lect.* x. 304 Initiated in the thearchic mysteries.

**Thearchy** (þī·āɹki). [ad. eccl. Gr. θεαρχία, f. θεός God + -αρχία a ruling.]

**1.** The rule or government of God or of a god; a theocracy.

1643 *Subject of Supremacie*, etc. 42 There ends Monarchy as a Thearchie, or divine dynastie. *c* 1643 *Maximes Unfolded* 8 Thearchie, or Gods Government in Families, a Nation, and all Nations. 1863 WHYTE MELVILLE *Gladiators* I. 254 His [the Jew's] belief in that direct thearchy, to which he was bound by the ties of gratitude.

**2.** An order or system of deities. (Cf. HIERARCHY 1, 3.)

1839 BAILEY *Festus* i. (1852) 11 From rank to rank in Thearchy divine, We angel raylets gladden in thy sight. 1876 GLADSTONE *Homeric Synchr.* 245 Pan was one of the younger gods in the Hellenic thearchy. 1899 *Literary Guide* 1 Dec. 178/1 When Jesus entered upon his ministry, the Olympian thearchy..was already tottering to its fall.

**Thear(e, Thearme**, obs. ff. THERE, THARM.

**Theat** (þīt). *Sc.* Also 5–9 thete, 6 theatt, (tyghte), 8–9 theet. [Etymology obscure: derivation from ON. *þétt-r* tight, has been suggested; cf. *tyght* in quot. 1573.] *pl.* 'The ropes or traces, by means of which horses draw in a carriage, plough, or harrow' (Jam.): now chiefly of the plough.

1496 *Acc. Ld. High Treas. Scot.* I. 293 Item, for xiij stane and a pund of towis to be thetis. 1513 DOUGLAS *Æneis* XII. ix. 77 The renis and the thetis, Quharwyth hys stedis ȝokkit war in thretis. [1573 *Lanc. Wills* (Chetham Soc.) III. 61 Twoo payre of tyghtes or trases for horses wᵗʰ withes of iren.] 1599 *Aberdeen Regr.* (1848) II. 183 Cutting with his knyff the theattis of the said pleucht. 1792 *Statist. Acc. Scot.* IV. 395 The rashen theats [are supplanted] by the iron traces. 1844 STEPHENS *Bk. Farm* II. 694 The sort of harness with which he is first invested is that of the plough, consisting of a bridle, collar,..and back-band and chains, or theats, as these are called in some parts of the country.

**b.** In fig. and allusive expressions: cf. *traces*. *Out of theats* (also *out of theet*), out of bounds: see quot. 1710, and cf. 'to kick over the traces' (KICK *v.*¹ 1 c).

1682 PEDEN in *Life & Proph.* (1868) 13 Good Lord, cut their theets, that their swingle-trees may fall to the ground. 1710 RUDDIMAN *Gloss. Douglas* s.v. *Thetis*, Ye are out of theet, i.e. ye are extravagant or in the wrong. 1731 T. BOSTON *Mem.* v. 53 They were going to call a new upstart, one that broke the thetes. 1871 W. ALEXANDER *Johnny Gibb* ii, Keep baith laird an' tenan' straucht i' the theets.

**Theater**, variant spelling of THEATRE.

Hence † **Theate·rian**, one connected with the stage; an actor (*obs.*).

1602 DEKKER *Satirom.* Wks. 1873 I. 244 One of these part-takers..(Players I meane) Theaterians, Stage-walkers.

**Theatine** (þī·ătəin), *sb.* (*a.*) *R. C. Ch.* Also 7 Tiatine, 7–9 Theatin. [ad. mod.L. *theatinus*, f. *Teate*, ancient name of *Chieti* in Italy: see -INE¹. So F. *théatin*, obs. It. *theatini* pl. (Florio).] A member of a congregation or order of 'regular clerks' founded in 1524 by St. Cajetan in conjunction with John Peter Caraffa (till then Archbishop of Chieti, whence the name, and later Pope Paul IV). A corresponding order of nuns was founded *c* 1600.

1597–8 BP. HALL *Sat.* IV. vii. 32 Like to a false dissembling Theatine. 1632 LITHGOW *Trav.* x. 472 The Tiatines would twice a day visite mee. 1658 PHILLIPS, *Theatins*. 1686 tr. *Bouhours' St. Ignatius* II. 136 The great correspondence which Ignatius held with Caraffa,..thence..the People in those times called Ignatius and his Companions, Theatins. 1736 CHANDLER *Hist. Persec.* 291 Those who are to die have two monks or Theatins, as they call them, walking by them. 1889 BRIDGETT & KNOX *Q. Eliz. & Cath. Hierarchy* ix. 215 The aim of the Theatines was the reformation of the secular clergy and the sanctification of the faithful.

**b.** as *adj.* Of or pertaining to the Theatines.

1693 tr. *Emilianne's Hist. Monast. Ord.* xviii. 186 They had in some countries the name of Theatin Jesuits. 1885 *Cath. Dict.* 793/1 The Theatine nuns were founded by the B. Ursula Benincasa. 1903 *Eng. Hist. Rev.* Apr. 277 The terrible personality of the Theatine bishop.

**Theatral** (þī·ătrăl), *a.* Now *rare*. [ad. L. *theātrāl-is*, f. *theātrum* THEATRE: see -AL. So F. *théâtral* (16th c.).] Of, pertaining to, or connected with the theatre; theatrical; dramatic.

1594 R. ASHLEY tr. *Loys le Roy* 76 They pardoned Roscius, the Authour of the law Theatral. 1665 BRATHWAIT *Comment Two Tales* 23 He [Absolom]..in Theatral actions personates Herod in his Majesty. 1755 in JOHNSON. 1904 *Times* 16 Aug. 5/2 Impressiveness..depends..on the vast extent and theatral disposition of the whole.

Hence **The·atralize** *v.*, *trans.* to adapt for performance on the stage.

1825 CARLYLE *Schiller* App. 270 Schiller had engaged to theatralize his original edition of the *Robbers*.

**Theatre, theater** (þī·ătəɹ), *sb.* Forms: 4–5 teatre, 4– theatre, 5– theater. [ad. (directly, or through OF.) L. *theātrum*, a. Gr. θέατρον, a place for viewing, esp. a theatre, f. θεᾶσθαι to behold (cf. θέα sight, view, θεατής a spectator). The word was completely naturalized in L., whence It., Sp. *teatro*, Pg. *theatro*, OF. *teatre, theatre* (12–13th c.), whence perh. the ME. forms, mod.F. *théâtre*; also Ger., Du., Da. *thea·ter*, Sw. *tea·ter*.

The earliest recorded Eng. forms, *c* 1380, are *theatre* and *teatre*; from *c* 1550 to 1700, or later, the prevalent spelling was *theater* (so in Dictionaries from Cawdrey to Kersey), but *theatre* in Holland, Milton, Fuller, Dryden, Addison, Pope; Bailey 1721 has both, '*Theatre, Theater*': and between 1720 and 1750, *theater* was dropped in Britain, but has been retained or (?) revived in U.S. The pronunciation (þiˌē·təɹ), or its accentuation, appears in Lydgate, and is still in vulgar use; *thē·ater* is found as early as 1591.]

**1.** *Gr.* and *Rom. Antiq.* A place constructed in the open air, for viewing dramatic plays or other spectacles.

It had the form of a segment of a circle; the auditorium was usually excavated from a hill-side, the seats rising in tiers above and behind one another; the orchestra, occupied by the chorus, separated the stage from the auditorium.

*c* 1374 CHAUCER *Boeth.* I. pr. i. 2 (Camb. MS.) Comune strompetes of swich a place þat men clepyn the theatre. 1382 WYCLIF *Acts* xix. 29 Thei maden a sawt with oon ynwit, or wille, in to the teatre [*gloss* or comune biholdyng place]. 1412–20 LYDG. *Chron. Troy* III. 5442 In compleynynge, pitously in rage, In þe theatre, with a ded visage. 1540–1 ELYOT *Image Gov.* 69 Many woulde resorte to the common houses called Theatres, and purposing some matter of philosophy, wold there dispute openly. 1591 SPENSER *Ruins of Time* 92 High towers, faire temples, goodly theaters. 1697 POTTER *Antiq. Greece* I. viii. I. 37 Ὠδεῖον was a Musick-Theater, Built by Pericles. 1840 ARNOLD *Hist. Rome* xxxvii. II. 477 The whole Tarentine people were assembled in the theatre.

† **b.** An amphitheatre. *Obs.*

*c* 1386 CHAUCER *Knt.'s T.* 1027 Swich a noble Theatre as it was, I dar wel seyn in this world ther nas. *a* 1548 HALL *Chron., Hen. IV* 2 b, Then he graunted them the battaill & assigned the place to be at the citee of Coventree..where he caused a sumpteous theatre and listes royal..to be prepared.

**c.** A natural formation or place suggesting such a structure.

1652 *Donne's Epigr.*, Poems 102 O wilt thou be Diana, haunt these fields, This Theater both woods and fountains yeelds? 1667 MILTON *P. L.* IV. 141 Shade above shade, a woodie Theatre Of stateliest view. 1697 DRYDEN *Æneid* V. 377 A native theatre, which rising slow, By just degrees o'erlook'd the ground below. 1727–46 THOMSON *Summer* 720 Mid the central depth of blackening woods, High-rais'd in solemn theatre around. 1818 BYRON *Ch. Har.* IV. xlviii, Girt by her theatre of hills. 1886 RUSKIN *Præterita* I. ix. 288 In Jura is a far retiring theatre of rising terraces.

† **d.** A circular basin of water. *Obs.*

1645 EVELYN *Diary* 5 May, A streame precipitating into a large theater of water. *Ibid.*, In one of these theaters of water is an Atlas spouting up the streame to a very great height.

**2.** In modern use, An edifice specially adapted to dramatic representations; a playhouse.

Its essential parts, as in sense 1, are the stage for the actors, and the auditorium (the latter consisting of ranges of seats, one above another); the stage is furnished with movable scenes and more or less elaborate stage machinery for their production and removal. In 16–17th c. the building was only partially roofed; it is now entirely under cover.

At first apparently the proper name of a particular playhouse in Shoreditch, outside the City of London, built 1576: see Arber, *Gosson's School of Abuse*, Introd. 8, and early quots.

*Patent theatre*, a theatre established or licensed by royal letters patent (the first two of which were granted in 1603). Their exclusive privileges were abolished in 1843. *Saloon theatre*, *Variety theatre*: see quots. 1892, 1902. *Picture theatre*, a hall in which kinematographic pictures are exhibited, a 'picture palace'.

1577 NORTHBROOKE *Dicing* (1579) 29 b, Those places..which are made vp and builded for suche Plaies and Enterludes, as the Theatre and Curtaine is. 1578 J. STOCKWOOD *Serm. Paul's Cross* 24 If you resorte to the Theatre, the Curtayne, and other places of Playes in the Citie. *Ibid.* 134 The gorgeous Playing place erected in the fieldes..as they please to haue it called, a Theatre. 1593 SHAKS. *Rich. II*, V. ii. 23 As in a Theater, the eyes of men After a well grac'd Actor leaues the Stage, Are idlely bent on him that enters next. 1603 DRAYTON *Odes* vii. 56 Till with shrill Claps the Theater doe shake. *a* 1658 CLEVELAND *Christchurch Windows* 215 Those that before our Glass Scaffolds prefer Would turn our Temple to a Theater. 1701 *Lond. Gaz.* No. 3750/4 The Patentees of the Theater-Royal in Covent-Garden. 1788 *Act 28 Geo. III*, c. 30 Such Trajedies, Comedies,..Plays, or Farces, as now are, or hereafter shall be acted, performed, or represented at either of the Patent or Licensed Theatres in the City of Westminster. 1864 DORAN *Ann. of Stage* II. xi. Suppl. 186 List of the principal Dramatic Pieces produced at the Patent Theatres, from the Retirement of Garrick to the End of the Eighteenth Century. 1888 WILLIAMS in *Encycl. Brit.* XXIII. 227/1 In the provinces patent theatres were established at Bath by 8 Geo. III. c. 10. *Ibid.* 227/2 The exclusive rights of the patent theatres were also recognized in the Music Hall Act of 1752. **1892** *Daily News* 26 Sept. 2/4 To erect a roomy theatre of varieties—which seems to be modern English for music hall. **1902** *Encycl. Brit.* XXXI. 45/2 (s.v. *Music Halls*) The 'saloon theatres' of the 'thirties were the music halls of to-day, and they owed their form and existence to the restrictive action of the patent theatres. *Ibid.* 46/2 The saloon theatres rarely offended the patent houses, and when they did the law was soon put in motion. **1911** *London Opinion* 13 May 248/1 A picture theatre [where] such films as Foxhunting..the Boat Race..or the Derby are being shown.

†**3.** *transf.* **a.** The stage or platform on which a play is acted. *Obs.*

**1589** RIDER *Bibl. Schol.* 1484 A theater, or scaffold whereon musitions, singers, or such like shew their cunning, *orchestra.* **1647** TRAPP *Comm. Rom.* i. 20 Clearly seen: As in a mirrour, or as on a theatre. **1659** STANLEY *Hist. Philos.* III. III. 23 Some plead in the Forum, others act on the theatre. *a* **1774** GOLDSM. *Nat. Hist.* (1776) IV. 93 Like the ghost on a theatre.

**b.** A theatreful of spectators; the audience, or 'house', at a theatre. (Cf. HOUSE *sb.* 4 g.)

**1602** SHAKS. *Ham.* III. ii. 31 The censure of the which One [the judicious], must in your allowance o'reway a whole Theater of Others. **1634** HEYWOOD *Maidenhead lost* 1. Wks. 1874 IV. 112 'Twas a glorious sight, Fit for a Theater of Gods to see. **1894** GLADSTONE *Hor., Odes* xvii. [xx.] 29 The theatre thrice clapped you then.

**c.** Dramatic performances as a branch of art, or as an institution; the drama.

**1668** DRYDEN *Ess. Dram. Poesy* Ess. (ed. Ker) I. 56 By his encouragement, Corneille, and some other Frenchmen, reformed their theatre, which before was as much below ours, as it now surpasses it. *a* **1859** L. HUNT *Shewe Faire Seeming* v. Poems (1860) 178 For much the stage he lov'd, and wise theatre. **1880** *Scribner's Mag.* June 286 Their chief delight is the theater or opera.

**d.** Dramatic works collectively.

**1640** C. G. in Brome *Antipodes* To Censuring Criticks, He [Jonson] was often pleas'd, to feed your eare With the choice dainties of his Theatre. **1703** ADDISON *Prol. to Steele's Tender Husb.* 9 But now Our British Theatre can boast Drolles of all kinds, a Vast Unthinking Hoast! **1880** *Cornh. Mag.* Aug. 156 Any two plays in the whole Shakespearian theatre. **1881** SAINTSBURY *Dryden* iii. 38 Except in Congreve's two editions and in the bulky edition of Scott, Dryden's theatre is unattainable.

**4.** A temporary platform, dais, or other raised stage, for any public ceremony.

**1587** FLEMING *Contn. Holinshed* III. 1334/1 It was found better for them by the aduise of the prince of Orange..to tarie for his highnesse vpon a theater which was prepared for him. [**1621** *Execution at Prague* in *Harl. Misc.* (Malh.) III. 410 The theatrum, or scaffold of timber, which was to be erected, and whereupon the..execution of the prisoners ..was to be performed.] **1680** *Lond. Gaz.* No. 1475/3 Then his Lordship conducted their Royal Hignesses to the Hall, at the South end whereof, was erected a Theater of 42 Foot in length, and 40 in breadth, covered with Carpets and rising five steps from the ground. **1696** PHILLIPS (ed. 5), *Theater*,..said in general, of any Scaffold erected for the performance or sight of any publick Ceremony. **1820** A. TAYLOR *Glory of Regality* 178 A large platform called the Theatre; in the midst of this are placed the royal thrones. **1838** *Order Coron. Q. Vict.*, The Queen..passes up through the Body of the Church,..and so up the Stairs to the Theatre. **1902** *Westm. Gaz.* 11 Aug. 4/2 According to the original order of service the King and Queen would have ascended the steps to the 'Theatre'—a square platform which had been erected in the central space under the 'Lantern'.

**5.** A room or hall fitted with tiers of rising seats facing the platform, lecturer's table, or president's seat, for lectures, scientific demonstrations, etc.

*The* (*Sheldonian*) *Theatre* (at Oxford), the building in which the great assemblies of the University are held, and honorary degrees are given at the annual Commemoration.

**1613** PURCHAS *Pilgrimage* VI. xi. 521 That is now rather become a Sepulcher of Sciences, then a Theater, there being not above five Students. **1641** EVELYN *Diary* 28 Aug., I was much pleased with a sight of their Anatomy schole, theater, and repository adjoyning. **1669** WOOD *Life* 9 July (O. H. S.) II. 165 Theater consecrated. The Archbishop's [Sheldon's] letter in English (read in Convocation) wherby he tells the vice-chancellor and Convocation that he had layd by 2000 li. for a purchase to keep the Theater in repayr. **1721** Sheldonian theatre [see TERRÆ FILIUS 2]. **1766** ENTICK *London* IV. 264 The surgeons erected a theatre in the Old-bailey. **1910** *Kelly's Directory of Oxford* 52 Of the many ceremonials and receptions which have taken place in the theatre, the most imposing..were the visit of the allied sovereigns in 1814, and the installation of the last five chancellors. *Ibid.* 37/2 The Radcliffe Infirmary and County Hospital...A new operating theatre was erected in 1898.

**6.** *fig.* Something represented as a theatre (in sense 1 or 2) in relation to a course of action performed or a spectacle displayed; *esp.* a place or region where some thing or action is presented to public view (literally or metaphorically).

**1581** in *Confer.* II. (1584) K iv, They..are set before all mens eyes, and in the middest of the Theatre of the whole world. **1600** SHAKS. *A. Y. L.* II. vii. 136 This wide and vniuersall Theater Presents more wofull Pageants then the Sceane Wherein we play in. **1639** FULLER *Holy War* v. x. 246 Asia, the theatre whereon they were acted, is at a great distance. **1684** T. BURNET *Th. Earth* I. 173 Earth was the first theater upon which mortals appear'd and acted. **1713** YOUNG *Last Day* I. 51 Wide theatre! where tempests play at large. **1769** ROBERTSON *Chas. V*, XI. III. 267 A theatre on which he might display his great qualities. **1798** WASHINGTON *Lett.* Writ. (1893) XIV. 21 The propriety..of my again appearing on a Public theatre, after declaring the sentiments I did in my Valedictory Address. **1855** BREWSTER *Newton* II. xvi. 104 An event..which.. placed him in a noble position on the theatre of public life. **1877** BRYANT *Ruins of Italica* ii, A tragic theatre, where Time Acts his great fable.

**b.** A place where some action proceeds; the scene of action. Cf. SCENE, STAGE.

**1615** G. SANDYS *Trav.* Ded. A vj, The most renowned countries and kingdomes:..the theaters of valour and heroicall actions. **1654** tr. *Martini's Conq. China* 198 Which Country was the Theater of all his Brutalities. **1720** OZELL *Vertot's Rom. Rep.* II. XI. 194 The Theatre of a Civil War. **1774** J. ADAMS in *Fam. Lett.* (1876) 26 To-morrow we reach the theatre of action. **1830** LYELL *Princ. Geol.* I. 199 The theatre of violent earthquakes. **1879** MENDELL *Art of War* iii. 75 The theater of operations of an army embraces all the territory it may desire to invade and all that it may be necessary to defend.

†**7.** A book giving a 'view' or 'conspectus' of some subject; a text-book, manual, treatise. (Chiefly in titles of such books.) *Obs.*

?**1566** J. ALDAY tr. *Boaystuau* (*title*) Theatrum Mundi, the Theatre or rule of the world, wherein may be sene the running race and course of euerye mans life, as touching miserie and felicity. **1599** R. ALLOT (*title*) Wits Theater of the little World. **1611** SPEED (*title*) The Theatre of the Empire of Great Britaine: Presenting an exact Geography of the Kingdomes of England, Scotland, Ireland, and the Iles adioyning. **1640** PARKINSON (*title*) Theatrum Botanicum, The Theater of Plantes, or An Universall and Compleate Herball. **1657** S. PURCHAS (*title*) A Theatre of Politicall Flying-Insects. **1704** R. MONTEITH (*title*) A Theater of Mortality; Or, the Illustrious Inscriptions..upon the several Monuments..within the Grey-friars Church-Yard [etc.] of Edinburgh.

†**8.** *transf.* A thing displayed to view; a sight, scene, spectacle; a gazing-stock.

**1606** SYLVESTER *Du Bartas* II. iv. I. *Tropheis* 343 All cast their eyes on this sad Theater. **1640** *Petit. A. Leighton* in Chandler *Hist. Persec.* (1736) 370 He was made a Theatre of Misery to Men and Angels. **1646** EVANCE *Noble Ord.* 38 If there be any that are made a Theature unto the world,.. it is such as Paul [cf. 1 *Cor.* iv. 9].

**9.** *attrib.* and *Comb.*, as *theatre-bill, coat, hat, -house, -haunter, -light, -pit, -poster, -ticket, -train, -tram, -wrap*, etc.; *theatre-like* adj. and adv.

**1577** T. W[ILCOCKS] *Serm. Pawles Crosse* 46 Beholde the sumptuous Theatre houses. **1611** COTGR., *Coeste*,..vsed by the auncient Grecians in their Theater combats. **1626** BACON *Sylva* § 253 Some hills that stand encompassed theatre-like. **1846** THACKERAY *L. Blanchard* Wks. 1900 XIII. 477 The young fellow,..theatre-stricken, poetry-stricken. **1856** KINGSLEY *Misc., Plays & Purit.* (1859) II. 137 Theatre-haunters were turning Romanists. **1873** *Routledge's Yng. Gentl. Mag.* Apr. 282/2 Theatre lights are lime-light jets fitted into square boxes. **1897** *Globe* 18 Feb. 6/3 Very handsome theatre coats and jackets are worn at the play in London. *Ibid.*, The fashionable theatre bodice. **1905** *Longm. Mag.* Apr. 501 The people you meet in buses and trams and theatre-trains.

**b.** Special combs.: **theatre-floor**: see quot.; **theatre-goer**, one who frequents theatres; so **theatre-going** *sb.* and *adj.*; **theatre-land**, the district of a town (spec. of London) in which most of the theatres are situated; **theatre-party** (*U.S.*), a party in which the guests, besides being entertained at dinner or supper, are taken to a theatre; **theatre-seat**, a seat of which the bottom is made to fold back when not occupied, so as to leave a wider passage; a tip-up seat used in theatres, also on tram-cars, etc.

**1895** *Funk's Stand. Dict.*, *Theater-floor, an inclined floor in a public building, as a lecture-hall, affording a better view of the platform from rear seats. **1874** *Macm. Mag.* Aug. 281 *Theatre-goers..who have long winced over the pale and unwholesome jokes of patchy vaudevilles. **1853** *Household Words* VI. 63 The Parisians..are evidently a more *theatre-going people than the Londoners. **1883** *Harper's Mag.* June 126/1 Theatre-going and..card-playing are..permitted. **1905** *Daily Chron.* 28 Dec. 4/7 [St. Martin's parish] Bishop Burnet described as 'the greatest cure in England'. '*Theatreland' we name it now. **1907** H. WYNDHAM *Flare of Footlights* xxxvi, The comfortable little house [the Sheridan theatre], situated in the very heart of theatre-land. **1885** A. FORBES *Souvenirs of Continents* 239 A New York '*theatre party'. **1903** *Smart Set* IX. 145/1 I've given theatre-parties to them, and watched them rustle in and fill box after box.

Hence **The·atre** *v., intr.* to go to the theatre; **The·atredom**, the domain or sphere of things theatrical and persons connected therewith; also, the district in which theatres are situated; **The·atreful**, as many as a theatre will hold; **The·atreless** *a.*, without a theatre or theatrical entertainments; **The·atrewards** *adv.*, towards a theatre; **The·atrewise** *adv.*, in the manner of a theatre.

**1896** *Pall Mall Mag.* 495 If a woman dances, and drives, and *theatres,..she keeps herself too chronically tired to think. **1906** *Daily Chron.* 26 June 4/7 Our round of entertainments..[does] not cease till we have lunched, motored, tea'd, dined, theatred, and supped. **1890** *Daily News* 29 Dec. 3/1 London *theatredom,..—if we may be allowed the expression—is, roughly speaking, about ten miles wide by six miles deep. **1904** *Westm. Gaz.* 5 May 1/3 Those versed in the inner life of London theatredom. **1902** *19th Cent.* Aug. 284 Get together a *theatreful of people to hear it. **1853** *Chamb. Jrnl.* XX. 409/2 The dreary prospect of a supperless, *theatreless Lent. **1897** *Daily News* 3 May 8/6 Walking slowly *theatrewards. **1629** MAXWELL tr. *Herodian* (1635) 164 A goodly spacious Plaine..lying under a row of Hills, *Theatre wise. **1737** [S BERINGTON] *G. di Lucca's Mem.* (1738) 227 Two Rows of young Men and Women, placed Theatre-wise one above another.

**Theatric** (þiˌæ·trik), *a.* (*sb.*) [ad. late L. *theātric-us*, ad. Gr. θεατρικός, f. θέατρον THEATRE: see -IC. So F. † *theatrique* (15–16th c. in Godef.).]

**1.** Of, belonging to, or of the nature of the theatre; = THEATRICAL *a.* 1.

**1706** STEELE *Prol. Vanbrugh's Mistake* 29 By him theatric angels mount more high, And mimic thunders shake a broader sky. **1809** W. IRVING *Knickerb.* VI. ii. (1849) 318 Two buskined theatric heroes. **1812** *Examiner* 21 Sept. 603/1 Theatric amusements might be made objects of taxation. **1855** MILMAN *Lat. Chr.* XIV. iv. (1864) IX. 183 Councils denounced these theatric performances [the Mysteries].

**b.** Resembling a theatre or amphitheatre in shape or formation.

**1764** GOLDSM. *Trav.* 108 Its uplands sloping deck the mountain's side, Woods over woods in gay theatric pride. **1781** MASON *Eng. Gard.* IV. 225 Two broad Piazzas in theatric curve. **1819** W. S. ROSE *Lett.* I. 27 Imagine.. a city with something of a theatric form. **1819** WORDSW. *Malham Cove*, Oh, had this vast theatric structure wound With finish'd sweep into a perfect round.

**2.** = THEATRICAL *a.* 2.

**1816** J. GILCHRIST *Philos. Etym.* 208 A poor, dull, servile, imitative, theatric set of artificial creatures, strutting about the stage of life in pompous insignificance.

**3.** Suggestive of the theatre; = THEATRICAL *a.* 3.

**1656** *Artif. Handsom.* 168 What is there in any civill order ..which doth not put on something Theatrick and pompous? **1760** WALPOLE in *Four C. Eng. Lett.* (1880) 267 It was very theatric to look down into the vault, where the coffin was, attended by mourners with lights. **1788** MME. D'ARBLAY *Diary* (1876) IV. IV. 343 So theatric an attitude. **1879** MCCARTHY *Own Times* II. xxii. 139 He was picturesque and perhaps even theatric in his dress and his bearing.

**B.** *sb.* In *pl.* = *theatricals* (THEATRICAL *sb.* 2).

**1807** W. IRVING *Salmag.* (1824) 9 Our theatrics shall take up but a small part of our paper.

Hence **Thea·tricable** *a.* (*nonce-wd.*), capable of being made theatric, i. e. dramatized.

**1901** HOWELLS in *N. Amer. Rev.* CLXXII. 798 It is the subordinate affair of the actor to adapt himself to the poet's conception, and find it theatricable.

**Theatrical** (þiˌæ·trikăl), *a.* [f. as THEATRIC + -AL: see -ICAL.]

**A.** *adj.* **1.** Pertaining to or connected with the theatre or 'stage', or with scenic representations.

**1558** PARKER in Burnet *Hist. Ref.* (1681) II. *Collect. Records* II. III. viii. 355 To dispense God's Word..in poor destitute Parishes..more meet for my decayed Voice..than in Theatrical and great Audience. **1603** HOLLAND *Plutarch's Mor.* 19 The straunge fables and Theatricall fictions. **1637–50** ROW *Hist. Kirk* (Wodrow Soc.) 6 There were also some theatricall playes. **1730** A. GORDON *Maffei's Amphith.* 335 The Power and Extent of the Theatrical Law. **1905** A. C. BENSON *Upton Lett.* (1906) 72 He drifts up to London and joins a theatrical company.

†**b.** = THEATRIC *a.* 1 b. *Obs*

**1766** AMORY *Buncle* (1770) IV. 22 In a theatrical space of about two hundred acres, which the hand of nature cut, or hollowed out, on the side of a mountain.

**2.** That 'plays a part'; † representing or exhibiting in the manner of an actor (*obs.*); that simulates, or is simulated; artificial, affected, assumed.

**1649** J. H. *Motion to Parl. Adv. Learn.* 37 Man in businesse is but a Theatricall person, and in a manner but personates himselfe. **1691** BOYLE *Greatn. Mind* I. 6 Philosophers..can easily distinguish betwixt that real Greatness.. and that Theatrical one, that Fortune may have annext to his Condition. **1711** SHAFTESB. *Charac.* VI. iii. (1737) III. 368 The good Painter must..take care that his Action be not theatrical, or at second hand; but original and drawn from Nature her-self. **1830** MACAULAY *Ess., Moore's Byron* (1887) 169 How far the character in which he [Byron] exhibited himself was genuine, and how far theatrical, it would probably have puzzled himself to say.

**3.** Having the style of dramatic performance; extravagantly or irrelevantly histrionic; 'stagy'; calculated for display, showy, spectacular.

**1709–10** STEELE & ADDISON *Tatler* No. 136 ¶ 3 His Theatrical Manner of making Love. **1751** *Affect. Narr. of Wager* 60 [He] read it to the Captain in a theatrical Tone. **1856** FROUDE *Hist. Eng.* II. viii. 277 The signal..was given with a theatrical bravado. **1883** MRS. OLIPHANT *Sheridan* ii. 57 Sheridan's art, from its very beginning, was theatrical, if we may use the word, rather than dramatic.

**B.** *sb.* **1.** *pl.* The performance of stage plays; now, dramatic performance by amateurs, usually in a private house (*private theatricals*). Also *fig.* doings of a theatrical character; 'acting', pretence.

**1657–83** EVELYN *Hist. Relig.* (1850) II. 291 Turning their ..services and ceremonies into theatricals. **1804** *Miniature* No. 21 (1806) I. 280 Private theatricals, when many of the first personages in the land choose to make themselves fools for the good of a large company. **1808** HAN. MORE *Cœlebs* (1809) II. xxxiii. 116 What the news-papers pertly call *Private Theatricals.* *a* **1849** H. COLERIDGE *Ess.* (1851) II. 12 If Charles had not carried his love of theatricals to church. **1897** MRS. E. L. VOYNICH *Gadfly* (1904) 30/2 It's only the usual theatricals, because he's ashamed to face us.

**2.** *pl.* Matters pertaining to the stage and acting; in quot. 1855 *concr.* = stage properties.

**1815** W. H. IRELAND *Scribbleomania* 106 *note*, He.. dedicated his mind to the study of theatricals. **1829** *Censor* 224 The depressed state of theatricals. **1855** DICKENS *Lett.* (1880) I. 397, I have some theatricals at home.

**3.** A professional actor.

**1859** SALA *Gaslight & D.* ii. 18 How hard-working..and persevering theatricals..generally are. **1863** DICKENS *Let.* 1 May in Holman-Hunt *Pre-Raphaelitism* (1905) II. 238 That half-gipsy life of our theatricals. **1888** *Harper's Mag.* Nov. 945/2 All the theatricals went there.

**Thea·tricalism.** [f. prec. + -ISM.] The practice of what is theatrical; theatrical style or character; 'staginess'.

1854 LD. COLERIDGE in *Life* I. 220 The dangers of sentimentalism and theatricalism in religion. 1884 J. W. HALES *Notes & Ess. Shaks.* 73 There is nothing normal or calm, but incessant eccentricity and theatricalism. 1908 *Westm. Gaz.* 18 Apr. 2/3 The phrase has just enough of the declamatory quality in it to give it that touch of theatricalism which was dear to the heart of the man who spoke it.

So †**Thea·tricalist** *nonce-wd.*, one who takes part in private theatricals.

1802 in *Spirit Pub. Jrnls.* VI. 181 Pic-nic Theatricalists.

**Theatricality** (þiˌæ:trikæ·lĭti). [See -ITY.]

**1.** The quality or character of being theatrical; theatricalness. With *a* and *pl.* an instance of this.

1837 CARLYLE *Fr. Rev.* II. I. ix, By act and word he strives to do it; with sincerity, if possible; failing that, with theatricality. 1880 R. L. NETTLESHIP *Hellenica* 112 A tendency to theatricality and effusiveness. 1889 *Times* 27 Feb. 9/2 The absurd theatricalities with which the.. campaign is now mainly carried on.

**b.** *transf.* A theatrical personage.

1840 CARLYLE *Heroes* ii, This Mahomet..we will in no wise consider as an Inanity and Theatricality. 1892 *Review of Rev.* Jan. 657 Two such theatricalities as Lord Beaconsfield and Lord Lytton.

**2.** A theatrical matter; a dramatic performance.

1866 CARLYLE *Remin.* (1881) II. 164, I remember once taking her to Drury Lane Theatre...Of the theatricality itself that night, I can remember absolutely nothing.

**Theatricalize** (þiˌæ·trikăləiz), *v.* [f. THEATRICAL + -IZE.]

**1.** *trans.* To make or render theatrical.

1778 MME. D'ARBLAY *Diary* Sept., I shall occasionally theatricalize my dialogues. 1899 *Westm. Gaz.* 2 June 2/1 The scene in which the unhappy hero has his epaulettes.. torn from him, and his sword broken, though a little too 'theatricalised', is really very moving. 1909 *Daily Chron.* 9 Sept. 5/3 As Lamb has said, any attempt to theatricalise the grandeur of Shakespeare's conception must fail.

**2.** *intr.* **a.** To act on the stage. **b.** To attend or frequent theatrical performances.

1794 COLERIDGE *Lett., to Southey* (1895) 86 It is an Ipswich Fair time, and the Norwich company are theatricalizing. 1833 E. FITZGERALD *Lett.* (1889) I. 20 He and I have been theatricalizing lately. We saw an awful Hamlet the other night.

Hence **Thea·tricaliza·tion**, the process of making theatrical; dramatization; also *fig.*

1875 HOWELLS *Foregone Concl.* iii, Ferris was an uncompromising enemy of the theatricalisation of Italy. 1890 *Judy* 1 Oct. 160/1 *Ravenswood*, as Herman Merivale calls his dramatization, or theatricalization, of the story of 'The Bride of Lammermoor'.

**Theatrically** (þiˌæ·trikăli), *adv.* [f. as prec. + -LY [2].]

**1.** In a theatrical manner or style; in relation to the theatre; dramatically; as a public spectacle.

1647 TRAPP *Comm. Epistles* 637 The Pharisees..did all theatrically, histrionically, hypocritically, 'to be seen of men'. 1669 BP. HOPKINS *Serm.* 1 *Pet.* (1685) 71 Here royal and sacred blood is theatrically spilt. *c* 1702 POPE *Imit. Earl Dorset, Artemisia* iii, Her voice theatrically loud. 1813 *Examiner* 29 Mar. 205/1 Whether good taste considers such a deformity as theatrically picturesque. 1878 BOSW. SMITH *Carthage* 407 Some forty years after Caius Marius had so theatrically taken his seat amidst its ruins.

†**2.** In rising terraces, like an amphitheatre. *Obs.*

1768 *Misc.* in *Ann. Reg.* 174/2 It has a strong appearance of benches; which never rise theatrically in these buildings abroad. 1778 *Eng. Gazetteer* (ed. 2) s.v. *Woburn*, On one side of this water..there are high hills, that are planted theatrically with evergreens.

**Theatricalness** (þiˌæ·trikălnĕs). [f. as prec. + -NESS.] The quality or condition of being theatrical.

1727 BAILEY vol. II, *Theatricalness*, the being according to the Custom or Manner of the Theatre. 1865 BAGEHOT in *Fortn. Rev.* No. 1. 15 A change of government..is one of those marked events which by its suddenness,..its theatricalness, impresses men more even than it should. 1890 *Spectator* 8 Feb., The thorough reality and absence of affectation in her character make an admirable foil for the innate theatricalness of that of her *fiancé*.

**Theatricism** (þiˌæ·trisiz'm). [f. THEATRIC *a.* + -ISM.] A mannerism or mode of action suited to the stage; artificial manner; = THEATRICALISM.

1872 *Daily News* 12 Apr. 4/6 The superb theatricisms (if we may employ such a word) of the elder Pitt, and the sonorous solemnities of the younger. 1880 MᶜCARTHY *Own Times* IV. lxi. 357 The monstrous excesses, the preposterous theatricism of the Paris Commune.

So **Thea·tricize** *v., trans.* to make or render theatric or 'stagy'; to make like stage scenery.

1852 *Fraser's Mag.* XLV. 664 Theatricized Stolzenfels is a glaring example of the monstrosity which may be bred from restoration, with its pasteboard battlements and tawdry gothic ornaments.

**Theatrize** (þī·ătrəiz), *v.* [ad. Gr. θεατρίζ-ειν to make a spectacle of, f. θέατρον in the sense 'show, spectacle'; also intr. as in 2: see -IZE.]

†**1.** *trans.* To make a spectacle or show of. *Obs.*

1678 J. BROWN *Life of Faith* (1824) I. i. 13 They were exposed to..public shame..when made open spectacles and theatrized. 1679 *Ibid.* II. xiv. 297 We read of some..who were theatrized, brought to open scaffolds. 1711 HICKES *Two Treat. Chr. Priesth.* (1847) I. 279 He endeavours to expose and theatrize us.

**2.** *intr.* To act theatrically, play a part.

1839 *Watchman* 18 Sept., The Pope's militia..can splendidly theatrize in Protestant England.

**3.** *trans.* To make theatrical or dramatic: to dramatize. *rare.*

1888 *Scribner's Mag.* Oct. 439/1 It became necessary to 'theatreize' or idealize history.

**Theatro-** (þī·ătro, þiˌæ·tro), combining form of Gr. θέατρον THEATRE. **Theatro·cracy** [Gr. θεατροκρατία], absolute power exercised by the ancient Athenian democracy, as exhibited at their assemblies in the theatre; ochlocracy. **The·atrograph** [-GRAPH]: see 2nd quot. **The:atroma·nia** [-MANIA: cf. Gr. θεατρομανής mad after plays], excessive fondness for theatre-going; so **The:atroma·niac,** one who is 'mad' on theatre-going. **The·atrophil** [-PHIL], a lover of the theatre; a theatre-goer. **The:atropho·bia** [-PHOBIA], horror of theatres and theatre-going. **The·atrophone** [-PHONE]: see quot. 1891. **Theatro·polis** [Gr. πόλις city], a town or district famous for its theatres. **The·atroscope** [-SCOPE] = KINEMATOGRAPH.

1820 T. MITCHELL *Aristoph.* I. p. cxi, They form the best comment on what Plato somewhere calls the *theatrocracy of Athens. 1877 RUSKIN *Fors Clav.* lxxiii. 18 Instead of aristocracy..rose up a certain polluted theatrocracy. 1896 *Daily Chron.* 23 Mar. 3/4 At Olympia..the large audiences have been greatly pleased with Mr. Paul's '*Theatrograph', comprising realistic scenes from popular plays. 1896 *Daily News* 2 Dec. 10/5 The theatrograph, now so popular at the music-halls...The effect of the theatrograph is produced by means of an ingenious apparatus, which causes an intermittent light to fall upon the living performers, who thus assume the hazy, tremulous appearance of the animated pictures. 1891 *Cent. Dict.*, *Theatromania. 1903 *Times, Lit. Supp.* 17 July 226/2 Your theatromania will lead to the production of the very worst type of bad play. *Ibid.*, Lamb was a *theatromaniac..without the dramatic faculty. 1901 *Referee* 26 May 7 (Cass. Supp.) A point for *theatrophiles. 1839 DARLEY in *Beaum. & Fletcher's Wks.* I. Introd. 29, I must acknowledge this sect justified..in its most reasonable *theatro-phobia. 1891 *Pall Mall G.* 29 May 6/2 The *theatrophone (writes a Paris correspondent) is intended to transmit, by means of a clever adaptation..of the ordinary telephone, everything audible which goes on upon the stage of the various..theatres. *Ibid.* 10 Dec. 6/3 The theatrophone has found its way from Paris to London, and a preliminary trial has been made at the Savoy Hotel with complete success. 1897 'OUIDA' *Massarenes* xviii, A modern woman of the world. As costly as an ironclad and as complicated as a theatrophone. 1899 E. CALLOW *Old Lond. Tav.* II. 302 The Gaiety commences what may be termed the *Theatropolis of London. 1904 *Edin. Rev.* Oct. 298 Paris has not been theatropolis all these years for nothing. 1896 *Daily News* 31 Mar. 7/6 A *theatroscope, the animated photography of which gives the audience specimens of burlesque, contortionist, and other scenes.

†**Theatry.** *Obs.* [app. an erroneous formation for *theatre.*] = THEATRE.

1513 DOUGLAS *Æneis* IV. viii. 128 Or lyk Orestes, son of Agamemnone On theatreis, in farcis mony one. *Ibid.* v. vi. 7 A playing place wes markit on the ground, Sic as that clepit bene a theatry. 1567 FENTON *Trag. Disc.* i. (1898) I. 47 The monument of your vertues being..advanced to the height of the highest theatrey in the worlde. 1571 *Satir. Poems Reform.* xxvii. 121 The throne of tryall and theatrie [*v.rr.* trettie, theatre] trew Is ffor to reigne.

**Theats,** traces: see THEAT.

**Theave, thaive** (þīv, þēɪv). *local.* Forms: *α.* 6 thayffe, 7 theafe, 8 theaf, thief. *β.* 7–9 theave, 8–9 thaive, 9 thave. *Pl.* 5–6 theyves, 6–7 theves, 7 theives, 6– theaves. [Known from 15th c.: etymology unascertained.] The name given in the midland and some southern counties of England to a female sheep of a particular age: most generally applied to a ewe of the first or second year, that has not yet borne a lamb; in some parts to a ewe between the first and second shearing: see quotations.

In Eng. Dial. Dict. cited in use from S.W. Yorkshire to the Thames, and from Hereford to Essex; also in Berks, Wilts, Dorset. In some districts app. identified with *teg* or *hog*, in others with the age succeeding this.

1465 *Paston Lett.* III. 437 Item,..iiijˣˣ hoggys and xl theyves. 1517 in *Eng. Hist. Rev.* (1897) XII. 234, 60 young ewes or theaves. 1523 FITZHERB. *Husb.* § 53 The ewes by them-selfe, the share-hogges and theyues by them selfe. 1544 (Dec. 13) *Will of J. Borow of S. Stoke* (MS.), A thayffe youe. 1596 *Unton Invent.* (1841) 9 Two hundred tegges and theves. 1607 TOPSELL *Four-f. Beasts* (1658) 495 The first year we call it in English a Lamb.., the second year, a Hog, Lam-hog, or Teg if it be a female, the third year, Hoggrils and Theives. 1614 MARKHAM *Cheap Husb.* III. i. (1668) 87 The second year the male is a Weather, and the female a Theafe, and then she may be put to the Ram; but if you let her go over that year also, then she is a double Theafe. 1669 WORLIDGE *Syst. Agric.* (1681) 323 A *Theave*, an Ew of the first year. [So 1691 RAY *S. & E. C. Words*, Essex.] 1736 W. ELLIS *New Exper. Husb.* 52 (E.D.S.) The first year we call the ewe a lamb; the second year a ewe pug or teg; the third year a thaive; and the fourth year a sheep. 1799 A. YOUNG *Agric. Lincoln.* 314 Theaves; ewe hogs. 1841 *Penny Cycl.* XXI. 356/1 After being shorn, she is a *shearing ewe* or *gimmer*, or *theave* or double-toothed ewe; and after that, a *two* or *three* or *four shear ewe* or *theave*. 1844 STEPHENS *Bk. Farm* II. 39 Gimmers are called theaves until they bear the first lamb. 1863 MORTON *Cycl. Agric.* (E.D.S.), *Theaves* (*West Engl.*), ewes that have been shorn once. 1879 MISS JACKSON *Shropsh. Word-bk.* 437 *Thave*, a ewe sheep of the first year. 1886 C. SCOTT *Sheep-Farming* 18 From first to second shearing... Gimmer, Theave, Shearling ewe. 1904 *Eng. Dial. Dict.*, *Theave. Wiltsh.* A ewe of the third year. *Dorset.* A sheep three years old and therefore having six incisors.

**Theba·ia.** *Chem.* [f. Gr. Θῆβαι Thebes + -IA [1] (after *ammonia*): see THEBAIC [2].] = THEBAÏNE.

1857 MILLER *Elem. Chem.* III. 282 *Thebaia, or *Paramorphia* ($C_{38}H_{21}NO_6$). This alkali crystallizes from its solution in alcohol or in ether, in square plates of silvery lustre, which have a styptic, acrid taste. 1869 *N. Syd. Soc. Bienn. Retrospect* 443 Thebaia is the first of the opium alkaloids in toxic activity.

**Thebaic** (þĭbē^ɪ·ik), *a.*[1] [ad. L. *Thēbaic-us*, ad. Gr. Θηβαϊκός, f. Θῆβαι, Θήβη Thebes.] Of or pertaining to the ancient city of Thebes on the Nile, formerly a centre of Egyptian civilization; *spec.* noting the Sahidic version of the Bible.

*Thebaic marble, stone*, the syenite of Thebes and Upper Egypt, famed in ancient times as material for columns, pillars, vases, etc.

1687 A. LOVELL tr. *Thevenot's Trav.* I. 123 The Vault [in old wall towers of Alexandria] is supported by great Pillars of Thebaick Stone. 1773 *Gentl. Mag.* Aug. 399/1 Thebaic stone, from waste ev'n yet secure, With hieroglyphic learn'd inwrought. 1830 TATTAM *Egypt. Gram.* Pref. 7 The terms Coptic and Sahidic have been adopted in this work, instead of Memphitic and Thebaic. 1839 *Civil Eng. & Arch. Jrnl.* II. 453/1 It seems to be the Syenite of the ancients, or perhaps..their Thebaic marble. 1884 H. M. SCOTT in *Chicago Advance* 31 Jan., Two, perhaps three, translations of the Scriptures, the Memphitic, for the Lower Egyptian Churches, and the Thebaic, for those of Upper Egypt.

**Theba·ic,** *a.*[2] *Pharm. Chem.* [f. as prec., in reference to the fact that Egypt is a chief source of the opium of commerce.] Of or derived from opium; *thebaic extract, tincture*, laudanum.

1746 H. PEMBERTON *Dispensatory* 153 Opium strained, otherwise called the Thebaic Extract. 1783 W. KEIR in *Med. Commun.* I. 129 An eighth part of thebaic tincture. 1797 *Encycl. Brit.* (ed. 3) XIV. *Pharmacy* § 558 Thebaic powder. *Ibid.* § 604 Thebaic electuary.

So **Theba·ïcine,** *Chem.*, a yellow amorphous alkaloid, described by Hesse 1870, formed by boiling thebaïne with concentrated hydrochloric acid; **Thebaïne** (þī·beˌəin) [-INE [5]], a highly poisonous alkaloid, $C_{19}H_{21}NO_3$, obtained in colourless leaflets or prisms from opium; formerly also called *paramorphine* and THEBAIA; also *attrib.* **Thebaïsm** (þī·beˌiz'm), *Path.*, the toxic action of thebaïne; **The·benine,** *Chem.*, an amorphous crystalline alkaloid, isomeric with thebaïne, from which it is formed by boiling with hydrochloric acid.

1875 WATTS *Dict. Chem.* VII. 1152 *Thebaïcine. 1894 MUIR & MORLEY *Watts' Dict. Chem.* IV. 681 Boiling [in] dilute $H_2SO$ converts it [Thebaïne] into thebenine and thebaïcine. 1835 *R. D. & T. Thomson's Rec. Gen. Sc.* II. 381 Ammonia is next poured into the purified liquid, by which means, Morphine and *Thebaine are precipitated. 1868 WATTS *Dict. Chem.* V. 759 Thebaine-salts do not crystallise from aqueous solution. 1871 ROSCOE *Elem. Chem.* 429 It appears that thebaine is the most powerful of the alkaloids. 1875 WATTS *Dict. Chem.* VII. 1153 *Thebenine.

**Thebaïd** (þī·beˌid), *a.* and *sb.* [ad. Gr. Θηβαΐς, -ιδ-, L. *Thēbaïs, -id-.*] **a.** *adj.* Pertaining to Thebes; usually **b.** *sb.* the territory belonging to (*a*) Egyptian, or (*b*) Bœotian Thebes; the name of certain poems, esp. that of Statius relating to Bœotian Thebes.

[1687 LOVELL tr. *Thevenot's Trav.* I. 175 Captos, a Town of the Thebais (the Ruines whereof are still to be seen betwixt Cossir and Chana).] 1727–41 CHAMBERS *Cycl.*, *Thebaid, Thebais*, a famous heroic poem of Statius. 1776 MICKLE tr. *Camoens' Lusiad* Introd. 146 The Iliad, the Eneid, and all those poems which may be classed with the Thebaid. 1839 *Civil Engin. & Arch. Jrnl.* II. 453/2 Thebaid [porphyry] red ground, with yellow spots. 1854 WHITTIER *Hermit of Thebaid* 115 Its holiest saint the Thebaid lost, And found a man! 1876 GLADSTONE *Homeric Synchr.* 241 Ammon was the god especially of the Thebaid.

**Theban** (þī·băn), *a.* and *sb.* (Also 7 -ean, 8 -æan.) [ad. L. *Thēbān-us*, f. *Thēbæ*, Gr. Θῆβαι, Thebes.]

**A.** *adj.* **1.** Of or belonging to Thebes, capital of ancient Bœotia in Greece.

*c* 1374 CHAUCER *Anel. & Arc.* 85 This theban knyght..Was yonge. *c* 1374 — *Troylus* v. 601 So cruwel..vn-to þe blood Thebane. 1746 FRANCIS tr. *Horace, Art Poetry* 533 Thus rose the Theban Wall; Amphion's Lyre, And soothing Voice the listening Stones inspire. 1762 FALCONER *Shipwreck* III. 227 To curb thy spirit with a Theban chain. 1861 PALEY *Æschylus* (ed. 2) VII. *Agst. Thebes* 240 *note*, The association of Theban gods..Pallas, Hera, Artemis,..Poseidon, Aphrodite, &c.

**2.** Of or belonging to Thebes, ancient capital of Upper Egypt; = THEBAIC *a.*[1]

*Theban drug*, opium or laudanum; *Theban marble, porphyry* = THEBAIC *stone*; *Theban year*, the Egyptian year of 365¼ days.

1645 EVELYN *Diary* 21 Feb., The architrave of the portico [of the Roman Pantheon] sustain'd by 13 pillars of Theban marble. [1753 CHAMBERS *Cycl. Supp.*, *Thebanus ophites*.. that species of the..serpentine marble more commonly called *ophites niger*, the black serpentine.] 1768 C. SHAW *Monody* xvi, Come, Theban drug, the wretch's only aid, To my torn heart its former peace restore. 1831–3 E. BURTON *Eccl. Hist.* xxviii. (1845) 596 The martyrdom of the Theban legion ..may be said to have taken place about the year 286, when Herculeus was on his march into Gaul. 1839 *Civil Eng. & Arch. Jrnl.* II. 435/2 Theban Porphyry was black with yellow spots.

**B.** *sb.* (also †**Thebien**). A native or inhabitant of Bœotian Thebes, a Bœotian.

*c* 1374 CHAUCER *Anel. & Arc.* 60. *c* 1386 — *Knt.'s T.* 1712 Thise two Thebans vp on either side. *c* 1420 *Wars Alex.* (Prose) 34 Þe Thebienes also þat were so wyse, and so grete exercyse hadde in armes. 1605 SHAKS. *Lear* III. iv. 162 Ile talke a word with this same lerned Theban. 1770 LANGHORNE *Plutarch* (1851) I. 320/2 They proclaimed liberty to the Thebans. 1822 T. Mitchell *Aristoph.* I. 103 Flute-music .. was stigmatised as Theban-like, and consequently unfit for a gentleman. 1880 Swinburne *Study Shaks.* 183 To the simpler eyes of less learned Thebans than these—Thebes, by the way, was Dryden's irreverent name for Cambridge.

**Thebe**, *dial.*: see Feaberry, gooseberry.

**Thebenine**: see Thebaic².

† **Thebes**, *sb. pl. Obs.* Also 5 Tebes, (Thebies). [? a. OF. **Thebes*, f. L. *Thēbæ, -ās*, the city *Thebes*.] = Thebans; see Theban *sb.*

13.. *K. Alis.* 2819 Mawgre the Thebes everichon. *Ibid.* 2824 Theo Thebes stoden aboute his harme. *a* 1400-50 *Wars Alex.* 2333 (MS. A.) Þe Thebies [*MS. D.* tebes] þam tiȝt þe toun to defende.

**Thebesian** (þibī·siăn), *a. Anat.* [f. *Thebesius*, name of a German anatomist (1686–1732) + -an.] Applied to structures in the heart discovered or investigated by Thebesius:

*Thebesian foramina*, small openings into the right auricle, believed to be the orifices of the Thebesian veins; *Thebesian valve*, the coronary valve; *Thebesian veins*, small veins bringing blood from the substance of the heart into the right auricle.

1871 Huxley *Anat. Vertebr. Anim.* 407 In the heart [of the porpoise] the fossa ovalis is distinct, but there is neither Eustachian nor Thebesian valve.

**Thebolactic** (þībolæ·ktik), *a. Chem.* [f. Theb-aic *a.*² + Lactic.] In *thebolactic acid*: see quots. Hence **Thebola·ctate**, a salt of this acid.

1867 *N. Syd. Soc. Bienn. Retrospect* 477 Messrs. T. and H. Smith give directions for the preparation of thebolactic acid, a new body discovered by them in opium...The process depends on the ready solubility of the thebolactate of lime. 1874 Garrod & Baxter *Mat. Med.* (1880) 191 Thebolactic acid ($C_3H_6O_3$), isomeric, or perhaps identical with lactic acid. Turkey opium contains 2 per cent. of it.

‖ **Theca** (þī·kă). Pl. **thecæ** (þī·sī). [L., ad. Gr. θήκη case, cover.]

**1.** A receptacle, a cell; *spec.* (*Eccl.*) = Burse 1 b.

1662 J. Bargrave *Pope Alex. VII* (1867) 121 Some of these underground streets were for their burials,..the corps were ..immurall'd in *thecas*, or, as it were, in hollow shelves dug into the wall. 1682 Lister tr. *Gœdart's Insects* 95 In this Nest they [Bees] make a *Theca*, or small Cell...Every Bee lays 9. little Worms in this *Theca*, or Cell.

**2.** *Bot.* A part of a plant serving as a receptacle; a sac, cell, or capsule; *spec.* (*a*) an anther cell, containing pollen; (*b*) a vessel containing spores in various cryptogamous plants, as the capsule of a moss, the sporangium of a fern, or the fructification in certain lichens.

1676 Grew *Anat. Flowers* ii. iii. § 9 These Parts [anthers] are all hollow; each being the Theca or Case of a great many extream small Particles. 1829 Loudon *Encycl. Pl.* (1836) 874 *Musci*...Thecæ many-seeded, solitary, furnished with an operculum and columella. *Ibid.* Gloss., *Thecæ*, the cases that contain the sporules of Cryptogamic plants. 1830 Lindley *Nat. Syst. Bot.* 307 *Sporules*, which are enclosed in particular cases called *thecæ*. 1880 Gray *Struct. Bot.* vi. § 6 (ed. 6) 251 The best technical name for anther-sac is that of *Theca*. 1897 Willis *Flower. Pl. & F.* I. 77 The anther has typically two main lobes or thecae.

**3.** *Zool.* and *Anat.* A case or sheath enclosing some organ or part: as

(*a*) the horny case of an insect pupa; (*b*) the loose sheath investing the spinal cord; (*c*) one of the fibrous sheaths in which the digital tendons glide; (*d*) the sheath of the proboscis of dipterous insects; (*e*) a cup-like or tubular structure in corals, containing a polyp.

1665-6 *Phil. Trans.* I. 89 It becomes a *Papilio* or Butter-fly, in the *Theca* or Case. 1670 *Ibid.* V. 2099 Some of these Maggots I took out of their *Theca* or bagg. 1807 *Med. Jrnl.* XVII. 308 The theca or sheath which encloses the femoral artery, nerve and vein. 1826 Kirby & Sp. *Entomol.* III. xxxiv. 467 In all [mouths of Dipterous insects], the *theca* or sheath is present. 1840 E. Wilson *Anat. Vade-M.* (1851) 239 In the thecæ of the fingers several small tendinous fasciculi are generally found. 1875 Huxley in *Encycl. Brit.* I. 130/2 In the simple aporose corals the calcification of the base and side walls of the body gives rise to the cup or *theca*. 1899 *Allbutt's Syst. Med.* VII. 536 The water-cushion which surrounds the cord within the spinal theca.

Hence **The·cal** *a.*, of, pertaining to, or of the nature of a theca; **The·cate** *a.*, having a theca, sheathed.

1847 Druitt *Surg. Vade M.* (ed. 4) 544 The tendinous whitlow, or thecal abscess. 1861 J. R. Greene *Man. Anim. Kingd., Cœlent.* 160 A thecal corallum, in other *Actinozoa*, at length comes to be formed. 1876 Tomes *Dental Anat.* 107 The tissue whence the dentine papillæ arise blends insensibly with that making up the substance of the thecal fold. 1877 Huxley *Anat. Inv. Anim.* iii. 159 The thecal canals of the Millepores. 1891 *Cent. Dict.*, Thecate.

**Thecaphore**, etc., erron. forms: see Theco-.

**Theche, theche**, obs. forms of Thatch.

**Theci-** (þī·si), combining form of L. theca, esp. in botanical words. **Theci·ferous** [-ferous], † **Theci·gerous** [-gerous] *a.*, bearing thecæ or asci. **The·ciform** *a.*, having the form of a theca.

1860 Mayne *Expos. Lex.*, Thecigerous. 1877 Huxley *Anat. Inv. Anim.* iii. 152 The theciform projections of the Graptolite stem. 1891 *Cent. Dict.*, Theciferous.

‖ **Thecitis** (þīsai·tis). *Path.* [f. Thec-a + -itis.] Inflammation of a tendon and its sheath; = Tenosynovitis. 1857 in Dunglison *Med. Lex.*

‖ **Thecium** (þī·siŏm). *Bot.* [mod.L., a. Gr. θηκίον, dim. of θήκη Theca.] The Hymenium of a lichen.

1882 J. M. Crombie in *Encycl. Brit.* XIV. 554/1 The two principal parts of which an apothecium consists are the *hypothecium* and the *thecium*. *Ibid.* 554/2 The thecium, or as it is more frequently termed the *hymenium*, is that part of the apothecium which contains the organs of the fruit.

**Theck**, Sc. variant of Theek, to thatch.

**Theclan** (þe·klăn), *a. Entom.* [f. mod.L. *Thecla*, generic name + -an.] Belonging to the genus *Thecla* of butterflies, comprising the Hair-streaks.

1884 *Stand. Nat. Hist.* (1888) II. 478 Among the grandest of the group are *T[hecla] coronata*, *T. imperialis*, and *T. regalis*, which are Brazilian species, and, as their names imply, are the regnant beauties of the Theclan court.

**Theco-** (þīko), erroneously **theca-**, combining form of Gr. θήκη case, receptacle (see Theca), used in Botany and Zoology. **Thecoda·ctyl(e** [Gr. δάκτυλος digit], *a.* having thick toes whose transverse scales furnish a sheath for the claw, as in some lizards; *sb.* a gecko of this type (Ogilvie 1882); so **Thecoda·ctylous** *a.* **Thecoglo·ssate** *a.* [Gr. γλῶσσα tongue], having a smooth tongue furnished with a sheath, as the *Thecoglossæ*, a group of lizards. **The·cophore** [-phore], (*a*) a surface or receptacle bearing a theca or thecæ (Webster 1864); (*b*) the stalk which in some flowers supports the ovary; = Gynophore 1. **Thecoso·mate, Thecoso·matous** *adjs.* [Gr. σῶμα body], belonging to the *Thecosomata*, a group of pteropods having the body sheathed in a mantle-skirt; so **The·cosome**, a thecosomatous pteropod. **The·cospore**, a spore produced in a theca, an ascospore; hence **Theco·sporal** *a.*, pertaining to a thecospore; **The·cospored, Theco·sporous** *adjs.*, having thecospores. **The·costome** [Gr. στόμα mouth], the orifice of the hydrotheca in calyptoblastic hydroids. **Theco·stomous** *a.*, having the sucking parts of the mouth enclosed in a sheath.

1891 *Cent. Dict.*, *Thecodactylous .. *Thecoglossate. 1832 Lindley *Introd. Bot.* i. ii. § 10. 139 Sometimes the ovarium..is seated upon a long stalk... This stalk is often called the *thecaphore or gynophore. 1878 Bell *Gegenbaur's Comp. Anat.* 321 The velum is largest in the Gastropoda and the *thecosomatous Pteropoda. 1888 Pelseneer in *Challenger Rep.* XXIII. 2 The Habits of the Thecosomatous Pteropods. 1890 *Athenæum* 12 July 66/2 The *thecosomes being tornatellids modified for a swimming life. 1891 *Cent. Dict.*, *Thecasporal. 1858 Carpenter *Veg. Phys.* § 405 The Lichens produce conceptacles,.. called apothecia,..which develope in their interior little bodies, called *thecaspores. 1882 J. M. Crombie in *Encycl. Brit.* XIV. 555/2 In various *thecaspored fungi. 1879 Webster *Supp.*, **Thecasporous*. 1883 *Challenger Rep.* VII. xx. 7 On either side of the hydrotheca, nearly on a level with its orifice or *thecostome. 1891 *Cent. Dict.*, *Thecostomous.

**Thecodont** (þī·kŏdǫnt), *a.* and *sb. Zool.* [f. Theco- + Gr. ὀδούς, ὀδοντ- tooth.] **a.** *adj.* Of or belonging to the *Thecodontes*, an extinct family of saurians having the teeth fixed in sockets in the jaw-bone. **b.** *sb.* A saurian having this character.

1840 Owen *Odontogr.* ii. iv. § 110. 266 (*heading*) Thecodonts. *Ibid.*, A third mode of fixation is presented by some extinct Saurians,..the teeth being implanted in sockets..: these may be termed the 'thecodont' Lacertians: the most ancient of all Saurians belong to this group. 1876 Page *Adv. Text-bk. Geol.* xv. 282 The thecodont saurians seem peculiar to the Permian. 1877 Le Conte *Elem. Geol.* iii. (1879) 404 In the coal, are also found now some Thecodont (socket-toothed) reptiles, allied to Crocodilians.

So **The·codontosau·rian**, *adj.* belonging to or characteristic of the thecodont saurians; *sb.* a member of this genus.

[1840 Owen *Odontogr.* ii. iv. § 112. 267 In the same formation as contained the jaw and teeth of the *Thecodontosaurus*.] 1869 Huxley in *Q. Jrnl. Geol. Soc.* XXVI. 44 The Thecodontosaurian ilium. *Ibid.*, I shall speak of the bones as those of Thecodontosaurians.

‖ **Thecomedu·sa.** *Zool.* [f. Theco- + Medusa.]

1878 Bell *Gegenbaur's Comp. Anat.* 98 The Thecomedusæ are polypoid Coelenterata provided with a test, and allied to the Hydriformes.

**Theddre**, obs. form of Thither.

† **Thede.** *Obs.* Forms: 1 þiod, 1–3 þeod, 2 þiode, 2–4 þeode, þede, 4–5 thede, (4 þedd, 5 *Sc.* theid). [OE. *þiod, þéod* = OS. *thioda, thiod*, OFris. *thiade*, OHG. *diota*, MHG. *diet*, ON. *þióð*, Goth. *þiuda*:—OTeut. **þeudō*, by Verner's Law:—Indo-Eur. **teutā-* fem.; cf. Lith. *tautà*, OIr. *túath*, Osc. *touto*, Sabine *touta* people.]

**1.** A people, race, nation.

855 *O. E. Chron.* an. 627 Her Edwine kyning wæs ȝefulwad mid his þeode on Eastron. *a* 1000 *Hymns* viii. 9 (Gr.) We þe..þanciað, þioda waldend. *c* 1000 *Ags. Gosp.* Luke xxi. 10 Þeod arist aȝen þeode. *a* 1175 *Cott. Hom.* 237 Þurh false godes þe ælc þiode ham selfe macede. *c* 1175 *Lamb. Hom.* 115 Wa þere þeode þer þe king bið child. *c* 1200 Ormin 3438 Tatt þeod wass hæþene þeod. *Ibid.* 16057 To spekenn wel Wiþþ alle þede spæchess. *c* 1250 *Gen. & Ex.* 2302 Quene he comen in vnkinde ðeden. *a* 1300 *Cursor M.* 4177 (Cott.) Marchands of an vncuth thede. *c* 1400 *Melayne* 1008 The chefe of hethyn thede.

**b.** *pl.* (biblical.) The nations, the Gentiles.

*c* 975 *Rushw. Gosp.* Matt. x. 18 To kyningum & ȝeroefum ȝe bioþ ȝelædde..in cyþnisse [h]eora & þeodum. *c* 1000 Ælfric *Hom.* I. 96 Se þeoda lareow Paulus. *a* 1175 *Cott. Hom.* 241 Ur hlaford sanctes paulus þe is þeoden lareaw.

**2.** The district occupied by a people; a country.

*c* 888 K. Ælfred *Boeth.* xxxv. § 7 An hearpere wæs on ðære ðiode ðæt Đracia hatte. *a* 1300 *Cursor M.* 5792 (Cott.), I sal þam bring..In-till a land, a wonsun thede. 13.. *K. Alis.* (Bodl. MS.) 7947 Þou shalt haue Perce, & Mede, And Babiloyne, þis riche þede. *a* 1400-50 *Alexander* 1803 In thorps & in many thede þar ȝe þurȝe ride. *c* 1470 *Golagros & Gaw.* 174 All the wyis and welth he weildis in theid.

**3.** *Comb.*, as **thede-folk** (OE. **þéod-folc*), people of a country, natives. (The OE. combinations and derivatives were very numerous.)

*c* 725 *Charter of Nunna* in Birch *Cart. Sax.* I. 211 On ðeodweȝ norð ofer þone weȝ. *a* 1000 *Boeth. Metr.* xxix. 92 Þæt hi þiowien swilcum þiodfruman. *c* 1205 Lay. 26494 Þusende of þan þeod-folke.

**Thede**, obs. form of Thead.

**Thedam, thedom**, varr. Theedom *Obs.*

**Theder, -ere, -ir(re, -ur, -yr**, obs. ff. Thither.

† **Thee**, *sb. Obs. rare*⁻¹. [f. Thee *v.*¹] *Evil thee*: Evil speed; bad luck. (Cf. Theedom b.)

1509 Barclay *Shyp of Folys* (1570) 25 Downe he commeth with an euill thee.

**Thee** (ðī, ði, ðĭ), *pers. pron.* Forms: 1 (acc.) þec (*Northumb.* ðeh, ðech); 1–6 (dat. and acc.) þe, 3 (te), þeo, 3–4 þi, 4–5 þee, 4–7 the, 4– thee (7 *dial.* they). For mod. dialect forms see *Eng. Dial. Dict.* [(1) Acc. OE. *ðec, ðeh*, later *ðē, þē* = OFris. *thi*, OS. *thic, thî* (MDu. *di*, MLG. (*dik, dek*) *dî*, LG. *dî*), OHG. *dih* (MHG., Ger. *dich*), ON. *þik* (Norw. *deg, de*, MSw. *þik, tik, tig, thig*, MDa. *thek, theg, deg*, Sw., Da. *dig*), Goth. *þuk*:—OTeut. **þekᵉ*, pre-Teut. **tege*: cf. L. *tē*, Gr. σέ, Doric τέ. (2) Dat. (later also acc.) OE. *ðē, þē* = OFris. *thi* (NFris. *di*, WFris. *dy*), OS. *thî* (MDu., MLG., LG. *dî*); (dative only) OHG. (MHG., Ger.) *dir*, ON. *þér* (Norw. *deg* (*der*), MSw. *þær, þir*, Sw., Da. *dig*), Goth. *þus*:—OTeut. **þez*, pre-Teut. **tes*. The original OE. acc. *ðec* still remained in Mercian in the 9th c. and in North Anglian (*þec, þeh, þech*) late in the 10th; in WSax. it ran together early with the dative *ðe, þe*, and thenceforth (as in LG. and Scand.) the two cases have had the same form, so that the direct and indirect object are only distinguishable by position or by context. On the original endings of the acc. and dat., cf. Me. The *e* was orig. short, but was lengthened under stress.]

**1.** The objective case of the pronoun Thou, representing the OE. accusative and dative.

As to restriction of use see note to Thou *pers. pron.* 1.

**a.** *Accusative*, as direct object of a verb.

*c* 825 *Lorica Prayer* in *O. E. Texts* 174 Đonne ȝehereð he ðec ðorh hiora ðingunge. *c* 888 K. Ælfred *Boeth.* xxvii. § 2 Ic asciȝe ðe..hwi þu swa maniȝfeald yfel hæfde? *c* 950 *Lindisf. Gosp.* Mark v. 31 Đu ȝesiist ðæt ðreat ðringende ðec. *c* 1160 *Hatton Gosp.* ibid., Þas meniȝeo..þrungen þe. *c* 1200 Ormin 670 To beldenn & to frofrenn þe ȝiff he þe seþ forrglopp-nedd. *a* 1225 *Ancr. R.* 98 Hwo haueð ihurt te, mi deore? *c* 1375 *Cursor M.* 5064 (Fairf.), I saghe þe [*Cott.* yow] neuer be-for þis day. 1382 Wyclif *Matt.* v. 41 Whoeuere constrayneth thee a thousand pacis, go thou with hym other tweyne. *c* 1440 *Jacob's Well* 258 Þe feende schal pursewe þe, & sle þe in soule. 1535 Coverdale 1 *Sam.* viii. 7 They haue not refused the, but me. 1548-9 (Mar.) *Bk. Comm. Prayer, Communion*, We praise thee, we blesse thee, we worship thee, we glorifie thee. *a* 1660 *Contemp. Hist. Irel.* (Ir. Archæol. Soc.) II. 157 They [= thy] credulitie bringe they [= thee] within distance of his reache. 1784 Cowper *Task* v. 460 Thee I account still happy. 1842 Tennyson *Locksley H.* 30 Dost thou love me, cousin?..I have loved thee long.

**b.** *Dative*, as indirect object = to thee; also in dependence on certain impersonal verbs.

*c* 825 *Vesp. Psalter* cxix. 3 Hwet bið sald ðe oððe hwet bið toseted ðe? *c* 1000 *Ags. Gosp.* John viii. 53 Hwæt þincð þe þæt þu sy? *c* 1200 Ormin 210 Hiderr amm icc sennd to þe þiss blisse þe to kiþenn. *a* 1225 *Ancr. R.* 12 Ich chulle scheawe þe soðlice hwat is God. *a* 1300 *Cursor M.* 4424 Ful iuel es yolden þe [*Gött.* ye] þi mede. *Ibid.* 20185, I sai it te [*v. r.* þe]. 1423 Jas. I *Kingis Q.* cxxix, Gif the ne list on lufe thy vertew set. *c* 1430 *Two Cookery-bks.* 6 As þe semyth best. 1584 R. W. *Three Ladies Lond.* in Hazl. *Dodsley* VI. 323 What avantageth it thee to win the world, and lose thy soul withal? 1610 Shaks. *Temp.* i. ii. 248 I haue..Told thee no lyes, made thee no mistakings. 1743 Francis tr. *Hor., Odes* i. xxxviii. 1, I tell thee, boy, that I detest The grandeur of a Persian feast. 1808 Scott *Marmion* vi. xiv, And, Douglas, more I tell thee here..I tell thee, thou 'rt defied! 1864 (*dial.*) Tennyson *N. Farmer, O. Style* 68 Git ma my aäle I tell tha.

**c.** As object of a preposition.

In OE. *accus.* or *dative*.

*c* 950 *Lindisf. Gosp.* Luke i. 35 Gaast haliȝ ofer-cymeð on ðeh [*Rushw.* ðec]. *c* 1000 *Ags. Gosp.* John iii. 26 Se ðe mid þe [*Lind.* ðec] wæs. *a* 1200 *Vices & Virtues* 35 Ȝif godd wuneð on ðe. *c* 1275 *Passion our Lord* 138 in *O. E. Misc.* 41 Þeyh alle of-schomed beo Ne schal me neuer schomye louered for þeo. 13.. *Cursor M.* 27483 If þou man gas þin offrand to mak, And þi broþer haf gain þi [*v. r.* þe] sak. 1470-85 Malory *Arthur* i. xxiii. 70 Ther maye no knyght ryde this way but yf he Iuste wyth the. 1535 Coverdale *Isa.* lx. 2 His glory shal be sene in the. 1592 Shaks. *Rom. & Jul.* iv. v. 57 By cruell, cruell thee, quite ouerthrowne. 1656 in *Jrnl. Friends' Hist. Soc.* (1911) VIII. 20 To..lay before yᵉ Henry Cromwell: who art Commander in Cheife ..the ground of my Sufferings. 1667 Milton *P. L.* iv. 35 To thee I call, But with no friendly voice, and add thy name. 1733 Pope *Ess. Man* iii. 31 Is it for thee the lark ascends and sings? 1820 Shelley *To Skylark* 1 Hail to thee, blithe Spirit! Bird thou never wert.

**2.** *Reflexive*: = thyself. **a.** *Accus.*, as direct object.

*c*950 *Lindisf. Gosp.* Matt. iv. 6 ȝif sunu godes arð ðu send ðeh [*Rushw.* þec] ufa hidune. *c* 1000 *Ags. Gosp.* ibid., Asend þe þonne nyðer. *a* 1225 *Ancr. R.* 104 Holt te i þine chaumbre. *a* 1300 *Cursor M.* 529 If þow wil þe vm-think. 13.. *Ibid.* 26575 Sua þou mate noght wasch þi [*v.r.* þee] wite. *a* 1518 SKELTON *Magnyf.* 303 Go shake the, dogge. 1560 BIBLE (Genev.) *Matt.* xvi. 23 Get thee behinde me, Satan. 1594 SHAKS. *Rich. III*, I. iii. 143 High thee to Hell..Thou Cacodemon. 1678 OTWAY *Friendship in F.* 26 Get thee gone for an Arch-wagg. 1887 *S. Cheshire Gloss.* 69 Get thee dressed wheil I wesh me.

**b.** *Dative*, as indirect object; or as object of a preposition.

*a* 1000 *Cædmon's Gen.* 518 (Gr.) Nim þe þis ofæt on hand. *a* 1100 *Leg. Rood* 15 Þu ȝetuȝe to þe ealle þa sawla. *c* 1300 *Harrow. Hell* (MS.L.) 103 Heouene ant erþe tac to þe. *c* 1470 HENRY *Wallace* I. 395 Thow sall haiff leiff to fysche, and tak the ma. 1599 SHAKS. *Much Ado* II. i. 20 Thou wilt neuer get thee a husband, if thou be so shrewd of thy tongue. 1611 BIBLE I *Kings* xx. 25 Number thee an armie like the armie that thou hast lost.

**c.** After some intr. verbs of motion and posture; esp. *sit*; see SIT *v.* 30.

1593 SHAKS. 3 *Hen. VI*, III. iii. 16 Be thou still like thy selfe And sit thee by our side. 1599 — *Much Ado* III. i. 1 Good Margaret runne thee to the parlour, There shalt thou finde my Cosin [etc.]. 1606 — *Ant. & Cl.* IV. vii. 16 Come thee on. 1867 E. WAUGH *Tufts* 252 Sit tho deawn. 1892 WRIGHT *Gram. Windhill* 120 Kum forəd lad ən sit ðe dān.

**3.** Used as *nominative*, instead of *thou*.

Often so used dialectally, and, in recent times, usually by Quakers, esp. with vb. in 3rd pers. sing.; but *thĕ* or *thă* unemphatic often represents both *thou* and *thee*.

*c* 1375 *Sc. Leg. Saints* vi. (*Thomas*) 617 Þe venys þat my god wrath wil be with me. *c* 1470 HENRY *Wallace* II. 93 Go hens, the Scot, the mekill dewill the speid. *a* 1590 *Marr. Wit & Wisd.* (1846) 12 Didest the nere se man before? 1596 SHAKS. 1 *Hen. IV*, I. ii. 127 How agrees the Diuell and thee about thy Soule? 1605 — *Lear* I. iv. 204 And yet I would not be thee, Nunckle. 1684 BUNYAN *Pilgr.* II. 83 What canst thee earn a day, quoth he? 1687 W. HITCHCOCK in *Jrnl. Friends' Hist. Soc.* IV. 74 If thee canst sell 250 acres of it & ye house. 1852 MRS. STOWE *Uncle Tom's C.* xiii, 'What does thee want, father?' said Rachel. *Ibid.* xvii, Friend, thee isn't wanted here'. 1861 E. WAUGH *Birtle Carter's T.* 15 An' mind te tells no lies abeawt th' lad i' thy talk.

**4.** As *sb.* **a.** The person or 'self' of the individual addressed. Cf. THOU *pron.* 2 a.

*c* 1600 SHAKS. *Sonn.* vi, That's for thy selfe to breed an other thee. 1831 CARLYLE *Sart. Res.* I. ix, A warm movable House, a Body round thy Body, wherein that strange Thee of thine sat snug. 1859 E. FITZGERALD *Rubáiyát* xxxiv, Then of the Thee in Me who works behind The Veil, I lifted up my hands to find A Lamp amid the Darkness.

**b.** The word itself as used in addressing a person; esp. in phr. *thee and thou*. Also *attrib.* in *thee and thou Quaker*.

1694 [see THOU 2 b]. 1774 J. ADAMS *Diary* 7 Sept., This plain Friend and his plain though pretty wife, with her Thees and Thous, had provided us the most costly entertainment. 1847 LONGF. *Evang.* II. v. 13 Her ear was pleased with the Thee and Thou of the Quakers. 1894 HALL CAINE *Manxman* 405 When he spoke it was always with the thees and thous and in the high pitch of the preacher. 1896 *Peterson Mag.* VI. 265/1 Whose head-master was Benjamin Hallowell, a 'thee' and 'thou' Quaker of the strictest sect.

† **Thee** (þī), *v.*[1] *Obs.* Forms: 1 **þion**, 1–3 **þeon**, 3–4 **þen**, **þe**, 4–5 **then**, 4–6 **the**, 5 **thene**, **theen**, 5–6 **þee**, (6 **thye**), 4– **thee**. *Pa. t.* 1 **þah**, **þaȝ**, **þæh**, 1–2 **þeah**, 1–3 **þeh**, 2–3 **þeaȝh**, 3 **þeȝ**, **þeu**, (5 **thee**); *pl.* 1 **þungon**; **þiȝon**; **þuȝon**. *Pa. pple.* 2–3 **þungen**; **þiȝen**; **þoȝen**, **þowen**, **þowuen**, 4 **thowen**. [OE. *þíon*, *þéon*, contr. from **þîhan* (:—**þîohan*, **þéohan*) = OS. *thîhan*, *thêh—thigun*, *githigan* (Du. *gedigen*), OHG. (*gi*)*dîhan*, *dêh—digun*, *digan* (MHG. (*ge*)*dîhen*, G. *gedeihen*), Goth. *þeihan—þáih—þaihun—þaihans* to thrive:—OTeut. **þinχ-*, earlier **þenχ-* (**þanχ-*, **þunχ-*) of the 3rd ablaut series :—Indo-Eur. root *tenk*. With the elimination of the nasal before χ the verb came in prim. Germ. to be assimilated to the 1st ablaut series (*ī—ai—i—i*); but traces of the primitive conjugation survive in the OS. pa. pple. *githungan*, and the OE. forms *þungon*, *-en*. The OE. contracted form *þéon* began to follow the inflexional type of *téon* :—**teuhan* (TEE *v.*[1]), whence *þéah*, *þuȝon*, *þoȝen*.]

**1.** *intr.* To grow; to thrive, prosper (*arch.* in 16th c. use).

*Beowulf* 8 He..weox under wolcnum, weorð-myndum þah. *c* 888 K. ÆLFRED *Boeth.* xix, Þeah hwa wexe..and þeo on eallum welum. *c* 1000 ÆLFRIC *Hom.* II. 104 His wæstmas ȝenihtsumlice þuȝon. *c* 1000 *Ags. Gosp.* Luke ii. 52 Se hælend þeah on wisdome and on ylde. *a* 1050 *Liber Scintill.* lxxxi. 221 Sume soþlice on æȝþrum þeoþ. *c* 1200 *Trin. Coll. Hom.* 161 And hit wacxs and wel þeaȝh. *Ibid.* 177 Here tuder swiðe wexeð and wel þieð. *c* 1250 *Gen. & Ex.* 2012 Vnder ioseph his welðe ðeȝ. *c* 1275 LAY. 24272 Þe borh suþþe ne þeh. 1297 R. GLOUC. (Rolls) 240 Þe child wax & wel iþeȝ [*v.rr.* thee, ythei]. *Ibid.* 7086 Þis chyld wax so wel & þeu. *c* 1300 *Beket* 149 He fond his sone..Þeoinge [*pr.* Theoinge] fair and manliche. *a* 1310 in Wright *Lyric P.* 23 Ʒef he beth thryven ant thowen in theode. 13.. *Pol. Rel. & L. Poems* 238 Ho þat me louit ssal þe no more. *c* 1400 *Gamelyn* 234 Come þou ones in my hond þou shalt neuer the. 1426 AUDELAY *Poems* 4 Thai schal have grace to thryve and thene. *c* 1440 *Promp. Parv.* 490/1 Theen, or thryvyn, *vigeo*. 1509 BARCLAY *Shyp of Folys* (1874) II. 94 [He] is seldome sen to thye. *a* 1518 SKELTON *Magnyf.* 862 Abusyon Forsothe I hyght;..That vseth me,—He can not thee. 1573 TUSSER *Husb.* (1878) 19 Giue ouer to sudgerne, that thinkest to thee.

**b.** In imprecations and asseverations.

*a* 1300 *Cursor M.* 5150 'Sais þou soth?' 'yaa, sa mot i the'. 13.. *Sir Beues* 2753 A swor, alse he moste þen, He nolde him neiþer hire ne sen. ? *a* 1366 CHAUCER *Rom. Rose* 1067 Wel yvel mote they thryve and thee, And yvel achyved mote they be. 1377 LANGL. *P. Pl.* B. v. 228 Ac I swere now, so the ik, þat synne wil I lete. *c* 1386 CHAUCER *Can. Yeom. Prol. & T.* 376 By cause our firne was nat maad of Beech, That is the cause, and oother noon, so theech. *c* 1425 *Seven Sag.* 1548 (P.) Quod the kyng, 'So mot I the, Astow wylt hyt schal bee. *c* 1450 *Mankind* 297 in *Macro Plays* 12 Gode let hym neuer thene! [*rime* sene]. 1586 FERNE *Blaz. Gentrie* 22 Full ill mought they both thee. 1598 E. GILPIN *Skial.* (1878) 19 (*Lydia*) So mote I thee thou art not faire, A plaine brownetta when thou art at best. ? *a* 1600 *Old Robin of Portingale* xiv. in Child *Ballads* III. (1885) 241/1 If it be not true,..God let me neuer thye. 17.. in Ritson *Songs* (1794) II. 132 He that spares, ne'er mote he thee. *a* 1800 in *Edinb. Mag.* June (1819) 527/1 But wearie fa' the fairy wicht..May he never thee.

**2.** *trans.* To cause to prosper; to prosper. *Obs.*

*c* 1250 *Prayer* in *Rel. Ant.* I. 22 Þe lavird þieh þe in hevirilk place.

Hence †**Thowen**, **þoȝen**, **þowun** *ppl. a.*, thriven; grown up, adult.

*c* 1200 *Trin. Coll. Hom.* 39 Mid-niht ðe bilimpeð to frumberdligges, hanecrau þe bilimpeð þowuene men. *Ibid.* 41 Ðese herdes..wakieð biforen euen, þanne þe childre wuel þewuen..he þo ful þoȝene turneð to godes bihouþe. *Ibid.* 127 Alse wat se he was þoȝen on wintre and on wastme.

**Thee** (ðī), *v.*[2] [f. THEE *pron.*] To use the pronoun 'thee' to a person: see THOU *v.* Also *to thee and thou* (cf. F. *tutoyer*). **a.** *trans.* **b.** *intr.* (or *absol.*). Hence **Thee·ing** *vbl. sb.*

**a.** 1662 TATHAM *Aqua Tri.* 6 Though I Thee Thee, and Thou Thee, I am no Quaker. *a* 1690 G. FOX *Jrnl.* (1827) I. 103, I was required to Thee and Thou all men and women, without any respect to rich or poor, great or small. *a* 1739 JARVIS *Quix.* I. IV. li, With the utmost arrogance he would thee and thou his equals and acquaintance. 1836 T. HOOK *G. Gurney* v, There I saw..two quaker children playing about the place, thee'ing and thou'ing each other, with perfect French familiarity. 1884 A. DOHERTY *N. Barlow* 28 Familiarly he 'thee'd' and 'thou'd' the men, And cheekily they 'thee'd' and 'thou'd' again.

**b.** 1679 [see THOU *v.* b]. 1696 C. LESLIE *Snake in Grass* p. xv, This was the Bottom upon which the Quakers first set up, to run down all worldly Honour..; to Thee and Thou; to call no Man Master, or Lord, and not to take off their Hats, or Bow to any. 1760 J. RUTTY *Spir. Diary* (ed. 2) 148 At meeting..was seen my insincerity in Theeing, inconsistent with my writing. 1894 DU MAURIER *Trilby* I. (1901) 19/2 There were ladies too *en cheveux*..some of whom thee'd and thou'd with familiar and friendly affection.

**Thee**, obs. and dial. form of THIGH.

† **Thee·dom, thedom.** *Obs.* Also 4 **þeodam**, 5 **thedam**, **-dame**, **þeedom**. [f. stem of THEE *v.*[1] + -DOM.] Thriving; prosperity.

1362 LANGL. *P. Pl.* A. x. 105 Þruft or þeodam with hem selden is I-seye. 1393 *Ibid.* C. VIII. 53 And ȝede a-bowte in my ȝouthe and ȝaf me to no þedom. *c* 1430 *How the Good Wife*, etc. 209 (*Babees Bk.* 47) Now þrift and þeedom mote þou haue. 1522 *World & Child* in Hazl. *Dodsley* I. 261 My thedom is near past.

**b.** *Evil theedom*, ill success, bad luck: used as a maledictory phrase.

*c* 1386 CHAUCER *Shipman's T.* 405 What! yuel thedam [*v.r.* thedom] on his Monkes snowte. *c* 1450 *Cov. Myst.* xiv. (Shaks. Soc.) 139 Evyl Thedom com to thi snowte!

**Theef(e**, obs. forms of THIEF.

**Theek, theik** (þīk), *v.* *Sc.* and *north. dial.* Forms: 4–7 **theke**, 5 **thicke**, 6 *Sc.* **thik**, **thyk**, 6–9 *Sc.* **theik**, **thick**, 7–9 **theak(e**, **thake**, 8–9 *Sc.* **theck**, **theek**. [A collateral form of THATCH *v.* in use before 1400, of somewhat uncertain history. Perhaps from OE. *þęccan*, the forms of the imperative *þece* and the 2nd and 3rd pers. sing. present *þecest*, *þeceð* being extended to the verb as a whole: cf. *streek*, Sc. and north. form of STRETCH, OE. *stręccan*.]

†**1.** *trans.* To roof (a building) *with* stone, slate, tiles, shingles, lead, or the like. *Obs.*

1387 *Charters &c. of Edinb.* (1871) 35 (St. Giles) The forsayde v chapellys sal be thekyt abovyn with stane. *c* 1400 MAUNDEV. (Roxb.) x. 38 A full faire kirk..thekid wele with leed. 1535 STEWART *Cron. Scot.* (Rolls) II. 568 Rycht clene thickit was than all this tour, Weill gilt with gold. *Ibid.* III. 190 Sanct Androis kirk..That thekit wes with coper in tha dais. 1559 *Burgh Rec. Edinb.* (1875) III. 57 To thik the southe syde of the towlbuyth with new sklait. 1572 *Satir. Poems Reform.* xxxiii. 192, I se ȝour tempills cassin downe and reuin: The maist part are bot theikit with the heuin. 1628 *Extracts Burgh Rec. Glasgow* (1876) I. 365 [To] theik the samyn [ruiff] with leid. 1710 SIBBALD *Hist. Fife* II. v. § 2. 78 They (as the Proverb has it) tirr'd the Kirk, to theek the Quire. 1777 J. ROBERTSON in McKay *Kilmarnock* (1880) 177 Water is gude for mony a purpose, although ye're a' aware we canna theek Kirks wi't.

**b.** *spec.* To cover the roof of (a house) *with* thatch of straw or the like; also, to protect the top of (a corn or hay rick) with straw laid so as to carry off the rain.

1399 *Mem. Ripon* (Surtees) III. 130 In vxx travis de stramine ordii emp. 5s.,..in salario j hominis tegentis,..thekand prædictam domum per v dies. *c* 1440 *Pallad. on Husb.* I. 474 Thy berne also..to thicke hit, thou ne lette. *c* 1450 *Life St. Cuthbert* (Surtees) 7649 And thekyd it with hay and thak. 1513 DOUGLAS *Æneis* VIII. xi. 30 Quhais rufis laitly full rouch thykyt war Wyth stra or gloy by Romulus the wycht. 1637–50 Row *Hist. Kirk* (Wodrow Soc.) 417 The fabrick of the kirk wes in so evill a condition, being theiked with heather. 1672 T. WHITTINGHAM *Diary* 30 Aug. in Best *Farm. Bks.* (Surtees) 138 *note*, Wheatley of Saiston ye theaker is to theake Leonords' Barn. 1721 RAMSAY *Bessy Bell & Mary Gray* i, They bigg'd a bower..And theck'd it o'er with rashes. 1863 MRS. TOOGOOD *Yorks. Dial.*, I want you to theak my rick. 1895 CROCKETT *Men of Moss-Hags* 283 The roof was daintily theeked with green rushes and withes.

**2.** *transf.* To cover in general (but often with allusion to thatching a roof).

1667 in Campbell *Balmerino* (1899) 414 To men that thickit a holl in the kirk with divite. 1719 RAMSAY *To Arbuckle* 117, I theck the out, and line the inside Of mony a douce and witty pash. *a* 1800 *Twa Corbies* iv. in Scott *Minstr. Scot. Bord.*, Wi' ae lock o' his gowden hair, We'll theek our nest when it grows bare. *a* 1810 TANNAHILL *Rab Roryson's Bonnet* Poems (1846) 116 This bonnet that theekit his wonderful head. 1896 CROCKETT *Cleg Kelly* xlii. 283 A pump theekit frae the frost wi' strae rapes.

**3.** *absol.* or *intr.* (from 1 or 2).

*a* 1518 SKELTON *Magnyf.* 1027 For it is I that other whyle Plucke down lede and theke with tyle. 1876 *Whitby Gloss.* s. v., 'You mun theeak weel, this caud weather', put on extra clothing.

Hence **Thee·ked**, **-it** *ppl. a.*, thatched; **Thee·king** *vbl. sb.*, the action (*concr.* the material or product) of thatching; *ppl. a.*, that thatches or covers.

1792 BURNS *Bessie & her Spinnin Wheel* ii, On ilka hand the burnies trot, And meet below my *theekit cot. *a* 1801 R. GALL *Poems* (1819) 28 She reached the theeked byre. 1393 *Regist. de Aberbrothoc* (Bann.) II. 43 For the quhilkis *thekyn and gutteryn the abbot..sal pay till hym xxxv marcis. 1579 *Burgh Rec. Edinb.* (1882) IV. 104 Wynd tycht, watter tycht, in thyking, slating,..and vther necessaris 1617 *Mem. St. Giles', Durham* (Surtees) 47 To Nycholas Sparke for thekin 4 days, viij a day. *a* 1835 HOGG *Tales, Sheph. Cal.* xvii, Bread for the belly and theeking for the back. 1846 BROCKETT *N. C. Words* (ed. 3) s. v. *Theaker*, A 'theaking snow' quietly but continuously falling, so as to cover thickly, as a thatch does, a house.

**Theeker** (þī·kəɹ). *Sc.* and *n. dial.* [f. THEEK *v.* + -ER[1].] A thatcher; in early use, a roofer of houses.

14.. *Voc.* in Wr.-Wülcker 650/27 *Hic architector*, thekare. 1483 *Cath. Angl.* 382/2 A Theker, *architector*, *tector* (A.). 1554–5 *Burgh Rec. Edinb.* (1871) II. 360 Item, to ane thekar to theik the thre choippis,..xijs. 1658 *N. Riding Rec.* VI. 4 To a Theaker by the day...With meate 6d. Without meate 12d. 1887 J. SERVICE *Dr. Duguid* I. xx. 132 Robin Rigging the theeker. 1904 in *Eng. Dial. Dict.* (from Caithness to N. Lincolnsh.).

**Theeself** (þe self, etc.): see THYSELF.

**Theetsee**, var. THITSI, black-varnish tree.

† **Thef.** *Obs. rare.* In 3 **ðef.** [a. ON. *þefr* smell, mod.Icel. *þefur*, Fær. *tev*, Norw. dial. *tev*, Sw. dial. *täv*, Da. *tǿv*. Cf. THEVE *v.*] A smell.

*c* 1250 *Gen. & Ex.* 3340 To dust he it [the manna] grunden and maden bread, ðat huni and olies ðef he bead.

**Theft** (þeft). Forms: *α.* 1 **þéofð**, **þíefð**, **þýfð**; 2–4 **þeofþe**, **þefþe**, 3–5 **þufþe**(*ü*), 4 (*Ayenb.*) **þiefþe**, **þyefþe**, 5 **thifthe**. *β.* 1 **þýft**, **þéoft**, 4–5 **þift**, **þeft**, 4–7 **thift**, 5 **thyft**, 6 **theaft**, **thieft**, 4– **theft**; 3–5 **þefte**, 4–6 **thefte**, (4 **þifte**, **þyfte**, 5 **theefte**, 6 **thifte**). [OE. WSax. *þíefð*, *þýfð*, later *þýft*, non-WSax. *þéofð*, later *þéoft*, = OFris. *thiufthe*, *thiufte* (obs. Du. *diefte*), ON. *þýfð*, later *þýft*, Goth. **þiubiþa* :—OTeut. **þeubiþā*, f. **þeuboz*, THIEF + suffix-*iþa* = L. *-itāt-em*: see -TH[1] b, -T[3] b. OE. showed two main dial. types: WSax. *þíeþþ*, later *þýfþ* with umlaut; non-WS. *þéofþ*. In both, final *þ* after *f* became *t* by dissimilation; *þeoft* became *þeft*, *theft*. In ME. the various forms often had final *-e* from the oblique cases; north. dial. and Sc. had *þift*, *þyft*, *thift* from ON. *þýfð*, *þýft*.]

**1.** The action of a thief; the felonious taking away of the personal goods of another; larceny; also, with *a* and *pl.*, an instance of this.

*α.* 688–95 *Laws of Ine* c. 28 Be þeofes onfenge æt ðiefðe [*MSS. B., H.* ðyfðe]. *Ibid.* c. 73 ȝif hit bið niht eald þiefð, ȝebeten þa þone gylt þe hine ȝefengon. 695–6 *Laws of Wihtræd* c. 25 ȝif man leud ofslea an þeofðe, licge buton wyr-gelde. *c* 1000 *Sax. Leechd.* III. 186 Þyfð ȝestrangað. *c* 1175 *Lamb. Hom.* 13 Ne do þu þeofðe. *a* 1225 *Ancr. R.* 202 Þe Vox of ȝiscunge haueð þeos hweolpes: Tricherie & Gile, Þeorðe, Refiac. *c* 1290 *Beket* 445 in *S. Eng. Leg.* I. 119 Ʒif a clerk hath ane Man a-slawe, oþur strong þeffþe i-do. 1297 R. GLOUC. (Rolls) 10361 Þe king..let prisouns vorþ bringe, þat uor þufþe were inome, & uor oþer þinge. 1340 *Ayenb.* 37 Þe oþer boȝ of auarice ys þyefþe. 1393 LANGL. *P. Pl.* C. III. 92 In bargeyns and in brocages with þe borghe of þufþe [*v.rr.* þefþe, þefte]. *a* 1450 *Knt. de la Tour* (1906) 60 The theef dothe..delite hem in thifthe tille thei be taken and putte to dethe.

*β.* *c* 1250 *O. Kentish Serm.* in *O. E. Misc.* 31 Þo grete sennen þet biedh diadliche Ase so is..þefte. *a* 1300 *Cursor M.* 15973 Iudas..Of his thift and his felunni, His moder al he tald. 1382 WYCLIF *Matt.* xv. 19 Of the herte gon out yuel thouȝtis, mansleayngis, auoutries, fornicaciouns, theftis. 1387 TREVISA *Higden* (Rolls) V. 383 Mauricius.. fondede to forbede his knyȝtes þifte [*v.rr.* þefþe, þeofþe]. *c* 1450 *Brut* 443 For treason & for þift þat thei had done to þe Kynge & to his liege peple. 1489 CAXTON *Faytes of A.* IV. ix. 251 To haue committed a smal theefte. 1552 HULOET, Theaft in stealynge cattell, *abigeatus*. 1570 LEVINS *Manip.* 52/44 Theft, *furtum*. *Ibid.* 118/5 Thift, *furtum*. 1577 HOLINSHED *Chron., Hist. Scot.* I. 440/1 Accused of theft, and of receiuing and maintening of theeues. 1605 SHAKS. *Mach.* II. iii. 151. 1629 SIR W. MURE *True Crucifixe* 1133 To hide the thift.

1771 *Junius Lett.* lxv. (1820) 328 The thief was taken in the theft. 1909 *Q. Rev.* July 176 His borrowings were not thefts but prolific suggestions.

† **b.** *By theft*, stealthily, furtively, by secret craft. *Obs. rare*⁻¹.

*c* 1470 HENRY *Wallace* XI. 592 Thai be thyft hecht to put Wallace doun.

**2.** *concr.* That which is or has been stolen; the proceeds of thieving. Now *rare*.

962–3 *Laws of Edgar* IV. c. 2 § 2 To ðy þæt..þeof nyte, hwær he þyfþe [*MS. C.* þeofte] befæste. *c* 1175 *Lamb. Hom.* 57 Ne þu naȝest for to stele, Ne nan þefþe for to heole. *a* 1300 *Cursor M.* 6754 Þat he mai yeild again his thift, He sal be saald. 1340 *Ayenb.* 38 Þe þyeues be uelaȝrede byeþ þo þet parteþ of þe þyefþe. 1413 *Pilgr. Sowle* (Caxton 1483) III. v. 53 The theft which they haue stolen ye haue you self receyued. 1530 TINDALE *Exod.* xxii. 4 Yf the thefte [WYCLIF, that that he hath stoln] be founde in his hande alyue..he shall restore double. 1665 G. HAVERS *P. della Valle's Trav. E. I.* 145 We found the theft in his breeches ty'd to his naked flesh. 1864 KINGSLEY *Rom. & Teut.* x. 284 If a free man be caught thieving,..he replaces the theft, and pays 80 solidi, or dies.

**3.** *attrib.* and *Comb.*, as *theft-guilty* adj.

1613–16 W. BROWNE *Brit. Past.* II. i, What store of houres theft-guilty night had spent. 1907 *Westm. Gaz.* 19 Oct. 9/2 The Police Commissioner..gave it as his opinion that the theft theory was the most probable.

**Theft-boot, -bote.** *Obs.* exc. *Hist.* Also 3, 6 thef-, 6 theefe-, 6–7 theif(e-. [orig. *thef-bote*, f. *thef*, THIEF + *bote*, BOOT *sb.*[1] Afterwards altered (app. first by Scottish writers) to *theftbote*: cf. THEFTDOM, THEFTLY.

The early form suggests an OE. **þéof-bót*, but this has not been found; the nearest equivalent in the Ags. Laws being *þéof-gyld* in Laws of Æthelred I. c. 1 § 2, III. c. 4, and of Cnut II. c. 30 § 1.]

The taking of some payment from a thief to secure him from legal prosecution; either the receiving back by the owner of the stolen goods or of some compensation, or the taking of a bribe by a person who ought to have brought the thief to justice.

Nichols (1865) in *Britton*, in note to quot. 1292, suggests that the word 'originally signified the legal *bote* or composition for theft', and was then 'applied to the illegal compounding of theft, or taking money to maintain or connive at such offenders'. But all our quotations refer to illegal payment, a form of compounding a felony.

α. 1284 *Stat. Wall.* an. 12 Edw. I, c. 4 De Thefbote, hoc est de emenda furti capta sine consideracione Curiæ Domini Regis. 1292 BRITTON I. xxi. § 11 Et puis soit enquis de ceux qi ount pris thefbote. 1369 *Liber Assisarum* § 5 (1606) 258 b, Et les Iustices disoient q' vn home q' reprist son chattel emblee dun laron ne fuit pas thefbote, eins thefbote fuit proprement ou vn home prist ses chattels dun laron de luy fauourer & mainteiner, et nemy auterment. 1579 *Expos. Termes Law* 177 b/2 *Thefbote*, is when a man taketh any goodes of a theefe to fauour and mainteine him. And not when a man taketh his owne goodes that were stollen from him &c.

β. *a* 1450 *Sc. Acts Robt. I*, c. 9 (1844) I. 109/2 (*heading*) Of þe takyn of thyftbute [*orig.* rechatum de latrone]. 1515 *Sc. Acts Jas. V* (1814) II. 282/2 Gif this complenar..wald concord with the said theif and tak thiftbute and put him fra the Law, in that caice he sall vnderly the Law. 1597 [see next]. 1619 DALTON *Country Just.* cviii. (1630) 288 Some other seeme to take this for theeftboot and so to be punishable..onely by ransome and imprisonment. 1678 SIR G. MACKENZIE *Crim. Laws Scot.* I. xx. § i. (1699) 106 Theft-boot is committed by securing a Thief against the punishment due by Law. 1745 *Univ. Spect.* 10 Aug., Yorkshire Tom was committed to Clerkenwell-Bridewell..for Theft-boot, accepting of 17 Guineas and a half, not to prosecute John Ditcher, a notorious Pick-pocket. 1769 BLACKSTONE *Comm.* IV. x. 133 The offence of theftbote, which is where the party robbed not only knows the felon, but also takes his goods again, or other amends, upon agreement not to prosecute. 1814 SCOTT *Wav.* xv, The Bailie opined that this transaction would amount to theftboot, or composition of felony. 1885 *Law Times* LXXX. 115/2 The offence of compounding a felony was really the old crime of theft-bote.

**The·ftdom.** *Sc.* [Altered from **thefdom*, THIEFDOM.] The action or practice of stealing; theft; thievery.

1566 *Sc. Acts Jas. I*, c. 154 That nouther Lord of Regalitie, Schiref, Barrone, na vthers sell ony theif, or fyne with him of thiftdome done [*Record ed.* (1814) of thift done]. 1597 SKENE *De Verb. Sign.* s.v. *Bote*, Thieft-bote..quhen ony sellis onie thiefe, or finis with him for thieft-dome done, or to be done. 1854 MRS. OLIPHANT *Magd. Hepburn* I. 221 Gentle or simple maunna tell me that God's will is for villany and theftdom.

† **The·ftfully**, *adv. Obs. rare.* In 5 thift-. [f. THEFT + -FUL + -LY[2].] By stealth: = THEFTLY.

*c* 1400 *Sc. Trojan War* II. 1391 Vlixes..frome Troy is passit thiftfully With all þaim of his company.

**Thefthorn**, variant of THEVE-THORN *Obs.*

**The·ftless**, *a. rare.* [f. THEFT + -LESS.] **a.** That is not a theft. **b.** Not liable to be stolen.

1656 S. H. *Gold. Law* 68 How punisht he poor Achan for a theftless theft to see to? 1803 LEYDEN *Scenes Infancy* iv. 362 Teviot's sons..devoid of fear Bind to the rush by night the theftless steer.

† **The·ftly**, *adv. Sc.* and *north. dial. Obs.* [Altered from ME. *þefly*, THIEFLY.] By stealth, furtively.

*c* 1400 *Sc. Trojan War* II. 271 He gyffande thiftely ws till The palladinar at our will. *Ibid.* 623 Bycause þe palladinar was Out of þe temple tone thyftly. *a* 1485 *Promp. Parv.* (MS. S), Stelyngly (theftely), *ffurtiue, latrocinaliter.* 1498 *Reg. Privy Seal Scot.* I. 23/1, ix catell thiftly tane fra Thomas Sowtar. 1515 *Nottingham Rec.* III. 343 Reyseyvng off oder menys goodes theyftely.

**Theftuous** (þe·ftiu,əs), *a.* Originally *Sc.* Forms: α. 5 thiftwis, 5–6 thiftuis, 6 thiftewus. β. 6–7 thifteous, (7 thiefteous, 6 thiftius). γ. 6 thiftuus, 6–7 -uous, 7 theftous, 6– theftuous. [ME. *thiftwis*, f. THEFT + WISE *sb.*: cf. RIGHTEOUS from *rihtwis*.]

**1.** Of the nature of theft, thievish.

*c* 1400 [implied in THEFTUOUSLY]. 1491 *Reg. Privy Seal Scot.* I. 2 For the thiftwis owtputtin and awaytakin of the gudis. 1502 *Ibid.* 117/1 The thiftewus distruction of Johne Mans gudis. 1569 *Reg. Privy Council Scot.* II. 22 In thiftuous maner. 1593 *Sc. Acts Jas. VI* (1814) IV. 43/2 Pairtakaris in thair thifteous and wicked deidis. 1678 SIR G. MACKENZIE *Crim. Laws Scot.* I. xx. § 3 (1699) 108 Whosoever..assists them in their theftous Stealings. 1837 B. H. HODGSON in *Jrnl. Asiat. Soc. Bengal* VI. 367 It is..remarkable..for its theftuous propensities. 1880 MUIRHEAD *Gaius* Digest 506 Theftuous removal of property.

**b.** *transf.* Furtive, secret, sneaking.

1881 MASSON *De Quincey* xi. 138 A theftuous hope to amuse an hour for you after dinner.

**2.** Of the nature of a thief; given to theft.

1632 LITHGOW *Trav.* (1906) 363 The Hungarians have ever beene thiftuous, treacherous and false. 1859 M. NAPIER *Visct. Dundee* I. p. x, That theftuous animal a cheap bookseller's hack. 1883 *Century Mag.* XXVII. 183 Pettily theftuous, like the English gypsies. 1885 *St. James' Gaz.* 28 Mar. 6/1 No man ever saw the most theftuous sparrow ashamed of himself.

**b.** *fig.* Said of an animal or vegetable parasite.

1883 H. DRUMMOND *Nat. Law in Spir. W.* (ed. 2) 342 By means of its twining and theftuous roots it [*Sacculina*] imbibes automatically its nourishment ready-prepared from the body of the crab. 1883 R. TURNER in *Gd. Words* July 470/2 Some [plants]..living by theftuous practices alone.

**Theftuously** (þe·ftiu,əsli), *adv.* Chiefly *Sc.* [f. prec. + -LY[2].] In a theftuous manner; by or as by theft; stealthily, secretly.

*c* 1400 *Sc. Trojan War* II. 1637 Vlixes stall thiftuisly Away, as grauntand him gilty. 1567–8 *Reg. Privy Council Scot.* I. 609 The leid upoun the Cathedrall Kirkis..is thiftuouslie stowin and takin away. 1653 URQUHART *Rabelais* II. xiv, One little villainous Turkie..rogue came thiefteously to snatch away some of my lardons. 1880 MUIRHEAD *Ulpian* vii. § 2 If a husband have theftuously abstracted anything of his wife's in prospect of divorce. 1882 *Chamb. Jrnl.* XIX. 73 On a late occasion, the tomb of a noble family was theftuously rifled of its contents.

**Thefysch**, obs. f. THIEVISH. **Thegh**, obs. f. THOUGH, THIGH. **Thegither**, Sc. f. TOGETHER.

**Thegn** (þēⁱn). *Hist.* A form used by some recent historians to represent the OE. *þegn* (*þegen*, *þén*), THANE[1], in its sense of tenant by military service, and as a term of rank below the *ealdorman* or *eorl* and above the *ceorl*, corresponding in its various grades to the post-conquest *baron* and *knight*.

The purpose of this spelling is to distinguish the Anglo-Saxon from the Scottish use of THANE[1] (sense 4), made familiar by Shakspere.

1848 LYTTON *Harold* I. i, A Thegn forfeited his rank if he lost his lands. 1867 FREEMAN *Norm. Conq.* I. vi. 428 *note*, The signatures are no doubt those of local Thegns. 1874 STUBBS *Const. Hist.* I. vi. 155 Closely connected with the *gesith* is the *thegn*...The thegn seems to be primarily the warrior *gesith*; in this idea Alfred uses the word as translating the *miles* of Bede. But he also appears as a landowner. *Ibid.* 156 The name of thegn covers the whole class which after the Conquest appears under the name of knights, with the same qualification in land and nearly the same obligations. 1890 GROSS *Gild Merch.* I. 185 The merchant who made three voyages across the ocean at his own cost became a thegn.

Hence **The·gn-born** *a.*, of noble or gentle birth. **The·gndom**, the position or rank of thegn. **The·gnhood**, the condition or position of a thegn; the order of thegns, thegns collectively. **The·gn-land**, land held by a thegn. **The·gnly**, *a.* and *adv.* [OE. *þegnlic*, *-lice*], **a.** *adj.* of or pertaining to, or becoming a thegn; **b.** *adv.* in a manner becoming a thegn. **The·gn-right**, the legal rights and privileges of a thegn. **The·gn-ship** [OE. *þegnscipe*], the office, function, or position of a thegn (in various senses). **The·gn-wer** [OE. *þegnwer*], the wer-gild of a thegn. **The·gn-worthy** *a.*: see quot.

?*c* 935 *Dunsæte* c. 5 in Liebermann *Gesetze* (1903) 376 Sy he *ðeȝenboren, sy he ceorlboren. 1874 STUBBS *Const. Hist.* I. vi. 156 The thegn-born are contrasted with the ceorl-born. 1897 RAMPINI *Hist. Moray & Nairn* i. 46 The principle of comradeship..underlay English *thegndom. 1867 FREEMAN *Norm. Conq.* I. iii. 95 The growth of the *Thegnhood was, on the whole, depressing to the Ceorls. 1881 S. R. GARDINER *Introd. Stud. Eng. Hist.* ii. 34 The thegnhood pushed its roots down, as it were, amongst the free classes. *a* 1100 *Charter of Will. II* in *Tabularis Ramesiensi* clxxviii (Du Cange), Si terra de Isham..si vero *Teinlanda tunc fuisse inveniatur. 1628 COKE *On Litt.* 86 In the book of Domesday land holden by knight's service was called *Tainland.* 1876 DIGBY *Real Prop.* i. § 2 (ed. 2) 13 Tain- or thegn-land. This seems to mean not a particular species of tenure, but land which was as a fact held or owned by a king's thegn. *c* 1000 ÆLFRIC *Hom.* I. 586 Andreas..is ȝereht *ðeȝenlic. *a* 1038 *Charter of Eanwene* in Kemble *Cod. Dipl.* IV. 55 Heo..to ðam þeȝnon cwæð: Doð þeȝnlice and wel! Abeodað mine ærende to ðam ȝemote. 1876 FREEMAN *Norm. Conq.* V. xxiv. 450 The words of Eanwene, when she bade the Scirgemōt of Herefordshire to 'do thegnly and well. 1897 MAITLAND *Domesday & Beyond* 53 The men..are usually men of thegnly rank. *Ibid.* 165 Each..will be entitled to a thegnly wergild and swear a thegnly oath. *c* 1000 *Oaths* in Liebermann (1903) 464 Se mæssepreost..bið *þeȝenrihtes wyrþe. 1872 E. W. ROBERTSON *Hist. Ess.* 118 None could pretend to the privileges of full thegn-right without the possession of at least a township. 959–62 *Laws of Edgar* III. c. 2 Se dema, se ðe oðrum on woh ȝedeme..þolige a his *þeȝnscipes. *c* 1000 ÆLFRIC *Saints' Lives* (1890) II. 82 Beoð nu ȝehyrte..and healdað mid ðeȝen-scipe ða halȝan Godes æ. 1897 MAITLAND *Domesday & Beyond* 163 We begin by thinking of thegnship as a relation between two men...Then the thegnship becomes more than a relationship, it becomes a status. 1008 *Laws of Ethelred* V. c. 9 Þæt he sy *þeȝenweres & þeȝenrihtes wyrðe. 1874 STUBBS *Const. Hist.* I. vi. 155 The ceorl who has acquired five hides of land,..with other judicial rights, becomes *thegnworthy; his oath and protection and wergild are those of a thegn.

**Thei, þei**, obs. f. THEY, THOUGH.

**Theic** (þī·ik). [f. mod.L. *the-a* TEA + -IC 3: cf. THEISM[2].] One addicted to immoderate tea-drinking, or who suffers from such excess; a tea-drunkard.

1886 *Medical News* (U.S.) XLIX. 305 It is possible to be a 'theic' by profession or a 'theic' by passion. 1899 in *Syd. Soc. Lex.*

**Theid**, Sc. var. THEDE *Obs.* **Theie, theiȝe**, obs. f. THIGH. **Theif**, obs. f. THIEF.

**Theiform** (þī·ifǭm), *a.* [ad. mod.L. *theiform-is*, f. *thea* TEA: see -FORM.] Resembling the tea-plant.

1846 WORCESTER, *Theiform*, being in the form of tea. *Everest.* 1860 in MAYNE *Expos. Lex.*

**Theigh, þeiȝ, þeigh, þeiȝt**, obs. ff. THOUGH. **Theight**, obs. f. TIGHT. **Theign(e**, obs. ff. THANE, THEINE *v.* **Theik**, var. THEEK, to thatch. **Theil**, var. THAIL, tael. **Theim**, obs. ff. THEM. **Thein, þein**, obs. f. THANE; var. THYNE *Obs.*, thence.

**Theine** (þī·əin), *sb. Chem.* Also † thei·na. [f. mod.L. *thea* TEA + -INE[5].] A vegetable alkaloid, originally thought to be a principle peculiar to tea, but found to be identical with CAFFEINE.

1838 T. THOMSON *Chem. Org. Bodies* 295 Oudry has..announced that he has discovered in tea a salifiable basis, to which he has given the name of *theina.* 1842 *Penny Cycl.* XXIV. 304/2 Thein, or Theina, the peculiar principle of tea. 1853 URE *Dict. Arts* II. 834 Theine was obtained from coffee by the same process slightly altered. 1863–72 WATTS *Dict. Chem.* I. 707 Oudry.., in 1827, found in tea a crystalline substance, which he called theine. 1881 A. GRIFFITH in *Science Gossip* No. 203. 248 Tea contains from a half to five per cent. of theine.

† **Theine, theign**, *v. Obs.* Forms: 1–2 þeȝnian (1 ðæȝn-), þénian, 2 þeiȝnen, 3 þæinen, þeine(n. [OE. *þegnian*, f. *þeign*, THANE = ON. *þegna*, OHG. *deganōn*:—OTeut. **þegnōjan*, f. **þegno-* THANE.] *intr.* To be a servant or minister, to perform the duties of an office. With *dative*: To minister to, wait or attend upon, serve (a person); hence, quasi-*trans.*

*Beowulf* 561 Ic him þenode deoran sweorde swa hit ȝedefe wæs. *a* 900 tr. *Bæda's Hist.* III. xvii. [xxiii.] (1890) 232 Þa he ða moniȝ ȝer..biscophad þeȝnade. 971 *Blickl. Hom.* 33 He wæs soþ God, þe him englas þeȝnedon. *c* 975 *Rushw. Gosp.* Matt. viii. 15 Hiu aras & ðæȝnade heom. *c* 1000 *Ags. Gosp.* ibid., Ða aras heo & þenode him. *c* 1160 *Hatton Gosp.* ibid., Þa aras hyo & þeiȝnede hym. *a* 1175 *Cott. Hom.* 239 Mid al þan þe..laȝelice her him þenið. *c* 1175 *Lamb. Hom.* 109 Vnwurðe bið þe on elde þet him oðer men þenien. *c* 1205 LAY. 24595 Þer weoren a þusen cnihtes bald..þat þeineden þan kinge. *Ibid.* 24621 A þusend hire eode biuore..to þæinen þere quene. *a* 1225 *St. Marher.* 23 Þeos þreo in an iþeinet of engles. *a* 1250 *Prov. Ælfred* 499 in *O. E. Misc.* 132 Loke þat þu him þeine mid alle þeuues þines.

Hence † **Theining** (þeiȝnung, þening), ministration, service, office.

*c* 888 K. ÆLFRED *Boeth.* xxxvii. § 1 ȝif him mon þonne awint of pa claþas, & him oftihð þara þenunga & þæs anwealdes. *a* 900 tr. *Bæda's Hist.* II. xiv. [xvi.] (1890) 144 Næniȝ..hrinan dorste ne ne wolde buton his nedþearflicre þeȝnunge. 971 *Blickl. Hom.* 209 Englas beoð to ðeȝnunge gæstum fram Gode hider on world sended. *c* 1000 *Ags. Gosp.* Matt. xxvi. 19 Hiȝ ȝe-ȝearwodon him easter-þenunga. *a* 1175 *Cott. Hom.* 233 His water [us werpð] drench and fiscynn his fer manifeald þeninge.

**Their** (ðē^ə^ɹ), *poss. pron.* Forms: see below. [In existing form *their*, in Ormin *þeȝȝre*, a. ON. *þeir(r)a*, genitive pl. of simple demonst. *sá*, *sú*, *þat* (= OE. *se*, *séo*, *þæt*), used in ON. also as pl. of 3 pers. pron. The β-forms *þer*, *þar*, *þere*, etc., were prob. due mainly to the unstressed pronunciation of *their*, *thair*, confused sometimes with that of the adv. *þær*, *thare*, THERE; but they may sometimes represent OE. *þæra*, late form of *þára*, gen. pl. of *þá* those, substituted for the same case of the personal pronoun. Cf. THEM.]

**A.** Illustration of Forms.

α. 3 (*Orm.*) þeȝȝre, (teȝȝre), 4 þeir(e, þeyr, þayre, þayire, þaier, 4–5 þair, þaire, 5 þeire; 4–5 thaire, 5 thayre, 5–7 theire, theyr, 6 thayr, (thier, 6–7 yair), 4– *Sc.* thair, 5– their.

*c* 1200 ORMIN Ded. 84 All þurrh þeȝȝre sinne. *Ibid.* 3933 Þatt teȝȝre genge shollde ben þurrh hallȝhe sawless ekedd. 1303 R. BRUNNE *Handl. Synne* 874 Þarefore þat day al holy cherche þeyr seruyse of here þey werche. 13.. *Cursor M.* 794 (Cott.) Al þaier kin. *Ibid.* 21800 (Edin.) Mani man..Þate thair [*v. r.* þair] hele hauis getin bare. *a* 1340 HAMPOLE *Psalter* lxxvii. 51 He gaf..þaire trauails til þe locust.

*c* 1400 *Destr. Troy* 6738 Menelaus, and Thelamon, .. with theire tite batels. *c* 1440 *Pallad. on Husb.* I. 116 Oute of thaire [*v.r.* their] kynde eke seedes wol renewe. 1470–85 MALORY *Arthur* VII. xviii. 240 All they felle vpon their knees. 1522 *Rutland Papers* (Camden) 84 To putt all thier stuf of householde in euery office. 1538 STARKEY *England* I. iv. 120 To tempur and refrayne thayr malyce. 1549 *Baxter-bks. St. Andrews* (1903) 5 Thomas mortowne To be yair Decane. *a* 1568 *Wyfe of Auchtermuchty* xii, That straik dang baith thair harnis owt. 1620 SIR R. NAUNTON in *Fortescue Papers* (Camden) 139 Theyr general aunswer to his Majesties commandement. 1641 BEST *Farm. Bks.* (Surtees) 126 Holes, of that bignesse that one may thrust in theire neafe.

*β.* (1 þæra, þeora) 4 þer, þar, (þur), 4–5 þere, 4–6 þare, thar, 5 thare, 5–6 ther, 6–8 there, 7 thir (used by Milton as unstressed form of *their*).

[? *a* 1100 *O. E. Chron.* (Laud MS.) an. 449, On þeora dagum ʒelaðode Wyrtʒeorn Angelcin hider. *Ibid.* an. 1086, þæt þa godan men niman æfter þeora godnesse.] *c* 1330 R. BRUNNE *Chron.* (1810) 127 Þe popille him bisouht þer kyng forto be. 13.. *Cursor M.* 476 (Cott.) Þat sithen þar [*v. rr.* þair(e, her] sted was neuer sene. *Ibid.* 666 Bath he sette in þare [*v. rr.* þair(e, her] fre will. *Ibid.* 13900 Moyse þur lagh þaim broght. *c* 1400 *Destr. Troy* 12467 Trees, thurgh tempestes, tynde hade þere leues. *c* 1450 *Godstow Regr.* 491 Ther heires lawfully I-be-gote of ther bodies. *c* 1460 *Towneley Myst.* ix. 119, I shalle fownd to crak thare crowne. 1513 DOUGLAS *Æneis* IV. ix. 33–4 The ryning fludis thar wattir stop can scho mak, And eik the sternis turne ther cours abak. 1526 There [see B. 1]. 1533 BELLENDEN *Livy* II. xix. (S.T.S.) I. 205 Þai obeyit weill eftir to þare capitanis. 1663 CHAS. II in Julia Cartwright *Henrietta of Orleans* (1894) 139 They will shew there affections to me. 1671 MILTON *P. R.* II. 235 He ceas'd, and heard thir grant in loud acclaim. 1757 MRS. GRIFFITH *Lett. Henry & Frances* (1767) I. 56 Rogueries.. which, they thought, brought a disgrace on there bruteships.

**B.** Signification.

**1.** *Poss. adj.* (orig. *gen. pl.* of *pers. pron.*) Of, belonging, or pertaining to them; also *refl.* of or belonging to themselves.

*c* 1200 ORMIN 127 Naffdenn þeȝȝ þurrh þeȝȝre streon Ne sune, child, ne dohhterr. *c* 1330 R. BRUNNE *Chron. Wace* (Rolls) 1115 Brutus wiþ his folk.. wente þer weye. 1340 HAMPOLE *Pr. Consc.* 3884 Prelats.. Sal account yhelde.. Of þair suggets undir þair powere. 1526 TINDALE *Matt.* vi. 5 Vereley I saye vnto you they have there rewarde. 1589 PUTTENHAM *Eng. Poesie* I. vi. (Arb.) 27 Vnder the conduict of Totila and Atila and other their generalles. 1617 MORYSON *Itin.* II. 219 Consider the inward motiues of their crauing mercy. 1640 tr. *Verdere's Rom. of Rom.* I. xviii. 78 With that they tooke their leaves of her. 1774 GOLDSM. *Nat. Hist.* (1776) VI. 222 The great agility of these animals prevents their often being taken. 1797 GODWIN *Enquirer* I. vi. 41 We must dwell upon their every word. 1847 DE QUINCEY *Orthogr. Mutineers* Wks. 1860 XIV. 105 When.. he [Milton] wishes to direct a bright jet of emphasis upon the possessive pronoun *their*, he writes it as we now write it. But when he wishes to take off the accent, he writes it *thir*. [Cf. A. *β.* 1671.] 1853 M. ARNOLD *Empedocles* II. 19 With men thou canst not live; Their thoughts, their ways, their wishes, are not thine. 1858 O. W. HOLMES *Aut. Breakf.-t.* iv, Long after the frost and snow have done their worst with the orchards. 1864 TENNYSON *Aylmer's F.* 383 These old pheasant-lords.. Who had mildew'd in their thousands, doing nothing Since Egbert.

**b.** *Obj. gen.* Of (for, to) them. (Cf. HIS B. 2.)

1553 T. WILSON *Rhet.* (1580) 77 For a tyme your grace muche bewailed their lacke. 1579 [see 5]. 1590 SPENSER *F. Q.* III. iii. 43 Shall.. quite from off the earth their memory be raste? 1607 TOPSELL *Four-f. Beasts* (1658) 66 Yet can there not be in any nation a neglect of oxen; and their reverence was so great that, in ancient time [etc]. 1780 BECKFORD *Biog. Mem.* 108 Humanity pleads strongly for the abridgment of their relation. *Mod.* We mourn their loss.

**c.** Const. with gen. pl. of *all*, *both*: *their aller*, *their bother*, *beyre* (obs.); also *all their*, *their both*, *both their*, *each of their* (arch.): meaning 'of all, both, or each of them'. See ALL D. 4, BOTH 4 b, BO *a.* c.

*a* 1250 *Owl & Night.* 1584 Þe louerd.. Vareþ vt on þare beyre neode. *a* 1300 *Cursor M.* 18766 He stei up in þair aller sight. *c* 1380 WYCLIF *Serm.* Sel. Wks. I. 289 Þe fend .. is þer alþer kyng. *c* 1465 *Eng. Chron.* (Camden) 48 Be thair bothe assent. 1559 *Mirr. Mag.* (1563) D v, Lo thus fond hope dyd theyr both lyues abrydge. *a* 1568 [see A. *α*]. 1589 PUTTENHAM *Eng. Poesie* I. viii. (Arb.) 35 Saying thus in all their hearings. 1654–66 EARL ORRERY *Parthen.* (1676) 550 With both their helps I was carried to a Chamber. 1672 TEMPLE *Misc.* I. 64 According to each of their hunger or need. 1874 SWINBURNE *Bothwell* II. i, Mine and all their free and sovereign king.

**2.** Used of a thing with which a number of persons have to do, or which is assumed to be the common possession of a class; e. g. 'These boys know their Greek syntax'. Cf. HIS *poss. pron.* 1 b.

1785 BURNS *Halloween* ii, To burn their nits, an' pou their stocks, An' haud their Halloween. 1905 *Daily Chron.* 2 Sept. 3/1 All those who love their Devon and especially their Dartmoor.

**3.** Often used in relation to a singular sb. or pronoun denoting a person, after *each*, *every*, *either*, *neither*, *no one*, *every one*, etc. Also so used instead of 'his or her', when the gender is inclusive or uncertain. Cf. THEY *pron.* 2, THEM *pron.* 2; NOBODY 1 b, SOMEBODY. (Not favoured by grammarians.)

13.. *Cursor M.* 389 (Cott.) Bath ware made sun and mon, Aiþer wit þer ouen light. *c* 1420 *Sir Amadace* (Camden) l, Iche mon in thayre degre. 14.. *Arth. & Merl.* 2440 (Kölbing) Many a Sarazen lost their liffe. 1533 [see THEMSELVES 5]. 1545 ABP. PARKER *Let. to Bp. Gardiner* 8 May, Thus was it agreed among us that every president should assemble their companies. 1563 WINȜET *Four Scoir Thre Quest.* liv, A man or woman being lang absent fra thair party. 1641 [see A. *α*]. 1643 TRAPP *Comm. Gen.* xxiv. 22 Each Countrey hath their fashions, and garnishes. 1749 FIELDING *Tom Jones* VII. xiv, Every one in the House were in their Beds. 1771 GOLDSM. *Hist. Eng.* III. 241 Every person .. now recovered their liberty. *a* 1845 SYD. SMITH *Wks.* (1850) 175 Every human being must do something with their existence. 1848 THACKERAY *Van. Fair* xli, A person can't help their birth. 1858 BAGEHOT *Lit. Studies* (1879) II. 206 Nobody in their senses would describe Gray's 'Elegy' as [etc.]. 1898 G. B. SHAW *Plays* II. *Candida* 86 It's enough to drive anyone out of their senses.

†**4.** After a sb. (usually a proper name), instead of the genitive inflexion. Cf. HIS *poss. pron.* 4, HER *poss. pron.* 3*rd pl.* 3. *Obs.* or *rare arch.*

1551 ROBINSON tr. *More's Utop.* II. (1895) 172 Vntyll the vtopians their creditours demaunde it. 1600 *Shakspere's Titus A.* (title-p.), As it hath sundry times beene playde by the Right Honourable the Earle of Pembrooke,.. and the Lorde Chamberlaine theyr Seruants. 1642 FEATLEY *Dippers Dipt* (1646) 11 These travellers their report, and the testimony of those witnesses. 1642 DRUMM. OF HAWTH. *Skiamachia* Wks. (1711) 193 An answer to the parliament of England their declaration. 1667 PEPYS *Diary* 3 Jan., The House of Lords their proceedings in petitioning the King. 1681 R. BURTHOGGE *Argt. for Inf. Bapt.* (1684) 6 From the Children of Believers their being Abraham's Spiritual Seed.

**5.** Serving as antecedent to a following relative; equivalent to 'of those'. (Now usually avoided.)

1579 TOMSON *Calvin's Serm. Tim.* 134/2 Under their obedience whome God hath set ouer us. 1593 in J. Morris *Troubles Cath. Forefathers* Ser. III. (1877) 124 The chiefest favour must be procured by their means that have spoiled us before. 1655 FULLER *Ch. Hist.* IX. vii. § 14 This prediction .. yet miss'd their meaning, who both first reported, and most believed it.

†**6.** *absol.* = THEIRS. Cf. HER *poss. pron.* 3*rd pers. pl.* 4. *Obs.*

13.. *Cursor M.* 7465 (Cott.) A man o þair gains an of vr. 1592 G. HARVEY *Four Lett.* Wks. (Grosart) I. 216, I offer them my hande: and request their. 1618 WITHER *Motto* Ciij b, My clothing keeps me full as warm as their [*rime* are]. *Ibid.* C iv, And my esteeme I will not change for their.

**Their**(**e**, obs. ff. THERE, THIR *dem. pron.*, etc. = these.

† **Theirkin**, *a. Obs.* Their kind of, of their kind. (Cf. THAKIN, THISKIN.)

13.. *Cursor M.* 12346 (Cott.) Þe leons.. Honur him on þairkin wise [*F.* þaire kin; *G.* opon þair wise].

**Theirn**, a midl. and south. dial. form for THEIRS, on the analogy of *ourn*, *yourn*, *hisn*, *hern*. See *Eng. Dial. Dict.*

**Theirs** (ðēᵊɹz), *poss. pron.* Forms: 4–5 þayres, thayres, þair(e)s, thaires, 4–6 þairis, thairis, þeires, theires, 5 þers, therys, 5–6 theyr(e)s, theyr's, 6 therse, 8–9 their's, 5– theirs (*Sc.* thairs). [In form a double possessive, f. THEIR + -*es* (cf. *hers*, *ours*, *yours*). Of northern origin.] The form of the possessive pron. THEIR, used when no sb. follows, i. e. either absolutely or predicatively: That or those belonging to them. (= F. *le*, *la leur*, *les leurs*; G. *der*, *die*, *das ihrige*, *die ihrigen*.)

*a* 1300 *Cursor M.* 22578 (Edinb.) Vntil hir channel sal sco [the sea] turne And als til þayres [*Cott.* þairs, *Gött.* þairis, *Trin.* hores, *Laud* heris] ilk a burne. *Ibid.* 14132 A castel was bath his and þairs [*Fairf. & Gött.* þairis, *Trin.* þeires]. 13.. *R. Brunne's Chron. Wace* (Rolls) 11632 (Lamb. MS.) Þer nis no power to þeires liche [*Petyt MS.* non is þer pere ne to þam]. 13.. *E. E. Allit. P.* B. 1527 Heyred hem as hyȝly as heuen wer þayres. 1375 BARBOUR *Bruce* III. 745 That thai and thairis.. Suld be in all thing at his will. 1425 *Rolls of Parlt.* IV. 296/2 Yat any of the said parties, by yayme or yaires, procede. *c* 1430 *Life St. Kath.* (1884) 27 Folowe our faders lyke as þey blessedly folewede thayres. *c* 1440 *Generydes* 2989 This day is therys, A nother shalbe ourez. 1484 CAXTON *Fables of Æsop* v. iii, Telle to them that it is thyn and not theyrs. 1526 TINDALE *Matt.* v. 10 Theirs ys the kingdome off heven. 1674 BOYLE *Excell. Mech. Hypothesis* 7 [They] have no recourse to any peculiar agency of theirs to account for Eclipses. 1719 DE FOE *Crusoe* (1840) II. iii. 50 The island was theirs. 1853 WHEWELL *Grotius* III. 377 Theirs is the sounder opinion, who hold that such a grant continues. 1855 TENNYSON *Charge Light Brigade* ii, Their's not to make reply, Their's not to reason why, Their's but to do and die.

**b.** *Of theirs*: see OF 44.

*c* 1400 *Laud Troy Bk.* 3521 That he scholde euere be on of thaires. *c* 1400 LOVE *Bonavent. Mirr.* xxxix. (1908) 197 A frende of theires. 1555 EDEN *Decades* 134 A childe of therse. 1564 *Brief Exam.* ⁎⁎, This gaye booke of theyrs. 1692 BENTLEY *Boyle Lect.* ii. 63 These Atoms of theirs. 1831 *Society* I. ii. 16 An old acquaintance of theirs.

†**c.** Used instead of THEIR (*rare*); in 17–18th c. when followed by another possessive, e. g. 'theirs or our country', now 'their country or ours'. *Obs.*

*c* 1200 ORMIN 2506 And all onn ane wise fell Till eȝȝþerr þeȝȝress herrte. 1560 *Inchaffray Charters* (S.H.S.) 167 Als fre as.. ouris or thairis granitaris or chalmirlanis.. Josit brukit or intromettit with. 1562 TURNER *Baths* Ded., For theyrs sake that are honest and vertuous men. 1652 GAULE *Magastrom.* 274 The event fell out contrary to theirs, and according to the Apostles prediction. 1667 MARVELL *Corr.* lxxviii. Wks. (Grosart) II. 223 Upon the importation.. into theirs or our country. *a* 1774 GOLDSM. tr. *Scarron's Com. Romance* (1775) II. 54 He thought it both theirs and his duty to mount immediately.

†**d.** *Maugre theirs*: in spite of them, against their will: see MAUGRE *prep.* 1 c. *Obs.*

*c* 1330 R. BRUNNE *Chron. Wace* (Rolls) 12811 Maugre þeires he dide þem go In to þe wode. *Ibid.* 15336. 1375 BARBOUR *Bruce* x. 118 Magre thairis he it wan. 1480 *Coventry Leet Bk.* 427 Wheder we shall make the people to abide styll here.., magre theirs, or els let hem departe.

**Theirself, -selves**: see THEMSELVES III.

**Theis**, *adv.* [Cf. THIS *adv.* and DYCE.] THUS.

*a* 1818 M. G. LEWIS *Jrnl. W. Ind.* (1834) 5 Sea terms.—.. *theis* (*thus*) you are near enough.

**Theism** [1] (þī·iz'm). [mod. f. Gr. θε-ός god + -ISM. Cf. F. *théisme* (Voltaire).] **a.** *gen.* Belief in a deity, or deities, as opposed to *atheism*. **b.** Belief in one god, as opposed to *polytheism* or *pantheism*; = MONOTHEISM. **c.** Belief in the existence of God, with denial of revelation: = DEISM. **d.** *esp.* Belief in one God as creator and supreme ruler of the universe, without denial of revelation: in this use distinguished from *deism*.

1678 CUDWORTH *Intell. Syst.* Pref., Nor indeed out of a meer Partiall Regard to that Cause of Theism neither, which we were engaged in. 1711 SHAFTESB. *Charac.* (1737) II. 209, I consider.. that to be a settled Christian, it is necessary to be first of all a good theist. For theism can only be oppos'd to polytheism, or atheism. *a* 1774 TUCKER *Lt. Nat.* (1834) II. 323 We find the introduction of theism, that is, the doctrine of an intelligent Agent, the Author of nature,.. claimed for Pythagoras. 1841 ELPHINSTONE *Hist. India* I. 163 The theism inculcated by the Védas.. has been supplanted by a system of gross polytheism and idolatry. 1877 R. FLINT *Theism* i. 18 Theism is the doctrine that the universe owes its existence, and continuance.. to the reason and will of a self-existent Being... It is the doctrine that nature has a Creator and Preserver. 1888 F. L. PATTON *Syllabus Lect. Theism* 1 (Funk) Theism may be considered religiously [as embracing] polytheism, pantheism, monotheism (theism par excellence).

**Theism** [2] (þī·iz'm). *Path.* [f. mod.L. *the-a* TEA + -ISM.] A morbid condition characterized by headache, sleeplessness, and palpitation of the heart, caused by excessive tea-drinking.

1886 *Science* VIII. 132 It is customary to speak of acute, subacute and chronic 'theism', a form that has no connection with theological matters. 1906 *Daily News* 14 Sept. 6 It is well to keep an eye on 'acute caffeism' and 'chronic theism'.

**Theist** [1] (þī·ist). [mod. f. Gr. θε-ός god + -IST. Cf. F. *théiste* (Voltaire).] One who holds the doctrine of theism: in earlier use = DEIST; in later use, esp. as distinguished from this: see note s. v. DEIST.

1662 E. MARTIN *Five Lett.* 45 To have said my office.. twice a day.. among Rebels, Theists, Atheists, Philologers, Wits, Masters of Reason, Puritanes [etc.]. *a* 1679 W. OWTRAM *Serm.* (1682) A v, What theist was ever known to live according to the principles of natural religion? *a* 1734 NORTH *Exam.* III. viii. § 11 (1740) 590 He [Oates] did but use the Privilege of a Theist or Freethinker, of which Crew, or worse, he plainly declared himself. 1820 POLWHELE in *Lavington's Enthus. Meth. & Papists* Introd. 135 The highly-polished preacher, whose audience are theophilanthropists or theists. 1870 J. H. NEWMAN *Gram. Assent* v. § 2. 120 No one is to be called a Theist, who does not believe in a Personal God.

**b** *attrib.* and *Comb.*

1711 HICKES *Two Treat. Chr. Priesth.* (1847) I. 267 His atheist-ridden, or theist-ridden.. mind. 1755 AMORY *Mem.* (1766) II. 107 The writings of the old theist philosophers.

**The·ist** [2]. *nonce-wd.* [f. mod.L. *thea* TEA: cf. THEISM [2].] A person addicted to tea-drinking.

*c* 1818 SHELLEY in Medwin *Life* (1847) II. 47 [Shelley.. was a lover of tea, calling himself.. humourously a] Theist.

**Theistic** (þiˌi·stik), *a.* [f. THEIST [1] + -IC.] **1.** Of or pertaining to theists or theism.

1780 WARTON *Sir T. Pope* vi. (ed. 2) 208 From an abhorrence of superstition, he appears to have adopted the most distant extremes of the theistic system. 1875 VOYSEY *Revised Prayer Bk.* (ed. 2) Pref., This modest attempt to adapt the Liturgy of the venerable Church of England to a purely Theistic worship. 1876 GLADSTONE in *Contemp. Rev.* June 5 Those who, professedly rejecting all known expressions of dogma, are nevertheless believers in a moral Governor of the Universe... I denominate the Theistic school.

**2.** Used in the sense: Of or pertaining to a god or gods; divine. *rare.*

1854 BRIMLEY *Ess.*, *Comte's Pos. Philos.* 324 A region of phenomena where Will.., quite apart from all consideration of theistic interference, introduces a disturbing element that baffles the provisions of science. 1878 GLADSTONE *Prim. Homer* vi. § 2. 66 Zeus.. combines, more than any other deity, the human and the theistic quality.

**Theistical** (þiˌi·stikăl), *a.* [f. as prec. + -AL: see -ICAL.] = prec. 1. Hence **Thei·stically** *adv.*, in a theistical manner.

1697 C. LESLIE *Short Meth. w. Deists* I. § 11 (1699) 45 *note*, The Theistical Clubb have set this up as a Principle. 1738 WARBURTON *Div. Legat.* III. ii. 304 That future State, which, I suppose, the Theistical Philosophers did not believe. 1841 ELPHINSTONE *Hist. India* I. 223 The work of Patanjali.. is the text-book of the theistical sect.

**Theive**, obs. form of THEAVE, THIEVE.

**Theivil**, Sc. var. THIVEL, pot-stick.

**Theke** (þīk). *Bot.* [ad. Gr. θήκη.] = THECA 2.

1872 TUCKERMAN *N. Amer. Lichens* 30 [Spores] occurring in eights in the thekes. 1882 *Ibid.* I. Introd. 8 The hymenium, consisting of thekes (thecæ, the spore-bearing organs). 1900 in B. D. JACKSON *Gloss. Bot. Terms.*

**Theke**, obs. form of THEEK, THILK.

**Thel, thele**, variants of THEAL *Obs.*, a board.

† **Thelema·tic**, *a. Obs. rare.* [f. Gr. θεληματ-, stem of θέλημα will + -IC.] Of or pertaining to will or volition; voluntary.

1813–21 BENTHAM *Ontology* Wks. 1843 VIII. 207/2 Thelematic [motions], those in the production of which volition.. is seen to be concerned.

**Thelemite** (þe·lĭməit). *rare.* [a. F. *thelemite* (Cotgr.), f. Gr. θέλημα will + -ITE 1, with reference to the abbey of Thélème in Rabelais, the only law of which was *Fay ce que vouldras*, Do what thou wilt.] (See quots.)

1656 BLOUNT *Glossogr.*, *Thelemite*, a libertine, one that does what he list. 1908 *Nation* 24 Oct. 144/1 We will.. take our oath to observe the Thelemite rule of 'Do what thou wilt', because, as its founder said, 'men that are free, well-born, well-bred, and conversant in honest companies have naturally an instinct and spur that prompts them unto virtuous actions'.

**Thelephoroid** (þī·le-fŏroid), *a. Bot.* [f. mod.L. *Thelephora* (f. Gr. θηλή a teat + -φορος bearing) + -OID.] Resembling or having the form of the genus *Thelephora* of hymenomycetous fungi. So **Thelepho·reous** *a.*, of or pertaining to this genus.

1860 MAYNE *Expos. Lex.*, *Thelephoreus*,..applied by Persoon to a Family.. of the *Exosporii Sarcomyci*..: thelephoreous. 1891 *Cent. Dict.*, Thelephoroid.

**Thelke**, obs. form of THILK.

† **Thellich**, *a.* and *pron. Obs.* Forms: α. 1 **þyslic, þyllic, þillic, þilic,** 2 **þellic,** 3 **þullich**(*e*), **þulli** (*e*), 4 **þellich.** β. 1 **þylc, þilc.** [OE. *þyllic*, by assimilation from *þyslic* (beside *þuslic*, *þullic*), f. *þus*, *þys*, THUS + *-lic*, -LY 1. See also THILK.]

**A.** *adj.* Of this or such a kind; suchlike, such.

*Beowulf* 2637 ʒif him þyslicu þearf ʒelumpe. *a* 890 tr. *Bæda's Hist.* II. ix. [xii.] (1890) 130 Se ðe þyslice ʒife & swa micle..forecwiþ. *c* 897 K. ÆLFRED *Gregory's Past. C.* xliii. 314 Ðyllic fæsten ic ʒeceas. *c* 1000 ÆLFRIC *Saints' Lives* xxxiii. 142 Ac þyllic lif nis na ʒewunelic on ure ceastre. *c* 1000 *Ags. Gosp.* Matt. xviii. 5 Swa hwylc swa anne þyllicne [*v.r.* þylcne, þilicne, *Hatt. G.* þellicne, *Lindisf.* ðuslic] lytling on minum naman onfehþ, se onfehþ me. — Mark vii. 8 Maneʒa oþre þyllice [*v.r.* þylce, *Hatt. G.* þellice] ðing ʒe doð. *c* 1050 *Liber Scintill.* 33 Ac swyþe feawa synd þa þylce ʒebedu habban. *Ibid.* 80 Þes þylc fela spycð. *a* 1225 *Ancr. R.* 8 Þeos & swuche oþre [*MS. C.* þullich oðere] beoð alle ine freo wille to donne. *c* 1230 *Hali Meid.* 9 Þe þohtes þat..leareð þe and eggeð toward þulli þeowdom. *a* 1240 *Sawles Warde* in *Cott. Hom.* 255 Of þulliche nesche wepnen ich mahte carien summes weis. *Ibid.* 265 Sikere ha beoð of al þis of þulli lif, of þulli wit, of þulli luue..ant of þulli blisse. 1340 *Ayenb.* 27 Of þelliche þinges him gledeþ ine his herte.

**B.** *pron.* [absol. or ellipt. use of the adj.] A thing or things of this, that, or such a kind; such.

*a* 890 tr. *Bæda's Hist.* III. xvi. [xxii.] (1890) 228 Þyslic wæs seo syn, þe se cyning fore ofsleʒen wæs. *c* 893 K. ÆLFRED *Oros.* IV. iv. § 2 Nu Romane him self þyllic writon. *a* 1000 *Ecgbert's Confess.* c. 15 ʒif..he awiht þylces do. *c* 1000 ÆLFRIC *Colloquy* in Wr.-Wülcker 96/42 Þylces fela, *his similia.* *c* 1000 *Ags. Gosp.* Luke ix. 9 Hwæt is þes be þam ic þilc [*Hatt.* þellic, *Lind.* ðuslico] ʒehyre? *a* 1225 *Leg. Kath.* 849 Low! þullich is al þæt ʒe þencheð to dei for to weorrin me wið. 1340 *Ayenb.* 7 Þe þridde heste is þellich.

**Thelphusian** (þelfiū·siăn), *a.* (*sb.*) *Zool.* [f. mod.L. *Thelphūsa* + -IAN.] Of or pertaining to the genus *Thelphusa* of fresh-water crabs, as *T. fluviatilis*, which burrows in river banks. **b.** *sb.* A crab of this family.

1842 *Penny Cycl.* XXIV. 305/2 *Thelphusa*, *Thelphusians*, M. Milne Edwards's name for a tribe of brachyurous crustaceans belonging to his family of *Catometopes*. *Ibid.*, Many of the Thelphusians.

**Thelyblast** (þe·li-, þī·liblæst). *Biol.* [f. Gr. θῆλυς female + -BLAST.] The female element of a sexual cell. Hence **Thelybla·stic** *a.*

1877 C. S. MINOT in *Proc. Boston Soc. Nat. Hist.* XIX. 170 The sexual generation may be called *genoblasts*, the male *arsenoblasts*, the female *thelyblasts* (direction cells, nucleoli of Infusoria and spermatozoa). 1890 BILLINGS *Nat. Med. Dict.*, *Thelyblasts*, term proposed by Minot to include mature ova and sperm-blastophores or seminal mother-cells.

‖ **Thelycum** (þī·li-, þe·likŏm). Pl. **thelyca.** [mod.L., ad. Gr. θηλυκόν, neuter of θηλυκός feminine, f. θῆλυ-ς female.] Name for a structure on the ventral surface of the thorax in the female of certain macrurous crustaceans.

1888 C. S. BATE in *Challenger Rep.* XXIV. 244 The ventral plate or thelycum in the female [*Penæus canaliculatus*]. *Ibid.* 245 The peculiar formation of the complementary external female apparatus which I propose to call thelycum.

**Thely·genous,** *a. Bot.* [f. Gr. θῆλυ-ς female + -GEN + -OUS.] Producing the female element.

1900 B. D. JACKSON *Gloss. Bot. Terms* 270/1 *Thelygenous*, inducing the female element, as thelygenous castration, the production of pistils in the male-flowers of a host by *Ustilago*.

**Thelykaryotic** (þe·li-, þī·likærio·tik), *a. Biol.* [irreg. f. Gr. θῆλυ-ς female + κάρυον nut, kernel + -OTIC, after *mitotic*.] Having a female nucleus.

1909 J. W. JENKINSON *Experim. Embryol.* 267 In the two-celled stage one blastomere has a male and a female nucleus, ..while the other has only a female (thelykaryotic).

† **Thelyphtho·ric,** *a. Obs. nonce-wd.* [f. mod. L. *thelyphthora* (M. Madan 1780), f. Gr. θῆλυ-ς female + φθορά corruption: cf. Gr. φθορικός corrupting.] That corrupts or ruins women.

[1780 M. MADAN (*title*) Thelyphthora; or, A Treatise on Female Ruin, in its Causes, Effects, Consequences, Prevention, and Remedy.] 1794 MATHIAS *Purs. Lit.* I. 160 Must I with Madan, bent on gospel truth, In Thelypthoric lore instruct our youth.

**Thelytokous** (þĭli·tŏkəs), *a. Zool.* Also *erron.* **thelyotokous** (-ǫ·tŏkəs). [f. Gr. θηλυτόκος bearing females (f. θῆλυ-ς female + -τόκος bearing) + -OUS.] Producing only female offspring, as the parthenogenetic females of some species: opposed to *arrenotokous*. So **Thely·toky** (also **thelyo·toky**), the production of females only in parthenogenesis.

1877 HUXLEY *Anat. Inv. Anim.* vii. 446 The terms arrenotokous and thelytokous have been proposed by Leuckart and Von Siebold to denote those parthenogenetic females which produce male and female young respectively. 1895 D. SHARP *Cambr. Nat. Hist.* V. iv. 141 The result of parthenogenesis in some species is the production of only one sex, which in some Insects is female, in others male; the phenomenon in the former case is called by Taschenberg Thelyotoky, in the latter case Arrhenotoky. *Ibid.* xxii. 498 Thelyotokous parthenogenesis is common in sawflies.

**Them** (ðem, ðĕm), *pers. pron.* Forms: see below. [Three types are found in ME. α. *þeȝȝm*, *þeym*, a. ON. *þeim* 'to those', 'to them', dat. pl. of the demonst. *sá*, *sú*, *þat*, the plural of which also supplies that of the 3rd pers. pron. (see THEY). This came down to the 16th c. in Eng. in the form *theim*, and still exists in north. dial. and in Sc. as *thaim*. β. Northern Eng. *þam*, app. bef. 1300; this appears to represent *þæm*, *þám*, dat. pl. of OE. *se*, *séo*, *þæt*, pl. *þá* (see THAT, THO), found already as accus. in the Rushworth Gospels, where Lindisf. has *hía*, Ags. Gosp. *híg*, Hatton *hyo*, all in the sense 'them'. This came down in Sc. as *thame* to 16th c. γ. The existing form *them*, found in R. Brunne *c* 1330. This may have originated as an unstressed form (ðĕm, ðăm) of *þeim* or (?) *þam*, or it may actually have represented the OE. Anglian *þæm* of the Rushworth Gospels.

Although the form from Norse is not known before Ormin, it must have been current in the Danelaw much earlier, since it was only dative in Norse, and must have been taken into OE. as dative, and have shared in the peculiar English change by which the accusative and dative of the pronouns were levelled under the dative form. In the singular *hine*, *him*, instances of this change are seen in the Rushworth Gospel Gloss *c* 975 (see HIM 1 d); and it is noteworthy that the same Gloss shows the use of *þæm* as acc., = *hia*, *hig*, *hyo*, as mentioned above. This use of *þæm* as pers. pron. may itself have been due to Norse influence, the OE. word being used in the same sense as the Norse *þeim*.

The commoner pron. of 3rd pers. pl. obj. (dat. and acc.) in OE. and ME. was HEM, surviving colloq. and dial. as *'em*.]

**A.** Illustration of Forms.

α. 2–3 (*Orm.*) **þeȝȝm,** 4–6 **þeym, þeim, theym**(e, **theim,** 6 **theime**; 4 **þaime, þaym,** 4–6 **þaim,** (4 **þaem,** 4–5 **taim**), 4–6 (4– *Sc.*) **thaim,** 4–6 **thaym**(e, 6 **thaime.**

*c* 1200 ORMIN 1751 Þatt he þeȝȝm ȝife blisse. *Ibid.* 1768 And hellpe þeȝȝm..To winnenn eche blisse. *a* 1300 *Cursor M.* 47 (Cott.) A saumpul her be þaem [*Gött.* þaim, *F.* ham, *T.* hem] I say. *Ibid.* 19378 (Edin.) Þai lerid at taim to suffer harde. *c* 1330 R. BRUNNE *Chron. Wace* 13072 Wawayn.. smot aboute, & made þeym rounn. *c* 1375 *Sc. Leg. Saints* xxvii. (*Machor*) 724 He betwene þaym pes can ma. *c* 1400 tr. *Secreta Secret.*, *Gov. Lordsh.* 58 Worschippe..þayme þat þou seez þat doon to be worschipped. 1523 LD. BERNERS *Froiss.* I. clxxxvi. 220 A stryfe fell bytwene theym and they of Parys. 1533 GAU *Richt Vay* (S.T.S.) 3 Thay quhilk red thayme or buyr thaime. 1534 CROMWELL in Merriman *Life & Lett.* (1902) I. 374 They..make not so muche for your purpose as ye allege thaim for. 1536 WRIOTHESLEY *Chron.* (Camden) I. 43 Great lamentation that the poore people made for theim. 1537 *Adm. Crt. Exemplif.* I. No. 174 Seeing a ship coming somewhat rome with theym. 1565 ALLEN *Def. Purg.* xv. 272 Sumwhiles by thabasing of theime. 1873 Thaim [see B. 5].

β. 1 **þæm,** 3–4 **þam,** 4–6 **þame** (6 **yame**), 4–7 **thame, tham.**

*c* 975 *Rushw. Gosp.* Matt. xx. 25 Hælend þa ceiʒde þæm [*Lind.* hia, *Ags.* hiȝ, *Hatt.* hyo] to him. 13.. *Cursor M.* 4900 (Cott.) Þe sargantz..Ran and ouertok þam [*Gött.* þaim] þare. *Ibid.* 7120 A redel þam vndo he badd. *c* 1330 R. BRUNNE *Chron.* (1810) 2 Iuor & Ini were disconfite þat day, Þe Iris & þe Wals with þam fled away. 1357 *Lay Folks Catech.* (MS. T.) 39 That..suld teche thame. *Ibid.* 65 To lere tham. *a* 1400 *Isumbras* 122 For thame es alle my kare. 1513 DOUGLAS *Æneis* XIII. x. 88 Gyf thame happynis careit for to be Tyll ony wther sted. 1577 HOLINSHED *Chron.*, *Hist. Scot.* I. 371/2 To yame that receyuit thy noble father yᵉ Duke of Longcastell. 1641 in Row *Hist. Kirk* (Wodrow Soc.) p. xliii, Being found qualifeit be thame.

γ. 4 **þem,** 4– **them,** (5–6 **theme**).

*c* 1330 R. BRUNNE *Chron. Wace* (Rolls) 15336 Oure kynde ..Schal do þem bowe, maugre þayres. 13.. *Cursor M.* 13725 (Cott.) Him for to tak bituix þem tua. *c* 1430– Them [see B. 4]. 1482 in *Eng. Hist. Rev.* XXV. 123 If ye wylle not, we bene purveyde of theme yat wylle. 1573 *Satir. Poems Reform.* xl. 21 To theme that was his fais.

**B.** Signification. **I.** Personal pronoun.

**1.** As pronoun of the third person plural, objective, direct and indirect (accusative and dative) of THEY. Also as antecedent pron. followed by relative, or prepositional phrase, and having then a demonstrative function, equivalent to *those* but less emphatic.

**a.** Direct object or accusative. (= L. *eos*, *illos*, G. *sie*.)

*c* 975 [see A. β]. *c* 1200 [see A. α]. *a* 1300 *Cursor M.* 1228 He þam for-soke in all þer nedis. *Ibid.* 8118 He heild þam to þaim for to kys. *c* 1330 [see A. γ]. 1470–85 MALORY *Arthur* x. lxix. 533 The grene knyghte hath..beten all them of Orkeney. 1474 *Coventry Leet Bk.* 389 To bye theym in þe Croschepyng. 1552 LYNDESAY *Monarche* 4822 Unoccupyit thay hald thame in thare neif. 1560 BIBLE (Genev.) 1 *Sam.* ii. 30 Them that honour me, I wil honour. 1586 T. B. *La Primaud. Fr. Acad.* I. (1589) 383 Have them in great estimation and admiration. 1667 MILTON *P. L.* IX. 420 By Fountain or by shadie Rivulet He sought them both. 1864 J. H. NEWMAN *Apol.* iv. (1904) 125/1 Charges..which..I fully believed at the time when I made them.

**b.** Indirect object or dative. (= L. *eis*, *illis*, G. *ihnen*.)

*c* 1200 ORMIN 1142 Þatt he þeȝȝm..Forrȝæfe þeȝȝre gilltess. *a* 1300 *Cursor M.* 667 Witte and wisdam he þam gaue. 1375 BARBOUR *Bruce* I. 79 Þis ordynance þaim thocht þe best. *c* 1400 *Rule St. Benet* 20 And by-kenne it taim þat best can serue god & te cuuent. *c* 1500 *Merch. & Son* 269 in Hazl. *E. P. P.* I. 151 The maryage of them ij. ys made. 1523 LD. BERNERS *Froiss.* I. ccxli. 353 He sent..and made alyaunces with them thre. 1535 COVERDALE *Jer.* xxxv. 2 Geue them wyne to drynke. 1656 EARL MONM. tr. *Boccalini's Advts. fr. Parnass.* I. i. (1674) 2 If their Lord..do but cast an artificial smile them, they take it as..a reward. 1779 *Mirror* No. 23 ⁋ 2 To show them what they are to understand. 1812 CRABBE *Tales* xviii, Men..whose pains, Credit, and prudence, brought them constant gains. *Mod.* I give them credit for good intentions.

**c.** As the object of a preposition.

*c* 1300 *Harrow. Hell* 29 (MS. E) Crist loked þaim vnto. *c* 1340 HAMPOLE *Prose Tr.* 28 Þou will noghte tente to thaym. 1474 CAXTON *Chesse* 7 Take not from them that is theyres. 1535 COVERDALE *Ps.* xvii[i]. 48 Thou shalt lift me vp from them that ryse agaynst me. 1663 GERBIER *Counsel* f viij, Letters, which the Ægiptians did attribute unto them. 1780 *Mirror* No. 96 ⁋ 2 They are neither of them niggardly. 1847 TENNYSON *Princess* Concl. 68 Too solemn for the comic touches in them. *Mod.* What will he do with them?

**d.** Sometimes *indefinitely*, as objective case of THEY 3. *colloq.* or *dialectal.*

**2.** Often used for 'him or her', referring to a singular person whose sex is not stated, or to *anybody*, *nobody*, *somebody*, *whoever*, etc. Cf. THEY 2.

1742 RICHARDSON *Pamela* III. 127 Little did I think..to make a..Complaint against a Person very dear to you,..but dont let them be so proud..as to make them not care how they affront everybody else. 1853 MISS YONGE *Heir of Redclyffe* xliv, Nobody else..has so little to plague them. 1874 DASENT *Half a Life* II. 198 Whenever any one was ill, she brewed them a drink.

**3.** Used for the nominative *they*. **a.** As antecedent or demonstrative pronoun: = THOSE. Now only *dial.* or *illiterate*.

*c* 1489 CAXTON *Sonnes of Aymon* iii. 78 All the foure brethern, and all theym of theyr companye arayed them selfe. *c* 1530 LD. BERNERS *Arth. Lyt. Bryt.* 393 Blessyd be them that hath brought that about. 1581 MARBECK *Bk. of Notes* 150 Such are them to whom yᵉ Lord doth giue his holy spirit. 1632 LITHGOW *Trav.* VII. 333 In a moment, them of the Villages came downe on horse and foote. 1873 MURRAY *Dial. S. Scotl.* 184 Thaim at dyd it. 1891 BARRIE *Little Minister* iii, Them as says there's no has me to fecht. *a* 1825 FORBY *Voc. E. Anglia* Introd. 141 Them are the women I meant. 1877 L. J. JENNINGS *Field Paths* iii. 47 Them be my two children. 1901 N. LLOYD *Chronic Loafer* i. 11 Them wasn't our only troubles.

**b.** As personal pronoun after *than*, *as*, and in the predicate after the verb *to be*. Common *colloq.*, but considered incorrect grammatically.

1654–66 EARL ORRERY *Parthen.* (1676) 708 It was an impossibility that these could be them. 1777 MICKLE *Cumnor Hall* xix, How far less blest am I than them! 1845 E. WARBURTON *Crescent & Cross* I. 331 It was not them we wanted. 1888 'J. S. WINTER' *Bootle's Childr.* xiv, It was them told me about her. 1888 'R. BOLDREWOOD' *Robbery under Arms* xxxiv, It was them or us..now. 1901 THEO. W. WILSON *Bacca Queen* xi. 89 Such as them enjoys thersells.

**II. 4.** As reflexive pron. = themselves. (= L. *se*, *sibi*, G. *sich*.)

As direct or indirect obj. of vb. (*arch.*), or obj. of prep.

13.. *Cursor M.* 1713 Þe meke be þam ai tua and tua, Þe wild do be þam-self al-sua. *Ibid.* 15757 (Cott.) Þai fell þaim don vn-to þe grund. 1375 BARBOUR *Bruce* I. 205 Gyff þat ony man þaim by Had ony thing þat wes worthy. *c* 1430 *Syr Tryam.* 770 The knyghtes gysed them fulle gay, And proved them fulle preste. 1535 COVERDALE *Exod.* xxxii. 8 They haue made them a molten calfe. *a* 1550 *Christis Kirke Gr.* xi, To dans thir damysellis thame dicht. 1565 COOPER *Thesaurus*, *Rubriceta*,..roset colour that women vse to paynte them. 1794 MRS. RADCLIFFE *Myst. Udolpho* lvii, Superior attainments of every sort bring with them duties of superior exertion. 1848 J. H. NEWMAN *Loss & Gain* II. xx. (1904) 254 What a way those fellows have with them! 1855 MACAULAY *Hist. Eng.* xxii. IV. 697 They then bethought them of a new expedient.

**III. 5.** As demonstr. adj. = THOSE. Now only *dial.* or *illiterate*.

**a.** Qualifying an objective (direct or indirect). Also strengthened by adding *there* (*'ere*, *air*).

1596 H. CLAPHAM *Bible Hist.* 92 To Samaria and them partes. 1598 BARRET *Theor. Warres* I. i. 4 The warres and weapons are now altered from them dayes. 1621 AINSWORTH *Annot. Pentat.* Gen. xviii. 6 Foure of them Logs make a Kab. 1726 CAVALLIER *Mem.* III. 231 If I had but one of them Hangmen. 1809–12 MAR. EDGEWORTH *Absentee* xii, I hope, then, the agent will give you encouragement about them mines. 1840 THACKERAY *Catherine* vii, It was a rare rise we got out of them chaps. 1878 MRS. STOWE *Poganuc P.* i, He don't believe in keeping none of them air prayer-book days.

**b.** Qualifying a nominative.

1607 TOPSELL *Four-f. Beasts* (1658) 126 Them few [dogs] which be kept must be tyed up in the day time. 1610 HEALEY *Vives' Comment St. Aug. Citie of God* XII. xvi, Augustine..saith that them times were called eternall. 1778 J. CRANE in F. Chase *Hist. Dartmouth* (Mass.) *Coll.* (1891) I. 389 The major part tories, or them sort of creatures called neuters. 1842 S. LOVER *Handy Andy* xxviii, Them ribbons of yours cost a trifle, Kitty. 1889 TENNYSON *Owd Roä* viii, 'Faaithful an' True' Them words be i' Scriptur. 1901 M. E. FRANCIS *Fiander's Widow* II. v. 255 'Them there legs o' yourn should be pretty well stretched by now.'

‖ **Thema** (þe·mă, þī·mă). Pl. **themata** (þe·mătă). [mod.L. *thema*, a. Gr. θέμα THEME.]

†**1.** The theme or subject of a declamation or discourse; a position to be maintained or demonstrated; a thesis. *Obs.*

**1531** ELYOT *Gov.* I. xiv, A case is appoynted to be moted by certayne yonge men, contaynyng some doubtefull controuersie, which is in stede of the heed of a declamation called *thema*. *a* **1734** NORTH *Exam.* I. i. § 8. (1740) 18 His grand *Thema* or Historical Position is, That King Charles II. was a concealed Papist. *Ibid.* ii. § 47. 53 Another of the Author's *Themata* or Positions.

**2.** The stem-form of a word; = THEME 5.

**1615** BEDWELL *Arab. Trudg.*, *Alkoran*, the thema is not *Karana*, .. as they would make vs beleeue: but *Kara*, which signifieth, to reade. **1883** *Athenæum* 6 Jan. 15/2 Scholars are still divided as to what thema or base to refer certain forms [of Icelandic nouns].

**3.** *Mus.* = THEME 4.

**1801** BUSBY *Dict. Mus.* **1871** GRAEME *Beethoven* ii. (1876) 27 Beethoven..requested a thema for an improvisation.

**4.** A dissertation or thesis submitted for a degree; cf. THEME 3.

**1888** *Athenæum* 28 July 129/3 'The Conflict of East and West in Egypt'..appears to be an enlargement of a *thema* for the doctorate of Columbia College.

**Thematic** (þīmæ·tik), *a.* (*sb.*) [ad. Gr. θεματικός, f. θέμα THEME: see -IC.] Of or pertaining to a theme or themes.

**1.** Of or pertaining to a subject or topic of discourse or writing. *rare.*

**1871** tr. *Lange's Comm. Jer.* 104 These introductory verses thus acquire a thematic character.

†**b.** *Logic.* Relating to or connected with the matter or subject of thought. *Obs.*

**1697** tr. *Burgersdicius his Logic* I. i. 2 A System of Logical Precepts consists of two Parts, Thematick and Organic. ..The first is that which is imploy'd about Theams, and their various Affections, and second Notions, as about the Matter of the Instruments of Logick.

**2.** *Mus.* Of, pertaining to, or constituting themes or subjects (see THEME 4); relating to themes and their contrapuntal development. In *thematic catalogue, index, summary*, = containing the opening themes or passages of musical pieces.

**1864** *Reader* 21 May 660 A handy thematic summary of the work is given in the 'Orchestra' for last week. **1878** C. F. POHL in Grove *Dict. Mus.* I. 66/2 The thematic catalogue which Mozart himself had kept of his works. **1906** *Athenæum* 1 Sept. 250/2 The thematic material has been carefully chosen, and its treatment shows thought and skill.

**3.** *Gram.* Of or pertaining to the theme or stem-form of a word: see THEME 5.

*Thematic vowel*, a vowel which comes between the root and the inflexions in a verb or sb., as the ε and ο in φέρ-ο-μεν, φέρ-ε-τε, the *i*, *e*, and *a* in OE. *ber-i-þ*, *ber-e-þ*, *luf-a-ð*.

**1861** GOLDSTÜCKER *Pánini* 257 There must be reasons for this variety of thematic forms which constitute the declension of the same base. **1877** PAPILLON *Man. Comp. Philol.* viii. (ed. 2) 167 Curtius..explains the vowel in question as a 'thematic vowel', i.e. a suffix to or increase of the stem or 'theme' previous to the reception of the inflections. **1887** COOK *Sievers' O. E. Gram.* 143 The thematic *w* being sometimes retained and sometimes lost. **1888** KENNEDY *Revised Lat. Primer* § 148 (1900) 94 Verbs...In which the Verb-Stem was formed by a so-called Thematic vowel added to the root.

**B.** as *sb.* That part of logic which deals with themes or subjects of thought. **1891** in *Cent. Dict.*

So **Thema·tical** *a.* = *thematic*; **Thema·tically** *adv.*, in a thematic manner; with respect to a theme or themes; † **The·matism** *Obs. nonce-wd.* [ad. Gr. θεματισμός a laying down], a placing, arrangement; **The·matist**, one who composes or writes themes (Ogilvie, 1882).

**1890** *Athenæum* 3 May 579/1 The *thematical material in the four movements of the work is..interesting, and..the music is pleasantly unconventional. *Ibid.* 25 Jan. 125/2 Structurally as well as *thematically we note a welcome advance towards clearness. **1729** SHELVOCKE *Artillery* v. 334 The first then shall be the **Thematism* (from the Greek Word θεματισμός) which signifies the Decorum and Gracefulness of any Pile.

**Theme** (þīm), *sb.* Forms: *α.* 4–6 teme, (4–5 teeme, 5 teem, 5–6 tyme). *β.* 4– theme, (6–7 theame, 6–8 theam). [a. OF. **teme* (not in Godef.: but cf. *tesme*, with graphic *s* indicating vowel-length (13th c. in Godef. *Compl.*); also *teume, thieume*); in *β* conformed to L. *thema*, a. Gr. θέμα proposition, f. θε-, root of τιθέναι to put, set, place, lay down. In 16–17th c. commonly spelt *theam* (þēm). Cf. ANTETHEME.]

**1.** The subject of discourse, discussion, conversation, meditation, or composition; a topic.

*α.* *a* **1300** *Cursor M.* 18495 (Cott.) Bot lenthius yald up his teme Bath to ioseph and to nichodeme. **13..** *E. E. Allit. P.* C. 358 Þe trwe tenor of his teme he tolde on þis wyse. *c* **1380** WYCLIF *Serm.* Sel. Wks. I. 306 Crist..toke þe same word for his teme þat Baptist toke whanne he prechide.

*β.* **13..** *E. E. Allit. P.* A. 943 Þe nwe [Ierusalem] þat lyȝt of godez sonde, Þe apostel in apocalyppce in theme con take. *c* **1386** CHAUCER *Pard. Prol.* 5 My theme [teeme, teme, teem, tyme] is alwey oon and euere was Radix malorum est Cupiditas. **1485** CAXTON *Paris & V.* Prol., I vndertake this theme..because I haue all my life taken pleasure in the reading of Romances. **1570** GOOGE *Pop. Kingd.* IV. 44 b, Now to my theame again. *a* **1600** [see THESE *sb.*]. **1649** MILTON *Eikon.* ix, The overworn theme, and stuffing of all his discourses. **1708** *Brit. Apollo* No. 18. 3/2 And Love and Pleasure be my Endless Theam [*rime* name]. **1804** WELLINGTON in Gurw. *Desp.* (1837) III. 81 His Highness's notorious treachery,..the theme of all the public dispatches. **1870** BRYANT *Iliad* VI. I. 200 A theme of song for men in time to come.

†**b.** *transf.* A subject treated by action (instead of by discourse, etc.); hence, that which is the cause *of* or *for* specified action, circumstance, or feeling; matter, subject. *Obs.*

**1588** SHAKS. *Tit. A.* v. ii. 80 See heere he comes, and I must play my theame. **1602** — *Ham.* v. i. 289 *Ham.* Why I will fight with him vppon this Theme...*Qu.* Oh my sonne, what Theame? *Ham.* I lou'd Ophelia [etc.]. **1634** SIR T. HERBERT *Trav.* 110 An infallible Theame of endlesse troubles. **1713** SWIFT *Cadenus & Vanessa* 298 In vain..You form'd this project in your brain..Nor shall Vanessa be the theme To manage thy abortive scheme. **1806** H. SIDDONS *Maid, Wife, & Widow* I. 179 His son grew up to man's estate, and gave him farther theme for uneasiness.

†**c.** *Logic.* That which is the subject of thought.

**1620** T. GRANGER *Div. Logike* 1 The externall is euery Theme, or matter propounded, whereof a man discourseth, or may discourse by his reason. **1697** tr. *Burgersdicius his Logic* I. ii. 2 A Theme is whatsoever may be propos'd to the Understanding to be known. Themes are either Simple or Composed. **1725** WATTS *Logic* I. ii. § 1 Every object of our idea is called a theme, whether it be a being or not-being; for not-being may be proposed to our..thoughts, as well as that which has a real being.

†**2.** *spec.* The text of a sermon; also, a proposition to be discussed. *Obs.* (or merged in 1).

*α.* **1362** LANGL. *P. Pl.* A. III. 86 A Sarmoun he made,..And tolde hem þis teeme [*v.r.* teme]. *Ibid.* VIII. 122 Thou mihtest preche whon þe luste, *Quoniam literaturam non cognoui* mihte be þy Teeme! *c* **1440** *Promp. Parv.* 488/1 Teme, of a sermone, *thema.* **1513** MORE *Rich. III*, Wks. 60/2 He toke for his tyme *spuria vitulamina non agent radices altas.* That is to say bastard slippes shal neuer take depe roote. **1530** PALSGR. 281/1 Tyme of a sermonde, *thesme.*

*β.* **1387** TREVISA *Higden* (Rolls) VIII. 151 (MS. *a*) He took a theme [L. *sumpto themate*] of holy writt, and gan to preche. **1432–50** tr. *Higden* ibid., This theme of scripture. *c* **1530** L. COX *Rhet.* (1899) 44 The theme of Tullyes oracyon or plee for Milo was thys, that he had slayne Clodius laufully. **1560** DAUS *Sleidane's Comm.* 367 The deuines had Themes geuen them to discusse and reason vpon. *c* **1566** *Merie Tales of Skelton* S.'s Wks. 1843 I. p. lxi, He dyd take that for hys antethem, the which of late dayes is named a theme, and sayde, *Qui se exaltat* [etc.]. **1594** T. B. *La Primaud. Fr. Acad.* II. 590 In the ende all woulde be but vanitie, according to Salomons theame, which hee handleth in his booke of the Preacher. **1618** HALES *Rem.*, *Lett. fr. Synod of Dort* II. 50 He took for his Theme the 122. Psalm.

**3.** An exercise written on a given subject, *esp.* a school essay; an exercise in translation. Now *rare.*

**1545–7** in *Archæologia* XXXIV. 41 After none they [form III] have a theme to be made in Laten. **1581** PETTIE *Guazzo's Civ. Conv.* II. (1586) 59 Like a schoolemaister, which doth dictate or rehearse to his schollers some Theame or Epistle. **1644** MILTON *Areop.* (Arb.) 56 The theam of a Grammar lad. **1739** CIBBER *Apol.* (1756) I. 7, I remember I was once whipp'd for my theme. **1824** in Grant *Burgh Sch. Scotl.* (1876) II. iv. 154 The Rector dictated an English theme to be translated into Latin. **1878** BOSW. SMITH *Carthage* 263 In Juvenal's time Roman schoolboys declaimed upon it in their weekly themes.

**4.** *Mus.* The principal melody, plainsong, or *canto fermo* in a contrapuntal piece; hence, any one of the principal melodies or motives in a sonata, symphony, etc.; a subject; also, a simple tune on which variations are constructed.

[**1597** MORLEY *Introd. Mus.* 86 Your plainsong is as it were your theme, and your descant as it were your declamation.] **1674** PLAYFORD *Skill Mus.* III. 2 It was usual with them to have a Tenor as a Theam, to which they were compelled to adapt their other Parts. **1854** *Cherubini's Counterpoint* 63 The subject, or theme of the fugue, should neither be too long nor too short. **1866** ENGEL *Nat. Mus.* iii. 103 A manifold and clever treatment of the motives of which the theme consists, contributes especially to the oneness and clearness of a musical composition.

**5.** *Philol.* The inflexional base or stem of a word, consisting of the '*root*' with modification or addition; thus in Gr. λείπειν and τέμνειν, the roots are λιπ, τεμ, the present themes or stems λειπ-, τεμν-; in τέκνον, the root is τεκ, the theme τεκνο-.

Formerly applied to the 1 pers. sing. pres. indic. of a verb; later identified with *root* (as in Greek); the modern application began with Curtius.

**1530** PALSGR. Introd. 31 The fyrst [conjugation]..hath his thre chefe rotes..his theme, his preterit participle, and his present infynityve ever of many syllables. *Ibid.*, The thyrde [conjugation] hath his theme most commenly in *S*.. as *je voys..je prens..je dis.* **1580** HOLLYBAND *Treas. Fr. Tong*, I call the Theame, speaking to the vnskilfull in the Latine tong, whereby we begin to decline a Verbe. **1615** BEDWELL *Index Assurat.* O iij, The theame or roote, as they call it, from whence it [*Koran*] is deriued, is..*Kara'*, to reade. **1741** WATTS *Improv. Mind* I. vii. § 6 In reducing the words to their original or theme. **1870** F. A. MARCH *Compar. Gram. Ags.* § 60 The variable final letters of a noun are its case-endings, the rest is its theme. **1875** WHITNEY *Life Lang.* x. 207 In the derivative theme or base.

**6.** *Astrol.* The disposition of the heavenly bodies at a particular time, as at the moment of a person's birth. Cf. HOROSCOPE *sb.* 1.

**1652** GAULE *Magastrom.* 293 Augustus had..such a confidence in this fatidical praesagition, that he divulged his natalitial theme. **1727–41** CHAMBERS *Cycl.*, *Theme*, among astrologers, denotes the figure they construct when they draw the horoscope; representing the state of the heavens for a certain point, or moment required; *i.e.* the places of the stars, and planets, for that moment. **1775** ASH *Dict.*, *Theme*,..a horoscope in astrology. [**1819** WILSON *Dict. Astrol.*, *Thema cœli*, a figure of the heavens.]

**7.** *Anc. Hist.* Each of the twenty-nine provinces into which the Byzantine empire was divided.

**1788** GIBBON *Decl. & F.* xlviii. V. 13 The Anatolian *theme* or province. *Ibid.* liii. 464 An accurate survey of the provinces, the *themes*, as they were then denominated, both of Europe and Asia. **1864** BRYCE *Holy Rom. Emp.* ix. (1889) 135 Nicephorus demanded the 'theme' or province of Rome as the price of compliance.

**8.** *attrib.* and *Comb.*, as *theme-maker.*

*a* **1661** HOLYDAY *Juvenal* To Rdr., Surely thou wilt acknowledge Juvenal to be a poet, but Horace to be some poor theme-maker.

Hence **Theme** *v. trans.*, to furnish with a theme or subject; **The·meless** *a.*, without a theme, having no theme; **The·mer**, one who sets or proposes a theme; **Themester** (þī·mstəɹ), one who labours at a theme (*contemptuous*).

**1594** R. SOUTHWELL *St. Peters Compl.*, etc. To Rdr., This *theames my heavie penne to plaine in prose. **1641** J. JACKSON *True Evang. T.* I. 10 [Points] capable to be spread out so as to theame the Preachers speech. **1840** GALT *Demon of Destiny* VI. 41 The *themeless babble of his idiot child. **1611** TARLTON *Jests* (1844) 28 Such commendations Tarlton got, that hee supt with the bailiffe that night, where my *theamer durst not come, although he were sent for. **1843** *Blackw. Mag.* LIV. 105 Where now, base *themester?

**Theme**, obs. f. TEAM (sense 8); also of THEM.

**Themel, -elle**, obs. forms of THIMBLE.

‖ **Themis** (þe·mis, þī·mis). [a. Gr. Θέμις, goddess of law and order, Justice personified.]

**1.** Name of the ancient Greek goddess of law and justice; hence, Law or Justice personified.

**1656** BLOUNT *Glossogr.*, *Themis*, the Godesse of Justice, that gave out Oracles at Bœotia. **1784** COWPER *Task* III. 257 Such thine, in whom Our British Themis gloried with just cause, Immortal Hale. **1880** J. PAYN *Confid. Agent* iv, She found a rival, not in Themis, but in Isabel Thurlow.

**2.** *Astron.* Name of the twenty-fourth of the Asteroids, discovered 5 April 1853 by De Gasparis.

**Themistian** (þīmi·stiăn). *Ch. Hist.* [f. *Themisti-us*, name of the founder of the sect (see quot. 1882–3) + -AN.] In plural: A sect of the MONOPHYSITES who attributed to Christ imperfect knowledge. Cf. AGNOITES.

**1874** in BLUNT *Dict. Sects, Heresies, &c.* **1882–3** *Schaff's Encycl. Relig. Knowl.* I. 36 The second sect (founded in the sixth century by Themistius, deacon of Alexandria), sometimes called the Themistians. **1883** *Cath. Dict.* (1885) 598/1 The Themistians, or Agnoetæ, held that the human element in Christ before his resurrection was subject to ignorance.

**Themselves** (ðĕmse·lvz), *pron. pl.* Forms: see THEM and SELF. [The original construction was nom., acc. *hī, hēo selfe*, dat. *heom selfum*, whence ME. *hemselve(n*, etc. In 14th c. this was superseded in north. dial. by *þaim self(e*, *þaim selven*, and in Standard Eng. *themself* was the normal form to *c* 1540, but disappeared *c* 1570. *Themselfs, themselves* appears *c* 1500, and became the standard form *c* 1540. For *theirself, theirselves*, see III.]

**I.** Emphatic. = Those very persons or things.

**1.** Standing in apposition with the pronoun *they* (rarely *them*), or with a sb., or adj. used subst.

*α.* **13..** *Cursor M.* 3708 (Cott.) All þaa þat blisses þe Sal þam-self blessed be. *Ibid.* 8131 (Gött.) Þaim-selue again þai tok þair sty [*Cott.* þamself a-gain tok þai sti], And went þaim þan to ethiopy. *c* **1460** *Towneley Myst.* xxx. 566 Thare neghburs thai demyd Thaym self as it semyd. **1533** MORE *Apol.* 7 b, They se full well them selfe, that they saye not trew.

*γ.* **1502** in *Lett. Rich. III & Hen. VII* (Rolls) II. 107 Thei them selves coulde not acertayne us of the tyme. **1555** EDEN *Decades* To Rdr. (Arb.) 53 More monstrous then the monsters theim selues. **1561** T. HOBY tr. *Castiglione's Courtyer* II. (1577) I vij b, Oftentimes to them themselues, they thrust out filthy and most dishonest wordes. **1651** HOWELL *Venice* 143 Approv'd of by the Popes Breve's themselfs. **1779** *Mirror* No. 54 ▸7 You tell us the effects of your feelings, child; but you don't distinguish the feelings themselves. **1810** CRABBE *Borough* ii. 110 Monuments themselves memorials need. **1872** HARDY *Under Greenw. Tree* Pref., Music-paper (which they mostly ruled themselves). **1876** GLADSTONE *Glean.* (1879) II. 295 Themselves knowing nothing of difficulty, or of obscurity,..they are liable to be intolerant of other men who stumble.

**2.** Used alone for emphasis as a simple nominative. *arch.*

*α.* **1512** *Helyas* in Thoms *Prose Rom.* (1828) III. 30 Thiniuries that them self had made. **1549** COVERDALE, etc. *Erasm. Par. Rom.* 38 Vnlearned people.., whiche thinke nothing rightful, but that them selfe do.

*β.* **13..** *Cursor M.* 23517 (Edin.) God..louis þaim als his auen sonis, Mar þan þaim-selwin lof þair driht [*Cott.* Mare þan þam-seluen luue þai dright].

*γ.* **1542** UDALL *Erasm. Apoph.* 105 Theimselfes by great pielage..dooe growe dayly & encrease in welthe. **1624** BEDELL *Lett.* x. 135 Themselues doe vtterly denie it. **1701** SWIFT *Contests Nobles & Com.* Wks. 1755 II. I. 51 To remember how themselves sate in fear of their persons. **1853** LYNCH *Self-Improv.* ii. 44 People's timorousness.. shows how insecurely grounded themselves are.

**b.** *To be themselves*: to be in their normal condition of mind, body, or behaviour: see SELF D. 1.

**1698** LISTER in *Phil. Trans.* XX. 247 They came so out of their Fits, that they were also well and as much themselves as ever. **1698** FRYER *Acc. E. India & P.* 379 Yet those..are always as lean as Skeletons, and seldom themselves.

**3.** As emphatic objective. Now chiefly as object of a preposition.

**1375** BARBOUR *Bruce* XIII. 234 Ane of them-selwyne that wes thar Capitane of thame all thai maid. *c* **1400** *Destr. Troy* 1582 To selle and to se as þaim selfe lyked. *c* **1430** LYDG. *Min. Poems* (Percy Soc.) 108 But yt move of themselfe, for sothe they thynke yt ryghte nowghte. **1711** ADDISON *Spect.* No. 26 ¶ 5 The Monuments of their [Dutch] Admirals .. represent them like themselves. **1764** REID *Inquiry* i. § 1 If we would know the works of God, we must consult themselves with attention and humility. **1825** SCOTT *Betrothed* xxvi, They have .. sacked the houses of the Flemings, spoiled their goods, misused their families, and murdered themselves. **1827** — *Surg. Dau.* iv, You are one of themselves, you know—Middlemas of that Ilk.

**II.** Reflexive: = L. *sibi, se*; F. *se, soi*; G. *sich*.

**4.** As direct obj. (accusative), indirect obj. (dative), or object of a preposition.

α. **13..** *Cursor M.* 386 (Cott.) Alkin things grouand..in þam self þaire seding bere. *Ibid.* 16455 Þai ches þaim-self dampnacion. *c* **1489** CAXTON *Sonnes of Aymon* xxiv. 518 They putte themself so to flighte. **1493** *Beverley MSS.* in *Rep. Hist. MSS. Comm.* XLVI. 620 That the Drapers shall have a confraternite emong thame self..as other crafts hafe. *a* **1548** HALL *Chron., Edw. IV* 239 Hys heyres and successors..by them self, or their deputie should offer a hart of lyke weight and value. *c* **1550** R. BIESTON *Bayte Fortune* B iv b, All men..Enforce them selfe to please him.

β. **13..** *Cursor M.* 801 (Gött.) Þan þai sau þaim seluen bare. *Ibid.* 3455 (Cott.) Til þay had o þam seluen might [*Gött.* þaim seluen; *Fairf.* ham-seluen; *Trin.* hem self]. **1375** BARBOUR *Bruce* I. 502 Fayn to mak thaim-selwyn fre. **1419** in Ellis *Orig. Lett.* Ser. II. I. 73 Thay kepe this good emonge thaim selven.

γ. **1502** in *Lett. Rich. III & Hen. VII* (Rolls) II. 107 Thei wold confesse them selves to be there as commissioners. *a* **1548** HALL *Chron., Hen. VIII* 135 b, The remnant..lept ouer the castle wal, and so saued themselfes. **1565** STAPLETON tr. *Bede's Hist.* 163 [They] did cast lotts equally amongst them selfs. **1611** BIBLE *Gen.* iii. 7 They..made themselues aprons. **1617** MORYSON *Itin.* III. 70 The dores..by waights are made to shut of themselves. **1647** TRAPP *Comm.* 2 *Thess.* iii. 11 Whose whole life is to eat..and laugh themselves fat. **1779** *Mirror* No. 17 ¶ 15 Not to make fools of themselves. **1818** SCOTT *Rob Roy* xxvi, These Hielands of ours..are but a wild kind of warld by themsells. **1885** *Manch. Exam.* 16 Sept. 5/2 The points on which they differ among themselves.

**5.** In concord with a singular pronoun or sb. denoting a person, in cases where the meaning implies more than one, as when the sb. is qualified by a distributive, or refers to either sex: = himself or herself. Cf. THEY 2, THEM 2.

α. **1464** *Rolls of Parlt.* V. 513/2 Inheritements, of which any of the seid persones..was seised by theym self, or joyntly with other. *c* **1489** CAXTON *Sonnes of Aymon* i. 39 Eche of theym sholde .. make theymselfe redy. **1533** MORE *Apol.* 55 b, Neyther Tyndale there nor thys precher..hath by theyr maner of expounynge..wonne them self mych wurshyp.

γ. **1600** SHAKS. *Lucr.* 125 Euery one to rest themselues [*ed.* 1594 himselfe] betake. **1654–66** EARL ORRERY *Parthen.* (1676) 147 All that happened, which every one assured themselves, would render him a large sharer in the general joy. **1874** DASENT *Half a Life* 3 Every one likes to keep it to themselves as long as they can.

**III.** From the 14th c. there has been a tendency to treat *self* as a sb. (= person, personality), and substitute *their* for *them* (cf. *his self*, HIMSELF IV.).

This is prevalent dialectally, but in literary Eng. has place only where an adj. intervenes, as *their own, sweet, very selves*. See SELF C. 1 a, and cf. OURSELF, OURSELVES.

α. **13..** *Cursor M.* 5378 (Cott.) To ches þam ware þair-self will neuen. *Ibid.* 6968 (Fairf.) Ilka kinrede of þa twelue Had an ouer-man be þaire [*v. rr.* ham, þaim, hem] selue. *c* **1440** *Alphabet of Tales* 110 Þai þat will commend þer selfe vnto þe devull. *c* **1490** CAXTON *Rule St. Benet* xxxiii. 129 Nor it is leefull ony to haue a thyng to theyrself propre. **1545** ASCHAM *Toxoph.* (Arb.) 101 They may hit a nother I trow and neuer take blow theyr selfe. *Mod. Sc.* Thai offert to dui't thersel.

β. **13..** *Cursor M.* 3708 (Fairf.) Alle þa atte blessis þe Sal þaire-seluen [*Cott.* þam-self, *Gött.* þaim seluen] blessed be.

γ. **1500–20** DUNBAR *Poems* xxiii. 27 Quhen thair baggis ar full thair selfis ar bair. **1525** LD. BERNERS *Froiss.* II. 473 They had gret desyre to prove their selfes. *c* **1560** A. SCOTT *Poems* (S.T.S.) xxx. 20 Till thay mischeif þair sellis. *a* **1568** ASCHAM *Scholem.* (Arb.) 97 Liking it well their selues. **1659** GAUDEN *Slight Healers* (1660) 47 To commend their skill to the publique, by giving some good experiments on their selves. **1728** MORGAN *Algiers* I. Pref. 22 They aver that they theirselves have been no less scandalized than I myself. *a* **1836** BOOTHROYD *Bible* Ps. xxxvii. 2 They theirselves stumbled and fell. *Mod. Sc.* Thai beikit thersel's in the sun.

**Themyl, -ylle,** obs. (ME.) ff. THIMBLE.

**Then** (ðen), *adv.* (*conj., adj., sb.*) Forms: see below. [OE. *þanne, þonne, þænne, þenne*, ME. *þenne, þan, þen*, = OFris. *thenne, thanne, than*, OS. *thanna, than* (MDu. *danne, dan*, Du. *dan*), OHG. *danne, denne* (MHG. *danne, denne*, G. *dann*); cf. also Goth. *þan*; adverbial formations from the demonstr. root *þa-*: cf. THAT, THE.

See also THAN *conj.*, orig. the same word, which in both senses varied in ME. and 16th c. between *then* and *than*. So Mod. Ger. now has *dann* adv. 'then', *denn* conj. 'than'. Du. has *dan* in both senses. The history in OTeut. presents many points of difficulty: see Per Persson in *Indog. Forsch.* II. 206, Van Helten in *Paul & Br. Beitr.* XXVIII. 564–5.]

**A.** Illustration of Forms.

α. **1–3 (5) þonne.**

**898** Þonne [see B. 1]. **971** *Blickl. Hom.* 11 Ond þæt ȝeweorþeþ on domes dæȝe..Þonne forhtiaþ ealle ȝesceafta. *c* **1205** LAY. 711 Þonne [*c* 1275 wane] men gað to bedde. [*a* **1425** *Cursor M.* 7961 (Trin.) Dauid gat ȝitt a son þonne [*rime* salomonne].]

β. **1–5 þanne,** (3–4 **tanne**), **3–4 þane, 4 thane, 4–5 thanne.**

**871–89** *Charter of Ælfred* in *O. E. Texts* 451 Þanne ȝeselle he cc peninga eȝhwylce ȝere. *Ibid.* 452 Ðanne ann ic ðem..alles mines erfes to brucenne. *c* **1200** ORMIN 221, & tanne comm he siþþenn ut. *Ibid.*, Þanne [see B. 1]. *c* **1205** LAY. 1546 Þane [*c* 1275 wane] he wule..scaðe wrec wrchen. *a* **1300** *Cursor M.* 153 (Cott.) Hit sal be reddynn þanne [*G.* þane, *F.* þan]. *Ibid.* 21618 (Edin.) Ilke paskis..Þis croce was tanne man wont to se. *c* **1330** *Assump. Virg.* 767 But þei sawe in þat stede þana Liand as it were amana [= manna]. *c* **1375** *Sc. Leg. Saints* xii. (*Mathias*) 353 Þane kyste [= cast] þai cuttis til assay. *c* **1440** *Jacob's Well* (E.E.T.S.) 191 Þanne þis heued preyere doth þe no profyȝt.

γ. **1–3 þænne.**

*c* **1000** *Ags. Ps.* (Th.) xcv[i]. 5 Heofonas þænne worhte haliȝ Drihten. *a* **1050** *Byrhtferth's Handboc* in *Anglia* VIII. 306 Swa fela tida beoð þænne on þam dæȝe & on þære nihte. *c* **1205** LAY. 9521 Þænne beoð hit þe wurse.

δ. **2–5 þenne,** (**3 þeonne**), **4 þene, 4–6 thenne, 5 þeyne, þynne, thynne, theynne.**

*c* **1175** *Lamb. Hom.* 135 Ðenne þeȝs folkes larþew his sed wule sawen. *c* **1205** LAY. 12037 [They] iseȝen scipen an & an..þeonne [*c* 1275 þan] feowere þenne fiue. *c* **1375** *Sc. Leg. Saints* xxxi. (*Eugenia*) 106 Þe oure-men þat þe cite gouernyt þene. *c* **1420** *Avow. Arth.* xxx, Thenne waknut the king. *c* **1420** *Chron. Vilod.* 2078 Alle þey þenne for hurre gret sorwe þey made. *Ibid.* 2095 And sore weptone and snobbedone þeyne. *Ibid.* 3253 He was kyng of Englonde ȝet þynne. **1600** *St. Papers Eliz., Domestic* CLXXVIII. No. 78 (P.R.O.) Thenne he was at the same play.

ε. **2–4 þann, 3–4 þan (tan), 4–7** (*dial.* **–9**) **than** (**5 þon**); **4–5 þen, 5– then.**

*c* **1200** ORMIN 4197 Domess daȝȝ, Þann all mannkinn shall risenn. *c* **1275** LAY. 6396 Morbidus þe bolde warþ þan a-bolwe. **13..** *Cursor M.* 367 (Gött.) Þe world..Þat ȝeit was þan [*Cott.* tan] of forme vnschapin. *Ibid.* 3086 (Cott.) Fra þan [*c* 1375 *F.* þen] wit laban duelled he. *c* **1400** *Ywaine & Gaw.* 805 Hastily þan went þai all And soght him. *a* **1425** *Cursor M.* 6152 (Trin.) Þei were whenne þei to go bigon Six hundride þousonde fote men þon [*all other MSS.* bigan ..þan]. *c* **1440** Then [see B. 4]. *c* **1450** *St. Cuthbert* (Surtees) 1503 It falles oft þen and þen. *a* **1568** ASCHAM *Scholem.* Pref. (Arb.) 17, I was glad than and do rejoice yet. **1643** DENHAM *Cooper's H.* 135 Than did Religion in a lazy Cell, In empty, aery Contemplations dwell.

**B.** Signification.

* *Demonstrative adverb of time.*

**1.** At that time. (Referring to a specified time, past or future: opposed to NOW 1.)

† *Then as*, at the time that, when (= sense 6): see AS B. 27.

*Beowulf* 1456 Næs þæt þonne mætost mæȝen-fultuma þæt him on ðearfe lah ðyle hroð-gares. **898** *O. E. Chron.* an. 894 Swa hit þonne fierdleas wæs. *c* **1200** ORMIN 4200 Whase þanne [at doomsday] wurrþiȝ beoþ To takenn eche blisse. *a* **1300** *Cursor M.* 14506 (Cott.) Biscops war þai þan [*Trin.* þo] a-bute. *c* **1330** R. BRUNNE *Chron.* (1810) 2 In Westsex was þan a kyng, his [name] was Sir Ine. **1424** in Picton *L'pool Munic. Rec.* (1883) I. 22 That we should go with him to Liverpull, then as the said congregation and riots were ordained to be. *c* **1449** PECOCK *Repr.* I. xi. 55 The al hool Bible was not thanne. **1582** ALLEN *Martyrd. Campion* (1908) 85 Naming one but newly cummen then into the realme. **1605** SHAKS. *Macb.* I. vii. 49 When you durst do it, then you were a man. **1632** LITHGOW *Trav.* X. 492 Sir Walter Aston, then Leiger Ambassadour there. **1763** J. BROWN *Poetry & Mus.* v. 67 Melody had then its greatest Power, when the Melody was most confined in its Compass. **1796** LAMB *Let. to Coleridge* 13 June, I hope to be able to pay you a visit (if you are then at Bristol) some time in..August. **1857** BUCKLE *Civiliz.* I. xiii. 717 History, as it was then written.

†**b.** Strengthened by *as* preceding: see AS B. 34 a.

**1456** SIR G. HAYE *Law Arms* (S.T.S.) 126 The autoritee of the grete officer slokis as than..the autoritee of the smallare officer. *c* **1470** HENRY *Wallace* I. 375 Off that labour as than he was nocht sle. **1523–1653** [see AS B. 34 a].

**c.** At the time defined by a relative or other clause (with verb in pres. tense). (Cf. NOW 4.)

**1340** HAMPOLE *Pr. Consc.* 468 Þan has a man les myght þan a beste When he es born. **1456** SIR G. HAYE *Law Arms* (S.T.S.) 120 It folowis nocht na the vertu of force.. is alswele in his curage than as before. **1567** MAPLET *Gr. Forest* A vij, As it is with yse which dissolueth, then when it vanisheth away. *a* **1644** QUARLES *Sol. Recant.* Sol. xii. 49 Give him the firstlings of thy strength, even than When fading Childehood seeks to ripen man Vpon thy downy cheeks. **1772** TOPLADY *Hymn*, '*Your harps, ye trembling saints*' vii, When we in darkness walk,..Then is the time to trust our God. **1908** [MISS E. FOWLER] *Betw. Trent & Ancholme* 43 Then is the time to turn our backs upon the sun.

**d.** *Then and there* († *then there*), at that precise time and place; immediately and on the spot. (Also *there and then*: see THERE *adv.* 13.)

**1436** *Rolls of Parlt.* IV. 498 Ye said William..putte hir in a stronge chaumbre till nyght; and yen yere..felonously.. ravysshed ye said Isabell. **1442** *Ibid.* V. 42/1 Which entre ..was thenne and there graunted. **1587** in Picton *L'pool Munic. Rec.* (1883) I. 63 It was then and there concluded by a general consent. **1600** ABP. ABBOT *Exp. Jonah* 220 To be brought to the pits brinke, and then and there to be stayed. **1825** SCOTT *Betrothed* xxxi, The Constable De Lacy ..was then and there to deliver to the Flemings a royal charter of their immunities. **1889** JEROME *Three Men in Boat* 212 We had insisted..that the things should be sent with us then and there.

**2.** *Now and then*, † *then and then* (obs.), at one time and at another, at various times, at intervals, occasionally (cf. *here and there*). *Now..then..*, at one time..at another time. (See also NOW 6 b, 7 b.)

*c* **1205** [see A. δ]. **13..** *Cursor M.* 1848 (Fairf.) Þai..wende ay þan and þan to droun. **1398** TREVISA *Barth. De P. R.* XI. vii. (Bodl. MS.) lf. 108 b/2 It [rain]..comeþ doune thanne and thanne. *c* **1450** *St. Cuthbert* (Surtees) 1467 He walde it tell' þan and þan. *c* **1550** R. BIESTON *Bayte Fortune* B iij, The ryche peraduenture oppresseth nowe and than. *a* **1555** PHILPOT *Exam. & Writ.* (Parker Soc.) 334 If that those at any time, then and then, be deceived. **1670** EACHARD *Cont. Clergy* 26 Now and then in an age, one miraculously, beyond all hopes, proves learned. **1763** C. JOHNSTON *Reverie* II. 239 She listened to him.., asking him every now and then such questions as should [etc.]. *a* **1825** FORBY *Voc. E. Anglia* s.v. *Tan, Than*..loses the aspirate in one phrase only, 'now and *tan*' for 'now and *then*'. **1894** BARING-GOULD *Deserts S. France* II. 245 Restive, now sullen, then in boisterous revolt.

** *Of sequence in time, order, consequence, incidence, inference.*

**3.** At the moment immediately following the action, etc. just spoken of; upon that, thereupon, directly after that; also in wider application, indicating the action or occurrence next in order of time: next, after that, afterwards, subsequently (often in contrast to *first*).

Sometimes, in narrative, introducing a speech with ellipsis of *said* (now *poet.* or *rhet.*).

**971** *Blickl. Hom.* 21 Se mon se þe gód onginneþ & þonne ablinneþ. *a* **1000** *Phœnix* 216 Bæl bið onæled þonne brond þeceð heoredreorȝes hus. *a* **1225** *Ancr. R.* 36 Þeonne valleð adun, & siggeð, 'Christe audi nos', twie. **13..** *Cursor M.* 3904 (Cott.) Rachell bare..First ioseph, þan beniamin. **1362** LANGL. *P. Pl.* A. XII. 139 And þanne I kneled on my knes and kyste her wel sone. *a* **1400–50** *Alexander* 95 Þen Anec onane riȝt efter þire wordis, A lowde laȝter he loȝe. *c* **1440** *Alphabet of Tales* 196 And þe bisshop sayd; 'Nay, son, þer is none now in all þis land'..And þan þis Malchus: 'In þis I hafe a great mervayle, ffor [etc.]'. **1526** TINDALE *Mark* iv. 28 First the blad, then the eares, after that [*R.V.* **1881** then] full corne in the eares. *a* **1533** LD. BERNERS *Huon* lxxxvii. 277 He..sayd how he wolde slee Huon, & than haue Esclaramounde to his wyfe. **1627** HAKEWILL *Apol.* (1630) 214 He cast high in the aire, then received it againe in his armes. *a* **1654** SELDEN *Table-T.* (Arb.) 49 First we Fast, and then we Feast. **1776** *Trial of Nando-comar* 23/1 He was at first very ill, then got better; he is now worse. **1859** TENNYSON *Enid* 300 Then Yniol, 'Enter therefore and partake [etc.]'. **1895** *Law Times Rep.* LXXIII. 21/2 The annuity was regularly paid up to 1878, then Mr. Harle got into difficulties.

**b.** In the next place, next (in a series of any kind, or esp. in order of narration); beyond that, more than that, in addition, besides.

*c* **1290** *St. Michael* 511 in *S. Eng. Leg.* I. 314 Þat fuyr is hext,..þe eir is þanne next bi-neothe. **1297** R. GLOUC. (Rolls) 64 Viue & þritti ssiren..Barcssire, & hamptessire, & þanne middelsex. **1588** PARKE tr. *Mendoza's Hist. China* III. xxvi. 406 Then forwards on there are other two small kingdoms. **1596** SHAKS. *Tam. Shr.* II. i. 358 First,..my house within the City Is richly furnished.. then at my farme I haue a hundred milch-kine. **1652** NEEDHAM tr. *Selden's Mare Cl.* 32 Then, it is added next, concerning the West-border [etc.]. **1707** FARQUHAR *Beaux Strat.* I. i, *Aim[well]*...What other company have you in Town? *Bon[iface]*. A power of fine Ladies; and then we have the French Officers. **1828** SCOTT *F. M. Perth* vi, Then there are the minstrels, with their romaunts and ballads. **1847** C. BRONTE *J. Eyre* xvi, And then she had such a fine head of hair.

**4.** In that case; in those circumstances; if that be (or were) the fact; if so; when that happens. Often correl. to *if* or *when*. *What then?* (ellipt.) what happens (or would happen) in that case? what of that?

**695–6** *Laws of Wihtræd* c. 26 ȝif man frigne man..ȝefo, þanne wealde se cyning ðreora anes [etc.]. **971** *Blickl. Hom.* 41 ȝif ȝe þonne ȝelyfaþ..þonne biþ hit eow nyt ȝeseald. *c* **1175** *Lamb. Hom.* 137 Ðenne bið þes monnes wile ibeht mid þere elmisse. *c* **1205** LAY. 9521 Þænne beoð hit þe wurse. *a* **1250** *Owl & Night.* 508 (Cott.) Wane þi lust is ago, Þanne is þi song ago also. *c* **1374** CHAUCER *Troylus* II. 536 (585) Be ȝe wys as ȝe ben fayr to se, Wel in þe ringe than is the ruby set. *c* **1440** *York Myst.* iv. 69 An ye do, then shall ye dye. **1533** GAU *Richt Vay* (S.T.S.) 32 For quhy if he is owr fader thane ar we his barnis and aris. **1564** *Brief Exam.* ****ij, What then? Did he not appoynt temperall rites? **1593** SHAKS. *Lucr.* 380 O had they in that darkesome prison died, Then had they seene the period of their ill. *a* **1677** HALE *Prim. Orig. Man.* I. iii. 86 Then he could never have ridden out an eternal period. **1782** MISS BURNEY *Cecilia* v. ix, Suppose you..had never a farthing but of your own getting; where would you be then? **1826** *Art of Brewing* (ed. 2) 203 The screw is sometimes made of wood, and then it is mostly nine or ten inches diameter.

**b.** *But then..*: but, that being so; but at the same time; but on the other hand, but: introducing a statement (rarely a phrase) in some way contrasted with or limiting the preceding.

**1445** in *Anglia* XXVIII. 279 But than thi soule..right benygne to othir, A Juge grevous for shamefastnes is felt vnto thi selfe. **1599** SHAKS. *Much Ado* v. i. 205 He is then a Giant to an Ape, but then is an Ape a Doctor to such a man. **1672** VILLIERS (Dk. Buckhm.) *Rehearsal* III. i, It is not very necessary to the Plot..But then it's as full of Drollery as ever it can hold. **1774** GOLDSM. *Nat. Hist.* (1776) VI. 286 The Fishing Frog..very much resembles a tadpole or young frog, but then a tadpole of enormous size. **1826** DISRAELI *Viv. Grey* I. iv, There was..some difficulty in keeping all things in order, but then Vivian Grey was such an excellent manager! **1887** BIRRELL *Obiter Dicta* Ser. II. *Pope* Ess. 1899 I. 182 Pope knew next to no Greek, but then he did not work upon the Greek text.

**c.** *Or then* = or, if not, then..; or failing that; or else, or otherwise; or even. *Sc.*

**1375** BARBOUR *Bruce* I. 217 Gud Knychtis.. For litill

enchesoune or than nane, Thai hangyt be the nekbane. **1513** DOUGLAS *Æneis* I. vi. 43 Quhiddir thou be Dyane,..Or than sum goddes of the nymphis kynd. **1596** DALRYMPLE tr. *Leslie's Hist. Scot.* (S. T. S.) I. 7 Verie conuenient to feid horse or nout, or flockis of scheip or gait, or than grett harte and hyne. **1634** RUTHERFORD *Lett.* (1881) 500 Pray Him to tarry, or then to take us with Him. **1636** *Ibid.* 320 They are..valuing Him at their unworthy halfpenny or else exchanging and bartering Christ with the miserable old fallen house of this vain world, or then they lend Him out upon interest. **1825** JAMIESON s.v., Come hame sune, or than I'll be angry.

**5.** (As a particle of inference, often unemphatic or enclitic.) That being the case; since that is so; on that account; therefore, consequently, as may be inferred; so. *Now then*: see Now 9 b.

**971** *Blickl. Hom.* 39 Us is þonne mycel nedþearf þæt we ʒebuʒon to him. *c* **1230** *Hali Meid.* 5 Nis ha þenne sariliche..akast & in to þewdom idrahen. **1297** R. GLOUC. (Rolls) 2491 Sire graunte me þanne..As moche place as mid a þuong ich may aboute tille. **13..** *Cursor M.* 5987 (Gött.) Wend on þann, siþen ȝe wil ga. *c* **1400** *Apol. Loll.* 4 It is certayn þan, þowe he be his seruaunt. ? *a* **1500** *Wycket* (1828) p. v, Why shoulde it then be taken awaye frome us. **1539** BIBLE (Great) 2 *Sam.* iii. 18 Now then do it. **1598** SHAKS. *Merry W.* II. ii. 35 *Fal.* Good-morrow, good-wife. *Qui.* Not so, and't please your worship. *Fal.* Good maid then. **1600** — *A. Y. L.* IV. iii. 176 Well then, take a good heart, and counterfeit to be a man. **1668** MILTON *P. L.* The Verse, This neglect then of Rime so little is to be taken for a defect..that [etc.]. **1773** GOLDSM. *Stoops to Conq.* v. ii, *Hast.* This is a riddle. *Tony.* Riddle me this then. **1821** SCOTT *Kenilw.* xx, 'Ha!' said the Countess, hastily; 'that rumour then is true, Janet'. **1884** W. C. SMITH *Kildrostan* 86 We give up our cruise, then, after all?

*** *As relative or conjunctive adv. of time.*

† **6.** At the time that; when. *Obs.*

**971** *Blickl. Hom.* 17 Þonne se mona wanað, þonne tacnað he ure deaþlicnesse. *c* **1000** ÆLFRIC *Colloq.* in Wr.-Wülcker 102/13 Swyþe waxʒeorn eart þu, þonne [L. *cum*] þu ealle þingc etst. **1056-66** *Inscr. Kirkdale Ch., Yorks.*, Orm..bohte scs Gregorivs minster ðonne hit wes æl tobrocan & tofalan. *c* **1175** *Lamb. Hom.* 35 Ne beo he nefre swa riche, forð he scal þenne is dei cumeð. *c* **1200** ORMIN 8401 He wass, þanne he þiderr for, Neh off an ȝeress elde. *a* **1250** *Owl & Night.* 420 (Cott.) Þu forbernest welneȝ for onde Þane ure blisse cumeþ to londe. *c* **1300** *Harrow. Hell* (MS. E.) 37 Þan ihesu hadde spilt his blod For our sinnes on þe rode, He nam him þe riȝt way Vnto helle. *c* **1425** *Eng. Conq. Irel.* 4 Than hir lord hit herde, he was ther-of tened swith stronge. *a* **1440** *Sir Eglam.* 286 Then hys howndys began to baye, That harde [= heard] the jeant there he laye.

**** *As sb. or adj.*

**7.** Preceded by a preposition, as *by, since, till*, etc. (= by, etc. that time). (Cf. Now 13.)

*a* **1300** *Cursor M.* 10953 (Cott.) Als he forwit [*Gött.* bifore] þan was wont. **1340** HAMPOLE *Pr. Consc.* 4647 Fra þan Til þe day of dome. *a* **1400** *R. Glouc.'s Chron.* (Rolls) App. G. 258 King belin after þan to þis lond gan wende. *c* **1430** *Chev. Assigne* 143 By þenne was þe hermyte go in-to þe wode. **1509** BP. FISHER *Funeral Serm. C'tess of Richmond* Wks. (E.E.T.S.) I. 294 The matynes of our lady, which kepte her to then. **1667** MILTON *P. L.* I. 93 Till then who knew The force of those dire Arms? **1794** MRS. RADCLIFFE *Myst. Udolpho* xlii, All the time between then and now seems as nothing. **1884** *Punch* 26 Apr. 197/2, I used your Soap Two Years ago; since then I have used no other. **1905** *Daily News* 5 Jan. 6 The little man..had by then recovered himself.

**b.** *By then that*, by the time that; ellipt. *by then* (as relative), by the time: see BY A. 21 c. Now *arch.* or *dial.*

? *a* **1400** *Morte Arth.* 99 By than that endyd was the fight, The fals were feld. **1470-85** MALORY *Arthur* I. x. 49 By than they were redy on horsbak, there were vij C knyghtes. *c* **1500** *Robin Hood* 1737 By than the yere was all agone, He had no man but twayne. **1634** MILTON *Comus* 540 This evening late by then the chewing flocks Had ta'n their supper on the savoury Herb..I sate me down. **1788** T. TAYLOR *Proclus' Comm.* (1792) I. 12 By then he was twenty-eight years of age he composed a multitude of works. **1863** READE *Hard Cash* I. v. 157 By then he had folded and addressed it, she returned. **1906** *Graphic* 29 Dec. 892/1 By then ye've been church-cried, I'll be in t' chimney corner like any proper old gaffer.

**8.** That time; the time referred to (esp. a past time): often contrasted with *now*. Cf. NOW 14, 15.

**1549-50** PAGET *Let.* 22 Feb. in Strype *Eccl. Mem.* II. App. II, The tyme is tourned: then was then, and now is now. **1601** SHAKS. *All's Well* III. ii. 62 When thou canst get the Ring vpon my finger, which neuer shall come off,..then call me husband: but in such a (then) I write a Neuer. **1674** N. FAIRFAX *Bulk & Selv.* 161 God could bring forth the world at that *then*, wherein or when he had cast with himself the world could afterwards be made. **1847** W. THOM in *Whistlebinkie* (1890) II. 234 Companion of my happy then! **1901** *Daily News* 19 Mar. 6/3 He reveals a corresponding contrast between the then and the now.

**9. a.** In sense 1, followed by a participle or adjective forming an adj. phrase, as *the then existing system* = the system then existing. (See also 10 a.)

**1653** BAXTER *Saints' R.* II. vi. § 2 (ed. 4) 257 That the extirpation of Piety was the then great design. **1827** SCOTT *Highl. Widow* ii, The then unwonted circumstance..of a passenger being seen on the high-road. **1870** LOWELL *Among my Bks.* Ser. I. (1873) 6 The trivium..and the quadrivium ..of the then ordinary university course. **1888** BRYCE *Amer. Commw.* (1889) I. xlvi. 548 The then existing Constitution.

**b.** *attrib.* or as *adj.* That existed or was so at that time; *the then ruler* = the ruler that then was. (Cf. NOW 16.)

**1584?** SIDNEY *Earl of Leicester* Misc. Wks. (1829) 263 He saith they are no gentlemen, affirming, that the then duke of Northumberland was not born so. **1620** E. BLOUNT *Horæ Subs.* 367 To the then Bishop of Rome. *a* **1647** PETTE in *Archæologia* XII. 255 The most noble prince, my then master. **1765** BLACKSTONE *Comm.* I. ii. 157 A bill..was countenanced by the then ministry, for limiting the number of the peerage. **1876** L. STEPHEN *Hist. Eng. Th.* 18*th C.* I. 203 In the then state of critical enquiry.

***** **10.** *Comb.* **a.** *advb.*, with pples. or adjs., as *then-instant, -ruling, -united* (cf. 9 a); **b.** *attrib.*: † **then-skill**, a reason belonging to the particular time or occasion (cf. SKILL *sb.* 3): *for a then-skill*, for the occasion; **then-time**, the time that was then, the past time referred to.

**1602** WARNER *Alb. Eng.* Epit., The said Edmund (whom the Duke's faction for a then-Skill surnamed Crook backe). **1605** SYLVESTER *Du Bartas* II. iii. III. *Law* 198 While the then-Time's hideous face and form Boads them (alas!) nothing but wrack and storm. **1621** G. SANDYS *Ovid's Met.* VIII. (1626) 165 Whose waues..That then-vnited masse of earth dis-ioyne. *a* **1656** BP. HALL *Rev. Unrevealed* § 11 The expectation of the then-instant appearing of Christ. **1848** C. C. CLIFFORD *Aristoph., Frogs* 40 Without the leave Of the then-ruling powers.

Hence **Then** *v.* (*nonce-wd.*), in phr. *to now it and then it*: see NOW.

**Then**, obs. f. THAN; obs. inflexion of THAT, THE.

**Then**, variant of THENNE *Obs.*, thence.

**Thenabouts** (ðe·năbau·ts), *adv. rare.* [f. THEN *adv.*, after *thereabouts*.] About that time.

**1589** PUTTENHAM *Eng. Poesie* I. vi. (Arb.) 27 For then aboutes began the declination of the Romain Empire. **1842** R. OASTLER *Fleet Papers* II. 344, I was mentioned more than once thenabouts. **1844** TUPPER *Crock of G.* xxiv, Then, or thenabouts, the devil hinted 'steal it'.

**Thenad** (þe·n-, þī·næd), *adv. Anat.* [f. THEN-AR + *-ad*: see DEXTRAD.] Towards the thenal aspect.

**1803** BARCLAY *New Anat. Nomencl.* 166 Ulnad will signify towards the ulnar aspect...Thenad..towards the thenal. **1808** — *Muscular Motions* 397 The pronators rolling them thenad and radiad. **1857** DUNGLISON *Med. Lex.*, *Thenad* is used adverbially..to signify 'towards the thenal aspect'.

**Then-a-days** (ðe·nădēˈz), *adv. rare.* [f. THEN *adv.*, after *nowadays*.] In those days, at that (past) time.

**1688** R. L'ESTRANGE *Brief Hist. Times* III. 9 At Length, through a Wonderful Providence (as Providence went Then-a-Days) both these Wants were supply'd. **1768** Ross *Helenore* II. 87 'Bout then a days we never met wi' cross. **1844** *N. Brit. Rev.* II. 56 Then-a-days one could acquire a very complete knowledge of chemistry..in a very short space of time. **1898** M. B. EDWARDS in *Westm. Gaz.* 20 July 2/3 Then-a-days, ah! then-a-days, All the months were merry Mays.

† **Then a·fter, thena·fter**, *adv. Obs.* After then, after that time: = THEREAFTER.

**1470-85** MALORY *Arthur* x. i. 494 And thenne after he gaf hym a drynke. **1485** *Rolls of Parlt.* VI. 285/2 Unabled fro thenceforth for ever, to claime, have or enjoy, any of the premisses, by him thenne after. **1605** T. SPARKE *Brotherly Perswasion* (1607) 6 Homilies then published and authorised, or to be then after published and authorised. **1791** *Selby Bridge Act* 14 At all times for ever thenafter.

So † **Then afterward(s** *adv. phr.* in same sense.

*a* **1485** FORTESCUE *Wks.* (1869) 486 Thanne afterward he ..destroied the Reame of Assury. **1597** BEARD *Theatre God's Judgem.* (1612) 99 He..was condemned for an Heretike by the Nicene Councell, and his books burned: and then afterwards making shew before Constantine the Emperour, with a solemne oath to recant his old errours. **1671** H. M. *Erasm. Colloq.* 226 What didst thou then afterward?

**Thenal** (þī·năl), *a. Anat.* [f. THEN-AR + -AL.] Of or pertaining to the thenar.

**1803** BARCLAY *New Anat. Nomencl.* 125 We may use the terms Radial and Ulnar to signify the two lateral parts... To the other two sides we may give the epithets Anconal and Thenal. **1808** — *Muscular Motions* 398 Being thenal flexors of the carpus. **1823** J. LIZARS *Syst. Anat. Plates* I. v. 94 The muscles on the palmar or thenal aspect.

**Thenar** (þī·nāɹ). *Anat.* Also 8 tenar, thenor, tenor. [mod.L., a. Gr. θέναρ palm of the hand, sole or flat of the foot. Cf. OHG. *tenar*, MHG. *tener*; F. *thénar* (16th c.).] The ball of muscle at the base of the thumb; the palm of the hand; the sole of the foot.

**1672** SIR T. BROWNE *Let. to Friend* § 10 The Thenar or Muscle of the Thumb. **1704** J. HARRIS *Lex. Techn.* I, *Tenar*,..*Thenor*, or *Tenor*, according to some, is the Name for an abducent Muscle which draws the Thumb from the Fore-finger. **1857** DUNGLISON *Med. Lex.*, *Thenar*, the palm of the hand, or sole of the foot.

**b.** *attrib.* or as *adj.* *Thenar muscles*, the muscles which form the *thenar eminence*, the ball at the base of the thumb.

**1857** DUNGLISON *Med. Lex.*, *Thenar* or *Thenal Muscle*, Riolan and Winslow give this name to the fleshy mass, formed of the abductor brevis. **1898** P. MANSON *Trop. Diseases* xiv. 224 So may the thenar, the hypothenar, and the arm muscles [be found tender]. **1899** *Allbutt's Syst. Med.* VII. 209 A distinct flattening of the thenar eminence.

**Thenardite** (þenā·ɹdəit, ten-). *Min.* [Named in honour of L. J. Thénard, French chemist: see -ITE [1].] Anhydrous sodium sulphate occurring in white or brown translucent crystals.

**1842** *Penny Cycl.* XXIV. 310/2 Thenardite—(Anhydrous Sulphate of Soda)—occurs crystallized...It is used in the preparation of carbonate of soda. **1868** DANA *Min.* 616 The water exudes during winter from the bottom of a basin, and becoming concentrated in the summer season, deposits crystals of thenardite.

† **Thena·smon**, var. TENASMON *Obs.*

*c* **1400** *Lanfranc's Cirurg.* 290 Þou schalt acese þe akynge wiþ þis medicyn, & is good for thenasmon.

**Thence** (ðens), *adv.* Forms: 3-4 **þannes**, 4 **þ-, thennus**, 4-5 **þ-, thennes, -is, -ys, þens**, 4-6 **thens**, 5 **þenns**, 5-6 **thense**, 6- **thence**. [ME. *þannes, þennes*, f. THENNE *adv.*, with adverbial genitive suffix *-es, -s*. The later spelling *thence* for *thens* was to preserve the breath sound of *s* when final inflexional *s* became (z); as in *hence, pence, defence, once, twice, mice, price*, etc.]

**1.** From that place; from there. (Now chiefly *literary*.)

*c* **1290** *S. Eng. Leg.* I. 50/137 And bad heom of þulke holie bodi: Þat huy it þannes bere. **1340** *Ayenb.* 12 Ha [Christ] wente into helle..uor to draȝe þannes..þe zaules of þe holi uaderes. **1340-70** *Alex. & Dind.* 98, I..am temted ful tid to turne me þennus. **13..** *Cursor M.* 164 (Gött.) Hu þat he was þennis [*Trin.* þennes; *Cott.* theþen] ledd. *c* **1386** CHAUCER *Frankl. T.* 232 Er they thennes [*v.rr.* þennes, þens, thens] wente..They fille in speche. *c* **1400** *Brut* 103 Þat men myȝt hit nouȝt remeve ne bere þenns. *Ibid.* 114 Or he departede þens. **1526** TINDALE *Mark* vi. 1 He departed thens and cam in to his awne countre. **1536** WRIOTHESLEY *Chron.* (Camden) I. 51 The Kinge with his companye departed thense. **1667** MILTON *P. L.* I. 12 If Sion hill Delight thee more,..I thence Invoke thy aid. **1867** LADY HERBERT *Cradle L.* iv. 123 Thence..the pilgrims came to the beautiful low shrine. **1895** *Law Times Rep.* LXXIII. 156/2 The 'Kirkmichael' left Liverpool..on a voyage thence to Melbourne.

**b.** Preceded by redundant *from* (†*fro*).

**1382** WYCLIF *Mark* vi. 1 And Jhesus gon out thennis [*v. r.* fro thennes]. **1388** *Ibid.*, And he ȝede out fro thennus. *c* **1400** *Destr. Troy* 13270 To a perellus place past I fro thens. **1535** COVERDALE *Baruch* vi. 2 After that wil I bringe you awaye peaceably from thence. **1609** HOLLAND *Amm. Marcell.* XXI. x. 177 He commanded Victor the Hystoriographer, whom he saw at Sirmium, to come from thence unto him. **1703** POPE *Thebais* 383 Begin from thence, where first Alpheus hides His wand'ring stream. **1867** GEO. ELIOT in Cross *Life* (1885) III. 9 Making our way homeward from thence by easy stages.

† **c.** As relative (also *thence that*): From which place, whence. *Obs. rare.*

*a* **1450** *Knt. de la Tour* (1906) 36 Y must to the erthe thennes that y come fro.

**2.** At a place distant or away from there; distant; absent. Now chiefly in stating distance.

*c* **1290** *Beket* 1780 in *S. Eng. Leg.* I. 157 To longe ich habbe þannes i-beo. *c* **1384** CHAUCER *H. Fame* II. 530 Lat a man stond..A myle thens and here hyt route. **1450-1530** *Myrr. our Ladye* 28 Though they..haue leue to be thense yet yt suffysyth not. **1489** CAXTON *Faytes of A.* IV. x. 257 True proues that all that day he was ferre thens. *a* **1548** HALL *Chron., Edw. V* 13 While one manne is there, which is neuer thence. *Mod.* Two miles thence is a fine waterfall.

**3.** From that time or date; thenceforward; thenceforth. Mostly with *from*. ? *Obs.*

*c* **1374** [see THENCEFORTH 1]. **1382** WYCLIF *Isa.* xvi. 13 The wrd that the Lord spac to Moab fro thennys [1388 fro that tyme]. *c* **1449** PECOCK *Repr.* II. ix. 197 He seid that peple schulde frothens after worschipe. **1606** G. W[OODCOCKE] *Hist. Justine* xx. 78 That no subiect of Carthage should from thence learne Greeke letters. *a* **1751** BOLINGBROKE *Stud. Hist.* (1752) I. vi. 236 From thence down to the present day. *a* **1832** BENTHAM *Mem. & Corr.* Wks. 1843 X. 62, I must have seen him..more than once at Romilly's, and thence afterwards at my own house.

**4.** From that, as a source, origin, or cause; (as an inference) from those premisses or data; therefrom. Also preceded by *from*.

**1652** NEEDHAM tr. *Selden's Mare Cl.* 2 Next are premised som things, for explaining the terms of the Question, that it may bee clearly thence understood. **1692** E. WALKER *Epictetus' Mor.* ix, Weigh every Circumstance, each Consequence, And usual Accident arising thence. **1796** H. HUNTER tr. *St.-Pierre's Stud. Nat.* (1799) II. 409 It would thence follow, that..the number of women would daily go on [etc.]. **1817** JAS. MILL *Brit. India* II. v. ix. 702 They could present to parliament every thing which favoured their own purposes, keep back every thing which opposed them; and thence more effectually deceive the nation.

**Thence-a·fter.** *rare.* After that time; thereafter.

**1593** *Tell-Troth's N. Y. Gift* (1876) 18 Thence after they must sit no more in the shoppes. **1864** NEALE *Seaton. Poems* 187 Those blessed feet, thenceafter nailed Fast to the bitter cross!

**Thenceforth** (ðe·nsˌfōᵊɹþ, ðensˌfōᵊ·ɹþ), *adv.* [Orig. two words: THENCE and FORTH *adv.*]

**1.** From that time onward. Also with *from* (†*fro*).

*c* **1374** CHAUCER *Boeth.* IV. Pr. iii. 86 (Camb. MS.) For no wiht as by Ryht fro thennes forth þat hym lakketh goodnesse ne shal ben clepyd good. **1526** TINDALE *John* xix. 12 From thence forthe sought Pilate meanes to loose hym. **1536** WRIOTHESLEY *Chron.* (Camden) I. 55 To be observed and kept from thencefourth through all this realme. **1590** SPENSER *F. Q.* I. ii. 40 Thensforth I tooke Duessa for my Dame. **1812** SOUTHEY *Omniana* II. 231 He makes a law, that from thenceforth there shall be only two lawyers in England. **1870** MORRIS *Earthly Par.* I. i. 396 Thenceforth her back upon the world she turned.

**2.** From that place or point onward. *rare.*

*c* **1449** PECOCK *Repr.* v. xi. 540 Rede there and frothens forth into the eende of the argument. **1887** MORRIS *Odyss.* XII. 429 Night-long thenceforth was I carried.

**Thencefo·rward**, *adv.* [Orig. two words: THENCE and FORWARD *adv.*] = prec. Also with *from* (†*fro*).

**1457** *Cal. Anc. Rec. Dublin* (1889) 294 Fro thens forward al thos that ben abyll to be jurys. **1472-3** *Rolls of Parlt.* VI. 30/2 To be from thensforward true Liegemen. **1677** CARY *Chronol.* II. II. III. ii. 226 From thence-forward they might safely betake themselves to their Labours. **1732** BERKELEY *Alciphr.* IV. § 14 As an artist leaves a clock, to go thenceforward of itself for a certain period. **1856** FROUDE *Hist. Eng.* II. x. 430 No monks, thenceforward, were to leave the precincts of the monastery.

† **Thencefo·rwards,** *adv. Obs.* [f. as prec. + FORWARDS.] = prec.

**1684** T. BURNET *Th. Earth* I. 180 A new order then setled in nature, which should continue thence forwards so long as the earth endur'd. **1727** *Bradley's Fam. Dict.* s.v. *Hen,* Let them continue so for two Days without touching them, and from thenceforwards to the twentieth turn them.

**Thence-from,** *adv. arch.* [An inversion of *from thence*: cf. *hence-from.*] From that place or source; thence.

*a* **1618** SYLVESTER *Wood-man's Bear* lxxi, Thence-from crafty Cupid shot All the Arrows of his quiver. **1666** J. SMITH *Old Age* (1676) 240 They flow not thence-from. **1856** PATMORE *Angel in Ho.* II. II. i, My life is hid with him in Christ, Never thencefrom to be enticed.

† **Thence-ou·t,** *adv. Obs.* [f. THENCE + OUT *adv.*] Out of that place; out from there.

**1614** RALEIGH *Hist. World* II. 401 Adad..inuaded Damascus, and thrust Rezon thence-out.

† **The·nceward,** *adv. Obs.* [f. THENCE *adv.* + -WARD.] From that direction; thence.

*c* **1440** CAPGRAVE *St. Kath.* III. 1015 (MS. Arundel) But this noble Adryan..had blisse I-now assigned to his part, He had so moche he was ful looth thens-wart. *c* **1440** *Alphabet of Tales* 291 He delyverd þe Holie Lande oute of Saracens handis, and come fro thens-ward be Constantynople. **1600** ABP. ABBOT *Exp. Jonah* 566 Whatsoever was to come, being to come from thence-ward.

**Thenche, þenche,** obs. ff. THINK *v.*[1] and [2].

**Thend, -e,** pr. pple. of THEE *v.*[1], to prosper.

**Thene, þene,** obs. forms of THAN, THEN; obs. acc. sing. masc. of THAT, THE.

**Thenforth, -forthward**: see THENNE.

**Thenk(e, þenk(e,** obs. ff. THINK *v.*[1] and [2].

† **Thenne, then,** *adv. Obs.* Forms: α. 1 þanon(n)e, þonane, þonone, 2–3 þonene, 2–5 þanane, 3 þanene, þeonene, þenene. β. 3 þonne, 3–4 þanne, þeonne (3 þeone), 3–5 þenne (3 þene), 4–5 thenne. γ. 1 þanan, -on, -un, þonan, -on, 2 þenen, þeonen, 2–3 þanen. δ. 1 þona. ε. 4–5 þen, þan, 5 then. See also THYNE. [OE. *þanone, þanon, þonan,* etc. = OFris. *thana,* OS. *thanana, thanān,* ODu. **þanna* (MDu. *danne, dan,* Du. *dan*), OHG. *thanana, than(n)ân, dan(n)ân* (MHG., Ger. *dannen*), Goth. type **þanana*: all formed by the addition of particles to the stem *þa-* of the demonstrative THAT.

As to the relations of the OE. forms, the β group may have arisen from the α, with loss of the middle vowel: *þan(o)ne, þanne,* etc. From the β forms, loss of the final *e* gave *than, then,* as in THEN *adv.* The δ *þona* is app. the northern form of *þonan* in γ. But the prehistoric development in OTeut. and the relation of the preh. forms to those of THEN, is very obscure: see the articles referred to under THEN.]

**1.** Of motion: **a.** From that place; = THENCE 1.

α. *a* **900** CYNEWULF *Judith* xi. 132 Eodon ða geȝnum þanonne þa idesa ba ellenþriste. *c* **1000** *Ags. Gosp.* Matt. v. 26 Ne gæst þu þanone [*Lindisf.* ðona, *Rush.* þonan, *Hatton* þanen] ær þu aȝylde þone ytemestan feorðlingc. *c* **1175** *Þe Lesse Crede* in *Lamb. Hom.* 217 Þonene he kumeð to demen ðe quike and ðe deade. *c* **1205** LAY. 235 Sone he þonene [*c* **1275** þanene] iuatte. *Ibid.* 1297 Þeonene [*c* **1275** þanene] he ferde forð. **1297** R. GLOUC. (Rolls) 1050 Brut..þat his fader slow, & þeruore was þenene [*later v. rr.* þenne, þanne, þens, þennys] idriue.

β. *c* **1205** LAY. 654 Nolde he þonne [*c* **1275** þanne] fare. *Ibid.* 5971 Þæ Belin þeonne [*c* **1275** þanne] wende. *Ibid.* 31362 To fleomen hine þenne. *c* **1230** *Hali Meid.* 43 Þeone godd warp hire. *a* **1250** *Owl & Night.* 132 Euer he cuþ þat he comme þenne [*v.r.* þonne]. *c* **1300** *Havelok* 1185 Þer to dwellen, or þenne to gonge. **1362** LANGL. *P. Pl.* A. I. 71 Er heo þeonne ȝeode. *c* **1440** *Pallad. on Husb.* XII. 325 Pike all the filthes thenne.

γ. *Beowulf* (Z.) 1806 Wolde feor þanon cuma collen-ferhð ceoles neosan. *c* **725** *Corpus Gloss., Illinc,* þanan. **971** *Blickl. Hom.* 67 He..þa halȝan sauwla þonon alædde. *c* **1000** *Ags. Gosp.* Matt. xi. 1 He for þanun [*c* **1160** *Hatton G.* for þanen]. *a* **1131** *O. E. Chron.* an. 1123, Þeonen he ferde to Wudestoke. *Ibid.*, Ða ferde se kyng þenen to Portesmuðe. *a* **1175** *Cott. Hom.* 241 Þanen hit was ibroht up into heofene.

δ. *c* **950** *Lindisf. Gosp.* Luke xii. 59 Ne gæs ðu ðona oðð [etc.].

ε. **13..** *Cursor M.* 8945 (Cott.) Þe tre þai vte o þe temple drogh..þai drou it þen [*v.rr.* þeiþen, þennes]. *c* **1425** *Ibid.* 6676 (Laud) Men shall hym þan draw to die. *Ibid.* 16908 Er they then went. *c* **1420** *Chron. Vilod.* 3000 Þat þulke relekes nolde neuer go þen a-way.

**b.** With redundant *from*: = THENCE 1 b.

**1297** R. GLOUC. (Rolls) 7743 Fram salesburi to wiȝt He wende & fram þanene to normandie riȝt. *Ibid.* 8224 Fram þanene hii wende.

**c.** As a relative adverb: Whence, from where.

*c* **950** *Lindisf. Gosp.* Matt. xii. 44 Ic willo cerre in hus min ðona [L. *unde*] ic cuom. **13..** *Cursor M.* 2768 (Cott.) Loth..Gayns þam ras fra þen [*v.r.* þar] he sate.

**2.** Of position: = THENCE 2.

**1297** R. GLOUC. (Rolls) 5845 A toun..þat bote þre myle þanne nas. **13..** *Coer de L.* 2947 Saladyn was ten myle thenne. *a* **1375** *Joseph Arim.* 25 Neuer more come aȝeyn whon þei weore enes þenne. *c* **1450** LOVELICH *Merlin* 9866 Wers wylen they don, and we ben thenne.

**3.** = THENCE 3. (Only OE.)

*c* **888** K. ÆLFRED *Boeth.* xxx. § 2, & þonan wyrð anæþeled oð ðæt he wyrð unæþele. *a* **1000** *Gloss.* in Wr.-Wülcker 220/43 *Dehinc, i. deinde, abhinc, rursum,..dein, uel* þonane, *uel* forþan.

**4.** From that source, origin, cause; = THENCE 4.

*Beowulf* 1265 Þanon woc fela ȝeo sceaft gasta. *Ibid.* 1961 Þonon ȝeomor woc, hæleðum to helpe. *c* **897** K. ÆLFRED *Gregory's Past. C.* xl. 289 Ðonne wierð ȝehnescad ðonone sio ðreaung ðæs anwaldes. *c* **1000** *Ags. Ps.* (Th.) lxvii[i]. 8 Þanon eorðe byð eall onhrered. *c* **1400** *Rule St. Benet* 4 Þanane byhouis þam feȝte þam ane, at god es tar best help.

Hence † **Thenforth, -forthon** *adv.* = THENCEFORTH; † **Thenforthward** *adv.* = THENCEFORWARD; † **Thenward, -wards** *adv.* = THENCEWARD.

*c* **875** *Sax. Genealogies* 23 in *O. E. Texts* 179 *Ðonan forð. *a* **1023** WULFSTAN *Hom.* I. (1883) 1 He ða syððan..þanonforð ȝeseon ne mihte. **13..** *Cursor M.* 6357 (Cott.) Fra þan forth heild sir moyses þis wandes bath. **1426** in *Surtees Misc.* (1888) 9 Þat þe sayd John Lyllyng fra þan furth suld be of gude governaunce. *c* **1477** CAXTON *Jason* 6 Fro *thenne forthon he named him his broder. **1484** — *Fables of Æsop* III. xx. *c* **1200** *Trin. Coll. Hom.* 189 And *þanenforðward he bereȝeð him wið sinne. *a* **1225** *Ancr. R.* 296 Hie him so *þeoneward, & ascur him so scheomeliche. *c* **1230** *Hali Meid.* 43 As ha nuste hwuch wei ha come þeneward; ne con ha neauer ifinden na wei aȝainward. **13..** *S. Eng. Leg.* (MS. Bodl. 779) in Herrig's *Archiv* LXXXII. 313/40 Franceys al naked þenwardis gan gon.

**Thenne, þenne,** obs. form of THAN, THEN, THIN.

† **Then-tofo·re,** *adv. Obs. rare.* [f. THEN *adv.*, after *theretofore.*] Before then, before that time: = THERETOFORE.

**1626** L. OWEN *Spec. Jesuit.* (1629) 7 According to many graces and priuiledges then-tofore granted. **1706** *Col. Rec. Pennsylv.* II. 268 Complaints made of the excessive charge thentofore of obtaining Lycences. **1785** J. DISNEY *Mem. A. A. Sykes* 130 Bishop Atterbury had thentofore written largely in support of the power of the convocation.

**Thenward,** *adv.*: see under THENNE *adv.*

**Theo, þeo**: see THE, THIGH, THO *pron.* and *a.*

**Theo-** (þīo), or, before a vowel, **the-**, repr. Gr. θεο-, stem of θεός God; in many compounds adopted from, or formed on the analogy of, Greek, or from Greek (rarely Latin or other) elements. See in their alphabetical places THEANTHROPIC, THEOCRACY, THEOLOGY, THEOSOPHY, etc. **The:o-anthropomo·rphic** *a.*, pertaining to gods in human form; so **The:o-anthropomo·rphism**: cf. *anthropomorphic, anthropomorphism.* **The:o-astrolo·gical** *a.*, of or pertaining to astrology theologically treated. **Theoce·ntric** *a.*, centring or centred in God; having God as its centre. **Theochri·stic** *a.* [Gr. θεόχριστ-ος], anointed by God (Webster 1864). **The:o-colle·ctivist,** of the nature of collectivism as divinely instituted. **The:o-demo·cracy,** a democracy under divine rule. **Theodra·ma,** a drama in which the actors are gods. **The:ogeolo·gical** *a.*, of or pertaining to geology as accommodated to theological tenets. **Theogno·stic** [after AGNOSTIC; cf. Gr. θεόγνωστος known of God], one who holds that God is knowable. **Theohu·man** *a.*, both divine and human; that is God as well as man. **Theoktonic** (-ktǫ·nik) *a.*, of or pertaining to theoktony. **Theoktony** (þīǫ·ktŏni) [Gr. θεοκτονία (*Eccl.*)], killing or death of the gods. **Theoma·mmonist** (see quot.). **Theoma·nia** [Gr. θεομανία madness caused or inspired by God], religious mania; also, demonomania. **Theoma·niac,** one affected with theomania. **Theoma·stix** [-MASTIX], the scourge of (i.e. appointed by) God. **Theo·metry** [-METRY], measurement or estimation of God. **Theomicrist** (þīǫ·mikrist) [Gr. μικρός little], one who belittles God. **The:o₁misa·nthropist** (*nonce-wd.*, after THEOPHILANTHROPIST), one who hates God and man. **Theomo·nism,** a monism which recognizes God. **Theopa·nphilist** (see quot.). **Theopa·ntism** [Gr. πᾶς, παντ- all], (*a*) see quot. 1864; (*b*) the doctrine that God is all that exists: = PANTHEISM. **The·ophile** [Gr. θεοφιλής dear to the gods], one beloved of God; also, one who loves God; so **Theo·philist.** **The:o₁philoso·phic** *a.*, that applies philosophy to theology. **Theophoric** (-fǫ·rik), **Theophorous** (þīǫ·fŏrəs), *adjs.* [Gr. θεοφόρος, f. φέρειν to bear], bearing or containing the name of a god. **Theophy·sical** *a. nonce-wd.*, physical, but ordered by God. **Theo₁psy·chism** [Gr. ψυχή soul], ascription of a divine nature to the soul. **Theotau·rine** *a.* [Gr. θεόταυρος god-bull, a title of Zeus], of or pertaining to a god in the form of a bull. **The:o₁teleo·logy,** the doctrine of the divine direction of nature to an appointed end; hence **The:o₁teleolo·gical** *a.*

**1873** FAIRBAIRN *Stud. Philos. Relig. & Hist.* (1876) 349 The Hellenic mind..created those *theo-anthropomorphic doctrines. *Ibid.* 348 The one contributed the Monotheism, the other the *Theo-anthropomorphism, which lie at the basis of Christianity. **1833** *Fraser's Mag.* VIII. 572 Their *theo-astrological mythologies, and their symbolical mysteries. **1886** M. VALENTINE in *Homilet. Rev.* Oct. 283 The old *Theocentric Calvinism, in which every thing was made to revolve about the divine sovereignty. **1893** FAIRBAIRN *Christ in Mod. Theol.* II. i. 301 This theology must..be as regards source Christocentric, but as regards object or matter Theocentric. **1901** *Daily Chron.* 30 Aug. 3/4 Massachusetts with its township government centreing round the church, its *theo-collectivist modes of thought. **1830** *Hist. Eur.* in *Ann. Reg.* 244/2 The cajolery or intimidation ..employed by the priests to make their flocks join the faction of (what one of them called) the *theo-democracy. **1853** LIEBER *Civil Liberty* xxiv. 242 The Mormons themselves call their government a theo-democracy. **1801** W. TAYLOR in Robberds *Mem.* I. 389 A *theo-drama or..an epic poem, where all the actors are gods. **1852** R. KNOX *Gt. Artists & Gt. Anat.* 43 A theory or two was forced on him [Cuvier] by the *theo-geological school of England, which were not his. **1898** *Chicago Advance* 14 Apr. 491/3 Is man by..his powers..an Agnostic or a *Theo-gnostic? **1839** BAILEY *Festus* x. (1852) 139 Thou art and livest, man-god, Christ!.. The *Theohuman Being. **1875** R. B. ANDERSON *Norse Mythol.* iii. 60 The Eddas have a *theoktonic myth. *Ibid.*, Ends with a *theoktony (death of the gods). **1804** COLERIDGE *Lett., to T. Poole* (1895) 455 Such men I aptly christen *Theo-mammonists, that is, those who at once worship God and Mammon. **1857** DUNGLISON *Med. Lex.*, **Theomania,* demonomania. **1890** BILLINGS *Nat. Med. Dict.*, *Theomania,* religious monomania. **1879** SWINBURNE *Stud. Shaks.* iii. 214 The brutallest unwashed *theomaniac of the Thebaid. **1633** T. CAREW *Cœl. Brit.* Wks. (1824) 154 My offices and title are, supreme *theomastix, hupercrittique of manners. **1881** ROSSETTI *Soothsay* xii, The Power that fashions man Measured not out thy little span For thee to take the meting-rod In turn, and so approve on God Thy science of *Theometry. **1834** DE QUINCEY in *Tait's Mag.* I. 688 He had defended Christianity against the vile blasphemers and impotent *theomicrists of the day. **1831** SOUTHEY in *Q. Rev.* Jan. 113 Those who (in reference to the appellation of a sect, not more presumptuous, and somewhat less impious) deserve to be called the *Theomisanthropists. **1906** F. BALLARD (*title*) *Theomonism True: God and the Universe in Modern Light. **1908** *Daily News* 7 Feb. 4/2 Mr. Ballard.. calls it sometimes theism and sometimes theomonism. **1833** *Fraser's Mag.* VIII. 570 The *initiati* called themselves *Theopanphilists, those who believed in the universal exhibition of the Divinity in characters of love. **1864** N. WEST in *Homilet. Rev.* (1886) May 407 It is true to teach *Theopantism, or that God is in all things. **1873** FAIRBAIRN *Stud. Philos. Relig. & Hist.* (1877) 392 It may evolve an Akosmism or Theopantism which is but the apotheosis of nature. *c* **1645** HOWELL *Lett.* (1650) II. xlii. 54 Afflictions are the portion of the best *Theophiles. **1677** GALE *Crt. Gentiles* II. III. 84 Virtuose persons..are *Theophilists, or beloved of God. **18..** MILMAN is cited by Worcester as using **theophilosophic.* **1901** W. MACINTOSH *Rabbi Jesus* 182 With the dawn of Christianity the theophilosophic train of thought was carried onward and upward into a higher, nobler, purer channel. **1891** CHEYNE *Orig. Psalter* vi. 303 Such shortened forms of *theophoric names as Ahaz for Jehoahaz. **1903** *Expositor* May 323 We are left for conjecture to the *theophorous names of her kings. **1908** *Ibid.* Jan. 95 Yahu..is familiar enough from Hebrew theophorous names. **1775** ADAIR *Amer. Ind.* 129 By the time that this *theo-physical operation is performed on a patient [i.e. breaking his neck on pretence that it is the Divine will]. **1896** DK. OF ARGYLL *Philos. Belief* vi. 253 It may be said..that '*theopsychism' attributed to man, is the real explanation of what is called the anthropomorphism attributed in the Hebrew scriptures to the mind and will of God. **1814** SOUTHEY *Lett.* (1856) II. 368 When..prepared for the food of man, it..resembleth entirely in its appearance the *theo-taurine compost from whence it sprung. **1903** L. F. WARD *Pure Sociol.* III. xvi. 465 A doctrine that afterwards took the name of *teleology*,.. would be better called **theoteleology,* since it simply postulates a power outside of nature directing it toward some end.

‖ **Theobroma** (þīobrō·mă). *Bot.* [mod.L., f. Gr. θεός god + βρῶμα food.] A genus of low trees, of which one species, *Theobroma Cacao,* a native of tropical America, and now naturalized in other warm countries, is the source of cocoa and chocolate. Hence **Theobro·mic** *a. Chem.* in *theobromic acid*: see quots.; **Theobromine** (þīobrō·məin), a bitter volatile alkaloid, $C_7H_8N_4O_2$, resembling caffeine, contained in the seeds of the cacao tree.

[**1737** LINNÆUS *Genera Plant.* 367 Polyadelphia. I. Pentandria. *Theobroma.] **1760** LEE *Introd. Bot.* App. (1788) 331/2 Chocolate-nut, *Theobroma.* **1785** MARTYN *Rousseau's Bot.* xxxi. (1794) 478 In..Theobroma, or Chocolate..it [the nectary] is Bell-shaped. **1871** GARROD *Mat. Med.* (ed. 3) 194 Oil of Theobroma...Cacao Butter. A concrete oil obtained by expression and heat from the ground seeds of Theobroma Cacao. **1878** KINGZETT in *Jrnl. Chem. Soc.* XXXIII. 44, I propose for it the name of **Theobromic acid,* which recalls the source from which it is obtained, namely, the fat of the seeds of *Theobroma Cacao.* **1881** WATTS *Dict. Chem.* VIII. 1922 *Theobromic acid,* $C_{64}H_{128}O_2$. This acid, the highest known member of the fatty series, has been obtained..from cacao-butter. **1842** *Penny Cycl.* XXIV. 313/2 The analysis of *Theobromine by Wosresensky shows .. that this article [chocolate]..must be highly nutritious. **1887** MOLONEY *Forestry W. Afr.* 165 They contain a very appreciable quantity of theobromine, which assists the action of caffein and possesses similar properties to that base.

**Theocracy** (þi₁ǫ·krăsi). Also 7 -craty, 7–8 -crasie, -crasy. [ad. Gr. θεοκρατία (Josephus): see THEO- and -CRACY: cf. F. *théocratie* (1704 in Hatz.-Darm.).] A form of government in which God (or a deity) is recognized as the king or immediate ruler, and his laws are taken as the statute-book of the kingdom, these laws being usually administered by a priestly order as his ministers and agents; hence (loosely) a system of government by a sacerdotal order, claiming a divine commission; also, a state so governed: esp. applied to the commonwealth of Israel from the exodus to the election of Saul as king.

**1622** DONNE *Serm.* (ed. Alford) V. 209 The Jews were only under a Theocracy, an immediate Government of God.

*a* 1652 J. SMITH *Sel. Disc.* VII. iv. (1821) 346 Josephus..properly calls the Jewish government θεοκρατιαν, 'a theocracy', or 'the government of God himself'. 1737 WHISTON *Josephus, Agst. Apion* II. § 17 (1814) IV. 340 He [Moses] ordained our government to be what, by a strained expression, may be termed a Theocracy [ὡς δ' ἄν τις εἴποι, βιασάμενος τον λόγον, θεοκρατίαν]. 1741 WARBURTON *Div. Legat.* v. ii. II. 365 Thus the Almighty becoming their King, in as proper a Sense as he was their God, the Republic of the Israelites was properly a Theocracy; in which the two Societies, Civil and Religious, must .. be intirely incorporated. 1811 PINKERTON *Mod. Geog., Peru* (ed. 3) 694 The government of the incas was a kind of theocracy. 1836 J. H. NEWMAN *Par. Serm.* (ed. 2) II. xxi. 283 When they tired of the Christian Theocracy, and clothed the church with 'the purple robe' of Cæsar. 1863 STANLEY *Jew. Ch.* vii. 155 The 'Theocracy' of Moses..was a government by God Himself, as opposed to the government by priests or kings. 1864 BURTON *Scot Abr.* I. v. 276 It [the Church of Calvin] was a theocracy, dictating to all men the rule of the Deity as to their daily life. 1878 MACLEAR *Celts* ii. (1879) 17 The Druids were at once the ministers of a theocracy and the judges and legislators of the people.

b. *transf.* A priestly order or religious body exercising political or civil power.

1825 WELLINGTON *Desp.* (1867) II. 597 The Roman Catholic clergy, nobility, lawyers, and gentlemen having property, form a sort of theocracy in Ireland, which in all essential points governs the populace.

**Theocrasy** (þī·oˌkrēˈsi, þiˌǫ·krăsi). [ad. Gr. θεοκρᾶσία, f. θεό-ς god + κρᾶσ-ις mingling: see -Y.]

1. *Anc. Mythol.* A mingling of various deities or divine attributes into one personality; also, a mixture of the worship of different deities.

1816 G. S. FABER *Orig. Pagan Idol.* II. 248 The mystic theocrasy of the old mythologists, by which all their deities were ultimately resolved into one person. 1831 KEIGHTLEY *Mythol.* I. ii. 16 The system of theocrasy..or mixing up, as we may call it, of the gods together.

2. (See quot.)

1842 BRANDE *Dict. Sc.*, etc., *Theocrasy*, in ancient Philosophy, a term invented to signify the intimate union of the soul with God in contemplation, which was considered attainable by the newer Platonists.

Hence **Theocrasical** (-kræ·sikăl) *a.*, pertaining to or involving theocrasy.

1816 G. S. FABER *Orig. Pagan Idol.* I. p. xxxviii, Theocrasical identity of Osiris and Typhon.

**Theocrat** (þī·okræt). [f. next: see -CRAT. Cf. mod.F. *théocrate* (Littré).]

1. One who rules in a theocracy as the representative of the Deity; a divine or deified ruler.

1827 G. S. FABER *Orig. Expiat. Sacr.* 234 This mode of administering temporal sanctions on the part of the temporal theocrat of Israel. 1854 MILMAN *Lat. Chr.* VI. iii. (1864) III. 482 Admirers of the great theocrat [Pope Gregory]. 1852 *Westm. Rev.* Jan. 269 Mahomet gradually degenerated.. ultimately into a voluptuous tyrant and oppressive theocrat. 1874 REYNOLDS *John Baptist* viii. 490 The haughty theocrats of Persia dared to call on their subjects to adore them.

2. One who believes in or favours theocratic government; an advocate of theocracy.

1843 EMERSON *Misc. Papers, Carlyle* Wks. (Bohn) III. 313 Though no theocrat..Mr. Carlyle..finds the calamity of the times not in bad bills of Parliament, nor the remedy in good bills. 1895 *Q. Rev.* Oct. 355 Disraeli..was a born theocrat. 1897 GOLDW. SMITH in *Amer. Hist. Rev.* Oct. 138 For all but the aristocracy and extreme theocrats they must have been about the best years that Scotland had known.

¶ b. See quot. (? erroneous use).

1864 WEBSTER, *Theocrat*, one who obeys God as his civil ruler. 1882 OGILVIE (Annandale), *Theocrat*, one who lives under a theocracy; one who is ruled in civil affairs directly by God.

**Theocratic** (þīokræ·tik), *a.* [f. Gr. θεοκρατία THEOCRACY + -IC: cf. *aristocratic*, etc.] Of, pertaining to, or of the nature of theocracy.

1741 WARBURTON *Div. Legat.* v. ii. II. 375 The true Reasons of the Theocratic Form of Government. 1841 TRENCH *Parables* ii. (1877) 29 We may say generally of the parables..that St. Matthew's are more Theocratic; St. Luke's more ethical. 1865 LECKY *Ration.* (1878) II. 120 This Church and State theory..forms the last vestige of the old theocratic spirit that marks the earlier stages of civilisation.

**Theocratical** (þīokræ·tikăl), *a.* [f. as prec. + -AL: cf. *aristocratical*.] = prec.

1690 C. NESSE *O. & N. Test.* I. 180 A new common-wealth with a theocratical government. 1755 WARBURTON *Div. Legat.* v. iv. Wks. 1788 III. 123 Temporal rewards and punishments administered by the hand of God, followed, as a consequence, from the Jewish Government's being Theocratical. 1837 *Foreign Q. Rev.* XIX. 187 The prophetic books were preserved in writing by a theocratical people. 1853 E. V. NEALE *Anal. Th. & Nat.* 201 The original form of all governments appears to have been theocratical.

**Theocra·tically,** *adv.* [f. prec. (or THEOCRATIC): see -ICALLY.] In a theocratic manner; from a theocratic point of view.

1827 G. S. FABER *Orig. Expiat. Sacr.* 234 Even the precept of a perfect love to God, when viewed theocratically, was part and parcel of the statute law of Israel.

**Theod, theode,** var. THEDE *Obs.*, people.

**Theo-democracy**: see THEO-.

**Theodicy** (þiˌǫ·disi). Also 9 theodice, -ee. [ad. F. *théodicée*, the title of a work of Leibnitz (1710), f. Gr. θεό-ς God + δίκη justice.] The, or a, vindication of the divine attributes, esp. justice and holiness, in respect to the existence of evil; a writing, doctrine, or theory intended to 'justify the ways of God to men'. Cf. OPTIMISM I.

1797 D. STEWART in *Encycl. Brit.* (ed. 3) XI. 481/2 Metaphysical theology, which Leibnitz and some others call theodicy. 1825 COLERIDGE *Aids Refl.* (1848) I. 120 All the theodices ever framed by human ingenuity, before and since the attempt of the celebrated Leibnitz. 1875 WHITE *Life in Christ* v. xxix. (1878) 500 Their theodicy is based on the belief that out of all evil God will bring eternal good.

Hence **Theodice·an,** one who frames or maintains a theodicy.

1873 MORLEY *Rousseau* I. 322 All things are for the best, said Rousseau and the theodiceans.

**Theodidact** (þī·oˌdidækt), *a.* and *sb.* [f. THEO- + Gr. διδακτ-ός taught.] **a.** *adj.* Taught by God. **b.** *sb.* One taught by God.

1715 M. DAVIES *Athen. Brit.* I. 66 Pretended Theodidacts, and self-knowing Gnosticks. 1865 tr. *Strauss's New Life Jesus* I. I. xxx. 262 The young Theodidact was able.. to give some advice to the most learned. 1894 LOUISE S. HOUGHTON tr. *Sabatier's St. Francis* Introd. 16 Owing nothing to church or schools he [St. Francis] was truly theodidact.

†**The·odisc,** *a.* *Obs. rare.* [OE. *þéodisc* = OS. *thiudisc*, OHG. *diutisc*:—OTeut. **þeudisko-z*, f. OE. *þéod*, THEDE. Cf. DUTCH. If the word had survived in later ME., its form would have been **theedish*.] Of or belonging to a nation or people; native, national, popular; in biblical use, Gentile; in quot. 1715 used for Old German.

*c* 1000 *Aldhelm Gl.* viii. 350 in Napier *O. E. Gloss.*, *Gentiles*, þeodisce. *c* 1205 LAY. 5838 Wende þa þeodisce men [*c* 1275 þe Romanisse] þat Belin wolde þenne. 1715 M. DAVIES *Athen. Brit.* I. 197 Who turn'd the Gospels into Theodisck or Old Francick Rhyme.

**Theodolite** (þiˌǫ·dŏləit). Forms: 6–7 theodelitus, 7 theodelite, -dolit, -dilit, 8 -dolet, 7– theodolite. [Origin unknown: see Note below.]

A portable surveying instrument, originally for measuring horizontal angles, and consisting essentially of a planisphere or horizontal graduated circular plate, with an alidad or index bearing sights; subsequently variously elaborated with a telescope instead of sights, a compass, level, vernier, micrometer, and other accessories, and now often with the addition of a vertical circle or arc for the measurement of angles of altitude or depression.

The original *theodelitus* of Digges was for horizontal angles only, and many quots. down to 19th c. use the name in this sense; Digges also describes a compound instrument having also a vertical semicircle for taking altitudes, but he calls that his *topographicall instrument*, restricting the name *theodelitus* to the horizontal circle.

1571 DIGGES *Pantom.* I. xxvii. H iij, The composition of the instrument called Theodelitus. It is but a circle diuided in 360..degrees, or a semicircle parted in 180 portions, and euery of those diuisions in 3 or rather 6 smaller partes... The index of that instrument with the sightes &c. are not vnlike to that whiche the square hath: In his backe prepare a vice or scrue to be fastned in the top of some staffe. *Ibid.* I ij, [In the figure] GEFO [is] *Theodelitus*, GF his *Alhidada* or index with sightes. *Ibid.* xxix. I j b, Describing also within the same square the Planisphere or circle called Theodelitus. 1607 J. NORDEN *Surv. Dial.* III. 127 It [Circumferentor] is a new name giuen to the very Theodelite, used in a sort otherwise then the Theodelite. 1611 A. HOPTON *Speculum Topogr.* vi. 27 The Theodelitus is an instrument consisting of a Planisphere and an Alhidada. *Ibid.* Table D d 2b, To take a plat at one station by the Theodelite. 1669 STURMY *Mariner's Mag.* II. 46 Any Instrument, as the Plain Table, the Theodolit or Circumferenter. 1701 MOXON *Math. Instr.* 20 *Theodolet*, a whole Circle made of Brass, containing 360 degrees, diagonally or otherwise divided, with an Index and sights moving on the Center, and a box and Needle in the middle. 1790 ROY in *Phil. Trans.* LXXX. 136 It is a brass circle, three feet in diameter, and may be called a great theodolet, rendered extremely perfect. 1833 HERSCHEL *Astron.* ii. § 155 The zenith sector and the theodolite are peculiar modifications of the altitude and azimuth instrument. 1842 *Penny Cycl.* XXIV. 314/2 *Theodolet*, or *Theodolite*...the name generally given to the instrument used for measuring horizontal angles. [*Ibid.* 315/2 The problem is to measure the horizontal angle between two objects. *Ibid.* 316/2 If the vertical angles are to be measured as accurately as the horizontal angles, the instrument becomes an altitude and azimuth circle.] [Cf. ALTAZIMUTH.]

**b.** *attrib.*, as **theodolite-goniometer**, a goniometer with horizontal and vertical graduated circles; **theodolite-magnetometer**, an instrument for measuring magnetic declination, and for observations of magnetic force; **theodolite-needle**, the needle of the compass of a theodolite.

1820 SCORESBY *Acc. Arctic Reg.* I. 333 A theodolite needle..performed ten vibrations in sixty seconds. 1877 KNIGHT *Dict. Mech.*, Theodolite-magnetometer. 1909 *Cent. Dict. Suppl.*, Theodolite-goniometer.

Hence **Theodoli·tic** *a.*, of, pertaining to, done or made with a theodolite (Webster 1864).

[*Note.* The name, alike in the Latinized form *theodelitus* and the vernacular *theodelite* (subseq. *-dolite*), originated in England, and is not known in French and German until the 19th c. Its first user, and probable inventor, L. or T. Digges, has left no account of its composition, as to which various futile conjectures, incompatible with its early history and use, have been offered; such is the notion that it arose in some way out of *alhidada* or its corruption *athelida* occurring in Bourne's *Treasure for Travailers* 1578, which an examination of the works of Digges and Bourne, where both words occur in their proper senses, shows to be absurd. *Theodelite* has the look of a formation from Greek; can it have been (like many modern names of inventions) an unscholarly formation from θεάομαι 'I view' or θεῶ 'behold' and δῆλος 'visible, clear, manifest', with a meaningless termination ?]

**Theodom**: see THEOWDOM.

**Theodosian** (þīodōu·siăn, -dōu·ʃiăn), *a.* and *sb.* [f. the name *Theodosi-us*: see -AN.]

**A.** *adj.* Of or pertaining to one named Theodosius; *esp.* of or pertaining to the Roman emperor Theodosius II (A. D. 408–450).

*Theodosian code*, a collection of laws made by direction of Theodosius II, and published A. D. 438.

1765 BLACKSTONE *Comm.* I. Introd. iii. 81 Which Theodosian code was the only book of civil law received as authentic in the western part of Europe till many centuries after. 1802 RANKEN *Hist. France* II. II. iii. § 2. 251 The Gothic gave way to the Theodosian code. 1833 *Encycl. Brit.* (ed. 7) V. 713/2 In the novel which sanctions the Theodosian Code, the emperor evidently admits that the compilers whom he had employed were not mere copyists. 1864 BRYCE *Rom. Emp.* iii. (1889) 29 Revised editions of the Theodosian code were issued by the Visigothic and Burgundian princes.

**B.** *sb.* **1.** A follower of Theodosius, a rhetorician of Alexandria, who became (A.D. 535) the leader of a division of the MONOPHYSITES.

1788 GIBBON *Decl. & F.* xlvii. IV. 611 *note*, The Gaianites and Theodosians. 1797 *Encycl. Brit.* (ed. 3) I. 797/2 Theodosians..held that the persons of the Trinity are not the same; that none of them exists of himself, and of his own nature; but that there is a common god or deity existing in them all, and that each is God, by a participation of this deity. 1874 J. H. BLUNT *Dict. Sects* (1886), *Theodosians*, the Alexandrian section of the sect of the Phthartolatræ.

**2.** A member of a sect founded by Theodosius, a Russian monk: see quot. 1860.

1860 J. GARDNER *Faiths World*, *Theodosians*, a sect of dissenters from the Russo-Greek Church who separated some years since from the Pomoryans, partly because they neglected to purify by prayer..articles..purchased from unbelievers. 1874 in J. H. BLUNT *Dict. Sects*, etc.

**Theodotian** (þīodōu·ʃiăn, -dōu·tiăn). [f. the name *Theodot-us*: see -IAN.] A follower of Theodotus ('the Tanner') of Byzantium, who (*c* 200 A. D.) taught the antitrinitarian doctrine of the MONARCHIANS; also, a follower of Theodotus ('the Banker') who promulgated a similar heresy in the 3rd c. A.D. Hence **Theodo·tianism.**

1853 W. E. TAYLOR *Hippolytus* II. iv. 102 Disputes occurring among the Theodotians, he became the head of a new sect. 1874 J. H. BLUNT *Dict. Sects, Heresies*, etc. (1886) s.v., Epiphanius writes that the Theodotians held Christ to be a mere man, and begotten of the seed of man... Hippolytus and Theodoret state that they had their beginning from Theodotus the Banker. 1876 A. PLUMMER tr. *Döllinger's Hippolytus & Callistus* iv. 287 *note*, A full denial of the divinity of Christ or Theodotianism.

**Theo-drama**: see THEO-.

**Theody** (þī·odi). [ad. It. *teodia*, ad. L. **theōdia*, *Gr. θεῳδία, f. θεό-ς God + ᾠδή song: cf. MELODY.] A song of praise to God; a psalm.

1867 LONGF. *Dante, Paradiso* xxv. 73 '*Sperent in te*', in the high Theody He sayeth, 'those who know thy name' [*orig.* Sperino in te, nell'alta Teodia, dice, color che sanno il nome tuo].

**Theof, Theofthe,** obs. ff. THIEF, THEFT.

**Theogeological, -gnostic**: see THEO-.

†**Theo·gonal,** *a.* [irreg. f. THEOGONY.] = next.

1727 A. HAMILTON *New Acc. E. Ind.* I. p. vii, Opportunities to know some topographical, historical, and theogonal Parts of this Work, from the Natives. *Ibid.* p. xxi, The theogonal and moral Parts may without Doubt, deserve some serious Thoughts or Attention.

**Theogonic** (þīogǫ·nik), *a.* [f. as next + -IC.] Of or pertaining to theogony; of the nature of theogony. So **Theogo·nical** *a.*

1840 tr. *C. O. Müller's Hist. Lit. Greece* xvi. § 4. 234 They show that by this time the character of the *theogonic poetry had been changed, and that Orphic ideas were in vogue. 1846 GROTE *Greece* I. xvi. I. 493 The acts described in the old heroic and theogonic legends. 1880 GLADSTONE in *19th Cent.* Apr. 720 The probable forms of theogonic and anthropomorphic evolution. 1854 MILMAN *Lat. Chr.* (1863) II. 30 To reconcile the doctrines of the Gospel with the *theogonical system of Asia.

**Theogonist** (þiˌǫ·gŏnist). [f. next + -IST. (In sense 2, f. Gr. θεόγονος born of God.)]

**1.** One who is versed in or treats of theogony.

1678 CUDWORTH *Intell. Syst.* I. iii. § 13. 114 Such Theologers as these, who were Theogonists, and Generated all the Gods..out of Sensless and Stupid Matter. 1845 MAURICE *Mor. & Met. Philos.* in *Encycl. Metrop.* (1847) II. 635/1 Plato, the cosmogonist and theogonist, is another man altogether from Plato the seeker of hidden truths in the facts which lay before him. 1880 E. MYERS *Æschylus* in E. Abbott *Hellenica* 16 If Pindar and Aeschylus treated the primitive theogonies with reverence, it was not the reverence of a primitive theogonist.

¶ **2.** *erron.* One who is born of God.

1833 *Fraser's Mag.* VIII. 570 [In] Genesis..it is..stated that the aboriginal races of just men distinguished themselves by this..title, Alibenim, theogonists, or God's sons, from the atheistical Sathanists, or evil-seekers.

So **Theo·gonism,** a system or theory of theogony; **Theo·gonite** = sense 2.

1678 CUDWORTH *Intell. Syst.* Pref. 34 That strange kind of Religious Atheism, or Atheistick Theogonism, which asserted..Beings..called by them Gods;..Generated at First out of Night and Chaos..and Corruptible again into the same. *Ibid.* Contents I. v. 726 A certain kind of Atheistick Theism, or Theogonism, which acknowledging a God or Soul of the World,..supposed Him..to have emerged out of Night and Chaos. 1831 *Fraser's Mag.* IV. 94 He [Lord Brougham] assumes too much of the theogonite to be wise.

**Theogony** (þiˌǫ·gŏni). Also 8–9 *erron.* -geny.

[ad. Gr. θεογονία generation or birth of the gods, f. θεός god + -γονία a begetting. So F. *théogonie.*] The generation of the gods; *esp.* an account or theory, or the belief or study, of the genealogy or birth of the deities of heathen mythology.

1612 SELDEN *Illustr. Drayton's Poly-olb.* xi. 183, I imagine many of their descents were iust as true as the Theogonie in Hesiod. 1656 BLOUNT *Glossogr., Theogonie,* the beginning or generation of the gods. 1748 HARTLEY *Observ. Man* II. ii. 87 There were many Cosmogonies and Theogonies current amongst the Pagans. 1853 MAX MÜLLER *Chips* (1880) I. iii. 73 In the Veda,..a theogony of which that of Hesiod is but the last chapter. 1859 I. TAYLOR *Logic in Theol.* 253 Theogenies, and theories of the universe.

**Theohuman, theoktonic, -ny**: see THEO-.

**Theolatry** (þiˌǫ·lătri). [ad. Gr. θεολατρεία worship of God, f. θεός God + λατρεία worship: see -LATRY.] The worship of a deity or deities.

1806 *Edin. Rev.* VII. 487 The distinction between herolatry and theolatry, or the sacred rites of heroes and the sacred rites of Gods, was perfectly well known in Greece. 1887 J. C. MORRISON *Service of Man* 265 The worship of deities has passed into the service of man. Instead of Theolatry we have anthropolatry.

**Theolepsy** (þī·olepsi). *rare.* [ad. Gr. θεοληψία, f. θεός god + -ληψία, f. λῆψις seizure, f. λαμβάνειν, root λαβ- to take.] Seizure or possession by a deity, inspiration. So **Theole·ptic** [Gr. θεοληπτικ-ός adj.], one possessed or inspired by a deity.

1881 W. ALEXANDER *Speaker's Comm. N. T.* IV. 332/2 The streets of Ephesus were full of theoleptics and convulsionaries. 1886 MAUDSLEY *Nat. Causes & Supernat. Seemings* 222 The incoherent utterances which..the theoleptic..poured out under divine compulsion. *Ibid.* 315 Neither theolepsy, nor diabolepsy, nor any other lepsy in the sense of possession of the individual by an external power.

**Theolog**, obs. form of THEOLOGUE.

**Theologal** (þiˌǫ·lŏgăl), *a.* and *sb.* [a. F. *théologal* adj. and sb. (14th c. in Hatz.-Darm.), f. Gr.-L. *theolog-us* theologian: see -AL.]

†**A.** *adj.* in *theologal virtues* [OF. *vertus théologales* (14th c.)]: see THEOLOGICAL *a.* 1. *Obs.*

1484 CAXTON *Chivalry* 71 Of the seuen vertues thre ben theologale or deuyne and the other four ben cardynal. The theologal ben fayth, hope and charyte. 1502 *Ord. Crysten Men* (W. de W. 1506) I. v. 48 There ben thre vertues theologales & infuses. 1610 DONNE *Pseudo-martyr* 190 Theologall vertues, Faith, Hope, and Charity, are infus'd from God. *Ibid.* 210 This is not meant onely of Charitie, as it is a Theologall vertue.

**B.** *sb.* *R. C. Ch.* A lecturer on theology and Holy Scripture attached to a cathedral or collegiate church. Also called *theologus* and *canon theologian.*

1638 BAKER tr. *Balzac's Lett.* (vol. III) 173 To Monsieur Senne, Theologall of the Church of Saints. 1872 JERVIS *Gallican Ch.* I. xi. 389 *note,* The theologal enjoyed a canonry by virtue of his office.

†**Theo·logant.** *Obs. rare*⁻¹. [ad. med.L. *theologānt-em,* pres. pple. of *theologāre, -ārī* (Du Cange) to theologize: see -ANT.] = THEOLOGER.

1678 MARVELL *Def. J. Howe* Wks. (Grosart) IV. 1169 The Theologants of former and later times..have attempted to clamber [etc.].

**Theologaster** (þiˌǫlŏgæ·stəɹ). [a. med.L. *theologaster* (Luther 1518), f. *theolog-us* theologian: see -ASTER.] A shallow or paltry theologian; a smatterer or pretender in theology.

1621 BURTON *Anat. Mel.* II. ii. III, The like measure is offered unto God himself by a company of theologasters. 1642 H. MORE *Song Soul* Interpr. Words, Superficiall conceited Theologasters..having but the surface and thin imagination of divinity. 1744 WARBURTON *Rem. Occas. Refl.* I. App. 134 This sorely distresses our Theologaster. 1888 SCHAFF *Hist. Chr. Ch.* VI. III. lix. 322 The furious decree of the Parisian theologasters.

Hence **Theologa·stric** *a.*, of or pertaining to a theologaster; in quot. as *sb.* a theologaster.

1894 FROUDE *Erasmus' Life & Lett.* iv. 65, I am speaking merely of the theologastrics of our own time, whose brains are the rottenest.

**Theologate** (þiˌǫ·lŏgĕt). *R. C. Ch.* [ad. mod. L. *theologāt-us,* f. *theolog-us* theologian: see -ATE¹.]

**1.** The course in theology prescribed for candidates for the priesthood.

1889 in WORCESTER *Suppl.*

**2.** A theological college or seminary.

1884 *Mrs. Calderwood's Jrnls.* v. 169 *note,* The Jesuit College at Liège, the theologate of the English Province. 1898 *Month* Oct. 439 The Professor of Holy Scripture at the great Jesuit Theologate of Woodstock. 1906 *Tablet* 15 Sept. 401 Ditton Hall, not far from Liverpool, where the exiled German province then had its theologate.

**Theologe**, obs. form of THEOLOGUE.

**Theologer** (þiˌǫ·lŏdʒəɹ). Now *rare.* [f. stem of Gr.-L. *theolog-us* or Eng. *theolog-y* + -ER¹: see -LOGER.] One who studies or busies himself with theology; = THEOLOGIAN (but now with less implication of scholarship). **a.** In reference to Christianity or other monotheistic religion.

1588 J. HARVEY *Disc. Probl.* 37 After which last maner may our diuines, or Theologers be termed prophets, but not otherwise. 1653 H. MORE *Conject. Cabbal.* (1713) 39 Supposing them [conclusions] true,..till such time as some able Philosopher or Theologer shall convince me of their falshood. 1756 AMORY *Buncle* (1770) II. 126 To make me a theologer, that I might be an able defender of the Creed of St. Athanasius. 1849 O. BROWNSON *Wks.* VII. 16 The theological speculations of theologers, as he [Dr. Bushnell] contemptuously calls them.

**b.** In reference to pagan religions.

1609 HOLLAND *Amm. Marcell.* 166 That..Goddesse Themis, whom..the antient Theologers have shrined in the verie bed and throne of Jupiter. 1678 CUDWORTH *Intell. Syst.* Pref. 38 The Pagan Theologers..acknowledged one Sovereign..Deity, from which all their other Gods were Generated or Created. 1724 COLLINS *Grounds Chr. Relig.* I. xi. 83 Allegory was in use among the Pagans; being cultivated by many of the Philosophers themselves as well as by Theologers. 1876 BLACKIE *Lang. & Lit. Highl. Scotl.* ii. 79 The 'Works and Days' of the old Bœotian theologer [Hesiod].

**Theologian** (þīolōu·dʒiăn). Also 5–6 -yen. [a. F. *théologien* (14th c. in Hatz.-Darm.), f. *théologie* or L. *theologia* THEOLOGY; subseq. assimilated to L. spelling: see -LOGIAN.] One who is versed in theology; *spec.* one who makes a study or profession of theology; a divine. Also *attrib.*

1483 CAXTON *Cato* F j b, The phycycyen was..ryght good Theologyen or knowyng the dyuyne scryptures. 1509 FISHER *Funeral Serm. C'tess Richmond* Wks. (1876) 303 Whiche thinge not onely the theologyens wytnesse, but the phylosophers also. *a* 1627 HAYWARD *Edw. VI* (1630) 84 Some theologians..desteining their professions..by publishing odious vntruths. 1667 MILTON *P. L.* v. 436 The common gloss Of Theologians. 1769 ROBERTSON *Chas. V,* XI. III. 352 The abilities or zeal of theologians long exercised in disputation. 1836 H. ROGERS *J. Howe* ii. (1863) 23 Professed theologians were not the parties for whom the Bible was exclusively, or even principally intended. 1897 *Scotsman* 26 May 10/6 My theologian judges and my lay judges.

**b.** In reference to pagan religions: = THEOLOGER b. *rare.*

1603 HOLLAND *Plutarch's Mor.* 1047 The olde Theologians and Divines..have put into the hands of the images of the gods, musicall instruments. 1904 BUDGE *3rd & 4th Egypt. Rooms Brit. Mus.* 127 Under the New Empire the votaries of Rā formed a numerous and powerful body, and their theologians and priests endeavoured to impress their views on the country in general.

**c.** *Canon theologian* (R. C. Ch.) = THEOLOGAL B.

1885 *Cath. Dict.* (ed. 3) s.v. *Canon Theologian,* The Council of Trent directed..that..in..cathedral..or even collegiate churches..a Canon Theologian..should be appointed.

**Theologic** (þīolǫ·dʒik), *a.* (*sb.*) [ad. F. *théologique* (14th c. in Hatz.-Darm.), ad. L. *theologic-us,* a. Gr. θεολογικός, f. θεολογία THEOLOGY.]

**1.** Of or belonging to theology; = next, 2.

1477 EARL RIVERS (Caxton) *Dictes* 78 Aristoteles..lerned of plato..Ethikes and the iiij sciences theologikes. 1669 GALE *Crt. Gentiles* I. Introd. 4 Plato..derived the choisest of his contemplations, both Physiologic, and Theologic..from the Jewish Church. 1678 CUDWORTH *Intell. Syst.* I. iv. 323 It was customary with the Egyptian Priests, to entitle their own Philosophick and Theologick Books, to Hermes. 1780 H. WALPOLE *Let. to Cole* 4 July, I hate theologic or political controversy. *a* 1876 M. COLLINS *Th. in Garden* (1880) II. 237 These young theologic adepts fancy they know everything.

†**2.** = THEOLOGICAL *a.* 1. *Obs. rare.*

1605 DRAYTON *Man in Moone* 488 Those Hierarchies..Whose Orders..Make up that holy Theologike nine: Thrones, Cherubin, and Seraphin [etc.]. 1637 HEYWOOD *London's Mirr.* Wks. 1874 IV. 314 The Theologicke vertues, the three Graces, And Charities have here their severall places.

**B.** *absol.* as *sb.* (*pl.*) Theological matters. *rare.*

1728 YOUNG *Love Fame* v. 374 These..who thus excell In Theologicks.

**Theological** (þīolǫ·dʒikăl), *a.* (*sb.*) [ad. med. L. *theologicālis* (Duns Scotus *a* 1308), f. L. *theologicus* (see prec.) + *-ālis,* -AL: see -ICAL.]

**1.** Of or pertaining to the word of God, i. e. the Bible; scriptural: cf. THEOLOGY 2; in *theological virtues* [*virtutes theologicæ,* Albertus Magnus], applied to faith, hope, and charity (1 Cor. xiii. 13), as distinct from the earlier four *cardinal virtues* of Plato and the Stoics (cf. TEMPERANCE, *Note*).

(From the contemporary senses of *theologia,* this seems to have been the original meaning; but other reasons for and explanations of the name were current from Aquinas onward: see the quots.; cf. also *c* 1380 WYCLIF *De Eccl.* ii. Sel. Wks. III. 340 Þes two godliche virtues [faith and hope]. The ancient pre-Christian virtues were called *virtutes cardinales* A.D. 379, by Ambrose *Exc. Satyri* i. 57.)

[1484: cf. THEOLOGAL.] 1526 *Pilgr. Perf.* (W. de W. 1531) 142 The rofe yᵗ coureth all is the theologicall vertue, hope. 1588 A. KING tr. *Canisius' Catech.* 184 The vertues (quhilk I hawe called theological and cardinal). 1607–12 BACON *Ess., Goodness* (Arb.) 198 Goodnes aunswares to the Theologicall vertue, Charitie, and admittes not excesse, but errour. 1616 BULLOKAR *Eng. Expos., Theologicall vertues,* Faith, Hope and Charity are so called, because they haue their obiect and end in God. 1660 R. COKE *Power & Subj.* 14 By Theological virtues I do not mean onely those three most eminent virtues of Faith, Hope, and Charity, but all those actions of obedience due to them..; to whom I owe my obedience not by any Law of Nature, but as commanded by God in the Scriptures. 1875 MANNING *Mission H. Ghost* iii. 82 Faith is called a theological virtue, because it unites the soul with its Maker. 1909 OTTLEY *Chr. Ideas & Ideals* I. vi. 98 Faith, hope, and love are commonly called 'theological virtues', for reasons which Aquinas briefly enumerates. They have, he says, God for their object; they [etc.].

**2.** Of, pertaining to, or of the nature of theology; dealing with or treating of theology.

1603 HOLLAND *Plutarch's Mor.* 1304 The Theologicall interpretations that the Stoicks give out: for they holde, that the generative and nutritive Spirit, is Bacchus. 1664 JER. TAYLOR *Dissuas. Popery* II. I. ii. (1667) 89 It is cited..in the decrees of the Popes, and in the Theological sums of great Divines. 1780 HARRIS *Philol. Enq.* Wks. (1841) 541 Among their [the Arabians'] theological works, there are some upon the mysteries of the mystic divinity. 1780 BENTHAM *Princ. Legisl.* Introd. ii. § 18 The theological principle; meaning that principle which professes to recur for the standard of right and wrong to the will of God. 1833 HT. MARTINEAU *Charmed Sea* i, Frederick was a theological student in the university at Wilna. 1861 STANLEY *East. Ch.* i. (1869) 23 The Athanasian controversy ..is, strictly speaking, theological; unlike the Pelagian or the Lutheran controversies, it relates not to man, but to God. 1904 *Times* 4 May 2/6 The abolition of all theological tests and sectarian teaching during school hours.

**B.** *sb.* †**1.** *pl.* The theological virtues. *Obs.*

1600 W. WATSON *Decacordon* (1602) 138 Three speciall *principia* or causes..called of Diuines the three Theologicals,..faith,..charitie,..hope.

†**2.** *pl.* Theological matters or principles. *Obs.*

*a* 1626 W. SCLATER *Exp. 4th ch. Rom.* Ep. Ded., The greatest patterne, and example for men to live by:..whether in your Naturalls, or in your Morals, or in your Theologicalls. 1774 J. HUTTON in *Mme. D'Arblay's Early Diary* (1889) I. 303, I have found much pleasure in Madame de Maintenon's Letters (except in Theologicals and Spirituals).

**3.** A man trained at a theological college.

1866 S. B. JAMES *Duty & Doctr.* (1871) 18 University clergy are rarer, and theologicals and literates more numerous.

**Theologically** (þīolǫ·dʒikăli), *adv.* [f. THEOLOGICAL + -LY².] In a theological manner; from a theological point of view; according to the principles of theology; as regards theology.

1611 COTGR., *Theologalement,* Theologically, diuinely. 1617 MORYSON *Itin.* II. 165 To speake theologically, God preserves us, but stil in our waies. 1681 FLAVEL *Meth. Grace* v. 95 Though a man be physically a living man,..yet his soul having no union with Christ, he is theologically a dead man. 1773 JOHNSON 7 May, in Boswell, He may be morally or theologically wrong in restraining the propagation of opinions, which he thinks dangerous, but he is politically right. 1845 FORD *Handbk. Spain* I. 70 It was long a disputed point in Spain whether chocolate did or did not break fast theologically. 1874 P. BAYNE in *Contemp. Rev.* Oct. 708 He liked them to be theologically in sympathy with the Reformation. 1905 W. SANDAY *Crit. Fourth Gosp.* v. 145 The simple peasants of Galilee needed moral teaching; whereas the theologically minded inhabitants of Judaea called out more of a theology.

**Theologician** (þiˌǫlodʒi·ʃăn). Now *rare.* Also 7 -itian. [f. L. *theologic-us* THEOLOGIC + -IAN: see -ICIAN.] = THEOLOGIAN.

*c* 1560 in 500 *Yrs. Chaucer Criticisms* (Chaucer Soc.) 95 Geffery Chaucer..was a sharpe Logician, a sweete Rhetorician, a pure Poett, a graue Philosopher, and a sacred theologician. 1647 W. BROWNE tr. *Polexander* I. III. 60 Though I am a weake Theologitian I dare assure my selfe [etc.]. 1757 MRS. GRIFFITH *Lett. Henry & Frances* (1767) II. 110 The same error..which theologicians attribute to the heathen Romans. 1848 ADAMSON *Life J. Morison* XV. 171 Mr. Meikle was pre-eminently the theologician of the group.

**Theologico-** (þīolǫ·dʒiko), combining form from Gr. θεολογικό-ς THEOLOGICAL: 'theologically-, theological and ..'; as in *theologico-astronomical, -ethical, -historical, -metaphysical, -military, -moral, -natural, -political* adjs.; also with sbs., as in *theologico-politician.*

1800 COLERIDGE *Lett., to Southey* (1895) 323 A *theologico-astronomical hypothesis. 1837 LEWIS *Lett.* (1870) 85 *Theologico-ethical opinions. 1842 BARHAM *Ingol. Leg.* Ser. II. *Lay St. Cuthbert* Introd., The extracts..may be considered as *theologico-historical. 1897 *Daily News* 21 Oct. 8/3 A *theologico-metaphysical speculator of no mean capacity. 1827 G. S. FABER *Sacr. Calend. Prophecy* (1844) III. 229 The *theologico-military exploits of the Saracens and the Turks. *c* 1644 *An Enquiry,* etc. in *Harl. Misc.* (Malh.) V. 498 The *theologico-moral design of convincing unnatural sinners. 1782 BECKFORD *Italy,* etc. (1834) I. iii. 330 A *theologico-natural history of birds, beasts, and fishes. 1680 R. MANSELL *Narr. Popish Plot* Addr. bj b, These *Theologico-Political Quacks. 1657–83 EVELYN *Hist. Relig.* (1850) II. 271 The *Theologico-politician Spinosa.

**Theologism** (þiˌǫ·lŏdʒiz'm). [f. THEOLOGIST or THEOLOGIZE: see -ISM; cf. F. *théologisme* (Littré).] The action or product of theologizing; theological speculation or system: usually in a derogatory sense.

1867 WESTCOTT in *Contemp. Rev.* VI. 407 The potential creed of the mass, springing out of spontaneous polytheism and tending to theologism. 1901 J. K. INGRAM in *Academy* 28 Sept. 256/2 Theologism, especially in its monotheistic form. 1908 *Hibbert Jrnl.* July 924 Dr. White's book..has opened Mr. Tyrrell's eyes to all the vileness of theologism.

**Theologist** (þiˌǫ·lŏdʒist). [ad. med.L. *theologista* (Luther 1519 *Wks.* (1884) II. 161), agent-n. f. *theologizāre*: see THEOLOGIZE and -IST.]

A professed theologian. **a.** In reference to heathen religions: = THEOLOGER b. (Used of ancient or modern writers on these.) Now *rare.*

*a* 1638 MEDE *Apostasy Later Times* (1641) 19 Their Theologists bring in another kinde of Daemons more high and sublime. *a* 1638 — *Wks.* (1672) 626, I take the word Δαιμόνιον..in the better..sense, as it was..taken among the Theologists and Philosophers of the Gentiles. 1755 *Gentl. Mag.* XXV. 58/1, I am informed by a most learned..theologist, that Tantalus did not incur the displeasure of Jupiter till after the accident which happened to his son. 1816 G. S. FABER *Orig. Pagan Idol.* II. 102 The other philosophizing theologists of the east.

**b.** In reference to Christianity or other monotheistic religion: = THEOLOGER a.

1641 EARL MONM. tr. *Biondi's Civil Warres* v. 109 The

schoole of Theologists who say that by sinning hee lost what hee had received by favour. **1668** Franco *Truth Springing* 1 The generally-received Opinion amongst the Jews Theologists, .. That the Lord governeth onely the people of Israel with his peculiar and particular Providence. **1774** Warton *Hist. Eng. Poetry* I. Diss. II. 42 Anselm, an acute metaphysician and theologist. *Ibid.* 75 These visionary theologists never explained or illustrated any scriptural topic. **1857** Baden-Powell in *Oxford Ess.* 181 The generality of these later natural theologists.

**c.** In derogatory sense: cf. Theologism.

**1900** A. M. Christie tr. *Hist. Germ. People Mid. Ages* III. 57 His opponents were not theologians but theologists.

‖ **Theologium** (þīolo₁dʒəi·ɒ̆m). *Gr. Antiq.* Also in Gr. form **theologeion** (-gəi·ǫ̆n). [mod. L., ad. Gr. θεολογεῖον (see def.), f. θεο-, Theo- + λογεῖον speaking-place.] In the ancient theatre, a small balcony above the stage, from which those impersonating the gods spoke.

**1888** in *Cassell's Encycl. Dict.* **1889** A. E. Haigh *Attic Theatre* iv. § 8. 193 Another appliance for exhibiting gods in a supernatural manner was the theologeion.

**Theo:logiza·tion.** *rare.* Also 6 -sacioun. [f. as next, perh. through a med.L. *theologizātio: see -ation.] The action of theologizing.

*a* **1529** Skelton *Replyc.* Wks. 1843 I. 209 The tetrycall theologisacioun of these demy diuines, and Stoicall studiantes.

**Theologize** (þi₁ǫ·lŏdʒəiz), *v.* [In sense 1, ad. med.L. *theologizāre* (Albertus Magnus *c* 1250; also in Aquinas, Duns Scotus, Wyclif, etc.), f. *theologia* Theology: see -ize. So F. *théologiser* (Godef. *Compl.*). But the trans. senses may have been formed later directly from *theology*.]

**1.** *intr.* To play the theologian; to discourse or reason theologically; to speculate in theology.

**1656** Blount *Glossogr.*, *Theologize*, to preach or play the Divine. **1662** H. More *Philos. Writ.* Pref. Gen. (1712) 6 My Design, which is not to Theologize in Philosophy. **1721** Earl Nottingham *Answ. to Whiston* 57 As we Christians have been taught to Theologize of Him. **1826** G. S. Faber *Diffic. Romanism* (1853) 158 Justin..theologises in manner following. **1875** E. White *Life in Christ* Pref. (1878) 4 When they do theologise..on the question whether the existing human race owes its being to law or to grace.

**2.** *trans.* To render theological; to conform to theology; to treat theologically.

**1649** V. Weigelius (*title*) Astrologie Theologized: wherein is set forth what Astrologie, and the light of Nature is. **1873** H. Rogers *Orig. Bible* vii. (1875) 295 Voltaire said that Pascal had illustrated..his genius..by theologising two things that seemed not made for theology—wit and pleasantry.

† **3.** To attribute divinity to; to treat as of divine or spiritual nature. Also *intr.* or *absol.* *Obs.*

**1678** Cudworth *Intell. Syst.* I. i. § 33. 40 The same persons did..both Atomize in their Physiology, taking away all Substantial Forms.., and also Theologize or Incorporealize, asserting Souls to be a Substance really distinct from Matter and Immortal. *Ibid.* iv. § 17. 298 In which Orphick Fables, not only the Things of Nature, and Parts of the World were all Theologized, but also all manner of Humane Passions.. attributed to the Gods.

Hence **Theo·logizing** *vbl. sb.* and *ppl. a.*; also **Theo·logizer**, one who theologizes, a theologer.

**1685** Boyle *Enq. Notion Nat.* iv. (1686) 93 The ancient Ægyptian *Theologizers..look'd upon the Sun and Moon.. as the chief Gods. **1693** J. Edwards *Author. O. & N. Test.* 92 Epicharmus, Thales, Plato, and all the Greek theologizers. **1857–8** Sears *Athan.* 8 Theologizers of the school we describe. **1677** Gale *Crt. Gentiles* II. III. 136 Origen's allegoric mode of *Theologising. **1833** J. H. Newman *Arians* II. iv. (1876) 190 The introduction of a subtle and irreverent question, whenever the theologizing Sophists should choose to raise it. **1881** G. A. Simcox in *Academy* 7 May 330 An instructive contrast to much fashionable theologising.

**Theologo-** (þi₁ǫ·lŏgo), combining form repr. Gr. θεολόγο-ς a theologian: as in **theo·logo-inquisito·rial** *adj.*, of or pertaining to a theological inquisitor; **theo·logo-ju·rist**, a jurist who treats of theology.

**1802–12** Bentham *Ration. Judic. Evid.* (1827) I. 555 The character of theologo-inquisitorial despotism. *a* **1843** Southey *Doctor* clxxii. (1848) 448/2 'The title of Christ to Eternal Life is become absolute,—by absolute',—says this theologo-jurist [J. Asgill],—'I mean discharged from all tenure or condition, and consequently from all forfeiture'.

‖ **Theologoumenon** (þīǒlogau·mènǫ̆n, -gū·mènǫ̆n). Pl. **-a** (-ă). [a. Gr. θεολογούμενον, neut. of pr. pple. pass. of θεολογεῖν to theologize, f. θεολόγος theologian.] A theological statement or utterance on theology: distinguished from an inspired doctrine or revelation.

**1891** *Brit. Weekly* 29 Oct. 1 What gives this dubious theologoumenon its importance in Dr. Dale's system is the connection into which he brings it with the doctrine of propitiation. **1895** J. Denney *Stud. Theol.* iii. 52 His utterances on this point may be disregarded as private theologoumena. **1906** D. W. Forrest *Author. Christ* VI. ix. 330 It can only rank as a theologoumenon of Peter.

**Theologue** (þī·ǒlǫg). Also 5–7 **theologe**, 6–9 **theolog.** [ad. L. *theolog-us*, a. Gr. θεολόγος one who treats, or gives an account, of the gods (e. g. Hesiod, Orpheus), or of God; f. θεός God + λέγειν to discourse: see -logue. Before *c* 1600 app. only Sc.: cf. Astrologue.]

**1.** = Theologian. Now *rare.*

*c* **1425** Wyntoun *Cron.* IX. xxi. 2237 (MS. Cott.) Master Henry of Wardlaw..A theologe solempneȝ was he Kende, and knawyn of gret bownte. *c* **1470** Henryson *Orpheus & Eur.* 422 Doctor nycholas Quhilk in his tyme a noble theologe was. **1508** Dunbar *Lament for Makaris* 38 Art, magicianis, and astrologgis, Rethoris, logicianis, & theologgis. **1605** Timme *Quersit.* Ded. 1 Moses, that auncient theologue. **1682** H. More *Annot. Glanvill's Lux O.* 62 The dry Dreams..of earthly either Philosophers or Theologs. **1693** *Phil. Trans.* XVII. 807 A bad Astronomer, a worse Theologe, and the worst of all Physiologers. *a* **1734** North *Exam.* III. ix. § 7 (1740) 652 It is not for a Layman to act the Theologue. **1859** I. Taylor *Logic in Theol.* 147 The writings of the great theologue of Bethlehem, Jerome.

**2.** A theological student. *U. S. colloq.*

(Prob. after Ger. *theolog.*)

**1663** Blair *Autobiog.* ii. (1848) 42 My refusal would very much grieve all the young theologues. **1810–16** O'Conor *Columbanus' Lett.* vi. 111 Barrister Theologues of the poddle! **1884** *Jrnl. Educ.* XIX. 327 The theologs who graduate from Lombard will stand high in their profession.

**Theology** (þi₁ǫ·lŏdʒi). Also 4 **teologye**, 4–7 **theologie** (5 -i, 6 -ye). [a. F. *théologie* (14th c. in Hatz.-Darm.), ad. L. *theologia*, a. Gr. θεολογία, abstr. sb. f. θεολόγ-ος: see prec. and -logy. For the early sense-history see Note below.]

**1.** The study or science which treats of God, His nature and attributes, and His relations with man and the universe; 'the science of things divine' (Hooker); divinity.

*Dogmatic theology*, theology as authoritatively held and taught by the church; a scientific statement of Christian dogma. *Natural theology*, theology based upon reasoning from natural facts apart from revelation. *Pastoral theology*, that branch of theology which deals with religious truth in its relation to the spiritual needs of men, and the 'cure of souls': see Pastoral *a.* 4.

**1362** Langl. *P. Pl.* A. XI. 136 Bote Teologye [B. x. 180, C. XII. 129 theologie] haþ teoned me ten score tymes; For þe more I muse þeron þe mistiloker hit semeþ. *c* **1386** Chaucer *Pars. T.* ¶ 969 The exposicion of this hooly preyere ..I bitake to thise maistres of Theologie. **1552** Abp. Hamilton *Catech.* (1884) 1 Doctours of Theologie and Canon law. **1594** Hooker *Eccl. Pol.* III. viii. § 11 The whole drift of the scripture of God, what is it but only to teach Theologie? Theologie, what is it, but the Science of things Divine? *c* **1698** Locke *Cond. Underst.* xxii, Theology, which, containing the knowledge of God and His creatures, our duty to him and our fellow-creatures, and a view of our present and future state, is the comprehension of all other knowledge, directed to its true end. **1742** Young *Nt. Th.* IV. 73 Were I as plump, as stall'd theology, Wishing would waste me to this shade again. **1837** Hallam *Hist. Lit.* (1847) I. i. § 81. 72 Peter Lombard, the founder of systematic theology in the twelfth century. **1845** Corrie *Theol.* in *Encycl. Metrop.* 857/1 Under the..term Theology we comprehend all the knowledge which man can obtain respecting God, whether concerning His nature and attributes, or concerning the relation in which man stands to Him. **1874** J. Duncan *Pulpit & Commun. Table* 73 Polemical theology is the defence, Practical theology the application, of Dogmatic theology, which again rests upon Exegetical.

**b.** A particular theological system or theory.

**1669** Gale *Crt. Gentiles* I. III. iv. 53 Aristotle wonderfully agrees with the Mosaic Theologie herein. **1796** H. Hunter tr. *St.-Pierre's Stud. Nat.* (1799) III. 734 Among those questions, two hundred referred to the theology of the Hebrews. **1830** Mackintosh *Eth. Philos.* Wks. 1846 I. 81 Clarke..considered such a scheme as the only security against Hobbism, and probably also against the Calvinistic theology. **1837** Hallam *Hist. Lit.* (1847) I. i. § 18. 13 The scholastic theology..was, in its general principle, an alliance between faith and reason. **1874** J. B. Brown *Higher Life* xx. 408 There lies a meaning in these glorious words..for which there is no room that I can see in any of our theologies. **1899** C. K. Paul *Mem.* iv. 130 There [at Eton] in 1841 [some] of us..became conscious of the great stir which was going on at Oxford; a few of our masters were falling under the influence of the new theology. **1907** *Standard* 19 Jan. 9/4 Latest development of 'New Theology'.

**c.** Applied to pagan or non-Christian systems.

**1662** Stillingfl. *Orig. Sacr.* I. ii. § 8 Had we no other demonstration of the greatness of mans Apostacy and degeneracy, the Ægyptian Theology would be an irrefragable evidence of it. **1677** Gilpin *Demonol.* (1867) 201 The Gentile theology of demons is the thing which Paul prophesies should be introduced into Christianity. **1712** Addison *Spect.* No. 471 ¶ 8 Our Forefather, according to the Pagan Theology, had a great Vessel presented him by Pandora. **1841** Elphinstone *Hist. India* II. iv. (1845) I. 211 Their theology, mythology, philosophy, .. are almost entirely of the Hindú family.

† **2.** Rarely used for Holy Scripture. So late Gr. θεολογία (Pseudo-Dion. *de Cæl. Hier.* 9 § 3), med.L. *theologia*. *Obs.*

[Cf. *a* **1149** *Hugo de S. Victore* (in Migne 1091 C), Theologia, id est divina scriptura.] **1494** Fabyan *Chron.* VII. ccxx. 242 This Lamfranke..was perfytely lerned in the scyence of theologie or holy wrytte. [Cf. **1653** Milton *Hirelings* (1659) 98 The study of Scripture (which is the only true theologie).]

† **b.** Hence, *Virtues of theology* (also *vertues theologyes*, (?) *theologycs*) = 'theological virtues': see Theological 1. *Obs.*

**1422** tr. *Secreta Secret., Priv. Priv.* 124 The prologe of the iiij$^{e}$. Cardynale vertues, declarynge the .iij$^{e}$. vertues of theologie, and foure maner of goodis. *Ibid.* 145 Ther byth thre Vertues pryncipalle of theologi or dyuynte, y-callid in lateyne Fides, Spes, Caritas. **1502** *Ord. Crysten Men* (W. de W. 1506) II. i. 85 The thre vertues theologyes or diuynes.

† **3.** Metaphysics. (See Note below.) *Obs*

**1390** Gower *Conf.* III. 86–7 Theorique..stant departed upon thre, The ferste..Is cleped in Philosophie The science of Theologie, That other named is Phisique, The thridde is seid Mathematique. Theologie is that science Which unto man yifth evidence Of thing which is noght bodely. *c* **1425** (?) Lydg. *Assembly of Gods* 859 Arsmetry, Geometry with Astronomy, .. Nobyll Theology, and Corporall Physyk.

[*Note.* Gr. θεολογία meant 'an account of the gods, or of God (whether legendary or philosophical)'. Varro, following the Stoics, distinguished three kinds of *theologia*, mythical, natural (rational), and civil, the last being the knowledge of the due rites and ceremonies of religion. This threefold division is referred to also by Tertullian and St. Augustine. In Christian Greek, the vb. θεολογεῖν was used = 'to speak of as God, to attribute deity to', whence θεολογία had the specific sense of 'the ascription of a divine nature to Christ', in contrast to οἰκονομία, the doctrine of his incarnation and human nature. Another patristic Gr. use, arising out of the primary sense, was 'the account of God, or record of God's ways, as given in the Bible', whence the late Gr. and med.L. use of *theologia* for the Scriptures themselves. In the 12th c. (1121–40) Abelard applied the term to a philosophical treatment of the doctrines of the Christian religion, which, though at first strongly condemned, became current, and, in this sense, 'theologia' came to designate a department of academic study, the text-books of which were the Bible and the Sentences (from the Fathers) of Peter Lombard. Hence the earliest Eng. use. (The passage from Gower in sense 3 is derived ultimately from Aristotle's division of the theoretic forms of philosophy into μαθηματική, φυσική, θεολογική, the last being what we should call metaphysics, which included his doctrine of the divine nature.)]

† **The·olony.** *Obs. rare*$^{-1}$. [ad. med.L. *theolōneum* tax, impost, corruption of late L. *telōnium* (*-eum*), in Vulg., ad. Gr. τελώνιον toll-house, custom-house.] Payment of taxes, tolls, or imposts.

**1610** W. Folkingham *Art of Survey* III. iv, Immunities and Exemptions from Theolonie, Pontage, Picage, Murage [etc.].

**Theomachy** (þi₁ǫ·măki). Also 6 in Gr.-L. form **theomachia** (þīomæ·kiă). [ad. Gr. θεομαχία, f. θεός god + -μαχία fighting.]

† **1.** A striving or warring against God; opposition to the will of God. **b.** *spec.* See quot. *Obs.*

**1570–6** Lambarde *Peramb. Kent* (1826) 327 The whole religion of Papistrie..is Theomachia and nothing else. **1598** Bacon *Sacr. Medit.* xi. (Arb.) 127 Atheisme and Theomachie rebelleth and mutineth against the power of God. **1633** T. Adams *Exp. 2 Peter* ii. 3 A theomachy, a desperate war against heaven. **1690** C. Nesse *O. & N. Test.* I. 134 This theomachy or rebelling against God.

**b.** **1656** Blount *Glossogr.*, *Theomachy*, a warring or fighting against the gods, as the old Giants are feigned to have done.

**2.** A battle or strife among the gods: esp. in reference to that narrated in Homer's Iliad.

**1858** Gladstone *Homer* II. ii. 77 When we come to discuss the position of Latona, both generally and in the Theomachy. **1865** — *Farewell Addr. Edin. Univ.* 29 Xanthos, a river god, appears in the Theomachy. **1878** — *Prim. Homer* vi. § 27. 83 Artemis .. is sorely belaboured, in the Theomachy, by the strong arm of Hera.

Hence [or from Gr. θεομάχ-ος] **Theomachist** (þi₁ǫ·măkist), one who fights against God.

**1794** Mathias *Purs. Lit.* (1798) 18 The continued labours of the arch Theomachist of the age, .. that..conflict which he maintained, during..a long and impious life, against the spiritual 'kingdoms of God and of his Christ'. **1871** T. Hardy *Desperate Remedies* viii, To resist fate with the vindictive determination of a Theomachist.

† **Theoma·gic,** *a.* (*sb.*) *Obs. rare.* [f. Theo- + Magic.] Of or pertaining to magic claiming to be wrought by divine aid. **b.** **Theoma·gics** *sb. pl.*, the principles and practice of 'theomagic' art. So † **Theoma·gical** *a.*; † **Theomagi·cian,** one who practises 'theomagics'.

**1650** H. More *Observ.* in *Enthus. Tri.*, etc. (1656) F j, The ..Magicall Multiplication, or Theomagical fecundity of your Divine Writings. *Ibid.* 72 Anthroposophus would be a rare Theomagician indeed. *Ibid.* 76 We will set the saddle on the right Horse; and this Theomagick jade shall bear the blame. *Ibid.* 127 His strange mysteries of his Theomagick stone. **1651** — *Second Lash* ibid. 170 A publick professor of Theomagicks. **1656** Blount *Glossogr.*, *Theomagical*, pertaining to the wisdome of God, or that works wonders by his help.

**Theomammonist**: see Theo-.

**Theomancy** (þī·omænsi). [ad. Gr. θεομαντεία spirit of prophecy, f. θεός god + μαντεία divination: see -mancy.] A kind of divination: see quots.

**1651** Hobbes *Leviath.* I. xii. 56 These kinds of foretelling events were accounted Theomancy, or Prophecy. **1807** Robinson *Archæol. Græca* III. xii. 257 Theomancy is distinguished from oracular divination, which was commonly limited to a fixed and stated time, and always to a certain place; whilst the θεομάντεις were free and unconfined, and able to offer sacrifices, and perform other prophetic rites, at any time, and in any part of the world. **1842** Brande *Dict. Sc.*, etc., *Theomancy*, a name..given to that species of divination which was drawn from the responses of oracles.., or from the predictions of sibyls and others supposed to be immediately inspired by some divinity.

Hence **Theoma·ntic** *a.*, pertaining to theomancy.

**1620** Middleton & Rowley *World Tost at Tennis* 258 Strike, by white art, a theomantic power, Magic divine. **1684** tr. *Agrippa's Van. Arts* xlvii. 122 This part..is twofold: Arithmantick..and Theomantick, which searches into the mysteries of the Divine Majesty.

**Theomania, -iac,** to **Theomonism**: see Theo-.

† **Theomeny.** *Obs. rare*$^{-0}$. [ad. Gr. θεομηνία the wrath of God, f. θεός God + μῆνις wrath.]

**1623** Cockeram, *Theomenie*, the wrath of God. **1656** Blount *Glossogr.*, Theominy.

**Theomorphic** (þīomǭ·ɹfik), *a.* [f. Gr. θεόμορφος of divine form (f. θεό-ς god + μόρφη form) + -ic.] Having the form or likeness of God; of or pertaining to theomorphism.

**1870** J. H. Blunt *Dict. Theol.* 324/2 Although the Creator thus made man theomorphic, we are not to think of God as anthropomorphic. **1889** A. Moore *Christian Doctr. God* in *Lux Mundi* 64 A theomorphic view of man is of the essence of his faith. **1894** J. R. Illingworth *Personality Hum. & Div.* viii. (1895) 214 Our anthropomorphic language follows from our theomorphic minds. **1897** Ottley *Aspects O. Test.* vii. 340 Mosaism recognizes, so to speak, the theomorphic structure of man.

So **Theomo·rphism,** the doctrine that man has the form or likeness of God; **Theomo·rphize** *v., trans.* to form in the image of God.

**1886** Mivart in *Fortn. Rev.* Jan. 63 A natural and innocuous Anthropomorphism of the intellect—which..may be more properly called Theomorphism. **1897** T. Stephens in *Evang. Mag.* June 289 Theomorphism in the doctrine of man has gone on side by side with anthropomorphism in the doctrine of God. **1905** J. Orr *Probl. O. Test.* v. 118 God, in creating, theomorphises man.

**The:o-mytho·logy.** [f. Theo- + Mythology. (Cf. Gr. θεομυθία divine lore, mythology.)] A combination of theology and mythology. Hence **The:o-mytho·loger.**

**1858** Gladstone *Homer* II. i. 2 That which, following German example, I have denominated the Theo-mythology of Homer. By that term it seems not improper to designate a mixture of theology and mythology. *Ibid.* v. 366, I have a lively conviction that Homer was (so to speak) the theomythologer who moulded these materials into system. **1868** — *Juv. Mundi* ix. (1870) 349 The will and power of the Olympian deities..may be described, from its mixed character of truth and fable, as the Theomythology of the poet.

**Theonomy** (þiˌǫ·nǒmi). [f. Gr. θεό-ς God + -νομία, -nomy, after Ger. *theonomie* (1838 in Heyse).] Administration or government by God; the condition of being ruled or governed by God.

**1890** J. F. Smith tr. *Pfleiderer's Developm. Theol. since Kant* i. 14 His autonomy must therefore..be an actual (not merely subjectively conceived) theonomy. **1905** P. T. Forsyth in *Contemp. Rev.* Oct. 578 The God who rules us in Christ is not a foreign power. Theonomy is not heteronomy. He, our law, becomes also our life.

**Theopanphilist, -pantism**: see Theo-.

**Theopaschite** (þīopæ·skəit). *Ch. Hist.* Also 6 **-paschit,** 7 **-passit.** [ad. eccl. L. *theopaschīta*, ad. Gr. θεοπασχίτης, f. θεό-ς god + πάσχ-ειν to suffer: see -ite[1] 1 a.] A member of a Monophysite sect of the 6th c., who held that the divine nature of Christ suffered on the Cross.

**1585** T. Rogers 39 *Art.* ii. § 2 (1625) 11 Most wicked were the opinions of those men which held..that..Christ had a bodie without a soule; as thought..the Theopaschites. *Ibid.* § 4. 14 That Christ really and indeed, hung not on the crosse: for his passion was in showe onely, said the Cerdonites..and the Manicheans: and another man, saide the Theopaschits,..suffered, and hung on the crosse. **1625** Gill *Sacr. Philos.* iv. 32 The errours..of the Theopaschites, who held that the God-head of Christ did suffer, while His body was nayled on the Crosse. **1874–86** J. H. Blunt *Dict. Sects*, etc., *Theopaschites*, a sect of the Monophysites who maintained that Christ having only one Nature, and that the Divine, it was therefore the Divine Nature which suffered..at the Crucifixion. **1882–3** *Schaff's Encycl. Relig. Knowl.* III. 2346 Theopaschites..a by-name applied to such as accepted the formula, that..'God had suffered and been crucified'.

Hence **Theopaschitally** (-pæ·skităli) *adv.*, in the manner of, or in accordance with the doctrine of the Theopaschites; **Theopaschitic** (-pæski·tik) *a.*, of or pertaining to the Theopaschites or their doctrine; **Theopaschitism** (-pæ·skitiz'm), the doctrine or tenets of the Theopaschites. So **Theopaschist** (-pæ·skist), a Theopaschite.

**1887** Richter *Levana* ix. 154 Theologians are active *Theopaschists. **1882** Cave & Banks tr. *Dorner's Chr. Doctr.* 209 In this respect it speaks quite *Theopaschitally. **1893** E. K. Mitchell tr. *Harnack's Hist. Dogma* 299 The carrying out of the *theopaschitic formula. **1882–3** *Schaff's Encycl. Relig. Knowl.* I. 463 A revival of..Patripassianism, or *Theopaschitism.

**Theopathetic** (þīoˌpăþe·tik), *a.* (*sb.*) [f. Theopathy, after *pathetic*.] Of, pertaining to, or characterized by theopathy: see quots.

**1748** Hartley *Observ. Man* ii. iii. § 7. 316 To deduce practical Rules concerning the Theopathetic Affections, Faith, Fear, Gratitude, Hope, Trust, Resignation, and Love. **1830** W. Taylor *Hist. Surv. Germ. Poetry* II. 5 All these publications..tend to assuade a benevolent sensibility, theopathetic affections, and evangelical doctrines. **1856** R. A. Vaughan *Mystics* (1860) I. i. v. 27 There are three kinds of mysticism, theopathetic, theosophic, theurgic. *Ibid.* 31 The mystic of the theopathetic species is content to contemplate, to feel, or to act, suffering under Deity, in his sublime passivity. **1878** Dowden *Stud. Lit.* 197 Studying the phenomena of morbid theopathetic emotion.

b. *sb.* (See quot.)

**1860** Gardner *Faiths World* II. 899/2 *Theopathetics*, those mystics who have resigned themselves more or less passively to an imagined divine manifestation.

**Theopathic** (þīopæ·þik), *a.* [f. next.] = prec.

**1846** Worcester cites *Q. Rev.* **1864** *Edin. Rev.* July 249 One of those rare beings..whose temperament, so to speak, is theopathic. **1899** *Q. Rev.* July 101 The theopathic and contemplative quietism of the East.

**Theopathy** (þiˌǫ·păþi). [f. Theo- + -pathy. Cf. Gr. θεοπάθεια the suffering of God.] Sympathetic passive feeling excited by the contemplation of God; susceptibility to this feeling; sensitiveness or responsiveness to divine influence; pious sentiment. Cf. Theopathetic.

**1748** Hartley *Observ. Man* i. iv. § 5. 486 The Pleasures and Pains of Theopathy: under this Class I comprehend all those Pleasures and Pains, which the Contemplation of God and his Attributes, and of our Relation to Him, raises up. **1816** Southey *Ess.* (1832) I. 235 In the order of nature, what Hartley calls theopathy, is not, and ought not, to be looked for, as the predominant feeling of youth. **1837** Hallam *Hist. Lit.* iii. ii. § 73 The writings..of St. Teresa..are..full of a mystical theopathy. **1881** *Ch.Q. Rev.* 60 The Sufi School, the 'Methodists of the East', as Martyn calls them, in reference to their creedless theopathy.

**Theophagous** (þiˌǫ·făgəs), *a.* [f. Theo- + -phagous.] God-eating. So **Theo·phagy** (-dʒi), the eating of God (in the mass or communion rite); **Theo·phagite** (-dʒəit), a God-eater (in quot. *attrib.*). All *nonce-wds.* (mostly dyslogistic).

**1805** *Monthly Mag.* XX. 35 The theophagite cannibalism of the communion-rite. **1880** Swinburne in *Fortn. Rev.* June 762 In the bosom of a deicidal and theophagous Christianity. *Ibid.*, A creed..based on deicide and sustained on theophagy. **1907** *Hibbert Jrnl.* Apr. 684 The origin of the rites of Theophagy or Communion.

**Theophany** (þiˌǫ·făni). [ad. L. *theophania* (*c* 400 in Rufinus), a. Gr. θεοφάνεια and θεοφάνια (neut. pl.), f. θεός god + φαίνειν to show: see -phany. So F. *théophanie*. Cf. Tiffany.] A manifestation or appearance of God or a god to man.

*a* **1633** Austin *Medit.* (1635) 56 First, the Starre manifested him..from the Heavens. That's, the Epiphany: Secondly, it manifested him from God (in Trinity): for hee sent the Starre. There's, the Theophany. And lastly; It manifested him on Earth (in Domo):..There's the Bethphany. **1677** Gale *Crt. Gentiles* II. iii. 193 Neither was the name Theophanie, which signifies the apparitio[n] of God or the Gods, unusual even among the Gentiles. **1854** Milman *Lat. Chr.* viii. v. III. 352 The universe is but a sublime Theophany, a visible manifestation of God. **1894** F. Watson *Genesis a true Hist.* vi. 141 In the records of the Theophanies to Joshua, Gideon, and Manoah. *Ibid.*, The Theophany to Elijah at Horeb.

b. A festival celebrating the manifestation of a deity. (Sometimes spec. applied to Christmas.)

**1745** A. Butler *Lives Saints* (1836) I. 26 *note*, The Greeks still keep the Epiphany with the birth of Christ on Christmas-day, which they call *Theophany*, or the manifestation of God. [**1753** Chambers *Cycl. Supp.*, *Theophania*, θεοφάνεια, ..a festival observed by the Delphians upon the day whereon Apollo first manifested himself to them.]

Hence **Theopha·nic** *a.*, of or pertaining to theophany; **Theo·phanism,** theophany; **Theo·phanous** *a.*, characterized by theophany.

**1882–3** *Schaff's Encycl. Relig. Knowl.* III. 2346 No vision is without a *theophanic element. **1886** C. A. Briggs *Messianic Proph.* i. vi. § 10. 20 It is the theophanic manifestation of God in forms of time and space and the sphere of physical nature. **1849** Lady Wilde tr. *Meinhold's Sidonia Sorc.* iii. xiii. II. 184 *note*, All the *theophanisms (God-manifestations) recorded in the Old Testament. **1909** *19th Cent.* Oct. 676 This *theophanous land.

**Theophilanthropist** (þī:oˌfilæ·nþrǒpist). [f. Theo- + Philanthropist, after F. *théophilanthrope*, erron. employed to express 'loving God and man', though etymologically it ought to mean 'a divine philanthropist'.] A member of a sect of Deists which appeared in France in 1796.

**1797** W. Taylor in *Monthly Rev.* XXIV. 554 It is satisfactory to observe how nearly the Theophilanthropists agree with the more thinking Christians. **1798** Hel. M. Williams *Tour Switzerl.* I. v. 79 This sect, distinguished by the name of Theophilanthropists, the friends of God and man. **1801** Belsham *Geo. III*, an. 1797 (R.), The Directory gave great encouragement to a new sect recently established under the name of theo-philanthropists.—These religionists, rejecting all revelation, confined their worship to one Supreme Being. **1897** *Daily News* 16 Jan. 6/2 The Society of Theophilanthropists, whose first public meeting was held in Paris, January 16, 1797, was of purely religious origin.

*attrib.* **1823** Southey in *Q. Rev.* XXVIII. 502 The proffered service of the Theophilanthropist lecturers. **1882–3** *Schaff's Encycl. Relig. Knowl.* III. 2347 God, virtue, and the immortality of the soul, formed the three articles of the Theophilanthropist creed.

So **Theophi·lanthrope** [as in F.] in same sense; **The:ophilanthro·pic, -ical** *adjs.*, of or pertaining to theophilanthropy or theophilanthropists; **The:ophila·nthropism** = next.

**1803** in *Spirit Pub. Jrnls.* VII. 254 We give and bequeath to our friend the Elector of Bavaria, the Bible of the *Theophilanthropes. **1843** tr. *Custine's Empire of Czar* III. 64 Their whole adjustment reminds one of the theophilanthropes of the French republic. **1797** W. Taylor in *Monthly Rev.* XXIII. 560 The illuminated or *theophilanthropic sect..who are supposed to reject the Old and to socinianize the New Testament. **1895** Péronne *Veil of Liberty* 389 Jean..had now transformed his Huguenot church into a Theophilanthropic temple. **1804** Larwood *No Gun Boats* 32 Having revolted from the Goddess of Reason, and the scheme of *Theophilanthropism. **1860** Gardner *Faiths World* II. 899/2 An attempt was made by Lamennais to revive Theophilanthropism in 1840, but it utterly failed.

**The:ophila·nthropy.** [a. F. *théophilanthropie*, intended to express 'love to God and man': cf. prec.] The deistic system of the theophilanthropists, based on a belief in the existence of God and in the immortality of the soul.

Theophilanthropy was adopted in France as a substitute for Roman Catholicism. It died out *c* 1801–2.

**1798** W. Taylor in *Monthly Rev.* XXVII. 500 The rise of Martinism and of Theophilanthropy. **1847** J. Hare *Vict. Faith* 7 His Christianity..has been stunted and enervated, ..into a sort of sentimental theophilanthropy. **1895** Péronne *Veil of Liberty* 395 The pastor of Versailles closed his church..and reopened it to preach Theophilanthropy.

**Theophile, -ist, -philosophic**: see Theo-.

‖**Theophobia** (þīoˌfōu·biă). [f. Theo- + -phobia. Cf. F. *théophobie* (*a* 1784 in Littré *Suppl.*).] Anxious fear of God; dread of divine anger; rarely, aversion to or hatred of God. So **Theophobist** (-ǫ·fǒbist), one who is affected with theophobia.

**1870** O. W. Holmes *Mechanism* (1888) 105 Pascal, whose reverence amounted to *theophobia. **1885** Swinburne *Misc.* (1886) 239 His..masterpiece of *Cain*,..might seem to a devout spirit to have been dictated by actual theophobia. **1899** *Expositor* Oct. 317 Those men laboured under a terrible disease—it is called Theophobia. **1885** Mrs. H. Ward tr. *Amiel's Jrnl.* II. 134 A *theophobist, whom faith in goodness rouses to a fury of contempt.

**Theophoric, -ous, -physical**: see Theo-.

**Theophylline** (þīofi·ləin). *Chem.* [irreg. f. mod.L. *thea* Tea + Gr. φύλλον leaf + -ine[5].] A colourless alkaloid, $C_7H_8N_4O_2$, found in tea-leaves.

**1894** in Morley & Muir *Watts' Dict. Chem.* IV. 682/2. **1899** *Syd. Soc. Lex.*, *Theophyllin*,..an alkaloid discovered in tea. It is isomeric with the base obtained from cacao (theobromine) and with paraxanthin, but differs from them in its reactions.

**Theopneust** (þī·opniūst), *a.* [ad. Gr. θεόπνευστος, f. θεό-ς God + -πνευστος inspired, f. stem πνευ- of πνεῖν to breathe, blow.] Divinely inspired.

**1647** Hammond *Power of Keys* iii. 30 Which delivers down all the books which make up our Canon of Scripture, for Canonicall, and Theopneust. **1806** G. S. Faber *Diss. Prophecies* (1814) II. 314 The promotion of image-worship, the purpose for which this misnamed *theopneust assembly* met together. **1885** tr. *Wellhausen's Hist. Israel* i. iii. 48 Their polemic is a purely prophetic one, i.e. individual, theopneust,..independent of all traditional..opinions.

So **Theopneu·stic** *a.* in same sense; **Theopneu·sty** [Ger. *theopneustie* (Heyse 1837), F. *théopneustie* (Littré)], ‖ **Theopneu·stia** [Gr. θεοπνευστία], divine inspiration; also **Theopneustian.**

**1660** S. Fisher *Rusticks Alarm* iv. i. Wks. (1679) 592 Denying any such *Theopneustian [*sic*], Divine Inspiration, Revelation, Motion, immediate Mission. **1894** *Thinker* VI. 67 According to this theory, the writers of the books of Kings and Chronicles needed and received less of *theopneustia than the prophet Isaiah or the Evangelist John. **1827** Hare *Guesses* Ser. i. (1873) 209 Its [Christianity's] anthropomorphism is *theopneustic. **1847** J. W. Donaldson *Vind. Protest. Princ.* 50 If man is, in his higher nature, a theopneustic being. **1847** Webster, **Theopneusty*, divine inspiration.

**Theopo·litics,** *sb. pl. rare.* [f. Theo- + Politics.] Politics based on the law of God. So **Theopoliti·cian,** one who bases his politics on conformity to the will of God or the divine law; † **Theopo·lity,** a polity based on the law of God.

**1736** Bailey (folio) Pref., *Theopoliticks*..godly or divine Politics. *Ibid.*, *Theopolity*..a godly or divine Administration of the Republick. **1867** *Union Rev.* July 346 He is not so much a politician as a theopolitician.

**Theopsychism**: see Theo-.

**Theor** (þī·oɹ). *Gr. Antiq.* Also in L. form **theo·rus.** [mod. ad. Gr. θεωρ-ός spectator, one who travels in order to see things, also an envoy, ambassador: see Theory[2].] An ambassador or envoy sent on behalf of a state, esp. to consult an oracle or perform a religious rite. (Cf. Theory[2].)

**1847** Grote *Greece* ii. ix. III. 37 The Theors or sacred envoys..appeared with ostentatious pomp. **1849** *Ibid.* ii. lv. VII. 73 The tent which the Athenian theôrs provided for their countrymen visitors to the games. **1873** Symonds *Grk. Poets* iii. 90 He went as a Theorus to the shrine of Delphi.

**Theorbo** (þiˌǭ·ɹbo). Also 7 **theorboe,** 7–8 **-orba;** 7 **theorb',** 7–8 **-orb,** 8–9 **-orbe.** [ad. F. *téorbe, théorbe* (17th c.), ad. It. *tiorba* 'a kind of musicall instrument used among countrie people' (Florio 1598), Sp. *tiorba*. The spelling with *th* appears first in Eng. (prob. after the Theo- group); the ending *-o* for It. and Sp. *-a* occurs in other words: see -ado. Origin of the It. word unknown: some suggest that it was named after the inventor.] A large kind of lute with a double neck and two sets of tuning-pegs, the lower holding the melody strings and the upper the bass strings; much in vogue in the 17th century. (Cf. Archlute.)

**1605** Chapman *All Fooles* Plays 1873 I. 144 *Cor.* Take thy Theorbo for my sake a little. *Val.* By heauen, this moneth I toucht not a Theorbo. **1611** Coryat *Crudities* 252 Two singular fellowes played together vpon Theorboes. **1652** Benlowes *Theoph.* i. lv, There sweet Religion strings and tunes, and skrues The Souls Theorb', and doth infuse Grave Dorick Epods. **1690** Shadwell *Am. Bigot* iv. i, I had provided this drum to sing to, which is better than a Theorb, or Harpsychord. **1697** tr. *C'tess D'Aunoy's Trav.* (1706) 258, I never saw any Virginals or Theorba's here. **1899** E. Gosse *J. Donne* i. 28 A madrigal for the theorbo. **1906** *Blackw. Mag.* Sept. 338/2 The whole household purchased Theorbes.

*attrib.* and *Comb.* **1657** J. Gamble (*title*) Ayres and Dialogues. To be Sung to the Theorbo-Lute or Bass-Viol. **1676** T. Mace *Musick's Monum.* 236 A Stop..which my Work-man calls the Theorboe Stop. **1688** Playford (*title*) Harmonia Sacra..: with a Thorow-bass for the Theorbo-Lute, Bass-Viol, Harpsichord, or Organ. **1880** Shorthouse *J. Inglesant* xxii, He found a young man,..playing on a double-necked theorbolute.

Hence **Theo·rboed** (-ōud) *ppl. a.*, converted into a theorbo; **Theo·rbist,** a player on the theorbo.

**1611** Coryat *Crudities* 252 These two Theorbists concluded the night's musicke. **1889** A. J. Hipkins in Grove *Dict. Mus.* IV. 100/2 Early in the 17th century many large lutes had been altered to theorbos by substituting double necks for the original single ones...The theorbo engraved in

Mersenne's 'Harmonie Universelle' (Paris, 1636) is really a theorboed lute.

**Theorem** (þīˑōrĕm), *sb.* Also 6–7 -eme. [ad. late L. *theōrēma* (Gellius), a. Gr. θεώρημα, -ματ-, spectacle, speculation, theory, (in Euclid) a proposition to be proved, f. θεωρεῖν to be a spectator (θεωρός), to look at, inspect. Perh. directly a. F. *théorème* (*téorème* in Rabelais).]

A universal or general proposition or statement, not self-evident (thus distinguished from an AXIOM), but demonstrable by argument (in the strict sense, by necessary reasoning); 'a demonstrable theoretical judgement' (Abp. Thomson).

**a.** In Mathematics and Physics; *spec.* in Geometry, a proposition embodying merely something to be proved, as distinguished from a PROBLEM (sense 4), which embodies something to be done.

Particular theorems are usually named after their discoverers or investigators, as *Boole's*, *Carnot's*, *Cauchy's*, *Cayley's*, *Clifford's*, *Euler's*, *Fermat's*, *Feuerbach's*, *Galileo's*, *Lagrange's*, *Lambert's*, *Maclaurin's*, *Newton's*, *Pappus's*, *Pascal's*, *Ptolemy's*, *Riemann's*, *Sylvester's*, *Taylor's*, *Wallis's*, *Wilson's* (etc.) *theorem*; sometimes by defining adjectives, as the BINOMIAL, EXPONENTIAL, MULTINOMIAL *theorem*.

**1551** RECORDE *Pathw. Knowl.* Argts., The Theoremes, (whiche maye be called approued truthes) seruinge for the due knowledge and sure proofe of all conclusions .. in Geometrye. **1570** BILLINGSLEY *Euclid* I. Introd. 8 A Theoreme, is a proposition, which requireth the searching out and demonstration of some propertie..of some figure. **1612** SELDEN in Drayton *Poly-olb.* A iij, His Geometricall Theorem in finding the squares of an Orthogonal triangles sides. **1752** FRANKLIN *Lett.* Wks. 1887 II. 253, I thank you for communicating the illustration of the theorem concerning light. **1806** HUTTON *Course Math.* I. 2 A Theorem is a demonstrative proposition; in which some property is asserted, and the truth of it required to be proved... A set or collection of such Theorems constitutes a Theory. **1816** tr. *Lacroix's Diff. & Int. Calculus* 22 This formula is called Taylor's Theorem, from the English geometer by whom it was discovered. **1862** H. SPENCER *First Princ.* II. xvi. § 136 Geometrical theorems grew out of empirical methods.

**b.** In general sense, or in reference to any particular science or technical subject. (In quot. 1697 applied to an axiom.)

**1597** HOOKER *Eccl. Pol.* v. lxxvi. § 2 The first being a Theoreme both vnderstood and confest of all, to labour in proofe thereof were superfluous. **1615** CROOKE *Body of Man* 27, I call it a Science, because it hath vniuersall or generall Theoremes or Maximes, and common Notions. **1649** JER. TAYLOR *Gt. Exemp.* I. Ad Sect. vi. 105 Christian Princes cannot be restrained [from war] with the engagements and peaceful Theoremes of..a holy Religion. **1676** COLEY *Astrol.* 143 Note that by the word Theorem is understood a Speculation or an undoubted Rule or Principle in any Science or Art, and is that which respects Contemplation more than Practice. **1697** tr. *Burgersdicius his Logic* I. xxii. 90 *Ax*[*iom*] 10...*Ax.* 11... These Theorems..the Sense of them is manifest enough. **1766** BECCARIA *Ess. Crimes* xiv. (1793) 51 The following general theorem is of great use in determining the certainty of facts. **1835** I. TAYLOR *Spir. Despot.* iii. 101 In working the abstract theorem of a church polity. **1864** BOWEN *Logic* xi. 374 A demonstrable judgment, or one which is announced as needing proof, if theoretical, is called a Theorem.

Hence **Theˑorem** *v., trans.* to express in or by means of a theorem.

**1840** CARLYLE *Heroes* i. (1872) 23 They are matters which refuse to be theoremed and diagramed. **1891** G. MEREDITH *One of our Conq.* I. vii. 121 Euclid would have theorem'd it out for you at a glance.

**Theorematic** (þīˑōrĕmæˑtik), *a.* [ad. Gr. θεωρηματικός, f. θεώρηματ-, THEOREM + -ικος, -IC. Cf. *problematic.*] Pertaining to, by means of, or of the nature of a theorem. Also † **Theoremaˑtical** *a.* Hence **Theoremaˑtically** *adv.*, in the way of or by means of a theorem. So **Theorematist** (-eˑmătist), one who discovers or formulates a theorem. Also † **Theoreˑmic** *a.* = *theorematic*; † **Theˑoremist** = *theorematist.*

**1656** BLOUNT *Glossogr.*, **Theorematick* or *Theoretick*, belonging to a theoreme, or to contemplation. **1879** W. E. FORSTER in T. W. Reid *Life* (1888) II. 224 The old principle was the Theorematic rule of the Sultan. **1908** *Hibbert Jrnl.* Oct. 102 Theorematic Demonstration. **1730** BAILEY (folio), **Theorematical*, of Theorems. **1755** JOHNSON, Theorematical, Theorematick, Theoremick. **1652** URQUHART *Jewel* Wks. (1834) 291 *Theorematically to infer consequences from infallible maximes. **1788** T. TAYLOR *Proclus* I. 109 We ought to conceive all those theorematically, but not problematically. **1727** BAILEY vol. II, **Theorematist*,..a Finder out or Producer of Theorems. **1701** GREW *Cosm. Sacra* II. v. 52 *Theoremick Truth, or that which lies in the Conceptions we have of Things. **1656** BLOUNT *Glossogr.*, **Theoremist*, a professor of Theoremes.

**Theoretic** (þīoreˑtik), *a.* (*sb.*) [ad. late L. *theōrētic-us* (*a* 397 Ambrosius *Examerōn* I. 5 § 17, *theoreticæ artes* opposed to *actuosæ*), a. Gr. θεωρητικός contemplative, f. θεωρητ-ός that may be seen, f. θεωρεῖν to look at, contemplate, inspect. So F. *théorétique* (1721 in Hatz.-Darm.).]

†**1.** Speculative. *Obs.*

**1656** STANLEY *Hist. Philos.* v. (1701) 180/2 Of Theoretick Philosophy one part enquires into things immutable..and the first causes of things. **1706** PHILLIPS, *Theoretick, Theorical*, or *Theorick*, belonging to Theory; Speculative.

**2.** (Rendering Gr. θεωρητικός in Aristotle.) Contemplative, as opposed to active or practical (πρακτικός): cf. CONTEMPLATIVE A. 3. *rare.*

**1907** J. SETH in *Hibbert Jrnl.* Oct. 117 In Aristotle we find the affirmation of the superior value..of the 'theoretic' or spiritual life to the practical life.

**3.** = THEORETICAL 2.

*a* **1661** FULLER *Worthies, Cornw.* (1662) I. 202 Attaining to great perfection in the Theoretick, and practicall parts of those professions. **1750** JOHNSON *Rambler* No. 77 ¶ 7 Few men, celebrated for theoretick wisdom, live with conformity to their precepts. **1773** *Life N. Frowde* 65, I soon reduced my Theoretic Knowledge to Practice. **1862** TYNDALL *Mountaineer.* ii. 10 Our master minds built their theoretic edifices upon the rock of fact.

**b.** = THEORETICAL 2 b.

**1790** BURKE *Fr. Rev.* Wks. V. 234 Is it then true, that.. it was of absolute necessity the whole fabrick should be.. pulled down, and the area cleared for the erection of a theoretick experimental edifice in its place? **1837** CARLYLE *Fr. Rev.* II. I. ii, Plots which cannot be executed; which are mostly theoretic. **1856** EMERSON *Eng. Traits, Universities* Wks. (Bohn) II. 91 Seven years' residence is the theoretic period for a master's degree.

**c.** Of persons, their minds, etc.: Versed in or proceeding by the scientific theory of the subject; opposed to *empirical*; also, Given to theories; speculative; theorizing: sometimes opp. to *practical*; = THEORETICAL 3 a, b.

**1727–41** CHAMBERS *Cycl.* s.v., The theoretic physicians were such as went on the foot of reason, in opposition to the empirical physicians, who went wholly on experience. **1783** POTT *Chirurg. Wks.* II. 435 To which theoretic and whimsical people have assigned this disease. **1872** GEO. ELIOT *Middlem.* i, Her mind was theoretic, and yearned by its nature after some lofty conception of the world. *Ibid.* lxxxvi, Distinguished in his side of the county as a theoretic and practical farmer.

**4.** Relating to the moral perception of beauty.

(Used in this sense by Ruskin, in preference to *æsthetic*: see quot., and cf. THEORIA 2.)

**1846** RUSKIN *Mod. Paint.* II. III. I. i. § 10 The Theoretic faculty is concerned with the moral perception and appreciation of ideas of beauty. And the error respecting it is.. calling it Æsthetic, degrading it to a mere operation of sense.

**B.** *sb.*

**1.** Usually *pl.*: Theory (as opposed to *practic*, practice); theoretical matters (= next, B.).

**1656** STANLEY *Hist. Philos.* v. (1701) 180/1 The Science of things that are is called Theoretick; of those which pertain to Action Practick. **1706** PHILLIPS (ed. Kersey), *Theoreticks*, those things that belong to the Speculative part of Physick. **1860** H. B. WILSON in *Ess. & Rev.* 160 Morals come before contemplation, ethics before theoretics. **1865** HODGSON *Time & Space* II. ix. § 68. 566 The three functions are conation, cognition, and feeling. The three branches of knowledge founded on these are Technic, Theoretic, and Teleologic.

**2.** A person devoted to a life of contemplation. (See quot.; cf. 2 above, and THEORIC *sb.* 4.)

*a* **1832** BENTHAM *Deontology* (1834) I. 54 A band of men, whom..he [the Moralist] calls theoretics. These men look ..to contemplation alone for the summum bonum...To reach the summit of human felicity, a man has nothing to do but to contemplate. Who would not be a theoretic?

**Theoretical** (þīoreˑtikăl), *a.* (*sb.*) [f. as prec. + -AL: see -ICAL.]

†**1.** (In sense of Gr. θεωρητικός, L. *theōrēticus*.) Of or pertaining to contemplation, contemplative.

**1616** BULLOKAR *Eng. Expos.*, *Theoreticall*, that which belongeth to contemplation or inward knowledge of a thing. **1623** COCKERAM, *Theoreticall*, belonging to studie or contemplation.

**2.** Of, pertaining or relating to theory; of the nature of or consisting in theory. Often opp. to *practical.*

*a* **1652** J. SMITH *Sel. Disc.* vi. 207 They fall into great confusions in many theoretical matters of no small moment. **1700** C. NESSE *Antid. Armin.* (1827) 99 The persons.. had merely escaped..through a theoretical knowledge of the Lord. **1727–41** CHAMBERS *Cycl.* s. v. *Theoretic*, The sciences are ordinarily divided into theoretical, as theology, philosophy, &c., and practical, as medicine, law, &c. **1770** COOK *Voy. round World* II. x. (1773) 477 The theoretical arguments which have been brought to prove that the existence of a southern continent is necessary to preserve an equilibrium between the two hemispheres. **1830** MACKINTOSH *Eth. Philos.* Wks. 1846 I. 177 In the strictly theoretical part his exposition is considerably fuller. **1860** MAURY *Phys. Geog. Sea* (Low) viii. § 381 These observations agree with the theoretical deductions. **1860** ABP. THOMSON *Laws Th.* § 129. 274 Judgments that relate to speculation only are called theoretical; those which refer to practice are practical.

**b.** That is such according to theory; existing only in theory, ideal, hypothetical.

**1826** HENRY *Chem.* II. 699 The theoretical numbers not agreeing with the experimental results, which are those of Dr. John Davy. **1883** SIR N. LINDLEY in *Law Rep.* 11 Q. B. Div. 556 The attachment was granted for something more than a mere theoretical contempt. **1883** GILMOUR *Mongols* xvii. 204 A man..whose existence is evidently.. theoretical.

**3. a.** Of the mind or intellectual faculties: Having the power of forming theories; speculative.

*a* **1652** J. SMITH *Sel. Disc.* iv. 115 As for the mind and theoretical power. **1863** E. V. NEALE *Anal. Th. & Nat.* 117 The intuitions of space and time, and the conceptions of relation drawn from the theoretical reason.

**b.** Of persons: Addicted to theory; constructing or dealing with theories; speculative.

**1840** CARLYLE *Heroes* vi. (1872) 211 What is to be done?.. a question which theoretical constitution-builders may find easy to answer. **1859** DARWIN *Orig. Spec.* i. (1860) 12 Doubts have been thrown on this principle only by theoretical writers. **1902** J. DENNEY *Death of Christ* iii. 121 The simplest preacher and the most effective is always the most absolutely theoretical.

**B.** *sb.* (*pl.*) Theoretical points or matters.

**1860** H. B. WILSON in *Ess. & Rev.* 181 It is..strange..to expect all ministers..to be of one opinion in theoreticals.

**Theoreˑtically**, *adv.* [f. prec. + -LY [2].] In a theoretic or theoretical manner.

**a.** In the way of or by means of theory; in relation to theory. (In quot. 1701 perh. = contemplatively, speculatively.)

**1701** NORRIS *Ideal World* I. v. 235 As they [the Divine Ideas] are thus independent upon the existence of things in nature, so also upon all mind or understanding.., that is, I mean, as conceptive, or theoretically considered. **1748** HARTLEY *Observ. Man* I. iii. 343 This lessens the Difference theoretically also. **1831** BREWSTER *Optics* xxxiii. § 163. 274 Huygens..investigated the subject, both experimentally and theoretically. **1886** *Manch. Exam.* 6 Jan. 3/1 Questions which are theoretically interesting to thoughtful people and practically interesting to every one.

**b.** According to theory, in theory, ideally; hypothetically (as opp. to actually).

**1790** C. C. PINCKNEY in Sparks *Corr. Amer. Rev.* IV. 341 One great advantage, that might not attend a Constitution theoretically perfect. **1853** LYTTON *My Novel* III. ix, The position was not quite so pleasant as, theoretically, he had deemed it. **1875** WHITNEY *Life Lang.* iv. 67 The possible number of human articulations is theoretically infinite.

**Theoretician** (þīoretiˑʃăn). [f. THEORETIC + -IAN: see -ICIAN.] One who treats of or studies the theoretical side of a subject; = THEORIST 1.

**1886** *Q. Rev.* Jan. 284 Not a mere theoretician or 'statist'. **1891** *Athenæum* 29 Aug. 299/2 Among musical theoreticians Mr. Prout occupies a distinguished position.

**Theoretico-** (þīoreˑtiko), combining form from Gr. θεωρητικό-ς THEORETIC, THEORETICAL, as in **theoreˑtico-praˑctical** *a.*, pertaining to or skilled in the theory as well as the practice of a subject.

**1832** AUSTIN *Jurispr.* (1879) II. 1122 A theoretico-practical lawyer extensively versed in law..and in the sciences related to law.

‖ **Theoria** (þiˌōˑriă). *rare.* [a. Gr. θεωρία a looking at, contemplation, f. θεώρειν to look at.]

†**1.** ? Contemplation, survey. *Obs. rare.*

**1590** MARLOWE *2nd Pt. Tamburl.* IV. iii, My love, In whom the learned Rabbis of this age Might find as many wondrous miracles As in the theoria of the world!

**2.** The perception of beauty regarded as a moral faculty. (Used in this sense by Ruskin, in contra-distinction to *æsthesis*: cf. THEORETIC *a.* 4.)

**1846** RUSKIN *Mod. Paint.* II. III. I. ii. § 1 The impressions of beauty..are neither sensual nor intellectual, but moral; and for the faculty receiving them..no term can be more accurate..than that employed by the Greeks, 'Theoretic', which I pray permission..to use, and to call the operation of the faculty itself, Theoria. *Ibid.* § 6 The mere animal consciousness of the pleasantness I call Æsthesis; but the exulting, reverent, and grateful perception of it I call Theoria.

**Theoric** (þīˑorik), *sb.* and *a.*[1] *Obs.* or *arch.* Also 4–5 -ik, 4–7 -ike, 4–9 -ique, 5–6 -yke, -yque, 6–7 -icke, -icque, 6–8 -ick. [ME. *theorique* in Gower, a. OF. *theorique* (13th c. in Godef., opposed to *pratique* practice), prob. repr. a med.L. *theōrica*, Gr. θεωρική (not recorded in this sense): cf. med.L. *theōricus* adj. (13th c. in Du Cange) in *vita theorica* the contemplative life. The place of the stress, as in *caˑtholic*, is due to Fr. derivation.

(L. **theōricē* sb., attributed in the Dicts. to Jerome, is now eliminated as an error, the word being θεολογικήν.)]

**A.** *sb.* **1.** = THEORY [1] 4, 5: chiefly in sense 4 b; often opposed to *practic* or *practice*. *Obs.* or *arch.*

**1390** GOWER *Conf.* III. 85 The nature of Philosophie, Which Aristotle..Declareth..As of thre points in principal. Wherof the ferste in special Is Theorique. **1483** CAXTON *Gold. Leg.* 389 b/2 Phylosophye is deuyded in thre in theoryque in practyque and in logyque. **1565** J. HALLE *Hist. Expost.* (Percy Soc.) 42 Chirurgerye cannot be perfectlye learned wythoute theorike. **1599** SHAKS. *Hen. V*, I. i. 52 So that the Art and Practique part of Life, Must be the Mistresse to this Theorique. **1601** HOLLAND *Pliny* II. Explan. Words, *Theoricke*, or *Theoretique*, contemplative knowledge without action and practise. **1604** SHAKS. *Oth.* I. i. 24. **1720** STRYPE *Stow's Surv.* (1754) I. I. vi. 32/2 The great French Philosopher Des Cartes..telling us, that, from the Theorique of the Moon, the Moon moves so in her elliptical Orb [etc.]. **1830** MISS MITFORD *Village* Ser. IV. 195 These..matters..may rather be termed the theorique than the practique of reform. **1853** [see PRACTIC *sb.*[1] 1].

†**b.** A theoreˑtical treatise or discourse. *Obs.*

*c* **1391** CHAUCER *Astrol.* Prol. 3 The .4. partie shal ben a theorik to declare the Moeuynge of the celestial bodies with [þe] causes.

†**c.** *pl.* **Theorics**: theoretical statements or notions; theory; often opp. to *practics* or *practice.*

**1551** RECORDE *Pathw. Knowl.* I. Defin., As they in theyr theorikes (which ar only mind workes) do precisely vnderstand these definitions. **1602** BLUNDEVILLE (*title*) The Theoriques of the seuen Planets, shewing all their diuerse motions. **1637** WOTTON *Lett.* (1907) II. 371 He was..a rare mathematician even..in algebra and the theoriques. *a* **1661** FULLER *Worthies, Cornw.* (1662) I. 202 Atwell..was well seen in the Theoricks of Physick, and happy in the practise thereof.

†**2.** A (mental) view or survey; a conspectus.

**1591** LAMBARDE *Eiren.* Proheme 2 A summarie consideration & Theorique of the whole office belonging to this Iustice. *Ibid.* I. 4 (*heading*) The First Booke, conteining a Theoricque [*ed.* 1602, or insight] of the office of the Iustices of Peace.

†**3.** A mechanical device theoretically representing or explaining a natural phenomenon. *Obs.*

**1592** DEE *Comp. Rehears.* (Chetham Soc.) 28 Divers other instrumentes as the theorick of the eighth spheare, the nynth and tenth, with an horizon and meridian of copper. **1594** BLUNDEVIL *Exerc.* VI. Introd. (1636) 608 In the Limbe of the backe part is described the Theorique of the Sun, to know therby in what signe and degree the Sun is every day ..by laying the Diopter thereto. **1657** W. RAND tr. *Gassendi's Life Peiresc* I. 145 He caused a mechanicall Theoric [*printed* Theorie; the L. is *theoricen mechanicam*] or Instrument to be made..that..the Places of the..Stars might be calculated.

†**4.** A man devoted to contemplation or speculation; a member of a contemplative sect of Essenes. (Cf. PRACTIC *sb.*[2]) *Obs.*

**1625** T. GODWIN *Moses & Aaron* I. xii. 62 Of these Essenes there were two sorts, some Theorikes, giuing themselues wholly to speculation; others Practicks, laborious..in.. handy-crafts. *a* **1641** BP. MOUNTAGU *Acts & Mon.* vii. (1642) 430 The one sect hee names Theoriques or Contemplators. **1798** W. TAYLOR in *Monthly Rev.* XXVII. 212 To the theorics, or instructors, a supper only.

†**B.** *adj.* **1.** = THEORETIC 3, THEORETICAL 2. (Often opp. to *practic* = practical.) *Obs.*

**1551** RECORDE *Pathw. Knowl.* I. Defin., This exactnes of definition is more meeter for onlye Theorike speculacion, then for practise and outwarde worke. **1662** PLAYFORD *Skill Mus.* I. i. (1674) 5 A true Rule of the Theorick part of Musick. **1726** *Adv. Capt. R. Boyle* (1768) 25 Gardening..I always took Delight in, both Theoric and Practic. **1804** W. TAYLOR in *Crit. Rev.* Ser. III. III. 528 These were daily instructed ..both in the theoric and practic parts of the Pythagorean philosophy.

†**2.** Knowing or studying the theory of things; theorizing; contemplative, speculative; = THEORETIC *a.* 2, 3 c, THEORETICAL 1, 3. *Obs.*

**1599** B. JONSON *Cynthia's Rev.* II. iii, According to our subdivision of a courtier, elementary, practique, and theorique. Your courtier theoric, is he that hath arrived to his farthest, and doth now know the court rather by speculation than practice. **1602** PLAT *Delightes for Ladies* Epist. (1605) 3 By fancie framde within a theorique braine. **1632** MASSINGER & FIELD *Fatal Dowry* II. i, A man but young, Yet old in judgment; theoric and practic In all humanity.

**Theoric** (þiˌǫ·rik), *a.*[2] *Gr. Antiq.* [ad. Gr. θεωρικός pertaining to spectacles, f. θεωρία viewing, beholding.] Pertaining to or connected with public spectacles, religious functions, and solemn embassies: applied esp. to a fund provided for these purposes from the public treasury at Athens. (Cf. THEORY [2].)

**1727-41** CHAMBERS *Cycl.* s.v., By the law of Eubulus, it was made a capital crime to pervert the theoric money to any other use; even to employ it in the occasions of war. **1852** GROTE *Greece* II. lxxv. IX. 526 The Theoric Board, or Paymasters for the general expenses of public worship and sacrifice. **1884** *Q. Rev.* Oct. 342 Pericles..by his theoric largesses, helped to swell the city mob of idlers.

†**Theo·rical,** *a. Obs.* [f. as THEORIC *a.*[1] + -AL: see -ICAL.]

**a.** = THEORIC *a.*[1] I. (Often opp. to *practical.*)

**1571** DIGGES *Pantom.* Epist. *ij b, A Discourse Geometricall..containing sundry Theoricall and practicall propositions. *a* **1619** FOTHERBY *Atheom.* II. viii. § 5 (1622) 292 Wee must..ioyne theorical and practicall vertues together. **1651** BIGGS *New Disp.* § 230 Theoricall or practicall phlebotomy. **1730** MALCOLM (*title*) A new system of Arithmetick Theorical and Practical.

**b.** = THEORETICAL 3.

**1594** PLAT *Diuerse new Sorts Soyle* 26, I thinke that those ..did not obteine thisskil by any true theoricall imagination, but..they did fynde the same without any seeking. **1663** COWLEY *Verses & Ess., Disc. O. Cromwell* (1669) 76, I see you are a Pedant, and Platonical Statesman, a Theorical Common-wealths-man, an Utopian Dreamer. **1730** MALCOLM *Syst. Arith.* Pref. 6 The Theorical writers have treated Arithmetick as a Science.

**c.** Contemplative, speculative. *rare.*

**1612** T. TAYLOR *Comm. Titus* i. 15. 281 Their cheife and eminent inward parts are defiled, whether we consider the theoricall part, that is, the minde and vnderstanding,..or the practicall facultie (included in the conscience). **1734** WATERLAND *Doctrine Holy Trinity* 513 That Three-fold Method of commenting which St. Jerome lays down; namely, the Historical, Tropological, and Theorical; or, in more familiar Terms, the literal, moral, and sublime.

†**Theo·rically,** *adv. Obs.* [f. prec. + -LY [2].] In theory; = THEORETICALLY a.

**1571** DIGGES *Pantom.* IV. xxv. Ggj, Hitherto haue I onely intreated of the fiue regulare bodies, Theorically and practically opening sundrie meanes to search out the proportion [etc.]. **1640** QUARLES *Enchirid.* 22 It is most requisite for a Prince to prepare against..Warre, both Theorically in reading Heroick Histories; and practically, in maintaining Martiall discipline. **1680** AUBREY *Lives, W. Holder* (1898) I. 404 He is very musicall, both theorically and practically.

**Theorician** (þiōri·ʃǎn). [f. (after F. *théoricien*) on THEORIC *sb.* + -IAN; cf. *logician, physician,* etc.] A holder of a theory; = THEORIST.

**1841** *Blackw. Mag.* L. 16 To examine Mr. Porter the statistician, to discover a decisive refutation of Mr. Porter the free-trade theorician. **1895** *Westm. Gaz.* 1 Oct. 3/1 Some editors..believed, at the promptings of jealous theoricians, that the Pasteur system was a fallacy. **1905** *Athenæum* 16 Sept. 365/1 Two other poets..are..considered in these pages; and then some theoricians.

‖**Theoricon** (þiˌǫ·rikǫn). *Gr. Antiq.* Also -kon. [a. Gr. θεωρικόν, neut. of θεωρικός THEORIC *a.*[2]] The theoric fund in ancient Athens: see THEORIC *a.*[2]

**1828** tr. *Boeckh's Public Econ. Athens* I. 294 The payment of the Theoricon out of the public money was first introduced by Pericles...This distribution of the Theoricon filled the theatre. **1842** BRANDE *Dict. Sc.*, etc., *Theoricon*, in ancient Attic History, the name given to that portion of the revenue of the state which was..reserved for the purpose of theatrical representations. **1850** GROTE *Greece* II. lxvi. VIII. 424 The manager of the Theôrikon or religious festival-fund.

**Theorism** (þī·ŏriz'm). *rare.* [f. as next + -ISM.] Theorizing, speculation.

**1856** H. R. REYNOLDS in *Life* v. (1898) 125 The lynx-eyed theorism of Lepsius. **1906** *Contemp. Rev.* July 60 Dead, dry-as-dust theorism.

**Theorist** (þī·ŏrist). [f. THEORY (or its Gr. or L. source) + -IST.]

**1.** An adept in the theory (as distinct from the practice) of a subject. Often with mixture of sense 2.

**1594** CAREW *Huarte's Exam. Wits* xii. (1596) 177 It is a miracle to find out a Phisition, who is both a great Theorist, and withall a great Practitioner. **1664** POWER *Exp. Philos.* Pref. 16 The Theorists in Conical Sections. **1784** *Cook's Voy. Pacific Ocean* v. vii. III. 144 *note*, Burney..perhaps the greatest musical theorist of this or any other age. **1855** MACAULAY *Hist. Eng.* xx. IV. 492 It is..curious..that a man who, as a theorist, was distinguished..by the largeness of his views..should, in practice, have been distinguished..by the obstinacy with which he adhered to an ancient mode of doing business.

**2.** One who theorizes; one who frames or propounds a theory or theories, a theoretical investigator or writer; one who holds or maintains a theory; sometimes, a framer or maintainer of a mere hypothesis or speculation (cf. THEORY [1] 6).

**1646** SIR T. BROWNE *Pseud. Ep.* 115 That a Brock or Badger hath his legs of one side shorter then of the other,.. an opinion..received not only by theorists and unexperienced beleevers, but assented unto by most who..behold and hunt them dayly. **1692** BENTLEY *Boyle Lect.* vii. 204 It [gravitation] is lately demonstrated..by that very excellent and divine theorist Mr. Isaac Newton. **1735** JOHNSON *Lobo's Abyssinia, Descr.* x. 106 Some of these Theorists have been pleas'd to declare it as their favourite Notion. **1884** *Spectator* 4 Oct. 1309/1 As a theorist on law, he has a distinctive place of his own.

**Theorize** (þī·ŏrəiz), *v.* [f. as prec. + -IZE: cf. med.L. *theōrīzāre* (Scotus Erigena *a* 880).]

†**1.** *trans.* To contemplate, survey. *Obs. rare.*

**1638** SIR T. HERBERT *Trav.* (ed. 2) 223 Hitherto wee have beene practicall; let mee now draw your eyes to theorize in generall the severall properties and fashions of this great Empire.

**2.** *intr.* To form or construct theories.

**1638** SIR T. HERBERT *Trav.* (ed. 2) 6 Let us theorize a little upon the Mathematiques. **1797** GILLIES *Aristotle's Ethics* x. vii. I. 397 Even unassisted and alone, though perhaps better with assistants, he [the sage] can still think and theorize. **1809-10** COLERIDGE *Friend* I. iv. (1865) 118 The meanest of men has his theory, and to think at all is to theorize. **1845** JEBB *Gen. Princ. Law* in *Encycl. Metrop.* II. 677/1 He did not theorize without regard to facts and experience. *a* **1862** BUCKLE *Misc. Wks.* (1872) I. 16.

**3.** *trans.* To construct a theory of or about.

*a* **1848** W. A. BUTLER *Hist. Anc. Philos.* (1856) I. 40 [Mechanics] theorizes the forces and motions of the masses; [Chemistry] the intimate structure of each.

**b.** To suppose, or assume, in the way of theory. (With simple obj. or obj. clause.)

**1838** G. S. FABER *Inquiry* 107 We can scarcely theorise a lower depth than this glaring and scandalous prostitution of justice. **1863** COWDEN CLARKE *Shaks. Char.* xx. 507 He theorised that the difference between a pea and nothing could make no difference to the poor beast.

**c.** To make or constitute in theory; to bring *into* or *out of* some condition theoretically.

**1843** *Blackw. Mag.* LIII. 697 He had..theorized himself into the future husband of his ward. **1864** LOWELL *McClellan's Rep.* Prose Wks. 1890 V. 97 The one thing that cannot be theorized out of existence..is a lost campaign. **1886** J. KER *Serm.* Ser. II. (1887) xi. 171 Men theorise it into a thing of natural growth.

Hence **The·orizing** *vbl. sb.* and *ppl. a.*; also **Theoriza·tion**, the action of theorizing, construction of a theory or theories; **The·orizer**, one who theorizes.

**1820** JEFFERSON *Writ.* (1830) IV. 325 The misconstructions, interpolations, and *theorizations of..fanatics. **1854** E. G. HOLLAND *Mem. J. Badger* 417 Men who have no tendency to speculative theorization. **1829** CARLYLE *Crit. & Misc. Ess., Novalis* (1872) II. 197 A great and original plan, very different..from that of our idle *theorisers and generalizers. **1870** PROCTOR *Other Worlds* 3 Not..the mere fanciful theoriser.., but men of the highest eminence in science. **1818** HALLAM *Mid. Ages* (1872) I. Pref. 6 A fault too common,..that of *theorising upon an imperfect induction. **1849** NOAD *Electricity* (ed. 3) 127 One fact is worth a volume of theorizing. **1792** J. BELKNAP *Hist. New Hampsh.* III. 229 The inconsistent conclusions of these *theorising philosophers. **1891** *Athenæum* 5 Dec. 753/2 We find the utmost scorn expressed [by Moltke] for..theorizing demagogues.

**Theory**[1] (þī·ŏri). Also 7 -ie, -ee. [ad. late L. *theōria* (Jerome in Ezech. XII. xl. 4), a. Gr. θεωρία a looking at, viewing, contemplation, speculation, theory, also a sight, a spectacle, abstr. sb. f. θεωρός (:—*θεαορός) spectator, looker on, f. stem θεα- of θεᾶσθαι to look on, view, contemplate. In mod. use prob. from med.L. transl. of Aristotle. Cf. It. *teoria* (Florio 1598 *theoría*), F. *théorie* (15.. in Godef. *Compl.*).]

†**1.** A sight, a spectacle. *Obs. rare.*

**1605** BP. ANDREWES *Serm., Passion* (1631) 365 Saint Luke ..calleth the Passion θεωρίαν a Theory or Sight...Of our blessed Saviour's whole life or death, there is no part but is a Theorie of it selfe, well worthie our looking on.

†**2.** Mental view, contemplation. *Obs.*

[**1598-1611** FLORIO, *Theoría*, contemplation, speculation, deepe study, insight or beholding.] **1611** COTGR., *Theorie*, theorie, contemplation, deepe studie; a sight, or beholding, speculation. **1643** SIR T. BROWNE *Relig. Med.* I. § 45 Nor can I thinke I have the true Theory of death when I contemplate a skull, or behold a Skeleton with those vulgar imaginations it casts upon us. **1646** — *Pseud. Ep.* VII. xix. 385 As they encrease the hatred of vice in some, so doe they enlarge the theory of wickednesse in all. **1653** W. HARVEY *Anat. Exercit.* Pref. ⁋ v, All their theory and contemplation (which they count Science) represents nothing but waking mens dreams, and sick mens phrensies. **1710** NORRIS *Chr. Prud.* ii. 65 Speculative Knowledge contemplates Truth for itself, and accordingly stops and rests in the Contemplation of it, which is what we commonly call Theory.

**3.** A conception or mental scheme of something to be done, or of the method of doing it; a systematic statement of rules or principles to be followed.

**1597** HOOKER *Eccl. Pol.* v. xxix. § 8 If they had been themselves to execute their owne Theorie in this Church. **1643** BP. HALL *Devout Soul* i, It will hardly be believed, how far some of their contemplative men have gone in the theory hereof. **1674** DRYDEN *Prol. Univ. Oxford* 11 Your theories are here to practice brought, As in mechanic operations wrought. **1798** MALTHUS *Popul.* III. ii. (1806) II. 103 A theory that will not admit of application cannot possibly be just. **1832** AUSTIN *Jurispr.* (1879) II. 1133 Theory of what is and theory of what ought to be are perpetually confounded. **1853** BRIGHT *Sp. India* 3 June (1876) 4 The theory of the old Government of India was one which could not be defended. **1879** M. PATTISON *Milton* xiii. 219 Even the calm and gentle author of the Christian Year..deliberately framed a theory of Poetic for the express purpose, as it would seem, of excluding the author of Paradise Lost from the first class of poets.

**4.** A scheme or system of ideas or statements held as an explanation or account of a group of facts or phenomena; a hypothesis that has been confirmed or established by observation or experiment, and is propounded or accepted as accounting for the known facts; a statement of what are held to be the general laws, principles, or causes of something known or observed.

**1638** SIR T. HERBERT *Trav.* (ed. 2) 127 Or whether from subterranean fires,..I dare not conclude, but leave such theories to those that study Meteors. **1684** BURNET (*title*) The Theory of the Earth. **1706** PHILLIPS (ed. Kersey), *Theories of the Planets*, certain Hypotheses, or Suppositions about the Motions of the Heavens, according to which, Astronomers explain..the Phænomena or Appearances of the Planets. **1727-41** CHAMBERS *Cycl.* s. v., We say..theory of the rainbow, of the microscope..the motion of the heart, the operation of purgatives, etc. **1812** PLAYFAIR *Nat. Phil.* (1819) I. 3 A theory is often nothing else but a contrivance for comprehending a certain number of facts under one expression. **1850** GROVE *Corr. Phys. Forces* (ed. 2) 105 Were a theory open to no objection it would cease to be a theory, and would become a law. **1879** M. PATTISON *Milton* xiii. 180 The Copernican theory, which placed the sun in the centre of our system, was already the established belief of the few well-informed. **1890** A. R. WALLACE *Darwinism* 7 The truest and most complete theory would not enable us to solve all the difficult problems which the whole course of the development of life upon our globe presents to us.

**b.** That department of an art or technical subject which consists in the knowledge or statement of the facts on which it depends, or of its principles or methods, as distinguished from the *practice* of it.

**1613** R. CAWDREY *Table Alph.* (ed. 3), *Theorie*, the contemplation, or inward knowledge of any art. **1626** BACON *Sylva* § 327 The means, hitherto propounded, to effect it, are in the practice, full of error and imposture, and in the theory, full of unsound imaginations. **1660** R. COKE *Power & Subj.* Pref. 5 A Musitian, who Composes well, yet understands but little in the theory of Musick. **1795** HUTTON *Math. Dict.* s. v., To be learned in an art, &c., the Theory is sufficient; to be a master of it, both the Theory and practice are requisite. **1827** WHATELY *Logic* (ed. 2) 205 Logic being concerned with the theory of Reasoning. **1884** GROVE *Dict. Mus.* IV. 101/1 *Theory*, a term often used..to express the knowledge of Harmony, Counter-point, Thorough-bass, etc., as distinguished from the art of playing, which is ..called 'Practice'.

**c.** A systematic statement of the general principles or laws of some branch of mathematics; a set of theorems forming a connected system: as *the theory of equations, of functions, of numbers, of probabilities.*

**1799** W. FREND (*title*) The Principles of Algebra..; or the true Theory of Equations established by mathematical demonstration. **1806** [see THEOREMA]. **1811** P. BARLOW (*title*) An Elementary Investigation of the Theory of Numbers. **1838** [see PROBABILITY 3]. **1893** FORSYTH (*title*) Theory of Functions.

**5.** In the abstract (without article): Systematic conception or statement of the principles of something; abstract knowledge, or the formulation of it: often used as implying more or less unsupported hypothesis (cf. 6): distinguished from or opposed to *practice* (cf. 4 b). *In theory* (formerly *in the theory*): according to theory, theoretically (opp. to *in practice* or *in fact*).

**1624** T. MACARNESSE in Capt. Smith *Virginia* Pref., That thou mightest read and know and safely see, What he by practice, thou by Theoree. **1692** SIR W. HOPE *Fencing-Master* (ed. 2) 164 Theorie without Practice will serve but for little. **1769-72** *Junius Lett.* Pref. (1820) 17 Theory is at variance with practise. **1776** J. Adams *Wks.* (1854) IX. 375 It is certain, in theory, that the only moral foundation of government is, the consent of the people. **1821** J. Q. Adams in Davies *Metr. Syst.* III. (1871) 175 A compromise between philosophical theory and inveterate popular habits.

**6.** In loose or general sense: A hypothesis proposed as an explanation; hence, a mere hypothesis, speculation, conjecture; an idea or set of ideas about something; an individual view or notion. Cf. 4.

**1792** Burke *Corr.* (1844) IV. 13 Whether I am right in the theory or not,..the fact is as I state it. **1794** Paley *Evid.* (1825) II. 347 Theories which have, at different times, gained possession of the public mind. **1829** Jas. Mill *Hum. Mind* (1869) II. xxv. 403 The word theory has been perverted to denote an operation..which..consists in supposing and setting down matters supposed as matters observed. Theory in fact has been confounded with Hypothesis. **1864** Bowen *Logic* xi. (1870) 375 A Theory, sometimes incorrectly used as a synonyme for Hypothesis. **1867** Lady Herbert *Cradle L.* iii. 95 So varied are the theories as to the origin of these wonderful sepulchres. **1880** T. A. Spalding *Eliz. Demonol.* 35 This was not a mere theory, but a vital active belief.

**7.** *Comb.*, as *theory-bigoted* adj., *-building*, *-monger*, *-spinning*; **theory-blind** *a.*, (*a*) blinded by a theory, so as to be unable to see the facts truly; (*b*) blind to a theory, i. e. unable to see or apprehend it (cf. *colour-blind*); **theory-man** (*nonce-wd.*), a theorist; **theory-tailor**, contemptuously for a shaper of theories.

**1884** *Q. Rev.* Apr. 337 More *theory-bigoted than Mr. ——. **1892** W. S. Lilly *Gt. Enigma* 230 You cannot help recognising, unless you are *theory-blind,..the law of correlation. **1902** *Q. Rev.* Apr. 359 No one who is not theory-blind—a very common form of blindness. **1780** *Mirror* No. 107 ⁋ 2 There is something..so delightful in this art of *theory-building. **1727** De Foe *Syst. Magic* I. i. (1840) 9 What our learned *theory-men insist to have been the causes of the deluge. **1905** *Academy* 4 Feb. 105/1 It is high time that protest be made..against the master's works being made the prey of *theorymongers. **1904** Windle *Prehist. Age* Pref. 13 There has been a vast amount of *theory-spinning in connexion with the early epochs. **1876** Meredith *Beauch. Career* xxxvii, These men are *theory-tailors not politicians.

**Theory**[2] (þī,ōᵊ·ri). *Gr. Antiq.* [ad. Gr. θεωρία, the same word as in Theory[1], in a specialized sense.] A body of Theors sent by a state to perform some religious rite or duty; a solemn legation.

**1842** *Smith's Dict. Grk. & Rom. Antiq.* s.v. *Salaminia*, They conveyed theories, despatches, &c. from Athens. **1850** Grote *Greece* II. lv. VII. 72 Curiosity..to see what figure the Theôry of Athens would make as to show and splendour. **1853** *Ibid.* II. lxxxiii. XI. 38 He sent thither his Theôry, or solemn legation for sacrifice, decked in the richest garments.

**Theos**, early ME.: see This, These.

**Theosoph** (þī·ǒsǫf). [= Fr. *théosophe* (*a* 1784 Diderot in Littré), ad. med.L. *theosophus* (Scotus Erigena *a* 880), a. late Gr. θεόσοφ-ος (*a* 500, Pseudo-Dionysius *De Div. Nom.* § 6) wise concerning God, f. θεός God + σοφός wise.] One who pursues Theosophy (sense 1).

(The med.L. *theosophus* was often used for *theologian*, in contrast with *philosophus*.)

**1822** Southey in *Q. Rev.* Jan. 37 This Theosophe was too poor, too religious, and too insane to have any share in establishing the seminary..at Avignon. **1838** *Fraser's Mag.* XVII. 27 The Theosophs were right in separating entirely the mind from the soul. **1878** Morley *Diderot* I. v. 203 The article on Theosophs would hardly have been so disproportionately long as it is, merely for the sake of Paracelsus. **1880** *Chambers's Encycl.* IX. 400/1 Within the Christian period we may number among Theosophs, the Neo-Platonists..; the Hesychasts of the Greek Church [etc.].

**Theosopheme** (þi,ǫ·sǒfīm). *rare.* [ad. Gr. type *θεοσόφημα: cf. *philosopheme*.] A theosophical speculation or conclusion.

**1856** C. J. Ellicott in *Cambr. Ess.* 162 Some appear to have been gospels..others the wildest and most unhistorical theosophemes. **1873** Symonds *Grk. Poets* vii. 231 The colossal theosophemes of Aeschylus called for profound reflection.

**Theosopher** (þi,ǫ·sǒfəɹ). [f. Theosoph(y, or med.L. *theosoph-us* (Scotus Erigena *a* 880) Theosoph + -er[1]: cf. Philosopher.] = Theosophist. (Applied spec. to Jacob Boehme, 'the Teutonic Theosopher', and his followers.)

**1647** Ward *Simp. Cobler* (1843) 18 Have an extraordinary care..of the late Theosophers, that teach men to climbe to heaven upon a ladder of lying figments. **1653** H. More *Conject. Cabbal.* (1713) 72 Laying down such Conclusions as the Naturalists and Theosophers in all Ages have looked upon as the choicest and most precious. **1755** Amory *Mem.* (1766) II. 73 *note*, Jacob Behemen, the reverend theosopher. **1782** *Gentl. Mag.* LII. 329/1 The true and infallible ground of what he there advanced was to be found in the Teutonic Theosopher, in his three first Properties of Eternal Nature. **1850** Maurice *Mor. & Met. Philos.* I. viii. § 2. 234 These books..which have procured him [Boehme] the name of the Theosopher. **1881** Overton *W. Law* 269 Hitherto Law has been presented to us in this chapter rather as a theosopher than as a mystic proper.

**Theosophic** (þīosǫ·fik), *a.* [f. Theosoph(y + -ic. Cf. F. *théosophique* (Diderot).] Of, pertaining to, or of the nature of theosophy; versed in theosophy. (Chiefly in reference to the school of Boehme; more recently = Theosophical b.)

**1649** Ellistone tr. *Behmen's Epist.* vii. § 24 He is a young companion of the Theosophic school. **1691** E. Taylor (*title*) Jacob Boehmen's Theosophick Philosophy Unfolded. **1710** R. Ward *Life H. More* 128 Such most Noble Truths, and Theosophick Mysteries are deliver'd in it. **1828** Carlyle *Misc., Werner* (1872) I. 79 His French scepticism had got overlaid with wondrous theosophic garniture. **1856** R. A. Vaughan *Mystics* I. v. (1860) I. 31 The mysticism I term theosophic aspires to know and believes itself in possession of a certain supernatural divine faculty for that purpose. **1902** *Encycl. Brit.* XXVII. 60/2 Christian Science, a system of theosophic and therapeutic doctrine, ..was originated..about 1866 by Mrs. Mary Baker Eddy.

**Theosophical** (þīosǫ·fikăl), *a.* [f. as prec. + -al: see -ical.] = prec.

**1642** H. More *Song of Soul* I. ii. III. iii. Argt., That th' earth doth move, proofs Physicall Unto us do descrie; Adde reasons Theosophicall, Als' adde Astronomie. **1697** *State Philadelph. Soc.* 13 The Title Page of the Theosophical Transactions. **1830** Pusey *Hist. Enq.* II. 351 To the theosophical fanatics, or a D. Hoffman, such a man, as he was, could not possibly assent. **1866** G. Macdonald *Ann. Q. Neighb.* xii, He had..often some theosophical theory to bring forward. **1886** *Manch. Exam.* 17 Feb. 3/3 Boehme is anything but a dealer in mere theosophical enigmas.

**b.** Of or belonging to Theosophy, in sense 2. *Theosophical Society*, an association founded at New York, 1875, by Col. H. S. Olcott, Madame Blavatsky, and W. Q. Judge, its professed objects being: 1. to form the nucleus of a universal brotherhood; 2. to promote the study of Aryan and other Eastern literature, religions, and sciences; 3. to investigate the unfamiliar laws of nature and the faculties latent in man.

**1881** Sinnett *Occult World* 35 Assisted by some other persons whose interest in the subject was kindled by occasional manifestations of her extraordinary powers, and notably by Colonel Olcott, its life-devoted President, she [Madame Blavatsky] founded the Theosophical Society. **1885** Olcott *Theosophy* Pref. 10 The Theosophical spirit of conceding to the people of all creeds the right of enjoying their religious convictions unmolested.

**Theoso·phically**, *adv.* [f. prec. + -ly[2].] In a theosophical manner; by means of theosophy.

**1689** Tryon (*title*) A Treatise of Dreams and Visions, wherein The Causes Natures and Uses of Nocturnal Representations, and the Communications both of Good and Evil Angels, as also departed Souls, to Mankinde, Are Theosophically Unfolded. **1855** Smedley, etc. *Occult Sciences* 135 The doctrine of Bœhmen,..worked out theosophically.

**b.** By means of or in accordance with theosophy (in sense 2).

**1896** *Columbus* (Ohio) *Dispatch* 21 July 4/3 C. B...says: Theosophically I know that W. J. Bryan is the reincarnation of Andrew Jackson, and spiritually I see around him the forms of Washington, Lincoln and the lamented Polk.

**Theosophico-** (þīosǫ·fiko), combining form of assumed Gr. *θεοσοφικό-s theosophic.

**1851** Carlyle *Sterling* I. viii. (1872) 50 The moaning singsong of that theosophico-metaphysical monotony.

**Theosophism** (þi,ǫ·sǒfiz'm). [f. as Theosoph + -ism. Cf. F. *théosophisme* (Diderot).] The theory and practice of theosophy; theosophizing.

**1791** Enfield *Hist. Philos.* IX. iii. II. 489 Many traces of the spirit of Theosophism may be found through the whole history of philosophy; in which nothing is more frequent, than fanatical and hypocritical pretensions to divine illumination. **1797** W. Taylor in *Monthly Rev.* Dec. 526 The ardent, zealous, and exalted enthusiast aspires to superhuman excellence, and clings to the prospects of theosophism.

**b.** In reference to Theosophy in sense 2.

**1896** *Chicago Advance* 1 Oct. 449 Theosophism, spiritualism, Christian Science,..are all modern instances of ways in which men are led astray.

**Theosophist** (þi,ǫ·sǒfist). [f. as prec. + -ist.]

**1.** One who professes or believes in Theosophy (in sense 1). **a.** With specific reference to Boehme. **b.** In a more general sense.

**a.** **1656** H. More *Enthus. Tri.* a viij, A promiscuous Collection of divers odd Conceits out of severall Theosophists and Chymists. *Ibid.* 40 This disease many of our Chymists and several Theosophists, in my judgement, seem very obnoxious to, who dictate their own Conceits and Fancies so magisterially and imperiously, as if they were indeed Authentick messengers from God Almighty. **1791** Enfield *Hist. Philos.* IX. iii. II. 488 The Theosophists..neither contented with the natural light of human reason, nor with the simple doctrines of scripture understood in their literal sense, have recourse to an internal supernatural light, superior to all other illuminations, from which they profess to derive a mysterious and divine philosophy, manifested only to the chosen favourites of heaven. **1817** Coleridge *Biog. Lit.* I. ix. 139 How dare I be ashamed of the Teutonic theosophist, Jacob Behmen?

**b.** **1814** Shelley *Deism* Pr. Wks. 1880 II. 77 The God of the rational Theosophist is a vast and wise animal. **1834** Southey *Doctor* ccix. (1862) 562/1 Certain theologians, and certain theosophists, as men who fancy themselves inspired sometimes affect to be called. **1837–9** Hallam *Hist. Lit.* (1847) II. III. ii. § 74. 361 The principal mystics or theosophists have generally been counted among philosophers. **1856** Vaughan *Mystics* I. v. (1860) I. 31 The theosophist is one who gives you a theory of God, or of the works of God, which has not reason, but an inspiration of his own for its basis. **1882** *Pall Mall G.* 30 Aug. 4 Of late years we have heard and learned a great deal about that interesting Oriental theosophist, the ideal Buddhist.

**2.** A professor or adherent of Theosophy (in sense 2); a member of the Theosophical Society; name of a magazine, the organ of that society.

**1881** *Sat. Rev.* 3 Sept. 298/2 The *Theosophist* is full of translations from the works of ancient 'theurgists'. **1881** Sinnett *Occult World* 37 The natives [of India] were flattered at the attitude towards them taken up by their new 'European' friends, as Madame Blavatsky and Colonel Olcott were no doubt generally regarded in spite of their American nationality, and showed a shallow eagerness to become Theosophists. **1885** Olcott *Theosophy* Pref. 11 We are..the same thing to all men—viz., Theosophists, who believe in the essential identity of all men, race, caste, and creed to the contrary notwithstanding. *Ibid.* 144 The Theosophist is a man who, whatever be his race, creed, or condition, aspires to reach this height of wisdom and beatitude by self-development.

**Theosophistic** (þi,ǫsofi·stik), *a.* [f. prec. + -ic.] Of the nature of or pertaining to a theosophist or theosophy (in sense 1).

**1849** Lady Wilde tr. *Meinhold's Sidonia Sorc.* III. xiii. II. 184 *note*, The theosophistic, cabalistic Dr. Joel. **1856** C. J. Ellicott in *Cambr. Ess.* 169 The main facts of Christianity..interwoven with the theosophistic speculations, the mystical doctrines..that were so dear to the hybrid Christian of Alexandria. **1857** — *Comm. Col.* Introd. (1861) 111 To warn the Colossians against a system of false teaching, partly Oriental and Theosophistic in its character, and partly Judaical and ceremonial. **1897** *Daily News* 5 Feb. 6/7 The theurgic and theosophistic obscurities of Kabbalistic writings.

**b.** Of or pertaining to Theosophy (in sense 2).

**1886** *Athenæum* 9 Jan. 68/3 Mr. Cumberland..in India is studying theosophistic philosophy on the spot.

So **Theosophi·stical** *a.*, in same sense (but with disparaging implication).

**1814** Shelley *Refut. Deism* Prose Wks. 1888 I. 292 To shew how much the cause of natural and revealed Religion has suffered from the mode of defence adopted by Theosophistical Christians. **1894** *Westm. Gaz.* 16 Nov. 4/2 The disingenuousness of this very Theosophistical letter.

**Theosophize** (þi,ǫ·sǒfəiz), *v.* [f. as Theosoph + -ize.] *intr.* To practise or pretend to theosophy; to reason or discourse theosophically. Hence **Theo·sophizing** *ppl. a.*

**1846** in Worcester citing M. Stuart. **1858** *Chamb. Jrnl.* X. 265/2 We owe, indirectly, the greatest scientific impetus of the modern world to a theosophising shoemaker [Behmen]. **1875** M. Arnold in *Contemp. Rev.* XXVI. 685 These things are not at all in the manner of Jesus. Jesus never theosophized.

**Theosophy** (þi,ǫ·sǒfi). [ad. med.L. *theosophia* (Scotus Erigena *a* 880), a. late Gr. θεοσοφία (*a* 500 Pseudo-Dion. *Myst. Theologia* i. § 1) wisdom concerning God or things divine, abstr. sb. from θεόσοφος Theosoph. So F. *théosophie* (18th c. in Littré).]

The word was revived early in the 17th c. in Latin and vernacular forms, to denote a kind of speculation, such as is found in the Jewish Cabbala and is illustrated by the writings of Cornelius Agrippa (1486–1535), Paracelsus, Robert Fludd, and others, which sought, usually by the doctrine of the macrocosm and microcosm, to derive from the knowledge of God contained in sacred books, or traditions mystically interpreted, a profounder knowledge and control of nature than could be obtained by the methods of the Aristotelian or other current philosophy. The name *theosophy* was often applied specifically to the system of Jacob Boehme (1575–1624), which, though not claiming to the same degree traditional authority, was largely expressed in language borrowed from writers of the school in question. The word has then and since been applied to more ancient and more recent views having more or less affinity to those already mentioned.

**1.** Any system of speculation which bases the knowledge of nature upon that of the divine nature: often with reference to such authors as those above mentioned, and more particularly to Boehme.

**1650** 'Eugenius Philalethes' (= T. Vaughan) *Anthroposophia Theomagica*, Author to Reader 13 The Ancient, reall Theosophie of the Hebrewes and Egyptians. **1678** Cudworth *Intell. Syst.* I. iv. § 20. 377 Xenophanes, philosophizing concerning the supreme Deity, was wont to call it ἓν καὶ πᾶν, *one and all*...Xenophanes his Theosophy, or divine philosophy, is most fully declared by Simplicius. **1681** H. More in Glanvill *Sadducismus* I. Postscr. (1726) 29 The sound Principles of Theosophy and true Divinity. **1691** E. Taylor *Behmen's Theos. Philos.* 171 What is all Sacred Theosophy, but the very understanding of a certain Divine Art? **1831** Carlyle *Early Germ. Lit.* in *Misc. Ess.* (1872) III. 194 That..devout temper, now degenerating into abstruse theosophy..was awake in this era. **1837** Hallam *Hist. Lit.* I. I. vii. § 17. 397 His own models were the oriental reveries of the Cabbala, and the theosophy of the mystics. *Ibid.* § 20 The theosophy of Paracelsus. **1841** W. Spalding *Italy & It. Isl.* III. 19 The Italians furnished few converts to the theosophy of Lepaux, they numbered very many quiet and contemptuous unbelievers. **1852** Conybeare & Howson *St. Paul* I. xiii. 483 There was a strong affinity between the Neo-Platonic philosophy of Alexandria and the Oriental theosophy which sprang from Buddhism and other kindred systems. **1856** R. A. Vaughan *Mystics* I. v. (1860) I. 30 Among the Germans I find mysticism generally called *theosophy* when applied to natural science. Too narrow a use of the word, I think. **1871** Farrar *Witn. Hist.* iii. 102 Porphyry and Hierocles met them with haughty mysticism and intellectual theosophy. **1877** E. Caird *Philos. Kant* ii. 17 The philosophies or theosophies that close the record of Greek speculation.

**2.** Applied to a system of recent origin, resembling the above in its claim to a knowledge of nature profounder than is obtained from empirical science, and contained in an esoteric tradition of which the doctrines of the various historical religions are held to be only the exoteric expression. Sometimes called Esoteric Buddhism. See *Theosophical Society*, under Theosophical b.

**1881** Sinnett *Occult World* 172 They have shown that Theosophy, or Occult Philosophy, is no new candidate for the world's attention, but is really a restatement of principles which have been recognized from the very infancy of mankind. **1884** *Chr. World* 16 Oct. 788/3 Theosophy is really another name for Esoteric Buddhism. **1885** Olcott *Theosophy* Pref. 13 Theosophy is the complement both of science and of philosophy, and as such is entitled to the respectful examination of the *savant* and the theologian. *Ibid.* 256

That priceless knowledge of divine things which we call Theosophy. **19..** MRS. BESANT *Meaning of Theosophy* 1 What is the essence of Theosophy? It is the fact that man, being himself divine, can know the Divinity whose life he shares. *Ibid.* 4 Theosophy has no code of morals, being itself the embodiment of the highest morality.

**3.** In etymol. sense: Wisdom or knowledge concerning things divine. *nonce-use.*

**1836–7** SIR W. HAMILTON *Metaph.* I. 416 An organ of Imagination is intimately connected with that of Theosophy or Veneration.

**Theotaurine**: see THEO-.

**Theotechny** (þīˈotekni). [f. Gr. θεός god + τέχνη art.] The introduction of divine or supernatural beings in the construction of a drama or epic; such beings collectively.

**1858** GLADSTONE *Homer* II. iii. 268 It is not difficult to understand why..Dionysus does not appear in the theotechny of the Iliad. **1869** — *Juv. Mundi* vii. 206 The personages of the Homeric Theotechny, under which name I include the whole of the supernatural beings, of whatever rank, introduced into the Poems. *Ibid.* xiv. § 1. 491 The Theotechny, or divine movement of the Poem [the Iliad].

So † **Theoteˑchnal** *a. Obs. rare*⁻¹, of the nature of divine art; **Theoteˑchnic** *a.*, pertaining to the invention or making of gods; also, belonging to theotechny; **Theoteˑchnist**, one who invents gods.

**1651** BIGGS *New Disp.* Pref. 9 Those Arts we speak of are Theotechnal, the Arts of God. **1874** PIAZZI SMYTH *Inher. Gt. Pyramid* v. (ed. 2) 64 At Thebes..those temples and tombs..speak lamentably to human theotechnic inventions. *Ibid.* xxii. 425 The original inventor and theotechnist of animal and other gods for his countrymen. **1878** GLADSTONE *Prim. Homer* vi. (1889) 67 Behind the complex and ever-active theotechnic machinery of the poem,. there is still the presence and operation of an august personage.

**Theoteleological, -logy**: see THEO-.

† **Theoten**, *v. Obs.* Forms: 1 **ðeotan, ðiotan, ðutan,** 3 **þeoten,** (*Orm.*) **þutenn.** [OE. *þéotan*, (pa. t. *þéat, þuton*) = ON. *þjóta* to whistle, etc., OHG. *diozan* to howl:—OTeut. **þeutan* (*þaut-, þut-*). OE. had also another pres. stem *þútan*, whence *þútende* pr. pple. and *þutenn* in Ormin; so Da. *tude*:—**þúta* to howl. Cf. *búgan*, Bow *v.*[1]] *intr.* To howl.

*c* **888** K. ÆLFRED *Boeth.* xxxviii. § 1 Sume wurdon to wulfan; þa ðuton, þon hi sprecan sceoldon. *a* **1000** *Boeth. Metr.* xxvi. 80 Ac hio þræʒmælum ðioton ongunnon. *c* **1000** ÆLFRIC *Hom.* I. 374 Ðeotende swa swa wulf. *c* **1000** *Ags. Gloss.* in Wr.-Wülcker 195/17 *Bombosa*, hlowende, þutende. *a* **1225** *St. Marher.* 22 Þa bigunnen to þeoten ant to ʒellen. *a* **1225** *Ancr. R.* 120 Ne deð heo bute þeoteð.

**b.** *trans.* To howl at.

*c* **1200** ORMIN 2034 Mann wollde tælenn þatt & hutenn hire & þutenn. *Ibid.* 4875 Icc hutedd amm & þutedd.

**Theothe**, etc., for *teoþe*, obs. f. TITHE, etc.

‖ **Theotokos** (þiˌǫˈtǒkǫs). [a. Gr. θεοτόκος adj., f. θεό-ς God + -τοκος bringing forth, f. stem τεκ-, τοκ- of τίκτειν to bear.] A title of the Virgin Mary as 'Mother of God'; = DEIPARA.

**1874** PUSEY *Lent. Serm.* 206 By this the lowly Virgin became Theotokos, 'the Mother of God'. **1879** SIR G. G. SCOTT *Lect. Archit.* xvii. II. 257 The Church of the Holy Theotokos, or of the Mother of God, is of much later date. **1896** *Trans. St. Paul's Eccles. Soc.* IV. I. 175 The devout orison to our Lady..said in honour of the Blessed Theotokos.

So **Theoˑtoky,** the divine motherhood of Mary.

**1899** *Westm. Gaz.* 24 Apr. 4/3 The Mysteries of..the Virginity of the Blessed Virgin, the Theotoky.

**Theow, thew,** *sb.* and *a.* Now only *Hist.* or *arch.* Forms: *α.* 1 **þeow** (*fem.* **þeowe,** *pl.* **þeowas**), **ðiow,** 2–3 **þeu,** 3 **þeou,** (*Orm.*) **þeoww, þeww,** (9 **theow(e).** *β.* 1 **þeowa** (*fem.* **þeowe,** *pl.* **þeowan**), **ðiowa, ðiuwa, ðiua, ðeua, ðea,** 2–3 **þeowe,** 3 **þeue,** 4 **þewe.** [OE. *ðíow, þéow, þéo*, str. masc., = OHG. *deo, dio*, ON. (Runic) *þewaʀ*, Goth. *þius*:—OTeut. **þewoᶻ*; beside OE. *þeow* str. fem., = OS. *thiu, thiwi*, OHG., MHG. *diu*, ON. *þý*, Goth. *þiwi*:—OTeut. **þewjô*. Also weak sbs. *þéowa* (masc.), *þéowe* (fem.); cf. OS. *thiwa*. *þéowa, -e* have the weak inflexion of the adj.]

**A.** *sb.* A slave, bondman, thrall.

*c* **893** K. ÆLFRED *Oros.* I. i. § 22 Þa þeowan drincað medo. *c* **897** — *Gregory's Past. C.* Pref. 4 Micel meniʒu Godes ðeowa [*Hatton MS.* ðiowa]. *a* **950** *Rituale Dunelm.* (Surtees) 170 Besih ofer vsiʒ ðea ðino [L. *famulos tuos*]. *c* **950** *Lindisf. Gosp.* Matt. viii. 9 Ic cueðo..ðeua [*Rushw.* ðeow] minum do ðis & does. *c* **1000** *Ags. Gosp.* Matt. xviii 28 Þa se þeowa [*Hatton* þeowe] ut-eode he ʒemette hys efenþeowan. *Ibid.* xx. 27 Sy he eower þeow [*Lindisf.* ðea *vel* ðegn, *Rushw.* esne]. *c* **1200** *Trin. Coll. Hom.* 181 Ðus was adam þeu, þo godes muð cursede eorðe. *c* **1200** ORMIN Introd. 31 Adam wass wurrþenn deofless þeoww. *Ibid.* 7454 An defless þeww. *c* **1205** LAY. 29390 Þenne moste he libben þeou a þisse londe. *c* **1320** *Cast. Love* 249 Þeuwe and þral may not craue þorw riht non heritage to haue.

*Hist.* and *arch.* **1819** SCOTT *Ivanhoe* xxxii, Theow and Esne art thou no longer. **1839** KEIGHTLEY *Hist. Eng.* I. 75 Beneath these orders of freemen were the Theowes or slaves...This word *ðeow* seems to have left no trace in the modern languages. **1865** LECKY *Ration.* II. vi. 260 All the civil laws for the protection of the theows, or Saxon slaves, appear to have been preceded by, and based upon, the Canon law. **1874** STUBBS *Const. Hist.* I. v. 78 The *theow* or slave simple, whether *wealh*—that is, of British extraction..or of the common German stock.

**b.** A female slave, a bondwoman.

*a* **900** tr. *Bæda's Hist.* IV. xii. [ix.] (1890) 290 Seo foresprecene Cristes þeowe. *c* **950** *Lindisf. Gosp.* Matt. xxvi. 69 An ðiua [*Rushw.* menen *vel* þeowæ] cueð. — Luke xii. 45 ʒife..esne..onginneð..slaa ða cnæhtas & ðiuwas [*Rushw.* ða ðiowe, *Vulg.* pueros et ancillas]. **1398** TREVISA *Barth. De P. R.* VI. xii. (Tollem. MS.), Sche is þewe and þralle er he be bore.

† **B.** *adj.* [OE. *þéow*, pl. *þéowe*; later pl. *þewe, thue.*] Servile, slavish; 'bond'. *Obs.*

*c* **888** K. ÆLFRED *Boeth.* xli. § 2 ʒif him sceolden þiowe men þenian. *c* **893** — *Oros.* III. vi. § 3 Hit þurh ænne þeowne mon ʒeypped wearð. *c* **1000** ÆLFRIC *Gram.* ix. (Z.) 67 *Hic manceps*, þes ðeowa mann. *Ibid.* xv. 101 *Meis mancipiis diuido denarios*, minum ðeowum mannum ic dæle peneʒas. *a* **1023** WULFSTAN *Hom.* xxxix. (Napier) 181 Þeowemen þa ðriʒ daʒas beon weorces ʒefreode. *c* **1205** LAY. 334 Al heo weren þeowe [*c* **1275** þeue]. *a* **1225** *St. Marher.* 4 Cuð me..ʒef þu art foster of freo monne oðer þeow wummon. *c* **1290** *Beket* 279 in *S. Eng. Leg.* I. 114 Þat word was sone wide couth a-mong þeuwe and freo. **1297** R. GLOUC. (Rolls) 9657 Þuman ne may nowʒt be imad aʒen is louerdes wille fre. *c* **1300** *Havelok* 2205 Alle samen, þeu and fre. *c* **1400** *St. Alexius* (Laud 463) 2 ʒong & olde, thewe & freo.

† **Theow, thew,** *v. Obs.* Forms: 1 **þeowian,** 1–2 **þewian,** 2 **þowie, þeowien,** 3 **þiwien.** [OE. *þéowian*, f. *þéow*, THEOW *sb.*] *trans.* To be a serf or servant to; to serve, minister. (In OE. *intr.* with *dat.*, or *absol.*)

*c* **888** K. ÆLFRED *Boeth.* xxi. § 1 Þa ðeowiað ealle þa þe ðeowiað, ʒe ða þe cunnon ʒe þa þe ne cunnon. *Ibid.* xxxix. § 13 Hi ne mihton elles bion, ʒif hi ne ðiowedon hiora fruman. *c* **975** *Rushw. Gosp.* Matt. iv. 10 To dryhtne þinum gode ðu to ʒebidde & him anum ðewiʒe. *c* **1000** *Ags. Gosp.* Luke xvi. 13 Ne mæʒ nan þeow twam hlafordum þeowian [*c* **1160** *Hatton G.* þewian]. *a* **1175** *Cott. Hom.* 241 Nan ne mai twan hlaforde..samod þowie. *c* **1205** LAY. 10015 Heo him wolden þiwien [*c* **1275** be þeouwe].

**Theowˑdom, thewˑdom.** *Obs.* exc. *Hist.* Also 4 **þedome,** 5 **theudome,** 7, 9 **theodom.** [OE. *þéowdom*, f. *þéow*, THEOW *sb.* + -DOM.] The condition of a 'theow' or slave; slavery, bondage, thraldom. (In OE. also in sense 'service', without connotation of servility.)

*c* **893** K. ÆLFRED *Oros.* I. x. § 6 Þæt men hie mehten aliesan mid feo of þeowdome. *a* **950** *Rituale Dunelm.* (Surtees) 6 In nedhernisse vel in ðeadome ic beʒo. *c* **1000** ÆLFRIC *Hom.* II. 524 Eʒe is twyfeald, and ðeowdom is twyfeald. *c* **1122** *O. E. Chron.* an. 675 (Laud MS.), Hi hit heafden ʒefreod .. of ealle þewdom. *Ibid.* an. 963, Hi hit freodon..wið ealle weoruld þeudom. *c* **1175** *Lamb. Hom.* 99 Men weren alesde from deofles ðeowdome. *c* **1200** ORMIN 3611, I þeowwdom unnderr laferrd. *Ibid.* 14779 Ut off þewwdomess bandess. *c* **1205** LAY. 454 Dardanisc kun ..woneð in þisse londe..inne þeowe-dome [*c* **1275** þeudome]. *a* **1225** *Ancr. R.* 32 Summe ine prisune, summe ine alse muchele ðeudome alse oxe is oþer asse. *c* **1320** *Cast. Love* 247 Whon he him serwede in þewdome [*v.rr.* thewdome, þedome]. *c* **1425** *Eng. Conq. Irel.* 138 Nether al to be vndone, ne fully I-broght yn-to theudome. [**1658** PHILLIPS, *Theodom* (Sax.), servitude. **1833** GALT in *Fraser's Mag.* VIII. 497 Too fond of literature to relish the distasteful theodom of a tutor.]

† **Theowˑlike, thewˑlike,** *a. Obs. rare.* [f. THEOW *sb.* + -LIKE.] Servile, slavish; base.

*c* **1200** ORMIN 4177 Itt iss Resstedaʒʒ Off all þewwlike dede. *Ibid.* 4181 Uss birrþ wel uss ʒemenn..All fra þewwlike dede, Þatt iss, fra sinnfull word & werrc.

† **Theowˑten,** *v. Obs. rare.* In Ormin **þeowwtenn, þewwtenn.** [f. OE. *þeowot, -(e)t* service, f. THEOW *sb.*] *trans.* and *intr.* To serve, minister.

*c* **1200** ORMIN Introd. 43–4 Forr all swa summ þu þeowwtesst himm, Swa shall þin sune himm þeowwtenn. *Ibid.* 546 To þewwtenn i þe temmple.

**Thepe,** dial. var. *fape*: see FEABERRY, gooseberry.

**Ther,** inflexion of THARF *v.*; obs. f. DARE *v.*[1] (A. 9); obs. f. THEIR, THERE; obs. var. THIR; obs. inflexion of THAT, THE.

‖ **Therapeusis** (þerăpiūˑsis). [mod.L., a. Gr. type **θεράπευσις* healing, f. θεραπεύειν to tend, heal (a sick person).] Therapeutic treatment.

**1857** DUNGLISON *Dict. Med. Sci.*, *Therapeusis*, therapeutics. **1875** H. C. WOOD *Therap.* (1879) 679 In regard to therapeusis, the first point to be determined in acute cases is..when to commence electrical treatment. **1897** *Allbutt's Syst. Med.* IV. 211 Effecting a more scientific and direct therapeusis.

‖ **Therapeutæ** (þerăpiūˑtī), *sb. pl.* Also 9 in anglicized form **therapeuts.** [eccl. L., a. Gr. θεραπευταί servants, attendants, ministers.] A sect of Jewish mystics residing in Egypt in the first century A.D., described in a book attributed to Philo.

**1681** S. PARKER *Demonstr. Law Nat.* II. xviii. 247 These Therapeutæ read the ancient Writings of the Authours of their Sect. **1856** R. A. VAUGHAN *Mystics* (1860) I. 53 The *Therapeutæ*, a sect similar to the Essenes, number many among them whose lives are truly exemplary. **1865** tr. *Strauss's New Life Jesus* I. I. xxix. 235 He took the Egyptian branch of the Essenes, the so-called Therapeuts, for regular Christians.

**Therapeutic** (þerăpiūˑtik), *sb.* Also 6 tera-. [In sense 1, ad. mod.L. *therapeutica*, a. Gr. θεραπευτική (sc. τέχνη) the art of healing, fem. sing. of θεραπευτικός: see THERAPEUTIC *a.* In Fr. *thérapeutique* (16th c.). In senses 2 and 3 recent absolute uses of the adj.]

**1.** That branch of medicine which is concerned with the remedial treatment of disease; the art of healing. **a.** In the singular. Now *rare.*

(Quot. 1890 may belong to 2 b.)

**1541** R. COPLAND *Galyen's Terap.* 2 A j, The fourth boke of the Terapeutyke or Methode curatyfe of Claude Galyen. **1547** BOORDE *Brev. Health* Pref. 2 b, Galen, prince of phisicions, in his Terapeutike doth reprehende and disproue [it]. **1625** HART *Anat. Ur.* I. ii. 19 Who did likewise deuide Physicke..into two parts, to wit, that which we commonly call Therapeuticke..: and..that part which we call Diagnosticke. **1890** S. P. LAMBROS in *Athenæum* 30 Aug. 294/2 The modern therapeutic is far from having used all the sources of the ancients.

**b.** Now usually in the plural **Therapeutics.**

**1671** SALMON *Syn. Med.* III. i. 324* The Therapeuticks, or active part of Physick, is either Material, or Relative. **1707** FLOYER *Physic. Pulse-Watch* p. ii, The Chinese also have made that a part of their Therapeutics. **1843** MILL *Logic* VI. vi. § 1 Students in politics..attempted to study the pathology and therapeutics of the social body, before they had laid the necessary foundation in its physiology.

**2. a.** A curative agent. **b.** A medical man.

**1842** ABDY *Water Cure* (1843) 123 M. Roche acknowledges..that cold water has long been known as a therapeutic. **1858** HOGG *Life Shelley* II. 429 Medical society... Some of the therapeutics were tolerably good company.

**3.** *pl.* = THERAPEUTÆ. *rare.*

**1847** WEBSTER, *Therapeutics*,..a religious sect described by Philo. They were devotees to religion.

**Therapeuˑtic,** *a.* [In sense 1, ad. mod.L. *therapeutic-us*, a. Gr. θεραπευτικός, f. θεραπευτής, agent-n. from θεραπεύ-ειν to minister to, treat medically, f. θέραψ, θεραπ- attendant, minister. In sense 2, from the name of the *Therapeutæ.*]

**1.** Of or pertaining to the healing of disease.

**1646** SIR T. BROWNE *Pseud. Ep.* IV. xiii. 23 Therapeutick or curative Physick, we term that, which..taketh away diseases actually affecting. **1678** PHILLIPS (ed. 4) s. v., The Therapeutick part of Medicine, is that which treats of the healing or curing of diseases. **1800** *Med. Jrnl.* III. 577 Here the fundamental therapeutic principles are proposed. **1857** MILLER *Elem. Chem.* (1862) III. 196 It has long been used as a therapeutic agent.

**2.** Of or pertaining to the Therapeutæ.

**1681** S. PARKER *Demonstr. Law Nat.* II. xviii. 248 Philo affirms that this Therapeutick Sect prayed onely twice a day. **1727–41** CHAMBERS *Cycl.* s. v. *Therapeutæ*, Josephus.. does not say one word of the *Therapeutæ*, or the therapeutic life. **1875** *Expositor* 429 Members of the Essene or Therapeutic communities.

**Therapeutical** (þerăpiūˑtikăl), *a.* (*sb.*) [f. as prec. + -AL.] = prec. 1. (In first quot. *absol.*)

**1605** DANIEL *Queen's Arcadia* III. ii, We must now Descend unto the Therapeutical. **1640** CHILMEAD tr. *Ferrand's Love Melanch.* xxxvii. 336 This Remedy .. should rather be Prophylacticall, for Prevention of the disease, then Therapeuticall, for the Cure of it. **1657** [see PROPHYLACTICAL]. **1703** T. S. *Art's Improv.* p. xxv. **1843** R. J. GRAVES *Syst. Clin. Med.* Introd. Lect. 21 Observation of the progress of symptoms and the effects of therapeutical agents.

**b.** *sb.* A therapeutic substance, a medicine.

**1845** FORD *Handbk. Spain* II. xiii. 967/2 Mineral therapeuticals still remain a..dead letter.

Hence **Therapeuˑtically** *adv.*, in a therapeutic manner; in relation to therapeutics.

**1875** H. C. WOOD *Therap.* (1879) 97 Dr. Leand affirms that the oxide of manganese is therapeutically equivalent to the preparations of bismuth excepting in that it does not constipate. **1885** G. H. TAYLOR *Pelv. & Hern. Therap.* 28 The local parts are by no means independent, therapeutically, as local therapeutics seem to imply.

**Therapeuˑtism.** [f. THERAPEUT-Æ + -ISM.] The system or practice of the Therapeutæ.

**1854** MILMAN *Lat. Chr.* I. 129 The Essenism or Therapeutism of the Jews.

**Therapeutist** (þerăpiūˑtist). [f. THERAPEUT-IC *sb.* + -IST. Cf. F. *thérapeutiste.*] One skilled in therapeutics; a physician.

**1816–30** BENTHAM *Offic. Apt. Maximized, Extr. Const. Code* (1830) 63 This little work of the illustrious Therapeutist. **1886** W. T. GAIRDNER in *Life Sir R. Christison* II. vii. 138 Many..are now accomplished therapeutists.

**Theraphim, -in, -ym, -yn,** obs. ff. TERAPHIM.

**Theraphose** (þeˑrăfōus), *a.* and *sb.* *Zool.* [f. mod.L. *Thĕrăphōsæ* (Walckenaer), irreg. f. Gr. θηράφιον a little 'beast' or insect, f. θήρ beast.] **a.** *adj.* Of or pertaining to the *Theraphosæ*, a division of latebricole spiders, as the mygalids and trap-door spiders. **b.** *sb.* A spider of this group. So **Theraphoˑsid** *a.* and *sb.*; **Theraphoˑsoid** *a.*

**1891** *Cent. Dict.*, Theraphose. **1898** *Proc. Zool. Soc.* 29 Nov. 892 A characteristic feature in these arboreal Theraphosids .. the long feathery fringes on the legs. **1895** *Funk's Standard Dict.*, Theraphosoid.

**Theˑrapist.** *rare.* [f. Gr. θέραψ, θεραπ- attendant (see THERAPEUTIC *a.*), or f. THERAP(Y + -IST.] = THERAPEUTIST.

**1886** *Medical News* (U.S.) XLIX. 510 The results..will be much more satisfactory to the therapist.

‖ **Therapon** (þeˑrăpǫn). *Ichthyol.* [mod.L., a. Gr. θεράπων attendant.] A genus of fishes, the type of the family *Theraponidæ*, allied to the perch; a fish of this genus. So **Theˑraponid,** a member of the *Theraponidæ*; **Theˑraponoid** *a.*, resembling the *Theraponidæ*.

**1891** *Cent. Dict.*, Theraponoid. **1895** *Funk's Standard Dict.*, Theraponid.

**Therapy** (þeˑrăpi). [ad. mod.L. *therapīa*, a. Gr. θεραπεία healing: cf. θεραπεύ-ειν to attend medically. Cf. F. *thérapie.*] The medical treatment of disease; curative medical treatment.

**1846** WORCESTER cites *Month. R.* **1873** WAGNER tr.

Teuffel's Hist. Rom. Lit. II. 26 The second [treats] of ..general pathology and therapy. 1881 Virchow in Nature 11 Aug. 348/1 It will be pointed out to us..that therapy is to be replaced by hygiene. 1894 Lancet 3 Nov. 1044 Serum therapy..is a discovery belonging to M. Behring.

**Therdde**, obs. form of Third.

**There** (ðēᵊɹ, *unstressed* ðěɹ), *adv.* (*a.*, *sb.*) Forms: see below. [OE. *þǽr*, *þár*, *þér*, cognate with OS. *thâr*, OFris. *thēr*, *dēr*, MLG. *dār*, MDu. *daer*, Du. *daar*, OHG. *dār* (MHG. *dār*, *dā*, Ger. *da*); cf. also Goth. *þar*, ON. *þar* (Sw., Da. *der*); all derivatives of the demonstrative stem *þa-*, pre-Teut. *to-* (That, The). The adverbial suffix *-r* appears also in OE. *hwǽr*, *hwér*, *hwar*, Where.

Besides *þǽr*, etc., OE. had also a rare form *þāra*, prob. an emphatic deriv., like OHG. *dāra*, *dāre*, and not cognate with OHG. *dara*, MHG. *dare*, *dar*, 'thither'. In ME. all the variants *þār*, *þǽr*, *þēr*, *þōr* appear also with final *-e*, perh. taken from the advb. *-e* in *inne*, *uppe*, *ūte*, *fore*, etc. The later forms *thare* and *there* may represent ME. *þāre*, *þēre*, or the final *e* may merely indicate the long vowel.]

**A.** Illustration of Forms.

α. 1 þára.

c888 K. Ælfred Boeth. xxxiii. § 5 Ac hit is þeah þara. c1000 Ags. Gosp. Mark xiv. 15 ȝe ȝe-earwiað us þara [Hatton þare, Lindisf. & Rushw. ðer].

β. 1–3 þǽr, 2 þǽre.

c888 K. Ælfred Boeth. xxxiii. § 5 Swa is eac þær fyr on ðam stanum and on ðam wætere. a900 tr. Bæda's Hist. i. i. (1890) 28 Swa þæt ðær seldon snau leng liȝeð þonne ðry daȝas. c1000 Ags. Gosp. Matt. xiv. 23 He wæs ana þær. a1131 O. E. Chron. an. 1123, Ða..ferde se king to Winceastre and wæs ealle Eastren tyde þære. c1200 Ormin 2789 Þe laffdiȝ Marȝe comm Till Zacariȝess bottle, And spacc þær wiþþ Elysabæþ.

γ. 1–2 þár, 2–5 þar, þare, 3–5 *north.* þaire, 4–6 thar, thare (4–5 tare), 6 *Sc.* thair, yare, yair.

c893 K. Ælfred Oros. i. i. § 22 ȝyf þar man an ban findeð unforbærned. c1000 Ags. Gosp. Matt. xxi. 17 He..lærde hi þar [A. þær, Hatt. þar, Lind. ðer, Rushw. þær] be godes rice. c1275 Lay. 27474 Cnihtes þar aswalten; blodes vt hurnen. Ibid. 25651 Þare. 13.. Cursor M. 5420 (Cott.) Iacob þaire [Gött. þar] lied seuenten yeir. Ibid. 21655 (Edin.) Thare dide him driȝtin to resune. ?a1400 Morte Arth. 3603 Thare the false men fletyde, and one flode lengede. c1400 Rule St. Benet 21 Þai sal be broht by-fore þe cuuent and tare amende hir faute. 1483 Cath. Angl. 381/2 Thare, ibi, ibidem, illic. 1535 Stewart Cron. Scot. (Rolls) I. 33 Greit slauchter oftymes wes maid yair. 1562 Reg. Privy Council Scot. I. 226 Williame Gordoun in Wigtoun, Johne Martine thair, Robert Johnestoun thair.

δ. 1–2 þér, 3–5 þer, þere (4 tere), 5 þeer, theer, 4–6 ther, 4– there.

c950 Lindisf. Gosp. Matt. v. 24 Forlet ðer [Rushw., Ags. G., Hatt. þær] ðing ðin to wiȝbed. — Mark iv. 15 Seðe ymb woeȝ ðer [Ags. Gosp. þar, Hatt. þær] bið ȝesauen. c1205 Lay. 10 Þer he bock radde [c1275 þer heo bokes radde]. Ibid. 25651 Nes he þere [c1275 þare] buten ane niht. Ibid. 29876 Alle..þa þer icumen weoren. c1275 Ibid. 8 Merie þer [c1205 þar] him þohte. Ibid. 582 Þere [c1205 þer] Brutus nam Antigo[num]. 1297 R. Glouc. (Rolls) 1796 An vrninde water þat ȝut is þer, ich wene. Ibid. 3519 Þere he huld is parlement. 13.. Cursor M. 21104 (Cott.) His bodi is birid tere [rime sper; other MSS. þere]. c1400 Destr. Troy 3719 Ermonia þe myld maynly was ther. 1412–20 Lydg. Chron. Troy ii. 4189, I was not þere. c1420 There [see B. 12]. a1425 Cursor M. 22980 (Trin.) Men wene þe doom shal be þeer. 1430–40 Lydg. Bochas ix. xxxi. (1558) 32 b, Clement theer concludyng if he may. 1432–50 tr. Higden (Rolls) VII. 401 The sedes..whiche hade bene sawen þer of olde tyme. c1440 There [see B. 9].

ε. (variants of δ *þer, there*) 2 þeor, 3 þear, þiar, 5–7 their, 6 thear, 6– *dial.* theare.

a1200 Moral Ode 273 (Lamb. MS.) Þeor beð naddren and snaken. c1200 Ibid. 165 (Trin. Coll. MS.) Ne sal þeih no man samie þiar. c1205 Lay. 607 Brutus hefde þa men..idon into þan castle & þear heom quic heolde. a1225 Leg. Kath. 8 Constantin..wunede summe hwile þear. c1425 Cursor M. 10042 (Laud) Their buxumnes holt her state. 1535 Coverdale Josh. xxi. 45 Their myssed nothinge of all the good that the Lorde had promysed. 1563 B. Googe Cupido Eglogs, etc. (Arb.) 117 And..thear, for succour thus doth call. 1570 — Pop. Kingd. ii. (1880) 13 Togither stande they theare [rime weare]. 1616 Purchas Pilgrimage, India (1864) 49 Three of the Gallions driuen on ground, ..and had beene their left but for the Frigates. 1655 Stanley Hist. Philos. i. 53/2 For their's no order in Equality.

ζ. 3–4 þór, 3–5 þore, 4–5 thôre.

c1250 Gen. & Ex. 1844 He droȝ ðider and wunede ðor. Ibid. 2270 Ðat riche louerd ðore. c1300 Havelok 922 Go þu yunder and sit þore [rime more]. Ibid. 1044 For neuere yete ne saw he or Putten the stone, or þanne þor. c1300 Harrow. Hell (Harl. MS.) 30 Ihesu crist..seide he wolde vacche hem thore [rime sore]. c1330 R. Brunne Chron. Wace (Rolls) 1021 He..wende haue founde Brutus þore. c1380 Sir Ferumb. 544 Þe Sarsyn þat was þor. c1420 Chron. Vilod. 2040 To make alle thyngus redy þore [rime byfore]. a1425 Cursor M. 409 (Trin.) He vs ȝaf ensaumple þore [rime more; earlier MSS. þare .. mare]. c1470 Harding Chron. iii. iv, Seleucus than was the first kynge þore [rime afore].

**B.** Signification.

**I.** As a demonstrative adverb.

* *Expressing locality or position.*

**1.** In or at that place; in the place (country, region, etc.) pointed to, indicated, or referred to, and away from the speaker; the opposite of *here*.

c888 [see A. α, β]. a900 [see A. β]. c950 [see A. δ]. c1050 Byrhtferth's Handboc in Anglia (1885) VIII. 303 Þonne beoð þær swa fela concurrentes. c1205 Lay. 716 Þær þu findest seouen houndred. c1400 Three Kings Cologne 118 Þei ȝede to þe cite of Sewill..and þere þei leuyd .ij. ȝere. 1523 Ld. Berners Froiss. I. cv. 126 The erle of Derby went to Pelagrue, and ther was sixe dayes. 1673 Ray Journ. Low C. 23 At our being there it was held with a strong Garrison. 1786 Cowper Let. to Lady Hesketh May, I have walked there, but have never walked thither. 1827 Scott Highl. Widow iii, The cloudberry..which is only found on very high hills, and there only in very small quantities. 1874 Bosw. Smith Mohammed, etc. (1876) 322 There if anywhere, will be the Armageddon of Islam.

**b.** *There* (in emphatic use) may be defined by a relative clause, following or preceding, introduced by *where* († *there*) or an equivalent.

c950 Lindisf. Gosp. Matt. vi. 21 Ðer vel huer forðon is strion ðin ðer is and hearta ðin. c1000 Ags. Gosp. ibid., þær ðin gold is þær is ðin heorte. a1300 Cursor M. 20258 Þar i sal be, quar mi sun is. c1500 Melusine xxxvi. 294 There where he passed by he enquyred after guedon. 1591 Harington Orl. Fur. Pref. ¶ ij b, Where the hedge is lowest, there doth euery man go ouer. 1810 Crabbe Borough iii. 195 Where Time has plough'd, there Misery loves to sow. 1850 McCosh Div. Govt. ii. i. (1874) 138 Wherever we find law, there we see the certain traces of a lawgiver. 1850 Tennyson In Mem. cxxiii, There rolls the deep where grew the tree.

**2.** Appended, unstressed, to the name of a person or thing to whose presence attention is called: = Who or that is there, whom or which you see there.

1590 Shaks. Com. Err. v. i. 275 He din'de with her there, at the Porpentine. 1606 — Tr. & Cr. ii. i. 91, I would haue peace.., but the foole will not: he there. 1611 — Wint. T. ii. iii. 160 You that haue beene so tenderly officious With Lady Margerie, your Mid-wife there. 1794 Mrs. Radcliffe Myst. Udolpho xlii, There she lay,..her face was upon the pillow there! Mod. Hand me that book there, please.

**b.** As a brusque mode of address (often in commands) to a person or persons in the place or direction indicated; = you (that are) there.

a1596 Sir T. More i. ii. 97 Silence there, hoe! 1605 Shaks. Lear iv. vii. 25 Louder the music there! a1619 Fletcher Mad Lover iii. ii, Put to the doors a while there. 1676 Dryden Aurengzebe ii. i. 24 Your fury hardens me:..A Guard there; seize her. 1859 Habits Gd. Soc. v. 200 He will..use some such phrase as: 'May I trouble you for that ball, sir?' not 'Bail, you there', as one sometimes hears it. Mod. Hurry up there! Do you hear there? Pass along there, please!

**c.** Emphatically appended to the demonstrative *that. dial.* and *vulgar*. (Cf. Here *adv.* 1 d.)

Also *that 'ere, that 'air.*

1742 Richardson Pamela III. 404 On leaving yours and Mr. B.'s hospitable House, because of that there Affair. 1778 Miss Burney Evelina (1791) II. xxxvii. 244 Did you ever get a ducking in that there place? Ibid. 245 'For the matter of that there', said the Captain, 'you must make him a soldier'. 1818 Scott Hrt. Midl. xli, That trunk is mine, and that there band-box, and that pillion mail. 1825 J. Neal Bro. Jonathan I. 244 Is that 'air fellow gone yet? 1840 Thackeray Catherine vi, How came you by that there horse? 1863 Literary Times 20 June, The 'this here' and 'that there' (euphonically contracted into 'that 'ere') of the Cockney.

**3.** Pointing to something as present to the sight or perception, chiefly in *there is, there are* (ðēᵊ·rɪz, ðēᵊɪz; ðēᵊ·rǎɪ); also, calling attention to something offered (often *absol.*; cf. 7).

1535 Lyndesay Satyre 1355 Tak, thair, ane vther [i.e. blow] vpon thy peild harne-pan. 1597 Shaks. 2 Hen. IV, v. ii. 117 There is my hand, You shall be as a Father, to my Youth. 1601 — Twel. N. iv. i. 27 And. Now sir, haue I met you again: ther's for you. Seb. Why there's for thee, and there, and there. 1728 Ramsay There's my Thumb ii, There's my thumb I'll ne'er beguile thee. 1742 Richardson Pamela IV. 375 There's for you, dear Sir! See what a Mother can do, if she pleases! 1890 'L. Falconer' Mlle. Ixe v, There was that lazy Mr. Lethbridge lounging in the doorway. Mod. There is the dinner-bell; make haste. See, there comes the train. Hark! there goes the bugle.

**b.** Pointing out a person or object with approval or commendation, or the contrary. Also in anticipatory commendation of the person addressed; cf. That *dem. pron.* B. I. 1 b.

1595 Shaks. John ii. i. 163 It grandame will Giue yt a plum, a cherry, and a figge; There's a good grandame. 1596 — Tam. Shr. v. ii. 180 Why there's a wench: Come on, and kisse mee Kate. 1741 Richardson Pamela II. 224 There's a Word for a Lady's Mouth! 1780 Mirror No. 97 ¶ 26 'Quantity of syllables', exclaimed the Captain, 'there is modern education for you!' 1825 T. Hook Sayings Ser. ii. Man of Many Fr. I. 191 Tom,..go and fetch the wine for your sister, there's a dear love. 1870 Dickens E. Drood ii, Don't moddley-coddley, there's a good fellow. 1872 'L. Carroll' Through Looking-Glass vi. 123 There's glory for you! Mod. There's a fine horse! all skin and bones.

**4.** Used unemphatically to introduce a sentence or clause in which, for the sake of emphasis or preparing the hearer, the verb comes before its subject, as *there comes a time when*, etc., *there was heard a rumbling noise*. In interrogative sentences *there* comes between the verb and subject, as *Breathes there the man*, etc.?, or follows the first word of a compound verb, as *Does there breathe a man?*, *Shall there be any notice taken of it?* The same order was formerly observed after an introductory adv. or clause, as *Then came there a voice, Soon shall there arise a prophet.*

Grammatically, there is no difference between *There comes the train!* and *There comes a time when*, etc.; but, while in the former *there* is demonstrative and stressed, in the latter it has been reduced to a mere anticipative element occupying the place of the subject which comes later. Preceding or following a main verb, or following any verb, *there*, thus used, is stressless (proclitic or enclitic: e.g. *there-ca'me, brea'thes-there, i's-there, wi'll-there*), but preceding *be* or an auxiliary, *there* has a slight stress, and the verb is enclitic (e.g. *the're-is, the're-was, the're-will*).

**a.** with intransitive verbs.

c888 K. Ælfred Boeth. iii. § 1 Þa com þær gan in to me heofencund Wisdom. c1000 Ags. Gosp. Matt. vii. 25 Þa com þær ren and mycele flod and þær bleowun windas. c1250 Gen. & Ex. 3863 And ðer ros wreððe and strif a-non Aȝen moysen and aaron. a1300 Cursor M. 19867 Als petre þan bigan til hon [Fairf., Gött. hone] þar com anoþer voice alson. c1320 Cast. Love 736 In þulke derworþe feire tour Þer stont a trone wiþ muche honour. c1386 Chaucer Melib. ¶ 537 Ne neuere cam ther a vileynous word out of his mouþ. 1470–85 Malory Arthur i. xxiii. 70 Ther maye no knyght ryde this wey but yf he Iuste with the. c1477 Caxton Jason 22 For to sle a man..ther belioueth but one stroke wel sette. c1566 J. Alday tr. Boaystuau's Theat. World K viij b, There died an infinite number of people. 1590 Spenser F. Q. ii. ix. 59 There chaunced to the Princes hand to rize An auncient booke. 1609 Holland Amm. Marcell. 47 In these Cottian Alpes..there peaketh up a mightie high mount. 1611 Bible Numb. xxiv. 17 There shall come a starre out of Iacob, and a Scepter shall rise out of Israel. 1761–2 Hume Hist. Eng. (1806) V. lxx. 247 There want not sufficient materials on which to form a true judgment. 1805 Scott Last Minstr. vi. i, Breathes there the man with soul so dead, Who never [etc.]? 1812 Byron Ch. Har. ii. lxxxii, Lurk there no hearts that throb with secret pain? 1857 Buckle Civiliz. I. vii. 399 From all these things there resulted consequences of vast importance.

†**b.** with transitive verbs: usually before an auxiliary of tense or mood. *Obs.*

13.. Cast. Love (Halliw.) 306 Withoute these..Ther may no kyng lede gret lordship. 1387 Trevisa Higden (Rolls) I. 223 When it was ones i-tend..þere couþe no man it aquenche wiþ no craft. 14.. Hoccleve Compl. Virgin 54 Ther may no martirdom me make smerte. 1548 Udall, etc. Erasm. Par. Acts 43 b, Peter, knowing..that there woulde some Iewes reproue this his doing.

**c.** with a verb in the passive voice.

a1533 Ld. Berners Huon cxi. 385 There coude not be founde a more goodlyer man. 1584 R. Scot Discov. Witchcr. x. vii. (1886) 147 Whilest the treasure is a digging, there must be read the psalmes [etc.]. 1691 T. H[ale] Acc. New Invent. 99 There's nothing said herein. 1877 Ruskin St. Mark's Rest i. § 4 There were no plenipotentiaries sent to the East, and back again. Mod. Here, there were found various relics of Franklin's expedition.

**d.** especially with the verb *to be*: cf. Be B. 1, 1 b, 5 b. *There is, there are*, are equivalent to F. *il est, il y a*, Ger. *es ist, es sind, es giebt*, Sp. *hay*. (For such phrases as *there is no saying* = 'it is impossible to say', see No *a.* 4.)

c893 K. Ælfred Oros. i. i. § 22 Þær is mid Estum an mæȝð. 1297 R. Glouc. (Rolls) 7551 Þer nas prince in al þe world of so noble fame. a1300 Cursor M. 17787 Vp risen [he] es, dut es þar nan. Ibid. 20123 Ne was tar noiþer seke ne fere. 13..Cast. Love (Halliw.) 275 Ther wes a kyng of myche myȝht. c1330 R. Brunne Chron. Wace (Rolls) 5467 Waster [was there] non þat wolde hym feyne. c1380 Wyclif Wks. (1880) 147 As þouȝ þer were no lif but only in þis wrecchid world. a1415 Lydg. Temple of Glass 179 And some þer were..That pleined sore. 1456 Sir G. Haye Law Arms (S.T.S.) 1 Into the quhilk buke thare salbe foure partis. 1485 Caxton Malory's Arthur Pref., Dyuers men holde oppynyon that there was no suche Arthur. 1531 in J. Bulloch Pynours (1887) 59 Considering thair has bene and is dalie besynes and ado with the pynouris. 1605 Shaks. Lear ii. iv. 305 For many Miles about There's scarce a Bush. 1657–83 Evelyn Hist. Relig. (1850) I. 79 Epicurus and his scholars of old..make this an argument of there being no God. 1782 Cowper Alex. Selkirk 2 My right there is none to dispute. 1823 F. Clissold Ascent Mt. Blanc 22 There being no moon. 1842 Tennyson Lady Clare xi, I will know If there be any faith in man.

**e.** When a relative clause follows, the relative pron. (*that, who,* or *which*) is often omitted. Now chiefly *colloquial* or *archaic*, as in ballad style.

Cf. That *rel. pron.* 10, of which this is a case.

?a1366 Chaucer Rom. Rose 1239 Ther is no cloth sitteth bet On damiselle, than doth roket. 1470–85 Malory Arthur xiii. iii. 616 There was no knyȝt knewe from whens he came. 1596 Shaks. 1 Hen. IV, ii. iv. 568 There are two Gentlemen Haue in this Robberie lost three hundred Markes. 1806 Wordsw. Address to Child 8 But how he will come, and whither he goes, There's never a scholar in England knows. Mod. colloq. There's a man at the door wants to see you.

**f.** The antecedent, when a simple pronominal word (usu. pl., e.g. *they, those, some*, rarely sing., e.g. *he, she, that*), is sometimes omitted. (App. a Latinism, after *sunt qui dicunt*, and the like.) Cf. That *rel. pron.* 3.

c1400 Destr. Troy 12860 There come out of castels & of cloise townes..þat hom bale wroght. 14.. Why I can't be a Nun 244 in E. E. P. (1862) 144 There weren that dyd not so. a1533 Ld. Berners Gold. Bk. M. Aurel. K k iv, There were that saied, that this ambassadour should be chastised. 1560 Bible (Genev.) Prov. xi. 24 There is that scatereth, and is more increased. 1569 J. Sanford tr. Agrippa's Van. Artes 101 b, There are of them whiche accompte it a greate offence to touche monie. 1628 Feltham Resolves ii. [i.] xiii. 35 There are, to whom Death doth seeme no more then a blood-letting. 1657–83 Evelyn Hist. Relig. (1850) I. 9 There have been..who pretend [etc.]. 1736 Welsted Wks. (1787) 455 There are, I know, who have strong prejudices to opinions of this sort. a1849 H. Coleridge Ess. (1851) I. 236 Waller called Milton the old blind schoolmaster, and there are who have spoken of Wordsworth as the stamp-master. 1864 Browning Abt Vogler v, There wanted not who walked in the glare and glow.

**5.** At that point or stage in action, proceeding, speech, or thought; formerly sometimes referring to what immediately precedes or follows: at that juncture; on that; on that occasion; then.

a1400 Relig. Pieces fr. Thornton MS. 77 At myn endynge ..I pray þe lady helpe me þare. a1450 Le Morte Arth.

2388 The kynge Arthur Answerys thore Wordys that were kene and throo. *Ibid.* 3480 'A ! false traytor' he sayd thore. **1596** SHAKS. *Merch. V.* II. viii. 46 And euen there his eye being big with teares, Turning his face, he put his hand behinde him. **1602** — *Ham.* II. i. 19 And there put on him What forgeries you please. **1647** MAY *Hist. Parl.* I. vii. 76 There we are at this instant. **1706** FARQUHAR *Recruit. Officer* I. i, Brother ! hold there, friend ; I am no kindred to you that I know of yet.

**b.** *And there('s) an end*: and that is the end of the matter or the last word on the subject ; 'and that's all'. *Obs.* or *arch.*

**1591, 1615** [see END *sb.* 23]. **1596** SHAKS. I *Hen. IV*, v. iii. 64 If not, honour comes vnlook'd for, and ther's an end. **1650** TRAPP *Comm. Exod.* vii. 25 As the dog, who getting out of the water, shakes his ears, and there's an end. **1872** RUSKIN *Fors Clav.* xvi. § 5 Confirmed by the signature of any person whom the Queen might appoint.., and there an end.

**6.** † **a.** In that case ; then. *Obs.*

*c* **888** K. ÆLFRED *Boeth.* xvi. § 2 Hu ne is se anweald þon þær nauht? **1362** LANGL. *P. Pl.* A. IX. 32 Þer [B. VIII. 37 þanne] weore þe Monnes lyf I-lost þorw lachesse of himselue.

**b.** In that thing, matter, or business; in that fact or circumstance ; in that respect, as to that.

*c* **1386** CHAUCER *Prol.* 259 In loue dayes ther koude he muchel helpe, For there he was nat lyk a Cloystrer. **1585** T. WASHINGTON tr. *Nicholay's Voy.* II. xx. 57 b, If the moneye ordayned for the poore is not there bestowed. **1592** SHAKS. *Rom. & Jul.* III. iii. 137 Thy Iuliet is aliue,..There art thou happy. **1602** — *Ham.* III. i. 65, I, there's the rub. **1605** — *Lear* IV. vi. 148 Oh ho, are you there with me? **1613** — *Hen. VIII*, III. ii. 408 There was the waight that pull'd me downe. **1855** BROWNING *Bp. Blougram's Apol.* 85 You would be all, I would be merely much ; you beat me there. **1884** H. JAMES in *Eng. Illustr. Mag.* Dec. 248/2 It was beastly awkward certainly ; *there* I could quite agree with him. **1896** *Daily News* 17 June 5/4 There is where the Japanese differ from us.

**c.** Referring to something said or done: In those words, in that act.

*a* **1596** *Sir T. More* I. i. 176 *Wil.* My maisters..lets.. sweare true secrecie vppon our liues. *Geo.* There spake an angell. Come, let vs along, then. **1603** SHAKS. *Meas. for M.* III. i. 86 There spake my brother : there my fathers graue Did vtter forth a voice. **1829** *Blackw. Mag.* XXV. 558 There you have hit the nail on the head, James. *Mod. colloq.* You have me there ! I cannot tell you.

**7.** Used interjectionally, usually to point (in a tone of vexation, dismay, derision, satisfaction, encouragement, etc.) to some fact, condition, or consummation, presented to the sight or mind.

**1535** COVERDALE *Ps.* xxxiv. [xxxv.] 21 They gape vpon me with their mouthes, sayenge : there, there [1611 Aha, aha !]: we se it with oure eyes. **1596** SHAKS. *Merch. V.* III. i. 87 Why there, there, there, there, a diamond gone cost me two thousand ducats. **1606** — *Tr. & Cr.* v. v. 43 *Ajax.* Troylus, thou coward Troylus. *Diom.* I, there, there. **1788** J. O'KEEFFE *Prisoner at large* I. vi, There, sir, the bed's ready. **1824** SCOTT *St. Ronan's* xxx, 'There now', said Touchwood, 'there was a rencontre between them—the very thing I wanted to know'. **1856** MRS. CARLYLE *Lett.* (1883) II. 295 There ! I have put my foot in it ! **1872** *Routledge's Ev. Boy's Ann.* 514/1 'There, there', my poor father answered, 'it is not that'. **1876** STEVENSON *Lett.* (1901) I. iii. 115 There, that's your prophecy did that ! **1878** BROWNING *La Saisiaz* 49 There, the dread descent is over. **1888** 'J. S. WINTER' *Bootle's Childr.* ix, And, indeed—but there, what's the good of talking about it. **1893** BURRELL & CUTHELL *Indian Mem.* 210 But there ! I was not going to tell you how you felt. **1894** 'J. S. WINTER' *Red-Coats* 55 My life's my own to do what I like with, and I'm going to 'em now; so there ! **1903** *Daily Chron.* 28 Oct. 7/1 She showered blows upon the lad's head and shoulders, with the words,..'There now, how do you like it ?'

*** Expressing motion to a place.*

**8.** To that place : now taking in ordinary use the place of THITHER.

*There and back*, to that place and back again. *To get there* (colloq. or slang) : see GET *v.* 31 c.

*a* **900** *O. E. Chron.* an. 894, Wæs Hæsten þa þær cumen mid his herʒe. *c* **1205** LAY. 29876 Alle ut wenden þa þer [*c* 1275 þider] icumen weoren. **13..** *Cursor M.* 1780 (Gött.) Quen þai cam þar [*v. rr.* þare, þere] was þar na bote. *a* **1425** *Ibid.* 9929 (Trin.) Waried wiʒt comeþ þere neuer. *c* **1440** *Alphabet of Tales* 122 Þis clerk denyed hym & sayd he come nott þer. **1592** SHAKS. *Ven. & Ad.* 780 And will not let a false sound enter there. **1610** — *Temp.* II. i. 99 And the rarest that ere came there. **1663** GERBIER *Counsel* 41 Strangers that come there. **1858** J. H. NEWMAN *Mission Bened. Ord.* Sel. Ess. 211 When St. Hubert was brought there. **1871** MRS. H. WOOD *Dene Hollow* xxviii, We shall go only there and back, grandpapa. **1907** *Westm. Gaz.* 7 June 12/1 The 'there-and-back' distance between 'Auld Reekie' and Inverness is but eight miles less. *Mod.* Going to the meeting?—I am on my way there.

**II.** As a relative or conjunctive adverb.

† **9.** In, on, at, or into which place ; = WHERE.

**a.** with a sb. as antecedent.

*a* **800** *O. E. Chron.* an. 755, On þære byriʒ..þær se cyning ofslæʒen læʒ. *c* **950** *Lindisf. Gosp.* Matt. vi. 20 Strionas.. iuh striona in heofnum, ðer [*Rushw.* þær] ne hrust ne ec mohðe ʒespilles. *c* **1000** *Ags. Gosp.* John xviii. 20 Ic lærde ..on temple þar [*Hatt.* þær] ealle iudeas togædere comon. *c* **1175** *Lamb. Hom.* 91 Bi þere stret þere petrus forð-eoðe. *a* **1272** *Luue Ron* 122 in *O. E. Misc.* 97 Hit stont vppon a treowe mote þar hit neuer truke ne schal. **1297** R. GLOUC. (Rolls) 7683 In þe tresorie at westmunstre þere it ʒut is. *c* **1300** *Cursor M.* 2904 (Cott.) Þai sink in þat wele þar neuer man sank þat was o sele. *c* **1386** CHAUCER *Frankl. T.* 347 In to hir owene dirke Regioun Vnder the ground ther Pluto dwelleth Inne. *c* **1440** *Pallad. on Husb.* I. 21 In places there thow wilt have the culture. **15..** *Merch. & Son* 92 in Hazl. *E. P. P.* I. 139 The erthe tremelyd there Wyllyam stode.

**b.** with *there* also as antecedent : *there there* = there where, in that place where.

*c* **1000** ÆLFRIC *Gen.* ii. 21 God .. ʒefilde mid flæsce, þær þær þæt ribb wæs. *c* **1000** ÆLFRIC *Saints' Lives* xiii. 67 Man mot..hine ʒebiddan, beo þærþær he beo. *c* **1175** *Lamb. Hom.* 85 He..scal þer þer hit is ful, makien hit clene. *a* **1250** *Owl & Night.* 295 Loke þat þu ne beo þare þar changling beoþ. *a* **1400** *Relig. Pieces fr. Thornton MS.* 24 Lecherye..mase manes herte to melte, and to playe thare þare his herte lykes.

**c.** with *there* serving as both antecedent and relative : (In) the place in which; = mod. *where*, as in 'I found it where I left it'.

*c* **888** K. ÆLFRED *Boeth.* xxxii. § 1 He nænne ne mæʒ ʒebringan þær he him ʒehet. *c* **1175** *Lamb. Hom.* 35 Ga to þine feder burinesse oðer þer eni of þine cunne lið in. *c* **1220** *Bestiary* 10 Ðe leun..Draʒeð dust wið his stert ðer he steppeð. **1303** R. BRUNNE *Handl. Synne* 851 And þere men haunted þat custome lest, Falleþ oft tyme grete tempest. *c* **1340** HAMPOLE *Prose Tr.* 5 For þare he es he sekes hym noghte. **13..** *Cursor M.* 2768 (Gött.) Again þaim he ras fra þar [*Trin.* þere] he sate. *c* **1400** *Laud Troy Bk.* 2926 Thei sayled alle on a rawe, Til thei were come ther thei were knawe. *c* **1440** CAPGRAVE *St. Kath.* I. 506 Wyth a G set there C shuld stond. *c* **1500** *God Speed the Plough* 22 Than cometh the clerk..To haue A shef of corne there it groweth. *a* **1533** LD. BERNERS *Huon* lxiv. 221 It had been better for hym to haue taryed there he was. **1594** T. BEDINGFIELD tr. *Machiavelli's Florentine Hist.* (1595) 182 Your laughing there you are, is the occasion I weep not where I am.

† **10.** In the very case or circumstances in which ; where on the other hand, or on the contrary ; whereas, while. (Cf. 6.) *Obs.*

*c* **1200** *Trin. Coll. Hom.* 219 For nu is euerihc man ifo þare he solde fren[d] be. *c* **1380** WYCLIF *Wks.* (1880) 32 Þei han..welfare of mete and drynk, þere þei myʒtten unneþe before have bene-bred and watir or feble ale. *c* **1380** *Antecrist* in Todd 3 *Treat. Wyclif* 134 Þei putten grete penaunce unto men þere Cristis charge is liʒt. **1393** LANGL. *P. Pl.* C. XVII. 88 For pouerte haþ bote pokes to putten yn hus goodes, Ther auarice haþ almaries and yre-bounden cofres.

**III. 11.** as *sb.* That place; the (or a) place yonder.

**1588** R. PARKE tr. *Mendoza's Hist. China* 202 They.. kneeled downe right ouer against there whereas the Viceroye sate in a chaire. **1857-8** SEARS *Athan.* 19 [Motion] requires a here and a there. **1888** J. MARTINEAU *Stud. Relig.* I. I. i. 68 In the Space-field lie innumerable other theres that never have been here. **1907** *Outlook* 16 Mar. 339/2 We..draw, laboriously, a small circle in the dark and say, 'We are here', forgetful that there is no 'here' nor 'there'. *Mod.* We shall stay in Birmingham overnight, and go on from there next day. He left there last night.

**IV.** Phrases. (from I.)

**12. a.** *To be there* : to be at or in the place in question ; to be present or at hand.

*a* **1300** *Cursor M.* 1248 Þou wat þat i was neuer þare. *c* **1400** *Brut* ccxxv. 295 He wolde be þer him-self in al þe haste þat he myʒt. *c* **1420** *Avow. Arth.* xxiii, Kay callut on Gauan, ʒorne Asshes 'Quo is there?' **1600** *St. Papers Eliz., Domestic* CLXXVIII. No. 78 (P.R.O.), Whether S[r] John davyes were ther or not thys examinate can not tell. **1602** SHAKS. *Ham.* I. i. 1 Who's there? **1722** RAMSAY *Three Bonnets* II. 43 Ha, ha ! ye Judas, are ye there ? **1818** LADY MORGAN *Autobiog.* (1859) 49 The Duke of Sussex was there, with Lady Arran,..and the whole family of Gore. **1881** LADY HERBERT *Edith* 17 The 'little rift within the lute' was still there.

**b.** *To be all there* (colloq.): to have all one's faculties or wits about one ; to be smart or on the alert ; hence, *not all there* = not quite right in the head.

**1864** MRS. GATTY *Parab. fr. Nat.* Ser. IV. 3 Hans Jansen was what is commonly called *not all there.* **1883** PAYN *Thicker than Water* xx, It was his excusable boast..that when anything was wanted he was 'all there'. **1889** MRS. L. B. WALFORD *Stiff-necked Generation* 325 'Was he there after dinner last night?' 'Very much there'. **1900** *Daily News* 23 Apr. 8/1 But they were of the real Lancashire type, and were, as the phrase goes, 'all there'.

**13. a.** *There and then* († *there then*), at that precise place and time ; on the spot, forthwith. Also *attrib.* (Also *then and there* : see THEN *adv.*[1] 1 d.)

**1428** in *Surtees Misc.* (1888) 8 And þar þan he was asked. **1496** *Coventry Leet Bk.* 580 Wheruppon þe seid Laurence was there & then commyt vnto þe Flete. **1600** ABP. ABBOT *Exp. Jonah* 564 Although God do not say before, that there and then he will strike. **1848** MRS. GASKELL *M. Barton* xxxviii, Going on the search there and then. **1908** *Daily Chron.* 16 July 3/5 Happily..a there-and-then agreement was come to on their behalf.

**b.** *Here and there, here .. there, here, there and everywhere, neither here nor there* : see HERE *adv.* 9–12.

**14.** *There or* († *and*) *thereabouts* : primarily in the literal local sense; hence also = that or very nearly that (amount) ; something like that; approximately. See also THEREABOUTS.

*a* **1696** AUBREY *Lives* (1898) II. 226 (*Shakspere*) He left 2 or 300*li.* per annum there and thereabout to a sister. **1819** SCOTT *Leg. Montrose* xiii, 'Speak plainly, will there be five thousand men ?' 'There and thereabouts', answered Dalgetty. **1825** T. HOOK *Sayings* Ser. II. *Passion & Princ.* i. II. 248 A close, or field, containing eight acres, there or thereabouts. **1890** 'R. BOLDREWOOD' *Col. Reformer* (1891) 431 You'll mostly find him there or thereabouts, as long as he's alive. **1890** BP. LIGHTFOOT in *Expositor* Feb. 91 Forty-six years there or thereabouts had actually elapsed.

**15.** *There he* (or *she*) *goes, there you, they, go*, is primarily literal, the person going being pointed to (as in 3) ; but it also calls attention to the way in which a person goes on, acts, talks, etc., usually expressing surprise or disapproval. *There it goes !* is a common exclamation when a thing falls, disappears, goes off, breaks, bursts, or the like.

**1780** *Mirror* No. 97 ⁋ 32 'There she goes, the travelled lady', cried the Captain ; 'she must always have a fling at her catechism'. **1837** DICKENS *Pickw.* ii, 'They're beginning up-stairs..fiddles tuning—now the harp—there they go'. The various sounds..announced the commencement of the first quadrille.

**16.** *There you are!* (*colloq.*) (*a*) = *there you go !* in 15 ; (*b*) expressing or drawing attention to the simplicity or ready consummation of a process or action ; = There it is for you, there you have it, the thing is done.

**1907** *Westm. Gaz.* 22 May 3/1 Tables, setting out in a there-you-are ! fashion the declining percentage to the total of British imports into certain countries for two contrasted decades. *Mod.* Can't find the waiter ? That's quite easy ; just press that button and there you are ! Accidents are common in Alpine ascents ; one false step, and there you are !

**V. 17.** *There* (in branch I) in combination with adverbs and prepositions.

For the history of these, see note s. v. HERE *adv.* 16. 'The compounds of *there* meaning *that*, and of *here* meaning *this*, have been for some time passing out of use, and are no longer found in elegant writings, or in any other than formulary pieces' (Todd's *Johnson* 1818, s.v. *Therewithall*). But see the Main words THEREABOUT, THEREAFTER, etc.

**a.** With adverbs, as *there all-about, there east, there-without* ; † **there-gates**, in that manner; † **there-thence**, thence; † **there-whyne** (*-quhyne*), from whence. Also THEREAWAY, etc. **b.** With prepositions : = that, that place, matter, etc., as *there-among* († *-imong*), *there-below, there-between* ; **thereamid** († *-emid*), amid that ; † **therebout** (*-buten*) = THEREABOUT ; † **therebove** (*-buve(n)* = THEREABOVE ; † **therenext**, next to that ; † **there-offen** = THEREOFFE ; † **thereouten**, out of that ; † **there-ovenon** (*-ufenen*), above that ; † **there-toforn**, before that (time). Originally mostly written as two words. See also the main words from THEREABOUT to THEREWITHIN.

**1422** tr. *Secreta Secret., Priv. Priv.* 198 Noone god of al that weryn *ther al aboute in al regions. *a* **1300** *Cursor M.* 11988 Mani childer was *þar emid. *c* **1220** *Bestiary* 601 He ðe swiken *ðer imong. **1899** *Westm. Gaz.* 18 Apr. 2/1 It is a real joy to know that the pilot-fish does hide itself within the capacious throat, or some snug harbourage *therebelow, when danger threatens. **1876** MORRIS *Sigurd* III. 194 And lingering flecks of the cloud-host are tangled *there-between. **1885-94** R. BRIDGES *Eros & Psyche*, *October* 9 She..sweeping therebetween a passage wide, Made clear of corn and chaff the temple space. *c* **1250** *Gen. & Ex.* 3625, .vii. moneð *ðor buten he ben. **1297** R. GLOUC. (Rolls) 11614 Bruggen hii breke oueral hii ne beleuede ssip non..þer boute [*C.* aboute]. *c* **897** K. ÆLFRED *Gregory's Past. C.* viii. 52 *Ðærbufan is ʒetealđ hwelc he beon sceol. *a* **1300** *Floriz & Bl.* 294 Aboue þe walle stant a treo..lef and blosme beoþ þer buue. **1639** BAILLIE *Lett.* 28 Sept. (Bann. Club) I. 201 The Tables *there East thought meet they should not conjoyne, bot divided them in foure. *c* **1440** *York Myst.* xii. 48 Þus may *þer-gatis be mente. **13..** *Cursor M.* 141 (Cott.) *Þar neist [*F.* þar next] sal be sythen tald How þat ioseph was boght and sald. **1387** TREVISA *Higden* (Rolls) VII. 71 Under a treen brugge þat was þere next. *c* **1450** LOVELICH *Merlin* 6294 The wheche child to hire schal ben browht; but *there-offen the peple may weten nowht. *c* **1250** *Gen. & Ex.* 3364 And he smot wið his wond ðor on, And water gan *ðor vten gon. *c* **1205** LAY. 12423 Heo bigunnen..ane swiðe deope dich & *þer ouen on ouer al ænne strongne stanene wal. *Ibid.* 17696 Þer ufenen he hæfde Ane ladliche here. *c* **1475** *Partenay* 3125 *Ther thens to uavuent [Vauvent] A man sent in message, Which full courtois was, inly wise also. *a* **1425** *Cursor M.* 12479 (Trin.) [He] wende þe maistir were of lyue As oþere *þer to forn were. **1456** SIR G. HAYE *Law Arms* (S.T.S.) 77 And *thairquhyne cumis this? *a* **1500** *Flower & Leaf* 71 Al tho that yeden *there without.

**There**, obs. gen. and dat. sing. fem. of THE ; obs. var. of THEIR, THIR ; inflexion of THARF *v. Obs.*

**Thereabout** (ðēᵊrăbau·t, ðēᵊ·răbaut), *adv.* Forms : see THERE and ABOUT. [OE. *þær abútan*, two words, viz. *þær*, THERE 17 and *abútan*, ABOUT.]

**1.** About (orig. outside) or near that place : = THEREABOUTS 1.

*a* **925** *O. E. Chron.* an. 917 (Parker MS.) Æt Hocneratune, and þær onbutan. *c* **1000** ÆLFRIC *Saints' Lives* xxv. 595. *c* **1000** *Ags. Gosp.* Mark xiv. 69 Heo ongan cweðan to þam þe ðar abutan stodon. **1131** *O. E. Chron.* an. 1124 (Laud MS.) Ealla þa casteles ða þær abuton wæron. *c* **1290** *Beket* 2126 in *S. Eng. Leg.* 167 And al round þare a-bouten it lay. *c* **1400** MAUNDEV. (Roxb.) Pref. 3 Ierusalem, and the haly placez þat er þare aboute. **1451** *Paston Lett.* I. 196 To all yowr frendes and tenauntes ther abowtyn. **1517** TORKINGTON *Pilgr.* (1884) 56 The Cityes in the Countre ther a bowght. **1562** *Reg. Privy Council Scot.* I. 220 To remane within the samin and foure mylis thairabout. **1692** RAY *Disc.* II. v. (1732) 215 The Alteration of the sea thereabout. **1864** BURTON *Scot Abr.* I. iii. 120 Quartered in the different villages thereabout. **1908** [MISS E. FOWLER] *Betw. Trent & Ancholme* 67 From somewhere thereabout our garden gravel came.

† **b.** Around that object (a pillar, or the like).

**1340-70** *Alex. & Dind.* 1136 He bad bulden of marbre A piler..& þat þei wrouhten a wrytte & writen þer aboute.

**c.** *fig.* About that; near to that state or action : cf. THEREABOUTS 1 c. *Obs.* or *rare.*

**1664** DRYDEN *Rival-Ladies* IV. iii, *Amid.*..I feel already My stout Heart melts. *Hip.* Oh ! Are you thereabout ?

**2. a.** About or somewhere near that time or date. **b.** About that number, quantity, size, space of time, etc. = THEREABOUTS 2. (Chiefly after *or*.)

**1297** R. GLOUC. (Rolls) 8984 Hit biuel þer aboute þat þe erl thebaud..destourbede þe peys. **1465** J. PASTON in *P. Lett.* II. 236 The xxii yere of Kyng Herry or ther abought. **1534** in *Rep. Hist. MSS. Comm., Var. Coll.* IV. 217 Amountyng to the some of 30*l.* or therabout. **1564** *Brief Exam.* ***** ij b, Referred to the Prophetes tymes, and thereabout. **1612** DAVIES *Why Ireland*, etc. (1787) 15 A company of volunteers, in number four hundred, or thereabout. **1727** DE FOE *Syst. Magic* I. ii. (1840) 51 At the distance of less than two hundred years, or thereabout. **1908** [MISS E. FOWLER] *Betw. Trent & Ancholme* 369 She has walked 221,490 miles, or thereabout.

**3.** About, concerning, or with reference to that matter or business; thereanent. *To go* or *be thereabout*, to occupy or busy oneself therewith: cf. ABOUT B. 10, 11. Now *arch.* or *rare*.

*a* **1300** *Cursor M.* 22885 (Edin.) Þe mar man swink him þar aboutin Fra sped þe ferre he sal ben outin. *c* **1350** *Will. Palerne* 972 But i were busi þer a-boute to blame i were. *c* **1386** CHAUCER *Somp. T.* 129 What wol ye dyne? I wol go ther-aboute. *c* **1400** *Ywaine & Gaw.* 2698 Thar-obout wil i be bayn. *c* **1440** *Jacob's Well* 56 Here resonable expensys þere abowte awȝte ferst to be takyn vp. **1450–1530** *Myrr. our Ladye* 51 All that wyll do theyr besynes there aboute. **1534** MORE *Treat. Passion* Wks. 1289/2 How much payn so euer himselfe tooke thereabout. **1611** BIBLE *Luke* xxiv. 4 They were much perplexed thereabout. **1657** W. RAND tr. *Gassendi's Life Peiresc* II. 77 Peireskius ..congratulated with him thereabout.

**Thereabou·ts**, *adv.* [f. prec. with advb. *-s*. Of later appearance than prec., but now in southern Eng. more frequent in senses 1 and 2.]

**1.** About, or in the neighbourhood of, that place; in the district, region, etc. round about there.

*c* **1400** MAUNDEV. (Roxb.) xiv. 63 Þare aboutes er many gude hilles and faire. **1522** *Rutland Papers* (Camden) 83 The noblemen belongyng to themperor that be lodged in the chanons howses of Paules and ther aboutes. **1585** T. WASHINGTON tr. *Nicholay's Voy.* I. xii. 14 Theeues..there abouts do lye secretly hidde too entrappe them that came therabouts. **1662** J. DAVIES tr. *Olearius' Voy. Ambass.* 6 Flies, Gnats, and Wasps, which the Fens thereabouts produce in such quantity. **1797** MME. D'ARBLAY *Let. to Burney* 13 Sept., It is the best house thereabouts..in a broad street. **1860** HAWTHORNE *Marb. Faun* xvi, A homeless dog, that haunted thereabouts. **1909** *Times* 23 July 10/1 In the streets thereabouts men and women gathered in crowds.

†**b.** After a preposition. *Obs. rare.*

**1491** CAXTON *Vitas Patr.* (W. de W. 1495) I. xxxvi. 38 b/1 All the others..departed all fro there abowtes. **1568** GRAFTON *Chron.* II. 673 In the Countie of Yorke, and other places, nere therabouts. **1654** EARL MONM. tr. *Bentivoglio's Warrs Flanders* 427 The Town of Groll is not far from thereabouts.

**c.** *fig.* About that; near to that state or action: see ABOUT *adv.* 13. *Obs.* or *rare.*

**1606** SHAKS. *Ant. & Cl.* III. x. 29, I, are you thereabouts? Why then goodnight indeede. **1611** — *Wint. T.* I. ii. 378. **1697** VANBRUGH *Æsop.* II. i, *Euph.* Unlace me, or I shall swoon. *Dor.* Unlace you! why, you are not there abouts, I hope? **1732** FIELDING *Debauchees* II. iv, Hoity-toity— Are you thereabouts, good father?

**2.** Transferred to time, quantity, quality, degree, etc. Mostly preceded by *or*.

**a.** About or near to a specified date or time.

**1561** T. NORTON *Calvin's Inst.* I. viii. 17 Cyrus was borne in the hundreth yere or there aboutes after the death of Esaie. **1631** WEEVER *Anc. Fun. Mon.* 139 Which happened since the dissolution here in England, or much what thereabouts. **1769** BURKE *Corr.* (1844) I. 177 The meeting is put off until ..the twelfth of September, or thereabouts. **1878** HUXLEY *Physiogr.* 10 From the year 1660 or thereabouts.

**b.** About or not far different from a stated number, sum, quantity, space of time, degree, condition, etc.; very nearly so; approximately so. *There or thereabouts*: see THERE *adv.* 14.

**1413** *Pilgr. Sowle* (Caxton 1483) IV. xvii. 64, I wyl that man lyue in..tribulacion fyue thousand yere or neyhe ther aboutes. **1581** in *Cath. Rec. Soc. Publ.* V. 20 William Tharley aged thirtie yeares or therabouts. **1601** SHAKS. *All's Well* IV. iii. 171 Fiue or six thousand horse I sed..or thereabouts. **1704** *Lond. Gaz.* No. 3987/4 A lighter Bay, 13 hands and half high, or thereabouts. **1719** DE FOE *Crusoe* (1840) II. viii. 191 In three hours, or thereabouts. **1794** SULLIVAN *View Nat.* II. 17 Mont Blanc is 15,562 feet or thereabouts. **1818** KEATS *Lett.* Wks. 1889 III. 127 Write to me and tell me that you are well, or thereabouts. **1878** HUXLEY *Physiogr.* 210 The pavement..was at the sea-level or thereabouts. **1898** *Pall Mall G.* 20 Jan. 2/2 You may be sure the original statement was thereabouts, if not quite there.

†**3.** About or concerning that; = prec. 3. *Obs.*

**1586** DAY *Eng. Secretary* II. (1625) 71, I would haue you to conferre with my Cosen T. R. thereabouts. **1611** W. SCLATER *Key* (1629) 306 Colour..cannot be said to be *obiectum actu*, till some act of sight be exercised thereabouts. **1631** GOUGE *God's Arrows* III. § 61. 298 Mens conjectures thereabouts are various. **1657** W. RAND tr. *Gassendi's Life Peiresc* I. 178 He concludes a passage thereabouts in these words.

**Thereabove** (ðēərăbɒ·v), *adv.* [Orig. two words, THERE 17 and ABOVE *adv.*] †**a.** Above or on the top of that (*obs.*). †**b.** Above or more than that (*obs.*). **c.** Up above there; up yonder (in heaven). *rare.*

**1382** WYCLIF 1 *Kings* vii. 35 In the cop..was a maner roundnes,..so forgid, that the watir ressel myȝte be sette there aboue. **1439** in *Fenland N. & Q.* July (1905) 221 To the somme of xl. mˡ. marc or yer above. **1891** C. E. NORTON *Dante's Hell* i. 5 That Emperor who reigneth thereabove [I. 124 quello Imperador, che lassù regna]. **1892** — *Paradise* i. 4 Beatrice was standing with her eyes wholly fixed on the eternal wheels, and on her I fixed my eyes from thereabove removed [I. 66 Le luci fisse di lassù rimote].

**Thereafter** (ðēərɑ·ftəɹ), *adv.* [OE. *þǽr æfter*, two words, viz. *þǽr*, THERE 17 and *æfter*, AFTER; ME. *þer after*. Cf. OS. *thar after* (Du. *daarachter*); ON. *þar epter* (Sw., Da., Norw. *derefter*).]

**1.** After that in time, order, or sequence; subsequently; afterwards. (Now somewhat formal.)

*c* **897** K. ÆLFRED *Gregory's Past. C.* xix. 144 Hie..ne ondrædað ðone dom þe ðær æfter fylȝeð. *c* **1000** *Sax. Leechd.* III. 244 Þonne byð se sunnan dæȝ þær æfter easter dæȝ. **1154** *O. E. Chron.* an. 1132 (Laud MS.) Was it noht suithe lang þer efter þatte king sende efter him. *c* **1205** LAY. 1220 He gon slomnen & þer æfter to slepen. **1297** R. GLOUC. (Rolls) 8277 Ȝut sone þer after an oþer com al so. **1375** BARBOUR *Bruce* I. 591 And the King A parlyament Gert set thareftir hastely. **1445** in *Wars Eng. in France* (1861) I. 465 At Witsontide next thereaftere. **1535** COVERDALE *Luke* xv. 13 Not longe therafter, gathered the yonger sonne all together. **1632** LITHGOW *Trav.* III. 84 A little thereafter the Generall of the Galleys came to the Monastery. **1760–72** H. BROOKE *Fool of Qual.* (1809) III. 50 This prerogative.. was thereafter..discontinued. **1898** *Allbutt's Syst. Med.* V. 513 A year thereafter she must be re-examined.

†**b.** After that in place or position. *Obs.*

*c* **1000** *Ags. Gosp.* Matt. xxi. 9 Ðæt folc þæt þar beforan ferde, and þæt þar æfter ferde. *c* **1250** *Gen. & Ex.* 3644 Ðat briȝte skie bi-foren hem fleȝt, And ðis folc ðor after teȝ.

†**2.** Conformably thereto, accordingly; *thereafter as*, according as; *to be thereafter*, to be conformable or agreeable thereto. *Obs.*

*c* **1175** *Lamb. Hom.* 133 Euric mon þe lusteð luueliche godes wordes and ledeð his lif rihtliche þer efter. *c* **1200** *Vices & Virt.* 65 Þis is godes ȝiue, ȝif ðu ðus ðe beþencst and ðar after wercst. *c* **1380** WYCLIF *Sel. Wks.* III. 360 ȝif oþer men wolden be preestis, lyve þei þerafter. **1470–85** MALORY *Arthur* IV. xii. 134 Ye shalle be a knyghte of myne, and yf your dedes be there after I shall so proferre yow [etc.]. *a* **1533** LD. BERNERS *Huon* xlii. 140 He was .xvii. fote of length, & of bygnes he was therafter. **1535** COVERDALE *Ps.* cx. 10 A good vnderstondinge haue all they that do thereafter. **1551** T. WILSON *Logike* (1580) Epist., The presente of a true faithfull subiecte, whiche would haue brought better if his power had been thereafter. **1584** COGAN *Haven Health* (1636) 198 The Physitian, in dyeting, should regard chiefly two things..and thereafter to prescribe lesse or more to be received. **1597** SHAKS. 2 *Hen. IV*, III. ii. 56. **1618** BP. HALL *Righteous Mammon* Wks. (1628) 723 Because these are but flowers,..wee regard them thereafter. **1671** MILTON *P. R.* II. 321. **1727** GAY *Begg. Op.* II, That, Madam, is thereafter as they be.

†**3.** With verbs const. with *after*, as *cry, gaze, look, wish, yearn*: cf. AFTER B. 5 e. *Obs.*

*c* **1200** *Trin. Coll. Hom.* 5 Alle bileffulle men þe waren þo and ðar biforen wissede swiðe ðar after. *a* **1300** *Cursor M.* 486 For godd aght not gif þam mercy, Þat þar efter wil not cri. **1393** LANGL. *P. Pl.* C. VIII. 225 Leue hem in þy lift hand and loke nouht þer-after.

**4.** quasi-*adj.* (with n. of action). Subsequent.

**1830** GALT *Lawrie T.* IV. xii, Supposing no thereafter increase.

**Therea·fterward**, *adv. rare.* [f. THERE *adv.* 17 + AFTERWARD.] = prec. 1.

**1867** LONGF. *Dante's Paradiso* XXIV. 70 And I thereafterward; 'The things profound [etc.]'. **1884** J. PAYNE *1000 Nts.* VIII. 8 The day thereafterward for weariness thou'lt pine.

†**Thereagain**, *adv. Obs.* Forms: *α.* 1 þæronȝen, 3 þer aȝen, (*Orm.*) þær onnȝæn, 4 þer aȝeyn(e, þer oȝein. *β.* 3–4 þar again, -egain, -agayn(e, 4 þer agayn(e, again, 5 therageyn. [OE. *þǽr ongé(a)n*, two words, viz. *þǽr*, THERE 17 and *ongéan*, ME. *onȝen, aȝen*, subseq. *ogain*, AGAIN.]

**1.** = THEREAGAINST 1.

*α.* [*a* **1023**: see 2.] *c* **1200** ORMIN 5304 Þa birrþ þe stanndenn þær onnȝæn. **1297** R. GLOUC. (Rolls) 8881 Þis mayde was þer aȝen, & wiþ sede it longe. *a* **1300** *Cursor M.* 3094 (Cott.) We sal neuer do þer again [*F.* þar a-gayne, *G.* þar egain, *T.* þer aȝayn]. **13..** *Guy Warw.* (A.) 977, & who so þer oȝain sey ouȝt. **1387** TREVISA *Higden* (Rolls) VII. 157 It is byholdinge to hym..þat he goo þere agayne wiþ tonge and hond. **1393** LANGL. *P. Pl.* C. XXI. 312 And neuere was þer aȝeyn. *a* **1425** *Cursor M.* 17054 (Trin.) Þer is no mon..may say þer aȝeyne. **1430–40** LYDG. *Bochas* IX. xviii. (MS. Bodl. 263) 422/1 Yet ther was sume that gruchched therageyn.

**2.** = THEREAGAINST 2.

*a* **1023** WULFSTAN *Hom.* xlviii. (Napier) 248 Englas..cyðað þine dæda..and deofol awrit þæronȝen ealle þine misdæda. **13..** *Cursor M.* 20789 (Fairf.) Bot þar againe [*C.* þar egain] sais Ieronim He wille take na charge on him. *a* **1350** *St. Stephen* 109 in Horstm. *Altengl. Leg.* (1881) 29 Bot þarogayn to þam he kend On thre maners þaire mys to mend.

**3.** = THEREAGAINST 3.

*c* **1330** *Arth. & Merl.* 5152 Wawain it seiȝe sone on hast, His scheld þer oȝein gan cast.

**Thereagainst** (ðēərăge·nst, -ăgē̆ⁱ·nst), *adv.* Now *arch.* Forms: *α.* 4 þerageyns, 5 ther-ayeines, -ayeynes, þer-aȝens, þar-agaynys, there aȝens. *β.* 5 ther agenst, ageynste, ther(e-ayenst(e, 6 ther agenst, -ageinst, 6– there-against. [f. THERE 17 + *againes*, AGAINST *prep.*]

**1.** Against or in opposition to that.

*α.* *c* **1380** WYCLIF *Sel. Wks.* III. 367 No mon may distrie hit, or dispense þerageyns. *c* **1402** LYDG. *Compl. Bl. Knt.* 533 Ther ayeines shal I never stryve. *c* **1449** PECOCK *Repr.* 75 If the gretter laboure be mad thereaȝens.

*β.* **1450–1530** *Myrr. our Ladye* 10 Remedyes..to be used there ageynste. *Ibid.* 69. **1528** TINDALE *Obed. Chr. Man* 93 b, I will not stryue nor saye thar agenst. *c* **1647** SANDERSON *Episcopacy* (1673) 9 Remedy provided there-against by an Act of Parliament. **1870** MAGNÚSSON & MORRIS *Völsunga Saga* xx. 71 But thereagainst I vowed a vow, that never would I wed one who knew the name of fear.

†**2.** As a set-off thereto; contrariwise; on the other side. *Obs.*

*a* **1400–50** *Alexander* 1264 Ser Beritinus þe bald þai bretned to dethe, And Sampson on þis side was slay þar agaynys. *c* **1407** H. SCOGAN *Moral Ballad* 158 Seeth, there ayenst, how vertuous noblesse..Dryveth away al vyce. **1422** tr. *Secreta Secret., Priv. Priv.* 141 Of the wynde comyth good. ..But ther ayeynes dyuers Perillis..and destourbaunce fallyth. **1558** PHAER *Æneid.* II. E iv b, In his purpose still he fixt remaindy fast. We therageinst with streaming teares.

**3.** In pressure or impact against that.

**1863** SALA in *Temple Bar Mag.* VII. 496 From the bobbing and rasping of watch-spring crinolines there-against. **1884** C. T. DAVIS *Manuf. Bricks & Tiles*, etc. ix. (1889) 285 Its ends are passed through the side pieces of the frame and tightened there-against by nuts.

**Thereamong** (ðēərămɒ·ŋ), *adv.* Now *rare* or *arch.* [Orig. two words, THERE 17 and AMONG *prep.*] Among that, those, or them.

**1399** LANGL. *Rich. Redeles* Prol. 57 If ȝe ffynde ffables or ffoly þer amonge. **1482** *Rolls of Parlt.* VI. 222/1 And thereamonge put Thokes and broken belyed fissh. **1836** *Fraser's Mag.* XIII. 12 There is neither fruit, nor appearance of fruit, there-among. **1869** TENNYSON *Pelleas* 92 Three knights were thereamong; and they too smiled.

So **Thereamo·ngst** *adv. rare*, in same sense.

**1599** A. M. tr. *Gabelhouer's Bk. Physicke* 10/1 Mixe theramongste Cubebes, Mace, Cloves. **1606** G. W[OODCOCK] *Hist. Ivstine* II. 11 b, They might perceiue a multitude of women to be there amongst.

**Thereanent** (ðēərăne·nt), *adv.* Orig. and chiefly *Sc.* and *north.* [Orig. two words, THERE 17 and ANENT *prep.*] About, concerning, or in reference to that matter, business, etc.; relating thereto.

*c* **1340** *Cursor M.* 20789 (Gött.) Bot þar enent [*v. r.* thereagain], sais Ieronim, He wil noght take þe boke on him. **1562** *Reg. Privy Council Scot.* I. 218 For satisfying of hir Hienes thairanent. **1578** *Ibid.* II. 700 Ordour to be takin thairanent with expeditioun. **1681** *Sc. Acts Jas. II* (1820) VIII. 243/2 According to the tenour of the respective acts of Parliament thereanent provided. **1726** *Wodrow Corr.* (1843) III. 243 To hear the state of this affair..and bring in an overture thereanent. **1819** SCOTT *Leg. Montrose* xii, I will gage my life upon his making my words good thereanent. **1853** C. BRONTË *Villette* xxi, The reader would not care to have my impressions thereanent. **1868** VISCT. STRANGFORD *Select.* (1869) II. 311 The public prints of an earlier date in this year..may be consulted thereanent with propriety.

Hence (with advb. genitive) †**Thereane·nts** (-anentis, -anendes) *adv.*, in same sense; in quot. *c* 1400 app. = THEREABOUTS 1.

*c* **1400** MAUNDEV. (Roxb.) viii. 30 It [þe Reed See] is þer anentes vi. myle brade. **1552** *Reg. Privy Council Scot.* I. 133 [We sall] leif nocht behind that lyis in our possibiliteis thairanentis. **1564** *Child-Marriages* 26 Procured the Counselles lettres theranendes. *c* **1568** REG. MURRAY in H. Campbell *Love Lett. Mary Q. Scots* (1824) 218 My Lord of Argyll..spak largely..theiranents to the Queen herself.

†**Thereas**, *conj. Obs.* [Originally a conjunctive phrase: see THERE 9, 10 and AS 27.]

**1.** In that place (or case) in which; where; = THERE 9.

*a* **1225** *Ancr. R.* 12 Þer ase þeos þinges beoð þer is riht religiun. **13..** *Cast. Love* (Halliw.) 444 Þes ne bydyth in no londe, Ther as were is nyȝh-honde. **1493** *Festivall* (W. de W. 1515) 6 To go to an hous ther as is a corps. **1550** COVERDALE *Bk. Death* II. i. 178 The comfortable promes of Chryst, there as he sayth: I am the resurreccion and yᵉ lyfe.

**2.** Whereas; = THERE 10.

*c* **1385** CHAUCER *L. G. W.* 1282 (*Dido*) Sche hath..hire reame ȝeuyn In to his hand, there as she myghte haue been Of othere landys than of cartage quien. *c* **1460** FORTESCUE *Abs. & Lim. Mon.* xix. (1885) 155 Þer as oþer kynges haue ffounded byshopriches..þe kyng shall þan haue ffounded an holl reaume. **1470–85** MALORY *Arthur* XX. xi. 815 There as ye say I haue slayn your good knyghtes, I wote wel that I haue done soo, and that me sore repenteth.

**Thereat** (ðēəræ·t), *adv.* Now *formal* or *arch.* [OE. *þǽr æt*, two words: see THERE 17 and AT.]

**1.** At the place, meeting, etc., mentioned; there.

*a* **900** tr. *Bæda's Hist.* IV. vii. § 2 Monige untrume..þær æt hælo onfengon. **1297** R. GLOUC. (Rolls) 9526 Hii hulde a parlement..& þe king him sulf was þerate. **13..** *Seuyn Sag.* (W.) 2358 Whan he com to Rome yate, And wolde wenden out therate. *c* **1400** MAUNDEV. (Roxb.) xvi. 74 Sum saise þai hafe bene þare att. **1526** TINDALE *Matt.* vii. 13 Many there be which goo yn there att. **1611** SHAKS. *Wint. T.* IV. iv. 500 Not for Bohemia, nor the pompe that may Be thereat gleaned. **1885** *Act* 48 & 49 *Vict.* c. 78 § 30 He shall..hold a sitting..and shall thereat take and receive any evidence..offered.

**b.** With a verb of motion or aim: cf. AT 13.

**1517** TORKINGTON *Pilgr.* (1884) 27 He cast a stonne ther att.

**c.** Expressing attachment to a thing: cf. AT 7.

**1566** tr. *Sc. Acts Jas. III*, c. 87 Our Souerane Lord..annexis till his Crowne the Erldome of Ros with the pertinentis, to remane thairat for euer. **1567** in *6th Rep. Hist. MSS. Comm.* 643/2 Ane tabled hyngand with ane gryit rubye and ane gryit hingand perle thairatt. **1650** BULWER *Anthropomet.* xi. 109 A broad plate..and the Jewel they hang thereat. **1688** R. HOLME *Armoury* III. 161/2 A Leather Girdle..with a strong Rope..hanging thereat.

**2.** On the occasion or occurrence of that, thereupon, because of that: cf. AT 34, 35.

*a* **1300** *Cursor M.* 2722 Sarra..Herd þis word and logh þar at. *a* **1450** *Knt. de la Tour* 98 His wyff..dysdeyned thereatte, and had scorne therof. **1490** CAXTON *Eneydos* xviii. 68 For to take theratte som comforte. **1590** SPENSER *F. Q.* II. vii. 34 Thereat the feend his gnashing teeth did grate. **1605** SHAKS. *Lear* IV. ii. 75 Bending his Sword To his great Master, who, thereat enrag'd Flew on him. 1869

TENNYSON *Pass. Arthur* 462 Thereat once more he moved about. **1870** MORRIS *Earthly Par.* II. III. 253 Thereat the silver trumpet's tuneful blare Made music strange.

**3.** At or in connexion with the thing or process on which action is brought to bear: cf. AT 17.

**13..** *Cursor M.* 11674 (Fairf.) My hande þer at may naþing do. *c* **1440** *Alphabet of Tales* 198 When he fand gude wyne on a tyme, he seld his slavyn & drank it þer-att. *c* **1556** R. COCKES in *Archæologia* XXXV. 20, I trust this weke that cometh we shall do a good chare therat [at the hay-making]. **1581** *Exch. Rolls Scot.* XXI. 551 The saidis parties oblissis thame to..abyid thairat bot any reclaming.

† **Thereatou·r,** *adv. Sc. Obs.* In 5 tharatour, 5–6 thairattour. [f. THERE 17 + ATOUR *prep.*] Over or beyond that; about or concerning that: see THEREOVER.

**1457** *Sc. Acts Jas. II,* c. 25 (1814) II. 51/1 Gif he dois ony thing þairattour furth with to arreist his persoun. **1473** *Rental Bk. Cupar-Angus* (1879) I. 173 Tharatour tha sal do thar det lelaly and truly to our myl..bath in fre multur and thyrl. **15..** *Priests Peblis* I. in Pinkerton *Scot. Poems* (1792) I. 14 Than spak the King, your conclusion is quaint; And thairattour ye mak to us a plaint.

**Thereaway** (ðēᵊ·răwēⁱ), *adv.* Chiefly *Sc.* and *north. dial.* [Orig. two words, THERE 17 and AWAY *adv.*]

†**1.** Of motion: Away thither, or in that direction. *Hereaway, thereaway*: see HEREAWAY. *Obs.*

**1375** BARBOUR *Bruce* x. 32 (MS. E.) For gif the king held thar away, He thoucht he suld soyn vencust be. *c* **1400** MAUNDEV. (Roxb.) v. 15 Schippes..commes þer away for to fraght þam with þat salt. *c* **1450** *Life St. Cuthbert* (Surtees) 5102 Þare away to fare. *a* **1500** *Smith & his Dame* 30 in Hazlitt *E. P. P.* III. 202 Ovr lorde came there away. **1549, 1793,** etc. [see HEREAWAY 2]. **1601** in Foley *Rec. Eng. Prov. S. J.* (1880) VI. 735 For such English as come thereaway to Loreto. **1659** W. GUTHRIE *Chr. Gt. Interest* II. vi. (1724) 207 Confirming the same by many mighty Works in Scripture tending there-away.

**2.** Of situation: Away in that direction or region; in those parts; thereabouts.

**1551** R. ROBINSON *More's Utop.* II. (1895) 253 There be fewe warres there awaye, wherin is not a greate numbre of them in bothe partyes. *c* **1670** PENN *Let.* in *Life* Wks. 1726 I. App. iii. 156 Among the Carnal and Historical Christians there-away. **1816** SCOTT *Bl. Dwarf* viii, All evil comes out o' thereaway..and we'll e'en away there. **1840** CAROLINE FOX *Old Friends* (1882) 60 The Duke of Wellington..in some mighty action thereaway showed his wondrous power in animating masses.

**3.** Somewhere about that (number, amount, age, etc.); = THEREABOUTS 2.

**1824** SCOTT *Redgauntlet* ch. xi, Swaggering about the country..for five or six months, or thereaway. **1830** MISS MITFORD *Village* Ser. IV. 328 An old batchelor of fifty-five, or there-away. **1862** MRS. GROTE *Coll. Papers* 261 A hundred thousand pounds or there-away.

Hence † **Thereaway-abouts** *adv.*, thereabouts.

**1828** MOIR *Mansie Wauch* xxii. (1849) 169 The martyrs had been buried thereaway-abouts.

**The·reaways,** *adv.* Now *dial.* [f. prec. with advb. genitive *-s*: cf. AWAYS.] = prec.

**1575** *Gamm. Gurton* IV. ii, He intends this same night to slip in there awayes. **1682** in *Jrnl. Friends' Hist. Soc.* IV. 151, I would have yᵉ to mynd my love to friends thereawayes and at Darnton. **1791** 'G. GAMBADO' *Ann. Horsem.* xvii. (1809) 137 Come from Lapland, or thereaways. *a* **1825** FORBY *Voc. E. Anglia* s.v., Is the horse worth twenty pounds? There and there-aways. **1902** BUCHAN *Watcher by Threshold* 73 What's taking ye thereaways?

† **The·rebefo·re,** *adv. Obs.* Forms: see THERE and BEFORE. [Late OE.; two words.]

**1.** Before that in position or order; in front.

*c* **1000** *Ags. Gosp.* Matt. xxi. 9 Ðæt folc þæt þar beforan [*c* **1160** *Hatton Gosp.*, þær be-fore] ferde.

**2.** Before that (time); formerly, previously.

*c* **1200** [see THEREAFTER 3]. *c* **1275** *Passion our Lord* 218 in *O. E. Misc.* 43 As vre louerd þer by-vore heom iseyd hedde. *c* **1386** CHAUCER *Man of Law's T.* 99 In sterres many a wynter ther biforn Was writen the deeth of Ector Achilles. *c* **1430** *Freemasonry* 302 Ȝef he nulle okepye hem no more, As he hath y-done ther by-fore. **1592** in J. Morris *Troub. Cath. Forefathers* (1877) 34 And the priest there before dead.

**Therebe·n,** *adv. Sc.* [See BEN *adv.* c.] 'Ben' there, within there.

[**13..** *Cursor M.* 2721 (Cott.) Sarra þar bin quare sco satt Herd þis word and logh þar-at.] *c* **1500** ROWLL *Cursing* 124 in *Bannatyne Poems* (Hunter. Cl.) 302 And thow art scho that stall the hen And put hir in the pot thair ben. *a* **1568** *Wowing Jok & Jynny* 21 ibid. 388 Ane pig, ane pot, ane raip thair ben. **1604** *Acts Sederunt* 11 Jan. (1790) 36 For removing of that impediment of proceeding in the Utterhouse, (that the procurator is thair ben) it is appointit..that [etc.]. **1728** RAMSAY *Monk & Miller's Wife* 144 'Hout I', quoth she, 'ye may well ken, 'Tis ill brought but [= out] that 's no there-ben'.

**Therebesi·de,** *adv.* Now only *arch.* and *poet.* [Orig. two words: see THERE 17, BESIDE *prep.*] By the side of that; next to that; near by.

*a* **1250** *Owl & Night.* 25 Þo stod on old stoc þar biside. **13..** in Horstmann *Altengl. Leg.* (1875) 91 He hedde þer is asse an is oxe, iteiȝed þer biside In a cracche. *c* **1400** MAUNDEV. (Roxb.) iii. 9 Þare be syde es a fayre place ordaynd for iustyng. **1470–85** MALORY *Arthur* II. xvi. 94 Ther besyde satte a fayr knyght on the ground. **1870** MORRIS *Earthly Par.* III. IV. 339 When I stood therebeside Methought its likeness ever would abide Within my mind.

So †**The·rebesi·des** *adv.*, in same sense.

**1470–85** MALORY *Arthur* I. x. 48 There bysydes were viij knyghtes that aspyed them.

**Therebinthe,** obs. form of TEREBINTH.

**Thereby** (ðēᵊɹbəi·, ðēᵊ·ɹbəi), *adv.* Forms: see THERE and BY. [OE. *þærbi*, f. *þær*, THERE 17 + *bi*, BY *prep.* Cf. G. *dabei*, Du. *daarbij*.]

**1.** By that; by means of, or because of, that; through that. Cf. BY A. 30–33, 36.

*c* **897** K. ÆLFRED *Past. C.* v. 42, ȝif he ðonne bearn ðærbiȝ [*v.r.* -bie, *Hatt.* -biȝ] ȝestriene. *a* **1225** *Ancr. R.* 160 He..feste..one iðe wildernesse vorte scheawen þerbi þet [etc.]. *a* **1300** *Cursor M.* 107 Þar bi man mai hir helping kenn. **1413** *Pilgr. Sowle* (Caxton) IV. xxxviii. (1859) 63 Supposyng therby for to geten honoure and fame. **1551** CRANMER in Strype *Life* (1694) App. 158 God shal therby be glorified. **1588** A. KING tr. *Canisius' Catech.* i vij, Ye sall haiff yairby ye hicht of ye æquinoctiall lyne. **1600** HAMILTON *Facile Tr.* in *Cath. Tractates* (S.T.S.) 220 Desyrous to ressaue thairbe, thair eternel felicitie in heauin. **1607** TOPSELL *Four-f. Beasts* (1658) 83 They cannot abide the savour of ointments, but fall mad thereby. **1703** MOXON *Mech. Exerc.* 126 Of the Ten-foot Rod, and thereby to measure and describe the Ground-plot. **1809** PINKNEY *Trav. France* 93 The rooms were so full as to render our stay unpleasant, and we thereby lost an anatomy lecture. **1896** R. S. S. BADEN-POWELL *Matabele Campaign* vi, For fear of having my attention distracted ..and of my thereby losing my bearings.

**2.** Beside, adjacent to, or near that. (In quot. *c* 1220, Up against that.) Now *arch.* and *dial.*

*c* **1220** *Bestiary* 634 A tre he sekeð..ðat is strong..and leneð him..ðer bi. *c* **1250** *Gen. & Ex.* 3361 It was a stede henden ðor bi, On a syde of munt synay. *a* **1300** *Cursor M.* 13765 Þar bi lai many [man] vn-fere. *c* **1449** PECOCK *Repr.* II. iii. 151 Ȝondir is the Holi Goost and therbi is Marie with Seint Peter. *c* **1450** *St. Cuthbert* (Surtees) 3915 He duelt in a place þare by. **1590** SPENSER *F. Q.* II. vii. 32 A couetous Spright..Who thereby did attend. **1641** HEYLIN *Hist. Episc.* I. (1657) 23 The twelve fountaines of Elim, and the seventy Palmes that grew thereby. **1719** DE FOE *Crusoe* (1840) II. iv. 94 At the foot of a tree thereby. **1875** MORRIS *Æneid* Proem 2 Fields that are thereby. **1888** ELWORTHY *W. Somerset Wordbk.* s.v., Nif I baint there, you'll vind me thereby.

**b.** With verbs of motion, in sense of BY A. 16.

*a* **1300** *Cursor M.* 15634 Quer i sal þis calice drinc, Or i sal pass þar bi. **1526** *Pilgr. Perf.* (W. de W. 1531) 3 Whan my glory shall passe therby, thou shalt se my hynder partes. **1606** G. W[OODCOCKE] *Hist. Ivstine* IV. 21 The tales of Scylla and Charibdis, which made men beleeve in sailing thereby that they heard the continuall barking of doggs.

**c.** *To come thereby* = to 'come by' or get possession of that: see COME *v.* 39 b and BY A. 15.

*c* **1386** CHAUCER *Wife's T.* 128 Whan that he saugh he myghte nat come therby This is to seye what wommen loue moost. *c* **1430** [see COME *v.* 39 b]. **1567** *Gude & Godlie B.* (S.T.S.) 27, I traist eternall glore to se; Christ grant that I may cum thairby.

†**3.** Besides, together with, or in addition to that.

**13..** *Minor Poems fr. Vernon MS.* xxxii. 524 Wȝuche ben þe seuen synnes dedly, And þe seuen vertuwes þerby. **14..** *Tundale's Vis.* 803 All ȝif god be fulle of mercye, Ryghtwysnesse behoves go þer by. ?*a* **1500** *Chester Pl.* (E.E.T.S.) 428 That he would revive them sone in hye, With flesh and Sinew and Skynn therby, Which sone he can them geue.

**4.** In reference to a number or quantity: Very nearly so; somewhere about that; = THEREABOUTS 2, 2 b. *Sc.*

[*c* **1425** WYNTOUN *Cron.* IX. xiv. 1568 A thousande and thre hundyr ȝhere Nynti and v. or þar by nere.] **1557–75** *Diurn. Occur.* (1833) 82 At xij houris at evin or thairby. **1563** *Reg. Privy Council Scot.* I. 245 To the nowmer of fourtie personis or thairby. **1582–8** *Hist. Jas. VI* (1804) 172 Thair were takin prisoneris 9 scoire and ten gentillmen or thairby. **1726** *Wodrow Corr.* (1843) III. 271 The spurious paper.. dully written, two years or thereby after Mr. Henderson's death. **1821** SCOTT *Kenilw.* x, There was one maiden of fifteen or thereby. **1863** A. B. GROSART *Small Sins* Pref. (ed. 2) 8 It is my intention..to print half-a-dozen or thereby of small books.

†**5.** With reference thereto; *apropos* of that; thereanent. *Obs.*

*a* **1250** *Owl & Night.* 244 Aday [= by day] þu art blynd oþer bisne, Þar by men seggeþ a vorbisne. **1303** R. BRUNNE *Handl. Synne* 3909 Seynt Gregory telleþ a tale þar by.

**b.** *Thereby hangs a tale*: see TALE *sb.* 3.

†**6.** In accordance with that. *Obs.*

**1512** *Act 4 Hen. VIII,* c. 19 *Preamble,* The seid Frensche kyng..the Decree of the enterdiccion dispysyng will not therby reforme himself.

**7.** quasi-*adj.* Consequent. *nonce-use.*

**1661** FELTHAM *Resolves* II. xl. 262 The chiefest Knowledg that we get, is that of our thereby guilt and misery.

†**Theredow·n,** *adv. Obs.* [In ME. two words, THERE 17 and DOWN *adv.* q.v. for Forms.] Down there; down: in reference to direction or position.

**1297** R. GLOUC. (Rolls) 9791 Þe brain orn al abrod in þe pauiment þer doune. *Ibid.* 9797 Nou he liþ þer doune. *c* **1305** *St. Kenelm* 206 in *E. E. P.* (1862) 53 And falsliche as heo com anheȝ, also heo ful [= fell] þerdoune. *c* **1325** *Poem Edw. II* 37 in *Pol. Songs* (Camden) 325 Certes holi churche is muchel i-brouht ther doune. **1375** BARBOUR *Bruce* XI. 300 The sykis alswa thair doune Sall put thame to confusioune. *a* **1550** *Freiris of B.* 178 in *Dunbar's Poems* (S.T.S.) 291 All that thay did thair doun he micht weill se.

**Therefore** (ðēᵊ·ɹfǭɹ, -fəɹ), **therefor** (ðēᵊɹfǭ·ɹ), *adv.* (*sb.*) Forms: *α.* 2–3 ðer-, 2–5 þerfore, (2 þaruore, 2–4 þeruore, 3 ðor-, þar-fore, 3–4 þervore), 5–6 therfore, (6 *Sc.* thair-, yair-, theirfore). *β.* 2–5 þerefore, (2–3 þereuore, 4 þarefore), 5– therefore. *γ.* 3–5 þerfor, (3 þeruor, 4 þar-, tarfor, 4–5 þer-for, yarfor), 5–7 therfor, (6 *Sc.* thair-, yairfor, -foir, 7 therfoer). *δ.* 6– therefor, (9 there-for). [Early ME. *þerfore*, *þerefore* (often written as two words), f. *þær-*, *þer-*, THERE + *fore*, OE. and early ME. collateral form of *for*: see FORE *adv.* and *prep.* After final *e* became mute, *fore* prep. was gradually levelled with *for*, and *ther(e)fore* was often written *therfor, therefor.* In mod. Eng. (since *c* 1800) *therefore* and *therefor* are almost always differentiated in spelling and stress in accordance with meaning: see below.]

**I.** (Now stressed ðēᵊɹfǭ·ɹ, and usu. spelt *therefor* for distinction from 2.) *formal* or *arch.*

**1.** For that (thing, act, etc.); for that, for it.

**a.** In various senses of FOR *prep.*

*c* **1175** *Lamb. Hom.* 9 His festen..and chirc-ȝong and god to donne þeruore. *c* **1220** *Bestiary* 377 God giueð ðer fore mede. *a* **1300** *Cursor M.* 610 (Cott.) He gaf it him, als in heritage, To yeild þerfor [*v.rr.* þare fore, þar for, þerfore] na mar knaulage. *c* **1386** CHAUCER *Sqr.'s T.* 169 Born anon in to the heighe Tour, With certeine officers ordeynd therfore [*v.rr.* ther fore, there fore, þerfore]. *c* **1440** *Alphabet of Tales* 97 Sho answerd agayn & sayd..sho wold not delyver it or he & his felow bothe samen come þerfor. **1477** EARL RIVERS (Caxton) *Dictes* 1 To gyue therfore synguler louynges & thankes. **1561** NORTON & SACKV. *Gorboduc* v. i, Speede must we vse to levie force therefore. **1622** CALLIS *Stat. Sewers* (1647) 86 To erect new Walls, Banks and other Defences, and what sums of Money to Raise and Levy therefore. **1824** MEDWIN *Convers. Byron* II. 186, I.. have..continued here..in the hope of seeing things reconciled, and have done all in my power there-for. **1856** R. A. VAUGHAN *Mystics* VI. iv. (1860) I. 184 If the emperor sins, he must give account to God therefor. **1861** *Evening Star* 4 Oct., 100lbs. of potatoes or a substitute therefore thrice a week. **1870** MORRIS *Earthly Par.* II. III. 344 The love I had therefor. **1877** F. HALL *Eng. Adj. in -able* 39 Argument being at an end, recourse was then had to the common substitute therefor, ridicule. **1885** *Act 48 & 49 Vict.* c. 70 § 7 He shall supply a copy of such report..on payment of the sum of one shilling therefor.

**b.** By reason of that; for that reason, on that account: cf. FOR *prep.* 21, 22.

*c* **1175** *Lamb. Hom.* 5 Þa ȝe [*MS.* þaȝ] habbe wele to ouer stohwennesse on þisse liue ne beo þu þereuore prud. *c* **1200** *Trin. Coll. Hom.* 143 Þaruore hire sinne hire bicome swiðe laðe. *c* **1220** *Bestiary* 509 Vt of his ðrote it smit an onde,..ðer-fore oðre fisses to him draȝen. *c* **1250** *Gen. & Ex.* 1215 Ysmael pleide hard gamen; Sarra was ðor-fore often wroð. **1297** R. GLOUC. (Rolls) 5348 Vre louerd mid is eyen of milce on þe lokeþ þerfore. *a* **1300** *Cursor M.* 287 Þerfor is he cald trinite For he es anfald godd in thre. **13..** *Ibid.* 2894 (Gött.) God forbede ȝe do þat sin Þat ȝe in hell þarfor [*Trin.* þerfore] brin. *c* **1385** CHAUCER *L. G. W.* 1863 (*Lucrece*) That Tarquyny shulde ybanysshed be ther-fore. **1533** MORE *Debell. Salem* Wks. 954/1 When he saith himself that they haue punished many therfore, that is to wit, for thesame cause. **1605** CAMDEN *Rem.* 181 If that any Iew did buy any Christian for his slave, hee should bee fined therefore. **1805** SCOTT *Last Minstr.* IV. vi, They crossed the Liddle..And burned my little lonely tower; The fiend receive their souls therefor! **1848** LOWELL *Lett.* (1894) I. 151 Tell Briggs that his ticket came safely, and that I am thankful therefor. **1868** HAWTHORNE *Amer. Note-Bks.* (1879) II. 173 They would all be ..healthier men therefor. **1899** F. T. BULLEN *Log Sea-waif* 149 The ill-used crew promptly refused to do any more in her, and were, of course, clapped in jail therefor.

**II.** (Now always spelt *therefore*, and stressed ðēᵊ·ɹfǭɹ.)

**2.** In consequence of that; that being so; as a result or inference from what has been stated; consequently. Formerly sometimes unemphatic (esp. in versions of N. T.) = THEN 5.

In early use often indistinguishable from 1 b, where see earlier examples; now distinguished as expressing a general relation of consequence or inference. Sometimes classed as a conjunction.

*a* **1400** *Prymer* (1891) 45 Lo ther fore alle generations schulle seye y am blessed. **1526** TINDALE *Matt.* xiii. 18 Heare ye therfore the similitude off the sower. **1533** CRANMER *Misc. Writ.* (Parker Soc.) II. 260. I trust, therefore, you will not so hardly regard my first request herein. **1548–9** (Mar.) *Bk. Com. Prayer, Communion,* It is very mete..that we shoulde ..geue thankes to thee, O Lorde...Therefore with Angelles and Archangels..we laud [etc.]. **1552** HULOET, Therfore,.. *cum accent. in penult., eo, ergo, idcirco, ideo, igitur,..propterea, propter hoc.* **1555** EDEN *Decades* 202 Manate..is the thyrde [fish] whereof I haue promysed to entreate. Manate therefore, is a fysshe of the sea, of the byggest sorte [etc.]. *c* **1600** SHAKS. *Sonn.* xli, Gentle thou art, and therefore to be wonne, Beautious thou art, therefore to be assailed. *Ibid.* cxxiii, Our dates are breefe, and therefor we admire, What thou dost foyst vpon vs that is ould. **1611** BIBLE *John* iv. 6 Now Iacobs Well was there. Iesus therefore [TINDALE then], being wearied with his iourney, sate thus on the Well. **1660** BARROW *Euclid* I. xv. Schol., Because the angle AEC+ AED+CEB+DEB = 4 right angles, therefore the angle AEC+AED=CEB+DEB = to two right angles, therefore CED and AEB are strait lines. **1735** BERKELEY *Freethink. in Math.* § 2 Things obscure are not therefore sacred. **1845** M. PATTISON *Ess.* (1889) I. 15 The Franks were the stronger, and therefore the masters. **1849** MACAULAY *Hist. Eng.* vi. II. 80 The refugees were zealous for the Calvinistic discipline...James therefore gave orders [etc.].

**B.** as *sb.* The word 'therefore' as marking a conclusion; an expressed conclusion or inference.

**1641** 'SMECTYMNUUS' *Vind. Answ.* xiii. 144 Let him first answer our *Therefores*, and wee will quickly answer his *Wherefores*. **1674** HICKMAN *Hist. Quinquart.* (ed. 2) 185 The Article having made a (*therefore*), its strange that any one should draw any other conclusion from it, than what it self hath drawn. **1874** GEO. ELIOT *Coll. Breakf. P.* in *Jubal*, etc. 232 A faith Defying sense and all its ruthless train Of arrogant 'therefores'.

†**Therefo·rne,** *adv. Obs.* In 3–4 þer-, þar-. [app. an alteration of THEREFORE, in imitation of

words in *-forne* from OE. *-foran*, e.g. *beforne.*] = THEREFORE 1.

*a* **1300** *E. E. Psalter* xvii[i]. 3 Mi schelder..And mi fonger ai þer forne. *Ibid.* xxxi[i]. 4, I am torned in mi sorw þar forn, Whiles þat pricked es þe thorn. **13..** *Gaw. & Gr. Knt.* 1107, & quat chek so ȝe acheue, chaunge me þer forne. *c* **1400** *Cato's Mor.* 260 in *Cursor M.* p. 1672 (Fairf.) If þi gode be lorne Sorou noȝt þar forne To double þi harme.

† **Therefo·rth,** *adv. Obs.* [f. THERE 17 + FORTH *adv.*]

**1. a.** Forth from thence; away from that place. **b.** Along that way; by that place.

**1297** R. GLOUC. (Rolls) 5704 Þis king also at glastingbury as he þeruorþ com, Seint aþelwold þat was þere monek, out of þe house he nom. **1387** TREVISA *Higden* (Rolls) V. 299 Þe kyng passede þerforþ, and wolde wite what it were. *c* **1450** LOVELICH *Grail* xliii. 312 Hem he took vpe thanne Everychon, and with hym bar þereforth Anon.

**2.** Out, outside; in the open; = THEREOUT 2.

**1536** BELLENDEN *Cron. Scot.* II. xi. (1541) 17 b/1 He punist theiffis..and othir criminabyll personis with sic seuerite.. that the bestiall & gudis lay thairfurth but ony trubyl. *Ibid.* v. iv. 56 b/1 Thay wer ane rude vndantit pepill, and lay thair furth all wynter nochtwithstanding ye cauld frostis.

† **Therefro·,** *adv. Obs.* Also *Sc.* **þar-fra.** [Orig. two words, THERE 17 and FRO *prep.*] = next.

**13..** *Cursor M.* 1316 (Gött.) Þar fra [*C.* þat oute of, *F.* þer-out] renis four grete stremis. **1340** HAMPOLE *Pr. Consc.* 5214 Lo! here þe sepulcre a lytil þar fra. ? *a* **1366** CHAUCER *Rom. Rose* 1660 Whan I was not fer therfro. *c* **1380** WYCLIF *Wks.* (1880) 364 With-owten addynge þer to or abregynge þer fro. **1413** *Pilgr. Sowle* (Caxton 1483) IV. x. 62 The juse that yssueth ther froo. **1565** in *Reg. Mag. Sig. Scot.* 1575. 656/1 Passand thairfra up ane dyke betuix Kippelaw and Bowdane. **1588** A. KING tr. *Canisius' Catech.* g viij b, Bot in this our age throwch ye anticipation of ye æquinoxe is distant yairfra almaist 4 dayes. **1622** MABBE tr. *Aleman's Guzman d'Alf.* II. 59, I would..desist there-fro. **1678** SIR G. MACKENZIE *Crim. Laws Scot.* II. xxiii. § 4 (1699) 248 They are not excluded therefrae by the foresaid act of Parliament.

**Therefrom** (ðēəɹfrǫ·m), *adv. arch.* or *formal.* [Orig. two words, THERE 17 and FROM *prep.*] From that; from that place; away from there.

*a* **1250** *Owl & Night.* 137 Þeyh he beo þar from bicume He cuþ hwenene he is icume. *c* **1300** *St. Brandan* 512 The ȝut hi were fur ther fram. **1387** TREVISA *Higden* (Rolls) VIII. 89 Þe schap of þe cros was i-seie forsake þe baner and passe somwhat of space þerfrom [*MS.* γ. þarvram]. *c* **1610** SIR J. MELVIL *Mem.* Author to Son (1735) 18 Debarring therefrom all honest, true, and plain Speakers. **1660** SHARROCK *Vegetables* 24, I much doubt of any effect therefrom. **1728** CHAMBERS *Cycl.* s.v. *Circus,* They took their name therefrom. **1850** NEALE *Med. Hymns* (1867) 102 The streams that flow therefrom. **1885** *Law Times* LXXX. 132/1 Nor was the doctrine contended for..logically deducible therefrom.

† **Theregai·n,** *adv. Obs.* Forms: 3 **ðor ȝen, þer yen,** 5 **ther geyn.** [f. THERE 17 + GAIN *prep.* Cf. THEREAGAIN.] Against or in opposition to that.

*c* **1250** *Gen. & Ex.* 2797 If he it werne and be ðor ȝen, Ic sal ðe techen hu it sal ben. *c* **1300** *Havelok* 2271 Þer yen ne wolde neuer on striue. *c* **1400** *Rom. Rose* 6555 If men wolde ther geyn appose The naked text.

So † **Theregai·ns** *adv.* [GAINS], on the side opposite to that; over against there.

*c* **1330** R. BRUNNE *Chron. Wace* (Rolls) 13538 O syde toke þe Romayns, & Arthur þat oþer euen þer gayns.

**Therehence,** *adv. Obs.* exc. *dial.* Forms: α. 4–5 **þerhenne,** (4 **therhanne**). β. 4 **þer hannes,** 6– **there(-)hence,** (6 **therence** (9 *dial.*), **therehens,** 7 **therhence**). [f. THERE 17 + HEN, HENNE *adv.*, and *hennes, hens,* HENCE *adv.*]

**1.** From or out of that place; from there: = THENCE 1. Now *dial.*

α. *c* **1300** *Beket* 1145 Therhanne he wende to Eystrie. ? *a* **1400** *Arthur* 591 Muche folke þerhenne he toke þo.

β. *c* **1400** *R. Gloucester's Chron.* (Rolls) App. AA. 2 He nolde þer hannes passi. **1548** UDALL *Erasm. Par. Luke* viii. 89 Therehens as..out of a chaire or pulpite he taught the multitude. **1600** HAKLUYT *Voy.* (1904) X. 101 The famous voyage of Sir Francis Drake into the South sea, and therehence about the whole Globe of the earth, begun in 1577. **1724** R. WELTON *Chr. Faith & Pract.* 367 The waves toss the ships up to the very clouds, and the winds therehence drive them to the deep abyss. **1898** T. HARDY *Wessex Poems* 46 Stone deaf therence went many a man.

† **2.** From that source or origin; from that fact or circumstance: = THENCE 4. *Obs.*

**1528** TINDALE *Parable Wicked Mammon* 16 *Hamon,* in the Ebrewe speche sygnyfyeth a multytude or abundaunce. ..And therhence commeth *mahamon* or *mammon,* abundaunce or plenteousnes of goodes or ryches. **1597** J. KING *On Jonas* (1618) 10 Therehence, they say, he was named the son of Amittai; that is, the sonne of truth. **1623** W. C. *Fatall Vesper* 4 Those vnreuealed attributes, which doe flow therehence. **1718** SWIFT *To Sheridan* 3, I have a great esteem for Plautus; And think your boys may gather there-hence More wit and humour than from Terence.

† **3.** Distant from that place: = THENCE 2. *rare.*

**1611** CORYAT *Crudities* 10 A countrey village..fourteene miles therehence distant. *Ibid.* 68 A parish tenne miles therehence.

**Therein** (ðēəri·n), *adv.* Now *formal, arch.*, or *dial.* Forms: see THERE and IN; also 3 **þrin.** [OE. *þǽrin*, f. *þǽr* THERE 17 + IN *prep.*]

**1.** In that place or (material) thing.

*a* **1000** *Boeth. Metr.* xi. 4 Wealdend..heofones & eorðan ..& ealra ðara þe ðærin wuniað. *a* **1300** *Cursor M.* 15895 (Cott.) A knaun freind he had þare in [*v. rr.* þar ine, þerin]. **1398** TREVISA *Barth. De P. R.* XIII. xxvi. (Bodl. MS.), Þerin is a maner kinde of beestes Dolphyns wiþ rugge itoþed as a sawe. *c* **1450** *St. Cuthbert* (Surtees) 789 Þai sailed þar in merualously. **1535** COVERDALE *Ps.* xxiv. 2 The compasse of the worlde, and all yt dwell therin. **1676** RAY *Corr.* (1848) 123 If you have observed any errors or mistakes therein. **1875** JOWETT *Plato* (ed. 2) III. 688 The universe, and the things that are and move therein. **1911** *Act 1 Geo. V*, c. 1 Sched. (Paisley Corp. Order Confirm. Act), The late Robert Brodie..by his trust disposition..conveyed his entire property to trustees therein named.

**b.** In or during that time.

**1539** BIBLE (Great) *Exod.* xxxi. 14 Kepe my Sabbath.. whosoeuer worketh therin, the same soule shalbe roted out from amonge hys people.

**2.** In that affair or matter; in that thing, circumstance, or particular.

*c* **1230** *Hali Meid.* 3 Maken þe to þenchen hwuch delit were þrin. *a* **1300** *Cursor M.* 13759 (Cott.) Lok þi will bi noght þar in. **1526** *Pilgr. Perf.* (W. de W. 1531) 2 That ye neuer..be besy to attempte ony persone therin. *c* **1555** HARPSFIELD *Divorce Hen. VIII* (Camden) 83 Therein we do find no fault. **1588** A. KING tr. *Canisius' Catech.* 130 All perdition had the beginning thairin [in pride]. **1631** HEYWOOD *2nd Pt. Maid of West* IV. Wks. 1874 II. 391 Thou therein hadst much hyperboliz'd. **1882** SPURGEON *Treas. Dav.* Ps. cxix. 17 The more will he be driven towards God for help therein.

**3.** Inside, in the house, within doors. *mod. Sc.*

**1822** HOGG *Perils of Man* III. vii. 202 Bessy Chisholm —Heh! Are ye therein? **1828** BUCHAN *Ballads* I. 113 If ye'll work therein as we thereout, Well borrow'd shou'd your body be.

**4.** Into that place or (material) thing.

*a* **1240** *Sawles Warde* in *Cott. Hom.* 263 Þu most al gan þrin ant al beon bigotten þrin, for in þe ne mei hit nanesweis neomen in. *a* **1300** *Cursor M.* 8852 Þair in [*Trin.* þerynne] þan was þair relikes don. **1398** TREVISA *Barth. De P. R.* III. xviii. (W. de W. 1495) 65 Somtyme grauel and powder falleth therin. **1526** R. WHYTFORD *Martiloge* 135 b, Than made they a grete fyre..and cast therin pytche and rosyne. **1747** WESLEY *Prim. Physick* (1762) 90 Smell to a Spunge dipt there-in.

† **5.** = THEREON 2: cf. IN *prep.* 31 a. *Obs.*

**1535** COVERDALE 1 *Sam.* xxxi. 4 Then toke Saul ye swerde, and fell therin. [Cf. *Germ.* (Luther) fiel darein; *Vulg.* super eum; *next verse has* vpon his swerde.]

† **6.** As *relative adv.*: In which; into which; = WHEREIN. *Obs.*

**971** *Blickl. Hom.* 73 He wæs on Simones huse..þærin ʒeat þæt wif þa deorwyrþan smerenesse on his heafod. **13..** *Cast. Love* (Halliw.) 56 This castel Marie bodi wes, Therin he alyght and his in ches [chose his inn]. **13..** *Cursor M.* 396 (Gött.) In þe heiest element of all, þar in þe fire has his stall. **1422** tr. *Secreta Secret., Priv. Priv.* 167 The Seete therin as he was woned to sitte.

**7. Therein a·fter, therein befo·re, therein u·nder,** = after, before, below in that document, statute, etc. (Usually written as single words: cf. *herein after*, etc., s. v. HEREIN.)

**1818** CRUISE *Digest* (ed. 2) II. 276 Upon trust to preserve the contingent remainders thereinafter limited. **1827** JARMAN *Powell's Devises* (ed. 3) II. 105 A general residuary devise of real and personal estate not thereinbefore disposed of. **18..** A. BAIN in B. Stewart *Conserv. Force* (1873) viii. 221 He gave 'mental work' as one heading, but declined to make an entry thereinunder.

† **There,i·nne,** *adv. Obs.* Forms: see THERE and INNE: also 4–5 **thrynne.** [OE. *þǽrinne*, f. *þǽr*, THERE 17 + INNE.] = THEREIN.

(In late instances perh. only a var. spelling of *therein.*)

*c* **897** K. ÆLFRED *Gregory's Past. C.* xvi. 100 He wæs ðærinne ʒetoʒen to ðære godcundan sceawunge, & ðærute [*v. r.* ðærut] he wæs abisʒod ymb ðæs folces ðearfe. *c* **1200** *Vices & Virt.* 137 All ðat folk ðe þerinne was. *c* **1200** ORMIN 1651 ȝiff þatt iss þatt mann wile itt don Wiþþ witt & skill þærinne. *c* **1250** *Gen. & Ex.* 1104 Non ðing ne mai ðor inne liuen. **1382** WYCLIF *Luke* xix. 45 He..bigan to caste out men sellinge ther ynne and biggynge. *c* **1400** *Gamelyn* 314, I wil not that this compaignye parten a-twynne, And ye wil doon after me, whil eny sope is thrynne. *c* **1400** *Sowdone Bab.* 335 Thai slough all, that were ther Inne. *c* **1450** *Merlin* i. 10 She wende to haue founde hym thar ynne.

† **There,inti·ll,** *adv. Sc. Obs.* [f. THERE 17 + INTILL.] Therein; thereinto.

**1507** in *Charters, &c. Edinb.* (1871) 192 To mak ony stop or impediment to thame thairintill. **1533** BELLENDEN *Livy* II. xiii. (S.T.S.) I. 175 The faderis, quhen þis mater wes brocht afore þame, mycht nocht ordourlie gif þare consultacioun þareintill. **1650** *Acts Sederunt* 29 Jan. (1790) 66 All bands and actis of caution..heirefter, shall bear this clause insert thereintill. **1700** in A. McKay *Kilmarnock* (1880) 61 To give furth and pronounce..sentences thereintill.

**Thereinto** (ðēəːrintū·, ðēəri·ntu), *adv. arch.* [f. THERE 17 + INTO.]

**1.** Into that place, matter, condition, etc.

*a* **1300** *Cursor M.* 23222 (Edinb.) Cald sa ken..þat þoh a firin fel war mad, And þoru a chance þar into slad [etc.]. **1611** BIBLE *Luke* xxi. 21 Let not them..enter thereinto. **1652** KIRKMAN *Clerio & Lozia* 178 No Victualls could be carried thereinto. **1695** WOODWARD *Nat. Hist. Earth* Pref., The Ways whereby I got Light thereinto. **1867** KINGSLEY in *Life* (1877) II. 249, I have been drawn thereinto because I find every one talking about it [Darwinism]. **1887** MORRIS *Odyss.* XI. 36 And the black blood flowed thereinto.

† **2.** = THEREIN 2. Cf. INTO 22. *Obs.*

**1581–2** *Reg. Privy Council Scot.* III. 452 The said compliner hes differrit the samin unto the tyme he knew his Hienes and Lordschippis myndis thairinto. **1676** OWEN *Nat. & Causes Apost.* Wks. 1851 VII. 4 On such principles of difference in judgment as have no considerable influence thereinto.

† **The·re-mid, ther-mid,** *adv. Obs.* [Orig. two words, THERE 17 and MID *prep.*[1]] With or by means of that; = THEREWITH 3.

*c* **888** K. ÆLFRED *Boeth.* xvi. § 2 (MS. B.) Þa forceaw he his aʒene tungan and wearp hine ðær mid on ðæt neb foran. *c* **1000** ÆLFRIC *Saints' Lives* xxiii B. 767 Ongan þa þær mid delfan. *c* **1175** *Lamb. Hom.* 63 We hit aȝen to ȝeme and god solf þer mid iqueme. *c* **1330** R. BRUNNE *Chron. Wace* (Rolls) 16450 ȝyf any had leyd a cors in pyt, Hym self fel þanne ded þer myt [the plague]. **1393** LANGL. *P. Pl.* C. IV. 253 To do þer myd here beste.

† **Ther(e)-mide, -mydde,** *adv. Obs.* [f. as prec. + *-e*, after THEREINNE, etc.]. **a.** Along with that; together with that; at the same time. **b.** = prec.

**a.** *c* **1175** *Lamb. Hom.* 75 Ic ou wile seggen word efter word and þermide hwat þet word bi-queþ. **1377** LANGL. *P. Pl.* B. XVI. 262 Þe pouke it hath attached, And me þere myde. *c* **1425** *Seven Sag.* (P.) 2171 He went don a[nd] bare uppe a cole, And a torche up ther myde.

**b.** *c* **1220** *Bestiary* 615 Siðen he bigeten on, and two ȝer he ðer mide gon. *a* **1250** *Prov. Ælfred* 392 in *O. E. Misc.* 126 Ne myhte he þar myde his lif none hwile holde. *c* **1250** *Gen. & Ex.* 2656 Hise tunges ende is brent ðor mide. *c* **1350** *Will. Palerne* 5358 Eche man þer mide miȝt hold him a-paied. **1377** LANGL. *P. Pl.* B. VI. 69 Make hem mery þere mydde.

**Therence,** variant of THEREHENCE.

**Thereness** (ðēəːɹnės). *rare.* [f. THERE + -NESS.] The condition or quality of being there; existence in a defined place. (Usually opposed to *hereness.*)

**1674** N. FAIRFAX *Bulk & Selv.* 11 The all-fillingness of God, the herenesses and therenesses of ghosts, have been too much interwoven and twisted together. *Ibid.* 45 The thereness or hereness was nothing belonging unto God. **1887** W. JAMES in *Mind* XII. 18 Could that possibly be the feeling of any special whereness or thereness? **1899** J. CAIRD *Fundamental Ideas Chr.* II. ix. 13 Hereness and thereness are incessantly passing out of and into each other.

† **There-ni·gh,** *adv. Obs.* Forms: see THERE and NIGH. [OE. *þǽr néah*: *þǽr*, THERE 17, *néah* near, NIGH.] Near that place or thing.

**971** *Blickl. Hom.* 139 Ceʒende ealle hire maʒas þa þe þær neah wæron. *c* **1175** *Lamb. Hom.* 43 Þar neh ne mihte nan liuiende mon gan. *c* **1290** *Beket* 929 in *S. Eng. Leg.* I. 133 Ich ov hote þat ȝe þare neiȝ ne beon. *a* **1300** *Cursor M.* 767 (Cott.) If we com þer nei [*F.* þer neye; *G.* þar ney; *T.* þer nyȝe]. **13..** *Ibid.* 7589 (Cott.) Þe sarzins war þar neigh be-side All fled.

**Thereof** (ðēəɹǫ·f, ðēəɹǫv *with shifting stress*), *adv.* Now *formal* or *arch.* Forms: see THERE and OF; also 3 **þrof (trof),** 5 **throf.** [OE. *þǽr of*: see THERE 17 and OF.]

**1.** Of that or it: in various current senses of OF.

*c* **1000** *Sax. Leechd.* I. 196, ʒenim þas ylcan wyrte, wyrc clyþan þærof. *c* **1200** ORMIN 9867 Þa staness þatt he spacc þæroff, Þeȝȝ wærenn rihhte staness. *a* **1240** *Sawles Warde* in *Cott. Hom.* 253 To a rudden him ut þrof. *Ibid.* 265 Þat tu hauest ibeo þear ant soð hauest iseid trof. **13..** *Cursor M.* 22722 (Cott.) Þar of wit trout he broght þam vte. *c* **1400** MAUNDEV. (Roxb.) v. 16 Men makes þeroff gude glasse. **1486** *Bk. St. Albans* C v, Make throf .iij. pellettis. **1526** *Pilgr. Perf.* (W. de W. 1531) 116 A sage persone..wyll be well ware therof. **1588** SHAKS. *L. L. L.* III. i. 130, I..in lieu thereof, impose on thee nothing but this. **1599** HAKLUYT *Voy.* II. 186, I..tooke oute thereof a iarre of oyle. **1611** BIBLE *John* vi. 50 That a man may eate thereof, and not die. **1678** WANLEY *Wond. Lit. World* v. ii. § 79 Having lived about fifty two years, and thereof Reigned thirty one. *a* **1761** LAW *Comf. Weary Pilgr.* (1809) 61 But instead thereof, he was left solely to the light and spirit of this world.

**b.** = *of it*, as objective genitive.

*c* **1175** *Lamb. Hom.* 3 Þe lauerd haueð þar of neode. *c* **1250** *Gen. & Ex.* 1132 Maniman ðor of holdet litel tale. *a* **1300** *Cursor M.* 1287 (Cott.) Quen [he] þar of son had a sight. *c* **1380** WYCLIF *Wks.* (1880) 69 Þei ben consenteris & fautouris þer of. *c* **1400** *Ywaine & Gaw.* 762 For tharof had he grete myster. **1568** GRAFTON *Chron.* II. 105 To the spedy execution thereof. **1590** SHAKS. *Com. Err.* IV. i. 38 Disburse the summe, on the receit thereof. **1600** J. PORY tr. *Leo's Africa* II. 62 At last [he] vsurped the gouernment thereof. **1665** in De Foe *Plague* (1840) 41 Give notice thereof to the examiner of health. **1698** TYSON *Anat. Opossum* 3 Find out some Name, that might be most expressive thereof. **1818** CRUISE *Digest* (ed. 2) III. 304 Nor should the heir be occupant thereof.

**c.** = *of it, its*, as possessive genitive.

Many examples in Biblical use; a few occur in the later Wycliffite version; they increase in the 16th c. versions, and become very numerous in the Rhemish and in 1611.

**1388** WYCLIF 2 *Kings* ii. 12 The chare of Israel, and the charietere therof [1382 of it; Cov. and his horsmen; *Genev.*, **1611**, and *R. V.* and the horsemen thereof]. — *Prov.* iii. 16 Lengthe of daies is in the riȝthalf therof, and richessis and glorie ben in the lifthalf therof [1382 [1]his, [2]of it]. — *Matt.* ii. 16 And slowe alle the children, that weren in Bethleem, and in alle the coostis therof [1382 in alle the eendis of it; TINDALE in all the costes there of; *Genev., Rhem.* therof; **1611** thereof; **1881** *R. V.* in all the borders thereof]. **1594** SHAKS. *Rich. III*, I. iii. 154 As little ioy you may suppose in me, That I enioy, being the Queene thereof. **1611** BIBLE *Joshua* xv. 47 Vnto the riuer of Egypt and the great sea and the border thereof. [So R. V.] **1623** COCKERAM III, *Ignavus*..He runneth up trees, and his desire is to sit there on the tops thereof. **1632** SANDERSON *Serm.* 129 Esay, speaking of Christ and his kingdome, and the righteousnesse thereof. **1825** J. NEAL *Bro. Jonathan* III. 401 He tottered away to a rock as to..an altar; clung to it, as to the horns thereof. **1910** *Act 10 Edw. VII*, c. 38 § 3 The schedules ..shall be deemed to be part of this Act in the same manner as if they had been contained in the body thereof.

**2.** From or out of that, as source or origin.

*c* **1230** *Hali Meid.* 5 Al þat muchele lure þat ter of ariseð. **1399** *Rolls of Parlt.* III. 451/2 So mykel harme and meschief felle therof. *c* **1400** MAUNDEV. (Roxb.) Pref. 2 Þeroff þai hafe grete solace and comforthe. *c* **1440** *Pallad. on Husb.* I. 5 What cam therof? **1542** UDALL *Erasm. Apoph.* 324 It is thought that one Caluus a poete brought it firste vp on Pompeius, & thereof the same to haue been taken vp in a prouerbe. **1590** SHAKS. *Com. Err.* v. i. 68 And thereof came it, that the man was mad. **1667** MILTON *P. L.* XII. 476 Much more good thereof shall spring. **1883** RICKABY

*Moral Philos.* I. x. 181 Better is the activity..than the pleasure which comes thereof.

†**3.** Answering to various obsolete uses of Of: in quots. = *thereat, therefor, therefrom, thereanent,* etc.

*a* **1200** *Vices & Virt.* 29 And ðanke ðerof gode swiðe ʒierne. **13..** *Guy Warw.* (A.) 4656 Now, sir, take þerof pite. *c* **1386** Chaucer *Pars. T.* ⁋ 240 For soothly he..sholde..yeuen his body and al his herte to the seruice of Ihesu crist and ther-of doon hym hommage. **1390** Gower *Conf.* I. 112 Gret offence He tok therof. *c* **1400** Maundev. (Roxb.) xxix. 131 Þai meruailed þam gretely þeroff. *c* **1400** *Brut* ccxxv. 293 Þe lordez of eny toun..shulde ansuere to þe King þerof. *c* **1440** *Alphabet of Tales* 113 He þankid almighti God þeroff. *c* **1450** *Godstow Reg.* 424 Doyng therof seruyce as hit is I-conteyned in the Charter. *c* **1500** *Melusine* xxiv. 183 By my feyth, lady,..doo your wyll therof. **1594** Carew *Huarte's Exam. Wits* (1616) 99 If Lazarus had carried to him a pitcher of fresh water, hee should haue taken great refreshment thereof. **1669** Marvell *Corr.* Wks. (Grosart) II. 276 If there be any particular that may more nearly relate to your affaires, you will be pleas'd to consider thereof.

Hence †**There-o·ffe, thero·ffe** *adv.* [with final *-e*, after Thereinne, etc.], in same senses.

*c* **1400** Maundev. (1839) ii. 13 He þat bereth A braunche.. þereoffe. *Ibid.* xiv. 156 So cold þat noman may drynke þere-offe. *a* **1461** *How Gd. Wif taught hir Doughter* 53 in Hazl. *E. P. P.* I. 183 Mesurely take ther offe [*v.r.* (*Babees Bk.* 36) þer-of], that the falle no blame.

**Thereology** (þeri,ǫ·lŏdʒi). *rare*⁻¹. [erron. f. Gr. θέρ-ειν to heat, in Nicander 'to foment or apply a fomentation to (a wound)', hence θέρων is glossed by a scholiast by ἰώμενος healing, curing: see -ology.] The healing art. (See quot.)

**1841** R. Park *Pantology* xii. iii. (1847) 418 In the branch of Thereology, we include the study of diseases, and the practice of Medicine. The name is derived from the Greek, Θερεω, I cure, or take care of.

So **Thereolo·gist**, one skilled in thereology.
**1882** in Ogilvie (Annandale).

**Thereon** (ðēᵊrǫ·n, ðēᵊ·rǫn), *adv. formal* or *arch.* Forms: see There and On; also 3 þron, 4 þran. [OE. *þǽron*, f. *þǽr*, There 17 + On *prep.*]

**1.** Of position, *lit.* or *fig.*: On or upon that or it.

**971** *Blickl. Hom.* 71 His þegnas..læddon him to þone eosol, & ʒedydon þæt he þær on ʒesittan mihte. *c* **1220** *Bestiary* 83 Ðanne goð he to a ston, and he billeð ðer on. *a* **1300** *Cursor M.* 2472 (Cott.) Quar-for þar on [*T.* þeron] godd tok his wrac. *c* **1400** *Lanfranc's Cirurg.* 181 If þe place be whijt & neische and miche moisture þeron. *a* **1533** Ld. Berners *Huon* lxxxiii. 259 He toke his cuppe and made theron .iii. crosses. **1606** Shaks. *Ant. & Cl.* v. ii. 133 If thereon you relye. I'll take my leaue. **1786** Jefferson *Wks.* (1859) I. 570 To confer with him thereon. **1809–10** Coleridge *Friend* i. iv. (1865) 125 All our notion of right and wrong is built thereon. **1896** *Law Times* C. 358/2 After payment of all charges thereon.

†**b.** as *relative adv.* On which: = Whereon.

*c* **1330** *Assump. Virg.* (B.M. MS.) 600 Foure of þe apostles schal bere þe beere Ther on schal ligge me modre deere.

**2.** Of motion or direction: On or upon that or it; onto that.

*a* **1300** *Cursor M.* 10776 A duu..þare lighted dun, and þar on lend. *c* **1315** Shoreham iii. 158 Þenche þou most wel bysyly, And þy wyʒt þran by-stowe. *c* **1400** Maundev. (Roxb.) ii. 7 Þe Iews..sett a coroun on his heued and thrast it þeron so fast þat þe blude ran doune. *c* **1475** *Rauf Coilʒear* 374 Thairun my lyfe dar I layd [= lay it]. **1593** Shaks. *Lucr.* 1139 Who, if it winke, shall thereon fall and die. **1728** Chambers *Cycl.* s.v. *Glass*, By reason of the Sand strew'd thereon. **1887** Morris *Odyss.* xi. 591 When up reached the elder his hands thereon to lay.

**3.** As soon as that happened, was done, or was said; immediately after that; = Thereupon 2 b.

*a* **1300** *Cursor M.* 5871 (Cott.) And taron [*v.rr.* þar on, þer on] sett he men at ask Of ilk dai to yeild þair task. **1618** Wither *Motto, Nec Curo* Wks. (1633) 545, I care not greatly what succeed thereon. **1783** in Cruise *Digest* (1818) V. 319 Any non-claim which had ensued thereon. **1870** Morris *Earthly Par.* II. iii. 243 Slowly thereon he gat unto his feet.

†**4.** From some obsolete uses of On: **a.** In that, therein. **b.** Into that, thereinto. **c.** About that, thereof. **d.** At that, thereat. *Obs.*

**a.** *c* **897** K. Ælfred *Gregory's Past. C.* li. 399 Hio is an lytel [burʒ], & ðeah ic mæʒ ðæron libban. *c* **1000** Ælfric *Hom.* II. 410 Aplanta þæron þa soðan lufe. *c* **1205** Lay. 7275 Þer Bruttus bi-com and to his liue he wunede þer an. *c* **1290** *St. Michael* 453 in *S. Eng. Leg.* I. 312 Men seoth þar on liʒt. **1513** Douglas *Æneis* i. iii. 82 Bid Eolus..clois the presoun of wyndis, and tharon ring. **1525** Ld. Berners *Froiss.* II. xxvi. 71, I had brought with me a boke...And euery night after supper I reed theron to hym. **b.** *c* **1000** Ælfric *Deut.* xxxii. 52 Þu scealt ʒeseon þæt land and þu ne cymst þær on. *c* **1275** Lay. 7274 Þar on Brutus bicom. **c.** *c* **1000** Ælfric *Gen.* xxxix. 23 He ne cuðe nan þing þar on. **d.** *c* **1400** *Brut* lxviii. 64 He wondrede þeron gretly, what it myʒt bitoken.

Hence † **There,o·nne** (þerone, also 3 þronne) *Obs.* [after *þærinne*, etc.; in later use sometimes only a variant spelling of *thereon*] = Thereon.

*c* **1200** Ormin 957 Þa twellfe namess ec þatt wærenn don þæronne. *c* **1200** *Trin. Coll. Hom.* 89 Ure helende rod þerone. *Ibid.* 217 Ich wille ew segge þat ich þronne understonde. *c* **1400** *Rowland & O.* 416 Ther-one was sett a Sercle of golde. *c* **1420** *Anturs of Arth.* 171 Þere one hertly take hede. *a* **1425** *Cursor M.* 1938 (Trin.) Noe..let reise an autere swiþe, Þeronne [*C.* þar-on] made he sacrifise.

Also **Thereo·nto** *adv.*, onto or upon that. *rare.*

**1898** *Blackw. Mag.* Mar. 406 Thereonto throw nine hairs from the head.

**Thereout** (ðēᵊrau·t), *adv.* Forms: 1 þǽr út(e, ME. þar, þer out(e: also 4-5 (9 *Sc.*) throut(e. [OE. *þærút(e*: see There 17 and Out, Oute.]

**1.** Outside of that place, etc.; without. Now *rare.*

*c* **893** K. Ælfred *Oros.* ii. viii. § 4 Nahton hie naþer ne þærinne mete ne þærute freond. *c* **897** [see Thereinne]. *c* **1000** *Ags. Gosp.* Mark iii. 31 His modor and his ʒebroðra ..þar ute stodon. *c* **1175** *Lamb. Hom.* 33 Þe mon þe leie .xii. moneð in ane prisune nalde he ʒefen al þet he efre mahte biʒeten wið þet he moste .xii. beo ðer ut of. *c* **1205** Lay. 1179 Brutus ferde in to þere temple..& lette al his folc bilæuen þer vte. *a* **1300** *Cursor M.* 1333 (Cott.) He..stod þer oute [*v.rr.* þar oute, þar vte], And sagh þe thing. *Ibid.* 15934 He..Fain wald ha ben þer vte. *c* **1470** Henry *Wallace* iv. 488 The ʒett he wor..; he held na man tharout. **1881** J. T. Bent *Genoa* vi. 127 A..story current in Roman Catholic circles, but not much accredited thereout.

**2.** Out of doors; in the open. Now *Sc.*

*a* **1300** *Cursor M.* 3928 Iacob..On þe feild þar oute he lai. *c* **1325** *Body & Soul* 114 in *Map's Poems* 349 For alle owre toures heye, ligge we shule throute In forstes ant in snowes. *c* **1400** Maundev. (Roxb.) xxvii. 125 Þe comouns..er all hird men and lyez þeroute in logez. *c* **1440** *Pallad. on Husb.* i. 896, x crabbes yf thou kest With watir in an erthen potte ywrie, Ten dayis throut [L. *subdivo*], vntil the vapur die. **1483** *Cath. Angl.* 382/1 Tharovte, *subdiuo .i. sub nudo Aere.* **1572** *Satir. Poems Reform.* xxxiii. 300 Lang time thay lay thairout. **1808–18** Jamieson s.v., *To lie thairout*, to lie in the open air during night.

**b.** Abroad; in existence; = Out 26 c. *Sc.*

*a* **1300** *Cursor M.* 1977 Quils þou may se mi rainbou þar oute, Of suilk a flod haue man na doute. *c* **1560** A. Scott *Poems* (S.T.S.) xxxiv. 25 The wysest woman þairout Wᵗ wird may be wyllit To do þe deid. **1725** Ramsay *Gentle Sheph.* iii. ii, Greater liars never ran thereout.

**3.** Of motion: Out of that; out from that place, etc.; forth from thence. Now *Sc.*

*a* **1300** *Cursor M.* 4542 Þe boteler to þe prisun lep, And suith þar-out he broght ioseph. **13..** *Ibid.* 2567 (Fairf.) Come now þer-oute, Be-halde þou þe lift a-boute. *c* **1489** Caxton *Sonnes of Aymon* xvi. 371 He went to the couffres, and toke there-out all the treysour. **1533** Gau *Richt Vay* (S.T.S.) 4 Blissit be god quhilk hes helpit me thair owt. *c* **1750** J. Nelson *Jrnl.* (1836) 58 They had better never have known the way of salvation than, after knowing it, be turned thereout.

**4.** From or out of that (it, them), as source or origin; thence. *arch.*

*c* **1375** *Sc. Leg. Saints* i. (*Petrus*) 391 Þe fals fend in his liknese Vith þe pupill wald spek þarowte [out of the figure]. **1535** Coverdale *Ps.* lxxii[i]. 10 And there out sucke they no small auauntage. **1650** Earl Monm. tr. *Senault's Man bec. Guilty* 36 They teare up the bowels of the earth to learn secrets thereout. **1788** Jefferson *Wks.* (1859) II. 353 On condition that he may retain thereout one hundred and eighty thousand guilders. **1865** Kingsley *Herew.* ix, With the divine instinct of freedom, and all the self-help and energy which spring thereout. **1871** B. Taylor *Faust* (1875) I. viii. 120 As oft as he drank thereout.

**Thereover** (ðēᵊrōᵘ·vəɹ), *adv. arch.* [OE. *ðǽrofer*, ME. *þer, þar ouer*: see There 17 and Over *prep.*]

**1.** Over or above that, in position (or in transit; also in charge, rank, number or amount).

*c* **897** K. Ælfred *Gregory's Past. C.* xlv. 336 Ne he self nanne wæstm ðærofer ne bireð. *c* **1000** *Ags. Gosp.* Matt. xxvii. 35 Hiʒ to-dældon hys reaf and wurpon hlot þær ofer. *c* **1220** *Bestiary* 64 Ðer ouer he fleʒeð. *a* **1300** *Cursor M.* 4157 Þer ouer standes a mikel tre. *c* **1400** Maundev. (Roxb.) xviii. 85 He berez it to þe kyng and makes þar ower many blissings. **1535** Coverdale *1 Chron.* xxiv. [xxiii.] 17 But yᵉ children of Rehabia were many therouer. **1558** Phaer *Æneid* vi. Qj, Therouer dare no bird attempt to flie, for deadly dout. **1870** Morris *Earthly Par.* III. iv. 235 In a dark blue kirtle was he clad, And a grey cloak thereover. **1905** *Contemp. Rev.* Feb. 208 To drive Man out of Paradise, and to keep watch thereover.

**2.** *fig.* In reference to that (which is under consideration or observation, or is the object of occupation, discourse, or attention: see Over *prep.* 4).

**1535** Coverdale *Ecclus.* xxxiv. 12, I..came oft in parell of death therouer, tyll I was delyuered from it. — *John* vi. 41 Then murmured the Iewes ther ouer, that he sayde: I am yᵗ bred which is come downe from heauen. **1870** Morris *Earthly Par.* II. iii. 355 He..smiled to see his deep-set eyes and grave Gleam out with joy thereover.

**Thereright** (ðēᵊɹ,rəi·t), *adv. Obs.* exc. *dial.* [OE. *þǽr rihte* (two words): see There 17 and Right *adv.* 7 b. Cf. Hereright.] Straightway, forthwith; there on the spot.

**971** *Blickl. Hom.* 221 Þa eode he ðær rihte biʒ on sume stowe. *c* **1000** Ælfric *Gram.* xxxviii. (Z.) 233 *Statim*, þar rihte. *c* **1205** Lay. 25676 Nu fulle feowertene niht þe foren heo hafueð ihaldet þer riht [*c* 1275 forþ riht]. **1628** Hobbes *Thucyd.* (1822) 92 Because their virtue was thought extraordinary [they] were therefore buried thereright. *a* **1656** Ussher *Ann.* vi. (1658) 392 And they with their naked swords threatened to kill them there-right, unless they returned to the fight. **1675** Hobbes *Odyss.* 112 On me..Bestow'd a ram, which on the sand there-right I made a sacrifice to mighty Jove. **1896** *Cheltenham Exam.* 12 Feb. 8 (E.D.D.) Er picked un up thurrite un went. **1898** T. Hardy *Wessex Poems* 204 Till he comes to the orchet, when crooping thereright..His lonesome young Bartree appears.

So †**Thereri·ghts** *adv.*, OE. **þǽr rihtes** [with advb. genitive], in same sense.

*a* **1100** *Ags. Hymns* (Surtees) 92 Pacemque dones protinus [*gloss*] & sibbe þu selle þær rihtes. *Ibid.* 113 Ascendant ..protinus Ad thronum..[*gloss*] Astiʒan..þær rihtes to þrymsetle. *c* **1175** *Lamb. Hom.* 33 Þerihtes he ne bið.

**Theresian**, variant of Teresian.

†**Therete·ken, þerte·ken**, *adv. Obs.* [OE. *þǽr tó éacan*, i.e. *þǽr*, There 17 and *tó éacan*, Teke, teken.] In addition to that; besides that.

*c* **1000** Ælfric *Hom.* II. 84 Hu he urum gyltum miltsað, and ðær to eacan þæt heofenlice rice behæt. *a* **1120** *O. E. Chron.* an. 1091, þær to eacan. *a* **1225** *Ancr. R.* 174 Þe nome of Hester ne seið nout one, 'abscondita',..ah ðeð þer teken, 'eleuata in populis'. *a* **1300** *Havelok* 2878 She is fayr, and she is fre,..Þertekene she is wel with me.

**Therethrough** (ðēᵊɹþrū·), *adv. arch.* Forms: see There and Through. [Early ME. *þer þurh*: see There 17, Through *prep.*]

**1.** Of place: Through that, it, or them.

*c* **1175** *Lamb. Hom.* 83 Þet gles..þe sunne schineð þer þurh. *a* **1325** *MS. Rawl. B.* 520 lf. 32 b, [They] sullen wite þe toune..ʒif ani vncouz passez þere þoru sal be aresteid for te amorue. **13..** *Cursor M.* 12872 (Gött.) Þe fader steuen þar thoru it brast, Right als it war a thonir blast. **1495** *Trevisa's Barth. De P. R.* v. v. (W. de W.) g iv/1 The glasy humour [of the eye] is..bryghte as glasse, soo yᵗ we maye se ther thorugh. **1594** Blundevil *Exerc.* iii. ii. xxvii. (1636) 423 To make therethrough a navigable passage. **1672** Marvell *Reh. Transp.* I. 55 Its Waters would not mix with this Lake ..but ran theere thorow without ever touching it. **1870** Morris *Earthly Par.* II. iii. 232 He hurried on until he reached again The outer door, and, sighing, passed therethrough. **1873** M. Collins *Miranda* I. 73 The musical moan of the water as the ship cuts its way therethrough.

**2.** By means, or by reason, of that; thereby.

*c* **1200** *Trin. Coll. Hom.* 189 Þat he haueð þer þurh forloren heuene wele. *c* **1200** Ormin 2325 Þatt ʒho..shollde wurrþenn Wiþþ childe swa þatt ʒho þærþurrh Ne shollde nohht ben wemmedd. *c* **1300** *Beket* 75 And therthurf me taʒte hire the wei: so that heo thider com. *c* **1412** Hoccleve *De Reg. Princ.* 2667 His lorde þe kyng withe venym wolde he fede, So þat ther-þurgh he steruen shulde nede. **1535** Coverdale *Ecclus.* Prol., Therfore they that..reade it, shulde not onely them selues be wyse there thorow, but serue other also with teachinge and wrytinge. **1678** R. Barclay *Apol. Quakers* v. xxi. 161 Every Man..may come therethrough to believe. **1818** Scott *Hrt. Midl.* xliii, Ye maun be minded not to act altogether on your ain judgment, for therethrough comes sair mistakes. **1894** F. T. Ellis *Reynard Fox* 257 Winning renown and fame therethrough.

**Theretill** (ðēᵊɹti·l), *adv. north. dial.* and *Sc.* [ME. *þar till*: see There 17 and Till *prep.*] = Thereto (in all its senses).

*a* **1300** *Cursor M.* 887 'Þe worm', sco said, 'me draf þar till'. *Ibid.* 15638 All þi wil it sal be dun, Þar til i am redi. *a* **1300** *Havelok* 1443 Castles ten, And þe lond þat þor til longes. *c* **1330** R. Brunne *Chron.* (1810) 110 Heyre was he non, no þertille had resoun; Þe Emperice sonne Henry he had right þertille. *c* **1400** Maundev. (Roxb.) vii. 26 By cause of þe perilous wayse þertill. *c* **1425** Wyntoun *Cron.* iii. ix. 1080 A thousand and thre hundyr yhere And ten thare tyll. *c* **1470** Henry *Wallace* v. 516 Gret strenth he has, bathe wyt and grace thartill. **1562** Bp. Pilkington *Burn. Paules Ch.* § 7 It is a commen true sayinge: he that wil do no yl, must do nothinge that longes there til. *a* **1577** Gascoigne *Dan Bartholomew* Wks., *Hearbes, Weedes, &c.* (1587) 96 And signe it with my simple hand and set my seale theretil. **1819** Tennant *Papistry Storm'd* ii. (1827) 63 Wi' angry bill, and wing theretill. **1832** Henderson *Scot. Prov.* 158 A shower of rain in July..Is worth a plough of owsen, and a' belangs theretill.

**Thereto** (ðēᵊɹtū·, ðēᵊ·ɹtu), *adv.* Now *formal* or *arch.* [OE. *þǽr tó, þǽrtó*: see There 17 and To *prep.*] To that (or those things), to it (or them).

**1.** To that place, thing, affair, etc. in various senses of To *prep.*

*c* **1000** Ælfric *Hom.* II. 378 Þæt he us ʒebringe to his ecan ʒebeorscipe, seðe þurh his to-cyme us ðærto ʒelaðode. *c* **1000** — *Saints' Lives* xxv. 227 Mathathias..ofsloh..þæs cyninges ðeʒn þe hine ðær to neadode. *a* **1225** *Ancr. R.* 6 Hwoa se nimeð þing on hond and bihat hit..to donne, heo bint hire þerto. *a* **1250** *Owl & Night.* 103 His nest..þar to þi stele in o day & leydest þar on þi fule ey. **1377** Langl. *P. Pl.* B. xviii. 178 Moyses and meny mo mercy shullen synge; And I shal daunce þer to. *c* **1400** *Apol. Loll.* 34 Ne to put more þer to, ne to draw þer fro. *c* **1440** *Pallad. on Husb.* i. 40 Smell also therto in cas it stynke. **1445** tr. *Claudian* in *Anglia* XXVIII. 275 Where he þat is worthy is callid therto. *a* **1533** Ld. Berners *Huon* lxxxi. 247 Nere therto there was a lytell wode. **1538** Starkey *England* i. ii. 53 Such as haue byn long vsyd therto. **1611** Bible *Isa.* xliv. 15 He maketh it a grauen image, and falleth downe thereto. **1794** G. Adams *Nat. & Exp. Philos.* IV. xxxviii. 59 The edge of the disk will be perpendicular thereto. **1875** F. Hall in *Lippincott's Mag.* XVI. 749/2 All circumstances of the provocation thereto being dispassionately considered. **1892** *Law Times Rep.* LXV. 582/1 The posts..are fixed thereto by iron dogs and dowels.

**2.** With words denoting pertinence, suitability, etc., expressed or implied: (Belonging, pertinent, suitable, needful) to that matter or thing; (according) therewith; for that matter, purpose, etc.

*c* **1000** Ælfric *Hom.* II. 494 On oðre healfe stod ðæs monan cræt..and ða oxan ðærto. *c* **1000** — *Saints' Lives* xxix. 129 Ures hælendes ʒerip mæniʒ-feald is..and feawa wyrhtan þær-to. *c* **1305** *St. Andrew* 33 in *E. E. P.* (1862) 99 Hou miʒte hit beo, þat his wille were þerto? *c* **1425** *Eng. Conq. Irel.* 6 His hert was mych there-to. **1454** *E. E. Wills* (1882) 133 My bed of grene sylke, wiþ þe testour & Canape ther-to. *c* **1485** *Digby Myst.* i. 24 If our cunnyng be ther-too. **1539** Tonstall *Serm. Palm Sund.* (1823) 86 Hauynge tyme therto. **1556** *Aberdeen Regr.* (1848) I. 294 All materiallis neidfull therto. **1626** Gouge *Serm. Dignity Chivalry* § 4 Preparation for Warre, Exercises thereto. **1748** G. White *Serm.* (MS.), Nothing more is needful thereto. **1871** Browning *Pr. Hohenst.-Schw.* 643 Now for the means thereto.

**3.** Added to that, in addition to that; besides, also, moreover. Now *arch.* and *poet.*

*a* **900** tr. *Bæda's Hist.* iii. xiv. [xvii.] (1890) 202 Nowiht aʒnes..butan his cyricean and þær to feower æceras. *c* **1000** Ælfric *De Vet. Test.* (Gr.) 14 Ic ʒesett hæbbe..wel feowertiʒ larspella on Engliscum ʒereorde and sumne eacan þær to. *a* **1121** *O. E. Chron.* an. 1102, Se eorl Rotbert.. hæfde þone eorldom her on lande on Scrobbesbyriʒ..&

micel rice pær to. c 1175 *Lamb. Hom.* 67 His apostles.. and monie oðre þere to. c 1386 CHAUCER *Prol.* 153 A Prioresse..Hir mouth ful smal, and ther to softe and reed. *Ibid.* 353. — *Squire's T.* 11. a 1450 *Knt. de la Tour* 103 To falle from richesse into lowe astate, and thereto pouerte. 1587 GOLDING *De Mornay* xi. (1592) 160 Man reasoneth and discourseth, because he is Man: and were he thereto vnchangeable, he were a God. 1633 P. FLETCHER *Purple Isl.* XI. xlvi, Thereto of substance strange, so thinne and slight. 1830 TENNYSON *Talking Oak* 196, I would have paid her kiss for kiss, With usury thereto. 1887 MORRIS *Odyss.* XI. 287 As Cromius and Nestor,..And thereto the glorious Pero.

**Theretofore** (ðēəːɹˌtufōəˑɹ), *adv.* Now *formal.* [ME. *þer tofore*: see THERE 17 and TOFORE *adv.*] Before that time; previously to that.

c 1350 *Will. Palerne* 2611 Þei..wist þat þai in wast wrouȝt þer to-fore. 1430-40 LYDG. *Bochas* VIII. i. (MS. Bodl. 263) 368/2 Emperors reknid for ther toforn was non. 1791 in Picton *L'pool Munic. Rec.* (1886) II. 205 The By-laws theretofore made. 1851 GLADSTONE *Glean.* (1879) VI. 4 A judgment that alienated dissenting endowments from purposes to which they had theretofore been applied. 1894 *State Trials* (N.S.) VI. 410 According to the canonical practice theretofore observed in England.

**Theretoˑward,** *adv. rare.* [ME. *pertoward*, f. THERE 17 + TOWARD *prep.*] Toward that (place, thing, matter, etc.).

a 1225 *Leg. Kath.* 1484 Þat alle þat ter bi gað..buhe þer toward. a 1225 *Ancr. R.* 52 Eue..turnde hire lust þer toward, & nom & et þerof, & ȝef hire louerd. 1908 *Daily News* 29 Feb. 4 The matter of Signor Nasi's conduct, with the popular attitude theretoward.

† **Theretoyeˑns,** *adv. Obs.* Forms: 1 þær toȝeanes, þar toȝenes, 3 þer to ȝenes, þertoȝeines, þerteyens. [Orig. two words: OE. *þǽr*, THERE 17, *toȝenes*, TO-GAINS; if the compound had survived till 15th c. it would have become *theretogainst.*]

**1.** Against or in opposition to that.

c 1000 ÆLFRIC *Hom.* I. 236 Swilce hi wislice sprecon! Ac we cweðað þær toȝeanes, þæt God is Ælmihtiȝ. a 1225 *Ancr. R.* 80 Nu we schullen sumhwat speken..aȝein vuel speche þæt ȝe þertoȝeines tunen ower earen. 1340 *Ayenb.* 11 Huo þet deþ þerteyens be his wytinde zenȝeþ dyadliche.

**2.** In return for that; in exchange therefor.

1066-9 in Thorpe *Charters* (1865) 436 We habbaþ heom ȝeunnen ..and hi us þar toȝenes ȝifeþ. c 1200 *Trin. Coll. Hom.* 203 Ech man þe for mine name..folȝeð me he shal fon þer to ȝenes hundredfeld mede.

**Thereunder** (ðēərʊˑndəɹ), *adv.* Now *formal.* [OE. *ðærunder*: see THERE 17 and UNDER *prep.*]

**1.** Under that or it; below or beneath that.

c 897 K. ÆLFRED *Gregory's Past. C.* xviii. 130 Ealle ða þe ofer oðre beoð, beoð heafdu ðara þe ðærunder beoð. c 1220 *Bestiary* 314 He draȝeð ðe neddre of ðe ston..for it wile ðerunder gon. 13.. *Cursor M.* 28731 Þe berer..behouis it [the burden] cast him fra, Quen he mai noght þar vnder ga. c 1440 *Sir Gowther* 313 There under he made his sete. 1579 W. WILKINSON *Confut. Family of Love, Heret. Affirm.* b b, Not that they should alwayes remaine as subject thereunder. 1630 SANDERSON *Serm.* (1681) II. 311 There is no way but to submit, and to humble our selves thereunder. 1862 SMILES *Engineers* III. 358 A contract with owners of land..for the working of the coal thereunder.

**2.** Under that title, heading, etc.; under the provisions, or by the authority, of that.

1617 MINSHEU *Ductor* Title-p., The Nature, Propertie, Condition..of things there-vnder contayned. 1640 BP. HALL *Episc.* I. v. 21 The cause of those, who there-under have reformed France. 1706 in *Parish Accts. St. Julian's, Shrewsbury* II. 43 (MS.) The Assessors thereunder named or the major part of them. 1885 H. REED in *Law Rep.* 15 Q. B. Div. 160 The intention is that s. 125..and the rules to be made thereunder shall constitute a complete and separate code. 1908 *Times* 6 May 17/3 Royalties paid thereunder were to be paid to the publishers.

**3.** Under or less than that (number, age, etc.).

1535 COVERDALE 1 *Chron.* xxvii. 23 Them that were twentye yeare olde and there vnder.

† **Thereuntiˑll,** *adv. Obs.* [f. THERE 17 + UNTIL *prep.*] = THEREUNTO.

13.. *Cursor M.* 1066 (Gött.) Vr lauerd loked noght þar vntill [*Cott.* þar till].

**Thereunto** (ðēərʊntūˑ, -ʊˑntu), *adv. arch.* [f. THERE 17 + UNTO *prep.*]

**1.** Unto or to that place; unto that thing, matter, subject, etc.

13.. *Cursor M.* 3717 (Gött.) Hir moder consail was þar vnto [*rime* do; *v.r.* þar to]. 1474 *Rolls of Parlt.* VI. 113/1 The said sommes..shuld be restored..to every persone.. that had payed therunto. 1568 GRAFTON *Chron.* II. 395 To make the offense the greater, he added much therevnto. a 1661 FULLER *Worthies, Surrey* (1662) III. 87, I am affraied that our Infidel Age will not give credit thereunto. 1713 WARDER *True Amazons* (ed. 2) 105 Many cannot attain thereunto. 1875 MYERS *Poems* (ed. 4) 89 When God had brought me thereunto.

† **2.** In addition to that; = THERETO 3. *Obs.*

1567 DRANT *Horace, Epist.* To Rdr. *v, A sillye translator rythmical and thervnto an harde wryter. 1678 WANLEY *Wond. Lit. World* v. ii. § 79. 472/1 Of an exceeding courage and strength, of a sharp wit, and thereunto very fortunate.

† **Thereuˑp,** *adv. Obs.* Forms: see THERE and UP; also 3 þruppe. [Late OE. *þǽr uppan* (*þǽr* there, *uppan* upon, on) would give ME. **þer uppen, þeruppe*, and in 14th c. *þerup*; but these might also be new formations from *uppe*, UP.]

**1.** Up on that, upon that (place or thing); up in or into that place; up there, up above. In quots. c 1230, above (on the page or in the document).

α. c 1000 ÆLFRIC *Saints' Lives* xxx. 200 Him wæs his myxen forlæten þæt he þær uppan sittan mihte. c 1230 *Hali Meid.* 39 Ich habbe ihalden mine beheaste þruppe. *Ibid.*, Forsac þi fader hus as hit is þeruppe iopenet. c 1250 *Gen. & Ex.* 1609 Ðe louerd ðor uppe a-buuen Lened ðor on. c 1300 *St. Brandan* 123 Bord and cloth i-sprad, And bred and fisch ther uppe. c 1315 SHOREHAM i. 41 Howe mey þat be? wo dar þer oppe steiȝe?

β. 1572 BUCHANAN *Detect. Q. Mary* U iij, I haue wakit laiter thairvp [Fr. *là haut*] then I wald haue done, if it had nat bene [etc.]. 1829 A. CLARKE in *Life* xiii. (1840) 478 Collectors..to take silver from all who should go thereup.

**2.** = THEREUPON 2, 3.

α. a 1225 *Ancr. R.* 42 Hwo se wule mei a-stunten þeruppe anon rihtes efter þe uorme ureisun. c 1290 *Beket* 447 in *S. Eng. Leg.* I. 119 Heo wollez þanne mis-don al day and beon þare-oppe wel bolde. 1297 R. GLOUC. (Rolls) 8084 [Robert] borewede þer uppe [*v.r.* c 1400 þer vpon] of him an hondred þousend marc. a 1325 *MS. Rawl. B.* 520 lf. 32 Þat a non riȝt..be i-mad so uers siute þer oppe fram toune to toune.

β. 1375 (*MS.* 1487) BARBOUR *Bruce* x. 433 Sic melle tharup can he mak. 1430 W. PASTON in *P. Lett.* I. 30 And there up to graunte your worthy lettres.

**3.** Over and above that, in addition to that.

1297 R. GLOUC. (Rolls) 716 Ȝif þou wole ȝut þer vppe more esse [= ask] & wite of me. *Ibid.* 1085 Þanne aȝt it be inou ..Loue & frendssipe to aski us..þei þou ne askedest þer vppe þralhede euere mo.

**Thereupon** (ðēərʊ̆pǫˑn, ðēəˑrʊ̆pǫn), *adv.* Forms: see THERE and UPON. [In ME. two (or three) words.]

**1.** Upon that or it (of position or motion, *lit.* or *fig.*). *arch.* or *formal.*

c 1175 *Lamb. Hom.* 53 Þes riche men..liggeð þer uppon alse þe tadde deð in þere eorðe. a 1225 *St. Marher.* 21 Cume þe sunfule mon ant legge his muð þer up on. a 1300 *Cursor M.* 18565 Þar apon þai did þair sele. c 1400 *Brut* 103 Þat euery man miȝt..þereoppon loke. c 1400 *Destr. Troy* 8447 Yche lede, þat leuys þerapon. 1588 A. KING tr. *Canisius' Catech.* h ij b, Ye sonday..callit ye day of our Lord, because of his resurrection yairvpon. 1716 *Lond. Gaz.* No. 5480/1 The Goods and Merchandizes laden thereupon. a 1774 TUCKER *Lt. Nat.* (1834) II. 679 If any man thinks he has ..formed his own speculative plan thereupon.

† **b.** Alongside of that. *Obs.*

c 1275 LAY. 12423 Hii bi-gonne..anne swiþe deope dich, and þar vp on oueral one stonene wal. 1652 NEEDHAM *Selden's Mare Cl.* To Rdr., Divers Potent Princes..who have..large territories lying thereupon [on the sea].

† **c.** = THEREABOUTS 2 b. *Sc. Obs.*

1649 BP. GUTHRIE *Mem.* (1702) 72 Standing in the Close, with 60 Gentlemen or thereupon about him.

**2.** Upon that (in time or order); on that being done or said; (directly) after that.

13.. *Cursor M.* 4945 (Gött.) Mete and drinck i gaf þaim bath,..And þar apon [*C.* þar on] stale [*C.* þai] þus mi thing. c 1400 [see THEREUP 2, quot. 1297]. 1499 BP. R. FOX in *Lett. Rich. III & Hen. VII* (Rolls) II. 85 [He] wilbe with you at Michaelmas or soone thereupon. 1526 *Pilgr. Perf.* (W. de W. 1531) 1 b, Thervpon I begon after my poore maner to wryte in latyn. 1651 HOBBES *Leviath.* II. xxvii. 159 If thereupon he accept Duell. 1891 *Law Times* XCII. 104/2 For the purposes of the argument and the decision following thereupon.

**b.** On that ground; in consequence of that. *arch.*

1534 STARKEY *Let. to Cromwell* in *England* (1878) p. x, So therapon wyth your beneuolent mynd you may set forward somewhat better my purpos. 1590 SHAKS. *Com. Err.* v. i. 388, I was tane for him, and he for me, And thereupon these errors are arose. 1766 BLACKSTONE *Comm.* II. xviii. 281 In some particular countries, by local custom, where other trees [than oak, ash, and elm] are generally used for building, they are thereupon considered as timber. 1851 RUSKIN *Stones Ven.* I. Pref. 5 It had been fitted up for somebody's reception, and been thereupon fresh painted.

**3.** On that subject or matter; with reference to that (it, them); thereanent. *arch.* or *formal.*

1414 *Rolls of Parlt.* IV. 22/2 That ther never be no Lawe made ther uppon. 1439 in *Archæologia* XXI. 35 After þe ..Kynges lettres patentz ther upon made. a 1557 *Diurn. Occur.* (1833) 34 The erle Bothwell..tuke thame to Abirlady, and disponit thairvpone at his pleasour. 1695 *Enq. Anc. Const. Eng.* 39 Upon a legal process issued out thereupon. 1781 H. GATES in Sparks *Corr. Amer. Rev.* III. 420, I should have been happy to know your sentiments thereupon. 1905 *Sat. Rev.* 23 Dec. 814/2 As the..reports ..interest..teachers I venture to address you thereupon.

† **Therewhiˑle,** *adv. Obs.* Forms: see THERE and WHILE. [ME. *þer hwile*, analysis not certain, but app. repr. an OE. (*on*)*þǽre hwíle* 'in that time', and thus, practically = the more usual *the while*, OE. *þá hwile*.

*þer hwile* had evidently come to be apprehended as a whole, and taken as an adv. before 1250, when it appears with advb. genitive *-es, -s*: see next. Cf. *the while* (OE.), *the whiles* c 1300, and the later *while, whiles*, advbs., both c 1300.]

**a.** During the time that; whilst; so long as. **b.** During that time; the while; meanwhile.

c 1220 *Bestiary* (in *O.E. Misc.*) 784 Ne dar he stiren, ne noman deren, Ðer wile he laȝe and luue beren. 1340 *Ayenb.* 213 Þer huile þet ich me solaci an playe, iche ne þenche none manne kuead. a 1400-50 *Alexander* 157 Many was þe bald berne at banned þar quile Þat euer he dured þat day. c 1430 *Life St. Kath.* Cont. (1884) 3 How þe Emperour .. ther whyle sent pryue lettres. 1575 Q. ELIZ. in *Harington's Nugæ Ant.* (ed. Park 1804) I. 126 Their-while I prepair my selffe to welcome deathe. 1617 HIERON *Wks.* II. 66 What becommeth of the Spirit of God therewhile? Is it lost?

† **Therewhiˑles, -whiˑlst,** *adv. Obs.* [f. prec. with *-s* of advb. genitive, subseq. made *-st*: see WHILST.] = prec.

α. c 1250 *Gen. & Ex.* 1282 Ðor quiles he wunede in bersabe, So was ysaaces eld [etc.]. c 1320 R. BRUNNE *Medit.* 367, Y kepte hem þyrwhylys y was with hem. 1340 *Ayenb.* 194 Offre to god worþi offringe þerhuyls þet þou leuest. 1377 LANGL. *P. Pl.* B. VI. 8 What sholde we wommen worche þere whiles? c 1491 CAXTON *Chast. Goddes Chyld.* 28 There whiles he may not be unied to god by cause he liueth in all contraryousnes. a 1557 MRS. M. BASSET tr. *More's Treat. Passion* M.'s Wks. 1376/2 Which is priuely emplied in euery thing he doth therwiles.

β. a 1541 WYATT *Penit. Ps.* xxxvii. 57 Therewhilst shall fail these wicked men therefore. 1587 FLEMING *Contn. Holinshed* III. 976/1 The lord Greie..bad him repeat his message, and therwhilest made a clearke..to write the same *Verbatim.* 1603 FLORIO *Montaigne* I. xxx. (1632) 103 Their women busie themselves therewhil'st with warming of their drinke.

**Therewith** (ðeəɹwiˑþ, ðēəɹwið *with shifting stress*), *adv.* Now *formal* or *arch.* [OE. *þǽr wiþ*, *ðærwið*, f. *þǽr*, THERE 17 + *wið*, WITH *prep.*]

† **1.** Against that (or those); in opposition to that; in return for that. *Obs.*

c 1000 ÆLFRIC *Gen.* xlvii. 16 Drifað hider eowre orf,..and ic sylle eow þær wið mete. a 1200 *Moral Ode* 300 Warnie [elc man] æc his frend þer wid so ic habbe mine. c 1220 *Bestiary* 383 Mikel ned, ðat we ðar wið ne dillen. c 1300 *Cursor M.* 28109, I said not ans þar wit nai.

**2.** With that (or those) as accompaniment, adjunct, etc.; together or in company with that (and in allied senses of *with*).

c 888 K. ÆLFRED *Boeth.* xxxiii. § 5 Swaþeah hi sint ðærwið ȝemengde. a 1300 *Cursor M.* 7262 [Samson] slogh his faas, him-self þar with. 1340 HAMPOLE *Pr. Consc.* 1751 Þai sal fele þar many a ded brayde, Bot þai sal ay lyf þar with. 1599 DAVIES *Immort. Soul* I. xxiii, All things.. We seeke to know, and how therewith to do. 1885 *Law Rep.* 14 Q. B. Div. 246 At right angles therewith. 1886 SPURGEON *Treas. David* Ps. cxxxii. 10 Every person connected therewith. 1907 ILLINGWORTH *Doctr. Trin.* iii. 44 The..historical accuracy of the Acts has been amply revindicated.., and therewith the value of its evidence. 1910 *Act* 10 *Edw. VII*, c. 38 Sched. B, For Old Age Pensions..and for certain Administration Expenses in connection therewith £500,000.

**b.** In addition to that; besides, withal.

a 1300 *Cursor M.* 2204 Nembrot..O babilon king, stijf in stur, And þer wit [*v. rr.* þar-wid, -wiþ] was he gret werrur. c 1400 MAUNDEV. (Roxb.) xii. 50 Þe water of þis see es full bitter and salt þarwith. 1886 KIPLING *Departm. Ditties*, etc. (1899) 41 Pagett, M.P., was a liar, and a fluent liar therewith.

**c.** With that (word, act, or occurrence); that being said or done; thereat, thereupon, forthwith.

c 1369 CHAUCER *Dethe Blaunche* 275 Y fil aslepe, and therewith evene Me mette so ynly swete a swevene. 1377 LANGL. *P. Pl.* B. XIX. 479 Þe vyker..toke his leue, And I awakned þere with. a 1425 *Cursor M.* 10462 (Trin.) Vtayne þer wiþ [*G.* wid þis word] gon to tene. 1512 R. COPLAND *Helyas* (1827) 76 Therwith the king and the quene went and kyssed theyr sonne Helias. 1517 TORKINGTON *Pilgr.* (1884) 33 And ther with they com ner hym. 1868 MORRIS *Earthly Par., Man born to be King* 107 Therewith he rose And led the way unto a close.

**3.** With that as instrument; by means of that.

c 1250 *Gen. & Ex.* 379 Two pilches weren..to Adam and to Eue broȝt, Ðor wið he ben nu boðen srid, And here same sumdel is hid. 1297 R. GLOUC. (Rolls) 3828 Is suerd he drou þere Vor to asaile him þerwiþ. c 1400 *Brut* ccviii. 238 Þai toke stone, and made þerwiþ þe tour. 1526 TINDALE *Jas.* iii. 9 The tonge..Therwith blesse we God the father and therwith cursse we men which are made vnto the similitude off God. 1579 LANGHAM *Gard. Health* (1633) 437 Whether fish or birds be taken therewith. 1725 *Bradley's Fam. Dict.* s. v. *Mint*, If you bathe the affected Part therewith.

**b.** With that as cause or occasion; on account of or because of that; in consequence of that.

c 1440 *Jacob's Well* 300 Whan þe flesch sufferyth penauns or hardnesse, it grucchyth þer with. c 1500 *Melusine* 360 Hys bretheren and the baronnye þere were abasshed therwith. 1526 TINDALE 1 *Tim.* vi. 9 When we have fode and rayment, let vs theirwith be content. 1579 SPENSER *Sheph. Cal.* Mar. 94 Therewith affrayd I ranne away. 1792 COWPER *Let. to J. Johnson* 5 Nov., I have finished the Sonnet..and sent it to Hayley, who is well pleased therewith.

**Therewithal** (ðēəɹwiðǭˑl), *adv. arch.* [Orig. two words, THERE 17 and WITHAL *adv.*]

**1.** Along with or together with that; besides, or in addition to that (fact, circumstance, etc.); with all that; over and above that; = THEREWITH 2, 2 b.

c 1330 R. BRUNNE *Chron. Wace* (Rolls) 11915 Nys non on lyue...Þat semeþ so wel his beryng, Ne so curteys þer wyþ-al. c 1386 CHAUCER *Wife's Prol.* 773 And ther with al he knew of mo prouerbes Than in this world ther growen gras or herbes. 1490 CAXTON *Eneydos* xxix. 112 A whyte coloure, with a bryght hew there with alle. 1591 SHAKS. *Two Gent.* IV. iv. 90 Giue her that Ring, and therewithall This letter. 1620 VENNER *Via Recta* vi. (1637) 113 A couple of potched Egges,..eating therewithall a little Bread and Butter. 1809 MALKIN *Gil Blas* XI. xi. (Rtldg.) 414 He was to make a voyage, and as he hoped, his fortune therewithal. a 1850 ROSSETTI *Dante & Circ.* I. (1874) 250 False hopes, true poverty, and therewithal The blinded judgment of a host of friends.

**2.** That being said or done; = THEREWITH 2 c.

a 1300 *Cursor M.* 1117 Caym..wend [h]a scaped þar wit alle [*G.* þar wid all]. 1375 BARBOUR *Bruce* v. 252, 'I grant', he said; and thar with all He lowtit, and his leyf has tane. c 1475 *Rauf Coilȝear* 151 He stakkerit thair with all Half the breid of the hall. c 1570 *Pride & Lowl.* (1841) 20 What then?..Quoth he; and therewithal he swore an oath. 1663 BLAIR *Autobiog.* iii. (1848) 55 Therewithal, stretching out both his arms, drew in my head to his bosom. 1801 WORDSW. *Troilus & Cr.* 8 And therewithal to cover his intent A cause he found into the Town to go. 1879 BUTCHER & LANG *Odyss.* xv. 255 He had signed silently to the woman and therewithal gat him away to the hollow ship.

† **3.** With that; = THEREWITH 3. *Obs.*

1490 CAXTON *Eneydos* lx. 159 He toke hys hand fulle of erthe..and fylled hys throte therwithalle. 1577 B. GOOGE

*Heresbach's Husb.* I. (1586) 43 Make plaister, and washe therewithall the walles within. **1656** EARL MONM. tr. *Boccalini's Advts. fr. Parnass.* I. xxvi. (1674) 28 [He] throwing off his Royal Cloak..would therewithall have covered that beautiful Lady.

**Therewithin** (ðɛəɹwiðiˑn), *adv. arch.* [Early ME. two words, *þer wiðinnen, wiþinne*, = THERE 17 and OE. *wiðinnan*, WITHIN: cf. THEREINNE, THEREIN.] Within or into that place; within there.

*c* **1200** *Trin. Coll. Hom.* 115 Þe engles þe þer wiðinnen weren. *c* **1320** *Cast. Love* 771 Neuer synne þer wiþ Inne com. **1375** BARBOUR *Bruce* III. 446 Þai na mete þar within had. **1447** *Shillingford Lett.* (Camden) 104 Eny persone dwelling there withynne. **1885** TENNYSON *Prol. to Gen. Hamley* 15 Therewithin a guest may make True cheer. **1892** C. E. NORTON *Dante's Paradise* v. 27.

**Therf, Therf-cake**: see THARF, THARF-CAKE.

**Therfor(e, -fro, -from, (-geyn), -hence,** obs. ff. THEREFORE, -FRO, -FROM, -GAIN, -HENCE.

**Theriac** (þɪəˑriæk), *sb.* (*a.*) *arch.* Forms: α. (1 tyriaca); 6- theriaca, 7–8 theriace. β. 5 tiriake, tyriake. γ. 6- theriac, 7 -ack, -aque. See also THERIACLE. [a. late L. *thēriaca, thēriacē* (med.L. *thēriacum*), a. Gr. θηριακή (ἀντίδοσις), θηριακόν (φάρμακον), fem. and neut. of θηριακός pertaining to wild beasts or poisonous reptiles, f. θηρίον, dim. of θήρ wild beast, poisonous reptile. So F. *thériaque* (16th c. in Godef.), whence the last γ form; It., Sp. *teriaca*, Sp. *triaca*, Pr. *tiriaca*; MHG. *triak*, G. *theriak*, Du. *teriaak*: see also THERIACLE.] An antidote to poison, esp. to the bite of a venomous serpent; = TREACLE *sb.* 1.

The flesh of the viper was formerly held to be a necessary ingredient of the antidote to its bite (see quot. 1608); hence many references in the fig. uses of *theriac* and *treacle*.

α. [*c* **1000** *Sax. Leechd.* II. 175 Tyriaca is god drenc wiþ innoþ tydernessum. *Ibid.* 290 Nime þonne ane lytle snæd þæs tyriacan & ʒemenge.] **1562** BULLEYN *Bulwark, Dial. Soarnes & Chir.* (1573) 59 Take Theriaca of the making of Andromachus, .. which is a Triacle incomperable. **1601** HOLLAND *Pliny* XXIX. i. 348 See what account there is made of a composition called Theriace [*mispr.* Theriall: *corrected in list of errata*]. **1608** TOPSELL *Serpents* (1658) 810 *Theriace*, or Triacle, not only because it cureth the venomous bitings of Serpents, but also because the Serpents themselves are usually mingled in the making thereof. **1765** *Univ. Mag.* XXXVII. 237/1 He..took..a large dose of theriaca with wine. [**1811** HOOPER *Med. Dict.* s. v., *Theriaca Andromachi*, the Venice or Mithridate treacle... *Theriaca communis*, common treacle, or molasses... *Theriaca Londinensis*, a cataplasm of cummin seed, bay-berries, germander, snakeroot, cloves and honey.]

β. *c* **1440** *Pallad. on Husb.* III. 1100 Vyn tiriake [*v. r.* Vyntariake] is also now to make..The bite of euery best me shal escape. *Ibid.* 1118 Also tiriake [*v. r.* Tyriake] Ys good to take and..Heeld on theyr rootes ofte.

γ. **1568** SKEYNE *The Pest* (1860) 24 One half vnce of guid auld theriac. **1658** ROWLAND *Moufet's Theat. Ins.* 1005 Oyl of Quinces is commended as the certain Theriack for this disease. **1665–6** *Phil. Trans.* I. 160 The great number of Vipers, brought to the Grand Duke of Toscany for the composing of Theriac or Treacle. **1674** JEAKE *Arith.* (1696) bij b, As when the skilful Artist to compose His mighty Theriaque; Weighs the Critick Dose. **1751** *Student* II. 344 When the disease was young, it was mitigated with.. crabs eyes;..theriac and vinegar. **1852** BEVERIDGE *Hist. India* I. I. v. 108 Tiriak of Khutta, a medicine..then in high repute as an antidote. **1890** *Athenæum* 19 Apr. 496/3 Such tisane or theriac as the science of the time could furnish.

**B.** *adj.* = THERIACAL.

*c* **1440** Vyn tiriake [= med.L. *vinum tiriacum*; see β above]. **1857** DUNGLISON *Med. Lex.* s.v. *Theriaca*, 'Theriac' and 'Theriacal' have been used adjectively for 'medicinal'.

**Theriacal** (þirɔ̄iˑăkăl), *a.* [f. THERIAC + -AL. Cf. F. *thériacal* (15th c. in Godef. *Compl.*).] Pertaining to or of the nature of theriac; antidotal.

**1603** HOLLAND *Plutarch's Mor.* 703 Who confound and mixe together minerals, herbs, theriacall trochists, made of the parts of venemous serpents, for the composition of their treacles. *Ibid.* Explan. Words, *Theriacal Trochisks*, Trosches made of vipers flesh. **1607** TOPSELL *Four-f. Beasts* (1658) 215 The heart of a Hare hath in it a theriacal virtue also. **1756–7** tr. *Keysler's Trav.* (1760) II. 131 To carry a spunge moistened with spirits of wine and a theriacal vinegar, and often to smell to it. **1857** [see prec. B].

Hence † **Theriacaˑlity**, theriacal quality. *rare*⁻¹.

**1657** TOMLINSON *Renou's Disp.* 331 Mesucus uses it in the Electuary..because there is some theriacality in it.

† **Theriˑacle.** *Obs.* Forms: 5 tiriacle, 6 tyriakle, 7 theriacle, -cal. [a. OF. *tiriacle, ter(i)acle* (15th c. in Godef. *Compl.*), beside OF. *triacle* (12th c.); popular alterations of *tiriaque, thériaque*, THERIAC: see also TREACLE.] = THERIAC, TREACLE *sb.* 1.

*c* **1400** MAUNDEV. (Roxb.) xxi. 94 Tiriacle may noȝt helpe ne nan oþer medecyne. **1561** HOLLYBUSH *Hom. Apoth.* 29 Geue him..a penyweyght of fyne Tyriakle. **1647** TRAPP *Comm. Acts* xxviii. 5 A wholesome theriacle.., or treacle, as we call it. **1681** tr. *Willis' Rem. Med. Wks.* Vocab., *Theriacal*, or treacle, a medicine..invented against poysons. **1730–6** BAILEY (folio), *Theri'aca, Theri'ace, Theri'acle*, Treacle.

[**Therial**, in recent Dicts., error for THERIAC.

Founded upon a misprint in Holland's *Pliny*, corrected in the *Errata* and in subseq. editions, but correction missed by Richardson: see quot. 1601 in THERIAC a.]

**Thericlean** (þeriklīˑăn), *a.* [f. L. *Thēriclē-us* adj., a. Gr. Θηρίκλει-ος made by Thericles, a famous Corinthian potter: see -AN.] Of Thericles; of the form or kind made by Thericles, as a cup.

**1692** R. L'ESTRANGE *Josephus, Antiq.* IX. i. (1733) 278 Vessels that Nebuchadnezzar carry'd away from the Temple at Jerusalem to be sent back and restor'd; that is to say.. fifty golden Vessels all thericlean Cups, and four hundred silver ones. **1703** ROWE *Ulyss.* Prol. 13 They sent her Billets doux, and presents many Of ancient Tea and Thericlean China. [**1857** BIRCH *Anc. Pottery* (1858) II. 107 The *Thericleios* was a kind of cup invented by Thericles, a Corinthian potter, the contemporary of Aristophanes.]

‖ **Theridion** (þiriˑdiǫn), **-ium** (-iŭm). *Zool.* [mod.L. a. Gr. θηρίδιον little animal, dim. of θήρ wild beast.] A genus of spiders, many of which spin webs of irregularly intersecting threads.

**1861** HULME tr. *Moquin-Tandon* II. v. ii. 261 Spiders... The most important are—1, the Mygales;..2, the Clubiones;..3, the Theridions, especially the Malmignatte of Corsica and Italy, and the Mactans of South America.

**Therin, -inne,** etc.: see THEREIN.

**Therio-** (þɪəriо), before a vowel **theri-** (þɪəri), representing Gr. θηριο-, combining form of θηρίον, dim. of θήρ wild beast; forming the first element in some scientific and other words. **Therianthroˑpic** *a.* [Gr. ἄνθρωπος man], combining the form of a beast with that of a man; of or pertaining to deities represented in the combined forms of man and beast, as dog- or eagle-headed divinities. **Theriaˑnthropism**, representation or worship of therianthropic deities (*Funk's Stand. Dict.* 1895). **Theˑriodont** [Gr. ὀδούς, ὀδοντ- tooth], a fossil reptile with teeth of a mammalian type, *spec.* one of the order *Theriodontia*; also *attrib.* or as *adj.* **Therioˑlatry**, the worship of beasts, or of theriomorphic deities. † **Theriolo·gic,** † **-ical** *adjs. rare*, of or pertaining to the scientific study of beasts; zoological. **Theˑriomancy** [-MANCY], divination from the movements of animals. **Therioma·niac**, *nonce-wd.*, one who has a mania for hunting wild beasts. **Theˑriopod** *a.* and *sb.* = THEROPOD (*Cent. Dict.* 1891). **Therioˑtomy** [Gr. τομή cutting], the dissection or anatomy of beasts; zootomy. **Theriotroˑphical** *a.* [Gr. τροφικ-ός nursing], concerning the nursing or rearing (of man) by beasts. **Theriozoˑic** *a.* [ZOIC], of or belonging to a period in human history anterior to the domestication of animals.

**1886** C. P. TIELE in *Encycl. Brit.* XX. 367/2 Religions, in which animistic ideas still play a prominent part, but which have grown up to a *therianthropic polytheism. **1876** OWEN in *Q. Jrnl. Geol. Soc.* XXXII. 352 (*title*) Evidences of *Theriodonts in Permian Deposits elsewhere [etc.]. *Ibid.* 356 It is to the Theriodont, not the Labyrinthodont order that such humerus must be referred. **1877** LE CONTE *Elem. Geol.* (1879) 410 Remarkable reptiles,..which from some mammalian characters, especially in the teeth, he [Owen] calls Theriodonts (beast tooth). **1905** *Athenæum* 25 Feb. 246/3 On..the Anatomy of a Theriodont Reptile. **1897** *Edin. Rev.* July 239 He rightly declines to trace back all *theriolatry to totemism. [**1620** ALSTED *Encycl.* 625 Physiognomia *theriologica est bestiarum.] **1697** EVELYN *Numism.* viii. 296 Compares this Theriologic Physiognomy and resemblance of Brutes. **1653** R. SANDERS *Physiogn.* b ij, I have dispatcht all the parts of Physiognomie except the *Theriological part. **1652** GAULE *Magastrom.* xix. 165 *Theriomancy, [divining] by Beasts. **1845** FORD *Handbk. Spain* II. xi. 751/2 Portraits of *theriomaniac Austrian royalty. **1857** DUNGLISON *Med. Lex.*, **Theriotomy*, zootomy. **1845** FORD *Handbk. Spain* I. vii. 535/1 These *theriotrophical legends are of all countries; thus Habis, king of Spain, was reared by a doe. **1898** SIR H. HOWORTH in *Nat. Sc.* Apr. 269 To separate the *Theriozoic beds into two series.

**Theriodic** (þɪəriǫˑdik), *a. rare*⁻⁰. [f. Gr. θηριωδία brutality, savagery + -IC.] Of ulcers, etc., Malignant.

**1899** in *Syd. Soc. Lex.* **1909** in *Cent. Dict., Suppl.*

**Theriomorphic** (þɪəri͵mǭˑɹfik), *a.* [f. THERIO- + Gr. μορφή form + -IC: cf. MORPHIC.] Having the form of a beast; also *transf.* of or pertaining to a deity worshipped in the form of a beast.

**1882** *Sat. Rev.* 21 Jan. 71 The process by which Theriomorphic became Anthropomorphic Gods is..sufficiently illustrated in early religions. **1884** E. H. PLUMPTRE in *Expositor* July 4 The 'abominations' of the Egyptian theriomorphic worship. **1890** L. R. FARNELL in *Oxf. Phil. Soc. Tr.* 7 Feb. 9 The perfectly human God, the transition from a..vaguer and often theriomorphic conception of him. **1898** *Q. Rev.* July 103 An elaborate cult of bestial gods, or at least a theriomorphic ritual.

So **Theriomorphosis** (-mǭˑɹfǫsis, -mǫɹfōˑsis), transformation into the shape of a beast; **Therioˑmoˑrphous** *a.*, **a.** = THERIOMORPHIC; **b.** *Zool.* of or pertaining to the *Theriomorpha*, in Owen's classification, a suborder of *Batrachia*; also in *Palæont.* resembling a quadruped or mammal, as 'the theriomorphous reptiles of the Permian period'.

**1865** BARING-GOULD *Werewolves* x. 172 The phase of transition from theriomorphosis to anthropomorphosis.

† **Therk,** *a. Obs.* Forms: 3 ðherk, 4–5 þerke, 5 therk, thirke, thyrke, 7 thurck, thurk. [app. a variant of ME. *derk*, DARK; but the change of initial *d* to *ð, þ*, is abnormal and unexplained: cf. however OS. *thimm*, beside OE. *dim(m)*, OFris. *dimme* DIM.] = DARK *a.*

*c* **1250** Ðherk [see THERKNESS below]. **13..** *Sir Beues* (A.) 2790 Til it was þe þerke niȝt. *c* **1430** LYDG. *Min. Poems* (Percy Soc.) 204 Your byl clothyd thirke and on clene. *c* **1440** *Jacob's Well* 219 Ffyve cytees schal be in þe lond of thirknes spekyng wyth a chaungyng tunge. Þis is for to saye, ffyve citees schal be in the therk body of man. *c* **1450** *Cov. Myst.* xvii. (1841) 170 To marre ȝow in a thyrke myste. *a* **1682** SIR T. BROWNE *Tracts* viii. (1684) 146 Words..of common use in Norfolk..as..*Thurck*. **1691** RAY *S. & E. C. Words*, *Tharky* adj., 'very *tharky*', very dark. *Suff... Thurk*, *Norf. Ibid.* Pref. 5 *Thurk* is plainly from the Saxon *deorc*, dark.

Hence † **Therk** *v. Obs.* (3 þirk) = DARK *v.*; † **Theˑrkness** *Obs.*, darkness.

*c* **1275** LAY. 11973 Þirkede vnder sonne Þustrede þe wolkne. *c* **1250** *Gen. & Ex.* 3102 Ðhikke ðherknesse cam on ðat lond. *c* **1440** [see above]. *c* **1485** *Digby Myst.* III. 773 Owt of þe ded slep of therknesse de-fend vs aye!

**Therl**, obs. form of THIRL *sb.*[1] and *v.*[1]

**Therm**[1] (þɜɹm). *arch.* Also 6–8 therme. [prob. a. F. *therme* (13th c. in Godef. *Compl.*) in pl., ad. L. *thermæ*, a. Gr. θέρμαι hot baths, pl. of θέρμη heat.] A public bath or bathing establishment.

**1549** THOMAS *Hist. Italie* (1549) 28 b, A noumbre of hotehouses in euerie Therme. **1606** SYLVESTER *Du Bartas* II. iv. I. *Trophies* 1112 O cleer Therms, If so your Waves be cold; what is it warms, Nay burns my heart? **1613** DANIEL *Hist. Eng.* I. 25 Britaine..could not but partake of the magnificence of their goodly structures, Thermes, Aquaductes, High wayes. **1629** MAXWELL tr. *Herodian* (1635) 175 The Theaters, Therms, and all the splendor and glory thereof. **1726** LEONI *Alberti's Archit.* II. 74/1 A public Bath or Therme. **1890** BRIDGETT *Blunders & Forg.* ii. 32 The same author describes the therms at Paris.

**Therm**[2] (þɜɹm). *Physics.* [mod. f. Gr. θερμός hot, warm, θέρμη heat.] A proposed unit of heat: the quantity of heat required to raise the temperature of one gramme of water at its maximum density one degree centigrade. (Not generally accepted.)

**1888** *Rep. Brit. Assoc.* 56 It was resolved, on the motion of Mr. W. H. Preece, to adopt the name 'Therm' for the Gramme-Water-Degree-Centigrade Unit of Heat. **1888** *Nature* 13 Dec. 159 *Electrical Notes*...The term 'therm', in place of *calorie*, for the unit of heat in the C. G. S. system, has not met with general approbation. **1889** *Rep. Brit. Assoc.* 514 The *Therm* as the unit of heat..did not commend itself to the French members [of the Electrical Congress in Paris, 1889]. They preferred for the present to retain the word *Calorie*. **1899** EDSER *Heat for Adv. Students* Pref. 1 Following the nomenclature used in the *Smithsonian Physical Tables* the term *therm* has been [here] used [etc.].

**Therm**[3], erron. f. TERM *sb.* (sense 15): see quot.

**1727–41** CHAMBERS *Cycl.*, *Terms, Termes, Termini*...Some write the word *thermes*, from *hermes*, a name the Greeks gave the god Mercury; whose statue..was placed in several of the cross-ways. **1811** W. COOKE *Thames* Sign. 39, lf. 3 The first object is the bust of Flora, on a therm. **1846** WORCESTER, *Therm*.., a pedestal increasing upwards for the reception of a bust.

**Therm**, obs. and Sc. form of THARM, intestine.

‖ **Thermæ** (þɜˑɹmī), *sb. pl. Cl. Antiq.* [L. = 'baths': see THERM[1].] One of the public bathing establishments of the ancient Romans and Greeks; also, hot springs (? *obs.*).

**1600** HOLLAND *Livy, Summ. Mar.* IV. xxv. 1382 Those places where they built these baines and hote houses, they call Thermæ. **1695** WOODWARD *Nat. Hist. Earth* III. i. 144 Thermæ, Natural Baths, or Hot-Springs. **1832** GELL *Pompeiana* I. iv. 47 The baths or thermae. **1908** *Westm. Gaz.* 31 Dec. 4/1 Unlike the thermæ of the *élégants* of Pompeii..the R.A.C. baths will have ample window space.

‖ **Thermæsthesia** (þɜ̄ɹmĕsþīˑsiă). *Path.* [mod. L., f. Gr. θέρμη heat + αἴσθησις perception.] Sensitiveness to heat or cold; the sense of heat. Hence **Thermæsthesioˑmeter**: see quot. 1885.

**1885** *Buck's Handbk. Med. Sc.* I. 85/2 *Thermæsthesiometer*, for measuring the sensibility to differences of temperature, Weber used two long glass phials filled with oil. *Ibid.* 86/1 In 1866, Eulenburg described his thermæsthesiometer. **1899** *Allbutt's Syst. Med.* VIII. 169 Thermæsthesia.—There are two disorders of subjective sensation of heat and cold.

**Thermal** (þɜ̄ˑɹmăl), *a.* [= F. *thermal* (Buffon), f. Gr. θέρμη heat + -AL.]

**1.** Of, pertaining to, or of the nature of *thermæ* or hot springs; of a spring, etc., (naturally) hot or warm; also, having hot springs.

**1756** C. LUCAS *Ess. Waters* III. 69 These thermal waters are absolutely colorless. **1800** W. SAUNDERS *Min. Waters* Pref. 17 The thermal waters of Bath or Buxton. *Ibid.* iv. 352 Enriched with several thermal springs. **1859** R. F. BURTON *Centr. Afr.* in *Jrnl. Geog. Soc.* XXIX. 81 Detached boulders, blackened, probably, by the thermal fumes. **1876** M. COLLINS *From Midn. to Midn.* III. ix. 169 The thermal city's [Bath's] superb crescents. **1898** *Allbutt's Syst. Med.* V. 1000 Simple thermal baths at 90° F. or under commonly tend to reduce the pulse-rate.

**2.** Of or pertaining to heat; determined, measured, or operated by heat.

The *thermal capacity* of a body (cf. CAPACITY 1 c, HEAT *sb.* 2 d) is measured by the quantity of heat required to raise its temperature one degree; the *thermal efficiency* of an engine, by the ratio of the work done by it to the heat supplied to it. *Thermal storage*: a system of storing water at high pressure and temperature in vessels above the boilers during hours of low load in electric generating stations. *Thermal unit*: a unit of heat; the *British thermal unit* (abbrev. *B. Th. U.*) is the amount of heat required to raise the temperature of a pound of water at its maximum density through one degree Fahrenheit.

**1837** BREWSTER *Magnet.* 267 The thermal and the magnetic equators are connected..with the thermal and magnetic poles. **1870** TYNDALL *Lect. Electr.* § 10 To produce both magnetic and thermal phenomena. **1876** *Catal. Sci.*

*App. S. Kens. Mus.* § 1056 The heat is calculated as follows, either in calories or British thermal units. **1884** KNIGHT *Dict. Mech., Suppl.* 891/1 Thermal Alarm for Hot Boxes. **1910** J. G. HORNER in *Encycl. Brit.* IV. 148/2 In some cases where the work required is very intermittent, thermal storage is employed. **1910** H. L. CALLENDAR *ibid.* V. 61/1 The specific heat of a substance is sometimes defined as the thermal capacity of unit mass. *Ibid.* XIII. 137/1 English Engineers usually state results in terms of the British Thermal Unit (B. Th. U.). *Ibid.* 138/1 The improvement in thermal efficiency obtained by expansive working.

**3.** *fig.* Heated with passion; erotic, passionate, impassioned.

**1866** *Lond. Rev.* 18 Aug. 178 Instead of the establishment in England of a thermal school of poetry; instead of the revivification of a grand (and wicked) old Paganism.

Hence **Therma·lity,** thermal condition; **The·rmally** *adv.*, in a thermal manner; by means of or with regard to heat.

**1884** tr. *L. Brachet's Aix-les-bains* I. 74 We must pay special attention to the thermality, which is the sole bond of union [etc.]. **1871** TYNDALL *Fragm. Sc.* (1879) I. xvii. 449 The experiments proved rock-salt to be coloured thermally.

**Thermammeter** (þəɹmæ·mĭtəɹ). [f. THERM(O- + AMMETER.] A device whereby the ampere-strength of an electric current is measured by the quantity of heat that it generates.

**1891** in *Cent. Dict.*

‖**Thermanæsthesia** (þɜ̄ımænėsþī·siă). *Path.* [mod.L. f. as prec. + ANÆSTHESIA.] Absence or loss of heat-perception; insensibility to heat.

**1885** *Buck's Handbk. Med. Sc.* I. 86/2 By extremes of heat or cold a thermanæsthesia is produced. **1899** *Allbutt's Syst. Med.* VII. 355 Cases..in which there have been complete analgesia and thermanæsthesia.

**Therma·ntic,** *a.* (*sb.*) *Med.* Now *rare* or *Obs.* [ad. Gr. θερμαντικός, f. θερμαίνειν to heat. Cf. F. *thermantique* (15th c. in Hatz.-Darm.).] That promotes warmth; heating, calefacient.

**1748** tr. *Renatus' Distemp. Horses* 175 The Animal must be warmed with thermantick Drenches. **1768** [W. DONALDSON] *Life Sir B. Sapskull* II. xii. 81 He then pulled out of his pocket a large phial of thermantic ingredients, which he had prepared..the night before. **1860** MAYNE *Expos. Lex.*, *Thermanticus*, promoting warmth;..thermantic.

**B.** as *sb.* A heating medicine, a calefacient.

**1706** PHILLIPS (ed. Kersey), *Thermanticks*, Medicines that cause Heat.

**Thermantidote** (þəɹmæ·ntidǫ̈ut). [f. Gr. θέρμη heat + ANTIDOTE.] An antidote to heat.

**1.** A rotating fan fixed in a window-opening and incased in wet tatties, used in India to drive in a current of cooled air. (Introduced in 1831.)

'[It] is in fact a winnowing machine fitted to a window aperture' (Yule).

**1840** W. G. OSBORNE *Crt. & Camp Runjeet Sing* 132 The thermometer at 112 all day in our tents, notwithstanding tatties, thermantidotes, and every possible invention.. to lessen the stifling heat. **1898** P. MANSON *Trop. Diseases* xii. 214 Rooms should be kept dark during the day, and cooled by means of punkahs, thermantidotes, tatties.

**2.** *Med.* A cooling medicine. *rare*—⁰.

**1860** MAYNE *Expos. Lex.*, *Thermantidotum*, term for a medicine..: a thermantidote. **1890** BILLINGS *Med. Dict.*, *Thermantidote*, a remedy against excessive heat or fever.

**Thermatology** (þɜ̄ımătǫ·lŏdʒi). *rare*—⁰. [f. Gr. θέρμα, θερματ- = θέρμη heat: see -LOGY.] Properly = THERMOLOGY; but given in Dicts. as = *thermotherapy* (see THERMO-).

**1891** in *Cent. Dict.* **1899** *Syd. Soc. Lex.*, *Thermatology*, science of treatment of disease by heat, or specifically by thermal baths.

**Therme,** obs. form of THARM, THERM [1].

†**Thermefy,** *v.* *Obs.* *rare*—⁰. [irreg. f. Gr. θερμ-ός hot + -FY.]

**1656** BLOUNT *Glossogr.*, *Thermefy*, to chafe or make one hot with outragious eating and drinking hot things.

**Thermelæometer**: see THERMO-.

**Thermic** (þɜ̄·ımik), *a.* [f. Gr. θέρμη heat + -IC: cf. F. *thermique.*] Of or pertaining to heat; of the nature of heat; = THERMAL 2.

*Thermic balance* = BOLOMETER. *Thermic fever*, fever resulting from external heat, esp. heat-stroke, insolation.

**1846** GROVE *Corr. Phys. Forces* 39 The definite thermic effects produced by chemical changes, have been lately much studied. **1849** MRS. SOMERVILLE *Connex. Phys. Sc.* xxv. 266 Those rays of the spectrum, whether luminous or thermic. **1890** BILLINGS *Med. Dict.*, *Thermic fever*, heat-stroke. **1896** *Allbutt's Syst. Med.* I. 499 In thermic fever or insolation the object is to reduce the temperature. **1897** *Ibid.* II. 313 Simple continued, thermic, and enteric fevers. **1899** *Ibid.* VIII. 706 Tactile, thermic, and pain sensibility.

So **The·rmical** *a.* in same sense; hence **The·rmically** *adv.*, in a thermic manner; thermally.

**1851** CARPENTER *Man. Phys.* (ed. 2) 44 This Power..manifests itself in those phenomena which we call electrical, magnetical, chemical, thermical, optical, or mechanical. **1859** R. F. BURTON *Centr. Afr.* in *Jrnl. Geog. Soc.* XXIX. 261 There are no unhealthy exhalations.., no thermical extremes nor surprises. **1877** ROSENTHAL *Muscles & Nerves* 109 A portion of the nerve may be heated, that is, it may be thermically irritated.

**Thermid**: see THEREMID *adv.*

**Thermidor** (þɜ̄ımidǭɹ, ‖tęrmidor). [Fr. (1793), f. Gr. θέρμη heat + δῶρον gift.] The eleventh month of the French revolutionary calendar, extending (in 1794) from July 19 to August 17.

**1827** SCOTT *Napoleon* Introd., The 9th Thermidor, or 27th July. **1842** BRANDE *Dict. Sc.*, etc. s.v. *Thermidor*, It was the month signalized by the overthrow of Robespierre and the Reign of Terror; thence commonly called the Revolution of Thermidor, and those who boasted of having participated in it called themselves Thermidorians.

**Thermidorian** (þɜ̄ımidǭ·riăn), *sb.* and *a.* Also -ean. [a. F. *thermidorien*, f. THERMIDOR + *-ien*, -IAN.]

**A.** *sb.* *Fr. Hist.* One of those who took part in the overthrow of Robespierre on the 9th Thermidor (27 July) 1794.

**1827** SCOTT *Napoleon* Introd., The *Thermidoriens*, as the actors in Robespierre's downfall termed themselves. *Ibid.* III. 58 The Thermidoreans, who had killed Robespierre and now reigned in his stead. **1842** [see THERMIDOR].

**B.** *adj.* **a.** Of, pertaining, or appropriate to the month Thermidor. **b.** Of or pertaining to the Thermidorians: see A.

**1891** T. HARDY *Tess* xxii, June passed, and the Thermidorean weather which came in its wake seemed [etc.]. **1895** *Edin. Rev.* Oct. 391 The Thermidorian leader [Barras].

**Thermite** (þɜ̄·ımait). Also thermit. [ad. Ger. *thermit*, f. Gr. θέρμη heat, θερμός hot + *-it* = -ITE [1].] A mixture of finely divided aluminium and oxide of iron or other metal, which produces on combustion a very high temperature (*c* 3000° C.)

Invented by Mr. Claude Vauten of London; named subsequently by Dr. H. Goldschmidt of Essen.

**1900** *Engineering Mag.* XIX. 756/2 A mixture called 'thermit' consisting essentially of iron oxide and aluminium. **1901** *Westm. Gaz.* 2 May 4/2 The application of 'thermite', as the mixture has been named, to welding steel tubes and rails was illustrated. **1901** *Nature* 8 Aug. 362/1 To this mixture the name of 'thermit' has been given, and several varieties of it, adapted to various kinds of work, are used. **1906** *Dundee Advertiser* 26 June 10/1 The neat developed in the combustion of thermit,..which makes it possible to mend iron castings weighing tons.

**Thermo-** (þɜ̄·ımo), before a vowel usually **therm-** (but often in full form), repr. Gr. θερμο-, combining form of θερμό-s hot, θέρμη heat; entering into many scientific and technical terms, as THERMOCHEMISTRY, THERMODYNAMIC, THERMOGRAPH, THERMOMETER, THERMOSCOPE, etc., q. v., and their derivatives; also in the following words of less frequent use or more recent formation. (In some of these *thermo-* is used as an abbreviation of THERMO-ELECTRIC.)

**The·rmelæo·meter** [Gr. ἔλαιον oil: see -METER], an apparatus for measuring the heat evolved by mixing concentrated sulphuric acid with various fixed oils. ‖ **The·rmo-æsthe·sia** = THERMÆSTHESIA. ‖ **The·rmo-anæsthe·sia** = THERMANÆSTHESIA. **Thermoa·queous** *a.*: see quot. **Thermoba·rograph,** an instrument which simultaneously records temperature and atmospheric pressure. **Thermobaro·meter,** a name given to two distinct modifications of the barometer: see quots. **Thermo-ba·ttery,** short for *thermo-electric battery*. **Thermo-ca·lcite** [CALCITE], a name for non-crystalline limestones. **The·rmo-call,** (*a*) a fire-alarm operated by a thermo-electric battery; (*b*) an electric fire-alarm in which the circuit is closed automatically when the temperature reaches a certain point. **Thermo-cau·tery,** any form of actual cautery; *spec.* a hollow platinum cautery in which heat is maintained by means of benzine or gasolene vapour. **The·rmo-cell,** a thermo-electric cell or couple. **Thermochao·tic** *a.*, of or pertaining to disintegration or dissolution by heat. **The·rmocline** [Gr. κλίνειν to incline], a temperature gradient; *esp.* an abrupt temperature gradient occurring in a body of water. **The·rmo-couple,** short for *thermo-electric couple* (see COUPLE *sb.* 12). **The·rmo-current,** the electric current produced in a thermo-electric battery; also (*nonce-use*) a stream of warm air or water. **Thermo-diffu·sion,** diffusion of heat. **The·rmodynamo·meter,** a sensitive thermometer in which the thermometric substance is the saturated vapour of some volatile liquid supporting a column of mercury. **Thermo-ela·stic** *a.*, pertaining to elasticity in connexion with heat. **The·rmo-electro·meter,** an instrument for measuring the heating power of an electric current, or for determining the strength of a current by the heat produced. **The·rmo-electromo·tive** *a.*, of, pertaining to, or of the nature of electromotive force produced by heat; = THERMO-ELECTRIC I. **Thermo-ele·ctroscope,** an instrument for indicating temperature electrically, as a thermopile. **The·rmo-e·lement,** a thermo-electric couple as an element of a battery. **Thermo-exci·tory** *a.*: see quot. 1899. **Thermo-expa·nsive** *a.*, expanding under the influence of heat. **Thermo-fo·cal** *a.*, of or pertaining to the focal length of a lens as influenced by heat. **Thermo-galvano·meter,** a thermo-electric instrument for measuring small electric currents. **The·rmo-gauge,** a form of pyrometer (*Cent. Dict., Suppl.*). **Thermo-geogra·phical** *a.*, pertaining to the geographical distribution and variation of temperature; so **Thermogeo·graphy,** the study of this. **Thermo-hydro·logy** [Gr. ὕδωρ water], the scientific study of thermal waters. **Thermo-hydro·meter,** a combined instrument showing the temperature and density of a liquid. **Thermo-hy·grograph** [Gr. ὑγρός moist], a combined instrument recording the temperature and the humidity of the air. **Thermo-hy·groscope** [-SCOPE], a combined instrument indicating the temperature and humidity of the air. **Thermo-inhi·bitory** *a.*, pertaining to the prevention of undue heat in the body; applied to a part or function of the nervous system (Billings 1890). **Thermo-i·sopleth** [Gr. ἰσοπληθ-ής equal in quantity, number, etc.]: see quot. **The·rmo-ju·nction,** the junction of two metals in a thermo-couple. **Thermokinema·tics,** the theory of the motion of heat. **The·rmo-lamp**: see quot. **Thermo-lumine·scence,** luminescence resulting from exposure to high temperature; hence **Thermo-lumine·scent** *a.*, characterized by or pertaining to thermo-luminescence. **Thermo-magne·tic** *a.*, pertaining to or of the nature of thermo-magnetism. **Thermo-ma·gnetism,** magnetism caused or modified by the action of heat. **Thermo-mano·meter** [MANOMETER], an instrument for measuring at the same time the temperature and elasticity of vapour. **Thermo-metamo·rphic** *a.*, of or pertaining to thermo-metamorphism. **Thermo-metamo·rphism,** *Geol.*, metamorphism produced by the action of heat. **Thermo-mo·tive** *a.*, of, pertaining to, or caused by heat applied to produce motion, as in a thermo-motor. **Thermo-mo·tor,** an engine driven by the expansive power of heated air or gas. **Thermo-neutra·lity,** neutrality in relation to temperature. **The·rmo-pair** = *thermo-couple*. **Thermo-palpa·tion**: see quot. 1899. **Thermopegology** (-pīgǫ·lŏdʒi) [Gr. πηγή spring], the scientific study of thermal springs. **Thermo·phagy** [-PHAGY]: see quot. 1899. **The·rmophore** [-PHORE], a portable heating apparatus: see quots. **Thermophyllite** (-fi·lait), *Min.* [Gr. φύλλον leaf; A. E. Nordenskiöld, 1855, in Swedish], a light brown variety of serpentine which exfoliates when heated, found in aggregate masses of small scaly crystals. **Thermopla·stic** *a.*, capable of being moulded or bent by heat. ‖ **Thermoplegia** (-plī·dʒiă) *Path.* [Gr. πληγή stroke], heat-stroke. **Thermo-radio·meter**: see quot. **Thermo-re·gulator,** an apparatus for regulating temperature; a thermostat. **Thermosy·nthesis,** chemical combination due to the action of heat. **Thermosysta·ltic** *a.*, of or pertaining to systaltic motion due to heat. **Thermote·lephone,** a thermo-electric telephone. **Thermo-te·nsile** *a.*, of or pertaining to cohesive power as affected by temperature. **Thermo-te·nsion,** tension or strain applied to material at a specified temperature to increase or test its tensile power. **Thermo-the·rapy** (also in Gr.-L. form -therapei·a) [Gr. θεραπεία medical treatment], treatment of disease by heat. **Thermoto·xin,** a poison developed in the body by heat. **The·rmo-unsta·ble** *a.* = THERMOLABILE. **Thermo-volta·ic** *a.*, of or pertaining to the thermal effects of voltaic electricity, or to heat and voltaic electricity.

**1890** *Jrnl. Soc. Chem. Industry* IX. 113 The heat evolved by mixing the oil with sulphuric acid is determined by means of the..apparatus named by the author [F. Jean in *J. Pharm. Chim.* (1889) XX. 337] '*Thermeleometer'. **1909** *Cent. Dict.* Suppl., *Thermoæsthesia. **1890** BILLINGS *Nat. Med. Dict.*, *Thermo-anæsthesia. **1899** *Allbutt's Syst. Med.* VII. 47 There was complete thermo-anæsthesia below the second rib. **1881** RAYMOND *Mining Gloss.*, **Thermo-aqueous*, produced by, or related to, the action of heated waters. **1891** *Cent. Dict.*, *Thermobarograph. **1864** WEBSTER, **Thermobarometer*, a barometric instrument graduated for giving altitudes by the boiling point of water. **1868** WATTS *Dict. Chem.* V. 761 *Thermobarometer*...Applied by Belloni to a syphon-barometer having its two wide legs united by a narrow tube, so that it could be used either in its ordinary position as a barometer, or in the reversed position as a thermometer. **1849** NOAD *Electricity* (ed. 3) 427 In order to effect the decomposition of water, Mr. Watkins employs a massive *thermo-battery, with pairs of bismuth and antimony. **1888** *Cassell's Encycl. Dict.*, *Thermo-calcite. **1895** *Funk's Standard Dict.*, *Thermo-call. **1902** SLOANE *Stand. Electr. Dict.*, *Thermo Call*, (*a*) An electric alarm or call bell operated by thermo-electric currents...(*b*) See *Thermo-electric Call.* **1879** BRYANT *Pract. Surg.* II. 6 The galvano-caustic or *thermo-cautery is superior to any. **1907** *Daily News* 13 Nov. 11/1 The adoption of this method of telephony was made possible by the invention of a *thermo-cell for use in the receiving circuit. **1895** *Funk's Stand. Dict.*, *Thermochaotic. **1898** *Nat. Science* May 297 As regards the production of the *Thermocline, Prof. Birge believes that, in Lake Mendota at least, it is due to the concurrence of gentle winds and hot weather. **1902** *Nature* 6 Nov. 16/1 Throughout the circulating water above the thermocline, oxygen was abundant, but carbonic acid was absent...Just below the thermocline both gases were present. **1890** *Lond., Edin. & Dubl. Philos. Mag.* Feb. 141 A practical method for the calibration of *thermocouples by aid of boiling-points. **1901** *Nature* 23 May 92/2 The temperatures were measured with the thermocouple. **1849** NOAD *Electricity* (ed. 3) 428 Dr. Andrews..succeeded in obtaining chemical decompositions, by this peculiar *thermo-current. *a* **1859** G. WILSON *Relig. Chem.* (1862) 16 A sleeper in a confined chamber could gain nothing from the winds, or thermo-currents, or the far-off sea. **1899** *Syd. Soc. Lex.*, **Thermo-diffusion*, diffusion (of gas) by inequalities of temperature. **1909** *Cent. Dict.*, Suppl., *Thermodynamometer. **1903** *Science Abstracts* VI. 130 To represent the *thermo-elastic properties of gases, liquids, and solids as the statical properties of monocyclic systems. **1842** FRANCIS *Dict. Arts*, etc., *Clarke's* ..**Thermo-Electrometer*,..an instrument which professes to ascertain the deflagrating, or heating power of an electric current. **1849** NOAD *Electricity* (ed. 3) 247 The instrument employed was a Harris's thermo-electrometer. **1890** *Lond., Edin. & Dubl. Philos. Mag.* Feb. 146 *Thermoelectromotive forces are..expressed in terms of a fixed standard, the torsional rigidity of the platinum wire. **1895** *Funk's Stand. Dict.*, *Thermo-electroscope. **1888** *Cassell's Encycl. Dict.*, *Thermo-element. **1891** *Cent. Dict.*, *Thermo-excitory. **1899** *Syd. Soc. Lex.*, *Thermo-excitory*, having the function of exciting the production of heat. **1854** J. SCOFFERN in *Orr's Circ. Sc., Chem.* 118 A *thermo-expansive material. **1903** *Science* 27 Feb. 333 A study of the *thermo-focal changes in long focus lenses. **1867** *Chambers' Encycl.* IX. 401/2 Special galvanometers..in which the coil wire is short..and thick..are called *thermo-galvanometers. **1902** SLOANE *Stand. Electr. Dict.* App., *Thermo-Galvanometer*, a galvanometer whose needle is suspended in a special form of thermo-electric couple.. used to measure small amounts of radiant energy. **1895** C. L. MADSEN (*title*) *Thermo-geographical Studies: General Exposition of the Analytical Method applied to Researches on Temperature and Climate. **1897** *Ibid.* Advt., Articles on the subject of *Thermo-Geography will be most thankfully received. **1881** PEALE in *12th Rep. U. S. Geol. & Geog. Survey* II. (1883) 355 *Thermo-hydrology. **1884** *Athenæum* 16 Aug. 211/2 The chapters on 'Thermo-hydrology' give evidences of a thoroughly scientific observer. **1894** *Brit. Jrnl. Photogr.* XLI. 43 Mr. W. E. Hales exhibited Fletcher's *Thermo-hydrometer. **1901** *Pop. Sc. Monthly* Dec. 186 An interesting figure shows the '*thermo-isopleths' for Berlin, these lines indicating, in one drawing, both the diurnal and the annual march of the air temperature. **1889** *L. E. & D. Philos. Mag.* Sept. 213 If the heat generated were immediately communicated to the *thermo-junction. **1903** *Times* 10 Sept. 10/4 A number of thermo-junctions of the platinum metals for use up to the highest temperatures have also been studied. **1871** CLERK MAXWELL *Heat* Introd. 9 The theory of the equilibrium of heat might be called Thermostatics, and that of the motion of heat *Thermokinematics. **1828** WEBSTER, **Thermolamp*, an instrument for furnishing light by means of inflammable gas. *Med. Repos.* **1897** J. J. THOMSON in *Smithsonian Rep.* (1898) 158 The phenomenon called by its discoverer, Prof. E. Wiedemann, *thermoluminescence. **1898** SIR W. CROOKES *Addr. Brit. Assoc.* 22 Fluor-spar, which by prolonged heating has lost its power of luminescing when re-heated, regains the power of thermo-luminescence when exposed to Röntgen rays. **1906** J. B. BURKE *Orig. Life* xiii. 241 Many substances, when warmed, possess the power of radiating energy which they had previously stored up in some other way: a phenomenon which is known as Thermoluminescence. **1899** A. S. HERSCHEL in *Nature* 11 May 29/2 A very moderate degree of heat suffices to expel completely from minerals..all the store of *thermo-luminescent energy which..they more or less abundantly possess. **1823** T. S. TRIALL in *Ann. Philos.* N. S. VI. Dec. 449 Having been lately engaged in some *thermomagnetic experiments. **1860** MAYNE *Expos. Lex.*, **Thermo-magnetism*, the same as Thermo-electricity. **1864** in WEBSTER. **1883** *Athenæum* 9 June 736/1 The use of a *thermo manometer, which would indicate whether the vapour pressure is below that to be expected from the temperature of the water. **1889** HARKER in *Geol. Mag.* VI. 17 The interpolation of *thermo-metamorphic rocks. *Ibid.* 16 High temperature and low pressure (**thermo-metamorphism*). **1881** WATTS *Dict. Chem.* VIII. 985 The term *thermo-neutrality is employed..to express the fact that the quantity of heat evolved or absorbed when a salt is dissolved in water already containing equivalent quantities of other salts, is, for the most part, the same that it would be if the former salt were dissolved in pure water. **1807** JOYCE *Sci. Dial., Electr.* vi. (1846) 424 Delicate *thermo-pairs have been used to obtain the temperature of the human body. **1891** *Cent. Dict.*, *Thermopalpation. **1899** *Syd. Soc. Lex.*, *Thermo-palpation*, palpation of the surface of the body, with a view of determining local or general variations of temperature. **1888** *Cassell's Encycl. Dict.*, *Thermo-pegology. **1860** MAYNE *Expos. Lex.*, *Thermophagy. **1899** *Syd. Soc. Lex.*, *Thermophagy*, the habit of swallowing very hot food. **1900** *Brit. Med. Jrnl.* 5 May 1105 To sterilise this instrument [i. e. a catheter].. with a small pocket *thermophore. **1901** *Lancet* 9 Nov. 1297/2 The introduction of a ring-shaped thermophore. **1868** DANA *Min.* 465 *Thermophyllite. **1883** *Fisheries Exhib. Catal.* 63 *Thermoplastic Splints, likewise Splints for Fractures and Broken Bones. **1909** *Cent. Dict.* Suppl., *Thermoplegia. **1876** *Catal. Sci. App. S. Kens. Mus.* § 1056 *Thermo-radiometer, [an instrument] for measuring losses of heat by radiation from walls of furnaces, sides of steam boilers, etc. **1875** WATTS *Dict. Chem.* VII. 1153 An automatic *thermo-regulator for use in the preparation of nitrous oxide and other gases. **1899** CAGNEY *Jaksch's Clin. Diagn.* x. (ed. 4) 446 Of these [thermostats] the author uses the thermo-regulator of L. Meyer. **1895** *Funk's Standard Dict.*, *Thermosystaltic. **1899** *Syd. Soc. Lex.*, *Thermosystaltic*, muscular contraction due to heat. **1884** KNIGHT *Dict. Mech.* Suppl., *Thermo-telephone. **1891** *Cent. Dict.* s. v. *Thermotensile*, Elaborate *thermotensile experiments on iron and steel, especially with reference to boiler-iron. **1847** WEBSTER, *Thermotension. **1860** E. WILSON (*title*) *Thermo-therapeia: the heat cure. *Ibid.* 3 Thermo-therapeia is the application of atmospheric air at a high temperature to the surface of the body, for the relief of pain and disease. **1899** *Syd. Soc. Lex.*, *Thermotherapy. **1902** W. WINTERNITZ (*title*) Hydrotherapy, Thermotherapy, Heliotherapy, and Phototherapy. **1902** *Brit. Med. Jrnl.* 5 Apr. 846 To demonstrate two very different forms of complement—one a *thermo-unstable, and the other a thermo-stable. **1895** *Funk's Stand. Dict.*, *Thermo-voltaic.

**Thermo-æsthesia** to **-chaotic**: see THERMO-.

**Thermoche·mistry.** [f. THERMO- + CHEMISTRY.] That branch of chemical science which deals with the quantities of heat evolved or absorbed when substances undergo chemical change or enter into solution; e. g. the amount of heat evolved when hydrogen burns in oxygen or when sodium hydroxide is neutralized by sulphuric acid. Also sometimes used in a wider sense to include all relations of heat to substances, such as conductivity, specific heat, etc.

**1844** JOULE in *L. E. & D. Philos. Mag.* (1845) May 382 The phænomena described in the present paper, as well as most of the facts of thermo-chemistry, agree with this theory. **1880** CLEMINSHAW *Wurtz' Atom. The.* 330 It is useless to bring forward in opposition to the hypothesis of atoms considerations drawn from thermo-chemistry. **1901** *Westm. Gaz.* 16 Dec., Up to the war of 1870 his [Berthelot's] time was mainly spent on researches in the region of physical chemistry, culminating in the foundation of a new science—that of thermo-chemistry.

So **Thermoche·mic, Thermoche·mical** *adjs.*, of or pertaining to thermochemistry; **Thermoche·mically** *adv.*, by means of or with reference to thermochemistry; **Thermoche·mist**, one who is skilled in thermochemistry.

**1871** THOMSEN in *Jrnl. Chem. Soc.* XXIV. 878 On the Inaccuracy of Favre and Silbermann's *Thermochemical Determinations made with the Mercury Calorimeter. **1880** CLEMINSHAW *Wurtz' Atom. The.* 330 Thermo-chemical facts agree perfectly with the atomic hypothesis. **1901** *Nature* 24 Oct. 644/1 A thermochemical comparison of the action of acids upon oxide of silver before and after the action of hydrogen peroxide. **1890** *Ibid.* 18 Dec. 165/2 *Thermochemists..attempt to draw an impossible distinction between chemical and physical changes.

**Thermochrosy** (þɜːmǫkrǭusi, þɜːmǫ·krǭsi). Also thermochrose (*erron.* -crose), -chro·sis. [f. THERMO- + Gr. χρῶσις colouring. Cf. F. *thermochrose* (Melloni).] The 'coloration' of heat-rays; the property possessed by radiant heat of being composed of waves of different lengths and degrees of refrangibility (thus corresponding to the different colours of light-rays). So **Thermochro·ic** *a.*, of or pertaining to thermochrosy; **The:rmochro͜o·logy**, the science of thermochrosy.

**1847** WHEWELL *Hist. Induct. Sc.* x. i. § 8 (ed. 2) II. 594 M. Melloni..has proposed for this part of thermotics the name Thermochroology. **1864** WEBSTER, *Thermochrosy*. **1866** ATKINSON tr. *Ganot's Physics* (ed. 2) § 379 Different luminous rays being distinguished by their colours, to these different obscure calorific rays Melloni gave the name of thermocrosis [*ed.* 1877 thermocrose] or heat coloration. **1867** MILLER *Elem. Chem.* I. 296 Thermochrosis or calorific tint .. is analogous to a difference in colour. **1895** *Funk's Standard Dict.*, Thermochroic. **1899** *Syd. Soc. Lex.*, *Thermo-chroic*, pertaining to a quality of certain substances that transmit some thermal radiations, but absorb or change others. **1909** *Cent. Dict.* Suppl., *Thermochroic*, of or pertaining to the differences in wave-length of heat-waves, and to the phenomena resulting therefrom.

**Thermocline** to **-current**: see THERMO-.

**Thermod** (þɜ̄·ɹmǫd, -ǭud). [f. THERM(O- + OD [2].] The odic or odylic force of heat; heat 'od': see OD [2] b. **1891** in *Cent. Dict.*

**Thermodin** (þɜ̄·ɹmǫdin). *Pharm.* [? Arbitrarily f. Gr. θερμώδης lukewarm + -IN.] Trade-name: see quot.

**1899** *Syd. Soc. Lex.*, *Thermodin*, acetyl-para-ethoxy-phenylmethane. (Not official.) It forms colourless crystals, almost insoluble in cold, and very slightly soluble in warm water. It is recommended..as a mild antipyretic.

**The:rmodyna·mic** (see DYNAMIC), *a.* [f. THERMO- + DYNAMIC.] Of or relating to thermodynamics; operating or operated by the transformation of heat into motive power.

**1849** THOMSON (Ld. Kelvin) in *Trans. R. Soc. Edin.* XVI. 545 A perfect thermo-dynamic engine. **1851** *Ibid.* XX. 261 In some conceivable 'thermo-dynamic' engines. **1853** RANKINE in *Phil. Trans.* (1854) 125 Third Corollary (of Thermo-Dynamic Functions). *Ibid.* 126 This function which I shall call a Thermo-dynamic Function. **1875** J. D. EVERETT *C. G. S. Syst. Units* ix. 54 By thermodynamic principles, the heat converted into mechanical effect in the cycle of operations is [etc.]. **1882** G. H. DARWIN in *Nature* 16 Feb. 361/1 He shows that the sun and earth together constitute a thermodynamic engine whereby the earth's rotation is accelerated.

So **Thermodyna·mical** *a.*, in same sense; **The:rmodyna·mically** *adv.*, in a thermodynamical manner; **The:rmodynami·cian, The:rmodyna·micist, Thermody·namist**, one versed in thermodynamics.

**1860** MAURY *Phys. Geog. Sea* (Low) ii. § 129 By no means the only body of warm water that the *thermo-dynamical forces of the ocean keep in motion. **1901** *Nature* 27 June 210/2 If the equilibrium between the jelly substance and the water was of a purely thermodynamical character. **1889** THURSTON in *Jrnl. Franklin Inst.* Dec. 467 The quantity so wasted varies with the weight of steam worked *thermodynamically each stroke. **1892** *Cambr. Univ. Corresp.* 15 Mar. 14/1 He failed to make any mark as a '*thermodynamician' during his lifetime. **1889** *Academy* 26 Oct. 273/3 The mechanical equivalent of heat—the familiar 'J.' of *thermodynamicists. **1901** THURSTON in *Smithsonian Rep.* (1902) 267 Prof. De Volson Wood, the greatest of American *thermodynamists of the nineteenth century.

**Thermodyna·mics,** *sb. pl.* [f. as prec. + DYNAMICS.] The theory of the relations between heat and mechanical energy, and of the conversion of either into the other.

**1854** *Phil. Trans.* 116 (*heading*) Mr. Macquorn Rankine on Thermo-dynamics. [Word not in article.] **1854** THOMSON (Ld. Kelvin) in *Trans. R. Soc. Edin.* XXI. 123 Fundamental Principles of General Thermo-dynamics recapitulated. **1867** MURCHISON *Siluria* xx. (ed. 4) 499 The principles of thermo-dynamics. **1871** CLERK MAXWELL *Heat* viii. 152 The principle of the conservation of energy, when applied to heat, is commonly called the First Law of Thermodynamics.

**Thermodynamometer, -elastic**: see THERMO-.

**The:rmo-ele·ctric,** *a.* (*sb.*) [f. THERMO- + ELECTRIC.]

**1.** Of or pertaining to thermo-electricity; characterized or operated by an electric current produced by difference of temperature. *Thermo-electric battery, current, pair, pile*: see quot. 1876.

**1823** CUMMING in *Ann. Philos.* Sept. 177 (*heading*) A List of Substances arranged according to their Thermoelectric Relations, with a Description of Instruments for exhibiting Rotation by Thermoelectricity. **1832** *Nat. Philos.* II. *Electro-Magnet.* xiii. § 305. 93 (Usef. Knowl. Soc.) The electrical current thus excited has been termed Thermo-electric, in order to distinguish it from the common galvanic current. **1842** FRANCIS *Dict. Arts*, etc., Thermo-Electric Circuit,.. Piles,..Thermometer. **1863** TYNDALL *Heat* i. (1870) App. 77 A thermo-electric pair or couple. *c* **1865** J. WYLDE in *Circ. Sc.* I. 29/1 We observe the thermo-electric battery. **1876** PREECE & SIVEWRIGHT *Telegraphy* 298 A current of electricity will continue to flow so long as a difference of temperature is maintained between the junction and the extremities. This current is named a thermo-electric current, and the two metals form what is known as a thermo-electric pair; a combination of these pairs forms the thermo-electric pile or battery. **1878** GURNEY *Crystallogr.* 115 Crystals sometimes acquire different electrifications when two ends are..differently heated..These crystals are called thermo-electric. **1902** SLOANE *Stand. Electr. Dict.*, *Thermo-electric Telephone*, a telephone transmitter including a thermo-electric battery placed in circuit with the line.

**2.** Of or pertaining to heat and electricity; *thermo-electric alarm* or *call*, a device in which a rise or fall of temperature to a pre-arranged point closes an electric circuit so as to cause a bell to ring.

**1877** KNIGHT *Dict. Mech.*, *Thermo-electric-Alarm*, an apparatus designed to indicate the rise of temperature in bearings for shaftings, or in any kind of machinery or any branch of manufacture where a fixed temperature is desirable. **1902** SLOANE *Stand. Electr. Dict.*, *Thermo-electric Call*, a thermostat arranged to ring a bell or give some indication when the temperature rises or falls beyond certain points.

†**B.** *sb.* (See quot. 1842.) *Obs.*

**1823** CUMMING in *Ann. Philos.* Sept. 179 The motion of the thermoelectrics on the approach of a magnet. **1842** FRANCIS *Dict. Arts*, etc., *Thermo-Electrics*, metallic bodies, the union of which show[s] the effects attributed to thermo-electricity.

So **Thermo-ele·ctrical** *a.*; hence **Thermo-ele·ctrically** *adv.*, in a thermo-electric manner; by means of thermo-electricity.

**1830** *Edinb. Encycl.* XVIII. 584/1 Professor Oersted has proposed to call the current discovered by Dr. Seebeck the thermo-electrical current. **1878** CHRYSTAL in *Encycl. Brit.* VIII. 94/2 A thermoelectric series, any metal in which is thermoelectrically related to any following one. **1881** *Athenæum* 29 Jan. 169/3 A thermo-electrical pile, one end of which is exposed to the heat, the other end being kept cool.

**The:rmo-ele:ctri·city.** [f. THERMO- + ELECTRICITY.] Electricity generated in a body by difference of temperature in its parts; *esp.* an electric current produced in a closed circuit composed of two dissimilar metals when one of the points of union is kept at a temperature different from that of the rest of the circuit. Also, that branch of electrical science which treats of currents produced by means of heat.

**1823** [see THERMO-ELECTRIC 1]. **1827** CUMMING *Man. Electro-Dynamics* 189 On the electro-dynamic effects of heat, or thermo-electricity. **1830** HERSCHEL *Nat. Philos.* 341 The curious relations of electricity to heat, as exhibited in the phenomena of what has been called thermo-electricity. **1834** *Edin. Rev.* LIX. 167 The new branches of magneto-electricity and thermo-electricity. **1871** TYNDALL *Fragm. Sc.* (1879) II. xiv. 347 In 1826 Thomas Seebeck discovered thermo-electricity.

**Thermo-electrometer** to **-gauge**: see THERMO-.

†**The·rmogen.** *Obs. rare*—[0]. [f. THERMO- + -GEN.] A name for the fluid formerly supposed to exist as the material substance of heat; = CALORIC 1. **1847** in WEBSTER.

**Thermogenesis** (þɜːmo͜idʒe·nĭsis). [f. THERMO- + GENESIS.] The generation or production of heat, esp. in the animal body.

**1891** in *Cent. Dict.* **1896** *Allbutt's Syst. Med.* I. 143 The nervous system presides over thermogenesis no less directly than over thermolysis. **1899** *Nature* 10 Aug. 360/1 Thermogenesis and use of energy by man in raising and lowering his own weight.

So **Thermogene·tic, Thermoge·nic** *adjs.*, of or pertaining to thermogenesis; **Thermogenous** (-ǫ·dʒĭnəs) *a.*, produced by or producing heat; **Thermo·geny**, thermogenesis (*Cent. Dict.*, Suppl. 1909).

1860 MAYNE *Expos. Lex.*, *Thermogenus, Min.*, applied by Haüy to a quartz agate which is deposited near the sources of silicious thermal springs..: thermogenous. 1877 FOSTER *Phys.* II. v. (1878) 377 Indications of the existence of what may be called 'thermogenic' nerves and thermogenic nervous mechanisms. 1879 WEBSTER Suppl., *Thermogenous*, producing heat. 1896 *Allbutt's Syst. Med.* I. 151 The thermogenetic chemical processes to which the taking in of food gives rise. 1899 *Ibid.* VIII. 244 In these children thermogenic powers are deficient. 1898 SALTER tr. *Lafar's Techn. Mycol.* I. 165 Thermogenic Bacteria.

**Thermo-geographical**, etc.: see THERMO-.

**Thermogram** (þɜ·ɹmǒgræm). [f. THERMO- + -GRAM: cf. next.] = next, 2.

1883 R. H. SCOTT *Elem. Meteorol.* 38 The thermograms, as such curves are called, are measured every hour. 1901 *Nature* 28 Mar. 522/2 During each winter the Vienna thermograms show some anomalous jumps of temperature, amounting to 3° to 5° C.

**Thermograph** (þɜ·ɹmǒgrɑf). [f. as prec. + -GRAPH: cf. F. *thermographe*.]

1. A figure or tracing produced by the action of heat, esp. of the heat-rays of the spectrum upon a prepared surface.

1840 HERSCHEL in *Proc. Roy. Soc.* 3 Mar. 209 He has discovered a process by which the calorific rays in the solar spectrum are made to affect a surface properly prepared.. so as to form what may be called a *thermograph* of the spectrum. 1865 *Reader* 28 Jan. 105/2 His drying paper presented to him a thermograph of the spectrum, and showed the heating power to extend far beyond the red. 1871 TYNDALL *Fragm. Sc.* (1879) I. ii. 48 The light is cut away,.. but an invisible thermograph remains. 1906 *Athenæum* 23 June 768/3 Such experiments..will yield valuable 'thermographs', as the resulting parti-coloured 'prints' are named.

2. A graphic record of variations of temperature; a heat register: = THERMOGRAM.

1843 *Mech. Mag.* XXXIX. 128 Obtained..by the aid of the pyrometer,..with the addition of the thermograph, or heat-register, which I have added to it. 1878 T. BRYANT *Pract. Surg.* I. 55 These points are well seen in the following thermographs.

3. A thermometric instrument which automatically records variations of temperature; a self-registering thermometer.

1881 *Nature* 15 Sept. 470/2 Bowkett's New Thermograph, ..an instrument for recording changes of temperature, which are measured by the action of heat upon a hollow circular metallic ring connected with a circular vessel. 1883-4 *Med. Ann.* 78 *Thermograph*—an ingenious instrument..for recording in permanent diagrams all variations in temperature occurring in any patient.

**Thermographic** (-græ·fik), *a.* [f. as prec. + -GRAPHIC, or f. prec. + -IC.] Of, pertaining to, or obtained by a thermograph or thermography.

1848 *Art-Union Jrnl.* Mar. 72 We have much satisfaction in recording the Thermographic processes. 1879 *St. George's Hosp. Rep.* IX. 688 In none..was there anything specially remarkable in the thermographic tracings.

**Thermography** (þɜɹmǫ·grăfi). [f. as prec. + -GRAPHY: cf. F. *thermographie*.] Any process of writing or drawing effected or developed by the influence of heat.

1840 HUNT in *Philos. Mag.* Oct. 268 A new.. field of .. inquiry, which may .. end in .. the establishment of the new art of Thermography. 1842 *Ibid.* Dec. 466, I..proposed the name of Thermography, to distinguish it from Photography. 1848 *Art-Union Jrnl.* Mar. 71 From the circumstance that all the results..exhibit a very close relation between the surfaces employed and their powers of radiating heat, the term *Thermography* or Heat-drawing has been employed. 1875 *Ure's Dict. Arts*, etc. (ed. 7), *Thermography*, a term proposed..to express the 'Art of Copying Engravings, &c. on Metal Plates'; the effect being due..to the influence of heat-radiations. 1883 J. F. CAMPBELL *Thermography* i. § 3. 11. *Ibid.* 12 Because light does not act upon the materials used, dark cameras are not needed in thermography.

**Thermo-hydrology** to **-kinematics**: see THERMO-.

**Thermolabile** (þɜ̄ɹmǒlæ·bil, -lē·bil), *a.* [f. THERMO- + LABILE.] Liable to destruction at moderately high temperatures, as certain toxins and serums: opposed to *thermostable*. Hence **The:rmolabi·lity**, thermolabile quality.

1904 *Brit. Med. Jrnl.* 10 Sept. 557 [see THERMOSTABLE]. *Ibid.* 561 The hæmolysis being due to the co-operation of a thermolabile complement—also called alexin—and thermostable immune body, otherwise amboceptor. *Ibid.* 563 This thermolabile serum feast preparer is called by Wright and Douglas opsonine. *Ibid.* 561 Buchner has drawn special attention to the characters of the alexins—their thermolability [etc.]. 1907 *Jrnl. Med. Research* May 288 (C. D., Suppl.) The digestive ferment of these organs in solution is ..thermolabile at 56° C.; the entire extract..is thermolabile at slightly higher temperatures.

**Thermology** (þɜɹmǫ·lŏdʒi). [ad. F. *thermologie*: see THERMO- and -LOGY.] The science of heat; that department of physics which treats of heat; thermotics.

1840 WHEWELL *Philos. Induct. Sc.* I. p. lxxii, The science which treats of heat has hitherto had no special designation. ..M. Le Comte terms it *Thermology* (i.e. the science of heat). In the History of the Sciences, I have named it *Thermotics*. 1843 MILL *Logic* II. iv. § 5 (1846) I. 246 Thus mechanics, hydrostatics, optics, acoustics, and thermology, have successively been rendered mathematical. 1858 H. SPENCER *Ess.* I. 215 Thus acoustics was arrested until thermology overtook and aided it.

Hence **Thermolo·gical** *a.*, of or pertaining to thermology.

1871 PROCTOR *Sun* iv. 193 So high an authority in meteorological and thermological questions.

**Thermo-luminescence**, etc.: see THERMO-.

**Thermolysis** (þɜɹmǫ·lisis). [f. THERMO- + Gr. λύσις loosing, solution, etc., after Ger. *thermolyse* (F. Mohr, 1874).]

1. *Chem.* The separation of a compound into its elements by the action of heat; decomposition or dissociation by heat.

1875 WATTS *Dict. Chem.* VII. 636 Decomposition by heat. Dissociation—Thermolysis (F. Mohr, Ann. Ch. Pharm. clxxi. 361). *Ibid.* 637 An essential condition of thermolysis is that the constituents of the compound shall, in combining, have given out heat. 1884 A. DANIELL *Princ. Physics* xiii. 319 The heat..has the effect of throwing the molecule into such agitation that the mutual affinity of the atoms cannot retain them in union. This is the process of Dissociation or Thermolysis.

2. *Physiol.* The dissipation or dispersion of heat from the body.

1896 *Allbutt's Syst. Med.* I. 143 [see THERMOGENESIS]. *Ibid.* 159 In Dr. Macalister's..Goulstonian Lectures on Fever it is suggested that thermogenesis, thermolysis, and thermotaxis must be regarded as three separate functions of the nervous system. 1899 *Syd. Soc. Lex.*, *Thermolysis*, the dissipation of heat.

Hence **Thermoly·tic** *a.*, pertaining to or producing thermolysis; *sb.* a thermolytic agent or substance; **The·rmolyse, -yze** *v.*, *trans.* to subject to thermolysis; to decompose by the action of heat.

1890 BILLINGS *Nat. Med. Dict.*, *Thermolytic*, heat-discharging. 1896 *Allbutt's Syst. Med.* I. 150 Able to influence 'thermolytic' or thermogenetic processes. 1891 *Cent. Dict.*, Thermolyze. 1899 *Syd. Soc. Lex.*, *Thermolytic*, ..[also] an agent promoting the discharge of heat from the body.

**Thermo-magnetic** to **-metamorphism**: see THERMO-.

**Thermometer** (þəɹmǫ·mĭtəɹ). Also 7 -tre. [mod. f. Gr. θέρμ-η heat, θερμό-ς hot + μέτρον measure: see -METER. In F. *thermomètre* (1624).

The name *thermoscopium* appears somewhat earlier: see THERMOSCOPE.]

An instrument for measuring temperature (see TEMPERATURE 7) by means of a substance whose expansion and contraction under different degrees of heat and cold are capable of accurate measurement.

For the history of the instrument and its names, see H. C. Bolton *The Evolution of the Thermometer* (Easton Pa. 1900), Renou *Hist. du Thermomètre* (Versailles 1876), Burckhardt *Zur Geschichte des Thermometers*, 1902.

The earliest form was an air-thermometer invented and used by Galilei *a* 1597, for indicating the temperature of the atmosphere; alcohol thermometers were used *c* 1650; the device of a fixed zero (orig. the freezing-point) was introduced by Hooke, 1665. The fixing of the zero at an arbitrary point below the freezing point is attributed to FAHRENHEIT of Amsterdam, who made mercurial thermometers *c* 1720, and his scale has been in general use in England since *c* 1724. The zero of REAUMUR (1730), and of the CENTIGRADE thermometer of Celsius (1742), now largely used in science, is (like that used by Hooke and Sir I. Newton) the freezing-point. The ordinary form is now a slender hermetically sealed glass tube with a fine bore, having a bulb at the lower end filled with mercury, or with alcohol or other liquid, and adjusted to a graduated scale; variations of temperature being indicated by the varying heights of the column of liquid in the tube, due to its expansion and contraction.

*Air-, Centigrade, Clinical, Differential, Fahrenheit, Gas-, Maximum-, Minimum-, Réaumur, Register thermometer*: see the first elements. *Metallic* (or *bimetallic*) *thermometer*, a thermometer which indicates temperature by differential expansion and contraction of composite metal bars.

[1624 'H. VAN ETTEN' (J. Leurechon) *Récréation mathématique* (1626) 99 Thermomètre ou instrument pour mesurer les degrez de chalour ou de froidure qui sont en l'air.] 1633 W. OUGHTRED tr. *van Etten's Math. Recr.* 110 Of the Thermometer: or an instrument to measure the degrees of heat and cold in the aire. 1646 SIR T. BROWNE *Pseud. Ep.* 227 The same is evident from the Thermometer. 1665 HOOKE *Microgr.* vii. 38 Sealed Thermometers, which I have, by several tryals, at last brought to a great certainty and tenderness: .. for graduating the stem, I fix that for the beginning of my division where the surface of the liquor in the stem remains when the ball is placed in..water, that is so cold that it just begins to freeze..(which I mark with an [o] or nought). 1687 A. LOVELL tr. *Thevenot's Trav.* II. 30 It is very hot in Aleppo,..the first day of June at Noon I found by my Thermometre, that the heat was at the thirtieth Degree. 1744 *Phil. Trans.* XLIII. 32 Fahrenheit,..so well known by his Mercurial Thermometers. 1782 *Phil. Trans.* LXXII. I. 72 Account of an improved Thermometer. By Mr. James Six. 1799 *Monthly Rev.* XXX. 9 In Pennsylvania, on the 14th of March, .. Fahrenheit's thermometer stood at 65° at noonday, though it had been at 14° but a week before. 1820 Register thermometer [see REGISTER *sb.*[1] 12]. 1878 HUXLEY *Physiogr.* 71 Dry-and-wet bulb Thermometers...One of the instruments has its bulb free, whilst the other is covered with muslin. *Ibid.* 199 If a thermometer be buried in the ground.., it is found to be affected by all superficial changes of temperature. 1898 P. MANSON *Trop. Diseases* viii. 158 The tongue now begins to moisten, the pulse-rate and the thermometer to fall.

b. *fig.*

1801 A. HAMILTON *Wks.* (1886) VII. 224 No bad thermometer of the capacity of our Chief Magistrate for government is furnished by the rule which he offers for judging of the utility of the Federal Courts. 1824 BYRON *Juan* XVI. xlviii, Taste..now-a-days is the thermometer By whose degrees all characters are class'd. 1883 H. SMITH in J. G. Butler *Bible Work* II. 825/1 The true missionary spirit in the Church is..the test and thermometer of her piety.

c. *attrib.* and *Comb.*, as *thermometer bulb, piece, reading, scale, tube*; **thermometer-gauge**, a steam-gauge which indicates the pressure in a boiler by the expansion of a fluid at the temperature due to the pressure; **thermometer-stove**, a stove automatically regulated by means of a thermometer.

1784 WEDGWOOD in *Phil. Trans.* LXXIV. 367 Some of the clay thermometer pieces were set on end upon the silver piece. 1834 MRS. SOMERVILLE *Connex. Phys. Sci.* xv. 125 A glass tube of extremely fine bore, such as a small thermometer-tube. 1838 *Civil Eng. & Arch. Jrnl.* I. 129/2 The self-regulating fire, or thermometer-stove. 1841 *Ibid.* IV. 13/1 The four instruments employed..to determine the pressure of steam,..the barometer-gauge, the air-gauge, the thermometer-gauge, and the spring-gauge or indicator. 1901 *Daily Chron.* 26 Nov. 5/1 The downward tendency in yesterday's thermometer readings.

**Thermometric** (þɜ̄ɹmǒme·trik), *a.* [f. prec. + -IC: cf. Gr. μετρικός of or for measuring. So F. *thermométrique* (18th c.).] = next.

1784 *Phil. Trans.* LXXIV. 367 The stage of extension.. always precedes the thermometric diminution. 1826 HENRY *Chem.* I. 86 The absolute zero, or point of total privation of heat on the thermometric scale. 1860 TYNDALL *Glac.* II. xiii. 296 His own thermometric experiments show us that the body of the glacier is at a temperature of 32° Fahr.

**Thermometrical** (þɜɹmǒme·trikăl), *a.* [f. as prec. + -AL: see -ICAL.] Of or pertaining to the thermometer or its use; made with or involving the use of the thermometer.

1664-5 BOYLE *Exper. & Obs. Cold* (heading), New Thermometrical Experiments and Thoughts. 1715 CHEYNE *Philos. Princ. Relig.* v. § 21 (ed. 2) 233 His Heat raises the Liquor in the Thermometrical Tubes. 1820 SCORESBY *Acc. Arctic Reg.* I. 352 A series of thermometrical observations, continued through the space of a few years. 1880 HAUGHTON *Phys. Geog.* iii. 90 Marking so many fixed points on the earth's thermometrical scale.

b. That acts as a thermometer; indicating rise or fall of temperature.

1823 J. BADCOCK *Dom. Amusem.* 40 Thermometrical Ink.

Hence **Thermome·trically** *adv.*, according to or by means of the thermometer or its indications.

1828 in WEBSTER. 1856 G. WILSON *Let.* 10 Apr., in *Mem.* x. (1860) 427 For a month..the wind has blown geographically from Araby the blest, but thermometrically from Iceland the accursed. 1881 SULLIVAN in *Macm. Mag.* XLIV. 342 A very heated term, thermometrically speaking.

**Thermometrograph** (þɜ̄ɹmǒme·trǒgrɑf). [f. THERMOMETER + -GRAPH.] A self-registering thermometer.

1837 MACDOUGALL tr. *Graah's E. Coast Greenland* 20 Mr. Vahl, having..let down his thermometrograph, found the temperature of the sea, at the depth of 110 fathoms, to be 5°·50, while that at the surface was 6°·3. 1877 KNIGHT *Dict. Mech.*, *Thermetograph* [*sic*], a self-registering thermometer, recording the maximum and minimum of temperature in a given time.

**Thermometry** (þəɹmǫ·mĕtri). [f. THERMO-METER: see -METRY.] The department of science which deals with the construction of thermometers; the scientific use of the thermometer; the measurement of temperature.

1858 LARDNER *Hand-bk. Nat. Phil.*, etc. 240 Chap. II. Thermometry. 1871 MAXWELL *Theory of Heat* Pref., The whole science of heat is founded on Thermometry and Calorimetry. 1878 LOCKYER *Stargazing* 376 He attaches a thermopile to his telescope and establishes a celestial thermometry.

**Thermo-motive, -motor**: see THERMO-.

**The:rmo-mu·ltiplier.** [f. THERMO- + MULTIPLIER 4.] Early name for a THERMOPILE: so called in reference to the multiplying effect of the numerous cells in the battery.

1835 FARADAY tr. Melloni in *Philos. Mag.* VII. 475 In order to experiment under these circumstances, it is clearly necessary to employ an extremely delicate thermoscope, such as well-constructed thermomultipliers. 1854 J. SCOFFERN in *Orr's Circ. Sc.*, *Chem.* 276 The thermo-multiplier of Nobili consists of about fifty pairs of antimony and bismuth bars. 1879 NEWCOMB & HOLDEN *Astron.* 495 In the case of the brighter stars the heat radiated has been made sensible in the foci of our telescopes by means of the thermo-multiplier.

So **The:rmo-mu·ltiple** in same sense.

1895 in *Funk's Stand. Dict.*

**Thermonatrite** (þɜ̄ɹmo,nē·trəit). *Min.* [a. Ger. *thermonatrit* (Haidinger 1845), 'because it results from the drying out of natron' (Chester), f. THERMO- + NATRON: see -ITE [1].] Hydrous carbonate of soda, found in various saline lakes, about some mines and volcanoes, and as an efflorescence in many dry regions.

1859 PAGE *Handbk. Geol. Terms* s.v., According to Haidinger, a saturated solution of soda at a temperature of 77° to 99° Fahr., and cooling slowly, forms crystals of thermonatrite. 1863-72 WATTS *Dict. Chem.* I. 795 $Na_2CO_3$+aq. formed from the deca-hydrate by efflorescence, is found native as thermonatrite, in the same localities as natron.

**Thermo-neutrality**, etc.: see THERMO-.

**The·rmonous**, *a. rare*[—1]. [a. Gr. θερμό-νους heated in mind, f. θερμός hot + νοῦς mind.]

1888 G. MEREDITH *Reading of Earth* Poems 1898 II. 200 Not as Cybele's beast will thy head lash tail So præter-determinedly thermonous.

**Thermophil, -phile** (þɜ̄·ɹmǒfil), *a.* and *sb.* [f. THERMO- + -PHIL.] **a.** *adj.* Requiring a high temperature for development, as certain bacteria. **b.**

*sb.* A thermophil organism. So **Thermophilic** (-fi·lik), **Thermophilous** (-ǫ·filəs) *adjs.*

1896 *Allbutt's Syst. Med.* I. 513 There is a class of microbes which refuse to grow at any temperature below 50° C.; such organisms are called 'thermophile'. 1899 *Nature* 15 June 147/1 Facts regarding the existence of thermophilous organisms. 1900 *Ibid.* 22 Feb. 388/2 Thermophilic bacteria..are specially important as regards the fermentation in ensilage and the digestion of cellulose.

**Thermophone** (þɔ̄·ɹmǝfōun). [f. as prec. + Gr. φωνή voice, sound, after TELEPHONE.] An apparatus in which sonorous vibrations of a diaphragm are produced by heat-rays.

1878 TH. WIESENDANGER in *Engineer* XLVI. Nov. 335 The Thermophone. A new source of sound for the telephone. 1881 A. G. BELL in *Nature* 12 May 44/1 We have decided to adopt the term 'radiophone'..limiting the words thermophone, photophone, and actinophone to apparatus for the production of sound by thermal, luminous, or actinic rays respectively. 1902 SLOANE *Stand. Electr. Dict.* 537 *Thermophone*, an apparatus for reproducing sounds telephonically by the agency of heat; a receiving-telephone actuated by heat.

Thermophore, etc.: see THERMO-.

**Thermopile** (þɔ̄·ɹmǒpəil). [f. THERMO- + PILE *sb.*[3] 5.] A thermo-electric battery, used in connexion with a galvanometer, for measuring minute quantities of radiant heat; also called THERMO-MULTIPLIER.

1849 NOAD *Electricity* (ed. 3) 424 Thermo-piles are now constructed by soldering together at their alternate edges, bars of antimony and bismuth, with squares of cardboard or thick paper intervening. 1871 B. STEWART *Heat* § 165 A square block, containing altogether 25 couples of bismuth and antimony is generally employed, and such an arrangement is called a thermo-pile. 1891 *Times* 2 Oct. 3/1 A thermopile..is an apparatus for direct conversion of heat into electricity.

‖ **Thermopolion, -ium** (þɔɹmopǭu·liǫn, -iǫ̆m). *Antiq.* [a. Gr. θερμο-πώλιον (L. *thermopolium*, Plaut.) a tavern where hot drinks were sold.] (See quot. 1753.) Hence † **Thermo·polist**: see quot. 1656; **Thermo·polite**, the keeper of a thermopolion.

1656 BLOUNT *Glossogr.*, *Thermopolist*.., a Cook that sells hot meat. 1753 CHAMBERS *Cycl. Supp.*, *Thermopolium*, a name for a sort of public houses among the ancients, in which hot liquors were sold. 1832 GELL *Pompeiana* I. i. 8 The shops of a thermopolite. *Ibid.* II. xii. 10 An ordinary wine shop or thermopolion.

† **The·rmopot, -pote.** *Obs. rare*—°. [ad. Gr. θερμο-πότης drinker of hot liquids, f. θερμο-, THERMO- + πότης drinker.] (See quot.)

1727 BAILEY vol. II, *Thermopote*, a Drinker of hot Liquors.

So ‖ **Thermopotis** (þəɹmǫ·potis), *Class. Archæol.* [a. Gr. θερμο-πότις cup for hot drinks].

1857 BIRCH *Anc. Pottery* (1858) II. 90 The thermopotis was a vase also used for warming wine.

**Thermo-radiometer, -regulator**: see THERMO-.

**Thermos** (þɔ̄·ɹmǫs). [a. Gr. θερμός warm, hot.] A registered trade term noting a flask, bottle, or the like capable of being kept hot by the device (invented by Sir James Dewar) of surrounding the interior vessel with a vacuum jacket to prevent the conduction of heat.

Patented 1904, No. 4421; not named. Name (Trade Mark No. 289,470) adv. in *Trade Marks Jrnl.* 20 March, 1907.

1907 *Eng. Mech.* 18 Oct. 246 This invention [of Sir James Dewar] is utilised in the thermos flask. 1909 *Ladies' Field* 28 Aug. 511/2 A Thermos bottle filled with hot coffee was not forgotten. 1909 *Westm. Gaz.* 16 Sept. 5/2 Lieutenant Shackleton testified to the fact that the Thermos flask helped him to perform his wonderful feats in the Antarctic. 1910 *Repts. Patent Cases* XXVII. 396 This was the *Dewar* vessel...In 1904 it occurred to a Mr. Burger that this vessel could be adapted for use as a flask..the result..was the production of the well known *Thermos* flask.

**Thermoscope** (þɔ̄·ɹmǒskoup). [ad. mod.L. *thermoscopium* (Bianconi, 1617): see THERMO- and -SCOPE. Cf. F. *thermoscope.*] An instrument for indicating changes of temperature, of which there are various forms.

**a.** An early name for the thermometer, esp. in its earlier forms. **b.** Count Rumford's name for a differential thermometer for detecting minute differences of temperature. **c.** An electric or magnetic apparatus, as a thermopile, for detecting and measuring minute differences of temperature. **d.** Any substance or device used to indicate excessive heat in machinery, variations of bodily temperature, rate of radiation of heat, or the like.

**a.** [1617 GIUS. BIANCONI *Sphæra Mundi, seu Cosmographia Demonstrativa*...Thermoscopium.] 1656 tr. *Hobbes's Elem. Philos.* (1839) 531 This organ is called a thermometer or thermoscope, because the degrees of heat and cold are measured and marked by it. 1672 BOYLE in *Phil. Trans.* VII. 5110 The Air by the seal'd Thermoscope appeared hot for the season. 1778 *Phil. Trans.* LXVIII. 484 The first inventors..called..their instruments..Baroscopes, Thermoscopes, Microscopes. 1790 DE LUC *ibid.* LXXXI. 32 The thermoscopes of quicksilver and water. 1842 BRANDE *Dict. Sc.*, etc. s. v. *Thermometer*, The thermometer of Drebbel and Sanctorio..had no scale, and was therefore merely an indicator of changes of temperature, or a thermoscope.

**b.** 1804 CT. RUMFORD in *Phil. Trans.* XCIV. 101 An instrument I contrived for measuring, or rather for discovering, those very small changes of temperature in bodies, which are occasioned by the radiations of other neighbouring bodies, which happen to be at a higher, or at a lower temperature. This instrument..I shall take the liberty to call a thermoscope. 1842 BRANDE *Dict. Sc.*, etc. s. v., The modification of the air thermometer, called by Leslie a differential thermometer, was claimed by Count Rumford as one of his own inventions, under the name of thermoscope. 1850 GROVE *Corr. Phys. Forces* (ed. 2) 42 With the most delicate thermoscope, he could detect no indications of transmitted heat. 1860 MAYNE *Expos. Lex.*, *Thermoscopium*, term for an instrument by Rumford for measuring the difference of temperature by dilatation of dry air contained in two balls, which a long tube, twice bent, separates from each other: a thermoscope.

**c.** 1835 [see THERMO-MULTIPLIER]. 1879 tr. *Du Moncel's Telephone* 195 It is therefore a microphone as well as a thermoscope. 1881 *Nature* 17 Feb 372/2 The magnetic thermoscope is intended to indicate differences of temperature by showing differences between the magnetic moments of steel magnets.

**d.** 1877 KNIGHT *Dict Mech* 2550/1 Barker and Mayer's thermoscope..is designed to indicate..the existence of excessive heat in journal-bearings...Marcy's thermoscope..is particularly designed for experiments on animal heat. 1884 *Ibid.* Suppl. 892/2 The varied changes of tint..may serve..as a rough index of the temperature of surrounding bodies, thus constituting the little instrument a thermoscope.

**Thermoscopic** (þɔɹmǫskǫ·pik), *a.* [f. prec. + -IC.] Of, pertaining to, or of the nature of a thermoscope.

1730 *Phil. Trans.* XXXVI. 254 The Severity of the Weather did not cease:..the Spirit of Wine, in the English Thermometer, in a Morning always stood at, or under the 8oth Deg. of the Thermoscopick Scale. 1843 GROVE *Corr. Phys. Forces* (1846) 17 Of which heat no evidence can be afforded by any thermoscopic test. 1854 J. SCOFFERN in *Orr's Circ. Sc.*, *Chem.* 121 Thermometric and thermoscopic instruments.

So **Thermosco·pical** *a.*, in same sense; whence **Thermosco·pically** *adv.*

1670 *Phil. Trans.* V. p. iv, The Thermoscopical Measures of Warmth and Frigidity. 1730 *Ibid.* XXXVI. 254 From Thermoscopical Observations. 1895 *Funk's Stand. Dict.*, Thermoscopically.

**Thermo-si·phon.** [f. THERMO- + SIPHON.] A siphon attachment by which the circulation in a system of hot-water pipes is increased or induced. Also *attrib.*

1834 LOUDON *Encycl. Gard.* § 2142 Fowler's method of circulating hot water in his thermosiphon. 1906 *Daily Chron.* 3 Mar. 3/6 Water from a reservoir is circulated around the cylinder, in the water-jacket, either by a pump worked by the engine, or on the thermo-syphon system.

**Thermostable** (þɔ̄rmostǟ·b'l), *a.* [f. THERMO- + STABLE *a.*] Retaining its character or active quality at moderately high temperatures: opposed to *thermolabile*. Hence **Thermostabi·lity,** the quality of being thermostable.

1904 *Brit. Med Jrnl.* 10 Sept. 557 The killing of the bacteria is associated with the presence in the serum of an immune animal, of two substances, one thermolabile (complement) which naturally occurs in the serum of the animal species involved, and the other thermostable (immune body), which either is present in normal serum in very small amount or is altogether absent. *Ibid.* 561 [see THERMOLABILE]. 1907 *Science* 13 Sept. 346 The high stability of opsonins against desiccation and the high thermostability of dried opsonins are very striking.

**Thermostat** (þɔ̄·ɹmostæt). [f. THERMO- + Gr. στατός standing: cf. HELIOSTAT.] An automatic apparatus for regulating temperature; *esp.* a device in which the expansive force of metals or gas acts directly upon the source of heat, ventilation, or the like, or controls them indirectly by opening and closing an electric circuit.

1831 URE in *Proc. Roy. Soc.* 16 June 67 On the Thermostat or Heat Governor, a self-acting physical Apparatus for regulating Temperature. 1835 — *Philos. Manuf.* 26 The instrument, for which I have obtained a patent, under the name of the heat-governor, or thermostat. 1877 W. THOMSON *Voy. Challenger* I. i. 34 The size of the iron frame was arranged so as to receive one of Bunsen's thermostats in ordinary use in laboratories. 1899 CAGNEY *Jaksch's Clin. Diagn.* ii. (ed. 4) 107 The test-tube containing the infected serum is now placed in a thermostat, maintained at 36·5°—37° C.

**b.** An apparatus which gives notice of undue increase of temperature; an automatic fire-alarm.

1881 *Philad. Record* No. 3462. 4 The thermostat, which gives an alarm as soon as the temperature of the room where it may be rises to 100°. 1908 *Daily Chron.* 24 Aug. 6/3 The thermostat is usually attached to the ceiling, and immediately an abnormal and dangerous rise of temperature occurs the metal bars expand.

So **Thermosta·tic** *a.*, of, pertaining to, or of the nature of a thermostat; **Thermosta·tically** *adv.*, by means of a thermostat; **Thermosta·tics** *sb. pl.* [after *hydrostatics*], name suggested for the theory of the equilibrium of heat.

1839 URE *Dict. Arts*, etc. 1237 A single thermostatic bar, consisting of two or more bars or rulers of differently expansible solids..firmly riveted or soldered together, face to face...A thermostatic hoop. 1871 Thermostatics [see *thermokinematics*, THERMO-]. 1877 KNIGHT *Dict. Mech.*, *Thermostatic Alarm*, a device to give a signal when a certain temperature is attained. 1883 *Cassell's Fam. Mag.* Aug. 537/2 Frost tell-tales..can be readily constructed by employing a thermostatic spring. 1891 *Cent. Dict.* s.v., A thermostatically adjusted radiator.

**Thermosynthesis, etc.**: see THERMO-.

**Thermota·ctic,** *a.* [f. as next + Gr. τακτικ-ός arranging, f. τακ-, root of τάσσ-ειν to arrange: see next.] Of or pertaining to thermotaxis.

1896 *Allbutt's Syst. Med.* I. 150 To this [the nervous] system must be assigned the thermotactic function. *Ibid.* 151 The question where the thermotactic centre or centres are to be found, and how they act in fevers. 1899 *Ibid.* VI. 860 The so-called heat fibres, that is the thermotactic.

‖ **Thermotaxis** (þɔɹmotæ·ksis). [mod.L., f. THERMO- + Gr. τάξις arrangement: see TAXIS.]

**1.** *Physiol.* That function of the nervous system on which the normal temperature of the body depends; the regulation of the bodily heat.

1891 in *Cent. Dict.* 1896 *Allbutt's Syst. Med.* I. 150 It may be assumed that thermotaxis is conducted by a 'centre' or 'centres'. *Ibid.* 156 What they do not prove is that fever is nothing more than a disorder of thermotaxis. 1899 *Ibid.* VII. 341 The tuber cinereum, which he regards as the true centre of thermotaxis.

**2.** *Biol.* Movement or stimulation in a living body caused by heat: cf. TAXIS 6.

1900 B. D. JACKSON *Gloss. Bot. Terms*, *Thermotaxis*, changes produced by warmth. 1902 MAX VERWORN in *Encycl. Brit.* XXXI. 715/1 Cases of directive stimulation..have been designated..positive or negative Chemotaxis, Phototaxis, Thermotaxis, Galvanotaxis, and so forth.

Hence **Thermota·xic** *a.* = THERMOTACTIC.

1877 FOSTER *Phys* II. v. (1878) 378 This at first sight looked like the indication of a thermotaxic mechanism, rendered inactive by the condition of fever. 1899 *Syd. Soc. Lex.*, *Thermotaxic*, same as *Thermotactic*.

**Thermotelephone, etc.**: see THERMO-.

**Thermotic** (þəɹmǫ·tik), *a.* [f. Gr. θερμωτικός (Plutarch *Q. Conv.* 715 C) warming, calorific: used in modified sense to match *acoustic, optic,* etc.] Of or pertaining to heat; *esp.* relating to thermotics. So **Thermo·tical** *a.*, in same sense (hence **Thermo·tically** *adv.*); **Thermo·tics** *sb. pl.*, the science of heat, thermology.

1837 WHEWELL *Hist. Induct. Sc.* VIII. Introd. II. 293 Acoustics, Optics, and Thermotics. *Ibid.* x. Introd. 465, I employ the term Thermotics, to include all the doctrines respecting Heat. *Ibid.* x. i. § 4. 481 They require the light of thermotical calculations. 1858 BUCKLE *Civiliz.* (1869) II. vii. 362 Fourier..employed himself in raising thermotics to a science. 1874 tr. *Lommel's Light* 201 In the spectrum of a flint-glass prism the apex of the thermotic curve is situated outside the apparent spectrum in the ultra-red region. 1879 S. HIGHLEY in *Cassell's Techn. Educ.* IV. 234/1 Optical, acoustic, and thermotic demonstrations in the lecture-room. 1895 *Funk's Stand. Dict.*, Thermotically.

**Thermotropic** (þɔ̄ɹmotrǫ·pik), *a. Bot.* [f. Gr. θερμο-, THERMO- + -τροπ-ος turning + -IC: cf. HELIOTROPIC.] Turning or bending under the influence of heat; of, pertaining to, or exhibiting thermotropism.

1885 GOODALE *Physiol. Bot.* (1892) 394 Curvatures dependent upon temperature are called thermotropic.

**Thermotropism** (þəɹmǫ·trǒpiz'm). *Bot.* [f. as prec. + -ISM.] The property possessed by growing plant-organs of turning or bending towards (*positive thermotropism*) or away from (*negative thermotropism*) the sun or other source of heat. In *Biology*, The bending or growth of any organism dependent upon temperature (*Cent. Dict.*, *Suppl.*).

1898 tr. *Strasburger's Text-Bk. Bot.* I. ii. 263 Thermotropism..and Aerotropism..stand in direct relations to certain vital requirements of plants.

**Thermotype** (þɔ̄·ɹmǒtəip). [f. THERMO- + -TYPE.] Name proposed for an impression obtained from an object by means of heat. Hence **Thermoty·pic** *a.*, of or pertaining to thermotypes or thermotypy; **The·rmotypy,** the process or art of making thermotypes.

1864 WEBSTER, Thermotype; Thermotypy. 1877 KNIGHT *Dict. Mech.*, *Thermotype*, an impression (as of a slice of wood) taken by means of wetting with dilute acid, pressing on the object, and subsequently heating the impression. 1909 *Cent. Dict.* Suppl., Thermotypic.

**Thermo-unstable, -voltaic**: see THERMO-.

† **Therne.** *Obs.* Also 4 tharne, (tarne), þierne. [a. ON. *þerna* (Sw. *tärna*, Da. *terne*) = OS. *thiorna* (Du. *deern*), OHG. *diorna* (MHG. *dierne*, Ger. *dirne*).] A girl, maid, young woman.

*c* 1300 *Havelok* 298 Sholde ic yeue a fol, a þerne, Engelond, þou sho it yerne? 1303 R. BRUNNE *Handl. Synne* 7353 Two vnweddyd..sengle knaue and sengle tarne [*v.r.* tharne]. *c* 1315 SHOREHAM *Poems* i. 1726 Þet knaue child fortene ȝer Schel habbe, ane tuel þe þerne. 1340 *Ayenb.* 129 Þe þierne [of] saynt abraham [i. e. Hagar].

**Thero-** (þī·ero), repr. Gr. θηρο-, combining form of θήρ wild beast; hence THEROID, THEROPOD, etc.; also the following: **Therocephalian** (-sǐfē̆·liǎn) [Gr. κεφαλή head], *a.* belonging to an extinct order of carnivorous reptiles having a skull of the mammalian type; *sb.* a reptile of this order. **Therocrotaphous** (-krǫ·tăfəs) *a.* [Gr. κρόταφος the temple], having the temporal bone resembling that of mammals. **The·rodont** *sb.* and *a.*, = *Theriodont* (*Cent. Dict.* 1891): see THERIO-. **Thero·latry** [-LATRY], beast-worship, worship of animals. **The·romorpholo·gical** *a.*, of or pertaining to the morphology of the lower animals.

1904 *Amer. Nat.* Feb. 103 These cynodonts have lost several of the other more primitive characters of the 'therocephalians, such as teeth in the palate. 1907 *Science* 6 Dec. 796 Three new Therocephalian genera have been discovered in beds which are probably Middle Permian. *Ibid.*, The discovery of this new reptile, *Galechirus*, strongly favors the descent of the Therocephalians from an early Rhynchocephaloid ancestor. **1907** WILLISTON in *Proc. U.S. Nat. Mus.* XXXII. 488 The plesiosaurs have a larger temporal vacuity, larger indeed than is to be found in any other reptiles of the *therocrotaphous (I coin the word) type. **1873** W. CORY *Lett. & Jrnls.* (1897) 311 Mahomet's alteration of a national character, the complete obliteration of *therolatry. **1885** HARTMANN *Anthropoid Apes* iii. 111 Virchow and W. Gruber have agreed in representing this frontal process as *theromorphological—that is, as a characteristic of the lower animals, and more especially of apes.

**Theroid** (þīᵊroid), *a.* [f. THERO- + -OID; cf. Gr. θηροειδής.] Like or having the form of a brute; of bestial nature or character.

**1867** MAUDSLEY *Physiol. Mind* 291 The theroid degenerations of mankind are pathological specimens. **1870** — *Body & Mind* 47 There is a class of idiots which may justly be designated theroid, so like brutes are the members of it. **1886** N. PEARSON in *19th Cent.* Sept. 353 The animal mind of the theroid idiot is accompanied by appropriate animal peculiarities of body.

**Therology** (þirǫ·lŏdʒi). [f. THERO- + -LOGY. Proposed as a substitute for the irregular but established *mammalogy*.] The science of beasts or mammals; mammalogy. Hence **Therologic** (þīᵊrolǫ·dʒik), **Therolo·gical** *adjs.*, of or pertaining to therology, mammalogical; **Thero·logist**, one versed in therology; a mammalogist.

[Cf. **1620** ALSTED *Encycl.* 572 Irrationale animal est, quod formâ brutâ est præditum, & dicitur bestia. Ejus doctrina dicitur Therologia.] **1877** *Academy* 25 Aug. 199/3 A gentleman who, to use a newly-coined transatlantic word, is certainly one of the first 'therologists' of his country. **1882** OGILVIE (Annandale), Therology. **1891** *Cent. Dict.*, Therologic, Therological, Therology.

**Theromorous** (þīᵊromōᵊrəs), *a. Palæont.* [f. mod.L. *Thērомōra* (see def.), f. Gr. θηρο-, THERO- + μωρ-ός sluggish, stupid, foolish: see -OUS.] Of or belonging to the *Theromora* (Cope), a synonym of *Theromorpha* (see next). So **Theromo·ran** *a.*, in same sense.

**1889** NICHOLSON & LYDEKKER *Palæontol.* liii. II. 1053 Theromorous Branch.—The Reptiles included in this branch or alliance. **1895** *Funk's Stand. Dict.*, Theromoran.

**Theromorph** (þīᵊrǫmǭɹf). *Palæont.* [f. mod. L. *Thērōmorpha* neut. pl. (see def.), f. Gr. θηρο-, THERO- + μορφή form.] A reptile of the extinct order *Theromorpha*, of Permian and Trias age, having certain mammalian characters. So **Thero-mo·rphic** *a.*[1], **Theromo·rphous** *a.*, belonging to or having the characters of the *Theromorpha.*

**1887** COPE *Orig. Fittest* xi. 317 The Mammalia have been traced to the theromorphous reptiles through the Monotremata. **1891** *Cent. Dict.*, Theromorph, Theromorphic. [**1901** H. GADOW in *Cambr. Nat. Hist.* VIII. viii. 303 Many of the Theromorpha reached a considerable size, massive skulls of one foot in length being not uncommon. *Note.* Cope, the inventor of this most appropriate name (Theromorpha, or 'beast-shaped' animals), soon changed it, unnecessarily, into Theromora.]

‖ **Theromorphia** (þīᵊromǭ·ɹfiă). [mod.L. a. Gr. θηρομορφία = θηριομορφία, f. θηριόμορφος having the form of a beast: see prec.] (See quot. 1890.) So **Theromo·rphic** *a.*[2], of or pertaining to theromorphia; **Theromo·rphism** = *theromorphia*.

**1890** BILLINGS *Nat. Med. Dict.*, *Theromorphia*, an abnormity in human anatomy resembling the normal structure in lower animals. **1891** *Cent. Dict.*, Theromorphic. **1899** *Syd. Soc. Lex.*, *Theromorphism*, an apparent reversion to an animal of lower type in the human subject.

**Theropodous** (þirǫ·pŏdəs), *a. Palæont.* [f. mod.L. *Thēropoda* neut. pl. (f. Gr. θηρο-, THERO- + πούς, ποδ- foot) + -OUS.] Of or belonging to the *Theropoda*, an order of carnivorous dinosaurs in Cope's classification, having feet like those of mammals. So **Theropod** (þīᵊrǫpǫd), *a.* = *theropodous*; *sb.* a dinosaur of this order.

**1889** *Q. Jrnl. Geol. Soc.* XLV. i. 44 Axis of a (? Theropodous) Dinosaur from the Wealden. **1891** *Cent. Dict.*, Theropod. **1901** H. GADOW in *Cambr. Nat. Hist.* VIII. x. 425 The whole hind-limb of the Theropodous *Compsognathus* is far more ornithic than that of any three-toed Ornithopoda.

**Therosaur** (þīᵊrŏsǭɹ). *Palæont.* [f. Gr. θηρο-, THERO- + σαῦρος lizard.] One of the *Therosauria*, an extinct order of herbivorous dinosaurs having the mammalian form and bird-like feet. Hence **Therosau·rian** *a.*, of or pertaining to the *Therosauria*, or having their characters; *sb.* a dinosaur of this order.

**Therrepylle**, obs. f. THRIPPLE, cart-shelving.

**Thers, therse**, obs. forms of THEIRS.

**Thersitical** (þəɹsi·tikăl), *a. rare.* [f. Gr. Θερσίτης Thersites ('the Audacious'), an ill-tongued Greek at the siege of Troy + -ICAL.] Like Thersites in language or address; abusive, reviling, scurrilous. So **Thersitean** (þəɹsitī·ăn) *a. rare*[−1].

**1650** BULWER *Anthropomet.* 4 With a Thersitical head and heart. **1767** STERNE *Tr. Shandy* IX. xiv, There is a pelting kind of Thersitical satire, as black as the very ink 'tis wrote with. **1908** *Daily Chron.* 28 July 4/4 Adding a string of Thersitean scurrilities unfit for publication.

**Therst(e**, obs. form of THIRST.

**Therst(e**: see DARE *v.*[1] A. 9, THARF *v.*

**Therve-cake**: see THARF-CAKE.

**Therwe, þerwe**, obs. form of THROUGH.

† **Thes**, *adv.* (*conj.*). *Obs.* Forms: 1–3 þæs, 2–4 þes, þas, 3 (*Orm.*) þess. [OE. *þæs*, gen. sing. masc. and neut. of *se, séo, þæt*: see THE A. 4 a, THAT A. 1. Retained in certain adverbial and conjunctive uses, after its simple genitive use became obsolete.]

**1. a.** Because of or on account of that; because. **b.** From that time, after that; from the time that, after. **c.** In the way that, according as, as. **d.** To that extent, so: cf. THAT *dem. adv.*

**a.** *c* **897** K. ÆLFRED *Gregory's Past. C.* xlix. 379 Waa me ðæs [L. *quia*] ic swiȝode. *c* **1205** LAY. 2743 Wa wes Lumbardisce folc þes [*c* **1275** þas]. *Ibid.* 5989 Wel wes Romanisce folc þæs [*c* **1275** þas]. *a* **1300** *XI Pains of Hell* 208 in *O. E. Misc.* 153 Þat weren her, wo is ham þes. **b.** *c* **893** K. ÆLFRED *Oros.* IV. vi. § 12 Þæs ymb iii ȝear..þa consulas foran..on Africe. *a* **900** *O. E. Chron.* an. 894, Þæt wæs ymb twelf monað þæs þe hie ær hider..comon. *a* **900** tr. *Bæda's Hist.* I. ix. [xii.] (1890) 44 Sona þæs ðe hi on þis ealond comon. *c* **1380** *Sir Ferumb.* 1387 Olyuer wax hol sone þas. **c.** *c* **888** K. ÆLFRED *Boeth.* xxiv. § 3 Men secað anfealde eadiȝnesse ðæs ðe him ðincð. *a* **900** tr. *Bæda's Hist.* I. xiv. [xxv.] (1890) 60 Þæs þe me ȝeþuht is & ȝesewen. *c* **1000** ÆLFRIC *Gen.* xliii. 7 We him andswaredon þæs þe he us axode. *c* **1000** *St. Andrew & Veronica* 26 Ðæs ðe bec secgaþ. **d.** *a* **1000** *Cædmon's Gen.* 832 Nære flod þæs deop, nære stream þæs micel.

**2.** *Thes the, þes þe* (*þess te*), before a comparative: For that the (more, etc.); so much the (more, etc.); = OHG. *desde*, MHG. *deste*, Ger. *desto* (*mehr*, etc.).

*c* **897** K. ÆLFRED *Gregory's Past. C.* xvii. 123 Sio wund bið ðæs ðe wierse. *c* **1000** *Ags. Gosp.* Matt. xx. 31 Þa clypodon hiȝ þæs þe ma. *c* **1160** *Hatton Gosp.* ibid., Þa clepedon hyo þæs þe mare. [So Mark x. 48.] *c* **1200** ORMIN 444–5 Þatt hise frend mihhtenn off himm All þess te mare blissenn, & tatt te follc all þess te bett Hiss lare sholde follȝhenn. *a* **1275** *Prov. Ælfred* 436 in *O. E. Misc.* 129 Þanne sal þe child þas þe bet worþen.

**Thes**, obs. f. THESE; gen. sing. of THAT, THE.

† **The·saur, -aure.** Chiefly *Sc. Obs.* [ad. L. THESAURUS: cf. Prov. *thesaur*, OCat. *tesor*, Sp., It. *tesoro*, Pg. *thesouro*.] = TREASURE.

**1491** *Sc. Acts Jas. IV* (1814) II. 230/1 Stelaris [and] concelaris, of the said gold or thessaure. *a* **1510** DOUGLAS *K. Hart* II. 340 Quhair is the thesaure now that ȝe have woun? **1532** *Addr. fr. Convoc.* (MS. Cleop. E. VI. lf. 274 b), The thesaure of this realme hath beene carried and conueyhed beyond the mountaines to the coort of rome. **1596** DALRYMPLE tr. *Leslie's Hist. Scot.* (S.T.S.) I. 7 Mony hidd thesauris. *Ibid.* v. 303 Quhat proffit sa euir cumis of that feild..sall cum in to the kingis Thesaur.

**b.** *Comb.* **The·saurhouse**, treasury.

**1488** *Acc. Ld. High Treas. Scot.* I. 85 *margin*, Thir boxis put in the Thesaurhous in the grete kist nerrest the windo. **1596** DALRYMPLE tr. *Leslie's Hist. Scot.* x. (S.T.S.) 264 The palice of Halyruidhous..theThesaurhous, and vtheris places.

**Thesaurarial** (þisǫrēᵊ·riăl), *a.* [f. L. *thēsaurāri-us* (see next) + -AL.] Of or pertaining to the office of treasurer.

**1881** *Athenæum* 2 July 15/2 He was invariably to be found..in his thesaurarial chair at the evening meetings. **1896** *Trans. Roy. Hist. Soc.* X. 42 The addition of the judicial to the thesaurarial functions..of the Court of Exchequer.

† **Thesau·rary, -ie.** Chiefly *Sc. Obs.* [ad. med.L. *thēsaurāria* 'thesaurarii dignitas' (Du Cange), fem. of *thēsaurāri-us* adj., f. *thēsaur-us* treasure: see -ARY[1]; cf. Pr. *thezauraria*, Sp. and It. *tesoreri·a*, mod.F. *trésorerie* treasury.]

**1.** The office of treasurer; treasurership. *Sc.*

**1473–4** *Acc. Ld. High Treas. Scot.* I. 1 Compt of a reuerennd fader in God..of the office of Thesaurary. *a* **1557** *Diurn. Occur.* (1833) 11 Archibald was depryvit of the thesaurarie. **1596** DALRYMPLE tr. *Leslie's Hist. Scot.* x. (S.T.S.) 291 The Cardinal..put him fra the office of the Thesaurarie.

**2.** *transf.* A treasury; also = THESAURUS 2.

**1592** *Sc. Acts Jas. VI* (1814) III. 558/1 The ordinar fies ..sall nawayis be gevin out of his Maiesties thesaurarie. **1597** A. M. tr. *Guillemeau's Fr. Chirurg.* C iij b/2 The end of the thesaurarye or storehouse of the Instrumentes of Chyrurgerie.

**3.** *attrib.* **Thesaurary house**, treasury.

**1495** *Acc. Ld. High Treas. Scot.* I. 268 To turs it to the Thesaurary hous in the Castell.

† **The·saurer.** Chiefly *Sc. Obs.* Also 5–6 **thesaurair, -are**, 5–7 **-ar**, 6 **thesorar, -uerer, -awrar**, 7 **-orer.** [ad. L. *thēsaurārius* treasurer, f. *thēsaurus* treasure: see -AR[2], -ER[2] 2. Cf. Pr. *thesaurier*, Sp. *tesorero*, It. *tesoriere*; also TREASURER.] An officer in charge of treasure, or of a treasury; = TREASURER. *Thesaurer deput*, deputy treasurer: see quot. 1708.

*c* **1450** HOLLAND *Howlat* 209 Apon the sand ȝit I sawe, as thesaurer tane, .. schir Gawane the Drak. **1473** *Acc. Ld. High Treas. Scot.* I. 32 Pait be the Thesaurair. **1489** *Ibid.* 125 Takyne be the Kyng .. out of the Thesorarris purs. **1544** in Gross *Gild Merch.* II. 75 The othir halfe to the thesuerer of the sayde sytty [Dublin]. **1557–75** *Diurn. Occur.* (1833) 180 Iohne Cunnynghame..wes maid half thesaurer, with Mr. Robert Ritchartsone that wes thesaurer of befoir. **1685** *Lond. Gaz.* No. 2031/1 The Earl of Kintore Lord Thesaurer Deput. **1707** *Narr. Jas. Nimmo* (1889) 103, I was chosen Town Thesaurer. **1708** J. CHAMBERLAYNE *St. Gt. Brit.* II. II. iv. (1737) 376 The Officers of State [of Scotland] before the late Union...The Lord Thesaurer Depute, whose Commission ran in the same Terms with that given to the Thesaurer Principal, or the Commissioners of Thesaury. **1711** *Countrey-Man's Let. to Curat* 21 The Lord Thesaurer Burleigh and Sir Francis Walsingham Secretary,..were professed Friends to the Non-conformists.

**b.** *attrib.* **Thesaurer house**, treasury.

**1489** *Acc. Ld. High Treas. Scot.* I. 110 Item, the thrid da of May, takin be the King furth of the Thesaurare Houss himself, foure score of demyss, lvj li.

† **The·saurize**, *v. Obs.* [ad. late L. *thēsaurizāre*, ad. Gr. θησαυρίζ-ειν, f. θησαυρ-ός treasure: see -IZE; cf. F. *thésauriser* (14th c. in Godef. *Compl.*).] *trans.* To hoard, as treasure. Mostly *fig.*

**1594** *Zepheria* vi, My heart prepares anew to thesaurize Sighs and loue options. *a* **1610** SIR J. SEMPLE in *S. Ballatis* (1872) 244, I was resoluit to thesaurize my greeife. *Ibid.* 247 Ȝet durst I not behold [? be bold]..But thesawriz'd my hiddin harmes. **1623** COCKERAM, *Thesaurize*, to gather riches. (Also in BLOUNT, BAILEY, etc.)

‖ **Thesaurus** (þisǭ·rɒs). Pl. **-i.** [L., a. Gr. θησαυρός a store, treasure, storehouse, treasury.]

**1.** *Archæol.* A treasury, as of a temple, etc.

**1823** in CRABB *Technol. Dict.* **1846** in WORCESTER. **1847** GROTE *Greece* II. ix. III. 44 Myrôn..built at the same holy place [Olympia] a thesaurus..for the reception of commemorative offerings.

**2.** A 'treasury' or 'storehouse' of knowledge, as a dictionary, encyclopædia, or the like.

[**1565** COOPER (*title*) Thesaurus Linguæ Romanæ et Britannicæ [etc.]. **1736** AINSWORTH (*title*) Thesaurus Linguæ Latinæ compendiarius; or..Dictionary of the Latin Tongue.] **1840** MILL *Diss. & Disc.* (1859) II. 461 A thesaurus of commonplaces for the discussion of questions. **1852** ROGET (*title*) Thesaurus of English Words and Phrases classified and arranged [etc.]. **1862** MARSH *Lect. Eng. Lang.* iii. 49 In a complete thesaurus of any language, the etymology of every word should exhibit both its philology and its linguistics. **1906** *Westm. Gaz.* 18 Dec. 2/2 This work is one of five thesauri published under the auspices of Kang Hsi, the second Emperor of the present dynasty. **1910** *Spectator* 20 Aug. 279/2 A thesaurus of critical learning.

† **The·saury.** Chiefly *Sc. Obs.* [ad. med.L. *thēsauria* 'locus ubi thesaurus reconditur, gazophylacium' (Du Cange), f. THESAUR-US + *-ia*: see -Y.] The treasury; the treasurership.

*a* **1639** SPOTTISWOOD *Hist. Ch. Scot.* VII. (1677) 517 His Uncle..was made Deputy in the Office of Thesaury. **1688** *Addr. Sc. Privy C.* in *Lond. Gaz.* No. 2388/2 They..have got Pay for the Month of October instant out of Your Majesties Thesaury. **1708** [see THESAURER].

† **These**, *sb. Sc.* [a. F. *thèse* (1579 in Godef. *Compl.*), or ad. med.L. *thesis*.] = THESIS 4, 5.

*a* **1600** MONTGOMERIE *Sonn.* lxiv. 11 Fy! I refuse sik filthie these or theam. **1640** R. BAILLIE *Canterb. Self-Convict.* 29 The Authour..avowes..that the These alleadged, and all the rest of his booke doeth perfectly agree with the English Articles. **1648** — *Lett. & Jrnls.* (1841) III. 63 The generall These which he professed to maintain.

**These** (ðīz), *dem. pron.* and *adj.* (*plural*). Forms: see below. [This word has a complicated history. The OE. pl. of *ðes, ðéos, ðis*, was *ðás*, less commonly *ðǽs* (:—OTeut. **þai-se, -si*), dat. *ðiosum, ðis(s)um*, gen. *ðissa, ðisra*. The form *ðás* remained in ME. as *þās*, which was duly retained in the north, and by regular phonetic development became *þōs* in midland and south. The OE. *ðǽs* gave ME. *þǣs, þēs, þeos*, and their local variants, including s. w. *þüs*. A frequent form of *þēs* from the 12th to the 16th c. was *þis*, identical with the sing.: see γ below. The two forms *þēs* and *þās* became differentiated in use after 1250–1300, *þēs* and its variants remaining in the south as plural of THIS, while *þās* became synonymous with *þā*, the plural of *se, séo, þæt*, THAT. This was prob. due to assimilation, *þēs, þis*, etc. being more like the singular and the dat. and gen. pl., while *þās* was in vowel like *þat* and *þā*. Apparently the assumption of *þās* as pl. of *þat* began in the north, and slowly spread to the south in the form *þōs*: see THOSE. But from the 12th c. there was evidently a tendency in the midl. dialects to differentiate the plural of *this* by adding *-e*, as in the plural of adjs. (*al, alle, sum, sume, his, hise*, etc.), so that from *c* 1200 to 1500 a frequent midland form was *þis-e* (2 syllables in Ormin, etc.); in e. midl. also *þese* appears *c* 1200. Even the s. w. *þüs* varied with *þüse*. Of all these varieties, *these* was the survivor. Also, of *thō* and *thōs*, the two plurals of *that*, the former was finally dropped in the course of the 16th c.; so that there now remain in standard English only the two forms *these* and *those* (*thoos, thōs*)—both in their origin plurals of *this*; the original plural of *that* being lost in standard English, though in Scotland and the northern counties of England it survives dialectally as *thae, theä, theeä*: see THAE. In the same district *these* has been superseded by THIR (*thur, thor*). (The original pl. *þās, þōs* is treated under THOSE, to which it belongs in form, though in meaning it belongs here.)]

**A.** Illustration of Forms.

[**α.** 1–3 **ðás, þás, þōs**: see THOSE.]

**β.** 1 **ðǽs**, 1–3 **þǽs**, 2–5 **þēs**, 3 **ðēs**, 3–4 **þeos**, (**teos, þeors**), 5 **þies, thees**, 5–6 **thes, thies**, 6 **thyes, thez, theis.** *Early inflexions*: *dat.* 1 **ðisum**; **ðiosum, ðissum, ðassum**, 2 **þison, -an**, 2–3 **þissen, þisse**, 2–4 **þisen**, 3 **þesse**. *gen.* 1 **ðissa**; **ðeossa, ðassa þisra**, 2–3 **þisse, þissere.**

*c* 888 K. ÆLFRED *Boeth.* xxxii. § 2 Hwelc þæs flæslican good sien. 971 *Blickl. Hom.* 5 Þeos haliȝe fæmne..brohte eallum ȝeleaffullum þæs bletsunga. *c* 1175 *Lamb. Hom.* 11 Moyses þe hehte heom feste þes daȝes uppon þe munte of synai. *c* 1200 *Trin. Coll. Hom.* 19 Nu ich eu habbe opened þes fif word...Hereð nu þes oðre. *c* 1205 LAY. 1038 Þæs [*c* 1275 þeos] tiðende him weren læðe. *Ibid.* 4621 We.. nuten næuere þæs gume [*c* 1275 þis gomes]. *c* 1230 *Hali Meid.* 5 Þeos þohtes warp ut of þin heorte. *c* 1250 *Gen. & Ex.* 1643 Iacob ðes hirdes freinen gan. *a* 1375 *Lay Folks Mass Bk.* App. iv. 175 Þeos Auctours alle. *c* 1380 WYCLIF *Serm.* Sel. Wks. II. 113 Studie þes wordis. *c* 1400 *Destr. Troy* 1454 All thies maters. 1490 CAXTON *Eneydos* xvi. 65 By what wayes he maye notyfye thees thynges to Dydo. *c* 1500 *New Not-br. Mayd* 235 Ayenst thyes thre. 1529 CDL. WOLSEY in *Four C. Eng. Lett.* (1880) 10 Thes thyngs consyderyd. 1556 *Chron. Gr. Friars* (Camden) 74 Theis iiij. knyghttes. *a* 1596 *Sir T. More* II. ii. 26 Fier the howses Of theis audatious strangers.

*dat.* *c* 825 *Vesp. Psalter* xvii[i]. 18 From ðissum ða fiodon me. *c* 893 K. ÆLFRED *Orosius* II. ii. § 2 He þa Romulus æfter þiosan underfeng Cirinensa ȝewinn. *c* 897 — *Gregory's Past. C.* xviii. 138 Betweox ðissum. *Ibid.* xxi. 162 Be ðiosum ȝit is swiðe ryhtlice ȝecweden. *c* 1000 *Ags. Gosp.* Matt. iii. 9 Of þysum stanum. *Ibid.* xxvii. 21 Hwæþerne.. of þisum twam? [*c* 1160 *Hatt. G.* ibid. of þisen stanen..Of þisan twam?]. *c* 1175 *Lamb. Hom.* 11 On þisse gastliche daȝen. *Ibid.* 37 Summe of þisse þinge. *c* 1200 *Trin. Coll. Hom.* 217 On þesse fewe litele wored...Ac ich ne mai ne ich ne can þesse [*pr.* þosse] on openi. *c* 1205 LAY. 26356 No aȝæf þissen [*c* 1275 to þeos] eorlen. 1340 *Ayenb.* 218 Of þisen we habbeþ ane uorbisne ine þe godspelle.

*gen.* *c* 897 K. ÆLFRED *Gregory's Past. C.* xiv. 82 Mid nanum ðissa. *c* 950 *Lindisf. Gosp.* Matt. xxi. 3 Hlaferd ðisra nytt hæfeð. *c* 1000 ÆLFRIC *Lives of Saints* xxiii. 137 Menn..þisra seofona ȝeorne heddon. *c* 1000 *Ags. Gosp.* Matt. xiii. 22 Leasung þissa woruld-welena. *c* 1160 *Hatton Gosp.* ibid., Leasunge þissere worlde welen. *c* 1205 LAY. 14829 Ich æm þissere leodene king.

γ. 2–5 **þis**, 5–7 **this**, (5–6 **thys**).

*c* 1200 *Trin. Coll. Hom.* 211 On þis fuwer laȝes. 1297 R. GLOUC. (Rolls) 320 Þes men of þis wilde bestes slowe & caȝte inowe. 1477 EARL RIVERS (Caxton) *Dictes* 30 Thou hast ben in all this dangers. 1534 in *Lett. Suppress. Monasteries* (Camden) 11 Yn thys thynges I desyryd you to do that you thowht metyst. 1622 S. WARD *Christ All in All* (1627) 13 This Eagles feathers will not abide blending with others.

δ. 3–5 **þus** (*ü*), **þuse**, **thus(e**.

1297 R. GLOUC. (Rolls) 11950 Þus sixe iwis. *a* 1300 *Fragm. Pop. Sc.* (Wright, 1841) 135/124 Of thuse four elementz ech quik best y-maked is. *c* 1300 *Beket* 890 Thuse kniȝtes ich lovie more. *c* 1380 *Sir Ferumb.* 1012 Þus þay prikede, þuse two baroun hure frendes to rescowe. *c* 1420 *Chron. Vilod.* 41 And hade þuse foure in his gouernynge. *Ibid.* 1359 And dred þus laudable wordus.

ε. 2–5 **þise**, 4–5 **thise**, 5 **thyse**.

*c* 1200 ORMIN 4573 Whas itt iss þatt follȝheþþ wel & filleþþ þise mahhtess. *c* 1220 *Bestiary* 514 Ðis cete ðanne..ðise fisses alle in sukeð. *c* 1386 CHAUCER *Wife's Prol.* 560 Thise wermes, ne thise Motthes, ne thise mytes. *c* 1450 *Merlin* i. 23 Whan alle thise thynges were don. 1494 FABYAN *Chron.* VII. 359 The best men of y^e cytie by thyse ryotous persones were spoyled & robbid.

ζ. 3 **ðese**, 4–5 **þese**, 4– **these**, (4 **þeose**, **þiese**, 5 **þeese**, 6 **theese**, **theise**).

*c* 1200 *Trin. Coll. Hom.* 13 Ðese six werkes..ben cleped lihtes scrud. *c* 1250 *Gen. & Ex.* 3697 Forð was gon al ðese oðer ȝer. 13.. *Cursor M.* 16767+65 (Cott.) These ilk wordez said he. *c* 1425 *Ibid.* 4597 (Trin.) Þeese oþere seuen woful neet. *c* 1550 *Disc. Common Weal Eng.* (1893) 139 In consideration of theese thinges. *Ibid.*, At theise days.

**B. Signification.**

The plural of THIS *pron.* and *adj.*

**I.** Demonstrative pronoun.

**1.** Denoting things or persons actually or ideally present or near; esp. those that have just been mentioned.

**a.** things: plural of THIS B. I. 1 a.

*c* 893 [see A. β]. *c* 1205 LAY. 26044 Ær þe king hæfde þæs ful isæide. 1303 R. BRUNNE *Handl. Synne* 11112 Þese are þo yche twey verse Þat to holynes are reuers. 1340 *Ayenb.* 97 Þise byeþ þe seve ruieles of holy lyf þet þe soþe salomon tekþ to his children. *a* 1425 *Cursor M.* 10115 (Trin.) Lecchory and gloteny, Þourȝe pese am I doun dryuen. 1474 *Coventry Leet Bk.* 397 If he do the contrary to any of thies his fyne is at every tyme xl d. 1581 CAMPION in Allen *Martyrd.* (1908) 2 These are the wordes of S. Paule. 1624 WOTTON *Archit.* in *Reliq.* (1651) 211 Such conceipts as these seem somewhat too fine among this Rubbage. 1790 BURKE *Fr. Rev.* 56 For want of these, they have seen the medicine of the state corrupted into its poison. 1862 RUSKIN *Unto this Last* iv. § 78 (1901) 158 His [man's] race has its bounds also; but these have not yet been reached.

**b.** persons.

Still used without the restriction to which the singular *this* is now subject: see THIS B. I. 1 b.

*c* 825 [see A. β]. 1297 R. GLOUC. (Rolls) 547 Þes were as þre kinges. *c* 1330 R. BRUNNE *Chron. Wace* (Rolls) 13395 Bifore Arthur schuld þeos alle wende. 1382 WYCLIF *Rev.* vii. 13, 14 Who ben thes..and of whennus camen thei? ..Thes ben thei, that camen fro greet tribulacioun. *c* 1400 *Destr. Troy* 14022 (heading) Thez Paris slogh in the ffeld. *c* 1440 *Gesta Rom.* lxiii. 274 (Harl. MS.) Þees ben þei, that sleith hire soulis. 1526 TINDALE *John* xxi. 15 Lovest thou me more then these? 1610 SHAKS. *Temp.* II. ii. 91 These are diuels; O defend me. *a* 1715 BURNET *Own Time* (1823) I. 342 One of these being taken, and apprehending he was in danger. 1869 TENNYSON *Coming of Arthur* 52 He..rode a simple knight among his knights, And many of these in richer arms than he.

**c.** Referring to things mentioned or enumerated immediately after: pl. of THIS B. I. 1 d; cf. II. 1 b.

*a* 1225 *Ancr. R.* 36 Þe vreisuns beoð þeos. 'Deus qui sanctam crucem' [etc.]. *c* 1380 *Lay Folks Catech.* 349 These ben also þy fyue Inwyttys, Wyl, Resoun, Mynd, ymaginacioun, and thogth. *c* 1400 tr. *Secreta Secret., Gov. Lordsh.* 68 Þes er þe tokenys of a good stomak—lightnes of body, clernes of vnderstondynge, stiryng appetyt. 1526 TINDALE *Gal.* v. 19 The dedes of the flesshe are manyfest, which are these, advoutrie, fornicacion [etc.]. 1678 BUNYAN *Pilgr.* I. 190 Such sayings as these: All our righteousnesses are as filthy rags [etc.]. 1847 TENNYSON *Princess* II. 55 Then an officer Rose up, and read the statutes, such as these: Not for three years to correspond with home [etc.].

**2.** In opposition to †*tho*, *those* (of things or persons); sometimes *spec.* = 'the latter': plural of THIS B. I. 3, 3 b. Also †*these*..*they* = some.. others (quot. *c* 1450).

*c* 893 K. ÆLFRED *Oros.* I. xi, ȝeþence þonne þara tida and nu þissa. *c* 1450 in Aungier *Syon* (1840) 266 Other sustres ..nowe these, now thei, owe of pyte..to visitte suche prysoners. 1611 BIBLE *Ezek.* i. 21 When the liuing creatures were lift vp from the earth, the wheels were lift vp... When those went, these went, and when those stood, these stood. 1674 tr. *Scheffer's Lapland* 15 The Russians are generally tall, the Laplanders..very short; those are fat and corpulent, these lean and slender. 1734 POPE *Ess. Man* IV. 22 Some place the bliss in action, some in ease, Those call it Pleasure, and Contentment these. 1902 *Westm. Gaz.* 20 Feb. 2/1, I left the skaters flitting to and fro, these with their hockey sticks, those with their sledges.

**II.** Demonstrative adjective.

**1.** Indicating things or persons present or near (actually, or in thought, esp. as having just been mentioned): plural of THIS B. II. 1.

*c* 888, etc. [see A. β]. *c* 1175 *Lamb. Hom.* 107 Hu þes halie mihten ouercumað þa sunnan. *c* 1205 LAY. 29786 Þæs [*c* 1275 þeos] tiðende come to Austine sone. *c* 1290 *Beket* 308 in *S. Eng. Leg.* I. 115 Þis wise men þat weren is Messagers. 1340 *Ayenb.* 7 Þise þri hestes diȝteþ ous to gode specialliche. 1390 GOWER *Conf.* I. 34 Yet these clerkes alday preche And sein, good dede may non be. 1411 *Rolls of Parlt.* III. 650/2, I..dyd assemble thise persones that here been. *c* 1440 *Alphabet of Tales* 42 Nowder of þies two did itt; I did it my selfe. 1526 TINDALE *Matt.* xx. 21 These my two sonnes. 1557 NORTH *Gueuara's Diall Pr.* 50 This daungerous and perillous warres. 1653 WALTON *Angler* ii. 69 I'l give you another dish of fish one of these dayes. 1869 LOWELL *Yussouf* ii, His who buildeth over these Our tents His glorious roof of night and day. 1872 TENNYSON *Gareth & Lynette* 798 Well that ye came, or else these caitiff rogues Had wreak'd themselves on me.

**b.** Referring to something immediately following: plural of THIS B II. 1 b.

*a* 1225 *Ancr. R.* 16 Efter þis ualleð acneon..mid teos vif gretunges. 'Adoramus te Christe [etc.]'. *c* 1275 LAY. 688 And þeos [*c* 1205 þas] word seide: Brutus þe sele, Niþinc þou art dead. 1377 LANGL. *P. Pl.* B. Prol. 184 A mous..to þe route of ratones reherced þese wordes: 'Thouȝ we culled þe catte [etc.]'. *c* 1420 *Chron. Vilod.* 2454 And þuse wordus to hym dude say. 1589 PUTTENHAM *Eng. Poesie* III. iv. (Arb.) 159 Also ye finde these words, *penetrate, penetrable, indignitie*. 1678 BUNYAN *Pilgr.* I. 80 Then was he glad, and that for these reasons: First [etc.]. 1737 *Gentl. Mag.* VII. 182/2 Under the Inscription are these Words, in Greek Letters, *Kairos 'o Pandamatōr.*

**c.** Referring to things or persons familiarly known, esp. to the whole class of such things or persons: plural of THIS B. II. 1 d.

*c* 1325 *Poem Times Edw. II* 49 in *Pol. Songs* (Camden) 326 Thise ersedeknes that ben set to visite holi churche. *c* 1386 CHAUCER *Frankl. Prol.* 1 Thise olde gentil Britons. 1591 SHAKS. 1 *Hen. VI*, I. ii. 123 These women are shrewd tempters with their tongues. 1602 — *Ham.* II. ii. 223 These tedious old fooles. *a* 1704 T. BROWN *Misc., Match for Devil* Wks. 1711 IV. 149 These Husbands are such very Drones. 1766 GOLDSM. *Vic. W.* iv, These rufflings, and pinkings, and patchings, will only make us hated. 1820 BYRON *Mar. Fal.* IV. ii. 17 These city slaves have all their private bias. *Mod.* Do you approve of these old age pensions? Who are these Manchu's in China?

**d.** Used instead of *this* with a sing. noun of multitude (formerly with *company, number*; now only with collectives in pl. sense, as *vermin*); or esp. with *kind, sort* (†*form*, †*manner*) followed by *of* with pl. sb. (cf. KIND *sb.* 14 b, THOSE II. 2 c).

*a* 1533 LD. BERNERS *Gold. Bk. M. Aurel.* Let. xii. (1535) Oo ij b, As I say of these smalle nombre, I myght say of many other. 1583 STUBBES *Anat. Abus.* I. (1879) 147 Then, marche these heathen company towards the Church. *a* 1643 J. SHUTE *Judgem. & Mercy* (1645) 108 All the land was covered with these vermin. 1796 SOUTHEY *Lett. fr. Spain* (1799) 328 A faithful picture of these vermin.

**e.** With a numeral (definite or indefinite) in expressions of time referring to a period immediately past or immediately future.

*c* 1386 CHAUCER *Merch. Prol.* 22, I haue ywedded bee Thise Monthes two. 1552 ASCHAM in *Lett. Lit. Men* (Camden) 11 Any thing that hapt vnto me, thies many years. 1600 SHAKS. *A. Y. L.* IV. i. 180 For these two houres Rosalinde, I wil leaue thee. 1641 R. BAILLIE *Lett. & Jrnls.* (1841) I. 313 These three or four years bygone. 1655 *Nicholas Papers* (Camden) II. 209 Att the French Court they expect not the conclusion these 4 monthes. 1738 SWIFT *Pol. Conversat.* 44 Where has the Wench been these Three Hours? 1764 FOOTE *Patron* III. Wks. 1799 I. 357, I warrant he won't shew his head for these six months. 1782 COWPER *Gilpin* ii, Though wedded we have been These twice ten tedious years. 1852 THACKERAY *Esmond* II. x, Dan Chaucer's, who's dead these ever so many hundred years. 1865 WHEWELL in *Life* (1881) 549 As I have done any time these twenty years and more.

**2.** In opposition to *those*: pl. of THIS B. II. 2.

1641 HINDE *J. Bruen* xxxiii. 104 O how great is the difference betwixt those holy exercises of Religion..and these prophane exercises of corruption and lust! 1660 BARROW *Euclid* v. xv, The number of these parts is equal to the number of those. 1810 CRABBE *Borough* iv. 54 And these fair acres, rented and enjoy'd, May those excel by Solway-moss destroy'd. *Mod.* Do you think these scissors sharper than those you had yesterday?

**III.** *Comb.* **These-like** *a.*, like these, such as these: cf. *this-like* s. v. THIS B. III.

1644 MILTON *Areop.* (Arb.) 57 Every acute reader upon the first sight of a pedantick licence, will be ready with these like words to ding the book a coits distance from him, I hate a pupil teacher [etc.]. 1819 KEATS *Hyperion* I. 50 Some mourning words, which in our feeble tongue Would come in these like accents.

**Thesean** (þisīˑăn), *a.* [f. L. *Thēsē-us* adj. + -AN.] Of or belonging to Theseus, a legendary hero-king of Athens. So **Theseid** (þīsīˑid) [ad. L. *Thēsēis, -idem*, Gr. Θησηΐς, -ΐδα], the title of a poem on the exploits of Theseus; *transf.* a poem of the same character as the 'Theseid of hoarse Codrus' referred to by Juvenal. **Theseium** (þīsīˑǝ̆m), **Theseum** (þisīˑǝ̆m), **Theseion** (þisəiˑǫn) [a. L. *Thēsēum*, Gr. Θησεῖον], the temple of Theseus at Athens, or the Doric building to which the name is now applied (generally held to be the temple of Hephæstus).

1902 *Speaker* 26 June 370/1 These..should go far to explain the old *Thesean legends. 1725 *Pope's Odyss.* I. *View Epic Poem*, etc. iv. 10 Poets..who composed their *Theseids, Heracleids, and the like. *a* 1822 SHELLEY *Def. Poetry* Ess. & Lett. (Camelot) 39, I confess myself..unwilling to be stunned by the Theseids of the hoarse Codri of the day. 1873 HAYMAN *Odyss.* XI. 260 *note* II. 205 An Amazon of the Theseid legend. 1819 E. DODWELL *Tour Greece* I. xii. 362 The *Theseion impresses the beholder more by its symmetry than its magnitude. 1837 *Antiq. Athens* 68 Unlike the lavish decoration of the temple of Minerva, the *Theseium was ornamented with a sparing hand. 1854 tr. *Hettner's Athens & Peloponnese* 152 The monument of Aristion in the *Theseum at Athens.

† **Thesial**, *a.* *Obs. rare*—[1]. [irreg. f. THESI-S + -AL.] Relating to a thesis or theses.

1654 VILVAIN *Epit. Ess.* App. 191 One hundred Thesial Verses are here entred.

**Theˑsicle.** *nonce-wd.* [f. THESIS + *-cle*, dim. suffix: see -CULE.] A little insignificant thesis.

1863 RUSSELL *Diary N. & S.* I. 232 Their paltry thesicles on the divine origin and uses of slavery. 1864 in WEBSTER.

**Thesis** (þīˑsis, þeˑsis). Pl. **theses** (þīˑsīz). [a. Gr. θέσις putting, placing; a proposition, affirmation, etc., f. root θε- of τι-θέ-ναι to put, place.]

**I.** In *Prosody*, etc.: opposed to ARSIS.

**1.** Originally and properly, according to ancient writers, The setting down of the foot or lowering of the hand in beating time, and hence (as marked by this) the stress or *ictus*; the stressed syllable of a foot in a verse; a stressed note in music.

[1855 WEIL & BENLOEW *Théorie générale de l'accentuation latine* 98. 1861 R. WESTPHAL *Fragm. der griech. Rhythmiker* 98. 1880 P. PIERSON *Métrique Naturelle du Lang.* 32.] 1864 HADLEY *Ess.* (1873) 81 The name *feet* for rhythmic elements, *arsis* (raising of the foot), *thesis* (setting down of the foot), have primary reference to orchestic. 1891 *Cent. Dict.*, *Thesis*...In musical rhythmics, a heavy accent, such as in beating time is marked by a down-beat.

**2.** By later Latin writers (e.g. Martianus Victorinus *a* 400, Priscian *c* 500) used for the lowering of the voice on an unstressed syllable, thus practically reversing the original meaning; hence in prevalent acceptation (from the time of Bentley, 1726): The unaccented or weak part of a foot in verse (classical or modern), or an unaccented note in music.

1398 TREVISA *Barth. De P. R.* XIX. cxxxi. (1495) 941 *Arsis* is rerynge of voys and is the begynnyng of songe. *Thesis* is settynge and is the ende. [1726 BENTLEY *Terence* p. i.] 1830 J. SEAGER tr. *Hermann's Metres* I. ii. 4 After the example of Bentley, we call that time in which the ictus is, the *arsis*, and those times, which are without the ictus, the *thesis*. ..Other writers on metres, together with ancient musicians,..call that thesis which we call arsis, and that arsis, which we call thesis. 1844 [see ANACRUSIS]. 1846 KEIGHTLEY *Notes Virg.*, *Bucol.* I. 47 (Fŏrtūnātĕ sĕnĕx, ĕrgŏ tŭă rūră mănēbūnt!) He [Wagner] adds, that the emphasis should therefore be on *tua*, and not on *manebunt*. But this was not possible to a Roman, for *tua* here (like *mea* ix. 4) is in the *thesis* of a dactyl. 1876 KENNEDY *Pub. Sch. Lat. Gram.* § 258 Each simple Foot has two parts, one of which is said to have the ictus upon it, and is called arsis. ; the other part is called thesis. 1879 OUSELEY in Grove *Dict. Mus.* I. 95/2 The terms arsis and thesis may be regarded as virtually obsolete, and are rarely used in these days.

‖ **3.** *Mus.* *Per arsin et thesin* (= 'by raising and lowering'): used of a fugue, canon, etc. in which the subject or melody is inverted, so that the rising parts correspond to the falling ones in the original subject and *vice versâ*: the same as *by inversion*.

1597 MORLEY *Introd. Mus.* II. 114 If therefore you make a Canon *per arsin & thesin*, without anie discorde in binding maner in it. 1706 PHILLIPS (ed. Kersey) s. v. *Arsis*, A Point being inverted or turned, is said, To move *per Arsin* and *Thesin*, that is to say when a Point rises in one Part, and falls in another; or on the contrary, when it falls in one Part, and rises in another. 1879 [see ARSIS 3].

**II.** In *Logic, Rhetoric*, etc.

**4.** A proposition laid down or stated, esp. as a theme to be discussed and proved, or to be maintained against attack (in *Logic* sometimes as distinct from HYPOTHESIS 2, in *Rhetoric* from ANTITHESIS 2); a statement, assertion, tenet.

1579 DIGGES *Stratiot.* a iv, The vulgare Thesis of the Earthes Stabilitie. 1600 W. WATSON *Decacordon* Pref.

(1602) A v b, By way of a Quodlibet or Thesis proposed. **1651** *Life Father Sarpi* (1676) 8 He was sent to dispute against the Theses that were then given in. **1697** tr. *Burgersdicius his Logic* II. xxiii. 112 A Thesis, whose Truth is not known by the meer Signification of the Words only; but by the Judgment of the Senses, or some other way of Declaration. **1727–41** CHAMBERS *Cycl.* s. v., The maintaining a thesis, is a great part of the exercise a student is to undergo for a degree. *Ibid.*, Every proposition may be divided into thesis and hypothesis, thesis contains the thing affirmed or denied, and hypothesis the conditions of the affirmation or negation. Thus,..If a triangle and parallelogram have equal bases and altitudes (is the hypothesis), the first is half of the second, the thesis. **1833** COLERIDGE *Table-t.* 3 July, The style of Junius is a sort of metre, the law of which is a balance of thesis and antithesis. **1860** COLLIER *Gt. Events Hist.* vi. 182 [Luther] Shaping his belief on the subject of the indulgences into ninety-five theses or propositions. **1879** FARRAR *St. Paul* II. 96 In the Epistle to the Romans he established the thesis that Jews and Gentiles were equally guilty.

**b.** *spec.* distinguished from HYPOTHESIS 1, q. v. quots. 1620–*a* 1647.

**c.** A theme for a school exercise, composition, or essay.

*a* **1774** TUCKER *Lt. Nat.* (1834) II. 624 Whether among the theses given to declaim upon, it might not be profitable sometimes to choose those wherein the boys will be heartily interested. **1786** JEFFERSON *Writ.* (1859) II. 42 On such a thesis, I never think the theme long.

**5.** A dissertation to maintain and prove a thesis (in sense 4); esp. one written or delivered by a candidate for a University degree.

**1653** *Munim. Univ. Glasgow* (1854) II. 323 Theologicall theses. **1659** OWEN *Consid. Bibl. Polygl.* 205 The Thesis prefering this or that translation above the originall. **1673** RAY *Journ. Low C.* 36 He makes Theses upon the Subject he intends to answer, which Theses are printed. **1741** WATTS *Improv. Mind* I. xiii. § 3 It is the business of the respondent to write a thesis..or short discourse on the question proposed. **1837** LOCKHART *Scott* vi, Scott's thesis was, in fact, on the Title of the Pandects, 'Concerning the disposal of the dead bodies of criminals'. **1864** BURTON *Scot Abr.* I. v. 266 There was an instruction that each should write his name on his thesis.

**6.** *Comb.*: **thesis-play**, a play composed with the purpose of maintaining a thesis, a tendency-play; so *thesis-playwright*.

**1902** *Edin. Rev.* July 199 The conscious, deliberate thesis-playwright was Dumas *fils*. **1904** *Ibid.* Oct. 299 The use of 'thesis play' as a term of reproach is not without a certain justification. **1905** *Daily Chron.* 14 June 5/2 'L'Adversaire' is one of those brilliantly specious thesis-plays with which M. Capus has been wont to astonish both the philosophic and dramatic worlds.

**Thesmo·philist.** *nonce-wd.* [f. Gr. θεσμός law (f. root θε- to lay down) + -φιλ-ος, -PHIL + -IST.] A lover of law.

**1644** SIR E. DERING *Prop. Sacr.* e iij b, His Bishop [Bp. Wren], that great Thesmophilist.

**Thesmophoric** (þesmǫfǫ·rik), *a. Gr. Antiq.* [f. Gr. (τὰ) θεσμοφόρια, neut. pl. (f. θεσμοφόρος, f. θεσμός law + -φορος -bearing, an epithet of the goddess Demeter) + -IC.] Of or pertaining to the *Thesmophoria*, an ancient Greek festival held by women in honour of Demeter. So **Thesmopho·rian** *a.*, in same sense.

**1884** W. M. RAMSAY in *Encycl. Brit.* XVII. 127/2 The Thesmophoric rites are so obscure that no sure idea can be gained of the relation between them and the simpler Arcadian cultus. **1891** *Cent. Dict.*, Thesmophorian.

**Thesmothete** (þe·smoþīt, -þet). Also in Gr. form **thesmothetes** (þesmǫ·þėtīz), *pl.* -thetæ. [ad. Gr. θεσμοθέτης, pl. -θέται (see def.), f. θεσμός law + -θετης, forming agent-nouns from root θε- to place, lay down.] Each of the six inferior archons in ancient Athens, who were judges and law-givers; hence *transf.* one who lays down the law.

**1603** HOLLAND *Plutarch* Explan. Words, *Thesmothetæ*, were six of the nine Archontes or chiefe rulers in Athens during their free popular estate. **1727** BAILEY vol. II, *Thesmothete*, a Law-giver. **1819** H. BUSK *Tea* 18 Without thee thesmothetes their laws enacted. **1874** T. HARDY *Far fr. Madding Crowd* x, Then this small thesmothete stepped from the table, and surged out of the hall.

**Thesocyte** (þe·sosəit). *Biol.* [irreg. f. Gr. θέσις putting, deposit + -CYTE.] (See quot.)

**1887** SOLLAS in *Encycl. Brit.* XXII. 420/2 Reserve cells or *thesocytes* have been described in several sponges as well as amylin and oil-bearing cells.

**Thesorar, -er**, variant of THESAURER *Obs.*

**Thespian** (þe·spiăn), *a.* and *sb.* [f. Gr. proper name Θέσπις + -AN.]

**A.** *adj.* Of or pertaining to Thespis, the traditional father of Greek tragedy (6th c. B. C.); hence, of or pertaining to tragedy, or the dramatic art; tragic, dramatic.

**1675** COCKER *Morals* 39 Nectar, Ambrosia, and the Thespian Spring, May all avant, for Mony is the Thing. **1748** THOMSON *Cast. Indol.* I. 463 Oft they snatch the pen, As if inspir'd, and in a Thespian rage; Then write and blot, as would your ruth engage. **1847** (*title*) Theatrical Times, a Weekly Magazine of Thespian Biography. **1855** KINGSLEY *Westw. Ho* ii, To extemporise a pageant,..or any effort of the Thespian art. **1906** *Athenæum* 3 Mar. 256/2 The Chorus was a reminiscence of the old Thespian drama.

**B.** *sb.* A tragedian; an actor or actress.

**1827** W. KENNEDY *Poems* 42 The Thespian's outward guise Of happiness, her secret mood belies. **1864** DORAN *Ann. Eng. Stage* I. v. 121 The..Lord Chamberlain..clapped the unoffending Thespian..in the Gate House.

**Thessaure**, var. THESAUR *Obs.*, treasure.

**Thessel, -downe**, obs. form of THISTLE, -DOWN.

† **Thester**, *sb. Obs.* Forms: 1 ðiostru, -tro, þeostru, ðiestru, þystru, -o, 2 þeostre, 3 þuster, 4 þustre, 4 þestri, þester, 4–5 thestre, 5 thestur. [OE. *ðíestru*, *þéostru*, fem. (orig. of the *-ī* decl.) = OS. *thiustrī*; also OE. *ðíestre*, *þéostre*, pl. *-ru*, neut.; f. THESTER *a.*] Darkness. *lit.* and *fig.*

*Beowulf* 87 Seþe in þystrum bad. *c* **897** K. ÆLFRED *Gregory's Past. C.* xxxv. 244 Se dæȝ bið ierres dæȝ & ðiestra ðæȝ. *a* **900** tr. *Bæda's Hist.* v. xiii. [xii.] (1890) 426 He mec forlet in middum þæm þeostrum. *c* **1000** *Ags. Gosp.* Matt. xxii. 13 Wurpaþ hyne on þa uttran þystro [*c* **1160** *Hatton G.* þeostran, *Rushw.* ðiostre, *Lindisf.* ðiostrum]. *c* **1175** *Lamb. Hom.* 131 He ledde heom of þeostran and of scadewe. *a* **1250** *Owl & Night.* 230 Hit luuyeþ þuster & hateþ lyht. *c* **1315** SHOREHAM v. 130 Þaȝ hyt were þustre of nyȝt. **13..** *E. E. Allit. P.* B. 1775 Þay þrongen þeder in þe þester. *c* **1400** *Destr. Troy* 4629 Thunret in the thestur throly with all. *a* **1400–50** *Alexander* 4627 Quen it walows & wannes all oure thestres.

Hence † **The·sterful, þeosterful** *a.*, full of darkness; † **Theosterleyk** (*Orm.* **þeossterrleȝȝc**), darkness.

*c* **1000** ÆLFRIC *Hom.* II. 350 Se engel me lædde..to anre þeostorfulre stowe. *c* **1000** *Ags. Gosp.* Matt. vi. 23 Eall þin lic-hama byð ðysterfull [*c* **1160** *Hatton G.* þeosterful]. *c* **1200** ORMIN 2964, I þiss lifess þeossterrleȝȝc.

† **Thester**, *a. Obs.* Forms: 1 ðiostre, *ðiestre, þystre, þiostor, 1–2 þeoster (-or, -ur), 1–3 þeostre, 2 þiestre, þostre, 2–3 þestre, 2–4 þester, 3 þuster, -re, þestere, (*Orm.* þessterr), 4 þyestre, þister, þyster, 4–5 thester, -ir, 5 thestur. [OE. *þíostre*, *þéostre*, in WS. (with umlaut) *þíestre*, *þýstre*, = OS. *thiustri*, OFris. *thiustere*, MDu. *dûster* (Du. *duister*, MLG., LG., G. *düster*), :—OTeut. **þiustr-jo*. Ulterior etymology uncertain.] Dark. *lit.* and *fig.*

*Beowulf* 2332 Breost innan weoll þeostrum ȝeþoncum. *a* **900** tr. *Bæda's Hist.* v. xiii. [xii.] (1890) 426 Under ðæm scuan þære ðeostran nihte. *c* **1000** *Ags. Ps.* (Th.) xvii[i]. 11 Þa hangode swiðe þystru wæter on þam wolcnum. *a* **1175** *Cott. Hom.* 233 H[e] sweueð hus mid þiestre nicht. *c* **1200** *Trin. Coll. Hom.* 39 Al þis lif..is to nihte iefned, for þat it is swa þester of ure ateliche synnes. *c* **1200** ORMIN 16774 Nicodem, Þatt comm till ure Laferrd O þessterr nahht. ? *a* **1300** *XI Pains Hell* 121 in *O. E. Misc.* 150 Þe stude is þustrore þene þe nyht. *Ibid.* 225 Þustrur þane þe nyht. *c* **1315** SHOREHAM v. 146 Be hyt þyster, be hyt lyȝt. **1340** *Ayenb.* 45 Þise zelleres of cloþ þet chieseþ þe þyestre stedes huer hi zelleþ hare cloþ. *c* **1400** *Destr. Troy* 2362 He þrong into þicke wodes, þester within. ? *a* **1500** *Chester Pl.* (Shaks. Soc.) I. 226 He maie goe no thester waie.

† **Thester**, *v. Obs.* Forms: 1 ð-, þeostrian, þiestrian, þystrian, 2 þestrian, 2–3 þ(e)ostren, 3 þustren, 4 þester. [OE. *þéostrian*, *þíestrian*, f. *þéostre*, THESTER *a.* Cf. G. *düstern.*]

**1.** *intr.* To become dark, grow dim.

*a* **900** tr. *Bæda's Hist.* v. xiii. [xii.] (1890) 426 Þa ȝeseah ic ..onginnan ðeostrian ða stowe. *c* **1000** ÆLFRIC *Gen.* xlviii. 10 Israheles eaȝan þystrodon for þære micclan ylde. **1154** *O. E. Chron.* an. 1135 (Laud MS.) Þa þestrede þe dæi ouer al landes. *c* **1175** *Lamb. Hom.* 143 Steorren sculen þeostren. *c* **1205** LAY. 4574 Þeostrede [*c* **1275** þustrede] þa wolcne.

**2.** *trans.* To make dark, darken; to dim.

*c* **888** K. ÆLFRED *Boeth.* xxxviii. § 5 Se dæȝ blent & þiostrað heora eaȝan. *c* **950** *Lindisf. Gosp.* Mark xiii. 24 Sunna bið ȝe-ðiostrod. *a* **1225** *Ancr. R.* 94 Þet heo her þeostreð nu ham suluen.

† **The·sterly**, *a.* and *adv.* Forms: 1 þeosterlic (*adj.*), 4 þiesterliche (*adv.*). [f. THESTER *a.*: see -LY [1], [2].] **a.** *adj.* Dark. **b.** *adv.* Darkly.

*c* **1000** ÆLFRIC *Hom.* I. 504 Þæs muntes cnoll mid þeosterlicum ȝenipum eal oferhangen wæs. **1340** *Ayenb.* 244 Þe clene of herte þet hier ssolle ysy him be byleaue, ac alneway þiesterliche.

† **The·sterness.** *Obs.* Forms: see THESTER *a.* [OE. *þéosternes*, etc., f. *þéostre*, THESTER *a.* + -NESS.] Darkness. *lit.* and *fig.*

*c* **888** K. ÆLFRED *Boeth.* xxxiv. § 8 Þesternes. *c* **893** — *Oros.* VI. ii. § 3 Wearð micel þeosternes ofer eallne middanȝeard. *c* **1000** *Ags. Hom.* (ed. Assmann 1889) 203 Þa com..þære nihte þysternys. *c* **1175** *Lamb. Hom.* 61 Þe engles a-dun follon in to þe þosternesse hellen. *a* **1200** *Moral Ode* 277 Eure þer is vuel smech, þusternesse and eie. *c* **1200** ORMIN 16737, & menn ne lufenn nohht te lihht Acc lufenn þessterrnesse. *c* **1250** *Gen. & Ex.* 1942 Quiles he slep, In ðis ðisternesse, old and dep. *c* **1300** *Havelok* 2191 Gon was þisternesse of þe nith. **1377** LANGL. *P. Pl.* B. XVI. 160 On a thoresday in thesternesse þus was he taken. ? *a* **1500** *Chester Pl.* ii. 12 Twynned shalbe throughe my mighte the lighte from Thesternes.

† **Thestri**, *a. Obs.* Forms: 1 ðiostriȝ, þystriȝ, 3 þeostri, 4 thestri. [OE. *þíostriȝ*, f. *þíostre*, *þéostre*, THESTER *a.* + *-iȝ*: see -Y.] Dark (*lit.* and *fig.*); = THESTER *a.*

*a* **900** WÆRFERTH *Gregory's Dial.* (1900) 76 Þonne bið þin lichama eall þystriȝ. *c* **950** *Lindisf. Gosp.* Mark viii. 17 Ðiostriȝ..ȝie habbað hearta iuer. *a* **1240** *Ureisun* in *Cott. Hom.* 200 Aliht mine þeostri heorte. *c* **1325** *Body & Soul* in *Map's Poems* (Camden) 346 In a thestri stude y stod.

**Thesuerer**, variant of THESAURER *Obs.*

**Thet, þet**, obs. f. THAT; obs. neut. sing. of THE.

**Theta** (þī·tă). [a. Gr. θῆτα: see def.] The eighth letter of the Greek alphabet, Θ, θ (see TH).

In ancient Greece, on the ballots used in voting upon a sentence of life or death, θ stood for θάνατος, death; hence in allusive use.

**1603** DANIEL *Def. Ryme* H iv, Setting his *Theta* or marke of condemnation vppon them. **1616–61** HOLYDAY *Persius* iv. 317 And the black theta, signe of deadly shame, Thou can'st prefix 'fore an offenders name. **1682** SIR T. BROWNE *Chr. Mor.* I. § 22 At the Tribunal..wherein iniquities have their natural Theta's, and no nocent is absolved by the verdict of himself. **1789** M. MADAN tr. *Persius* (1795) 103 Able to fix the black theta to vice.

**b.** *attrib.* and *Comb.*, as *theta-sounding* adj.; **theta-function**, in *Math.*, a name for two different functions: (*a*) the sum of a series from $n = -\infty$ to $n = +\infty$ of terms denoted by $\exp(n^2a + 2na)$; also extended to a similar function of several variables; (*b*) a function occurring in probabilities, expressed by the integral $\int e^{-t^2}dt$; **theta-phi diagram**, the temperature-entropy diagram, which represents the heat-units converted into work per pound of working fluid ($\theta$ = absolute temperature, and $\phi$ = entropy).

**1871** M. COLLINS *Mrq. & Merch.* III. iii. 88 You [English] are a theta-sounding people. **1879** CAYLEY *Coll. Math. Papers* X. 475 We have thus an addition-with-subtraction theorem for the double theta-functions. **1901** *Pract. Engineer Pocket Bk.* 166 The temperature-entropy diagram is usually called the θφ (theta-phi) diagram.

**Thetch** (þetʃ). *dial.* [A dial. form of *fetch* = VETCH: cf. *thane* [2], and see TH (6).]

**1733** W. ELLIS *Chiltern & Vale Farm.* 50 Waggon Loads of Peas, Thetches, Chaff and other Grain. **1759** in *Q. Jrnl. Economics* Nov. (1907) 77 To be sowed Wheat as soon as the thetches are tyed off. **1893** *Wilts. Gloss.*, *Thetches*, *Thatches*, vetches. *Lent thetches* are an early spring kind.

**Thetch(e**, obs. variants of THATCH.

**Thete** (þīt). *Gr. Antiq.* [ad. Gr. θής, θητ-, orig. a villein, slave.] In ancient Athens, by the constitution of Solon, a free man of the lowest class, whose property in land was assessed at less than 150 medimni.

**1652** L. S. *People's Liberty* ix. 17 Such whose revenue amounted not to so much as 200 measures of aride and liquide fruicts (who were called Thetes). **1846** GROTE *Greece* I. xx. II. 131 Poor freemen called Thetes, working for hire. *Ibid.* 132 The condition of a slave under an average master may have been as good as that of the free Thête.

**Thete**, variant of THEAT.

**Thethe, Thething**, erroneous spelling of *tethe*, *tething*, = TITHE, TITHING.

† **Thethen**, *adv. Obs.* Forms: 2–3 (*Orm.*) þeþenn, 3 ðeðen, 4 þi-, þei-, þeyþen, þeiþin, thythen, þeden, -in, 4–5 þeþen, -þin, -thyn, theþen, -then, -thyn, 5 þ-, thethin, -thyne. [Early ME., a. ON. *þeðan*, Icel. *þaðan* (MSw. *thædhan*, obs. Da. *deden*), f. root of THE with suffix of 'motion from', as in HETHEN, WHETHEN; cf. Gr. -θεν.] From that place; = THENCE.

*c* **1200** ORMIN 1098 Siþþenn ȝede he þeþenn ut. *c* **1220** *Bestiary* 727 in *O. E. Misc.* 23 Ðeðen he sal cumen eft. *a* **1300** *Cursor M.* 6190 Þai suld his banes þeþen bring. *Ib.* 8945 (G.) Þai drow it þeþin [*F.* þeiþen]. *c* **1400** *Melayne* 519 The myghte of god..Had broghte tham thethyn a way. *c* **1450** *St. Cuthbert* (Surtees) 548 Sho hyed her þeþin fast.

**b.** Preceded by *fro* (= from).

**1340** HAMPOLE *Pr. Consc.* 1018 Þe ayre fra þeþen, and þe heat of þe son Sustayns þe erthe here, þar we won. *c* **1400** *Destr. Troy* 8790 Fro thethen the lycour belyue launchit doun evyn. *c* **1420** *Wars Alexander* (Prose) 66 Fra thethyn, Alexander remowede his Oste & come to þe ȝates of Caspee.

Hence † **The·thenforth** *adv.* = THENCEFORTH; † **The·thenward** *adv.* = THENCEWARD.

*c* **1200** ORMIN 10786 Iwhillc mann þatt.. Iss laȝhelike fullhtnedd Birrþ stiȝhenn dun fra þeþennforþ Off modiȝnessess lawe. *Ibid.* 18176, & teþennforþ þewwtenn Crist. *c* **1200** *Trin. Coll. Hom.* 69 Ðe ðeðen forð shal wexen alse he seide. **13..** *Cursor M.* 6357 (Fairf.) Fra þeiþen forþ sir moises þer wandes bare. *Ibid.* 14557 (Cott.) In effraym dueld he..And þeþen ward son can he funde.

**Thether, -ur**, obs. forms of THITHER.

† **Thethey**, obs. ? scribal error for TEETHY *a.*[1]

*c* **1400** *Rowland & O.* 1032 Gude sir, ryde my lemmane nere, the knyghte es full thethey.

**Thethorn**, variant of THEVE-THORN *Obs.*

**Thethy**: see TETHY.

**Thetic** (þe·tik), *a.* (*sb.*) [ad. Gr. θετικ-ός such as is placed or is fit to be placed; positive, affirmative, f. θέτος placed, f. root θε- to place.]

**1.** Characterized by laying down or setting forth; involving positive statement: cf. THESIS 4.

**1678** GALE *Crt. Gentiles* III. Pref., To render our Discourse the lesse offensive, we have cast it into a thetic and dogmatic method, rather than agonistic and polemic. **1837** E. BICKERSTETH *Life Francke* iv. 61 Thetic and historical divinity were not the fields which Francke had chosen to lecture upon. **1882** A. M. FAIRBAIRN in *Contemp. Rev.* Dec. 862 His [Mohammed's] genius was not thetic, but synthetic, not creative but constructive.

**2.** *Pros.* That bears the thesis; stressed.

**1815** J. GRANT in *Monthly Mag.* XXXIX. 303 The first syllable of each being thetic or emphatic and the remainder of the foot being in arsis or remiss.

**b.** 'Beginning with a thesis' (*Cent. Dict.* 1891).

**B.** *sb.* (*pl.*) **Thetics** (nonce-wd.), the art of laying down principles or putting forth propositions.

**1864** CARLYLE *Fredk. Gt.* XVI. v. (1873) VI. 182 Polemics, Thetics, Exegetics.

**Thetical** (þe·tikăl), *a.* [f. as prec. + -AL: see -ICAL.] Of the nature of or involving direct or positive statement; laid down or stated positively or absolutely; positive; dogmatic; arbitrary.

1653 H. MORE *Conject. Cabbal.* (1713) 66 This Law..was merely Thetical or Positive, not Indispensable and Natural. 1678 CUDWORTH *Intell. Syst.* Pref. 2. 1718 J. CHAMBERLAYNE *Relig. Philos.* Pref. (1730) 4 The Thetical Way..must not appear imperfect to them. 1873 W. HUMPHREY *Div. Teacher* p. iii, A thetical exposition of the Catholic doctrine.

**Thetically** (þe·tikăli), *adv.* [f. THETICAL + -LY [2].] In a thetical manner; by way of assertion or positive statement; positively.

1657 W. MORICE *Coena quasi Κοινὴ* v. 58 Why should the same thing be true when proposed thetically, generally.., and false when applyed hypothetically, particularly? 1697 G. K. *Disc. Geom. Problems* 12, [I] have proposed it rather Problematically than Thetically. 1870 M. J. EVANS *Oosterzee's Theol. N. T.* 305 The doctrine of justification is in the Epistle to the Romans presented more thetically (i. e. by way of statement), in Galatians more polemically.

**Thetis** (þe·tis). [a. Gr. Θέτις, proper name.] **1.** *Gr.* and *Rom. Mythology.* One of the Nereids or sea-nymphs, the mother of Achilles; poetically, the sea personified.

1422 LYDG. *Min. Poems* (Percy Soc.) 14 Thetes wiche is of water chef Goddes. c 1620 T. ROBINSON *Mary Magd.* 14 Neptune too, and Thetis greene, In my palace may bee seene. 1711 SHAFTESB. *Charac.* (1737) II. 396 The bridegroom-doge, who in his stately Bucentaur floats on the bosom of his Thetis, has less possession than the poor shepherd, who from a hanging rock..admires her beauty. 1840 BARHAM *Ingol. Leg.* Ser. I. *Witches' Frolic* 87 If.. he laid his head In Thetis's lap beneath the seas.

**2.** *Astron.* Name of the seventeenth asteroid.

Hence †**The·tisie**, *obs. nonce-wd.*, the abode of Thetis and the Nereids; the watery realm.

1600 TOURNEUR *Transf. Metam.* xl, The Treasure-house of Neptune's Thetisie. *Ibid.* lxxiv, When fatall Neptune.. hal'd him to his Thetisie.

**Thetsee**, var. THITSI, black-varnish tree.

**Theu, theue**, var. THEOW, THEW.

**Theurgic** (þi,ǖ·ɹdʒik), *a.* (*sb.*) [ad. L. *theurgicus*, a. Gr. θεουργικός magical: see THEURGY and -IC. So F. *théurgique* (14th c.).] Of or pertaining to theurgy.

1610 HEALEY *St. Aug. Citie of God* x. ix. 371 Certaine Theurgike consecrations called *Teletae*. 1718 BP. HUTCHINSON *Witchcraft* 35 A Golden Image of Jupiter, prepared by the Theurgic Art. 1834 LYTTON *Pompeii* II. viii. [see GOETIC A.]. 1861 — *Str. Story* (1862) I. 313 Every secret ..which the nobler, or theurgic, magic seeks to fathom. 1895 FARRAR *Gathering Clouds* ii. 38 Whatever skill..of medicine he possessed, he eked it out with theurgic pretences.

†**B.** *sb.* A theurgist. *Obs. rare.*

1610 HEALEY *St. Aug. Citie of God* x. xvi. (1620) 362 Let the Platonists, Theurgiques (or rather Periurgikes..) or any other Philosophers answer. *Ibid.* 395 They whom the malicious Theurgike bound from purging the soule of the good one.

**Theurgical** (þi,ǖ·ɹdʒikăl), *a.* [f. as prec. + -AL: see -ICAL.] = prec. adj.

1569 [see THEURGY 1]. 1610 HEALEY *St. Aug. Citie of God* 395 The true Angels..differ from them that descend unto men that use Theurgicall conjurations. 1652 [see GOETICAL]. 1678 CUDWORTH *Intell. Syst.* I. iv. § 16. 286 This Divine Magick of Zoroaster..degenerated..into the Theurgical Magick. a 1834 COLERIDGE *Lit. Rem.* (1839) III. 159 A corrupt mystical theurgical pseudo-Platonism.

Hence **Theu·rgically** *adv.*

1854 MAURICE *Mor. & Met. Philos.* II. 71 The author proposes to discuss..theurgical [questions] theurgically.

**Theurgist** (þi,ǖ·ɹdʒist). [f. THEURG(Y + -IST. Cf. F. *théurgiste* (18th c.).] One who practises or believes in theurgy; a magician.

1652 GAULE *Magastrom.* xxvi, The sacrilegious theurgist will consecrate my head to the crows. 1678 CUDWORTH *Intell. Syst.* I. iv. § 15. 269 One of those more refined [magicians], who have been called by themselves Theurgists. 1856 R. A. VAUGHAN *Mystics* (1860) I. I. iv. 24 The mysticism of the theurgist, which will pass the bounds of the dreaded spirit world..to seize one of its thrones.

**Theurgy** (þi,ǖ·ɹdʒi). [ad. L. *theūrgia*, a. Gr. θεουργία sorcery, f. θεός god + -εργος working. So F. *théurgie* (14th c. in Godef. *Compl.*).]

**1.** A system of magic, originally practised by the Egyptian Platonists, to procure communication with beneficent spirits, and by their aid produce miraculous effects; in later times distinguished as 'white magic' from GOETY or 'black magic'.

1569 J. SANFORD tr. *Agrippa's Van. Artes* 59 b, Porpherie who doth muche dispute of this Theurgie or Magicke of thinges deuine doth finally conclude that with Theurgicall consecrations mans minde may be made apte to receaue Spirites and Angels. 1584 R. SCOT *Discov. Witchcr.* xv. xlii. (1886) 392 There is yet another art, which is called Theurgie; wherein they worke by good angels. 1652 GAULE *Magastrom.* xxvi, Of ceremoniall magick there are two parts, goetie and theurgie. 1751 [see GOETY]. 1899 W. R. INGE *Chr. Mysticism* vii. 267 The turbid streams of theurgy and magic flowed into the broad river of Christian thought by two channels—the later Neo-platonism, and Jewish Cabbalism.

**2.** The operation of a divine or supernatural agency in human affairs; the effects produced among men by direct divine or spiritual action.

1858 GLADSTONE *Homer* III. 564 We stand here at a juncture in the poem, where its theurgy supersedes its human mechanism. 1873 M. ARNOLD *Lit. & Dogma* (1876) 167 The constant tendency of popular Christianity to add to the element of theurgy and thaumaturgy, to increase and develope it. 1878 GLADSTONE *Prim. Homer* 86 The Olympian court is the masterpiece of the whole theurgy of Homer,

**Theutonicke**, obs. form of TEUTONIC.

†**Theve**, *sb. Obs. rare*[−1]. The first element of THEVE-THORN, of uncertain derivation: app. Brushwood, bush, shrub; = BRUSH *sb.*[1] 2.

c 1440 *Promp. Parv.* 490/2 Theve, brusch [*v. r.* brush: no Latin equivalent given].

†**Theve**, *v. Obs.* Also 4 thef. [ME. a. ON. *þefa* to smell, to sniff. Cf. THEF.] *trans.* To smell.

13.. *Cursor M.* 23456 (Gött.) In þis lijf has man gret liking..Suete spiceri to theue [*Edin.* thef, *Cott.* fell (= fele), *F.* tast] and smell.

**Theves**, obs. pl. of THEAVE, THIEF.

†**The·ve-thorn, the·-thorn.** *Obs.* Forms: 1 thebanthorn, þefan-, þeofe-, þife-, þyfe-, 1–3 þefeþorn, 3–5 theve-, 4 theoue, thef-, 4–5 thethorn(e; (5 thewe-, threw-thorn). [Cogn. with OHG. *depandorn* (*Ahd. Glossen* I. 237, 34). Etymology of first element uncertain.

Grimm, *Kl. Schr.* I. 246, renders *depandorn* 'brenndorn', comparing '*deba, diba* incendium', in the Malb. Gloss. This might refer to thorns used for burning or kindling a fire. See also Van Helten in *P. & B. Beitr.* XXV. 348.]

Name of some thorny shrub.

**a.** In OE. and ME. glossaries commonly rendering L. *rhamnus*, which was sometimes in late and med.L. applied to the bramble or blackberry-bush, and was sometimes glossed by whitethorn or hawthorn.

The sense 'bramble' or 'blackberry-bush' is supported by L. *mōrus* in *Metr. Voc.* (which has this sense sometimes in Pliny, and still in Romanic langs.); that of 'hawthorn' by the *red* fruit of *Sinon. Barthol.* (*Thevethorn* could not be buckthorn, the late botanical identification of *Rhamnus* with buckthorn being merely a caprice of Linnæus, without any ancient warrant.)

a 700 *Epinal Gloss.* (O. E. T.) 880 *Ramnus*, thebanthorn. c725 *Corpus Gloss.* 1710 *Ramnus*, ðeofeðorn. c 1000 *Sax. Leechd.* II. 312 Wiþ bite wyrc sealfe; nim..þefan þorn. *Ibid.* III. 56 Nim..ðefeþorn. c 1000 *Ags. Voc.* in Wr.-Wülcker 269/21 *Ramnus*, coltetræppe, þefanðorn. c 1000 ÆLFRIC *Voc.* ibid. 139/20 *Ramnus*, þifeþorn. *Ibid.* 149/32 *Ramnus, uel sentix ursina*, ðyfeþorn. a 1300 *E. E. Psalter* lvii[i]. 10 Ar-til þai undre-stande bi-forn Of youre thornes of thevethorn [1382 WYCLIF theue thorne, Vulg. *rhamnum*]. 13.. *Heber MS.* 8336 in *Promp. Parv.* 490 *note*, Nym the floures of theoue-thorn. a 1340 HAMPOLE *Psalter* lvii. 9 Rammyn, þat þai call thefthorne, has swilke a kynd, þat it is first soft, and sithen turnys it in til thornes. a 1387 *Sinon. Barthol.* (Anecd. Oxon.) 36 *Rampnus* est frutex spinosus ferens rubeos fructus, i. thethorne. 1388 WYCLIF *Judg.* ix. 14 And alle trees seiden to the ramne [*gloss* ether theue thorn; *Vulg.* ad rhamnum; 1382 to the thorn], Come thou, and be lord on vs. 14.. *Metr. Voc.* in Wr.-Wülcker 629/6 *Morus*, thewe-thornys. 14.. *Nom.* ibid. 715/35 *Hec ramnus*, ..a thethorntre. c 1450 *Medulla* in *Cath. Angl.* 382 *note*, *Ramnus*, a whyte thorne or a thepe [? theve] bushe. 1483 *Cath. Angl.* 382/2 A Thethorne, *rampnus*.

**b.** Sometimes applied to the gooseberry.

In Ps. lvii. 9, the two 12th c. Anglo-Norman Psalters (ed. Fr. Michel, 1860, 1876) render *rhamnus* by *groseiller, groselier*, gooseberry, and this identification is found in some ME. glossaries, and was also adopted by Theodore Gaza, c 1450. Cf. also FEABERRY, DAYBERRY, possibly dialectal alterations of *the-berry* from *thethorn*.

c 1265 *Voc.* in Wr.-Wülcker 558/29 *Ramni, i.* [Fr.] grosiler, *i.* [Eng.] þefeþorn. c 1450 *Alphita* (Anecd. Oxon.) 156 *Rampnus, gallice* griseler, *anglice*, threwthorn. [1862 WRIGHT *Hist. Domest. Mann.* 296 In the dialect of Norfolk, gooseberries are still called *theabes*.] [Cf. *Thapes, thepes* gooseberries (Eng. Dial. Dict.).]

†**The·vis ne·k.** *Sc. Obs.* = 'Thief's neck', one fit for the gallows: a term of opprobrium.

In quots. represented as the cry of the tewhit or lapwing.

c 1450 HOLLAND *Howlat* 823 The Tuchet and the gukkit Golk...Callit him [the Rook] thryss thevisnek, to thrawe in a widdy. 1549 *Compl. Scot.* vi. 39 The tuechitis cryit theuis nek, quhen the piettis clattrit.

**Thew** (þiū), *sb.*[1] Forms: 1–3 þeaw, þeau, (1 ðeow), 2–3 þæw, 2–5 þew, þewe, 3 þeauw, þeuw, þeæw, þeu, 4 theaw, 4–5 theu, thue, 4–9 thewe, (5 thegh), 4– thew. [OE. *þéaw* = OS. *thau* usage, custom, habit, OHG. *thau* (*dau*) discipline. Not recorded outside WGer. langs. Ulterior etymology uncertain.]

†**1.** A custom, usage, general practice (e. g. of a people, community, or class). *Obs.*

*Beowulf* 360 Cuþe he duȝuðe þeaw. c893 K. ÆLFRED *Oros.* I. x. § 2 Siþþan wæs hiera þeaw. c950 *Lindisf. Gosp.* John xix. 40 Sua ðeau Iudeum [*Rushw.* ðeow iudea, *Ags. Gosp.* iudea þ[e]aw, *Hatton G.* iudea þæw] is bybyrȝe. c 1200 *Trin. Coll. Hom.* 47 Wich þeau was on þe olde laȝe. *Ibid.*, Swich þeu wes bi þan daȝen.

†**b.** *pl.* Customs ordained; ordinances. *Obs.*

13.. *E. E. Allit. P.* B. 544 In de-voydynge þe vylanye þat venkquyst his þewez. *Ibid.* 755. 1624 QUARLES *Job* vii. 7 Thy sacred Thewes, and sweet Instructions, did Helpe those were falling, rays'd up such as slid.

†**2.** A custom or habit of an individual; manner of behaving or acting; hence, a personal quality (mental or moral); a characteristic, attribute, trait. Chiefly in *pl. Obs.*

c 888 K. ÆLFRED *Boeth.* xxvii. § 2 Wisdom..ælces godes þeawes he ȝesylð þone þe hine lufað. c893 — *Oros.* VI. xiv. § 1 He wæs swiþe yfel monn ealra þeawa. 971 *Blickl. Hom.* 217 Wæs he swiðe ȝeþungen on his ðeawum. c 1000 ÆLFRIC *Gen.* xxxi. 5 Ic ȝeseo on eowres fader þeawum, þat he nys swa wel wið me ȝeworht. c 1200 ORMIN 7328, I dærne unnclene þohht & þæw. c 1205 LAY. 6361 Morpidus.. Monnene strengest Of maine and of þeauwe. c 1230 *Hali Meid.* 3 Euch meiden þat haueð meidene þeawes. a 1300 *Cursor M.* 1947 (Cott.) To doghty thues lok þou þe gif. 1382 WYCLIF 1 *Cor.* xv. 33 Forsoth yuele spechis corumpen (or distroyen) goode thewis (or vertues). 1422 tr. *Secreta Secret., Priv. Priv.* 211 A man may not fynde in no beste, custume ne thegh, wyche is noght in a man. 1456 SIR G. HAYE *Law Arms* (S.T.S.) 120 The vertues cardinalis..reule of all vertues and gude thewis as kingis. 1508 DUNBAR *Tua Mariit Wemen* 119 Full of eldnyng..and anger, and all euill thewis. 1559 *Mirr. Mag., Dk. Clarence* xviii, In vertuous thewes. 1590 SPENSER *F. Q.* II. x. 59 Helena..in all godly thewes and goodly prayse Did far excell. 1805 SOUTHEY *Madoc* II. xviii, In martial thewes and manly discipline, To train the sons of Owen.

†**b.** Without qualification: A good quality or habit; a virtue; courteous or gracious action. *Obs.*

c 1205 LAY. 300 Þis child leuede & wel iþei, & þeweas [c 1275 þeuwes] hit luuede. a 1225 *Ancr. R.* 278 Þes þeau [humility] is alre þeauwene moder. c 1250 *Gen. & Ex.* 2757 Hu a ȝunge man, at te welle[n] Ðewe and wursipe hem dede. 13.. *Cursor M.* 20996 (Cott.) A man o mekenes and o theu. 1357 *Lay Folks Catech.* 406 The third vertu or thew is charite. c 1400 *Emare* 58 She thawȝth [= tawȝt] hyt curtesye and thewe, Golde and sylke for to sewe. 1575 GASCOIGNE *Notes Instr.* in *Steele Gl.* etc. (Arb.) 37 This poeticall license..turkeneth all things at pleasure, for example, *ydone* for *done..thewes* for good partes or good qualities.

**3.** *pl.* Physical good qualities, features, or personal endowments. †**a.** *generally* (e. g. the fair features or lineaments of a woman). *Obs.*

1567 TURBERV. *Ovid's Epist.* xv. N iv b, Doost thou thinke ..that doltish silly man, The thewes of Helens passing forme, may iudge, or throughly scan? *Ibid.* xviii. Q vj, I leaue her thewes vntoucht, Wherein she may compare With heauenly peeres, such feature fals On earthlie creatures rare.

**b.** The bodily powers or forces of a man (L. *vires*), might, strength, vigour; in Shaks., bodily proportions, lineaments, or parts, as indicating physical strength; in modern use after Scott, muscular development, associated with *sinews*, and hence materialized as if = muscles or tendons.

1566 NUCE tr. *Seneca's Octavia* I. iv. B iij b, Ere while thilke wretch recoyleth backe againe, And to my thews for ayde retyres amaine. 1597 SHAKS. 2 *Hen. IV*, III. ii. 276 Care I for the Limbes, the Thewes, the stature, bulke, and bigge assemblance of a man? giue mee the spirit. 1601 — *Jul. C.* I. iii. 81 Romans now Haue Thewes, and Limbes, like to their Ancestors. 1602 — *Ham.* I. iii. 12 Nature cressant does not grow alone, In thewes and Bulke. 1791 COWPER *Odyss.* XVII. 271 He should on bulkier thewes Supported stand [cf. POPE *ibid.* 264 If any labour those big joints could learn]. 1818 SCOTT *Rob Roy* iii, My fellow-traveller, to judge by his thewes and sinews, was a man who might have set danger at defiance. 1843 LYTTON *Last Bar.* I. vi, A man who values his kind mainly by their thews and their sinews. 1850 TENNYSON *In Mem.* ciii. 31, I felt the thews of Anakim, The pulses of a Titan's heart. 1887 MISS BRADDON *Like & Unlike* i, Nature has been kinder to your brother in the matter of thew and sinew.

**c.** *fig.* Applied to cords or ropes.

1851 MELVILLE *The Whale* xvi. I. 111 (*Descr. of a ship*), Bulwarks..garnished..with the long, sharp teeth of the sperm whale..to fasten her old hempen thews and tendons to. Those thews ran not through base blocks of land wood, but deftly travelled through sheaves of sea-ivory.

†**Thew** (þiū), *sb.*[2] *Obs.* Also 3–4 theu, 3–6 thewe. [Known before 1250: etymology obscure; app. from THEW *v.*, in sense 'chastise'; but OE. *þýwan, þéowan* 'to press, squeeze, compress' is also a possible source. The forms are identical with contemporary ones of THEW *sb.*[1]]

Name of an instrument or apparatus of punishment ordained, instead of the pillory, for women; often identified with the CUCKING-STOOL. Also in comb. *thewpenny* (cf. BURGHAL-PENNY).

The med.L. equivalent was *collistrigium*, i. e. an iron collar compressing and confining the neck.

1275 *Rot. Hundred.* (1818) II. 302/2 (Bassetlaw, Notts) Tempore domini Walteri de Gray [a 1256]..levatum fuit le theu primo in villis ejusdem Archiepiscopi..jam xxx annis elapsis. 1287 *Plac. de Quo Warranto* (1818) 11/1 Ibi habet tantummodo tumberellum et thewe. *Ibid.* 11/2 Cum soca et saka ..boruhapeny et theupeny. 1290–1 *Ipswich Domesday* lxxiv. in *Blk. Bk. Admir.* (Rolls) II. 164 Femmes qe sunt communs tenceresses..seyent eles chastiez par la juyse qe [est] apele le theu. 1364 *Lett.-Bk. G. London* lf. 137 Consideratum fuit..quod præfata Alicia subhiat judicium cullistr' pro mulieribus inde ordinat' vocata la Thewe [tr. Riley *Mem.* (1868) 319 That the said Alice should undergo the punishment of the pillory for women ordained, called the thewe.] 1391 *Ibid. H.* lf. 258 b, Quod eadem Isabella ponatur super le Thewe pro mulieribus ordinat'..ibidem moratura per unam horam diei [tr. *ibid.* 526, that she should be put upon the thewe, for women ordained, for one hour of the day]. c 1440 *Promp. Parv.* 490/2 Thewe, or pylory, *collistrigium*. c 1450 *Surtees Misc.* (1888) 60 Y^e sayd Burgese schall..ordan a pelory and a thew, lawfull and strang. 1483 *Cath. Angl.* 382/2 A Thewe, *tripotheum* (A. *Collistrigium, et cetera*). 15.. in *MS. Harl.* 2115 lf. 77 Punire per iudicium de Thewe, hoc est ponere eas super Scabellum vocatum Cokestolle. 1533 *Surtees Misc.* (1888) 34 She shalnot chyde ne flyte,..oppon ridyng of the jebit, or thew, aboute the towne. 1577 HARRISON *England* II. xix. (1877) I. 310 It is not lawfull for anie subiect..to..set vp furels, tumbrell, thew, or pillorie. 1696 PHILLIPS (ed. 5), *Thew*, an old Word for a Cucking Stool.

**Thew**, *sb.*[3] and *v.*[1] ME. form of THEOW *sb.* and *v.*

†**Thew**, *v.*[2] *Obs.* In early ME. þæwen, pa. pple. i-þæwed, i-þeuwed. [app. f. OE. *þéaw*, THEW *sb.*[1]] *trans.* To instruct in morals or manners; to discipline, train, instruct, chastise.

(In quots. a 1225 and c 1305 it may possibly represent or be influenced by OE. *þýwan, þýȝan, þéowan* to press, oppress, repress, threaten, rebuke, which otherwise does not appear to have come down into ME.)

*c* 1200 ORMIN 6217, & ȝunnc birrþ nimenn mikell gom To þæwenn ȝunnkerr chilldre. *a* 1225 *Ancr. R.* 268 (MS. T.) Tu ne schuldest nout tuhten, ne chasten þi meiden uor hire gultes, ne þeawe þine servanz. *c* 1305 *Pilat* 57 in *E. E. P.* (1862) 112 Þo þ'emperour ihurde þat he miȝte þat liþere folc so þewe, He ne huld non so queynte man as he huld þe schrewe. *c* 1422 HOCCLEVE *Learn to Die* 83 And thee the bettre for to thewe, The misterie of my lore y shal the shewe. 1625 GILL *Sacr. Philos.* iv. 53 Although some Fathers were no better Cosmographers then to think this; yet for the most part they were better thewed [?instructed, or mannered].

**Thewed** (þiūd), *ppl. a.* Also 2 **þeaud**, 3–4 **þeu(e)d**, 3 **i-þæwed, i-þeuwed.** [Orig. pa. pple. of THEW *v.*, but app. often treated as f. THEW *sb.*[1] + -ED[2].]

†**1.** Trained, instructed in morals or manners; having qualities or manners (of a specified kind). Chiefly in compounds, as *ill-thewed*, WELL-THEWED, etc., -mannered, -conditioned, -natured.

*c* 1200 *Trin. Coll. Hom.* 41 Þe wise man and þat wel þeaud child habbeð boðe on laȝe. *c* 1205 LAY. 6536 He wes swiðe soðfest and swiðe wel iðæwed [*c* 1275 i-þeuwed]. *c* 1374 CHAUCER *Compl. Mars* 180 My lady is..so wel fortuned and thewed That thorow the worlde her goodnesse is yshewed. *c* 1440 *Pallad. on Husb.* IV. 856 [Foals] So thewed that from high quyete & reste Anoon they may be stered forto prike. 1456 SIR G. HAYE *Law Arms* (S.T.S.) 150 Men..full of vicis, ryotous and evil thewit. 1590 SPENSER *F. Q.* II. vi. 26 Yet would not seeme so rude, and thewed ill As to despise so curteous seeming part. 1596 — *Hymne in Hon. Beautie* 138 A beauteous soule, with faire conditions thewed.

†**b.** *spec.* Having good qualities or manners.

*a* 1300 *Cursor M.* 8425 Þe child es theud [*v. rr.* theued, þewed] and mild o mode, Lok þat he haf maister god. 13.. *Ibid.* 27632 (Fairf.) If þou be þewed al-so curtaise, Þen atte first I wille þe praise. 13.. *E. E. Allit. P.* B. 733 A.a.! blessed be þow,..so boner & þewed. [*a* 1601 ? MARSTON *Pasquil & Kath.* III. 16 Nay, good Thewte hart: good kind Iacke, stay.]

**2.** Having thews or muscles (of a specified kind).

1864 WEBSTER s.v., A well-thewed limb. 1865 SWINBURNE *Chastelard* I. ii. 34 Do you know that lord With sharp-set eyes? and him with huge thewed throat? *Ibid.* IV. i. 116 You have a heart thewed harder than my heart. 1881 C. DE KAY *Vis. Nimrod* iv. 71 A fearful beast..Amazing thewed, with fourfold plate-like horns.

†**Thew·edly,** *adv. Obs. rare*[−1]. [f. prec. + -LY[2].] In a well-mannered way; virtuously.

13.. *Cursor M.* 28663 (Cott.) Charite..biddes vs bath in gode and ill Theudli [*v. r.* trewly] thole vr lauerds wille.

†**Thew·ful,** *a. Obs.* [f. THEW *sb.*[1] + -FUL.] Full of or characterized by good qualities; good, virtuous, moral.

*c* 1205 LAY. 1797 Heo godd thonkeden mid þeu-fulle worden. *a* 1225 *Ancr. R.* 422 Talkeð mid ouer meidenes and mid þeaufule talen schurteð ou to-gederes. *c* 1230 *Hali Meid.* 45 Wiðute oðer god & þawfulle mihtes. 13.. *Cursor M.* 2337 (Cott.) For [Abram] was theuful [*F.* curtays, *G., Tr.* meke] bath and hind. *Ibid.* 2665 A theuful [*G., Tr.* holy] takynyng for to ken At tuin yow wit fra oþer men.

**Thewless** (þiū·lės), *a.* Now only *Sc.* [f. THEW *sb.*[1] + -LESS. Cf. THOWLESS.]

†**1.** Destitute of morals or virtue; vicious, immoral: = THOWLESS 1. *Obs.*

*a* 1327 *Pol. Songs* (Camden) 255 For lust hath leve, the lond is theweles. 1513 DOUGLAS *Æneis* IV. Prol. 163 Sic thewles lustis [sall returne] in bittir pane and wo.

**2.** Without energy, inert, spiritless: = THOWLESS 2.

1895 CROCKETT *Men of Moss-Hags* I, He was a quiet, thewless, pleasantly conforming man. 1896 SNOWDEN *Web of Weaver* vi. 72, I seemed to stand thewless. 1900 C. MURRAY *Hamewith* 85 Like some puir dwinin' thewless wicht Wi' death in view. 1904 *Dundee Advertiser* 13 June 8/1 That the 'thewless' and 'wastrel' class be relegated to labour colonies there to work out their own salvation.

**Thew·ness.** *rare.* [f. THEW *sb.*[1] + -NESS.] †**a.** Virtue. *Obs.* **b.** Vigour, robustness.

*c* 1200 *Trin. Coll. Hom.* 177 Wunderful is ure louerd on þeunesse. 1860 W. J. C. MUIR *Pagan or Christian* 274 Real wealth lies in the sinewy force of moral thewness.

**Thewtill,** obs. variant of THWITTLE.

**Thewy** (þiū·i), *a. rare.* [f. THEW *sb.*[1] 3 b + -Y.] Having well-developed thews; muscular, brawny.

1845 S. JUDD *Margaret* I. x, There were..broad, hard hands in kid gloves; thewy, red elbows..in lace ruffles.

**They** (ðē^i), *pers. pron.* Forms: see below. [Early ME. *þei* (in Ormin *þeȝȝ*), a. ON. *þei-r*, nom. pl. masc. of the simple demonstrative *sá, sú, þat* (= OE. *þá*, ME. *þā, þō*), which in ON. filled the place of the lost plural of the 3rd pers. pron.: cf. Norw., MSw., Sw., MDa., Da. *de*, 'they'. In OE. the 3rd pers. pron. had its own plural *hí, híe, híg, héo*, which continued in extreme southern dialect to about 1400, and in the oblique cases a century longer: see HI[2], HEM *pron.*, HER *poss. pron.*[2] But even in OE. the function of *hí* was largely shared by the pl. demonstrative *þá* 'those', ME. northern *þā*, midl. and south. *þō*: see THO *dem. pron.* 1. The Trin. Coll. Homilies, *c* 1200, have both *hie* and *þei*, but only *hem, her(e* for 'them, their'. Ormin, *c* 1200, has always *þeȝȝ* in the nom., but often *hemm* and *heore, here*, beside *þeȝȝm* and *þeȝȝre*. Between 1200 and 1500 the Norse forms gradually displaced the original pronominal: in Caxton's earlier works we find *thei, hem, hir*, and in the later *thei, theim, their*. See HE, HI[2], THO *dem. pron.*]

**A.** Illustration of Forms.

3 (*Orm.*) **þeȝȝ,** (**teȝȝ**), 3 **ðei,** 3–5 **þei, þai** (**tai**), **þey,** 4 (**þi, þy**), 4–6 **thei, thai** (*unstressed* **þe, the**), 4–7 (*Sc.* –9) **thay,** (5 **þeȝe, dey,** 5–6 **yei,** 6–7 **thee**), 4– **they.**

*c* 1200 ORMIN 125–7, & swa þeȝȝ leddenn heore lif Till þatt teȝȝ wærenn alde, Þatt naffdenn þeȝȝ þurrh þeȝȝre streon Ne sune child ne dohhterr. *c* 1200 *Trin. Coll. Hom.* 189 For þan þe þei nehȝie wunien. *c* 1250 *Gen. & Ex.* 573 Mete quorbi ðei miȝten liuen. *a* 1300 *Cursor M.* 19044 (Edin.) Ilkane als tai saȝ mistir haue. *c* 1300 *Havelok* 414 In þe castel..þer þei sperd wore; Þer he greten ofte sore. *c* 1300 *E. E. Psalter* xxi. 5 Oure fadres in þe hoped þai. *c* 1330 R. BRUNNE *Chron. Wace* (Rolls) 2745 Þey ȝede spiande her & þer. *Ibid.* 2747 Þay wyste alle at ones. *c* 1375 *Cursor M.* 2243 (Fairf.) Quen thay..had fest þe gronde, Þe werke thai raised. 1382 WYCLIF *Matt.* vi. 5 Thei han resseyued her meede. *c* 1386 CHAUCER *Prol.* 40 To telle yow al the condicion Of ech of hem..whiche they were and of what degree. *c* 1400 *Rule St. Benet* 10 Yeme þaim, þat tay folȝ þe wordis of god. *c* 1400 *Brut* 83 Thei of Normandye, Gascoigne & Spaigne. *c* 1400 *Destr. Troy* 8008 When the knewen all the cause, þo kynges bydene, All denyede it anon. *a* 1425 *Cursor M.* 5042 (Trin.) Into egipte soone coom þey. 14.. in *Hist. Coll. Citizen London* (Camden) 213 To set the pavys where the lykyd. *c* 1440 *Generydes* 2633 So fought y^ei still. *c* 1550 CHEKE *Matt.* xxvi. 15 Yei appointed him 30 silverlinges. 1559 BP. SCOT in Strype *Ann. Ref.* (1709) I. App. vii. 12 Thei be joyned as in one. *c* 1560 A. SCOTT *Poems* (S. T. S.) ii. 101 Than to Dalkeith thai maid thame boun. *a* 1584 MONTGOMERIE *Cherrie & Slae* 541 Thay get na credit quhair we come.

**B.** Signification.

**I. 1.** As pronoun of the third person plural, nom. case; the plural of *he, she*, or *it*: The persons or things in question, or last mentioned.

*c* 1200– [see A.]. *c* 1200 *Trin. Coll. Hom.* 39 Here orf þe þei leswueð on halie larspelle. *c* 1330 R. BRUNNE *Chron. Wace* (Rolls) 4990 Þritty oþer wyþ hym þey went. 13.. *Cursor M.* 800 (G.) For scham þay stode bath and quakid. *c* 1489 CAXTON *Sonnes of Aymon* xii. 301 Lete theym shyfte hardely, they two togyder. *c* 1550—*a* 1584 [see A.]. 1707 E. WARD *Hud. Rediv.* II. v. 27 They're Rogues, as sure as Light's in Heaven. 1838 RUSKIN *Ess. Music & Paint.* § 24 Wks. 1903 I. 285 If others do not follow their example, —the more fools they. 1846 GROTE *Greece* I. xxi. II. 175 They two were the framers of all Grecian theogony. 1909 J. W. JENKINSON *Experim. Embryol.* 28 The plane in which they all lie.

**b.** Sometimes used where literary Eng. has the objective THEM. Now only *dial.* or *illiterate.*

[*c* 1380 WYCLIF *Wks.* (1880) 391 No man lawfully may.. minystre hem save þai. Cf. SAVE *prep.* 1 b.] 1681 T. FLATMAN *Heraclitus Ridens* No. 37 (1713) I. 239 An Officer, who is sworn not to permit any Person to speak with them, or they with any Body. 1688 LD. DELAMER *Wks.* (1694) 27 That will only tend to render both you and they uneasie. 1890 A. GISSING *Vill. Hampden* I. iv. 102, I don't understand anything about they. 1890 A. C. BICKLEY *Surrey Hills* I. i. 12 It 'ud be a sight better if 'ee kept they to hissen.

†**c.** *They are* (or *were*) was formerly used (instead of the earlier *it are, it were*, mod. *it is, it was*: see IT B. 2) to introduce a plural sb. about which some statement is made by a relative clause following.

*a* 1716 SOUTH *Serm.* (1823) I. 437 The scripture vouches Solomon for the wisest of men: and they are his Proverbs that prove him so. *Ibid.* IV. 420 They were the sins and apostasies of their souls, for the reformation of which he plagued them. 1748 RICHARDSON *Clarissa* (1811) IV. 375 They are the abandoned people in the house who keep thee up to a resolution against her. *a* 1838 PUSEY *Paroch. Serm.* (1883) III. 223 They are our own self-chosen employments, ..which hinder prayer.

**2.** Often used in reference to a singular noun made universal by *every, any, no*, etc., or applicable to one of either sex (= 'he or she').

See Jespersen *Progress in Lang.* § 24.

1526 *Pilgr. Perf.* (W. de W. 1531) 163 b, Yf..a psalme scape ony persone, or a lesson, or else y^t they omyt one verse or twayne. 1535 FISHER *Ways perf. Relig.* ix. Wks. (1876) 383 He neuer forsaketh any creature vnlesse they before haue forsaken them selues. 1749 FIELDING *Tom Jones* VIII. xi, Every Body fell a laughing, as how could they help it. 1759 CHESTERF. *Lett.* IV. ccclv. 170 If a person is born of a gloomy temper..they cannot help it. 1835 WHEWELL in *Life* (1881) 173 Nobody can deprive us of the Church, if they would. 1858 BAGEHOT *Lit. Stud.* (1879) II. 206 Nobody fancies for a moment that they are reading about anything beyond the pale of ordinary propriety. 1866 RUSKIN *Crown Wild Olives* § 38 (1873) 44 Now, nobody does anything well that they cannot help doing. 1874 [see THEMSELVES 5].

**3.** As indefinite pronoun: People in general; any persons, not including the speaker; people. (Cf. ONE *pron.* 21, and OE. *man*, ME. *men, me*, G. *man*, F. *on.*) Often in phrase *they say* = people say, it is said.

Much used colloquially and dialectally instead of the passive voice.

1415 SIR T. GREY in 43 *Dep. Kpr.'s Rep.* 583 A man..yay calle Skranby toke me a lettre. 1565 COOPER *Thesaurus* s.v. *Basis*, Suche a foote as they set chafing disshes on. 1582 ALLEN *Martyrd. Campion* (1908) 111 Sent to prison upon suspition of Papistry, as they terme the Catholike faith. 1599 SHAKS. *Much Ado* IV. i. 254 To strange sores strangely they straine the cure. *a* 1637 B. JONSON *Good-wife's Ale* (*Athenæum* 1 Oct. 1904), My pock-hold Face, they say, appeard to some Just like a dry and burning hony combe. 1671 LADY MARY BERTIE in 12*th Rep. Hist. MSS. Comm.* App. v. 23 They say the King hath put out a Proclamation to forbid maskerades. 1756–7 tr. *Keysler's Trav.* (1760) II. 64 They still shew here the three cells in which Cosmo..used frequently to retire. 1884 *Manch. Exam.* 17 May 5/1 In India and in Holland they 'cure' tobacco fairly well. 1896 M. FIELD *Attila* II. 49 He shall be scourged With the iron-knotted lash they use for slaves. *Mod.* They do the passage to America now in 5 days.

**II. 4.** As demonstrative pronoun, chiefly as antecedent: = THOSE I. 2, 4. Somewhat *arch.*

1382 WYCLIF *Matt.* v. 10 Blessid be thei that suffren persecucioun for riȝtwisnesse, for the kyngdam of heuenes is herun. *c* 1400 *Brut* lxxiii. 69 Þai wiþin kepte þe toune. 1470–85 MALORY *Arthur* XVII. i. 689 They within were putte to the werse. 1539 BIBLE (Great) 2 *Kings* vi. 16 For they that be with vs, are moo then they that be with them. 1630 *R. Johnson's Kingd. & Commw.* 130 The shops..nothing so full of wares, nor so rich, as they of London. 1691 tr. *Emilianne's Observ. Journ. Naples* 290 They are they that have all the Nobility at command. 1803 WORDSW. *Rob Roy's Grave* 39 The good old rule Sufficeth them, the simple plan, That they should take, who have the power, And they should keep who can. 1847 TENNYSON *Princess* I. 143 And they that know such things..would call them masterpieces.

**b.** Also obj., instead of *them*: cf. 1 b. (Now *dial.*)

*c* 1489 CAXTON *Sonnes of Aymon* iii. 90 Reynawde..made all they that were wyth hym..to be hanged. *a* 1553 UDALL *Royster D.* III. v. (Arb.) 57 And as for all they that woulde do you wrong. 1900 NORWAY *Parson Peter* iv. 108 The devil damn they that keeps me here.

**5.** As demonstrative adj. = THOSE II. 2, 4; but often in weaker sense, = THE (*pl.*). Now *dial.* (In the Sc. quots. perh. meant for *þa, tha*, mod.Sc. THAE.)

**a.** Qualifying a sb. in the nominative case.

1297 R. GLOUC. (Rolls) 2091 So þei [*v.r.* þe] ssrewe robeours abbe hor wille. 13.. *Cursor M.* 1423 (Cott.) Stil ai stod þai [*G.* þa, *T.* þo] wandes thre. *c* 1375 *Sc. Leg. Saints* v. (*Johannes*) 180 Þai men..Þat sa set þar appetyte In Riches. 1567 *Satir. Poems Reform.* iv. 76 How that thay bucheouris blew me in the air. 1877 L. J. JENNINGS *Field Paths* iii. 45 They rooks as you see on bärson's pläce.

**b.** Qualifying a sb. in the objective case.

*c* 1375 *Sc. Leg. Saints* iv. (*Jacobus*) 324 And folow þai bese [oxen], till þai blyne Of þar awne wil. *c* 1400 *Destr. Troy* 1024 Þen he lacches his leue and þai lordes þonkit. 1422 tr. *Secreta Secret., Priv. Priv.* 160 Fore thay thre causis, I leue of that matiere. 1456 SIR G. HAYE *Law Arms* (S.T.S.) 82 For the occasioun of thai weris. *c* 1470 HENRY *Wallace* I. 57 Thai landis thane he clamde as heretage. 1552 *Reg. Privy Council Scot.* I. 136 He suld be Commissar in they pairtis. 1596 DALRYMPLE tr. *Leslie's Hist. Scot.* (S.T.S.) I. 10 The inhabitours of thay pairtes. 1885 G. M. FENN *Patience Wins* (1886) 130 A set o' fullish boys as plays they tricks. 1905 F. YOUNG *Sands Pleas.* I. iii, Some o' they Cockney labourers began grumbling.

**They,** obs. f. THIGH, THOUGH. **Theyf,** obs. f. THIEF. **Theyfage,** error for *theyfish*, THIEVISH.

†**Theyght,** i.e. the eighth: see TH-, TH' I.

1536 *Cal. Anc. Rec. Dublin* (1889) 400 Kyng Henri theyght.

**Theyn(e, theynne,** obs. ff. THANE, THEN.

**Theynt, þ-,** obs. 3rd pers. sing. of THINK *v.*[1]

**Theyrd, Theyves:** see THIRD, THEAVE.

**Thi, þi,** obs. form of THE, THEY, THIGH, THY.

**Thiacetate** to **Thiamine:** see THIO-.

‖ **Thiasus, thiasos** (þəi·ăsŏs, -ǫs). *Gr. Antiq.* [L. *thiasus*, a. Gr. θίασος the Bacchic dance.] A company assembled to celebrate the festival of one of the gods (esp. of Bacchus) with dancing and singing. So **Thiasarch** (þəi·ăsāɹk) [ad. Gr. θιασάρχης], the leader of the thiasus; **Thi·asite** (-əit), **Thi·asote** (-ǭut) [ad. Gr. θιασίτης, θιασώτης], a member of the thiasus.

1820 W. TOOKE tr. *Lucian* I. 569 *note*, The president of it was styled a thiasarch. 1850 LEITCH tr. *C. O. Müller's Anc. Art* § 390 (ed. 2) 507 Representations of Dionysus and his thiasotes..were got up. *Ibid.* § 367. 460 Dionysus bringing back Hephæstus in the thiasus (at which are also Marsyas and Comœdia). 1873 *Contemp. Rev.* XXI. 568 The 'eranists' are termed 'thiasotes' or 'thiasites'.

**Thibet, Thibetan:** see TIBET, etc.

**Thible,** dial. variant of THIVEL.

**Thic,** obs. form of THICK; dial. var. of THILK.

**Thich, Thicht,** Sc. forms of THIGH, THIGHT.

**Thick** (þik), *a.* (*sb.*) Forms: 1 **ðicce,** (3 **þihk**), **ðikke, þeck,** (9 *dial.* **theck**), 3–5 **þ-, thikke,** 3–6 **þ-, thycke,** 3–7 **þ-, thicke,** 4 **thic, thikc,** 4–5 **þ-, thyk(e, thykke, þik,** 4–6 **thik, thikk,** 5 **thek, þ-,thike,** 5–6 **thyck,** (7 **thigge**), 4– **thick.** [OE. *þicce* = OS. *thikki* (Du. *dik*), OHG. *dicchi* (G. *dick*), ON. *þykkr*, beside *þjokki* (Da. *tyk*, Sw. *tjok, tjock*), Goth. **þiqus*:—O Teut. **þik(k)uz*, fem. *þik(k)wī-*; cf. Ir., Gael. *tiugh* (< **tigu-*); ulterior etymology uncertain.]

**I. 1.** Having relatively great extension between the opposite surfaces or sides; of comparatively large measurement through: as a thick wall, board, or plank, a thick stem, post, or stick; a thick stratum or seam of coal, a thick layer of fat or coating of paint, thick cloth, etc. Opposed to *thin*; distinct from *long* and *broad*: cf. sense 2.

*c* 888 K. ÆLFRED *Boeth.* xxxv. § 4 Hi woldon witan hu heah hit wære to ðæm heofone, & hu ðicce se hefon wære & hu fæst. *c* 1000 *Sax. Leechd.* II. 200 Leȝe on þone þiccestan clað oþðe on fel. *c* 1020 *Rule St. Benet* lv. (Logeman) 91 Culam [= cowl] on wintre þicce on sumere þinne. *a* 1225 *Ancr. R.* 50 Þe blake cloð..is þiccure aȝein þe wind. *c* 1375

*Sc. Leg. Saints* vii. (*Jacobus*) 753 He saw a wal wes fow thyke. *c* 1440 *Promp. Parv.* 490/2 Thykke clothe. 1535 COVERDALE 1 *Kings* xii. 10 My litle fynger shall be thicker then my fathers loynes. 1552 HULOET, Thicke leafe, *carnosum folium*. 1687 A. LOVELL tr. *Thevenot's Trav.* I. 6 The Grapes that grow there .. have a thick skin. 1776 WITHERING *Brit. Plants* (1796) III. 206 Stems several, the central one thickest; leafy. 1809 *Med. Jrnl.* XXI. 335 The individuals belonging to the Austrian branch have thick lips. 1845 TALFOURD *Vac. Rambles* I. 174 The dull gleam through the thick glass of my small round peep-hole.

*fig.* *a* 1571 JEWEL *Sacram.* in *Serm.* etc. (1583) X v b, I neede not speake more hereof, the errour is so grosse, so thicke, so sensible and palpable.

†**b.** Extending far down from the surface; deep.

*c* 893 [see sense 2]. 1676 W. ROW *Contn. Blair's Autobiog.* ix. (1848) 138 Riding the water of Belfast, it being thicker than he apprehended. 1693 EVELYN *De la Quint. Compl. Gard.* II. 58 A thick Frost would kill the Roots, as well as the Head.

**c.** Of a person or animal: Thickset, stout, burly. *Obs.* exc. *dial.*

*a* 1250 *Owl & Night.* 580 Ne þu nart þikke ne þu nart long. 1297 R. GLOUC. (Rolls) 8570 Þikke mon he was ynou, round & noȝt wel long. *c* 1385 CHAUCER *L. G. W.* 1198 (*Dido*) Vp on a thikke palfrey..Sit Dido. 1486 *Bk. St. Albans* a vj b, A longe hawke, a short thike hawke. 1570 FOXE *A. & M.* (ed. 2) 2252/1 She was..of a very litle and short stature, somwhat thicke. 1643 BAKER *Chron., Will. II* 49 He was but meane of stature, thick and square bodied. 1819 W. TENNANT *Papistry Storm'd* ii. (1827) 69 Thick Jamie Bud, lang Sandy Kay.

†**d.** *transf.* Having substance all through; solid, not hollow. *Obs. rare*⁻¹.

*a* 1400–50 *Alexander* 4073 Imagis..He made his pepill þaim to perse, to proue þam with-in, Quethire þai ware hologhe or hale, & hale he þam fyndis, Saȝe þaim thike þurȝe-out.

**2.** Used (with words of measurement, or in the comparative or superlative) to express the third dimension of a solid, which has a direction at right angles at once to the length and the breadth: Having a (specified) thickness. (Sometimes equivalent to *deep*, but not now said of a body of water or other fluid.) Commonly following the words stating the measure, as *ten feet thick*, *paper* $\frac{1}{10}$ *of a millimeter thick*.

In this sense not opposed to *thin*; for the thinnest substance has some thickness, as the shortest line has some length, and the narrowest surface some breadth or width.

*c* 893 K. ÆLFRED *Oros.* I. iii. § 1 Ælce ȝeare þæt land middeweard oferfleow mid fotes þicce flode. *Ibid.* IV. xiii. § 2 Se weall wæs xx fota ðicce, & xL elna heah. *c* 1384 CHAUCER *H. Fame* III. 245 Men myght make of hem a bible xxti foote thykke. 1493 *Litt. Red Bk. Bristol* (1900) II. 134 Whiche wall we Fynde xxij yenchis thycke by the grownde. 1602 SHAKS. *Ham.* v. i. 214 Let her paint an inch thicke, to this fauour she must come. 1682 WHELER *Journ. Greece* I. 70 The Front is thick Fourteen foot. 1703 MOXON *Mech. Exerc.* 88 One Inch thick, and three Inches broad. 1812 *New Bot. Gard.* I. 61 Some very rotten dung put in the bottom six inches thick. 1825 J. NICHOLSON *Operat. Mechanic* 69 When a sheet of water is not a quarter of an inch thick before it meets the float [of a mill-wheel].

†**b.** Standing one behind the other; = DEEP *a.* 2 b. *Obs.*

1604 E. GRIMSTONE *Hist. Siege Ostend* 56 They discouered their Gabions nine thicke. 1605 B. JONSON *Volpone* I. i. ad fin., There is a guard of spies ten thick upon her. 1650 RUDD *Geom. Questions* 130 The Pikes are invironed with shot four men thick, round about.

**3.** *fig.* Excessive in some disagreeable quality; too much to manage or to stand; *spec.* too gross, indecent, or indelicate. Often in phrase 'a bit thick'. Cf. 'to lay it on thick'. *slang.*

1884 *Standard* 6 June 6/3, I know it is thick in Brum. [Birmingham] for you, so that we must meet in London. 1902 *Daily Chron.* 9 Sept. 7/3 Guardsmen who have been drinking are a thick lot,..and gentle methods will not always prevail with them. 1907 H. WALES *The Yoke* xii, They hinted more than once that Christopher was 'a bit thick'. 1907 H. WYNDHAM *Flare of Footlights* x, 'By the way, what's the piece like?'..'A bit thick, my dear? I should just think it was! It's an adaptation from the French, you know'. *Ibid.* xxii, 'It's a bit thick', he said indignantly, 'when a man of my position is passed over for a beginner like young Merrick'.

**II.** In general sense of *dense*.

**4.** Closely occupied, filled, or set with objects or individuals; composed of numerous individuals or parts densely arranged; dense, crowded. Of hair: Bushy, luxuriant.

*c* 888 K. ÆLFRED *Boeth.* xxxv. § 5 Ðu..lædst me hidres & ðidres on swa þicne wudu. *a* 900 *O. E. Martyrol.* 148 Þa ȝewat he in þone þiccestan wudu. *c* 1000 *Sax. Leechd.* II. 156 ȝif hær to þicce sie, ȝenim [etc.]. *c* 1205 LAY. 27525 Amidden þan þrunge þer heo þihkest weoren. *a* 1250 *Owl & Night.* 17 In ore vaste þikke hegge. 13.. *K. Alis.* 4067 (Bodl. MS.) Of þe draweyng of bowȝes & stykke, Þe eyre bicom trouble & þicke. *c* 1330 R. BRUNNE *Chron. Wace* 13925 Mikel was þe pres, ful þykke þe þro. *c* 1400 *Destr. Troy* 12496 A thoner and a thicke rayne þrublet in the skewes. *c* 1440 *Promp. Parv.* 490/2 Thykke, as wodys, gresse, or corne, or other lyke, *densus.* 1500–20 DUNBAR *Poems* xxxiii. 89 Thik was the clud of kayis and crawis. 1612 *Proc. Virginia* 61 in *Capt. Smith's Wks.* (Arb.) 424 He had a thicke blacke bush beard. 1620 T. GRANGER *Div. Logike* 166 A thick multitude of people. 1658 DRYDEN *Stanzas to O. Cromwell* xiv, Thick as the galaxy with stars is sown. 1711 ADDISON *Spect.* No. 56 ⁋ 3 A thick Forest made up of Bushes, Brambles, and pointed Thorns. 1855 MACAULAY *Hist. Eng.* xii. III. 199 The women .. were seen amidst the thickest fire serving out water and ammunition to their husbands and brothers. 1872 TENNYSON *Last Tourn.* 213 Then fell thick rain. 1899 *Westm. Gaz.* 24 Nov. 8/2 After..the high grass and thick country is entered.

*fig.* 1387 TREVISA *Higden* (Rolls) I. 355 Þey makeþ.. melody wiþ wel þicke tunes, werbeles, and nootes. 1655 FULLER *Ch. Hist.* III. iv. § 24 His reign was not onely long.. but also thick for remarkable mutations happening therein.

**b.** Const. *with*, †*of*.

*c* 1386 CHAUCER *Knt.'s T.* 217 A wyndow thikke of many a barre Of Iren. 1535 COVERDALE *Ps.* lxiv. [lxv.] 13 The valleys stonde so thicke with corne yt they laugh and synge. 1558 PHAER *Æneid* VII. S iij, This Laurel bushe full thick of browse. 1660 F. BROOKE tr. *Le Blanc's Trav.* 22 The Red Seas coast towards Aden is thick of good towns. 1700 DRYDEN *Sigism. & Guiscardo* 102 A mount of rough ascent, and thick with wood. 1871 FREEMAN *Norm. Conq.* IV. xviii. 154 The whole range of walls and towers was thick with defenders.

**5.** Of the individual things collectively: Existing or occurring in large numbers in a relatively small space, or at short intervals; densely arranged, crowded; hence, numerous, abundant, plentiful. (Usually *predicative*, rarely *attrib.*)

*c* 893 K. ÆLFRED *Oros.* I. i. § 9 Heo ȝedeð mid þæm flode swiþe þicce eorþwæstmas on Ægypta lande. *c* 1386 CHAUCER *Wife's T.* 12 Hooly freres..As thikke as motes in the sonne beem. *c* 1400 MAUNDEV. (Roxb.) xxxiv. 152 Gude tounes er þare so thikk þat [etc.]. *c* 1400 *Destr. Troy* 6626 He segh þe troiens so tore, & turnyt so þik, All pyght in a place on a playn feld. 1560 DAUS tr. *Sleidane's Comm.* 136 Rotman ..running amonges his ennemies where they were thickest was slayne. 1667 MILTON *P. L.* I. 303 His Legions..Thick as autumnal leaves that strow the brooks In Vallombrosa. 1726 LEONI tr. *Palladio's Archit.* (1742) I. 97 Thick columns ..distant from each other .. at the most two diameters. *c* 1813 MRS. SHERWOOD *Stories Ch. Catech.* xxxvi. (1816) 367 We are pretty thick..in this berth. 1836 BROWNING *Paracelsus* v. 369 Lay me..within some narrow grave..But where such graves are thickest. 1849 MACAULAY *Hist. Eng.* v. I. 629 Among the thick graves of unquiet and aspiring statesmen, lie more delicate sufferers.

†**b.** Of actions: Occurring in quick succession; rapid, frequent. Also *transf.* of an agent. *Obs.*

*c* 1450 *St. Cuthbert* (Surtees) 8319 Þe bischops prayers þik Made him to take þe bischopryk. 1552 HULOET, Thycke speaker, *tolutiloquus*. *Ibid.*, Thycke speakynge, *tolutiloquentia*. 1573–80 BARET *Alv.* T 154 A thicke and feeble beating of the pulse. 1611 SHAKS. *Cymb.* I. vi. 67 He furnaces The thicke sighes from him. *a* 1631 DONNE *Lett.* (1651) 149 If you make not so thick goings as you used. 1665 DRYDEN *Ind. Emperor* I. ii, Thick breath, quick Pulse and heaving of my Heart.

**6.** Having great or considerable density, either from natural consistence or from containing much solid matter; dense, viscid; stiff. (Said of liquids, semi-liquids, and plastic or easily liquefiable solids; formerly sometimes of solids generally.)

*c* 888 K. ÆLFRED *Boeth.* xxxiii. § 5 Sio eorþe þon is hefigre & þiccre þon oðra ȝesceafta. *c* 897 — *Gregory's Past. C.* xliv. 329 Ðonne ðæt mon gadriȝe ðæt ðicce fenn on hiene. *c* 1000 *Sax. Leechd.* II. 74 Wæter..swa þicce swa huniges tear. *Ibid.* 314 Hrer on blede oþ þ hit sie þicce swa þynne briw. 1377 LANGL. *P. Pl.* B. xix. 398, I can..drawe..at on hole þikke ale and þinne ale. 1398 TREVISA *Barth. De P. R.* xix. lxiii. [xlviii.] (Bodl. MS.), Þe more þik melke is þe more chese is þerin. *c* 1440 *Promp. Parv.* 490/2 Thykke, as lycure, *spissus*. 1552 HULOET, Thicke as dregges, *turbidus*. 1605 SHAKS. *Macb.* IV. i. 32 Make the Grewell thicke, and slab. 1674 N. FAIRFAX *Bulk & Selv.* 86 So as the surface might not be some airsom body, but all such thick or fast body. 1875 DARWIN *Insectiv. Pl.* v. 78 A mixture about as thick as cream. 1877 HUXLEY *Physiogr.* x. 161 Not..a clear bright spring, but..a thick stream laden with detritus. 1893 HODGES *Elem. Photogr.* (1907) 106 It should solidify into a thick jelly.

*fig.* 1596 SHAKS. *Tam. Shr.* v. ii. 143 A woman mou'd, is like a fountaine troubled, Muddie, ill seeming, thicke, bereft of beautie. 1602 — *Ham.* IV. v. 82 The people muddied, Thicke and vnwholsome in their thoughts.

**b.** Of air: Foul from admixture of fumes, vapours, etc., stuffy, close; also, dense, not rare or thin. Now *rare* or *Obs.* (Cf. 7.)

1626 BACON *Sylva* § 143 When the Aire is more Thin,.. the Sound pierceth better; But when the Aire is more Thicke, (as in the Night) the Sound spendeth and spreadeth abroad lesse. 1756–7 tr. *Keysler's Trav.* (1760) I. 330 Thick fogs..continually rising from the Po, and other waters, by which the air is rendered thick and moist, and consequently unhealthy. 1819 SHELLEY *Peter Bell the Third* III. xxiii, They breathe an air Thick, infected, joy-dispelling.

**7.** Of mist, fog, smoke, etc.: Having the component particles densely aggregated, so as to intercept or hinder vision. Hence of the weather, etc.: Characterized by mist or haze; foggy, misty.

*a* 1000 *Boeth. Metr.* v. 6 Se þicca mist þynra weorðe. *Ibid.* xx. 264 Todrif þone þiccan [mist]. *c* 1000 ÆLFRIC *Exod.* xix. 16 Liȝetta & þunor & þicce ȝenip [*nubes densissima*] oferwreh þone munt. *c* 1290 *St. Michael* 621 in *S. Eng. Leg.* 317 Þanne freost þe þicke Myst, and cleouez an heiȝ on þe treo. *c* 1384 CHAUCER *H. Fame* II. 400 Or ellis was the aire so thikke That y ne myght not discerne. *c* 1400 *Song Roland* 848 Thik, and clowdy, and evyll wedur thene. 1594 T. B. *La Primaud. Fr. Acad.* II. 211 Like to a thick smoke ascending out of a great fire which would dim the eies. 1654 WHITELOCKE *Jrnl. Swed. Emb.* (1772) II. 328 The fogge.. was so thicke, that we could not see two ships length before us. 1745 P. THOMAS *Voy. S. Seas* 18 The Weather proving thick and hazy. 1836 MARRYAT *Midsh. Easy* xxvi, The horizon was so thick that the vessels ahead were no longer to be seen. 1884 Q. VICTORIA *More Leaves* 128 A very dull, dark thick morning..Still, no rain.

**b.** *transf.*, esp. of darkness: Difficult to penetrate; dense, deep, profound.

*a* 900 tr. *Bæda's Hist.* v. xiii. [xii.] (1890) 426 Ða þeostro.. swa micel & swa ðicco wæron, þæt ic noht ȝeseon meahte. *c* 1000 ÆLFRIC *Hom.* II. 194 Ðicce ðeostru and eȝeslice. *c* 1250 *Gen. & Ex.* 3102 Ðhikke ðherknesse cam on ðat lond. 1340 HAMPOLE *Pr. Consc.* 6566 Swa mykel myrknes, Þat it may be graped, swa thik it es. 1605 SHAKS. *Macb.* I. v. 51 Come thick Night, And pall thee in the dunnest smoake of Hell. 1611 BIBLE *Exod.* xx. 21 Moses drew neere vnto the thicke darkenes, where God was. 1781 *Sc. Paraphrases* I. ii, Thick darkness brooded o'er the deep.

**III.** In transferred senses.

**8.** Of the voice, etc.: Not clear; hoarse; having a confused or husky sound; indistinct, inarticulate; also, of low pitch; deep; guttural; throaty.

1398 TREVISA *Barth. De P. R.* XIX. cxxxi. (1495) 942 The voyces ben fatte and thycke whanne moche spyryte comyth out as the voys of a man. 1556, etc. [implied in THICK *adv.* 4]. 1748 J. MASON *Elocut.* 17 To cure a thick confused cluttering Voice. 1844 MRS. CARLYLE *Lett.* (1883) I. 283 His speech is..so thick that I have great difficulty in catching what he says. 1881 ROSSETTI *Ballads & Sonn.* (1882) 325 The young rooks cheep 'mid the thick caw o' the old. 1887 HALL CAINE *Deemster* xxxiii, The thick boom of the sea that came up from the rocks. 1889 MORFILL *Gram. Russian Lang.* 4 The sound of the vowel ы is a thick guttural *e*.

**9. a.** Of or in reference to hearing: Dull of perception; not quick or acute. Also of sight. (See also *thick-eyed* in 12 b, THICK-SIGHTED.) Now *dial.*

1526 TINDALE *Acts* xxviii. 27 The hert off this people is wexed grosse and their eares wexe thycke of hearinge. 1594 T. B. *La Primaud. Fr. Acad.* II. 81 Many become deafe by hearing ouergreat soundes, whereof wee haue experience in Smithes, amongest whome many are thicke of hearing. 1597 SHAKS. 2 *Hen. IV*, III. ii. 336 His Dimensions (to any thicke sight) were invincible. 1601 — *Jul. C.* v. iii. 21 My sight was euer thicke. 1720 *Col. Rec. Pennsylv.* III. 97 But we find their Ears are thick. 1888 ELWORTHY *W. Somerset Gloss.* s. v., 'Thick o' yearin'' (hearing).

**b.** Of mental faculties or actions, or of persons: Slow (or characterized by slowness) of apprehension; dense, crass, thick-headed; stupid, obtuse. Now *dial.*

(In quot. 1597 with play on sense 6.)

1597 SHAKS. 2 *Hen. IV*, II. iv. 262 Hang him Baboone, his Wit is as thicke as Tewksburie Mustard. 1603 HAYWARD *Answ. to Doleman* iv. M j, I omit your thicke error in putting no difference betweene a magistrate and a king. 1670 PENN *Liberty of Consc.* v. 32 What if you think our Reasons thick, and our ground of Separation mistaken? *a* 1800 PEGGE *Suppl. Grose*, *Thick*...Also stupid. North. 1824 BYRON *Juan* XVI. lxxxiii, To hammer a horse laugh from the thick throng.

**IV. 10.** (*fig.* from 5.) Close in confidence and association; intimate, familiar; often in similes (with allusion to other senses), e.g. *as thick as glue*, *as inkle-weavers*, *as peas in a shell*, *as* (*two*) *thieves*, *as three in a bed*, etc. *colloq.*

*c* 1756 BP. LAW in J. Nichols *Lit. Aneca.* 18*th C.* (1812) II. 70 'Yes', said he, 'we begin now, though contrary to my expectation, and without my seeking, to be pretty thick; and I thank God who reconciles me to my adversaries'. 1781 TWINING in *Select. Papers T. Family* (1887) 100 He and I were quite 'thick'. We rode together frequently. 1803 LAMB *Let. to Manning* Feb., Are you and the first consul thick? 1820 SCOTT *Monast.* Introd. Ep., That's right, Captain,..you twa will be as thick as three in a bed an ance ye forgather. 1833 T. HOOK *Parson's Dau.* II. ii, She and my wife are as thick as thieves, as the proverb goes. 1836 LADY GRANVILLE *Lett.* (1894) II. 199 He is thick with all the new Ministers. 1869 *Routledge's Ev. Boy's Ann.* 593 We soon grew as thick as inkle-weavers.

**V. 11.** Phrases. *Thick and threefold*: see THICK *adv.* 6; THICK AND THIN, q. v.

**12.** Combinations. Chiefly parasynthetic adjectives; these can be formed at pleasure; the following are specimens: *thick-ankled* (having thick ankles), *-barred* (having thick bars), *thick-billed*, *-blooded*, *-bodied*, *-bottomed*, *-brained* (in sense 9 b), *-coated*, *-fleeced*, *-foliaged*, *-haired*, *-hided* (hence *-hidedness*), *-knobbed*, *-legged*, *-necked*, *-ribbed*, *-rinded*, *-shelled*, *-soled*, *-stemmed*, *-topped*, *-voiced*, *-walled*. Also *thick-looking* (looking or seeming thick). See also THICK-HEADED, -SKINNED, -SKULLED, etc.

1853 TENNYSON in Ld. Tennyson *Mem.* (1897) II. 505 [In these, he would say] 'Wordsworth seemed to him *thick-ankled'. 1753 YOUNG *Brothers* v. i, Ye *thick-barr'd sunless passages for air. 1855 J. R. LEIFCHILD *Cornwall Mines* 96 Slate abounding in tin is uniformly of a *thick-bedded, deep-blue colour. 1783 LATHAM *Gen. Syn.* III. 148 *Thick-billed Gr[osbeak]. Size of a Bulfinch: length five inches three quarters. 1897 W. R. OGILVIE-GRANT *Game-Birds* II. 151 The Thick-billed Partridges. Genus Odontophorus. 1888 DOUGHTY *Arabia Deserta* I. 471 A little of that *thick-blooded unforbearing, which was in her family, with her own elder son. 1752 J. HILL *Hist. Anim.* 110 The long-legged and *thick-bodied, small, green Lacerta. 1868 *Rep. U. S. Commission. Agric.* (1869) 314 Small, thick-bodied butterflies. 1844 MRS. BROWNING *Duchess May* Concl. v, Though in passion ye would dash..Up against the *thick-bossed shield of God's judgment in the field. 1619 DRAYTON *Sacr. Apollo* vii, The *thick-brained audience lively to awake. 1620 VENNER *Via Recta* vi. 106 It..is for them that be short and *thicke breathed, the .. greatest remedy. 1626 BACON *Sylva* § 318 A Pomegranate or some such *thick-coated fruit. 1828 P. CUNNINGHAM *N. S. Wales* (ed. 3) II. 170 Clumps of *thick-foliaged trees. *c* 1386 CHAUCER *Knt.'s T.* 1660 Somme helden with hym with the blake berd, Somme with the balled, somme with the *thikke hered. *c* 1611 CHAPMAN *Iliad* II. 40 The thick-hair'd Greeks. 1861 KINGSLEY in *Lett.*, etc. (1877) II. 132 But the mass will not have ——'s courage or *thick-hidedness. **1689** *Lond. Gaz.* No. 2415/4 A Young Slender Horse 5 years old,..*thick Jawed. **1861** DICKENS *Gt. Expect.* xxviii, Their keeper..carried a *thick-knobbed bludgeon. **1849** *Sk. Nat. Hist., Mammalia* III. 197 Forster's Sea-Lion..everywhere equally *thick-looking, as Buffon describes it, like a great cylinder. **1591** PERCIVAL *Sp. Dict.*, *Cervigudo*, *thicke necked. **1840** CARLYLE *Heroes* v. (1872) 176 There is the same burly thick-necked strength of body as of soul. **1603** SHAKS. *Meas. for M.* III. i. 123 To recide In thrilling Region of *thicke-ribbed Ice. **1590** GREENE *Orl. Fur.* Wks. (Rtldg.) 95/2 And *thickest-shadow'd groves. **1649** G. DANIEL *Trinarch.* The Author 8 To stoope at the *thick-Shell'd Dorrs of Obiection. **1804** BEWICK *Brit. Birds* (1847) II. 272 The female..lays..six or seven thick-shelled white eggs. **1815** SCOTT *Guy M.* l, His rough coat and *thick-soled boots. **1851** MANTELL *Petrif.* i. § 3. 70 *Thick-toed tridactylous birds. **1552** HULOET, *Thycke tothed, or stronge tothed, *dentatus*. **1859** CORNWALLIS *New World* I. 63 A very stout, thick-set, *thick-voiced Yorkshireman. **1875** BENNETT & DYER *Sachs' Bot.* 484 The very *thick-walled mother-cells do not become isolated.

**b.** Special combinations and collocations: **thick-back**, a species of sole, *Solea variegata* (*Cent. Dict.* 1891); **thick-bill**, a local name of the bullfinch; **thick coal**: see quot.; hence *thick-coalman*; **thick end**, the greater part *of* anything (*dial.*); **thick-eyed** *a.*, having obscure vision, dim-sighted; **thick intestine**, *Entom.*, in some insects, a dilatation of the posterior end of the ileum, forming a large blind sac turned back towards the ventricules; **thick-leaf**, a name of plants of the genus *Crassula*; †**thick letter** *Typogr.*, type cast too thick: see quot.; †**thick listed** *a.* [LIST *sb.*[1]], hard of hearing; **thick register**, the lowest register of the voice; **thick seam**, a seam of 'thick coal'; also *attrib.*; **thick-stamen** (see quot.), a small genus of prostrate euphorbiaceous plants, the Alleghany Mountain Spurge; **thick-stuff**: see quot. *c* 1850; **thick tea**, high tea (*local*); **thick-tongued** *a.*, speaking thickly; **thick wind**, in *Farriery*, laborious breathing, usually due to previous inflammation; hence *thick-winded* adj. Also THICK-HEAD, THICK-KNEE, etc.

**1847–78** HALLIWELL, **Thick-bill*, the bullfinch. *Lanc.* **1883** GRESLEY *Coal Mining Gloss.*, **Thick Coals* or *Thick Seams*, coal seams of greater thickness than (say) 8 or 10 feet...The *Thick coal* of South Staffordshire is about 28 or 30 feet thick. **1894** *Daily News* 7 May 8/4 The new scale will give 1d per ton rise in *thick-coalmen's wages for every 1½d advance in the price of thick coal. **1847–78** HALLIWELL s.v., 'The *thick-end of a mile'. *Linc.* **1865** W. WHITE *E. Eng.* II. 66 When he spoke of the *thick end of a mile*, it reminded me of the 'thick league of a certain rustic whom I once accosted on the sandy wastes of Friesland. **1877** *N. W. Lincs. Gloss.* s. v., I've gotten th' thick end o' th' job finished wi'. **1596** SHAKS. 1 *Hen. IV*, II. iii. 49 *Thicke-ey'd musing, and curst melancholly. **1684** *Lond. Gaz.* No. 1976/4 A gray Horse, Milk white about the Mouth and Tail,..all his Paces, thickeyed. **1884** MILLER *Plant-n.*, **Thick-leaf*, the genus *Crassula*. **1683** MOXON *Mech. Exerc., Printing* 392 A Fount of Letter that Rubs not high enough into the Neck is called **Thick Letter*; and consequently will Drive out Matter. [*c* **1200** *Trin. Coll. Hom.* 129 Deue we ben, oðer *þicke liste, þanne we heren speke godes word and nimeð þer to litel geme.] **1579** TWYNE *Phisicke agst. Fort.* II. xcvii. 289 They that are thicke listed, seeme in a maner to be out of their wittes. **1905** J. HEYWOOD *Music in Churches* 17 Average choir boys cannot recite on a low note without being liable to use the thick register or chest voice instead of the medium register, and the use of their lower mechanism is usually accompanied with..coarseness of tone. **1883** *Thick seam [see *thick coal*]. **1892** *Daily News* 25 Jan. 2/6 The leading thick-seam pits are sending a large tonnage to Hull and Grimsby. **1878** T. MEEHAN *Native Fl. & Ferns U. S.* I. 30 The stamens have remarkably thick filaments, and this suggested its botanical name Pachysandra, which is the Greek for '*thick-stamen'. **1884** MILLER *Plant-n.*, American Thick-stamen, *Pachysandra procumbens*. **1769** FALCONER *Dict. Marine* (1789) H iij, The **thick stuff*, or strong planks of the bottom withinboard. *c* **1850** *Rudim. Navig.* (Weale) 155 *Thickstuff*, a name for sided timber exceeding 4 inches, but not being more than 12 inches, in thickness. **1893** *Daily News* 1 June 5/2 Perhaps something might have been said for the compromise of a *thick tea. **1896** *Ibid.* 18 Dec. 3/6 The 'thick teas' of Lancashire have long been celebrated for their eccentricity. **1887** *Poor Nellie* (1888) 370 Though *thick-tongued still, she spoke more clearly. **1831** [YOUATT] *Horse* x. 193 *Thick-wind consists in short, frequent, and laborious breathing, especially when the animal is in exercise. *a* **1694** *Life M. Robinson* (1856) 35 He was *thickwinded and ungovernable. **1704** *Lond. Gaz.* No. 3981/4 A..Mare,..thick Winded. **1831** [YOUATT] *Horse* x. 193 Heavy draught-horses are..thick-winded.

**B.** *absolute* use of *adj.*, passing into *sb.*: That which (rarely, one who) is thick, in any sense.

**I.** Only in *sing.* **1.** The most densely occupied or crowded part (*of* a wood, an assemblage, etc.).

*a* **1250** *Owl & Night.* 1626 Me may vppe smale sticke Me sette a wude ine þe þikke. *c* **1400** MAUNDEV. (1839) xxi. 226 3if ony of hem had ben hid in the thikke of the wodes. *a* **1548** HALL *Chron., Edw. IV* 221 Some fledde for succor in the thyck of the parke. *a* **1610** KNOLLES (J.), In the thick of the dust and smoke presently entered his men. **1637** RUTHERFORD *Lett.* (1671) 28 If I could yoke in amongst the thick of Angels, and Seraphims. **1714** *Spect.* No. 625 ⁋ 22 In the Anti-chamber, where I thrust my Head into the thick of the Press. **1857** LADY CANNING in Hare *Two Noble Lives* (1893) II. 328 The Residency buildings and its gardens are in the thick of the town. **1890** C. MARTYN *W. Phillips* 192 Mr. Phillips was constantly out in the thick and throng of the world.

**b.** *fig.* The position, time, stage, or state in which activity is most intense; the midst, the height (of an action). Always *in the thick of.*

**1681** FLAVEL *Meth. Grace* x. 214 Something they enjoy.. in the very thick of troubles. **1821** BYRON *Sardan.* III. i. 111 Where a soldier should be. In the thick of the fight. **1849** C. BRONTE *Shirley* i, They are in the thick of a revival. **1870** BURTON *Hist. Scot.* (1873) V. lv. 105 The bishop was in the thick of these splendid projects. **1885** DUNCKLEY in *Manch. Exam.* 15 June 6/2 We are now in the thick of a Cabinet crisis.

**2.** The more turbid or viscid part of a liquid, which usually subsides to the bottom. *rare.*

?*c* **1400** LYDG. *Æsop's Fab.* ii. 39 He was wont my water here to trouble, To meue þe thyk, þat lay low doune. **1707** MORTIMER *Husb.* (1721) I. 78 This he dissolved in Water, and poured off the thick into another Bason, till all was gone but the Sand.

**3.** The thick part of a limb or of the body.

*c* **1400** *Destr. Troy* 9021 He..braid out a big sword,..& derit hym full euyll Throgh the thicke of the thegh. **1470–85** MALORY *Arthur* VII. xxii. 248 He smote hym with a foyne thorou the thycke of the thy3. **1880** TENNYSON *Northern Cobbler* xv, An' blacksmith 'e strips me the thick ov 'is airm, an 'e shaws it to me.

**4.** So **thi·ckest** (the superl. adj. used *absol.* as *sb.*): the thickest part (in any of prec. senses).

*c* **1470** HENRY *Wallace* II. 56 Throuch oute the thikest of the pres he 3eid. **1548** UDALL *Erasm. Par. Luke* iii. 37 Puttyng himself in coumpaignie emong the thickest of the people. **1617** MORYSON *Itin.* II. 24 Valiantly fighting among the thickest of the Rebels. **1868** FREEMAN *Norm. Conq.* II. viii. 259 Henry was..soon again in the thickest of the fight.

**II.** *sb.* with *pl.* **5.** (from 1) = THICKET. Now *rare.*

*c* **825** *Vesp. Psalter* xxviii [xxix]. 9 Stefn dryhtnes 3earwienden heoretas & biwrah ða ðiccan [*Vulg.* revelavit condensa]. *c* **1430** *Pilgr. Lyf Manhode* II. cxxxii. (1869) 126 He may not sette the wacches in the thikke ther thei ben. *a* **1547** SURREY *Æneid* IV. 708 Among the bushy thickes of bryar. **1612** DRAYTON *Poly-olb.* iii. 118 Where mists and rotten fogs Hang in the gloomie thicks, and make vnstedfast bogs. **1812** *Sporting Mag.* XXXIX. 200 A fox..made good his retreat to Sir Thos. Beauchamp's thicks. **1836** L. HUNT in *New Monthly Mag.* XLVII. 20 The lusty bee..dances in the bloomy thicks with darksome antheming.

**6.** *School slang.* A thick-headed or stupid person.

**1857** HUGHES *Tom Brown* I. vii, What a thick I was to come! *Ibid.* II. viii, I'm such a thick, I never should have had time for both. **1891** WRENCH *Winchester Word-bk.* s. v., He is not a thick, but he won't mug.

**Thick** (þik), *adv.* Forms: see the adj. [OE. *þicce* = OS. *thikko*, OHG. *diccho*: see THICK *a.*] In a thick manner, thickly. (After many verbs as *come, fall, lie, stand, sow*, etc., when *thick* expresses the accompanying or resulting condition, it is often rather an adj. than an adv.; cf. L. *pinus prona cadit*; *supinus cadere.*)

**1.** So as to be thick; to a great depth.

*c* **1000** ÆLFRIC *Voc.* in Wr.-Wülcker 151/22 *Pauidensis*, ðicce 3ewefen hræ3el. *a* **1300** *Cursor M.* 3377 (Cott.) Suilk er in þis liue ful thikc, Forgetes þe deid for þe quick. **1670** H. STUBBE *Plus Ultra* 136 We found the passage crusted very thick. **1713** ADDISON *Cato* I. iii, Cato has piercing eyes, and will discern Our frauds, unless they're cover'd thick with art. **1860** TYNDALL *Glac.* I. x. 67 The snow..lay thick upon the glacier.

†**b.** *fig.* Deeply, severely. *Obs. rare.*

**13..** *E. E. Allit. P.* C. 6 Quo for þro may no3t þole, þe þikker he suffers.

**c.** *To lay it on thick*, (*fig.*) to do something with vehemence or excess. Cf. LAY *v.*[1] 55 f.

**1806–7** J. BERESFORD *Miseries Hum. Life* (1826) I. Introd., Lay it on thick, I beg, while your hand is in. **1818** SCOTT *Br. Lamm.* xi, Lay it on thick, and never mind expenses. **1888** MRS. H. WARD *R. Elsmere* xviii, Henslowe lays it on thick —paints with a will.

†**d.** After a sum of money: To the extent of (so much), 'deep'. *Obs.*

**1570** FOXE *A. & M.* (ed. 2) 2142/2 Which then cost the Vniuersitie an hundreth pound thicke. **1592** GREENE *Blacke Bks. Messenger* Wks. (Grosart) XI. 31 My couetous maister is cheated fortie or fiftie pound thick at one clap. **1592** — *Repentance* ibid. XII. 177.

**2.** In a thick, dense, or crowded state; closely, densely, compactly; in crowds or throngs; numerously, abundantly. (See also *thick and threefold* in 6.)

**971** *Blickl. Hom.* 203 Ða flu3on þa le3etu swylce fyrene strælas..toðæm þicce þæt [etc.]. *c* **1000** *Sax. Leechd.* III. 234 Eall swa þicce is þeo heofon mid steorrum afylled on dæ3 swa on niht. *a* **1175** *Cott. Hom.* 237 Of þe folce we sigge\ð þat hit..elce de3ie þicce þringeð. *c* **1290** *S. Eng. Leg.* I. 26/72 Þut folk a-boute heom cam ase þicke ase huy mi3ten go. *c* **1305** *St. Lucy* 12 in *E. E. P.* (1862) 101 Þat folc wende þider þicke. *c* **1400** *Brut* lxxviii. 79 Þai deide wonder þik wiþin the citee for hunger. *c* **1500** *Melusine* 289 Quarelles & arowes, that flewh so thyk. **1523** FITZHERBERT *Husb.* § 12 The beste propertie..is, to sowe all maner of corne thycke ynough. *a* **1687** PETTY *Pol. Arith.* (1690) 73 When England shall be thicker peopled. **1772–84** *Cook's Voy.* (1790) V. 1683 The woods in many places..so thick intersected with boughs and matted with leaves. **1855** MACAULAY *Hist. Eng.* xiv. III. 454 Doubts came thick upon him.

**3.** In close or rapid succession; frequently; quickly; fast. Often *thick and fast.* (See also *thick and threefold* in 6.)

*a* **1000** *Cædmon's Gen.* 684 (Gr.) Hio spræc him þicce to. *c* **1385** CHAUCER *L. G. W.* 655 (*Cleopatras*) Ffor strokys whiche that wente as thikke as hayl. *c* **1450** in Aungier *Syon* (1840) 255 She schal nothing say butte '*Mea culpa*, I wylle amende', whiche sche schal reherse thykke and many tymes. **1540** *Act* 32 *Hen. VIII*, c. 43 The sayd apparaunce & attendaunce commeth so often and thicke together. **1573** TUSSER *Husb.* (1878) 165 Cock croweth at midnight, times few aboue six,.. At three a clock thicker. **1642** FULLER *Holy & Prof. St.* III. xxi. 210 Great talkers discharge too thick to take alwayes true aim. **1706** E. WARD *Wooden World Diss.* (1708) 98 He and his Brother-Jacks..toss Jests and Oaths about as thick and fast as Boys do Squibs. **1729** LAW *Serious C.* xx. (1732) 378 It will perhaps be thought.. that these hours of prayer come too thick. **1869** FREEMAN *Norm. Conq.* III. xi. 66 Thick and fast indeed came the events.

**4.** With confused and indistinct articulation; also, with a husky or hoarse voice.

**1556** W. TOWRSON in Hakluyt *Voy.* (1589) 102 These wordes they speake very thicke. **1597** SHAKS. 2 *Hen. IV*, II. iii. 24 Speaking thicke (which Nature made his blemish) Became the Accents of the Valiant. **1686** *Lond. Gaz.* No. 2143/4 He speaks so thick that he is scarce to be understood. *a* **1791** *Tom Line* xiii. in Child *Ballads* (1884) II. 343/2 Out then spak her father dear, He spak baith thick and milde.

**5.** With density or thick consistence; densely.

*a* **1711**, **1746** [implied in *thick-clouded, -streaming* in 7]. *Mod. colloq.* The syrup runs thick. The porridge stirs thick.

**6.** Phrases. *To lay it on thick*: see 1 c. *Thick and fast*: see 3. **Thick and threefold**, *advb.* (*sb.*, *adj.*) *phr.* **a.** In large numbers; in quick succession; with rapid iteration. *arch.* and *dial.*

*a* **1548** HALL *Chron., Hen. VIII* 186 When mo newe Testamentes were Imprinted thei came thicke and threfold into Englande. **1560** DAUS tr. *Sleidane's Comm.* 134 There dwell deuylles thycke and threfolde. *a* **1592** GREENE *Alphonsus* I. Wks. (Rtldg.) 225/2 How that such clients cluster'd to thy court, By thick and threefold. **1613** DAY *Dyall* ix. (1614) 218 Our Antipodes of Rome that so much boast of the Fathers, and how they are theirs, thicke and threefold. **1710** tr. *Werenfels's Disc. Logom.* 3 Scoffs and Reproaches come thick and threefold. **1872** DE MORGAN *Budget of Paradoxes* 163 A..writer..who threw aspersions on his opponents thick and threefold.

†**b.** With vehemence; fervently, ardently, impetuously. *Obs. rare*[−1].

**1627** W. SCLATER *Exp.* 2 *Thess.* (1629) 295 So thicke and threefold he falls vpon his deuotion.

†**c.** as *adj.* Abundant and frequent. *Obs.*

**1614** DAY *Festivals* xi. (1615) 302 The Commendations given Anna here are thicke and threefold. **1809** MALKIN *Gil Blas* V. i. ⁋ 4 This thick and threefold companionship with [the] birch was not the only rub.

**7.** In combination with participles (with hyphen, or as single words); forming adjs., usually of obvious meaning, unlimited in number; as **a.** in sense 1, as *thick-blown, -plied, -spread, -woven, -wrought*; **b.** in senses 2 and 3, as *thick-beating, -coming, -drawn, -flaming, -growing, -jewelled, -laid, -packed, -rustling, -spreading, -starred*, etc.; **c.** in sense 4, as *thick-speaking*; **d.** in sense 5, as *thick-clouded, -streaming.*

**1690** DRYDEN *Don Sebast.* IV. i, The trampling of *thick-beating feet. **1725** RAMSAY *Gentle Sheph.* I. ii, The *thick-blawn wreaths of snaw. *a* **1711** KEN *Edmund* Poet. Wks. 1721 II. 355 Your now *thick-clouded Mind. **1605** SHAKS. *Macb.* V. iii. 38 Troubled with *thicke-comming Fancies. **1715–20** POPE *Iliad* III. 6 With piercing frosts, or *thick-descending rain. **1777** J. MOUNTAIN *Poet. Reveries* (ed. 2) 6 His children watch his *thick-drawn breath. **1757** DYER *Fleece* IV. Poems (1761) 184 While flames, *thick-flashing in the gloom. **1865** TROLLOPE *Belton Est.* xxxi, Wide fields and *thick-growing woods. **1593** SHAKS. 3 *Hen. VI*, III. i. 1 Vnder this *thicke growne brake. **1833** TENNYSON *Lady of Shalott* III. iii, All in the blue unclouded weather *Thick-jewell'd shone the saddle-leather. **1698** NORRIS *Pract. Disc.* (1707) IV. 191 So *thick-laid are the Temptations of the World. **1599** SHAKS. *Much Ado* I. ii. 10 Walking in a *thick pleached alley. **1840** CARLYLE *Heroes* vi. (1872) 204 The *thick-plied perversions which distort our image of Cromwell. **1861** W. F. COLLIER *Hist. Eng. Lit.* 114 The *thick-speaking, shambling,..pedant. **1740** SOMERVILLE *Hobbinol* I. 9 On the large Bough Of a *thick-spreading Elm. **1676** DRYDEN *Aurengzebe* I. i, Of *thick-sprung Lances in a waving Field. *c* **1391** CHAUCER *Astrol.* II. § 23 In some wynters nyht, whan the firmament is clere & *thikke-sterred. **1860** EMERSON *Cond. Life, Worship* Wks. (Bohn) II. 408 Thick-starred Orion was my only companion. **1746** FRANCIS tr. *Hor., Sat.* I. viii. 47 They..fill'd a magic Trench profound With a black Lamb's *thick-streaming Gore. **1738** WESLEY *Psalms* CXVIII. iv, Hosts of Enemies Vexatious as *thick-swarming Bees. **1595** *Locrine* II. v. 39 Amongst the dangers of the *thick througd pikes. *c* **1410** *Master of Game* (MS. Digby 182) ii, Whan þe heed is of gret beemes and is wele afeted and *thike tynded. **1671** MILTON *P. R.* IV. 246 Where the Attic Bird Trills her *thick-warbl'd notes. **1865** *Q. Rev.* Apr. 329 The *thick-wove paper, and the brilliant type. **1667** MILTON *P. L.* IX. 437 Now hid, now seen Among *thick-wov'n Arborets and Flours. **1743** FRANCIS tr. *Hor., Odes* I. vii. 28 Whether..Tibur holds thee in its *thick-wrought Shade.

**Thick** (þik), *v.* Now *rare* or *Obs.* (In the current senses THICKEN is the usual verb.) [OE. *þiccian*, f. *þicce*, THICK *a.* (cf. OHG. *dicchên*, MHG. *dicken*).]

**1.** *trans.* To make dense in consistence. *arch.*

*c* **1000** ÆLFRIC *Gram.* xxxvii. (Z.) 220 *Denso*..and *denseo*.., ic ðicci3e. **1398** TREVISA *Barth. De P. R.* IV. ii. (Tollem. MS.), It [melancholy] þikkeþ þe blood, þat it fleteþ nou3t from digestion by clernesse and þinnesse. *c* **1440** *Anc. Cookery* in *Househ. Ord.* (1790) 430 Let hit boyle and thyck hit with floure of ryse. **1526** *Grete Herball* cxliv. (1529) I ij b, A moysture that by the heet of the sonne is thycked, ..and torned to a gommy substaunce. **1611** SHAKS. *Wint. T.* I. ii. 171 Thoughts, that would thick my blood. **1642** H. MORE *Song Soul* I. I. xxvii, You thick that veil, and so your selves array With visibility. **1798** COLERIDGE *Anc. Mar.*

III. xi, The Night-Mare Life-in-Death was she, Who thicks man's blood with cold.

† **2.** To make (cloth, etc.) close in texture by fulling; = THICKEN 5. *Obs.*

**1482** *Rolls of Parlt.* VI. 223/2 Made, wrought, fulled and thikked, by the myghte and strengh of men. **1511–12** *Act* 3 *Hen. VIII*, c. 6 § 1 The Walker and Fuller shall truely walke fulle thikke and werke every webbe of wollen yerne. **1566** *Act* 8 *Eliz.* c. 11 § 2 That no person..shall thicke or full in any Myll..any Cappe vntyll suche tyme as the same Cappe be first..half thicked..in the Footestocke. **1719** D'URFEY *Pills* VI. 92 The Water..over-thicks my Cloth.

**3.** *intr.* To become thick, in various senses; = THICKEN *intr.* Now *dial.* or *arch.*

*a* **1000** *Gloss.* in Wr.-Wülcker 219/7 *Densescit, spissat*, þiccaþ. *c* **1290** *St. Michael* 714 in *S. Eng. Leg.* 320 Hit þickez to Nye dawes..þanne it tornez formest to flesch. **13..** *K. Alis.* 3841 (Bodl. MS.) Þe erþe quaked of her rydyng: Þe weder þicked of her crieyng. *c* **1450** *Two Cookery-bks.* 91 Lete hit not boyle til hit thikke. **1579** SPENSER *Sheph. Cal.* Mar. 115 But see the Welkin thicks apace. **1876** *Mid-Yorks. Gloss.* s. v., T'day's thicking (getting cloudy). **1879** J. D. LONG *Æneid* II. 374 The sounds grow clear, The noise of battle thicks.

† **b.** ? To become frequent or prevalent. *Obs.*

**13..** *Cursor M.* 17476 (Cott.) Ful wa þam was þaa wreches wick, Quen þis tiþand bigan to thik.

† **4.** *intr.* To move thickly or in crowds; to flock, crowd. *Obs. rare.*

*c* **1000** in Cockayne *Shrine* (1864) 38 Þa þiccodan þider semninga þa ismaheli. **1513** DOUGLAS *Æneis* VI. v. 30 Als gret number thiddir thikkit in feir As..Levis of treis. *Ibid.* x. vii. 31 Quhar ȝondir sop of men thikkis in a rout.

† **5.** *refl.* [f. THICK *sb.* 5.] To get into the thick of any place; to hide. *Obs. rare*[−1].

**1574** HELLOWES *Gueuara's Fam. Ep.* (1584) 144 Hauing past three daies and three nightes, forsaking al high wayes, thicked myself in the great desart, and being vtterly tyred with great and extreame heat.

Hence **Thicked** (þikt) *ppl. a.*, thickened; † fulled; **Thi·cking** *vbl. sb.*, thickening; † fulling.

*c* **1440** *Anc. Cookery* in *Househ. Ord.* (1790) 435 Stere hit tyl hit be thyk, and in the thikkynge do the rosted felettes therto. **1482** *Rolls of Parlt.* VI. 223/2 To forfaite and lose xl *s.*, as ofte as eny such persone shall putt to fullyng or thikkyng, or to sale, eny suche Huers, Bonettes or Cappes. **1552–3** *Act* 7 *Edw. VI*, c. 8 (*title*) An Acte for the true fulling and thicking of Cappes. **1604** *Compt Bk. D. Wedderburne* (S.H.S.) 45, xij ellis & a quarter bred thicket blew worzet clayth. **1759** *Compl. Letter-writer* (ed. 6) 53 The thicking or fulling-mill.

**Thick**, Sc. var. THEEK, to thatch; dial. var. THILK.

**Thick and thin, thi·ck-and-thi·n**, *phr.* Also **thick or thin, (neither) thick nor thin.**

Cf., for the mere collocation, *a* **1000** *O.E. Riddles* xli. 36 Eal ic under heofones hwearfte recce..þicce and þynne.

**A.** as *sb.*

**1.** Phr. *Through thick and thin* († *in thick and thin*): through everything that is in the way; without regard to or in spite of obstacles or difficulties; under any circumstances. *lit.* and *fig.* (app. orig. with reference to 'thicket and thin wood'.)

*c* **1386** CHAUCER *Reeve's T.* 146 The hors..gynneth gon.. Forth with wehee, thurgh thikke and thurgh thenne [*v. r.* thurgh thikke and thenne]. **1426** LYDG. *De Guil. Pilgr.* 22682 A smale posterne I may pace, And, thorough thykke and thynne trace. *c* **1450** J. METHAM *Wks.* 41/1101 Forth yn thyk and thyn He gan lepe. **1543** GRAFTON *Contn. Harding* 544 Kyng Richard..purposed to goo thorow thicke and thinne in this mater. **1590** SPENSER *F. Q.* III. i. 17 His tyreling Jade he fiersly forth did push Through thicke and thin, both over banck and bush. **1627** DRAYTON *Mooncalf* 1317 And tag and rag through thick and thin came running. **1681** DRYDEN *Span. Friar* v. ii, A thorough-paced liar, that will swear through thick and thin. **1782** COWPER *Gilpin* 40 Six precious souls, and all agog To dash through thick and thin. **1894** HALL CAINE *Manxman* v. vi, There's five hundred men here to back you up through thick and thin.

**2.** *sb.* Adherence to some course, principle, or party, under all circumstances. **b.** *attrib.* or *adj.* (usually hyphened): That adheres or is ready to follow in all circumstances; constant, steadfast, unwavering. **c.** Hence **thick-and-thinnite** (*nonce-wd.*), one who supports a 'thick-and-thin' or resolute policy regardless of consequences. (*Political* and *journalistic slang.*)

**1884** *Pall Mall G.* 14 Feb. 1/1 He would have been denounced as a traitor by the hidebound partisans of thick and thin. **1886** J. PAYN *Heir of Ages* xxxv, It would have been difficult to find a more thick-and-thin admirer of its excellences. **1890** *Spectator* 18 Oct. 515/2 In his thick-and-thin advocacy of the democratic policy. **1898** DR. FARQUHARSON *Sp. Ho. Com.* 9 May, [On these matters he was a] thick and thin-ite. **1900** A. J. BALFOUR *Sp. Manchester* 9 Jan., I felt as if I was before this speech tarred with the brush of being a 'thick-and-thinnite'. **1900** *Westm. Gaz.* 11 Jan. 2/2 There does not exist a thick-and-thinner party man than Mr. Balfour.

† **B.** as *adv. Either thick or thin*: in any case, under any circumstances; *neither thick nor thin*, in no circumstances. *Obs. rare.*

**1486** *Bk. St. Albans* e vij b, Thyk nor thynne [see GARGILON]. **1546** *St. Papers Hen. VIII*, XI. 254 The Dolphyn spared not, thyck nor thynne.

**C.** as *adj.* **1.** *Naut.* Of a tackle-block: Having one sheave larger than the other; cf. FIDDLE-*block.*

**1815** BURNEY *Falconer's Dict. Marine* s. v. *Block, Thick and thin*, or, *Quarter Block*, is a double block with one sheave thicker than the other, and is used to lead down the topsail-sheets and clew-lines. **1841** DANA *Seaman's Man.* Gloss., *Thick-and-thin Block*, a block having one sheave larger than the other. Sometimes used for quarter-blocks.

**2.** See A. 2 b.

**Thicke**, obs. form of THEEK, THICK, THILK.

**Thicken** (þi·k'n), *v.* [f. THICK *a.* + -EN 5. Cf. ON. *þykkn-a*, f. *þykk* adj. THICK.] To make or become thick or thicker.

**1.** *trans.* To make dense in consistence; to coagulate, inspissate. Also *fig.*

*c* **1425** tr. *Arderne's Treat. Fistula* 30 Vnto þat þe watrynes of þe Iuyse be somewhat þikned. **1552** HULOET, Thycken or congeale, *congelo.* **1616** SURFL. & MARKH. *Country Farme* 64 Heat doth safegard and thicken the milk. **1698** FRYER *Acc. E. India & P.* 353 By indulging his Body he thickens his Understanding. **1771** MRS. HAYWOOD *New Present* 44 It is a very good thing to thicken gravy with. **1801** C. DIBDIN *Tour* I. 356 The illuminati, who generally thicken in the clear, so as to confound the business, that a man of plain sense can make nothing out of them. **1866** ROGERS *Agric. & Prices* I. xiii. 221 Oatmeal was used scantily, but generally for thickening soup.

**b.** *intr.* To increase in density or consistence; also, to become turbid or cloudy. Also *fig.*

**1598** *Epulario* I j b, Set it all night to thicken..in a cold place. **1660** F. BROOKE tr. *Le Blanc's Trav.* 19 A licquor, or gumme, which thickens of it selfe. **1718** PRIOR *Solomon* I. 355 Water stopt gives birth To grass and plants, and thickens into earth. **1888** BESANT 50 *Years Ago* vii. 121 There comes a time when the brow clouds, and the speech thickens, and the tongue refuses to act.

**2.** *intr.* To become dark, obscure, or opaque; of the weather: to become misty.

**1605** SHAKS. *Macb.* III. ii. 50 Light thickens,.. Good things of Day begin to droope, and drowse. **1606** — *Ant. & Cl.* II. iii. 27 Thy Luster thickens, When he shines by. **1670** DRYDEN *1st Pt. Conq. Granada* II. i, I'll face this Storm that thickens in the Wind. **1784** *Cook's Voy. Pacific* VI. iii. III. 239 The weather still thickening, and preventing a nearer approach to the land. **1860** TYNDALL *Glac.* I. xxv. 189 As we approached the summit the air thickened more and more.

**3.** *trans.* To make close or dense in disposition of parts or in texture; to fill up the interstices or intervals of. ? *Obs.*

**1575** LANEHAM *Let.* (1871) 8 Seauen posts on a side, that stood a twelue foot a sunder, thikned betweene with well proportioned Pillars turnd. **1620** T. GRANGER *Div. Logike* 30 The clouds are not thickned in the skie: therfore it will not be raine. **1755** JOHNSON *Dict.*, *Thicken*, v.,..to make frequent, to make close or numerous. **1812** BRACKENRIDGE *Views Louisiana* (1814) 116 It is perhaps good policy in our government..to thicken the frontier, and to suffer the intermediate space to fill up gradually.

**4.** *intr.* To become crowded, numerous, or frequent; to gather thickly. Also † To move in great numbers, to flock, troop (*obs. poet.*).

**1726** POPE *Odyss.* XVIII. 49 Well pleased they spring Swift from their seats, and thickening form a ring. **1771** *Junius Lett.* liv. (1820) 286 Honours shall..thicken over him. **1789** MME. D'ARBLAY *Diary* 19 Nov., The crowd every instant thickening. **1838** DICKENS *Nich. Nick.* liv, Misfortune and discovery are thickening about your head.

**5. a.** *trans.* To increase the substance between opposite surfaces of; to make thicker in measurement.

*c* **1611** CHAPMAN *Iliad* XIII. 123 Lance was lin'd with lance; Shields thickned with opposed shields. **1777** SHERIDAN *Trip to Scarborough* I. ii, The calves of these stockings are thicken'd a little too much. **1858** GLENNY *Gard. Every-day Bk.* 244/1 The earth in the alleys [is to be] thrown up to thicken the soil above them a little. **1884** BOWER & SCOTT *De Bary's Phaner.* 229 In most cases the walls are thickened by spiral fibres.

**b.** *intr.* To become thicker in measurement; to increase in girth or bulk.

**1763** MILLS *Syst. Pract. Husb.* IV. 35 That their roots.. may have full room to thicken and run downward. **1805** PIKE *Sources Mississ.* (1810) 42 Ice in the river thickening. **1872** R. B. SMYTH *Mining Statist.* 21 The seams..thicken in one place and thin out in another.

**c.** *trans. fig.* To make more substantial; to strengthen, confirm.

**1604** SHAKS. *Oth.* III. iii. 430 This may helpe to thicken other proofes, That do demonstrate thinly. **1893** C. W. WENDTE in *Reasonable Relig.* 73 The philosophers..are thickening up their systems..with scientific facts.

**6.** *intr. fig.* To become more complex or intricate (esp. said of a plot); to increase in intensity.

**1671** VILLIERS (Dk. Buckhm.) *Rehearsal* III. ii. (Arb.) 81 Ay, now the Plot thickens very much upon us. **1697** DRYDEN *Æneid* IX. 908 The combat thickens, like the storm that flies. **1810** SCOTT *Lady of L.* I. ii, The cry, That thickened as the chase drew nigh. **1859** KINGSLEY *Misc.* I. i. 16 As the quarrel thickened and neared.

Hence **Thickened** (þi·k'nd) *ppl. a.*, that is made thick or thicker, in various senses.

*c* **1611** CHAPMAN *Iliad* XIX. 368 A bright thickned bush of golden haire. **1667** MILTON *P. L.* XI. 742 The thick'nd Skie Like a dark Ceeling stood. **1697** DRYDEN *Virg. Georg.* IV. 386 Mix it with thicken'd Juice of sodden Wines. **1861** BENTLEY *Man. Bot.* 401 Plants with succulent or thickened leaves. **1900** *Daily News* 17 Apr. 7/4 With solids and pneumatics [tyres], both of the wired-on and thickened-edge varieties.

**Thickener** (þi·k'nəɹ). [f. prec. vb. + -ER[1].] That which (or one who) thickens; in *Dyeing*, a substance used to increase the consistence of the colours or mordants.

**1652** FRENCH *Yorksh. Spa* iv. 46 The body is to be annointed with oyle, with spissaments or thickeners. **1732** ARBUTHNOT *Rules of Diet* in *Aliments*, etc. 261 Thickeners of the Humours. **1883** R. HALDANE *Workshop Receipts* Ser. II. 206/2 The next step..is the removal of the thickeners.

**Thickening** (þi·k'niŋ), *vbl. sb.* [f. as prec. + -ING[1].] The action of the verb THICKEN; the process of making or becoming thick or thicker; *concr.* the result of this action or process; a thickened substance or part.

**1580** HOLLYBAND *Treas. Fr. Tong*, *Espessissement*, a thickening. **1603** HOLLAND *Plutarch's Mor.* 998 Mists, fogs, and clouds are no congealations, but onely gatherings, and thickenings of a moist and vapourous aire. **1822** J. PARKINSON *Outl. Oryctol.* 159 A subglobose univalve; the opening longer than wide;..no thickening of the left lip. **1893** TUCKEY tr. *Hatschek's Amphioxus* 154 He was misled by a thickening of the alimentary canal in front of the gland. **1899** *Allbutt's Syst. Med.* VIII. 511 Eczema of the palms very frequently leads..to great thickening of the epidermis. *c* **1900** *Beeton's Everyday Cookery Bk.* 209/2 By the addition of various store sauces, thickening and flavouring, good stock may be converted into good gravies.

**b.** A substance used to thicken something; *spec.* in *Dyeing.* = THICKENER.

**1839** URE *Dict. Arts*, etc. 222 Several circumstances may require the consistence of the thickening to be varied. **1874** W. CROOKES *Dyeing & Calico-print.* ii. 17 Only two mineral thickenings are at present employed, namely, kaolin and pipe-clay.

**c.** *Foundry* = THICKNESS 8.

**1872** ELLACOMBE *Bells of Ch.* i. 200 When thoroughly dried, the outer mould is removed, and the thickening (the *fac-simile* of the bell) destroyed.

**d.** *Bot. Thickening layer, mass, ring* (Ger. *verdickungsring*): see quots.

**1875** BENNETT & DYER tr. *Sachs's Bot.* 27 A wider cavity, which is bounded on the sides by the narrow part of the thickening-masses, on the outside by the primary cell-wall. *Ibid.* 108 Generating ring of tissue, corresponding to Sanio's thickening ring. **1900** B. D. JACKSON *Gloss. Bot. Terms* 270/2 *Thickening Layer*, an apparent layer of cellulose on the inner face of a cell-wall; *Thickening Ring*, Sanio's term for a ring of meristem in which the first fibro-vascular bundles originate.

**Thickening** (þi·k'niŋ), *ppl. a.* [f. as prec. + -ING[2].] That thickens: **a.** That grows thicker; **b.** That makes something thick or thicker.

**1721** J. DART *Westminster Abbey* 57 When Learning was with thick'ning Mists o'erspread. **1784** COWPER *Task* IV. 330 Earth receives Gladly the thickening mantle [snow]. **1860** TYNDALL *Glac.* I. xii. 88 At the close of the day thickening clouds warned me off. **1880** BROWNING *Dram. Idyls, Pan & Luna* 10 Fast-thickening poppy-juice. **1895** *Model Steam Engine* 69 The thickening piece is soldered to the boiler.

† **Thi·cker.** *Obs.* [f. THICK *v.* + -ER[1].] One who 'thicks' or fulls cloth; a fuller. Also as second element in comb., as *cap-thicker, say-thicker.*

**1520** WHITINTON *Vulg.* (1527) 16 b, In the strete vpon the backe halfe, be drapers..cappers, thyckers of cappes. **1570** FOXE *A. & M.* (ed. 2) 944/2 One Walker a thicker of S. Clementes. **1641** Saye-Thickers [see SAY *sb.*[1] 3].

**Thicket** (þi·kėt). Also 1 **þiccet**, 6 **thykette**, 7 **thickett.** [OE. *þiccet*, neut., f. *þicce* thick + *-et*, denominative suffix (as in *emn-et* plain, *rýmet* space).] A dense growth of shrubs, underwood, and small trees; a place where low trees or bushes grow thickly together; a brake. Cf. THICK *sb.* 5.

*a* **1000** *Ps.* (Spelm.) xxviii[i]. 9 Stefn drihtnes awrihþ þiccettu [*Lamb.* þiccetu]. **1530** TINDALE *Gen.* xxii. 13 A ram caught by the hornes in a thykette. **1530** PALSGR. 280/1 Thicket or a forest, *boscaige.* **1555** EDEN *Decades* 57 They founde a greate thicket of reedes. **1593** SHAKS. 3 *Hen. VI*, IV. v. 3 Leaue off to wonder why I drew you hither, Into this cheefest Thicket of the Parke. **1667** MILTON *P. L.* IV. 681 How often from the steep Of echoing Hill or Thicket have we heard Celestial voices to the midnight air.. Singing. **1711** ADDISON *Spect.* No. 56 ⁋ 3 This huge Thicket of Thorns and Brakes was designed as a Kind of Fence. **1855** KINGSLEY *Heroes* III. (1868) 32 They sang like nightingales among the thickets.

**b.** *transf.* and *fig.*

**1582** STANYHURST *Æneis* II. (Arb.) 54, I run forward too rush throgh thicket of armoure. **1612** WEBSTER *White Devil* II. i. 79 I'le meete thee Even in a thicket of thy ablest men. **1657** S. PURCHAS *Pol. Flying-Ins.* xvii. 111 They are quickly be-wildred in a thicket of errors. **1698** FRYER *Acc. E. India & P.* 45 A Thicket of twenty Sail of our Enemies were discovered. **1821** SCOTT *Kenilw.* xiii, His wild and overgrown thicket of beard was now restrained to two small mustachios. **1866** J. MARTINEAU *Ess.* I. 52 We entangle ourselves in a thicket of ever-growing problems.

**c.** *attrib.* and *Comb.*, as *thicket-maze, -haunting.*

**1813** SCOTT *Rokeby* IV. ii, Where the thicket-groupes recede. **1837** STANLEY *Gipsies* 136 Or track old Jordan through his thicket maze. **1850** ALLINGHAM *Poems, Music-master* II. xv, The thicket-tangling, tenderest briar-rose. **1892** *Guardian* 11 May 706/2 Along the courtly mere of thicket isles.

Hence **Thi·cketed** *a.*, occupied or covered by thickets; **Thi·cketful**, as many or as much as fills a thicket; **Thi·ckety** *a.*, abounding in thickets.

*c* **1624** CHAPMAN *Homer, Hymn to Bacchus* 140 In ivies and in baies All over *thicketed. **1835** W. IRVING *Tour Prairies* xxxiii, The same kind of rough, hilly, thicketed country. **1887** J. SERVICE *Dr. Duguid* 270 Sweet sounds.. From out the *thicketful of singing throats. **1846** MRS. MARSH *Emilia Wyndham* (1848) 349 Very fine timber and *thickety woods. **1865** W. G. PALGRAVE *Arabia* I. 238 Broken and thickety ground in front.

† **Thi·ckfold**, *adv.* (*adj.*) *Obs.* Chiefly *north.* [f. THICK *a.*: see -FOLD.] Thickly together; in great numbers, in crowds.

*a* **1300** *Cursor M.* 11258 Þas oþer [angels] lighted dun thic-fald. *c* **1400** *Rowland & O.* 1108 Full thikke folde gan Sarazenes dy. *c* **1440** *Bone Flor.* 871 Many myrakyls for hur he wroght, Many a oon and thyck folde **1513** DOUGLAS *Æneis* XIII. ii. 68 O ȝe my feris..Throu mony hard perrellis and thikfald..Hiddir now careit to this cost with me. **1535** STEWART *Cron. Scot.* (Rolls) III. 98 Thikfald to him all in the tyme tha drew.

**Thi·ck-head.** One who or that which has a thick head.

**1.** One who is dull of intellect; a blockhead.

**1871** CARLYLE in *Mrs. Carlyle's Lett.* (1883) I. 103 *note*, Ambitious thickhead. **1882** H. SEEBOHM *Siberia in Asia* 32 One of the greatest thickheads that I have ever met with.

**b.** *attrib.* or *adj.* = THICK-HEADED b.

**1873** BROWNING *Red Cott. Nt.-cap* II. 235 Who ever has his speech in readiness For thick-head juvenility at fault. **1894** F. S. ELLIS *Reynard Fox* 187 I'll shortly sow strife among Those thick-head folks.

**2.** A name given in different localities to various birds: e.g. **a.** Any bird of the subfamily *Pachycephalinæ*, the Thick-headed Shrikes of the Australian region. **b.** A scansorial barbet of the subfamily *Capitoninæ* (*Cent. Dict.* 1891).

**1837** SWAINSON *Nat. Hist. Birds* II. 250 Vireoninæ.. Pachycephala..Thickhead. **1890** *Victorian Stat., Game Act* Sched. iii. (Morris), Thick-heads. [Close season] From the first day of August to the twentieth day of December. **1894** NEWTON *Dict. Birds* 621 Native-Thrush, *Pachycephala olivacea* (Thickhead). **1896** *Ibid.* 958 The name Thickhead is..given in other parts of the world to very different birds, and in South Africa especially to *Œdicnemus capensis*.., the Stone-Curlew of that country.

**Thi·ck-hea·ded,** *a.* [Parasynthetic f. prec. + -ED[2].] Having a thick head. **a.** *lit.*; esp. in names of animals, as **Thick-headed Mullet,** *Moxostoma congesta*; **Thick-headed Shrike** = THICK-HEAD 2 a.

**1707** MORTIMER *Husb.* (1721) I. 314 Make a Trail..so as to bring it near some thick-headed Tree. **1752** J. HILL *Hist. Anim.* 569 The thick-headed Hippopotamus, with no tail. The Copy-Bara.

**b.** *fig.* Dull of intellect; slow-witted, obtuse.

**1801** MAR. EDGEWORTH *Gd. French Gov.* (1895) 7 He was so 'thick-headed at his book', that Mrs. Grace..affirmed that he never would learn to read. **1860** GEN. P. THOMPSON *Audi Alt.* III. cxxv. 80 A thick-headed idea of law is, that it is a machine for getting men hanged. **1891** LOUNSBURY *Stud. Chaucer* II. vi. 481 Something of the feeling..which represents the members of the nobility as being good-hearted but also thick-headed.

Hence **Thickhea·dedness,** obtuseness, crassness.

**1889** *Voice* (N. Y.) 14 Feb., He..failed to estimate the thickheadedness of the party addressed. **1892** *Spectator* 23 Jan. 126/2 Bumptious, bullying thickheadedness.

**Thicking,** *vbl. sb.*: see THICK *v.*

**Thickish** (þi·kiʃ), *a.* [f. THICK *a.* + -ISH[1].] Somewhat thick.

**1545** RAYNOLD *Byrth Mankynde* 141 Also her vryne waxeth spysse and thyckysshe. **1713** *Lond. Gaz.* No. 5178/4 Thickish of Hearing. **1737** BRACKEN *Farriery Impr.* (1757) II. 23 Horses that are a little thickish about the Shoulders. **1894** *Cornh. Mag.* Mar. 269 Two thickish quarto volumes.

**Thick-knee** (þi·kˌnī). Also **thicknee.** A name for any bird of the genus *Œdicnemus*, esp. the Stone Curlew, Norfolk or Great Plover, *Œ. scolopax* (*Œ. crepitans*, Temminck); so called from the enlargement of the tibio-tarsal joint.

**1816** LEACH *Cat. Mamm. & B. in Brit. Mus.* 28 *Fedoa Œdicnemus* Common thicknee, Wiltshire. **1840** *Penny Cycl.* XVI. 402/1 The..Thick-knee, Thick-kneed Bustard. **1866** OWEN *Vertebr. Anim.* xiv. II. 26 The 'Thick-knees'..and Bustards..have the four-notched sternum. **1896** *List Anim. Zool. Soc.* 520 *Œdicnemus grallarius*, Australian Thicknee. ..*Œ. superciliaris*, Peruvian Thicknee.

So **Thi·ck-knee·d** *a.*, having thick knees; esp. in *thick-kneed bustard* or *plover*, the Stone Curlew.

**1776** PENNANT *Zool.* (ed. 4) I. 244 Bustard, thick-kneed. **1840** [see THICK-KNEE]. **1893** NEWTON *Dict. Birds* 129 The Curlew of inlanders, or Stone-Curlew—called also..most wrongly..the Thick-knee or Thick-kneed Bustard.

**Thi·ck-leaved** (-līvd), **-leafed** (-līft), *a.* [See LEAVED, LEAFED.] **a.** Having or covered with dense foliage; thickly set with leaves.

**1582** STANYHURST *Æneis* I. (Arb.) 28 Shaded with thickleaued arbours. **1660** BLOUNT *Boscobel* 32 The colonel made choice of a thick-leafed oak. **1847** TENNYSON *Princess* III. 159 The thick-leaved platans of the vale.

**b.** Having thick fleshy leaves.

**1707** MORTIMER *Husb.* (1721) I. 31 Where thick-leav'd Weeds are amongst the Grass, they will need more drying than ordinary Grass doth. **1860** *Merc. Marine Mag.* VII. 199 A thick leafed..plant.

**Thick-lipped** (þi·kˌli·pt: stress var.), *a.* Having thick or full lips.

*a* **1529** SKELTON *E. Rummyng* 467 She was vgly hypped, And vgly thycke lypped. **1588** SHAKS. *Tit. A.* IV. ii. 175 Come on you thick-lipt-slaue. **1682** *Lond. Gaz.* No. 1685/4 John Wilmote,..of a pretty Ruddy Complexion, and somthing thick Lipped. **1838** JOHNSTON in *Proc. Berw. Nat. Club* I. No. 6. 171 *Mugil chelo*,.. the Thick-lipped Grey Mullet. **1867** BAKER *Nile Tribut.* xx. (1872) 352 A real thick-lipped flat-nosed nigger.

So **Thi·ck-lips,** one who has thick lips; a contemptuous appellation for a negro.

**1604** SHAKS. *Oth.* I. i. 66 What a full Fortune do's the Thicks-lips owe If he can carry't thus?

**Thickly** (þi·kli), *adv.* [f. THICK *a.* + -LY[2].] In a thick manner; so as to be thick, in various senses; densely; closely; abundantly; frequently; deeply; obscurely, indistinctly.

*c* **1400** *Laud Troy Bk.* 5672 Thei died thanne thikly. *c* **1430** *Pilgr. Lyf Manhode* II. lvii. (1869) 98 Sum time thou shalt see me thikkeliche and derkeliche. **1573–80** BARET *Alv.* T 151 Thicklie: groslie: clubbishlie, or blockishlie. *c* **1611** CHAPMAN *Iliad* XV. 440 His helmet, thickly plum'd. **1630** DRAYTON *Noah's Flood* 83 Your sins..so thickly throng. **1770** COOK *Voy. round World* III. ii. (1773) 519 Lofty hills, all thickly clothed with wood. **1860** TYNDALL *Glac.* I. xviii. 123 Mont Cervin gathered the clouds more thickly round him. **1883** LD. R. GOWER *My Remin.* I. iii. 35 The walls of the principal apartments are thickly hung with paintings.

**b.** In comb. with ppl. or other adjs.

**1797** T. PARK *Sonn.* 7 Clouds, thickly-driving, veil the face of day. **1832** MOTHERWELL *Poet. Wks.* (1847) 8 Those thickly-timbered shores. **1900** *Westm. Gaz.* 7 Sept. 4/1 A thickly-inhabited district.

**Thicknee,** variant of THICK-KNEE.

**Thickness** (þi·knės). [OE. *þicness* = OHG. *dicnissa*, f. THICK *a.* + -NESS.]

**I.** The quality or condition of being thick.

**1.** Relatively large measurement through, or between opposite surfaces; stoutness, bulkiness; the opposite of *thinness* or *slenderness*. Also *fig.*

*c* **1000** *Ags. Gloss.* in *Haupt's Zeitschr.* (1853) IX. 519 *Elephantina callositate*, hreoflicre þicnesse. **1538** ELYOT, *Crassamentum*, thyckenesse. .. *Crassities & crassitudo*, fatnesse, thicknes, grossenes. **1577** B. GOOGE *Heresbach's Husb.* II. (1586) 80 b, The equall medley of .. thicknesse and thinnes. **1613** HAYWARD *Norm. Kings* 23 As he grew in yeeres, so did he in thicknesse and fatnesse of body. **1641** EVELYN *Diary* 7 Aug., Walls..of prodigious thicknesse. **1885** J. PAYN *Luck of Darrells* xx, His companion's astounding thickness of skin [cf. THICK-SKINNED 2].

**2.** Measurement or extension of anything between its opposite surfaces; the third (and commonly least) dimension, distinct from length and breadth.

*a* **900** WÆRFERTH *Gregory's Dial.* (1900) 44 He ʒewænde þæs wæteres ʒecynd on eles þicnesse. **1387** TREVISA *Higden* (Rolls) I. 45 Þe þiknesse of þe erþe þorw oute is almest sexe þousand and fyue hondred myle. **14..** *Tundale's Vis.* (Wagner) 1314 Fourti cubytes on brede he hadde And nine on theknes was he made. *a* **1548** HALL *Chron., Hen. VIII* 33 The Frenchmen came on in .iii. ranges, xxxvi. mens thickenes [i. e. thirty-six deep]. **1570** BILLINGSLEY *Euclid* I. def. ii. 2 A point..neither hath length, breadth, nor thickenes. **1683** MOXON *Mech. Exerc., Printing* xxiv, It is Quadrat high, of several Thicknesses, viz. a Nonparel, Brevier, Long-primmer, Pica, etc. **1735** JOHNSON *Lobo's Abyssinia, Descr.* x. 103 The Crocodile is very ugly, having no Proportion between his Length and Thickness. **1815** J. SMITH *Panorama Sc. & Art* I. 7 In half an hour it will scarcely be the thickness of a sixpence. **1854** *Pereira's Polariz. Light* 134 The resulting tint depends on the difference of the thicknesses. **1884** BOWER & SCOTT *De Bary's Phaner.* 411 They there attain a thickness which amounts to ½ or even more than ⅔ of the entire thickness of the leaf.

**3.** The quality or condition of being consistent or viscous (also, degree of consistence); of the air, the condition of being laden with impurities.

*c* **1000** *Sax. Leechd.* I. 126 Cnuca mid wine on huniʒes þicnysse. **1398** TREVISA *Barth. De P. R.* III. xvii. (W. de W. 1495) d iv b/1, Yf it is all clere & wᵗout thyknesse as the ayere is, thenne yᵗ is not seen. *c* **1425** tr. *Arderne's Treat. Fistula* 36 Medled togidre in suche þiknes þat it may be ʒetted in by a nastare of tree. **1663** GERBIER *Counsel* 27 Morter..unequall in thicknesse. **1737** WHISTON *Josephus, Antiq.* II. xiv. § 5 Whereby their sight being obstructed, and their breathing hindered by the thickness of the air, they died miserably. **1747** WESLEY *Prim. Physick* (1762) 109 Mix juice of Celandine with Honey to the Thickness of Cream.

**4.** Of the air, etc.: Misty or hazy condition; obscurity, opacity.

*c* **1000** *Ags. Ps.* (Spelm.) xcvi. 2 ʒenipu and þicnæs, *nubes et caligo.* *c* **1000** *Sax. Leechd.* III. 232 We ne maʒon for ðære fyrlynan heahnysse & þæra wolcna ðicnysse .. hi næfre ʒeseon. **1426** LYDG. *De Guil. Pilgr.* 11036 And off the owgly ffoul thyknesse,..Thow shalt lese the syht off me.

**5.** Dense or crowded condition; closeness of collocation or growth.

**1398** TREVISA *Barth. De P. R.* v. xv. (Bodl. MS.), Þiknes of berd is signe and tokenne of heete and of substancial humour and of strengþe. **1433** LYDG. *St. Edmund* II. 838 A couert, shrowded with thyknesse Of thornys sharpe. *c* **1440** *Promp. Parv.* 491/1 Thykkenesse, as of wodys, gresse, corne, or other lyke, *densitas.* **1825** SCOTT *Talism.* vi, His hair in thickness might have resembled that of Samson.

**6.** Want of clearness in breathing, hearing, or utterance; indistinct articulation.

**1538** ELYOT *Dict.* Addit., *Daseia*, thyckenes of brethe. **1669** HOLDER *Elem. Speech* 168 Being at sometimes subject to thicknes of Hearing. **1686** BURNET *Lett.* (1708) 249 Her Nurse had an extraordinary Thickness of Hearing. **1863** A. M. BELL *Princ. Speech* 183 The inarticulate confusion of speech which results is commonly called 'thickness'. **1908** R. BAGOT *A. Cuthbert* iii, His few observations being characterised by a decided thickness of utterance.

**II.** That which is thick or has thickness.

**7.** That which is thick, in any sense; the part (of anything) which is thick; the thick (of anything); the space between opposite surfaces (e. g. of a wall).

*c* **1000** *Ags. Gloss.* in *Haupt's Zeitschr.* (1853) IX. 499 *Sulphureis flammarum globis*, sweflenum þicnyssum. *a* **1000** *Lambeth Ps.* cxviii[i]. 27 On þyccetum *vel* on ðicnessum, *in condensis.* **1382** WYCLIF *Isa.* ix. 18 It shal be brend vp in the thickenes of the wilde wode. **1560** BIBLE (Genev.) *Ezek.* xlii. 10 The chambres were in the thickenes of the wall of the court. **1687** A. LOVELL tr. *Thevenot's Trav.* II. 82 They go down..by steps made in the thickness of the Walls. **1796** MORSE *Amer. Geog.* II. 477 Incumbered with unwholesome marshes..and impenetrable thicknesses. **1859** JEPHSON *Brittany* vii. 93 The wall is here about five yards thick, and in its thickness are stone benches. **1905** R. BAGOT *Passport* iii. 19 There was only the thickness of a floor between them.

**8.** A layer (of cloth, paper, etc.). In *Foundry*, A layer of loam in a mould which represents the object to be cast (e. g. a pipe, bell), and is broken away from the completed mould to make room for the molten metal.

**1815** J. SMITH *Panorama Sc. & Art* II. 807 Place several thicknesses of paper upon the glass. **1853** SIR H. DOUGLAS *Milit. Bridges* (ed. 3) 325 The whole six thicknesses of planks..are then well drawn together, and fastened to each other, by the trenails. **1884** N. E. SPRETSON *Casting & Founding* 215 In the absence of patterns, however, for these and for other varieties of short piping, they are swept up in loam, the core within the 'thickness'. **1889** *Anthony's Photogr. Bull.* II. 237 On top..a single thickness of common felt cloth is placed.

Hence **Thi·cknessing** *vbl. sb.*, the action of reducing (boards, etc.) to a given thickness.

**1870** *Eng. Mech.* 4 Feb. 497/2 That side of the machine employed for tenoning, planing, thicknessing, or moulding. **1901** *Daily Chron.* 9 May 1/6 Planing and Thicknessing Machine, 20in.

**Thicksell,** dial. variant of THIXIL, an adz.

**Thick-set,** *a.* and *sb.* [f. THICK *adv.* + *set*, pa. pple. of SET *v.*]

**A.** *adj.* (Stress variable, ·– ·, :–·, ·–:; cf. note under ILL *adv.* 3.)

**1.** Composed of individuals or parts arranged in close order; thickly studded or planted (*with* something).

?*a* **1366** CHAUCER *Rom. Rose* 1419 By the stremes..Sprang up the gras, as thikke sette And softe as ony velvet. **1610** HOLLAND *Camden's Brit.* (1637) 627 Thicker set with high Hilles. *c* **1665** MRS. HUTCHINSON *Mem. Col. Hutchinson* (1846) 22 His hair of light brown, very thick set in his youth. **1697** DRYDEN *Æneid* I. 617 Thick-set with trees, a venerable wood. **1869** TOZER *Highl. Turkey* II. 220 A wild hilly country..thick-set with bushes of prickly palluria.

*c* **1410** *Master of Game* (MS. Digby 182) xxiv, He [a hart] bereth a thykesette hede [HEAD *sb.* 6]. **1638–48** G. DANIEL *Eclog.* ii. 2 The Covert of yond' thickset Thorne. *a* **1700** DRYDEN *Ovid's Met.* XIII. *Acis*, etc. 156 A thick-set underwood of bristling hair. **1819** CRABBE *T. of Hall* VI. 132 That thickset alley by the arbour closed.

**2.** Set or placed close together; closely arranged.

**1570–6** LAMBARDE *Peramb. Kent* (1826) 181 The place hath in it sundry villages, although not thicke set, nor much inhabited. **1765** *Museum Rust.* V. xxiv. 118 Its flowers are yellow, and thick-set.

**1612** DRAYTON *Poly-olb.* i. 447 Where Corineus ran With slaughter through the thick-set squadrons of the foes. **1848** BUCKLEY *Iliad* 457 They made a great fence around, with thick-set stakes.

**3.** Having a dense or close-grained nap: cf. B. 2. **b.** *Thick-set wheat*: see quot. 1808.

**1709** *Lond. Gaz.* No. 4608/4 A pair of thickset Fustian Breeches. **1769** *Public Advertiser* 25 Sept. 3/1 Dressed in Fustian or Thickset Cloaths. **1808** BATCHELOR *Agric.* 362 Velvet-eared wheat, which is called in this county white-chaffed led wheat, and thick-set wheat.

**4.** Of close compact build; *esp.* short and strongly made; square-built; stocky.

**1724** *Lond. Gaz.* No. 6251/3 He is a thick-set Boy. **1777** *Charact.* in *Ann. Reg.* 43/1 A short thick-set man, with a very honest ingenuous countenance. **1824** L. M. HAWKINS *Annaline* I. 86 Distinguished by thickset limbs. **1830** MARRYAT *King's Own* xix, He was short and thick-set.

**B.** *sb.* (þi·kˌset).

**1.** A thicket; a thick-set plantation.

**1766** AMORY *Buncle* (1825) III. 108 The first spring of this water is..in the middle of a thick-set of shrubs. **1844** *P. Parley's Ann.* V. 191 Tungee had more than once threaded this maze of wood and thickset.

**2.** A stout twilled cotton cloth with a short very close nap; a kind of fustian; also, a garment of this material. ? *Obs.*

**1756** TOLDERVY *Hist. 2 Orphans* II. 105 The latter having on his back his common grey frock, and the former a Manchester thickset. **1796** MORSE *Amer. Geog.* I. 440 Jeans, fustians, denims, thicksets, velvets. **1822** GALT *Sir A. Wylie* i, His breeches, of olive thickset, were..carefully preserved from stains. **1882** BECK *Draper's Dict.* 142 Corduroy and thickset are also coarser varieties of fustian.

**b.** Short for *thick-set wheat* (see A. 3 b).

**1875** *Encycl. Brit.* I. 354/1 The red-straw white [wheat] and Piper's thick-set have properties similar to the Fenton.

**Thi·ck-si·ghted** (stress var.), *a.* ? *Obs.* Not seeing clearly; having obscure or dim vision.

**1592** SHAKS. *Ven. & Ad.* 136 Were I..Thick-sighted, barren, leane, and lacking iuyce. **1628** FELTHAM *Resolves* II. [I.] xcii. 269 Shee is thick-sighted, and cannot see them. **1775** SHERIDAN *St. Patr. Day* II. iii, We are but blind guessers. .. Thick-sighted mortals. **1863** MRS. GASKELL *Sylvia's Lovers* xxi, Too thick sighted to see through a board.

**Thickskin** (þi·kˌskin). One who has a thick skin; a person dull or slow of feeling. Also *attrib.*

**1582** STANYHURST *Æneis* Ded. (Arb.) 9 What thinck you of thee thick skyn, that made this for a fare wel for this mystresse? **1597** BP. HALL *Sat.* I. i. 8 Nor can I bide to pen some hungry Scene For thick-skin eares, and vndiscerning eyne. **1611** COTGR., *Ceruelle à double rebras*, a.. ioulthead, thicke-skinne, dull fellow. **1893** H. M. DOUGHTY *Wherry in Wendish L.* 53 We..should have made a fair distance but for those slugs and thickskins of bridge-keepers.

**Thi·ck-ski·nned** (-skind: stress var.), *a.*

**1.** Having a thick skin; of plants, fruits, etc., having a thick outer coat or peel.

**1545** ELYOT, *Callosus*, thicke skynned. **1601** HOLLAND *Pliny* I. XI. xxxix. 346 Men..who are thicke skinned..be more grosse of sence and understanding. **1813** SIR H. DAVY *Agric. Chem.* (1814) 152 In the South of Europe, hard or thin-skinned wheat is in higher estimation than soft or thick-skinned wheat. **1831** CARLYLE *Sart. Res.* II. ii, Did not these bristly thick-skinned beings [hogs] here manifest intelligence? **1884** BOWER & SCOTT *De Bary's Phaner.* 38 The superficial position of the stomata is the rule for herbaceous less thick-skinned parts.

**2.** *fig.* Dull of sensation or feeling; obtuse, stolid; now *esp.* not sensitive to criticism or rebuff; the opposite of *thin-skinned.*

**1602** *2nd Pt. Return fr. Parnass.* III. iv. 1383 The Seruile current of my slyding verse, Gently shal runne into his thick skind eares. **1658** SIR T. BROWNE *Hydriot.* Introd. (1736) 8 They who are so Thick-skinned as still to believe the Story of the Phœnix. **1828** SCOTT *Jrnl.* 26 June, He would be thick-skinned if he stands the clamour. **1885** *American* IX. 387 He is too thick-skinned to mind eloquent and indignant criticism.

**Thi·ck-sku·lled** (-skʊld: stress var.), *a.* Having a thick skull; hence *fig.* slow or dull of apprehension; dense, dull-witted; = THICK-HEADED.

*a* **1653** G. DANIEL *Idyll.* v. 140 As the thick-Skull'd Turke ..It baffles vs, with our owne Instrument. **1673** *Ess. Educ. Gentlewom.* 32 Every thick-skull'd Fellow that babbles this out, thinks no Billingsgate Woman can Answer it. **1755** SMOLLETT *Quix.* I. IV. xxi. (1803) II. 258 Is it possible that your worship can be so thick-skulled and brainless, as not to perceive the truth of what I alledge? **1821** SCOTT *Let. to Cunningham* 27 Apr., The common class of readers..are thick-skulled enough. **1860** EMERSON *Cond. Life, Fate* Wks. II. 317 Thick-skulled, small-brained, fishy..quadruped.

So **Thi·ck-skull,** a thick-skulled person.

**1755** JOHNSON, *Dolt,* a heavy stupid fellow; a blockhead; a thickscul; a loggerhead. **1838** JAS. GRANT *Sk. Lond.* 223 Says I, 'You lie, you stupid thickskull!' **1894** CROCKETT *Raiders* 346 Such a thick-skull was I.

**Thi·ck-sow·n,** *a.* Also 8 **thick-sowed.** Sown thickly or with little interval between the seeds. Also *fig.* So **Thick-sow** *v.* (*rare*), to sow thickly.

**1683** NORRIS *Coll. Misc.* (1687) 429 A little Plot of ground thick-sown. **1712** ADDISON *Spect.* No. 285 ⁋ 8 Metaphors are not so thick sown in Milton. **1728** MORGAN *Algiers* I. Pref. 14 Many were more inclined to fall on the well-laden thick-sowed English than any others. **1742** YOUNG *Nt. Th.* IX. 1234 To count The thick-sown glories in this field of fire. **1896** *Harper's Mag.* Apr. 671/2 The distances, thick-sown with the faint yellow candle-flames. **1898** *Westm. Gaz.* 7 Oct. 3/1 It is useless to thick-sow your dialogue with 'ess fay' and 'thicky', and 'pretty vitty', ..and omit the breath of life and..expression of character.

† **Thi·ckways,** *adv. Obs. rare.* [f. THICK *a.* + -WAYS.] In the direction of the thickness.

**1644** DIGBY *Nat. Bodies* xviii. § 1. 158 The ayre..not ..admitting to be diuided thickewayes so much as is necessary to fill the first growing distance, between the two stones. *Ibid.* xxv. § 2. 227 If the externe causes had pressed vpon this droppe, only broadwayes and thickewayes..then it would haue proued a cylinder.

**Thi·ck-wi·tted** (stress var.), *a.* Having 'thick' wits; dull of intellect, stupid.

**1634** W. WOOD *New Eng. Prosp.* To Rdr., I decline this sort of thick-witted readers. **1642** MILTON *Apol. Smect.* Wks. 1851 III. 256 The conceit that all who are not Prelaticall, are grosse headed, thick-witted, illiterat, shallow. **1821** SCOTT *Kenilw.* xxxv, He is..thick-witted enough to adopt any belief that is thrust on him.

So **Thi·ckwit,** a thick-witted person.

**1904** M. HEWLETT *Queen's Quair* III. ii. 376 She cheapened herself in Love's honour and was held cheap by Scotch thickwits.

† **Thi·cky,** *a. Obs.* [f. THICK *a.* + -Y.] Of a thick nature; inclined to be thick.

**1587** A. DAY *Daphnis & Chloe* (1890) 112 Since Ceres first the thickie groues pursued. **1590** GREENE *Mourn. Garm.* Wks. (Rtldg.) 304/2 It was near a thicky shade, That broad leaves of beech had made. **1598** Q. ELIZ. *Plutarch* iv. 26 Fly thou this darke and thikky mysty folded Cloude.

**Thicky,** *dem. adj.* (*dial.*): see THILK.

**Thidder, -ir,** etc., obs. ff. THITHER.

**Thie,** obs. form of THIGH.

**Thief** (þīf). *Pl.* **thieves** (þīvz). Forms: 1 **theb, þiof, þéof,** (**þéaf, þæf**), 2 **þof** (*dat.* **þove**), 2–5 **þeof,** (3 *dat.* **þeve**), 3–4 **þief,** 3–5 **þef, þeef,** 4 **þyef, þefe,** 4–5 **thef, -ff, thif, theyf,** 4–6 **thefe,** 4–7 **theif, theef, -ffe,** 5 (**þeue**), **thife, thyf(e,** 5–6 **theyff,** 5–7 **theefe,** 6 **theaf, theiff, thieffe,** 6–7 **thiefe,** 6– **thief.** *Pl.* also 4 **þewes; þeifs, þefs, theffes,** 4–6 **thefes.** [OE. *þíof, þéof* (North. *þéaf*). Com. Teut.; in OFris. *thiaf,* OS. *thiof* (MDu., Du. *dief,* MLG. *dief, dêf,* LG. *dêf,* pl. *dêven*), OHG. *diob, diup* (MHG. *diep,* Ger. *dieb*); ON *þiófr* (Sw *tiuf,* Da. *tyv*), Goth. *þiufs, þiuƀ-*:— OTeut. **þeuƀoz*, pointing to an Indo-Eur. ablaut-series **teup-, toup-, tup-*: cf. Lith. *tupēti* to crouch down.

The final consonant represents an unvoicing of the stem consonant, which appears in the inflected forms and the derivatives, as pl. *thieves, thievery,* etc.]

**1.** One who takes portable property from another without the knowledge or consent of the latter, converting it to his own use; one who steals.

**a.** *spec.* One who does this by stealth, esp. from the person; one who commits theft or larceny.

**688–95** *Laws of Ine* c. 12 ʒif ðeof sie ʒefongen. ?*a* **900** *Durh. Adm.* in *O. E. T.* 176 Wið netena unʒetionu & ðiofum. *c* **975** *Rushw. Gosp.* Matt. vi. 19 Ne hydeþ eow hord..þær ðiofes [*Lindisf.* ðeafas, *Ags. Gosp.* ðeofas, *Vulg.* fures] adelfaþ ne forstelaþ. *c* **1000** *Ags. Gosp.* John x. 1 Se þe ne gæð æt þam gete into sceapa falde, ac styhþ elles ofer he is þeof [*Lind.* ðeaf, *Rush.* ðæf] & sceaða [*Vulg.* fur et latro]. *c* **1175** *Lamb. Hom.* 29 Rubberes and þa reueres and þa þeoues. *a* **1200** *Moral Ode* 43 (Lamb. MS.), For þer ne þerf he bon of-dred of fure ne of þoue [*v. r.* þeve]. *c* **1200** *Trin. Coll. Hom.* 61 Oðer þurh fur, oðer þurh þiefes, oðer þurh roberie. *c* **1250** *Gen. & Ex.* 1773 Ðu me ransakes als an ðef. *a* **1300** *St. Gregory* 997 in Herrig's *Archiv* LVII. 69 Þou þeefes fere, Þou ne dost bote make men of þe speke. *a* **1300** *Cursor M.* 4891–2 (Cott.) Yon er theues we lelmen wend, And theif [*v. rr.* thif, thefe, þeof] es he þam hider send. *Ibid.* 15970 Iudas was iesu aumnere, Bath theif [*v. r.* þeef] and traitur bald. *c* **1386** CHAUCER *Doctor's T.* 83 A theef [*v. rr.* theefe, þeef, þef, þeof] of venyson..Kan kepe a fforest best of any man. **1390** GOWER *Conf.* I. 52 So that an yhe is as a thief To love, and doth ful gret meschief. *c* **1420** *Chron. Vilod.* 2923 Bot þe Iaylardes folowedone þis theff fulle fast. *a* **1425** *Cursor M.* 7234 (Trin.) Þer is noon so myche may greue As traitour derne & priue þeue. **14..** *Nom.* in Wr.-Wülcker 694/1 *Hic. fur,* a theffe. *c* **1470** HENRY *Wallace* II. 392, I trow thow be sum spy, Or ellis a theyff. **1532–3** *Act 24 Hen. VIII,* c. 5 An Acte where a Man kyllyng a Theffe shall not forfayte his Goodes. **1596** SHAKS. *Merch. V.* III. i. 97 The theefe gone with so much, and so much to finde the theefe, and no satisfaction, no reuenge. **1605** CAMDEN *Rem.* 229 When thou commest into a strange place, thinke all men there to be theeves. **1643** SIR T. BROWNE *Relig. Med.* I. § 46 How comes He then like a theefe in the night? **1678** BUNYAN *Pilgr.* I. 163 Thou art a Theif and a Robber. *Ibid.* 165 He did hang his head like a Thief. **1769** COOK *Voy. round World* I. x. (1773) 100 The people of this country [Otaheite]..are the errantest thieves upon the face of the earth. **1878** STUBBS *Const. Hist.* III. xviii. 243 There is more spirit and a better heart in a robber than in a thief. **1879** JEFFERIES *Wild Life in S. C.* 160 The robin is accused of being a terrible thief of currants.

**b.** In more general sense, comprehending such as rob with violence; e.g. robbers, freebooters, pirates, etc.; now *rare* exc. as a general designation of one who obtains goods by fraudulent means, over-reaching, deceit, etc.

*Border thieves,* the freebooters of the Scottish Border, whose depredations were so notorious in the 16th century. † *Thief of the sea,* a pirate, SEA-THIEF.

In the Revised Version of the N. T., in all cases where *thief* in the 1611 version renders λῃστής, Vulg. *latro,* it is changed to *robber,* and *thief* only retained where it renders κλέπτης, Vulg. *fūr.*

*a* **700** *Epinal Gloss.* (O.E.T.) 630 *Mimoparo,* thebscib. *c* **950** *Lindisf. Gosp.* Matt. xxi. 13 ʒie worhton ða ilca cofa (*vel* græfe) ðeafana [*Vulg.* latronum; *c* **975** *Rushw. Gosp.* ibid., ʒescræfe ðiofas (*vel* scaþena), *c* **1000** *Ags. Gosp.* þeofa cote]. *c* **1000** *Ags. Gosp.* Matt. xxvi. 55 Eall-swa to þeofe [*Lindisf.* mor-sceaðe, *Rushw.* scaþe, *Vulg.* latronem] ʒe synt cumene mid swurdum. — John xviii. 40 Witodlice barrabbas wæs þeof [*Lindisf.* morsceaða, *Rushw.* sceaða, *Vulg.* latro, Gr. λῃστής, WYCLIF, *Rhem.* theef, theefe, TINDALE, 1611 robber]. *c* **1200** *Vices & Virt.* 51 Betwenen twa þieues. *a* **1300** *Cursor M.* 10297 (Cott.) Stalworth men..Þat moght again þe theues [*v. r.* thefes] fight. *c* **1330** R. BRUNNE *Chron. Wace* (Rolls) 6631 Þise Sarsynes þeues þey drof awey. **1340** *Ayenb.* 37 Þer ys a þyef open and a þyef ywreʒe, a þief priue and a þyef uelaʒe. **13..** *E. E. Allit. P.* B. 1142 Hit were rafte wyth vnryʒt & robbed wyth þewes. **1382** WYCLIF *Matt.* xxvii. 38 Thanne two theeues [*Vulg.* latrones] ben crucified with him. **1387** TREVISA *Higden* (Rolls) I. 329 Þe men of þat lond beeþ schipmen and þeues of þe see. **1436** *Libel Eng. Policy* in *Pol. Poems* (Rolls) II. 164 The grettest rovers and the grettest thevys That have bene in the see many oone yere. **1533** GAU *Richt Vay* (S.T.S.) 93 The tirannis and oppressours and theyffis. **1567** SIR R. MAITLAND *Complaynt* i, Of Liddisdaill the commoun theifis Sa pertlie steillis now and reifis, That nane may keip Hors, nolt, nor scheip: Nor yit dar sleip, For thair mischeifis. *Ibid.* iv, Thay thiefis have neirhand herreit haill Ettricke forest and Lawderdaill. **1651** HOBBES *Leviath.* I. x. 45 Till there were constituted great Common-wealths, it was thought no dishonour to be..a High-way Theefe. **1678** R. L'ESTRANGE *Seneca's Mor.* II. vii. (1705) 150 Nothing is more Common, than for Great Thieves to ride in Triumph, when the Little ones are punish'd. **1712** tr. *Arab. Nights* (1785) 561/2 The Story of Ali Baba, and the Forty Thieves. **1892** KIPLING *Ballad of East & W.* 24 Who rides at the tail of a Border thief, he sits not long at his meat.

**c.** In proverbial expressions.

*c* **1230** *Hali Meid.* 17 Man seið þat eise makeð þeof. **1539** TAVERNER *Erasm. Prov.* (1552) 65 Aske my felowe if I be a thefe. **1546** J. HEYWOOD *Prov.* (1867) 20 A paterne, as meete as a rope for a theefe. **1562** *Ibid.* 151 When theeues fall out, trewe men come to their goode. **1670** RAY *Prov.* 129 Opportunity makes the thief. *Ibid.* 148 Set a thief to take a thief. **1791** BENTHAM *Panopt.* Wks. 1843 IV. 225 A sort of honour may be found (according to a proverbial saying) even among thieves. **1833** [see THICK *a.* 10].

**d.** *fig.* That which steals or furtively takes away.

**1742** YOUNG *Nt. Th.* I. 393 Procrastination is the thief of time. **1838** L. HUNT *Rondeau* 3 Time, you thief, who love to get Sweets into your list, put that in.

**2.** As a general term of reproach or opprobrium: Evil man, villain, scoundrel. (Still *dial.*)

**1297** R. GLOUC. (Rolls) 5621 Þis þef þat lay bi neþe..smot þen king..in þe brust. *a* **1300** *K. Horn* 323 Hennes þu go, þu fule þeof. **13..** *Cursor M.* 786 (Fairf.) He sayde þaire ioy walde be mykel Þis fals þefe þat was so fikel. *c* **1400** *Laud Troy Bk.* 15271 This wicked theff Achilles Thi bretheren hath sclayn with-oute les. *c* **1425** *Cast. Persev.* 1137 in *Macro Plays* 111 For ilke man callyth oþer 'hore & thefe'. *a* **1548** HALL *Chron., Hen. IV* 12 b, Thou trayter thefe, thou hast bene a traitour to kyng Richard. **1653** HOLCROFT *Procopius, Goth Wars* III. 107 These Theeves alledge, to provoke you to a War, our holding Syrmium, and some other places in Dacia. *a* **1800** PEGGE *Suppl. Grose, Thief,* a general term of reproach, not confined to stealing. **1893** STEVENSON *Catriona* ix. 102 Yon thief of the black midnight, Simon Fraser.

**b.** *Old* (*auld*), *ill thief*: the Devil. *Sc. dial.*

**1789** BURNS *To Dr. Blacklock* ii, The ill-thief blaw the Heron south! **1822** HOGG *Perils of Man* III. 38 Cuffed about by the 'auld thief' as they styled him. **1893** *Westm. Gaz.* 21 Feb. 9/2 What does D stand for?—The first letter o' the Auld Thief's name.

**3.** *transf.* † **a.** Applied to a goshawk (*obs.*). † **b.** A kind of wild bee said to rob hives (*obs.*). **c.** A shoot from the root of a vine, rose-bush, or other trained shrub, which robs the main stem of its strength. **d.** *Mod. slang.* A horse that does not run up to form in a race.

**1486** *Bk. St. Albans* d ij, A Goshawke shulde not flie to any fowle of the Ryuer with bellis in no wise, and therfore a Goshawke is calde a theef. **1608** TOPSELL *Serpents* (1658) 650 Some have thought that Theeves are one proper sort of Bees, although they be very great, and black, having a larger belly or bulk then the true Bee, and yet lesser then the drones. **1658** ROWLAND *Moufet's Theat. Ins.* 920 The Theeves being naturally odious to the Bees, steal upon their labours when they are absent, wasting and spoyling their provision of honey. **1669** J. ROSE *Eng. Vineyard* (1675) 28 Rubbing off the thieves which sprung from the roots of the plant. **1896** J. PORTER *Kingsclere* 127 Gay Hampton..turned out a terrible 'thief', and a savage.

**4.** 'An excrescence in the snuff of a candle' (J.) which causes it to gutter and waste.

**1628** MAY *Virg. Georg.* I. 436 Theeues about the snuffe doe grow. *a* **1633** FLETCHER & SHIRLEY *Night-Walker* II. i, Methinks the light burns blew, I prethee snuff it, There's a thief in't I think. **1642** HOWELL *For. Trav.* (Arb.) 77 If there bee a theefe in the Candle, (as wee use to say commonly) there is a way to pull it out. **1665** BOYLE *Occas. Reflect.* II. x, Upon a Thief in a Candle. **1796** MME. D'ARBLAY *Camilla* II. 407 [He] perceived a thief in the candle, which made it run down..over his hand and the sleeve of his coat. **1824** LAMB *Let. to Barton* 9 Jan., My wick hath a thief in it, but I can't muster courage to snuff it.

**5.** *attrib.* and *Comb.*, as *thief-catching, -colony, -craft, -detector, -maker*; *thief-proof, -resisting, -stolen* adjs.; **thief and reever bell**: see quots.; **thief-bote**: see THEFT-BOOT; **thief-catcher,** (*a*) one who catches thieves; = THIEF-TAKER; (*b*) a device used formerly in apprehending thieves; **thief-key,** a skeleton key; † **thief-land,** a name for Botany Bay; † **thief-leader,** a thief-taker; **thief-tube**: see quot.; † **thef-wyke**: see quot. Also with *thieves'*, as **thieves' cat**: see quots.; **thieves' hole,** a dungeon reserved for thieves; **thieves' Latin,** cant used by thieves; **thieves' vinegar,** an infusion of rosemary tops, sage leaves, etc. in vinegar, formerly esteemed as an antidote against the plague. Also THIEF-LIKE, -TAKER.

**1777** BRAND *Pop. Antiq.* 17 A Bell, usually called the *Thief and Reever Bell, proclaims our two annual Fairs. **1825** BROCKETT *N. C. Words, Thief and Reever-Bell,* the name given to the tolling of the great bell of Saint Nicholas, Newcastle, which is rung at 8 o'clock of the evening preceding every fair. **1732** *Hist. Litteraria* IV. 83 The Draper, to engage the *Thief-catcher to his Interests, made him a Present of a Suit of Clothes. **1891** *Daily News* 6 Nov. 3/1 The thief-catcher..is a shrewd piece of work, from which no head, leg, or arm could extricate itself once caught. **1737** *Gentl. Mag.* VII. 592/1, I do not know that the Army has ever been employed in any sort of *Thief-catching, except with respect to those Thieves called Smugglers. **1786** A. DALRYMPLE (*title*) A Serious Admonition to the Publick, on the Intended *Thief-Colony at Botany Bay. **1859** W. ANDERSON *Disc.* (1860) 291 Adepts in the fashionable *thief-craft. **1909** *Cent. Dict.* Suppl., **Thief-detector*..a delicate microphone designed for seismological studies, but so arranged by Milne that it gives notice of tremors produced by the gentlest footstep in its neighborhood. **1820** *Examiner* No. 614. 39/2 Insurious unliterary *Thiefland. **1692** R. L'ESTRANGE *Fables* cccclxvii. 441 A Wolf had the Fortune to pass by, as the *Thief-Leaders were Dragging a..Fox to the Place of Execution. **1856** G. PRICE (*title*) A Treatise on Fire & *Thief-proof Depositories. **1904** *Daily Chron.* 29 Sept. 1/6 Safes.., fire and *thief-resisting. **1551** ROBINSON tr. *More's Utop.* I. (1895) 66 The Kynge; whome they thynke to haue no more ryghte to the *thefe stolen thynge than the thieffe himselfe hath. **1611** SHAKS. *Cymb.* I. vi. 5 Had I bin Theefe-stolne. **1877** KNIGHT *Dict. Mech.*, **Thief-tube,* a tube for withdrawing of liquids from casks, etc. A sampling-tube; a ve-linche. *c* **1350** in *Eng. Gilds* (1870) 350 Þer sholde be twey baylyues y-swore in þe Citee, and treweleche þe *þefwyke wytye.

**1867** SMYTH *Sailor's Word-bk.*, **Thieves' Cat,* a cat-o'-nine-tails having knots upon it..used for the punishment of theft. **1899** *Daily News* 19 Sept. 6/3 The 'cat' used at Macquarie Harbour..was called 'the thief's cat', or 'double cat o' nine-tails'. **1578** *Burgh Rec. Edinb.* (1882) IV. 86 For..dichting of the new wall, clenging of the *thevis hoill, and the vther the commoun affaris. **1864** A. MCKAY *Hist. Kilmarnock* (1880) 45 A loathsome dungeon called the Thieves'-hole. **1821** SCOTT *Kenilw.* xxix, A very learned man..and can vent Greek and Hebrew as fast as I can *thieves'-Latin. **1840** *Comic Lat. Gram.* 16 Thieves' Latin, more commonly known by the name of slang...Examples, to prig a wipe—to steal a handkerchief [etc.]. **1802** MRS. J. WEST *Infidel Father* III. 5 Conversation was for some days confined to ipecacuanha, *thieves' vinegar, and smoked tobacco.

**Thiefdom, thievedom** (þī·fdəm, þī·vdəm). [f. THIEF + -DOM.]

**1.** The practice of theft; thieving, robbery. *rare.*

*α.* **1548** HOOPER *Declar. Commandm.* xi. 180 The grettist thyffdomme of all is Sacrilege, in robbing of the goodes appointid to an holye vse.

*β.* **1562** PHAER *Æneid* x. Dd iij, Who did their league by theuedom breke? **1887** P. M'NEILL *Blawearie* 153 A' we made by our thievdom, was—I lost a tooth and had my dowg's tail destroyed.

**2.** The realm or domain of thieves.

*α.* **1864** *Sat. Rev.* 27 Aug. 272/1 A narrative illustrative of London thiefdom. **1888** A. WARDROP *Poems & Sk.* 193 Literary thiefdom and Yankeedom are now synonymous.

*β.* **1862** *Cornh. Mag.* Nov. 645 A fiddler to play at the thievedom carnivals. **1870** H. W. HOLLAND in *Gd. Words* 1 June 391/2 In the interior of thievedom they have public-houses, beer-houses, shops, and lodging-houses, almost entirely to themselves.

**Thief-like** (þī·flaik), *a.* and *adv.* [f. THIEF + LIKE *a.* and *adv.*] **a.** *adj.* Like or resembling a thief. **b.** *adv.* In the manner of a thief.

**1621** FLETCHER *Pilgrim* II. ii, But since thou stealst upon me like a spie, And thief-like thinkst that holy case shall carry thee Through all my purposes. **1760–72** H. BROOKE *Fool of Qual.* (1809) IV. 25 Each of them, thief-like, wished to steal an unobserved gaze at the other. **1847** EMERSON *Poems* (1857) 143 And thief-like step of liberal hours Thawing snow-drift into flowers.

† **Thie·fly,** *a.* and *adv.* *Obs.* [ME. *þeoflich(e, þevelich*: –OE. **þéoflic, -líce*: see THIEF and -LY [1, 2].]

**A.** *adj.* Thief-like, stealthy, underhand.

**1395** PURVEY *Remonstr.* (1851) 11 It is theefli, fals and symonient. *c* **1422** HOCCLEVE *Learn to Die* 115 Ful vnwaar was Y of thy theefly breid.

**B.** *adv.* In a thievish or thief-like manner; by stealth; stealthily, furtively.

*c* **1290** *St. Brandan* 284 in *S. Eng. Leg.* I. 227 ȝwan it is ov i-brouȝt, þane ȝe it þeofliche nomen. **1377** LANGL. *P. Pl.* B. XVIII. 336 Theuelich þow me robbedest. **1382** WYCLIF *Gen.* xl. 15 Theuelich [**1388** theefli] Y am had a wey fro the loond of Hebrew. **1387** TREVISA *Higden* (Rolls) VI. 63 (MS. *a*) Seynt Oswald his arm..was þeefliche [*v. rr.* þeeve-lich, þuefliche; CAXTON theefly] i-stole out of þe olde restynge place. **1568** SKEYNE *The Pest* A ij b, Ane feuir most wikit quietlie and thieflie strikis the patient.

**Thieft, thiefthe,** obs. forms of THEFT.

**Thie·f-ta:ker.** One who detects and captures a thief; *spec.* one of a company who undertook the detection and arrest of thieves.

**1535** STEWART *Cron. Scot.* (Rolls) I. 87 The theif takar suld haif the forder spald. **1700** T. BROWN *Amusem. Ser. & Com.* viii. (1709) 84 Serv'd the State in the Quality of Marshal's Men, and Thief-Takers. **1718** C. HITCHIN (*title*) A True Discovery of the Conduct of Receivers and Thief-takers in and about the City of London. **1761** *Chron.* in *Ann. Reg.* 76/2 Two thief-takers, in hopes of entrapping the highwayman.., set out..like travellers. **1840** DICKENS *Barn. Rudge* lxi, A body of thief-takers had been keeping watch in the house all night.

So **Thief-taking** (in quot. *attrib.*).

**1771** SMOLLETT *Humph. Cl.* (1815) 188 He had been for some time in the snares of the thief-taking society.

**Thiefteously,** obs. form of THEFTUOUSLY.

**Thien, þien,** var. THYNE *adv. Obs.*, thence.

**Thier,** obs. form of THEIR, THIR (these).

**Thiethe,** obs. erron. form of TITHE.

**Thieve** (þīv), *v.* [In OE. *þéofian*, f. *þéof*, THIEF. The verb is rare in OE., after which it does not appear till the 17th c. The vbl. sb. *thieving* occurs from 1530. (For the *v* see note to THIEF.)]

**1.** *intr.* To act as a thief. commit theft, steal.

[*a* **901** *Laws of Ælfred* c. 6 ȝif hwa on cirican hwæt ȝeðeo-fiȝe.] *c* **920** in Thorpe *Charters* (1865) 177 Se ðe..ða are þænce to þeofiȝenne. **1530, 1598** [see THIEVING *vbl. sb.* and *ppl. a.*]. **1627** DRAYTON *Mooncalf* 1067 And there this monster sat him down to thieve. **1656** S. H. *Gold. Law* 11 Thus to Traytorize, Murther, and Thieve it. **1691–2** WOOD *Life* 13 Jan. (O. H. S.) III. 380 Foot-soldiers..rob and theeve in Oxon. **1848** DICKENS *Dombey* xxii, I never did such a thing as thieve.

**2.** *trans.* To steal (a thing).

*a* **1695** WOOD *Oxford* (O. H. S.) III. 172 A brass plate having been theeved away. **1760–72** H. BROOKE *Fool of Qual.* (1809) IV. 7 He endeavoured to thieve from me the only friend I had. **1867** *Pall Mall G.* 27 July 9 The prisoner..said it was the first time he had 'thieved' anything. **1901** *Academy* 23 Mar. 243 Goods to the value of a quarter of a million..were annually thieved out of ships in the Pool.

Hence **Thie·vable** *a.*, that may be stolen; **Thie·ver,** one who thieves, a thief.

**1615** J. STEPHENS *Ess. & Char.. Warrener*, Where he hath many night-spels, to the hazard of much Pullen, and indeed all things thieve-able. **1899** LUMSDEN *Edinburgh Poems & Songs* 105 Wha hack'd an' hash'd an' stole, Like reivers an' thievers.

**Thievedom**: see THIEFDOM.

**Thieve-friend.** *nonce-wd.* A friend of thieves. So **Thie·veland,** a land of thieves; a district full of thieves; whence **Thie·velander** [-ER [1] 1].

**1599** PORTER *Angry Wom. Abingd.* I iij, Let not this theefe friend misty vale of night, Incroach on day. **1642** SHIRLEY *Sisters* I. i, Ye are all valiant, honest Thievelanders, And I will be your prince again.

**Thieveless** (þī·vlės), *a.* *Sc.* [Of uncertain origin; first in Ramsay, ? misreading of earlier *theueles*, THEWLESS, to which it answers in sense.] Void of energy, ineffectual, aimless; spiritless, not serious; cold, without warmth of manner.

**1725** RAMSAY *Gentle Sheph.* I. i, She cam wi a right thieve-less errand back. **1786** BURNS *Brigs of Ayr* 89 Wi' thieve-less sneer to see his modish mien, He, down the water, gies him this guid-e'en. **1835** CARRICK *Laird of Logan* 289 (E.D.D.) She answered in a gay thieveless-like way. **1897** R. M. FERGUSSON *Vill. Poet* xiii. 80 He..appeared listless, or, as he himself expressed it, 'rale thieveless'.

**b.** 'Applied to weather in a sort of intermediate or uncertain state. Thus, a thieveless day is one that has no decided character, neither properly good nor bad' (Jamieson, s. v. *Thewles*).

**Thievely,** variant of THIEFLY *Obs.*

**Thievery** (þī·vəri). [f. THIEF, *thiev-* (see note in etym. s. v.), or THIEVE *v.* + -ERY.]

**1.** The committing or practice of theft; stealing. With *a* and *pl.*, An act of thieving.

**1568** FULWELL *Like Will to Like* E j b, Yet better it is to beg moste shamefully, Then to be hanged and to theeuery our selues frame. **1580** *Apol. Pr. Orange* in *Phœnix* (1721) I. 479 Their Thieveries and Sackings. **1623** T. SCOT *Highw. God* 21 But the Theefe proceedes in his theeuery till he brings himselfe to the gallowes. **1722** DE FOE *Col. Jack* vii, They were whipped so for picking pockets, and other petty thieveries. **1840** CARLYLE *Heroes* iv. (1872) 138 We do not 'tolerate' Falsehoods, Thieveries, Iniquities. **1871** R. ELLIS *Catullus* xlvii. 2 The greedy Piso's Tools of thievery, rogues to famish ages.

**2.** The result or produce of thieving; stolen property. Cf. PILFERY 3.

**1583** STOCKER *Civ. Warres Lowe C.* IV. 23 b, The Spaniardes departed Mastright, with their butin and theeuerie. **1606** SHAKS. *Tr. & Cr.* IV. iv. 45 Now with a robbers haste Crams his rich theeuerie vp, he knowes not how. **1873** BROWNING *Red Cott. Nt.-cap* II. 720 A veriest trap of twigs On tree-top, every straw a thievery.

**Thieving** (þī·viŋ), *vbl. sb.* [app. f. THIEVE *v.* + -ING [1]; but perh. f. THIEF *sb.*]

**1.** The action of a thief; the committing of theft; stealing. Also *attrib.*

**1530** PALSGR. 699/2 A nyghtes he gothe a thevyng. **1571** GOLDING *Calvin on Ps.* x. 8 They made royall palaces theyr theeuing-places, too cut sillie mens throtes in. **1634** SIR T. HERBERT *Trav.* 185 These Mallabars..excell in theeuing. **1892** SYMONDS *Michel Angelo* (1899) II. xi. 54 Your failure to discharge your obligations is regarded as an act of thieving.

**2.** *concr.* A thing obtained by theft.

**1861** THORNBURY *Turner* (1862) I. 328 The Louvre, at that time full of Napoleon's magnificent thievings.

**Thie·ving,** *ppl. a.* [f. as prec. + -ING [2].] That thieves or acts like a thief.

**1598** MARSTON *Pygmal.* v 157 Theeuing Mercury That euen in his new borne infancy Stole faire Apollos quiuer. **1823** SCOTT *Quentin D.* vi, I will teach these misbelieving, thieving sorcerers, to interfere with the King s justice. **1897** MARY KINGSLEY *W. Africa* vi. 107 Canoes..drawn up out of the reach of the ever-mischievous, thieving sea.

†**b.** *Thieving nutmeg*; see quots. *Obs.*

**1668** *Phil. Trans.* III. 863 The Nutmeg called Theeving; because that being put among a whole room full of good Nutmegs, though it be but one, it will corrupt them all. **1681** GREW *Musæum* IV. iii. 376 The Fruit..of..the Thieving-Nutmeg, because it infects and spoils the good ones where it lies. **1693** SIR T. P. BLOUNT *Nat. Hist.* 45.

Hence **Thie·vingly** *adv.*, by way of thieving, theftuously.

**1880** RUSKIN *Fors Clav.* lxxxix. 144 Every pleasure got.. cheaply, thievingly, and swiftly.

**Thievish** (þī·viʃ), *a.* Forms: *α.* 5 thef-, 6 theaffish. *β.* 5–6 theu-, 6 thev-, 6–7 theeu-, 6–8 theev-, 6– thievish. [f. THIEF, *thiev-* (see note in etym. s. v.) + -ISH [1].]

†**1.** Infested or frequented by thieves. *Obs.*

**1483** *Cath. Angl.* 382/2 Thefyische (*A.* A Thefis place), *crebrifurus, spoliatorium.* **1535** COVERDALE 1 *Macc.* i. 35 Thus became it a theuysh castell. **1541** BIBLE (Cranmer) *Ps.* x. 8 He syteth lurkyng in yᵉ theuish corners of the stretes. **1592** SHAKS. *Rom. & Jul.* IV. i. 79 Or walke in theeuish waies. **1632** LITHGOW *Trav.* VII. 335 Three French murderers set vppon me in a theeuish Wood.

**2.** Inclined or given to thieving; dishonest.

**1538** ELYOT, *Furax, acis*, theuyshe, a great picker. **1552** HULOET, Theaffyshe and thieuyshe, *furax, cis.* **1555** EDEN *Decades* 300 A theeuysshe kynd of men. **1575** *Gamm. Gurton* v. ii, A theeuisher knaue is not on liue. **1634** SIR T. HERBERT *Trav.* 236 Rashboots a theeuish but valiant people in India vnder the Mogul. **1748** *Anson's Voy.* III. x. 414 Their Magistrates are corrupt. their people thievish. **1883** J. GILMOUR *Mongols* xxxi. 363 The Mongol is despised as ignorant, dirty, stupid, and thievish.

**3.** Of, pertaining to, or characteristic of a thief or thieves; thief-like; furtive, stealthy.

*c* **1450,** *c* **1460** [implied in THIEVISHLY, -NESS]. **1587** TURBERV. *Trag. T.* (1837) 152 Yet wrought it not so well, For all their theevish pace. **1600** SHAKS. *A. Y. L.* II. iii. 33 Enforce A theeuish liuing on the common rode. *c* **1600** — *Sonn.* lxxvii, Times theeuish progresse to eternitie. **1691** HART-CLIFFE *Virtues* 95 According to the manner of Thievish War, the Conqueror by Proclamation gave away the Houses and Possessions of such as were vanquished. **1735** THOMSON *Liberty* III. 399 Corruption's Thievish Arts. **1837** W. IRVING *Capt. Bonneville* III. 8 Their extortion, and their thievish propensities.

**Thievishly** (þī·viʃli), *adv.* [f. prec. + -LY [2].] In a thievish manner; as a thief; furtively, by stealth.

*c* **1450** in Aungier *Syon* (1840) 265 Any instrumente,..by the whiche sche myghte escape theueschely oute of pryson. **1628** WITHER *Brit. Rememb* IV. 664 Some, theevishly, pur-loyned from the sick. **1708** *Brit. Apollo* No 64. 2/2 A Woman so thievishly inclined. **1855** SINGLETON *Virgil* I. 128 Fire..thievishly beneath the fatty bark At first con-cealed, hath on the timber seized.

**Thievishness** (þī·viʃnės). [f. as prec. + -NESS.] The quality or condition of being thievish.

*c* **1460** METHAM *Wks.* 94 Yt sygnyfyith onstabylnes and ontrwth and theuyschnes. **1727** BAILEY Vol. II, *Thievish-ness*, Addictedness to Stealing. **1907** *19th Cent.* Apr. 567 Attacking the spite, frivolity, vanity,.. thievishness and similar endearing qualities of the sex.

†**Thie·vously,** *adv. Obs.* = THIEVISHLY.

**1658** BROMHALL *Treat. Specters* I. 92 [They] thievously stole to the shore through rough and hard rocks.

**Thif(e, Thift(e, -th(e,** obs. ff. THIEF, THEFT.

**Thife-thorn,** variant of THEVE-THORN *Obs.*

**Thig** (þig), *v.* Now *Sc.* Forms: 1 þicg(e)an, 2 þigg(i)en, 3–5 thigge, 3–8 thigg, 4–5 thygg, 5–6 thyg, (6 thige), 4– thig. [OE. *þicg(e)an, þeah, þáh-, þǽgon, þegen* to take, esp. as food; also as a weak vb., pa. t. *þig(e)de.* ME. *thigge*, a. ON. *þiggja, þá-, þágum, þágum, þegen* to receive (Sw. *tigga*, Da. *tigge* to beg); cf. OS. *thiggian* to beg, OHG. *dikken*, etc. (MHG. *digen*) to beg; :–OTeut. **þigjan* (with *j* suffix as in **ligjan* LIE *v.*[1], **sitjan* SIT *v.*), f. root **þig- : þag- : þǣg-* :–Indo-Eur. **tegh : togh- : tēgh.*

The OE. vb., which would have given *thidge* or perh. *thie, thy* in mod. Eng. (cf. LIE, SAY), was lost *a* 1150, and its place was taken in the north by the Norse form, with modification of sense.]

†**1.** *trans.* To take, receive, accept; *esp.* to take (food), to consume by eating or drinking.

*a* **864** *O. E. Chron.* an. 755 (Parker MS.) And hiera se æþeling ȝehwelcum feoh and feorh ȝebead and hiera næniȝ hit ȝeþicgean [*Laud MS. c* **1100** þicgan] nolde. *c* **1000** *Ags. Gosp.* Mark vii. 5 Hwi..þine leorning-cnihtas..besmitenum handum hyra hlaf þicgað [*c* **1160** *Hatton Gosp.*, þiggieð]. *c* **1000** *Sax. Leechd.* III. 92 Þiȝe þar of anne cuppan fulle on ærne morȝe and oþerne an niht. *c* **1175** *Lamb. Hom.* 105 Temperantia þet is metnesse on englisc, þet mon beo imete on alle þing and to muchel ne þigge on ete and on wete.

**2.** To receive by begging; to beg (alms, one's food, etc.); in mod. *Sc.*, to solicit gifts on special occasions, esp. on setting up housekeeping, etc.: cf. THIGGING *vbl. sb.* quots. 1827, 1872.

*c* **1300** *Havelok* 1373 He haueth me do[n] mi mete to thigge, And ofte in sorwe and pine ligge. *c* **1375** *Sc. Leg. Saints* xxiv. (*Alexis*) 169 [He] Ilke day thigyt his lyf-led. *c* **1400** *Destr. Troy* 13549 Now me bus, as a beggar, my bred for to thigge. **1561** *Maitl. Club Misc.* III. 282 My brother is and salbe Vicar of Crayll quhen thow sal thyg thy mayt fals smayk. **1887** J. SERVICE *Dr. Duguid* III. iv. 262 He gaed to the gaits' hoose to thig 'oo' [= wool]. **1894** P. H. HUNTER *J. Inwick* xi. 145 Syne thig a' they can get aff the pairish.

**b.** *intr.* To beg, cadge.

*a* **1300** *E. E. Psalter* cviii. [cix.] 10 Drecchand his sones be outborne awai, And thigg mote þai, night and dai. *c* **1470** HENRYSON *Mor. Fab.* IV. (*Fox's Conf.*) xiv, I eschame to thig, I can not wirk. **1665** J. FRASER *Polichron.* (S.H.S.) 281, I will not goe begg nor thigg amongst my friends. **1818** SCOTT *Rob Roy* xxvi, Lang-legged Hieland gillies that.. maun gang thigging and sorning about on their acquaintance. *Note. Thigging* and *sorning* was a kind of genteel begging, or rather something between begging and robbing, by which the needy in Scotland used to extort cattle, or the means of subsistence, from those who had any to give. **1895** CROCKETT *Men of Moss-Hags* 166 Ye see it's treason to hae sic a thing, and rank conspiracy to thig and barter to get it back.

**c.** *trans.* To take, borrow (as a quotation).

**1728** RAMSAY *Epist. to D. Forbes* xi, I'll frae a Frenchman thigg a fable, And busk it in a plaid. **1728** — *Adv. to Mr.* —— *on his Marriage* 22 And blaw ye up with windy fancies, That he has thigit frae romances.

†**3.** To crave, request, ask (a boon, a favour, leave); in quot. *c* 1470 [2] with the person as obj. *Obs.*

*c* **1450** *St. Cuthbert* (Surtees) 3565 Bot of thi grace we thyg To vouche safe with us to ligg. *c* **1470** HENRY *Wallace* II. 260 Scho..thyggyt leiff away with him to fayr. *c* **1470** HENRYSON *Mor. Fab.* IX. (*Wolf & Fox*) xiii, Thocht we wald thig ȝone verray Churlische chuf, He will not gif vs ane hering of his Creill. **1513** DOUGLAS *Æneis* VII. x. 75 Thay thyg vengence at the goddis. *a* **1568** BALNAVES in *Bannatyne Poems* (Hunter. Cl.) 391 To tar and tig, syne grace to thig, That is ane petouss preiss.

†**b.** *intr.* *Obs.*

*c* **1375** *Sc. Leg. Saints* l. (*Katerine*) 1144 Graunt þaim þar bowne, I thig at þe. *a* **1578** LINDESAY *Chron. Scot.* (S.T.S.) I. 125 They war faine to thige and cry for peace.

Hence **Thig** *sb.*, begging, mendicancy.

**1898** *Blackw. Mag.* July 82/1 Master Brown sat..studying through horn specks the tale of thig and theft which the town officer had made up a report on.

**Thigger** (þi·gəɹ). *Sc.* [f. THIG *v.* + -ER [1].] One who thigs; a beggar, a cadger; an exactor of contributions; one who plants himself on others for assistance; 'one who draws on others for sub-sistence in a genteel sort of way' (Jamieson); a gaberlunzie or licensed beggar who went his regular rounds, and received a night's lodging and food at particular houses; also, any one who begged or solicited presents on certain recognized occasions, e. g. wedding-presents.

**1424** *Sc. Acts Jas. I* (1879) II. 8 Þat na thiggar be thollyt to thyg noþer in burghe nor to land. *a* **1733** *Shetland Acts* 4 in *Proc. Soc. Ant. Scot.* (1892) XXVI. 196 That all thiggers of wool, corn, fish and others be apprehended wherever they come. **1822** SCOTT *Pirate* v, Ye wadna have me waste our substance on every thigger or sorner that has the luck to come by the door in a wet day? **1824** MACTAGGART *Gallovid. Encycl.*, *Thiggers*..are those who beg in a genteel way; who have their houses they call at in certain seasons, and get corn, and other little things. **1828** SCOTT *F. M. Perth* ix, Such exaction, which more resembles the masterful license of Highland thiggers and sorners.

So **Thi·gster** [-STER] in same sense.

**1710** *Dict. Feudal Law* 151 *Thigsters*, are a sort of gentle Beggars.

**Thigging** (þi·giŋ), *vbl. sb.* [f. THIG *v.* + -ING [1].] The action of the verb THIG; begging.

**1331** *Chester Plea Roll* 4 & 5 *Edw. III* m. 15 (P.R.O.) Bedelli non debent habere offringes thiggynges fulcenale nec aliquod aliud proficuum nisi tantummodo puturam de illis certis tenementis que vocantur warelondes. *c* **1440** *Promp. Parv.* 490/2 Thyggynge, or beggynge, *mendicacio.* **1513** DOUGLAS *Æneis* VIII. Prol. 74 Scho..waistis hir tym In thiggin, as it thrift war. **1827** J. ANDERSON *St. Soc. & Knowl. in Highlands* 73 note, Sometimes the young people [about to be married] made the round of their relatives and neighbours to try fortune's smiles. This was called *thigging*. **1872** MICHIE *Deeside T.* xv. 132 The bridegroom gaed a thiggan' among the friends, an got presents o' corn an' ither gear in token o' their well wishes.

So **Thigging** *ppl. a.*, that thigs.

*a* **1300** *E. E. Psalter* xxxix. 18 [xl. 17] And thiggand and pouer am I [WYCLIF, I forsothe a beggere am and pore].

**Thigh** (þəi), *sb.* Forms: see below. [OE. *þíoh, þéoh*, Anglian *þéh* = OFris. *thiach*, neuter, OLG. **thioh*, ODu. *thio* (MDu. *dië, diege, dieghe, dijge*, Du. *dij*), ON. *þjó*, OHG. *dioh* (MHG. *diech*) :—OTeut. **þeuh-oᵐ*, from Indo-Eur. ablaut-series **teuk-, tauk-, tuk-*; cf. Lith. *taukas*, OSlav. *tukŭ*, Russ. *tukⁿ* fat of animals, Lith. *tukti* to become fat. The regular representative of OE. *þéoh* was ME. *þeh, þeȝ, þee*, which still remains as *thee* in Sc. and north. dialect; but in the 12–13th c. *þeȝ* became narrowed to *þiȝ, thigh* (as *heȝ, neȝ, deȝen* became *hiȝ, niȝ, diȝen, high, nigh, die*).]

**1.** The upper part of the leg, from the hip to the knee (in man).

*α.* 1 **théoh, þéoh, þíoh** (**ðeeoh, þyoh**), *Angl.* **thegh, 1–3 þeh, þeo, 3 þeȝ, 3–5 þe, 4–5 þee, thegh, 4–6 they, the, 5 þeie, theȝe, theiȝe; 4–7** (*Sc.* and *north.* -9) **thee.** Pl. 1 **þéoh, 2–3 þeȝ, 2–þeos,** etc.

*c* **725** *Corpus Gloss.* (O.E.T.) 556 *Coxa*, thegh. *a* **800** *Erfurt Gloss.* 295 Theoh. *c* **893** K. ÆLFRED *Oros.* I. vii. § 1 Hy crupon þæm mannum betuh þa þeoh. *c* **897** — *Gregory's Past.* C. lvi. 433 Be his ðio. *a* **900** *O. E. Martyrol.* 130 Wund on oðrum þeo. *c* **1000** *Lorica Gl.* in *Sax. Leechd.* I. Pref. 70 Ðeeoh, *bathma*. *Ibid.* 74 Þyoh. *Ibid.* I. 78 ȝif men his ðeoh acen. *c* **1200** ORMIN 8079 Fet & þeos Tobollenn. *c* **1250** *Hymn to God* 24 in *Trin. Coll. Hom.* 258 Bind him honden, fet, & þeȝ. *c* **1275** LAY. 30581 He cutte his owe þeh. *a* **1300** *Havelok* 1903 He broken shankes, he broken thes. *a* **1300** *Cursor M.* 3941 Þe maister sinu of his the. *a* **1340** HAMPOLE *Ps.* xliv. 4 With þi swerd abouen þi thee. *c* **1375** *Sc. Leg. Saints* xxviii. (*Margaret*) 430 Vpwart til his theis. **1422** tr. *Secreta Secret., Priv. Priv.* 177 Woundid in the thegh. *c* **1450** *St. Cuthbert* (Surtees) 1525 In his þe þar was a byle. *c* **1475** *Pict. Voc.* in Wr.-Wülcker 750/28 *Hoc femur*, a they. **1513** DOUGLAS *Æneis* II. viii. [vii.] 56 Ane Gregioun swerd doun by his thee. **1685** *Lintoun Green* (1817) 168 The miller..stands Wi' his untheeked thees. *a* **1869** C. SPENCE *Fr. Braes of Carse* (1898) 71, I wade the ditches to the thees.

*β.* **2–3 þih, 2–4 þi, þy, 4–5 þiȝ, þiȝe, þigh(e, þyghe, þyhe, thyȝe, 4–6 þie, þye, thie, 5–6 thy, thyghe, 5–7 thye, 6 thighe,** *Sc.* **thich, 6– thigh.** Pl. 2–3 **þih; 3–6 þyes,** etc.; **6– thighs.**

**11..** *Fragm. Ælfric's Gram.* (1838) 2 *Femur* vel *coxa*, þih. *c* **1200** *Trin. Coll. Hom.* 211 Þih and shonkes and fet. *c* **1275** *Passion Our Lord* 490 in *O. E. Misc.* 51 Þat heore þyes beon to-broken. **13..** *Minor Poems fr. Vernon MS.* xxv. 337 Þi boþe þiȝes. *c* **1380** WYCLIF *Serm.* Sel. Wks. I. 143 Þe knyȝtis broken not Cristis þies. **1387** TREVISA *Higden* (Rolls) I. 425 As hit were a manis þyghe. *Ibid.* II. 203 Somme haueþ þighes with oute hammes. *a* **1400** *R. Gloucester's Chron.* 4921 + 110 (Harl. MS.) A gret pece of ys owe þy [*v. rr.* þiȝ, þiȝe, thyȝe, þye] he kerf out wyþ a knyf. **1484** CAXTON *Fables of Avian* xiii, He..hytte hym on the thye. *c* **1532** DU WES *Introd. Fr.* in *Palsgr.* 903 The thighe, *la cuisse*. **1545** T. SCALON *Treat. Astron.* (MS. Ashm. 391), Mars the hed, Sol the thyg[h]es or hamme. *a* **1584** MONTGOMERIE *Cherrie & Slae* 114 By his naked thyis. **1590** SPENSER *F. Q.* III. v. 20 The wicked steele stayd not till it did light In his left thigh. **1596** DALRYMPLE tr. *Leslie's Hist. Scot.* VIII. (S.T.S.) 125 His thich bane is brokne. **1615** CHAPMAN *Odyss.* XVIII. 105 Through his thin Garment, what a Thigh he showes. **1865** KINGSLEY *Herew.* x, Hereward..owned..no mistress save the sword on his thigh.

†**b.** The part of a garment covering the thigh.

**1533** *Acc. Ld. High Treas. Scot.* VI. 184 To draw the theis of the saidis gray hois. **1550** *Ibid.* IX. 405 Theis of hose.

**2.** In lower vertebrate animals, The part of the hind leg which is homologous with the human thigh, or which is popularly regarded as corresponding to it in position or shape; in certain quadrupeds, as the horse, applied to the tibia; in birds to the tarsus; hence in insects, etc., the third section of the leg.

*a* **1300** *Thrush & Night.* 68 in Hazl. *E. P. P.* I. 53 Fowel, me thinketh thou art les, They thou be milde and softe of thes. **1387** TREVISA *Higden* (Rolls) V. 355 Liche to mares wiþ white legges up to þe þiȝes. *c* **1440** *Promp. Parv.* 490/2 Thy, lymme of a beeste, *femur*. **1604** DRAYTON *Owle* 121 Each Bee with Honey on her laden thye. **1737** *Ochtertyre House Bks.* (1907) 66 For a thigh of beefe for the hawks £0. 1. 1. **1834** McMURTRIE *Cuvier's Anim. Kingd.* 374 The posterior thighs are strongly inflated in one of the sexes, where the antennæ are usually long and smaller at the extremity. **1866** B. W. HAWKINS *Anat. Horse* 23 The bones of the leg ('thigh' of horsemen) are the *tibia* and *fibula*.

**3.** *transf.* e.g. the stem of a plant, the lower trunk of a tree, the lower slopes of a mountain.

*c* **1440** *Pallad. on Husb.* III. 255 About his thegh let no thyng growyng be, But if hit axe to be reuocate. **1758** *Phil. Trans.* L. 632 Ribs, like what we call the thighs of certain trees. **1889** C. EDWARDES *Sardinia* 232 The burly thighs of [mount] Gennargentu as an impenetrable barrier between us and the south.

**4.** *attrib.* and *Comb.*, as *thigh-ache, -joint, -muscle, -percussion-sound, -socket, -wound*; *thigh-born, -deep, -fraughted, -high, -long*, adjs.; †**thigh-belly-less** *a.*, having neither thighs nor belly (*nonce-wd.*); **thigh-boot,** a boot with uppers reaching to the thigh; **thigh-hole,** †(*a*) the groin (*obs.*); (*b*) a hole for the thigh in bathing-drawers or the like; **thigh-piece** (**† the-pess**), a piece of armour for the thigh; **thigh-tongue**: see quot.

*c* **1000** *Sax. Leechd.* II. 6 Læcedomas wiþ *þeohece. **1579** LANGHAM *Gard. Health* (1633) 655 Thighache, anoint with sheepes doung and vineger often. *a* **1649** DRUMM. OF HAWTH. *Shadow Judgm.* Wks. (1711) 34 *Thigh-bellyless, most gastly to the sight. **1840** DICKENS *Barn. Rudge* lxiv, Great *thigh-boots smoked hot with grease and blood. **1630** J. TAYLOR (Water P.) *Triumphall Verses* Wks. III. 122/2 His braine-bred Daughter, and his *thigh-borne Sonne. **1655** tr. *Com. Hist. Francion* v. 7 Bacchus the thigh-born Infant. **1851** MAYNE REID *Scalp Hunt.* xli, We fought *thigh-deep in the gathering flood. **1615** BRATHWAIT *Strappado* (1878) 87 When the *thigh-fraughted Bee gathered her thyme. **1893** *Scribner's Mag.* June 734/1 Bamboo grass, *thigh-high. *c* **1425** tr. *Arderne's Treat. Fistula* 11 Þe armeholes, þe *þeholes, þe chawellez, &c. **1899** *Allbutt's Syst. Med.* VII. 191 The knee-jerk is uniformly absent when the *thigh-muscles are paralysed. **1853** MARKHAM *Skoda's Auscult.* 10 The completely empty percussion-sound—the *thigh-percussion-sound—heard at any yielding part of the walls of the thorax, or the abdomen. *c* **1470** HENRY *Wallace* VIII. 265 On the *the pess a felloun strak him gaiff. **1828** TYTLER *Hist. Scot.* (1864) I. 322 Arm-plates, thigh-pieces, greaves for the legs. **1812** A. PLUMTRE *Lichtenstein's S. Afr.* I. 97 The great muscle of the thigh [of the eland] smoked...These..from the resemblance they then bear to bullocks' tongues, are called *thigh-tongues.

† **Thigh** (þəi), *v. Obs.* [f. THIGH *sb.*]

**1.** *trans.* To carve (a small bird): see quots.

*c* **1470** in *Hors, Shepe, & G.* etc. (Caxton 1479 Roxb. repr.) 33 Alle smale birdes thyed. **1508** *Bk. Keruing* A j, in *Babees Bk.* 265 Thye that pegyon..thye that wodcocke, thye all maner of small byrdes. **1675** HAN. WOOLLEY *Gentlewom. Comp.* 113 In cutting up all manner of small Birds, it is proper to say, Thigh them. **1796** MRS. GLASSE *Cookery* xxvi. 382 So you thigh curlews, plover, or snipe.

**2.** *intr.* To cower down, squat. *rare*—⁰.

**1611** FLORIO, *Accosciare*, to thigh, to coure down [1598 to ioyne thighes].

**Thi·gh-bone.** Also 5 *north.* **the-bane.** The bone of the thigh; the femur; in quot. 1825 as an emblem of death: cf. *cross-bones*.

*c* **1450** *St. Cuthbert* (Surtees) 5849 Men wend his the bane had bryst. **1615** CROOKE *Body of Man* 999 On the foreside at the roote of the necke the thighbone is large and rough. **1825** J. NEAL *Bro. Jonathan* III. 295, I begin to see a thighbone or two, now. **1889** MIVART *On Truth* 148 The girdle to which the thigh-bones are articulated.

**Thighed** (þəid), *a.* Also 7 **thyght.** [f. THIGH *sb.* + -ED².] Having thighs (of a specified kind); often in parasynthetic combinations.

*c* **1600** HARINGTON *Nugæ Ant.* (1779) II. 181 To seeme.. smaller wasted, and fuller thyght, then wee are. **1737** BRACKEN *Farriery Impr.* (1757) II. 38 If he [a horse] is Thigh'd down to the Hough, as the Expression is. **1860** RUSKIN *Mod. Paint.* V. IX. iii. 220 Thighed and shouldered like the billows. **1881** R. BUCHANAN *God & Man* I. 160 Bee-hives, with gold thighed swarms hovering near them.

*transf.* *c* **1440** *Pallad. on Husb.* III. 226 Diuerse kynde of vynys: The best is lyke a bosh ythied breef [cf. THIGH *sb.* 3, quot. *c* 1440].

**Thight** (þəit), *a.* Now *dial.* Forms: 4 **thycht** (*Sc.*), 5 **thyght, thyht,** 6 **thicht** (*Sc.*), (**theight**), 7 (9 *dial.*) **thite, thyte,** 7–8 (9 *dial.*) **thight,** (9 *dial.* **theet, theat**). [Found *c* 1375: the earlier form of the word TIGHT. App. a. early ON. **þéhtr*, in later ON. *þéttr* tight, water-tight, close in texture, solid (Norw. *tjett, tett*, Sw. *tät*, Da. *tæt* tight, compact, close). Corresponding in form and meaning to WFris. *ticht*, MDu. and MLG. *dicht* (whence also mod. Ger. *dicht* in same sense), also to MHG. *dîhte* close (whence mod. Ger. dial. *deicht* in Livonia and Esthonia). Not known in the earlier stage of any WGer. lang., but would be in OHG. **dîht*, OS. and OFris. **thicht*, OE. **þîht*, Goth. **þeihts* :—OTeut. **þîhto*ᶻ from earlier **þiŋχto*ᶻ, f. verbal root **þiŋχ*- to grow: see THEE *v.*¹ Though not evidenced before 1375, the word was doubtless in use in the Danelaw from early times. See also TIGHT.]

**1.** Set or growing closely together; thick-set, dense: said of rain, growing crops, reeds in a marsh, etc. Now *dial.*

*c* **1375** *Sc. Leg. Saints* xl. (*Ninian*) 574 Þare-with fel þe rane sa thycht, Þat [etc.]. **1787** W. MARSHALL *Norfolk* Gloss., *Thight*, applied to turneps or other crops,—close, thickset. [*Ibid.* I. 271 There are men who are fully aware that the 'proof' of their turnep-crop depends more on its thightness than on the size of the plant.] **1895** EMERSON *Birds*, etc. *Norfolk Broadland* I. xx. 56 The happy pair [of reed-pheasants] fly about the 'thyte (thick) reed', plucking reed-feathers.

†**2.** Solid, not hollow, whole. *Obs.*

*c* **1440** *Promp. Parv.* 491/2 Thyht, hool fro brekynge, not brokyn.., *integer*. Thyht, not hool wythe-in, *solidus*. *Ibid.*, Thyhtyn, or make thyht, *integro, consolido, solido*.

†**3.** Close, compact, or dense in structure or texture, as a membrane. *Obs.*

In quot. 1539 the sense differs little from 1. In some uses also with the notion of being impermeable to moisture, as in 4.

**1539** *Will T. Samson* (Somerset Ho.), A thyght nett. **1615** CROOKE *Body of Man* 86 It is harder then the true skin and more thight. [*Ibid.* 88 Wherefore they referre the cause of the concretion or congealing with Aristotle, to the fastnesse and thightnesse of the Membranes.] *Ibid.* 387 The coates of the veines are thicke and thight, that nothing but that which is very thinne may sweate out. **1678** PHILLIPS (ed. 4), *Thight*, (old word) well compacted or knit together.

**4.** So close in texture or structure as to keep water out; *esp.* of a ship or boat, so closely compacted and well caulked as to be water-tight. Now *dial.*

**1501** *Acc. Ld. High Treas. Scot.* II. 24 Item, for vij pund of rosait to mak the clath thicht..xiiij *d.* **1587** GREENE *Penelope's Web* Wks. (Grosart) V. 150 Causing his weather beaten shippes to be warped out of the Hauen as soone as they were made theight. *a* **1625** *Nomenclator Navalis* (Harl. MS. 2301) s. v., When the Shipp is staunch and makes but little water, she is thight. **1628** DIGBY *Voy. Medit.* (Camden) 27 Shee was so leakie as was a great cumber..till shee were vnladen and mended thyte. *Ibid.* 37 The boate seemed to be a fine one and thite, but with long driuing was halfe full of water. *a* **1825** FORBY *Voc. E. Anglia*, *Thite*, compact, not leaky, water-tight. **1866** EDMONDSTON *Gloss. Shetl. & Orkney*, *Thight*, close, so as not to admit water. **1877** *Holderness Gloss.* s. v., A theet roof, a theet cask.

**5.** Tight, close-fitting, as apparel. *dial.*

*a* **1825** in FORBY *Voc. E. Anglia*.

Hence † **Thi·ght** *v.*, *trans.* to make 'thight'; **Thi·ghtness,** closeness, denseness, tightness.

*c* **1440** Thyhtyn [see 2]. **1615, 1787** Thightness [see 3, 1].

‖ **Thigmotaxis** (þigmotæ·ksis). *Biol.* [mod. L. f. Gr. θίγμα touch + τάξις arrangement, disposition.] The way in which an organism moves or disposes itself in response to a touch stimulus, i. e. by being attracted (positive thigmotaxis) or repelled (negative thigmotaxis).

**1900** B. D. JACKSON *Gloss. Bot. Terms* 270/2 *Thigmotaxis*..is a synonym [of Thigmotropism]. **1905** *Nature* 31 Aug. 426/2 The 'Thigmotaxis' exhibited by an oxytrocha moving round a spherical egg, unable to leave its surface. **1909** J. W. JENKINSON *Experim. Embryol.* 272 Thus we have positive and negative heliotropism, galvanotaxis, geotropism, galvanotropism, thigmotaxis, and so on.

So **Thigmota·ctic** *a.* [Gr. τακτικ-ός pertaining to arrangement], of, pertaining to, or exhibiting thigmotaxis; hence **Thigmota·ctically** *adv.*

**1900** in *Amer. Jrnl. Psychol.* XII. 141 One is the thigmotactic reaction. Starting with the moving infusorian, we find that it reacts to contact with solid bodies of a certain physical texture by suspending part of the usual ciliary motion. **1901** *Ibid.* 229 A definite rat-hole consciousness that acts, as it were, thigmotactically. **1903** *Science* 8 May 738 The ventral surface of planarians is strongly positively thigmotactic, whereas the dorsal surface is negatively thigmotactic.

**Thigmotropism** (þigmǫ·trǒpiz'm). *Biol.* [f. Gr. θίγμα touch + τρόπη a turning + -ISM.] The movement of some part of any organism in response to a touch stimulus; the habit of turning towards or away from a foreign body on coming into contact with it. So **Thigmotro·pic** *a.*, of, pertaining to, resulting from, or exhibiting thigmotropism.

**1900** B. D. JACKSON *Gloss. Bot. Terms* 270/2 *Thigmotropism*, curvature induced in climbing plants by the stimulus of a rough surface. **1908** M. F. WASHBURN *Animal Mind* iii. § 12. 57. **1909** J. W. JENKINSON *Experim. Embryol.* 275 The outgrowth of the ciliated ring into the arms is due to a stimulus—thigmotropic, perhaps,—exerted by the tip of the spicule.

**Thik,** var. THEEK, THILK; obs. form of THICK.

**Thilc, þ-,** variant of THELLICH *Obs.*

† **Thild.** *Obs.* [ONorthumb. *þyld* (= general OE. *geþyld*) = OHG. *dult*, :—OTeut. **þul-di-*, nominal derivative of verb-stem **þul-* in Goth. *þulan* to endure: see THOLE *v.*] Patience, endurance.

*c* **950** *Lindisf. Gosp.* Luke xxi. 19 On ðyld [*Rushw.* ðylde] iuera ȝie byeð sauelo iuero. *c* **1200** ORMIN 2613 For þild birrþ ben wiþþ iwhillc mahht To beoldenn itt & strengenn. *a* **1300** *E. E. Psalter* ix. 19 Þild ofe pouer [WYCLIF the pacience of pore men] ouer alle Noght in ende forworth salle.

Hence †**Thi·ldi** (OE. **þyldiȝ,** early ME. **þuldi**(*ü*)) *a.*, patient; whence †**Thi·ldiliche** *adv.*, patiently.

*a* **950** *Rituale Dunelm.* (Surtees) 101 Crist' ðv ðe arð doeme soðfæst strong and *ðyldiȝ. *a* **1225** *Leg. Kath.* 177 Ha wes þuldi and þolemod. *c* **1200** ORMIN 1186 Ure Laferrd Jesu Crist..Toc *þildiliȝ wiþþutenn bracc, Þatt mann himm band wiþþ woȝhe. *a* **1225** *Ancr. R.* 106 He þolede þuldeliche þet te Giws dutten..his deorewurde muð mid hore dreori fustes. *a* **1225** *Juliana* 28 Þuldeliche heo hit þolede.

**Thilk** (ðilk), *dem. adj.* and *pron. arch.* or *dial.* Forms: *α.* **3–5 þilke, 3–7 thilke, 4–5 þylke, þilk, 4–7 thylke, 5 thylk, (6 thailk), 4– thilk.** *β.* **3–5 þulke**(*ü*), **5 þulk, 4–5 þelke.** *γ.* **3–5 þike, 4 þyke, þeke, þuke, 4–5 thike, thyke, theke, 5 thik, 6 þieke; 9** *dial.* **thik, thic, thick, thek, thuck, thicky.** [ME. *þilke*, known *a* 1300; app. f. *þe*, THE + *ilce*, ILK same, meaning *the* or *that same*; in some of the quots. *þe ilke* or *þet ilke* occurs as a MS. variant.

This analysis suits the form *þilke*, but does not explain the early southern *þülke* and the Kentish *þelke*, which naturally indicate an OE. **þylce*. Can there have been a confusion in the south between *þilke* and late OE. *þylc* for *þyllic*, THELLICH?

(*Thick* (ðik) is in dialect use from Cornwall and Hants to Worcester and Hereford; and also in Pembroke, Glamorgan, and Wexford. In many parts it has also the form *thicky, thickee*, or *thicka*. It generally means 'that', but in some parts 'this', in which case it is contrasted with *thuck, thock*, or *thack* = that. It is sometimes indefinite, and has to be made definite, as *thick here*, this, *thick there*, that. In Somerset and Dorset, *thick* and *theäse* are used only of individual shaped things, as a man or tree, while *that* and *this* are used of formless substances in the mass, as flour, milk, marble. See *Eng. Dial. Dict.*)]

**A.** *adj.* The very (thing, person, etc.) mentioned or indicated; the same; that; this.

*a* **1225** *Ancr. R.* 68 Iðen ilke huse [*MS. C.* in þilke hus]. *a* **1300** *Floriz & Bl.* 54 So blisful him þuȝte þilke steuene. *c* **1330** R. BRUNNE *Chron. Wace* (Rolls) 381 Ascaneus..gat a child Cycillius; Þylke Cycylli gat þat man Brutus. *c* **1374** CHAUCER *Boeth.* III. pr. x. 73 (Camb. MS.) It semeth þat þilke same thing be most desyred. *a* **1425** *Cursor M.* 11386 (Trin.) And comen to crist þilke day [*C., G.* þat ilk dai]. *c* **1449** PECOCK *Repr.* 235 Neither in thilk hil neither in Ierusalem. **1513** DOUGLAS *Æneis* I. Prol. 134 Thilk werk tuelf ȝeris first was in making eik. **1579** SPENSER *Sheph. Cal.* Jan. 61, I loue thilke lasse, (alas why doe I loue?). *a* **1643** CARTWRIGHT *Ordinary* II. ii, Dan Cupido Sure sent thylke sweven to mine head. **1724** DE FOE *Mem. Cavalier* (1840) 236 Says he, in a broad north-country tone, 'whar hast thou thilk horse?'

*β. c* **1290** *St. Brandan* 519 in *S. Eng. Leg.* 234 Þo tornede þe wynd in-to þe North,..In þulke side stronge Inouȝ. *a* **1300** *Floriz & Bl.* 432 Þulke terme him þuȝte long. *c* **1315** SHOREHAM vii. 133 And þelke sone ȝet naþeles Ryȝt ase þe fader hys endeles. **1387** TREVISA *Higden* (Rolls) V. 83 (MS. γ) Þulke Decius. *Ibid.* VI. 303 Unlawful wedlok.. with þelke Iuditha. *c* **1400** *R. Gloucester's Chron.* (Rolls) 3771 Þe men of norweye..adde ymade anoþer mon king of þe [*MS. α* þelke] londe. *a* **1425** *Cursor M.* 11417 (Trin.) Þulke [*Laud* thilk, *Cott. & Gött.* þis ilk] sterre hem coom to warn.

*γ.* **1303** R. BRUNNE *Handl. Synne* 6151 Syn þat þyke pore ermyte was yn drede for so lyte. *c* **1320** *Cast. Love* (Halliw.) 747 Ne never wes but thyke [*v.r.* þulke] oon. *c* **1410** *Master of Game* (MS. Digby 182) xxxv, Hemm þat shulde haue parte of þike deere. **1432–50** tr. *Higden* (Rolls) II. 449 Theke parte scholde haue þe victory. **1439** in *Ancestor* July (1904) 16 That every day in thik month the vij tapres brenne. *c* **1440** LOVELICH *Merlin* 12104 The tothyr cyte..hindicam hyghte at thyke tyme tho. **1553** *Respublica* III. iii, Þieke same waie goeth the hare. **1820** COBBETT *Gram. Eng. Lang.* xvii. (1847) 109 When we hear a Hampshire ploughboy say '[She] have giv'd I thick handkercher'. **1874** T. HARDY *Far fr. Madding Crowd* II. 289 To ho and hanker after thik woman in the way a do. **1898** E. PHILLPOTTS *Child. of Mist* I. iii. 28 'Tis thicky auld Muscovite duck, roostin' on his lil island. **1909** *Westm. Gaz.* 7 Aug. 2/2 Do 'ee mind thic time, Daddy, when you an' me catched gert lobsters?

† **b.** With plural sb.: These; those. *Obs.*

*c* **1275** LAY. 1284 Þe strengest þe weren in þilke daies [*c* **1205** o þon dawen]. **1387** TREVISA *Higden* (Rolls) I. 49 Of þilke mouþes þe see of myddel erþe bygynneþ. *c* **1420** *Chron. Vilod.* 3000 Þat þulke relekes nolde neuer go þen a-way. *c* **1489** CAXTON *Sonnes of Aymon* xxviii. 577 Wythoute ye had more helpe than thilke knaves.

**B.** *pron.* That (or this) person or thing.

*c* **1275** *Passion our Lord* 110 in *O. E. Misc.* 40 Mayster am ich þilke þat þe wile so dyhte. *c* **1300** *Harrow. Hell* 135 Þilke þat nulleþ aȝeyn hem stonde. *c* **1386** CHAUCER *Pars. T.* ¶ 32 Pryuee penaunce is thilke that men doon alday for priuee synnes. **1413** *Pilgr. Sowle* (Caxton) I. xix. (1859) 19 Ful oftymes haue I warned the..as thylk that oueth the. *c* **1449** PECOCK *Repr.* II. xx. 273 Therfore chese the reder..whether this or thilk or bothe he wole holde. **1867** ROCK *Jim & Nell* vii, Britting o' thick an' crazing thack. **1880** JEFFERIES *Gt. Estate* x. 188 Thuck's our feyther's. **1885** *Househ. Words* 20 June 141/2, I cowd ha' sold thee thilk.

† **b.** *pl.* Those. *Obs.*

*c* **1330** R. BRUNNE *Chron. Wace* (Rolls) 7341 Þulke of twenty wynter elde. **1370–80** *XI Pains of Hell* 113 in *O. E. Misc.* 226 Þo þat weren vp to þe briȝes In þat flod.. Þulke weore glade of þe mischeef. **1401** J. SKYDMORE in Ellis *Orig. Lett.* Ser. II. I. 20 To all thilke that ye suppose wol take this mater to hert. *a* **1450** MYRC *Par. Pr.* 687 Al thilk that with hold eny fredomes.

**Thill** [1] (þil). Also 5 þylle, thyl, 6 thyll. Cf. also FILL *sb.*[2] [Of uncertain origin: the 14th c. *þille*, *þylle* is identical in form with OE. *þille*, glossed *tabulāta*, *tabulāmen*, *tabulāmentum*, i.e. 'board, deal, boarding, flooring', but the sense 'pole or shaft' is so different that, without further evidence, it seems unsafe to connect them.

For the OE. *þille* see THEAL: none of the cognate words there cited show any approach to the mod. sense of *thill*.]

The pole or shaft by which a wagon, cart, or other vehicle is attached to the animal drawing it, *esp.* one of the pair of shafts between which a single draught animal is placed. Applied (*a*) in *sing.* to the single pole, rarely to the pair of shafts (*obs.*); (*b*) in *pl.* to the pair of shafts.

(*a*) **14..** *Voc.* in Wr.-Wülcker 615/35 *Temo*, a thylle. **14..** *Metrical Voc.* ibid. 628/20 *Reda*, thylle. *c* **1440** *Promp. Parv.* 491/1 Thylle, of a carte, *temo*. **1530** PALSGR. 280/2 Thyll of a carte, *le lymon*. **1611** COTGR., *Alimonner*, to put into..the thill of a cart. *Ibid.*, *Limon*,..the Thill of a waine, wagon, &c.; In which sense (because a Thill consists of two beames) it is most vsed in the Plurall number. **1688** R. HOLME *Armoury* III. xviii. (Roxb.) 139/1 The two side shafts make one thill. **1770** LANGHORNE *Plutarch* (1879) I. 256/2 That piece of wood with which they supported the thill of a waggon.

(*b*) *c* **1325** *Gloss. W. de Bibbesw.* in Wright *Voc.* 168 *Les lymouns*, the thilles. *c* **1400** *Laud Troy Bk.* 12820 Fals fortune of him now filles, He put him riȝt In hir thilles. *c* **1425** *Voc.* in Wr.-Wülcker 665/30 *Hic limo*, thyllys. **1707** MORTIMER *Husb.* (1721) I. 360 If the fore Wheels were as high as the hinder Wheels, and if the Thills were fixed under the Axis. **1890** O. CRAWFURD *Round the Cal. in Portugal* 104 The mule and the horse work between the thills of the cart and of the plough.

**b.** *attrib.* and *Comb.*, as *thill hame, harness, pin*; **thill-coupling, -jack, -tug**: see quot. 1877; **thill-saddle** = SADDLE *sb.* 3. Also THILL-HORSE.

**14..** *Nom.* in Wr.-Wülcker 727/33 *Hic limarillum*, a thylpyn. **1549** *Rutland MSS.* (1905) IV. 570 Thill hames, xl pare. **1776** in Hughes *Scour. White Horse* v, The same time a Thill harness will be run for by Cart-horses, &c. **1807** A. YOUNG *Agric. Essex* (1813) I. 107, 3 thill saddles, breechins, cruppers, &c. **1859** HUGHES *Scour. White Horse* v, Varmer Mifflin's mare..won a new Cart-saddle and thill-tugs. *Ibid.* vi, The great horses in their thill harness. **1877** KNIGHT *Dict. Mech.*, *Thill-coupling*, a device for fastening the shafts to the fore-axle. *Ibid.*, *Thill-jack*, a tool for attaching the thills of a carriage to the clips of the axle. *Ibid.*, *Thill-tug*, a leathern loop depending from the harness saddle to hold the shaft of a carriage.

**Thill** [2] (þil). [A local term of unknown origin; cf. TILL *sb.*, boulder-clay.] The thin stratum of fire-clay, etc. usually underlying a coal-seam; underclay; the floor or bottom of a seam of coal.

**1329–30** *Durham Acc. Rolls* (Surtees) 515 Quatuor bayardours portantibus Thill et focale in abbathiam per x septimanas, xxiij s. vj d. **1454–5** *Ibid.* 634 Operanti circa le ryddyng ac adquisicione de le Thill pro eodem furno. **1500–1** *Ibid.* 657 Pro iiij[or] plaustr. de lez thillstone, xvj d. **1708** J. C. *Compl. Collier* (1845) 39 Sometimes a Pit may happen to have a Hitch or Dipping of the Thill or Bottom of the Way. **1851** GREENWELL *Coal-trade Terms Northumb. & Durh.* 54 *Thill*, the floor of a seam of coal. **1867** W. W. SMYTH *Coal* 25 The floor, thill, or seat.., of the coal is an underclay. **1878** LEBOUR *Geol. Northumberland & Durh.* (1886) iii. 12 There is a strict analogy between these peat-marls and clays and the 'thills' or 'underclays' of many coals. **1881** *Borings & Sinkings* II. 4 (E.D.D.) Grey thill with water. **1887** WOODWARD *Geol. Eng. & Wales* (ed. 2) 179 The Underclay is known as 'Spavin' in Yorkshire; as 'Thill' in Durham; as 'Warrant' or 'Seat-earth' in Lancashire; and as 'Bottomstone' or 'Pouncin' in South Wales. **1894** HESLOP *Northumb. Gloss.* s.v., The underlayer of a coal seam frequently consists of a thin bed of fireclay; hence thin strata of that material are called *thill*, irrespective of their position with regard to a seam of coal.

**Thiller** (þi·ləɹ). Also 9 *dial.* **tiller**: see also FILLER [2]. [f. THILL [1] + -ER [1].] = next. Also *attrib.*

**1552** HULOET, Thyller of a carte, *veredus, di.* **1573** TUSSER *Husb.* (1878) 36 Hole bridle and saddle, whit lether and nall, With collers and harneis, for thiller and all. **1607** TOPSELL *Four-f. Beasts* (1658) 330 His Thiller fell and put his shoulder clean out of joynt. **1640** HEXHAM *Princ. Art Milit.* III. 5 A halfe Canon..vpon its carriage, drawne with seven couple of horse, and a Thiller horse. **1733** TULL *Horse-Hoeing Husb.* xxiii. 363 Limbers,..also called Shafts, Sharps, and Thills; from whence the Horse that goes in them is call'd a Thiller. **1893** *Stratford-on-Avon Herald* 24 Feb. 4/2, 3 Sets of Harness, Thillers' and Trace Gears.

**Thill-horse** (þi·l,hǭɹs). See also *fill-horse* s.v. FILL *sb.*[2] [f. THILL [1] + HORSE.] The shaft-horse or wheeler in a team.

*c* **1325** *Gloss. W. de Bibbesw.* in Wright *Voc.* 168 En lymouns [*gl.*] thilles va ly limounere [*gl.*] the thillo-hors. *c* **1425** *Voc.* in Wr.-Wülcker 665/32 *Hic uiredus*, thylhors. **1483** *Funeral Edw. IV* in *Lett. & Pap. Rich. III*, etc. (Rolls) I. 7 Upon the fore horse, and the thil horse sat ij chariot men. **1543** *Will J. England* (Somerset Ho.), Oon Carte, a Tyll horsse & foure Oxen. **1704** W. DERHAM in *Phil. Trans.* XXV. 1583 The Thill-Horse in Charles's Wain, called Alioth. **1876** BROWNING *Pacchiarotto* xxi, A Spare-Horse? Be rather a thill-horse.

**Thi·lly**, *a.* [f. THILL [2].] Of the nature of thill.

**1894** HESLOP *Northumbld. Gloss.* s.v. *Thill*, Any stone partaking of the nature of indurated clay is called *thilly*.

**Thimble** (þi·mb'l), *sb.* Forms: *α.* 1 **þýmel**, 5–6 **thymelle, -yl(le, thyme, themel, -elle, -yl(le, (5 thomelle, timmele), 9** *dial.* **thimmel.** *β.* 5 **thymbyl(l, thomble, 6 thymble, -bel(l, -bil(l, thumble, (tymble), 6–7 thimbell, 6– thimble.** [OE. *þýmel*, f. *þúma* THUMB + *-el*, -LE, suffix forming names of instruments: cf. *handle*. The later Eng. form has developed a *b* after *m*, as in *humble*, *nimble*, etc. ON., *þumall* meant the thumb of a glove; perh. a leather thumbstall was the earliest form of thimble; metal thimbles were app. introduced in the 17th c.]

† **1.** A sheath or covering for the thumb or finger; a fingerstall. *Obs.* (Only OE.)

*c* **1000** *Sax. Leechd.* II. 150 Wyrc þonne þymel to.

**2.** A bell-shaped sheath of metal (formerly of leather) worn on the end of the finger to push the needle in sewing.

*Tailor's, upholsterer's*, etc. *thimble*, a similar metal sheath open at both ends; *sail-maker's thimble* = PALM *sb.*[2] 5. *Knight of the thimble*, a tailor: see KNIGHT *sb.* 12 c.

*α. c* **1412** HOCCLEVE *De Reg. Princ.* 682 Look whedir In þis purs þer be any croyse or crouche, Sauf nedel and þrede, & themel [*MS. Reg.* thymelle] of leþer. **14..** *Voc.* in Wr.-Wülcker 578/29 *Digitale*, a themyl. **1483** *Cath. Angl.* 383/1 A Themelle (*A.* Thymbylle, Thymle). **1488** *Acc. Ld. High Treas. Scot.* I. 80 A thing of gold with a top like a timmele. *a* **1568** in *Bannatyne Poems* (Hunter. Cl.) 396 With elwand, scheir and thymmill.

*β. c* **1440** *Promp. Parv.* 491/1 Thymbyl, *theca*,..*digita*. **14..** *Debate Carpenter's Tools* 18 in Hazl. *E. P. P.* I. 80 3is, 3is, seyd the wymbylle, I ame als rounde as a thymbyll. **1530** PALSGR. 280/2 Thymble to sowe with, *deyl*. **1591** FLORIO *2nd Fruites* 5, I haue neither needle, thred, nor thimble. **1664** POWER *Exp. Philos.* I. 5 The Common Fly.. her eyes are..most neatly dimpled with innumerable little cavities like a small grater or thimble. **1700** CONGREVE *Way of World* III. iii, Hast thou ne'er a brass thimble clinking in thy pocket? **1793** *Girlhood M. J. Holroyd* (1896) 253, I have worked with my Thimble, and like it extremely. **1812** [see KNIGHT *sb.* 12 c]. **1841** MOORE *Young Jessica* i, The safest shield against the darts Of Cupid, is Minerva's thimble.

**b.** *Thimble and Bodkin Army* (Eng. Hist.): a nickname of the Parliamentary Army of the Civil War: see quots.

**1647** MAY *Hist. Parl.* II. vi. 97 The poorer sort, like that Widow in the Gospel, presented their Mites also; insomuch that it was a common Jeer of men disaffected to the Cause, to call it the Thimble- and Bodkin-Army. **1884** DOWELL *Taxes in Eng.* II. i. 3 On the parliamentary side the subscriptions of silver offerings included even such little personal articles as those that suggested the term, the 'Thimble and Bodkin' army.

**c.** A thimble or similar article as used by a thimblerigger: see THIMBLERIG 1.

**1716** GAY *Trivia* II. 166 Nor try the Thimble's Cheats. **1742** FIELDING *Jos. Andrews* II. iii, A person travelling to a neighbouring fair with the thimble and button. **1838** DICKENS *Nich. Nick.* l, Gathered round a pea and thimble table. **1909** *Q. Rev.* July 173 A conjuror..astonishing a simple audience with the pea-and-thimble trick.

**3.** The ring or socket in the heel of a gate which turns on the hook or pin in the gate-post. *local.*

**1550** *Hawkhurst Ch. Acc.* in *Archæol. Cantiana* V. 64 For a thymble to the churche gate ij[d]. **1627** *MS. Acc. St. John's Hosp., Canterb.*, For ij thimbles for the beane garden gate xvj d. **1804** *Trans. Soc. Arts* XXII. 83 The upper thimble should be fixed..nearer the farther side of the heel of the gate than the lower thimble. **1881** *Leicestersh. Gloss.*

**4.** *Naut.* A broad ring of metal, having a concave outer surface, around which the end of a rope is spliced, so that the thimble forms an eye to the rope.

**1711** W. SUTHERLAND *Shipbuild. Assist.* 132 Thimbles, large..34. Ordinary..118. **1775** FALCK *Day's Diving Vessel* 50 Each cable has a large thimble spliced in at one end, through which each alternate cable is reeved. **1860** *Merc. M. Mag.* VII. 113 A leach-line is..carried through thimbles.

**5.** In various technical applications. **a.** *Mech.* A ring, tube, or similar part, e.g. a sleeve, bushing, ferrule, etc.; often in comb., as *thimble-coupling*, *-joint*, etc.: see 9. **b.** The outer casing of a rifle-ball. **c.** *Pottery*: A rest for placing the ware during glost-firing. **d.** *Dentistry*: see quot. **e.** A cone of fat-free paper used in a fat-extraction apparatus. **f.** = *thimble-rubber* in 9. **g.** See quot.

**a. 1789** *Trans. Soc. Arts* VII. 179 Thimbles made of wire, twisted in the slit of the harpoon. **1831** J. HOLLAND *Manuf. Metal* I. 184 Fitting into the holes bushes or thimbles to give them the greater strength. **1877** KNIGHT *Dict. Mech., Thimble*...3. (*Machinery*.) *a.* A sleeve or tube through which a bolt passes, and which may act as a stay. *b.* A ferrule to expand a tube; specifically, a ferrule for boiler-tubes. 4. A sleeve around a stove-pipe when it passes through a wall or ceiling. **1881** GREENER *Gun* 84 The charge is put in a small steel thimble. **b.** *c* **1860** H. STUART *Seaman's Catech.* 11 The thimble expands and rifles the ball. **1900** *Brit. Med. Jrnl.* No. 2053. 1156 The thimble or shell of the Mauser and Lee-Metford. *Ibid.*, The core is of hardened lead, and the thimble composed of copper and nickel. **c. 1901** [see *thimble-picker* in 9]. **1910** *Rep. Lead Comm.* (Parl. Pap. Eng.), Placing the ware on rests with pointed projections..'Thimbles' similar in shape to a sewing thimble,..provided with a single horn. **d. 1877** KNIGHT *Dict. Mech.* 2554/1 The extension thimble of the dentist is a prong on the end of the thimble, used to reach into the mouth to hold the foil or a compress, while operating on the teeth. **e. 1901** *Jrnl. Exper. Med.* 25 Mar. 515 This residue was then ground up with sand, placed in a fat-extraction thimble and extracted again. **f. 1909** *Cent. Dict. Suppl.*, *Thimble*,..*pl.*, a trade-name for crude india-rubber from the lower Kongo and Loanda in small balls of a gray color, darker outside. **g. 1541** R. COPLAND *Guydon's Quest. Chirurg.* Liij, Thyrdly a seame incarnatyfe is made with egal themylles made of towe well wrythen & sklenderly.

**6.** Applied (usually in *pl.*) to certain flowers and plants, or parts of them, e.g. (*a*) the Foxglove, also known as *Fairy* or *Witches' Thimbles*; (*b*) the Sea Campion; (*c*) the Harebell; (*d*) the cup of an acorn. See also *Lady's Thimble*, LADY *sb.* 17 b.

**1873** BROWNING *Red Cott. Nt.-cap* I. 150 Nor its fine thimble fits the acorn top. **1878** BRITTEN & HOLLAND *Plant-n.*, Fairy Thimbles, *Digitalis purpurea*. **1881** J. A. SIDEY in *Mod. Scot. Poets* 396 Whaur the witch thummles bloom. **1886** BRITTEN & H. *Plant-n.*, *Thimble*, (1) *Digitalis purpurea*..(2) *Silene maritima*. **1894** *Daily News* 28 Apr. 6/5 The tall foxglove, with its graduated 'thimbles'.

**7.** *Thieves' slang.* A watch.

**1812** in J. H. VAUX *Flash Dict.* **1834** W. H. AINSWORTH *Rookwood* III. v, My thimble of ridge. **1901** W. S. WALKER *In the Blood* xiii. 138 Silver money, and a watch and chain, or, in thieves' language, 'white-lot' and 'thimble and slang'.

**8.** = THIMBLEFUL.

**1841** HOOD *Tale of Trumpet* xii, [They] never swallowed a thimble the less Of something the Reader is left to guess. **1865** BUSHNELL *Vicar. Sacr.* Introd. (1868) 24 Such thimbles of meaning as can be confidently managed.

**9.** *attrib.* and *Comb.*, as *thimble-case, -finger, -maker, -top*; *thimble-crowned, -like, -sealed, -shaped, -sized* adjs.; **thimble-belt**, a kind of cartridge-belt; **thimble-berry** (**thimble blackberry**), the black raspberry of America, *Rubus occidentalis*, so called from the shape of its receptacle; **thimble-coupling**: see quot.; **thimble-grater**, a species of gastropod shell; **thimble-joint**: see quot.; **thimble lily**, a name of the Australian liliaceous plant *Blandfordia nobilis*, with flowers in racemes; **thimble-limpet**, a West Indian species of limpet, so called from its shape; **thimble - man** = THIMBLERIGGER; **thimble-picker**, a young person employed in a pottery to pick from among the used thimbles (see sense 5 c) those that can be used a second time: so *thimble-picking*; **thimble-pie**: see quots.; **thimble-plating**, the formation of a cylindrical boiler-shell or a flue by successive slightly overlapping rings of plate; **thimble-rubber**: see quots.; **thimble-shift, -shifting**, the shifting of the pea from one thimble to another by a thimblerigger; also *fig.*; **thimble-skein**, a skein for an axle made in tubular form; **thimble-surface**, *Ceramics*, a surface of raised dots produced by closely pitting the interior of the mould; **thimble-weed**: see quot.

**1901** *N. Amer. Rev.* Feb. 231 The *thimble belt, used only by the Americans, is still preferred to the cartridge pouches of the others. **1854** Thoreau *Walden* xiv. (1886) 262 Strawberries, raspberries, *thimble-berries. **1883** Stevenson *Silverado Sq.* iii, A bower of green and tangled thicket ..where thimbleberry played the part of our English hawthorn. **1715** Lady M. W. Montagu *Basset-Table* 34 A myrtle foliage round the *thimble-case. **1882** Ogilvie, **Thimble-coupling*...In *mach.* a kind of permanent coupling, of which the coupling-box consists of a plain ring of metal, supposed to resemble a tailor's thimble. **1876** H. Gardner *Sunflowers, Dream of Noon* 48 Then she Raising a slender finger, *thimble-crowned, Beckoned him onwards. **1796** Burney *Mem. Metastasio* III. 277 A whitloe in the stitching or *thimble finger. *c* **1711** Petiver *Gazophyl.* vi. liv, Borneo *Thimble Grater... The outside is rough like a Grater, and hollow like a Cap or Thimble. **1877** Knight *Dict. Mech.*, **Thimble-joint*, a sleeve-joint, with an interior packing to keep the joints of pipes tight during expansion and contraction. **1899** *Allbutt's Syst. Med.* VIII. 602 The minute honey-combed, *thimble-like appearance of its surface. **1883** Guilfoyle *Catal. Plants Melbourne Bot. Gard.* 22 *Blandfordia nobilis*..*Thimble Lily. *c* **1711** Petiver *Gazophyl.* Dec. viii. Tab. 80 Barbadoes *Thimble Limpet. **1654** *Nicholas Papers* (Camden) II. 116 For other his undertakinges [he] is a *thimble-maker.., a meere cheat that rambles up and doun, not worth on farthing. **1830** Gen. P. Thompson *Exerc.* (1842) I. 192 The army of *thimble-men from Doncaster is upon you. **1901** *Scotsman* 28 Mar. 9/1 Persons are returned ..as *thimble-pickers, without mentioning that they are directly engaged in making..earthenware. **1828** *Craven Gloss.*, **Thimble-pie*, a fillip with the thimble. **1882** Mozley *Remin.* II. cviii. 245, I had to sit under the lady's three-legged work table, receiving 'thimble-pie', that is a sharp rap with a thimble on the crown of my head. **1881** *Rep. Kew Gardens* 39/2 W. African rubber..appears as ..agglutinated masses of small cubes of which there are specimens in the Kew Museum under the name of *Thimble rubber. **1840** Thackeray *Catherine* i, The dirty scrap of paper, *thimble-sealed. **1867** *Thimble-shaped [see Thimble-eye]. **1905** *Daily News* 1 Aug. 4 [A bee's] thimble-shaped cell. **1834** *Hist.* in *Ann. Reg.* 90/1 About twenty per cent. was to be deducted from the tithe-owner [etc.]. This was *thimble-shift the first. **1834** Stanley in *Hansard's Parl. Deb.* 4 July XXIV. 1154 How was this deficiency to be made good to the State? Here, then, was one instance of his right hon. friend's *thimble-shifting. **1895** Clive Holland *Jap. Wife* (ed. 11) 121 The little silver pipe with its *thimble-sized bowl. **1874** Knight *Dict. Mech.* 144/2 *Arm*..the *axle-spindle*. When of wood, it is strengthened by metallic straps called skeins, and sometimes by a conical sheath called a *thimble-skein. **1879** H. Drummond in *Life* vii. (1899) 166 The spurts come up in little domes, some only the size of a *thimble-top. **1860** Bartlett *Dict. Amer.*, **Thimble-weed.* (*Rudbeckia.*)..Like the Thimble-berry, its receptacle resembles a thimble.

Hence **Thi·mble** *v.*, *intr.* to use a thimble, to sew; **Thi·mbling** *vbl. sb.* and *ppl. a.*, using a thimble in sewing; also = *thimblerigging*.

**1659** H. M. *Pair Spectacles Nation* 4 Cobling Hewson, Cooper, thimbling Barkstead, Bury, and the rest of their Confederates. **1780** Beckford *Italy* (1834) I. v. 38 Pretty sempstresses, warbling melodious hymns as they sat needling and thimbling at their windows above. **1856** J. Ballantine *Poems, Wee Raggit Laddie* xiv, Ilk thimblin' thievin' gamblin' diddler..Chase thee like fire. **1857** Borrow *Rom. Rye* xliv, If you have not sufficient capital, why do you engage in so deep a trade as thimbling?

**Thimbled** (þi·mb'ld), *a.* [f. Thimble + -ed [2].] Having, or furnished with, a thimble; in *thieves' slang*, wearing a watch.

**1812** J. H. Vaux *Flash Dict.*, *Thimbled*, having or wearing a watch. **1851** Hawthorne *Snow Image* (1879) 21 With her thimbled finger. **1884** *Pall Mall G.* 10 Dec. 3/2 Long before either Dutch or English thought of thimbles Chinese ladies were thimbled when they worked at their embroidery.

**Thimble-eye** (þi·mb'l,əi). [f. Thimble + Eye.] **a.** *Naut.* See quots. 1867, 1877. **b.** A fish, the Chub Mackerel, *Scomber colias*. So **Thimble-eyed** *a.*, having eyes like thimbles, as this fish.

**1867** Smyth *Sailor's Word-bk.*, *Thimble-eyes*, are thimble-shaped apertures in iron-plates where sheaves are not required; frequently used instead of dead-eyes for the top-mast-rigging, futtock-plates, and backstays in the channels. **1877** Knight *Dict. Mech.*, *Thimble-eye*,..an eye in a plate through which a rope is rove without a sheave. A dead-eye. **1888** Goode *Amer. Fishes* 196 The only other spotted fish which has been known to frequent our coast is the 'chub mackerel' or 'thimble eye'. **1891** *Cent. Dict.*, *Thimble-eyed*,..used of the chub-mackerel.

**Thimbleful** (þi·mb'l,ful). [f. Thimble + -ful.] As much as a thimble will hold; hence, a small quantity, esp. of wine or spirits; a dram; also *fig.* of something immaterial.

**1607** Markham *Caval.* ii. (1617) 120 Take halfe a thimble-ful of Gunpowder. **1622** Mabbe tr. *Aleman's Guzman d'Alf.* i. 23 By eating by ounces, and drinking by thimblefuls, they liue by drams. **1760** Foote *Minor* i. Wks. 1799 I. 248 Wou'd you take another thimbleful, Mrs. Cole? **1789** Wolcott (P. Pindar) *Expost. Odes* xi, Now can't I give a thimblefull of Praise. **1889** Jessopp *Coming of Friars* ii. 93 Cordials were..on special occasions dealt out in thimblefuls. **1894** Helen M. Gougar in *Voice* (N.Y.) 31 May, Anybody with a thimbleful of political or reform sense knows.

**Thimblerig** (þi·mb'l,rig), *sb.* [f. Thimble + Rig *sb.*[5] 2; *lit.* 'thimble-trick'.]

**1.** A swindling game usually played with three thimbles (see Thimble 2 c) and a pea which was ostensibly placed under one of them; the sharper then challenging the bystanders to guess under which the pea had been placed, and to bet on their choice; a cheat similar to the *three-card trick*.

**1825** Hone *Every-day Bk.* I. 768 An unfair game known among the frequenters of races and fairs by the name of 'the thimble rig'. **1836** T. Hook *G. Gurney* vii, I will start alone, and appear to know no more of you, than one of the cads of the thimble-rig knows of the pea-holder. **1856** J. D. Chambers *Strictures on Judgm. in Westerton v. Liddell* 139 *note*, The manipulations of a sharper with cups and balls on his gambling table, commonly called *thimblerig*. **1893** Leland *Mem.* I. 13.

*attrib.* and *Comb.* **1834** Littleton in *Hansard's Parl. Deb.* 4 July, XXIV. 1206 His right hon. friend (Mr. Stanley) ..had chosen to describe him (Mr. Littleton) as a thimble-rig player, in consequence of the changes that he had made in the clauses of that Bill. **1856** T. A. Trollope *Girlhd. Cath. de Med.* Notes 352 A good deal of confusion as to the dates of these thimblerig-like transactions exists in the narratives of the historians. **1886** C. E. Pascoe *London of To-day* xviii. (ed. 3) 157 Epsom Downs... There are.. tumblers, jugglers, boxers, thimble-rig men.

**2.** = Thimblerigger.

**1839** *Fraser's Mag.* XX. 355 Greatly applauded by all the thimblerigs of the fauxbourgs.

**Thi·mblerig**, *v.* [f. prec.: app. first used in vbl. sb. and pr. pple.] *intr.* To practise the cheat of the thimblerig; also *fig.* to cheat in a juggling manner or as with sleight of hand. **b.** *trans.* To manipulate (a matter or thing) in this manner. So **Thi·mblerigged** (-rigd) *ppl. a.*, duped by the game of thimblerig; disturbed or affected by thimblerigging, as a market; = Rigged *ppl. a.*[2]; **Thi·mblerigging** *vbl. sb.* and *ppl. a.*

**1839** Thackeray *Catherine* i, Don't let us have any juggling and thimblerigging with virtue and vice. **1840** — *Cruikshank* Wks. 1900 XIII. 310 The different degrees of rascality, as exhibited in each face of the thimblerigging trio. *Ibid.*, Is any man so blind that he cannot see the exact face that is writhing under the thimblerigged hero's hat? **1887** Frith *Autobiog.* I. xxi. 271 Gambling tents and thimble-rigging..had not then been stopped by the police. **1889** Mivart *Orig. Hum. Reason* 92 That 'intellectual thimble-rigging' which all men of the sensist school..must perform. **1892** *Labour Commission* Gloss., *Thimblerigged*, an expression in general use descriptive of speculative operations in the stock, produce, or other markets by combination for other than legitimate trade or market requirements. **1899** *Daily News* 31 Jan. 5/3 M. Lebret passes quickly over the legal aspect of the case—thimblerigs it so to speak.

**Thimblerigger** (þi·mb'l,ri:gəɪ). [f. Thimblerig *sb.* + -er [1].] A professional sharper who cheats by thimblerigging; also *transf.* one who cheats by means of tricks, or juggles with phrases, etc.

**1831** *Lincoln Herald* 7 Oct. 4/4 An altercation took place between some countrymen and the thimble-riggers, on a charge of cheating. **1871** L. Stephen *Playgr. Eur.* ix. (1894) 202 A cross between a prizefighter and a thimble-rigger. **1891** T. Hardy *Tess* xviii, A firm believer—not as the phrase is now elusively construed by theological thimble-riggers in the Church and out of it.

Hence **Thi·mbleri·ggery**, thimblerigging.

**1841** *Blackw. Mag.* L. 178 Lying and thimbleriggery assume high privilege. **1841** R. Oastler *Fleet Papers* I. l. 399 The noble art of 'thimble-riggery'.

**Thimbling**, *vbl. sb.* and *ppl. a.*: see Thimble *v.*

**Thime**, obs. form of Thyme.

**Thin** (þin), *a.* (*sb.*) and *adv.* Forms: 1 þynne, þinne, þyn, þin, 3–5 þunne, 3–6 thyn, 4 þenne, 4–6 thynne, (4 thyne, 5 thynn), 4–7 thinn(e, (4–5 thine), 6– thin. [OE. *þynne* = OFris. *thenne, *thinne (WFris. *ten, tēn, tin*); OLG. **þunni* (MLG. *dunne*, MDu. *dunne, dinne*, Du. *dun*), OHG. *dunni* (MHG. *dünne*, G. *dünn*), in Gothic **þunnu-s*, ON. *þunnr* (Sw. *tunn*, Da. *tynd*):—OTeut. **þunnu-z*, fem. **þunnī*, with *nu* from *nw*, in Indo-Eur. **tnús*, fem. **tnwī*, from weak grade of ablaut stem *ten-, ton-, tn-* to stretch (cf. Skr. *tanús*, L. *tenuis*).]

**A.** *adj.*

**I. 1.** Having relatively little extension between opposite surfaces; of little thickness or depth. Opposed to Thick *a.* 1.

*a* **900** tr. *Bæda's Hist.* v. vi. (1890) 400 Stan..mid ðinre tyrf bewrizen. *c* **1000** *Sax. Leechd.* I. 238 Ðeos wyrt.. hafað þynne leaf. *c* **1020** *Rule St. Benet* lv. (Logeman) 91 Culam on wintre þicce on sumere þinne. *a* **1300** *Cursor M.* 1673 (Cott.) Wit pike þou lok it be noght thyn [*v. rr.* þinne, thine, þynne]. *a* **1310** in Wright *Lyric P.* x. 37 Betere is were thunne boute laste, Then syde robes ant synke into synne. **1387** Trevisa *Higden* (Rolls) I. 405 Brood cakes, round and þynne. **1508** Dunbar *Tua Mariit Wemen* 23 With curches..of kirsp cleir and thin. **1530** Palsgr. 280/2 Thyn skynne, *tenue peau*. **1638** Junius *Paint. Ancients* 227 We doe not make our plate so thinne as to break it. **1710** J. Clarke *Rohault's Nat. Phil.* (1729) I. 215 A Glass that is thinner in the Middle than at the Edges. **1802** Playfair *Illustr. Hutton. Th.* 294 The thinnest part of that rock ..is still covered by the strata. **1887** B. V. Head *Hist. Numorum* 697 The coins of the Sassanian monarchs are thin, flat, and neatly executed.

**b.** Of small cross section in proportion to length; slender, tenuous, attenuated. (Usually said of a thing more or less cylindrical, as a wire, rod, branch, stem, stock, trunk, limb.)

*a* **1425** tr. *Arderne's Treat. Fistula* 59 If it be bi reson of þe membre, þat is for þe membre is to ouer þinne. **1570** Levins *Manip.* 133/24 Thinne, *gracilis, tenuis*. **1665** Sir T. Herbert *Trav.* (1677) 303 Their Harquebuz is longer than ours, but thinner. **1776** Withering *Brit. Plants* (1796) IV. 118 Branches..of equal thickness, nay rather thinner at their origin. **1884** Bower & Scott *De Bary's Phaner.* 426 In the cortex of the thin stem. **1885** Watson & Burbury *Math. Th. Electr. & Magn.* I. 95 The connection between them being a very thin wire.

**c.** *spec.* Having little flesh; lean, spare, not fat or plump. Also of ears of corn.

*c* **1000** *Sax. Leechd.* II. 206 Ne mæȝ him se lichoma batian ac he bið blac & þynne & acolod. *c* **1050** *Gloss.* in Wr.-Wülcker 415/27 *Galbus*, þynne monn. *a* **1327** *Maximon* iv. in *Rel. Ant.* I. 120 Care and kunde of elde Maketh mi body felde..Ant mi body thunne Such is worldes wunne. **1382** Wyclif *Gen.* xli. 6 Seuene eerys..thinne and smytun with meldew, weren growun. **1535** Coverdale *Gen.* xli. 3 Seuen kyne,..thynne, euell fauoured, and leenfleshed. **1617** Moryson *Itin.* ii. 46 His face grew thinne, his ruddy colour failed. **1697** Dryden *Virg. Past.* iii. 156 My Flocks..yet look so thin, Their Bones are barely cover'd with their Skin. **1794** Mrs. Radcliffe *Myst. Udolpho* xlix, You look so pale now, and so thin, too. **1805–6** Coleridge *Three Graves* iv. xi, Oft she said, I'm not grown thin! And then her wrist she spanned. **1865** Miss Braddon *Sir Jasper* iv. 37 To have long thin white hands, all aglitter with diamond rings.

**d.** Penetrable by light or vision, like a thin veil; *fig.* easily 'seen through', transparent, flimsy, as a pretext or excuse. (Cf. some uses in 4 a.)

**1613** Shaks. *Hen. VIII*, v. iii. 125, I come not To heare such flattery now, and in my presence They [commendations] are too thin. **1662** Hibbert *Body Div.* i. 252 A lie is of a thin and transparent nature. **1851** Brimley *Ess., Wordsw.* 103 Under a thin disguise of name. **1860** Tyndall *Glac.* i. xiv. 94 Over the glacier hung a thin veil of fog. *a* **1904** A. Adams *Log Cowboy* xviii, He put up a thin excuse just like the rest. Any one could see through it.

**II. 2.** Consisting of or characterized by individual constituents or parts placed at relatively large intervals; not thick, dense, or bushy. Opposed to Thick *a.* 4.

**849** in Birch *Cart. Sax.* II. 40 In..sceaȝan ðær he ðynnest is. *c* **1000** Ælfric *Hom.* II. 466 Oft of ðinnum renscurum flewð seo eorðe. *c* **1290** *S. Eng. Leg.* I. 48/44 Bote þornes and þunne boskes. *c* **1400** Maundev. (Roxb.) xxvi. 126 Þe Tartarenes hase..lytill berdes and thynne. *c* **1440** *Promp. Parv.* 491/1 Thynne, as gresse, corne, wodys, ..*rarus*. **1573–80** Baret *Alv.* T 166 Thinne,..not thicke growen, or set,..*rarus*. **1617** Moryson *Itin.* ii. 45 [Lord Mountjoy's] haire was..thinne on his head. **1796** Morse *Amer. Geog.* I. 77 Indian population is thin; vast tracts.. are uninhabited. **1894** Doyle *Mem. S. Holmes* 49 A thin rain began to fall.

†**b.** Of the members of a collective group or class: Not numerous or abundant; scarce, rare, few, scanty. Opposed to Thick *a.* 5. *Obs.*

**1508** Kennedy *Flyting w. Dunbar* 350 Corspatrik..Thy forefader maid Irisch and Irisch men thin. **1573–80** Baret *Alv.* T 166 Thinne:..seld and not often, *rarus*: to waxe thin, to waxe a small number. **1638** Junius *Paint. Ancients* 188 Artificers also grew thinner and thinner, till none at length were left. *c* **1645** Howell *Lett.* (1650) I. 95 Gentry amongst them is very thin,..and coming to dwell in towns, they soon mingle with the merchants, and so degenerate. **1725** T. Thomas in *Portland Papers* VI. (Hist. MSS. Comm.) 109 Churches are very thin in this part of the World. [**1863** W. C. Baldwin *Afr. Hunting* ix. 405 Game of all sorts is as thin as deal boards.]

†**c.** Of a place: Sparsely occupied or peopled; with *of*, sparsely furnished or supplied with; thinly occupied or attended by. *Obs.*

**1621** Burton *Anat. Mel.* Democr. to Rdr. (1628) 52 Many Kingdomes are fertile, but thin of inhabitants. **1673** *Essex Papers* (Camden) I. 65 How thinn of Soldrs are ye Few Garrisons we keepe. **1693** *Humours Town* 51 You must be content with such as your thin Neighbourhood affords. **1711** Swift *Jrnl. to Stella* 24 Aug., The town being thin, I am less pestered with company. **1733** Tull *Horse-Hoeing Husb.* xi. 124 Both these Rows were Thin of Plants. **1797** *Encycl. Brit.* (ed. 3) VII. 528/1 Galicia..is but thin of people. **1800** Ht. Lee *Canterb. T.* (ed. 2) III. 89 Summer was now fast approaching, and the town was thin.

**d.** Of an assembly or body of people: Scantily furnished with members; thinly attended; not full.

**1647** Clarendon *Hist. Reb.* v. § 361 What had been..in a full House, rejected, was many times in a thin House.. resumed, and determined contrary to the former conclusions. **1660** Pepys *Diary* 2 Oct., There I found but a thin congregation already. **1703** *Lond. Gaz.* No. 3904/1 Their Battalions are thin and sickly. **1713** S. Sewall *Diary* 27 Oct., Buried with a very thin Funeral. **1746** Francis tr. *Horace's Art Poetry* 297 The little Theatre..To which a thin and pious Audience came. **1860–70** Stubbs *Lect. Europ. Hist.* i. ix. (1904) 119 In a very thin meeting, Ferdinand stated his view.

**3.** Of a liquid or a pasty substance: Of slight density or consistence; fluid; of air or vapour: not dense; rare, tenuous, subtile. Opp. to Thick *a.* 6.

*a* **900** tr. *Bæda's Hist.* iii. xix. [xxvii.] (1890) 244 Nemne medmicel hlafes mid þinre meolc. *a* **1000** *Boeth. Metr.* v. 6 Ær se þicca mist þynra weorðe. *c* **1000** *Sax. Leechd.* II. 314 Hrer on blede oþ þ hit sie þicce swa þynne briw. *c* **1375** *Sc. Leg. Saints* xxxii. (*Justin*) 735 Vndir it a fyre gert ma Til þat mater [pitch and brimstone] wes moltyne thyne. *c* **1430** *Two Cookery-bks.* 12 Late it be nowt to þikke ne to þinne, but as potage shulde be. **1530** Palsgr. 280/2 Thyn cloude in the ayre. **1621** Burton *Anat. Mel.* ii. ii. i. i. (1651) 232 Pure, thin, light water. **1667** Milton *P. L.* viii. 348 Fish..cannot change Thir Element to draw the thinner Aire. **1744** Berkeley *Siris* § 121 An exceeding thin volatile oil. **1850** *Young's Patent* in *Law Times Rep.* X. 862/1 Chalk, ground up with a little water into a thin paste.

**b.** *transf.* and *fig.* Wanting body or substance; unsubstantial; intangible.

**1610** SHAKS. *Temp.* IV. i. 150 These our actors..were all Spirits, and Are melted into Ayre, into thin Ayre. **1705** ADDISON *Italy* 3 The lab'ring Plow-man oft with Horror spies Thin airy Shapes that o'er the Furrows rise. **1724** R. WELTON *Chr. Faith & Pract.* 120 All the thin and airy delights of the world. **1892** WESTCOTT *Gospel of Life* 108 Man cannot live in the thin atmosphere of abstractions. **1907** *Edin. Rev.* Oct. 402 Logic is too thin and bloodless a thing to govern life.

**c.** Wanting depth or intensity; faint, weak, dim, pale. Formerly of light (*arch.*): in mod. use, of colours, painting, or the like.

**1649** LOVELACE *Poems* 90 Yet its Glory did appeare But thinne, because her eyes were neere. **1655** STANLEY *Hist. Philos.* II. (1701) 61/2 The Moon hath a light of her own: but very thin. **1875** FORTNUM *Maiolica* xiv. 156 The use of a bright yellow..in imitations of the golden lustre, and a thin green. **1893** HODGES *Elem. Photogr.* (1907) 102 Thin and rather weak negatives. **1894** *Athenæum* 3 Mar. 285/3 The figures are half-lengths, and executed in a thin, hard, and laborious manner.

**d.** Of sound: Wanting fullness, volume, or depth; weak and high-pitched; shrill and feeble.

**16..** DRYDEN (J.), I hear the groans of ghosts; Thin, hollow sounds, and lamentable screams. **1726** POPE *Odyss.* XXIV. 8 Trembling the Spectres glide, and plaintive vent Thin, hollow screams. **1824** LAMB *Elia* Ser. II. *Capt. Jackson*, Be dumb, thou thin accompanier of her thinner warble! *a* **1895** W. MORRIS in Mackail *Life* (1899) II. 314, I heard.. the trowels fall Upon the stone, a thin noise far away. **1901** *Scotsman* 15 Mar. 7/4 The possessor of the thinnest treble in the Irish quarter..piped tremulously.

**4.** *fig.* Deficient in substance or quality; poor; unsubstantial. **a.** Of immaterial things: Wanting in fullness, breadth, force, or vigour; scanty, insufficient; weak, feeble; slight; of little worth.

[*a* **900** tr. *Bæda's Hist.* v. xvii. [xix.] (1890) 462 Nemne ðynre eðunge anre ætywde þæt he lifes wæs. *c* **1000** *Sax. Leechd.* II. 84 Hwilc þ mægen sie & sio ȝecynd þæs lichoman, hwæþer hio sie strang.., þe hio sie hnesce & mearwe & þynne.] *a* **1225** *Ancr. R.* 144 Vre god þet is þunne—vre sunnen þet beoð so monie. *c* **1315** SHOREHAM iii. 272 Hare wyȝt [= wit] hys al to þenne. *c* **1330** R. BRUNNE *Chron. Wace* (Rolls) 113 My witte was oure thynne So strange speche to trauayle in. *c* **1374** CHAUCER *Boeth.* II. Met. vii. 47 (Camb. MS.) The thynne fame yit lastynge of hir ydel names, is marked with a fewe letterys. *c* **1425** ? LYDG. *Assembly of Gods* 1591 My brayne ys so thynne. **1545** ASCHAM *Toxoph.* (Arb.) 28 As thinne invention, as other poore men. **1580** H. GIFFORD *Posie Gillowflowers, Merrie Jest*, Yet was her wit but thin. **1658–9** *Burton's Diary* (1828) IV. 65 They are gallant in their persons, but thin in relations. **1844** KINGLAKE *Eöthen* vii. (1878) 96 Engaged in very thin conversation. **1888** *Daily News* 9 July 4/8 The apology is a very lame one—what our American cousins call 'thin'. **1890** *Spectator* 16 Aug. 221/2 This is about the thinnest travel-book we have ever read. **1894** *Westm. Gaz.* 5 Feb. 1/2 Really, has not this laudation of the old at the expense of the new become a little too thin?

**b.** Of diet or supplies: Scanty, meagre, spare; not full or rich; poor, low. Now *rare.*

*c* **1374** CHAUCER *Former Age* 36 Ther as vitayle is ek so skars and thinne [*v. r.* thynne]. *c* **1450** *St. Cuthbert* (Surtees) 5264 Bot vytayls were ful thynn. *c* **1485** *Digby Myst.* III. 1733 Yower spendyng is thyn. **1535** STEWART *Cron. Scot.* (Rolls) II. 618 Becaus he wes in his substance so thyn. **1596** SHAKS. *Tam. Shr.* IV. iv. 61 At so slender warning, You are like to haue a thin and slender pittance. **1648** CRASHAW *Steps to Temple* Wks. (1904) 82 Nor hath God a thinner Share. **1707** FLOYER *Physic. Pulse-Watch* 196 In these Fasting is necessary, or a thin Diet. **1826** DISRAELI *Viv. Grey* VI. i, Thin entertainment here, kind Sir.

**c.** *spec.* Of liquor: Without body; not strong or rich; of low alcoholic strength; weak. (Cf. 3.)

[**1377** LANGL. *P. Pl.* B. XIX. 398, I can selle Bothe dregges & draffe, and drawe it at on hole, þikke ale and þinne ale.] *c* **1440** *Alphabet of Tales* 6, I may not drynk your thyn ale. **1560** PILKINGTON *Expos. Aggeus* (1562) 90 Loke howe many of youre poore neighbours..drink thin drink. **1597** SHAKS. *2 Hen. IV*, IV. iii. 134 To forsweare thinne Potations, and to addict themselues to Sack. **1691** RAY *N. C. Words* 138 Thin drink, small Beer, *Cerevisia tenuis.* **1859** DICKENS *T. Two Cities* II. xv, Monsieur Defarge sold a very thin wine at the best of times.

**B.** *absol.* as *sb.*: mostly elliptical or nonce-uses. *Thin and thick*: see THICK AND THIN.

*c* **1350** *St. Jacob* 173 (xix.) in Horstmann *Altengl. Leg.* (1881) 99/1 Þai suld noght leue for thin ne thik Till þai war broght bath ded or quik. **1426** LYDG. *De Guil. Pilgr.* 11135, I [Youth] passe bothe thorgh thynne & thykke. **1895** G. ALLEN *Woman who did* (1906) 184 This very fact that she had always lived in the Thick of Things made a change to the Thin of Things only the more enchanting.

**C.** *adv.* **1.** = THINLY 1. † *To go thin*: to wear thin clothing, to be thinly clad (*obs.*).

*a* **1250** *Owl & Night.* 1529 Wel þunne isrud & ived wroþe. *a* **1610** HEALEY *Theophrastus* (1636) 11 Why hee goes so thinne, and why hee will not go better cloth'd? *a* **1631** DONNE *Serm.* xlv. 450 Spread we this a little thinner, and we shall better see through it. **1633** HERBERT *Temple, Praise* vii, My heart, Though press'd, runnes thin. **1652–62** HEYLIN *Cosmogr.* IV. (1682) 31 The people go extreme thin in the sharpest Winter. **1738** SWIFT *Pol. Conversat.* p. xliii, They ought to be husbanded better, and spread much thinner. **1806** A. HUNTER *Culina* (ed. 2) 194 Cut the chops very thin.

† **b.** In a poor or sparing manner. *Obs.*

**1607** TOPSELL *Four-f. Beasts* (1658) 325 Let the Horse be thin dieted, during his curing time.

**2.** = THINLY 2.

**1375** BARBOUR *Bruce* IV. 685 Bot þai prophetis so thyn ar sawin, Þat [etc.]. *c* **1386** CHAUCER *Knt.'s Prol.* 679 But thinne it lay, by colpons oon and oon. **1573–80** BARET *Alv.* T 167 Seldome: not oft: thinne: not thicke, *rare.* **1649** BLITHE *Eng. Improv. Impr.* (1653) To Husbandm., The earlier thou sowest, the thinner thou maiest sow thy winter corn. **1707** MORTIMER *Husb.* (1721) I. 34 To sow something thinner than ordinary. **1886** C. SCOTT *Sheep-Farming* 37 The thinner sheep are pastured the healthier they are.

**D.** Combinations. **I.** Of the adj.

**a.** Chiefly parasynthetic adjectives, as *thin-bedded, -bladed, -brained* (in sense A. 4 a), *-cheeked, -faced, -flanked,* † *-gaskined* (GASKIN[1] 2), *-haired, -leaved, -lipped, -rinded* († *rined*), *-soled, -stemmed,* etc. See also THIN-GUTTED, -SKINNED, -WALLED.

**1859** MURCHISON *Siluria* iv. (ed. 3) 75 We reach the *thin-bedded..flags. **1855** WHYTE MELVILLE *Gen. Bounce* ix, A *thin-bladed knife and two-pronged fork. **1598** MARSTON *Sco. Villanie* III. x, *Thin-brain'd Idiots, dull, vncapable. **1596** R. L[INCHE] *Diella* (1877) 74 In my *thin-cheekt face thou well maist see. **1633** T. ADAMS *Exp. 2 Peter* ii. 1 Away with that *thin-dawned profession. **1601** SHAKS. *Twel. N.* v. i. 213 A *thin fac'd knaue, a gull. **1899** CROCKETT *Kit Kennedy* xii. 88 A thin-faced..woman, with an air of being perpetually tired. **1649** G. DANIEL *Trinarch., Hen. V* clxiv, The *thin-film'd Bladder breakes. **1737** BRACKEN *Farriery Impr.* (1757) II. 102 Some Horses are so *thin Gascoign'd, that they will never look plump. **1398** TREVISA *Barth. De P. R.* XVIII. xv. (Bodl. MS.), The Bugle is..*þynne hered. **1697** DRYDEN *Virg. Georg.* II. 96 The *thin-leav'd Arbute Hazle Graffs receives. **1897** *Daily News* 2 Oct. 2/3 Cranes and herons and ibis and other *thin-legged water fowl. **1681** GREW *Musæum* I. VI. i. 130 The *Thin-Lip'd Wilk. **1907** H. WYNDHAM *Flare Footlights* vii, An unpleasant smile playing about the corners of his thin-lipped mouth. **1677** YARRANTON *Eng. Improv.* 120 Our Wheat is large, full-brested, and *thin-rined. **1805** DICKSON *Pract. Agric.* I. 572 The most plump and thinnest-rinded grain. **1682** OTWAY *Venice Preserved* III. ii, Cathars and Tooth Ach got By *thin-sol'd shoos. **1869** TOZER *Highl. Turkey* I. 315 An Albanian with his long *thin-stocked gun.

**b.** Special combinations and collocations: **thin-belly**, one who has a thin belly; in quot. *attrib.*; so **thin-bellied** *a.*, lean, hungry-looking; **thin coal**, coal found in shallow beds or seams: cf. *thick coal* s.v. THICK *a.* 12 b; **thin-headed** *a.*, having a thin or narrow head; *fig.* shallow-pated, silly; **thin miner, thin seam** (also *attrib.*), see quots.; **thin-worn** *a.*, made thin by wear.

**1588** SHAKS. *L. L. L.* III. i. 19 Your armes crost on your *thinbellie doublet. **1591** PERCIVAL *Span. Dict.*, *Trasijado*, lanke, *thinne bellied. **1855** J. PHILLIPS *Man. Geol.* 188 Strata and *thin coals. **1900** *Engineering Mag.* XIX. 717 In days gone by thin seams were worked by special thin coal miners. **1603** DEKKER *Wonderfull Yeare* A iij b, *Thin-headed fellowes that liue vpon the scraps of inuention. **1804** SHAW *Gen. Zool.* V. 237 Thin-headed Carp, *Cyprinus Leptocephalus.* **1892** *Labour Commission* Gloss., **Thin miners*, miners who get coal out of thin seams. **1883** GRESLEY *Gloss. Coal-mining*, **Thin Seams*,..coal seams (say) less than 3 feet in thickness. **1887** *Pall Mall G.* 5 Sept. 12/1 The coal-mining industry in the thin-seam districts. **1823** MRS. GRANT *Mem. & Corr.* (1844) III. 31 Easily she threw off the *thin-worn robe of mortality.

**II.** Of the adverb: with participles or adjectives, to which *thin* is now joined by a hyphen, or as a single word; forming adjs., usually of obvious meaning, unlimited in number, as, in sense 1, *thin-clad, -cut, -frozen, -laid, -lined, -pervading, -veiled, -wrought*; in sense 2, † *thin-bred, -descending, -flowing, -grown, -officered, -peopled, -set, -shot,* etc. See also THIN-SOWN, THIN-SPUN.

*a* **1400–50** *Alexander* 320 A berd as a besom with *thyn bred haris. **1690** LOCKE *Hum. Und.* IV. xvii. § 4 'Tis not safe..to go abroad *thin clad. **1851** CARLYLE *J. Sterling* I. ii. (1872) 11 A light *thin-flowing style of mirth. **1865** W. J. LINTON 3 *Englishmen, Alfred*, He..breaks a way through the *thin-frozen sludge. **1908** *Westm. Gaz.* 29 Sept. 4/2 Prices that need not stand in the way of the *thinnest-lined of purses. *a* **1687** PETTY *Pol. Arith.* i. (1690) 11 In *thin peopled places. **1647–9** G. DANIEL *Poems* Wks. (Grosart) II. 130 Hee, poore Swaine, in bare And *thin-Set Shades did Sing. **1812** CRABBE *Tales* x. 351 The burning sand, the fields of thin-set rye. **1642** H. MORE *Song of Soul* II. iii. I. xxiii, Their *thin-shot shadowings And lightned sides. **1538** ELYOT *Dict.*, *Leuidensis*, *thynne wrought, and of small substance.

**Thin** (þin), *v.*[1] [OE. *þynnian*, f. *þynne*, THIN *a.* Cf. OHG. *dunnên*, Ger. *dünnen*, MLG. *dunnen*, MDu. *dunnen, dinnen*, Du. *dunnen*, ON. *þynna* to thin.]

**1.** *trans.* To make thin; to reduce in thickness or depth; to spread or draw *out* in a thin layer or thread. *To thin off, down*: to diminish gradually to vanishing point.

*c* **900** *Bede Glosses* 80 in *O. E. Texts* 182 *Obtenuerað* (*t*), ðynnade. *c* **1000** ÆLFRIC *Saints' Lives* xxxiii. 236 And ne oncneow hi na for-þam heo wæs swiðe ȝeþynnod. **1482** *Monk of Evesham* (Arb.) 41 For the stature and forme of some of them was as hyt had be lessyd or thynnyde by tormentys. **1608** TOPSELL *Serpents* (1658) 616 To smooth and thin the skin. **1684** R. WALLER *Nat. Exper.* 117 The battered Silver (which being so little Ductile did not at all thin, and distend it self). **1727** *Philip Quarll* (1816) 56 Having resolved, as the summer approached, to thin his clothing by degrees. **1793** *Trans. Soc. Arts* V. 204 The two ends are to be thinned off in form of a wedge. **1891** G. MEREDITH *One of our Conq.* III. iv. 66 She..had thinned her lips for utterance of a desperate thing.

**b.** *fig.* (In quot. 1382 a literalism of translation.)

**1382** WYCLIF *Jer.* xxx. 19, Y shal glorifie them, and thei shuln not be thynned [*Vulg.* non attenuabuntur]. **1670** EACHARD *Cont. Clergy* 33 By this means he has usually so thinn'd his judgment. **1787** JEFFERSON *Writ.* (1859) II. 117 Real friends, whose affections are not thinned to cob-web. **1874** H. R. REYNOLDS *John Bapt.* viii. 497 To thin down the distinction between the mission, character, education, and position of John and those of Christ.

**2.** *intr.* To become thin or thinner; to decrease in thickness or depth. *To thin out* (*off, away*): to become gradually thinner until it disappears, as a layer or stratum. Also *fig.*

**1804** COLERIDGE *Lett., to D. Stuart* (1895) 475 A rock which thins as it rises up. **1830** LYELL *Princ. Geol.* I. 341 When a number of beds thin out gradually, and at different points. **1833** HERSCHEL *Astron.* viii. 256 The half-moon becomes a crescent, which thins off. **1851** *Jrnl. R. Agric. Soc.* XII. II. 473 In which direction the boulder clay appears to thin off. **1874** HARDY *Far fr. Madding Crowd* xxii, Men thin away to insignificance and oblivion. **1899** J. HUTCHINSON in *Arch. Surg.* X. 155 Their usual course is to cause the nail over them to thin and break down.

**b.** *spec.* To lose flesh; to become spare or lean.

**1870** *Pall Mall G.* 7 Sept. 11 During this troubled period he had thinned so as to seem a different man. **1893** *Chamb. Jrnl.* 19 Aug. 523/2 Her fresh comeliness left her; her face thinned down.

**3.** *trans.* To render less crowded or close by removing individuals; hence, to reduce in number.

**a.** With an assemblage of individuals as object.

*c* **1440** *Promp. Parv.* 491/1 Thynnyn, or make thynne, as wodys, cornys, gresse. **1687** DRYDEN *Hind & P.* II. 243 As when the cause goes hard, the guilty man Excepts, and thins his jury all he can. **1699** S. SEWALL *Diary* 28 Dec., Our Meeting was pretty much thin'd by it. **1832** HT. MARTINEAU *Homes Abroad* i. 12 To thin our population. **1855** MACAULAY *Hist. Eng.* xvi. III. 681 The malady which had thinned the ranks of Schomberg's army at Dundalk.

**b.** With the individuals as object.

**1697** DRYDEN *Virg. Georg.* II. 554 T' unload the Branches, or the Leaves to thin, That suck the Vital Moisture of the Vine. **1786** ABERCROMBIE *Gard. Assist.* 257 Hoe and thin turneps. **1850** *Florist* Aug., Thin out superfluous shoots. **1856** DICKENS *Lett.* (1880) I. 439 Your friend..has thinned the trees. **1890** *Spectator* 19 Apr., For reducing the new expenditure on drink, and for thinning-off the public-houses in the rural districts.

**c.** To render (a place) less closely or numerously occupied by the removal *of* occupants.

**1743** BLAIR *Grave* 213 Who..in a cruel wantonness of power Thinn'd states of half their people. **1774** GOLDSM. *Nat. Hist.* (1776) III. 400 It would soon thin the forest of every other living creature. **1856** MERIVALE *Rom. Emp.* IV. xl. 507 The Forum and other public places were deliberately thinned of their overgrowths of sculpture. **1905** *Daily Chron.* 24 Aug. 4/7 A head already thinned of hair.

**4.** *intr.* Of a place: To become less full or crowded; of a crowd: to become less numerous.

**1779** EARL CARLISLE in Jesse *Selwyn & Contemp.* (1844) IV. 180 The town begins to thin, though Parliament is still sitting. **1805** HAN. MORE in Roberts *Mem.* (1835) III. 240 No resident minister;..the church of course thins. **1828** *Examiner* 129/1 The band..is steadily thinning. **1848** DICKENS *Dombey* iv, 'The streets have thinned', as Mr. Gills says, 'very much'. *c* **1860** FABER *Hymn*, '*After a Death*' xvii, My world of friends thins round me fast. **1897** H. DRUMMOND *Ideal Life* 101 The crowd thinned.

**5.** *trans.* To make less thick, dense, or viscid; to dilute. Also *fig.*

*c* **1000** *Sax. Leechd.* II. 194 Þæt ofstandene þicce slipiȝe horh þu scealt..wyrman & þynnian. *a* **1340** HAMPOLE *Psalter, Cant.* 497 Myn eghyn ere thynyd, that is..purgid of vile lustis..and made sutil. *c* **1440** *Promp. Parv.* 491/2 Thynnyn, or make thynne, as lycurys, *tenuo.* **1605** TIMME *Quersit.* III. 182 This water..cutteth and thinneth grosse matters. **1796** MRS. GLASSE *Cookery* xxi. 336 Mix half a pound of best flour, and thin it with damask-rose-water. **1880** J. CAIRD *Philos. Relig.* ii. 60 By thinning down the idea of God to an abstraction which would embrace under a common head the rudest fetishism and the spiritual theism of Christianity. **1890** ABNEY *Photogr.* (ed. 6) 76 The..liquid is..thinned down to proper fluidity.

**6.** *intr.* To become less dense or consistent; to grow fluid, tenuous, or rare.

**1834** M. SCOTT in *Blackw. Mag.* XXXV. 900 Gradually the figure, without changing its position, thinned, and anon ..the stars were seen through it. **1884** S. COX *Miracles* 63 The haze of difficulty which enshrouds them thins.

† **Thin**, *v.*[2] *Obs. rare.* [f. OE. *þennan* (*þænnan*) and *þenian* = OS. *thenian*, OHG. *dennen, denen* (G. *dehnen*), ON. *þenja*, Goth. *uf*)*þanjan* :—OTeut. **þanjan-*, factitive vb. from Indo-Eur. root **ten-* to stretch.] *trans.* To stretch out, extend.

The existence of this in ME. is doubtful: the OE. form would properly give ME. *þenne* or *þene*; *þinne* is perh. an error.

*c* **1000** *Ags. Ps.* (Th.) cxlii[i]. 6 Ic mine hande to þe holde þenede. *c* **1000** *Sax. Leechd.* III. 22 Þænne þone swiðran earm swa he swiþast mæȝe. *a* **1300** *E. E. Psalter* cvii. 10 [cviii. 9] In Ydume sal i þinne [WYCLIF strecchen] mi scho.

**Thin**, obs. f. THINE; var. THYNE, *Obs.*, thence.

**Thine** (ðəin), *poss. pron.* Forms: 1–4 **ðín, þín,** 4–5 **þyn, þine, þyne, thin, thyn,** 4–6 **thyne,** (2, 4 **tin,** 3 **ten,** 3–4 **tine,** 5 **tyn**), 4– **thine.** [OE. *ðín, þín*, used as genitive case of *ðú*, THOU, and as possess. adj. = OFris., OS *thîn* (MDu. *dijn*, MLG., LG. *dîn*), OHG. *dîn* (MHG. *dîn*, G. *dein*), ON. *þín* (*þín-n*, etc.) (Norw., Sw., Da. *dîn*), Goth. gen. *þeina*, poss. pron. *þeins*, etc.:—OTeut. **þîno-*, deriv. of stem *þe-*: see THEE.]

For restriction of use see note to THOU *pron.* 1.

† **I. 1.** Genitive case of the pronoun THOU: = of thee, thee. *Obs.*

**971** *Blickl. Hom.* 233 Hie woldon to eorþan astiȝan, & þin þær onbidan. *c* **1300** *Havelok* 1128 Ye sholen ben weddeth, And, maugre þin, to-gidere beddeth. *Ibid.* 1789. *c* **1500** *Lancelot* 115 Al magre thine a seruand schal yow bee.

**II.** The possessive adjective or pronoun of the second person sing.: Belonging to thee.

In OE. an adj. *þīn, þīne, þīn*, with strong inflexions, remains of which survived in Early ME., as sing. masc. acc. *þīnne (þīne)*, dat. *þīnum (-an, -en, -e)*, gen. *þīnes*; f. nom. *þīne*, gen. and dat. *þīnre (þīre, þīne)*; pl. nom., acc. *þīne*, dat. *þīnum (-on, -en, -e)*, gen. *þīnra (-re, þīre)*. The final *n* of *þīn* began to be dropped before a cons. *a* 1200, leaving *þī*, later written *þy*, THY, q. v. At last *thin, thine*, was restricted to the position in which the possessive is not followed by a sb. Cf. MINE.

**2.** *Attributively* (= Ger. *dein*, F. *ton*). Now *arch.* or *poet.* before a vowel or *h*, or when following the sb.: otherwise superseded by THY.

*c* **825** *Vesp. Psalter* ci[i]. 29 Bearn ðiowa ðinra ineardiað ðer. *Ibid.* cxviii[i]. 125 Ðiow ðin ic eam. *c* **1000** *Ags. Ps.* (Th.) xlix. 21 [l. 20] Þu sæte onȝean þinne broþor, and tældest hine. *c* **1000** *Ags. Gosp.* Matt. vi. 10 ȝewurþe ðin willa on eorðan. *c* **1175** *Lamb. Hom.* 13 Þenne beoð þine daȝes ilenged.. in eorðan. *c* **1200** ORMIN 6727 Þurrh þine gode þæwess. *c* **1205** LAY. 3093 Þine sustren sculen habben mi kinelond. *a* **1240** *Ureisun* 149 in *Cott. Hom.* 199 Uor ðire mild-heortnesse. *a* **1250** *Owl & Night.* 43 Al so þu dost on þire side. *c* **1250** *Gen. & Ex.* 3556 Go ðu nu dun ðin folc to sen. *a* **1300** *Cursor M.* 923 (Cott.) Al þe dais on þin eild. *Ibid.* 11340 (Gött.) Do me to rest nu seruand þine. *Ibid.* 24675 (Edin.) For qui his moder was tin ant. **1382** WYCLIF *Matt.* vi. 22 3if thin eiȝe be symple, al thi body shal be liȝtful. **14..** *Chaucer's Astrol.* II. § 2–3 (MS. L.) To knowe the degre of thyn sonne in thyn zodiak. *c* **1440** *Pallad. on Husb.* I. 56 No doute is in thi watir ner thyn aier. **15..** HUNNIS *Psalms* vi. 59 Yet, O Lord, in rigour thine Forbeare thy heauie stroke. **1615** BEDWELL *Moham. Imp.* II. § 47, I am amazed at this thine answer. **1616** B. JONSON *Forest, To Celia* i, Drink to me only with thine eyes. **1784** COWPER *Task* v. 782 Thine eye shall be instructed, and thine heart, Made pure, shall relish [etc.]. **1864** PLUMPTRE *Hymn*, Thine arm, O Lord, in days of old Was strong to heal and save.

**3.** *Predicatively.* (= Ger. *der deinige*, F. *le tien.*)

*c* **1000** *Ags. Gosp.* John xvii. 6 Hiȝ wæron þine [*Lind.* ðino ueron]. *a* **1240** *Wohunge* in *Cott. Hom.* 271 Al is tin mi sweting. *a* **1300** *Floriz & Bl.* 4 Whil he is þin ne dute noþing. **13..** *Cursor M.* 2601 If ani barn of hir war þine. **13..** HAMPOLE *Medit. Passion* Wks. 1895 I. 93 Swete Ihesu, I biseche þee to..make me al þin. **1390** GOWER *Conf.* I. 74 Fro this day forth I am al thin. *c* **1475** *Rauf Coilȝear* 56 Sum part salbe thyne. **1534** TINDALE *Matt.* vi. 13 For thyne is the kyngedome and the power, and the glorye. **1605** SHAKS. *Lear* I. i. 265 Let her be thine. **1667** MILTON *P. L.* v. 154 Almightie, thine this universal Frame. **1707** WATTS *Hymn*, '*Come let us join*' iii, And blessings more than we can give Be, Lord, for ever thine. **1869** TENNYSON *Grail* 449 'Take thou my robe', she said, 'for all is thine'.

**4.** *Elliptically*, equivalent to THY with a sb. to be supplied from the previous context.

*c* **1430** *Freemasonry* 328 Ny by thy felows concubyne [lie], No more thou woldest he dede by thyne. *c* **1440** *Alphabet of Tales* 316, I thank þe at þou hase giffen me my son agayn, & behold, lo, I bryng þe thyne agayn. **1601** LYLY *Love's Met.* I. ii, Of what colours or flowers is thine made of, Niobe? **1749** CHESTERF. *Lett.* (1792) II. 220 *S.* Tastes are different, you know... *E.* That's true; but thine's a devilish odd one.

**5.** *absol.* **a.** That which is thine; thy property. (= Ger. *Deines, das deinige*, F. *le tien.*)

*a* **1000** *Cædmon's Gen.* 2144 (Gr.) Nis..sceat ne scilling, þæs ic..þines ahredde. *c* **1175** *Lamb. Hom.* 79 3if þu mare spenest of þine, hwan ic aȝen cherre al ic þe ȝelde. **13..** *Cursor M.* 2428 (Cott.) O þine wil i not haue a dele. *Ibid.* 10777 Of þin wil i neuer a dele. **1555** EDEN *Decades* 17 b, That amonge them [Cubans], the lande is as common as the sonne and water: And that Myne and Thyne (the seedes of all myscheefe) haue no place with them.

**b.** (*pl.*) Those who are thine; thy people, family, or kindred. (= Ger. *die deinigen*, F. *les tiens.*)

*c* **1000** *Ags. Gosp.* John xvii. 10 Ealle mine synt þine & þine synt mine. *c* **1000** *Sax. Leechd.* I. 328 Þonne þu & þine beod alysde. *a* **1300** *Cursor M.* 2386 (Cott.) Abram þis es þi land þar þou and tine [*v. r.* þine] sal be weldand. *c* **1440** *Jacob's Well* 201 To restoryn as myche as was don harme be þe or be þine. **1593** SHAKS. *Lucr.* 1630 Lasting shame On thee and thine this night I will inflict. **1776** TOPLADY in *Sacr. Poetry* (1868) 109 Thou Feeder and Guardian of Thine.

**c.** *Of thine*: that is (or are) thine; belonging to thee: see OF *prep.* 44.

**1390** GOWER *Conf.* I. 47 Ma dame, I am a man of thyne, That in thi Court have longe served. **1526** *Pilgr. Perf.* (W. de W. 1531) 300 b, Spyttynge in that blessed face of thyne. **1605** SHAKS. *Macb.* v. iii. 16 Those Linnen cheekes of thine Are Counsailers to feare. **1877** TENNYSON *Harold* I. ii, Thou hast misread this merry dream of thine.

**Thine, þine**, var. THYNE *adv. Obs.*, thence.

**Thing** (þiŋ), *sb.*[1] Forms: 1–3 **ðing**, 1–5 **þing**, 3–4 **þyng**, 4–5 **þinge**, **þynge**, (**thyngge**), 4–6 **thyng**, 5–6 **thinge**, **thynge**; 4– **thing**. (β. 1 **þingc**, **þincg**, 3 **þinc**, 3–4 **þink**, 4 **þynk**, 4–6 **think**, 5–6 **thynk(e)**. Pl. 1–3 **ðing**, **þing**, 3–5 **þinges** (3 **þingues**), 5–7 **thinges**, 5– **things**. [OE. *þing* (see below), Com. Teut.: cf. OFris. *thing, ting* assembly, council, suit, matter, thing (WFris., NFris. *ting* assembly); OS. *thing* assembly for judicial or deliberative purposes, conference, transaction, matter, affair, thing, object (MDu. *dinc* court-day, suit, plea, concern, affair, thing, Du. *ding* thing; MLG. *ding, dink*, LG. *ding* affair, thing, object); OHG. *ding, dinc* public assembly for judgement and transaction of business, law-court, lawsuit, plea, cause, matter, affair, thing, mod.G. *ding* affair, matter, thing; ON. *þing* public assembly, meeting, parliament, council; also in pl., objects, articles, valuable things, Norw. *ting* neut. public assembly, creature, being; masc. affair, thing, object, Sw. *ting* assize, thing; Da. *ting* court, court of justice, thing. Gothic had the cognate *þeihs* n.:—**þiŋχ-s* fixed time, time appointed for something, whence it is thought by some that the original sense of N. and WGer. *þing* was 'day of assembly'. With the sense-history, as shown in OE. and more fully in the cognate langs., cf. that of Ger. *sache*, Du. *zaak* affair, thing, orig. strife, dispute, lawsuit, cause, charge, crime, and F. *chose*, It., Sp. *cosa* thing, from L. *causa* judicial process, lawsuit, cause; also L. *rēs* affair, thing, also a case in law, lawsuit, cause.]

**I.** †**1.** (Only in *OE.*) A meeting, assembly, *esp.* a deliberative or judicial assembly, a court, a council. Phr. *þing gehégan*, to hold a meeting.

**685–6** *Laws of Hlothær & Eadric* c. 8 ȝif man oþerne sace tihte and he þane mannan mote an medle oþþe an þinge. *Beowulf* 426 [Ic] nu wið Grendel sceal..ana ȝeheȝan ðing wið þyrse. *a* **800** CYNEWULF *Christ* 926 Þonne he frean ȝesihð ealra ȝesceafta andweardne faran mid mæȝen-wundrum monȝum to þinge. *a* **1000** *Andreas* 157 Swa hie symble ymb þritiȝ þing ȝehedon nihtȝerimes. *a* **1000** *Gnomic Verses* 18 Þing sceal ȝeheȝan frod wið frodne, bið hyra ferð ȝelic.

†**2.** A matter brought before a court of law; a legal process; a charge brought, a suit or cause pleaded before a court. *Obs.* or passing into 3.

*a* **1000** *Ags. Psalms* (Th.) xxxiv. 22 [xxxv. 23] Drihten, min God, aris to minum þinge. *Ibid.* cviii. 30 [cix. 31] Þær he þearfendra þinga teolode. *c* **1122** *O. E. Chron.* an. 1022 (Laud MS.) [He] hine þær ælces þinges ȝeclænsode þe him mann on sæde. [**1534** CROMWELL in Merriman *Life & Lett.* (1902) I. 387 Ye..shall repayre hither to answer unto suche thinges as then shalbe leyed and objected to you. *a* **1548** HALL *Chron., Hen. VI* 151 The duke..sufficiently answered to all thynges to hym obiected.]

†**b.** Hence, Cause, reason, account; sake. *Obs.*

*c* **1000** ÆLFRIC *Saints' Lives* xxxiii. 129 Þonne nimð he me neadunga þanon for mines bryd-guman þingan. *c* **1000** *Ags. Gosp.* Luke viii. 47 For hwylcum þinge heo hit æthran. *c* **1175** *Lamb. Hom.* 67 Luue him for godes þing. *a* **1250** *Owl & Night.* 434 Ech wiht is glad for mine þinge. **13..** *Guy Warw.* (A.) 7306+st. 86 Wiltow fiȝt for mi þing..? *c* **1386** CHAUCER *Prol.* 276 He wolde the see were kept for any thyng Bitwixe Middelburgh and Orewelle. *c* **1425** *Eng. Conq. Irel.* 8 Robert was a trew man, & for no tynge wold do thynge wher-of he myght be þer-after I-wyted of wntrowth. **1581** [see NOTHING A. 9 a].

**3.** That with which one is concerned (in action, speech, or thought); an affair, business, concern, matter, subject; *pl.* affairs, concerns, matters. (In early use sometimes *sing.* in collective sense.)

*c* **897** K. ÆLFRED *Gregory's Past. C.* xviii. 128 Sio ȝeornfulnes eorðlicra ðinga abisȝað ðæt ondȝit. **971** *Blickl. Hom.* 13 No on ȝesundum þingum anum, ac..on wiðerweardum þingum. *c* **975** *Rushw. Gosp.* Matt. xviii. 19 ȝif tweȝen eower ȝeþafiȝaþ on eorþan be æniȝum þinge. *c* **1200** ORMIN 3640 All þiss middellærdess þing Aȝȝ turneþþ her & wharrfeþþ Nu upp, nu dun. *Ibid.* 8954 Me birrþ beon hoȝhefull Abutenn hise þingess. **1375** BARBOUR *Bruce* XX. 142 Quhill [=till] thai had wit to steir thar thing. *c* **1400** *Laud Troy Bk.* 2724 That thei with Paris to Grece schulde wende, To brynge this thyng to an ende. **1550** *Acts Privy Counc.* (1891) III. 84 The Lord Admirall desired licence to go into Lincolnshire for a moneth to see his thinges that he had not seen of a long tyme. **1598** SHAKS. *Merry W.* IV. v. 126 You shall heare how things goe. **1622** MABBE tr. *Aleman's Guzman d'Alf.* I. 11 These things (I meane your Law-suites) will require a great deale of care. **1743** BULKELEY & CUMMINS *Voy. S. Seas* 190 He acquainted us, that the Brigadier had order'd Things in another Manner. **1844** DICKENS *Mart. Chuz.* xii, How have things gone on in our absence? **1867** FREEMAN *Norm. Conq.* I. iv. 252 *note*, Things changed greatly in the course of a year.

**4.** That which is done or to be done; a doing, act, deed, transaction; an event, occurrence, incident; a fact, circumstance, experience. (*The*) *first thing* (advb.): as that which is first done or to be done; in the first place, firstly: see FIRST A. 1 f. So (*the*) *next thing*, in the next place, next; (*the*) *last thing*, in the last place, lastly.

*c* **1000** ÆLFRIC *Exod.* ix. 5 Tomorȝen deþ Drihten þas þing on eorþan. *c* **1000** *Sax. Leechd.* I. 112 Drince þonne fæstende niȝon daȝas, binnan þam fæce þu onȝytst on ðam wundorlic ðingc. *c* **1205** LAY. 265 Vnder-ȝetene weren þe þinges þat þeo wimon was mid childe. *Ibid.* 16042 Sæie me of þan þinge þe me to cumen sonden. **1382** WYCLIF 1 *Cor.* xvi. 14 Be alle ȝoure thingis don in charite. **1449** in *Calr. Proc. Chanc. Q. Eliz.* (1830) II. Pref. 55 In witnes of which thyng the forseid parties to these endentures chaungeable haue sette her seales. **1525** LD. BERNERS *Froiss.* (1812) II. cciv, The fyrst thynge he dyd he wente to the Church of saynt Peter. **1651** HOBBES *Leviath.* III. xl. 252 When two of them Prophecyed in the Camp, it was thought a new and unlawfull thing. **1712** STEELE *Spect.* No. 284 ¶ 4, I hate writing, of all Things in the World. **1809** MALKIN *Gil Blas* I. xvii. ¶ 9 Have not I done the thing genteelly? **1841** HELPS *Ess., Pract. Wisd.* (1842) 4 Men who have done great things in the world. **1871** *Routledge's Ev. Boy's Ann.* June 370 He often goes round the last thing..to make sure that all is right. **1875** JOWETT *Plato* (ed. 2) V. 512 Theft is a mean, and robbery a shameless thing. **1902** *Munsey's Mag.* XXVI. 602/2 The great thing was to get there. *Mod.* A pretty thing to have your own children wounding on you!

**5.** That which is said; a saying, utterance, expression, statement; with various connotations, e. g.: a charge or accusation made against a person (see 2); † a form of prayer (*pl.* prayers, devotions); a story, tale; a part or section of an argument or discourse; a witty saying, a jest (usu. *good thing*).

**13..** *Cursor M.* 17288+375 (Cott.) In alle thinkez þat þe prophetz han spoken. *c* **1386** CHAUCER *Pard. Prol.* 39 Lat hym telle vs of no ribaudye Telle vs som moral thyng. — *Shipm. T.* 91 Dann Iohn..hath hise thynges [prayers, offices] seyd ful curteisly. **1551** T. WILSON *Logike* (1580) 40 This manne is no Rhetoricien, because he can not place his thynges in good order. **1686** tr. *Chardin's Trav. Persia* 122 The first thing she said to me. **1738** SWIFT *Pol. Conversat.* i. 34, I never heard a better Thing. **1766** GOLDSM. *Vic. W.* xvi, All the good things of the high wits. **1771** *Misc. Ess.* in *Ann. Reg.* 184/2 This Greek spoke many handsome things of Marseilles, and of our colonies. **1859** SALA *Tw. round Clock* (1861) 132 The people who went about saying things. **1909** *Nation* 3 Apr. 13/2 The right thing will say itself—and will say itself with awful precision.

**b.** That which is thought; an opinion; a notion; an idea.

**1765** A. DICKSON *Treat. Agric.* (ed. 2) 76 With equal reason we may infer the same thing of earth. **1842** TENNYSON *Dora* 56 Mary sat..and thought Hard things of Dora. **1885** ANSTEY *Tinted Venus* i. 8 Putting things in the poor girl's head.

†**6.** Formerly used *absol.* (without article or qualifying word), also *a thing*, in indefinite sense: = anything, something. (With various meanings: see prec. senses.) *Obs.*

*a* **1300** *Cursor M.* 14952 Þai wil me neuer luue, i-wiss, For thing i mai þam tell. **1382** WYCLIF 1 *Sam.* xiv. 12 Stieth vp to vs, and we shulen shewe ȝou a thing. **1413** *Pilgr. Sowle* (Caxton 1483) IV. xxv. 70 Neuer ne dyde the body thyng withouten thyn assent. *c* **1500** *Melusine* 24, I pray you to telle it to me, yf it is thinge that I may knowe. **1525** LD. BERNERS *Froiss.* II. lxxxvi. [lxxxii.] 255 They neuer dyd thynge that they wolde haue ben gladder. **1588** SHAKS. *L. L. L.* v. i. 152 Shall I tell you a thing? **1678** BUNYAN *Pilgr.* I. 142 Ho, turn aside hither, and I will shew you a thing.

**II.** An entity of any kind.

**7.** That which exists individually (in the most general sense, in fact or in idea); that which is or may be in any way an object of perception, knowledge, or thought; a being, an entity. (Including persons, when personality is not considered, as in quots. *c* 888, 1380, 1539, 1597, 1732.) **a.** In unemphatic use: mostly with adj. or other defining word or phrase (the two together corresponding to the absol. use of a neuter adj. in Latin or Greek). Cf. also *anything, nothing, something*, in 17.

*c* **888** K. ÆLFRED *Boeth.* xxxiii. § 1 Þonne þa fif þing..eall ȝegaderode bioð, þonne bið hit eall an þing, & þæt an ðing bið God. **1044–7** *Charter of Eadweard* in Kemble *Cod. Dipl.* IV. 115 On ealweldendes drihtnes naman ðe ealle þing ȝewrohte. *c* **1200** ORMIN 1839 Niss nani þing þatt muȝhe ben Wiþþ Godd off efenn mahhte. *c* **1250** *O. Kentish Serm.* in *O. E. Misc.* 28 Wer-bi we moue hatie þo ileke þinges þet he hatedh,..and luuie þo ilek þinkes þat he lued. *a* **1300** *Cursor M.* 695 Ilkin thing, on serekin wise ȝeld til Adam þar seruise. **1380** *Lay Folks Catech.* 530 Þer ys but O god in trinite. This god is most myȝty þyng þat may be. **1388** WYCLIF *Ps.* cxlviii. 5 For he seide, & þingis weren maad; he comaundide, & þingis weren maad of nouȝt. **1539** TONSTALL *Serm. Palme Sund.* (1823) 8 He said in the tenth chapiter of John, I and my father are one thynge, that is to say, one substance. **1549** LATIMER *5th Serm. bef. Edw. VI* (Arb.) 147 All thynges are solde for mony at rome. **1594** GREENE *Selimus* I. Aiij b, He knowes not what it is to be a King, That thinks a scepter is a pleasant thing. **1597** SHAKS. 2 *Hen. IV*, v. v. 60 Presume not, that I am the thing I was. **1667** MILTON *P. L.* II. 922 To compare Great things with small. **1732** BERKELEY *Alciphr.* I. § 11 A man of parts is one thing, and a pedant another. **1788** J. MILNER in *Life I. Milner* iv. (1842) 44 Regencies are generally turbulent things. **1818** KEATS *Endym.* I. 1 A thing of beauty is a joy for ever. **1843** MILL *Logic* I. iii. § 5 What is an action? Not one thing but a series of two things: the state of mind called a volition, followed by an effect. **1879** GEO. ELIOT *Theo. Such* xiii. 266 The latest thing in tattooing.

**b.** Applied to an attribute, quality, or property of an actual being or entity; hence sometimes (in such phrases as *in all things*) = point, respect.

**971** *Blickl. Hom.* 13 Þa wæs heo on eallum þingum þe eaþmoddre. *c* **1200** *Trin. Coll. Hom.* 15 Dre þing ben þat elch man habben mot..þat on is rihte bileue, þat oðer is fulohtninge, þe þridde þe faire liflode. *a* **1300** *Cursor M.* 295 In þe sune þat schines clere Es a thing and thre thinges sere; A bodi rond, and hete and light. **1340** *Ayenb.* 194 Þe oþer þing þet behoueþ ine elmesse is þet me hit do zone and hasteliche. *c* **1520** BARCLAY tr. *Sallust* (ed. 2) 47 Their enmies myght lytell thynge preuayle agaynst them. **1558** KNOX *First Blast* (Arb.) 26 Augustine defineth ordre to be that thing, by the whiche God hath appointed and ordeined all things. **1644** EVELYN *Diary* 10 Nov., The whitenesse and smoothnesse of the pargeting was a thing I much observ'd. **1705** BERKELEY *Commonplace Bk.* Wks. 1871 IV. 420, I side in all things with the mob. **1838–9** FR. A. KEMBLE *Resid. in Georgia* (1863) 132 Ignorance is an odious thing.

**c.** Used indefinitely to denote something which the speaker is not able or does not choose to particularize, or which is incapable of being precisely described; a something, a somewhat.

**1602** SHAKS. *Ham.* I. i. 21 What, ha's this thing appear'd againe to night? **1804** WORDSW. *To Cuckoo* iv, No Bird, but an invisible thing, A voice, a mystery. **1822** BYRON *Heaven & Earth* I. iii, Thou..awful Thing of Shadows, speak to me! **1842** TENNYSON *Walking to the Mail* 36 'Yes, we're flitting,' says the ghost (For they had pack'd the thing among the beds). **1893** STEVENSON *Catriona* xv, Wi' the bang and the skirl the thing had clean disappeared.

**d.** In emphatic use: That which has separate or individual existence (e. g. as distinct on the one and from the totality of being, on the other rom attributes or qualities). See also 8.

1817 COLERIDGE *Biog. Lit.* xii. I. 267 An infinite independent hing, is no less a contradiction, than an infinite circle or a ideless triangle. 1820 BYRON *Mar. Fal.* v. i. 288 True words re things, And dying men's are things which long outlive, and often times avenge them. 1862 H. SPENCER *First Princ.* . iii. § 15 (1875) 47 While, on the hypothesis of their objectivity, space and Time must be classed as things, we find, on experiment, that to represent them in thought as things is mpossible. 1884 tr. *Lotze's Logic* 58 The doctrine of Kant, who represented the relation of a thing to its property, or of ubstance to its accident, as the model upon which the mind connects *S* and *P* in the categorical judgment. 1910 CHRISTIE in *Contemp. Rev.* Feb. 194 'Things'..are, as Lotze ried to show, but the activities of the One everlasting Spirit.

**8.** *spec.* **a.** That which is signified, as distinguished from a word, symbol, or idea by which it s represented; the actual being or entity as opposed o a symbol of it. †*In thing*, in reality, really, actually (opposed to *in name* = nominally).

*c*1450 *Bk. Curtesye* 343 (Oriel MS.) His [Chaucer's] longage was so feyre and pertinent, That semed vnto mennys heryng, Not only the worde, but verrely the thing. 1482 *Rolls of Parlt.* VI. 208/2 That the Deane..and Chanons..be oon body corporat in thyng and name. *a* 1533 FRITH *Answ. More* (1548) G iij, But the thinge it selfe, whose sacrament thys is, is receyued. 1534 MORE *Treat. Passion* Wks. 332/2 The thyng of a sacrament is properly called that holye thinge that the sacrament betokeneth. 1663 BUTLER *Hud.* I. i. 804 Bear-baiting..is an Antichristian Game Unlawful both in thing and name. 1705 BERKELEY *Commonplace Bk.* Wks. 1871 IV. 440 The supposition that things re distinct from ideas takes away all real truth. 1725 WATTS *Logic* I. iv. § 1 The World is fruitful in the Invention of Utensils of Life, and new Characters and Offices of Men, yet Names entirely new are seldom invented; therefore old Names are almost necessarily us'd to signify new Things. 827 ROBINSON *Archæol. Græca* x. (ed. 2) p. lxiii, The philosophy of Aristotle is rather the philosophy of words than of hings. 1850 TENNYSON *In Mem.* lxxv. 6 What practice owsoe'er expert In fitting aptest words to things..Hath power to give thee as thou wert? 1876 JEVONS *Logic Prim.* i. 22 The meaning of a word is that thing which we think bout when we use the word.

**b.** *esp.* A being without life or consciousness; n inanimate object, as distinguished from a person or living creature. (See also 11. 12.)

1689–90 TEMPLE *Ess. Learn.* Wks. 1731 I. 302 Things.. uch as have been either of general Use or Pleasure to Mankind. 1729 LAW *Serious C.* iv. (1732) 47 Things..are ll to be used according to the Will of God. 1766 [see 12 b]. 840 DICKENS *Barn. Rudge* iii, Consideration of persons, hings, times and places. 1850 LYNCH *Theo. Trin.* viii. 149 He that getteth a wife getteth a good thing'; that is at east, if his wife be more than a *thing*. 1853 MAURICE *Proph. & Kings* xvi. 279 The human being was sacrificed; he *person* was given up for the *thing*.

**9.** Applied (usually with qualifying word) to a iving being or creature; occasionally to a plant.

*c*1000 *Sax. Leechd.* II. 146 For þon þonne ealle æterno ing fleogaþ. *c* 1000 ÆLFRIC *Gen.* vii. 22 Ælc þing, þe lif æfde. *c* 1275 LAY. 25656 He saide þat þar was icome A uþer þing to londe..A wel loþliche feond. *a* 1300 *Cursor M.* 385 Alkin things grouand sere..in þam self þaire seding pere. *c* 1440 *Pallad. on Husb.* I. 935 For eddris, spritis, monstris, thyng of drede. 1580 FRAMPTON *Monardes' Med. Hgst. Venome* 138 Least any venomous thing fall therein, as pyders. 1667 MILTON *P. L.* IX. 194 When all things that breath,..send up silent praise To the Creator. 1819 SHELLEY *Prometh. Unb.* I. 305, I wish no living thing to suffer pain. 1858 GLENNY *Gard. Every-day Bk.* 120/1 Nemophila, Coreopsis, and other free-growing things.

**10.** Applied to a person, now only in contempt, reproach, pity, or affection (esp. to a woman or child); formerly also in commendation or honour. Cf. CREATURE 3 b, c. **a.** with qualifying word.

*c*1290 *St. Lucy* 150 in *S. Eng. Leg.* I. 105 Ʒwan he ne miȝte his clene þing [St. Lucy] ouer-come mid al is lore. *a* 1300 *Cursor M.* 2077 Fle me fra, þou wared thing. *Ibid.* 7285 Samuel..was a selcuth dughti thing, Þe first þat smerld man to king. *c* 1330 *Arth. & Merl.* 6482 Þe kinges steward ..wedded þat swete þing. *c* 1450 *Guy Warw.* (C.) 26 A may thynge, The Erlys doghtur, a swete thynge. 1533 J. HEYWOOD *Play Wether* (1903) 1097 A goodly dame, an ydyll thynge wys. 1542 UDALL *Erasm. Apoph.* 241 b, Augustus beeyng yet a young thyng vnder mannes state. *a* 1568 ASCHAM *Scholem.* I. (Arb.) 53 If he be bashefull, and will soone blushe, they call him a babishe and ill brought vp thyng. 1607 SHAKS. *Cor.* IV. v. 122 But that I see thee heere Thou noble thing, more dances my rapt heart [etc.]. 1689 MRS. BEHN *Novels* (1871) I. 70 The worst-natur'd, incorrigible, thing in the world. 1711 STEELE *Spect.* No. 4 ⁋ 5 At a Play.. looking..at a young thing in a Box before us. 1758 JOHNSON *Idler* No. 13 ⁋ 3 My wife often tells me that boys are dirty things. 1838 DICKENS *Nich. Nick.* xxvii, Why don't you go and ask them to walk up, you stupid thing? 1898 FLOR. MONTGOMERY *Tony* 12 The very smallest and youngest thing that had ever worn an Eton jacket. *Mod.* Poor thing! I pity her.

**b.** without qualification, in contempt or reproach, implying unworthiness to be called a person: cf. 8 b. 1610 SHAKS. *Temp.* III. ii. 63 Reuenge it on him, (for I know Thou dar'st) But this Thing dare not. 1611 — *Wint. T.* II. i. 82 O thou Thing. 1633 BP. HALL *Occas. Medit.* (1851) 143 What can we make of this thing? man, I cannot call him. 1756 LADY M. W. MONTAGU *Let. to C'tess of Bute* 8 Nov., By what accident they have fallen into the hands of that thing Dodsley I know not. 1860 MOTLEY *Netherl.* ii. I. 37 To accept the sovereignty of a thing like Henry of Valois.

**11.** A material object, a body; a being or entity consisting of matter, or occupying space. (Often, a vague designation for an object which it is difficult to denominate more exactly.)

971 *Blickl. Hom.* 91 Heofon & eorþe, & sæ, & ealle þa þing þe on þæm syndon. *c* 1200 ORMIN 18825 Þatt arrke þatt iss wrohht off tre..iss whilwendlike þing. *a* 1300 *Signa ante Judicium* 102 in *E. E. Poems* (1862) 10 Þe iren sul blede..Þe þing þat bodi no flesse naþ non. *a* 1300 *Cursor M.* 9383 Al-king thing was þan..Wel pithier þan þai ar now. *c* 1400 *Lanfranc's Cyrurg.* 141 Woundis..maad wiþ a swerd or wiþ sum dinge ellis þat woundiþ. 1547 HOOPER *Declar. Christe* viii. H vij, Mens yeyes be obedient unto the creatour that they may se on think and yet not a nother. 1570 BILLINGSLEY *Euclid* I. post. i. 7 Thinges equall to one and the selfe same thyng are equall also the one to the other. *c* 1595 CAPT. WYATT *R. Dudley's Voy. W. Ind.* (Hakl. Soc.) 16 Leavinge behinde us certaine letters inclosed in a thinge of wood provided of purpose. 1709 BERKELEY *Ess. Vision* § 135 Things perceivable by touch. 1719 DE FOE *Crusoe* (1840) I. xvi. 273 A three-cornered..thing, like..a shoulder-of-mutton sail. 1842 TENNYSON *Vis. Sin* IV. vii, Callest thou that thing a leg? 1875 JOWETT *Plato* (ed. 2) III. 509 Stones and shells and things of earth and rock.

**b.** A material substance (usually of a specified kind); stuff, material; in mod. use chiefly applied to substances used as food, drink, or medicine.

*c* 1000 *Sax. Leechd.* II. 210 Eal þa wætan þing..& eall swete þing..ȝe þa scearpan afran þing sint to fleonne. 13.. *E. E. Allit. P.* B. 819 Loth þenne..his men amonestes mete for to dyȝt, Bot þenkkez on hit be þrefte what þynk so ȝe make, For wyth no sour ne no salt seruez hym neuer. *c* 1400 *Destr. Troy* 7856 Þai wold stuf hom full stithly..with mete..& mony othir thinges. *a* 1500 in Arnolde *Chron.* (1811) 91 Yf ony persone caste or put ony rubyes, dunge ..or ony other noyos thinge in Thamys at Walbrok. 1589 J. CHILTON in Hakluyt *Voy.* 590 Annele..is a kinde of thing to dye blew withall. 1631 R. BYFIELD *Doctr. Sabb.* 204 We drinke some warme thing. 1694 SALMON *Bate's Dispens.* (1713) 169/1 It is a most excellent Thing in Fevers. 1737 WHISTON *Josephus, Antiq.* XI. viii. § 7 Accused by those at Jerusalem of having eaten things common. *Mod.* Sour things are bad for the stomach.

**c.** *euphem.* Privy member, private parts.

*c* 1386 CHAUCER *Wife's Prol.* 121. *c* 1440 *Voc.* in Wr.-Wülcker 632/12. 1508 DUNBAR *Tua Mariit Wemen* 389. 1610 B. JONSON *Alch.* V. i. 1700 FARQUHAR *Constant Couple* IV. iii. 1762 BRIDGES *Burlesque Homer* (1772) 62.

**12.** †**a.** A collective term for that which one possesses; property, wealth, substance. *Obs.*

*c* 1000 ÆLFRIC *Hom.* II. 506 Him eallum wæron heora ðing ȝemæne. *a* 1200 *Moral Ode* 263 Þer inne boð..Þe þet is oðers monnes þing loure. *c* 1200 ORMIN 4520 Þatt tu nan oþerr manness þing Ne ȝeorne nohht to winnenn. *c* 1250 *Gen. & Ex.* 3378 He let bi-aften de more del, To kepen here ðing al wel. 1297 R. GLOUC. (Rolls) 10196 Persones þing he solde men þat mest wolde þeruore ȝiue. 13.. *Minor Poems fr. Vernon MS.* xxxvii. 719 For he wolde haue offryng And liue bi oþur mennes þing. 1432–50 tr. *Higden* (Rolls) I. 35 Composicion of a commune thynge, the disposicion of a thynge familier. 1513 DOUGLAS *Æneis* VI. xiv. 93 That art full mychty bot of lytle thing.

**b.** A piece of property, an individual possession; usually in *pl.*, possessions, belongings, goods; *esp.* (*colloq.*) those which one has or carries with one at the time, e. g. on a journey; *impedimenta*.

*Things real, things personal* (in Law) = real property, personal property: see REAL *a.*[2] 6, PERSONAL *a.* 6 b.

*c* 1290 *S. Eng. Leg.* I. 14/459 Mid þat gold and þe riche þingues þat he fond al-so þere Þe churchene..þare-with he liet a-rere. *c* 1460 *Towneley Myst.* vi. 83 Where ar oure thyngis, ar thay past Iordan? 1481 CAXTON *Godeffroy* xlv. 85 They had born theder alle theyr thynges. 1560 DAUS tr. *Sleidane's Comm.* 119 b, The parson and vicar wyll haue for a mortuary..the best thynge that is about the house. 1585 T. WASHINGTON tr. *Nicholay's Voy.* I. v, [They] lost the most part of theyr apparrel, & things. 1603 KNOLLES *Hist. Turks* (1621) 599 Busie in packing vp his things against his departure. 1662 J. DAVIES *Mandelslo's Trav.* 17 We.. went..to the Custome House to have our things search'd by the Officers there. 1759 JOHNSON *Let. to Miss Porter* 23 Mar., in *Boswell*, I have this day moved my things, and you are now to direct to me at Staple-inn. 1766 BLACKSTONE *Comm.* II. ii. 16 The objects of dominion or property are things, as contradistinguished from persons: and things are by the law of England distributed into two kinds; things real, and things personal. 1865 TROLLOPE *Belton Est.* xxvi, She packed up all her things.

**c.** *spec.* (*pl.*) Articles of apparel; clothes, garments; *esp.* such as women put on to go out in, in addition to the indoor dress. *colloq.*

1634 W. WOOD *New Eng. Prosp.* (1865) 56 A long coarse coate, to keepe better things from the pitched ropes and plankes. 1713 STEELE *Guardian* No. 10 ⁋ 5, I know every part of their dress, and can name all their things by their names. 1748 RICHARDSON *Clarissa* (1811) V. xxiv. 257 But having her things on, (as the women call every thing)..she thought it best to go. 1774 FOOTE *Cozeners* I. Wks. 1799 II. 157, I have had but just time to huddle on my things. 1833 T. HOOK *Parson's Dau.* (1847) 239 Take off your things—and we will order..tea. 1885 ANSTEY *Tinted Venus* vi. 66, 'I haven't bought my winter things yet', said Matilda. 1902 R. BAGOT *Donna Diana* viii. 100 Diana left the room to put on her things for driving.

**d.** *pl.* Implements or equipment for some special use; utensils. Chiefly *colloq.*

1698 VANBRUGH *Prov. Wife* III. i, Here, take away the things; I expect company. 1738 *Ochtertyre House Bks.* (1909) 154 For mending the Kitchen things. 1844 *Mem. Babylonian Princess* II. 304 With the breakfast things the waiter brought the morning paper. 1891 C. JAMES *Rom. Rigmarole* 156, I hadn't any proper hunting things. 1898 G. B. SHAW *Plays* II. *Man of Destiny* 160 Clearing the table and removing the things to a tray on the sideboard.

**13.** An individual work of literature or art, a composition; a writing, piece of music, etc.

*c* 1386 CHAUCER *Prol.* 325 Ther-to he [the Sergeant of the Law] koude endite and make a thyng. — *Sqr.'s T.* 70 Herknynge hise Mynstrals hir thynges pleye. 1581 PETTIE *Guazzo's Civ. Conv.* I. (1586) 17 b, Yᵗ they haue imploied all their time in reading some good thing or other. 1589 PUTTENHAM *Eng. Poesie* III. xxii. (Arb.) 265 One of our late makers who in the most of his things wrote very well. 1591 SHAKS. *Two Gent.* IV. ii. 71 You would haue them alwaies play but one thing. 1731 SWIFT *Let. to Pope* 12 June, I have a thing in prose, begun above twenty-eight years ago, and almost finished. 1831 *Examiner* 213/2 A dozen things of Handel's;..some things of Avison's, one of the poorest of musicians. 1902 BESANT 5 *Yrs. Tryst* 26 You'll pass your exams with distinction; you'll get appointments; you'll write things.

**III.** Phrases, special collocations, and combinations.

**14. a.** ... *and things* (colloq., unstressed): and other things of the same kind; and the like, *et cetera*. **b.** *For one thing*: as one point to be noted; in the first place. So *for another thing*. **c.** *To make a good thing of*: to turn to profit, make gain out of. **d.** *No great things* (used predicatively, usually of a person or thing): nothing great, nothing much, of ordinary quality or character. *colloq.* or *dial.* (Cf. *no great shakes.*) **e.** *Thing in itself* (rendering Ger. *ding an sich* (Kant)), *Metaph.*: a thing regarded apart from its attributes; a noumenon. **f.** *To know a thing or two*: see KNOW *v.* 15; so *to learn, to show* (a person) *a thing or two*.

**a.** 1596 SHAKS. *Tam. Shr.* IV. iii. 56 With Ruffes and Cuffes, and Fardingales, and things. 1841 S. C. HALL *Ireland* I. 30 Grace would mend her father's nets and things. 1894 *To-day* 13 Jan. 14 The Japanese supper with the Japanese room and mats and things. **b.** 1790 *Bystander* 139 For one thing, he [Garrick] knew that in delivering the text of an author, if he endeavoured to give his meaning a new colouring,..it would be considered as pedantic. 18.. KEBLE [see FOR *prep.* 19 d]. 1878 MORLEY *Diderot* I. v. 173 For one thing, physical science had in the interval taken immense strides. *Mod.* I didn't care much for his speech; for one thing, his delivery was very bad; for another thing, the subject was not particularly interesting. **c.** 1819 SHELLEY *P. Bell the Third* VI. xxxv, I have found the way To make a better thing of metre Than e'er was made. 1873 GREENWOOD in *St. Paul's Mag.* XII. 657 These dealers in ragged merchandize make a good thing of it. **d.** 1816 'QUIZ' *Grand Master* VII. 184 Now I shall give,—'the Governor,'—He's no great things, between us, Sir. 1842 THACKERAY *Miss Tickletoby's Lect.* vi, His scholarship..I take it, was no great things. 1890 'R. BOLDREWOOD' *Col. Reformer* (1891) 352 That old place at Bowning..I don't believe it was any great things. **e.** [1659 H. MORE *Immort. Soul* I. ii. § 2. 6 What ever things are in themselves, they are nothing to us, but so far forth as they become known to our..Cognitive powers.] 1867 [see NOUMENON]. 1871 FRASER *Life Berkeley* ii. 41 He recognises substance, or, as we might say, the thing-in-itself. *a* 1881 A. BARRATT *Phys. Metempiric* (1883) 39 We have had to conclude that the doctrine of Realism or Things-in-themselves cannot be proved. 1891 E. B. BAX *Outlooks fr. New Standp.* III. 182 This is the truth at the bottom of the 'thing-in-itself', so much decried by the orthodox Hegelians. **f.** 1792, 1817 [see KNOW *v.* 15]. 1856 READE *Never too late* lii, Jackey showed Robinson a thing or two. 1859 THACKERAY *Virgin.* xviii, I think I have shown him that we in Virginia know a thing or two. 1897 MARY KINGSLEY *W. Africa* 673 Does any one..feel inclined to tell me that those old palm-oil chiefs have not learnt a thing or two during their lives?

**15.** *The thing* (colloq., emphatic). **a.** (predicatively) The correct thing; what is proper, befitting, or fashionable; also of a person, in good condition or 'form', 'up to the mark', fit (physically or otherwise).

1762 GOLDSM. *Cit. W.* lxxvii, [The silk] is at once rich, tasty, and quite the thing. 1775 MME. D'ARBLAY *Early Diary* 3 Apr., Mr. Bruce was quite the thing; he addressed himself with great gallantry to us all alternately. 1781 JOHNSON 12 Apr., in *Boswell*, Why, Sir, a Bishop's calling company together in this week [Passion Week] is, to use the vulgar phrase, not the thing. 1802 MRS. J. WEST *Infidel Father* II. 123 This behaviour was certainly the very thing. 1841 THACKERAY *Gt. Hoggarty Diamond* ii, He really looked quite the genteel thing. 1864 MEREDITH *Sandra Belloni* xix, Wilfrid took his arm and put it gently down on the chair, saying: 'You're not quite the thing to-day, sir.' 1897 *Boston* (Mass.) *Jrnl.* 12 Jan. 5/1 They are used in the long gold chains which are so pre-eminently the thing. 1901 'L. MALET' *Sir R. Calmady* v. vii, I am not quite the thing this morning.

**b.** The special, important, or notable point; *esp.* what is specially required.

1850 THACKERAY *Pendennis* lxxv, But he has got the rowdy, which is the thing. 1873 M. ARNOLD *Lit. & Dogma* Pref. 11 The question [of a state church]..is..so absolutely unimportant! The thing is, to recast religion. 1892 SYMONDS *Michel Angelo* (1899) I. VI. x. 290 The thing about Michel Angelo is this: he is not..at the head of a class, he stands apart by himself.

**16.** †**a.** *All thing* (obs.): everything, all things; also *advb.* altogether, wholly: see ALL A. 3, C. 2 b. **b.** *That* (*this, what*, etc.) *kind* (or *sort*) *of thing*: see KIND *sb.* 14, SORT *sb.* **c.** *A thing of nothing* or *of nought*: see NOTHING A. 3 b, NOUGHT A. 4 c. †**d.** *Public thing, thing public* (obs.) = L. *res publica*: see PUBLIC *a.* 2 a. **e.** *Such a thing, no such thing*: see SUCH.

**17.** *Any thing, every thing, no thing, some thing* (in which *thing* is an unemphatic stressless use of sense 7 or 11), are now written each as one word (see ANYTHING, EVERYTHING, NOTHING, SOMETHING).

**18.** *attrib.* and *Comb.*, as *thing-aspect, -element*;

*thing-creating* adj.; *thing-like* adj., like a material or impersonal thing (hence *thing-likeness*).

1663 BOYLE *Usef. Exp. Nat. Philos.* I. 123 Matter cannot move it self, but requires to be mov'd by a Tectonic thing-creating Power. *c* 1854 FABER *Old Labourer* iii, Such a thing-like person. 1895 POLLOCK & MAITLAND *Hist. Eng. Law* II. iv. § 6 II. 133 Annuities.. in course of time.. assumed the guise of merely contractual rights; but in the earlier Year Books their thinglikeness is visible. 1909 G. TYRRELL in *Q. Rev.* July 108 Those..who, as priests..are interested in the 'thing-aspect' of religion. *Ibid.*, His tendency to cleave to this 'thing-element' in religion.

Hence (all *rare* or *nonce-wds.*) **Thingal** (þi·ŋăl) *a.*, pertaining to things (= REAL *a.*[2] 7 b); in first quot. *absol.*; **Thi·nghood**, the state or character of being a thing (in quot. 1888, as distinct from a person); existence as a thing, reality, substantiality; **Thinginess** (þi·ŋinės), the quality of being *thingy* (see below); (*a*) reality, actuality, objectivity; (*b*) devotion to things, practical or matter-of-fact character; **Thingish** (þi·ŋiʃ) *a.*, having the nature of a thing: = *thingy* (*a*); **Thingless** (þi·ŋlės) *a.*, destitute of the character of a thing, insubstantial (whence **Thi·nglessness**); **Thinglet** (þi·ŋlėt), a little thing, a diminutive object or creature; **Thingliness** (þi·ŋlinės), the quality of being *thingly*; existence as a thing, essence; **Thingling** (þi·ŋliŋ) = *thinglet*; **Thingly** (þi·ŋli) *a.*, having the nature of a thing: = *thingy* (*a*); **Thi·ngness**, the fact or character of being a thing (in quot. 1902, as distinct from a person); reality; so † **Thi·ngship**, † **Thi·ngsomeness**; **Thingy** (þi·ŋi) *sb. Sc.* [-Y, dim. suff.; cf. -IE], a little thing; **Thingy** *a.*, (*a*) having the nature or character of a thing; real, actual, objective, substantial; in quot. 1894, ? consisting of separate, independent, or unconnected things; (*b*) devoting oneself to or concerned with actual things, practical, matter-of-fact.

1857 J. HINTON in *Life* vii. (1885) 132 This love might lead us away from thoughts of the real or *thingal. 1884 *Mind* July 398 What he [James Hinton] would probably call 'thingal beauty'. 1865 J. GROTE *Moral Ideals* ii. (1876) 28 Any form of *thinghood or reality. 1872 *Contemp. Rev.* XX. 76 The conception of an external thinghood, and.. of a permanent substantiality as basis of the qualities. 1880 *Mind* V. 141 Thinghood, Substantiality, Existence, are synonymous terms. 1888 L. ABBOTT in *Century Mag.* Aug. 624/1 The materialism that puts thinghood above manhood. 1891 *Cent. Dict.*, **Thinginess.* 1890 *Open Court* (U. S.) 5 June 2316/2 Yet is space no *thingish entity, no tangible object. 1599 T. M[OUFET] *Silkwormes* 1 What breth embreath'd these almost *thingles things. 1874 F. H. LAING in *Ess. Relig. & Lit.* Ser. III. 270 How thing came out of *thinglessness. 1890 *Australian Girl* I. xv. 203 Creatures on foot and on wing—*thinglets that fly one moment and fall down helplessly the next. 1662 J. CHANDLER *Van Helmont's Oriat.* 69 That man was ignorant of the *thingliness of a Gas..and..of the properties of cold in the Air. *Ibid.* 343 The essential thingliness of a thing. 1652 BENLOWES *Theoph.* v. xxiv, Poor *thingling Man! 1900 *Westm. Gaz.* 25 July 2/3 The words 'real presence' (he adds) meant originally the presence of (*res*) a thing—if one may say so, a '*thingly' presence—*i.e.*, presence as a thing. 1896 FRASER *Philos. Theism* Ser. II. vi. 150 Personality instead of *thingness is the highest form under which man..can conceive of God. 1902 GREENOUGH & KITTREDGE *Words* 35 *note*, A New-England philosopher was much ridiculed for using the 'thing-ness of the here' for 'the actuality of the present'. 1697 J. SERGEANT *Solid Philos.* 239 We can have.. a Notion of the Thing..precisely according to its *Thingship (as we may say) or Reality. 1674 N. FAIRFAX *Bulk & Selv.* 19 He that gives it a little reality or *thingsomeness, cannot..be so sparing as to..give it no more. 1888 BARRIE *When a Man's Single* (1900) 11/2 A speerity bit *thingy she was. 1891 *Cent. Dict.*, *Thingy, *adj.* 1894 M. SCHUYLER in *Forum* (N. Y.) July 617 The government buildings have become more and more 'thingy', more and more compilations of 'features' that fail to make up a physiognomy.

**Thing** (þiŋ), *sb.*[2] Also ting. [a. ON. *þing* (mod.Scand. *ting*); the same word as THING *sb.*[1], but taken independently from ONorse.]

**1.** In Scandinavian countries (or settlements, as in parts of England before the Conquest): A public meeting or assembly; *esp.* a legislative council, a parliament; a court of law. Cf. ALTHING, STORTHING. (Usually with capital T.)

1840 *Iceland, Greenland*, etc. 99 They had been accustomed to assemble at the *Thing*, near the idol temples. 1857 DUFFERIN *Lett. High Lat.* xii. (ed. 3) 387 These landed proprietors were called the Bonders...On stated occasions they met together, in a solemn assembly, or Thing, (*i.e.* Parliament,)..for the transaction of public business. 1860 LONGF. *Wayside Inn, Saga K. Olaf* XVII. vi, The Swedish King Summoned in haste a Thing, Weapons and men to bring In aid of Denmark. 1861 PEARSON *Early & Mid. Ages Eng.* 150 Next year, 1014 A.D., while Sweyn, in the midst of his ting, was blaspheming St. Edmund, the saint appeared armed. 1865 KINGSLEY *Herew.* xxvii, We shall see what thou sayest to all this, in full Thing at home in Denmark. 1886 CORBETT *Fall of Asgard* I. xi. 137 He was proclaimed King of Norway by the Thing. *Ibid.* II. vii. 92 The judges went out to try the causes...It was the greatest suit of which notice had been given for that Thing.

*transf.* 1888 *Pall Mall G.* 3 Oct. 11/1 This morning..the twenty-eighth Church Congress began work...Those who remember..the third Congress..are remarking how the great Thing of the Church-folk has grown in popularity.

‖ **2.** (See quot.)

1874 STUBBS *Const. Hist.* I. iii. § 26 Iceland is divided into four fiordungs [ON. *fjorðungar*] or quarters...Each fiordung was divided into three things, and each thing into three godords or lordships.

**3.** *attrib.* and *Comb.*: **thing-day**, a day on which a Thing is held; **thing-dues**, fees payable to a chief who presides at a Thing; **thing-field, -hall, -hill, -stead**, a field, hall, hill, or place where a Thing meets. See also THINGMAN.

*c* 1856 *Denham Tracts* (1895) II. 207 The thingstead for determining the controversies among the rude tribes. 1886 CORBETT *Fall of Asgard* I. xiii. 168 They skirted the Thing-field. *Ibid.* II. i. 7 All that were gathered that day upon the Thing-hill. *Ibid.* vii. 98 Till the end of the Thing-days. *Ibid.* ix. 127 Thorkel found himself rich. Nor was it from the Thing-dues alone. *Ibid.* xiv. 195 To Olaf's great Thing-hall went Thorkel,..on the day appointed.

**Thing**, *v.* [OE. *þingian*, as sense 1 below, also to make terms, come to terms, settle, determine, speak, discourse, address; Com. Teut. = OFris. *thingja* to plead (WFris. *tingen*, NFris. *tingje*), OS. *thingôn* to confer, transact business, deal (MDu. *dinghen*, Du. and LG. *dingen* to bargain, etc.), OHG. *dingôn* to hold a court, conduct a process or suit, negotiate, come to an agreement, arrange a compromise or terms of peace, to stipulate, etc. (Ger. *dingen* to discuss, bargain, hire, engage on terms), ON. *þinga* to hold a (public) meeting, confer, consult, discuss terms (Sw. *tinga* to agree as to terms, engage, Da. *tinge* to bargain, etc.):—OTeut. *þingōjan*, f. *þingom* THING *sb.*[1], the original sense being more distinctly retained in the vb.]

† **1.** *intr.* To plead a cause, supplicate, intercede, make intercession (with *dative* = for); *trans.* to bring to reconciliation. *Obs.*

*a* 1000 *Ecgberti Poenitentiale* IV. c. 62 Gif he wyle..him sylfum þingian [L. *supplicare*]. *c* 1000 *Cædmon's Satan* 510 Ic [Christ] eow þingade, þa me on beame beornas sticedon. *c* 1200 *Trin. Coll. Hom.* 15 Þe lauerd sainte poul..þingie us to þe holie fader of heuene, þat he geue us mihte. *Ibid.* 43 Do we ec mid ure wel dede þingen us wið ure helende. *c* 1200 ORMIN 8097 To þingenn uss wiþþ ure Godd Þurrh bedess & þurrh lakess. *Ibid.* 18124 Ure Laferrd Jesu Crist Iss Prest..Hiss folc to þingenn wel inoh Towarrd Drihhtin off Heffne.

**2.** To represent by things, i. e. concrete objects. Hence **Thinger** (þi·ŋəɹ).

1883 G. MASSEY *Nat. Genesis* I. i. 16 Symbolism was not a conscious creation of the human mind; man..did not begin by thinging his thoughts in intentional enigmas of expression. *Ibid.*, Things were pourtrayed before thoughts by those who were thingers rather than thinkers.

**Thing**, obs. form of THINK *v.*[1] and [2].

**Thingal** to **Thingly**: see after THING *sb.*[1]

**Thinger**: see THING *v.* 2.

**Thingman** (þi·ŋmæ̆n). Pl. **-men.** [ad. ON. *þingmaðr*, in pl. *þingmenn*.] A member of a Scandinavian Thing; *spec.* = HOUSECARL.

[1862 LD. BROUGHAM *Brit. Const.* x. 137 The Danish Princes..keeping on foot a guard called *Thingmann* or *Thinglate*, of 3,000 men.] 1870 FREEMAN *Norm. Conq.* (ed. 2) I. vi. 440 Cnut now organized a regular paid force...These were the famous Thingmen, the Housecarls. 1886 CORBETT *Fall of Asgard* II. x. 130 The bonders came and laid their hands in Thorkel's, swearing themselves his Thingmen. 1890 HALL CAINE *Bondman* III. iv, Who were these men? They were Thingmen..the law-makers.

**Thingness** to **Thingsomeness**: see after THING *sb.*[1]

**Thingum** (þi·ŋəm). *colloq.* ? *Obs.* exc. *dial.* Also 9 thing'em. [f. THING *sb.*[1], with meaningless suffix.] = THINGUMMY. (In first quot. in reduplicated form *thingum thangum*: cf. CRINKUM-CRANKUM.)

1680 OTWAY *Atheist* IV. i, With a deep Point Thingum Thangum over her Shoulders. 1681 T. FLATMAN *Heraclitus Ridens* No. 45 (1713) II. 38 Is there no News from the Thingum in the Old Baily? 1741 CHESTERF. *Let. to Son* 6 Aug., To speak of Mr. What-d'ye-call-him, or Mrs. Thingum, or How-d'ye-call-her, is excessively awkward and ordinary. 1793 FITZGERALD in *Europ. Mag.* XXIII. 387 All your bunch of thingums. 1808 MRS. C. KEMBLE *Day after Wedding* 11 What were you saying, Mr. Thing'em?

So in extended forms **Thingumary** (þi·ŋəmări), (**thingummarie, thing-a-merry**), **Thingumajig** (þi·ŋəmădʒig), (**thingymyjig, etc.**). See also next two words.

1819 'R. RABELAIS' *Abeillard & Heloisa* 146 Deep pond'ring—in a reverie On some dubious thingummarie. 1827 HONE *Every-day Bk.* II. 58 That clever fellow, 'Thing-a-merry', or that stupid dog, 'What-d'ye-call-um'. 1876 'L. CARROLL' *Hunting of Snark* I. ix, He would answer..To 'What-you-may-call-um?' or 'What-was-his-name!' But especially 'Thingum-a-jig!' 1889 *Century Mag.* Apr. 913/1 He got ther critter propped up an' ther thingermajig stropped on ter 'im. 1902 ELIZ. L. BANKS *Newspaper Girl* 149, I would drive through Hyde Park in a victoria,..and everybody would say, 'There goes the editress of the Thingymygig Magazine!'

**Thingumbob** (þi·ŋəmbǫb). *colloq.* Also 8–9 thing(-)em(-)bob, 9 thing'em bob, thingamobob, thingumebob. [Arbitrary extension of prec., the last syllable now meaningless.] = next.

1751 SMOLLETT *Per. Pic.* ii, In a laced doublet and thingumbobs at the wrists. 1778 MISS BURNEY *Evelina* (1791) II. xxxvii. 240 Pray, is one Miss Anville in any of them thingembobs? 1788 BENTHAM *Mem. & Corr.* Wks. 1843 X. 181 One is composed of the thingumbobs called Cinq-foils, which you will find in your seal. 1832 LYTTON *Eugene A.* I. ii, A lonely grey house with a thingumebob at the top; a serv tory they call it. 1870 MISS BRIDGMAN *Rob. Lynne* II. v. 1 We're going to try him for thingamobob—bigamy.

**Thingummy** (þi·ŋəmi). *colloq.* Also 8 thing o-me, thing-o'-me, 9 thing-o-my, thingam -ammy, -ummie, -umy. [f. THINGUM + -Y (?dim.) Used (in undignified speech) to indicate vaguely thing (or person) of which the speaker cann at the moment recall the name, or which he is a loss or does not care to specify precisely; a 'wha you-may-call-it'.

1796 MME. D'ARBLAY *Camilla* III. 259 Poor miss thin o'-me's hat is spoilt already. 1803 FESSENDEN *Terr. Tracto* IV. (ed. 2) 174 *note*, The little whalebone thingamy whic the Duke of Queensbury run at New Market. 1807 W IRVING *Salmag.* (1824) 38, I mean only to tune up tho little thing-o-mys, who represent nobody but themselve 1819 'R. RABELAIS' *Abeillard & Heloisa* 101 A passport to brilliant court Where all great thingummies resort. 18 THACKERAY *Philip* viii, What a bloated aristocrat Thingam has become! 1904 *Times* 11 Jan. 12/2 Mr. So-and-so has 'entrusted' its little carcase to Mr. Thingummy, birdstuffe

† **Thi·n-gut.** Now *Obs.* or *vulgar.* [f. THIN *a* + GUT *sb.*] One who has a thin belly; a lea starved-looking person; a starveling.

1602 MIDDLETON *Blurt, Master Constable* I. ii, Sirrah thi gut, what's thy name? 1607 ROWLANDS *Diog. Lanth.* 6 'T Mounsieur Vsury, what a leane lanke thin-gut it is. 16 MASSINGER *Believe as You List* III. ii, Does it soe, yo thinnegut? Thou thinge without moysture.

So † **Thi·n-gu·tted** *a.*, thin-bellied, lank, lean.

1625 MASSINGER *New Way* I. ii, I am out of charity Wit none so much as the thin-gutted squire. 1735 R. GAL in *Mem. W. Stukeley* (Surtees) III. 111 A thin-gutted do like a grey-hound. 1746 FRANCIS tr. *Hor., Sat.* I. v. 9 Methinks, a single Pound of Bread a day Might such a slee thin-gutted Rogue content.

**Thingy**: see after THING *sb.*[1]

† **Thi·nhead.** *Obs. rare*—°. [f. THIN *a.* + *-hede* -HEAD.] = THINNESS.

*c* 1440 *Promp. Parv.* 491/1 Thynnesse, or thynhede c licurys, as ale, water, and oþer lyke, *tenuitas.*

† **Think**, *v.*[1] *Obs.* (exc. in METHINKS, q. v. Forms: see below. [OE. *þync(e)an, þúhte, geþúh* = OS. *thunkian, thûhta* (Du. *dunken*), OHG. *dun chan, dûhta* (MHG. *dunken*, G. *dünken, däuchte*) ON. *þykkja, þótta* (:—**þuŋkja*, **þúhta*) (Sw. *tycka* Da. *tykkes*), Goth. *þugkjan, þūhta*;—OTeut. **þuŋk jan*, **þuŋχta* to seem, appear. Although in Gothi and all the Teutonic langs. *þuŋkjan* is inflected a weak verb, with forms parallel to those of *þaŋkjan* (THINK *v.*[2]), it is generally held to have bee originally a strong vb., the present stem of whic was formed with *-ja* suffix, like **ligjan*, **sitjan* etc., on the weak grade of an original ablaut serie **þiŋk-*, **þaŋk-*, **þuŋk-* (see THINK *v.*[2]), whic subseq. passed into the first class of weak vbs. (cf *brūkjan, brûhte, bugjan, bauhte*, etc.). In OE., a in the cognate langs., the forms of this vb. an THINK *v.*[2] remained quite distinct; but in ME. owing to the fact that both *þync-* and *þenc-* gav ME. *þink-*, and both *þúht* and *þóht* appeared in ME. as *þouȝt, thought*, they became confused an finally fell together. The contiguity of sense als helped: see THINK *v.*[2]]

**A.** Illustration of Forms.

**1.** *Inf.* and *Pres. t.* α. 1 **þyncan, -cean**; *3r pers. sing.* 1 **ðynceþ, ðynceþ**, 4 **thunceth**(*ii*); **þunceþ** (**þunþ**).

*a* 800 CYNEWULF *Elene* 541 (Gr.) Do swa þe þynce. *c* 89 K. ÆLFRED *Gregory's Past. C.* xxxvi. 255 Hwelc wite sceal us ðonne to hefig ðyncan [*v. r.* ðynceán]? *a* 1250 *Owl & Night.* 1592 Ek steape hire þun[c]þ a mile. *Ibid.* 1649 M þunch, 1672 þuncþ [*Jesus MS.* þinkþ].

β. 1 **þincan, þincean**, 3–5 **þink(e, 4 þynke, thinc, 4–6 thynk(e, 4–7 thinke, 5 thynck, 6 thincke**, 4–6 (7–9 *arch.* in METHINKS) **think**; *3rd pers. sing.* 1 **þinþ**, 1–3 **þincþ**, 3 **þinkþ**, **thinkt**; 3 (*Orm.*) **þinnkeþþ**.

*c* 888 K. ÆLFRED *Boeth.* xxxiii. § 2 ʒif he hine þonne beʒit, þonne þincð him þæt he næbbe ʒenoʒ. *c* 1000 *Sax. Leechd.* II. 74 Swa micel swa þe þince. *c* 1200 ORMIN 11807 N þinnke ʒuw nan wunnderr. *c* 1325 *Spec. Gy Warw.* 58 Þouh þe þinke, hit greue þe. *c* 1350 *Will. Palerne* 38 Lordes, lusteneþ her-to, ʒif ʒou lef þinkes. 13.. *Cursor M.* 18966 (Gött.) Gret selcuth here-of thinces vus. *Ibid.* 260 (Fairf.) Me walde þink þat hit ware myne. *a* 1400 HYLTON *Scala Perf.* (W. de W. 1494) I. xxxiv, Hym shall thynke that his synnes are..so fowle. *c* 1400 MAUNDEV. (1839) xxvii. 278 Þanne wolde hem thinken gretter delyt. 1531 *Dial. on Laws Eng.* I. xxix. 70 It thynketh more resonable. 1577 HARRISON *England* II. i. (1877) I. 18 Adding what him thinketh good of his owne knowledge.

*Irreg.* 13.. *Cursor M.* 225 (Cott.) Notful me thinc it ware to man. *Ibid.* 16389 Selcuth vs thinc o þe. *c* 1400 MAUNDEV. (Roxb.) xxi. 96 Þis think me ane of þe grettest meruailes. 1530 CROME in Strype *Eccl. Mem.* (1721) III. App. x. 20 But my thynk theye hurt purgatorye sore. *c* 1572 GASCOIGNE *Fruites Warre* Wks. (1831) 212 Me thinke if then their cause be rightly scande.

γ. 2–3 **þinche(n, 2–4 þunche(n**; 3 **þenche(n, 4 thynche(n.**

*c* 1175 *Lamb. Hom.* 33 Nalde hit þe þinchen na mare bute [etc.]. *Ibid.* 35 ʒet hit wald me þunchen þet softeste beð.. þat ic efre ibad. *Ibid.* 69 Þet þunched gode swiðe god. *a* 1200 *Moral Ode* 62 Eiðer to lutel and to muchel scal þunchen [*v. r.* þunche] eft hom baþe. *c* **1230** *Hali Meid.* 7 Þah hit þunche oðre men þat ha drehen harde. *c* **1250** *A Lutel soth Sermun* 80 in *O. E. Misc.* 190 An eue to go mid him Ne þunchet [*v.r.* þincheþ] hire no schome. *c* **1300** *Harrow. Hell* (Harl. MS.) 140 Me þuncheþ he is a coward. **1399** *Pol. Poems* (Rolls) I. 397, I say ffor my self, and schewe, as me thynchith.

δ. 3–4 **þenke(n**, 4–5 **thenke(n**, 5 **thenck**; *3rd pers. sing.* 4 **thenkth**. (Belonging in form to THINK *v.*²)

*c* **1330** [see B. 3]. *c* **1374** CHAUCER *Anel. & Arc.* 105 But no thing thenkith þe fals as doth the trewe. **1390** GOWER *Conf.* II. 8 So that him thenketh of a day A thousand yer, til he mai se The visage of Penolope. **1419** in *Proc. Privy Council* (1834) II. 247 Þus us thenkiþ þer was grete negligence in sum persone.

ε. *3rd pers. sing.* 3–4 **þingþ**, 4 **thingth**; 5 **thyngyt**; **thing**.

*a* **1300** *Fragm. Pop. Sc.* (Wright) 96 The sonne is more than the mone, . . The mone thinȝth the more, for heo so neȝ ous is. **1340** *Ayenb.* 166 Suo dede þe martires ase hit þingþ ine hare liue. *c* **1420** *Anturs of Arth.* xxv, Vs thing [*v.r.* thynke] a masse als squete, As any spyce that euyr thou ete.

**2.** *Pa. t.* α. 1–3 **þuhte**, 3 **þuȝte**, **ðhuȝte**, (*Orm.*) **þuhhte**, 4 **þuȝt**, 5 **thught**.

*a* **800** CYNEWULF *Christ* 1424 Lytel þuhte is leoda bearnum. *c* **1200** *Trin. Coll. Hom.* 119 Hit þuhte here ech sunderlepes þat it was his landes speche. *c* **1200** ORMIN 15324 Itt himm þuhhte swiþe god. *c* **1250** *Death* 186 in *O. E. Misc.* 180 Hit þuȝte [*v. r.* þuhte] þe ful god. *c* **1250** *Gen. & Ex.* 1849 To sen de werld ðhuȝte hire god. **13..** *Cursor M.* 750 (Fairf.) If ham gode þuȝt [*v.rr.* thoght, þouȝt].

β. 3 **þohte**, 3–4 **þoȝte**, 3–5 **þouȝte**, 4 **thoȝte**, **þoȝt**, **þoht**, **thouht**, (**þouȝth**), 4–5 **þouȝt**, **thoght**, 4–6 *Sc.* **thocht**, 5 **thoghte**, **thoȝt**, **þowht**, *Sc.* **thoucht**, 5–7 (8–9 *arch.* in *methought*) **thought**; 3–4 **þoute**, 4 **thout**, (**thouth**), 4–5 **þout**, 5 **thowt**. (Coinciding in form with THINK *v.*²)

*c* **1290** *St. Kenelm* 123 in *S. Eng. Leg.* I. 348 Him þouȝte he clam op-on þat treo. *a* **1300** *Cursor M.* 19040 (Edin.) Þar of to don quat taim god þoȝte [*C.*, *G.* thoght, *L.* thoȝt, *Tr.* þouȝt]. *Ibid.* 1339 (Cott.) Him thoght [*Gött.* thout, *F.* þoȝt, *Tr.* þouȝte] . . þat to þe sky it raght þe toppe. **13..** *E. E. Allit. P.* B. 562 Hard hit hym þoȝt. **1375** BARBOUR *Bruce* I. 79 Þis ordynance þaim thocht þe best. *c* **1430** *Hymns Virg.* 83 Al þat y dide, it þouȝte me swete. **1513** DOUGLAS *Æneis* XI. vi. 15 The Goddis wraik, hym thocht, Schew that by fait Ene was thiddir brocht. **1632** HOLLAND *Cyrupædia* 205 Him thought that one came unto him.

**B.** Signification. *intr.* To seem, to appear.

**1.** With expressed subject (sometimes *it*) and complement; often also with dat. pron.

*c* **888** K. ÆLFRED *Boeth.* xxxii. § 2 Þonne ne ðuhte he him no innon swa fæȝer swa he utan þuhte. *c* **897** [see A. 1 α]. *c* **975** *Rushw. Gosp.* Matt. xvii. 25 Hwæt ðynceþ þe simon petre? *a* **1000** *Boeth. Metr.* xxviii. 63 Ne þincð þæt wundor micel monna æneȝum. *c* **1175** *Lamb. Hom.* 119 Monie þewas beoð . . þe monnen þuncheð rihte. *c* **1200** *Trin. Coll. Hom.* 109 Þe sunne þinkeð ful of liht . . þe sunne þincheð ful of hete. *c* **1275** *Woman of Samaria* 19 in *O. E. Misc.* 84 Hwat artu þat drynke me byst, þu þinchest of iude-londe. *c* **1386** CHAUCER *Knt.'s T.* 2183 Thanne is it wysdom, as it thynketh me To maken vertu of necessitee. **1437** EARL WARWICK in *Wars Eng. in France* (Rolls) II. Pref. 67 Such as shall think unto youre lordship necessarie and sufficient. *a* **1450** *Le Morte Arth.* 3829 That lyffe hym thought no-thyng longe.

**2.** Impersonal, i.e. without expressed subject, or with following clause as implicit subject: It seems. (Always with dat. pron., *me*, *him*, *her*, etc.)

After *c* 1300 sometimes irreg. put into the person or number of the dative pron., by confusion with THINK *v.*²: thus *me-think*, for *methinks*, after *I think*. Cf. A. 1 β. *irreg.*

**a.** With complement, as in 1; also with following inf. clause as implicit subject.

*Beowulf* 1748 Þinceð him to lytel þæt he lange heold. *c* **888** K. ÆLFRED *Boeth.* xiv. § 2 Ac þincð him ȝenoȝ on þam þe hi binnan heora æȝenre hyde habbað. *c* **1200** ORMIN 5030 Ȝiff himm þinnkeþþ god, he maȝȝ Þe ȝifenn heoffness blisse. *a* **1300** *Cursor M.* 636 (Cott.) Þar for thoght þam þen na scham. *Ibid.* 868 Vs thoght scam þe to bide. *c* **1425** *Ibid.* 16827 (Laud) Dothe hym doune as you thenckyth best. *c* **1460** *Towneley Myst.* ii. 158 Cry on, cry, whyls the thynk good. *c* **1520** BARCLAY *Jugurth* (1557) 28 b, Whan he had . . such companí as him thought competent for an army. **1556** *Aurelio & Isab.* (1608) D iv, Take that nombre of men and women as shall thincke you goode.

**b.** Followed by a sb. clause (constituting the logical subject), or parenthetic. See also METHINKS.

*c* **888** K. ÆLFRED *Boeth.* xxix. § 1 Him selfum ðincð þæt he nænne næbbe. *c* **1200** ORMIN 10299 Hemm þuhhte þatt he mihhte ben Helysew þe profete. **1297** R. GLOUC. (Rolls) 7597 To bete þulke robberie, þat him þoȝte he adde ydo. *c* **1386** CHAUCER *Knt.'s T.* 100 Hym thoughte þat his herte wolde breke. *c* **1470** HENRY *Wallace* v. 998 Say quhat ye will, this is the best, think me. **1530** TINDALE *Pract. Prelates* I vij, The maryage of the brother with the sister is not so greuouse agenst the lawe of nature (thinketh me) as the degrees aboue rehersed. **1635** HEYWOOD *Hierarch.* IV. 198 Him thought that in his depth of sleepe he saw A Souldier arm'd.

**c.** With adverb (*as*, *how*, *so*, *thus*), usually representing a clause.

[*Beowulf* 1341 ȝe feor hafað fæhðe ȝestæled þæs þe þincean mæȝ þeȝne moneȝum.] *c* **1000** *Ags. Gosp.* Matt. xxi. 28 Hu þincð eow? *a* **1300** *Cursor M.* 639 (Cott.) 'Adam', he said, 'how thinkt [*v.rr.* thinkes, þinkeþ] þe, In þis stede es fair to be?' *c* **1385** CHAUCER *L. G. W.* Prol. 248 Therfore may I seyn, as thynketh me, This songe in preysyng of this lady fre. *c* **1440** *Alphabet of Tales* 175 We hard a grete noyse of armyd men, & as vs thoght, of harnessid hors.

**1570–6** LAMBARDE *Peramb. Kent* (1826) 333 The which may (as me thinketh) be broken in-to foure severall portions.

**3.** Phr. *Think long*, to seem long, to be wearisome (to one): cf. THINK *v.*² 10 c.

*a* **1000** *Boeth. Metr.* x. 66 Þeah hit lang ðince. *c* **1200** *Trin. Coll. Hom.* 183 Hire þuncheð lang, þat hie on him bileueð. *c* **1330** *Assump. Virg.* (B. M. MS.) 121 Alle him þenkeþ swiþe longe Til þou comest hem amonge. *c* **1430** *Hymns Virg.* 9/49 After his loue me þenkiþ long.

**Think** (þiŋk), *v.*² Pa. t. and pple. **thought** (þǭt). Forms: see below. [OE. *þenc(e)an*, *þóhte*, (*ge*)*þóht*, = OFris. *thinka* (WFris. *tinkje*, *tinze*); OS. *thenkian*, *thāhta* (Du., LG. *denken*), OHG. *denchen*, *dāhta* (MHG., Ger. *denken*, *dachte*), ON. *þekkja*, *þátta* (**þeŋkja*, **þáhta*), (Sw. *tänka*, Da. *tænka*), Goth. *þagkjan*, *þāhta* (:—**þaŋχta*). In form, a factitive vb. f. *þaŋk-*, strong grade of ablaut series *þiŋk-*, *þaŋk-*, *þuŋk-*:—pre-Teut. **teng-*, **tong-*, **tng-*: cf. THINK *v.*¹ The original meaning may thus have been 'to cause (something) to seem or appear (to oneself)'. In ME., *þenk* (as was normal with the groups *-eng*, *-enk*) became *þink*, with the result of confusing this in the present stem with the prec. vb., of which the pa. t. *þúhte* was also from 13th c. written *þoughte*, *thought(e*, so that the forms of the two verbs became completely identical. The practical equivalence of sense between *me thinks*, *him thought*, etc., and *I think*, *he thought*, etc., also contributed to this result, there being no difference of import between 'such companí as *him thought* [= OE. *him þúhte*] competent' (see THINK *v.*¹ B. 2 a) and 'such company as *he thought* [= OE. *he þóhte*] competent'.]

**A.** Illustration of Forms.

**1.** *Inf.* and *Pres. t.* α. 1 **þencan**, 2 **þence**, 2–4 **þenken**, (3 *Orm.* **þennkenn**, **ðenke(n**, 4 **þengke**), 4–5 **þenke**, **thenke**, **þenk**, 4–5 **thenk**.

*c* **888** Hwæt he þencð [see B. 1]. ? *a* **1100** *O. E. Chron.* an. 995 (MS. F) Nan mann ne mihte ðencan embe naht elles butan. *a* **1175** Þence [see B. 8 b]. *c* **1200** *Trin. Coll. Hom.* 49 Þe man þe . . ne þencð no þing. *c* **1250** *Gen. & Ex.* 2072 Of me ðu ðhenke ðan it sal ben. *Ibid.* 3563 And ðenk, louerd, quat ben bi-foren Abram, and ysaac, and iacob sworen. *c* **1290** *St. Gregory* 50 in *S. Eng. Leg.* I. 357 Þou þencst . . with þi conseil al rome to bi-traiȝe. **1382** Thenk [see B. 2]. *c* **1440** *Promp. Parv.* 490/2 Thenkyn, *cogito*.

β. 2–3 **þenchen**, 3–4 **þenche**, 4 **thenche**.

*c* **1175** *Lamb. Hom.* 61 Þet we ne þenchen ufel to don. *c* **1200** *Moral Ode* 118 (Trin. Coll. MS.) He sal hit þenche þanne. *c* **1205**, *c* **1275** Þench, þinche [see B. 2 b (*b*)]. *c* **1330** *Arth. & Merl.* (Kölbing) 6534 Eten & drink men schal on benche And after mete in chaumber þenche. *c* **1386** Thenche [see B. 4].

γ. 4 **þink-**, **þinc-**, **thinc-**, 4–5 **þinke**, 5 **þynke**; 4–6 **thynk**, **thynke**, (**thincke**), 4–7 **thinke**, (**thinck**, 6 **thyncke**), 4– **think**.

**13..** *Cursor M.* 14187 (Cott.) Sir quat thinckes þou? *Ibid.* 21630 (Edin.) Mar . . Than ani man mai þinc [*Cott.* thing] in thoȝt. *a* **1340** HAMPOLE *Psalter* cxlv. 1 Þe purere part of mannys saule, þat thynkis þe wisdom of god. *c* **1425** *Eng. Conq. Irel.* 22 Other, that wors is . . vs tynken vndo that god shild. **1552** HULOET, Thyncke often, *reputo, as.* **1648** tr. *Senault's Paraphr. Job* 360 To thinke . . on their domesticke affaires. **1653** Thinck [see B. 2 b (*b*)].

δ. 3–4 *imper.* **þeng**, 4 *inf.* **thing**.

*a* **1275** *Prov. Ælfred* 518 in *O. E. Misc.* 133 Ne þeng þu neuere þi lif. **13..** Thing [see γ]. *a* **1400** Þeng [see B. 5 a].

**2.** *Pa. t.* 1–4 **ð-**, **þóhte**, 3 **þoȝte**, (**þochte**, **þoute**, **þuhte**, *Orm.* **þohhte**), 3–5 **þouȝte**, **þouȝt**, 4 **þouhte**, **þoughte**, **þoȝt**, **þoght**, (**þout**, **þuȝt**), **thoȝte**, **thoȝt**, **thouȝte**, *Sc.* **thowcht**, 4–5 **þought**, *Sc.* **thoucht**, 4–6 **thoght**, 4– *Sc.* **thocht**, 5 **þowȝt(e**, (**þowȝth**), **thouȝt**, **thowght(e**, (**thught**), 6 **thoughte**, (*dial.* 8–9 **thoft**, 9 **thowt**), 4– **thought**.

**971** Ðohte [see B. 2 b]. *c* **1200** ORMIN 7312 Herode . . þohhte þohh to cwellenn himm. *c* **1205** LAY. 1255 He þoute [*c* **1275** þohte] of his swefne. *Ibid.* 24190 Þuhte [see B. 10]. **1297** R. GLOUC. (Rolls) 2652 Hengist þoȝte þe king & is bytraye. **13..** *Cursor M.* 3352 (Cott.) He . . thoght on thing he had to done. *Ibid.* 2039 (Fairf.) Þe ȝonger broþer þuȝt ful wa. *c* **1350** *Will. Palerne* 855 Sche þout þroly in herte þat leuer hire were. **13..** *Gaw. & Gr. Knt.* 848 Wel hym semed for soþe, as þe segge þuȝt. *c* **1375** *Sc. Leg. Saints* iii. (*Andreas*) 928 Fore-þi I thowcht I wald nocht dwell. **1375** BARBOUR *Bruce* II. 69 He Thoucht that suld pass ane othir way. *c* **1400** *Destr. Troy* 3189 Fele of þe folke febull it thughten. **1450** W. LOMNER in *Four C. Eng. Lett.* (1880) 4 He thowghte he was desseyvyd. **1535** STEWART *Cron. Scot.* (Rolls) I. 90 Tha thocht it greit folie. **1604** E. G[RIMSTONE] *D'Acosta's Hist. Indies* III. ix. 146, I thought good to speak this. **1749** FIELDING *Tom Jones* VII. xiii, I thoft he had been an officer himself. **1864** MRS. LLOYD *Ladies Polc.* 102 I thoft, if so be you would be so handsome as to spake a word for me. **1864** TENNYSON *Northern Farmer, Old Style* v, I niver knaw'd whot a meän'd but I thowt a 'ad summat to saäy.

**3.** *Pa. pple.* 3 **iþoht**, **-e**, (**yþout**), **þoht**, (*Orm.* **þohht**), 3–4 **iþoȝt**, 4 **i-þouȝt**, **yþouȝt**, **i-thought**, **þoȝt**, **-e**, **þouȝte**, *Sc.* **thowcht**, **thocht**, 4–5 **thoght**, 5 **þouȝt**, **þought**, 5–6 **thowght**, 6–7 *Sc.* **thocht(e**, 7 **thoughte**, (5–9 *dial.* **thoft(e)**, 5– **thought**.

*c* **1200** *Trin. Coll. Hom.* 71 Ure ateliche sinnes þe we hauen don and queðen and þoht. *c* **1200** ORMIN 2364 Wel haffde þohht to libbenn. *c* **1205** LAY. 13468 Þat he hæfde iþoht ær. **13..** *Cursor M.* 20092 (Edin.) Quat hauis tu þoȝte [*v. r.* thoght]? *c* **1330** *Arth. & Merl.* 513 Ich haue y-þouȝt. *c* **1375** *Sc. Leg. Saints* ii. (*Paulus*) 380 To do þis, hafe I thowcht. *Ibid.* x. (*Mathou*) 135 As men . . thocht had. **1377** LANGL. *P. Pl.* B. XIII. 268 Þis wil be þouȝte longe. **1387–8** T. USK *Test. Love* I. ii. (Skeat) l. 162 If I coud haue made chere to one, and ithought an other. **1482** *Ord. Gild Exeter* in *Eng. Gilds* (1870) 314 To have a sustenans . . as cane be thofte . . resounabyll. **1560** DAUS tr. *Sleidane's Comm.* 276 This was thought to be done for this intent.

**B.** Signification. **I.** To conceive in the mind, exercise the mind, etc.

**1.** *trans.* To form in the mind, conceive (a thought, etc.); to have in the mind as a notion, an idea, etc.; to do in the way of mental action.

**a.** with simple obj. (sb. or pron.).

*c* **888** K. ÆLFRED *Boeth.* xxxix. § 9 Þeah hwa mæȝe onȝitan hwæt oðer do, he ne mæȝ witan hwæt he þencð. *a* **1200** *Moral Ode* 79 He wat wet þenkeð and hwet doð alle quike wihte. **13..** *Cursor M.* 27101 (Cott.) Vr thoghtes ar þai be thoght. *c* **1400** *Rom. Rose* 2541 They in herte cunne thenke a thing And seyn another, in hir speking. *a* **1548** HALL *Chron.*, *Edw. IV* 224 Whatsoeuer he thought in his Imaginacion. **1596** SHAKS. *Merch. V.* II. vii. 50 To thinke so base a thought. **1651** HOBBES *Leviath.* II. xxx. 180 Any man that sees what I am doing, may easily perceive what I think. **1871** SMILES *Charac.* i. (1876) 22 They think great thoughts. **1895** *Cornh. Mag.* Mar. 303 Don't begin to think hard things now.

**b.** with a direct statement, question, or exclamation as obj. (For constructions with indirect statement, etc., see 2 b, 4 a, 5 a, 8 a, 9.)

**971** *Blickl. Hom.* 21 Þæt mæȝ beon þæt sume men þencan oþþe cweþan, 'hu mæȝ ic secan þæt gastlice leoht [etc.]?' *c* **1386** CHAUCER *Man of Law's T.* 939 Parfay, thoghte he, fantome is in myn heed. *c* **1440** *Gesta Rom.* xxxi. 112 (Harl. MS.) And he thought to him selfe 'how may this be . . ?' **1611** BIBLE 2 *Kings* v. 11, I thought, He will surely come out to me. **1634** MILTON *Comus* 566 O poor hapless Nightingale thought I. **1692** BENTLEY *Confut. Atheism* III. (1693) 16 If any one shall think with himself, How then can any thing live in Mercury and Saturn? **1832** TENNYSON *Miller's Dau.* 93 My mother thought, What ails the boy? **1842** — *Dora* 4 He . . often thought, 'I'll make them man and wife'.

**c.** To conceive, feel (some emotion): as, † *to think wonder* (*ferly*), to wonder (*obs.*); *to think scorn* (*of*, or *to do* something), to scorn (*arch.*); *to think shame*, to be ashamed (now *dial.*). See also SCORN *sb.* 4, SHAME *sb.*

*a* **1300** *Cursor M.* 10601 (Cott.) Hir freindes . . Thoght ferli hou sco þider wan. *c* **1425** *Eng. Conq. Irel.* 16 Many hadden gret enuy, and mych wonder toght of Robert de barr. *c* **1430** [see SCORN *sb.* 4]. *c* **1440** *Alphabet of Tales* 85 When þe preste hard þis, onone he thoght shame. *a* **1533** LD. BERNERS *Huon* lxxxiii. 259 He thinkes scorne to speke to me. **1681** R. KNOX *Hist. Ceylon* 49 These gifts . . he thinks scorn to receive. *a* **1791** GROSE *Olio* (1796) 108 He ought to think shame of himself for such treatment. **1886** STEVENSON *Kidnapped* i, Can you forget . . old friends . . ? Fie, fie; think shame!

†**2.** (with simple obj.) To meditate on, turn over in the mind, ponder over, consider. *Obs.*

*c* **1000** *Ags. Ps.* (Th.) cxviii. [cxix.] 117 And ic þine soðfæstnysse symble þence. *c* **1200** *Moral Ode* 118 (Trin. Coll. MS.) Al þat a fri man haueð idon . . he sal hit þenche þanne. *a* **1300** *E. E. Psalter* i. 2 And his lagh þincke he night and dai. **13..** *Cursor M.* 24064 (Cott.), I thinc it euer and ai. **1382** WYCLIF 1 *Tim.* iv. 15 Thenk thou thes thingis. **1486** *Bk. St. Albans* e ij b, Thynke what I say my sonne nyght and day. **1605** SHAKS. *Macb.* II. ii. 33 These deeds must not be thought After these wayes.

**b.** with indirect question as obj.: (For const. with direct question see 1 b.) (*a*) in reference to a fact or possibility.

**971** *Blickl. Hom.* 7 Maria . . ðohte hwæt seo halettung wære. *a* **1300** *Cursor M.* 1323 (Cott.) Seth bigan to thinc for-qui, þat þis tre bi-com sua dri. **1881** TROLLOPE *Dr. Wortle's School* v. iv, Mrs. Wortle began to think whether the visitor could have known of her intended absence.

(*b*) In reference to something to be done, with implication of purpose or design. (Cf. 7, 8.)

**971** *Blickl. Hom.* 241 And hie þohton hu hie hine acwellan meahton. *c* **1205** LAY. 8555 And þench [*c* **1275** þinche] mid wulche deden þu miht werien þine leoden. *c* **1386** CHAUCER *Melib.* ¶ 761 Thinkinge how she myghte brynge this nede vnto a good conclusion. **1474** CAXTON *Chesse* IV. viii. (1883) 184 He began to thynke in what maner he myght escape the deth. **1653** HOLCROFT *Procopius* I. 10 Thinck Sir! how you may avenge us and the Persians. **1778** MISS BURNEY *Evelina* (1791) I. xxxiii. 178 A-thinking what he should do. *Mod.* I am thinking what to do next.

**c.** To have one's thoughts full of, imbued with, or influenced by; to think in terms of.

**1821** BYRON *Diary* 29 Jan., They . . think and dream Dante. **1859** *Habits Gd. Soc.* Pref., A horse-dealer . . if he thinks nothing but horses, he cannot be good society. **1865** KINGSLEY *Herew.* ii, Unless thou hast been drinking beer and thinking beer. **1889** *Pall Mall G.* 24 Oct. 7/2 The present generation of Greeks talks French but thinks German.

**3.** *intr.* To exercise the mind, esp. the understanding, in any active way; to form connected ideas of any kind; to have, or make, a train of ideas pass through the mind; to meditate, cogitate. (The most general verb to express internal mental activity, excluding mere perception of external things or passive reception of ideas.)

*Think aloud*: to express one's thoughts by audible speech as they pass through the mind.

*c* **1000** ÆLFRIC *Gen.* xxiv. 63 Þe eode ut on þæt land þencende. *c* **1320** *Cast. Love* 17 He leue vs þenche and worchen so, þat he vs schylde from vre fo. **1382** WYCLIF 1 *Cor.* xiii. 11 Whanne I was a litil child . . I thouȝte as a litil child. **1552** HULOET, Thinke muche, *reputo*. **1603** SHAKS. *Meas.*

*for M.* II. iv. 1 When I would pray, and think, I thinke, and pray To seuerall subiects. **1673** DRYDEN *State Innocence* II. i, That I am I know, because I think. **1690** LOCKE *Hum. Und.* II. i. § 10 There is something in us, that has a Power to think. *c* **1714** POPE *Lett.* (1735) I. 151 The Freedom I shall use in this Manner of Thinking aloud. **1764** GOLDSM. *Trav.* 372 Those who think must govern those that toil. **1864** BOWEN *Logic* i. 10 To think is to make clear through Concepts something already otherwise represented or known to consciousness.

**b.** with *about*, *of*, (*on*, *upon* arch.), *over*, †*to* (obs. rare): To exercise the mind upon, or have the mind occupied with; to meditate on; to consider, attend to mentally, apply the mind to.

**971** *Blickl. Hom.* 57 Myccle swiðor we sceolan þencan be þæm gastlicum þingum. *c* **1000** *Ags. Ps.* (Th.) cxvii[i]. 8 God ys on Dryhten ʒeorne to þenceanne. *c* **1000** *Institutes of Polity* c. 14 Riht is þæt munecas..a to Gode þencan and ʒeornlice clypian. *c* **1200** *Vices & Virt.* 17 Ac ðu..noldest þenchen of ðine for[ð]siðe. *a* **1300** *Floriz & Bl.* 32 Ac floriz þencheþ al on oþer. *c* **1340** HAMPOLE *Prose Tr.* 36 Thow may..thynke ouer thi synnes be-fore donne. **13..** *Cursor M.* 15612 (Gött.) To thinc apon his care. *a* **1380** *Minor Poems fr. Vernon MS.* xxxix. 138 Nou is deþ a wonder þing And grislich for to þenken on. *a* **1425** *Cursor M.* 9977 (Trin.) [She] þouȝte neuer to wicked dede. **1477** EARL RIVERS (Caxton) *Dictes* 11 Think & loke wele vpon your werkis without hasting you. **1641** EVELYN *Diary* 2 Jan., Who now thought of nothing but the pursuite of vanity. **1706** E. WARD *Wooden World Diss.* (1708) 100 It makes him think upon Pay-Day. **1782** MISS BURNEY *Cecilia* VIII. vi, Think of it well ere you proceed. **1804–6** SYD. SMITH *Mor. Philos.* (1850) 89 He began thinking about lances. *Mod.* I'll think over the matter, and let you know my decision in a day or two. [Cf. 16.]

**4.** To form or have an idea of (a thing, action, or circumstance, real or imaginary) in one's mind; to imagine, conceive, fancy, picture. **a.** *trans.* with simple obj. or obj. cl.; also *absol.* in colloq. phrases *only think! you can't think!*

*c* **1200** ORMIN 1761 Unnseȝȝenndlike mare inoh þann aniȝ wihht maȝȝ þennkenn. *a* **1300** *Cursor M.* 647 Es nan..wit hert mai think,..þe hert may ioy þat þam es lent. *c* **1386** CHAUCER *Miller's T.* 67 There nas no man so wys þat koude thenche So gay a popelote, or swich a wenche. **1415** *Rolls of Parlt.* IV. 85/1 As free..as hert may thynk, or eygh may see. **1590** SHAKS. *Mids. N.* V. i. 431 Thinke but this..That you haue but slumbred heere. **1656** STANLEY *Hist. Philos.* VIII. (1701) 303/1 Thou seest not what thou thinkst before thy eye. **1782** MME. D'ARBLAY *Diary* 8 Dec., You can't think how I'm encumbered with these ruffles! **1864** MRS. CARLYLE *Lett.* III. 220 Only think! I get my new milk again, at eight.

**b.** *intr.* with *of* (*on* obs. or arch.), in same sense. (Often imperative in colloq. phrases.)

*a* **1300** *Cursor M.* 18802 (Cott.) Quat hert mai thinc o suilk honur. *c* **1400** MAUNDEV. (1839) xxvii. 278 He had..all maner of foules & of bestes that ony man myghte thenke on. **1598** SHAKS. *Merry W.* III. v. 116 And then to be stopt in like a strong distillation with stinking Cloathes, that fretted in their owne grease: thinke of that, a man of my Kidney; thinke of that. **1653** WALTON *Angler* ii. 41 The gloves of an Otter are the best fortification for your hands against wet weather that can be thought of. **1741** H. WALPOLE *Lett. to Mann* (1834) I. vi. 12 Do but think on a duel between Winnington and Augustus Townshend. **1842** TENNYSON *Locksley Hall* 73 Can I think of her as dead? **1844** E. FITZGERALD *Lett.* (1889) I. 125 Think of the *rococity* of a gentleman studying Seneca in the middle of February 1844 in a remarkably damp cottage. **1861** J. PYCROFT *Agony Point* xlvi, Think of me ever being rich! **1875** JOWETT *Plato* (ed. 2) IV. 264 The ancient philosophers ..thought of science only as pure abstraction. **1885** J. PAYN *Talk of Town* I. 7 She always thought of him..as a very young man.

**c.** *trans.* with simple obj. To form a definite conception of (something real) by a conscious mental act; to picture in one's mind, apprehend clearly, cognize (with or without direct perception).

**1864** BOWEN *Logic* i. 5 We..are thus enabled *to think* the landscape as a whole. **1885** J. MARTINEAU *Types Eth. Th.* (ed. 2) I. I. xi. § 8. 212 When you think this equation [surface of a sphere = area of circle of twice its diameter]. **1890** W. JAMES *Princ. Psychol.* II. xx. 203 We think the ocean as a whole by multiplying mentally the impression we get at any moment when at sea.

**II.** To call to mind, take into consideration.

**5. a.** *trans.* (with obj. clause, often indirect interrogative): To call to mind; to consider, reflect upon; to recollect, remember, bear in mind.

*c* **1020** *Rule St. Benet* lxiii. (Logeman) 104 Ac he þænce simle þæt he be eallum his domum & weorcum be his is to ʒildanne. *c* **1230** *Hali Meid.* 3, & maken þe to þenchen hwuch delit were þrin. *a* **1400** *Pol. Rel. & L. Poems* (1903) 258 Þeng wat þou art, & wat þou was. **1474** CAXTON *Chesse* I. iii. (1883) 15 Yf thou be a man thinke that thou shalt dye. **1605** SHAKS. *Macb.* II. ii. 51, I am afraid, to thinke what I haue done. **1667** MILTON *P. L.* VI. 135 Fool, not to think how vain Against th' Omnipotent to rise in Arms. **1818** SHELLEY *Rosalind & Helen* 188 Helen smiled..To think that a boy as fair as he..The like sweet fancies had pursued.

**b.** *intr.* To consider the matter; to reflect.

*Beowulf* 290 Æʒ hwæþres sceal scearp scyld-wiʒa ʒescad witan worda & worca seþe wel þenceð. *a* **1800** COWPER *Inscr. Tomb Hamilton* 1 Pause here, and think. **1842** TENNYSON *Dora* 27 Consider, William: take a month to think. **1862** E. FITZGERALD *Lett.* (1889) I. 286, I somehow fancy a line of nonsense will catch you at Ely: and yet, now I come to think, you will have left Ely, probably. **1910** G. F. HILL in *Archæologia* LXII. 140, I confess that had I come across this MS. at the beginning of my search, I should have thought twice before going on.

**c.** *intr.* with *of* (arch. *on*, *upon*), or *inf.*: To call to mind, remember, bethink oneself (of), hit upon mentally. (See also 7 b.)

*c* **1175** *Pater Noster* 96 in *Lamb. Hom.* 59 He walde þet he of him þohte. *a* **1300** *Cursor M.* 1860 (Cott.) Our lauerd þan on noe thoght. *c* **1400** *Emare* 951 The emperour.. þowȝt on hys synne; Of hys þowȝtyr Emare, That was putte yn-to þe see. *a* **1536** TINDALE *Declar. Sacraments* a vj b, God ..promysed that thei shuld be thoght vpon before the lord yir god & saued from their enemies. **1552** HULOET, Thynke vpon me, *memento mei*. **1611** SHAKS. *Wint. T.* IV. iv. 547 Haue you thought on A place whereto you'l go? **1613** — *Hen. VIII*, II. ii. 138 The most conuenient place, that I can thinke of..is Black-Fryers. **1712** ARBUTHNOT *John Bull* II. iv, There is a small concern of a thousand pounds; I hope you think on it, Sir. **1844** MACAULAY *Ess.*, *Earl Chatham* (1887) 838 In his distress, he thought on Pitt. *Mod.* Did you think to ask him how his father is? No, I didn't think of it.

**d.** *intr.* with *on* (adv.), To remember. Now *dial.*

**1671** H. M. tr. *Erasm. Colloq.* 226, I much wonder that now thou thinkest on at last to ask me that. *a* **1800** PEGGE *Suppl. Grose*, *Think on*, think of it, as I will if I think on. **1828** *Craven Gloss.*, *Think-on*, to remember. 'Be sure to mind to think-on'.

**e.** *refl.* To bethink oneself. *rare.*

**1556** *Aurelio & Isab.* (1608) G j, I thinckes me never the lesse that you have saide an exemple of the peacocke. **1890** W. A. WALLACE *Only a Sister* 325, I thought me at last of the vestry window.

**f.** *To think better of*: see BETTER *adv.* 6.

**6.** To take into consideration, have regard to, consider. †**a.** *trans.* with simple obj. *Obs. rare.*

*c* **1175** *Lamb. Hom.* 15 Þet we sculden þenchen nu ʒef we weren iseli. **1382** WYCLIF *Prov.* iii. 6 In alle thi weies thenc [1388 thenke on] hym. *c* **1450** tr. *De Imitatione* I. xxiv. 32 Þenke no þinge but þi soule helþe; charge onely þo þinges þat longiþ to þi soule.

**b.** *intr.* with *of*, arch. *on* (*upon*).

*a* **1300** *Cursor M.* 10435 (Cott.) Qui ne wil þou on þi seluen thinc, Þat þou wil noiþer ete ne drinc? **1340** HAMPOLE *Pr. Consc.* 2652 And whyles he lyffes..Thynk he suld ay of his lyfes hende. *c* **1380** WYCLIF *Serm.* Sel. Wks. I. 65 Wolde God þat preelatis wolde þenke on þis now. **1387** TREVISA *Higden* (Rolls) V. 181 To þinke [*v.r.* þengke] on þe comyn profit. **1532** TINDALE *Expos. Matt. v–vii* vii. 11. 89 If thou repente..he promyseth that he will not thynke on thy synnes. **1735** JOHNSON *Lobo's Abyssinia, Descr.* xi. 112 Nothing was thought of, but how to save ourselves, and the little goods we had. **1827** SCOTT *Surg. Dau.* x, 'That is the last matter to be thought on', said Hartley. **1875** JOWETT *Plato* (ed. 2) IV. 35 If..we begin by thinking of ourselves first, we are easily led on to think of others.

**7.** To bethink oneself of something in the way of a plan or purpose; to find out or hit upon (a way to do something) by mental effort; to contrive, devise, plan, plot. (Cf. *think out*, 15. See also 8.) **a.** *trans.* with simple obj. or inf.

*c* **1330** R. BRUNNE *Chron. Wace* (Rolls) 1075 Brutus by-þoughte hym of queintise: Queyntise bihouede [*v.r.* behoues] hym nedly þenke, Þat his enemys schold waite a blenk. **1483** CAXTON *Gold. Leg.* 181 b/1 Thou cursyd wretche now thynke to saue thy lyf. **1602** MARSTON *Antonio's Rev.* IV. v, Let's thinke a plot. **1852** THACKERAY *Esmond* I. ix, It was this lady's disposition to think kindnesses..and to scheme benevolence.

**b.** *intr.* with *of* (*on*, *upon*, obs. or arch.).

**1598** SHAKS. *Merry W.* IV. iv. 46 What shall be done with him? What is your plot? *Mist. Pa.* That likewise haue we thought vpon. **1630** in Picton *L'pool Munic. Rec.* (1883) I. 158 His Majesty..hath thought of a way. **1699** LISTER *Journ. Paris* 49 'Tis..their Misfortune not to have Thought of an Alphabet. *a* **1715** BURNET *Own Time* (1766) II. 31 She..took all the ways she could think on to ruin him. *a* **1774** GOLDSM. *Surv. Exp. Philos.* (1776) II. 121 Derham ..was the first who thought upon this method of measuring the heights..by the barometer.

**8.** To conceive or entertain the notion of doing something; to meditate, contemplate, intend, purpose, design, mean, 'have a mind', 'have thoughts (of)'. In early use often not distinguishable from 7; in later use mostly denoting an imperfect, temporary, or ineffective intention: cf. THOUGHT *sb.* 3 d. **a.** *trans.* with *inf.* or *obj. cl.*

*Beowulf* 1536 Swa sceal man don þonne he æt guðe ʒegan þenceð long-sumne lof. **971** *Blickl. Hom.* 151 Þa Iudeas.. þohton þæt hie woldan ofslean þa apostolas. *c* **1175** *Lamb. Hom.* 61 Þet we ne þenchen ufel to don. *c* **1220** *Bestiary* 455 He..ðoȝte he wulde him fordon. **1297** R. GLOUC. (Rolls) 1181 Iulius þe emperour..þoȝte to sle al þat folc. **1375** BARBOUR *Bruce* XI. 532 To the castell thai thoucht to fair. *c* **1400** *Brut* xii. 16 Ferst he þougt assaye whiche of ham louede him most and best. **1535** COVERDALE *2 Chron.* ii. 1 Salomon thoughte to buylde an house vnto the name of the Lorde. **1585** ABP. WHITGIFT in *Lett. Lit. Men* (Camden) 44 This Paper..which I had thowght to have delivered unto you my self yesterday. **1681** DRYDEN *Abs. & Achit.* 510 With them joined all the haranguers of the throng, That thought to get preferment by the tongue. **1833** TENNYSON *Lady Clara V. de Vere* i, You thought to break a country heart For pastime. **1878** T. HARDY *Ret. Native* IV. ii, He..thought he would send for his mother; and then he thought he would not.

**b.** *trans.* With simple obj. (usually an action).

*a* **1175** *Cott. Hom.* 221 Ne yfel to þence, ne to donne. *c* **1220** *Bestiary* 449 Wo so seieð oðer god, & ðenkeð iuel on his mod, Fox he is & fend iwis. *a* **1300** *Cursor M.* 4124 To stint wald he..Þe foly þat his breþer thoght. *c* **1320** *Cast. Love* 1 Þat good þenkeþ, good may do. *a* **1450** *Le Morte Arth.* 1655 How in an Appelle he dede the galle And hadde it thought to syr gawayne. **1553** ASCHAM in *Lett. Lit. Men* (Camden) 14 To whom yow never intended to think any harm. **1667** MILTON *P. L.* I. 661 Peace is despaird, For who can think Submission? **1819** SHELLEY *Cenci* I. i. 97 While yet Manhood remained to act the thing I thought.

**c.** *intr.* with *of* (also *upon*, ?arch. or dial.).

**1698** FRYER *Acc. E. India & P.* 9 We began to think of returning. **1749** FIELDING *Tom Jones* Ded., It was by your Desire that I first thought of such a Composition. **1760–72** H. BROOKE *Fool of Qual.* (1809) III. 138 You must no think of going till you take..dinner with us. **1812** CRABBE *Tales* xviii, Each thought of taking to himself a wife. **186**[illegible] KINGSLEY in *Lett. & Mem.* (1877) II. 133, I hear you think of getting into Parliament. **1894** J. T. FOWLER *Adamnan* Introd. 60 He thought of going to Rome and Jerusalem and did go to Tours.

**d.** *spec.* with *of*: To consider (a person) in view of some vacancy, or *esp.* of marriage; to cherish the notion or intention of marrying.

**1670** LADY CHAWORTH in *12th Rep. Hist. MSS. Comm.* App. v. 17 Lady Exeter..could heartily wish that you thought of her niece Lady Betty. **1802** MAR. EDGEWORTH *Moral T.* (1816) I. xx. 187, I trust to your prudence, not to think of Flora..; for you can't..marry a girl with so small a fortune. **1856** PATMORE *Angel in Ho.* II. II. iii, You, with your looks and catching air, To think of Vaughan!

†**e.** *intr.* or *ellipt.* To purpose or intend to go; to direct one's course. *Obs.*

*c* **893** K. ÆLFRED *Oros.* IV. ix. § 2 He þara ælces ehtende wolde beon,.. þe þæs wordes wære þæt from Romebyrg þohte. *a* **1023** WULFSTAN *Hom.* xlii. (Napier) 200 On ða wisan, þe man hors ʒewæpnað, þonne man to wiʒe þenċð. *c* **1330** R. BRUNNE *Chron. Wace* (Rolls) 12501 [Arthur] passed Burgoyne..Vntil Hostum, þyder he þought. **1377** LANGL. *P. Pl.* B. XVI. 175, I frayned hym..of whennes he were, and whider þat he þouȝte. *a* **1400–50** *Alexander* 1121 Now airis he furthe with his ost, to Egist he thinkes.

†**f.** *fig.* To seem likely (*to do* something): *thought to* = 'was like to', was on the point of, nearly did... Cf. F. *penser à*. *Obs.*

**1578** N. BAXTER *Calvin on Jonah* 9 The shyppe thought to be broken. **1585** T. WASHINGTON tr. *Nicholay's Voy.* II. xi. 45 b, A Northerly wynde..thought to haue made vs turne backe agayne. **1599** NASHE *Lenten Stuffe* 46 With so ill a will hee went, that hee had thought to haue topled his burning carre..into the sea (as Phaeton did).

**III.** To be of opinion, deem, judge, etc.

**9.** *trans.* with *obj. cl.* (or pronoun substitute), or parenthetic: To be of opinion, hold the opinion, believe, deem, judge, apprehend, consider; usually, to believe without any great assurance, to regard it as likely, to have the idea, to suppose; in reference to a future event, to expect (coinciding partly in sense with 12).

*Who do you think? What do you think?* (colloq.) phrases used, esp. parenthetically, to introduce a surprising statement.

*Beowulf* 691 Næniʒ heora þohte þæt he þanon scolde eft eard lufan æfre ʒesecean. *c* **1175** *Lamb. Hom.* 67 Þos ilke bode, wisliche þing, of oðre is ful festning. *a* **1300** *Cursor M.* 950 Þou sal thinc þou liues to lang. *c* **1386** CHAUCER *Sompn. T.* 322 Thanne thoughte they it was the beste reed To lede hem bothe to the Iuge agayn. **1450** W. LOMNER in *Four C. Eng. Lett.* (1880) 4 He thowghte he was desseyvyd. *a* **1548** HALL *Chron.*, *Hen. VIII* 170 Who would haue thought that our Uncle of Englande would haue made warre on vs? **1592** MORYSON *Let.* in *Itin.* (1617) I. 25 Each of vs went to our taske, he (as I thought) to goe, I to sleepe. **1601** HOLLAND *Pliny* (1634) I. 188 Thrason was the first builder of towne wals: of towers & fortresses, the Cyclops, as Aristotle thinketh. **1610** SHAKS. *Temp.* I. ii. 40 Canst thou remember..? I doe not thinke thou canst. **1615** G. SANDYS *Trav.* 38 Fresh water, some say brought thither by art, I rather think from a naturall fountain. **1616** B. JONSON *Epigr.*, *Voyage itself* 135 But 'mongst these Tiberts, who do you think there was? Old Banks the juggler. **1726** SWIFT *Gulliver* I. vii, A country, governed, as I thought, by very different maxims from those in Europe. **1849** MACAULAY *Hist. Eng.* vi. II. 15 It was thought that the flocks, thus separated from the evil shepherds, would soon return to the true fold. **1875** JOWETT *Plato* (ed. 2) I. 97, I think that I understand him. *Nursery Rime*, There was an old woman; and what do you think? She lived upon nothing but victuals and drink.

**b.** *I don't think* (slang): used after an ironical statement, to indicate that the reverse is intended.

**1837** DICKENS *Pickw.* xxxviii, 'You're a amiably-disposed young man, sir, I don't think', resumed Mr. Weller, in a tone of moral reproof. **1853** 'C. BEDE' *Verdant Green* III. iv, 'Well! you're a grateful bird, I don't think!' said Mr. Bouncer. **1857** HUGHES *Tom Brown* II. ii, Hark how he swears, Tom. Nicely brought-up young man, ain't he, I don't think. **1911** KEBLE HOWARD *Cheerful Knave* xvi, Breakfast? Yer a credit to yer calling, I don't think.

**c.** *intr.* To hold the opinion (indicated by context). *To think so*, to be of that opinion; *to think from* (quot. 1625), to dissent from, to disagree with; *to think with*, to be of the same opinion as.

*a* **1200** *Moral Ode* 149 Al he walde and oðerluker don and oðerluker þenchen Wenne he bi-þohte on helle fur. **1552** HULOET, Thyncke contrarye, *absentio, is.* **1560** DAUS tr. *Sleidane's Comm.* 425 b, He said he spake as he thought. **1591** SHAKS. *Two Gent.* II. vii. 62, I feare me it will make me scandaliz'd. *Luc.* If you thinke so, then stay at home. **1625** F. MARKHAM *Bk. Hon.* I. vi. § 2 The Holy Ghost (from whose rule we dare not thinke) mentioneth but two Sonnes. **1820** BYRON *Mar. Fal.* II. i. 302, I did not Think with him, but would not oppose the thought. **1877** *Smith & Wace's Dict. Chr. Biog.* I. s.v. *Atticus*, Those who thought with him found in him a warm friend.

**10.** *trans.* with complement (with or more often without *inf.*): To believe, consider, or suppose (to be..); to look upon as.

† Also (quot. 1607) with *for* (cf. *take for*, and 12 d).

*c* **1205** LAY. 24190 For he heom þuhte wurðe. *a* **1250** *Prov. Ælfred* 60 in *O. E. Misc.* 106 We [*read* þe] hine her on worlde wrþie þencheþ [*c* **1275** þenket]. **1340** HAMPOLE *Pr. Consc.* 4250 He sal thynk hym loverd of alle. *c* **1459** *Regist. de Aberbrothoc* (Bann. Cl.) II. 107 Thynkand it onkyndle tyll thole ane nominatioun of lardschipe of sic ane man. *a* **1548** HALL *Chron.*, *Hen. VII* 7 They were thought to haue been confederates. **1593** SHAKS. *Rich. II*, v. ii. 26 Thinking his prattle to be tedious. **1607** — *Cor.* IV. v. 62 If..not yet thou know'st me, and..dost not thinke me for the man I am. **1610** — *Temp.* IV. i. 120 May I be bold To thinke these spirits? **1651** HOBBES *Leviath.* II. xxv. 135 Some, that have the ambition to be thought eloquent. **1728** YOUNG *Love of Fame* VI. 205 Think nought a trifle, tho' it small appear. **1834** JAMES *J. Marston Hall* vii, Lord Masterton thought himself bound to act the part of an elder brother. **1865** RUSKIN *Sesame* ii. § 94 You think that only a lover's fancy.

**b.** with complement immediately following (with ellipsis of obj. *it*, or with inf. or clause as obj. placed after the complement). Now chiefly in *think fit* (see FIT *a.* 2 b), *think proper.*

*c* **1375** *Cursor M.* 14096 (Fairf.) Martha þuȝt il ho [Mary] ne help hir walde. *c* **1400** *Laud Troy Bk.* 3426 Wherfore I rede, if ȝe thenke right, That we sende som messanger To Delos. *c* **1460** SIR R. ROSS *La Belle Dame* 190 Whan he þought tyme to daunce with her. *a* **1500** *Debate Carpenter's Tools* 208 in Hazl. *E. P. P.* I. 86 Alle the ȝerne that I may spynne, To spend at ale he thinkes no synne. **1560** in Feuillerat *Revels Q. Eliz.* (1908) 51 As the said Edmunde.. shall thinke behoofefull & expedient. **1611–1875** [see FIT *a.* 2 b]. **1692** SIR T. P. BLOUNT *Ess.* 37, I thought good to go to the Philosophers. **1831** SCOTT *Chron. Canongate* Introd., The little narrative which I thought proper to put forth in October, 1827.

**c.** *Think* (*it*) *long*: to grow weary with waiting; to weary, to be impatient; to long, yearn. In quot. *c* 1380 *think long by* = to weary of. See also LONG *a.*[1] 9 b. *Obs.* exc. *dial.*

A perversion of the earlier *think long* (THINK *v.*[1] B. 3) 'to seem or appear long to', by substituting the nom. for the (uninflected) dative. In the first quot. 'þat Crist þouȝte longe' may be = that to Christ seemed long (cf. 'that him thoughte long').

*c* **1380** WYCLIF *Serm.* Sel. Wks. II. 59 Þe Jewis þouȝten þat Crist þouȝte longe bi his liif, and wolde..slee himsilf. **1450** MARG. PASTON in *P. Lett.* I. 178, I thynk ryth longe tyll I have some god tydyngys fro yow. *a* **1533** LD. BERNERS *Huon* xciii. 303 My wyfe..thynkethe longe for my comynge. **1592** G. HARVEY *Four Lett.*, etc. Sonn. xviii, These hungry wormes thinke longe for their repast. **1631** RUTHERFORD *Lett.* (1862) I. 75 Behold I come..; think not long. I shall be with you at once. **1650** TRAPP *Comm. Exod.* x. 3 God think's long of the time that men misspend ..in wicked courses. **1788** CLARA REEVE *Exiles* I. 195 We think long till we see you. **1895** FRASER *Whaups* xi. 152 Ye maunna bide lang away, for I'll be thinkin' lang till I see ye again.

†**d.** *Think* (*it*) *much*: to think it a great or serious matter; to make objection, object, grudge; to be shy, hesitate (*to do* something, or *of* something); to be surprised, wonder (*that*...). See also MUCH B. 2 g, and cf. 11. *Obs.*

Perh. altered from 'it thinks me much' (THINK *v.*[1]).

**1610** SHAKS. *Temp.* I. ii. 252 Thou..thinkst it much to tread y^e^ Ooze Of the salt deepe. **1656** EARL MONM. tr. *Boccalini's Advts. fr. Parnass.* I. i. (1674) 1 Menante thinks not much to acquaint you here with the chiefest of them. **1669** R. MONTAGU in *Buccleuch MSS.* (Hist. MSS. Comm.) I. 465 Mr. Grey nor Mr. Treasurer will not think much of my sharing with them. **1678** TILLOTSON *Serm.*, 1 *John* v. 3 I. 221 If we consider our infinite obligations to God, we have no reason to think much to sacrifice to him our dearest interests.

†**e.** *pass.* To seem, appear (*to* a person): = THINK *v.*[1]; also *ellipt.* to seem good. *Obs.*

Perh. originally for THINK *v.*[1]: 'it thinks (= appears) to the king' being changed by way of correction to 'it is thought to the king'; hence the retention of *to*.

**1425** *Rolls of Parlt.* IV. 290/2 Hit is thoght to the Kyng.. that there is provision. **1427** *Ibid.* 326/2 Alleggyng..such groundes..as it was þought to youre discretion. **1558** Q. MARY in J. M. Stone *Life* (1901) 512 As to hys godly wysdome shall be thowght mete and convenyent. **1577** J. KNEWSTUB *Confutation* (1579) 86 It was thought good vnto almighty God, that the Scriptures shoulde be penned.

**11.** *intr.* To have a (good, bad, or other) opinion with regard to a person or thing; to value or esteem something (highly or otherwise). Const. with adv. (*much, little, well, ill*, etc.), or adverbial accusative (in fig. phrases, as *to think the world of, small beer of*, etc.: see also the sbs.); and with *of* († *by*, † *on*, † *at*, dial. *to*) before the name of the person or thing.

*c* **1375** *Cursor M.* 14669 (Fairf.) Þai loked on him & loured grim & heþeli þai þuȝt be him. *c* **1489** CAXTON *Sonnes of Aymon* xii. 298 'What thynke you by hym?' 'Certes', sayd rowlande, 'reynawd is a sage knyght'. **1535** COVERDALE *Haggai* ii. 3 But what thinke ye now by it? **1579** TOMSON *Calvin's Serm. Tim.* 111/1 To constraine vs to thinke better on our selues. **1581** MULCASTER *Positions* iii. (1887) 11 This man wrote thus, and was verie well thought of. **1598** SHAKS. *Merry W.* II. i. 85 What doth he thinke of vs? **1601** — *Twel. N.* IV. ii. 59, I thinke nobly of the soule. **1711** STEELE *Spect.* No. 104 ⁋ 1 To be negligent of what any one thinks of you, does not only shew you arrogant but abandoned. **1813** *Sk. Character* (ed. 2) I. 55, I didn't think much of her. **1902** O. WISTER *Virginian* ix, Mrs. Tayler..thought the world of her. [*Midl. dial.* I don't think much to him. What do you think to the book?]

**b.** *Think nothing of*: (*a*) to have a very low opinion of, set no value upon, esteem as worthless; (*b*) to make light of, make no difficulty or scruple about (cf. *make nothing of*, NOTHING 11 a); so *to think no more of..than.*

[**1640** DK. NEWCASTLE *Country Capt.* II. i, Betweene, us too, what thinke you of a wench? *Court.* Nothinge.] **1802** BEDDOES *Hygëia* VIII. 76 A pint of wine in two hours is nothing thought of. **1872** O. W. HOLMES *Poet Breakf.-t.* v, The Lady thanked him..but said she thought nothing of the walk. **1888** *Harper's Mag.* Mar. 565/2 The Western people..think no more of throwing down a railroad..than a conservative Easterner does of taking an unaccustomed walk across country.

**12.** To believe possible or likely; to suspect; to expect, anticipate. **a.** *trans.* with simple obj.

*c* **1400** *Destr. Troy* 11837 Priam..& his prise knightes, Sweryn all swiftly, & no swyke thoghtyn. **1604** SHAKS. *Oth.* III. iii. 339, I saw't not, thought it not: it harm'd not me. **1719** DE FOE *Crusoe* (1840) I. ii. 25 He, thinking no harm, agreed.

**b.** with *inf.* To expect.

*c* **1400** *Ywaine & Gaw.* 549 He thoght to be wele on hys way Or it war passed the thryd day. **1597** SHAKS. 2 *Hen. IV*, IV. v. 92, I neuer thought to heare you speake againe. **1613** — *Hen. VIII*, III. ii. 429 Cromwel, I did not thinke to shed a teare In all my Miseries. **1765** G. COLMAN *Terence, Step-Mother* IV. vi, And do you think To find a woman without any fault? **1769** BICKERSTAFFE *Dr. Last* III. xi, O, don't think to humbug me so. **1823** SOUTHEY *Lett.* (1856) III. 392, I thought to have seen you ere this. *Mod.* I little thought to find you here!

**c.** *intr.* with *of*, † *on* (*upon*), † *to*: To have a notion, anticipation, or expectation; to suspect; to expect, look for.

**1483** CAXTON *G. de la Tour* d iv b, She..answerd withoute remembrynge her ne thynkyng to no harme. **1594** SHAKS. *Rich. III*, I. iv. 244 When that our Princely Father..Blest his three Sonnes.., He little thought of this diuided Friendship. **1650** GENTILIS *Considerations* 234 He stumbles at some evill which hee did not think upon. **1706** E. WARD *Wooden World Diss.* (1708) 98 He may meet with both when he least thinks on 't. *fig.* **1868** MORRIS *Earthly Par.*, *Man born to be King* 298 Staring out into the night Where yet the woods thought not of light.

**d.** *intr.* with *for* († *of*, † *on*), after *as* or *than*, and with the preposition at the end of the clause: To expect, suppose. (Cf. *look for*, LOOK 15 a.)

*c* **1530** LD. BERNERS *Arth. Lyt. Bryt.* 239, I thinke ye should not reioyse her so easily as ye thynke of. **1596** SHAKS. *Tam. Shr.* IV. iii. 163 Oh sir, the conceit is deeper than you think for. **1658** GURNALL *Chr. in Arm.* verse 14. ix. (1669) 93/2 A godly Servant is a greater blessing than we think on. **1751** R. PALTOCK *P. Wilkins* (1884) I. 141, I have not made so bad a hand of my time as I thought for. **1821** SCOTT *Kenilw.* xv, They hear farther than you think of. **1852** LYTTON *My Novel* XII. xiv, It is of more importance to him than I even thought for.

**13.** *trans.* To judge or consider to exist; to believe in the existence of. *rare.*

**1532** CROMWELL in Merriman *Life & Lett.* (1902) I. 351 He ..percase might thinke sum unkyndenes and also presumpcyon in yow so to handell hym. **1671** MILTON *Samson* 295 Unless there be who think not God at all. **1872** *Contemp. Rev.* XX. 92 Whatever its limits in a given percept be, there must be thought corresponding limits in its external sphere.

**IV.** With adverbial extension.

**14.** *trans.* To bring by thinking, or in thought, into or out of some specified condition.

**1599** SHAKS. *Much Ado* III. iv. 84 Indeed I cannot thinke, if I would thinke my hart out of thinking, that you are in loue. **1666** SOUTH *Serm., Tit.* ii. 15 (1715) I. 199 He that thinks a Man to the Ground, will quickly endeavour to lay him there. **1784** COWPER *Task* VI. 85 Meditation here May think down hours to moments. **1849** *Tait's Mag.* XVI. 376/2 He thinks away every proposition he has been taught to believe. **1865** BUSHNELL *Vicar. Sacr.* II. iv. (1868) 187 We hardly dare think them into our finite molds.

**15.** *Think out*: (*a*) To find out, devise, or elaborate by thinking, to construct intellectually; (*b*) to arrive at a clear understanding of by continued thinking; to solve by a process of thought; (*c*) to think to the end, finish or complete in thought.

**1382** WYCLIF *Ecclus.* xvii. 31 Or what wers than that flesh thoȝte out and blod? [*Vulg.* quid nequius quam quod excogitavit caro et sanguis?] **1847** HELPS *Friends in C.* I. iii. 40 Too mean a subject for despair, or, at least, unworthy of having any remedy..thought out for it. **1849** MACAULAY *Hist. Eng.* iv. I. 519 He meditated deeply on the philosophy of trade, and thought out by degrees a complete..theory. **1862** MISS BRADDON *Lady Audley* xxxiii, She did not finish the thought in words. She did not even think out the sentence. **1885** ANSTEY *Tinted Venus* ii. 25 Oh, don't bother me... I don't want to be uncivil, but I've got to think this out.

**16.** *Think* (a thing) *over*: to give continued thought to (it); to apply the mind steadily to, with the view of coming to a decision.

**1847** MARRYAT *Childr. New Forest* ix, He would think the matter over. **1873** BLACK *Pr. Thule* xxii, She had thought it well over beforehand. **1884** [see OVER *adv.* 12].

**17.** *Think up*: to make up or compose by thinking. ? *U. S. colloq.*

**1885** *Century Mag.* XXIX. 350/1, I believe she is thinking up another poem.

**Think,** *sb. dial.* or *colloq.* [f. THINK *v.*[2]]

**1.** An act of (continued) thinking; a meditation.

**1834** *Tait's Mag.* I. 426/1 We lie lown yonder..and have time for our ain think. **1870** MRS. WHITNEY *We Girls* ii, Ruth did talk..when she came out of one of her thinks. **1891** FENN *Mahme Nousie* II. v. 73 Let's have a cigar and a quiet think.

**b.** *nonce-use.* An idea, a thought.

**1886** MAUDSLEY *Nat. Causes & Supernat. Seemings* 33 To every one a thing is..what he thinks it—in effect, a think. **1887** G. MACDONALD *Home Again* iv, A thing must be a think before it be a thing.

**2.** What one thinks about something; an opinion.

**1835** LADY GRANVILLE *Lett.* (1894) II. 187 My own private think is that he will execute another voluntary. **1861** J. BROWN *Horæ Subs.* Ser. II. 355 The cobbler..dispenses his 'think'..to all comers on all subjects.

**3.** *attrib.* and *Comb.* (*nonce-wds.*), as **think-ache,** pain of thought, mental suffering; **think-room,** a room or apartment for meditation.

**1892** BRIDGER *Depression* p. v, Each separate thinkache enumerated by my depressed patients. **1906** *Month* July 72 Castle, work-room, think-room.

**Think, þink,** obs. form of THING.

**Thinkable** (þi·ŋkăb'l), *a.* [f. THINK *v.*[2] + -ABLE. Cf. UNTHINKABLE *c* 1430, etc.]

**1.** Capable of being thought; such as one can form a notion or idea of; cogitable.

**1854** H. SPENCER in *Brit. Q. Rev.* July 137 A corresponding progress in language, by which greater varieties of objects are thinkable and expressible. **1883** H. DRUMMOND *Nat. Law in Spir. W.* Introd. (1884) 3 To marshal the discrete materials..into thinkable form.

**2.** That can be deemed real or actual; conceivable or imaginable as an existing fact.

**1805** CARLYLE *Fredk. Gt.* XX. vi. (1872) IX. 109 How charming that you should make thinkable to us..what we were all inclined to think. **1908** *Times* 10 Sept. 8/4 It is thinkable that considerate driving may render legal enactments unnecessary.

Hence **Thi·nkableness.**

**1895** A. J. BALFOUR *Found. Belief* 286 'Ultimate' scientific ideas may be unthinkable without prejudice to the 'thinkableness' of 'proximate' scientific ideas.

†**Thi·nkative,** *a. Obs.* [f. THINK *v.*[2] + -ATIVE: cf. *talkative.*] Consisting in mere thinking, speculative.

**1662** J. CHANDLER *Van Helmont's Oriat.* 343 The knowledge of Observation, doth not introduce an understanding into the essential thingliness of a thing, but erecteth only a thinkative knowledge.

**Thinker** (þi·ŋkəɹ). [f. THINK *v.*[2] + -ER[1].]

**1.** One who thinks. **a.** *gen.* A person or being engaged in thinking, or having the power to think; also, one who thinks out or devises something.

*c* **1440** *Promp. Parv.* 490/2 Thenkare, *cogitator, pensator.* **1548** UDALL, etc. *Erasm. Par. Matt.* xii. 73 Noysome onely vnto the thynker. **1678** CUDWORTH *Intell. Syst.* I. v. § 2. 761 The Democriticks and Epicureans did indeed suppose all humane cogitations to be caused..by the incursion of corporeal atoms upon the thinker. **1841** SPALDING *Italy & It. Isl.* III. 208 He stands forth..as the thinker, the inventor, the actor of the scene. **1879** J. COOK *Lect. Conscience* vi, The universe exhibits thought. There cannot be thought without a thinker.

**b.** with qualifying adj.: One who thinks in the way expressed by the adj.; with commendatory words (e. g. *able, deep, original*, etc.) often practically coinciding with next sense.

*c* **1698** LOCKE *Cond. Underst.* § 4 You may as well hope to make a good..Musician..by a Lecture..in the Arts of Musick..as a coherent Thinker, or strict Reasoner, by a Set of Rules. **1703** ATTERBURY *Serm.* (1734) IV. iv. 114 He was able..to delude a superficial Thinker with his new Terms and Reasonings. **1807** G. CHALMERS *Caledonia* I. II. i. 227 Lloyd ..was an original thinker, rather than the collector of the opinions of others. **1874** L. STEPHEN *Hours in Library* (1892) I. ix. 300 Two of the ablest thinkers whom America has yet produced. **1903** *Church Times* 11 Dec. 749/3 Mr. Spencer showed another weakness of the abstract Thinker.

**c.** *spec.* One who has special or well-trained powers of thought, esp. abstract thought; a person of skilled or powerful mind; also, one who devotes himself to thinking, as distinguished from action or practical affairs.

**1830** CARLYLE in Froude *Life* (1882) II. 128 Neither is his [Jeffrey's] arguing like that of a thinker, but of the advocate. **1849** MACAULAY *Hist. Eng.* I. i. 20 English thinkers aspired to know, or dared to doubt, where bigots had been content to wonder and to believe. **1880** E. WHITE *Cert. Relig.* 50 Not one of them makes the slightest pretension to be a scholar or a thinker.

**2.** *Theatr. colloq.* An actor who plays in 'thinking parts' (see THINKING *vbl. sb.* 3).

**1886** *Stage Gossip* 70 The gentlemen who play the most subordinate parts are..called 'thinkers' on account of their having little or nothing to say and lots of time wherein to think.

**3.** *nonce-use.* That which thinks; thinking organ or faculty; mind.

**1835** ANN F. TYTLER *Mary & Fl.* i. 6 What should we do about our thinkers? would one thinker do for two Tongues? **1883** J. PARKER *Tyne Ch.* 279 'If God did not intend I should think, why did He give me a "thinker"?' Probably a more childish inquiry was never made by a full-grown man. **1899** MISS A. ROBERTSON in *Educat. Rev.* Aug., So this unnecessary 'finger accuracy' is really the result of a sluggish unwillingness to use one's 'thinker'.

**Thinkful** (þi·ŋkfŭl), *a. rare.* [f. THINK *v.*[2] + -FUL; cf. *wakeful.*] Full of or given to thinking; thoughtful. Hence **Thi·nkfulness,** quality or faculty of thinking.

**1674** N. FAIRFAX *Bulk & Selv.* 16 As sure, as I am of my own thinkfulness. **1910** *Weekly Westm. Gaz.* 23 Apr. 6/3 A thinkful man, and one of eloquent silences.

**Thinking** (þi·ŋkiŋ), *vbl. sb.* [f. THINK *v.*[2] + -ING[1].] The action of THINK *v.*[2]

**1.** Thought, cogitation, meditation, mental action or activity, etc.: see various senses of the verb.

*a* **1300** *E. E. Psalter* xviii. 15 [xix. 14] And thinginge of herte mine, Ever mare in sight þine. **1382** WYCLIF *ibid.*, The swete thenking of myn herte in thi siȝte euermore. *c* **1460** ASHBY *Dicta Philos.* 16 Bethink in the nyght of goode ordennance, And in the day execute thy thynkyng. **1598** SHAKS. *Merry W.* III. ii. 31 Has Page any braines? Hath he any eies? Hath he any thinking? **1690** LOCKE *Hum. Und.* II. ix. § 1 Thinking..signifies that sort of operation of the Mind about its Ideas, wherein the Mind is active. **1802** WORDSW. *Sonn.*, '*O Friend! I know not*', etc., Plain living and high thinking are no more. 1885 J. Martineau *Types Eth. Th.* I. i. i. § 3. 159 Thinking is the very essence of mind, as extension is of matter.

**b.** *pl.* Thoughts; meditations, courses of thought. 1382 Wyclif *Isa.* lxv. 2 A puple..that goth in a wei not good, after ther thenkingus. 1491 Caxton *Vitas Patr.* (W. de W. 1495) ii. 192 b/2 So oryson with fastyng casteth out..the foule thoughtes & vayne thynkynges. 1548 Udall *Erasm. Par. Luke* v. 70 The secrete thinkynges of theyr hertes. 1601 Shaks. *All's Well* v. iii. 128, I am wrap'd in dismall thinkings. 1812 Southey *Lett.* (1856) II. 283 Put together all your recollections and memoranda, I will put together my gleanings and thinkings. 1840 Dickens *Old C. Shop* viii, All these sayings and doings and thinkings.. affected him not in the least.

†**c.** *spec.* Imagination, fancy; idle fancy. *rare.* c 1420 *Chron. Vilod.* 1702 Þe sweuene Of þe tweyn appullon þat fellon from þe tre in to þe water in his thenkyng. 1502 *Ord. Crysten Men* (W. de W. 1506) i. iii. 23 These wordes..be not made for no thynge and with thynkynge.

**d.** With various constructions: see the verb. *There is no thinking*, one cannot or need not think. 1638 Baker tr. *Balzac's Lett.* (vol. II.) 111 There is no thinking therefore to deceive you by a shew of good. 1669 R. Montagu in *Buccleuch MSS.* (Hist. MSS. Comm.) I. 436 Without her ever thinking of it. 1849 Clough *Dipsychus* ii. ii. 105 My pleasure of thought is the pleasure of thinking How pleasant it is to have money.

**2.** The holding of an opinion or opinions; judging, mental viewing; opinion, judgement, belief; phr. *to* († *after, in*) *my thinking* = in my opinion. c 1410 *Master of Game* (Digby MS. 182) Prol. 13 What shalbe in euery sesoun moste durable and, to my thynkynge, ..oftenest most desportfull of all games. 1490 J. Kay tr. *Caoursin's Siege of Rhodes* (1870) ₱ 10 That hyt was jmpossible, after hys thynkyng, to fynde in all the world such instruments of werre. 1597 Shaks. *2 Hen. IV*, v. v. 114, I heare a Bird so sing, Whose Musicke (to my thinking) pleas'd the King. 1599 Dallam in *Early Voy. Levant* (Hakl. Soc.) 11 In my thinkinge it seemed not to be above 3 myles. c 1775 Burke *Addr. to King* Wks. IX. 177 In.. opposition to the..confirmed sentiments and habits of thinking of an whole people. 1879 B. Taylor *Stud. Germ. Lit.* 143 Frauenlob, the last, and, to my thinking, the poorest of the Minnesingers.

**3.** *attrib.* and *Comb.*, as *thinking-party, -place, process, -room, -substance*; **thinking-cap** (see Cap *sb.*[1] 9, and cf. *considering-cap*, Considering *vbl. sb.* 2 b); **thinking part** (*Theatr. colloq.*), a part in which the actor has no words to speak, a silent part; **thinking-shop** (*humorous*), a building or institution for study, as a university; **thinking-time, -while**, time to think, a short space of time. 1874 Coues *Birds N. W.* 527 Startled in his retreat while his *thinking-cap is on, he [the bittern] seems dazed, like one suddenly aroused from a deep sleep. 1903 *Daily Chron.* 21 Jan. 5/4 It is satisfactory to know that the Post Office Department has its 'thinking-cap' on. 1898 *Daily News* 12 Mar. 6/3 The great Benefit which is to be given to Nellie Farren next week at Drury Lane...Some of the most famous [actresses] are content with what are humorously called good '*thinking' parts. 1908 *Greenroom Bk.* 667 He made his professional debut in 1867 in a 'thinking part'. 1897 *Q. Rev.* Apr. 348 That remarkable series of reading-parties (or more truly of *thinking-parties). 1883 Jefferies *Story of my Heart* 74 This..was a favourite *thinking-place. 1899 *Allbutt's Syst. Med.* VII. 423 These kinæsthetic images..play only a small part in *thinking processes. 1862 Thoreau *Yankee in Canada* i. (1866) 13 When every house..will have not only its sleeping-rooms, and dining-room, and talking-room or parlor, but its *thinking-room also. 1836–48 B. D. Walsh *Aristoph., Clouds* i. ii, I am come To be a Scholar in the *Thinking-shop. 1890 *Spectator* 19 Apr., It turned Oxford into an aristocratic boarding-school from a democratic thinking-shop. 1884 J. Tait *Mind in Matter* (1892) 99 The etherialised medium of force, which probably connects the brain with the *thinking-substance. 1667 Dryden & Dk. Newcastle *Sir Martin Mar-all* v. i, I'll put you upon something, give me but a *thinking time. *Ibid.* iii. i, As a whiff of tobacco ..[used] in the midst of a discourse for a *thinking-while.

**Thi·nking**, *ppl. a.* [f. as prec. + -ing[2].]

**1.** That thinks; having, or exercising, the faculty of thought; cogitative. 1678 Dryden & Lee *Œdipus* iii. i, A thinking soul is punishment enough. 1709 Steele & Addison *Tatler* No. 111 ₱ 1 What was the proper Employment of a thinking Being? 1800 *Med. Jrnl.* III. 281 According to the laws of the thinking faculty, the understanding and reason. 1864 Bowen *Logic* i. 2 The Thinking or Elaborative faculty,—i.e. the Understanding.

**2.** Given to thinking; habitually exercising one's mind; having special or well-trained powers of thought; thoughtful, reflective, intellectual. (Cf. Thinker 1 c.) 1681 *Let. to Person of Hon.* in *Select. Harl. Misc.* (1793) 461 To have an account of the sense of the thinking-men about the town concerning it. 1779 *Mirror* No. 16 ₱ 3 Those moments of deeper pensiveness to which every thinking mind is liable. 1837 W. Irving *Capt. Bonneville* III. 225 The senior chief..was a thinking man, and a man of observation.

**3.** *fig.* Said of very life-like sculpture: cf. Breathing *ppl. a.* b. 1732 M. Green *Grotto* 57 The thinking sculpture helps to raise Deep thoughts, the genii of the place.

Hence **Thi·nkingdom** (*nonce-wd.*), a realm of thinking persons; **Thi·nkingly** *adv.*, in a thinking manner, in the way of thought; with thought, consciously, deliberately; in (one's own) thought or supposition (quot. 1894); **Thi·nkingness**, thinking quality; thoughtfulness, intellectuality; the essence of a thinking being (quot. 1865). 1880 *Q. Rev.* Oct. 415 Christendom..is far enough as yet from having been replaced by the Utopian *Thinkingdom (*Cogitantenthum*), to which one of the modern German apostles of materialism..looks forward. 1847 Webster, *Thinkingly, by thought. 1887 Mary Linskill *In Exchange for Soul* xlviii, Quite thinkingly he sent the message in his wife's name. 1673 O. Walker *Educ.* v. 43 Contrary to that seriousnes and *thinkingnes requisite to prudence and gallantry of spirit. 1838 *New Monthly Mag.* LIII. 118 All men say..good things of the courage of Englishmen, the chastity of English women, the thinkingness of both sexes. 1865 J. Grote *Explor. Philos.* i. 140, I recognise two manners of existence,..thinkingness and thoughtness.

**Thinkling** (þi·ŋkˌliŋ). *nonce-wd.* [f. Think *v.*[2] + -ling.] A petty or inferior thinker. 1815 J. Gilchrist *Labyrinth Demolished* 22. 1816 — *Philos. Etym.* 247 A proper Etymological Dictionary, which petty thinklings—quackish pretenders affect to despise.

**Thi·nk-so.** *nonce-wd.* [The phr. (*I*) *think so* (Think *v.*[2] 9 c) used as a sb.] A mere opinion. 1666 Bunyan *Grace Ab.* § 97 How if all our Faith, and Christ, and Scriptures, should be but a Think-so too? 1675 — *Saved by Grace* Wks. (1692) I. 568/1 He thinks former encouragements were Fancies, Delusions or meer Think-so's. 1887 Hall Caine *Deemster* xxxix, All the dread I had felt hitherto..was no more than a thinkso.

**Thin-laid, -leaved**, etc.: see Thin *a.* D.

**Thinly** (þi·nli), *adv.* [f. Thin *a.* + -ly[2].] In a thin manner.

**1.** With little thickness or depth; with thin clothing. Also *fig.* 13.. *K. Alis.* 5906 (Bodl. MS.) Thynnelich hy beþ y-hatered. 1746 Francis tr. *Hor., Sat.* ii. vi. 94 This Morning Air is very bad For them, who go but thinly clad. 1770 *Phil. Trans.* LXI. 334, I covered the bottom with it thinly. 1855 Macaulay *Hist. Eng.* xxi. IV. 570 The scheme of assassination, thus thinly veiled, was communicated to James. 1859 Gullick & Timbs *Paint.* 229 Pictures in oil ..may, of course, be thinly painted throughout.

**b.** *fig.* Poorly, meagrely. ? *Obs. rare.* 1537 Cromwell in Merriman *Life & Lett.* (1902) II. 75 Your neighbours, without whom..all the rest of you would live full thynnely.

**2.** With large intervals of space or time; sparsely; not closely or thickly. c 1545 in Dugdale *Monast.* (1821) III. 283, v. acrez di. thinly growyne with olde bechez and some oke. 1667–8 Sir T. Browne *Brampton Urns* Wks. 1835 III. 500 Great ones were but thinly found. a 1727 Newton *Chronol. Amended* i. (1728) 178 He found that country..peopled but thinly. 1827 Hone *Every-day Bk.* II. 106 The market was..thinly attended.

**3.** In combination with pa. pples. or adjs. used attributively; now usually hyphened. 1757 Dyer *Fleece* i. Wks. (1761) 60 The thinly-scatter'd meal. 1797 Godwin *Enquirer* ii. xii. 454 Ten thinly printed pages. 1862 Ansted *Channel Isl.* i. ii. (ed. 2) 26 Thinly-bedded grey rocks. 1890 'R. Boldrewood' *Col. Reformer* (1891) 70 An open, thinly-timbered, well-grassed country. 1902 *Daily Chron.* 25 Jan. 3/2 He makes thinly-veiled love to the young lady.

†**Thi·nmost**, *a.* *Obs. rare*$^{-1}$. [f. Thin *a.*: see -most.] Thinnest. 1644 Nye *Gunnery* (1670) 83 If this Peece were fortified.. onely so much, as the thinnest part of the metall is.

**Thinned** (þind), *ppl. a.* [f. Thin *v.*[1] + -ed[1].] Made thin or less thick, in senses of Thin *v.*[1]; reduced in thickness, density, frequency, number, etc. 1710 J. Clarke *Rohault's Nat. Phil.* i. xxvii. (1729) I. 210 The Superficies of the thinned Body, where it is of any one Thickness. 1857 Ld. Dufferin *Lett. High Lat.* xii. (ed. 3) 359 The thinned ranks on board the '*Iron Beard*' are constantly replenished. 1899 *Allbutt's Syst. Med.* VIII. 695 Pigment is irregularly accumulated in the thinned epidermis.

**Thi·nner.** [agent-n. from Thin *v.*[1]: see -er[1].] One who thins. 1832 *Planting* 63 in *Libr. Usef. Knowl., Husb.* III, Leaving them to press upon each other more severely than vigorous thinners would permit. 1889 *Pall Mall G.* 2 July 2/2 The case of the little turnip-thinners in Saxony.

**Thinness** (þi·nˌnės). [f. Thin *a.* + -ness.] The quality or condition of being thin.

**1.** Narrowness of dimension between opposite surfaces; absence of thickness or depth. 1577 B. Googe *Heresbach's Husb.* ii. (1586) 80 b, Fulnesse and emptinesse, or thicknesse and thinnes. 1617 Moryson *Itin.* iii. 175 Cotton cloth..for thinnesse not vnlike our boulting cloths. 1715 Desaguliers *Fires Impr.* 113 Where you cannot dig in the Back-Wall of a Chimney by reason of its thinness. 1807 Vancouver *Agric. Devon* (1813) 54 The thinness of the seam [of coal]. 1863 Lyell *Antiq. Man* iii. 34 The extreme thinness of the film of matter.

**b.** Lean or spare habit of body; spareness. 1827–35 Willis *Leper* 65 There, alone, Wasted to ghastly thinness, Helon knelt.

**c.** *fig.* Deficiency, poverty, meagreness, feebleness; lack of depth or fullness. c 1000 *Sax. Leechd.* I. 134 Hit ȝehælð þa þynnysse þære ȝesihðe. 1623 W. Balcanqual *Serm. St. Maries Spittle* 98 The thinnesse of our Ioy, because we did sowe our teares too thin. 1903 *Daily Chron.* 20 Feb. 3/6 That there was much 'intellectual thinness' among young men.

**2.** The condition of being thinly arranged, occupied, or attended; want of fullness; sparseness. c 1440 *Promp. Parv.* 491/1 Thynnesse, of wodys, cornys, and oþer lyke, *raritas.* 1573–80 Baret *Alv.* T 166 Thinnesse: seldomnesse, *rarité.* 1690 Locke *Govt.* ii. vi. § 74 The Thinness of People gives Families Leave to separate into unpossessed Quarters. 1774 A. Gib *Pres. Truth* II. 40 None of these brethren opened a mouth about the thinness of the meeting. 1826 F. Reynolds *Life & Times* II. 200 Expressing my surprise at the..thinness of the house.

**3.** Absence or lack of density, consistence, or viscosity; fluidity, tenuity, rarity. c 1000 *Sax. Leechd.* II. 199 Þonne þara metta meltung biþ & þynnes. 1398 Trevisa *Barth. De P. R.* xi. i. (Tollem. MS.), Eyer haþ more þinnesse and clerenesse þan oþer elementis. c 1440 *Promp. Parv.* 491/1 Thynnesse, or thynhede of licurys. 1582 Stanyhurst *Æneis* i. (Arb.) 37 From earthly thicknesse, too thinnesse vannished ayerie. 1684–5 Boyle *Min. Waters* 26 Of the thinness or viscosity of the Mineral Water. a 1854 Caroline B. Southey *Poet. Wks.* (1867) 67 Milk..tempered down To wholesome thinness.

†**Thi·nnify**, *v.* *Obs. rare*$^{-1}$. [f. Thin *a.* + *-ify*, -fy.] *trans.* To make thin; = Thin *v.*[1] 5. a 1693 *Urquhart's Rabelais* iii. iv. 49 The Heart doth in its left side Ventricle so thinnifie the Blood.

**Thi·nning**, *vbl. sb.* [f. Thin *v.*[1] + -ing[1].] The action of Thin *v.*[1], in various senses; reduction or decrease in thickness, closeness, number, density, etc. Also with *out, off, away, up*, etc. c 1000 *Sax. Leechd.* II. 260 Læcedomas þa þe þynnunge mæȝen hæbben. 1398 Trevisa *Barth. De P. R.* xix. xi. (Bodl. MS.), White mater is igendred of thynnynge and spredinge of aier. 1799 J. Robertson *Agric. Perth* 257 Weeded down by various thinnings. 1839 Ure *Dict. Arts* 1269 The thinning up, or quantity of turpentine required to bring it to its proper consistence. 1851 Carpenter *Man. Phys.* (ed. 2) 268 By the thinning-away of its wall at its most projecting part. 1868 *Rep. U. S. Commissioner Agric.* (1869) 423 Upon thinning out, enough plants were cast away to have run at least twelve rows additional.

**b.** *concr.* usually *pl.* That which is removed in the process of thinning. (Cf. *sweepings*.) 1771 *Usef. Proj.* in *Ann. Reg.* 115/2 Sir John..never receives less than a guinea an acre in thinnings throughout his plantations. 1805 R. W. Dickson *Pract. Agric.* I. Pl. xxx. 110 A fir paling of the horizontal kind, made from the thinning of trees of that kind. 1893 *Jrnl. R. Agric. Soc.* Dec. 826 Thinnings and rubbish should be immediately removed and burnt.

**Thi·nning**, *ppl. a.* [f. Thin *v.*[1] + -ing[2].] That thins, in various senses of the verb. 1550 Bale *Eng. Votaries* ii. 81 To confirme the thynynge shewe of hypocresye. 1790 Wolcott (P. Pindar) *Rowland for Oliver* 92 Art thou a Doctor? Yes, of thinning skill. 1888 *Pump Court* 31 Oct. 5/2 His gradually thinning hair. 1899 Mackail *Life Morris* II. 154 A mere thinning remnant between two divergent and increasing camps.

**Thinnish** (þi·niʃ), *a.* [f. Thin *a.* + -ish[1].] Somewhat thin; tending to thinness. 1545 Raynold *Byrth Mankynde* 139 Her vryne shall appeare whyte and thynnyssh. 1780 C. A. Burney in *Mme. D'Arblay's Early Diary* (1889) II. 289 The Masquerade at the Pantheon was rather thinnish. 1827 F. Cooper *Prairie* I. ii. 30 They told us..we should find settlers something thinnish hereaway. 1884 *Century Mag.* XXIX. 138/1 My somewhat slight figure and thinnish legs.

**Thinnye**, obs. form of Tunny.

**Thinocorine** (þəinǫ·kŏrəin), *a.* *Ornith.* [f. mod.L. *Thinocorus* (properly *-ys*), f. Gr. θίς, θῖν- beach, sea-shore + κόρυς lark: see -ine[1].] Of, pertaining to, or characteristic of the *Thinocoridæ* or quail-snipes, a family of South American wading birds, typified by the genus *Thinocorus*. 1885 *Stand. Nat. Hist.* IV. 92 The Thinocorine palate, in which the vomer is connected with the nasal cartilages in a manner recalling that of the Ægithognathæ.

**Thinolite** (þəi·nŏləit). *Min.* [f. Gr. θίς, θῖν- (see prec.) + λίθος stone: see -lite.] 'A variety of calcite, occurring in pseudomorphous crystals, the original mineral being still in doubt' (Chester *Dict. Min.* 1896). 1879 C. King *Geol. 40th Parallel* I. 508 (Chester).

**Thin-skinned** (-skind: stress var.), *a.*

**1.** Having a thin skin or rind. 1598 Chapman *Blinde Begger of Alexandria* Wks. 1873 I. 11 Round faces and thinne skinde are happiest still. 1707 Mortimer *Husb.* (1721) II. 155 Chuse the large, round, white, and thin-skinned ones. 1875 Bennett & Dyer *Sachs' Bot.* 539 A stony endocarp surrounding the thin-skinned seed.

**2.** *fig.* Sensitive to criticism, ridicule, or abuse; easily hurt or offended; touchy. 1680 Baxter *Answ. Stillingfl.* lxxviii. 99, I..never was so thin Skin'd as to be unable to bear a Cholerick breath. 1771 Smollett *Humph. Cl.* 8 June, My apothecary, who is a proud Scotchman, very thin skinned. 1818 Cobbett *Pol. Reg.* XXXIII. 311 The professional gentlemen in Pennsylvania are..extremely thin-skinned, when they are the party attacked. 1894 Froude *Life & Lett. Erasmus* xvii. 328 Erasmus..was thin-skinned as ever.

Hence **Thi·n-ski·nnedness**, the condition or quality of being thin-skinned; sensitiveness. 1882 Sala *Amer. Revis.* (1883) I. iii. 43 *note*, A very gratifying proof of the diminution of what may be termed 'thin-skinnedness'. 1897 *Spectator* 23 Oct. 552/1 This thin-skinnedness among experienced public men.

**Thin-sown** (þi·nˌsōun: stress var.), *a.* Also 7 thin-sowed. Sown or planted thinly; *lit.* said of plants, or a crop; *fig.* scattered at wide intervals, scarce; also, of a field or territory: scantily furnished *with* († *of*). 1589 R. Harvey *Pl. Perc.* (1590) 18 Good deeds, which are now both thin sowne.., and thinner growne. a 1631 Donne *Lett.* (1651) 159 This Countrie is so thin sowed with such persons, as he comes to seek; that he will scarce know, where to find a corn to peck at. 1698 Norris *Pract. Disc.* IV. 60 Very good Men..were always very thin sown. a 1846 in J. Baxter *Libr. Pract. Agric.* (ed. 4) II. 398 In the early stages..the appearance of thick-sown corn is much superior to that of the thin-sown.

**Thi·n-spu·n,** *a.* (stress var.) Spun thinly; drawn out in spinning to a slender thread. Also *fig.*

**1637** MILTON *Lycidas* 76 Comes the blind Fury with th' abhorred shears, And slits the thin spun life. **1642** H. MORE *Song of Soul* II. iii. IV. ix, Thin-spun reason and exile discourse. **1821** CLARE *Vill. Minstr.* I. 93 How thin-spun clouds glide swiftly by. *Ibid.* 120 Nor broken seam, nor thin-spun screen.

**Thi·n-walled** (-wǭld), *a.* Having thin walls.

**1854** OWEN *Skel. & Teeth* (1855) 7 The thinnest-walled and widest air-bone of the bird of flight was first solid. **1875** BENNETT & DYER *Sachs' Bot.* 90 Alternate layers of narrow thick-walled and broad thin-walled cork-cells are formed. **1875** HUXLEY & MARTIN *Elem. Biol.* (1877) 184 Posteriorly, the oviducts dilate into capacious thin-walled chambers.

**Thio-** (þəi,o), also before a vowel **thi-**, repr. Gr. θεῖον sulphur; a formative element in names of things containing or connected with sulphur.

**1.** in *Chem.* (See also THIOL-, THION-.) In names of compounds containing sulphur = *sulpho-*.

In systematic nomenclature restricted to those in which one or more atoms of sulphur take the place of one or more of oxygen in the substance designated by the rest of the name; e. g. *thiacetic* acid $C_2H_3O.SH$, from acetic acid $C_2H_3O.OH$, *tri-thiocarbonic* acid $H_2CS_3$, from carbonic acid $H_2CO_3$. So *thio-acid, -alcohol, -aldehyde, -ether, -salt*; also *thio-antimo·nic, -antimo·nious, -arse·nic, -arse·nious, -lactic, -phosphoric, -phosphoryl, -stannic, -tungstic*, etc. But many names do not conform exactly to this systematic use.

The following are the chief combinations of *thio-*.

**Thia·cetate,** a salt of thiacetic acid. **Thiace·tic** *a.*, in *thiacetic acid* ($C_2H_3O.SH$), a colourless liquid boiling at 93° C. **Thi-a·cid** = *thio-acid.* **Thia·ldine** [ALD(EHYDE + -INE[5]], a crystalline substance, $NH:2(CHCH_3.S):CHCH_3$, produced by passing hydrogen sulphide into a solution of aldehyde ammonia. **Thi·alol** [AL(COHOL + -OL 3], a name for diethyl disulphide, $(C_2H_5)_2S_2$, a colourless oily compound, having an odour like garlic. **Thi·amide,** generic name for substances formed by replacing the oxygen of an amide by sulphur, as *thiacetamide*, $CH_3CS.NH_2$, from acetamide, $CH_3CO.NH_2$. **Thi·amine,** generic name for amines containing the group NHSH, as *ethylthiamine*, $C_2H_5.NHSH$. **Thiazole** [AZO- + *-ole*, -OL 3], N⟨CH.S / CH:CH⟩, a liquid boiling at 117° C. **Thi·enyl** [contr. of *thiophenyl*, proposed 1883 by V. Meyer], the radical $C_4H_3S$ contained in *thiophene*, $C_4H_4S$. **Thi·o-a·cid, thi·-a·cid,** an acid in which oxygen is replaced by sulphur. **Thio-a·lbumose,** a deutero-albumose containing a large amount of sulphur. **Thio-a·lcohol,** a compound of the nature of an alcohol in which sulphur takes the place of oxygen, as mercaptan, $C_2H_5.SH$, analogous to ethyl alcohol, $C_2H_5.OH$. **Thioca·rbamate,** a salt of thiocarbamic acid. **Thiocarba·mic** *a.*, in *t. acid*, $NH_2.CO.SH$ and $NH_2.CS.OH$: now distinguished as *thiolcarbamic* and *thioncarbamic* acids: see THIOL-, THION-. **Thioca·rbamide,** $CS(NH_2)_2$ or $HS.C(NH_2):NH$, a crystalline substance melting at 170° C. **Thioca·rbonate,** a salt of thiocarbonic acid. **Thiocarbo·nic** *a.*, in *t. acid*: in derivatives, as *mono-, di-, tri-thiocarbonic acid*: the last, $H_2CS_3$, is a dark yellow strongly smelling oil, very easily decomposed by heating into $CS_2$ and $H_2S$; esters of *dithiocarbonic acid*, $H_2COS_2$, and of *monothiocarbonic acid*, $H_2CO_2S$, are known. **Thioca·rbonyl,** the radical (CS)″, in which the oxygen of carbonyl (CO)″ is replaced by sulphur. **Thioca·rbylamine** = *iso-thiocyanic* acid, CHNS, = C☰N.SH. **Thiocresol** (þəi,o,kre·sǫl), a compound with the formula $CH_3:C_6H_4SH$, of which there are three modifications, two crystalline and one liquid. **Thiocy·anate,** a salt of thiocyanic acid. **Thiocya·nic** *a.*, in *t. acid*, N⋮C.SH = cyanic acid, N⋮C.OH, in which oxygen is replaced by sulphur; a liquid with a penetrating odour. **Thiocya·nogen,** the radical CNS of thiocyanic acid; in comb. *thiocyano-*. **Thiofo·rmic** *a.*, in *t. acid*, $H_2COS$, a crystalline substance melting at 120° C. **Thiona·phthene,** a colourless crystalline compound, $C_8H_6S$, consisting of benzene, $C_6H_6$, of which two atoms of H are replaced by CH:CH.S. **Thionic** (þəi,o·nik) *a.*, in *t. acids*, group name for the acids represented by the formula $H_2S_nO_6$, where n = 2, 3, 4, 5, and perhaps 6. These acids are called *dithionic, trithionic, tetrathionic, pentathionic*, and *hexathionic* acid. **Thi·onine,** a brownish-black dye, $SC_{12}H_9N_3$, crystallizing in plates, called *phenylene violet*, or *Lauth's v.*, and largely used to stain microscopic objects. **Thionu·rate,** a salt of thionuric acid. **Thionuric** (þəi,o̜niū͡ə·rik) *a.* [f. Gr. θεῖον + URIC], in *thionuric acid*, $CO:2(NH.CO):CH.NH.SO_3H$, formed by the action of ammonia and sulphurous acid on alloxan in aqueous solution. **Thi·onyl** [-YL], the radical (SO)″: so named in 1857 by Schiff (*Annalen der Chem. und Pharm.* CII. 113). **Thi·ophene,** $C_4H_4S$, a colourless liquid with an odour like benzene, occurring in benzene from coal-tar to the extent of about 0·5 per cent.; hence **Thiophe·nic** *a.*, in *thiophenic acid*, $C_4H_3S.CO_2H$, derived from thiophene. **Thiophe·nol,** a colourless liquid, $C_6H_5SH$ (= PHENOL with S in place of O), with the odour of garlic. **Thio·phthene** [NA)PHTHENE], a colourless oily compound, $C_6H_4S_2$, obtained by the distillation of citric acid with $P_2S_3$. **Thi:oreso·rcin,** also **Thioreso·rcinol,** $C_6H_4(SH)_2$, a yellowish-grey substance, used medicinally as a substitute for iodoform. **Thi·osalicy·lic** *a.*, in *t. acid*, $HOC_6H_4CO(SH)$, a brownish-yellow amorphous substance, used in medicine as an antiseptic. **Thio-salt,** a salt of a thio-acid, as a thiosulphate. **Thiosi·namine** [L. *sinapis* mustard + AMINE] = *allyl-thio-urea*, $C_3H_5NH.CS.NH_2$, a crystalline substance produced by the action of ammonia on allyl mustard oil. **Thiosu·lphate,** a salt of thiosulphuric acid; formerly called *hyposulphite*. **Thiosulphu·ric** *a.*, in *t. acid*, $H_2S_2O_3$, an acid only known in solution and soon decomposing, the salts of which are stable, and are applied in bleaching and photography; it is sulphuric acid, $H_2SO_4$, in which one atom of oxygen is replaced by sulphur; formerly called *hyposulphurous* acid. **Thioto·luene** [TOLUENE] = *methylthiophene*, $C_4H_3(CH_3)S$, a colourless oily compound, found as an impurity in crude toluene; two isomeric forms are known. **Thio-urea** (þəi,o,iū͡ə·riă), $CS(NH_2)_2$ or $HS.C(NH_2):NH$ = *thiocarbamide.* **Thioxa·nthone** [XANTHONE], $C_{13}H_8OS$, crystallizing in yellow needles. **Thioxene** (þəi,o·ksīn), **Thioxylene** (þəi,o·ksilīn) [named *thioxene* by Victor Meyer (*Ber. Deut. Chem. Ges.* 1884, XVII. 789)] = *dimethylthiophene*, $C_4H_2(CH_3)_2S$, found as an impurity in xylene; there are several isomeric forms.

**1854** KEKULÉ in *Proc. Roy. Soc.* VII. 38 **Thiacetic Acid,—Sulphuretted Acetic Acid*—has been obtained by me by acting on monohydrated acetic acid with tersulphide of phosphorus. **1847** WÖHLER & LIEBIG in *Mem. Chem. Soc.* III. 303 A new organic alkali free from oxygen..which we call *thialdine..contracted from θεῖον and aldehyde. **1881** WATTS *Dict. Chem.* VIII. 1952 *Thiamides..may be conveniently prepared by the action of phosphorus sulphide ..on amides. **1888** HANTZSCH & WEBER in *Jrnl. Chem. Soc.* LIV. 256 *Thiazole is the name given to [these] isomeric compounds. **1885** PETER *Ibid.* XLVIII. 141 **Thiënylmethylacetoxime* $C_4H_3S.CMe:NOH$..forms a white crystalline mass. **1882** WILL *Ibid.* XLII. 1088 *Thiocarbamates...A continuation of the author's researches. **1878** GUARESCHI *Ibid.* XXXIV. 860 **Thiocarbamide* $CS(NH_2)_2$ [etc.] when oxidised by permanganate likewise yield all their sulphur in the state of sulphuric acid. **1891** *Anthony's Photogr. Bull.* IV. 397 Prof. J. E. Reynolds, who was the original discoverer of the rinsing sulphur urea, now known as *thio-carbamide.* **1883** *Jrnl. Chem. Soc.* XLIV. 405 The use of potassium *thiocarbonate as a remedy against phylloxera. **1887** *Ibid.* LI. 272 The conversion of *thiocarbonyl chloride into thiocarbonyl tetrachloride by the assimilation of two atoms of chlorine takes place at ordinary temperatures. **1877** *Ibid.* XXXII. 869 *Thiocyanates of the acid radicles are prepared by the action of acid chlorides on dry lead thiocyanate. **1877** *Ibid.* XXXII. 423 Action of Nascent *Thiocyanic Acid on Alcohol. **1857** *Ibid.* IX. 185 *Thioformic acid crystallises from formic acid, or from boiling alcohol, in slender needles. **1880** *Ibid.* XXXVII. 593 A qualitative reaction, by which pentathionic acid is clearly distinguished from any other of the *thionic acids. **1839** THOMSON *British Ann.* 377 *Thionurate of zinc. *Ibid.*, *Thionuric acid. **1874** WATTS *Dict. Chem.* V. 779 Thionuric acid..forms a crystalline mass, consisting of fine needles. *Ibid.* 780 *Thionyl. SO.—The radicle of the sulphurous compounds: e. g., sulphurous chloride, $(SO)''Cl_2$ = chloride of thionyl. **1883** MEYER in *Jrnl. Chem. Soc.* XLIV. 1091 A substance contained in Coal-tar Benzene..to which the author has given the name of **thiophene.* **1899** *Syd. Soc. Lex.*, **Thiophenol*,..phenyl mercaptan. *Ibid.*, **Thioresorcin*,.. a popular substitution of resorcin...Used as a dusting powder. **1853** URE *Dict. Arts* I. 32 *Thiosinnamine. **1881** PIESSE & STANSELL in *Jrnl. Chem. Soc.* XL. 207 *Thiosinamine* is an oily substance at 100°, but gradually solidifies when cold. **1873** WATTS *Fownes' Chem.* 198 The solution of a *thiosulphate. **1874** *Jrnl. Chem. Soc.* XXVII. 771 The close relation between the thiosulphates and sulphates is shown by the formulæ—$SO_2{}^{SNa}_{ONa}$ and $SO_2{}^{ONa}_{ONa}$ **1873** WATTS *Fownes' Chem.* 204 *Thiosulphuric Acid is scarcely known. **1874** *Jrnl. Chem. Soc.* XXVII. 770 On the Constitution of Hyposulphurous (Thiosulphuric) Acid. **1885** *Ibid.* XLVIII. 251 A Simple Method of obtaining *Thiotolene. **1894** MUIR & MORLEY *Watts' Dict. Chem.* IV. 710 Formed by adding Br to an alcoholic or cold aqueous solution of *thio-urea. **1885** *Jrnl. Chem. Soc.* XLVIII. 251 A simple method of obtaining..*thioxylene.

**2.** In pharmaceutical and other terms.

**Thiobacte·ria,** name proposed by Migula for sulphur and iron bacteria mostly found in seawater and soils. **Thi·ocamph** [CAMPH(OR)], a fluid disinfectant, used for fumigation, formed by the action of sulphur dioxide on camphor. **Thi·ocol** [GUAIA)COL], a preparation of guaiacol, used in lung diseases. **Thi·oform** [after *chloroform*], trade-name of a basic bismuth di-thiosalicylate, as an antiseptic for wounds. **Thioge·nic** *a.* [-GEN 1 + -IC], producing sulphur, *spec.* applied to bacteria which produce free sulphur by the oxidization of sulphuretted hydrogen. **Thio·genol,** trade-name of a solution of sodium sulphonate as a medical wash. **Thi·olin** [L. *līnum* flax], trade-name of a dark-green substance prepared from linseed oil by the action of sulphur; hence **Thioli·nic** *acid.* **Thiosa·piol, -sapol** [L. *sapo* soap], **-sa·vonal,** trade-names of soap containing sulphur in chemical combination. ‖ **Thi·othrix** [Gr. θρίξ hair], a genus of sulphur bacteria found in sulphur springs.

**1900** A. C. JONES tr. *Fischer's Str. & Funct. Bacteria* 65 The sulphur bacteria, **Thiobacteria*, whose cells are often crammed full of spherical refringent masses of pure sulphur, occur in nature in places where free sulphuretted hydrogen is present. *Ibid.*, Thiobacteria can be found at any time of the year, but are most abundant in the early spring and late autumn. **1899** *Syd. Soc. Lex.*, **Thiocamph*..on exposure evolves sulphur dioxide in steady fumes. *Ibid.*, **Thioform* ..a light yellowish powder, without odour or taste..has.. been introduced into surgery with promising success. **1910** BRICKDALE *Guide Newer Remedies* 60 A dithiosalicylate ..has been..named Thioform. **1894** REMINGTON *Pract. Pharm.* (ed. 3) 1433 **Thiolin.* Salts of thiosulphonic acid. Salt of thiolinic acid. Sulphonated and sulphurated linseed oil. **1899** *Syd. Soc. Lex.*, Thiolin, thiolinic acid. *Ibid.*, **Thiosa·piol*, a sulphuretted soap, containing 10 per cent. of sulphur, obtained by heating sulphur and oleic acid together...A successful application to many skin diseases.

**Thiol-** (þəi·ǫl). *Chem.* [arbitrarily f. THIO-.] A name for the group SH in combination, analogous to hydroxyl, OH.

It indicates the presence of an -SH group (or an -SR group, where R is an alkyl radical), as in *methyl-thiolcarbamate*, $H_2N.CO.SCH_3$, as distinguished from *methyl carbamate*, $H_2N.CO.OCH_3$, and also from *methyl-thioncarbamate*, $H_2N.CS.OCH_3$: see THION-. Also, in those cases in which *hydroxy-* would mean the presence of an -OH group, *thiol-* indicates the presence of an -SH group; and where *methoxy-*, *ethoxy-*, etc., would indicate $CH_3O$-, $C_2H_5O$-, RO- groups, *methylthiol-*, *ethylthiol-*, *R-thiol-*, indicate $CH_3S$-, $C_2H_5S$-, RS- groups; thus, the sulphur compound corresponding to *sodium ethoxyacetate* $C_2H_5O.CH_2.CO_2Na$ is *sodium ethylthiolacetate* $C_2H_5S.CH_2.CO_2Na$. Cf. THION-.

**1899** *Jrnl. Chem. Soc.* LXXVI. I. 797 The authors adopt the Geneva nomenclature, *thion* being used to denote compounds containing the group .CS.OR, and *thiol* those containing the group .CO.SR. **1905** *Ibid.* LXXXVIII. I. 626 α-Thiolbutyric acid, $SH.CHEt.CO_2H$, is an oil boiling at 118–122° under 19 mm. pressure.

**Thion-** (þəi·ǫn). *Chem.* [a. Gr. θεῖον sulphur: cf. THIO-.] A name for sulphur taking the place of oxygen in a compound and joined by two bonds to carbon.

e. g. in *methyl thioncarbamate*, $H_2N.CS.OCH_3$, as distinct from methyl carbamate and methyl-thiolcarbamate: see THIOL-. (Certain words beginning with *thion-* do not conform to this system: see THIONIC, etc. under THIO-.)

**1899** *Jrnl. Chem. Soc.* LXXVI. I. 797 [see THIOL-]. **1904** *Ibid.* LXXXVI. I. 990 The crude ester..is best converted directly into thionoxanilic acid, $NHPh.CS.CO_2H$.

**Thir** (ðir, ðǝ̄i), *dem. pron.* and *adj. Sc.* and *north. dial.* Forms: 3?, 4– thir; also 4 (**þeir, þier**), **þer(e, þar(e, there,** 4–5 **þir(e,** 4–7 **ther,** 5 **thire, theire, thair,** (8–9 *north. dial.* **ther, thor, thoor, thur**). [Origin obscure. The introduction of the word app. coincided with the change of *þās* in the north from being plural of *this* to being synonymous with *þā*, pl. of *that*: see THESE, THOSE, THO. The earliest evidence is that of Cursor Mundi and the northern works of 1300–1350, in which *þās* and *þā* appear as plural of *that*, and *thir* in various spellings is the established plural of *this*, = southern *thēs*, midland *thise*, *these*. Some suggest its adoption from ON. *þeir*, *þǽr* 'those', pl. masc. and fem. of the simple demonstrative *sá*, *sú*, *þat*, of which the plural was used also as 3rd pers. pron. pl. 'they'. Others have suggested a combination of *þe* with *hēr* 'here', as if = the here, those here. Both suggestions present difficulties. See Note.]

**A.** *pron.* = THESE *dem. pron.*

**13..** *Cursor M.* 6291 (Cott., Gött.) Þir [*F.*, *Tr.* þes] er þe folk of israel. *Ibid.* 6481 (Cott.) Þir [*F.* þer, *G.* þis, *Tr.* þese] er þe coma[n]mentes ten. *Ibid.* 23053 (Edin., Gött.) Gret lauerdschip sal þir [*Cott.* þar, *F.* ham] be lent. *Ibid.* 23643 (Edin., Gött.) Þir sal worsip al creature. *a* **1340** HAMPOLE *Psalter* iii. 2 Þere ere leghers, and þai say to bigile þe. **13..** *Evang. Nicod.* 28 in Herrig's *Archiv* LIII. 392 We, whatkyn godes er þire [*rimes* syre, ire, desyre]? *c* **1450** *St. Cuthbert* (Surtees) 3521 Þir [five onions], he saide, has bene my mete. **1456** SIR G. HAYE *Law Arms* (S.T.S.) 85 Of all thir, thare is nane sa gude as..defens of gude rycht. **1552–3** *Reg. Privy Council Scot.* I. 137 Thir ar the artikills of the Lordis. **1637–50** Row *Hist. Kirk* (Wodr. S.) 197 Any one of thir requyrs a wholl man. **1825** BROCKETT *N. C. Words*, *Thur*, these. **1828** *Craven Gloss.*, *Thur, thir*, these.

**B.** *adj.* = THESE *dem. adj.*

**13..** *Cursor M.* 4085 (Cott.) Þeir [*Gött.* þir, *F.* þes, *T.* þese] breþer, þat i said of are. *Ibid.* 5938 'Yee prai your lauerd', he said, 'þat he Wald do þier frosses [*F.* þere froskis, *G.* þir froskis, *T.* þese frogges] a-wai fra me'. *Ibid.* 19391 Þir [*F.* þer, *Tr.* þese] seuen were Sett be-fore þe aposteles sere. **1340** HAMPOLE *Pr. Consc.* 1682 Als þir clerkes fyndes writen. *c* **1400** MAUNDEV. (Roxb.) Pref. 2 Þir werldly lordes. *c* **1420** *Anturs of Arth.* 575 Witturly ther weys [*Douce MS.* þes wighte mene] thayre weppuns thai weld. **1423** JAS. I *Kingis Quair* li, I..said thir versis sevin. *c* **1440** *Alphabet of*

*Tales* 55 He lukid evur when þir fendis suld com agayn. 1490 *Exch. Rolls Scotl.* X. 663 To quhais knauleg thire our letterris salcum greting. 1553 Kennedy *Compend. Tract.* in *Wodrow Soc. Misc.* (1844) 109 Sen the tyme of the Apostolis to thir our dayis. 1678 *Contract* in *Proc. Soc. Ant. Scot.* (1896) XXX. 21 Both pairties are content that ther present[s] be insert. 1715 *Wodrow Corr.* (1843) II. 33 Thir two men have bred trouble enough. 1790 Burns *Tam o' Shanter* 155 Thir breeks o' mine, my only pair. 1790 Mrs. Wheeler *Westmld. Dial.* Pref. 11 Thor Men hed been at a College, coad Cambridg.

[*Note.* Difficulties of derivation from ON. *þeir, þær* are: (1) The retention of inflexional *-r*, otherwise unexemplified, and the fact that *þei-r* had already been adopted in its pronominal sense as *þeȝȝ, they, thei*, in the north *þai, þay*, and was in full use in Cursor M. and other northern works: see They. Moreover, neither *thir* nor *ther* appears to represent *þei-r* phonetically, as Ormin's *þeȝȝ* and E. Midl. *þei* did. (2) The sense is quite different; the ON. word means 'those' or 'they', distinct from *þesser, -ar* 'these'; while *thir* has been from the beginning emphatically 'these', as distinct from *þā, þās* 'those'. The explanation 'the here', 'those here' suits the sense; but (1) no trace has been found of these in an uncombined form; and (2) the addition of *here* to a demonstrative, common in the midlands and south of England (see Here 1 d), is not known as a northern idiom.]

**Thir**, obs. unstressed form of Their.

**Third** (þɔ̄ɹd), *a.* (*adv.*), *sb.* Forms: see below. [OE. *þridda, -e, þird(d)a, -e*, Comm. Teut. and Indo-Eur.; = OFris. *thredda*, OS. *thriddio* (MLG. *drudde, derde*, Du. *derde*), OHG. *dritto* (MHG., G. *dritte*), ON. *þriðe, -i* (Sw. *tredje*, Da. *tredie*), Goth. *þridja*, :—OTeut. **þridjô-*, :—Indo-Eur. **tritjo's*: cf. Gr. τρίτος, L. *tertius*, Skr. *tṛtīyas*.
The metathesis of *third* for *thrid* appears already in ONorthumb. *c* 950, but *thrid* was the prevalent type down to the 16th c.]

**A.** Illustration of Forms.

α. 1 (3) **þridda, 2–5 þridde, 3 þride, 4 þryd(e, threid, þred, 4–5 thrydde, thride, þrid, thridd, 4–6 thridde, thryd, thredde, 4–7 thred, 4–6, *Sc.* –8 thrid, 5 thryde, thrudde, (tryd).**

*a* 800 Cynewulf *Christ* 726 Wæs se þridda hlyp. *c* 1000 *Sax. Leechd.* II. 298 Þridde mæȝen is. *c* 1200 Ormin Ded. 6 Broþerr min i Godess hus, ȝet o þe þride [*elsewhere* þridde] wise. *c* 1250 *Gen. & Ex.* 3516 Ðe ðridde moneð in is cumen. *a* 1300 *Cursor M.* 8471 (Cott.) Þe thride boke efter þa tua. *Ibid.* 16892 To rise þe thrid [*Gött.* thred] dai. *Ibid.* 18646 To þe thrid [*G.* threid] morn. 13.. *E. E. Allit. P.* B. 300 The Iolef Iapheth watz gendered þe þryd. 1382 Wyclif *Acts* xx. 9 He ledd by sleep fel down fro the thridde stage. *c* 1450 *Two Cookery-bks.* 113 (Laud MS.) Ye thrudde perty shal be sugar. 1588 A. King tr. *Canisius' Catech.* Kalendar 1 Feb., S. Ignatius bischop of Antioch threid efter S. Peter. 1606 *Sc. Acts Jas. VI* (1816) IV. 279/2 The thrid day of this instant. *c* 1730 Thrid [see B. I. 1].

β. 1 (*Northumb.*) **ðirda, ðirdda, 2 þerdde, 4 þirde, 5–6 thyrd(e, 5–7 thirde, 6 theyrd, thurd, 5– third.**

*c* 950 *Lindisf. Gosp.* Luke xii. 38 ȝif on ða ðirdda wacan ȝe-cymeð. *a* 1200 *Moral Ode* 138 (Lamb. MS.) Nolde he for al middenerd þe þerdde [*v.r.* þridde] [dei] þer abiden. 1393 Langl. *P. Pl.* C. xxii. 264 And matheu þe þirde. 1446 Lydg. *Nightingale Poems* i. 299 Ye that are in the third age Of your lyfe ande passed morow & prime. 1473 Warkw. *Chron.* (Camden) 3 In the thyrde ȝere of the reygne of Kynge Edwarde. 1552 Huloet, Thyrde fayre or market proclaymed.

**B.** Signification. **I.** *adj.*

As with other ordinals, usually *the third*: see The *def. art.* B. 18.

**1.** The ordinal numeral corresponding to the cardinal three: last of three; that comes next after the second. **a.** with sb. expressed.

*a* 800 [see A. α]. 971 *Blickl. Hom.* 15 Þy þriddan dæȝe he of deaþe ariseþ. *a* 1225 *Ancr. R.* 14 Þe þridde dole. 1340 Hampole *Pr. Consc.* 1664 Here bigynnes þe thred part. 1497 *Naval Acc. Hen. VII* (1896) 141 The thryde day of Marche. 1533 Bellenden *Livy* iii. xi. (S. T. S.) I. 292 To be haldin þe thrid day eftir þe nundinis. 1552 Huloet, Thyrde sillable, *ante penultima*. 1597 A. M. tr. *Guillemeau's Fr. Chirurg.* 30/1 The finger called *Medicus*, or thirde finger. *c* 1730 Burt *Lett. N. Scotl.* (1818) I. 20 Inquire for such a launde.., where the gentleman stayd, at the thrid stair, that is three stories high. 1847 Helps *Friends in C.* I. vi. 92, I prefer real life..where there is no third volume [as in a novel] to make things straight.

**b.** Following the names of sovereigns, popes, etc.: cf. Second A. 1 b.

1414 *Rolls of Parlt.* IV. 59/2 Kyng Henry the Thridde. 1550 Bale *K. Johan* (Camden) 42 Pope Innocent the thred. 1735 Johnson *Lobo's Abyssinia, Descr.* v. 73 King John the Third [of Portugal].

**c.** with sb. understood.

*c* 950 *Lindisf. Gosp.* Matt. xxii. 26 ȝelic ðe æftera..& ðe ðirda [*Rushw.* þridde]. *c* 1175 *Lamb. Hom.* 133 Ðreo þing.. þet oðer is goddes word and þet ðridde is weldede. *a* 1300 *Cursor M.* 358 (Cott.) Þe thrid es air, and fir þe ferth. 1382 Wyclif *Dan.* v. 7 Shal be the thrid in my rewme. *c* 1440 *Gesta Rom.* xv. 51 (Harl. MS.) And so he wrote to the thrid, þat seid she lovid him. 1552–3 *Inv. Ch. Goods, Staffs.* in *Ann. Lichfield* (1863) IV. 70, iij vestements, one of whyte fustian, another of blacke chamblet, & the thryd of blewe sarsynet. 1662 Playford *Skill Mus.* ii. (1674) 92 Six strings,..the first ..is called the Treble; the second, the Small Mean; the third, the Great Mean. 1821 Scott *Kenilw.* xxxviii, 'Hush! thou knave!' said a third; 'how know'st thou who may be within hearing?'

**d.** *Gram.* In *third person*: see Person *sb.* 8. Also in *third declension, conjugation*, and in names of tenses, as *third future, preterite*, where the reference is to a conventional order of enumeration adopted by grammarians.

1530 Palsgr. 93 In verbes of theyr thyrde conjugation I fynde a litell more difficultie. *a* 1586 Sidney *Arcadia* ii. (Sommer) 137 He had..forgotten in speaking of him selfe to vse the third person. 1764 W. Primatt *Accentus Rediv.* 111 Provided they were third persons plural. 1848 J. T. White *Xenophon's Anab.* ii. iv. § 5 Notes (1872) 116 Sometimes..the third future is used, instead of the common future, to point out more forcibly all but immediate occurrence of some future action. 1857 Williams *Sanskrit Gram.* § 415 Fortunately..the third preterite occurs but rarely in the better specimens of Hindū composition.

**2.** Additional to and distinct from two others already known or mentioned. *Third person* (in *Law*) = Third party. †*Third place*, a place which is neutral ground to two persons (*obs.*).

*c* 1290 *Beket* 415 in *S. Eng. Leg.* I. 118 Þat þridde þing ȝeot mest of alle and sonest in wraþþe hem brouȝte. *c* 1400 *Apol. Loll.* 3 And þe þrid, if he be most obedient to God and to His lawe. 1579 W. Wilkinson *Confut. Familye of Loue* 17 b, Incorporall and immateriall essences cannot be coupled in the same third matter. 1709 E. Ward tr. *Cervantes* 189 Any thing is easily believ'd that is to the Disreputation of a third Person. 1757 Chesterf. *Lett.* 31 Dec., I could neither visit, nor be visited by, the Ministers of those two Crowns: but we met every day, or dined at third places. 1818 Cruise *Digest* (ed. 2) I. 444 The clause.. extends..to third persons only; not to the persons conveying, or those to whom lands are conveyed to uses. 1865 Kingsley *Herew.* xvii, Martin Lightfoot..was as a third hand and foot to him all day long. 1878 Stewart & Tait *Unseen Univ.* iv. § 122. 133 There can be no third thing besides body and void. [Cf. Tertium quid.]

†**b.** *Third tongue*, a backbiter; a slanderer. Used by Wyclif and Coverdale to render *lingua tertia* of the Vulgate, in LXX. γλῶσσα τρίτη. *Obs.*

1382 Wyclif *Ecclus.* xxviii. 16 The thridde tunge manye men stirede. 1388 *Ibid.* 19 *margin*, The tunge of the preuey bacbiter is clepid the thridde tunge..and the bacbiter him silf hath the thridde tunge, for he, as the thridde, makith debate betwen a man and his neiȝbore. 1535 Coverdale *Ecclus.* xxviii. 14–15 The thirde tonge hath disquieted many one, and dryuen them from one londe to another...The thirde tonge hath cast out many an honest woman, and robbed them of their labours.

**3.** *Third part* = B. II. 1. Now *rare*: see Part *sb.* 5.

*a* 1300 *Cursor M.* 973 (Cott.) Þe half parte gladli or þe thrid We wil þe giue. 1375 Barbour *Bruce* ii. 305 Þe thrid part went to þe forray. 1483 *Cath. Angl.* 385/2 Þe Thryd parte of a halpeny, *trissis*. 1570–6 Lambarde *Peramb. Kent* 228 The Monkes should enioy the whole tongue, and two third partes of the rest of the body. 1611 Bible *Rev.* viii. 8 The third part of the sea became blood.

**4.** The last of each successive group of three; one in every three, i. e. one third of the whole. *Third penny*: one third of the whole sum; *spec.* (see quot. 1706). *Third sheaf and teind*: see *third and teind*, II. 1.

*c* 1400 Maundev. (Roxb.) xix. 87 Sum..at ilke a thridd passe knelis doune apon þe erthe. 1423 *Cal. Letter Bk. I. Lond.* (1909) 295 Have he, for his labour, the tryd peny that shal be recovered. *a* 1578 Lindesay (Pitscottie) *Chron. Scot.* (S. T. S.) II. 315 Thair come in be sie sa meikill victuallis that it come downe the thrid penny. 1597 [see Every 1 e (*c*)]. 1627 *Rep. Parishes Scotl.* (Bann. Cl.) 3 Ten landis..payis presentlie the thrid scheiff and teind led. 1706 Phillips (ed. Kersey), *Third-penny*, the third part of Fines and Profits, arising from Law-Processes, which in every County was heretofore allow'd to the Sheriff; the other two Parts being appointed for the King's Use. 1727 Swift *Poisoning E. Curll* Wks. 1755 III. i. 152 You shall have your third share of the Court poems. 1904 [see Quartan A. 1, def.].

**b.** *Third-day ague*, tertian ague.

1817–18 Cobbett *Resid. U. S.* (1822) 319 You would frighten him into a third-day ague.

**5.** Combinations, collocations, or phrases with special meaning (some of which may be used *attrib.* or as *adj.*), as *third base, cousin, cousinship, degree, form* (hence *third-former*), *heir, magnitude, person, story, term* (hence *third-termery*): see the sbs.; **third ague**, tertian ague; **third best**, third in point of quality, that is next inferior to the Second best; **third-day**, the Quaker name for Tuesday, as being the third day of the week; **third estate**, the Commons: see Estate *sb.* 6; **third floor**, (*a*) in England, the floor or story of a building separated by two from the ground floor; (*b*) in *Sc.*, *U. S.*, etc., the third story, counting the ground floor as the first; **third hour**, (*a*) among the Jews, the third of the twelve equal divisions of time between morning and evening; the hour between 8 and 9 a.m.; (*b*) in *R.C.Ch.*, the hour of Tierce; **third house**, (*U.S. polit. slang*): see quot.; **third man**, *Cricket*, a fielder placed between point and short slip, but further out; an additional short slip; also, the position occupied by him; **third order**: see Tertiary A. 5; **third penny**: see 4 above; † **third place**: see 2 above; **third point**, *Arch.* = Tierce *point*: see quot.; **third rail**, in some systems of electric railways, an additional rail which conveys the current; **third rime, rhyme**, = Terza rima; **third season man**, = *third year man*; **third staff**, = *third stave*; † **third state**, = *third estate*; **third stave**: see quot.; † **third tongue**: see 2 b above; **third ventricle**, that portion of the central cavity of the brain that lies between the optic thalami; **third year man**, a student who has entered upon the third (often the last) year of a course of study.

1674 N. Fairfax *Bulk & Selv.* 131 In the very fit of a *Third Ague. 1375 Barbour *Bruce* xiii. 321 He was the *thrid best knycht, perfay, That men wist liffand in his day. 1859 *Habits Gd. Soc.* iii. 155, I am wondering whether everybody arranges his wardrobe as our ungrammatical nurses used to do ours, under the heads of 'best, second-best, third-best', and so on. 1901 *Daily News* 31 Jan. 7/3 The *third-cousinships of German Princes. 1677 in Penn *Trav. Holland* (1694) 9 A Monthly Meeting..upon the third *third day of the Month. 1901 *Scotsman* 5 Apr. 6/4 In the *third degree in [Free] Masonry a skull and cross-bones are employed. 1604 in Rymer *Fœdera* XVI. 562/1 Knightes and Burgesses..doe present the Bodie of the *Thirde Estate. 1855 F. B. Wells tr. *Thierry* (*title*), The Formation and Progress of the Tiers État, or Third Estate in France. 1875 Stubbs *Const. Hist.* II. xv. 185 That portion of the third estate which was represented by the knights of the shire. 1908 *Daily Chron.* 14 Aug. 8/6 Immediately after the arrival of the *third-floor-back lodger a transformation takes place. 1687 Settle *Refl. Dryden* 63 So old a Phrase,..that it has been in twenty *third-Form School-Boys Exercises. 1869 Blackmore *Lorna D.* ii, A *third-former nearly six feet high. *c* 1400 *26 Pol. Poems* xxvi. 208 Men seyen 'good geten vntrewly, The *iij^de eyre browke hit ne may'. 1484 Caxton *Fables of Auian* xviii, Of the thynge wrongfully and euylle goten, the thyrd heyre shalle neuer be possessour of hit. 1382 Wyclif *Acts* ii. 15 It is the *thridde our of the day. 1706 tr. *Dupin's Eccl. Hist. 16th C.* II. v. 43 Called Tierce, because it began at the Third Hour of the day. 1889 Farmer *Dict. Amer.* s. v. *Lobby*, The lobby is also called the '*Third House'. 1905 *Westm. Gaz.* 13 Feb. 10/1 In the constellation of the Twins, near the *third-magnitude star Mu. 1871 Hoppe, **Third man*, einer der *fielders* im Cricket. 1881 *Standard* 14 June 3/8 The catch that dismissed him was an easy one at third man. 1891 W. G. Grace *Cricket* 260 Third man must ask the bowler whether he should stand rather fine or square. 1629 Wadsworth *Pilgr.* vii. 72 There is besides another Nunnery of the *third Order of St. Francis. 1753 Challoner *Cath. Chr. Instr.* 184 Besides these there are the..Nuns of the third Order of St. Francis. 1908 *Westm. Gaz.* 24 Dec. 6/3 The..version of the Rule of the Third Order found..in the Capistran Convent in the Abruzzi. 1727–41 Chambers *Cycl.*, **Third Point*, or *Tierce-point*, in architecture, the point of section in the vertex of an equilateral triangle. Arches or vaults of the third point..are those consisting of two arches of a circle, meeting in an angle a-top. 1901 *Westm. Gaz.* 23 July 4/3 A new electric railway..built on the '*third rail' system, which is believed to represent a great economy as compared with the overhead system. 1905 *Daily Chron.* 2 Feb. 3/4 Avoiding the dangers which had been experienced with the third-rail system. 1656 H. Phillips *Purch. Patt.* (1676) A iv b, An house of the *third rate. 1820 Byron *Let. to Murray* Wks. (1846) 505/1 You will find ..in *third rhyme (*terza rima*),..Fanny of Rimini. *a* 1860 Alb. Smith *Lond. Med. Stud.* (1861) 17 His mentor is ready in the shape of a *third-season man. 1667 E. Chamberlayne *Pres. St. Eng.* i. xix. (1684) 322 Of the *Third State, or Commons of England. 1898 Stainer & Barrett *Dict. Mus. Terms*, **Third Stave*, a name given to the stave upon which pedal music is written for the organ. 1679 Moxon *Mech. Exerc.* vii. 130 Your Ground-plot, or second or *third Story. 1890 *Cincinnati Commerc. Gaz.* 30 June, There would be no *third termery in it, as he [Pres. Cleveland] had not two consecutive terms.

**II.** *sb.*

**1.** A third part (B. I. 3) *of* anything; any one of three equal parts into which a whole may be divided.

*Third and teind*, one-third of the produce and one-tenth of the remainder (making two-fifths of the whole) paid as rent.

1382 Wyclif 1 *Macc.* x. 29 Nowe Y assoile ȝou..of tributis, and I forȝeue to ȝou the pricis of salt, and forȝeue crownys, and the thriddis [1388 thridde part] of seed. 1479 *Act. Dom. Conc.* (1839) 32/2 Þat þe schiref..deliuer þe said vmfra & his tennandis ane evinly thrid þarof. 1611 Shaks. *Cymb.* v. iv. 19 Men, Who of their broken Debtors take a third, A sixth, a tenth, letting them thriue againe. 1705 Addison *Italy* 136 No Sentence can stand that is not confirm'd by Two Thirds of this Council. 1799 J. Robertson *Agric. Perth* 139 In most parts of Strathallan, the land is kept in thirds, (i.e.) one third in tillage for three year, and two thirds always grass. 1852 R. F. Burton *Falconry in Vall. Indus* vi. 71 One will require at least a third more breaking than another. 1884 J. Tait in *U. P. Mag.* Apr. 156 The Master was to have the third and teind shorn and set up. 1893 *Law Times* XCIV. 504/1 Whether such a gift..would be divisible into moieties or thirds.

**2.** *Law.* (Mostly *pl.*) The third of the personal property of a deceased husband allowed to his widow. Also, the third of his real property to which his widow might be legally entitled for her life (*obs.* exc. *Hist.*). Cf. Terce 2.

1396 in *Scott. Antiq.* XIV. 318 Swa mykyl as pertenys to the modyr of the forsaid Erle..be resone of hir thryd. 1540 *Test. Ebor.* (Surtees) VI. 106 She [the wife] to be fullie content with hir thirds. 1596 Bacon *Use of Law* Wks. 1879 I. 585/1 By this course of putting lands into use there were many inconveniences, as..The wife was defrauded of her thirds; the husband of being tenant by courtesy [etc.]. 1609 Skene *Reg. Maj.* i. 113. 1636 in *Crt. & Times Chas. I* (1848) II. 239 Having renounced her jointure and thirds, she may be so utterly undone. 1664 *Early Rec. Groton, Mass.* (1880) 145 Vnto which alienation the wiues of them both doe giue their consent to the giuing vp their thirds. 1709 S. Sewall *Diary* 18 Nov., 30*l.* more to Grace, and 12. to her Brother, to come out of their Mothers Thirds now to be divided. 1767 [see Dower *sb.*² 1]. 1864 Thoreau *Maine W.* (1894) 207 There you are never reminded that the wilderness which you are threading is, after all, some villager's familiar wood-lot, some widow's thirds.

†**3.** A third of the proceeds of captures, or of certain fines, forfeitures, etc., of which two thirds were due to the king. *Obs.*

1429 in Rymer *Fœdera* X. 422 Eny Thriddes, or other Gaines of Werre. 1444 in *Coll. Hist. Staff.* (1891) XII. 319 The thrides of the thrides of all maner Prisoners, Prises, and wynynges. 1627 in *Crt. & Times Chas. I* (1848) I. 234 A commission to proceed against recusants for their thirds due to his majesty by law.

**4.** *Sc. Eccl. Hist.* See quot. 1838.

1573 *Satir. Poems Reform.* xlii. 812 Thir thriddis, I say, but stopping ony, The Kirkis Collectouris suld vptane, Syne vnto the Excheker gane. *c* 1575 *Balfour's Practicks* (1754) 143 The teindis, landis, maillis, fermis, and dewteis of landis assumit in the thriddis of benefices. 1586 in *Dunfermline Regr.* (Bann. Cl.) 449 The haill prelaceis of our reallme ar bund and obleissit to warrand their thridis to ws fra thair awin deidis. 1838 W. Bell *Dict. Law Scot.*, *Thirds*... Before the annexation of the year 1587, the King, in order to prevent the entire abstraction of their provisions from the acting clergy,..assumed into his own hands a third of the revenues of all ecclesiastical benefices, which he intrusted to the Commissioners of Plat, who assigned to the ministers respectively sufficient provisions, and reserved the remainder for the King. [See Plat *sb.*[3] 6.]

†**5.** *pl.* The sum paid by an incoming freshman for the furniture, etc. of his college rooms, usually assessed at two thirds of the amount paid by the preceding tenant. *Obs.*

1687 Wilding in *Collect.* (O. H. S.) I. 255 Reced of my Chum for thirds. 1826 C. Wordsworth *Let.* in *Ann. Early Life* I. 38 Tell my father that I expect he will hear something about 'the thirds' which we pay for furniture, &c. 1853 'C. Bede' *Verdant Green* I. iv, Mr. Filcher then explained the system of thirds, by which the furniture...was to be paid for. 1858 Hogg *Shelley* I. 69 Transferring the.. movables to the successor on payment of thirds, that is, of two-thirds of the price last given.

**6.** *Mus.* A note three diatonic degrees above or below a given note (both notes being reckoned); also (usually) the interval between this and the given note, equivalent either to two tones (*major third*), or to one tone and one diatonic semitone (*minor third*); also, the harmonic combination of two such notes.

*Diminished third*, an interval equal to two diatonic semitones, being less by a chromatic semitone than a minor third.

1597 Morley *Introd. Mus.* 70 Which distances make a Concord or consonant Harmony?..A third, a Fift, a Sixt, and an eight. 1662 Playford *Skill Mus.* I. v. (1674) 20 You will tune from Sol to Mi which is a Third. 1752 tr. *Rameau's Treat. Musick* 34 Those Notes, which are a Third above, are deemed Thirds. 1855 Browning *Toccata of Galuppi's* vii, Those lesser thirds so plaintive. 1855 — *Lovers' Quarrel* xviii, We shall have the word In a minor third There is none but the cuckoo knows. 1884 Parry in Grove *Dict. Mus.* IV. 102 *Third*, one of the most important intervals in modern music...Three forms are met with in modern music—major, minor, and diminished.

**7.** The third of the subdivisions of any standard measure or dimension which is successively subdivided in a constant ratio; the subdivision next below seconds: see Prime *sb.*[2] 2. †Formerly, in Scotland, a weight of account = the 13,824th part $(1 \div 24^3)$ of a grain (*obs.*).

1594 J. Davis *Seaman's Secr.* (1643) D j b, Euery degree.. doth containe 60 minutes, and euery minute 60 seconds, and euery second 60 thirds, &c. 1604 in Moryson *Itin.* I. (1617) 282 (Table of Scottish Weights of Coins), xx. s. [sterling] = 06 pennyweights, 10 graines, 16 mites, 18 droits, 10 periots, English Weight; 07 deniers, 21 graines, 07 primes, 01 seconds, 09 thirds, 19 fourths, Scottish Weight. 1694 Holder *On Time* ii. 32 To divide.. an Hour into 60′ (Minutes), a Minute into 60″ (Second Minutes), a Second Minute into 60‴ (Thirds). 1840 Lardner *Geom.* 56 This system of division is sometimes carried even further, a second being divided into sixty equal parts called thirds; but it is more usual to express small angles or arcs in decimal parts of a second.

†**b.** In decimal fractions: see quots. *Obs.*

1660 J. Moore *Arith.* 10 Some call their Tenth part Primes, the Hundereth parts Seconds, the 1000 parts Thirds. 1766 Hutton *School Master's Guide* 55 The 1st, 2d, 3d, 4th, &c. places of decimals..are denominated the places of primes, seconds, thirds, and fourths, &c. respectively.

**8.** *Comm. pl.* Goods of the third degree of quality.

1823 J. Badcock *Dom. Amusem.* 163 Flour or bread,..of the usual London manufacture, as *seconds*, *thirds*, and *browns*. 1832 G. R. Porter *Porcelain & Gl.* 186 Crown glass is sold, according to its quality, under four different denominations —firsts, seconds, thirds, and fourths. 1888 *Times* (weekly ed.) 14 Sept. 19/1 Fruit should be sorted into bests and seconds and in some cases into thirds. 1903 *Daily Chron.* 21 Apr. 2/6 Cork butter.—Firsts, 86s.; seconds, 80s.; thirds, 78s.

**9.** Elliptical uses of the adj. passing into sb.

**a.** *Third of kin* (*Sc.*): one related in the third degree of consanguinity.

1535 Stewart *Cron. Scot.* (Rolls) III. 260 The erle of Arrane, lord of Hammiltoun, Evin thrid and thrid to him [that] weiris the croun. 1569 *Reg. Privy Council Scot.* II. 39 The said Erll and the said umquhile Johnne Suthirland quha wes slane thrid and ferdis of kin [the Earl's father was cousin to John's grandmother]. 1583 *Ibid.* III. 622 Quha and he ar secundes and thriddes of kin. 1892 G. Stewart *Shetland Fireside T.* ix. (ed. 2) 71 Auld Ibbie Bartley, dat wis thrids o' kin to my wife's foster midder, an' her oey.

**b.** Elliptical for third person (in Grammar); third day (of the month); third chapter (of a book of the Bible); third year (of a reign).

1530 Palsgr. Introd. 33 The thyrde syngular [endeth].. most commenly in T. 1536 Cromwell in Merriman *Life & Lett.* (1902) II. 1 From Eltham thridde of Janua[ry]. 1539 Tonstall *Serm. Palm Sund.* (1823) 86 It is written in the thirde of Matthewe. 1747 *Gentl. Mag.* May 247/1 On Sunday the 3d of May. 1857 Williams *Sanskrit Gram.* § 330 It is the only conjugation that rejects the nasal in the 3d. plur.

**c.** A card of the third size; also *thirds card*: see quots.

1891 *Cent. Dict.* s. v., *Thirds card*, a card $1\frac{1}{2}$ by 3 inches, the size most used for a man's visiting-card. (Eng.). 1892 *Chiswick Press Calendar*, Sizes of Cards..Extra Thirds $3 \times 1\frac{5}{8}$. Thirds $3 \times 1\frac{1}{2}$ in.

**d.** *Third of exchange*: the last of a set of three bills of exchange of even tenor and date: see Exchange *sb.* 5.

**e.** Generally, the word omitted being usually obvious from the context; esp. in familiar use.

*a* 1635 Sibbes *Confer. Christ & Mary* (1656) 104 He must be a friend or enemy; there is no third in God. 1859 *Habits Gd. Soc.* (new ed.) 44 In the third [class railway-carriage] he will have to sit next to an odoriferous ploughboy. 1864 Bowen *Logic* iii. 49 The Axiom which is usually called the Law of Excluded Third. 1889 Linskill *Golf* iii. (1895) 15 Odd No. 1. 'Stroke a hole'...Sometimes a 'third' is given, which means the application of Odd No. 1 at every third hole. 1891 *Cent. Dict.*, *Third*...In *base-ball*, same as *third base*. 1900 *Monthly Rev.* I. 46 The Russian peasant who travels third is not accustomed to luxuries. 1903 *Westm. Gaz.* 30 Dec. 11/1 It is of course the Third Preference stock which is directly affected...Some operators are anticipating that the Thirds will get a half per cent. more than for last year. *Mod.* Mr. A. did badly; he only got a third in Greats.

**Third,** *v.* [f. prec.]

**1.** *trans.* To divide (anything) into three equal parts; to reduce to one third of the number or bulk.

1455 *Sc. Acts Jas. II* (1814) II. 44/2 þ[t] na man gang away w[t] na maner of gudis quhill it be thriddyt, and partyt befor þe chiftane. 1612 *Two Noble K.* I. ii, What man Thirds his owne worth? 1747 Franklin *Lett.* Wks. 1887 II. 97 That celerity doubled, tripled, &c., or halved, thirded, &c. 1874 Furnivall in *10th Rep. Committee E. E. T. S.* 16 Such a course would have halved or thirded the number of our subscribers.

†**b.** To buy or sell (college furniture, etc.) at two thirds of its last selling price: see Third *sb.* 5. *Obs.*

1811 [R. Fenton] *Tour Genealogy* 157 The same..tale..is always worse told by him that tells it last; till like college furniture, too often thirded, it becomes too threadbare for credit.

**2.** To speak in favour of (a motion, proposition, etc.) as third speaker; to support the seconder.

1656 *Burton's Diary* (1828) I. 90 It has been firsted, seconded, and thirded. 1707 Luttrell *Brief Rel.* (1857) VI. 233 A motion of the lord Wharton, seconded and thirded by the lords Somers and Hallifax. 1893 E. H. Baker in *King's Business* (New Haven, Conn.) 174 That resolution ..was seconded by a theological professor...It was thirded by a pastor in the Episcopal Church.

†**b.** To support or back up in the third place: cf. Second *v.* 2. *Obs.*

1602 Carew *Cornwall* 84 b, The next Captains should forthwith put themselves with their companies into their assigned sea coast townes, whom the adjoyning land-forces were appoynted to second and third.

†**3.** To hoe (turnips), clean (wheat), etc., the third time. *Obs.*

1683 J. Erskine *Jrnl.* 20 Sept. (1893) 17, I was winding and thirding some corn. 18.. *Moor's Suffolk MS.* (Halliw.), 'Ar them there tahnups done woth?' 'No, we are thirding 'em.'

**Thi·rdborough, thri·dborrow.** *Obs.* exc. *Hist.* Also 5–6 (7–8) **thrid-,** 6 **thred-, thur-, thar-,** 6–7 **therd-;** 5 **-borro,** 6 **-bourogh(e, -borow(e,** 6–7 **-barow(e, -barrow,** 7 **-borrow, -bearer.** [In 15th c. *thridborro*, 16th c. *thridborowe*, later *third-borow*; and with both elements variously corrupted. Early evidence of origin scanty; but, as pointed out by Professor Skeat, prob. a ME. corruption of *fridborgh* :—OE. *friðborg* peace-pledge, peace-surety: see Frithborh, Frank-pledge. The corruption may have been due to Norman scribes, but not necessarily so: cf. Th (6). See Note below, and cf. Borrowhead, Borsholder, Headborough.]

Formerly, The head man of a frithborh or frankpledge; hence, the conservator of peace or peace-officer of a tithing, the petty constable of a township or manor.

?*c* 1475 *Hunt. Hare* 199 Jac of Bonam he was constabull. ..Hobb Andrw he was thridborro; He bad hom, 'Pesse! God gyff hom sorro! For I may arrest yow best'. 1512 *Act 4 Hen. VIII*, c. 19 § 6 Preceptes to the Constables Hedbouroghes Thirdbouroghes Subconstables Tythingmen Borsalders. 1523 Fitzherb. *Surv.* 20 b, The othe of all maner of Offycers generally...I shall true constable be, trewe thridborowe, trewe reue, trewe frankelege [etc.]..and truely and duely do and kepe all thynges that belongeth to myne offyce to do. 1536 *Act* 28 *Hen. VIII*, c. 10 § 6 Euery ..Hedborowe,Thredborough, Borsolder, and euery other Lay Officer. 1547 in J. H. Glover *Kingsthorpiana* (1883) 84 If any customery tenant or suter..do rebuke, revyle, or dysobey the constables, thurbarowes, ale-tasters, haywarde, or other officers sworne in doyinge their offyce. 1581 Lambarde *Eiren.* I. iii. (1588) 15 Where each third Borow only hath a Constable, there the officers of the other two Borowes, be called Third-borowes. 1588 Shaks. *L. L. L.* I. i. 185, I my selfe reprehend his owne person, for I am his graces Tharborough. 1596 — *Tam. Shr.* Induct. i. 12 *Host.* I know my remedie, I must go fetch the Head-borough. *Beg.* Third, or fourth, or fift Borough, Ile answere him by Law. 1607 Cowell *Interpr.*, *Thridborow*, is vsed for a constable.. which seemeth to be corruptly vsed for the Saxon *freoborh* i. *ingenuus fideiussor.* 1610 Norden *Spec. Brit., Cornw.* (1728) 30 The hundreds haue Constables, Tythinges haue Therd-barows, in some places Hedborows, in some Borowsheds, and in the weste partes a tythingman. *a* 1625 Sir H. Finch *Law* (1636) 336 The conseruator of peace..is called..In a Tything, a petie Constable, Borsholder, Headborough, Thirdborough, Boroughhead, Tything-man, or Chiefe pledge. 1634–5 *Althorp MS.* in Simpkinson *Washingtons* (1860) App. p. lxix, March 5. To the third bearers of Brington for cryeing and prayseing a baye straye nagg taken up. 1645 *MS. Rec. Court Leet Castle Donington, Leicester.* 25 Apr., They present R. R., J. B., R. W. and T. T. to serve the kinge and the lord of this mannor in the office of Thirdborrow for one whole year which they refused. 1658 Phillips, *Thridborough* or *Thirdborough*, a word used in some old Acts, for a Headborough or Constable. 1755 Johnson, *Thirdborough*,.. an under-constable. 1831 Carlyle *Sart. Res.* III. i, Some prospect of..an honourable Mastership in Cordwainery, and perhaps the post of Thirdborough in his Hundred.

[*Note.* The *friðborh* or *frithborgh* was orig. the 'association of ten men in common responsibility' to prevent crime and breach of the peace. In ME. legal use the word was worn down to *fridborgh*, *friborg*, and *freoborg*, and, the first element being associated with *freo* 'free', was rendered in Anglo-Fr. *frankplege*, Anglo-L. *francum plegium*. The head man of the frithborh was in the 12th c. called *friðborg-heved* or *frithborges heved*, 'head of the frithborh' (*Laws of Edw. Conf.* 20 (or 19), § 3), and was later known as *bor(r)ow-head*, *head-bor(ou)gh*, *bor(h)s-holder*, and *burrow-elder* (:—**borh-ealdor*), also in Anglo-L. *plegius capitalis* 'head or chief pledge'. In Fleta I. xlvii. § 10, it is said, 'frithborgh [*printed* frich-] est laudabilis homo astrarius testimonii... per quem omnes iuxta ipsum commorantes firmiori pace sustententur sub stabilitate fideiussionis eius vel alterius per denarium numerum, unde quilibet est quasi plegius alterius'. In this we see the transition of *frithborh* from the association to its individual members, and esp. to the headborough. In certain cases the latter acted with two of his fellows, 'duos de melioribus suorum frithborgorum' (*Laws of Edw.* 20 (or 19), § 3), and this association of three may have contributed to the change of name from *fridborgh* to *thridborgh* and *thirdborough*. The probable connexion of *thridborow* with *freoborh* was suggested by Cowell: see quot. 1607.]

**Third class, third-class,** *phr.* (*sb.* and *a.*)

**1.** *sb. phr.* The class next below the second; esp. of railway carriages; also in an examination list; hence, a place in the third class in an examination.

1845 *Bradshaw's Railway Guide* Aug. 5 Fares between London and Brighton..by..third class, 5*s.* *Mod.* Mr. A. got a third class in History.

**2.** *attrib.* or *adj.* Of or belonging to the class next below the second.

1839 *Bradshaw's Railway Time Table* 19 Oct., Children under seven years of age.. for Second Class Carriages [charged] Third Class price. 1840 *Bradshaw's Railway Comp.*, Third class passengers are conveyed by the 6 a.m. and 8 p.m. Down Trains. 1852 R. S. Surtees *Sponge's Sp. Tour* (1893) 76 The introduction of railways, whose worst third-class accommodation is far better than the old coaches' best. 1859 *All Year Round* No. 30. 78 The third-class carriages, as a rule, were the mere seatless and unsheltered cattle-trucks that still linger on the road from London to Greenwich. 1871 M. Collins *Marq. & Merch.* III. iv. 127 The train was third class. 1886 C. E. Pascoe *London of To-day* xix. (ed. 3) 186 The economical traveller will find many a worse resting-place than its third-class carriages provide. 1891 *Cent. Dict.*, *Third-class matter*, in the postal system of the United States, printed matter other than newspapers or periodicals, sent through the mails by the publishers.

**3.** quasi-*adv.* By a third-class conveyance.

1864 Trevelyan *Compet. Wallah* (1866) 24 Natives almost invariably travel third-class.

†**Thi·rdel.** *Obs.* Forms: 3 thriddedel, 4 þridde deel, 5 thryddele, 6 thirdle, thirdel. [ME. *thriddedel* :—OE. *þridda dǽl* third part: see Deal *sb.*[1] Cf. Ger. *drittel.*] A third part (*of* anything); = next.

1297 R. Glouc. (Rolls) 283 Þe þriddedel mi kinedom ich ȝiue þe to be mi fere. 1387 Trevisa *Higden* (Rolls) III. 169 Þe quene hadde i-sent hire ȝong sone wiþ þe þridde deel [*MS. β.* thriddel, Caxton thryddele] of heere oost aȝenst Cirus. 1542 Recorde *Gr. Artes* K vj b, There bee tertians (that is to say thirdles) of pypes, of hogges heddes, and of barels. *Ibid.* L iij, Take awaye 2 thyrdeles frome any summe, and you muste needes graunt, that that whyche remayneth, is 1 thyrdele of the summe laste before.

†**Thi·rdendeal.** *Obs.* Forms: 1 **þriddan dǽl;** 4 **þridden-,** 4–5 **thridden-,** 5 **threden-, thredden-, thryden-, thyrdyn-,** 6 **thirdin-, thyrden-,** (**thirding-,** 7 **thurron-**), 6–8 **thirden-;** 4–5 **-del,** 5–7 **-dele,** 6 **-deale, deall,** 7 **-dell,** 7–8 **-deal;** 4–6 (9 *dial.*) **-dale.** [OE. (*þone*) *þriddan dǽl*, accus. case of (*se*) *þridda dǽl* the third part (see Thirdel, Deal *sb.*[1], Dale[2]). Cf. Halfendeal, Farthingdeal.]

**1.** The third part of anything; a third.

*c* 1000 *Sax. Leechd.* I. 98 Seoþe on wætere to þriddan dæle. *Ibid.* II. 120 Bewyl oþ þriddan dæl. 13.. *Guy Warw.* (A.) 7306 + st. 65 Þriddendel his lond haue he schold. 14.. *E. E. Misc.* (Warton Cl.) 72 With the thyrdyndele of gume, and twyse so mych of water. *a* 1500 in Arnolde *Chron.* (1811) 147 Euery Sonday a soule out of purgatory and the thredden dele of al synnes releced. 1558 Warde tr. *Alexis' Secr.* I. i. (1580) 37 b, Drinke thereof two thirdendales of a glassefull. 1581 J. Bell *Haddon's Answ. Osor.* 459 b, A thyrdendeale of the Crowne of Thornes is shewed at Paris in the Holy Chappell there.

**2.** A third of a tun; = Tertian B. 2.

1423 *Rolls of Parlt.* IV. 256/1 Thredendels and hoggeshedes so aftur lesse mesure. 14.. *MS. Cantab. Ff.* 5. 48, lf. 55 *b* (Hartshorne *Anc. Metr. T.* (1829) 54), Hit holdis a gode thyrdendele Ful of wyne euery mele.

**3.** (See quots.)

1571 in *Shaks. Jahrbuch* (1896) 142 The hooped pot commonly called a thirdindeale and a half thirdindeale. 1590 [TARLTON] *News Purgat.* (1844) 114 When Tapsters..Fill thirdingdeall pots till the drinke run ouer. 1620 MELTON *Astrolog.* 32 Many of them dare not goe to bed without a Thurrondell Pot of six shillings Beere. 1678 PHILLIPS (ed. 4), *Thirdendeal*, a Liquid Measure used in Salisbury containing three Pints. 1721 in BAILEY.

**Thi·rder.** *rare*⁻¹. [f. THIRD *sb.* + -ER [1].] In *thirder and teinder*, one who pays by way of rent the 'third and teind' (see THIRD B. II. 1).

1884 J. TAIT in *U. P. Mag.* Apr. 156/2 Another case resembles the arrangement of thirders and teinders described by Arthur Young as existing in some parts of France.

**Third hand, third-hand.** [THIRD B. 1 and HAND *sb.* 10 c, after SECOND-HAND.]

**1.** In advb. phrase *at* (†*the*) *third hand*: from a second middleman or intermediary; at the second remove from the original source.

1553 *Reg. Privy Council Scot.* I. 141 Na maner of gudis can be had nor coft bot at the thrid hand. *a* 1635 SIBBES *Confer. Christ & Mary* (1656) 67 We have it at the third hand. 1895 in *Bookman* Oct. 23/1 The illustrations..were reproduced from inferior German copies at third-hand.

**2.** *attrib.* or as *adj.* Obtained, copied, or imitated from a second-hand source; further away from the original source, and so more stale, less authoritative, etc., than the second-hand.

1599 MARSTON *Sco. Villanie* I. iv, Laboring with third-hand iests, and Apish skips. 1862 LATHAM *Channel Isl.* III. xiv. (ed. 2) 348 The second-hand and third-hand text-books. 1866 *Macm. Mag.* Apr. 521 Resting on mere second-hand, nay, often third-hand information.

**b.** *Third-hand dealer*, one who deals in third-hand articles.

1864 TREVELYAN *Compet. Wallah* (1866) 104 Cheated in the purchase of his first buggy by a third-hand dealer in Calcutta.

†**Thi·rding,** *sb. Obs. rare*⁻⁰. [f. THIRD *sb.* + -ING [3].] = RIDING *sb.*: cf. TRITHING.

1847–78 HALLIWELL, *Thirdings*, the Ridings. This word is given by Urry, in his MS. Additions to Ray.

**Thi·rding,** *vbl. sb.* [f. THIRD *v.* + -ING [1].] (See quots.)

1670 BLOUNT *Law Dict.*, *Thirdings*, the third part of the Corn or Grain growing on the Ground at the Tenants death, due to the Lord for a Heriot within a certain Mannor, ..belonging to the Chappel of Turfat in Com. Heref. [So 1706 in PHILLIPS; 1721 in BAILEY; and in mod. dicts.] 1847–78 HALLIWELL, *Thirding*..(2) A custom practised at the universities, where two thirds of the original price is allowed by the upholsterers to the students for household goods returned to them within the year.

**Thirdling** (þǝ·ɹdliŋ). *nonce-wd.* [f. THIRD *a.* + -LING.] Something that comes third.

1884 BROWNING *Ferishtah* Prol. 18 First, food—then, piquancy—and last of all Follows the thirdling.

**Thirdly** (þǝ·ɹdli), *adv.* [f. THIRD *a.* + -LY [2].] In the third place.

1509 HAWES *Past. Pleas.* viii. (Percy Soc.) 30 Thyrdly, they had suche a fantasy In this hyghe arte to be intelligible. 1662 STILLINGFL. *Orig. Sacr.* I. ii. § 12. 1877 A. MACEWEN *Serm.* xvii. 217 Thirdly, we need a firm conviction of the sufficiency of Divine grace.

**Thi·rd pa·rty.** A party or person besides the two primarily concerned, as in a law case or the like. Also *attrib.*

1818 SCOTT *Rob Roy* xiii, Speak as you would to an unconcerned third party. 1853 MAURICE *Proph. & Kings* xx. 343 It appears to be a narrative written by a third party. 1883 *Wharton's Law Lex.* s.v., 'A Third party' may be introduced into an action by a defendant claiming an indemnity, or any other remedy over against him, under Jud. Act, 1873, s. 24. sub. 3, and Order XVI., Rules 17, 19. 1883 *Law Times* 20 Oct. 407/2 The rules relating to third-party procedure..are a great improvement upon the former rules. 1905 *Daily Chron.* 12 Sept. 3/2 The largest third-party vote, with one exception, since the Civil War.

**Thi·rd-ra·te,** *a.* and *sb.* [See RATE *sb.*[1] 9, 9 b.]

**A.** *adj.*

†**1.** Of the third 'rate' (esp. of ships). *Obs.*

1649 CROMWELL *Let.* 14 Nov. in *Carlyle*, The Garland, one of your third-rate ships, coming happily into Waterford Bay. 1666 PEPYS *Diary* 9 Mar., Mr. Castle's new third-rate ship, which is to be called the Defyance. 1693 *Lond. Gaz.* No. 2857/3 This day was Launched a New Third Rate Ship of 80 Guns, called the *Norfolk*.

**2.** Of the third class in point of quality; usually *depreciative*, below 'second-rate'; of decidedly poor or inferior quality.

1838 THIRLWALL *Greece* V. xliv. 327 An actor of third-rate parts. 1850 GROTE *Greece* II. lxi. VII. 491 A town of second-rate or third-rate magnitude. 1855 MACAULAY *Hist. Eng.* xix. IV. 354 The poor thoughts and poor words of a thirdrate pamphleteer.

**B.** *sb. Naut.* A war-vessel of the third rate.

1666 PEPYS *Diary* 4 July, Ten great ships..none to be under third-rates. 1695 *Lond. Gaz.* No. 3061/1 A Third Rate of 62 Guns. 1790 BEATSON *Nav. & Mil. Mem.* I. 65 The fleet.., consisting of but one third rate, five fourth rates, and one sixth rate.

Hence **Thi·rd-ra·teling, Thi·rd-ra·ter,** a third-rate person or thing.

1816 SOUTHEY *Ess.* I. 245 The second and third-ratelings compose works of perishable stuff. 1820 *Blackw. Mag.* VIII. 89 Where is there a Whig in England..that, as a literary man, is fairly out of the class of third raters?

**Thirdsman** (þǝ·ɹdzmæ̆n). A third person or party; *esp.* one called in as an intermediary, mediator, or arbiter.

1818 SCOTT *Hrt. Midl.* xxiv, There was risk of Andro Ferrara coming in thirdsman. *Ibid.* xlviii, If I come in thirdsman among you at the kirk-sessions, you will be all in a tamn'd pad posture indeed. 1887 SAINTSBURY *Hist. Elizab. Lit.* x. (1890) 386 Herrick and Carew..with Crashaw as a great thirdsman, called themselves 'sons' of Ben Jonson.

†**Thi·rdsome,** *a. Obs. rare.* In 5 thryd-, þridde-, thyrd(e)-. [f. THIRD *a.* + -SOME.] Being one of three; accompanied by two others.

*c* 1425 *Eng. Conq. Irel.* 14 Othere thwey cantredes he yaf heruy of Mountmorthy,..a knyght þat com in that same flote, hym þriddesum [*v. r.* thyrdesum] of knyghtes. *Ibid.* 32 Heruy of Mountmorthy, that to ham was ycome, hym thyrdsome [*v. r.* thyrdsome] of knyghtes.

†**Thi·rkin,** *a. Obs.* [f. THIR + KIN *sb.*[1] 6 b. Cf. THAKIN: which is the antithetic word.] These kind of; of this kind.

13.. *Cursor M.* 28576 Man þat o þirkin sinn es scriuen, on seuen maners ar þai for-giuen.

**Thirl** (þǝɹl), *sb.*[1] Now *dial.* Forms: 1 þyrel, -il, þyrl, 3 þirl, þurl, 4 therl, 9 thurl, 4– thirl. See also THRILL *sb.*[1] [OE. *þyrel*, for older **þyrhil*, **þurh-il*, f. *þurh* THOROUGH + -EL [1]. Cf. OHG. *dur(i)hhil*, MHG. *dürchel*, *dürkel*, OE. *þyrel* adjs., pierced, perforated.]

**1.** A hole, bore, perforation; an aperture.

*a* 900 tr. *Bæda's Hist.* IV. iii. (1890) 272 Þonne is on þæm medmicel þyrel ȝeworht. *c* 950 *Lindisf. Gosp.* Matt. xix. 24 Ðerh ðyril nedles. *c* 1000 ÆLFRIC *Voc.* in Wr.-Wülcker 113/29 *Orificium*, ælces kynnes muð *vel* ðyrl. *a* 1225 *Ancr. R.* 292 He..þet lette makien swuche þurles in him uorte huden us inne. *a* 1300 *Cursor M.* 528 Mans hefd has thirls seuen. 1513 DOUGLAS *Æneis* VII. x. 59 A thyrll or aynding stede Of terribyle Pluto. *a* 1640 JACKSON *Creed* XI. xxxviii. § 10 They could not peck the least hole in the mitre, or make the least thirl in the surplice, without working [etc.]. 1866 BROGDEN *Provinc. Wds. Lincoln.* s.v., Fetch a nail passer and make a thirl through this board.

**b.** Each of the two holes or orifices of the nose; a nostril: see NOSE-THIRL.

*a* 1350 *St. Barthol.* 89 in Horstm. *Altengl. Leg.* (1881) 120 His nese es euyn, with thirles small. 1382 WYCLIF *Job* xli. 11 Of his nose therlis goth forth smoke. 1513 DOUGLAS *Æneis* XII. Prol. 29 The flambe owtbrastyng at his neys thyrlys. 1560 DAUS tr. *Sleidane's Comm.* 222 b, With her wyde mouthe and nose thirlles. 1828 *Craven Gloss.*, *Thirl*, the orifice of the nose; nose-thirl, alias nostril.

**2.** An aperture or opening in a wall or the like; e.g. a door or window in a house (*obs.*), a sheep-hole in a wall, etc. Also *fig.*

*a* 1050 *Liber Scintill.* xxxviii. 140 Hwæt framað þæt onȝean feonda searwa eal ceaster byþ ȝehealden ȝif an þyrl open byð forlæten. *a* 1225 *Ancr. R.* 62 Þe kerneaus of þe castel beoð hire huses þurles. *Ibid.* 96 3if eni..worpe his hond forð touward þe þurl cloð, swiftliche anonriht, schutteð al þet þurl [*MS. T.* windohe] to, & letteð hine iwurden. 1340 *Ayenb.* 204 Huerby þe dieuel geþ in ofte ine þe vif þerles of þe house. 14.. *MS. Lincoln A. i. 17*, lf. 241 (Halliw.) If..alle the thirlles, dores and wyndows ware stokyne that na sone myght enter. 1794 W. HUTCHINSON *Hist. Cumbld.* I. 64 *Thirl*..of common acceptation in the north, for an opening left in moor fences, for sheep to pass to and from the commons adjacent to inclosed grounds. 1904 *Eng. Dial. Dict.* s.v. (n. Yorks.), A lot o' sheep..wantin' to go threw a thirl at yance.

†**3.** A small cavity or recess; in quot. a closet.

*a* 1300 *E. E. Psalter* civ. [cv.] 30 He forth-broght froskes þe land of þa, In thirles [L. *in cubilibus*] of þar kinges ma.

**4.** See quots. and cf. THIRLING *vbl. sb.*[1] 2.

1847–78 HALLIWELL, *Thurl*, a long adit in a coal-pit. 1871 *Trans. Amer. Inst. Mining Engin.* I. 304 These would be thurled (cross-cut) at every forty or sixty feet, or at such a distance as the air could be induced to pass the last thurl made. 1899 PREVOST *Cumbld. Gloss.*, *Thirls*, openings made between a pair of exploring places or drifts, for the purpose of ventilation.

**5.** = THRILL *sb.*[3] 1.

1879 J. WHITE *Jottings* 226 (E. D. D.) Yer sang..gied me a thirl. 1897 W. BEATTY *Secretar* xlii. 343 'I kend that', she said with a thirl of gladness in the words.

**Thirl** (þǝɹl), *sb.*[2] *Sc.* Also 6 thyrile, thyrll, 6–8 thirle. [f. THIRL *v.*[2]]

**1. a.** Astriction (usually to a particular mill; in quot. 1564 to a smithy): see THIRLAGE 2. **b.** The duty and liability of tenants in thirlage. **c.** The astricted lands or district, = SUCKEN.

1564 in *Reg. Mag. Sig. Scot.* (1586) 301/2 Cum astrictione fabricandi ferrum infra terras suas de Angus (the haille thirle of the irne werk of oure landis of Angus uist and wont). 1582 *Calr. Laing Charters* (1899) 258 In primis, The thyrile, the haile toun..to haif twa chaldyr of schilling. *Ibid.* 259 This is the just thyrll that we fermoraris of Crummy aw to our mile. 1681 STAIR *Inst. Law Scot.* xvii. § 19. 351 A Clause of thirlage granted by a Town to a Miln ..found to be extended to all Corns Kilned or Steeped within the Thirle. *a* 1722 FOUNTAINHALL *Decisions* (1759) I. 276 That the building a mill within his thirle could be interpreted to be done with no other design but *in aemulatione vicini*. 1773 ERSKINE *Inst. Law Scot.* II. ix. § 20 The astricted lands are called *the thirl*, or *the sucken*; and the persons subjected to the astriction get the name of *suckeners*. 1821 SCOTT *Pirate* xi, Plaguing themselves about baron's mills, and thirls.

**2.** A bondsman, a thrall. *rare.*

1871 WADDELL *Ps.* lxxix. 11 Lat the sigh o' the weary thirl win ben afore yer sight.

**3.** *Comb.* **thirl-band,** chain or bond of servitude; **thirl-folk,** bondmen; **thirl-man,** bondman, serf; **thirl-service** (see THIRL *v.*[2] 2, quot. 1609).

1871 WADDELL *Ps.* ii. 3 Lat's rive their thirlbans syndry. *Ibid.* lxxxix. 50 O Lord, hae min' o' yer thirlfolk's pine. *Ibid.* lxxviii. 70 He lightit on David his thirlman.

**Thirl** (þǝɹl), *a. Sc.* [? attrib. use of THIRL *sb.*[2] 1.] Bound in thirlage *to*.

1582 *Calr. Laing Charters* (1899) 258 Ouir mile that we ar thyrll to. 1897 SARAH TYTLER *Witch-wife* vi. 82 Malt and meal from the mill to which he was 'bound thirl'.

**Thirl** (þǝɹl), *v.*[1] *Obs.* exc. *dial.* and *local.* Forms: 1 þyrlian, þirlian, 2–4 þurle(n (*ü*), 3–4 þorle, 4 þerle, thirll, 4–5 therle, þirle, thurle, 4–7 thyrl(e, 4–8 thirle, 5 thorle, 5–6 thyrll, 7–9 thurl, 4– thirl. See also THRILL *v.*[1] [OE. *þyrlian*, f. *þyr(e)l* THIRL *sb.*[1]: cf. MHG. *dürkeln*.]

**1.** *trans.* To pierce, to run through or into (a body) as a sharp-pointed instrument does; to pierce (anything) with such an instrument; to bore a hole in or through; to perforate.

*c* 1000 ÆLFRIC *Exod.* xxi. 6 Þirlie his eare mid anum æle. *c* 1205 LAY. 4541 Þer wes moni breoste mid brade spere i-þurlud [*c* 1275 iþorled]. *c* 1320 *Cast. Love* 1151 He lette boþe þurlen his feet and honden. *c* 1386 CHAUCER *Knt.'s T.* 1852 Namely oon That with a spere was thirled his brest boon. 1398 TREVISA *Barth. De P. R.* XVIII. cvi. (Bodl. MS.), These wormes beþ icleped Terodenes for þey þorleþ & eteþ trees. *c* 1440 *Pallad. on Husb.* I. 925 They thurle a nutte, and stuffe hit so withynne With brymstoon, chaf, and cedria, this thre. 1578 in *Scot. Poems 16th C.* (1801) II. 127 Remember the speir that thirlit my hart. 1674 RAY *N. C. Words*, To *Thirl*, to bore a hole. 1706 SIBBALD *Hist. Picts* in *Misc. Scot.* I. 118 Being thirled or pierced in many places. 1825 BROCKETT *N. C. Words*, *Thirl*, to pierce, to perforate. 1878 *Cumbld. Gloss.*, *Thirl*, *Thurl*, to bore through.

†**b.** With the weapon or instrument as object.

*a* 1400 *Prymer* (1891) 41 A spere in to his syde was therled of a knyȝt. *a* 1400 *Stac. Rome* 568 There is..A thorne thyrlyd in crystis hed, when he suffyrde for us.

**c.** To make (a hole) by piercing, to bore. *Obs.*

1609 HOLLAND *Amm. Marcell.* XXIV. ii. 244 The forcible and violent push of the Ram had thirled an hole through a corner-tower.

†**d.** To fix with a nail or the like; to transfix.

*c* 1450 *Mirour Saluacioun* 2506 Thai..thirlid thaym to the crosse with one naille cruwelly.

**e.** *fig.* To 'pierce'.

*c* 1315 SHOREHAM iv. 194 Hy beþ men,..Wyþ sennes al þorȝ-þerled. *a* 1340 HAMPOLE *Psalter* xliv. 7 Þi wordis ere sharpe þat thirlis mennys thoghtis. *c* 1470 HENRY *Wallace* x. 394 The pytuous payn so sor thyrllyt his thocht. *c* 1560 A. SCOTT *Poems* (S. T. S.) xviii. 34 Throw langour of my sueit So thirlit is my spreit. 1742 R. FORBES *Ajax* xxix, Whare now thy groans in dowy dens The yerd-fast stanes do thirle.

†**2.** *transf.* To pass right through, penetrate, traverse (anything). *Obs.*

*c* 1175 *Lamb. Hom.* 85 Þet corn þet þurleð þe wind, þet smal chef þet flið forð mid þe winde. *a* 1350 *Peter & Paul* 492 in Horstm. *Altengl. Leg.* (1881) 50 Goddes sun now hardily es he; He thyrles heuyn. 1496 *Dives & Paup.* (W. de W.) I. xv. 47/2 The prayer of hym that loweth hym in his prayer thyrleth the clowdes. 1541 R. COPLAND *Guydon's Quest. Chirurg.* F ij b, The Meri otherwyse called Ysophagus..commeth out of the throte and thyrleth the mydryfe vnto yͤ bely or stomacke. *c* 1560 A. SCOTT *Poems* (S. T. S.) xiv. 1 Rycht as þe glass bene thirlit thruͭ wͭ bemis Off Phebus..visage bricht.

†**3.** To make a hole in (the earth); to excavate.

*a* 1000 *Voc.* in Wr.-Wülcker 201/32 *Cauantur, euacuantur*, þyrliaþ. 1577 STANYHURST *Descr. Irel.* in *Holinshed* (1808) VI. 9 The toad..began to thirle and as it were to dig the earth, where finding an hole, it slunke awaie.

**4.** *spec. Coal Mining.* To cut through (a wall of coal, etc.). Also *absol.* or *intr.*

1686, 1797 [cf. THIRLING *vbl. sb.*[1] 2]. 1839 URE *Dict. Arts* 987 The stenting walls 6 or 8 yards thick,..are holed or thirled at such a distance as may be most suitable for the state of the air. 1871 [see THIRL *sb.*[1] 4]. 1881 MISS JACKSON *Shropsh. Word-bk.* s.v., We'n thirled out o' our Top-end into Smith's Level to-day. 1883 GRESLEY *Coal Mining Gloss.*, *Thirl*,..to cut away the last web of coals, etc., separating two headings or other workings.

†**5.** *intr.* or *absol.* To pierce, penetrate (as a sharp instrument). Also *fig. Obs.*

*c* 1374 CHAUCER *Anel. & Arc.* 214 So thirlleþe with þe poynt of Remembraunce þe swerde of sorowe. 1398 TREVISA *Barth. De P. R.* VIII. xxviii. (Bodl. MS.), Light is a bodilich substaunce..moste meuable and passinglich þorling. *Ibid.* IX. xix, Þis moneþ [November] for his coldenes þorleþ inward and greueþ bodies wele sore. 1513 DOUGLAS *Æneis* x. viii. 114 Quhill throu the cost thyrlit the deidly pryk. *Ibid.* XI. xvii. 26 A wofull wyfly cry Went to the starnys and thyrlyt throw the sky. *a* 1600 MONTGOMERIE *Misc. Poems* xv. 26 Ten thousand dairts..Thirlis throu my hevy hart.

†**6.** *intr.* To pass through or penetrate (*into* or *to* a place or thing). *Obs.*

*a* 1300 *Cursor M.* 21098 (Cott.) Thomas..soght þat estrin thede, And thirlid intil haiþen-hede. 1398 TREVISA *Barth. De P. R.* IV. ii. (Tollem. MS.), Þat oon abideþ wiþ blood, and þurleþ þerwith in to þe membris. *Ibid.* v. v. (Bodl. MS.), For þe spirite of siȝt may not þurle and come þereto, for þe lette þat is bitwene. 1565 GOLDING *Ovid's Met.* III. (1567) 31 The piercing dart..Whereas the ioynts doe knit the backe it thirled through the skin.

**7.** = THRILL *v.*[1] in various constructions. *dial.*

1725 RAMSAY *Gentle Sheph.* I. ii, His words they thirle like music thro' my heart. 1785 BURNS *Epist. to J. Lapraik* iii, It thirl'd the heart-strings thro' the breast, A' to the life. 1819 R. ANDERSON *Cumbld. Ball.* 60 A single luik will thirl ye thro; A single word ensnare ye! 1868 J. SALMON *Gowodean* I. iv. 27 Yon roof-tree, which had sae often dirled As Willie's gladsome voice around it thirled.

Hence **Thirled** *ppl. a.*[1], pierced, perforated.

*c* 1200 *Trin. Coll Hom.* 199 Neddre..cumeð to ane

þurlede ston, and criepeð nedlinge þureh nerewe hole, and bileueð hire hude baften hire. 1398 TREVISA *Barth. De P.R.* XVII. cxcvi. (1495) X iv b/1 Not thyrllyd nother hoolyd. *c* 1440 *Pallad. on Husb.* IV. 821 Their nasis thorlid wide and patent be. *c* 1560 A. SCOTT *Poems* (S.T.S.) xviii. 26 My thirlit hairt dois bleid. 1610 HOLLAND *Camden's Brit.* I. 387 And now the pipes of thyrled box On euery side resound.

**Thirl** (þɜːl), *v.*[2] Chiefly *Sc.* Also 6 **thirll**, 6–7 **thirle.** [A metathetic variant of THRILL *v.*[2]]

†**1.** *trans.* To reduce to or hold in bondage or servitude; to enslave (a person, country, etc.).

1535 STEWART *Cron. Scot.* (Rolls) I. 538 This land..wes thirlit and ouirthrawin Be this tirrane that now is laitlie deid. 1536 BELLENDEN *Cron. Scot.* (1821) I. 109 That daye, behuffit thay othir to recover thair liberte, or ellis be thirlit to perpetual servitude. 1567 *Gude & Godlie B.* (S. T. S.) 35 Father gif me my part of geir,..I will na mair be thirlit heir.

†**b.** To subject or bind *to* some condition. *Obs.*

1541 BELLENDEN *Descr. Albion* i. in *Cron. Scot.* B j b, All thyngis (quhilkis ar comprehendit within the speir of the mone) ar sa thirlit to deith & alteration, yᵗ [etc.]. 1586 *Reg. Privy Council Scot.* IV. 102 To..thirll him to the pament of certane ministeris stipendis to be modifeit be thame.

**2.** *Sc. Law.* To bind or astrict (lands or tenants) to a servitude, esp. *to* a particular mill (usually that of the landlord or superior) for the grinding of their corn: see THIRLAGE 2.

[1480: see THRILL *v.*[2] 2.] 1574 *Reg. Privy Council Scot.* II. 384 Quhilk haill lordschip is thirlit to the mylne of Mabroule. 1609 SKENE *Reg. Maj.* I. 113 No..Fermour may thirle his Lord of his frie tenement, althought he within his time haue done thirle seruice [*seruicium*]..not aught be him...For the law sayes, that the deedes of the Fermour may not thirle, nor make prejudice to his Lords right. 1773 ERSKINE *Inst. Law Scot.* II. ix. § 21 Thirlage..may be constituted..by the proprietor thirling his tenants to his own mill. 1805 G. BARRY *Orkney Isl.* (1808) 356 Mills, to which almost all the lands are thirled or astricted.

*fig.* 1834 *Tait's Mag.* I. 428/2 Earnest-money given by the Church, in sign that he has thirled himself to her mill.

**b.** with the corn as object.

1881 J. RUSSELL *Haigs of Bemersyde* v. 115 On the other part, Robert Haig [in contract of 1592]..'thirles' the whole of the corns of the lands of Bemersyde to the mill of Dryburgh,..the said corns to be thirled for all time coming.

†**3.** To mortgage (land, etc.). *Obs.*

1582 *Reg. Privy Council Scot.* III. 521 Thay..have spendit and warit thair commoun gude and rentis that the samin ar yit thirlit and not fre. 1582–3 *Ibid.* 554 His saidis landes ..wilbe altogither thirlit and engadgit. 1587 *Ibid.* IV. 170 Thay have thirllit ane uthir parte of thair commoun gude.

**4.** To bind or oblige (a person) to give his work, service, or custom to one particular party.

1871 A. S. HARVEY in *Gd. Words* 614 Till this account is cleared off, the hapless knitter is hopelessly bound or 'thirled' to the merchant. 1890 H. HALIBURTON *In Scot. Fields* 125 The inhabitants were not, of course, 'thirled' to any particular tailor, as they used to be to a district mill.

**b.** *fig.* To bind, confine, or restrict in service or action *to* (some party or thing); to tie *to*.

1864 W. ARNOT *Parab. our Lord* iv. (1874) 119 The serpent, as a metaphor, was in practice as completely thirled to the indication of evil, as leaven had been. 1888 BRYCE *Amer. Commw.* IV. lxxix. (1889) II. 266 Great is their power, because they are deemed to be less 'thirled' to a party or leader, because they speak from a moral standpoint. 1902 *Union Mag.* June 246/2 We don't 'thirl' ourselves enough to our duties. 1903 W. DICKIE *Chr. Ethics Soc. Life* 18 God does not encourage us to be thirled to this world and its material things.

Hence **Thirled** (þɜːld) *ppl. a.*[2], bound in servitude, service, or duty.

1567 *Gude & Godlie B.* (S. T. S.) 59 Till Christ..I gif my thirlit hart in gouernance. *a* 1722 FOUNTAINHALL *Decisions* (1759) I. 276 The defender ought not to have built a mill upon the thirled lands. 1898 CROCKETT *Standard Bearer* iv. 36 As a thirled labourer serves for his meat.

†**Thirl,** *v.*[3] *Obs.* [Chiefly of 16th c.: origin obscure. Sense 1 might possibly arise out of THIRL *v.*[1], and give origin to the intr. sense 2. But sense 3 appears to have some connexion with *whirl*: cf. note in etym. of THIRLEPOLL.]

**1.** *trans.* To hurl (a missile, etc.), esp. with spinning or revolving motion. Hence **Thirled** *ppl. a.*[3]

1567 TURBERV. *Epitaphs*, etc. C ij b, First shall you see the shiuering shafts and vewe the thirled darts. 1587 *Mirr. Mag.* (1610) 477 These..who deem'd themselues in skies to dwell, She [Fortune] thirleth downe to dread the gulfes of gastly hell. 1603 FLORIO *Montaigne* I. iv. (1632) 9 On whom a Moore hath thirl'd his slinged speare. *Ibid.* xlviii. 157 With monstrous buzzing came a fire-dart thirled, As if a thunder-bolt had there beene whirled.

**2.** *intr.* To pass or fly with darting or spinning motion.

1565 GOLDING *Ovid's Met.* VIII. 98 b, He tooke the Chaplet from hir head, and vp to Heauen it threw, The Chaplet thirled through the Aire [l. 179 *tenues volat illa per auras*] and as it gliding flew [etc.]. 1567–*a* 1593 [see THIRLING *ppl. a.*[2]].

**3.** *trans.* To whirl, twirl, roll or wind round.

1582 STANYHURST *Æneis* II. (Arb.) 59 [The adder] hym self now youthfulye bleacheth, His tayle smoog thirling, slyke breast to Titan vpheauing [*Lubrica convolvit sublato pectore terga*]. 1594 NASHE *Unfort. Trav.* 16 Like a countrie huswiues banskin, which she thirles her spindle on.

†**Thirl,** *v.*[4] *Sc. Obs.* [Dialectal form of FURL *v.*: see TH initial (6).] *trans.* = FURL *v.* 1.

1549 *Compl. Scot.* vi. 41 Tak in 3our top salis, and thirl them. 1632 LITHGOW *Trav.* VII. 328 [We] thirle our Sailes, if Pirats but appeare.

†**Thi·rlable,** *a. Obs. rare*⁻⁰. [f. THIRL *v.*[1] + -ABLE.] That may be thirled or pierced; penetrable.

1483 *Cath. Angl.* 383/2 Thirleabylle, *penetrabilis.*

**Thirlage** (þɜːlėdʒ). *Sc.* [A metathetic variant of THRILLAGE. Cf. THIRL *v.*[2]]

†**1.** Thraldom, bondage, servitude; also, thirlservice. *Obs.*

1513 DOUGLAS *Æneis* XI. iv. 61 This mysfortoun is myne of ald thirlage. 1536 BELLENDEN *Cron. Scot.* (1821) I. 170 The Romanis contending to saif thaim fra thirlage of barbar pepill. 1549 *Compl. Scot.* xi. 93 3e sal lyf in mair thirlage nor brutal bestis. 1560 ROLLAND *Crt. Venus* Prol. 171 To hald thair Realme and land out of thirlage. 1578 *Gude & Godlie B.* (S.T.S.) App. 236, I haue the fred from all thirlage. 1609 SKENE *Reg. Maj.* I. 113 Gif any frie-halder..does to that ilk Ladie any service..or for her lifdayes does any thirlage.

†**b.** A lien on land or property; mortgage. *Obs.*

1578 *Sc. Acts Jas. VI* (1814) III. 100/2 The said vmquhile erll of Mar..spendit and debursit.., besydis the thirlage of his awin Leving, and the rentis of his proper dependance for the advancement of our souerane Lordis seruice.

**2.** *Sc. Law.* A condition of servitude or state of obligation, in which the tenants of certain lands, or dwellers in certain districts, are bound to restrict their custom to a particular mill, forge, or the like. In later times, spec. the obligation to grind their corn at a particular mill (orig. that of the lord or his assignee), and pay the recognized consideration (multure), or at least to pay the dues in lieu thereof.

In early times there were other forms of thirlage, e. g. the obligation on tenants to get all their ironwork done at a particular forge or smithy: see THIRL *sb.*[2] 1, quot. 1564.

1681 STAIR *Inst. Law Scot.* xvii. § 15. 348 The chief and most frequent Servitude in Scotland is Thirlage, or a restriction of Lands to Milns, wherein the Miln is Dominant, and the Lands astricted are servient. 1773 ERSKINE *Inst. Law Scot.* II. ix. § 18 Thirlage is that servitude by which lands are astricted or thirled to a particular mill, to which the possessors must carry the grain of the growth of the astricted lands to be grinded. 1799 J. ROBERTSON *Agric. Perth* 396 Thirlage is a grievous bondage; and its pernicious influence on the improvement of the country is severely felt, in every place where it prevails. 1812 SIR J. SINCLAIR *Syst. Husb. Scot.* I. 5 A recent law, by which the servitude of thirlage, or bondage to any particular mill, may be legally commuted. 1820 SCOTT *Monast.* xiii, Those of the *Sucken*, or enthralled ground, were liable in penalties, if, deviating from this thirlage,..they carried their grain to another mill.

**b.** The multure exacted under this system.

1799 J. ROBERTSON *Agric. Perth* 396 At every mill, the present amount of the thirlage is by far more than an adequate value for the labour, to which it is supposed to be the price. 1898 CROCKETT *Red Axe* (ed. 4) 235 The smile of a shrewd miller casting up his thirlage upon the mill door when he sees the fields of his parish ripe to the harvest.

†**Thi·rldom.** *Sc. Obs.* [A metathetic variant of THRILDOM: cf. THIRL *v.*[2], THIRLAGE.] Thraldom, bondage, servitude.

1489 *Barbour's Bruce* I. 236 (MS. E.) The angyr, na the wrechyt dome, That is cowplyt to foule thyrldome [*Ibid.* 265 threldome; 269 thryldome]. 1552 ABP. HAMILTON *Catech.* (1884) 23 Thair..miserable thirldome in Babylone [*Ibid.* 38 thrildome]. 1567 *Gude & Godlie B.* (S. T. S.) 114 On the sauch treis our harpis we hang, Quhen thay requyrit vs ane sang, That held vs in sic thirldome. 1609 SKENE *Reg. Maj.* I. 24 Gif he be made ane professed Monke, he sall be made frie from bondage and thirldome.

**Thirled,** *ppl. a.*[1], [2], [3]: see THIRL *v.*[1], etc.

†**Thirlepoll, -pole, -poole.** *Obs.* Forms: *a.* 5 **thorle-, thurlepolle,** 6 **thurle-, thyrlepole, thirlepolle, -poole.** *β.* 6 **thir-, thorpole.** *γ.* 7 **thorn(e)pole, thornpool.** See also WHIRLPOOL. [perh. f. THIRL *sb.*[1] + POLL *sb.*[1], from the blowholes or nostrils in the head: cf. quot. 1603.

If this was the etymology the name would be applicable to the Cetacea generally, although from the quots. it was, at least often, specifically applied. But the etymology is itself rendered doubtful by the synonyms WHIRLPOOL (1552: see quot. 1538) and HURLPOOL (1556), which show that in the 16th c. the first element was sometimes taken as THIRL *v.*[3] to hurl, whirl, and the name thus app. identified with WHIRLPOOL, a vortex, from the commotion caused by its spouting or blowing. See however THURLHEAD.]

A whale, or some species or kind of whale.

*c* 1460 J. RUSSELL *Bk. Nurture* 837 Salt Thurlepolle, salt whale, is good with egre wyne. 1513 *Bk. Keruynge* in *Babees Bk.* (1868) 281 Samon, congre, sturgyon, turbot, thorpole, thornebacke, hounde-fysshe, & halybut. 1533 ELYOT *Cast. Helthe* (1541) 67 b, Greatte fysshes of the sea, as thurlepole, porpyse, and sturgeon. 1538 — *Dict.*, *Balæna*, a greatte fishe, whiche I suppose to be a thurlepoll [*edd.* 1545, 1548 thirlepole; 1552 whirlepoole]. 1550 BALE *Eng. Votaries* II. 105 By the sea coast a she fish was founde of a wonderfull greatnesse, called a thirlepole. 1570 LEVINS *Manip.* 160/41 A Thirlepoole, *balena.* A Hurlepoole, *idem.* 1577–87 HOLINSHED *Chron.* (1807) II. 390 There were eleauen whales or thirlepooles cast on land. 1591 HARINGTON *Orl. Fur.* VI. xxxvi, The Dolphin strong, the Tunny good of tast..With Porpose, Seales, and Thornpooles. 1603 OWEN *Pembrokeshire* (1892) 127 The thornepole is of like forme.. to the Porpisse..having a great round hole in the pole of his head, thoroughe the wᶜʰ he vseth to spoute out water.

†**Thi·rler.** *Sc. Obs.* [f. THIRL *v.*[2] + -ER[1].] A person under thirlage.

1656 *Burgh Rec. Culross* 18 Aug., They war his thirleris this hundrethe and halfe yeir.

**Thirling** (þɜːliŋ), *vbl. sb.*[1] Forms: see THIRL *v.*[1] [f. THIRL *v.*[1] + -ING[1].]

**1.** The action of THIRL *v.*[1]; piercing, boring.

*a* 1225 *Ancr. R.* 166 Þet, 3if 3e weren iðe worldes þrunge, mid a lutel hurlunge [*MS. T.* hurtlinge; *MS. C.* þurlunge] 3e muhten al uor leosen. 1443 *Durham Acc. Rolls* (Surtees) 713 Cum thirlyng unius shafte, ut patet per bill. 10 *li.*

**2.** *Coal Mining.* See quots. and cf. THIRL[1] 4.

1686 PLOT *Staffordsh.* 148 Between the wallings there were ribbs left, and passages through them called thurlings. 1797 *Encycl. Brit.* (ed. 3) V. 101/1 The workings called rooms, turned off at right angles from the others,..the workings called *throughers* or *thirlings*, 9 feet wide, wrought through at right angles from one room to another. 1839 URE *Dict. Arts* 976 Let fig. 840 be a small portion of the pillars, rooms, and thirlings formed in a coal-field.

**Thirling** (þɜːliŋ), *vbl. sb.*[2] [f. THIRL *v.*[2] + -ING[1].] A bringing into subjection or bondage.

1535 STEWART *Cron. Scot.* (Rolls) II. 444 Rycht hevelie he buir into his hart The grit ouirthraw and thirling of his ring [= realm]. 1871 A. S. HARVEY in *Gd. Words* 615 As in the hosiery trade, so in the fishery, the 'thirling' begins with the boy, and is never subsequently thrown off.

**b.** *Thirling mill*, a mill to which certain lands, etc. are astricted in thirlage.

1773 FERGUSSON *Farmer's Ingle* xi, How big a birn maun lie on bassie's back, For meal and multure to the thirling mill. 1824 MACTAGGART *Gallovid. Encycl.* s. v. *Thirlage*, All [mills] erected by such compactions are thirling mills.

**Thirling** (þɜːliŋ), *ppl. a.*[1] [f. THIRL *v.*[1] + -ING[2].] That thirls; piercing.

*c* 1380 WYCLIF *Sel. Wks.* III. 27 Þoru li3t of þin arrowis, þat is, of þi þurlinge wordis. 1398 [see THIRL *v.*[1] 5]. *a* 1547 SURREY *Æneid* IV. 91 [The hind which] the Shepheard smiteth at unwares And leaves unwist in her the thirling head. 1566 DRANT *Horace, Sat.* iii. F vij, What thirlinge thrawes doth twitche thy harte? *a* 1618 DAVIES *Eglogues* Poems (1772) 116 To let in thirling notes of noted laies. 1801 W. BEATTIE *Parings* (1873) 28 Really this night's thirlin'; I never maist fan sic a frost.

†**Thi·rling,** *ppl. a.*[2] *Obs.* [f. THIRL *v.*[3] 2 + -ING[2].] Flying like something hurled; darting; whirling.

1567 TURBERV. *Ovid's Epist.* 22 Where thou with thy nymble arme a thyrling launce doth cast. 1579 *Remedy agst. Love* B iij b, To hunt, to hawke, to throwe the thyrling darte. *a* 1593 MARLOWE *Hero & Leander* I. 108 Nor that night-wandering, pale, and watery star (When yawning dragons draw her [Diana's] thirling car From Latmus' mount up to the gloomy sky).

†**Thirl-mu·lture.** *Sc. Law. Obs.* Also 5 **thrill-, thryl-, threll-.** [See THIRL *sb.*[2], THRILL *sb.*[2], and MULTURE.] The insucken multure paid by tenants of astricted lands to the mill having the right of thirlage; also, the right to exact this multure.

*a.* 1423 *Charters, &c. of Edinb.* (1871) 55 With the suckins, thryl multuris, and al freedomes langand thairto. 1471 *Acta Audit.* (1839) 21/1 The actioune .. twiching þe thrill multer of þe landis of Carnfyne & Carnebro. 1488 *Ibid.* 124/2 Þe wrangwis withalding of þe threll multure & sukkin awing to þe said Alexandris myine.

*β.* 1537 *Reg. Mag. Sig. Scot.* 374/1 Astricta multura, vulgariter *thirle multer*. 1617 *Sc. Acts Jas. VI* (1816) IV. 579/2 His Maiestie..dissolvis fra the Croun..the said Burgh of Abirdene with all and sindrie thair landis,..salmond fischeingis..milnes, thirle multeris [etc.]. 1882 J. WALKER *Scot. Poems* 122 Quoth the man o'dust an' thirl-mouter.

**Thirs, thirse,** var. THURSE *Obs.*, goblin.

**Thirse,** obs. form of THYRSE.

**Thirsill,** obs. Sc. form of THISTLE.

**Thirst** (þɜːst), *sb.* Forms: *a.* 1–4 **þurst,** 3–5 **þorst,** 4–5 **thurste,** 4–6 **thurst;** 3 (*Orm.*) **þirrst,** 3–5 **þirst,** 4 **þerst(e,** 5 **þirste,** 5–6 **thyrst(e,** 6 **thirste,** 4– **thirst.** *β.* 3 (*Orm.*) **þrisst,** 3–5 **þrist,** 4 **threist, threste, þrust(e, þrest (þrast),** 4–5 **thrist, thryst,** 4–6 **thriste, thrust, thruste,** 4–7 **thrist,** 5 **þreste,** 5–6 **thryste.** *γ.* 4 **first, ferst, furst, vurste.** [OE. *þurst* = OFris. **thurst*, **thorst* (mod.Fris. *torst*, *toarst*, EFris. *thurst*), OS. *thurst* (Du. *dorst*), OHG. (G.) *durst*:—OTeut. **þurs-tus*; cf. ON. *þorsti* masc. (Sw., Da. *törst*), Goth. *þaurstei* fem.; all formed, with nominal suffix, from a verbal stem **þurs-* (cf. Gothic *þaurseiþ mik* I thirst):—Indo-Eur. **trs*, weak grade of **ters* : **tors* : **trs*. Cf. L. *torrēre* to dry, Skr. *trš* to thirst.

The change from *thurst* to *thirst* was prob. an assimilation of the sb. to the form of the vb. The metathetic *thrist*, *thrust*, was in use from *c* 1200 to 1590.]

**1.** The uneasy or painful sensation caused by want of drink; also, the physical condition resulting from this want.

*a. c* 1000 *Sax. Leechd.* II. 192 Do þis wið ma3an bryne & þurste. *c* 1050 *Byrhtferth's Handboc* in *Anglia* (1885) VIII. 336 Win & beor eall to ecum þurste awend. *c* 1175 *Lamb. Hom.* 79 He hefde þurst and hunger. *c* 1200 *Trin. Coll. Hom.* 75 He ne mai þolen hunger ne þirst ne oðer pine. *c* 1200 ORMIN 14602 Þatt ma33 þe slekkenn wel þin þirrst. *a* 1225 *Ancr. R.* 114 He..mende him ase of þurst. *c* 1330 R. BRUNNE *Chron. Wace* (Rolls) 10176 Þey deyde for hunger & þirst. 1340 *Ayenb.* 139 He soffreþ and honger an þorst. 1377 LANGL. *P. Pl.* B. XX. 19 He dronke at eche diche ar he for thurste deyde. *c* 1380 *Sir Ferumb.* 2810 Feynt & pal for hungre & for þerst. *c* 1440 *Promp. Parv.* 491/2 Thyrste, or thryste, *sitis*. 1489 CAXTON *Faytes of A.* I. xiii. 34 They ouercome theyre enemyes more by thurst than by armes. 1508 FISHER *Penit. Ps.* cii. Wks. (1876) 179 That may suffre & endure grete labours, watchynge, pouerte, thurst, hungre, colde, & hete. 1697 DRYDEN *Virg. Georg.* III. 470 Let thy Goats..be..led to living Streams, to quench their Thirst. 1738 GRAY *Propertius* iii. 89 The long thirst of Tantalus allay. 1858 O. W. HOLMES *Aut. Breakf.-t.* ix. 79 Thirst belongs to humanity, everywhere, in all ages.

β. *c* 1200 Ormin 1615, & pinenn þær þi bodiȝ a Wiþþ chele & þrisst & hunngerr. *c* 1220 *Bestiary* 320 He haueð ðrist. *c* 1300 *Harrow. Hell* 50 (MS. E.) Seþþen haue y fond & wist Hot & cold, hunger & þrest. 13.. *Sir Beues* (A.) 2791 Beues hadde þanne swich þrast. *a* 1340 Hampole *Psalter* cxlii. 7 Slokyn my threst. *c* 1375 *XI Pains of Hell* 156 in *O. E. Misc.* 215 Þai schil haue hongir and þrust wereeuer þai gon. *c* 1400 Maundev. (Roxb.) viii. 30 Þai made murmuracion agaynes him by cause of thrist. *c* 1440 *Jacob's Well* 147 Be þe weye thedyrward, he hadde thrust. 1530 Palsgr. 163 *Soyf*, thrust. 1535 Stewart *Cron. Scot.* (Rolls) II. 219 Vter drank for to cuill his thrist. 1590 Spenser *F. Q.* ii. vi. 17 Him..that..Will die for thrist, and water doth refuse.

γ. 13.. *S. Eng. Leg.* in Herrig's *Archiv* LXXXII. 395/68 For drede of gret hongir & ferst. *c* 1325 *Song of Mercy* 53 in *E. E. P.* (1862) 120 Ne neuer my furst ne woldestou slake. 1387 Trevisa *Higden* (Rolls) VI. 269 He brende for first [*v. r.* vurste].

†**b.** (See quot.) *dial. Obs.*

1741 *Compl. Fam.-Piece* iii. (ed. 3) 504 Swine..are subject to a Distemper which is called the *Thirst*, or *Lungs*, according to some Farmers.

**c.** Short for *thirstland*: see 3.

1906 *Blackw. Mag.* Sept. 394/2 Getting a span of oxen through the long 'thirsts', as the waterless stretches of road are expressively called.

**2.** *fig.* A vehement desire (*of* (arch.), *for*, *after* something, *to do* something).

*c* 1200 Ormin 5688 All hiss hunngerr & hiss þrisst Shall ben þurrh Drihhtin sleckedd. *c* 1374 Chaucer *Boeth.* ii. met. ii, The more ay brenneth in Hem the thurst of hauynge. *c* 1450 *Mirour Saluacioun* 219 Thi thrust to shedde mans blode was neuer wery. *a* 1541 Wyatt *Penit. Ps.* cxxx. 27 To quench of sleep the thrust. 1554 Knox *Faythf. Admon.* D vj, An earnest thirst..of your saluacion. 1607 Shaks. *Cor.* i. i. 25 Not in thirst for Reuenge. 1669 Gale *Crt. Gentiles* i. i. i. 2 Those infinite thirsts after truth. 1751 Johnson *Rambler* No. 83 ⁋ 1 That thirst after curiosities, which often draws contempt and ridicule upon itself. 1812 Cary *Dante, Paradise* iv. 121 Our mind can satisfy her thirst to know. 1831 Scott *Ct. Robt.* xiii, The more lofty-minded..despise the thirst of gold. 1849 Macaulay *Hist. Eng.* v. I. 657 It may be distinctly traced..either to thirst for money or to thirst for blood. 1851 Dixon *W. Penn* xxxi. (1872) 296 In his thirst for knowledge he was in the habit of studying every sect.

**3.** *attrib.* and *Comb.*, as *thirst-fever*, *-longing*, *-quencher*; *thirst-abating*, *-creating*, *-inducing*, *-quenching*, *-scorched*, *-tormented* adjs.; **thirst-country, -land**, a waterless tract of country, spec. in S. Africa; **thirst-serpent** (see quot.).

1708 J. Philips *Cyder* ii. 63 The Root For *Thirst-abating Sweetness prais'd. 1895 J. G. Millais *Breath fr. Veldt* (1899) 170 If you are in a '*Thirst' country, you take, of course, a water-bottle. 1781 Cowper *Conversat.* 262 The riotous abuse Thy *thirst-creating steams at length produce. 1829 T. Hook *Bank to Barnes* 49 These cows had just finished their *thirst-inducing meal. 1895 J. G. Millais *Breath fr. Veldt* (1899) 184 We entered the great forest *Thirstland...In this expanse of some hundred square miles there is but one waterhole. 1908 J. Wells *Stewart of Lovedale* xviii. 182 Without crossing the Karoo and great Thirst-land of Unbelief. *c* 1614 Campion *Wks.* (1909) 179 A heate I finde, Like *thirst-longing, that doth bide Where they say my heart doth moue. 1908 *Daily Chron.* 3 Jan. 3/6 He prefers pure water as a *thirst-quencher. 1895 *Westm. Gaz.* 19 Mar. 8/2 This orange wine is most refreshing and *thirst-quenching. 1861 W. F. Collier *Hist. Eng. Lit.* 443 In view of the *thirst-scorched seamen. 1731 Medley tr. *Kolben's Cape G. Hope* II. 165 The Dipsas or *Thirst-Serpent is so call'd from its bite causing a burning thirst.

**Thirst** (þɔ̄ɹst), *v.* Forms: *α.* 1 ð-, þyrst-, 2–4 þirst-, 3–4 þurst- (*ü*), (4 furst-), 4–6 thurst-, 5–6 thyrst-, 5– thirst. *β.* 4 þryst-, þrist-, þrest-, 4–6 thrust-, 5 thryst-, 5–6 threst-, thrist-. [OE. *þyrstan*, f. *þurst* Thirst *sb.* Cf. OS. *thurstian* (Du. *dorsten*), OHG. *dursten* (G. *dürsten*), ON. *þyrsta* (Sw. *törsta*, Da. *törste*).]

†**1.** *impers.* as in *me thirsteth*, 'it thirsts me', I am thirsty. (In OE. with accus. of person and gen. of thing, or with dat. of person.)

*c* 897 K. Ælfred *Gregory's Past. C.* ii. 30 Ðeah ðæt folc ðyrste ðære lare. *c* 1000 *Ags. Gosp.* John xix. 28 Þa cwæð he, me þyrst. *c* 1000 *Sax. Leechd.* II. 194 Þa men ne þyrst. *c* 1200 Ormin 14603 Ȝiff þatt iss þatt te þirrsteþþ. *c* 1200 *Trin. Coll. Hom.* 199 Hire þurst swiðe. *a* 1300 *Cursor M.* 23085 Me thristed sare, drinc yee me broght. *c* 1386 Chaucer *Monk's T.* 49 So thursted hym, that he Was wel ny lorn. *c* 1440 *York Myst.* xxxvi. 221 A! me thristis sare.

**2.** *intr.* To feel or suffer thirst; to be thirsty. Also *transf.*, e.g. of parched ground or plants. Somewhat *arch.*

*c* 950 *Lindisf. Gosp.* John xix. 28 Cuoeð ic ðyrsto. *c* 975 *Rushw. Gosp.* John iv. 14 Seðe wutudlice drinceð of wætre dæt ic selo him ne ðyrstet in ecnisse. 1340 Hampole *Pr. Consc.* 5771, I thrested, and yhe me na drynk bedde. 1382 Wyclif 1 *Cor.* iv. 11 We hungren, and thirsten, and ben nakid. 1398 Trevisa *Barth. De P. R.* v. xliv. (Bodl. MS.), Euerich beeste with lunges þrusteþ moche. 14.. *Lybeaus Disc.* (1890) 1426 Sir Libeaus þursted sore And seide..To drinke let me go. 1530 Palsgr. 757/1, I Thrust, I want drinke. 1577 B. Googe *Heresbach's Husb.* iii. (1586) 146 You shall gyue them water as oft as they thirst. 1611 Bible *Isa.* lv. 1 Ho, euery one that thirsteth, come ye to the waters. 1649, 1770, 1820 [see Thirsting *ppl. a.*]. 1871 R. Ellis *Catullus* lxviii. 79 Bloodless of high sacrifice, Now thirsts each desolate altar! 1875 [see Thirsty 1].

**3.** *fig.* To have a longing, craving, or strong desire. Const. in OE. with gen., = of; later *after*, *for* († *to*) something, *to do* something.

*c* 893 K. Ælfred *Oros.* ii. iv. § 10 Þu þe þyrstende wære monnes blodes. *c* 1375 *Sc. Leg. Saints* xlii. (*Agatha*) 87 Scho thristyt..for til cume til hewynnis kyng. 1388 Wyclif *Ps.* lxii. 2 [lxiii. 1] Mi soule thirstide to thee; my fleisch thirstide to thee ful many foold. 1419 in Sharpe *Lond. & Kingd.* (1894–5) III. 363 Your poure lieges þat have loong thrusted after knowlech of your prosperite. *a* 1548 Hall *Chron., Hen. VII* 25 b, The Frenche nacion..thrusted for the blood..of the poore Brytones. 1601 R. Johnson *Kingd. & Commw.* (1603) 157 The Turkish Emperor..thirsting to open a way into Moscouie. 1791 Burke *App. Whigs* Wks. VI. 203 It is not necessary to teach men to thirst after power. 1858 G. Macdonald *Phantastes* v. (1878) 75, I entered, thirsting for the shade which it promised.

†**4.** *trans.* To desire vehemently; to long for. *Obs.*

*c* 950 *Lindisf. Gosp.* Matt. v. 6 Eadȝe biðon ða ðe hyncgrað & ðyrstas soðfæstnisse. *c* 1000 *Ags. Gosp.* ibid., Eadiȝe synt þa ðe rihtwisnesse hingriað & þyrstað. *c* 1050 *Liber Scintill.* x. 49. *a* 1340 Hampole *Psalter, Cant.* 506 Erthly kyngis þat threstis mannys blode. 1382 Wyclif *Matt.* v. 6 Blessid be thei that hungren and thirsten riȝtwisnesse, for thei shuln ben fulfillid. 1432–50 tr. *Higden* (Rolls) III. 471 Ye thruste golde..and couette honoure. 1527 Tindale *Obed. Chr. Man* To Rdr. 20 b, Sufficient vnto them that thirst the trueth. 1593 Q. Eliz. *Boeth.* i. iv. 11 Wicked men, that thursted the blud of all the senate. 1718 Prior *Solomon* i. 203 He seeks his keeper's flesh, and thirsts his blood.

Hence †**Thi·rsted** *ppl. a.*, longed for.

*c* 1611 Chapman *Iliad* xxii. 277 His bright and sparkling eyes..sought through all that prise The next way to his thirsted life.

**Thirster** (þɔ̄·ɹstəɹ). [f. Thirst *v.* + -er [1].] One who thirsts; *fig.* one who craves or longs (*for*, *after* something).

1382 Wyclif *Isa.* xxxii. 6 Drinc to the thristere he shal don awei. *a* 1578 Lindesay (Pitscottie) *Chron. Scot.* (S.T.S.) I. 100 Ane fallis wngodlie thrister of innocent bloode. 1624 F. White *Repl. Fisher* 112 The Pope was..an insatiable..thirster after monie. 1779–81 Johnson *L. P., Prior* Wks. III. 139 He was by nature no thirster for blood. 1883 *Cambridge Staircase* ii. 28 The thirster after knowledge.

**Thirstful** (þɔ̄·ɹstfŭl), *a. rare.* [f. Thirst *sb.* + -ful.] Full of thirst; thirsty.

1865 *Reader* No. 151. 568/1 A dry, arid, thirstful land. 1871 G. Meredith *H. Richmond* xxix, My other eager thirstful self I shook off like a thing worn out.

**Thirstily** (þɔ̄·ɹstĭli), *adv.* [f. Thirsty + -ly [2].] In a thirsty manner; with thirst. Also *fig.*

1549 Coverdale, etc. *Erasm. Par.* 1 *Peter* 7 Not to be supped lothesomly, but gredily, yea and thrustily. *a* 1586 Sidney *Arcadia* iii. Wks. 1724 II. 427 Which she..had drunk up thirstily. *c* 1665 Mrs. Hutchinson *Mem. Col. Hutchinson* (1846) 408 A kinsman of his who thirstily aspired after preferment. 1831 Carlyle *Sart. Res.* ii. iii, From such Fountain he draws, diligently, thirstily.

**Thirstiness** (þɔ̄·ɹstinės). [f. Thirsty + -ness.] The quality or condition of being thirsty; thirst.

1583 Golding *Calvin on Deut.* clxvii. 1035 There is no man but he is vexed with diuerse chaunges and sortes of thirstinesse. 1619 R. Harris *Drunkard's Cup* 3 It..causes a dropsie and..thirstinesse. 1649 Blithe *Eng. Improv. Impr.* (1653) 107 That Thirstiness in me after the Common good. 1872 *Daily News* 15 July, Streams of sightseers, whose curiosity is accompanied by a general thirstiness. 1897 *Ibid.* 19 July 3/1 The terrible and undoubted thirstiness of the season.

**Thirsting** (þɔ̄·ɹstiŋ), *vbl. sb.* [f. Thirst *v.* + -ing [1].] The condition denoted by the verb Thirst; thirst; *fig.* longing, craving.

*c* 1500 Kennedy *Passion of Christ* 739 Bitter wyne myxt with gall..þai him gaif to slokin his thristing. 1653 Cromwell *Sp.* 14 July in *Carlyle*, We have had many desires, and thirstings in our spirits, to find out ways and means. 1701 Stanhope *Augustine's Medit.* xxxv. 82 What impatient thirstings ought I to bring! 1861 *Times* 22 Aug., A thirsting for political liberty.

**Thi·rsting,** *ppl. a.* [f. as prec. + -ing [2].] That thirsts, thirsty; *fig.* longing.

1382 Wyclif *Prov.* xxv. 25 Cold watir to the threstende soule. 1552 Huloet, Thyrstynge, or beynge a thyrste, *sitiens*. 1649 Blithe *Eng. Improv. Impr.* (1653) 25 Keep thy Land rather in a thirsting condition. 1770 Wesley *Jrnl.* 26 June, They drank in the words of life, just as the thirsting earth the showers. 1820 Shelley *Cloud* i, I bring fresh showers for the thirsting flowers. 1857–8 Sears *Athan.* ii. iii. 195 His marvellous tale..has fallen into thirsting ears.

Hence **Thi·rstingly** *adv.*, longingly.

1619 W. Sclater *Exp.* 1 *Thess.* (1630) 570 The will..so thirstingly inclined to wickednesse.

**Thirstless** (þɔ̄·ɹstlės), *a.* [f. Thirst *sb.* + -less.] Having no thirst; not thirsty.

1591 Sylvester *Du Bartas* i. vii. 648 Th' officious Kids..sip (self thirst-less) of the River's brink, Which in their mouthes they bring them [their Parents old] home to drink. 1856 Dobell *Lyrics in War Time, Home Wounded*, Among the thirstless dead. 1883 *Half-hours in Many Lands* 4 This great thirstless teetotal abstainer [the camel].

**b.** Not impelled by thirst. *nonce-use.*

1706 Baynard in Sir J. Floyer *Hot & Cold Bath.* ii. 330 Unnecessary and thirstless Epotations.

Hence **Thi·rstlessness.**

1822–34 *Good's Study Med.* (ed. 4) I. 102 Cases of thirstlessness are not by any means frequent.

†**Thi·rstlew,** *a.* [f. Thirst *sb.* + -lewe.] Thirsty.

*c* 1425 *Orolog. Sapient.* i. in *Anglia* X. 327/9 Þe whiche qwenchede not fullye here thriste, but hit..made hem more thristlewe. *c* 1430 Lydg. *Min. Poems* (Percy Soc.) 75 Drye in the see, and wete upon the stronde;..In reveris thurstlew, and moyst upon the londe. 1430–40 — *Bochas* i. xv. (MS. Bodl. 263) lf. 69/2 He was..wonder thrustleuh afftir trauailyng.

**Thirsty** (þɔ̄·ɹsti), *a.* Forms: see Thirst *sb.* [OE. *þurstig*, *þyrstig*, f. *þurst*, Thirst *sb.* + *-ig*, -y. Cf. OS. *thurstig*, OHG. *durstag*.]

**1.** Having the sensation of thirst; feeling desire or craving for drink.

*c* 950 *Lindisf. Gosp.* Matt. xxv. 35 Ic wæs ðyrstiȝ and ȝe saldon me dringe. *c* 1000 *Ags. Ps.* (Th.) lxi[i]. 4 Wide urnon; þurstiȝe muðe. *c* 1200 Ormin 6163 Forr þe birrþ fedenn hunngriȝ mann & þrisstiȝ ȝifenn drinnke. *a* 1300 *Cursor M.* 1020 (Cott.) Suld he neuer thresti [*F.* þristy, *G.* thristi, *Tr.* fursti] be. 1426 Audelay *Poems* 7 The thorste ȝif dryng. *c* 1440 *Alphabet of Tales* 460 Hym thoght in his slepe þat hym was passand thrustie. *a* 1533 Ld. Berners *Huon* xxii. 66, I fele my selfe nother hungry nor thrusty. 1549 *Compl. Scot.* v. 34 Quhen ve ar thirsty, ve seik drynk. 1590 Spenser *F. Q.* i. x. 38 His office was the hungry for to feed, And thristy give to drinke. 1697 Dryden *Virg. Past.* v. 38 The thirsty Cattel..abstain'd From Water. 1703 Maundrell *Journ. Jerus.* 79 The Fountain being..very inviting to the thirsty Passenger. 1875 Jowett *Plato* (ed. 2) III. 319 The thirsty one, in that he thirsts, desires only drink.

**b.** *transf.* Of earth or plants: Greatly wanting moisture; dry, parched, arid.

1388 Wyclif *Isa.* xxxv. 7 That that was drie, is maad in to a poond, and the thirsti..in to wellis of watris. 1471 Ripley *Comp. Alch.* iii. iv. in Ashm. *Theat. Chem. Brit.* (1652) 140 Dry up thyne Erth tyll hyt be thrysty. 1577 B. Googe *Heresbach's Husb.* ii. (1586) 80 b, The salte, bitter, and thirstie ground. *c* 1586 C'tess Pembroke *Ps.* lxxiv. xiv, Thou wondrously didst cause..From thirsty flynt a fountayne flow. 1743 Francis tr. *Hor., Odes* i. xxii. 16 The tawny lion reigns Fierce on his native Afric's thirsty plains. 1878 Bosw. Smith *Carthage* 254 The country was parched and thirsty.

**2.** *fig.* Having or characterized by a vehement desire or craving; eager, greedy.

*c* 888 K. Ælfred *Boeth.* xii, Swa swylc seo ȝitsung þa dreosendan welan..forþam hio hiora simle bið þursteȝu. *c* 1400 tr. *Secreta Secret., Gov. Lordsh.* 56 It semys bettir þat þe eres of þe folk be thristy to þe wordes of þe kyng. 1577 Harrison *England* ii. i. (1877) i. 17 The thirstie desire of the people..to heare the word of God. 1697 Dryden *Virg. Georg.* iii. 727 When the thirsty Fire had drunk Their vital Blood. 1760 Franklin *Lett.* Wks. 1840 VI. 230 She has a mind thirsty after knowledge. 1831 Lamb *Elia, Newspapers 35 Yrs. ago*, Refreshing to the thirsty curiosity of the traveller.

**3.** *transf.* That causes thirst. (Now *colloq.*)

1599 Sandys *Europæ Spec.* (1632) 152 Troubled with the dropsie..caused..or accompanied with a thirstie infirmitie. 1603 Shaks. *Meas. for M.* i. ii. 134 Our Natures doe pursue Like Rats that rauyn downe their proper Bane, A thirsty euill, and when we drinke, we die. 1812 W. Tennant *Anster F.* iv. xlviii, Slices of the thirsty ham. 1897 F. T. Jane *Lordship*, etc. i. 2 A thirsty walk up and down terrible bad roads. *Mod.* Thirsty weather and thirsty work.

**4.** *Comb.*, as *thirsty-cupped*, *thirsty-looking* adjs.; **thirsty frog, thirsty snake**: see quots.

1567 Maplet *Gr. Forest* 70 b, There is.. fiue kindes of Aspis. The first named *Dipsas* in Greeke, in Latine *Situla*, Thristie Snake. 1802 Shaw *Gen. Zool.* III. 115 Thirsty Frog, *Rana Sitibunda*..Native of desert places about the river Ural:..has the habit of a toad. 1875 Lanier *Poems, Symphony* 132 Marsh-plants, thirsty-cupped for rains. *Mod.* A thirsty-looking man standing outside a public-house.

**Thirteen** (þɔ̄·ɹtīn, þɔ̄ɹtī·n: see -teen). Forms: *α.* 1 þreotiene, -tene, -tyne, þreottene, -tyne, 1–4 þrettyne, 2–5 þrit-, 3 þre-, þreat-, 4 thrat-, þrot-, thrittene, þritten, 4–7 thret-, 5 throt-, (thred-), thryttene, thretten, 6 thretene, 7 threteen(e, thretteín. *β.* 5 þirt-, 5–6 thyr-, thurtene, 6 thirtene, -tine, thurteyn, 6–7 thirteene, 8 therteen, 7– thirteen. [OE. *þréotiene*, *-téne* = OS. *thriutein*, *thrutein*, OFris. *threttine* (MLG. *druttein*, Du. *dertien*), OHG. *drîzehan* (G. *dreizehn*), ON. *þrettán* (Da. *tretten*, Sw. *tretton*); f. *þréo*, Three + *tíene*, *téne*, pl. -teen, Ten.] The cardinal number composed of ten and three, represented by the symbols 13 or xiii.

**A.** *adj.* **1.** In concord with a sb. expressed.

*α.* *a* 900 tr. *Bæda's Hist.* i. xiii. [xxiii.] (1890) 54 Þreotteno ȝer & syx monað & tyn daȝas. *Ibid.* iv. xxiv. [xxiii.] 342 Þær seondon betweoh þæm mynstrum twæm þreottyne mila ametene. *c* 1200 Ormin 11071 Ȝe muȝhenn uppo ȝure ȝer þrittene moneþþ findenn. *c* 1205 Lay. 7771 Þreottene monðes wunede Julius in Oðeres. *a* 1225 *Ancr. R.* 234 Seinte Sare, nes heo fulle þreattene ȝer itented of hire vlesche. 1297 R. Glouc. (Rolls) 652 Brut is sone king was þrettene [*v. rr.* þrottene, thryttene] ȝer. 13.. *Guy Warw.* (A.) 7305 + st. 279 For þritten pouer men & ȝete mo. 1610 *Mem. St. Giles's Durham* 39 Everie housholder shall pay to the bakehouse man for everie threteene cakes one cake and no more. 1661 *Reg. Privy Counc. Scotl.* I. 26 Threttein.

*β.* *c* 1430 *R. Gloucester's Chron.* (Rolls) 8666 (MS. ε.) He adde be kyng þirttene ȝer. 1531 in *Sel. Cases Crt. Requests* (1898) 34 To haue for his waiges only thurteyn shillinges and foure pence by the yere. 1538 Elyot, *Tredecim*, thyrtene. 1561 Daus tr. *Bullinger on Apoc.* Pref. (1573) 14 Thirtine yeares past. 1588 *Holy Bull*, etc. (title-p.), Pardon and Indulgence of their Sinnes: and that for..two Spanish Realls, viz. Thirteen Pence. 1659 Baxter *Key Cath.* xxxii. 205 One Kingdom hath thirteen Arch-bishops. 1901 *N. Amer. Rev.* Feb. 162 Fines amounting to thirteen times the amount of the indemnity.

**2.** Absolutely (or sb. implied in context).

*c* 1000 *Menologium* (Gr.) 116 Ymb þreotyne [tida lange]..tyn mihtum eac. 1297 R. Glouc. (Rolls) 10377 In þe ȝer of grace ywis Tuelf hundred & þretene ido was al þis. 1362 Langl. *P. Pl.* A. v. 128, I..putte hem in a pressour..Til ten ȝerdes oþer twelue tolden out þrettene. 1562 in W. H. Turner *Select. Rec. Oxford* (1880) 289 Called before the Mayre and the thurtene. 1725 in Warden *Burgh Laws Dundee*, etc. (1872) 356 Non shall give no more butt therteen for the duson of bread, except that it be to Baxteris or Baxters wifs. 1865 S. Evans *Bro. Fabian's MS., Charm* v, If thirteen sit down to sup And thou first have risen up, Goodman, turn thy money! 1884 *Harper's Mag.* Nov. 889/1, I do not know as to their feelings regarding thirteen at table.

† **3.** As ordinal: = THIRTEENTH. *Obs.*

*c* **1375** *Sc. Leg. Saints* ii. (*Paulus*) 72 [He] prechit þare.. till of nero þe thrattene ȝere. *c* **1430** *Freemasonry* 239 The threttene artycul..Ys [etc.]. **1503** *Rolls of Parlt.* VI. 527/2 The thretene day of Marche. **1551** RECORDE *Pathw. Knowl.* I. Defin., In the thirtene conclusion. **1603** KNOLLES *Hist. Turks* (1638) 30 He..died the thirteen of November, Anno 1142. **1640–1** *Kirkcudbr. War-Comm. Min. Bk.* (1855) 60 The threttene day of October, 1640.

**4.** *Comb.*, forming attrib. phrases, as *thirteen-day, -inch, -stone*; *thirteen-ringed, -square* adjs.; † **thirteen-penny** *sb.* = B. 2.

**1517** TORKINGTON *Pilgr.* (1884) 30 A fayer Tower xiij Sqware. **1798** *Hull Advertiser* 6 Oct. 2/1 The two thirteen-inch mortars. **1828** LANDOR *Imag. Conv.* Wks. 1846 I. 305/2 A half-crown contents me..and, just for the peg-polisher, a thirteen-penny. **1897** MARY KINGSLEY *W. Africa* 263 Getting these twelve to thirteen-stone gentlemen up. **1898** P. MANSON *Trop. Diseases* xxxvii. 589 A thirteen-ringed larva is hatched out from each egg. **1904** *Westm. Gaz.* 8 Feb. 5/2 The thirteen-story Continental Trust building.

† **b.** *Thirteen-pence-halfpenny*, alleged to have been the wage of a hangman. *Thirteen-pence-halfpenny piece*, the name of the Scottish merk (= 13*s.* 4*d.* Scots money) current during the 17th century. *Obs.*

[*c* **1470** *Miners' Laws* in C. Walters *Bygone Somerset* (1897) 41 If any..doth pick or steal any lead or Oare to the value of thirteen pence halfpenny the lord or his Officers may Arrest all his Lead-works.] **1604** DEKKER *2nd Pt. Honest Wh.* Wks. 1873 II. 171 Why should I eate hempe-seed at the Hangmans thirteene-pence halfe-penny Ordinary? **1608** DAY *Hum. out of Br.* IV. F iij, He could not hang me for't; tis not worth thirteen pence halfe penny. **1722** DE FOE *Col. Jack* (1840) 46 A paper of old thirteen-pence-halfpenny pieces, half and quarter pieces, with nine-pences, and four-pence-halfpennies, all old crooked money, Scotch and Irish coin. **1796** PEGGE *Anonym.* (1809) 460 Thirteen-pence halfpenny is Hangman's wages, because there was a piece of money of this sort, as likewise six-pence three-farthings, the half of it, both of them Scotch pieces, brought to us by James the First. I have seen them both.

**B.** *sb.* (With plural *thirteens*.)

**1.** The abstract number; also, a symbol or the figures representing this.

That the number is unlucky is a widespread superstition (cf. quots. 1865, 1884 in A. 2); hence such applications as *thirteen club*: see quots. 1883, 1905.

*a* **1400** in Halliwell *Rara Mathem.* (1841) 30 Nombrys ..componyd of a digyt and of an articule as fourtene fyftene thirttene and suche other. **1599** MINSHEU *Span. Dict.* s. v. *Tréze*, *Estárse en sus Tréze*, to be in his thirteenes, to be obstinate, to stand still in his purpose. **1883** *St. James's Gaz.* 26 Oct., The social crusade against the venerable superstition respecting the number 13...Last year, a Thirteen Club was established [in America]. **1905** *Daily News* 6 Feb. 9 Where is the Thirteen Club and its campaign to shame the superstitious public out of their dread of the number 13?

**b.** A thing distinguished by the number thirteen, as an article of a certain size so called.

**1799** *Hull Advertiser* 20 Apr. 2/3 Wine bottles, thirteens, fourteens, and fifteens, at 2s. 6d. per dozen. *Mod.* This gentleman takes a thirteen in boots.

† **2.** The name formerly current in Ireland for a silver shilling, as being worth thirteen pence of Irish copper currency. *Obs.*

*c* **1720** SWIFT *Dean's Answ.* 8 Restore..My twelve thirteens and sixpence ha'penny. **1762** FOOTE *Orators* II. (1780) 57 I'll wager you three thirteens to a rap, that it is no such matter at all, at all. **1810** *Naval Chron.* XXIV. 151 Oft was his pocket without a thirteen. **1830** MARRYAT *King's Own* xxi, 'He says that it's two thirteens that must be paid for it'... 'Have you two shillings?'

**Thirteener** (þɔːɪtīˑnəɪ). [f. prec. sb. + -ER [1].]

**1.** A silver shilling; = THIRTEEN B. 2. *Thirteener and a baubee*: see prec. A. 4 b.

**1762** *Naval Chron.* XXIV. 369 Cheat the sheriff out of his thirteener and a baubee! **1811** *Henry & Isabella* I. 289, I have scraped together a few thirteeners honestly, for my old age. **1836** T. HOOK *G. Gurney* ii, Says the padré, 'tip us the thirteeners, and you are as clean as a whistle for the next twelve months'.

**2. a.** *Cricket.* A hit for thirteen runs. **b.** See quot. 1891.

**1893** *Black & White* 29 July 139/2 Of cricket there are anecdotes galore; how a 'thirteener' was once run out on the Marlborough ground. **1900** *Westm. Gaz.* 5 July 3/2 But F. P. Miller once hit a 'thirteener' at single wicket, which is considered a record. **1891** *Cent. Dict.*, *Thirteener*, ..the thirteenth one of any number of things; specifically, in whist, the last card of a suit left in the hands of a player after the other twelve have been played.

**Thirteenth** (þɔːɪtīˑnþ, þɔˑɪtīnþ: see -TEEN), *a.*, *sb.* (*adv.*). Forms: see below. [Of this there have been many forms, the earlier reflecting the various types of TENTH, the later the two types of THIRTEEN. In OE. (Anglian **þrīteogeða, -e, -tegða*) WSax. *þrie-, þreótéoða*, etc., whence early southern ME. *þrettethe*. Northern ME. had *þrett-, þrittend(e* from ON. *þrettánde*. From these arose *a* 1400 *þrett-, þrittenþ(e*, and by metathesis (as in *thirteen*), *ther-, thyr-, thirtenth*, and finally in 16th c. *thirteenth*, as if formed at once from *thirteen* + -TH [2]. Cf. in the cognate langs. OFris. *threttinde* (Du. *dertiende*), OHG. *drittozehanto* (Ger. *dreizehnte*), ON. *þrettánde* (Sw. *trettonde*, Da. *trettende*).]

**A.** *adj.* in concord with sb. expressed or implied. **1.** The ordinal numeral belonging to the cardinal thirteen: the last of thirteen.

**α.** 1 **þreoteȝþa, þrie-, þreo-, þryteoða,** 1–3 **þreott-, þrytteoða,** 3 **þrett-, þritteþe.**

*a* **900** *O. E. Martyrol.* 13 Mar. 38 On þone þreoteȝðan dæȝ þæs monðes. *c* **1000** *Ags. Gosp.* Matt. xi. 20 *margin*, On þære þrytteoðan wucan ofer pentecosten. *c* **1000** ÆLFRIC *Hom.* II. 520 Paulus is se ðreotteoða ðyses heapes. *c* **1275** *Shires & Hundreds* in *O. E. Misc.* 146 Þe þreotteoþe on lyncholne. **1297** R. GLOUC. (Rolls) 5933 In þe þritteþe [*MS. α.* þretteþe] ȝer.

**β.** 3 (*Orm.*) **þrittennde,** 4 **thritt-, thretend(e, thritteind, thritend,** 4–5 **þrettend(e.**

*c* **1200** ORMIN 11062 Itt iss þe þrittennde daȝȝ. *a* **1300** *Cursor M.* 11373 (Cott.) Fra he was born þe dai thritteind. *Ibid.* 29330 (Cott. Galba) Þe thritend case. **1447** BOKENHAM *Seyntys* (Roxb.) 34 Of Octobyr the thrеttend day.

**γ.** 4 **þrett-, þrittenþe, þritteneþ,** 4–5 **threttenethe;** 6 **threttent.**

*c* **1380** WYCLIF *Serm.* Sel. Wks. II. 268 Þe þrittenþe condicioun. *c* **1420** *Chron. Vilod.* 2395 Þe threttenethe ȝere. *a* **1425** *Cursor M.* 22671 (Trin.) Þe þretteneþe day shal be snelle. **1581** N. BURNE *Disput.* in *Cath. Tractates* (S. T. S.) 142 Gregorius the threttent quha is nou bischop of Rome.

**δ.** 5 **þirttenth (þirdtenth), thertenth (-tenst),** 6 **thyrd-, thyr-, thirtenth,** 6– **thirteenth.**

**1483** CAXTON *Gold. Leg.* 78 b/2 The thertenst day. **1530** PALSGR. 372/1 *Treiziesme*, thyrteenth. **1538** ELYOT, *Terdenus, na, num*, the thyrdtenth. **1552** HULOET, Thyrtenth. **1579** FULKE *Heskins' Parl.* 180 The thirteenth Chapter. **1624** BEDELL *Lett.* i. 42 This thirteenth Article, of the thirteenth Apostle...it seemes you haue learned. **1711** *Lond. Gaz.* No. 4903/2 On the Thirteenth the Artillery..was discharg'd. **1759** *Walton's Angler* ii. (ed. 7) 38 The wise Statutes made in the 13th of Edward the First. **1878** VILLARI *Machiavelli* (1898) II. ii. 73 The literature of the thirteenth century.

**2.** *Thirteenth part*: one of thirteen equal parts into which anything may be divided.

**1790** BURKE *Fr. Rev.* 178 About a thirteenth part of their clear income. **1857** MILLER *Elem. Chem.* (1862) III. 157 Exactly twelve thirteenth parts of an equal measure of distilled water.

**B.** *sb.* **1.** A thirteenth part.

**1611** COTGR., *Treziesme*, a thirteenth. *Mod.* A lunar month is very nearly a thirteenth of a year.

**b.** *Eng. Hist.* A thirteenth part of the value of movables, or of the rent of the year, formerly granted or levied as a tax.

[**1206–7** *Patent Roll* 8 *John* m. 3 dorso in *Lanc. & Chesh. Rec. Soc.* (1893) XXVII. 35 M. CC. vij, Hoc anno assisa de terciodecimo facta est ad opus regis universaliter a clericis et laicis et per vim laicalem.] **1893** J. A. C. VINCENT *ibid.* 36 The method of collecting this thirteenth is laid down in the king's letters patent. Every layman to give 12-pence out of every mark's (13*s.* 4*d.*) worth of annual rent, or out of such moveable chattels of like value as he had on the Octaves of the Purification (9 February), being the date of the council. **1874** STUBBS *Const. Hist.* I. xiii. 586 The assessment of the thirteenth in A. D. 1207 was..not made by juries, but by the oath of the individual payer taken before the justices; the contribution of the clergy being a matter of special arrangement made by the archdeacons.

**2.** *Music.* A note thirteen diatonic degrees above or below a given note (both notes being counted); the interval between, or consonance of, two notes thirteen diatonic degrees apart; a chord containing this interval.

**1597** MORLEY *Introd. Mus.* 71 Which distances do make vnperfect consonants?..A third, a sixt, and their eightes: a tenth, a thirteenth [etc.]. **1609** DOULAND *Ornith. Microl.* 79 An eight doth agree in sound with an vnison,..and a thirteenth with a sixt. **1880** STAINER *Composition* § 14 The third degree of the scale..also forms part of the well-known cadential $\frac{6}{4}$ chord, and dominant thirteenth.

**C.** *adv.* Thirteenthly.

**1526** *Pilgr. Perf.* (W. de W. 1531) 292 b, Thyrtenth, they be mortifyed from all property of wyll.

Hence **Thirteeˑnthly** *adv.*, in the thirteenth place; also as *sb.* (*nonce use*) the thirteenth head or section of a discourse, etc.

*a* **1642** SIR W. MONSON *Naval Tracts* III. (1704) 322/1 Thirteenthly, They ought to take a yearly account. **1887** J. SERVICE *Life & Recoll. Duguid* iii. 22 Mr. McClumpha ..was toilin' on to his thirteenthly. **1893** STEVENSON *Catriona* xvi, Thirteenthly, my brethren,..the law itself must be regarded as a means of grace.

**Thirtieth** (þɔˑɪti,eþ), *a.* (*sb.*) Forms: **α.** 1 **ðrítiȝoða, þrittiȝoþa, þríteȝoða, þritteoȝoða, þreotteoȝaþa, þríteȝoð,** 2–3 **þrittuþe,** 3–4 **þrittiþe,** (3 **-teþe**), 4 **þrittyþe, thretyd,** (*Ayenb.*) **prittaȝte,** 4–5 **thrittyde, threttithe, -yth,** 5 **thrydtythe, thryddyþ.** **β.** (5 **thyrttyest**), 6 **thyrteth, -ieth, thirteth, -ith, therttieth,** 6– **thirtieth.** [OE. *þrítigoða, -e*, f. *þrítig* + *-oða, -oðe* (see -TH [2]), becoming in ME. *þrittyþe, threttyth*, in 16th c., by assimilation to the current form of the cardinal, *thirtith, therttieth, thirtieth*. Cf. ON. *þrítugande, -tugunde, -tegunde*, later *þrítugti*. The WGer. langs. have a form in *-ësta, -esta*, OFris. *thrítegesta*, OHG. *drîzugôsto*, Ger. *dreissigste*; so mod. Icel. *þrítugasti*: cf. Caxton's *thyrttyest*.]

**A.** *adj.* The ordinal numeral belonging to the cardinal thirty; the last of thirty. *The thirtieth man*, the last man, or any one man, of thirty. *Thirtieth part*, one of the thirty equal parts into which anything may be divided.

*a* **900** tr. *Bæda's Hist.* v. xxii. [xxiii.] (1890) 482 Þy ðritiȝoðan [ȝere mines lifes]. *a* **900** *Martyrol.* 88 On þone an ond þriteȝðan dæȝ. *c* **1000** ÆLFRIC *Gram.* xlix. (Z.) 283 *Tricesimus*, se þrittiȝoða [ðritoȝoða, þritteoȝoða]. *c* **1200** *Trin. Coll. Hom.* 47 On þe two and þrittuðe dai. **1297** R. GLOUC. (Rolls) 9129 In þe sixe & þrittiþe ȝer. *c* **1330** R. BRUNNE *Chron. Wace* (Rolls) 1418 Þe þrittyþe day, lesse ne mo. **1340** *Ayenb.* 234 Þo þet byeþ ine spoushod..habbeþ þet þrittaȝte frut. *c* **1375** *Sc. Leg. Saints* xxvi. (*Nycholas*) 560 He..syne þe thretyd psalme can say. *c* **1400** MAUNDEV. (Roxb.) xxxiv. 155 In þe foure and thrittyde ȝere. *c* **1420** *Chron. Vilod.* 2182 In þe same thryddyþ day. **1483** CAXTON *Gold. Leg.* 350 b/2 The monke that was dede appierid on the thyrttyest day. **1530** PALSGR. 372/2 *Trentiesme*, thyrteth. **1579** FULKE *Heskins' Parl.* 390 The thirtieth Chapter beginneth the exposition. **1587** GOLDING *De Mornay* xvi. (1592) 258 Which of all the beastes hath so much as the thirtith part of them in his body? **1596** DALRYMPLE tr. *Leslie's Hist. Scot.* (S.T.S.) I. 167 The threttieth ȝeir of his regne. *Mod.* Term ends on the thirtieth of June.

**B.** *sb.* A thirtieth part; in *Eng. Hist.* a thirtieth part of movable goods payable as an aid.

**1800** YOUNG in *Phil. Trans.* XCI. 59 A thirtieth of an inch. **1825** J. NICHOLSON *Operat. Mech.* 662 An addition of one-twentieth or one-thirtieth to the mass. **1893** J. A. VINCENT in *Lanc. & Chesh. Rec. Soc.* XXVII. 44 The great council, in which the king required a Thirtieth from the whole nation.

**Thirtover**, dial. form of THWARTOVER.

**Thirty** (þɔˑɪti), *a.* and *sb.* Forms: **α.** 1 **ð-, þrítiȝ, þrittiȝ, ðrít(e)ih, ðrittih,** (2 **þrihti**), 2–3 **þrittiȝ, þritti,** 3 **þrittie, þrytti, þriȝti,** 3–4 **pritty,** 3–5 **þrytty,** 4 **þritte, þrutty, thriti,** 4–5 **thritte, thritti,** 4–6 **thritty**; also 4 **þretti, þretty, threti, threiti,** 4–5 **thretti,** 5 **threty,** 6–7 **threttie,** 4–6 (–9 *dial.*) **thratty.** **β.** 5 **thirtti (derty),** 5–6 **thyrty,** 6 **thurty, thyrtye,** 6–7 **thirtie,** 6– **thirty.** [OE. *þrítig*, f. *þri*, THREE + *-tig* (= Goth. **tigus* decade: see -TY); = OFris. *thritich*; OS. *thrîtig* (LG. *dörtig*, Du. *dertig*); OHG. *drîzzug* (MHG. *drîzec*, G. *dreissig*); ON. *þrírteger* (*-tigir*), later *þrjátigi*, *þrjátíu* (Sw. *trettio*, Da. *tredive*); Goth. *þreis tigjus* 'three tens'. The metathetic form *thirty* appears in literature in 15th c. and has prevailed since 16th c.

In the oldest Eng., *ðrítig* was a neuter sb. sing. construed with a genitive pl., e. g. *he genam þritig þegna* he took (a) thirty (of) thanes (Beowulf 123), *he wæs ðritiges geara eald* he was of (a) thirty (of) years old (*Past. C.* xlix). Later it was construed as an adj. pl., with dat. *þrittigum*, gen. *þrittig(r)a*, e. g. *þara þrittigra manna* of those thirty men. Few traces of these inflexional forms remained in early ME.]

**A.** *adj.* **1.** The cardinal number equal to three tens, represented by the symbols 30, or XXX, xxx. In concord with a sb. expressed or implied.

**α.** *Beowulf* 123 [He] ȝenam þritiȝ þeȝna. *c* **950** *Lindisf. Gosp.* Luke iii. 23 Hælend wæs onginnende suelce wintra ðrittih [*Rushw.* ðritiȝ, *Ags. G.* þrit[t]iȝ, *Hatt.* þrittiȝ(e. *c* **1000** ÆLFRIC *Gen.* vi. 15 Þreohund fæðma..on lenge.. and þrittiȝ on heahnisse. *Ibid.* xviii. 30 Hwæt, ȝif þær beoð þritiȝ? *a* **1175** *Cott. Hom.* 225 Þritti fedme [*OE.* þrittiȝ fæðma] heah. *c* **1200** ORMIN 3207 Neh Off þrittiȝ winnterr elde. *c* **1205** LAY. 26631 After þan þreom cnihten þritti þer comen; after þan þrittie heo iseȝen þreo þusende. **1297** R. GLOUC. (Rolls) 7055 He was fleme & frendles mo þan þritty [*MS. B.* þrutty, *C.* þretty] ȝer. **13..** *Cursor M.* 1216 (Fairf.) Vs telles of adam þis story Of sones he had ful þretty [*Cott.* thirtti, *G.* thritti, *Tr.* þritty]. **1375** BARBOUR *Bruce* IX. 640 Quhar ay for ane thai var thretty. *c* **1400** *Apol. Loll.* 53 Judas sold Him onis..for þritty penies. *a* **1450** MYRC *Festial* 22 And duret soo þrytty wyntyr. *c* **1489** CAXTON *Blanchardyn* xxi. 71 Hath he not taken this daye..threty coursers? **1579** SPENSER *Sheph. Cal.* Feb. 17 Selfe haue I worne out thrise threttie yeares. **1818** SCOTT *Hrt. Midl.* xii, 'Ye may ca' the twenty punds thretty', said Dumbiedikes.

**β.** **1413** *Pilgr. Sowle* (Caxton) v. v. (1859) 76 The sterres.. were sette by thyrty and by thyrty, in suche a maner wyse, that in euery thyrty was sette a grete sonne. **1526** TINDALE *Luke* iii. 23 And Iesus..was about thirty yere of age when he began. **1530** PALSGR. 367/2 *Trente*, thurty, xxx. **1552** HULOET, Thyrtye tymes, *tricies*. **1671** MILTON *Samson* 1197 Your ill-meaning Politician Lords..Appointed to await me thirty spies. **1837** HT. MARTINEAU *Soc. Amer.* II. 33 Lenders of money into Vermont received thirty per cent. interest from farmers.

**b.** In comb. with the numerals *one* to *nine*, to express numbers between thirty and forty, as *thirty-one, thirty-six*, also (now less commonly) *one-and-thirty, six-and-thirty*, etc., and the ordinals *thirty-first, thirty-second, thirty-ninth*, etc., now less usually *one-and-thirtieth, five-and-thirtieth*, etc. Also as a multiple of higher numbers, as *thirty thousand, thirty-six millions*.

**971** *Blickl. Hom.* 35 Ne bið þara fæstendaȝa na ma þonne syx & þritiȝ. *c* **1000** *Ags. Gosp.* John v. 5 Ðær wæs sum man eahta and þrittiȝ [*c* **950** *Lind.* ðrittih, *c* **975** *Rushw.* ðritiȝ] wintra on his untrumnysse. *c* **1200** *Vices & Virt.* 51 Þrie and þrihti wintre and an half. **13..** *Sir Beues* (A.) 4532 Þe nombre was, veraiment, To and þretti þosent. **13..** *Cursor M.* 2158 (Gött.) Thre hundrid and eyt and thriti ȝere. *c* **1425** *Craft of Nombrynge* (E.E.T.S.) 5 Rede forth þus, 9 thousand sex hundryth thritty & foure. **1536** CROMWELL in Merriman *Life & Lett.* (1902) II. 26 In the yere of our Lorde god a thousande five hundreth syxt and thrittey. **1610** HOLLAND *Camden's Brit.* (1637) 696 Thirty thousand Englishmen were that day left dead in the field. **1711** *Lond. Gaz.* No. 4903/2 On the Thirty-first of the last Month. **1731** MILLER *Gard. Dict.* s.v. *Aloe*, The fifth,..thirty-fourth, and thirty-fifth Sorts require a greater Share of Heat. **1797** *Encycl. Brit.* (ed. 3) XVIII. 659/1 In the 39th degree of latitude. 1837 SOUTHEY *Let.* 24 Nov., The difference of five and thirty years between me and Bertha. 1884 *Harper's Mag.* Feb. 471/2 One-thirty-sixth of their..area.

**c.** Phrases. *The Thirty (Tyrants)*: the thirty magistrates imposed by Sparta upon the Athenians at the end of the Peloponnesian war (403 B.C.). *The Thirty Years' War*: the religious wars of 1618–48 fought chiefly on German soil.

1842 *Penny Cycl.* XXIV. 382/1 This conquest was the last important event of the Thirty Years' War, which began and ended at Prague. 1875 JOWETT *Plato* (ed. 2) I. 266 Anytus ..had joined Thrasybulus in the conflict with the Thirty.

**2.** *spec.* (*ellipt.*) **a.** The age of thirty; thirty years (of age, old, etc.). So *thirty-one*, etc.

*c* 1000 in *Anglia* XI. 3/77 Se hælend wæs þrittiȝ þa hine mann fullude. 1618 CHAPMAN *Hesiod's Georg.* II. 486 Thy selfe, if well in yeares; thy wife take home, Not much past thirtie; nor haue much to come. *a* 1715 BURNET *Own Time* III. (1724) I. 373 A cooler and elder man than I was, being then but thirty. 1780 MME. D'ARBLAY *Diary* 7 Apr., Conversable as he could have been at thirty-two. 1859 GEO. ELIOT *A. Bede* xxxi, She might well die o' th' inflammation afore she war thirty.

**b.** In stating the time of day, thirty minutes; as in *six-thirty* = 6.30 o'clock, half-past six; also *attrib.* as *the* 6.30 *train*.

1870 MISS BRIDGMAN *Rob. Lynne* xvi, Mr. Lynne had come down..by the 7.30, and departed by the 9.45. 1899 *Westm. Gaz.* 23 Dec. 6/3 He who came a moment after eleven-thirty stood very small chance of getting anywhere near the carriage door.

†**3.** As ordinal: = THIRTIETH. So *thirty-two* for *thirty-second*, etc. *Obs.*

*c* 1380 WYCLIF *Last Age of Chirche* p. xxiv, Þe þre and þritty sermon. 1540 HYRDE tr. *Vives' Instr. Chr. Wom.* (1592) Cc vij, In the hundred and thirtie Psalme. 1594 *Contention* I. i. 50 Ere the thirty day of the next month. 1606 G. W[OODCOCKE] *Lives Emperors* in *Hist. Ivstine* Ff ij, He died the thirty two year of his age. 1609 SKENE *Reg. Maj., Stat. K. William* 3 The sextene veshell, or the tuentie or threttie.

**B.** *sb.*

**1.** The abstract number; also, a symbol representing this. So *thirty-one*, *thirty-six*, etc.

*c* 1050 *Byrhtferth's Handboc* in *Anglia* (1885) VIII. 302 Fif siðon seofon beoð fif & þrittiȝ. *c* 1425 *Craft of Nombrynge* (E.E.T.S.) 4 The figure of 3...betokens ten tymes more þen he schuld & he stode þere þat þe figure of 4. stondes, þat is thretty. 1501 in *Exch. Rolls Scotl.* XII. 236 *note*, The nomir threttynyne. *Mod.* A Roman thirty is written thus: xxx. Twice thirty are sixty.

**2.** *The thirties*: the years of which the numbers begin with 30; the fourth decade of a century.

1880 G. MEREDITH *Tragic Com.* xvi, His forty years.. matched the twenties and thirties of other men. 1883 SEELEY *Expansion Eng.* 288 Dating only from about the thirties of the present century. 1892 A. E. LEE *Hist. Columbus, Ohio* II. 73 The company..maintained its primary organization until some time in the early thirties.

**3.** (See quot.)

1895 *Funk's Standard Dict.*, *Thirty*..among printers and telegraphers, the last sheet, word, or line of copy or of a despatch; the last; the end.

**4.** *Thirty* and its compounds in elliptical uses: e.g. *thirty-four*, port-wine of the year 1834; *thirty-two*, a thirty-two-pound gun; a flower-pot of which there are 32 in a 'cast' (see CAST *sb.* 15): see also THIRTYTWOMO.

1802 W. FORSYTH *Fruit-Trees* viii. 114 *note*, [Flower] pots are denominated by the number contained in what the Potters call a Cast...[The] 5 [size, of] 32 [in the Cast is called] Thirty-two's. 1860 *All Year Round* No. 66. 378 'Toasts are almost out of date', I replied; 'but the 'thirty-four must pay for this'. 1870 *Routledge's Ev. Boy's Ann.* Feb. 85 They..could knock the thirty-twos about in the style characteristic of British sailors. 1903 D. MCDONALD *Gard. Companion* Ser. II. 70 They choose pots of various sizes—those called thirty-twos (6 in.) seem to be most liked.

**C.** *Comb.* **a.** With sbs. forming attrib. phrases, as *thirty-acre*, *-day*, *-foot*, *-hour*, *-knot*, *-pound*, *-ton*, *-word*, *-year*; hence *thirty-footer*, *-miler*, *-tonner*, etc. (a ... of thirty feet, miles, tons, etc.). So with the compounds *thirty-one*, *thirty-nine*, etc., as *thirty-two-horse* (power), *-months-old*; *thirty-three-year*; *thirty-two-celled*, *thirty-four-seated*, *thirty-eight-volumed* adjs.; *thirty-five-tonner*, *thirty-six-pounder*, etc. (a ... of thirty- ... tons, pounds, etc.).

1666 J. DAVIES *Hist. Caribby Isles* 200 These French Servants, by reason of the three years service they are engaged to, are commonly called the *Thirty-six-months-men*. 1733 TULL *Horse-Hoeing Husb.* xiv. 176 Drill Double Rows with Eight-Inch Partitions, and Thirty-Inch Intervals. 1775 *Chron.* in *Ann. Reg.* 163/2 They are about the size of a thirty-six shilling piece. 1825 J. NICHOLSON *Operat. Mechanic* 491 The great wheel..pulley on its axis, over which the cord goes (as in a common thirty-hour clock). 1876 BLACKMORE *Cripps* xxxv, A May cold is a thirty-day cold. 1890 W. J. GORDON *Foundry* 13 Where the mighty thirty-five-tonner is shaking the earth. 1907 *Westm. Gaz.* 21 Mar. 9/1 The working expenses of thirty-four-seated petrol motor-omnibuses. 1909 *Ibid.* 8 Mar. 12/2 A thirty-six holes match has been arranged between..one-armed golfers. 1909 *Times, Lit. Suppl.* 18 Mar. 101/2 This thirty-eight-volumed behemoth.

**b.** Special Combs.: †**thirty-cross**, one of the transverse bars of a cross staff, viz. that used for about 30°; **thirty-penny nail**, a size of nail: see PENNY 10; †**thirty-perforce**, name of an old card game: see quot.; **thirty-pounder**, a gun throwing a shot of thirty pounds: so *thirty-six-pounder*, etc.; †**thirty-pound knight**, one alleged to have obtained his knighthood for a payment of thirty pounds; **thirty-second-note** (*Mus.*), a note of the length of $\frac{1}{32}$ of a semibreve, a demisemiquaver.

1726 G. ROBERTS *Four Yrs. Voy.* 102 They left my Fore-staff, with only the *Thirty-cross, having as I suppose, flung the other Crosses over-board. *c* 1850 *Rudim. Navig.* (Weale) 135 Nails of sorts are..30, and 40-penny nails. 1599 MINSHEU *Sp. Dict.* Dial. iii. 25 Behold here are the cards, let vs play at *thirtie perforce, or Albures [*Sp.* juguemos treinta por fuerça, o los albures], for these are good plaies. 1812 R. HALL in *Examiner* 12 Oct. 648/1 Two batteries of..*thirty-six pounders commanded the beach. 1769 FALCONER *Dict. Marine* (1789) I iv, A thirty-two-pounder. 1605 CHAPMAN, etc. *Eastward Hoe* IV. i. F j b, I ken the man weel, hees one of my *thirty pound knights.

† **Thi·rty-day.** *Obs.* A commemoration of a deceased person thirty days after his death: = MONTH'S MIND 1.

1479 *Bury Wills* (Camden) 51, I will that euery poure man that comyth to my threty day haue j d. 1537 *Ibid.* 129 A thyrty daye kepte wythe mete..money, and a yere daye lekwyse. 1546 LANGLEY *Pol. Verg. De Invent.* VI. viii. 128 In England the custome is to kepe the thirty daie or moneth mynde with like Obites, as wer dooen on the buriall daies.

**Thi·rtyfo:ld,** *a.* (*adv.*) [See -FOLD.] Thirty times as great or as much; increased thirty times.

*c* 1000 *Ags. Gosp.* Matt. xiii. 8 Sume..sealdon weastm sum hund-fealdne..sum þrittiȝ-fealdne. *c* 1230 *Hali Meid.* 23 Wedlac haueð hire frut þrittifald in heuene. 1382 WYCLIF *Matt.* xiii. 8 Sume an hundred fold, another sexti fold, another thritti fold. 1871 PROCTOR *Light Sci.* 132 An increase of width not less than thirtyfold. 1898 *Allbutt's Syst. Med.* V. 450 Mixing..equal volumes of, say, thirty and forty-fold diluted normal acid and titrating with the resulting thirty-five-fold acid solution.

**Thirty-one.** The name of a game (or games) of cards. Also *one-and-thirty*: see ONE 2 b.

Cf. F. *trente et un*: 'il consiste à compléter 31 points; qui passe perd' (Littré).

[1549 LATIMER *5th Serm. bef. Edw. VI* (Arb.) 149 It is like he gaue one to his man for his laboure to make vp the game, and so ther was xxxi. 1596, 1632, 1654: see PIP *sb.*[2] 1 b.] 1834–43 SOUTHEY *Doctor* cxlii. (1848) 356/1 A Frenchman..published a Treatise upon the game of Thirty-One. 1903 in Hoffmann *Card & Table Games* (ed. 3) 249 Thirty-one (the German *Schnautz*)...The primary object of the game is to hold three cards of the same suit, which shall together make 'thirty-one'; the ace counting eleven, court cards ten each.

**Thirtytwomo** (-tū·mo). [English reading of the symbol 32mo or XXXIImo, for L. (*in*) *tricesimo secundo*: cf. *twelvemo*, *sixteenmo*.] The size of a book, or of a leaf of a book, formed of sheets each folded five times, making thirty-two leaves; hence, a book of this size. Also **Thirty-twos.** So **Thirtysi·xmo** (**thirty-sixes**).

1771 LUCKOMBE *Hist. Print.* 403 Sixteens, Twenty-fours, Thirty-two's, are but the Octavo's and Twelves doubled, or twice doubled and Imposed in Half Sheets. *Ibid.* 424 A half sheet of thirty-six's without cutting. 1787 *Smith's Printer's Gram.* 210 A Sheet of Thirty-twos, with Four Signatures. 1841 SAVAGE *Dict. Printing* 796 A sheet of paper folded into thirty-six leaves, seventy-two pages, is termed thirty-sixmo.., a sheet of paper folded into thirty-two leaves, sixty-four pages, is termed thirty-twomo.

**This** (ðis), *dem. pron.* and *adj.* Pl. THESE, q.v. [Orig. the sing. neuter, nom. and acc., now the sole singular form of the OE. demonstrative *þes*, *þéos*, *þis*, corresp. to OFris. **this*, *thius* (*thisse*), *thit*, OS. **these*, *thius* (*thesu*), *thit*, OHG. *dese*, *-er* (later *diser*, *dirro*), *desiu* (*disiu*), *diz*, ON. m. and f. *þesse*, *þessi*, neut. *þetta*; a Norse and WGer. formation, produced by adding *se*, *si* (prob. = Goth. *sai* 'see, behold') to the simple demonstrative represented by THE and THAT, as shown by the early ON. Runic forms *sá-si*, *sú-si*, *þat-si*, acc. sing. *þan-si*, *þá-si*, *þat-si*, dat. *þaim-si*, pl. neuter *þau-si*. Later the compound was felt as a single word and inflected at the end, the initial *þ* being also extended to the m. and f. nom. sing., making **þá-si*, **þú-si*, in ON. *þesse*, *-i*, in OE. *þe-s*, *þío-s* or *þéo-s*. Gothic expressed the sense differently, viz. by adding to the demonstrative *sa*, *sô*, *þata*, the strengthening particle *-uh*, making *sah*, *sôh*, *þatuh*, pl. m. *þáih*. The OE. nom. pl. was *þás*, less commonly *þǽs*, ME. *þēs*; the former now represented by THOSE (which functions as pl. of *that*), the latter by THESE q.v. In OE. the word was thus inflected:

| SING. | MASC. | FEM. | NEUT. | PLURAL. |
|---|---|---|---|---|
| *Nom.* | þes | þéos, þíos | þis | þás, þǽs |
| *Acc.* | þisne | þás | þis | þás, þǽs |
| *Dat.* | þis(s)um | þisse | þisum | þisum |
| *Gen.* | þis(s)es | þisse | þis(s)es | þissa |
| *Inst.* | þýs, þís | | þýs, þís | |

In ME. these forms were gradually eliminated or reduced, until by 1200 in some dialects, and by 15th c. in all, *þis* alone remained in the sing.]

**A.** Forms and Inflexions. (For plural see THESE.)

**1.** *Sing. Nom.* **a.** *masc.* 1–4 **þes**, (1 **þæs**, **þis**), 2–3 (*Orm.*) **þiss**, **-tiss**, 3–5 **þis**, (3 **þus**, 4 **þeos**); 4– **this**. **β.** *neut.* 1–3 **þis**, (1 **þæs**), (*Orm.*) **þiss**, **-tiss**, 3–4 **þes**. **γ.** *fem.* 1 **ðíos**, (**ðius**, **ðyus**), 1–4 **þéos**, 2 **þies**, **þyos**, 2–3 **þas**, 3–4 **þis**, 4 **þues**.

α, β. ?670 *Bewcastle Column* in *O. E. Texts* 124 Þis sigbecn þun setton. *a* 800 *Beowulf* 1703 Þæt ðes eorl wære ȝeboren betera. *c* 950 *Lindisf. Gosp.* John i. 30 Ðæs is of ðæm ic cuæð. *Ibid.* vi. 42 Ahne is ðis se hælend? *c* 1175 *Lamb. Hom.* 49 Þes put bitacneð deopnesse of sunne. *Ibid.* 81 Nu is þes prest uorþe. *c* 1205 LAY. 16937 Þa þus [*c* 1275 þes] dom wes isæid. 1297 R. GLOUC. (Rolls) 1902 Þoru þes signe. 1340 *Ayenb.* 41 Þes boȝ heþ manie tuygges. 1387 TREVISA *Higden* (Rolls) III. 253 (MS. γ) Þeos Salon his lawes.

γ. *c* 825 *Vesp. Psalter* cviii[i]. 27 Ðæt witen ðætte hond ðin ðeos is. *c* 950 *Lindisf. Gosp.* John xii. 30 Ne fore mec stefn ðius [*Rushw.* ðios] cuom. *a* 1000 *Boeth. Metr.* xx. 118 Þios eorðe. *c* 1000 *Ags. Gosp.* John xii. 30 Þeos stefen. *c* 1160 *Hatton Gosp.* ibid., Þyos stefne. *Ibid.* vii. 36 Hwæt ys þies spræce þe he sprecð? *c* 1175 *Lamb. Hom.* 35 Nis þas weorld nawiht. *Ibid.* 103 Ðeos sunne fordeð eiðer ȝe saule ȝe lichoma. *c* 1205 LAY. 261 Þeos ȝunge wiman. *Ibid.* 2061 Þus is þas burh i-uaren. 1297 R. GLOUC. (Rolls) 5579 To wonye þer as in hor owe, & a þis alf [*MS.* α (*c* 1350) a þeos half] noȝt. 1387 TREVISA *Higden* (Rolls) III. 13 (MS. γ) Þeos queene. *Ibid.* VI. 421 In preysinge of þis [γ þues] Elfleda.

**2.** *Accus.* **a.** *masc.* 1–4 **þisne**, (1 **þysne**, **þeosne**), 2–3 **þesne**, 3 **þusne**, 4 **þerne**. **β.** *neut.* as nom.; (also 3 **þæs**). **γ.** *fem.* 1–3 **þás**, 3 **þes**, (*Orm.*) **þiss**.

α, β. *c* 897 K. ÆLFRED *Gregory's Past. C.* xliv. 324 ȝehieren men ðisne cwide. 971 *Blickl. Hom.* 11 He ȝefylde þysne middanȝeard. *Ibid.* 15 Eal þæt folc þe þis wundor ȝeseah. *c* 1000 ÆLFRIC *Saints' Lives* (1890) II. 38 Oþ þeosne andweardan dæȝ. *c* 1122 *O. E. Chron.* an. 1012, Þet hi woldon þisne eard healdan. *c* 1175 *Lamb. Hom.* 5 Al þe hebreisce folc..sungun þisne lofsong. *Ibid.* 27 Þesne mon ic habbe itaken. *c* 1205 LAY. 216 Asscanius heold þis drih[t]liche lond. *Ibid.* 827 Iche wlle þesne king læden mid me seolfan. *Ibid.* 4081 Þis wes þe feiruste mon þe æuere æhte ær þusne kinedom. 1297 R. GLOUC. (Rolls) 5104 Þis auisyon þat þe aungel him sede. *c* 1315 SHOREHAM vii. 716 For þou areredst þerne storm. 1340 *Ayenb.* 94 Þerne gardyn zette þe greate gardyner þet is god þe uader. 13.. *R. Gloucester's Chron.* (Rolls) App. H. 145 Þe king..þisne heiȝe man igrop.

γ. *c* 897 K. ÆLFRED *Gregory's Past. C.* 2 (*heading*) Hu S. Gregorius ðas boc ȝedihte þe man Pastoralem nemnað. *c* 975 *Rushw. Gosp.* Matt. xv. 15 Arecce us ȝelicnisse þas. *a* 1175 *Cott. Hom.* 235 Þer efter arerde god þas laȝe. *c* 1205 LAY. 2044 Þas [*c* 1275 þes] burh he luuede swiðe.

**3.** *Dative.* **α, β.** *masc.* and *neut.* 1 **þisum**, **þysum**, **ðissum**, 2 **þisen**, **ðise**, **þis**, 2–3 **þissen**, **þisse**, 3–5 **þis**. **γ.** *fem.* 1–3 **þisse**, **þissere**, (**þysse**), 1–2 **þisser**, 2 **þesser**, **þeser**, 2–4 **þusse**, 3 **þese**, **þis**, 3–4 **þise**, 4 **þyssere**.

α, β. *c* 1000 *Ags. Gosp.* Matt. xxi. 21 Eac þeh ȝe cweþan to þisum [*Lindisf.* ðissum, *Hatton* þisen] munte, Ahefe þe upp. *a* 1131 *O. E. Chron.* an. 1124, Sende se papa of Rome to ðise lande. *c* 1205 LAY. 9912 A þisse londe.

γ. *c* 1000 *Ags. Gosp.* Matt. xii. 32 Ne on þisse worulde ne on þære toweardan. *a* 1175 *Cott. Hom.* 235 Wið-ute þeser laȝe. *Ibid.*, Ærndraces of þisser laȝe. *Ibid.*, An þesser laȝe. *c* 1175 *Lamb. Hom.* 9 Heo is unbunden in þisse newe laȝe. *Ibid.* 91 On þissere tide. *a* 1200 *Moral Ode* 342 Fared bi þusse strete. *c* 1200 *Trin. Coll. Hom.* 59 On þese wise. *c* 1205 LAY. 5320, I þissere [*c* 1275 þisse] burh. *c* 1290 *S. Eng. Leg.* I. 292/148 Criede in þusse place. *c* 1315 SHOREHAM *Poems* i. 1449 Inne þe elde lawe þe ordre a-gan, Ine tokne of þyssere newe. *a* 1325 *MS. Rawl. B. 520* lf. 48 On þusse manere ant in þilke forme sal þe writ ben idressed.

**4.** *Genitive.* **α, β.** *masc.* and *neut.* 1 **þises**, **þys(s)es**, 1–3 **þisses**, 3 **þesses**, 4 **þisis**. **γ.** *fem.* 1–2 **þisse**, 2–3 **þissere**.

α, β. *c* 893 K. ÆLFRED *Oros.* I. i. § 1 Þisne ymbhwyrft þises middanȝeardes. *a* 1000 *Boeth. Metr.* xxiv. 3 Ofer heane hrof heofones þisses. *c* 1200 *Trin. Coll. Hom.* 230 Wið þesses wreches woreldes luue. *c* 1205 LAY. 823 Ich habbe þisses [*c* 1275 þis] folkes king. *a* 1225 *Ancr. R.* 198 Þisses hweolpes nurice. 1382 WYCLIF *Tobit* vii. 5 Tobie, of the whiche thou askest, is thisis fader [1388 the fadir of this man].

γ. *c* 975 *Rushw. Gosp.* Matt. xiii. 22 Be-hyȝdnis weorulde þisse. *c* 1000 *Ags. Gosp.* ibid., Eornfullness þisse worulde. *c* 1175 *Lamb. Hom.* 21 For þisse weorlde lewnesse. *Ibid.* 105 Þa sorinessen þissere sterke worlde.

**5.** *General uninflected form.* 3 (*Orm.*) **þiss**, **tiss**, 3–5 **þis**, (3–4 **tis**, **þes**, 4–5 **thus**, 4–6 **thys**), 4– **this**.

*c* 1200 ORMIN Ded. 95, & whase wilenn shall þiss boc Efft oþerr siþe writenn. *Ibid.* 303, & tohh þatt tiss Elysabæþ.. Wass þuss off Aaroness kinn. *Ibid.* 411, & ȝet tiss Goddspell seȝȝþ off hemm [etc.]. *c* 1220 *Bestiary* 88 Al is man so is tis ern. *Ibid.* 276 Ðis little wile ðe we on ðis werld wunen. *a* 1440 *Sir Degrev.* 387 Her is comen to thus walle...Sire Degrevvant the gode knyȝt. 1478 J. PASTON in *P. Lett.* III. 219 To handyll well..thys mater now thys Lent. 1551 R. ROBINSON tr. *More's Utopia* Transl. Ep., This my poore present. 1552 HULOET, Thys, *hic*, *hæc hoc*.

**B.** Signification.

**I.** Demonstrative Pronoun.

**1.** Indicating a thing or person present or near (actually in space or time, or ideally in thought, esp. as having just been mentioned and thus being present to the mind); *spec.* as being nearer than some other (hence opposed to *that*, or in earlier and dial. use to *yon*: see 3, also THAT B. II. 2).

**a.** a thing (concrete or abstract).

Sometimes, for emphasis (in mod. use), placed (as subj.) after the noun (as pred.) with ellipsis of *is*: cf. THAT B. I. 1 a.

*a* 900 tr. *Bæda's Hist.* Pref. i. (1890) 2 For þinre ðearfe & for þinre ðeode ic þis awrat. *c* 1000 *Ags. Gosp.* Mark i. 27 Hwæt ys þis? 1056–66 *Inscr. on Dial Kirkdale Ch. Yorks.*, Þis is dæȝes sol merca. 1297 R. GLOUC. (Rolls) 110 Al þis was ȝwile icluped þe march of walis. *a* 1300 *Cursor M.* 22476 (Edin.) Þe toþer day..it sal be wel wer þan þiis. 1477 *Paston Lett.* III. 186 Thes beyng the vj. letter that I have send yow. *a* 1575 *Wife lapped*, etc. 1100 in Hazl. *E. P. P.* IV. 225 This yong man was glad, ye may be sure, That he had brought hys wyfe to this. **1610** SHAKS. *Temp.* II. ii. 148 O Stephano, ha'st any more of this? **1622** FLETCHER *Beggar's Bush* III. iii, This is the wood they live in. **1654–66** EARL ORRERY *Parthen.* (1676) 131 The greatness of its horror had this of advantageous, that it made Death a Comparative Good. **1699** VANBRUGH *False Friend* II. i, A very humdrum marriage this. **1748** RICHARDSON *Clarissa* (1811) VIII. lxxvi. 362 This of Bavaria is a gallant and polite court. **1809** WINDHAM *Let.* 23 July, in *Sp.* (1812) I. 108 Terrible news this from Germany! **1837** CARLYLE *Fr. Rev.* III. III. v, It has grown to be no country for the Rich, this. **1864** TENNYSON *Aylmer's Field* 240 A gracious gift to give a lady, this! *Mod.* This is what I like.

**b.** a person. Now indicating a person actually present, and always as subj. of the verb *to be*, with the person as predicate; in which position the neuter *þis* was used in OE. (so Ger. *dies* ist mein bruder). (Cf. THAT B. I. 1 b.)

† *He this, she this*, this man, this woman: see also 3. *Obs.*

*c* **825** *Vesp. Psalter* xxiii[i]. 5 Ðes onfoeð bledsunge from dryhtne. *c* **950** *Lindisf. Gosp.* Matt. iii. 17 Ðis is sunu min leof [*c* 975 *Rushw.* þis is min sune]. *Ibid.* xxi. 10–11 Hua is ðis?..ðis is ðe hælend. *c* **1000** *Ags. Gosp.* ibid., Hwæt is þes?..þis ys se hælend. *Ibid.* xiv. 2 Þes [*Lind., Rushw.* þis, *Hatton* þes] is iohannes se fulluhtere. *c* **1275** *Passion our Lord* 244 in *O. E. Misc.* 44 Þer arysen tweyne and bigunne to speke, Þes seyde hwat he wolde þe temple al to-breke. *a* **1300** *Cursor M.* 11351 Quen þat sco þis can iesus se. *Ibid.* 18209 A ded man suilk als tis es an. *c* **1374** CHAUCER *Troylus* III. 855 (904) This is so gentil and so tender of herte. *c* **1380** WYCLIF *Serm.* Sel. Wks. II. 52 More þan Jonas is he þis. *c* **1400** MAUNDEV. (Roxb.) vi. 19 He þis, by cause he was ane aliene,..was putte oute of þe land. **1451** CAPGRAVE *Life St. Gilbert* 77 And þis þat schuld be his successour he lerned for to do lich as he saide. **1588** SHAKS. *L. L. L.* v. ii. 640 Hector was but a Troyan in respect of this. **1601** — *Jul. C.* I. ii. 299 What a blunt fellow is this growne to be! *c* **1633** MILTON *Arcades* 5 This, this is she To whom our vows and wishes bend. **1808** SCOTT *Marm.* I. xxiv, Here is a holy Palmer come...This were a guide o'er moor and dale. **1864** TENNYSON *En. Ard.* 28 This is my house and this my little wife. *Mod.* This is our new inspector.

**c.** Referring to a fact, act, or occurrence, or a statement or question, mentioned or implied in the preceding context. (Cf. THAT B. I. 1 c.)

*c* **893** K. ÆLFRED *Oros.* I. viii. § 1 Þa þis ʒedon wæs. *Ibid.* II. i. § 3 On þæm ilcan ʒeare þe þiss wæs. *a* **1123** *O. E. Chron.* an. 1101, And þis þa mid aðe ʒefæstnodan. *c* **1200** ORMIN 1340 All þiss wass don forr heore ned. *a* **1300** *Cursor M.* 14776 (Cott.) Quen iesus had said tis [*other MSS.* þis] and mare, He left all his disciplis þar. *c* **1425** WYNTOUN *Cron.* IX. xxv. 2910 Fore þis þane rais þe gret debaite. *c* **1500** *Melusine* 368 Euer thinking vpon this that Melyor had said to hym. **1591** SHAKS. *Two Gent.* v. ii. 49 Why this it is, to be a peeuish Girle. **1693** J. EDWARDS *Author. O. & N. Test.* 152 They said this as a jeer to the Jews. **1825** L. MURRAY *Eng. Gram.* (ed. 5) I. 325 Bodies which have no taste, and no power of affecting the skin, may, notwithstanding this, act upon organs which are more delicate. **1868** BROWNING *Ring & Bk.* VI. 234 This was years ago, Four hundred, full.

**d.** Pointing to a statement, proposal, or question which immediately follows. Cf. II. 1 b.

*c* **1000** *Ags. Gosp.* Luke viii. 11 Soðlice þis is þæt biʒspell, þæt sæd ys godes word. **1297** R. GLOUC. (Rolls) 8719 He bihet god & þat folc an biheste þat was þys, To alegge alle luþer lawes..& þe betere make. *c* **1400** *Gamelyn* 603 My reed is now this, Abide we no longer. **1451** CAPGRAVE *Life St. Aug.* 42 The question disputed amongis hem was þis, Fro whens þat euel comith. **1535** COVERDALE *Dan.* v. 25 This is the scripture, that is written vp: Mane, Thetel, Phares. **1602** SHAKS. *Ham.* I. iii. 78 This aboue all: to thine owne selfe be true. **1664** BUTLER *Hud.* II. II. 255 Yet all of us hold this for true, No faith is to the Wicked due. **1858** M. ARNOLD *Merope* 895, I speak no word of boast, but this I say: A private loss here founds a nation's peace.

**e.** After various prepositions (*after, before, by, ere*, etc.), = 'this time'; i.e. either, the present time, the time of speaking or writing; or, in narrative, the time just mentioned. (Cf. THAT B. I. 1 d; also NOW 13, THEN 7.)

*c* **897** K. ÆLFRED *Gregory's Past. C.* Pref. 6 Hu sio lar Lædenʒeðeodes ær ðysum [*Hatt. MS.* ðissum] oðfeallen wæs. *a* **900** tr. *Bæda's Hist.* I. vii. (1890) 40 Ða wæs se dema æfter ðyssum..ʒedrefed. *c* **1000** *Ags. Ps.* (Th.) cxx. 7 Of þisson forð awa to woruldе. *c* **1250** *Gen. & Ex.* 925 After ðis spac god to abram. *a* **1300** *Floriz & Bl.* 430 Ihc wulle fonde what i do may Bituene þis and þe þridde day. *a* **1300** [see BY *prep.* 21 b]. **13..** *Cursor M.* 7252 (Fairf.) Be þis [*Cott.* wit þis] his hare was waxin new. **1390** GOWER *Conf.* I. 21 For it hath proeved ofte er this. **1571–2** *Reg. Privy Council Scot.* II. 130 Frome this furth I sall and will beare fayth and trew allegeance. **1607** SHAKS. *Cor.* IV. iii. 43, I shall betweene this and Supper, tell you most strange things. **1654–66** EARL ORRERY *Parthen.* (1676) 683 My Soldiers having (during this) taken a little refreshment. **1719** DE FOE *Crusoe* (1840) II. i. 17 Some time after this,..they fired three muskets. **1818** KEATS *Endym.* I. 988 By this the sun is setting.

**f.** After a preposition, or as obj. of a verb: = 'this place'. (Now (in colloq. use) more usually *here*: cf. HERE *adv.* B.)

*c* **1460** [see HERE *adv.* 1 d]. **1535** LYNDESAY *Satyre* 2191 Betwixt this and Dumbartane. **1802** JEFFERSON *Writ.* (1830) III. 496, I shall leave this on the 21st. **1841** LYTTON *Money* II. v, The finest player..between this and the Pyramids. **1868** W. S. GILBERT *Bab Ballads, Bob Polter* xiv, You filthy beast, get out of this.

**g.** Strengthened by *here* immediately following (cf. II. 1. i): see HERE *adv.* 1 d. *dial.* and *vulgar.*

†**2.** In OE. and early ME., used (like THAT) with the verb *to be* in the plural in reference to a plural predicate.

(This was a collective use of the singular neuter.)

*c* **888** K. ÆLFRED *Boeth.* iii. § 4 Sint þis nu þa god & þa edlean þe þu ealne weʒ ʒehete. *c* **893** — *Oros.* III. i. § 7 þiss wæron ealle Creca leode. *c* **1000** ÆLFRIC *Exod.* i. 1 Thys synd Israela bearna naman. *c* **1205** LAY. 25387 Þis weoren þa sixe.

**3.** In contrast to *that*: now almost always of things; esp. in phr. *this and* (*or*) *that* = one thing (or person) and (or) another. So † *he this..he that* = this (or the one) man..that (or the other) man (quot. 1426). Also occas. *this..this* = one thing (or person)..another; also *this..the other.*

[**13..** *Cursor M.* 8502 (Cott.) Þat [the forbidden] tre was ded [*v. r.* deþ], þis sal be lijf.] **1390** GOWER *Conf.* II. 210 In ech of hem he fint somwhat That pleseth him, in this or that. **1426** LYDG. *De Guil. Pilgr.* 20110 He thys ys wroth, he that ys glad. **1526** TINDALE *Jas.* iv. 15 For that ye ought to saye: yff the lorde will.., let vs do this or thatt. **1581** E. CAMPION in *Confer.* II. (1584) L iv, It shalbe reported that I sayd this and that, and my wordes shalbe depraued. **1629** DONNE *Serm.* xxxi. (1640) 308 A Ruby will conduce best to the Expressing of This & an Emeraud of This. **1693** DRYDEN *Persius' Sat.* iv. 19 This is not fair; nor profitable that; Nor t'other Question proper for Debate. **1800** MRS. HERVEY *Mourtray Fam.* II. 227 Because one man did this, that truly I must do that. **18..** M. ARNOLD *Epil. to Lessing's Laocoon* 116 This through the Ride upon his steed Goes slowly by, and this at speed. **1870** MORRIS *Earthly Par.* I. I. 381 At their..feast they sat Thinking their thoughts, and spoke of this or that.

**b.** *spec.* (after Latin idiom.) The latter: in contrast to *that* = the former (THAT B. I. 3 b).

*c* **1440** *Pallad. on Husb.* IV. 21 Ffor sunne & wynde hem make a tegument, Lest they in this be shake, in that to brent. **1591** FRAUNCE (*title*) The Countesse of Pembrokes Yuychurch. Conteining the affectionate life, and vnfortunate death of Phillis and Amyntas: That in a Pastorall; This in a Funerall. **1627–47** FELTHAM *Resolves* I. lxxxvii. 271 Travaile..makes a wise man better, and a foole worse. This gains nothing but the gay sights, vices,..and the Apery of a Countrey. **1740** BERKELEY *Siris* § 72 Warm water..mixed with hot and cold, will lessen the heat in that, and the cold in this. **1868** S. J. STONE *Hymn*, '*The old year's long campaign is o'er*' ii, Go forth! firm faith in every heart, Bright hope on every helm, Through that shall pierce no fiery dart, And this no fear o'erwhelm.

**c.** With *That*, as quasi-proper names (with capital T), indefinitely denoting one person and another. So 'No. [= number] This..No. That'.

**1824** BYRON *Juan* XVI. xliv, Miss That or This, or Lady T'other. **1864** J. H. NEWMAN *Apol.* i. (1904) 9/2 He..placed me between Provost This and Principal That.

**d.** As quasi-*sb.*: *a this or a that* = one thing or another (in quot. 1656, one or other person of consequence); also nonce-pl. *thises and thats.*

**1656** CROMWELL *Sp.* 17 Sept., in *Carlyle*, A company of mean fellows,..not a lord, nor a gentleman, nor a man of fortune, nor a this nor that, among them. **1865** RUSKIN *Ethics of Dust* v. (1883) 100 You..begin to think that it is a chastisement or a warning, or a this or that or the other of profound significance. **1895** *Harper's Mag.* Nov. 952/1 There were many thises and thats put together.

**4.** Phrases. *All this*: cf. *all that* s. v. THAT B. I. 5 b; *for all this*, notwithstanding this: cf. FOR 23 a. *Like this*, of this kind; in this manner, thus: cf. *like that* (LIKE *a.* 1 ¶, *adv.* 1; THAT B. I. 5 b).

*c* **1122** *O. E. Chron.* an. 1006 (Laud MS.), Ac for eallum þissum se here ferde swa he sylf wolde. *c* **1250** *Gen. & Ex.* 3791 For al ðis, oðer day ðor was nest, Aʒenes moyses and is prest Gan al ðis folc wið wreðe gon. *a* **1774** GOLDSM. *Surv. Exp. Philos.* (1776) I. 288 Yet the friction shall not for all this become four times as great. **1858** J. H. NEWMAN *Sel. Ess.* 213 The monks were not so soft as all this, after all. **1881** DUFFIELD *Don Quix.* II. 548 To go like this..is like looking for..the bachelor in Salamanca. **1881** W. S. GILBERT *Patience* II, You hold yourself like this, You hold yourself like that, By hook or crook, you try to look, both angular and flat. **1889** C. C. R. *Up for Season* 76 Of what could we talk on an evening like this?

**II.** Demonstrative Adjective.

**1.** Used in concord with a sb., to indicate a thing or person present or near (actually or in thought), esp. one just mentioned: cf. I. 1.

The use before a possessive pron. (e.g. *this my son*) is *arch.*, the periphrasis with *of* being now substituted, as with *that*: cf. THAT B. II. 1.

*This morning, this afternoon, this evening* now always mean 'the morning (etc.) of to-day' (whether past, present, or future): cf. MORNING *sb.* 3 d.

*c* **893** K. ÆLFRED *Oros.* II. viii. § 1 Þysne nyttan cræft, þeh he arlic nære, funde heora tictator, Camillis hatte. *c* **897** — *Gregory's Past. C.* 3 (Hatton MS.) *heading*, Ðeos boc sceal to wioʒora ceastre. *a* **900** tr. *Bæda's Hist.* I. v. (1890) 32 Þes casere framlice rehte ða cynewisan. *c* **1000** *Ags. Gosp.* Matt. xiv. 15 Ðeos stow ys weste. **1154** *O. E. Chron.*, On þis gær wærd þe king Stephne ded. *c* **1200** *Trin. Coll. Hom.* 141 Þes wimmannes name. *c* **1200** ORMIN 473, & he, þiss Zakaryas, wass Bitwenenn oþre prestess..to serrfenn sett. *a* **1240** *Ureisun* in *Cott. Hom.* 199 Ich habbe i-sungen þe ðesne englissce lai. *c* **1250** *Gen. & Ex.* 3951 Al-so leun is miʒtful der, So sal ðis folc ben miʒtul her. **1340** *Ayenb.* 12 Þis article zette saynt andreu. **1382** WYCLIF *Luke* xv. 24 For this my sone was deed, and hath lyued aʒen. *c* **1400** *Brut* 100 Þis Elfride hade a sone þat me callede Edwynne. **1432–50** tr. *Higden* (Rolls) II. 285 Whiche consuetude peple of that cuntre vse to this tyme presente. **1518** in *Peebles Burgh Rec.* (1872) 46 This last Sonday he send his..men. **1554** J. CHRISTOPHERSON in Maitland *Ess.* (1849) 302 He had bene better a great deale to have lived amonge Turkes & Saracenes then amonge this kind of folke. **1600** SHAKS. *A. Y. L.* II. i. 15 And this our life exempt from publike haunt. **1632** SIR T. HAWKINS tr. *Mathieu's Unhappy Prosperitie* 163 This five yeares Consulship intoxicated him. *a* **1648** LD. HERBERT *Hen. VIII* (1683) 471 To omit the same for this present. **1711** ADDISON *Spect.* No. 18 ¶ 1 It is my Design in this Paper to deliver..a faithful Account of the Italian Opera. **1772** *Sheridaniana* (1826) 47, I have this moment heard that Sheridan is returned. **1819** SCOTT *Ivanhoe* xliv, To do battle for her in this her cause. **1851** TENNYSON *To the Queen* v, Take, Madam, this poor book of song.

**b.** Referring to something which is mentioned immediately after. (Cf. the use of *that* for something mentioned before: see THAT B. II. 1.)

*c* **897** K. ÆLFRED *Gregory's Past. C.* xliv. 324 ʒehieren men ðisne cwide: Hald ðine ælmessan, ðylæs ðu hie forweorpe. *a* **1175** *Cott. Hom.* 225 Ic wille settan mi wed betwuxe me and eow to þisan behate, þat is [etc.]. *a* **1225** *Ancr. R.* 44 And sigge, stondinde, þesne vreisun. Uisita quesumus, Domine, habitationem istam'. *c* **1440** *Alphabet of Tales* 186 He began to syng þis antem, 'O! pastor eterne'. **1509** HAWES *Past. Pleas.* xxxv. (Percy Soc.) 180 In a russet banner..There was wrytten this worde, Detraction. **1681–6** J. SCOTT *Chr. Life* (1747) III. 48 Upon this account indeed they had great cause to rejoice, because now they knew they had a sure Friend in Heaven. **1703** THORESBY *Let. to Ray* (E.D.S.), This additional list of local words is larger than I expected. **1864** J. H. NEWMAN *Apol.* 63, I..confine myself to this one consideration, viz. [etc.].

**c.** In phrases denoting or referring to the present state or stage of existence; esp. *this life*, THIS WORLD (q. v.).

*c* **1000**– [see LIFE *sb.* 12 b]. *c* **1200** *Trin. Coll. Hom.* 187 To freurende þo forsineʒede of þis wrecche woreld. **1526** TINDALE 1 *Cor.* xv. 53 For this corruptible must putt on incorruptibilite: and this mortall must put on immortalite. **1709** KEN *Hymn*, '*All Praise to Thee my God this night*' iii, That this vile Body may Rise Glorious at the awful day.

**d.** Referring to something as known, talked about, or (as in quot. 1610) inferred; esp. to something now in vogue or recently introduced. (Cf. THAT B. II. 1 b.)

**1533** BELLENDEN *Livy* I. viii. (S.T.S.) I. 46 Numa, this civil and Illustar prince. **1582** ALLEN *Martyrd. Campion* (1908) 16 Raised and upholden by this new religion. **1585** T. WASHINGTON tr. *Nicholay's Voy.* II. xiii, This lamentable losse of Constantinople. **1596** SHAKS. *Tam. Shr.* I. ii. 160 Oh this learning, what a thing it is. **1599** — *Much Ado* III. iv. 73 Get you some of this distill'd *carduus benedictus.* **1610** — *Temp.* v. i. 280 Where should they Finde this grand Liquor? *Mod. colloq.* What do you think of this wireless telegraphy? This railway strike is a serious business.

**e.** Used before a date, esp. (now only) in legal or formal documents.

**1582** L. KIRBY in Allen *Martyrd. Campion* (1908) 77, I bid you farewell, this x of Januarie, 1582. **1603** PARSONS *Let.* 6 July, in *Cath. Rec. Soc. Publ.* (1906) II. 218 And with this I byd you most hartely farewell..this 6 of July 1603. **1648** CROMWELL *Procl.* in Carlyle *Lett. & Sp.* (1871) II. 55 Given under my hand, this 20th September, 1648. **1739** in J. O. Payne *Rec. Eng. Cath. of 1715* (1889) 53, I, William Plowden, being this 31st March, 1739, full 70 years of age.

**f.** Used instead of THESE in concord with a plural sb. or numeral; esp. (now only) with a plural treated as a singular (e.g. *means, odds*), or with a numeral expression denoting a period of time taken as a whole (in this case usually = 'just past or completed', or more rarely 'just beginning'). So also *this many a day* (*year*, etc.) = these many days, this period of many days (etc.) just past.

The earlier evidence is often doubtful from the fact that *this* was long one of the forms of *these*: see THESE A γ.

[*c* **1275** LAY. 26320 Þis [*c* 1205 þeos] þreo cnihtes bolde.] *c* **1420** *Avow. Arth.* lxix, Thoȝhe ȝe sege this seuyn ȝere, Castelle gete ȝe none here. *c* **1450** *Cov. Myst.* xiv. (1841) 132 More ..Than evyr ther was this thowsand ȝere. **1523** LD. BERNERS *Froiss.* I. ix. 7 Whan the quene hard thys tidyngis. **1550** CRANMER *Defence* To Rdr., Where-with they haue this many yeares deluded and bewitched the world. **1578–1600** *Scot. Poems 16th C.* II. 164 This lang and mony ane day. **1592** SHAKS. *Rom. & Jul.* v. ii. 25 Within this three houres will faire Iuliet wake. **1596** DANETT tr. *Comines* (1614) 206 Which will bleed this many a yeare. **1779** *Mirror* No. 55. ¶ 7 By this means..even the worthiest men..may be led into fatal errors. **1810** SOUTHEY *Ess.* (1832) I. 9 Unless there be something to weigh against this fearful odds. **1867** RUSKIN *Time & Tide* xv. § 86 (1904) 109 The silence has kept my own heart heavy this many a day. **1883** L. OLIPHANT *Altiora Peto* II. 261 This last six months.

†**g.** *This bearer* (*bringer*) = the bearer of this.

**1493** *Plumpton Corr.* (Camden) 106, I pray you that I may be answered by my servant, this bearer. *c* **1495** *Ibid.*, I desire..you to send me a copple with my servant, this bringer. **1533** CRANMER *Let. to Ld. Rochford* in *Misc. Writ.* (Parker Soc.) II. 259 This bringer P. M. sueth unto me to write unto you in his favour. **1623** USSHER *Lett.* (1686) 91, I received your Graces Letter brought by this Bearer. **1630** W. BEDELL *ibid.* 440 These things I write now in exceeding post-haste, in respect that this Bearer goes away so presently.

**h.** *This once*; *this same* (*ilk*); *this side*: see ONCE 9 c, SAME A. 5, B. 2, 4 (ILK), SIDE *sb.* 13 b.

**13..** *Cursor M.* 15928 (Cott.) Þis ilk es an of his felauscep for-soth. *c* **1375** *Sc. Leg. Saints* xxxiii. (*George*) 931 Þis sammyne aray, þat now þou seis me haf. **1513** DOUGLAS *Æneis* IV. vi. 36 This ilk cursit fame. *c* **1542** UDALL in Flügel *Neuengl. Leseb.* I. 352 Be good maister to me this oons. **1769** *De Foe's Tour Gt. Brit.* I. i. 4 A little on this Side the Whalebone, a Place so called, because [etc.].

**i.** Strengthened by *here* immediately following: see HERE *adv.* 1 d. (Cf. *that there*, THERE B. 2 c.) Now *dial.* or *vulgar.*

*c* **1380** WYCLIF *Sel. Wks.* III. 203 God forbede þat ony Cristene man understonde, þat þis here synsynge and criynge..be þe beste servyce of a prest. **1762**– [see HERE *adv.* 1 d].

†**j.** *This other* = 'the other' (OTHER A. 3 b).
**1300–1596** [see OTHER A. 3 b (*b*), (*c*)].

**2.** In contrast to *that*: properly denoting the nearer of two things, but often vaguely indicating one thing as distinct from another, esp. in phr. *this and* (*or*) *that* .. = one and (or) another .. So also †*this* .. *this* .. (quots. *c* 1460, 1624); *this* .. *the other* .. (quot. 1717); *this* .. *the next* .. (quot. 1768). Cf. I. 3 above.

*c* **1460** *Towneley Myst.* ii. 251 Thou wold I gaf hym this shefe, or this sheyfe. **1551** T. WILSON *Logike* (1580) 33 Shewyng it to be true in this substaunce, and that substance. **1560** DAUS tr. *Sleidane's Comm.* 40 b, The cause of this or that precept. **1588** SHAKS. *L. L. L.* v. ii. 942 You that way; we this way. **1597** A. M. tr. *Guillemeau's Fr. Chirurg.* cj b, Those turne this way and that way in the hande. **1624** DONNE *Serm.* ii. (1640) 16 How Rheubarb, or how Aloes came by this, or this vertue, to purge this, or this humour. **1697** DRYDEN *Æneid* I. 82 This way and that the impatient captives tend. **1717** PRIOR *Alma* III. 494 This man pursues What if he gain'd he could not use: And t'other fondly hopes to see What never was, nor e'er shall be. **1732** BERKELEY *Alciphr.* I. § 16 Truth .. must not be measured by the convenience of this or that man. **1768** GOLDSM. *Good-n. Man* I. i, He laughs this minute with one, and cries the next with another. **1842** [see DIVIDE *v.* 8 e]. **1867** FREEMAN *Norm. Conq.* I. iii. 128 The temporary .. superiority of this or that Bretwalda.

**III.** Combinations and special collocations.

† **This gate,** (in) this way, thus (cf. THUS-GATE); † **thi·s half** (*obs.*), this side (HALF *sb.* 1, 2); *a* (*on*) *this half* = on this side of (see also A-THIS-HALF); **thi·s-how** *adv.* (*nonce-wd.* after *somehow*), in this manner, thus (in quot. as sb.); **thi·s-like** *a.*, like this, such as this, of this kind (cf. *these-like*, THESE, B. III); **thi·s-way-ward** *adv.*, towards this way, in this direction; † **this while** *advb. phr.* (also †*this whiles*), during this time, or the time in question; meanwhile; the while. See also THISKIN, THISWISE, THIS WORLD.

**1513** DOUGLAS *Æneis* XII. xi. 28 Turnus, lat ws persew Troianys *this gayt. **1872, 1893** [see GATE *sb.*[2] 2]. *c* **1205** LAY. 14018 A *þas hælf [*c* **1275** a þis half] þere Humbre. **1387–8** T. USK *Test. Love* I. ix. (Skeat) l. 39 Is not euery thyng a thiss-halfe God; Made buxome to mannes contemplacion? **1476** SIR J. PASTON in *P. Lett.* III. 162, xij myle on thysehalff Roome, the Lorde Ryverse was robbyd off alle hys jowelles. **1868** BROWNING *Ring & Bk.* I. 706 The somehow may be *thishow. **1880** W. WATSON *Prince's Quest* Poems 1905 II. 153 The passion .. voiced itself in *this-like monotone. **1662** PEPYS *Diary* 7 May, He left the Queen and fleet in the Bay of Biscay, coming *this wayward. **1594** CAREW *Huarte's Exam. Wits* xiii. (1596) 236 A thousand inconueniencies come into his fancie, which hold him in suspense, and *this-while the occasion of the remedie passeth away. **1644** DIGBY *Nat. Soul* Concl. 455 Making roome for this soule rauishing contemplation, by remouing this whiles all other images of things farre from me. **1660** F. BROOKE tr. *Le Blanc's Trav.* 3 This while the greatest part of us perished on the shallowes.

**This** (ðis), *adv.* [In I. prob. OE. *þýs*, *þís*, instrumental case of THIS *dem. pron.*; in II. app. advb. use of accus. sing. neuter (cf. THAT *adv.*). In some instances, perhaps an alteration of THUS *adv.*]

**I.** †**1.** In this way or manner; like this; thus.

*c* **1375** *Sc. Leg. Saints* i. (*Petrus*) 729 And þis he ȝalde þe spyrit. *c* **1420** *Chron. Vilod.* 3123 When þis lomb had þis y-ron þrye þe tomb abouȝt. *a* **1518** SKELTON *Magnyf.* 1043, I wyll not haue it so, I wyll haue it this. *a* **1578** LINDESAY (Pitscottie) *Chron. Scot.* (S. T. S.) I. 368 And this the King of Scotland depairtit out of France. **1592** SHAKS. *Ven. & Ad.* 205 What am I that thou shouldst contemne me this?

**II.** †**2.** To this extent or degree; as much as this; thus. *Obs.* exc. as in b. (Cf. THAT *adv.*)

*c* **1460** *Wisdom* 936 in *Macro Plays* 66 To clense þe soull wyche ys þis fowll. ? *a* **1500** *Chester Pl.* (Shaks. Soc.) II. 11 Elles this boulde durste he not be, To make such araye. **1523** LD. BERNERS *Froiss.* I. ccclxxviii. 631 Let vs go forwarde, let vs nat be this a colde to make warr. **1567** *Gude & Godlie B.* (S.T.S.) 60 This vmbeset I am on eurie syde.

**b.** Qualifying an adj. or adv. of quantity, now chiefly in *this much* (where *this* is perh. felt as the pronoun = 'as much as this'). (Cf. THAT *adv.* b.)

*c* **1460** *Wisdom* 982 in *Macro Plays* 67, I be-gyn awake, I that þis longe hath slumberyde in syne. **1586** SIR F. WALSINGHAM in *Leycester's Corr.* (Camden) 230 This myche have I receyved from her majestye. **1596** DALRYMPLE tr. *Leslie's Hist. Scot.* (S.T.S.) I. 62 And this far of the Iles called Hebrides. **1675** BAXTER *Cath. Theol.* II. viii. 190 Having said this much preparatorily. **1763** C. JOHNSTON *Reverie* I. 23 He might have spared himself the trouble even of this much. **1877** RUSKIN *Fors Clav.* lxxxii. 324 Perhaps this much of Plato is enough for one letter. **1884** J. P. NORRIS in *Shakespeariana* May 181 None of the portraits mentioned by Walpole are dated this early. **1885** J. J. MURPHY in *Brit. Q. Rev.* July 100 The Agnostic argument .. must go this far if it is to be valid.

**Thisan**(e, obs. var. PTISAN, barley-water, etc.

**Thisen, this-en**: see THISSEN.

† **Thi·skin,** *a. Sc. Obs.* Also thiskins. [f. THIS *dem. a.* + KIN *sb.*[1] 6 b; repr. an OE. **þises cynnes*, early ME. **þis cunnes* = L. *hujus generis*.] Of this kind; *on thiskin wise*, on this wise, in this way.

*a* **1300** *Cursor M.* 3292 (Cott.) He .. said til hir o þiskin wise. **1375** BARBOUR *Bruce* XVI. 49 Kyng robert, upon thiskyn wiss, In-till Irland arivit is. *c* **1420** *Sir Amadace* (Camden) xxix, Qwen he was gone on this kin wise, Thenne iche mon sayd thayre deuise.

**Thisne**: OE. and ME. inflexion of THIS.

**Thisness** (ðiˑsnės). [f. THIS + -NESS: rendering med. (Scholastic) L. *hæcceitās*.] The quality of being 'this' (as distinct from anything else): = HÆCCEITY.

**1643** [see THATNESS]. **1837** WHEWELL *Hist. Induct. Sc.* (1857) I. 244 Which his school called Hæcceity or thisness. **1895** RASHDALL *Universities* II. 532 An individuating form called by the later Scotists its *hæcceitas* or 'thisness'.

**Thissell-cok**: see THROSTLE-COCK.

**Thissen** (ðiˑs'n), *adv. dial.* Also 9 **this'ne, this(-)en, thisn, this'ns.** [perh. reduced from THISKIN: cf. dial. *siccan* = *swilk-kin*, *that'n what'n* = WHATKIN.] In this way or manner. Usually *a thissen* or *thissens*, in this way, thus.

(Some so understand Bottom's *Thisne* in SHAKS. *Mids. N.* I. ii. 54.)

*a* **1652** BROME *Eng. Moor* III. ii, *Ed.* An Idiote is it. *Buz.* Yes: A very natural; and goes a thissen. **1707** MRS. CENTLIVRE *Platonick Lady* IV. i, If old Roger Dowdy were alive and zeen me thissen. **1790** MRS. WHEELER *Westmld. Dial.* 89 Tae gang on a thisen is a fearful Thing. *a* **1825** FORBY *Voc. E. Anglia*, *This'ns, thus'ns, that'ns* .. in this or that manner.

**Thister, þister,** variant of THESTER *Obs.*, dark.

**Thistle** (þiˑs'l), *sb.* Forms: 1 **thistil, þistel, þystel,** 4–6 **thistel, thystle,** 5 **thestel, thystelle, -tylle,** 5–6 **thistell, thystell,** 6 **thystel, thistyll, thessel,** 7 **thissel,** 5– **thistle.** β. (chiefly *Sc.*) 5 **thristelle,** 5–7 **thrissill(e,** 6 **thirsill, thyrsill,** 6–9 **thrissel, thrisle,** 8–9 **thrissle,** 9 **thristle.** γ. 9 *dial.* **fissle, fistle.** [OE. *þistil*, *-el* m. = OHG. *distil* masc., *distila* fem. (MHG. *distel* m., f., Ger. *distel* f.), Du. *distel*, ON. *þistell*, *-ill* m. (Sw. *tistel*, Da. *tidsel*). Modern dialects point to an original long *ī* in the stem-syllable (cf. Somersetsh. *dəis'l*, *deif'l*, *dāf'l*; also LG. *diestel*, *dīstel*, *dīssel*, beside *dəistələ*, *deussl*, *duissl*, in various German dialects. Of OTeut. **þīstil-oz* m., **þīstil-a* f., the ulterior history is unknown.

Sc. *thristell* may have been influenced by *thrist* vb.]

**1.** The common name of the prickly herbaceous plants of the genus *Carduus* (N.O. *Compositæ*, suborder *Cynarocephalæ*) and several closely allied genera (*Cnicus*, *Cirsium*, *Onopordum*, etc.), having the stems, leaves, and involucres thickly armed with prickles, the flower-heads usually globular, and the flowers most commonly purple; many species are abundant as weeds.

Formerly (and in scriptural or rhetorical language) applied vaguely, including various prickly plants: cf. 2, 3.

*c* **725** *Corpus Gloss.* (O.E.T.) 384 *Carduus*, þistel. *a* **800** *Erfurt Gloss.* 271 *Carduus*, thistil. *c* **1050** *Gloss.* in Wr.-Wülcker 379/23 *Carduus orrens*, se onscunienda þystel. *a* **1327** *On Dreams* in *Rel. Ant.* I. 264 Ȝef thou etest of thystles ȝurne, Thy fomon the freteth on uche hurne. *c* **1400** *Rom. Rose* 1835 Thornes sharpe .. Ther were, and also thistels thikke, And breres, brimme for to prikke. **1481** CAXTON *Reynard* xxxii. (Arb.) 86, I haue nothyng but thystles and nettles. **1535** COVERDALE *Gen.* iii. 18 Cursed be yͤ earth for thy sake .. Thornes and thistles shall it beare vnto the. **1562** TURNER *Herbal* II. 145 b, Spina in Latin is properly called a thistel. **1650** BAXTER *Saint's R.* I. vii, Doubts are like the Thistle, a bad weed, but growing in good ground. **1758** R. BROWN *Compl. Farmer* II. (1760) 31 Thistles, docks, and all sorts of rank weeds. **1890** A. R. WALLACE *Darwinism* 28 Hundreds of square miles of the plains of La Plata are now covered with .. species of European thistle.

β. *c* **1400** MAUNDEV. (1839) xi. 130 A gode contree to sowen Inne thristelle & breres & broom & thornes. **1503** DUNBAR *Thistle & Rose* 129 Vpone the awfull Thrissill scho beheld. **1548** H. BALNAUES *Conf. Faith* (1584) 132 May yee gather grapes of thornes, or figges of thrisles? **1806** A. DOUGLAS *Poems* 145 (E.D.D.) Nae thrisles here your thumbs to prick. **1815** SCOTT *Guy M.* iii, The thristles by the road-side.

γ. **1809** T. BATCHELOR *Orth. Anal. Eng. Lang.*, *Bedford Words* 123/2 Provincial Pronunciations, *fislz*. **1848** B. EVANS *Leicestersh. Words*, *Fistle*, var. pron. of 'thistle'. **1886** BRITTEN & HOLLAND *Plant-n.*, *Fissle*, *Fistle*, a thistle.

**b.** As the heraldic emblem of Scotland; also, a figure of a thistle as such. Cf. ROSE *sb.* 6 b, 12 c.

**1488** *Acc. Ld. High Treas. Scot.* I. 85 A couering of .. purpir tartar browdin with thrissillis and a vnicorne. **1507** *Ibid.* III. 261 Thre thrissilles of coppir gilt. **1562** A. SCOTT *Poems* (S.T.S.) i. 3 Welcum, oure thrissill with þe Lorane grene! **1786** BURNS *Earnest Cry & Prayer* vii, Paint Scotland greeting owre her thrissle. **1831** SCOTT *Cast. Dang.* xiii, She seeks the Black Douglas, or some such hero of the Thistle. **1853** [see ROSE *sb.* 12 c].

**c.** As a part of the insignia of the *Order of the Thistle*, the distinctively Scottish order of knighthood (instituted by James II in 1687 and revived by Queen Anne in 1703) conferred on noblemen of that country; hence *transf.* the order itself, or membership in it.

**1687** *Lond. Gaz.* No. 2251/2 His Majesty having been Graciously Pleased the 29th of May last, to Sign a Patent to be past under the Great Seal of Scotland, for Reviving and Restoring [*sic*] the most Ancient and most Noble Order of the Thistle. **1710** *Ibid.* No. 4694/3 The Earl of Stair was invested .. with the most Noble Order of the Thistle. **1852** THACKERAY *Esmond* III. iv, Having the Thistle already originally bestowed on him by King James the Second, his Grace was now promoted to the honour of the Garter. **1898** *Westm. Gaz.* 10 Jan. 1/1 The Duke of Argyll .. received his Thistle from Lord Palmerston in 1851.

**d.** *transf.* Something resembling a thistle in form or appearance.

**1891** J. W. HARRISON *Mackay of Uganda* i. 2 Thistles of frost garnished the window-panes.

**e.** *fig.* or in figurative context, with reference to the thistle as a noxious or prickly weed.

**1563** WINȜET *Vincent. Lirin.* xxviii. Wks. (S.T.S.) II. 59 God forbid that the rose plantis of the catholik sense be turnit in thirsillis and thornis! **1642** FULLER *Holy & Prof. St.* V. xiv. 415 He snatcheth at the thistle of a project, which first pricks his hands, and then breaks. **1797–1803** FOSTER in *Life & Corr.* (1846) I. 163 Adversity! thou thistle of life. **1840** CARLYLE *Heroes* ii, His knowledge is a pedantry, and dead thistle, otherwise.

†**2.** Applied (definitely) to other prickly plants, as artichoke, sea-holly (*Eryngium*), teasel, etc.

**1398** TREVISA *Barth. De P. R.* XVII. cxxvii. (Bodl. MS.), Paliurus is a þistel moste rowȝe & scharp with prikkes and growiþ .. wiþ certeyne hedes ful of certeyne prickes. **14..** [see TEASEL *sb.* 1]. **1545** ELYOT, *Scolymus*, a thystell nowe called Arkechoke, of some men is taken for the .. cowethystell. **1577** B. GOOGE *Heresbach's Husb.* II. (1586) 64 A Thistell is the Hartichoch; that euerie where dooth grow. **1578** LYTE *Dodoens* IV. lviii. 519 The first kinde of these Thistels is called .. in Latine *Eryngium*: .. in Englishe, .. Sea Holly. *Ibid.* lx. 522 Of the Teasel .. This kinde of Thistel is called .. in Englishe, Fullers Teasel, Carde Thistell.

**b.** = TEASEL *sb.* 2.

**1839** URE *Dict. Arts* 1322 The large side [of the frame], against which the tops of the teasels rest, is hollowed out .. There are .. cross-bars, which serve .. to form short compartments for keeping the thistles compact.

**3.** With qualifying words, applied to various species of *Carduus* and allied genera, and to some prickly plants of other orders: as

**Bull thistle,** a local name (in Ireland and U.S.) for *Carduus lanceolatus*; **Canada thistle** (*U.S.*), **Corn-thistle, Creeping thistle, Cursed thistle,** *Carduus arvensis* (*Cirsium arvense*), a troublesome weed with creeping rootstocks; **Dog thistle,** 'apparently *Carduus arvensis*' (Britten & Holland); **Dwarf thistle,** *Carduus* (*Cnicus*) *acaulis*; **Gentle thistle,** *Carduus anglicus*; **Green thistle, Herring-bone thistle** (also called *fish-bone thistle*: see FISH *sb.*[1] 7), *Chamæpeuce* (*Cirsium*) *Casabonæ*; **Holy thistle,** (*a*) *Centaurea benedicta* (*Cnicus benedictus*), with yellow flowers and weak prickles on the leaves, formerly in repute as an antidote; also called *blessed thistle*; (*b*) erron. applied to *Carduus Marianus*, with white veins on the leaves; also called *Our Lady's thistle* or *milk thistle*; **Hundred-headed thistle** (abbrev. *hundred thistle*), *Eryngium campestre* (N.O. *Umbelliferæ*); **Jersey thistle,** *Centaurea Isnardi* (*C. aspera*); **Mexican thistle,** a prickly composite plant, *Erythrolæna conspicua*, cultivated in gardens, having yellow florets surrounded with scarlet involucral scales; **Russian thistle** (*U.S.*), a species of saltwort, *Salsola Tragus*, with prickly stems, introduced from Russia into S. Dakota with flax-seed, and now abundant as a weed in that and neighbouring States; **Scotch thistle,** a name for the species supposed to be that figured as the emblem of Scotland, variously identified as the spear-thistle (*Carduus lanceolatus*), the musk thistle (*C. nutans*), the milk thistle (*C. Marianus*), and the cotton-thistle (*Onopordum Acanthium*); **Silver thistle,** a name for the cotton-thistle; **Smooth thistle,** a name for SOWTHISTLE (*Sonchus*); **Syrian thistle,** *Notobasis Syriaca*; **Welted thistle,** *Carduus acanthoides*; **Woolly thistle,** the cotton-thistle; **Woolly-headed thistle,** *C. eriophorus*; **Yellow thistle,** (*a*) a species of thistle with pale-yellow or purple flowers (*Cnicus horridulus*), found in the eastern U.S.; (*b*) a name for the prickly poppy (*Argemone mexicana*): see POPPY *sb.* 3. See also ARGENTINE *thistle*, *St.* BARNABY'S *t.*, BLESSED *t.*, BOAR *t.*, BUR *t.*, CARD *t.*, CARLINE *t.*, COTTON-THISTLE, DISTAFF *t.*, FRIAR'S *t.*, FULLERS' *t.*, GLOBE *t.*, GOLDEN *t.*, GUM *t.*, HARE'S *t.*, HEDGEHOG *t.*, HORSE *t.*, LADY'S THISTLE, *St.* MARY'S *t.*, MELANCHOLY *t.*, MELON *t.*, MILK *t.*, MUSK *t.*, OAT *t.*, PINE *t.*, PLUME *t.*, SAFFRON *t.*, SEA-THISTLE, SOWTHISTLE, SPEAR *t.*, STAR-THISTLE, SWINE'S *t.*, THOWTHISTLE, TORCH *t.*, WAY *t.*, WOLF'S *t.*

**1878** BRITTEN & HOLLAND *Eng. Plant-n.*, *Bull Thistle, *Carduus lanceolatus*. *Irel.* (Belfast). **1884** MILLER *Plant-n.*, *Cirsium arvense*, *Canada Thistle, Creeping Thistle, 'Cursed Thistle', of N. America. **1878** BRITTEN & HOLLAND *Eng. Plant-n.*, *Corn Thistle, *Carduus arvensis*. **1845** *Gard. Chron.* 20 Dec. 864/1 Will any of your correspondents inform me the most effectual way to eradicate the *Dog Thistle? **1846** SOWERBY *Eng. Bot.* (ed. 3), *Dwarf Thistle, *Carduus acaulis*. **1760** J. LEE *Introd. Bot.* App. 329 *Gentle Thistle. **1882** *Garden* 3 June 391/3 A large oval-shaped bed of Ricinus Gibsoni .. edged with Chamæpeuce Casabonæ or *Green Thistle. **1884** MILLER *Plant-n.*, *Chamæpeuce Casabonæ*, Fish-bone or *Herring-bone Thistle. **1587** MASCALL *Govt. Cattle*, *Horses* (1627) 190 Take the soft downe of the stalks of the hearb *Cardus Benedictus*, called the *holy-thistle, and therewith fill the wounds. **1599** SHAKS. *Much Ado* III. iv. 80 Get you some of this distill'd *Carduus benedictus* .., it is the only thing for a qualm .. I meant plaine holy thissell. **1793** A. B[ISANI] *Pict. Tour Europe*, etc. 52 Sciato .. The hills .. are covered with holy thistle, centaury, thyme, sage, and calamint. **1866** *Treas. Bot.* 222 The Holy Thistle (*Carduus Marianus*) is well marked by the white veins on its large shiny leaves. **1893** MCCARTHY *Red Diamonds* II. 42 Here was holy thistle, which of old its admirers called Benedictus for its supposed astonishing virtues. **1578** LYTE *Dodoens* IV. lviii. 519 The other kinde is called .. the *Hundred headed Thistel .. This without doubt is a kinde of Eringium. **1880** BRITTEN & HOLLAND *Eng. Plant-n.*, Hundred Thistle, *Eryngium campestre*. **1866** *Treas. Bot.* 468 *E*[*rythrolæna*] *conspicua* .. was introduced to English gardens about 1838, and is commonly known as the Scarlet *Mexican Thistle. **1705** tr. *Cowley's Plants* Wks. 1711 III. 367 Whilst the *Scotch Thistle, with audacious Pride, Taking Advantage, gores your bleeding Side. **1861** MISS PRATT *Flower. Pl.* III. 240 The handsome Cotton Thistle .. is often cultivated under the name of the Scotch Thistle. **1888** *Encycl. Brit.* XXIII. 307/1 The common *C*[*arduus*] *lanceolatus* seems to be the most suitable prototype for the Scotch Thistle. **1578** LYTE *Dodoens* IV. lxiv. 526 In Latine *Acanthium*: .. in Englishe White Cotton Thistell, Wilde white Thistell, and Argentine, or *Siluer Thistel. **1633** *Gerarde's Herbal* II. xx. 292 The stalk of Hares Lettuce or *smooth-Thistle. **1866** *Treas.*

*Bot.* 794 The *Syrian Thistle, *N[otobasis] syriaca*,.. is distinguished from other thistles by the central florets of the flower-head only being fertile. **1846** SOWERBY *Eng. Bot.* (ed. 3) *Welted Thistle, *Carduus crispus*. **1884** MILLER *Plant-n.*, Thistle, Welted, *Carduus acanthoides*. **1760** J. LEE *Introd. Bot.* App. 329 Thistle, *Woolly, *Onopordon*. **1867** BABINGTON *Man. Brit. Bot.* (ed. 6) 200 *C[arduus] eriophorus*...Heads very large; involucre covered with a dense white web...*Woolly-headed Thistle. **1866** *Treas. Bot.* 1145 Thistle.., *Yellow, *Argemone mexicana*.

**4.** *attrib.* and *Comb.*, as *thistle-flower*, *thistle-topped* adj.; **thistle-ball**, the globular head of feathery seeds of the thistle; **thistle-beard** = THISTLE-DOWN; **thistle-bird**, a bird that feeds on thistle-seeds (cf. THISTLE-FINCH); *spec.* the American goldfinch, *Chrysomitris* (*Spinus*) *tristis*; **thistle-butterfly**, the 'painted lady', *Vanessa* (*Pyrameis*) *cardui*, whose larva feeds on the thistle; **thistle-cock** (*dial.*), the corn bunting, *Emberiza miliaria*; (see also THROSTLE-COCK); **thistle-cropper** = *thistle-eater* (*b*); **thistle-crown**, (*a*) a name for a Scottish gold coin of James VI, bearing the figure of a thistle on the reverse, and worth about 4 shillings; cf. *thistle noble*; (*b*) the flower-head of the thistle; **thistle-cutter**, a machine for cutting down thistles or other weeds; **thistle-digger**, a tool for rooting up thistles; **thistle dollar**, (*a*) a name for a Scottish silver coin of James VI, also called *double merk*, bearing the figure of a thistle on the reverse, and worth 26*s.* 8*d.* Scotch (2*s.* 2⅔*d.* English); (*b*) a silver coin of the reign of Charles II; **thistle-eater, thistle-feeder**, (*a*) a bird that eats thistle-seeds (cf. THISTLE-FINCH); (*b*) a beast that eats thistles, as a donkey; so **thistle-feeding** *a.*; **thistle-fly**, an insect (*Urophora cardui*) infesting a species of thistle; **thistle funnel**, a kind of funnel used in chemical operations, having a large bulb between the conical flaring part and the tube, so as to suggest the form of a thistle-head upon its stalk; **thistle-gall**, a gall produced by the *thistle-fly* or **thistle-gall fly**; **thistle-head**, the flower-head or *capitulum* of the thistle (in quot. 1839, that of the teasel = 2 b above); **thistle-like** *a.*, resembling a thistle; also, of the thistle kind, of the suborder *Cynarocephalæ* of *Compositæ*, comprising the thistles and allied plants; **thistle merk** [MARK *sb.*[2]], collectors' name for a Scottish silver coin of James VI, bearing the figure of a thistle on the reverse, and worth 13*s.* 4*d.* Scotch (13⅓*d.* English); **thistle noble**, a Scottish gold half-merk of James VI, bearing the figure of a thistle on the reverse; **thistle-plume** [PLUME *sb.* 5], *U. S.*, 'a plume-moth, *Pterophorus carduidactylus*, whose larva feeds on thistle-heads' (*Cent. Dict.*); **thistle-saffron**, the safflower = *saffron-thistle* (see SAFFRON 6 c); **thistle-seed**, the feathery or pappose 'seed' or achene of the thistle; **thistle-spud** = *thistle-digger*; **thistle-stamped** *a.*, stamped with the figure of a thistle; **thistle-teasel** = TEASEL *sb.* 2; **thistle-top**, (*a*) = THISTLE-DOWN; (*b*) = *thistle-head*; **thistle-tube** = *thistle funnel*; **thistle-tuft** = THISTLE-DOWN; **thistle-whipper** (*Hunting slang*), a nickname for a hare-hunter.

**1855** BROWNING *Two in Campagna* xi, Must I go Still like the *thistle-ball..Onward, whenever light winds blow? **1797** COLERIDGE *Foster-mother's T.* 20 A baby wrapt in mosses, lined With *thistle-beards. **1872** COUES *N. Amer. Birds* 131 American Goldfinch. Yellowbird. *Thistlebird. **1893** *Scribner's Mag.* June 763/1 The goldfinch or wild canary is seen, perched on a thistle-top...'Thistle bird' is another name that he bears, on account of his fondness for thistle-seeds as food, and thistle-down for the lining of his nest. **1836** PRICHARD *Phys. Hist. Man.* (ed. 3) I. 58 The *thistle-butterfly, termed 'La Belle Dame'. **1866** EDMONSTON *Shetl. & Orkney Gloss.* 127 *Thistle-cock, common bunting (*Emberiza miliaria*). **1726** LEAKE *Nummi Brit. Hist.* 83 *Thistle Crowns..4*s.* 4½*d.* **1878** M. A. BROWN *Nadeschda* 20 Plucked a thistle-crown and fastened it As a breast-knot. **1899** *Daily News* 12 July 8/3 To watch the goldfinch clinging to the silken thistle-crown. **1901** *Dundee Advertiser* 30 June 3 A capital display of the *thistle cutter's powers on a rank growth of bracken.., the rapidly whirling knives..made short..work of the bracken. **1877** KNIGHT *Dict. Mech.* s.v. *Spade*, The *thistle-digger is a pronged tool, intended to catch the root below the crown, and then pry out the plant. **1562** TURNER *Herbal* II. 145 b, Aristotel..wryteth ..: τὰ δὲ τοιὰ ἀκανθοφάγα...That is to saye, these are spiniuora, that is *thistel eaters...Aristotell sayeth that Linetes and Goldfinches, and Grenefinches, are acanthophage. **1904** *Daily News* 20 June 5, I did not see either the bullfinch or the goldfinch,..either the detested bud-plucker or the pretty *thistle-feeder. **1906** *Outlook* 24 Mar. 404/2 In Hertfordshire, a county notable for the high-farming that was supposed to have exiled the *thistle-feeding birds, goldfinches were singing about their nests. **1552** HULOET, *Thystle floure, *scholymos*. **1908** [Miss FOWLER] *Betw. Trent & Ancholme* 107 No Thistle flowers as yet. **1753** CHAMBERS *Cycl. Supp.*, **Thistle Fly*, a small fly produced from a fly-worm, hatching in the protuberances of the carduus hæmorrhoidalis. **1849** D. CAMPBELL *Inorg. Chem.* 17 Sometimes a small funnel (called a *thistle funnel) passes through the cork, and reaches nearly to the bottom of the bottle. **1753** CHAMBERS *Cycl. Supp.*, **Thistle-Galls*, a name given..to the protuberances on the stalks of a species of Thistle, called.. *carduus hæmorrhoidalis*, from these tubercles, which are supposed to resemble those of the hæmorrhoidal veins. **1864–5** WOOD *Homes without H.* xxvi. (1868) 505 The Thistle-gall Fly (*Urophora Cardui*)..produces large and hard woody galls upon the thistle. **1839** URE *Dict. Arts* 1322, 16 frames bearing the teasels which are to act upon the cloth,..their breadth only large enough to contain two *thistle-heads set end to end. **1896** *Spectator* 31 Oct. 588/2 He [a bee] returned to the inviting thistle-head. **1857** HENFREY *Bot.* 320 The *Cynareæ*, or *thistle-like Compositæ. **1866** *Treas. Bot.* 225 *Carlina*, a genus..distinguished among the thistle-like group of compound flowers by having the inner leaves of the..involucre coloured. **1590–1** *Reg. Privy Council Scot.* IV. 574, [200 oz. weight of] utter fyne gold [shall be coined] in the *thrissill noblis. **1603** *Ibid.* VI. 529 Thrissill noblis of gold. **1782** COWPER *Progr. Err.* 555 They..Like *thistle-seeds, are sown by every wind. **1896** MRS. CAFFYN *Quaker Grandm.* 105 Why should Mr. Ince lag behind with the dogs, and his *thistle-spud? **1882** J. WALKER *Jaunt Auld Reekie* 41 *Thistle-stampit auld Scotch bodles. **1835** URE *Philos. Manuf.* 202 Preparing *thistle-teasels for the workman. **1552** HULOET, *Thystle toppe, whych is lyke plume, *pappus*. **1606** [see THISTLEWARP]. **1893** [see *thistle-bird* above]. **1903** *Westm. Gaz.* 29 Dec. 10/1 Carved thistles ornament his dining-room chairs; and a *thistle-topped railing lends novelty to the front of the house. *a* **1847** ELIZA COOK *Song of Wind* iii, I grasped an airy *thistle-tuft. **1801** *Sporting Mag.* XIX. 114 This North-Country *ThistleWhipper. **1856** 'STONEHENGE' *Brit. Sports* (ed. 2) § 1 A brace of hares, or a single fox, will serve for the amusement of a large field of fox-hunters or thistle-whippers.

Hence **Thi·stle** *v.*, *trans.* to clear of thistles, to weed out the thistles from (whence **Thi·stling** *vbl. sb.*); **Thistled** (þi·s'ld) *a.*, covered or overgrown with thistles; adorned with figures of thistles; **Thi·stlery** (þi·s'lri), a plantation of thistles; **Thi·stlish** *a.*, resembling or suggesting a thistle.

**1766** *Compl. Farmer* s.v., In France, a farmer may sue his neighbour who neglects to *thistle his land at the proper seasons. **1745** in Motherwell *Harp of Renfrewshire* (1819) 319 The *Thistled banners far were streaming. **1797** MRS. M. ROBINSON *Walsingham* I. 72 The upland mead, and thistled down. **1893** CHR. G. ROSSETTI *Poems* (1904) 123/2 Our thorned and thistled plot. **1889** MARY E. BAMFORD *Up & Down Brooks* 97 Do not his folk make such '*thistleries' in Paraguay that robbers can hide among them? **1766** *Compl. Farmer*, **Thistling*, the action of cutting or pulling up thistles. **1858** MOTLEY *Corr.* 17 June, Like his tongue and his mind, it [his visage] is eminently Scotch, sharp, caustic, rugged, *thistle-ish.

**Thistle**, obs. variant of THIXEL, an adz.

**Thistle-down** (þi·s'l,daun). [f. THISTLE *sb.* + DOWN *sb.*[2]] The down or pappus which crowns the 'seeds' or achenes of the thistle, and by means of which they are carried along by the wind: either collectively, or that of a single 'seed'.

**1561** [see c]. **1585** HIGINS *Junius' Nomencl.* 112/1 *Pappus*, the downe of flowers which the wind bloweth about: as thistle downe. **1591** SPENSER *M. Hubberd* 634 As a thistle-downe in th' ayre doth flie. **1723** MANDEVILLE *Fab. Bees* 277 If it were a hard Winter, they mingled some Thistle down with their Rushes to keep them warm. **1879** JEFFERIES *Wild Life in S. Co.* 206 Thistledown is sometimes gathered to fill pillow-cases. **1894** MISS F. WILLARD in *Chicago Advance* 4 Oct., One sees a thistledown borne on the breeze.

**b.** As a type of lightness, flimsiness, or instability; hence *fig.*

**1868** W. CORY *Lett. & Jrnls.* (1897) 251 The thistle-down of sentiment hung about me all the time. **1904** R. HICHENS *Gard. Allah* x, Forgive my malice...It was really a thing of thistledown. **1908** *Outlook* 27 Nov. 880/1 That is not to say that Christianity is to be a thistledown to be blown hither and thither at the breath of every fad and whim.

**c.** *attrib.* Of or like thistle-down (*lit.* and *fig.*).

**1561** *Will M. Langrygge* (Somerset Ho.), Thesseldowne bed. **1889** *John Bull* 2 Mar. 149/3 The train was of thistle-down brocade, that being the design brocaded, or rather embossed, upon the snowy surface of the silk. **1897** *Westm. Gaz.* 12 Feb. 2/1 The thistle-down character of Miss Hart.

**Thi·stle-finch.** [f. as prec. + FINCH; cf. G. *distelfink*, OHG. *distilvinko*, Du. *distelvink*.] Any one of several species of finches which feed on the seeds of the thistle; *spec.* the goldfinch, *Carduelis elegans*.

**1589** FLEMING *Virg. Georg.* III. 48 The singing thistle-finch. **1678** RAY *Willughby's Ornith.* 256 The Goldfinch, or Thistle-finch. **1736** AINSWORTH *Lat. Dict.* III. s.v. *Aëdon*, She is feigned to have died for grief, and to be turned into a linnet, or thistlefinch. **1851** BRODERIP *Leaves fr. Note Bk. Nat.* (1852) 230 The goldfinch or thistlefinch passes much of its time among flowers.

† **Thi·stle-tack.** *Obs.* exc. *Hist.* [Origin obscure: connexion with THISTLE *sb.* is doubtful; the second element is TACK *sb.*[2]] The name in some localities of a due levied upon the owners of pigs by the lord of the manor, as a charge for pannage. Cf. quot. 1523 for *tack-swine*, s.v. TACK *sb.*[2] 6.

**1303–5** *York Vac. Roll* (Ministers Accts. 1144/1, P.R.O.), Et de xs. vijd. de operibus custumariorum..cum pannagio quod dicitur thistiltak. **1327** *Inquis. Death Thomas Earl Lancaster* (I. P. M. Edw. III, File 6 (m. 3), P. R. O.) (Yorks., Soureby), Et de quadam consuetudine porcorum ibidem vocata Thisteltack ad terminum Sancti Andree xviij d. **1377** *Halymote of Halton*, etc. (Court Rolls 50 Edw. III, Bundle 2. No. 27), Et de iij s collectis de pannagio vocato Thisteltak pro porcis diversorum tenencium domini apud Runkorn. **1419** *Excheq. Accts.* 7 *Hen. V*, Bundle 131. No. 14 (Forest of Galtres, Yorks.) Sed de Thistiltak nichil quia nullum tale proficuum accidit hoc anno.

¶ The following accounts of the term are given by 17th c. writers:

**1677** THOROTON *Nottinghamshire* 308/1 If any Native or Cottager [at Fiskerton, Nottinghamshire] having a Swine above a year old, should kill him, he was to give the Lord 1d. and it was called Thisteltak. **1691** *Blount's Law Dict.* (ed. 2), *Thistle-take*,..a Custom in the honor of Halton, ..That if in driving Beasts over the Common, the Driver permits them to graze or take but a Thistle, he shall pay a half-peny a Beast to the Lord of the Fee. **1906** N. J. HONE *Manor & Manor. Recds.* 112 'Thistle-take' was claimed by the lords [of Manors] in Lancashire and Yorkshire, as an acknowledgment of the hasty crop taken by droves of beasts passing over a common, and similar payments.

(The statement in quot. 1691 (whence in 1906) was evidently 'popular etymology'.)

† **Thi·stlewarp.** *Obs.* [f. THISTLE *sb.* + WARP *v.*, to throw, turn, twist; cf. MOULDWARP.] The goldfinch: = THISTLE-FINCH.

**1606** MARLOWE & CHAPMAN *Hero & Leander* VI. 277 Neptune for pity..Flung them into the air, and did awake them Like two sweet birds, surnamed th' Acanthides, Which we call Thistle-warps, that..feed on thistle-tops. **1624** BURTON *Anat. Mel.* II. iii. VII, An asse flung downe a Thistlewarpes neast, the little bird pecked his gaul'd backe in revenge.

**Thistly** (þi·s'li), *a.* [f. THISTLE *sb.* + -Y.]

**1.** Of the nature of or resembling a thistle; spiny, prickly; consisting of or constituted by thistles. (In 1611, made of 'thistles', i. e. teasel-heads.)

**1598** SYLVESTER *Du Bartas* II. ii. IV. *Columnes* 625 That shell [of the chestnut] incas't in a thick thistly fell. **1611** COTGR., *Applaneur de draps*, the Cloathworker; who with his thistly cards doth smooth, and stroake down clothes. **1784** COWPER *Task* VI. 768 The land..Exults to see its thistly curse repealed. **1845** G. STRUTHERS in *Ess. Chr. Union* vii. (1851) 416 The plant of schism has put forth its thistly spines wherever it has been carried.

**2.** Full of, abounding or overgrown with thistles.

**1710** *Tusser Redivivus* in *T.'s Husb.* (1878) 129 *note*, Where the Wheat is thistly. **1727–46** THOMSON *Summer* 1658 Wide o'er the thistly lawn, as swells the breeze, A whitening shower of vegetable down Amusive floats. **1900** HUDSON *Nat. in Downland* 41 Thistly and weedy wastelands.

**3.** *fig.* (from 1 and 2).

**1784** COWPER *Task* IV. 335 A world, so thorny,..where none Finds happiness..Without some thistly sorrow at it's side. **1866** HOWELLS *Venet. Life* 342 Converted into a fortress..all thistly with bayonets. **1889** *Harper's Mag.* Mar. 661/1 Wandering..into thistly byways of dissent.

† **Thi·stolow.** *Obs. rare.* Altered form of *fistolow*, FISTULA: see TH (6).

**1684** HANNAH WOOLLEY *Queen-like Closet* (ed. 5) Supp. 25 When you dress any Wound or Thistolow with it, you must warm it very hot. *Ibid.*, I did cure a Gentlewoman of a Thistolow in the Eye with it.

**Thiswise** (ði·s,waiz), *adv.* Now *rare.* [Short for *a* (*on*) *this wise*.] In this manner, thus.

*13..* *Cursor M.* 11971 (Cott.) 'Sun', sco said, '[wirk] noght þis wise'. **1509** BARCLAY *Shyp of Folys* (1570) 244 Howe darest thou wretched men this wise abuse? **1530** TINDALE *Answ. More* Wks. (1572) 254/2 Whiche text may this wise be vnderstand. **1846** H. W. TORRENS *Rem. Milit. Hist.* 166 This-wise they slowly pursued their journey.

**This world.** The present world; the present state or stage of existence, as distinguished from another, esp. a future one. (Cf. OTHER WORLD.)

*c* **950** *Lindisf. Gosp.*, Luke xvi. 8 Suno ðisses woruldes [*c* **1000** *Ags. Gosp.* ðisse worulde bearn]. *a* **1175** *Cott. Hom.* 231 He cumð an ende þisser wrld. *c* **1175** *Lamb. Hom.* 7 Þeos world is whilende. **1382** WYCLIF *John* xvi. 11 The prince of this world is now demyd. **1470–85** MALORY *Arthur* XIII. vii. 621 They alle shalle neuer mete more in thys world. **1583** J. MUNDEN in J. B. Wainwright *Two Eng. Mart.* (C.T.S.) 24 Biddinge you farewell for ever in this worlde. **1705** STANHOPE *Paraphr.* III. 332 The perishing possessions of this World. **1883** MISS BRADDON *Gold. Calf* xiv, What higher office can a man hold in this world than to form the minds of the rising generation?

**b.** *attrib.* Pertaining to this world; mundane.

**1889** J. TITSWORTH in *Chicago Advance* 7 Feb., [To] appreciate the this-world sphere of the Kingdom of Heaven.

Hence (*nonce-wds.*) **Thi·s-wo·rldian**, a man of this world, a worldling; **Thi·s-wo·rldism, Thi·s-wo·rldliness**, devotion to the things of this world.

**1830** COLERIDGE *Ch. & St.* (1839) 77 Those..that separate the Christian from the this-worldian. **1872** HOWELLS *Wedd. Journ.* (1892) 269 A spiritual-worldliness which was the clarified likeness of this-worldliness. **1883** W. M. ADAMSON in *Evang. Union Worthies* 319 This-worldism ignored God, if it did not deny His existence. **1887** *Pall Mall G.* 19 Oct. 2/1 The Need of 'This-worldliness'...Evangelical Christians have been too often guilty of 'other-worldliness'.

**Thite**, obs. and dial. form of THIGHT.

**Thither** (ði·ðəɹ), *adv.* (*a.*) Forms: see below. [OE. *ðider*, *þider*, earlier *þæder* (Lindisf. *ðadder*): corresp. in form to ON. *þaðra* there; f. *þa-*, stem of THAT, THE + suffix, denoting motion towards, Goth. *-drē*, Vedic *-trā*: cf. *hither*, OE. *hider*, Goth. *hidrē*, and *whither*, OE. *hwider*:—*hwæder*, Goth. *hwadrē*; a form corresp. to OE. *þæder* is wanting in Goth. (which uses *jaindrē* thither, yonder); cf. Vedic *tatrā* there, thither. The OE. *þæder*, *hwæder* became *þider*, *hwider*, app. under the influence of *hider*, HITHER, in which the *i* was original. For the later ME. *-ther* for *-der* in all three words (first in MSS. of *Cursor Mundi*, but rare bef. 1525), as in *gather*, *mother*, etc., see TH (6), and Note s. v. FATHER. In Sc. *thidder* came down to 1600. The extended ME. *þidere*, *þidre*, was app. influenced by ordinary adverbs in *-e*.]

**1.** To or towards that place (with verb of motion expressed or implied). (Now almost exclusively literary; in ordinary speech superseded by THERE.)

*α.* 1 **þæder, ðadder.**

*a*900 *O. E. Martyrol.* 190 On merȝen com se biscop þæder. *Ibid.* 222 þa Thome þæder ineode. *c*950 *Lindisf. Gosp.* John vii. 35 Ðadder ðes færende is [*mistr.*]. *c*1000 ÆLFRIC *Exod.* xxxii. 34 Ga þu and læde þis folc þæder, þe ic þe ær sæde.

*β.* 1–3 **ðider,** (1 **ðieder**), 1–4 **þidder,** 1–5 **þider,** 3 (*Orm.*) **þiderr (tiderr),** 4 **thidur, þyder, -ir,** (**tyder**), 4–5 **þidur, -ir, thider,** 5 **thidir, -yr, thyd(d)ur,** 5–6 **thyder,** 6 **thidder, -ir.**

*a*900 tr. *Bæda's Eccl. Hist.* III. vi. [viii.] (1890) 174 þæt ȝyldne mynet..þætte þider of Cent cwom. *c*950 *Lindisf. Gosp.* John xi. 8 Eftersona ðu faeris ðidder [*c*975 *Rushw.* ðider]. *c*1000 ÆLFRIC *Deut.* i. 37 Ne færst þu þider. *c*1175 *Lamb. Hom.* 61 Crist us ȝife þider to cumen. *c*1200 ORMIN 17924, & tiderr comm þe follc till himm. *c*1250 *Gen. & Ex.* 1959 Ðan ruben cam ðider a-ȝen. 13.. *Cursor M.* 746 (Fairf.) Selcuþ was how he þidder [*v.r.* þider] wan. *c*1375 *Sc. Leg. Saints* iii. (*Andreas*) 23 He knew nocht [t]hydir þe way. *Ibid.* 1008 þare-for had he þidder socht. *c*1386 CHAUCER *Frankl. T.* 763 They ne wiste why she thider wente. 1388 WYCLIF *John* xviii. 3 He cam thidur with lanternys, and brondis, and armeris. 14.. *Voc.* in Wr.-Wülcker 588/46 *Illuc*, thydur. *c*1450 *St. Cuthbert* (Surtees) 347 How þe kyng sent hir thider. 1559 *Mirr. Mag.* (1563) H iv, Thyder they came wyth kynge Henry out of Skotlande. *a*1600 MONTGOMERIE *Misc. Poems* xi. 28 Thidder did I drau For to refresh my werynes.

*γ.* 1 **þyder,** 3–5 **þuder(ü).**

*Beowulf* 3086 Wæs þæt ȝifeðe to swið þe ðone þyder ontyhte. 971 *Blickl. Hom.* 29 Þæt he þyder come..mid his wyllan. 12.. *Moral Ode* 396 (Egerton MS.) Crist ȝyue us..þat we moten þuder [*v.r.* þider] come. 1297 R. GLOUC. (Rolls) 2509 þis king com þuder priueliche. 1387 TREVISA *Higden* (Rolls) III. 455 Moche folk was iflowe þider [*MS. γ.* þuder]. *Ibid.* IV. 445 Men..com þider [*γ.* þuder].

*δ.* 4–5 **þedir, -yr,** 4–6 **þeder,** 5 **-ur, þeoder.**

13.. *Cursor M.* 1700 (Cott.) Al þeir filth sal þedir [*Gött.* þeder] fall. *c*1350 *Will. Palerne* 2235 Whanne þei þeder come. *c*1400 *R. Gloucester's Chron.* 8078 (MS. *a*) Hii þeoder ne wende. *c*1400 *Destr. Troy* 13454 Thedur kynges wold come. 1447 BOKENHAM *Seyntys* (Roxb.) 165 Of hire thedyr goyng this was the entent. 1464 *Nottingham Rec.* II. 375 At their first ridyng thedir. 1536 WRIOTHESLEY *Chron.* (Camden) I. 50 After dynner the Kinges grace came theder in a maske.

*ε.* 4 **þeþir,** 5 **thethur,** 6–7 **thether.**

*a*1400 *Cursor M.* 17566 (Gött.) Þat iesus be noght rauist þeþir [*Cott., Trin.* þider]. *c*1420 *Avow. Arth.* xxii, Wold ȝe thethur be bowne. 1526 *Pilgr. Perf.* (W. de W. 1531) 14 By bothe wayes man may come thether. 1560 DAUS tr. *Sleidane's Comm.* 307 b, Thether came none at all; and hether but very fewe. 1653 HANE *Jrnl.* (1896) 1 A ship.. which I made use of for my transportacion thether.

*ζ.* 4 **þiþer, -ir,** 6 **thyther,** 6– **thither.**

*a*1400 *Cursor M.* 13692 (Gött.) þiþer [*v. rr.* þidder, þidur] ȝode he ai..þar to prai. 1523 LD. BERNERS *Froiss.* I. ccliii. 376 Thyther syr Eustace was ryght wellcome to all the company. 1548–9 (Mar.) *Bk. Com. Prayer, Collect Ascension Day*, We may also in heart and mind thither ascende. 1585 T. WASHINGTON tr. *Nicholay's Voy.* I. iv, Merchauntes comming thyther too lade salte. 1605 SHAKS. *Macb.* II. iv. 36 Will you to Scone? ..No, Cosin, Ile to Fife...Well, I will thither. 1709 STEELE & ADDISON *Tatler* No. 88 ⁋ 12 The Gentlewoman of the next House begged me to step thither. 1872 JENKINSON *Guide Eng. Lakes* (1879) 256 The road thither leaves the main road at right angles.

*η.* 3–4 **þidere, þudere(ü),** 4 **þedirre, þid(d)ire, þeodre,** 4–5 **þ-, thedere, þ-, thidere,** 5 **thed(d)re, thidre, thidyre,** 6 **thiddre.**

*c*1205 LAY. 8171 He wes þudere icumen. 1340–70 *Alex. & Dind.* 2 Rydinge þedirre. *Ibid.* 156 Drawen hem þiddire. 1393 LANGL. *P. Pl.* C. VIII. 292 Now most ich þudere, To loke how me lykeþ hit. *c*1400 *R. Gloucester's Chron.* (Rolls) 827 (MS. *a*) Pur meseise him þeodre [*v.r.* theder] drof. *Ibid.* 5721 Þe monekes out of abendone verst were þedere yuet. *c*1400 MAUNDEV. (1839) ii. 13 Grete Lordes that comen thidre. 1448 *Lett. Marg. Anjou & Bp. Beckington* (Camden) 101 To resorte thedre. 1473 WARKWORTH *Chron.* (Camden) 9 The Lorde Scales..was sent thedere. 1483 *Cath. Angl.* 382/2 Thidyre, *illo, illuc.* 1490 CAXTON *Eneydos* xxii. 81 Yf she went thidre. 1492 in 10*th Rep. Hist. MSS. Comm.* App. v. 323 Nor to goo theddre. 1507 in Leadam *Sel. Cas. Star Chamber* 252 He..resorted thiddre.

*θ.* (chiefly *north.*; perh. scribal errors.) 4 **didir dydur, dedur,** 5 **-yr;** 4 **diþer, deþir(e, -er, -ur.**

*a*1400 *Cursor M.* 2383 (Gött.) Als suith als þai diþer cam. *Ibid.* 14573 For didir gas sua mani man. *Ibid.* 14596 Deþir. *Ibid.* 17352 Deþire. *a*1400 *Stac. Rome* 66 To alle þat wylle deþur goo. 1482 *Monk of Evesham* (Arb.) 75 Al that.. whent not dedyr.

*ι.* 4 *Sc.* **yd(d)ir, -yr(e, -ire.** (app. for *þdir*, etc.)

*c*1375 *Sc. Leg. Saints* xvi. (*Magdalena*) 784, & yddir ewinely can hyr mark. (So xxxii. 352, xxxiii. 65, xl. 119; xxix. 347 ydir; xviii. 864 ydyr; vii. 616 yddyre; xvi. 384 yddire.)

†**b.** Followed by *in, out*: In or out thither.

971 *Blickl. Hom.* 207 Hie þyder inwæron to ðæm lofsangum ȝesamnode. *c*1000 ÆLFRIC *Saints' Lives* xxiii B. 500 Ic becom to sanctes iohannes cyrcan..and ic me þyder inneode. *c*1205 LAY. 31599 Ah Pendan ga þider ut anon. *a*1300 *Cursor M.* 22643 It sal..dump þe deuls þider in.

**c.** Defined by a relative clause introduced by *þe* or *þæt* (see 2), *whither, where*, or equivalent.

The relative clause with *whither*, etc., often precedes.

[*c*897, 1393, 1496: see 2.] *c*1380 WYCLIF *Serm.* Sel. Wks. II. 37 Wherever þe bodi be, þiþir shal þe eglis be giderid. For whidir ever comeþ Cristis bodi, þidir shal his seintis come. 1482 *Monk of Evesham* (Arb.) 35 They wondrid howe..he myght comme thedyr to that place, where the couent was. 1548–9 (Mar.) *Bk. Com. Prayer, Communion*, That where he is, thither might we also ascende. 1650 T. B. *Worcester's Apoph.* 27 The meanes of bringing her thither, where now she had but little way to go. *a*1700 DRYDEN *Ceyx & Alcyone* 440 She..thither by her destiny was brought, Where last he stood.

**d.** *Hither and thither*: see HITHER *adv.* 5.

†**2.** With relative *particle* (*þe, that, as*) = WHITHER *rel. adv.* (See THE *particle* 2, THAT *conj.* 6, AS 27.)

*c*897 K. ÆLFRED *Gregory's Past. C.* xi. 65 (Hatton MS.) Ðonne ne maȝon ðider fullice becuman ðā stæpas ðæs weorcas ðieder ðe he wilnað. 1393 LANGL. *P. Pl.* C. II. 119 For þider as þe fend flegh, hus fote for to sette, Ther he failede & ful. 1496 *Dives & Paup.* (W. de W.) VI. v. 237/1 Theder that the hede ledeth thyder sholde the bodye folowe.

†**3.** *transf.* **a.** Up to that time; until then. **b.** To or towards that end, purpose, result, or action.

13.. *Cursor M.* 5181 (Cott.) Yee sal ha lijf langer þen þider. 1600 SHAKS. *A. Y. L.* I. i. 179 This wrastler shall cleare all: nothing remaines, but that I kindle the boy thither.

**B.** *adj.* Lying on that side or in that direction, i.e. the side or direction away from *this*; the farther or more remote (of two things). A recent use, introduced as the opposite of HITHER *a.*

1830 LAMB *Let. to Wordsworth* 22 Jan., These all came in..on the thither side of innocence. 1857–8 SEARS *Athan.* 5 Death is not a transition to another existence on the thither side of nature. 1868 HAWTHORNE *Amer. Note-Bks.* (1879) II. 166 Between the hither and the thither row of houses. 1890 KIPLING in *Fortn. Rev.* XLVII. 165, I doubt that a double is to be found on the thither side of hell.

**Thi·ther,** *v.* Used in 'to hither and thither': see HITHER *v.*

1837 MRS. CARLYLE *Let. to Carlyle* 29 Aug. in *Lett. & Mem.* (1903) I. 61 Waiting for certainties; hithering and thithering being a condition under which I find it almost impossible to write. 1856, 1864 [see HITHER *v.*].

**Thitherto** (ðiðəɹtū·, ði·ðəɹtu), *adv.* [f. THITHER *adv.* + To *prep.*: after *hitherto.*]

**1.** Up to that time; until then. Now *rare.*

*c*1449 PECOCK *Repr.* I. iv. 19 The Iewis weren chargid with alle the lawis..with whiche the peple fro Adam thidir to weren chargid. 1529 MORE *Dyaloge* III. Wks. 205/2 All the men in effecte yt any faith had from Adam thetherto. 1654–66 EARL ORRERY *Parthen.* (1676) 655 Usage..which thitherto I had considered as an invitation. 1822 O'CONOR *Chron. Eri* I. p. vi, The thitherto one and only language. 1900 H. G. GRAHAM *Soc. Life Scot.* in 18*th C.* XIII. i. (1901) 476 Young men who had thitherto thronged to Holland.

†**2.** To that condition, point, or result. *Obs.*

1659 WHARTON *Cabal 12 Ho. Astrol.* Wks. (1683) 208 Although it be indeed new, and hitherto unheard of, yet it is firmly established upon Physical Reasons, and..is thitherto reduced. 1662 J. CHANDLER *Van Helmont's Oriat.* 313 The manner of comming thitherto..is moreover far remote.

**Thitherward** (ðiˑðəɹwǫ̈ɹd), *adv.* (*a.*) *arch.* [OE. *þiderweard*: see THITHER and -WARD.]

**1.** Towards that place; in that direction; thither.

*Hitherward and thitherward*: see HITHERWARD.

*c*893 K. ÆLFRED *Oros.* I. i. § 20 Ða he þiderweard seȝlode. *c*1000 ÆLFRIC *Josh.* x. 7 Iosue þa ferde mid his fyrde þiderweard. *c*1205 LAY. 1662 Swiðe he fusde þider ward kene his ferde. 1297 R. GLOUC. (Rolls) 9183 Anon he wende þuderward wiþ vair compainie. *a*1300 *Cursor M.* 9908 (Cott.) Þe man þat þider-werd [*v. rr.* þiþer-ward, thedirward] es fledd. 1340 HAMPOLE *Pr. Consc.* 979 Þider sal we com..If we þederward hald þe right way. 1393 LANGL. *P. Pl.* C. VIII. 205 This ys þe heye weye þyderwarde. 1433 *Rolls of Parlt.* IV. 425/1 His passage from hens thitherward. *a*1533 LD. BERNERS *Huon* lx. 208 Huon..saw a shyppe comynge thether warde. 1560 BIBLE (Genev.) *Jer.* l. 5 They shal aske the waye to Zion, with their faces thetherward. 1624 CAPT. SMITH *Virginia* v. 196 He.. instantly made thitherward in person. 1823 SCOTT *Quentin D.* viii, Were thy vocation in truth thitherward! 1884 ROE *Nat. Ser. Story* viii, All eyes turned thitherward.

†**2.** On the way thither; going thither. *Obs.*

*c*1000 ÆLFRIC *Saints' Lives* xxx. 200 Þa he ðyderweard wæs, ȝeseah he þæt an wulf ȝenam þæt [child]. *c*1175 *Lamb. Hom.* 3 Þa wes hit cud..þet þe helind wes þiderward, heo urnen on-ȝein him. *a*1300 *Cursor M.* 2956 (Cott.) Þiderward þair wonnyng was. *a*1400 *Stac. Rome* 242 ȝyf þou dye dydurward, Heuenne blys shalle be þy part. 1634 SIR T. HERBERT *Trav.* 28 He dared not to..plead his defence..in our Company and thitherward.

**B.** quasi-*adj.* Moving or directed thither. *rare.*

1795 SOUTHEY *Joan of Arc* VI. 49 The sentinel, soon as he heard Thitherward footsteps,.. Challenged the darkling travellers.

**Thi·therwards,** *adv. arch.* [f. prec.: see -WARDS.] = prec. 1.

*c*888 K. ÆLFRED *Boeth.* xxxix. § 5 He..tiohhode hit ðeah þiderweardes. *c*1000 ÆLFRIC *Saints' Lives* xxiii B. 724 Heo..ofer þa hnescan yða þæs wæteres eode swa swa heo ær dyde þyder-weardes. 13.. *Sir Beues* (A.) 125 Þederwardes he gan gon Wiþ outen demere. 1484 *Cely Papers* (Camden) 149 On Tewysday nexte they schall departe theder warddes. 1592 MARLOWE *Edw. II*, v. ii, So, now away! post thitherwards amain. 1756 *Phil. Trans.* LV. 189 The air of the lower regions [is] flowing thitherwards. *a*1850 ROSSETTI *Dante & Circ.* I. (1874) 40, I had occasion to..go thitherwards where she abode. 1886 *Cornh. Mag.* July 43 A number of rough labouring men..strolling thitherwards.

†**Thi·therways,** *adv. Obs. rare.* [f. THITHER + -WAYS: cf. *sideways*, etc.] On the way thither, in that direction, thitherwards.

1630 *R. Johnson's Kingd. & Commw.* 41 Suppose an enemie..be discovered at Sea upon the coast of Kent, thitherwayes presently make the Land forces.

[**Thitling,** spurious word; a misprint for TITHING, cited by Richardson from an ed. of Milton's Prose Wks., and thence in recent American Dictionaries.]

‖**Thitsi, thitsee** (þi·tsī). *East Ind.* Also thet-, theet-, thietsee, thyt-si. [Burmese *pitsī*, *þissī* (written *sachchē*), f. *þit* tree, wood + *asī*, in comb. *-sī* gum: cf. *sē* to be sticky.] The 'black varnish tree', *Melanorrhœa usitatissima*, N.O. *Anacardiaceæ*, of Burma and Pegu; also applied to the varnish obtained from it.

1832 DON *Gen. Syst. Gard.* II. 67/1 *M*[*elanorrhœa*] *usitata.* ..Native of Hindostan..where it is called *Theet-tsee* or *Zitsi.* 1839 ROYLE *Bot. Himalayan Mts.* I. 178 *Melanorrhœa usitata* of Dr. Wallich,..the *theet-see*, or varnishing-tree of the Burmese,..abounds in a thick and viscid, greyish-brown fluid, which turns black soon after coming into contact with the air. 1858 HOGG *Veg. Kingd.* 244 The Black Varnish-Tree..grows..in the Burmese empire, on the banks of the Irrawadi, where it is called Theet-tsee, or Zit-si. 1858 SIMMONDS *Dict. Trade*, *Thetsee*, a varnish obtained from *Melanorrhœa usitata*, in Arracan, and used for lacquering. 1890 HALLETT 1000 *Miles* 284 A plain in which many great *thyt-si* (black-varnish trees) were growing.

**Thiuret** (þəi·iuret). *Chem.* [f. Gr. θε-ῖον sulphur (see THIO-) + -URET.] A light odourless crystalline powder, $C_8H_7N_3S_2$, used as a substitute for iodoform as an antiseptic.

1899 *Syd. Soc. Lex.* s.v., Sulphur separates out from thiuret in presence of alkalies, even at low temperatures. It owes its antiseptic properties to the separation of sulphur in a nascent state.

**Thivel, thible** (þi·v'l, þəi·v'l; þi·b'l, þəi·b'l). *Sc.* and *north. dial.* Forms: *α.* 5 **thyvelle,** 6 **thyvil,** 7– **thivel,** (9 *dial.* **thyvel, theevil, thieval,** etc.); *β.* 7– **thible,** (9 *dial.* **thibble, thybel,** etc.); *γ.* 9 *dial.* **thavel, thaivel, thabble,** etc.; *δ.* 9 *Sc.* **theedle**; for other forms see E. D. D. [Of obscure origin and history. The forms with *v* are app. the original, being found two centuries earlier, and used both in Scotland and the north of England, while the later forms with *b* are confined to n. Engl. The stem vowel is found variously as i, ī, e, ē, a, ā, ǭ, and əi; the earliest spellings have *y* (? i or ī), but the phonological development is not easy to trace.

In form, *thīvel* seems to correspond to OE. *þyfel* 'bush, leafy plant', but no links of connexion between this and the modern sense have been found. In its various current forms the word is in use from N. of Scotl. to S. Lancashire, W. and E. Yorksh.; this localization suggests a Norse origin, and it has been referred to OIcel. *þefja* (þe·vya); but this is a very rare word of doubtful standing, and in any case meant 'to thicken by beating or stamping' rather than 'to stir'. The actual ONorse name for a stirring-stick was *þvara*, between which and *thivel* there is of course no connexion.]

**1.** A stick for stirring porridge or anything cooked in a pot; a potstick. (See also quot. 1876, *γ.*)

*α.* 1483 *Cath. Angl.* 383/2 A Thyvelle, *spatula, vertimella.* 1570 LEVINS *Manip.* 126/17 A Thyuil, *rubicula.* 1768 ROSS *Helenore* 138 The thivel on the pottage pan, Shall strick my hour to rise. 1785 *Spanish Rivals* 8 He's a queer stick to make a thivel on. 1815 G. BEATTIE *John o' Arnha* (1826) 35 An' ay's they steer'd them wi' a thivel, They mummelt 'crowdy for the devil'. 1880 EDWARDS *Mod. Scot. Poets* I. 362 Soup ladles and theevils. 1889 BARRIE *Window in Thrums* vi, Nearly a foot having been cut..from the original ..to make a porridge thieval. 1894 HESLOP *Nthbld. Gloss.*, *Thivel, Thybel*, a round stick,..about fifteen inches long and three-quarters of an inch in diameter; used to stir porridge.

*β.* 1674 RAY *N. C. Words*, *A Thible or Thivel*, A Stick to stirre a Pot. 1764 ELIZ. MOXON *Eng. Housew.* (ed. 9) 109 With a paste-pin or thible stir in your flour to the butter. 1847 EMILY BRONTË *Wuthering Heights* xiii, The quicker the thible ran round..the faster the handfuls of meal fell into the water. 1863 E. WAUGH *Lancash. Songs* 54 Wi' th' edge o' th porridge thible [*rime* Bible].

*γ.* 1876 *Whitby Gloss.*, *Thabble*, the plug in the leaden milk-trough, which draws out and lets off the milk, while the cream is left behind.

*δ.* 1864 A. LEIGHTON *Myst Leg. Edinb.* (1886) 68 The stirring utensil called a 'theedle'. 1884 C. ROGERS *Soc. Life Scot.* I. vii. 233 Stirred with a wooden spurtle or theedle.

†**2.** = DIBBLE *sb. Obs.* (perh. an error in Ray).

1691 RAY *N. C. Words*, *Thible, Thivel*...Also a dibble, or setting-stick. Hence 1787 in GROSE *Provinc. Gloss.*

**Thixel, thixle** (þi·ks'l). Now *dial.* Forms: 4 **þixil, -el,** 5 **thyxyl, -le, -ill, -ille, -elle, (tyxhyl, tixil), thyxtyll, -ill, thistill,** 7 **thistle,** 8–9 **thi-, thyzle,** 9 **thixle, thicksell.** [ME. *þixil, þixel*, known *c*1300, not yet found in OE. = MDu. *dessel, dissel* (Du. *dissel*, LG. *dessel*), OHG. *dehsala, dehsla*, MHG. *dehsel, dichsel*, Ger. *deichsel*, in Upper Ger. dialects *dechsel, dächsel*; from OTeut. root **þehs-* (by-form **þihs-*), Indo-Eur. **teks-*: cf. OSlav. *tes-ati* to hew, *tesla* ax, Lith. *tasz-ȳti* to hew or shape with the ax. See Kluge *Etym. Wbch.*, and Schade.] An adz.

*c*1300 *E. E. Psalter* lxxiii. 7 [lxxiv. 6] Als in wodes of trees ..In ax and in thixil [*MS. E.* þixel] þai ite dounecaste. 1404 *Durham Acc. Rolls* (Surtees) 396, j thyxyll..j thyxtyll goug. 14.. *Nom.* in Wr.-Wülcker 726/37 *Hec acia*, a thyxylle. *c*1440 *Promp. Parv.* 491/2 Thyxyl, instrument (*S.* twybyle, *P.* thyxill), *ascia.* 1468 *Medulla Gram.* (MS. Cant.), *Ascia*, a thyxelle...*Celtes*, a cheselle or a thyxelle [*Harl. MS.* tixil]. 1562 *Wills & Inv. N. C.* (Surtees) I. 207, j mattoche, j thistill,..iij woumbles. 1611–12 *Knaresb. Wills* (Surtees) II. 34 One thistle, all my chissils. 1796 PEGGE *Derbicisms* (E.D.S.), *Thizle*, an adze. 1847–78 HALLIWELL, *Thixille*, an axe, or hatchet. 1888 *Sheffield Gloss.*, *Thicksell*, an adze. ..It has a crooked handle, and is used by wheelwrights, and for making spouts hollow, etc. [*E.D.D.* gives the forms thixle, thicksell, thizle, thyzle.]

‖ **Thlaspi** (þlæ·spi). *Bot.* Also 7 thlaspe, 8 thlaspy. [mod.L., a. Gr. θλάσπι, -ις, 'a sort of cress, the seed of which was bruised and used like mustard' (L. and Sc.).] A genus of cruciferous plants (tribe *Thlaspideæ*), containing about thirty species, chiefly annuals, bearing insignificant white, pink, or purplish flowers, succeeded by flattened orbicular seed-pods. *T. arvense,* Penny-cress, was formerly in repute for its medicinal qualities.

Formerly including *Capsella* or Shepherd's Purse, and loosely applied to Candytuft, etc.

**1562** TURNER *Herbal* II. 152 Thlaspi is named..in English triacle mustard, boures mustard, or dishe mustarde. **1579** LANGHAM *Gard. Health* (1633) 634 Thlaspi seeds eaten, purge choller. **1597** GERARDE *Herbal* II. xix. 207 The seede of Thlaspi..helpeth the sciatica. **1640** PARKINSON *Theat. Bot.* VII. xii. 839 That Thlaspi that the best do allow for the truest Thlaspi to be used in Treakle and Mithridate. **1725** *Bradley's Fam. Dict.* s. v. *Shepherds Purse*, Somewhat like the Leaves of Thlaspi. **1842** *Penny Cycl.* XXIV. 384/2 The genus Thlaspi is known by its silicles being emarginate at the apex with the valves winged at the back.

‖ **Thlipsis** (þli·psis). *Path.* [a. Gr. θλῖψις pressure, compression, from θλῑβ-ειν to press, squeeze.] (See quots.)

**1693** tr. *Blancard's Phys. Dict.*, Thlipsis. **1704** J. HARRIS *Lex. Techn.* I, *Thlipsis*, is a Compression of the Vessels, in an Animal Body. **1857** DUNGLISON *Med. Lex.*, *Thlipsis*, compression, and especially constriction of vessels by an external cause. Oppression. [Hence in mod. Dicts.]

So ‖ **Thlipsencephalus** (þli:psense·fălŭs) [Gr. ἐγκέφαλος brain]: see quot.; hence **Thli:psence·phalous** *a.*, of or pertaining to a thlipsencephalus.

**1857** DUNGLISON *Med. Lex.*, *Thlipsencephalus*,..a monster in whom the skull is open, not merely in the frontal and parietal, but also in the occipital regions. **1860** MAYNE *Expos. Lex.*, Thlipsencephalous.

**Thlummery**, obs. variant of FLUMMERY.

**Thnetopsychism** (þnĭtopsəi·kiz'm). [f. eccl. Gr. θνητόψυχος maintaining the mortality of the soul (f. θνητός mortal + ψυχή soul) + -ISM.] The doctrine (based on 1 *Tim.* vi. 16, 'who only hath immortality') held by the *Thnētopsȳchitæ*, a Christian sect which arose in Arabia in the third century, who believed that the soul dies with the body, and is recalled to life with it at the Day of Judgement.

[**1625** GILL *Sacr. Philos.* IV. 63 The *Thnatopsychitæ*, which thought that the soule of man came to nought, as the soules of the beasts.] **1882–3** W. F. TILLETT in *Schaff's Encycl. Relig. Knowl.* III. 2218 The still grosser error of soul-death, or thnetopsychism.

† **Tho**, *dem. pron.* and *adj.* (*rel. pron.*), *pl. Obs.* Forms: see below. [OE. *þá*, nom. and acc. pl. of *se, séo, þæt*, simple demonstrative, THAT, and definite article, THE; = OFris. *thâ*, OS. *thia* (also m. *thie, the*, f. *the*, n. *thiu*, OHG. m. *die, dia, dê*, f. *dio, dia, dê*, n. *diu, dei*, ON. m. *þeir*, f. *þær*, n. *þau*, Goth. m. *þai*, f. *þôs*, n. *þô*. The original form *þá, thā* remained in the northern dialect, where it still exists as Sc. *thae, theae*, N. Yorksh. *theeä*: see THAE. In midl. and south of England *þā* became regularly *þō* (found in Kentish *a* 1200), and remained in use as *tho* (*thoo, thoe*) to *c* 1550. As early as 1300 it began to be supplanted in the north by *þās*, and later in the south by *þōs*, which finally took its place in Standard Engl. as THOSE, q. v.]

**A. Illustration of Forms.**

**α.** 1–3 **ðá**, 1–5 **þá**, (3 **þæ**), 4 **þaa**, 4–6 **tha**, *Sc.* **þai, thai, thay** [6– *Sc.* THAE, q. v.]. *Early inflexions*: *dat.* 1 **þǽm, þám**, 2–3 **þan, þon**, 3 **þen**. *gen.* 1 **þára, þǽra, ðeara**, 2–3 **þare, þere**.

*c* **825** *Vesp. Psalter* ii. 10 Alle ða ðe doemað eorðan. *c* **1000** *Ags. Gosp.* Mark iv. 10 þa twelfe þe mid him wæron. *c* **1200** ORMIN 429 Swa ne didenn nohht ta twa þatt we nu mælenn ummbe. *Ibid.* 2796 þa menn þatt wel himm follʒhenn. *c* **1205** LAY. 9180 Seoððe him comen þæ [*c* 1275 þe] tiðinde of Crist godes childe. **1340** HAMPOLE *Pr. Consc.* 6435 Aparty of þa paynes sere. **13..** *Cursor M.* 6448 (Cott.) To þaa þat gret birþin bar. *c* **1375** *Sc. Leg. Saints* iv. (*Jacobus*) 317 To þai discipulis þe kynge Had granttit.. þar askine. *c* **1560** A. SCOTT *Poems* (S. T. S.) ii. 16 Tha stalwart knychtis. [**1583**–: see THAE.]

*dat.* *c* **893** K. ÆLFRED *Oros.* I. i. § 7 Betux þæm twæm ean sindon þas land Arocasia & Parthia. *Ibid.* II. vii. § 2 On þæm daʒum. *c* **1000** *Ags. Gosp.* Matt. iii. 1 On þam [*Rushw.* In þæm] daʒum com iohannes se fulluhtere. *c* **1160** *Hatton Gosp.* Matt. v. 44 Doð wel þan [*Ags. G.* þam] þe eow yfel doð. *c* **1200** *Trin. Coll. Hom.* 47 Swich þeu wes bi þan daʒen. *c* **1205** LAY. 747 Cuð he wes þen cnihten [*c* 1275 þeos cniþtes]. **1340** *Ayenb.* 11 To alle þon þet wyleþ by yborʒe. *Ibid.* 30 Of þan þet hi byeþ yhealde uor te amendi.

*gen.* *c* **825** *Vesp. Psalter* xiii. 3 Ðeara [L. *quorum*] muð awergednisse & bitterniss ful bið. *c* **893** K. ÆLFRED *Oros.* I. i. § 16 Þara wæron syx stælhranas. *c* **1000** *Ags. Ps.* (Th.) ii. (*heading*) Ælc þæra þe þysne sealm sincgð. *c* **1175** *Lamb. Hom.* 135 On ðere monne heorte. *c* **1205** LAY. 1776 Þere Freinsce monnen [*c* 1275 of þe Frense mennene]. *Ibid.* 3346 Heo sende..to þare cnihtene inne. *a* **1250** *Owl & Night.* 1584 (Cott.) On þare beire nede.

**β.** 2–3 **þeo.**

*c* **1175** *Lamb. Hom.* 47 Alle þeo þe ihereð godes weordes. *c* **1205** LAY. 9056 Þeo cudden Kinbeline. *a* **1225** *Leg. Kath.* 360 Cleopest þeo [*MS. C.* þoa] þinges godes. *c* **1300** *Beket* 721 Nameliche theo for alle other.

**γ.** 2–4 **þo**, (3 **to**), 3 **þoa**, 4 **þoo**, 4–6 **tho, thoo**, (5 **thow**), 6 **thoe.**

*c* **1175** *Lamb. Hom.* 79 Þo þet weren imakede engles. *c* **1200** *Trin. Coll. Hom.* 139 And bi þo daʒes luuede herodes ..his broðer wif. **1388** WYCLIF *Prov.* iv. 22 For tho ben lijf to men fyndynge thoo. *c* **1460** *Wisdom* 689 in *Macro Plays* 58 Now wyll we thre do make a dance Off thow þat longe to owur retenaunce. **1521** FISHER *Wks.* (1876) 316 In thoo causes that perteyne vnto god. **1526** TINDALE *Rev.* ii. 10 Feare none off thoo [COVERD. tho; *Gt. Bible* those] thynges which thou shalt soffre. **1553** BECON *Reliques of Rome* (1563) 238 All thoe that fraunches of holye Churche breake.

**B. Signification.**

**I.** Dem. pron.: pl. of THAT B. I.; = THOSE I. (they, them).

Often indistinguishable from 3rd pers. pron. *they*. The ME. north. and Sc. *þa* often ran together with *þai, þay*, they.

**1.** In general sense.

*c* **893** K. ÆLFRED *Oros.* I. i. § 21 Þa habbað him sylf cyning. *Ibid.* I. i. § 11 Binnan þæm sindon moneʒa þeoda. *c* **1000** *Sax. Leechd.* I. 290 Heo hafaþ leaf sinewealte and ða bittere on byrgincge. [Cf. THOSE I. 2 b.] *c* **1205** LAY. 6403 Þeo [*c* 1275 hii] fihten wið þone duke. *a* **1300** *E. E. Psalter* cxxiii[i]. 6 Þat noght gaf us swa In taking of tothe of þa. *a* **1310** in Wright *Lyric P.* vii. 29 Ne lete for non of tho. **13..** *Cursor M.* 8817 (Gött.) Þus þa [*C., F.* þai, *Tr.* þei] proued it thre days. **1388** WYCLIF 1 *Kings* vi. 12 If thou..kepist alle my comaundementis, and goist bi tho [1382 hem; L. *per ea*]. **1390** GOWER *Conf.* I. 52 Tho be proprely the gates, Thurgh whiche..Comth alle thing. **1434** MISYN *Mending Life* II. vi. 116 Be þame þa wote endles lyfe to wynn. *c* **1440** *Generydes* 888 Peraventour I myght be on of thoo. **1573** *Satir. Poems Reform.* xlii. 231 Quhair ar tha? **1596** DALRYMPLE tr. *Leslie's Hist. Scot.* x. (S.T.S.) II. 298 Sa tha facht that betueine thame was amissing a thousand or thairabout. *a* **1600** MONTGOMERIE *Misc. Poems* xiv. 9, I am not one of tho.

**2.** As antecedent pronoun followed by a relative clause or its equivalent: = THOSE B. I. 4.

*c* **825** *Vesp. Psalter* cxxxiv. 2 Ða ðe stondað in huse dryhtnes. *c* **1000** *Ags. Ps.* (Th.) v. 5 Þu hatast ealle þa þe unriht wyrcað. *a* **1175** *Cott. Hom.* 219 Heo ʒescop ʒesceafte þaða he wolde. *c* **1200** ORMIN 53 Þa þatt wærenn gode menn. *c* **1205** LAY. 6420 Þeo [*c* 1275 þaie] þat hit iseʒen. *a* **1225** *Ancr. R.* 32 Habbeð reouþe of þeo þet beoð ine. *c* **1300** *Harrow. Hell* 82 Alle þo þat bueþ heryne. *c* **1330** R. BRUNNE *Chron. Wace* (Rolls) 13903 Seide Arthur þen to þo þer ware. **13..** *Cursor M.* 1529 (Cott.) Þaa [*v.rr.* þai, þei] þat þa [þer, þir] wonders werkes wroght. *c* **1385** CHAUCER *L. G. W.* 1531 (*Hypsiphyle*) Alle tho that lyuyn & been dede. *c* **1400** *Rule St. Benet* 12 Of þe þridde maner o mekenes spekys sain benet to þa in his reul wyl be. *c* **1400** MAUNDEV. (Roxb.) iii. 10 Þa þat schafes þaire berdes. **1463** *Bury Wills* (Camden) 29 The chymes, as wel tho that been in Seynt Marie stepill as tho that been [etc.]. *c* **1475** *Rauf Coilʒear* 802 The maist man of all tha That euer he had sene. **1509** FISHER *Wks.* (1876) 271 Blessyd are tho whiche haue made vertuous ende. *a* **1533** LD. BERNERS *Huon* lvii. 193 All tho in your company. **1553** BECON *Reliques of Rome* (1563) 238 b, All thoe y[t] be common robbers.

**II.** Dem. adj.

**3.** Plural of THAT B. II.; = THOSE II.

*c* **893** K. ÆLFRED *Oros.* I. i. § 16 Þa deor hi hatað hranas. *Ibid.* § 17 On þæm morum eardiað Finnas. *a* **1123** *O. E. Chron.* an. 1119, Þa tweʒen cyngas..mid heoran folcan. *c* **1200** *Trin. Coll. Hom.* 51 Þo word muneʒeð us. *c* **1330** R. BRUNNE *Chron. Wace* (Rolls) 461 Custume was bi þo dawes. **13..** *Cursor M.* 2590 (Cott.) Als it was hight be-for þaa [*v.rr.* þa, þas] dais. *c* **1386** CHAUCER *Prol.* 500 Out of the Gospel he tho wordes caughte. **1412–20** LYDG. *Chron. Troy* I. 1755 Al-þei he were a paynym in þo dawes. **1502** ARNOLDE *Chron.* (1811) 146 Whoo kysseth thoo crosses hath v. C. yere of pardon. **1526** TINDALE *Acts* xviii. 17 Gallio cared for none of tho thynges. **1553** KENNEDY *Compend. Tract.* in *Wodrow Soc. Misc.* (1844) 108 The juge that wes in tha dayis.

**b.** In concord with a sb. antecedent to a relative.

*c* **893** K. ÆLFRED *Oros.* I. i. § 22 Ealle ða menn ðe swyftoste hors habbað. *Ibid.* § 25 Þa land þe man hæt Gallia Bellica. *c* **1000** *Ags. Ps.* (Th.) iii. (*heading*), Ælc þæra manna þe þisne sealm singð. **1122** *O. E. Chron.*, Ealle þa gersumes þe þær binnen wæron. *c* **1175** *Lamb. Hom.* 125 Ða songes þa we nu singeð. **1382** WYCLIF *Prov.* i. 22 Tho thingus that ben noʒesum to them. **1418** HEN. V in *Proc. Privy Counc.* (1834) II. 244 Al þoo personnes þat been oure sugettes. *c* **1450** tr. *De Imitatione* III. i. 64 Blessid be þo eres þat receyueþ of goddys rounynge. **1526** [see A. γ]. **1579** SPENSER *Sheph. Cal.* Sept. 32 In tho countryes, whereas I haue bene.

**4.** Plural of definite article THE.

*c* **825** *Vesp. Psalter* v. 6 Ne ðorhwuniað ða unrehtwisan biforan eʒum ðinum. *c* **850** *O. E. Chron.* an. 2, And þa cild on Bethlem of slæʒene wærun for Cristes ethnesse from Herode. *c* **893** K. ÆLFRED *Oros.* I. i. § 15 Þa Finnas, him þuhte, and þa Beormas spræcon neah an ʒeþeode. *c* **1000** *Ags. Gosp.* Matt. v. 5 Eadiʒe synt þa liðan [*Lindisf.* ða milde], forþam þe hi eorðan aʒun. *a* **1123** *O. E. Chron.* an. 1116, Eallæ þa husas. *Ibid.* an. 1117, Þurh þa renas. *c* **1175** *Lamb. Hom.* 11 Þa halie daʒes. *c* **1200** *Moral Ode* (Egerton MS.) 192 He scal deme þo quike and to dede. *a* **1300** *Cursor M.* 861 (Cott., Gött.) He wend to hide him amang þa [*F., Tr.* þe] tres.

**III. 5.** Relative pron., plural of THAT *rel. pron.*

*c* **825** *Vesp. Psalter* viii. 4 Steorran ða ðu ʒesteaðulades. *c* **1000** *Ags. Ps.* (Th.) cxliii. 9 Fremdra bearna, and frecenra, þara [L. *quorum*] muðas sprecað man-idel word. *c* **1175** [see 3 b]. *c* **1200** *Trin. Coll. Hom.* 21 Us..and alle þo nede habbeð. *c* **1205** LAY. 7121 For uncuðe leoden þeo þis londe habbeð bi-wunnen. *Ibid.* 6415 Alle þa [*c* 1275 þe] he funde. *Ibid.* 7789 He sette reuwen stronge & hæʒen þo fengen þa lond-gauel. **1422** tr. *Secreta Secret., Priv. Priv.* 160 His Sonnes tha wickyd men were. *a* **1425** *Cursor M.* 5237 (Trin.) Manassen and effraym þo [*earlier MSS.* þat] in egipte his wif him bare whiche [*v.rr.* þat, þe quilk] þe kyng had geten him þare.

**Tho**, *adv.* (*conj.*) *Obs.* exc. *dial.* Forms: 1–4 **þá**, (1 **ðá, tha**), 2–5 **þo**, (5 **þoo**), 3 **þeo, þeoa, ðoa** (**ta, to**), 4 **þaa, þae**, 4–5 **thoo**, 4–7 (*dial* –9) **tho**, (5–6 **thoe**). [OE. *ðá, þá* = ON. *þá* (Norw. *daa*, Sw. *då*, Da. *da*) then, when; orig. a case-form of the demonstr. stem *þa-* of THE, THAT; either the actual acc. sing. fem., OE. and ON. *þá*, or (as some think) a stressed form of the orig. acc. masc.; meaning 'that time', the sb. being omitted: cf. L. *tum, tam.* (But cf. also the sense-equivalent OS. *thō, thuo*, OHG. *dô, duo.*) In ME. *þā* remained in the north, but *c* 1200 regularly became *þō, thō* in midland and south. *Tho, thoa* still remains = then, at that time, in the south-west.]

**1.** As demonstrative adv.: Then. **a.** At that time: = THEN *adv.* 1. Now *dial.* (In quot. *c* 1385 preceded by a prep.: = THEN *adv.* 7.)

*c* **893** K. ÆLFRED *Oros.* I. i. § 14 Þa for he norþryhte be þæm lande. *c* **897** — *Gregory's Past. C.* 2 Hu ʒesæliʒlica tida þa wæron ʒeond Angelcynn. *c* **1000** ÆLFRIC *Hom.* II. 378 Hit mæʒ eow nu fremian swa micclum swa hit ða mihte. *c* **1200** *Trin. Coll. Hom.* 51 Nimeð forbisne efter þe olde men þe þo weren. *a* **1225** *Juliana* 9 As me luuede þa. *a* **1300** *Cursor M.* 6383 (Cott.) Þis mete þat þai war fed of þaa [*v. rr.* þo, þan] þai cald it..manna. *c* **1330** R. BRUNNE *Chron. Wace* (Rolls) 7936 Þe kyng þankede God þo. *Ibid.* 16261 Þider cam nought þo Osewy. *c* **1385** CHAUCER *L. G. W.* 1060 (*Dido*) The queene..had herde ofte of Eneas er thoo. **1390** GOWER *Conf.* I. 6 Tho was the lif of man in helthe, Tho was plente, tho was richesse. *c* **1420** *Chron. Vilod.* 46 Fiue maner of pepull here dwellyd þo. **1513** DOUGLAS *Æneis* I. vi. 68 As was the maner tho. **1549–62** STERNHOLD & HOPKINS *Ps.* lxxviii. 6 They and their posteritie, Which were not sprong up tho. **1600** *Sheph. Slumber* in *Eng. Helicon* (1887) 222 In peascod time..I went to gather strawberries tho. **1888** ELWORTHY *W. Som. Words*, *Tho*, adv. of time, then. Still the usual form here...'Her told'n he should have his money, but her 'adn a-got it *tho*.'

† **b.** (Next) after that, upon that, thereupon: = THEN *adv.* 3. *Obs.*

*c* **700** CÆDMON *Hymn* 7 He aerist scop..heben til hrofe.. Tha middunʒeard [etc.]. *c* **893** K. ÆLFRED *Oros.* I. ii. § 1 Þa æt nyhstan he wæs feohtende wið Sciððie. *a* **1000** *Juliana* 594 Þa se dema wearð hreoh & hyʒegrim. **1131** *O. E. Chron.* (Laud MS.) an. 1127, Siððen þa nam he þes kynges wifes swuster of France to wife. *a* **1175** *Cott. Hom.* 225 Þo warð god toðan swiðe ʒegremed þurh mannamandede. *c* **1200** ORMIN 225, & ta þeʒʒ wisstenn sone anan Forr whatt he dwelledd haffde. *a* **1225** *Ancr. R.* 428 Ette mete no word, oðer lut, & þeo beon stille. *c* **1275** LAY. 3616 Þo [*c* **1205** þon] nam Leir þe king his leofeste cnihtes. *c* **1386** CHAUCER *Sompn. T.* Prol. 18 Vn-to this Angel spak the frere tho. **1470–85** MALORY *Arthur* XVII. i. 689 Whanne Galahad had rescowed Percyual..he yede tho in to a waste foreste. **1579** SPENSER *Sheph. Cal.* Jan. 11 Tho to a hill his faynting flocke he ledde. **1642** H. MORE *Song Soul* I. II. xxxv, Tho I gan closely on his person look.

† **2.** As relative or conjunctive adv.: When, at the time that. (Often correlative to *þa* in sense 1.)

*Beowulf* (Z.) 462 Ða hine gara cyn,..habban ne mihte. *c* **893** K. ÆLFRED *Oros.* I. i. § 20 Ða he þiderweard seʒlode..þa wæs him on þæt bæcbord Denamearc. **971** *Blickl. Hom.* 19 Hwæt he dyde þa hine seo meneʒo þreade. **1154** *O. E. Chron.*, Þa þe king was ded, þa was þe eorl beionde sæ. *c* **1175** *Lamb. Hom.* 11 Þa ten laʒe þe þa israelisce folc sceolde halden þa he heom ledde of egipte londe. *a* **1225** *Ancr. R.* 314 He was lutel child þeoa he hit dude. *a* **1250** *Owl & Night.* 1690 Ah hit was unker uoreward, Þo we come hiderward. *c* **1250** *Death* 20 in *O. E. Misc.* 168 We weren poure þa we hider come. **13..** *K. Alis.* 1648 (Bodl. MS.) Afterward þoo it was niʒth, Hij founden [etc.]. **1377** LANGL. *P. Pl.* B. Prol. 176 Ac þo þe belle was ybouʒt..Þere ne was ratoun..Þat dorst haue ybounden þe belle aboute þe cattis nekke. *c* **1425** *Seven Sag.* (P.) 183 Uppon morwen, tho it was day, The childe awakid.

† **b.** Also followed by *the* conj. (*þa þe*), in same sense: = When that, when. See THE *particle* 2 a.

*c* **1000** *Ags. Psalter* (Surtees) xlviii. 21 Ða ðe he in are wæs. *a* **1175** *Cott. Hom.* 219 Þaðe hi wolde mid modinesse beon betere þonne he ʒesceapen were. *Ibid.* 223 Þaðae he slep þa ʒename he ribb of his sidan. *c* **1175** *Lamb. Hom.* 79 Þa þe he heuede scome aʒeines his scuppende þa he hefde þurst and hunger.

**Tho, þo**, obs. inflexions of THE.

**Tho, tho'**, abbrev. forms of THOUGH.

**Thoan** (þōu·ăn), *a. Zool.* ? *Obs.* [f. THO-US + -AN.] Of or pertaining to canine beasts of or akin to the subgenus *Thous*; in a restricted application including certain African jackals, but often extended as in THOOID.

**1839** C. H. SMITH *Dogs* I. iv. 193 The Thoan group represents in form the wolf on a reduced scale. **1842** *Penny Cycl.* XXIV. 240/2 A race of..dogs..in Arabia..of Thoan form.

**Thoch, thocht**, obs. Sc. forms of THOUGH.

**Thocht**, Sc. f. THOUGHT [1], and pa. t. and pple. of THINK *v.*[1] and [2]; so **Thochtful, Thochty.**

† **Thode.** *Obs. rare.* Forms: 1 **þoden**, 3 **þode, þodde**, 7 **thode**, (9 **thod**). [OE. *þoden* str. masc., ? f. stem *þud-* of OE. *þyddan* (:—**þudjan*), pa. t. *þudde*, to strike, thrust, push, THUD.] A violent wind, a whirlwind. With quot. 1684 cf. THUD *sb.* 1.

*c* **725** *Corpus Gloss.* (O. E. T.) 136 *Alcanus* [? Altanus], þoden. *c* **897** K. ÆLFRED *Gregory's Past. C.* xviii. 128 Sio ʒeornfulnes..ablent ðæs modes eaʒan..suæ suæ dust deð ðæs lichoman eaʒan on sumera mid ðodene [*v. r.* ðodne]. *a* **1000** *Ags. Voc.* in Wr.-Wülcker 203/5 *Ceruleis turbinibus*, laʒeflodum þodenum. *c* **1000** ÆLFRIC *Gram.* ix. (Z.) 37 *Turbo*, ðoden. *c* **1012** *O. E. Chron.* an. 793 (MS. D.) Her wæron reðe forebecna cumene ofer Norðanhymbra land... þ[æt] wæron ormete þodenas & liʒrescas. *c* **1205** LAY. 27645 He þraste to þan fihte swa þode [*c* **1275** þodde] doþ on felde. **1684** BUNYAN *Seasonable Counsel* 206 Those thodes, gusts, blasts, or battering storms that beat against thy wall. [**1867**

SMYTH *Sailor's Word-bk.*, *Thods*, an old northern term for sudden gusts of wind.]

**Thoe**, var. THO *pron., adj.*, and *adv. Obs.*

**Thoes**, pl. of THOS, a canine beast; obs. f. THOSE.

**Thof(e, thoff(e**, obs. or dial. ff. THOUGH.

**Thof, thoft**, obs. and dial. ff. THOUGHT [1]; see also THINK *v.*[2]

**Thoft** (þǫft). Now *north. dial.* Forms: 1 þofta, 4 thoffte, 4– thoft, 9 *Sc.* thaft (*Shetl.*, *I. of Man* taft, taff). [OE. *þofte* (wk. fem.), = ON. *þopta* (Norw., Da. *tofte*), OHG. *dofta*; MLG., LG. *ducht*, whence Ger. *ducht* (*duft*), MDu. *dofte, dochte*, Du. *doft*:—OTeut. **þuftô*:—Indo-Eur. **tuptā*, f. root **tup* to squat, sit low. Also Gaelic *tobhta* from Lowland Sc. or Norse. See also THOUGHT [2].

*þofta* in quot. *c* 1000 is either a scribal error for *þoftan*, or pl. of a str. fem. *þoft*.

It is remarkable that this word, which must have lived on in the north, should appear only once between 1336 and the 19th c.]

A rower's bench; = THWART *sb.*[2]

*c* 1000 ÆLFRIC *Voc.* in Wr.-Wülcker 166/17 *Transtra*, scipsetl. *Transtra*, uel *juga*, þofta. *c* 1050 *Suppl. Ælfric's Voc.* ibid. 182/5 *Transtra*, þoftan. 1307–8 *Acc. Exch. K. R.* Bd. 14 No. 14 (P. R. O.), In .C. bordis estricis emptis..ad faciendum inde Thoftes, Hurdys, et cotes pro dicta Bargia ..xv. s...In .vj. bordis emptis ..ad ponendum sub Thoftis.. iij. s. 1336 *Acc. Exch. K. R.* Bundle 19. No. 31. m. 6 Et in xiiij lignis emptis pro Thofftes inde faciendis precium cuiuslibet .vj. d. 1513 DOUGLAS *Æneis* v. iii. 63 (Camb. MS.) The remanent of ye rowaris.. Apon yair scyttis and thoftis all atanys Yair placis hynt. [Cf. Virg. v. 136 *considunt transtris.*] 1808–18 JAMIESON, *Thafts*, the benches of a boat, on which the rowers sit. 1827 *Blackw. Mag.* XXI. 859 This waterman on one 'thoft' presenting the breadth of his oar before the wind and with the stream. 1834 H. MILLER *Scenes & Leg.* xvii. (1857) 251 One of the poor fellows tumbled over the thaft. 1876 *Whitby Gloss.*, *Thofts*, the thwarts, or plank-seats across a boat. 1885 RUNCIMAN *Skippers & Sh.* 21 Leapt lightly on the thoft. 1887 T. E. BROWN *Doctor* 18 (I. of Man) Sortin them out On the taff. 1891 BURGESS *Rasmie's Büddie* 51 (Shetl.) Strik rouwin faider frae his taft. 1904 *Eng. Dial. Dict.* s.v. (Shetl.), In a boat the thoft where the mast stands is called the sailing thoft.

*Comb.* 1847–78 HALLIWELL, *Thoft-fellow*, a fellow oarsman. [Cf. 1874 VIGFUSSON *Icel. Dict.*, *þôpti*, a bench-fellow.]

**Thoȝen, þoȝen**, pa. pple. of THEE *v.*[1] *Obs.*

**Thogh, þoȝ, þogh, thoght**, obs. ff. THOUGH.

**Thoght, þoȝt**, etc., obs. ff. THOUGHT [1]: see also THINK *v.*[1] and [2].

**Thoil(l**, obs. Sc. f. THOLE *v.*; erron. f. TOLL *sb.*

**Thoke** (þōᵘk), *a.* and *sb.* Now *dial.* [Late ME.; origin unascertained.]

†**A.** *adj.* Not firm or solid; unsound. *rare*—⁰.

*c* 1440 *Promp. Parv.* 491/2 Thoke, as onsadde fysche, *humorosus.*

**B.** *sb.* †**1.** An unsound fish: see quots. *Obs.*

1482 *Rolls of Parlt.* VI. 222/1 That tale fish shuld not be pakked with the lesse fish called Grilles, nor there shuld be pakked therwith neither Thokes nor broken belied fissh. [Cf. 1482–3 *Act 22 Edw. IV*, c. 2 § 3 Saunz mixture & pakkur dez chosez et [*v. r.* thokes ou] pessons rompez le ventre.] 1494–5 *Act 11 Hen. VII*, c. 23 Without medling and packing of Thokys or broken belied fisshe with the seid tale fisshe or small fisshe. 1758 *Descr. Thames* 259 Of barrelled Fish. Grills, Thokes, &c.

**2.** *dial.*, *School slang.* (See quots.)

[*a* 1485 *Promp. Parv.* (Winch. MS., ed. 1908) 97 Cowerde, herteles, long choke [*suggested reading* 582 thoke], *vecors.*] 1891 WRENCH *Winchester Word-bk.*, *Thoke*,..a rest, a lying in bed, an idling.

Hence **Thoke** *v.* 'to lie late in bed, to be idle; *thoke on*, to look forward to; **Tho·kester**, an idler' (*Winchester Word-bk.*); **Tho·kish, Thoky** *adjs. dial.*: see quots.

*a* 1682 SIR T. BROWNE *Tracts* viii. (1684) 146 Words..of common use in Norfolk..as..Thokish. 1691 RAY *S. & E. C. Wds.* Pref. *ad fin.*, *Cothish*, morose, and *thokish*, slothful, sluggish, I have no account to give of. 1847–78 HALLIWELL, *Thokish*, slothful; sluggish. *East.* In Lincolnshire it is usually *thoky.*

†**Tho·lance.** *Sc. Obs.* [f. THOLE *v.* + -ANCE; cf. *sufferance.*] Sufferance, toleration; cf. THOLING *vbl. sb.* 2.

1456 SIR G. HAYE *Law Arms* (S.T.S.) 171 Throu the permissioun and tholaunce of God. 1470 *Regr. Aberbrothoc* (Bann. Cl.) 162 Suppos the said abbot and conuent dois ws fauor in the sasyng of the said anwellis.., of thar gracious tholance and prestance. 1479 *Act. Dom. Conc.* (1839) 39/1 Gife..his predecessouris occupijt þe said acris..,and quheþir as malaris, or tholance or propirte to þe chapellanery. ?15.. *Brechine Reg.* lf. 92 (Jam.) Hed ony richt to the said tak bot allanerly off tholance.

**Thole** (þōᵘl), *sb.*[1] Forms: 1 thol, ðoll, þol; 5–6 tholle, 6–8 thoule, 7–8 thowle, 8 thoul, 9 thowel(l, thowl, (thauel), 7– thole. [OE. *þol(l*, corresp. to ON. *þollr*, Norw. *toll, tulle*, Sw. (*år*) *tull*, Da. (*aar*) *tol*; MLG. *dolle, dulle, dole, doule*, LG. (Brem. Wbch.) *dolle, dulle*, EFris. *dolle, dol*, MDu. *dolle*, Du. *dol(l.* Ulterior etymology uncertain. In ON. *þollr* was also 'fir-tree', poet. 'tree' generally: the connexion of sense is not clear. The history of the Eng. word also shows a hiatus during nearly the whole ME. period.

The late altered forms *thoule, thowle*, and 19th c. *thowel*, may be influenced by *doule, dowle*, DOWEL.]

**1.** A vertical pin or peg in the side of a boat against which in rowing the oar presses as the fulcrum of its action; *esp.* one of a pair between which the oar works; hence, a rowlock.

*c* 725 *Corpus Gloss.* (O. E. T.) 1820 *Scalmus*, thol. *c* 1000 *Voc.* in Wr.-Wülcker 289/9 *Scalmus*, ðoll. 1611 COTGR., *Scalme*, a Thowle; the little peg whereby the oare of a Skiffe is staied. 1624 CAPT. SMITH *Virginia* 62 In stead of thoules wee made sticks like Bedstaues. 1697 DAMPIER *Voy. round World* (1699) 35 Straps..through which they put their Oars in rowing, instead of tholes or pegs. 1769 FALCONER *Dict. Marine* (1789), *Autarelles*, the thoules or rowlock-pins of a galley. 1827 ROBERTS *Voy. Centr. Amer.* 178 These oars are secured to the thowel by straps of raw hide. 1847 LONGF. *Evang.* II. ii. 102 The sound of their oars on the tholes had died in the distance. 1857 P. COLQUHOUN *Comp. Oarsman's Guide* 29 The row-lock is composed of 3 parts; the thauel, against which you row [etc.]. 1862 WHITTIER *Cry Lost Soul* iv, The guide.. drops his oar against the gunwale's thole.

**2.** A pin or peg in general: *spec.* **a.** A pin by means of which the shafts are fastened to the carriage or axle of a cart, etc. **b.** The handle or 'nib' of a scythe-snathe.

*c* 1440 *Promp. Parv.* 492/1 Tholle, carte pynne (or tolpyn, *infra*), *cavilla.* 1530 PALSGR. 280/2 Tholle a cartpynne, *cheuille de charette.* 1707 SLOANE *Jamaica* I. p. lii, The use of..drums made of a piece of a hollow tree, covered on one end with any green skin, and stretch'd with Thouls or Pins. 1828 WEBSTER, *Thole*, 2. the pin or handle of a sythe-snath. 1880 R. S. CHARNOCK *Essex Gloss.*, *Thole*, the two pieces or handles of a scythe. 1910 H. BELLOC *Mr. Clutterbuck's Election* iv, The woodwork..was designed in the Cheshire fashion, with drawpins, tholes, and spring-heads tinctured to a sober brown.

†**Thole**, *sb.*[2] *Obs. rare*—¹. [f. THOLE *v.*] Patience, forbearance, endurance.

*c* 1250 *Gen. & Ex.* 3496 Ic am god, gelus and strong, Min wreche is hard, min ðole is long.

†**Thole**, *sb.*[3] *Obs. rare.* [Anglicized f. L. *thol-us*: see THOLUS.] See quot. 1656, and cf. THOLUS.

1633 [J. FISHER] *True Trojans* III. ii. E ij, Let Altars smoake, and Tholes expect our spoiles. 1656 BLOUNT *Glossogr.*, *Thole* (*tholus*),..that place in Temples, where donaries and such gifts as were presented there, are hung up.

**Thole** (þōᵘl), *v.* Now *north. dial.* or *arch.* Forms: 1 þolian, 2–3 -ien, (2 þale(n), 2–4 þolye, -ie, -en, 3 (*Orm.*) þolenn, 3–4 -yen, 4 þoole, tholen, -y, 4–5 þole, tholie, 4– thole. (Also 4, 6 *Sc.* thol, 4 (5–6 *Sc.*) thoile, 4–6 *Sc.* thoill, 5 þoliȝe, þol(l, thoole, thowle, tholl, 6 (7–8 *Sc.*) thoell, 8 *n. dial.* thoyl, 6– *Sc.* and *n. dial.* thoil.) [OE. *þolian* = OS. *tholôn, tholian*, OHG. *dolôn, dolên* (MHG. *dolen, doln*; cf. Ger. *gedul-d*), ON. *þola* (Da. *taale*, Sw. *tåla*), Goth. *þulan*, f. OTeut. stem **þul-*:—weak grade of root **tel*: **tol*: **tl* to bear, suffer: cf. L. *tuli, tol-erare, toll-ere*, Gr. τλῆναι.]

**1.** *trans.* To be subjected or exposed to (something evil); to be afflicted with; to have to bear, suffer, endure, undergo.

*Beowulf* 832 Hie..for þreanydum þolian scoldon torn un-lytel. *c* 897 K. ÆLFRED *Gregory's Past. C.* xxviii. 197 Dauid..lange ær his [Saul's] ehtnesse earfoðlice ðolode. *a* 1000 *Cædmon's Gen.* 2240 (Gr.) Þeowdom þolian. 1154 *O. E. Chron.* (Laud MS.) an. 1137, Suilc & mare þanne we cunnen sæin we þoleden xix wintre for ure sinnes. *c* 1175 *Lamb. Hom.* 75 His halie fif wunden þa he þolede for us ine þe halie rode. *c* 1200 ORMIN Ded. 201 He ȝaff hiss aȝhenn lif..To þolenn dæþþ o rodetre. *c* 1290 *Beket* 2316 in *S. Eng. Leg.* I. 173 Þis holi man..þolede martyrdom. *c* 1320 *Cast. Love* 410 He schal euere þolyen deþ. 13.. *Cursor M.* 9636 (Cott.) Ded he aght to thole. 1375 BARBOUR *Bruce* IV. 659 Feill anoyis thoill ȝhe sall. *c* 1386 CHAUCER *Friar's T.* 248 So muche wo as I haue with yow tholed. *c* 1450 *Mirour Saluacioun* 212 All yᵉ oure lord Ihū soeffred in his passionne Oure ladie tholed in sawle. 1530 LYNDESAY *Test. Papyngo* 175 Off bitter deth now mon I thole the schouris. 1599 PORTER *Angry Wom. Abingd.* in Hazl. *Dodsley* VII. 370 What a winter of cold fear I thole. 1717 RAMSAY *Elegy on Lucky Wood* i, What loss, what crosses dost thou thole! 1884 FREEMAN in Stephens *Life* (1895) II. x. 321 They that believed nothing were to thole all revealed punishments. [*Affected archaism.*]

*absol.* 1357 *Lay Folks Catech.* 132 [Christ] tholed [*v.r.* suffryd] bodily for synful man kynd. *c* 1394 *P. Pl. Crede* 90 Þe cros þat crist opon þolede. *c* 1430 LYDG. *Min. Poems* (Percy Soc.) 227 How ever thou thole ore thryfe, Alwey thonk God of alle. 1718 RAMSAY *Christ's Kirk Gr.* III. xvi, Ye's thole for this, ye scaul. 1880 A. FORBES in 19*th Cent.* Jan. 190 To be told how our countrymen..toil and thole.

**b.** *To thole an assize, judgement, the laws*, etc., to undergo trial. *Sc.*

1425 *Sc. Acts Jas. I* (1814) II. 9/2 Þe king..forbiddis þat ony man..be aponne his assise þat sall thole þe law. 1508 DUNBAR *Flyting* 78 For quhilk, brybour, ȝit sall thow thoill a breif. *a* 1578 LINDESAY (Pitscottie) *Chron. Scot.* III. iv. (S.T.S.) I. 223 The lordis..quhilk was..thair to thoill ane syse conforme to thair ditta. 1609 SKENE *Reg. Maj.* I. 93 b, It is statute, that na man sould thoill judgement, or be judged, be ane man of inferiour estate then his awin peir. 1678 SIR G. MACKENZIE *Crim. Laws Scot.* I. xx. § 4 (1699) 108 The Receptor with us cannot be punished, or thole an Assize, till the principal Thief be first convict. 1886 *St. James' Gaz.* 16 Dec. 3 Mr...would probably by this time have tholed an assize before the High Court of Justiciary.

**2.** To endure without resistance or complaint; to submit with patience to; to bear with, 'abide'; to put up with, tolerate. Also with *inf.* or *subord. cl.*

*c* 950 *Lindisf. Gosp.* Mark ix. 19 Ða huile mið iuh ic beom, ða huile iuih ic ðola. *a* 1000 *Cædmon's Gen.* 597 (Gr.) Þæt is micel wundor þæt hit ece god æfre wolde, þeoden, þolian. 1297 R. GLOUC. (Rolls) 9479 So luþer & prout heo was, þat me ne miȝte it þolie noȝt. *c* 1330 R. BRUNNE *Chron. Wace* (Rolls) 15976 Al þer trauaille & al þer ylle Þat þey had þoled wiþ gode wille. 1393 *Rec. Elgin* (New Spald. Cl.) I. 7 Þis as before wyt al men we wil nocht thole. *c* 1430 *Syr Gener.* (Roxb.) 8490 He might the betre thoole Thurgh gile to les a little ring, Whan [etc.]. 1552 ABP. HAMILTON *Catech.* (1884) 81 Thai that tholis nocht thair father and mother, suppose thai do thame iniuris and be cummersum. 1584 HUDSON tr. *Du Bartas' Judith* III. 179 For thee, we frankly shall pursue and thole Th'eternall heat and colde of either Pole. 1786 BURNS *Twa Dogs* 96 Poor tenant bodies, scant o' cash, How they maun thole a factor's snash. *c* 1800 *Newcastle Prov.* in Brockett *N. C. Gloss.* (1846) II. 178 He that has a good crop may thole some thistles. 184. in *Contemp. Rev.* (1905) July 64 'I com' away,' said he, 'for I couldn't thoil to see good food wasted.' 1889 BARRIE *Window in Thrums* 38, I canna thole 'im.

*absol.* 1154 *O. E. Chron.* an. 1140 § 6 (Laud MS.) Þa hi ne leng ne muhten þolen, þa stali hi ut & fluȝen. *c* 1200 *Trin. Coll. Hom.* 79 Þe man..þe þoleð and forbereð and ne wile seche after wreche. *a* 1340 HAMPOLE *Psalter* ix. 41 Þaire hert redy to serue þe and to thole. *c* 1470 HENRY *Wallace* VIII. 663 Ȝeit Wallace tholyt, and leit thaim say thar will. 1560 ROLLAND *Seven Sages* 77 Better it is to thoill heir patientlie, Nor euer mair in hell condampnit be. 1880 A. FORBES in 19*th Cent.* Feb. 234 The British soldier can thole as well as can the Russian soldier.

†**b.** To endure or bear without giving way; to withstand; to stand. *Obs.*

*c* 1200 ORMIN 9399 Þa maȝȝ itt [the eye] siþþenn þolenn wel Þe sunness brihhte leome. 13.. *Cursor M.* 7312 (Gött.) It es wel worthi þat qua May thole na wele, to thole þe wa. *c* 1400 *Destr. Troy* 9674 No buerne vpon bent his buffettes might thowle. 14.. *Songs Costume* (Percy Soc.) 60 Her mantill of humilitie, To tholl bayth wind and weit.

**c.** To bear, stand, admit of, be capable of; to have room for; esp. in phrase *to thole amends*, to admit of improvement. *dial.*

1770 JAS. WATT *Let. to Small* 3 Jan., Health and spirits beyond what I commonly enjoy..; though they would still thole amends. *a* 1774 FERGUSSON *Cauler Oysters* Poems (1845) 7 Fling owre your craig sufficient doses; You'll thole a hunder. 1808 SCOTT *Let. to G. Ellis* 23 Feb., in *Lockhart*, The style would..*thole amends*, i. e. admit of improvement. 1871 in *N. & Q.* 4th Ser. VIII. 156/2 It'll thole a drap mair watter.

†**3.** To allow, suffer, permit. (With obj. clause, obj. and inf., or equivalent pron.) *Obs.*

*c* 1070 *Charter of Leofgifu* in Kemble *Cod. Dipl.* IV. 269 Ic bidde mine leuedien for Godes louen ðat ðu [ne] þolie ðat ani man mine quide awende. *c* 1175 *Lamb. Hom.* 71 Þole us to bi-wepen ure sunne. *c* 1200 ORMIN 12089 Ȝiff Crist itt nollde þolenn himm Naffde he þærto nan mahhte. 1297 R. GLOUC. (Rolls) 1583 Þe toun folc.. nolde namore þolie þan ssrewe among hom a wede. 13.. *Gaw. & Gr. Knt.* 1859 Þenne he þulged with hir þrepe, & þoled hir to speke. *c* 1400 *Apol. Loll.* 59 Þei be þolid to minister prestly oþer sacraments. 1466 *Dunfermline Regr.* (Bann. Cl.) 356, I sall nocht thole, graunt nore gyff leiffe.. to na man..to draw na drauchtis of wateris throu my landis. 1513 DOUGLAS *Æneis* IX. vii. 89 Thoil me to trubble this gret rout of men. 1552 ABP. HAMILTON *Catech.* (1884) 35 God will nocht thoile you want your dailie sustentatioun. 1575 CHURCHYARD *Chippes* (1817) 193 God would not thoell, for one mans sake alone: That broyles should cause a million make their mone. 1721 RAMSAY *Prospect of Plenty* 83 They'll never thole this great design to tak.

**4.** *intr.* To be patient, have patience, wait patiently. *dial.*

1674 RAY *N. C. Words* 48 *Thole* a while, i.e. stay a while. 1766 A. NICOL *Poems* 58 (E. D. D.), I do bid them thole a while Till ance the spring come in again. 1896 [J. LUMSDEN] *Poems* 7 (ibid.) Great is our drouth—but thole a wee.

**5.** *trans.* To bear to give; to afford or grant willingly. *dial.*

1703 THORESBY *Let. to Ray* Gloss. (E. D. S.), *Thoyl*, to afford. 1828 *Craven Gloss.* s. v., I could thole him t' meat out o' my mouth. 1863 MRS. TOOGOOD *Yorksh. Dial.* (MS.), He is so covetous he cannot thoil his servants enough food.

**Thole**, obs. erron. f. TOLL, in *thole and theam*, 'toll and team'.

†**Tho·leburde**, *a. Obs. rare.* Forms: 1 þolebyrde, (þoli-, þolo-), 3 þoleburde. [Late OE. *þolebyrde*, f. stem of THOLE *vb.* + *byrd* bearing.] Bearing patiently; forbearing, submissive. Hence †**Tho·leburdness** *Obs. rare*, patience, submission.

*a* 1050 *Liber Scintill.* i. 3 To þolibyrdnysse þrowunga strange, *ad tolerantiam passionum fortes. Ibid.* ii. 13 Þolobyrde mann, *patiens homo. Ibid.*, Wer soðlice þolebyrde, *uir enim patiens.* *c* 1200 *Trin. Coll. Hom.* 79 [To] ben swo þoleburde to-ȝenes his wissinge to forleten þat he forbet, and don þat he bit. *Ibid.*, *Tanta est uirtus paciencie*.., swo holie mihte is þoleburdnesse. *a* 1250 *Orison* 51 in *O. E. Misc.* 140 Ihesuc ich þe grete..For þe muchel þoleburne [? -burnesse]..Þat þu schawedest mon-kunne, þo þu þoledest deþ.

†**Tho·lemode**, *a.* and *sb. Obs.* Forms: 1–4 þolemod, þolmod, (1 þolo-), 2–4 þolemode, 4 tholemod, tholmod, -moud, -mud, (-mound), 4–5 tholemode, tholmode; *Sc.* 5 tholemude, 6 thoilmude, -muide, (8 tholemoody). [OE. *þolemód*, f. *þole-* (see prec.) + *mód*, MOOD *sb.*[1] Cf. ON. *þolin-móðr*, Da. *taal-modig.*]

**A.** *adj.* Patient, submissive, meek.

*c* 1000 *Ags. Hom.* (Assmann) 127 (Gr.) Heo wæs þolemod and ȝestæðþiȝ on hire ȝebæran. *c* 1000 ÆLFRIC *Saints' Lives* xvii. 56 And beo ȝesibsum, ȝeðyldiȝ and ðolmod. *a* 1050 *Liber Scintill.* ii. 8 Þolomod, *patiens.* *a* 1100 *O. E. Glosses* (Napier) I. 1319 *Longanimem*, þolemod. *c* 1175 *Lamb. Hom.* 105 Þet þe mon beo iþuldi and þolemod. *a* 1225 *Leg. Kath.* 177 Ha wes þuldi & þolemod. *a* 1300 *Cursor M.* 10187 (Cott.) Was neuer..nan tholmoder in chastite. *c* 1450 *Mirour Saluacioun* 4607 In alle aduersitees y^t I so tholemode ay be. 1513 DOUGLAS *Æneis* v. vii. 48 In vane that name thow beris,..Geif thow,sa tholimuide, sufferis leid away Sa greit a price. 1710 RUDDIMAN *Gloss. to Douglas' Æneis, Tholmude*, Scot. Bor. say *tholemoody*, i. e. patient.

**B.** *sb.* = THOLEMODENESS. *rare.*

*c* 1000 ÆLFRIC *Saints' Lives* xvi. 334 (MS. D.) Se feorðe mihte is patientia, þæt is ðolmod ȝecweden. *c* 1175 *Pater-noster* 266 in *Lamb. Hom.* 69 Edmodnesse and þolemod þet þuncheð gode swiðe god.

† **Tho·lemodely,** *adv. Obs.* [f. prec. + -LY ².] Patiently, submissively, meekly.

*a* 1225 *Ancr. R.* 46 Nime hire sicnesse nout one þolemod-liche, auch do swuð gledliche. *a* 1340 HAMPOLE *Psalter* xxiv. 2 All þat tholmodly beris þe birþin of tribulacioun. *c* 1375 *Sc. Leg. Saints* iii. (*Andreas*) 403 Gyf þu wil her me tholmodly. *c* 1450 *Mirour Saluacioun* 3195 The swerde of sharpest tonges herd of crist tholemodely.

† **Tho·lemodeness.** *Obs.* [f. as prec. + -NESS.] Patience, submissiveness, meekness.

*c* 1000 ÆLFRIC *Saints' Lives* xvi. 334 (MS. J.) Patientia þæt is ȝeðyld and þolmodnys ȝecwæden. *a* 1225 *Ancr. R.* 276 Wreððes salue [is] þolemodnesse. 1303 R. BRUNNE *Handl. Synne* 5831 Moche he louede þolmodnesse. *c* 1375 *Sc. Leg. Saints* xxxvi. (*Baptista*) 433 Of tholmudnes als sic wes he þat he with-stud in na degre Agane þame þat..til hyme mysded. 1456 SIR G. HAYE *Law Armys* (S.T.S.) 285 The prince suld be..of gude tholemudenes, to suetely here the caus.

**Tho·le-pin.** Forms: see THOLE *sb.*¹; also 5 tolpyn. [f. THOLE *sb.*¹ + PIN *sb.*]

**1.** A peg used as a fastening; = THOLE *sb.*¹ 2.

*c* 1440 *Promp. Parv.* 496/1 Tolpyn, *idem quod* tholle, *supra.* 1881 *Isle of Wight Gloss., Thole-pin*, the pin that goes into the shafts of the roller by which the horse draws. 1884 *19th Cent.* Feb. 244 A coffin..having a thong-hinged cover..fastened by a thole pin. 1893 INGLIS *Ain Folk* vii, The thole-pin which kept the loft folding-door in position.

**2.** = THOLE *sb.*¹ 1.

1598 FLORIO, *Schelma*..a..peg in a boate whereat the rowers stay their oares when they rowe, called a thoule pin. 1725 DUDLEY in *Phil. Trans.* XXXVI. 264 An Oar..not so much as lifted up out of the Thole-Pin. 1859 W. H. GREGORY *Egypt* I. 293 It scorched our hands to touch at midday the iron plates in which the thowl-pins were fastened.

**Tholing** (þōᵘ·liŋ), *vbl. sb.* [f. THOLE *v.* + -ING ¹.]

**1.** The action of THOLE *v.*; suffering, enduring.

*a* 1300 *Cursor M.* 15684 (Cott.) Thoru mi bodi most it pass þe tholing o þis pine. *c* 1400 *Apol. Loll.* 5 Petir..fillid þe office of Crist, in liuing, and in teching, and in þoling. 1562 TURNER *Baths* 10 b, According to the complexion of the sicke, and after the suffrance or tholling of the stomack. 1884 FREEMAN in Stephens *Life & Lett.* II. x. 322 But then that entitles me to the unrevealed tholings [*affected archaism*].

† **2.** Sufferance, permission, allowance, leave. *Obs.*

*c* 1375 *Sc. Leg. Saints* xxx. (*Theodera*) 6 Þo þar-to he haf mycht Thru godis tholyne & gret slycht. 1457 *Dunfermline Regr.* (Bann. Cl.) 344 Rechart be goddis tholyng Abbote of Donfermlyn. 1466 *Ibid.* 356, I giff and grauntis..full leiffe and tholing and gude will to þe saidis Abbot..to mak land stell and Dame forganis my said landis.

**Tho·ling,** *ppl. a.* [f. THOLE *v.* + -ING ².] That tholes; enduring; patient.

1340 *Ayenb.* 167 Þe holy gost..him makeþ strang and þolyinde uor to þolye huanne hi comeþ. *c* 1425 tr. *Arderne's Treat. Fistula* 58 Men now of daiez bene vnpacient and yuel tholyng.

**Tholl,** obs. erron. f. TOLL *sb.*

**Tholnie, tholoney,** var. TOLNE *Sc. Obs.*, toll.

**Tholobate** (þǫ·lŏbēⁱt). *Arch.* [f. Gr. θόλ-ος THOLUS + -βατης one who goes, f. βαίνειν to go.] (See quots.)

1831 HOSKING in *Encycl. Brit.* (ed. 7) I. 471/1 *Tholobate*, ..that on which a dome or cupola rests...A term not in general use...What is generally termed the attic above the peristyle and under the cupola of St. Paul's, would be correctly designated the tholobate. A tholobate of a different description..is the circular substructure to the cupola of the London University. 1838 BRITTON *Dict. Archit.* 457. 1845 PARKER *Gloss. Archit.* (ed. 4), *Tholobate*, the substructure on which a dome or cupola rests.

**Tholsel, -l,** var. TOLSEL, TOLZEY. *Obs.*

‖ **Tholus** (þōᵘ·lŏs). *Arch.* Pl. **tholi** (-əi). Also in Gr. form **tholos** (þǫ·lǫs), pl. **tholoi** (-oi). [L. *tholus*, a. Gr. θόλος a round building with a conical or vaulted roof.] A circular domed building or structure; a dome, cupola; a lantern.

1644 EVELYN *Diary* 7 Nov., A pretty odd fabriq, with a Tribunal, or Tholus within. *a* 1668 LASSELS *Voy. Italy* (1698) I. 188 On the top of it [the Domo of Florence] stands mounted a fair Cupola (or Tholus). 1730-6 BAILEY (folio), *Tholus*, the Roof of a Temple or Church, the Centre, Scutcheon, or Knot in the middle of an arched Roof, the Lanthorn or Cupola of a publick Hall. 1832 GELL *Pompeiana* I. iv. 47 A circular or polygonal tholos. 1841 *Civil Eng. & Arch. Jrnl.* IV. 117/2 The tholus, or concave dome.

**b.** *Gr. Antiq.* An excavated circular tomb of the Mycenæan age, domed and lined with masonry.

1885 *Athenæum* 12 Dec. 773/2 Mr. Pullan..was astonished to find that the lower cell of the so-called prison of St. Peter at Rome was part of a tholus. 1896 Tholoi [see DROMOS]. 1910 *Edin. Rev.* Apr. 479 Among the forms sepulchre are the great bee-hive *tholos* [etc.].

*attrib.* 1902 R. C. BOSANQUET in *Ann. Brit. Sch. at Athens* VIII. 305 Tholos-burial was introduced in eastern Crete towards the close of the Minoan Age.

**Thomæan** (tomī·ăn), *a.* and *sb.* Also **Thomean.** [app. f. med.L. *Thōmæ-us* (f. the name *Thōmā-s*) + -AN.] **a.** *adj.* Of or pertaining to the Christian church traditionally said to have been founded by St. Thomas the Apostle, which has existed from early times on the Malabar coast. **b.** *sb.* A member of this church. Also called *Thomite, Christian of St. Thomas.*

1727-41 CHAMBERS *Cycl., Thomæans, Thomeans, Thomites*, or *Christians of St. Thomas*, a people of the East-Indians, who, according to tradition, received the gospel from the apostle St. Thomas. *Ibid.*, A great part of the Thomæan church relapsed, and thus still continues partly Roman, partly Thomæan. 1842 BRANDE *Dict. Sci., Lit.*, etc., *Thomæans*, or *Thomites.*

**Thomaism,** variant of THOMISM, q. v.

**Thoman, -and,** obs. variants of TOMAN.

**Thomas** (tǫ·măs). [a. L. *Thōmās*, Gr. Θωμᾶς.]

**1.** A Greek, Latin, and common Christian name; well known as that of the 'doubting apostle' (see John xx. 25), and hence used allusively; also used as a representative proper name for one of the populace taken at random. Familiarly abbreviated to TOM, the dim. or pet form of which is TOMMY.

*c* 1000 *Ags. Gosp.* John xx. 24 Thomas an of þam twelfon þe ys ȝecweden didimus..næs mid him þa se hælend com. *c* 1275 *O. E. Misc.* 90 Haly thomas of heoue[n]riche. *c* 1412 HOCCLEVE *De Reg. Princ.* 5080 ȝe, so I drede me, by seynt Thomas. *c* 1620 ROBINSON *Mary Magd.* 1519 O, that I might, with waueringe Thomas, dippe The finger of my faith within his side. 1656 BLOUNT *Glossogr., Thomas (Hebr.)* signifies twin, or as some will have it, bottomlesse deep. 1848 MRS. GASKELL *M. Barton* xii, Mary, don't let my being an unbelieving Thomas weaken your faith. 1883 *Harper's Mag.* June 93/1 Doubting Thomases, who will only believe what they see, must wait awhile.

**2.** Generic name for a footman or waiter.

1846 MRS. GORE *Eng. Char.* (1852) 78 The gossip of one fashionable dinner-table alone, within ear-shot of three or four first-rate Thomases, is sufficient to disperse throughout the town rumours enough to set a hundred families of consideration into a ferment. 1901 *Daily Graphic* 23 Feb., The 'men' are not any less 'splendid' because they are known by this diminutive term [Tommy], any more than waiters are heroic because we give them their full title of 'Thomas'.

**3. Thomas Atkins** (also *Thomas*): a familiar name for the typical private soldier in the British Army; arising out of the casual use of this name in the specimen forms given in the official regulations from 1815 onward: see quots.

In some of the specimen forms other names are used; but 'Thomas Atkins' being that used in all the forms for privates in the Cavalry or Infantry, is by far the most frequent, and thus became the most familiar. Now more popularly TOMMY ATKINS or TOMMY q.v.

1815 (Aug. 31) War Office, *Collection of Orders, Regulations, etc.* 75 (Form of a Soldier's Book in the Cavalry when filled up). Description, Service, &c. of Thomas Atkins, Private, No. 6 Troop, 6th Regt. of Dragoons. Where Born... Parish of Odiham, Hants...Bounty, £6. Received, Thomas Atkins, his × mark. *Ibid.* 76 Clothing Account of Thomas Atkins, Private, No. 6 Troop, 6th Dragoons...Clothing Account of William Jones, Trumpeter, No. 2 Troop, 9th Light Dragoons...Clothing Account of John Thomas, Serjeant, No. 8 Troop, 15th Hussars. [So Forms on pp. 78-81 all 'Thomas Atkins, Private'.] *Ibid.* 82 Form of Soldier's Book in the Infantry, when filled up. Description, Service, etc. of Thomas Atkins, Private, No. 6 Company, 1st Batt. 23d Regt. Foot. Where born [etc.]...Bounty £7 7s. Received, Thomas Atkins, his × mark. [So Forms on pp. 83-87, all signed 'Thomas Atkins, his × mark'.] 1837 (June 1) *King's Regulations & Orders for the Army* 204, Form No. 2, No. 55 Thomas Atkins, Serjeant, Born in the Parish of St. Mary in or near the Town of Portsmouth, in the County of Hants, by Trade a Labourer. *Ibid.* 206-9 [Various Forms, all filled up or subscribed 'Thomas Atkins' (who no longer signs by 'his mark')]. *Ibid.* 210 Character: Thomas Atkins has been a well-conducted Soldier; was wounded at ——, and has distinguished himself by several acts of bravery. Signed ——, Commanding Officer. 1864 *Stand. Orders Roy. Reg. Artill.* 89 Thomas Atkins. Enlisted..on the 9th April, 1857. *Ibid.*, We certify that the above is a correct Statement of the Services of Thomas Atkins, to the 10th June 1887. 1890 *Times* 6 Dec. 12/4 Mr. Thomas Atkins..can break it [a rifle] down in half-a-dozen ways in the course of his musketry instruction. 1897 *Allahabad Pioneer* in *Westm. Gaz.* 14 Dec. 7/3 'You take my advice, Bill', remarked one Thomas to another,..'don't you never stand near no white stone or yet near no horcifer'.

**4. St. Thomas'**, in composition. **St. Thomas' balsam** = *balsam of* TOLU. † **St. Thomas' coin** (also **St. Thomas**), ? an East Indian coin. **St. Thomas' tree**, *Bauhinia tomentosa* or *B. variegata* of the E. Indies, the pale yellow petals of which are spotted with crimson, fabled to be the blood of St. Thomas. **St. Thomas worsted**: see SAINT *a.* 4 c.

1559 in Marsden *Court Adm.* (Selden) II. 110 Novem pecias auri vulgo dictas *Saintte Thomas coyne. 1698 FRYER *Acc. E. India & P.* 53 Their Coins are of Gold; a St. Thomas, 10s. a Fanam, 7 and ½ of which go to a Dollar, or Petacha. 1866 *Treas. Bot.*, *St. Thomas' Tree, *Bauhinia tomentosa.* 1887 MOLONEY *Forestry W. Afr.* 332 St. Thomas' Tree...Shrub or small tree. 1518 *N. C. Wills* (Surtees 1908) 95 A jaket of tawny *Saint Thomas worsted.

**Thomasing** (tǫ·măsiŋ). *dial.* [f. THOMAS + -ING ¹.] The begging of alms on St. Thomas's day (21 Dec.). Also called *corning, doling*, or *gooding.*

1847-78 HALLIWELL, *Thomasing*, a custom in Derbyshire, going from house to house on St. Thomas's day with a basket and can to beg milk, wheat, oatmeal, or flour. 1866 W. HENDERSON *Folk Lore* ii. 50 The widows ask and commonly receive at the farmers' houses a small measure of wheat, and they call it 'going a Thomasing'. 1900 *Daily Chron.* 3 Nov. 3 (Cass. Supp.) The maying, processioning, Thomasing, carolling, and other junketings.

**Thomasite** (tǫ·măsəit). [f. as prec. + -ITE ¹.] = CHRISTADELPHIAN, from the name of the founder, Dr. John Thomas. 1888 in *Cassell's Encycl. Dict.*

**Thomb(e, thome,** obs. forms of THUMB.

**Thomble, thomelle,** obs. forms of THIMBLE.

**Thomble-toe,** etc.: see THUMBLE-TOE.

**Thomism** (tōᵘ·miz'm). *Theol.* [f. THOM-AS + -ISM. So F. *thomisme* (Roquefort, 1829).] The doctrines of Thomas Aquinas or of the Thomists.

1727-41 CHAMBERS *Cycl., Thomism*, or *Thomaism. Ibid.*, The Thomism..which Alvarez embraces, admits a physical premonition, or predetermination. 1731 BAILEY vol. II, *Thomism*, the doctrine of Thomas Aquinas,..chiefly with respect to his opinions on predestination and grace. 1883 *Schaff's Encycl. Relig. Knowl.* III. 2354 The Jesuits opposed Thomism,..but it prevailed at the Spanish Universities of Salamanca, Coimbra, and Alcala.

**Thomist** (tōᵘ·mist), *sb.* (*a.*) *Eccl.* [ad. med.L. *Thōmista* (Wyclif, 1359), f. *Thōm-ās*: see below. Cf. F. *thomiste* (Pascal).] A follower of Thomas Aquinas (known as 'The Angelical Doctor'), a scholastic philosopher and theologian of the 13th c. (Cf. SCOTIST.)

[1359 WYCLIF *Wks.* (1905) 127 Thomiste qui sanctum Thomam secuntur.] 1533 TINDALE *Supper of Lord* B iij *margin*, Thomistes be the schole docters. 1669 T. GALE *True Idea Jansenisme* 58 No doubt there are such small Graces, as the Thomists call sufficient. 1709 POPE *Ess. Crit.* 444 Scotists and Thomists now in peace remain Amidst their kindred cobwebs in Duck-lane. 1842 BRANDE *Dict. Sc.*, etc. s. v., The Thomists continued as a sect to the commencement of the 17th century. 1882-3 *Schaff's Encycl. Relig. Knowl.* I. 658 The controversy between Thomists and Scotists..concerning the exemption of Mary from hereditary sin.

**b.** *attrib.* or as *adj.*

1845 S. AUSTIN *Ranke's Hist. Ref.* I. 485 She was that same thomist aristotelic church, with which he was engaged in a mortal struggle. 1884 *Mind* IX. 159 The Thomist philosophy, now again authoritatively proclaimed to be the sheet-anchor of Catholic doctrine.

**Thomistic** (tomi·stik), *a.* [f. prec. + -IC.] Of or pertaining to the Thomists or their doctrines.

1881 *Nature* XXIII. 235 On the recent restoration of the scholastic and tomistic philosophy. 1882-3 *Schaff's Encycl. Relig. Knowl.* I. 358 [Cajetan] was generally considered the real head of the Thomistic school. 1889 E. H. DERING (*title*) On Universals: an Exposition of Thomistic Doctrine. By Father Matteo Liberatore, S.J.

So **Thomi·stical** *a.* = prec.; **Thomi·sticate** *v.* (*nonce-wd.*) *intr.* to argue or discourse in the manner of the Thomists; to 'split hairs', use over-refined arguments.

1533 TINDALE *Supper of Lord* C v b, Howe farre lo, M. More is thys your straunge *thomystical sense from the flate letter? 1642 J. EATON *Honey-c. Free Justif.* 120 The Thomisticall distinctions of the Schoolemen. 1715 M. DAVIES *Athen. Brit.* I. 171 The rigorous Calvinistical and Thomistical Opinion of Predestination. 1730 LEWIS *Life of Fisher* (1855) I. 194 In defence of the mass's being a sacrifice, the king thus *Thomisticates.

**Thomite** (tōᵘ·məit). *rare*—⁰. [f. THOM-AS + -ITE ¹.] = THOMÆAN *sb.* (q.v. quot. 1727-41).

**Thomsenolite** (tǫ·msĕnələit). *Min.* [Named, 1868, after Dr. Julius Thomsen of Copenhagen: see -LITE.] Hydrous fluoride of aluminium, calcium, and sodium, found with pachnolite on the cryolite of Greenland.

1868 DANA *Min.* 129 Thomsenolite..was first noticed by Dr. Julius Thomsen of Copenhagen, the originator of the cryolite industry, after whom it is here named. 1883 *Science* I. 331/2 It is distinguished from thomsenolite by its absence of water.

**Thomsen's disease.** *Path.* [Named after Dr. Thomsen of Schleswig-Holstein, who first described it, from his own case.] See quot. 1890. So **Tho·msen-like** *a.*

1890 BILLINGS *Nat. Med. Dict.*, *Thomsen's disease, Myotonia congenita*, a peculiar congenital affection characterized by inability to relax the muscles immediately after contraction. 1899 *Allbutt's Syst. Med.* VI. 471 The Thomsen-like contractions are due to the action of phosphate of soda on the muscular fibres themselves.

**Thomsonian** (tǫmsōᵘ·niăn), *a.* (*sb.*) [f. *Thomson*, proper name (see definitions) + -IAN.]

**1.** Of or pertaining to the system of medicine practised by Dr. Samuel Thomson, of Massachusetts (1769–1843). Also as *sb.* One who follows this system. (Often erroneously spelt *Thompsonian.*)

1833 C. THOMSON (*title*) A plain historical Statement of facts respecting the Thomsonian plan of medicine, as originated by Samuel Thomson. 1857 DUNGLISON *Med. Lex., Thompsonian*, one who practises or believes in Thompsonianism. *Ibid.* s.v., *Thompsonianism*, The Thompsonians are Botanical Doctors. 1860 BARTLETT *Dict. Americanisms, Thompsonian Doctor*, a physician who follows the Thompsonian practice; also called Steam Doctor. *Thompsonian Practice*, a peculiar treatment of diseases.

**2.** Of, pertaining to, or characteristic of the poet James Thomson, author of 'The Seasons'.

1890 TENNYSON in *Mem.* (1897) I. i. 11, I covered two sides of a slate with Thomsonian blank verse in praise of flowers. 1908 *Westm. Gaz.* 5 Feb. 4/2 One is apt..to over-estimate the difference between the Wordsworthian 'Nature' and the Thomsonian 'Nature'.

Hence **Thomso·nianism,** the Thomsonian medical system: see sense 1.

1857 [see sense 1 above]. 1890 BILLINGS *Nat. Med. Dict.*, *Thomsonianism.* 1894 *Outing* (U.S.) XXIV. 332/1 Do you believe in the mind cure—Thompsonianism—metallic tractors—Christian science? **1899** *Syd. Soc. Lex.*, *Thomsonianism*.., a form of empiric medicine introduced by Samuel Thomson (1769–1843), of Massachusetts. Sweating, lobelia, and capsicum, were the principal agencies relied on.

**Thomsonite** (tǫ·msənəit). *Min.* [Named, 1820, after Dr. Thomas Thomson (1773–1852), professor of chemistry at Glasgow: see -ITE [1].] Hydrous silicate of aluminium, calcium, and sodium, found often in fibrous radiated masses, white to reddish-brown in colour; = COMPTONITE.

**1820** H. J. BROOKE in *Ann. Philos.* Sept. 193, I shall call the Auvergne variety, Mesotype; that from Iceland and Ferro, Needlestone; and that from Dumbarton, Thomsonite, after the editor of this journal [Dr. T. Thomson]. **1843** PORTLOCK *Geol.* 215 Thomsonite..is rarely met in Irish trap. **1869** PHILLIPS *Vesuv.* x. 294 Thomsonite, or Comptonite [occurs] in ejected blocks of gray lava.

**Thon** (ðǫn), *dem. pron.* and *a.*, *dial.* [app. a comparatively recent alteration of *yon*, the initial consonant being assimilated to *this* and *that*. (A suggestion that it arose from misreading the written *y* as the compendious form of *th*, as in *y^e*, *yis*, *yat*, *yem*, *yairof*, etc., is, in view of the wide popular diffusion of *thon* and *thonder*, inadequate.)] = YON: the demonstrative pron. and adj., pointing to something more remote in place or time than *that*: = L. *ille*, Sp. *aquello*.

Used in Scotland, Ulster, and the four northern English counties. Written examples not found before 1800; app. not in Ramsay nor in Burns.

**1804** TARRAS *Poems* 96 (Jam.) Leuk down the gate, what squabble's thon, That ca's the thrang's attention? **1808** JAMIESON *Sc. Dict.*, *Thone*, yonder, yon. **1818** MISS FERRIER *Marriage* I. ii. 18 'Hoose!' repeated the driver, 'ca' ye thon a hoose? Thon's gude Glenfern Castle'. **1886** R. L. STEVENSON *Lett.* (1901) II. viii. 39 Strange conduc' o' thon man Rankeillor. **1893** — *Catriona* 136 I'll no forget thon of the cinnamon water. **1894** HESLOP *Northumbld. Gloss.* 727 Whe's thon? Whe's thon chep? De ye see thon hoose ower there? [**1904** in *Eng. Dial. Dict.* from Scotland (Aberdeen to Roxb.), Ulster, Northumberland, Durham.]

So **Thonder** (ðǫ·ndəɹ) *adv.* and *a. dial.* (also **thaander, thander, thender, thinder**) = YONDER.

Used in Scotland, Ulster, England from north border to Hereford, Leicester, E. Anglia.

*a* **1825** FORBY *Vocab. E. Anglia*, *Thinder*, adv., v. Yinder. *c* **1847** [Common in Roxburghsh.] *Thonder* adv. **18..** ROBSON *Bards of Tyne* (1863) 441 Then at last, aw heard her say, O! thonder is the Gardens. **1854** MISS BAKER *Northampt. Gloss.* s.v., He lives over thender. **1876** BOUND *Provinc. Herefordsh.* (E.D.D.), Thander one is the man. **1879** MISS JACKSON *Shropsh. Word-bk.* Introd. 50 Yander, thander, *adj.* **1887** DARLINGTON *Folk-sp. S. Cheshire* 70 *Yonder* has the forms *yondur*, *yaandur*, and *dhondur*. **1899** *Blackw. Mag.* Feb. 168, (*Sc.*) I didna mak verra muckle o' the fairming up-bye thonder.

**Thon, þon**, obs. f. THAN, THEN; obs. inflexion of THE. **Thonder, -dre**, etc., obs. ff. THUNDER.

†**Thone**, coalesced form of *the one*, frequent in 16th c.: see TH-, TH'.

Chiefly used in contrast with THOTHER = the other.

**1542** UDALL *Erasm. Apoph.* E.'s Pref., He had mingled the saiynges..thone with thother. *c* **1566** *Meric Tales of Skelton* in *Wks.* (1843) I. p. lix, If any scoler had fallen out thone with thother, the one woulde call thother Swanborn. **1594** WEST *2nd Pt. Symbol.* § 43 Because thone hath trespassed more than thother, he shall pay to thother, x. s.

**Thoner, Thonewonge**, obs. forms of THUNDER, THUNWANG.

**Thong** (þǫŋ), *sb.* Forms: *α.* 1 **ðwong, ðuong, ðwange, þwæng, ðuuencg**, 1–3 **þwang**; 4 **thuang**, 4–5 (*Sc.* and *north.* –9) **thwang** (5 **thwange, twange**, 6 **thwangue**), 5–7 *Sc.* **thwayng** (*dial.* 7–9 (with *hw*, *wh*-, for *þw*-) **whaing, whang**). *β.* 3–4 **þwong, þuong(e**, 4–5 **thwong(e** (*dial.* **twonge**). *γ.* 3–5 **þong**, 4– **thong**, (4–5 **þonge, thongh**, 6–7 **thonge**, 6 **thongue**). *δ.* 5 **thownge, thowyng**; *dial.* 8–9 **thung, thunk, thonk**. [OE. *þwang*, *þwǫng* str. masc. (also fem.); also, ONorthumb. pl. *ðuuencgu*, N. Anglian *þwænga*, agreeing with ON. *þvengr* (:—*þvangi^z*); all from ablaut stem **þwing-*, **þwang-*, **þwung-*, to restrain:—Indo-Eur. root **twenk*: cf. Ger. *zwingen*: see TWING, TWINGE *v.*, and cf. the dial. form WHANG.]

**1.** A narrow strip of hide or leather, for use as a lace, cord, band, strap, or the like.

In early use, esp. the lace or 'latchet' of a shoe.

*α.* *c* **950** *Lindisf. G.* John i. 27 Ic ne am wyrðe þætte ic undoe his ðuong scoes [*Rushw.* ðwong ȝiscoes, *Ags. Gosp.* sceoþwang]. *c* **1000** *Ags. Gosp.* Mk. i. 7 His sceona þwanga [*Lindisf.* ðuongas scóe his, *Rushw.* þwongas ȝescoas his]. *c* **1000** ÆLFRIC *Gen.* xiv. 23 (Gr.) Þæt ic ne underfo furðon anne þwang of eallum þisum þingum. *c* **1050** *Gloss.* in Wr.-Wülcker 379/32 *Corrigie*, olþwongas. *a* **1100** *Ibid.* 332/12 *Corrigia*, ðwangc. *c* **1275** LAY. 22295 Somme makede þwanges. *a* **1300** *Cursor M.* 12823 (Cott.) To lese þe thuanges of his sco. *c* **1425** WYNTOUN *Cron.* VIII. xxviii. 4599 A royne lanȝhare..And schare a thwayng at all laysere. **1513** DOUGLAS *Æneis* IX. xi. 5 Dartis..Quhilk thai with lyamis and thwangis lang owt threw. **1570** LEVINS *Manip.* 23/42 A Thwangue, *lorum*. **1641** *Ferguson's Sc. Prov.* No. 647 Mony ane tines the haff-merk whinger for the halfpenny whang. **1703** THORESBY *Let. to Ray* Gloss. (E.D.S.), 'A thwang for a shoe', the latchet. **1894** HESLOP *Northumbld. Gloss.* 779 The end..of a flail is lashed to the wood with a whang.

*β.* *c* **1200** *Trin. Coll. Hom.* 137 Ich nam noht ne for ðen wurðe þat ich un-cnutte his sho þuong. *c* **1205** LAY. 22295 Sum makede þwonges. **1297** R. GLOUC. (Rolls) 2492 As moche place as mid a þuong ich may aboute tille. **13..** *Gaw. & Gr. Knt.* 194 Syþen þrawen wyth a þwong a þwarle knot alofte. **1387** TREVISA *Higden* (Rolls) I. 369 Þey usede hiȝe schone unto þe kne, i-slitte to fore, and i-laced wiþ þwonges. **1485** CAXTON *Paris & V.* 27 Henge a lytel keye by a thwonge.

*γ.* *c* **1205** LAY. 14221 Þa al islit wes þe þong he wes wunder ane long. *c* **1350** *Will. Palerne* 1720 Sche..festened hire in þat fel wiþ ful gode þonges. **1480** CAXTON *Chron. Eng.* lvi. 40 Engyst prayd hym..of as moche place as he myght compasse with a thong of a skynne. **1563** GOLDING *Cæsar* V. (1565) 138 He aduised him to tie the letter to the thong of a Iaueling, & so to throw it into his camp. **1570** LEVINS *Manip.* 167/2 A Thongue, *lorum*. **1610** HOLLAND *Camden's Brit.* (1637) 339 A beasts hide cut into thongs. **1649** G. DANIEL *Trinarch.*, *Hen. V* clxxix, Another girds his Frock, with a sure Thonge [*rime* strong]. **1703** MOXON *Mech. Exerc.* 179 The Noose of a Leather Thong. **1867** PARKMAN *Jesuits N. Amer.* xvii. (1875) 246 Subsisting on the bark of trees or the thongs of raw hide.

*δ.* *c* **1425** *Eng. Voc.* in Wr.-Wülcker 656/1 *Hec corigia*, thowyng. *c* **1440** *Promp. Parv.* 492/1 Thownge, or lanere. *a* **1800** PEGGE *Suppl. Grose*, *Thunk*, Lancashire pronunciation of Thong. **1881** MISS JACKSON *Shropsh. Word-bk.* s.v. *Thung*, 'I give the cobbler a penny fur two thunks'. **1886** *Cheshire Gloss.*, *Thonk*, a thong, a bootlace; also *Thunk*.

†**b.** A phylactery. Only OE. *rare*.

*c* **950** *Lindisf. Gosp.* Matt. xxiii. 5 Hia ȝebrædas forðon ðuuencgu hiora. *c* **975** *Rushw. Gosp.* ibid., þwænga.

**c.** Such a strip used as an instrument of flagellation; also as the lash of a whip; hence *spec.* a whip-lash of plaited hide.

**1592** LYLY *Midas* IV. iii, A boy was beaten on the taile with a leathern thong. **1728–46** THOMSON *Spring* 809 The trembling steed..Nor heeds the rein, nor hears the sounding thong. **1782** COWPER *Progr. Err.* 360 Man's coltish disposition asks the thong. **1832** LYTTON *Eugene A.* II. vi, A gentleman..left the whip to have a new thong put to it. **1876** GRANT *Burgh Sch. Scot.* II. v. 195 Horace prayed for a settled standard of punishment, lest any one should be subjected to the horrible thong, who is only deserving of a slight whipping.

**d.** *transf.* A similar strip of other material, as a tough pliant plant-stem, etc.

**1665** HOOKE *Microgr.* 6 Bound together with thongs of Brambles. **1838** T. THOMSON *Chem. Org. Bodies* 696 Take a thong of this substance [india-rubber]. **1875** T. W. HIGGINSON *Yng. Folks' Hist. U.S.* iii. 17 The edges were sewed with thongs cut from the roots of the cedar.

**e.** *fig.*; esp. in phrase *to cut a large thong* (or *large thongs*) *of another man's leather*, *thongs of other men's hides*, to be lavish with that which is another's.

*c* **1380** WYCLIF *Serm.* Sel. Wks. I. 76 Þis ordre is a þuonge to bynde mennis willes togidere. **1465** MARG. PASTON in *P. Lett.* II. 226 Men cut large thongs here of other mens lether. **1784** COWPER *Task* III. 26 What chance that I..Should speak to purpose, or with better hope Crack the satiric thong? **1865** KINGSLEY *Herew.* i, As long as I could cut long thongs out of other men's hides. **1878** *Masque Poets* 149 The silken tie became a thong Wherewith she pinioned him in bondage strong.

**2.** *attrib.* and *Comb.*, as *thong-point*, *-wearer*; *thong-hurled* adj.; **thong-drill**, a drill rotated by means of a thong or cord wound round its stem; **thong-man**, a man who wields the thong or lash; in quot., a critic; **thong-seal**, a name sometimes given to the bearded seal, *Erignathus barbatus*, the hide of which is cut into a continuous strip for use as a line.

**1865** TYLOR *Early Hist. Man.* ix. 242 The *thong-drill with the mouthpiece. **1685** COTTON tr. *Montaigne* (1877) I. 23 The bear, made fiercer by the wound from the Lybian's *thong-hurled dart. **1876** G. MEREDITH *Beauch. Career* xxxiv, Self-appointed *thongmen who walk up and down our ranks flapping their leathern straps. **1897** *Blackw. Mag.* Nov. 593/2 A leather sporran tagged with *thong points tied in knots. **1901** *Athenæum* 2 Nov. 589/1 It is the cord-wearer [Franciscan] rather than the *thong-wearer [Dominican] who is the hero of the more scandalous anecdotes.

Hence **Thongy** (þǫ·ŋi) *a. dial.*: see quots.

**1847–78** HALLIWELL, *Thongy*, ropy, viscid. *Somerset*. **1885** *Reports Provinc.* (E.D.D.), Cider is often said 'to be thongy', when it gets into the peculiar state known as 'reamed' or 'ropy'.

**Thong** (þǫŋ), *v.* Forms: see prec. [f. THONG *sb.* Cf. ON. *þvengja* (*skó*) to furnish (shoes) with a thong.]

**1.** *trans.* To furnish with a thong; to fasten or secure with a thong or thongs; to bind with thongs.

*a* **1225** [implied in THONGED]. **1483** *Cath. Angl.* 388/1 To Thwange [*v.r.* Twange], *corrigiare*. **1723** R. MILLAR *Hist. Propag. Chr.* II. vii. 302 Their Habits are Sheep Skins undressed thonged together. **1861** *Life of Bacon* xx. 414 He too is thonging the scourge for his own back.

**2.** To flog or lash with a thong. Also *absol.*

**1746** *Exmoor Scolding* 77 (E.D.S.) Chell [=ich will] thong tha,..chell pummel tha,..chell lace tha. **1855** THACKERAY *Newcomes* I. ii. 23 Mrs. Newcome thonged him with the lash of her indignation. **1866** *Cornh. Mag.* Dec. 743 'Stick to them, my lads', shouts Captain Blake, double-thonging with a hunting-whip like a maniac. **1890** 'R. BOLDREWOOD' *Miner's Right* vii, He..was quite capable of raising a wale upon that epidermis which it suited him to thong.

**3.** *dial.* (See quot.)

**1888** *Berksh. Gloss.*, *Thong*, to twine or twist together.

**4.** *dial. intr.* To become viscous or 'ropy'.

**1847–78** HALLIWELL, *Thong*, to rope; to stretch out into viscous threads or filaments.

Hence **Thonged** (þǫŋd) *ppl. a.*, furnished or fastened with thongs; **Tho·nging** *vbl. sb.*, flogging with a thong.

*a* **1225** *Ancr. R.* 362 And me ne mei nout..two þongede scheon habben, wiðuten buggunge. *a* **1847** J. T. HURLOCK in *Essex Rev.* XVII. 56 Scourge not with thonged whips. **1860** THACKERAY *Round. Papers*, *Small-beer Chron.*, Is there no enemy who would be the better for a little thonging? **1880** BROWNING *Dram. Idyls* II. *Echetlos* 22 The large limbs thonged and brown.

**Thonir**, obs. f. THUNDER. **Thonk(e**, obs. ff. THANK. **Thonne, þonne**, obs. f. THEN, THENNE.

†**Thonneliche, þ-**, *adv.* *Obs. rare*⁻¹. [f. ME. *þonne*, THEN + *-liche*, -LY [2]. (The modern form, if the word had survived, would be *thenly*.)] In that case: = THEN 4.

**1340** *Ayenb.* 31 Kueade anginnynge heþ þe sleuuolle be zix zennes. Þe uerste is þonneliche huanne þe man loueþ lite and lheuc.liche oure lhord.

**Thonner, thonor**, etc., obs. ff. THUNDER.

**Thonwange, -wonge**, var. THUNWANG *Obs.*

**Thoo, þoo**, variant of THO *pron.* and *adv. Obs.*

**Thooid** (þōu·oid), *a.* (*sb.*) *Zool.* [f. Gr. *θώ-ς*, THOUS + -OID.] Resembling in form, or related to, the sub-genus *Thous*; in an extended use applied to a division of the genus *Canis* including the wolf, dog, and jackal; as distinct from the alopecoid, typified by the fox. **b.** *sb.* A beast of this division.

**1880** HUXLEY in *Proc. Zool. Soc.* 6 Apr. 278 Thooids and Alopecoids, similar to those which exist at present, inhabited Europe during the Quaternary epoch. *Ibid.* 286, I am disposed..to regard *Otocyon* and the Thooid and Alopecoid series respectively as genera, retaining for the two latter the old names of *Canis* and *Vulpes*. **1891** FLOWER & LYDEKKER *Mammals* xi. 548 Thooid or Lupine Series [of Canines].

**Thoole, þoole**, obs. forms of THOLE *v.*

**Thoom**, obs. and dial. form of THUMB.

**Thor** (þǭɹ). *Mythol.* [a. ON. *þórr* :—*þunro^z* thunder: see THURSDAY.] The proper name of the strongest and bravest of the Scandinavian deities, the god of thunder, whose weapon was a hammer; his belt doubled his strength; hence in allusive use.

*a* **1020** WULFSTAN *Hom.* xlii. (21 a) Napier 197 Þór and Owðen, þe hæðene men herjað swiðe. **1605** VERSTEGAN *Dec. Intell.* 74 Description of the great Idol Thor. **1817** BYRON *Beppo* lxi, Crush'd was Napoleon by the northern Thor, Who knock'd his army down with icy hammer. **1841** EMERSON *Ess.* Ser. I. ii. (1876) 63 Let us enter into the state of war, and wake Thor and Woden, courage and constancy, in our Saxon breasts. **1898** *Daily News* 6 May 8/1 The din of a thousand Thors at their forges, the hubbub of the workshop.

**b.** *attrib.*, as *Thor-hammerer*; *Thor-like* adj.; **Thor-barley** (see quot. 1755).

**1755** tr. *Pontoppidan's Nat. Hist. Norway* I. iv. § 5. 105 This barley..the peasants term Thor-barley, possibly from the opinion of the ancients, who..imagined this corn to be fit for the banquets of the gods. **1865** DE MORGAN in *Athenæum* 14 Oct. 729/2 The Thor-hammerer does nothing but grumble. **1866** M. C. TYLER *Glimpses Eng.* (1898) 159 The splendor of his [John Bright's] Thor-like eloquence.

**Thor**, dial. variant of THEIR, and THIR, these.

**Thora**, variant of TORAH, the Mosaic law.

**Thoracabdominal**, etc.: see THORACO-.

**Thoraci-** (þorǣ·si), combining form of L. *thōrāx*, *-ācem*, in same sense as THORACO-. **Thora·ciform** *a.*, having the form of a thorax, thorax-shaped. **Thora·cipod** [Gr. *ποδ-* foot] *a.*, of or pertaining to the *Thoracipoda*, a division of crustaceans having ambulatory thoracic limbs; *sb.* a crustacean of this division; so **Thoraci·podous** *a.* (*Cent. Dict.* 1891). **Thora·cispi·nal** *a.*, pertaining to the thoracic portion of the spinal column.

**1826** KIRBY & SP. *Entomol.* IV. xlvi. 331 Orismology... Mesothorax...β. Dorsolum. *Thoraciform,..when it forms the principal part of the upper surface of the trunk. **1887** COUES in *Cent. Dict.*, *Thoracispinal. **1899** *Syd. Soc. Lex.*, Thoracispinal.

**Thoracic** (þorǣ·sik), *a.* (*sb.*). Also 7 thorachique, -cique. [ad. med.L. *thōrācic-us*, a. Gr. *θωρᾱκικ-ός*, f. *θώρᾱξ*, *θωρακ-*: see THORAX and -IC. In Blount from obs. F. *thorachique* (A. Paré in Cotgr.).]

**1.** *Anat.* Of, pertaining to, or contained in the thorax; pectoral.

*Thoracic aorta* (also called *pectoral aorta*), that part of the aorta which traverses the thorax. *Thoracic artery*, any one of the branches arising from the axillary artery. *Thoracic cage*, the skeleton of the thorax with its ligaments (Billings, 1890). *Thoracic cavity*, the space enclosed by the ribs, spine, and diaphragm, containing the heart, lungs, etc. *Thoracic duct*, the main trunk of the lymphatic system, through which the chyle and lymph are conveyed to the blood. *Thoracic limb*, in a vertebrate, a fore-limb; in man, the arm; in quadrupeds, the fore-leg; in birds, the wing; in fishes, a thoracic or pectoral fin; in invertebrates, a member appended to the thorax. *Thoracic vertebra*, a vertebra which articulates with a rib; a dorsal vertebra.

**1656** BLOUNT *Glossogr.*, *Thorachique*,..belonging to the breast or stomack. *Ibid.* s.v. *Vein*. **1658** PHILLIPS, *Thoracique*,..belonging to the stomack or brest. **1727–41** CHAMBERS *Cycl.* s.v., The thoracic arteries...Thoracic veins... Thoracic duct..is..a continuation of the exit or mouth of the receptaculum chyli. **1793** BEDDOES *Lett. Darwin* 56 No sooner does it touch the lungs than..the functions of all the thoracic organs go on easily and pleasantly again. **1793** M. BAILLIE *Morb. Anat.* Pref. (1807) 10 The thoracic and abdominal viscera. **1876** BRISTOWE *The. & Pract. Med.* (1878) 13 In our own country, thoracic inflammations are most frequent during the cold seasons of the year.

**b.** Pertaining to, attached to, or forming part of the thorax (of an insect or crustacean).

**1817** KIRBY & SP. *Entomol.* (1818) II. 413 The light emitted by the two thoracic tubercles alone is so considerable [etc.]. **1880** HUXLEY *Crayfish* i. 22 The crayfish..walks by means of the four hinder pairs of thoracic limbs.

**2.** *Ichthyol.* Having the ventral fins situated directly beneath the pectoral; belonging to the *Thōrăcicī*, the third order of fishes in the Linnæan system. Cf. ABDOMINAL *a.* 3.

**1769** PENNANT *Zool.* III. 216 That section of bony fish, termed Thoracic. **1774** GOLDSM. *Nat. Hist.* (1862) II. III. i. 294 The ventral fins placed directly under the pectoral fins, ..and then it is called a Thoracic fish. **1854** OWEN *Skel. & Teeth* in *Orr's Circ. Sc.* I. *Org. Nat.* 183 The fins called 'ventral'..indicate by their position the orders of fishes called 'abdominal', 'thoracic', and 'jugular', by Linnæus.

**3.** Having a thorax (as a distinguishing character); belonging to the *Thoracica*, a sub-order of cirripeds, in which the body consists of six thoracic segments, with a rudimentary abdomen. **1891** in *Cent. Dict.*

**4.** As a specific distinction in *Nat. Hist.*: Having the thorax conspicuously marked or coloured.

*c* **1812** SHAW *Natur. Misc.* XXII. 969 Thoracic Wagtail [*Motacilla thoracica*]. **1819** STEPHENS in Shaw *Gen. Zool.* XI. 322 Thoracic Francolin [*Francolinus thoracicus*].

**5.** Comb., as **thoracic-abdominal** *a.*, of the combined thorax and abdomen.

**1835–6** *Todd's Cycl. Anat.* I. 214/1 A..band which commences at the thoracic-abdominal constriction. **1854** OWEN *Skel. & Teeth* in *Orr's Circ. Sc.* I. *Org. Nat.* 191 The ribs ..do not encompass the thoracic-abdominal cavity.

**B.** *sb.* †**1.** A medicine acting on the thorax; a pectoral. *Obs.*

[**1706** PHILLIPS (ed. Kersey), *Thoracica*, medicines proper for Diseases of the Breast.] **1710** T. FULLER *Pharm. Extemp.* 249 In a word it is a most excellent Thoracic.

**2.** A thoracic fish: see 2 above.

**1828** WEBSTER, *Thoracics*,..an order of bony fishes,..the ventral fins are placed underneath the thorax, or beneath the pectoral fins.

**3.** A thoracic organ or structure.

**1857** DUNGLISON *Med. Lex.* s.v., *First of the Thoracics*, mammary superior external artery.

† **Thora·cical,** *a.* *Obs.* [f. as prec. + -AL: see -ICAL.] = THORACIC.

**1664** POWER *Exp. Philos.* III. 191 We had yet never known the Mesenterical and Thoracical *Lacteæ*. **1669** W. SIMPSON *Hydrol. Chym.* 65 The thoracical vessels. **1830** *Fraser's Mag.* I. 354 Medicinal in all matters thoracical, if I may use the expression.

**Thoracico-** (þoræ·siko), combining form of THORACIC *a.*, used to form adjs. in sense 'pertaining to the thorax and (some other part)', as *thoracico-abdominal* (also *thoracicabdominal*: see also THORACIC 5), *thoracicoacromial* (also *thoracicacromial*), *thoracico-humeral*, *thoracico-lumbar*.

**1870** ROLLESTON *Anim. Life* 30 The internal aspect of the *thoracico-abdominal cavity. **1891** *Cent. Dict.*, *Thoracicacromial. **1895** *Funk's Standard Dict.*, Thoracicoacromial. **1891** *Cent. Dict.*, *Thoracicohumeral. **1899** *Syd. Soc. Lex.*, **Thoracico-lumbar*, pertaining to the thoracic and lumbar regions.

†**Thora·cious,** *a.* *Obs. rare*⁻¹. [irreg. f. L. *thōrāx, thorāci-*, THORAX + -OUS.] = THORACIC *a.* 1.

**1681** tr. *Willis' Rem. Med. Wks.* Voc., *Thoracious*, belonging to the breast or thorax, or medicines good to help the diseases of the thorax.

‖ **Thoraco-** (þorē·ko), before a vowel **thorac-**, combining form of Gr. θώραξ, θωρακ-, THORAX; used in forming terms of anatomy, zoology, etc. **Thoracabdo·minal** *a.* = *thoracico-abdominal*. **Thoracacro·mial** *a.* = *thoracico-acromial*. **Thoracente·sis** = *thoracocentesis*. ‖ **Thoracetron** (-sī·trǫn) [Gr. ἦτρον abdomen], Owen's name of the second division of the body in certain crustaceans, as the king-crab (cf. PLEON [1]); hence **Thorace·tral** *a.*, of or pertaining to the thoracetron. **Thora:co-acro·mial** = THORACICO-ACROMIAL. ‖ **Thoraco-centesis** (-sentī·sis) [Gr. κέντησις pricking], the perforation of the chest-wall to draw off morbid accumulations of fluid. ‖ **Thoracocyllosis** (-silōᵘ·sis) [Gr. κύλλωσις curvature], deformity of the thorax (Billings, 1890). ‖ **Thoracocyrtosis** (-səitōᵘ·sis) [Gr. κύρτωσις crookedness], abnormal curvature of the chest. ‖ **Thoracodynia** (-di·niă) [Gr. ὀδύνη pain], pain in the thorax; also in English form † **Tho·racodyne.** **Thoracometer** (-kǫ·mĭtəɪ), an apparatus for measuring the movement of the chest-wall in respiration; a stethometer. **Thoracopagous** (-ǫ·păgəs) *a.*, pertaining to or of the nature of a thoracopagus. ‖ **Thoraco·pagus** [Gr. πάγος that which is fixed, f. πηγνύναι to fasten], a double or twin monster joined at the thorax. **Thoracopathy** (-ǫ·păþi), disease in the thoracic region. **Tho·racopla·sty** [-PLASTY]: see quot. **Thora·cosco·pe** [-SCOPE], an instrument for sounding the chest, a stethoscope. **Thoraco·scopy,** the sounding or exploration of the chest. **Thoraco·stracous** [Gr. ὄστρακον hard shell] *a.*, of or pertaining to the *Thoracostraca*, a division of crustaceans, including the Decapoda and other series, having a cephalo-thoracic shield and (usually) stalked eyes. ‖ **Thoracothe·ca** *Entom.* [THECA], that part of the pupa-case which covers the thorax of the pupa (*Cent. Dict.* 1891). **Thoraco·tomy** [Gr. τομή cutting], incision into the thorax.

**1891** *Cent. Dict.*, *Thoracabdominal. **1899** *Syd. Soc. Lex.*, *Thoracabdominal*, pertaining to, or common to, the thorax and abdomen. **1887** COUES in *Cent. Dict.*, *Thoracacromial. **1857** DUNGLISON *Med. Lex.*, *Thoracentesis. **1866** A. FLINT *Princ. Med.* (1880) 147 Thoracentesis..is admissible whenever the pleural cavity remains filled with liquid after a brief trial of the measures designed to promote absorption. **1872** OWEN in *Trans. Linnean Soc.* XXVIII. 467 The succeeding *thoracetral appendages are 4-articulate. *Ibid.* 465 This segment..belongs to the category of 'thoracetral' plates: it is cephaletral only by confluence. *Ibid.* 463, I venture to hope that the term 'cephaletron' may meet with some acceptance.., and that the term '*thoracetron' may have the same fortune in relation to the second division of the body. *Ibid.* 467 The ventral surface of the thoracetron. **1857** DUNGLISON *Med. Lex.*, *Thoracocentesis. **1903** *Westm. Gaz.* 10 July 7/1 Professor Rossoni..and Dr. Mazzoni went to the Vatican at half-past eight this morning, and repeated the operation of thoraco-centesis. **1860** MAYNE *Expos. Lex.*, *Thoracocyrtosis. **1857** DUNGLISON *Med. Lex.*, **Thoracodyne*, pleurodynia. **1860** MAYNE, Thoracodyne, Thoracodynia. **1877** S. GEE *Auscult. & Percuss.* I. ii. (ed. 2) 35 Instruments which have been invented for registering the respiratory movements and powers: stethographs, stethometers, *thoracometers, spirometers, pneumatometers. **1886** A. GAMGEE in *Encycl. Brit.* XX. 477/1 Apparatuses for measuring the excursion of a given point of the chest wall during respiration are called thoracometers or stethometers. **1894** BATESON *Variation* xxiv. 560 Eichwald examined the evidence as to *thoracopagous double monsters. **1902** *Brit. Med. Jrnl.* 15 Mar. 672 The Greeks in their deity-construction seem to have made no use of the various types of united twins—for example, the thoracopagous and dicephalic monstrosities. **1894** BATESON *Variation* xxiv. 560 There are..a few cases even of *thoracopagi where neither body exhibits any transposition. **1890** BILLINGS *Nat. Med. Dict.*, **Thoracoplasty*, plastic operation on the thorax, as excision of portions of ribs to close an abscess; Estlander's operation. [**1857** DUNGLISON *Med. Lex.*, **Thoracoscopium*, stethoscope.] **1895** *Funk's Standard Dict.*, Thoracoscope. **1890** BILLINGS *Nat. Med. Dict.*, **Thoracoscopy*, exploration of the chest. **1902** *Cassell's Encycl. Dict.* Suppl., *Thoracostracous. **1857** DUNGLISON *Med. Lex.*, **Thoracotomy*, thoracocentesis. **1890** BILLINGS *Nat. Med. Dict.*, *Thoracotomy*, cutting into the chest; Estlander's operation.

**Thorah,** variant of TORAH, the Mosaic law.

† **Thora·kial,** *a.* *Obs. rare*⁻¹. [f. Gr. θωρακ-, THORAX + -IAL.] = THORACIC *a.* 1. *T. canal*, the thoracic duct.

**1716** M. DAVIES *Athen. Brit.* III. *Diss. Physick* 5 Speaking more at large of the Thorakial Canal, than a Roman Physician..near an Age before.

† **Tho·ral,** *a.* *Obs. rare.* [f. *thor-us* (cf. '*Thoral, thorāle*, culcitra' in Du Cange), med. spelling of L. *torus* couch, marriage + -AL.] Of or pertaining to the marriage-bed.

**1696** PHILLIPS (ed. 5), *Thoral Line*, otherwise call'd in Palmistry the Mensal Line, or the Line of Venus. **1726** AYLIFFE *Parergon* 48 The second Punishment..is a Thoral Separation or a Dissolution of Matrimony.

**Thorax** (þōᵊ·ræks). Pl. **tho·raxes** (*rare*), or in L. form **thoraces** (þorē·sīz). [a. L. *thōrāx*, a. Gr. θώραξ breast-plate, cuirass, also breast, chest.]

**1.** *Anat.* and *Zool.* That part of the body of a mammal between the neck and the abdomen, comprising the cavity enclosed by the ribs, breast-bone, and dorsal vertebræ, and containing the chief organs of circulation and respiration; the chest; also the corresponding part in the lower vertebrates, as birds, serpents, and fishes.

*c* **1400** *Lanfranc's Cirurg.* 161 Thorax is maad of .vij. boonys & euery boon at þe eende is cartilaginosum. **1548–77** VICARY *Anat.* vii. (1888) 54 The Brest or Thorax is the Arke or Chest of the spirituall members of man. **1653** H. MORE *Antid. Ath.* II. xii. § 5 Enlarging the Thorax, that the Lungs may have play. **1692** LOCKE *Educ.* (1693) 12 The Thorax, wherein is placed the Heart and Seat of Life. **1704** F. FULLER *Med. Gymn.* (1711) 7 Laughing..proves so beneficial by the playing of the Muscles of the Thorax. **1855** HOLDEN *Human Osteol.* (1878) 228 The Thorax is the framework which contains the heart and lungs.

**2.** *Zool.* The middle region of the body of an arthropod, between the head and the abdomen.

In insects, the thorax consists of three somites, the prothorax, mesothorax, and metathorax, and bears the legs, and wings if any exist. In arachnids and some crustaceans, the thorax is joined to the head, forming the CEPHALOTHORAX.

**1750** *Phil. Trans.* XLVII. viii. 40 The thorax drops its breast-plate, and then the legs quit their crustaceous coverings. **1842** BRANDE *Dict. Sc.*, etc., *Thorax*, the second segment of insects is so called by Latreille and Audouin; the term is restricted to the upper surface of the trunk by Linné and Fabricius. **1868** DUNCAN tr. *Figuier's Insect World* Introd. 7 The thorax, the second primary division of the body of insects, plays almost as important a part as the head. **1888** ROLLESTON & JACKSON *Anim. Life* 491 A head region..either remains distinct..or becomes continuous with a part or whole of the thorax, forming a cephalo-thorax... A thorax is not marked off in the *Myriapoda*.

‖ **3.** *Gr. Antiq.* A cuirass, corselet: see quots.

**1842** BRANDE *Dict. Sc.*, etc., *Thorax*, in Grecian Antiquities, a piece of defensive armour consisting of two parts, one defending the back, and the other the belly; called *lorica* by the Romans. **1845** C. H. SMITH in *Kitto's Cycl. Bibl. Lit.* s.v. *Arms*, In Egypt..a more ancient national form [of cuirass] was a kind of thorax, tippet, שריון *shereyon*, or square, with an opening in it for the head, the four points covering the breast, back, and both upper arms. **1857** BIRCH *Anc. Pottery* (1858) I. 410 They wear Corinthian helmets, often crested; *thoraces*, or breast-plates, under which is a tunic, and greaves.

Hence **Thoraxed** (þōᵊ·rækst) *a.*, having a thorax (of a specified kind).

**1907** *Nation* 24 Aug. 923/1 The yellow-thoraxed species [of insects].

† **Thore.** *Obs. rare*⁻¹. App. an anglicization of *thorus*, med. spelling of L. *torus* nuptial couch.

**1649** LOVELACE *Lucasta* Ded. 7 To the Taper of the Thore Which the God himselfe but bore; To the Sea of Chast Delight Let me cast the Drop I write.

**Thore,** obs. var. of DARE *v.*[1] (A. 9).

**Thore, þore,** obs. 3 pl. indic. pres. of THARF *v.*, to need; obs. f. THERE.

† **Thores even, ene.** *Obs.* [After *Thores-day* THURSDAY.] The eve of (Holy) Thursday (Ascension Day).

**1297** R. GLOUC. (Rolls) 394 Hii bygonne an holy Thore's ene þen toun asaly þere. *Ibid.* 8120 An hal[i] þores euen [*v.rr.* þois, þours, þorsdai, Thursday eue].

**Thorfe,** inflexion of THARF *v.*, to need. **Thorgh, þorgh, -ȝ, thorght, Thorghoute,** obs. ff. THROUGH, THROUGHOUT.

‖ **Thoria** (þōᵊ·riă). *Chem.* [f. as THORIUM + -*a*, after *alumina, magnesia, silica*, etc.] An oxide of thorium, $ThO_2$; a very heavy white substance discovered in the mineral thorite by Berzelius, 1828, and named by him in Swedish, *Thorjord*, Ger. *Thorerde*, lit. Thor-earth. Now important in the manufacture of incandescent gas mantles. Also *attrib.*

**1847** in WEBSTER. **1881** WATTS *Dict. Chem.* VIII. 1967 Thorium Oxide, or Thoria,..is insoluble in dilute acids. **1899** *Westm. Gaz.* 10 June 6/3 The expiry of the master patent this year, and the thoria patent next spring. **1904** *Ibid.* 16 Apr. 7/1 About [1888] experiments on incandescent mantles gave to thoria considerable commercial value. A mantle of pure thoria gives a very little light; but, on the other hand, it gives a stability to the fragile mantle which no other body yet discovered is able to do.

**Thorianite** (þōᵊ·riănəit). *Min.* [f. **thorian* (f. THORIA) + -ITE [1] 2 b.] A mineral consisting chiefly of the oxides of thorium, uranium, and other rare metals, found in 1904 in the south-west of Ceylon, in small brownish-black crystals having a resinous lustre; a variety of pitch-blende.

**1904** DUNSTAN in *Nature* 31 Mar. 510 This mineral appears to be new, and I suggest for it the name of *thorianite*. **1907** *Daily Chron.* 5 Jan. 2/5 The discovery of deposits of the very valuable mineral thorianite, containing something like 80 per cent. of the rare earth thoria, which is used in the manufacture of incandescent gas mantles.

**Thoric** (þōᵊ·rik), *a.* *Chem.* [f. THOR(IUM + -IC.] Of or derived from thorium. **1891** in *Cent. Dict.*

† **Thorina** (þorəi·nă). *Chem. Obs.* [ad. F. *thorine*, 1817, a bad representation of Berzelius's name *Thorjord*, Ger. *Thorerde*: see THORIA.

In the *Annales de Chemie*, etc. 1817, V. 5, the form *thorine* is erroneously attributed to Berzelius himself ('une nouvelle terre à laquelle M. Berzelius a donné le nome de thorine'). Misled by this, English chemists long used *thorina* and *thorinum* for *thoria* and *thorium*.]

**1.** The name given at first to a substance found by Berzelius in 1815 in various Swedish and Norwegian minerals, and named by him *Thorjord*, which afterwards proved to be yttrium phosphate.

**1818** W. PHILLIPS *Outl. Min. & Geol.* (ed. 3) 29 The discovery of a new Earth by Berzelius a Swedish Chemist, has lately been announced...This earth has been named.. Thorina, from the Scandinavian deity Thor. **1826** HENRY *Elem. Chem.* II. 695 A farther investigation by Berzelius of the substance to which, in 1815, he had given the name of Thorina [*ought to be* Thorjord].., has now satisfied him that it is merely a sub-phosphate of yttria.

**2.** The name formerly given to the earth or oxide to which Berzelius in 1828 transferred the name *Thorjord*, now called THORIA.

**1831** T. P. JONES *Convers. Chem.* xvii. 180 Thorina [is found] in one mineral only, in Norway. **1836** BRANDE *Chem.* (ed. 4) 847 Thorina..after having been heated to redness, is white, and insoluble in the acids, with the exception of the sulphuric. **1839** URE *Dict. Arts*, etc. 1239 Pure thorina is a white powder, without taste, smell, or alkaline reaction on litmus. **1877** WATTS *Fownes' Chem.* (ed. 12) 397 Thorinum Oxide or Thorina, $ThO_2$.

† **Thori·nic,** *a.* *Chem. Obs.* [f. next + -IC.] = THORIC.

**1868** WATTS *Dict. Chem.* V. 786 A precipitate of thorinic hyposulphite is then formed.

‖ **Thorinum** (þorəi·nǒm). *Chem. Obs.* [f. F. *thorine* and Eng. THORINA, in accordance with L. names of metals in *-um*, as *aurum, cuprum, plumbum*.]

**1.** The name originally given to a hypothetical metal of which THORINA (sense 1) was (erroneously) supposed by Berzelius, 1815, to be the oxide.

**1819** CHILDREN *Ess. Chem. Anal.* § 76 Oxide of Thorinium, or Thorina. **1820** URE *Dict. Chem.*, *Thorinum*, the supposed metallic basis of the preceding earth [THORINA 1], not hitherto extracted. **1826** HENRY *Elem. Chem.* I. 635 *Thorinum.* Nothing is known of the metallic base of this earth [thorina], and it is only from analogy that it is supposed to be constituted of such a base united with oxygen.

**2.** The name given in France and England, for several years after 1828, to the metallic element THORIUM, q. v.

**1836** BRANDE *Chem.* (ed. 4) 847 Thorinum..was discovered by Berzelius in 1828, in a rare and complex mineral, found in the Syenitic rock of the Isle of Lövon, near Brevig, in Norway. It contained about 58 per cent. of thorina. *Ibid.*, By passing a current of dry chlorine over a mixture of thorina and charcoal-powder, a crystalline chloride of thorinum is obtained, which is easily decomposed by potassium, and the product is thorinum. It is of a gray colour, metallic lustre, and apparently malleable. **1873** WATTS *Fownes' Chem.* (1877) I. 397 Thorinum forms but one class of compounds, in all of which it is quadrivalent.

**Thorite** [1] (þōᵊ·rəit). *Min.* [a. Swed. *thorit* (Berzelius, 1828–9), f. *Thor* (as in *thoria, thorium*) + -ITE [1] 2 b.] Hydrous silicate of thorium, occurring crystalline, massive, and compact, orange-yellow (ORANGITE) to brownish-black or black, with a vitreous or resinous lustre.

**1832** [see THORIUM]. **1839** URE *Dict. Arts* 1239 It [thorina] was extracted from the mineral thorite, of which it constitutes 58 per cent. **1868** DANA *Min.* 413 The brownish-black and black variety, from Lövö, Norway, was the mineral from which Berzelius obtained the metal thorium, and which received the name thorite.

**Thorite** [2] (þōᵊ·rəit). [f. THOR + -ITE [1] 4.] An explosive of the ammonium nitrate class.

**1899** *Westm. Gaz.* 13 July 7/2 Thorite, a new explosive invented by Dr. Tuttle, of Tacoma,..stood severe tests...A red-hot iron was plunged into a can of thorite, but it merely ignited the particles that touched the iron.

‖**Thorium** (þōᵊ·riŏm). *Chem.* [f. THOR, the Norse deity + -IUM in other names of metals.

So named by its discoverer Berzelius 1828–9: see *Kongl. Vetenskaps-Acad. Handlingar* 1829, p. 1. The French having called the earth *thorine* (see THORINA) named the metal THORINUM, which prevailed also in England for many years.]

A rare metallic element discovered by Berzelius in the mineral thorite, and subsequently found in small quantities in some other rare minerals. Symbol Th. Also *attrib.*

Now noted as one of the radio-active elements.

**1832** *Encycl. Brit.* (ed. 7) VI. 401/2 Thorina, which constitutes an oxide of thorium, has been hitherto found only in a black mineral.., thorite. *Ibid.* 402/1 The only known compound of thorium and oxygen is thorina. **1868** WATTS *Dict. Chem.* V. 785 *Thorinum*, or *Thorium.* Atomic Weight, 115·72; Symbol, Th. **1881** *Ibid.* VIII. 1967 Thorium ..is not isomorphous with any other known element. *Ibid.*, Thorium Oxide [$ThO_2$]..Chloride [$ThCl_4$]..Nitrate..Sulphate [etc.]. **1898** SIR W. CROOKES *Addr. Brit. Assoc.* 24 Rays..emitted by thorium and its compounds. The thorium rays affect photographic plates through screens of paper or aluminium, and are absorbed by metals and other dense bodies. **1903** *Daily Chron.* 27 Nov. 8/3 He [Sir W. Ramsay] pointed out that the thorium emanations were an ephemeral gas which in two minutes ceased to exist. **1907** *Athenæum* 31 Aug. 244/2 Thorium..gives no fewer than seven radio-active products, in the following order: mesothorium, radiothorium, thorium X, thorium emanation, and thorium A, B, and C.

**Thorle, þorle**, obs. form of THIRL *v.*[1]

**Thorlepolle**, variant of THIRLEPOLL *Obs.*

**Thorn** (þǫɹn), *sb.* Forms: 1–3 ðorn, 1–5 þorn, (2 þeorn, 3 (*Orm.*) þorrn, 4 thorun), 4–5 þorne, 4–8 thorne, 4– thorn. [OE. *þorn* = OS. *thorn* (Du. *doorn*), OHG. *dorn* (MHG., G. *dorn*), ON. *þorn* (Sw., Da. *torn*), Goth. *þaurnus*, :–OTeut. **þurn-uz*; :–Indo-Eur. **trnus*: cf. OSlav. *trŭnŭ* thorn.]

**I. 1.** A stiff, sharp-pointed, straight or curved woody process on the stem or other part of a plant; a spine, a prickle.

*a* **800** CYNEWULF *Crist* 1445 Þa hi hwæsne beaȝ ymb min heafod heardne ȝebyȝdon..se wæs of þornum ȝeworht. *c* **950** *Lindisf. Gosp.* Matt. xxvii. 29 Ða cempo..ymbworhton ða beȝe of ðornum, ȝesetton ofer heafud his. *c* **1000** *Ælfric's Voc.* in Wr.-Wülcker 139/21 *Spina*, þorn. *Ibid.* 139/22 *Tribulus*, þorn. *c* **1200** *Trin. Coll. Hom.* 207 He hadde..þornene helm, and þe þornes swiðe prikeden. *a* **1300** *Cursor M.* 17136 (Cott.) Þe thornnes o mi hede standes. *Ibid.* 17774 (Cott.) Wit thorns crund als was he. **1382** WYCLIF *Prov.* xxvi. 9 If a thorun [1388 thorn] be growen in the hond of the drunken. *c* **1400** *Lanfranc's Cirurg.* 166 Of woundis of þornis. **1484** CAXTON *Fables of Æsop* III. i, As he ranne, a thorne entred into his foote. **1593** SHAKS. 3 *Hen. VI*, III. ii. 175 Like one lost in a Thornie Wood, That rents the Thornes, and is rent with the Thornes. **1667** MILTON *P. L.* IV. 256 Flours of all hue, and without Thorn the Rose. **1671** GREW *Anat. Plants* iv. App. § 1 Thorns are of two kinds, Lignous and Cortical. **1776** WITHERING *Brit. Plants* (1796) II. 104 Capsules..awl-shaped, scored, tapering and ending in a double thorn or awn. *Ibid.* 350 Fruit-stalks forming bunches: thorns 3 together. **1867** J. HOGG *Microsc.* II. i. 324 Thorns, such as those of the rose, are aborted branches. **1880** GRAY *Struct. Bot.* iii. § 3 (ed. 6) 55 A Spine or Thorn is usually..the termination of a stem or branch, indurated, leafless, and attenuated to a point. *Prov.* There is no rose without a thorn.

**2.** *fig.* (or in fig. context): Anything that causes pain, grief, or trouble; in various metaphors, similes, and proverbial expressions, as *a thorn in the flesh* or *side*, a constant affliction, a source of continual grief, trouble, or annoyance; (*to be, sit, stand, walk*) *on thorns*, (to be, etc.) in a painful state of anxiety or suspense.

*c* **1230** *Hali Meid.* 9 Ha lickeð huni of þornes: ha buggen al þat swete wið twa dale of bittre. *c* **1374** CHAUCER *Troylus* III. 1055 (1104) Ye, Nece, wole ye pulle out þe þorn [*v.r.* thorne] That stiketh in his herte. **1500–20** DUNBAR *Poems* xii. 14 Welth, warldly gloir, and riche array, Ar all bot thornis laid in thy way. **1561** T. HOBY tr. *Castiglione's Courtyer* II. (1900) 114 The poore gentilwoman stood upon thornes, and thought an houre a thousande yeare, till she were got from him. *c* **1580** JEFFERIE *Bugbears* III. ii. in *Archiv Stud. Neu. Spr.* (1897), I sytt all on thornes till that matter take effect. **1602** SHAKS. *Ham.* I. v. 87 Those Thornes that in her bosome lodge. **1611** BIBLE 2 *Cor.* xii. 7 Least I should bee exalted aboue measure.. there was giuen to me a thorne in the flesh [1526 TIND. vnquyetnes of, 1557 *Gen.* a pricke in the fleshe], the messenger of Sathan to buffet me. *a* **1698** TEMPLE *Hist. Eng.* 93 No Prince ever came so early into the Cares and Thorns of a Crown. **1768** EARL CARLISLE in Jesse *Selwyn & Contemp.* (1843) II. 316, I should have been upon thorns till you had wrote. **1775** SHERIDAN *Rivals* v. i, Virtuous love..shall pluck the thorn from compunction. **1822** GALT *Provost* xlv, The perverse views.. of that Yankee thorn-in-the-side, Mr. Hickery. **1864** BRYCE *Holy Rom. Emp.* xii. (1875) 191 The Eastern Church was then, as she is to this day, a thorn in the side of the Papacy. **1886** C. E. PASCOE *Lond. of To-day* xxx. (ed. 3) 274 Not far from the grave of Elizabeth and Mary is that of the former's thorn in life, Mary of Scotland.

**3. a.** A spine or spiny process in an animal.

*c* **1300–** [implied in THORNBACK 1]. *c* **1711–56** [implied in THORNY 1 b]. **1860** [see *thorn oyster* in 8].

**b.** *Histology.* (See quots.)

**1899** *Allbutt's Syst. Med.* VI. 490 The dendrons are possessed of numerous minute lateral projections, gemmules, spines, or 'thorns' as they have been variously called. *Ibid.* VIII. 325 Dr. Alexander Hill believes the so-called 'thorns' to be organic structures, which are not shewn in their entirety by the chrome-silver method; and that a thorn is really the cell-end of an unstainable nerve filament, surrounded by a film of staining cell plasm.

**c.** *pl.* In *Lace-making*, Pointed projections used to decorate the cordonnet, etc., in point-lace.

**1874** *Queen Lace Bk.* I. 18 Little loops, knots, or knobs.. called Pearls, Thorns, or Picots. **1882** CAULFEILD & SAWARD *Dict. Needlework*, *Thorns*, used in Needlepoints to decorate the cordonnets and raised parts of the lace. See *Spines*.

**II. 4.** A plant which bears thorns or prickles; a bramble or brier; a prickly bush, shrub, or tree; a thorn-tree or thorn-bush; esp. any species of the genus *Cratægus*; in England, *spec.* the Hawthorn or White-thorn (*C. Oxyacantha*).

In early OE. *þyrne* wk. fem.:—**þurnjōn*.

*a* **700–** [implied in HAWTHORN]. *c* **725** *Corpus Gloss.* (O. E. T.) 1834 *Sentes*, ðornas. *c* **888** K. ÆLFRED *Boeth.* xxiii, Swa hwa swa wille sawan westmabære land, atio ærest of ða þornas & þa fyrsas & þ fearn & ealle þa weod. *c* **950** *Lindisf. Gosp.* Matt. xiii. 7 Oðro uutedlice ȝefeollon in ðornum..& woxon ða ðornas..& underdulfon ða. *c* **1000** ÆLFRIC *Gen.* iii. 18 Þornas and bremelas heo asprit þe. **1045** *Charter Edward* in Kemble *Cod. Dipl.* IV. 98 On ðane greatan þorn ðe stynt wið Grimes dic. *c* **1200** ORMIN 9219 Þurrh þorrness & þurrh breress þær shulenn beon ridinngess nu. *c* **1250** *Gen. & Ex.* 1334 Faste in ðornes he saȝ a sep. **1382** WYCLIF *Judg.* ix. 14 And alle the trees seiden to the thorn, Com, and comaund thow vpon us. *c* **1450** *Godstow Reg.* 34 Fowre burdyns of thornys of her wood of Cumnore. **1545** BRINKLOW *Lament.* (1874) 92 Do briers bringe forth figges, and thorns grapes? **1615** W. LAWSON *Orch. & Gard.* (1623) Pref., Curious conceits..inoculating Roses on Thornes, and such like. **1750** GRAY *Elegy* 116 Grav'd on the stone beneath yon aged thorn. **1800** WORDSW. *Hart-leap Well* 33 Dismounting, then, he leaned against a thorn. **1866** *Treas. Bot.* 344/2 The thorns [*Cratægus*] are natives of Europe, North America, and the temperate regions of Asia and Africa. **1882** *Garden* 24 June 419/1 Thorns, white, pink, and crimson..have been very beautiful.

**b.** (*without article*). Thorn bushes or branches collectively; also, the wood of a thorn-tree.

*a* **1300** *Cursor M.* 924 (Cott.) Brembel and thorn it sal te yeild. *Ibid.* 16437 Þai crond him wit þorn. *c* **1330** R. BRUNNE *Chron.* (1810) 14 Sibriht,..Þat a suynhird slouh vnder a busk of thorn. **1377** LANGL. *P. Pl.* B. XII. 228 Þe pyes..þere þe þorne is thikkest..buylden and brede. **1508** DUNBAR *Tua Mariit Wemen* 15 Throw pykis of the plet thorne I presandlie luikit. **1592** SHAKS. *Rom. & Jul.* I. iv. 26 It is too rough, Too rude, too boysterous, and it pricks like thorne. **1615** CHAPMAN *Odyss.* XIV. 17 The inner part..Which with an hedge of Thorn he fenc't about. **1712** POPE *Messiah* 73 Sandy vallies once perplexed with thorn. *Mod.* Thorn is a hard wood, and makes good cudgels.

**c.** *fig.* (or in figurative language). Sometimes alluding to the parable of the sower, Matt. xiii. 7.

*a* **1340** HAMPOLE *Psalter* xxxii. 12 Full of thornes & brers of synnes. **1735** JOHNSON *Lobo's Abyssinia, Descr.* i. 47 Little besides the Name of Christianity is to be found here, and the Thorns may be said to have choaked the Grain. **1819** SHELLEY *Ode West Wind* 54, I fall upon the thorns of life! I bleed! **1850** W. IRVING *Goldsmith* xxxvii. 358 The thorns which beset an author in the path of theatrical literature.

**5.** With qualifying words used to distinguish species and varieties of *Cratægus*, and to designate various other thorny plants: as

**Aronia thorn**, *Cratægus Aronia*; **Buffalo thorn**, *Acacia latronum*, an Indian tree; **Egyptian thorn**, *Acacia vera*, one of the trees which produce gum-arabic; **Elephant thorn**, *Acacia tomentosa* (*Treas. Bot.* 1866); **Evergreen thorn**, *Cratægus Pyracantha*, an ornamental evergreen bearing a profusion of red berries in clusters during winter; **Jerusalem thorn**, *Parkinsonia aculeata*, a spiny shrub found in tropical regions; **Mysore thorn**, *Cæsalpinia sepiaria*, a leguminous plant; **Spanish hedgehog thorn**, some species of the genus *Anthyllis*. See also BLACKTHORN, BOX-*t.*, BUCKTHORN, CAMEL'S-*t.*, CHRIST'S *t.*, GLASTONBURY *t.*, GOAT'S-*t.*, HAWTHORN, LILY *t.*, MOUSE-*t.*, ORANGE *t.*, PURGING *t.*, SALLOW *t.*, SCORPION'S *t.*, WHITE-THORN.

**1882** *Garden* 12 Aug. 145/3 The *Aronia Thorn..is a moderate-growing tree. **1866** *Treas. Bot.*, *Buffalo Thorn, *Acacia latronum.* **1731** MILLER *Gard. Dict.*, *Acacia*, *Egyptian Thorn or Binding Bean Tree. **1860** MAYNE *Expos. Lex.*, Egyptian Thorn,..*Acacia vera*, the gum-arabic tree. **1731** MILLER *Gard. Dict.* s.v. *Mespilus*, The Pyracantha or *Ever-green Thorn. **1866** *Treas. Bot.* 847/2 *P[arkinsonia] aculeata*, called in Jamaica the *Jerusalem Thorn. **1814** ROXBURGH *Hort. Bengal.* 32 *Cæsalpinia sepiaria*, *Mysore Thorn. **1760** J. LEE *Introd. Bot.* App. 329 Thorn, *Spanish Hedgehog, *Anthyllis.*

**6.** (Short for *thorn-moth.*) Collectors' name for various geometrid moths.

Applied originally to species whose larvæ feed on the hawthorn or kindred plants.

**1832** RENNIE *Conspectus Butterfl. & Moths* 105 Geometra (Leach)...The September Thorn (*G. erosaria*). *Ibid.* 106 The Angled Thorn (*G. angularia*). **1869** NEWMAN *Brit. Moths* 57 The September Thorn (*Ennomos erosaria*).

**III. 7.** The name of the Old English and Icelandic runic letter Þ þ (= th); named, like other runes, from the word of which it was the initial.

*c* **1000** *Runic Poem* iii. (Gr.), Þorn byð þearle scearp. *c* **1400** MAUNDEV. (Roxb.) xv. 71 Þ and ȝ, whilk er called þorn and ȝok. **1885** E. M. THOMPSON in *Encycl. Brit.* XVIII. 160/1 The English letter thorn, *þ*, survived and continued in use down to the 15th century.

**IV. 8.** *attrib.* and *Comb.* **a.** Attributive, as *thorn-acacia, avenue, -bed* (BED *sb.* 8), *-cover* (COVER *sb.*[1] 4), *fence, -fire, forest, grove, -holt, jungle, kloof, -prick, -puncture, scrub, stick, -sting, thicket*; objective, etc., as *thorn-bearer, -eater*; *thorn-like, -proof, -resisting* adjs.; instrumental, as *thorn-bound, -covered, -encompassed, -marked, -pricked, -set, -strewn, -wounded, -wreathed* adjs. **b.** Special combs.: †**thorn-beak**, the garfish, *Belone vulgaris*; **thorn-bill**, a humming-bird of the South American genus *Rhamphomicron*; **thorn-bird**, a South American bird, *Anumbius acuticaudatus* (allied to the OVEN-BIRD), which builds a large domed nest of thorny twigs (Webster, 1890); **thorn-bit**, ? a bit with a sharp projection which pricks the horse's mouth; also *fig.*; †**thorn-broom**, (*a*) the petty whin, *Genista anglica*; (*b*) the common furze; †**thorn-but** [BUTT *sb.*[1]], ? = THORNBACK 1; **thorn-catcher**, a device attached to a bicycle or motor-car, to extract thorns and the like from the tire as the wheel rotates; **thorn-devil**, name of an Australian lizard, *Moloch horridus*; = MOLOCH 2; **thorn-fly** (also *hawthorn-fly, thorn-tree fly*), a kind of artificial fly; †**thorn-garth**, an enclosure protected by a thorn-hedge; †**thorn-grape**, the gooseberry; **thorn-head** (Webster, 1890), **thorn-headed worm**, one of the *Acanthocephala*, intestinal parasitic worms having the proboscis furnished with hooks or spines; †**thorn-hog**, a hedgehog; **thorn-hopper**, a tree-hopper, *Thelia cratægi*, which frequents thorny shrubs (*Cent. Dict.* 1891); **thorn house**, in salt-making by the graduation method, a structure in which weak brine is caused to trickle over piles or high walls of thorns and brushwood giving a large surface for evaporation; **thorn-letter**, the runic letter þ: = sense 7; **thorn-lizard** = *thorn-devil*; **thorn-locust**, the common honey-locust tree of N. America, *Gleditschia triacanthos*; **thorn-moth** = sense 6; **thorn-mussel**, a pinna; **thorn oyster**, popular name of bivalves of the family *Spondylidæ*, in which the older specimens have the lower valve spiny; also *thorny oyster*; **thorn-quick**, a young thorn-plant for a hedge; †**thorn-rone**, a brake or undergrowth of thorns; **thorn-shell**, a spiny shellfish; **thorn-stone**, a concretion deposited on the faggots in a *thorn house* (see quot. 1848); **thorn-swine**, a porcupine (*Cent. Dict.* 1891); **thorn-tail**, popular name of the humming-birds of the South American genus *Gouldia*, distinguished by a long pointed tail; **thorn-tailed** *a.*, having a tail resembling a thorn, or with thorn-like processes; *thorn-tailed agama*, an agamoid lizard of the genus *Uromastix*, having the tail cased with rings of spiny scales; **thorn-wall**, in salt-making: cf. *thorn house*; **thorn-wood**, (*a*) a wood of thorns; (*b*) (*thornwood*) a South African tree (perh. *Acacia Natalitia*, the South African Wattle); also *attrib.* See also THORN-APPLE, THORN-BUSH, etc.

**1570** LEVINS *Manip.* 207/6 A Hornbeak, fish...A *Thornbeak. **1894** G. ALLEN in *Westm. Gaz.* 8 May 2/1 They [nettles] make a practice of sheltering themselves under.. stouter and taller *thorn-bearers. **1844** STEPHENS *Bk. Farm* I. 374 The ditch is thus marked out ready for the formation of the *thorn-bed. **1861** GOULD *Humming Birds* III. Pl. 188 *Ramphomicron Ruficeps*—Red-capped *Thorn-Bill. **1870** GILLMORE tr. *Figuier's Rept. & Birds* 471 The Thornbills..are American birds. **1886** KIPLING *Departm. Ditties*, etc. (1899) 90 The colt who is wise will abstain from the terrible *thorn-bit of Marriage. **1578** LYTE *Dodoens* VI. ix. 668 *Genistilla*, Furze or *thorne Broome groweth in vntoyled places. **1597** GERARDE *Herbal* III. xviii. 1140 In English Furze, Furzen bushes, Whinne, Gorsse, and

Thorne Broome. 1668 CHARLETON *Onomast.* 149 *Rhombus* ..Qui est vel *Aculeatus*, the *Thorn-but. 1736 AINSWORTH *Lat. Dict.*, The thornbut, *Rhombus aculeatus.* 1901 *Daily Chron.* 1 June 8/7 A great many punctures can be nipped in the bud, so to speak, by employing *thorn-catchers. 1850 R. G. CUMMING *Hunter's Life S. Afr.* (1902) 158/2 We halted..beside several acres of *thorn-cover. 1642 MILTON *Apol. Smect.* v. Wks. 1738 I. 119 This obscure *thorn-eater of Malice and Detraction, as well as of Quodlibets and Sophisms. 1799 G. SMITH *Laboratory* II. 310 *Thorn-fly. Dubbing of black lamb's wool [etc.]. *a* 1340 HAMPOLE *Psalter* lxxxviii. 39 Thou distroyd all his *thorne garthis. 1578 LYTE *Dodoens* VI. xix. 681 *Vua spina*, whiche may be Englished, *Thorne grape. 1886 FAGGE & PYE-SMITH *Princ. Med.* (ed. 2) II. 234 An acanthocephalous or *thornheaded worm, Echinorrhynchus sp., has only once been certainly discovered in the human intestine. 1340 *Ayenb.* 66 Þe *þorn-hog þet ys al ywryȝe myd prikyinde eles. *c* 1450 *Godstow Reg.* 208 Half a rode of lond, liyng in the *thorneholte in the feldes of halso. 1866 *Tomlinson's Cycl.* II. 552/1 [At Moutiers] There are four evaporating houses called *Maisons d'Épines* or *thorn-houses.* 1879 G. GLADSTONE in *Cassell's Techn. Educ.* IV. 353/1 Thorn houses..are gigantic erections consisting of a skeleton of timber filled in with thorn bushes.. the water trickles down over the ends of the twigs. 1902 SKEAT in *Athenæum* 22 Nov. 684/1 The words 'that' and 'this' and 'the' all begin, in the MS., with the usual *thorn-letter. 1899 CAGNEY *Jaksch's Clin. Diagn.* viii. 413 The resulting cultivation is marked with..*thorn-like processes projecting from it. 1860 WRAXALL *Life in Sea* vi. 143 The great *Thorn-mussel (*Pinna*) of the Mediterranean. *Ibid.* viii. 208 They [species of Spondyli] are distinguished by bright colours, but more especially by the long thorns and spurs with which they are covered, and for this reason they are also called *Thorn Oysters. 1858 CHR. ROSSETTI *Fr. House to Home* 63, I felt no *thorn-prick when I plucked a flower. 1565 JEWEL *Repl. Harding* (1611) 417 That *Thorn-prickt, Nail-boared, Speare-pierced, and otherwise wounded, rent, and torne Bodie. 1908 *Daily Chron.* 25 Apr. 9/5 A Beeston Humber bicycle, of roadster type, fully equipped with special *thorn-proof tyres and a metal gear-case. 1755 *Forfeited Estates Papers* (S.H.S.) 92 [He] has raised..since 1740 no less than 1,676,147 *Thorn Quicks. *a* 1400 *Sc. Trojan War* II. 2437 And has bot one small hole but dout In-to þat *thorne-rone, richt secre. 1757 DYER *Fleece* I. 115 Haughty trees.. that weaken *thorn-set mounds. 1860 WRAXALL *Life in Sea* viii. 209 A wondrously beautiful *Thorn Shell. 1857 HUGHES *Tom Brown* I. ii, A stout *thorn stick in his hand. 1848 *Knapp's Chem. Technol.* I. 266 The thorns become gradually covered with a thick coating (*thorn-stone*), consisting of carbonates of lime, magnesia, manganese, and protoxide of iron. 1885 C. G. W. LOCK *Workshop Receipts* Ser. IV. 153/1 [The fagots] have to be changed every 2 years or so, on account of a deposit of calcium carbonate ('thornstone') which coats them. 1783 LATHAM *Gen. Syn. Birds* IV. 463 *Thorn-tailed Warbler... Inhabits Terra del Fuego. 1888 *Cassell's Encycl. Dict.* s.v. *Uromastix*, Thorn-tailed Agamas..from the south of Russia..and Central India. 1866 *Tomlinson's Cycl.* II. 554/1 The Saxon method of graduation by the use of *thorn-walls. 1850 R. G. CUMMING *Hunter's Life S. Afr.* (1902) 147/1 Reducing with adzes a *thornwood tree, which was to serve as a beam. 1863 W. C. BALDWIN *Afr. Hunting* vi. 148 A beautiful country of dense thornwood. 1819 SHELLEY *Prometh. Unb.* I. 598 Let that *thorn-wounded brow Stream not with blood.

**Thorn** (þǭɹn), *v.* Now *rare.* [f. prec. sb.]

**1.** *trans.* To make thorny, to furnish with thorns; *esp.* to protect (a newly planted quick-set hedge or the like) with dead thorn-bushes. Also *absol.*

1483 *Cath. Angl.* 384/1 To Thorne, *dumare, spinare, dumere esse vel fieri, -escere.* 1541 *Nottingham Rec.* III. 382 For thorns and for thornyng of wylo settes. 1579 *Mem. St. Giles, Durham* (Surtees) 1 Payde..for thornynge the wicke for saufegayrde of the shepe. 1784 ROBINSON *Let.* in *N. & Q.* 3rd Ser. IV. 342/2, [I] set a man to hedge and thorn. 1875 BROWNING *Aristophanes' Apol.* 630 Vowel-buds thorned about with consonants.

**2.** To prick with or as with a thorn; to vex.

1590 C'TESS PEMBROKE *Antonie* 226 And thousand thousand woes Our heau'nly soules now thorne. *Ibid.* 917 This grief, nay rage,..thornes me still. 1778 *Saberna* 16 A ruffian he!..Who stole a rose, and thorn'd the heart it blest! 1811 COLERIDGE *Let.* in J. P. Collier *Seven Lect.* (1856) p. lvii, The perplexities with which..I have been thorned and embrangled. 1877 TENNYSON *Harold* I. i. 243, I am the only rose of all the stock That never thorn'd him.

**†3.** To attach or pin together with thorns. *Obs.*

1598 SYLVESTER *Du Bartas* II. i. IV. *Handie-crafts* 140 With their sundry locks, thorn'd each to other, Their tender limbs they hide.

**Thoˑrn-aˑpple.** The common name of *Datura Stramonium*, N.O. *Solanaceæ* (see DATURA), a coarse annual plant bearing large funnel-shaped white flowers, succeeded by large four-celled capsules covered with prickly spines; also the capsule or fruit itself. Also formerly called *thorny apple.*

1578 LYTE *Dodoens* III. lxxxvii. 440 Fruite, round as an apple.., beset rounde about with many prickley thornes, and therefore they call it Thorne apple. 1694 W. SALMON *Bate's Dispens.* (1713) 680/2 Fresh Leaves of Strammonium bearing Thorn Apples. 1846 LINDLEY *Veg. Kingd.* 619 The Thorn-apple.. is a violent narcotic when taken internally. 1898 *Allbutt's Syst. Med.* V. 415 Crenation of the red-corpuscles, giving rise to the so-called mulberry and thorn-apple forms.

**Thornback** (þǭɹnbæk). Forms: see THORN *sb.* and BACK *sb.*[1]; also 5 -bagge, 7 -bage, -bagg.

**1.** The common ray or skate (*Raia clavata*) of British seas, used as food, distinguished by having several rows of short sharp spines arranged along the back and tail. Also called †*thorny-back* (obs.).

*c* 1300 *Havelok* 759 Þe Butte, þe schulle, þe þornebake. *Ibid.* 832. 1392 *Earl Derby's Exp.* (Camden) 155 Pro vj thornebakkes, iiij d. *c* 1440 *Anc. Cookery* in *Househ. Ord.* (1790) 469 A codlynge or whitynge, or thornbagge, or hadok. 1594 NASHE *Unfort. Trav.* 16 My cape cloake..ouer-spreading my backe like a thorne-backe. 1605 *Shuttleworths' Acc.* (Chetham Soc.) 170 One thornbage and fyve flokes vj[d]. 1653 H. COGAN tr. *Pinto's Trav.* xxiv. (1663) 89 We saw Fishes in the Shape of Thornbacks, that were four fathoms about, and had a Muzzle like an Ox. 1859 *Yarrell's Brit. Fishes* II. 582 The Thornback and its female the Maid. 1861 HULME tr. *Moquin-Tandon* II. III. i. 106 The Thornback.., from the shores of the Mediterranean, is of a brown colour, spotted with white and black. The body attains a length of twelve feet.

**b.** As the name of other species of ray: see quots.

1731 MEDLEY *Kolben's Cape G. Hope* II. 202 The Cape Thornback is a broad flat fish from three quarters of an inch to an inch thick. 1898 MORRIS *Austral Eng.*, *Thornback*, Name for one of the Stingrays, *Raia lemprieri*, Richards.

**†c.** *fig.* Opprobriously applied to a person.

1599 NASHE *Lenten Stuffe* (1871) 101 To be held a flat thornback, or sharp pricking dog-fish to the public weal.

**2. a.** Short for *thornback crab*: see 4.

1891 in *Cent. Dict.*

**b.** Provincial name of the stickleback.

1859 *Yarrell's Brit. Fishes* (ed. 3) II. 75 Rough-tailed Stickleback. Pinkeen..Thornback. *c* 1904 E. SMITH (*MS.*) *Warwick. Gloss.* (E.D.D.), *Thorn-back*, a small fish with a strong back fin. It abounds in the Avon, but it is not the stickleback.

**†3.** An old maid. *slang. Obs.*

The female young of the thornback is called *maid* (MAID *sb.*[1] 7), and *maiden-skate* (*Sc.*).

1694 MOTTEUX *Rabelais* v. iv, Whether when they were Maids, or Thornbacks, in their Prime, or at their last Prayers. 1709 *Brit. Apollo* II. No. 70. 2/2 Meeting with three Thornbacks.., I treated them. 1898 *Daily News* 14 Mar. 4/7 After 25, young ladies were called 'thorn-backs' by the much marrying Puritans of New England.

**4.** *attrib.*, as **thornback crab**, a species of spider-crab or sea-spider, *Maia squinado*, called also in U.S. king-crab; † **thornback dog**, a kind of dog-fish or shark of the genus *Galeus*; **thornback ray** = sense 1; **thornback skate** (see quot.).

1668 WILKINS *Real Char.* II. v. § 3. 132 Thornback Dog, [margin] *Galeus spinax.* 1862 COUCH *Brit. Fishes* I. 99 Thornback Ray, Ray-maid...This is one of the commonest of the Rays, and the most valued. 1875 *Melbourne Spectator* 28 Aug. 201/3 A thornback skate [*Raia rostrata*],.. weighing 109 lbs., has been caught..at North Arm.

Hence † **Thoˑrnbackly** *a. Obs.*, of the nature of a thornback: cf. 1 c above.

1605 *Tryall Chev.* v. ii. in Bullen *Old Pl.* (1884) III. 350 The Thornbackly slave!

**Thoˑrn-bush.** Any bush that bears thorns; e. g. a hawthorn, a bramble. Also *attrib.*

*c* 1330 R. BRUNNE *Chron.* (1810) 9 A suynhird smote he to dede vnder a thorn busk. 1483 *Cath. Angl.* 384/1 A Thorne buske, *spinetum.* 1535 COVERDALE *Judg.* ix. 15 Then sayde all the trees vnto the thorne buszshe: Come thou, and be kynge ouer vs. 1590 SHAKS. *Mids. N.* v. i. 263, I, the man in the Moone; this thorne bush, my thorne bush; and this dog, my dog. 1896 BADEN-POWELL *Matabele Campaign* xi, I lay up during the heat of the day with a waterproof sheet spread over a thorn-bush as a shelter from the sun. 1902 *Westm. Gaz.* 3 Nov. 3/1 Crossing this thick thorn-bush country in the face of the opposition of a numerous army elated by recent success.

**Thoˑrn-crown.** A crown or fillet of thorns: chiefly in reference to that placed in mockery on the head of Christ (Matt. xxvii. 29, etc.).

?*c* 1400 *Warres of Jewes* (Laud MS. 22) in Warton *Hist. Eng. Poetry* (1840) II. 106 A strange thorn crown was thraste on his hed. 1859 LD. LYTTON *Wanderer* (ed. 2) 420 The thorn-crown hath blossom'd on my brow. 1902 *Lindsey Star* 12 July 2/2 He wore the thorn-crown on His brow.

So **Thoˑrn-crowned** *a.*, crowned with thorns, wearing a crown of thorns.

1609 J. DAVIES *Holy Roode* G j, We learne..by his Thorne-crowned head, How to adorne vs. 1792 R. CUMBERLAND *Calvary* (1803) II. 101 His thorn-crown'd head upon his breast reclin'd. 1903 *Month* Aug. 127 The thorn-crowned figure of the Redeemer.

**Thorne**, variant of THARN *v. Obs.*, to lack.

**Thorned** (þǭɹnd), *a.* [f. THORN *sb.* + -ED[2].] **a.** Having or provided with thorns. **b.** Overgrown with thorn-bushes.

1893 CHR. ROSSETTI *Songs for Strangers*, etc., Poems (1904) 123/2 Our crooked ground, our thorned and thistled plot. 1895 *Pop. Sci. Monthly* Feb. 499 The thorned plants that inhabit them. 1903 *Daily Chron.* 21 Mar. 8/4 Long trails of thorned rose stems.

**†Thoˑrnel.** *Obs. rare*—[1]. [Corruption of dial. German *darndel* = *darrling*, f. *darr-en* to dry, parch, roast.] Silver or copper ore which remains unreduced in smelting.

1683 PETTUS *Fleta Min.* I. xxviii. § 9. 75 Let the Silver be dry, and when the Thornels (if there be any) and the Silver hath taken hold on the Ashes, they must be beaten down with a Hammer. *Ibid.* II. 125 *Thornels*,..a term of Art, for that which remains of the roasted Oar, unmelted.

**Thornen** (þǭˑɹnĕn), *a. Obs.* exc. *dial.* Forms: 1 ð-, þyrnen, 2 þernen; 2–4 þornen, 4 (9 *dial.*) thornen, 9 *dial.* tharnin. [In OE. *þyrnen* = OHG. *durnîn*, Goth. *þaurneins*, :—OTeut. **þurnînoz*, f. **þurn-us* THORN: see -EN *suffix*[4]. ME. *þornen* (without umlaut) was assimilated to the sb.; so Ger. *dornen.*] Of thorns or thorn; thorny.

*c* 897 K. ÆLFRED *Gregory's Past. C.* xxxvi. 260 He ȝeðafode ðæt him mon sette ðyrnenne beaȝ on ðæt heafod. *c* 1000 ÆLFRIC *Hom.* II. 252 His cempan..mid þyrnenum helme his heafod befengon. *c* 1160 *Hatton Gosp.* Mark xv. 17 Þa cempen..him on setten þernene helm awundene. *c* 1175 *Lamb. Hom.* 121 Mid þornene crune his heaued wes icruned. *c* 1400 *Trevisa's Higden* (Rolls) VI. 427 He feng a party of þe holy crosse, and som of þe crowne of þorne [*MSS. a, γ*, þornene crowne; *β*, þornen coroun]. 1859 HUGHES *Scour. Wh. Horse* iv, The tharnin tree..As is called King Alferd's tharn. 1863 BARNES *Poems* III. 29, I pass'd the maid avore the spring, An' shepherd by the thornen tree.

**Thoˑrn-heˑdge.** A hedge of thorny shrubs; *spec.* a hedge composed of hawthorn 'sets'. Hence **Thoˑrn-heˑdged** *a.*, furnished with or enclosed by a thorn-hedge.

1560 BIBLE (Genev.) *Micah* vii. 4 The most righteous of them is sharper then a thorne hedge. *a* 1732 T. BOSTON *Crook in Lot* (1805) 33 It is like a thorn-hedge..in the way which that bias inclines him to. 1854 *Zoologist* XII. 4286, I discovered in a thorn-hedge the first nest that I had seen that year. 1892 A. M. CLERKE *Fam. Stud. Homer* iii. 73 Odysseus..approached the thorn-hedged enclosure.

**Thornily** (þǭˑɹnili), *adv.* [f. as next + -LY[2].] In a thorny manner; so as to be thorny.

1887 BLACKMORE *Springhaven* xvi, Thornily crested with good stout furze.

**Thorniness** (þǭˑɹninės). [f. THORNY + -NESS.] Thorny quality or condition, prickliness; *fig.* acerbity of manner, roughness, ruggedness.

1674 R. GODFREY *Inj. & Ab. Physic* 87 The Thornyness, or bad Character imprinted on the stomach,..might be obliterated. 1721 BAILEY, *Spinosity*, thorniness, difficulty. 1868 A. R. WALLACE *Malay Archip.* 158 The most characteristic feature of the jungle was its thorniness. 1895 *Current Hist.* (Buffalo, N. Y.) V. 753 The historian's rude sallies and general thorniness. 1906 *Athenæum* 7 July 5/2 The thorniness of metre which this poet shares with Browning.

**†Thoˑrnish**, *a. Obs. rare.* [f. THORN *sb.* + -ISH[1].] Thorny, prickly.

1426 LYDG. *De Guil. Pilgr.* 11234 Me thouthe I sawh a fforkyd weye Partyng at an heg on tweyne, Thykke and thornyssh in certeyne. 1577 FRAMPTON *Joyful News* II. (1596) 79 The fruite of a tree very great, after the maner of Thornish Chestnuts.

**Thornless** (þǭˑɹnlės), *a.* [f. THORN *sb.* + -LESS.] Having no thorns; free from thorns; without a thorn.

1776 WITHERING *Brit. Plants* (1796) II. 461 [*Mespilus germanica*] Thornless: leaves spear-shaped, cottony underneath: flowers solitary, sitting. 1803 VISCT. STRANGFORD *Poems of Camoens, To Night* (1810) 66, I..Have never yet been one of those Whose love has prov'd a thornless rose! 1825 H. ALFORD in *Life* 17 Perennial and thornless flowers bloom only in the Paradise above.

Hence **Thoˑrnlessness.**

1857 LIVINGSTONE *Trav.* xviii. 345 The thornlessness of the vegetation is especially noticeable.

**Thornlet** (þǭˑɹnlėt). [f. THORN *sb.* + -LET.] **a.** A diminutive thorn-bush. **b.** A minute thorn.

1865 E. BURRITT *Walk Land's End* xii. 419 The Rifle Corps fired a volley over the consecrated thornlet. 1882 SLADEN in *Jrnl. Linn. Soc.* XVI. 201 The spinelets..appear like well-developed thornlets.

**Thornpole, -pool**, var. *thorlpoll*, THIRLEPOLL.

**Thoˑrn-tree.** A tree having or bearing thorns; in Great Britain, usually a hawthorn tree.

1483 *Cath. Angl.* 384/1 A Thorne tree, *mespula, rampnus.* 1850 R. G. CUMMING *Hunter's Life S. Afr.* (1902) 60/1 A clump of tangled thorn-trees. 1856 STANLEY *Sinai & Pal.* x. 363 The 'Nabk', or thorn-tree,..here breaks out along the hill-sides in thick jungles. 1895 *Atlantic Monthly* July 61 The thorn-tree before me was perhaps fifteen feet high.

**b.** *attrib.* **Thorn-tree fly**, a March trout-fly, a thorn-fly or HAWTHORN-FLY, q. v.

1676 COTTON *Walton's Angler* II. vii. (1881) 285 There is also for this month [March], a fly, called the Thorn-tree fly; the dubbing is..black, mixed with eight or ten hairs of Isabella-coloured mohair. 1787 BEST *Angling* 99 March. The Thorn or Hawthorn Tree fly. 1909 *Westm. Gaz.* 4 May 2/3 Scant thorn-tree shade where white sheep flock.

**Thorny** (þǭˑɹni), *a.* [OE. *þorniȝ*, f. THORN *sb.* + *-iȝ*, -Y. Cf. MHG. *dornic.*]

**1.** Abounding in, characterized by, or consisting of thorns or spines; spiny, prickly.

*a* 1023 WULFSTAN *Hom.* xlviii. (Napier) 246 ȝeheȝa þine earan mid þorniȝum heȝe. *a* 1225 *Ancr. R.* 134 Heo makieð frommard hore nest—softe wiðuten, & þorni wiðinnen. 1398 TREVISA *Barth. De P. R.* XVIII. xix. (Bodl. MS.), Þe Cameles mete is þorny and harde. 1456 *Coventry Leet Bk.* 291 Weryng þe Thorny crowne yn worship of Jhesu. 1596 SHAKS. *Tam. Shr.* Ind. ii. 59 Daphne roming through a thornie wood. 1697 DRYDEN *Virg. Georg.* III. 490 On Shrubs they browze, and..thorny Brambles crop. 1850 TENNYSON *In Mem.* lxix. 6, I found a wood with thorny boughs.

**b.** Of an animal (or a part of one): Having thorn-like organs or appendages; spiny. See also 4.

*c* 1711 PETIVER *Gazophyl.* VI. lx, Sea Porcupine...This thorny Fish is a sort of Sea Hedge-hog. 1743 ZOLLMAN in *Phil. Trans.* XLII. 463 Those Caterpillars which, from the Figure and the Stiffness of their Hairs, have been called the Thorny ones. 1756 AMORY *Buncle* (1825) I. 250 The perch [with] the thorny fins on its back.

**2.** Abounding in thorn-bearing or prickly plants; overgrown with thorns or brambles. Also *fig.*

*Thorny ground*, fig. after the parable of the sower, Matt. xiii. 7, etc. Often *attrib.*

*c* 1000 ÆLFRIC *Hom.* I. 342 Se yrðling lufað ðone æcer, ðe æfter ðornum..wæstmas aȝifð, swiðor þonne he lufiȝe ðone ðe ðorniȝ næs, ne wæstmbære ne bið. *c* 1325 *Metr. Hom.* 52 This gat es stany and thornye. *c* 1440 *Gesta Rom.* viii. 19 (Harl. MS.) Þe wey toward þe Cite was stony, þorny, and scroggy. 1593 SHAKS. 3 *Hen. VI*, v. iv. 67 The thornie Wood, Which..Must by the Roots be hew'ne vp yet ere Night. 1657 J. WATTS *Dipper Sprinkled* 93, I was a High-way side Hearer, a Thorny-ground Auditor. 1735 SOMERville *Chace* I. 259 He..in the thorny Brake Torn and embarrass'd bleeds. **1799** Mary Titherington *Diary* in *Life* 13, I am but too much a thorny-ground hearer. **1863** W. C. Baldwin *Afr. Hunting* vi. 150 There are lots of game here, and a nice thorny country.

**3.** *fig* **a.** Pricking or piercing to the mind; full of points painful or wounding to the feelings; painful, distressing; harassing, vexatious, irritating.

*a* **1340** Hampole *Psalter* xvii. 36 All þe thorny & þe lairy besynes of þis warld. *a* **1586** Sidney *Arcadia* III. (R.), It was easily seen it was a very thorny abode he made there. **1600** Shaks. *A. Y. L.* II. vii. 94 The thorny point Of bare distresse, hath tane from me the shew Of smooth ciuility. **1728** Young *Love Fame* v. 252 Thorny care, and rank and stinging hate. **1868** Lynch *Rivulet* CXL. vi, That thorny cares may yield sweet fruits.

**b.** Full of points of contention or difficulty; difficult to handle; delicate, ticklish.

**1653** tr. *Hales' Dissert. de Pace* x. 48 In these so subtil and thorny explications, if they..chance to erre, shall they presently be termed the enemies of God and Christ? **1675** Traherne *Chr. Ethics* 25 Prudence is that knowledge, by which we guide our selves in thorny and uncertain affairs. **1793** Burke *Corr.* (1844) IV. 133 This American is an ugly and thorny affair. **1831** Scott *Jrnl.* 13 Mar., I have finally arranged a thorny transaction. **1907** *Athenæum* 25 May 638/1 Several of the thorniest questions which have perplexed both ancient and modern logicians.

**4. a.** In the names of species or varieties of plants, animals, or shells, characterized by having thorns or spines: prickly, spiny; as *thorny acacia, asparagus, clam, germander, lobster, rest-harrow*.

Also **thorny apple** = Thorn-apple; **thorny broom,** (*a*) the petty whin, *Genista anglica*, (*b*) the common whin, furze, or gorse; **thorny oyster** = *thorn-oyster* (Thorn *sb.* 8); **thorny palm**, the prickly palm of the W. Indies, *Bactris Plumierana*; **thorny trefoil**, a thorny shrub of the Mediterranean region, *Fagonia Cretica*; **thorny woodcock,** a shell of the Indian Ocean, *Murex tenuispina*, with long thin closely-set spines. (See also 5 b.)

**1834** Pringle *Afr. Sk.* vii. 239 An open grassy meadow ..bordered by willow trees and groves of the *thorny acacia [*A. horrida*, Dornboom]. **1578** Lyte *Dodoens* III. lxxxvii. 441 The Names..*Thornie apples, Prickle apples, and *Stramonia*. **1832** *Veg. Subst. Food Man* 187 The *thorny asparagus,..beset with sharp spines. **1597** Gerarde *Herbal* III. xviii. 1140 This *thorney Broome is taken for Theophrastus his *Scorpius*, which Gaza nameth *Nepa*. **1822** *Hortus Anglicus* II. 81 T[*eucrium*] *Spinosum*, *Thorny Germander. **1833** *Encycl. Brit.* (ed. 7) VII. 502/1 The *Palinurus vulgaris*, or *thorny lobster, sometimes also termed cray-fish. **1666** J. Davies *Hist. Caribby Isles* 35 The Prickly or *Thorny-Palm, having that name from the prickliness of it. **1822** *Hortus Anglicus* II. 233 *O*[*nonis*] *Spinosa*. *Thorny Rest Harrow. **1760** Lee *Introd. Bot.* App. 353/1 *Thorny Trefoil, of Candia, *Fagonia*. **1842** *Penny Cycl.* XXII. 55/1 *Murex Tribulus* (Common *Thorny Woodcock).

**b.** In other collocations, as † **thorny marrow**, the spinal marrow.

**1662** J. Chandler *Van Helmont's Oriat.* 195 It is made motive in the thorny marrow or *Spina Medullæ*.

**5.** *Comb.* as *thorny-edged, -pointed, -pricking, -thin, -twining* adjs.

**1594** Kyd *Cornelia* II. 269 Whose loftie Towers (like thorny-pointed speares). **1596** *Edw. III*, I. i, Feruent desire,..Is farre more thornie pricking than this blade. **1705** Petiver in *Phil. Trans.* XXV. 1952 The Thorny-edged Carolina Crab. **1735** Somerville *Chace* II. 166 The thorny-twining Hedge. **1885** Hel. G. Cone in *Atlantic Monthly* Apr. 451 What lifeless laughter, crackling thorny-thin?

**b.** Special Combs.: **thorny-back**, (*a*) the thornback; (*b*) the stickleback; (*c*) the river perch; **thorny-ribs** (see quot.); **thorny-shell**, a univalve mollusc, *Voluta spinosa*.

**1810** P. Neill *List Fishes* 28 (Jam.) *Thorny-back (*Raia clavata*). **1869** *Chater's Tyneside Alm.* 13 (E.D.D.) Here may be fund the thorney-back, the Poheed an' Tommy Lodjor. *c* **1711** Petiver *Gazophyl.* VIII. lxxviii, Limington *Thorney-ribs...A sort of Fossil Murex. **1713** Petiver *Aquat. Anim. Amboinæ* Tab. iii, *Voluta spinosa*..River *Thorney-shell.

**Thoro**, obs. form of Thorough.

**Thoro-** (þōᵊ·ro), combining form of Thorium, in names of compound salts, minerals, etc. e. g. **Thorogu·mmite** *Min.* [Gummite: see quot. 1889], a hydrated thorosilicate of uranium; **Thorosi·licate** *Chem.*, a silicate in which part of the silicon is replaced by thorium.

**1889** *Amer. Jrnl. Sc. & Art* XXXVIII. 481 We name this mineral *thoro-gummite*, because it is a gummite in which the water has been replaced by the thorite molecule. *Ibid.* 480 It seems better to regard the mineral as a hydrated thoro-silicate of uranium, rather than as a urano-silicate of thorium. **1909** *Cent. Dict. Supp.*, Thorogummite..like other native compounds of thorium and uranium, has marked radio-active properties.

**Thorough** (þʌ·rŏ, þʌ·rə), *prep.* and *adv.* Chiefly *archaic* or *Obs.* Forms: see below. [A disyllabic development of OE. *þurh*, Through, when fully stressed, which appeared already in later OE. as *þuruh* (cf. OHG. *duruh, durah, durih*, OS. *thuru*), and has regularly become *thorough* in mod.Eng., as *burh* became *buruh, borough, furh furrow, borh borrow, sorh sorrow, mearh marrow. Thorough* is thus the direct representative of the full-stressed OE. *þurh*; and it is owing to the fact that *þurh* was chiefly a preposition, and thus usually proclitic and stressless, that it is now, in this use, represented by *through* (unstressed þru, new-stressed þrū). The stressed form was naturally used when *þurh* was a separate word, i. e. an adv., adj., or sb., or the stressed part of a compound, as in *tho·roughfare*; and, as prepositions were sometimes emphatic and stressed, the *þuruh, thorough* form remained also as a prep. beside the unstressed *pŭrh, þŭr, þrŭh, þrŭ*, etc.; on the other hand, the new-stressed form *through* (þrū) of the prep. has in more recent times been taken also by the adv., while *thorough* remains in both as an archaic form, and as that of the derived adj. and sb. In the adverb its function is largely taken over by its derivative *thoroughly*.

As both *thorough* and *through* are existing words, distinct in spelling and still more in pronunciation, it seems best to make two articles, placing under Through the various monosyllabic forms, including the obsolete *þurh, thurgh, þurþ, þurth*, and the now dialectal *thruff*, and treating under Thorough the less numerous disyllabic variants. This entails some duplication of the definition, but appears preferable to treating *thorough* merely as a variant of *through*. It must be remembered however that both *þruh*, through, and *þuruh*, thorough, developed by insensible gradations out of *þurh, thurgh*, and that therefore the *a*-forms under Through belong, down to 1300 and 1400, really as much to the history of *thorough*.]

**A.** Illustration of Forms.

**α.** 1–3 **þuruh**, 3 **þureh**, **puregh**, 3–5 **þoruȝ**, 4 **þoruh**, **þoruhe**, **þoroȝ**, **þorogh**, **thorogh**, 4–5 **þorouȝ**, **thoruȝ**, 4–6 **thorugh**, 5 **thoruh**, **thorowh**, **-owgh**, **-ughe**, **-oughe**, 5– **thorough** (8– **thoro'**). **β.** 3–4 **þuru**, **þoru**, 4 **thoru**, **þorou**, 4–5 **thoro**, **thorou**, **þorow(e**, 4–6 **thorowe**, 4–8 (9 in comb.) **thorow**, (5 **thurow**, **thurrowe**, 5–6 **dorow**, 6 **thurrou(ly)**, **thorro**, 6–7 **thorrow**); **γ.** 3–4 **þorw**, 4 **þurw**, **þourw**, **thorw**, 4–5 **þorwe**; 4 **þoruth** (in *þoruthlike*, Thoroughly).

*c* **1000** *Ags. Ps.* (Th.) lxv. 11 We þuruh fyr farað, and þuruh floda þrym. *c* **1200** *Trin. Coll. Hom.* 199 Oðer kinnes neddre..crieþeð nedlinge þureh nerewe hole. *Ibid.* 33 Þuregh [see B. I. 6]. **1297** R. Glouc. (Rolls) 8513 Þoru godes wille. *a* **1300** *Cursor M.* 151 How crist com thoro [*v.rr.* þorow, thoru, þourȝe] propheci. **13..** *Ibid.* 20698 (B. M. Add. MS.) Þorwe [*v.rr.* thoru, þorou, þourȝe] þe toun. **1377** Langl. *P. Pl.* B. IX. 151 Þus þourw cursed caym cam care vppon erthe. *Ibid.* XIV. 300 Þorw þe pas of altoun Pouerte myȝte passe with-oute peril of robbynge. *c* **1380** Þorouȝ [see B. I. 1 b]. *c* **1430** *Hymns Virg.* 123 Longeus hym stonge dorow þe syde. *c* **1449** Pecock *Repr.* I. i. 7 Weelnyȝ thoruȝ al the chapiter. **1456** Thurrowe [see B. I. 6]. **1467, 1482** Thorow [see B. II. 3]. **1474** Thorough [see B. II. 4]. **1484** Caxton *Fables of Æsop* I. xiv, Deceyued thoroughe fals counceylle. **1485** — *Chas. Gt.* I. II. v. 30 Thorugh hys empyre. **1556** *Chron. Gr. Friars* (Camden) 40 Browte..to the tower thorrow Smythfelde and in at Newgat, rydynge soo thorrow Chepe-syde. *Ibid.* 56 Prechyng thorro alle Ynglonde agayne the sacrament of the auter. **1590** Shaks. *Mids. N.* II. i. 3 Over hill, over dale, Thorough [*folios* Through] bush, thorough brier. **1672**, *a* **1713** Thorow [see B. II. 1]. **1725** S. Sewall *Diary* 17 Mar., Much Water passes thorow the three Spaces left for that purpose. **1850, 1893** Thorough [see B. I. 1, 2].

**B.** Signification.

**I.** *prep.* (Still in poetic or archaic use.)

**1.** From side to side or end to end of; = Through *prep.* 1. *arch.*

*c* **1000**, *c* **1200** [see A.]. **1297** R. Glouc. (Rolls) 4277 Þe erl ..mid is launce þoru þe þrote smot on. *a* **1300** *Cursor M.* 7809 Thoru his licam mi suerd i draif. **1377** [see A.]. *c* **1450** *ME. Med. Bk.* (Heinrich) 204 Let hyt renne þorow a fayre cloþ. *a* **1540** Barnes *Wks.* (1573) 212/2 You ryde thorowe streetes, and townes. **1684** R. Waller *Nat. Exper.* 121 An hole thorough the bottom of the Vessel. **1712** tr. *Pomet's Hist. Drugs* I. 149 Such as will pass thorow an Iron Ring. **1850** Blackie *Æschylus* I. 191 Thorough my heart, Thorough my liver, Keen as the cold ice Shot through the river.

**b.** Of transmission of light or sight. *Obs.* or *arch.*

*c* **1380** Wyclif *Serm.* Sel. Wks. I. 142 As þe sunne comeþ þorouȝ þe glas. **1585** T. Washington tr. *Nicholay's Voy.* II. iii. 33, I saw these bathes thorow a great hole. *a* **1636** Lynde *Case for Spect.* (1638) 45 You begin to looke asquint thorow your Spectacles at the reformed Churches. **1705** Stanhope *Paraphr.* II. 599 The Truth never shines so bright, as when the Oppositions, that strive to darken it, are plainly seen thorow.

† **c.** In reference to the passage of the voice through the throat, etc.: = Through *prep.* 1 d.

**1668** [see Through B. I. 1 d].

† **d.** Of passage between the individual things of a group; = Through *prep.* 1 e. *Obs.*

**1535** Fisher *Wks.* (1876) 365 He must..creepe thorowe the thicke bushes. **1684** Bunyan *Pilgr.* II. 39 The man that cut his way thorough his Enemies.

† **e.** In phrase *thorough one's hands* = Through *prep.* 1 f. *Obs.*

**1660** F. Brooke tr. *Le Blanc's Trav.* 19 The Jewes..are such cheates, they sophisticate all that comes thorough their hands. **1710** Prideaux *Orig. Tithes* v. 268 Lawyers, whose hands it passed thorough.

† **f.** In various fig. applications: see Through *prep.* 1 g. *Obs.*

**1543** [see Thick and thin A. 1]. **1581** Pettie *Guazzo's Civ. Conv.* II. (1586) 58 b, Those of Piemount, who with the shrilnesse of their wordes goe thorow ones eares. **1619** Hieron *Wks.* II. 16 Good points of doctrine runne thorow vs as thorow a pipe. **1680** Burnet *Rochester* (1692) 127 Which the strength of his Mind would soon break thorough.

† **g.** *Thorough and thorough* = Through *prep.* 1 h. *Obs.*

**13..** *Cursor M.* 24381 (Fairf.) A squorde sulde stike ouer-thwert þorou and þorou [*Gött.* Toru and thoru] þine awen hert. *c* **1489** Caxton *Sonnes of Aymon* i. 56 He shoued hym thorughe and thorughe his body.

**2.** Along (to any distance) within. Without implication of traversing from end to end. *arch.*

*c* **1050**, etc. [see Through B. I. 2]. *c* **1430** *Chev. Assigne* 95 He wente þorow a foreste fowre longe myle. **1646** Sir T. Browne *Pseud. Ep.* v. xvi. 257 The Picture of St Christopher..with a staff in his hand, wading thorow the water. **1893** Symonds in H. T. Wharton *Sappho* (1895) 60 Pinion on pinion, thorough middle ether Down from heaven hurried.

**3.** Over the whole extent of, in or to all parts of; throughout; = Through *prep.* 3. Also **b.** sometimes following the sb. *arch.* and *poet.*

*c* **1000** [see Through B. I. 3]. ? *a* **1366** Chaucer *Rom. Rose* 1366 Fyges, and many a date tree There wexen.. Thorough the gardyn in length and brede. **1485** Caxton *Chas. Gt.* I. II. v. 30 Charles..sente oueral thorugh hys empyre. **1535** Coverdale *Acts* xiv. 23 Whan they had ordeyned them Elders by eleccion thorow all the congregacions. *a* **1635** Bp. Corbet *Poems* (1807) 12 Send of this stuffe thy territories thorough To Ireland, Wales and Scottish Eddenborough. **1678** Cudworth *Intell. Syst.* I. iv. § 18. 343 Which Supreme Incorporeal Deity, was..said to be All Things, because it diffused it self thorough All. **1803** Wordsw. *Yarrow Unvisited* v, O'er hilly path and open Strath We'll wander Scotland thorough.

† **c.** Phrase. *Thorough all thing*: see Through *prep.* 3 c. *Obs.*

**1297** R. Glouc. (Rolls) 7549 Þis noble duc willam him let crouny king At londone amidwinter day, nobliche þoru alle þing. *c* **1380** *Sir Ferumb.* 1926 Charlis, þat is of fraunce kyng..Hoteþ þe þorw alle þyng to leuen þyn errour.

**4.** From beginning to end of a space of time; = Through *prep.* 4. Also following the sb.

*a* **1000**, etc. [see Through B. I. 4]. **1535** Coverdale *Ps.* lxxvii. 14 All the night thorow with a light of fyre. **1608** Dod & Cleaver *Expos. Prov.* ix–x. 7 Thorow the whole yeere. **1896** A. E. Housman *Shropshire Lad* xvii, Twice a week the winter thorough [*rime* sorrow] Here stood I.

† **5.** From beginning to end of a process, action, writing, etc., *esp.* to the very end of; = Through *prep.* 5, 5 c. *Obs.*

*c* **1449** Pecock *Repr.* I. i. 7 Weelnyȝ thoruȝ al the chapiter, Poul meeneth [etc.]. **1628** Wither *Brit. Rememb.* 243 At the last God brought me thorow all My doubts and feares. **1632** Sanderson *Serm.* 61, I foresaw we should not haue time to goe thorow all that was intended.

**6.** Indicating intermediation, means, agency, instrumentality; = Through *prep.* 7. *arch.* or *Obs.*

*a* **800–1154** [see Through B. I. 7]. *c* **1200** *Trin. Coll. Hom.* 33 Þe engel..seweð a whilche wise and þuregh hwam þis blisse cumen sholde. *a* **1300** *Cursor M.* 1395 Thoro birth of a blisful child. **1377** [see A.]. **1456** *Coventry Leet Bk.* 289 The blessyd babe..Thurrowe whom pece & tranquilite shall take þis reme on hand. **1535** Coverdale *Josh.* xxiv. 12 Not thorow thy swerde, ner thorow thy bowe. **1671** Flavel *Fount. Life* xiii. 37 By Vertue of the Mediator and thorow the Benefit of his Death. **1847** Emerson *Poems, Sphinx*, Thorough a thousand voices Spoke the universal dame.

† **b.** Indicating the agent after a passive verb; = Through *prep.* 7 b. *Obs.*

*a* **900**–*c* **1000** [see Through B. I. 7 b]. *c* **1290** *Beket* 374 in *S. Eng. Leg.* I. 117/374 Þe churche..þat..was..a-rerd þoruȝ henri þe oþur kingue. *a* **1325** *MS. Rawl. B.* 520 lf. 32 b, Hit is icomaunded þoru þe King þat eche man habbe in house wepne. **1393** Langl. *P. Pl.* C. IV. 2 Þorw bedeles and bailifs brouht by-fore þe kynge.

† **7.** Indicating cause, reason, or motive; = Through *prep.* 8. *Obs.*

*a* **1000**–*c* **1460** [see Through B. I. 8]. **1297** R. Glouc. (Rolls) 11320 Þe king hadde þer to gode wille þoru frerene rede. *c* **1374** Chaucer *Anel. & Arc.* 271 Þe swerde of sorowe byte My woofull harte þorowe your creweltee. **1596** Danett tr. *Comines* (1614) 236 He ended his life thorow a sickenes. **1666** H. Stubbe *Mirac. Conform.* 3 His life seemed burthensome to him thorough the violence of the..temptation.

**II.** *adverb.* (Now *arch.* or *dial.*)

**1.** From side to side, from surface to surface, from end to end (of a body or space); = Through *adv.* 1.

*a* **1000**–*c* **1400** [see Through B. II. 1]. *a* **1300**, **1330** [see *thorough-bear, -bore* in Thorough- 1]. *c* **1493** *Epitaffe*, etc. in *Skelton's Wks.* (1843) II. 392 Thorow thrylled and persyd with payne. **1638** Junius *Paint. Ancients* 227 We doe not make our plate so thinne as to..cut it quite thorough with engraving. **1672** Marvell *Reh. Transp.* I. 42 If he meet them in the dark, he runs them thorow. *a* **1713** Ellwood *Autobiog.* (1765) 184, I walked it thorow in a Day. **1883** Swinburne *Cent. Roundels, Sorrow* ii, One thought lies close in her heart gnawn thorough [*rime* furrow] With pain.

† **b.** To the end of the journey, all the way; = Through *adv.* 1 b. *Obs.*

**1684** Bunyan *Pilgr.* II. 73 You should have begged me of him to have gon quite thorough with you. *Ibid.* 176 How he got thorow to whither he intended.

**2.** From beginning to end (of a time, process, action, work, book); = Through *adv.* 2. *arch.*

*a* **1225** [see *thorough-fill* in Thorough- 1]. **1513** More in Grafton *Chron.* (1568) II. 777 Sithence he had once begonne, he would stoutly go thorowe. **1548–9** (Mar.) *Bk. Com. Prayer, Concern. Service*, They were onely begon, and neuer read thorow. **1670–1** Marvell *Corr.* Wks. (Grosart) II. 371 The Committee of Conventicles have..gone thorow with their Bill. **1748** Chesterf. *Lett.* 26 July, They..never consider it in all its different views; and, in short, never think it thorough. **1843** Carlyle *Past & Pr.* III. xv. (tr. Goethe), The Future hides in it Gladness and sorrow; We press still thorow.

† **3.** Predicatively, after the vb. *to be*, indicating settlement; = Through *adv.* 3 b. *Obs.*

**1467** J. Paston in *P. Lett.* II. 299 He is owtlawyd at Sir John Fastolfys swte..notwithstanding he is thorow with Sir T. Howys for Sir John Fastolf. **1482** *Cely Papers*

Camden) 88, I gawhe the exchetter xls for ws bothe and so whe be thorow with hym for aull matters.

**4.** Qualifying pa. pple. or adj.; = THROUGH *adv.* 4 a. *Obs.* or *dial.*

Now usually expressed by THOROUGHLY, except when hyphened to a pa.pple., as *thorough-bred*; see THOROUGH- 1. In 17-18th c. also hyphened to adjs.

**a 1240** *Ureisun* 123 in *Cott. Hom.* 197 Mid swuþe luðere lasten mi soule is þuruh bunden. **1474** *Coventry Leet Bk.* 401 Þat it be thorough tannyd and thorowe Coryed. **1531** TINDALE *Exp.* 1 *John* i. (1538) 14 b, Yet is it neuer thorow whole vntyll the houre of death. **1594** PLAT *Jewell-ho.* II. 38 When it is thorough hot. **1620** VENNER *Via Recta* vii. 120 The sweet Grapes..being thorow ripe. **1622** MABBE tr. *Aleman's Guzman d'Alf.* I. 37 When he [the patient] saw that he was thorow well. **1640** FULLER *Joseph's Coat, David's Punishm.* (1867) 239 Thou art not yet so thorough worn with age. **1692** R. L'ESTRANGE *Fables* ccii. (1714) 219 The Lion himself was not Thorough-Proof against this Fantastical Alarum. **1702** C. MATHER *Magn. Chr.* III. III. (1852) 560 They had thorow-good reasons for doing so. **1710** PRIDEAUX *Orig. Tithes* iv. 208 A Veteran and thorough settled Constitution of this Kingdom. **1729** BUTLER *Serm.* Wks. 1874 II. 82 A thorough honest man would..have repeated his former answer. **a 1774** GOLDSM. *Hist. Greece* II. 112 He had a thorough good opinion of himself. **1796** C. MARSHALL *Garden.* xiv. (1813) 192 Till the earth is got thorough warm again. **1853** MISS YONGE *Heir of Redclyffe* xliv, He is a thorough great man.

† **5.** *Thorough and thorough* = through and through: see THROUGH *adv.* 5. *Obs.*

**1470-85** MALORY *Arthur* I. xvi. 58 With his swerd he broched the hors.. thorow and thorow. **1526** TINDALE *John* xix. 23 The coote was with out seme woven vppon thorowe and thorowe. **1658** CLEVELAND *Rustick Ramp.* Wks. (1687) 446 Richard might have been struck thorough and thorough.

† **6.** With ellipsis of *go, get, pass*, or other vb. of motion; = THROUGH *adv.* 6. *Obs.*

**1573** TUSSER *Husb.* (1878) 31 Trench hedge and forrow, that water may thorow. **1670** COTTON *Espernon* II. VII. 339 We are now come too far..to return.., we must either thorow, or dye.

**Thorough** (þʊ·rŏ, þʊ·rə), *adj.* and *sb.* [attrib. use of prec. adv.]

**A.** *adjective.*

**1.** Used chiefly with sbs. of action or position, being a kind of elliptical use of the adv. = 'going, passing, or extending through', as *thorough passage* = passage through, *thorough heat* = heating through; cf. THROUGH *a.* 1. *Obs.* exc. in special applications. (See also THOROUGH- *in comb.* 2.)

**c 1489** [see sense 2]. **c 1566** SIR H. GILBERT in Hakluyt *Voy.* (1600) III. 20 He had heard a Fisherman..say..that he sayled very farre towards the Southeast, finding no end of the Sea: whereby he hoped a thorow passage to be that way. **1776** G. SEMPLE *Building in Water* 47 Very large Stones carefully bedded.., to guard the thorough Foundation between the Piers from..being displaced. **1799** G. SMITH *Laboratory* I. 186 Give it by degrees a thorough heat. **1843** R. J. GRAVES *Syst. Clin. Med.* v. 62 The bed-room..should be well aired, but without what is termed thorough air. *Ibid.* xxi. 251 The patient caught a fresh cold from being exposed to the thorough air of our too well ventilated ward. **1884** F. J. BRITTEN *Watch & Clockm.* 101 The holes for the train pivots are termed 'thorough holes'.

**2. a.** Of an action, etc.: Carried out through the whole of something; thoroughgoing; fully executed; applied to or affecting every part or detail. Hence, *gen.* That is fully what is expressed by the noun; thoroughgoing, complete, perfect, downright, entire. † In quot. 1581, Completely apt or suitable. (See also THROUGH *a.* 2.)

Formerly sometimes hyphened to the following sb., being treated as the adv. in combination (cf. THOROUGH-2, THROUGH-).

**c 1489** SIR S. HAMERTON in *Plumpton Corr.* (Camden) 63 To make a thorow search for my matter. **a 1500** in C. Trice-Martin *Chanc. Proc. 15th C.* (1904) 6 [To] make a thurgh ende with the said Piers Hous and pay hym .xx. marcs. **1581** SIDNEY *Astr. & Stella* lvii, He forc't them out to find The thorowest words, fit for woes selfe to grone. **1615** LATHAM *Falconry* (1633) 92 To give her a thorough scowring. **1617** HIERON *Wks.* II. 110 To bring vs to this thorow and effectuall vnderstanding. **1678** BUTLER *Hud.* III. II. 850 Those who laid the first Foundation Compleat the thorow Reformation. **1719** DE FOE *Crusoe* I. 214 In the Morning, even before it was thorow Day-light. **1766** GOLDSM. *Vic. W.* xxv, A thorough knowledge of the world. **1780** in Jesse *Selwyn & Contemp.* (1844) IV. 383 Mr. Mathews..proposed a thorough resolution..to stand by you. **1862** BURTON *Bk. Hunter* 102 The thoroughest test of active scholarship. **1893** W. LEWIN in *Bookman* June 85/2 His knowledge of English literature is extensive and thorough.

**b.** Of a person in reference to his action or quality.

**1655** GURNALL *Chr. in Arm.* verse 13. viii. § 4 (1669) 144/1 The soul effectually brought out of the love of sin as sin, will never be thorow-friends with it again. **a 1700** DRYDEN (J.), A thorough translator must be a thorough poet. **1726** LEONI *Alberti's Archit.* II. 96/2 He is a thorow master of those elements of Painting. **1829** LYTTON *Disowned* xlii, He was the finest and most thorough gentleman I ever saw. **1850** MRS. CARLYLE *Let.* (1883) II. 129 Servants who give themselves out for 'thorough'. **1884** 'RITA' *Vivienne* I. iii, Blanche de Verdreuil was a thorough coquette.

**B.** *sb.* [Elliptical or absolute uses of THOROUGH *a.* or *adv.*].

**1.** Thorough-going action or policy: in *Eng. Hist.* (with capital T) applied to that of Strafford and Laud in the reign of Charles I, and sometimes to that of Cromwell as Lord Protector.

**c 1634** LAUD in *Strafford Papers* I. 111 And for the state, indeed, my lord, I am for Thorough. **1849** MACAULAY *Hist. Eng.* i. I. 92 And now Wentworth exulted in the near prospect of Thorough. **1874** GREEN *Short Hist.* viii. § 5 The dark gloomy countenance, the full heavy eye, which meet us in Strafford's portrait are the best commentary on his policy of 'Thorough'. **1900** MORLEY *Cromwell* IV. vi. 354 They had set up the Commonwealth without lords or monarch. They were deep in all the proceedings of Cromwellian Thorough.

† **2.** A channel artificially cut or dug; a trench, esp. *Agric.* one made for draining a field; = THROUGH *sb.*[2] 1. *Obs.*

**a 1555** BRADFORD *Wks.* (Parker Soc.) I. 303 If any man would alter the natural course of any water to run a contrary way, he shall never be able to do it with dams... Therefore the alteration must be from the head, by making other thoroughs and devices. **1581** *Coventry Leet Bk.* 824 Vp a thorowe betwene two Landes in the middes of the feild by certain meare-stones there sett.

**3.** A furrow; *water-thorough*, a 'thorough' made for surface-draining; a water-furrow. *Agric.*

The *Eng. Dial. Dict.* has in sense 'furrow', *thurrow*, Yorksh. to Herts and Essex, also locally written *thorough, thurrough, thurrar.* Cf. TH, the initial, (6).

**1733** W. ELLIS *Chiltern & Vale Farm.* 5 The Ignorance and Idleness of the Plowman, who either goes so shallow, or plows his Thoroughs so wide, or misses Part of the Ground. *Ibid.* 22 Sow them in four Thoroughs. **1744-50** — *Mod. Husbandm.* I. I. 16 The ploughman..goes on plowing throughout the field, without making any..water-thoroughs. **1766** *Compl. Farmer* s.v. *Lucern*, Then ploughing it very narrow and sharp, he made water thoroughs with the plough. **1796** W. MARSHALL *Midl.* Gloss., *Thorough*, an interfurrow, between two ridges. **1888** *Sheffield Gloss.*, *Thurrow*, a furrow of land.

† **Tho·rough,** *v.*[1] *Obs. rare*^−1. [f. THOROUGH *adv.*] *trans.* To pass through, pierce, penetrate.

**1578** BANISTER *Hist. Man* I. 32 The superiour [part] is thorowed on ech side, with a large & ample hole.

**Tho·rough,** *v.*[2] *local.* [f. THOROUGH *sb.*] *trans.* To make 'thoroughs' or furrows in; see THOROUGH *sb.* 3. Hence **Tho·roughed** *ppl. a.*; **Tho·roughing** *vbl. sb.*

**1733** W. ELLIS *Chiltern & Vale Farm.* 28 Plough them in very shallow,..thorough and harrow well. *Ibid.* 106 The Ground may be so gathered into a four Thorough'd-stitch or Ridge. **1744-50** — *Mod. Husbandm.* V. I. 87 The land ..should be back-bouted, or what we call thoroughed-down. **1759** — *Pract. Farmer* (ed. 5) Gloss. 5 Four-thoroughing of Land is not Clean Ploughing, but running up four Thoroughs close together with the Plough. *Ibid.*, Thoroughing down is drawing the plough once through the bought, to lay it plain for wheat or barley.

**Thorough-** in combination. (See also THOROUGH *a.* 2, and THROUGH- *in comb.*)

**1.** Combinations of THOROUGH *adv.* with verbs, pples., or adjs.: † **tho·rough-bea·r** *v.* [BEAR *v.*[1] 35], *trans.* to 'bear' through, pierce, transfix, stab; **tho·rough-bi·nd** *v.*, *trans.* to bind or fasten (a wall, etc.) by a stone or iron, passing through from side to side (cf. *thorough-band* in 2); **tho·rough-bo·re** *v.* [OE. *þurhborian*], *trans.* to bore through, perforate; † **tho·rough-clea·nsing** *a.*, cleansing throughout or thoroughly; † **tho·rough-de·villed** *ppl. adj. Obs., nonce-wd.*, completely possessed by a devil; **tho·rough-dre·ss** *v.*, *trans.* to dress or manure (ground) thoroughly; **tho·rough-dry·** *v.*, *trans.* to dry thoroughly; **tho·rough-fe·lt** *pa. pple.*, felt throughout; † **tho·rough-fi·ll** (*þuruh fullen*) *v.*, to fill up, complete; **tho·rough-fou·ght** *ppl. a.*, fought through or to the end; **tho·rough-go-ni·mble** (*slang* or *dial.*): see quots.; † **tho·rough-hu·mble** *v.*, *trans.* to humble thoroughly or completely; † **tho·rough-li·ned** *ppl. a.*, lined throughout; † **tho·rough-ma·de** *ppl. a.*, thoroughly made, made with full determination; **tho·rough-ri·pe** (**throu·gh-ripe**) *a.*, ripe throughout, thoroughly ripe; † **tho·rough-ru·n**, *v. trans.* to run through, pierce, penetrate; † **tho·rough-sea·soned** *ppl. a.*, seasoned throughout or thoroughly; † **tho·rough-sho·t** *ppl. a.*, shot through, transfixed as with an arrow; † **tho·rough-si·ping** *ppl. a.* [SIPE *v.*], oozing or trickling through; **tho·rough-spe·d** *ppl. a.* (? *obs.* exc. *dial.*), thoroughly accomplished or developed; perfect, thoroughgoing, thorough-paced; † **tho·rough-stai·n** *v.*, *trans.* to stain thoroughly. See also THOROUGHBRED, etc.

(In early use the adv. was often written separately before a vb., as it still is when it follows the vb.)

**a 1300** *Cursor M.* 7624 Þe king smat til him wit a sper In breth he wald him *thoru ber. **c 1400** *Laud Troy Bk.* 16431 Echon other al to-bet, Sclow, & wounded, & thorow-bare. **1884** L. OLIPHANT *Haifa* (1887) 189 The crusaders used them [granite pillars] to *thorough-bind their walls. **1900** *Union Mag.* Oct. 457/2 Ancient columns are built into the walls of later castles, to thoroughbind the masonry. **c 1000** in Cockayne *Narrat.* (1861) 20 Het hie þa *þurhborian. **c 1330** R. BRUNNE *Chron. Wace* (Rolls) 16184 Handes, armes, þey dide þorow bore. **1703** T. N. *City & C. Purchaser* 4 They then thorough bore their Poles. **1642** H. MORE *Song Soul* II. i. I. xxi, *Thorough-cleansing virtue. **1604** PARSONS *3rd Pt. Three Convers. Eng.* 279 They were indeuilled, superdeuilled, and *thorowdeuilled. **1733** W. ELLIS *Chiltern & Vale Farm.* 31 Their vast Crops of Straws, and great Numbers of Cattle, make such Returns of Dung, as enables most of them to *thorough-dress their own Grounds. **1707** MORTIMER *Husb.* (1721) I. 184 Firing..must be long continued to *thorough-dry so many together. **1817** MOORE *Lalla R.*, *Fire-worsh.* iv. 115 How deep, how *thorough-felt the glow Of rapture. **a 1225** *Ancr. R.* 404 Heo..*þuruh fulleð, onont hire, Godes pine o rode. **1585-6** EARL LEYCESTER *Corr.* (Camden) 427 A gallant and a *thorow-fought assault. **1822** SCOTT *Pirate* xv, The small beer of the college, commonly there termed *thorough-go-nimble'. **1825** BROCKETT *N. C. Words*, *Thorough-go-nimble*, a diarrhœa. **1617** HIERON *Wks.* II. 77 To bring Dauid to these two specialties: first, of *thorow-humbling himselfe; secondly, of making an acknowledgement. **1605** SYLVESTER *Du Bartas* II. iii. III. *Law* 1006 A cloak of clouds, all *thorough-lin'd with thunder. **1649** LOVELACE *To Deare Bro. Col. F. L.* v, One gallant *thorough-made Resolve Doth Starry Influence dissolve. **1669** WORLIDGE *Syst. Agric.* (1681) 153 They get more in the *through-ripe Hop by the weight, than they loose in the colour. **1707** MORTIMER *Husb.* (1721) II. 347 Cyder pressed from pulpy, or thorough-ripe, or mellow Fruit. **1658** A. FOX *Würtz' Surg.* I. iv. 18 If..sharper things should be used, they would *thorough-run the Wound. **1598** SYLVESTER *Du Bartas* II. i. I. *Eden* 62 The *thorough-seasoned But Wherein the tears of death-prest Grapes are put. **1649** LOVELACE *Poems* 50 Thee and thy wounds I would bemoane Faire *thorough-shot Religion. **1642** H. MORE *Song Soul* I. III. xxiv, Here fifty Sisters in a sieve do draw *Thorough-siping water: Tantalus is here. **1730** SWIFT *Vind. Ld. Cartaret* ⁋ 28 Our *thoroughsped republic of Whigs. **1898** T. HARDY *Wessex Poems* 63 Never upon me Had she thrown look of love so thorough-sped. **1593** NASHE *Christ's T.* Wks. (Grosart) IV. 216 Spotting and *thorow-stayning thy deere bought Spyrit.

**2.** Combinations with sbs. or derived adjs. (cf. THOROUGH *a.*): **tho·rough-ba·nd** (**throu·gh-band**), a stone, etc., extending through the breadth of a wall or dyke so as to bind the sides together (cf. *band-stone*, BAND *sb.*[1] 15); also *attrib.*; **thorough-blood** *a.*, of pure breed (said of a horse); cf. FULL-BLOOD; **tho·rough-door**, a door leading through; the door of a passage; **tho·rough-draught** (**throu·gh-draught**), a draught or current of air passing through a room, etc. (in quot. 1866, a channel or passage for a draught of air); **tho·rough-edged** *a.*, thoroughly or perfectly edged; keen-edged; **tho·rough-foot**, a disarrangement in a tackle caused by one or both of the blocks getting entangled in the fall (cf. *thorough-put*); **tho·rough-hearted** *a.*, whole-hearted, entirely devoted; hence *thorough-hea·rtedness*; **tho·rough-joint** (*Anat.*), a perfectly movable joint or articulation (cf. DIARTHROSIS); **tho·rough-put**, a knot or tangle upon a rope formed by putting one part of it through a loop in another (cf. *thorough-foot*); † **tho·rough-road** = THOROUGHFARE *sb.* (in quot. *attrib.*); **tho·rough-shot, tho·rough-stem**: see quots.; † **tho·rough-touch** († **throu·gh-touch**), a touch that penetrates the soul, a deep spiritual impression; **tho·rough-winded** *a.* (of a horse), sound in 'wind' or breathing; not broken-winded. See also THOROUGHBASS to THOROUGHWORT.

**1805** DICKSON *Pract. Agric.* I. Pl. xxix, The *through band turf..being first lightly laid. **1810** S. SMITH *Agric. Surv. Galloway* vi. 88 It is essential to the durability of a dyke..that the two sides be well bound together by long stones laid across, termed throughbands. **1844** STEPHENS *Bk. Farm* III. 1007 It tends much to the stability of a dyke to have what is called a thorough-band stone..placed across it. **1829** *Sporting Mag.* XXIII. 271 Our nearly *thorough-blood hunter and carriage horses. **1827** G. DARLEY *Sylvia* 32 But you may catch his sullen roar More loud when opes the *thorough-door. **1866** HOWELLS *Venet. Life* iii, The narrow streets are bitter *thorough-drafts. **1868** *Rep. U.S. Commissioner Agric.* (1869) 438 The windows are closed and matted, and no thorough-draught is allowed. **1905** *Daily Chron.* 22 July 8/5 The drawing-room is..spared the desecrating through-draught. **1830** TENNYSON *Isabel* ii, The intuitive decision of a bright And *thorough-edged intellect to part Error from crime. **1867** *Thorough-foot [see *thorough-put*]. **1887** *Athenæum* 31 Dec. 883/3 The *thorough-heartedness with which Barnes threw himself into this. **1882** COUES (Cent. Dict.), *Thorough-joint. **1829** GEN. P. THOMPSON *Exerc.* (1842) I. 112 Knots, of different degrees of complexity, from a simple *thorow-put, to a complication of loops and twists [etc.]. **1867** SMYTH *Sailor's Word-bk.*, *Thorough-puts*, or *Thorough-foots*, are kinks or tangles in a rope; or parts of a tackle not leading fair by reason of one of the blocks having been passed round part of the fall. **a 1661** FULLER *Worthies, Lond.* (1662) II. 224 He built at Buntingford (a *thorow-road market..) a neat and strong Chappel. **1891** *Cent. Dict.*, *Thorough-shot*, same as *thorough-pin*. *Thorough-stem*, same as *thorough-wort*. **1607** HIERON *Wks.* I. 459 Nothing which may argue a *through-touch, or a comfortable expectation of Gods fauour. **1617** *Ibid.* II. 72 Whether we haue receiued any such thorow-touch as is the..fruit of true repentance. **1737** BRACKEN *Farriery Impr.* (1757) II. Pref. 11 You shall hear many a Horse praised for being a *thorow-winded one.

**Thorough-band** to **-bore**: see THOROUGH-.

**Thoroughbass** (þʊ·rŏbēⁱs). *Mus.* [f. THOROUGH *prep.* or *adv.* + BASS *sb.*[5]; cf. BASSO *continuo.*] A bass part extending through a piece of music, and written by itself, with figures indicating the chords or harmonies to be played with it; a figured bass, *basso continuo*; *esp.* (formerly) an accompaniment thus written or played; hence *loosely*, an accompaniment in general (also *fig.*). Also, the method of indicating harmonies by a figured bass, or the art of playing from it; *loosely*, the science of harmony in general.

**1662** PALYFORD *Skill Mus.* I. ii. (1674) 36 The Figures usually placed over Notes in the Thorough-Bass of Songs or Ayres. **1685** EVELYN *Mem.* 10 Mar., She had an excellent voice, to which she play'd a thorough bass on the harpsichord. **1731** KELLER in *Holder's Harmony* 159 Rules for Playing a Thorow-bass. **1778** H. WALPOLE *Let. to H. S. Conway* 8 July, Tumults would be a dreadful thorough bass to speeches. **1845** E. HOLMES *Mozart* 258 He..wrote a treatise on thorough bass. **1875** STEDMAN *Vict. Poets* i. 3 Full-throated, happy minstrels, like Béranger or Burns, need no knowledge of thorough-bass and the historical range of composition.

¶ **b.** *erron.* A loud or deep bass.

**1749** FIELDING *Tom Jones* v. ix, He found..his nurse snoring..at the bed's feet. He immediately took the only method of silencing this thorough bass, whose music he feared might disturb Mr. Allworthy. **1835** W. IRVING *Crayon Misc.* (1849) 30 He..had..a whiffling double voice, shifting abruptly from a treble to a thorough-bass.

**Thorough-bolt**: see *through-bolt*, THROUGH- 2.

**Thoroughbrace** (þʊ·rŏbrēᵊs). *U. S.* [f. THOROUGH *prep.* or *adv.* + BRACE *sb.*[2] 11.] Each of a pair of strong braces or bands of leather connecting the front and back C-springs and supporting the body of a coach or other vehicle. Hence **Tho·roughbraced** (-brēⁱst) *a.*, suspended by thoroughbraces.

**1837** HT. MARTINEAU *Soc. Amer.* II. 175 Half a mile before reaching the place..the thorough-brace broke, and we had to walk..to the inn. **1858** O. W. HOLMES *Deacon's Masterp.* 22 In building of chaises..There is always somewhere a weakest spot,—In hub, tire, felloe, in spring or thill,..In screw, bolt, thoroughbrace. **1884** S. O. JEWETT *Country Doctor* 19 The old-fashioned thorough-braced wagon.

**Thoroughbred** (þʊ·rŏbred), *a.* (*sb.*) Also 8 through-bred. [f. THOROUGH *adv.* + BRED *ppl. a.*[1]]

**1.** Thoroughly educated or accomplished; hence, complete, thorough, out-and-out. (Now regarded as *fig.* from 2: cf. 2 b.)

**1701** GREW *Cosm. Sacra* II. vii. 77 A through-bred Soldier weighs all present Circumstances, and all possible Contingents. **1721** AMHERST *Terræ Fil.* No. 47 (1754) 253 Nothing can restrain a thorough-bred gamester. **1874** L. STEPHEN *Hours in Library* (1892) I. ix. 300 A thorough-bred utilitarian, full of sagacity. **1882** MISS BRADDON *Mt. Royal* III. i. 20 He never handled a gun like a thoroughbred sportsman.

**2.** Of a horse: Of pure breed or stock; *spec.* applied to a race-horse whose pedigree for a given number of generations is recorded in the stud-book. Also of a dog, bull, etc.

**1796** J. LAWRENCE *Treat. Horses* iv. 166 Thorough-bred hacks are the most docile and quiet, and the least liable to shy. **1825** N. H. SMITH *Breeding for Turf* 5 The pedigree of Eclipse affords a singular illustration of the descent of our thorough-bred horses from pure Eastern blood. **1840–70** BLAINE *Encycl. Rur. Sports* § 930 The term thorough-bred, as relating to a horse..is neither critically nor conventionally definite. **1856** *Farmer's Mag.* Jan. 29 There are some men who prefer the cross-bred animal—the best I believe to be between the Hampshire Down and Cotswold; but..I must give a decided preference to the thorough-bred. **1887** SIR R. H. ROBERTS *In the Shires* i. 18 Mounted upon a thoroughbred..bay mare.

**b.** *transf.* Applied to human beings or their attributes: sometimes implying characteristics like those of a thoroughbred horse, as gracefulness, energy, distinction, etc. (Cf. B. 2.)

**1820** BYRON *Juan* v. cvi, More thorough-bred or fairer fingers. **1864** TREVELYAN *Compet. Wallah* (1866) 345 It is hardly possible for a man brought up amidst European.. associations to realize the idea conceived of him..by a thorough-bred Hindoo.

*Comb.* **1882** MISS BRADDON *Mt. Royal* ix, Who the deuce is that thoroughbred-looking girl?

**B.** *sb.* **1.** A thoroughbred animal, esp. a horse.

**1842** THACKERAY *Fitz-Boodle Pap.* Pref., I can't afford a thorough-bred, and hate a cock-tail. **1887** 'H. SMART' *Cleverly Won* i, Three or four thorough-breds that he had reared.

**2.** *transf.* and *fig.*: A well-born, well-bred, or thoroughly trained person. Also, a first-rate motor-car, bicycle, or other vehicle.

**1894** H. GARDENER *Unofficial Patriot* 15 There is rather a paucity of thoroughbreds among the Methodists. **1894** *Outing* (U.S.) XXIV. 281/2 An air..that made you feel sure that she could play tennis or sail a boat. In fact, she looked a thoroughbred. **1901** *Pall Mall Mag.* Sept. 67/2 A vehicle running a race must in some mysterious way be a thoroughbred. **1908** *Daily Chron.* 21 Nov. 9/4 This machine [bicycle] and all the thorough-breds..are now..treated before enamelling to the special Coslett non-rusting process, which preserves the metal from all corrosion.

Hence **Tho·roughbre·dness.**

**1894** ELIZ. L. BANKS *Camp. Curiosity* 127 As regards the thorough-bredness of my black poodle.

**Thorough-cleansing**, etc.: see THOROUGH-.

**Tho·rough-drain**, *v. Agric.* [f. THOROUGH *adv.* (or *sb.* 3) + DRAIN *v.*] *trans.* To drain (a field) by means of water-thoroughs or -furrows; also, to drain thoroughly.

**1844** STEPHENS *Bk. Farm* I. 489 As by this kind of draining [surface-draining] the land is thoroughly or effectually drained, it has been most appropriately called thorough-draining. *Ibid.* 593 A farmer..thorough-drained one-half of a 4-acre field. *Ibid.* 662 The subsoil will afford a sufficient quantity of stones, to thorough-drain the ground. **1847** RAYNBIRD in *Jrnl. R. Agric. Soc.* VIII. II. 311 The term thorough-draining is perhaps derived from the old word 'thorrow', which Bradley mentions as 'a distinguishing character for a trench cut purposely for carrying off of water'.

**Thoroughfare** (þʊ·rŏfēᵊɹ), *sb.* (*a.*) Forms: 4–5 thurghfare, 5 thurghe-; thoruȝ faar, thoruhfare, 6 thorowe, thoroughe, thorough fare, 6–8 thorowfare, 7–8 thorow-, thorough-fare, (7 thorow-faire, thorough fair, 7–8 thorow-, thorough-fair, 8 thorowfair, 8–9 thorofare), 7– thoroughfare. *β.* 5 *Sc.* throchtfayr, 6 throwfare, *Sc.* throuchfair, throuche fair, 6–7 through fare, through-fare, 7–9 throughfare. [In ME. *thurghfare*, 15th c. *thoruȝ faar*, f. *þurh*, *þuruh*, THROUGH + FARE *sb.*[1], OE. *faru* passage, way, track: cf. THOROUGH- 2. Cf. Du. *doorvaart* (*deurvaerd*, Kilian) passage, esp. passage for ships (cf. 1 d below), LG. *dörfard*, MHG. *durchvart*, G. *durchfahrt*.]

**1.** A passage or way through.

**a.** In general sense; also *fig.* Now usually merged in sense c, exc. in phr. *No thoroughfare*, no public way through or right of way here.

*c* **1386** CHAUCER *Knt.'s T.* 1989 This world nys but a thurghfare ful of wo, And we been pilgrymes, passynge to and fro. **1430–40** LYDG. *Bochas* I. i. (MS. Bodl. 263) lf. 11/2 This world is a thoruhfare [*ed.* 1554 throwfare] ful of wo. **1596** SHAKS. *Merch. V.* II. vii. 41 The Hircanion deserts, and the vaste wildes Of wide Arabia are as throughfares now For Princes to come view faire Portia. **1601** WEEVER *Mirr. Mart.* B iv, Yet makes the wood my through-fare into heauen. **1641** HINDE *J. Bruen* lviii. 195 You..rather glory to have your house made a through-fare of profane persons. **1797–1802** G. COLMAN *Br. Grins, Elder Bro.* (1819) 117 Making their throats a thoroughfare for wine. **1822** BYRON *Juan* VII. xi, To hint, at least, 'Here is no thoroughfare'. **1856** EMERSON *Eng. Traits, Ability* Wks. (Bohn) II. 41 They have made the island a thoroughfare; and London a shop .. inviting to strangers. **1893** HUXLEY *Sci. & Chr. Tradit.* Pref. (1894) 8 Before me stood the thorny barrier with its comminatory notice-board—'No Thoroughfare. By order. Moses'.

† **b.** *spec.* A town through which traffic passes; a town on a highway or line of traffic. *Obs.*

*c* **1440** *Promp. Parv.* 493/2 Thurghfare, *oppidum.* *c* **1449** PECOCK *Repr.* v. vii. (Rolls) 521 Whi in a town which is a thoruȝ faar toward Londoun ben so manye ostries clepid innes? **1530** PALSGR. 200/1 Borowe or thorowe fare, *bourc. Ibid.* 281/1 Throwfare, *bourgade, bourc.* *a* **1552** LELAND *Itin.* IV. 131 From Uxbridge to Southall a Village about 6 Miles. Thence to Acton a pretty Through-Fare a 4 Miles. **1619** DALTON *Country Just.* vii. (1630) 32 In Towns which are no thorow-fare the Justices shall..be sparing of allowing of any alehouse. **1769** *De Foe's Tour Gt. Brit.* I. 87 New-market..being a Thorough-fare, reaps no small Advantage by that Means, as well as from the Races. **1829** SCOTT *Anne of G.* vii, The little castle and town of Ferette..served as a thoroughfare to the traffic of Berne and Soleure.

**c.** A road, street, lane, or path forming a communication between two other roads or streets, or between two places; a public way unobstructed and open at both ends; *esp.* a main road or street, a highway.

**1540** *Act* 32 *Hen. VIII*, c. 17 Chauncerie lane...And.. Fewter lane, being thorough fares and passages from Fletestrete into Holborne. **1628** WITHER *Brit. Rememb.* IV. 251 The Strand, that goodly thorow-fare betweene The Court and City. **1658** W. BURTON *Itin. Anton.* 2 Those publick Through-fares, or Waies, which the Souldiers raised. **1796** W. MARSHALL *W. England* II. 54 It is a large inland Market Town; but has no thorofare to support it. **1843** BETHUNE *Sc. Fireside Stor.* 275 One of the thoroughfares to the metropolis passed through the place.

**d.** A piece of water, as a strait or river, affording passage for ships, etc.; an unobstructed channel. (In definite application to a particular channel, chiefly *U.S.*; otherwise a special case of the general sense.)

**1699** ROBERTS *Voy. Levant* 32 There is a Thoroughfare between the Mainland..and this Isle. **1712** E. COOKE *Voy. S. Sea* 127 There is a Thorough-Fare in the Midst of it, where we rode with our Ships. **1739** *Descr. Windward Passage* (ed. 2) 6 A Thorough-fare for Shipping between some Islands, or other Land, as .. the Gulf of Messina between the Island of Sicily and Italy. **1856** STANLEY *Sinai & Pal.* ii. 113 The Mediterranean was not yet the thoroughfare—it was rather the boundary..of the eastern nations. (*b*) **1848** THOREAU *Maine W.* (1894) 46 After one mile of river, or what the boatmen call 'thoroughfare'—for the river becomes at length only the connecting link between the lakes,—..we entered the North Twin Lake. **1896** *Trans. Roy. Soc. Canada* II. ii. 210 *Thoroughfare*, a passage between lakes on the same level.

**e.** 'A strait of water, or neck of land connecting two bodies of water, habitually traversed by wild fowl in migrating or passing to and from their feeding-grounds' (Hallock *Sportsman's Gazetteer* 1883, Gloss.).

**2.** The action of going or passing through, or the condition of being passed through or traversed; passage. Now *rare* or *Obs.*

**1667** MILTON *P. L.* x. 393 Ye..have..made one Realm Hell and this World, one Realm, one Continent Of easie thorough-fare. **1668** CULPEPPER & COLE *Barthol. Anat.* I. x. 23 Made hard and callous, by the continual thoroughfare of the Chylus. **1810** *Sporting Mag.* XXXVI. 57 Till custom had grown into a right of thoroughfare. **1868** STANLEY *Westm. Abb.* i. 4 The River Thames..here widening to an almost majestic size, yet not too wide for thoroughfare.

**3.** *attrib.* or *adj.* That is a thoroughfare; passed or travelled through by traffic; chiefly in *thoroughfare town* = sense 1 b.

[Cf. OE. *þurhfere* passable, in *Ags. Hymnar.* (Surtees) 112, 9 (Bosw.-T.) ȝeat þurhfere.]

**1553** *Reg. Privy Council Scot.* I. 143 All villages and throuchfair townis of this realme. **1564** *Yorks. Chantry Surv.* (Surtees) 264 [Boroughbridge] being one thoroughffare towne of the Kinges strete. **1592** *Sc. Acts Jas. VI* (1814) III. 576/1 At the principall throuche fair townis and paroche kirkis. *a* **1661** FULLER *Worthies, Hartford.* (1662) II. 25 William of Ware born in that thorough fair Town twenty miles from London. **1674** N. FAIRFAX *Bulk & Selv.* 146 The two ends of the Earths throughfare line or diameter. **1841** LANE *Arab. Nts.* I. 76 Most of the great thoroughfare streets. **1908** *Westm. Gaz.* 10 June 2/1 How seldom must these ancient [Italian] walled villages communicate with the thoroughfare-valleys, or the railway, or distant Rome!

**Tho·roughfare,** *v. rare.* [In early use, OE. *þurhféran* (also *þurhfaran* str. vb.) to pass through, traverse: cf. Du. *doorvaren* (*deurvaeren*, Kilian), LG. *dörfaren*; OHG. *durahfaran*, Ger. *durchfahren*. In 2 from (or after) prec. sb.]

**1.** *trans.* To go, pass, or travel through.

*a* **900** tr. *Bæda's Hist.* IV. ii. (1890) 258 He sona ðurhferde eall Breotone ealond. *a* **1225** *Leg. Kath.* 1147 Hu mei he helpen oðre..þe þurhferde deað as heo doð? [**1674**, **1895**: see *thoroughfaring* below.]

**2.** To pass through or traverse, as a road; to form a thoroughfare in or across.

**1886** LOWELL *Progr. World* in *Latest Lit. Ess.* (1891) 163 Those..slits that thoroughfared the older town.

So † **Tho·roughfared** *a. Obs.* [f. prec. sb. + -ED[2]], having a thoroughfare or passage, perforated; † **Tho·rough-farer** (**throu·gh-farer**) *Obs.*, one who goes or travels through, a wayfarer; **Tho·rough-faring** (**throu·ghfaring**), a going, passing, or travelling through; **Tho·roughfaresome** (**throu·gh-faresome**) *a.*, (*a*) capable of being passed through, penetrable; (*b*) relating to passing through.

**1668** CULPEPPER & COLE *Barthol. Anat.* II. vii. 111 When the Ventricles are dilated above the *thorough-far'd Septum ..the little holes would be shut up. **1626** in *10th Rep. Hist. MSS. Comm.* App. v. 474 [To] intertaine *through-farers and passengers. **1674** N. FAIRFAX *Bulk & Selv.* 90 There would be..no *throughfarings of the least steams or reekings of bodies. **1895** A. NUTT *Voy. Bran* I. 301 A road worn with much thoroughfaring. **1674** N. FAIRFAX *Bulk & Selv.* 138 All body being as *throughfaresom to ghost, as tis stopping to body. **1863** DE MORGAN *Let. to Whewell* in *Life* (1882) 319, I feel helped by the word διιέναι, because it is a very thoroughfaresome word...It is used for going *through* a country, or for running a man *through* the body.

**Thorough-felt** to **-fought**: see THOROUGH-.

† **Tho·roughgate.** *Obs.* In 5 throgat, 6–7 thorowgate. [f. THOROUGH *adv.* + GATE *sb.*[2]] A passage through: = THOROUGHFARE *sb.* 1.

**1456** *Burgh Rec. Peebles* (1872) 117 The throgat sal serf tham bath vp throu and don throu. **1598** R. BERNARD tr. *Terence, Adelphi* IV. ii, That corner is no thorow gate [*angiportum non pervium*]. **1639** HORN & ROB. *Gate Lang. Unl.* lviii. § 617 Lanes most commonly are unpassable, and have no thorow-gate.

**Thoroughgoing** (þʊ·rŏgōᵘiŋ), *a.* [f. THOROUGH *adv.* + *going*, pr. pple. of GO *v.* See also THROUGHGOING.] Going the full length; doing things thoroughly; acting with completeness; uncompromising, thorough, extreme, out-and-out. (Of persons, actions, etc.)

**1819** SCOTT *Leg. Montrose* xiii, A thoroughgoing friend that understands a hint is worth a million! **1838** THIRLWALL *Greece* IV. xxxi. 194 They now proceeded to bolder and more thorough-going measures. **1856** R. A. VAUGHAN *Mystics* (1860) II. 18 What seems..the thorough-going madness of the fiery Persian. **1888** BRYCE *Amer. Commw.* I. 120 Jefferson..was a thorough-going party leader.

Hence **Tho·roughgo·ingly** *adv.*; **Tho·rough-go·ingness.** So **Tho·roughgo·er**, a thorough-going person or animal; **Tho·roughgo·ing** *sb.*, the action or habit of doing things thoroughly.

**1895** *Outing* (U.S.) 388/1 The horses [polo-ponies] are such *thoroughgoers in the field that it is difficult to say this or the other is best. **1851** J. D. BURNS *Jrnl.* in *Mem.* iv. (1869) 66 Much..is said about *thoroughgoing and decision of character. **1886** *New Eng. Dict.* s.v. *Boot sb.*[3] 1 b, *Like old boots*: vigorously, *thoroughgoingly. **1865** M. ARNOLD *Ess. Crit.* ii. 65 The newspaper, with its party spirit, its *thorough-goingness. **1867** PEARSON *Hist. Eng.* I. 35 The Roman sword did its work..with terrible thorough-goingness.

**Thorough-go-nimble** to **Thorough-lined**: see THOROUGH- *in comb.* 1, 2.

**Tho·roughleaf.** ? *Obs.* In 6 thorow-. [f. THOROUGH *adv.* + LEAF *sb.*] = THOROUGHWAX.

**1578** LYTE *Dodoens* I. xcv. 136 Of Thorowwaxe, or Thorowleafe. Thorowleafe hath a round, slender stalke ful of branches, yᵉ branches passing, or going thorow the leaues. **1597** [see THOROUGHWAX]. **1866** *Treas. Bot.* 181 *Bupleurum.* Hare's-ear, Thorow-wax, or Thorow-leaf.

**Tho·rough-light.** Now *rare* or *Obs.* Also throu·gh-light.

**a.** *pl.* Windows on opposite sides of a room, so that the light passes right through.

**1625** BACON *Ess., Building* (Arb.) 551 And let all three Sides, be a double House, without Thorow Lights, on the Sides, that you may haue Roomes from the Sunne, both for Fore-noone, and Afternoone. **1642** FULLER *Holy & Prof. St.* III. vii. 167 Thorow-lights are best for rooms of entertainment, and windows on one side for dormitories. **1697** DRYDEN *Æneid* VIII. 349 The doors, unbarr'd, receive the rushing day; And thorough lights disclose the ravish'd prey. **1745** P. THOMAS *Jrnl. Anson's Voy.* 230 The Houses have thorough Lights.

**b.** *fig.* (*sing.* and *pl.*) in reference to the 'light' of knowledge or discovery.
**1605** BACON *Adv. Learn.* II. ii. § 13 This great Building of the world had neuer through lights made in it till the age of vs and our fathers. **1642** FULLER *Holy & Prof. St.* II. xxi. 137 [Drake] returned safe into England, and landed at Plimouth, (being almost the first of those that made a thorow-light through the world). **1646** TRAPP *Comm. John* i. 5 The former [light of nature] is but a dim half-light...The latter [light of Scripture] is a clear thorough-light. **1698** NORRIS *Pract. Disc.* IV. 44 All shall be then open,..every Man's Heart a thorough-light to every Man. **1841** EMERSON *Lect.* '*Times*' Wks. (Bohn) II. 256 Paving the earth with eyes, destroying privacy, and making thorough-lights.
So **Tho·rough-lighted** (**through-**) *a.*, having thorough-lights; having the light passing through.
**1624** WOTTON *Archit.* in *Reliq.* (1651) 286 Rooms windowed on both ends, which we call through-lighted. **1703** T. N. *City & C. Purchaser* 260 Rooms are said to be Through-lighted when they have Windows on both ends. **1842–76** GWILT *Archit.* Gloss., *Thorough lighted Rooms*, such as have windows on opposite sides.

**Thoroughly** (þʊ·rŏli), *adv.* [f. THOROUGH *adv.* or *adj.* + -LY [2]. See also THROUGHLY.]
†**1.** In a way that penetrates or goes through; right through, quite through. *Obs. rare.*
With quots. 1633, 1703 cf. THROUGHLY *adv.* 2.
*c* **1300** *Havelok* 680 Godard..lokede on him þoruth-like, with eyne grim. **1633** W. MUISHO in *Buccleuch MSS.* (Hist. MSS. Comm.) I. 273, I would have gone home (wet thoroughly). **1703** MAUNDRELL *Journ. Jerus.* (1732) 9 Thorowly soaked with the wet.
**2.** In a thorough manner or degree; in every part or detail; in all respects; with nothing left undone; fully, completely, wholly, entirely, perfectly.
**1473** *Rolls of Parlt.* VI. 66/1 In cas all other things were thoroughly passed and concluded betwixt his Highnes and theym. **1522** MORE *De Quat. Nouiss.* Wks. 76/2 We know them..yet not so very thorowly as we might peradueuture. **1593** SHAKS. *2 Hen. VI*, II. i. 202 To looke into this Businesse thorowly. **1643** BURROUGHES *Exp. Hosea* iv. (1652) 77 This promise is not yet thoroughly fulfilled. **1736** BUTLER *Anal.* II. vi. 224 Whoever will weigh the Matter thoroughly. **1846** RUSKIN *Mod. Paint.* (1851) I. II. I. vii. § 10 The thoroughly great men are those who have done everything thoroughly. **1878** HUTTON *Scott* iii. 35 She had a thoroughly kindly nature.

**Thoroughness** (þʊ·rŏnės). [f. THOROUGH *a.* + -NESS.] The quality of being thorough or of doing things thoroughly; the condition of being done thoroughly; completeness of execution or treatment; completeness in general, perfectness.
**1843** PRESCOTT *Mexico* (1850) I. 152 A book of the highest authority, for the perspicuity, fidelity, and thoroughness, with which the multifarious topics in it are discussed. **1848** MILL *Pol. Econ.* I. vii. § 3 The thoroughness of their application to work. **1862** DANA *Man. Geol.* II. 245 The exception to the thoroughness of the extinction in the Eastern border region. **1897** E. K. CHAMBERS in *Bookman* Jan. 113/1 He has emulated the Teutonic thoroughness without the Teutonic pedantry.

**Thoroughoute**, etc., obs. forms of THROUGHOUT.

**Thorough-paced** (þʊ·rŏpēist), *a.* Also *β.* 7 **through-paced.** [f. THOROUGH *adv.* + PACED.]
**1.** *lit.* Of a horse: Thoroughly trained; having all his paces. *rare.* ? *Obs.*
*a* **1661** FULLER *Worthies, Huntington.* (1662) II. 51 It is given to thorough-paced-Naggs, that amble naturally, to trip much whilest artificial pacers goe sure on foot.
*β.* **1668** *Lond. Gaz.* No. 272/4 A Baye Mare,..flat ribb'd, Roach back'd, through paced.
**2.** *fig.* Thoroughly trained or accomplished, perfectly skilled or versed (*in* something); hence, thoroughgoing, complete, perfect, thorough.
**1646** JENKYN *Remora* 18 The thorow-pac'd Politician borrows this of the Atheist. **1678** CUDWORTH *Intell. Syst.* I. iv. § 30. 382 Anaxagoras..was severely taxed..as one not thorough-paced in Theism. **1710** PALMER *Proverbs* 114 A thoro'-pac'd villain. *a* **1715** BURNET *Own Time* an. 1681 (1823) II. 278 Men of a thorough-paced obsequiousness. **1823** LAMB *Elia* Ser. II. *Old Margate Hoy*, A hearty thorough-paced liar. **1850** GROTE *Greece* II. lvi. VII. 132 Introducing more thorough-paced oligarchy into the already oligarchical Sikyônian government. **1893** *Spectator* 28 Jan. 101/2 A thorough-paced English gentleman.
*β.* **1655** FULLER *Church Hist.* I. iv. § 13 Constantius was a through-paced Christian. **1658** PHILLIPS *Dict.* Ded., An universally through-pac't Dictionary. *a* **1661** FULLER *Worthies, Huntington.* (1662) II. 50 He was through-paced in three Tongues, Latine, Greek..and Hebrew. **1691** WOOD *Ath. Oxon.* I. 535 Robert Burton..was..a thro-pac'd Philologist.
So † **Tho·rough-pace** *v. Obs. intr.* of a horse; † **Tho·rough-pa·cer**, a horse having all his paces.
**1684** *Lond. Gaz.* No. 1945/4 A bay Nag..seven years old, a thorough pacer. **1690** *Ibid.* No. 2545/4 A light sorrel Gelding,..walks, thorough-paces and gallops.

**Thorough-passage**: see THROUGH-PASSAGE.

**Thorough-pierce**: see *through-pierce*, in THROUGH- I.

**Thorough-pin** (þʊ·rŏ₁pin). *Farriery.* [f. THOROUGH- + PIN *sb.*[1] (cf. sense 10).] A swelling in the sheath of the tendon of the flexor perforans muscle in a horse's hock, appearing on both sides so as to suggest a pin passing through; also a similar swelling in the carpal joint of the fore-leg. Cf. earlier *through-serewe*, etc.: s.v. THROUGH- 2.
**1789** *Bath Jrnl.* 22 June Advt., [A pony] with a spavin and thorough pins. **1831** YOUATT *Horse* 265 We have spoken of wind-galls...A similar enlargement is found above the hock...As from its situation it must necessarily project on both sides of the hock, in the form of a round swelling, it is called a thorough-pin. **1906** *Daily News* 20 Apr. 6 Amitie, a very well-bred mare, is marred by a thorough-pin.

**Thoroughpost**: see THROUGHPOST.

**Thorough-put** to **-run**, etc.: see THOROUGH-.

† **Thorough-see·**, *v. Obs.* [OE. *þurh sēon*, f. *þurh* THOROUGH, THROUGH *adv.* + *sēon* to SEE: cf. OHG. *durhsehen*, Ger. *durchsehen.*] *trans.* To see through (*lit.* and *fig.*: cf. SEE *v.* 24). Hence † **Thorough-see·ing** *vbl. sb.*, the action of this vb.; *ppl. a.* that sees through; † **Thorough-see·able** *a.*, capable of being seen through, transparent.
*c* **888** K. ÆLFRED *Boeth.* xli. § 1 He ᵹeseohð & þurhseohð ealle his ᵹesceafta ændemest. *a* **1200** *Moral Ode* 90 (Lambeth) He þurþ-sicheþ uches monnes þonc [*v.r.* þurh-sihð elches mannes þanc]. *a* **1225** *Ancr. R.* 50 Þe blake cloð.. is þiccure..& wurse to þurhseon. **1553** GRIMALDE *Cicero's Offices* (1556) 7 Whoso thorowseeth moste what in everye case is truest. *Ibid.* 68 So desireful of thorow seing and learning the nature of things. **1561** T. HOBY tr. *Castiglione's Courtyer* IV. (1577) X viij b, The eyes of the minde..then beginne to be sharp and thorough seing, when the eyes of the body lose the floure of theyr sightlynesse. **1562** TURNER *Herbal* II. 151 The rosin or turpentine [of Terebinthus]..is clere, & thorow seable, whyte, like a glasse & blewish gray.

**Thorough-seek, -shining**: see THROUGH-SEEK, -SHINING.

**Tho·rough-stitch, through-stitch,** *sb.*, *adv.*, and *adj. Obs.* exc. *dial.* [f. THOROUGH *adv.* + STITCH *sb.*]
† **A.** *sb.* ? A stitch drawn right through the stuff; hence *fig.* in reference to thoroughness of action: cf. B. *Obs. rare.*
*a* **1569** KINGESMYLL *Man's Est.* xv. (1580) 124 Now there fore to knitte vppe the knot, and to make a through stitch. **1663** COWLEY *Cutter Colman St.* II. viii, When I do a business, I'm for through-stich; I'm through pac'd.
**B.** *adv.* Right through, through to the end; thoroughly, completely; almost always in phr. *to go thorough-stitch* (*with*), to perform something thoroughly, carry it out completely and effectually, go through with: 'a tailor's expression for finishing any thing once begun' (Egan *Slang Dict.* 1823).
**1579** GOSSON *Sch. Abuse, Apol.* (Arb.) 68 Philippe of Macedon tooke vpon him to reason with a new Musition.. and was not able to go thorowe stitche. **1596** NASHE *Saffron Walden* 37 That wee might haue made round worke, and gone thorough stitch. **1634** FORD *Perkin Warbeck* II. iii, He that threads his needle with the sharp eyes of industry shall in good time go throughstitch with the new suit of preferment. **1685** EVELYN *Diary* 22 May, The..Cheif Justice Jefferies..went thorough stitch in that tribunal. **1694** R. L'ESTRANGE *Fables* cxxxiii. (1714) 150 'Tis Perseverance alone that can carry us Thorough-Stitch. **1723** MANDEVILLE *Fab. Bees* (1725) I. 216 A Man of Honour enters into a Conspiracy with others to murder a King; he is obliged to go thorough Stich with it. **1824** *Blackw. Mag.* XV. 147 We have gone too far to retreat,..we must e'en go thorough-stitch. **1904** *Eng. Dial. Dict.* s.v. *Thorough*, She's means to do the place up thorough-stitch.
**C.** *adj.* Thoroughgoing, out-and-out. ? *Obs.*
*c* **1685** in *Verney Memoirs* (1907) II. 396 A thorough-stitch enemy to the crown. **1786** A. GIB *Sacr. Contempl.* 402 It may not suit with his courage or his prudence to be thorough-stitch with it. **1825** HAZLITT *Spirit of Age* 335 He..must make thorough-stitch work of it. **1828** WILSON in *Blackw. Mag.* XXIII. 785 [He] seems to have no thorough-stitch advocate in the London press.
Hence † **Tho·rough-stitched, through-stitched** *a.* = C.
**1682** MRS. BEHN *City Heiress* 35 You are resolv'd to make a through-stitcht Robbery on't. **1799** T. TWINING in *Recreat. & Stud.* (1882) 233 What a painstaking, thorough-paced, thorough-stitched man you are when you set about anything!

**Thorough-stone**: see THROUGH-STONE [2].

**Thoroughte**, obs. form of THROUGHOUT.

**Thorough-toll**: see THROUGH-TOLL.

**Thorough-touch**: see THOROUGH- 2.

**Thoroughwax** (þʊ·rŏwæks). Also 6– **thorow-**, 6 **thorowe-**, 7 **through-**, 6–7 **waxe**, 6– **-wax.** [f. THOROUGH *prep.* and *adv.* through + WAX *v.* to grow, after G. *durchwachs*; from the branches appearing to grow through the leaves.] A name for the umbelliferous herb *Bupleurum rotundifolium*, also called *hare's-ear*, having roundish-oval perfoliate leaves, and small greenish-yellow flowers with conspicuous bracts.
**1548** TURNER *Names Herbes* 85 Perfoliata is an herbe wyth a leafe lyke a pease...The Germans cal it Durchwassz. It maye be called in englishe Thorowwax, because the stalke waxeth thorowe the leaues. **1578** LYTE *Dodoens* I. xcv. 137 This herbe is now called..in English Thorowwaxe and Thorowleafe. **1597** GERARDE *Herbal* II. clxviii. § 1. 429 Thorowe waxe or Thorowe leafe, hath a..stalke, diuided into manie small branches, which passe or go thorow the leaues. **1678** PHILLIPS (ed. 4), *Thorough-wax*,..a Martial Herb, somewhat bitter and astringent and good against Ruptures. **1828** J. E. SMITH *Eng. Flora* II. 93 *B*[*upleurum*] *rotundifolium.* Common Hare's-ear. Thorow-wax.

**Thorough-winded**: see THOROUGH- 2.

**Thoroughwort** (þʊ·rŏwɔ̄ɹt). [f. THOROUGH *prep.* or *adv.* + WORT, after THOROUGHWAX.] A North American composite plant, *Eupatorium perfoliatum*, having opposite leaves, each pair united at the base so that the stem appears to grow through them (connate-perfoliate), and large corymbs of numerous white flowers; valued for its tonic properties; also called *boneset* or *crosswort.*
**1828** in WEBSTER. **1845–50** MRS. LINCOLN *Lect. Bot.* 185 Florets tubulous, without rays; as, boneset, or thoroughwort (Eupatorium). **1857** GRAY *First Lessons Bot.* (1866) 100 Cases of real leaves growing together.., those of the common Thorough-wort, and the upper pairs in Woodbines or Honeysuckles. **1893** F. P. HUMPHREY *New Eng. Cactus* 27 Aromatic herbs, pennyroyal, thoroughwort, and catnip.
†**b.** = THOROUGHWAX. *Obs. rare*[−1].
**1597** GERARDE *Herbal, Table*, Throughwoort and his kinds.

**Thorow**, obs. f. THOROUGH. **Thorowout, thorowte**, etc., obs. ff. THROUGHOUT.

**Thorp** (þǭɹp). *arch.* and *Hist.* Forms: *α.* 1 **ðrop** (**þrep**), 1–5 **þrop**, (4–5 **throop-e, þroup**), 4, 9 *dial.* **throp** (5 **thrope**). *β.* 1–2, 4–5 **þorp**, 5– **thorpe**, 5, 7– **thorp.** [OE. and ME. *þrop* and *þorp* hamlet, village, farm, or estate; Com. Teut. = OFris. *thorp*, *therp* village, mod.Fris. *terp* village, village-mound (see TERP); OS. *thorp* (MLG., LG., MDu., Du. *dorp*, LG. and EFris. *dörp*); OHG. (MHG., Ger.) *dorf* village (locally 'gathering of people, meeting'); ON. *þorp* village, hamlet, farmstead (Norw. *torp*, Sw. *torp* cottage, little farm, Da. *torp* farmstead, hamlet, borough), Goth. *þaurp* estate, land, field:—OTeut. **þorpo*[m]. Ulterior etymology doubtful; original sense and its development in the Teutonic languages not clear.
ON. has (app. thence derived) *þyrpast* to crowd, throng, *þyrping* crowd; and *þorp* is by many referred to same root as L. *turba*, Gr. τύρβη crowd, tumult. Others compare L. *tribus* tribe, and OCelt. **treb* subdivision of a people, W. *tref* town. For other suggested cognates, cf. Kluge, Franck, Doornkaat-Koolman.]
A hamlet, village, or small town; in ME. *esp.* an agricultural village: see quots.
Not a frequent word in OE., being chiefly found in Glosses and Vocabularies, in form *þrop*, which was also the prevailing form in ME. down to 1400. *Þorp* appears once in late OE. and in the north in 14th c., and may really be due to Norse influence. In various forms as *Thorpe, Throop, Thrupp*, the word occurs as a place-name, and it is a frequent second element in these in the forms *-thorpe, -thrup, -trup*, chiefly in the Danelaw district. It appears to have been a 'common noun' to Langland and Chaucer; but in Caxton to be a literalism of translation. As a separate word it has been used occasionally from 1600, but is app. only literary or archaic, rarely dialectal: see *Eng. Dial. Dict.*
*α.* *c* **725** *Corpus Gloss.* (O.E.T.) 557 *Conpetum* [= cross-ways, Carfax], tuun, þrop. *a* **800** *Erfurt Gloss.* 307 *Conpetum*, tuun, *vel* ðrop. *a* **1000** ÆLFRIC *Voc.* in Wr.-Wülcker 147/5 *Fundus* [= farm, piece of land], þrop. *a* **1000** *Ags. Gloss.* ibid. 207/14 *Competum*..i. *uilla, uel* þingstow, *uel* þrop. *c* **1200** *Trin. Coll. Hom.* 89 Bethfage, Swo hatte þe þrop þe preste one wunien, bi sides ierusalem. *c* **1350** *Will. Palerne* 2141 To seche eche cite & alle smale þropes. **1362** LANGL. *P. Pl.* A. II. 47 For lewede, for lerede, for laborers of þropes [*v. rr.* þrepis, þorpes]. **1393** *Ibid.* C. I. 219 As barouns & burgeis and bondemen of þroupes [*v. rr.* þropus, þropes, thorpys]. *c* **1386** CHAUCER *Wife's T.* 15 Citees, burghes, castels, hye toures, Thropes, bernes, shipnes, dayeryes, This maketh that ther been no ffairyes. — *Clerk's T.* 143 Noght fer..There stood a throope [2 *MSS.*, throop 1, thrope 3, thorpt 1] of site delitable, In which that poure folk of that village, Hadden hir beestes and hir herbergage. *c* **1440** [see *β*].
*β.* *a* **1122** *O. E. Chron.* an. 963 (Laud MS.), Sce. Petres mynstre Medeshamstede..and ealle þa þorpes þe ðærto lin. **13..** *E. E. Allit. P.* B. 1178 He wast wyth werre þe wones of þorpes. *c* **1381** CHAUCER *Parl. Foules* 350 (MS. Gg. 4. 27) The kok that orloge is of thorpis lyte. *c* **1440** *Promp. Parv.* 492/1 Tho(r)pe, thrope, lytylle towne. **1481** CAXTON *Reynard* viii. (Arb.) 15 The worde anone sprange oueral in the thorpe [*Orig. Flem.* die mare die spranck over al den dorp]. **1485** — *St. Wenefryde* 18 He reteynynge his felawe with hym abode that nyght in a thorpe. **1600** FAIRFAX *Tasso* XII. xxxii. 219 Within a little thorpe I staid at last. **1613** W. BROWNE *Brit. Past.* II. iii, About whose Thorps that night curs'd Limos went. **1814** WORDSW. *Excursion* VIII. 101 Welcome, wheresoe'er he came—Among the tenantry of thorpe and vill. **1855** TENNYSON *Brook* 29, I hurry down..By twenty thorps, a little town, And half a hundred bridges. **1864** — *En. Ard.* (end), The little thorp had seldom seen A costlier funeral.
Hence † **Tho·rpsman**, a villager. *Obs. rare.*
**1674** N. FAIRFAX *Bulk & Selv.* To Rdr., The inbred stock of more homely women and less filching Thorps-men. **1876** *Whitby Gloss.*, *Thorpsmen*, villagers. Old local print.

**Thorpole**, variant of THIRLEPOLL *Obs.*

**Thorrocke, Thorsday**, obs. ff. THURROCK, THURSDAY. **Thorst**, obs. f. THIRST; obs. var. *durst*, pa. t. of DARE *v.*[1]

**Thort**, obs. pa. t. of THARF; Sc. f. THWART.

**Thorter** (þǭ·ɹtəɹ, *Sc.* þo·rtər), *adv.*, *prep.*, *adj.*, *sb. Sc.* Forms: 5 **thwortour, thuortour, thourtour**, 5–6 **thortour**, 6 **-oure, -yr, -ir, -ar**, (**thortwart**), 7 **thorture**, 6– **thorter.** [In early forms *thwortour, thuortour, thortour*, Sc. forms of THWARTOVER: cf. Sc. *a-thort* = *a-thwart.* The second element has been so weakened as to appear a mere suffix, as in *easter, wester*, etc. *Thortwart* is a deformation.]
†**A.** *adv.* Athwart, across, crosswise. *Obs. rare.*
*c* **1470** HENRY *Wallace* V. 1110 Feill off thaim dede fell thwortour in [= into] the fyr.
**B.** *prep.* Athwart, across, overthwart.
**1533** BELLENDEN *Livy* I. vi. (S.T.S.) I. 39 Incontinent þe buschment foresaid come thortoure þare gate. **1609** *Sc. Acts Jas. VI* (1816) IV. 443/2 Landis..beginnand at þe watter of Tarress.. To rowaneburne and thorter Ingreis

ȝeattis by the fute of magilwod. **1897** LD. E. HAMILTON *Outlaws* xviii. 209 You daurna show your face thorter the water.

**C.** *adj.* Crossing, lying athwart, transverse. *Thorter land*, land lying across or beyond a certain area, outer land; *thorter way*, a cross-way; so *thorter lane, road*, etc.

*c* **1470** HENRY *Wallace* IV. 540 A cleuch thar was, quharoff a strenth thai maid With thuortour treis. *Ibid.* IX. 1632 A thourtour bande, that all the drawcht wpbar, He cuttyt it. *c* **1475** *Rauf Coilȝear* 569 In ane thourtour way, Seir gaitis pas thay,..Thus partit thay twa. **1533** BELLENDEN *Livy* II. xvi. (S.T.S.) I. 194 Sic thingis done, he past fordwart with thortoure passage in [= into] þe latyne way. **1535** *Aberd. Reg.* XV. (Jam.), To remoif, red, & flit out of the said inland thortyrland, yard, & forentres. **1580** *Burgh Rec. Edinb.* (1882) IV. 185 To caus mak sufficient thorter barris of irne, and infix thaim in the window of the mid hous. **1814** *North. Antiq.* 404 (Jam.) To look through an elf-bore in wood, where a thorter-knot..has been taken out. *Mod.* Forming part of local names: there is in Dundee a 'Thorter Row', which 'crosses' between the Nethergate and Overgate; in Hawick 'ThorterDykes', beyond the Loan-head, etc.

† **b.** Coming athwart; obstructing, opposing.

**1533** BELLENDEN *Livy* I. v. (S.T.S.) I. 35 The sabyne ladyis ..be preiss of þair thortwart cuming devidit & put sindry þe armit oistis. **1536** — *Cron. Scot.* III. iv. (1541) 27/1 Sa agill of thair bodyis, that thay may dant all thortour and difficill gatis.

† **D.** *sb.* Opposition, obstruction, resistance.

**1581** J. MELVILL *Diary* (Wodrow Soc.) 124 The thrid thortar and debat quhilk he haid was with the provist, bailyies, and counsall..about their ministerie. **1598** *Ibid.* 532 Anent quhatsoevir the thorteris and accidentis fallin out.

Hence **Tho·rter** *v. trans.* and *intr.*, to cross the path or way of; to thwart or oppose (a person); hence **Tho·rtering** *vbl. sb.*, thwarting, resisting; † **Tho·rtersome** *a.*, tending to thwart, obstructive.

**1608** JAS. VI *Let.* in Calderwood *Hist. Ch. Scot.* (1678) 581 Their willingness..hath been ever *thortered and impeded by too many..Advocations. **1671** M. BRUCE *Gd. News in Evil Times* (1708) 46 There is much Thortering with, and Murdering of Light in Scotland now, but Thortering of Light shall be the drearysomest Sin that ever Scotland had. **1890** J. SERVICE *Thir Notandums* xiv. 101 They [witches] made wee maiks oot o' clay..of them that had thortered them, stappin' the maiks fu o' preens. **1606** BIRNIE *Kirk-Buriall* (1833) 30 The passage so impeshed with *thortersome throughes.

**Tho·rter-i·ll.** *Sc.* Also **thwarter-.** [f. prec. + ILL *sb.*] A disease of sheep, characterized by distortion of the neck; louping-ill.

**1791** *Statist. Acc. Scot.* I. 138 Palsy, called trembling, or thorter ill, to which those fed on certain lands are peculiarly subject. **1808** *Sporting Mag.* XXXII. 195 A sheep which had died of disease (the thorter ill) and was at the time in a state of putrescence. **1829** HOGG *Tales, Sheph. Cal.* xvi, The thwarter-ill (a sort of paralytic affection) came among them [the sheep].

† **Tho·rtron,** *a. Sc. Obs. rare.* [f. THORTER: cf. *southron*.] Having a transverse direction.

*c* **1580** *Balfour's Practicks* (1754) 439 Thortron burnis in monthis hie Sall stop na heid roume, thoch thay be.

† **Thorty,** obs. form of THIRTY.

**1538** *Sel. Cas. Star Chamb.* (Selden) II. 60.

**Thoru, þoru, thorugh, thorw,** etc., obs. ff. THOROUGH, THROUGH *sb.*[1]

‖ **Thos** (þōus). Pl. **thoes** (þōu·īz). [L. *thōs*, pl. *thōes*, a. Gr. θώς, pl. θῶ-ες, a beast of prey of the dog kind.] The Greek and Latin name of a beast of the canine group; probably a jackal of some species; but variously identified or imagined by 17th c. translators. See also THOUS.

**1601** HOLLAND *Pliny* x. lxiii. I. 303 Wolves, Panthers, and Thoes, kindle their young before they can see. *Ibid.* lxxiv. 308 The Thoes and the Lions doe foulely jarre and disagree. **1607** TOPSELL *Four-f. Beasts* (1658) 581 The lesser kinde of Thoes are the best, for some make two kinde of Thoes, and some three...We will therefore take it for confessed, that the Thoes is a beast engendered betwixt a Wolf and a Fox, whereof some are greater and some are smaller. **1706** PHILLIPS (ed. Kersey), *Thos*,..a Lynx, a Creature resembling a Wolf, but spotted like a Leopard. **1753** CHAMBERS *Cycl. Supp.*, *Thos*,..a name given to an animal of the wolf kind, but larger than the common wolf. **1839** C. H. SMITH *Dogs* I. v. 207 It may be, that one of the smaller Thoes of Aristotle is the true Jackal.

**Thos, þos,** obs. form of THOSE, THUS.

**Thoscan,** obs. form of TUSCAN.

**Those** (ðōuz), *dem. pron.* and *adj.* (*pl.*) Forms: *α.* 1–3 **ðás,** 1–4 **þás,** 4 **þaas, þais,** 4–5 **þase,** (5 **þaes**); 5 **thas, thase,** 5–6 **thais.** *β.* 3–4 **þos** (3 **þosse**), 4–5 **þose, thoos,** (5, 7 **thoes,** Scotticized **thoise, thoys**), 6 **thoose**; 4– **those.** [OE. *þás, þās*, ME. *þōs*, pl. of THIS, which during the ME. period became synonymous with *þā*, THO, pl. of *that*, which it at length superseded, and thus came to be used in its current sense. The identification of *þās* (*þaas, þase, þais(e)* with *þā* began in the north, where it is evidenced *c* 1300–1340; the use of *þōs* (*thoos, those*) for *þō*, in midld. and south, came later. Chaucer has only *tho*; and most of the examples of *thos(e* before 1475 occur either in midld. versions of northern poems, such as the *Anturs of Arthur* and *Sir Perceval*, where the scribe transliterated *thas(e* into *thos(e*, or in the works of northern men, as Wyclif, whose native dialect had *thas(e*. In Eng. literature *those, thoos, thoes*, became common first in works printed by Caxton, and thenceforth *those* and *tho* continued to be used in the same sense, *tho* gradually becoming rarer, till *c* 1550.

The early southern ME. *þōs* = THESE, appears to have been retained longest in Kentish: see quot. 1340 in. I. 1. It was of course obsolete in Midld. Eng. before *thos, thoos, those* in the modern sense was accepted. It is doubtful whether *thase* ever found a footing in Scotland, where *þā* continued in use, and still exists as THAE pl. of *that*.]

**I.** Demonstrative pronoun.

† **1.** Plural of THIS B. I = THESE B. I. *Obs.*

*c* **825** *Vesp. Psalter* xliii. 18 [xliv. 17] Ðas all cwomun ofer usic. *a* **900** K. ÆLFRED *Laws* Introd. c. 49 § 9 Ic ða Ælfred cyning þas togædere ȝegaderode. *a* **900** tr. *Bæda's Hist.* III. xix. [xxvii.] 242 Betweoh þas wæron tweȝen ȝeonge æðelingas. *c* **1000** *Ags. Gosp.* Matt. iv. 9 Ealle þas ic sylle þe. *c* **1200** *Trin. Coll. Hom.* 217 Ac ich ne mai ne ich ne can þosse [i. e. words] on openi. **1340** *Ayenb.* 10 Vor alle þos byeþ ualse wytnesses. *Ibid.* 39 Þise makeþ þe ualse mariages. Þise benimeþ þe heritages. Þos doþ zuo moche kuead..and al þis hi doþ be hare greate couaytise.

**2.** Plural of THAT: indicating things or persons pointed to or already mentioned: see THAT B. I. 1.

**1340** HAMPOLE *Pr. Consc.* 6556, I fynde wryten paynes fourtene,.. And whilk þas er I sal yhow telle. *a* **1400** *K. Alis.* 4913 (Bodl. MS.) A folk woneþ biside þoos, Þat beeþ ycleped Farangos. **1477** EARL RIVERS (Caxton) *Dictes* 33 He made diuers bookis of phisik..and of thoos, xij the most be studyed by ordre. **1591** SHAKS. *Two Gent.* III. i. 225 A Sea of melting pearls, which some call teares: Those at her fathers churlish feete she tenderd. **1599** — *Hen. V*, III. vii. 74 The Armour that I saw in your Tent to night, are those Starres or Sunnes vpon it? **1611** BIBLE *Eccl.* vii. 28 A woman among all those haue I not found. **1653** WALTON *Angler* ii. 65 *Milk.* What Song was it, I pray? was it, Come Shepherds deck your heads: or, As at noon Dulcina rested: or Philida flouts me? *Pisc.* No, it is none of those. *a* **1822** SHELLEY *Serchio* 36 Melchior and Lionel were not among those. *Mod.* Who are those passing? Those are our neighbours Smith and Jones. I looked at all the books on the top shelf, but it was not one of those.

**b.** Preceded by *and*, introducing an additional qualification of the things or persons mentioned in the previous clause: plural of THAT I. 2 a.

**1545** ASCHAM *Toxoph.* II. (Arb.) 162 Other and those very good archers in drawyng, loke at the marke. **1590** RYTHER tr. *Ubaldino's Disc. Span. Invasion* 5 Through penurie of many and those necessarie things. **1601** HOLLAND *Pliny* (1634) I. 529 If the vineyard lie pendant vpon the hanging of an hill, it requireth deeper ditches, and those raised vp well with earth. **1697** DRYDEN *Virg. Georg.* IV. 189 Lord of few Acres, and those barren too. **1701** NORRIS *Ideal World* I. ii. 53 Other figures..and those perfect ones. *Mod.* I have only three, and those not of the best.

**3.** In opposition to *these*; sometimes *spec.* = 'the former': plural of THAT B. I. 3, 3 b. For quots. see THESE B. I. 2, II. 2. Also in contrast to (*the*) *others.*

**1653** WALTON *Angler* iv. 116 Palmer flies, not only those rib'd with silver and gold, but others that have their bodies all made of black. **1655** STANLEY *Hist. Philos.* I. I. 6 Those affirming they had bargain'd onely for the fish, the others that they bought the draught at a venture.

**4.** As antecedent pronoun, followed by a defining word or phrase, viz. a relative clause (with relative expressed or understood), a participle (or other vbl. adj.), or a preposition (esp. *of*) with a sb. which serves to qualify or particularize *those*: plural of THAT B. I. 6–8. (= Ger. *diejenigen* or *die*, F. *ceux, celles.*)

**a.** In general sense: chiefly, now only, of persons: *those who* = the people who; *those of* = the people of, etc. Plural of THAT B. I. 6 a, c, 8 b.

**1340** HAMPOLE *Pr. Consc.* 7510 Alle þase þat wille þair syn forsake. *c* **1400** MAUNDEV. (Roxb.) xv. 67 Þase þat trowes perfitely in Godd sall be sauf. *c* **1440** *Alphabet of Tales* 296 Þase at sulde bere hym myght gett hym no ferrer. **1477** EARL RIVERS (Caxton) *Dictes* 115 Thoos that be nedy. *Ibid.* 129 Thoes that blame. **1535** COVERDALE *Prov.* viii. 12, I am louynge vnto those that loue me. **1548** FORREST *Pleas. Poesye* 55 Of thoise that they had too them made subiugate. **1554–9** T. WATERTOUNE in *Songs & Ball.* (1860) 11 All thoys that have years this vndarstande. **1590** SHAKS. *Com. Err.* III. i. 48 Who are those at the gate? **1598** — *Merry W.* v. v. 57 Those as sleepe, and thinke not on their sins. **1605** — *Macb.* II. iii. 106 Those of his Chamber, as it seem'd, had don't. **1610** — *Temp.* I. ii. 398 Those are pearles that were his eies. **1613** — *Hen. VIII*, III. i. 167 Pray thinke vs, Those we professe, Peace-makers, Friends, and Seruants. **1777** ROBERTSON *Hist. Amer.* (1783) II. 216 Those who appeared more gentle and tractable. **1790** BURKE *Fr. Rev.* 50 Those from whom they are descended. **1856** GEO. ELIOT *Ess.* (1884) 232 Those among our painters who aim at giving the rustic type of features. **1896** *Law Times* C. 410/1 Any person other than himself and those claiming under him. *Mod.* Of those expected only a few turned up.

**b.** Referring to things or persons mentioned immediately before, and equivalent to *the* with the pl. sb.; e. g. in quot. 1593, *those* = 'the storms'. Plural of THAT B. I. 6 b, 8 a.

**1477** EARL RIVERS (Caxton) *Dictes* 31 Diuerse opinions, And in especial thoos of plato. **1593** SHAKS. *Lucr.* 1589 These watergalls..Foretell new stormes to those alreadie spent. **1611** BIBLE *Josh.* iii. 16 The waters which came downe from aboue, stood and rose vp vpon an heape..and those that came downe toward the sea of the plaine..failed, and were cut off. **1774** GOLDSM. *Nat. Hist.* (1790) VII. 51 The oysters..are by no means so large as those found sticking to rocks. **1779** *Mirror* No. 6 ¶ 10 The classical writers..were those from whose works he felt the highest pleasure. **1797** *Encycl. Brit.* (ed. 3) IV. 778/2 The larvæ, which resemble those of the wasp. **1819** KEATS *Ode Grecian Urn* ii, Heard melodies are sweet, but those unheard Are sweeter. **1874** DASENT *Half a Life* II. 76 His laws being like those of the Medes and Persians.

**II.** Demonstrative adjective.

† **1.** Plural of THIS B. II = THESE B. II. *Obs.*

*a* **900** K. ÆLFRED *Laws* Introd., Dryhten wæs sprecende ðas word to Moyse. *c* **1000** *Ags. Gosp.* Matt. vi. 32 Ealle þas þing þeoda seceað. *c* **1175** *Lamb. Hom.* 11 (*De Quadragesima*) Þas daȝes beoð iset us to muchele helpe..al swa moyses..feste þes daȝes. *c* **1200** *Trin. Coll. Hom.* 185 Ðos feawe word..seide ure drihten. *c* **1205** LAY. 672 Brutus hine bi-þohte..& þas [*c* 1275 þeos] word seide. *a* **1250** *Owl & Night.* 139 (Cott.) Þos [*Jes.* þeos] word aȝaf þe niȝtingale.

**2.** Plural of THAT B. II. 1.

*α.* **13..** *Cursor M.* 2590 (Gött.) As it was hite [*v. r.* hight] bifor þas [*C.* þaa, *F.* þa] dais. *Ibid.* 4948 (Cott.) Þan spak ruben, þe eildest broiþer, Stilli menand til þas [*F.* þase] oþer. *Ibid.* 8187 (Cott.) He tok þaas [*G.* þa] wandes in his hand. *Ibid.* 19859 Quen petre þais [*G.*, *F.* þa: *Tr.* þo] vnbestes sagh. *c* **1440** *Alphabet of Tales* 82 With all þase candels he cursid þis fend & entirditid hym.

*β.* *c* **1375** *Cursor M.* (Fairf.) 7254 Bi a piler was he sette to glew þos [*C.* þaa] gomis at mete. *c* **1380** WYCLIF *Serm.* Sel. Wks. II. 112 Bifore þat tyme weren þos wordis spoken of Crist. *a* **1400** *Sir Perc.* 229 Fyftene wynter and mare He duellede in those holtes hare. **1477** EARL RIVERS (Caxton) *Dictes* Pref. 3 Ony of thoos bookes. *Ibid.* 27 Whiche was a Cyte in thoos dayes. **1491** in *Lett. Rich. III & Hen. VII* (Rolls) I. 99 Bring the said Sir Robert and thoes other oure rebelles and traitours. **1526** TINDALE *Luke* i. 39 Mary arose in thoose [COVERD. & *Gt. Bible* those] dayes. **1595** SHAKS. *John* III. iv. 61 Binde vp those tresses. **1639** *Hamilton Papers* (Camden) 90 So many men..with thoes I haue heir, as will make up that number. **1741–2** CHALLONER *Mission. Priests* (1803) II. 19 John Sugar was born at Womborn.. of a noted family in those parts. **1845** M. PATTISON *Ess.* (1889) I. 14 A living stirring picture of the Church and State of those days.

**b.** Indicating things or persons as known to be such as described: plural of THAT B. II. 1 b.

**1590** SHAKS. *Mids. N.* III. ii. 140 Thy lips, those kissing cherries. **1678** CUDWORTH *Intell. Syst.* I. ii. 61 As for those Romantick Mongrammous Gods of Epicurus. **1753** CHALLONER *Cath. Chr. Instr.* 178 Those two great Lights of the Church, St. Gregory Nazianzen and St. Basil. **1822** SHELLEY *Question* 10 Daisies, those pearled Arcturi of the earth. **1855** MACAULAY *Hist. Eng.* xx. IV. 494 Those worst enemies of the nation.

**c.** Used instead of *that* with a sing. noun of multitude (now only with collectives in pl. sense, as *clergy, foot* (foot-soldiers), *horse, vermin*); and esp. with *kind, sort*, followed by *of* with pl. sb. (see KIND *sb.* 14 b). Cf. THESE B. II. 1 d.

*Those kind* (or *sort*) *of men*, is put for 'men of that kind (*or* sort)', L. *ejus generis homines*, and is grammatically anomalous: cf. THAKIN.

**1560** WHITEHORNE *Ord. Souldiours* (1588) 9 b, Behind the said teeth to place those number of men which first were taken out. **1601** SHAKS. *Twel. N.* I. ii. 10 You, and those poore number saued with you. **1692** O. WALKER *Grk. & Rom. Hist.* 266 He..chased away those Vermin of Courtiers. **1875** GLADSTONE *Glean.* VI. 126 Some of those clergy who are called Broadchurchmen.

**1565** J. SPARKE in Hawkins *Voy.* II. (Hakl. Soc.) 51 Those sorte of men are eaters of the flesh of men, as well as the Canibals. **1577** NORTHBROOKE *Dicing* (1843) 99 From whence those kinde of playes had their beginning. **1608** DOD & CLEAVER *Expos. Prov.* xi–xii. 150 In those kind of trees, the root cannot defend the branches, nor bodie. **1761** H. WALPOLE *Let. to H. Zouch* 3 Jan., The little regard shown ..to those sort of things. **1798** JANE AUSTEN *Lett.* (1884) I. 187 Those kind of foolish and incomprehensible feelings. **1887** RIDER HAGGARD *Jess* 126 Those sort of reflections.

**3.** In opposition to *these*: plural of THAT B. II. 2; cf. I. 3 above. For quots. see THESE B. II. 2.

**4.** In concord with a noun which is the antecedent to a relative (expressed or omitted), or which is further defined by a participle: pl. of THAT B. II. 3.

*c* **1175** *Lamb. Hom.* 13 Þas .x. bebode þe godalmihti seolf idihte. **1526** TINDALE *Eph.* v. 12 Those thynges which are done of them in secrete. — *Jude* 10 Those thinges which they knowe not. In tho thynges which they knowe naturally they corrupte them selves [so COVERD. & *Gt. Bible*]. **1539** BIBLE (Great) *Rev.* i. 3 And kepe those [TINDALE & COVERD. thoo] thynges which are written therin. **1563** WINȜET *Four Scoir Thre Quest.* § 35 Wks. (S.T.S.) I. 100 Gif ze be nocht admittit be thais Kirkis, quhome ze serue. **1599** SHAKS. *Hen. V*, IV. viii. 96 The Names of those their Nobles that lye dead. **1631** MILTON *Epitaph Marchioness Winchester* 43 Those Pearls of dew she wears. **1779** *Mirror* No. 30 ¶ 2 Those national boasts which are always allowable. **1780** *Ibid.* No. 79 ¶ 5 Those useful chronicles of facts, called newspapers. **1859** GEO. ELIOT *A. Bede* xlix, Brethren and sisters..who have none of those comforts you have.

**5.** = Such: plural of THAT B. II. 4. Now *rare.*

**1605** SHAKS. *Lear* I. i. 99, I returne those duties backe as are right fit. **1611** — *Cymb.* v. v. 338 Those Arts they haue, as I Could put into them. **1632** MASSINGER & FIELD *Fatal Dowry* III. i, Obnoxious to those foolish things As they can gibe at. **1689** LUTTRELL *Brief Rel.* (1857) I. 567 The town ..was reduced to those straights, that if not releived..it must have surrendred in two daies time. **1827** DISRAELI *Viv. Grey* v. vi, He spoke of you in those terms that make me glad that I have met the son.

† **Thost(e.** *Obs.* [OE. *þost* = OHG. *dost.*] Dung, excrement; a turd.

*c* **1000** *Sax. Leechd.* I. 364 Scinseocum men wyrc drenc of hwites hundes þoste on bitere leȝe. *a* **1300** *E. E. Psalter* lxxxii[i]. 11 [10] Þai for-worthed in Endor, Þai ere made als thoste of erthe þar-for. *a* **1327** *Pol. Songs* (Camden) 237 Alle weren y-haht Of an horse thoste. **1387** TREVISA *Higden* (Rolls) IV. 423 Alle men þrewe on hym drit and thost. *c* **1425** *Cast. Persev.* 2413 in *Macro Plays* 149 Al oure fare is not worth a thost. *c* **1440** *Pallad. on Husb.* IV. 348 Asse vryne & swynes thost. *c* **1440** *Promp. Parv.* 492/1 Thoste (or toord), *stercus*.

† **Tho·ther**, coalesced form of *the other*, frequent from 14th to 17th c.; in later time also written *th' other*: see TH-, TH'.

Often used in contrast to THONE = the one: see THONE, ONE 18, 19, and TOTHER.

*c* **1300** *Beket* 466 Tho were thothere glad ynouȝ. *c* **1400** *Trevisa's Higden* (Rolls) III. 65 (MS. γ) Þooþer wys men. **1534-5** *MS. Rawl. D.* 777 lf. 67 b, One of them in [etc.] and thoder in the hawpace. **1556** *Knaresborough Wills* (Surtees) I. 73 To my children thother half. **1633** T. STAFFORD *Pac. Hib.* I. i. (1821) 11 On thother part.

**Thou** (ðau), *pers. pron., 2nd sing. nom.* Forms: 1-3 **ðu**, 1-5 **þu**, (2-3 tu, tou, -te), 3 (þe, þeou), **ðhu**, 3-5 **þou**, 3-6 **thu**, (4 **þouȝ**), 4-5 **þow**, (-tow), 4-6 **thow**, 4, 6 (9 *dial.*) th-, th', (5 thowe), 4- thou. (*Mod. dial.* thau, thaw, thah, tha; theau, theow, thoo, thu; tau, taw, ta, tay; teau, teaw, teu, too, tou, tow; doo, dou, du, etc.: see *Eng. Dial. Dict.*) [OE. *ðŭ*, *þŭ*; Com. Teut. and Indo-Eur.; = OFris. *thŭ* (*du*), OS. *thŭ* (MDu., MLG., LG. *du*), OHG. *dŭ* (MHG., Ger. *du*), ON. *þú* (Norw., Sw., Da. *du*), Goth. *þu*:— OTeut. *þŭ* = pre-Teut. *tŭ*: = L. *tu*, Ir. *tu*, Welsh *ti*, Gr. σύ, Doric τύ, Lith. *tu*, OSlav. *ty*, Skr. *twa-m*. The oblique cases, and the possessive, are formed on a stem *þe-* = pre-Teut. *te-*: see THEE, THINE. The pl. YE, in OE. *gé*, is from a different root, to which also belonged a dual *git*, YIT, 'ye two', still used after 1200 in ME. The acc. and dat. sing. were levelled in OE. under the dat. form: see THEE. The OE. genitive was identical in form with a possessive adj. *þín*: see THINE, THY. The paradigm of *thou* is therefore as follows:

*Old English.*

| | SINGULAR. | DUAL. | PLURAL. |
|---|---|---|---|
| *Nom.* | þú, þu | ȝit | ȝé, ȝe, ȝie |
| *Acc.* | þec; þē, þe | incit; inc | ēowic; ēow (iuih, iuh) |
| *Dat.* | þē, þe | inc | ēow |
| *Gen.* / *Poss. Pron.* | þín | incer | ēower |

*Middle English.*

| | | | |
|---|---|---|---|
| *Nom.* | þū, þou, þow | ȝit, ȝet | ȝe, ȝie, yhe, ye |
| *Dat. Acc.* | þē, þee | inc, ȝinc, ȝunc | eow, eou, ou, ow, ȝiu, ȝu, ȝou, yhu (etc.) |
| *Gen.* | þīn | inker, ȝunker, unker | eower, eour, ower, ȝure, ȝour(e |
| *Poss. Pron.* | þīn, þī | inker, ȝunker, unker | |

*Modern English.*

| | | | |
|---|---|---|---|
| *Nom.* | thou | [*obs.*] | ye, you |
| *Dat. Acc.* | thee | " | you |
| *Poss. absol.* | thine | " | yours |
| *Pron. adj.* | thy | " | your.] |

**1.** The pronoun by which a person (or thing) is addressed, in the nominative singular; the pronoun denoting the person (or thing) spoken to.

*Thou* and its cases *thee, thine, thy*, were in OE. used in ordinary speech; in ME. they were gradually superseded by the plural *ye, you, your, yours*, in addressing a superior and (later) an equal, but were long retained in addressing an inferior. Long retained by Quakers in addressing a single person, though now less general; still in various dialects used by parents to children, and familiarly between equals, esp. intimates; in other cases considered as rude. In general English used in addressing God or Christ, also in homiletic language, and in poetry, apostrophe, and elevated prose. For details of dialect use, see Wright, *Eng. Dial. Dict.*, *Thou* II, *Eng. Dial. Gram.* § 404.

In ME. freq. combined with its verb when this precedes, the *þ* being then absorbed in the preceding *t*, as *artow* = art thou, *hastow* = hast thou. The initial *þ* also became *t* after *s*, *t*, or *d*, as *hauis tu* = hast thou, *þat tu, and tu*: see T 8.

*Beowulf* 507 Eart þu se Beowulf? *c* **825** *Vesp. Psalter* ix. 15 Ðu uphest mec of ȝeatum deaðes. *c* **1205** LAY. 690 Niðing þou ært al dead.. Bote þu min lare do. *Ibid.* 2978 Þeou [*c* **1275** þou] ært leouere þene mi lif. *a* **1225** *Ancr. R.* 240 Þench ec hwat tu owust God, uor his god deden. *a* **1240** *Ureisun* in *Cott. Hom.* 199 So þu dest and so þu schalt. *c* **1250** *Gen. & Ex.* 361 For ðhu min bode-word haues broken, ðhu salt ben ut in sorȝe luken, In swinc ðu salt tilien ði mete. **1297** R. GLOUC. (Rolls) 6371 Þou ne ssalt of þin liflode neuere carie noȝt. *a* **1300** *Cursor M.* 19585 (Edin.) Hauis tu [*v.rr.* þu, þou] na parte.. here. *Ibid.* 1253 (Gött.) In þat way sal yu [*Cott.* þou] find forsoth þi moþer. *Ibid.* 8306 (Fairf.) Werrour artow [*Cott.* art þow] gode in fiȝt. *c* **1391** CHAUCER *Astrol.* I. § 13 Thanne hastow a brod Rewle. *c* **1440** *Pallad. on Husb.* I. 42 The better may thowe with that water holde. **1535** COVERDALE *Ps.* lxiv. [lxv.] 1 Thou, O God, art praysed in Sion. **1592** SHAKS. *Rom. & Jul.* I. v. 9 Good thou, saue mee a piece of Marchpane. **1597** — *2 Hen. IV*, II. ii. 17 How many paire of Silk stockings yͧ haste. **1671** H. M. tr. *Erasm. Colloq.* 326 Why shouldest thou do so, seeing how thou wast not far from thine own shore? **1715-20** POPE *Iliad* XII. 69 Oh thou! bold leader of the Trojan bands, And you, confederate chiefs from foreign lands! **1741** RICHARDSON *Pamela* II. 273, I dare say thou'lt set the good Work forward. *a* **1835** MRS. HEMANS *Graves of Househ.* viii, Alas, for love! if thou wert all, And nought beyond, O Earth. **1872** TENNYSON *Gareth & Lyn.* 1210 Thou—Lancelot!—thine the hand That threw me?

*Dialectal.* **1579** SPENSER *Sheph. Cal.* July 33 Syker, thous but a laesie loord. **1607** BEAUMONT *Woman Hater* III. i, Heres ta, and tha [Hearest thou, if thou] wants lodging, take my house, 'tis big enough. **1802** R. ANDERSON *Cumberld. Ball., Sally Gray* iv, Had tou seen her at kurk, man, last Sunday, Tou couldn't ha'e thought o' the text. **1861** E. WAUGH *Birtle Carter's T.* 32 Well neaw, mind ta does do. **1876** *Whitby Gloss.* 171/2 If thoo will gan, sithence be 't. **1886** HALL CAINE *Son of Hagar* I. i, What sayst tha, Reuben?

**b.** Used in apposition to and preceding a sb. in the vocative: in reproach or contempt often emphasized by being placed or repeated after the sb.

*c* **888** K. ÆLFRED *Boeth.* xxvii. § 2 Ic asciȝe ðe, þu Boetius. **13..** *Cursor M.* 13632 (Gött.) 'Hald ȝe to him', said þai, 'þu caitiue'. *c* **1350** *Will. Palerne* 312 A! gracious gode god! þouȝ grettest of alle! *c* **1425** ? LYDG. *Assembly of Gods* 1394 'What' seyde Ryghtwysnes, 'thow olde dotyng foole'. *c* **1485** *Digby Myst.* III. 1399 Loke þat we have drynke, boy þou. **1590** SHAKS. *Mids. N.* V. i. 177 Thow wall, o wall, o sweet and louely wall. **1601** — *Jul. C.* IV. iii. 301 Sleepe againe Lucius: Sirra Claudio, Fellow, Thou: Awake. **1610** — *Temp.* III. ii. 52 Thou lyest, thou iesting Monkey thou. **1756** HOME *Douglas* III. ii, Thou riddler, speak Direct and clear. **1820** WORDSW. *Ch. San Salvador* I Thou sacred Pile! whose turrets rise.. Guarded by lone San Salvador. **1850** (Westmorland), Get oop, thoo lile ligabed!

**2.** As *sb.* **a.** The person or 'self' of the individual addressed. Cf. THEE *pron.* 4 a.

**1693** DRYDEN *Persius' Sat.* I. 249 Thou, if there be a Thou, in this base Town, Who dares, with angry Eupolis, to frown. **1831** CARLYLE *Sart. Res.* II. ix, Because the Thou (sweet gentleman) is not sufficiently honoured, nourished, soft-bedded.

**b.** The word itself: see also THEE *pron.* 4 b.

**1655** BAXTER *Quaker Catech.* 27 The Quakers.. call out for a formal Righteousnesse.., consisting in such things as these following, to wit,.. That we say (*Thou*) and no (*You*) to him we speak to. **1694** PENN in *G. Fox's Jrnl.* (1827) I. Pref. 15 They also used the plain language of Thou and Thee to a single person. **1827** HARE *Guesses* (1859) 119 When *you* came into use among the higher classes, the lower were still addrest with *thou*. **1905** *Daily Chron.* 16 Feb. 5/1 Among the concessions.. is that the men shall be addressed in the second person plural, not as is usual throughout Russia, in the case of the working classes, in the singular 'thou' (a mark of inferiority).

**Thou** (ðau), *v.* [f. THOU *pron.*] To use the pronoun 'thou' to a person: familiarly, to an inferior, in contempt or insult, or as done (formerly universally, now less frequently) on principle by Quakers: cf. note to THOU *pers. pron.* 1. Often in phr. *to thou and thee, to thee and thou*: cf. also THEE *v.*[2] **a.** *trans.* **b.** *intr.* (or *absol.*). Hence **Thouing** *vbl. sb.* (Cf. THOWT(E *v.*)

**a.** *c* **1440** *Promp. Parv.* 492/1 Thowtyn, or seyn thow to a mann (*A.* thowyn or sey þu), *tuo*. **14..** *Voc.* in Wr.-Wülcker 618/7 *Tuo*, to thuy. *c* **1450** in Aungier *Syon* (1840) 297 None of hyghenesse schal thou another in spekynge. *c* **1530** *Hickscorner* (1905) 149 Avaunt, caitiff, dost thou thou me! I am come of good kin I tell thee! **1564-78** BULLEYN *Dial. agst. Pest.* (1888) 5 He thous not God, but you[s] hym. **1603** COKE in Hargrave *State Trials* (1776) I. 216 All that Lord Cobham did was by thy instigation, thou viper; for I thou thee, thou Traitor! **1664** PEPYS *Diary* 11 Jan., She [a Quakeress] thou'd him [the king] all along. **1682** R. WARE *Foxes & Firebrands* II. 103 He.. Quaker-like, thou'd and thee'd Oliver. **1805** tr. *Lafontaine's Hermann & Emilia* I. 110 When she heard the young people *thou* and *thee* each other. **1888** *Liversedge, Yorks. Dial.*, Shoo said, Art thah goin'? Yo' knaw shoo al'us thah's ma. We're owd mates.

**b.** **1679** *Establ. Test* 23 A.. Iesuit takes a Lodging at a Quakers, can thou and thee, and yea and nay, as well as the best of them. **1697** *State Philadelph. Soc.* 2 They were not so silly as to place Religion in Thouing and Theeing. **1883** *Globe* 24 Mar. 1/5 In this country 'thouing' is a lost art.

**Thou** (þau), *sb.*, a colloquial and familiar shortening of the word *thousand*; *esp.* a thousand pounds sterling; but also in other senses: see quots.

**1869** tr. *Sue's Myst. Paris* I. xxvi, The annual amount of his betting-book reached to two or three 'thous'. **1897** *Speaker* 13 Nov. 531 The writer did not demean himself by fixing his price at so much 'per thou'. **1899** *Daily News* 23 Feb. 6/2 Fancy Wellington and Nelson coaxed for copy at the rate, say, of five hundred pounds a 'thou'. **1902** *Westm. Gaz.* 30 June 3/3 In engineering we divide the inch into one thousand parts, and the expression of dimensions in 'thous', as they are called in workshops, is far more convenient than the expression of the same dimensions in parts of millimètres.

**Thou, þou, thouch(t**, obs. forms of THOUGH.

**Thoucht**, obs. Sc. f. THOUGHT *sb.*[1]; also of *thought* pa. t. of THINK *v.*

**Though** (ðōᵘ), *adv.* and *conj.* Forms: see below. [OE. had *ðéah, þéah, þéh*, corresp. to Goth. *þauh* (= *þau* 'in that case' + *h* = L. *-que* 'also'), OFris. *thâch* (Saterl. *dach*); OS. *thôh* (MDu., Du., LG. *doch*), OHG. *doh* (shortened fr. *dôh*), ON. *þó* (contr. fr. **þauh*), MSw., MDa. *þo, tho*. Of the numerous ME. forms, those in *α* and *β* were developments of OE. *þéah, þæ̂h, þâh*, with various treatment of the diphthong, and early shortening of the vowel in unstressed position (cf. Ormin's *þĕhh*, Lamb. Hom. *păch*), with subseq. stress-lengthening, as *þeih, they*, and *þauch, thau, thaw*. The *γ* forms were from Norse, representing an ON. **þôh* (intermediate to *þauh* and *þó*), shortened in Ormin to *þŏhh*, with subseq. stress-lengthening to *þōuȝ, though, thō*. The Norse form gradually gained over the native *α* and *β* forms, which disappeared from literature before 1500. The *δ* forms show the same development of *f* from *ȝ, gh* (χʷ), as in *laugh, cough, tough*; *thof* was occasional in literature as late as 1750, and is still prevalent in many varieties from Yorksh. and Lancash. to Hampsh. and Devon: see Wright *Eng. Dial. Gram.* In Scotl. and north of Engl. *though* is pronounced (þō); the Hampsh. and WSom. *thof* also is (þof), not (ðof).]

**A.** Illustration of Forms.

*α.* 1 **þéah, ðéah**, 1-3 **þéh, ðæch, þæh**, 2-3 **þech**, (**þehȝ**), (*Orm.*) **þěhh, þeih**, 3-4 **þeigh**, 3-5 **þei, þey**, 4 **þeiȝh**, 4-5 **þeyȝ, þeyh, þeiȝ, thegh, thei**, 5 **þeiȝt, theigh(e, they (the)**. Also 3 **þaih, þaiȝ, þayh, þayȝ, þay**, 4 **þai**.

*c* **888** K. ÆLFRED *Boeth.* xix. § 1 Hu neara þære eorðan stede is, þeah heo us rum þince. *c* **950** *Lindisf. Gosp.* Mark xiv. 29 ȝif *vel* ðæh alle ȝeondspyrand see. ah.. næfre ic. — John iv. 2 Ðæch se hælend ne fuluuade. **971** *Blickl. Hom.* 37 Þeah [see B. I]. *Ibid.* 55 Þeh he ȝeornlice ȝehyre þa word. *c* **1175** *Lamb. Hom.* 77 He [Christ] nis nawiht alle monne lauerd, þech alle men bon on his onwald. *c* **1200** *Vices & Virt.* 9 Þeih me niede me to ðan aðe, me ne net me noht te forsweriȝen, ac soð te seggen of ðan ðe ic am bicleped. *c* **1200** *Trin. Coll. Hom.* 83 Þeh [see B. II. 4]. *Ibid.* 159 Al þat man doð.. þehȝ hie ben don ec for godes luue. *c* **1200** ORMIN 395 Þatt teȝȝ.. sinndenn þohh swa þehh i þohht. *c* **1205** LAY. 13002 He þus sæide, soð þæh [*c* **1275** þoh] hit nære. *Ibid.* 22736 Wunder þæh [*c* **1275** þeh] hit þunche. *c* **1290** *S. Eng. Leg.* I. 260/148 Þei he fader and moder a-slouȝ. *c* **1350** *Will. Palerne* 689 As þeiȝh he gyled were. **1387** TREVISA *Higden* (Rolls) I. 213 Þeyȝ þou nygh all fallynge be. *c* **1394** *P. Pl. Crede* 69 Þeiȝ his felawes fayle good. **1398** TREVISA *Barth. De P. R.* III. iii. (Tollem. MS.), Þey [L. *quamvis*] þe soule be onid to a body. *c* **1400** *Brut* 49 As þeiȝt Vortiger hade nouȝt wiste þerof. **1400** in *Roy. & Hist. Lett. Hen. IV* (Rolls) 38 Thegh John Welle hath doon as thu aboven has certefied. *c* **1425** *Seven Sag.* (P.) 1741 He loved hit wel, the hit were bad. *a* **1450** *Le Morte Arth.* 1985 What wondyr theighe hys herte were wo. *c* **1450** LOVELICH *Grail* lv. 298 As they Alle they in the world hadde ben there. *c* **1205** LAY. 2513 Þaih he bere ræd gold. *c* **1250** *Hymn Virgin* 62 in *Trin. Coll. Hom.* 257 Betere ne miȝte he þaiȝ he wolde. **1297** R. GLOUC. (Rolls) 3284 Þei [*v. r.* þay] ȝo were wif.

*β.* 1-3 **þah** (3 **tah**), 2 **þach, þaȝh**, 3-4 **þaȝ**, 5 **þagh, thaȝ, thaghe, thaȝhe**; 2-5 **þau**, 3 **þaue**, 3-4 **þauh** (**tauh**), 4-5 **þauȝ, þaw**, 5 **þawe, thau**.

*c* **950** *Lindisf. Gosp.* Luke xviii. 4 Ðah god ne ondredo ic ne monno sceomiȝo. *c* **1175** *Lamb. Hom.* 15 Þaȝh [see B. II. 2]. *Ibid.* 147 Þach his likame swiche pine ne þole. *c* **1205** LAY. 244 Þa com his lifes ende, lað þah him were. *a* **1225** *St. Marher.* 4 Freo wummon ich am ant tah godes þeowe. *a* **1240** *Ureisun* in *Cott. Hom.* 203 [He] beieð adun toward þe his.. heaued, ase þauh [*v. r. Ibid.* 189 þah] he seide [etc.]. *a* **1250** *Owl & Night.* 1274 Þah he habbe neole. *c* **1320** Þauȝ [see B. I]. **1340** Þaȝ [see B. II. 3]. **1362** LANGL. *P. Pl.* A. I. 132 No dedly sunne to do dyȝe þauȝ þou scholdest. *c* **1420** *Sir Amadace* xxviii, Quat wundur were hit, thaȝhe him were wo? **1426** AUDELAY *Poems* 15 Thaȝ Kayme his borne broder were cursid. *a* **1450** MYRC *Par. Pr.* 91 And thaghe þe chylde bote half be bore.

*γ.* 3 (*Orm.*) **þohh** (**tohh**), 3-4 **þoh** (**þoch**, 3 **ðhoȝ**), 4 **þoȝ, þhoh, þho, þouh, þouȝh, þouhȝ, þowh, þowgh**, 4-5 **þowȝ, þouȝ, -e, þou, þogh, þow** (**dow**), **þo**, 4-6 **thow**, 5 **þowe, thoȝe, thouȝ, thowh, thowgh, thou**, *Sc.* **thouch**, 5-6 **thoughe**, 5-7 **thogh**, 6 *Sc.* **thoch**, 5- **though**; 5-9 **tho**, 6- **tho'**, (7 **thô**).

*c* **1200** ORMIN Ded. 155 Þohh þatt teȝȝ all forrwerrpenn itt. *Ibid.* Introd. 23, & itt wass þohh full mikell rihht. *c* **1275** LAY. 2345 He seide, soþ þoh [*c* **1205** þeih] hit neare. *Ibid.* 4264 Þoh [*c* **1205** ȝef] he hadde man islaȝe. **13..** *Cursor M.* 21818 (Edin.) Þat tu fande þoȝ [*Cott.* þof, *Gött.* þou] I walde it noȝte. *Ibid.* 24590 Þho þu wald þai birid þi barn. *Ibid.* 73 (Gött.) Þou i sumtime be untrewe. *Ibid.* 4763 (Fairf.) Þo þai had siluer and golde rede. *Ibid.* 10941 (Gött.) And dow þai þar-fore murnand were. **1377** LANGL. *P. Pl.* B. VI. 40 And þowgh ȝe mowe amercy hem, late mercy be taxoure. *c* **1380** WYCLIF *Sel. Wks.* III. 328 Þouȝ men ben nevere so opynly cursid. *c* **1425** *Seven Sag.* (P.) 576 Hit his no wondir tho me be wo. *c* **1425** tr. *Higden* (Rolls) VII. App. 519 (MS. *β*) Thouȝ that tale teller were as huge as a geaunt. *c* **1449** PECOCK *Repr.* II. ix. 195 ȝhe, thou tho gouernauncis.. be weel ynouȝ. **1456** SIR G. HAYE *Law Arms* (S.T.S.) 81 Thouch thai be feble of corps. *c* **1489** CAXTON *Sonnes Aymon* xxii. 481 Thoughe he dothe wronge to leve me here. *a* **1529** SKELTON *Agst. Garnesche* 124 Thow a Sarsens hed ye bere. *a* **1540** BARNES *Wks.* (1573) 281/1 Though all the worlde say naye. *a* **1550** *Christis Kirke Gr.* xvi, Thoch he wes wight, he wes nocht wyss. **1615** HIERON *Wks.* I. 628 Thogh He do not alwaies shew it. **1643** DENHAM *Cooper's H.* Poems (1703) 12 Tho deep, yet clear, tho gentle, yet not dull. **1711** SHAFTESB. *Charac.* (1737) II. 149 Tho the impatience of abstaining be greater. **1741** Tho' [see B. II. 1].

*δ.* 4 **þowf**, 4-5 **þof** (**of**), **þofe, thofe, thoffe**, 5 (**yof**), **þaf, þuff**, 5-6 **thaff**, 5-7 (*dial.* -9) **thof**, 8 *dial.* **thoff.**

**13..** *Cursor M.* 698 (Cott.) Þowf he was euer wittur. *Ibid.* 19648 And þof a smitt moght he not se. *c* **1340** HAMPOLE *Prose Tr.* 7 'Thoffe I ware', quod he. *Ibid.* 21 Thoffe I be a wrech and vnworthi. *c* **1440** Þof, yof [see B. II. 1]. *c* **1440** *Lay Folks Mass Bk.* (MS. E.) 7 Þaf a Mˡᵉ [= thousand] clerkus dyd noght ellus. *c* **1440** *Alphabet of Tales* 64 Þuff all he lefte it. *c* **1450** Thof [see B. II. 2]. **14..** *Kyng & Hermit* 158 in Hazl. *E. P. P.* I. 19 Thaff thou were sych thre. *a* **1565** J. HEYWOOD *Dial. Wit & Folly* (Percy Soc.) 8 As thowghff he knewe th' end of thing at begynnyng. **1695** CONGREVE *Love for L.* III. xv, A Sailor will be honest, thof mayhap he has never a Penny of Money in his Pocket. **1748** Thof [see B. II. 1]. **1803** MARY CHARLTON *Wife & Mistress* II. 149, I never mintioned it before, thof I knowed it all along!

ε. (Chiefly *Sc.*) 4–5 þocht, (4 þoght, thowcht), 4–6 thoucht, 4–7 thocht, 5–7 thoght, 6 thought, thouȝght, thoᵗ.

**1303** R. BRUNNE *Handl. Synne* 969 Y wlde nat leue for here to werche þoght men rong noun at þe cherche. *c* **1375** *Sc. Leg. Saints* Prol. 166 Thowcht god chesit Androw firste To be ane apostill. **1375** (MS. 1489) BARBOUR *Bruce* I. 264 ȝe may weile se, thoucht nane ȝow tell. *c* **1470** HENRY *Wallace* VI. 24 Thocht Inglismen was grewyt at his repayr, ȝeit [etc.]. **1530** in W. H. Turner *Select. Rec. Oxford* (1880) 78, I wolde it had ben uppon the constabyll, thouȝght it had ben worse. **1535** Thocht [see B. II. 1]. *c* **1560** A. SCOTT *Poems* (S.T.S.) ii. 147 Thoᵗ I had rycht noᵗ bot a rok. **1567** *Ps.* li. in *Gude & Godlie B.* (S.T.S.) 122 Thocht *v. r.* thoght] thow..be Jugeit thus Full fals and wrangouslie.

B. Signification.

An adversative particle expressing that relation of two opposed facts or circumstances (actual or hypothetical) in which the one is inadequate to prevent the other, and therefore both concur, contrary to what might be expected.

I. *adv.* For all that; in spite of that; nevertheless, howbeit, however, yet. Now *colloq.*; usually enclitic, as 'he did though' (*hi di·d ðo*).

**971** *Blickl. Hom.* 37 Ne maȝon þis þeah ealle men don. *c* **1175** *Lamb. Hom.* 119 Monie þewas beoð..þe monnen þuncheð rihte, ac hi þah ledað to deðe on ende. *a* **1225** *Ancr. R.* 10 Ich am blac & tauh hwit, heo seið. *Ibid.* 422 Ancre ne schal nout.. turnen hire ancre hus to childrene scole. Hire meiden mei, þauh, techen sum lutel meiden. *c* **1320** *Cast. Love* 1296 Persones þreo in þrillihod, And o God þauȝ in on-hod. **13..** *Cursor M.* 5750 (Gött.) Þe tre ..semid to brine, And þou [*Fairf.* ȝet] þar was na fir widin. **1590** SHAKS. *Mids. N.* III. ii. 343 Your hands then mine, are quicker for a fray, My legs are longer though to runne away. **1672** DRYDEN *Assignation* Prol. 3 Prologues like bells to Churches toll you in With chiming verse,.. With this sad difference though, of pit and pew, You damn the poet, but the priest damns you. **1741** RICHARDSON *Pamela* I. xxv. 30 Is there no Constable nor Headborough, tho', to take me out of his House? **1872** BROWNING *Fifine at the Fair* lxvii. 13 It did its duty, though. **1885** ANSTEY *Tinted Venus* vii. 81 It was in a note, but I've lost it. She told me what was inside though.

II. *conj.* (or *conjunctive adv.*).

1. Introducing a subordinate clause expressing a fact: Notwithstanding that; in spite of the fact that, although. (Formerly with verb in subjunctive, where the indicative is now used.)

*c* **888** [see A. α]. **971** *Blickl. Hom.* 21 [He] bið þonne undeaþlic, þeah he ær deaþlic wære. *c* **1175** [see A. α]. **12..** *Moral Ode* 356 Ne mai non vuel..beon inne godes riche ðeh þer beð wunienges fele. **13..** *E. E. Allit. P.* B. 233 For-þy þaȝ þe rape were rank, þe rawþe watz lyttel. **13..** *Gaw. & Gr. Knt.* 69 Ladies laȝed ful loude, þoȝ þay lost haden. **1362** LANGL. *P. Pl.* A. I. 10 Ich was a-ferd of hire face þauh heo feir weore [*B.* þeiȝ she faire were]. *c* **1440** *York Myst.* xxx. 45 My-selffe yof I saye itt. *Ibid.* xlviii. 344 Helpe ne holde, Hadde I none of you, þof I quaked. **1535** STEWART *Cron. Scot.* (Rolls) II. 590 The duke..Treittit him weill thocht he was far fra hame. **1610** SHAKS. *Temp.* II. ii. 135 Though thou canst swim like a Ducke, thou art made like a Goose. **1701** DE FOE *True-born Eng.* II. 314 They are no kings, though they possess the crown. **1746** FRANCIS tr. *Horace, Art Poet.* 414 The hone Gives edge to razors, though itself has none. **1748** SMOLLETT *Rod. Rand.* vi, The French..are very civil, thof I don't understand their lingo. **1840** DICKENS *Old C. Shop* xv, A gentle hand..rough-grained and hard though it was. **1857** BUCKLE *Civiliz.* I. xi. 647 Though they rallied, the effort cost them dear.

b. With ellipsis in the subordinate clause: usually directly preceding an adj., pple., sb., or adj. phr. qualifying the subject of the main clause, or an adv. or adv. phr. qualifying the verb.

**1592** WARNER *Alb. Eng.* IX. xlvi. (1602) 216 It was objected, though untruely, That they were ydle. **1599** SHAKS. *Much Ado* II. i. 215 The base (though bitter) disposition of Beatrice. **1711** SHAFTESB. *Charac.* I. III. ii. (1737) I. 48 Favourable to a few, tho for slight causes. **1812** CRABBE *Tales* xv. 268 For the zealous Youth Resolved, though timid, to profess the truth. **1875** JOWETT *Plato* (ed. 2) I. 256 One who, though a foreigner, has often been chosen their general. **1896** *N. & Q.* 8th Ser. IX. 160/1 Though marred by eccentricities and extravagances of language, the play has genuine dramatic fibre.

2. Introducing a subordinate clause expressing a supposition or possibility: Even if; even supposing that; granting that. (With verb in subjunctive.)

*c* **888** K. ÆLFRED *Boeth.* xiii, Hwæt hæfst þu..æt ðæm welan, þeah hy nu ece wæron? *c* **1175** *Lamb. Hom.* 15 Þaȝh we suneȝhie nu on þisse liue ne scal us na mon uuelien þer uore. *a* **1300** *Cursor M.* 4296 Strengh o luue..nan mai stere, þof his hert al stillen were. *a* **1450** MYRC *Par. Pr.* 358 For þaȝ a preste be but a fonne Aske hys teyþynge welle he conne. *c* **1450** in Aungier *Hist. Syon Monast.* (1840) 385 None shal enclyne to other, thof it be the abbes that passethe by them. **1539** BIBLE (Great) *Job* xiii. 15 Though he slaye me, yet wyll I put my trust in hym. **1610** SHAKS. *Temp.* I. i. 62 Hee'l be hang'd yet, Though euery drop of water sweare against it. **1714** ADDISON *Spect.* No. 557 ¶ 2 He would not accept of one [witness], tho' it were Cato himself. **1884** *Leisure Hour* Oct. 611 Though knots be tied in the sunshine..they're meant to hold in a gale.

b. With ellipsis (as in 1 b).

**1591** SHAKS. *Two Gent.* III. i. 102 Though nere so blacke, say they haue Angells faces. **1703** ROWE *Fair Penit.* II. ii, No Place, tho' e'er so holy, shou'd protect him. **1792** CHARLOTTE SMITH *Desmond* III. 346 If she looks pale, though only from slight cold or..fatigue, I fancy her about to be ill. **1875** J. P. HOPPS *Princ. Relig.* x. (1878) 32 Though punished by the rulers, [he] may be rewarded by the ruled.

3. Introducing an additional statement restricting or modifying the preceding: And yet, but yet, but still, nevertheless, however. Sometimes preceding the main statement. (Coinciding in sense with I, but differing in construction, being conjunctive.)

*a* **1240** *Ureisun* 105 in *Cott. Hom.* 197 Ful wel þu me iseie þauh þu stille were. **1340** *Ayenb.* 9 Þet is on of þe zeuen dyadliches zennes, þaȝ þer by zome bronches þet ne byeþ naȝt dyadlich zenne. *c* **1400** *Destr. Troy* 1312 Tho þat left were on lyue þogh þai lite were. **1526** *Pilgr. Perf.* (W. de W. 1531) 2 Though it be necessary to all maner of religyous persones, yet moost expedient it is to prelates. **1678** BUNYAN *Pilgr.* 178 Glad shall I be, if I meet with no more such brunts, though I fear we are not got beyond all danger. **1774** MITFORD *Ess. Harmony Lang.* 16 Tho what has been printed on both sides is little red. **1810** CRABBE *Borough* vii. 48 To show the world what long experience gains, Requires not courage, though it calls for pains. **1894** *Solicitors' Jrnl.* XXXIX. 2/2 The..report..must state that fraud has been committed, though the guilty person need not be specified.

4. In more or less weakened or modified sense, often nearly coinciding with *if*, but usually retaining some notion of opposition. †a. After negative or interrogative phrases with *wonder*, *marvel*, *be sorry*, *care*, etc., where *if* or *that* is now substituted.

*c* **1200** *Trin. Coll. Hom.* 117 He forbed his apostles, þat hie neren noht sorie, þeh he hem forlete lichamliche. **1340** HAMPOLE *Pr. Consc.* 9585, I rek noght, þogh þe ryme be rude. **13..** *Cursor M.* 4122 (Gött.) Na wonder þan þow [*Fairf.* if] him was wa. **14..** *Beryn* 953 No mervell þouȝe his herte wer in grete mournyng. **1557** NORTH *Gueuara's Diall Pr.* 295, I do not mervel though they are ful of dyseases when they are old. **1637** GILLESPIE *Eng. Pop. Cerem.* Ep. A ij b, He cares not though the Church sinke.

b. In phr. *as though*: as if; as would or might be the case if; so as to suggest the supposition that. (With verb in past subjunctive (also with ellipsis), or with inf. of purpose: cf. *as if* s. v. IF 8 c.) In quot. 1297, with ellipsis of *as* (obs.).

Here the opposition is not between the two suppositions actually denoted by the main and subordinate clauses, but between two facts, one expressed by the main clause, and the other implied; e. g. in quot. 1598, 'I thank you as much as though I did', = 'I thank you as much as I would thank you if I did eat (though I do not)'.

*c* **1200** *Trin. Coll. Hom.* 7 Sainte powel wrot þo a writ,.. and dude him seluen mid hem þaron, alse þeih he sunful were. **1297** R. GLOUC. (Rolls) 165 Vpe þe hul of þe pek þe wind þere iwis Vp of þe erþe ofte comþ of holes þei hit were. **13..** *Cursor M.* 19088 (Edin.) Qui wondir ȝie..Als þoȝ þis war don wiþ ur miȝt? *c* **1400** *Brut* 238 Buriede in þat sande, as þauȝ þai hade bene hondes. **1509–10** *Act 1 Hen. VIII*, c. 18 § 2 The Quene [shall] have like Habilitie..as though she had orygynally ben borne within this Realme. **1583** STUBBES *Anat. Abus.* II. (1882) 72 This is as though a man should despise meane fare, bicause he cannot come by better. **1598** SHAKS. *Merry W.* I. i. 291 I'faith, Ile eate nothing: I thanke you as much as though I did. **1632** LITHGOW *Trav.* VI. 298 The Camell..hath a most slow and lazy pace.., as though he were weighing his feete in a ballance. **1794** MRS. RADCLIFFE *Myst. Udolpho* iii, I have reason to love him as though he was my own son. **1864** DASENT *Jest & Earnest* (1873) II. 239 This looks as though Magnus was more afraid of Harold than of Sweyn. *Mod.* He shaded his eyes as though dazzled by the light. He raised his hand as though to take off his hat.

†c. *simply.* If, supposing that. *Obs. rare.*

**1526** TINDALE *Acts* xxiii. 9 Though a sprete or an angell hath apered to hym, lett vs not stryue agaynst God.

5. With special constructions (in sense 1, 2, or 3). †a. Followed by *that* (in OE. *þe*): see THAT *conj.* 7, THE *particle* 2. *Obs.*

*c* **1050** *Byrhtferth's Handboc* in *Anglia* (1885) VIII. 302 Ðeah ðe ealle daȝas ælce ȝeare habbon heora concurrentes. *c* **1200** ORMIN Ded. 155 Icc hafe hemm wrohht tiss boc To þeȝȝre sawle nede, þohh þatt teȝȝ all forrwerrpenn itt. *a* **1300** *Cursor M.* 1803 Bot þof þat noe was in quert, He was noght al at es in hert. *c* **1386** CHAUCER *Prol.* 729, I pray yow.. That ye narette it nat my vileynye Thogh that I pleynly speke. *c* **1475** *Rauf Coilȝear* 166 Thocht that I simpill be, Do as I bid thee. **1595** SHAKS. *John* III. iii. 57 Though that my death were adiunct to my Act, By heauen I would doe it. **1605** — *Lear* IV. vi. 219 Though that the Queen on special cause is here Her Army is mou'd on. **1711** in *10th Rep. Hist. MSS. Comm.* App. v. 160 It appears to be a mock-siege; tho' that Ginckle gained the town in earnest.

b. Strengthened by *all*, following (see ALL C. 10 a) or preceding. *Obs.* (exc. in comb. ALTHOUGH). Also by *even* preceding: see EVEN *adv.* 9 c.

*Even though* is not used by Shakspere nor in Bible of 1611. *c* **1325** *Song Mercy* 168 in *E. E. Poems* (1862) 123 Al þauȝ i kouþe, yf þat i wolde. *c* **1330** R. BRUNNE *Chron. Wace* (Rolls) 16055 Þowh al he hadde Crysten feyþ, To þo Crysten he dide ouer leyþ. **13..** *Cursor M.* 4246 (Gött.) Al þou þair treuthes sundri ware. *a* **1400** in *Hampole's Wks.* (1896) I. 200 Þofe-all they know me noghte for þi sone. *c* **1400** MAUNDEV. (Roxb.) Pref. 2 John Mawndevyle, Knyȝt, þof all I be vnworthy. *c* **1450** *St. Cuthbert* (Surtees) 107 Þof all' he be with outen gylte. **1697, 1791** [see EVEN *adv.* 9 c]. **1856** J. H. NEWMAN *Serm. Var. Occas.* i. (1881) 12 Nor, even though it be told to her, can she enter into it.

†6. Ormin has the combination *þohh swa þehh*, lit. 'though so though', 'though so yet', in the sense 'nevertheless', 'notwithstanding'. Cf. THOUGH-WHETHER in same sense.

This is the only use of the form *þehh* in Ormin.

*c* **1200** ORMIN 9717, & teȝȝre name þohh swa þehh Bitacneþþ rihhtwisnesse. *Ibid.* 395 [see A. α], 1104, 9713.

III. as *sb.* The word used as a name for itself, or an utterance of it. *nonce-use.* (Cf. IF B.)

**1634** CANNE *Necess. Separ.* (1849) 255 To answer his ifs & thoughs & whats particularly.

†**Thoughless, þaȝles,** *adv.* or *conj. Obs.* [f. *þaȝ*, THOUGH + -LESS *adv.*] Nevertheless.

**1340** *Ayenb.* 6 Oure lhord..ous uorbyet..þet me ne zuerie, ..þaȝles ine guode skele me may zuerie wyþ-oute zenne. *Ibid.* 8 Þis heste uorbyet þet non ne ssel slaȝe oþren...Þaȝles uor to slaȝe þe misdoeres,..hit is guod riȝt by þe laȝe. *Ibid.* 9.

**Thought**[1] (þǭt). Forms: 1–3 ðoht, 1–4 þoht, 2–4 þouht, 3–4 þoȝt, 3–5 þouȝt, 5– thought; also 3 þoucht, (*Orm.*) þohht (ðhoȝt), 3–4 þoȝte, 4 thouȝt, (thouht, thouth, thout, toght); 4–5 þoght, thoȝt, (þout, þouth, thoȝth), *Sc.* thoucht; 4–7 thoght; 5 þowȝt, þouȝte, thoȝte, (thowhte, þowȝth, þowth, towyth (? towȝth), 5–6 thoughte, thowte, thowthe, 6 thowghte, thoft), 4– *Sc.* thocht. [OE. *þoht*, shortened from **þóht*, :—**þaŋχt-*, from stem of *þencan* THINK *v.*[2] + -T *suffix*[3]. Cf. OS. *githâht* (Du. *gedachte*), OHG. *gidâht*; also ON. *þótti*, *þóttr*, Goth. *þûhtus* (:—**þuŋχtus*). In most of the senses *thought* corresponds not so much to OE. *þoht*, as to the compound *geþoht*, which survived in the 12th c. as *iþoht*: see sense 2.]

1. The action or process of thinking; mental action or activity in general, esp. that of the intellect; exercise of the mental faculty; formation and arrangement of ideas in the mind.

In quot. *c* 1250, thinking in a specified way; nearly = feeling, emotion.

*a* **839** *Laws of Ecgbert* c. 5 Mid þohtes wilnunga.. besmiten. *c* **1250** *Gen. & Ex.* 2254 Quanne Iosep hem alle saȝ, Kinde ðoȝt in his herte was ðaȝ. **1377** LANGL. *P. Pl.* B. V. 513 Þise Ribaudes..repente hem..Þat euere þei wratthed þe..in worde, þouȝte, or dedes. *c* **1425** *Craft of Nombrynge* (E.E.T.S.) 28 Here he teches þe to multiplie be þowȝt figures in þi mynde. *c* **1440** *Promp. Parv.* 492/1 Thowhte, or thynkynge, *cogitacio.* **1530** PALSGR. 280/2 Thought, the laboryng of the mynde, *cogitation, pensee.* **1637** MILTON *Lycidas* 189 With eager thought warbling his Dorick lay. **1704** NORRIS *Ideal World* II. iii. 102 Whether Brutes are capable of thought? **1794** PALEY *Evid.* III. viii. (1817) 393 Thought..can be completely suspended and completely restored. **1853** KINGSLEY *Hypatia* xiv. 166 The pale..student, oppressed with the weight of careful thought. **1875** JOWETT *Plato* (ed. 2) IV. 270 Psychology..analyses the transition from sense to thought.

b. As a function or attribute of a living being: Thinking as a permanent characteristic or condition; the capacity of thinking; the thinking faculty; in early use often nearly = mind.

*c* **950** *Lindisf. Gosp.* Matt. xxii. 37 Lufa drihten..of alle hearte ðine & of alle sauele ðine & in alle ðoht ðinne [L. *in tota mente tua*]. — Mark v. 15 Sittende ȝecladed..& hales ðohtes [L. *sane mentis*]. [*c* **1175** *Lamb. Hom.* 99 He onlihte ure mod mid seofanfald ȝife, þet is mid wisdom, and angite mid iðohte, and streinde [etc.].] *c* **1200** *Trin. Coll. Hom.* 71 We hauen on ure þoht, to shewen him ure sinnes. *a* **1300** *Cursor M.* 22166 (Edin.) Þai sale be studiand in þair þoȝte [*Gött.* thouth] Queþir þate he be criste our nai. *Ibid.* 25598 Do wickednes vte of vr thoght. *c* **1386** CHAUCER *Wife's T.* 227 Greet was the wo the knyght hadde in his thoght. *c* **1400** *Emare* 223 Alle hys hert & alle hys þowȝth, Her to loue was yn browght. *c* **1460** *Wisdom* 959 in *Macro Plays* 67 Put yt, Lorde, in-to my thowte. *c* **1470** HENRY *Wallace* I. 251 With hewy cheyr and sorowfull in thoucht. **1605** SHAKS. *Lear* IV. vi. 45 Had he bin where he thought, By this had thought bin past. **1830** TENNYSON *Deserted House* i, Life and Thought have gone away. **1877** E. R. CONDER *Bas. Faith* i. 8 Thought, feeling, will, are the three strands of the triple cord of life.

c. The product of mental action or effort; what one thinks; that which is in the mind (sometimes, as expressed in language: cf. quot. 1702).

*c* **1200** ORMIN 2577 Forr hire þohht & hire word & hire weorrc was clene. *c* **1250** *Hymn to God* 12 in *Trin. Coll. Hom.* 258 Þu þe wost al ure þoucht. *c* **1290** *Beket* 1188 in *S. Eng. Leg.* I. 140 He rounede in is wiues ere, and tolde hire al is þouȝt. *c* **1375** *Sc. Leg. Saints* i. (*Petrus*) 424 Cum furth, and say þi thoucht and ded but delay. *c* **1400** MAUNDEV. (Roxb.) xiii. 59 Oure Lord takes mare hede to thoȝt þan to word. **1560** BIBLE (Genev.) *Ps.* cxxxix. 2 Thou vnderstandest my thoght afarre of. **1702** ADDISON *Dial. Medals* i. Wks. 1721 I. 439 One..may often find as much thought on the reverse of a Medal as in a Canto of Spenser. **1732** POPE *Hor. Sat.* II. ii. 129 Thus Bethel spoke, who always speaks his thought. **1822** 'B. CORNWALL' *Flood Thessaly* II. 553 Those wondrous letters..By which bright thought was in its quick flight stopp'd And saved from perishing. **1865** TYLOR *Early Hist. Man.* iv. 68 Thought is not even present to the thinker, till he has set it forth out of himself.

d. In a collective sense (with defining adj.): The intellectual activity or mental product characteristic of the thinkers of a particular class, time, or place; what is or has been thought by the philosophers or learned men of some specified country, etc.

*a* **1853** ROBERTSON *Lect.* (1858) 228 Wordsworth is the type of English thought. **1856** *N. Brit. Rev.* XXVI. 39 How old is Modern Thought?—a few years only:—we think ten years—in this country, will include the time within which this peculiar tendency and feeling has distinctly shown its characteristics...Modern Thought, regarded as the opposite and the antagonist of an unexceptive submission to the authority of Holy Scripture. **1884** F. TEMPLE *Relat. Relig. & Sc.* v. (1885) 132 The leaders of scientific thought. *Mod.* Plato and Aristotle, the leaders of Greek thought.

2. (with *a* and *pl.*) A single act or product of thinking; an item of mental activity; something that one thinks or has thought; a thing that is in the mind; an idea, notion. (Sometimes, as expressed in writing: as in quots. 1645, 1709, 1875.)

*c* 975 *Rushw. Gosp.* Matt. ix. 4 And þa ʒeseende ðohtas heora cwæþ to heom forhwon þencaþ ʒe yfel in heortum eowrum? [*c* 1175 *Lamb. Hom.* 109 Ðan alden his to warniene wið uuele iðohtas.] *c* 1200 *Vices & Virt.* 11 Oðer of ðouhtes oðer of wordes oðer of weorkes. 13.. *Cursor M.* 27101 (Cott.) Vr thoghtes ar þai be thoght..he seis. 1451 CAPGRAVE *Life St. Gilbert* 86 Occupied with orisones and meditaciones to avoyde euel þoutes. 1557 N. T. (Genev.) 2 *Cor.* x. 5 Wherwith we..bringe into captiuitie euery thoght, to the obedience of Christe. *a* 1568 KING H. STEWARD in *Bann. Poems* (Hunter. Cl.) 706 Gif cairfull thoftis restoir My havy hairt. 1604 SHAKS. *Oth.* III. iii. 161 *Oth.* Ile know thy Thoughts. *Iago.* You cannot, if my heart were in your hand, Nor shall not, whil'st 'tis in my custodie. 1645 FULLER (*title*) Good Thoughts in Bad Times. 1709 POPE *Ess. Crit.* 354 The last..couplet fraught With some unmeaning thing they call a thought. 1754 GRAY *Progr. Poesy* III. iii, Thoughts that breathe, and words that burn. 1803–6 WORDSW. *Intim. Immort.* xi, Thoughts that do often lie too deep for tears. 1824 L. M. HAWKINS *Annaline* I. 344, I will collect my scattered thoughts. 1864 BROWNING *Abt Vogler* viii, One scarce can say..That he even gave it a thought. 1875 JOWETT *Plato* (ed. 2) V. 28 A similar thought is repeated in the Laws. 1891 'J. S. WINTER' *Lumley* i, Here I'm idle and haven't a thought in my head—there my brain positively teems with ideas.

**b.** *spec.* An idea suggested or recalled to the mind; a reflection, a consideration.

*a* 1240 *Ureisun* in *Cott. Hom.* 203 Hwi ne bi-hold ich þis euer in mine heorte, and þenche ðet hit was for me...þis þoht wolde sikerliche ontenden so soð luue on me. 1593 SHAKS. *Rich. II*, v. v. 28 Like silly Beggars, Who sitting in the Stockes, refuge their shame That many haue, and others must sit there; And in this Thought, they finde a kind of ease. 1665 BOYLE *Occas. Refl.* v. v, This..is onely to tell us, what you observ'd, not what Reflections you made upon it, and..that which I was inquisitive after, was your Thoughts. 1818 SCOTT *Hrt. Midl.* xxxvii, The thoughts that ye hae intervened to spare the puir thing's life will be sweeter in that hour..than [etc.]. 1835 J. H. NEWMAN *Par. Serm.* (1837) I. i. 15 Though this thought should not make a man despair to-day, yet it should ever make him tremble for to-morrow.

**c.** *Second thoughts*: ideas occurring subsequently; later and maturer consideration (usu. in phr. *on* or *upon second thoughts*). So *first thoughts*.

1642 CHAS. I *Mess. to Both Houses* 28 Apr. 4 Second thoughts may present somewhat to your considerations which escaped you before. 1667 MILTON *P. L.* IX. 213 Now advise Or hear what to my mind first thoughts present. 1687 BP. CARTWRIGHT in *Magd. Coll.* (O. H. S.) 139 Are you ..willing upon better and second thoughts to submit? 1711 HICKES *Two Treat. Chr. Priesth.* (1847) II. 396, I desire you to send your second thoughts and reflections upon it. 1838 J. H. NEWMAN *Par. Serm.* (1842) IV. ii. 41 It is often said that second thoughts are best; so they are in matters of judgment, but not in matters of conscience. 1864 TENNYSON *Sea Dreams* 65 Is it so true that second thoughts are best? Not first, and third, which are a riper first?

**3.** Proverbial Phrases (from 1 and 2): **a.** *As swift as thought*, etc.; so *at*, *like*, *upon*, or *with a thought*, in an instant, immediately, at once. **b.** *Thought is free*: one is at liberty to think as one will.

*a* 1225 *Ancr. R.* 94 Ase swifte ase is nu monnes þouht, & ase is þe sunne gleam. 1572 FORREST *Theophilus* 342 in *Anglia* VII, Made in vocation, And was present in manner, at a thought. 1588 SHAKS. *L. L. L.* v. ii. 261 Fleeter then arrows, bullets, wind, thought. 1610 — *Temp.* IV. i. 164 Come with a thought; I thank thee Ariell: come. 1611 — *Wint. T.* IV. iv. 565 Faster then Thought, or Time. 1845 GOSSE *Ocean* iv. (1849) 168 The whole herd are gone like a thought, leaving their unhappy comrade to his fate. 1885 C. F. HOLDER *Marvels Anim. Life* 230 Quick as thought the skipper hurled his weapon.

**b.** 1580 LYLY *Euphues* (Arb.) 281 Thought is free my Lord quoth she. *a* 1600 [see THRALL $a.^1$ 1 (*b*)]. 1601 SHAKS. *Twel. N.* I. iii. 73. 1673 KIRKMAN *Unlucky Citizen* 185, I would tell him that thought was free, and I should not tell him what I thought. 1690 DRYDEN *Amphitryon* II. i, I dare say nothing, but thought is free.

**4.** In various specialized senses (from 1 and 2): cf. various senses of THINK $v.^2$

**a.** Consideration, attention, heed, care, regard. *To take thought*, to consider, meditate (how to do something, etc.). In quot. 1602 implying indecision.

*a* 1250 *Owl & Night.* 492 He ne rekþ noht of clennesse, Al his þouht is of golnesse. *a* 1300 *Cursor M.* 1563 (Cott.) On al thinges was mare þair thoght [*G.* thout] þan was on drightin þat al wroght. *c* 1385 CHAUCER *L. G. W.* 373 (*Balade*) This schulde a ryghtwys lord han in his thouȝt. 1509 *Payne Evyll Marr.* 125 And wyll take thought, and often muse How he myght fynde [etc.]. 1567 *Reg. Privy Council Scot.* I. 519 Na persoun..takkis thocht quhat unhappy deid he sall tak upoun hand. 1602 SHAKS. *Ham.* III. i. 85 And thus the Natiue hew of Resolution Is sicklied o're, with the pale cast of Thought. 1684 EARL ROSCOMMON *Ess. Transl. Verse* 162 Pride..Proceeds from Ignorance, and want of Thought. 1742 GRAY *Ode Eton Coll.* x, Thought would destroy their paradise. *a* 1845 HOOD *Lady's Dream* xvi, Evil is wrought by want of Thought, As well as want of Heart! 1862 F. HALL *Hindu Philos. Syst.* 109 To realize his own wretchedness, so that he may take thought how to escape from it.

**b.** Meditation, mental contemplation; † perplexity, puzzled condition of mind (quot. 1387, and cf. 5); † *transf.* subject of meditation (quot. *c* 1300).

*a* 1300 *Floriz & Bl.* 34 On blauncheflur was al his þoȝt. *c* 1300 *E. E. Psalter* cxviii[i]. 97 Hou luued i, lauerd, þi lagh ai; Mi thoghte es it al þe dai. 1387 TREVISA *Higden* (Rolls) I. 311 To brynge here hertes out of þouȝt þat hereþ speke of laborintus, here I telle what laborinthus is to menynge. *c* 1420 *Sir Amadace* (Camden) xx, On the dede cors, that lay on bere, Ful myculle his thoȝte was on. 1611 SIR W. MURE *Misc. Poems* ii. 13 Perceauing me in thot perplex'd. 1715 POPE *2nd Ep. Miss Blount* 33 In pensive thought recall the fancy'd scene. 1842 TENNYSON *Lord of Burleigh* 21 From deep thought himself he rouses. *Mod.* She was lost in thought.

**c.** Conception, imagination, fancy.

*a* 1300 *Cursor M.* 21630 (Edin.) Mar miȝtis hauis ur lauerd wroȝt Than ani man mai þinc in thoȝt. 1413 *Pilgr. Sowle* (Caxton 1483) III. x. 56 The grete horrour therof may not be ..declared by..thought of mannes herte. 1593 SHAKS. *Lucr.* 288 Within his thought her heauenly image sits. 1602 MARSTON *Ant. & Mel.* I. Wks. 1856 I. 15, I long, beyond all thought, To know the man. 1671 MILTON *Samson* 117 O change beyond report, thought, or belief! 1742 COLLINS *Ecl.* ii. 50 When thought creates unnumber'd scenes of woe. 1832 TENNYSON *Miller's Dau.* 237 With blessings beyond hope or thought. 1850 — *In Mem.* lxx. 8 In shadowy thoroughfares of thought.

**d.** The entertaining of some project in the mind; the idea or notion of doing something, as contemplated or entertained in the mind; hence, intention, purpose, design; *esp.* an imperfect or half-formed intention; with negative expressed or implied = not the least intention or notion of doing something. Also in *pl.* as '*to have thoughts* (*of*)'. Cf. THINK $v.^2$ 8.

*c* 1250 *Gen. & Ex.* 1153 Ðis maidenes deden it in god ðhoȝt. *c* 1320 *Cast. Love* 4 For nas neuere good werk wrouȝt Wᵗ-oute biginninge of good þouȝt. *c* 1425 *Cast. Persev.* 581 in *Macro Plays* 94 Of worldly good is al his þouth. 1535 COVERDALE *Jer.* xxix. 11, I knowe, what I haue deuysed for you...My thoughtes are to geue you peace, & not trouble. 1610 SHAKS. *Temp.* IV. i. 220, I do begin to haue bloody thoughts. *a* 1771 GRAY *Tophet* 6 Satan's self had thoughts of taking orders. 1818 SCOTT *Hrt. Midl.* xlix, Knock says his Grace has no thought to buy it. 1849 MACAULAY *Hist. Eng.* vi. II. 76 All thought of returning to the policy of the Triple Alliance was abandoned. *Mod.* I had some thought of going, but found I could not manage it. I had no thoughts of it then.

**e.** Remembrance, 'mind'. † *To hold in thought*, † *to have thought on*, to keep in mind, remember. *Obs.* or merged in the general sense.

1297 R. GLOUC. (Rolls) 6553 Of alle is proute dedes i ne may uorbere noȝt, Þat i ne mot ȝou telle of on, nou it comeþ in mi þoȝt. 13.. *Cursor M.* 24042 (Gött.) To domes-dai liue if i moght, Ne ȝode it neuer vte of mi thoght. 13.. *Minor Poems fr. Vernon MS.* l. 66 Hold hem in þi þouht. *c* 1400 *Gamelyn* 474 Adams wordes he held in his thoght. *c* 1475 *Rauf Coilȝear* 257 Haue gude thocht on my Name. 1611 SHAKS. *Cymb.* IV. iv. 33, I and my Brother are not knowne; your selfe So out of thought,..Cannot be question'd.

**f.** Mental anticipation, expectation. (Now mostly with negative expressed or implied.)

*a* 1307 in *Pol. Songs* (Camden) 220 Tho [= when] he wes in Scotland, lutel wes ys thoht Of the harde jugement that him wes bysoht In stounde. 1597 SHAKS. 2 *Hen. IV*, I. iii. 30 Flatt'ring himselfe with Proiect of a power, Much smaller, then the smallest of his Thoughts. 1611 BIBLE *Ps.* xlix. 11 Their inward thought is, that their houses shall continue for euer. 1677 HALE *Contempl.* II. 127, I had thoughts to find repose there. *Mod.* I had no thought of meeting him there.

**g.** An opinion or judgement; a belief or supposition; what one thinks of or about a thing or person.

1596 SHAKS. 1 *Hen. IV*, III. ii. 131 Heauen forgiue them, that so much haue sway'd Your Maiesties good thoughts away from me. 1606 — *Tr. & Cr.* IV. i. 53 Who in your thoughts merits faire Helen most? 1613 WEBSTER *Devil's Law-Case* II. i, You are false To the good thought I held of you. 1786 BURNS *Twa Dogs* 221 The Ladies arm-in-arm.. As great an' gracious a' as sisters; But hear their absent thoughts o' ither. 1831 SCOTT *Ct. Robt.* xxvii, What, then, are thy thoughts of the Emperor? 1855 BROWNING *Childe Roland* i, My first thought was, he lied in every word.

**†5.** Anxiety or distress of mind; solicitude; grief, sorrow, trouble, care, vexation. *To take thought*, to trouble oneself, grieve, be anxious or distressed. *Obs.* (exc. *dial.*: see Eng. Dial. Dict.).

*c* 1220 *Bestiary* 682 in *O. E. Misc.* 22 He suggeden & sorȝeden & weren in ðoȝt, Wu he miȝten him helpen ovt. *c* 1250 *Gen. & Ex.* 1433 Ysaac..wunede ðor in ðoȝt and care, For moderes dead and sondes fare. *c* 1330 R. BRUNNE *Chron.* (1810) 85 Þe kyng had fulle grete þouht, his reame ageyn him ros. *c* 1425 *Cast. Persev.* 292 in *Macro Plays* 86, I stonde & stodye, al ful of þowth. 1485 CAXTON *Paris & V.* 46 Paris kyssed Vyenne wyth grete syghes and thoughtes. *c* 1500 *Nutbrown Maid* 119 in Hazlitt *E. P. P.* II. 277 To make thought, Your labur were in vayne. 1523 LD. BERNERS *Froiss.* I. ccxxxiii. 324 His wyfe..toke moche thought for his departyng. 1526 TINDALE *Matt.* vi. 31 Therfore take no thought saynge: what shall we eate? 1556 BP. PONET *Treat. Politic Power* I iij b, Wriothesley..either poisoned himself, or pyned awaye for thought. 1608 E. GRIMSTONE *Hist. France* (1611) 270 Valentine, Duchesse of Orleans (seeing her paines lost..) dies for thought within few daies after. 1613 PURCHAS *Pilgrimage* (1614) 871 Soto died of thought in Florida.

**b.** *transf.* A cause of distress or anxiety, a 'trouble'. *Obs.* exc. *Sc.* and *dial.*

1649 CROMWELL in Carlyle *Lett. & Sp.* (1871) II. 188 How many considerable ones we have lost, is no little thought of heart to us. 1887 *Suppl. to Jamieson, Addenda*, s.v., That wild son has been a sair thocht..to his mother. 1895 CROCKETT in *Cornh. Mag.* Dec. 569 So mony bairn's things were just a cumber and a thocht to me.

**6.** A very small amount, a very little, a trifle. (Usually, now always, adverbial.)

1581 MULCASTER *Positions* xxxix. (1887) 204 The prince is a thought aboue him for all he be his brother in respect of old Adam. 1599 SHAKS. *Much Ado* III. iv. 14, I like the new tire..if the haire were a thought browner. 1617 HIERON *Wks.* II. 207 A wound may be giuen in a thought of time, which yet may be in healing aboue a yeere. 1628 GAULE *Pract. The. Panegyr.* 49 They are not currant, if they want the least Thought of a Graine. 1727 SWIFT *Let. to Sheridan* 12 Aug., My giddiness seized me,..I think I am a thought better. 1818 SCOTT *Rob Roy* iv, He seems a thought rash. 1897 G. ALLEN *Type-writer Girl* xvii, The champagne..was a thought too dry.

**7.** *attrib.* and *Comb.* **a.** attrib., as *thought-accent* (accent of thought), *thought-box*, *-coop*, *-defect*, *-form*, *-life*, *-line*, *-manufactory*, *-part*, *-production*, *-seed*, *-shop*, *-sign*, *-system*. **b.** objective and obj. gen., as *thought-abhorring*, *-exceeding*, *-giving*, *-inspiring*, *-reviving*, *-shaming*, *-sounding*, *-stirring*, *-straining*, *-tracing*, *-transcending* adjs.; *thought-catcher*, *-conductor*, *-maker*, *-sprinkler*, †*-taking* (see 5). **c.** instrumental, as *thought-bewildered* (bewildered by thought), *thought-burdened*, *-fed*, *-laden*, *-pressed*, *-unsounded*, *-winged*, *-working*, *-worn*; locative, as *thought-bound* (bound in thought), *thought-fixed*, *-free*, *-set*, *-tinted*; similative, as *thought-swift*; *thought-worthy* (worthy of thought). **d.** Special Combs.: **thought-body** (*Psychics*), see quot.; **thought-consciousness**, consciousness in the state in which it is during the process of thought; **thought-counter**, a current symbol of a thought; **thought-executing** *a.*, (*a*) in quot. 1605, 'doing execution with the swiftness of thought' (Aldis Wright); (*b*) executing the thought or intention of a person; † **thought-sick** *a.*, sick with 'thought' or thinking; **thought-sign**, a symbol of thought or judgement, the copula of a predication; † **thoughtswift-flying** *a.*, that flies as swift as thought: † **thought-taking** *sb.*, the taking of thought; **thought-tra·nsfer**, **-transference** (*Psychics*), transference or communication of thought from one mind to another apart from the ordinary channels of sense; telepathy; **thought-transfe·r** *v.*, *trans.* to convey by thought or telepathically; hence **thought-transfere·ntial** *a.*, pertaining to thought-transference; **thought-wave**, (*a*) in *Psychics*, a 'wave' or undulation of a hypothetical medium of thought-transference; (*b*) a 'wave' or impulse of thought passing simultaneously through a crowd of persons or other living beings; **thought-word**, a word conceived in the mind but not uttered; **thought-writing**, the recording of thought by graphic symbols directly denoting ideas; ideography. See also THOUGHT-READING.

1835 *Woman* I. 104 An idle set, a *thought-abhorring crew. 1897 ANWYL *Greek Gram.* § 40 The *Thought-Accent is the stress or emphasis laid upon a word or syllable, in order to bring out the meaning of the sentence. 1796 COLERIDGE in J. Cottle *Early Recoll.* (1837) I. 199, I wandered on so *thought-bewildered, that it is no wonder I became way-bewildered. 1893 H. R. HAWEIS in *Fortn. Rev.* Jan. 121–2 Assume that there is something personal about us able to manifest and arrange matter, and thus assert itself after death..suppose we call that something our *thought-body. ..Consider then the evidence; first, for the thought-body as Double, and second, for the thought-body as Ghost. 1886 TUPPER *My Life as Author* 145 The emptying out of my *thought-box.., a most necessary relief. 1892 SYMONDS *Michel Angelo* II. XII. viii. 31 This terrible *thought-burdened form. 1584 LYLY *Campaspe* v. iv, I am no *thought catcher, but I gesse vnhappily. 1889 SIR W. F. BUTLER *C. G. Gordon* vii. (1899) 188 This lightning *thought-conductor [the electric telegraph] had been used..to disseminate lies and foster gambling in stocks or horses. 1901 E. B. TITCHENER *Exper. Psychol.* I. i. 1 A *thought-consciousness, our mind as it is when we are arguing something out. 1870 LOWELL *Study Wind.* (1886) 309 His importation of the French theory of the couplet as a kind of *thought-coop did nothing but mischief. 1899 *Allbutt's Syst. Med.* VII. 423 The auditory and visual images of words which constitute our habitual *thought-counters. 1637 NABBES *Microcosm.* I. B iv b, Dispute not..your owne *thought-defects. 1593 NASHE *Christ's T.* Wks. (Grosart) IV. 61 *Thought-exceeding glorification. 1605 SHAKS. *Lear* III. ii. 4 You Sulph'rous and *Thought-executing Fires. 1819 SHELLEY *Prometh. Unb.* I. i. 387 Trampled down By his thought-executing ministers. 1874 GEO. ELIOT *Coll. Breakf. P.* 472 The thrill ..Of *thought-fed passion. 1773 BEATTIE *Tri. Melancholy* lii, The *thought-fix'd portraiture, the breathing bust. 1892 *Month* Jan. 10 The *Thought-forms with which he has surrounded himself. 1626 SHIRLEY *Brothers* v. iii, To clear myself *thought-free From any promise. 1729 SAVAGE *Wanderer* III. 167 *Thought-inspiring Woe. *a* 1847 ELIZA COOK *Summer is Nigh* iv, My *thought-laden brow. 1884 J. PARKER *Apostolic Life* III. 267 The writing..is a kind of body in which his *thought-life lives for ever. 1909 J. WELLS *Stewart of Lovedale* xxxiv. 371 His strenuous life had deepened the *thought-lines on his strong face. 1855 *Pict. Chr. Heroism* 244 Pictures of the *thought-maker at his work. 1860 RUSKIN *Mod. Paint.* V. VIII. i. § 14. 164 From the time of the Aristophanes thought-shop to the great German establishment, or *thought-manufactory. 1796 T. TOWNSHEND *Poems* 69 The musing *thought-prest head. 1884 J. TAIT *Mind in Matter* (1892) 114 Tunnelling out a theory of *thought-production. 1825 D. L. RICHARDSON *Sonn.* 24 A calm and *thought-reviving sound. 1839 BAILEY *Festus* xx. (1848) 245 He would his brain had died ere it conceived One half the *thought-seeds that took life in it. 1813 HOGG *Queen's Wake* 225 Still his *thought-set eye was raised To Ettrick mountains. 1605 SYLVESTER *Du Bartas* II. iii. I. *Abraham* 373 Your *thought-shaming acts. 1598 J. DICKENSON *Greene in Conc.* (1878) 109 *Thought-sicke louers haue onely reason their soueraigne refuge. 1602 SHAKS. *Ham.* III. iv. 51. 1854 S. NEIL *Elem. Rhet.* 34 The *thought-sign *is*, also possesses its own specific signification.

1598 SYLVESTER *Du Bartas* II. i. IV. *Handie-crafts* 304 Rein-searching God, *thought-sounding Judge. *a* 1774 TUCKER *Lt. Nat.* (1834) II. 506 *Thought-straining fervours of prayer and devotion. 1595 MARKHAM *Sir R. Grinvile* xiv, In that same myd-daies hower came sayling in A *thought-swift-flying pynnase. 1900 *Month* Sept. 236 The Church has used..whatever other *thought-system she has found in vogue. 1615 HIERON *Wks.* I. 661 Exercised with a world of cares and *thought-takings. 1668 WILKINS *Real Char.* II. viii. 201 Anxiety, Discontent, thought-taking, dump, trouble, anguish. *a* 1845 HOOD *Two Peacocks* xv, As if *thought-tinted by the stains Of gorgeous light through many-colour'd panes. 1791 COWPER *Yardley Oak* 158 The *thought-tracing quill. *a* 1711 KEN *Hymnarium* Poet. Wks. 1721 II. 101 O Great I am, enthron'd on high, Of *Thought-transcending Majesty. 1898 *Month* Sept. 232 Other perplexing instances are tortured into cases of *thought-transfer. 1901 *Westm. Gaz.* 8 Jan. 4/2 The Psychic has only got to thought-transfer his desire for telescopic verification. 1884 E. GURNEY in *Pall Mall G.* 29 May 2/2 Our conclusion as to genuine *thought-transference. 1886 MYERS *Phantasms Living* I. Introd. 43 It was thus..that thought-transference, or telepathy, was first discovered. 1905 A. R. WALLACE *My Life* II. 310 Thought, or brain-vibrations, may be carried by the ether to other brains, and thus produce thought-transference. 1890 O. LODGE in *Proc. Soc. Psych. Research* Dec. 461 The hypothesis of a direct *thought-transferential means of obtaining information. 1878 SWINBURNE *In the Bay* xxxix, The *thought-unsounded sea. 1891 *Cent. Dict.*, *Thought-wave. 1901 *Daily Chron.* 18 Sept. 3/2 The Greek idea of a thought-wave, or wind of thought, sweeping through crowds. 1818 SHELLEY *Lines Euganean Hills* 207 The sun floats up the sky, Like *thought-winged Liberty. 1889 MIVART *Orig. Hum. Reason* 106 Expressing a voluminous perception by a sudden gesture far too rapid even for *thought-words. 1906 *Hibbert Jrnl.* Jan. 277 The doctrine of the Logos, the Thought-Word in the Cosmos. 1816 L. HUNT *Rimini* IV. 88 His *thought-working head. 1846 MRS. GORE *Eng. Char.* (1852) 127 Sparing and *thought-worn, there is nothing in his gravity of brow to encourage indiscreet encroachment. 1859 LEVER *Davenport Dunn* ii, Thoughts of what alone is *thought-worthy. 1890 *Smithsonian Rep.* 50 The monographs on sign language and pictography, having as their text the attainments of the North American Indians..may contribute to the understanding of similar exhibitions of evanescent and durable *thought-writing.

Hence (chiefly *nonce-wds.*) † **Thou·ghtive** *a.*, addicted to or engaged in thought, thoughtful; **Thou·ghtkin, Thou·ghtlet, Thou·ghtling,** a small or insignificant thought; **Thou·ghtsman** (*nonce-wd.*, after *draughtsman*, etc.): see quot.

1654 GAYTON *Pleas. Notes* I. ii. 5 If he be *thoughtive or cogitabund,..his lips, his eyes, his hands, goe as well as his legs. *Ibid.* IV. iii. 187 The Don is indeed a more thoughtive, inward, close, and conceal'd Cocksome. 1867 CARLYLE *Remin.* (1881) II. 148 That little *thoughtkin stands in some of my books. 1858 H. W. BEECHER *Life Th.* (1859) 74 Mosses and inconspicuous blooms hidden in the grass—*thoughtlets, the intents of the heart. 1863 *Reader* 22 Aug., Mere vendors of what may be called carefully-connected thoughtlets. 1832 J. P. KENNEDY *Swallow B.* x, A little nest of *thoughtlings about the eyes. 1842 MIALL *Non-conf. Sketch-bk.* 255 One whom we shall venture to designate a *thoughtsman for the rest..whose..business it shall be..to make himself..acquainted with truth..for the common benefit.

**Thought** [2], **thaught** (þǭt). Now *dial.* Also 7 **thougt, thoat,** 8 **thout,** 9 **thawt,** *dial.* **thowt.** [Altered from the earlier THOFT, q. v. with change of (f) to (χ), (the converse of what occurs in *thoft* for *thought*, THOUGHT [1] and pa. t. THINK *v.*[2], and *thof* for THOUGH). Cf. also MDu. *dochte* and *dofte*, Du. *doft*, MLG. and LG. *ducht*, whence mod. Ger. *ducht*, beside dial. *duft* from OHG. *dofta*. See also the modern equivalent *thwart*.] A rower's bench; = THWART *sb.*[2]

1622 SIR R. HAWKINS *Voy. S. Sea* liv. 129 His boate fitted with Sayle, Oares, thougts, tholes, dauyd, windles and rother. 1627 CAPT. SMITH *Seaman's Gram.* vi. 27 Thoughts are the seats whereon the Rowers sit. 1633 T. JAMES *Voyage* 57 It did breake two thoughts of our Boat. 1688 R. HOLME *Armoury* III. xv. (Roxb.) 27/1 The thaughts and seats they sit on to rowe. 1697 DAMPIER *Voy. round World* (1699) 118 These Canoas were fitted with Thoats or Benches. 1704 J. HARRIS *Lex. Techn.* I, *Thaughts*, or *Thoughts*. 1725 DE FOE *Voy. round World* (1840) 341 Three muskets which were lashed under their thouts, or benches of the canoe. 1823 MOOR *Suffolk Wds.* 428 *Thowts*, the seats of rowers in a boat—the *thwarts* perhaps; or what go across. 1867 SMYTH *Sailor's Word-bk.*, *Thought*, an old spelling of *thwart*. 1886 R. C. LESLIE *Sea-painter's Log* 172 We turned-to and lashed the nets down from thawt to thawt.

**Thought** (þǭt), pa. t. and pple. of THINK *v.*[1] and [2]. **Thought,** obs. Sc. form of THOUGH.

**Thoughted** (þǭ·tėd), *a.* [f. THOUGHT [1] + -ED [2].] **1.** Having thoughts (of a specified kind): esp. in parasynthetic combinations, as *deep-*, *high-*, *low-*, *solemn-thoughted*, etc.: see the first element.

1592, 1631 Sick-thoughted [see SICK *a.* 11]. 1599 R. LINCHE *Fount. Anc. Fict.* I ij, They should not grow insolent, prowd,..or ouer-highly thoughted. 1643 *True Informer* 23 Most of the moderate and well-thoughted Members were retired to their rest. 1886 SWINBURNE *Stud. Prose & Poetry* (1894) 167 The same high-thoughted harmony of primal and ideal emotions.

**2.** *Sc.* (thochtit) Affected with grief or anxiety; anxious, concerned. (Cf. THOUGHT [1] 5.)

1869 [MCLENNAN] *Peas. Life* Ser. I. 19 She can see ne'er a door at a' for hirin', and she's sair thochted for it. *a* 1884 J. SERVICE *Dr. Duguid* II. v. (1887) 209, I was geyan thochted 'estreen, when I heard the win' risin' the way it did. *c* 1890 *Let. to Editor*, Old Scotch folks say *Thoughted* for 'sicklied o'er with the pale cast of thought'.

† **Thou·ghten,** *a. Obs. rare*[−1]. [irreg. form of *thought*, pa. pple. of THINK *v.*[2]; cf. *boughten*.] Having a (specified) thought or belief; thinking.

1608 SHAKS. *Per.* IV. vi. 115 For me be you thoughten That I came with no ill intent.

**Thoughtful** (þǭ·tfŭl), *a.* [f. THOUGHT [1] + -FUL.] Full of or characterized by thought, in various senses.

**1.** Given to, disposed to, or engaged in thinking; absorbed in thought; meditative, contemplative; pensive, musing; full of thoughts, preoccupied in mind, hence, in quot. 1656, absent-minded. Also *transf.* of personal attributes, actions, etc.

*c* 1200 ORMIN 3423 Ure laffdiȝ Marȝe toc All þatt ȝho sahh & herrde,..& leȝȝde itt all tosamenn aȝȝ I swiþe þohhtfull heorrte. 1552 HULOET, Thoughtfull, *cogitabundus*, *meditabundus*. 1656 STANLEY *Hist. Philos.* IV. (1701) 152/2 He was so thoughtful, that going to put Incense into a Censer, he put it besides. 1704 POPE *Windsor Forest* 249 Wand'ring thoughtful in the silent wood. 1722 — *1st Chorus Trag. Brutus* 7 War, horrid war, your thoughtful walks invades. 1805 H. K. WHITE *Lett., to B. Haddock* 18 Oct., My silent and thoughtful cup of tea. 1873 BLACK *Pr. Thule* iii, Her calm and thoughtful look.

**b.** Disposed to think about or consider matters; prudent; reflective. Also *transf.* Characterized by reflection; manifesting thought or consideration.

13.. *Cursor M.* 11404 (Cott.) Þai ordeind tuelue, þe thoghtfulest a-mang þam-selue. *a* 1533 LD. BERNERS *Gold. Bk. M. Aurel.* x. (1535) F ij b, This emperour was so thoughtfull in the orderynge and teachynge of his children, that [etc.]. 1736 BUTLER *Anal.* II. viii. Wks. 1874 I. 292 Objections, which may appear very material to thoughtful men. 1879 FROUDE *Cæsar* xiv. 200 Thoughtful persons.. had heard of these doings with uneasiness. 1884 F. TEMPLE *Relat. Relig. & Sc.* i. (1885) 5 Not beyond the reach of thoughtful inquiry.

**c.** With *inf.*, *dependent cl.*, or *of*: (*a*) Careful, heedful; (*b*) Having the intention or purpose, aiming at or desirous *of* something; (*c*) Thinking about or meditating on something; mindful. Now *rare* or *Obs.* (See also 3.)

[*c* 1375 *Sc. Leg. Saints* xvi. (*Magdalena*) 552, I..prays [= pray] þe þat þu wil thochtful one me be.] 1597 SHAKS. *2 Hen. IV*, IV. v. 73 For this, they haue beene thoughtfull, to inuest Their Sonnes with Arts, and Martiall Exercises. 1621 T. WILLIAMSON tr. *Goulart's Wise Vieillard* 105 They are much more thoughtfull of their minde. 1715 J. CHAPPELOW *Rt. Way Rich* (1717) 138 The believer..is thoughtful to have a..fuller view of him [Christ]. 1726 LEONI *Alberti's Archit.* I. 93/2 A Prisoner always thoughtful of his liberty and safety. 1821 *Examiner* 252/1 Thoughtful of enjoyments for ever left behind.

† **2.** Full of mental trouble; anxious; sorrowful, melancholy, moody. Also *transf. Obs.*

*a* 1300 *Cursor M.* 11140 He wex thoghtful and likand ill. 1387–8 T. USK *Test. Love* II. ix. (Skeat) l. 185 For her bast thou suffred many thoughtfull diseases. *c* 1430 *Diatorie* 6 in *Babees Bk.* 54 Not pensif ne þouȝtful for ony sodein chaunce. *c* 1500 *Melusine* 26 In this dolour & woo was Raymondyn a longe space of tyme, & was moche þoughtfull & wroth. 1627–77 FELTHAM *Resolves* I. v. 6 The merry soul is freer from intended mischief than the thoughtful man. 1744 M. BISHOP *Life & Adv.* viii. 117 Something to divert my Mother and Wife who were both prodigiously thoughtful.

**3.** Showing thought or consideration for others; considerate, kindly.

1851 BRIMLEY *Ess.*, *Wordsw.* 155 Rich in thoughtful affection. 1863 MRS. GASKELL *Sylvia's L.* iii, In his thoughtful wish of escorting them through the streets of the rough, riotous town. *Mod.* She is very unselfish and thoughtful of others.

† **4.** Capable of thought; conscious, intelligent. *Obs. rare*[−1].

1674 N. FAIRFAX *Bulk & Selv.* 134 To think, that body may be thoughtful too, and any ways aware.

**5.** *Comb.*, as *thoughtful-browed*, *-looking*.

*a* 1849 MANGAN *Lay Bell* Poems (1859) 35 He alone is thoughtfulsouled. 1904 *Westm. Gaz.* 9 Dec. 6/3 Great, round, thoughtful-looking heads.

**Thoughtfully** (þǭ·tfŭli), *adv.* [f. prec. + -LY [2].] In a thoughtful manner; with thought or consideration; meditatively, musingly; reflectively; considerately, kindly.

1611 COTGR., *Songneusement*, carefully, thoughtfully. 1746 FRANCIS tr. *Horace, Epist.* I. xviii. 163 The Modest oft too dark appear, The Silent thoughtfully severe. 1860 TYNDALL *Glac.* II. App. 431 Right or wrong, a theory thus thoughtfully uttered has its value. 1885 S. H. PRESTON in *Law Times* LXXIX. 335/1 Many of the persons entitled could not be traced..so the company very thoughtfully issued advertisements.

**Thou·ghtfulness.** [f. as prec. + -NESS.] The quality or state of being thoughtful.

† **1.** Anxiety, concern, melancholy. *Obs.*

1574 tr. *Marlorat's Apocalips* 113 The scripture calleth vpon vs to lay away..all thoughtfulnesse for this present life. 1685 BAXTER *Paraphr. N. T.* Matt. vi. 27 Your self-troubling distrustful care and thoughtfulness. 1742 RICHARDSON *Pamela* III. 418 If he but sees the least Thoughtfulness upon my Brow, studying..to dispel it.

**2.** Meditativeness, pensiveness; reflectiveness; considerateness.

1697 BURGHOPE *Disc. Relig. Assemb.* Ded., These are the men that I wou'd awaken into sober thoughtfulness. 1737 WHISTON *Josephus, Antiq.* XVI. ix, Herod was silent and in great thoughtfulness. 1809 W. IRVING *Knickerb.* 85 The honest burghers smoked their pipes in profound thoughtfulness. 1876 MISS BRADDON *J. Haggard's Dau.* III. 101 A countenance as mysterious in its solemn thoughtfulness as the head of Memnon. 1880 'OUIDA' *Moths* II. iv. 89 Reared in tender thoughtfulness to the poor.

**Thoughtiness**: see after THOUGHTY.

**Thoughtive, Thoughtkin**: see after THOUGHT [1].

**Thoughtless** (þǭ·tlės), *a.* [f. THOUGHT [1] + -LESS.] That is without thought, in various senses: the opposite of THOUGHTFUL.

**1.** Not taking thought, acting without thought or reflection; unreflecting, heedless, imprudent.

1592 KYD *Sp. Trag.* IV. i. 40 Nor thinke I thoughtles thinke vpon a meane, To let his death be vnreueng'd at full. 1611 FLORIO, *Inpensierato*, thoughtlesse, carelesse. *a* 1704 T. BROWN *Sat. agst. Woman* 39 Weak curses..For thoughtless crimes, which come out of thy kind. 1736 BUTLER *Anal.* I. ii. Wks. 1874 I. 42 Youth may be alleged as an excuse for rashness and folly, as being naturally thoughtless. 1849 B. TAYLOR in *Life & Lett.* I. vii. 149, I shall neither be rash nor thoughtless.

**b.** With *of* or dependent clause: Not thinking; unmindful, forgetful; heedless, careless; unsuspecting. Now *rare*.

1615 CHAPMAN *Odyss.* v. 19 He..Finds you so thoughtlesse of him, and his birth. 16.. ROGERS (J.), Without remorse for the past, and thoughtless of the future. 1697 DRYDEN *Virg. Georg.* III. 668 A Snake..Leaving his Nest ..thoughtless of his Eggs. 1725 POPE *Odyss.* IV. 716 The Royal guest, Thoughtless of ill, accepts the fraudful feast. 1742 YOUNG *Nt. Th.* IV. 365 Men homage pay to men, Thoughtless beneath whose dreadful eye they bow.

† **c.** Free from care or anxiety. Also *transf. Obs.*

1742 GRAY *Eton Coll.* v, The thoughtless day, the easy night. 1764 GOLDSM. *Trav.* 255 So blest a life these thoughtless realms display. 1789 BLAKE *Songs Innoc.*, *Night* 17 They look in every thoughtless nest.

**d.** Wanting in consideration for others; inconsiderate.

1794 BLAKE *Songs Exper.*, *Fly* 3 Little fly, Thy summer's play My thoughtless hand Has brush'd away. *Mod.* It was very thoughtless of you to disturb her.

**2.** Deficient in or lacking thought; not given to thinking; stupid, senseless, dull-witted; destitute of ideas. Now *rare*.

1682 DRYDEN *Mac Flecknoe* 26 Shadwell never deviates into sense.., his goodly fabric..seems designed for thoughtless majesty. 1714 POPE *Epil. Jane Shore* 7 As a blockhead rubs his thoughtless skull, And thanks his stars he was not born a fool. 1879 B. TAYLOR *Stud. Germ. Lit.* 194 He was an earnest thinker in a thoughtless time.

† **b.** Of inanimate things: Devoid of thought.

1691–8 NORRIS *Pract. Disc.* (1711) III. 22 Bodies have no Thought, therefore they produce none:..for how can a thoughtless Principle produce a Thought? *c* 1705 BERKELEY *Commonpl. Bk.* Wks. 1871 IV. 469 Extension to exist in a thoughtless thing (or rather in a thing void of perception..), is a contradiction.

**Thou·ghtlessly,** *adv.* [f. prec. + -LY [2].] In a thoughtless manner; without thought or consideration; unreflectingly, carelessly, inconsiderately.

1714 GARTH *Dispensary* v. 59 In restless Hurries thoughtlessly they live. 1792 V. KNOX *Serm.* vi. 133 He who runs on thoughtlessly in the mad career of pleasure. 1806 HUTTON *Course Math.* I. 152 One thoughtlessly spends 10*l.* a year more than his pay. 1890 GROSS *Gild Merch.* I. 104 The arbitrary interpretation..which came to be thoughtlessly accepted as a fact.

**Thou·ghtlessness.** [f. as prec. + -NESS.] The quality of being thoughtless; want of thought or consideration; carelessness, inconsiderateness.

*a* 1704 T. BROWN *Praise Pov.* Wks. 1730 I. 96 The remains of the night [they spend] in sleep, idleness, thoughtlessness [etc.]. 1775 ADAIR *Amer. Ind.* 420 Dry wood, with which they..provide themselves, but only from day to day, through their thoughtlessness of to-morrow. *a* 1862 BUCKLE *Misc. Wks.* (1872) I. 27 Vice is often cunning and wary; but thoughtlessness is always profuse and reckless. 1884 *Manch. Exam.* 1 Oct. 3/1 The thoughtlessness of some of her actions is only equalled by their stupidity.

**Thoughtlet, Thoughtling**: see after THOUGHT [1].

**Thoughtness** (þǭ·tnės). *rare.* [f. *thought*, pa. pple. of THINK *v.*[2] + -NESS.] The fact or quality of being thought or mentally discerned.

1865 J. GROTE *Explor. Philos.* I. 140, I recognise two manners of existence,..thinkingness and thoughtness, and it is the latter which, when we believe the thought correct or justified, we call phenomenal existence or matter. 1905 *Athenæum* 11 Mar. 306/3 In the dead-alive fashion of the functions of a thinking apotheosized as a thoughtness.

**Thought-out** (þǭ·tˌau·t: stress variable), *ppl. a.* [pa. pple. of *think out* (see THINK *v.*[2] 15) used as adj.] Elaborated, constructed, or arrived at by thinking or mental labour; thoroughly considered.

1870 J. H. FRISWELL *Mod. Men of Lett.* vii. 129 'Paracelsus', and other hard thought-out dramatic pieces. 1907 BP. ROBERTSON in *Trans. Devon Assoc.* XXXIX. 44 A weighty and thought-out survey of the scope and nature of scientific truth.

**Thou·ght-rea·ding,** *sb.* The reading of another person's thoughts; direct perception by one mind of what is passing in another, independent of ordinary means of expression or communication: a power alleged to be possessed by certain persons or by persons in certain psychic states. Hence allusively. So **Thou·ght-read** *v.*, *trans.* to read a person's thoughts (with the person or the thought as obj.); *intr.* to practise thought-reading; **Thou·ght-rea·der,** one who practises or professes thought-reading; **Thou·ght-rea·ding** *a.*, that practises thought-reading.

1855 Smedley, etc. *Occult Sc.* 258 Thought-reading, in certain experiences of the somnambulist. 1880 Mrs. Forrester *Roy & V.* I. 30 Did you ever hear of people being thought-readers? 1883 *Fortn. Rev.* 1 Aug. 275 The most recently refurbished mystery in the guise of science, viz. that of so-called 'Thought-reading'. 1891 Mrs. Riddell *Mad Tour* 111 No thought-reader could have imagined the topic that was engaging Bobby's mind. 1892 *19th Cent.* Jan. 37 These thought readings and foretellings. 1898 L. A. Tollemache *Talks w. Gladstone* 166 One would like to have seen, or (better still) to have thought-read, Carlyle. 1899 *Daily News* 9 Dec. 6/4 Do you think your thought-reading gift could be turned to practical service in detective work—a thought-reading Sherlock Holmes? 1906 *Pall Mall G.* 4 Jan. 2 He thought-read the conditional intentions of the British commander.

**Thoughtsman**: see after Thought[1].

† **Thou·ghtsome,** *a. Obs. rare.* [f. Thought[1] + -some.] **a.** Addicted to thought; thoughtful. **b.** Of the nature of thought, or having the faculty of thought; mental, spiritual. Hence † **Thou·ghtsomeness.**

1611 Cotgr., *Mental*,..mentall, thoughtsome, belonging to the mind. *c* 1627 Scudder *Chr. Daily Walk* ix. § 1 (1637) 219 If men report evill of you..Be not so much inquisitiue who raised it, or thought-some how to bring him to his answer. 1674 N. Fairfax *Bulk & Selv.* 82 A ghost being in it self not roomthy, it cannot bear any roomthy behaviour towards bodies that are so, any more than bodies that are bulky, can bear immaterial respects or thoughtsom behaviours towards ghosts that are so. *Ibid.* 34 Thoughtsomness setting full as close to the very stamp or inmostness of a thinking Being, as boak or roomthyness does to the Being that is Bodysom.

**Thou·ghty,** *a. Obs.* exc. *Sc.* Forms: see Thought[1]. [f. as prec. + -y.] Given to thought, thoughtful. **a.** Heedful, attentive, intent. † **b.** Pensive, melancholy, anxious.

*c* 1375 *Sc. Leg. Saints* xxvii. (*Machor*) 706 Besy.. Til infourme ȝu in cheryte, And in sawle-hele thochty to be. 1387–8 T. Usk *Test. Love* ii. ix. (Skeat) l. 21 Euer is their contemplacion in ful of thoughty study to plesaunce. *c* 1412 Hoccleve *De Reg. Princ.* 80 Who so þat thoghty is, is wo-be-gon. *c* 1425 Wyntoun *Cron.* vi. xvi. 1608 As he past apon a day In til huntynge..On his gamyn al thouchty. *c* 1430 *Pilgr. Lyf Manhode* i. cxl. (1869) 73, I was ther of wonderliche abashed and thouhti. 1823 Corbett *Petticoat T.* II. 110 (Jam.) Fanny is two years younger than I am, and not so thoughty, as Philip says.

Hence † **Thou·ghtiness,** melancholy, pensiveness.

1707 J. Nimmo *Narr.* (1889) 4 My father was resolved to use authoretie q[eh] was not pleasing to me and increased my thoghtiness.

† **Though-whether,** *adv. Obs.* Forms: 1 þeah-hwæþere, 2 þeah-, þæh-, þahwhweðre, -weþere, -weðer, 3 þohhwheþþre (*Orm.*), þeih hweðere, þohqueþer, -ir, 4 þoh-, þo-, do-, þou-, þof-, þe-queþer, -ir, though whethir. [OE. *þéah-hwæþere*, f. *þéah* Though + *hwæðere* Whether. Cf. OHG. *thoh uuidaru, thoh thiu uuidoro* (Tatian), *dhoh dhiu huuedheru* (Isidore). The analysis of the combination is not clear.] Notwithstanding, nevertheless, howbeit, however.

*c* 897 K. Ælfred *Gregory's Past. C.* xxi. 151 Moniȝe sint ..ðe mon sceal wærlice licettan, and ðeahhwæðre eft cyðan. 971 *Blickl. Hom.* 31 Nam he fif stanas..& þeah-hweþere mid anum he þone gigant ofwearp. *a* 1175 *Cott. Hom.* 223 Se lichame is deadlic..ac þeahweðer god arerð eft þane licame to ecene þingum. *c* 1175 *Lamb. Hom.* 37 Þa hweþere þine saul feren scal in to eche pine. *Ibid.* 131 Þah hweðre his saule wes in helle. *c* 1200 Ormin 2459 Þatt ȝho þohhwheþþre shollde ben Maȝȝdenn all þwerrt utt clene. *c* 1200 *Moral Ode* 131 (Trin. MS.) Þeih hweðere we hit leueð wel. 13.. *Cursor M.* 22934 (Edin.) Þohqueþir we sal understand þat [etc.]. *Ibid.* 19546 (Cott.) Thar naman þof-queþer wene. 1357 *Lay Folks Catech.* (MS. T.) 93 Though-whethir noght twa goddes the fadir and the son.

**Thoul(e, Thoume,** obs. ff. Thole *sb.*[1], Thumb.

**Thoundre, thouner,** obs. forms of Thunder.

**Thour, þour, thourch, thourgh, þourȝ, thourh, þourh, thourth,** obs. ff. Through.

**Thourt,** variant pa. t. of Tharf *v. Obs.*

‖ **Thous** (þōu·ǒs). *Zool.* [mod.L., a. Gr. θώς, θω-ός: see Thos.] A species or group of species of the extended genus *Canis*, canine beasts, natives of Africa and Asia; including *Thōus* (or *Canis*) *anthus* (the North African Jackal), and *T. mesomelas*, *variegatus*, and *Senegalensis*, African jackals.

1839 C. H. Smith *Dogs* I. iv. 193 Section IV. Thous. *Ibid.* v. 207 By separating our group of Thous from the true Jackals, much confusion..is removed.

**Thousand** (þau·zənd), *sb.* and *a.* Forms: 1–3 þusend, 2–3 -ent, (*Orm.*) -ennd, 3 -and, -und, þousunt, 3–4 -end, 3–6 thousande, 4 thus(s)-, thos(s)and(e, 4–5 þous-, þows-, thous-, thows-, -and(e, -ant(e, -aund, -end, -ent, -ind(e, -ond(e, -ynd, 4–7 thowsand, 5 þou-, þow-, thouzand; 4– thousand (*mod. Sc.* thoozan(t). [OE. *þúsend*, sb. fem. and neut. = OFris. *thûsend*, OS. *thûsundig*, *thûsind* (Du. *duizend*), OHG. *dûsunt* (MHG. *tûsent*, G. *tausend*), Salfrank. *þûschunde*, ON. *þúsuna* (*þúshund*, *þúshundrað*, Sw. *tusen*, Da. *tusind*), Goth. *þûsundi* sb. fem. and neut. Generally held to be cognate with Lith. *túkstanti-s*, Lett. *tûkstûts*, OPruss. **tûsimta* (acc. pl. *tûsimtons*), OSlav. тысѧщта *tysęšta*, -ęšta, Russ. тысяча *ty·sjatša*, Pol. *tysiac*, Czech *tisíc*, pointing to an orig. Slavo-Teut. **tūssontiā* or *tussntjā*, whence also OTeut. **þūsundi*. The first element is considered by many to be an Indo-Eur. **tūs* meaning 'multitude, force'; cf. Skr. *tawa's* 'strong, force'; as to the rest of the word etymologists differ.

The general result is that *þúsundi* was prob. an indefinite term for a 'great multitude' (cf. Gr. μυριάς, -αδ-, in its indefinite, and *myriad* in its common English use), which was used as the available equivalent of Gr. χίλιοι and L. *mille*, themselves prob. originally indefinite words, there being no general Indo-Eur. word for 'thousand'.]

**1.** The cardinal number equal to ten times one hundred: denoted by the symbols 1000 or M (for L. *mille*), formerly often by m̄, or [m], as xxx[m].

**a.** As sb. or quasi-sb., with plural. (*a*) In singular. Usually *a thousand*, emphatically or precisely *one thousand*.

971 *Blickl. Hom.* 119 Nis..næniȝ mon þe..wite..hwæþer þis þusend sceole beon scyrtre ofer þæt þe lengre. *c* 1000 *Ælfric's Vocab.* in Wr.-Wülcker 110/12 *Ciliarcus*, þusendes ealdor. *c* 1205 Lay. 21401 Bi þusund & bi þusend þer feollen [*sc.* Sexes] æuere in þene grund. 1340 Hampole *Pr. Consc.* 7490 Men and wymmen, many a thousand. 1398 Trevisa *Barth. De P. R.* xix. cxxiii. (1495), Ten hundryd makyth a thousande. 1583 Stocker *Civ. Warres Lowe C.* iv. 49 A thousande fiue hundred seuentie and nine. 1668 R. Steele *Husbandman's Calling* x. (1672) 256 A thousand to one, they have..some gnawing care..that defeats their comfort. *Mod.* Bricks are sold by the thousand.

(*b*) In plural *thousands* (OE. *þúsendu*, -*o*, -*a*, ME. -*e*, -*es*).

In *Arith.* often *ellipt.* for the digits denoting the number of thousands: cf. *units, tens, hundreds.*

*Beowulf* 2196 He..him ȝesealde seofan þusendo. *c* 893 K. Ælfred *Oros.* v. iv. § 2 Þider for mid moneȝum þusendum. *c* 1000 Ælfric *Josh.* vii. 3 Ac twa þusenda oððe þreo læt faran. *a* 1120 *O. E. Chron.* an. 694 (Laud MS.) Cantwara.. him ȝesealdon xxx þusenda. *c* 1205 Lay. 545 Þider in iwenden moni þusunde [*c* 1275 mani þusend]. *c* 1275 *Ibid.* 465 Ich habbe..in þan mountes mani þusendes. *a* 1300 *Cursor M.* 19134 (Edin.) Þare was conuertid thusandis [*Gött.* thousandes] v. *c* 1425 [see (*c*)]. 1542 Recorde *Gr. Artes* 120 Then adde I y[e] thousandes together. 1615 Mure *Misc. P.* xiv. 12 Metamorphos'd his thowsands in milleounes. 1771 *Hist. Eur.* in *Ann. Reg.* 24/2 They amounted in all to some thousands. 1877 H. Spencer in *Min. Evid. Copyright Comm.* (1878) 258 Now I simply have to print additional thousands as they are demanded.

(*c*) After another numeral the singular is now commonly used as a collective plural. (Cf. *dozen, hundred.*)

But in OE. the plural form was usual: see (*b*).

*c* 1000 Ælfric *Gram.* (Z.) 282 Tweȝen ias, ȝetitelode ĪĪ, ȝetacniað twa þusend. *c* 1205 Lay. 83 Hire weoren..hund þousunt deade. *Ibid.* 465 Ich habbe in þane munten monie þusund [*c* 1275 þusendes]. 1297 R. Glouc. (Rolls) 1789 Þe brutons sywede after,..& slowe mani þousend. 1382 Wyclif *Luke* xiv. 31 If he may with ten thousynd go aȝens him that cometh to him with twenty thousynd. *c* 1425 *Crafte Nombrynge* (E. E. T. S.) 29 In þe 5 place [he schuld betoken] sexty þowsant...In þe 8 place sexty þowsant thowsantes. 1587 Golding *De Mornay* xviii. (1592) 288 For one that triumpheth, a hundred thousand are led in captiuitie. *Mod.* How many followers has he? He claims to have fifty thousand. The hall will seat four thousand.

(*d*) As a sb. it takes after it *of*, representing the OE. genitive pl. Now after a numeral only as a unit of quantity by which things are sold.

(*A thousand of, thousands of*, are used partitively as in the case of other numerals.)

*c* 893 K. Ælfred *Oros.* i. x. § 4 On an scip mæȝe an þusend manna. *Ibid.* ii. v. § 2 Hie acuron endlefan þusend monna. *c* 1000 Ælfric *Hom.* II. 334 Ða ȝehyrde he..sang ..maneȝa ðusenda engla. *c* 1050 *Byrhtferth's Handboc* in *Anglia* (1885) VIII. 311 Eahta þusend tida. *c* 1175 *Lamb. Hom.* 35 Moni þusent monne mahte libben fele ȝere mare þenne he do. *c* 1275 *Shires & Hund.* 58 in *O. E. Misc.* 146, xxvi. þusend hida.

*c* 1250 *Gen. & Ex.* 4078 Godes wreche ðor haueð of-slaȝen xx.iii. ðusent of daȝen. 1398 Trevisa *Barth. De P. R.* i. (1495) A iv/2 He fedde many thousandes of peple wyth fewe looues of brede. *c* 1449 Pecock *Repr.* (Rolls) 540 Many hundrid thousind of soulis. *c* 1450 tr. *De Imitatione* iii. xi. 78 What shal I ȝeue þe for all þese þousand of godes? *c* 1475 *Rauf Coilȝear* 327 Ane thousand and ma of fensabill men. 1596–7 in Ducarel *Hist. Croydon* App. (1783) 153 Four loads of flinte..will well save one thousand of bricke. 1606 G. W[oodcocke] *Lives Emperors* in *Hist. Ivstine* Iij, The King of Persia with his wife Cæsarea and many thousand of their followers. 1663 Gerbier *Counsel* 52 Twenty Thousand of Bricks. 1671 S. Clarke (*title*) A Mirrour, or Looking-Glass, both for Saints and Sinners, held forth in some Thousands of Examples. 1748 in Waghorn *Cricket Scores* (1899) 41 Some thousands of pounds were depending on this match. 1880 C. R. Markham *Peruv. Bark* 51 Thousands of arrobas were..obtained.

**b.** As adj. or quasi-adj., followed immediately by a plural (or collective) noun.

*c* 1000 Ælfric *Hom.* II. 458 Iob..wæron eft forȝoldene ..þusend ȝetyme oxena and þusend assan. *a* 1123 *O. E. Chron.* an. 1101, Rotbert..sceolde..þreo þusend marc seolfres habban. *c* 1200 *Vices & Virt.* 115 Mani þusend hali saules. *c* 1200 Ormin 15510 He fedde fif þusennde menn Wiþþ fife barrliȝ lafess. *c* 1290 *S. Eng. Leg.* I. 8/243 More þane a þousend ȝer. *c* 1380 Wyclif *Wks.* (1880) 465 Þis þousinde wynter & more. 1489 Wriothesley *Chron.* (Camden) I. 2 Manye knightes with seaven thowsand men. 1523 Ld. Berners *Froiss.* I. 672 He brought over the mountaynes a xxx. thousande fyghtinge men. 1553 T. Wilson *Rhet.* 66 b, Him..that was once worthe three thousande pounde, and is not nowe worthe the three grotes. 1650 Baxter *Saints' R.* ii. vii. (1654) 269 So many thousand Christians so barbarously murdered. 1891 Kipling *Light that Failed* xiv. (1900) 263 You've lost about a thousand pounds' worth of sketches.

**2.** Often used vaguely or hyperbolically for a large number: cf. *hundred.*

So *ten thousand, thousands, thousands of thousands.*

*c* 1000 *Ags. Ps.* (Th.) iii. 5 Ic me nu na ondræde þusendu folces. *a* 1300 *Cursor M.* 10090 Þe sunn o rightwisnes,.. Hir mad a thusand sith sa bright. *c* 1385 Chaucer *L. G. W.* 1 A Thousent sythis haue I herd men telle That there is Ioye in heuene. 1549 Coverdale *Erasm. Par. Epist.* Ded. 2 What vayne pylgremages, what offerynges and lyghtes to stockes and stones,..with thousandes moe inconueniences. 1638 R. Baker tr. *Balzac's Lett.* (vol. III.) 37, I give you a thousand thanks. 1700 T. Brown *Fresny's Amusem.* v. 49 Some of them [*sc.* ladies] having Scab'd, or Pimpled Faces, wear a Thousand Patches to hide them. 1713 Young *Last Day* iii. 159 Ten thousand thousand fathoms still remain. 1779 *Mirror* No. 67 ¶ 11 You may do good to thousands. 1786 tr. *Beckford's Vathek* 157 A thousand ridiculous stories were propagated, at his expence. 1821 Byron *Juan* iii. lxxxvi. *Isles of Greece* iv, And ships, by thousands, lay below, And men in nations;—all were his! 1842 *Dumfries Herald* Oct., Clean them from the worms of the thousand-and-one flies that feed on them. 1880 W. S. Gilbert *Pirates of Penzance* i, You will find me a wife of a thousand. *a* 1895 in Baring-Gould *Nursery Songs & Rhymes* vii. 17 Ten thousand parks where deer run, Ten thousand roses in the sun.

**3.** Elliptical uses. **a.** A thousand of some weight, measure, or quantity; e. g. acres, pounds, cubic feet, years, pieces, packages, etc. according to the nature of the commodity, etc.

*a* 900 *O. E. Chron.* an. 648 (Parker MS.), Her Cenwalh ȝesalde Cuþrede his mæȝe iii þusendo londes be Æsces dune. *c* 1000 *Ags. Ps.* (Th.) cxviii[i]. 72 Me is micle betere, ..þonne mon me ȝeofe ȝeara ðusende goldes and seolfres. *a* 1300 *E. E. Psalter* ibid., Ouer thousandes ofe siluer ore golde. 1443 *Acts Privy Counc.* (1835) V. 281 To delivere Johan Dawnsonn maister of þordenaunces of my Lorde of Somerset iiij[ml] salpetre iij[ml] sulphure. 1482 in *Charters, &c. Edinb.* (1871) 169 Of the thousand irne ij s. 1840 Thackeray *Cox's Diary* May, Instead of looking twenty, he looked a thousand. 1884 *Sat. Rev.* 7 June 758/1 He dines at 6, plays [billiards] a thousand-up by gaslight. 1901 *Daily Express* 28 Feb. 4/6 The price of gas in London in 1876 was 3*s*. 9*d*. per thousand.

**b.** A thousand pounds sterling.

1547–64 Bauldwin *Mor. Philos.* (Palfr.) 65 A merchant's compters, that is to day worth thousands. 1588 *Marprel. Epist.* (Arb.) 5 Come downe you bishopps from your thousands, and content you with your hundreds. 1609 B. Jonson *Sil. Wom.* iv. v, A man of two thousand a yeere. 1826 Disraeli *Viv. Grey* ii. xiii, A clear rental of five-and-twenty thousand per annum. 1852 Thackeray *Esmond* i. ix, A merchant on 'Change,..having lost his thousands, embarks a few guineas upon the next ship.

† **4.** As ordinal: = Thousandth. *Obs.*

*c* 1400 Maundev. (Roxb.) xvi. 74 He knew noȝt þe thowsand parte of his gude. 14.. *Tundale's Vis.* 1923 (Edinb. MS.) Not by an hvndryþe þowsand part. 1600 Shaks. *A. Y. L.* iv. i. 46 Breake but a part of the thousand part of a minute in the affairs of loue. 1680 N. Lee *Cæsar Borgia* Ep. Ded., My best Merits are not the ten thousand part of his smallest labours.

**5.** *Comb.* Forming (*a*) attrib. compounds with a sb., as *thousand-acre, -dollar, -guinea, -mile, -pound, -round, -year* (hence *-year-long, -year-old*, etc.); (*b*) parasynthetic combs., as *thousand-eyed* (having a thousand eyes), *-footed, -handed, -headed, -hued, -sided, -souled, -voiced*, etc. adjs.; also **thousand-feet, -legs,** a millepede or centipede; **thousand-yearist,** nonce-rendering of Chiliast.

1895 *Daily News* 30 Nov. 3/4 The attempt to turn England into a rural arcadia of *thousand acre farms. 1871 Alabaster *Wheel of Law* 171 There the *thousand-eyed Lord..is attended by thousands of houris. *Ibid.* 209 The thousand-eyed is a common epithet of Indra. 1704 in Churchill *Collect. Voy.* III. 828/2 *Thousand Feet, called *Millepie* by the Portugueses. 1858 O. W. Holmes *Aut. Breakf.-t.* vii, To take shelter..under one of the *thousand-footed bridges. 1894 Du Maurier *Trilby* II. 111 Princes.. who pay them *thousand-guinea fees. 1870 Emerson *Soc. & Solit.* vii. 133 This *thousand-handed art. *a* 1618 Sylvester *Miracle of Peace* xxiv, Thou *thousand-headed head-lesse Monster-most. 1839 Bailey *Festus* xxxi. (1852) 490 Fluttering its wings in lightnings *thousand-hued. 1807 Young *Agric. Essex* I. 392 The *thousand legs eats and makes them [potatoes] scabby. 1898 *Westm. Gaz.* 17 June 5/1 A *thousand-pound projectile..tore a gaping hole in the emplacement. 1902 *Lond. Mag.* June 484/1 Accused of systematically uttering forged Bank of England thousand-pound notes. 1704 Norris *Ideal World* ii. ix. 387 Four, five, or a *thousand-sided figures..are capable of a greater number of relations..than simple triangles are. 1838–9 Hallam *Hist. Lit.* III. iii. vi. § 49. 313 Coleridge has most felicitously applied to him a Greek epithet.. μυριόνους, the *thousand-souled Shakspeare. 1898 *Westm. Gaz.* 2 Sept. 5/1 Amidst the *thousand-voiced tumult. 1886 Kipling *Departm. Ditties*, etc. (1899) 45 So I fled with steps uncertain On a *thousand-year long race. 1610 Healey *St. Aug. Citie of God* 798 The worde [Chiliasts] is greeke, and may bee interpreted, Millenaryes, or *Thousand-yere-ists.

Hence **Thousandai·re** (*nonce-wd.* after *millionaire*), one who has a thousand pounds; † **Thou·sandly** *adv.*, thousandfold.

1896 *Eclectic Mag.* Mar. 350 To prevent their possessor from ever becoming even a thousandaire. *c* 1450 *Mirour Saluacioun* 4920 Now shalle I the rewarde innoumbrable thovzandly.

† **Thou·sandel.** *Obs.* [Contr. of the phr. *by a thousand deal* (Deal *sb.*[1] 1 e).] A thousand times.

13.. *Guy Warw.* (A.) 4265 More riches þe worþ bi a þousandel Boþe of cites & of riche castel,..Þan þerl Rohaut haþ. 1390 Gower *Conf.* I. 66 For in good feith, this lieveth wel, Mi will was betre a thousendel.

**Thousandfold** (þau·zəndfōuld), *a.*, *adv.*, and *sb.* [OE. *þúsendfeald*: see THOUSAND and -FOLD.]

**A.** *adj.* One thousand times as much or many; consisting of a thousand parts; a thousand times repeated or multiplied.

c 1000 ÆLFRIC *Hom.* II. 576 Salomon..ȝeoffrode him.. þusendfealde onsæȝednyssa æt anre offrunge. a 1023 WULFSTAN *Hom.* xlvii. (Napier) 243 Ðæt þusendfeald ȝetæl is fulfremed. c 1200 *Trin. Coll. Hom.* 191 Mid þusendfeld wrenches he þe herte to-wendeð. 1840 CARLYLE *Heroes* i, How such light will then shine out, and with wondrous thousandfold expansion spread itself. 1858 HAWTHORNE *Fr. & It. Note-Bks.* (1872) I. 45 This bustle and babble; this thousand-fold talk.

**B.** *adv.* A thousand times (in amount); a thousand times as much. (Usually *a thousandfold.*)

a 1225 *Leg. Kath.* 2323 Þæt þing..schal arisen, þurh þæt fal, a þusentfalt te fehere..to lif undeðlich. c 1374 CHAUCER *Troylus* I. 819 A guerdoun..A þowsand folde more þan he kan deserue. ? a 1500 *Chester Pl.* i. 144 Brighter then god a thowsand fould. 1586 A. DAY *Eng. Secretary* II. (1625) 86 Thou hast..heaped mischiefe a thousandfold to thy selfe. 1681–6 J. SCOTT *Chr. Life* II. i. § 3 Our sincere Compliance with the immutable Obligations of Piety and Vertue, is a Thousandfold more acceptable to God, than [etc.]. 1872 MORLEY *Voltaire* i. (1886) 10 The sacrifice may repay itself a thousand-fold.

† **b.** A thousand times (in succession). *rare*—[1].

1500–20 DUNBAR *Poems* xlix. 37 War the fox tane a thousand fawd, And grace him gevin als oft for frawd.

**C.** *sb.* A thousand times the amount or number.

a 1711 KEN *Sion* Poet. Wks. 1721 IV. 370 The Son ador'd and nurs'd by the sweet Maid, A thousand-fold of Love for Love repaid.

Hence **Thou·sandfo:ldly** *adv.* = B. *rare*—[1].

1829 COLERIDGE *Improvisatore* Poems II. 130 In the person of a thousand-foldly endeared partner.

**Thousandth** (þau·zəndþ), *a.* and *sb.* [f. THOUSAND + -TH. Not found before 16th c.: cf. THOUSAND 4.] The ordinal numeral belonging to the cardinal THOUSAND.

**A.** *adj.* **1.** Coming last in order of a thousand successive individuals.

1552 HULOET, Thousandth, *millesimus.* 1656 tr. *Hobbes' Elem. Philos.* (1839) 100 Though our computation reach the fixed stars, or the ninth or tenth, nay, the thousandth sphere. 1732 POPE *Ess. Man* I. 246 From Nature's chain whatever link you strike, Tenth or ten thousandth, breaks the chain alike. 1875 BRYCE *Holy Rom. Emp.* (ed. 5) vi. 77 Modern Germany proclaims the era of A. D. 843 the beginning of her national existence, and celebrated its thousandth anniversary thirty-two years ago.

**2.** *Thousandth part*: one of a thousand equal parts into which anything may be divided.

1561 T. HOBY tr. *Castiglione's Courtyer* I. K ij, Ye felt not the thousandeth part of yᵉ delite. 1710 BERKELEY *Princ. Hum. Knowl.* § 127 The ten thousandth part of that line. 1782 HERSCHEL in *Phil. Trans.* LXXII. 165 Pinions ..so evenly divided as..to be depended upon..to perhaps the two, three, or four thousandth part of an inch. 1836 J. H. NEWMAN *Lyra Apost.* (1849) 231 Lord! Who Thy thousand years dost wait To work the thousandth part Of Thy vast plan.

**B.** *sb.* A thousandth part.

1793 YOUNG in *Phil. Trans.* LXXXIII. 174 In the ox's eye, the diameter of the crystalline is 700 thousandths of an inch. 1867 DENISON *Astron. without Math.* 6 Inches about a thousandth longer than our inches.

**Thousandweight** (þau·zəndˌwēɪt). *rare.* A weight of a thousand pounds.

1538 ELYOT, *Milliarius, a, um,* of a thousande weight. 1552 HULOET, Thousande weyght, *millepondium.* 1559 W. CUNNINGHAM *Cosmogr. Glasse* 176 Sulphure is there so plentifull that you may for the 4. part of a ducate, haue a thousande weight. 1667 PRIMATT *City & C. Build.* 99 A thousand weight of Lead taken up in Pipes, Gutters, and in Ridges. 1685 *Lond. Gaz.* No. 2064/4, 40 thousand weight of Powder. 1768 *Chron.* in *Ann. Reg.* 113/2 The Sherborne waggon was stopped by the populace, and about a thousand weight of butter taken away.

**'Thout**, aphetic form of *athout*, WITHOUT.

**Thout, þout, thouth**, obs. ff. THOUGHT [1] and [2].

**Thow**, obs. f. THOU *pron.*; also, occasional copyist's error for *you.* **Thow, þow(e**, var. THO *dem. pron.*; obs. form of THOUGH.

**Thowcht**, obs. Sc. form of THOUGH, THOUGHT.

**Thowel(l, thowl(e**, obs. ff. THOLE *sb.*[1] and *v.*

**Thowen, þoȝen, þowun**, pa. pple. of THEE *v.*[1]

**Thowght, þowȝt, þowht**, etc., obs. ff. THOUGHT.

**Thowless** (þau·lės, þōu·lės), *a. Sc.* Forms: 4–5 **thowles**, 5 **-lace**, **-las**, **-lys**, **thoulass**, 8– **thowless.** [app. a collateral Sc. form of THEWLESS, with which it agrees in sense; but the phonology is unexplained.]

† **1.** Without morality or virtue; wanton, dissolute, profligate; also, thoughtless. *Obs.*

1375 [implied in THOWLESSNESS]. c 1425 WYNTOUN *Cron.* VIII. xxii. 3292 (MS. Cott.) He was thowlace [*v. r.* wantoun], and had in won,..oftsyis to ly Oþir syndry women by. *Ibid.* xxxiii. 5933 Weil waxyn vp..And thowles þan, for his ȝoutheide To þat natur walde hym leide. 14.. *How the Good wife*, etc. 260 in *Barbour's Bruce* 534 And chasty thame quhen thai do myss, Or [*MS.* our] rekles thoulass wantoun is. a 1500 *Ratis Raving* I. 1264 This eild is thowles & wnswere, And ȝarnis play, and al blytht chere. a 1500 *Thewis Gd. Women* 145 in *Ratis Raving*, etc. 107 Women that has a thowlas hart.

**2.** Devoid of energy or spirit; inert, inactive; spiritless, listless.

1721 RAMSAY *Prospect of Plenty* 128 A poor and haughty drone, Wha thowless stands a lazy looker-on. 1728 — *Tea-t. Misc., Widow* vi, Fortune..ruins the woer that's thowless and cauld. 1801 MACNEILL *Poems* (1844) 111 Thowless, he tint his gate deep 'mang the snaw. 1818 SCOTT *Br. Lamm.* xii[i], You, ye thowless jade, to sit still and see my substance disponed upon to an idle, drunken, reprobate, worm-eaten serving man. a 1875 J. MURRAY in *Mod. Scot. Poets* (1881) III. 150 The kye stand thowless on the croft.

Hence **Thow·lessness**, † evil or immoral conduct, bad behaviour; wantonness, vice (*obs.*); also, want of energy, ineffectiveness.

1375 BARBOUR *Bruce* I. 333 And till swylk thowlesnes he ȝeid, As the courss askis off ȝowtheid. c 1425 WYNTOUN *Cron.* VI. iii. 268 That thai suld noucht for ydilnes Fall intill iwill thowlysnes. 1885 'J. STRATHESK' *More Bits* xi. (ed. 2) 206 She did not quite like some of Bell's remarks about 'wasterfu'ness' and 'thowlessness', possibly because they were only too true.

**Thowmbe, thowme**, obs. Sc. ff. THUMB.

**Thown, Thownyr**, obs. ff. TOWN, THUNDER.

† **Thowt(e**, *v. Obs.* [f. *thow*, THOU *pers. pron.* Cf. MHG. and Ger. *dutzen, duzen*, F. *tutoyer*, It. *tuizzare, tizzare*, med.L. *tuāre, tuisāre.*] *trans.* To address with the singular pronoun *thou*, to thou. Hence † **Thow·ting** *vbl. sb.*

c 1440 *Promp. Parv.* 535/2 Þowton, or thowton [*v. rr.* þowtyn, yowtyn], *tuo.* *Ibid.*, Þowtynge, or thowthynge, *tuacio, vel tuatus.*

**Thowt(e**, obs. or dial. ff. *thought*: see THINK *v.*[1] and [2]; obs. ff. THOUGHT [2], rower's bench.

**Thow·thistle.** Now *dial.* [OE. *þúðistel*, = OHG. *dúdistel*, MHG. *du-, dau-distel* (Grimm). Etymology of first element obscure. Perh. the original name, subseq. changed to SOWTHISTLE: see E. Schröder, *Götting. Gelehrte Nachr.* 1908, p. 28.] A herb; the sowthistle, or perh. formerly the wild lettuce.

a 700 *Epinal Gloss.* (O.E.T.) 601 *Lactuca*, þuþistel. c 725 *Corpus Gl.* 1175 *Lactuca*, þuðistel. c 1265 *Voc. Names Plants* in Wr.-Wülcker 559/5 *Andiuia*, *i.* letrun, *i.* þuȝe-þistel. c 1440 *Promp. Parv.* 492/1 Thowthystylle, herbe (or sowthystyle). 1888 *Sheffield Gloss.*, *Sowthistle*..also called a thow-thistle, or thoo-thistle.

**Thra**, variant of THRO *sb.*, *a.*, *adv.*

**Thra, thraa**, dial. forms of THROW *v.*

**Thrack** (þræk), *v.* Now *dial.* Also 9 *dial.* **thrag.** [Etymology obscure.] *trans.* To pack full, fill, cram; to load. Also *intr.* for *passive.*

1655 GURNALL *Chr. in Arm.* verse II. I. v. § 3 (1669) 33/2 Bags that are thracked full with money. a 1716 SOUTH *Serm.* (1744) VIII. vi. 176 The strait gate is too narrow for any man to come bustling in, thrack'd with great possessions. 1809 BATCHELOR *Anal. Eng. Lang.* 145 *Thrag*, to throng. 'As full as it could thrag'. 1854 MISS BAKER *Northampt. Gloss.* II. 337 *Thracked*...Used..for a hamper of apples. 'It was thracked full'. 1904 in *Eng. Dial. Dict.* s.v. *Thrag*, The streets were thragged with people.

† **Thracksat.** *Obs. rare.* [Origin obscure: perh. f. prec. + *sat* for *set* = 'set in compact mass'.] (See quot.)

1678 PHILLIPS (ed. 4), *Thracksat*, a Chymical term for a Metal, which is yet in the Mine. [Hence (printed *-scat*) in Bailey, Crabb, Worcester, Cassell, etc.]

**Thraf, thrafe, thraif**, obs. forms of THRAVE.

**Thraf caike**, obs. f. THARF-CAKE.

† **Thra·ftly**, *adv. Obs.* Forms: 3 **þræfliche**, 6 **thraftly.** [perh. f. OE. *þræft* quarrel, contention, chiding (= ON. *þrapt* quarrel: cf. OE. *þrafian* to urge, press, rebuke, censure) + -LY [2].] ? Angrily; surlily.

c 1205 LAY. 27797 Ah Bruttes him þrungen to þræfliche [c 1275 wroþliche] swiðe. a 1578 LINDESAY (Pitscottie) *Chron. Scot.* XXI. xxxvi. (MS. F. Advoc. Libr.; ed. 1728, 171), Where they were bot thraftlie receaved of the King.

† **Thra·fully**, *adv. Obs.* [f. **thraful* adj. (f. THRO, THRA *sb.* + -FUL) + -LY [2].] Violently.

1535 STEWART *Cron. Scot.* (Rolls) I. 144 With sic ane reird quhill all the rochis rang, So thrafullie togidder that tha thrang.

[**Thragge**, in Halliwell's ed. of Nares, misquotation of Huloet's *shragge*, SHRAG *v.*, copied in Latham's *Johnson* and some later Dicts.]

† **Thrail.** *Obs.* [Alteration of *frail*: see TH (6).] = FRAIL *sb.*[1]

1694 WESTMACOTT *Script. Herb.* 164 Matt-Reed..of which also are made Matts, and Frailes, or Thrailes.

**Thraip**, obs. and dial. variant of THREAP.

**Thraldom** (þrǭ·ldəm). Forms: see next. [f. next + -DOM.] The state or condition of being a thrall; bondage, servitude; captivity. **a.** *lit.*

c 1205 LAY. 29156 Summe heo fluȝen to Irlonde..and þer wuneden þeouwe inne þraldome. c 1250 *Gen. & Ex.* 2322 Driuen In-to ðraldom, euermor to liuen. 1377 LANGL. *P. Pl.* B. XVIII. 103 And ȝowre Fraunchise, þat fre was fallen is in thraldome. 1450–1530 *Myrr. our Ladye* 331 Theyr delyuerance oute of the thraldome of Egypte. 1590 WEBBE *Trav.* (Arb.) 14 In the midst of my thraldom in Turkie. 1617 MORYSON *Itin.* II. 25 Tyrone was among the Irish celebrated as the Deliverer of his Country from thraldome. 1756 HUME *Hist. Eng.* II. xli. 432 Elizabeth..would have been sure to detain him in perpetual thraldom. 1872 YEATS *Techn. Hist. Comm.* 165 Shoemakers were among the first to rescue themselves from the thraldom of the lords of the soil.

**b.** *fig.*

c 1175 *Lamb. Hom.* 139 Alle oðer daȝes of þe wike beoð to þreldome to þis dei. c 1380 WYCLIF *Serm.* Sel. Wks. II. 53 Þe moost þraldom and worst of alle is þe þraldom of synne. c 1450 tr. *De Imitatione* II. xii. 58 To chastise þe body, to bring it in þraldom. 1561 T. NORTON *Calvin's Inst.* I. xv. (1634) 74 This miserable estate whereunto man is now in thraldome. 1755 YOUNG *Centaur* iii. Wks. 1757 IV. 170 This thraldom to their pleasures. 1875 JOWETT *Plato* (ed. 2) I. 461 She may deliver herself up again to the thraldom of pleasures and pains.

**Thrall** (þrǭl), *sb.*[1] (*a.*[1]). Now *arch.* or *Hist.* Forms: *α.* 1 **þræl**, 2–4 **þrēl** (*pl.* **þrēles, þrelles**), 4 **þrell, þrelle, threll.** *β.* 2–3 **þral** (*pl.* 3–5 **þrāles, þralles**), (4 **þrale**), 4–5 **þrall**, 4–8 **thral**, 4– **thrall** (6 **thrawl, thraule**, *Sc.* **thraill**). *γ.* 4–5 **tharl**, 5 **tharlle.** See also THRILL *sb.*[2] [OE. *þræl*, a. ON. *þræll* (Da. *træl*, Sw. *träll*), perh. :— prehist. ON. **þrāhilaR* :—OTeut. **þrăhilo*ᶻ, f. OTeut. root *þreh-* to run. Cf. OHG. *dregil, drigil* 'servant', prop. 'runner'. Branch II is from THRALL *v.*: cf. M.Da. and Norw. *træl* drudgery, f. *trælle* to drudge.]

**I. 1.** One who is in bondage to a lord or master; a villein, serf, bondman, slave; also, in vaguer use, a servant, subject; *transf.* one whose liberty is forfeit; a captive, prisoner of war.

*α.* c 950 *Lindisf. Gosp.* Mark x. 44 And sua huæ seðe wælle in iuh forðmest wosa bie allra ðræl. 991 *Laws of Æthelred* II. c. 5 § 1 ȝyf Englisc man Denisc ne ðræl ofslea, ȝylde hine mid punde. c 1175 *Lamb. Hom.* 47 Heo [i.e. Sunday] on eorðe ȝeueð reste to alle eorðe þrelles, wepmen and wifmen of heore þrel weorkes. *Ibid.* 123 Herien we ure drihten þe ..makede us freo of þeowan and of þrelan his ahȝene bern. a 1225 *Ancr. R.* 130 'Hwon ȝe habbeð al wel idon' he seið, ..'siȝȝeð þæt ȝe beoð unnute þrelles'. 1340 *Ayenb.* 19 He deþ manhode to þe dyeule and becomþ his þrel. 1375 BARBOUR *Bruce* I. 274 Nane can tell The halle condicioun off A threll. *Ibid.* III. 220 Serwandis and threllis mad he fre.

*β.* c 1200 *Vices & Virt.* 17 Ðe ðe hlauerd betahte his þralle. c 1200 *Trin. Coll. Hom.* 121 To lesen þe þrales of þralshipe. 1297 R. GLOUC. (Rolls) 3010 Þe king..Nom of him sikernesse to be is þral euere mo. 1415 HOCCLEVE *To Sir J. Oldcastle* 98 Where is thy knyghtly herte, art thow his thral? 1566 DRANT *Wail. Hierim.* v, Our yonge men, lyke to vylaine thrawles, in drudgerie did grinde. 1612 T. TAYLOR *Comm. Titus* I. 4 (1619) 68 A Redeemer, purchasing us being captiues, and thralls to Sathan. 1748 THOMSON *Cast. Indol.* I. xi, Outcast of Nature, Man! the wretched thrall Of bitter-dropping sweat. 1867 BURTON *Hist. Scot.* (1873) I. xi. 362 The thralls or personal slaves.

*γ.* a 1500 *Spir. Remedies* in Halliwell *Nugæ Poet.* 65 Lorde, sende it unto the syke tharlle.

**b.** *fig.* One who is in bondage to some power or influence; a slave (*to* something).

c 950 *Lindisf. Gosp.* John viii. 34 Seðe wyrcas synne ðræl is synnes. c 1230 *Hali Meid.* 5 Þeos as flesches þralles beoð in worldes þeowdom. 1340 *Ayenb.* 86 Þet hi ne byeþ þrelles ne to gold ne to zeluer ne to hare caroyne. 1571 GOLDING *Calvin on Ps.* xxxvi. 5 They willingly yeelde themselves thralls to wickednes. 1605 SHAKS. *Macb.* III. vi. 13 Slaues of drinke, and thralles of sleepe. 1821 LAMB *Elia* Ser. I. *Imperfect Sympathies*, The veriest thrall to sympathies, apathies, antipathies.

**II. 2.** The condition of a thrall; thraldom, bondage, servitude; captivity.

13.. *Cursor M.* 6304 (Fairf.) Quen moises þe folk had lad..out of þe þralle of pharaon. 14.. *Chester Pl.* I. 129 If that yow in thrall yow bringe. a 1578 LINDESAY (Pitscottie) *Chron. Scot.* (S.T.S.) II. 44 The nyght in prosperatie, the morne in thraill. 1592 TIMME *Ten Eng. Lepers* A ij b, To bring this noble Realme of England to thraule. 1607 DEKKER & WEBSTER *Sir T. Wyatt* Wks. 1873 III. 111 You free your Countrie from base spanish thrall. 1791 BURNS *Lament Mary Q. Scots* ii, In love and freedom they rejoice, Wi' care nor thrall oppress. 1842 TENNYSON *Sir Galahad* ii, For them I battle till the end, To save from shame and thrall.

*fig.* 1576 *Thanksgiving* in *Liturg. Serv. Q. Eliz.* (1847) 559 Thou didst set us free from thrall. 1633 G. HERBERT *Temple, Church-porch* xx, When wanton pleasures becken us to thrall. 1800–24 CAMPBELL *Jilted Nymph* iv, A suitor, Whose heart I have gotten in thrall. 1856 MISS MULOCK *J. Halifax* xii, The Anonymous Friend: who held him in such fascinated thrall.

† **3.** Oppression, trouble, misery, distress. *Obs.*

1560 ROLLAND *Seven Sages* 25 It is better..we all seuin suld die..Or this ȝoung man suld suffer ony thrall. 1609 DANIEL *Civ. Wars* VIII. xciv, Sit downe, And rest you, after all this passed thrall. c 1796 MISS J. GRAHAM in Chambers *Scott. Songs* (1829) 15 As yet you've met with little thrall. a 1829 in Roby *Trad. Lanc.* (1867) II. 26 In my trouble and thrall.

**III. 4.** *attrib.* and *Comb.*, as *thrall-folk, -man* [ON. *þræl-monni*], *-woman, -work* [ON. *þræl-verk*]; *thrall-like* adj.

c 1175 Þrel weorkes [see 1 *α*]. c 1205 LAY. 455 Þat Dardanisc kun..woneð..inne þeowe-dome Þrel-werkes [c 1275 þralle-workes] doð. 1641 MILTON *Reform.* I. 2 Instead of..cheerful boldness..came servile and thrallike fear. 1886 CORBETT *Fall of Asgard* I. 35 She was a wild-looking thrall-girl. *Ibid.* 86 The thrall-woman came to answer for herself. 1887 MORRIS *Odyss.* XI. 190 A-winter he sleeps in the feast-hall whereto the thrall-folk seek.

**B.** *adjective.* [attrib. use of the sb.]

**1.** That is a thrall; subject, captive, enslaved, in bondage. **a.** in the predicate, or following the sb. (*a*) *lit.*

1297 R. GLOUC. (Rolls) 4074 To bringe hom vnder þe þat þe wolde makie þral. c 1330 R. BRUNNE *Chron.* (1810) 51 Hardknoute of Danmark..he was born thralle. c 1430 LYDG. *Chichev. & Byc.* in *Min. Poems* (Percy Soc.) 132 For we ben thralle and they be free. c 1510 BARCLAY *Mirr. Gd. Manners* (1570) D iij, Sparing the Citizens to him subiect and thrall. 1633 HEYWOOD & ROWLEY *Fort. by Land &*

*Sea* IV. Wks. 1874 VI. 418 We now are captives that made others thrall. **1862** BARING-GOULD *Iceland* (1863) 252 Male or female—free or thrall.

(*b*) *fig.*

*a* **1225** *Ancr. R.* 370 Hweðer is betere, ine secnesse uorte beon Godes freo child, þen i flesches heale uorte beon þrel under sunne? *a* **1300** *Cursor M.* 16940 (Cott.) Thoru a tre ..was al mankind mad thrall. **1477** EARL RIVERS (Caxton) *Dictes* 1 To be subgette and thral vnto the stormes of fortune. **1548** UDALL *Erasm. Par. Luke* vi. 75 To be thrall to no vice. *a* **1600** *Scot. Poems 16th C.* (1801) II. 216 Sen word is thrall, and thoght is only free. *a* **1628** F. GREVIL *Mustapha* III. i, Those silly natures, apt to louingnesse, Which euer must in others power liue, With doubt become more fond, with wrong more thral. **1845** E. HOLMES *Mozart* 167 It would seem that he was soon thrall to the court taste.

† **b.** preceding the sb. *Obs.*

**1450–1530** *Myrr. our Ladye* 213 For the delyuerance of hys thrall seruante. **1526** *Pilgr. Perf.* (1531) 208 As thrall synners bounde in captiuite. **1554–9** in *Songs & Ball.* (1860) 3 Beyng slaves to Sathan, and thrall captyves vyle.

† **2.** Belonging to or characteristic of thraldom; slave-like, slavish, servile. *Obs.*

**1398** TREVISA *Barth. De P. R.* II. xii. (1495) b vj b/2 To put of thrall drede & torne to god. **1528** ROY *Rede me* (Arb.) 69 Rid vs from antichristis bondes so thrall. **1535** in Strype *Eccl. Mem.* (1721) I. App. lxiii. 155 To perceive the thral captivity under the usurped power of the Bishop of Rome.

† **Thrall**, *sb.*[2] *Obs.* [app. corruption of *thraw*, THROW *sb.*[1]] A space of time, a while.

*c* **1450** *Cov. Myst.* xxxv. (1841) 351, I pray ȝow alle Abyde stylle a lytyl thralle. **1535** STEWART *Cron. Scot.* (Rolls) II. 522 He..schew to him into that samin thrall, Far moir kyndnes nor ony of thame all.

**Thrall, thrawl** (þrǭl), *sb.*[3] *dial.* Also 7 **throale.** [Origin uncertain: ? an application of THRALL *sb.*[1]] A stand or frame for barrels, milk-pans, etc.

**1674** *Inv.* in *New Shaks. Soc. Trans.* (1881–3) App. II. 14†, In the Sellars..Throales, hogsheads..and Tubbs. *a* **1800** PEGGE *Suppl. Grose*, *Gantril*, a stand for a barrel. North. Called also a *Thrawl*. **1843** *Jrnl. Roy. Agric. Soc.* IV. II. 497 A barrel thrawl, or stillion, of cast-iron, furnished with a..lever apparatus for tilting casks without shaking their contents. **1859** GEO. ELIOT *A. Bede* vi, The dairy thralls, I might ha' wrote my name on 'em. **1884** *Vaughan's Patent* No. 14432 A thrall or stand and tilter for casks.

**Thrall**, *a.*[1]: see THRALL *sb.*[1]

† **Thrall**, *a.*[2] *Obs. rare.* [Etymology obscure.] ? Strenuous, hard, severe.

*c* **1430** *Syr Gener.* (Roxb.) 3947 [Generides] was in hert thral; His shelde he made from him to fall. *c* **1525** in *Rel. Ant.* II. 118 At Beverley a sudden chaunce did falle, The parish church stepille it felle At evynsonge tyme, the chaunce was thralle, Fourscore folke ther was slayn thay telle.

**Thrall** (þrǭl), *v. arch.* [Early ME. *þrallen*, f. THRALL *sb.*[1]] *trans.* To bring into bondage or subjection; to deprive of liberty; to hold in thraldom, enthrall, enslave; to take or hold captive. **a.** *lit.*

*c* **1205** LAY. 11205 He sloh þæ eorles & þrallede þæ chærles. **13..** *Cursor M.* 9485 (Cott.) Quils he es thralled in his seruis He ne mai be fre. *Ibid.* 17209 Þus am i thrald to ma þe fre. *c* **1450** *Mirour Saluacioun* 3311 The childere of Israel be pharao thralde hoegely. *a* **1612** HARINGTON *Ps.* CXXXVII. in Farr *S. P. Eliz.* (1845) I. 116 They that thralle us thus by wrong, Amid our sorrowes aske a song. **1872** TENNYSON *Gareth & Lyn.* 348 Yet lo! my husband's brother had my son Thrall'd in his castle, and hath starved him dead.

**b.** *fig.*

? *a* **1366** CHAUCER *Rom. Rose* 882 The God of Love..can wel these lordis thrallen. *c* **1412** HOCCLEVE *De Reg. Princ.* 4658 He þat auaricious is, is thralled To moneie. *a* **1533** FRITH *Disput. Purg.* Pref. (1829) 91 Fleshly lust..would subdue..and hold us thralled under sin. *a* **1649** DRUMM. OF HAWTH. *Sonn.* I. iv, That bright Cherubine which thralls my Thought. *a* **1651** CALDERWOOD *Hist. Kirk* (1843) II. 391. **1835** *Court Mag.* VI. 216/1 What right had he..to thrall her promise, and waste away her young life?

**c.** *refl.* To enslave, bind, or submit oneself.

*a* **1300** *Cursor M.* 23787 (Edin.) We thrall vs til vr ful fa In prisun for to life in wa. *c* **1412** HOCCLEVE *De Reg. Princ.* 2959 They wolden nat hem to þo lawes thralle.

Hence **Thra·lling** *ppl. a. rare*, enthralling.

**1871** J. HAY *Pike County Ball.* (1880) 88 Wrapped in thralling memories.

**Thralled** (þrǭld), *ppl. a.* [f. prec. vb. + -ED[1].] Made a thrall, enslaved, held in bondage; also *transf.* thrall-like, servile.

**1527** *St. Papers Hen. VIII*, I. 230 For the delyveraunce of Your Grace out of the thraulde, pensif, and dolerous lif that the same is in. *a* **1586** SIDNEY *Arcadia* II. (1622) 103 With the most submissiue behauiour that a thralled heart could expresse. **1665** *Surv. Aff. Netherl.* 179 The English spirit, that prefers an honourable death to a thralled life. **1859** A. MACMILLAN *Lett.* (1908) 11 Italy is the thralled place she is, owing to her indulgence in that luscious enfeebling vein of literature.

**Thraller** (þrǭ·ləɪ). *rare*—⁰. [f. as prec. + -ER[1].] One who enthralls.

**1887** in *Cassell's Encycl. Dict.*

† **Thralless** (þrǭ·lės), *sb. Obs. rare.* [f. THRALL *sb.*[1] + -ESS.] A female thrall; a bondwoman.

**1382** WYCLIF *Deut.* xxviii. 68 There thow shalt be sold to thin enemyes, into thrallis and thrallessis. — *Isa.* xiv. 2 And shal welden hem the hous of Irael..in to thralles and thrallesses [1388 in to seruauntis and hand maidis].

**Thralless** (þrǭ·l,lės), *a.* [f. THRALL *sb.*[1] + -LESS.] Having no thrall; without bondmen.

**1847** in WEBSTER.

† **Thra·llful**, *a. Obs. rare*—¹. [f. THRALL *sb.*[1] + -FUL.] Full of misery: cf. THRALL *sb.*[1] 3.

**1615** SYLVESTER *Job Triumphant* IV. 686 Also the Lord accepted Job, and staid His Thrall-full State.

† **Thra·llhead, -hood.** *Obs.* [f. THRALL *sb.*[1] + -HEAD, -HOOD.] = THRALDOM.

**1297** R. GLOUC. (Rolls) 3013 An place..To wonie þer inne in þralhede vnder þe king. *a* **1300** *Cursor M.* 18372 (Cott.) All þi peple for to bring Vte of thralhed til þi chosling. *a* **1300** *K. Horn* 439 (MS. C) Þanne is mi þralhod [*MSS. L, O*, þralhede] I went in to kniȝthod.

† **Thra·lship.** *Obs.* [See -SHIP.] = THRALDOM.

*c* **1200** *Trin. Coll. Hom.* 37 Þe shepisse and þe netisse men beð under cristes þralshipe. *Ibid.* 101 Ure louerd hadde maked hem fre of þe deules þralsipe. *a* **1400** *R. Glouc.'s Chron.* (Rolls) 1085 (MS. *a*) Þei þou ne askedest þer vppe þralschipe [*MSS. β.* -scheep, *δ.* -schype, *γ.* thralschyppe; *A.* þralhede] euere mo.

**Thraly, Thraness**, var. THROLY, THRONESS.

**Thrammel**, Sc. and dial. variant of TRAMMEL.

**Thraneen**, Irish var. TRANEEN. **Thrang**, pa. t. of THRING *v. Obs.*; Sc. and n. dial. f. THRONG.

**Thranite** (þrǣ·nəit). *Gr. Antiq.* [ad. Gr. θρανίτης, f. θρᾶνος bench.] In the ancient trireme, a rower in one of the tiers, as generally supposed, the uppermost tier, which had the longest oars and hardest work; but the actual arrangement is disputed. Also *attrib.*

**1842** BRANDE *Dict. Sc.* etc., *Thranite*, the uppermost (or, according to some arrangements of the classical galley, the foremost) of the three classes of rowers in an Athenian trireme. **1869** 'W. BRADWOOD' *The O. V. H.* xxx, Look at that tall, sloping-shouldered, brown-bearded thranite. **1894** *Athenæum* 29 Sept. 426/3 If..the oarsmen sat in a rectangular gallery..it would seem to be impossible to have more oarsmen on the thranite bank than on the other banks. **1904** KIPLING *Traffics & Discov.* 38 The thranite now and the thalamite are [steam] pressures low and high.

Hence **Thrani·tic** *a.*, of or pertaining to the thranites.

**1886** WARRE in *Encycl. Brit.* XXI. 807 Supernumerary oars..probably slightly exceeding the thranitic oars in length. *Ibid.*, About the level of the thranitic benches.

**Thrap**, *v.* [Error for or dial. var. of *frap*: cf. TH (6).] *trans.* To bind tightly; = FRAP *v.*[2]

**1813** SOUTHEY *Nelson* I. 150 The hull was so damaged, that it had for some time been secured by having cables served or thrapped round.

**Thrapple**, Sc. dial. form of THROPPLE.

**Thrash** (þræʃ), **thresh** (þreʃ), *v.* Forms: see below. [OE. *þerscan* (pa. t. *þærsc*, *þurscon*, pa. pple. *þorscen*), rarely and late *þrescan*, *þryscan*; a Common Teutonic verb, = OLG. **þerscan* (MLG., MDu., Flem. *derschen*; also MDu., Du., LG. *dorschen*, LG. *drosken*, EFris. *dörsken*); OHG. *dreskan* (MHG., Ger. *dreschen*); ON. *þreskja*, weak vb. (Norw. *treskja*, Da. *tærske*, Sw. *tröska*); Goth. *þriskan* (pa. t. **þrask*, **þruskans*):—OTeut. **þresk-*:—Indo-Eur. **tresk-*, exemplified also in Lith. *traszkėti* to rattle, make a noise, Russ. трескать *treskatĭ* (refl.) to burst, crash, crackle: cf. OSlav. трескъ sb. a crash. The metathesis *þersk-* for *þresk-* is found in OE., LG., Du., and Da. The meaning in OTeut. was prob. 'to tramp or stamp heavily with the feet', including both the action and the noise, as shown by the senses in which the word was taken into Romanic: Prov. *tresc-ar*, *dresc-ar*, It. *tresc-are*, OF. *trescher* to dance, Sp., Pg. *trisc-ar* to make a noise with the feet (see Diez s. v. *trescare*). The word came to be applied esp. to the act of treading out corn by the feet of men or oxen, and thus to the action of threshing by this or any later method. This is the only sense known in Gothic, OHG., and ONorse; but within historical times the chief mode of threshing was beating with the flail, whence the word came to be applied fig. to knocking, beating, or striking generally, and esp. of a person in battle or in punishment. In English this appears already in the OE. period; in German it is later (Grimm). The historical form in Eng. is *thresh*; a dialectal variant *thrash*, faintly represented in early times, came into literary use near the end of the 16th c., and became established in the 17th c., esp. in the sense 'to beat, flog, or belabour', for which it is now the ordinary form, while *thresh* is still largely retained in reference to corn. By this means, *to thresh* (corn) and *to thrash* (an offender or an opponent) have become to a considerable extent differentiated, so as almost to be felt as distinct words, esp. since the use of the flail has become so much superseded by mechanical means. Another form *throsh*, with the vowel of the pa. pple. as in Du. and LG., was frequent in late ME., but is now only dialectal.]

**A.** Illustration of Forms.

**1.** Present stem.

*α.* 1 **þersc(e)an, þirsc-, ðærsc-, ðerhs-, ðearc-, ðearsc-, þearcs-, þrex-, ðryscan**; 3 **þreoschen,** 3–4 **þressh-,** 4 **threisch-, threissch-,** 4–5 **þresch-, þressch-e(n,** 4–6 **thresshe, thresche, -yn, threshe, thresse, -yn,** 5 **thraissh,** 6–7 **threash,** 6– **thresh** (*dial.* 6 **tress, drayse, draysche,** 8–9 **draish, dresh**).

*a* **800** CYNEWULF *Elene* 358 (Gr.) Ða wereȝan neat, þe man ..drifeð and þirsceð. *a* **850** Ðeh ðu þercce [? þersce] [see B. 1]. *c* **897** Ðerscað ðone weall [see B. 4]. *c* **950** *Lindisf. Gosp.* Mark v. 5 Cliopende & ðærscende hine to stanum. *Ibid.* xiv. 65 Ongunnun..mið fystum *vel* dyntum hine ȝeslaa *vel* ȝeðearsca [*c* 975 *Rushw.* ðarsca]. *c* **1000** To þerscenne, *a* **1100** Ðerhsan [see B. 1 b]. *a* **1100** in Napier *O. E. Glosses* 212/1 *Territat*, þearcs. *a* **1100** *Aldhelm Gloss.* I. 3433 ibid. 91/2 *Triturandos*, to þrexen[n]e. *a* **1225** *Ancr. R.* 306 Þet seoruwe þreosche him wiðinne þe heorte. **1377**, **1382**, *c* **1386** Thresche, threshe, threischinge, thresshe, þressche [see B. 1 b]. **14..** *Tretyce* in *W. of Henley's Husb.* (1890) 50 Let yo^r^ threshers be sworne to thresse it clene. *c* **1440** *Promp. Parv.* 492/2 Threschyn, *trituro, flagello.* **1530** PALSGR. 755/2, I thresshe corne in a barne. **15..** Thressyn [see B. 1 b]. **1552** HULOET, Threshe, *flagello*, .. *trituro.* **1570** LEVINS *Manip.* 91/32 To Thresh, *triturare.* **1596** DALRYMPLE tr. *Leslie's Hist. Scot.* I. (S. T. S.) I. 95 Thay thresche na stuf. **1693**, **1764**, etc. Thresh [see B. 1].

*β.* (1 **ðarscan**), 5 **thrassh,** 6– **thrash** (8–9 *dial.* **drash**).

*c* **975** Ðarsca [see *α*, quot. *c* 950[2]]. **1591** SPENSER *M. Hubberd* 264 To..thrash, to thetch, to mowe. **1662** J. DAVIES tr. *Olearius' Voy. Ambass.* 390 The men bring it [corn] into the barn, but the women thrash and sell it. **1746** *Exmoor Scolding* 94 Chell baste tha, chell stram tha, chell drash tha. **1795** WOLCOTT (P. Pindar) *Royal Visit Exeter* II. xiv, He did zo drash about his brain, That was not over stor'd.

*γ.* 5 **throsch(e,** 5–6 **throsh(e, throsshe, throszshe,** (8–9 *dial.* **drosh**).

**14..** *Chaucer's Prol.* 536 (MS. Cambr. Gg 4, 27) He wolde throsche. **1486** [implied in Throsheris: see THRASHER[1] 1]. **1495** *Trevisa's Barth. De P. R.* XVIII. xiv. aa viij b/1 They ledyth them [oxen] abowte vpon corne to breke the strawe in throsshyng and tredynge the flour. **1526** TINDALE 1 *Cor.* ix. 10 He which throssheth in hope shulde be part taker of his hope. **1535** COVERDALE *Hab.* iii. 12 Thou trodest downe the londe..and didest throsshe the Heithen.

**2.** Past tense.

*α.* 1 **ðærsc**, *pl.* **ðurscon, -un (þurcson, þurhsun),** 2 *pl.* **þurscen,** 5 *pl.* **throsshen**; 8–9 *Sc.* **thruish, threush(***ö***).**

*a* **900** *O. E. Martyrol.* 7 Mar. 36 He..corn þærsc ond þæt windwode. *c* **950** *Lindisf. Gosp.* Mark xii. 5 Sume ðurscun oðero æc ofsloȝon. *c* **1000** *Ags. Gosp.* Luke xxii. 64 Þa.. ofer-wruȝon hys ansyne & þurhsun [*v. r.* þurcson, *c* **1160** *Hatton G.* þurscen] his nebb. *c* **1430** *Pilgr. Lyf Manhode* I. lxxiv. (1869) 43 Manye..throsshen it and fanned it. **1815** Threush [B. 3 b]. *Mod. Sc.* He thruish aa' day i' the barn.

*β.* (*weak conj.*) 4–5 **threschéd,** 6 **threashed, (throszshed),** 6– **threshed, thrashed.**

*c* **1400** Threschéd [see B. 4 b]. **1535** COVERDALE 1 *Chron.* xxii. [xxi.] 20 Arnan throszshed wheate. **1560** BIBLE (Genev.) *Judg.* vi. 11 Gideon threashed [**1611** threshed] wheat. **1577** HOLINSHED *Chron.* II. 639/1 Sundrie..came to theyr Barnes, threshed vp theyr grayne. **1633** Thresht [see B. 2].

**3.** Past participle.

*α.* 1 ***þorscen,** 2 **iþor[s]chen;** 3 **i-ðrosschen, (***Orm.***) þrosshenn,** 4 **ithrosshen, i-þrosschen, y-þorsse, throsshe,** 5 **throsshen, (trosshyn),** 6 **throshen,** 9 *Sc.* **thruishen(***ö***).**

*c* **1175** Iþor[s]chen [see B. 2]. *c* **1200** ORMIN 1530 Þa winndwesst tu þin þrosshenn corn. *a* **1225** Iðrosschen [see B. 5]. **1340** Y-þorsse [see B. 1, 4]. **13..** *Propr. Sanct.* (Vernon MS.) in Herrig's *Archiv* LXXXI. 83/26 Hit is brouht hom til a Berne, Hard I-þrosschen in an hurne. **1584** *Shuttleworths' Acc.* (Chetham Soc.) I. 21 When the same [corn] was throshen xiij^d^. *Mod. Sc.* When the last stack was thruishen.

*β.* 5–6 **thresshen,** (5 **(i)thresshe, ythrysshe),** 6 **threshoone,** 7 *Sc.* **threaschin,** 8 *Sc.* **threshen.**

**1426** LYDG. *De Guil. Pilgr.* 5412 Tyl the thressherys.. Hadde thys greyn ythrysshe & bete. *c* **1450** *Godstow Reg.* 649 The corn that is wonyd to be gyf I-thresshe. *c* **1450** *Oseney Reg.* 144, I and myne heyres schall make it to Be thresshe. **1523** FITZHERB. *Husb.* § 13 Whan it is thresshen, there is moche lyght corne. **1599** *Nottingham Rec.* IV. 251 All the corne..threshoone and vnthreshoone. **1629** *Orkney Witch Trial* in *County Folk-Lore* (1903) III. 77 Edward Rendall..said thair was nane [corn] threa[s]chin. **1720** T. BOSTON *Fourfold St.* (1797) 135 The corn of my floor threshen in the floor of wrath.

*γ.* (*weak conj.*) 4 **threschid, threischid,** 6 **(tressyd), thresht(e,** 6– **threshed, thrashed** (7 **thrasht**).

**1382** Threschid [see B. 2]. **1538** in *Lett. Suppress. Monasteries* (Camden) 176 Sum is threshte,..and mych is yit to threshe. **1544** in I. S. Leadam *Sel. Cases Crt. Requests* (1898) 76 The said Baylyf causyd the same pease to be tressyd. *a* **1625** Thrasht [see B. 5 *β*].

**B.** Signification.

**I.** To thresh (thrash) corn, etc. and directly derived senses.

**1.** To separate by any mechanical means, e. g. rubbing, shaking, trampling, stamping, beating, or intermittent pressure, the grains of any cereal from the husks and straw; esp. by beating with a flail; now (from the latter part of the eighteenth century) also by the action of revolving mechanism in a mill or machine. Also, to shake out or separate in the same way the seed of any plant.

The verb was in early times applied to the trampling and stamping of oxen, or the dragging of heavy rugged things, over the corn laid on a smooth surface or 'floor'.

**a.** *trans.*

*α.* *a* **850** *Kentish Gloss.* in Wr.-Wülcker 83/35–7 Ðeh ðu þercce [*for* þersce] swa berecorn ðerccedum [*for* ðerscendum]. *c* **1200** ORMIN 1500 Þa þresshesst tu þin corn wiþþ fleȝȝl. **1340** *Ayenb.* 139 Of þe hyeape of huete y-þorsse, þe cornes byeþ beneþe and þet chef above. *c* **1450** LYDG. *Secrees* 1436 Afftir hervest .. men thresshe shevys. **1530,** **1596** [see A. 1 a]. **1693** EVELYN *De la Quint. Compl. Gard.* II. 163 Cutting off all the Seed stems, and when they are dried, threshing out the Seed. **1764** *Museum Rust.* II. lxxvi. 260 How he lets his corn to thresh by the great. **1845** FORD *Handbk. Spain* I. 25 The modern system of threshing grain in Spain is extremely ancient, classical, and Oriental. **1880** W. NEWTON *Serm. Boys & Girls* (1881) 219 He had a number of men engaged in threshing wheat.

*β.* **1588** SHAKS. *Tit. A.* II. iii. 123 First thrash the Corne, then after burne the straw. **1603** HOLLAND *Plutarch's Mor.* 1008 Husbandmen are affraid to thrash their wheat upon a dry and sandy floore, because of ants. **1662** [see A. 1 *β*]. **1846** *J. Baxter's Libr. Pract. Agric.* (ed. 4) II. 337 The [turnip] seed may then be .. stacked and thrashed when wanted. **1877** KNIGHT *Dict. Mech.* 2555/2 Doura, sorghum, or flax was thrashed by drawing across a comb-like instrument.

**b.** *absol.* or *intr.*

*a.* *c* **1000** *Ælfric's Voc.* in Wr.-Wülcker 147/14 *Area*, breda þiling, *uel* flor on to þerscenne. *a* **1100** *Gerefa* in *Anglia* (1886) IX. 261 Mænige inweorc wyrcean, ðerhsan, wudu cleofan. *a* **1300** *Cursor M.* 4744 (Cott.) Ioseph þat was ful o pite Did thresche [*v.rr.* þresshe, threche] son in þat contre. **1377** LANGL. *P. Pl.* B. v. 553 Some tyme I sowe and some tyme I thresche. **1382** WYCLIF *Micah* iv. 13 Ryse thou, and threshe, douȝter of Syon. — 1 *Cor.* ix. 9 Thou schalt not bynde the mouth of the oxe threischinge [1388 that threischith]. *c* **1386** CHAUCER *Prol.* 536 He wolde thresshe [*v.rr.* throsche, þressche] and ther to dyke and delue. **15..** *Ragman Roll* 53 in Hazl. *E. P. P.* I. 72 Who so lyst may thressyn in your berne. **1758** JOHNSON *Idler* No. 70 ▸ 10 He, whose task is to reap and thresh.

*β.* **1591** [see A. 1 *β*]. **1755** JOHNSON, To thrash, *v.n.*

**c.** *intr.* for *pass.* Of corn: To bear threshing; to be threshed.

**1760** R. BROWN *Compl. Farmer* II. 72 The weeds..will.. cause it [rye] not to thrash well. *Ibid.* 81.

**2.** *fig.*; in earlier use sometimes with reference to ancient modes of threshing. *To thresh* (*thrash*) *straw*, to work at what is unproductive or unprofitable; also *to thresh over old straw*.

*c* **1175** *Lamb. Hom.* 85 In þe deie of liureisun hwense god almihtin wule windwin þet er wes iþor[s]chen. **1382** WYCLIF *Isa.* xxv. 10 Threschid shal ben Moab vnder hym, as ben to-treden strawes in a wayn. **1633** P. FLETCHER *Purple Isl.* XI. xxiv, She..Drove farre their flying troops, and thresht with iron flail. **1777** GARRICK *Prol. Sheridan's Sch. Scand.* 11 All night at cards when threshing Strong tea and scandal. **1857** PUSEY *Real Presence* i. (1869) 144 Bruick said,..'as to the King himself [Hen. VIII] it was to thresh an empty ear'. **1871** B. TAYLOR *Faust* (1875) I. iv. 73 Why plague thyself with threshing straw forever? *a* **1876** *Binorie O an Binorie* iii. in Child *Ballads* I. (1882) 133/1 O sister, O sister, will ye go to the dams, To hear the blackbird thrashin oer his songs?

**b.** *To thresh* (*thrash*) *out* (*a subject*, etc.), to discuss (a matter) exhaustively, to argue thoroughly; to get at the truth of (a question) by discussion or argument.

**1882** PEBODY *Eng. Journalism* xxiii. 186 There is hardly a question..that is not now completely thrashed out in the Press long before it reaches Parliament. **1884** *Law Times* 15 Mar. 353/1 Every case thoroughly thrashed out. **1885** SIR C. S. C. BOWEN in *Law Rep.* 29 Ch. Div. 810 That point had been threshed out before Mr. Justice Pearson. **1893** *Spectator* 18 Mar. 349 The matter should have been thoroughly threshed out.

**3.** *transf.* To beat or strike as with a flail: see quots. and cf. 5.

*a.* **1573** TUSSER *Husb.* (1878) 180 At Shroftide to shrouing, go thresh the fat hen. **1707** J. STEVENS tr. *Quevedo's Com. Wks.* (1709) R ij, Condemn'd to thresh the Sea, that is to the Gallies. **1867** F. FRANCIS *Angling* v. (1880) 153 The angler goes on threshing the water.

*β.* **1638** SIR T. HERBERT *Trav.* (ed. 2) 171 Swarms of Gnats, Mus-ke-toes, and such like.., stung and pesterd us..; they biting us, we thrashing them like mad folks. **1697** DRYDEN *Virg. Past.* II. 73 Myself will..thrash the Chesnuts in the Neighb'ring Grove. **1823** F. COOPER *Pioneers* i, The black ..began thrashing his arms together, in order to restore the circulation.

**b.** *intr.* To deliver or inflict blows as with a flail; to strike or beat *on* or *at*. (With quot. 1693 cf. BEAT *v.*[1] 26 b.)

**1693** DRYDEN *Juvenal's Sat.* x. 194, I rather wou'd be Mævius, thrash for Rhimes Like his,..Than that Philippique ..should be mine. **1815** G. BEATTIE *John o' Arnha'* (1826) 33 He scourg'd the water wi' his tail, An' threush on John as wi' a flail. **1905** F. YOUNG *Sands Pleas.* III. ii, Richard ..walked out of the graveyard, threshing at the nettles with his stick.

†**4.** *trans.* To beat, batter, strike, knock. Also *fig. Obs.* exc. as in 3.

*c* **897** K. ÆLFRED *Gregory's Past. C.* xxi. 160 Send ðærto ȝefylceo, & ðerscað ðone weall mid rammum. *a* **950** *Rituale Eccl. Dunelm.* (Surtees) 6 Svæ ic fehto no svoelce lyft ðerscende [*non quasi æram* (Vulg. *aerem*) *verberans*]. *a* **1000** *Sal. & Sat.* (Kemble) 148 Se ðunor hit ðrysceð mid ðære fyrenan æcxe. **1340** *Ayenb.* 266 Vram þo lyȝte byeþ y-þorsse mine eȝen. *a* **1400-50** *Alexander* 1326 He laschis out a lange swerde..Threschis doun in a thrawe many threuyn dukis.

†**b.** *intr.* To strike, inflict blows *on*. *Obs.*

**13..** *Gaw. & Gr. Knt.* 2300 Wy þresch on, þou þro mon, þou þretez to longe. *c* **1400** *Laud Troy Bk.* 16912 Echon on other dong & thresched.

**II.** To beat a person, an army, etc. Now commonly **thrash.**

**5.** *trans.* To beat by way of punishment; to chastise by or as by beating; to flog, orig. with a stick, cudgel, whip, etc.; in mod. use also to pommel with the fists. Also *transf.* and *fig.*

*a.* *a* **950** *Rituale Eccl. Dunelm.* (Surtees) 43 Ðv ðe rehtlice ðv ðersces synfvllo [*qui juste verberas peccatores*]. *a* **1225** *Ancr. R.* 186 Hendi children þet cusseð þe ȝerden þet he haueð ou mid iðrosschen. *a* **1400** *Octouian* 764 With a staf Y wol the thressche. **1647** TRAPP *Comm. Epistles* 366 Gideon by threshing the men of Succoth, taught them [etc.]. **1806-7** J. BERESFORD *Miseries Hum. Life* XXI. xvii, Learning to box, too—i.e. feeing a great raw-boned fellow to thresh you as long as he can stand over you.

*β.* *a* **1625** FLETCHER *Nice Valour* III. iii, Oh gentlemen y'are welcom: I have been thrasht i' faith. .. Never was Shrove-tuesday Bird So cudgel'd gentlemen. **1733** FIELDING *Mock Doctor* iv, Take a good cudgel, and thrash him with it. **1739** 'R. BULL' tr. *Dedekindus' Grobianus* 168 A Wife, an Ass, a Walnut-tree ('tis thought) Except they're thrash'd, are never good for ought. **1833** MARRYAT *P. Simple* x, O'Brien..was very kind to me in general, and allowed nobody to thrash me but himself. **1866** GEO. ELIOT *F. Holt* i, I always meant to..thrash a lord or two who thrashed me at Eton. **1885** *Manch. Exam.* 11 Nov. 3/3 The deacon..thrashes him for wasting his time.

**b.** In colloq. phrases, as *to thrash one's jacket*, *to thrash the life out of* (cf. BEAT *v.*[1] 15).

**1687** T. BROWN *Saints in Uproar* Wks. 1730 I. 74 I'll substantially thrash your jacket for you. **1873** BLACK *Pr. Thule* xvii, If you were half-a-dozen years older, I would thrash the life out of you.

**6.** To beat completely or thoroughly (BEAT *v.*[1] 10); to defeat or overcome with severe loss in war or fighting, or *at* a game or contest.

*a.* **1606** SHAKS. *Tr. & Cr.* II. i. 50 Thou scuruy valiant Asse, thou art heere but to thresh Troyans. **1721** AMHERST *Terræ Fil.* No. 13. (1754) 66 They could either thresh corn, or their country's enemies.

*β.* **1778** LADY SARAH LENNOX *Lett.* (1901) I. 279 Send them home to thrash the French. **1796** NELSON in Nicolas *Disp.* (1845) II. 256, I shall..take my chance of helping to thrash Don Langara. **1841** LEVER *C. O'Malley* lxxii, We had been attacked by the French in force and devilishly well thrashed. **1863** KINGSLEY *Water Bab.* i, [He] could have thrashed Mr. Grimes himself in fair fight. **1890** 'R. BOLDREWOOD' *Col. Reformer* (1891) 276 The Colonel..has just been thrashing me at billiards. **1903** *Westm. Gaz.* 14 Apr. 2/3 [incident of June 1815] It touched land, and a man jumped out waving his hat and exclaiming, 'Hurrah, Wellington has thrashed Boney!'

**III.** Transferred uses, often referring to both I and II. Usually **thrash.**

**7.** *intr. Naut.* To force or work one's way against opposing wind, tide, etc.; = BEAT *v.*[1] 19; said of a ship or of mariners. Also *trans.* with *way*.

*a.* **1857** DUFFERIN *Lett. High Lat.* v. (ed. 3) 28 We had to return..to our old practice of threshing to windward.

*β.* **1830** COL. HAWKER *Diary* (1893) II. 15 Hard labour to ..thrash for an hour through blocks of ice before we could get out. **1855** KINGSLEY *Westw. Ho* xx, The ship thrashed close-hauled through the rolling seas. **1890** CLARK RUSSELL *Marriage at Sea* xiii, The steamer was thrashing through it at an exhilarating speed. **1900** *Daily News* 15 Oct. 6/7 The Nuddea encountered the typhoon some distance to the southward of Hong Kong, and..had to thrash her way through it.

**b.** *trans.* To force (a ship) forward, esp. against contrary wind or sea. Cf. BEAT *v.*[1] 19 d.

*a.* **1886** *Daily Tel.* 23 Apr. 2/1 The captain threshes his great structure through the deep.

*β.* **1891** KIPLING *Light that Failed* xv. 310 The screw began to thrash the ship along the Docks. **1893** — *Many Invent.* 365 Carry on and thrash her out with all she'll stand.

**8.** *intr.* To make wild movements like those of a flail or a whip; to lash out; to throw oneself (or itself) to and fro with violence; to toss, plunge; of hair, branches, or anything free at one end: to flap, whip, lash. Also *trans.* (*refl.*) with *into*.

**1850** SCORESBY *Cheever's Whalem. Adv.* v. (1858) 74 [A whale] blindly thrashed and rolled about in great agony. **1875** LD. SHAFTESBURY in *Life* (1886) III. xxxiii. 354 He [a preacher] thrashed with his arms, as though he were about to strike. **1883** C. F. HOLDER in *Harper's Mag.* Jan. 186/2 The shark squirmed out, thrashing about and snapping its jaws. **1891** KIPLING *Light that Failed* i. 13 A night-wind thrashed along the bents of the foreshore. *Ibid.* xiii. 244 The red-haired girl threshed distressfully across the sheets. **1896** *Boston* (Mass.) *Jrnl.* 11 Jan. 4/8 The wounded bears were kicking and thrashing around me. **1897** CROCKETT *Lad's Love* xxiii, The wind unloosed the banded hair and blew it about.., till it threshed in the man's face and annoyed him. **1900** N. MUNRO in *Blackw. Mag.* Nov. 656/1 They saw the boughs thrash and the tree tops rise and fall like billows round the village.

*refl.* **1865** BUSHNELL *Vicar. Sacr.* III. v. (1868) 327 A broken engine by running will only thresh itself into a more complete wreck.

Hence **Thrashed, threshed** *ppl. a.*

[*c* **1200** Þrosshenn corn: see A. 3 *a*.] **1707** MORTIMER *Husb.* (1721) I. 147 They..put some of the Chaff in first, and then their thrashed Wheat. **1805** DICKSON *Pract. Agric.* I. 48 A large quantity of thrashed grain is seldom kept. **1867** F. FRANCIS *Angling* vi. (1880) 193 One of our well-threshed streams.

**Thrash, thresh,** *sb.*[1] [f. prec. vb.]

†**1.** ? A threshing implement, a flail: cf. THRESHEL.

**1669** PENN *No Cross* xviii. § 10 (1682) 368 That the Cart, the Plough, the Thrash should be in that continual Severity laid upon Nineteen parts of the Land, to feed the inordinate Lusts and delicious Appetites of the Twentieth.

**2.** An act or the action of thrashing or threshing; a blow, stroke, knock; a beat or beating.

**1840** HOOD *Kilmansegg, Fancy Ball* iii, Tories like to worry the Whigs,..Giving them lashes, thrashes, and digs. **1898** *Blackw. Mag.* Sept. 376 It [a boat's progress] was a long monotonous thresh for the rest of the afternoon. **1899** CROCKETT *Black Douglas* xlii. 305 The thresh of the rain upon the lattice casement. **1902** J. MASEFIELD *Salt-Water Ball., D Avalos' Prayer* iii, The wash and thresh of the sea-foam. **1906** *Outlook* 20 Oct. 511/2 A thrash of rain.

**b.** *fig.* A dash.

**1870** J. K. HUNTER *Life Stud. Charac.* xxxv, I appeared in the court..wi' a thrash, and had the case settled in a jiffy.

**c.** In reduplicated form *thresh-thresh*, representing the continuous sound of threshing.

**1904** *Blackw. Mag.* Apr. 485 A rhythmic thresh-thresh that had accompanied but hardly broken the silence, suddenly ceased.

**Thrash, thresh,** *sb.*[2] *Sc.* Also 7 **thrush.** [corrupt. of *rash*, *resh*, OE. *risc*, RUSH *sb.*[1]] A rush. Also *attrib.*, **thresh-bush**, a clump of rushes.

**1697** CLELAND *Poems* 30 (Jam.) Their bare preaching now Makes the thrush-bush keep the cow. **1795** A. WILSON *Spouter* in *Poems & Lit. Prose* (1876) II. 335 Green thrashes were strewed on the floor. **1822** R. WILSON *Poems, Twa Mice* (E.D.D.), Wi' their teeth green threshes chackit. **1850** J. STRUTHERS *Life* vi. Poet. Wks. I. p. cxiv, The shelter of a few well-grown thresh-bushes. **1871** H. S. RIDDELL *Poet. Wks.* II. 127 (E.D.D.) Threshes formed the theekin.

**Thrashel**, dial. form of THRESHEL.

**Thrasher**[1], **thresher** (þræ·ʃəɹ, þre·ʃəɹ). Forms: see THRASH *v.*; also 6-7 **tres(s)her.** [f. THRASH, THRESH *v.* + -ER[1].] One who or that which thrashes or threshes.

**1.** One who separates grain from the straw by beating with a flail, or otherwise. (More usually spelt *thresher*.)

**1380** in Thorold Rogers *Oxford City Doc.* (1891) 39 *De Waltero* le thressher. *c* **1400** *Laud Troy Bk.* 9333 Echon on other ffaste doth bete, Ryght as threscheres doth on whete. *c* **1440** *Promp. Parv.* 492/2 Threschare, *triturator*, *flagellator*. **1486** *Bk. St. Albans* F vj b, A Thraue of Throsheris. **1535** COVERDALE *Isa.* xxi. 10 O my felowe throsshers and fanners. **1593** SHAKS. 3 *Hen. VI*, II. i. 131 A lazie Thresher with a Flaile. **1616** SURFL. & MARKH. *Country Farme* 18 Your Barne, with his great dore..to giue light to the Threshers. **1632** MASSINGER *City Madam* II. ii, To sit like a fool at home, and eye your thrashers. **1641** BEST *Farm. Bks.* (Surtees) 143 Others..give to theire thrashers 5d. a quarter for oates. **1707** MORTIMER *Husb.* (1721) I. 36 A good Thrasher can thrash out but about six Gallons in a Day. **1784** COWPER *Task* I. 356 We may discern the thresher at his task. Thump after thump resounds the constant flail. **1859** JEPHSON *Brittany* iii. 23 The threshers..struck the corn alternately. **1864** H. AINSWORTH *John Law* v. ix, I lays about me right and left like a thrasher.

**b.** (*a*) Each of the beaters in a threshing-machine. (*b*) A threshing-machine.

**1805** DICKSON *Pract. Agric.* I. 30 If the unthrashed corn goes in sideways or irregularly, the thrashers can have but little power upon it. **1877** KNIGHT *Dict. Mech.* 2554/1 Meikle..invented a machine in 1786, which is the type of modern thrashers. **1884** *Manchester Exam.* 30 Sept. 5/7 Teams of horses draw the corn to the thrasher. **1891** T. HARDY *Tess* xlvii, The hum of the thresher..increased to a raving whenever the supply of corn fell short of the regular quantity.

**2.** A sea-fox or fox-shark, *Alopias vulpes*; so called from the very long upper division of the tail, with which it lashes an enemy. Also called *thresher-* or *thrasher-fish*, *-shark*.

*a.* **1609** *Newes fr. Bermudas* July, in Force *Hist. Tracts* II. 22 The Threasher keepeth above him, & with a mighty great thing like unto a flaile, hee so bangeth the whale, that hee will roare as though it thundered. **1630** DONNE *Progr. Soul* 351 The Flail-finn'd Thresher, and steel-beak'd Sword-fish. **1758** BORLASE *Nat. Hist. Cornw.* xxiii. § 3. 265 The sea-fox, *Vulpecula*, or *Simia marina*..; this shark we call the Thresher, from the motion of its long fox-like tail with which it strikes or threshes its larger and less agile enemy the grampus. **1845** GOSSE *Ocean* iii. (1849) 146 Another Shark, often called the Thresher,..is said to use its muscular tail..to inflict terrible slaps on the Whale.

*β.* **1638** DAVENANT *Madagascar* Wks. (1673) 206 The martiall Musick might incite The Sword-fish, Thrasher, and the Whale to fight. **1712** E. COOKE *Voy. S. Sea* 173 The Spaniards say the Thrashers and Sword-Fishes often kill the Whales. **1860** J. COUCH *Brit. Fishes* I. 38 Instances are reported where a Sword fish on the one hand and a Thrasher on the other, have persecuted a large Whale.

**3.** One who thrashes or beats another.

**1907** *Daily Chron.* 21 Mar. 5/5 A Bill..introduced..into the Legislature of Pennsylvania legalising the thrashing of editors..who wrongfully comment on individuals. The Bill makes the proof of publication of a libel a complete defence if the editor sues the thrasher for assault and battery.

**4.** *attrib.* and *Comb.*, as *thresher-fish*, *-shark* = 2; **thresher-** or **thrasher-whale**, a grampus or killer, as *Orca gladiator*.

**1865** DE MORGAN in *Athenæum* No. 1981. 504/2 As the thresher-fish behaves towards the whale. **1888** *Ayr Advertiser* 5 July 6 A very large specimen of the fox or 'thresher' shark was recently caught..at Port-na-Luing. **1905** *Daily Chron.* 5 July 6/6 A thrasher whale, measuring 10ft., and weighing 2 cwt. **1906** *Ibid.* 11 June 5/5 Three Southwold fishermen have secured in the bay a thresher fish.

**Thrasher**[2] (þræ·ʃəɹ). Also **thresher, thrusher.** [Perh. a survival of *thrusher*, *thresher*, an Eng. dialectal name of the THRUSH (*Turdus musicus*), in U. S. assimilated to prec.; but chronological evidence is wanting.

Cf. **1881** *Oxfordsh. Gloss., Suppl.* (E.D.S.), *Thresher* or *Thrusher*, a thrush.]

A bird of the North American genus *Harporhynchus*, resembling the Song Thrush; esp. *H.* († *Turdus*) *fuscus*, the best known of the species, of the north-eastern U. S., called also *brown thrasher*, *brown thrush*

1808–14 A. Wilson *Amer. Ornith.* (1832) I. 233 The Brown Thrush, or Thrasher, of the middle and eastern states. *Ibid.* 235 The Thrasher is a welcome visitant in spring. 1845 S. Judd *Margaret* i. vi, She sings round after dark, like a thrasher. 1883 Newton in *Encycl. Brit.* XVI. 541/1 Known in the United States as Threshers..very Thrush-like in their habits. 1896 — *Dict. Birds* 958 *Thrasher, Thresher*, or *Thrusher*,..a bird well known in the eastern part of North America, the *Turdus fuscus* of the older and *Harporhynchus fuscus* of later ornithologists.

**Thrashing, threshing** (þræ·ʃiŋ, þre·ʃiŋ), *vbl. sb.* [f. Thrash, thresh *v.* + -ing [1].] The action of the verb Thrash or thresh in various senses. (For the status of the spellings, see the vb.)

I. 1. Beating with or as with a flail; *esp.* the separation of grain from the straw by beating or otherwise.

1382 Wyclif *Hos.* x. 11 Effraym a cow calf, tauȝt for to loue thresshyng. 1393 Langl. *P. Pl.* C. ix. 199 In þresshynge, in þecchynge, in thwytynge of pynnes. 1601 Holland *Pliny* xviii. xxx. I. 602 The good redbearded wheat Far..commeth hardly out of the huske, and asketh some painefull thrashing. 1877 Talmage *Serm.* 378 In Grace, as in farming, there is a time for threshing. 1898 *Westm. Gaz.* 31 Jan. 2/1 No break or variety in the low, dark clouds, or the steady threshing of the rain.

b. That which is threshed; the grain obtained by threshing.

1382 Wyclif *Isa.* xxi. 10 My thressing, and the doȝter of my cornflor. 1898 *Westm. Gaz.* 21 Apr. 2/1 The British farmer who has not yet sold last year's thrashing will thus reap the benefit of the higher prices.

II. 2. Beating or flogging, esp. by way of punishment; an instance of this. (Regularly *thrashing*.)

1843 Bethune *Sc. Fireside Stor.* 111 The benefit of the instructions and thrashings of..the parish schoolmaster. 1863 P. Barry *Dockyard Econ.* 53 Gifts of that kind..are viewed in the light of schoolboy indulgences after a severe thrashing. 1875 A. R. Hope *Schoolboy Friends* 80 I'll give you the greatest thrashing you ever had.

b. A defeat in battle or in any contest.

1815 Ld. Apsley in Stocqueler *Wellington* (1853) II. App. 340, I think the French will get such a thrashing as they have seldom had. 1885 *L'pool Daily Post* 1 June 5/4 The county suffered a 'one innings' thrashing [at cricket] at the hands of their antagonists.

3. *transf.*: see senses 7 and 8 of the verb.

1886 R. C. Leslie *Sea Painter's Log* 115 Much thrashing to and fro in the chops of the Channel. 1895 *Outing* (U.S.) XXVII. 50/1, I knew from the thrashing going on..that the game was mine.

4. *attrib.* and *Comb.*, as *thrashing-* or *threshing-barn, -flail*, etc.

1382 Wyclif *Gen.* l. 10 Thei camen to the thresshyng feelde of Adad. 1560 Bible (Genev.) *Amos* i. 3 Thei haue threshed Gilead with threshing instruments of yron. 1609 Bible (Douay) *Isa.* xli. 15, I have made thee as a new threshing wayne, having teeth like a saw. 1812 Sir J. Sinclair *Syst. Husb. Scot.* i. 15 The threshing-barn..must be sufficiently spacious to contain one stack of grain in the straw. *Ibid.* 72 The threshing-mill has generally one set of fanners attached to it, driven by a belt from the end of the axle of the threshing drum. 1844 Stephens *Bk. Farm* II. 267 No corn should be presented until the mill has acquired its proper momentum, the *thrashing-motion*, as it is termed. 1865 Miss Cary *Ball. & Lyrics* 140 The..farmer-boy Who cut my name upon his thrashing-flail. 1877 Knight *Dict. Mech.* 2557/1 Rollers which carry the grain in the straw from the feed-board to the thrashing cylinder.

**Thra·shing, thre·shing**, *ppl. a.* [f. as prec. + -ing [2].] That thrashes or threshes; *esp.* that threshes corn, etc. In quot. 1706 in sense 'great', 'big': cf. Thumping *ppl. a.*

1591 *Troub. Raigne K. John* (1611) 28 Base heardgroom, coward, peasant, worse than a threshing slaue. 1670 Eachard *Cont. Clergy* 71 He observes, that the worm Jacob was a threshing worm [cf. Isa. xli. 14, 15]. 1706 E. Ward *Wooden World Diss.* (1708) 30 In one Twelve-Month he comes to be an able, roaring, threshing Fellow. 1887 G. Meredith *Ballads & P.* 74 Chosen warriors, keen and hard; Grains of threshing battle-dints.

**Thra·shing-, thre·shing-floor.** A prepared hard level surface on which corn is threshed: cf. Floor *sb.*[1] 6.

α. 1398 Trevisa *Barth. De P. R.* xvii. clvi. (Bodl. MS.), Þe greyne þat is loweste in þe þresschinge floore is beste to sede. *Ibid.* clxxv, Feeldes and þresschinge flores. 1611 Bible *Gen.* l. 10 They came to the threshing floore [1885 *Revised* threshing-floor] of Atad. 1839 Longfellow *Village Blacksmith* iv, The burning sparks that fly Like chaff from a threshing-floor.

β. 1697 Dryden *Virg. Georg.* i. 278 In vain the Hind shall vex the Thrashing-floor, For empty Chaff and Straw will be thy Store. 1805 Dickson *Pract. Agric.* I. 47 The size of the thrashing-floors of barns must vary according to circumstances.

**Thra·shing-, thre·shing-machi·ne.** A power-driven machine for separating grain or other seed from the straw or husk. Also in *Comb.*

α. 1812 Sir J. Sinclair *Syst. Husb. Scot.* i. 78 Oxen are at least equal..to horses, for working threshing-machines. 1812 *Examiner* 21 Dec. 813/1 W. Forrest, Shiffnal, Salop, threshing-machine-maker. 1848 Mill *Pol. Econ.* i. ix. § 4 It may not answer to a small farmer to own a threshing machine, for the small quantity of corn he has to thresh.

β. 1797 *Encycl. Brit.* (ed. 3) XVIII. 505/2 The first thrashing machine attempted in modern times..was invented in Edinburgh..about the year 1732. 1834–6 Barlow in *Encycl. Metrop.* (1845) VIII. 92/1 Where the thrashing machine supplies the place of the flail. 1861 *Times* 24 Sept., The fine farm-steading, with its stalls, barns, 12-horse fixed steam engine, thrashing machine, saw-mill, bone-mill, &c.

**Thra·shing-, thre·shing-mill.** A fixed threshing-machine; usually, one driven by water or wind power (though the name was also given to those driven by a horizontal wheel drawn round by horses or oxen).

1797 *Encycl. Brit.* (ed. 3) XVIII. 506/1 Such was the thrashing mill invented by Mr. Michael Stirling..1758. 1816 J. Scott *Vis. Paris* (ed. 5) 308 The Scotch threshing mill seems to be entirely unknown in France. 1825 J. Nicholson *Operat. Mechanic* 86 A considerable fall of water..used to give motion to a thrashing mill. 1902 R. C. Maclagan *Evil Eye in W. Highl.* 64 They had no threshing-mill and did it all with flails.

**Thraskist, -ite**, obs. ff. Traskist, -ite.

‖ **Thraso** (þrēi·so). Pl. **-os, -oes**, also as L., **Thrasones** (-ōu·nīz). [L., ad. Gr. Θράσων, name of a braggart soldier in Terence's *Eunuchus*, f. θρασ-ύς bold, spirited.] A braggart, a boaster.

[1563 B. Googe *Eglogs* (Arb.) 85 In Countreye Venus hath defecte, In Countreye Thraso hath no grace.] *a* 1576 Pilkington *Expos. Nehem.* iv. 14 (1585) 62 b, These big boasting Thrasones and vaunting *Milites gloriosi*. 1580 Hollyband *Treas. Fr. Tong*, *Vn Tevot*, a Thraso. 1650 French tr. *Sandivogius' Alchymie* Pref. A iij b, Vapouring Thrasoes or Letter-learned scoffers. 1716 Bolingbroke *Refl. on Exile* (1777) 351 Philosophy has her Thrasos as well as war.

**Thrasonic** (þrĕsǫ·nik), *a.* [f. L. *Thrasōn-*, stem of Thraso + -ic.] = next.

1657 H. Pinnell *Philos. Ref.* 154 With a..Thrasonick boasting they brag that they can perfectly cure all diseases. 1778 Jefferson *Corr.* Wks. 1859 I. 207 Thrasonic accounts of victories they have never won. 1843 *Blackw. Mag.* LIV. 52 The last extravagance of thrasonic and impotent national arrogance. 1903 *Contemp. Rev.* Aug. 178 The 'Thrasonic' verbiage of German nautical enthusiasts.

**Thrasonical** (þrĕsǫ·nikăl), *a.* [f. as prec. + -al: see -ical.] Resembling Thraso or his behaviour; given to or marked by boasting; bragging, boastful, vainglorious.

1564 Coverdale tr. *Ridley* in *Lett. Mart.* 76 In comparison of this Thrasonicall and glorious ostentation. 1590 [see Gnathonical]. 1600 Shaks. *A. Y. L.* v. ii. 34 Cesars Thrasonicall bragge of I came, saw, and ouercame. 1755 Carte *Hist. Eng.* IV. 130 *note*, It is too thrasonical to deserve any credit. 1877 Morley *Crit. Misc.* Ser. ii. 374 Ocular arrogance, and a rather too thrasonical complacency. 1893 McCarthy *Dictator* II. x. 3 Unlike the ordinary soldier of fortune, he was not in the least thrasonical.

Hence **Thraso·nically** *adv.*, in a thrasonical manner.

1591 Greene *Farewell to Folly* Wks. (Grosart) IX. 249 Such..as Thrasonically countenance themselues wt the title of a souldior. 1626 L. Owen *Spec. Jesuit.* (1629) 59 These ..fathers doe very Thrasonically brag, that their society or order, was diuinely ordained. 1755 Johnson s.v. *Rodomontade*, To brag thrasonically, to boast like Rodomonte. 1862 Beveridge *Hist. India* II. v. viii. 509 General Stuart ..had rashly and thrasonically pledged himself, that..'the army might and must move'.

† **Thra·sonism.** *Obs. rare.* [f. L. *Thrasōn-*, stem of Thraso + -ism.] Thrasonic conduct; boastfulness. So † **Thra·sonist**, a boaster, a swaggerer; † **Thra·sonize** *v. intr.* (in quot. const. with *it*), to play the Thraso, to boast, brag.

1596 Nashe *Saffron-Walden* Wks. (Grosart) III. 200 Hath he (as with his Thrasonisme) infected them all with his methode of Lenuoyes, Post-scripts and Preambles. 1619 H. Hutton *Follie's Anat.* 48 Warres austere God, with stout Achilles lance..doth Thrasonize it, rage. 1626 T. H[awkins] *Caussin's Holy Crt.* 74 These little Thrasonists are no sooner out of the shell, but instantly they establish a iurisdiction in the family.

**Thrassel**, obs. form of Throstle.

**Thrast, -e**, early var. and pa. t. of Threst *v.*

**Thrat, thratte, -en**, obs. pa. t. of Threat *v.*

**Thratch**, dial. variant of Fratch *v.* and *sb.*

**Thratle, thrattell, thrattle**, obs. ff. Throttle.

**Thrau(e, thrauwe**, obs. forms of Throw *v.*

† **Thrau·pis.** *Obs.* [a. Gr. θραυπίς.] A species of finch mentioned by Aristotle as feeding on thistles; generally taken to be the Siskin.

1600 Surflet *Countrie Farme* vii. lxx. 900 The *Thraupis* [F. *tarin*] is of the continuance of sixe yeeres or there about, according as she is kept better or woorse...Her singing is but yrkesome and tedious. 1910 Thompson tr. *Aristotle's Hist. Anim.* 592 The following and the like feed on thistles; to wit, the linnet, the thraupis, and the goldfinch.

**Thrave, threave** (þrēiv, þrīv). Chiefly *Sc.* and *north. Eng.* Forms: α. 1 *pl.* þreues; 4–6, 9 threve, 5 threfe, 6 threff, threif(f, threafe, 7 *Sc.* thref, 8 *Sc.* threive, 9 *Sc.* thrief, thrieve, 7– threave. β. 5 *Sc.* thraf, 5–6 thraue, thrafe, *north.* thrawe, 6 thrayf, thravffe, *Sc.* thraif, 9 thraive, 5– thrave. γ. *Sc.* and *north.* 3 traue, 5 trawe, 6 (9 *dial.*) trave, 9 *dial.* traeve. [Of Scandinavian origin; in α, a. West Scand. **þrefi*, Icel. *þrefi*, Norw. *treve, træve*; in β, a. East Scand. **þrafe*, MSw. *þrave*, Sw. *trafve*, Da. *trave* (whence NFris. (Sylt.) *traav*). **þrefe* and **þrafe* were prob. ablaut variants.]

1. Two shocks or stooks of corn (or pulse), generally containing twelve sheaves each, but varying in different localities; hence used as a measure of straw, fodder, etc.

α. 963–84 in Birch *Cart. Sax.* III. 367 Swa man ær simle dide tioþunge æt ælcere sylh an foðer cornes þe eahte þreues cornes on weron. 1483 *Cath. Angl.* 384/2 (MS. A.) A Threfe [*v.r.* thrave] of corne, *traua*. 1512–13 *Durham Acc. Rolls* (Surtees) 106 Pro xl threff straminis. 1556 *Records of Elgin* (N. Spalding Cl.) I. 30 The threafe or fodder, viij d. 1572 in *Reg. Mag. Sig. Scot.* 1576. 708/2 For ane threif of custome stray. 1618–19 *N. Riding Rec.* II. 189 A Thirske woman presented for stealing six threaves of Hempe value 10/. 1716 *Parochial Rec. Stonehouse* 17 July, To cause pull sixtie threive of heather for thatching. 1812 Sir J. Sinclair *Syst. Husb. Scot.* i. 330 A threave of wheat, consisting of twenty-eight sheaves, each sheaf measuring thirty inches round,..a threave of barley, oats, or pease, of twenty-four sheaves, each thirty inches round. 1822 *Lights & Shadows of Sc. Life* 214 (Jam.), I have thrashed a few thrieves in the minister's barn. 1851 *Jrnl. R. Agric. Soc.* XII. i. 129 An acre of good oats generally averages 32 threves (768 sheaves).

β. 1423 *Act 2 Hen. VI*, c. 2 *Endowé..dun Thrave des blees aprendre annuelment de chescun charue*...Endowed ..of a thraue of corn to be taken yerely of euery ploughe. *c* 1462 *Wright's Chaste Wife* 245 A thrafe of flex. 1537 *Stanlowe Cell Inv.* (Publ. Rec. Office), vj Thrayf of vnthrashen Barlycorne. 1551 in *Wills & Inv. N. C.* (Surtees) I. 134 A c. thrave of wheit and rye at ijs. vjd. a thrave. 1584 *Shuttleworths' Acc.* (Chetham Soc.) 19 Eighte thravffe of stroue sould at Houle viijd. 1679 Filmer *Freeholder* 54 Their Living..consisted chiefly upon the having of a Thrave of Corn of every Plow-land. 1865 W. White *E. Eng.* I. 289, Reapers got sixpence a thrave for their reaping.

γ. 1284 *Acc. Exch. K. R.* Bd. 97 No. 3 Pro .lxxij. Trauis litere emptis..pro eisdem [horses]. *c* 1447 in *Jarrow & Wearmouth* (Surtees) 242 Tho trawes and other arrerage of the said corn. 1504–5 *Durham Acc. Rolls* (Surtees) 251 Pro xxxij trave de lyng. 1868 Atkinson *Cleveland Gloss.*, *Thrave, pron.* trave, treeav. 1900 *Shetland News* 22 Sept. (E.D.D.), What mak's doo o' da twartree [= two or three] traeve o' bare.

2. *transf.* and *fig.* A large number; a company; a multitude, a 'heap', a 'lot'.

α. 1377 Langl. *P. Pl.* B. xvi. 55, I have þouȝtes a threve of þis þre piles, In what wode thei woxen. 1610 B. Jonson *Alch.* v. ii, Gallants..[have] beene seene to flock here In threaues. 1635 J. Jones *Adrasta* iii. i. G j, Come, gi' me a threave of kisses. 1825 Scott *Betrothed* xxi, Minstrels singing ballads by the threave.

β. 1486 *Bk. St. Albans* f vi b, A Thraue of Throsheris. 1500–20 Dunbar *Poems* lxvi. 55 Sum with ane thraif playis passage plane. *a* 1656 Bp. Hall *Rev. Unrevealed* § 8 Tidings ..of a thrave of Jews newly converted.

† 3. A bundle or handful tied up like a small sheaf. *Obs.*

1606 Chapman *Gentleman Usher* ii. i. Plays 1873 I. 273 Lay me vm [rushes] thus In fine smoothe threaues, look you sir, thus, in threaues. 1656 Sir J. Mennis *K. Oberon's Apparel* in *Musarum Del.* 34 His Belt was made of mirtle leaves, Plaited in small curious threaves.

Hence **Thra·ver, threa·ver**, a reaper who is paid according to the number of thraves he cuts; **Threa·ving** *vbl. sb.*, the practice of paying reapers at so much for the thraves.

1812 Sir J. Sinclair *Syst. Husb. Scot.* i. 329 About six years ago, another practice took place in that district, which ..is called threaving. 1813 G. Robertson *Agric. Surv. Kincard.* 264 (Jam.) While a reaper cuts..at the rate of nine threaves a-day, a threaver will..cut ten threaves in the same time. 1844 Stephens *Bk. Farm* III. 1053 Threavers..have a strong inducement to cut the straw near the ground.

**Thraw** (þrǭ), *v.*, the earlier form of Throw *v.*[1], retained in northern dialect in all senses of the verb, and preserving in Scottish use a group of senses in which *throw* is not in English use, or, when occasionally used by English writers, is taken in the Sc. form as a distinct word; viz. the senses: To turn, twist, turn awry, contort, distort (esp. to make a wry face or mouth, cf. Thrawn *ppl. a.*); to wrest, warp, strain, or distort (words or their meaning); to wrench; to extort; to cross, thwart, vex, manifest opposition or ill temper. For these see Throw *v.*[1], senses 1 to 5 b. So **Thraw** *sb.*, northern and Sc. form of Throw *sb.*[2]: see esp. senses 1, b, c.

**Thraw** (þrǭ), *a.* *Sc.* and *n. dial.* [app. shortened form of Thrawn.] Twisted, turned awry. Also in *comb.* = Wry-, as **thraw-gabbit** *a.*, wry-mouthed, peevish; **thraw-necked** *a.*, having the neck twisted.

1501 Douglas *Pal. Hon.* i. 437 Thir megir bellis, Sum round, sum thraw. 18.. Joanna Baillie *Hooly & Fairly* i, My wife..ca's me a niggardly thraw-gabbit carlie. 1884 Mrs. J. H. Riddell *Berna Boyle* xi, There was nothing in his offer the best gentleman in the land need have drawn a thraw mouth over. 1894 Lang *Poems* 41 (E.D.D.) Our present Duke's nae thraw man. 1898 Ld. E. Hamilton *Mawkin* xx. 275 A pair of poor thraw-neckit corpses.

**Thraw**, obs. f. or var. Thro, Throe, Throw *sb.*[1]

**Thraward** (þrǭ·wǫ̆rd), *a.* *Sc.* Also 5–9 **thrawart**, 6 **thrauard** (**threwart**), 7 **thrawert**. [app. altered from the earlier *fraward* (*c* 1200), Froward, perh. under the influence of Thraw *v.*, Thrawn, etc. But cf. mod. Sc. dial. *thra, thrae*, for *fra, frae*.]

1. Disposed to turn aside from the proper way; froward, refractory, perverse, adverse. *arch.*

*c* 1470 Henryson *Mor. Fab.* xii. (*Wolf & Lamb*) vii, His exhorbetand and thrawart [*ed.* 1570 frawart] pleid. 1508 Dunbar *Flyting* 108 In sic is sett thy thraward appetyte. *a* 1600 Montgomerie *Sonn.* xxxiii. 2 Vhom suld I warie bot my wicked weard, Vha span my thriftles thrauard fatall threed? 1795 Macneill *Will & Jean* 1, Such was Jean when Will first, mawing, Spied her on a thrawart beast. 1818 Scott *Hrt. Midl.* xiii, Mony a thrawart job I hae had wi' her first and last. 1901 J. Molleson *Poems* 48 The maister ne'er gae them a thrawart look.

2. *dial.* Twisted, crooked, wry, 'thrawn'.

**1814** W. NICHOLSON *Poems* 118 Yon todlin' burn.. Still presses owre ilk thrawart turn. **1827** J. WATT *Poems* 15 (E.D.D.) Man's life's..A chain o' mony thrawart links. **1894** A. REID *Sangs Heatherland* 72 His nosie..Sae hookit, and thrawart.

Hence **Thra·wartly** *adv. Sc.*, frowardly, perversely. So **Thra·wart-like** *adv.*

**1533** BELLENDEN *Livy* II. xxv. (S.T.S.) I. 232 Þe armye consauit na litill Ire and Indignatioun in þare myndis.. and did all thingis sa thrawartlie..that [etc.]. **1768** Ross *Helenore* I. 30 Very thrawart like, I yeed in by.

**Thra·wardness.** *Sc.* [f. prec. + -NESS.] Frowardness, perversity, 'thrawnness'.

**1567** *Reg. Privy Council Scot.* I. 515 Hir Hienes clemency is commounlie abusit and recompansit with threwartnes and ingratitude. *a* **1600** *Scot. Poems 16th C.* (1801) I. 70 Remoue from mee all thrawardnesse, Als well in mynde, as into deid. **1609** SKENE *Reg. Maj., Stat. Will.* 4 b, Gif he quha leides bot ane beast.. be thrawertnes, passes throw them, quha drives the many horse. *a* **1651** CALDERWOOD *Hist. Kirk* (1843) II. 538 A pitifull caus,..and yitt led by the thrawardnesse of time and our unhappe.

**Thrawcrook,** variant of THROW-CROOK.

**Thrawe,** obs. f. THRAVE, THRO, THROE, THROW.

**Thrawl,** obs. f. THRALL *sb.*[1], dial. var. *sb.*[3]

**Thrawn** (þrǭn, þrân), *ppl. a. Sc.* Also 6-9 thrawin, (6 throwin). [Sc. and north. dial. form of THROWN; used in senses in which *thrown* is not now used in English. Cf. THRAW *v.*]

**1.** Twisted, crooked, bent from the straight; mis-shapen, drawn awry, distorted.

**1513** DOUGLAS *Æneis* II. ii. (i.) 70 In jonyngis of the thrawin wame of tre Festinyt the lance. **1715** RAMSAY *Christ's Kirk Gr.* II. x, A thrawn knublock hit his heel. **1752** *Rec. Elgin* (New Spald. Cl.) I. 465 All..sowms, thramels, rigwoodies, tethers, wallropes, thrawn wawns [wands] and all other wood or work of wood, straw, bent, or rushes. *a* **1824** *Ld. Saltoun & Auchanachie* vi. in Child *Ball.* VIII. (1892) 348/1 He's bowed on the back, and thrawin on the knee. **1871** G. LAWRENCE *Anteros* xv, She had seen the husband..brought home a corpse stiff and thrawn. **1897** Thrawn thrapple [see THREAP *sb.* 2]. **1901** *Westm. Gaz.* 9 Apr. 3/1 'Dramatic idyls'..peopled by the stark 'thrawn' figures of the Pre-Raphaelite world.

**b.** Of the mouth or face: Drawn awry or distorted by anger, ill-temper, or the like; frowning.

**1513** DOUGLAS *Æneis* III. ix. 89 His mekle E, That lurkit allane vnder his thrawin front. *Ibid.* VII. viii. 23 Alecto her thrawin vyssage dyd away. *a* **1585** POLWART *Flyting w. Montgomerie* 784 Iock Blunt, thrawin frunt! **1719, 1897** [see 3].

**2.** *fig.* Perverse, contrary; cross-grained, ill-tempered, crabbed, peevish, cross.

*c* **1450** HOLLAND *Howlat* 918 Thus wycit he the walentyne thraly and thrawin. *c* **1470** HENRY *Wallace* x. 593 Thar salusyng was bot boustous and thrawin. *c* **1475** *Rauf Coilȝear* 129 Sa mot I thriue, I am thrawin, Begin we to threip. **1585** JAS. I *Ess. Poesie* (Arb.) 39 Lyke the curr,.. sparing alwaies those are to him knowin, To them most gentle, to the others throwin. **1718** RAMSAY *Christ's Kirk Gr.* III. i, Greedy wives wi' girning thrawn, Cry'd lasses up to thrift. **1719** — *To Arbuckle* 109 Wishing thrawn parties wad agree. **1737** — *Sc. Prov.* v. (1750) 15 A thrawin question should have a thrawart answer. **1816** SCOTT *Bl. Dwarf* xviii, Though he was thrawn and cankered in his converse, he likeit dumb creatures weel. **1862** *Leisure Hours in Town* 13 The expressive Scotticism which says of a perverse and impracticable man that he is a thrawn person; that is, a person who has got a thraw or twist. **1889** BARRIE *Window in Thrums* xix, He cried it oot fell thrawn. **1893** CROCKETT *Stickit Minister* 117 A grummle from that thrawn stick o' a registrar.

**3.** *Comb.* as **thrawn-faced, -gabbit, -mowit** *adjs.*, having a 'thrawn' face or mouth (see 1, 1 b); hence, crabbed, ill-tempered, snarling.

**1578** *Inv. Royal Wardr.* (1815) 249 Ane moyane of fonte thrawin mowit without armes maid be Hanis Cochrane. **1719** RAMSAY *2nd Answ. to Hamilton* vii, Thrawn-gabbit sumphs that snarl At our frank lines. **1897** CROCKETT *Lad's Love* iii, Ye thrawn-faced, slack-twisted muckle haythen ye.

Hence **Thraw·nly** *adv. Sc.*, awry; perversely, ill-temperedly; **Thraw·nness** *Sc.*, perversity, obstinacy, cantankerousness.

**1513** DOUGLAS *Æneis* VII. vii. 133 Wyth bludy ene rowing full thrawinly. **1825** JAMIESON, *Thrawinness*, perverseness, obstinacy. **1862** *Leisure Hours in Town* 18 Perversity, or general Unpleasantness and Thrawn-ness. **1883** STEWART *Nether Lochaber* lii. 328 A perverseness of disposition and a thrawnness of temper.

**Thre,** obs. form of THREE.

† **Threa,** *v. Obs.* Forms: 1 ðréaȝan, þréawian, 1-4 ðrean, þrean, 3 þraih-, þhray-, þrayh-, þrah-, þraghen; 2 *pa. t.* þreadde, þredde. [OE. *þréag(e)an*, wk. vb., contr. *þréan*, pa. t. *þréade* = OHG. *drewen, drouwen* (MHG. *dröuwen, drouwen*, Ger. *dräuen*), Goth. **þraujan*:—OTeut. **þrawjan*; f. OE. *þrawu, þréa* sb. threatening, rebuke, chastisement, OHG. *drô*, ON. *þrá*: OTeut. **þrawā*: cf. Falk & Torp, s. v. *Traa* II.] *trans.* To rebuke, reprove, chastise; to punish; to torment, afflict.

*c* **897** K. ÆLFRED *Gregory's Past. C.* ii. 30 Forðon hi nan mon ne dear ðreaȝean ðeah hi agylten. *Ibid.* xxi. 150 Swiðe wel Dryhten ðreade Iudeas. *a* **900** tr. *Bæda's Hist.* II. vi. (1890) 114 Mid hu miclum swingum he þread..wæs. *c* **950** *Lindisf. Gosp.* Luke xxiii. 22 Ic ðrea..forðon hine & ic forleto. *c* **1000** *Ags. Gosp.* Matt. xvii. 18 Þa þreade [*c* **1160** *Hatton G.* þredde] se hælend hyne. *c* **1160** *Hatton Gosp.* Luke xxiii. 40 Þa andswerede se oðer & hine þreadde. *a* **1300** *E. E. Psalter* lxxii[i]. 14 In vghteninges mi þhraying ai. *Ibid.* cxvii[i]. 18 ȝraihand [*v.rr.* þraghand, ȝrayhand] lauerd me ȝrahed he [*castigans castigavit me Dominus*].

**Thread** (þred), *sb.* Forms: 1-3 þrǽd (1 ðréd), 2 þread, 3-5 þred, 4-5 þreed, 4-7 (9 *dial.*) threed, (5 tredde), 5-6 threde, 5-8 thred, 6 threade, thredde, thride, 6-7 threede, *Sc.* threid, 6-8 thrid, 7 thrydd, 5- thread. [OE. *þrǽd* = OLG. **thrâd* (MDu. *draet*, Du. *draad*), OHG., MHG. *drât* (G. *draht*), ON. *þráð*r (Da. *traad*, Sw. *tråd*):—OTeut. **þrǣ-đuᶻ*, pre-Teut. **trētús*; f. **þrǣ-* to twist (see THROW *v.*[1]) + dental suffix. Cf. *bread, seed.*]

**1.** A fine cord composed of the fibres or filaments of flax, cotton, wool, silk, etc. spun to a considerable length; *spec.* such a cord composed of two or more yarns, esp. of flax, twisted together; applied also to a similar product from glass, asbestos, a ductile metal, etc.

*c* **725** *Corpus Gloss.* (O. E. T.) 876 *Filum*, ðred. *c* **888** K. ÆLFRED *Boeth.* xxix. § 1 Hwæt ðæt bið ȝesæliȝ mon þe him ealne weȝ ne hangað nacod sweord ofer ðæm heafde be smale þræde. *c* **1000** *Sax. Leechd.* I. 218 Cnyte mid anum ðræde on anum clænan linenan. *c* **1205** LAY. 14220 Nes þe þwong..buten swulc a twines þræd [*c* **1275** twined þred]. *c* **1400** *Sowdone Bab.* 1999 He teyde a tredde on a pole. *c* **1425** tr. *Arderne's Treat. Fistula* 9 It hath..an yȝe like a nedel by whiche þredes ow to be drawen agayn by middez of þe fistule. **1508** DUNBAR *Gold. Targe* 62 Thair brycht hairis.. wyppit wyth goldyn thredis. **1535** COVERDALE 1 *Kings* vii. 23 A threde of thirtie cubites longe. **1641** W. GASCOIGNE in *Nat. Philos.* III. *Hist. Astron.* xiii. (1834) 66/2 (Usef. Knowl. Soc.), I am fitting my sextant for all manner of observations, by two perspicills with threads. **1720** WELTON *Suffer. Son of God* II. xxii. 594 From these little Threads..such strong Cables are form'd. **1828** J. M. SPEARMAN *Brit. Gunner* (ed. 2) 150 Hawsers (Machine made). ..Of 4 Inches, or 108 Threads..Of 10 Inches, or 648 Threads. **1832** G. R. PORTER *Porcelain & Glass* ix. 231 Glass may be spun into very long and minute threads.

**b.** The sacred thread with which Brahmins and Parsees are invested at initiation: see quots.

**1582** N. LICHEFIELD tr. *Castanheda's Conq. E. Ind.* I. xvi. 42 b, Vpon their left sholders they had certaine number of thrids, which came vnder their right shoulders. **1860** J. BATEMAN *Life Bp. D. Wilson* I. xii. 341 Several Brahmins being manifested by their 'thread'. **1874** J. H. BLUNT *Dict. Sects*, etc. 405/2 (*Parsees*) The investiture at initiation with the sacred thread. **1903** *Times* 5 Mar. 3/5 Mrs. Ruttonjee Tata..was..invested with the sacred thread and *sudra* of the Parsees.

† **c.** *spec.* A fishing-line. (In quot. 1622 *fig.*) *Obs.*

**1602** CAREW *Cornwall* 31 b, For catching of Whiting and Basse, they vse a thred, so named because it consisteth of a long small lyne with a hooke at the end. **1622** BACON *Hen. VII* 137 Thinking, that the King (what with his Baits, and what with his Nets) would draw them all vnto him,.. diuers came away by the Thred, sometimes one, and sometimes another.

**2.** Each of the lengths of yarn which form the warp and woof of a woven fabric; hence, any one of these as an ultimate constituent of such a fabric, and thus of one's clothing; the least part of one's dress; esp. in the phrase *not a* (*one*) *dry thread on one.* Also *fig.*

*c* **1200** *Vices & Virt.* 39 Ðar behoued to maniȝe þreades ær hit bie full wroht. *c* **1374** CHAUCER *Boeth.* I. pr. i. 2 (Camb. MS.) Hyr clothes weeren maked of riht delye thredes. *c* **1380** WYCLIF *Wks.* (1880) 316 Ilche þreed of siche cloþis þat ben tuo wast & too costliche. **1382** — *Gen.* xiv. 23 Fro a threed of the weeft vnto a garter of an hoos I shal not take of alle thingis that ben thin. **1470-85** MALORY *Arthur* xv. ii. 699 It shalle not lye in your power nor to perysshe me as moche as a threde. *a* **1500** *Flower & Leaf* 370 The ladies ne the knightes nade o threed Drie on them. **1550** VERON *Godly Sayings* (1846) 141 Howe can you..come to this roial feast and banket not having one thrid of this wedding rayment..upon you? **1600** HAKLUYT *Voy.* III. 83 Hee that had fiue or sixe shifts of apparell had scarce one drie threed to his backe. **1610** SHAKS. *Temp.* IV. i. 3. **1610** B. JONSON *Alch.* III. ii, Your threescore minutes Were at the last thred. **1726** LEONI *Alberti's Archit.* III. 13/2, I take a veil made of the finest threds..: this I divide into..squares ..by some bigger threds parallel to each other. **1815** SCOTT *Guy M.* xl, There will no be a dry thread amang us or we get the cargo out. **1844** G. DODD *Textile M.* vi. 201 Plain silks, as well as most woven fabrics, consist of threads crossing each other at right angles. **1879** JEFFERIES *Wild Life in S. C.* 133 The costume is true to a thread. **1908** in *Westm. Gaz.* 1 Apr. 12/1 Till April's dead, change not a thread.

**b.** *Bare* or *worn to the thread*, etc. = THREADBARE.

**1483-4** *Act 1 Rich. III*, c. 8 *Preamble*, Suche course Clothes, beyng bare of threde. **1615** CHAPMAN *Odyss.* XVII. 254 His garments to a thred All bare, and burn'd. **1882** STEVENSON *New Arab. Nts.* i. 23 The furniture was scanty, and the coverings worn to the thread.

**c.** *Thread and thrum*, each length of the warp-yarn, and the tuft where it is fastened to the loom; hence *fig.* the whole of anything; good and bad together. Also, *threads and thrums*, ends of warp threads, miscellaneous scraps or waste fragments.

**1590** SHAKS. *Mids. N.* V. i. 291 O Fates! come, come: Cut thred and thrum. **1648** HERRICK *Hesper.*, *Upon some Women*, Learne of me what woman is. Something made of thred and thrumme; A meere botch of all and some. **1654** GATAKER *Disc. Apol.* 93 By those thrums and threds that he hath pickt and puld out of it.., the Reader may judge of the whole. **1833** CARLYLE *Diderot* in *Misc. Ess.* (1872) V. 2 The confused and ravelled mass of threads and thrums, ycleped Memoirs.

**d.** A lineal measure of yarn: the length of a coil of the reel, varying in amount according to the material, and also with the locality (see quots.).

**1662** *Act 14 Chas. II*, c. 5 § 6 Every Reel staff shall containe fourteen Leas and every Lea fourty threads. **1688** R. HOLME *Armoury* III. vi. 288/2 A knot is a Hundred Threds round the Reel. **1696** PHILLIPS (ed. 5) s. v. *Lea*, Every Lea of Yarn at Kidderminster shall contain 200 Threds reel'd on a Reel four yards about. *a* **1825** FORBY *Voc. E. Anglia*, *Lea*, forty threads of hemp-yarn. **1858** SIMMONDS *Dict. Trade*, *Thread*,..a yarn-measure, containing in cotton-yarn 54 inches; in linen-yarn 90 inches; in worsted yarn 35 inches. On the Continent 85½ Ermland inches make one thread. **1875** TEMPLE & SHELDON *Hist. Northfield, Mass.* 161 A run of yarn consisted of twenty knots, a knot was composed of forty threads, and a thread was seventy-four inches in length, or once round the reel.

**e.** *fig.* A single element interwoven with others in any composite fabric, mental, moral, social, political, or the like.

**1836** J. GILBERT *Chr. Atonem.* vii. (1852) 190 In this, as in almost all theories,..there is indeed a thread of truth. **1851** HELPS *Comp. Solit.* xiii. (1874) 248 The threads of our poor human affairs..might yet be interwoven harmoniously with the great cords of love and duty. **1859** KINGSLEY *Misc.* (1860) II. ii. 29 The only threads of light in the dark web of his history are clerical and theurgic. **1879** STAINER *Music of Bible* 168 The pleasure which accrues to a trained musician when he grasps in his mind many threads of delicious melody, and traces the composer's genius in interlacing them.

**3.** Without *a*, as name of the substance of which the above-mentioned things are composed, or of these things taken in the mass; woollen, silk, linen, cotton, or other fibre, or fine-drawn metal, spun into material for weaving, knitting, sewing, or fastening: often with distinctive word, as *gold* or *silk thread*; sometimes *spec.* flaxen or linen thread as distinct from silk or cotton; in *pl.*, kinds of thread.

*c* **1386** CHAUCER *Monk's T.* 485 Nettes of gold threed hadde he greet plentee. *c* **1400** *Rom. Rose* 7369 A large coverechief of threde She wrapped alle aboute hir hede. *c* **1400** *Laud Troy Bk.* 6775 Of his hors fel that kynge, As it were a clewe of thred. *c* **1400** *Lybeaus Disc.* (Kaluza) 940 As selke þrede. **1529** MORE *Dyaloge* II. x. Wks. 195/1 He thankinge the monke for the thrid, desired him to teache him how he should knit it. **1545** *Rates of Customs* c vij b, Threde called wotenall threde. **1552-3** *Inv. Ch. Goods, Staffs.* in *Ann. Lichfield* (1863) IV. 48, ij vestements, one of grene chamblet, another of threde. **1576** in Feuillerat *Revels Q. Eliz.* (1908) 264 For a quartern of black threede. **1584** *Ibid.* 370 For iii li. of thrid of all cullers. **1588** PARKE tr. *Mendoza's Hist. China* 320 They take out of this plant..a kinde of thride or yarne. **1596** DALRYMPLE tr. *Leslie's Hist. Scot.* I. (S.T.S.) I. 94 Wᵗ threid of silke..al the partes of the sarke ..thay sewit. **1560** F. BROOKE tr. *Le Blanc's Trav.* 184 They have also thread from another tree called Langir. **1806** *Gazetteer Scotl.* (ed. 2) 555/2 The principal manufacture is that of linen yarn, thread, and brown linens. **1887** *Daily News* 19 Oct. 2/8 Linens and threads maintain the improvement lately reported.

† **b.** *fig.* The material or 'fibre' of which anything is composed; 'texture', quality, nature. *Obs.*

**1632** SANDERSON *Serm.* 268 Hypocrisie is spunne of a fine threed, and is not easily discerneable. **1635** A. STAFFORD *Fem. Glory* (1869) 134 Of the same pure thred with the rest of her life. **1659** O. WALKER *Instruct. Oratory* 19 That the Oration may seem Continuous and all of one thread. **1718** OCKLEY *Saracens* (1848) II. Introd. 24 The language must be all of the same thread. **1746** FRANCIS tr. *Hor., Sat.* II. iv. 14 The Matter nice, and wrought of subtle Thread.

**4.** Something having the slenderness or fineness of a thread: e. g. a fine ligament, an animal or vegetable fibre, a hair, a filament of a cobweb or of the byssus of a shell-fish.

**1398** TREVISA *Barth. De P. R.* XVIII. xi. (Bodl. MS.), Þe spiþer..drawiþ and bringeþ ofte aȝen his þrede þwarte ouer fro pointe to pointe. *c* **1400** *Lanfranc's Cirurg.* 263 Þer is a þreed vndir sum mannes tunge þat he mai not put out his tunge as he schulde, & also it lettiþ him to speke. **1541** R. COPLAND *Galyen's Terap.* 2 A iij b, A spyder threde. **1686** GOAD *Celest. Bodies* I. ii. 2 A Fog which sometimes casts it self into Threds or Ropes, and..furls up into Gossamere. **1693** EVELYN *De la Quint. Compl. Gard.* II. 57 Producing the least Thread of a capilar Root. **1774** GOLDSM. *Nat. Hist.* (1776) VII. 45 These threads, which are usually called the beard of the muscle. **1776** WITHERING *Brit. Plants* (1796) I. 365 The Seeds, with the elastic threads to which they are attached. *Ibid.* IV. 129 Threads when dry uniting into stiff sharp points. Conferva amphibia.

**b.** A 'string' of any viscid substance; a thin continuous stream of liquid, sand, etc.; a narrow strip of space; a fine line or streak of colour or light; a 'thin' continuity of sound; *spec.* in glass-making: see quot. 1832.

**1593** NASHE *Christ's T.* (1613) 126 Why breake not thunder bolts through the Clowdes in steade of thrids of raine? **1626** BACON *Sylva* § 24 Stillicides of Water..will Draw themselues into a small thred. **1674** N. FAIRFAX *Bulk & Selv.* 121 What a long thread of sand passes the neck-hole of an hour-glass in that same time. **1710** J. CLARKE *Rohault's Nat. Phil.* (1729) I. 22 If it be a fat Liquor, it will go on in a long Thread, whose Parts are uninterrupted. **1830** *Trans. Nat. Hist. Soc. Northumb.*, etc. I. 186 Sandstone roofs [in coal-mines] are subject to fissures of various sizes and extent, called threads and gullets by the colliers. **1832** G. R. PORTER *Porcelain & Gl.* 248 The name of threads is usually given to fibrous appearances in the body of the glass, which result from the vitrification of clay. **1837** P. KEITH *Bot. Lex.* 56 The infusions were absorbed by the roots, and carried up to the very summit of the stem, leaving..traces of their ascent in the form of longitudinal streaks or threads. **1868** GLADSTONE *Juv. Mundi* xi. (1869) 432 The Trojan elders, whose volubility, and their shrill thread of voice, Homer compares to the chirp of grasshoppers. **1884** J. H. HOLLOWELL in *Congregationalist* June 498 The pale Aare..winds its white thread through the valley. **1899** *Westm. Gaz.* 6 Apr. 2/1

Using her pleasant thread of voice agreeably. **1904** *Daily Chron.* 17 Oct. 8/1 The amazing thing is that so much good work should be done in such a mere thread of space. **1907** *Outlook* 16 Nov. 661/1 A little thread of unfrozen water which tinkles feebly over the rocks.

**c.** Applied to the apparent action of a feeble pulse: see quot., and cf. THREAD-LIKE b, THREADY 4.

**1899** *Allbutt's Syst. Med.* VI. 49 A mere tightened thread being felt under the finger.

**d.** A degree of stickiness reached in boiling clarified syrup for confectionery: see quot.

**1862** J. THOMAS *How to mix Drinks* 104 There are nine essential points, or degrees, in boiling sugar. They are called Small Thread, Large Thread, Little Pearl, Large Pearl [etc.]. *Ibid.*, The sugar forms a fine thread which will break at a short distance...This is termed the 'Small Thread'. *Ibid.*, A somewhat longer string will be drawn. This is termed the 'Large Thread'. **1883** R. HALDANE *Workshop Receipts* Ser. II. 152/1.

**5.** *transf.* The spiral ridge winding round the shank of a screw; also, each complete turn of this.

**1674** PETTY *Disc. Dupl. Proportion* 116 The Force must be increased at every Turn or Thred of a Screw-Press. **1733** TULL *Horse-Hoeing Husb.* xxiv. 402 Taper Screws made with Iron, having very deep Threads, whereby they hold fast when screw'd into Wood. **1829** *Nat. Philos.* I. *Mechanics* II. xi. 48 (U. K. S.) Hunter's screw..gives an indefinitely slow motion, without requiring a very exquisitely fine thread. **1902** MARSHALL *Metal Tools* 63 For pipes and tubes a special thread termed a gas thread is employed.

**II. 6.** *fig.* Something figured as being spun or continuously drawn out like a thread. **a.** The continued course of life, represented in classical mythology as a thread which is spun and cut off by the Fates.

**1447** BOKENHAM *Seyntys* (Roxb.) 8 Wil..Attropos..My fatal threed a sundyr smyte. *Ibid.* 43 Or than deth the threed untwyne Of oure fatal web. **1563** *Mirr. Mag., Induct.* xliii, His vitall threde. **1596** SPENSER *F. Q.* IV. ii. 48 Sad Clotho held the rocke, the whiles the thrid By griesly Lachesis was spun with paine, That cruell Atropos eftsoones undid, With cursed knife cutting the twist in twaine. **1643** SIR T. BROWNE *Relig. Med.* I. § 42 For my owne part, I would not..beginne againe the thred of my dayes. **1696** TATE & BR. *Ps.* xc. 10 So soon the slender Thread is cut. **1704** SWIFT *Batt. Bks.* ¶ 25 Her Son..to whom the Fates had assign'd a very short Thred. **1829** SCOTT *Anne of G.* xvii, Why I should spare my own almost exhausted thread of life. **1846** H. G. ROBINSON *Odes of Horace* II. iii, While..the three Sisters' sable thread Allows you still the power. **1907** DILLON in *Contemp. Rev.* Nov. 705 So long as three such Parcae have the threads of Macedonia in their hands.

**b.** In various other applications: see quots.

*c* **1586** C'TESS PEMBROKE *Ps.* LXXXV. ii, Wilt thou of thy wrathfull rage Draw the threed from age to age? **1588** SHAKS. *L. L. L.* V. i. 19 He draweth out the thred of his verbositie finer then the staple of his argument. **1608** D. T[UVIL] *Ess. Pol. & Mor.* 88 b, I will stretch the thred of my subiect to a further length. **1645** *City Alarum* 19 Consider first what a thred of time the German wars have spun out. **1670** EACHARD *Cont. Clergy* 32 Fearing he should break the thread of your patience, he concludes. **1719** DE FOE *Crusoe* (1840) II. vii. 159, I cut the thread of all his comforts, and shortened his days. **1736** BUTLER *Anal.* II. vii. 362 To make up a continued thread of history of the length of between three and four thousand years. *a* **1774** TUCKER *Lt. Nat.* (1834) II. 664 Drawing out the threads of argumentation, preventing them from entangling.

**7.** A thread in various mythological or legendary tales (esp. that of Theseus in the Cretan Labyrinth) is mentioned as the means of finding the way through a labyrinth or maze: hence in many figurative applications: That which guides through a maze, perplexity, difficulty, or intricate investigation: cf. CLEW *sb.*[1] 3, CLUE 2.

**1580** LYLY *Euphues* (Arb.) 312 Neither Ariadnes thrid, nor Sibillas bough, nor Medeas seede, may remedy thy griefe. **1582** T. WATSON *Centurie of Loue* lv, My guiding thrid by Reason spunne. **1589** *Pasquil's Return* A iij, Hauing gotten this thred by the end, I neuer left winding til I came to the paper that made the bottom. *c* **1614** SIR W. MURE *Dido & Æneas* I. 6 Path'd wayes I trace, as Theseus in his neid, Conducted by a loyal virgin's threid. **1672** STERRY *Freed. Will* (1675) C iij, What a golden-thread of Harmony guides us through the nature of things! **1711** W. KING tr. *Naude's Ref. Politics* i. 11 Having in my hand that thread of knowledge, which might extricate me thence.

**8.** That which connects the successive points in anything, esp. a narrative, train of thought, or the like; the sequence of events or ideas continuing through the whole course of anything; train.

**1642** HOWELL *For. Trav.* (Arb.) 23 If one read skippingly and by snatches, and not take the threed of the story along, it must needs puzzle and distract the memory. **1687** DRYDEN *Hind & P.* III. 278 The matron..then Resumed the thrid of her discourse again. **1738** SWIFT *Pol. Conversat.* Introd. 64 After a Pause, the grave Companion resumes his Thread,..'Well, but to go on with my Story'. **1782** MME. D'ARBLAY *Diary* Dec., We laughed so violently..that he could not recover the thread of his harangue. **1844** THIRLWALL *Greece* VIII. lxii. 201 We resume the thread of Grecian history.

**9.** Some continuous or persistent feature which runs through the pattern of anything, or combines with other features to form a pattern or texture.

**1685** MRS. EVELYN *Let.* in *E.'s Diary* (1827) IV. 440 A thred of piety accompanyed all her actions. **1823** LAMB *Elia* Ser. II. *Some Sonn. of Sydney*, An historical thread runs through [Sydney's Sonnets]. **1875** JOWETT *Plato, Introd. Phaedrus* (ed. 2) II. 86 The continuous thread which appears and reappears throughout his rhetoric. **1892** SYMONDS *Michel Angelo* (1899) I. VII. vii. 343 A pleasant thread runs through Michel Angelo's correspondence.

†**10.** A (fine) dividing line or boundary line. *To cut* (*to*) *a thread* (*between*), to strike the exact line of division, to 'draw the line'. *Obs.*

**13..** *Gaw. & Gr. Knt.* 1771 Þat prynce of pris depresed hym so þikke, Nurned hym so neȝe þe þred, þat nede hym bi-houed, Oþer lach þer hir luf, oþir lodly re-fuse. **1567** MAPLET *Gr. Forest* 28 To twine vp this threde of deuision [the division of plants into kinds] vpon some bottome. *c* **1591** W. DAVIES in Pollen *Acts Eng. Mart.* (1891) 131 It was come to that now, that a thread divided my life and death. **1598** MANWOOD *Lawes Forest* xx. § 11 (1615) 180 Within the lists or bounds of the Forest, or within the threed (as they call it) of the Forest. **1647** WARD *Simp. Cobler* (1843) 52 To cut an exquisite thred between Kings Prerogatives, and Subjects Liberties. **1650** B. *Discolliminium* 19, I know no harder task..than..to cut a just thread between Gods Providence, and Mans Improvidence. **1692** R. L'ESTRANGE *Fables* ccccxvi. 393 The Art of Pleasing is..the Skill of Cutting to a Thrid, betwixt Flattery and Ill Manners.

**11.** The central line of the current of a stream, esp. as a boundary line. [Rendering med. L. *filum aquæ*: cf. F. *fil de l'eau.*]

**1691** *Blount's Law Dict.*, *Filum Aquæ* is the Thread or Middle of the Stream, where a River parts Two Lordships. [? 17.. tr. *Commission to ordain Ways to Hull*, The Jurors say that from the thread of the Water of Hull [1302 *de filo aque de Hull*] there is a certain way ordained next Alexander Cook's Mill. — tr. *Charter 25 Hen. VI* (1447) All lands between the said ditch as far as the middle thread of the water of Humbre [*usque medium fili acque de Humber*].] **1815** J. SMITH *Panorama Sc. & Art* II. 110 One part of a river is generally observed to flow with much greater velocity than any other part, and is therefore called the thread or channel of the river, which is very rarely in the middle, or at any regular distance from the banks. **1848** WHARTON *Law Dict.* 255. **1886** H. AUSTIN *Farm Law* 135 (Cent. Dict.).

**12.** That by which something is suspended, or upon which things hang. *To hang by* (*on, upon*) *a thread*, to be in a precarious condition. Often with reference to the legend of Damocles.

[*c* 888: see sense 1.] **1538** STARKEY *England* I. iv. 121 But thys hangyth only apon the wyl of the prynce—a veray weke thred in such a case. **1560** DAUS tr. *Sleidane's Comm.* 63 b, There hangeth assuredly a wounderfull daunger ouer you, as a sworde dependynge ouer your neckes by a twhyne threde. **1607** H. RAYMOND *Ode* in Farr *S. P. Jas. I* (1848) 360 Life, ioy, and euery pleasant weede, Scarce hangeth by a slender threede. **1804** JEFFERSON *Writ.* (1830) IV. 19 My evening prospects now hang on the slender thread of a single life. **1869** J. MARTINEAU *Ess.* II. 94 Hair-bridges, suspending you by a thread of logic.

**13.** In reference to other functions of a thread; esp. as a means of connecting or holding together.

Sometimes with mixture of sense 6 or 7.

**1818** SCOTT *Hrt. Midl.* xxxvii, She kept in her hands the thread of many a political intrigue. **1844** A. W. WELBY *Poems* (1867) 58 She was the golden thread that bound us In one bright chain together here. **1849** ROBERTSON *Serm.* Ser. I. xv. (1866) 260 A thread runs through all true acts stringing them together. **1861** TULLOCH *Eng. Purit.* i. 84 So was snapped the last feeble thread of negotiation. **1875** JOWETT *Plato* (ed. 2) IV. 123 Many threads join together in one the love and dialectic of the Phædrus. **1904** JESSIE WESTON in *Romania* XXXIII. 334 *note*, A thread uniting all the different parts of our legend.

**14.** *attrib.* and *Comb.* **a.** General. (*a*) Simple attrib., 'of thread', as *thread-end*, *-mill*, *-spool*, etc. (*b*) in sense 'made of linen or cotton thread' = THREADEN, as *thread bodice, girdle, glove, net, point, ribbon, shoe, stocking*, etc. (often hyphened). (*c*) Objective and obj. genitive, as *thread-maker*, *-manufacturer*, *-twister*, *-winder*, etc.; *thread-cutting*, *-making*, *-spinning*, *-twisting*, *-winding*, etc. sbs. and adjs.; similative, parasynthetic, etc., as *thread-line*; *thread-lettered*, *-shaped* adjs.

*c* **1665** in *Verney Mem.* (1907) II. 275 A black *thread bodice. **1884** KNIGHT *Dict. Mech.* Suppl., **Thread-cutting machine* ..for cutting threads in bolts, etc. **1900** W. H. HUDSON *Nat. Downland* 53 Slender dry bents standing out like pale yellow *thread-ends. *a* **1604** HANMER *Chron. Irel.* (1633) 80 A linnen or *threed Girdle. **1851** *Illustr. Catal. Gt. Exhib.* 201 Fast cotton dyeing for Lisle *thread gloves. **1858** SIMMONDS *Dict. Trade*, *Lisle-gloves*, fine thread gloves. **1873** *Routledge's Yng. Gentl. Mag.* Jan. 83/2 The specific name *filigrammaria*, or *thread-lettered. **1890** JUL. P. BALLARD *Among Moths & Butterfl.* 122 The quickness of the parting and closing of this narrow *thread-line. **1695** J. EDWARDS *Perfect. Script.* 237 Where had they thread, when the *thread-makers trade was not invented? **1878** J. WATSON (*title*) Art of Spinning and *Thread-Making. **1895** ZANGWILL *Master* I. vii, A *thread-net confined her hair. **1635** *Voy. Foxe & James* (Hakl. Soc.) I. 42 He gave every one of them a *Threed point [= needle]. *c* **1645** HOWELL *Lett.* (1650) II. 34 Calicoes, *threed-ribbands, and such polldavy ware. **1713** *Lond. Gaz.* No. 5173/4 A *Thread-Sattin Night-Gown, striped red and white. **1760** LEE *Bot.* (1778) 56 An amentaceous aggregate Flower has a Filiform, *Thread-shaped Receptacle. **1660** F. BROOKE tr. *Le Blanc's Trav.* 184 Strings which they pull out to make..*thread shooes after the Spanish manner. **1870** EMERSON *Soc. & Solit.* Wks. (Bohn) III. 42 Out of blocks, *thread-spools, cards, and checkers, he [the child] will build his pyramid. *c* **1665** in *Verney Mem.* II. 275 Stirrup *thredd stockins. **1697** tr. *C'tess D'Aunoy's Trav.* (1706) 3 They..presented me with Gloves, and Thread-Stockings, most delicately knit. **1711–12** SWIFT *Jrnl. to Stella* 9 Jan., I hide my purse in my thread stocking between the bed's head and the wainscot. **1725** *Lond. Gaz.* No. 6384/7 Gabriel Beale, .. *Thread-Twister. **1877** KNIGHT *Dict. Mech.* 2560 *Thread-winding Guide..Thread-winding Machine.

**b.** Special Combs.: **thread-animalcule**, a vibrionine animalcule; **thread-board**, in a ring-frame, a board placed over the spindles to hold the thread-guides; **thread-carrier**, a guide through which the yarn passes in the knitting-machine (Knight *Dict. Mech.* 1877); **thread-cell**, (*a*) a stinging cell in cœlenterates; a nematocyst; (*b*) a spermatozoon (*Cent. Dict.*); **thread-counter**, a magnifying-glass used in counting the threads within a given space in a texture; **thread-cutter**, (*a*) a small blade attached to a sewing-machine or the like for severing a sewing-thread; (*b*) a tool or machine for cutting screw-threads; **thread-drawing**, the process of ornamenting a textile fabric by drawing out some of the threads so as to form a pattern; cf. DRAWN-WORK; **thread-feather**: see quot.; **thread-fin** = *thread-fish*, (*a*); **thread-finisher**, a machine by which a smooth glossy surface is given to thread (Knight, 1877); **thread-fish**, (*a*) a polynemoid fish; (*b*) the West Indian cobbler-fish, *Blepharis crinitus*; (*c*) the cutlass-fish or silvery hair-tail, *Trichiurus lepturus*; **thread-flower**, (*a*) a name for plants of the genus *Poinciana*, N.O. *Leguminosæ*, section *Cæsalpinieæ*, so called from their long thread-like stamens; (*b*) a plant of the S. American genus *Nematanthus*, N.O. *Gesneraceæ*, of climbing shrubs, bearing crimson flowers pendent on long stalks; **thread-foot**, a name of the herb *Podostemon ceratophyllus*, in reference to its finely-divided linear leaves; **thread-frame**, a machine in which linen or cotton yarn is doubled and twisted into thread; **thread-gauge**, a gauge for ascertaining the number of turns to the inch in, or the accuracy of, a screw-thread (Knight, 1877); **thread-guide**, a device in a sewing- or spinning-machine for directing the thread (ibid.); **thread-herring**, popular name of (*a*) *Dorosoma cepedianum*, also called the mud-shad or gizzard-shad (*local, U. S.*); (*b*) a clupeoid fish, *Opisthonema thrissa*, of the Atlantic coast of N. America, in which the last ray of the dorsal fin is thread-like; **thread-indicator**, a device for the accurate measurement of plant-growth, in which a thread attached to the plant passes over a pulley and actuates a registering apparatus; **thread-leaved** *a.*, having narrow filiform leaves; **threadman**, a maker or seller of thread; **thread-mark**, a distinguishing mark consisting of a highly coloured thread, incorporated in bank-note paper to prevent counterfeiting by photography; **thread-mill**, a factory actuated by water or steam power in which thread is made; **thread-moss**, a moss of the genus *Bryum* or one of its allies; **thread-oiler**, an oil vessel through which the thread was conducted in some sewing machines (Knight, 1877); **thread-petalled** *a.*, having filiform petals; **thread-plant**, any plant from which fibre for thread-making is obtained (Ogilvie, 1882); **thread rush**, *Juncus filiformis*; **thread-sister** [SISTER 7 d], the stool on which the thread-lace pillow is placed; **thread-tangle**, the seaweed *Chorda filum*, having long cylindrical fronds; sea-laces; **thread-waxer**: see quot.; **thread-wire**, a wire thread-guide in a spinning-machine; **thread-woman**: see *thread-man*; **thread-work**, (*a*) a fabric consisting of or resembling threads; ornamental work formed of threads, lace-work; *drawn thread work*: see DRAWN-WORK; (*b*) *pl.* a thread-making establishment; **thread-worn** *a.*, worn to the thread, threadbare; also, of a screw, having a worn thread. See also THREADBARE, -LACE, etc.

**1892** NASMITH *Cotton Spinning* ix. 328 The yarn is taken through the wire eyes fixed in hinged boards known as '*thread boards'. **1859** HUXLEY *Oceanic Hydrozoa* 82 The distal division remains short, and acquires only small *thread-cells. **1871** ALLMAN *Monogr. Gymnoblastic Hydroids* I. p. xiv, *Thread-cells*, peculiar bodies consisting of a containing capsule and contained filament destined for urtication. **1911** *Thread-counter [see *texture-counter* s.v. TEXTURE *sb.* 7]. **1877** KNIGHT *Dict. Mech.*, **Thread-cutter*, a small blade attached to a thimble, to a thread-stand, or to a sewing-machine, to cut off a sewing-thread. **1872** COUES *N. Amer. Birds* 4 Filoplumes (*filoplumæ*), or *thread-feathers..have an extremely slender, almost invisible, stem. **1885** HORNADAY 2 *Yrs. in Jungle* xxxii. 386 All but three were *thread fishes, a strange species of *Polynemus*..distinguished by the..thread-like filaments..attached to the pectoral fins. **1884** MILLER *Plant-n.*, Crimson *Thread-flower, *Poinciana* (*Cæsalpinia*) *Gilliesii*. *Ibid.*, *Thread-foot, *Podostemon ceratophyllus*. **1839** URE *Dict. Arts*, etc. 1239 The doubling and twisting of cotton or linen yarn into a compact thread..is performed by..the *thread-frame. **1888** GOODE *Amer. Fishes* 409 In the Chesapeake region it is known as the 'Mud-Shad',..in North Carolina as the 'Hairy-back' or the '*Thread Herring'. **1875** BENNETT & DYER *Sachs' Bot.* 747 The *Thread-indicator..in which..a horizontal needle..moves freely over a graduated scale as the end of the thread which is fixed to the plant rises with its growth. **1884** MILLER *Plant-n.*, *Drosera filiformis*, *Thread-leaved Sun-dew. **1663** *Canterbury Marriage Licences* (MS.), Stephen Ward of Maidstone, *thredman. **1711** *Lond. Gaz.* No. 4932/4 Benjamin Cutlove, of London,

Threadman. 1799 *Hull Advertiser* 23 Feb. 3/2 A..fire broke out .. which entirely consumed nine *thread-mills. 1907 *Daily Chron.* 2 Oct. 6/6 Exciting scenes..in connection with the Paisley thread mill strike. 1864 M. G. CAMPBELL in *Intell. Observ.* No. 33. 155 The *thread-mosses are an interesting and numerous tribe. 1899 *Daily News* 7 Dec. 11/1 Spidery kinds [of chrysanthemums] include the *thread-petalled Mrs. Carter. 1861 MISS PRATT *Flower. Pl.* V. 291 *Thread Rush, or Slender Rush..is remarkable for its thread-like stems. 1721 C. KING *Brit. Merch.* I. 285 *Thred Sisters. 1844 STEPHENS *Bk. Farm* II. 416 The *Chorda filum*, or *thread-tangle. 1877 KNIGHT *Dict. Mech.*, **Thread-waxer*, a bowl of heated shoemaker's wax, through which the thread is conducted in sewing-machines for boots, shoes, and leather. 1825 J. NICHOLSON *Operat. Mechanic* 398 When either of the threads break, the *thread-wire through which it passes falls down. 1753 *World* No. 4. ⁋ 5 'The happiest in the world, madam', returned the *thread-woman. 1856 R. A. VAUGHAN *Mystics* (1860) II. VIII. ix. 97 The deftly-woven *threadwork of the tissues. 1861 LYTTON *Str. Story* (1862) II. 185 Pillows edged with the thread-work of Louvain. 1906 *Daily Chron.* 10 May 9/4 Mill girls employed in the thread works joined this organisation. 1888 *Dublin Rev.* July 69 The subject..is *threadworn.

**Thread** (þred), *v.* Forms: 4–6 threde, 6 threede, 6–7 thred, 7 threed, 7– thread; also 6– thrid. Pa. t. and pple. threaded; also 9 (*arch.*) thrid (*pa. pple.* thridden). [f. THREAD *sb.*: independently in various senses.

The spelling *thrid* is still quite common in some of the transf. and fig. uses.]

**1.** *trans.* To pass one end of a thread through the eye of (a needle) in order to use it in sewing; to furnish (a needle) with a thread; also, to treat (any perforated object) in the same way (as in quot. 1607).

?*a* 1366 CHAUCER *Rom. Rose* 99 A sylvre nedle forth I droughe,..And gan this nedle threde anon. 1530 PALSGR. 755/2, I threde a nedell to sowe with, *je enfile*. 1570 LEVINS *Manip.* 52/29 To Threede, *acum filo inducere*. 1607 TOPSELL *Four-f. Beasts* (1658) 307 Thread all the other rings with the loose end of the rope. 1676 C. HATTON in *H. Corr.* (Camden) 124 Good for nothing but to sit in ladyes chambers and thred their needles. 1709–10 STEELE *Tatler* No. 141 ⁋ 2 The Girl can scarce thread a Needle. 1840 HALIBURTON *Letter Bag* i. 14 He threaded my needle for me.

**b.** *transf.* To cause (something) to pass through something else, as a thread through the eye of a needle.

1851 MANTELL *Petrifact.* iii. § 7. 341 The graphic simile ..that the Plesiosaurus might be compared to a serpent threaded through the shell of a turtle. 1894 H. GARDENER *Unoff. Patriot* 27 Nature built these mountains, and threaded that little river over the stones. 1901 WATERHOUSE *Conduit Wiring* 3 Size of Conductors which can be threaded through Simplex Conduits. 1902 *Westm. Gaz.* 28 Apr. 5/2 The [foot-]ball was..threaded in and out among the Southampton players.

**c.** *fig.* To pass through, make a hole through, penetrate, pierce.

1670 PETTUS *Fodinæ Reg.* 2 When the Miners by these Shafts or Adits do strike or threed a Vein of any Metal. 1896 *Pall Mall Mag.* May 12 Tom out here will have leave to thrid you with bullets. 1899 B. CAPES *Lady of Darkness* xvi, Thridding Ned's brain as they passed with a receding sound like that made by pebbles hopping over ice.

**2.** To fix (anything) upon a string or wire that passes through it; *esp.* to connect (a number of things) by passing a thread through each, to string together on or as on a thread. Also *fig.*

1633 G. HERBERT *Temple, Sunday* v, The Sundaies of mans life, Thredded together on times string. 1650 EARL MONM. tr. *Senault's Man bec. Guilty* Ep. Ded., If you will adde Charity enough..to pardon the faults escaped in the Presse, I shall thread it to the rest of my Obligations. *a* 1668 DAVENANT *Song* Wks. (1673) 321 Thy Teares to Thrid instead of Pearle, On Bracelets of thy Hair. 1705 F. HAUKSBEE in *Phil. Trans.* XXIV. 2166 Amber..beads, about the bigness of small Nutmegs, and Threaded. 1809 SCOTT *Let.* 14 Sept., The sight of our beautiful mountains and lakes..[has] set me to threading verses together. 1867 F. FRANCIS *Angling* vii. (1880) 268 Threading the bait upon the hook. 1874 SPURGEON *Treas. David* Ps. ciii. 3 He selects a few of the choicest pearls.., threads them on the string of memory. *Mod.* The girl was threading beads on a string of catgut.

**b.** To make or embellish with or as with things strung on or fastened together by a thread.

1796 MRS. M. ROBINSON *Angelina* I. 230 No blithesome groups, thridding the roseate wreath, Or tripping in fantastic measures by. 1877 S. LANIER *Tampa Robins* II, I Will ..thrid the heavenly orange-tree With orbits bright of minstrelsy.

**3.** *fig.* To run or pass like a continuous thread through the whole length or course of; to pervade.

1830 *Examiner* 485/2 The melody which threads the first duet. 1858 *Eclectic Rev.* Ser. VI. III. 413 The burr of which [consonants]..thridding the open music of the vowel-sounds. 1871 EARLE *Philol. Eng. Tongue* 259 One spirit and purpose threads the whole, and gives a sort of unity. 1905 *Westm. Gaz.* 13 Oct. 1/3 A haunting mystical vision that always threaded my slumbers.

**b.** *intr.* for *refl.* To connect itself as by a thread.

*a* 1848 R. W. HAMILTON *Rew. & Punishm.* ii. (1853) 78 It has been seen how thought can thrid with thought, and feeling flow into feeling.

**4.** *trans.* To make one's way through (a narrow place, a passage presenting difficulties or obstacles, a forest, a crowd, or the like); to pass skilfully through the intricacies or difficulties of. *To thread out*, to pick out and follow, to trace (a path).

1593 SHAKS. *Rich. II*, v. v. 17 It is as hard to come, as for a Camell To thred the posterne of a Needles eye. 1607 — *Cor.* III. i. 127 They would not thred the Gates. *a* 1619 FLETCHER *Bonduca* IV. ii, See where he thrids the thickets. 1633 G. HERBERT *Temple, Vanitie* i, The fleet Astronomer can bore, And thred the spheres with his quick-piercing Minde. 1751 SMOLLETT *Per. Pic.* xcvi. (1779) IV. 175 A captain of the guards, who..had threaded every station in their community. 1809 MALKIN *Gil Blas* I. vi. ⁋ 3, I threaded all the windings of this new labyrinth. 1832 LYTTON *Eugene A.* IV. x, Events thicken, and the maze is nearly thridden. 1863 GEO. ELIOT *Romola* i, A labyrinth of narrow streets ..rarely threaded by the stranger. 1866 DORA GREENWELL *Ess.* 219 A land intersected and thridden by the channels of benevolence.

**b.** *To thread one's way, course*, etc. in same sense.

1825 COLERIDGE *Aids Refl.* (1848) I. 323 He..thrids his way through the odorous and flowering thickets into open spots of greenery. 1868 E. EDWARDS *Ralegh* I. x. 179 He ..proceeded to thread his course amidst the tortuous.. channels. 1887 BOWEN *Æneid* II. 634, I..through foemen and flames, by the goddess's grace Thrid my way.

**c.** *intr.* = b.

1660 F. BROOKE tr. *Le Blanc's Trav.* 5 The other [stream] ..threds through the middle of the Town. 1872 JENKINSON *Guide Eng. Lakes* (1879) 68 Bend to the left..and thread in an up-and-down course amongst the bare, rugged rocks. 1893 STEVENSON *Catriona* xi. 119, I..threaded through the midst of it [the wood], and returned to the west selvage. *Ibid.* xxii. 260 We thrid all the way among shoals.

†**d.** *trans. To thread the difference*: to trace out or follow the narrow dividing line. *Obs. rare.*

1627 WREN *Serm. at Whitehall* 17 Feb. 15 The Epidemiall prophanation of our times, that will thrid you a difference now betwixt this feare and perfect worship.

**5.** *intr.* To move in a thread-like course or manner; to flow in a slender stream; to creep, twine, wind.

1611, 1626 [see THREADING *vbl. sb.*]. *a* 1879 T. ORMOND in *Mod. Sc. Poets* II. 356 Gracefully the ivy green Did round the craprods thread.

**6.** *trans.* To weave as a thread into the texture of something; to interweave.

1853 ROCK *Ch. of Fathers* III. II. 25 These old 'tropes' ..used to be twined and threaded into the words of the daily service.

**b.** *passive.* To be penetrated, permeated, or interspersed as with threads.

1861 DORA GREENWELL *Poems* 215 The thrice refined gold Was thrid with baser clay. 1875 — *Liber Human.* 108 The elements which, mixed and threaded with whatever imaginable alloy, go to make up man's moral nature. 1891 ZANGWILL *Bachelor's Club* 21 His tawny hair, too, began to be threaded with silver.

†**7.** To bring on or induce gradually, as by the gentle drawing of a thread or line; to lead on. *Obs.*

1709 WODROW *Corr.* (1842) I. 48 Our corruptions, and so our desolation for a season, are like to be threaded in gradually upon us. *Ibid.* 61 Provided we be not gradually threaded in to greater encroachments on the Church's rights this way. 1716 *Ibid.* II. 202 We are like to be threaded out of the exercise of our power as to fasts and thanksgivings by the Assembly.

**8.** To stretch threads across or over; to intersperse with threads so stretched.

1884 *Chr. Commw.* 20 Mar. 536/2 The devil's long lines of temptation, with which the stream of life is so thickly threaded. 1907 *Westm. Gaz.* 25 Feb. 2/3 Heavy spraying.. and threading [fruit-trees]..he has found to be a failure. *Mod.* I am obliged to thread my crocuses and polyanthuses every spring to protect them from destructive birds.

**9.** To form a screw-thread on; to furnish (a bolt or the like) with a screw-thread.

1858 SIMMONDS *Dict. Trade* s.v. *Screw*, Threading is effected by a saw which [etc.]. 1877 KNIGHT *Dict. Mech.* 2074/1 Screw-threading machine. 1888 HASLUCK *Model Engin. Handybk.* (1900) 46 The extreme end is threaded for a nut, as shown in the section of cylinder. 1893 *Brit. Jrnl. Photogr.* XL. 801 A hole is bored in the neck and threaded, and the valve is screwed..in.

**Threadbare** (þre·dbēᵊɹ), *a.* Also 5 *Sc.* thred bar, (8 thread-bear), 5– thread(-)bare. [f. THREAD *sb.* + BARE *a.*]

**1.** Of a garment, etc.: Having the nap worn off, leaving bare the threads of the warp and woof; worn to the thread; shabby; worn-out.

1362 LANGL. *P. Pl.* A. v. 113 But ȝif a lous couþe lepe I con hit not I-leue Heo scholde wandre on þat walk hit was so þred-bare. *c* 1386 CHAUCER *Prol.* 260 He was nat lyk a Cloystrer With a thredbare cope as is a poure scoler. *c* 1470 HENRY *Wallace* VI. 449 Thi ald hud, becaus it is thred bar. 1590 SPENSER *F. Q.* I. iv. 28 Thred-bare cote, and cobled shoes, hee ware. 1693 BOWLES *Juvenal* v. 193 Will any Freedom here from you be born, Whose Clothes are thread-bare? 1711 ADDISON *Spect.* No. 42 ⁋ 2 Dresses and Clothes that were thread-bare and decayed. 1824 W. IRVING *T. Trav.* I. 196 Wit and coin are always doubted with a thread-bare coat.

**2.** *fig.* Resembling a threadbare garment; hence, poorly furnished or provided; meagre, scanty, poor, beggarly; contemptible, 'sorry'.

*c* 1412 HOCCLEVE *De Reg. Princ.* 1431 Som person is so threde-bare of konnynge. 1462 MARG. PASTON in *P. Lett.* II. 83 Yelverton is a good thredbare frend for yow. *c* 1518 SKELTON *Magnyf.* 223 Welth and Wyt, I say, be so threde bare worne. *a* 1550 *Fane wald I luve* 19 in *Dunbar's Poems* (S.T.S.) 308 Sum strykis down a threid bair cheik. 1586 DAY *Eng. Secretary* I. (1625) 44 With bad attire, and thred-bare dyet, he lived with him a pretty season. 1676 MARVELL *Mr. Smirke* 10 What Power they have, they will not wear it thred bare. 1704 SWIFT *T. Tub* Introd. ⁋ 25 A conscience thread-bare and ragged with perpetual turning. 1864 PUSEY *Lect. Daniel* (1876) 438 We should often have had but a threadbare history.

**b.** *esp.* Having lost its influence, freshness, or force by much use; trite from constant repetition; commonplace, stale, hackneyed.

1598 E. GILPIN *Skial.* (1878) 26 So long he hath vsde to cry, *oh rare*, That now that phrase is growne thin & thredbare. 1657 J. WATTS *Vind. Ch. Eng.* 107 A trite, and thredbare exception. 1746 CHESTERF. *Lett.* (1870) 23 The trite, threadbare jokes of those who set up for wit without having any. 1825 SCOTT *Let.* 29 Apr., If this quotation is rather threadbare. 1891 MRS. OLIPHANT *Jerusalem* I. iv. 157 A strange sermon upon..the fallacy of the hopes of men, which is a threadbare subject.

**3.** Of persons: Wearing threadbare clothes; shabby, seedy; hence, impecunious, hard up; down-at-heel, out-at-elbows. Now *rare* or *Obs.*

1577 R. WRIGHTE in Ellis *Orig. Lett.* Ser. II. III. 75 He shall not onley be thrid bare but ragged. 1628 EARLE *Microcosm., Prison* (Arb.) 82 Onely to be out at elbowes is in fashion here, and a great Indecorum, not to be thredbare. 1672 SHADWELL *Timon* I. Wks. 1720 II. 298 Honesty, Thou foolish, slender, thread-bare, starving thing. 1713 STEELE *Englishm.* No. 16. 108 You shall see him..in close Whisper with a thread-bare Philosopher. 1760–72 H. BROOKE *Fool of Qual.* (1809) IV. 136 [He] took the thread-bare Longfield ..under the arm, and carried him away.

**4.** *Comb.*, as *threadbare-genteel* (cf. *shabby-genteel*).

1849 CLOUGH *Amours de Voyage* I. 130 Some Threadbare-genteel relations.

**Threa·dbareness.** [f. prec. + -NESS.] The state or quality of being threadbare.

1530 PALSGR. 280/2 Threde bareness, *deureur*. ?*c* 1600 *Distr. Emperor* I. i. in Bullen *O. Pl.* (1884) III. 169 Thou that hast worne thy selfe and a blewe coate To equall thryddbareness. 1771 MACKENZIE *Man Feel.* xxi. (1886) 60 His look..spoke of the sleekness of folly and the threadbareness of wisdom. 1870 LOWELL *Among my Bks.* Ser. I. (1873) 355 A little threadbareness in the similes.

So **Threadba·rity** *nonce-wd.*, in same sense.

1892 BESANT *Ivory Gate* 69 The rags and duds and threadbarity too often enter largely into the picturesque.

**Threaded** (þre·dėd), *ppl. a.* [f. THREAD *v.* (and *sb.*) + -ED.]

**1.** Furnished with a thread (as a needle); strung on or as on a thread (as beads); interlaced, twined; consisting of or ornamented with threads.

1541 COPLAND *Guydon's Quest. Chirurg.* L iij, In puttyng threded nedles in to theym [wounds]. 1758 J. S. *Le Dran's Observ. Surg.* (1771) 274, I supported the Compress with a threaded Dossil. 1821 *Sporting Mag.* VIII. 262 She [a mare] had large corns on each foot, one of which was what is termed a threaded corn. 1821 JOANNA BAILLIE *Wallace* liv, Tissue of threaded gems is worn. 1856 BRYANT *West Wind* i, And hear the breezes of the West Among the threaded foliage sigh. 1876 GEO. ELIOT *Dan. Der.* IV. xxx, Standing with her arms thrust down and her fingers threaded. 1904 FARRER *Gard. Asia* viii. 74 A threaded chain of lakes.

**2.** Having or furnished with a screw-thread.

1844 *Civil Eng. & Arch. Jrnl.* VII. 153/2 On approaching the farther or opposite end they are made irregular, commonly called 'drunken threaded'. 1884 C. G. W. LOCK *Workshop Receipts* Ser. III. 288/1 The shank and threaded part of the tap. 1898 *Cycling* 49 Working upon the threaded end of the axle.

**3.** [f. THREAD *sb.*] As the second element in parasynthetic combinations, as *bare-*, *gold-*, *grey-*, *small-threaded*.

1616 J. DEACON *Tobacco Tortured* 66 They make..well bred Gentlemen, but bare thredded Yeomen. 1617 MINSHEU *Voc. Hisp. Lat.*, *Aranuelo*,..a small threaded net to catch birds. 1896 *Godey's Mag.* Feb. 211/2 Long opera wraps..of gold-threaded brocade.

**Threaden** (þre·d'n), *a.* Now *arch.* or *dial.* Forms: see THREAD *sb.*; (also 5 therdyn). [f. THREAD *sb.* + -EN [4].] Composed or made of thread; *spec.* made of linen thread.

*c* 1400 *Laud Troy Bk.* 8351, I ȝeue not a threden lace Off thyn euel wil and thi manace! 1499 *Croscombe Churchw. Acc.* (Som. Rec. Soc.) 23 A therdyn cerchewe. 1590 LODGE *Euphues' Gold. Leg.* 59b, A dosen of new thredden points of medley coulour. 1594 WILLOBIE *Avisa* (1880) 76 Not worth in proofe a threden poynt. 1610 B. JONSON *Alch.* I. i, A thin thredden cloake. 1688 R. HOLME *Armoury* III. 224/1 They went always covered with Threaden Caps or Hoods. 1780 WARNER *Let.* 24 Aug., in Jesse *Selwyn & Contemp.* (1844) IV. 366 Of his threaden sails [he] has made wings to our riches wherewith to fly away. *a* 1825 FORBY *Voc. E. Anglia* s.v., Within our memory 'threaden stockings' were an article of Sunday apparel for village servants and apprentices. 1870 ROCK *Text. Fabr.* Introd. v. 127 Very fine threaden cloths..for liturgical purposes.

**Threader** (þre·dəɹ). Also 5 thredere, 9 thredder. [f. THREAD *v.* + -ER [1].] One who or that which threads; *spec.* **a.** a person employed to keep the shuttles threaded in weaving; **b.** a bodkin for threading tape or ribbon through interstices in a garment or the like; see also quot. 1877.

*c* 1430 *Pilgr. Lyf Manhode* IV. lviii. (1869) 204 My mooder Charitee was cordere and thredere [Fr. *fillaciere*]. 1877 KNIGHT *Dict. Mech.*, *Threader*, a device for guiding the thread into the eye of a needle. See *Needle-threader*. 1908 *Daily News* 1 Aug. 5/1 He went, at the age of ten, into a lace mill, where he advanced from the position of a 'jacker off' to that of a 'thredder'. 1911 *Ibid.* 3 May 8 Inspecting automatic threaders and inquiring into their adaptability.

**Threa·diness.** *rare.* [f. THREADY + -NESS.] The quality of being thready; in quot., stringiness.

*c* 1425 tr. *Arderne's Treat. Fistula* 82 Arsenic & auripigment bene boþe one,..but auripigment is..more disesy for to grynde for his þredinez. 1864 in WEBSTER.

**Threa·ding**, *vbl. sb.* [f. THREAD *v.* + -ING [1].] The action of the verb THREAD in various senses; an instance of this.

**1611** COTGR., *Filet d'huyle*, a small drop, or threading of oyle. **1626** BACON *Sylva* § 293 We see in Liquors, the thredding of them in Stillicides. **1852** R. S. SURTEES *Sponge's Sp. Tour* (1893) 118 The collar..exhibited all the stitchings and threadings incident to that department of the garment. **1887** E. GURNEY *Tertium Quid* II. 45 Accurate thridding of labyrinthine things. **1889** *Pall Mall G.* 25 Nov. 7/1 The machine which does the threading [of screws] is complicated and slow. **1908** R. W. CHAMBERS *Firing Line* xxviii, Another woman awoke to take up the ravelled threadings of her life again.

†**Threa·dish**, *a. Obs. rare*$^{-1}$. [f. THREAD *sb.* + -ISH [1].] Resembling a thread; thread-like.

**1578** LYTE *Dodoens* II. i. 147 The roote is tender & of threddish strings.

**Threa·d-lace.** Lace made of linen or cotton thread as distinguished from silk lace.

**1581** *Acc. Bk. W. Wray* in *Antiquary* XXXII. 117 A grose white thred lace, vs. vj d. **1785** in *Home Counties Mag.* (1902) IV. 226 One of the best thread lace-makers in England. **1821** J. SMYTH *Pract. of Customs* 118 No Thread Lace can be imported in a less quantity than 12 yards, unless of the value of £2 per yard or upwards. **1861** GEO. ELIOT *Silas M.* i, Great ladies, clothed in silk and thread-lace.

**Threadle** (þre·d'l), *v. dial.* Also 9 **threddle, thriddle.** [f. THREAD *sb.* + -LE 3.] = THREAD *v.*

**1746** BOWLKER *Art Angling* (1833) 52 Threadle this gudgeon. **1767** J. BICKERSTAFFE *Love in City* I. ii, Here threadle my needle. **1881** *Isle of Wight Gloss.*, *Threadle*, to thread; to string. **1887** BOWEN *Æneid* II. 454 A passage adjoined Thriddling the inner palace. **1888** *Berks. Gloss.* s.v., To 'threddle' a needle is to pass thread through the eye of it ready for sewing.

**Threadless** (þre·dlės), *a.* [f. as prec. + -LESS.] **1.** Without a thread; having no thread; unthreaded.

**1822** *Blackw. Mag.* XII. 711 Threadless, knotless, endless, useless mysteries, tragedies, and dramas. **1866** T. BRUCE *Summer Queen* 14 Fancy lost in threadless maze Was running to and fro.

**2.** Having no screw-thread.

**1886** *Cyclist* 4 Aug. 1081/1 It [a bicycle]..is made with Clarke's patent threadless spokes.

**Threadlet** (þre·dlėt). [f. as prec. + -LET.] A minute thread; a slender filament.

**1882** J. PARKER in *Homil. Mag.* (N. Y.) May 459 By what threadlets is he lifted up? **1887** C. L. MORGAN *Anim. Biol.* iii. 29 A delicate dark thread, from which minute threadlets pass off.

**Thread-like** (þre·dləik), *a.* [f. as prec. + -LIKE.] Like a thread; also, like that of a thread.

**1774** MRS. DELANY in *Life & Corr.* Ser. II. (1862) II. 47 A little brassish, copperish, goldish thread-like stuff adhering to a bit of slate or coal. **1814** SOUTHEY *Roderick* XVII. 50 The stream's perpetual flow..with its..Dimples and thread-like motions infinite. **1835–6** *Todd's Cycl. Anat.* I. 604/1 Cellular tissue formed of white thread-like filaments. **1901** *Scribner's Mag.* XXIX. 433/2 Ridges over which the white tracks wind, thread-like, toward the hazy rim of mountains.

**b.** Of the pulse: = THREADY 4.

*a* **1829** in *Good's Study Med.* (1829) II. 612 Difficulty of swallowing; thread-like pulse. **1897** *Allbutt's Syst. Med.* II. 818 The heart's action becomes extremely feeble, and the pulse threadlike and uncountable. *Ibid.* IV. 389 It may be found that a pulsation of thread-like smallness will pass in spite of almost any pressure which the finger can apply.

†**Threa·dmeal**, *adv. Obs. rare.* [f. as prec. + -MEAL.] Thread by thread.

**1565** COOPER *Thesaurus*, *Filatim*,..threade meale: threade by threade. *Ibid.* s.v. *Distraho*, *Filatim distrahi*, to be pulled a sunder threadmeale.

**Threa·d-nee·dle.** Also **thread-the-needle; threadthe (my) needle-eye, my grandmother's, the tailor's needle**; *dial.* **grandy needles.** [f. THREAD *v.* + NEEDLE.]

**1.** A children's game, in which, all joining hands, the player at one end of the string passes between the last two at the other end, the rest following.

**1751** *Advent. G. Edwards* 140 (Halliwell) Eight people..joining hands like children at thread-needle. **1797–1805** S. & HT. LEE *Canterb. T.* III. 450 Children..playing thread my grandmother's needle. **1825–7** HONE *Every-day Bk.* I. 692 The prettiest sight..was a game at 'Thread my needle', played by about a dozen lasses. **1856** MISS MULOCK *J. Halifax* xxv, From top to bottom, the young men and women were running in a long 'Thread-the-needle'.

**2. Thread the needle,** as *verb phrase*: (*a*) in dancing, denoting the movement in which the lady passes under her partner's arm, their hands being joined; (*b*) to pass in and out in a winding course; (*c*) in shooting: see quot. 1895 [2].

**1844** DICKENS *Christmas Carol* ii, Advance and retire, both hands to your partner, bow and curtsey, corkscrew, thread-the-needle, and back again to your place. **1895** *Daily News* 12 June 7/2 The toiling oarsman..might then have to 'thread the needle' (inshore for the boat, outside for the punt, close astern). **1895** *Funk's Standard Dict.* s.v., *To thread the needle* (*Western U.S.*), to fire a rifle-ball through an auger-hole barely large enough to allow the ball to pass without enlarging the hole.

**Threa·d-pa·per.** A strip of thin soft paper folded in creases so as to form separate divisions for different skeins of thread; the paper so folded forming a long and narrow strip.

**1761** STERNE *Tr. Shandy* III. xli, What is become of my wife's thread-paper? **1796** MME. D'ARBLAY *Camilla* II. 404 [She] had lost the thread-paper from which she was to mend her gown. **1880** *Plain Hints Needlework* 57 It should be cut at each end of the skein and folded securely into a 'thread paper'.

**b.** *fig.* A person of slender or thin figure.

**1824** MISS MITFORD *Village* Ser. I. 153 So tall and so limp, bent in the middle—a thread-paper, six feet high! **1833** MARRYAT *P. Simple* xxix, If the common sailors were ..such little thread-papers as you. **1881** HUXLEY in *Life* (1900) II. ii. 35, I was a thread paper of a boy myself.

**c.** *attrib.* Having the attributes of a thread-paper; long and narrow slender, attenuated; limp, feeble, flimsy.

**1746–7** MRS. DELANY in *Life & Corr.* (1861) II. 450, I expect soon to see the other extreme of thread-paper heads and no hoops, and from appearing like so many blown bladders, we shall look like so many bodkins stalking about. **1803** *Naval Chron.* X. 510 Bonaparte's thread paper flotilla. **1882** P. FITZGERALD *Recreat. Lit. Man* (1883) 186 [Landing from a Calais steamer] Singers, actresses, ladies of quality, princesses, queens, all reduced to the common thread-paper level. **1884** STEVENSON *New Arab. Nts.* 308 She was a thread-paper creature.

**Threadworm** (þre·dwɒɹm). A worm of thread-like form, as the GUINEA WORM, HAIR-WORM, etc.; *esp.* the pin-worm, *Oxyuris* (*Ascaris*) *vermicularis*, parasitic in the human rectum, chiefly in children.

**1802** BINGLEY *Anim. Biog.* (1813) III. 400 The Indian thread-worm, or guinea-worm,..enters the naked feet of the slaves. **1822–34** *Good's Study Med.* (ed. 4) I. 274 The head of the thread-worm is subulate, nodose, and divided into three vesicles. **1879** WRIGHT *Anim. Life* 582 The Thread Worm (*Gordius aquaticus*) is viviparous, and the young differ in form from the mother. **1899** *Allbutt's Syst. Med.* VIII. 512 [Eczema] may follow the irritation of thread worms.

**Thready** (þre·di), *a.* [f. THREAD *sb.* + -Y.]

†**1.** Full of or covered with thread. *Obs.*

**1594** WILLOBIE *Avisa* 37 b, When threedy spindle full was grown. **1757** DYER *Fleece* III. 135 The thready shuttle glides along the lines.

**2.** Of thread-like texture; composed of fine fibres; stringy, fibrous.

*c* **1425** [implied in THREADINESS]. **1715** tr. *Pancirollus' Rerum Mem.* I. I. iv. 12 Its threaddy Substance may be weav'd into a Web. **1750** tr. *Leonardus' Mirr. Stones* 71 Amianton is a stone of a lucid colour, and thready, like feathered alum. **1797** *Encycl. Brit.* (ed. 3) XII. 371/2 The bark [of the mulberry tree]..is rough, thick, thready, and fit for being made into ropes. **1809** tr. *Landt's Descr. Feroe Isl.* (1810) 141 Compact, thready, or radiant zeolite. **1826** CARLYLE *Early Lett.* (1886) II. 350 Abundance of grand thready peats.

**b.** Of liquid: Forming strings; viscid, ropy.

**1733** *Ordinary of Newgate* No. 1 Advt., Urine foul, slimy, thready. **1846** G. E. DAY tr. *Simon's Anim. Chem.* II. 182 The mucus will become very tough, and almost thready. **1897** *Allbutt's Syst. Med.* IV. 435 [The fluid of a pyonephrosis] is more or less thready and glairy.

**c.** Of a plant: Bearing thread-like fibres or parts; filamentous, hairy. *rare*$^{-1}$.

**1804** CHARLOTTE SMITH *Conversations*, etc. II. Notes 204 Thready Yucca, an Aloe, I believe.

**d.** Having thread-like markings; veined.

**1601** HOLLAND *Pliny* (1634) I. 493 Ioyners doe chuse the mistresse threadie grain that is most streight.

**e.** Threadbare; showing the threads.

**1910** *Nation* 15 Jan. 639/2 The envelope fluttered to the thready carpet.

**3.** Of the nature of, consisting of, or resembling a thread or a mass of loose threads; thread-like, hair-like; of a root: fibrous.

**1597** GERARDE *Herbal* I. ii. § 4. 3 The roote is threddie. **1621** T. GRANGER *Comm. Eccles.* xii. 6. 325 The small and threddie rootes of a tree. **1671** MARTEN *Voy. Spitzbergen* in *Acc. Sev. Late Voy.* II. (1694) 92 Her Feathers are thready or hairy. **1698** J. PETIVER in *Phil. Trans.* XX. 405 Its Style is thready, and about an Inch long. **1733** W. ELLIS *Chiltern & Vale Farm.* 231 Here it will twist and fasten its thready Entanglements to them almost from top to bottom. **1879** G. MACDONALD *Sir Gibbie* i, Her black hair..would have revealed a thready glitter of grey. **1882** — *Castle Warlock* xxviii, Many a thready weed.

**4.** Of the pulse: see quot. 1899.

**1753** N. TORRIANO *Gangr. Sore Throat* 109 A frequent, and very thready Pulse. **1764** *Phil. Trans.* LIV. 239 His pulse was too quick..and withall low and thready. **1860–1** FLOR. NIGHTINGALE *Nursing* 80 The pulse becomes quick, perhaps 130, and so thready, it is not like a pulse at all, but like a string vibrating just underneath the skin. **1897** *Allbutt's Syst. Med.* III. 621 The pulse becomes small, sharp, wiry or thready. **1899** *Syd. Soc. Lex.*, *Thready pulse*, a small, scarcely perceptible pulse found in the terminal stages of fatal diseases.

**5.** Of the voice, etc.: Dry and thin; wanting in fullness. (Cf. THREAD *sb.* 4 b.)

**1860** *All Year Round* No. 41. 344 Incapable of knowing how exceedingly high he is pitching his thready old voice. **1874** LISLE CARR *Jud. Gwynne* I. iii. 92 Sickly pianos and thready harps. **1902** MISS BROUGHTON *Lavinia* (ed. Tauchn.) 235 A fuller sound in the thready voice.

**Threap** (þrīp), *sb.* Now *Sc.* and *north. dial.* Forms: 3–4 **þrep**, 4–5 **þrepe**, **threp**, 4–6 **threpe**, 6 **threip**, **threype**, 7 **threape**, 8–9 **threep**, 8– **threap.** [f. THREAP *v.*]

**1.** The action of threaping; contradiction, contention, argument, discussion; controversy, dispute; strife, quarrel, contest.

*a* **1300** *Cursor M.* 13310 (Cott.) Wit-vten threp [*Gött.* ani threpe] or strijf. *Ibid.* 27609 O pride bicums throues o thrett, Hething, threp [*v. r.* þrepe], and athes grett. **13..** *E. E. Allit. P.* B. 350 Enter in þenne..& haf þi wyf with þe, Þy þre sunez with-outen þrep & her þre wyuez. *c* **1400** *Destr. Troy* 5246 Þai hade no strenght to withstonde þe striff of þe pepull, Þat were þro men in threpe. **1418** *26 Pol. Poems* xiv. 78 Stryf wiþ comons, threp, and thro, To brynge þat in amendement. **1535** STEWART *Cron. Scot.* (Rolls) I. 37 We sall mak threip ȝit or we ar ouirthrawin. **1794** *Har'st Rig* lxi, They stop at last, but still look laith The threap to yield. **1866** CARLYLE *Let.* Apr. in Froude *Life in L.* (1884) II. xxviii. 308, I had privately a kind of threap that the brandy should be yours. **1886** *S. W. Linc. Gloss.* s.v., We had a bit of a threap about it.

**2.** An act of threaping; a contradictive or pertinacious assertion; a hostile charge or accusation.

**1538** CROMWELL in Merriman *Life & Lett.* (1902) II. 128 To desire to conquer me by shrowde wordes, to vanquishe me by sharpe threpes of scripture. *a* **1699** J. FRASER in *Wodrow Soc. Sel. Biog.* (1847) II. 214 Let us..hear patiently all assertions and threaps. **1742** R. FORBES *Ajax* viii, At threeps I am na' sae perquire, Nor auld-farren as he. **1768** ROSS *Helenore* III. 111, I nae mair sall say this threap about,..That on my side the bargain did na fa'. **1864** CARLYLE *Fredk. Gt.* XV. xv. (1872) VI. 119 He had taken a threap that he would have it finished. **1897** SNAITH *Fierceheart* vi. 67 The threep was fause, an he..got a thrawn thrapple for a deed he didna dae.

**b.** Phr. *To keep (to) one's threap.*

**1756** MRS. CALDERWOOD *Jrnl.* (1884) 318 Encouraging her to keep to her threap. **1818** SCOTT *Br. Lamm.* xxvii, Lady Ashton..will, as Scotchmen say, keep her threep.

†**3.** Reproof, rebuke. (Cf. THREAP *v.* 1.) *Obs. rare.*

**1636** JAMES *Iter Lanc.* 276, I leaue thy heape Of bloodie crimes to God's revendge and threape.

**4.** *Comb.* **threap-ground, threap-land(s**, land of disputed ownership, debatable land; *spec.* applied to the Debatable Lands of the Border.

**1259** *Registr. Aberdon.* (Maitl.) I. 26 Super quadam terra que dicebatur threpland inter terram de Bondyngton..et terram de Newton. **1449** in Rymer *Fœdera* XI. 245/1 As touching the Landez callid Batable Landez or Threpe Landez in the West Marchez. **1568** in H. Campbell *Love-Lett. Mary Q. Scots* App. (1824) 15 The contraversy yerely arising by occasion of certein grounds upon the frontiers in the east marches, commonly called the threap-land, or debatable. **1825** E. MACKENZIE *Hist. Northumbld.* II. 257 A long tract of land..which was formerly Debateable Land, or Threap Ground; but which, in 1552, was divided by agreement between the proper officers of both nations. **1858** DENHAM *Folk-Lore* 55 (E.D.D.) Part of Wooler Common is still undivided, owing to disputes respecting it. It is called Threap-ground. **1894** HESLOP *Northumbld. Gloss.*, *Threap-lands, Threap-ground*,..land the ownership of which is disputed.

**Threap** (þrīp), *v.* Now *Sc.* and *north. dial.* Forms: 1 **ðreapian**, 3 **þreape**, (*Orm.*) **þræpenn**, 3–5 **þrepe**, 3–7 **threpe**, 4–6 **threppe**, (4–5 *pa. t.* **þrappit, þreppit**), 5–6 **threip**, 6 **thraip**, 6–7 **threape**, 6–9 **threep**, 6– **threap.** [OE. *þréapian* to rebuke, reprehend: of uncertain history.]

**1.** *trans.* To rebuke, reprove, chide, scold, blame.

*c* **897** K. ÆLFRED *Gregory's Past. C.* xxi. 165 Ðonne he to suiðe & to ðearllice ðreapian wile his hieremenn. *a* **1300** *E. E. Psalter* xciii[i]. 10 Þat vndretakes genge, noght threpe mon, Þat leres man wisedome to kun? **1582** STANYHURST *Æneis* IV. (Arb.) 106 Let not mee falslye be threpped. **1682** SHADWELL *Lanc. Witches* V. 71 Who threped and threped, and aw to becaw'd me. **1787** GROSE *Provinc. Gloss.*, *Threap*, or *Threapen*, to blame, rebuke, reprove, or chide. **1877** *N. W. Linc. Gloss.* s.v., I wen't be threp by a bairn like thoo. **1879** CLOUGH *B. Bresskittle* 14 (E.D.D.) Th' owd lass.. threap'd me foinly.

†**b.** *To threap* (a person) *with kindness* = *to threap kindness upon*: see 4 b. *Obs.*

**1567** JEWEL *Let. to Harding* in *Def. Apol.* Rrr j b, Yee threape her Maiestie fondely with kindenesse.

**2.** *intr.* To contend in words; to inveigh *against*; to argue, dispute; to quarrel, bicker, disagree; to wrangle about terms, haggle.

*c* **1200** ORMIN 5744 Acc himm birrþ þræpenn aȝȝ wiþþ skill Onnȝæness alle sinness. **1303** R. BRUNNE *Handl. Synne* 4352 Whan ȝe aȝens þe prechur þrepe. *Ibid.* 6065 Aȝens mokerers wyl y þrepe. *c* **1400** *Destr. Troy* 2152 Than ..priam..þonket hom þroly, þrappit no lengur. *Ibid.* 12235 He þroly with þrong wil þreppit agayn. *c* **1475** *Rauf Coilȝear* 79 Thank me not ouir airlie, for dreid that we threip. **1535** STEWART *Cron. Scot.* (Rolls) III. 454 The erle of Craufurd that same tyme and he,..Begouth to threip quha than that war best peiris. **15..** *Ballad, Take thy old cloak about thee* 67 It's not for a man with a woman to threape Unless he first gave oer the plea. **1755** JOHNSON, To *Threap*, a country word denoting to argue much or contend. **1847** C. BRONTË *J. Eyre* xxix, They were so agreeable with each other—never fell out nor 'threaped'. **1871** [see THREAPING *vbl. sb.*]. **1873** LYTTON *Parisians* IX. iii, Threep and argue as we may.

†**b.** *intr.* To fight, struggle, strive, contend. *Obs.*

**13..** *Gaw. & Gr. Knt.* 504 Bot þenne þe weder of þe worlde wyth wynter hit þrepez. ? *a* **1400** *Morte Arth.* 930 Of the nyghtgale notez the noisez was swette, They threpide wyth the throstilles, thre hundreth at ones! *c* **1400** *Destr. Troy* 2003 Þre dayes þroly þai þrappit with stormys. *Ibid.* 10098 Mony thoghtes full þro þrappit in his hert. *Ibid.* 12134 In þronge and in þraldom þrepe with þe werld.

**3.** *trans.* (usu. with *obj. cl.*) To persist in asserting (something contradicted or doubted); to affirm positively or pertinaciously; to maintain obstinately or aggressively.

*c* **1386** CHAUCER *Can. Yeom. Prol. & T.* 273 Sol gold is and Luna siluer we threpe. *c* **1475** *Rauf Coilȝear* 199 Thay threip that I thring doun of the fattest. **1509** FISHER *Wks.* (1876) 299 Some other threpe that he hathe forgoten theym. **1656** BLOUNT *Glossogr.*, *Threpe*,..to affirme positively, or to face one down with confidence; still used in the North. **1728** RAMSAY *Cameleon* 26, I say he's blue; He threaps, he's green: now what say you? *a* **1774** FERGUSSON *Drink Ecl.* Poems (1845) 53 Will ye your breedin' threep ye mongrel loun? **1816** SCOTT *Antiq.* xxiv, He threeps the castle and lands are his ain as his mother's eldest son. **1887** P. M'NEILL *Blawearie* 50 A group o' miners..threepit doon my throat that the grave..was only about four feet deep.

**b.** *To threap* (a person) *out of*: to move or do (him) out of (something) by persistent assertion.

**1677** Gilpin *Demonol.* (1867) 168 Thus are men threaped out of their own persuasions. **1885** J. Hartley *Clock Alm.* 40 (Yorks.) (E.D.D.) Shoo tried to threap me aght on it.

**c.** with *inf.* To insist on or persist in doing something. *rare*⁻¹.

**1827** Scott *Surg. Dau.* i, She threeps to keep on a black fause-face, and skirls if we offer to take it away.

**4.** *To threap* (something) *upon* (a person): †**a.** To impose (an assertion) upon; to lead or try to lead one to believe by persistent assertion. *Obs.*

*c* **1440** *Alphabet of Tales* 482 When his servandis wolde eatt any gude meate, þai wolde threpe vppon hym at he was seke. **1530** Palsgr. 755/2, I threpe a mater upon one, I beare one in hande that he hath doone or saide a thing a mysse..This terme is..farre northren. He wolde threpe upon me that I have his penne. **1608** Hieron *2nd Pt. Def. Ministers' Reas. Refusal Subscription* 72 Slaundring the Ministers and threaping one and the same..slaunder vpon them.

†**b.** To impute, attribute, ascribe (something) to a person. *To threap kindness* or *love upon* (also *of*): to attribute kindness, etc. to; to give (one) credit for love or goodwill, to urge to the exercise of kindness. (See also 1 b.) *Obs.*

**1559** Bercher *Nobylytye Wymen* (1904) 104 In dede..you threape kindenes vppon me, and surely..I can well a way wth yor prayse. **1579** W. Wilkinson *Confut. Familye of Loue* 65 It is but a vayne kyndnes, which Theophilus in this place threapeth on God. **1589** R. Bruce *Serm.* (1843) 129 Thou suld threep kindness of him. **1596** Nashe *Saffron Walden* 152 The baudie rymes he threapes vpon me. *a* **1603** T. Cartwright *Confut. Rhem. N.T.* (1618) 231 You do but threap kindnesse of the Hereticks, as you call them; for they acknowledge no such miracles to be done by your reliques. **1648** J. Beaumont *Psyche* v. ccxxvii, Behold how gross a Ly of Ugliness They on my face have threaped. **1660** Dickson *Writings* (1845) I. 42 If any wilt threap love upon God, they shall not be disappointed. **1730** T. Boston *Serm. Song of Sol. ii. 17* Wks. 1855 V. 552 It will make men very peremptory for Christ, that they will not take a refusal, to threap kindness on him and special interest in him.

**c.** To thrust, obtrude, press (something) upon a person; to urge upon him acceptance of or acquiescence in.

**1571** Golding *Calvin on Ps.* xviii. 3 If Sathan threpe any feare uppon us, it may be kept farre of from enterance. **1690** C. Nesse *O. & N. Test.* I. 68 Araunah had a princely spirit..but generous David threaps upon him fifty shekels. **1816** Scott *Antiq.* xv, Monkbarns had threepit on them to gang in till 't to see the wark o' the monks lang syne. **1869** 'Ouida' *Puck* xlii, Look'ee here! These arena goods to threap.

**5.** *To threap down*: to put down or silence by vehement or pertinacious assertion; also, with double object (sb. and clause), *to threap* (a person) *down* (*that*...): to try to force a statement upon (a person) by strength of assertion or insistent reiteration.

**1599** Nashe *Lenten Stuffe* (1871) 51 Bolingbroke,..at his removing..into banishment, as Father Froissart threaps down, was accompanied with forty-thousand men, women, and children weeping. **1674** N. Fairfax *Bulk & Selv.* 83 You may as well threap one down, that a ghost is heavier or lighter, colder or hotter,..whiter or blacker than a body. **1841** R. W. Hamilton *Nugæ Lit.* 340 A man will say of a clamorous talker, he did not convince me, but he threaped me down. **1877** Leigh *Cheshire Gloss.* s. v., He thraped me down it were noine, but I knowed it were a dozen.

Hence **Threa·ping** *vbl. sb.* and *ppl. a.*; **Threa·per**, one who 'threaps' or persistently asserts.

*c* **897** K. Ælfred *Gregory's Past. C.* xxi. 167 ʒif him mon to unʒemetlice mid ðære ðreapunga oferfylʒð. **13..** *E. E. Allit. P.* B. 183 For þeft, & for þrepyng, vnþonk may mon haue. *c* **1400** *Destr. Troy* 10847 A thowsaund full þro, þrepand in wer. *c* **1440** *York Myst.* xl. 105 Thei thraste hym full thraly, þan was þer no threpyng. *c* **1460** *Towneley Myst.* xxviii. 19 Do way youre threpyng! are ye wode? **1785** [W. Hutton] *Bran New Wark* 38 Naa brawling or threaping is heard. **1871** W. Alexander *Johnny Gibb* i, Johnny offered 'sax poun'..after much 'threepin' as his ultimatum. **1871** P. H. Waddell *Ps.* xxxv. 11 Thar raise amang them threepers o' ill. **1899** *Leeds Merc., Suppl.* 18 Feb. (E.D.D.), Ah niver knew sich a threaper as thee.

**Threa·pen,** *v. Obs.* exc. *dial.* [app. f. Threap *v.* + -en⁵; but, in sense 1, perh. for *threaten*.]

†**1.** To threaten (*trans.* and *intr.*). *Obs.*

**1340** *Ayenb.* 84 Naʒt ne habbeþ more of myʒte aye uirtues kueade mysfalles and zorʒes ne al þet fortune may þreapny and do: more þanne þer byeþ dropen of rayn ine þe ze. *Ibid.* 97. *Ibid.* 162 Hardyesse uor to þolie alle þe kueadnesse þet þe wordle may þreapni. **1559** Bercher *Nobylytye Wymen* (1904) 128 Yf they be threpned [It. *se sono minacciate*] they langwyshe, yf they be cheryshed they be prowde.

**2.** To blame, rebuke, chide, reprove: = prec. 1.

*a* **1667** Skinner *Etymologicon* (1671), To Threap or Threapen, *vox agro Linc. usitatissima*, ab AS. *Þreapian, Redarguere, vel Þrafian, Urgere.* **1691** Ray *N. C. Words, Threap, Threapen*, to blame, rebuke, reprove, chide. **1904** *Eng. Dial. Dict.* (E. Yorks.), *Threapen*, to reprove, rebuke, chide.

Hence **Threa·pening** *vbl. sb.*

**1340** *Ayenb.* 65, vij. oþre boʒes. Huer-of þe uerste is strif, þe oþer chidinge, þe þridde missigginge, þe uerþe godelinge, þe uifte atwytinge, þe zixte þreapninge, þe zeuende vnonynge arere. *Ibid.* 66 Efterward zuo comeþ þe þreapnynges and beginneþ þe medles and þe werres.

**Threat** (þret), *sb.* Forms: 1–3 **þreat,** (1 **ðreot(t, ðreatt),** 2 **þreatt,** 3 **þræt,** 3–4 **þrat,** 4 **þret, thrett,** 4–5 **þret(e, thret(e,** 6 **threttte,** 6– **threat.** [OE. *þréat* masc. (With sense 2 cf. ON. *þraut* fem. struggle, labour, trouble) :—OTeut. **þrauto-*, *-ā*, from ablaut-series **þreut-, þraut-, þrut-* (cf. OE. *þréotan* to trouble, weary, Goth. *us-þriutan* to trouble, threaten, OHG. *ir-drioʒan*, MHG. *ver-drieʒen*, Ger. *ver-drieszen*, Du. *verdrieten* to trouble, vex; cf. L. *trūdĕre* to press, thrust). Sense 1 has the same form as 2 in OE. and early ME., and is commonly considered the same word; it appears to go back, like 'throng' and 'press (of people)', to the radical sense 'to press'.]

**I.** †**1.** A throng, press, crowd, multitude of people; a troop, band, body of men. *Obs.*

*Beowulf* 2406 Se wæs on ðam ðreate þreotteoða secg. *a* **800** Cynewulf *Elene* 329 Hio..þrungon..on þreate. *c* **950** *Lindisf. Gosp.* Mark iii. 32 gesætt ymb hine ðreat [*c* **975** *Rushw. G.* ðe ðreatt, L. *turba*]. *Ibid.* viii. 2 Ic milsa ofer ðreat [*R.* ðreott]. *c* **1205** Lay. 9791 Riden ut to-some..þritti þusend þe þræt wes þa mare. *Ibid.* 26294 Hit is feole ʒere þat heore þrættes [*c* **1275** þretes] comen here.

**II.** †**2.** Painful pressure, oppression, compulsion; vexation, torment; affliction, distress, misery; danger, peril. *Obs.*

*a* **800** Cynewulf *Juliana* 465 Is þeos þraʒ ful strong, þreat ormæte; ic sceal þinga ʒehwylc þolian. **971** *Blickl. Hom.* 119 Hie seoþþan ealle worlde wean & ealle þreatas oforhoʒodan. *c* **1200** *Trin. Coll. Hom.* 61 Listeð nu wich þreat dauid setted uppen us bute [we] lesten ure bihese. **13..** *E. E. Allit. P.* B. 55 Þenne þrat moste I þole. *c* **1330** R. Brunne *Chron.* Prol. (1810) p. xcviii, With mykelle wo, In sclaundire, in threte & in thro. **13..** *Minor Poems fr. Vernon MS.* xliv. 36 And þretes—þo beoþ vuele þre, ffurst and hunger and þesternesse. *c* **1450** Lovelich *Grail* xiii. 606 They wenden han put him to gret thret.

**3.** A denunciation to a person of ill to befall him; *esp.* a declaration of hostile determination or of loss, pain, punishment, or damage to be inflicted in retribution for or conditionally upon some course; a menace. Also *fig.* an indication of impending evil.

The radical sense appears to be 'pressure applied to the will by declaration of the harm that will follow non-compliance'. It is thus indirect compulsion.

It is doubtful whether quots. *c* 1000 belong here or to sense 2.

*c* **1000** Ælfric *Saints' Lives* xxv. 220 Ac mathathias nolde ..godes æ forgæʒan for his [the king's] gramlican ðreate. *Ibid.* xxviii. 105 Ða hæþenan..heton hine secgan mid swyðlicum þreate hweþer he cristen wære. *c* **1200** *Vices & Virt.* 87 Oðerhwile cumeð maniʒe þohtes of godes þreatt of helle pines. *a* **1250** *Owl & Night.* 58 Ne recche ich nouht of þine þrete. *c* **1325** *Song of Yesterday* 148 in *E. E. P.* (1862) 137 ʒif þi neiʒebor þe manas Oþer to culle oþer to bete..þou wold drede þi neiʒebores þrete. **1526** *Pilgr. Perf.* (W. de W. 1531) 14 b, Wherby he myght scape the menasses and threttes of god. **1601** Shaks. *Jul. C.* iv. iii. 66 There is no terror Cassius in your threats. **1750** Gray *Elegy* 62 The threats of pain and ruin to despise. **1874** Green *Short Hist.* vii. § 1. 348 He met the hostility of the nobles with a threat which marked his power. **1884** *Manch. Exam.* 19 Feb. 5/4 Clouds full of the threat of rain.

**Threat** (þret), *v. arch.* and *dial.* Forms: see below. [OE. *þréatian* weak vb., pa. t. *þréatode*, f. *þréat*, Threat *sb.* :—OTeut. type **þrautōjan*.]

**A.** Illustration of Forms.

**1.** *Pres. stem.* α. 1 **þreatian,** 3 **-en, -in, þretie(n, þræten, þreat,** 3–5 **þrete,** 5 **þreete,** 5–6 **threte,** 6 **threete,** 6–7 **threate,** 6– **threat.**

*c* **888** K. Ælfred *Boeth.* xxxvii. § 1 Þa..þreatiað eal moncynn mid hiora þrymme. *a* **1225** *Leg. Kath.* 623 Me ham walde þreatin & leaden unlaheliche. *a* **1225** *Juliana* 13 Nulle ich þe her onont þreate se þu þreate buhe ne beien. *a* **1250** *Owl & Night.* 1609 Me myd stone & lugge þreteþ. **1483** *Cath. Angl.* 385/2 To Threte, *minari.* **1530** Palsgr. 755/2, I threete, or I thretten one to do hym harme, *je menasse.* **1600** Threat [see B. 5].

β. 4–6 **thret, thrette,** 4–7 **thrett.**

**13..** *Cursor M.* 18247 Nu þai thrett [*v. r.* thret] vs sare. *Ibid.* 19181 Þar-for sal we thret þam herd. *c* **1375** *Sc. Leg. Saints* xliii. (*Agatha*) 147 Gyf be fyre þu threttis me. **1523** Ld. Berners *Froiss.* I. clx. 194 Whan ye be at Parys..ye do thret thenglysshmen. *a* **1533** — *Gold. Bk. M. Aurel.* (1546) Gg iij b, She..thretteth them that be absent.

γ. 3 **þrattien, -en.**

*c* **1205** Lay. 20341 Swiðe heo gunnen þrattien [*c* 1275 þretie] Arður þene king. *Ibid.* 18738 Þrattest [see B. 4 a].

**2.** *Past tense.* α. 1 **th-, þreatade, -ode,** 2 **-ede,** 3 **þreated, þræted, þret-, þrætt-, þrettede,** 4 **þreted,** 5–6 **thretid,** 6– **threated.**

*c* **725**–*c* **1000** [see B. 1]. *c* **1160** [see B. 2]. *c* **1205** Lay. 504 Þe king þræted [*c* **1275** þretede] Brutun. *Ibid.* 27131 Summe þrætteden [*c* **1275** þrettede] heore ueond. *c* **1250** Þreated [see B. 3]. **13..** *Minor Poems fr. Vernon MS.* liv. 33 Harde þei þreted me in her þouʒt. *c* **1440** Thretid [see B. 3]. *a* **1529** Skelton *Wofully Araid* 13 The Jewis me thretid. **1673** Wood *Life* 14 July (O.H.S.) II. 266, I threated to geld the translator.

β. 3–4 **þrette,** 4 **þret,** 4–5 **thrett,** 4–6 **thret, threttte,** 5 **threte,** (**thred**).

*c* **1250** Þrette, *c* **1300** Þrette [see B. 5]. **13..** *Cursor M.* 19603 Saulus..thrett [*v. rr.* þrette, þret] All þe cristen. *c* **1330** R. Brunne *Chron.* (1810) 44 Þe corsaynt & þe kirke he threttte for to brennyng. *c* **1400** *Laud Troy Bk.* 10493 He chased the Troiens & thret. *c* **1440** *Alphabet of Tales* 81 And þan he thred hur. *c* **1440** *Generydes* 500 She threte hym sore. **1523** Ld. Berners *Froiss.* I. ccclxxxiii. 645 They thret them of London.

γ. 2–4 **þratte,** 4 **þrat,** 5 **thrat(t,** 5–6 **thratte,** 6 **thrate.**

*c* **1200** Ormin 15514 He þratte stirne wind o sæ & itt warrþ stille & liþe. **13..** *E. E. Allit. P.* B. 937 Þe aungelez hasted þise oþer & aʒly hem þratten. **13..** *Gaw. & Gr. Knt.* 1980 Fele þryuande þonnkkez he þrat hom to haue. *c* **1400** *Laud Troy Bk.* 6907 Thei thrat him alle, tho he was tan. **1589** R. Robinson *Gold. Mirr.* (Chetham) 37 Albion Isle he thrate.

**3.** *Pa. pple.*: 3 **i-ðrat,** 4–5 **þret, -tt, -tte**; 4–6 **threted,** 7 **threat,** 5– **threated.**

*a* **1225** *Ancr. R.* 304 Ich was ined [*MS. T.* iðrat] þerto. **13..** *Gaw. & Gr. Knt.* 1725 Þer he watz þreted, & ofte þef called. *a* **1400–50** *Alexander* 707 Þik & þrathly am I thret. **1470–85** Malory *Arthur* x. lxii. 520 Ful sore are we threted. **1472** Sir J. Paston in *P. Lett.* III. 38 That poor woode is soor manashed and thrett. **1631** Threat [see B. 3].

**B.** Signification.

†**1.** *trans.* To press, urge, try to force or induce; esp. by means of menaces. (With clause or inf.)

*c* **725** *Corpus Gloss.* (O.E.T.) 1275 *Maceratus*, þreatende. *Ibid.* 2169 *Urguet*, threatade. *a* **900** *O. E. Martyrol.* 18 Apr. 58 Adrianus se caser[e hine] þreatade þæt he Criste wiðsoce. *c* **950** *Lindisf. Gosp.* Matt. v. 42 Ðæm nedende *vel* ðæm ðreatende [*Vulg.* uolenti] huerfa ðec ne acerre. *c* **1000** Ælfric *Hom.* I. 416 Þa cempan..hine ðreatodon þæt he ðære deadan anlicnysse his lac offrian sceolde. *a* **1225** *Ancr. R.* 248 Ne mei he [the devil] buten scheawe þe uorð sumhwat of his apeware, & oluhnen, oðer þreaten þet me bugge þerof. **13..** [see A. 2 γ]. *c* **1470** Ashby *Dicta Philos.* 308 Who that wol nat be feire entreted, Must be foule & rigorously threted. **1501** *Plumpton Corr.* (Camden) 157 Ever they thratte me that I shold goe to London. **1638** *Hamilton Papers* (Camden) 4 They..thrett privatt men to singe the Covenatt.

†**2.** To rebuke, reprove. *Obs.* Cf. Threap *v.* 1.

*a* **1000** *Ags. Ps.* (Th.) lxvii. 27 [lxviii. 30] On wuda þu wildeor wordum þreatast. *c* **1160** *Hatton Gosp.* Luke ix. 55 And he be-wente hine and hyo þreatede. *c* **1200** [see A. 2 γ]. *a* **1300** *E. E. Psalter* vi. 1 Lauerd, ne threte me in þi wreth.

**3.** To hold out threats against; = Threaten 2.

*a* **1000** *Ags. Ps.* (Th.) ix. 29 [x. 8] And þreatað þone earman mid his eaʒum. *c* **1205** Lay. 641 He..þreateð þene castel & þat folc þer inne. *c* **1250** *Gen. & Ex.* 4125 And wrot an canticle..Ðat ðreated ðo men bitter-like Ðe god ne seruen luue-like. **1428** in *Surtees Misc.* (1888) 3 Wham he thret with bodily harm. *c* **1440** *Alphabet of Tales* 439 Sho apperid vnto hym & thretid hym att he was ferd for hur. *c* **1489** Caxton *Sonnes of Aymon* xvii. 390 It becometh not to suche a knighte as ye be, for to threte me thus. **1526** *Pilgr. Perf.* (W. de W. 1531) 66 He that thretteth a dogge for his barkyng prouoketh hym to more felnesse. **1631** R. H. *Arraignm. Whole Creature* x. § 2. 84 The Apostles glad, that they were threat, and beat for the Name of Christ. **1781** *Hist. Europe* in *Ann. Reg.* 25/2 The Spaniards sent out so great a force..as seemed sufficient..to threat the British fleets and islands with the most imminent danger. **1848** Lytton *Harold* i. iv, Send for me if danger threat thee.

**b.** With inf. or clause as complement.

*a* **1330** *Otuel* 736 Hou þei..þratten roulond to die. *c* **1330** R. Brunne *Chron. Wace* (Rolls) 8294 [The Britons] þretten Hengist to wake hys wough. *c* **1440** *Alphabet of Tales* 32 Þe devull come aforn hym with a byrnand stake, and thretid hym þat he sulde þruste itt in at his mouthe. **1461** *Paston Lett.* II. 25 She is thret if that she myght be take, she shuld be slayne. *a* **1517** in G. P. Scrope *Castle Combe* (1852) 295 He..thret hym that he schulde make hyme aper before my lordys grase. **1611** *Coryat's Crudities* Panegyr. Verses c iij, All the Sophists he did threat Their problemes to confound. **1642** J. Eaton *Honey-c. Free Justif.* 475 It would be a foolish part to set it [a kettle] beside the fire, and then charge it to be hot, and to threat it that else it shall be spilt.

**c.** *fig.* Said of things; = Threaten 4.

**1422** [see Threating *vbl. sb.*]. *c* **1590** Marlowe *Faust.* vii. 18 A sumptuous temple..That threats the stars with her aspiring top. **1634** Milton *Comus* 39 This drear Wood, The nodding horror of whose shady brows Threats the forlorn and wandring Passinger. *a* **1717** Parnell *Bookworm* 70 To see what dangers threat the year. **1800** Coleridge *Piccolom.* i. iii. 46 This tempest, which..threats us from all quarters. **1832** *Fraser's Mag.* IV. 764 The fate which threats kingdoms.

**4.** To hold forth (something) by way of a threat; = Threaten 3. **a.** with inf. or clause as obj.

*c* **1205** Lay. 17300 He gon þretien swiðe þat al he wolde heom to-driue. *Ibid.* 18738 Þu..þrattest hine to slænne. *c* **1250** *Lutel Soth Sermun* 82 in *O. E. Misc.* 190 Hire sire & hire dame þreteþ hire to bete. **1375** Barbour *Bruce* vi. 536 Vmbeset With fayis þat to slay hym thret. *c* **1557** Abp. Parker *Ps.* D ij, If the adversaries flocke to-gether..and threate to destroy the house of God. **1633** Bp. Hall *Hard Texts, O. T.* 413 Who is this..that threats to sweep all before him? **1681** Dryden *Abs. & Achit.* 801 If ancient fabrics nod and threat to fall. **1724** Ramsay *Royal Archers* 25 And seems to threat,..'No man unpunish'd shall provoke my rage'.

**b.** With sb. or pron. as obj.

*c* **1386** Chaucer *Parson's T.* ⁋ 572 He threttith more þan he may parfourme. **1526** *Pilgr. Perf.* (1531) 61 What payne & turment is threttte to the wycked & euyll lyuers. **1581** Mulcaster *Positions* vi. (1887) 47 Where thickning threates harme, there thinning fines the substance. **1594** Shaks. *Rich. III*, v. iii. 205 Euery one did threat To morrowes vengeance on the head of Richard. **1633** Bp. Hall *Hard Texts, N. T.* 17 Let the Tyrants..threat what they please. **1795** Burns *Dumfries Volunteers* i, Does haughty Gaul invasion threat? **1821** Clare *Vill. Minstr.* I. 4 Where black neglect..threats her constant winter cold and chill.

**5.** *absol.* or *intr.* To offer threats; = Threaten 5.

*c* **1250** *Gen. & Ex.* 2023 Often ʒhe ðrette, often ʒhe scroð. *c* **1300** *Havelok* 1163 Sho was adrad, for he so þrette. **1390** Gower *Conf.* III. 57 Bot they with proude wordes grete Begunne to manace and threte. *c* **1491** *Chast. Goddes Chyld.* 14 She..spekyth somtyme sharply somtyme she threteth. *a* **1541** Wyatt *Penit. Ps.* vi. 30 That drede of deathe, of deathe that ever lastes, Threateth of right. **1600** Holland *Livy* viii. xxxii. 304 Some were heard to intreat, others to threat. **1605** Shaks. *Macb.* ii. i. 60 Whiles I threat, he liues. **1725** Pope *Odyss.* ii. 231 Threat on, O prince! elude the bridal day, Tnreat on, till all thy stores in waste decay. **1822** Byron *Werner* II. ii. 266 Threat'st thou? **1901** Savage-Armstr. *Ball.* 64 (E.D.D.) Whun danger threats, return.

Hence †**Threat** *ppl. a.*, obtained by threats, forced, compulsory.

*c* **1375** *Cursor M.* 26944 (Fairf.) Wiseli loke þou be shriuin & noȝt wiþ strenght þer-to driuen For þret shrift mai haue na mede. *c* **1375** *Sc. Leg. Saints* xi. (*Symon & Judas*) 1338 God wald one na wyse Of ony man haf thret seruice.

**Threaten** (þre·t'n), *v.* Forms: 1 **þreatnian**, 3 **þret(t)ne(n, þretni**, 4–5 **þret(t)en**, 4–6 **threten, thretne**, 6 **thretten**, *Sc.* **threiten**, (6–8 **thretn-**), 6– **threaten.** [OE. *þréat-n-ian*, f. *þréat*, Threat *sb.* + -en [5] 2.]

†**1.** *trans.* To press, urge, force; = Threat *v.*[1] 1. Only in OE.

*c* **1000** Ælfric *Hom.* I. 424 Neadað se deofol eow þæt ȝe cristene men to his biȝgengum ðreatniað?

**2.** To try to influence (a person) by menaces; to utter or hold out a threat against; to declare (usually conditionally) one's intention of inflicting injury upon (in quot. 1816, one's certainty that some specified injury will fall upon); to menace. Const. *with* the thing; also with compl. clause (with finite vb. or inf.).

*c* **1290** *S. Eng. Leg.* I. 35/41 He þrettnede faste hermogenes. **1297** R. Glouc. (Rolls) 2391 Þe picars were wroþe ek & þretnede him ynou. **1387** Trevisa *Higden* (Rolls) III. 419 Alisaundre þretteneþ þe Iewes. **14..** *Sir Beues* 3341 (MS. N.) He me thretenyd for to slen. [**15..** *Ibid.* (Pynson) 3001 He threteneth me to be slayne.] **1474** Caxton *Chesse* II. v. (1883) 68 A tyrant dide do tormente Anamaximenes & thretenyd hym for to cutte of his tonge. **1526** *Pilgr. Perf.* (W. de W. 1531) 177 b, Traian commaunded hym to speke no more of it, thretnynge hym, that yf he dyd, he sholde lese his heed. **1651** Hobbes *Leviath.* II. xxxi. 186 Threatning them with Punishment. **1715** De Foe *Fam. Instruct.* I. iv. (1841) I. 83, I won't be threatened neither. **1816** Scott *Old Mort.* xliv, In vain his wife..hung by his skirts, threatening him with death..for meddling with other folks' matters. **1834** *Picture of Liverpool* 39 All classes were threatened to be overwhelmed in one universal ruin.

†**b.** To charge or command with threats of punishment or displeasure; to command sternly or strictly. (Chiefly in biblical versions.) *Obs.*

**1382** Wyclif *Mark* viii. 30 And he thretenyde hem, that thei schulden nat seie to ony man of him. **1526** Tindale *Acts* iv. 17 Lett vs threten and chaurge them that they speake hence forth to noo man in this name. **1555** Eden *Decades* 158 They..threatned them to auoyde the lande excepte they woolde bee distroyed euery manne. **1582** N.T. (Rhem.) *Mark* i. 25 And Iesvs threatened him, saying, Hold thy peace, and goe out of the man.

**c.** *fig.* (chiefly of impersonal agents or objects): To be likely to injure; to be a source of danger to; to endanger actively.

**1638** R. Baker tr. *Balzac's Lett.* (vol. II.) 34 Perhaps the tempest that threatens my head will fall but at my feet. **1725** De Foe *Voy. round World* (1840) 302 The wind..blew very hard, threatening us with a storm. **1781** Gibbon *Decl. & F.* xix. II. 139 The Persian monarch, elated by victory, again threatened the peace of Asia. **1835** Thirlwall *Greece* x. I. 381 Where one threatens the existence of another. **1877** Froude *Short Stud.* (1883) IV. I. ii. 23 France and England had been..drawn together by a special danger which threatened Christendom.

**3.** To hold out or offer (some injury) by way of a threat; to declare one's intention of inflicting. **a.** with infin. or clause as obj.

**1297** R. Glouc. (Rolls) 11209 Þe burgeis were þo bolde, & þretnede to nime mo. **1567** *Satir. Poems Reform.* vi. 71 The Propheit threitnit..That war and battell sould his land pas throw. **1649** Bp. Reynolds *Serm. Hosea* iv. 59 God threatneth terribly to shake the earth. **1682** Bunyan *Holy War* 49 They threatned also what men they would be. **1748** *Anson's Voy.* II. iii. 146 Threatning to murder all who should oppose them. **1855** Macaulay *Hist. Eng.* xxi. IV. 663 He was at last forced to threaten that he would immediately make the whole matter public.

**b.** with sb. or pron. as obj.

**1297** R. Glouc. (Rolls) 9383 Mid word he þretneþ muche & lute deþ in dede. *c* **1450** *R. Gloucester's Chron.* (1724) 483/1 *note* (MS. Coll. Arms), He meketh prout men, and he thretneth werre. **1590** Marlowe *2nd Pt. Tamburl.* v. iii, These cowards..threaten conquest on our sovereign. **1649** Bp. Reynolds *Serm. Hosea* i. 43 They..should unwillingly suffer what he threatneth. **1774** Burke *Corr.* (1844) I. 498 The party that has lost the election threatens a petition. **1844** H. H. Wilson *Brit. India* II. xii. II. 585 Reluctant to inflict the penalty that had been threatened.

**4.** *fig.* Of things, conditions: To give ominous indication of (impending evil); to presage, portend.

**1611** Shaks. *Wint. T.* III. iii. 4 The skies looke grimly, And threaten present blusters. **1644** Evelyn *Diary* 22 Oct., Another pendant Towre like that at Pisa, always threatning ruine. **1818–20** E. Thompson tr. *Cullen's Nosol. Method.* (ed. 3) 247 A sense of hunger threatening syncope. **1853** W. C. Baldwin *Afr. Hunting* viii. 339 The weather constantly threatens rain.

*intr.* (for *pass.*). **1850** D. G. Mitchell *Reveries Bachelor* 175 Hostilities would sometimes threaten between the school and village boys.

**b.** with infin.: To appear likely *to do* some evil.

**1780** *Mirror* No. 81 ¶ 9, I am sometimes..frightened with dangers that threaten to diminish it [my estate]. **1848** Dickens *Dombey* iv, It threatens to be wet to night. **1899** 'A. Hope' *King's Mirr.* ix, Age had not bent, but it threatened to break him. *Mod.* The new drainage scheme threatens to be an expensive undertaking.

**5.** *absol.* or *intr.* To utter or use threats; to declare one's intention of injuring or punishing in order to influence. **a.** *lit.* (absol. use of 2 or 3).

**1297** R. Glouc. (Rolls) 10308 Nou sir clerc quaþ þe king ȝe mowe þretni ynou. *c* **1450** tr. *De Imitatione* III. xviii. 86 Þou shalt not þreten euerlastingly. **1602** Shaks. *Ham.* III. iv. 57 An eye like Mars, to threaten or command. **1774** Goldsm. *Nat. Hist.* (1776) VII. 221 If too closely pursued, they [snakes] hiss and threaten. **1864** in Ellacombe *Ch. Bells Devon*, etc. (1872) 267 Do not threaten,..never let down your dignity by one single word of violence.

**b.** *fig.* (absol. use of 2 c or 4). To portend evil.

**1610** Shaks. *Temp.* v. i. 178 Though the Seas threaten they are mercifull. **1725** Pope *Odyss.* II. 6 A two-edged faulchion threatened by his side. **1793** Mann in *Lett. Lit. Men* (Camden) 437 Our political horizon blackens and threatens more and more. *Mod.* The weather threatens.

¶ **6.** *To threaten kindness* (*upon* a person): app. an altered form of the phrase *to threap kindness*: see Threap *v.* 4 b. *Obs.*

**1560** Daus *Sleidane's Comm.* 247 The byshop of Rome sendeth his letters to the Swisses, & threatning vpon them kindnes, for the frenship that had ben betwene them & his predecessours. **1577–87** Holinshed *Chron.* (1807) II. 249 The moonks being overcome with the kings words, threatning kindnesse upon them, fulfilled his request. **1579** Lyly *Euphues* (Arb.) 84 Philautus..threatneth such kindenesse at my handes, and suche curtesie at yours, that he shoulde accompt me his wife before he woe me.

Hence **Threa·tenable** *a.*, that may be threatened.

**1841–4** Emerson *Ess., Exper.* Wks. (Bohn) I. 186 The chagrins which the bad heart gives off..take form..and threaten or insult whatever is threatenable and insultable in us.

**Threatened** (þre·t'nd), *ppl. a.* [f. prec. + -ed [1].]

**1.** That is the object of a threat; assailed by menaces. Proverb *Threatened men live long.*

**1533** Lady Eliz. Wheathell in Mary A. E. Wood *Lett. Roy. & Illustr. Ladies* (1846) II. 91 There is an old saying, —'threatened men live long'. *a* **1642** Sir W. Monson *Naval Tracts* II. (1704) 287/1 It is an old Saying, That a threaten'd Man eats Bread. **1855** Macaulay *Hist. Eng.* xx. IV. 401 He took his post near Louvain, on the road between the two threatened cities. **1894** *Westm. Gaz.* 27 Nov. 5/3 The best-hated and the most threatened man in Germany.

**2.** Of evil: Held out or presented as impending.

**1567** Golding *Ovid's Met.* vi. (1593) 129 Neptunus standing striking with his long threatned blade Upon the ragged rocke. **1660** South *Interest Deposed* (title-p.) In the threatned and expected Ruin of the Laws. **1794** Mrs. Radcliffe *Myst. Udolpho* xxxi, She determined to brave the threatened vengeance. **1831** Scott *Ct. Robt.* xxiv, The Turks..had resolved to prevent the threatened attack of the crusaders.

**Threatener** (þre·t'nəɹ). [f. as prec. + -er [1].] One who threatens.

*a* **1541** Wyatt *Song of Iopas* 46 The starre of Saturne olde, A threat'ner of all liuing things with drought. **1595** Shaks. *John* v. i. 49 Threaten the threatner, and out-face the brow Of bragging horror. **1630** *R. Johnson's Kingd. & Commw.* A ij b, That Enemie and Threatner of our English Nation. **1748** Richardson *Clarissa* (1810) III. ii. 10 Threateners..were seldom to be feared. **1867** Jean Ingelow *Story Doom* vii. 140 A feeble threatener with a foolish threat.

**Threatening** (þre·t'niŋ), *vbl. sb.* [f. as prec. + -ing [1].] The action of the verb Threaten; menacing; also, an instance of this, a threat.

*c* **1290** *St. Kenelm* 242 in *S. Eng. Leg.* I. 352 So gret þretningue for him heo made. **1388** Wyclif *Acts* iv. 29 And now, Lord, biholde in to the thretnyngis [1382 thretingis] of hem. **1489** Caxton *Faytes of A.* I. xvi. 46 By thretnyng he shal also fraye hem. *a* **1548** Hall *Chron., Hen. IV* 7 b, The said kyng..menaced theym with sore thretenynges. **1611** Bible *Eph.* vi. 9 Doe the same things vnto them, forbearing threatning. **1719** De Foe *Crusoe* (1840) II. iii. 54 The Spaniards, despising their threatening. **1865–6** H. Phillips *Amer. Paper Curr.* II. 12 The threatenings of war were then only heard at a distance.

**Threa·tening,** *ppl. a.* [f. as prec. + -ing [2].] That threatens; conveying or indicating a threat or menace; portending some impending evil.

**1530** in W. H. Turner *Select. Rec. Oxford* (1880) 83 Gevyng hym many thretenyng and opprobryous words. **1656** Earl Monm. tr. *Boccalini, Pol. Touchstone* (1674) 287 With threatning countenances they said [etc.]. **1724** De Foe *Mem. Cavalier* (1840) 48 If Tilly did but write a threatening letter. **1829** Scott *Anne of G.* xxx, There muster yonder in the west some threatening clouds. **1898** *Allbutt's Syst. Med.* V. 118 The fever is high, and the condition of the patient is threatening.

**Threa·teningly,** *adv.* [f. prec. + -ly [2].] In a threatening manner; menacingly.

**1601** Shaks. *All's Well* II. iii. 85 The honor sir that flames in your faire eyes, Before I speake too threatningly replies. **1819** Wordsw. '*Departing summer hath assumed*' vii, Woe! woe to Tyrants! from the lyre Broke threateningly. **1857** W. Collins *Dead Secret* v. iii, The booming of the surf sounding threateningly near in..the fog.

So **Threa·teningness.**

**1891** Atkinson *Last of Giant Killers* 239 The suddenness of the action, and the threateningness of it.

†**Threa·ter.** *Obs. rare*[−0]. [f. Threat *v.*[1] + -er [1].] = Threatener.

*c* **1440** *Promp. Parv.* 492/2 Thretare, *minator.*

**Threatful** (þre·tfŭl), *a. rare.* [f. Threat *sb.* + -ful.] Full of threats; threatening.

*c* **1557** Abp. Parker *Ps.* E iij, The thretfull warninges of the judgement. **1611** Speed *Hist. Gt. Brit.* ix. viii. (1623) 582 By their threatfull letters. **1760–72** H. Brooke *Fool of Qual.* (1809) IV. 129 A threatful and agile whirl of his staff. **1882** Farrar *Early Chr.* II. 6 Not the threatful Law of Moses,..but the royal Law, the perfect Law of liberty.

Hence **Threa·tfully** *adv.*, threateningly.

**1565** Stapleton tr. *Bede's Hist. Ch. Eng.* 50 S. Austen thretfully proficied, that, if they would not take peace.. with their brethern, they should receaue..warre from their enemies. **1634** Sir T. Herbert *Trav.* 190 [A] flaming Semiter (threatfully held against him). **1822** Hood *Lycus* vi, The spirits of sin..that..threatfully warr'd with the light.

**Threating** (þre·tiŋ), *vbl. sb. Obs.* or *arch.* [f. Threat *v.*[1] + -ing [1].] The action of the verb Threat; threatening; a threat.

**1046** *O. E. Chron.* (MS. D), On þam ȝeare ȝegaderade Eadward cyng mycele scypferde on Sandwic þurh Magnus þreatunge on Norwegon. *a* **1225** *Ancr. R.* 156 Vre Louerd hefde ifuld him of his þreatunge. **1382** [see quot. 1388 s. v. Threatening *vbl. sb.*]. **1422** tr. *Secreta Secret., Priv. Priv.* 152 Seneca..wriet the hede atte the t[h]retyngis of the Swerde. **1482** *Monk of Evesham* (Arb.) 96 Whenne he herde..this thretyng he was sore aferd. **1562** J. Heywood *Prov. & Epigr.* (1867) 129 Not to wag their beardes in brawlyng and threatyng. **1643** Bp. H. Leslie *Serm. St. Mary's, Oxford* 9 Feb. 4 None of his threatings could fall to the ground.

**Threa·ting,** *ppl. a. Obs.* or *arch.* [f. as prec. + -ing [2].] That threats; threatening, menacing.

**13..** *K. Alis.* 930 (Bodl. MS.) Wiþ cryeyng & þretyng wordes. **1483** *Cath. Angl.* 385/2 Threthynge, *minans, minax.* **1510** *Sel. Cas. Crt. Star Chamber* (Selden) 205 With thretyng wordes [they] Caused the Carpynders to leve ther werke. **1641** A. Scott *Journ.* in *Sc. Hist. Soc. Misc.* (1904) 278 The threating danger of the Scottish mist.

**Threatless** (þre·tlės), *a. rare.* [f. Threat *sb.* + -less.] Devoid of threats; not threatening.

**1605** Sylvester *Du Bartas* II. iii. IV. *Captaines* 201 Threat-lesse their brows, and without braves their voyce.

**Threave,** variant of Thrave.

**Thred(e, thredde,** obs. ff. Third, Thread.

**Three** (þrī), *a.* and *sb.* Forms: see below. [OE. *þrí* (*þríe*), *þrío*, *þréo*, Com. Teut. and Indo-Eur.; = OFris. *thre* m., *thria* f., *thriu*, *thria* n.; OS. *thrie* (*thria*, *threa*) m., *threa* f., *thrua* (*thriu*, *thria*) n. (MLG., LG. *drê*, *dru* n., MDu., Du. *drie*); OHG. *drî*, *drio*, *driu* (MHG. *drî(e*, Ger. *drei*); ON. *þrír*, *þrjár*, *þrjú* (Norw., Sw., Da. *tre*); Goth. **þreis*, *þrija*; :—OTeut. **þrīz* (:—**þrijiz*), **þrijā* :—Indo-Eur. *treies*, *treja*. Cf. Skr. *trayas*, Zend *θri*, Gr. τρεῖς, τρία, L. *trēs*, *tria*, Lith. *trýs*, OSlav. *trĭje*, *trije*, Irish and Welsh *tri*. The masc. has the form of a plural *-i* stem.]

**A.** Illustration of Forms.

*α. nom.* and *acc.* 1 masc. **þrí, þríe, þrý** (**þréo**), fem. and neut. **þrío, þréo,** (*ONorth.* **ðríu, ðría, ðréa**); 2–4 **þreo,** 1–5 **þre,** (2 **þru** (? *ü*), 2–3 **þri, þro,** 2–4 **þrie**), 4 **þree,** (**tre**), 4–6 **thre** (6 **threy, thrie**), 5– **three.**

**803** *Charter Cuðred* in *O. E. T.* 442 Þisses londes earan ðrie sulong. *c* **825** *Vesp. Hymns* v. (*O. E. T.* 405), Ðreo foeðan [*ternos statores*]. *c* **891** *O. E. Chron.* an. 891, Þrie Scottas comon. *c* **950** *Lindisf. Gosp.* Mark viii. 2 Ðrio doȝor ȝe-abidas mec. *Ibid.* ix. 5 Ðrea [*c* **975** *Rushw.* ðria] husa. — Luke xi. 5 Sel me ðreo [*Rushw.* ðria] hlafas. **971** *Blickl. Hom.* 145 Þa þre fæmnan. *c* **1000** Ælfric *Gen.* xl. 12 Þa þreo clystru þæt sind..þri daȝas. *c* **1000** *Ags. Gosp.* Matt. xii. 40 Þry daȝas and þreo niht. **11..** *Sax. Leechd.* III. 134 Leȝe þarto þru dæȝes & þre niht. *a* **1175** *Cott. Hom.* 237 Þri ampres were an mancyn. *c* **1175** *Lamb. Hom.* 73 Þro þing boð þet ech Mon habbe mot. *c* **1200** *Trin. Coll. Hom.* 3 On þesse þre wuken. *Ibid.* 27 Þese þrie þing. *c* **1205** Lay. 53 Þa þre boc. *Ibid.* 391 He ȝef Assaracun .. þreo [*c* **1275** þre] castles. *c* **1275** *Ibid.* 16589 Þreo daȝes and þreo niht. **13..** *Cursor M.* 5469 (Cott.) Þar of tre yeir was him wan. *Ibid.* 9192 (Gött.) Þat was vmgang jornays thrie. **1340** *Ayenb.* 88 Þe þri greteste guodes. **1362** Langl. *P. Pl.* A. I. 20 Þreo [**1377** B. Þree, **1393** C. Þre] þinges. **1483** *Cath. Angl.* 385/1 Three, *tres & tria.* **1552–3** *Inv. Ch. Goods Staffs.* in *Ann. Lichfield* (1863) IV. 46 Stoles & fannes for threy vestiments. **1596** Thrie [see B. I. 3]. **1600** in *Shaks. Cent. Praise* (Shaks. Soc.) 36 The L. montegle with some thre more.

*β. dative*, 1 **þrim, þrym, þriim, þrém,** 1–3 **þréom** (3 **þrom**); *genitive*, 1 **þríora, þréora.**

*c* **893** K. Ælfred *Oros.* Contents IV. vi, On þriora consula dæȝe. *Ibid.* III. ix. § 5 On ðæm þrim ȝearum..on þrim folc ȝefeohtum. *c* **950** *Lindisf. Gosp.* Matt. xxvi 61 Æfter ðrim [*c* **1000** *Ags. Gosp.* þrym; *c* **1160** *Hatt. Gosp.* þrem] daȝum. — Mark xv. 29 On ðriim daȝum. *c* **1000** *Ags. Gosp.* John ii. 6 Ælc wæs on tweȝra sestra ȝemete oððe on þreora. *c* **1100** *O. E. Chron.* an. 1078, Þreom nihton ær Candelmæssan. *c* **1205** Lay. 8059 Þas dæies æn þreom [*c* 1275 a þreo] wiken. *Ibid.* 10034 Wið innen þan þrom ȝeren.

**B.** Signification.

The cardinal number next above two, represented by the symbols 3, III, or iii.

**I.** as *adj.* **1.** In concord with a sb. expressed.

**803–***c* **1000** [see A]. *c* **1175** *Lamb. Hom.* 11 Nu weren þas þreo laȝe ȝe-writen inne þa oðre table breode sunderlipes. *c* **1250** *Gen. & Ex.* 557 Noe and hise ðre sunen. *a* **1300** *Cursor M.* 182 Fiue thossand men..he Fedd wyt fiue laues and fisses thre. *c* **1412** Hoccleve *De Reg. Princ.* 1801 Of thre conclusions moot I cheese one: Or begge, or stele, or sterue. *c* **1460** *Wisdom* 293 in *Macro Plays* 45 Ye haue iij enmyes:..The worlde, þe flesche, & þe fende. **1526** *Pilgr. Perf.* (W. de W. 1531) 1 This treatyse..is..diuyded in to thre bokes. **1753** Challoner *Cath. Chr. Instr.* 2 The three Divine Virtues of Faith, Hope and Charity. **1775** Sheridan *Rivals* IV. ii, Like Cerberus, three Gentlemen at once. **1871** Tyndall *Fragm. Sci.* (1879) I. xii. 358 Rocksalt cleaves in three directions.

**b.** Standing alone as predicate, or in concord with and following a pronoun, or pronominal adj.

*c* **1050** *Charter of Eadwine* in Kemble *Cod. Dipl.* IV. 260 Ðise write sinden þre. *c* **1200** Ormin 18657, & tohh þeȝȝ sinndenn alle þre An Godd. **1362** Langl. *P. Pl.* A. IX. 100 As þei þreo assenten. **13..** *Pol. Rel. & L. Poems* 228

Reuthþe and treuthþe and charite, Beþ out of lond alle þreo. *c* 1470 *Golagros & Gaw.* 400 Our souerane Arthour.. Has maid ws thre as mediatour. *a* 1548 HALL *Chron., Edw. IV* 199 b, Wee were all three one mannes sonnes. 1678 DRYDEN & LEE *Œdipus* III. i, *Tir[esias]*.. By the Fates that spun thy thread! *Cho[rus]*. Which are three. 1845 BROWNING *How they brought the Good News* 2, I galloped, Dirck galloped, we galloped all three.

**c.** Forming compound numerals with multiples of ten; originally placed first, as *three and thirty* (rarely *thirty and three*), now usually *thirty-three*. So also *three and thirtieth* (arch.: now *thirty-third*), etc.

*c* 1000 ÆLFRIC *Exod.* xxxii. 28 Þreo and twentiȝ þusendra manna. *c* 1205 LAY. 3870 Þer of he wes lauerd þro and þritti wintere. *c* 1380 WYCLIF *Sel. Wks.* III. 340 Aboute þree and þritti ȝeer. *c* 1470 *Golagros & Gaw.* 247 The roy rekinnit on raw Thretty and thre. 1579 FULKE *Heskins' Parl.* 204 The three and twentieth Chapter endeth the exposition. 1588 PARKE tr. *Mendoza's Hist. China* 301 So they departed..the three and twentie day of Ianuarie. 1725 DE FOE *Voy. round World* (1840) 168 A true oriental pearl ..I sold it for three-and-fifty pounds.

**d.** Followed by *dozen, score,* and by *hundred, thousand*, etc., or the ordinals of these.

971 *Blickl. Hom.* 75 To þrim hunde peneȝa. *a* 1123 *O. E. Chron.* an. 1101, Rotbert..sceolde..þreo þusend marc seolfres habban. *c* 1220 *Bestiary* 616 Ðre hundred ȝer. 1388–[see THREESCORE]. *c* 1475 *Rauf Coilȝear* 757 Ilk ȝeir thre hundreth pund assigne the I sall. 1483 *Cath. Angl.* 385/1 Threhundrethe, *tricentesimus*. 1634 SIR T. HERBERT *Trav.* 205 Seuenty Temples, in one of which are set three thousand three hundred thirty three gilded Idols. 1839 URE *Dict. Arts* 583 With about.. a three-thousandth part of arsenic. *Mod.* I can find room for three dozen begonias.

**e.** *Three fourths*: three out of four equal parts or portions into which a whole is or may be divided; three quarters. Often *loosely* or *hyperbolically*, the greater part, most *of*.

1600 HOLLAND *Livy* VIII. ii. 289 Two acres in the Latine countrie, with a supplement of three foure parts out of the Privernates land to make up the whole. 1777 ROBERTSON *Hist. Amer.* (1783) III. 279 About three-fourths..of it belongs to the holder of the grant. 1779 *Mirror* No. 23 ¶ 5 He was called a good-hearted man by three-fourths of his acquaintance. 1849 D. J. BROWNE *Amer. Poultry Yd.* (1855) 28 They do not get perfectly feathered till they are three fourths grown. 1866 FROUDE in Sir H. Brackenbury *Some Mem. My Spare Time* (1909) 41 The sailor's rule for grog—three-fourths spirit and all the water you add spoils it—applies pre-eminently to writing on practical questions. 1890 *Anthony's Photogr. Bull.* III. 200 A block of wood has a three-fourth inch hole bored in it.

† **f.** Rarely used for the ordinal THIRD. *Obs.*

1521 in *Test. Ebor.* (Surtees) VI. 4 Witnesses, Rober Gibson..and many other, the three daye of Auguste. 1598 SHAKS. *Merry W.* I. i. 142 The three party is..mine Host of the Garter.

**g.** In special collocations. *Problem of three bodies* (Dynamics): the problem of ascertaining the movements of three particles attracting one another under the law of gravitation (as yet only approximately solved for special cases). *The three chapters* (Ch. Hist.), the writings, etc., condemned by an edict of Justinian issued 544 A.D.: see quot. † *The three tongues*, the three inscribed on the Cross, and primarily requisite to the theologian, viz. Latin, Greek, and Hebrew. † *Three trees*, the gallows. *Three vowels* (slang), an I O U. Also *three* († *blue, golden*) *balls* (BALL *sb.*[1] 20); *the three (Holy) Children* (CHILD *sb.* 2 b); *the three F's* (F III. 2); *three faces under a (one) hood* (FACE *sb.* 1 d); *the three kings* (KING *sb.* 1 c); *the three L's* (L 7); *the three Persons* (PERSON *sb.* 7); *the three R's* (R II. 2 b); *three sheets in the wind* (SHEET); *the three sisters* (SISTER *sb.* 4 b); *three sticks* (STICK *sb.*)

1816 PLAYFAIR *Nat. Phil.* II. 263 Mayer has also sought to determine the Sun's parallax from one of the lunar equations, as deduced from the solution of the problem of the *three bodies. 1858 CAYLEY *Math. Papers* III. 97 The problem of three or more bodies is considered by Sir W. R. Hamilton in his two..memoirs on a general method in Dynamics, *Phil. Trans.* 1834 and 1835. 1885 *Cath. Dict.* s.v. *Three Chapters*, The condemnation of the *three chapters means the condemnation of (1) Theodore of Mopsuestia, his person, and his writings, (2) of Theodoret's writings against Cyril and the Ephesine Council, (3) of a letter from Ibas to Maris the Persian, also against Cyril and the Council. 1582 ALLEN *Martyrd. Campion* (1908) 36 He was also very skilful in the *three tongues. 1561 T. HOBY tr. *Castiglione's Courtyer* II. (1577) M iij, To play your Comedye yee shall neede..as much wood as is in Sclauonia..and for preparation of the Tragedie *three trees is enough. 1582 BRETON *Toyes Idle Head* (Grosart) 28/2 For commonly, such knaues as these Doe ende their lyves vpon three trees. 1822 SCOTT *Nigel* xvii, The captain, who was in the habit..of paying his losses with *three vowels.

**2.** Used vaguely for a small or trifling number; a few. So *three or four*. Cf. TWO *or three*.

1534 MORE *Comf. agst. Trib.* III. Wks. 1247/2 So very a childishe fantasy, that in a matter almost of three chippes ..neuer should mooue any man. 1596 HARINGTON *Apol. Ajax* (1814) 39 After they have roved three or four idle wordes. 1638 R. BAKER tr. *Balzac's Lett.* (vol. II) 39 If they have but three words of latin. 1825 T. HOOK *Sayings* Ser. II. *Man of Many Fr.* I. 182 But as to his anger..I don't care three of his sugar-loaves. 1842 BORROW *Bible in Spain* xli. (Pelh. Libr.) 283, I but said three words to the alcayde of the prison.

**3.** Absolutely or with ellipsis of sb. (most often *persons*; otherwise to be supplied from context). More specifically, short for *three years* (of age); *three tines* (of a stag's horns); also for *three pounds, shillings, pence, farthings, inches*, etc., as *three ten* = £3. 10; *three and three* = 3*s.* 3*d.*; *one and eleven-three* = 1*s.* 11¾*d.*; *three foot three* = 3 ft. 3 in.

1382 WYCLIF *Matt.* xviii. 20 For where two or three shulen be gedrid in my name, ther am I in the midil of hem. 1412–20 LYDG. *Chron. Troy* IV. 4640 Þis þre han made a suggestioun Vn-to þe kyng touchynge þe trete. *c* 1489 CAXTON *Sonnes of Aymon* xvi. 377 The other thre he broughte to the dongeon. 1596 DALRYMPLE tr. *Leslie's Hist. Scot.* (S.T.S.) I. 13 Fresche water lochis..; that abundes in mony kyndes of fische, cheiflie in thrie, Killine, Skait, and Makrell. 1675 *Essex Papers* (Camden) I. 319 That Trear. had lately procured from King thirteen thousand pounds for Essex, of which Trear. was to have three for himselfe. 1683 J. MASON *Spir. Songs* XXIII. iv, The Three, when Christ did make the Fourth, Found Fire as meek as Air. 1688 R. HOLME *Armoury* II. 131/2 Hares, 2 a Brase, 3 a Lease. *Mod.* Which three do you choose? Any three you please.

*c* 1425 *Seven Sag.* (P.) 55 Er ther passe thre and fyve, Yf he have wyt and his on lyve. 1840 THACKERAY *Barber Cox* Jan., Sold in pots at two-and-three, and three-and-nine. 1872 H. KINGSLEY *Hornby Mills*, etc. II. 40 'How much money have you got, my lord?'..'Three-and-sixpence'. 1884 JEFFERIES *Red Deer* iv. 69 At the upper end the antler divides into three points, called three on top. 1906 C. MANSFIELD *Girl & Gods* v, You told me yesterday you could not afford a pug bitch you wanted, and she was only three ten. 1909 *Lady's Realm* Mar. 554/2 The chubby, dirty-faced child of three.

**II.** *sb.* (With plural *threes*.)

**1.** The abstract number.

*c* 1200 ORMIN 11266 ȝiff þu sammnesst þreo till þreo þa findesst tu þær sexe. *a* 1300 *Cursor M.* 21747 O four and thre qua tels euen He sal þe numbre mak o seuen. 1387–8 T. USK *Test. Love* III. i. (Skeat) l. 3 Among all nombres thre is determined for moste certain. 1588 SHAKS. *L. L. L.* v. ii. 495 By Ioue, I alwaies tooke three threes for nine. 1597 HOOKER *Eccl. Pol.* v. lxxix. § 7 Three, being the mysticall number of Gods unsearchable perfection within himselfe. 1825 T. HOOK *Sayings* Ser. II. *Passion & Princ.* vi. III. 53 It would be..useless..to expatiate upon the qualities attributable to the number Three, or quote the Graces, the Fates [etc.].

**b.** The figure (3) denoting this number.

1895 *Outing* (U. S.) XXVII. 204/1 Granted control of the outside and inside edges, and the many eights, threes, loops, etc. are simplified at once.

**2.** A group or set of three things or persons. *spec.* **a.** A card, a domino, or the side of a die marked with three pips or spots. † *Three, two, and ace*: name of an old card game. **b.** *Cricket.* A hit for which three runs are obtained.

*c* 1540 J. HEYWOOD *Four P. P.* E ij, Take thre of the yongest and thre of the eldest...And when all these threes be had a sunder, Of eche three, two..Shall be founde shrewes. 1578 TIMME *Caluine on Gen.* 196 By seven and seven, understand not so many pairs of every kind, but threese, to the which one beast is added over and above. 1587 SAUNDERS *Voy. Tripolie* B iv b, Wee were cheaned three and three to an oare. 1599 MINSHEU *Span. Dict.*, *Dial.* iii. 25 Games of chiefest price, as the Reynado, the three, two and ace, still trumpe. 1607 SHAKS. *Cor.* II. iii. 47 We are..to come by him where he stands, by ones, by twoes, and by threes. 1755 JOHNSON, *Kayle*, a kind of play..in which nine holes ranged in three's are made in the ground. 1830 LINDLEY *Nat. Syst. Bot.* 137 Flowers solitary, or in pairs or threes. 1836 in 'Bat' *Cricket Man.* (1850) 100 Threes, fours, and fives appear as easy for him to get. 1870 HARDY & WARE *Mod. Hoyle* 77 Fifteen can be made in several ways [in cribbage]; for example, ten and five,..three fours and a three.

**c.** in military drill, when each three men form a unit for the purpose of wheeling.

1796 *Instr. & Reg. Cavalry* (1813) 63 When a division wheels to a flank rank by three's. 1832 *Regul. Instr. Cavalry* 14 The Threes wheel at once, upon the word 'Threes Right', 'Threes Left', or 'Threes about'. 1847 *Infantry Man.* (1854) 61 The company..may form threes.

**3. a.** *ellipt.* for *three parts* or *divisions*; as *to divide a thing in(to) three*.

13.. *Cursor M.* 10178 (Gött.) In thre [*Cott.* thrin] his godis did he dele. *c* 1400 *Destr. Troy* 1146 Þat oþer part of our pupull put we in thre! *c* 1425 WYNTOUN *Cron.* I. ix. 534 As men may be a roundall se Merkit to be delt in thre. *c* 1435 *Torr. Portugal* 686 He brast hys schyld on thre. *c* 1450 *Songs, Carols*, etc. (E. E. T. S.) 20/79 They clave my harte in III. 18.. G. MACDONALD *Ballads, Leg. Corrievrechan* xiii, The hemp was broken in three.

**b.** With omission of *hours* (of the day): *three o'clock* (also *attrib.*), also simply *three*; *half-past three*; *three fifteen*, 3.15 = a quarter past three.

*c* 1460 *Wisdom* 797 in *Macro Plays* 61 At þe parvise I wyll be,..be-twyn ij and iij. 1530 PALSGR. 714/1 We shal nat set in tyll to morowe thre of the clocke. 1762 FOOTE *Orator* I. Wks. 1799 I. 191 We shall be sure to find them at three at the Shakspeare. 1814 SCOTT *Diary* 17 Aug., in *Lockhart*, On board at half-past three. 1902 ELIZ. L. BANKS *Newspaper Girl* 42, I want you to go out at once and report that three o'clock meeting at the Methodist Church. *Mod.* Our train starts at three fifteen.

**c.** In phrases and specific uses. *Three in One* = the Trinity, the Triune God (also *One in Three*, and simply *Three*). *Three to one*, three chances to one; † in the ratio of three to one, three times (in amount) (quot. 1683). *Three times three*, i.e. cheers; hence as a verb (*nonce-use*), to utter nine times. *Rule of three*: see RULE *sb.* 8 b.

*a* 1711 KEN *Hymnarium* Poet. Wks. 1721 II. 68 Most holy, holy, holy *Three, Harmonious Unity. 1849 ROBISON *Hymn*, Three in One, and One in Three, Ruler of the earth and sea. 1683 PENN *Let. to Comm. Free Soc. Traders Pennsylv.* 1 The Back-Lands being generally *three to one Richer than those that lie by Navigable Waters. 1766 EARL MARCH in Jesse *Selwyn & Contemp.* (1843) II. 28 The odds are three to one on my side. 1813 *Chron.* in *Ann. Reg.* 51/2 Next followed 'The King', drank standing, and with *three times three. 1850 TENNYSON *In Mem.* Concl. xxvi, Again the feast, the speech, the glee,..The crowning cup, the three-times-three. 1829 E. ELLIOTT *Jacobin's Prayer* iv, And when pale Freedom's champions fell, He three-times-three'd his carnage yell.

**d.** *Threes*, short for three per cent stock, or THREE PER CENTS (so *three-and-a-halfs*); for three-quarter-backs (in Football); for three-pennyworth (of liquor).

1850 THACKERAY *Pendennis* xxxvi, I'm told she has six hundred thousand pounds in the Threes. 1891 *Daily News* 27 Apr. 3/2 People who had 'threes' of beer and 'large lagers', both of which were over half a pint. 1895 *Ibid.* 30 Sept. 2/6 French Threes rose on the day 15 c., to 101 for money. *Ibid.* 30 Dec. 7/4 Three-and-a-Halfs declined 25 c., to 105.45 for money. 1905 *Westm. Gaz.* 12 Dec. 9/2 Another run by the Cambridge 'threes' took them down to the Oxford line once more.

**III.** Combinations (unlimited in number, of which the following are examples):

**1. a.** Adjectives formed of *three* and a sb. (usually in singular), meaning 'of, pertaining to, consisting of, containing, measuring, etc. three of the things named', as *three-act* (consisting of three acts), *three-bout* (formed by three bouts of the plough), *three-bushel, -class, -colour, -cylinder, -day, -fathom, -foot (-feet), -guinea, -hand, -horse, -hour (-s), -line, -mile, -minute, -month (-s), -phase* (PHASE 3), *-pint, -plait, -ply, -point, -pound, -rail, -row, -shilling, -speed, -stairs, -story, -strand, -throw, -tier, -volume, -wheel*. **b.** Parasynthetic adjs. formed on similar collocations + -ED [2], = 'having or characterized by three of the things named', as *three-aisled* (having three aisles), *three-angled, -armed, -bladed, -bodied, -bolted, -branched, -chinned, -coloured, -coned, -corded, -crowned, -dayed, -dropped, -eared, -eyed, -faced, -fingered, -floored, -formed, -grained, -groined, -handed, -hooped, -lettered, -mouthed, -necked, -nooked, -phased, -pointed, -pronged, -ribbed, -roomed, -shaped, -soled, -storied, -stranded, -suited, -syllabled, -tailed, -tiered, -toothed, -wheeled, -wormed*, etc.; *spec.* in botanical and zoological adjs., as *three-capsuled, -celled, -fibred, -flowered, -jointed, -lobed, -nerved, -petalled, -seeded, -valved*, etc. (now largely superseded by terms derived from Latin, as *tricapsular, trilocular, trivalvular*, etc.); also with other endings, as † *three-dayen* (of three days), *three-dimensional*, † *three-shapen, three-weekly*. **c.** Parasynthetic sbs. in *-er* [see -ER [1] 1], as *three-miler* (one who goes three miles), *three-mover* [MOVER [1] 7], *-railer, -tonner, -volumer, -wheeler*.

1905 CHESTERTON *Heretics* 280 Some absurd shrill and affected voice, such as we only hear from a duchess in a *three-act farce. 1766 ENTICK *London* IV. 204 Making a *three-isled cathedral. 1865 *Cornh. Mag.* July 34 The thrice *three-angled beech nut shell. *c* 1830 *Glouc. Farm Rep.* 32 in *Libr. Usef. Knowl., Husb.* III, Cut with a *three-bladed knife. 1574 HELLOWES *Gueuara's Fam. Ep.* (1577) 336, I giue my condemned soule and life to the infernall *three bodyed Pluto. 1667 MILTON *P. L.* VI. 764 Beside him hung his Bow And Quiver with *three-bolted Thunder stor'd. 1770–4 A. HUNTER *Georg. Ess.* (1803) IV. 38 Suppose..the field to be formed into *three-bout ridges. 1617 HIERON *Wks.* II. 352 This treble or *three-branched sufficiencie. 1860 *All Year Round* No. 69. 448 A hectolitre contains a trifle more than a *three-bushel English corn-sack. 1881 C. E. TURNER in *Macm. Mag.* XLIV. 307 A gray riding-coat, with a *three-caped collar. 1793 MARTYN *Lang. Bot.*, *Three-celled Pericarp. 1898 *Daily News* 15 Oct. 6/3 A very cheap way of producing..necessary blocks for *three-colour printing. 1902 *Daily Chron.* 10 Jan. 6/6 Methods of colour-photography,..the 'three-colour process' invented by Professor Lippman. 1741 *Compl. Fam.-Piece* II. iii. 403 *Three colour'd Violet or Heart's Ease. 1649 *Lanc. Tracts* (Chetham Soc.) 277 A *three-corded scourge. 1604 HIERON *Wks.* I. 576 To maintaine the state Of your *three-crowned potentate. 1904 *Westm. Gaz.* 28 Dec. 3/1 The best work on the Midland [Railway] was accomplished with *three-cylinder compounds. 1890 *Pall Mall G.* 18 Aug. 2/1 Whether you go by a two-day or a *three-day coach. 1422 tr. *Secreta Secret., Priv. Priv.* 200 God Sente..Ionas to the grete Cite of Nynyvee, wyche was a *thre-dayen Iornay. 1618 CHAPMAN *Hesiod, Georg.* II. 426 A *three-ear'd tripod. 1598 Q. ELIZ. *Plutarch* x. 30 Axing for..*thre yead men. 1689 *Lond. Gaz.* No. 2510/4 A *Three faced Steel Seal. 1828 G. W. BRIDGES *Ann. Jamaica* II. xiv. 183 *Three-fingered Jack, the notorious rebel. 1793 MARTYN *Lang. Bot.*, *Three-flowered Peduncle. 1861 MISS PRATT *Flower. Pl.* V. 298 Three-flowered Rush. 1567 GOLDING *Ovid's Met.* VII. (1593) 157 Our *threeformed Goddesse. 1766 *Compl. Farmer* s.v. *Meadow*, With a shovel, hoe, or *three grained fork. 1719 HAMILTON *Ep. to Ramsay* 24 Aug., in *R.'s Poems*, The pleasure..snoovt away like *three-hand ombre. 1680 COTTON *Compl. Gamester* x. 83 Some play at two handed, or *three handed Whist. 1593 SHAKS. 2 *Hen. VI*, IV. ii. 72 The *three hoop'd pot, shall haue ten hoopes. 1812 SIR J. SINCLAIR *Syst. Husb. Scot.* I. 75 A *three-horse power does very well for potatoe-oats, when the corn is fed in by a careful hand. 1906 KROPOTKIN *Mem. Revolutionist* (1908) I. v. 23 A three-horse carriage. 1592 SHAKS. *Rom. & Jul.* III. ii. 99, I, thy *three houres wife. 1837 *Penny Cycl.* IX. 13/2 [The antennæ] are generally..*three-jointed. 1653 R. SANDERS *Physiogn.* 69 The *three-lettered name of the 72 Angels. 1793 MARTYN *Lang. Bot.*, *Three-lobed leaf. 1833 *Penny Cycl.* I. 77/1 Leaves..,three-lobed. 1895 *Outing* (U. S.) XXVI. 459/1 In the *three-mile run England has a decided advantage. 1899 *Daily News* 19 July 6/5

The *three-milers were the next to appear. **1697** DRYDEN *Virg. Georg.* IV. 692 The gaping *three-mouth'd Dog forgets to snarl. **1891** *Athenæum* 31 Jan. 148/2 The current runs ..in favour of short [chess] problems; nothing beyond *three-movers is even looked at. **1799** H. GURNEY *Cupid & Psyche* XX. (1800) 51 Charm the *three-neck'd dog of Hell! **1793** MARTYN *Lang. Bot.*, *Three-nerved Leaf. **1606** SHAKS. *Ant. & Cl.* IV. vi. 6 The *three nook'd world. **1892** *Lightning* 3 Mar. *Gloss. Electr. Terms*, **Three phase system*, a system of distribution of electrical energy in which three alternating currents, each differing from the two others by one third of the period, are used. **1522** in *Bury Wills* (Camden) 115 A *thre pynt pott of pewter. **1868** *Rep. U. S. Commissioner Agric.* (1869) 51 Carpets, treble ingrain, *three-ply, and worsted chain Venetian. **1797** *Encycl. Brit.* (ed. 3) XIV. 606/1 One dog-tooth, and five or six *three-pointed grinders. **1866** CRUMP *Banking* x. 223 Edward VI. Gold. *Three-pound piece, sovereign [etc.]. **1711** *Lond. Gaz.* No. 4915/4 A small *three prong'd silver Fork. **1890** 'R. BOLDREWOOD' *Col. Reformer* (1891) 283 The Colonel..rode his horse over a stiff *three-railer [fence]. **1828** SIR J. E. SMITH *Eng. Flora* II. 93 Partial bracteas five, ovate, acute, *three-ribbed. **1844** *Port Phillip Patriot* 11 July 1/3 A *three-roomed hut. **1593** G. HARVEY *Pierce's Super.* 109 The *three-shapen Geryon. **1640–1** *Kirkcudbr. War-Comm. Min. Bk.* (1855) 149 The inch of *thrie-solled schoes, of the best leather, be sold at twa shillings twa pennies. **1902** *Daily Chron.* 21 Nov. 11/4 The Sturmey-Archer *three-speed gear,..an elaboration of the well-tried 'Hub' two-speed gear, is exhibited by the Raleigh Cycle Company. **1852** W. WICKENDEN *Hunchback's Chest* 330 In his *three-stairs back, Grove Street. **1814** SCOTT *Diary* 22 Aug., in *Lockhart*, There is a decent *three-storied house, belonging to the laird. **1832** G. LONG *Egypt. Antiq.* I. ix. 199 To the height of 60 feet, which is considerably above the ordinary elevation of *three-story houses. **1841** CATLIN *N. Amer. Ind.* I. xxi. 147 Its string was *three stranded. **1605** SHAKS. *Lear* II. ii. 16 A base,.. beggerly, *three-suited, hundred pound, filthy woosted-stocking knaue. **1802–12** BENTHAM *Ration. Judic. Evid.* (1827) I. 11 A *three-tailed instead of a five-tailed bandage. **1848** THACKERAY *Bk. Snobs* iii, A three-tailed Pasha. **1822** GALT *Provost* xliii, Wearing..a white *three-tiered wig. **1883** J. D. J. KELLY in *Harper's Mag.* Aug. 445/2 Diminutive *three-tonners..were cruising. **1382** WYCLIF 1 *Sam.* ii. 13 The child..hadde a flesh hook *thre tothid in his hoond. **1793** MARTYN *Lang. Bot.*, *Three-valved pericarp. **1877–84** F. E. HULME *Wild Fl.* p. viii, Capsule obtusely three-angled and three-valved. **1834** R. P. WARD *Chatsworth* I. 115 The fee-simple of his estate in *three-volume-noveldom. **1889** *Athenæum* 10 Aug. 184/3 He has made clear the distinction between the 'racionabilis secta' and suit to the *three-weekly court. **1656** EARL MONM. tr. *Boccalini's Advts. fr. Parnass.* I. xxxi. (1674) 35 A *three-wheel'd Charret. **1886** *Cyclist's Tour. Club Gaz.* IV. 123 The safeties and *three-wheelers [tricycles]. **1683** MOXON *Mech. Exerc.*, *Printing* xi. ¶ 1 A *Three-Worm'd Spindle.

**2.** Special combinations and collocations: †**three-aged** *a.*, living through three generations; **three-awned** *a.*, having three awns, as in *three-awned grass*, the name of several American grasses of the genus *Aristida*; also called *beard-grass* (*Cent. Dict.* 1891); **three-banded** *a.*, having three bands, as in *three-banded armadillo*, an armadillo of the genus *Tolypeutes*, distinguished by the shell consisting of three bands; **three-bar** *a.*, *Geom.* applied to a curve generated by the motion of three bars pivoted together; **three-bearded** *a.*, having three beards (BEARD *sb.* 3 a) or barbels, as *three-bearded cod* or *rockling* (see ROCKLING); **three-birds**, (*a*) a showy garden species of toad-flax, *Linaria triornithophora*, from Spain; (*b*) name of two American orchids, *Pogonia pendula* and *Triphora trianthophora*, also called *nodding cap* (*Cent. Dict.* 1891, and *Suppl.* 1909); **three-bottle** *a.*, applied to one who can drink three bottles of wine at a sitting; **three-card** *a.*, pertaining to or played with three cards, as *three-card monte* (see MONTE); *three-card trick*, a trick popular with race-course sharpers, also known as *find the lady*, in which a queen and two other cards are spread out face downwards, and bystanders invited to bet which is the queen; **three-cleft** *a.*, cleft or divided into three segments, trifid; **three-coat** *a.*, requiring three coats, as work in plastering and painting; **three-cocked** *a.*, having three cocks, as *three-cocked hat* (COCKED *ppl. a.*[2]); also absol. as *sb.*; † **three-corned** [CORNED[2] 2], three-cornered; **three-day(s) fever** = DENGUE; **three-eight** (usually $\frac{3}{8}$) *Mus.*, denoting a 'time' or rhythm with three quavers in a bar; **three estates**: see ESTATE *sb.* 6, 7; †**three-fallow** *v.*, to fallow threefold: cf. THRY-FALLOW; **three-field** *a.*, noting a method of agriculture in which three fields are worked on a three-course system of two crops and a fallow; **three-four** (usually $\frac{3}{4}$) *Mus.*, denoting a 'time' or rhythm with three crotchets in a bar; **three-high** *a.*: see quots.; **three-holes**, a boys' game of marbles; **three-horned** *a.*, having three horns; esp. applied to particular species of animals; **three-in-hand**, three horses drawing a vehicle, driven by one person; **three-iron** *a.*, welded together from three strands of iron; **three-life** *a.*, applied to a system of tenure under which (till 1854) land (esp. ecclesiastical and college estates) was held during the joint lives of three persons or the longest liver of them; **three-light**, (*a*) *adj.* having three lights: see LIGHT *sb.* 10; (*b*) *sb.* 'a chandelier or candelabrum with three lamps for candles' (*Cent. Dict.* 1891); †**three-like** *a.*, having three equal sides, equilateral (of a triangle); **three-line, three-lined** *a.*, having, consisting of, or marked with three lines; in *Printing*, extending through three lines, as a large capital letter; **three-pounder**, a thing weighing three pounds; a gun firing a three-pound ball; †**three-shafted** *a.* [cf. Ger. *dreischäftig*], of cloth, woven with treble web-shafts (see SHAFT), three-stranded; **three-shear**, a sheep between its third and fourth shearing; **three-spined** *a.*, having three spines, as *three-spined stickleback*, the commonest species of STICKLEBACK; **three-spot**, a three-pipped playing card; **three-thorned** *a.*, having three thorns, or triple thorns, as *three-thorned acacia*, a name for the honey-locust (*Gleditschia triacanthos*), a N. American tree having thorns in groups of three; †**three-threads**, a mixture of common ale, porter, and double (or twopenny) beer, popular *c* 1700: see quots.; **three-throw** *a.*, having three throws (see THROW *sb.*[2] 2), as a *three-throw crank*; hence, having such a crank, as *three-throw pump* or *engine*, one worked by a three-throw crank-shaft; **three-two** (usually $\frac{3}{2}$) *Mus.*, denoting a 'time' or rhythm with three minims in a bar; **three-up**, a game resembling pitch and toss; **three-water** *a.*, *Naut.* diluted with three times its bulk of water, as *three-water grog* or *rum*; also *absol.*; **three-went way**, *dial.* a point where three roads meet without intersecting; cf. FOUR-WENT; **three-wire** *a.*, applied to a system of distributing electric power, involving three mains and two dynamos, the two outer mains being joined to the free terminals of the dynamos, and the central main to a conductor joining the two.

**1697** CREECH tr. *Manilius* I. 30 Great Atreus Sons,.. With *three-ag'd Nestor. **1800** SHAW *Gen. Zool.* I. 188 *Three-banded Armadillo..may be considered..as the most elegant of the whole genus;..it is a native of Brazil. **1875** S. ROBERTS in *Proc. Lond. Math. Soc.* 11 Nov. 14, I propose to extend ..to general *three-bar motion a discussion..of some particular cases. **1876** CAYLEY *Math. Papers* IX. 551 The Three-Bar Curve is derived from the motion of a system of three bars..pivoted to each other, and to two fixed points. **1806** SURR *Winter in Lond.* III. 121 Metamorphosed from a*three-bottle man to the image of temperance. **1854** T. PARKER in Weiss *Life* (1863) II. 134 *Three-card-monte men, and gambling-house keepers. **1887** LOWELL *Tariff Reform* Wks. 1890 VI. 187 They..play their three-card trick. **1793** MARTYN *Lang. Bot.*, *Three-cleft, *trifidus*. *Ibid.*, Three-cleft-palmate leaf. **1875** MORRIS *Æneid* II. 475 Three-cleft tongue. **1842** BRANDE *Dict. Sc.*, etc., **Three-coat work*. In Architecture. **1877** KNIGHT *Dict. Mech.*, *Three-coat Work.* (Plastering.) The first is called *pricking-up* on lath...The second coat is called *floating*; the third, *set* or *finishing-coat*. **1813** LD. PALMERSTON in *Parl. Deb.* 8 Mar., To see the troops in the small *three cocked hats which they formerly wore. *a* **1608** DEE *Rel. Spirits* I. (1659) 83 The books be green, bright, and they be *three-corned. **1897** *Allbutt's Syst. Med.* II. 376 Synonyms [of Dengue] ..polka fever (Brazilian), *three days fever. **1577** B. GOOGE *Heresbach's Husb.* I. (1586) 22 b, For some seede, you must not only twyfallowe and *threefallowe your ground, but also fourefallow it. **1868** *Rep. U.S. Commissioner Agric.* (1869) 156 The Polish *three-field farming. **1907** M. C. F. MORRIS *Nunburnholme* 251 Supposing the three-field system to be adopted. **1902** *Westm. Gaz.* 14 June 4/3 The new waltz,..the 'Military Dip', is in *three-four waltz time, and has one dip to each three counts. **1877** KNIGHT *Dict. Mech.*, **Three-high Roll* (Metal-working), a rolling-apparatus in which three rollers are arranged in a vertical series. **1881** RAYMOND *Mining Gloss.*, *Three-high train*, a roll-train composed of three rolls, the bar being entered on one side between the bottom and the middle roll, and on the other side between the middle and the upper roll. **1853** LYTTON *My Novel* I. xi, Keep off the other boys from..playing *three-holes and chuck-farthing. **1681** GREW *Musæum* I. vii. § 2. 163 The little *Three-Horned Beetle, *Scarabæus Triceros minor*. **1887** MORRIS *Odyss.* XII. 135 Unto the Three-horned island she sent them aloof to dwell. **1816** 'QUIZ' *Grand Master* VII. 198 When Jove had found that *three in hand This Jehu did not understand. **1892** GREENER *Breech-Loader* 5 Processes of Barrel Welding. (1) *Three-Iron Damascus; (2) Two-Iron Damascus. **1898** A. F. LEACH *Beverley Act Bk.* I. p. xlv, In 1300, one of the Canons leased, on the usual *three-life system, some of the lands of his prebend. **1618** in Willis & Clark *Cambridge* (1886) I. 208 One *three light window and two single light windowes. **1551** RECORDE *Pathw. Knowl.* I. Defin., That the Greekes doo call *Isopleuron*, and Latine men *æquilaterum*: and in english it may be called a *threlike triangle. **1683** MOXON *Mech. Exerc.*, *Printing* xxii. ¶ 5 He begins his Chapter.. with a..*Three or Four-lin'd Letter. *Mod.* A three-lined whip has been issued for to-night's division in the House of Commons. **1684** J. PETER *Siege Vienna* 109 *Three pounders of Iron. **1872** H. KINGSLEY *Hornby Mills*, etc. II. 232 One three-pounder is worth fishing all day for. **1876** BANCROFT *Hist. U.S.* V. xx. 568 The Hessians captured two brass three-pounders, which had lately arrived from France. *c* **1440** *Promp. Parv.* 492/2 (MS. A.) *Thre schaftyd clothe, *trilix*. **1770–4** A. HUNTER *Georg. Ess.* (1803) IV. 593 Under the necessity of wintering some of their *three-shears before they are marketable. **1886** C. SCOTT *Sheep-Farming* 18 After the third shearing, three-shear or four-shear, three or four year olds, are the definitions employed. **1822** *Hortus Angl.* II. 573 *Gleditschia Triacanthos.* *Three thorned Acacia, or Honey Locust Tree. **1698** W. KING tr. *Sorbière's Journ. Lond.* 35 He had a thousand such Sort of Liquors, as.. *Three Threads, Four Threads. *a* **1700** B. E. *Dict. Cant. Crew*, *Three-threads*, half common Ale, and the rest Stout or Double Beer. **1802** [see ENTIRE A. 2 b]. **1829** *Nat. Philos.* I. *Hydraulics* ii. 12 (Usef. Knowl. Soc.) Keeping two or..three pumps constantly at work by what is called a triple or *three-throw crank. **1900** *Engineering Mag.* XIX. 726 Three-throw ram pump for dip workings. **1851** MAYHEW *Lond. Labour* I. 12/1 'Shove-halfpenny' is another game played by them [costermongers]; so is 'Three up'. **1840** *P. Parley's Ann.* I. 295 A large lump of salt beef, with some *three water grog. **1905** *Daily Chron.* 25 May 4/7 Rum and water came to be called 'grog' likewise, being 'two-water' or 'three-water' grog, according to the proportions of the mixture. **1787** *Kentish Trav. Comp.* 49 He gets to a *three-went way. **1898** *Westm. Gaz.* 9 July 7/2 There was some discussion as to the particular kind of electrical equipment to be used, but eventually the *three-wire system was adopted.

**Three·-co:rner** (stress var.), *a.* Of or pertaining to three corners (quot. *a* 1548); having three corners, three-cornered, triangular.

*a* **1548** HALL *Chron.*, *Hen. VI* 122 The Frenche kyng, perceiuyng this toune [Laigny], to be the thre corner key, betwene the territories of the Englishemen, the Burgonyons, and his awne. **1683** WOOD *Life* 3 Dec. (O. H. S.) III. 84 He pointed to the dore, and bid me 'be gone', with his three corner cap. **1902** MARSHALL *Metal Tools* 38 Three-corner files are very useful for cleaning out the sharp corners of square holes,..for sharpening saw teeth, or for filing nicks in a piece of steel before breaking it off.

So **Three-cornerism** (*nonce-wd.*), the fact or system of having 'three-cornered' constituencies; **Three-corner-ways, -wise** *advs.*, with three corners, triangularly.

**1884** *Edin. Rev.* Jan. 294 No diagnosis will discover *three-cornerism to be the cause of the disease. **1796** MRS. GLASSE *Cookery* xiv. 234 Toast some thin slices of bread cut *three-corner-ways. **1862** T. A. TROLLOPE *Marietta* I. xii. 228 Kerchief folded *three-cornerwise.

**Three-cornered** (þrīˌkǭ·ɹnəɹd: str. var.), *a.*

**1.** Having three corners or angles; triangular (in plan or in cross-section).

*c* **1400** MAUNDEV. iii. 15 Costantynoble..is iij cornered. *c* **1400** *Lanfranc's Cirurg.* 36 Haue a nedle þre cornerid. **1594** BLUNDEVIL *Exerc.* III. I. (1636) 274 Of Triangles or three-cornerd figures. **1668** CULPEPPER & COLE *Barthol. Anat.* I. xviii. 49 Somtimes they are three-corner'd, seldom round. **1833** T. HOOK *Parson's Dau.* II. i, Immediately following..came a three-cornered note from Lady Gorgon. **1855** O. W. HOLMES *Poems* 86 The old three-cornered hat.

**b.** *transf.* Applied to a constituency represented by three members.

Such constituencies were a feature of the electoral system for the House of Commons from 1867 to 1885; each elector having the right to vote for not more than two candidates, which enabled a strong minority to elect one of the representatives.

**1882** OGILVIE, Three-cornered constituency. **1883** *Manch. Guard.* 22 Oct. 5/2 What shall be done with the three-cornered constituencies?

**c.** Applied to a contest, discussion, or the like, between three persons.

**1891** KIPLING *Light that Failed* xii. (1900) 197 Let us rather ..consider whether Torp's three-cornered ministrations are exactly what Dick needs just now. **1894** H. GARDENER *Unoff. Patriot* 59 They had a three-cornered fight with Bradley's mulatto, Ned. *Mod.* The election in Kilmarnock Burghs was a three-cornered fight.

**2. a.** Of a horse: Awkwardly shaped. *colloq.*

**1861** WHYTE MELVILLE *Mkt. Harb.* iv. 28 The grey..and the bay, with a little three-cornered jumping hack. **1890** 'R. BOLDREWOOD' *Col. Reformer* (1891) 386 And the horses? Sell every three-cornered wretch of 'em.

**b.** *fig.* Awkward, cross-grained, peevish; cf. ANGULAR *a.* 4. (Also quasi-*adv.*)

*c* **1850** E. FARMER *Scrap Bk.* (1869) 96 Matters run three-cornered. **1876** GEO. ELIOT *Dan. Der.* xxxiii, A three-cornered, impracticable fellow. **1879** F. W. ROBINSON *Coward Consc.* III. xviii, This hard, three-cornered family.

Hence **Three·-co:rneredness**, triangularity; **Three·-co:rneredwise** *adv.*, triangularly.

**1682** T. FLATMAN *Heraclitus Ridens* No. 68 (1713) II. 169 A Place in Egypt, call'd *Delta*, from the Three-corner'dness of its Shape. **1580** HOLLYBAND *Treas. Fr. Tong*, *Triangulaire*, three cornerdwise, or after three corners.

**Three·-deck**, *a. rare.* = next.

**1692** LUTTRELL *Brief Rel.* (1857) II. 636, 3 three deck ships were lately launched at Brest. **1708** *Lond. Gaz.* No. 4423/7 The Boyn, a three Deck Ship of 80 Guns. **1797** *Encycl. Brit.* (ed. 3) XVII. 403/1 The middle deck in three-deck ships.

**Three·-decked** (-dekt), *a. rare.* Having three decks; *three-decked ship* = next, 1.

**1692** DELAVAL in *Lond. Gaz.* No. 2769/3, I found 3 three Deck'd Ships of the Enemies. **1834** *Encycl. Metrop.* (1845) VI. 343/1 The Royal Navy is divided into the following classes and denominations. 1. Rated ships, *viz. First rate*, all three-decked ships.

**Three·-de:cker.** [f. *three-deck*: see DECKER[2].]

**1.** A three-decked ship; formerly *spec.* a line-of-battle ship carrying guns on three decks.

**1795** Three deckers [see DECKER[2]]. **1797** *Encycl. Brit.* (ed. 3) XVII. 403/1 In three-deckers it [the fire hearth] is.. on the middle deck. **1855** TENNYSON *Maud* I. I. xiii, If..the rushing battle-bolt sang from the three-decker out of the foam.

**b.** *fig.* Applied to a thing (or person) of great size or importance.

**1835** E. FITZGERALD *Lett.* (1889) I. 34 Pray do write to me: a few lines soon are better than a three-decker a month hence. **1836** E. HOWARD *R. Reefer* xlv, Three deckers—words of Latin or Greek derivation. **1877** BLACK *Green Past.* xxiv, He went over to Mrs. Blythe,..and sat down by that majestic three-decker. **1886** Dowden *Shelley* (1887) I. iii. 115 Some great three-decker of orthodoxy.

**2.** *transf.* Something consisting of three ranges or divisions: *spec.* **a.** Nickname for the three-storied pulpit formerly in use, consisting of the desk for the clerk, the reading desk, and the pulpit proper, one above another. **b.** A skirt with three flounces. **c.** A three-volume novel.

**1874** Micklethwaite *Mod. Par. Churches* 56 The Georgian three-decker, the few surviving examples of which are now such objects of scorn. **1895** *Westm. Gaz.* 26 Apr. 2/1 The long-winded novel of our forefathers—what you may call the old three-decker of fiction. **1909** *Daily Chron.* 3 May 7/4 That graceful form of skirt, which consists of three flounces (known sometimes to the irreverent as a 'three-decker'). **1910** Gathorne-Hardy *Mem. 1st Earl Cranbrook* I. 115 In the place now occupied by the present one [chancel arch] the old 'three-decker' stood [in 1858].

**3.** *attrib.* (in senses 1 b and 2).

**1860** O. W. Holmes *Prof. Breakf.-t.* ii, A boy..with a three-decker brain. **1890** *John Bull* 5 Apr. 229/1 In the latter part of the eighteenth and first part of the nineteenth centuries .. great 'three-decker' pulpits blocked up the chancels. **1898** *Daily News* 29 Sept. 3/4 The 'three-decker' skirt is supplemented by a three-decker cape. **1904** *Daily Chron.* 27 Apr. 7/4 The winding rope attached to the three-decker cage parted, and it dropped a distance of 2,000ft.

†**Three·-dou·ble,** *a. Obs.* 'Doubled' or folded in three; consisting of three layers, courses, thicknesses, etc.; threefold.

**1541** R. Copland *Guydon's Quest. Chirurg.* Q j, Ouer that a lynnen cloth thre dowble. **1613** *Uncasing of Machivils Instr.* 16 A Falling-band, or a three-double ruffe. **1653** H. Cogan *Pinto's Trav.* xxxii. (1663) 129 Having a chain of Pearl three double about his neck. **1658** J. Rowland *Moufet's Theat. Ins.* 953 Terrible for biting,..piercing through a three double stocking and boots likewise.

So †**Three-double** *v.*, to treble; †**Three-doubled** *a.*, threefold, triple.

**1558** Phaer *Æneid* vii. U iij b, Threedubbeld shyrtes Of golde. **1580** Hollyband *Treas. Fr. Tong*, *Tripler*, to three double.

**Three·-e·dged** (-edʒd: stress var.), *a.* Having three edges. Also *fig.*

**1398** Trevisa *Barth. De P. R.* xvii. xxxv. (Bodl. MS.), Segge..is acounted amonge kindes of rissches, as Sias seiþ, and cleped it a þre egged ruyssche. **1541** R. Copland *Guydon's Quest. Chirurg.* L iij b, Nedles..euen and smoth, and thre edged at the poynte. **1685** *Lond. Gaz.* No. 2085/4 Lost.., a large Silver Hilted Sword, with..a long three edged blade. **1793** Martyn *Lang. Bot.*, Three-cornered or Three-edged, *trigonus*. **1898** G. W. E. Russell *Collect. & Recoll.* xix. (1903) 178 This three-edged compliment has seldom been surpassed. **1900** B. D. Jackson *Gloss. Bot. Terms* 270/2 *Three-edged*, with three sides,..and three acute angles, triquetrous.

**Three·-fa·rthings.** In the literal sense: see Farthing. Also, money of the value of three farthings; hence the name of a silver coin of that value issued by Queen Elizabeth.

**1561** Q. Eliz. *Proclam.* 15 Nov., Because a halfpeny cannot be made of such finenesse to beare any conuenient bulke, an other small peece shall also be coyned of three farthynges..whiche..shalbe of meere fine starling syluer. **1588** Shaks. *L. L. L.* iii. i. 140 Remuneration, O, that's the Latine word for three-farthings. *Ibid.* 150 Threefarthings worth of Silke. **1598** B. Jonson *Ev. Man in Hum.* ii. i, He values me at a crack'd three-farthings, for aught I see. *a* **1616** Beaum. & Fl. *Scornf. Lady* iii. i, Whip'd and then crop'd, For washing out the roses in three farthings, To make 'em pence. **1898** G. B. Rawlings *Brit. Coinage* 65 The threefarthings..was the least of all the coins having a rose behind the ear. *Ibid.* [see Three-halfpence].

Hence **Three-fa·rthing** *a.*, of the value of three farthings; hence, paltry, insignificant.

*c* **1600** *Timon* iii. v. (Shaks. Soc.) 56 Away, away, thou poore three farthing Iacke! **1656** Earl Monm. tr. *Boccalini, Pol. Touchstone* (1674) 276 They had put to arbitriment the salvation of mens souls upon a three-farthing business. **1822** tr. *Aristoph., Plutus* 15 Do you suppose the despotism ..would be worth a three-farthing piece, were you [Plutus] to recover? **1898** G. B. Rawlings *Brit. Coinage* 64 Two new denominations in silver are introduced in this [Elizabeth's] reign, namely, the threehalfpenny and threefarthing pieces. *Mod.* A three-farthing bun.

**Threefold** (þrī·fōuld), *a.*, *adv.* (*sb.*) Forms: see Three and -fold. [OE. *þrífeald*, *þrýfeald*: = OFris. *thrifald*, obs. Du. *drijvoud*, OHG., MHG. *drivalt*, ON. *þrífaldr*: see Three and -fold.]

**A.** *adj.* **1.** Consisting of three combined in one, or one thrice repeated; comprising three kinds, parts, divisions, or branches; triple.

*c* **1000** Ælfric *Hom.* II. 606 Nis se Ælmihtiȝa God na ðryfeald, ac is Ðrynnys. *c* **1200** *Twelfth Cent. Hom.* 136 Crist arerde þreo men of deaþe to life, & þa þreo tacnoden þene ðreofealde deaþ þare sunfule sawle. *c* **1200** *Trin. Coll. Hom.* 65 God bad us turnen to him, and þat us bihoueð to don on þrefold wise. **13..** *Cursor M.* 25943 (Cott.) And for we sin on maners thre, Vr scrift aght thrifald for to be. **1434** Misyn *Mending Life* i. 107 Þis is þe threfold rope þat vnnethis may be brokyn. *a* **1600** *Scot. Poems 16th C.* (1801) II. 192 His popish pride, and threefald crowne. *c* **1709** Prior *1st Hymn Callimachus* 66 The three-fold empire Of Heaven, of ocean, and deep hell beneath. **1793** Martyn *Lang. Bot.*, *Terna folia*, three-fold leaves, in threes, or three and three. **1857** Toulmin Smith *Parish* 104 Highways, bridges, and military defence, constituted the three fold conditions (*trinoda necessitas*) always..attached to the tenure of land.

**2.** Three times as great or numerous.

*c* **1200** Ormin 14034 Twafald oþerr þrefald mett Þa fetless alle tokenn. **1858** Lardner *Hand-bk. Nat. Phil.* 158 If the compressing force be increased in a threefold proportion, the volume of the air compressed will be diminished in a threefold proportion. **1870** Bryant *Iliad* I. v. 140 A threefold courage now Inspired him.

**B.** *adv.*

**1.** In a threefold manner, triply; †in threes, three together (*obs.*); †in three ways (*obs.*); in or into three parts (now *rare*).

*c* **1020** *Rule St. Benet* i. (Logeman) 10 Þa twyfealde þreofealde oððe soðes anlepie gangende butan hyrde. **13..** *Cursor M.* 26069 (Cott.) Als þe sin es wroght Thre-fald, wit word, dede, and thoght. **1486** *Bk. St. Albans, Her.* C vij b, Rather it shall be calde a cros threfolde pärtitid flurri. **1558** Phaer *Æneid* iv. Lj, On the threefoldshapen dame, And on Diana's virgins faces three she doth exclame. **1855** Tennyson *Brook* 73 The chestnut, when the shell Divides threefold to show the fruit within.

**2.** Three times, thrice (in amount); three times or thrice as much. See also Thick *adv.* 6.

*c* **1400** *Brut* 299 ȝet were þey threfold so meny of hem as of Englisshe men. **1591** Shaks. *Two Gent.* i. i. 116 'Tis threefold too little. **1594** — *Rich. III*, ii. ii. 86 Alas! you three, on me threefold distrest: Power all your teares.

**C.** *sb.* A name for the plant buckbean (*Menyanthes trifoliata*), from its threefold leaves. *dial.*

**1788** W. Marshall *Yorksh.* II. Gloss. (E.D.S.), *Threefold*, *Menyanthes trifoliata*, bogbean, buckbean. **1876** in Robinson *Whitby Gloss.*

Hence **Three·fol:ded** *a.* (*rare*), threefold (whence **Threefo·ldedness** = *threefoldness*); **Three·foldly** *adv.*, in a threefold manner; **Three·foldness,** the quality or condition of being threefold.

**1528** Roy *Rede me*, etc. (Arb.) 29 Fye on his golden *three folded crowne. **1553** T. Wilson *Rhet.* 6 b, Quintilian giueth warnyng to vse this threfolded order. **1905** *Chr. Progress* Feb. 22 The word Trinity means *Threefoldedness. *a* **901** *Laws of Ælfred* c. 39 § 2 ȝif syxhyndum þissa hwæðer ȝelimpe, *ðriefealdlice arise be ðære cierliscan bote. **13..** *Cursor M.* 25939 (Cott.) Man he sinnes threfaldli, Þat es in thoght, in word, in wark. *c* **1450** *Mirour Saluacioun* 1591 How the feend temptede crist threfaldelye. **1901** R. C. Moberly *Atonem. & Person.* viii. 154 The Three Persons [in the Trinity] are neither Three Gods, nor Three parts of God. Rather they are God Threefoldly. **1856** Faber *Creator & Creature* ii. i. (1886) 110 The *Threefoldness of Persons and the Unity of Essence.

**Three·-foot,** *a.* †**a.** = Three-footed. *Obs.* **b.** Measuring three feet in length, breadth, or other dimension.

**1590** Shaks. *Mids. N.* ii. i. 52 The wisest Aunt..Sometime for three-foot stoole, mistaketh me. **1675** Hobbes *Odyss.* 155 A caldron, or a three-foot pot of brass. **1870** Mrs. Riddell *A. Friars* iv, The usual three-foot passage leading from the front door to the kitchen. **1880** A. A. Common in *Mem. Roy. Astron. Soc.* XLVI. 173 Particulars of the Mounting of a Three-Foot Reflector.

**Three·-foo·ted,** *a.* Having three feet; *esp.* having three supports, tripod, as a *three-footed stool*.

*c* **1000** Ælfric *Gram.* xlix. (Z.) 287 *Tripes*, þryfete [*MS. W.* þrifotede]. — *Voc.* in Wr.-Wülcker 124/6 *Trisilis*, þryfotad fæt. *c* **1425** *Cast. Persev.* 2599 in *Macro Plays* 154 Worldis wele is lyke a iij-foted stole; It faylyt a man at hys most nede. **1555** Eden *Decades* 195, I named the mountayne where these trees grow, the mountayne of three footed trees. **1671** H. M. tr. *Erasm. Colloq.* 436 If we believe Oedipus, there are found fourfooted, and threefooted, and twofooted men. **1821** Scott *Kenilw.* x, So saying he approached to the fire a three-footed stool.

**Three·-forked** (-fǭˑɹkt, *poet.* -fǭˑɹkėd), *a.* Having three forks or prongs; trifurcate.

**1535–1887** [see Forked *ppl. a.* 1 f]. **1615** Crooke *Body of Man* 375 Within these vesselles are certaine values or leafegates...Some of these are three-forcked, some like halfe Moones. *a* **1678** Marvell *Horatian Ode*, Like the three-forked lightning. **1822** *Hortus Angl.* II. 165 *C. Tricuspidatus.* Three-forked Stock. Leaves lyre-shaped; pods three toothed at the tip.

**Three-halfpence** (þrīhēˑpĕns). Money of the value of three halfpennies, or a penny and a halfpenny ($1\frac{1}{2}d.$); a silver coin of this value issued by Queen Elizabeth; also, a silver coin of William IV and Victoria, issued for use in Ceylon.

**1483** *Cath. Angl.* 385/1 Threhalpenys, *trissis* (A.). **1562** J. Heywood *Prov. & Epigr.* (1867) 151 They take three halfpence. **1654** Whitlock *Zootomia* 181 To the Philosopher, three halfpence. **1872** *Punch* 9 Mar. 105/1 The fee for the hire of a chair with arms will be reduced to three-halfpence. **1898** G. B. Rawlings *Brit. Coinage* 65 The sixpence, threepence, threehalfpence, and threefarthings [of Q. Elizabeth], are distinguished by having a rose behind the head.

**Three-halfpenny** (-hēˑpĕni), *a.* (*sb.*) That is worth, or costs, three-halfpence; often a depreciatory epithet of anything held in small esteem: paltry, vile, contemptible. Also *sb.* a three-halfpenny piece: see prec.

**1552** Gilpin *Serm.* in *Life*, etc. (1636) 258 A great number ..keep them [the livings] as their owne lands, and give some three halfe-peny Priest a Curates wages. **1587** Fleming *Contn. Holinshed* III. 1287/1 To let it perish in threehalfepenie pamphlets, and so die in obliuion. **1638** Sanderson *Serm.* (1657) 142 We laugh't at the silliness of the poor Indians..for parting with a massie lump of Gold-ore for a three halfpenny knife. **1726–31** Tindal *Rapin's Hist. Eng.* xvii. (1743) II. 157 The Three Half-penny Piece (coined by this queen only). **1898** G. B. Rawlings *Brit. Coinage* 66 The threehalfpennies, pennies and threefarthings have as their obverse legend E D G *Rosa sine spina*. *Ibid.* 200 William IV also coined silver three-halfpenny pieces for Ceylon and the West Indies.

**Three-halfpennyworth,** usually contr. **ha'porth** (-hēˑpəɹþ). [Cf. Halfpennyworth.] As much as is worth, or costs, three-halfpence.

*c* **1440** *Promp. Parv.* 492/2 Thre halpworthe, *trissis*. **1692** Southerne *Wives Excuse* i. i, Three halfperth of farthings. **1901** *Essex Weekly News* 15 Mar. 6/1 Deceased only had three ha'porth of beer.

†**Three·head.** *Obs.* [f. Three + -head.] The being three (in one); trinity.

*a* **1225** *Juliana* 78 Þet rixleð in þreohad & þah is an untweamet. *a* **1240** *Sawles Warde* in *Lamb. Hom.*, etc. 267 His hali milce..rixleð in þreo-had a buten ende. *a* **1400** *Relig. Pieces fr. Thornton MS.* 59 A God and ane Lord yn threhed, And thre persons yn anehed.

**Three-headed** (þrīˑhe·dėd), *a.* [f. *three head*(*s* + -ed [2].] Having three heads.

*c* **1000** Ælfric *Gram.* ix. (Z.) 67 *Triceps*, þryheafdede. *c* **1400** *Destr. Troy* 300 He highyt vnto helle yates, A þre hedet hounde in his honnd coght. **1567** Golding *Ovid's Met.* vii. (1593) 157 And thou three-headed Hecat. **1839** Bailey *Festus* xxvi. (1852) 456 The dog three-headed, by the gates of woe. **1905** W. T. Pilter *Bible & Babylon* 116 The woman was first tempted by the three-headed Serpent.

**Three·-inch,** *a.* Measuring three inches in length, thickness, etc. (in first quot. *humorous*). Also in *comb.*, as *three-inch-thick*, *-wide*. So **Three-inched** (-inʃt) *a. rare.*

**1596** Shaks. *Tam. Shr.* iv. i. 27 Away you three inch foole, I am no beast. **1626** Capt. Smith *Accid. Yng. Seamen* 9 All the Orlope to be layd with square three inch planck. **1839** Ure *Dict. Arts*, etc. 927 A three-inch-thick plank. **1845** Stocqueler *Handbk. Brit. India* (1854) 399 A formidable knife..tapering from a three-inched hilt to the finest point. **1846** *J. Baxter's Libr. Pract. Agric.* (ed. 4) I. 153 In Suffolk they are hoed.. with three-inch hoes, having handles not above two feet in length.

†**Three·-leaf.** *Obs.* [f. Three + Leaf: cf. Trefoil.] A three-leaved or trifoliate plant. **a.** The wood-sorrel; so called from its ternate leaves. **b.** A species of orchid (? *Habenaria*) with three root-leaves.

*c* **1000** Ælfric *Voc.* in Wr.-Wülcker 133/22 *Trifolium*, ȝeacessure, *uel* þrilefe. **1562** Turner *Herbal* ii. 128 Satyrion whiche som call Threleafe, because it hath thre leaues, bowing doune toward the earth.

**Three·-leaved** (-līvd), *a.* Also -leafed. [See Leaved and Leafed.] Having three leaves, or leaves consisting each of three leaflets; trifoliate. **Three-leaved grass**, an old name for clover; in quot. 1634 app. wood-sorrel (cf. prec. a); **three-leaved ivy**, an American name for the poison ivy (*Rhus toxicodendron*); **three-leaved rush,** *Juncus trifidus*.

**14..** *Voc.* in Wr.-Wülcker 595/33 *Melilotum*, thre-leued-gras. **1562** Turner *Herbal* ii. 41 Among so many threleued herbes as we haue. **1634** Sir T. Herbert *Trav.* 13 Such as haue the Scuruy,..eat three-leafed-grasse, fresh meate, or the like. **1772** Forster in *Phil. Trans.* LXII. 55 The threeleaved Hellebore. **1861** Miss Pratt *Flower. Pl.* V. 296 Three-leaved Rush. .. This rare species,.. has crowded, erect, thread-like stems, from four to six inches high. **1884** J. Tait *Mind in Matter* (1892) 329 Saint Patrick..employed the three-leaved clover to illustrate the Unity of Nature, and Plurality of Persons in the Deity.

**Three·-legged** (-legd, -le·gėd), *a.* Having three legs, as *a three-legged stool*.

†*Three-legged mare*, a nickname for the gallows; *three-legged race*, a race run by couples, the right leg of one person being bound to the left leg of the other; †*three-legged staff*, a tripod for supporting surveying instruments, etc.

**1596** Shaks. *Tam. Shr.* i. i. 64 To combe your noddle with a three-legg'd stoole. **1685** T. Brown *Advice Dr. Oates* 26 From Fear Of being mounted on a Three-legg'd-Mare. **1694**, **1834** [see Mare [1] 2 a]. **1701** Moxon *Math. Instr.* 21 *Three-Leg'd Staff*, made with Joynts to shut together, and take off in the middle for the better carriage: to support Instruments for Astronomy, Surveying, etc. **1764** Maskelyne in *Phil. Trans.* LIV. 350 The wooden three-legged stand, which supports the sector. **1863** W. C. Baldwin *Afr. Hunting* i. 3 Quill-driving was not my particular vocation, nor a three-legged stool the..range to which I was willing to restrict myself. **1909** *Mission Field* July 118 How the boys did enjoy the 'three-legged' race and the sack races!

**Three·lihood.** *nonce-wd.* [app. f. Three + -ly [1] + -hood; perh. after ME. Thrillehod.] The Trinity; threefoldness.

**1839** Bailey *Festus* xx. (1848) 250 To shew the holy God, in three scenes, first And last in Threelihood, and midst in One.

**Three·-man,** *a.* Requiring three men; managed, worked, or performed by three men; esp. in *three-man('s) song*, *glee* (also *three men's song*), a convivial part-song for three men; a trio for male voices. (Corrupted to *freeman's song*: see Freeman 4.)

*c* **1425** *Cast. Persev.* 2336 in *Macro Plays* 147, xxx[ti] thousende..Þat had leuere syttyn at þe ale, iij mens songys to syngyn lowde, Þanne to-ward þe chyrche for to crowde. *c* **1440** *Promp. Parv.* 492/2 Thre mannys songe, *tricinnium*. **1597** Shaks. 2 *Hen. IV*, i. ii. 255 If I do, fillop me with a three-man-Beetle. **1611** — *Wint. T.* iv. iii. 44 Three-man song-men, all, and very good ones. **1600** Heywood *1st Pt. Edw. IV*, Wks. 1874 I. 51 Weele haue a three-men song, to make our guests merry. **1857** Kingsley *Two Y. Ago* xxi, An old seventeenth-century ditty, of the days of 'three-man glees'. **1865** — *Hereward* v.

**Three·-mast,** *a.* Having three masts. So **Three-ma·sted** *a.*; **Three-ma·ster** [Master *sb.*[2]], a three-masted ship.

**1775** Dalrymple in *Phil. Trans.* LXVIII. 392 Two three-mast vessels with latine sails. **1839** Marryat *Phant. Ship* vi, A three-masted vessel. **1883** De Forest in *Harper's Mag.* Mar. 519/2 This ghost of a great three-master.

**Three-mo·nthly,** *a.* (*sb.*) Of or pertaining to three months; appearing every three months, as a periodical; quarterly. **b.** *sb.* A quarterly magazine or review.

**1818** Byron *Juan* I. ccxi, Magazines,..Daily, or monthly, or three monthly. **1830** Gen. P. Thompson *Exerc.* (1842) I. 233 Writing in a three-monthly Review. **1846** Mrs. Gore *Eng. Char.* (1852) 13 Convinced that all the weekly, monthly, and three-monthly critics cannot be in the wrong. **1885** Tupper *My Life as Author* 179, I was editor..of an extinct three-monthly, the *Anglo-Saxon*.

**Threen,** obs. form of Threne.

**Threeness** (þrī·nės). [f. Three + -ness; cf. OE. *þrynes, þrignes*: see Thrinness.] The fact, quality, or condition of being three or threefold; *spec.* said of the Godhead.

[*a* 900 tr. *Bæda's Hist.* IV. xix. [xvii.] (1890) 312 We ondettað ..þrignisse in Annisse efenspedelice, ond Annesse in þære þrignesse.] **1829** Jas. Mill *Hum. Mind* (1869) II. 92 Abstract terms merely; in place of which, the words oneness, twoness, threeness, might be substituted. **1855** Lynch *Lett. to Scattered* v. (1872) 65 That in the Oneness there is Threeness, that the One God is Triune. **1899** *Month* Jan. 14 Threeness in person with oneness in nature.

**Three-one,** *a.* (*sb.*) Being three in one, triune. **b.** *absol.* or as *sb.* The triune God, the Trinity.

**1638–56** Cowley *Davideis* I. 371 Who shall describe thy throne, Thou great Three-One? **1719** J. T. Philipps tr. *Thirty-four Confer.* 174 This glorious Three-One God had created all Things. **1772** T. Olivers *Hymn*, '*The God of Abraham praise*', Before the great Three-One They all exulting stand. **1802** J. Jamieson *Use Sacr. Hist.* II. III. ii. 53 The love of a three-one God is displayed.

**Threep,** variant of Threap.

**Three·-pair,** *a.* In full, *three pair of stairs* (see Pair *sb.*[1] 6 b). Of or belonging to the third floor, as in *three-pair room, back, front, window*.

**1788** *Phil. Trans.* LXXVIII. 217 Out of a three-pair-of-stairs window. **1818** Scott *Hrt. Midl.* xli, Like a squirrel in his cage, hung out of a three pair of stairs window. **1838** Dickens *Nich. Nick.* xxi, In the two-pair back of the house.. or in the three-pair front. **1883** Mrs. Plunkett in *Harper's Mag.* Jan. 236/2 Kate was established in the little 'three pair back'.

**Three-part,** *a.* (*adv.*) Containing, consisting of, having, or involving three parts.

**1854** *Cherubini's Counterpoint* 20 It is prohibited in three-part-counterpoint, as in two-part-counterpoint, to make concealed fifths. **1884** F. J. Britten *Watch & Clockm.* 255 [A] Three Part Clock [or] Three Train Clock..[is] a clock with three trains: the going train, the striking train, and the quarter or chiming train. **1910** Tovey *Encycl. Brit.* III. 129/2, 15 three-part symphonies.

**b.** *adv.* (in comb.) = Three-parts.

**1840** Blaine *Encycl. Rur. Sports* § 1282 A three-part-bred mare.

So **Three-parted** *a.*, divided into or having three parts, tripartite.

**1553** Grimalde *Cicero's Offices* III. (1558) 117 A threeparted deuision. **1793** Martyn *Lang. Bot.*, Three-parted leaf,.. divided into three parts down to the base, but not entirely separate. **1900** Jackson *Gloss. Bot. Terms* 270/2.

**Three parts.** Three out of four equal parts, three quarters. Hence as *advb. phrase*, To the extent of three quarters; well-nigh, almost.

**1711** Swift *Jrnl. to Stella* 30 June, Patrick comes early, and wakes me.., though I am three parts asleep. **1842** Borrow *Bible in Spain* vii. 45 He was half-intoxicated, and soon became three-parts so. **1871** M. Collins *Mrq. & Merch.* x, He rides a three-parts thorough-bred. **1877** Browning *La Saisiaz* 72 There's the stoppage at the inn Three-parts up the mountain. **1887** Stevenson *Mem. & Portraits* xv. 250 Conduct is three parts of life, they say; but I think they put it high.

**Threepence** (þri·pĕns, þre·pĕns). [f. Three + Pence, collective pl. of Penny.]

**1.** A sum of money equal in value to three pennies.

**1605** B. Jonson *Volpone* II. i, What monstrous..circumstance Is here, to get some three or four gazettes, Some three-pence in the whole! **1701** Cibber *Love makes Man* v. ii, *Ang*...Fortune, once again, is kind; but how it comes about— *D. Lew.* Does not signify Three pence. **1849** *Sk. Nat. Hist., Mammalia* IV. 12 In Pennsylvania an old law existed offering threepence a head for every squirrel destroyed.

**2.** A silver coin of this value; a threepenny piece. (Now the smallest silver coin of Great Britain.)

**1589** *Hay any Work* (1844) 11 A round threepence serueth the turn. **1675** *Lond. Gaz.* No. 987/4 One Purse.., and therein..about 18 new Groats, Three-pences, and Two-pences. **1712–13** Swift *Jrnl. to Stella* 23 Jan., Dr. Pratt and I..with the Bishop of Clogher,..played at ombre for threepences. **1824** Miss Mitford *Village* Ser. I. (1863) 235, I would venture the lowest stake of gentility, a silver three-pence, that [etc.]. **1898** G. B. Rawlings *Brit. Coinage* 53 Edward VI coined..a silver crown, half-crown, sixpence, and threepence.

**Threepenny** (þri·pėni, þre·pėni), *a.* (*sb.*)

**1.** Of the value or price of threepence. **a.** *Threepenny nail*, a nail of the size which originally cost threepence a hundred. (See Penny 10.)

**1429–30** *Rec. St. Mary at Hill* 73 Also for d^e iij peny nayll. j d ob. **1481, 1484** [see Penny 10]. **1486** *Naval Acc. Hen. VII* (1896) 16, ccc iij peny nailes ix^d. **1494–5** in Swayne *Sarum Churchw. Acc.* (1896) 43 De clauis vocatis threpenynayle precii centene iij d.

**b.** *Threepenny bit* (Bit *sb.*[2] 8 c), *piece* = Threepence 2; also *fig.* (in reference to the size of the coin) something very small. Also ellipt. *threepenny*.

**1729** *Evelyn's Kal. Hort.* 199 A Leaf as broad as a Three-penny Piece. **1879** *St. George's Hosp. Rep.* IX. 311 Pieces of..bone, varying in size from that of a threepenny-piece to half-a-crown. **1884** W. Black in *Harper's Mag.* Dec. 21/2 A small threepenny-bit of a creature. **1892** A. Maclaren *Paul's Prayers*, etc. (1893) 289 Only a threepenny bit and not a talent. **1905** *Daily Chron.* 8 Nov. 6/7 Threepennies, indeed, are as characteristic of the provinces as the farthing is peculiar to London.

**c.** Costing or involving an outlay of threepence.

**1698** *Christ Exalted* 55 No more shaken than a pair of Three-penny Bellows can shake down the Monument. **1712–13** Swift *Jrnl. to Stella* 17 Feb., I play but threepenny ombre. **1825** T. Hook *Sayings* Ser. II. *Passion & Princ.* viii. III. 126 The letter which had arrived by the threepenny post from Hackney. **1902** *Westm. Gaz.* 25 Apr. 7/3 The 7.3 from Hoe-street, Walthamstow, commonly known as 'the last threepenny train' (largely used by workmen).

**d.** *transf.* Of or pertaining to threepence or to something worth threepence; able or willing to pay threepence.

**1630** J. Taylor (Water P.) *Navy Land Ships* Wks. I. 79/1 Some Men (being borne vnder a threepeny planet) can neither by paines..or any industry be worth a groat. **1895** *Daily News* 13 Dec. 7/1 Consigned to the threepenny boxes of the second-hand booksellers. **1898** *Daily Chron.* 14 Oct. 3/4 What in magazine parlance may be called..the 'threepenny' public. **1899** J. Pennell in *Fortn. Rev.* LXV. 113 It is useless to discuss any matter with the threepenny populace.

**2.** *fig.* as a disparaging epithet: Of little worth; trifling, paltry, cheap, worthless.

**1613** Rowland *Four Knaves* (Percy Soc.) 47 Like threepenie watch-men..Each with a rustie browne-bill in his hand. **1651** C. Cartwright *Cert. Relig.* I. 76 Such men.. were permitted to excommunicate for a threepeny matter. **1823** Scott *Peveril* xxvii, Down to that three-penny baggage, Mistress Nelly.

**Threepennyworth** (þri·pe·niwɒ̆ıþ), contr. **three-penn'orth** (-pe·nəıþ). The quantity that is worth, or costs, threepence.

[**1340** *Ayenb.* 37 Hi habbeþ þri paneworþes of worke uor ane peny.] **1617** *MS. Acc. St. John's Hosp., Canterb.*, For thre penneard of wax candelles iij d. **1700** Congreve *Way of World* v. i, With your Three-penny-worth of small Ware. **1865** Dickens *Mut. Fr.* III. x, 'Threepenn'orth Rum', said Mr. Dolls.

**Three· per ce·nt,** *adj.* and *sb. phr.*

**A.** as *adj.* **a.** Yielding 3 per cent. interest (see B.). **b.** Containing three parts in every hundred.

**1753** *Bank of Eng. Dividend Bk.* 5 Jan., 3 per cent. consolidated annuities. **1796** Cnt. Rumford in *Phil. Trans.* LXXXVII. 215 In the three per cent. consolidated public funds of this country. **1880** Barwell *Aneurism* i. 12, I.. placed them in a three-per-cent. solution of carbolic acid.

**B.** as *sb.* (*absol.* use of A. a). In pl. **three per cents,** the Government securities of Great Britain, consolidated in 1751 into a single stock paying 3 per cent. interest: see Consolidated b.

In 1888 the interest on the consolidated stock (*consols*) was reduced to 2¾ per cent., and in 1903 to 2½ per cent., so that the name, so long familiar, ceased to be applicable.

**1794** G. Rose *Diaries* (1860) I. 195 We borrow in the Three Per Cents. **1823** Scott *Quentin D.* Introd., There were two thousand three per cents as much lost to my family as if the sponge had been drawn over the national slate. *a* **1839** Praed *Poems* (1864) I. 266 Annuities and Three per Cents., Little cares he about them. **1905** *Harmsw. Encycl.* 1562/2 In 1888..the 3 per cents. outstanding were ..£549,094,000.

**Three·-pi·le,** *a.* (*sb.*) [See Pile *sb.*[5] 2.] Applied to velvet in which the loops of the pile-warp (which constitutes the nap) are formed by three threads, producing a pile of treble thickness; so of carpets; also *absol.* or as *sb.* = three-pile velvet.

[**1603** Shaks. *Meas. for M.* IV. iii. 11 Master Three-Pile the Mercer.] **1607** Dekker *Westw. Hoe* I. i. Wks. 1873 II. 283 My..maister hath sent you a veluet gowne heare:..three pile. **1611** Shaks. *Wint. T.* IV. iii. 14, I haue seru'd Prince Florizell, and in my time wore three pile. **1827** Hare *Guesses* Ser. I. (1847) 1 A cloak should be of three-pile, to keep its gloss in wear. **1844** Willis *Lady Jane* I. 208 This delicate alarum is worth while, More 'specially with carpets of three-pile.

**Three·-piled** (-paild), *a.*[1] [f. prec. + -ed[2]. Cf. Piled *ppl. a.*[3] 2.]

**1.** = Three-pile. Also *transf.* of grass, Growing thickly with a soft surface like velvet.

**1603** Shaks. *Meas. for M.* I. ii. 35 Thou art good veluet; thou'rt a three pild peece I warrant thee. **1605** *Lond. Prodigal* I. i. 140 Sixe peeces of vellet...a peece of Ash-colour, a three pilde blacke [etc.]. **1610** *Chester's Tri.* (Chetham Soc.) 41 Our verdant pastures three pil'd greene in graine. *a* **1861** Mrs. Browning *Nature's Remorses* ii, On three-piled carpet of compliments.

**2.** *fig.* Of the highest quality, refined, exquisite; also, of very great degree, excessive, extreme, intense (cf. *threefold, treble, triple*). ? *Obs.*

**1588** Shaks. *L. L. L.* v. ii. 407 Taffata phrases, silken tearmes precise, Three-pil'd Hyperboles. *a* **1616** Beaum. & Fl. *Scornf. Lady* III. i, You, tender sir, whose gentle blood..makes you snuff at all But three-piled people. **1690** Dryden *Don Sebastian* III. ii, She has made my pious father a three-piled cuckold.

**Three·-piled,** *a.*[2] [See Piled *ppl. a.*[2]] Consisting of three things piled one upon another; also *fig.* threefold.

**1656** J. Harrington *Oceana* (1700) 59 As under Herod, Pilat, and Tiberius, a threepil'd Tyranny. **1661** Cowley *Disc. Cromwell* Wks. 1710 II. 637 The Son of Earth,..Upon his three-pil'd Mountain stands, 'Till Thunder strikes him. **1908** *Daily Chron.* 21 Nov. 9/5 The work under the mark of the three piled arms of the B.S.A. Co.

**Three-qua·rter, -qua·rters,** *sb., adj.,* and *advb. phr.*

**A.** as *sb.* **1.** *Three quarters*, three of the four equal parts into which anything is or may be divided; *loosely*, the greater part of anything.

**1470, 1650** [see Quarter *sb.* 1]. **1886** C. E. Pascoe *London of To-day* i. (ed. 3) 29 A modest luncheon of grilled chops and boiled potatoes is ordered. In three-quarters of an hour these appear. **1900** Stoddard *Evol. Eng. Novel* 191 That three-quarters of life which is called conduct.

**2.** *Three-quarter* (pl. *-quarters*), in *Football*, short for *three-quarter back* (see D.).

**1889** H. Vassall *Rugby Football* 13 If he [the captain] is playing four three-quarters and finds that his eight forwards are swamped by the opposing nine, he must make his extra three-quarter go forward. **1897** *Whitaker's Alm.* 645/1 The English halves and three-quarters were run out before they had a chance of getting away.

**B.** as *adj.* *Three-quarter* (rarely *-quarters*). Amounting to three quarters of the whole; one quarter less in magnitude or dimension than that which is complete or full; three-fourths of the ordinary; also vaguely (cf. A. 1).

**1677** *Lond. Gaz.* No. 1239/4 A middle sized Fox Beagle,.. white breast, and her legs whitish, with three quarter sterne. **1684** J. Peter *Siege Vienna* 204 Three quarter Cannons, of each 36 pound. **1700** T. Brown *Acc. Journ. Exon* Wks. 1709 III. II. 101 As if he had been riding three-quarter-speed. **1766** Entick *London* IV. 448 Adjoining to the walls are ten three-quarter columns. **1837** *Civil Eng. & Arch. Jrnl.* I. 33/1 Secured with three-quarter inch bolts. **1867** Aug. J. E. Wilson *Vashti* xxii, A three-quarter moon was staring down at her own image.

**b.** *spec.* Of portraits, etc. (*a*) Originally applied to a canvas measuring 30 inches by 25 (about three-fourths of the area of a kitcat, 36 in. × 28). (*b*) Now usually applied to a portrait showing three-fourths of the figure (in full, *three quarter(s length)*. (Also to a lady's coat of similar length.) (*c*) *Three-quarter-face* (esp. in *Photogr.*), the aspect intermediate between full face and profile.

**1712–13** Swift *Jrnl. to Stella* 27 Feb., I have a very fine picture of lady Orkney,..by sir Godfrey Kneller, three quarters length. **1831** Williams *Life & Corr. Sir T. Lawrence*, 1769–1830, I. 77 The last prices received by Sir Thomas Lawrence. For a head-size, or three-quarters, 210*l.*; for a kit-kat, 315*l.*; for a half-length, 420*l.*;..and for a full-length, 630*l.* *c* **1850** *Catalogue of Wm. Macgill, Edinb.* 10 Canvasses on Frames kept in Stock..24 by 20, head size; 30 by 25, ¾ size; 36 by 28, Kitcat,..50 by 40, half-length [etc.]. **1865** Miss Braddon *Sir Jasper* ii, There were several sketches of the Baronet's elder daughter; now a three-quarter face..; now a profile..; now a full face. **1882** J. Ashton *Soc. Life Reign Q. Anne* xxvii. II. 42 Wollaston, a portrait painter, who could only command five guineas for a three-quarters canvas. **1894** H. Gamlin *G. Romney* 202 Lady Susan Murray is a beautiful three-quarter standing figure. **1911** *Queen* 4 Nov. Suppl. 14/3 A three-quarter length [coat] comes out at only 5 guineas.

**c.** *ellipt.* Measuring or relating to three quarters (of a yard) in Cloth Measure, or three fourths of any quantity indicated by context; *spec.* of a coal seam, three quarters of a yard thick.

**1708** J. C. *Compleat Collier* (1845) 16 The 3 Quarter Coal about 3 Quarters thick or more. **1838** *Civil Eng. & Arch. Jrnl.* I. 381/2 A half-inch service pipe will fill a cistern in one-third the time now taken by the three-quarter cock. **1846** McCulloch *Acc. Brit. Empire* (1854) I. 75 The principal beds of coal are one of 6 feet thick, and a lower one called the three-quarter bed. **1894** Heslop *Northumbld. Gloss.*, *Three quarter-coal*, a seam of coal about three-quarters of a yard in thickness. *Mod.* The three-quarter chimes.

**C.** as *adv.* To the extent of three quarters.

*a* **1584** Montgomerie *Cherrie & Slae* 110 That little God of Loue..With bow thrie quarteris scant. **1832** *Regul. Instr. Cavalry* III. 106 The..Troops wheel three-quarters left about. **1869** 'Lewis Carroll' *Phantasmagoria* 106 Prone to the dust he bent his head, And lay like one three-quarters dead.

**D.** Spec. Comb. and Collocations: **three-quarter back,** in *Rugby Football* (also in *Hockey*), one of two, three, or four players stationed between the half-backs and the full-backs; **three-quarter binding,** a style of bookbinding having more leather than half-binding: see quot.; **three-quarter-bred** *a.*, having three quarters of pure blood; **three-quarter cleft (clift),** *dial.* a person three-quarters 'cracked': cf. Quarter-cleft 2; **three-quarters face,** *Mil.* three quarters of a full 'face' or turn; **three-quarter fiddle**: see quot.; **three-quarter plate (watch)**: see quot.

**1880** *Daily Tel.* 20 Dec., One of the Northern *three-quarter backs sustained an injury to his leg. **1889** H. Vassall *Rugby Football* 10 This led to the increase in the number of three-quarter-backs, first, from one to two, with two full-backs, and then to three, with one full-back—in other words, three-quarter-back became the main line of defence against the rush of opposing forwards. **1890** Cresswell *Hockey* 10 The three-quarter-backs, generally two in number. **1897** *Let. to Editor*, *Three quarter binding is a very wide back and large corners. The sides may be of anything, paper, cloth [etc.]. **1902** Bodkin *Shillelagh* 32 The fast *three-quarter bred mare between the shafts. **1843** Carleton *Traits Irish Peas.* I. 5 'A *three-quarter clift' of a fellow—half knave, half fool. **1833** *Regul. Instr. Cavalry* I. 14 The recruit..makes a *three quarters face. **1889** E. J. Payne in Grove *Dict. Mus.* IV. 813/1 *Violino Piccolo* (..*Dreiviertel-geige*, *Three-quarter fiddle), a violin of small size, but of the ordinary parts and proportions, differing in this respect from the pochette or kit. **1884** Britten

*Watch & Clockm.* 199 In *three-quarter plate watches there is a piece cut out of the top plate sufficiently large to allow the balance to move in the same horizontal plane.

So **Three-quartered** *a.*, † **a.** made in three sections (*obs.*); **b.** *Her.* of an animal as a bearing: turned so as to be nearly affronté, but showing a part of the flank.

*c* 1450 LOVELICH *Grail* xxxv. 535 There-Inne stoden peleris of Marbil stones..thre-qwarterid they weren Of Gold & Asure And Of Silver. *c* 1828 BERRY *Encycl. Her.* I. Gloss., *Three-quartered*, showing three-fourths of an animal; termed, also, *trian-aspect*, as an eagle, &c. in a *trian-aspect*. 1889 in ELVIN *Dict. Her.*

**Threes**, obs. form of THRICE.

**Threescore** (þrīˈskōᵊɹ, þrīskōᵊɹ), *a.* (*sb.*) *arch.* Forms: see THREE and SCORE *sb.* [SCORE *sb.* 16.] Three times twenty; sixty. (Formerly sometimes written in Roman numerals, iij^xx.)

1388 WYCLIF *Lev.* xii. 5 Thre scoor and sixe daies. 1470–85 MALORY *Arthur* VI. viii. 194, I wil delyuer al the prysoners that I haue that is thre score and foure. 1535 COVERDALE *Ps.* lxxxix. [xc.] 10 The dayes of oure age are iij. score yeares & ten. 1599 in *Thanes of Cawdor* (Spald. Club) 218 Violentlie cuttit doun iij^xx dussonis young growand treis. 1610 HOLLAND *Camden's Brit.* (1637) 529 Almost threescore miles in length. 1699 DRYDEN *Epist. J. Driden* 91 But we their sons, a pamper'd race of men, Are dwindled down to threescore years and ten. 1741 CHESTERF. *Lett.* (1792) I. 216 Very long ships, rowed by oars, some of forty, some of fifty, and threescore oars.

**b.** *absol.* with ellipsis of *years*, in reference to age; hence as *sb.* the age of sixty years, or *transf.* a person of this age. So *threescore* (*years*) *and ten*, seventy years.

1605 SHAKS. *Macb.* II. iv. 1 *Old man.* Threescore and ten I can remember well. 1719 YOUNG *Revenge* II. 18 And reverend Grey Threescore is but a Voucher. 1764 GOLDSM. *Trav.* 254 The gay grandsire..Has frisk'd beneath the burden of threescore. 1822 GALT *Provost* xl, The worthy man was hale and hearty, not exceeding three score and seven. *Mod.* He has long passed the three score and ten.

† **c.** Used as ordinal numeral (*threescore and one* = sixty-first). *Obs.*

1596 DANETT tr. *Comines* (1614) 219 The King..when he died was well forward in the threescore and one yeere.

Hence † **Threescorth** *a. Obs.* [-TH ²], sixtieth.

1571 GOLDING *Calvin on Ps.* xlv. 1 The threescorthe Psalme is intytled (A Lilly). 1657 *North's Plutarch, Add. Lives* (1676) 38 Acacanius the threescorth King of the Scots.

**Three·-si·ded** (stress var.), *a.* Having three sides, trilateral (either as a plane figure or flat body with three edges, triangular; or as a solid figure or body with three lateral surfaces, trihedral); *fig.* having three parts or aspects.

1601 HOLLAND *Pliny* (1634) II. 489 In the triumph..he made a shew of three-sided tables, cup-bourds, and bourds, supported by one foot all of brasse. 1793 MARTYN *Lang. Bot.*, *Three-sided stem*,..having three plane sides. 1823 H. J. BROOKE *Introd. Crystallogr.* 115 Dodecahedrons with triangular planes, appearing as three-sided pyramids on the planes of the tetrahedron. 1878 H. H. GIBBS *Ombre* 8 One of those three-sided tables with pits in them to hold the counters. 1901 *Westm. Gaz.* 5 Feb. 10/1 The taste of Queen Victoria in books was..a three-sided taste.

**Threesome** (þrīˈsǫ̆m), *sb.* and *a.* (*adv.*) Chiefly *Sc.* Also 4–6 **thresum**, 6 **thriesum.** [f. THREE + -SOME.] **A.** *sb.* Three persons together; three forming a company.

1375 BARBOUR *Bruce* III. 420 It [boat] sa litill wes, þat It Mycht our þe wattir bot thresum flyt. 1549 *Compl. Scot.* xv. 131 It is nocht possibil to gar thresum keip consel. *a* 1578 LINDESAY (Pitscottie) *Chron. Scot.* (S.T.S.) I. 275 Mccleine ..eschapit and thriesum with him. 1816 SCOTT *Bl. Dwarf* viii, The rest disperse by twasome and threesome through the waste, and meet me at the Trysting Pool. 1893 STEVENSON *Catriona* xxix, We..sat down to meat, we threesome.

**B.** *adj.* Consisting or composed of three; performed by three together; threefold, triple.

1839 *New Monthly Mag.* LVII. 42 Any thing like a country-dance, or a threesome or foursome reel. 1872 MORRIS *Love is Enough* (1873) 8 To have seen Your nimble feet tread down the green In threesome dance. 1875 — *Æneid* v. 580 Then..they..in threesome order slip Their cloven ranks. 1878 H. H. GIBBS *Ombre* 4 Tresillo means a threesome game. *Mod. Sc.* A threesome cluster of nuts. She does her back-hair in a threesome plait.

**b.** quasi-*adv. nonce-use*: cf. FOURSOME 1 b.

1875 MORRIS *Æneid* VII. 639 Mail-coat threesome laid Of golden link.

Hence **Three·someness** *nonce-wd.*, the quality of existing in threes, triplicity.

1853 *Athenæum* 15 Oct. 1216 What may be called the threesomeness of everything in the moral world.

**Three·-squa·re**, *a.* Now *dial.* or *techn.* [f. THREE, after *four-square*; cf. *five-square*, *six-square*.] Having three equal sides; equilaterally triangular. Also *fig.* threefold, triple.

*c* 1440 *Jacob's Well* 119 Þis wose of coueytise is thre sqware. Þe firste sqware is..desyre..to haue..wordly ryches. 1527 ANDREW *Brunswyke's Distyll. Waters* b ij, Ye must haue x or xii fyltes..beyng thresquare, a fote of length. 1590 SPENSER *F. Q.* I. vi. 41 Catching up in hast his three-square shield And shining helmet. 1642 FULLER *Holy & Prof. St.* I. iv. 10, I intend not to range over all his life as he stands threesquare in relation, Husband, Father, Master. 1683 MOXON *Mech. Exerc.*, *Printing* xiii. ¶ 2 For ..Triangular Punches, I commonly reserve my worn out three square Files. 1766 J. BARTRAM *Jrnl.* 9 Feb. in W. Stork *Acc. E. Florida* 63 A good sort of rush to bottom chairs with, much better than the..bull-rush or the three-square ones. 1873 *Routledge's Yng. Gentl. Mag.* July 502/1 Take a triangular file, three-square file it is called.

† **Three·-squared**, *a. Obs.* [f. as prec. + -ED.] = prec.

*c* 1400 MAUNDEV. (1839) xiv. 160 Summe [diamonds] ben .vj. squared, summe iiij. squared, and summe iij. as nature schapeth hem. [*Fr.* Et totes sont quarrez et ont pointes de lour nature; et ascuns sont a vj. quarrez et ascuns a iiij. et ascuns a iij., si come nature les fourme.] 1577 *Wills & Inv. N. C.* (Surtees) I. 415 One dosen three-squarde fyles. 1585 LUPTON *Thous. Notable Th.* (1675) 144 A hole made..with a three squared stake. 1701 *Lond. Gaz.* No. 3708/4 Lost.., a Three-squared turning Seal, with 3 Stones.

**Three·-stringed** (-striŋd), *a.* Having three strings: usually of a musical instrument.

1599 SANDYS *Europæ Spec.* (1632) 145 The whole Realme ..hath beene scourged with a three stringed whip, Warre, Ill-governement, and Injustice. 1611 BIBLE 1 *Sam.* xviii. 6 *margin*, Three stringed instruments. 1752 NEWTON *Note Milton's L'Allegro* 94 Rebeck is a three-stringed fiddle. 1843 *Penny Cycl.* XXVI. 346/1 Medals..representing Apollo playing on a three-stringed instrument.

**Threete**, obs. form of THREAT *v.*

**Three·-tined** (-təind), *a.* Having three tines or prongs, three-pronged.

1558 PHAER *Æneid* II. E iij b, The God Neptune..With forck thretinde the walles vprootes. 1587 FLEMING *Contn. Holinshed* III. 1339/1 Neptune with his threetined mace, riding ouer waues vpon a dolphin. 1706 *Lond. Gaz.* No. 4259/3, 6 Silver three-tined Forks. 1904 *Daily News* 7 Nov. 4 A three-tined dinner fork.

**Three·-toed** (-tōᵘd), *a.* Having three toes; in *Zool.* a descriptive epithet of particular species of animals.

1752 SIR J. HILL *Hist. Anim.* 562 The three-toed Armadilla. 1772 FORSTER in *Phil. Trans.* LXII. 388 Three-toed Woodpecker. 1879 E. P. WRIGHT *Anim. Life* 211 The Three-toed Sloth..is a native of Brazil, Para, and Rio Janeiro. 1906 *Westm. Gaz.* 24 Jan. 12/1 That the three-toed horse became extinct ages ago—geologically speaking.

**Three·-tongued** (-tɒŋd), *a.* Having three tongues; also, knowing or using three languages, trilingual.

1594 CAREW *Huarte's Exam. Wits* xi. (1596) 152 The vowels, and phrases of speech hold a very different signification from that which the vulgar and three-tongued men do know. 1690 C. NESSE *O. & N. Test.* I. 18 That Doeg aforesaid..was *trilinguis*, three-tongued. 1743 FRANCIS tr. *Hor.*, *Odes* III. xi. 22 From his three-tongu'd Jaws the Poison flow'd.

**Three·-way**, *a.* Having, or connected with, three ways, roads, or channels; situated where three ways meet. *Three-way cock, valve*, one with an inlet and two alternative outlets.

1587 FLEMING *Contn. Holinshed* III. 1338/2 His highnesse passing foorth still beyond the place called the Threewaieleet, came to the street named Hwiuetterstreet, that is to say, the chandellors street. 1603, 1608, 1674–91 [see LEET *sb.*³]. 1633 AMES *Agst. Cerem.* II. 325 To have set up Altars of devotion at every three-way-leet. 1838 *Civil Eng. & Arch. Jrnl.* I. 189/2 Five three-way cocks and their appendages. 1884 COUES *Key N. Amer. Birds* (ed. 2) 190 This curious extra-vestibular chamber, which may be named the *trivia*, or 'three-way' place. 1888 LOCKWOOD *Dict. Mech. Engineering Terms*, *Three-way cock*..for diverting the liquid from the inlet branch into two different directions at pleasure. 1907 *Installation News* June 11/2 This necessitates a three-way distribution board.

**Three·-years, -year**, *a.*

**1.** Of or pertaining to, or lasting for, three years; of the age of three years.

1665 PEPYS *Diary* 7 Apr., We having already..spent one year's share of the three-years tax. 1727 [DORRINGTON] *Philip Quarll* (1816) 37 They set sail for a three years voyage. 1798 COLERIDGE *Anc. Mar.* I. iv, The Wedding-Guest stood still, And listens like a three years child.

**2. Three·-year-o·ld**, of the age of three years; *spec.* of horses; also, of three years' standing, that has been such for three years. Also *three years old.*

1825 BENTHAM *Offic. Apt. Maximized, Observ. Peel's Sp.* (1830) 10 Exclusion of all Barristers but three-year-old ones. *Ibid.* 13 Three years old Barristers. 1838 *Penny Cycl.* XII. 307/2 A three-year-old colt. 1894 *Field* 9 June 850/3 A three-year-old animal may have all the permanent incisors well up. 1910 *Westm. Gaz.* 2 Apr. 7/3 A strange story of an alleged three-year-old treaty between Russia and China.

**b.** *absol.* or as *sb.*; also *attrib.*

1617 in *T. Pont's Topogr. Acc. Cunningham* (Maitland Cl.) 200 Saxtein auld kye...Item, thrie thrie-yeir-aldis. 1825 BENTHAM *Offic. Apt. Maximized, Observ. Peel's Sp.* (1830) 18 Turn now to the three year olds [i. e. barristers]. 1856 'STONEHENGE' *Brit. Sports* II. (ed. 2) § 119 By Training the three-year-old is understood the preparation of the colt for racing as a three-year-old, in his fourth year. 1882 *Daily News* 26 Dec. 3/5 Not only in the three-year-old prizes did the fillies make their mark.

So **Three-yea·rling** *a.* = *three-year-old.*

1621 AINSWORTH *Annot. Pentat.* (1639) 58 Take unto thee a three-yeerling heiffer and a three-yeerling she goat.

**Thref(e, threff**, obs. ff. THRAVE, THRIFT.

**Threies, Threin, Threip, Threist**: see THRICE, THRIN, THREAP, THIRST.

**Threit, -en**: see THREAT, THRETE, THREATEN.

**Threll**, var. THRILL *sb.*² *Obs.*, obs. f. THRALL *sb.*

**Threll multure**: see THIRL-MULTURE.

**Thremmatology** (þremătǫ·lŏdʒi). *Biol.* [f. Gr. θρέμμα (-ατ-) nursling + -LOGY.] That part of biology which treats of the propagation or breeding of domestic animals and plants.

1888 E. R. LANKESTER in *Encycl. Brit.* XXIV. 802/1 The area of biological knowledge..which relates to the breeding of animals and plants, their congenital variations, and the transmission and perpetuation of those variations..may be called thremmatology. *Ibid.*, Darwin's introduction of thremmatology into the domain of scientific biology. 1889 *Athenæum* 12 Jan. 47/2 The second subdivision, 'Bionomics', includes..thremmatology—a word coined for the subjects of variation, heredity, and the breeder's lore.

**Threne** (þrīn), *sb.* Forms: 5–6 **trene**, 7 **threen**, 6– **threne**. [ad. Gr. θρῆνος funeral lament. So obs. F. *thrène* (1526 in Godef. *Compl.*).] A song of lamentation; a dirge, threnody; formerly *spec.* (in *pl.*) the Lamentations of Jeremiah (LXX θρῆνοι Ἰερεμίου, Vulgate *Threni*).

1432–50 tr. *Higden* (Rolls) III. 85 The seide Ieremy.. made also the trenes, that is to say, the lamentaciones. 1493 *Festivall* (W. de W. 1515) 7 Ye paynfull deth of our sauyour..of the whiche is made mencyon in the fyrst chapytre of Trenys. 1593 SOUTHWELL *St. Peter's Compl.* 2 My threnes an endlesse Alphabet doe finde. 1601 SHAKS. *Phœnix & Turtle* 49 Whereupon it made this threne To the phœnix and the dove. 1651 BP. H. KING in *Ussher's Lett.* (1686) 567 Some of these Psalms may serve as Threnes and Dirges to lament the Present Miseries. 1811 LAMB *Guy Faux* Misc. Wks. (1871) 372 The tears and sad threnes of the matrons in universal mourning.

So **Threne** *v.* [cf. Gr. θρηνεῖν], to compose or sing a threne; **Threne·tic, Threne·tical** *adjs.* [Gr. θρηνητικός], pertaining to a threnody; mournful.

1890 *Univ. Rev.* Dec. 540 Her voice grew strangely low as she *threned. 1656 BLOUNT *Glossogr.*, *Threnetick.. mournful, lamentable. 1850 MURE *Hist. Lang. & Lit. Greece* III. 325 Threnetic odes are also ascribed to Sappho. 1829 CARLYLE *Misc.*, *Voltaire* (1872) II. 152 *Threnetical discourses.

† **Threng**, *sb. Obs.* [variant of THRING *sb.*¹, assimilated to THRENG *v.*] A crowd, throng; = THRING *sb.*¹

*c* 1275 LAY. 2229 Among þe þrenge of sipmen hii funde þeos maydenes. 13.. *K. Alis.* 2533 (Bodl. MS.) Abouten hij gonnen goo Par force smyten in to þe þrenge And duden beastes from oþere drenge. *c* 1330 *Arth. & Merl.* (Kölbing) 6099 Of Sarazins gret þreng About our Cristen made reng.

† **Threng**, *v. Obs.* Pa. t. **threngde.** [Early ME. *þrengen*, wk. vb.; in form a factitive from THRING *v.*:—OTeut. **þrangian* (cf. MHG. *drengen*, Ger. *drängen* to press, throng, late ON. *þrøngva*, *-gja*, Icel. *þrengja*, Sw. *tränga*, Da. *trænge* to press), in signification not differing from THRING *v.*]

**1.** *trans.* To press or crush into a narrow space; to force into confinement: = THRING *v.* B. 5 c.

*a* 1154 *O. E. Chron.* an. 1137, Sume hi diden in crucethus ðæt is in an cæste þat was scort and nareu and undep..and þrengde þe man þær inne ðæt him bræcon alle þe limes. *c* 1380 WYCLIF *Wks.* (1880) 473 Anticrist wolde faste to men godis of fortune bi coueytise, þat shulden drenge a man to helle. [But perh. this is for *drenche* = sink.]

**2.** *intr.* To go in a crowd or throng, press *in*, *out*, etc.: = THRING *v.* B. 1.

*c* 1200 ORMIN 16182 Þatt he swiþe mikell follc Draf all ut off þe temmple...Swa þatt te33 alle þrenngdenn ut Off all þatt miccle temmple.

**Threnode** (þrī·nōᵘd). [Alteration of next, after *ode*.] = next.

1858 KINGSLEY *Misc.*, *Chalk-stream Stud.* I. 167 The threnodes of a certain peevish friend who literally hates a mountain. 1876 STEDMAN *Victorian Poets* 99 As a threnode nothing comparable to [Arnold's *Thyrsis*] had then appeared since the *Adonais* of Shelley. 1903 *Daily Chron.* 16 June 3/2 In death the old wailing of the threnode is still raised, and sometimes Charon's penny is still put under the tongue.

**Threnody** (þre·nŏdi, þrī·n-). [ad. Gr. θρηνῳδία dirge, f. θρῆνος THRENE + ᾠδή song.] A song of lamentation; *spec.* a lament for the dead, a dirge.

1634 SIR T. HERBERT *Trav.* 10 They repaire vnto the Sepulchre,..vsing Thrænodies and dolorous complaints. 1647 FARINDON *Serm.* 34 (L.) The most powerful eloquence is the threnody of a broken heart. 1827 CARLYLE *Misc.*, *Richter* (1872) I. 4 Next came threnodies from all the four winds. 1876 STEDMAN *Victorian Poets* 168 This elegiac poem [*In Memoriam*], the great threnody of our language.

So **Threnodial** (þrĭnōᵘ·diăl), **Threno·dian, Threnodic** (-ǫ·dik), **Threno·dical** *adjs.*, of or pertaining to a threnody, mournful; **Thre·nodist**, one who composes or utters a threnody; **Thre·nody** *v.*, *trans.* to mourn in a threnody.

1817 SOUTHEY *Lett.* (1856) III. 81, I would..fain be excused from any *threnodial service. 1837 — *Doctor* cxxxiii. IV. 352 This was pretty well for a threnodial flight. But Dr. Watts went farther. 1624 QUARLES *Funeral Elegies* Poems (1717) 416 If this *Threnodian story Intend her honour with thy loss of glory. 1891 *Cent. Dict.*, *Threnodic. 1881 *Nation* (N. Y.) XXXII. 188 The brief *threnodical essay published at the time of Irving's death. 1827 CARLYLE *Misc.*, *Richter* (1872) I. 4 To think of laughing over these unhappy *threnodists and panegyrists. 1832 DE QUINCEY *Cæsars* Wks. 1862 IX. 5 Peace, then, rhetoricians, false threnodists of false liberty! 1893 G. ALLEN *Scallywag* III. 254 Mr. Solomons, thus *threnodied by the appointed latter-day bards,..was buried.

‖ **Threnos** (þrī·nǫs). Also in Lat. form **threnus**. [a. Gr. θρῆνος, L. *thrēnus*.] = THRENE, THRENODY.

1601 SHAKS. *Phœnix & Turtle* (heading), Threnos. 1840 tr. *C. O. Müller's Hist. Lit. Greece* iii. § 5. 21 These singers of the threnos were at the burial of Achilles represented by the Muses themselves, who sang the lament. 1850 MURE *Hist. Lang. & Lit. Greece* III. 97 The Threnus of Homer's bards..was probably in dactylic measure. 1903 *Speaker* 28 Feb. 539/1 A lad..whose short life may be likened to a threnos.

**Thre·noˌthria·mbics.** *humorous nonce-wd.* [f. Gr. θρῆνο-ς THRENE + θριαμβικ-ός triumphal (f. θρίαμβος a hymn to Bacchus).] Verses in which lamentation and triumph are combined.

**1673** *S' too him Bayes* 57 In such lamentable threnothriambicks that you would think Nineve were going to be destroy'd immediately.

**Threo, Threottene,** obs. f. THREE, THIRTEEN.

**Threp, threpe,** obs. ff. THREAP.

**Threpel, -il,** obs. ff. TRIPLE *v.*

**Threpso·logy.** *rare*—°. [irreg. for **threpsiology*, f. Gr. θρέψις nutrition + -LOGY.] See quot.

**1857** DUNGLISON *Dict. Med. Sc.*, *Threpsology*,..the doctrine of, or a treatise on, the nutrition of organized bodies. **1860** in MAYNE *Expos. Lex.*

**Threptic** (þre·ptik), *a.* *rare*—¹. [ad. Gr. θρεπτικ-ός able to feed, f. τρέφειν to nourish.] Of or pertaining to nutrition.

**1845** MAURICE *Mor. & Met. Philos.* (1850) I. vi. § 6. 199 We may define all the faculties which can exist in any living creature to be these: first, the faculty of receiving nourishment (θρεπτική); secondly, [etc.]... The threptic faculty is the lowest of these, and is present in all cases.

**Thresch, Threser,** obs. f. THRESH, TREASURE.

**Threschefold, threschwald,** etc., obs. ff. THRESHOLD.

**Thresh,** *v.*, the earlier and etymological form of the vb. now also written THRASH, q. v.; still frequent in the sense of beating out corn; so **Thresh** *sb.*, **Threshing,** etc.: see THRASH, etc.

**Threshal, -el, fold,** etc., varr. THRESHOLD.

**Threshel** (þre·ʃ'l). Now *dial.* Forms: 1 **þerscel, þyrscel**; 7–9 **threshal, -all, -el,** (7 **thressal, threshold,** 9 **-le**), 9 *dial.* **thrashel, drashel,** etc.: see *Eng. Dial. Dict.* [OE. *þerscel*, f. *þersc-an*, THRASH, THRESH *v.* + -EL¹; cf. OHG. *driscil*, MHG., G. *drischel*.] A flail.

*a* **1000** *Ags. Gloss.* in Wr.-Wülcker 192/3 *Bainus*, þerscel. *c* **1000** *Ælfric's Voc.* ibid. 107/2, 141/16 *Tritorium*, þerscel. **1674** FLAVEL *Husb. Spir.* I. xix. 159 As they have threshals of different sizes, so they bestow on some grain more, on other fewer, strokes. *Ibid.* 161 He little regards whether it be bruised and battered to pieces by the threshold or no. **1685** R. DUNNING *Plain & Easie Method* 5 By his Threshall, Mattock, and the like, he now gains his Meat and Drink. **1688** R. HOLME *Armoury* III. 333/1 A Threshall or Flail [to Thrash or Thresh the Corn]. **1813** T. DAVIS *Agric. Wilts.* Gloss. s. v., A pair of threshles or drashols, or flyals, a flail. **1881** MISS JACKSON *Shropsh. Word-bk.*, *Thrashal*, *Thrashat*, ..a flail. **1882** JAGO *Cornw. Gloss.*, *Drashel*, a flail.

† **b.** A mediæval weapon: see quot., and cf. FLAIL *sb.*² and MORGENSTERN. *Obs.*

**1688** R. HOLME *Armoury* III. xvi. (Roxb.) 88/1 A round Iron or Lead Ball sett on all sides with spike nayles, or sharp pointed Irons, hung in a chaine, to the end of a staffe or cudgell...Some terme it a slinged Galthrope, others Waring thressal.

**Thresher**¹: see THRASHER¹.

**Thre·sher**². (With capital T.) A member of an Irish political organization instituted in 1806, which issued manifestos signed 'Captain Thresher'.

**1806** LD. PLUNKET *Sp.* 5 Dec. in Howell *State Trials* (1822) XXX. 7 For some time past the peace of the county [Sligo] has been infested by a set of persons assuming the name of 'Threshers'. **1808** *Hist.* in *Ann. Reg.* 1806. 263 Disturbances..occasioned by a banditti, who went about in the night time under the name of Threshers, committing every sort of crime and outrage. **1812** *Chron.* ibid. 31/1 The spirit of party broke out between several of the lower orders, styling themselves Threshers on the one side, and Orangemen on the other.

**Thresher,** var. of THRASHER², a N. Amer. bird.

**Threshold** (þre·ʃo͡ld). Forms: see below. [OE. *þerscold, -wold, þerxold, -wold, þrexold, -wold* = ON. *þreskjǫldr, -kǫldr*, nom. pl. *þreskeldir*, mod. Icel. *þröskuldr*, Norw., Sw. *tröskel*, Da. (*dør*)*tærskel*; cf. OHG. *driscûfli* neuter, MHG. *drischuvel, durschufel*, Ger. dial. *drischaufel*, etc. The first element is generally identified with THRESH *v.* (? in its original sense 'to tread, trample'), the forms of which it generally follows; but the second is doubtful, and has in English, as in other langs., undergone many popular transformations.]

**1.** The piece of timber or stone which lies below the bottom of a door, and has to be crossed in entering a house; the sill of a doorway; hence, the entrance to a house or building.

α. 1 **þresc-, þrex-, þerxold,** 5 **thresshhold,** 6 **threshhold, thressald, threzsh-, tresholde,** 6–7 **thresholde,** 6– **threshold.**

*c* **1000** ÆLFRIC *Exod.* xii. 22 And dippað ysopan sceaft on þam blode, þe ys on þam þerxolde. — *Deut.* vi. 9 And write þa on þinum þrescolde. *c* **1000** Ðrexold [see β]. **1513** DOUGLAS *Æneis* VI. i. 100 To the dur thressald cumin ar thai. **1530** PALSGR. 280/2 Thresholde, *seuil de huys* [*l'uis*]. **1535** COVERDALE 1 *Sam.* v. 5 They..treade not vpon the threszsholde of Dagon. — *Prov.* xxvi. 14 Like as the dore turneth aboute vpon the tresholde. **1553** BECON *Reliques of Rome* (1563) 256 b, At euery time the bishop shal come vnto yᵉ church dore & strike yᵉ threshold thereof with his Crossier staffe. **1607** SHAKS. *Cor.* IV. v. 124. **1727** GAY *Fables* xxiii. 30 The horse-shoe's nail'd (each threshold's guard). **1837** LYTTON *E. Maltrav.* I. i, A tall figure crossed the threshold.

β. 1 **þrex-, þræx-, þreox-, ðærsc-, þersc-, þeorsc-, þercs-, þer(e)xwold, þrexwald, -weald, þersc-, þærsc-, þirscwald,** 2 **þreoxwold,** 4 **þrex-, thresshe-, thresh-, threswold, thers-, þreis-, thrys-, throssche-, treswald,** 5 **thrys-, threschwolde, thris-, thresche-, thryshwald,** 6 **threskwolde** (9 *dial.* **thresh-wood**).

[*c* 888 þeorscwold: see sense 2.]

**971** *Blickl. Hom.* 207 Of ðæs portices dura..ðærscwolde wæs ȝesyne þæt [etc.]. *c* **1000** ÆLFRIC *Gram.* ix. (Z.) 40 *Limen*, ofersleȝe oððe þerexwold [*v.rr.* þræx-, þreox-, þerxwold, ðrexold]. *c* **1000** *Sax. Leechd.* II. 142 Ofer þa duru, & under þone þerxwold. *c* **1000** *Ags. Voc.* in Wr.-Wülcker 280/15 *Limen*, perscwald. **11..** *Voc.* ibid. 551/32 *Limen*, ofersleie, *uel* þreoxwold. *c* **1325** *Gloss. W. de Bibbesw.* in Wright *Voc.* 170 *La lyme*, the therswald. **1362** LANGL. *P. Pl.* A. v. 201 He þrompelde atte þrexwolde [*v.rr.* þresshewold, þreschfold, throschfold] and þreuh to þe grounde. *c* **1375** *Sc. Leg. Saints* xviii. (*Egipciane*) 579 Quhen we come to þe thryswald. *Ibid.* 593, I..furth can gange to þe treswald. **1382** WYCLIF 1 *Kings* xiv. 17 Whanne she wente in the threshwold of the hows, the child dyede. *c* **1386** CHAUCER *Clerk's T.* 232 (Lansd.) And as sche wolde ouer þe þresshewolde gon [*Camb.* throswald, *Petw.* thressholde, *Ellesm.*, *Heng.*, *Corp.* thresshfold, *Harl.* þreisshfold]. *c* **1400** *Ywaine & Gaw.* 3222 He come to the thriswald. **14..** *Nom.* in Wr.-Wülcker 733/8 *Hoc limen*, *-nis*, thryswold. *c* **1440** *Promp. Parv.* 492/2 Threschwolde, *limen*. **1444** in J. R. Boyle *Hedon* (1875) App. 184 Thryshwald. **1483** *Cath. Angl.* 385/1 A Threschewalde, *limen*. **1511** *Nottingham Rec.* III. 333 Makyng ye seid doore and leyeng of ij. threskwoldes. **1825** J. BRIGGS *Rem.* 215 (E.D.D.) Upon this thresh-wood..cross straws were laid.

γ. 4 **þreschefolde, threshfoold, þreshe-, thressh-, þresch-, threissh-, threis-, throschfold,** 5 **thresh-, thresfold(e** (9 *dial.* **thresh-fod**).

*c* **1374** CHAUCER *Boeth.* I. pr. i. 3 (Camb. MS.) They passeden sorwfully the thresshfold [*B. M. MS.* þreschefolde]. **1382** WYCLIF *Ezek.* ix. 3 At the threshfoold [**1388** threisfold] of the house. **1393** LANGL. *P. Pl.* C. VII. 408 He thrumbled at þe þreshefold [*v. rr.* þresshfold, þrescwolde, treshfold]. **1413** *Pilgr. Sowle* (Caxton 1483) III. ix. 56 Not by the dore but vnder the threshfold drawen oute. **14..** *Voc.* in Wr.-Wülcker 592/47 *Limen*, a thresfolde. **1828** *Craven Gloss.*, *Thresh-fod*, threshold.

δ. 6 **thressholl,** 7–8 **threshal,** 9 *dial.* **threshel, thrashel (drashel).**

**1593** Thressholl [see 2 b]. **1607** CHAPMAN *Bussy d'Ambois* IV. G ij b, Ile make th' inspired threshals of his Court Sweat with the weather of my horrid steps Before I enter. *c* **1645** HOWELL *Lett.* (1688) IV. 494 He dragg'd her Body to the Threshal of the Door. **1787** in *Coll. Sc. Poems* 12 (E.D.D.) Luckie out o'er the threshal goes. **1898** MACMANUS *Bend of Road* 90 The house crammed..from the threshel to the backstone. **1900** G. WILLIAMS *Fairmner's Tint Laddies* iv. (E.D.D.), To cross the thrashel o' oor hoose.

ε. *dial.* 7 **treshwart,** 9 **threshwort, threshut**; 9 **freshwood**: cf. TH- (6).

**1608** *Vestry Bks.* (Surtees) 151 Pᵈ to John Lamb for mendinge of the treshwart of the portch, iiijd. **18..** BRIERLEY *Out of Work* x. (E.D.D.), Mind thou doesno' tumble o'er that threshut. **1888** W. DICKINSON *Lit. Rem.* 234 (E.D.D.) The threshwort's worn quite hollow down.
**1825** J. BRIGGS *Rem.* 201 (E.D.D.) The entrance from the front door was called the freshwood. **1879** SIMMONS *Lay Folks Mass Bk.* Notes 399, I bids thee..never again set thy foot over my freshwood. **1892** HESLOP *Northumbld. Gloss.*, *Fresh-wood*, the threshold, or foot-beam of the front door.

¶ **b.** (*erron.*) The upper horizontal part of a door-case; the lintel. *rare.*

[Cf. *c* **1000** in 1 α, 1 β. **1382**: see OVERTHRESHOLD.] **1821** CLARE *Vill. Minstr.* I. 11 The rural sports of May, When each cot-threshold mounts its hailing bough. **1834** HT. MARTINEAU *Demerara* iv. 52 Cassius stood, leaning his forehead against his low threshold.

**2.** *transf.* and *fig.* **a.** Border, limit (of a region); the line which one crosses in entering.

*c* **888** K. ÆLFRED *Boeth.* xxi, Se ilca [*sc.* Godes miht] forwyrnð þæræ sæ þæt heo ne mot þone þeorscwold oferstæppan þære eorþan. *a* **900** tr. *Bæda's Hist.* v. vi. (1890) 398 Forðon þe he mæc..from deaðes þirscwalde wæs aceȝende. **1642** FULLER *Holy & Prof. St.* III. iv. 159 Know most of the rooms of thy native countrey before thou goest over the threshold thereof. *a* **1863** FABER *Hymn, 'The happy Gate of Heaven'* ii, Fair are the thresholds of blue sea. **1899** *Westm. Gaz.* 2 Sept. 2/1 On what is known as 'the threshold of England', the Sussex coast.

**b.** In reference to entrance, the beginning of a state or action, outset, opening. (In quot. 1659, in reference to going out or leaving, close, end.)

*c* **1586** C'TESS PEMBROKE *Ps.* (1823) cxix. R. i, Right wonderfull thy testimonies be,..Their very threshold gives men light. **1593** Q. ELIZ. *Boeth.* II. pr. iv. 28 The thressholl of thy felicitie. **1659** *Clarke Papers* (Camden) IV. 297, I.. shall be moste glad to heare that you are gott over the thresholde of your present troublesome stay in London, the country being the most proper place for [etc.]. **1834** L. RITCHIE *Wand. by Seine* 8 The youth, stepping proudly upon the threshold of manhood. **1877** FOSTER *Phys.* III. i. (1878) 389 We are..met on the very threshold of every enquiry [etc.].

**c.** *Psychol.*: esp. in phr. *threshold of consciousness*: see quots., and cf. LIMEN, SUBLIMINAL.

**1874** SULLY *Sensation & Intuition* 47 There is a certain limit below which our several sensibilities are unable to discriminate. This boundary..Fechner calls the 'threshold' (*die Schwelle*). **1886** GURNEY, etc. *Phantasms of Living* I. 453 A telepathic disturbance may take place below the threshold of consciousness. **1886** WARD in *Encycl. Brit.* XX. 47/2 We do not distinguish or attend separately to presentations of less than a certain assignable intensity. On attaining this intensity presentations are said to pass over the threshold of consciousness, to use Herbart's now classic phrase ['*Schwelle des Bewusstseins*' (*Psychol. als Wissenschaft* (1824) § 47)].

† **d.** An obstacle, stumbling-block. *Obs.*

**1601** SIR W. CORNWALLIS *Ess.* iv, Makes his imagination build blockes and thresholds, in the plainest and most beaten way. **1705** HICKERINGILL *Priest-cr.* II. vii. 70, I hope it was left by chance, and not on purpose to be a Threshold, or Stumbling-block at the Church Door. *Ibid.* viii. 91.

**3.** *attrib.* and *Comb.*

**1535** COVERDALE 2 *Kings* xxii. 5 The money that is brought vnto yᵉ house of yᵉ Lorde (which the tresholde kepers haue gathered). *a* **1661** HOLYDAY *Juvenal* vi. (1673) 95 The hangings too, and threshold-boughs yet green. **1678** OTWAY *Friendship in F.* v. i, Let all the Doors be barr'd.., and Gunpowder under each Threshold-place. **1805** SCOTT *Last Minstr.* I. i, No living wight, save the Ladye alone, Had dared to cross the threshold stone. **1842** TENNYSON *St. Simeon Styl.* 188 His footsteps smite the threshold stairs Of life.

**Threskite,** obs. form of TRASKITE.

**Thresorer, -ory, -our,** obs. ff. TREASURER, TREASURY, TREASURE.

† **Threst, thrast,** *sb. Obs.* [f. OE. *þrǽstan*: see next.]

**1.** Torment, affliction, trouble, hardship.

**13..** *Cursor M.* 4283 (Cott.) For o quat pine es herder threst Þen tharn þe thing men luues best. *Ibid.* 11829 Ydropsi held him sua in threst, Þat him thoght his bodi suld brest. *Ibid.* 29168 Þai sal..Bren in þe fier of purgatori,..Bot efter-ward þat herd threst, Sal þai be borun in to rest. **1340** *Ayenb.* 121 Þe yefþe of drede is þe doreward to þe greate þreste, þet is..to þe greate þreapninge of godes dom. *Ibid.* 183 Þe guode kniȝt..þet..heþ y-byine uele þrestes mid grat wil and grat honger.

**2.** A thrust, a sharp stroke; the stroke or dart of lightning, a thunderbolt.

**13..** *E. E. Allit. P.* B. 952 Þe þik þunder þrast þirled hem ofte. **13..** *Gaw. & Gr. Knt.* 1443 For þre at þe fyrst þrast he þryȝt to þe erþe. *a* **1400–50** *Alexander* 554 Þe liȝt lemand late laschis fra þe heuyn, Thonere thrastis ware thra thristid þe welkyn.

† **Threst, thrast,** *v. Obs.* Forms: α. 1 **þrǽstan,** 3 **þræsten, þreaste,** 3–4 **þreste(n,** 4 **þrest,** 4–5 **threste,** 4–6 **threst.** β. 3 **þrasten,** 4 **þrast,** 5–6 **thrast,** *Sc.* **thraist.** *Pa. t.* α. 3 **þreaste (þærste),** 3–4 **þreste,** 4 **threste,** 4–5 **threst,** 5–6 **þrested.** β. 3–4 **þraste** (3 **þarste**), 4–6 **thraste, thrast** (5 **tharst**). *Pa. pple.* 1 **þrǽst, þrǽsted,** 4–5 **þrast,** 5 **(y)threst,** 5–6 **thrast(e** (5 **threstyd**), 6 **threst.** [OE. *þrǽstan* to writhe, twist, torture, torment, constrain, representing an OTeut. type **þraistjan*, not known in the other Teut. languages.

OE. *þrǽstan* had no etymological connexion with THRUST, early ME. *þrusten, þrysten, þristen*, from ON. *þrýsta* (OTeut. **þrûstjan*), nor did the original senses of the two agree. But, app. from the contiguity of the two forms *þrest*, and *þrist*, and possibly from the development in both vbs. of the notion of constraint or pressure, the OE. vb. appears to have been, by 1200, identified with the Norse vb., so that in ME. they were treated more or less as parallel forms of one and the same word, and actually appear in some cases as variant MS. readings. In ME., *thrust, thrist* was esp. northern and north midland, and *threst* predominantly southern, where it still survived in 1542. The past tense *thraste* is here placed under *threst*, to which in form it belongs; but it is possible that it was also used by some whose present tense was *thrist*, or *thrust*.]

(The OE. senses 1. *intr.* to twist, writhe, 2. *trans.* to torture, torment, plague, afflict, 3. to compress, constrain, compel, did not come down into ME.)

**1.** *intr.* To press (*in, out, together*, etc.); to push one's way; to crowd; = THRUST *v.* 3.

α. *c* **1205** LAY. 23372 Mine cnihtes balde scullen þræsten [*c* **1275** þreaste] bi-foren me. *a* **1225** *St. Marher.* 9 In his ihurnd heauet..þreaste smeorðrinde smoke ut. *a* **1225** *Ancr. R.* 220 (MS. C) 'Irruerunt super me' þet is, heo þresten in uppon me. *Ibid.* 314 One schipe þet haueð monie þurles, þer þet water þrest in. **13..** *Sir Beues* (A.) 4157 So harde þai þreste to gedre þo, Þat here gerþes borste ato. *c* **1386** CHAUCER *Knt.'s T.* 1754 He thurgh the thikkeste of the throng gan threste. *c* **1500** *Melusine* 289 The valyaunt geffray..smote his hors with his sporys, & thrested in to myddes of his enemys.

β. *c* **1205** LAY. 26318 Moni þusenden þrasten [*c* 1275 þreste] ut of telden. *Ibid.* 26633 Þer after comen þrasten [*c* 1275 comen þreaste] þritto þusen[d] anan. *c* **1375** *Cursor M.* 19462 (Fairf.) Þen sulde alle to him þrast. *c* **1380** *Sir Ferumb.* 1977 Forþ sche þraste among hem alle. *c* **1386** CHAUCER *Doctor's T.* 260 But right anon a thousand peple in thraste To saue the knyght. *a* **1400–50** *Alexander* 2939 ȝit he threw to þe thrid & thrast inn þare-eftir. *c* **1440** *Partonope* 7053 Forth into the Reynes he tharst And aboute hym leyde on fast.

**2.** *trans.* To pierce, stab; to give (one) a thrust; = THRUST *v.* 5.

*c* **1205** LAY. 30853 He com him baften and imong al þan þrunge þærsten him in þan ruge. **1508** FISHER 7 *Penit. Ps.* xxxii. Wks. (1876) 30 Lyke as he hadde ben thraste thrugh the herte with a thorne. **1526** R. WHYTFORD *Martiloge* 138 After all she was thrast unto the herte with a swerde. **1532** — *Werke for Househ.* G iij, One of the sowdyours made a wounde in his syde, and thraste him to the herte with a spere.

**3.** To push forcibly or violently; = THRUST *v.* 1, 6.

*c* **1275** LAY. 1898 Gemagog..þraste [*c* 1205 þudde] Corineum framward his breoste. *c* **1325** *Song of Yesterday* 69 in *E. E. P.* (1862) 135 Þenne schal vr bodies in eorþe be þrast. **13..** *K. Alis.* 3326 Beste He can his launce thorugh threste [*Bodl. MS.* þrest]. **1340** *Ayenb.* 204 Hy þresten out hare eȝen. *c* **1374** CHAUCER *Troylus* II. 1106 (1155) And yn here bosom þe lettre doun he þraste. *c* **1400** *Rom. Rose* 6825 By my treget, I gadre and threste The gret tresour into my cheste. *c* **1430** *Syr Gener.* (Roxb.) 8740 The cheke in twoo he brast, And his neke on sondre thrast. **1484**

CAXTON *Fables of Auian* ii, The Egle..thrested his clowes in to the tortoses bely. **1508** FISHER 7 *Penit. Ps.* cii. Wks. (1876) 171 Now we be thraste downe in to a very streyght angyll. *c* **1510** MORE *Picus* Wks. 22 As a thefe betwene two theues threst. *c* **1530** L. COX *Rhet.* (1899) 61 He thrast his hande into the fyre. **1534** WHITINTON *Tullyes Offices* III. (1540) 131 In no wyse he ought to threst downe that man that proueth maystryes with hym.

**4.** To press, squeeze; to crush; = THRUST *v.* 4.

*c* **1410** *Master of Game* (MS. Digby 182) xxiv, If..þe foote and þe knees haue ythrest doune wele þe erth and ypressede þe grasse a doune,..it is a grete deere and an heuy. *a* **1450** *Tundale's Vis.* (Wagner) 1357 He thrust [*MS. A*, thrast] hem, as men dose Grapes, to wryng out the wose. **1494** FABYAN *Chron.* VII. 417 At whiche coronacion was so excedynge prease, that a knyght, called sir Iohn Bakwell, was threstyd to deth.

**b.** To crowd; to cram; = THRUST 3 c.

*c* **1400** *Destr. Troy* 4129 Two and thretty thried shippes þrast full of pepull. **1542** UDALL *Erasm. Apoph.* 49 b, [They] poure their throtes and bealies thrasting full.

**c.** *fig.* To oppress, vex.

**1513** DOUGLAS *Æneis* I. v. 58 Sen sic thochtis the thraistis [*rime* traistis].

Hence †**Thresting** *vbl. sb.*, pressing, squeezing, crushing.

**1481** CAXTON *Reynard* xli. (Arb.) 111 The threstyng that he suffred in his colyons made hym so faynt. **1483** — *Gold. Leg.* 245/2 The deken fyll [= fell]..by thympulsion and threstyng of the paynems.

**Threst(e**, obs. ff. THIRST. **Threstel, -yll**, obs. ff. THROSTLE. **Threstle**, obs. f. TRESTLE. **Threswold**, obs. f. THRESHOLD.

**Thret, threte**, obs. forms of THREAT.

† **Threte**, *sb. Sc. Obs.* In 6 threit, *pl.* thretis. Origin and meaning obscure. Occurs app. only in Douglas's *Æneis*, where it is expletive, answering to nothing in the Latin. Referred in Ruddiman's *Glossary*, 1710, to THREAT *sb.*, and explained as 'a throng, crowd, haste, speed'.

Jamieson takes it in the first quot. as 'throng, crowd' (which does not suit the context); the second and third examples he renders 'in haste, eagerly', the fourth 'in pairs, in couples'. In all the passages we have perhaps strained applications of THREAT *sb.* sense 2, 'pressure, etc.' introduced for the sake of rime.

**1513** DOUGLAS *Æneis* II. [x.] ix. 33 Scho..Him towart hir hes brocht, but ony threte. *Ibid.* V. ii. 117 Sum vthir..the colis hett Wndir the speitis swakkis, to roist in threit The raw spaldis ordanit for the muld meit. *Ibid.* XII. xii. 141 The rynnyng hund dois hym [the hart] assail in threte Baith with swyft raise and with his questis grete. *Ibid.* XII. ix. 78 That this Murranus the renis and the thetis Quharwyth hys stedis ȝokkit war in thretis Vndyr the quhelis hes do weltit doun.

† **Threte**, *v. Obs. rare.* Pa. t. in 5 thret. [a. ON. *þræta* (*þrætta*) to quarrel, dispute, wrangle, Sw. *träta* Da. *trættes* refl. to quarrel, strive, contest. (See Falk & Torp s.v. *Trætte*.)] *intr.* To dispute, contend; to quarrel, wrangle.

13.. *E. E. Allit. P.* A. 560, I hyred þe for a peny a grete, Quy bygynnez þou now to þrete? *c* **1430** *This World but Vanyte* 20 in *Hymns Virgin* (1867) 83 Þe kinde of childhode y dide also, Wiþ my felawis to fiȝte and þrete. *c* **1450** *St. Cuthbert* (Surtees) 7110 Þai were stonyd what þis moght mene, What þai suld do þai thret þaim betwene. **1513** DOUGLAS *Æneis* VIII. Prol. 17 So thochtis thretis in thra our breistis ourthwort. [Probably belongs here.]

**Threten, thretne, thrett(e**, etc., obs. ff. THREAT, THREATEN. **Thretinde**, obs. f. THREETINED. **Threttene, -tende, -tethe, -ty**, obs. ff. THIRTEEN, -TEENTH, THIRTIETH, -TY.

**Threu**, obs. form of THREW, THROUGH.

**Threuch, threwgh**, obs. ff. THROUGH *sb.*[1], tombstone, etc. **Threuth**, obs. form of TRUTH.

**Threve**, obs. and dial. form of THRAVE.

**Threw**, pa. t. of THROW *v.*

**Threw**, obs. form of THROUGH *prep.*, TRUE.

**Thrice** (þrəis), *adv.* Forms: *α.* 3 (*Orm.*) þriȝess, 3–4 þries, thryese, 4 þryys, 4–5 thries, 4–6 thryes, -is, 5 threes, threies, thryess, 6 *Sc.* thryiss. *β.* 4 þrys, þriis, thrijs, 4–5 thrys, threys, 4–6 thris, 4–7 thrise, thryse, 5 thrisse, 5–6 thryss, 7 thryce, 6– thrice. [ME. *þriȝes*, *þriës*, *þryës*, f. *þrië*, *þryë*, THRIE + -*s* of advb. genitive, after ME. *anes*, *ones*, ONCE: cf. *twice*.

From *c* 1600 spelt *thrice*, to indicate the long vowel and the breath sound of *s*, as in *dice*, *mice*, *nice*, *twice*, etc.]

**1.** Three times (in succession); on three successive occasions.

*c* **1200** ORMIN 1149 Ure Laferrd..Badd hise bedess þriȝess. *a* **1225** *Ancr. R.* 106 He weop himsulf þries mid his feire eien. *c* **1275** LAY. 26066 And so Arthur..bi-vrne hit þries [*c* 1205 þreie]. *a* **1300** *Cursor M.* 20973 (Cott.) Paule..Scipbreging he suffurd thrise [*v. rr.* þries, thrijs]. *c* **1330** R. BRUNNE *Chron. Wace* (Rolls) 11340 Was þer no knyght of so hey blod..Þat þer fore scholde be holde in pris, But he in dede were proued þrys. **1350–1400** *Sir Beues* (MS. E.) 4313 + 208 Þryys sche ffyl doun to þe grounde. *c* **1375** *Lay Folks Mass Bk.* (MS. B.) 308 At þo ende [he] sayes sanctus thryese. *c* **1400** MAUNDEV. (Roxb.) xi. 45 Þare denyed Petre oure Lord thryess. *a* **1400–50** *Alexander* 2279 Þus fall þou thrisse. *c* **1400** *Brut* cxciv. 214 [He] felle adoun..and þries [1480 CAXTON thryes] cussede þe grounde. **1425** in Entick *London* (1766) IV. 354 Threies seaven Ave Marias, with xv Pater Nosters and thre credes. *a* **1450** *Knt. de la Tour* (1906) 83 The king sent vnto her onis, tuyes, thries, and she denied not to come. **1456** SIR G. HAYE *Law Arms* (S.T.S.) 170 Israel was discomfyte twys, or thris. **1548–9** (Mar.) *Bk. Com. Prayer, Baptism*, Namyng the childe, [he] shall dyppe it in the water thryse. *a* **1550** *Freiris of Berwik* 356 in *Dunbar's Poems* (S.T.S.) 297 He turnit him abowt Weill thryiss. **1563–7** BUCHANAN *Reform. St. Andros* Wks. (1892) 16 Twyss or thryis in the ȝeir. **1611** BIBLE *Mark* xiv. 30 Before the cocke crowe twise, thou shalt deny me thrise [TIND. thryse]. **1732** ARBUTHNOT *Rules of Diet* in *Aliments*, etc. 418 A Spoonful or two of Canary Wine twice or thrice a day. **1842** BORROW *Bible in Spain* xxxiv. (Pelh. Libr.) 246 Though I left it thrice, it was of my own free will.

**2.** Three times as much as (in number, amount, or value). Often vaguely or hyperbolically: Many times (as much).

Usually preceding a numeral, or const. with *as*, or with comparative (now *rare* or *obs.*).

*a* **1300** *Cursor M.* 430 Angels..Þat suld of ordres haf thris thre. **1427** in *10th Rep. Hist. MSS. Comm.* App. v. 295 Threes as much as he..shall losse. *c* **1460** *Wisdom* 649 in *Macro Plays* 56 More þan I take, spende I threys iij. **1528** in *Exch. Rolls Scotl.* XV. 666 Bot giff the personis..be vailȝeand in gudis wortht thryss the gudis at ar pundit. **1552** HULOET, Thrise as muche, *triplaris, e.* *c* **1600** SHAKS. *Sonnets* lvi. 14 Which..Makes Sommers welcome thrice more wish'd, more rare. **1605** *1st Pt. Ieronimo* (1901) I. i, I haue a hart thrice stronger then my years. *a* **1771** GRAY *Death Hoel* 12 Thrice two hundred warriors. **1849** MACAULAY *Hist. Eng.* iii. I. 344 A sum more than thrice as great as the whole income of the English crown in 1685. **1859** TENNYSON *Geraint & Enid* 557 With some surprise and thrice as much disdain.

†**b.** In three manners or respects. *Obs.*

**1607–12** BACON *Ess., Great Place* (Arb.) 278 Men in great place, are thrice seruauntes; Servauntes of the Sovereigne, or State, Servauntes of fame, and seruauntes of businesse.

**3.** Combined with a pa. pple., forming an attrib. phrase or compound adj. (in senses 1 and 2).

**1508** KENNEDIE *Flyting w. Dunbar* 30 Thryse scheild [? sealed] trumpir. **1600** SHAKS. *A. Y. L.* III. ii. 2 Thou thrice crowned Queene of night. **1693** J. DRYDEN in *D.'s Juvenal* xiv. (1697) 353 A Dish Of thrice-boil'd Beans. **1742** YOUNG *Nt. Th.* IV. 37 Like a thrice-told tale. **1864** PUSEY *Lect. Daniel* v. 283 A hundred millions thrice-told.

**b.** Similarly with any adjective, used vaguely or hyperbolically (as in 2): Very, highly, greatly, extremely (cf. L. *ter*).

**1579** G. HARVEY *Letter-bk.* (Camden) 60 Howe will my right worshipfull and thrisevenerable masters of Cambridge scorne at the matter? *Ibid.* 61 Thrishonorable. **1593** SHAKS. 2 *Hen. VI*, III. ii. 157 This thrice-famed Duke. **1631** WEEVER *Anc. Fun. Mon.* 536 This thrice-noble family of the Percies. **1667** MILTON *P. L.* III. 570 Thrice happy Isles. **1850** TENNYSON *In Mem.* xxxii. 13 Thrice blest whose lives are faithful prayers.

**4.** As quasi-*adj.* Thrice performed; threefold, triple (*rare*); in first quot. vaguely: Very great.

**1470–85** MALORY *Arthur* IV. xix. 143 Ther were many knyghtes that ouermatched syr gawayne for alle the thryes myghte that he had. **1600** W. WATSON *Decacordon* (1602) 44 S. Peter..after his relapse with thrise denial and forswearing of him. **1619** DRAYTON *Heroic Ep., E. Cobham to Dk. Humphrey* Argt. 9 For which, she her thrice-Penance was assign'd. *a* **1866** NEALE *Sequences, Hymns*, etc. 21 Till the thrice Confession Blot the thrice Denial out.

**Thricche, thrich(e**, obs. forms of THRUTCH.

**Thrid**, var. THREAD, esp. the vb.; obs. f. THIRD.

**Thridace** (þri·dēs). *Pharm.* Also *erron.* thridach. [ad. mod.L. *thridacium*, f. Gr. θρίδαξ lettuce. Cf. F. *thridace*.] The inspissated juice of lettuce, used as a sedative; = LACTUCARIUM.

**1831** J. DAVIES *Manual Mat. Med.* 313 Thridace... Juice furnished during the time of fructification by the Garden Lettuce, *Lactuca sativa*. **1836** J. M. GULLY *Magendie's Formul.* (ed. 2) 164 The *lactucarium* of Dr. Duncan, and the thridach of Dr. François, are nothing more than the white, viscid juice of the garden lettuce..at the flowering time of the plant. **1857** DUNGLISON *Dict. Med. Sc., Thridace.*

**Thridde, Thriddendele**, obs. ff. THIRD, THIRDENDEAL. **Thride**, obs. f. THIRD, THREAD.

†**Thrie, thrye**, *adv. Obs.* Forms: *α.* 1 þriwa, ðriȝa, ðriȝe, ðria, 2 þreowe, 3 þreie, 3–4 þrie, 4–5 þrye, thrie, (4 thry), 5 thrye. *β.* 3 þrien, þreoien, 4 thrien. [OE. *þríwa*, *ðríga* = OFris. *thrî(i)a*, OS. *thrîuuo*, *thrîo*. Like *twíwa*, etc., not found outside the Saxon-Frisian group of WGer., and of obscure formation. They seem to have the form of genitival advbs., *twi-a*, *þri-a*, with the gap between *i* and *a* variously filled up by *w* and *g* (again lost in ME.), and lengthened by assimilation to *þri*, THREE. See further under TWIE.] Three times; thrice.

*α.* *c* **950** *Lindisf. Gosp.* Mark xiv. 30 Ðria [*Rushw.* ðriȝe] mec ðu bist onsæcc. *c* **1000** *Ags. Gosp.* ibid., Þriwa [*c* **1160** *Hatton Gosp.*, þreowe] wiðsæcst min. *c* **1020** *Rule St. Benet* ix. (Logeman) 38 Oðer siðon þriwa is to singanne. *c* **1205** LAY. 17432 Þrie he eode abuten. *Ibid.* 26066 Arður & þe scucke biurnen hit þreie a-buten. **1297** R. GLOUC. (Rolls) 10056 Þer on he smot þrie þe wrecche to gret pine. *c* **1375** *Cursor M.* 13627 (Fairf.) Quy quarto sulde I tel ȝou mare? Twy or thry I talde ȝou are. *c* **1460** *Compl. Criste* 88 in *Pol. Rel. & L. Poems* 164 The devylle me tempttyd neuer but thrye, But þou me temptyst frome day to daye. ? *a* **1500** *Chester Pl.* (Shaks. Soc.) II. 25 Or the cocke have crowen thrye Thou shalte forsake my companye. *β.* *c* **1205** LAY. 14338 Þenne cusseoð heo þreoien. — 14352 Þat maide..þrien hine custe. **13..** *Judas* 33 in *Rel. Ant.* I. 144 Thou wolt fursake me thrien, ar the coc him crowe.

**Thrie, þrie**, obs. form of THREE.

**Thrief, -ve, Thriep**, obs. ff. THRAVE, THREAP.

**Thries, þries**, obs. form of THRICE.

**Thrift** (þrift), *sb.*[1] Also 3–5 þrift(e, (4 þruft, þreft, þref), 4–5 þryft, 4–6 thryft(e (threft), 5–6 thrifte (6 thryfft). [f. THRIVE *v.* + -T *suffix* 3 a: cf. *drift*, *gift*, *rift*, *weft*, etc.; also ON. *þrift*, occasional synonym of *þrif* thriving condition, well-doing, prosperity, which may have reinforced the word in the north of England.]

†**1.** The fact or condition of thriving or prospering; prosperity, success, good luck; in early use sometimes = fortune (good or bad); luck: cf. THRIVE *v.* 1. *Obs.*

*c* **1305** *St. James* 70 in *E. E. P.* (1862) 59 Sorewe him mote bifalle And liþer þrift vpon his heued. **13..** *Cursor M.* 4439 (Cott.) He ferd ai wit so mikel thrift þat al was don als he wald scift. **1362** LANGL. *P. Pl.* A. x. 105 And men þat Cunne mony Craftes..Þruft or þeodam with hem selden is I-seye. *c* **1380** *Sir Ferumb.* 2017 Mahoun ȝyue þe euele þref. *c* **1386** CHAUCER *Reeve's T.* 129 By my thrift [*v. rr.* þreft, thryft], yet shal I blere hir eye. *c* **1412** HOCCLEVE *De Reg. Princ.* 386 Now good thrifte come vn-to þe, sone dere! *c* **1440** *Promp. Parv.* 490/1 Thedam (or thryfte), *vigencia*. **1549** COVERDALE, etc. *Erasm. Par. Phil.* 5 The entrie vnto immortall thrifte is throughe losse of transitorie thynges. *a* **1625** FLETCHER & MASSINGER *Laws of Candy* IV. i, I could wish All thrift to his affections. **1679** BUNYAN *Fear of God* Wks. (ed. Offor) I. 485 Every grace is nourished by the Word, and without it there is no thrift in the soul.

**b.** Means of thriving; industry, labour; profitable occupation. Now *dial.*

*c* **1580** LODGE *Reply Gosson's Sch. Abuse* (Hunter. Cl.) 3 You are..a man of the letter little sauoring of learning, your giddy brain made you leaue your thrift, and your abuses in London some part of your honestie. **1596** SPENSER *State Irel.* Wks. (Globe) 662/1 To fall to thrifte, as I haue seene manye souldiours after the service to proove verye good husbandes. **1612** DEKKER *If it be not good* Wks. 1873 III. 270 Dread King of Ghosts, weele plye our thrift so well, Thou shalt be forc'd to enlarge thy Iayle of Hell. **1612** R. CHURTON (*title*) An Old Thrift newly Revived, wherein is declared the manner of Planting..and Husbanding Young Trees. **1721** RAMSAY *Ode to Mr. F——* 17 Poor Vulcan hard at thrift, Gets mony a sair and heavy lift. **1816** SCOTT *Antiq.* xxvi, With her distaff..and her spindle..she plied..the old fashioned Scottish thrift, according to the old fashioned Scottish manner.

**c.** Prosperous growth, physical thriving.

*c* **1230** *Hali Meid.* 37 His waxunge se lat & se slaw his þrifti [? þrift; *v. r.* þriftre]. **1615** W. LAWSON *Country Housew. Gard.* (1626) 22 Manie trees stand so thicke, that one could not thriue for the throng of his neighbours... Hence small thrift, gals, wounds. **1857–8** SEARS *Athan.* viii. 66 The outward bark..scaling off that the tree may expand with more thrift and freedom.

**d.** Growing-pains. *dial.*

*a* **1800** PEGGE *Suppl. Grose*, *Thrift*, the pain which young persons feel in growing. Lanc. **1886** *Chester Gloss.* s. v., What ails thee, pooin thi face? It's nowt bu' th' thrift that tha's getten. **1887** *S. Chesh. Gloss.*, *Thrift*, 'thriving' or growing pains.

**2.** Savings, earnings, gains, profit; acquired wealth, estate, or substance. *arch.* (Cf. FRUGALITY c.)

*a* **1310** in Wright *Lyric P.* xv. 47 In luthere lastes y am layn, That maketh myn thryftes thunne. **1436** *Eng. Policy* in *Pol. Poems* (Rolls) II. 174 They bere the golde owte of thys londe, And souketh the thryfte awey oute of oure honde. **1508** KENNEDIE *Flyting w. Dunbar* 443 Thou drank thy thrift, sald and wedsett thy clais. **1530** PALSGR. 280/2 Thrifte gayne, *proufit*. **1605** *Play Stucley* in Simpson *Sch. Shaks.* (1878) I. 195 He that drinks, or spends his thrift at dice. **1805** HOLCROFT *Bryan Perdue* III. 264 Our worldly thrift was more than equal to all our wants. **1893** CHR. G. ROSSETTI *Poems* (1904) 223/2 If much were mine, then manifold Would be the offering of my thrift.

†**b.** That which is saved (*of* something); savings. *Obs.*

In quot. 1387 rendering L. *nucleus*; sense intended doubtful.

**1387** TREVISA *Higden* (Rolls) II. 15 Þe þrift of þe fatnesse drieþ himself þeryn. **1519** HORMAN *Vulg.* 159 Mynse all the thryfte [L. *compendium*] of the flesshe: and mengle it with the spice.

**3.** Economical management, economy; sparing use or careful expenditure of means; frugality, saving; † euphemistically, parsimony, niggardliness (*obs.*).

**1553** *Respublica* v. iii. 1343 As..bodylye foode is never founde to bee so pleasaunte nor so goode As whan fretting hongre and thrift hathe pincht afore. **1570** LEVINS *Manip.* 118/6 Thrift, *frugalitas, atis*. **1600** J. PORY tr. *Leo's Africa* II. 58 These people are well given to thrift and good husbandry. **1608–11** BP. HALL *Medit.* 99 So devotion is counterfaited by superstition, good thrift by niggardliness. **1784** COWPER *Task* IV. 398 With all this thrift they thrive not. **1849** LONGF. *Kavanagh* 152 The air of comfort and plenty, of neatness, thrift, and equality, visible everywhere. **1876** GREEN *Stray Stud.* 26 The true cure for pauperism lies in the growth of thrift among the poor.

**4.** A name given to various plants.

†**a.** Said by Turner to have been a name for the Stone Orpine (*Sedum reflexum*). *Obs. rare.*

**1538** TURNER *Libellus* s. v. *Sedum*, Sedum minus puto esse herbam quam uulgus appellat Thryft; aut Stoncrop. **1548** — *Names of Herbes* (1881) 72 The seconde kynde is called in English thryft or stoncroppe. **1562** — *Herbal* II. 133 The lesse Semperuiuum, that we call thrift or great stone crop, groweth in walles, rockes, mudwalles, .. it hath manye stalkes comming from one root.

**b.** The plant *Armeria maritima* (*vulgaris*), a well-known sea-shore and alpine plant bearing rose-pink, white, or purple flowers on naked stems growing from a dense tuft of grass-like radical leaves. Also called *sea-pink*, *sea gillyflower*, *sea-grass*, and *ladies' cushion*.

**1592** GREENE *Upst. Courtier* (1871) 5 The weed they so wrangled for was a little dapper flower, like a ground honey-suckle, called thrift. **1597** GERARDE *Herbal* II. clxxvii. 483 Called..in English Thrift, Sea grasse, and our Ladies Cushion. **1688** R. HOLME *Armoury* II. 64/1 Thrift..is only set in Gardens to keep up Borders. **1814** WORDSW. *Excursion* I. 722 Daisy-flowers and thrift Had..straggled O'er paths they used to deck. **1856** DELAMER *Fl. Gard.* (1861) 104 Thrift...The English name is derived from its thriftiness in towns and confined situations, though its native home is on the grassy tops of cliffs whose base is washed by the waves. **1862** BARING-GOULD *Iceland* (1863) 242 The thrift with its rose coloured flower heads was very abundant.

**c.** Hence extended to other species of *Armeria*: e.g. Great Thrift, *A. Cephalotes*, of the Mediterranean region; Plantain Thrift, *A. plantaginea*, found in Jersey; also to plants of allied genera or similar habit, as **Lavender Thrift**, *Statice Limonium*; **Prickly Thrift**, *Acantholimon glumaceum*, a pretty garden rock-plant.

**1776–96** WITHERING *Brit. Plants* (ed. 3) II. 320 Lavender Thrift. Sea banks near Walton, Essex. **1866** *Treas. Bot.* 1147 Prickly Thrift, *Acantholimon*.

**5.** *attrib.* and *Comb.*, as (in sense 3) *thrift club*, *society*, etc.; (in sense 4) *thrift edging*; **thrift-box, -pot**, a box or pot in which savings are put.

**1777** BRAND *Pop. Antiq.* 164 *note*, A Thrift-Box..is put up against the Wall, and every Customer puts in something. **1786** ABERCROMBIE *Gard. Assist.* 95 Box and thrift edgings. **1835** *Fair-Day* 82 You could break your thrift-pot..and get to the money. **1897** *Daily News* 8 May 7/4 It [a mission] has established thrift societies [etc.]. **1899** *Ibid.* 5 June 4/3 Round these 'schools' have grown thrift clubs, and benevolent societies. **1902** *Daily Chron.* 27 Mar. 7/6 Unregulated shop clubs or thrift funds.

**Thrift**, *sb.*[2] [Origin obscure. Cf. ON. *þrífa* to grip: but connecting links are unknown.] The handle (usu. wooden) of a mill bill, which is fixed in a mortise in the thick head of the handle.

*c* **1900** *Circular of Bryan Corcoran Lim.*, Mill Bill in Wood Thrift..Iron Thrift, Steel Thrift. *Ibid.*, Model Mill Bill stone dressing machine..the thrift is set in a ball hinge. ..Like in ordinary hand dressing, the thrift is worked to give the blow.

**Thrift**, *v.* [f. THRIFT *sb.*[1]] *trans.* To save thriftily, to economize.

**1869** BLACKMORE *Lorna D.* ii, Not that I ever bore much wealth, but because I had been thrifting it for this time. **1885** L. LEVI in *Pall Mall G.* 13 Jan. 6/2 The earnings of agricultural labourers..if well thrifted, leave a surplus.

**Thriftily** (þri·ftili), *adv.* Also 4–5 *Sc.* **thryftly**, 5–6 **thriftly**, 6 **thriftely**. [f. THRIFTY + -LY [2].]

†**1.** In a becoming or seemly manner, properly; worthily, handsomely, finely; hence, thoroughly, soundly, well. *Obs.*

*c* **1374** CHAUCER *Troylus* III. 162 (211) She toke here leue at hem ful þryftyly. *c* **1375** *Sc. Leg. Saints* xiii. (*Marcus*) 128 Þe byschape anany did his office ful thryftly. *c* **1386** CHAUCER *Prol.* 105 A sheef of pecok arwes bright and kene Vnder his belt he bar ful thriftily. *c* **1449** PECOCK *Repr.* (Rolls) 43 If thei schulen thriftili serue to God. *a* **1586** SIDNEY *Arcadia* III. Wks. 1724 II. 704 Thou..hast sung well and thriftily. **1638** EARL STRAFFORD *Lett. & Disp.* (1739) II. 208 Nor that they will..be brought into their right Wits, till they be well and thriftily cudgelled back into them.

**2.** Frugally, sparingly, economically, carefully.

**1581** PETTIE *Guazzo's Civ. Conv.* III. (1586) 140 It..doth him good to see his wife so thriftely giuen. **1599** HAKLUYT *Voy.* II. II. 108 That they might..husband it more thriftily. **1694** FALLE *Jersey* iii. 96 Our Kings heretofore did use to dispose of this Revenue more thriftily than they now do. **1712** STEELE *Spect.* No. 430 ⁋ 1 A blind Beggar..with a Needle and Thread thriftily mending his Stockings. **1883** S. C. HALL *Retrospect* II. 315 They could neither order a household thriftily, nor cut out a gown.

**3.** Thrivingly, flourishingly; vigorously.

**1865** E. BURRITT *Walk Land's End* vii. 215 Two of the largest and oldest California pines are growing most thriftily in these gardens. **1894** A. G. ROBINSON in *Amer. Missionary* Sept. 330 The seed..is growing thriftily, and..will bear a harvest.

**Thriftiness** (þri·ftinės). [f. as prec. + -NESS.] The state or quality of being thrifty.

†**1.** Thriving condition, prosperity. *Obs. rare*[−1].

*c* **1530** *Proper Dyaloge* in *Rede me*, etc. (Arb.) 137 They haue brought the lande to beggery And all thryftynes clene awaye swepte.

**2.** The quality of being frugal or saving; economy, good husbandry: cf. THRIFT *sb.*[1] 3.

**1552** ELYOT *Dict.*, *Frugalitas*..thriftines. **1576** FLEMING *Panopl. Epist.* 225 A minde..contented with perseuerance, with frugalitie or thriftinesse. **1645** USSHER *Body Div.* (1647) 304 Parsimony or thriftiness; whereby we honestly keep and preserve our goods. **1782** KNOX *Ess.* lxxxvii. II. 22 The qualities distinguished by the homely titles of thriftiness and good housewifery. **1826** F. REYNOLDS in *Life & Times* II. 83 [He was] a compound of liberality and thriftiness. **1884** *Brit. Almanac & Comp.* 65 The actual increase of national thriftiness.

**Thriftless** (þri·ftlės), *a.* [f. THRIFT [1] + -LESS.]

†**1.** Not thriving or prosperous; unsuccessful; unfortunate. *Obs.*

*c* **1400** *Brut* ccxiii. 249 Longe berde hertles, peyntede Hode witles, Gay cote graceles, makeþ Englissheman þriftles. **1467** *Songs Costume* (Percy) 56 Ye prowd galantts hertlesse, With your hygh cappis witlesse, And your schort gownys thriftlesse. *a* **1585** MONTGOMERIE *Flyting* 387 This thriftlesse [infant] is meit for vs. **1591** *Troub. Raigne K. John* (1611) 39 As they shoulder thee from out thine owne,.. So heauens crosse them with a thriftless course. **1592** WARNER *Alb. Eng.* VIII. xli. (1612) 197 A thriftles Mariage with the trustles King of Spaine.

†**b.** Not flourishing (in physical condition).

**1693** OWEN *Glory Chr.* II. Wks. 1852 I. 442 If men will neglect their daily food..it is no wonder if they be weak and thriftless.

**2.** Unprofitable, worthless, useless. Now *rare.*

**1568** T. HOWELL *Arb. Amitie* (1879) 87 Pleasant sights begin to growe, among the thriftles thornes. **1601** SHAKS. *Twel. N.* II. ii. 40 What thriftlesse sighes shall poore Oliuia breath? *a* **1619** FOTHERBY *Atheom.* I. vi. § 4 (1622) 47 The most thriftles and vnprofitable part of all the whole Tree. **1750** SHENSTONE *Rural Elegance* 65 E'en thriftless furze detains their wand'ring sight. **1840** CARLYLE *Heroes* v, A man must not complain of his 'element', of his 'time', or the like; it is thriftless work doing so.

**3.** Devoid of thrift; without frugality or economy; wasteful, improvident, spendthrift.

**1576** GASCOIGNE *Philomene* 9 These thriftles birds..which spend the day, In needlesse notes. **1593** SHAKS. *Rich. II*, v. iii. 69 He shall spend mine Honour, with his Shame; As thriftlesse Sonnes, their scraping Fathers Gold. **1647** SANDERSON *Serm.* (1657) II. 291 The unjust Steward; a faithless, and a thriftless man. **1702** *Guide for Constables* 101 The thriftless poor. **1862** SIR B. BRODIE *Psychol. Inq.* II. iii. 105 The artisans in crowded cities..to a great extent indulging in intemperate and thriftless habits.

Hence **Thri·ftlessly** *adv.*, wastefully; **Thri·ftlessness**, wastefulness, improvidence.

**1846** WORCESTER, Thriftlessly (citing LEE). Thriftlessness (citing CHALMERS). **1847** R. W. HAMILTON *Disq. Sabbath* v. (1848) 188 They cannot spare thus thriftlessly moments which claim each its duty. **1858** *Sat. Rev.* 20 Nov. 494/2 Lords P—— and C—— seem rather to have copied the thriftlessness of Esau. **1862** W. W. STORY *Roba di R.* xii. (1864) 228 The usual thriftlessness of the people, who live from hand to mouth and from day to day.

†**Thriftre.** *Obs. rare*[−1]. [If a genuine word, f. THRIFT (or THRIVE), with an uncertain suffix (cf. *laughter*, *slaughter*); but perh. a scribal error of some kind.] = THRIFT *sb.*[1] 1 c.

*c* **1230** *Hali Meid.* (Bodley MS.: E.E.T.S. ed. 2) 50 His waxunge se lat & se slaw his þriftre [*MS. Titus* þrifti].

**Thrifty** (þri·fti), *a.* [f. THRIFT *sb.*[1] + -Y.]

(In many early quotations, it is not possible to fix the meaning of this adj.; two or three senses equally well suiting the context.)

**1.** Characterized by success or prosperity (see THRIFT *sb.*[1] 1); thriving, prosperous, well-to-do, successful, flourishing; fortunate.

*c* **1400** *Destr. Troy* 5454 A thousaund þro men þrifte in armys. *c* **1440** *Generydes* 1134 Now A dayis I lese all that I wanne, Where here before I was a threfty man. **1545** ELYOT s.v. *Res*, *Rem augere*, to waxe thryfty. **1634** FORD *Perkin Warbeck* v. iii, May he prove more thrifty In this world's just applause, not more desertful. **1697** DAMPIER *Voy.* I. xvii. 487 The Ships crew were not so thrifty in bargaining..as single persons. **1860** HOLLAND *Miss Gilbert* xxi. 371 The family generally has been getting thrifty in the world. **1865** E. BURRITT *Walk Land's End* x. 339 This is a thrifty, modern-looking town. **1876** GREEN *Stray Stud.* 27 Both had become zealous florists, and thrifty, respectable men. **1883** J. W. SHERER *At Home & in India* 24 No one was in thrifty and independent comfort.

†**2. a.** Of a person: Worthy, worshipful, estimable, respectable, well-living. Cf. THRIVEN 2, THRIVING *ppl. a.* 1. *Obs.*

*c* **1374** CHAUCER *Troylus* I. 1081 The gentileste and ek þe most fre The þriftieste and oon þe beste knyght That yn his tyme was. *c* **1456** PECOCK *Bk. Faith* (1909) 202 Ech thrifti sad clerk in logik. **1463** *Bury Wills* (Camden) 26 Sum thrifty man of seynt Marie paryssh to be at the selyng. **1467** in *Eng. Gilds* (1870) 377, ij thrifty comyners, trewe, sufficiant, and feithfulle men. **1556** OLDE *Antichrist* 196 That we may be founde ready, like thriftye servauntes, at the Lordes commyng. **1596** DALRYMPLE tr. *Leslie's Hist. Scot.* IV. (S.T.S.) I. 235 A thryftie man, and profitable ennimie to gluttonie and al vice.

†**b.** Of an action or concrete thing: Respectable, decent, becoming, proper, as it should be. *Obs.*

*c* **1386** CHAUCER *Man of Law's Prol.* 46, I kan right now no thrifty tale seyn. *c* **1386** — *Wife's Prol.* 238, I sitte at hoom, I haue no thrifty clooth. *c* **1430** *Two Cookery-bks.* 31 Draw vppe a þrifti Mylke of Almaundys y-blaunchyd. *Ibid.* 34 Make a gode þryfty Syryppe. *c* **1449** PECOCK *Repr.* (Rolls) 160 The yuel .. is pareable and kutteable awey bi good and thrifti bisynes therto sett.

**3.** Thriving physically; growing with vigour; in good or healthy condition; flourishing.

*c* **1440** *Promp. Parv.* 492/2 Thryfty, *vigens.* *c* **1440** *Generydes* 280 This lady..Brought furth a sonne whiche was a threfte child. **1667** WATERHOUSE *Fire Lond.* 171 Thrifty Oaks, though fleeced of under boughs, yet if not headed, may thrive. **1707** MORTIMER *Husb.* (1721) II. 83 In many Forests and Woods, where you have one thrifty Tree, you have twenty unthrifty Ones. **1862** B. TAYLOR *Home & Abroad* Ser. II. 251 A small but thrifty specimen of the Sequoia, or California tree. **1886** C. SCOTT *Sheep-Farming* 143 A lot of lambs which .. have a fresher and thriftier appearance. **1890** MARY E. WILKINS *Humble Rom., Bar Lighth.* (1891) 279 The bush really looked wonderfully thrifty, considering its many drawbacks to growth.

**4.** Characterized by thrift or frugality; economical, careful of expenditure, sparing, saving; provident.

**1526** *Knaresborough Wills* (Surtees) I. 20, I wyll, if none of my sonnes be thryftie nor woll thryve,..the land to thuse of our ladie aulter. **1647** BOYLE in *Life* Wks. 1772 I. p. xix, Thrifty he was extremely, and very skilful in the slights of thrift. **1666** — *Orig. Formes & Qual.* II. vii, Tis no very thrifty way of Transmutation. **1688** — *Final Causes Nat. Things* iv. 205 Sometimes God's wisdom seems to be as it were thrifty and solicitous not to bestow on an animal..more than is necessary for the use for which 'tis designed. **1726** SWIFT *Gulliver* II. viii, I told my wife she had been too thrifty, for I found she had starved herself and her daughter. **1746** FRANCIS tr. *Hor.*, *Sat.* II. vi. 167 Thrifty he was, and full of cares To make the most of his affairs. *a* **1768** SECKER *Serm.* (1770) III. v. 104 They who are sparing in their younger Days seldom fail to be much more thrifty in their Decline. *c* **1827** SCOTT *Verses* in Lockhart lxxiv, I've heard your knowing people say, Disown the debt you cannot pay, You'll find it far the thriftiest way. **1859** SMILES *Self-Help* ii. (1860) 35 He was honest,..thrifty and hard-working; and his trade prospered. **1872** YEATS *Growth Comm.* 3 Wealth would accumulate in the hands of the thrifty.

†**b.** Well-husbanded. *Obs. rare.*

**1600** SHAKS. *A. Y. L.* II. iii. 39, I haue fiue hundred Crownes, The thriftie hire I saued vnder your Father.

†**c.** *transf.* (?) Of scanty or meagre dimensions.

**1599** B. JONSON *Cynthia's Rev.* III. ii, Nor can my weak imperfect memory Now render half the forms unto my tongue, That were convoked within this thrifty room.

**Thriis, þriis,** obs. forms of THRICE.

†**Thrildom,** *Sc. Obs.* Also 4 **threl-, thryldome.** [f. THRILL *sb.*[2] + -DOM. Cf. THIRLDOM.] = THRALDOM.

**1375** BARBOUR *Bruce* I. 265 ȝe may weile se .. How hard A thing þat threldome Is. *Ibid.* 269 Thryldome is weill wer þan deid. *c* **1375** *Sc. Leg. Saints* xxii. 377 Fore til deliuer ws of thryldome. **1552** ABP. HAMILTON *Catech.* (1884) 38 In a house of miserable thrildome & bondage.

†**Thri·le, thri·li,** *a. Obs.* [OE. *þrili*, *þrielig* = OHG. *drilîh*, MHG. *drilich*, *drilch*, mod.Ger. *drillich*, app. WGer. ad. L. *trilīx*, *trilīc-em* woven with three threads, f. *trēs*, *tri-* three + *līcium* a thread of a web, a thrum. Cf. Ger. *zwillich*, TWILL.] Woven with three threads; threefold, triple; three in one.

*c* **725** *Corpus Gloss.* (Hessels) *Interpr.* 322 *Trilex*, ðrili. *a* **800** *Leiden Gloss.* (O.E.T.) 158 *Triplex*, drili. *a* **1000** *Ags. Glosses* in Wr.-Wülcker 279/3 *Triligium*, þrieliȝ hræȝil. *a* **1225** *St. Marher.* 11 Þrumnesse þreo fald..þrile i þreo hades. *a* **1225** *Ancr. R.* 26 ȝif me on, almihti God, þrile ine [*printed* me] þreo hodes, þeos ilke þreo þinges.

†**Thrill** (þril), *sb.*[1] *Obs.* [A metathetic form of THIRL *sb.*[1]; originally northern.] A hole or aperture; *esp.* a NOSE-THIRL, nostril.

**1382** Noose thrillis, *c* **1400** Nose thrilles [see NOSE-THIRL β]. *c* **1400** *Destr. Troy* 3045 Hir nose..With thrilles noght thrat, but thriftily made. *a* **1400–50** *Alexander* 4073 Hale he þam [images] fyndis..& aithire thrill stoppis. **1634** SIR T. HERBERT *Trav.* 211 Her [dodo's] bill is crooked downwards, in midst is the thrill.

*Comb.* **1618** BRATHWAIT *Descr. Death* xiv, Naked his scalpe, thrill-open is his Nose.

†**Thrill,** *sb.*[2] *Sc. Obs.* Also 4 **threll, thryll, thril.** [OE. *þrǣl*, ON. *þræll*, THRALL *sb.*[1], app. became in Sc. *threll*, which was later narrowed to *thrill*. Cf. THIRL *sb.*[2] 2.] One who is bound in servitude; a thrall. *Comb.* †**Thrillman**, bondman.

**1375** BARBOUR *Bruce* I. 243 He þ[t] thryll Is has nocht his, All þ[t] he has enbandownyt Is Till hys lord. *Ibid.* 274 Schortly to say, is nane can tell Þe halle condicioun off A threll. *Ibid.* III. 220. *c* **1375** *Sc. Leg. Saints* ii. (*Paulus*) 974 To..pure men, to thrillmen & to women. *Ibid.* v. (*Johannes*) 202 Riche man is thril alway to twa: þe tane, is riches. *Ibid.* l. (*Katerine*) 220 Be þe body giff þu will Gowerne þe, þu beis a thrill. *c* **1470** *Golagros & Gaw.* 435 Our doughty elderis has bene endurand Thriuandly in this thede, vnchargit as thril.

**Thrill** (þril), *sb.*[3] [f. THRILL *v.*[1]]

**1.** A subtle nervous tremor caused by intense emotion or excitement (as pleasure, fear, etc.), producing a slight shudder or tingling through the body; a penetrating influx of feeling or emotion.

*a* **1680** GLANVILL *Serm.* vii. (R.), Joy warms the..blood, and sends it about with a pleasant thrill through all the channels of its motion. **1799** HT. LEE *Canterb. T.*, *Frenchm. T.* (ed. 2) I. 240 Those communications..shot cold thrills through his frame. **1852** MRS. STOWE *Uncle Tom's C.* xxii, St. Clare would feel a sudden thrill, and clasp her in his arms. **1867** SMILES *Huguenots Eng.* xi. (1880) 195 The intelligence caused a thrill of indignation to run throughout England.

**b.** Thrilling property (of a play, novel, narrative, speech, etc.); sensational quality; *transf.* (*slang*), a literary work having this property, a sensational story, a 'thriller'.

**1886** *Westm. Rev.* Oct. 382 The sensational title of a shilling thrill. **1891** E. KINGLAKE *Australian at H.* 97 Relevancy..is apparently not a matter of so much consequence as thrill, as the man says in Mark Twain's book. **1894** MRS. H. WARD *Marcella* I. 14 Whatever had been spoken by him had grace, thrill, meaning.

**2.** The vibrating or quivering of anything tangible or visible; acute tremulousness, as of a sound; a vibration, throbbing, tremor.

**1817** MOORE *Lalla R.*, *Veiled Prophet* (1854) 96 While a thrill Lives in your sapient bosoms. **1825** SCOTT *Talism.* xiv, As the thrill of a nerve, unexpectedly jarred, will awaken the sensation of agony. **1865** BARING-GOULD *Werewolves* xiv. 240 Listening to the harplike thrill of the breeze in the old grey tree-tops. **1874** LOWELL *Agassiz* I. i, The electric nerve, whose instantaneous thrill Makes next-door gossips of the antipodes. **1892** TYNDALL in *Times* 3 Feb. 5/6 The sudden..dropping and lifting of an opaque screen over the electric light, thus producing vivid thrills upon the fog.

**b.** *Phys.* and *Path.* A vibratory movement, resonance, or murmur, felt or heard in auscultation.

**1822–34** *Good's Study Med.* (ed. 4) I. 544 That vibratory thrill [of the pulse] which has been called wiriness. **1877** ROBERTS *Handbk. Med.* (ed. 3) II. 9 Thrill or purring tremor..indicate the special character of a peculiar vibratory sensation conveyed to the fingers. **1879** KHORY *Princ.*

*Med.* 56 Besides impulse we have another movement of the heart, known as thrill. **1897** *Allbutt's Syst. Med.* III. 58 He..has a well-marked pre-systolic thrill and a loud pre-systolic murmur at the cardiac apex.

**Thrill,** *sb.*[4] *dial.* Corruption of THILL[1].

**1688** R. HOLME *Armoury* III. xviii. (Roxb.) 139/1 The shafts, are the side of the thrill or thill. **1772** *Sterne's Tr. Shandy* VII. xv. Wks. V. 93 (Jod.) The thrillhorse [*edd.* 1765, 1776 thill-horse] trotting. **1886** *Cheshire Gloss.* s. v. *Cart*, Two longitudinal pieces, known as *thrill bars* or *mid thrills*, are morticed into the binders, and these support the boards which form the bottom of the cart. **1887** *S. Cheshire Gloss.* s. v. *Cart*, The shafts are also called *thrills*..; hence we speak of '*thrill-gears*'.., 'a good *thrill-hoss*'...But the simple word *thrill*, though still universally understood, is less commonly used than formerly.

**Thrill** (þril), *v.*[1] Forms: 4 thril, 4–5 þrill(e, þrulle(*ii*), 4–6 thrille, 5 thryl(le, 5–6 thryll, 4– thrill. [A metathetic form of THIRL *v.*[1]]

I. Of the action of material bodies.

†**1.** *trans.* To pierce, bore, penetrate; = THIRL *v.*[1] 1. Also *intr.* with *through* (quot. 1387[1]).

*a* **1300** *Cursor M.* 11824 Þe fester thrild his bodi thurgh. *c* **1330** R. BRUNNE *Chron.* (1810) 30, & scharp lance þat thrilled Ihesu side. *a* **1340** HAMPOLE *Psalter* iii. 4 Þe fors of fire of luf..þat makis his prayere to thrill heuen. **1387** TREVISA *Higden* (Rolls) I. 339 A torf..i-doo aboute a worme sleeþ hym oþer makeþ hym þrulle þoruȝ þe erþe [*terram penetrare*] for to scape a way. *Ibid.* VII. 349 A grym strook of liȝtnynge..þrulled þe wal. **1530** PALSGR. 755/2, I thrill, I perce or bore thorowe a thyng...This terme is olde and nowe lytell used. **1605** SYLVESTER *Du Bartas* II. iii. I. *Vocation* 115 Through Corslets, Rivets, Jacks, and Shirts of Mail His shaft shall thrill the Foes that him assail. **1634** A. RHEAD *Descr. Body Man* C vj/2 A roughnesse where there is a hole, but not thrilled through. **1661** *Merry Drollery* 13 The sword..doth nimbly come to the point.., Thrilling, and drilling, And killing, and spilling.

†**b.** To break or penetrate through (an enemy's line). Also *intr.* with *through*. *Obs.*

**1375** BARBOUR *Bruce* XVI. 430 [Thai] thrillit thame [the ynglis rout] weill neir throu-out. **1470–85** MALORY *Arthur* IX. iv. 343 Thorou the thyckest prees he thrulled thorou them.

†**2.** *intr.* To penetrate or pass through, proceed (*into* or *to* a place); = THIRL *v.*[1] 6. *Obs. rare.*

**13..** *Cursor M.* 21098 (Edin.) Thomas..he soȝte þat estern thede, And þrillid [*v. rr.* þirled, thirlid] intil haiþinhede.

†**3.** *trans.* To cause (a lance, dart, or the like) to pass; to dart, hurl (a piercing weapon). *Obs.*

(Perhaps sometimes including a notion of the quivering motion of the missile.)

**1609** HEYWOOD *Brit. Troy* XIII. lxx, He thrild a Iavelin at the Dardans brest. **1624** QUARLES *Sion's Elegies* ii. 4 Darts, thrill'd from heaven, transfixe my bleeding hart. **1637** HEYWOOD *Dial., Pelopæa & Alope* Wks. 1874 VI. 301 Our well-tride Nymphs,..thrild their arrowie Iavelins after him. **1646** G. DANIEL *Poems* Wks. (Grosart) I. 77, I am..deeply strucke, and beare The fatall Iaveline, with me everie where; Into the Marrow thrill'd.

†**b.** To hurl, to send (persons) flying. *Obs. rare.* (Cf. THIRL *v.*[3] 1, quot. 1587.)

**1606** WARNER *Alb. Eng.* XIV. lxxxv. (1612) 353 But leauing Romaines thrilled thence, and Brutes by Rome opprest, What hapt meane while betwixt the Picts and Scots shall be digest.

II. Of the action of non-material forces.

†**4.** *fig.* from 1: To pierce, penetrate (as a sound, or an emotion). *Obs.* (passing into 5).

*a* **1300** *Cursor M.* 17738 Of his ded als þe sorful ord Sal thril þin hert thoru als a suord. *c* **1375** *Sc. Leg. Saints* xxxvi. (*Baptista*) 131 Þi word thrillit myn ere. *c* **1440** *Gesta Rom.* xlv. 177 (Harl. MS.) Synne in twynkelynge of an ye þrillithe alle the erþe. **1590** SPENSER *F. Q.* I. viii. 39 With percing point Of pitty deare his hart was thrilled sore. **1629** MILTON *Ode Nativity, Hymn* x, Such sound..the Airy region thrilling. **1642** H. MORE *Song Soul* I. I. vi, Which in their sprights, may cause sweet agony, And thrill their bodies through with pleasing dart.

†**b.** *intr.* with *through*. *Obs* (passing into 5 b).

**1526** *Pilgr. Perf.* (W. de W. 1531) 258 b, Many moo sorowes dyd teare & thryll thorowe her herte. **1590** SPENSER *F. Q.* I. viii. 6 Eger greedinesse through every member thrild. **1592** [see 5 b].

**5.** *trans.* To affect or move with a sudden wave of emotion.

**1605** SHAKS. *Lear* IV. ii. 73 A Seruant that he bred, thrill'd with remorse, Oppos'd against the act. **1718** POPE *Iliad* XIX. 266 Greece around sat thrill'd with sacred awe. **1791** MRS. RADCLIFFE *Rom. Forest* ii, A kind of pleasing dread thrilled her bosom. **1805** WORDSW. *Waggoner* II. 34 His ears are by the music thrilled. **1842** TENNYSON *Sir Galahad* ii, Me mightier transports move and thrill.

**b.** *intr.* To produce a thrill, as an emotion, or anything causing emotion; to pass with a thrill *through*.

**1592** SHAKS. *Rom. & Jul.* IV. iii. 15, I haue a faint cold feare thrills through my veines. *a* **1719** ADDISON *Milton's Style Imitated* 124 A sudden horror..Ran through each nerve, and thrill'd in ev'ry vein. **1823** SCOTT *Quentin D.* xii, When some peculiar feeling of hope, or perhaps of remorse, happened to thrill across his mind. **1854** J. S. C. ABBOTT *Napoleon* (1855) II. xx. 356 In tones which thrilled upon every heart. **1874** GREEN *Short Hist.* viii. § 5. 513 The news of Hampden's resistance thrilled through England.

**c.** *intr.* (? for *pass.*) To feel, or be moved by, a thrill of emotion. Often const. *at*, *with*.

**1595** SHAKS. *John* v. ii. 143 To thrill and shake, Euen at the crying of your Nations crow, Thinking this voyce an armed Englishman. **1596** — 1 *Hen. IV*, II. iv. 407 Art not thou horrible afraid? Doth not thy blood thrill at it? **1825** T. HOOK *Sayings* Ser. II. *Passion & Princ.* x. III. 179 He ..read over..the 'last words' of his adored Fanny, till the blood thrilled in his veins. **1874** GREEN *Short Hist.* viii. § 3. 488 England was thrilling with excitement at the thought that her own hour of deadly peril might come again.

**6.** *intr.* To move tremulously or with vibration; to quiver, vibrate. (Said esp. of sound or light.)

**1776** MICKLE tr. *Camoens' Lusiad* IX. 396 Here..The solemn harp's melodious warblings thrill. **1816** SCOTT *Bl. Dwarf* iii, Exhausting his voice in shrieks and imprecations, that thrilled wildly along the waste heath. **1827–35** WILLIS *Absalom* 79 My pulses thrill, Like a rich harp-string. **1862** TYNDALL *Mountaineer.* i. 8 Watching the lightning thrilling behind the clouds. **1878** T. HARDY *Ret. Native* v. vi, The great valley of purple heath thrilling silently in the sun.

**b.** *trans.* To send forth or utter tremulously.

**1647** CRASHAW *Music's Duel* 57 Her supple breast thrills out Sharp airs. **1868** FARRAR *Silence & V.* ii. (1875) 35 The spirit within us thrills its glad response to the noble utterance.

**c.** To cause to quiver; to throw into vibration.

**1800** MOORE *Anacreon* lviii, Sweet [are] the sighs that thrill the lyre. **1860** FARRAR *Orig. Lang.* i. 12 The air is thrilled with the voice of birds. **1872** O. W. HOLMES *Poet Breakf.-t.* v. (1885) 124 An earthquake thrills the planet.

†**Thrill,** *v.*[2] *Sc. Obs.* [f. THRILL *sb.*[2]]

**1.** *trans.* To make a thrall of, enthrall, enslave; = THIRL *v.*[2] 1.

**1456** SIR G. HAYE *Law Arms* (S.T.S.) 157 It is..na to be tholit..sen he [Christ] has maid man free, he suld thrill his brother. **1536** BELLENDEN *Cron. Scot.* (1821) I. 73 To thrill us to maist schamefull servitude.

**2.** To bind or engage (lands) in thirlage: = THIRL *v.*[2] 2.

**1480** *Act. Dom. Conc.* (1839) 70/2 Þ[t] þe said Robert..sall be na maner of way thrill þa landis bot deliuer þaim fre as said is.

†**Thrill,** *v.*[3] *Obs.* [Cf. DRILL *v.*[2], TRILL *v.*] *intr.* To flow in a small stream or in drops; to trickle, percolate; to drip; = DRILL *v.*[2] 1.

**1545** RAYNOLD *Byrth Mankynde* 22 Water passing and thrilling through y[t] narow conduit. *Ibid.* 79 Y[e] bloud.. penetratith, thryllith, and yssuyth furth the soner. **1607** WALKINGTON *Opt. Glass* xiii. (1664) 137 They razed his Skin with a Razor till the Bloud thrilled down. **1615** BRATHWAIT *Strappado* (1878) 220 No streams of grace, Thrilling or trickling from thy blubber't face.

†**Thri·llage.** *Sc. Obs.* Also 5 -ege. [f. THRILL *sb.*[2] + -AGE.] Thraldom, bondage, subjection; = THIRLAGE 1.

**1375** BARBOUR *Bruce* I. 101 Þat he put to swylk thrillage, That þai..Suld ryn on fute, as rebaldaill. *c* **1400** *Sc. Trojan War* II. 984 They askede thame to be, As worthy, of all thrillege fre. *Ibid.* 2784 And frome all thrillege be maid fre. *c* **1470** HENRY *Wallace* I. 136 He thocht ay till hald hym in thrillage.

†**Thrillant,** *a. Obs. rare.* [irreg. f. THRILL *v.*[1] + -ANT[1].] = THRILLING *ppl. a.* 1.

**1590** SPENSER *F. Q.* I. xi. 20 His thrillant speare. *Ibid.* II. iv. 46 One of his thrillant darts he threw. **1594** ? GREENE *Selimus* 1784 Pierce my poor heart with thy thrillant steel.

**Thrilled** (þrild), *ppl. a.* [f. THRILL *v.*[1] + -ED[1].] †**a.** Pierced, penetrated. *Obs.* **b.** Affected by a thrill of emotion. **c.** Caused to vibrate.

**1615** SYLVESTER *Job Triumphant* IV. xxxiv, My thrilled Wound Is past all cure. **1850** ROBERTSON *Serm.* (1872) III. 116 Incoherent utterances and thrilled sensibilities. **1900** *Daily News* 19 Feb. 2/1 When the thrilled listener has refreshed the tale-teller. **1908** *Daily Chron.* 16 July 5/6 There was no thrilled and electrified populace such as in the old Greek Games packed the amphitheatre.

†**Thri·llehod, thrillihod.** *Obs.* [f. ME. *þrille-*, *þrilli-* for *þrile-*: see THRILE and -HOOD.] Threefold condition; trinity.

*c* **1320** *Cast. Love* 9 God ffader and Sone and Holigost,.. Þat O God art and þrilli-hod. *Ibid.* 129 Þrilli-hod. *Ibid.* 1239 Persones þreo in þrille-hod And o God cleped in on-hod.

**Thriller** (þri·ləɹ). [f. THRILL *v.*[1] + -ER[1].] One who or that which thrills; *spec.* (*slang* or *colloq.*) a sensational play or story (cf. SHOCKER).

**1889** *Pall Mall G.* 1 July 6/1 It is always painful to see clever actors..wasting their energies on a worthless play... It is seldom that we are treated to a more bald and empty production than this invertebrate 'thriller'. **1896** *Pall Mall Mag.* Nov. 380 Fullblown detectives..the sort you read of in the thrillers!

**Thrillful** (þri·lfŭl), *a.* [f. THRILL *sb.*[1] + -FUL.] Full of thrills, thrilling.

**1887** J. ASHBY STERRY *Lazy Minstrel* (1892) 234 O lilt of leaves! O song of sea! O mingled thrillful harmony! **1893** E. L. WAKEMAN in *Columbus* (Ohio) *Dispatch* 15 June, We ..passed a thrillful hour at a genuine Whitechapel 'penny gaff'.

**Thrilling** (þri·liŋ), *vbl. sb.* [f. THRILL *v.*[1] + -ING[1].] The action of THRILL *v.*[1], in various senses; an instance of this. Also *attrib.*

**1526** *Pilgr. Perf.* (W. de W. 1531) 241 As though we bare the same stonges thryllynges & persyng turmentes that he suffred. **1747** HERVEY *Medit.* II. 104 From the Thrillings of polluted Joy, to the Agonies of eternal Despair. **1748** HARTLEY *Observ. Man* I. ii. 120 A Thrilling or Shivering may be felt to run along the Skin. **1835–6** *Todd's Cycl. Anat.* I. 241/2 On laying the finger on it [the vein], a peculiar thrilling sensation is perceptible. **1879** J. D. LONG *Æneid* IX. 806 Go to the heights of Dindymus, And list the thrilling of the pipe.

**Thrilling** (þri·liŋ), *ppl. a.* [f. as prec. + -ING[2].] That thrills, in various senses.

†**1.** Penetrating, piercing. Also *fig. Obs.*

**1579** SPENSER *Sheph. Cal.* May 208 A thrilling throbbe from her hart did aryse [*gloss, A thrilling throb*, a percing sighe]. **1590** — *F. Q.* I. iii. 42 He perced through his [the lion's] chaufed chest With thrilling point of deadly yron brand. **1621** G. SANDYS *Ovid's Met.* VIII. (1626) 160 Æsonides then threw his thrilling lance [L. (l. 412) *Misit et Æsonides jaculum*]. **1718** POPE *Iliad* XV. 528 Through his fair neck the thrilling arrow flies.

**b.** Piercing or penetrating, as cold; causing shivering or shuddering.

**1603** SHAKS. *Meas. for M.* III. i. 123 To recide In thrilling Region of thicke-ribbed Ice. **1753** *Scots Mag.* Oct. 516/1 Attended with a thrilling coldness. **1760–72** H. BROOKE *Fool of Qual.* (1809) II. 59 A thrilling sort of chillness would run through my blood. *c* **1820** S. ROGERS *Italy, Campagna of Rome* 91 Regions of thrilling ice.

**2.** Producing a sudden wave of excitement or emotion; piercing the feelings.

**1761** GRAY *Odin* 24 The thrilling verse that wakes the Dead. **1821** JOANNA BAILLIE *Metr. Leg., Columbus* xix, A thrilling, fearful joy. **1867** LADY HERBERT *Cradle L.* viii. 220 Nazareth, a place of such deep and thrilling interest to every reader of the Gospel history.

**3.** Quivering, vibrating.

**1850** KINGSLEY *Alt. Locke* xi, Insects..that poised themselves motionless on thrilling wings. **1871** TYNDALL *Fragm. Sc.* (1879) I. ii. 78 Let us look for a moment at this thrilling medium.

Hence **Thri·llingly** *adv.*; **Thri·llingness.**

**1825** SOUTHEY *Tale Paraguay* III. xl, So thrillingly attuned the cadence fell, That with the music..She moved herself to tears. **1847** WEBSTER, *Thrillingness.* **1863** COWDEN CLARKE *Shaks. Char.* iii. 71 How thrillingly grand is all this! **1891** *Blackw. Mag.* CL. 637/2 Emotions..of unexpected thrillingness.

**Thrill-multure**: see THIRL-MULTURE.

**Thrilly** (þri·li), *a. rare.* [f. THRILL *sb.*[1] + -Y. Cf. *chilly.*] **a.** Affected with a thrill. **b.** Having a thrilling quality.

**1893** *Illustr. Sporting & Dram. News* 25 Feb. 848/1, I felt somewhat 'thrilly' about the heart region. **1896** *Punch* 21 Mar. 133/3 Oh the feeling sweet and thrilly.

**Thrimble, thrimmel,** etc.: see THRUMBLE.

**Thrimlar** *Sc. Obs.*: see THRUMBLER.

†**Thri·mness.** *Obs.* Forms: 2 þrimnis, þreomnes, 2–3 þrem-, þrim-, (*Orm.*) þrimmnesse, 3 þrum- (*ii*). [Early ME. alteration of OE. *þrines*, *þrinnes*, THRINNESS. The change may have been due to association with OE. *þrymm* THRUM *sb.*[1], majesty, glory, and its compounds, as *þrymsetl* throne, *þrymsittende* (cf. 'seo þrynis þrymsittende', 'the Trinity sitting in glory'); but in that case we should have expected the form with *þrym* to have appeared in OE.] The Trinity. Cf. THREENESS.

*a* **1175** *Cott. Hom.* 219 Þeos þrimnis is an god. *c* **1175** *Lamb. Hom.* 99 He scal ileafan on þa halȝa þreomnesse and on soðre annesse. *Ibid.* 101 Þere halȝan þremnesse. *c* **1200** ORMIN 11177 Þatt iss an Unnseȝȝenndliȝ þrimmnesse, Faderr, & Sune, & Haliȝ Gast. *c* **1200** *Trin. Coll. Hom.* 25 Þe holie þremnesse shop and biwalt alle shafte. *a* **1225** *St. Marher.* 11 Þrumnesse þreo fald ant anfaldte hweðere. *a* **1240** *Sawles Warde* in *Cott. Hom.* 259 Þe hali þrumnesse, feader ant sune ant hali gast.

**Thrimp,** *v. Sc.* and *north. dial.* In 6 thrymp; 9 *dial.* thrump. [? Akin to THRUM *v.*[1]] *intr.* and *trans.* To press; to push.

**1513** DOUGLAS *Æneis* XI. xii. 8 Apon thar strait born bridillis brankand fast, Now thrympand heyr, now thayr, thayr hedis can cast. **1825** JAMIESON, *Thrump*,..to press ..as in a crowd...To push; especially applied to school-boys, when they push all before them from the one end of a form to another. *a* **1828** T. BEWICK *Howdy* (1850) 10 His hands.. thrimpt owr his Thees. *Ibid.* 13 Mouny oh them thrimped in. **1894** *Northumberl. Gloss.*, *Thrimpt*, pressed closely.

**Thri·msa, thrymsa.** *Hist.* [repr. OE. *þrimsa*, *þrymsa*, late altered form of *trim(e)sa*, *trym(e)sa*, genitive pl. of *trimes*, *trymes*, **trims* (nom. pl. *trimsas*, *trymsas*), ad. L. *trēmis*, the third part of an aureus; also a weight, a drachma: cf. OHG. '*drimisa*, *trimisa* = dragma'. (Both in OE. and OHG. assimilated to *þri*, *dri*, three.) The genitive pl. is frequent in OE. Laws, etc., after a numeral, and has been erroneously taken by 17th c. antiquaries, and from them by later writers, for a nominative singular.]

An erroneous name for the OE. *trimes* or *trims*, a coin (or money of account) representing the Roman *trēmis*, the value of which varied in OE. times and is uncertain; also, as a weight, a drachma.

In early times the Merovingian gold *tremis* had circulation in England, where a few are said also to have been struck in the early 7th century; but in the 10th c. the name appears to have been applied to a small silver coin of similar size; perhaps in some districts to the *sceatt*; see quots.

*a* **954** *Norð-leoda laga* § 1 in Schmid *Gesetze* 396 Norðleoda cynges gild is xxx þusend þrymsa [*v. r.* þrimsa]. § 3 Biscopes and ealdormannes viii þusend þrymsa. *c* **950** *Lindisf. Gosp.* Matt. xvii. 27 [Staterem, *gl.* þæt wæs feor trymes *vel* viii [*Rushw. Gosp.* scilling, *Ags. Gosp.* ænne wecg, *Hatton Gosp.* ænne peniȝ]. **1614** SELDEN *Titles Hon.* II. ii. 204 A Thrymsa was a third part of their shilling; not three shillings as some much mistake. **1706** PHILLIPS (ed. Kersey), *Thrimsa*, an old German Coin, valued at the third part of a Shilling, or Four Pence. **1720** J. JOHNSON *Canons Eng. Ch.* (Laws Ethelstan an. 926 No. 2), In Mercia the common Man's Weregild is 266 Thrymsa, this is 200 Shillings. **1754** HUME *Hist. Eng.* (1761) I. App. I. 100 His weregild..was by law thirty thousand thrimsas, near 1,300*l.* of present money. **1860**

Hook *Lives Abps.* (1869) I. v. 243 A bishop was on the same footing as an ealdorman, reckoned at eight thousand thrymsas. **1875** Jevons *Money* viii. 71 The *mark*, the *ora*, and the *thrimsa* were other moneys of account used by the Anglo-Saxons.

**Thrin, thrinne,** *a.* (*sb.*) Forms: 1 þrinna, 3–4 þrinne, 3–5 thrinne, 4 þrynne, þrine, thrine, threin, thrijn, 5 thryn, 4 (9 *sb.*) thrin. [Late OE. *þrinna*, a. early ON. *þrinn-r* (later *þrenn-r*) triple, threefold; often = three (Sw. *trenne*, Da. *trende*), prob. :—OTeut. **þrizno-*, f. **þris* (Indo-Eur. **tris*, Skr. *tris*, Gr. *τρίς*) thrice, with adj. ending: cf. L. *trī-nus*, pl. *trī-nī* = *ternī*.] † Threefold, triple; also three kinds of, three. An adj., but sometimes best rendered by 'thrice' (cf. ON. *þrennar tylptir* 'triple twelves', i.e. 'thrice twelve'). *Obs.*

*a* **1012** *Laws Æthelred* III. c. 13 Ladiȝe hine mid þrinna XII [L. *cum ter XII*]; and se ȝerefa namiȝe þa lade. *c* **1200** Ormin 1144 Her habbe icc shæwedd þrinne lac Forr þrinne kinne leode. *a* **1300** *Cursor M.* 3381 Ysmael had wijfs thrin [*v. rr.* þrinne, thre]. *c* **1300** *Havelok* 716 Hauelok..he dide þer-inne, Him and his wif, hise sones þrinne, And hise two doutres. **13..** *E. E. Allit. P.* B. 1805 Þus vpon þrynne wyses I haf yow þro schewed.

*absol. c* **1330** R. Brunne *Chron. Wace* (Rolls) 385 Þey departed þys land in þrynne. **13..** *Cursor M.* 9815 (Cott.) His hert aght ar atbrest in thrin [*Gött.* o thrinne]. **13..** *E. E. Allit. P.* B. 1727 Mane, Techal, Pharez, merked in þrynne.

**B.** *sb.* (in *pl.*) [perh. a new formation after *twins*.] Three children at a birth. *dial.*

**1878** *Cumbld. Gloss.*, *Thrins*, three at a birth. **1887** *Indian Med. Gaz.* 1 Sept. 246 In the case of twins and thrins about three times more than in the case of singletons.

† **Thri·nfald,** *a.* (*adv.*) *Sc.* and *north. dial. Obs.* Also 4 thrine-, 5 thryn-, 6 trin-, trene-. [Assimilation of the earlier *thrifald*, OE. *þriefeald*, Threefold, to Thrin.] = Threefold *a.*; triple, treble.

In 1st quot. (Fairfax MS.) as *adv.* = Threefold B. 1.

**13..** *Cursor M.* 26986 (Cott.) Þis hope þan mai be thrinefald [*Fairf.* vnderstande þis hope þrinfalde]. *c* **1375** *Sc. Leg. Saints* vi. (*Thomas*) 390 God..in substance bot ane Is, & thrinfald in-to personis. *Ibid.* xxxvi. (*Baptista*) 463 He þe thrinfald crone sal euir bruk fore his wardone. *c* **1470** Henry *Wallace* VII. 141 The thrynfald buk is bot this brokyn land. **1513** Douglas *Æneis* IV. ix. 78 The thrinfald goddes Proserpina. **1552** Lyndesay *Monarche* 4407 Two and thretty gude papis..Ressauit the crown of Martyrdome, Bot nocht the Thrinfald Diadame. **1570** *Satir. Poems Reform.* xxi. 19 Thay trinfauld Tratours Hes steirit vp this stryfe.

† **Thring,** *sb.*[1] *Obs.* Forms: α. 3–4 þring, þ-, thryng, 4 thring. β. 3 þrung (*ii*). [f. OE. *geþring* neut. press, crowd, tumult, f. *þring-an* to press, crowd. The β-forms probably belong here.]

**1.** A crowd, press, or throng of people.

[*a* **1000** *Andreas* 368 (Gr.) Þæt hi þe eað mihton ofer yða ȝeþring drohtað adreoȝan.] *c* **1205** Lay. 12448 Heo comen to hustinge mid alle heore þringe. *Ibid.* 27524 Amidden þan þrunge [*c* **1275** þringe] þer heo þihkest weoren *a* **1225** *Ancr. R.* 160 Engel to mon ine þrunge ne scheawude him neuer ofte. *c* **1275** *Wom. Samaria* 72 in *O. E. Misc.* 86 Monye..vrnen vt of þe bureuh myd wel Muchel þrynge. **13..** *K. Alis.* 2533 Aboutyn heom they can go; Parforce smyten into the thrynge. **13..** *Sir Beues* (A.) 1365 Vnneþe i scapede among þat þring, For to bringe þe tiding!

**2.** Pressure, tightness; some kind of disease.

*a* **1300** *Cursor M.* 11821 (Cott.) Þe scab ouer-gas his bodi all, In his sides him held þe thring.

† **Thring,** *sb.*[2] *Obs.* [app. an altered or erroneous form of *dring* (also used by Layamon), *dreng*, perh. influenced by Thring *v.*] = Dreng.

*c* **1205** Lay. 6725 In to þere burh senden Æfter þon hehste þringe [*c* **1275** after on eorl] Þat he comen to þen kinge. *Ibid.* 31455 Þa þringes norðerne makeden hine to kinge. *Ibid.* 31740 Þer weoren niȝe þusunde ðringes norðerne islaȝen. **1861** Pearson *Early & Mid. Ages Eng.* 201 Drenghs or thrings, owing special service to ride as couriers or to keep horses or dogs, were settled on certain estates.

**Thring** (þriŋ), *v. Obs.* exc. *dial.* Forms: see below. [OE. *þringan, þrang* (pl. *þrungon*), *þrungen*. Com. Teut. = OS. *thringan* (MLG., MDu., Du. *dringen*), OHG. *dringan* (MHG., Ger. *dringen*), ON. *þryngva, -gja* (pa. t. *þrǫng, þrungom*, pa. pple. *þrungenn*), cf. Goth. *þreihan* (pa. t. *þraih, þraihum*, pa. pple. *þraihans*) :—OTeut. **þriŋh(w)-* : *þriŋg(w)-*; cf. Lith. *trènkti* to shake, strike, *trànksmas* uproar, scrimmage, Lett. *treekt* to shatter. The Gothic *þreihan* passed into a different conjugational class: cf. Thee *v.*[1] In ON. *þryngva* was displaced by the weak *þrǫ́ngva, -gja*: cf. Sw. *tränga*, Da. *trænge*.]

**A.** Illustration of Forms.

**1.** *Inf.* and *Pres. stem.* 1–5 þring- (2 dring-), 3–5 þryng- (3 þrung-), 4–6 thryng- (5 dryng-), 4–7 (*dial.* –9) thring.

*c* **888** K. Ælfred *Boeth.* xvi. § 1 Ne þurfon ȝe..him æfter þringan. *a* **1225** *Ancr. R.* 252 Dumbe bestes..hwon heo beoð asailed..heo þrungeð alle togederes. *a* **1250** *Owl & Night.* 796 An eiþer oþer faste þringe. *c* **1374** Chaucer *Troylus* IV. 38 (66) He gan in thrynge. **14..** *Lybeaus Disc.* (Kaluza) 2187 (MS. C.) Þyder þey gonne þrynge. *c* **1450** Drynge [see B. 2]. **1570** Levins *Manip.* 135/39 To Thring, *artare, stringere.* **1606** *tr. Rollock's Lect. on 1 Thess.* 30 (Jam.) How men and wemen did thring in. **1871** Waddell *Ps.* ii. 9 Ye sal thring them wi' a gad o' airn.

**2.** *Pa. t.* α. *sing.* 1–5 þrang, 3–5 thrange, 7 (9 *dial.*) thrung, 4– thrang; *pl.* 1 þrungon, 2–3 -en.

*a* **800** *Andreas* 126 (Gr.) Duguð samnade, hæðne hildfrecan heapum þrungon. *c* **1000** Ælfric *Hom.* II. 394 Þæt folc hine þrang. *a* **1225** *Juliana* 67 Þrungen euchan biuoren oðer. *c* **1375** *Cursor M.* 24359 (Fairf.) Þe nailis þat him þrange on rode. *c* **1400** *Destr. Troy* 11135 Two thawsaund full þroly, þai þrang out of lyue. **1470–85** Malory *Arthur* x. xli. 479 He thrange in to the thyckest prees. **1535** Thrang [see B. 5]. **1607** Dekker *Knt.'s Conjur.* (1842) 41 In therefore they thrung, some wading vp to the knees. **1904** Thrung [see B. 5].

β. 1 þrǫng, 3–5 þrong(e, (4 *pl.* þrongen), 4–6 thronge, 4–7 throng.

*c* **893** Þrong [see B 2]. **13..** *E. E. Allit. P.* B. 1775 Þay þrongen þeder. *c* **1374** Chaucer *Anel. & Arc.* 55 But [Mars] throng now here now there amongis hem both. *c* **1400** *Song Roland* 838 They preissid, and throng, And thrusten out. *c* **1400** Þronge, *a* **1440** thronge [see B. 5]. *c* **1520** *Adam Bel*, etc. 224 in Hazl. *E. P. P.* II. 147 To the gate faste he throng. **1526** Thronge [see B. 1 b].

**3.** *Pa. pple.* α. 1 þrunge, 3 i-þrunge, 3–4 thrungen (4 -un, 4–5 -yn, 4–6 -in(e); 5–7 thrung, 6 throung.

*a* **1250** *Owl & Night.* 38 Wonne þu art to me i-þrunge. *a* **1300** *E. E. Psalter* lxxii. 21 [lxxiii. 22] And i am to noghte ..Thrungen. **1377** Langl. *P. Pl.* B. v. 517 A thousand of men þo thrungen togyderes Criede vpward to cryst. *c* **1400** *Destr. Troy* 11723 Twenty thowsaund thristy, þrungyn togedur. **1513** Throung [see B. 5 b].

β. 4–5 þrong-en (-un), 5–6 throng(e.

**1382** Wyclif *Luke* viii. 42 The while he wente, he was throngun of the cumpeny. *c* **1400** Þrongen [see B. 1 c]. *c* **1400** *Hymns Virg.* 13 Whanne þou were in þraldom þrong. **1435** Thronge [see B. 3]. *a* **1550** Throng [see B. 1 c].

γ. 5 þryngid. *c* **1400** [see B. 5 *c*].

**B.** Signification.

† **1.** *intr.* To press, crowd, throng; to move or gather in a crowd; to assemble. Also *fig.* *Obs.*

*a* **800** [see A. 2 *a*]. *a* **1000** *Phœnix* 339 (Gr.) Ðonne fuȝla cynn on healfa ȝehwone heapum þringað..þone halȝan hringe beteldað flyhte on lyfte. *a* **1175** *Cott. Hom.* 237 Of þe folce we siggeð þat hit..elce deȝie þicce þringeð. *a* **1225** [see A. 1]. *a* **1300** *Cursor M.* 24637 (Gött.) Quen mi sun ras..All till his graue [*Cott.* thrugh] þai thrang. ?*a* **1366** Chaucer *Rom. Rose* 656 For there was many a brid singing, Throughout the yerde al thringing. *c* **1400** *Destr. Troy* 470 Mony thoughtes full thro thrange in hir brest. **1513** Douglas *Æneis* IV. vii. 58 The damecellis fast to thar lady thringis.

† **b.** *trans.* To crowd around or upon, to throng (a person). *Obs.*

*c* **1000** [see A. 2 *a*]. *c* **1000** *Ags. Gosp.* Mark v. 24 Him fyliȝde mycel meniȝeo and þrungon [*c* **1160** *Hatton Gosp.* þrungen] hine. — Luke viii. 45 Þas meneȝeo þe ðringað. **1382** Wyclif *Luke* viii. 45 Comaundour, cumpanyes thringen, and turmentyn thee. **1526** Tindale *Mark* v. 24 And moche people folowed hym, and thronge hym.

† **c.** *trans.* To press or crowd together (persons or things). Chiefly in *pa. pple.* (which may belong to a). *Obs.*

*c* **1400** *Destr. Troy* 5748 With seven thowsaund þro men þrongen to-gedur. *c* **1460** *Towneley Myst.* xii. 416 It was a mery song; I dar say that he broght foure & twenty to a long..so many he throng On a heppe. *a* **1550** *Hye Way to Spyttel Ho.* 171 in Hazl. *E. P. P.* IV. 30 Lyke as bestes togyder they be throng, Bothe lame, and seke, and hole them among.

**2.** *intr.* To press or push forward, as against or through a crowd, or against obstacles; to push or force one's way hastily or eagerly; to press, rush, hasten, push on. Now *dial.*

*c* **893** K. Ælfred *Oros.* v. xii. § 8 He for þære ondrædinge þæs þe swiþor on þæt weorod þrong. *c* **1205** Lay. 9421 Ouer þene wal heo clumben & binnen heo þrungen. *c* **1374** [see A. 1]. *c* **1400** *Destr. Troy* 2362 He þrong into þicke wodes, þester within. *c* **1450** *Hymns Virg.* 122 For alle the stonys grett and smale..All they schalle togedyr drynge, And eurychon to oþer dynge. *c* **1470** Henry *Wallace* IV. 454 Thrys apon fute he thrang throuch all the rout. **1470–85** Malory *Arthur* VII. xxxi. 262 He thrang here & there, & so with grete payne he gat out of the prees. **1607** [see A. 2 *a*]. **1638** Rutherford *Lett., to Lady Robertland* 4 Jan., That we may thring in, stooping low. **1823** Carlyle *Let.* in Froude *Life* (1882) I. xi. 194, I shall just thring on here till I get desperate.

† **3. a.** *intr.* To press hard, use oppression. **b.** *trans.* To oppress, harass, distress, afflict; to repress. *Obs.*

*c* **1175** *Lamb. Hom.* 43 He walde anuppon his underlinges mid wohe motien and longe dringan [? ðringan]. *c* **1205** Lay. 10652 Carrais him on þrong and mid spere him of-stong. *a* **1250** [see A. 1]. *c* **1375** *Cursor M.* 11821 (Fairf.) On his [Herod's] heued he has þe skalle, Þe scabbe ouer-gas his bodi alle, Fast þai be-gynne him to þringe. **1435** Misyn *Fire of Love* I. xviii. 40 Nouþer with resone it is restrenyd nor with drede it is thronge nor with dome tempyd. **1871** [see A. 1].

† **4.** *trans.* To press together, squeeze, compress; to crush, bruise. *Obs.*

**13..** *Cursor M.* 900 (Cott.) Þou sal waite womman for to sting, And sco sal yiet þi hede thring. **13..** *St. Mergrete* 220 in Horstm. *Altengl. Leg.* (1881) 231 Sche set hir fot in his nek, to þe erþe sche him þrong.

**5.** To thrust or drive with pressure or violence; to cast, throw, or fling violently; to hurl, dash, knock; usually with prep. or advb. extension, as *in, on, out, through, up.* Now *dial.*

*a* **1300** *E. E. Psalter* lxxvii[i]. 59 God herd..And to noghte he thrangge swythe Iraele. *c* **1330** R. Brunne *Chron.* (1810) 52 Þei did his iȝene out þring. *c* **1400** *Rom. Rose* 7419 In his sleve he gan to thringe A rasour sharpe & wel bitinge. *c* **1400** *Destr. Troy* 6516 Thretty of þe proest he þronge out of lyue. *a* **1440** *Sir Eglam.* 1023 He to the erthe theme thronge. *c* **1470** Henry *Wallace* XI. 621 About he turnd, and wp his armys thrang; On thai traytours with knychtlik fer he dang. **1483** *Cath. Angl.* 386/1 To Thrynge owte, *expremere.* **1500–20** Dunbar *Poems* lxxii. 46 Vneiss ..he mycht sustene That crowne, on thrungin with crueltie. **1535** Stewart *Cron. Scot.* (Rolls) II. 247 Ilk ane of thame out throw him thrang a knyfe,..Thair he la deid syne. **1557** *Peebles Burgh Rec.* (1872) 237 To thring him self throw the mercat becaus it wes thrang,..and [he] culd na vther wayis evaid vntuichit. **1584** T. Bastard *Chrestoleros* (1880) 97 Nature which headlong into life doth thring vs. **1904** M. Hewlett *Queen's Quair* II. x. 321 She..just let all go, and thrung herself face to the wall.

**b.** With *down*: To throw down by force, thrust or knock down, overthrow (*lit.* or *fig.*); to bring to ruin. (See also *down-thring* s. v. Down *adv.* 33.)

*c* **1375** *Sc. Leg. Saints* xxvii. (*Machor*) 1141 For sperer of his maieste fra his Joy sall donne thrungine be. *c* **1475** *Rauf Coilȝear* 199 Thay threip that I thring doun of the fattest [deer]. **1513** Douglas *Æneis* III. viii. 141 Doun throung vndir this mont Enchelades body..lyis half bront. **1549** *Compl. Scot.* i. 19 The souerane consel of the diuyne sapiens..doune thringis them fra the hie trone of ther imperial dominations. **1570** *Satir. Poems Reform.* xix. 35 Idolatrie but reuth he did down thring. **1584** T. Hudson *Du Bartas' Judith* I. in *Sylvester's Du B.* (1620) 695 The vassels of that onely King, That Thunder sends and scepters down doth thring. **1871** Waddell *Ps.* xlvii. 3 He sal thring down the folk aneth us.

† **c.** To thrust or crush (into a confined space); to shut up, confine, bind; *fig.* to confine, restrict (quot. *c* 1374); in quot. *c* 1400, to bind tightly. *Obs.*

*c* **1250** *Death* 176 in *O. E. Misc.* 178 Þu schal in þe putte faste beon iþrunge. *c* **1374** Chaucer *Boeth.* II. pr. vii. 44 (Camb. MS.) Yowre glorye þat is so narwh and so streyte Ithrongen in to so lytul bowndes. *c* **1375** *Sc. Leg. Saints* xxxvi. (*Baptista*) 930 Herrod..petre gert in presone thring. *c* **1380** Wyclif *Wks.* (1880) 319 Disciples of crist..weren not þringen in siche couentis. *c* **1400** *Song Roland* 290 His kneys coueryd with platis.., his thies thryngid with silk. *c* **1440** *Bone Flor.* 1370 They bonde the false..And in pryson caste them,..And ther yn can them thrynge.

† **6.** *intr.* To make way (*through* something) by pressure; to pierce, penetrate; to burst *out.* *Obs.*

*a* **1300** *Cursor M.* 16438 Þai crond him wit thorn, Þat thoru his hefd thrang. **13..** *Guy Warw.* (A.) 1509 Þat gode swerd þurchim þrang, Gwichard wald abide nouȝt lang. *c* **1400** *Destr. Troy* 9641 The ledis on the land..thrappit full throly, thryngyng thurgh sheldis. *c* **1460** *Towneley Myst.* xvi. 240 My guttys will outt thryng Bot I this lad hyng.

† **b.** *trans.* To pierce. *Obs.*

*c* **1485** *Digby Myst.* IV. 672 Se how his hede with thornys is thronge!

Hence **Thri·nging** *vbl. sb.*; also **Thri·nger,** one who 'thrings' (*downthringer*, an overthrower).

**1483** *Cath. Angl.* 385/2 A Thryngyn[g] downe, *articulus, pressura.* *a* **1572** Knox *Hist. Ref.* Wks. 1846 I. 73 The down thringars of God his glore,..doctouris in idolatrie. *a* **1584** Montgomerie *Cherrie & Slae* 935 With wringing and thringing, His hands on vther dang. **1637** Rutherford *Lett., to J. Gordon* 14 Mar., There is no little thrusting and thringing to thrust in at Heaven's gates.

† **Thri·nness.** *Obs.* [OE. orig. *þrines, þrynes, -nis, -nys* (in obl. case *-nesse, -nysse*) = OHG. *drinissa*, f. *þri-*, combining stem of *þré, þréo*, Three + -ness; later with *nn*, after Thrin, *þrinnes, þrynnys*; in ME. eventually Thrimness, q. v.] Threefold condition, threeness; the Trinity.

*a* **800** Cynewulf *Crist* 379 Heah and haliȝ heofon-cund þrynes. **8..** *Halsuncge* in *Rituale Dunelm.* 114 Ic eow halsiȝe..for ða haliȝan ðrinesse. *c* **900** tr. *Bæda's Eccl. Hist.* IV. xix. [xvii.] (1890) 312 We ondettað..Fæder & Sunu & Haliȝne Gast, Þriȝnisse in Annisse..ond Annesse in þære Þriȝnesse. **971** *Blickl. Hom.* iii. (1880) 29 Of þæm mæȝene þære Halȝan Þrynesse. *Ibid.* xix. (1880) 249 On þære Halȝan Þrynnysse. *c* **1000** Ælfric *Hom.* I. 10 Ðeos þrynnys is an God. *Ibid.* 288 Þæs mannes sawl hæfð on hire ȝecynde þære Halȝan þrynnysse anlicnysse. *a* **1300** *Athanasian Creed* in Hickes *Thesaurus* (1725) I. 233 Ðat o god inne þrinnesse And þrinness in onnesse Wurchip we þe more and lesse.

**Thrinter** (þri·ntəɹ), *a.* and *sb.* Now *dial.* Also 6 trynter, thrwnter, thrwenter, 9 thrunter (*Sc.* fronter, frunter). [In OE. *þri-winter*, three-winter-, three-year; but the word may have been formed anew in 16th c., after Twinter.] **a.** *adj.* Of three winters; three years old: said of cattle and sheep. **b.** *sb.* A sheep or bovine animal of three years or winters (now applied only to sheep).

[*c* **1000** Ælfric *Voc.* in Wr.-Wülcker 117/20 *Trimus, uel triennis, uel trimulus*, ðri-winter.] **1536** *Durham Acc. Rolls* (Surtees) 419, 4 Trynters, 7 Twynters,..20 Dynmontes, 23 Hogges. **1570** *Wills & Inv. N. C.* (Surtees) I. 341 Fyue thrwnter stotts at v[s] xiij[s] iiij[d]—iij thrwenter whyes at iiij[l]. **1577** in *Hist. Soc. Lanc. & Chesh.* LV–LVI. 27 Item. One other cowe...Item two thrinters. **1890** *Cornh. Mag.* Oct. 382 One of our thrunters, or three-winter-old ewes. *a* **1898** J. Shaw in R. Wallace *Country Schoolmaster* (1899) 339 'Twinters' and 'th[r]inters', sic like names for sheep.

**Thrip** (þrip), *sb. slang.* Also 7 threpps, 8 threps. Short for Threepence.

*a* **1700** B. E. *Dict. Cant. Crew*, *Threpps*, Three-pence. **1887** J. C. Harris *Free Joe*, etc. (1888) 60 A little boy who wanted to buy a thrip's worth of candy.

**Thrip** (þrip), *v. dial.* [app. echoic: cf. Flip *v.*] † **1.** *intr.* To make a noise with thumb and finger which resembles the whispering of 'thrip' or 'flip'; *trans.* to snap (the fingers). *Obs.*

**1594** Nashe *Unfort. Trav.* 33 He with clapping his

handes and thripping his fingers seemed to dance an antike. *Ibid.* 34 A fifth..thript with his finger and his thumbe.

**2.** *trans.* To jerk with a slight movement.

**1674** N. FAIRFAX *Bulk & Selv.* 125 A Watch or a Jack, by being only wown up without thripping the balance or flyer. **1901** 'ZACK' *T. Dunstable Weir* 190 Her zot under the big fig tree, thripping her lace-bobbins in and out.

† **3.** [Prob. the same word.] To spin. *Obs. dial.* Hence † **Thri·pping** *vbl. sb.*

*a* **1652** BROME *Eng. Moor* III. i, *Q.* But where about in Norfolk wert thou bred? *P.* At Thripperstown, Sir, near the City of Norwich. *Q.* Where they live much by spinning with the Rocks? *P.* Thripping they call it, Sir. *Ibid.* IV. v, Yes, he has learn'd to thrip among the Mothers.

**Thrip**, erron. sing. form of THRIPS.

**Thripell**, þ-, obs. or dial. form of TRIPLE.

**Thripple** (þri·p'l), *sb.* Now *local.* Also 5 þerrepyll, 7–8 **thriple.** [Origin not ascertained: the suffix appears to be -EL or -LE, as in *handle, shovel*, etc.] A movable framework fitted upon a cart, so as to project in every direction beyond its sides, and thus to extend its carrying surface when loaded with hay, etc.; a cart-ladder, shelving.

**14..** *Metr. Voc.* in Wr.-Wülcker 628/10 *Epredia*, the þerrepyllis. **1686** PLOT *Staffordsh.* 354 The Cart-ladder or thripple both before and behind being to be taken off at pleasure. **1688** R. HOLME *Armoury* III. 339/2 In an Oxe Teeame [the Cart Lathers] are termed Thriples. **1891** *Berrow's Worcester Jrnl.* 28 Mar. 7/2 His pair of thripples were new ones. He bought the thripples from defendant in exchange for some hay hauling he had done for him.

† **Thri·pple**, *v. Obs.* [Origin unknown: in form a dim. or freq.: see -LE 3.] *intr.* To practise small economies; to exercise mean thrift.

**1583** STUBBES *Anat. Abus.* M vj b, This makes many a one to thripple and pinch, to runne into debte and daunger.

**Thrippling**, *vbl. sb. Sc.* ? *Obs.* [app. f. RIPPLING *vbl. sb.*[1] with *thr-* for *r-*, as in *thresh, thrush*, for *rush.*] *Thrippling-comb*, a comb-like implement for cleaning flax or hemp; = RIPPLE *sb.*[1]

**1728** RAMSAY *Bob of Dunblane* i, Lend me your braw hemp heckle And I'll lend you my thripling kame. **1874** *Mem. Alloa* 74 His winsome thrifty dame Plyin' wi' eident han' her thriplin' kaim.

‖ **Thrips** (þrips). *Entom.* Often erron. taken as pl., with a false sing. **thrip**; the analogical Eng. pl. would be *thripses.* [L. *thrips* (Pliny), a. Gr. θρίψ, pl. θρῖπες a wood-worm.] **a.** The typical genus of the *Thripsidæ* or *Thripidæ*, the sole family of the order *Thysanoptera* (formerly called *Physopoda*), comprising minute insects with four fringed wings, many of which are injurious to various plants; an insect of this genus or family. **b.** Erroneously applied to any one of the *Jassidæ*, a hemipterous family of leaf-hoppers that feed on the grape-vine.

[**1658** ROWLAND *Moufet's Theat. Ins.* 1082 Those [worms] that are bred in..dry wood are called Thripes.] **1795** *Gentl. Mag.* LXV. II. 629/1 The whole genus of *thrips* is a perfectly innocent animal. **1829** J. L. KNAPP *Jrnl. Nat.* 299 The wireworm destroys the root, the thrips the germ of the wheat. **1844** DARWIN in *Life & Lett.* (1887) II. 30, I have seen a microscopic Thrips and a Cecidomya take flight from a flower..with pollen adhering to them. **1851** *B'ham & Midl. Gard. Mag.* Aug. 139 If thrip be troublesome, fine muslin bags should be fastened over the buds. **1869** *Rep. U. S. Comm. Agric.* 217 What insects are most injurious to the vine?..Wisconsin: The thrips to a small extent. **1881** E. A. ORMEROD *Injur. Insects* (1890) 97 The attack of Corn Thrips..often does a great deal of harm very quietly. **1892** E. P. DIXON *Seed Catalogue* 3 Sufficient moisture to keep the red spider and thrip at bay.

**Thris, thrise, thrisse**, obs. forms of THRICE.

**Thrissel, thristle**, etc., obs. or dial. ff. THISTLE, THROSTLE. **Thrist**, obs. f. THIRST, THRUST.

† **Thri·star.** *Sc. Obs.* [f. *thrist*, THRUST *v.* + -AR [3].] One who thrusts, a thruster.

**1500–20** DUNBAR *Poems* lxiii. 47 Thrimlaris and thristaris, as thay war woid, Kokenis, and kennis na man of gude.

† **Thriste**, *a. Obs.* [OE. *þríste* = OS. *thrīsti* (MLG., LG. *drīste*, whence Du. *driest*, Ger. *dreist*); not found elsewhere in Teutonic. Ultimate origin unknown: see suggestions in Kluge and Franck.] Bold, daring; audacious, presumptuous.

*c* **897** K. ÆLFRED *Gregory's Past. C.* Proem 23 Ðylæs..he to ðriste & to stið sie for ðy underfenge his lareowdomes. *a* **1023** WULFSTAN *Hom.* l. (Napier) 270 Ðencan þa nu, þe to þam þriste syn, þæt hiȝ god oferseoð. *c* **1175** *Lamb. Hom.* 117 Fela stuntnesse beoð..þer þe dusie mon bið þriste. *c* **1205** LAY. 25549 Næs þer nan swa þriste cniht under criste. *a* **1250** *Owl & Night.* 758 For ic can craft & ic kan lyste & þarfore ic am þus þriste.

**Thriste**, obs. f. THIRST, THRUST, TRIST.

**Thrithing, -er**, earlier ff. TRITHING, -ER: cf. also RIDING *sb.*

**Thrittene, -tende, -tethe, -ty**, etc., obs. ff. THIRTEEN, -TEENTH, THIRTIETH, -TY.

† **Thri·vage.** *Obs. rare*—[1]. [f. THRIVE *v.* + -AGE.] The quality or degree of thriving.

**1610** W. FOLKINGHAM *Art of Survey* I. iii. 6 In Grouth, the thriuage, verdure, fruitage, prematurance, &c. of particular Vegetables are regardable.

**Thrive** (þrəiv), *v.* Pa. t. **throve** (þrōuv); pa. pple. **thriven** (þri·v'n). Also pa. t. and pple. **thrived** (þrəivd). [ME. *þrīve*, first in Ormin (*þrifenn*), ad. ON. *þrífa-sk* refl., to thrive. So Sw. *trifvas*, Da. *trives* to thrive, flourish. No trace appears in English of the reflexive suffix, which must have been dropped before the word became naturalized. ON. *þrífa-sk* is in form the reflexive or passive of *þrífa*, recorded in the senses 'to clutch, grip, grasp, lay hold of with sudden effort'.

(For the sense-history Fritzner, Falk and Torp compare *taka-sk*, similarly used. The non-reflexive use may have started from the pa. pple *þrifinn*, thriven.)]

**A.** Illustration of Forms.

**1.** *Inf.* and *Pres. stem.* 3 (*Orm.*) þrifenn, 3–5 **þriue(n**, 4–5 **þryve**, 4–6 **thryfe, thryue** (5 **þr-, thrywe**), 5–6 **thrife, thryff(e**, 6 **thrif**, 4–7 **thriue**, 5– **thrive.**

*c* **1200** ORMIN 10868, & þrifenn aȝȝ & waxenn aȝȝ Inn alle gode þinge. *a* **1300** Þriue [see B. 1]. **13..** *Cursor M.* 12139 (Cott.) Als mot we thriue. *c* **1375** *Sc. Leg. Saints* xxv. (*Julian*) 365 Allace! I thocht nocht fore to thryfe. **1398** Þryue [see B. 1]. *c* **1400** *Destr. Troy* 4832 Þan thrive we þe bettur. *c* **1425** *Cast. Persev.* 548 in *Macro Plays* 93 Fast he gunne to thrywe. *c* **1460** Þrywe [see B. 1]. *c* **1500** *Debate Carpenter's Tools* in Halliw. *Nugæ Poet.* 14 He thouht ever fore to thryffe. **1508** DUNBAR *Tua Mariit Wemen* 488 That mai nought..thrif as thai wald. **1535** STEWART *Cron. Scot.* (Rolls) II. 398 We will nocht thryfe this ȝeir.

**2.** *Pa. t.* **a.** *north.* 3 þraf, 4 **thraf(e, thrave** (-we), 6 **thraif**, 9 **thrave** (also *arch.*).

*c* **1200** Þraf [see B. 1]. *a* **1300** Thraf, thrafe [see B. 2]. *c* **1375** *Sc. Leg. Saints* xxvii. (*Machor*) 49 He thrawe, þat wele fosterit was. *a* **1400** *Sir Perc.* 212 He wexe and wele thrafe. *a* **1578** LINDESAY (Pitscottie) *Chron. Scot.* (S.T.S.) II. 53 Fre that tyme fourtht the earle Bothewell thraif newer. *a* **1850** ROSSETTI *Dante & Circ.* I. (1874) 186 While yet my body thrave On earth. *a* **1910** T. DUNLOP in *Poets Ayrshire* 261 Brawer bairn..Never thrave.

*β.* 4 **þrof, -ff**, 4–5 **þroof**, 5 **þrofe, throf(e**, (6 *Sc.* **throueff**), 8– **throve.**

*c* **1330** R. BRUNNE *Chron. Wace* (Rolls) 1885 [The Britons] multeplyed, & wel þrof. *c* **1380** WYCLIF *Sel. Wks.* II. 411 In Cristis tyme..þroof þe Chirche. **1399** LANGL. *Rich. Redeles* III. 137 As he had þroff neuere. **1470–85** MALORY *Arthur* VI. vii. 192 He..smote doune twelue knyghtes, and the moost party of hem neuer throfe after. **1597** in *Spalding Club Misc.* (1841) I. 179 Fra that tyme furthe, the said Janet thrueff never. **1777** ROBERTSON *Hist. Amer.* I. I. 45 These throve prosperously. **1830, 1852** Throve [see B. 1, 1 b].

*γ.* 4 **þryued**, 7– **thrived.**

**13..** *E. E. Allit. P.* C. 521 Couþe I not þole bot as þou þer þryued ful fewe. **1614, 1647, 1790** Thrived [see B. 1 b]. **1622–1883** [see B. 2 b].

**3.** *Pa. pple.* **a.** 4 **þriuen**, 4–5 **þ-, thryuen, threuen**, 5 **thryffyn, threvyn**, 4–7 **thriuen**, 6– **thriven**; 5 **y-threve, thryve**, 6–7 **thriue** (þriv).

*c* **1330** R. BRUNNE *Chron. Wace* (Rolls) 6546 Gentil damysels.., Þat able to mennes companye were þryuen. **13..** *Cursor M.* 5641 (Gött.) Quen it [the child] was thriuen and sum del ald. *a* **1400** *Theophilus* ii. in *Eng. Studien* XXXII. 5 How wel þat he was threuen. **14..** *MS. Cantab. Ff.* ii. 38 lf. 128 (Halliwell) He ys welle y-threve. **1622** R. AYLETT in Farr *S. P. Jas. I* (1848) 202 By her when wee in life of grace haue thriue, With her we euer shall in glory liue. **1643** *Plain English* 16 The guard is thriven to an Army. **1830–3** LYELL *Princ. Geol.* III. xlii. (1868) II. 459 The ass has thriven very generally in the new world.

*β.* 8 **throve.**

**1758** *Herald* No. 21. II. 89 How very prosperously the shoots of your planting have throve.

*γ.* 4 **þriuid**, 7–9 **thrived.**

**13..** Þriuid [see B. 4]. **1622** MABBE tr. *Aleman's Guzman d'Alf.* I. 228 How haue you thriu'd this yeare? **1654** GAYTON *Pleas. Notes* III. xii. 155 He might have thriv'd better upon the Tanzies. **1901** *Munsey's Mag.* XXV. 335 All the protected species have thrived wonderfully at Nehasane.

**B.** Signification.

**1.** *intr.* To grow or develop well and vigorously; to flourish, prosper.

**a.** Of persons or plants: in early quots. (esp. Ormin) simply † To grow, to increase in some respect; also † to be successful or eminent in arms or war; in quot. 1711, † to grow stout (*obs.*).

*c* **1200** ORMIN 8973 Hire sune wex & þraf I wissdom & inn elde. *Ibid.* 10868. *a* **1300** *K. Horn* 620 (MS. C.) Ne miȝte þer non þriue. *c* **1300** *Havelok* 280 Þe kinges douther bigan þriue. *c* **1330** [see A. 3 *a*]. **1398** TREVISA *Barth. De P. R.* VIII. i. (Tollem. MS.), Ayer, by þe whiche all þinge þat haþ lyf breþeþ and þryueþ. *Ibid.* XVII. lxii. (Bodl. MS.), Fige treen þriueþ lasse in þe norþe contreies. *c* **1400** [see THRIVING *ppl. a.* 1]. *c* **1460** *Wisdom* 1021 in *Macro Plays* 69 As many roddys as myght grow or þrywe In þe space of a days Jornye. **1530** PALSGR. 756/1, I thrive, as a tree or herbe groweth and dothe well, *je vegete.* **1697** J. LEWIS *Mem. Dk. Glocester* (1789) 6 The young Prince continued there about twelve months, thriving apace. **1711** STEELE *Spect.* No. 32 ₱ 2 My Lady Ample..grudges herself meat and drink, for fear she should thrive by them. **1830** H. N. COLERIDGE *Grk. Poets* (1834) 357 The child throve wonderfully under this caustic treatment. **1886** CORBETT *Fall of Asgard* I. 50 In the clear mountain air he grew and thrived with marvellous rapidity.

**b.** *fig.* of immaterial things.

**1613** *Will. I* in *Harl. Misc.* (Malh.) III. 163 Two great impediments that valour cannot thrive. **1614** C. BROOKE *Ghost Rich. III* Poems (1872) 106 What? wilt thou..where once Wisdome thriu'd, let Folly grow? **1647** DIGGES *Unlawf. Taking Arms* 50 Those innocent times, when Christianity thrived upon suffering. **1790** REYNOLDS *Disc.* xv. (1876) 110 The manner of Michel Angelo thrived but little with them. **1852** MISS YONGE *Cameos* (1877) II. xxii. 239 The spirit of resistance throve the more. **1907** *Edin. Rev.* Oct. 406 Thought thrives on conflict.

**2.** Of a person or community: To prosper; to increase in wealth; to be successful or fortunate; in early use sometimes † To have (good or bad) fortune, to speed, fare, 'hap' (well or ill).

*a* **1300** *Cursor M.* 3911 (Cott.) Iacob wex riche, his childer thraf [*F.* thrafe, *T.* þroof]. ? *a* **1366** CHAUCER *Rom. Rose* 1067 Wel yvel mote they thryve and thee. *c* **1400** *Laud Troy Bk.* 16823 Ther schal but fewe—so mote I thryue!—Off he n passe away on lyue! *c* **1460** *Wisdom* 781 in *Macro Plays* 61 Ye! & ewyll be þou thryvande! **1530** PALSGR. 755/2, I thrive, I go forwarde in rychesse. **1593** SHAKS. *Rich. II*, IV. i. 78 As I intend to thriue in this new World. **1657** J. SERGEANT *Schism Dispach't* 225 Since he thriv'd best among the Gentiles. **1709** MRS. MANLEY *Secret Mem.* (1720) III. 250 He thriv'd in all his Pretences. **1883** TYNDALL in *Contemp. Rev.* XLIV. 52 Nations..and even villages thrive in proportion to the activity of their industry.

**b.** Of a thing: To be successful, turn out well.

**1587** *Mirr. Mag., Humber* xvii, God is iust, iniustice will not thrive. **1622** MABBE tr. *Aleman's Guzman d'Alf.* II. 240, I (kind foole) seeing the world thriu'd with me. **1640** E. DACRES tr. *Machiavel's Prince* 138 His coosenages all thriv'd well with him; for hee knew how to play this part cunningly. **1883** F. DAY *Indian Fish* 9 (Fish. Exhib. Publ.) A few years since, fisheries thrived along the Beloochistan coast.

† **3.** ? To be saved, to remain over. *Obs. rare.*

**1509** *Parl. Devylles* xlv, Twelue lepes of relefe therof dyde thryue, To men and chyldren that had nede.

† **4.** *trans.* (?) To cause to thrive; to prosper. *Obs. rare*—[1].

**13..** *Cursor M.* 22388 (Fairf.) Þat alle þat wille him [Antichrist] sal with-stande, Salle þriuid [*other MSS.* coround, cruned, crouned] be to life lastande.

† **Thrive**, *sb. Obs. rare.* [f. prec. vb. Cf. ON. *þrif* thrift.] Thriving; profit: = THRIFT *sb.*[1] 1, 2.

**1592** WYRLEY *Armorie, Capitall de Buz* ii, Such one as seeks not after gainfull thriue, But firmely doth his thoughts to honor bind. **1604** *Sc. Acts Jas. VI* (1816) IV. 263/2 The Sweitnes of the thrife, Peace, wealth, and felicitie.

**Thriveless** (þrəi·vlės), *a. poet.* [f. THRIVE *v.* or *sb.* + -LESS.] Not thriving; lacking prosperity or success; unsuccessful, profitless.

*c* **1520** *Treat. Galaunt* (1860) 16 This causeth our galauntes, by theyr nacyon Neuerthryfte and thryueles, noye euer vs so nere. **1620** QUARLES *Jonah* (1638) 25 The feeble Sailors ..Forbeare their thrivelesse labours. **1635** — *Embl.* I. xii, And thou, whose thrivelesse hands are ever straying Earths fluent Brests, into an empty Sive. **1835** BROWNING *Paracelsus* I. 255 The dull stagnation of a soul, content, Once foiled, to leave betimes a thriveless quest.

**Thriven** (þri·v'n), *ppl. a.* Forms: see THRIVE *v.* A. 3. [pa. pple. of THRIVE *v.* Cf. ON. *þrifinn.*]

**1.** Advanced in growth, grown; grown up. Now only in comb., as *ill-thriven* (Sc. *ill-three'n*).

**13..** *Cursor M.* 14806 (Cott.) And said, 'Fast es he throd and thriuen [*Fairf.* Þis man is wele þriuen], And mikel grace ai es him giuen'. **13..** *E. E. Allit. P.* B. 298 Hym watz þe nome Noe,..He had þre þryuen sunez. *c* **1400** *Destr. Troy* 13760 The child..Wex & wele threvan in winturs a few. *a* **1400–50** *Alexander* 2709 A heuy As..A thing threuyn is & thike. **1697** DRYDEN *Virg. Georg.* III. 743 The thriven Calves in Meads their Food forsake. **1806, 1843** Ill-thriven [see ILL- B.]. **1907** *Daily Chron.* 8 May 5/7 The pretensions of a neurotic, ill-thriven youth.

† **2.** As an epithet of commendation, esp. in the alliterative phrase *thriven and thro* (see THRO *a.*[2]): ? Eminent, excellent, worthy, honourable, noble. Cf. THRIFTY *a.* 2. *Obs.*

**13..** in Wright *Lyric P.* 23 ȝef he beth thryven ant thowen in theode. **13..** *E. E. Allit. P.* A. 1191 Þe perle me prayed þat watz so þryuen. **13..** *Gaw. & Gr. Knt.* 1740 Hir þryuen face & hir þrote þrowen al naked, Hir brest bare bifore, & bihinde eke. *a* **1400–50** *Alexander* 1326 (Ashmole MS.) He laschis out a lange swerde.., Threschis doun in a thrawe many threuyn dukis. *Ibid.* 3307 Twa hundreth thousand ..all of threuen kniȝtis.

**3.** That has thriven; successful, prosperous.

**1863** HAWTHORNE *Our Old Home* (1879) 114 The careful, thrifty, thriven man of property.

**Thriver** (þrəi·vəɹ). Now *rare.* [f. THRIVE *v.* + -ER [1].] One who or that which thrives.

**1573** TUSSER *Husb.* (1878) 25 Ill tithers ill thriuers most commonlie bee. ? **1601** BACON *Let. to Sir T. Lucy* Wks. 1879 II. 25/2 If my brother or myself were either thrivers, or fortunate in the queen's service. *c* **1613** MIDDLETON *No Wit like Woman's* I. iii, They're the best thrivers In turnips, hartichalks, and cabbishes. *c* **1659** *Elegy on Cleveland* 47 C.'s Wks. (1687) 278 Timists be only Thrivers: But a Brain That's freely Generous scorns Servile Gain.

**Thriving** (þrəi·viŋ), *vbl. sb.* [f. THRIVE *v.* + -ING [1].] The action of the verb THRIVE, in various senses; prospering; prosperity; vigorous growth.

*c* **1460** *How Gd. Wif taught Dou.* 164 in Hazl. *E. P. P.* I. 191 Make the nought to riche of other mannys thinge; The bolder to spende the worse thriuing. **1530** PALSGR. 276/1, I set up a man, I am the occasyon of his thrivynge, or avauncement. **1622** E. MISSELDEN *Free Trade* 79 This their better thriuing is because euery man is at libertie to be a Merchant at his pleasure. **1707** MORTIMER *Husb.* (1721) II. 81 If a Tree begins to abate of its thriving, lop off some of the Branches. **1878** J. TODHUNTER *Alcestis* (1879) 28 'Twas when he made processions through the land, To test his people's thriving.

**Thri·ving**, *ppl. a.* Also 5 *n. dial.* -and(e. [f. THRIVE *v.* + -ING [2].] That thrives, in various senses.

† **1.** In alliterative use: Excelling, excellent, worthy; = THRIVEN 2, THRIFTY 2. *Obs.*

**13..** *E. E. Allit. P.* B. 751 What if þretty þryuande be þrad in ȝon tounez **13..** *Gaw. & Gr. Knt.* 1980 Fele þryuande þonkkez he þrat hom to haue. *c* **1400** *Destr. Troy*

1482 Of his sonnes..The þrid was a þro knight, þrivand in Armys. *Ibid.* 5435, 5458, etc. *Ibid.* 4103 Machaon & Polidus ..triet shippes broght Two & thretty full thryuond, & þrong into prise. c 1470 *Golagros & Gaw.* 345 Ye ar thre in this thede, thriuand oft in thrang.

2. Growing vigorously; flourishing (physically).

c 1645 Howell *Lett.* (1650) II. x. 15 The dust of Martyrs were the thrivingst seeds of Christianity. 1681 Flavel *Meth. Grace* xxv. 438 The new creature is a thriving creature, growing from strength to strength. 1784 Cowper *Task* II. 714 Learning grew Beneath his care, a thriving vig'rous plant. 1848 Dickens *Dombey* iii, 'How is Master Paul, Richards?' 'Quite thriving, sir, and well.'

3. Prospering, doing well in business; successful, fortunate.

1607 Tourneur *Rev. Trag.* iv. iv, Aske but the thriuing'st harlot in cold bloud; Shee'd giue the world to make her honour good. 1710 Steele *Tatler* No. 200 ⁋ 2, I am not fond of a Man only for being of..a Thriving Temper. 1758 Johnson *Idler* No. 16 ⁋ 2 Ned was..considered as a thriving trader. 1849 Macaulay *Hist. Eng.* iii. I. 375 Two great towns, which have a large and thriving trade with each other. *Ibid.* vi. II. 135 The colonists were in a thriving condition.

**Thri·vingly**, *adv.* [f. prec. + -ly [2].]

†1. In a worthy or honourable manner; also, excellently, finely. *Obs.*

13.. *St. Erkenwolde* 47 in Horstm. *Altengl. Leg.* (1881) 267 A throghe of thykke stone, thryuandly hewene. 13.. *Gaw. & Gr. Knt.* 1080 Now I þonk yow þryuandely þur3 alle oþer þynge. a 1400-50 *Alexander* 3747 Scho lengis in oure bur3e, And is oure thewis of oure thede thryfandly enfourmed. c 1470 [see Thrill *sb.*[2]].

2. Prosperously, successfully, flourishingly.

1745 H. Walpole *Lett. to Mann* (1834) II. 22 Our coalition goes on thrivingly. 1833 *Fraser's Mag.* VII. 571 May my poor silly sheep go on thrivingly. 1837 Hawthorne *Twice-Told T.* (1851) I. xiv. 231 Others..grow thrivingly among brick and stone.

So **Thri·vingness** *rare*, thriving condition.

1818 in Todd. 1864 Kingsley *Let. to Mrs. K.* in *Life* (1879) II. 167 Thrivingness and improvement everywhere.

†**Thro, thra**, *sb. Obs.* Forms: 4 þro, 4–5 thro, throo, 5–6 *Sc.* thra. [ME. a. ON. *þrá*, neut. obstinacy, persistence in opposition, contrariety, 'hard struggle' (Vigf.); perh. confounded with *þrá* fem., painful or violent longing, eager yearning (cognate with OE. *þrawu* painful pressure): see Falk and Torp s. v. *traa* [2].]

1. Struggle, contest; trouble.

1303 R. Brunne *Handl. Synne* 10570 Þat tyme was mykyl þro, And ofte was boþe werre and wo. c 1330 — *Chron. Wace* (Rolls) 54 In sclaundire & threte, & in thro. *Ibid.* 13925 Mikel was þe pres, ful þykke þe þro. a 1400-50 *Alexander* 2282 He..Thringis to þe thrid time & þe thra [*Dubl. MS.* thro] wynnys [in wrestling].

2. Anger, wrath.

13.. *E. E. Allit. P.* B. 754 3et for þretty in þrong I schal my þro steke. a 1400 *Sir Perc.* 376, I hafe spokene with thame, I wene, Wordes in thro.

3. Eagerness, keenness, haste.

c 1470 Henry *Wallace* viii. 237 Our men on him thrang forthwart in to thra. c 1475 *Rauf Coil3ear* 801 He sa cummand in thra The maist man of all tha, That euer he had sene. 1513 Douglas *Æneis* viii. Prol. 17 Thochtis thretis in thra our breistis ourthwort.

†**Thro, thra**, *a.*[1] (*adv.*) *Obs.* Forms: 3–4 **þra**, (5–7 *Sc.*) **thra**, 4–5 **þro, thro, throo** (5 **throe**). [ME. a. ON. *þrá-r* 'stubborn, obstinate, unyielding, refractory, persistent, zealous, eager, keen', adj. cognate with *þrá* sb.: see prec.]

1. Stubborn, obstinate, persistent; reluctant to give way, or accede to a request.

(The spelling *throw* in quot. c 1500 is app. due to confusion with other words.)

a 1300 *Cursor M.* 5803 (Cott.) King pharaon..es ful thra [*Trin.* þro], Lath sal him think to let þam ga. 13.. *Ibid.* 28092 (Cott.) Vn-buxum haf i bene, and thra A-gayn my gastly fader al-sa. c 1400 *Destr. Troy* 5246 Þat were þro men in threpe, & thre-tymes mo. ? a 1500 *Chester Pl.* (Shaks. Soc.) II. 11 In this place, be you never so throe, Shall you no longer dwell. c 1500 *Smyth & his Dame* 317 in Hazl. *E. P. P.* III. 213 Be thov neuer so throw, I shal amende the sonne, I trow. c 1560 A. Scott *Poems* (S.T.S.) xiii. 31 Than be not thra 3our scherwand to confort. 1603 *Philotus* xl, Scho is sa ackwart and sa thra, That with refuse I come hir fra.

b. Of a corpse: Stiff, rigid.

a 1400-50 *Alexander* 4452 Graffis garnyscht of gold & gilten tombis Thurghis to thrawyn in quen 3e þraa worthe.

2. Stubborn in fight, sturdy, bold; fierce. Also *fig.*

c 1320 *Sir Tristr.* 777 Þei þou be þro, Lat mo men wiþ þe ride On rowe. ? a 1400 *Morte Arth.* 3757 They..thristis to þe erthe Of the thraeste mene thre hundrethe. c 1400 *Ywaine & Gaw.* 3570 Thir wordes herd the knyghtes twa, It made tham forto be mor thra. c 1400 *Destr. Troy* 6422 Merion.. With þre thousand þro men þrong hym vnto. *Ibid.* 6446, 6462, etc. c 1470 Henry *Wallace* ix. 846 Wallace with him had fourty archarys thra. 1513 Douglas *Æneis* viii. xii. 128 And Gelones, thai pepill of Sithya, In archery the quhilk ar wonder thra. 1535 Stewart *Cron. Scot.* (Rolls) I. 250 The Albionis, thocht tha war neuir sa thra, Out of the feild on force wer maid to ga.

3. Angry, wroth, furious, violent.

13.. *E. E. Allit. P.* A. 344 Anger gaynez þe not a cresse, Who nedez schal þole be not so þro. c 1375 *Sc. Leg. Saints* ii. (*Paulus*) 504 As he, þat firste wes cristis fa, And in thra will his men can sla. c 1380 *Sir Ferumb.* 3968 Wan þay come to þe dupe Ryuer, þat wilde was & thro, Entrye þanne ne darst hy no3t. c 1400 *Destr. Troy* 147 He bethought hym full thicke in his throo hert. c 1440 *Bone Flor.* 2075 Sche dyd me oonys an evyll dede, My harte was wondur throo. c 1475 *Sqr. Lowe Degre* 1017 With egre mode, and herte full throwe, The stewardes throte he cut in two.

4. Keen, eager, zealous, earnest.

a 1300 *Cursor M.* 14392 (Cott.) Ful deueli war þai Iuus thra Þair blisced lauerd for to sla. c 1320 *Sir Tristr.* 615 Rohand was ful þra Of tristrem for to frain. c 1350 *Will Palerne* 3264 Þre M. of men þat þro were to fi3t. c 1400 *Destr. Troy* 470 Mony thoughtes full thro thrange in hir brest. c 1425 Wyntoun *Cron.* v. vi. 1198 Sancte Gregor.. Made special and thra oryson þat God walde grant his saule to be..fre. ? a 1500 *Chester Pl.* (E.E.T.S.) 451 Falsehed to further he was euer throe. [1775 John Watson *Hist. Halifax* 547 A person is said to be thro about any thing, who is very keen or intent about it.]

b. *fig.* Of a thing: Ready, apt, disposed.

a 1425 *Cursor M.* 16560 (Trin.) Þei..cut þis tre in two ..What þei wolde þerof shape: Þerto hit was ful þro.

B. *adv.* Obstinately; vigorously; boldly.

a 1425 *Cursor M.* 5997 (Trin.) 3itt þe kyng hem helde ful þro For wolde he not lete hem go. c 1450 *St. Cuthbert* (Surtees) 6032 Oxen twenty and twa War drawand þis bell full thra. c 1470 *Golagros & Gaw.* 60 The berne bovnit to the burgh..and thrang in full thra.

†**Thro**, *a.*[2] *Obs.* Origin, status, and meaning uncertain; occurs in the alliterative phrase *thriven and thro*, always commendatory or honorific, and apparently meaning something like 'excellent'.

(It is not impossible that this may originally have been the same word as Thro *a.*[1] 2, and that 'thriven and thro' became a stock phrase which was vaguely used; cf. 'a þro knight, þrivand in armys', c 1400 in Thriving *ppl. a.* 1, and the other references there given. But there seems also to have been connexion in sense with Thro *v.*, as if it had been taken as 'grown, become great'; cf. the phrases 'throd and thriven' [*v. r.* 'wele þriuen'] c 1300 in Thriven *ppl. a.* 1, 'thryven ant thowen' [from Thee *v.*[1]] a 1310 *ibid.* 2.)

a 1310 in Wright *Lyric P.* 26 He is thrustle thryven in [?and] thro that singeth in sale. *Ibid.* 39 Wel were him that wiste hire thoht, That thryven ant þro. 13.. *E. E. Allit. P.* A. 867, I seghe, says Iohan, þe loumbe hym stande, On þe mount of syon ful þryuen & þro. a 1450 *Le Morte Arth.* 589 There is no lady of flesshe ne bone In this world so thryve or thro, Thoughe hyr herte were stele or stone, That might hyr loue hald hym fro.

†**Thro**, *v. Obs.* Pa. pple. **throd, throdd,** (**throded**). [Northern ME., app. ad. ON. *þróa-sk* refl. to thrive, wax, grow: cf. *þroskr* adj. full-grown, *þroska-sk* vb. to grow up to manhood; also dial. Ger. *drûhen, trûhen* (Grimm), *drôen, trühen* to thrive, prosper, grow.] *intr.* To grow, wax, increase in size or stature; to grow up.

Cf. dial. *Throdden* ppl. adj., fat, well-grown, in good condition, well-fed (Brockett, and E.D.D. Northumb., Yorksh.).

c 1325 *Metr. Hom.* 112 That ilke childe Was sa unthewed and sa wilde, That alle the schathe that he moht do, He did quen he bigan to thro. c 1330 R. Brunne *Chron.* (1810) 240 Now [MS. no] gynnes Dauid to thro. For now bigynnes Dauid to wax a wereour. 13.. *Cursor M.* 3077 (Cott.) For quen [ysmael] throded [*v. r.* waxyn] was to yoman. *Ibid.* 5641 Quen it [the child Moses] was throd [*F.* waxen, *G.* thriuen] and sumdel ald To kinges doghter sco it yald. *Ibid.* 14806 Fast es he [Jesus] throd [*G.* throdd] and thriuen, And mikel grace ai es him giuen.

b. ? To advance. (Perh. a different word.)

c 1330 R. Brunne *Chron. Wace* (Rolls) 10058 Al softly he bad hem go, Þat non schulde byfore oþer þro Til þey come vnto þe bataille.

**Thro, thro'**, early form and contraction of Through. **Throale**, obs. form of Thrall *sb.*[3]

**Throat** (þrōut), *sb.* Forms: 1 ð-, **þrote, þrotu,** 2–5 **þ-**, 2–7 **throte,** (3 **þorte**), 4–9 (mainly *Sc.*) **throt,** 5–6 (8 *Naut.*) **thrott,** (5 **troht,** 5–6 **throthe,** *Sc.* **throit**), 6–7 **throate,** 6– **throat.** [OE. *þrote, -u,* wk. fem., = OHG. *drozza* wk. f., MHG. *drozze* wk. f. or m. (whence mod. Ger. *drossel* wk. f., throat, Throttle); app. from OTeut. root **þrut-*, Indo-Eur. **trud-*: cf. OE. *þrútian* to swell, *þrútung* swelling, ON. *þrútna* to swell, *þrútinn* swollen, *þroti* a swelling; the name may have had reference to the external appearance of the throat. Beside this an OTeut. **strut-* is evidenced by OLG. *strota* wk. f., throat (MLG., LG. *strotte*, MDu. *strote*, Du. *strot* throat); cf. OFris. *strotbolla*, beside OE. *þrotbolla*, Throat-boll; also MHG. *strozze* wk. f. (whence It. *strozza* throat). The original relations between the stems *þrut-* and *strut-* are not determined, but both may have had the sense 'thrust out, project, swell'.]

I. The part of the body.

1. The front of the neck beneath the chin and above the collar-bones, containing the passages from the mouth and nose to the lungs and stomach. Also the corresponding part in vertebrates generally, and sometimes the analogous part in insects, etc.

(As 'round the neck' necessarily includes 'round the throat', 'throat' is sometimes said with the wider sense of the 'neck': cf. quot. 13..[2].)

a 700, etc. [implied in Throat-boll]. c 1000 Ælfric *Hom.* II. 250 Iudas..hine sylfne aheng sona mid grine, and rihtlice 3ewrað ða forwyrhtan ðrotan. a 1154 *O. E. Chron.* an. 1137, Me..diden an scærp iren abuton þa mannes throte. c 1290 *S. Eng. Leg.* I. 16/525 In þe þrote with a swerd he smot þe suete rode. 13.. *K. Alis.* 5952 He ne had noiþere nekke ne þrote His heued was in his body yshote. 13.. *Sir Beues* (A.) 218 Þow schelt ben hanged be þe þrote. 1340 *Ayenb.* 14 Þet bodi of þe beste wes ase lipard, þe uet weren of bere, þe þrote of lioun. a 1450 Myrc *Festial* 79 By ryght dome, þat þrote þat spake þe wordes of traytery a3eynys his Lord, þat þrote was ystrangled wyth þe grynne of a rope. 1553 Eden *Treat. Newe Ind.* (Arb.) 15 [The Elephant] his mouth is vnder his throte. 1573 *Satir. Poems Reform.* xxxix. 142 Thay schot gude Manfrild in athort the throit. 1741 Richardson *Pamela* (1824) I. 84 His throat sticking out like a wen. 1826 Kirby & Sp. *Entomol.* III. 367 External Anatomy of Insects... 2. *Jugulum* (the Throat). That part of the subface that lies between the temples. 1860 Tyndall *Glac.* I. xxii. 156 The cold smote my naked throat bitterly. 1878 Villari *Machiavelli* (1898) I. iii. viii. 143 Her throat is well turned but seems to me somewhat thin.

2. The passage in the anterior part of the neck, leading from the mouth and nose to the gullet and windpipe; also, either of these passages considered separately.

c 888 K. Ælfred *Boeth.* xxii. § 1 He is swiðe biter on muðe, & he þe tirð on ða þrotan. c 1000 Ælfric *Voc.* in Wr.-Wülcker 157/41 *Guttur*, þrotu. c 1220 *Bestiary* 507 in *O. E. Misc.* 16 Ut of his ðrote it [whale] smit an onde, Ðe swetteste ðing ðat is o londe. c 1375 *Sc. Leg. Saints* xx. (*Blasius*) 344 Quha-sa-euire in þare throt seknes has. 1398 Trevisa *Barth. De P. R.* v. xxiv. (Bodl. MS.) The þrote is þe pipes of þe lunges..Þe substaunce of þis pipe is grustely and hard. c 1425 *Voc.* in Wr.-Wülcker 635/17 *Nomina membrorum...Hec gula*, troht. c 1475 *Pict. Voc.* ibid. 748/13 *Hec gula, Hoc guttur, Hic jugulus*, a throthe. 1527 Andrew *Brunswyke's Distyll. Waters* A iij b, The same water.. gargoled in the throte..withdryueth the payne of the throte. 1602 Marston *Ant. & Mel.* iii. Wks. 1856 I. 31 Thou.. choakst their throts with dust. 1769 Cook *Voy. round World* I. v. (1773) 56 A sound exactly like that which we make to clear the throat when any thing happens to obstruct it. 1897 'Tivoli' (H. W. Bleakley) *Short Innings* v. 76 A huge piece of cake went down the wrong throat, and Carrots had to belabour him lustily to persuade it to take the right direction.

3. This part with its passages, considered in various capacities, whence various expressions.

a. Viewed as the entrance to the stomach; hence in figurative expressions, as

(*to fill, full*) *up to the throat*, to the limit of capacity; *to pour* (also *send*) *down the throat*, to waste or squander (property or money) in eating and drinking; *to cram, ram, thrust down one's throat*, to force (an opinion or the like) upon one's acceptance; *to jump down one's throat*, to interrupt one in his speech sharply or roughly; in quot. 1883, ? to give oneself up absolutely to a person.

a 1225 *Ancr. R.* 216 3if þe gulchecuppe weallinde bres to drincken, & 3eot in his wide þrote. 1340-70 *Alex. & Dind.* 677 Bacus þe bollere..3e callen him kepere of þe þrote. 1500-20 Dunbar *Poems* xxvi. 65 Ay as thay tomit thame of schot, Ffyendis fild thame new vp to the thrott. 1606 Shaks. *Ant. & Cl.* ii. v. 36 The Gold I giue thee, will I melt and powr Downe thy ill vttering throate. 1610 Holland *Camden's Brit.* (1637) 543 Who..delight to send their estates downe the throat. 1724 Ramsay *Vision* viii, Quha rammed, and crammed, That bargin down thair throts. 1829 Fonblanque *Eng. under Seven Administr.* (1837) I. 232 Since the Duke of Wellington..thrust the Emancipation Bill down his [Geo. IV's] royal throat. 1861 Dickens *Lett.* 3 Dec., A place already full to the throat. 1883 Mrs. Kennard *Right Sort* ix, I might have jumped down this gentleman's throat in my foolish admiration for his powers of equitation.

b. Considered as containing the vocal organs; hence *transf.* the voice.

†*To lay, set out,* (*set up*) *a* or *one's throat*, to raise one's voice; †(*to speak*) *with a full throat*, (to speak) loudly; hence *fig.* plainly, roundly; *at the top of one's throat*, at the top of one's voice: see Top *sb.*

a 1250 *Owl & Night.* 1721 Þe wrenne..hadde stefne small Heo hadde gode þrote [*v. r.* þorte] & schille. c 1369 Chaucer *Dethe Blaunche* 320 To fynde out of mery crafty notys They ne spared nat her throtes. a 1450 [see sense 1]. 1535 Coverdale *Ps.* cxiii. [cxv.] 7 Fete haue they, but they can not go, nether can they speake thorow their throte. 1567 *Gude & Godlie B.* (S.T.S.) 110 Thay can pronunce na voce furth of thair throtis. 1600 Holland *Livy* vii. ix. 255 As lowd as ever he could set out a throate, maketh this challenge. 1686 tr. *Chardin's Coronat. Solyman* 94 These Women made such a noise..set up their throats as they did before. 1742 Gray *Spring* i, The Attic warbler pours her throat, Responsive to the cuckow's note. 1819 Scott *Leg. Montrose* xi, Men..talking Earse at the top of their throats. 1869 Ruskin *Q. of Air* § 65 Into the throat of the bird is given the voice of the air.

c. In the repudiation of a statement as false, in phr. (*to give*, etc. *one the lie*) *in* († *down*) *one's throat*, regarded as the place of issue, to which the assertion is thrown back; also, with merely intensive force, *to lie in one's throat*, to lie foully or infamously.

1588 Shaks. *Tit. A.* ii. i. 55 Till I haue..Thrust these reprochfull speeches downe his throat, That he hath breath'd in my dishonour heere. 1601 — *Twel. N.* iii. iv. 172 Thou lyest in thy throat. 1602 — *Ham.* ii. ii. 600 Who..giues me the Lye i'th' Throate, As deepe as to the Lungs? 1616 J. Lane *Cont. Sqr.'s T.* ix. 198 Gave him home the lie, adowne his throte. a 1648 Ld. Herbert *Hen. VIII* (1683) 227 We say unto you, that you have lyed in your throat. 1805 Scott *Last Minstr.* v. xx, He lyes most foully in his throat. 1824 Byron *Let. to Murray* Wks. (1846) 433/1 Whoever asserts that I am the author.., lies in his throat.

d. Regarded as a vital part, and the most vulnerable point of attack; esp. in the phrase *to cut the throat*, to kill by this method; also *fig.*

Hence, *to cut one's own throat* (*with one's own knife*), to be the means of one's own defeat or destruction; *to cut the throat of* (a project, etc.), to defeat, destroy, put an end to: see Cut *v.* 46; *to cut one another's throats*, to be desperately at variance, quarrel violently; *mod. colloq.*, to engage in ruinous competition (cf. Cutthroat 6, quot. 1886); also *to have, hold, catch, take by the throat* (also *fig.*), †*to pull out, to fly at*, †*start into* (*unto*) *one's throat*.

c 1380 Wyclif *Sel. Wks.* III. 423 Þes apes..done more harm to men þen þof þei cutted hor throtes. c 1385 Chaucer *L. G. W.* 1803 (*Lucrece*) That hast hire by the throte with a swerd at herte. a 1400-50 *Alexander* 1812 Þai suld titly þam take & by þe to3e throtis, And for þaire souerayne sake þam send to þe galawis. *c* 1400 *Brut* 22 She come to here sone..wiþ ij knyfes, and þerwiþ cotte his þrote. **1583** GOLDING *Calvin on Deut.* lxxx. 490 They cut their own throtes with their own knife. **1596** DALRYMPLE tr. *Leslie's Hist. Scot.* IX. (S.T.S.) II. 197 Quha committis a sworde til an vnskilful persone, quhairwith, quhither he cut his awne throt, or hurt the cuntrie [etc.]. **1631** R. BYFIELD *Doctr. Sabb.* 111 That..cuts the throat of your solution. **1685** DK. BUCKHM. *Reason. Relig.* in *Phenix* (1708) II. 526 Perpetually quarrelling amongst themselves, and cutting one another's Throats. *a* **1722** FOUNTAINHALL *Decis.* (1759) I. 7 This interlocutor..knocked his cause..in the head, and cutted its throat. **1824, 1867** [see CUT *v.* 46]. **1884** RIDER HAGGARD *Dawn* xii, He had let him die; he had effectually and beyond redemption cut his own throat. *Mod.* Ready to fly at each other's throats.

†**4.** *fig.* The devouring capacity of any destructive agency, as death, war, etc.; cf. JAW *sb.*[1] 5, MAW *sb.*[1] 1 b, TEETH. *Obs.*

*a* **1578** LINDESAY (Pitscottie) *Chron. Scot.* (S.T.S.) I. 55 The maist walliezand men in the throt of the battell. **1594** SHAKS. *Rich. III*, V. iv. 5 He fights, Seeking for Richmond in the throat of death. **1730–46** THOMSON *Seasons, Autumn* 937 Calm and intrepid in the very throat Of sulphurous war.

**II.** Transferred senses.

**5.** A narrow passage, esp. in or near the entrance of something; a narrow part in a passage.

*a* **1584** MONTGOMERIE *Cherrie & Slae* 1551 A prettie spring: Quhois throt, sir, I wot, sir, ȝe may stap with ȝour neive. **1814** SCOTT *Diary* 17 Aug., in *Lockhart*, The access through this strait would be easy, were it not for the Island of Græmsay, lying in the very throat of the passage. **1823** BUCKLAND *Reliq. Diluv.* 141 The throat of the cave, by which we ascend from the mouth to the interior. **1837** EMERSON *Address Amer. Schol.* Wks. (Bohn) II. 186 One central fire, which flaming now out of the..throat of Vesuvius, illuminates the towers..of Naples. **1838** J. L. STEPHENS *Trav. Russia* 70/1 Field-pieces, whose throats once poured their iron hail against the walls within which they now repose as trophies. **1899** A. GRIFFITHS in *Fortn. Rev.* LXV. 312 Lang's Nek, the throat of the passage into the Transvaal.

**6.** *spec.* in technical use. **a.** *Archit., Building*, etc. †(*a*) The narrowest part of the shaft of a column, immediately below the capital; the hypotrachelium. (*b*) The neck of an outwork: = GORGE *sb.*[1] 6. (*c*) The part in a chimney, furnace, or furnace-arch immediately above the fire-place, which narrows down to the neck or 'gathering'. (*d*) A groove or channel on the under side of a coping or projecting moulding to keep the drip from reaching the wall.

**1663** GERBIER *Counsel* 32 The Freese, Gul or Throat. **1727–41** CHAMBERS *Cycl.*, *Throat*, in architecture, fortification, &c., see *Gorge*, and *Gula*. **1815** J. SMITH *Panorama Sc. & Art* I. 246 The throat is that part of the opening immediately above the fire, and contained between the mantle and the back. **1838** *Civil Eng. & Arch. Jrnl.* I. 364/1 The smoke..ascends vertically by the throat of the chimney into the flue. **1868** JOYNSON *Metals* 16 The opening at the top of the furnace, called the throat or trunnel-hole. **1895** *Jrnl. Roy. Instit. Brit. Archit.* 14 Mar. 351 If brick sills be used, see that they have a good, clean throat.

**b.** *Shipbuilding* and *Naut.* (*a*) The hollow of the bend of a knee-timber. (*b*) The outside curve of the jaws of a gaff; hence, the forward upper corner of a fore-and-aft sail; see also quot. 1867. (*c*) The amidships part of a floor-timber, esp. if it bulges and then tapers into the kelson. (*d*) The curve of the flukes of an anchor where they join the shank.

**1711** W. SUTHERLAND *Shipbuild. Assist.* 165 *Throat*, the inward bending of Knee-timber. **1776** FALCONER *Dict. Marine*, *Throat*, a name given to the inner end of a gaff, or to that part which is next to the mast. It is opposed to *peek*, which implies the outer extremity of the said gaff. *c* **1850** *Rudim. Navig.* (Weale) 142 They must be deeper in the throat or at the cutting-down. *Ibid.* 155 *Throat*,..the midship part of the floor-timbers. *c* **1860** H. STUART *Seaman's Catech.*, It is..bolted through the throat of each floor. **1867** SMYTH *Sailor's Word-bk.*, *Throt*, that part of the mizen-yard close to the mast. **1882** NARES *Seamanship* (ed. 6) 81 Hooked to a bolt in the throat of the gaff.

**c.** *Mech.*, etc. (*a*) Of a plough: see quot. 1807. (*b*) In a threshing-machine, the passage from the feed-board to the threshing-cylinder (Knight *Dict. Mech.* 1877). (*c*) The opening in the stock of a plane, in which the iron is set, and through which the shavings pass. (*d*) A contracted part of a spoke near the hub (Knight). (*e*) The angle between the running surface of a railway or tramcar wheel and its flange. *U.S.* (*f*) A tapered pipe connecting two tubes or sections of different diameters (*Cent. Dict., Suppl.* 1909).

**1807** A. YOUNG *Agric. Essex* I. 132 *The throat*,..the space from the share point to the junction or approach of the breast to the beam. **1805** DICKSON *Pract. Agric.* I. 4 The throat and breast, or that part which enters, perforates, and breaks up the ground.

**7.** *Bot.* The throat-like opening of a gamopetalous corolla at which the tube and the petals unite.

**1847** W. E. STEELE *Field Bot.* 8 Florets all tubular, with an inflated throat, generally spreading into a hemispherical head. **1880** GRAY *Struct. Bot.* vi. § 5 (ed. 6) 246 The line, or sometimes a manifest or conspicuous portion, between the limb and the tube..is called the Throat, in Latin Faux, pl. fauces. **1882** *Garden* 28 Jan. 66/3 The throat of the flower is unbearded.

**8.** *attrib.* and *Comb.* **a.** attrib. 'of, pertaining to, or affecting the throat', as *throat-ache, -disease, -muscle, -performer, -roar*, etc.; in sense 6 b (*b*), as *throat-bolt, -brail, cringle, -downhaul, halyard, lashing* (see these words, and quots. here); **b.** 'that is on, around, or near the throat', as *throat-bar, button, -cloth, -feather, -fringe, -patch, -wattle*; **c.** objective, obj. genitive, locative, etc., as *throat-clearing* sb. and adj., *-clutching, -slitting*; *throat-bursten, -cracking, -swollen* adjs. **d.** Special combs.: †**throat-brisk**, ? part of the brisket near the throat; **throat-chain**, in whaling, a chain passed through the throat and tongue of the whale; **throat-clutch**, a guttural catch or momentary closure; **throat-deafness**, deafness caused by a diseased condition of the throat; **throat-flap**, the epiglottis; **throat-full** *a.*, full to the throat, stuffed, crammed; **throat-jaws**, jaw-like pharyngeal bones in the lower vertebrates; **throat-letter**, a guttural; **throat-piece**, (*a*) in mediæval armour, a part of the helm protecting the throat; (*b*) the neck of a racket, where the ends of the rim are brought together upon the handle (*Cent. Dict., Suppl.* 1909); **throat-pipe**, the windpipe; also, the steam supply pipe in a steam-engine; **throat-pit**, a triangular depression at the front of the neck, between the collar-bones at the point where they articulate with the breastbone; **throat-plate**, the forward exterior plate of a locomotive fire-box (*Cent. Dict., Suppl.*); **throat-pouch**, a gular sac in certain birds and animals; **throat-register**, the lowest register of the voice; **throat-ring**, Waldeyer's name for the circular group of lymphatic bodies surrounding the beginning of the respiratory tract; **throat-room**, room for shouting; **throat-root**, an American hairy species of Avens, *Geum virginianum*; **throat-rupture**, goitre; **throat-seizing**, *Naut.*: see quot.; **throat-stopper**, the epiglottis: cf. *throat-flap*; **throat-strap** = THROAT-LATCH; **throat-sweetbread**, butcher's name for the thymus gland; also called *neck-sweetbread*; **throat-thong** = THROAT-LATCH; **throat-toggle**, a toggle with which the *throat-chain* is secured; **throat-vent**, the opening in a coking-oven for the escape of smoke, etc.; **throat-wash**, a medicinal gargle. See also THROAT-BAND, THROAT-BOLL, etc.

**1898** J. ARCH *Story of Life* x. 247 Head-aches and heart-aches and *throat-aches. **1872** COUES *N. Amer. Birds* 180 Chuck-will's-widow..a whitish *throatbar. **1867** SMYTH *Sailor's Word-bk.*, **Throat-bolts*, eye-bolts fixed in the lower parts of the tops, and the jaw-ends of gaffs for hooking the throat-halliards to. **1815** BURNEY *Falconer's Dict. M.*, **Throat-Brails*,..are those which are attached to the gaff close to the mast. **1615** CHAPMAN *Odyss.* III. 620 Apart flew either thie: That with the fat they dubd with art alone; The *throte-briske, and the sweet-bread pricking on. **1890** 'R. BOLDREWOOD' *Miner's Right* xxxiv, One button was missing between the upper or *throat button and the third. **1811** L. M. HAWKINS *C'tess & Gertr.* I. 78 A vast deal of *throat-clearing, face-stroking, and aukward hesitation. **1871** *Routledge's Ev. Boy's Ann.* Dec. 2 He invariably wore a white *throat-cloth or neckerchief. **1895** F. OSGOOD in *Forum* (N.Y.) June 507 Nerve-strain tends to the prevalence of the high vocal pitch and to the American fault—the *throat-clutch. **1895** *Outing* (U.S.) XXVI. 47/1 To bend a mainsail, shackle the *throat cringle to the eyebolt under the jaws of the gaff [etc.]. **1897** *Allbutt's Syst. Med.* IV. 778 Adult patients suffering since childhood from '*throat-deafness'. *Ibid.* 750 The so-called 'lithæmic diathesis' is a much more frequent cause of *throat-disease than is generally believed. **1877** KNIGHT *Dict. Mech.*, **Throat-down-hauls*..., ropes for rousing down the throat of a gaff. **1872** COUES *N. Amer. Birds* 162 Ravens, with *throat-feathers acute, lengthened, disconnected. **1683** A. SNAPE *Anat. Horse* IV. x. (1686) 165 The Epiglottis or *Throat-flap, that covers the chink of the Larynx. **1896** *Proc. Zool. Soc. Lond.* 1 Dec. 932 The narrowness and banded coloration of the *throat-fringe must likewise be noted. **1681** W. ROBERTSON *Phraseol. Gen.* (1693) 475 To dine, or eat till he be *throat-full. *a* **1800** COWPER *On Receipt of Hamper*, A bottle green Throat-full. **1762** FALCONER *Shipwr.* II. 389 The hallyards *thrott and peek are next apply'd. **1776** — *Dict. Marine* s.v. *Throat*, The ropes employed to hoist up, and lower a gaff,..are called the throat or peek haliards. **1893** PEMBERTON *Iron Pirate* 39 There being..no hand either at the peak halyards or the throat halyards. **1873** MIVART *Lessons Elem. Anat.* viii. § 18. 318 Moving those '*throat-jaws', the pharyngeal bones, which exist in so many of the lowest Vertebrate class. **1893** *Times* 13 June 12/1 A *throat lashing of steel rope. **1847** *Proc. Philol. Soc.* III. 116 A similar interchange between lip and *throat letters. **1875** HUXLEY & MARTIN *Elem. Biol.* (1877) 203 The *throat-muscles: through the broad thin muscle in front (mylohyoid) is seen the hypoglossal nerve. **1872** COUES *N. Amer. Birds* 195 Young birds lack..the crimson *throat-patch. **1776** BURNEY *Hist. Mus.* I. 340 The vociferous Stentor..the most illustrious *Throat-performer, or herald of antiquity. **1869** BOUTELL *Arms & Arm.* v. (1874) 79 His helm is ornamented..; the *throat-piece has thunderbolts..in hammer work. **1600** J. PORY tr. *Leo's Africa* III. 185 The inhabitants of this region haue the balles of their *throat-pipes very great. **1632** J. HAYWARD tr. *Biondi's Eromena* 29 She..stab'd her husband..in the face, thinking to strike him in the throat-pipes. **1824** R. STUART *Hist. Steam Engine* 72 The regulator valve [the 'throttle'], which opens or shuts the communication between the cylinder and boiler by the throat-pipe. **1660** *Albert Durer Revived* 4 A straight perpendicular line from the *Throat-pit down. **1672** SIR T. BROWNE *Let. Friend* § 10 Some are so curious as to observe the depth of the throat-pit. **1871** DARWIN *Desc. Man* II. xii. II. 33 In the genus Sitana, the males alone are furnished with a large *throat-pouch. **1872** COUES *N. Amer. Birds* 18 Pelicans, cormorants, etc., that have a naked throat-pouch. **1903** *Med. Record* 7 Feb. 228 The various lymphatic structures in Waldeyer's so-called lymphatic *throat ring. **1843** CARLYLE *Past & Pr.* III. xii, Let me have elbow-room, *throat-room, and I will not fail! **1858** *Hilpert's Eng.-Germ. Dict.*, *Throat-root. **1884** MILLER *Plant-n.*, *Geum virginianum*, Throat-root, White Avens. **1684** tr. *Bonet's Merc. Compit.* II. 44 One..had his neck wonderfully swelled with the *Throat-Rupture. **1867** SMYTH *Sailor's Word-bk.*, **Throat-seizing*, in blocks, confines the hook and thimble in the strop home to the scores. **1886** CORBETT *Fall of Asgard* II. 9 There will be some merry *throat-slitting. **1661** LOVELL *Hist. Anim. & Min.* Introd., Amongst Birds..The *throat stopper is in none, yet they temper the motion so, that nothing may fall into the throat. **1877** KNIGHT *Dict. Mech.*, **Throat-strap*, the upper strap of a halter that encircles the horse's throat; also called jaw strap. *a* **1661** HOLYDAY *Juvenal* x. 191 Nero did..ne're contract With one *throat-swoln, gor-bellied, or crump-back'd. **1611** COTGR., *Sousgorge d'une bride*, the *throat-thong, or throat-band of a bridle. **1874** SCAMMON *Marine Mammals* 232 The cutting gear..consists of toggles, spades, boarding and leaning knives,..*throat-toggle, head axes, etc. **1839** URE *Dict. Arts* 997 The *throat-vents..are then left open. **1901** *Lancet* 2 Nov. 1203/1 The application of an antiseptic *throat-wash. **1875** *Zoologist* X. 4686 It [a bird] has but one medial *throat-wattle.

**Throat** (þrōᵘt), *v.* [f. THROAT *sb.*]

†**1.** *trans.* To utter or articulate in or from one's throat; to speak in a guttural tone; *to throat out*, to cry out or shout from the throat. *Obs.*

*c* **1611** CHAPMAN *Iliad* XIII. 135 So Hector hereto throated threats, to go to sea in blood. **1622** MABBE tr. *Aleman's Guzman d'Alf.* II. 113 Throating it out, wheresoever he comes,..'I am an Alguazil'.

†**2.** To cut the throat of; to slaughter, slay. *Obs. rare.* (Cf also THROATING-*knife*.)

**1382** WYCLIF *2 Kings* x. 14 Whom when thei hadden taken alyve, thei throtyden [1388 strangliden, *Vulg.* jugulaverunt, LXX ἐσφαξαν] hem in the cystern, besyde the chaumbre.

†**b.** *Farming* (*local*). See quot. *Obs.*

**1750** [implied in THROATING *vbl. sb.*]. **1763** *Museum Rust.* (ed. 2) I. 236 Mons. de L'Isle's workman cuts the wheat against the bending, or, as an Aylesbury-vale man would say, throats it.

**3.** *Building.* To furnish with a throat; to groove or channel. (Chiefly in *pa. pple.* and *vbl. sb.*)

**1823** P. NICHOLSON *Pract. Build.* 311 [The fascia] is fluted or throated on its upper edge, to prevent the water from running over the ashlaring. **1876** *Encycl. Brit.* IV. 472/2 Sills are weathered and throated like the parts of a string course. **1881** YOUNG *Ev. Man his own Mechanic* § 1299 A dash-board..may be made out of a solid piece sloped at the top..and 'throated' or channelled on the under surface with a deep groove. **1883** *Specif. Alnwick & Cornhill Railw.* 5 Ashlar Copings..no stone is to be less than 2 feet 6 inches in length, and the whole are to be weathered and throated.

**Throatal** (þrōᵘ·tăl), *a.* [irreg. f. THROAT *sb.* + -AL.] Of or pertaining to the throat; guttural; cervical.

**1905** *Sat. Rev.* 1 Apr. 415/2 The loudest..click..comes at the end of the liquid, throatal noise. **1908** *Westm. Gaz.* 1 Aug. 15/2 The throatal band that separates the white from the light blue of the breast and under-parts.

**Throa·t-band.**

**1.** *Saddlery.* = THROAT-LATCH.

**1611** COTGR., *Sousbarbe*,..the throat-band of a bridle. **1794** W. FELTON *Carriages* (1801) II. 138 The Throat-Band [is] a narrow, short strap, with a buckle at each end. **1833** *Regul. Instr. Cavalry* I. 70 The throat-band must be..slack.

**2.** A band worn round the neck; also, a part of a garment encircling the neck; a neck-band.

**1903** *Daily Chron.* 9 May 8/4 *Rebats*, to give the new throat bands with their short hanging fronts their correct French name. **1904** *Daily Chron.* 12 Mar. 8/4 The collars ..in others..are simply throat-bands elaborated into shoulder straps. **1907** *Blackw. Mag.* July 501 The grimy throat-band, originally white, of a common regimental shirt.

†**Throa·t-boll.** *Obs.* Forms: see THROAT *sb.* and BOWL *sb.*[1] [OE. *þrotbolla*, f. *þrote*, THROAT + *bolla*: see BOWL *sb.*[1] and BOLL *sb.*[1] 5. Cf. OFris. *strotbolla* in same sense.] The protuberance in the front of the throat; the Adam's apple; hence, the larynx.

*a* **700** *Epinal Gloss.* (O.E.T.) 456 *Gurgulio*, throtbolla. *c* **725** *Corpus G.* 1000 & *a* **800** *Leiden G.* Ðrotbolla. *a* **901** *Laws K. Ælfred* c. 51 ȝif monnes ðrotbolla bið þyrel, ȝebete mid xii scill. *c* **1000** ÆLFRIC *Gram.* ix. (Z.) 35 *Gurgulio*, ymel oððe ðrotbolla. *c* **1250** *Death* 173 in *O. E. Misc.* 178 Þi þrote-bolle þat þu mide sunge. *c* **1386** CHAUCER *Reeve's T.* 353 By the throte bolle he caughte Alayn.. And on the nose he smoot hym with his fest. *c* **1450** *Two Cookery-bks.* 79 Take a Curlewe..; take awey the nether lippe and throte boll. **1529** RASTELL *Pastyme, Hist. Brit.* (1811) 292 One of them..cut his throte bolle a sonder with a dagger. **1548–77** VICARY *Anat.* ii. (1888) 19 It is necessarie in some meane places to put a grystle, as in the throte bowel for the sounde. **1565** GOLDING *Ovid's Met.* III. (1593) 57 His throte-boll sweld with puffed veines. **1575** *Gamm. Gurton* III. iii. C iij b, Trounce her, pull out her throte boule. **1611** COTGR., *Gueneau*, the throtle, or throat-boll.

**Throa·t-cu·tter.** Chiefly *Sc.* or *nonce-wd.* One who cuts throats; a cutthroat, an assassin.

**1535** STEWART *Cron. Scot.* (Rolls) III. 18 Of throt-cutteris and all sic cursit cryme, And murderaris of leill men be the way. **1567** *Satir. Poems Reform.* vii. 66 Bludy bucheouris and throtcutters. *a* **1598** ROLLOCK *Wks.* (Wodrow Soc.) II. xv. 172 Two vagabonds, two throat-cutters. **1840** THACKERAY

*Paris Sk. Bk.* Wks. 1900 V. 209 An executioner..had come ..to assist the professional throat-cutter.

So **Throa·t-cu·tting** *vbl. sb.*, the cutting of the throat; *ppl. a.*, that cuts the throat.

**1655** GURNALL *Chr. in Arm.* verse 14. I. iii. (1679) 7/2 He buys his Sleep dear, that pays his throat-cutting for it. **1840** GEN. P. THOMPSON *Exerc.* (1842) V. 23 Then come the murders, the throat-cuttings, the massacres of prisoners. **1859** *Habits Gd. Soc.* iii. 132 How difficult..has it been to abolish the stiff black hat and the throat-cutting collar.

**Throated** (þrōu·tèd), *a.* [f. THROAT *sb.* or *v.* + -ED.] Having or furnished with a throat; having a throat of a specified kind (chiefly in combination), as *deep-, dry-, large-, red-, white-throated.*

**1530** PALSGR. 327/2 Throted, *gorgé.* **1601** ? MARSTON *Pasquil & Kath.* I. 76 Yon same drie throated huskes Will sucke you vp. **1746** FRANCIS tr. *Hor., Sat.* II. ii. 53 Give me, the Harpy-throated Glutton cries, In a large Dish a Mullet's mighty Size. **1850** *Beck's Florist* Dec. 292 One of the best of the white-throated kinds [of Petunias]. **1880** W. WATSON *Prince's Quest* (1892) 102 Sooth-tongued singers, throated like the bird.

**b.** *Building.* Having a throat or groove; fluted, channelled, grooved.

**1847** SMEATON *Builder's Man.* 189 Bath proper sunk and throated sills.

**Throa·ter.** *local.* A throating-knife: see THROATING *vbl. sb.* d; also, a man who uses this knife in cutting off the heads of fishes.

**1891** *Cent. Dict.* cites from New Brunswick.

† **Throa·teral,** *a. Obs. nonce-wd.* [irreg. f. THROAT *sb.*, after *guttural.*] Guttural.

**1662** J. WILSON *Cheats* III. iii, Guttural, that is to say, throteral.

† **Throa·t-goll.** *Obs. rare.* [f. THROAT + ? *golle*, GULL *sb.* 4, throat, gullet.] The windpipe, or its upper part close to the epiglottis. (The word appears to have been somewhat vaguely used.)

**14..** *Sir Beues* (C.) 2753+102 Sethen he went to the skulle [of the dragon] And hewyd asonder the throte golle [*v. r.* þrote bolle]. **14..** *Nom.* in Wr.-Wülcker 676/25 *Hoc epiglotum*, a th[r]otegole. *c* **1440** *Promp. Parv.* 493/1 Throte golle, *epiglotum, frumen.* **1530** PALSGR. 281/1 Throtegole or throtebole, *neu de la gorge, gosier.*

† **Throat-hole,** occas. error for THROAT-BOLL.

**Throa·tily,** *adv.* [f. THROATY *a.* + -LY [2].] In a throaty manner; gutturally; hoarsely.

**1893** *Scribner's Mag.* XIV. 61 A tame cornet tenored it throatily. **1899** B. CAPES *Lady of Darkness* xvii, Charlot sniggered throatily. **1901** *Blackw. Mag.* Dec. 820/1 The wind..ranged throatily round the coast.

**Throatiness** (þrōu·tinès). [f. as prec. + -NESS.] The condition of being throaty (in either sense).

**1871** G. LAWRENCE *Anteros* xix, You might pick out..one or two clear cases of throatiness. **1883** G. STABLES *Our Friend the Dog* vii. 61 *Throatiness*, a term applied to loose skin about the throat, where none should exist, as in the Pointer. **1884** G. MOORE *Mummer's Wife* (1887) 163 In a few lessons I could get rid of that throatiness, and show her how to get a note or two from the chest. **1890** *Pall Mall G.* 25 Aug. 2/3 Influenza..The symptoms are always the same—rheumatism, throatiness, headache, and slight fever.

**Throating** (þrōu·tiŋ), *vbl. sb.* [f. THROAT *v.* + -ING [1].] The action of the verb THROAT. † **a.** *Farming* (*local*). (See quots.) *Obs.*

**1750** W. ELLIS *Mod. Husb.* V. I. 68 (E.D.S.) When they mow beans against their bending, they [in the Vale of Aylesbury] call it throating. **1763** *Museum Rust.* (ed. 2) I. 236 It is only when they chance to have a thin crop, that they venture to mow them against their own bending (this they call throating).

**b.** *Building*, etc. The cutting of a 'throat' or channel; the undercutting of a projecting moulding in order to prevent rain water from trickling down the wall; *concr.* the channel or groove thus cut: = THROAT *sb.* 6 a (*d*).

**1825** J. NICHOLSON *Operat. Mechanic* 543 In measuring strings, the weathering is denominated sunk work, and the grooving throatings. **1838** F. W. SIMMS *Public Wks. Gt. Brit.* 9 The coping shall [have] a throating of half an inch wide cut on its underside. *c* **1850** *Rudim. Navig.* (Weale) 160 *Wood-lock*, a piece of elm..in the throating or score of the pintle. **1898** *Speaker* 26 Feb. 264/1 Masses of greyish white—almost like a faint throating of snow.

**c.** *Shipbuilding.* The throat of a floor-timber.

**1869** SIR E. J. REED *Shipbuild.* ii. 28 Keep its upper edge level with the throating of the floors.

**d.** *attrib.*: **throating-knife**, a knife used for cutting the throats of fish; **throating-line** = *cutting-down line* (CUTTING *vbl. sb.* 9 b); **throating-machine**, a machine for shaping the throats of wheel spokes (*Cent. Dict., Suppl.* 1909).

**1883** *Fisheries Exhib. Catal.* 197 Cod splitting, ripping and throating knives.

**Throat-latch, throat-lash,** *sb. Saddlery.* [f. THROAT *sb.* + LATCH *sb.*[1] 1, LASH *sb.*[2] 1.] A strap passing under the horse's throat which helps to keep the bridle in position.

**1794** W. FELTON *Carriages* (1801) II. 167 Bearing-reins hung to the throat-band by throat-latch dees. **1829** *Sporting Mag.* XXIV. 175, I never saw a horse driven in the throat-latch in Germany. **1890** 'R. BOLDREWOOD' *Col. Reformer* (1891) 106 He..held on to the bridle-rein with such tenacity that the throat-lash giving way, it was jerked over the horse's head, leaving the reins in the rider's hands. *transf.* *a* **1825** FORBY *Voc. E. Anglia, Throat-latch*..2. The strings of a hat, cap, &c. fastened under the chin. *attrib.* **1794** [above]. **1901** G. W. CABLE *Cavalier* xix, He had a retreating chin, a throat-latch beard and a roving eye.

Hence **Throat-latch** *v. trans.*, to put a throat-latch upon.

**1829** *Sporting Mag.* XXIV. 175, I throat-latched him, and never drove a better leader.

**Throatless** (þrōu·tlès), *a.* [f. THROAT *sb.* + -LESS.] Without a throat; having no throat.

**1881** G. ALLEN *Evolutionist at Large* v. 49 A wasp whose head has been severed from its body and stuck upon a pin, will still greedily suck up honey with its throatless mouth. **1887** *Longm. Mag.* Sept. 539 Vast, featureless head, set throatless on a formless bust.

**Throatlet** (þrōu·tlèt). [f. as prec. + -LET.] An article of ornament or protection for the throat; a woman's necklet; a small boa, usually of fur.

**1865** LIVINGSTONE *Zambesi* v. 114 The Manjanga adorn their bodies [with] throatlets, bracelets and anklets of brass, copper, or iron. **1889** *Star* 29 Oct. 1/6 A throatlet of coral beads. **1896** *Echo* 15 Feb. 4/4 Capes, throatlets, and boas are the chief forms in which peltry seems to be worn.

**Throatwort** (þrōu·twɒɹt). [f. as prec. + WORT: see quot. 1597.] Name for the Nettle-leaved Bell-flower, *Campanula Trachelium*; also extended to other species, as *C. glomerata, latifolia*, and *Cervicaria*; also locally applied to the Foxglove, Figwort (*Scrophularia nodosa*), and American Button Snake-root (*Liatris spicata*).

**1578** LYTE *Dodoens* II. xx. 170 This Throtewurte or Haskwurte..is..of three sortes,..the great and the small, and the creeping kinde. **1597** GERARDE *Herbal* II. cx. 363 The thirde sort of Canterburie Bels, called likewise Throtewoorte, of his vertue in curing the diseases of the throte. **1766** *Museum Rust.* VI. 446 Lesser Throatwort, or Canterbury Bells. **1813** SCOTT *Rokeby* III. viii, Where..throatwort with its azure bell, And moss and thyme his cushion swell. *Note.* The Campanula latifolia, *Grand* [? error for *Giant*] *Throatwort*, or *Canterbury Bells*, grows in profusion upon the beautiful banks of the river Greta.

**Throaty** (þrōu·ti), *a.* [f. as prec. + -Y.]

**1.** Of vocal sounds, or of the voice: Produced or modified in the throat; guttural; hoarse.

*c* **1645** HOWELL *Lett.* (1650) II. lxxiii. 112 A rime of certain hard throaty words..accounted the difficultst in all the whole Castilian language. **1863** E. C. CLAYTON *Queens of Song* II. 108 In flexibility she was surpassed by few singers..but for purity of tone and volume, her organ..was throaty. **1874** HULLAH *Speaking Voice* 12 Qualities to which we apply, somewhat vaguely, the epithets thick, thin, throaty, mouthy, and the like. **1876** GEO. ELIOT *Dan. Der.* xlvi, A wonderful mixture of the throaty and the nasal. **1906** *Times* 8 Nov. 11/3 Parts of her voice are very throaty in quality.

**2.** Of an animal: Having the skin about the throat too loose and pendulous; having a prominent throat or capacious swallow.

**1778** *Reading Merc. & Oxf. Gaz.* 30 Nov., A little black Welch Bullock..with a white back, grizzle head and neck throaty. *a* **1843** SOUTHEY *Comm.-pl. Bk.* (1851) IV. 400/2 Some bulls of the middle-horned breed are reproached with being throaty, the skin too profuse and pendulous. **1897** *Outing* (U.S.) XXIX. 541/2 The Spanish pointer was huge of bone, coarse in head and muzzle, very throaty.

**Throb** (þrǫb), *sb.* [f. THROB *v.*] An act of throbbing; a violent beat or pulsation of the heart or an artery.

**1579** SPENSER *Sheph. Cal.* May 208 A thrilling throbbe from her hart did aryse. **1579** LYLY *Euphues* Wks. 1902 I. 264 As the throbbes and throwes in chyldbirth wrought hir payne. **1597** — *Wom. in Moon* I. i. 171 What throbs are these that labour in my brest? **1612** tr. *Benvenuto's Passenger* II. i. § 2. 361 Throbbes, yellings, teares. **1750** JOHNSON *Rambler* No. 76 ⁋ 6 Another lenitive by which the throbs of the breast are assuaged. **1827** SCOTT *Surg. Dau.* vii, The feverish throb of his pulsation was diminished. **1852** MRS. STOWE *Uncle Tom's C.* xii, Not one throb of anguish, not one tear of the oppressed, is forgotten by the Man of Sorrows. **1889** M. GRAY *Reproach of Annesley* VI. ii, His heart gave a strong throb.

**b.** Applied to a (normal) pulsation.

**1653** JER. TAYLOR *Serm. for Year* I. xvii. 231 Though it [the heart] strikes to one side by the prerogative of Nature, yet those throbs and constant motions are felt on the other side also. **1891** E. PEACOCK *N. Brendon* I. 230 The throb of the pulse in the temple.

**c.** *transf.* and *fig.*; cf. senses of THROB *v.* In first quot. used for a (formal) lamentation: cf. THRENE.

**1626** JACKSON *Creed* VIII. xxiii. § 5 The deepe straine of this particular threne or throb. **1836** W. IRVING *Astoria* I. 243 He..felt a throb of his old pioneer spirit, impelling him to..join the adventurous band. **1868** J. H. BLUNT *Ref. Ch. Eng.* I. 333 We hear the dying throbs of that sad devotion. **1889** DOYLE *Micah Clarke* 245 There were half-a-dozen throbs of flame in the mist behind, and as many balls sung among our rigging. **1892** GUNTER *Miss Dividends* (1893) 184 Every throb of the locomotive..bears him away from Erma Travenion.

**Throb** (þrǫb), *v.* Forms: 4 (*pr. pple.*) þrobbant, (6 frob), 6–7 throbbe, 6– throb. [The pr. pple. *throbbant* occurs in Piers Plowman, 1362; no other examples of the word are known till 1542, when *frob* occurs in a letter; *throbbe, throb* is known from 1553. Apparently echoic: no cognate word in Teutonic or Romanic.]

**1.** *intr.* Of the heart: To beat strongly, esp. as the result of emotion or excitement; to palpitate. Sometimes said of the pulse, bosom, temples, brain, or even of the blood in the vessels.

**1362** [implied in THROBBING *ppl. a.*]. **1542** *St. Papers Hen. VIII*, IX. 124 My hart frobbed exceedingly. **1553** *Respublica* I. iii. 157 But een as against suche a thing my harte wyll throbbe. **1588** SHAKS. *Tit. A.* v. iii. 95 Your hearts will throb and weepe to hear him speake. **1596** SPENSER *F. Q.* IV. x. 53 Whome soone as I beheld, my hart gan throb. **1738** POPE *Epil. Sat.* i. 103 No cheek is known to blush, no heart to throb. **1741** RICHARDSON *Pamela* (1824) I. 120 O my exulting heart! how it throbs in my bosom. **1825** J. NEAL *Bro. Jonathan* III. 206 His temples throbbed—his head rang. **1848** THACKERAY *Van. Fair* xxx, His pulse was throbbing and his cheeks flushed. **1860** TYNDALL *Glac.* I. xi. 81 At each pause my heart throbbed audibly. **1865** SWINBURNE *Rococo* 55 Throbs through the heart of pleasure The purpler blood of pain.

**b.** To beat as the heart does normally; to pulsate. *rare.*

**1653** [implied in THROB *sb.* b]. **1725** N. ROBINSON *Th. Physick* 27 The Hearts of several Animals..will throb and beat, some time after they have been exempted from the Body. **1831** SCOTT *Cast. Dang.* xx, Whose cause..the champions..were bound to avenge while the blood throbbed in their veins.

**c.** *transf.* Said of the emotion or the like which affects the heart. In quot. 1591 *trans. nonce-use* (cf. *weep* = bewail). Cf. PULSATE *v.* 1 b, PULSE *v.* 2 b.

**1591** *Troub. Raigne K. John* x. 21 Deepe sorrow throbbeth misbefalne euents. **1799** HT. LEE *Canterb. T., Frenchm. T.* (ed. 2) I. 233 Fear still throbbed over her frame. **1819** BYRON *Juan* II. cxxxiv, Not even a vision of his former woes Throbb'd in accursed dreams. **1820** W. IRVING *Sketch Bk.* I. 176 The simple affections of human nature throbbing under the ermine. **1881** H. JAMES *Portr. Lady* xv, A feeling of freedom..which..occasionally throbbed into joyous excitement.

**d.** *transf.* Of a person, a body of people, etc.: To feel or exhibit emotion; to quiver.

**1841–4** EMERSON *Ess., Love* Wks. (Bohn) I. 74 We..throb at the recollection of days when happiness was not happy enough. **1862** BURTON *Bk. Hunter* (1863) 8 The world throbs with the excitement of some wonderful criminal trial. **1863** KINGLAKE *Crimea* (1877) II. xi. 124 A vast empire was made to throb with the passions which rent the bosom of the one man Nicholas. **1878** R. W. DALE *Lect. Preach.* ix. 278, I like to have two or three hymns throbbing with emotion.

**2.** *gen.* To be moved or move rhythmically; to pulsate, vibrate, beat.

**1847** EMERSON *Woodnotes* ii, And God said, 'Throb!' and there was motion, And the vast mass became vast ocean. **1865** HOLLAND *Plain T.* ii. 74 Her whole being throbbed and sparkled like the sea. **1870** MORRIS *Earthly Par.* III. IV. 15 The very air..Throbbed with sweet scent. **1889** DOYLE *Micah Clarke* 59 One great beacon throbbed upon the summit of Bulster. **1905** R. GARNETT *Shaks.* 106 The verdant level and the slow canal Shall bristle with our pikes, throb with our drums.

**b.** esp. said of a steamship with reference to the beat of the engine. Also *trans.* with *way* as obj.

**1864** LOWELL *Fireside Trav.* 111 We embarked on the little steamer M., and were soon throbbing up the lake. **1873** BLACK *Pr. Thule* viii, Then the big steamer throbbed its way out of the harbour.

**3.** *trans.* To cause to throb or beat violently. *rare.*

**1606** WARNER *Alb. Eng.* xv. xciv. (1612) 376, I know not why, but sure it throbs my heart of late. **1821** CLARE *Vill. Minstr.* II. 200 That intense, enthusiastic glow That throbs the bosom. **1911** KILPATRICK *N. T. Evangelism* 105 Samuel Rutherford..whose passionate devotion throbs his letters.

**Throbbing** (þrǫ·biŋ), *vbl. sb.* [f. THROB *v.* + -ING [1].] The action of the verb THROB in various senses; an instance of this; pulsation, beating; vibration; rhythmic movement.

**1676** WISEMAN *Chirurg. Treat.* VI. vi. 430 In the depending Orifice there was a throbbing of the Arteriall bloud. **1758** J. S. *Le Dran's Observ. Surg.* (1771) 152 He felt frequent Throbbings or Shootings in the Tumour. **1889** DOYLE *Micah Clarke* 234 On every side of us sounded the throbbing of the sea.

**Thro·bbing,** *ppl. a.* [f. as prec. + -ING [2].] That throbs; beating, pulsating.

**1362** LANGL. *P. Pl.* A. XII. 48, I..þanked hure a þousand sypes with þrobbant hert. **1592** SHAKS. *Ven. & Ad.* 1186 My throbbing hart shall rock thee day and night. **1676** WISEMAN *Chirurg. Treat.* v. ii. 355 A throbbing pain in his Wound. **1746–7** HERVEY *Medit.* (1818) 152 When violent and barbarous blows..fixed every thorn deep in his throbbing temples. **1876** T. HARDY *Ethelberta* (1890) 155 Ethelberta ..was brimming with compassion for the throbbing girl so nearly related to her. **1898** *Allbutt's Syst. Med.* V. 577 Slight periodic throbbing pains in the joints.

**b.** *transf.* and *fig.*

**1633** G. HERBERT *Temple, Storm* ii, A throbbing conscience spurred by remorse Hath a strange force. **1746–7** HERVEY *Medit.* (1818) 24 Adapted to soothe the throbbing anguish of the mourners. **1847** EMERSON *Dæmonic Love*, The throbbing sea, the quaking earth. **1864** W. CORY *Lett. & Jrnls.* (1897) 140 The throbbing scarlet of the geraniums. **1890** 'R. BOLDREWOOD' *Col. Reformer* (1891) 154 A stately ocean steamer, with throbbing screw.., left a long line of smoke trailing behind her.

Hence **Thro·bbingly** *adv.*, in a throbbing manner; with throbbing; with heart beating strongly.

*a* **1693** *Urquhart's Rabelais* III. xlviii. 389 Nor was the rapt of Polyxena more throbbingly resented. **1871** *Daily News* 14 Sept., The gunners on foot could not keep up with their pieces, and panted throbbingly after them. **1885** G. MEREDITH *Diana of the Crossways* II. xiii. 334 Letters, formally worded..but throbbingly full.

**Throbless** (þrǫ·blès), *a.* [f. THROB *sb.* + -LESS.] Without a throb or throbs; that does not throb; without or destitute of feeling or emotion.

**1748** RICHARDSON *Clarissa* (1811) VI. xiii. 67 Every heart quaking; mine, in a particular manner, sunk throbless. **1821** BYRON *Sardan.* v. i. 162 Let me..fold that throbless heart To this which beats so bitterly. **1839** J. STERLING *Poems* 221 An hour in throbless quiet live.

**Throch, throcht,** obs. Sc. ff. THROUCH, THROUGH, TROUGH.

**Throck** (þrǫk). *dial.* [OE. *þroc*, of unknown origin.] In full *plough-throck*: The share-beam; = PLOUGHHEAD I.

*a* 1000 *Ags. Gloss.* in Wr.-Wülcker 219/6 *Dentale, s. est aratri pars prima in qua uomer inducitur quasi dens*, sule-reost, *uel* þroc. 1649 BLITHE *Eng. Improv. Impr.* xxviii. (1653) 190 For the Plough-head, some call them the Plough-throck, some the Plough-chip. 1688 R. HOLME *Armoury* III. 333/2 The Throck [of a Plow] is the piece of Timber on which the Suck is fixed. 1893 *S. E. Worc. Gloss.*, *Throck*, the lower part of a (wooden) plough. On the end of the throck the ploughshare is fixed.

**Throd, Throdden,** *pa. pple.*: see THRO *v.* Hence **Throdden** *v.*, *north. dial. intr.*, to grow, to thrive: see quots.

1641 BEST *Farm. Bks.* (Surtees) 5 Neyther will it [a lamb] throden (as the shepheardes say) till such time as the cowe milke bee all voyded. 1690 RAY *N. C. Words* 75 To *Throdden*; to grow, to thrive, to wax, to sturken. 1877 KATH. MACQUOID *Doris Barugh* i, T' stock throddens weel. 1894 *Northumb. Gloss.*, *Throdden*, to make grow, to thrive. Hence *throdden* and *throddy*, plump, fat, well thriven.

**Throe, † throw(e** (þrōu), *sb.* Forms: *α.* 3 (?) **þrahe,** 4–5 **þraue, þrawe, thrawe,** 4–6 **thrau(e,** (4 **traue**), 4–5 (*Sc.* 6–) **thraw** (þrǭ, þrā). *β.* 3–4 **þrowe,** 4–7 **throwe,** (4 **throghe**), 6–8 **throw.** *γ.* 7– **throe.** [*Throe* is a late alteration (noted first in 1615) of the earlier *throwe, throw* (which survived as late as 1733). The origin and history of ME. *þrowe* (found *c* 1200), and its northern form *þraw(e, þraw, thrau* (known *c* 1300, and still in use in Sc.) is not quite clear.

The normal source of an Eng. *ōw* : Sc. *aw*, as in *blow* : *blaw, crow* : *craw, snow* : *snaw*, is an OE. *áw*; this would lead us to see in *þrow(e* : *þraw(e*, an early derivative from the verb *þrowen* : *þrawen*, OE. *þráwan*, THROW *v.*[1], in its early sense 'to twist, rack, torture' (cf. THROW *v.*[1] I, quots. *c* 1000). Some suggest that the sb. represented OE. *þrawu*, 'painful infliction, affliction, plague, pang, evil' (Bosw.-Toller), which is perh. favoured by the instance *c* 1250 of *þrahes* riming with *lahes* 'laws' (if that belongs here). But *þrawu* would normally give in midland and southern Eng. not *throwe* but *thrawe* (cf. CLAW). On the other hand, a derivation (also suggested) from OE. *þrówian*, THROW *v.*[2] 'to suffer', which would suit Eng. *throw*, would not explain the northern *thraw*. If then the word was orig. the OE. *þrawu*, we should have to suppose that this by 1200 (under the influence of *þrówian* to suffer) became *þrōwe*, but remained in the north as *þrawe, thraw*, and eventually ran together with *thraw*, THROW *sb.*[2], from *thraw*, THROW *v.*[1]

The identity of *throe* with ME. *throwe*, makes its derivation from OE. *þrá*, ME. THRO, THRA *sb.* impossible. The change of *throw(e* to *throe* was app. merely quasi-phonetic; cf. *hoe, roe* (of fish) for earlier *howe, rowe*, also *bloe* as a 16th c. variant of *blow* sb., and on the other hand *slow-worm* for *slo-worm*, OE. *slá-wyrm*; *throe* would gain favour as making a distinction between this word and *throw* sb.[2] in its ordinary English use. In Scotland, on the other hand, where *thraw* vb. has kindred senses, *thraw* remains unchanged as the form of this sb., as in *deid-thraw* = death-throe.]

**1.** A violent spasm or pang, such as convulses the body, limbs, or face. Also, a spasm of feeling; a paroxysm; agony of mind; anguish.

**a.** In general sense.

*α.* *c* 1325 *Metr. Hom.* 36 Welthe to pride our hert draus, And wa geres us thol hard traues [*MS. C.* thrawes; *rime* draus]. ? *a* 1500 *Chester Plays* (E.E.T.S.) 438 Suffer I must many a hard Thraw. 1673 *Wedderburn's Vocab.* 19 (Jam.) *Tormen alvi*, a thraw in the bellie. 1793 BURNS *Blithe hae I been* ii, If she winna ease the thraws In my bosom swelling.

*β.* *c* 1374 CHAUCER *Troylus* v. 206 Troylus..his sorwes þat he spared hadde He yaf an yssue large..And in his þrowes frenetyk and madde He curssed loue. 1390 GOWER *Conf.* III. 273 And for thin ese..Thi love throghes forto lisse. 1549 J. CHEKE in *Lett. Lit. Men* (Camden) 8 How honorable is it to fli from honors throws. 1597 GERARDE *Herbal* I. xxi. § 2. 27 The throwes and gripings of the bellie. 1607 SHAKS. *Timon* v. i. 203 Their pangs of Loue, with other incident throwes That Natures fragile Vessell doth sustaine. 1719 DE FOE *Crusoe* (Hotten's repr.) 408 Frequent Throws and Pangs of Appetite, that nothing but the Tortures of Death can imitate.

*γ.* 1730–46 THOMSON *Autumn* 1322 His heart distends With gentle throes. 1787 BURNS *Let. to Earl of Glencairn*, I conjure your lordship, by the honest throe of gratitude. 1814 SCOTT *Ld. of Isles* II. i, But ask thou not..If the loud laugh disguise convulsive throe. 1860 C. SANGSTER *Hesperus*, etc. 166 Tumultuous throes Of some vast grief. 1870 DISRAELI *Lothair* lvi, In the very throes of its fell despair.

*spec.* **b.** The pain and struggle of childbirth; *pl.* labour-pangs.

*α.* *c* 1250 *Comp. Mariæ* in Napier *Hist. Rood-t.* 78 Nou þu moostes, lauedi, lere Wmmone wo þat barnes bere, Þa bitter and ta bale þrahes [*MS.* þrehes; *rime* lahes (laws)]. 13.. *K. Alis.* 606 Time is come the lady schal childe:.. The thrawes [*Bodl. MS.* þrowen] hire afongon.

*β.* *c* 1200 *Trin. Coll. Hom.* 181 Elch wimman..þan hie beȝ mid childe bistonden..nimeð hire stundmele so bittere þrowes. *Ibid.*, Ðat child on his burde þoleð ec bittere þrowe. *c* 1290 *S. Eng. Leg.* I. 472/354 Hire token ful strongue þrowes. 1390 GOWER *Conf.* III. 211 This hell [= hill] on his childinge lay, And whan the throwes on him come His noise..Was ferfull. *c* 1440 *Promp. Parv.* 493/1 Throwe, womannys pronge. 1613 PURCHAS *Pilgrimage* VIII. xiv. 685 All the throwes..of this hills monstrous trauells. 1690 C. NESSE *Hist. & Myst. O. & N. Test.* I. 52 The throws in birth be so torturing as no kind of torments can parallel. 1733 CHEYNE *Eng. Malady* II. x. § 3 (1734) 220 The *Fœtus*, by its Motion or Pressure, raises those Throws and Convulsions in the Mother.

*γ.* 1615 CHAPMAN *Odyss.* XIX. 565 Moane for my daughters yet vnended throes. 1621 QUARLES *Esther* Div. Poems (1717) 131 By throes, God sends a joyful birth. 1667 MILTON *P. L.* II. 780 My womb..Prodigious motion felt and rueful throes. 1715–20 POPE *Iliad* XVII. 6 Her new-fall'n young..Fruit of her throes. 1742 YOUNG *Nt. Th.* I. 241 In this shape, or in that, has fate entail'd The mother's throes on all of woman born.

**c.** The agony of death; the death-struggle, death-throe (Sc. *deid-thraw*).

*α.* *a* 1300 *Cursor M.* 24317 (Cott.) Wit hard thraus [*Ed.* thrauis, *F.* þrawes, *G.* thraues] þat he throu, Þai sagh þat he to ded drou. *Ibid.* 24726 (Edin.) Euir apon his þraues [*Gött.* passiun] þink. *Ibid.* 16762+64 (Cott.) For þe grete thraws of ded. *c* 1440 *Alphabet of Tales* 358 Hur husband lay in dead thrawis. 1549 *Compl. Scotl.* xiv. 121 Quhen darius vas in the agonya and deitht thrau. *a* 1823 G. BEATTIE *John o' Arnha'* (1826) 39 Some glowr'd an' thratch'd, in deadly thraws.

*β.* 13.. *K. Alis.* 720 (Bodl. MS.) In his deþ þrowe he was swowe. *c* 1330 *Asump. Virg.* 533 ȝif any..wille on his last þrowe Schryue him. 1590 SPENSER *F. Q.* I. x. 41 O man! have mind of that last bitter throw. 1629 SIR W. MURE *True Crucifixe* 1581 Death's tormenting throws.

*γ.* 1814 SCOTT *Wav.* lxix, The throes of a mortal and painful disorder. 1833 HT. MARTINEAU *Tale of Tyne* vi. 113 The agony of..outrage transcends the throes of dissolution.

**2.** *transf.* and *fig.* A violent convulsion or struggle preceding or accompanying the 'bringing forth' of something.

1698 CROWNE *Caligula* III. 18 For that poor chaff how will he thrash his brains, He is in throws before, but then he's eas'd. 1856 FROUDE *Hist. Eng.* (1858) II. ix. 373 When a nation is in the throes of revolution, wild spirits are abroad in the storm. 1860 TYNDALL *Glac.* I. viii. 59 A..scene, suggesting throes of spasmodic energy. 1878 MISS J. J. YOUNG *Ceram. Art* (1879) 125 The author is represented seated at a table..in the very throes of composition.

**3.** *attrib.* and *Comb.*

1835 STERLING in Carlyle *Life* II. ii. (1872) 101 The restless immaturity of our self-consciousness, and the promise of its long throe-pangs. 1839 BAILEY *Festus* xxxiv. (1852) 552 Awhile in dead throe-like suspense they stood. 1883 *Century Mag.* Oct. 819/1 The wild, throe-built, water-quarried rock gorges.

**Throe, † throw(e,** *v. rare.* [f. prec. sb.]

**† 1.** *trans.* To cause to suffer throes; to agonize as in childbirth; to torture. *Obs. rare.*

1610 SHAKS. *Temp.* II. i. 231 A birth..Which throwes thee much to yeeld. 1683 KENNETT tr. *Erasm. on Folly* 51 How many..pangs of a labouring mind ye are perpetually thrown and tortured with.

**2.** *intr.* To suffer throes; to agonize; to be convulsed, 'labour', struggle painfully.

*a* 1618 [see below]. 1880 L. WALLACE *Ben-Hur* (1887) 388 His memory began to throe and struggle.

Hence **Throeing** *vbl. sb.*

*a* 1618 SYLVESTER *Honour's Fare-well* 105 Soul's sad Repenting, and Heart's heavy Throeing, Are surest Fruits that in the World are growing.

**Throe,** obs. form of THRO *a.*, stubborn, etc.

**† Throll.** *Obs.* [app. related to THRILL *sb.*[1]] A nostril or breathing hole.

*c* 1430 *Bk. Hawkyng* in *Rel. Ant.* I. 301 But if it have hastely help it wol stop his nare throlles. 1555 *Douglas's Æneis* VII. x. 59 Ane horribill caue..ane throll [*ed. Small* thyrll], or aynding stede, Of terribill Pluto.

**† Thro·ly,** *a. Obs. rare.* [app. f. THRO, THRA *sb.* (or ? *a.*) + -LY [1].] Vehement, persistent, painful.

*c* 1350 *Will. Palerne* 612 Al comes of a þroly þouȝt þat þirles min hert. *Ibid.* 910. *Ibid.* 3518 Þe þroli þouȝt þat him meued..sone he let ouer-slide.

**† Thro·ly, thra·ly,** *adv. Obs.* Also 4 **þroliche, throle.** [f. THRO, THRA *a.* + -LY [2].] In a 'thro' manner; obstinately; angrily, furiously, fiercely, violently; eagerly, keenly.

13.. *Cursor M.* 196 (Cott.) Iuus iesu oft..for his sermon thrali thrette [so *F.*]. *Ibid.* 880 (C.) Mi fere, Þat þou me gaf mi wijf to be; Ful thrali [so *F.*; *G.* stiffli] first sco bedde it me. 1340–70 *Alisaunder* 215 Hee thought on this thing þroliche in hert. *c* 1350 *Will. Palerne* 103 He..þroliche þonked god mani þousand siþes. 1362 LANGL. *P. Pl.* A. IX. 107 Þroly we eoden Disputyng on Dowel. ? *a* 1400 *Morte Arth.* 1150 Þe theefe at þe dede thrawe so throly hyme thryngez, Þat three rybbys in his syde he thrystez in sundere. *a* 1400–50 *Alexander* 707 (Dubl. MS.) Thik & thraly [*MS. Ashm.* þrathly] am I thrett & thole must I sone Þe slauughter of my awne sonne. *c* 1400 *Destr. Troy* 1987 [It] Thonret full throly with a thicke haile. *Ibid.* 7040 Throly the þre men thronght hym aboute. *c* 1450 *St. Cuthbert* (Surtees) 5705 Þe man thraly Forth on his way he ȝode. 1535 STEWART *Cron. Scot.* (Rolls) I. 407 So thralie than togidder that thai thrist, That speiris brak.

**Throm,** obs. form of THRUM.

**Thro·mbase.** *Physiol. Chem.* [mod. f. Gr. θρόμβ-ος clot, THROMBUS + *-ase*, after *diastase.*] A synonym of thrombin (on the assumption that that is an enzyme).

1908 BAYLISS *Nature of Enzymes* 73 According to Morawitz there exists in circulating blood a body 'thrombogen', which can be converted by a 'thrombokinase' present in all tissues into a precursor of the enzyme which acts upon fibrinogen to form fibrin. This precursor, or prothrombase, is changed into the active thrombase by calcium ions.

**Thrombin** (þrǫ·mbin). *Physiol. Chem.* [mod. f. as prec. + -IN.] The substance which by interaction with fibrinogen gives rise to fibrin, and is hence the immediate cause of the clotting of shed blood; fibrin-ferment.

1898 *E. A. Schäfer's Text-bk. Physiol.* I. 160 Fibrin-ferment (thrombin) or its precursor (prothrombin) producing the formation of fibrin from fibrinogen. 1900 E. H. STARLING *Elem. Hum. Physiol.* iii. (ed. 4) 78 The coagulation of the blood is due to the conversion of a soluble proteid present in the plasma—fibrinogen, into an insoluble proteid—fibrin, under the agency of a ferment, which is known as fibrin ferment or thrombin.

**Thrombo-** (þrǫ·mbo), before a vowel **thromb-,** combining form of Gr. θρόμβο-ς THROMBUS, a formative in some pathological and chemical terms, as **Thro·mbo-arteri·tis,** arterial inflammation producing thrombosis; **Thro·mbocyst** [mod.L. *thrombocystis* (Dunglison, 1857)], a cyst surrounding a clot of blood; **Thro·mbogen,** a hypothetical substance in the blood which converts fibrinogen into fibrin; the proenzyme of the fibrin-ferment; hence **Thromboge·nic** *a.*, of or pertaining to thrombogen; producing coagulation; **Thro·mbokinase** (-kinēⁱs): see quot. s. v. THROMBASE; **Thrombophlebi·tis,** phlebitis due to obstruction of the vein by a thrombus.

1890 BILLINGS *Nat. Med. Dict.*, *Thromboarteritis. 1899 *Allbutt's Syst. Med.* VI. 205 An acute infective disease without anatomical lesions other than the thrombo-phlebitis, or thrombo-arteritis. 1860 MAYNE *Expos. Lex.* 1274/2 A cyst or membrane containing a clot of blood: a *thrombocyst. 1899 *Syd. Soc. Lex.*, **Thrombogen*, producing or giving rise to clots. *Ibid.*, **Thrombogenic enzyme*, an unorganised ferment having the power to cause clotting. 1908 Thrombogen, *Thrombokinase [see THROMBASE]. 1896 *Allbutt's Syst. Med.* I. 654 *Thrombo-phlebitis and localised abscesses are by no means uncommon.

**Thromboid** (þrǫ·mboid), *a. Path.* [f. Gr. θρόμβος clot of blood + -OID; cf. Gr. θρομβοειδής full of clots.] Resembling a thrombus.

1860 in MAYNE *Expos. Lex.* 1899 in *Syd. Soc. Lex.*

**Thrombolite** (þrǫ·mbolait). *Min.* [ad. Ger. *thrombolith* (Breithaupt, 1838), f. Gr. θρόμβ-ος in sense 'curd', in allusion to its appearance + -LITE.] A mineral, found in amorphous masses, containing the oxides of copper and antimony; perh. a mixture.

1844–68 DANA *Min.* (ed. 5) 562 Thrombolite...Amorphous. ..Color emerald-, leek-, or dark green...Found with malachite in a fine-grained limestone at Retzbanya, Hungary.

**Thrombosed** (þrǫ·mbōᵘzd), *a.* [f. implied vb. **thrombose* (f. THROMBOSIS) + -ED [1].] Affected with thrombosis.

1873 T. H. GREEN *Introd. Pathol.* (ed. 2) 327 These vessels communicate with the cavity of the thrombosed vessel. 1906 *Lancet* 27 Oct. 1142/1 The sinus was not thrombosed.

‖ **Thrombosis** (þrǫmbōᵘ·sis). [mod.L., a. Gr. θρόμβωσις a curdling, f. θρομβοῦσθαι to become curdled or clotted, f. θρόμβος THROMBUS: see -OSIS.] † A coagulation or curdling (*obs. rare*); *spec. Path.* a local coagulation of the blood in any part of the vascular system during life, the formation of a thrombus.

1706 PHILLIPS (ed. Kersey), *Thrombosis*, a congealing, or clotting together of any thing. 1866 A. FLINT *Princ. Med.* (1880) 28 The causes of thrombosis are, first, changes in the walls of the vessels, and, second, retardation of the circulation. 1891 *Lancet* 2 May 1003/2 In consequence of venous thrombosis in the right lower extremity. 1904 *Times* 20 Aug. 5/3 Lady H—— died..from an attack of pulmonary thrombosis.

**Thrombotic** (þrǫmbǫ·tik), *a.* [ad. Gr. type *θρομβωτικ-ός: see prec. and -OTIC.] Of, pertaining to, of the nature of, or caused by thrombosis.

1866 A. FLINT *Princ. Med.* (1880) 330 Portions of the granular or of the thrombotic deposits may be carried into the circulation as emboli. 1899 *Allbutt's Syst. Med.* VII. 224 The lesions were probably thrombotic.

‖ **Thrombus** (þrǫ·mbŏs). *Path.* [mod.L., a. Gr. θρόμβος lump, piece, clot of blood, curd of milk.] **† a.** A small tumour occasioned by the escape of blood from a vein into the adjacent cellular tissue, and its coagulation there. *Obs.* **b.** A fibrinous clot which forms in a blood-vessel and obstructs the circulation.

*Milk thrombus*, a tumour caused by accumulation of milk in the ducts during lactation (*Funk's Standard Dict.*, 1895).

1693 tr. *Blancard's Phys. Dict.* (ed. 2), *Thrombus*, the Coagulation of Blood or Milk into Clots or Clusters. 1706 PHILLIPS (ed. Kersey), *Thrombus*...Among Surgeons a small Swelling that arises after the Operation of Bloud-letting, when the Orifice is made too small. 1866 A. FLINT *Princ. Med.* (1880) 28 A coagulum formed during life in the heart or in the vessels is called a *thrombus.* 1873 RALFE *Phys. Chem.* 16 A thrombus blocks up a cerebral artery, and acute softening of the cerebral substance supplied by that artery is the result. 1901 OSLER *Princ. & Pract. Med.* i. 12 Inflammation of the arteries with thrombus formation has been frequently described in typhoid fever.

**Throme, thromm(e,** obs. ff. THRUM *sb.*[2]

**Thron, þron,** obs. contr. form of THEREON.

**Thronal** (þrōᵘ·năl), *a. rare.* [f. L. *thron-us* THRONE + -AL.] Of or pertaining to a throne; befitting or of the nature of a throne.

*a* 1711 KEN *Hymnotheo* Poet. Wks. 1721 III. 205 His Standard he erects of Thronal Light.

**Throne** (þrōᵘn), *sb.* Forms: *α.* 3–6 **trone,** (4 **tron, tronne,** 4–5 **troone,** 4–6 *Sc.* **trown, trowne,** 5 **troyne,** 5–6 *Sc.* **troune,** 6 *Sc.* **trune**). *β.* 3– **throne,** (4 **thron,** 6–7 **throan**). [a. OF. *trone* (12th c. in Godef. *Compl.*), mod.F. *trône*, ad. L. *thron-us*, a. Gr. θρόνος an elevated seat.]

**1.** The seat of state of a potentate or dignitary; *esp.* the seat occupied by a sovereign on state occasions; formerly often an elaborate elevated structure, richly ornamented; now a more or less ornate chair, with a footstool, usually placed upon a dais and standing under a canopy.

*α.* **a 1240** *Sawles Warde* in *Cott. Hom.* 259 Sitten in a trone se swiðe briht wid ȝimmes i-stirret. **c 1290** *S. Eng. Leg.* I. 93/35 Þe Aumperour sat In is trone. **a 1300** *Cursor M.* 9944 (Cott.) Wit-in þis tour..Es sett a tron [*Gött.* trone]. **c 1425** *Cast. Persev.* 459 in *Macro Plays* 91 *Mundus.* Now I sytte in my semly sale; I trotte & tremle in my trew trone...Kyng, knyth & kayser, to me makyn mone. **1535** STEWART *Cron. Scot.* (Rolls) I. 94 Brutell beistis set vp in ane trune [*rime* mune]. **a 1548** HALL *Chron.*, *Hen. VI* 177 The trone royall, vnder the clothe of estate.

*β.* **1390** GOWER *Conf.* III. 167 Wher he was in his real Throne. **c 1400** MAUNDEV. (1839) xx. 217 The Emperoures throne fulle high, where he sytteth at the mete. **1570** LEVINS *Manip.* 168/10 A Throne, *thronus, ni.* **1591** DRAYTON *Harmonie of Ch.* (Percy Soc.) 20 See where Salomon is set In royal throan. **1611** BIBLE *Matt.* xix. 28 Ye also shal sit vpon twelue thrones, iudging the twelue tribes of Israel. **1732** LEDIARD *Sethos* II. VII. 32 A throne of red wood, rais'd by five steps. **1855** PUSEY *Doctr. Real Presence* Note S. 390 Make thy left hand as if a throne for thy right.

**b.** The seat occupied by a pope or bishop on ceremonial occasions.

**c 1380** WYCLIF *Wks.* (1880) 457 Þe pope sittiþ in his troone & makiþ lordis to kisse his feet. **a 1533** LD. BERNERS *Huon* lxii. 216 They founde the pope set in his trone. **1726** AYLIFFE *Parergon* 121 In those Times, the Bishops preach'd on the Steps of the Altar.., having not as yet assum'd to themselves the Pride and State of a Throne. **1845** M. PATTISON *Ess.* (1889) I. 15 No chair of dignified ease was a bishop's throne in the sixth century. **1910** *Kelly's Directory of Oxford*, The Cathedral... The bishop's throne .. was erected as a memorial to the late Bishop Wilberforce.

**c.** A seat provided by portrait-painters for their sitters: see quot. 1859.

**1838** DICKENS *Nich. Nick.* x, A very faded chair raised upon a very dusty throne in Miss La Creevy's room. **1859** GULLICK & TIMBS *Paint.* 199 The Throne is the name portrait painters give the chair provided for their 'sitters', from the circumstance of its being placed on a raised daïs covered usually with red cloth.

**2.** As the seat of a deity, esp. of God or Christ. *The throne of grace* or simply *the throne*, the mercy-seat, the place where God is conceived as seated to answer prayer.

*α.* **a 1240** *Ureisun* in *Cott. Hom.* 191 Þu ert hore blostme biuoren godes trone. **c 1375** *Sc. Leg. Saints* xviii. (*Egipciane*) 794 Þu sittis with god in til his trowne. **1382** WYCLIF *Heb.* iv. 16 Therfore go we with trist to the trone of his grace. **1393** LANGL. *P. Pl.* C. II. 134 Þe trone þat trinite ynne sitteþ. **1398** TREVISA *Barth. De P. R.* I. (1495) 8 Cryste Iesus..syttyng in his trone of jugement. **1508** FISHER 7 *Penit. Ps.* vi. Wks. (1876) 9 Euery man & woman shall stande before the trone of almyghty god. **1526** TINDALE *Rev.* xiv. 5 They are with outen spott before the trone off God. **1559** *Mirr. Mag.* (1563) V iij, The trone of mighty Jove.

*β.* **c 1290** *Beket* 2304 in *S. Eng. Leg.* I. 172 Bi-fore ore louerd sone..ase he sat in is throne. **1552** *Bk. Com. Prayer, Morn. Pr., Exhort.*, The throne of the heauenlie grace. **1662** GURNALL *Chr. in Arm.* verse 17. xiii. III. 101 It sends them to the Throne of Grace. **c 1765** M. BRUCE *Hymn*, '*Where high* [etc.]' vi, With boldness, therefore, at the throne, Let us make all our sorrows known. **1849** W. K. TWEEDIE *Life J. MacDonald* 157 It was made a frequent errand to the throne. **1875** BP. BICKERSTETH *Hymn*, '*Peace, perfect peace*', Jesus we know, and He is on the throne.

**†3.** In the phrase *in* (*on*) *throne*: enthroned; esp. as said of God or Christ. *Obs.*

**a 1225** *Ancr. R.* 40 Þi swete blisfule sune..sette þe ine trone. **a 1340** HAMPOLE *Psalter* ix. 4 Þou sittis on trone þ[t] demys rightwisnes. **1340** — *Pr. Consc.* 5080 Hyde us Fra þe face of hym þat syttes in throne. **c 1380** *Sir Ferumb.* 162, Y swere by cryst in trone. **c 1440** *R. Gloucester's Chron.* (Rolls) App. XX. 446 To king he was iblessed at londone ywis & iset in trone [*v.r.* ine throne]. **c 1500** *New Notbr. Mayd* 464 in Hazl. *E. P. P.* III. 19 Ye syttynge in throne. **a 1600** MONTGOMERIE *Misc. Poems* xli. 44 With shyning bright shieldis [As] Titan in trone.

**4.** *fig.* A seat or position of dominion or supremacy; *spec.* in *Astrol.*: see quot. 1819.

**a 1548** HALL *Chron.*, *Hen. VI* 149 b, This Marques thus gotten vp, into fortunes trone. **1654** WHITLOCK *Zootomia* 361 The Pulpit a Throne of higher Authority..rewarding with Promises of far more elevating Hopes than any earthly one can. **1819** JAS. WILSON *Compl. Dict. Astrol.* s. v., Any part of a sign where a planet has two or more testimonies, *i. e.* essential dignities, is called its throne, chariot, of any other foolish name that comes to hand. **1855** BREWSTER *Newton* II. xiv. 23 [Leibnitz] had nearly placed himself on the throne which Newton was destined to ascend. **18..** B. TAYLOR *In the Meadows* Poems (1866) 299 The sun on his midday throne. **1892** HENLEY *Song of Sword*, etc. 45 We tracked the winds of the world to the steps of their very thrones.

**5.** *transf.* The position, office, or dignity of a sovereign; sovereign power or authority, dominion.

**a 1300** *Cursor M.* 22122 In þe temple o salamon Þan sal þat traitur sett his tron. **1387** TREVISA *Higden* (Rolls) III. 245 Artarxerses..saued his fader trone and his broþer lyf. **1474** CAXTON *Chesse* II. i. (1883) 20 Mysericorde and trouthe conserue and kepe the kynge in his trone. **1534** MORE *Comf. agst. Trib.* II. Wks. 1199/2, I will..set my trone on the sides of y[e] north. **1593** SHAKS. 3 *Hen. VI*, II. i. 193 The next degree, is Englands Royall Throne. **1696** PHILLIPS (ed. 5) s. v., *Throne* also Synecdochycally is taken for Supream Command, or Soveraign Authority of those that sit upon the Throne. **1750** GRAY *Elegy* 67 To wade through slaughter to a throne. **1848** W. H. KELLY tr. *L. Blanc's Hist. Ten Y.* II. 84 Worthy..of occupying the first place in the state beneath the throne. **1849** HELPS *Friends in C.* II. i. (1854) I. 267 Mighty thrones and distant empires.

**b.** *Throne and altar*, the civil and ecclesiastical systems as established; cf. *church and state* (CHURCH *sb.* 18); hence used *attrib.*

**1822** *Edin. Rev.* XXXVII. 420 The poetical representation of the..Throne-and-Altar class. **1885** *Pall Mall G.* 12 Jan. 4/2 Two currents ran through the auditory. Gentlemen of high life and throne and altar journalists were hostile. Radical journalists .. were brimful of sympathy. **1908** *Expositor* June 558 The guardian of the nation's throne and altar.

**6.** *transf.* Put for the occupant of the throne; the sovereign.

**1762** GOLDSM. *Cit. W.* xlii, 'Here', cried he, addressing himself to the throne. **1818** LD. ALTHORP in *Parl. Deb.* 21 A time when they had to offer their condolence to the throne.

**7.** (With capital T.) *pl.* In mediæval angelology, The third of the nine orders of angels (see ORDER *sb.* 5).

**13..** *Ipotis* 93 (Vern. MS.) in Horstm. *Altengl. Leg.* (1881) 342 Þe þridde [order] is cleped Trones. **1398** TREVISA *Barth. De P. R.* II. x. (1495) b vj/2 The thyrde Ordre [of angels] is the ordre of Thrones, and hath the name of the yefte of dome, for god syttyth in theym, and yeuyth his domes. **1584** R. SCOT *Discov. Witchcr.* xv. ii. (1886) 315 Twentie legions of divels, partlie of the order of vertues, & partlie of the order of thrones. **1667** MILTON *P. L.* v. 601 Thrones, Dominations, Princedoms, Vertues, Powers. **a 1711** KEN *Hymnotheo* Poet. Wks. 1721 III. 201 Thrones, who God's Judgments hear, and then proclaim. **c 1850** NEALE *Hymns East. Ch.* (1866) 134 Thrones, Principalities, Virtues, and Powers.

**8.** *attrib.* and *Comb.*, as *throne adversary, -bearer, -chair, -city, gallery, -power, -rail, -room, -seat*, † *-sitter, -step*; *throne-capable, -like, -shattering, -worthy* adjs.; **throne-born** *a.*, born of a sovereign parentage; of royal birth; **throne-name**, a name given on ascending the throne.

**1651** *Serm. Coron. Chas. II at Scoon* in *Phenix* I. 266 A word of Encouragement against *Throne Adversaries. Your Enemies are the Enemies of the Lord's Throne. **1855** BAILEY *Mystic* etc., *Spir. Leg.* 131 Some crowned and sword-girt conqueror *Throne-born. **1851** SIR F. PALGRAVE *Norm. & Eng.* I. 547 There was only one clearly acknowledged legitimate heir or *throne-capable representative of Charlemagne. **1814** SIR R. WILSON *Diary* (1861) II. 344 Murat was seated as a Sultan—princes and dukes all standing behind his *throne-chair. **1906** *Westm. Gaz.* 6 June 1/3 The procession then proceeds to the *throne gallery. **1894** *Ibid.* 30 June 5/1 Two *thronelike chairs of larger growth stood in the centre. **c 1875** *Queen's Printers' Bible-Aids* 139 The people make Shallum..King, he taking the *throne-name of Jehoahaz. **1864** SIR T. SEATON *From Cadet to Colonel* xvii. 361 The interior room is the King's *throne-room. **1889** *John Bull* 2 Mar. 149/2 The Queen.. entered the Throne-room shortly after three o'clock. **1816** J. WILSON *City of Plague* 51 Lurid stars Prophetic of *throne-shattering wars. **1552** HULOET, *Trone sytter, or he that sytteth in maiestie, *altitronus.*

**Throne** (þrōᵘn), *v.* [f. prec. sb.]

**1.** *trans.* To place on or as on a throne; esp. as symbolic of accession to sovereignty: = ENTHRONE.

**1377** LANGL. *P. Pl.* B. I. 131 Þer treuthe is in Trinitee and troneth [A. I. 122 corouneþ; *v. r.* tronen] hem alle. **1387–8** T. USK *Test. Love* I. ii. (Skeat) l. 94, I lefte it for no tene, till he was troned in my blisse for his seruice. **a 1400** *Pistill of Susan* 90 Turtils troned on trene. **1508** KENNEDIE *Flyting w. Dunbar* 400, I sall..with tresone trone the on the treis. **1549** LATIMER 2*nd Serm. bef. Edw. VI* (Arb.) 58 Thus was Salomon throned, by the aduise and wyl of hys father. **1599** B. JONSON *Cynthia's Rev.* Induct., Why, throne your selfe in state on the stage. **1601** SHAKS. *Twel. N.* II. iv. 22 The seate Where loue is thron'd. **1624** F. WHITE *Repl. Fisher* 56 He trode vpon the necke of kings, throning and dethroning, crowning and decrowning them. **1673** MILTON *True Relig.* 10 The Pope..Thrones and Unthrones Kings. **1715–20** POPE *Iliad* VIII. 551 Th' eternal thunderer sat thron'd in gold. **1792** *Anecd. W. Pitt* III. xliii. 154 Mercy can do no harm, it will seat the King where he ought to be, throned on the hearts of his people. **1815** SCOTT *Guy M.* xi, Mrs. Mac-Candlish, throned in a comfortable easy chair..was regaling herself..with a cup of genuine tea. **1864** R. S. HAWKER *Quest Sangraal* 16 Foremost sad Lancelot, throned upon his Steed. **1866** CONINGTON *Virg. Æneid* VII. 686 To throne him in the seat of power. **1884** TENNYSON *Becket* I. iii. 70 That the King Would throne me in the great Archbishoprick.

**2.** *intr.* To be enthroned; to sit on or as on a throne; to sit in state. Often *to throne it.*

**1607** SHAKS. *Cor.* v. iv. 26 He wants nothing of a God but Eternity, and a Heauen to Throne in. **1848** *Blackw. Mag.* LXIII. 768 He throned it always like a tragedy king. **1903** LD. R. GOWER *Rec. & Remin.* 358 After seeing my Shakespeare [group statue] throning it in the centre of the Palais d'Industrie [Paris]. **1904** R. J. FARRER *Garden of Asia* 139 The abbot of imperial blood no longer thrones among the pines of Uyeno. **1905** *Westm. Gaz.* 20 Mar. 2/2 The sofa on which she had throned.

Hence **Thro·ning** *vbl. sb.*, enthronement.

**c 1400** MAUNDEV. (1839) xvi. 175 The dedicacioun of the chirche, & the thronynge [*Roxb.* tronyng] of the ydole.

**Throned** (þrōᵘnd, *poet.* þrōᵘ·nėd), *ppl. a.*

**1.** [f. THRONE *v.* + -ED [1].] Seated on or as on a throne; enthroned. Also in comb., as *heaven-throned.*

**c 1440** *York Myst.* xxvi. 86 Oure tempill is þe toure Of his troned sire. **1596** SHAKS. *Merch. V.* IV. i. 189 [Mercy] becomes The throned Monarch better then his Crowne. **1606** — *Ant. & Cl.* I. iii. 28 Though you in swearing shake the Throaned Gods. **1621** G. SANDYS *Ovid's Met.* XI. (1632) 374 Ioue shunnes the bed Of Sea-thron'd Thetis. **1760–72** H. BROOKE *Fool of Qual.* (1809) IV. 14 Adam..had been constituted a throned lord and controller. **1839** BAILEY *Festus* xi. (1852) 136 Hear Thou, Heaven-throned! **1906** *Daily Chron.* 25 Sept. 3/4 In the song of the minor poet we often recognise the faint echo of a throned master.

**2.** [? f. THRONE *sb.*] (*a*) Having a throne; (*b*) Made like a throne.

**1801** S. TURNER *Anglo-Sax.* III. iii. II. 59 A work which pretends to give to Denmark a throned existence [before Christ]. **1852** THACKERAY *Esmond* II. vi, The old Dean on his throned stall.

**Thronedom** (þrōᵘ·ndəm). *rare.* [f. THRONE *sb.* + -DOM.] The dominion of a throne; the position implied by a throne.

**1820** J. H. WIFFEN *Aonian Hours* (ed. 2) 48 Of this frame Empires and thronedoms have been, and are made. **1859** SALA *Tw. round Clock* (1861) 165 The late Grand Duke of Tuscany..has been signally kicked off thronedom.

**Throneless** (þrōᵘ·nlės), *a.* [f. as prec. + -LESS.] Without a throne; deposed from a throne.

**1814** BYRON *Ode to Nap.* xiii, Thou throneless Homicide. **1846** W. E. AYTOUN *Lays Sc. Cavaliers* (1849) 213 Fitting for the throneless exile. **1897** TROTTER *Life J. Nicholson* x. (1908) 149 A throneless pensioner of the Indian Government.

**Thronelet** (þrōᵘ·nlėt). [f. as prec. + -LET.] A little or miniature throne.

**1648** HERRICK *Hesper.*, *Transfiguration*, When thou art set In thy refulgent thronelet.

**† Thro·nely,** *a. Obs. rare.* [f. as prec. + -LY [1].] Pertaining to the throne; applied to certain ranks of angels: see quots., and cf. THRONE *sb.* 7.

**1486** *Bk. St. Albans, Her.* a iv, Ther be ix orderys of angelis, v. Jerarchie & iiij. Tronly. *Ibid.* a iv b, The iiij. Tronli be theys Principatus Trony Cherubyn and Seraphyn. **1586** FERNE *Blaz. Gentrie* 143 The cullors in this Coate, namely, white blew & guoles..are referred to the orders of Angels which be Thronely.

**† Thro·neship.** *Obs. rare*⁻¹. [-SHIP.] Occupancy or tenure of a throne; sovereignty; reign.

**1599** NASHE *Lenten Stuffe* 10 That manner of prouostship or gouernment remained in full force and vertue all their fowre throneships, alias a hundred yeare.

**† Thro·ness, thra·ness.** *Obs. rare.* [f. THRO, THRA *a.* + -NESS.] The quality of being 'thro'; untowardness; obstinacy, reluctance.

**13..** *Cursor M.* 26964 (Fairf.) Ne for na þranes [*altered in MS. to* mekenes, *C.* mekenes] þat mai be þi-seluin say bot soþ of þe. *Ibid.* 27608 (Cott.) O pride bicums thrones [*pr.* throues; *F.* þranes, *pr.* þraues; *Cott.*, *G.* trauers] o threth, Hething, threp, and athes grett.

**Throneward** (þrōᵘ·nwǭɹd), *adv.* [f. as prec. + -WARD.] Towards the throne.

**1844** MRS. BROWNING *Dead Pan* xxvii, When His priestly blood dropped downward, And His kingly eyes looked throneward. **1886** LILLIAN B. FEARING *Sleeping World*, etc., My soul would gaze Throneward for God's dear blame or praise.

**Throng** (þrǫŋ), *sb.* Also *Sc.* and *north. dial.* **thrang.** [ME. *þrang, þrong*, prob. shortened from OE. *geþrang* throng, crowd, tumult, deriv. from verbal ablaut series *þring-, þrang-, þrung-*: see THRING *v.*: cf. MDu. *dranc(g-)*, Du. *drang*, MHG. *dranc* (earlier *gedranc*), Ger. *drang* throng, pressure, crowd; ON. *þrǫng* fem., throng, crowd. *Throng* sb., vb., and adj. appear about the 13–14th c., the adj. being the latest.]

**I. 1.** Oppression; distress, straits; trouble, woe, affliction; danger. Now *dial. rare.*

**13..** *Cursor M.* 2585 Þai þat suld hald þam in þat thrang [*Trin.* þrong]. *Ibid.* 2622 'Fra mi lauedi', sco said, 'i gang, For sco me halds fast in thrang' [*v.r.* ga .. wa]. *Ibid.* 21867 Mikel on erth sal be þe thrang, Þat sal be o men o-mang. **1375** BARBOUR *Bruce* VII. 251 His fayis hym haldis now in thrang. **c 1470** HENRY *Wallace* v. 931 Thaim to reskew that was in fellone thrang. **c 1470** HARDING *Chron.* XXI. v. (MS. Arch. Seld. B. 10. lf. 19 b), The maiden Castelle strong..That on a Roche ful high stonte oute of throng. **1596** DALRYMPLE tr. *Leslie's Hist. Scot.* VII. (S.T.S.) II. 43 Now in sik thrang, that sche nathing culde find radie at hand, to halde the dur fast. **1855** *Woman's Devotion* I. 278 We'll hae o'er-much joy, to be thinking o' past thrangs.

**†b.** The pain of childbirth: usually *pl.*; = THROE *sb.* 1 b. *Obs.*

**1545** RAYNOLD *Byrth Mankynde* Prol. D j, The laboryinge woman hath bene greatly conforted, and alleuiatyd of her throngs and trauell. *Ibid.* 49 The parels, dangeours, and throngs, which chanse to women in theyr labor. *Ibid.* 85 Yf..she feale greate thronge and payne.

**II. 2.** Pressing or crowding of people; an act of thronging or crowding; crowded condition.

**1303** R. BRUNNE *Handl. Synne* 947 As þey stode, & made grete þrong. **c 1440** *York Myst.* xxii. 2 Make rome be-lyve, and late me gang, Who makis here all þis þrang? **1556** *Aurelio & Isab.* (1608) P iv, Soddaineley all withe one thronge caste the poore Affranio to the grounde. **1600** J. PORY tr. *Leo's Africa* II. 88 The throng was so great at their entrance of the gates, that moe then fowerscore citizens were slaine therein. **1715** RAMSAY *Christ's Kirk Gr.* II. xv, He could get nae place.., For thrang that day. **1791** COWPER *Iliad* II. 63 Went the summons forth Into all quarters, and the throng began. **1870** FREEMAN *Norm. Conq.* (ed. 2) II. x. 502 Near to the great city, and yet removed from its immediate throng and turmoil.

**3.** *concr.* A crowded mass of persons actually (or in idea) assembled together; a crowd.

[**993** *Battle of Maldon* 299 He wæs on geþrange hyra þreora bana.] **c 1000** *Gloss.* in *Haupt's Zeitschr.* IX. 427/15 *Lixarum coetibus* (gl. *mercenariorum, qui aquam portant*), wæterberendra. *marg.* þran[gum]. **a 1300** *Cursor M.* 13462 Iesus..bi-held þat folk..Þat folud him til mikel thrang [*Trin.* þrong]. **13..** *E. E. Allit. P.* B. 754 Ȝet for þretty in þrong I schal my þro steke. **c 1470** HENRY *Wallace* IV. 247 Rudely fra him he reft it in that thrang. **1598** BARRET *Theor. Warres* IV. iv. 113 The people to passe foorth..not by thronges..but by litle and litle. **1665** MANLEY *Grotius'*

*Low C. Warres* 199 The whole Throng of Ecclesiastical Persons were beyond the Inspection of the Magistrates. **1784** COWPER *Task* IV. 196 The pent-up breath of an unsavoury throng. **1832** W. IRVING *Alhambra* II. 153 To draw fashionable throngs to their saloons. **1840** DICKENS *Old C. Shop* xix, The streets were filled with throngs of people.

**b.** A great number of things crowded together, either actually or in idea; a multitude.

**1549–62** STERNHOLD & H. *Ps.* lxxii. 16 The mighty mountaynes..Of corne shall beare such throng. **1602** MARSTON *Antonio's Rev.* II. iii, Throngs of thoughts crowde for their passage. *c* **1760** SMOLLETT *Ode to Sleep* 8 Attended by an airy throng Of gentle dreams. **1824** DIBDIN *Libr. Comp.* 205 A series, and almost throng, of Histories of England.

**4.** Pressure, or a pressing amount, *of* work or business. Now *dial.*

**1642** CHAS. I *Message to both Ho.* 28 Apr. 4 We hope this Animadversion will be no breach of your Priviledges in this throng of Businesse, and Distemper of Affections. **1707** J. WODROW in *Life* (1828) 181 My throng of work that fell in on me stopped me. **1730** T. BOSTON *Fourfold St.* IV. iv, A great throng of business, but a great scarcity of faith and holiness. **1778** [W. MARSHALL] *Minutes Agric.* 6 Feb. an. 1776 *note*, The principal objection to a dog-day's-fallow is, that it falls amid the throng of hay time and harvest. **1896** CROCKETT *Grey Man* lii. 349 With all this throng of business on hand.

**5.** 'Intimacy' (Jam.), company; *to keep throng*, to keep company, associate *with*. *Sc. dial.*

**1768** ROSS *Helenore* 11 It sets them well into our thrang to spy. **1843** BETHUNE *Sc. Fireside Stor.* 78 He keepit thrang wi' Jenny M'Intosh his Landlady's daughter.

**Throng** (þrǫŋ), *a.* (*adv.*) Now *Sc.* and *north. dial.* Also 4–5 þ-, thrange, 5–6, *Sc.* 6– thrang. [ME. *þrang*, *þrong*, from same root as prec. Cf. ON. *þrǫng-r*, narrow, close, crowded (Sw. *trång*, Da. *trang*), strait, narrow, close, tight.]

†**1.** In various early instances difficult to explain, all connected with THRING *v.* Among these may be distinguished the senses (*a*) Compressing; (*b*) Compressed, oppressed, distressed; (*c*) Pressing, earnest, eager. But in some cases the exact sense is uncertain; *thrange* may even be adverbial; cf. Ger. *gedrang(e* adv. and adj. *Obs.*

**13..** *E. E. Allit. P.* A. 17 Þat dotz bot þrych my hert þrange, My breste in bale bot bolne & bele. *a* **1400–50** *Alexander* 4813 Neȝe throtild with þe thik aire & thrange in þare andes. *c* **1400** *Destr. Troy* 12235 And he þroly with þrong wil þreppit agayn. **14..** *Siege Jerus.* 2 A þrange þornen croune was þraste on his hed. [*a* **1535** *Frere & Boye* 254 in Hazl. *E.P.P.* III. 72 The frere amonge the thornes was thronge [? pa. pple of THRING *v.*].]

**2.** Pressed or massed closely together as a crowd; crowded, thronged; †dense, close, thick (*obs.*).

*c* **1400** MAUNDEV. (Roxb.) xxvi. 124 When þai schall feight, þai hald þam so nere togyder and so thrang þat, whare þer er xx^m^ men, sum men wald suppose þer ware noȝt x^m^. *c* **1440** *Alphabet of Tales* 401 Nerehand all Rome was gadurd þedur, & þe peple was passand thrang. *c* **1500** *Lancelot* 3366 Thar was the batell dangerus and strong, Gret was the pres, bath perellus and throng. **1535** STEWART *Cron. Scot.* (Rolls) II. 379 Amang the Scottis, quhair tha war maist thrang, Or euir he wist wes closit thame amang. **1603** J. SAVILE *K. Jas.' Entertainm.* Introd. Bij b, The people were so throng. **1743** in Keble *Life Bp. Wilson* xxiv. (1863) 825 [The registry preserves the memorandum in the Curate's own hand of his having published this order in Rushen Church] in the presence of a throng congregation. **1770** *Lett. Jas. Murray, Loyalist* (1901) 134 As throng as three in a bed. **1896** PROUDLOCK *Borderland Muse* 269, I see the 'trouts' are 'rising' thrang.

**3.** Crowded with people, etc.; thronged; very fully attended or frequented.

**1660** H. MORE *Myst. Godl.* I. ix. 28 What a[n]..unsutable representation is it of this throng Theatre in Heaven, made up of Saints and Angels? **1711** RAMSAY *On Maggy Johnstoun* ii, The barn and yard was aft sae thrang, We took the green. **1766** REID *Wks.* (1863) I. 46/2 We have had a thronger College this year than ever before. **1822** GALT *Provost* xxxiii, The street was as throng as on a market day. **1890** HALL CAINE *Bondman* I. x, [The hut] was all but as throng of people as it had been..on the day of 'Liza Killey's wedding. **1894** P. H. HUNTER *Jas. Inwick* i. (1900) 14 Oor Kirk keepit as thrang as afore.

**4.** Of times, seasons, places, etc.: Into which much is crowded; full of work; busy.

**1568** *Satir. Poems Reform.* xlviii. 85 The merkit is thrang, and will no^t^ lest lang. **1615** BRATHWAIT *Strappado* (1878) 62 You Clients..that visit this throng Terme. **1715** *Wodrow Corr.* (1843) II. 75 The harvest is just at its throngest. **1764** *Museum Rust.* II. lxxvii. 265 The value of the time..in so throng a season as the summer, is very considerable. **1816** SCOTT *Old Mort.* iv, It will be hard for you to fill her place, especially on sic a thrang day as this. **1889** GRETTON *Memory's Harkb.* 111 It was wonderful to see..how way was made for him through the crowded streets at the afternoon throng hour. **1895** SNAITH *Mistr. D. Marvin* xlix, 'Tis a very throng time this week.

**5.** Of a person or persons: Closely engaged in work or business; pressed; fully employed, busy.

**1623** SANDERSON *Serm., Job xxix. 14* § 25 Great men..are as throng as ever in pulling down houses, and setting up hedges; in unpeopling towns and creating beggars. **1723** *Wodrow Corr.* (1843) III. 50, I have been so throng this day with my booksellers, that I was not in the Assembly. **1786** BURNS *Twa Dogs* 5 Twa dogs, that were na thrang at hame. **1804** TARRAS *Poems* 1 We see his sheep thrang nibblin on the height. **1863** MRS. GASKELL *Sylvia's L.* II. 8 When we're throng, I help Hester. **1896** BARRIE *Marg. Ogilvy* vi, 'I suppose you are terrible thrang', she says. 'Well, I am rather busy'.

**6.** Closely engaged together; intimately associated; 'thick'.

**1790** D. MORISON *Poems* 136 (Jam.) Syne hame we scour'd fu' cheery and fu' thrang. **1865** G. MACDONALD *A. Forbes* 51 Him an' oor Willie's unco throng.

**B.** *adv.* Earnestly; busily.

*c* **1400** *Destr. Troy* 3094 And thus ho thought full thrange in hir thro hert, þat so semely a sight ho se neuer before. **1786** BURNS *Dream* ii, I see ye're complimented thrang By mony a lord an' lady. *a* **1810** TANNAHILL *Ambitious Mite* 10 Some brushing thrang their wings and noses.

**Throng** (þrǫŋ), *v.* Also 4 (9 *dial.*) thrang. [ME. *þrange*, *þronge* wk. vb., in form a derivative from the stem of THRING *v.*, with which it agrees in sense. It may continue an unrecorded OE. **þrongian* = OHG. *drangôn*; or may be f. THRONG *sb.*: cf. *to crowd*. (A factitive from *thring* would have been in OE. **þręng(e)an*: cf. Ger. *drängen*, ON. *þrengva* (Sw. *tränga*, Da. *trænge*, wk. vbs.).]

†**1.** *trans.* To press or compress violently; to squeeze, crush. *Obs.*

**13..** *Cursor M.* 900 (Gött.) Þu sal waite womman to stang, And scho sal ȝeit þin hefde thrang. **1590** SPENSER *F. Q.* III. ix. 45 He [the Thames] raves With roring rage, and sore him selfe does throng. **1596** DANETT tr. *Comines* (1614) 223 *margin*, He was..thronged to death in the gate. **1601** HOLLAND *Pliny* (1634) I. 120 See into what great streights betweene both seas Asia is..as it were thronged. **1616** R. C. *Times' Whistle* v. 2141 This foolish prophesie, That, vnlesse throngd to death, thou ne're shalt die. **1825** BROCKETT *N. C. Words*, *Thrang*, to press, to thrust, to squeeze.

†**2.** *intr.* To push or force one's way, as through a crowd or against obstacles; to press. *Obs.*

? *a* **1400** *Morte Arth.* 3755 Thare they thronge in the thikke, and thristis to the erthe Of the thraeste mene thre hundrethe. *c* **1400** *Destr. Troy* 7040 Throly the þre men throngth hym aboute. **1560** DAUS tr. *Sleidane's Comm.* 343 b, The people, which striue, who may first thronge in. **1582** STANYHURST *Æneis* I. (Arb.) 32 Hee throngs..Through crowds of the pepil. **1593** SHAKS. *Lucr.* 1041 Her breath..thronging through her lips. **1603** KNOLLES *Hist. Turks* (1638) 90 The Enemy, thronging in as fast as he could. **1624** CAPT. SMITH *Virginia* III. ix. 80 Whereat they quickly thronged faster backe then before forward. *a* **1625** FLETCHER & MASSINGER *Laws of Candy* I. ii, Having taken breath, he throng'd before me, Renewed the fight.

**3.** *intr.* To assemble in a group or crowd; to collect in large numbers; to crowd; also, to go in a crowd.

**15..** *Adam Bel* 79 in Hazl. *E. P. P.* II. 142 They rysed the towne..And came thronging to Wyllyames house. **1603** HOLLAND *Plutarch's Mor.* 410 The Greekes who thronged about his pavilion doores. **1647** COWLEY *Mistr.*, *The Wish* v, Lest men..Should hither throng..And so make a City. **1710** PHILIPS *Pastorals* ii. 43 No more beneath thy Shade shall Shepherds throng. **1812** BYRON *Ch. Har.* II. lxvi, Childe Harold saw them..Thronging to war. **1832** W. IRVING *Alhambra* II. 277 The people thronged forth to see him with impatient joy. *a* **1839** PRAED *Poems* (1864) II. 164 We did not meet in courtly hall, Where birth and beauty throng.

*fig.* **1671** MILTON *Samson* 21 Restless thoughts, that like a deadly swarm Of Hornets..rush upon me thronging. **1803–6** WORDSW. *Intimations Immort.* iii, I hear the Echoes through the mountains throng.

†**b.** *indirect pass.* (cf. 4). *Obs.*

**1607** SHAKS. *Timon* IV. iii. 395 *Ape(mantus)*..Ile say th' hast Gold: Thou wilt be throng'd too shortly. *Tim.* Throng'd too? **1663** PEPYS *Diary* 13 June, To the Royall Theatre... Here we saw 'The Faithfull Sheepeardesse', a most simple thing, and yet much thronged after.

**4.** *trans.* To crowd round and press upon; to press upon as in a crowd, to jostle. Also *fig.*

**1534** TINDALE *Mark* v. 24 Moche people folowed him, and thronged him. **1593** SHAKS. *Lucr.* 1417 Here one being throng'd bears back. **1692** BENTLEY *Boyle Lect.* 217 That particles so widely disseminated could ever throng and crowd one another into a close and compact texture. **1704** J. TRAPP *Abra-Mulé* I. ii. 299 Not so he look'd when throng'd with Multitudes Of the applauding Soldiers. **1850** TENNYSON *In Mem.* xxi. 15 When more and more the people throng The chairs and thrones of civil power.

**5.** To bring or drive into a crowd, or into one place; to collect closely, to crowd; to press or drive in a crowd (quot. 1615). Chiefly in *pa. pple.*

**1578** BANISTER *Hist. Man* I. 7 Pericles..seemed..to throng and thunder out his wordes. *a* **1608** SIR F. VERE *Comm.* (1657) 6 The enemy coming..with ensigns displayed, very thick thronged together. **1615** HEYWOOD *Foure Prentises* I. Wks. 1874 II. 230 My Standerd..the sight whereof Will driue these stragglers in disordered rankes, And in a hurly burly throng them hence. **1652–62** HEYLIN *Cosmogr.* Introd. (1674) 8/2 Bochartus..hath thronged Joktan and his Sons into a little corner of Arabia Felix. **1677** SEDLEY *Ant. & Cl.* v. i, All she holds dear she has throng'd there but you, And now intreats that you will enter too. **1752** YOUNG *Brothers* II. i, Throngs the pride of ages in an hour. **1822** [see THRONGED 1].

**6.** To fill or occupy (a place, etc.) *with* a large number of things or persons, or quantity of something; to crowd, cram, stuff; to burden (quot. 1648).

**1607** SHAKS. *Cor.* III. iii. 36 Throng [*Theobald's correction*; *folios* Through] our large temples with the shows of peace, And not our streets with war. **1634** MILTON *Comus* 713 Thronging the Seas with spawn innumerable. **1648** J. BEAUMONT *Psyche* III. xxv, If..I throng my Darling with this massy store, 'Twill to a Burden swell my Courtesy. **1704** *Elegy Author True born Eng.* xx, Nature to make amends for want of Sense, Has throng'd his Head with clear Impertinence. **1817** LADY MORGAN *France* (1818) I. 90 The rehearsals..occupied and thronged the streets of Paris for some days. **1842** TENNYSON *Locksley Hall* 36 Her whisper throng'd my pulses with the fullness of the Spring. **1874** PUSEY *Lent. Serm.* 268 To occupy and throng your thoughts with cares..of your own seeking.

**b.** Said of a multitude of persons or things: To occupy completely, fill, crowd (a place, etc.).

**1819** SHELLEY *Prometh. Unb.* I. 2 All Spirits..who throng those bright and rolling worlds. **1853** C. BRONTE *Villett[e]* xxxviii, Gay dresses, grand equipages, fine horses..throng the bright streets. **1860** TYNDALL *Glac.* II. i. 229 Insect[s] which thronged the adjacent grass. **1873** 'OUIDA' *Pascare[l]* I. viii, Great multitudes..thronged every square and street.

**c.** *pa. pple.* Occupied by a crowd or multitude of persons or things; crowded, crammed, filled (const. *with*, or *absol.*). See also THRONGED 2.

**1594** DRAYTON *Idea* 649 With those the thronged Theater that presse, I in the circuit for the Laurell strove. **160[5]** SHAKS. *Per.* II. i. 77 A man throng'd vp with cold, my Veine[s] are chill. **1677** THORESBY *Diary* (1830) I. 4 The Glasshouse Lecture..was thronged. **1719** DE FOE *Crusoe* (1858) 33[.] We discovered the ship's boats..both thronged with people. **1772** BEDINGFIELD in *Lett. Lit. Men* (Camden) 405 The churches every where seemed well thronged. **1841** W. SPALDING *Italy & It. Isl.* I. iv. I. 149 The galleries of Italian palaces are still thronged with statues, as were the temples. **1894** HALL CAINE *Manxman* v. v, The streets were thronged.

**d.** *intr.* for *pass.* Now *dial.*

**1757** EDWARDS *Orig. Sin* viii. (1837) 75 Multitudes that the Christian world throngs with. **1844** W. JAMIE *Muse* 11 (E.D.D.) The whisky tents began to throng.

**Throng(e, -en**, obs. pa.t. and pple. of THRING *v.*

**Thronged** (þrǫŋd, *poet.* þrǫ·ŋėd), *ppl. a.* [f. THRONG *v.* + -ED[1].]

**1.** Closely packed, as a multitude of people or things; crowded.

**1652** BENLOWES *Theoph.* VII. iv, Those throng'd figures sun[g] not Thee. **1713** ADDISON *Cato* II. i, The thick array Of his thronged legions. **1822** J. MACDONALD *Mem. J. Benson* 463 He addressed a thronged audience. **1860** PUSEY *Min. Proph.* 270 The mariners..ask Jonah thronged questions. **1908** MRS. E. WHARTON *Hermit & Wild Wom.* 41 The air shone with thronged candle-flames.

**2.** Of a place, etc.: Closely packed with people or things; crowded.

**1594** [see THRONG *v.* 6 c]. **1613** W. BROWNE *Brit. Past.* II. v. 115 As vnder their [trees'] command the thronged Creeke Ran lessened vp. **1746–7** HERVEY *Medit.* (1818) 251 To slip away from the thronged city. **1831** SCOTT *Ct. Robt.* xxiii, A loud and varied murmur, resembling that of a thronged hive. **1889** GRETTON *Memory's Harkb.* 189 To me these thronged places are wearisome in the extreme.

**b.** Of time: Full of work or business; busily occupied; busy. *dial.*

**1791** ISABELLA WILSON in *Mem.* (1825) 36 We have had a thronged time with our harvest. **1832** *Yorkshire Dial.*, We had a very thronged day.

**Thronger** (þrǫ·ŋəɹ). [f. THRONG *v.* + -ER[1].] One who throngs: see the verb.

**1648** HEXHAM II, *Een dringer*, a Presser, a thronger, or a pusher. **1908** R. W. CHAMBERS *Firing Line* vii, The jewelled throngers of the horse-shows and motor-shows.

**Throngful** (þrǫ·ŋfŭl), *a.* [f. THRONG *sb.* + -FUL.] Full of a throng or crowd; crowded.

**1833** WHITTIER *Female Martyr* 44 Where The throngful street grew foul with death. **1866** — *Snow-bound* 743 Dreaming in throngful city ways Of winter joys his boyhood knew.

**Thronging** (þrǫ·ŋiŋ), *vbl. sb.* [f. THRONG *v.* + -ING[1].] The action of the verb THRONG; pressing; crowding.

**13..** *Cursor M.* 22683 (Cott.) Wit thranging sal þai samen threst. **1548** UDALL, etc. *Erasm. Par. Mark* v. 32 b, So was he payned with the throngyng of the people. **1581** MULCASTER *Positions* xxxix. (1887) 196 Why there is such thronging of all people that way. **1679** LUTTRELL *Brief Rel.* (1857) I. 7 Mr. Oates preached at Wood-street church..and there was great thronging. **1724** P. WALKER *Peden* in *Biogr. Presbyt.* (1827) I. 153 Such a Thronging to the fearful Pit.

**Thro·nging,** *ppl. a.* [f. as prec. + -ING[2].] That throngs; crowding or crowded; assembling or assembled in large numbers; going in a crowd.

**1582** STANYHURST *Æneis* II. (Arb.) 67 Theare weare the enymyes with thronging cluster asembled. **1600** HOLLAND *Livy* I. xiv. 11 All at once the enemies in thrunging manner sallied forth. **1697** POTTER *Antiq. Greece* I. viii. (1715) 41 Too weak to support the vast weight of thronging Multitudes. **1827** KEBLE *Chr. Y., S. Matt.* v, Such brief rest As thronging cares afford. **1871** R. ELLIS *Catullus* lxiv. 33 Thronging hosts uncounted, a company joyous approaching.

Hence **Thro·ngingly** *adv.*

**1624** GEE *Hold Fast* 52 A glorious spectacle..fit for vs to step out of our dores and throngingly to behold. **1731** BAILEY, *Throngingly*, crowdingly.

**Thro·ngly,** *adv. Obs.* or *dial.* [f. THRONG *a.* + -LY[2].] Thickly, densely; busily.

**1653** H. MORE *Conject. Cabbal.* ii. § 7 The World of Life, which is every where nigh at hand, and does very throngly inequitate the moist and unctuous Aire. **1727** BAILEY vol. II, *Throngly*..pressingly, crowdingly.

So **Thro·ngness**, the state of being 'throng' or crowded; crowdedness.

**1727** P. WALKER *Cameron* in *Biogr. Presbyt.* (1827) I. 276 When Prisons were more throng than ever, even in Dunnottar-Castle, where Eight-score and eight of us were driven into one Vault; and yet I never saw Throngness nor Irons marr any from writing.

†**Thronize,** *v. Obs. rare.* Also 5 tronyse. [prob. aphetic for ENTHRONIZE: cf. also Gr. θρονίζεσθαι to be enthroned.] *trans.* To enthrone, to seat on a throne.

**1494** FABYAN *Chron.* VII. 455 He was..tronysed in the sayd moneth of May. **1559** *Act 2 Eliz.* in Bolton *Stat. Irel.* (1621) 283 Everie person and persons being hereafter conferred, invested, and consecrated,..may from henceforth be thronized or installed. 1711 Hickes *Two Treat. Chr. Priesth.* (1847) II. 290 'To mount into his throne', or as we say to be thronized.

Hence †**Throniza·tion**, tron- [cf. Enthroniza-tion], enthronement. *Obs. rare*⁻¹.

1526 R. Whytford *Martiloge* 22 Feb. 21 At antioche the stallacion or tronizacyon of saynt Peter.

†**Throno·nical**, *a. nonce-wd.* [irreg. f. Throne *sb.*, perh. after *canonical.*] Of or pertaining to the throne.

1591 Horsey *Trav.* (Hakl. Soc.) 175 He [Ivan the Terrible] thonders owt his thrononicall threats to their ears.

†**Thro·nonize, tro·nonize**, *v. Obs. rare.* [irreg. f. as prec.: perh. after *canonize*; cf. also *intrononyzacion*, s. v. Enthronization, quot. 1517.] *trans.* To enthrone.

*c* 1470 Harding *Chron.* xvi. iii. (MS. Egerton 1992, lf. 14 b), Aftere his merites trononized [*so ed.* 1543; *other MSS.* inthronized, intronozed, in thronyed] high in trone. 1509 Hawes *Joyf. Medit.* xxii, O God aboue, tronoynsed in heuen. 1533-4 *Act* 25 *Hen. VIII*, c. 20 § 5 Every person..chosen ..and consecrate to the dignitie or office of any Archebishop or Byshop..shall..be trononysed or installed as the case shall require.

**Throo**, var. Thro, *Obs.* **Throomb**, obs. f. Thrum.

**Throp, thrope**, obs. and dial. ff. Thorp.

†**Throplet.** *Obs. rare*⁻¹. [f. Thropple *sb.* + -et.] The pharynx.

1720 W. Gibson *Dict. Horses* i. (ed. 2) 10 The Jaws should be..on the upper Part placed at a moderate Distance from each other, that the Head of the Pharynx or Throplet may easily fall between them.

**Thropple, thrapple** (þrǫ·p'l, þra·p'l), *sb. Sc.* and *north. dial.* Forms: α. 4–6 **throppill**, 6 **-il**, **-el**, 6–8 **throple**, 7 **throp(p)ell**, 6– **thropple**. β. 8– *Sc. dial.* **thrapple**. [In use from 14th c. chiefly in the North. Origin obscure: its date is against its being an altered form of Throttle *sb.*

A conjecture that it is a descendant of OE. *þrotbolla*, Throat-boll, does not fit phonology and local distribution.]

The throat; now *esp.* the windpipe or gullet. (More widely in use of a horse or other beast than of human beings.)

1375 Barbour *Bruce* vii. 584 [The king] hyt þe formast in þe hals, Till throppill and vassand [*v. r.* wesand] ȝeid in twa. 1533 Bellenden *Livy* i. x. (S.T.S.) I. 59 He straik this thrid brothir..in þe throppil. 1562 Turner *Herbal* ii. 164 b, The violet..swageth and softeneth the throple and the breste. 1562 — *Baths* 8 b, The diseases of the longes and winde pipe or throppel. 1570 Levins *Manip.* 126/19 A Throppil, *iugulum.* 1607 Markham *Caval.* iii. (1617) 15 The throppell, or neather part of the necke [of a horse] which goes from the vnder chappes to the brest. 1690 *Lond. Gaz.* No. 2527/4 A Light grey Mare,..one feather on each side her Thropple. 1755 Johnson, *Thrapple*, the windpipe of any animal. They still retain it in the Scottish dialect. *a* 1758 Ramsay *Address of Thanks* xviii, Bring to the warld the luckless wean, And sneg its infant thrapple. 1815 Scott *Guy M.* i, Sorrow be in your thrapple then! 1825 Brockett *N. C. Words, Thropple*, the windpipe, the throat. 'A bull's thropple'. 1894 Crockett *Raiders* (ed. 3) 218 That dry yeukin' in my thrapple.

**Thro·pple, thra·pple**, *v. Sc.* and *north. dial.* [f. prec. sb.] *trans.* To throttle, strangle.

1570 Levins *Manip.* 170/16 To Thropple, *iugulare.* 1674 Ray *N. C. Words*, To *Thropple*, to Throttle or strangle. 1806 J. Cock *Simple Strains* (1810) II. 136 (E.D.D.) Some were maistly thrappl't Wi' grips that night. 1899 J. Strang *Lass of Lennox* iii. 29 I could thrapple ye whaur ye staun'.

**Thro·ppled, thra·ppled**, *a.* [f. Thropple *sb.* + -ed ².] Having a thropple (of a specified kind). Chiefly used of horses.

1607 Markham *Caval.* iii. (1617) 15 Cock-throppled [see Cock-throppled]. 1614 — *Cheap Husb.* (1623) 47 A full eye, open nostrill, wide jawed, loose thropled, deepe neckt. 1725 *Bradley's Fam. Dict.* s. v. *Pursiness*, When the Horse is Cock-thropled, for that his Throple or Wind-pipe being so long, he is not able to draw it [breath] in and out with so much Ease and Pleasure as other Horses do that are loose thropled. 1834 Cock-thrappled [see Cock-throppled].

**Throsche, throsh**, obs. ff. Thrash, thresh.

**Throst, -er**, obs. forms of Throwst, -er.

**Throstle** (þrǫ·s'l). Forms: α. 1–3 **þrostle**, 4 **þrostel**, **-yl**, 4–5 **throstel(e**, 5 **-elle**, **-il**, **-yl(l**, 7 **throssel**, **throssle**, (**thrassel**), 5– **throstle**. β. 4 **þrustel(e**, 4–8 **thrustle**, 5 **-ille**, **-yll(e**, 5–6 **thrustel(l**, 6 **-ele**, 7 **thrussel**. γ. 4 **þrestel**, **thristill**, (5 **thyrstylle**), 6 **threstyll**, **thrissell**, 8 **thrissel**, **thristle**, **thrystle**. [OE. *þrostle* or ?*þrǫ́stle*, wk. fem. For *þrǫ́stle*, cf. MLG. *drǫ̂sle* (Low Ger. dial. *drǭssel*, *draussel*, *drausele*), app. pointing to an OTeut. **þramstala* (Kluge). For *þrostle*, cf. MHG. *drostel*, the root-form of which appears in ON. *þrǫstr* (Norw. *trost*, *trast*, Sw. *trast*, Da. *trost*):—OTeut. **þrastuz*, commonly referred to Indo-Eur. **trozdu-s*, whence L. *turdus* (**trzdo-*), OPruss. *tresde*, and Lett. *strazds*, Lith. *strãzdas*, all meaning 'thrush'. Cf. also OSlav. *drozgŭ* and Russ. *drozdŭ*. (See Suolahti, *Deutsche Vogelnamen* 1909, 51–54.)

App. in origin distinct from Thrush, though the derivative forms of the latter, *thruschel*, *thrusshill* in ME., *droschel*, *druschel* in Ger., come very near to *throstle*, *thrustle*, and MHG. *drostel*. The vocalization of ME. *thrustel*, *thristel*, *threstyl*, etc. seems also to have been influenced by that of *thrusche*, *thrysshe*, *threshe*, *thrishel*, etc.: see Thrush ¹.]

**1.** A thrush; *esp.* the song-thrush or mavis, *Turdus musicus.* Now only *literary* and *dial.*

In many ME. passages, esp. in alliterative verse, 'throstle' and 'thrush' are distinguished, and in several cases, e. g. quots. *c* 900, 1303, *c* 1440, and (?) 1601, *throstle* is applied to the blackbird. In quot. 1303, the original Fr. has in one MS. 'Le oysel est merle apelé, Neir est [*v. r.* Veu l'ay] en yuer & en esté'. Chaucer, also, in *Rom. Rose* 665 translates 'Melles [?merles] et mauvis', Thrustels, Terins, and Mauise.

*c* 725 *Corpus Gloss.* (O.E.T.) 2068 *Turdella*, ðrostle. *c* 900 Wærferth tr. *Gregory's Dial.* 100 Sum swyþe sweart & lytel fugel, se is on folcisc þrostle ȝehaten. 956 *Charter of Eadwig* in Birch *Cart. Sax.* III. 141 Of þam lea on þrostlan wyl. *a* 1250 *Owl & Night.* 1659 Þaruore anan to hire cherde Þrusche and þrostle and wudewale. 1303 R. Brunne *Handl. Synne* 7480 A fend of helle Yn a lykenes of a bryd. A 'þrostyl' ys þe name kyd. *c* 1350 *Will. Palerne* 820 Boþe þe þrusch & þe þrustele bi xxxti of boþe. 13.. *Minor Poems fr. Vernon MS.* xlvi. 181 Þe þrestel song ful schille. 1375 Barbour *Bruce* v. 4 Byrdis smale, As thristill and þe nychtingale. 1387 Trevisa *Higden* (Rolls) I. 237 Whan somer is hote þrostel syngeþ wiþ mery note. 1403 *Nottingham Rec.* II. 20, j. caige cum j. throstyll. *c* 1440 *Promp. Parv.* 493/1 Thrustylle, bryd (*P.* thrusshill or thrustyll), *merula.* *c* 1450 *Alphita* (Anecd. Oxon.) 188 *Turdus* auis est. g[allice] mauuys, an[glice] throstle. 1483 *Cath. Angl.* 386/2 A Throstelle, *mauiscus.* 1601 Holland *Pliny* (1634) I. 293 Agrippina the Empresse..had a Black-bird or a Throstle.. which could counterfeit mans speech. 1604 Drayton *Owle* 1259 The iocund Throstle, for his varying Note, Clad by the Eagle in a speckled Cote. 1661 Walton *Angler* i. (ed. 3) 10 How doth the Black-bird and Thrassel..bid welcome to the cheerful Spring! 1668 Charleton *Onomast.* 83 *Turdus*,.. the Thrush, Song-Thrush, Throssle, or Mavis. 1766 Pennant *Zool.* (1768) I. 226 The throstle is the finest of our singing birds. 1798 Wordsw. *Tables Turned* iv, And hark! how blithe the throstle sings! 1841 Browning *Pippa Passes*, Oh, Lark, be day's apostle To mavis, merle and throstle.

**2.** A spinning-machine for cotton, wool, etc., a modification of that originally called a *water-frame*; differing from a *mule* in having a continuous action, the processes of drawing, twisting, and winding being carried on simultaneously.

As to the reason of the name see quot. 1877.

1825 J. Nicholson *Operat. Mechanic* 387 This construction of a water spinning-frame is called a throstle. 1835 Ure *Philos. Manuf.* 110 Both systems of spinning, namely, the continuous or by throstles, and the discontinuous or by mules. 1876 J. Watts *Brit. Manuf.* III. 138 The throstle, an extension and modification of the original spinning-frame,.. is employed in the spinning of yarn for warps. 1877 Knight *Dict. Mech.* s. v., The throstle derived its name from the singing or humming which it occasioned.

**3.** *attrib.* and *Comb.* **a.** in sense 1, as *throstle-throat*, *-wing*; *throstle-like* adj.; **throstle-breast** (*Mining*): see quot.; **throstle-nest**, applied *attrib.* to a form of stag's horn (see quot. 1785). See also Throstle-cock.

1747 Hooson *Miner's Dict.*, **Throstlebrest*, a kind of Ore or rather Knockings, mixt with a brown Tuft. 1902 F. Campbell in *Temple Bar Mag.* CXXVI. 106 Mary's *throstle-like voice. 1785 Barker in *Phil. Trans.* LXXV. 354 Horns..which park-keepers in this part of the country call *throstle-nest horns,..the upper part..is branched out into a number of short antlers which form an hollow about large enough to contain a thrush's nest. 1898 *Westm. Gaz.* 5 Mar. 8/1 Antlers of the 'throstle nest' type. 17.. *Jolly Hind Squire* viii. in Child *Ballads* ii. (1884) 429/2 The *thristle-throat is the next that sings Unto the nightingale. 1681 Chetham *Angler's Vade-m.* xxxiv. § 14 (1689) 190 Feathers of..*Throstle-wing.

**b.** in sense 2, as *throstle-frame* (= 2), *-piecer* (Piecer 2), *-spindle*, *-spinner*, *-spinning*, *-yarn.*

1835 Ure *Philos. Manuf.* 23 The water-twist, or throstle cotton mills. *Ibid.* 40 A throstle frame made in the best manner. *Ibid.* 71 The throstle twist, which has been so largely exported of late years. 1844 G. Dodd *Textile Manuf.* i. 35 The roller principle, modified in a manner.. represented by the throstle machine, is that by which the strong and hard yarns are produced. 1862 *Illustr. Lond. News* XLI. 558/3 The Throstle Spinner..has an assistant, called the Throstle Doffer, a little girl or boy. 1884 W. S. B. McLaren *Spinning* viii. (ed. 2) 150 There are four methods of spinning worsted, three of which come under the head of throstle frames...The fourth is the mule.

**Thro·stle-cock.** The male throstle or song-thrush; *dial.* the male missel-thrush.

*c* 1300 *Thrush & Night.* 121 in Hazl. *E. P. P.* I. 55 Threstelkok, thou hauest wrong. *c* 1386 Chaucer *Sir Thopas* 58 (Harl.) The þrostilcok [*v. rr.* thrustel-, -il-] maad eek his lay. *c* 1430 Lydg. *Min. Poems* (Percy Soc.) 203 The thruschylcok nor the feldfare. 1530 Palsgr. 281/1 Thrustell cocke, *mauluis.* *a* 1600 Montgomerie *Misc. Poems* xli. 5 The thissell-cok [*sic*] cryis On louers vha lyis. 1604 Drayton *Owle* 220 The warbling Throstle Cocke. 1825 Jamieson, *Thrissel-cock*, the Missel-thrush or Shrite, Turdus viscivorus, Gesner; the *Throstle-cock* of the North of England. 1870 Morris *Earthly Par.* II. iii. 169 A throstle-cock beside him broke Into the sweetest of his song.

[**Throstling.** Probably in origin a misprint or other error for *throttling.* See quots.

1726 [? N. Bailey] *Dict. Rust.* (ed. 3), *Throstling*, a Disease in Black Cattle, which proceeds from humours gathering under their throats, which so dangerously swell the Glands, that the Beast will be choak'd if not relieved. 1753 in Chambers *Cycl. Suppl.* 1828–32 in Webster; and in later Dictionaries; but not known to Veterinary Surgery.]

**Throte, Throttene**, obs. ff. Throat, Thirteen.

**Throttle** (þrǫ·t'l), *sb.* Forms: 6 **throtal**, **throttil**, 7 *dial.* **thrattle**, 8 **throtle**, 6– **throttle**. [Has the form of a dim. of *throte*, Throat: cf. Ger. *drossel*, dim. of OHG. *drozza* throat. But the late appearance of the word (*c* 1550), its app. synonymy with the earlier Thropple (*c* 1375), and the earlier existence of Throttle *v.*, combine to make its actual history perplexing.

Sense 3, of 17th c., is evidently a noun of action from the vb., and might be treated as a distinct word.]

**1.** The throat. Now chiefly *dial.*

*a* 1547 Surrey *Æneid* iv. 361 Amid his throtal his voice likewise gan stick [L. *vox faucibus hæsit*, Douglas the voce stak in his hals]. 1570 Levins *Manip.* 126/18 A Throttil, *guttus, uris, hoc.* A Throppil, *idem, iugulum.* *c* 1720 Gibson *Farrier's Guide* i. iii. (1738) 28 This pipe is called the Trachea..which Name it obtains from the Throtle to the Lungs. 1806-7 J. Beresford *Miseries Hum. Life* xx. 238 The neck of each bottle She thrusts down her throttle. 1823 F. Cooper *Pioneers* xxxiv, Under the grasp which the steward held on his throttle. 1871 B. Taylor *Faust* (1875) I. vi. 109 Now, here's a bottle, Wherefrom, sometimes, I wet my throttle.

**b.** The larynx. Now *rare.*

1615 Crooke *Body of Man* 763 Because the actions of the Throttle or Larynx are performed with voluntary motion, Nature hath giuen it muscles. 1646 Sir T. Browne *Pseud. Ep.* iii. xxvii. 174 The windepipe..in this birde [bittern]..hath no Larinx or throttle to qualifie the sound. 1905 *Daily Chron.* 16 Mar. 3/4 He used to carry home to me..from his anatomy class..the throttles of all kinds of animals!—chickens, sheep and cows. You would imagine that these cartilaginous larynxes, red from the operating table, would have disgusted me.

**c.** *transf.* The throat or neck of a bottle.

*a* 1845 Hood *Public Dinner* ii, Certain bottles Made long in the throttles.

**2.** (See quot.)

*a* 1864 Gesner *Coal, Petrol.*, etc. (1865) 79 The throttles.. are small flues which distribute the heat around the still.

†**3.** The act of throttling or fact of being throttled; choking, suffocation. *Obs. rare*⁻¹.

1622 Mabbe tr. *Aleman's Guzman d'Alf.* i. 24 They cramme their crawes like so many Capons in a Coope, till they can swallow no more, and so die of the throttle.

**4.** Short for *throttle-valve* (see 5); also a similar valve in a motor engine.

1877 Knight *Dict. Mech., Throttle.* (*Steam.*) A name for the *Throttle-valve.* 1903 *Times* 30 Apr. 3/2 He had slowed down..the motor-cycle..and had almost closed the throttle. 1907 *Ibid.* 30 May 4/6 An experienced driver controlled the throttle and could pull up at once. 1908 *Ibid.* 6 Apr. 7/1 He was on watch in the engine-room and standing near the throttles.

**5.** *attrib.* and *Comb.*, as (in sense 1) *throttle bone*, *-pipe*, (in sense 4) as *throttle control*; **throttle damper**, an adjustable damper for a flue, etc. working like a throttle-valve; **throttle-lever**, a lever for opening or closing a throttle or throttle-valve; **throttle-valve** (probably from the vb.), a valve for regulating the supply of steam, esp. to the cylinder of a steam-engine.

1681 Grew *Musæum* i. ii. i. 11 The *Throttle Bone of a Male Aquiqui. 1910 *Westm. Gaz.* 10 Feb. 5/1 The *throttle control is well worth careful attention. 1884 Knight *Dict. Mech., Supp.* s. v., A *throttle damper, with arrow and quadrant, for regulating the passage of the flue and registering the same. 1864 Webster, *Throttle-lever. 1882 Scudder *Noah Webster* vi. 184 He seems..to have his hand close to the throttle-lever without knowing it. 1632 Brome *Northern Lass* iii. iii, I'le cut your *thrattle-pipe. 1824 R. Stuart *Hist. Steam Engine* 129 A cock or valve, called the *throttle-valve or regulator, placed on the pipe conveying the steam from the boiler. 1877 Knight *Dict. Mech.* 2564 Throttle-valve..in the Watt engine..a disk turning on an axis, and occupying in its transverse position the bore of the main steam-pipe..frequently an ordinary conical valve with a stem operated by a screw. 1899 F. T. Bullen *Log Sea-waif* 252 The grey-headed chief-engineer stood by the grunting machinery, his hand on the throttle-valve.

**Throttle** (þrǫ·t'l), *v.* Forms: 5 **throtel**, 5–6 **throtil**, 5–7 **throtle**, 6–7 **thrattle**, **thratle**, 7 **thrattell**, 7 **throatle**, 6– **throttle**. [Late ME. *throtel*, *-il*, perh. f. Throat + -le *suffix* ³.

App. not derived from Throttle *sb.*, which appears 150 years later. The Ger. *drosseln* (much later), now only in *erdrosseln*, is from *drossel* sb., so that *drosseln* and *to throttle* are not in their history parallel.]

**1.** *trans.* To stop the breath of by compressing the throat, to strangle; to kill in this way; *loosely*, to stop the breath of in any way, to choke, suffocate. The original meaning may have been 'to take or seize by the throat'. Also *refl.*

In some early quots. the meaning appears to be 'to kill by cutting or stabbing the throat' (rendering L. *jugulāre*).

*a* 1400-50 *Alexander* 4813 Þan come þai blesnand till a barme of a brent lawe, Neȝe throtild with þe thik aire & thrange in þare andes. *c* 1400 *Destr. Troy* 12752 Þan entrid this Engist,..And, with a thricche in the throte, throtlet the kyng. 1432-50 tr. *Higden* (Rolls) IV. 181 His felawes taken by Antonius,..caste in to prison, were throtelede [*strangulati*] in hit. *Ibid.* V. 321 Boecius..was throtelede [*eum jugulari fecit*] in the territory Mediolanense. 1564 Haward *Eutropius* iv. 44 This Aristonicus was thratled in prisone by the commandement of the Senate. 1582 N. T. (Rhem.) *Matt.* xviii. 28 He found one of his fellow-seruants ..and..thratled him saying Repay that thou owest. 1602 Rowlands *Greene's Ghost* 15 One of them thratled him so sore by the wind-pipe, that he could make no noise, but sodainly sunke to the ground. 1609 Holland *Amm. Marcell.* 349 Palladius..knit his necke in an halter, and so throtled himselfe, and died. 1693 Dryden *Persius' Sat.* iii. 199 His Throat half throtled with corrupted Fleam. 1730 Swift *Misc., True Eng. Dean* ix, Then throttle thy self with an Ell of strong Tape. 1816 Scott *Bl. Dwarf* vii, The dog..pulled down and throttled one of the hermit's she-goats. 1861 Geo. Eliot *Silas M.* i. iii, 'Hold your tongue..', said Godfrey,..'else I'll throttle you'.

**b.** *transf.* To tie something tightly round the neck of; to compress by fastening something round.
**1863** BRIERLEY *Waverlow* 228 The lower [portion of these figures] was..'throttled' in unyielding pantaloons. **1866** GEO. ELIOT *F. Holt* v, Let a man once throttle himself with a satin stock. **1869** BLACKMORE *Lorna D.* xxxv, I never had throttled a finger before, and it [the ring] looked very queer ..upon my great..hand.

**c.** *intr.* or *absol.*
**1837** CARLYLE *Fr. Rev.* III. III. iv, Party tugging and throttling with Party might have suppressed and smothered one another.

**2. a.** To check or break off (utterance) as if choking; † in qt. 1610, to utter in a choking voice.
**1582** STANYHURST *Æneis* IV. (Arb.) 108 Her talck in the mydel, with this last parlye, she throtled. **1590** SHAKS. *Mids. N.* v. i. 97, I haue seene them shiuer and looke pale,.. Throttle their practiz'd accent in their feares. **1610** TOFTE *Honours Acad.* I. 80 With a hollow voice, he thratled forth these few words. My dearest friends, let me intreat you [etc.].

**b.** *fig.* To stop forcibly the utterance of (a person or thing).
**1641** MILTON *Animadv.* ii. Wks. 1851 III. 205 And thus you throttle your selfe with your owne Similies. **1647** TRAPP *Comm. Mark* iii. 2 It is a brave thing to throttle envy, to stop an evil mouth. **1838** EMERSON *Address, Cambr., Mass.* Wks. (Bohn) II. 196 The injury to faith throttles the preacher. **1901** *Scotsman* 7 Mar. 6/2 If it were given any quarter, it would throttle Parliament.

**3.** *intr.* To undergo suffocation; to choke.
**1566** [implied in *throttling* ppl. a.]. *a* **1687** H. MORE in *Life R. Ward* (1710) 208 She dyed without any Fever,.. drawing her Breath a while as one asleep, without throatling. **1828–32** WEBSTER, *Throttle*..2. To breathe hard, as when nearly suffocated. **1909** *Westm. Gaz.* 21 Aug. 3/1 The child throttled and died in my arms.

**4.** *trans.* To check or stop the flow of (a fluid in a tube, etc.) esp. by means of a valve, or by compression; to regulate the supply of steam or gas to (an engine) in this way. (Cf. *throttle-valve* in prec. sb. 5.)
**1875** R. F. MARTIN tr. *Havrez' Winding Mach.* 75 It would be better to use the steam expansively, rather than to throttle it by means of the regulator. **1884** R. WILSON in *Pall Mall G.* 19 May 11/2 How..can the pressure be reduced from two inches or more to eight-tenths? By throttling the gas at the meter or at the burner. **1898** *Allbutt's Syst. Med.* V. 932 As the stenosis throttles the wave the increased velocity of the blood is counteracted by the rising pressure in the aorta. **1907** *Daily Chron.* 29 July 5/5 The [motor] bus started skidding. I throttled the engine and stuck to my seat as long as I could.

Hence **Throttled** (þrǫ·t'ld) *ppl. a.*, **Thro·ttling** *vbl. sb.* and *ppl. a.*; also **Thro·ttler,** one who or that which throttles: see also quot. 1895.
**1818** SCOTT *Br. Lamm.* ix, The huntsman then withdrew the hounds from the *throttled stag. **1906** *Westm. Gaz.* 14 Nov. 9/2 The motor-car..has grown out of knowledge. Pneumatic tyres, multiple cylinders, a throttled engine, electric ignition,..are a few of the leading improvements. **1859** MAX MÜLLER *Sc. Lang.* ix. (1861) 367 All who have seen..the statue of Laokoon..may realise what those ancients felt..when they called sin *anhas*, or the *throttler. **1889** — *Nat. Relig.* xv. 404 An enemy had been called a throttler. **1895** *Funk's Standard Dict.*, *Throttler*..2. A throttle-valve, or an engine having one. *a* **1687** *Throatling [see 3]. **1826** SCOTT *Jrnl.* 30 May, A sort of throttling sensation. **1863** GEO. ELIOT *Romola* xxii, [He] might easily check any rebellious movement by the threat of throttling. **1875** R. F. MARTIN tr. *Havrez' Winding Mach.* 79 The throttling of the steam at the regulator. **1566** STUDLEY tr. *Seneca, Agam.* E vij, The old mans *thratlyng throt I sawe (alas) I saw yborde With cruell Pirrhus blade [*senis in iugulo Telum Pyrrhi..tingui*]. **1700** DRYDEN *Pal. & Arc.* III. 406 The throttling quinsey 'tis my star appoints. **1830** SCOTT *Demonol.* i. 43 The broken cry of deer mangled by throttling dogs.

**Throu**, obs. form of THROUGH.

† **Throuch, through** (þrɒχ, þrɒχʷ). *Sc. Obs.* Also 6 thrugh, throch, throuche. [History and etymology unknown.
All the forms cited occur also as spellings of THROUGH *sb.*[1], but it is difficult to see any connexion with that word, unless it be that both are rectangular and flat.]
A sheet (of paper).
**1502** *Acc. Ld. High Treas. Scot.* II. 343 For xxj thrugh of ymagery to be patrownis to the broudstar,..xxj s. **1546** *Ibid.* VIII. 450 For xij throuchis of Lumbart paper to be patronis for chargeouris of gunnis,..ij s. **1556–7** *Edinburgh Burgh Rec.* 9 Jan., To tak the inuentar of the habilite of all personis and the quantite of thair substance, and wryting the samyn, quhilk was xxviij throch of paper. **1572** *Satir. Poems Reform.* xxxiii. Ded. 5 To quhome can I this lytill throuch propyne, Bot vnto ane of excellent ingyne? *a* **1578** LINDESAY (Pitscottie) *Chron. Scot.* (S.T.S.) I. 407 The Cardinal held ane throch of paper to the king and causit him wreit his handwreit thairon. **1590** in *Acts of Sederunt* (1790) 18 That all letteris that conteinis mair nor ane throuche of paper, that everie battering, and end of the throuche, sall be subscrivit be him. **1618** *Rec. Elgin* (New Spald. Cl.) I. 237 For writin of half ane through of paper.

**Through,** *sb.*[1] *Obs.* exc. *Sc.* and *north. dial.* (þrɒχʷ, þrɒf, þruf). Forms: 1 thru(u)ch, throuch, 1–3 þruh, (1 þryh), 4 throuȝ, þrouhwe, 4–5 þrugh, þrouȝ, 4–6 throgh(e, 4–6 (9 *Sc.*) thrugh, 5 thrughe, throw(e, throh, 6 threwgh, *Sc.* throch, throwch, throuche, throcht, throucht, 7 throughe, 6– through; 6– *Sc.* throuch, (9 threuch, thruch, throoch, *north. dial.* thruff). *β.* 4 thoru, 5 thorow, thorw, thurwhe, thwrwe, thurgh, 6 thorgh, thorowgh, 7 thorough. [OE. *þrúh*, a fem. cons. stem, oblique cases *þrýh*, cogn. with ON. *þró* fem. (pl. *þróer*) a receptacle hollowed out, a tube, chest, trough, whence *stein-þró* stone-chest, stone-coffin; cf. also OHG. *drûha*, *truhâ* (MHG. *trûhe*, *truche*, Ger. *truhe*), which agrees in sense, but not in the initial consonant: see Kluge *Etymol. Wörterb.*]

†**1.** (Only in *OE.*) A trough, pipe, channel for water. [So ON. *þró* trough, watering trough.]
*a* **700** *Epinal Gloss.* (O.E.T.) 1000 *Tubo*, thruu[c]h [*Corpus* ðruh, *Erfurt* thruch]. *Ibid.* 232 *Caractis* [*cataractes*], uua[e]terthruch [*Corpus* ueterþruh, *Erfurt* uaeterthrouch]. *a* **900** *O. E. Martyrol.* 2 Sept., Þa ȝesomnodon þa sticceo hi in þa þruh, þurh þa þe þæt wæter fleow; þa ne meahte þæt wæter flowan.

†**2.** A hollow receptacle for a dead body: orig. perh. a stone cist or coffin; hence a coffin generally, e. g. of wood; also a grave, tomb, sepulchre. *Obs.*
*a* **900** tr. *Bæda's Hist.* IV. xiv. [xi.] (1890) 296 Þa wæs se lichoma sponne lengra þære þryh. *c* **1000** ÆLFRIC *Hom.* I. 216 Tweȝen ȝelyfede men..bebyriȝdon his lic ær æfene, on niwere ðryh. *Ibid.* II. 262 Þa ȝedafode Pilatus þæt hi..ða ðruh ȝe-innseȝelodon. *c* **1275** *Passion of our Lord* 511 in *O. E. Misc.* 51 Ioseph..hyne leyde in one þruh of stone. *a* **1300** *Cursor M.* 24637 (Edin.) Al til his þruh þai þrang. **13..** *Ibid.* 17288 + 13 (Cott.) Our lord opend not his throgh when he ros at morne. **13..** *Guy Warw.* (A.) 7306 + st. 296 Þay tok a þrouȝ of marbel ston, & leyd his bodi þer-in anon. **13..** *Propr. Sanct.* 179 (Vernon MS.) in Herrig's *Archiv* LXXXI. 83 On domus-day, Al vre þrouhwes þen schul ouerþrowe. *c* **1400** *Laud Troy Bk.* 15570 Now he is ded & lith In throw [*rime* now]. *c* **1410** *Chron. Eng.* (Ritson) 747 Ant leggen in a throh of ston. **1483** *Cath. Angl.* 386/2 A Thrughe (*A.* Throghe), *mauseolum..cippus*;..*vbi* a grawe. *β.* **13..** *Cursor M.* 17390 (Cott.) Þan þai badd be-for ham call þat gett [*v.r.* kepte] þe thoru þe knightes all. *c* **1400** *Trevisa's Higden* (Rolls) VII. 535 (MS. *β*) On caas ȝe mowe kepe my body..lay hit in a thorow [*MS. γ*, þrouȝ] of stoon and heleth hit with a lidde of lede. *a* **1450** Thurghis [see THRO *a.*[1] 1 b].

**3.** A large slab of stone, etc. laid upon a tomb; a flat grave-stone or grave-cover; also, a table gravestone resting on feet. (See THROUGH-STONE[1].)
*a* **1350** *St. Nicholas* 384 in Horstm. *Altengl. Leg.* (1881) 16 Enterd he was in toumbe of stone And a marble thrugh laid him opon. **1523** *Test. Ebor.* (Surtees) V. 174 To lay oppon my body & Alicie my wif a conveniente thrughe of stone. **1560** in *Edinb. Burgh Rec.* 62 To reparrall the kirk, to lay the throwchis thairof of new and sparge the samyn. **1593** *Rites of Durham* (Surtees 1903) 15 Two lyons..artificially wrought and sett forth all in brasse marueilously beautifyinge the said through of marble. **1606** [see THORTERSOME]. **1630** *Vestry Bks.* (Surtees) 185 Through the ignorance or negligence of the sexton or others,..the throughs and flaggs have been brooke, and once taken up never so well laid downe. *a* **1663** BP. BRAMHALL *Will*, I to be buried in the middle alley within the church of Alhallowes in Pontefracte under the greate blewe through at the end of the Maior and Aldresses stall. **1777** *Bothkennar Par. Reg.* 8 July, in *N. & Q.* 9th Ser. II. 237/1 John Simpson, tenant in Crofthead, hath 2 lairs with throughs in the churchyard of Bothkennar. **1804** STAGG *Misc. Poems* (1808) 4 Then great Job Bruff gat on a thruff. **1804** W. CHAMBERS *Hist. Peebles.* 295 Throuchs or flat table-like stones.

**Through,** *sb.*[2]: see THROUCH.

**Through** (þrū), *sb.*[3] Also 8–9 *dial.* **thruff** (þrɒf). [f. THROUGH *adv.* or *adj.*, sometimes due to ellipsis of a sb.]

**1.** = THOROUGH *sb.* 2. *dial.*
**1778** [W. MARSHALL] *Minutes Agric.* 10 June an. 1777, Mixes it with the sand and marl, which is thrown out in making their elaborate thruffs,—or sub-drains.

**2.** = THROUGH-STONE[2].
**1805** [see THROUGH-STONE[2]]. **1828** *Craven Gloss.*, *Thruff*, a bond stone, or thorough stone. **1846** BROCKETT *N. C. Words* s. v. *Thruff-stone*, These walls being composed of fragments of all shapes and sizes, without mortar, the 'thruffs' are used as bond-stones and give great stability. **1892** J. T. BENT *Ruined Cities Mashonaland* iv. 97 Most of them [the stones] run back into the wall irregularly, acting in the same way as *throughs* in our dry-built walls.

**3.** A ladder-rung that goes through the sides. *local.*
**1899** *N. & Q.* 9th Ser. III. 76/2 Ladders are often made with three or four flat bars, longer than the rounded ones, and projecting sufficiently on each side to admit a wooden peg...These are called flat rungs, sometimes 'throughs' (thrufs).

**Through** (þrū), *a.* [attrib. use of THROUGH *adv.*, primarily used with verbal sbs., nouns of action, agent-nouns, and the like, derived from vbs. qualified by the adv., or with ellipsis of a pple. of such a verb, as in *through* (going) *way*; afterwards in various extended or transferred uses.]

**1.** That passes, extends, or affords passage through something. (See also THOROUGH *a.* 1; THROUGH- 2.)
*spec.* Of a bolt, rivet, etc.: Passing through the whole thickness of that in which it is fixed: see also *through-bolt* s. v. THROUGH- 2. *Through bridge*: see quot. 1877. *Through lights*: see THOROUGH-LIGHT.
**1523** [see *through-serewe*, *-spavin* in THROUGH- 2]. *a* **1578** [see THROUGH-PASSAGE]. **1596** SPENSER *State Irel.* Wks. (Globe) 614/1 Was there not a through way then made by the swoord for the imposing of lawes uppon them? **1605** BACON *Adv. Learn.* II. ii. § 14 The opennesse and through passage of the world..were appointed to be in the same ages. **1865** *Once a Week* 10 June 679/1 Building houses back to back without any 'through' ventilation. **1877** KNIGHT *Dict. Mech.*, *Through-bridge*, one in which the track rests on the lower stringer, in contradistinction to a *deck*-bridge. **1889** WELCH *Text Bk. Naval Archit.* iv. 74 The rivets are of two kinds, through (or clenched) and tap.

**b.** That goes, extends, or conveys through the whole of a long distance or journey without interruption, or without change; as a *through train*, *passenger*, *line of railway*, *fare*, *ticket*, *traffic*.
**1845** *Boston* (Mass.) *Transcript* 29 Nov. 3/2 Through tickets may be obtained for Montreal. **1846** *Boston* (Mass.) *Traveller* 2 July, Through trains from Boston. **1858** HAWTHORNE *Fr. & It. Note-Bks.* (1872) I. 1 Having taken through tickets to Paris by way of Folkestone and Boulogne. **1861** JEFFERSON DAVIS *Message to Confederate Congress Amer.* 18 Nov., The construction of this..line would give us a through route from North to South. **1861** *Sat. Rev.* 7 Sept. 236 The through traffic to Scotland has been carried on by eight independent Companies. **1884** *Gt. West. Railw. Time Tables* July 10 The direct Through Trains between Aldgate and Richmond. **1890** *Daily News* 12 Nov. 7/2 Any railway to which there is through booking from Aldershot. **1893** EARL DUNMORE *Pamirs* I. 83 A few merchants carry on a through trade between India and Turkestan. **1905** *Sat. Rev.* 21 Oct. 522/2 What with the through travellers and the..traffic, there was no lack of variety.

**c.** Of an organ-stop: Extending through the whole compass of the keyboard.
**1881** C. A. EDWARDS *Organs* 146 All the foundation..stops of a really good organ should be through stops.

†**2.** Going through or affecting the whole of something; = THOROUGH *a.* 2. *Obs.*
*Through coal*, or *through and through coal*, coal as it comes from the pit, i. e. large and small mixed indiscriminately.
**1542** UDALL *Erasm. Apoph.* 80 That thei might..haue a through sight in it. **1581** SIDNEY *Apol. Poetrie* (Arb.) 49 From a through beholding the worthines of the subiect. **1607** HIERON *Wks.* I. 462 To speake of a true and through reformation. **1647** CLARENDON *Hist. Reb.* III. § 211 There was not a Grievance..to which there was not a through Remedy applied. **1696** VANBRUGH *Relapse* Epil. 22 You never saw a through republican a finish'd beau. **1710** PRIDEAUX *Orig. Tithes* ii. 69 If on through search and examination they were approved of.

**Through,** *v. Sc. rare.* ? *Obs.* [f. THROUGH *prep.* and *adv.*: cf. THOROUGH *v.*[1]]

**1.** *trans.* To carry through, put through, carry into effect. Hence **Throu·ghing** *vbl. sb.*
**1638** R. BAILLIE *Lett. & Jrnls.* (1841) I. 74 His father's throughing of Perth articles. **1716** *Wodrow Corr.* (1843) II. 172, I am mistaken if this way they get their design throughed.

**2.** *intr.* To get through; to succeed. *To make to through*, to make good, prove.
**1786** BURNS *Brigs of Ayr* 175 Faith ye've said enough, And muckle mair than ye can mak to through. **1863** JANET HAMILTON *Poems & Ess.* 56 We've throught weel and thrivin this mony a year.

**Through** (þrū, þru), *prep.* and *adv.* From *c* 1700, abbreviated **thro'**; in 15–18th c., without ', **thro.** Forms: see below. [OE. *ðurh*, *þurh*, Northumb. *ðerh*, a Common WGer. prep. and adv.: cf. OFris. (from *thurch) *thruch*, *truch* (WFris. *troch*, NFris. *truch*, *troch*); OS. *thurh*, *thuru*, **thurih* (MLG. *dorch*, *dörch*, *dor*, *dör*, LG. *dör*, *dôr*, MDu. *door*, *dôre*, *döre*, *deur*, *dor*, *dur*, Du. *door*); OHG. *duruh*, *durih*, *duri*, *dur* (MHG. *durch*, *dürch*, *dur*, *dür*, Ger. *durch*, dial. *dur*, *dör*). Not in Scandinavian: in Gothic with different ablaut grade *þairh* (= *þerh*); prob. cases of a sb., belonging to a pre-Teut. ablaut-series **terk-*, *tork-*, *trk-* to bore: cf. Goth. *þairkô* hole, and OHG. *durhil*, MHG. *dürchel*, *dürkel*, OE. **þyrhil*, *þyrel* bored, perforated: cf. THIRL *sb.* OE. *þurh* with full stress became *þuruh*, now THOROUGH, as *burh* has become *borough*, *furh furrow*, etc.; when unstressed and proclitic, *þurh* became *þŭr*, and with metathesis *þrŭh*, *þrŭ*, *throŭ*, *thrŏ*. The unstressed forms naturally prevailed in proclitic prepositional use, and the stressed in the adverb, and its derived adj. and sb. But with the re-stressing of the prep. *thrŭ* as *through* (þrū), this form has also become possible as an adverb, while on the other hand the stressed THOROUGH also survives as an archaic form of the preposition beside the normal *through*. *Thurf* is an early phonetic development of *þurh*, and *thruf* a more recent one of *þruh*, similar to (rɒf) for *rough*, *dwarf* from *dwergh*, (bārf) for *Bargh*, (bruf) for *Burgh* (place-names), (ɪnɒ·f) for *enough*, (þǫf) for *though*, etc. The metathesis of *þruh* for *þurh* occurs already *c* 1300 in a s. w. text; but otherwise in ME. is usually northern. From Caxton onwards it was the standard English form.
See *Note* under THOROUGH *prep.* and *adv.*]

**A. Illustration of Forms.**
For disyllabic forms *þureh*, *þuruh*, *þurow*, etc.: see THOROUGH.
**a.** 1 **þurȝ** (þerh), 1–3 **þorh** (1 þorch), 1–4 **þurh,** 2–4 **þurch,** 3 *Orm.* **þurrh,** 3–4 **þurȝ, þorȝ, thurȝ,** 3–5 **þurgh,** 4 **þorgh, þorghe, þourh, þourȝ,** (**þour**), 4–5 **þourgh, thourgh, thurghe, thorgh,** 4–6 **thurgh,** 5 **thorȝ, þurȝe, þourȝe,** (**thour**), *Sc.* **thourch.** Also 3 **þurþ, þorþ,** 4 **þurth, þurȝth,** 5 **thourth,** (**dorth**); 4–5 **thurght, thorght,** 5 **þurght.**
(Final *þ*, *ð*, is frequently a scribal error for final ȝ, and *th*

a copyist's error for *ch*; in Scotch *t* was often added to *-ch*, *-gh*, or *-th*.)

*a* 700 *Epinal Gloss.* (O.E.T.) 741 *Per seudoterum*, þorh ludgaet. *Ibid.* 757 *Per anticipationem*, þorch [*Erfurt* dorh] obst. *a* 800 CYNEWULF *Elene* 289 Þurh witȝena wordȝeryno. *a* 900 Þurh [see B. I. 7 b]. *c* 950 *Lindisf. Gosp.* Mark xv. 10 Ðerh æfist [*Rushw.* ðærh æfeste] ȝesaldon hine. *c* 1000 *Fates 12 Apostles* 13 (Gr.) Þurȝ Nerones nearo-searwe. *c* 1000 *Ags. Gosp.* ibid., Ðurh andan hine sealdon. *a* 1175 *Cott. Hom.* 223 Ealle þing ȝeworhcte god þurch his worda. *a* 1200 *Moral Ode* 282 Þe suneȝe þurð sihte. *c* 1200 Þurrh [see B. I. 7]. 1297 R. GLOUC. (Rolls) 681, & regnede þritti ȝer wel þor [*v. rr.* þoru, þurgh, thorugh, þrough] alle þinge. 13.. *Cursor M.* 11070 (Gött.) All þe cunthre thurght. *c* 1350 *Will. Palerne* 4219 Þourh ȝour help. 13.. *Gaw. & Gr. Knt.* 310 Þurȝ ryalmes so mony. 1377 LANGL. *P. Pl.* B. I. 32 Thorw [*C.* Thorgh] wyn and þorw women þere was Loth acombred. 1393 *Ibid.* C. XXI. 399 So þat þorgh gyle was geten, þorwe grace is now y-wonne. *c* 1380 WYCLIF *Serm.* Sel. Wks. I. 392 Þourȝ Samarie and þe cuntre of Galile. *c* 1386 CHAUCER *Frankl. T.* 137 Eterne god that thurgh [*v. rr.* thour, þurgh, þourgh, þoruhe] thy purueiance Ledest the world. *c* 1410 Thourh [see B. II. 5 b]. *c* 1425 *Seven Sag.* (P.) 522 Thourth the emperours commandement. *c* 1440 Thorgh [see B. I. 2]. *c* 1450 *Merlin* ii. 32 He hadde resceyved deth thourgh me. *c* 1460 *Launfal* 1031 The lady rod dorth Cardevyle. *c* 1460 Thourth; 1521 Thurgh [see B. II. 1; B. I. 1].

**β. 3 þruh, 4 þrouȝ, 5 þroughe, throwȝe, thruȝ, thrughe, (drogh, trogh), 5–6 thrugh, throughe, 5–7 throgh, 6 throwgh(e, 5– through (8– *abbrev.* thro'); 4 thru, *Sc.* thrw, threu, threw, 4–7 (chiefly *Sc.*) throu, 4–8 (–9 *Sc.* or *dial.*) throw, 5 þro, 5–9 thro, 6 throwe, *Sc.* throuw; *Sc.* 4–6 throuch, 6 thruch, thrwch, throwch, 7 throche, 8 throch; 5 throght, (troght), 5–6 *Sc.* throcht, 6 thruȝht, *Sc.* thrucht, throucht.**

?*a* 1300 *Prayer to Virgin* 8 in *O. E. Misc.* (1872) 195 Bote þu þruh þin milde mod bringe me out of sunne. *Ibid.* 19. 13.. Thru, throu [see B. I. 1 b, 7 b]. *c* 1350 *Will. Palerne* 459 Mi wicked eyiȝen..lad myn hert þrouȝ loking þis langour to drye. 1375 BARBOUR *Bruce* I. 137 Throuch thar aller hale assent. *Ibid.* 533 Destroyit throw pwsoune. *c* 1375 *Sc. Leg. Saints* x. (*Mathou*) 52 Thrw sorcery & felone gyle. *Ibid.* xiii.[2] (*Marcus*) 49 Threw þe schewynge Of þe ewangele. *Ibid.* xxvi. (*Nycholas*) 806 Blyndyt threu gret cowatise. *c* 1400 *Sowdone Bab.* 2526 He..hade pardon Throgh prayere and specialle grace. *c* 1400 *Destr. Troy* 1129 Thrugh lemys of light. *Ibid.* 4977 Þro mony long chaumburs. *c* 1425 *Eng. Conq. Irel.* 18 The gret peril that myght be-fall hym..drogh the owt-comen folk þat was thus in-to the land I-com. *Ibid.* 26 Trogh al thynge. *Ibid.* 28 That thou ne hast y-done troght some grete lette. *c* 1470 HENRY *Wallace* VIII. 709 Throcht falsheid, and thar subtilite. 1484 CAXTON *Fables of Æsop* v. viii, The serpent..slewe the child through his venym. 1487–8 Throwȝe [see B. I. 4]. *c* 1489 Thrughe [see B. I. 1 h]. *a* 1500 *Cokwolds Daunce* 105 in Hazl. *E. P. P.* I. 43 Ffor that was thruȝht a chans. 1500–20 DUNBAR *Poems* xlii. 81 Thrucht Skornes noss thai put a prik. — Throucht [see B. I. 3]. 1508— *Gold. Targe* 28 Doun throu the ryce a ryuir ran. 1533 *Cal. Anc. Rec. Dublin* (1889) 396 Such merchunds..as cum throw Oxmantown. 1545–7 in *Archæologia* XXXIV. 41 Throwgh the weke. 1596 Throuch [see B. II. 4]. 1674 BREVINT *Saul at Endor* 140 [He] may fall..thro a broken bridge. *a* 1679 HOBBES *Rhet.* (1681) Pref., Throu the working of Belief. 1709 PRIOR *Despairing Shepherd* i, Wand'ring thro' the lonely Rocks. 1724 RAMSAY *Vision* i, Throch feidom, our Freedom Is blotit with this skore. *a* 1758 — *Bonny Tweedside* i, I'll awa' to bonny Tweed side, And see my deary come throw.

**γ. 3–4 þurf, 3–6 thurf, 8–9 (*dial.*) thruff.**

*c* 1290 *St. Brendan* 149 in *S. Eng. Leg.* I. 223 Þurf oure louerdes grace. *a* 1300 *Fragm. Pop. Sc.* (Wright) l. 11 Thurf dai & thurf niȝt. *a* 1500 *Childe of Bristowe* 520 in Hazl. *E. P. P.* I. 129 Thurf your good he is save. *a* 1800 PEGGE *Suppl. Grose, Thruff and thruff*, i.e. through and through. *Derb.* 1864 TENNYSON *North. Farmer, O. Style* xi, I..runn'd plow thruff it an' all. 1888 FENN *Dick o' Fens* 153 Go thruff yon reed-bed home.

**B. Signification.**

**I.** *prep.* The preposition expressing the relation of transition or direction within something from one limit of it to the other: primarily in reference to motion in space, hence in various derived senses.

**1.** From one end, side, or surface to the other or opposite end, side, or surface of (a body or a space) by passing within it; usually implying into, at one end, side, etc. and out of at the other.

(Expressing movement (or extension) either so as to penetrate the substance of a thing, or along a passage or opening already existing in it.) With various vbs. of motion forming prepositional phrases: cf. PASS *v.* 58 a, RUN *v.* 12–15, etc.

*a* 700 [see A. α]. *c* 950 *Lindisf. Gosp.* Matt. vii. 13 Inngeonges ðerh nearuo port. *c* 1000 *ibid.*, Gangað inn þurh þæt nearwe ȝeat. *c* 1400 *Destr. Troy* 4977 Led were þo lordes þro mony long chaumburs..þurgh mony gay Alys. 1446 *Registr. Aberdon.* (Maitl. Cl.) I. 245 A lonyng lyand þrow the mur betwix twa ald stane dykes. 1490 CAXTON *Eneydos* xv. 60 Fyres..sodaynly sente throughe the cloudes in grete tempeste and murmure. 1521 FISHER *Wks.* (1876) 315 To condyth that people thurgh the deserte. 1557 N. T. (Genev.) *John* iv. 4 He must nedes go through [1526 TINDALE thorowe] Samaria. 1605 CAMDEN *Rem.* 193 An extreame cold winde passed throgh his sides. 1708 *Constit. Watermen's Co.* xl, If any person Row..through London-Bridge, on the Flood-Tide. 1758 JOHNSON *Idler* No. 15 ⁋ 2 Sauntering about the Shop with her arms through her pocket-holes. 1848 THACKERAY *Van. Fair* xxxii, George..was lying..dead, with a bullet through his heart. *Mod.* There is a path through the wood.

**b.** Denoting transmission of light, or of sight, by an aperture or a transparent medium; also *fig.* (See also LOOK *v.* 20, SEE *v.* 24.)

13.. *Cursor M.* 11229 (Gött.) Þe sune beme gas thru [*Cott.* thoru] þe glas. *c* 1386 CHAUCER *Knt.'s T.* 217 Thurgh a wyndow..He cast his eye vpon Emelya. 1640 NABBES *Bride* III. ii, A pigmie that cannot be discerned but through a multiplying glas. 1704 POPE *Disc. Past. Poetry* § 5 Piety to the Gods should shine through the Poem. 1766 GOLDSM. *Vic. W.* xvi, These instances of cunning, which she thought impenetrable, yet which everybody saw through. 1852 DICKENS *Bleak Ho.* viii, Mrs. Pardiggle..had been regarding him through her spectacles.

**c.** In reference to a (more distant or fainter) sound heard simultaneously with another (nearer or louder) which does not 'drown' it or prevent it from reaching the ear.

1819 KEATS *Isabella* xxxvi, Languor there was in it, and tremulous shake,..And through it moan'd a ghostly undersong. 1847 TENNYSON *Princess* IV. 554 Thy voice is heard thro' rolling drums.

**d.** In reference to the passages traversed by the breath in the production and modification of vocal sound, as *to speak through the throat, the nose*, etc.

1588, 1741, 1850 [see NOSE *sb.* 3]. 1668 OWEN PRICE *Eng. Orthographie* 16 *Gh* soundes now like *h*, in *Almighty*, *although* [etc.]. *Note*, But the Ancients did, as the Welch, & Scots do still pronounce *gh*, thorow the throat.

**e.** With pl. (or collective) sb., expressing passage between or among things so as to penetrate the whole mass or body of them (without penetrating the individual things); through between. See also 2, and cf. THROUGH OTHER.

1535, 1684 [see THOROUGH B. I. 1 d]. 1709 PRIOR *Despairing Sheph.* i, Wand'ring thro' the lonely Rocks. 1712 ADDISON *Spect.* No. 327 ⁋ 6 [Raphael's] Flight thro' the Choirs of Angels is finely imaged. 1852 R. S. SURTEES *Sponge's Sp. Tour* (1893) 85 He was small and wiry, with legs that a pig could run through. 1890 'R. BOLDREWOOD' *Col. Reformer* (1891) 204 The slippery savage..was bounding through the trees. *Mod.* Walking through the long grass.

**f.** In phr. *through* (one's) *hands, through a machine*, etc., referring to something being handled, manufactured, subjected to some process, or dealt with in any way. (See also MILL *sb.*[1] 1 b.)

*c* 1320 *Sir Beues* (A.) 1035 Erst þow schelt pase þourȝ min hond. 1630 *R. Johnson's Kingd. & Commw.* 346 They are able in one day to make two hundred Harquibushes..although there be no Harquebush that goeth through lesse than ten hands at the least. 1641 in Cochran-Patrick *Rec. Coinage Scotl.* (1876) I. Introd. 31 They would putt 1000 stane [of copper] throw the yrons in the yeire. 1709 BAGFORD in *MS. Rawl. Lett.* 21, lf. 8 All of them from yᵉ Bookes themselues which haue run throw my handes. 1815 SCOTT *Guy M.* xxxix, I had her through hands once, and could then make little of her. 1874 GREEN *Short Hist.* vii. § 6. 408 Plot and approval alike passed through Walsingham's hands. *Mod.* It has passed through many hands since then.

**g.** In various directly figurative applications: e.g. (*a*) referring to the action upon the ears or nerves of a loud, shrill, harsh, or 'piercing' sound; (*b*) implying the overcoming of hindrance or obstruction (see also BREAK *v.* 55); (*c*) indicating connexion or transmission by an intermediate thing (or person) or a series of such, etc.

*To pay through the nose*: see NOSE *sb.* 11. *Through thick and thin*: see THICK AND THIN.

1543 [see THICK AND THIN A. 1]. 1581–1680 [see THOROUGH B. I. 1 f]. 1647 MAY *Hist. Parl.* II. vi. 127 Your Parliament, whose..undiscouraged endeavours..have passed thorow difficulties unheard of. 1766 GOLDSM. *Vic. W.* xxx, The circumstances of my unfortunate son broke through all efforts to dissemble. *a* 1784 JOHNSON in *Boswell* an. 1737 Knowledge of the world, fresh from life, not strained through books. 1849 MACAULAY *Hist. Eng.* v. I. 526 John Ayloffe, a lawyer connected by affinity with the Hydes, and through the Hydes, with James.

**h.** *Through and through*: repeatedly through; so as to penetrate both sides or surfaces of; right through, entirely through. Also *fig.* (Cf. II. 5.)

13.. [see THOROUGH B. I. 1 g]. *c* 1489 CAXTON *Sonnes of Aymon* xiv. 346 He shoved his swerde thrughe & thrughe his body. 1599 SHAKS. *Much Ado* v. i. 68 Thy slander hath gone through and through her heart. *a* 1716 SOUTH *Serm.* (1842) I. 321 His infinite, all-searching knowledge, which looks through and through the most secret of our thoughts. 1724 DE FOE *Mem. Cavalier* (1840) 227 He broke through and through them. 1745 P. THOMAS *Voy. S. Seas* 281 Our second Shot..went thro' and thro' her upper Works.

**i.** After an auxiliary verb, with ellipsis of *go*. Cf. II. 6; THROUGH *v.* 2.

1567 MAPLET *Gr. Forest* 85 If a mans iourney lieth so, that he must nedes through the Forrest. 1606 SHAKS. *Tr. & Cr.* v. x. 26 You vile abhominable Tents,..He through, and through you.

**2.** Of motion or direction within the limits of; along within; as in 1, 1 e, but not necessarily implying the traversing of the whole extent from end to end.

*c* 1050 *Byrhtferth's Handboc* in *Anglia* (1885) VIII. 298 Þurh þæne yrnð seo sunne. *a* 1300 *Cursor M.* 23412 (Edin.) Al þat þe witstandand es Thurȝ sal [þou] þirle wit sweftnes. *c* 1440 *Pallad. on Husb.* VI. 36 A forgh iij footes deep thy londes thorgh. 1591 SHAKS. *Two Gent.* v. ii. 38 As he in pennance wander'd through the Forrest. 1667 MILTON *P. L.* II. 663 The Night-Hag..riding through the Air. 1787 WINTER *Syst. Husb.* 82 Clouds, which being heavier than the air, of course fall thro' it. 1818 SHELLEY *Sonnet 'Lift not the painted veil'* 11 Through the unheeding many he did move, A splendour among shadows. 1819 KEATS *Eve St. Agnes* i, The hare limp'd trembling through the frozen grass. 1903 *Times* 14 Mar. 14/5 The Oxonians showed good form through choppy water.

**3.** Over or about the whole extent of, all over (a surface); so as to traverse or penetrate every part or district of; in or to all parts of (a region, or a body); throughout; everywhere in. (See also RUN *v.* 68 d.)

*c* 1000 *Ags. Gosp.* Luke xxiii. 5 He astyrað þis folc lærende þurh ealle iudeam. 13.. *Gaw. & Gr. Knt.* 243 Al stouned at his steuen..þurȝ þe sale riche. *c* 1350 *Old Usages Winchester* in *Eng. Gilds* (1870) 359 Lat crye þe ban þorghe þe town þe þridde day by-fore þe selynge. *c* 1450 *Merlin* i. 10, I sought thourgh my chamber. 1500–20 DUNBAR *Poems* lxxiv. 14 Leif creuelte..Or throucht the warld quyte losit is ȝour name. 1591 SHAKS. 1 *Hen. VI*, III. iii. 13 We will make thee famous through the World. 1659 *Termes de la Ley* 146 b/2 That there should be but one scantling of weights and measures through all the Realm. 1727–46 THOMSON *Summer* 1168 And Thule bellows through her utmost isles. 1860 TYNDALL *Glac.* II. vii. 260 Minute particles diffused through the atmosphere.

**b.** Placed after the sb. *arch.*, *poet.*

*a* 1300 *Cursor M.* 11070 Noght allan ierusalem burgh, Bot elles al þe contre thurgh [*v. rr.* thurght, thorogh, þourȝe]. *Ibid.* 11824 Þe fester thrild his bodi thurgh [*rime* scurf]. 1556 ROBINSON *More's Utop.* Shorte Meter (Arb.) 167 Platoes citie, Whose fame flieth the worlde throughe. *a* 1635, 1802 [see THOROUGH B. I. 3]. 1851 MRS. BROWNING *Casa Guidi Wind.* II. 266 A cry is up in England, which doth ring The hollow world through.

†**c.** Phr. *Through all thing* [cf. F. *partout*]: in every point, in all respects, thoroughly. *Obs.*

*c* 1205 LAY. 10966 Ich sugge þe þurh alle þing, ich sloh Asclepidiot. *c* 1290 *Beket* 252 in *S. Eng. Leg.* I. 113 Euere he was chaste þoruȝ alle þing. 1297, *c* 1380 [see THOROUGH B. I. 3 c]. *c* 1425 *Eng. Conq. Irel.* 26 A man full queynt, trow trogh al thynge, & stalwarth.

**4.** During the whole of (a period of time, or an action, etc., with reference to the time it occupies from beginning to end). See also GET *v.* 43 c.

*a* 1000 *Ags. Ps.* (Th.) lxxiii[i]. 21 [22] Þurh ealne dæȝ [*tota die*]. *a* 1250 *Owl & Night.* 447 (Cott.) And ich so dó þurȝ niȝt and dai. 1487–8 *Rec. St. Mary at Hill* 141 On euery sonday throwȝe þe yer. 1581 ALLEN *Apol.* 74 Al the Churches of Christ through al ages. 1593 SHAKS. *Lucr.* 718 Through the length of times he stands disgraced. 1667 MILTON *P. L.* x. 846 Thus Adam..lamented..Through the still Night. 1779 *Mirror* No. 37 ⁋ 5 The same sanguine temperament of mind which..has attended him through life. 1861 MRS. CARLYLE *Lett.* (1883) III. 81 A brass band plays all through our breakfast. 1896 T. F. TOUT *Edw. I*, iv. 80 All through his reign, the Lusignans helped him in Gascony.

**b.** Placed after a sb.; esp. preceded by *all*.

1535 [see THOROUGH B. I. 4]. 1864 MRS. GATTY *Parab. fr. Nat.* Ser. IV. 5 He was seldom seen without one [a flower] in his button-hole all the summer through. 1872 A. DE VERE *Leg. St. Patrick, Disbelief Milcho* 32 Fireless sits he, winter through. 1873 BLACK *Pr. Thule* iii, It will be like this all the night through.

**5.** From beginning to end of; in or along the whole length or course of (an action, an experience, a piece of work, etc.; also of a discourse, a book, etc.). See also GET *v.* 43, GO *v.* 63, PASS *v.* 58 b, RUN *v.* 68.

*c* 1449 [see THOROUGH B. I. 5]. 1578 TIMME *Caluine on Gen.* 326, I may not runne through vncertain speculations. 1766 GOLDSM. *Vic. W.* xiv, I had..put my horse through all his paces. 1774 MITFORD *Ess. Harmony Lang.* 93, I cannot find any thing like [it]..thro the whole essay. 1831 MACAULAY *Let.* in Trevelyan *Life* (1876) I. iv. 233, I should have liked to have sat through so tremendous a storm. 1886 AD. SERGEANT *No Saint* I. vi. 105 An old land surveyor ..put him through a long catechism.

**b.** with emphasis on the intervening or intermediate stage or condition. (Leading on to 7.)

1671 MILTON *P. R.* I. 5 Obedience fully tri'd Through all temptation. 1818 MOORE *Fudge Fam. Paris* vi. 103 They graduate Through job, red ribbon, and silk gown, To Chancellorship and Marquisate. 1837 DICKENS *Pickw.* lvii, Mr. Bob Sawyer, having previously passed through the Gazette, passed over to Bengal. 1870 W. MORRIS *Earthly Par.* III. *Story Rhodope* 20 The brown plain..Changed year by year through green to hoary gold. 1881 STANLEY *Chr. Instit.* vii. (1882) 131 In the new crisis through which the world was to pass.

**c.** with emphasis laid upon the completion: To the end of. (Leading on to 6.)

1628 [see THOROUGH B. I. 5]. 1744 BERKELEY *Siris* § 2 Seven children, who came all very well through the small-pox. 1824 *New Monthly Mag.* X. 19, I never could read through the Nouvelle Heloïse. 1843 MRS. CARLYLE *Lett.* (1883) I. 253, I seemed to be got pretty well through my sewing. *Mod.* When shall you get through your task? He has got through 'Smalls'.

**6.** Indicating a position or point ultimately reached. (Usually in predicate, after verb *to be*.) Cf. II. 3. **a.** *lit.* At a point beyond, or at the further end of. **b.** *fig.* Having reached the end of (a course of action, a book, etc.); having finished, completed, or done with. **c.** In reference to an examination, *to be through* is to have passed.

1791 JEFFERSON *Writ.* (1896) V. 330, I think I can be through them [a bundle of letters] by the end of the week. 1791 BURNS *Tam O'Shanter* 93 By this time he was cross the ford..And thro' the whins, and by the cairn. 1801 tr. *Gabrielli's Myst. Husb.* II. 267 They stopped at an inn nearly through the town. 1804 SOUTHEY in *Life* (1850) II. 262, I am half through the poem. 1894 *Outing* (U.S.) XXIV. 428/2 You may as well tell him that you're through taking lessons. *Mod.* Is he through his examination?

**7.** Indicating medium, means, agency, or instrument: By means of; by the action of, by (*obs.* or *arch.*) Now *spec.* By the instrumentality of.

*a* 800 [see A. α]. *c* 950 *Lindisf. Gosp.* Luke xvii. 1 Wæ ðæm ðerh ðone hia cymes. *c* 1000 *Fates 12 Apostles* 63 (Gr.) We þæt ȝehyrdon þurh haliȝe bec. 1154 *O. E. Chron.* an.

1132 (Laud), þurh Godes milce & þurh þe biscop of Seresberi. *c* **1200** ORMIN 13254 3a þurrh fulluhht, 3a þurrh hanndgang Att hadedd manness hande. **1258** *Proclam. Hen. III* 12 Oct., Henry thur3 godes fultome king on Engleneloande. *c* **1305** *Pilate* 89 in *E. E. P.* (1862) 113 He huld him bitrayd þurf felonie. **1375** BARBOUR *Bruce* I. 137 Throuch þar aller hale assent, Messingeris till hym þai sent. **1475** *Bk. Noblesse* (Roxb.) 16 A grete navy..ovyrcom throw myghty fyghtyng. **1579** W. WILKINSON *Confut. Familye of Loue* B iij, Abell was slayne..through the handes of his brother Cain. **1763** J. BROWN *Poetry & Mus.* vii. 151 This Event happened..thro' the Authority of the thirty Tyrants. **1793** BURKE *Corr.* (1844) IV. 153 The answer given to Monsieur Lesardier was through a young gentleman. **1849** MACAULAY *Hist. Eng.* vi. II. 123 [He] could not prevent the national sentiment from expressing itself through the pulpit and the press. **1883** SIR N. LINDLEY in *Law Rep.* 11 Q. Bench Div. 572 The..Society..seeks to do through him that which it cannot otherwise do. **1885** *Act* 48 & 49 *Vict.* c. 54 § 15 Every notice..sent through the post in a prepaid registered letter.

†**b.** Indicating the agent, after a passive verb: = BY *prep.* 33. *Obs.*

*a* **900** tr. *Bæda's Hist.* I. ix, Seo her3ung wæs þurh Alaricum..3eworden. **971** *Blickl. Hom.* 9 Heofonrices duru..sceal þonne þurh þe ontened beon. *c* **1000** *Ags. Gosp.* Matt. xxvi. 24 Wa þam menn þurh þone þe byþ mannes sunu be-læwed. **13..** *Cursor M.* 20909 (Cott.) In rome throu an þat hight neron .. Petre .. naild on þe rod he was. **1424** *Sc. Acts Jas. I* (1814) II. 5/1 Chargit be þe gret aithe throwe þe bischope. *c* **1425** *Eng. Conq. Irel.* 12 Vnnethes he was I-draw vp throgh his felowes, þat mych put har lyf in aduentur for to saw his lif. **1597** A. M. tr. *Guillemeau's Fr. Chirurg.* 43 b/1 The skinne beinge lift vp through some seruant, or through the Chyrurgiane with his Pinsers.

**8.** Indicating cause, reason, or motive: In consequence of, by reason of, on account of, owing to; from; for.

*a* **1000** *Cædmon's Gen.* 610 (Gr.) Þa se forhatena spræc þurh feondscipe. *c* **1000** *Ags. Gosp.* Matt. xxvi. 31 Þurh þæs hyrdes sle3e byð seo heord todræfed. **1154** *O. E. Chron.* an. 1127 (Laud), Þet wes eall ðurh þone kyng Heanri. *c* **1200** *Trin. Coll. Hom.* 191 Þurch onde com deað in to þe worelde. *c* **1460** *Oseney Regr.* 3 Þe paralytke man..heled of our lorde ..þroughe þe beleve off theyme þat bare hym. **1562** *Aberdeen Kirk Sess. Rec.* (Spald. Cl.) 9 Gryte thyft, committit throcht verray neid and necessite. **1671** MILTON *Samson* 369 If he through frailty err. **1697** DRYDEN *Virg. Georg.* II. 638 Thro' Wine they quarrell'd, and thro' Wine were slain. **1798** COLERIDGE *Anc. Mar.* II. xiii, Every tongue thro' utter drouth Was wither'd at the root. **1894** J. J. FOWLER *Adamnan* Introd. 56 The southern Picts..embraced the truth through the preaching of St. Ninian.

†**b.** In oaths and adjurations: By, in the name of. (Cf. BY *prep.* 2.) *Obs.*

*a* **1000** *Cædmon's Satan* 694 Ic þe hate þurh þa hehstan miht, þæt ðu hellwarum hyht ne abeode. *c* **1000** ÆLFRIC *Gen.* xxii. 16 Ic swerige þurh me sylfne, sæde se Ælmihti3a. *a* **1225** *Ancr. R.* 114 þurh þeo ilke neiles ich halse ou ancren,..holdeð our honden wiðinnen ouwer þurles. *c* **1290** *Edmund Conf.* 307 in *S. Eng. Leg.* I. 440 'Þurf oure louerdes passioun tel nou', he seide.

**II.** *adv.*

(For special combinations with verbs, as BREAK *through*, CARRY *through*, FALL *through*, GET *through*, GO *through*, PASS *through*, PULL *through*, PUT *through*, RUN *through*, etc., see the verbs.)

**1.** From end to end, side to side, or surface to surface (of a body or space) by passing or extending within; so as to penetrate: cf. I. 1.

*a* **1000** *Ags. Ps.* (Th.) lxxviii[i]. 15 [13] He sæ toslat, sealte yþa 3efæstnade, and hi foran þurh. *a* **1225** *Ancr. R.* 272 Heo þuruh stihten Isboset..into þe schere. *c* **1400** *Destr. Troy* 6780 Mony shalke þurgh shot with þere sharpe gere. **14..** *Tundale's Vis.* 327 Þo heyte of the fuyr dyd throw pas. *c* **1460** METHAM *Wks.* (E.E.T.S.) 91 Als strekyn thourth with oon lyne or with many lynes. *a* **1533** LD. BERNERS *Huon* lix. 205 Huon..strake hym with his spere clene throwe. **1719** WATTS *Hymns* II. lix. 2 Glory to God that walks the sky, And sends his blessing thro'. **1798** COLERIDGE *Anc. Mar.* I. xvii, The Ice did split with a Thunder-fit; The Helmsman steer'd us thro'! **1850** LEITCH tr. *C. O. Müller's Anc. Art* (ed. 2) § 337 A..garment..drawn..over the right arm, or else through beneath it towards the left arm.

**b.** In reference to travel or conveyance: Along the whole distance; all the way; to the end of the journey; to the destination.

[*a* **1425** *Cursor M.* 11741 (Trin.) Of þritty dayes Iourney þro þou shal haue but a day to go [*earlier MSS.* lang..gang].] **1617** J. BARGRAVE in *Buccleuch MSS.* (Hist. MSS. Comm.) I. 198 His packets sometimes fail when private letters go through. **1692** LUTTRELL *Brief Rel.* (1857) II. 376 He was accompanied part of the way by the queen ..and Essex, who went thro'. **1732** POPE *Ess. Man* II. 274 Hope travels thro', nor quits us when we die. **1858** *Penny Cycl.* 2nd Suppl. 565/2 A man may now 'book through' from London to so many continental cities. **1858** HAWTHORNE *Fr. & It. Note-bks.* (1872) I. 3 The great bulk of our luggage had been registered through to Paris. *Mod.* The train goes through to Edinburgh.

**c.** In reference to size: As measured from side to side; in diameter.

*a* **1687** PETTY *Treat. Naval Philos.* I. iv. § 5 A Mast above 30 inches through.

**2.** From beginning to end (of a time, course of action, life, trial, book, etc.); to the end or purposed accomplishment: cf. I. 4, 5.

*a* **1175** *Cott. Hom.* 237 He wes acende of þe clene mede þe efer þurh lefede mede. **1456** SIR G. HAYE *Law Arms* (S.T.S.) 85 Traistand in God, and in his gude rycht to bring him throuch. **1556** *N. C. Wills* (Surtees 1908) 239 Iff he helpe my executors through for the making of my accompte with the King. **1611** SHAKS. *Cymb.* v. v. 382 When shall I heare all through? **1790** BURKE *Fr. Rev.* 133 Who now reads Bolingbroke? Who ever read him through? **1865** SWINBURNE *Chasteland* I. i. (1894) 9 She must weep If she sing through. **1891** *Law Times* XCII. 18/2 Having heard the case through and seen the witnesses.

**3.** Predicatively, after the verb *to be*, indicating a position, point, or condition ultimately arrived at. **a.** *lit.* Having penetrated or traversed a body or space. **b.** More usually *fig.* Having completed or accomplished an action or process (*spec.* having passed an examination); completed, as an action, etc.; finished, at an end, 'done'. *To be through with*, to have finished or completed; to have done with, have no further dealings with; also, to have arranged matters or come to an agreement with (a person) (now *dial.*): cf. quot. *a* 1500 s. v. THOROUGH *a.* 2.

**1481–90** *Howard Househ. Bks.* (Roxb.) 480 My Lord is throughe with his servaunt Robert Worsley, for certayn men ..to be ready at all tymes at my Lordes wages. **1597** SHAKS. 2 *Hen. IV*, I. ii. 45 If a man is through with them in honest Taking-up, then they must stand vpon Securitie. **1607** — *Cor.* II. iii. 130, I am halfe through, The one part suffered, the other will I doe. **1840** R. H. DANA *Bef. Mast* xix. 57 We had just so much work to do, and when that was through, the time was our own. **1866** *Belgravia* Nov. 76 The examiners..are now consulting together as to who is 'through' and who is 'plucked'. **1869** *Lonsdale Gloss., To be through with any one*, to complete a bargain with him. **1896** *Daily News* 18 July 3/1 [He] did not arrive till the speech was half through. **1901** K. STEUART *By Allan Water* ii. 63 All knew that James Steuart was 'far through' [= near the end of his life]. *Mod.* I saw the train enter the tunnel; it must be through now.

**4.** Qualifying adjs. and pa. pples.: Through the whole extent, substance, or thickness; throughout; hence, entirely, completely, thoroughly. †**a.** Standing before a pple. or adj.; = THOROUGH *adv.* 4. *Obs.* Formerly often hyphened to the following word; cf. THROUGH- *in comb.* 1.

*a* **1240** [see THOROUGH B. II. 4]. *c* **1440** *Anc. Cookery* in *Househ. Ord.* (1790) 459 When thai byn thurgh hot, take hom up with a skymmour. **1472** in Swayne *Sarum Churchw. Acc.* (1896) 2, j playne Chalice with his patent both through gilte. **1578** LYTE *Dodoens* v. lxxx. 651 The grapes be through ripe in September. **1594** NASHE *Unfort. Trav.* 31 To haue him stand in the raine till he was through wet. **1596** DALRYMPLE tr. *Leslie's Hist. Scot.* (S.T.S.) I. 32 In wintir quhen thay ar throuch fatt. **1631** HEYWOOD *2nd Pt. Maid of West* III. i, Through satiate with the pleasures of this night. **1639** FULLER *Holy War* III. xxvi. (1647) 156 Once through-hot long in cooling. **1665** MANLEY *Grotius' Low C. Warres* 762 Materials being now through dry by the heat of the weather. [**1692–1853**: see THOROUGH B. II. 4.] **1901** HAYDEN *Round Our Vill.* 154 (E.D.D.) Come in, you must be through wet.

**b.** Now regularly after the adj. or pple., and only in reference to physical condition, as *wet through* (see also WET).

*a* **1766** MRS. F. SHERIDAN *Sidney Bidulph* IV. 53 He had been wet quite through. **1821** CLARE *Vill. Minstr.* I. 165 Thy..trunk is nearly rotten through. *c* **1825** *Houlston Juv. Tracts, Forethought* 3 It is of no use to put up your umbrella when you are wet through. **1892** G. HAKE *Mem. 80 Years* lxiii. 259 The natives get hot-through in the.. spring and summer months. *Mod.* This is a cold room; I am chilled through. It is barely warmed through.

**5.** *Through and through*: **a.** With repeated or complete penetration; through the whole thickness or substance; completely from beginning to end; right through, entirely through.

**1470–85** [see THOROUGH B. II. 5]. **1611** SHAKS. *Wint. T.* IV. iv. 112 You'ld be so leane, that blasts of Ianuary Would blow you through and through. *c* **1643** LD. HERBERT *Autobiog.* (1824) 19 The English shot her [the Spanish ship] through and through so often that she run herself aground. **1709** *Lond. Gaz.* No. 4521/2 Having our Ship's Sides in a great many places shot through and through. **1894** SIR J. ASTLEY *Fifty Yrs. Life* I. 166 We were all wet through and through.

**b.** In all points or respects; thoroughly, wholly, entirely, out and out.

*c* **1410** *Chron. Eng.* (Ritson) 554 An holi wommon thourh ant thourh. **1531** in Hall *Chron., Hen. VIII* (1548) 197 We ..searched and examined through and through..bothe the bookes of holy scripture, and also the moste approued interpreters of the same. **1600** SHAKS. *A. Y. L.* II. vii. 59, I will through and through Cleanse the foule bodie of th' infected world. **1746** FRANCIS tr. *Hor., Sat.* I. ix. 134 One who knew My sweet Companion through and through. **1888** RHYS *Hibbert Lect.* 458 The Thorsteinn story..not corresponding through and through to any of the Celtic ones. **1894** ROOSEVELT in *Forum* (N.Y.) July 557 They must act as Americans, through and through, in spirit and hope and purpose.

**6.** After an auxiliary vb., with ellipsis of *go, get, pass*, etc., in *lit.* or *fig.* senses (see above); thus functioning as a verb in the infinitive. (See also THROUGH *v.* 2.)

**1423** JAS. I *Kingis Q.* lxiii, Bot, hert! quhere as the body may noght throu, Folow thy hevin! *c* **1470** HENRYSON *Mor. Fab.* x. (*Fox & Wolf*) xiii, This will not throw, but greit coist and expence. **1573, 1670** [see THOROUGH B. II. 6]. **1644** NYE *Gunnery* (1670) 20 If you cannot sift it through the sieve, beat that again into powder which will not through. **1906** MARJ. BOWEN *Viper of Milan* xxi, We must pass, we must through this moment.

**Through**, obs. form of THROW, TROUGH.

**Through-**, in combination. (See THOROUGH-.)

**1.** Combinations of THROUGH *prep.* or *adv.* with verbs (pples., vbl. sbs.), or adjs. Chiefly *Obs.*

In OE. *through* qualifying a verb stood before it regularly in the infinitive and participles, and usually in the finite vb. in subordinate clauses. In such cases there was a tendency for it to be written in comb., as in mod. German *durchgehen, durchgehend, durchwachsen*. In some words this tendency became stronger in ME., and the combined form was used also in the finite verb. For these see the Main words below. The following illustrate the process, without any attempt to be exhaustive:

†**through-ca·rve** (-**kerf**) *v.*, *trans.* to cut through; hence **through-carved** *ppl. a.*, see quot.; † **through-ca·st** *v.* [CAST *v.* 57], *trans.* to plaster throughout; †**through-cu·t** *v.*, *trans.* to cut through, perforate by cutting; †**through-dri·ve** *v.*, *trans.* to drive a nail or spike through, to transfix; †**through-fi·cche** (**thurghe-fyche**) *v.* [FICCHE *v.*], *trans.* to pierce through, transfix; †**throu·gh-fo·rmed** *ppl. a.*, thoroughly formed, full-grown; †**through-ga·lled** *pa. pple.* [GALL *v.*[1] 5], thoroughly harassed or disabled; †**through-handling**, management of details; carrying through; transaction; †**through-lanced** *pa. pple.*, pierced as with a lance, transfixed; †**through-look** *v.*, *trans.* to look through, examine thoroughly; †**through-nailed** *pa. pple.*, transfixed with nails; †**through-nim** *v.*, *trans.* to 'run through', transfix; *fig.* to penetrate; †**through-pierce** (**thorough-pierce**) *v.*, *trans.* to pierce through, transfix; hence *through-, thorough-piercing* ppl. adj.; †**through-ride** (**thorough-ride**) *v.*, (*a*) *trans.* to ride through, make a raid through (cf. RIDE *v.* 2); (*b*) *intr.* to penetrate through (cf. RIDE *v.* 9); †**through-rive** *v.* (*pa. t.* **þurh-raf**) [RIVE *v.*], *trans.* to rive or tear through; †**through-run** (**thurh-ærn**) *v.*, *trans.* to overrun; †**through-shed** (**þur3sched**) *v.* (L. *perfundere*), *trans.* to suffuse; †**through-shoo·t** (*pa. t.* **þurh-, þor3schote**) *v.*, *trans.* to shoot through, pierce through; †**through-shove** *v.* (*pa. pple.* **þurgh-shove**), *trans.* to thrust through, transfix; †**through-swi·m** *v.*, *trans.* to swim through; †**through-thri·lled** *pa. pple.*, pierced through; *fig.* thrilled through; †**through-wa·xen** *pa. pple.* [*waxen*, pa. pple. of WAX *v.*], grown over; †**through-wo·n** *v.* [OE. *þurh-wunian*: see WON *v.*], *intr.* to abide, continue, or remain through; †**through-wou·nd** *v.*, *trans.* to wound through or deeply. See also THROUGH-BEARING, THROUGH-GO, etc. **b.** with adjectives: †**through-old** *a.*, extremely old; antiquated; †**throu·gh-wet** *a.*, wetted or wet through, saturated with moisture.

*c* **1330** *Arth. & Merl.* (Kölbing) 8141 Stel & yren his ax *þurchcarf Wher þurch mani starf. **1875** PARKER *Gloss. Archit., Through Carved-work*, .. in which the spaces between the ornamental parts are pierced entirely through. **1611** in Willis & Clark *Cambridge* (1886) II. 112 The whole passage to be *throughecast with lime and haire. *c* **1330** *Arth. & Merl.* 9286 Ich of hem on [o]þer hitt, Oþer heued ofsmot or bodi *þurch kitt. **1594** PLAT *Jewell-ho.* III. 34 How to graue any..deuise vpon an egge shel, & how to through-cut the same. *a* **1023** WULFSTAN *Hom.* iii. (Napier) 22 Him æ3ðer *þurhdraf mid isenum næ3lum 3e fet 3e handa. *a* **1225** *Leg. Kath.* 1204 Þurhdriuen upon þe rode. *Ibid.* 1943, & let þurhdriuen..þe spaken & te felien Mid irnene gadien. *c* **1340** HAMPOLE *Prose Tr.* 2 It has *thurghe-fychede my herte. **1664** H. MORE *Myst. Iniq.* Apol. 542 Who are so *through-formed Christians as cordially to believe all the Essential Parts of our Religion. **1594** KYD *Cornelia* v. 308 Scipio that saw his ships *through-galled, And by the foe fulfild with fire and blood. *a* **1586** SIDNEY *Arcadia* (1622) 177 (Skimming any thing that came before him) [He] was disciplined to leaue the *through-handling of all to his gentle wife. **1594** SPENSER *Amoretti* lvii, Seeing my hart *through-launced every where With thousand arrowes, which your eies have shot. *c* **1200** ORMIN Ded. 68, & te bitæche icc off þiss boc,..All to þurrhsekenn illc an ferrs, & to *þurrhlokenn offte. **1446** LYDG. *Two Nightingale P.* ii. 240 *Thurgh-nayled weren his holy handis tweyne. *c* **1205** LAY. 14711 Catiger þer com & mid his spere hine *þurh-nom. **1390** GOWER *Conf.* II. 249 Into wepinge Sche fell, as sche that was thurgh nome With love. **1639** FULLER *Holy War* II. xliv. (1647) 103 Then must he be a *through-old man. *Ibid.* v. xxix. 281 What credit there is to be given to that through-old if not doting prophecie. *c* **1330** *Arth. & Merl.* 7936, & wiþ gode hert & main fin þai *þurchperced þo Sarrazin. **1413** *Pilgr. Sowle* (Caxton) I. xiv. (1859) 11 Grete drede and heuynesse had thorughpercyd my herte. **1590** SPENSER *F. Q.* II. i. 38 Her tender hart was rent in twaine, Or thrild with point of thorough-piercing paine. **1609** HEYWOOD *Brit. Troy* XIV. xxv, Quite through-pierc'st the Greeke dropt down a corse. *c* **1205** LAY. 18082 He..smat hine i þere side þat þat spere *þurh-rade [*c* **1275** þorh-rod]. *c* **1330** R. BRUNNE *Chron. Wace* (Rolls) 14516 Þat alle landes he wolde þorow ryde.. Cristen men to struye & quelle. *c* **1400** *Destr. Troy* 5008 Thy..Rewme þurgh Riden, robbed þi goodis. *c* **1205** LAY. 23943 [He] smat i þere breoste þat þat spere *þurh raf [*c* **1275** þorh rof]. *Ibid.* 12129 Þat lond heo *þurh arnden & her3eden. *Ibid.* 16657 Þat lond heo gunne þurh-ærnen & þa tunes fur-bernen. **1382** WYCLIF *Esther* xv. 8 She forsothe *thur3shed [*Vulg.* perfusa] the chere with rose colour. **971** *Blickl. Hom.* 109 Þonne he his byrnsweord 3etyhþ & þas world ealle þurhslyhþ, & þa lichoman *þurh sceoteð. *c* **1330** R. BRUNNE *Chron. Wace* (Rolls) 4373 Þer sciaftes þorgh schoten body & schelde. *c* **1330** *Arth. & Merl.* 7959 Þer was mani wombe *þurchschoue & mani heued cleued aboue. *c* **1420** 26 *Pol. Poems* xvii. 189 His herte was wiþ a spere þurgh-shoue. **1615** CHAPMAN *Odyss.* VII.

184, I yet *through-swomme the waues, that your shore binds. *a* **1631** DONNE *Progr. Soule* xxvii, The net through-swome, she kept the liquid Path. **1605** SYLVESTER *Du Bartas* II. iii. I. *Vocation* 375 With our Swords and Lances ..*Through-thrilled (Villains) this shall be your last. **1608** *Ibid.* iv. IV. *Decay* 322 My heart's through-thrilled with your miseries. *c* **1205** LAY. 18338 Wes þe munt *þurh-wexen [*c* **1275** þorh-woxe] Mid ane wude feiren. **1583** T. WATSON *Centurie of Loue* xci, Then, hang your *throughwett garmentes on the wall. *c* **1000** *Ags. Gosp.* Matt. xxiv. 13 Witodlice seþe *þurhwunað oð ende, se byþ hal. *a* **1175** *Cott. Hom.* 227 Þaða hire time com hi acennede and þurh-wunede meden. *c* **1205** LAY. 1384 An lond he ferde sechinde Þer he mihte þurh-wunian Mid his wnfolke. *a* **1225** *Leg. Kath.* 662 Þe wið godd hehfeder, & wið þen hali gast, Þurhwunest in alre worlde world. *c* **1200** ORMIN 17443 Þa neddress.. Þeȝȝ tacnenn alle sinness, Þatt stingenn & *þurrh-wundenn all þatt bodiȝ, & tatt sawle.

**2.** Combinations with sbs. (cf. THROUGH *a.*): **throu·gh-a·rch** *Archit.* (also *attrib.*), see quot.; **throu·gh-blow·**, a blowing or current of air passing through; **throu·gh-bo·lt (thorough-bolt)**, a bolt passing through the objects fastened by it, and secured at each end; †**throu·gh-co·ld**, a penetrating or deep-seated cold or chill; **throu·gh-fang** [FANG *sb.* 6 a] = *through-tang*; †**throu·gh-fa·st** [FAST *sb.*[1] 1], a fast all through a period, e.g. the fast of Lent; **throu·gh-joi·nt**, a joint passing through the thickness of something; **throu·gh-key** [KEY *sb.*[1] 9], a key or pin fitting into a hole which passes right through the parts to be fastened by it; †**throu·gh-lock** (?): see quot.; **throu·gh-mo·rtise**, a mortise cut right through the timber; †**throu·gh-pa·th**, a path or way through something; **throu·gh-rod**, a rod passing or extending through or from end to end of some structure or piece of mechanism; †**through-serewe**, †**-spavin**, †**-splint**, names of diseases of the leg of the horse: see quots. and SEREWE, SPAVIN, SPLINT; also cf. THOROUGH-PIN; **throu·gh-tang**, a method of hafting knives, forks, etc. by inserting the tang in a hole drilled right through the handle and riveting it at the end; **throu·gh-work**, work extending through the thickness, or occupying the whole breadth of, some structure. See also THROUGH-STONE[2].

*a* **1878** SIR G. G. SCOTT *Lect. Archit.* I. vii. 283 The two systems may be distinguished as rere-arch windows and *through-arch windows—i. e., those in which the inner is distinct from the outer arch, and those in which the same arch runs through the wall, showing itself more or less similarly on its outer and inner faces. In thick walls and rich work there is often another order of through-arch within the tracery order, or rather the outer order re-appears within. **1908** *Times* 29 Dec. 4/5 No airing or '*through-blow' is possible in a..flat where the openings are all on one side. **1837** *Civil Eng. & Arch. Jrnl.* I. 33/1 The outer and inner rows of piling..are to be securely tied together, with two-inch wrought-iron *thorough bolts. **1864** *Daily Tel.* 19 Aug., The use of large-area solid plates [in ship-building], in combination with through bolts. **1874** KNIGHT *Dict. Mech.* s. v. *Bolt*, A *through-bolt* is one which goes through the pieces which are to be fastened together. Such are clinch-bolts, and bolts secured by nut and washer. **1601** HOLLAND *Pliny* (1634) II. 289 In drink, it dissolueth ventosities, riddeth away *through-colds, and namely the shiuerings..in cold agues. **1851-4** TOMLINSON *Cycl. Arts* (1866) I. 487/2 A very good method is what is called '*through-fang*', that is, to drill a hole completely through the handle, and to insert a..prong projecting from the blade, riveting it at the opposite end. **1652** FULLER *Comm. Christ's Tempt.* ii. in *Sel. Rem.* (1891) II. 26 'He had fasted forty days and forty nights.' The words contain the *through-fast of Christ. **1862** *Catal. Internat. Exhib.* II. x. 53 The *through-joints admit wet into the interior. **1548** *Acc. Ld. High Treas. Scot.* IX. 167 Thre gret *throuch lokes to the palice of Halyrudhous. **1632-5** CORBET *Sp. in aid St. Paul's* in Longman *Three Cathedrals* (1873) 60 Are we not beholding to it..for a prayer or a *throwpath? **1523** FITZHERB. *Husb.* § 96 Some horses haue a *throughe serewe on bothe sydes of the legge. *Ibid.* § 106 Some horses haue *throughe spauen, and appereth bothe within and without. **1565** BLUNDEVIL *Horsemanship* IV. cxxvii. (1580) 58 Of the wet Spauen, or through Spauen. This is a soft swelling growing on both sides of the hough, and seemes to go cleane through the hough, and therefore may be called a through Spauen. **1607** TOPSELL *Four-f. Beasts* 401 A Splent is a sorance of the least moment, vnlesse it bee on the knee, or else a *through Splent, both which cannot bee cured. **1687** MIÈGE *Gt. Fr. Dict.* I, *Sur-os chevillé*, serew or through-splent. **1833** J. HOLLAND *Manuf. Metal* II. 14 Hafting table knives by the insertion of that portion of the blade which has been properly drawn out, quite through the handle..is called '*through-tang*'. **1686** PLOT *Staffordsh.* 384 He also cuts wreath'd pillars with the same Engine (that are not *through-work).

**Through-band**: see *thorough-band* s. v. THOROUGH- 2.

**Throu·gh-bear,** *v. Sc.* [BEAR *v.*[1] II.] *trans.* To maintain, support. Hence **Throu·gh-bearing** *vbl. sb.* **a.** Support through (life), livelihood, maintenance. **b.** Supporting, upholding, maintaining (a cause).

**1680** D. HACKSTON *Let.* 25 July in *Cloud Witnesses* (1871) 45 He will perfect His work in me and by me, either to a remarkable delivery, or through-bearing (*i. e.* upholding) me as He sees most for His own glory. **1730** T. BOSTON *Mem.* vii. (1899) 151 God would provide things necessary for our through-bearing. **1786** A. GIB *Sacr. Contempl.* 296 It secures all the outward through-bearing, preservation and protection, leading and guiding. **1813** CHALMERS *Let.* 12 Oct. in *Life* (1850) I. xii. 343 A day of mortification. Everything went against us by the through-bearing of the opposite party. **1857** A. WALLACE *Gloaming of Life* i. (1875) 3 She opened a small shop as the means of securing an honest throughbearing.

**Through-bred**: see THOROUGHBRED.

**Through-cast** to **-drive**: see THROUGH-.

**Through-draught**: see *thorough-draught* s. v. THOROUGH- 2. **Throughe**, obs. f. THROW *v.*

**Througher** (þrū·ər). *Coal-mining.* [f. THROUGH *prep.* or *adv.* + -ER[1].] (See quots.)

**1797** *Encycl. Brit.* (ed. 3) V. 101/1 The workings called *rooms*..of the width of 12 feet;..the workings called *throughers* or *thirlings*, 9 feet wide, wrought through at right angles from one room to another. **1883** GRESLEY *Gloss. Terms Coal Mining*, *Througher*,..a thirl put through between two headings which are up-stoop.

**Through-fang** to **-galled**: see THROUGH-.

**Through-fare**, etc., see THOROUGHFARE, etc.

**Throu·gh-gang,** *sb. Sc. Obs.* or *rare.* [GANG *sb.* 4.] A way or road through; a passage; sometimes = thoroughfare.

**1463** *Burgh Rec. Edinb.* (1869) I. 22 The througang is set to William Met for 8s., on his own security. **1513** DOUGLAS *Æneis* II. viii. 80 Secrete throwgangis are schawin. **1587** *Reg. Privy Council Scot.* IV. 205 In the portche or throwgang of the said West Kirk dure. **1862** G. HENDERSON *Matt. in Lowland Scotch* vi. 2 (E. D. D.) Dinna toot a trumpet afore thee, as the hypocrites do in the throwgangs.

**b.** *attrib.* or *adj.* Allowing passage through.

**1523** *Acc. Ld. High Treas. Scot.* V. 220 For ane band to the throuchgang windo of the quenis chalmer. **1808** JAMIESON s.v., *A throwgang close* is an open passage, by which one may go from one street to another, as opposed to a blind alley.

So † **Through-ga·ng** *v.*, *Sc. trans.* to go through, to traverse. **Throu·gh-ganging** (also **throw-gaan'**) *a.*, that goes through any amount of work, active, energetic, thoroughgoing.

*c* **1000** *Ags. Ps.* (Th.) xc[i]. 6 Ne forhtast þu ðe on dæȝe flan on lyfte, þæt þu þuruh gangan garas on ðeostrum. *c* **1205** LAY. 1207 ȝif ich þat lond mai bi-ȝeten & mi folc hit þurh-gengen [*c* **1275** þorh-genge]. **1814** SCOTT *Wav.* xxxix, Ye.. should ken a horse's points; ye see that through-ganging thing that Balmawhapple's on. **1825** JAMIESON, *Through-ganging*, active, having a great deal of action; a term used by jockies.

†**Through-gi·rd,** *v. Obs.* [GIRD *v.*[2]] *trans.* To strike through, smite through, pierce with a cut or blow.

*c* **1386** CHAUCER *Knt.'s T.* 152 Thurgh girt with many a greuous blody wounde. *c* **1430** *Syr Gener.* (Roxb.) 5764 The king supposed..Generides he had thurgh girt. **1513** DOUGLAS *Æneis* II. viii. [vii.] 118 Hypanis eik, and Dymas ..War by thair fallowis throw gird baith twa. **1573** TWYNE *Æneid* x. Ee iij, Then Pallas soone Sir Rhoeteus..Through-girdes. *c* **1594** KYD *Sp. Trag.* IV. iv, Where hanging on a tree I found my sonne, Through girt with wounds.

†**Through-go·**, *v. Obs.* [OE. *þurhgán*, pa. t. *þurhéode*, f. *þurh* adv. THROUGH + *gán* to GO (cf. OHG. *durhgân*).] *trans.* To go through, pass through, traverse.

*c* **1000** *Pop. Treat. Sci.* (1841) 9 Seo eorðe byð mid þam winterlicum cyle þurh-gan. *c* **1000** ÆLFRIC *Hom.* II. 502 Ic wille ðurhgan orsorh ðone here. *c* **1200** ORMIN 12860 Þurrh þatt teȝȝ sholldenn all þurrh gan Þiss middellærd to spellenn Off himm. *a* **1300** *E. E. Psalter* civ. [cv.] 18 Irne thurghyhode his saule ful grim. *a* **1400** *Isumbras* 522 That alle a syde of a cunntre he hase thurgh gane.

So **Throu·ghgoing** *vbl. sb.*, passing through; a going through accounts, a taking to task; **Throu·ghgoing** (*Sc.* **throwgaun**) *ppl. a.*, that goes or passes through; that goes through any amount of work, pushing, active, strenuous: cf. THOROUGHGOING.

**1818** SCOTT *Rob Roy* xiv, The folk..gae him sic an awfu' throughgaun about his rinnin' awa. **1820** *Blackw. Mag.* Dec. 265/1 A plump and jocose little woman; gleg, blithe, and throwgaun for her years. **1822** GALT *Provost* xxxiii, Those mighty masses of foreign commodities, the throughgoing of which left..'goud in goupins'. **1841** *Penny Cycl.* XIX. 254/2 In the Dublin and Kingstown railway an attempt was made to ensure increased solidity by introducing *throughgoing* stone blocks..of granite, six feet long,.. stretched across the track. **1910** N. MUNRO in *Blackw. Mag.* Oct. 529/2 Maurice met her..in a through-going close.

**Through-handling** to **-look**: see THROUGH-.

†**Through-light** (þrū·ləit), *sb.* and *a. Obs.* **a.** *sb.*: see THOROUGH-LIGHT. **b.** *adj.* That lets light through; transparent. So **Through-lighted**: see THOROUGH-LIGHTED.

**1601** DONNE *Progr. Soul* Epist., If any coulors can deliver a minde so plaine and flatt and through-light as mine. **1612** .. *Funeral Elegy* 61 'Twas but a through-light scarfe, her mind t'enroule.

**Throughly** (þrū·li), *adv. arch.* [f. THROUGH *adv.* or *adj.* + -LY[2]. See also THOROUGHLY.]

**1.** Fully, completely, perfectly; = THOROUGHLY 2.

*c* **1440** *Generydes* 346, I prae yow..That ye will..teche hym throughely That att longith to hym to do. **1490** CAXTON *Eneydos* xxviii. 108 Lete vs loke to her wounde, and in her face, yf she is thrughly passed [gone, dead]. **1560** BIBLE (Genev.) *Ps.* li. 2 Wash me throughly from mine iniquitie. **1563** WINȜET *Four Scoir Thre Quest.* Wks. (S.T.S.) I. 68 Nocht throuchlie vnderstanding zour doctrine. **1596** SHAKS. *Merch. V.* IV. i. 173, I am enformed throughly of the cause. **1660** BOYLE *New Exp. Phys. Mech.* xl. 78 Throughly kindled Wood-coals. **1712** STEELE *Spect.* No. 264 ¶ 2 Throughly equipped from Head to Foot. *a* **1850** ROSSETTI *Dante & Circ.* I. (1874) 85 Mine inmost being then feels throughly quit Of anguish. **1885** DIXON *Hist. Ch. Eng.* III. 451 Hooper..swept his unfortunate garner so throughly.

**2.** Through the whole thickness, substance, or extent; through, throughout, all through, quite through. *arch.*, *poet.*

**1541** *Act* 33 *Hen. VIII*, c. 18 The kerseyes thereof made cannot be so certenly wroughte as the same..myght kepe any true or just certentye of lenghe or breadeth throughlye. **1577** HARRISON *England* II. vi. (1877) I. 156 Barleie..steeped in a cesterne..vntill it be throughlie soked. **1603** OWEN *Pembrokeshire* (1892) 93 Being thus dried throwlie. **1634** SIR T. HERBERT *Trav.* 150 When tis throughly tosted..they eat it. **1677** MOXON *Mech. Exerc.* I. 10 If it be not throughly welded at the first Heat. **1872** TENNYSON *Gareth & Lyn.* 1371 Then with a stronger buffet he clove the helm As throughly as the skull.

†**b.** Through, from beginning to end; for the whole length or time; all through. *Obs.*

**1563** FOXE *A. & M.* 807 He was not throughly presente at the Byshoppes sermon. *c* **1590** MARLOWE *Faust.* vi. 189 Take this book; peruse it throughly. **1692** E. WALKER *Epictetus' Mor.* x, Thou hast but begun The glorious Race, nor hast it throughly run.

**Through-mortise** to **-old**: see THROUGH-.

**Through other, throu·gh-other,** *adv. phr.* and *adj.* Chiefly *Sc.* Also 6 **throuch(e vther,** 7 **thorough other,** 8–9 **throw ither, throwither, thro'ither; throwther, thro'ther,** 9 **throuther**; also 7 **through others,** 9 **through-others.** [f. THROUGH *prep.* + OTHER B. 8: i. e. 'through each other'. Cf. Ger. *durcheinander.*]

**1.** *adv. phr.* (Mingled) through each other or one another; promiscuously; indiscriminately; in disorder.

**1596** DALRYMPLE tr. *Leslie's Hist. Scot.* x. (S.T.S.) II. 301 Captiues war numberit al throuch vther [L. *plus minus*] a thousand. **1632** LITHGOW *Trav.* III. 85 Figges, Orenges, Lemmons,.. growing all through other. **1637** MONRO *Exped.* I. 11 Having beene divers times Pell mel through others. **1637** RUTHERFORD *Lett.* (1862) I. 317 Hope and love, woven through other. *a* **1653** BINNING *Heart Humil.* xviii. Wks. (1735) 622/1 Sin and Judgment mixed in thorow other. **1768** ROSS *Helenore* II. 80 When she saw things had taken sick a cast, An' sae thro' ither warpl'd were. **1786** BURNS *Earnest Cry & Prayer* Postscr. iii, Till skelp—a shot —they're aff, a' throwther, To save their skin. **1818** SCOTT *Hrt. Midl.* xvi, They were a' speaking and gabbling through other.

**2. a.** In predicative use: Mingled or mixed up; in a medley; in confusion, in disorder. (In quot. 1630, Mixed up intimately.)

**1630** RUTHERFORD *Lett.* (1862) I. 52 O sweet communion, when Christ and we are through other and are no longer two! **1855** RUSKIN *Let.* in Collingwood *Life* (ed. 5) 159 With all the pages through-other and backside foremost. **1865** *Church Times* 25 Nov., Everything..is opened and dragged out, shirts and books,..clothes and letters, all topsy-turvy, and (to use that most expressive Scotch adjective) 'through-other'. **1894** HALL CAINE *Manxman* v. i, A face ..like a ghose's, and his hair all through-others.

**b.** *adj.* (in attrib. use). Confused, disorderly.

**1720** *Wodrow Corr.* (1843) II. 492 About half an hour after I despatched mine to you,..my rude and through-other draught.

**3.** Of persons or their attributes (*pred.* or *attrib.*): Disorderly; wild, reckless; disordered.

**1813** PICKEN *Poems* I. 62 (Jam.) Weel, tho' he was so sadly throu'ther, Since than he ne'er leuk'd o'er his shouther. **1853** *Whistle-Binkie* Ser. II. 10 He was idle and thro'ither, and drucken an' a'. **1863** J. BROWN *Horæ Subs.* (1882) 320 Leading a wild throughother life. **1880** *Jamieson's Dict.* s. v. *Through-ither*, Also used as an adj., implying rash, reckless, rattling; as, 'She's a wild, throwither lassie', *Clydes[dale]*. *Mod.* (*Sc.*, *Roxb.*) She was a very willing servant, but oh, so throwother! no sense o' order.

**Throughout** (þru₁au·t), *prep.*, *adv.*, *adj.* ME. forms (more than 70) in **þurh, þuruh, þurgh, þurȝe, þurf, þoru, þorw, þoruȝ, þorȝ, þorȝe, þorou, þorow(e, thairgh, thurf, thorgh, thorow, thorough, thorrow, thru, thro, throw,** etc. with **út(e, out(e, owt(e,** etc.; also contr. 2 **þurut,** 5 **þrowte, throute,** 5-6 **thorowte, throwt,** etc. A prevalent form in 6–7 was **thorow-out; through-out** noted first in 6. [In OE. two words, *þurh* THROUGH, *út* OUT, later gradually combined or hyphened. Cf. Ger. *durchaus* (16th c. in Grimm).]

**A.** *prep.* †**1.** Through and out at the other side; completely or right through (a material body, or a place); sometimes simply = THROUGH *prep.* 1, 2. *Obs.* (or *arch.*).

*c* **1066** *O. E. Chron.* an. 1066 (MS. C.), He for þurhut Eoferwic. *c* **1205** LAY. 315 He..ihitte his aȝene fader þurh ut þere broste. *c* **1305** *St. Lucy* 151 in *E. E. P.* (1862) 105 Þo heo [St. Lucy] was þurfout þe þrote ismyte þe bet heo spac ynouȝ. **13..** *Cursor M.* 1036 (Cott.) Þis flummes four..Thoru out all oþer contres rinnes. *c* **1380** *Sir Ferumb.* 4558 As liȝtliche as hit had ibeo wax, ran þe strok þanne of ys ax Chayne & tre þorȝoute. *c* **1400** MAUNDEV. (1839) v. 41 The Ryuere of Euphrate ran þorgh out the cytee. *c* **1420** *Anturs of Arth.* 315 (Thornton MS.) Me buse wende one my waye, thorowte this wode. *c* **1470** HENRY *Wallace* II. 56 Throuch oute the thikest of the pres he ȝeid. **1513** DOUGLAS *Æneis* VI. i. 121 The cald dreid ..Thirland throwout hard banis. *c* **1614** MURE *Dido & Æneas* I. 153 Throughout the streets her hurling chariots roll. **1629** WADSWORTH *Pilgr.* iv. 35 [He] gaue vs two broad sides.., shooting..our ships through, and through out.

**2.** Through the whole of (a space, region, etc.);

in or to every part of; everywhere in. (Cf. THROUGH *prep.* 3.)

† *Throughout all thing* (quot. *c* 1380), in all points: = *through all thing* (THROUGH *prep.* 3 c).

*c* **1205** LAY. 29537 Þa iwende seint Austin vorð..þurh ut Englelond. **1297** R. GLOUC. (Rolls) 8589 Þoru out al þat lond it [the wind] dude sorwe inou. **1340** HAMPOLE *Pr. Consc.* 4359 Thurgh-out þe world, ferre and nere. *c* **1380** *Sir Ferumb.* 1500 Wel y-armed þorw-out al þyng euerechone þey ware. **1399** LANGL. *Rich. Redeles* II. 5 So ryff as þey ronne ȝoure rewme þoru-oute. *c* **1440** *R. Gloucester's Chron.* 6901 (MS. δ) Throute al þe londe sone þys word drou. **1558** WARDE tr. *Alexis' Secr.* (1568) 40 b, That great and vehement plague in the yere 1348 which crepte thorowe oute all the worlde. **1583** STUBBES *Anat. Abus.* II. (1882) 21 In euery parish throughout the Realme. **1599** CHAPMAN *Hum. Dayes Myrth* Plays 1873 I. 51 Yet hath the morning sprinckled throwt the clowdes, But halfe her tincture. **1674** BREVINT *Saul at Endor* 247 Thro-out all the Catholic Countries. **1783** HAILES *Antiq. Chr. Ch.* ii. 31 The Jews throughout the empire. **1883** GILMOUR *Mongols* xviii. 213 Throughout the length and breadth of the country.

**b.** Through or during the whole of (a period of time or course of action); from beginning to end of. (Cf. THROUGH *prep.* 4, 5.)

*c* **1540** *Pilgr. T.* 195 in *Thynne's Animadv.* (1875) App. i. 82 And so thorow-out the hole story. **1591** SHAKS. *1 Hen. VI*, I. i. 42 Ne're throughout the yeere to Church thou go'st. **1641** MILTON *Church Govt.* I. i, There is not that thing in the world of more..urgent importance throughout the whole life of man, than is discipline. *a* **1672** WOOD *Life* 3 May an. 1661 (O.H.S.) I. 393 A. W...was present throut all the transactions. **1709** STEELE *Tatler* No. 78 ℙ 8 Hippocrates, who visited me throughout my whole Illness. **1799** NELSON in Nicolas *Disp.* (1845) III. 307 Throughout my command in the Levant seas. **1868** FREEMAN *Norm. Conq.* II. vii. 78 Harold and Swegen.., by their invasion of Denmark, gave him full occupation throughout the year.

† **3.** By means of, by the action of, by, from: = THROUGH *prep.* 7–8. *Obs. rare.*

*a* **1240** *Wohunge* in *Cott. Hom.* 271 Ich hit rewli fordide þurh-hut mine sunnes. **13..** *Cursor M.* 16317 (Cott.) Sai me nu qui þou ert als prisun tan, Thoruut þis biscop and his men? *c* **1400** *Rom. Rose* 3489 Thurghout my deming outerly, Than had he knowlege certeinly, That Love me ladde in sich a wyse.

**B.** *adv.*

† **1.** Right through, quite through, so as to penetrate completely. *Obs.*

*c* **1000** ÆLFRIC *Saints' Lives* xii. 55 Swa þæt þæt spere him eode þurh ut. *a* **1300** *Sarmun* xxxiv. in *E. E. P.* (1862) 5 Sei sinful man..wel aȝt þi hert þroȝ ute cleue. *a* **1450** *Le Morte Arth.* 3115 Fele men lyeth..With bryght brondys throw-owte borne. **1470–85** MALORY *Arthur* XIX. vi. 781 One of the barres of yron kytte the braune of his handes thurgh out to the bone. *a* **1533** LD. BERNERS *Huon* lv. 186 The shelde was perced through out.

† **b.** Right through from beginning to end (of a time, an action, a book, etc.); to the end of a journey without stopping. *Obs.*

*a* **1400–50** *Alexander* 4737 Þus thre daies in þat thede thurgh-out þai lengid. **1656** D'CHESS NEWCASTLE *Nature's Pict.* C ij, I never read a Romancy Book throughout in all my life. **1660** F. BROOKE tr. *Le Blanc's Trav.* 24 The Merchants..rest here in their journy to the Indies, whereas before they went throughout, without landing here.

**2.** Through the whole of a body, region, etc.; in or to every part, everywhere.

*c* **1175** *Lamb. Hom.* 27 Ane berninde glede þet hine al forbernað þurut to cole. *c* **1290** *St. Brendan* 476 in *S. Eng. Leg.* I. 232 Þoru-out swart and brenninde. *c* **1450** *Mirour Saluacioun* 1261 This virgine fulle of splendour and thorgh out lumynouse. **1544** *Test. Ebor.* (Surtees) VI. 210 A furde gowne lyned with foxe thorow-oute. **1607** SHAKS. *Timon* v. i. 212 Tell Athens, in the sequence of degree, From high to low throughout, that [etc.]. **1611** BIBLE *John* xix. 23 The coat was without seame, wouen from the top thorowout. *a* **1700** DRYDEN *Epit. on Sir P. Fairborne* 15 His youth and age..All of a piece throughout, and all divine. **1880** GEIKIE *Phys. Geog.* v. xxxi. 562 The plains of Central Europe..are clothed with a vegetation which has one common character throughout.

**b.** Through the whole of a time or course of action; at every moment or point; all through.

**1766** FORDYCE *Serm. Yng. Wom.* (1767) II. ix. 56 Act on these Principles throughout. **1833** HT. MARTINEAU *Berkeley the Banker* I. ix, Do not treat me as if I had not been your friend and adviser throughout. **1866** J. MARTINEAU *Ess.* I. 206 Mr. Spencer treats the two cases as parallel throughout. **1885** *Manch. Exam.* 22 Sept. 5/6 To-day has been beautifully fine throughout.

† **3.** Completely, entirely, thoroughly. *Obs.*

*c* **1200** *Vices & Virt.* 73 Ȝif ðu wilt..bien ðurhut god mann. *a* **1250** *Owl & Night.* 877 Þeyh summe men beon þurhut gode & þurhut clene on heore mode. *c* **1300** *Beket* 262 If he hadde of his owe flesch thurfout seignurye. **1470–85** MALORY *Arthur* VII. xxiii. 250 Ther was no man..sholde hele hym thorou oute of his wound.

† **C.** *adj. Obs.* **1.** Thorough, out-and-out.

**1387–8** T. USK *Test. Love* II. v. (Skeat) l. 105 Often, when there is a throw out shrewe, he coineth al the gold,..to haue in his bandon. *Ibid.* vi. l. 69 All the bodily goods..comen oft to throw out shrewes. **1670** BROOKS *Wks.* (1867) VI. 115, I cannot charge such throughout saints..with that horrid profanation of the Sabbath.

**2.** That is so throughout; permanent. *rare.*

**1701** BEVERLEY *Glory of Grace* 4 The uninterrupted, and throughout Efficiency of grace.

† **Throughou·tly**, *adv. Obs.* Forms: see prec.; also 5 **throughtly**. [f. prec. + -LY [2].] **a.** Completely, thoroughly: = prec. B. 3. **b.** In every part, all over: = prec. B. 2.

*c* **1200** ORMIN 5246 All Drihhtiness bodeword..Iss filledd þurrhutlike wel, ȝiff þatt soþ lufe iss filledd. **13..** *E. E. Allit. P.* A. 858 We þurȝ-outly hauen cnawyng. *c* **1475** *Partenay* 3075 So huge a stroke..That quite clene the arme share off throughtly. **1552** in J. O. Payne *St. Paul's Cath. Edw. VI* (1893) 11 Not throughoutlye platedd with silver but to the myddes onlye. **1647** WARD *Simp. Cobler* (1843) 35 If this..worke bee throughly and throughoutly dispatched.

**Through-paced**: see THOROUGH-PACED.

**Throu·gh-pa·ssage.** Also 6 **thorow-**. A passage through; a thoroughfare.

*c* **1566** [see THOROUGH *a.* 1]. *a* **1578** LINDESAY (Pitscottie) *Chron. Scot.* (S.T.S.) I. 333 Transses and throw passagis. **1615** CROOKE *Body of Man* 103 Albeit there be but one *ductus* or through-passage from the *pylorus* or mouth of the stomack. **1663** GERBIER *Counsel* 23 Free accesse to the double roomes, without making them through passage. **1684** S. G. *Anglorum Spec.* 483 Wind-again-Lane..in it there is no through-passage. **1886** WILLIS & CLARK *Cambridge* III. 187 The two large rooms..were thrown into one; the through-passage being placed at the east end.

**Through-pierce**: see THROUGH- 1.

† **Throu·ghpost.** *Obs.* Also **tho·roughpost.** [f. THROUGH- + POST *sb.*[2] 1.] An express messenger riding post the whole way to his destination: see POST *sb.*[2] 1. *To lay through posts*, to establish a line of posts at which fresh horses were supplied.

**1558** *Act Privy Counc.* 29 Aug., The Quenes Majestie must..seke some new meanes to be served from tyme to tyme with a through poste. **1592** *Ibid.* 18 Apr., We have auctorized this bearer Robert Gascoyns, postmaster for the court, to lay through postes betweene London and the court. **1603** in *Rep. Secr. Comm. Post Office* (1844) 39 Carriers or thorow-posts, riding in our affaires by speciall commission. **1609** *Ibid.*, Thorough Postes, through-posts [see POST *sb.*[2] 1]. **1696** in *Massachusetts Acts* (1895) VIII. 280 Such Master..shall provide Horses and furniture to let to hire unto all through posts and persons rideing in post.

**Through-ride** to **-rod**: see THROUGH-.

**Through-ripe**: see *thorough-ripe*, s.v. THOROUGH- 1.

† **Throughsee·k**, *v. Obs.* Forms: see THROUGH *prep.* and SEEK *v.* [OE. *þurhsécan*, f. *þurh*, THROUGH *adv.* + *sécan* to SEEK: cf. OHG. *durh-suohhan*, Ger. *durchsuchen*.]

**1.** *trans.* To seek or search through; to search or examine thoroughly.

*a* **1050** *Liber Scintill.* 209 *Conquirens*, þurhsecende. *c* **1200** ORMIN 242 Her endenn twa Goddspelless þuss, & uss birrþ hemm þurrhsekenn. *a* **1225** *Leg. Kath.* 520 Þa he hefde al þet lond ouergan & þurhsoht. **1340** HAMPOLE *Pr. Consc.* 2440 When alle þi life sal be thurgh soght. **1489** SKELTON *Dethe Erle Northumbld.* 179 Whose pere is hard to fynd, Algife Englond and Fraunce were thorow saught.

**2.** To penetrate; to imbue or saturate thoroughly; in quot. *a* 1450, to pierce, run through with a weapon.

*c* **1200** *Trin. Coll. Hom.* 191 He..mid te shene attre þurh sechėð al þe soule. *c* **1250** *Death* 54 in *O. E. Misc.* 170 And in euche lime Deþ us hafð þurh-soht. **1387–8** T. USK *Test. Love* I. i. (Skeat) l. 120 Purely mated with sorowe thorough sought. **1390** GOWER *Conf.* I. 106 His wit..is with pride so thurghsoght, That he alle othre set at noght. *a* **1450** *Le Morte Arth.* 2873 Thys qarell leve wyll I noght, Ne pees shall ther neuer be sayne Or thy sydes be throw sought.

**Through-shed**: see THROUGH- 1.

† **Throu·gh-shine,** *a. Obs.* [In OE. *þurh-*scíne, -scýne*, f. *scínan* to SHINE.] Through which light shines; transparent, translucent.

*c* **1000** ÆLFRIC *Voc.* in Wr.-Wülcker 148/7 *Specularis*, þurhscyne stan. *a* **1631** DONNE *To C'tess Bedford* 27 That wee May in your through-shine face our hart's thoughts see.

So † **Through-shi·ne** *v.* [f. SHINE *v.*: cf. OHG. *durhskînan*, Ger. *durchscheinen*], *intr.* to shine through; hence † **Throu·gh-, tho·rough-shi·ning** *ppl. a.*, shining through, translucent, transparent.

**1526** TINDALE *Rev.* xxi. 21 The strete of the cite was pure golde, as thorowe shynynge glasse. **1578** LYTE *Dodoens* I. xxxiv. 49 Rounde tender, thorough shining, and browne redde stalkes. **1603** FLORIO *Montaigne* I. xxv. (1632) 77 It ought to make her contentment to through-shine in all exteriour parts. **1634** PEACHAM *Gentl. Exerc.* I. xxvii. 95 Then buy the Goldsmiths red Ammell, which in any case let be very transparent and through-shining.

**Through-shoot, -shove**: see THROUGH- 1.

† **Through-sti·ng,** *v. Obs.* [OE. *þurhstingan*, f. *stingan* to STING.] *trans.* To stab or pierce through.

*c* **1000** ÆLFRIC *Deut.* xv. 17 Nim þonne anne æl, & þurhsting his ear æt þines huses dura. *c* **1200** *Trin. Coll. Hom.* 207 Þe honden and te fet weren mid irene nailen þurh stungen. *a* **1300** *Cursor M.* 17134 (Cott.) Brest, and hand, and fote thurghstungen [*v.r.* thorustongen]. *Ibid.* 24357 Wit spere þai stoked him wit wrang, Þat ilk min hert it thoru-stang. *c* **1330** *Arth. & Merl.* (Kölbing) 6630 Wiþ hors fete þai riden hem on & þurch stongen mani on.

**Through-stitch**: see THOROUGH-STITCH.

**Through-stone** [1] (þrū·χʷstǝun, þrʊ·f-). Now only *Sc.* and *north. dial.* [f. THROUGH *sb.*[1] (q. v. for Forms) + STONE *sb.*] A horizontal grave-stone or slab over a tomb: = THROUGH *sb.*[1] 3.

**13..** *Cursor M.* 16762+94 (Cott.) Throgh stones in sunder brast, And ded bodyes gon rise. *c* **1440** *Promp. Parv.* 493/2 Thurwhe stone, of a grave [*v.rr.* thwrwe ston, throwe or thorw ston, throwe or throwstone], *sarcofagus.* **1509** *Test. Ebor.* (Surtees) V. 5, I will have a thorgh ston of marbill to be laid uppon my grave. **1540** *N. C. Wills* (Surtees 1908) 167 Yt myne executoures shall bye a thr命wgh stone and laye upon my mother in Seynt Andrewes Church. **1593** *Rites of Durham* (Surtees 1903) 60 An other gentleman..was buryed in the said Garth..with a faire throwgh stone aboue hym. **1703** BP. W. NICOLSON *Misc. Acc.* (1877) 100 A couple of fair Freestone Monuments or Through-Stones. **1818** SCOTT *Br. Lamm.* xxiv, The muckle through-stane that stands on sax legs yonder. **1825** BROCKETT *N. C. Words*, *Thruff-stone.* **1848** *Edinb. Antiq. Mag.* Nov. 113 A group of beautiful 'throoch-stanes', *i.e.* the large flat stones on pillars. **1894** CROCKETT *Lilac Sunbonnet* 55 [He] set a big thruch stane ower his first wife.

**Through-stone** [2] (þrū·stǝun), **thorough-stone** (þʊ·rǒstǝun). *Building.* [f. THROUGH *prep.* + STONE *sb.*] A stone placed so as to extend through the thickness of a wall; a bond-stone.

**1805** DICKSON *Pract. Agric.* I. 112 Long stones should..be selected for the purpose of being placed occasionally across the wall, in order to bind it well together. These are termed *throughs*, or *through stones.* **1825** J. NICHOLSON *Operat. Mechanic* 538 In each course of ashlar facing..thorough-stones should occasionally be introduced. **1879** *Cassell's Techn. Educ.* II. 98 Thorough-stones or bond-stones. **1893** C. HODGES in *Reliquary* Jan. 9 The side walls..are built of large stones, as wide as the walls are thick, *i.e.* they are all through stones.

**Through-swim, -tang, -thrilled**: see THROUGH-. **Throught, -ly**: see THROUGHOUT, -LY.

**Throu·gh-to·ll.** Also 7 **thorough-**. [See TOLL.] A toll or duty levied on persons, animals, or goods passing through certain places, esp. through a town or territory. Also, a toll which passes one through two or more turnpike gates.

**1567–79** *Expos. Termes Law* s. v. *Tolle*, Through tolle, is where a Towne prescribes to haue tol for euery beast that goeth through their towne. **1610** HOLLAND *Camden's Brit.* (1637) 731 Bowes..where..the Earles of Richmond had..a certaine custome called Thorough-toll. **1611** COTGR., *Droict de Chemage*, the passage-toll, or through-toll, thats taken at Sens. **1636** PRYNNE *Rem. agst. Shipmoney* 8 This Tax..layes a farre greater charge on the Subject then any new office, Murage, Toll-travers, or thorough-toll. **1892** *Daily News* 6 Apr. 5/4 The amount received at Newcastle for through toll in one year amounts..to nearly 7,000 *l.*

**Through-touch**: see *thorough-touch* s. v. THOROUGH- 2. **Through-wax, -wort**: see THOROUGHWAX, -WORT.

**Through-waxen** to **-wound**: see THROUGH-.

**Throut(e**: see THEREOUT, THROUGHOUT.

**Throve**, past tense of THRIVE *v.*

† **Throw**, *sb.*[1] *Obs.* Forms: α. 1 **þráᵹ, þráh**, 3 **þraȝhe**, 4 **thrau(e**, 4–5 **þraw(e**, 4–6 **thraw**; 4 **trau, trawe**, (5 **drawe**). β. 3 **þroȝe**, 3–5 **þrowe**, 3–6 **throwe**, 5–6 **throw**; 5 **trowe**. γ. 5 **threwe**. [OE. *þrág, þráh* fem. a (point or space of) time, a season. Not found in the cognate langs.; if in OTeut., its form would naturally be **þraigā*, Goth. **þráiga*.]

**1.** The time at which anything happens; an occasion. *Many a throw*, many a time, often.

Like *minute, instant*, often used in advb. phrases with preposition omitted, as *that, this, any, the same throw.*

*Beowulf* 2884 Ferᵹendra to lyt þrong ymbe þeoden þa hyne sio þraᵹ becwom. *c* **888** K. ÆLFRED *Boeth.* xxxvii. § 1 Onwæcnað sio wode þraᵹ þære wrænnesse. **971** *Blickl. Hom.* 117 Nis þæt eower..þæt ᵹe witan þa þraᵹe & þa tide. *a* **1250** *Owl & Night.* 478 Blisse myd heom sume þrowe. *Ibid.* 1455, I singe myd heom one þrowe [*v. r.* þroȝe]. **1390** GOWER *Conf.* III. 36 This riche man the same throwe With soudein deth was overthrowe. **14..** HOCCLEVE *Compl. Virgin* 73 O thynke how many a throwe Thow in myn armes lay. *c* **1440** LOVELICH *Merlin* 9949 ȝoure Ryng to taken me jn this threwe, To ȝoure cosin le-ownces that j myhte it schewe. *c* **1460** *Towneley Myst.* xx. 380 Peter, thou shall thryse apon a thraw fforsake me, or the cok craw. **1513** DOUGLAS *Æneis* x. xiii. 53 The casting dart..Smate worthy Anthores the ilk thraw.

**2.** A space of time; a while; in later use always, a brief while, an instant, a moment.

*a* **1000** *Cædmon's Gen.* 1426 (Gr.) Þær se halᵹa bad sunu Lameches soðra ᵹehata lange þraᵹe. *a* **1000** *Juliana* 464 (Gr.) Is þeos þraᵹ ful strong,..ic sceal þinᵹa ᵹehwylc þolian. *c* **1175** *Lamb. Hom.* 33 Nis nawiht þeos weorld; al heo aȝeð on ane alpi þraȝe. *c* **1200** ORMIN 3475 Wass mikell weȝȝe till þatt land..& forrþi wass hemm ned to don God þraȝhe to þatt weȝȝe. *c* **1205** LAY. 640 He tah hine aȝein ane þrowe. *a* **1300** *Cursor M.* 3281 (Cott.) Had he noght rested bot a thrau [*v. rr.* þraw, þrowe]. **1375** BARBOUR *Bruce* VII. 34 He..said eftir a litill thraw, Þat he suld wenge in hy thar blude. *c* **1386** CHAUCER *Man of Law's T.* 855 Now lat vs stynte of Custance but a throwe [*v. r.* trowe]. **1423** JAS. I *Kingis Quair* xlv, Quhen I a lytill thrawe had maid my moon. *c* **1440** *Promp. Parv.* 493/1 Throwe, a lytyl wyle, *momentum.* *c* **1570** *Pride & Lowl.* (1841) 64 They were defaced in a throw. **1590** SPENSER *F. Q.* III. iv. 53 Downe himselfe he layd Upon the grassy ground to sleepe a throw.

**b.** *Be throwes*, by turns, time about. *rare.*

**1390** GOWER *Conf.* I. 55 After that cause and nede it ladde, Be throwes ech of hem it hadde.

**Throw** (þrōᵘ), *sb.*[2] Also 6–7 **throwe**, 6– *Sc.* **thraw.** [f. THROW *v.*[1]] The act expressed by THROW *v.*[1]; a twist; a cast.

**I.** A twist, a turn. * In Sc. form **thraw.**

**1.** An act of twisting or turning; the fact or condition of being twisted; a turn or twist round, or to one side, or out of the straight or regular line; a wrench, crook, warp; also the act of turning a key, or the like. Also *fig. In a throw*, crookedly, awry. *Sc.*

*a* **1585** POLWART *Flyting w. Montgomerie* 564 The bleared bucke..Hes right trim teeth, somewhat set in a thraw.

**1632** LITHGOW *Trav.* x. 465 Each torture consisting of three winding throwes of euery pinne; which amounted to twenty one throwes. *a* **1653** BINNING *Serm.* (1845) 68 Man's fall from God hath made a wretched thraw and crook in the soul. **1785** BURNS *Halloween* xxii, She turns the key wi' cannie thraw. **1814** SCOTT *Wav.* xlviii, Deil be wi' me if I do not give your craig [neck] a thraw. **1902** *Westm. Gaz.* 15 May 10/2 When the beacon took a 'thrawe' and his workmen fled into the tower, then almost finished, he sat unmoved reading his Bible.

**b.** *fig.* A perverse twist of temper or humour; a fit of perversity or 'thrawnness'. *mod.Sc.*

**1788** R. GALLOWAY *Poems* 93 (Jam.) Lasses were kiss'd ..Nor seem'd to tak it ill, Wi' thraw that day. **1814** J. TRAIN *Strains Mount. Muse* 113 (ibid.) Auld Lucky Nature..unto Miss Scotia, just out of a thraw, She gave a bleak wilderness, barren and raw. **1864** T. BRUCE in *Poets Ayrshire* (1910) 233 Agents an' corks, in ruthless thraw Sought out each scob an' tear.

**c.** Phrase. *Heads and thraws*, Sc.: see quot. 1825.

**1728** RAMSAY *To Robt. Yarde* 14 A laigh hut, where sax thegither Ly heads and thraws on craps of heather. **1765** *Museum Rust.* IV. cvi. 462 They lay root-ends and crop-ends together, or, as is commonly called, heads and thraws. **1819** SCOTT *Leg. Montrose* vi, The great barn would hold fifty more, if they would lie heads and thraws. **1825** JAMIESON, *Heads-and-thraws*, with the heads and feet, or heads and points, lying in opposite directions...*To play at heads and thraws*, to play at push-pin.

* * In Eng. form **throw**.

**2.** *Mech.* The action or motion of a slide-valve, or of a crank, eccentric, or cam; also, the extent of this measured on a straight line passing through the centre of motion; also, a crank-arm; a crank.

**1829** Three throw [see THREE III. 2]. **1864** in WEBSTER. **1874** KNIGHT *Dict. Mech.* s. v. *Crank*, A two-throw or three-throw crank-shaft is one having so many cranks set at different angles on the shaft. **1888** HASLUCK *Model Engin. Handybk.* (1900) 77 When the space between the bearings is limited, that part of the rod forming the crank throws, is made elliptical in section. **1904** LINEHAM *Text Bk. Mech. Engin.* 637 The eccentricity..must be measured from centre of eccentric sheave to centre of shaft. This amount we shall sometimes call the throw.

**b.** *Electr.* (See quot.)

**1902** O'CONOR SLOANE *Electr. Dict.*, *Throw*, in a galvanometer, the instantaneous deflection of the needle when the contact or closing of the circuit is instantaneous, or when the discharge is completed before the needle begins to move.

**c.** Deflection from the right line.

**1858** MALLET in *Rep. Brit. Assoc.* I. 94 The obliquity of throw of each of the balls..from their respective cardinal and vertical planes.

**3.** A twist of some fibre (e.g. silk). *rare*$^{-1}$.

**1873** BROWNING *Red Cott. Nt.-cap* IV. 857 That stalk whereto her hermitage She tacked by golden throw of silk.

**4.** A machine by which a rotary motion is given to an object while being shaped; a lathe, esp. one worked by hand: cf. *throw-lathe* in THROW- 1.

**1657** TOMLINSON *Renou's Disp.* 490 Boxes are..either made with a throwe, or composed of a thin broad chip. **1659** HOOLE *Comenius' Vis. World* (1777) 89 The turner sitting over the treddle, turneth with a throw. **1836-8** *Encycl. Metrop.* (1845) VIII. 454 The jigger, also called a throw, is larger than, yet much resembling a lapidary's wheel. **1879** HOLTZAPFFEL *Turning* IV. 29 The potter's lathe or 'throw'. ..The term throw, also applied to the clock throw.

**II. 5.** An act of throwing a missile, etc.; a forcible propulsion or delivery from or as from the hand or arm; a cast. Also *fig.* (As a fault in Cricket: see BOWL *v.*[1] 4 and cf. quots. 1901 here.)

*To have a throw at (fig.)*, to attack, have an attempt at; to have a 'fling' at.

**1530** PALSGR. 233/1 Hurle or throwe with a stone, *coup de pierre*. **1548** ELYOT *Dict.*, *Iactus*, a throwe, a hurle, a caste. **1590** SPENSER *F. Q.* II. v. 9 He hewd, and lasht, and foynd, and thundred blowes..Ne plate, ne male, could ward so mighty throwes. **1692** BENTLEY *Boyle Lect.* 157 It is so many million of millions odds to one against any single throw, that the assigned order will not be cast. **1698** COLLIER *Immor. Stage* iii. 101 The Old Batchelour has a Throw at the Dissenting Ministers. **1755** *Game at Cricket* 10 If in running a Notch, the Wicket is struck down by a Throw, it's out. **1884** *Mil. Engineering* (ed. 3) I. II. 45 Keep the shovellers back at least 10 feet from the edge of the excavation; otherwise they interfere with the throw of the diggers. **1895** CROCKETT *Men of Moss-Hags* l, We will hae a thraw at it, to see if we canna break through the Thieves' Hole. **1901** *Speaker* 5 Jan. 361/2 There is no satisfactory definition of a 'throw' [at Cricket]. What one man conscientiously regards as 'throwing', another..equally conscientiously passes as bowling. **1901** *Westm. Gaz.* 11 Jan. 5/2, I wonder what [he] would say if anyone told him he could not tell a throw from a fairly-bowled ball.

**6.** The distance to which anything may or is to be thrown: often qualified, as a *stone's throw*.

**1582** N. LICHEFIELD tr. *Castanheda's Conq. E. Ind.* I. lxvii. 138 The enimyes were come, within the throwe of a Dart. **1607** SHAKS. *Cor.* v. ii. 21 Like to a Bowle vpon a subtle ground I haue tumbled past the throw. **1704** SWIFT *Batt. Bks.* Misc. (1711) 252 The two Cavaliers had now approach'd within a Throw of a Lance. **1712** ARBUTHNOT *John Bull* I. ix, She stank so, that nobody durst come within a stone's throw of her. **1893** F. F. MOORE *I Forbid Banns* (1899) 16 The vessel steamed within a biscuit-throw of the southern cliffs.

**7.** *spec.* **a.** A cast at dice; the number cast. Also *fig.*

**1577** STANYHURST *Descr. Irel.* in *Holinshed* I. 84/1 Fall how it will, this throwe is for an huddle. **1596** SHAKS. *Merch. V.* II. i. 33 The greater throw May turne by fortune from the weaker hand. **1611** SPEED *Hist. Gt. Brit.* IX. xx. § 66 Freede from the awe of open challenges of the Crowne, and from throwes at his maine. *a* **1667** JER. TAYLOR *Serm. Ephes.* v. 32-33 Wks. 1831 I. 319 They..cast a die..of the greatest interest in the world, next to the last throw for eternity. **1702** *Lond. Gaz.* No. 3839/4 The most at Three Throws is to have him. **1710** PALMER *Proverbs* 368 A man's friends..on an ill throw don't care to go his halves. **1759** *Hist.* in *Ann. Reg.* 8/1 This able general, who never risques his fortune on a single throw, began to think of a retreat. **1850** ROBERTSON *Serm.* Ser. III. ii. (1872) 24 The gambler who improvidently stakes all upon a moment's throw. **1878** Bosw. SMITH *Carthage* 259 They had ventured their all, or nearly their all, on this one throw.

**b.** A cast of a net, a fishing-line, etc.; = CAST *sb.* 5, 5 c. Also *fig.*

**1548** UDALL, etc. *Erasm. Par. Acts* ii. 11 This was the firste caste and throwe of his nette. **1687** DRYDEN *Hind & P.* II. 20 With the self-same throw, To catch the quarry and the vermin too. **1851** NEWLAND *The Erne* 75 For the trout, the gillaroo, and the jenkin, the northern shore affords the best throws. **1867** F. FRANCIS *Angling* v. (1880) 159 When ..he can manage this throw.

**c.** *Wrestling.* The throwing down of an opponent, which finishes a bout or round: cf. FALL *sb.*[1] 13, CAST *sb.* 11.

**1819** *Sporting Mag.* IV. 236 The Irish trump again got the throw. **1861** PALEY *Æschylus* (ed. 2) *Choephoroe* 331 *note*, ἀτρίακτος, 'invincible,' from the three throws of a wrestler.

**d.** A felling of timber: cf. FALL *sb.*[1] 14; also, the direction in which a tree is caused to fall.

**1879** JEFFERIES *Wild Life in S. Co.* 289 While all these throws of timber have successively taken place, no attempt has been made to fill up the gaps. **1880** — *Gt. Estate* 173 The throw of oak that was going on in one part of the Chace.

**8.** *Geol.* and *Mining.* A dislocation in a vein or stratum, in which the part on one side of the fracture is displaced up or down; = FAULT *sb.* 9; also, the amount of vertical displacement so caused.

**1796** OUTRAM in *Phil. Trans.* LXXXVI. 351 A fault, throw, or break of the strata, which was filled with shale. **1828** *Craven Gloss.*, *Throw*,..a disrupture of the beds or strata. **1855** J. R. LEIFCHILD *Cornwall Mines* 86 The 'throw' or perpendicular distance between the corresponding strata on the opposites of a vein, varies from a few inches to thirty or forty, or even a hundred fathoms.

**Throw**, *sb.*[3], earlier form of THROE *sb.*

**Throw** (þrōu), *v.*[1] Pa. t. **threw** (þrū); pa. pple. **thrown** (þrōun). Forms: see below. [OE. *þráwan* (pa. t. *þréow*, pa. pple. *þráwen*) str. vb., to turn, twist; corresp. to OLG. **thrâjan*, MLG. *dreien*, LG. *draien*, *dreien*, MDu. *draeien*, Du. *draaien*, OHG. *drâen* (from **drâjan*), MHG. *dræjen*, *dræn*, Ger. *drehen*, weak vb., to twist, twirl, turn; wanting in Gothic, where it would have been a reduplicated vb. **þráian*, like *wáian*; OTeut. root *þrǣ-*, pre-Teut. *trē-*, *ter-* to turn; in Gr. and L., to bore. In Eng. the orig. sense 'twist, turn' remained in the north, and in certain technical uses (see branch I); otherwise it passed in ME. into that of branch II, = OE. *weorpan*, perh. through an unrecorded sense 'throw by a turn or twist of the arm, or with a sling'. Cf. note to CAST *v.*]

**A.** Illustration of Forms.

**1.** *Present stem.* **a.** 1 **ðráw-an**, 1–4 **þraw-**, 3–4 **þrauw-**, 3–7 **thrawe**, 5– *Sc.* **thraw**, (4 **þrau-**, 5–6 **thrau**, 9 *dial.* **thraa**, **thrah**, **thra**, **tra(a)** (see *Eng. Dial. Dict.*).

*c* **1000** Þrawan [see B. 1]. *a* **1300** Thrawe [see B. 8]. **1340** *Ayenb.* 17 God þrauþ doun prede. *c* **1450** *Two Cookery-bks.* 101 Thrawe it þorgh a streynour. *c* **1470** Thraw [see B. 1]. **1570** LEVINS *Manip.* 45/38 To Thrawe, cast, *iactare*, *mittere*. **1581** Thrau [see B. 3]. **1720** RAMSAY *Wealth* 141 I'll thraw my gab and gloom. **1787-1884** Thraw [see B. 5]. **1828** *Craven Gloss.*, *Thraa*, to throw; also to turn in a lathe.

**β.** 3–5 **þrōw-en**, 4–7 **throwe**, 6– **throw** (6–7 **through**, 7 **throughe**, **thro'**, 9 *dial.* **thro**, **trow**).

*c* **1250** *Long Life* 37 in *O. E. Misc.* 158 Weilawei, deþ þe schal adun þrowe. **1377** LANGL. *P. Pl.* B. XVI. 131, I shal ouertourne þis temple and adown throwe. **1387** Þrow [see B. 37 a]. *a* **1400** Þrowe [see B. 30]. **1552** HULOET, Throwe, *jacio*. **1580** Throw [see B. 15]. **1598** Through [see B. 14]. *c* **1614** SIR W. MURE *Dido & Æneas* II. 219, I, frome above, a tempest downe shall thro'. *c* **1620** Throughes [see B. 19].

**2.** *Past tense.* **a.** 1 **ðreow**, 1–3 **þreow**, (3 **þreuw**), 3–4 **þreou**, **þreu**, **þrew**, **-e**, 4 **þreuh**, **þruw**, **-e**, **threow**, **thrwe**, 4–6 **threwe**, 5– **threw**, (5 **threew**, **throwe**, 7 **thrue**).

*c* **1000** ÆLFRIC *Hom.* II. 510 He sona ðreow ðwyres. *c* **1205** LAY. 12321 Þa cheorles up þreowen [*c* **1275** þreuwen]. *Ibid.* 807 Þreou, aþreu [see B. 28]. *a* **1300** *K. Horn* 1162 Horn þreu [*v. r.* þrew] is ryng to grounde. **13..** *K. Alis.* 2427 Ded he threow him to grounde. **1362** LANGL. *P. Pl.* A. v. 201 He..þreuh [*texts B., C.* þreu, þrew, threwe, throwe] to þe grounde. *c* **1374** Thrwe [see B. 43]. **1387** TREVISA *Higden* (Rolls) VI. 11 Þe aungel..þrewe [*MS.* γ, þruw] þat cloop into þat fuyre. *a* **1400-50** Threw [see B. 46 a]. *c* **1422** Threew [see B. 48 a]. *c* **1449** PECOCK *Repr.* (Rolls) 260 Thou ..threwist doun hors and man. *c* **1470** HENRY *Wallace* v. 1020 Thom Haliday sone be the craig him threw. **1526** *Pilgr. Perf.* (W. de W. 1531) 304 The chyldren..toke vp stones & clay, & threwe them. **1618** Thrue [see B. 44 i].

**β.** (*dial.*) 7–9 **throwed**, 9 **thrawed**.

**1666** in Picton *L'pool Munic. Rec.* (1883) I. 315 Pt..hee throwed downe into the trench. **1820** Throwed [see B. 19]. **1871** Thrawed [see B. 2].

**3.** *Past pple.* **a.** 1–4 **þrawen** (3 **þrauwen**, 4 **y(þraw)**, 5–6 *Sc.* **thrawen** (5–7 **-in**, **-ne**), 6– *Sc.* **thrawn**, 9 *dial.* **thraan**. See also THRAWN.

*c* **1205** Þrauwen, **13..** Þrawen [see B. 1]. *c* **1330** Y-þrawe [see B. 40 c]. **1483** Thrawen [see THROWN]. **1513** DOUGLAS *Æneis* v. v. 66 [The adder] In lowpis thrawin. **1591** Thrawne [see B. 4]. **1645** *Shetland Witch Trial* in Hibbert *Descr. Shetl. Isl.* (1822) 597 Scho..cam scouring hame..having her head thrawin backward to her back. **1824** SCOTT *St. Ronan's* ix, He winna bide being thrawn.

**β.** 4–5 **þrowen**, (4 **i-þrowen**, 4–5 **i-þrow(e)**, 4–7 (9 *dial.*) **throwen**, (4 **throwyn**, **-un**, 4–5 **(y-)throwe**, **ytrowe**, **i-drow**, 6 **throwin**), 6–7 **throwne**, 7– **thrown**, (6 **trowne**, 9 *dial.* **threuwn**.)

*c* **1320** *Cast. Love* 739 Wiþ Cumpas I-þrowen and wiþ gin al I-do. **1382** WYCLIF *Acts* xxvii. 18 Vs throwun with greet tempest. **1387** TREVISA *Higden* (Rolls) III. 93 Þe body ..þat was so i-þrowe wiþ oute þe walles. *Ibid.* VII. 327 Þe knyȝt þat hadde i-þrow hym downe. **1399** Throwe [see B. 8]. *c* **1400** *Laud Troy Bk.* 3867 Riche Troye..Schal be brent and doun ytrowe. *c* **1425** I-drow [see B. 40 c]. **1482** *Monk of Evesham* (Arb.) 74 They..were greuysly caste and throwe fro one place to anothir. **1535** COVERDALE *Lam.* i. 13 He hath..throwne me wyde open. **1589** R. ROBINSON *Gold. Mirr.* (Chetham Soc.) Ep. to Rdr., Stones .. thou would have throwen. **1647** Thrown [see B. 42 a].

**γ.** 8–9 (now *dial.*) **throwed**, 9 *north.* **thrawed**.

**1727-41** [see THROWED]. **1878** Throwed [see B. 20]. **1896** Thrawed [see B. 1].

**B.** Signification.

**I.** To twist, to turn, and derived uses.

* *Sc.* in form **thraw**; * * *technical*, in form **throw**.

***1.** *trans.* To twist, to wring; to turn to one side (also *fig.*); to twist about, twine, wreathe; to turn (a key or the like); in OE. to torture on the rack. Now *Sc.* and *north. dial.*

*To thraw one's face, gab, mouth* (*Sc.*), to pull a wry face, to contort the face, e. g. in pain, anger, or passion.

*c* **1000** ÆLFRIC *Hom.* II. 308 [He het] hine hon on heardre hengene..and mid hengene ðrawan to langere hwile. *c* **1000** — *Saints' Lives* viii. 113 Þa wearð se arleasa ȝehathyrt, and het hi on hencgene a-streccan and ðrawan swa swa wiððan wælhreowlice. *c* **1000** ÆLFRIC *Gram.* xxvi (Z.) 155 *Contorqueo*, ic samod þrawe. *c* **1205** LAY. 27359 Heȝe hare-marken.. sixti þusende þrauwen mid winde. **13..** *Gaw. & Gr. Knt.* 194 Þe tayl..þrawen wyth a þwong a þwarle knot alofte. *c* **1470** HENRY *Wallace* VII. 410 Than xx$^{ty}$ men he gert fast wetheis thraw,..Than festnyt thai with wetheis duris fast. **1536** BELLENDEN *Cosmogr.* xiv, Apperit than ane multitude of wormis thrawing thaim self out of sindry hollis and boris of this tre. **1583** *Calr. Scott. Pap.* VI. 356 [They] forcit thame..be towis thrawin about their heidis [to reveal the money]. **1689** BURNET *Tracts* I. 82 He threw it which way he pleased. **1728** RAMSAY *Fable, Fox & Rat* 26 He threw his gab, and girn'd. ?**17..** *Young Redin* xiv. in Child *Ballads* II. 146 Ye'll thraw my head aff my hause-bane, And throw me in the sea. **1816** SCOTT *Bl. Dwarf* ix, To thraw the keys, or draw the bolts, or open the grate. **1823** HOGG *Sheph. Cal.* i. (1829) I. 4 Ye're something ill for thrawing your mou' at Providence now and then. **18..** *Sc. Proverb*, Thraw the widdie [= withy] while it's green Between three and thirteen. **1881** W. WALKER in *Mod. Scot. Poets* III. 104 Hoo his een are starin: hoo he thraws his mouth. **1894** CROCKETT *Raiders* 144 I'll thraw your neck for that, Jerry. **1896** — *Grey Man* i. 7 His countenance thrawed and drawn, his shrunk shanks twisted.

**2.** *intr.* To turn, twist, curl, twine, writhe; of a moored boat: to swing, sway. Chiefly *Sc.*

Quots. 1513, *a* 1650, appear to have the spec. meaning 'to writhe in death-throes'; they are closely connected with *thraw*, northern form of THROE *sb.*, and may perhaps be viewed as showing a Sc. form of THROE *v.* 2.

*c* **1000** *Gloss.* in *Haupt's Zeitschr.* IX. 435 *Crispantibus*, þrawendum *vel* cyrpisiendum, *marg.* cyrpsum loccum. *c* **1000** *Gloss.* in Wr.-Wülcker 527/2 *Rotante*, þrawende. *c* **1000** ÆLFRIC *Hom.* II. 510 Se liȝ..sona ðreow ðwyres wið þæs windes. *c* **1450** HOLLAND *Howlat* 823 Twa..fulis..Callit him thryss thevisnek, to thrawe in a widdy. **1513** DOUGLAS *Æneis* XII. vi. 48 Down strowand eik vnder fut in the plane Diuers otheris ȝit thrawand and half slane. *a* **1650** *Sir Eger & Sir Gryme* 1611 in Laing *Early Metr. T.* (1826) 55 Gray-Steel unto his death thus thrawes; He walters, and the grass updrawes. *a* **1699** BONNELL in W. Hamilton *Life* II. (1703) 85 We stomach..Injuries that we think are done to us; we fling and throw under them. **1818** SCOTT *Br. Lamm.* xxiii, If the dead corpse binna straughted, it will girn and thraw. **1871** ROSSETTI *Stratton Water* xxxvii, The empty boat thrawed i' the wind, Against the postern tied. **1881** PALGRAVE *Visions Eng.* 248 The strong branches cry And start and thraw in that fierce furnace-flame.

**3.** *trans.* (*fig.*) To wrest, warp, or pervert the meaning or intention of; to do violence to, strain; also, to distort the pronunciation of. *Sc.*

**1558** KENNEDY *Compend. Tract.* 6 Wrestand and thrawing the Scripture, contrare the godlie menynge of the samyn. **1581** HAMILTON in *Cath. Tractates* (S. T. S.) 77 The scripture, quhilk thaj thrau efter thair sensuall iugement. **1873** MURDOCH *Doric Lyre* 86 (E.D.D.) What though he thraw'd the law a wee? **1877** G. MACDONALD *Mrq. Lossie* xxviii, They dinna thraw the words there jist the same gait they du at Portlossie.

**b.** To change detrimentally the colour of, to discolour or cause to fade: cf. CAST *v.* 24.

*Mod. Sc. dial.* The sun has quite thrown my silk gown.

†**4.** To obtain or extract by twisting or wringing; to wrench; chiefly *fig.* to extort. *Sc. Obs.*

**1513** DOUGLAS *Æneis* XII. vi. 120 Owt of hys [an enemy's] rycht hand Richt austernly has he thrawin the brand. **1591** R. BRUCE *Serm.* R j b, When hee hath thrawne all these good turnes out of them. *a* **1598** ROLLOCK *Wks.* (1844) II. vi. 73 He throws another accusation out of the Jews.

†**b.** To force by torture or violence; to constrain. *Sc. Obs.*

**1599** JAS. I Βασιλ. Δωρον (1682) 96 Beware of thrawing or constraining them thereto.

**5.** To cross, thwart, frustrate. Chiefly *Sc.*

**1787** BURNS *When Guilford good*, etc. vi, Saint Stephen's boys, wi' jarring noise, They did his measures thraw. **1818** SCOTT *Rob Roy* xxvi, He's easy wi' a' body that will be easy wi' him; but if ye thraw him ye had better thraw the deevil. 1884 *Lays & Leg. N. Irel.* 11 If his Riv'rance released him he'd thraw him no more.

**b.** *intr.* To go counter, to act in opposition; to be at variance or awkward; to exhibit dislike or aversion; to quarrel or contend *with*. *Sc.*

*a* 1578 LINDESAY (Pitscottie) *Chron. Scot.* XXI. iv. (1728) 125 Bishop Forman had..caused the duke to thraw [*so* 3 *MSS.*; 2 *MSS.* stur(e] with him till he gave certain Benefices to the Duke to give unto his friends. 1807 HOGG *Laird of Lairistan* xxiii, Jealous of the Stuart race, The English lords begin to thraw. 1824 MACTAGGART *Gallovid. Encycl.* (1876) 214 At nature ay to girn and thraw..Is sure a sin infernal. 1888 D. GRANT *Scotch Stories* 10 Thraw wi' him, an' he was just as stubborn an' rampageous as a wild ox.

**6.** *trans.* To form or fashion by means of a rotary or twisting motion. **a.** To turn (wood, etc.) in a lathe; to shape (round pottery) on a potter's lathe or 'throwing-wheel'. Now *techn.* or *dial.*

*c* 1440 *Promp. Parv.* 493/1 Throwyn, or turne vessel of a tre, *torno*. 1570 LEVINS *Manip.* 45/39 To Thraw or turne, *tornare*. 1604 *Shuttleworths' Acc.* (Chetham Soc.) 159 To the disshe-thrower, ix days throwing disshes and bassenes..iij*s*. 1674 RAY *N. C. Words*, To *Throw*, to Turn as Turners doe. 1752 *Gentl. Mag.* Aug. 348 Rooms for throwing, turning, and stove drying the ware. 1755 JOHNSON s. v., Balls thrown in a lathe. 1839 URE *Dict. Arts*, etc. 1011 Throwing is performed upon a tool called the potter's lathe...The mass of dough to be thrown is weighed out or gauged by an experienced hand. 1900 *Daily News* 25 May 6/2 Further on a potter is 'throwing' pots on his wheel.

**b.** *Silk Manuf.* To prepare and twist (raw silk) into thread; *spec.* to form into thread by twisting two or more threads or 'singles' in the direction opposite to that of their component filaments.

1455 [implied in THROWSTER 1]. 1463-4 [implied in THROWN 2]. 1483 *Act* 1 *Rich. III*, c. 10 § 1 Calle sylk or coleyn silk throwen or wrought. 1670 BLOUNT *Law-Dict., Silk-thrower*,..a Trade, or Mystery, that winds, twists, and spins, or throws silk, thereby fitting it for use. 1796 *Trans. Soc. Arts* XIV. 328, I became convinced that Bengal Silk could be thrown in this country. 1839 URE *Dict. Arts*, etc. 1105 The raw silk..requires to be regularly wound upon bobbins, doubled, twisted, and reeled in our silk-mills. These processes are called throwing silk, and their proprietors are called silk throwsters. 1877 KNIGHT *Dict. Mech.* s.v. *Thrown Singles*, Silk filaments are twisted to form *singles*. Several of these are combined and twisted together (doubling) forming *dumb singles*. A number of the latter are associated and twisted together (throwing), forming *thrown singles*. 1897 *Daily News* 9 Dec. 10/5 Silk is still 'thrown' at Derby.

**c.** To make by twisting: cf. THROW-CROOK.

1896 P. A. GRAHAM *Red Scaur* v. 78 We began to throw straw ropes for them.

†**7.** To form, fashion, dispose, arrange; = CAST *v.* 45. *Obs. rare.*

*c* 1320 *Cast. Love* 739 A Trone..Of whit Iuori..Wiþ Cumpas I-þrowen and wiþ gin al I-do. *Ibid.* 807 Þe þreo baylys..þat wiþ þe cornels byth so feyre I-set, And throwen [*v.r.* I-cast] wiþ cumpas and walled abowte.

**II.** To project or propel through the air, and connected uses; to cast, fling, hurl, drive, shoot (away from the propelling agent).

**8.** *trans.* To project (anything) with a force of the nature of a jerk, from the hand or arm, so that it passes through the air or free space; to cast, hurl, fling; *spec.* to cast by a sudden jerk or straightening of the arm, esp. at the level of or over the shoulder (as distinguished from *bowl*, *pitch*, *toss*). Cf. CAST *v.* I.

Now the main sense of the word (= Fr. *jeter*, Ger. *werfen*, L. *jacĕre*, *jactāre*), which is contained or involved in all the later senses and applications; *throw* being the primary, most general, and most proper word for this action.

*a* 1300 *E. E. Psalter* cxxxix. [cxl.] 11 In fire sal tou thrawe þam swa. *a* 1300 *K. Horn* 1076 Horn þreu him ouer þe brigge. 1387 TREVISA *Higden* (Rolls) V. 9 Ignacius..was i-brouȝt to Rome, and i-þrowe to wylde bestes. 1399 LANGL. *Rich. Redeles* IV. 82 Ne had þei striked a strake ..or þe blast come, þey had be throwe ouere þe borde backewarde ichonne. *c* 1440 *Promp. Parv.* 493/1 Throwyn, or castyn, *jacto*. 1513 DOUGLAS *Æneis* XI. vi. 142 Ane lance towartis his aduersar thrawis he. 1530 PALSGR. 756/1, I threwe a potte at his head. 1567 *Satir. Poems Reform.* iii. 174 Jesabell, Quhome throw ane windo suirlie men did thraw. 1651 HOBBES *Leviath.* II. xxi. 108 When a man throweth his goods into the Sea for feare the ship should sink. 1724 DE FOE *Mem. Cavalier* I. 76 I'd throw it [money] all into the Elbe. 1818 SCOTT *Br. Lamm.* xxiv, He threw the fellow a dollar. *Ibid.* xxxiii, Throwing Craigengelt from him with such violence that he rolled down the steps. 1863 GEO. ELIOT *Romola* xx, There were practical jokes of all sorts, from throwing comfits to throwing stones. 1869 *Prov.* [see GLASS-HOUSE]. *Mod.* Throw me a rope.

**b.** *absol.* To hurl a missile, a weapon, etc.

13.. *Sir Beues* (A.) 3106 Þow miȝt nouȝt sen ariȝt to þrowe. 1869 *Temple Bar Mag.* VI. 283 Parr threw 109 yards, the soldier only three yards less. 1889 DOYLE *M. Clarke* 34 The turnip on a stick at which we used to throw at the fairs.

†**c.** *trans.* To assail *with* missiles, to pelt. *Obs. rare*$^{-1}$.

13.. *K. Alis.* 4702 (Bodl. MS.) Men hem þrew wiþ drytt & dunge [*v.r.* to heom throewe drit and donge].

**9.** *refl.* To fling or cast oneself; to precipitate oneself; † of a river, to precipitate itself, fall *into* another river, a lake, etc. (*obs.*) Also *fig.*

13.. *Sir Beues* (A.) 2179 Beues in to þe sadel him þrew. 1387 TREVISA *Higden* (Rolls) III. 411 Alisaundre..þrewe hym self into a water þat renneþ þere. 1576 FLEMING *Panopl. Epist.* 310 Another throweth himselfe headlong from the topp of an house, and breaketh his necke. *c* 1630 RISDON *Surv. Devon* § 220 (1810) 227 The river Thrushell..throws itself into Lyd. 1714 ADDISON *Spect.* No. 556 ¶ 6, I..threw myself into an Assembly of Ladies. 1794 MRS. RADCLIFFE *Myst. Udolpho* xl, 'This is too—too much!' exclaimed Valancourt,..throwing himself into a chair. 1795 BURKE *Corr.* (1844) IV. 324 If you throw yourself into one of the early coaches, you would be here very quickly. 1843 LEVER *J. Hinton* xi, He threw himself upon his horse.

**b.** *To throw oneself upon*: to attack with violence or vigour; to fall upon. (Cf. 28.)

1823 SCOTT *Quentin D.* iv, He threw himself upon the ragout, and the plate was presently vacant.

**10.** *trans.* To cast (dice) from the dice-box; to make (a cast) at dice; also *absol.* or *intr.* to cast or throw dice, to play at dice. Also *fig.*

† *To throw at all*: to stake or venture all one has (*obs.*).

1587 GREENE *Penelopes Web* Wks. (Grosart) V. 181 Least ..we set our rest on the hazard and so desperately throw at all. 1601 SHAKS. *All's Well* II. iii. 84, I had rather be in this choise, then throw Ames-ace for my life. 1605 — *Lear* I. iv. 136 Set lesse then thou throwest. *a* 1667 JER. TAYLOR *Wks.* (1835) I. 533 (Cent.) That great day of expense, in which a man is to throw his last cast for an eternity of joys and sorrows. 1698 *Act* 10 *Will. III*, c. 23 § 3 Every Person or Persons that..shall play throw or draw at any such Lottery..shall forfeite for every such Offence the Sum of Twenty Pounds. 1720 *Lond. Gaz.* No. 5872/6 The Winning Horse to be thrown for at 40 Guineas by the Contributors. 1848 THACKERAY *Van. Fair* xxii, George had thrown the great cast. 1892 *Monthly Packet* May 558 If I should throw doublets, we will share the stakes.

**b.** To play (a card) out of one's hand; *esp.* to discard.

1748 [see *throw away*, 37 c]. 1879 'CAVENDISH' *Card Ess.*, etc. 109 Throwing the ace of hearts to the last spade. 1891 *Harper's Mag.* Mar. 603/1 He can therefore safely throw his queen on the ace. 1891 *Field* 28 Nov. 842/3 We should throw four diamonds, and the seven of spades, but do not say it is the proper 'discard'.

**c.** To cast (a vote): = CAST *v.* 1 f.

1844 W. PHILLIPS in *Life of Garrison* (1889) III. iv. 99 No one can take office, or throw a vote for another to hold office. 1888 BRYCE *Amer. Commw.* I. v. 55 *note*, 37 additional presidential votes..all thrown for the Democratic candidate. 1890 *Spectator* 8 Mar., Their usual leaders do not know their thoughts, and until their votes are thrown, can form only guesses as to the way their sympathies are tending.

**11.** To hurl, project, shoot, as a missile engine does; also of a person using such an engine. Often *absol.* (esp. in reference to distance or direction).

1393 LANGL. *P. Pl.* C. XXI. 295 Sette mahon at þe mangonel and mulle-stones þroweþ. *a* 1400-50 *Alexander* 2218 Thre thousand of thra men to thraw with engynes. 1726 LEONI *Alberti's Archit.* I. 69/1 This will baulk the aim of the military engines, and make them throw over the wall. 1880 *Daily Tel.* 23 Dec., Although throwing only a 7lb. projectile, they [guns] are [etc.]. 1890 CLARK RUSSELL *Ocean Trag.* II. xviii. 106 That gun 'll throw about three quarters of a mile. 1900 POLLOK & THOM *Sports Burma* vi. 212, I tried the weapon, and found that both barrels threw considerably to the left.

**12.** To put forth with a throwing action (a fishing net, line, or bait); to cast, make a cast with. Also *absol.*

1841 LANE *Arab. Nts.* I. ii. 101 And threw his net. 1889 CROMMELIN & BROWN *Violet Vyvian* II. ix. 154 Violet.. learnt to throw a fly. 1891 *Sat. Rev.* 20 June 734/1 Good anglers..can throw to a hairbreadth and not miss.

**13.** Of the sea or wind: †**a.** To toss or drive violently about; also, to drive, send, impel (*obs. rare*); **b.** *esp.* to drive or cast with violence (on rocks or a coast); to cast away, wreck.

1382 WYCLIF *Matt.* xiv. 24 Sothely the boot in the mydil see was throwen [L. *iactabatur*] with wawis. 1423 JAS. I *Kingis Q.* xvii, My feble bote full fast to stere and rowe, ..the wynter nyght I wake, To wayte the wynd that furthward suld me throwe. 1659 D. PELL *Impr. Sea* Proœm. d ij b, They are thrown irrecoverably upon Rocks and Sands. 1879 MINTO *Defoe* ix. 142 [He] might have been thrown on a desert island. 1886 BURTON *Arab. Nts.* (abr. ed.) I. 126 A billow..threw me with a long cast on dry land.

**14.** To project (a ray, beam, light) *on*, *upon*, *over*, etc.; to emit (light); to project, cast (a shadow).

1598 B. JONSON *Ev. Man in Hum.* III. i, To through the least beame of regard upon such a [fellow]. 1600 FAIRFAX *Tasso* XVIII. xv, The morning's lusty queen, Begilding, with the radiant beams she threw, His helm. 1797 MRS. RADCLIFFE *Italian* vii, A nun, kneeling..beneath a lamp which threw its rays aslant her head. 1876 TAIT *Rec. Adv. Phys. Sc.* ix. (ed. 2) 213 Throwing the spectrum of light..on the screen. 1893 *Harper's Mag.* Jan. 280/2 The great mound ..threw a long shadow westward.

**b.** In *fig.* phrases, esp. *to throw* (*a*) *light on*, to contribute to the elucidation of, to make clearer or plainer; *to throw a lustre over*, to illuminate or render lustrous; also *to throw a shadow, cloud, gloom, over*: see the sbs.

1598 [see prec. sense]. 1769 [see LUSTRE *sb.*[1] 4]. 1774 GOLDSM. *Nat. Hist.* (1776) V. 78 The testimony of a single witness..will throw more light on the subject than the reasonings of an hundred philosophers. 1825 MOORE *Sheridan* I. 510 It was in the power of the orator..to throw a lustre over the historian. 1825 T. HOOK *Sayings* Ser. II. *Passion & Princ.* ix. III. 153 Showers of rain..threw a gloom over the gaieties. 1875 JOWETT *Plato* (ed. 2) I. p. xviii, Ancient and modern philosophy throw a light upon one another. 1890 SIR A. KEKEWICH in *Law Times Rep.* LXIII. 684/1 The defendants' evidence does not throw much light on the question.

**15.** To direct (words, an utterance) *towards*, etc., esp. in hostility or contempt; to hurl, cast; to cause (sound, or *fig.* a gesture) to pass or travel; to waft (a kiss), to cast (a nod).

1580 SIDNEY *Ps.* XXXI. ix, Those lips..Which..throw their words against the most vpright. 1600 SHAKS. *A. Y. L.* I. iii. 3 Not a word? *Ros.* Not one to throw at a dog. *a* 1748 WATTS (J.), There is no need to throw words of contempt on such a practice. 1822 SCOTT *Nigel* i, The poor youth had not a word to throw at a dog. 1831 — *Cast. Dang.* ii, 'Never fear me, Augustine,' said the old man,..throwing a kiss towards the boy. 1844 MRS. BROWNING *Drama of Exile* Poems 1850 I. 75 The blessed nightingale which threw Its melancholy music after us. 1892 *Field* 19 Nov. 771/2 The hideous yells that were thrown at him.

**b.** *To throw the tongue*: see TONGUE.

**16.** *To throw one's eye* or *eyes, a glance, a look*: to turn or direct one's gaze, to look; *esp.* to look hastily, rapidly, or cursorily; to glance: = CAST *v.* 7.

1590 SPENSER *F. Q.* III. i. 16 Still as she fledd her eye she backward threw. 1779 *Mirror* No. 17. ¶ 1 To throw your eye sometimes upon the inferior ranks of life. 1800 *Char.* in *Asiat. Ann. Reg.* 45/1 The mother lifting up her eyes,.. instantly threw them to the ground. 1885 FITZPATRICK *T. N. Burke* II. 35 Happening to throw his eye over the address delivered..at Boston. 1892 *Longm. Mag.* Jan. 276 Mrs. Duffield..threw inquiring glances across the table.

†**17.** To give, deliver (blows); also *absol.* or *intr.* to aim blows, strike. (Cf. to '*lay* about him'.) *Obs. rare.*

*c* 1470 *Golagros & Gaw.* 709 Thai threw in that thrang Stalwart strakis and strang. 1590 SPENSER *F. Q.* III. ix. 16 Then drew he his bright sword, and gan about him throw.

†**b.** *trans.* ? To deliver a blow at; to strike.

*c* 1470 HENRY *Wallace* IV. 252 That staff he had, hewy and forgyt new, With it Wallace wpon the hede him threw, Quhill bayn and brayn all in to sondyr ȝeid.

**18.** To perform, execute (a somersault or a leap, in which the body is thrown with force); also *to throw a fit*, to have a fit (*U. S. slang*).

1826 *Examiner* 585/1 Throw a somerset, leap a stick, tumble through a hoop. 1889 BADEN-POWELL *Pigsticking* viii. 39 Mr. Kingscote threw about three back somersaults. *Ibid.* xiii. 99 Don't be surprised to find your horse unexpectedly 'throwing leps'. 1897 FLANDRAU *Harvard Episodes* 132, I don't suppose the creature thought I was throwing a fit like that just for exercise.

**III.** Pregnant uses.

* = *throw down*; ** = *throw off*; *** = *throw out* or *up*.

***19.** *trans.* To cause to fall to the ground; to cast down, knock down, prostrate, lay low; *spec.* in *Wrestling*, to bring (one's opponent) to the ground, also with double object, *to throw one a fall*. Cf. *throw down*, 40.

13.. *K. Alis.* 2219 (Bodl. MS.) A riche kyng..smoot tholomewe þat he of his hors hym þrewe. Tholomeu on fote lep, And who hym þrewe he name gode kepe. 1530 PALSGR. 756/1 Wrestell nat with me, for I wyll throwe the on thy backe. *c* 1620 T. ROBINSON *Mary Magd.* 819 A newe delusion throughes Her pride as lowe as Phlegetonicke maine. 1820 *Sporting Mag.* VI. 177 Tom..throwed his opponent in masterly style. 1824 in *Examiner* 759/1 Cannon, grappling his man, threw him a tremendous fall. 1902 *Brit. Med. Jrnl.* No. 2154. 880 Three years ago [he] was thrown at football and hurt his knee.

**b.** *fig.* or in *fig.* context: To defeat in a contest; also, to be the cause of defeat to; to give or gain the verdict against in an action at law (*U. S.*): cf. CAST *v.* 14.

1850 TENNYSON *In Mem.* cix. 6 Seraphic intellect and force To seize and throw the doubts of man. 1887 in *Lisbon* (Dakota) *Star* 20 May 2/5, 'I am compelled to throw you in the cost', said a justice of the peace. 1888 *Poultry, Pigeons*, etc. 27 July 377 (Prize list) Third..a good black Red, but a little out of feather, which, no doubt, threw her. 1909 W. R. INGE *Faith* xi. (1910) 193 The sceptic cannot throw his opponent if his own feet are in the air.

**20.** To cause forcibly (a tree or structure) to fall; to bring, knock, break, or cut down; to fell. In *Coal-mining*: see quot. 1881.

1568 GRAFTON *Chron.* II. 139 Some of them, they threwe to the grounde and consumed with fire. 1878 JEFFERIES *Gamekeeper at H.* i. 14 In the spring when the oak timber is throwed [*dial. speech*]. *Ibid.* iii. 52 The entire wood is thrown and renovated. 1881 RAYMOND *Mining Gloss.*, *Throwing*,..the operation of breaking out the spurns, so as to leave the hanging coal unsupported, except by its own cohesion. 1908 *Daily News* 25 Jan. 9 Some 40 telephone wires had to be temporarily cut, in order to enable the [chimney] shaft to be 'thrown'.

**b.** *spec. To throw an ant-hill*: see quot. and cf. GELD *v.*[1] 3 d. *dial.*

1848 *Jrnl. R. Agric. Soc.* IX. I. 17 Ant-hills..are quickly checked by throwing, or gelding. *Ibid.* 25 [see GELD *v.*[1] 3 d].

****21.** Of a horse, etc.: To cause (the rider) to fall off; to unseat, shake off; = *throw off*, 42 a; also in passive *to be thrown* (from a horse or vehicle).

1531 ELYOT *Gov.* II. xiii, The courser..will stere and plonge and endeuour hym selfe to throwe hym. 1623 MASSINGER *Bondman* II. ii, This morning, As I rode to take the air, the untutored jade Threw me, and kicked me. 1748 *Anson's Voy.* II. xii. 265 One of their horses fell down and threw his rider. 1890 J. PAYN *Burnt Million* II. xxx. 248 He was thrown from his horse in the steeplechase. 1893 *Field* 4 Mar. 335/3 Had the [bicycle-]rider been thrown or killed.

**22.** Of a snake, a bird, etc.: To cast (the skin); to moult (feathers). Of a horse: to cast or lose (a shoe).

1590 SHAKS. *Mids. N.* II. i. 255 There the snake throwes her enammel'd skinne. 1765 *Treat. Dom. Pigeons* 41 If your Pigeons..stop in their molting, so that they don't throw their feathers well. **1821** SCOTT *Kenilw.* ix, To shoe my horse,..you may see that he has thrown a forefoot shoe. **1841** J. T. HEWLETT *Parish Clerk* I. 168 The post-boy..contrived to 'throw a shoe' [i. e. off his horse].

**23.** Of domestic animals: To produce as offspring; to give birth to, to drop. Also *absol.*, *to throw true*, to produce offspring true to the parent type. (Cf. also *throw back*, 38 d.)

**1845** *Jrnl. R. Agric. Soc.* V. II. 546 You cannot possibly tell what sort of foal your mare may throw. **1858** *Ibid.* XIX. I. 28 In a breeding sow for a dairy farm..we should have a disposition to throw large farrows and a good supply of milk. **1892** *Pall Mall G.* 16 June 2/3 Each of these [three varieties of the rabbit] has marked and unmistakable characteristics, and each of them, to use the naturalist's phrase, 'throws true'. **1903** *Times* 9 Jan. 5/2 In 1884 she threw a calf to a bison bull.

**b.** *gen.* To produce: see quots.

**1891** *Morning Post* 25 Dec. 6/5 Indian or Ceylon teas..throw a stronger liquor than the same amount of China tea would in double or treble the time. **1892** *Garden* 27 Aug. 194 Sown early and transplanted a good distance apart, the plants will throw immense heads of flowers.

*****24.** Of a fountain or pump: To eject or project (water); to discharge; also *absol.* Of a locomotive steam-engine: *to throw fire*, to discharge burning fuel from the funnel. Cf. *throw out*, *up*, senses 44, 48.

**1644** EVELYN *Diary* 27 Feb., The fountain of Laocoon is in a large square pool, throwing the water neere 40 feet high. **1697** DRYDEN *Virg. Georg.* III. 374 (*orig.* 241) The Waters boil, and belching from below, Black Sands, as from a forceful Engine throw. **1806** O. GREGORY *Mech.* (1807) II. 175 A machine by which water is thrown upon fires. **1864** *Jrnl. R. Agric. Soc.* XXV. II. 293 The pumps..throw daily 60,000 to 70,000 gallons. **1893** *Field* 4 Mar. 332/3 Bad stoking may be..the cause of a locomotive 'throwing fire'.

**25.** A horse is said to *throw* his feet, when he lifts them well in moving, esp. over rough ground. Also *transf.* (*slang*): see quot. 1900.

**1827** SCOTT *Chron. Canongate* ii, A famous piece of rough upland pasture, for rearing young colts, and teaching them to throw their feet. **1900** J. FLYNT *Tramping w. Tramps* IV. 397 *Throw the Feet*, to beg, 'hustle', or do anything that involves much action.

**26.** To form by throwing up with a spade or shovel; to cast up, raise (a mound, etc.). = *throw up*, 48 d. *rare.*

**1843** MARRYAT *M. Violet* xlii, Nearly all the hills in this part of New York were thrown by human hands.

**27.** To vomit; cf. *throw up*, 48 b. *Sc.* and *dial.*

**18..** WILSON *Tyneside Songs* (1890) 374 He retched an' he threw i' the hight oo his anguish. *Mod. Sc.* 'I no sooner get up but I begin to throw'.

**IV.** Intransitive senses related to II and III.

**28.** *intr.* To cast or fling oneself impetuously; to spring, start, leap, rush. *Obs.* exc. as in quots. 1812, 1891, and in sense 48 j.

(Allied in sense to 9, but found earlier, and app. not derived from it.)

*c* **1205** LAY. 807 Of his horse he þreou [*c* 1275 aþreu]. *Ibid.* 12321 Þa cheorles up þreowen [*c* 1275 vp þreuwen]. **1508** [see *throw out*, 44 o]. **1535** STEWART *Cron. Scot.* (Rolls) II. 192 Out of his wame ane meruelus multitude Of foule serpentis..thair threw. **1812** *Sporting Mag.* XXXIX. 186 Which she [the hare] was prevented doing by all the dogs throwing at her at the same time. **1891** ATKINSON *Moorland Par.* 83 The black dog, according to the expression used, 'threw at her'.

†**29.** *intr.* To fall with violence or force. *Obs.*

(Looks like an intrans. or passive of sense 19, but occurs earlier.)

**1297** R. GLOUC. (Rolls) 6831 Þe king bi an laddre to þe ssip clam an hey & þreu vp to doun in þe se. **1362** LANGL. *P. Pl.* A. v. 201 He þrompelde atte þrexwolde and þreuh [*v. rr.* fel, stey] to þe grounde.

**V.** Figurative and transferred senses.

**30.** *trans.* To cause to pass, go, or come into some place or position by some action likened to throwing; to put or place with haste, suddenness, or force; e. g. to put (a garment) *on* or *off* hurriedly, hastily, or carelessly.

(Many of these uses come very near the literal sense, and form a transition to the more fig. senses following.)

*c* **1384** CHAUCER *H. Fame* III. 235 And euery man Of hem ..Had on him throwen a vesture. *a* **1400** *Sir Beues* (E.) 3777+3 Euery kny3t and hys squyer Fayre queyntyse on hem ganne þrowe For no man scholde hem knowe. **1655** STANLEY *Hist. Philos.* III. (1701) 101/1 He is now coming to Athens, being thrown out of his House by the People. **1711** *Spect.* No. 116 ¶ 6 The Hare immediately threw them [the hounds] above a Mile behind her. **1722** STEELE in *Addison's Drummer* Ded., He only spoke it, and I took all the Pains of throwing it upon Paper. **1786** J. HUNTER *Treat. Venereal Dis.* VI. iii. § 2 (1810) 509 The quantity of mercury, to be thrown into the constitution..must be proportioned to the violence of the disease. **1799** *Med. Jrnl.* I. 424 No doubt but the father would have suffered equally with the son, had it [poison] not so soon been thrown off the stomach. **1806** COLERIDGE *Three Graves* xxxiii, Her arms Round Ellen's neck she threw. **1816** J. DALLAWAY *Stat. & Sculp.* 350 The paludamentum was a vestment..thrown over the cuirass and fastened over the shoulder with a golden clasp. **1843** R. J. GRAVES *Syst. Clin. Med.* vii. 84 *note*, I threw some common injection into the tibial arteries. **1859** *Musketry Instr.* 39 Throw the rifle smartly to the front of the right shoulder. **1891** A. GISSING *Moorland Idyll* II. iv. 102 To throw a hand to a drowning man.

**b.** In figurative uses of various phrases, as *to throw the reins on*, *to throw a veil over*, etc.; *to throw good money after bad*, to incur a further loss in trying to make good a previous one; *to throw oneself* or *be thrown at* (a man), of a woman, to put herself or be put designedly in the way of, so as to invite the attention of; *to throw oneself into the arms of*, to become the wife or mistress of.

*c* **1611** CHAPMAN *Iliad* I. 214 Throw Reins on thy passions, and serve us. **1825** SCOTT *Talism.* iv, That modest pride which throws fetters even on love itself. **1831** — *Ct. Robt.* xxxi, To be, without her own consent, thrown, as it were, at the head now of one suitor, now of another. **1833** J. H. NEWMAN *Arians* II. i. (1876) 147 However plausible may be the veil thus thrown over heterogeneous doctrines, the flimsy artifice is discomposed so soon as [etc.]. **1871** FREEMAN *Norm. Conq.* IV. xviii. 231 Their wives were throwing themselves into the arms of other men. *a* **1891** BESANT in J. M. Dixon *Idiom. Eng. Phr.* 336 As for the girls, Claire, they just throw themselves at a man.

**c.** With immaterial object (e.g. blame, influence, power, obstacles, etc.).

*c* **1620** T. ROBINSON *Mary Magd.* 301 So the bewitchinge oracle yᵗ throughes, About the maidens fancy, strange Deludinge showes. **1697** DRYDEN *Virg. Georg.* IV. 325 Thro' Heav'n, and Earth, and Ocean's Depth he throws His Influence round. **1718** POPE *Iliad* XIII. 291 On Greece no blame be thrown. **1753** MISS COLLIER *Art Torment.* II. ii. (1811) 129 Throw a languidness into your countenance;..appear so perfectly dejected and low-spirited, that [etc.]. **1856** *Jrnl. R. Agric. Soc.* XVII. II. 367 The carriage of materials is usually thrown upon the tenant. **1869** W. LONGMAN *Hist. Edw. III*, I. viii. 138 Philip threw every obstacle in the way of reconciliation. **1871** EARLE *Philol. Eng. T.* 133 They throw the accent often on the close of a word. **1890** TOUT *Hist. Eng. from 1689* 36 Skill in such arts gradually threw real power into the hands of a ring.

**d.** To put *into* as an addition; to add, incorporate; = *throw in*, 41 b.

**1676** LISTER in *Ray's Corr.* (1848) 125, I would either put them [observations] out separately,..or throw them into Mr. Willughby's store. **1862** *Temple Bar Mag.* VI. 503 The saddle being thrown into the bargain. *a* **1904** A. ADAMS *Log Cowboy* vii. 85 Flood's attention once drawn to the brand, he ordered them thrown into our herd.

**31.** *spec.* **a.** A person is said to be *thrown into prison*, etc. when roughly or forcibly imprisoned.

**1560** DAUS tr. *Sleidane's Comm.* 175 The Turke throweth his Ambassadoure in pryson. **1776** *Trial of Nundocomar* 73/1 When Maha Rajah was first thrown into confinement. **1849** MACAULAY *Hist. Eng.* v. I. 630 This impostor was thrown into prison for his fraud. **1892** GARDINER *Stud. Hist. Eng.* 285 Richard was carried to London and thrown into the Tower.

**b.** Troops, succour, supplies, or the like are said to be *thrown* into a besieged place, or a strategic position. Also *refl.*

**1617** MORYSON *Itin.* II. 119 The Town had beene carried ..if Sir Francis Vere had not throwne himselfe into it with one thousand sixe hundred English. **1693** *Mem. Cnt. Teckely* II. 145 A great number of Gentry who had thrown themselves into the place. **1736** LEDIARD *Life Marlborough* I. 157 The States..threw 12,000 Men into that Place. **1823** *Examiner* 95/2 Provisions had been thrown into Corinth previously to this incursion. **1836** ALISON *Hist. Europe* (1849–50) V. xxvii. § 68. 58 He threw six thousand men across the principal arm into a wooded island. **1844** H. H. WILSON *Brit. India* III. ii. III. 57 A detachment was thrown forward to Ramoo. **1869** T. HUGHES *Alfred* ix. 108 He throws himself into a castle or fort called Cynwith.

**c.** A bridge or arch is said to be *thrown* from one side to another of, or *over*, a river, passage, or space. Also *fig.*

**1751** J. BROWN *Shaftesb. Charac.* 74 This visionary arch which he hath..thrown over the depths of error. **1793** *Regal Rambler* 74 He proposes to throw a bridge over the Fleet-market. **1819** SCOTT *Ivanhoe* xlii. *note*, The skill to throw an arch,..or erect a stair. **1849** *Tait's Mag.* XVI. 16/1 A suspension bridge has been thrown over the river.

**32.** To cause to fall, pass, or come into or out of some condition or relation (or place or thing implying this); properly with the connotation of abruptness, suddenness, or force; to cast, force, drive, plunge, thrust. Usually with *prep.*

**1560** BECON *Chr. Knt.* Wks. II. 148 Adam & Eua, whom after thou haddest deceaued through thy lyenge, thou threwest them hedlonge into synne and death. *a* **1652** J. SMITH *Sel. Disc.* IX. viii. (1859) 442 God hath never thrown the world from Himself. **1705** in Hearne *Collect.* 28 Sept. (O.H.S.) I. 49 They..threaten'd to..throw me out of my Chaplain's place. **1766** GOLDSM. *Vic. W.* xviii, The fatigues I had undergone threw me into a fever. **1809** MALKIN *Gil Blas* XII. vii. (Rtldg.) 432 Chance threw me across him, as he came out of a printing-house. **1815** SCOTT *Guy M.* xviii, I do not suspect his equanimity of being so easily thrown off its balance. **1821** *Examiner* 386/1, I cannot let the land be thrown out of cultivation. **1869** W. LONGMAN *Hist. Edw. III*, I. iv. 63 The Scots were thrown into confusion. **1893** *Nat. Observ.* 7 Oct. 527/1 Recruited by men thrown idle by the selfish policy.

**b.** To put deftly into a particular form or shape; to express in a specified form (in speech or writing); to convert or change *into* some other form; to turn or translate *into* another language.

**1723** WATERLAND *2nd Vind. Christ's Div.* xxiii. Wks. 1823 III. 408, I have reason to complain of your..not throwing your disjointed materials into a more neat and regular order. **1740** J. CLARKE *Educ. Youth* (ed. 3) 177 A Master should be able to throw the Latin..into proper English. **1766** *Compl. Farmer* s. v. *Lucern*, A quarter of an acre; which we threw into fifty-four rows. **1789** MRS. PIOZZI *Journ. France*, etc. I. Pref. 6, I have not thrown my thoughts into the form of private letters. **1824** *Examiner* 362/1 Two dress boxes .. were thrown into one. **1892** H. R. MILL *Realm Nat.* xii. 233 The surface..is thrown into a sheet of ridges. **1893** TRAILL *Soc. Eng.* Introd. 30 Cædmon..throws Scripture into metrical paraphrase.

**c.** *To throw open* (*apart*, *asunder*): to set open (separate, break asunder) with a sudden or energetic impulse; hence *fig.* to make publicly accessible or available (also *to throw open the gates of*). *To throw open one's doors to*, to receive as a guest, to welcome.

**1709–10** ADDISON *Tatler* No. 116 ¶ 1, I had ordered the Folding-Doors to be thrown open. *c* **1790** IMISON *Sch. Art* I. 72 The explosion of the gun-powder will throw asunder the roof. **1827** ROBERTS *Voy. Centr. Amer.* 235 The depositories were not thrown open. **1830** *Examiner* 408/2 The railway .. will be thrown open .. in August. **1844** A. B. WELBY *Poems* (1867) 46 As the blossom waits the breeze Before it throws the leaves apart. **1850** *Tait's Mag.* XVII. 85/2 Labouring to throw open the gates of commerce. **1885** MRS. C. PRAED *Affinities* vi, He..threw open the shutters. **1890** T. F. TOUT *Hist. Eng. from 1689* 192 A University Reform Act..threw open the endowments.

**33.** *refl.* *To throw oneself on* or *upon*: to have urgent recourse to (some one) for succour, support, or protection; to commit oneself entirely to (his generosity, mercy, or the like). Also in *pass.* to be made or become dependent upon.

**1650** JER. TAYLOR *Holy Living* iv. I. 235 In time of temptation be not busie to dispute, but..throw your self upon God. **1801** CHARLOTTE SMITH *Lett. Solit. Wand.* I. 87 To throw myself into the protection of my only parent. **1812** *Examiner* 24 Aug. 534/1 They are obliged to throw themselves on the parish for aid. **1830** *Ibid.* 550/1 Thrown upon their own resources. **1877** MISS YONGE *Cameos* Ser. III. ix. 80 His wife threw herself upon James's mercy. **1891** *Temple Bar Mag.* Apr. 489, I must throw myself upon Ida's indulgence.

**34.** *To throw oneself into*: to engage in with zeal or earnestness.

**1868** in Q. Victoria *Life Highl.* Pref. 7 A mind..throwing itself..into the enjoyment of [etc.]. **1871** FREEMAN *Hist. Ess.* Ser. I. iv. 113 The faculty of throwing himself with a lively interest into times so alien to our own. **1881** GARDINER & MULLINGER *Stud. Eng. Hist.* I. v. 86 England threw herself..into a war of conquest against France. **1888** BURGON *Lives 12 Gd. Men* II. v. 46 He was..prepared to throw himself heart and soul into any project.

**b.** So *to throw one's soul*, *heart*, *life*, *spirit*, *energy*, *efforts*, etc. *into* a thing or action.

**1829** *Examiner* 373/2 She threw her whole soul into her voice. **1868** E. EDWARDS *Ralegh* I. iii. 43 He continued to throw all his energy into the distasteful duty. **1890** *Field* 8 Nov. 707/3 The Blackheath forwards threw great spirit into their play.

**VI.** In combination with adverbs.

**35. Throw about. a.** *trans.* See simple senses and ABOUT.

**1377** LANGL. *P. Pl.* B. xx. 163 This sleuthe..a slynge made, And threwe drede of dyspayre a dozein myle aboute. **1719** DE FOE *Crusoe* (1840) II. iii. 52 They..threw everything about in such a manner, that the poor men found..some of their things a mile off. **1885** *Manch. Exam.* 6 May 5/1 A policeman had seen him throwing his arms about.

**b.** *Naut.* *absol.* or *intr.* To turn about at once; to go directly upon the other tack; to go about, put about. Also *fig.* Also *to throw round.*

**1591** SPENSER *M. Hubberd* 80, I..meane for better winde about to throwe. **1757** CAPT. RANDALL in *Naval Chron.* XIV. 98 They threw about, and stood for us again. **1894** *Times* 10 July 11/1 When the vessels next met the American was far enough ahead to throw about on the Britannia's weather bow. **1894** *Daily News* 24 July 8/4 Shortly afterwards Vigilant threw round, and stood in.

**36. Throw aside. a.** *trans.* See simple senses and ASIDE.

**1530** PALSGR. 281/1 Throwyng asyde, disordring, *debaux.* **1695** TELFAIR *New Confut. Sadd.* (1696) 10 His dog catcht a Fulmard by the way, which Andrew threw aside when he came into the House. **1841** LANE *Arab. Nts.* I. i. 44 When thou atest the date, and threwest aside the stone, it struck my son. *Ibid.* ii. 79 He threw aside the jar. **1857** MILLER *Elem. Chem.* (1862) III. 162 When masses of the husk of the grape..are thrown aside, and allowed to ferment.

**b.** *spec.* To cast aside out of use, or as useless; *fig.* to discard, cease to use.

**1827** CLARE *Sheph. Cal.* 59 The old beechen bowl .. is thrown aside. **1857** MILLER *Elem. Chem.* (1862) III. 14 A little of the dried oxide of copper, which is thrown aside. **1880** FOWLER *Locke* viii. 128 He throws aside the technical phraseology of the schools.

**37. Throw away.** †**a.** *trans.* To cast away from oneself; to reject; to refuse to admit or accept. *Obs.*

**1382** WYCLIF *1 Sam.* xv. 23 Forthi .. that thow hast throwen aweye the word of the Lord, the Lord hath throwen awey thee, that thow be not kyng. **1387** TREVISA *Higden* (Rolls) VI. 12 Þrow not awey þat þou hast to forhonde approved.

**b.** To cast away out of one's hands or possession as useless or unneeded.

**1530** PALSGR. 756/2, I throwe awaye, as we do thynges that we care nat for.., *je deguerpis*,..*je desjecte.* *a* **1548** HALL *Chron.*, *Edw. IV* 204 b, The Lyncolnshyre men..threw away their coates, the lighter to runne away, and fled. *a* **1667** JER. TAYLOR (J.), He that will throw away a good book because not gilded, is more curious to please his eye than understanding. **1690** LOCKE *Hum. Und.* I. i. § 5 They will..throw away the Blessings their hands are fill'd with, because they are not big enough to grasp every thing. **1700** DRYDEN *Charac. Gd. Parson* 37 He melts, and throws his cumbrous cloak away. **1742** *Lond. & Country Brew.* I. (ed. 4) 64 A fresh Cask must be tapped..and the remaining Part of the other throw'd away. **1893** HODGES *Elem. Photogr.* (1907) 101 The used solution..is thrown away.

**c.** To spend or use without adequate return; to squander, waste; to bestow upon an unworthy object; also, to neglect to take advantage of (an opportunity, etc.); *spec.* at *Cards*, to play (a losing card) when one cannot follow suit, to discard.

1653 JER. TAYLOR *Serm. for Year* I. xxii. 294 We are pleased to throw away our time. 1714 *Spect.* No. 624 ⁋ 1 Advice..would be but thrown away upon them. 1748 HOYLE *Games Impr.* (1778) 56 Do not trump it, but throw away a losing Card, which makes room for your Partner's Suit. 1761 GRAY *Let. to Wharton* 9 May, I had rather Major G. throwed away his money than somebody else. 1798 WORDSW. *We are Seven* xvii, 'Twas throwing words away; for still The little Maid would have her will. 1861 *Temple Bar Mag.* II. 447 The Abbé's prayers will not be thrown away. *Mod.* Do not throw away your chance.

**d.** *refl. To throw oneself away*: chiefly said of a woman in reference to marriage.

1680 OTWAY *Orphan* I. i, Where Dilatory Fortune plays the Jilt With the brave noble honest gallant man, To throw her self away on Fools and Knaves. 1891 E. PEACOCK *N. Brendon* I. 243 She had thrown herself away on one utterly unworthy of her.

**38. Throw back. a.** *trans.* See simple senses and BACK *adv.*

*a* 1822 SHELLEY *A Juno* Wks. 1888 I. 410 The manner in which the act of throwing back one leg is expressed. 1831 SCOTT *Cast. Dang.* i, The reflection of the evening sun, sometimes thrown back from pool or stream. 1859 *Habits Gd. Soc.* iii. 148 The frock-coat should be ample and loose, and a tall well-built man may throw it back. 1890 GERARD *Sensitive Plant* (1891) III. III. xvi. 149 Each tall mirror threw back the image in the other.

**b.** To put back in time or condition; to delay, make late, throw behind; to retard or check in expected or desired progress; to reduce to a previous or lower condition.

1840 *Jrnl. R. Agric. Soc.* I. IV. 453, I..am not thrown back in getting the land sown. 1850 *Ibid.* XI. II. 419 Wet weather is what throws sheep back. 1858 *Ibid.* XIX. II. 294 The loss of that fortnight..throws an incoming tenant back a whole year. 1868 FREEMAN *Norm. Conq.* II. vii. 114 That..parliamentary life which..the Norman Conquest threw back for many generations.

**c.** With *upon*: to compel to fall back upon, or recur to; cf. FALL *v.* 81.

1851 J. H. NEWMAN *Cath. in Eng.* Ded., The violence of our enemies has thrown us back upon ourselves and upon each other. 1892 *Chamb. Jrnl.* 4 June 355/2 If there is no comic boy,..we are thrown back upon Checkley.

**d.** *intr.* To revert to an ancestral type or character not present in recent generations; to exhibit atavism. *colloq.* Also *fig.* (Cf. 23.)

1879 'CAVENDISH' *Card Ess.*, etc. 63 'Throwing back' more nearly..to the parent games, Poker..is invented. 1887 A. LANG *Myth, Rit. & Relig.* I. 195 Another child may be said in the language of dogbreeders to have 'thrown back'. 1893 *Standard* 22 Apr. 4/3 In politics Lord Derby 'threw back' to the family creed of an earlier generation. 1899 *Allbutt's Syst. Med.* VIII. 279 She 'throws back' to her savage ancestors. 1911 GALSWORTHY *Patrician* II. i. 176 He and his ideas throw back to the Middle Ages.

**e.** *intr.* To go back in date *to*, to have a history reaching back *to*; to hark back, cast back.

1892 *Sat. Rev.* 28 May 635/1 His Metaphysic..begin with Kant, and only 'throws back' to Kant's forerunners. 1892 *Illustr. Sporting & Dram. News* 17 Sept. 39/2 An old hostelry that throws back nobody knows how many centuries..; throwing back three quarters of a century, a hundred men mustered here.

**39. Throw by. a.** *trans.* To put aside with decision; to reject from present use; to discard.

1611 B. JONSON *Catiline* I. i, It can but shew Like one of Ivnoes..disguises..: and will..When things succeed, be throwne by, or let fall. 1674 FLAVEL *Husb. Spir.* ii. 27 My lazy heart throws by the shovel, and cryes, 'Dig I cannot!' 1770 *Hist.* in *Ann. Reg.* 39 Aly Bey..has thrown by the mask, and..boldly mounted the throne. 1825 J. NEAL *Bro. Jonathan* III. 187, I took another name. I threw by that of my father.

†**b.** To dismiss from consideration; to set aside.

1710 S. PALMER *Proverbs* 141 His best actions thrown by and lessen'd by false turns. 1710 HEARNE *Collect.* (O.H.S.) III. 36 They are very angry with him, and throw by what he has done as being against the Government.

**40. Throw down** (†**adown**). **a.** *trans.* See simple senses and DOWN *adv.*

*To throw down a horse*, (of a rider) to cause or allow it to fall.

*c* 1250 *Long Life* 37 in *O. E. Misc.* 158 Weilawei deþ þe schal adun þrowe Þer þu wenest heȝest to steo. *c* 1275 LAY. 12323 Þe cheorles..þa king icnewen and hine adun þreuwe. 1387 TREVISA *Higden* (Rolls) VII. 349 A grym strook of liȝtnynge smoot þe cherche tour..and þrew [*v. r.* þruw] doun þe crucifex,..and þrew doun oure Lady ymage. *a* 1586 SIDNEY *Arcadia* III. (1598) 361 After her song with an affected modestie, she threw downe her eye. 1660 F. BROOKE tr. *Le Blanc's Trav.* 371 The Mountains..throw down divers Rivers. 1714 *Spect.* No. 558 ⁋ 4 Another after a great deal of puffing, threw down his Luggage. 1787 'G. GAMBADO' *Acad. Horsem.* (1809) 44 Take care never to throw your horse down, it is an unlucky trick.

**b.** Expressing a symbolic action; as *to throw down one's arms*, to surrender; *to throw down one's brief* (of a barrister), to decline to go on with a case; so *to throw down one's pipe*, etc.

*To throw down the* GAUNTLET or GLOVE: see these words.

1700 S. L. tr. *Fryke's Voy. E. Ind.* 58 Most of them threw down their arms. 1711 STEELE *Spect.* No. 49 ⁋ 2 Mr. Beaver has thrown down his Pipe. 1833 DISRAELI *Cont. Flem.* I. i, I throw down the volume in disgust. 1855 MACAULAY *Hist. Eng.* xx. IV. 523 Williams threw down his brief.

**c.** To cause to fall, to overthrow, demolish (a building, etc.); also *fig.*

*c* 1330 *Arth. & Merl.* (Kölbing) 9306 Baners & castels adoun y-þrawe. 1340 *Ayenb.* 23 Þe grete wynd, þet þrauþ doun þe greate tours. *c* 1425 *Eng. Conq. Irel.* 18 Thay lay all I-drow a-doune and I-cast to grond. 1528 *Sel. Cas. Star Chamb.* (Selden) II. 19 That the sayd J. M. shuld throwe downe and avoyde the sayde enclosures from the sayd comon grownde. 1530 PALSGR. 756/2, I throwe downe to the grounde, or distroye a thynge. 1645 EVELYN *Diary* 8 Feb., The ruines of a very stately Temple or Theatre..throwne downe by an earthquake. 1713 ADDISON *Cato* II. v. 67 Must one rash word..Throw down the merit of my better years? 1766 FORDYCE *Serm. Yng. Wom.* (1767) I. vii. 302 The admiration raised..is often..thrown down. 1838 THIRLWALL *Greece* III. 101 The Athenians..ordered the Potidæans to throw down the walls of their town on the side of the Peninsula of Pallene.

**d.** To deposit or cause to be deposited from solution; to precipitate.

1812 SIR H. DAVY *Chem. Philos.* 120 Earths, and oxides, are usually thrown down from their solutions in union with water. 1838 T. THOMSON *Chem. Org. Bodies* 188 Alcohol throws it down from its aqueous solution. 1864 *Jrnl. R. Agric. Soc.* XXV. II. 566 Water that contains much lime on boiling throws down a white deposit.

**e.** *Agric.* (*a*) To plough (land) so as to level it down; opposed to *gather up* (GATHER *v.* 16). (*b*) To convert (arable land) into pasture; to lay down to grass. (Cf. LAY *v.* 51 m.)

1844 STEPHENS *Bk. Farm* I. 477 The mode of ploughing exactly opposite to twice-gathering-up is that of cleaving or throwing down land. 1891 S. C. SCRIVENER *Our Fields & Cities* 143 It is capable of being applied..to almost any land, including that 'thrown down' to grass.

**f.** *fig.* To put down with force; to lower in rank or station; to degrade, humiliate; to deject in spirits; also, to destroy the effect of, bring to nought.

*c* 1450 tr. *De Imitatione* III. xxi. 89, I am sone þrowen doun with litel aduersite. 1567 *Satir. Poems Reform.* vi. 23 God wil haue the pride of man doune thrawin. 1610 HOLLAND *Camden's Brit.* (1637) 725 Lifting and throwing downe Princes at her pleasure. 1729 G. ADAMS tr. *Sophocl., Antig.* v. i. II. 65 Fortune raises up, and throws down, makes one fortunate, and another miserable.

**g.** *slang.* To overcome; to prove too much for; to floor, 'give a fall' to.

1891 *Harry Fludyer* 98 (Farmer), I think I shall floor mine ['exam.'], and Dick's sure to throw his examiners down.

**h.** *U. S. slang.* To discard, throw off.

*Mod. U. S.* 'Is she still engaged?' 'Why no, she threw her beau down'.

**41. Throw in. a.** *trans.* See simple senses and IN.

13.. *K. Horn* 1176 (Harl. MS.) Þe ryng þat þou yn þrewe. 1679 M. RUSDEN *Further Discov. Bees* 91 Throwing in a few handsfull of peas. 1730 A. GORDON *Maffei's Amphith.* 303 The Window above that Stair throws the Light in. 1892 *Illustr. Lond. News* 21 May 634/3 He was thrown in with men who..had been intimately acquainted with the Zulu people. *Mod. Cookery Bk.* Throw in a bunch of sweet herbs.

**b.** To put in as a supplement or addition; to add, esp. to a bargain. Cf. 30 d.

1678 LADY CHAWORTH in *12th Rep. Hist. MSS. Comm.* App. v. 45 Lord Shrewsbery is like to marry Mr. Chiffens his daughter, who will be first and last made worth 40,000*l.* to him, and they talke as if the King should throw in a Dukedome. 1679 MRS. BEHN *Feign'd Curtizan* III. i, Cou'd you not..throw in a little Love and Constancy, to inch out that want of Honesty of yours? 1824 *Examiner* 471/2 Additional dialogue and incident should be..thrown in. 1892 *Black & White* 22 Oct. 476/1 [The] story turns..on murder and revenge, with a little love thrown in.

**c.** To introduce, insert, or interject in the course or process of something; *esp.* to interpose or contribute (a remark); to put in.

1704 NORRIS *Ideal World* II. xii. 509 A further reflection which it may be convenient to throw in to this explanatory account to make it more full and entire. 1739 tr. *Algarotti on 'Newton's Theory'* (1742) I. 7, I threw in, from Time to Time, little Digressions to vary the Conversation. 1821 CLARE *Vill. Minstr.* II. 85 The old dames..Throw in their hints of man's deluding ways. 1890 BARING-GOULD *Urith* xxxi, 'Not a grain', threw in Julian, hotly. 1891 *Harper's Mag.* Dec. 102/1, I wish to throw in a parenthesis.

**d.** In technical uses (often *absol.*). (*a*) *Fishing.* To make a cast (in quot. *fig.*). (*b*) *Hunting.* To start (hounds) upon the scent. (*c*) *Wrestling* and *Pugilism.* To toss one's hat into the ring as a challenge or acceptance; hence *fig.* to become a candidate, put in *for*. (*d*) *Football* and *Cricket.* Cf. *throw-in* sb. (THROW- 2).

1823 *Mirror* No. 14. I. 213/2 When you launch a good thing, which is only heard by the person next you, wait patiently for a pause, and throw in again. 1844 J. T. HEWLETT *Parsons & W.* liv, The hounds were thrown in. 1886 ELWORTHY *W. Somerset Word-bk.*, *Drow in*, to give or accept a challenge in a wrestling or cudgel-playing match. 1887 SHEARMAN *Athletics & Football* 348 [Association] The halves at the sides too must learn to throw in from touch, for this duty as a rule devolves upon them. 1889 H. VASSALL *Rugby Game* 27 There are endless ways of throwing in, and he must practise. 1892 *Field* 8 Oct. 553/3 [He] prefers the glory of winning the Cambridgeshire to throwing in for his chance of the £5000 to-morrow.

**e.** *To throw in one's lot with*: to enter into association with, so as to share the fortunes of (see LOT *sb.* 1 e); so with *fortune, interest.*

1867 [see LOT *sb.* 1 e]. 1870 ROGERS *Hist. Gleanings* Ser. II. 97 He would have thrown in his lot with the Hydes. 1889 MRS. C. CARR *Marg. Maliphant* III. xxx. 27 On which side do you suppose he would throw in his interest? 1890 *Eng. Illustr. Mag.* Dec. 173 He willingly threw in his fortune with theirs.

†**f.** *intr.* At the game of hazard: To throw a number the same as the main (MAIN *sb.*[3] 1: see none there) or which has a certain correspondence with it (see NICK *sb.*[1] 6); to win at hazard. *Obs.*

1880 *Encycl. Brit.* XI. 547/1 The player or 'caster' calls a 'main' (that is, any number from five to nine inclusive). He then throws with two dice. If he 'throws in', or 'nicks', he wins the sum played for from the banker or 'setter'..If the caster 'throws out' by throwing aces, or deuce ace (called crabs), he loses.

**42. Throw off. a.** *trans.* (*lit.* and *fig.*) See simple senses and OFF.

1447–8 J. SHILLINGFORD *Lett.* 2 Feb. (Camden) 36 How hit was procured and shortly throwen of. 1647 HAMMOND *Power of Keys* iii. 30 He had thus confidently thrown off these Epistles from being written by Ignatius. 1720 WATERLAND *Eight Serm.* 115, I was once inclinable to defer the Treating of it some time longer; thinking it most suitable..to throw it off to the last part of what I intend upon this Subject. 1726 LEONI *Alberti's Archit.* I. 15/1 The Covering..shou'd..incline of one side to throw off the Rain. 1747 FRANKLIN *Lett.* Wks. 1840 V. 182 To show that points will throw off as well as draw off the electrical fire. 1790 MRS. WHEELER *Westmld. Dial.* ii. 65 Bil Watson..flayd Galoway, et it set off a Gallop an thraad him off. 1823 J. BADCOCK *Dom. Amusem.* 52 A concave glass..will throw the objects off and reduce their size. 1892 *Sat. Rev.* 7 May 542/1 The pumps..were throwing off 7,000 gallons per minute.

**b.** To rid or free oneself by force from, to get rid of, shake off (a yoke, restraint, burden, etc.); to repudiate or reject the authority of; also, to cast off, disown (an associate).

1618 BOLTON *Florus* (1636) 131 The first who threw the yoake off, were the Macedonians. 1681 DRYDEN *Span. Friar* III. iii, 'Twould be better yet, Cou'd you provoke him to give you th' occasion, And then to throw him off. 1793 J. BOWLES *Real Ground Pres. War w. France* (ed. 5) 75 Throwing off every restraint of honour and principle. 1822 *Examiner* 229/2 The Spanish Colonies..have thrown off the yoke of the mother country. 1879 DOWDEN *Southey* iii. 64 Unless the disease were thrown off by regular exercise. 1899 *Allbutt's Syst. Med.* VIII. 156 An extraordinary power of throwing off fatigue.

**c.** To cast off, put off energetically (something put on or assumed, as a garment); to divest oneself of (a quality, character, habit, feeling, etc.); to lay aside quickly or decisively; to discard.

1681 DRYDEN *Span. Friar* IV. ii, Virtue must be thrown off; 'tis a coarse garment. 1697 J. LEWIS *Mem. Dk. Glocester* (1789) 8 To throw off childish toys, saying he was then a man. 1706 E. WARD *Wooden World Diss.* (1708) 41 He throws off his Gown and Hypocrisy together. 1872 C. E. MAURICE *S. Langton* i. 52 He throws off his chancellorship at once. 1885 *Manch. Exam.* 28 Sept. 5/3 If he should suddenly throw off his coat in a cold room. 1893 *Nat. Observ.* 7 Oct. 535/2 Monson threw off the pirate and appeared the king's officer.

**d.** To shake off or divert (a pursuer or competitor in a race); = *throw out*, 44 k; also, to throw off the scent.

1695 BLACKMORE *Pr. Arth.* I. 354 Reason..stops her pace, Is soon thrown off, and quits th' unequal Chase. 1891 *Blackw. Mag.* CXLIX. 468/1 He wasn't to be thrown off by a false scent. 1892 *Field* 2 Apr. 475/1 A check threw hounds off for a minute. 1893 *Ibid.* 11 Feb. 186/3 The leading hounds are very near him; he cannot throw them off.

**e.** *Hunting.* To free from the leashes, to start (hounds) in the chase; to let fly (a hawk, etc.). Now *esp. absol.* or *intr.*, of foxhunters or hounds: To begin hunting; hence *fig.* to make a beginning in anything; to begin.

1735 SOMERVILLE *Chase* II. 123 Where..the rank Mead Affords the wand'ring Hares a rich Repast; Throw off thy ready Pack. 1784 COWPER *Wks.* (1837) XV. 150 On Friday..we attended an attempt to throw off a balloon at Mr. Throckmorton's. 1825 SCOTT *Betrothed* xxiii, Each holding a hawk on his wrist, and anxiously adjusting the mode in which they should throw them off. 1892 *Field* 7 May 664/2 They threw off the hounds, found an otter, and, after two hours, killed.

*intr.* 1811 *Sporting Mag.* XXXVII. 88 They [hounds] throw off generally three times a week. 1818 COL. HAWKER *Diary* (1893) I. 162, I threw off in the great woods round Cold Henley. 1866 GLADSTONE in Morley *Life* (1903) II. v. ix. § 5. 156, I had to throw off in my new capacity. 1892 *Field* 26 Nov. 808/1 Many packs would not have thrown off at all on such a morning.

**f.** To eject, emit, give off, esp. from the body or system; *esp.* to expel or discharge (waste or morbid products); *rarely*, to vomit.

1737 BRACKEN *Farriery Impr.* (1756) I. 235 These Creatures throw off a vast deal from their Lungs in Respiration. 1747 tr. *Astruc's Fevers* 105 A crisis, or critical depuration of the humours, whereby the peccant matter is thrown off:..just as we see in the small-pox, measles, &c. 1829 *Examiner* 267/2 When he found anything disagreeing with his stomach, he retired and threw it off. 1846 *Jrnl. R. Agric. Soc.* VII. II. 308 Plants decompose carbonic acid, and throw off oxygen. 1862 *Temple Bar Mag.* VI. 474 Dense volumes of smoke are thrown off. 1864 *Gd. Words* 102/1 They exude, or throw off from themselves, the spent materials which are excrementitious. 1891 *Harper's Mag.* Aug. 357/1 From all parts of the living body living gemmules are being thrown off.

**g.** To produce and send forth (as offspring or the like); esp. of a hive of bees: to send forth (a swarm). Cf. 23. Also = *throw out*, 44 d.

1828 *Examiner* 541/2 A swarm of bees thrown off from

one of his scapes. **1842** J. AITON *Domest. Econ.* (1857) 268 The gray rabbit..generally throws off three, four, five, or six litters..by the first of June. **1862** *Temple Bar Mag.* IV. 548 A massive pillar..threw off rough branches of stone. **1892** *Gd. Words* Dec. 816/1 Its territory was small and it threw off many colonies.

**h.** To produce with speed and facility (a literary or artistic work or sketch); to execute in a ready and spontaneous manner.

**1761** *Ramsay's Ever-green* I. 5 *note*, That this Way of throwing off a Verse easily was first introduced by him. **1823** J. BADCOCK *Dom. Amusem.* p. iv, The new articles.. having been 'thrown off at a heat', stood particularly in want of re-revision. **1850** *Tait's Mag.* XVII. 115/2 Those exquisite works which..Chantrey so frequently threw off in marble. **1893** *Temple Bar Mag.* XCVIII. 518 Having thrown his compositions off at white heat.

**i.** *Printing.* To print off. (Often with mixture of the literal sense.)

**1803** SCOTT *Let. to Ballantyne* 21 Apr., in *Lockhart*, I have to thank you for the accuracy with which the Minstrelsy is thrown off. Longman and Rees are delighted with the printing. **1873** SPENCER *Stud. Sociol.* vi. 126 Its own immense edition is thrown off in a few hours every morning.

**j.** To deduct from the total; to knock off.

**1821** *Examiner* 383/2 An abatement of rent, Mr. S! Why ..last year I threw you off 200*l.* **1845** *P. Parley's Ann.* VI. 299 Perhaps, if you are a good girl, and pay regularly every week, I may throw you off something at the end of the year.

**43. Throw on. a.** *trans.* See simple senses and ON. **b.** To put on (apparel) hastily or carelessly: the opposite of *throw off*, 42 c. **c.** To put (hounds) on the scent. †**d.** ?To win (a main) at hazard (*obs.*); cf. *throw in*, *throw out*, 41 f, and 44 m.

*c* **1374** CHAUCER *Compl. Mars* 99 He threwe [*v. rr.* threw(e, throweth] on his helme of huge wyght. **1801** *Sporting Mag.* XVIII. 95 He once won 17,000*l.* at hazard, by throwing on, as it is called, fourteen successive mains. **1815** *Ibid.* XLV. 253 After the usual law, the hounds were thrown on. **1862** *Temple Bar Mag.* VI. 421 He throws on his colour at once, with a very evident freedom of pencil. **1873** J. RICHARDS *Wood-working Factories* 76 Watch persons trying to throw on a belt [upon a pulley]. .. The one will throw it on instantly.

**44. Throw out.** (See also OUT-THROW.) **a.** *trans.* See simple senses and OUT; *spec.* of frost, etc.: to force (young plants) out of the ground.

**1590** SPENSER *F. Q.* I. vi. 6 The pitteous mayden..Does throw out thrilling shriekes, and shrieking cryes. **1600** J. PORY tr. *Leo's Africa* II. 81 His theeues carcase is throwne out to be deuoured of dogs. **1706** E. WARD *Wooden World Diss.* (1708) 100 He..falls to throwing every Thing out at the Window. **1753** CHAMBERS *Cycl. Supp.* s.v. *Marygold*, The flowers of the common marygold..promote sweat, and are good to throw out the small-pox, or any other eruption. **1830** LYELL *Princ. Geol.* I. 406 [In an earthquake] Cones of sand, six or eight feet in height, were thrown out of the lands near the Runn [of Cutch]. **1840** *Jrnl. R. Agric. Soc.* I. III. 272 The wheat is usually only thrown out in severe frosts. **1847** *Ibid.* VIII. I. 66 The rolling and treading..prevent the plants being thrown out by alternate frosts and thaws. **1885** J. K. JEROME *On the Stage* 42 To make your voice 'carry', you have to throw it out, instead of letting it crawl out when you open your mouth.

**b.** To put out forcibly or suddenly from a place, office, or employment; to eject, expel, turn out.

**1526** *Pilgr. Perf.* (W. de W. 1531) 18 Whome..god suffreth ..vtterly to be throwen out from the kyngdome of glorye. **1710** HEARNE *Collect.* (O.H.S.) II. 348 Ld. Rialton..will be thrown out the next Election. **1780** WARNER in Jesse *Selwyn & Contemp.* (1844) IV. 382, I suppose it is not possible to throw Barrow out. **1826** *Examiner* 387/2 General Palmer has been thrown out for Bath.

**c.** *transf.* and *fig.* To put forth vigorously from within; to emit, radiate (heat or light); to exude; to produce, be the source of; to send out, put forth (buds, shoots, etc.).

**1750** tr. *Leonardus' Mirr. Stones* 99 It grows warm, and throws out a heat. **1756** P. BROWNE *Jamaica* 236 Wherever the trunk or larger branches of this tree are wounded, they throw out a thick resinous gum. **1838** T. THOMSON *Chem. Org. Bodies* 995 Plants, when exposed to the light, absorb carbonic acid, decompose it, and throw out again the greatest part of the oxygen. **1845** *Jrnl. R. Agric. Soc.* VI. II. 580 Artichokes..throwing out stems from 7 to 10 feet in length. **1850** LYNCH *Theoph. Trin.* xii. 235 Truth and goodness throw out a vivifying electric agency. **1880** C. R. MARKHAM *Peruv. Bark* xviii. 210 The plants..had begun to bud and throw out young leaves.

**d.** To cause to project, protrude, stretch out, or extend; *spec.* in Bookbinding, see quot. 1880.

**1849** THACKERAY *Pendennis* xxii, We'll throw a conservatory out, over the balcony. **1851** *Jrnl. R. Agric. Soc.* XXII. II. 352 Both ranges throw out spurs. **1880** ZAEHNSDORF *Bookbinding* 8 By mounting a map on a guard the size of the page it may be kept laid open on the table beside the book. This is technically called 'throwing out' a map. **1890** R. M. KETTLE *Old Hall* II. ii, The old trees..threw out giant branches.

**e.** To bring into prominence or relief, to cause to 'stand out'.

**1860** RUSKIN *Mod. Paint.* V. IX. viii. § 4. 283 The tone of the whole is dark and gray, throwing out the figures in spots of light.

**f.** *Mil.* To send out (skirmishers, etc.) to a distance from the main body. Also in *fig.* context.

**1834-47** J. S. MACAULAY *Field Fortif.* (1851) 265 The infantry will..throw out skirmishers, and..push on to support them. **1862** *Temple Bar Mag.* V. 373 Mamma throws out skirmishing parties among likely shops. **1863** LD. LYTTON *Ring Amasis* x, His senses, all on the alert, were throwing out scouts and outposts in every direction. **1893** FORBES-MITCHELL *Remin. Gt. Mutiny* 258 We bivouacked on the plain, strong piquets being thrown out.

**g.** To give utterance or expression to; now *esp.* to put forward tentatively, give (a hint or suggestion); also with obj. clause, to suggest.

**1611** BEAUMONT & FL. *Maid's Trag.* IV. ii, I have thrown out words That would have fetch'd warm blood upon the cheeks Of guilty men. **1633** EARLE *Microcosm.* lxxviii. (Arb.) 103 Not a jest throwne out, but he will make it hitt him. *a* **1763** W. KING *Polit. & Lit. Anecd.* (1819) 246 Such an infamous appellation, that I scarce believe the most fiery sectarist among us..would dare to throw out. **1793** *Trial of Fyshe Palmer* 33 He at first threw out that till these were totally abolished we would contend with them. **1869** A. W. WARD tr. *Curtius' Hist. Greece* II. III. ii. 392 Athens unhesitatingly accepted the challenge thrown out. **1891** *Cornh. Mag.* July 106 The hint of danger which Norbury threw out was the one thing needed.

**h.** To put forth visibly, display, exhibit; also †*refl.* to express oneself freely; to 'launch out'.

**1710** POPE *Lett.* (1735) I. 116, I Resume my old Liberty of throwing out myself upon Paper to you. **1763** J. BROWN *Poetry & Mus.* v. 85 His warlike Genius threw itself out, in Subjects that were grand and terrible. **1806** A. DUNCAN *Nelson* 32 The signal was thrown out for the.. fleet to prepare for action. **1890** MRS. R. JOCELYN *M.F.H.'s Daugh.* xvii, Belton's horse also threw out signs of distress.

**i.** To dismiss from acceptance, use, or consideration; to reject; to leave out of a reckoning; in *Écarté*, to discard, 'throw away'.

**1618** in Foster *Eng. Factories Ind.* (1906) 48 What I found grose I thrue out or cutt. **1660** MILTON *Free Commw.* Wks. (1847) 449/1 To us who have thrown it [monarchy] out, received back again, it cannot but prove pernicious. **1753** MISS COLLIER *Art Torment., Fable* 233 The letter L.. confined the competitors to the lion, the leopard, the lynx, and the lamb. The lamb, by almost general consent, was instantly thrown out, as knowing nothing of the subjects treated of. **1811** SIR WM. SCOTT *Dodson's Rep.* I. 31 Some circumstances stated on behalf of Captain Honeyman, which I may also throw out as immaterial. **1856** OLMSTED *Slave States* 241 They..made further clearings in the forest, and 'threw out', to use their own phrase, so much of the land as they had ruined. **1896** *Indianapolis Typogr. Jrnl.* 16 Nov. 407 When the contract expires, this newspaper will throw out its linotype machines.

**j.** Of a legislative assembly or a grand jury: To reject (a bill, etc.).

**1707** *Vulpone* 2 This Proposal..occasion'd very great Debates..and was Scandalously Treated and thrown Out. **1732** HEARNE *Diary* 27 Sept., His petition..was thrown out of the house. **1817** *Parl. Deb. Ho. Lords*, The grand jury..whose duty it was to find the bills had thrown them out. **1873** P. V. SMITH *Hist. Eng. Inst.* II. v. 175 The Ballot Bill..was thrown out by the Lords.

**k.** *Sporting.* To put out of place or order by leaving behind in a chase or race; to distance, outpace.

**1713** ADDISON *Cato* I. i, A Virtue that has cast me at a Distance, And thrown me out in the Pursuits of Honour. **1807** *Sporting Anecd.* 179 Jack was mounted on a hunter, which he assured me was never yet thrown out. **1823** SCOTT *Quentin D.* ix, I had been unluckily thrown out, and was riding fast, to be in my place. **1889** W. WESTALL *Birch Dene* III. xii. 202 More than once he threw them [his pursuers] out by a double.

**l.** To disturb (a person) from his self-possession, train of thought, normal or equable state of mind, or ordinary course of action (see OUT *adv.* 5); = *put out*, PUT *v.*[1] 47 f.

**1844** J. H. NEWMAN *Lett.* (1891) II. 442 He was surprised and thrown out by finding I did not seem to be what he had fancied. **1891** *Murray's Mag.* Apr. 551 Seeing her there acting the part of a governess..threw him out. **1891** *Field* 28 Nov. 837/3 The visitors kicked off, but the heavy ground at first seemed to throw them out.

†**m.** *absol.* In the game of hazard, To make a losing cast (see note s. v. MAIN *sb.*[3] 1). *Obs.*

*a* **1680** BUTLER *Satyr Gaming* 80 Although he..crucify his Saviour worse Than those Jew-Troopers that threw out, When they were raffling for his Coat. **1765** EARL MARCH in Jesse *Selwyn & Contemp.* (1843) I. 308, I am very sorry to hear that you are still throwing out [*note*, at hazard] as well as me.

**n.** *Cricket.* Of a fieldsman: To put (the batsman) 'out' by throwing the ball so as to hit his wicket. So in *Baseball*, to put (a base-runner) 'out' by throwing the ball to a player on or near a base.

**1871** HOPPE s.v. *Out, 'Out'* wird der einzelne Schläger.. wenn ein andrer der *fielders* während des *crossing* den Ball gegen das *wicket* werfen kann (*he is thrown out*). **1892** *Field* 11 June 870/3 Mr. Jackson threw him out from cover-point, when the batsmen were attempting a short run.

**o.** *intr.* (for *refl.*) †To turn out, throng or press out (*obs.*); to move outwards from a centre; to strike out with hands or feet; to let oneself go; to push out (as a root). Cf. sense 9.

**1508** DUNBAR *Flyting* 217 Off Edinburgh, the boyis as beis owt thrawis. **15..** *Peblis to the Play* v, Thai out threw Out of the townis untald. **1771** WOLLASTON in *Phil. Trans.* LXI. 561 The pendulum did not..throw-out so far by about 7′ as it generally did. **1798** J. T. DUCKWORTH in *Naval Chron.* (1799) I. 78 The wind throwing out caused me to anchor. **1798** in *Spirit Pub. Jrnls.* (1799) II. 296 He threw out and kicked a good deal. **1809** MALKIN *Gil Blas* III. iv. ⁋ 4 The fear of talking absurdly prevents you from throwing out at all. **1825** J. NICHOLSON *Operat. Mechanic* 518 The pallet A can throw out till it reach *a*,.. B will throw out as far on the other side. **1855** *Jrnl. R. Agric. Soc.* XVI. I. 176 Such soils turn up as a fine mould.. and the roots can throw out without impediment.

**p.** *intr.* or *absol.* Of a printing machine: To fail to register.

**45. Throw over. a.** See simple senses and OVER.

**1857** HUGHES *Tom Brown* II. viii, Jack Raggles is furious, and begins throwing over savagely to the further wicket.

**b.** To throw overboard (in *fig.* sense); to cast off (a lover, associate, or ally); to abandon.

**1836** T. HOOK *G. Gurney* II. 186, I was satisfied that Emma had thrown me over. **1874** STUBBS *Const. Hist.* I. vi. 163 *note*, Mr. Freeman..throws over the latter part of Palgrave's theory. **1890** T. F. TOUT *Hist. Eng. fr. 1689* 27 They threw over their allies.

**Throw round** (*Naut.*): = *throw about*, 35 b.

**46. Throw to.** †**a.** *trans.* To put quickly with something else which is already there. *Obs.*

*a* **1400-50** *Alexander* 2939 Anoþire boll was him broȝt, & bathe he deuoydid, And ȝit he threw to þe thrid, & thrast in þare-eftir.

**b.** To close (a door, etc.) with force.

**1741** RICHARDSON *Pamela* (1824) I. xv. 26, I made shift to get into it [the chamber], and threw-to the door, and it locked after me. **1892** *Chamb. Jrnl.* 23 July 473/1 The slamming of one of the church doors, as if thrown-to by a draught.

**47. Throw together. a.** *trans.* See simple senses and TOGETHER.

**1717** BERKELEY *Let. to Pope* Wks. 1871 IV. 82 A wonderful variety of hills, vales, ragged rocks, fruitful plains, and barren mountains, all thrown together in a most romantic confusion.

**b.** To put together hastily or roughly; to combine or collect without much care or finish. (Said in relation to literary work.)

**1711** ADDISON *Spect.* No. 105 ⁋ 3 On my retiring to my Lodgings, I could not forbear throwing together such Reflections as occurred to me upon that Subject. **1713** BERKELEY *Guard.* No. 88 ⁋ 3, I shall throw together some passages relating to this subject. **1748** *Anson's Voy.* III. ii. 308, I shall..throw together the most interesting particulars..in relation to..Tinian.

**c.** To bring (persons) casually into contact or association.

**1831** *Society* I. 207 They were to meet as old friends, when they were next thrown together in London. **1889** FROUDE *Two Chiefs Dunboy* xxi. 313 They had been thrown together as children, but had rarely met since.

**48. Throw up. a.** *trans.* See simple senses and UP. †*spec.* To throw open (a gate, etc.) (*obs.*).

*To throw up the sponge*, to give in, surrender: see SPONGE *sb.*, and cf. CHUCK *v.*[2] 2 b.

**14..** *Sir Beues* (M.) 1655+20 Anon the gates he gan up throwe. *c* **1422** HOCCLEVE *Jereslaus' Wife* 364 Vp he threew an heuy syk. **1675** BROOKS *Gold. Key* Wks. 1867 V. 511 You may throw up your caps at them, and bid them do their worst. **1780** COXE *Russ. Disc.* 253 The chain of islands here laid down may..be considered as thrown up by some late volcanos. **1797** *Encycl. Brit.* (ed. 3) XVI. 492/2 When the cable is finished, to shorten it two fathoms more, which our workmen call *throwing the turn well up*. **1833** J. HOLLAND *Manuf. Metal* II. vii. 189 The fresh coals..will throw up..a body of thick smoke. **1842** *Jrnl. R. Agric. Soc.* III. II. 171 Land..thrown up into very narrow ridges. **1850** *Ibid.* I. IV. 381 Milk..throws up less cream in glass than in wood. **1861** *Temple Bar Mag.* III. 221 She hastily threw up the window. **1893** *Argosy* Aug. 116 The seaweeds thrown up on his estate.

**b.** To discharge by vomiting; to vomit. Also (*slang*) *to throw up one's accounts*, in same sense (cf. CAST *v.* 83 b).

**1732** ARBUTHNOT *Rules of Diet* iii, It is easy to judge of the Cause by the Substances which the Patient throws up. **1763** C. JOHNSTON *Reverie* I. 135 Before he can be on the guard, hitting him a plump in the bread-basket, that shall make him throw up his accounts. **1822-34** *Good's Study Med.* (ed. 4) II. 449 Blood from the stomach..thrown up by vomiting.

**c.** To raise (the hands, eyes, etc.) quickly or suddenly; *spec.* in *Throw up your hands*, as a command to surrender: cf. *Hands up* (HAND *sb.* 54).

**1746** FRANCIS tr. *Hor., Sat.* II. vii. 54, I throw my Nose up to a savoury Steam. **1821** *Examiner* 524/1 Eternally throwing up their eyes to heaven. **1880** [see BAIL *v.*[3] 2]. **1887** I. R. *Lady's Ranche Life Montana* 37 He was suddenly aware of a horse galloping rapidly up behind him, and heard a shout: 'Throw up your hands!' **1890** FENN *Double Knot* III. i. 19 The woman threw up her hands and reeled. **1891** *Eng. Illustr. Mag.* No. 88. 306 Bail up, throw up your hands now, or I'll shoot every man jack of you.

**d.** To cast up (a heap or earthwork) with or as with the spade; to erect or construct hastily.

**1586** DAY *Eng. Secretary* I. (1625) A iij, The gardner, who first throweth vp his earth on a rude heape. **1709** STEELE *Tatler* No. 6 ⁋ 10 The Greeks threw up a great Intrenchment to secure their Navy. **1869** HUGHES *Alfred the Gt.* vi. 71 They..threw up earthworks, and entrenched themselves there. **1880** R. MACKENZIE *19th Cent.* III. ii. 287 Armed crowds began to appear, and barricades were thrown up.

**e.** To render prominent or distinct; to cause to 'stand out'; to make noticeable by contrast.

**1882** MRS. OLIPHANT *Lit. Hist. Eng.* I. 288 A..background to throw up and bring into full relief the figure. **1885** MONKHOUSE in *Mag. Art* Sept. 474/2 The dado is darker..and throws up the rest effectively. **1891** G. D. GALTON *La Fenton* vi, The black folds of her dress throwing up..the marble pallor of her face.

**f.** *Naut. To throw* (a ship) *up in* (*into, on*) *the wind*, to turn the vessel into the wind till she points almost directly to windward; also *absol.* said of the navigator.

**1769** FALCONER *Dict. Marine* (1789), *Donner vent devant*, to throw a ship up in the wind, or in stays. **1832** MARRYAT *N. Forster* xlvii, The Windsor Castle was thrown up on the wind. **1833** — *P. Simple* xvi, We threw up in the wind.

**g.** To cease definitely to do, use, or practise; to give up participation in, or the exercise or use of; to relinquish, abandon, quit, give up; originally in the phrase *to throw up the game* or *one's cards*, i. e. to place one's cards face upwards on the table on withdrawing from the game. Also *absol.*

1678 BUTLER *Hud.* III. III. 543 Bad Games are thrown up too soon, Until th' are never to be won. 1681 W. ROBERTSON *Phraseol. Gen.* (1693) 1225 To throw up his cards, *desistere a lusu.* a 1687 PETTY *Pol. Arith.* i. (1691) 33 To throw up their Husbandry, and make no use of their Lands, but for Grass [etc.]. 1731 *Gentl. Mag.* I. 539 The Evidence for the King being full and clear, the Defendant's Council threw up their Briefs. 1874 T. HARDY *Madding Crowd* xlvi, He..threw up his cards and forswore his game for that time and always. 1889 *Repentance P. Wentworth* II. xii. 261 He decided to throw up his practice at the Bar. 1894 *Times* (weekly ed.) 19 Jan. 49/1 When he was 20 he threw up his employment.

**h.** *To throw it up against, at, to one* (*low colloq.*): to cast it in one's teeth, to upbraid one (with obj. cl.). Cf. *cast up* (CAST *v.* 83 i).

1890 *Univ. Rev.* 15 Oct. 198 The children in the street throws it up against me I ain't got no father.

**i.** *intr.* Of hounds: To lift the head from the ground, the scent having been lost.

1856 'STONEHENGE' *Brit. Rur. Sports* I. VI. v. 128/1 Whenever it happens, and the hounds begin to throw up, and really *cannot* hunt, it is better to take them away. 1893 *Field* 4 Feb. 170/2 Hounds suddenly threw up in a most unaccountable manner.

**j.** *intr. Falconry.* See quots. (Cf. 28.)

1881 *Graphic* 5 Nov. 470/3, I [a falcon] stopped my downward course..spread my wings, and 'threw up' towards the upper air. 1900 MICHELL *Art Hawking* 128 Instead of throwing up high, as they would if they had missed, they check their flight quickly, and..descend rapidly on the panting or dazed foe. 1901 FISHER *Remin. Falconer* 96 No hawk stooping from a very high pitch can readily clutch or grasp her prey. She rushes upwards (i.e. throws up) impelled by her momentum..turns over, and is on the grouse directly. *Ibid.* 113.

**VII. 49.** In various proverbial, figurative, idiomatic, or colloquial phrases (beside those mentioned under the senses to which they belong), as *throw off one's* BALANCE, *over the* BAR, COLD WATER *on*, *a* DAMP *on*, DIRT, *the* GAUNTLET, *off one's* GUARD, *the* HELVE *after the hatchet* (so *the* HANDLE *after the head*, *the* ROPE *after the bucket*). *the* HOUSE *out at* (*of*) *the windows*, OVERBOARD, *off the* SCENT, *into the* SHADE, *the* STOCKING (at a wedding), *down the* STREAM, *in one's* TEETH, *to the* WINDS, etc.; as to which see the sbs.

For the verb-stem in combination: see THROW- in Comb.

† **Throw** (þrōu), *v.*[2] *Obs.* Forms: 1–2 **þrówian**, (2 **þrouwian**), 3 **þrowwenn** (*Orm.*), **þrowin**, **þruwen**, **ðhrow**. *Pa. t.* 1–3 **þrowode**, **-ede**, **-ude**. [OE. *þrówian* = OHG. *druoên* (Tatian *þruoên*), *drôên*, *trôên*, *truên*:—OTeut. **þrôwjan*, f. **þrôw-*, ablaut-grade of **þraw-* in OE. *þrawu* painful pressure: see THREA *v.*]

**1.** *trans.* To suffer, bear, endure.

*Beowulf* 2606 ȝeseah his mondryhten under here-griman hat þrowian. c888 K. ÆLFRED *Boeth.* xxxi. § 1 Swa swa bearneacen wif aceð bearn & ðrowað micel earfoðu. 971 *Blickl. Hom.* 93 Feallaþ ofor us.., þæt we ne þurfon þysne eȝe leng þrowian. c1000 ÆLFRIC *Gram.* xix. (Z.) 119 *Verbum* ys word..ȝetacniende oððe sum ðing to donne oððe sum ðing to þrowiȝenne. a1175 *Cott. Hom.* 229 He wolde for hus deað þrowian.

**2.** *intr.* (or *absol.*). To suffer, undergo suffering or pain.

*Beowulf* 2595 Nearo ðrowode fyre befongen seðe ær folce weold. 971 *Blickl. Hom.* 65 He wolde þrowian for ealra manna hæle. c1175 *Lamb. Hom.* 121 His ahȝenes þonkes he þrowede for us and binom ure sunnan. c1200 *Trin. Coll. Hom.* 101 Ure helende þrowede on þe holi rode. a1225 *Leg. Kath.* 1140 Hwi walde he þrowin as he dude, & þolien deð on rode?

Hence † **Throw·ing** *vbl. sb.*[2] [OE. *þrówung*], suffering; passion; *esp.* the Passion of Christ.

c897 K. ÆLFRED *Gregory's Past. C.* xviii. 136 Ic eom eower efnðeowa & Cristes ðrowunge ȝewiota. c1000 ÆLFRIC *Hom.* II. 506 On hwæs timan he ðrowunge underhniȝe. c1175 *Lamb. Hom.* 87 Nu is his þrowunge and his ariste ure ester tid. c1200 *Trin. Coll. Hom.* 81 His holie þroweȝunge þe he wolde þolien. c1200 ORMIN 15205 Inntill þrowwinnge & pine. a1225 *Ancr. R.* 372 Þuruh to stronge uondunges, soule þrowunge. c1250 *Gen. & Ex.* 1317 Wið-uten long ðhrowing and fiȝt. c1275 *Passion* 4 in *O. E. Misc.* 37 Cristes þruwinge þet he þolede her.

Here, apparently, belongs

†**Throw·and**, *pr. pple.* and *ppl. a. Sc. Obs.*, suffering the throes of death, struggling in death-agony.

1375 BARBOUR *Bruce* XV. 230 About him slayne lay his menȝe.. And he, redy to dey, throwand. 1513 DOUGLAS *Æneis* IV. xii. 60 Hir sistir An..Fast ruschis throw..the rout, And on the throwand [*morientem*]..Callis by name. *Ibid.* 102 Almychty Iuno..Hir maid Iris from the hevin hes send The throwand saull [*luctantem animam*] to lous. [Cf. a1547 SURREY *Æneid* IV. 927 From heauen she sent the Goddesse Iris downe, The throwing sprite and jointed limmes to loose.]

(Since Barbour and Douglas here use *throwand* and not *thrawand*, we seem obliged to refer their word, in form at least, to this verb; although difficulty is caused by the lateness of the use, long after the last examples known in English. It is probable that Surrey, in imitating Douglas's rendering, used *throwing* in the sense of THROE *v.* 2, of which the Sc. form would be *thrawand*: cf. THROW *v.*[1], sense 2 *note*.)

**Throw**: see THRO, THROE, THROUGH, TROW.

**Throw-** in Comb. [THROW *sb.*[2] or stem of THROW *v.*[1], in comb. with sbs. or advbs., forming sbs. or adjs.]

**1.** In comb. with sbs. **a.** (from branch I of the sb. or vb.) **throw-crank**, a crank which converts rotary into reciprocating motion; **throw-disk** (*Cent. Dict., Suppl.*), **throw-lever**, a disk-crank or a lever having a specified or adjustable throw (sense 2); **throw-lathe**, a lathe driven by hand; **thraw-mouse** (*Sc. dial.*), the shrew-mouse: see quot.; **throw-wheel**, the driving-wheel of a throw or lathe. **b.** (from branch II of vb.) **throw-bait**, bait thrown to attract fish to a place; **throw-line**, a fishing-line thrown out by hand, a hand-line. See also THROW-CROOK, THROW-STICK.

1867 URE *Dict. Arts*, etc. II. 783 A carrier, which is made to advance and recede alternately by means of a *throw-crank. 1877 KNIGHT *Dict. Mech.*, **Throw-lathe*, a small lathe which is driven by one hand, while the tool is managed by the other. 1904 *Brit. & Col. Printer* 10 Mar. 14/3 An intermediate adjustable or variable *throw lever. 1908 *Westm. Gaz.* 19 Sept. 10/2 One day when he was fishing off the rocks with *throw-lines. 1881 GREGOR *Folk-Lore N.-E. Scotl.* 127 The field mouse, called 'the *thraw mouse', running over the foot of a person, was supposed to produce paralysis in the foot. 1884 F. J. BRITTEN *Watch & Clockm.* (1886) 304 *Throw*, a clockmakers' 'dead centre' lathe...A gut connects the large *throw wheel with a small pulley rotating freely on the lathe centre.

**2.** In comb. with adverbs, forming sbs. expressing the action of the corresponding verbal phrases (see THROW *v.*[1] VI.); as *throw-in*, *-up* (an act of throwing in or up); **throw-away**, a printed sheet or work not intended for preservation after it has been read; also *attrib.*; **throw-down**, a fall, as in wrestling; a come-down; a defeat (*slang*); **throw-in**, in Football, an act of throwing the ball into play again after it has crossed one of the touch-lines; in Cricket, an act of throwing in the ball from the field to the wicket-keeper or bowler; **throw-on**, an act of throwing onwards or forwards; *spec.* in Rugby football: see quot.; **throw-out**, an act of throwing out, or a thing thrown out; anything discarded or rejected; also *attrib.* See also THROW-BACK, -OFF, -OVER.

1903 *Westm. Gaz.* 7 Oct. 12/2 Every now and then a little blue square of printed paper fluttered in the breeze. No one seemed to connect these little '*throw-aways' with the venerable figure on the front seat. 1905 *Daily Chron.* 20 Feb. 4/6 This present rag of a throwaway that you can get for a halfpenny. 1905 *Westm. Gaz.* 31 July 10/2 Lord Alverstone..vigorously denounced the 'sixpenny throw-away rubbish'. 1903 *Architect* 24 Apr. Suppl. 27/1 Any delay on the work is 'a *throw-down for the boss'. 1898 J. GOODALL *Assoc. Football* 61 The object of the Association was to make the *throw-in from touch a superficial benefit. 1909 *Westm. Gaz.* 8 Feb. 12/2 This umpire seems..somewhat ignorant of the throw-in rule. 1845 *Rules Footb. Rugby School* § 4 *A Knock on*, as distinguished from *a* '*throw on*, consists in striking the ball on with the arm or hand. 1894 *Blackw. Mag.* Sept. 426/2 Catching these little fish by means of what are known locally as '*throw out' lines. 1901 *Law Rep.* 2 K. B. Div. 698 Small lots of timber called in the trade 'throw-outs'. 1907 *Daily Chron.* 9 Apr. 8/4 A patch of narcissus which nobody takes the trouble to gather. They are the 'throw-outs' from the fields. 1911 *Daily Graphic* 16 Jan. 20/3 'Witney Blanket Rugs': Manufacturers' Throw Outs. 1832 *Examiner* 508/1 He answered with a bold front and an important *throw up of his head.

**Throwand**: see after THROW *v.*[2] prec. column.

**Throw·-back.** [f. phr. *to throw back*: see THROW *v.*[1] 38.] An act of throwing back.

**1.** A backward movement or direction given. Also *attrib. Throw-back indicator*, see quot. 1902 [2].

1901 *Blackw. Mag.* Aug. 192/1 Rob's head had a confident jerky throwback, like a gamecock's. 1902 *Daily Chron.* 19 Mar. 9/4 The Light Blues' throw-back of the bodies for the first catch is imposing. 1902 O'CONOR SLOANE *Stand. Electr. Dict.*, *Throw-back Indicator*, a drop annunciator, whose shutter or drop is electrically replaced.

**2.** An arrest or reverse in a course or progress; a check, set-back, relapse.

1856 H. R. REYNOLDS in *Life* v. (1898) 123 The little throw-back of my progress..was not such as to create any uneasiness. 1902 *Edin. Rev.* Oct. 286 The belief in popular principles held by most Englishmen before the great throw back of the French Revolution.

**3.** Reversion to an earlier ancestral type or character; an example of this. Chiefly *fig.*

1889 *Athenæum* 14 Sept. 351/3 By a not unusual freak of heredity she is personally a 'throw-back' to an angel. 1894 *Temple Bar Mag.* Mar. 454 Our feeble throw-back to savagery. 1904 W. H. POLLOCK *Anim. that have Owned us* vii. 98 He must have been a freak or a 'throw back'.

**Throwch**, obs. Sc. f. THROUGH *sb.* and *prep.*

**Throw·-crook**, *Sc.* & *n. dial.* **thraw·crook.** [f. THROW *v.*[1] + CROOK *sb.*] A hooked implement for 'throwing' or twisting coarse rope from hay, straw, or hair.

a1568 *Wowing of Jok & Jynny* 68 in *Bannatyne Poems* 389 Ane thrawcruk to twyne ane tedder. 1828 J. STRUTHERS *Hist. Scot.* II. 624 Ropes of hair twined upon the thraw-crook. 1829 BROCKETT *N. C. Gloss.* (ed. 2), *Thrawcrook*, an instrument acting on a swivel for twisting ropes. 1844 STEPHENS *Bk. Farm* III. 1092 The simplest instrument is the old-fashioned throw-crook.

**Throwe**, obs. f. THROE, THROUGH, THROW.

**Throwed** (þrōud), obs. or dial. pa. t. and pa. pple. of THROW *v.*[1]; in quot. as *ppl. a.* = THROWN.

1727–41 CHAMBERS *Cycl.* s.v. *Silk*, *Throwed or twisted silks* are such, as, besides their spinning and winding, have received their milling or throwing..: properly,..throwed silks are those wherein the threads are pretty thick throwed, and are twisted several times.

**Thrower** (þrōu·əɹ). Also 5 *Sc.* and *north. dial.* **thrawer.** [f. THROW *v.*[1] + -ER [1].] One who throws, in various senses.

**I. 1.** One who fashions something by a rotary motion. †**a.** One who fashions wooden objects on a lathe; a turner. *Obs.*

1483 *Cath. Angl.* 385/1 A Thrawer, *tornator.* 1620 *Shuttleworths' Acc.* (Chetham Soc.) 243 P'd to the thrower for the chessotts making. 1688 R. HOLME *Armoury* III. 269/2 A Turners, or Throwers Tools.

**b.** One who shapes pottery on a potter's wheel or throw; a potter.

1604 [see THROW *v.*[1] 6 a]. 1744 *Indenture J. Wedgwood* in Eliza Meteyard *Life* (1865) I. 222 To Learn his Art Mistery Occupation or Imployment of Thrower and Handleing which he the said Thomas Wedgwood now useth. 1790 in *Guide Mus. Pract. Geol.* (1859) 98 About 90 painters.. and about 200 throwers, turners, &c., were employed under one roof. 1881 *Guide Worcester Porcel. Wks.* (1906) 19 The man who works at the potter's wheel is called the thrower. 1894 SMILES *Wedgwood* iii. 22 The thrower is the person who sits in his shed, near the potter's wheel, and forms by hand from the moist clay as it revolves, the crock, the butter pot, the porringer or other such wares. 1903 *Daily Rec. & Mail* 1 July 4 The Potter's Wheel..is made of ash, and the thrower works upon it now in the same way as did the thrower thousands of years ago in Egypt.

**c.** One who twists filaments of silk into silk thread; a throwster.

1621 in Strype *Stow's Surv.* v. xiv. (1754) II. 321/1 To take Hearing and Consideration of the Petition of the Silk-throwers. 1662 *Act 14 Chas. II*, c. 15 § 5 There is a necessity lying upon the Silke throwers to deliver to theire Winders or Doublers considerable quantities of silke which being of good value is..many times..deceitfully and falsly purloined..to the great damage and sometimes the utter undoing of the Thrower whoe employes the said persons.

†**2.** (In form **thrawer.**) One who twists, wrests, or perverts; a perverter of the sense. *Sc. rare*—[1].

1563 DAVIDSON *Confut. Kennedy* in *Wodrow Soc. Misc.* (1844) 229, I wald we war judgit, quhidder we be thrawers of the Scripturs.

**II. 3.** One who (or that which) casts, hurls, flings, or pitches: see the senses of THROW *v.*[1] II–V.

1519 HORMAN *Vulg.* 253 b, Come nat vpon that horsebacke: for he is a great throware. 1552 HULOET, Thrower of a stone with a hole therin for exercise, *discobolus.* 1579–80 NORTH *Plutarch* (1676) 173 Throwers with slings, Archers, and other light armed men. 1677 PLOT *Oxfordsh.* 10 If it be thrown in an oblique line, it returns not to the thrower but to another place. 1850 'BAT' *Cricket. Man.* 44 Long Leg must..be occupied by a good thrower. 1892 RIDER HAGGARD *Nada the Lily* 198 It is the bold thrower who oftenest wins. 1911 *Times* 3 Mar. 8/3 The thrower of the bomb was immediately arrested.

**b.** With various adverbs: cf. THROW *v.*[1] VI.

c1450 tr. *De Imitatione* III. lx. 142 She is maistresse of trouþe..þrower doun, dryuer awey of sorowe. 1611 SHAKS. *Wint. T.* III. iii. 29 Since Fate..Hath made thy person for the Thrower-out Of my poore babe. 1719 LONDON & WISE *Compl. Gard.* vi. 19 The Autumn Winds, those throwers down of Fruits. 1773 J. ALLEN *Serm. St. Mary's, Oxford* 26 We have no Ahaz, no thrower down nor changer of altars. 1860 GEN. P. THOMPSON *Audi Alt. P.* III. cxxiv. 78 It may be late, but they have not been the throwers away.

**Throwing** (þrōu·iŋ), *vbl. sb.*[1] [f. as prec. + -ING [1].] The action of THROW *v.*[1]

**I. 1.** (In form **thrawing.**) Twisting, wringing; turning or bending to one side; also *fig.* crossing, thwarting; quarrelling. *Sc.*

a1585 MONTGOMERIE *Flyting* 376 They deemde, what death it sould die..'be throwing [*v.r.* thrawing] of the throate, Like a tyke ouer a tree'. 1785 BURNS *Halloween* xxiii, It chanc'd the stack..Was timmer-propt for thrawin'. 1816 SCOTT *Bl. Dwarf* viii, Speak him fair, Hobbie; the like o' him will no bear thrawing. 1897 *Daily Rec. & Mail* 17 Sept. 4 The present unsatisfactory condition of affairs is..due in great part to personal feeling and 'thrawing'.

**2. a.** The turning of objects from wood; the shaping of round pottery on a potter's wheel.

c1440 *Promp. Parv.* 493/1 Throwynge, or turnynge of vesselle, *tornacio.* 1483 *Cath. Angl.* 385/1 A Thrawynge, *to[r]natura.* 1797 *Encycl. Brit.* (ed. 3) XVII. 811/1 (Stoneware) The mixture..is beat..and then is in order for throwing. 1832 G. R. PORTER *Porcelain & Gl.* 45 The operation of throwing consists in shaping such vessels as have a circular form, and is performed upon a machine called a potter's lathe. a1882 SIR H. COLE *50 Yrs. Public Wk.* (1884) I. 105 Superintending the throwing, turning, modelling, and moulding of a tea service.

**b.** The twisting of raw silk into thread.

1621– [see SILK-THROWING]. 1662 *Act 14 Chas. II*, c. 15 § 9 The said Corporation of Silk throwers shall not..make any Orders Ordinances or By-Lawes to sett any Rates or Prices whatsoever upon the Throwing of Silk. 1844 G. DODD *Textile Manuf.* vi. 192 The next process, called *throwing*, by which the two, three, five or a dozen threads are twisted firmly one round another. 1868 *Rep. U. S. Commissioner Agric.* 288 The twisting or 'throwing' process is done by passing the thread of raw silk from an upright bottom through the eye of a craned wire flyer, which rapidly spins with the top of the bobbin revolving above.

**II. 3.** Projecting, casting, flinging, hurling (*lit.* or *fig.*). *Throwing at cocks*: = COCK-THROWING.

13.. *Cursor M.* 22683 (Edin. MS.) Þe stanis.. Wit þrawing [*Cott.* thrauing, *Fairf.* casting, *Gött.* wid strenth] sal tai samin þrist, þat al to pecis sal tai brist. 13.. *K. Alis.* 1614 With launceynge and with rydyng With throwyng [*Bodley MS.* þraweynge], and with nymyng. 1375 BARBOUR *Bruce* XIII. 156 Thar wes.. sic thrawing and sic thristing,.. That it wes hydwiss for till her. *c* 1440 *Promp. Parv.* 493/1 Throwynge, or castynge, *jactura, jactus.* 1639 DRUMM. OF HAWTH. *Answ. to Objections* Wks. (1711) 214 By throwing of oat-meal in the people's eyes. *c* 1770 (*title*) A friendly admonition against throwing at Cocks and of Cockfighting. 1833 NYREN *Yng. Cricketer's Tutor* 90 Walker.. began the system of throwing instead of bowling, now so much the fashion. At that time, it was esteemed foul play. 1897 *Daily News* 1 Nov. 5/2 The throwing nuisance, which has for years been the scandal of English cricket.

**4.** With adverbs, as *throwing about, back, down, in, off, out, up*: see THROW *v.*[1] VI.

*c* 1440 *Promp. Parv.* 493/1 Throwynge downe, fro hey place.., *precipicium.* 1518 *Sel. Pl. Star Chamb.* (Selden) II. 131 Yf they had known the throwyng downe of the seyd iij gappes. 1653 H. MORE *Antid. Ath.* III. ix. § 4 The watchmen of the Town.. heard.. the fallings and throwings of things about. 1772 WOLLASTON in *Phil. Trans.* LXIII. 68, I have set down the throwing-out of the pendulum,.. on a scale behind it. 1785 M. GARTHSHORE in *Med. Commun.* II. 39 It terminated by the throwing off of sloughs. 1851 *Jrnl. R. Agric. Soc.* XII. I. 88 These straining efforts are sometimes so energetic as to cause 'throwing down' of the uterus. 1869 TOZER *Highl. Turkey* II. 331 Throwing back the head (ἀνανεύειν) is still.. a negative answer.

**III. 5.** *attrib.* and *Comb.* **a.** for throwing pottery or silk: as *throwing-clay, -house, -machine, -room*; **throwing-engine**, applied by Nicholson to the driving-wheel of a potter's wheel; **throwing-mill**, (*a*) a building in which silk-throwing is carried on; (*b*) a machine for twisting raw silk into thread; **throwing-table**, a descriptive name for a potter's wheel: see quot.; **throwing-wheel**, a potter's wheel; sometimes, as in quot. 1825, applied to the driving-wheel. **b.** for casting, hurling, etc.: as *throwing-bat, -club, -hatchet, -knife, -net, -spear*; **throwing-balls**, the South American BOLAS; **throwing-board**, a spear-thrower, = THROWING-STICK a.; **throwing-iron**, a knife-like missile used by some African savages.

**a.** 1686 PLOT *Staffordsh.* 122 All which they call *throwing clays, because they.. will work on the wheel. 1825 J. NICHOLSON *Operat. Mechanic* 462 A strap is attached from the driven cone to the spindle of the *throwing-engine. 1733 P. LINDSAY *Interest Scotl.* 136 *Throwing Mills, after the Manner of that One at Darby. 1831 G. R. PORTER *Silk Manuf.* 201 Spinning or twisting the thread.. wound upon the bobbins, is performed with the throwing mill. 1851 L. D. B. GORDON in *Art Jrnl. Illustr. Catal.* p. ii**/2 The factories in which raw silk is spun into silk-thread for weaving are called throwing mills. 1881 *Guide Worcester Porcel. Wks.* 11 The *Throwing Room. 1877 KNIGHT *Dict. Mech.*, **Throwing-table*, a revolving, horizontal table on which earthen vessels are shaped by the potter. 1825 J. NICHOLSON *Operat. Mechanic* 461 The **throwing-wheel*, or, with greater propriety, the *throwing-engine*, consists of a large vertical wheel; having a winch or handle affixed to it, and a groove on the rim for the introduction of a cord [etc.]. **b.** 1891 *Cent. Dict.*, *Throwing-balls. 1845 C. H. SMITH in *Kitto's Cycl. Bibl. Lit.* s.v. *Arms*, Among these [instruments at first employed in the chase] were the club and the *throwing-bat. 1909 *Cent. Dict. Suppl.*, *Throwing-board. 1895 *Cornh. Mag.* Dec. 634 The soldiers.. had brought him down with *throwing-clubs. 1903 KIPLING in *Windsor Mag.* Sept. 370/1 Tegumai.. was holding his stone *throwing-hatchet in one hand. 1898 tr. *Ratzel's Hist. Mankind* III. 71 The indispensable weapon was the *throwing-iron, of which many carried several specimens,.. in sheaths of hide. *Ibid.* 72 *Throwing-knives are among the notable properties of the races of the Monbuttu type north of the Congo. 1902 L. LOAT in Boulenger *Zool. Egypt, Fishes Nile* Introd. (1907) 21 At Cairo.. the commonest net of all is a circular *throwing-net,.. with an average circumference of about 50 feet and a half-inch mesh. 1900 A. B. LLOYD in *Daily News* 18 July 6/2 Each carried either bow and quiver of arrows, or short *throwing-spears.

**Throwing,** *vbl. sb.*[2], suffering: see THROW *v.*[2]

**Throw·ing-stick.** **a.** A short wooden implement by which a dart or spear is thrown, in order to give increased velocity to it: = SPEAR-THROWER, WOOMERA. **b.** A short club used as a missile; = THROW-STICK a.

1770 COOK *Voy. round World* III. viii. (1773) 641 An instrument which we called a throwing stick. This is a plain smooth piece of a hard reddish wood, very highly polished, about two inches broad, half an inch thick, and three feet long, with a small knob, or hook at one end, and a cross piece about three or four inches long at the other. 1802 G. BARRINGTON *Hist. N. S. Wales* i. 26 The throwing-stick is used in discharging the spear. 1865 LUBBOCK *Preh. Times* 403 For throwing the harpoon they use a short handle or throwing-stick, about two feet long. 1885 H. H. HAYTER *Carboona* 24 Warrk Warrk, having a dart on his throwing-stick ready adjusted, hurled it. 1901 *Athenæum* 11 May 599/2 The throwing-stick of the Moki [Pueblo Indians] is closely related to the Australian boomerang, but does not return to the thrower.

**Thrown** (þrōun), *ppl. a.* [Pa. pple. of THROW *v.*[1], where see Forms. See also special Scotch senses under THRAWN.]

**I. 1. a.** Turned on a lathe, as woodwork. Now *dial.* **b.** Shaped on the potter's wheel. Cf. THROW *v.*[1] 6 a.

1483 *Cath. Angl.* 385/1 Thrawen (*A.* Thrawne), *tornalis.* 1495 *Nottingham Rec.* III. 40 Unam cathedram vocatam 'a throwen' cheyer'. 1535 COVERDALE 2 *Chron.* iii. 5 He.. ouerlayed it with the best golde, and made palme trees and throwne worke theron. 1600 *Acc. Bk. W. Wray* in *Antiquary* XXXII. 279 A throwne chaire. 1853 URE *Dict. Arts* II. 455 When the 'thrown ware' is sufficiently dry, it is transferred to the hands of the 'turner'. 1883 *W. Yorks. Gloss.*, *Thrown*, turned in a lathe (as bed-posts, &c.).

**2.** Of silk: Twisted into thread.

*Thrown silk*: silk thread consisting of two or more singles twisted together: = ORGANZINE. *Thrown singles*: silk thread consisting of a single strand of raw silk which has been cleaned, wound, and twisted: see quot. 1877 s. v. THROW *v.*[1] 6 b. Also (in trade) *absol.* as *sb.*

1463-4 *Rolls of Parlt.* V. 506/1 Wrought Silke, throwen Rybans and Laces. 1483 [see THROW *v.*[1] 6 b]. 1690 LUTTRELL *Brief Rel.* (1857) II. 45 An act for discouraging the importation of thrown silk. 1709 *Lond. Gaz.* No. 4523/4 Some Piemond Thrown Silk.. saved out of an Italian Ship. 1719 W. WOOD *Surv. Trade* 87 Oil, Wine, Thrown and Raw-silk, Wrought Silks. 1812 J. SMYTH *Pract. of Customs* (1821) 214 Raw Silk has only one thread: the thrown Silk is distinguished from it by having two threads. 1844 G. DODD *Textile Manuf.* vi. 184 Thrown singles, is silk which has been wound, cleaned, and thrown. 1883 *Times* 16 May 11 In silk.. Chinas have suffered from the reduced consumption of throwns. 1906 *Sat. Rev.* 13 Jan. 38/2 They buy their silk in the spun or thrown state.

† **b.** Twisted; in a state of torsion. *Obs.*

1674 N. FAIRFAX *Bulk & Selv. World* Contents, Open'd by the stirring of a watch, of thrown bodies, the springiness of an egge.

**II. 3.** Cast, pitched, hurled; unseated from a horse.

1833 HT. MARTINEAU *Berkeley the Banker* I. i. 18 The horse galloping away, and the thrown young lady lying on the ground. 1888 RUSKIN in *Mag. Art* Jan. 75/1 To put them together out of chance-thrown heaps.

**4.** With adverbs, as *thrown-back, -down, -on, -over, -up*, expressing the completed action of the corresponding verbal phrases (see THROW *v.*[1] VI).

1891 C. ROBERTS *Adrift Amer.* 146 They sat.. on the mound made of the thrown-up earth from the burrows. 1901 *Westm. Gaz.* 17 Oct. 2/2 The thrown-back front and sleeve both gave glimpses of their lining. 1903 *Ibid.* 8 Jan. 3/2 Some such thrown-on kind of wrap can be added for coming and going. *Ibid.* 4 June 5/2 One fire was caused by a thrown-down light.

**Throw-off.** [f. the vbl. phrase *to throw off* (THROW *v.* 42).] **a.** *Fox-hunting.* The throwing-off of the hounds, the start of a hunt; by extension, of a race; hence, a start generally. **b.** A shaking off, getting rid of or free from. **c.** A mechanism by which some part of a machine is disconnected, or its action suspended. **d.** That which is thrown off; something produced or given off, an offshoot.

1859 PALMERSTON in Lucas *Ld. Glenesk* (1910) 147 The throw-off is awkward, beginning with the insignificant word 'in'. 1864 WEBSTER, *Throw-off*, a start in a hunt or race. 1864 *Gd. Words* 104/2 These millions, these atoms of life—they are a free throw off from the Creative Beneficence. 1873 *Punch* 13 Sept. 107/1 Whither I had driven in order to see the throw-off. 1886 J. M. CAULFEILD *Seamanship Notes* 3 *Parts of the Capstan*,.. bar pins, throw off, spindle,.. entablature. 1889 *Nature* 22 Aug. 393/1 No micro-seismic shock can ever take place otherwise than as a throw-off from some violent disturbance more or less remotely located. 1891 *Melbourne Punch* 4 June 377/2, I received an invitation to see the throw off of the Ballarat hounds in the afternoon.

**Throw·-over.** [f. the verbal phrase *to throw over* (THROW *v.* 45).] The act or result of throwing over, in various senses; also, *concr.*, a wrap to throw over the shoulders; a loose outer garment.

1819 *Hermit in London* III. 212 They had practised what they technically termed a throw over. 1852 LEWIS *Lett.* (1870) 257 The complete and definitive throw over both of Protection and local burdens must loosen the hold of the Government upon the agricultural body. 1902 O'CONOR SLOANE *Stand. Electr. Dict.* App., *Throw-Over Switch*, a double throw knife switch designed to connect a three wire system in a building either to a three wire street main or to a single source on the two wire system. 1907 *Ladies' Field* 12 Jan. 3/2 White Foxaline long Stole or Throwover. 1909 *Westm. Gaz.* 3 Apr. 15/1 The nearest approach we have to the Marie Antoinette 'throw-over'—it cannot be called a tea gown..—is the Japanese kimono. *Ibid.* 16 Oct. 15/1 The drapery.. has grown in its proportions till now it resembles a shawl, and nothing could be more convenient as a throw-over, either for day or evening purposes.

† **Throwst,** *v. Obs.* Also 7–8 throst. [irreg. back-formation from THROWSTER.] *trans.* To throw silk; = THROW *v.*[1] 6 b. So **Throw·sting** *vbl. sb.*, silk-throwing; also attrib. *throwsting-machine, -mill.*

1691 W. SEWEL *Dutch Dict.* s. v. *Reeden, Zy-Reeden*, to Throst silk. 1825 J. NICHOLSON *Operat. Mechanic* 396 A representation of the throwsting-mills. *Ibid.* 399 The bobbins being thus filled with double or triple threads, are carried back to the throwsting-machine, and are there spun or twisted together. 1844 G. DODD *Textile Manuf.* vi. 196 The processes of silk-throwing, or 'throwsting', may now be said to be finished.

**Throwster** (þrōu·stəɹ). Forms: 5 throwestre, -er, 6 throwstar, (7–8 throster), 7– throwster. [f. THROW *v.*[1] 6 b + -STER.]

**1.** One who twists silk fibres into raw silk or raw silk into thread, a silk-throwster; originally, a woman who did this, a SILK-WOMAN (the earliest term). † Also extended to a worsted-spinner (*obs.*).

1455 *Rolls of Parlt.* V. 325/1 The Silkewymmen and Throwestres of the Craftes and occupation of Silkewerk. 1530 PALSGR. 281/1 Throwstar, *deuideresse de soye.* 1620 MIDDLETON & ROWLEY *World Tost at Tennis* 95 Job a venerable silk-weaver, Jehu a throwster dwelling i' the Spitalfields. 1678 PHILLIPS (ed. 4), *Throster*, one that twisteth Silk or Thred. 1716 *Lond. Gaz.* No. 5401/4 A Worsted-Throwster by Trade. 1734 SWIFT *Compl. Deafness* 16 A woman's clack, if I have skill, Sounds somewhat like a throwster's mill. 1846 McCULLOCH *Acc. Brit. Empire* (1854) I. 713 The throwsters of the metropolis were formed into a fellowship in 1562, but they were not incorporated till 1629. 1880 CHARL. M. MASON *Forty Shires* 95 English throwsters did their work as well as those of Italy.

**2.** *Pottery.* = THROWER 1 b: see quot. (? error).

1894 H. SPEIGHT *Nidderdale* 384 *note*, Throwsters and drysters were potters' craftsmen; the throwster being the man who works the wheel, and.. forms by the pressure of his hand the 'lining' for the dish or cup.

† **3.** A dice-thrower, a gamester. *Obs. rare.*

1832 J. WILSON *Noct. Ambr.* in *Blackw. Mag.* Sept. 388 A certain bold throwster had swept the pool.

**Throw·-stick.** [f. THROW *v.*[1] + STICK *sb.*] **a.** A heavy, usually curved, piece of wood used as a missile; an ancient kind of boomerang. **b.** A stick with which a spear or dart is thrown: = THROWING-STICK a.

1837 WILKINSON *Mann. & Cust. Anc. Egypt.* viii. III. 38 The use of the throw-stick was very general. 1857 — *Egypt. in Time Pharaohs* 80 Birds were felled with the throwstick, a weapon of hard wood,.. slightly curved.. like the boomerang. 1869 BOUTELL *Arms & Arm.* vi. (1874) 84 When the dart is discharged, the *wummera*, or throw-stick, .. remains in the warrior's hand. *c* 1875 H. B. TRISTRAM in *Queen's Printers' Bible-Aids* 57 In 1 Sam. xxvi. 20 allusion is made to chasing partridges on the hills with throw-sticks.

**Throwt**(e, obs. contr. of THROUGHOUT. **Throw-ther**: see THROUGH-OTHER. **Thru, thruch, thrucht, thruff, thrugh**: see THROUCH, THROUGH *prep.* and *sb.* **Thrub**, obs. var. DRUB. **Thrudde, Thrulle**, obs. ff. THIRD, THRILL *v.*[1]

† **Thrum,** *sb.*[1] *Obs.* Forms: 1 þrymm, 1–2 þrym, 3–4 þrum, 4 þrom, 4–5 throm, throme, 5 thrumme. [app. OE. *þrymm* a host, a great body of people, a multitude (also strength, might, majesty, glory); cf. OS. *thrumme* in *mid heruthrummeon* 'with hostile power or strength'; cf. OS. *thrimman* to swell; also Flemish *drommen* in THRUM *v.*[1]]

**1.** A company or body of people (or animals); a band, troop, crowd; *on a thrum*, in a body, in a crowd. Also, a bundle (of arrows, quot. *c* 1450). Also *attrib.* † **þrum-ferd** (FERD *sb.*[1] 3).

*a* 800 CYNEWULF *Christ* (Cod. Exon.) 1063 Se engla þrym. *c* 1000 ÆLFRIC *Saints' Lives* xxv. 841 Se hundredes ealdor.. com on ærne merȝen mid mycclum þrymme. *c* 1205 LAY. 1356 Þer heo leof folc funden feower þrum ferden. *c* 1330 *Arth. & Merl.* 211 Whiles þou were in our þrome, No were we neuer ouercome. *a* 1350 *St. Andrew* 209 in Horstm. *Altengl. Leg.* (1881) 6 Þe folk thrang efter al on a þrum. *c* 1400 *Laud Troy Bk.* 13236 Thei schal alle dye on a throme. *c* 1430 *Syr Gener.* (Roxb.) 2949 A hundred houndes on a throm He saw that were thider com. *c* 1450 *Ball. Death Robin Lyth* 48 (Ritson) Fowre and twenty goode arwys Trusyd in a thrumme.

**2.** Magnificence, splendour.

971 *Blickl. Hom.* 77 Emb þone þrym and þa fægernesse ðæs temples. *c* 1175 *12th Cent. Hom.* 130 Þenne beoð þa welæn & þa glengæ aȝotene, & þe þrym tobrocen.

**Thrum** (þrɒm), *sb.*[2] Forms: (1 þrum), 4–6 throm(e, 5 thrum(e, thrwme, 5–6 thromm(e, 5–7 thrumm(e, 6–7 thrumbe, (6 *Sc.* throomb), 6–9 thrumb, 6– thrum. [OE. *þrum* (in comb. in *tungeþrum* ligament of the tongue), ME. *thrum*, *throm*, = MDu. *drom*, Du. dial. *drom*, *drum* (in mod. Du. *dreum* m. 'thrum'), OHG., MHG. *drum* end-piece, remnant (in mod. G. *trumm* 'thrum', pl. *trümmer* remnants, ruins); cf. ON. *þrǫmr* edge, brim (Norw. *tröm, trumm, tram* edge, brim, Sw. dial. *tröm, trumm, trom* stump); formed, with various suffixes, from OTeut. ablaut-stem **þrum-*, **þram-*, :—Indo-Eur. **trmo-*; cf. L. *term-inus*, Gr. *τέρμ-α* end.

*a* 1000 *Lorica Gloss.* in *Sax. Leechd.* I. Pref. 70 *Sublinguæ*, tungeðrum [*Harl. MS.* ibid. 74 undertungeðrum].]

**1.** *Weaving.* Each of the ends of the warp-threads left unwoven and remaining attached to the loom when the web is cut off; usually in *pl.* (also *collect. sing.*) the row or fringe of such threads.

1429 *Rolls of Parlt.* IV. 360/2 The Weyvers.. have taken .. in common usage,.. what tyme yat yei have wroght a Clothe almost to ye end, to kitte away to yair singuler avauntage ye yerne yat leveth unwoven, and callen hit Thrommes [cf. Act 8 Hen. VI, c. 23 § 1]. 14.. *Nom.* in Wr.-Wülcker 728/17 *Hoc licium*, a throm. 1449 *Maldon, Essex, Crt. Rolls* (Bundle 29, No. 3), Ricardus Vyce petit xxd. pro xx lb. de Thromes empt. 1590 SHAKS. *Mids. N.* v. i. 291 O Fates! come, come: Cut thred and thrum. 1591 R. BRUCE *Serm.* I j b, The Webster doth cut off the web from the throombs of his beam. 1611 BIBLE *Isa.* xxxviii. 12 He will cut mee off with pining sicknesse [*marg.* from the thrum]. 1649 ROBERTS *Clavis Bibl.* 447 A weavers web brought unto the thrum, and ready to be cut off. 1725 *Bradley's Fam. Dict.* s.v. *Wound*, If the Shot be quite thorough the Wound, then take a few Weavers Linnen Thrums.. and dipping 'em first in Varnish, draw 'em through the Wound. 1847–78 HALLIWELL, *Thrum*, the extremity of a weaver's warp, often about nine inches long, which cannot be woven.

**2.** A short piece of waste thread or yarn (including the unwoven ends of the warp = 1); *pl.* or *collect. sing.* odds and ends of thread; also, a short or loose end of thread projecting from the surface of a woven fabric; a tuft, tassel, or fringe of threads at the edge of a piece of cloth, etc.

(In early quots. barely distinguishable from 1.)

1346 *Litt. Red Bk. Bristol* (1900) II. 5 Drap..estre fait de fil de lein appele thromes. 1439 *Deed* (Westm. Chapter Archives), Qui tunc dedit predicto Johanni Kirkeby capellum de thrummes fact[um] quod tunc temporis erat de noua coniectura. c 1440 *Promp. Parv.* 493/1 Thrvmm, of a clothe, *filamen,..villus fractillus*. 1519 Horman *Vulg.* 167 b, The baudy thrummys of the carpettis toke me faste by the feete. 1530 Palsgr. 158 *Vng payné*, a thrumme of a hatte or suche lyke. 1541–2 *Act* 33 *Hen. VIII*, c. 18 § 3 They..shall..[not] make..any manner Kerseyes with flockis, thrummes or other deceivable thinge or thingis. 1555 W. Watreman *Fardle Facions* II. x. 215 Thei [Tartars] make..litle pupettes of silke or of felte, or of thrumme. 1611 Cotgr., *Pesles*, thrummes; or that which hangs at the end of a peece of cloth like fringe. c 1645 Howell *Lett.* (1650) III. 33 The wrong side of a Turky carpet, which useth to be full of thrums and knots, and nothing so even as the right side. 1675 V. Alsop *Anti-Sozzo* 302 Tying both the Ends so handsomely together, that it may not Ravel out into Thrums. 1681 Colvil *Whigs Supplic.* (1751) 4 Like pictures on the wrong side of Arras hangings, spoiled with thrumbs and threads. 1878 Pater *Child in House* Misc. Stud. (1895) 174 Childish treasures, glass beads, empty scent-bottles still sweet, thrum of coloured silks.

**b.** *Naut.* (*pl.*, also *collect. sing.*) Short pieces of coarse woollen or hempen yarn, used for mops, etc.: cf. Thrum *v.*2 e, and Thrummed1 c.

1466 *Mann. & Househ. Exp.* (Roxb.) 346 Thrommes for pyche mapoltes. 1623 Whitbourne *Newfoundland* 75 Thrummes for Pitch mabs. 1848 [see Thrum *v.*2 e]. 1867 Smyth *Sailor's Word-bk.*, *Thrum*, any coarse woollen or hempen yarn. It is used for mops, &c., in the cabins.

**c.** *fig.*: *pl.* (or *collect. sing.*) Odds and ends, scraps.

1648—1833 Thread and thrum, Threads and thrums [see Thread *sb.* 2 c]. a 1653 G. Daniel *Idyll.* v. 180 Arguments For you to ravell; Thrumbs of Discontents: From the large Webbe of Care. 1872 Morley *Voltaire* III. (ed. 2) 147 It is this, which..makes life a whole instead of a parcel of thrums bound together by an accident.

†**3.** Short for *thrum cap* (see 7). *Obs. rare*−1.

1719 D'Urfey *Pills* IV. 158 The Monmouth Cap, the Sailor's Thrumb. *Ibid.*, The Sea-man with his Thrumb.

†**4.** Applied to various structures in plants or animals resembling small threads, or a tuft of these. **a.** *pl.* The florets of the disk in a composite flower, or the stamens in a simple flower; also, *sing.* the disk, the central petals of a double flower, or the stamens collectively. *Obs.* (exc. in comb. *thrum-eyed*: see 7).

1578 Lyte *Dodoens* II. xxxii. 189 Of Buphthalmos, or Oxe eye...The floure is of a fayre bright yellow colour, and large, with many small thrommes or yellow thredes in the middle, almost like to the floures of Marigoldes. 1657 W. Coles *Adam in Eden* ii. 4 Fair large red flours [of peony]..having..in the midst, yellow Threds or Thrums. 1668 Wilkins *Real Char.* II. iv. § 4. 81 Consisting of..a circle of Leaves, and a Thrumm of short stamina, close set together. 1671 Grew *Anat. Plants* v. § 17 The Florid Attire, is commonly known by the blind and rude Name of Thrums. 1694 Westmacott *Script. Herb.* (1695) 99 The Water-Lillies ..bearing a white flower, with yellow thrums in the middle. 1726 *Flower Gard. Displ.* (ed. 2) Introd., Thrums, Apices or Chives, when a great Number of them grow together in a Flower. 1812 *New Bot. Gard.* I. 33 The..cutting winds in March will often cause them [double Anemones] to blow single, by destroying the thrum that is in the middle of the flower.

†**b.** A tuft, bundle, or fringe of any threadlike structures, as hairs on a leaf, fibres of a root, etc.

1578 Lyte *Dodoens* IV. lxvii. 529 Of Carline Thistel...Upon [the] stemme groweth a round flat head,..thromde like Ueluet, and round about that Ueluet throm, or Crowne, standeth a pale or inclosure, of..small white leaues, whiche is the flower. 1597 Gerarde *Herbal* I. xxxvi. § 1. 51 A fringe or thrum downe the middle of the lower leaues. *Ibid.* II. xvii. § 3. 200 The roote is nothing else but as it were a thrum or bundell of threedes. 1688 R. Holme *Armoury* II. 61/2 Three [leaves]..each having a yellow freez, or thrum near the bottome.

†**c.** A bundle of minute blood-vessels, a plexus.

1615 Crooke *Body of Man* 431 A thrumbe of crisped vessels called *Plexus Choroides*.., wherein the Animal spirits receiue their preparation.

**5.** *Brewing.* (See quots.) *dial.*

1828 *Craven Gloss.*, *Thrum*, a bundle of birch or twigs in a mash tub, to prevent the malt from escaping and through which the liquor percolates. 1877 *N. W. Linc. Gloss.*, *Thrum*, a small utensil of wicker-work affixed to the hole in a mash-tub in brewing, to hinder the malt from escaping when the wort is run off.

†**6.** Applied jocularly or contemptuously to a person (? one meanly or raggedly dressed). *Obs.*

1610 B. Jonson *Alch.* I. i, You were once..the good, Honest, plaine, liuery-three-pound-thrum; that kept Your masters worships house..For the vacations. 1705 Elstob in Hearne *Collect.* 30 Nov. (O.H.S.) I. 108 He eyes ye greasy Rout, Of gaping thrums, stand listning round about. 1727 Somerville *Canidia's Epithal.* 9 Each sprightly soph, each brawny thrum, Spent his first runnings here.

**7.** *attrib.* and *Comb.* **a.** *attrib.* Made or consisting of thrums or waste threads of yarn (or something resembling it), or having thrums inserted in or projecting from it (cf. Thrum *v.*2, Thrummed1): as *thrum beard, bonnet, hat, mat, mop, night-cap*; pertaining to or dealing in thrums, as *thrum shop*. **b.** *Comb.*: †**thrum cap**, a cap made of thrums; *transf.* a person wearing a thrum cap; hence †**thrum-capped** (-kæpt) *a.*, wearing a thrum cap; **thrum-chinned** (-tʃind) *a.* (*jocular*), bearded; **thrum-eyed** (-əid) *a.*, applied by florists to the short-styled form of a flower (esp. of the genus *Primula*), which shows the boss of 'thrums' or anthers (cf. 4 a) at the top of the corolla-tube (opp. to Pin-eyed); so **thrum eye**; †**thrum-flower**, (of Petiver) *Astrocarpus Clusii*, a native of the western Mediterranean region; †**thrum-stone**, Grew's name for asbestos, as being a fibrous mineral. See also Thrumwort.

1577 Hanmer *Anc. Eccl. Hist.* (1619) 307 A long *thrum beard. 1827 Scott *Highl. Widow* i, Duncan with the *thrum bonnet, and the other lords of the..towers of Kilchurn. [*Thrum cap: cf. quot. 1439 in 2.] 1624 Massinger *Renegado* I. iii, A witch with a thrum cap, That sells ale underground. 1676 Lady Fanshawe in *Mem.* Feb. an. 1650 (1829) 93, I..desired him [the cabin-boy] to be so good as to give me his blue thrum cap he wore, and his tarred coat ..and putting them on..I..stood upon the deck by my husband's side. 1690 Dryden *Don Sebast.* I. i, Hold, my dear Thrum-cap: I obey thee cheerfully. 1720 Strype *Stow's Surv.* (1754) I. I. xxvi. 196/1 (The Blue Coat Hospital) Their habit being now..a round thrum Cap tied with a red band, yellow Stockings. 1708 W. King *Art Cookery* (1807) 73 Would our *thrum-cappd ancestors find fault, For want of sugartongs, or spoons for salt? 1608 Middleton *Trick to Catch Old One* IV. iii, [Widows] that will marry unfledged boys before comely *thrum-chinned gentlemen. 1888 *Pall Mall G.* 19 May 6/1 Auriculas..with their characters of grey or green edge, pin or *thrum eye, &c. 1861 Darwin in *Jrnl. of Linnæan Soc., Botany* VI. 77 Florists who cultivate the Polyanthus and Auricula..call those which display the globular stigma at the mouth of the corolla 'pin-headed' or 'pin-eyed', and those which display the stamens *thrum-eyed. c 1711 Petiver *Gazophyl.* VI. lii, Small Spanish Purple *Thrum-flower,..Grows a Span high on the stony Hills of Salamanca. 1543 *Acc. Ld. High Treas. Scot.* VIII. 180 Twa *thrum hattis of silk, price of the pece xiiij s. 1590 [Tarlton] *News Purgat.* (1844) 120 A thrumbe hat she had of red. 1770 Cook *Voy. round World* II. ix. (1773) 453 Ends..hanging out..like the shag or *thrumb matts which [etc.]. 1753 Hogarth *Anal. Beauty* vi. 74 The inelegant and inanimate figure of a *thrum mop or muff. 1768 Sterne *Sent. Journ.*, *The Husband*, He sits..in his *thrum night-cap. 1796 Colquhoun *Police Metropolis* p. viii, Petty Pilferers at Old Iron Shops,..Rag and *Thrum Shops. 1681 Grew *Musæum* III. I. v. 313 *Thrum-Stone, as I call it. *Amianthus Lapis & Asbestinus.*

**Thrum** (þrʌm), *sb.*3 [Echoic: cf. Thrum *v.*3] An echoic word representing various sounds, esp. the tones produced by 'thrumming' a guitar or similar instrument; also *dial.* the purring of a cat.

[a 1553 Udall *Royster D.* II. i, Anon to our gitterne, thrumpledum, thrumpledum thrum.] 1798 Lawrence *Treat. Horses* II. i. 18 That..affectionate domestic the cat,..its feet kneading in unison with the grateful thrum. 1814 *Sporting Mag.* XLIV. 128 The soft and melodious thrum evincing the happy state of his [a cat's] feelings. 1845 T. Cooper *Purgatory of Suicides* (1877) 110 Fear not Grimalkin! she doth sing 'three-thrum'. 1863 W. Miller *Willie Winkie* ii, The cat's singing grey thrums To the sleeping hen. 1883 Bertha Thomas *George Sand* 119 The distant thrum of guitars. 1884 *Pall Mall G.* 4 July 4/1 The thrum-thrum, ting-ting, tum-a tum-tum of their banjoes filled the air.

†**Thrum**, *v.*1 *Obs. rare.* [? Related to Thrum *sb.*1: cf. Flemish '*drommen = dringhen*, premere, pressare, stipare, *drom*, *ghedrom*, pressura' (Kilian).]

**1.** *trans.* To compress, condense.

c 1205 Lay. 54 Feþeren he nom mid fingren & fiede on boc-felle..& þa þre boc þrumde to are [*i. e.* to one].

**2.** To press or crowd in; to cram.

1603 Harsnet *Pop. Impost.* 52 The Devills they had cast, did rebound back againe..which by this provision of Thrumming in Devills at the first might..haue been avoided.

**Thrum**, *v.*2 Also 6 throm, 7–9 **thrumb**. See also Thrummed1. [f. Thrum *sb.*2]

*trans.* To furnish or adorn with thrums or ends of thread (or something similar); to cover with thrums or small tufts, raise a pile upon (cloth); to make shaggy. Now *dial.*

c 1525 *Harl. MS.* 4217 art. 11 Hattes thrommyd with silke of diuerse collours. a 1562 Cavendish *Wolsey* (1893) 88 His hosyn, frome the kne upward, was alltogether thrommed with sylke. 1598 Florio, *Irtare*, to thrum, to make rough, hairie or brislie. 1809 Southey in *Q. Rev.* II. 41 When the young king is first invested with the..red sash of royalty (which is made of net work, and thrummed with red and yellow feathers). 1887 *Suppl. to* Jamieson, *Thrum*, to raise a tufted pile on knitted or woven woollen stuffs, to cover woollen cloth with small tufts like thrums.

†**b.** *transf.* and *fig.* To fringe or clothe. *Obs.*

1589 R. Harvey *Pl. Perc.* 13 Leaue thrumming thy Pibault Iestes with Scripture, Iron and Clay will not be tempered togither. 1591 Sylvester *Du Bartas* I. vii. 27 A craggy Rocks steep-hanging boss (Thrumm'd half with Ivie, half with crisped Moss). 1630 Drayton *Muses' Elysium* iv. 82, I could wish..this bank were thickly thrumb'd with grass As soft as sleave or sarcenet ever was.

†**c.** To twist, curl, twine; also *intr.* To curl (as hair). *Obs.*

1598 Florio, *Cincinnare*, to curle, or thrum any haire. 1668 Culpepper & Cole *Barthol. Anat.* III. i. 128 So in Æthiopia by a peculiar thrumming of their hairs, they are defended from the heat.

†**d.** *To thrum caps*: *lit.* to cover caps with thrums; a proverbial phrase expressing trifling, or waste of work and time. Also *to thrum buttons*, and absol. *to thrum*. *Obs.*

1594 Nashe *Unfort. Trav.* 9 The King stood not long a thrumming of buttons there. 1602 *Narcissus* (1893) 160 Why stand wee heere, as it were cappes a thrumming? 1614 J. Cooke *Greene's Tu Quoque* H ij b, I'de nere stand thrumming of Caps for the matter. 1626 Middleton *Women Beware Wom.* III. iii, I'll not stand all day thrumming, But quickly shoot my bolt. 1644 Quarles *Judgm. & Mercy* 18 Are we born to thrum caps, or pick straws?

**e.** *Naut.* To sew or fasten bunches of rope-yarn over (a mat or sail) so as to produce a shaggy surface, suitable to prevent chafing or stop a leak.

1711 [see Thrummed1 c]. 1783 Capt. Inglefield *Narr. Loss Centaur* 16 All the officers, passengers and boys, who were not of the profession of seamen, had been employed thrumming a sail which was passed under the ship's bottom. 1820 Scoresby *Acc. Arctic Reg.* II. 448 *note*, By thrumbing the sail, that is, sewing long bunches of ropeyarn all over it. 1838 Poe *A. G. Pym* Wks. 1864 IV. 66 A sail was thrummed, and got under the bows. 1848 G. Biddlecombe *Art of Rigging* 36 *Thrumming*, interplacing, in a regular manner, through intervals of matting made by a fid, short pieces of thrums, or ropeyarn. 1867 Smyth *Sailor's Word-bk.* s. v., A vessel, when leaky, is thrummed by working some heavy spare sail, as the spritsail, into a thrummed mat, greasing and tarring it well, passing it under the bottom, and heaving all parts tight.

**Thrum**, *v.*3 Also 7–9 **thrumb**. [Echoic: going with Thrum *sb.*3]

**1. a.** *intr.* To play on a stringed instrument, as a guitar, harp, etc., by plucking the strings; to play on any stringed instrument in an idle, mechanical, or unskilful way; to strum.

1592 Greene *Disput.* 25 Neither had he any excellent quallities but thrumming on the gittron. 1669 Pepys *Diary* 12 Apr., After sitting a while, thrumming upon my viall, and singing. 1766 Goldsm. *Vic. W.* xvii, Sophy, love, take your guitar, and thrum in with the boy a little. 1822 W. Irving *Braceb. Hall* v, Sometimes he even thrums a little on the piano. 1872 Calverley *Fly Leaves* (1903) 72 Bang, twang, clatter and clang, Strum, thrum, upon fiddle and drum.

**b.** *trans.* To play (a stringed instrument, or a tune on it) idly, monotonously, or unskilfully; to strum upon; also, to pluck, twang (a string).

a 1625 [see *thrumming* below]. 1675 Covel in *Early Voy. Levant* (Hakl. Soc.) 215 A little pittifull instrument with three wire strings, which every fellow thrums ordinarily about the street. 1681 Dryden *Abs. & Achit.* 439 Th' old Harp on which he thrums his Lays. 1758 L. Temple *Sketches* (ed. 2) 28 The Productions of our present Italian Masters are thrummed over for a Season. 1782 [T. Vaughan] *Fashionable Follies* II. cci. 113 Thrumming his guittar under her window. 1841 Catlin *N. Amer. Ind.* I. xxii. 159 Bows were strung and thrummed to test their elasticity. 1866 Mrs. Stowe *Litt. Foxes* 117 They thrum a few tunes on the piano. 1873 'Ouida' *Pascarèl* II. 15 The violin of Toccò thrummed a gay melody.

**2.** *intr.* To sound as an instrument or string when thrummed; to sound monotonously; to hum.

1763 *Poetry* in *Ann. Reg.* 245 With dead, dull, doleful, heavy hums..The sober hurdy-gurdy thrums. 1887 Gunter *Mr. Barnes* xxii. 159 And so with mandolins thrumming at their head they finally come up the avenue. 1900 *Westm. Gaz.* 9 Oct. 2/3 Looms are full of woollen webs, spinning-wheels are thrumming.

**b.** Of a cat: To purr. *dial.*

a 1810 Tannahill *Poems* (1846) 30 Auld baudrons sits, and croodling thrums. 1841 *P. Parley's Ann.* II. 324 She began to cock her tail,..and to purr and thrum as if all her sorrows were entirely forgotten.

**3. a.** *trans.* To recite or tell in a 'sing-song' or monotonous way; also, to hum over (a melody).

1710 Steele *Tatler* No. 173 ¶ 1 Horace and Virgil must be thrummed by a Boy as well before he goes to an Apprenticeship as to the University. 1807 W. Irving *Salmag.* XII. v. (1824) 216 Who the fair..vex, By thrumming for ever their weakness of sex. 1816 Scott *Antiq.* xxi, And then siccan stories as Sanders had..; and eh! as he wad thrum them ower and ower..ayont the ingle at e'en. a 1845 Hood *Compass* xxi, And as he walk'd to self he talked, Some ancient ditty thrumming, In under tone.

**b.** *intr.* To speak or read monotonously, to 'drone', mumble.

a 1774 Tucker *Lt. Nat.* (1834) II. 681 To despise every old woman that thrums over good books all day,..because she does not understand Latin. 1825 [see *thrumming* below]. 1829 Scott *Jrnl.* 26 Mar., Boswell..has thrummed upon this topic till it is threadbare. 1858 Bailey *Age* 152 Shall every ninny who can thrum on rhyme, Break all our ear-drums without tune or time?

**4.** To strike something with the fingers as if playing on a musical instrument; to drum upon (a table, etc.). **a.** *trans.*

c 1750 Shenstone *Colemira* 28 How I long..To view those rosy fingers strike the lyre! For late when bees to change their clime began How did I see 'em thrum the frying pan. 1848 Thackeray *Van. Fair* lxiii, She..dashing the pin through the card on to the table, sat thrumming it for a while.

**b.** *intr.* with *on* or *upon*.

1820 W. Irving *Sketch Bk.* I. 265 While I sat..meditating ..I was thrumming with the other hand upon the quarto. 1842 Tennyson *Will Waterproof* xx, I sit, my empty glass reversed, And thrumming on the table. 1865 G. Meredith *Rhoda Fleming* xv, The squire was thrumming on the back of his chair.

**5.** *slang.* (*trans.*) **a.** To beat (a person). ? *Obs.*

1604 Dekker *Honest Wh.* I. vii, Flat-cap,..y'are a flat foole, an Asse, a Gull, and I'le thrum you. 1676 Shadwell *Virtuoso* I. i, 'Sdeath! you sawcy Jades,..I'll thrum you. 1823 [see *thrumming* below].

**b.** In obscene sense: see quots. ? *Obs.*

1611 Florio, *Accencire ūna dónna*, to thrum a wench. 1762 Brydges *Burlesque Homer* (1797) I. 138 How they had thrum'd the maids of Troy.

Hence **Thrummed** (þrʌmd) *ppl. a.*; **Thru·mming** *vbl. sb.* and *ppl. a.*

a 1625 Fletcher *Woman's Prize* I. i, Your mistress..

must think This single thrumming of a fiddle..but even poor sport. **1681** DRYDEN *Span. Friar* I. ii, The thrumming of a guitar. **1697** COLLIER *Mor. Subj.* II. (1709) 19 As for Thrumming upon a Fiddle, he left it to such Finical Sparks as they were. **1823** PYNE *Wine & Walnuts* (1824) II. xv. 208 The ushers..begged a half holiday for the whole school, ..and thus they escaped a thrumming. **1825** SCOTT *Let.* 29 Nov., I am writing in the Court..little..enlivened by the thrumming of two very dull pleaders. **1840** LADY C. BURY *Hist. of Flirt* vii, Thrumming generally leads to whispering and love-making. **1876** GEO. ELIOT *Dan. Der.* I, Little tinklings of mule-bells and whirrings of thrumbed strings.

†**Thru·mble**, *v.*[1] *Obs. rare*$^{-1}$. In 4–5 also þrompel thromle. *intr.* In quot., To stumble.

**1362** LANGL. *P. Pl.* A. v. 201 He þrompelde [*v.rr.* stumblide, stumblid] atte þrexwolde and þreuh to þe grounde. **1393** *Ibid.* C. vii. 408 He thrumbled [*v.rr.* thromlide, trobled, stombelde, etc.] at þe þreshefold.

**Thrumble** (þrʌ·mb'l), **thrimble** (þri·mb'l), *v.*[2] Chiefly, now only, *Sc.* and *north. dial.* Forms: *α.* 6– **thrumble**, (9 **thrummle**). *β.* 6 **thrimbil, thrymble, thrimle, thrymle, thrimmil,** 8 **thrimmle,** 9 **thrimal, thrimmel,** 7– **thrimble.** [app. a derivative of THRUM *v.*[1] Cf. obs. Du. or Flem. '*drommel*, res simul compactæ et densæ; res compactiles' (Kilian); Du. *in een drommel verzamelen*, to crowd together.]

**1.** *trans.* To press, compress, squeeze; to crowd or heap together.

*α.* **1589** BRUCE *Serm. Sacram.* iii. I v, Peter..sayis: Thou art thrumbled and thrusted be the multitude, and zit thou speeris quha hes twitched thee. **1600** HOLLAND *Livy* XXVI. xxxix. 614 So thrumbled [L. *conglobati*] they were and thrust togither disorderly. **1603** — *Plutarch's Mor.* 258 Wicked and leawd folke, who gather, thrumble, and heape up together all sorts of gaine.

*β.* **1513** DOUGLAS *Æneis* III. ix. 67 Twa bodeis of our sort he [Polyphemus] tuke and raif; Intill his hiddius hand thaim thrimbillit and wrang. *Ibid.* v. xiii. 93 The fers Achil..Chasand affrayit Troianis..The gret rowtis to the wallis thrymbland. **1596** DALRYMPLE tr. *Leslie's Hist. Scotl.* (S.T.S.) I. 49 Marr lyes on the costsyde neist, thrimmilit..as it war intil a narrow boundes, in ane parte, bot in ane vthir parte..braider. **1836** M. MACKINTOSH *Cottager's Dau.* 78 The cruel boot, too, I hae hane Thrice thrimal'd on my leg.

**b.** *intr.* To make one's way by pushing or jostling: to push, jostle.

**1500–20** [implied in *thrumbler* below]. *a* **1598** ROLLOCK *Serm.* Wks. 1849 I. 493 She thrumbleth and thrusteth in at the gates of heaven. **1638** ADAMSON *Muse's Threnodie* i. (1774) 23 With kind embracements did we thurst and thrimble, (For in these days I was exceeding nimble). **1901** W. MORRISON *Johnston of W.* vi. 37 Even with all their help they could scarce 'thrumble through'.

**2.** *trans.* To press or rub between the finger and thumb; to finger, handle.

**1632** SHERWOOD, To thrumble, *frotter entre les doigts.* **1789** DAVIDSON *Seasons* 36 Taylors, fain the gear to thrimmle Of coward coofs. **1828** *Craven Gloss., Thrimble*, to pull or draw out with reluctance, to press...' He thrimbl'd out his sixpence wi' a deal to do'. **1906** J. PATTERSON *Wamphray* iv. 104 [Others] after 'thrimmling' the money in their fingers paid part of what they owed.

Hence †**Thru·mbler**, in 6 thrimlar, *Sc. Obs. rare*$^{-1}$, one who thrumbles, or makes his way by pressing; a hustler; **Thru·mbling** *vbl. sb.*

**1500–20** DUNBAR *Poems* lxiii. 47 Thrimlaris and thristaris, as thay war woid, Kokenis, and kennis na man of gude. **1649** KENMURE *Sp.* in *Sel. Biog.* (Wodrow Soc.) I. 398 The Kingdom of Heaven is not gotten but with much seeking, thrumbling and thrusting.

†**Thru·mble**, *v.*[3] *Obs. rare*$^{-1}$. [app. a derivative of THRUM *v.*[3]] *intr.* = THRUM *v.*[3] 1 a (in quot. *fig.*).

**1685** CROWNE *Sir C. Nice* II. 11 No, Madam, he's the General Guitarre o' the Town... *Vio.* Well, I have provided one shall thrumble on him.

**Thrummed** (þrʌmd), *ppl. a.*[1] Also 6 **thrombyed, throm(m)ed, thromde,** *Sc.* **thrumit,** 6–7 **thrumd, thrumbd, thrumb'd,** 6–9 **thrumbed,** 7–8 **thrum'd.** [f. THRUM *sb.*[2] or *v.*[2] + -ED.]

Covered or decked with thrums; having a nap or shaggy surface; also, fringed. *Obs.* or *dial.*

**1535** *Bury Wills* (Camden) 126, I gyf and bequeth to Alys Mannyng,..iij s. iiij d. and on new thrombyed hate. **1546** *Aberdeen Regr.* (1844) I. 237 Ane blak thrumit hat. **1562** BULLEYN *Bulwark, Bk. Simples* 16 b, The flowers is like a Blewe or White thrummed hatte. **1578** in Feuillerat *Revels Q. Eliz.* (1908) 287 Hattes of crymson silk and sylver thrommed and wreythed bandes. **1602** *Inv.* in *Collect. Archæol.* (1863) II. 98 One thrummed blanquett xviij*d.* **1603** KNOLLES *Hist. Turks* (1621) 529 The common soldiors used thrumd caps. **1609–10** in Willis & Clark *Cambridge* (1886) III. 353 Item pro .12. thrummed quishions xliiij*s.* **1615** CROOKE *Body of Man* 94 So becomming a thrummed rugge to keepe warme the Membranous and vnbloody guts and stomacke vnder it. **1650** FULLER *Pisgah* IV. vi. 101 A fringe in Hebrew..represented the complication, or conjunction of Gods commandments among themselves,..as the threads in those thrummed fringes were woven together. **1656** *Artif. Handsom.* 44 Many..by a thrumb'd stocking, a bumbast or bolstered garment,..endeavour to redeem themselves. **1665** SIR T. HERBERT *Trav.* (1677) 223 Carpets of silks, silk and gold, and of course thrumd-wool.

†**b.** *transf.* and *fig.*; in quot. 1607 perh. used for 'thatched'. *Obs.*

**1577** KENDALL *Flowers Epigr.* 17 b, The sun, the starres, the thrunbed thrones with siluer perle and gold. **1578** LYTE *Dodoens* I. viii. 15 The sayde..knoppes do open and put forth a fayre purple, thromde, or veluet floure. **1607** MIDDLETON *Michaelm. Term* I. ii, Wouldst thou..live in a poor thrummed house i' th' country?

**c.** *Naut.* Of a mat or sail: Having pieces of rope-yarn sewn upon or stuck through it so as to produce a dense shaggy surface: see quot. 1900.

**1711** W. SUTHERLAND *Shipbuild. Assist.* 162 Paunch, thrum'd Mats. **1798** CAPT. TROUBRIDGE in *Naval Chron.* XXIII. 19 With thrummed sails [we] reduced the leak. **1835** SIR J. ROSS *Narr. 2nd Voy.* liii. 686 The men had each a bed place with a canvas bottom, and a thrummed mat for a bed. **1900** F. T. BULLEN in *Daily News* 7 Aug. 3/4 They must..lay loosely spread the collision mat, a mass of rope and thrummed yarn, about fifteen feet square, four inches thick, and weighing about a quarter of a ton.

**Thrummed,** *ppl. a.*[2]: see THRUM *v.*[3]

**Thrummer** (þrʌ·məɹ). [f. THRUM *v.*[3] + -ER [1].] One who thrums or strums on a stringed instrument; an idle or indifferent player.

**1706** E. WARD *Hud. Rediv.* I. x. 8 A Welsh Thrummer's slaving Ass, That carr's his Harp from Place to Place. *a* **1810** TANNAHILL *Wand. Bard* Poems (1846) 108 No, thou old intruding thrummer, Thou canst have no lodging here. **1850** S. DOBELL *Roman* vii, To the buttery-hatch, Ye strolling thrummers.

**Thrumming,** *vbl. sb.* and *ppl. a.*: see THRUM *v.*[3]

**Thrummy** (þrʌ·mi), *a.* Now *rare.* [f. THRUM *sb.*[2] + -Y.] Consisting of, characterized by, or resembling thrums; covered with thrums; shaggy, downy, velvety. Formerly of flowers with conspicuous anthers, of fibrous roots, etc. (cf. THRUM *sb.*[2] 4).

**1597** GERARDE *Herbal* I. xi. § 2. 13 His roote is..made of many thrummie threds. **1598** FLORIO, *Velutoso*, soft, woolly, thrummie, full of silke or veluet. *c* **1600** CHALKHILL *Thealma & Cl.* (1683) 102 In Furrs yclad, And on her Head a thrummy Cap she had. **1659** TORRIANO, *Filaccio*, course raw silk, thrummy yarn. **1697** J. PETIVER in *Phil. Trans.* XIX. 680 At the top of each Branch stand small thrummy Flowers. **1703** DAMPIER *Voy.* III. I. 158 A Columella thick set with thrummy *apiculæ* which argue this Plant to belong to the Malvaceous kind. **1909** A. REID *Kirriemuir* ii. 11 The weaver's dress was often very 'thrummy'.

**Thrumwort** (þrʌ·mˌwɒɹt). [f. THRUM *sb.*[2] + WORT.] A name for different plants having parts resembling thrums. **a.** The water-plantain, *Alisma Plantago* (or other species); also the allied star-fruit, *Actinocarpus Damasonium.* **b.** 'Love-lies-bleeding', *Amarantus caudatus.*

**1829** *Glover's Hist. Derby* I. 112 *Alisma ranunculoides*, lesser thrum wort...*Alisma lanceolata*, narrow-leaved thrum wort. **1866** *Treas. Bot.* 1147 Thrumwort, *Actinocarpus*; also *Amaranthus caudatus.* **1879** PRIOR *Names Brit. Plants, Thrum-wort*...The plant has its name from its long tassel-like panicles of red flowers, the florimer, *Amarantus caudatus.* **1886** BRITTEN & HOLLAND *Eng. Plant-n.*, Thrum-wort. (1) *Amaranthus caudatus*...(2) A book-name for *Actinocarpus Damasonium*...Thrumwort, Great, *Alisma Plantago.*

**Thrung, Thrunter**: see THRING *v.*, THRINTER.

**Thrus, thrusche**: see THRUSH, THURSE.

†**Thrusche,** *v. Sc. Obs.* [Etymology and meaning obscure; perhaps there are here two words.

In sense 2, possibly :—OE. *þyrscan in *ge-*, *of-þyrscan*, 'to press, press down, repress'; but this does not suit sense 1, for which some suggest identity with FRUSH *v.*, with *th* for *f*; but this also seems to fail to give the sense 'cut or cleave'.]

**1.** *trans.* ? To cut asunder, cleave.

*c* **1470** HENRY *Wallace* III. 190 The thrusande blaid his hals in sonder schayr. *Ibid.* XI. 252 His gud suerd..His body in twa it thurschyt euirlikdeill. **1483** *Cath. Angl.* 387/2 To Thrusche. [No Latin.]

**2.** To thrust, press.

**1600** *Sc. Acts Jas. VI* (1816) IV. 206/2 [He] pullit vp the brod of the windo Quhairvnto the said mr alexander had thrusschit his majesteis heid and schulderis. [Panton's *Dissert. Gowry Consp.* 1812, quotes the passage with *thrust.*]

**Thrush** [1] (þrʌʃ). Forms: 1 **ðræsce, þrysce, þryssce, þrisce,** 3 **þrusche** (*ü*), **þruysse** (*for* **þrüshe**), 4 **þrusch,** 5–6 **thrusshe, thrushe** (5 **thryshe, thrusche, thrus,** 7 **thresh**); 6– **thrush.** [Two ablaut-forms in OE.: *α.* *þrysce*, later *pryssce*, wk. fem. :—O. Teut. **þrûskjôn.* For the change of vowel in ME. *þrusche, thrush*, cf. *clutch, crutch, rush, thrutch*, with *u* (*v*) from *y* (*ü*); in 15th c., some dialects retained *þruysse* (= *prüshe*) and *thryshe*, and *thrice-cock* (for *thrȳshe-cock*) is still a dialect-name of the missel-thrush. *β.* OE. had *a* 800 Anglian *þræsce* = WSax. **þréasce* = OHG. *drôsca* :—OTeut. **þrauskôn.* Examples of this form are rare, and indeed not yet cited in ME., where it would be **presche*, **thresshe*; but *thresh* occurs in 17th c., and the derivative *thresher* is dialectal in Oxfordsh. and Berksh. Cf. also the U.S. *thrasher.* There are also the derivative forms *thrushel, thrishel, thrissel*, from the *a* type: see THRUSHEL.]

**1.** Historically, A name of two British and general European birds; (1) primarily, and without qualification, that also called *Throstle* and *Mavis*, distinctively *Song-thrush* (*Turdus musicus*); (2) the *Mistletoe thrush, Mistle-*, or *Missel-thrush* (*T. viscivorus*), a larger and less musical species. Thence extended (with qualifications) by ornithologists to other species of the genus *Turdus* (many of which, in vernacular language, have other names, and are not regarded as thrushes), or more widely, to all members of the family *Turdidæ.* By colonists, travellers, etc., transferred, with qualifications, to birds of other lands, allied to the European thrushes, or merely resembling these in general appearance or some feature; see b.

The song-thrush is locally known as THROSTLE and MAVIS, dialectally *thrushel, thrustle, thrusher, thrush-field, whistling thrush*; the missel-thrush, as *bull thrush, gawthrush, holm-t., horse-t., marble-t., Norman t., stone-t., wood-t., thrush-cock, throstle-cock, storm-cock*, etc. In OE. and ME., *thrush* and *throstle* are sometimes mentioned as distinct birds: see THROSTLE. Among the thrushes (*Turdi*) of ornithology, are the redwing, fieldfare, blackbird, ring-ouzel, of Great Britain, and the robin, veery, hermit-thrush, wood-thrush, and other species of North America.

*α.* *c* **1000** *Voc.* in Wr.-Wülcker 260/30 *Trutius*, þrisce. *c* **1000** *Voc.* ibid. 286/23 *Strutio*, þrysce. *a* **1250** *Owl & Night.* 1659 þruysse [*MS. Cott.* þrusche] & þrostle & wodewale. *c* **1350** *Will. Palerne* 820 Briddes þat bliþeliche song, Boþe þe þrusch & þe þrustele. **1413** *Pilgr. Sowle* (Caxton) v. v. (1859) 76, I bethought me vppon the byrdes as thrusshes, and thrustels, and stares whiche I haue sene. **14..** *Voc.* in Wr.-Wülcker 595/20 *Mauiscus, anglice* a thryshe. **14..** *Nom.* ibid. 702/39 *Hic garulus*, a thrus. *c* **1460** J. RUSSELL *Bk. Nurture* 438 Of quayle, sparow, larke,..pygeoun, swalow, thrusche, osulle. **1530** PALSGR. 281/1 Thrusshe a byrde, *gryue.* **1596** SPENSER *F. Q.* VI. iv. 17 Abrode to wend, To take the ayre and heare the thrushes song. **1624** CAPT. SMITH *Virginia* II. 27 There are..Thrushes and divers sorts of small Birds. **1658** CHARLETON *Onomast.* 83 *Turdus*,..theThrush, Song-Thrush, or Throssle, or Mavis. **1746** FRANCIS tr. *Horace, Epist.* I. xv. 51 A fat Thrush is most delightful Food, And a Swine's Paunch superlatively good. **1810** SCOTT *Lady of L.* III. ii, The blackbird and the speckled thrush Good-morrow gave from brake and bush.

*β.* *c* **725** *Corpus Gloss.* (O.E.T.) 2063 *Truitius*, ðræsce. *c* **1676** *Roxb. Ball.* (1886) VI. 305 'Oh!' says the squeaking little Thresh, 'My Sorrows now begin afresh'. [**1904** *Eng. Dial. Dict.* s.v. *Thrusher*, Also in form *thresher* Oxf., Bucks...The song-thrush.]

**b.** With qualifying words (indicating native country, colour, food, habits, etc.) applied to various species of the genus *Turdus* or family *Turdidæ*; also popularly to numerous species of other families (starlings, warblers, shrikes, etc.) more or less resembling the true thrushes: as **Babbling thrush**: = *thrush-babbler* in 3. **Chinese thrush,** *Trochalopterum canorum*; †**Golden thrush**: early name of the Golden Oriole. **Harmonic thrush,** *Collyriocincla harmonica*, of Australia. **Long-legged thrush,** any bird of Swainson's subfamily *Crateropodinæ*, also called *babblers*, formerly classed with the thrushes. **Migratory thrush,** the American robin. **New York thrush,** an American Water-thrush, *Seiurus nævius.* **Olive-backed thrush** = OLIVE-BACK. **Pacific thrush,** a Polynesian bird, *Lalage pacifica.* **Red thrush, Red-breasted thrush,** the American robin. **Shining thrush,** a W. African glossy starling, *Lamprocolius splendidus.* **Shrike-thrush**: see SHRIKE. **Songster thrush,** *Calornis panayensis*, of the Philippines. **Spectacle thrush,** *Garrulax perspicillatus*, of Southern China and Siam. **Varied thrush,** the Oregon robin, *Hesperocichla nævia.* **Whidah thrush,** a W. African starling, *Pholidauges leucogaster.* **Wilson's thrush,** the VEERY of N. America. **Wind-thrush,** local name of the REDWING. **Wine thrush,** a S. African species, *Turdus olivaceus.* See also ANT-THRUSH, GROUND-THRUSH, HERMIT-THRUSH, ROCK-THRUSH, WATER-THRUSH, WOOD-THRUSH.

*a* **1705** RAY *Syn. Avium & P.* (1713) 64 *Turdus viscivorus minor*.., the Mavis, Throstle, or Song-Thrush... *Turdus Iliacus*.., the Red-Wing, Swine Pipe or Wind-Thrush. **1731** MEDLEY *Kolben's Cape G. Hope* II. 160 The Wine-thrushes have their name from their loving of grape-stones. **1750** EDWARDS *Nat. Hist. Birds* III. 185 The Golden Thrush. Icterus...They are found in the Southern Parts of Europe all the Summer Season. **1754** CATESBY *Nat. Hist. Carolina* (ed. 2) I. 30 The red-leg'd Thrush, *Turdus viscivorus plumbeus.* *Ibid.* 31 The little Thrush (*Turdus minimus*). In shape and colour it agrees with the description of the European *Mavis*, or Song-Thrush, differing only in bigness. **1783** LATHAM *Gen. Synopsis Birds* II. I. 36 *Chinese Thrush*, less than a Redwing. *Ibid.* 61 *Spectacle Thrush*, a Trifle bigger than a Blackbird. *a* **1792** S. HEARNE *Journ. Northern Ocean* x. (1795) 418 The Red-breasted Thrushes, commonly called in Hudson's Bay..Red Birds. **1827** AUDUBON *Jrnls.* 2 May, The Red Thrush. **1843** *Ibid.* 27 May, This morning my ears were saluted by the delightful song of the Red Thrush. **1898** MORRIS *Austral Eng.*, *Thrush*,..applied in Australia and New Zealand to four [*sic*] different genera of birds, viz.—(1) *Collyriocincla*, the Shrike-Thrushes...(2) *Geocincla*, the Ground-Thrushes. (3) *Oreocincla*, the Mountain-Thrush. (4) *Pachycephala*; called Thrushes, but more often Thickheads. (5) *Turnagra* (the New Zealand Thrushes).

†**2.** *Sea-thrush, thrush-fish*, names given (after L. *turdus*) to various species of wrasse (*Labrus*), of which *L. turdus* is common in the Mediterranean; *L. maculatus* the Ballan wrasse, and *L. mixtus* the striped wrasse, are found also on the British coasts.

**1601** HOLLAND *Pliny* IX. xv. I. 244 Of Stone-fishes, such as live among rocks, the sea Thrush, the sea Merle, and the purple shell-fishes are not to be found. **1661** LOVELL *Hist. Anim. & Min.* 235 *Thrush-fish*...They are very difficultly concocted yet Pliny counteth them good. **1726** LEONI *Alberti's Archit.* I. 97/2 The Sea-thrush and Whiting feed best among the Rocks.

**3.** *Comb.* as *thrush-haunted, -like* adjs.; **thrush-babbler** = BABBLER 4; **thrush-blackbird,** a name for the Rusty Grackle, *Scolecophagus ferrugineus* (*Cent. Dict.* 1891); **thrush-breast** *a.*, speckled like a thrush's breast; †**thrush-fish** = *sea-thrush* (sense 2 above); **thrush-nightingale,** a nightingale (*Daulias philomela*) with a slightly speckled breast, found in central and eastern Europe; **thrush-tit**, a book-name for birds of the genus *Cochoa* (or *Xanthogenys*), inhabiting the Himalayas, China, and Java (*Cent. Dict.* 1891).

1878 P. ROBINSON *In my Indian Gard.* II. 83 The feeble-winged thrush-babblers were wrangling over worms. 1896 *Allbutt's Syst. Med.* I. 191 [The walls of the fatty heart] frequently present a 'tabby-cat' or '*thrush-breast' appearance. 1905 *Speaker* 9 Sept. 548 *Thrush-haunted woods and peaceful shades. 1842 *Penny Cycl.* XXIII. 173/1 The chief peculiarities of the grakles, viz. the strong *thrush-like bill [etc.]. 1872 COUES *N. Amer. Birds* 76 Aquatic thrush-like birds. 1840 *Penny Cycl.* XVI. 231/1 The *Thrush Nightingale.. inhabiting central Europe. 1904 *Westm. Gaz.* 30 Nov. 12/1 Known as the thrush nightingale, and in Germany as the 'Sprosser'.

**Thrush** [2] (þrɒʃ). [Not known in either sense before the 17th c., though the phonology of the word, with *þ* and *sh*, indicates English origin, and points to an OE. **þrusc*. The only continental cognates appear to be, in sense 1, Sw. and ODa. *törsk*, Da. *troske*, Sw. dial. *trosk*, which Falk and Torp refer to an ON. **þruskr*. See *Note* below.]

**1.** A disease, chiefly of infants, characterized by white vesicular specks on the inside of the mouth and throat, and on the lips and tongue, caused by a parasitic fungus (see *thrush-fungus* in 3); scientifically called *aphtha* or *parasitic stomatitis*.

1665 PEPYS *Diary* 17 June, He hath a fever, a thrush and a hickup. 1712 *Pomet's Hist. Drugs* I. 47 A Gargle of it cures the Thrush. 1828 MRS. BRAY *Protestant* xvii. (1884) 180 The thrush, colic, and other disorders incidental to children. 1877 ROBERTS *Handbk. Med.* (ed. 3) I. 289 Thrush is frequently associated with typhoid fever.

**2.** In the horse, An inflammation of the lower surface of the frog of the hoof, accompanied with a fetid discharge. Cf. FRUSH *sb.*[2]

1753 J. BARTLET *Gentl. Farriery* (1754) 319 Of the Running Thrush. Bathe the thrush with this, wherever there appears a more than ordinary moisture, and lay over the ulcer a little tow dipped in the same. 1810 *Sporting Mag.* XXXVI. 154 It had a thrush, spavins and contracted knees. 1831 [YOUATT] *Horse* xvi. 307 Thrush is a discharge of offensive matter from the cleft of the frog. It is inflammation of the lower surface of the sensible frog.

**3.** *Comb.*: **thrush-fungus**, the parasitic fungus *Saccharomyces albicans*, which causes thrush (sense 1); **thrush-lichen, thrush-moss**, a species of lichen, *Peltigera aphthosa*, found on moist alpine rocks, and used in Sweden boiled in milk as a cure for thrush (sense 1); **thrush-paste**, an astringent paste for curing thrush in horses (sense 2).

1759 STILLINGFL. *Misc. Tracts* (1775) 217 The countrey people taught us the virtues of the thrush-moss for sore throats. 1858 SIMMONDS *Dict. Trade, Thrush Lichen*, the *Peltidea apthosa*. 1888 *Cassell's Encycl. Dict.*, Thrush-lichen... Thrush-paste. 1899 CAGNEY *Jaksch's Clin. Diagn.* iii. (ed. 4) 113 In a few cases, thrush-fungus and vegetations have been found in the nose.

[*Note.* Norw. has *fresk, frosk* 'thrush', phonetically identical with *frosk* frog; cf. Norw. dial. *trausk* = *frausk*, 'frog', which seems to rest upon an old phonetic confusion of **þruskr* and *froskr*. Some would connect this with the fact that Gr. βάτραχος and L. *rāna, rānula*, 'frog', were also names of a disease in the mouth of cattle. The evidence of Eng. is however that **þrosc* = *ON. *þruskr*, was the orig. word for the disease in sense 1. The connexion of sense 2 is not explained; can it be connected with Da. *trøske* rotten or decayed wood, 'rottenness in the bones'?]

**Thrush**, variant of THURSE, goblin.

**Thrush, thrush-bush**: see THRASH *sb.*[2]

**Thrush-a-thrush.** *dial. rare.* Also **thrush.** Name of some boys' game.

1760–72 H. BROOKE *Fool of Qual.* (1809) I. 20 Leap-frog, and thrush-a-thrush. 1880 *Antrim & Down Gloss.*, Thrush.

**Thrushel** (þrɒ·ʃěl). Now *dial.* Also 5 **thruschyl, thrusshill**, 9 **thrishell** (*Devon*). [A derivative of THRUSH *sb.*[1], prob. dim.; cf. OHG. *drôscala*, dim. of *drôsca*, MHG. *drôschele*, dial. *droschel, druschel, drouschel*. Dialectally these forms tend to fall together with variants of THROSTLE and Ger. *drossel*.] A name, now local, of the thrush or song-thrush.

*c* 1430 LYDG., Thruschylcok [see THROSTLE-COCK]. 1499 *Promp. Parv.* (ed. Pynson), Thrusshill or thrustyll, *merula*. 1881 MISS JACKSON *Shropsh. Wordbk.* 441 *Thrushel*, same as *Throstle*: Bridgnorth. 1885 SWAINSON *Prov. Names Birds* 3 (Song Thrush) Thrusher (Berks and Bucks), Dirsh (Somerset), Thrushfield (Salop), Thrushel or Thrustle (Salop), Thirstle (Devon, Cornwall, Salop).

**Thru·shling.** *nonce-wd.* [See -LING.] A young thrush.

1899 P. ROBINSON in *Contemp. Rev.* 347 Surely a thrushling sitting on a tennis lawn.

**Thru·shy,** *a.* [f. THRUSH [2] 2 + -Y.] Pertaining to or affected with thrush (sense 2).

1831 [YOUATT] *Horse* xvi. 307 When the frog.. becomes.. diseased, the cleft.. penetrates even to the sensible horn within, and through this.. fissure the thrushy discharge proceeds. *Ibid.* 308 Turning out would be prejudicial rather than of benefit to thrushy feet.

**Thrust** (þrɒst), *sb.* Also 6– *Sc.* and *north. dial.* **thrist.** [f. THRUST *v.*, in various senses.]

**I. †1.** An act of pressing or pressure (see sense 4 of the verb); chiefly *fig.* 'pinch', hardship. *Obs.*

In phr. *heap and thrust*, app. used *attrib.* = heaped up and pressed down; cf. THRUTCH *sb.*, quot. 1678.

1513 DOUGLAS *Æneis* VI. ii. 33 Withdraw the from na perrellis, nor hard thrist. 1535 STEWART *Cron. Scot.* (Rolls) II. 548 Tak tent in tyme or ȝe be put in thrist. *a* 1600 MONTGOMERIE *Misc. Poems* xxiv. 76 Sen thou art thrald, think thou mon thole a thrist. 1670 CAPT. J. SMITH *Eng. Improv. Reviv'd* 91, 16000 Bushels of Chaff or Hulls worth 3 pence the Bushel heap and thrust.

**†2.** Pressure or pushing of a crowd, jostling, crowding; a crowd, throng, 'press'. *Obs.*

1565 COOPER *Thesaurus* s.v. *Arceo, Arctum theatrum* ..wherin is great thronge or thrust. 1588 PARKE tr. *Mendoza's Hist. China* 295 They were verie faint with the great thrust and throng of the people. 1600 FAIRFAX *Tasso* XX. xvii, What can he do..In that confusion, trouble, thrust and throng? 1615 CHAPMAN *Odyss.* III. 52 In thrust did all men draw About their entry. 1620 SHELTON *Quix.* (1746) IV. xx. 164 Two of them, bold Crack-ropes, came among the Thrust.

**3.** *Mech.*, etc. A pushing force exerted by one part of a structure, etc. upon another contiguous part: *spec.* (*a*) *Arch.*, etc. Such a force exerted laterally by an arch or other part of a building or structure against an abutment or support; (*b*) the driving force exerted by a paddle or propeller-shaft in a ship or aeroplane; (*c*) *Mining*: see quot. 1881; (*d*) *Geol.* a compressive strain in the earth's crust.

1708 J. C. *Compl. Collier* (1845) 30 [Lest it] bring a Thrust, or a general Crush in one of your Collieries. 1739 LABELYE *Short Acc. Piers Westm. Br.* 44 The lower an Arch is, in proportion to its Opening, the greater is the Thrust it exerts against its Piers. 1853 SIR H. DOUGLAS *Milit. Bridges* (ed. 3) 326 In.. truss-frame bridges.. there is no thrust or pressure against the abutments, as in arched bridges. 1869 SIR E. J. REED *Shipbuild.* i. 8 Intended to aid in distributing the thrust of the paddleshaft. 1881 RAYMOND *Mining Gloss.*, *Thrust*, the breaking down or the slow descent of the roof of a gangway. Compare *Creep*. 1903 *Nature* 12 Feb. 359/1 Local thrusts and shear slips took place again, fragmenting the previous thrust-masses and igneous intrusions. 1909 *Westm. Gaz.* 18 Mar. 4/1 The result of revolving a screw in water or air is to project a current.. in a direction approximately parallel to the axis of the screw, and the reaction from this in the opposite direction to which the current is flowing is called the 'thrust', and the aim of every designer is to obtain the greatest possible thrust from any given dimensions of propeller when working at its designed speed.

**b.** Short for *thrust-bearing*: see 7.

1875 BEDFORD *Sailor's Pocket Bk.* vi. (ed. 2) 211 Have every.. part of the engines carefully oiled, especially cylinders, slide-valves, eccentrics, cranks, and thrust.

**4.** = *thrustings*, THRUSTING *vbl. sb.* 2.

1877 KNIGHT *Dict. Mech.*, *Thrust*,.. the white whey which last leaves the curd in pressing.

**II. 5.** An act, or the action, of thrusting (in sense 1 of the vb.); a forcible push or pushing. Also *fig.*

1823 SCOTT *Quentin D.* xxii, 'Take away the carrion' (giving the bishop's corpse a thrust with his foot). 1860 TYNDALL *Glac.* I. iii. 26 The thrust of the descending glacier. 1866 J. MARTINEAU *Ess.* I. 151 A logical thrust of the ostrich-head into the sand.

**6.** An act of thrusting (in sense 5 of the vb.); a lunge or stab made with a weapon.

*a* 1586 SIDNEY *Arcadia* II. (1590) 153 b, Zelmane harkening to no more wordes, began with such wittie furie to pursue him with blowes and thrustes. 1592 SHAKS. *Rom. & Jul.* I. i. 120 While we were enterchanging thrusts and blowes. 1601 R. JOHNSON *Kingd. & Commw.* (1603) 203 Garments of cotten wooll so close and hard quilted that they woulde beare out the thrust of a lance or sword. 1687 A. LOVELL tr. *Thevenot's Trav.* I. 127 They were taught to bend the Bow, shoot exact, give a true thrust with a Launce. 1779, 1828 [see PARRY *sb.* 1]. 1840 DICKENS *Barn. Rudge* xvii, I made a thrust at him. 1879 G. MEREDITH *Egoist* xliii, He depended entirely on his agility to elude the thrusts that assailed him.

**b.** *transf.* and *fig.*

1668 H. MORE *Div. Dial.* I. xi. 41 There is one thrust at your pure pretended Mechanism. 1852 MRS. H. B. STOWE *Uncle Tom's C.* xxii, The faithful old heart felt a sudden thrust. 1859 MEREDITH *R. Feverel* xlii, White thrusts of light were darted from the sky. 1872 MORLEY *Voltaire* i. 8 Those shrewd thrusts, that flashing scorn, that relentless fire,.. with which.. Voltaire pushed on his work of 'crushing the Infamous'.

**c.** In phr. *Cut and thrust*: see CUT *sb.*[2] 2 c; *thrust and parry* (*lit.* and *fig.*).

1763–1875 [see CUT *sb.*[2] 2 c]. 1889 *Pall Mall G.* 18 Oct. 1/2 A rollicking candidate whose thrust-and-parry recalls the days of the hustings. 1894 A. BIRRELL *Men, Women & Bks.* (ed. 2) 209 Swaggering Bohemians, cut-and-thrust men. 1905 WARREN in Alderson *Asquith* ii. 20 In the rapid thrust and parry of passing repartee.

**†d.** A bout of thrusting; a contest or encounter with swords. *Obs.*

1602 EARL NORTHUMBLD. in Collins *Peerage* (1779) II. 413 They two should have a thruste together. 1816 SCOTT *Bl. Dwarf* xii, I should like well to have a thrust with him on the green turf.

**7.** *Comb.* **†thrust-bearer, thrust-bearing**, a bearing designed to receive a thrust in machinery; *spec.* the bearing in which revolves the foremost length of propeller-shafting in a screw steamer, its function being to transmit the thrust of the shaft to the hull of the ship; **thrust-block**, a block supporting a thrust-bearing; the casting or frame carrying or containing the bearings on which the collars of the propeller-shaft press; **thrust-box**, a box-bearing which sustains the end-thrust of a shaft (*Cent. Dict.*); **thrust-collar**, each of the series of collars on a propeller-shaft, through which the thrust of the shaft is transmitted to the thrust-block and thence to the hull of the ship; **thrust-fault** *Geol.*, a reversed fault: = OVERFAULT; **thrust-hoe**: see HOE *sb.*[2] 1 b; **thrust-mass** *Geol.*, the displaced mass of rock in an overfault; **thrust-movement**, movement caused by a thrust (3 *d*); **thrust-post**, a post so placed as to take the thrust from a load or force; **thrust-ring**, a brass ring made in two halves fitted in between the collars on the thrust-shaft to transmit the horizontal thrust of the shaft to the thrust-block; **thrust screw**, a thrusting-screw (THRUSTING *vbl. sb.* 3); see also quot. 1888; **thrust-shaft**, a propeller-shaft; *spec.* that part of the shaft on which are the thrust-collars. See also THRUST-PLANE.

1869 SIR E. J. REED *Shipbuild.* xv. 287 In a Screw steamship it is necessary to make some arrangement by means of which the thrust of the propeller shaft shall be transmitted to the ship, and the injurious effects prevented which would result from the direct action of the thrust upon the machinery. For this purpose *thrust-bearers are fitted. 1864 WEBSTER, **Thrust-bearing* (Screw-steamers). 1889 WHITHAM *Steam Engine Design* 264 Another form of thrust bearing often used consists of a single thrust collar, forged with the shaft. 1906 SENNETT & ORAM *Marine Steam Engine* 285 a, An ordinary plummer block should always be fitted close to the thrust bearing to take the weight of the shaft. 1893 *Pall Mall G.* 2 Jan. 5/2 The shaft in the *thrust-block is twenty-five inches in diameter, and of solid steel. 1906 SENNETT & ORAM *M. S. Eng.* 285 a, Thrust blocks are carried on strong plate bearers generally fixed to not less than three frames of the ship. 1889 *Thrust-collar [see *thrust-bearing*]. 1903 *Nature* 20 Aug. 375/1 The overfolding and repetition of strata by *thrust-faults. 1901 *Ibid.* 24 Jan. 294/2 Three higher tiers of *thrust-masses are present on the west of the Linth Valley. 1890 *Hardwicke's Sci. Gossip* XXVI. 238/1 An arch of Cambrian rocks.. repeatedly broken on the west side by *thrust-movements, causing newer beds to be driven over beds of various horizons, in some cases many thousands of feet apart in the succession. 18.. WHITHAM *Const. Steam Engin.* 102 *Thrust-ring. 1906 SENNETT & ORAM *M. S. Eng.* 285 a, Another form of thrust block.. containing separate brass thrust rings fitted in the bearing to form the rubbing surfaces. 1858 SIMMONDS *Dict. Trade*, *Thrust-screw. 1888 *Lockwood's Dict. Terms Mech. Engin.* 374 *Thrust Screw*, a screw with or without the power of endlong adjustment, which takes the thrust of a revolving spindle. Examples of thrust screws occur at the top of the drill spindles of some drilling machines, and in the back centres of the headstocks of lathes. 1893 *Daily News* 6 Feb. 6/3 The Cunard steamer Umbria.. will be placed in the graving dock.. and refitted with new *thrust shaft. 1906 SENNETT & ORAM *M. S. Eng.* 285 a, These horseshoe collars fit between the collars on the thrust shaft.

**Thrust** (þrɒst), *v.* Pa. t. and pple. **thrust.** Forms: see below. [Early ME. (*c* 1200) *þrusten* (*ü*), *þrysten*, a. ON. *þrýsta* to thrust, press, compress, force (Norw. *tryste*, Aasen, to press, squeeze). ON. *þrýsta* (:–*þrūstj-*) has been doubtfully referred to Indo-Eur. *trud-, trūd-*, in L. *trūdere* to thrust (Falk and Torp).]

**A.** Illustration of Forms.

**1.** *Inf.* and *Pres. stem.* α. 3 ***þrust-e** (*ü*), 3–6 **þrist-en**, 4 **þrist**, 4–6 **thrist**, 5 **thryste.**

*c* 1300 *Havelok* 1152, I shal hangen þe ful heye, Or y shal þristen vt þin eie. *c* 1330 Þrist [see B. 3]. 1388 WYCLIF *Mark* iii. 9 Lest thei thristen hym. 1483 *Cath. Angl.* 386/1 To Thryste downe, *oppremere*. 1510–20 *Everyman* in Hazl. *Dodsley* I. 138 Go, thrist thee into the ground. 1596 DALRYMPLE tr. *Leslie's Hist. Scot.* VII. (S.T.S.) II. 43 Sche thristis in her tender arme into the hole of the bar.

β. 5 **þrust-e**, 6–7 **thruste** (7 **thurst**), 6– **thrust.**

*c* 1440 *Alphabet of Tales* 347 Yisterday he thristid down þe erth, and þis day þe erth þrustis hym down. 1530, etc. Thrust [see B. 3, etc.]. 1560 DAUS tr. *Sleidane's Comm.* 216 b, He fortuned to thruste of a stone.

**2.** *Pa. tense.* α. 2–3 **þruste** (*ü*), 3–5 **þriste, þrist**, 4 **thryste**, 4–5 **thriste.**

[*c* 1175 *Lamb. Hom.* 131 He to-þruste þa stelene gate and to-brec þa irene barren of helle.] *c* 1205 LAY. 30341 Æiðer þratte oðer swiðe and þruste mid worde. *c* 1250 Ðrist, *c* 1290 Þruste [see B. 1]. *c* 1374 Þriste [see B. 6 b].

β. 5–6 **thruste** (5 **throste**, 6 **thurst**), 6– **thrust.**

*c* 1410 Thruste [see B. 5]. *c* 1470 HARDING *Chron.* XII. ii. (MS. Ashm. 34) lf. 12 b, This Gogmagog so throste [*v. rr.* thrast, -e] Coryneus. 1526, 1535– Thrust; 1560 Thruste [see B. 1, 1 c, etc.]. 1568 Thurst [see B. 6].

γ. 5 **thristid** (5–6 *Sc.* **-it**), 6 **thristed**; 7–8 **thrusted.**

*c* 1440 Thristid [see A. 1 β]. *c* 1475 Thristit [see B. 3]. 1560 ROLLAND *Crt. Venus* IV. 590 Swa in hir armis than scho him thristit. 1634 CANNE *Necess. Separ.* (1849) 194 He thrusted out Cain from the same. 1788 Thrusted [see B. 6 b].

**3.** *Pa. pple.* α. 4 **þryst**, 4–5 **thrist**, 5 **thriste, thryst, þirstyn.**

*c* 1330 R. BRUNNE *Chron. Wace* (Rolls) 8889 When þey ofte hadde put & þryst.. ȝit stirede þey nought þe leste ston. 13.. Thrist [see B. 6 quot. *a* 1300]. 14.. *Gosp. Nicodemus* (A.) 1443 And in thraldame thrist hym þou has. 1435 MISYN *Fire of Love* I. v. 11 To god þai ȝelde no deuocion, for þe byrdyn of riches with þe whilk þai ar þirstyn to þe erth. 1483 *Cath. Angl.* 386/1 Thriste downe, *oppressus*. 1495 Thryst [see B. 6 b].

β. 4, 6– **thrust** (6 **thurst**); 4 *Sc.* **thrustyne, thrussine.**

*c* 1375 *Sc. Leg. Saints* xviii. (*Egipciane*) 581 Bot I, vnhappy, thrustyne sare, A fut mycht nocht get forthyr-mare. *Ibid.* xxxvii. (*Vincencius*) 285 He.. wes.. thrussine done.

1382 WYCLIF *Judg.* vi. 38 [Dew] thrust out of the fleese [Vulg. *expresso vellere*]. 1573–80, 1577, etc. Thrust [see B. 5, 1 b, etc.].

γ. 4–5 þristed, 4 *Sc.* thristit, 7–9 thrusted.

*c* 1375 *Sc. Leg. Saints* xl. (*Ninian*) 516 His stafe..has he ..in þe maste hoile..thristit ful faste. *c* 1425 tr. *Arderne's Treat. Fistula* 65 Þat it may..be þristed out. 1665 Thrusted [see B. 1].

B. Signification.

**I. 1.** *trans.* To exert the force of impact upon or against (a body) so as to move it away; to push, shove, drive. Chiefly with adverb or advb. phr. (Now chiefly literary.)

[*c* 1175: see A. 2 *a*.] *c* 1250 *Gen. & Ex.* 2110, vii. lene [ears of corn]..ðe ranc he hauen ðo ouer-cumen,..and, on a stund, ðe fette ðrist hem to ðo grund. *c* 1290 *S. Eng. Leg.* I. 328/188 Seint Clement..in grete wrathþe hire pulte a-wei and to þe grounde upriȝt þruste. *a* 1400–50 *Alexander* 1407 Þai..Thristis ouir thikefald many threuyn bernes. 1526 TINDALE *Matt.* xxi. 39 They caught hym and thrust him out of the vyneyarde. 1587 TURBERV. *Trag. T.* (1837) 152 And up they thrust the same [door], And softly entred in. 1597 SHAKS. 2 *Hen. IV*, II. iv. 202 Thrust him downe stayres. 1665 HOOKE *Microgr.* vi. 23 Another Ladle thrusted four or five inches under water. 1719 DE FOE *Crusoe* (1840) II. ix. 203, I caused the boat to be thrust in. 1860 TYNDALL *Glac.* I. xix. 135 The glacier is forcibly thrust..against the projecting base of the mountain.

**b.** *transf.* and *fig.* Applied to action of any kind having an effect analogous to that of physical pushing or moving. Often in phr. *to thrust out*, to expel, eject.

*c* 1330 R. BRUNNE *Chron.* (1810) 217 Whan Sir Symon wist, þe dome ageyn þam gon, His felonie forth thrist. 1535 COVERDALE *Josh.* xxiv. 18 The Lorde thrust out before vs all the people of the Amorites. 1577 tr. *Bullinger's Decades* (1592) 161 Dionysius of Syracuse is reported for his tyranny to have been thrust beside his seate. 1598 SHAKS. *Merry W.* v. v. 156 Though wee would haue thrust vertue out of our hearts by the head and shoulders. 1610 HOLLAND *Camden's Brit.* (1637) 513 King Henry the Eighth thrust out the Monkes. 1655 JER. TAYLOR *Guide Devot.* (1719) 14 He only can preserve them in the same Being, and thrust them forward to a better. 1854 H. ROGERS *Ess.* (1860) II. 2 Thrusting aside all authority but that of Reason. 1855 MACAULAY *Hist. Eng.* xii. III. 222 They were now, without any trial, without any accusation, thrust out of their house.

**c.** *absol.* or *intr.* To push against something; to make a thrust. (*lit.* and *fig.*)

*c* 1205 [see A. 2 *a*]. *c* 1330 R. BRUNNE *Chron. Wace* (Rolls) 8886 Þey schouued, þey þriste, þey stode o strot. 1535 COVERDALE *Ps.* cxvii[i]. 13 They thrust at me, that I might fall. 1560 DAUS tr. *Sleidane's Comm.* 80 One of them with his staffe, thruste at the Image of a saincte, in so muche that it fell downe and brake. 1648 GAGE *West Ind.* 176 They still at the door thrusting.

†**2.** *intr.* To come *together* with force of impact; to strike together, collide. *Obs.*

13.. *Cursor M.* 22683 (Edin.) Al þe stanis þat er mad..Wit þrawing sal tai samin þrist [*other MSS.* threst, þrest], Þat al to pecis sal tai brist. 1500–20 DUNBAR *Poems* xxxv. 28 Thir terrible monsteris sall togidder thrist, And in the cludis gett the Antechrist.

**3.** *intr.* To push or force one's way, as through a crowd; to crowd *in*; to make one's way or advance as against obstacles; to press onwards or into a place, etc. Also *fig.*

*c* 1330 R. BRUNNE *Chron.* (1810) 277 Fleand fast þei þrist. *c* 1475 *Rauf Coilȝear* 694 He thristit in throw threttie all at anis. 1530 PALSGR. 757/1, I thrust in to a place thorowe a prease. 1611 SPEED *Hist. Gt. Brit.* IX. xvi. (1623) 854 It will be best abruptly to thrust into the narration. 1615 G. SANDYS *Trav.* 26 That night we came to Callipoly..and thrust into a little haven North of the towne. 1653 W. LAUSON in Arb. *Garner* I. 197 They thrust up little brooks to spawn. 1760 WESLEY *Jrnl.* 10 Aug., A person hugely daubed with gold thrust violently in. 1828 SCOTT *F. M. Perth* xii, She thrust in between them. 1865 KINGSLEY *Herew.* xvii, He thrust in with so earnest and sad a face that the servants let him pass.

†**b.** *trans.* To press upon or push against; to throng, to jostle. *Obs.*

*c* 1375 [see A. 3 *β*]. 1388 WYCLIF *Mark* v. 31 Thou seest the puple thristynge thee: and seist, Who touchide me? 1526 TINDALE *ibid.*, Thou seist the people thrustinge the on euery syde. 1589 BRUCE *Serm. Sacram.* iii. I v, Thou art thrumbled and thrusted be the multitude. 1642 [see THRUSTING *vbl. sb.* 1].

†**c.** To press (objects) into a confined space; also, to fill (a space) densely; to crowd, cram. *Obs.*

*c* 1380 [see THRUSTING *vbl. sb.* 1]. 1614 TOMKIS *Albumazar* I. iii, A Hall thrust full of bare-heads.

†**4.** *trans.* To press, compress, squeeze. *Obs.* (exc. in spec. reference to cheese-making: cf. THRUSTING *vbl. sb.* 2, *thrusting-screw*, *-tub*, ibid. 3).

1382 [see A. 3 *β*]. 1398 TREVISA *Barth. De P. R.* v. xxiv. (Bodl. MS.), With compressing and þrusting togederes þe wey of the breþe. *c* 1400 *Pety Job* 98 in 26 *Pol. Poems* 124 To thryste me doune, and me accuse. *c* 1440 *Promp. Parv.* 491/2 Thrystyn, or pressyn, *premo, comprimo.* 1530 PALSGR. 757/1, I thrust togyther, *je compresse*...He hath thrust the appell so moche togyder that it is naugth. 1539 BIBLE (Great) *Judg.* vi. 38 He..thrust the flece togeather, and wronge the dewe therout. *a* 1550 *Freiris of Berwik* 168 in *Dunbar's Poems* (S.T.S.) 290 He thristit hir hand agane richt prevely. 1794 WEDGE *Agric. Chester* 52 Thrusting or hand-pressing the Cheese in the Vat [cf. THRUSTING *vbl. sb.* 2].

**II.** †**5.** To strike with a pushing action; to stab or pierce *with* a pointed instrument. *Obs.*

*c* 1410 *Chron. Eng.* (Ritson) 671 The thef braid out is knyf anon, Ant to the heorte the kyng thruste. 1526 *Pilgr. Perf.* (W. de W. 1531) 305 b, They..with a sharpe speare..thrust the..vnto thy blessed herte. 1573–80 BARET *Alv.* T 218 It is Thrust through with a needle,..*traiectatur acu.* 1593 SHAKS. 2 *Hen. VI*, IV. vii. 10 He was thrust in the mouth with a Speare. *c* 1643 LD. HERBERT *Autobiog.* (1824) 91, I.. with my sword thrust him [a wild boar] twice or thrice without entering his skin. 1770 *Trial W. Spiggot*, etc. *Heref.* 3 That the said William Williams struck, thrusted, and stabbed him..with a certain sword.

**b.** *intr.* To make a thrust, stab, or lunge with a pointed weapon; *spec.* in *Fencing*. Also *fig.*

1596 SHAKS. 1 *Hen. IV*, II. iv. 223 These foure..thrust at me; I..tooke all their seuen points in my target. *c* 1643 LD. HERBERT *Autobiog.* (1824) 64–5 To strike or thrust as he shall see occasion;..to strike or thrust high or low as his Enemy doth. 1700 DRYDEN *Ovid's Met.* XII. 642 He next his Fauchion try'd, in closer Fight;..He thrust; the blunted Point return'd again. 1826 SCOTT *Woodst.* xxxvii, His sword had no more power than had he thrusted with a tobacco-pipe. 1869 BOUTELL *Arms & Arm.* ii. (1874) 23 This formidable weapon served equally well to deliver blows.. and to thrust with the point. 1871 B. TAYLOR *Faust* (1875) I. xix. 172 Thrust home! 1878 BROWNING *La Saisiaz* 404 Fancy thrust and Reason parry!

**6.** *trans.* To cause (anything, esp. something grasped in the hand) to enter, pierce, or penetrate some thing or place by or as by pushing; to put, drive, or force into some place or position.

*a* 1300 *Cursor M.* 557 (Cott.) Als prient of seel in wax es thrist. *c* 1375 *Sc. Leg. Saints* xix. (*Cristofore*) 264 Thrist it [the staff] fast done in þe grownd. 1526 TINDALE *Rev.* xiv. 15 Thruste in thy sycle and rype. *a* 1550 *Freiris of Berwik* 134 in *Dunbar's Poems* (S.T.S.) 289 Scho..thristit on fatt caponis to the speit. 1568 GRAFTON *Chron.* II. 24 He.. sodenly thurst his speare into the kinges left eye. 1591 SHAKS. 1 *Hen. VI*, III. ii. 23 By thrusting out a Torch from yonder Tower. 1647 WARD *Simp. Cobler* (title-p.), Coblers must thrust their awles up to the hefts. 1726 SWIFT *Gulliver* II. viii, I then fastened my handkerchief to a stick..and, thrusting it up the hole, waved it. 1832 HT. MARTINEAU *Ella of Gar.* i, A bunch of seabirds' feathers, which he thrust into Ella's hand. 1832 TENNYSON *Dream Fair Wom.* 259 You should have..thrust The dagger thro' her side.

**b.** To put forth, extend (a limb or member) into some place or in some direction; to put forth, throw out, or extend, as in the process of growth (a root, branch, or connected part) so as to project.

*c* 1374 CHAUCER *Troylus* III. 1525 (1574) With that his arm al sodeynly he þriste Vnder here nekke and at þe laste here keste. 1495 *Trevisa's Barth. De P. R.* VII. lii. (W. de W.), In the dropesye..yf ones fynger be thryst in to the fleesshe it makyth an hole other a pytte. 1593 SHAKS. *Rich. II*, V. i. 29 The Lyon dying, thrusteth forth his Paw. 1596 [see A. 1 *a*]. 1610 HOLLAND *Camden's Brit.* 189 From S. Michaels mount Southward, immediatly there is thrust forth a bi-land or demi-Ile. 1748 SMOLLETT *Rod. Rand.* xlvi, I perceived him thrust his tongue in his cheek. 1788 *Lond. Mag.* 240 Each..thrusted his head through a hole in the curtain. 1815 SCOTT *Guy M.* viii, Thrusting his hand in his pocket to find a half-crown. 1856 STANLEY *Sinai & Pal.* x. 353 Those hills are the western roots which Hermon thrusts out towards the sea. *Mod.* As a tree thrusts its roots deep into the soil and its branches high into the air.

**c.** *transf.* and *fig.* (See also 7.)

1588 SHAKS. *L. L. L.* v. ii. 398 Thrust thy sharpe wit quite through my ignorance. 1601 — *Jul. C.* v. iii. 74 Thrusting this report Into his eares. 1770 LANGHORNE *Plutarch* (1879) I. 1/1 Geographers thrust into the extremities of their maps, those countries that are unknown to them. 1795 BURKE *Corr.* (1844) IV. 285, I shall say more.. since you suffer me to thrust in my opinion. 1865 TYLOR *Early Hist. Man.* iii. 38 On the art of thrusting knowledge into the minds of such children.

**III. 7.** *fig.* To put (a person) forcibly *into* some condition or course of action (usually against his own will); *refl.* to put oneself rashly, 'plunge' (into danger, quot. 1639).

14.. [see A. 3 *a*]. 1639 in *Verney Memoirs* (1907) I. 186, I will not willfully thrust myself in danger. *a* 1649 DRUMM. OF HAWTH. *Prophecy* Wks. (1711) 179 To remedy our evils by the thrusting us into a civil war; and the medicine is worse than the disease. 1654 JER. TAYLOR *Real Pres.* iv. 75 Into the concession of this Bellarmine is thrust by the force of our argument. 1750 WHITEFIELD *Let. to Lady Huntingdon* 24 Mar., O that the Lord of the harvest would thrust out more labourers! 1879 FARRAR *St. Paul* (1883) 296 The very men who were now thrust into antagonism with his sentiments.

**b.** To put (something) improperly *into* some position; to insinuate (quot. 1574); esp. in phr. *thrust in*, to introduce irrelevantly, interpolate.

1574 tr. *Marlorat's Apocalips* 5 Prouoke vs to impaciencie, or thruste any douting of Gods promise into vs. 1654 JER. TAYLOR *Real Pres.* Ep. Ded. A iv, It is..suspected, that.. the tale..was a long time after..thrust in by some Monk in a place to which it relates not. 1861 PALEY *Æschylus* (ed. 2) *Supplices* 267 *note*, The MSS. have ἔχον δ', in which δ' seems to have been thrust in for the sake of the metre.

**8.** To put (a person) forcibly *into* some position (against the will of others concerned); to intrude (some one) *upon* (a person or persons).

1559 in Strype *Ann. Ref.* (1709) I. App. viii. 23 Stephen Langhton, thrust into the archebisshoppricke of Canterbury by the pope. 1583 STUBBES *Anat. Abus.* II. (1882) 92 Why would you not haue pastors to be thrust vpon the churches, whether the churches will or not? 1848 W. H. KELLY tr. *L. Blanc's Hist. Ten Y.* II. 586 He..conjured his friends not to vote for a candidate who would be thrust upon them by the Centre.

**b.** *refl.* To intrude oneself *into* any position, condition, or circumstances, or *upon* another person; to push oneself forward.

1530 PALSGR. 757/1, I thruste my selfe in to a prease or amongest a company. 1613 SHAKS. *Hen. VIII*, II. ii. 65 How dare you thrust your selues Into my priuate Meditations? 1651 HOBBES *Leviath.* IV. xliv. 336 A stranger that thrusteth himself into the throne. 1797 MRS. RADCLIFFE *Italian* xvii, They would thrust themselves into my company. 1855 MACAULAY *Hist. Eng.* xviii. IV. 185 He ceased to insist on his right to thrust himself between the First Lord and the Chancellor of the Exchequer. 1867 AUG. J. E. WILSON *Vashti* xiv, I should not feel justified thrusting myself into her presence.

**c.** To put (something) forcibly (*into* the hands of a person); to press, force, or impose the acceptance of (*upon* some one).

1593 SHAKS. *Rich. II*, II. ii. 110 How..to order these affaires Thus disorderly thrust into my hands. 1601 — *Twel. N.* II. v. 158 Some are born great, some atcheeue greatnesse, and some haue greatnesse thrust vppon em. 1865 TROLLOPE *Belton Est.* xxvii, She had no alternative but to assume the position which was thus thrust upon her.

**Thrust(e**, obs. forms of THIRST.

**Thrustel(l, -tille, -tle**, obs. ff. THROSTLE.

**Thruster** (þrʊ·stəɹ). [f. THRUST *v.* + -ER [1].]

**1.** One who or that which thrusts: see the verb.

1597 A. M. tr. *Guillemeau's Fr. Chirurg.* b iv b/2 The expulser or thruster out (of teeth). 1612 J. DAVIES *Muse's Sacr.* (Grosart) 34/2, I was sore thrust at,..But, thou o'erthrew'st my thrusters. 1794 *Hope's New Meth. Fencing* 221 After whatever Fashion the Thruster holds his Fleuret. 1825 *Chron.* in *Ann. Reg.* 4/2 The corves..were drawn to the shaft of the pit by several other men called hurriers, and a number of boys called thrusters [cf. THRUTCHER]. 1907 *Contemp. Rev.* Apr. 512 Brunetière was a keen thruster and never missed a parry.

**2.** *Hunting slang.* One who thrusts himself forward in the field, or rides too close to the hounds.

1886 *Field* 2 Jan. 3/1 His companion..chances to be a recognised thruster in the fullest sense of the term. 1892 *Ibid.* 9 Jan. 56/1 More than the average number of thrusters striving for a forward place. 1898 J. A. GIBBS *Cotswold Vill.* xiii. 305 That somewhat unpopular class of sportsmen, the 'thrusters' of the hunting field.

**Thrustful** (þrʊ·stful), *a.* [f. THRUST *sb.* + -FUL.] Characterized by thrusting; energetic, pushful. Hence **Thru·stfulness.**

1907 *Daily Chron.* 9 Sept. 9/3 Not an ideal centre forward,..but he is all vigour and thrustfulness. 1909 *Ibid.* 16 Feb. 8/8 The half-backs neither tackle nor follow up keenly enough, and the forwards were not sufficiently thrustful or accurate.

**Thru·sting**, *vbl. sb.* [f. THRUST *v.* + -ING [1].]

**1.** The action of the verb THRUST (in various senses).

1375 BARBOUR *Bruce* XIII. 156 With sic thrawing and sic thristing That it wes hydwiss for till her. *c* 1380 WYCLIF *Wks.* (1880) 319 Þristyng of ordris in oon cloystre or in oon hous. *c* 1440 *Alphabet of Tales* 297 His arm was als bla & als sare with þe thrustyng of Saynt Laurens as he had suffred it evyn on his body. 1552 HULOET, Thrustynge downe, *oppressio.* *a* 1584 MONTGOMERIE *Cherrie & Slae* 291 With wristing and thristing The faster still is scho. 1642 R. CARPENTER *Experience* III. iv. 17 That so many Angels may well stand together without much thrusting upon a needles point. 1794 *Hope's New Meth. Fencing* 224 Orderly and regular Parieing and Thrusting. 1859 GEO. ELIOT *A. Bede* ii, The thrusting out of his chin and stomach, and the twirling of his thumbs.

**2.** *concr.* in *pl. thrustings* = *thrutchings*: see after THRUTCH *v.*, and cf. quot. s. v. THRUST *sb.* 4.

1794 WEDGE *Agric. Chester* 38 In the process of making whey butter,..the 'thrustings', or white whey, is set in 'cream mugs', to 'carve', and acidulate for churning. 1885 *Cheshire Gloss.*, *Thrustings*, white whey, the same as *thrutchings*.

**3.** *attrib.* and *Comb.* Used in or worked by thrusting, as *thrusting-bridge*, *-pike*; **thrusting-screw**, a screw by which a press, esp. a cheese-press, is actuated and regulated; **thrusting-shaft**, a thrust-shaft (THRUST *sb.* 7); **thrusting-tub** (see quot.).

1761 STERNE *Tr. Shandy* III. xxv, He was determined..to have one [bridge] of that particular construction which is made to draw back horizontally..; and to thrust forwards again..: but my father advising my uncle..to have nothing more to do with *thrusting bridges.., he changed his mind. 1856 GROTE *Greece* II. xciv. XII. 326 Arming them with the short Macedonian *thrusting-pike. 1794 WEDGE *Agric. Chester* 52 In many dairies, a lever is used to thrust or press the cheese...In other dairies, they use *thrusting screws. 1906 *Westm. Gaz.* 3 Oct. 8/1 The arm was caught in the *thrusting-shaft of my machine. 1846 *J. Baxter's Libr. Pract. Agric.* (ed. 4) I. 207 The '*thrusting-tub', in which the curd has now to be pressed, is round, and is perforated with holes at the sides and bottom for the whey to escape through.

**Thru·sting**, *ppl. a.* [f. as prec. + -ING [2].] That thrusts: see the verb.

1898 *Allbutt's Syst. Med.* V. 981 The forcible heaving or thrusting movements of the ventricle. 1909 *Blackw. Mag.* Dec. 741/1 The bright thrusting blade of the sun seemed more endurable.

**b.** *Hunting slang.* That thrusts himself forward in the hunting-field: cf. THRUSTER 2.

1895 *Daily News* 22 Nov. 6/5 The difference between 'true sportsmen who "ride to hunt" and the thrusting steeplechasers who "hunt to ride"'. 1900 *Westm. Gaz.* 30 Nov. 4/3 There had been no need to request thrusting riders to 'Hold hard!'

**Thru·st-plane.** *Geol.* The plane of dislocation in an overfault, along which the dislocated strata have been driven.

1884 GEIKIE in *Nature* 13 Nov. 30/1 The most extraordinary dislocations..are those to which..we have given the name of Thrust-Planes. They are, strictly, reversed faults, but with so low a hade that the rocks on their up-throw side have been, as it were, pushed horizontally forward.

1884 Peach & Horne *ibid.* 33/2 At length this intricate system of faults and folds culminates in a great dislocation which,.. to distinguish it from the ordinary reversed faults, may be termed a Thrust-Plane. 1907 *Athenæum* 2 Nov. 554/3 The planes of disruption along which the masses travelled are known as thrust-planes.

**Thrutch** (þrʊtʃ), *sb.* Now *dial.* Forms: 4 þrich, 5 thricche, thrich, 7– thrutch. [f. next.] An act of 'thrutching'; a thrust, push, press, squeeze; also, *concr.* a narrow gorge or ravine (*local*).

13.. *Gaw. & Gr. Knt.* 1713 Þer þre þro [hounds] at a þrich þrat hym [a fox] at ones. c 1400 *Destr. Troy* 12752 Þan entrid this Engist,..And, with a thricche in the throte, throtlet the kyng. c 1425 Wyntoun *Cron.* v. iv. 606 [It] gert hym offt in thrichis [*v.rr.* thrystis, thryftis] thraw. 1678 Ray *Prov.* (ed. 2) 302 Maxfield measure, heap and thrutch [cf. Thrust *sb.* 1]. 1855 E. Waugh *Lanc. Life* (1857) 33 The last sylvan stronghold of the fairies; where they would remain impregnable, haunting wild 'thrutches' and sylvan 'chapels', in lonely deeps of its cloughs and woods. 1881 Westall *Old Factory* xi. I. 150 Try what a good thrutch ..will do first.

**Thrutch** (þrʊtʃ), *v.* Now *dial.* Forms: α. 1 þryccan, 4–5 thricche, þrich(e. β. 3 þrucche, 6, 8 thruch, 6– thrutch. *Pa. t.* and *pple.* 1 þryhte, þryht, 4 þryȝt, 4–5 thricchet, thrucchit; 5 thright. [OE. *þrycc(e)an* = OHG. *drucchen* (MHG., G. *drücken*) to press;—WGerm. *þrukkjan, nominal vb. f. *þrukki-, whence OHG. *druck* (MHG. *druc*, G. *druck*) pressure.]

1. *trans.* To press, squeeze, crush; to crowd, throng; *fig.* to oppress.

c 888 K. Ælfred *Boeth.* iv, Sittað manfulle on heahsetlum, and haliȝe under heora fotum þrycað. 13.. *E. E. Allit. P.* A. 17 Þat dotz bot þrych my hert þrange. *Ibid.* B. 135 He fande..A þral þryȝt in þe þrong unþryuandely cloþed. c 1400 *Destr. Troy* 13461 Mony holes in the howses..Ouergrowen with..thornes, Euyn thestur and thicke thricchet of wode. c 1440 *Anc. Cookery* § 438 in *Househ. Ord.* (1790) 471 When hit is sothen, thricche oute the water. 1546 Coverdale *Treat. Lord's Supp.* Transl. Pref. A iij, Thrutchyng vp into a corner yᵉ parte whiche no place can conteyne. c 1746 J. Collier (Tim Bobbin) *View Lanc. Dial.* 1 Yet I'm war thrutcht, between two arran Rogues. 1888 *Sheffield Gloss.*, *Thrutch*, to thrust, to squeeze.

b. *spec.* To press (cheese).

1688 R. Holme *Armoury* iii. viii. 335/1 Thruch them in the Cheese-Fate. 1818 Wilbraham *Cheshire Gloss.* 29 Squeezing or pressing the cheese is called thrutching it.

2. To thrust, push.

c 1205 Lay. 19483 He wænde mid his crucche us adun þrucche. 13.. *E. E. Allit. P.* A. 705 He..dyed Delfully þurȝ hondez þryȝt. 13.. *Gaw. & Gr. Knt.* 1443 For þre at þe fyrst þrast he þryȝt to þe erþe. c 1400 *Destr. Troy* 6732 He..wan to the knight, And xxx in the throng thrucchit to dethe. ? a 1500 *Chester Pl.* x. 406 When they their spears throughe him thright. 1885 *Cheshire Gloss.* s.v., I'st be thrutched off here.

3. *intr.* To push or press into a place; to jostle.

[a 1000 *Guthlac* (Exeter Bk.) 285 We þas wic maȝun fotum afyllan, folc in ðriceð meara þreatum and monfarum.] c 1837 in Stephens *Mem. R. Durnford* (1899) 75 'Thrutch him up' shouted some..malcontents at a..vestry meeting [at Middleton, Lancs.]...'Thrutch away, gentlemen', replied the young Rector, jumping on to an oak chest. 1848 T. Blezard *Westmoreld. Songs* 35 (E.D.D.) At last we thrutch'd into th' Ship Inn.

Hence **Thru·tching** *vbl. sb.* (in quot., squeezing, wringing); also *concr.* (in *pl.*): see quot. 1885. **Thru·tcher**, *Lancash.*: see quot. 1901.

c 1400 *Destr. Troy* 1522 All his wongys were wete for weping of teres,..with thricching of hondys. c 1746 J. Collier (Tim Bobbin) *View Lanc. Dial.* Wks. (1862) 68, I stown a lyte Wetur-podditch, an some Thrutchings. 1885 *Cheshire Gloss.*, *Thrutchings*, whey which is *thrutched* or squeezed out whilst the cheese is under pressure. 1901 F. E. Taylor *Folk-Sp. S. Lancs.* (E.D.D.), *Thrutcher*, specially applied to the pushers of a rush-cart, and to the boys who push the corves in a coal-pit.

**Thrutty**, obs. f. Thirty. **Thrw, thrwch**, obs. Sc. ff. Through. **Thrwenter, thrwnter**, obs. ff. Thrinter. **Thrwsse**, var. Thurse, goblin. **Thryd-e, thrydde**, obs. ff. Third. **Thrye, þrye**, var. Thrie *Obs.*, thrice. **Thryes(e, -ess, -is(s, thrys(e, thryss**, obs. ff. Thrice.

†**Thry·-fa·llow**, *v. Obs.* [app. f. Thrie, Thrye, thrice + Fallow *v.*, but perh. a later alteration of *three-fallow* (Three III. 2) after *twy-*, Twi-fallow.] *trans.* = Trifallow.

1573 Tusser *Husb.* (1878) 121 Thry fallow I pray thee, Least thistles bewray thee. 1641 *Terrier Plesheybury Manor, Essex* Sept. lf. 5 b, The tenaunt..to leave 10 acres of land sufficiently fallowed, twyfallowed, thryfallowed.

**Thryȝt**, obs. pa. t. and pple. of Thrutch *v.*

**Thryl, thryll(e**, obs. ff. Thrill. **Thrymsa**: see Thrimsa. **Thryn**, var. Thrinne *Obs.*, threefold. **Thryng(e**, obs. form of Thring *v.* **Thrynne, þrynne**, var. Thereinne *Obs.*, Thrinne *Obs.*

**Thryssce, thryshe**, obs. ff. Thrush. **Thryst(e**, obs. ff. Thirst, Thrust. **Thrystle**, obs. f. Throstle.

**Thryttene, -tende**, obs. ff. Thirteen, -teenth.

**Thryttethe, -ty**, obs. ff. Thirtieth, -ty.

**Thryve**, obs. form of Thrive, Thriven.

**Thuang**, variant of obs. *thwang*, Thong.

**Thuck**, dial. form of Thilk *dem. pron.*

†**Thucke.** *Obs. rare*$^{-1}$. [Origin uncertain. It anwers in sense to Ger. *tücke* fem., mischievous trick, MHG. *tuck*, also *duck*, blow, knock, cunning stroke, knavery; and *duck*, if the original form, would answer to an Eng. *þuck. Stratmann compares ON. *þykkr*, thwack, blow; OE. *tucian* to treat badly, harm, has also been compared; but that gave *tuke*, *tuc* in *Ancren R.*]

A malicious trick.

a 1225 *Ancr. R.* 326 He wule beon afered uorte don þe eft swuche þucke.

**Thud** (þʊd), *sb.* Orig. *Sc.* Also 6 thuid, thude. [Appears c 1513 along with Thud *v.*², q. v.]

1. A blast of wind or tempest; a gust; a squall. (In later quots. including the notion of sound.) *Sc.*

1513 Douglas *Æneis* i. i. 80 Aiax breist persit..Scho [Pallas] with a thuid [L. *turbine*] stikkit on ane scharp roike [= rock]. 1536 Bellenden *Cron. Scot.* (1821) II. 52 Quhen haistilie come sic ane thud of wind, that sail, mast, and taikillis wer blawin in the brim seis. 1606 tr. *Rollock's Lect.* 1 *Thess.* 121 (Jam.) All this worlde is full of tentations: the diuell blowes,..raising a storme: it is a stormie world, and all the thuds light on the sillie creature. 1724 Ramsay *Vision* ii, The air grew ruch with bousteous thuds. 1825 Jamieson s. v., 'The wind comes in thuds' when it comes in gusts; and especially when it strikes on any body that conveys the sound, as a door, &c. 1858 M. Porteous *Souter Johnny* 30 Wud as tempest thud.

†b. A loud sound, as of a clap of thunder, or the discharge of a cannon. *Sc. Obs.*

1535 Stewart *Cron. Scot.* (Rolls) I. 384 Thair scheildis rave and all thair speiris brak, With sic ane thude evin lyke ane thunder crak. a 1586 in Pinkerton *Anc. Scot. Poems* (1786) 246 Hir voice sa rank..Most lyik the thundring thuds of canoun din. 1796 Macneill *Waes o' War* iii. x, Loud the din o' streams fast fa'ing, Strak the ear wi' thundering thud.

2. A heavy blow; a thump with the fist. Also *fig.* a severe affliction, a 'blow'. *Sc.* and *n. dial.*

1787 W. Taylor *Scots Poems* 26 (E.D.D.) Wi' an etnach cud Than gae her Daddie sic a thud. 1790 Morison *Poems* 151 (Jam.) He cocks his hand, and gi's his wife a thud. 1806 Cock *Simple Strains* (1810) 136 (ibid.) Lusty thuds were dealt about. 1847 Emily Bronte *Wuthering Heights* xix, 'Noa', said Joseph, giving a thud with his prop on the floor. 1876 D. Gilmour *Paisley Weavers* ix. 91 Puir lass, it's a sair thud to thee.

3. A dull heavy sound without resonance, such as is produced when a heavy stone strikes the ground. (Orig. *north. dial.*)

1825 Brockett *N. C. Words*, *Thud*, the noise of a fall, a stroke causing a blunt and hollow sound. 1859 Geo. Eliot *A. Bede* iv, Lisbeth heard the heavy 'thud' of a running footstep on the turf. 1861 Hughes *Tom Brown at Oxf.* x, The thud thud of the eight-oar. 1878 Besant & Rice *Celia's Arb.* xi, The heavy thud of the steam-hammer. 1895 Clive Holland *Jap. Wife* (ed. 11) 13 The sound of a mousmé pattering barefoot, her quick, short steps making a gentle thud, thud on the matting.

b. As interjection or adverb: With a thud.

1880 Jefferies *Gt. Estate* 197 We heard an apple fall.. thud on the sward. 1890 L. C. D'Oyle *Notches* 71 Bill shot again and the ball went 'thud!' into the bear.

†**Thud**, *v.*¹ *Obs.* Forms: 1 þyddan, þiddan, 3 þudde (*ü*), 4 thud. *Pa. t.* 1 þydde, þidde, 3 þudde. *Pa. pple.* 3 iþud. [OE. *þyddan*, of uncertain origin. It would normally represent an OTeut. *þudjan, from a stem *þud-.]

1. *trans.* To strike or thrust with a weapon; to stab. Only in *OE.*

c 897 K. Ælfred *Gregory's Past. C.* xl. 294 Ða ðydde [L. *percussit*] Abner hiene mid hindewearde sceafte on ðæt smælðearme ðæt he wæs dead. *Ibid.* 296 Ðæt mon mid hindewearde sceafte ðone ðydde [L. *ferire est*] þe him oferfylȝe. c 1000 Ælfric *Judg.* iii. 21 Þa abræd Aoth..his swurd..and hine hetelice þidde, swa þæt þa hiltan eodon in to þam innoðe.

2. To thrust, press, push (a thing *to* or *into* a place, etc.). Also *fig.*

c 1000 Ælfric *Num.* xxii. 25 Se assa..þidde his hlafordes fot þearle to þam heȝe. c 1205 Lay. 1898 Geomagog.. þudde [c 1275 þraste] Corineum frommard his breoste. *Ibid.* 9159 Moni hundred þusend þe iþud beoð to hellen. a 1225 *St. Marher.* 14 Ant þenne þudde ich in ham luueliche þohtes. 1400 in *Ancestor* July (1904) 19 And anon as i be ded thud me in the erthe.

3. *intr.* To press with force.

a 1225 *St. Marher.* 12 Þa þudde ha uppon þe þurs feste wið hire fot.

**Thud** (þʊd), *v.*² Orig. *Sc.* [Occurs, with the corresp. sb., c 1513. Identity with the earlier Thud *v.*¹ is doubtful; formally it is quite possible; but there is a gap both of time and sense between the examples of the two. The present vb. and sb. may be purely echoic, imitating the sound which they express or imply; if historically connected with Thud *v.*¹, the vb. has changed its meaning under echoic influence, and a sb. of corresponding echoic meaning has arisen.]

1. *intr.* To come with a blast or gust, as the wind; sometimes including the notion of sound. *Sc.*

1513 Douglas *Æneis* xii. vi. 136 As the blastis with thar bustuus sovn..cumis thuddand doun On the deip sey Egean. a 1584 Montgomerie *Cherrie & Slae* 237 Throw cluddis so he thuddis so, And flew I wist not quhair. 1721 Ramsay *Ode to Ph—* vi, Then upo' sight the hailstains thud. 1796 Macneill *Waes o' War* i. xii, Loud and sair the cauld winds thud.

b. *trans.* in causal sense: To drive in blasts. *Sc.*

1728 Ramsay *Answer Ep. fr. Mr. Somerville* 59 Boreas nae mair thuds Hail, snaw, and sleet, frae blacken'd clouds.

2. *intr.* To produce a thud or dull heavy sound, as a falling or moving body by striking against something; to fall or impinge with a thud; also said of the body or surface struck.

1796, 1833 [see *thudding* below]. 1859 L. Oliphant *Earl Elgin's Mission to China* I. 127 Feeble rockets, barbed as arrows, thudded about and fizzed for a moment in the grass. 1862 Sala *Seven Sons* III. v. 120 The carriage came thudding by on the soft turf. 1885 Tennyson *Balin & Balan* 316 He felt the hollow-beaten mosses thud And tremble. 1893 *Harper's Mag.* Jan. 247/1 They heard his feet thudding upon the stairs. 1908 H. Wales *Old Allegiance* xvii. 305 A bullet thudded into the wall above me.

b. *trans.* To strike (something) so as to produce a thud.

1899 J. Lumsden *Edin. Poems & Songs* 259 Blow all your trumps! thud all your drums!

Hence **Thu·dding** *vbl. sb.* and *ppl. a.* (whence **Thu·ddingly** *adv.*); all from sense 2.

1796 A. Wilson in *Poems & Lit. Prose* (1876) II. 66 Cease, thou flighterin' thuddin' heart. 1833 M. Scott *Tom Cringle* i. (1859) 29 A puff of white smoak, then another,..followed by thudding reports. 1901 Lawson *Remin. Dollar Acad.* 87 A brilliant peroration accompanied by a thudding on the pulpit. 1904 Marie Corelli *God's Gd. Man* x, The quick gallop of hoofs echoed thuddingly on the velvety turf.

**Thuder(e, Thue**, obs. ff. Thither, Thew *sb.*¹

†**Thuelle**, obs. f. Tewel, tuel, chimney-pipe.

14.. *Pict. Voc.* in Wr.-Wülcker 777/13 *Hoc epicausterium*, a thuelle.

†**Thuet**, erron. var. *tewet*, *tewit*, Tewhit, lapwing. In quot. applied to the Hoopoe.

1688 R. Holme *Armoury* ii. 254/2 Some call this Bird [Upupa] a Thuet. It is born by the name of Thuet.

**Thuff, þuff**, obs. form of Though.

†**Thu·ften.** *Obs.* [OE. *þyften*, *þeften* (erron. *-an*), representing an OTeut. *þuftinī, doubtfully considered to be fem. of *gi)þuftô, in OE. *geþofta*, ON *þópti* a bench-fellow (cf. Thoft); the suffix being -en², as in OE. *þiwen* maidservant, *fyxen* Vixen, etc.] A maidservant; a handmaid, female slave.

a 1100 *Aldhelm Gloss.* i. 2349 (Napier *O. E. Gl.*) *Uernacula*: i. *ancilla* vel *serua*, þyftan. *Ibid.* 2716 *Uerna*, .i. *seruus*, þyften. a 1100 in *Haupt's Zeitschr.* IX. 461/2 *Vernacula* (gl. *servula*, *ancilla*), þeftan. a 1225 *Ancr. R.* 4 Þeos riwle nis bute vorto serui þe oðer. Þe oðer is ase lefdi: þeos is ase þuften. c 1230 *Hali Meid.* 45 Mi lauerd biseh his þufftenes mekelac.

**Thug** (þʊg, *prop.* tʰʊg), *sb.* Also 9 thag, theg, t'hug. [a. Hindī *ṭhag*, Mahr. *ṭhag*, *ṭhak* a cheat, swindler.] (With capital T.) One of an association of professional robbers and murderers in India, who strangled their victims; a p'hansigar. Also *attrib.*

Their methods were described already in Thevenot's *Voyages*, c 1665 (see Yule). They are mentioned under their more correct name of *p'hansigars* (*phanseegurs*), i. e. 'stranglers', by Forbes *Orient. Mem.* IV. 13 (1813), and as *Thugs*, *Thags*, or *Thegs* from 1810. Their suppression was rigidly prosecuted from 1831, and the system is now practically extinct.

1810 in *Hist. & Pract. Thugs* xxi. (1837) 329 It having come to the knowledge of Government, that several Sepoys ..have been robbed and murdered by a description of persons denominated 'Thugs', who infested the districts of the Docab and other parts of the Upper Provinces. 1816 in *Asiat. Res.* XIII. 287 The term '*Theg*' is usually applied, in the western provinces, to persons who rob and murder travellers on the highways, either by poison, or the application of the cord or knife. 1839 M. Taylor *Confess. Thug* (1873) 2 You know not the high and stirring excitement of a Thug's occupation. 1897 *Daily News* 22 Sept. 6/4 When the Prince of Wales was in India, a Thug criminal showed him how victims were strangled.

b. *transf.* A cutthroat, ruffian, rough. Now *U.S.*

1839 Carlyle *Chartism* i. 4 'Glasgow Thuggery', 'Glasgow Thugs'; it is a witty nickname. 1883 Cable in *Century Mag.* June 230/1 A few 'thugs' terrorized the city with.. beating, stabbing, and shooting. 1889 *Boston* (Mass.) *Jrnl.* 24 Apr. 1/8 Thugs, plug-uglies, and 'flash sports'. 1895 J. Burns in *Westm. Gaz.* 17 Jan. 2/1 They even engage 'knockers-out', who..belabour and disable voters as they are entering the booths...They are called 'election Thugs'.

Hence **Thug** *v.*, *trans.* to assassinate by thuggee; **Thu·gdom**, the domain of Thugs; **Thu·ggess**, a female Thug; **Thu·ggism**, the practice and principles of Thugs: = next.

1837 *Edin. Rev.* Jan. 369 If a single civilian or military man had been thugged, thuggee would have been abolished long ago. 1839 De Quincey *Murder* ad fin., At length came the toast of the day—Thugdom in all its branches. 1856 Froude *Hist. Eng.* I. ii. 155 What teachers of Thuggism would appear to ourselves, the teachers of heresy actually appeared to Sir Thomas More. 1859 Lang *Wand. India* 100 The victim, another Thuggess, was supposed to be sleeping when the operation was performed. 1903 *Daily Chron.* 4 Dec. 5/2 Lord William Bentinck is..known for his suppression of Thuggism, which made strangling a religious rite to the goddess Kali.

**Thuggee** (þʊgī·). Also -ie. [a. Hindī *ṭhagī*, abstr. sb. f. *ṭhag* Thug.] The system of robbery and murder practised by the Thugs. Also *attrib.*

1837 *Edin. Rev.* Jan. 358 These..people are known by the name of Thugs, and their profession is called Thuggee. 1859 Lang *Wand. India* 98 The suppression of Thuggee in the British dominions. 1898 *Speaker* 26 Nov. 641/1 Colonel Sleeman..had charge of the Thuggee inquiries. 1902 *Daily Chron.* 7 Aug. 3/5 Colonel Sir E. Bradford was appointed general superintendent of the operations for the suppression of 'thagi and dakaiti', as the India Office calls it.

**Thuggery** (þʊ·gəri). [f. Thug + -ery.] = prec.; also *transf.*

1839 [see Thug b]. 1849 E. B. Eastwick *Dry Leaves* 58 The Amirs had no more power to prevent the robberies and murders..than we have to extinguish the system of Thuggery or Dacoitism. 1865 *Reader* 26 Aug. 225/1 Ecclesiastical thuggery.

**Thught, þuȝt(e, þuhte,** obs. pa. t. and pple. of Think *v.*[1] and [2]. **Thuid,** obs. Sc. form of Thud.

‖ **Thuja** (þiū·dʒă). [mod.L. (Linnæus): see Thuya.] The more common English form of the name of trees or shrubs of the botanical genus now called Thuya, q. v., also of the wood of *T. occidentalis*, and of drugs derived from it.

*Oil of thuja*, an essential oil obtained by distilling the ends of the branches and the leaves of *T. occidentalis* with water.

1760 J. Lee *Introd. Bot.* (1788) 299 *Thuja*, Arbor Vitæ. 1865 Visct. Milton & Cheadle *Northwest Passage by Land* 287 There were pines and thujas of every size. 1866 *Treas. Bot.*, *Thuja occidentalis* is the American Arbor Vitæ. 1868 *Rep. U. S. Commissioner Agric.* (1869) 186 After ascending some distance the mountain sides.., the wood..consists particularly of a noble Thuja. 1884 Q. Victoria *More Leaves* 301 There are..a wonderful old laurel and thuja which have spread to an immense size. 1884 *Mag. of Art* Mar. 179/2 The richly carved ceiling of thuja and cedar.

Hence names of chemical compounds obtained from the species *Thuja occidentalis* (all in *Cent. Dict.* spelt *thuy-*): **Thu·jene** = *thujone*; **Thu·jenin** or **Thuji·genin, Thuje·tic** *acid*, **Thu·jetin, Thu·jin, Thu·jone**: see quots.

1868 Watts *Dict. Chem.* V. 789 *Thujetic acid*, $C_{28}H_{22}O_{13}$..is prepared: 1. by boiling thujetin with baryta-water [etc.]..2...by boiling thujin for some hours with baryta-water in an atmosphere of hydrogen. *Ibid.*, *Thujetin*, $C_{28}H_{28}O_{16}$... A compound obtained, together with crystallisable sugar, by heating thujin with dilute acids. *Ibid.* 790 *Thujigenin*, $C_{28}H_{24}O_{11}$...A compound occurring in..the green parts of *Thuja occidentalis*, and produced, together with sugar, when thujin is heated with hydrochloric acid. *Ibid.*, *Thujin*, $C_{20}H_{22}O_{12}$...A crystallisable glucoside, occurring in the green parts of *Thuja occidentalis*...Thujin forms shining lemon-yellow crystals, appearing under the microscope as four-sided tables. *Ibid.* 791 *Thujone*, a volatile hydrocarbon, obtained by the action of iodine on oil of thuja. 1873 — *Fownes' Chem.* 643 When heated..with hydrochloric acid, [thujin] yields..thujenin. 1894 Muir & Morley *Watts' Dict. Chem.* IV. 714 Thujone, $C_{10}H_{18}O$,..occurs, together with the terpene $C_{10}H_{16}$..in the essential oil of thuja.

**Thuk, þuke,** dial. variants of Thilk.

‖ **Thule** (þiū·lī). Forms: 1 Thila, 1, 4–5 **Tyle, Tile,** 7 **Thyle, Tule,** 6– **Thule.** [L. *Thūlē* (*Thȳle*) = Gr. Θούλη (Θύλη), proper name of unknown origin.] The ancient Greek and Latin name (first found in Polybius's account of the voyage of Pytheas) for a land six days' sail north of Britain, which he supposed to be the most northerly region in the world.

(*Thule* has been variously conjectured to be the Shetland Islands (so app. in Pliny and Tacitus), Iceland, the northern point of Denmark, or some point on the coast of Norway.

*c* 888 K. Ælfred *Boeth.* xxix. § 3 Oð ðæt iland þe we hatað Tyle. *c* 893 — *Oros.* I. i. § 27 Be westannorðan Ibernia is þæt ytemeste land þæt man hæt Thila. *a* 1000 *Boeth. Metr.* xvi. 15 An iȝlond..þ is Tile haten. *c* 1374 Chaucer *Boeth.* III. met. v. (Camb. MS.), Þe last Ile in þe see þat hyhte tyle [*v.r.* tile]. 1387 Trevisa *Higden* (Rolls) I. 325 Tyle is sixe dayes seillynge oute of Bretayne. 1598 Sylvester *Du Bartas* II. ii. IV. *Columnes* 230 From Africa to Thule's farthest Flood. 1613–16 W. Browne *Brit. Past.* I. v, Monster-breeding Nyle Or through the North to the unpeopled Thyle. 1665 Sir T. Herbert *Trav.* (1677) 2 The fortunate Islands..about which has been no small difference amongst Writers. Some placing them at the Azores..but the Commentator upon Horace near the *Ultima Thule*. *a* 1688 J. Wallace (*title*) An Essay Concerning the Thule of the Ancients. 1730–46 Thomson *Autumn* 864 Where, the Northern Ocean..Boils round the naked melancholy isles Of farthest Thule. 1847 Macaulay in Trevelyan *Life* (1876) II. 190 Where more than Thule's winter barbs the breeze.

**b.** *transf.* As the type of the extreme limit of travel and discovery, chiefly (after Latin usage) in the phrase *ultima Thule* (farthest Thule); hence *fig.* the highest or uttermost point or degree attained or attainable, the acme, limit.

1771 Smollett *Humph. Cl.* 3 Sept., I am now little short of the *Ultima Thule*, if this appellation properly belongs to the Orkneys or Hebrides. 1784–5 *Ann. Reg.* II. 12/1 An unknown coast, which he [Cook] named Sandwich Land, the *thule* of the Southern hemisphere. 1828 *Lights & Shades* II. 136 The caricature of a fop, the *ultima Thule* of extravagant frippery. 1878 *Times* 10 May (Stanf.), The expedition reached their Ultima Thule.

† **Thulge,** *v. Obs. rare.* [app. representing OE. (*ȝe*)*þyldȝian* to be patient, f. *ȝeþyldig* patient; but this would normally give in ME. (*ȝe*)*þuld*(*i*)*en*.] **a.** *intr.* To be patient, have patience, bear or put up *with*. **b.** *trans.* (only in OE.) To wait for.

[*c* 897 K. Ælfred *Gregory's Past. C.* xxxiii. 216 Ne mæȝ he ȝeðyldȝian ðæt he ðæt forhele. *a* 1000 *Ags. Ps.* (Spelm.) xxiv. 5 Ðe ic ȝeþyldȝode [Vulg. *te sustinui*] ealne dæȝ. *Ibid.* xci. 14 Wel þyldiȝende hi beoð [Vulg. *bene patientes erunt*].] 13.. *Gaw. & Gr. Knt.* 1859 Þenne he þulged with hir þrepe, & þoled hir to speke, & ho..bede hit hym swyþe.

**Thulite** (þiū·ləit). *Min.* [ad. Ger. and Sw. *thulit*: named by Ekeberg, 1820, f. Thule: see -ite [1].] A rose-red variety of Zoisite.

1820 Jameson *Syst. Min.* (ed. 3) I. 134 The rare blue variety [of the Pyramidal Garnet] is found..in Tellemark, in Norway, along with a hard peach-blossom coloured mineral named Thulite. 1888 Rutley *Rock-Forming Min.* 161 Thulite displays strong pleochroism.

**Thulk(e, Thulli(ch, (þ-):** see Thilk, Thellich.

**Thuman, þ-**: see Theow *a.*, quot. 1297.

**Thumb** (þʊm), *sb.* Forms: *α.* 1 th-, ð-, þuma, 3 þume, 3–4 þoume, 4–5 (6 *Sc.*) **thoume, thowme,** 4–6 **thome,** 5 **thomme,** 6 **thom,** 7–8 **thum,** 8–9 *Sc.* and *n. dial.* **thoum, thoom.** *β.* 3–4 **þoumbe,** 4 (6 *Sc.*) **thoumbe,** 4–5 **þombe,** 4–7 **thombe,** 5 **þ-, thowmbe,** 6–7 **thumbe,** 4– **thumb.** *γ.* 4–5 **tumb, toumbe.** [OE. *þúma* wk. masc. = OFris. *thūma, tūma, tumma*, WFris. *tumme, tomme*, Saterl. *tūme*, NFris. *tüm, tim*, OLG. **thūmo* (MLG. *dūme*, LG. *dūme, dūm*; MDu. *dūme*, Du. *duim*), OHG. *dūmo* (MHG. *dūme*, Ger. *daumen*); ON. wanting (deriv. *þumall* thumb of a glove); Norw. *tume, tumme, tome*, Sw. *tumme*, Da. *tomme* inch, *tommel*:—OTeut. **þūmon-*, pre-Teut. **tūmon-* the stout or thick (finger), f. root *tū-* to swell: cf. Zend *tūma* fat, Skr. *tūtumá* strong, *tumrá* fat, L. *tumēre* to swell. In ME. the excrescent *b* after *m* is found *c* 1290.]

**1.** The short thick inner digit of the human hand, opposable to the fingers, and distinguished from them by having only two phalanges; hence, *gen.*, the inner digit of a limb when opposable to and set apart from the other digits (as in the *Quadrumana* and opossums).

*a* 700 *Epinal Gloss.* 821 *Pollux*, thuma. *a* 901 *Laws K. Ælfred* c. 56 ȝif se ðuma bið ofaslæȝen, þam sceal xxx scill. to bote. *c* 1000 *Sax. Leechd.* III. 18 Swa greate swa ðin þuma. *a* 1225 *Ancr. R.* 18, & makieð on ower muþe mit te þume a creoiz. *c* 1290 *S. Eng. Leg.* I. 308/319 Strongue is þe þoumbe I-cleoped. *a* 1300 *Cursor M.* 21244 (Cott.) Men sais þat of his thumb [*G.* tumb, *F.* thowme, *T.* þombe] he smate, And þat was noght bot for to fle. *c* 1375 *Lay Folks Mass Bk.* (MS. B.) 158 Makes a cros vpon þo letter with his thoume. 13.. *Minor Poems fr. Vernon MS.* xxv. 296 Þi þhommes and þi ffyngres. *c* 1440 *Gesta Rom.* xxii. 72 (Harl. MS.) Tho anon he toke the thome of the dede man, and made him to seal hit [a charter] with a fals seal. *c* 1475 *Pict. Voc.* in Wr.-Wülcker 749/31 *Hic pollex*, a thumb. 1507 in Leadam *Sel. Cas. Star Chamber* (Seld.) I. 260 They hade maymed one William Thomson..& cutte of his right thom. 1596 Shaks. 1 *Hen. IV*, I. iii. 38 'Twixt his Finger and his Thumbe, he held A Pouncet-box. 1605 — *Macb.* IV. i. 44 By the pricking of my Thumbes, Something wicked this way comes. 1662 *Reg. Privy Council Scotl.* Ser. III. I. 237 They..tortured the women by waking, hanging them up by the thombes, burning the soles of their feet at the fyre. 1662 Stillingfl. *Orig. Sacr.* III. i. § 16 The thumb, which may equally joyn with any of the fingers in taking hold of any thing. 1712 tr. *Pomet's Hist. Drugs* I. 152 A round Stalk, the Thickness of two Thumbs. 1833 *Penny Cycl.* I. 183/2 The hinder extremities [of the chimpanzee] are..marked by a thumb—a finger opposed to the other fingers. 1840 *Ibid.* XVI. 458/1 s.v. *Opossum*, The whole of this subfamily [*Didelphidæ*] have the inner toe of the hind foot converted into a thumb. 1869 Hazlitt *Eng. Prov.* 373 The richer the cobbler, the blacker his thumb. 1893 Hodges *Elem. Photogr.* (1907) 78 Held between the thumb and finger of the left hand.

*fig.* 1895 Baring-Gould *Noémi* xxii, I must have more men. I dare not leave Domme [a fortress] without a thumb on it to hold it down.

† **b.** The corresponding digit of the foot; the great toe. *Obs.*

1432–50 tr. *Higden* (Rolls) II. 189 A thowmbe [L. *pollex*; Trevisa, greet too] in the ryȝhte foote of Pyrrhus kynge, the towchenge of whom ȝafe subsidy ageyne venom. 1535 Coverdale *Judg.* i. 6 They cut of the thombes of his handes and fete. *a* 1643 J. Shute *Judgem. & M.* 38 Adonibezek cut off the thumbs both of the hands and feet of seventy kings.

**c.** In the lower animals generally: The inmost digit of the fore-foot; in a bird, the first digit of the wing, bearing the bastard-wing or alula; also the hind toe, inner hind toe, or hallux; in insects: see quot. 1826.

1607 Topsell *Four-f. Beasts* (1658) 424 The Nut-mouse, ..upon his forefeet..hath four claws or distinct toes, for he wanteth a thumb. 1797 *Encycl. Brit.* (ed. 3) XIV. 612/1 The fore-feet [of a seal] are like the human hand, the middle toe being the longest and the thumb short. 1826 Kirby & Sp. *Entomol.* III. 370 *Pollex* (the Thumb). A small accessory joint, attached to the *Ungula* of the *Manus* in *Mantis*. 1828 Stark *Elem. Nat. Hist.* I. 116 [Lemming] Fore-feet pentadactylous; nail of the thumb short and rounded. 1854 Owen *Skel. & Teeth* in *Orr's Circ. Sc.* I. *Org. Nat.* 223 Those which are attached to the short outer digit,..erroneously called the 'thumb', are the..bastard feathers. 1860 Mayne *Expos. Lex.*, *Thumb*,..*Ornithol.*, applied to a small bone of the hand, or third portion of the anterior extremity..also to the shortest toe.., situated behind...*Zool.*, applied to the first finger of the anterior extremity, or forefoot of certain of the *Reptilia*. 1872 Coues *N. Amer. Birds* 30 The forefinger hand-bone sticks out a little from the side of the principal one, and bears on its end one finger-bone.. which is commonly, but wrongly, called the bird's 'thumb'. 1894 Newton *Dict. Birds* 737 *Pollex*, the thumb or first digit of the wing.

**2.** *transf.* The part of a glove or mitten which covers the thumb. 1888 in *Cassell's Encycl. Dict.*

**3.** A thing or part analogous to or in some way resembling a thumb; e.g. a projecting spur or stump of a woody plant, a tool, etc.; also (cf. *Tom Thumb*) a diminutive animal or object; see quots.

1745 tr. *Columella's Husb.* IV. ii, Having remarked the thumb of the former year [*superioris anni pollice*] one may leave one or two eyes from which it may germinate. 1778 [W. Marshall] *Minutes Agric.* 20 Sept. an. 1775, A corn-fork, without the thumb, is the best. 1854 *N. & Q.* 1st Ser. IX. 385/1 Three kinds..: the weasel, the stoat or stump, and the mousehunt or mousehunter, which is also called the thumb from its diminutive size. 1869 [Thumbs and fingers in *Colour-printing*: see Finger *sb.* 11 b]. 1901 *Chronicle* 25 Oct. (E.D.D., Staffs.), 'Tot', a small mug, that held a quartern, sometimes also called a thumb. 1904 *Science* 20 May 803 (Cent. Suppl.) The extremely acute 'thumbs' and pinnacles which surmount the trap plateau of different parts of Greenland.

**4.** As a measure (also more fully, *thumb's breadth*): The breadth of the thumb, taken as equal to an inch.

Formerly it was usual to allow a 'thumb' in addition to each yard (of cloth, etc.) measured; this is still the practice in the cloth trade.

[1611 Cotgr., *Poulcée*, an inch, or inch-measure; the breadth of a thumbe.] 1622 Malynes *Anc. Law-Merch.* 52 A thumbe or Inch is 6 Graines or Barleycornes. 1634 Sanderson *Serm.* 1 *Sam.* xii. 3 § 29 False weights, false measures, false thumbs, false lights, false marks. 1711 *Act* 10 *Anne* c. 16 § 4 One Table..with the Length of a Yard nailed or marked thereupon; to which shall be added one Inch more, which shall be used instead of that which is commonly called a Thumb's Breadth. 1812 J. Smyth *Pract. of Customs* (1821) 126 (*Linen*) The practice of allowing what is termed a Thumb is now discontinued by the Board's order [8th May, 1806].

**5.** Phrases. **a.** *Thumb of gold, a golden thumb, miller's thumb*: in reference either to the alleged dishonesty of millers or to the lucrative character of their trade. † **b.** *To bring* (a person) *above the thumb, to turn over the thumb*, to get or have under one's control; cf. 'to twist round one's finger'. *Obs.* **c.** *One's fingers all thumbs* (etc.): said of a person who is clumsy or wanting in dexterity. † **d.** *To hit* († *cross*) *one over* (*of, on*) *the thumbs*, to punish or reprove sharply, 'rap one's knuckles'. **e.** (*a*) *To bite one's thumbs*, as an indication of anger or vexation; (*b*) *to bite the thumb at*, as an insult: see Bite *v.* 16. † **f.** *Under* (*the*) *thumb*, secretly, confidentially. *Obs.* **g.** *Under the thumb of*, entirely at the disposal or direction of, completely subservient to. **h.** In expressions referring to the use of the thumb by the spectators in the ancient amphitheatre, to indicate approbation or the opposite: see quot. 1880.

**a.** *c* 1386—1876 [see Miller 1 b]. **b.** 1469 J. Paston in *P. Lett.* II. 356 Thow thou can begyll the Dwk of Norffolk, and bryng hym abow the thombe as thow lyst, I let the wet thow shalt not do me so. 1577 Northbrooke *Dicing* 48 The gaine gotten by this playe at Dice, where all is gotten with a trice ouer the thumbe. 1603 Dekker *Wonderfull Yeare* F iv, Shee would haue tickled them, and turned them ouer the thumbs. **c.** 1546 J. Heywood *Prov.* (1562) G iij b, Whan he should get ought, eche fynger is a thumbe. 1870 *Echo* 16 Nov., Your uneducated man is all thumbs, as the phrase runs; and what education does for him is to supply him with clever fingers. 1872 *Routledge's Ev. Boy's Ann.* 155/2 Whose fingers were reported..to be 'all thumbs'. **d.** 1522 Skelton, Thwartyng ouer thom [see Thwart *v.* 2]. *a* 1548 Hall *Chron.*, *Hen. VII* 33 In the later ende of hys oracion, he a litle rebuked the lady Margaret and hyt her of [Grafton on] the thombes. 1553 T. Wilson *Rhet.* (1580) 3 The Philosopher..did hit a yong man ouer the Thumbes verie handsomely, for vsyng ouer old, and ouer straunge woordes. *Ibid.* 137, I haue knowen some so hitte of the thumbes, that thei could not tell..whether [etc.]. 1591 Greene *Farew. to Follie* Wks. (Grosart) IX. 285 Peratio..thought to crosse Benedetto ouer the thumbs. 1594 Lodge & Greene *Looking Glasse* (Hunter. Cl.) 9 Well said Smith, that crost him ouer the thumbs. **e.** 1573 *Satir. Poems Reform.* xlii. 266 The Clerk was like to byte his thowmis. 1592 Shaks. *Rom. & Jul.* I. i. 49. [1596 Lodge *Wits Misery* 23 Giuing me the Fico with his thombe in his mouth.] 1608 Dekker *Dead Term* D iv b, What shouldering, what Justling, what Jeering, what byting of Thumbs to beget quarels. 1638 Randolph *Muses Looking-Gl.* III. iii, Daggs, and Pistolls! To bite his thumb at me? 1670 G. H. *Hist. Cardinals* II. II. 158 The Spaniards were nettled, and bit their thumbs..in private. 1863 *Chambers' Bk. Days* 11 Mar. I. 358 It is very probable that..the act of biting the thumb was not so much a gesture of insulting contempt as a threat. **f.** 1586 J. Hooker *Hist. Irel.* in *Holinshed* II. 89/1 Diuerse other secret vnderminers, who wrought so cunninglie vnder the thumbe..as if Kildare had prospered, ..their malice would not haue beene in manner suspected. 1596 Dalrymple tr. *Leslie's Hist. Scot.* II. (S.T.S.) I. 171 This consuetude..was, as we vse to speik, vndir thoume stil reteined. *a* 1693 *Urquhart's Rabelais* III. xxxvi. 299 Privily and under Thumb. **g.** 1754 Richardson *Grandison* IV. xxix. 181 She..is obliged to be silent. I have her under my thumb. 1809 Malkin *Gil Blas* VII. xiii. ⁋ 6 Authors..are under the thumb of booksellers and players. 1889 Jessopp *Coming of Friars* ii. 65 The lord was a petty king, having his subjects very much under his thumb. **h.** 1601 Holland *Pliny* XXVIII. ii. 297 To bend or bow downe the thumbes when wee giue assent unto a thing, or doe favour any person. 1693 Dryden *Juvenal's Sat.* iii. 68 Where..With Thumbs bent back, they popularly kill. 1880 Lewis & Short s. v. *Pollex*, To close down the thumb (*premere*) was a sign of approbation; to extend it (*vertere, convertere*; *pollex infestus*) a sign of disapprobation. 1887 R. Garnett *Life Carlyle* iv, They had unanimously turned their thumbs up. 'Sartor', the publisher acquainted him, 'excites universal disapprobation'. 1907 R. Y. Tyrrell in *Academy* 9 Mar. 234/1 'Thumbs down' means 'spare him..': the signal for death was 'thumbs up'.

**i.** *To get one's thumb out of* (a person's) *mouth*, to escape from, to get out of the clutches of. † *The finger next one's thumb*, one's closest friend. So † *to be finger and thumb*, to be on intimate terms.

† *A thumb under the girdle*: an expression denoting reserve or unsociableness. † *To a cow's thumb*, exactly, perfectly, to a hair. *There's my thumb* (Sc.), in asseveration, in allusion to the practice of licking the thumb in sealing a bargain; see *thumb-licking* in 6. *Above one's thumb* (Sc.), beyond one's reach or ability. *To fash one's thumb* (Sc.), to put oneself out, to worry or concern oneself. *To clap*, *put*, or *keep the thumb on* (Sc.), to keep secret. *To whistle on one's thumb* (Sc.): cf. *to pipe in an ivy-leaf* (see IVY-LEAF). *As easy as kiss my thumb.* See also RULE OF THUMB.

**1481** CAXTON *Reynard* xx. (Arb.) 49, I shal by my wille neuer more come in the kynges daunger, I haue now goten my thombe out of his mouth. **1579** LYLY *Euphues* (Arb.) 68 In yat thou crauest my aide, assure thy selfe I will be the finger next thy thombe. **1607** WALKINGTON *Opt. Glass* 130 Wee count a melancholicke man..the *aqua-fortis* of merry company, a thumb vnder the girdle. *a* **1613** OVERBURY *Charac., Old Man* (1614) E iij b, They call the thombe vnder the girdle grauitie. **1681** T. FLATMAN *Heraclitus Ridens* No. 40 (1713) II. 2 Let him alone, he'll trim their Whiskers and comb their Perukes for them to a Cow's thumb. **1722** RAMSAY *Three Bonnets* III. 104 There's my thumb That, while I breathe, I'se ne'er beguile ye. **1730–6** BAILEY (folio) s.v., They are Finger and Thumb, that is, they are so great together, there is no parting them. **1766** A. NICOL *Poems* 59 (E.D.D.) Your match is nane aboon your thumb. **1786** BURNS *Earnest Cry & Prayer* v, Speak out, an' never fash your thumb. **1818** SCOTT *Hrt. Midl.* xviii, We'll leave Mr. Sharpitlaw to whistle on his thumb. **1825** JAMIESON s.v., *To Clap or Put the Thoum on any thing*, to conceal it carefully,..keep it secret. **1838** W. BELL *Dict. Law Scot.*, *Licking of Thumbs*, a symbolical mode of indicating that a bargain has been concluded. **1891** A. J. MUNBY *Vulgar Verses* 101, I lay it's as easy as kiss-my-thumb, For to have my way wi' her.

**6.** *attrib.* and *Comb.* **a.** Simple *attrib.*, as *thumb-bone*, *-breadth*, *-joint*, *-knuckle*, *-unction*; **b.** in names of objects of comparatively diminutive size, as *thumb-book*, *-brush*, *-wren*; **c.** in names of mechanical devices operated by the thumb, or of parts on which the thumb presses in grasping, etc., as *thumb-catch*, *-cock*, *-ferule*, *-hole*, *-latch*, *-lever*, *-milling*, *-nut*, *-reel*, *-sneck*, *-switch*, *-wheel*; **d.** objective, instrumental, etc., as *thumb-sucking*; *thumb-like*, *-made*, *-worn* adjs. **e.** Special combs.: **thumb-ball**, the ball of the thumb (BALL *sb.*[1] 15); **thumb bird**, a local name for the Goldcrest; **thumb-bit, thumb-blue,** † **thumb-bolts** *sb. pl.*: see quots.; † **thumb-case**, a thumb-stall; **thumb-cleat** *Naut.*: see quot.; **thumb-finger**, the thumb; **thumb-fingered** *a.*, clumsy, not dexterous (cf. 5 c); **thumb-hand** *dial.*, the right hand; **thumb-index**, a reference-index consisting of grooves cut in the front edges of the leaves, or formerly of projecting tabs, or margins so cut as to show initial letters or titles, so that any division may be turned to by placing the thumb or finger on the proper initial, etc.; **thumb-kissing**, the kissing of the thumb with which the book is held instead of the book itself in taking an oath; **thumb-knot** = *overhand knot*: see OVERHAND *a.* 4; **thumb-lancet**, the usual form of lancet, having a broad two-edged blade; **thumb-licking** (*Sc.*), the licking and joining of thumbs by the parties concerned in token of the completion of a bargain; **thumb-lock**, (*a*) a kind of lock which is opened by pressing with the thumb; (*b*) *pl.* = THUMB-SCREW *sb.* 2; **thumb-loose** [LOOSE *sb.* 1] *Archery*, a method of releasing the bow-string with the thumb: cf. THUMB-RING c; † **thumb-measure**: see quot. and cf. 4; **thumb-mould**, a small mould usually having designs in intaglio, into which the clay is pressed with the thumb in making ornaments for the decoration of ware (*Cent. Dict., Suppl.* 1909); **thumb-pad**, a pad covering the inner metacarpal bone in some batrachians (*Cent. Dict.*, 1891); **thumb-pin** = *thumb-tack*; **thumb-piston** = PISTON 2 b; **thumb position**, in violoncello playing, a position in which the thumb serves as a movable 'nut'; **thumb-pot**, (*a*) a flower-pot of the smallest size; (*b*) see quot. 1885; **thumb print**, the impression or mark of the inner surface of the top joint of the thumb, made with ink or otherwise upon a receptive surface; **thumb-printing**, the use of 'thumbs and fingers' (see FINGER *sb.* 11 b) in the aquatint process; **thumb-read** *v.*, *trans.* to read cursorily; to turn the pages of (a book) with the thumb in glancing through it; **thumb-register** = *thumb-index*; **thumb-rule** = RULE OF THUMB; **thumb-tack**, a tack with a broad head, which may be pushed in with the thumb. See also THUMB-BAND, etc.

**1821** *Blackw. Mag.* VIII. 430 Along his *thumb-ball, Will his pen-knife tries. **1885** SWAINSON *Provinc. Names Birds* 25 Goldcrest (*Regulus cristatus*)... Miller's thumb (Roxburgh). *Thumb bird (Hants). **1847–78** HALLIWELL, **Thumb-bit*, a piece of meat eaten on bread, so called from the thumb being placed on it. [Cf. THUMB-PIECE b.] **1858** SIMMONDS *Dict. Trade*, **Thumb-blue*, a name for small knobs of indigo used by washerwomen. **1711** C. LOCKYER *Acc. Trade India* iv. 95, I understand *Congas* [= cangue] to be *Thumbolts. *c* **1375** *Sc. Leg. Saints* xxxvi. (*Baptista*) 882 A-pon þe autere scho saw ly As a *thoume-bane propirly. **1715** M. DAVIES *Athen. Brit.* I. 77 A little *Thumb-Book, or Pamphlet, call'd, 'The Office of the Virgin Mary'. **1846** BROWNING *Let.* 20 July, You can't write 'so many lines a day' any more than you can paint a picture by *thumb-breadths. **1597** A. M. tr. *Guillemeau's Fr. Chirurg.* 39 b/2 As touching the thumbe and the fingers, we must haue a *thumbcase. **1844** STEPHENS *Bk. Farm* I. 139, 2 shutters ..to open on hinges, and fasten inside with a *thumb-catch. **1867** SMYTH *Sailor's Word-bk.*, **Thumb-cleat*, in shape resembling a thumb. **1886** R. C. LESLIE *Sea-painter's Log* vi. 137 Clumsy thumb-cleats, with more clothes-line twining about them. **1826** *Sporting Mag.* XVIII. 326 The cap and the *thumb-ferrel on the four-horse whips. **1855** J. DAVIES *Races of Lanc.* in *Trans. Philol. Soc.* 276 *note*, A word I have occasionally heard in my boyhood, though now obsolete, *thumb-finger. **1906** *Westm. Gaz.* 11 Aug. 16/1 The inner flight feathers grow first, leaving the thumb finger free until the feathers have grown long enough. **1903** *Med. Rec.* 28 Feb. 335 Iridectomy must be skilfully and delicately performed. No *thumb-fingered tyro need attempt it with hope of success. **1750** *Student* I. 332 The third house of your *thumb-hand in Blow-Bladder-Street. **1907** *N. & Q.* 10th Ser. VII. 467/1 This remarkable expression..heard in the neighbourhood of Sheffield..'Ye mun go down there, and keep to t' thomb-hand side'. **1859** GULLICK & TIMBS *Paint.* 199 The '*thumb-hole' is, however, of recent introduction, and replaced projecting handles. **1902** *Daily Chron.* 24 Jan. 5/1, I was worrying about that palette of yours. Couldn't you have the thumb-hole in it padded? **1903** *Periodical* July 16 The *Oxford *Thumb-Index Bible* is the latest novelty. **1853** CARLETON *Traits*, etc. *Irish Peas.* (1860) II. 5 *Thumb-kissing is another feature in Paddy's adroitness. **1795** HUTTON *Math. Dict.* s.v. *Knot*, A **Thumb knot*..the simplest of all. It is used..by taylors &c. at the end of their thread. **1869** BLACKMORE *Lorna D.* ii, The Lord be with thee, Jan, and turn thy *thumb-knuckle inwards. **1903** *Med. Rec.* 30 May 853 At a time (1862) when the *thumb-lancet was hardly considered a necessity. **1801** NEMNICH *Waaren Lexicon* II. 686/2 **Thumb latches*, Thürklinken mit einem Drücker. **1844** STEPHENS *Bk. Farm* II. 167 The outer-door provided with a good thumb-latch, and lock and key. **1883** [see THUMB-PIECE a]. **1773** ERSKINE *Inst. Law Scot.* III. iii. § 5. 447 Decrees are yet extant in our records..sustaining sales upon summonses of *thumb-licking, upon this medium, That the parties had licked thumbs at finishing the bargain. **1895** S. S. BUCKMAN in *Pop. Sci. Monthly* Jan. 376 The big toe..reveals its former *thumblike use. **1801** NEMNICH *Waaren Lexicon* II. 686/2 **Thumb locks*, Feder-Thürschlösser die mit einem Schlüssel ohne Bart, aufgedrückt werden. **1882** J. TAYLOR *Sc. Covenanters* 88 They carried with them..iron fetters, and an instrument of torture called thumb-locks. **1844** STEPHENS *Bk. Farm* III. 979 It should be tied in bundles or sheaves with *thumb-made straw-ropes. **1611** COTGR. s.v. *Süant*, *A poulce süant*, by ynch, or *thumbe-measure; the breadth of a thumbe giuen betweene euerie yard in measuring. **1867** J. HOGG *Microsc.* I. iii. 204 The teeth answer the triple purposes of *thumb-milling, ratchet-stop, and graduation. **1794** *Thumb-nut [see THUMB-SCREW *sb.* 1]. **1904** HARRISON & H. *Restoration Durh. Cath. Organ*, The *Thumb-Pistons will be of solid ivory. **1889** E. J. PAYNE in Grove *Dict. Mus.* IV. 300/2 (*Violoncello-playing*) At present..the use of the *thumb positions is more restricted. **1851** *Beck's Florist* Dec. 267 As soon as they are sufficiently large to handle..pot them singly in small *thumb-pots. **1885** M. COLLINS in *Eng. Illustr. Mag.* 687/2 [Roman pottery] Many are still called 'thumb-pots', the sides being indented with the potter's thumb. **1900** *Literature* 15 Dec. 486/2 The *thumb-print of Kangali Charan..was compared with the magnified lines of the smudge. Identification was instant. **1906** *Daily Chron.* 2 May 7/5 To-day the photograph of his thumb prints was received from London. They exactly tally with Johnson's thumb-prints made here. **1869** S. T. DAVENPORT in *Eng. Mech.* 31 Dec. 377/2 This was effected by small inking-rubbers, known as thumbs and fingers, and the printing was called *thumb-printing. **1825** SOUTHEY *Let. to H. Hill* 22 Mar., I had merely *thumb-read his book as a whole. **1844** J. T. HEWLETT *Parsons & W.* xi, A..trolling-rod, and a large *thumb-reel. **1904** WORDSWORTH *Old Service-Bks.* 277 A kind of book-marker or *thumb-register, for finding the places in a book read in choir. **1906** *Westm. Gaz.* 2 July 2/2 The effect of this missionary work..is not to be measured by any *thumb-rule. *a* **1825** FORBY *Voc. E. Anglia* s.v. *Snack*, A *thumb-snack, in which the latch is lifted by pressing the thumb on the broad end of a short lever which moves it. **1897** *Allbutt's Syst. Med.* II. 1039 Finger-nails must be kept short and clean, and *thumb-sucking and nail-biting discouraged. **1908** *Daily Chron.* 27 Feb. 8/1 Fasten all securely to a flat surface..with pins or *thumb tacks. **1826** SOUTHEY *Vind. Eccl. Angl.* 497 Among all my books there is no other which bears such marks of *thumb-unction. **1863** *Ecclesiologist* XXIV. 338 The *thumb-worn binding..would be enough to scare a fashionable Englishman. **1908** W. CHURCHILL *Mr. Crewe's Career* xvii, Certain thumb-worn schedules were referred to. **1844** *Zoologist* II. 511 Common wren, '*Thumb-wren'. *Troglodytes europæus.*

**Thumb** (þɒm), *v.* [f. THUMB *sb.*]

**1.** *trans.* To feel with or as with the thumb; to handle.

† *To thumb the belt of*, to be in subjection to. *Sc. Obs.*

**1623, 1711** [see THUMBING *vbl. sb.*]. *a* **1758** RAMSAY *Addr. of Thanks* xxvii, They will be forc'd to thumb your belt At last, and a' knock under. **1765** E. THOMPSON *Meretriciad* (ed. 6) 30 None had the art To thumb the guineas. **1894** *Daily News* 17 Jan. 3/1 The ladies and children..stroke his moist nose..; the men punch his ribs and thumb his brisket. **1898** F. WHITMORE in *Atlantic Monthly* Apr. 501/1 He thumbed an edge-tool like an artist.

**2.** To play (a wind instrument, an air) with or as with the thumbs; to perform or manipulate clumsily. Also *intr.* with *it*.

**1593** G. HARVEY *New Lett. Notable Contents* C ij b, If the Princock must be playing vpon them, that can play vpon his warped sconce, as vpon a tabor, or a fiddle, let himselfe thanke himselfe, if he be kindly thummed. **1641** MILTON *Animadv.* ii. Wks. 1851 III. 209 If men should ever be thumming the drone of one plaine Song, it would bee a dull Opiat to the most wakefull attention. **1675** COTTON *Scoffer Scoft* 93 One winds a Horn..Another thumbs it on a Tabor. **1755** JOHNSON, *Thumb*, to handle awkwardly.

**3.** To soil or wear (esp. a book) with the thumbs in using or handling; hence, to read much or often.

**1644–7** CLEVELAND *Char. Lond. Diurn.* 1 The Emperick-Divines of the Assembly,..thumbe it accordingly. **1673** [R. LEIGH] *Transp. Reh.* 43 Romances are thumb'd more than St. Thomas. *c* **1720** PRIOR *Female Phaeton* 9 Shall I thumb holy books, confin'd With Abigails, forsaken? **1849** MACAULAY *Hist. Eng.* iii. I. 391 Within a week after it had arrived it had been thumbed by twenty families. **1878** ARBER *Pref. to Caxton's Reynard* p. xii, These early editions were thumbed out of existence.

**4. a.** To press, smooth, clean, spread, or smear with the thumb. **b.** To cover (the touchhole of a cannon) with the thumb; cf. THUMB-STALL d. (*Funk's Stand. Dict.*, 1895.)

**1768** ROSS *Helenore* III. 112 Honest Jean..thumb'd it [a cutty spoon] round and gae't unto the squire. **1856** J. BALLANTINE *Poems* 185 The tither cake, wi' butter thoom'd. **1899** B. CAPES *Lady of Darkness* iv. 220 A seed thumbed in too deep is often choked from sprouting. **1904** *Daily Chron.* 7 July 4/4 To thumb down the tobacco in his pipe.

† **Thu·mb-band.** *Obs.* A rope of hay or straw made by twisting the material round the thumb.

**1639** T. DE GRAY *Compl. Horsem.* 85 Take of the hay.. making a thum-band thereof, rowle it about the leg. **1707** MORTIMER *Husb.* (1721) II. 78 Tie Thumb-bands of Hay or Straw round them. **1725** *Bradley's Fam. Dict.* s.v. *String Halt*, Wisp him with a soft Thumb-Band of Hay, from the Pastern to the Top of the Hoof.

**Thu·mb-bottle.** ? *dial.* A small flask, a phial.

**1727** W. MATHER *Yng. Man's Comp.* 92 Put a Penny-worth of the Spirit of Vitriol in a Thumb Bottle. **1782** WOLCOTT (P. Pindar) *Odes R. Acad.* iii. 48 A walking thumb-bottle of aqua-fortis. **1830–3** CARLETON *Traits Irish Peas.* (1843) I. 44 If I don't cork you in a thumb-bottle for this, I'm not here.

**Thumbed** (þɒmd), *a.* [f. THUMB *sb.* and *v.* + -ED.]

**1.** *adj.* Provided with or having thumbs (of a certain kind); chiefly in comb. as *black-thumbed*.

*a* **1529** SKELTON *E. Rumming* 41 A man would haue pytty To se how she is gumbed, Fyngered and thumbed. **1663** BUTLER *Hud.* I. II. 421 The Knight of Greece..With whom his black-thumb'd Ancestor Was Comerade.

**2.** *ppl. a.* Of a book or the like: Having the pages soiled or worn by the thumbs of readers; showing signs of much use. Often preceded by an adverb, as *little*, *much*, *well-thumbed*.

*a* **1800** S. PEGGE *Anecd. Eng. Lang.* (1803) 232 Our old thumbed friend, Littleton's dictionary tells us [etc.]. **1837** LOCKHART *Scott* xxv, He produced a well-thumbed copy. **1883** SYMONDS *Shaks. Predec.* vii. (1900) 197 They [plays] perished in thumbed MSS...before arriving at the honours of the press. **1886** STEVENSON *Kidnapped* xxiii, An old, thumbed, greasy pack of cards.

**Thu·mb-flint.** A simple kind of prehistoric flint implement; = SCRAPER 4 e.

**1865** W. GREENWELL in *Archæol. Jrnl.* XXII. 101 Arrow-heads..and the so-called 'thumb-flints'. *Note.* The commonest type of the 'thumb-flint' is the round one..; an oval form is also frequent. **1896** SPURRELL *ibid.* LIII. 46 Thumb-flints, or slicking-knives. **1900** Thumbflint [see SCRAPER 4 e].

**Thumbikins, thumbkins** (þɒ·mikinz, þɒ·mkinz), *sb. pl.* *Sc.* Also 7 **thumbe-**, 7–8 **thummi-**, 7–9 **thumkins**, 8–9 **thumbikens**. [f. THUMB + -*i*)*kin* dim. suffix: cf. CUTIKIN.] = THUMB-SCREW 2.

**1684** *Reg. Privy Council Scotl.* 23 July, Whereas..ther is now a new inventione and Ingyne called the thumbekins ..[the Lords] ordaine that when any persone shall be (by ther order) put to torture that the saids thumbekins or bootes or both be applyed to them. **1684** (Aug. 7) FOUNTAINHALL *Hist. Notices* (Bann. Cl.) 548 Spence..is again tortured, and his thumbs crushed with pilliwincks or thumbikins: It's a new invention..discovered by Generalls Dalzeell and Drummond, they having seene them used in Musco[vy]. **1690** in M. Napier *Visct. Dundee* (1860) II. 119 Nevil Pain..put to the torture of the thumbkins, and of the boot upon one leg before the thumbkins were taken off. **1715** CARSTAIRS *Let.* in Wodrow *Hist. Ch. Scot.* III. viii. (1722) II. 389 The King's Smith was called in [5 Sept. 1684], to bring in a new Instrument to torture by the Thumbkins, that had never been used before...And under this Torture I continued near an Hour and a Half. **1793** *Statist. Acc. Scot.* V. 583 *Greenock*, [He] has in his possession the identical thumbikins, with which the Principal [Carstairs] was severely tortured. **1818** SCOTT *Hrt. Midl.* x, Dread of bloody rope..pain of boots and thumkins.

**Thumbing** (þɒ·miŋ), *vbl. sb.* [f. THUMB *v.* + -ING[1].] The action of the verb THUMB, in various senses; *spec.* in dicing: see quot. 1711; also, the stretching of a fabric in order to produce a soft pliable finish; in quot. 1847 the keeping of a subordinate under one's thumb.

**1623** FLETCHER & ROWLEY *Maid in Mill* v. ii, Miller, this is not for your thumming. **1711** PUCKLE *Club* 22 Gamesters have the top, the peep, eclipse, thumbing. [*Note.* Securing with the little finger a die on the outside of the box, Ditto with the thumb, when the person play'd with, sits on the right hand.] **1845** *Mech. Mag.* XLII. 14 It was a known practice to pull the cloth by hand, three or four persons being stationed on each side, for the purpose of 'thumbing' as it was termed. **1847–78** HALLIWELL, *Thumbing*, a Nottingham phrase, used to describe that species of intimidation practised by masters on their servants when the latter are compelled to vote as their employers please. **1889** JESSOPP *Coming of Friars* iii. 130 The perpetual thumbing and fingering would subject [books] to immense wear and tear.

**Thumble** (þʊ·mb'l), *v.*[1] *dial.* [f. THUMB *sb.*: cf. *handle.*] *trans.* To touch with or as with the thumb; to handle clumsily; to fumble.

**1623** *Wily Beguiled* C iv b, Stay quotha? To bee yauld and iauld at, and tumbled and thumbled [*ed.* 1606 tumbled and tumbled], and tost and turn'd as I am by an old Hagge. **1829** BROCKETT *N. C. Gloss.*, *Thrumble*, or *Thumble*, to handle awkwardly—to thumb.

† **Thu·mble,** *v.*[2] [? f. RUMBLE *v.*, influenced by THUNDER.] *intr.* To rumble as thunder.

*a* **1608** DEE *Relat. Spir.* I. (1659) 59 Now it thumbleth [so MS.] again very terribly, as though a whole town should fall down into a great Valley.

**Thumble,** obs. form of THIMBLE.

**Thumbless** (þʊ·mlės), *a.* [See -LESS.] Having no thumb or thumbs; destitute or deprived of thumbs; *spec.* applied to the African *Colobus* and to the American Spider-monkeys (*Ateles*) in which the thumb is rudimentary or functionless.

**1720** D'URFEY *Pills* VI. 351 And there'll be Bow-legg'd Bobby, And thumbless Kate's geud Man. **1859** OWEN *Classif. Mammalia* 48 The true Baboons..are African, as are the thumbless Monkeys (*Colobus*). **1870** J. ORTON *Andes & Amazons* xxi. (1876) 312 One genus, Ateles, 'the imperfect', is thumbless altogether. **1890** DOYLE *White Company* viii, Leaving the thumbless archer and his brood, the wayfarers struck through the scattered huts of Emery Down. **1906** *Westm. Gaz.* 24 Dec. 4/1 An African thumbless monkey is among the recent additions to the 'Zoo' menagerie.

**b.** *fig.* Clumsy; incompetent; cf. HANDLESS 2.

**1648** HERRICK *Hesper.*, *Leprosie in Houses*, When to a house I come and see..The servants thumblesse.

**Thumble-toe.** *north. dial.* In 5 thomble-, thomelle-, 9 *dial.* thummel-, -il-, etc. [a. ON. *þumal-tá* the great toe, f. *þumall* = OE. *þúma*, THUMB.] The great toe.

*c* **1440** *Alphabet of Tales* 13, I prikkid hur in hur thomble ta. *Ibid.* 14 Als sone as I prikkid in hur thomble ta sho wappid me in furris. **14..** *MS. Lincoln A. i. 17* lf. 301 (Halliw.) Thane blede one the fute..one the veyne that is bitwix the thomelle taa and the nexte. **1483** *Cath. Angl.* 384/1 A Thomelle too, *allux*. **1904** in *Eng. Dial. Dict.*, cited for Durh., Yorks., Lake Distr., etc.

**Thumbling** (þʊ·mliŋ). [f. THUMB *sb.* + -LING: cf. Ger. *däumling* in same sense.] A diminutive being; a dwarf, pigmy; a Tom Thumb or Hop-o'-my-thumb.

**1867** *Contemp. Rev.* Oct. 50 Thumblings and Fingerlings whom the Pygmies have enslaved. **1879** M. D. CONWAY *Demonol.* I. II. vi. 163 The skill with which some little Jack or Thumbling overcomes his adversary. **1884** MARG. B. PEEKE in *Chicago Advance* 26 June, It was well for the little thumbling that he did not see the smile on his sister's and brother's faces.

**Thu·mb-mark,** *sb.* A mark made with the thumb, esp. on the page of a book in turning the leaves; also, such a mark made with the inked thumb for identification of a person. Also *attrib.*

**1845** LONGF. *To Old Danish Song-bk.* iii, There are thumb-marks on thy margin, Made by hands that clasped thee rudely. **1866** G. MACDONALD *Ann. Q. Neighb.* xi, Thumb-marks I find very obnoxious. **1889** DOYLE *Micah Clarke* 185 It is impossible to get the thumb-marks of any two men to be alike. **1904** *Westm. Gaz.* 20 June 3/1 Thumb-mark impressions are to be taken—a precaution which in..England..is only taken in the case of criminals.

**b.** *transf.* (See quot.)

**1877** W. G. STABLES *Pract. Kennel Guide* iii. (ed. 3) 36 [Words used in the Fancy] *Thumb-mark*, an obliquely-shaped black mark crossing the foot of a well-bred Black-and-tan above the toes.

Hence **Thu·mb-mark** *v.*, *trans.* to make a thumb-mark upon; to mark with the thumb.

**1909** KIPLING *Actions & Reactions* 114 Captain Parnall thumbmarks and passes it to Mr. Geary.

**Thu·mb-nail.**

**1.** The nail of the thumb. Often in allusive expressions; with quot. 1604 cf. SUPERNACULUM.

**1604** DEKKER *1st Pt. Honest Wh.* I. v, *Cast.* Pledge him. ..*Flu.* So: I ha done you right on my thumb naile. **1648** HERRICK *Hesper.*, *To his Booke* (1869) 228 Be bold, my booke, nor be abasht, or feare The cutting thumb-naile, or the brow severe. **1727** SOMERVILLE *Sweet-scented Miser* 27 On his thumb-nail it might be wrote 'A penny sav'd's a penny got. **1841–4** EMERSON *Ess.*, *Nat.* Wks. (Bohn) I. 228 The whole code..may be written on the thumbnail.

**2.** *transf.* A drawing or sketch of the size of the thumb-nail; hence *fig.* a brief word-picture. Chiefly *attrib.*, as *thumb-nail sketch*.

**1900** D. WOODSIDE *Life H. Calderwood* ix. 208 Small ink-sketches of the thumb-nail order. **1901** *Daily Chron.* 3 Jan. 4 (Cass. Suppl.) The truth of Dickens's vignettes and thumb-nails of humanity. **1909** *Westm. Gaz.* 4 Jan. 1/3 There are also 'thumb-nails' of some French figures, and..little pencil portraits of well-known faces.

**Thumb-piece** (þʊ·m,pīs). **a.** The part of a handle, etc., intended to receive the thumb; a part of a mechanism operated by pressure of the thumb.

**1759** MOUNTAINE in *Phil. Trans.* LI. 290 A piece of the deal moulding..adjoining to the brass thumb-piece,..was splintered off. **1868** *Report Munitions of War* 63 The breech-block turns over and is secured in position, when closed, by a vertical bolt with a projecting thumb-piece at the side. **1883** ROMANES *Ment. Evol. Anim.* xx. 351 *note*, A cat which jumps at a thumb-latch, and while holding on to the curved handle beneath with one foreleg, depresses the thumb-piece with the other. **1894** *Proc. Soc. Antiq.* 22 Nov. 238 The lid [of a ewer]..has a thumb-piece.

**b.** (See quot.) *dial.*

**1882** *W. Worc. Gloss.*, *Thumb-piece*, a piece of bread with cheese or meat, held between the thumb and finger. **1897** *Daily News* 5 Nov. 10/7 Eating his dinner, which consisted of a thumb piece of fat pork and bread.

**c.** A covering for the thumb, as the leathern pad worn by needle-grinders; the thumb of a glove or mitten (= THUMB *sb.* 2).

**1891** in *Cent. Dict.* **1899** *Daily News* 15 July 7/4 The sleeves of this dress cover nearly half the hand, and can be made with thumb-pieces, like mittens.

**Thu·mb-ring.** **a.** A ring formerly worn on the thumb.

Often engraved with a seal, or inscribed with a posy.

**1596** SHAKS. *1 Hen. IV*, II. iv. 365, I could haue crept into any Aldermans Thumbe-Ring. **1639** GLAPTHORNE *Wit in a Constable* IV. i. (1640) F ij, An Alderman..has no more Wit then the rest oth' bench: what lies in's thumbe-ring. **1714** *Spect.* No. 614 ¶ 8 The large Thumb Ring,..given her by her Husband, quickly recommends her to some wealthy Neighbour. **1754** J. SHEBBEARE *Matrimony* (1766) I. 4 She was ..none of your meagre thin Things, which..might have been drawn through an Alderman's Thumb-Ring. **1877** *Smith & Wace's Dict. Chr. Biog.* I. 728/1 (*Cuthbert*) A plain massive thumb-ring, with a sapphire set in it. **1877** W. JONES *Finger-ring* 28 A thumb-ring of unusual magnitude and of costly material.

*attrib.* **1642** MILTON *Apol. Smect.* iii, Instead of well siz'd periods, he greets us with a quantity of thumring posies.

**b.** A ring for the thumb on the guard of a dagger or sword; also each of a pair of rings on the hilt of a dagger by means of which it may be fastened to a staff. **1891** in *Cent. Dict.*

**c.** *Archery.* (See quot. 1893.)

[**1727–41** CHAMBERS *Cycl.* s. v. *Larynx*, A ring which the Turks put on their thumb for the drawing of their bows.] **1893** *Smithsonian Rep.* 637 *Thumb ring*, a ring worn on the thumb in archery by those peoples that use the Mongolian release; called *sefin* by the Persians. **1907** PAYNE-GALLWEY *Projectile-Throwing Engines* II. 12, I can bend a strong bow much easier and draw it a great deal farther with the Turkish thumb-ring than I can with the ordinary European finger-grip.

**Thu·mb-rope.** Now *dial.* A rope made by twisting hay or straw on the thumb; cf. THUMB-BAND.

**1601** HOLLAND *Pliny* (1634) I. 501 To lap and wrap them about with wreaths and thumb-ropes of straw. **1601** DEACON & WALKER *Spirits & Divels* 83 Matters that cleaue together like thombe-roppes of sand. **1679** V. ALSOP *Melius Inquir.* II. ii. 212 A Thumb-rope of Sand will make an excellent Cable for Fishers-Folly. **1733** TULL *Horse-Hoeing Husb.* xxi. 300 Winding Thumb-Ropes of Straw about the Iron Circles of the Wheels, and about the Spokes. **1805** FORSYTH *Beauties Scotl.* II. 448 When ready for stacking, they are bound with thumb-ropes, and put on the carts. **1894** *Northumbld. Gloss.*, *Thoom-rope*, a short straw-rope, extemporized by twisting it on the thumb of the right hand whilst the length required is drawn evenly through the left hand.

**Thu·mb-screw, thu·mbscrew,** *sb.* [f. THUMB *sb.* + SCREW *sb.*; cf. Ger. *daumschraube*.]

**1.** A screw with a flattened or winged head, adapted for being turned with the thumb and fingers; a butterfly screw; also a small clamp adjusted by such a screw.

**1794** FELTON *Carriages* (1801) *Gloss.*, Thumb Nut or Screw. **1805** DICKSON *Pract. Agric.* I. Pl. xxiv, On the side of the tub is a thumb screw fixed to the lever underneath, which regulates the stones. **1888** *Lockwood's Dict. Mech. Engin.* s.v. *Screw Clamp*, Small screw clamps are sometimes called thumb screws. **1908** *Times* 22 Apr. 5/5 A thumb-screw securing the sashes had been removed.

**2.** An instrument of torture by which one or both thumbs were compressed; cf. THUMBIKINS; also called 'the screws' (SCREW *sb.*[1] 1 e).

[*a* **1715** BURNET *Own Time* xvi, Little screws of steel were made use of, that screwed the thumbs [etc.: see SCREW *sb.*[1] 1 e].] **1817** SCOTT *Old Mort.* xxxvi, An oaken table..on which lay thumb-screws, and an iron case, called the Scottish boot. **1832** G. DOWNES *Lett. Cont. Countries* I. 200 Such intellects as devised the rack and the thumb-screw. **1855** MACAULAY *Hist. Eng.* xiii. III. 290 The using of racks and thumbscrews for the purpose of forcing prisoners to accuse themselves. **1859** JEPHSON *Brittany* iii. 34 A grim functionary, whose countenance was suggestive of dungeons and thumbscrews.

**Thu·mb-screw, thu·mbscrew,** *v.* [f. THUMB *sb.* + SCREW *v.*, or f. prec.; evidenced earlier than the sb.] *trans.* To torture by screwing the thumbs; to torture with or as with thumb-screws. Hence **Thu·mb-screwing** *vbl. sb.* and *ppl. a.*

**1771** E. LONG in Hone *Every-day Bk.* (1827) II. 199 He must..be *thumb-screwed*. **1792** *Gentl. Mag.* LXII. I. 260/2 Think what tortures we endur'd,..Whipp'd, chain'd, thumb-screw'd. **1835** *Tait's Mag.* II. 377 We tax, distrain, screw, thumb-screw, incarcerate. **1882** *Standard* 9 Sept. 5/5 His Highness admits that a case of thumb-screwing has come to his knowledge. **1892** *Pall Mall G.* 22 Dec. 2/2 We have little sympathy with the thriftless borrowers, but less with the thumbscrewing Shylock.

**Thu·mb-stall.** **a.** A shoemaker's or sailmaker's thimble (see quot. 1794).

**1589** NASHE *Martin's Months Minde* Wks. (Grosart) I. 196 Farewell old shoes, thombe stall, and clouting lether. **1755** JOHNSON, *Thumstall*, a thimble. **1794** *Rigging & Seamanship* I. 90 *Thumb-stall*, a ferrule, made of iron, horn, or leather, with the edges turned up, to receive the thread in sewing. It is worn on the thumb to tighten the stitches. **1877** KNIGHT *Dict. Mech.*, *Thumb-stall*..2, a sailor's thimble used in sail-making.

**b.** A sheath worn on the thumb to protect it when injured.

**1654** GAYTON *Pleas. Notes* III. v. 97 Gloves cut into thumb-stals. **1792** BURNS *Let. to Creech* 16 Apr. (in *W. Brown's Catal.* Aug. (1905) 64), As much mine as the thumb-stall I have just now drawn on my finger, which I unfortunately gashed in mending my pen. **1904** *Eng. Dial. Dict.* s.v. *Thumb* 2, *Thumb-cap*, a thumb-stall or covering for the thumb.

**c.** *Eccl.* = POUCER: see quots.

**1849** ROCK *Ch. of Fathers* II. vi. 167 [The bishop's] thumbstal was put upon the right hand thumb that had been dipped into the chrism. **1872** SHIPLEY *Gloss. Eccl. Terms*, *Pouser*, a thumbstall of silver or other precious metal, used formerly by bishops for anointing in confirmation.

**d.** *Mil.* In obsolete artillery: see quot.

**1864** in WEBSTER. **1877** KNIGHT *Dict. Mech.*, *Thumb-stall* 1. (*Ordnance*), a stall of buckskin stuffed with hair, which a cannoneer wears on his thumb to cover the vent while the piece is being sponged and loaded.

**Thumby** (þʊ·mi). *colloq.* Also thummy, -ie. [f. THUMB *sb.* + -Y, dim. suffix.] A little thumb; a kind of pet-name for the thumb.

**1811** W. TENNANT *Anster Concert* in *Life* (1861) 26 He never fashed his thummie. **1859** LANG *Wand. India* 265 The little finger replied: 'Who told you so, Thummy, Thummy?' **1866** 'R. B. PAUL' *Let.* in *Mem.* xx. (1872) 353 Now thumby is beginning to make a grumble.

† **Thumerstone** (tū·mərstōun). *Min. Obs.* [ad. Ger. *thumerstein* (Werner, 1788), f. Thum, in Saxony, where found.] A synonym of AXINITE. So † **Thumite** (tū·məit), in same sense.

**1796** KIRWAN *Elem. Min.* (ed. 2) I. 273 *Thumerstone*,.. Glass Shorl. [*Ibid.* 274 It is found crystallized in Dauphiné .., and amorphous in Saxony, near Thum, whence Mr. Werner calls it Thumerstein. **1802** [see AXINITE].] **1868** DANA *Min.* 297 Axinite,..Thumerstein...Thumite.

† **Thu·mmart.** *Sc. Obs.* Also 7 thulmard, 9 thummert, thoumart. A dialectal alteration of FOUMART, polecat: see TH (6).

**1696** A. TELFAIR *True Relat.* 12 (Edinb. ed.) By the way his Dog Catched a Thulmard. **1785** BURNS *Twa Herds* vi, The thummart, wil'-cat, brock and tod, Weel kend his voice. **1850** J. D. BROWN *Ballads* (1856) 98 (E.D.D.) His cleidin was skins o' the thoumart and tod.

*transf.* **1822** GALT *Sir A. Wylie* x, There never was surely a droller like thummert o' a creature seen.

‖ **Thummim** (þʊ·mim). [a. Heb. תֻּמִּים *tummīm*, also (after וְ, הַ, etc.) *thummīm*, pl. of תֹּם *tōm*, completeness, integrity.] Used in the collocation *Urim and Thummim*, rarely *Thummim and Urim*: see URIM.

**1539** BIBLE (Great) *Deut.* xxxiii. 8 Vnto Leui he sayde: Thumim & vrim [COVERD. Thy perfectnesse and thy lighte] shalbe with the, & with euery one that is godly in the. **1616** BULLOKAR *Eng. Expos.*, *Thummim*, an Hebrew word signifying perfection. *Ibid.*, *Vrim*, an Hebrew word, which the high Priest of the Iewes wore with the word Thummim, in the plaits of the Rationall vpon his brest. **1623** COCKERAM, *Thummim*, perfection.

† **Thu·momancy.** *Obs. rare*—[1]. [ad. Gr. type *θυμομαντεία, f. θυμόμαντις prophesying from one's own soul, f. θυμός soul, spirit: see -MANCY.] Divination by one's own soul: see quot., and cf. PSYCHOMANCY 1.

**1651** HOBBES *Leviath.* I. xii. 56 Sometimes in their own hopes and feares, called Thumomancy, or Presage.

**Thump** (þʊmp), *sb.* [Goes with THUMP *v.*]

**1.** 'A hard heavy dead dull blow with something blunt' (J.), as with a club or the fist; a heavy knock; also, the heavy sound of such a blow (not so dull as a *thud*). Also *fig.*

**1552** HULOET, Bownce, noyse or thumpe, *bombus, crepitus*. **1563** B. GOOGE *Eglogs* iv. (Arb.) 43 Thou yat throwest the thunder thumps from Heauens hye, to Hell. *a* **1625** FLETCHER *Nice Valour* III. ii, Now your thump, A thing deriv'd first from your hemp-beaters, Takes a man's wind away, most spitefully. **1675** HOBBES *Odyss.* 262 Down with a thump he falls upon his face. **1716** ADDISON *Freeholder* No. 50 ¶ 4 Their Thumps and Bruises might turn to account,..if they could beat each other into good Manners. **1784** COWPER *Task* I. 357 Thump after thump resounds the constant flail. **1834** DICKENS *Sk. Boz*, *Steam Excurs.*, The unfortunate little victim..receiving sundry thumps on the head from both his parents. **1886** A. WINCHELL *Walks Geol. Field* 85 Heavy thumps sometimes heard before and during the action, in geyser-holes.

† **b.** *To cry thump*: to make a thumping sound; to thump. *Obs.*

**1601** B. JONSON *Poetaster* III. iv, How can I hold my fist from crying thump? **1604** DEKKER *1st Pt. Honest Wh.* I. vii, Did you not heare something crie thump?

**c.** Repeated, expressing a series of thumps.

**1850** BROWNING *Christmas-Eve* iv. 64 The thump-thump and shriek-shriek Of the train. **1835** FARGUS *Slings & Arrows* x. 193 The steady, monotonous thump, thump, thump of the engines. **1899** WERNER *Capt. of Locusts* 69 The thump-thump of the women's pestles pounding the maize in the grain-mortar.

**d.** *adverbially*: With a thump (also *fig.*).

**1704** N. N. tr. *Boccalini's Advts. fr. Parnass.* I. 56 Here Tacitus..bid him leave off his fulsome Preambles, and fall thump to the Business of the Impeachment. **1840** THACKERAY *Catherine* i, Which..made his heart to go thump—thump! against his side.

**2.** *spec.* **a.** A knocking or pounding of machinery arising from slackness at a joint where there is reciprocal motion. **b.** *pl.* A beating of the chest in the horse due to spasmodic contractions of the diaphragm, analogous to the hiccup in man.

**1903** *Rep. U.S. Dept. Agric.* (*On Dis. Horse* 140), Thumps or Spasm of the Diaphragm...Thumps is produced by causes similar to those that produce congestion of the lungs and dilatation or palpitation of the heart.

**Thump** (þʊmp), *v.* Also 6 thomp, 6–7 thumpe. [Only mod.Eng. (16th c.); of echoic formation. Parallel echoic formations are EFris. *dump* a knock, late Icel. *dumpa* to thump, Sw. dial. *dumpa* to make a noise, *dompa* to thump. The earliest evidence of the word-group in Eng. is in THUMPER 1. The following shows it as a mere imitation of a noise:

*c* 1550 BALE *K. Johan* (Camden) 53 Sedycyon *extra locum.* Alarum! Alarum! tro ro ro ro ro,..Thomp, thomp, thomp, downe, downe, downe, to go, to go, to go! *K. J.* What a noyse is thys..without the dore?]

**1.** *trans.* To strike or beat heavily, as with the fist, a club, or any blunt instrument, producing a dead, dull, somewhat hard sound; also, without reference to the sound produced, to hammer, pound, knock forcibly.

*To thump a cushion, the pulpit,* etc.: said of a preacher who uses violent gestures; cf. CUSHION-*thumper*.

*c* 1537 [implied in THUMPER 1]. 1548 ELYOT s.v. *Incurso, Pugnis aliquem incursare*, to renne on one to thumpe and beate hym with his fystes. 1565 COOPER *Thesaurus, Pertundo*, to beate with hammers: to thumpe, or knocke. 1582 STANYHURST *Æneis* I. (Arb.) 19 Thee pacient panting shee thumpt and launst wyth a fyrebolt. *a* 1635 CORBET *On Gt. Tom of Christ-Church* 1 Be dumbe ye infant Chimes, thumpe not your mettle. 1673 HICKERINGILL *Greg. F. Greyb.* 218 In thumping the pulpit..has frighted some from their seats. 1716 GAY *Trivia* I. 13 The sturdy Pavior thumps the ground. 1725 B. HIGGONS *Rem. Burnet* II. Hist. Wks. 1736 II. 79 He [Bp. Burnet] would..with greater Pleasure and Vehemence have thump'd a Cushion in that Congregation, we now call a Conventicle. 1807 CRABBE *Par. Reg.* I. 711 There was he pinch'd and pitied, thump'd and fed. 1907 *Q. Rev.* Apr. 393 It was left to the Navy League to thump the big drum.

**b.** With extension: To drive or force (*down, forward, off, out,* etc., or *into* some position or condition) by thumping.

1588 SHAKS. *Tit. A.* III. ii. 11 When my hart..Beats.., Then thus I thumpe it downe. 1596 SPENSER *F. Q.* VI. ii. 10 He with his speare,..Would thumpe her forward and inforce to goe. *c* 1611 CHAPMAN *Iliad* XVIII. 141 Thrice the feet the hands of Hector seized, And thrice th' Ajaces thumped him off. *a* 1677 BARROW *Serm.* Wks. 1716 II. 80 To think..a slow body may be thumpt and driven into passion..how can we..entertain such suppositions? 1821 CLARE *Vill. Minstr.* I. 4 Born to the flail and plough, To thump the corn out and to till the earth.

**c.** Of the feet, etc.: To beat or strike (the ground, etc.) heavily and noisily; also of a body: to impinge upon with a thump; to strike violently.

1582 STANYHURST *Æneis* I. (Arb.) 21 Downe the pilot tumbleth..headlong. Thrise the grauel thumping. 1596 SPENSER *F. Q.* VI. x. 10 A shrill pipe he playing heard on hight, And many feete fast thumping th' hollow ground. 1902 ELIZ. L. BANKS *Newspaper Girl* 173 His tail would thump the floor most vigorously.

**d.** With that which beats, strikes, or knocks as object. *To thump down,* to put or throw down with a thump.

1720 RAMSAY *Wealth* 72 While you may thump your Pows against the Wa'. 1821 CLARE *Vill. Minstr.* (1823) I. 9 And lumping knocks as one would thump a flail. 1852 HAWTHORNE *Blithedale Rom.* xvii, Baggage, which he thumped down upon the floors.

**2.** *fig.* To 'beat' (in a fight), to drub, lick, thrash severely. *colloq.*

1594 SHAKS. *Rich. III*, v. iii. 334 These bastard Britaines, whom our Fathers Haue in their owne Land beaten, bobb'd, and thump'd. 1797–1802 G. COLMAN *Br. Grins*, etc., *Knt. & Friar* I. i, In our Fifth Harry's reign, when 'twas the fashion To thump the French..to excess. 1827 SCOTT *Jrnl.* 14 Nov., We have thumped the Turks very well.

**3.** *intr.* To strike or beat with force or violence, with an abrupt dull noise; to knock or bump with force. Also *to thump it.*

1565 COOPER *Thesaurus* s.v. *Insulto, Insultare fores calcibus*, to thumpe or beate at the doore with heeles. *a* 1619 FLETCHER, etc. *Knt. Malta* III. i. song, Drums beat, Ensigns wave, and Cannons thump it. 1663 BUTLER *Hudibras* I. III. 520 Colon, chusing out a stone, Level'd so right, it thumpt upon His manly Paunch. 1691 E. TAYLOR *Behmen's Theos. Philos.* 340 That which melodiously ringeth in the Light, rumbleth and thumpeth in the dark. 1832 MARRYAT *N. Forster* xiii, I heard the boat thumping under the main channels. 1856 KANE *Arct. Expl.* I. vii. 72 The..floe-ice against which we were alternately sliding and thumping 1883 *Pall Mall G.* 20 Dec. 3/2 No one thinks a drummer-boy a giant because he thumps away upon a big drum.

**b.** To walk with heavy sounding steps, to stump noisily; also, of a thing, to move with thumps or noisy jolts.

1604 T. M. *Black Bk.* in *Middleton's Wks.* (Bullen) VIII. 28, I thumped down stairs with my cowheel. 1825 T. HOOK *Sayings* Ser. II. *Passion & Princ.* xv. III. 378 Along ..went the waggon, thumping and bumping up this hill and down that. 1894 MRS. DYAN *All in a Man's Keeping* 233 Long ropes.. which thumped with wet swishes over the slippery decks. 1899 J. LUMSDEN *Edin. Poems & Songs* 77 He thumpeth down the stony street.

**c.** Of the heart, etc.: To beat violently or audibly; to throb forcibly.

1784 COWPER *Task* IV. 47 Who patient stands till his feet throb, And his head thumps. 1841 THACKERAY *2nd Fun. Napoleon* iii, Everybody's heart was thumping as hard as possible. 1879 BROWNING *Ned Bratts* 282 Hearts heaved, heads thumped. 1880 — *Dram. Idyls* Ser. II. *Retio* 180 How my head throbs, how my heart thumps.

**4.** The verb-stem in combination with a sb.; as **thu·mp-cushion**, a preacher who thumps the cushion of the pulpit; in quot. *attrib.*

1827 G. DARLEY *Sylvia* 60 Grip him fast by his thump-cushion arm, lest he overdo the action.

† **Thu·mpatory**, *a. nonce-wd.* [f. prec. after words in *-atory*.] Characterized by thumping.

*a* 1693 *Urquhart's Rabelais* III. xx. 169 These thumpatory warnings.

**Thumper** (þʊ·mpəɹ). [f. THUMP *v.* + -ER [1].]

**1.** One who or that which thumps.

In quots. *c* 1537, *a* 1619, app. a cant name for some class of 'rogue', or for some coin. In quot. 1728, applied to the striking apparatus of a clock.

*c* 1537 *Thersites* in *Four Old Plays* (1848) 81 Tynckers,.. tryfullers, turners, and trumpers, Tempters, traytoures, trauaylers, and thumpers. *a* 1619 FLETCHER *Mad Lover* v. iv, *Chi.* (Takes out his purse, and shakes it.).. Here are thumpers, chequins, golden rogues. 1728 RAMSAY *To Starrat* 18 The thumper that tells hours upon the kirk. 1824 *New Monthly Mag.* XII. 344/2 The thumper on the great drum.

**2.** A thumping or heavy blow.

1682 T. FLATMAN *Heraclitus Ridens* No. 67 (1713) II. 163 I'll give you such a Thumper shall make your Shoulders ake.

**3.** Anything 'thumping' or strikingly big of its kind, *esp.* a 'thumping' lie; a 'whopper', 'whacker': cf. BOUNCER 3, 4. *colloq.*

1660 TATHAM *Charac. Rump* Dram. Wks. (1878) 287 You may call it the tail of the great dragon, and 'tis a thumper. 1677 W. HUGHES *Man of Sin* III. iii. 97 For Thumpers commend me to Abbot Bar, and St. Brendons Stories. 1711 SWIFT *Jrnl. to Stella* 8 Sept., You are apt to lie in your travels, though not so bad as Stella; she tells thumpers. 1804 J. COLLINS *Scripscrap.* 157 They gives me a Thumper of a Christmas Box. 1863 J. R. GREEN *Lett.* II. (1901) 125 His lies are such thumpers.

**Thumping** (þʊ·mpiŋ), *vbl. sb.* [f. THUMP *v.* + -ING [1].] The action of the verb THUMP in various senses; an instance of this.

1577 NORTHBROOKE *Dicing* (1843) 171 They daunce with.. monstrous thumping of the feete. 1657 THORNLEY tr. *Longus' Daphnis & Chloe* 84 Leaping Dolphins, with the thumping of their tails, loosened the planks. 1722 in Boulton *Amusem. Old London* (1901) I. 29 She may expect a good thumping. 1862 B. TAYLOR *Poet's Jrnl.* II. *Autumnal Dreams*, The drowsy air is startled With the thumping of the flail. 1892 SYMONDS *M. Angelo* (1899) I. v. ii. 187 He was cast forth.. with good round kicks and thumpings.

**b.** *attrib.*, as **thumping-board**, a loaded board placed across the keys of an organ just behind the part used by the fingers, to prevent an undue rising of the key when released by the finger.

1879 *Organ Voicing* i. 6 The *thumping-board* or *damper*, assists to keep the keys level. 1881 W. E. DICKSON *Organ-Build.* viii. 114 A heavy damper or 'thumping-board' should be laid across the key-board.

**Thu·mping**, *ppl. a.* [f. THUMP *v.* + -ING [2].]

**1.** That thumps, in various senses; beating; banging; throbbing.

1581 MULCASTER *Positions* xxvii. (1887) 107 The tumbling Cybistike, the thumping Pugillate, the buffeting Cestus. *a* 1597 PEELE *David & Bethsabe* III. ii, To scape the fury of their thumping beaks. 1859 *Habits Gd. Soc.* vi. 234 The loud, thumping style [of playing the piano] should be avoided. 1898 *Allbutt's Syst. Med.* V. 916 In slim, long-chested youths..a thumping or uncovered heart may well be mistaken for a hypertrophy.

**2.** *fig.* (*colloq.*) Of striking size, extent, or amount; exceptionally large or heavy; huge, 'whacking', 'whopping': cf. BOUNCING *ppl. a.*

1576 FLEMING *Panopl. Epist.* 402 He vseth great and thumping words. 1671 H. FOULIS *Hist. Rom. Treasons* (1681) 26 The thumping commendations of their Saints. 1719 D'URFEY *Pills* II. 48 Strong Wine, and thumping Glasses. *a* 1814 *He must be Married* III. i. in *New Brit. Theatre* IV. 268 A house-full of great, thumping, rosy-cheeked, boys and girls. 1826 W. E. ANDREWS *Crit. Rev. Fox's Bk. Mart.* II. 270 This is a thumping lie. 1855 THACKERAY *Newcomes* lv, Let us console that martyr.. with thumping damages. 1865 SIR S. NORTHCOTE in *Daily News* 29 May 3 Producing sensational effects by the utterance of what I may call good, stout, thumping lies. 1902 C. G. HARPER *Holyhead Road* II. 94 The electors returned both himself and the other Conservative candidate by thumping majorities.

Hence **Thu·mpingly** *adv.*

*a* 1693 *Urquhart's Rabelais* III. ix. 77 If I did not.. thumpingly bethwack her Gillets.

‖ **Thunbergia** (tʊnbə·rgiă, þʊnbɔ̄·ɹdʒiă). *Bot.* [mod.L., f. the name of C. P. Thunberg, a Swedish botanist and traveller (1743–1822).] A genus of herbaceous (mostly climbing) plants, N.O. *Acanthaceæ*, natives of tropical and sub-tropical parts of Africa and Asia, of which many species are cultivated in greenhouses for the beauty of their various-coloured flowers.

1842 *Penny Cycl.* XXIV. 411/2 Retzius named a genus of plants in the natural order Acanthaceæ, in honour of him [C. P. Thunberg], *Thunbergia.* 1893 MRS. C. PRAED *Outlaw & Lawmaker* II. 69 A trellis of Cape jasmine and thunbergia. 1898 J. D. REES in *19th Cent.* June 1017 The beautiful blue thunbergia.

**Thunche**, variant of THINK *v.*[1] *Obs.*, to seem.

**Thunder** (þʊ·ndəɹ), *sb.* Forms: *α.* 1 **þunor, -er**; 2–3 *dative* **þunre**, 3–5 **þonre**; 4 **thonir, -yr(e, -ure, thunure, thonner, -ere, -ir**, 4–5 **thoner, -or**, 5 **thonere, thonour, thouner, thownyr**, 6–9 *Sc.* and *north. dial.* **thunner.** *β.* 3 **ðhunder**, 3–4 **þondre**, 3–5 **þonder**, 3–6 **thundre**, 4 **þundir, thundir**, 4–5 **þunder, þondir, -ur**, 4–6 **thonder, thondre, thoundre** (6 **-ir**), 5 **þundre, thundyr, thwndur, thondour**, (**dondyr**), 5–6 **thondir**, *Sc.* **thwndyr**, 9 *s. w. dial.* **thinder**, 5– **thunder.** [OE. *þunor*, ME. *þoner*, etc. (later *þonder*, etc. with epenthetic *d*) = OFris. *thuner*, OS. *thuner*, (MDu., Du. *donder*), OHG. *donar* (MHG. *doner*, G. *donner*), ON. *þórr*, (:—**þonr-*: cf. Da. *torden*, Sw. *tordön* 'Thor's din'):—OTeut. **þonar-oz* f. Indo-Eur. ablaut series **ten, ton, tn* to stretch, resound, whence Skr. *tan* to sound, L. *tonāre* to thunder; cf. Skr. *stan* to sound, sigh, thunder, Gr. *στέν-ειν* to groan. (The *-on-* in ME. was the usual way of writing *-un-*, to avoid confusion.)]

**1.** The loud noise accompanying a flash of lightning (apparently following it, being heard after it at an interval depending on distance), due to the sudden violent disturbance of the air by the electric discharge; varying from a sharp report or crash to a prolonged roll or reverberation. Also, the unseen cause of the phenomenon, the meteorological condition or action (scientifically, the electric storm and discharge) from which the loud noise proceeds.

The popular use vaguely includes the phenomenon and its cause.

*α.* [*c* 725 *Corpus Gloss.* (O. E. T.) 1152 *Jovem*, þuner.] *a* 800 *Riddles* xlvii. 22 (Gr.) Stefne ðunures micles. *c* 950 *Lindisf. Gosp.* John xii. 29 Ðe here forðon ðio stod & ȝeherde cuoedun ðuner þætte auorden. *c* 1000 *Sax. Leechd.* III. 280 Swa hattra sumor, swa mara ðunor & liȝet on ȝeare. *c* 1175 *Lamb. Hom.* 43 Heore eþem scean swa deð þe leit a-monge þunre. *a* 1300 *Cursor M.* 22143 Thoner o-loft fal sal he gar. *c* 1325 *Gloss. W. de Bibbesw.* in Wright *Voc.* 160 *Tonere*, thonner. *a* 1340 HAMPOLE *Psalter* lxxvi[i]. 17 [18] Þe voice of þi thunure in whele. *c* 1400 MAUNDEV. (Roxb.) xxxi. 140 We ware..striken doune to þe erthe with grete hidous blastez of wind and of thouner. 1483 *Cath. Angl.* 384/1 A Thonour, *tonitruus.* *Ibid.* 387/2 A Thowнyr. 1500–20 DUNBAR *Poems* xxvii. 35 Ane rak of fartis lyk ony thunner. 1816 SCOTT *Old Mort.* xxxvii, Rather than ye suld ride on in the rain and thunner.

*β.* *c* 1250 Ðhunder [see b]. *c* 1290 *St. Brendan* 473 in *S. Eng. Leg.* I. 232 Gret betynge and noyse i-nouȝ, þondre ase þei it were. *c* 1384 CHAUCER *H. Fame* II. 100 The god of thonder Whiche that men callen Iupiter. *c* 1460 *Brut* 510 A gret tempest of thondre & lightenyng. *c* 1475 *Pict. Voc.* in Wr.-Wülcker 802/1 *Hic tonitrus*, thwndur. 1549 *Compl. Scot.* vi. 59 The thoundir is ane corrupt fume generit on the eird. 1595 SHAKS. *John* v. ii. 173 A drumme..That shall..mocke the deepe mouth'd Thunder. 1753 HOGARTH *Anal. Beauty* xii. 97 By the decreasing noise of thunder, we form the idea of its moving further from us. 1818 SCOTT *Br. Lamm.* viii. [ix.], The cloud..began now, by one or two distant peals, to announce the thunders with which it was fraught. 1858 STANLEY *Sinai & Pal.* ii. 124 The thunder, heard, not..in short and broken peals, but in one continuous roll. *Mod.* It is a sultry day; I think there must be thunder about. The farmer's wife says that the thunder turns the milk.

**b.** Regarded as the destructive agent producing the effects usually attributed to the lightning; (with *a* and *pl.*) a thunderstroke or 'thunderbolt'. Now only *poet.* or *rhet.* (exc. *fig.*).

*c* 893 K. ÆLFRED *Oros.* IV. ii. § 1 Þunor tosloȝ heora hiehstan godes hus. *Ibid.* VI. xxix, Hiene ofsloȝ an þunor. *c* 1250 *Gen. & Ex.* 1108 Oc siðen loth wente ut of hine, Brende it ðhunder, sanc it erðe-dine. 1390 GOWER *Conf.* I. 109 Fro the sky A firy thonder sodeinly He sende, and him to pouldre smot. *c* 1400 MAUNDEV. (Roxb.) ii. 7 Þer schall na thunder ne na maner of tempest dere him. *c* 1460 *Towneley Myst.* iii. 346 Thise thoners and levyn downe gar fall..Castels and towres. 1593 SHAKS. *Rich. II*, I. iii. 81 Let thy blowes..Fall like amazing thunder on the Caske Of thy amaz'd pernicious enemy. 1686 tr. *Chardin's Trav. Persia* 209 The Thunder had thrown down a good part of it. 1707 *Curios. in Husb. & Gard.* 243 The Thunder fell upon her, and kill'd her out-right. 1751 MACSPARRAN *Diary* (1899) 61 The Thunder struck Col. Northrup. 1769 COOK *Voy. round World* II. ii. (1773) 304 To acquaint them that we had weapons which, like thunder, would destroy them in a moment. 1820 SHELLEY *Vis. Sea* 61 Six the thunder has smitten, And they lie black as mummies.

**c.** (with *a* and *pl.*) A peal of thunder, a thunderclap. Now only *poet.* or *rhet.*

*c* 1000 *Sax. Leechd.* III. 280 Þa þuneras..on apocalipsin synd gastlice to understandenne. *a* 1300 *Cursor M.* 18124 Þar come a mikel steuen, Als it a thoner war of heuen. 1382 WYCLIF *Rev.* x. 3 Whan he hadde cried, seuen thundres spaken her voices. 1601 HOLLAND *Pliny* II. xliii. 21 Thunders are nothing els but the blows and thumps given by the fires beating hard upon the clouds. *c* 1665 BAXTER in *Reliq.* 23 Apr. an. 1661 (1696) 303 As they were returning from Westminster-hall, there was very terrible Thunders, when none expected it. 1700 DRYDEN *Cymon & Iphigenia* 334 The thunders roll, the forky lightning flies. 1842 TENNYSON *Talking Oak* 279 Low thunders bring the mellow rain. 1855 — *Maud* II. iv. 49 And a sullen thunder is roll'd.

**d.** (with *a* and *pl.*) A thunderstorm. *Obs.* exc. *dial.*

*a* 1300 *Cursor M.* 6019 Was a weder ful selcut snell, A thonor [*v.rr.* þondre, thoner, þondur] wit an haile sua kene. *c* 1400 MAUNDEV. (Roxb.) xiv. 65 In somer es þer grete thundres and leightens. *c* 1400 *Destr. Troy* 7619 A thondir with a thicke Rayn thrublit in þe skewes. 1470–85 MALORY *Arthur* VII. xxxi. 263 Thenne felle there a thonder and a rayne as heuen and erthe shold goo to gyder. 1623 BINGHAM *Xenophon* III. i. 42 It seemed to him, that in a thunder the bolt fell vpon his Fathers House. 1665 E. DIGGES in *Phil. Trans.* I. 26 Our Country of Virginia is very much subject to Thunders. 1892 HEWETT *Peas. Sp. Devon* 101, I zim arter thease mizzle us chell 'ave a thinder.

**2.** *transf.* Any loud deep rumbling or resounding noise. (Also with *a* and *pl.*)

1590 SHAKS. *Mids. N.* IV. i. 123, I was with Hercules and Cadmus once, When..they bayed the Beare With hounds of Sparta...I neuer heard So musicall a discord, such sweet thunder. **1595** — *John* I. i. 26 The thunder of my Cannon shall be heard. **1611** BIBLE *Job* xxxix. 25 He smelleth the battaile afarre off, the thunder of the captaines, and the shouting. *a* **1674** CLARENDON *Hist. Reb.* XVI. § 245 One continued thunder of Cannon. *c* **1800** H. K. WHITE *Poems* (1837) 143 Let the pealing organ play; And, while the harmonious thunders roll [etc.]. **1807–8** SYD. SMITH *Plymley's Lett.* vii. Wks. 1859 II. 162/2 Thunders of applause from the pit and the galleries. **1847** TENNYSON *Princ.* II. 452 The great organ..rolling thro' the court A long melodious thunder. **1887** BOWEN *Virg. Eclogue* V. 83 The thunder of surf on the shore.

**3.** *fig.* **a.** Threatening, terrifying, or strongly impressive utterance; awful denunciation, menace, censure, or invective, 'fulmination'; vehement or powerful eloquence. (*sing.* and *pl.*)

*c* **1380** WYCLIF *Wks.* (1880) 288 Drede we nouȝt þis þondir, for it turneþ aȝen & cursiþ þe welle þat it come fro. *c* **1540** NISBET *N. T. in Scot.* Prol. Romans (S.T.S.) III. 332 But the spret mon first cum,..and with the thwndyr of the lawe feare him. **1693** G. STEPNY in *Dryden's Juvenal* VIII. (1697) 197 Who felt the Thunder of the States Decree. **1712** ADDISON *Spect.* No. 407 ¶ 1 Pouring out the Thunder of his Rhetorick. **1781** GIBBON *Decl. & F.* xxi. (1869) I. 591 He directed the thunders of the church against heresy. **1852** MISS YONGE *Cameos* I. xxvii. 220 The barons..thought little of the thunders of the Pope. **1879** FARRAR *St. Paul* II. viii. (1883) 117 Something..made him [Stephen]..hurl in their faces the gathered thunder of his wrath and scorn.

**b.** In phrases denoting great force or energy (chiefly in versions or imitations of the Scriptures).

**1535** COVERDALE *Job* xxvi. 14 Who can perceaue and vnderstonde y^e thondre of his power? **1611** BIBLE *Job* xxxix. 19 Hast thou clothed his necke with thunder? **1754** GRAY *Poesy* 106 With necks in thunder cloath'd, and long resounding pace. **1796** ELIZA HAMILTON *Lett. Hindoo Rajah* (1811) I. 83 One of their ships of war, a huge edifice, whose sides were clothed with thunder. **1818, 1887** [see *thunder-maned, -shod* below].

**c.** *Struck with thunder* = THUNDERSTRUCK 2 a. *rare*$^{-1}$.

**1823** SCOTT *Quentin D.* xxiv, 'I am struck with thunder!' said Crèvecœur. 'Liege in insurrection!—..the Bishop murdered!'

**4.** *slang* or *colloq.* Used vaguely in exclamations, imprecations, and expletive or intensive phrases.

**1709–10** STEELE *Tatler* No. 137 ¶ 3 Thunder, Furies, and Damnation! I'll cut your Ears off. **1842** S. LOVER *Handy Andy* xxv, 'Thunder and turf!' said the drunken giant. **1891** C. ROBERTS *Adrift Amer.* 66 Why in thunder, if you were hungry, did you not come and tell me? **1894** A. ROBERTSON *Nuggets*, etc. 79 Where in thunder did he get the money?

**5.** *attrib.* and *Comb.* **a.** *attrib.* Of, as of, pertaining to, or connected with thunder, as *thunder-crash, -fire, -gloom, -place, -psalm, -rain, -roll, -scar, -sky, -tent, -volley, -weather*; violent, destructive, or (esp.) loud as thunder, as *thunder-blow, -bullet, -curse, -music, -shout, -voice, -yell.* **b.** objective, etc., as *thunder-thrower*; *thunder-breathing, -forging, -guiding, -ruling, -throwing, -wielding* adjs.; *thunder-delighting* (delighting in thunder), *-fearless, -free, -proof, -rejoicing* adjs.; *thunder-like* adj. and adv. **c.** instrumental, as *thunder-armed, -baffled, -charged, -fraught, -girt, -hid, -laden, -riven, -scarred, -scathed, -shod, -smitten, -splintered, -split, -splitten, -teeming, -thwarted, -tipped* adjs. **d.** parasynthetic and similative, as *thunder-footed, -maned, -tongued* adjs.

**1620** MIDDLETON & ROWLEY *World Tost at Tennis* 221 Imperial-crown'd, and *thunder-armèd Jove. **1819** SHELLEY *Prometh. Unb.* III. ii. 12 An eagle..his *thunder-baffled wings Entangled in the whirlwind. **1878** B. TAYLOR *Deukalion* I. iii. 28 We saw the *thunder-blows Given and taken. **1826** E. IRVING *Babylon* II. 380 Our *thunder-breathing ships. **1605** *Tryall Chev.* I. ii. in Bullen *O. Pl.* (1884) III. 276 Lov'dst thou a towne, Ide teach thee how to woo her With words of *thunder-bullets wrapt in fire. **1844** LEVER *Tom Burke* II. 162 A mass of heavy..clouds, dark and *thunder-charged. **1826** K. DIGBY *Broadst. Hon.* (1846) II. *Tancredus* 5 The *thunder-crash broke over our heads. **1650** WELDON *Crt. Jas. I* (1817) 31 This dreadful *thunder-curse or imprecation. **1839** BAILEY *Festus* xix. (1852) 305 As an angel when He hears the thunder-curse of demon foe. **1848** BUCKLEY *Iliad* 15 *Thunder-delighting Jove. **1608** BEAUM. & FL. *Four Plays in One* Induct., Low at your sacred feet our poor muse lays Her, and her *thunder-fearless verdant bayes. **1855** BAILEY *Spir. Leg.* in *Mystic*, etc. 115 Rooted out..with threefold *thunder-fires. **1839** — *Festus* xx. (1852) 343 The *thunder-footed coursers of the sun. **1779** R. POTTER tr. *Æschylus* (ed. 2) I. 106 The *thunder-forging Cyclopes. **1810** S. ROGERS *To old Oak* iv, Many a navy *thunder-fraught. **1841** BROWNING *Pippa Passes* II. 59 A Greek, in Athens,..Feasting, bay-filleted and *thunder-free. **1853** — *Johannes Agric.* 14 Ere stars were *thundergirt. **1848** LYTTON *Harold* VIII. iv, Some *thunder-gloom of thine own destiny. **1868** ALEX. SMITH *Last Leaves* 154 He could watch the purple thunder-gloom gathering on the distant hills. **1874** GEO. ELIOT *Coll. Breakf. P.* 314 Rule Of *thunder-guiding powers. *c* **1586** C'TESS PEMBROKE *Ps.* (1823) LXXXI. iii, *Thunder-hid I answer gave. **1865** tr. *Strauss's New Life Jesus* I. I. xliii. 373 The *thunder-laden Revelation. **1607** SHAKS. *Cor.* I. iv. 59 With thy grim lookes, and The *Thunder-like percussion of thy sounds. **1826** MRS. SHELLEY *Last Man* II. 73 A crash was heard. Thunderlike it reverberated through the sky. **1846** BROWNING *Let.* 7 Sept., How hot and thunder-like this oppressive air! **1818** MILMAN *Samor* 50 The *thunder-maned steed. **1850** TENNYSON *In Mem.* LXXXVII. ii, I..heard..*thunder-music, rolling, shake The prophets blazon'd on the panes. **1599** B. JONSON *Ev. Man out of Hum.* I. iii, Vnlesse his house and skin were *thunder-proofe. **1733** TULL *Horse-Hoeing Husb.* xiii. 149 The Giants found that even Mountains were not Thunder-Proof. **1822** SHELLEY *Chas. I,* iv. 58 Through palaces and temples thunderproof. **1821** — *Epipsych.* 465 The wingèd storms, chaunting their *thunder-psalm To other lands. **1826** MRS. HEMANS *Forest Sanctuary* I. xiv, Sounds of thickening steps, like *thunder-rain That plashes on the roof. **1848** BUCKLEY *Iliad* 45 In honour of *thunder-rejoicing Jove. **1831** CARLYLE *Sart. Res.* II. viii, The fire-baptised soul, long so scathed and *thunder-riven. **1844** MRS. BROWNING *Rhapsody Life's Progr.* v, Let the cloud meet the cloud in a grand *thunder-roll! **1749** G. WEST *Hymn of Cleanthes* 49 O great father, *thunder-ruling god! **1710** PHILIPS *Pastorals* 2 Yonder naked tree Which bears the *thunder-scar. **1842** SIR A. DE VERE *Song of Faith* 198 Cliffs..Wave-worn and *thunder-scarred. **1846** PROWETT *Prom. Bound* 18 His brawny force All *thunder-scathed and cindered. **1887** G. MEREDITH *Ballads & P.* 78 O for the time when *thunder-shod He champed the grain of the wrath of God. **1863** TYNDALL *Heat* vi. § 210 The Earth..rang with the *thunder-shout of the liberated prisoner. **1818** SCOTT *Br. Lamm.* ix. [x.], The heavy and gloomy appearance of the *thunder-sky. **1825** J. NEAL *Bro. Jon.* III. 395 The..bare, *thunder-smitten tree. **1810** SCOTT *Lady of L.* I. xi, A rocky pyramid, Shooting abruptly from the dell Its *thunder-splinter'd pinnacle. **1825** J. WILSON *Poems* II. 39 Like a *thunder-split oak-tree. **1818** SCOTT *Hrt. Midl.* xlv, The shattered and *thunder-splitten peaks of Arran. **1761** GLOVER *Medea* III. vi. 51 No *thunder-teeming cloud. **1818** KEATS *Endym.* III. 27 Ethereal things, that..Can..poise about in cloudy *thunder-tents. **1614** SYLVESTER *Bethulia's Rescue* I. 315 Vassals of the *Thunder-Thrower. **1605** — *Du Bartas* II. iii. IV. *Captaines* 920 God's *Thunder-throwing hand. **1855** BAILEY *Spir. Leg.* in *Mystic*, etc. 127 Black Babel's *thunder-thwarted pile. **1822** T. MITCHELL *Com. Aristoph.* II. 209 Speed With your tongues *thunder-tipt and tell Cleon our need. **1843** CARLYLE *Past & Pr.* I. v, It is Fact, speaking ..in miraculous *thunder-voice. *a* **1847** ELIZA COOK *Song Seaweed* iii, The *thunder-volley shakes. **13..** *K. Alis.* 3729 (Bodl. MS.) Hij holdeþ hem alle togidre So flok of dere in *þonder wedre. **1900** SUTCLIFFE *Shameless Wayne* xxiv. 301 This thunner-weather that's coming up. **1816** WORDSW. *Feelings of French Royalist*, The *thunder-wielding hands Of Justice. **1887** BOWEN *Virg. Æneid* I. 298 Still yelling her *thunder-yells to the blast.

**6.** Special Combs.: **thunder-ax**, a popular name in Cornwall for a celt (cf. THUNDERBOLT 3 b); **thunder-ball**, (*a*) the electric phenomenon called a fire-ball or globe-lightning; (*b*) *poet.* a thunderbolt; (*c*) the common red poppy (*Papaver Rhœas*) (*dial.*); **thunder-beat** *v.*, *trans.* 'to beat with thundering strokes' (Davies); so **thunder-beaten** *pa. pple.*; **thunder-beating** *vbl. sb.*, beating down by thunder-storms; **thunder-bird**, (*a*) a species of Australian shrike or thickhead (*Pachycephala gutturalis*); (*b*) a mythical bird thought by some savage tribes to cause thunder; †**thunder bounce** (*humorously bombastic*), a loud sudden noise like thunder; **thunder-bowl**, a metal bowl used in a theatre to imitate thunder; **thunder-carriage**, a name for the chariot of the god Thor in early Scandinavian art; †**thunder-clover** [OE. *þunorclafre*], a plant, of doubtful identity; †**thunder-dart**, a thunderbolt (in art); so †**thu·nder-da·rter**, the wielder of thunderbolts, **thu·nder-da·rting** *ppl. a.*; **thunder-dint** (*arch.*), a thunder-stroke; **thunder-dirt**, name for a gelatinous fungus, *Ileodictyon cibarium*, eaten by the natives of New Zealand; **thunder-drop**, one of the large scattered drops of rain which fall at the beginning of a thunder-shower; **thunder-drum**, (*a*) a drum used in a theatre to imitate thunder; (*b*) a fabulous drum represented as the source of thunder; **thunder-fish**, (*a*) a siluroid fish of African rivers, *Malapterurus electricus*, capable of inflicting electric shocks; (*b*) a European cyprinoid fish, *Misgurnus fossilis*, which burrows in mud, and comes to the surface before bad weather; also called *weather-fish*; **thunder-fit** (*nonce-wd.*), a shock or sound like thunder; †**thunder-flone** *Obs.* [*flone*, FLANE, arrow], a thunderbolt or thunderstroke; lightning; **thunder-flower**, a local name for three different plants: (*a*) the common stitchwort, *Stellaria Holostea*; (*b*) the corn poppy, *Papaver Rhœas*; (*c*) the white campion, *Lychnis vespertina*; **thunder-fly**, a name for the insects of the genus *Thrips*; **thunder-god**, the god of thunder; a deity supposed to rule or control the thunder, as Jove in the Roman, or Thor in the Norse mythology; **thunder-hammer**, a popular name for a celt or other prehistoric implement (cf. *thunder-ax*); **thunder-head**, a rounded mass of cumulus cloud seen near the horizon projecting above the general body of cloud, and portending a thunder-storm; hence **thunder-headed** *a.*, having, or of the nature of, a thunder-head; **thunder-house**, a small model of a house with electric conductors through which a discharge may be passed to illustrate the destructive effects of a thunderstroke; **thunder-master**, the master or lord of thunder, i. e. Jove; †**thunder-pad** (*dial.*): see quot.; **thunder-peal**, a peal or resounding clap of thunder; so **thunder-pealed** *pa. pple.*, uttered loudly as by a thunder-peal; **thunder-pick**, a local name for a belemnite (cf. THUNDERBOLT 3 a); **thunder-plant**, a name for the house-leek, *Sempervivum tectorum*; **thunder-plump**, chiefly *Sc.*, a heavy and sudden thunder-shower [cf. PLUMP *sb.*$^{3}$ 3]; **thunder-pump** = next, (*a*); **thunder-pumper**, (*a*) the American bittern, also called *pump-thunder*; (*b*) the American fish *Haplodinotus grunniens*, also called *fresh-water drum*, *croaker*, or *sheepshead*: in both cases from the sounds which they emit; †**thunder-rod**, a lightning-rod or lightning-conductor (see LIGHTNING 3 e); †**thunder-shot** *sb. Obs.*, thunderbolts collectively; lightning; †**thunder-shot** *pa. pple. Obs.*, struck by 'thunder' or lightning; **thunder-shower**, a shower of rain accompanied by thunder and lightning; **thunder-slain** *pa. pple.* (*obs.* or *dial.*), struck by 'thunder' or lightning; **thunder-smite** *v.*, *trans.* to smite as with thunder, to discomfit utterly; †**thunder-smith** *Obs.*, one who forges thunderbolts: applied to Vulcan, also *fig.*; **thunder-snake**, a name for snakes of the genus *Ophibolus* (also *thunder-and-lightning snake*), and for the common little worm-snake, *Carphiophis amœna*, of the U. S.; perh. from their being forced out of their holes by a thunder-shower; †**thunder-thump** *sb. Obs.*, ? a thunderbolt; †**thunder-thump** *v. Obs.*, *trans.* to thump or beat with thundering strokes; †**thunder-thumping** *ppl. a. Obs.*, (*a*) striking with thunder (*humorously bombastic*); (*b*) sounding like thunder when beaten, as a drum; also *fig.* of language, 'full of sound and fury'; **thunder-tube** = FULGURITE 1, *lightning-tube* (LIGHTNING 3 e); **thunder-worm**, 'an amphisbænoid lizard of Florida, *Rhineura floridana*: so called as forced out of its burrows by a thunder-shower' (*Cent. Dict.* 1891). See also THUNDER AND LIGHTNING, THUNDER-BLAST, etc.

**1602** CAREW *Cornwall* 82 There are also taken vp in such works certaine little tooles heads of Brasse, which some terme *Thunder-axes. **1865** TYLOR *Early Hist. Man.* viii. 223 The country folk..still hold that the 'thunder-axes' they find, once fell from the sky. **1686** GOAD *Celest. Bodies* II. xiv. 351 The *Thunderball..entred the Church. **1819** SHELLEY *Prometh. Unb.* IV. 355 Caves cloven by the thunder-ball. **1584** HUDSON *Du Bartas' Judith* V. 397 So he them *thunderbet wherso he went. **1669** WORLIDGE *Syst. Agric.* (1681) 297 Shores..*Thunder-beaten with the Floods. **1560** PILKINGTON *Expos. Aggeus* (1562) 125 Corn.. is subject to many daungers as..*thunder-beating, layde with a raine. *a* **1827** CALEY in *Trans. Linn. Soc.* XV. 239 This species is called *Thunder-bird by the colonists...The natives tell me, that, when it begins to thunder, this bird is very noisy. **1871** TYLOR *Prim. Cult.* I. ix. 328 Among Caribs, Brazilians,..Basutos, we find legends of a flapping or flashing Thunder-bird. **1875** F. PARKMAN in *N. Amer. Rev.* CXX. 40 The thunder-bird is offended,..thunder-storms are occasioned by his anger. **1628** FORD *Lover's Mel.* I. i, When blustering Boreas tosseth up the deep, And thumps a *thunder bounce! **1882** WORSAAE *Industr. Arts Denmark* 168 Another type of coarser work..represents Thor..on his *thunder-carriage. *c* **1000** *Sax. Leechd.* I. 374 ʒenim..*ðunorclafran blostman [etc.]. *c* **1265** *Voc. Names Plants* in Wr.-Wülcker 558/2 *Consolida media*, þundreclouere. **1569** SPENSER *Vis. Bellay* iv. in *Theatre Worldlings*, *Thunder dartes for Jove. **1591** SYLVESTER *Du Bartas* I. i. 272 Th' immortall, mighty *Thunder-darter. **1606** SHAKS. *Tr. & Cr.* II. iii. 11. **1601** B. JONSON *Poetaster* V. iii, You shall sweare By *thunder-darting Iove, the King of gods. *c* **1374** CHAUCER *Troylus* V. 1505 How cappaneus the proude With *thonder dynt was slayn. *c* **1440** *Jacob's Well* 100 He was smyten to deth, wyth leuenyng & wyth thunder-dynt. **1808** SCOTT *Marm.* I. xxiii, The Mount, where Israel heard the law, 'Mid thunder-dint, and flashing levin. **1883** R. TURNER in *Gd. Words* Sept. 590/1 The gelatinous [fungus] which the New Zealand natives know as '*thunder-dirt'. **1832** TENNYSON *Dream Fair Wom.* 122 As *thunder-drops fall on a sleeping sea. **1807–8** W. IRVING *Salmag.* (1824) 270 The great *thunder-drum has been new braced. **1876** BLACKIE *Songs Relig. & Life* 175 When Jove beats loud his thunder-drum. **1882** OGILVIE (Annandale), **Thunder-fish*, a species of fish.. found in the Nile, which, like the torpedo, can give an electric shock...The *Malapterurus electricus* of naturalists. **1886** *Nature* 25 Mar. 497/2 Additions to the Zool. Soc. Gardens..include..a Thunder Fish (*Misgurnus fossilis*) from Austria. **1798** COLERIDGE *Anc. Mar.* I. xvii, The ice did split with a *thunder-fit. *c* **1380** WYCLIF *Serm.* Sel. Wks. I. 186 Crist seiþ..þat he saiȝ Saþanas fallinge fro hevene, as þe *þunder floon falliþ fro þe cloude. *c* **1460** *Towneley Myst.* xii. 324 So bright as it shone, I wold haue trowed, veraly, it had bene thoner flone. **1853** G. JOHNSTON *Bot. E. Bord.* 30 About Wooler it [the corn-poppy] was wont to be called *Thunder-flower or Lightnings, and children were afraid to pluck the flower, for if..the petals fell off..the gatherer became more liable to be struck with lightning. **1886** BRITTEN & HOLLAND *Eng. Plant-n.*, Thunder-flower. (1) *Stellaria Holostea*...(2) *Papaver Rhœas.—E. Bord.* Bot. E. Bord...(3) *Lychnis vespertina.—W. Cumb.* **1854** A. ADAMS, etc. *Man. Nat. Hist.* 213 The tiny *Thunder-Flies which we often find during the summer in countless multitudes. **1840** CARLYLE *Heroes* i. (1872) 33 Thor the *Thundergod changed into Jack the Giant-killer. **1907** *Q. Rev.* July 193 Kari, the thunder-god, who kills the wicked by lightning. **1861** L. L. NOBLE *Icebergs* 138 An iceberg rises..after the figure of a *thunderhead. **1879** J. BURROUGHS *Locusts & W. Honey* 94 A growing storm or thunder-head in the horizon. **1773** HENLEY in *Phil. Trans.* LXIV. 135 The apparatus known, to electricians, by the name of the *thunder-house. **1887** GUMMING *Electricity treated Exper.* 147 An instructive experiment is that known as the Thunder House. **1611** SHAKS. *Cymb.* v. iv. 30 No more thou *Thunder-Master shew thy spight on Mortall

Flies. **1700** *Phil. Trans.* XXII. 453 These animals [tadpoles] are known by the vulgar sort of people by the name of *Thunder-pads. **1804** J. GRAHAME *Sabbath* (1808) 15 *Thunder-peals compelled the men of blood To couch within their dens. **1860** TYNDALL *Glac.* I. xi. 86 The breaking up of the weather was announced by a thunder-peal. **1878** BROWNING *La Saisiaz* 150 Truth is truth in each degree—'Thunder-pealed by God to Nature, whispered by my soul to me. **1801** *Med. Jrnl.* XXI. 85 A stone of the calcareous species, ..called by the common people *thunder-pick. **1866** *Treas. Bot.* 1148 *Thunder-plant, *Sempervivum tectorum.* **1821** GALT *Annals Parish* i. 22 It came on such a *thunder-plump, that there was not a single soul stayed in the kirk-yard to hear him. **1883** MRS. BISHOP in *Leisure Hour* 20/2 A heavy shower, like a 'thunder-plump', takes up a part of the afternoon. **1888** GOODE *Amer. Fishes* 142 The name..'*Thunder-pumper', also used for the bittern,..is heard along the Mississippi River. **1891** E. ROPER *By Track & Trail* xxi. 312 The gurgle and the wheeze and the final explosion of a 'thunder-pumper' [bittern]. **1824** *Mechanic's Mag.* No. 57. 10 A good kitchen fire has more efficacy in preventing a house from being struck than a whole magazine of *thunder-rods. **1605** SYLVESTER *Du Bartas* II. iii. I. *Vocation* 1304 Heav'n flings down nought but flashing *Thundershot. **1626** T. H[AWKINS] *Caussin's Holy Crt.* 130 Some haue beene.. *thunder-shot in a bath. *a* **1699** STILLINGFL. (J.), The conceit is long in delivering, and at last it comes like a *Thunder-shower, full of sulphur and darkness. **1766** WESLEY *Jrnl.* 13 July, We were met..by a furious thunder-shower. *c* **1440** *York Myst.* xi. 320 So are they threst and *thondour slayne. **1732** P. WALKER *Cargill* in *Biog. Presbyt.* (1827) II. 24 Frighted as if they were blasted or thunder-slain. **1875** BROWNING *Aristoph. Apol.* 1968 Hellas *thundersmote The Persian. **1592** G. HARVEY *Four Lett.* iii. 37 That terrible *Thundersmith of termes. **1593** — *Pierce's Super.* 190 Vulcan ..the..thundersmith of..Iupiter. **1800** LAMB *Let. to Manning* 16 Oct., Whip-snakes, *thunder-snakes, pig-nose-snakes. **1863** T. W. HIGGINSON *Army Life* (1870) 140 A thunder-snake, eight feet long. **1563** B. GOOGE *Eglogs* iv. (Arb.) 43 O thou yat throwest the *thunder thumps From Heauens hye, to Hell. **1637** BASTWICK *Litany* I. 11, I will soe *thunderthump Your Pautry Politans. *a* **1586** SIDNEY *Arcadia* (1598) 571 Now the *thunderthumping Ioue transfund his dotes into your excellent formositie. **1623** LISLE *Ælfric on O. & N. Test.* Ded. xii, The shriking trump, and thunder-thumping drum. **1679** V. ALSOP *Mel. Inquirend.* II. iii. 250 They cannot cloath their thoughts in thunder-thumping Phraseology.

**Thunder** (þʊ·ndəɹ), *v.* Forms: see the sb.; also 3 **þondri**, 4 **thonyre**; 5 *pa. t.* **thunret**. [OE. *þunrian*, in 13th c. *þondren*, f. *þunor*, THUNDER *sb.*; cf. Du. *donderen*, LG. *dönnern*, OHG. *donarôn*, MHG. *donren*, MG. *dunren*, Ger. *donnern*; Norw. dial. *tora*; Sw. *dundra*, Da. *tordne*, *dundre* (from LG.).]

**1.** *intr.* **a.** Impersonally: *it thunders*, thunder sounds, there is thunder.

*c* **888** K. ÆLFRED *Boeth.* xxxix. § 3 Hit hwilum þunrað, hwilum na ne onginð. *c* **1000** *Ags. Gosp.* John xii. 29 Seo menio..þæt ȝehyrde sædon þæt hyt þunrode. *c* **1290** *S. Eng. Leg.* I. 198/37 Þat weder..bi-gan to chaungie..hit bi-gan to þondri and hauli. *a* **1375** *Joseph Arim.* 235 Hit þester bi-gon and þonderde swiþe. *c* **1400** *Destr. Troy* 3691 Thunret full throly; thrappit the windes. **1526** TINDALE *John* xii. 29 Then sayde the people that stode by and herde, it thoundreth. **1616** SURFL. & MARKHAM *Country Farme* 25 If in Summer it lighten when it thundreth not. **1725** WATTS *Logic* III. ii. § 4 Thunder seldom comes without Lightning; but it thundered Yesterday; therefore probably it lightened also. **1890** DOYLE *White Company* xv, I can well remember that in Navarre one day it thundered on the left out of a cloudless sky.

**b.** With subject (the or a deity, heaven, the clouds, the sky, etc.): To cause or give forth thunder; to sound with thunder.

*a* **1000** *Ags. Ps.* (Th.) xxviii[i]. 3 He is mæȝen-þrymmes God, and he þunrað ofer maneȝum wæterum. *a* **1300** *E. E. Psalter* xvi[i]. 14 [13] And laverd thonered fra heuen. *a* **1340** HAMPOLE *Psalter, Cant.* 502 In heuyns he sall thonyre. **1535** COVERDALE *Ps.* lxxvi[i]. 17 Yᵉ cloudes thondered, and thy arowes wente abrode. **1582** STANYHURST *Æneis* I. (Arb.) 20 Thee skyes doo thunder. **1607** SHAKS. *Cor.* III. i. 257 He would not flatter..Ioue, for 's power to Thunder. **1810** SOUTHEY *Thalaba* VII. xxii, Then darkness cover'd all, Earth shook, Heaven thunder'd.

**c.** *trans.* (with various objects): To deal *out* or inflict by thunder; to strike *down* by thunder; to utter in thunder. *arch. rare.*

**1579** GOSSON *Sch. Abuse* (Arb.) 47 Beeing the Sonnes of Iupiter, they..thunder out plagues to the proude in heart. **1608** SYLVESTER *Du Bartas* II. iv. IV. *Schisme* 1193 The Heav'nly Powrs, Who thunder-down the high-aspiring Towrs. *a* **1625** JAS. I *Ps.* xxix. in Farr *S. P. Jas. I* (1848) 4 God doth thunder his uoyce.

**2.** *transf. intr.* To make a loud resounding noise like thunder; to sound very loudly; to roar. Sometimes connoting violent movement: To rush or fall with great noise and commotion.

*c* **1374** CHAUCER *Boeth.* II. met. iv. 31 (Camb. MS.) Al thowgh the wynde trowblynge the see thondre with ouerthrowynges. **1568** GRAFTON *Chron.* II. 1334 The great artillary began to thunder from either side. **1610** HOLLAND *Camden's Brit.* (1637) 705 The Danes like a mighty storme thundring from out of the North-East. **1718** POPE *Iliad* II. 1017 His fiery coursers thunder o'er the plains. **1749** FIELDING *Tom Jones* XIII. iv, A footman knocked, or rather thundered at the door. **1845** J. COULTER *Adv. Pacific* x. 124 A vast body of water passed down over a precipice about a hundred feet high, and thundered into the sea. **1855** TENNYSON *Light Brigade* iii, Cannon in front of them Volley'd and thunder'd. **1860** TYNDALL *Glac.* I. xxiv. 175 Avalanches thundered incessantly from the Aiguille Verte.

**b.** *trans.* (with various objects): To deal or inflict, drive or impel, sound or give forth, strike, attack, or bombard, put *down* or overwhelm, etc. with a loud noise or other action like thunder.

**1590** SPENSER *F. Q.* I. vi. 43 They gan..To thunder blowes, and fiersly to assaile Each other. *Ibid.* III. x. 33 Forth the Boaster..begonne His stolen steed to thunder furiously. **1601** B. JONSON *Poetaster* IV. v, Thou anger'st vs,..we will thunder thee in peeces. **1638** SIR T. HERBERT *Trav.* (ed. 2) 108 The English merchants ships thundred out his health by 200 great shot. **1687** RYCAUT *Hist. Turks* II. 322 The Town would be thundred with greater violence. **1759** W. WILKIE *Epigon.* VI. 173 Learn to dread My vengeance thund'red on your wretched head. **1839** BAILEY *Festus* xix. (1852) 304 Like to a foaming force, Which thunders down the echo it creates. **1894** HALL CAINE *Manxman* IV. xii, He pounded it [a drum], boomed it, thundered it.

**3.** *fig.* **a.** *intr.* To speak in the way of vehement threatening or reproof; to utter terrible menace or denunciation; to 'fulminate'; to inveigh powerfully *against*; sometimes, to speak bombastically, or with powerful eloquence. Also simply, to speak in a very loud tone, shout loudly, vociferate.

*a* **1340** HAMPOLE *Psalter* xvii. 15 Oure lord thonord, manaunsand pyne of hell til synful men. **1549** COVERDALE, etc. *Erasm. Par. Tim.* 13 Thunder not at him with cruell wordes. **1575** GASCOIGNE *Making of Verse* in *Steele Gl.*, etc. (Arb.) 31 It is not inough..to thunder in Rym, Ram, Ruff, by letter (quoth my master Chaucer). **1617** MORYSON *Itin.* I. 142 The Hoste so thundred among us like the bragging souldier. **1697** DRYDEN *Æneid* VI. 823 The queen of Furies ..thund'ring in their ears. **1722** DE FOE *Plague* (1754) 33 The Ministers..thundered against these, and other wicked Practices. **1863** W. PHILLIPS *Speeches* i. 9 James Otis thundered in this hall.

**b.** *trans.* To utter or publish in the way of terrible threatening, denunciation, or invective; also simply, to utter loudly, shout out, roar.

*c* **1380** WYCLIF *Wks.* (1880) 287 Cursyngis purchased of þe pope and oþere felle sensuris þondured ouere til Englond. **1548** UDALL, etc. *Erasm. Par. Matt.* xii. 74 Do not thunder sore threatenings. *c* **1590** MARLOWE *Faust.* vi. 20 Fearful echoes thunder in mine ears, 'Faustus, thou art damned!' **1592** GREENE *Groat's W. Wit* (1617) 27 The twelue labours of Hercules haue I terribly thundered on the Stage. **1604** ROWLANDS *Looke to it* 43 Thunder out Oathes, such as in Hell are bred. **1681** T. FLATMAN *Heraclitus Ridens* No. 31 (1713) I. 200 Adieu, ye Whigs, Poor Protestant Pigs, The Tories now will thunder us. *a* **1715** BURNET *Own Time* (1766) I. 274 Censures would have been thundered at Rome against all that should take any such test. **1839** THACKERAY *Fatal Boots* Mar., He thundered out so much of his abuse of me,..that the boys roared with laughter. **1887** BOWEN *Virg. Æneid* I. 747 Tyrians thunder applause.

**c.** To hurl or launch vehement threats or invectives against; to denounce violently; also, to drive or put *down* by denunciation. Now *rare* or *Obs.*

**1677** W. HUGHES *Man of Sin* II. vi. 103 S. Becket..thunders from off the Earth, and down as low as Hell, vast numbers of Clerks, Bishops, and Nobles. **1694** CROWNE *Married Beau* V. 62 Men thunder one another. *a* **1720** SEWEL *Hist. Quakers* (1795) I. IV. 331 If he had..thundered down deceit.

**Thu·nder and li·ghtning.**

**1.** For the literal use see THUNDER *sb.* 1.

**2.** *fig.* Denunciation, invective: cf. THUNDER *sb.* 3, *v.* 3.

**1638** CHILLINGW. *Relig. Prot.* I. Ep. Ded. 4 They speak nothing but thunder and lightning to us. **1883** J. PARKER *Tyne Ch.* 295 They assail with thunder and lightning the credulity..of official guides.

**3.** *transf.* †**a.** Applied to a cloth, app. of glaring colours, worn in 18th c., and perhaps later. **b.** *attrib.* (19th c.) Applied to articles of apparel of a 'loud' or 'flashy' style, or combining two strongly contrasted colours.

(Cf. **1815** NEMNICH *Britische Waaren Encycl.* s.v. *Thunder and Lightning*..ein Borat oder wollenes Zeug von grellem Ansehen. **1891** FLÜGEL *Eng. Germ. Dict.*, *Thunder and Lightning*, eine Art Borat oder wollenes Zeug aus Schwarz und Gelb gemischt [*i. e.* mixed of black and yellow] (plattdeutsch *Klütjenstoff* oder *Wederschall* [*Widerschein*] Nemn.)

**1766** GOLDSM. *Vic. W.* xii, He had on a coat made of that cloth they call thunder and lightning. **1837** DICKENS *Pickw.* xxxii, He wore a black velvet waistcoat with thunder-and-lightning buttons. **1839** THACKERAY *Fatal Boots* Mar., I recollect my costume very well: a thunder-and-lightning coat, a white waistcoat.., a pair of knee-breeches. **1857** HUGHES *Tom Brown* II. v, A tall fellow, in thunder-and-lightning waistcoat. **1868** YATES *Rock Ahead* I. i, Gorgeous in..thunder-and-lightning neckties.

**4.** *slang* and *dial.* (See quots.)

**1802** *Sporting Mag.* XX. 224 Thunder and lightning (i. e. gin and bitters). **1880** MISS BRADDON in *World* 3 Mar. 13 Treacle and clotted cream, alias thunder and lightning. **1904** *Eng. Dial. Dict.* s. v. *Thunder, Thunder-and-lightning*, (*a*) brandy-sauce when ignited; (*b*) bread spread over with cream and treacle.

**5.** *Thunder-and-lightning snake*: see *thunder-snake* s. v. THUNDER *sb.* 6.

**Thunderation** (þʊndərē¹·ʃən). *U. S. slang.* [f. THUNDER *sb.* + -ATION.] Used as a vague expletive or intensive: cf. THUNDER *sb.* 4.

**1887** *Century Mag.* Nov. 44/2 Everybody wants to know who in thunderation Rache will marry. **1901** *Munsey's Mag.* XXIV. 792/2 'I like you all to thunderation..', he said earnestly, dropping all reserve, 'but [etc.]'.

**Thu·nder-bea:rer.** The bearer of thunder, or of thunderbolts, i. e. Jupiter. So **Thu·nder-bea:ring** *a.*, that bears or carries thunder, laden with thunder; also *fig.*, bearing cannon.

**1605** SHAKS. *Lear* II. iv. 230, I do not bid the Thunder-bearer shoote, Nor tell tales of thee to high-iudging Ioue. **1661** ROSS *Silius Italicus* XVII. 68 Thunder-bearing Birds, descending from The Gods Abodes. **1731** C. JOHNSON *Medæa* III. i, O Thunder-bearing Jove, most ancient Cause. **1754** M. MORGAN *Philoclea* II. iii. (Jod.), And thou, great thunder-bearer Jove, look down. **1823** BYRON *Island* II. x, The thunder-bearing strangers came, In vast canoes, begirt with bolts of flame.

**Thu·nder-blast,** *sb.* Chiefly *poet.* **a.** A peal or clap of thunder. **b.** A stroke of 'thunder'. Also *fig.*

**13..** *Cursor M.* 18075 (Cott.) Þar come a steuen als thoner blast. *c* **1440** *Bone Flor.* 1643 Hys doghtur schulde be strekyn downe Wyth a thonder blaste. **1558** PHAER *Æneid* I. Cj b, My son, that of the thunderblastes of hye Ioue setst but light. **1839** BAILEY *Festus* xxiii. (1854) 414 Be still, ye thunderblasts and hills of fire! **1884** TENNYSON *Becket* III. iii, The Pope's last letters..threaten The immediate thunder-blast of interdict.

So **Thu·nder-bla:sted** *a.*, blasted with 'thunder', struck by lightning.

**1614** JACKSON *Creed* III. xvi. § 5 God will not haue true faith thunderblasted in the tender blade. **1818** SCOTT *Br. Lamm.* xi, Our thunder-blasted dinner. *a* **1849** POE *To One in Paradise* 19 The thunder-blasted tree.

**Thunderbolt** (þʊ·ndəɹbōᵘlt), *sb.* Forms: see THUNDER *sb.* and BOLT *sb.*[1]; (9 *dial.* **dunderbolt**).

**1.** A supposed bolt or dart formerly (and still vulgarly) believed to be the destructive agent in a lightning-flash when it 'strikes' anything; a flash of lightning conceived as an intensely hot solid body moving rapidly through the air and impinging upon something: in mythology an attribute of Jove, Thor, or other deity. Cf. BOLT *sb.*[1] 2.

In later use often a vague rhetorical or poetic expression for a destructive lightning-flash or thunderstroke.

*c* **1440** *Alphabet of Tales* 49 Þis womman was burnyd to dede with a thondre-bolte. **1535** [see BOLT *sb.*[1] 2]. **1560** DAUS tr. *Sleidane's Comm.* 462 In the beginning of..Ianuary ..were horrible tempestes, thondering, and lightening, and thonderboltes. **1632** LITHGOW *Trav.* II. 69 Men should dread the thunder-bolt, when they see the lightning. **1710** W. KING *Heathen Gods & Heroes* x. (1722) 33 All the rest [of the Giants]..fell by the Thunderbolts of Jupiter. **1890** W. E. NORRIS *Misadventure* xvii, The intelligence..had fallen upon him like a thunderbolt from a clear sky.

**b.** An imaginary or conventional representation of the above as an emblem of a deity, a heraldic bearing, etc.

**1727–41** CHAMBERS *Cycl.* s.v., On medals, the thunder-bolt is sometimes found to accompany the emperors heads; as that of Augustus. **1823** P. NICHOLSON *Pract. Build.* 489 The head of Medusa, or the Furies, thunderbolts, and other symbols of horror. **1894** *Parker's Gloss. Her.* s.v., Azure, a sun between three thunderbolts, winged and shafted or.

**2.** *fig.* Something very destructive, terrible, or startling; *esp.* an awful denunciation, censure, or threat proceeding from a high authority; some sudden or unexpected, and hence startling event or piece of news, usually untoward.

**1559** *Primer* in *Priv. Prayers* (1851) 91 To the thunderbolts of thy word put violence. **1591** SPENSER *Ruins of Rome* 150 To dart abroad the thunder bolts of warre. **1633** T. STAFFORD *Pac. Hib.* I. xv. (1821) 168 Terrified with the Priests Thunderbolts of Excommunication. **1787** MME. D'ARBLAY *Diary* 30 Jan., This information was a thunderbolt to her. **1860** READE *Cloister & H.* xxxviii, Awaking from the stupor into which this thunderbolt of tyranny had thrown him.

**b.** Applied to a person noted for violent or destructive action; one who acts with furious and resistless energy.

**1593** HARVEY *Pierce's Super.* Wks. (Grosart) II. 48 Oratours..infinitely ouermatched by this hideous thunderbolt in humanity. **1599** HAYWARD *1st Pt. Hen. IV* 2 Prince Edward the thunderbolt of warre in his time. **1708** MRS. CENTLIVRE *Busie Body* III. iii, I have done you a piece of Service; I told the old Thunderbolt, that the Gentleman that was gone in, was [etc.]. **1742** R. BLAIR *Grave* 123 Where are the mighty thunderbolts of war? The Roman Cæsars? **1847** EMERSON *Repr. Men, Napoleon* Wks. (Bohn) I. 372 A thunderbolt in the attack, he was found invulnerable in his entrenchments.

**3.** Locally applied to various stones, fossils, or mineral concretions, formerly or vulgarly supposed to be thunderbolts (sense 1): **a.** a belemnite or other fossil cephalopod; **b.** a flint celt or similar prehistoric implement; **c.** a mass or nodule of iron pyrites occurring in chalk.

**1613** LATHAM *2nd Bk. Falconry* (1633) 160 Take a thunder-bolt, the which is found most commonly in the fields, in some channell or watercourse,..put it into a hot fire and burne it well. **1634–5** BRERETON *Trav.* (Chetham Soc.) 41 The dart of a thunderbolt about the length and thickness of your little finger. **1712** STEELE *Spect.* No. 431 ¶ 3 Thunderbolts, a certain long, round bluish Stone, which I found among the Gravel in our Garden. **1814** SCOTT *Diary* 8 Aug., in *Lockhart*, The most superb collection of the stone axes.. called celts. The Zetlanders call them thunderbolts, and keep them in their houses as a receipt against thunder. **1826** POLWHELE *Trad. & Recoll.* ix. II. 607 For 'the reumatis'..I knew an old woman who used to boil a celt (vulgarly a dunderbolt or thunderbolt) for some hours, and then dispense her water to the diseased. **1862** *Athenæum* 30 Aug. 280 Go..into any of the more productive chalk-pits.., and the workmen will offer you fragmentary 'thunderbolts' (belemnites) and nautili.

**d.** Erroneously or by confusion applied to a meteoric stone or meteorite.

**1802** [see THUNDER-STONE 2]. **1830** HERSCHEL *Stud. Nat. Phil.* 120 These circumstances..long caused them to be confounded with an effect of lightning, and called thunderbolts.

**4.** Applied (chiefly locally) to various plants: **a.**

the corn poppy (= *thunder-flower* (*b*), THUNDER *sb.* 6); **b.** the bladder campion; **c.** the white campion; **d.** a species of iris, *Iris Xiphium*.

**1847–78** HALLIWELL, *Thunder-bolt*. (1) The corn poppy. *West.* **1886** BRITTEN & HOLLAND *Eng. Plant-n.*, Thunder Bolts. (1) *Lychnis vespertina*. Rutl. (2) *Papaver Rhœas*. ..(3) *Silene inflata*. Kent.., where the children snap the calyxes, which explode with a slight report. **1898** *Westm. Gaz.* 28 June 3/1 That strangely beautiful Spanish iris the Thunderbolt, a large flower of browns and yellows and greyish purples.

**5.** *attrib.* **Thunderbolt beetle**, a species of beetle, *Arhopalus fulminans*, with dark wing-cases crossed by zigzag grey lines; **thunderbolt-stone**: see quot., and cf. THUNDERBOLT 3.

**1871** TYLOR *Prim. Cult.* xvi. II. 238 They [Sioux Indians] consider the lightning entering the ground to scatter there in all directions thunderbolt-stones, which are flints, etc.

Hence **Thu·nderbolt** *v., trans.* (*a*) to strike with or as with a thunderbolt; to astonish, amaze, or terrify; (*b*) to hurl or dart like a thunderbolt; **Thu·nderbolted** *ppl. a.*, struck by a thunderbolt; charged with thunderbolts.

*a* **1586** SIDNEY *Arcadia* III. (1622) 304 Sorrow not being able so quickely to thunderbolt her heart thorough her senses. **1593** G. HARVEY *Pierce's Super.* **iv b, He brandisheth the whurlewinde .. And thunderbolteth fo-confounding shott. **1623** J. WODROEPHE *Marrow Fr. Tongue* 487/2 A culpable and indebted Man is alwayes thunder-bolted. **1819** W. TENNANT *Papistry Storm'd* (1827) 31 It beat the thunder-boltit leven. **1881** in Elworthy *W. Somerset Word-bk.* s. v., He (the tower) was thunderbolted about of a sixty year agone.

**Thu·nder-clap.** [f. THUNDER *sb.* + CLAP *sb.*[1]] A clap or loud crash of thunder; formerly also, a thunderstroke. Often allusively used: cf. c.

*c* **1386** CHAUCER *Pars. T.* ¶ 100 The Eyr..shal be ful of thonder clappes and lyghtnynges. *c* **1489** CAXTON *Blanchardyn* liv. 218 Since it hath pleased..God to terrifie with his thunderclaps our feeble hearts. **1598** HAKLUYT *Voy.* I. 60 He was afterward slaine by a thunderclap. **1686** tr. *Chardin's Trav. Persia* 45 This Answer was like a Thunderclap. **1758** BORLASE *Nat. Hist. Cornw.* 15 The Thunder-claps were within a few minutes of one another. **1861** SALA *Dutch Pict.* xi. 161 The massacre of Scio burst upon us like a thunder-clap. **1864** C. KNIGHT *Passages Work. Life* I. i. 17 The loudest thunder-clap..would produce such a concussion of the air.

**b.** *transf.* of other loud noises.

**1610** R. NICCOLS *Winter Nt.'s Vis., K. Arthur* xxx, The thunde. claps of clashing armes. **1711** ADDISON *Spect.* 40 ¶ 6 With what Thunder-claps of Applause he leaves the Stage.

**c.** *fig.* A sudden startling or terrifying occurrence, act, utterance, or piece of news. (Cf. THUNDERBOLT 2.)

**1610** HOLLAND *Camden's Brit.* (1637) 243 Untill that fatal thunder-clap [the Dissolution] overthrew all the Monasteries of England. **1665** SIR T. HERBERT *Trav.* (1677) 331 A thunderclap was heard..anathematizing Elharu-Esed. **1852** JERDAN *Autobiog.* II. v. 49 A thunder-clap burst open and astonished Europe; Buonaparte had escaped from Elba. **1886** G. ALLEN *Maimie's Sake* xxvii, It was as great a thunder-clap to me as to you.

**Thu·nder-cloud.** A storm-cloud charged with electricity, that sends forth thunder and lightning.

**1697** DAMPIER *Voy.* I. iv. 79 These Tornadoe's commonly come against the wind.., as our Thunder-Clouds are often observed to do. **1794** MRS. RADCLIFFE *Myst. Udolpho* l, The thunder-clouds, being dispersed, had left the sky perfectly serene. **1860** PUSEY *Min. Proph.* 155, God's judgments rolled round like a thunder-cloud. **1871** tr. *Schellen's Spectr. Anal.* § 7. 21 When the electric spark flashes from the thunder-cloud to the earth.

**b.** *fig.* Something threatening or dreadful figured as a cloud.

**1783** COWPER *Valediction* 76 To scenes where competition, envy, strife, Beget no thunder-clouds to trouble life. **1898** *N. & Q.* 9th Ser. II. 138/2 The black thunder-cloud of Spain overshadowed half the heavens.

**Thu·nder-crack.** *arch.* or *dial.* = THUNDER-CLAP. **a.** *lit.*

*c* **1440** *Jacob's Well* 203 þe feend, wyth a thunder-crakke, smote doun þe cherche to þe grounde. **1560** PILKINGTON *Expos. Aggeus* (1562) 180 The cloudes burstes, & the thunder-cracke comes. **1622** S. WARD *Life of Faith in Death* (1627) 79 Like fooles that feare the thunder cracke, and not the Bolt. *a* **1834** R. SURTEES *Poems* in Taylor *Life* 317 The sky looks..black, And so we get a thunder-crack.

†**b.** *transf. Obs.*

**1595** B. BARNES *Spir. Sonn.* xxxiii, Thrice puissant generall ..Whose voyce itselfe is dreadfull thunder-cracke.

†**c.** *fig. Obs.*

**1577** VAUTROUILLIER *Luther on Ep. Gal.* 25 The Pope.. rappeth out his thundercrackes and cursings against the miserable and terrified in conscience. **1624** MIDDLETON *Game at Chess* II. ii. 179 Those thunder-cracks of pride, Ushering a storm of malice. **1646** P. BULKELEY *Gospel Covt.* I. 68 Had they not heard those thundercrackes?

†**Thu·nderday, thu·ndurday.** *Obs.* A rare synonym of THURSDAY, q. v.

*c* **1460** *Oseney Reg.* 138 þe þundurday [orig. L. *die Iovis*] nexte after the ffest of þ^e Birth of owr lorde In the ȝere of the Reyne of Kynge Henry the v.

**Thundered** (þʋ·ndəɹd), *ppl. a.* [f. THUNDER *v.* or *sb.* + -ED.] **a.** Dealt or inflicted as by thunder. †**b.** Struck by 'thunder' or lightning (*obs.*). **c.** Uttered or sounded with a noise like thunder. **d.** Affected by thunder; turned sour (as milk) by atmospheric electricity.

**1600** FAIRFAX *Tasso* xx. ciii, So falles a thundred towre. **1819** SHELLEY *Masque Anarchy* xc, Like Oppression's thundered doom. **1823** BYRON *Juan* XI. xxix, Thunder'd knockers broke the..spell. **1877** BLACKIE *Wise Men* 326 Some, Like thundered milk, have turned the sweet to sour.

**Thunderer** (þʋ·ndərəɹ). [f. THUNDER *v.* + -ER[1].] One who or that which thunders.

**1.** He who thunders or causes thunder: applied to God, or to a deity, as Jupiter or Thor.

*c* **1374** CHAUCER *Boeth.* IV. met. vi. 111 (Camb. MS.) The lawes of the heye thonderere, þat is to seyn of god. **1552** HULOET, Thundrer, *altitonans, tis*, a name that the panyms gaue to God. **1611** SHAKS. *Cymb.* v. iv. 95 *Iupiter*...How dare you Ghostes Accuse the Thunderer? **1791** COWPER *Iliad* I. 492 Once the Gods..Conspired to bind the Thund'rer. **1870** BRYANT *Iliad* I. I. 23 Make my suit to Jupiter The Thunderer.

**b.** A person employed at a dramatic representation to imitate thunder by some mechanical means.

**1711** ADDISON *Spect.* No. 235 ¶ 2 Others will have it to be the Play-house Thunderer. **1807–8** W. IRVING *Salmag.* (1824) 270 It will be a further gratification to the patriotic audience to know that the present thunderer is a fellow-countryman.

**2.** *fig.* A resistless warrior; a powerful declaimer or orator, an utterer of violent invective, or the like; *spec.* as a sobriquet of the London *Times* newspaper.

**1586** T. B. *La Primaud. Fr. Acad.* (1589) 615 Who will not wish to have the surname of Aristides the just..rather than as many use to be called Conquerors, Besiegers, Thunderers? **1784** COWPER *Task* II. 221 To shake thy senate, and from heights sublime Of patriot eloquence to flash down fire Upon thy foes, was never meant my task: But I can feel thy fortunes..with as true a heart As any thund'rer there. **1840** CARLYLE *Let.* 13 June in *C. & Lond. Libr.* (1907) 58 Six and sixpence—for a *Times* advertisement, which the Thunderer dunned me for to-day! **1882** PEBODY *Eng. Journalism* xv. 114 It was the writing of Edward Sterling that gave the *Times* the name of the 'Thunderer'. **1884** W. M. DICKSON in *Harper's Mag.* June 64/1 He reappeared in the arena, again the thunderer of the scene.

**3.** Something that makes a noise like thunder; *spec.* a toy made of a flat thin piece of wood or an ox-rib with a string attached at one end, which makes a roaring noise when whirled round; a 'bull-roarer'.

**1860** TYNDALL *Glac.* II. xxv. 364 A new [shaft] is hollowed out, in which..the cataract plays the thunderer. **1908** [MISS E. FOWLER] *Between Trent & Ancholme* 81 'Thunderers', a bricklayer's thin lath, etc.

**Thunderful** (þʋ·ndəɹfŭl), *a. rare.* [f. THUNDER *sb.* + -FUL.] Full of or charged with thunder; *loosely*, thundering, sounding like thunder.

**1898** G. MEREDITH *Day of Daughter of Hades* ix, Legions of thunderful horse. **1910** *Westm. Gaz.* (weekly ed.) 30 Apr. 6/3 As clouds that are thunderful.

**Thu·nder-gust.** Chiefly *U.S.* A strong gust of wind accompanying a thunder-storm.

**1748** FRANKLIN *Lett.* Wks. 1840 V. 220 Hence thunder-gusts after heats, and cool air after gusts. **1817** SHELLEY *Revolt of Islam* IV. xx, Like a thunder gust Caught by some forest. **1824** W. IRVING *T. Trav.* (1849) 389 A terrible black thundergust was coming up. **1876** BANCROFT *Hist. U. S.* IV. xxxvii. 122 During a violent thunder-gust and rain, Ulloa landed, with civil officers, three Capuchin monks, and eighty soldiers.

**Thundering** (þʋ·ndəriŋ), *vbl. sb.* [f. THUNDER *v.* + -ING[1].] The action of the verb THUNDER.

**1.** *lit.* (see THUNDER *v.* 1); also in *pl.*: = THUNDER *sb.* 1, 1 c (now *rare* or *arch.*).

*a* **1100** *O. E. Chron.* an. 1086 [*miswr.* 1085], Swa stor þunring & læȝt wes, swa þæt hit acwealde maniȝe men. **1297** R. GLOUC. (Rolls) 7763 Tempestes þer come þondringe & liȝtinge ek þat slou men ilome. **1398** TREVISA *Barth. De P. R.* XI. i. (1495) 381 Ayre strongly meuyd makyth wyndes lyghtnynge and thondrynge drawe togyder. **1526** TINDALE *Rev.* xix. 6 As the voyce off many waters, and as the voyce off stronge thondrynges [so **1539** (Great), **1560** (Genev.), **1611**; 1881 *R. V.* thunders]. **1555** EDEN *Decades* 90 Soo many thunderinges, lyghtnynge, and tempestes wherwith they are soo often troubeled. **1727** [DORRINGTON] *Philip Quarll* (1816) 80 Great thundering and lightning. **1884** TAIT *Mind in Matter* (1892) 200 At the bidding of Moses, thunderings, lightnings, and hail, by divine command, exhibited [etc.].

**2.** *transf.* Loud resounding noise (see THUNDER *v.* 2): = THUNDER *sb.* 2.

**1560** DAUS tr. *Sleidane's Comm.* 414 b, Than..was the city [Metz]..beaten with shot,..the noise and Thondering thereof was hard ..iiii Dutche miles beyond the Rhine. **1633** P. FLETCHER *Purple Isl.* XI. iii, Raise my soft strain to high thundering. **1822** BYRON *Werner* V. i. 113 The thundering Of far artillery. **1866** DICKENS *Lett.* (1880) II. 254 The thundering of applause..was quite staggering.

**b.** Infliction of heavy and resounding strokes.

**1592** WYRLEY *Armorie, Ld. Chandos* i, Whom sound he hit with stagring steps doth reel, They knew it sure that his sad thundring feel.

**3.** *fig.* Vehement threatening, invective, or the like (see THUNDER *v.* 3): = THUNDER *sb.* 3.

**1564** KNOX *Bk. Com. Order* (1840) 158 Lawful excommunication (for the thunderings of that Roman antichrist are but vanity and wind). **1597** J. PAYNE *Royal Exch.* 42 What thundringe soever the scripture sownds agaynst yt. **1607** HIERON *Wks.* I. 183 The thundring out of the threatnings and terror of the law. **1893** E. L. WAKEMAN in *Columbus* (Ohio) *Dispatch* 11 May, By direst sacerdotal thunderings.

**4.** *attrib.* and *Comb.*, as **thundering-machine**, an apparatus for imitating thunder in a theatre.

**1826** *Museum Crit.* II. 214 [The Greeks] had..a βροντεῖον, or artificial thundering machine, consisting of a vessel filled with stones, which was rolled along a sheet of copper.

**Thu·ndering,** *ppl. a.* (*adv.*) [f. as prec. + -ING[2].] That thunders, in various senses.

**1.** *lit.* Causing or sending forth thunder; †of or characterized by thunder, thundery (*obs.*).

**1530** PALSGR. 281/1 Thundring, *altitonant*. **1573** TUSSER *Husb., Author's Belief* vii, That sendeth thundring claps, like terrours out of hell. **1621** in Foster *Eng. Factories Ind.* (1906) 242 We came to anchor.., and in a flat calme began to make thundering weather. **1751** J. BARTRAM *Observ. Trav. Pennsylv.*, etc. 56 A rainy thundering warm day. **1856** MASSON *Ess.* vi. 179 [He] resumed his place in the public eye as the thundering Jove of the Opposition.

**b.** *Thundering Legion*: see quots.

**1650** BAXTER *Saints' R.* II. vi. § 6 (1651) 264 Hence the Christian soldiers in their Army were called, the Thundering Legion. **1727–41** CHAMBERS *Cycl.*, *Thundering Legion*, *Legio Fulminans*, was a legion in the Roman army, consisting of Christian soldiers, who in the expedition of the emperor Marcus Aurelius against the Sarmatæ, Quadi, and Marcomanni, saved the whole army, then ready to perish of thirst, by procuring, with their prayers, a very plentiful shower thereon; and, at the same time, a furious hail, mixed with lightening and thunderbolts, on the enemy..: though some say, that the legion those Christians were of, was called the *thundering legion* before. **1831–3** E. BURTON *Eccl. Hist.* xix. (1845) 413. **1835** *Penny Cycl.* III. 105/1 Some unlucky legendist, not knowing that the 12th or Thundering Legion, which was engaged in this affair, had its name before it happened, took occasion to call it a Christian Legion, and to attribute the miraculous storm to the efficacy of its prayers.

**2.** *transf.* Making a noise like thunder, sounding very loudly; of sound, As loud as thunder.

† *Thundering gold*, see note s. v. FULMINATING *ppl. a.*[1]

**1576** GASCOIGNE *Spoyle of Antwerpe* B ij, The Castle had all this while, played at the Towne and trenches, with thundring shot. **1687** DRYDEN *Ode St. Cecilia's Day* iii, The double, double, double beat Of the thundring Drum. **1694** SALMON *Bate's Dispens.* (1713) 317/1 *Aurum Fulminans*: Lightning or Thundering Gold. *c* **1764** GRAY *Owen* 23 There the thund'ring strokes begin. **1845** J. COULTER *Adv. Pacific* iii. 25 A long, deep, regular sea, with a fine thundering crest on the top of the wave. **1871** L. STEPHEN *Playgr. Eur.* xii. (1894) 283 The thundering fall of the Handeck becomes [in winter] a gentle thread of pure water.

**3.** *fig.* in reference to terrible invective, threatening, etc., or to powerful eloquence; sometimes to bombastic or inflated language.

**1543** GRAFTON *Contn. of Harding* 463 The duke of Burgoyne..wrote sharpe letters of thretenyng..whose fyrye and thundryng wordes [etc.]. **1576** FLEMING *Panopl. Epist.* 357 To resist the..outragious rule of thundering Tyraunts. *a* **1674** CLARENDON *Hist. Reb.* XIII. § 15 Thundering Letters came from the Parliament, with great menaces what they would do. **1727** POPE *Shaks. Wks.* Pref. I. 5 The most pompous Rhymes, and thundering Versification. *a* **1797** WILKES in J. Almon *Mem.* (1805) V. 35, I hear of a thundering memorial against this country from Spain. **1883** J. PARKER *Apost. Life* II. 16 The thundering eloquence.

**4.** Very energetic or forcible, violent; hence as a mere intensive: Very great or big, excessive, immense, 'tremendous', 'terrific'. *colloq.* or *slang*.

**1618** T. ADAMS *Love's Copy* Wks. 1862 II. 420 He goes a thundering pace, that you would not think it possible to overtake him. **1632** LITHGOW *Trav.* x. 476 They all three left mee in a thundering rage. **1681** OTWAY *Soldier's Fort.* I. i, I warrant him a thundering Rogue. *a* **1704** T. BROWN *Aristænetus' Epist.* I. Wks. 1720 I. 249, I was drawing a thundring Fish out of the Water, so very large, that it made my Rod crack again. **1851** BORROW *Lavengro* xcix, What a thundering old fool you are! **1900** BARRIE *Tommy & Grizel* v, Such a thundering lie.

**b.** as *adv.* Excessively, immensely, 'tremendously'. *colloq.* or *slang*.

[**1839** THACKERAY *Fatal Boots* June, 'Open the Yard Door!' says he, with a thundering loud voice.] **1852** DICKENS *Bleak Ho.* xxi, I was a thundering bad son. **1887** BLACK *Sabina Zembra* 228 Don't you think that a thundering good licking would knock the laziness out of him? **1890** 'R. BOLDREWOOD' *Col. Reformer* (1891) 261 A thundering soft thing it is, in a general way.

Hence **Thu·nderingly** *adv.*, in a thundering manner; with a noise as of thunder; *fig.* violently, powerfully; with fierce denunciation; excessively (*slang* or *colloq.*).

**1680** *Honest Hodge & Ralph* 19 To take the Charge off from the Pope,..the more thunderingly to Clap it upon the Phanatick. **1759** H. WALPOLE *Let. to Mann* 10 May, It is well if he concludes this [campaign] as thunderingly as he did the last. **1885** C. GIBBON *Hard Knot* II. xxxiii. 229 It's thunderingly annoying.

†**Thunder-layt, -leit.** *Obs.* Also -leite, -leyt(e. [f. THUNDER + *leyt, lait*, etc., in OE. *leget* (see LAIT *sb.*[1]) lightning.] See THUNDERLIGHT.

**Thunderless** (þʋ·ndəɹlės), *a.* [f. THUNDER *sb.* + -LESS.] Unaccompanied by thunder (or noise like thunder).

**1855** G. MEREDITH *Shav. Shagpat* (1856) 371 Flashes of thunderless lightnings. **1880** TENNYSON *Voy. Maeldune* iii, The long waterfalls Pour'd in a thunderless plunge to the base of the mountain walls.

**Thu·nderlight.** *arch.* [Alteration of the earlier *thunder-layt, -leit* (see above) by substitution of *light* for *leit*. The earlier form occurs in some of the Chaucer MSS.] Light of thunder, lightning.

*c* **1374** CHAUCER *Boeth.* I. met. iv. 7 (MS. Camb. I i. 3. 21) Ne the wey of thonderlyht [*Add. MS.* þonder lyȝt; *MS. Camb.* I i. I. 38 thonder leit; *ed.* 1532 thonder leyte] þat is wont to smyten heye towres, ne shal not moeue þat man. *c* **1386** — *Pars. T.* ¶ 765 (Camb. MS.) After that he brende .v. ceteis with thundyr liȝth [*v. rr.* liȝt, lyht, lyght, lighte, *Ellesm.* leyt, *Harl.* layt]. **1815** L. HUNT *Feast of Poets*, etc. 149 What shall move his placid might? Not the headlong thunderlight. **1834**

LD. HOUGHTON *Mem. Many Scenes* (1844) 59 Under such a sky—Thus grave, thus streaked with thunderlight.

**Thunderous** (þʋ·ndərəs), *a.* Also 6 **thunderus,** 7–9 **thundrous.** [f. THUNDER *sb.* + -OUS.]

**1.** Full of or charged with thunder; of or pertaining to thunder; thundery.

**1582** STANYHURST *Æneis* I. (Arb.) 25 O God most puisaunt, whose mighty auctoritye..mankind skeareth with thunderus humbling. **1667** MILTON *P. L.* x. 702 Notus and Afer black with thundrous Clouds. **1726** POPE *Odyss.* XIX. 513 Nor winter's boreal blast, nor thund'rous show'r, Nor solar ray, cou'd pierce the shady bow'r. **1876** BLACK *Madcap V.* xiv, The lurid and sultry evening had died down into a gloomy and thunderous darkness. **1904** M. HEWLETT *Queen's Quair* III. x. 484 The 10th of June had been a thunderous day.

**2.** Resembling thunder in its loudness.

**1606** SYLVESTER *Du Bartas* II. iv. I. *Trophies* 370 Rushing with thundrous roar. **1820** KEATS *Hyperion* II. 8 Thunderous waterfalls and torrents hoarse. **1875** H. JAMES *R. Hudson* vii. 239 In a voice almost thunderous,..he repeated, 'Sit down!' **1876** GEO. ELIOT *Dan. Der.* vi, Herr Klesmer ..at the piano, struck a thunderous chord. **1892** *Times* 10 June 9/1 Which [motion] was carried amid thunderous applause.

**3.** *fig.* Suggestive of thunder; of threatening aspect, or charged with latent energy, like a thunder-cloud; violent, destructive, or terrifying like thunder.

**1844** MRS. BROWNING *Vis. Poets* xcix, Here, Homer, with the broad suspense Of thunderous brows. **1873** SYMONDS *Grk. Poets* vii. 218 Her [Medea's] fiery eyes and thundrous silence. **1874** BLACKIE *Self-Cult.* 57 The first Napoleon, in his thunderous career over our western world.

Hence **Thu·nderously** *adv.*, in a thunderous manner, with a noise like thunder, very loudly; with threatening aspect as if presaging thunder; **Thu·nderousness,** thunderous quality.

**1842** L. HUNT *Palfrey* I. 184 Shaking him and his saddle right thunderously. **1886** MRS. PHELPS *Burglars in Paradise* vii, Some one knocked thunderously at the back door. **1903** A. SMELLIE *Men of the Covt.* vii. (1904) 103 The skies hung still more thunderously over Presbyterian Scotland. **1904** *Westm. Gaz.* 17 Mar. 2/1 The great organ-voice of many waters sounding in mellowed thunderousness.

**Thunder-stone** (þʋ·ndəɹ,stōun).

**1.** = THUNDERBOLT 1. *arch.*

**1598** MARSTON *Pigmal.* iv, Enuie, let Pines of Ida rest alone, For they will growe spight of thy thunder stone. **1601** SHAKS. *Jul. C.* I. iii. 49, I..Haue bar'd my Bosome to the Thunder-stone. **1678** DRYDEN & LEE *Œdipus* IV. i, You merciless powers, Hoard up your thunder-stones. **1819** SHELLEY *Prometh. Unb.* IV. 341 Sceptred curse..sending A solid cloud to rain hot thunderstones. **1888** LOWELL *Heartsease & Rue* 70 Splintered with thunder-stone.

**2.** Applied to various stones, fossils, etc. formerly identified with 'thunderbolts', as celts, belemnites, masses of pyrites, meteorites: = THUNDERBOLT 3.

**1681** GREW *Musæum* III. I. i. 258 Thunder-Stone or hard Button-Stone. *Brontias.* So called, for that people think they fall sometimes with Thunder. **1703** MAUNDRELL *Journ. Jerus.* (1721) 52 Each tube had a small cavity in its Center, from which its parts were projected in form of rays, to the circumference, after the manner of the Stones vulgarly call'd Thunder-stones. *c* **1710** CELIA FIENNES *Diary* (1888) 218 Ye oare as its just dug Lookes like ye thunderstone. **1778** *Encycl. Brit.* (ed. 2) II. 1090/1 *Belemnites,* vulgarly called thunder-bolts or thunder-stones. **1796** MORSE *Amer. Geog.* II. 16 Norway produces..amethysts, agates, thunder-stones, and eagle-stones. **1802** HOWARD in *Phil. Trans.* XCII. 169 Because explosion and report have generally accompanied the descent of [meteorolites], the name of thunder-bolt, or thunderstone, has ignorantly attached itself to them. **1907** *Q. Rev.* July 176 The 'thunderstones' were of human workmanship.

**3.** *poet.* Applied to a (? stone) cannon-ball.

**1821** SHELLEY *Hellas* 370 The..allies Fled from the glance of our artillery Almost before the thunderstone alit.

**Thu·nder-storm.** A storm of thunder and lightning, usually accompanied with heavy rain.

**1652** BP. HALL *Invis. World* I. vi, A fearful thunder-storm arose. **1794** MRS. RADCLIFFE *Myst. Udolpho* xxxi, Along the open glen,..less dangerous than the woods in a thunder-storm. **1839** DARWIN *Voy. Nat.* iii. (1852) 62 In the year 1793 one of the most destructive thunder-storms perhaps on record happened at Buenos Ayres. **1865** 'L. CARROLL' *Alice in Wonderland* ix, There stood the Queen..frowning like a thunderstorm.

*transf.* **1877** M. PRIOR in *Daily News* 1 Oct. 6/3 No troops could..live in such a thunderstorm of leaden hail.

**Thunderstricken** (þʋ·ndəɹ,strik'n), *a.* [f. THUNDER + STRICKEN.]

**1.** *lit.* = THUNDERSTRUCK 1.

**1652** GAULE *Magastrom.* 310 Upon the Statue of Augustus there was inscribed Caesar. Now, it being thunderstriken, ..the letter C was thereby blotted out. **1818** BYRON *Ch. Har.* IV. lxxxviii, Thou the thunder-stricken nurse of Rome! She-wolf! **1845** G. MURRAY *Islaford* 37 A thunder-stricken corse was found.

**2.** *fig.* = THUNDERSTRUCK 2.

*a* **1586** SIDNEY *Arcadia* III. (1590) 291 b, She..stood as it were thunder-striken with amazement. **1780** MRS. THRALE *Let. to Johnson* 10 June, Mr. Thrale seems thunderstricken, he don't mind anything. **1890** L. C. D'OYLE *Notches* 135 When Mrs. Low hastily lighted the lamp..and saw nothing, she was thunderstricken.

**Thunderstrike** (þʋ·ndəɹ,strəik), *v.* Pa. t. and pple. **thunderstruck** (see also prec. and THUNDERSTRUCK). [prob. a back-formation from *thunderstricken,* that being taken as a pa. pple.]

**1.** *trans.* (*lit.*) To strike with 'thunder' or lightning (cf. THUNDER *sb.* 1 b). ? *Obs.*

**1613** HEYWOOD *Brazen Age* IV. Wks. 1874 III. 232 My father [Jove]..startles vp to thunder-strike the lad [Phaeton]. **1666** T. NEALE in *Phil. Trans.* I. 247 The Account..by the learned Dr. Charleton, concerning the boy that was Thunder-struck near Nantwich in Cheshire. **1710** W. KING *Heathen Gods & Heroes* liv. (1722) 186 Charybdis..was Thunder-struck by Jupiter, and transformed into a Sea-Monster. *a* **1711** KEN *Christophil* Poet. Wks. 1721 I. 442 Angels..Expected when Almighty Ire Shou'd Thunder-strike our guilty Sire. **1902** GREENOUGH & KITTREDGE *Words* 309 'Astonish' is literally 'to thunderstrike', and was once common in the physical sense of 'stun'.

**2.** *fig.* To strike as with 'thunder'. **a.** To strike with amazement, astonish greatly. *Obs.* exc. as in *thunderstricken, thunderstruck.*

**1613**– [see THUNDERSTRUCK 2 a]. **1721** G. ROUSSILLON tr. *Vertot's Rev. Portugal* 104 This message thunder-struck the Duke. **1789** M. NUBER *Let.* in *Ld. Auckland's Corr.* (1861) II. 324 This revolution thunder-strikes the keenest man. **1807** SOUTHEY *Espriella's Lett.* III. 183 The news.. thunderstruck all present.

**b.** To inflict severe or terrible vengeance, reproof, or the like, upon. In quot. 1818 in physical sense, to batter severely.

**1638** SIR T. HERBERT *Trav.* (ed. 2) 71 He had..thunder struck him, with a storme of mighty words. **1650** TRAPP *Comm. Exod.* xix. 16 To terrifie and thunder-strike offenders. **1699** CIBBER *Xerxes* v, To Thunder-strike thy Soul. **1818** BYRON *Ch. Har.* IV. clxxxi, The armaments which thunderstrike the walls.

**Thunderstroke** (þʋ·ndəɹ,strōuk). A stroke of 'thunder' (cf. THUNDER *sb.* 1 b); the impact of a lightning-flash.

*c* **1600** CHALKHILL *Thealma & Cl.* (1683) 5 The lofty Cedar, and the knotty Oak, Are subject more unto the thunder-stroak, Than the low shrubs. **1610** SHAKS. *Temp.* II. i. 204 They fell together..as by a Thunder-stroke. **1844** MRS. BROWNING *Dead Pan* vii, At the rushing thunderstroke would No sob tremble through the tree?

**b.** *transf.* and *fig.*

**1587** GOLDING *De Mornay* xxvi. (1592) 397 The others cutting words which are the thunderstrooks doubled. **1780** BENTHAM *Princ. Legisl.* xiii. § 4 During the first assault of passion as under a thunder-stroke the sentiments of virtue may yield for a moment. **1808** SCOTT *Marm.* II. i, When all the loud artillery spoke, With lightning-flash, and thunder-stroke. **1880** TREVELYAN *Early Hist. C. J. Fox* vi. (1910) 243 The thunder-stroke of such a confession..could not be parried.

**Thunderstruck** (þʋ·ndəɹstrʋk), *ppl. a.* Also 7 **-stroken, -strucken.** (Usually in participial const., as predicate; less commonly in attrib. const., before the sb. For the purely ppl. use with auxiliary, see THUNDERSTRIKE.) [Orig. a later equivalent of *thunderstricken.*]

**1.** *lit.* Struck by lightning: cf. THUNDER *sb.* 1 b. Now *rare* or *Obs.*

**1638** SIR T. HERBERT *Trav.* (ed. 2) 19 Falling downe as thunder-struck. **1676** *Phil. Trans.* XI. 648 Those Thunder-strucken ones [compasses] did never..recover their right positions. **1720** T. BOSTON *Fourf. St.* II. ii. (1784) 104 When a person is thunder-struck, oft-times there is not a wound to be seen in the skin. **1775** ADAIR *Amer. Ind.* 86 Esteeming thunder-struck individuals under the displeasure of heaven.

**2.** *fig.* **a.** Struck with sudden amazement, terror, or the like; greatly amazed, astonished, terrified, or confounded.

**1613** W. BROWNE *Brit. Past.* I. i, The Thunder-stroken Swaine lean'd to a tree, As void of sense as weeping Niobe. **1687** BOYLE *Martyrd. Theodora* v, Thunder-struck with this unexpected answer. **1711** ADDISON *Spect.* No. 60 ¶ 4 The Lover was thunder-struck with his Misfortune. **1775** SHERIDAN *Duenna* I. iii, I'm astonished! I'm thunder struck! here's treachery and conspiracy with a vengeance! **1855** MACAULAY *Hist. Eng.* xx. IV. 402 Luxemburg was thunder-struck. He expostulated boldly and earnestly.

**b.** in reference to ecclesiastical censure, etc.: cf. THUNDER *sb.* 3 a, THUNDERBOLT 2. *rare.*

**1649** BP. HALL *Cases Consc.* III. v. (1654) 202 How many famous Churches have beene..thunder-struck with direfull censures of Excommunication. **1680** H. MORE *Apocal. Apoc.* 132 Gregory the seventh, when he had excommunicated the Emperour Henry the fourth, said, he was *fulmine afflatus* thunder-struck by him.

**Thundery** (þʋ·ndəri), *a.* Also 6–8 **thundry.** [f. THUNDER *sb.* + -Y.]

**1.** Of or pertaining to thunder; characterized by or betokening thunder.

**1598** SYLVESTER *Du Bartas* II. ii. IV. *Columnes* 779 When (angry)..he throws down thundry storms. **1682** in Birch *Hist. Roy. Soc.* (1757) IV. 146 In thundry weather he [Mr. Hooke] supposed..hot sulphureous steams to issue out of the earth, which caused the sultriness that preceded. **1774** WHITE in *Phil. Trans.* LXV. 267 This bird [the Swift] is never so much alive as in sultry, thundry weather. **1894** *Daily News* 4 July 5/4 The sky..covered with heavy clouds of a very thundery type.

† **2.** Making a noise like thunder: = THUNDEROUS 2. *Obs.*

**1605** SYLVESTER *Du Bartas* II. iv. IV. *Decay* 648 As a Cannon's thundry roaring Ball.

**3.** *fig.* Threatening an explosion of anger or passion; gloomy, frowning.

**1824** MISS FERRIER *Inher.* xliv, Mr. R.'s brow looked rather thundery. **1845** CARLYLE *Cromwell's Lett. & Sp.* (1871) V. 40 *note,* That thundery countenance of yours. **1867** S. WILBERFORCE *Ess.* (1874) II. 85 A thundery state of the political and social atmosphere.

**Thung** (þʋŋ), *sb.* ? *dial.* [Echoic: cf. THUNGE; also Lancash. dial. '*thwang,* a great blow' (*Tim Bobbin* 1746).] A dull heavy sound, as of a blow with the fist, but with some resonance. So **Thung** *v., intr.* to make such a sound.

**1890** HALL CAINE *Bondman* x, The thud and thung of twenty hard fists on the table. **1894** — *Manxman* V. iv, Nancy went back to her kneading... Nancy looked up at her thumping and thunging. *Ibid.* VI. xii, He went roaring down the stairs, but came thunging up again in a moment.

**Thung, thunk,** dial. forms of THONG.

**Thunge** (þʋndʒ), *sb. dial.* [Echoic.] 'A loud, hollow sound'; 'a heavy blow or fall producing such a sound'. So **Thunge** *v.* (*Eng. Dial. Dict.*).

**1849** 'T. TREDDLEHOYLE' *Bairnsla Ann.* Feb. (E.D.D.), Sho wor startald wi a thunge at t' chaimber door. **1863** J. H. BURROW *Advent. Alfan* 350 He lay down..and listened to the thunges of the battering-ram. **1881** MISS JACKSON *Shropsh. Word-bk., Thunge*..(2) *sb.* a thump; a heavy fall. 'I come down sich a thunge'. **1887** *S. Cheshire Gloss., Thunge, s.* (1) a loud, hollow sound... It is the word always used to imitate the sound of a gun.

**Thunner, thunure,** Sc. and obs. ff. THUNDER.

**Thunny,** variant of TUNNY, fish.

† **Thu·nwang, -wange.** *Obs.* Forms: 1 **þun-,** 4 **thone-,** 5 **thun-,** (**thwn-, tun-**), **thon-,** (**thoun-**); 1–5 **-wong(e, -wang(e.** [OE. *þunwange, -wonge* (later also *-wang*), *þunwenge,* f. *þun-* (:—OTeut. **þunnu-*: see THIN) + *wang, -e* cheek, jaw; lit. 'thin cheek'. Cf. OHG. *dunwangi, -wengi* (MHG. *tunewenge,* LG. *dunninge, dünninge, dünnege, dunje* (Brem. Wbch.); also local G. *dünne, dünnung* temple, flank), ON. *þunnvangi, -vengi* (Sw. *tinning,* Da. *tinding*).] The temple (of the head).

*a* **1000** *Gloss.* in Wr.-Wülcker 228/7 *Dolor timporum,* þunwenga sar. *c* **1000** *Ælfric's Voc.* ibid. 156/17 *Timpus,* þunwang. *c* **1000** ÆLFRIC *Judg.* iv. 21 ȝelæhte seo wifman an þæra teldsticcena and..ȝesloh þa mid anum bytle bufan his þunwengan. *c* **1325** *Gloss. W. de Bibbesw.* in Wright *Voc.* 146 *Les temples,* thonewonges. *c* **1350** *Nom. Gall.-Angl.* 22 *Iowe temples et iernoun,* Cheke þonewonges and here-liste. *a* **1450** *Stockh. Med. MS.* ii. 76 in *Anglia* XVIII. 295 A playster of betonye..Is good on þe thonwongys for to leye. *c* **1450** *Mirour Saluacioun* 3265 Wham thorgh the thonwonges with a naile at last perced Jael. **1483** *Cath. Angl.* 387/2 A Thunwange (*A.* Thwnwynge), *tempus.*

**Thuong, Thuortour,** obs. ff. THONG, THORTER.

**Thur, þur,** obs. f. THEIR; dial. var. THIR.

† **Thural** (þiū·răl), *a. Obs. rare.* [ad. (rare) L. *tūrāl-is,* f. *tūs* (*thūs*), *tūr-* incense: see -AL.] Of, pertaining to, or of the nature of incense.

**1624** DARCIE *Birth of Heresies* xvi. 66 In this little Thurall Coffer lay the Odors which the Priest tooke. **1714** *Solomon's Song* in R. Steele *Poet. Misc.* 242 Ripe thural Fruits their Frankincense exhale.

**Thurbarow, -barrowe,** corrupt ff. THIRDBOROUGH. **Thurd,** obs. form of THIRD.

† **Thure.** *Obs. rare.* [ad. L. *tūs, thūs* (stem *t(h)ūr-*) incense: see THUS *sb.*: perh. immediately repr. L. *thūra* pl.] Incense, frankincense.

*c* **1425** tr. *Arderne's Treat. Fistula* 63 Mirre, thure, mastike, sadanum. *Ibid.* 66 Bole armoniac, sang dracon, thure, aloe, vitriol combust. *c* **1440** *Pallad. on Husb.* XI. 412 A vnce of mascul thure, Wel smellynge.

**Thurf, þurf,** obs. forms of THROUGH.

† **Thurfe,** *a. Obs. rare*⁻¹. [In Ormin *þurrfe,* app. a. ON. *þurfe, -a* wanting, in need, f. stem *þurf-* of THARF *v.*] Needed, needful, wanting.

*c* **1200** ORMIN 9628 Lare inoh Off all þatt hemm wass þurrfe.

**Thurfte, þurfte,** pa. t. of THARF *v. Obs.,* to need.

**Thurgh, þurȝ, þurgh,** etc., obs. ff. THROUGH.

**Thurible** (þiū·rib'l), *sb.* Forms: 5 **turrible, thoryble,** 7– **thurible,** (9 **thuribule**). [ad. L. *tūribulum, thūribulum* censer, f. *tūs, thūs, thūr-* incense: see THUS *sb.* So OF. *thurible* (Godef.).]

A vessel in which incense is burnt in religious ceremonies; a censer.

Now usually a metal vase with pierced cover, containing combustible material to burn the gums used as incense, which is swung in the hand (or suspended) by chains.

*c* **1440** *Promp. Parv.* 506/2 Turrible (or thoryble), *idem quod* sencere. **1660** JER. TAYLOR *Duct. Dubit.* II. ii. rule vi. § 10 Upon the shekel of the Sanctuary was impress'd the image of Aarons rod and a pot of Manna, or thurible. *a* **1668** LASSELS *Voy. Italy* (1698) II. 239 They shewed us..the great Candlesticks and Thurible of beaten gold. **1805** SOUTHEY *Madoc in W.* xiii, Sweet incense from the waving thuribule Rose like a mist. **1877** J. D. CHAMBERS *Div. Worship* 262 Burning Incense from pendant Thuribles.

*β.* Also in L. form **thuribulum** (þiuri·biŭlŏm).

**1706** PHILLIPS (ed. Kersey), *Thuribulum,* a Censer or Smoaking-Pot, to burn Incence in. **1851** D. WILSON *Preh. Ann.* II. III. ii. 73 The thuribulum is very carefully executed.

**b.** *Comb.* **thurible-boat** = BOAT *sb.* 2 b.

**1853** DALE tr. *Baldeschi's Cerem.* 159 They..deposit the thurible-boat and vase of holy water in the proper place.

Hence † **Thu·rible** *v.,* to cense.

*c* **1440** *Promp. Parv.* 506/2 Turryblon, or sencyn, *thurifico.*

**Thuribuler** (þiuri·biŭləɹ). Also 9 **thu·ribler.** [ad. med.L. *thūribulārius* (1312 in Du Cange), f. *thūribul-um* THURIBLE + *-ārius,* -ER [2] 2. So F. *thuribulier* (16th c. in Godef.).] An acolyte who carries the thurible; = next.

**1504** in *Ripon Ch. Acts* (Surtees) 295 The vicars, dekenez, thuribulers, and the choristers. **1546** *Yorks. Chantry Surv.* (Surtees) 530 In the saide collegiate churche bee..ij thuribulers. 1877 J. D. Chambers *Div. Worship* 111 When the Antiphon..is finished the Thuribler should retire. 1891 *Athenæum* 24 Oct. 544/1 The usual complement of..priests, deacons and subdeacons, choristers, thuribulers, and clerks.

**Thurifer** (þiūᵊ·rifəɹ). [a. mod.L. *thūrifer* 'incense-bearer', sb. use of *thūrifer* adj., f. *thūs, thūr-* incense (see Thus *sb.*) + *-fer* bearing. Med.L. had *thūriferārius* (Du Cange).] One who carries burning incense in religious ceremonies; = prec.

1853 Rock *Ch. of Fathers* III. II. xi. 80 In this procession walked..thurifers with their smoking censers. 1853 Dale tr. *Baldeschi's Ceremonial* 62 At the proper time the Thurifer should prepare fire in some convenient place. 1871 C. B. Pearson *Sarum Sequences* Pref. 6 A procession..consisting..of the deacon.., preceded by a thurifer, candle-bearer, and cross-bearer, and the subdeacon.

**Thuriferous** (þiuəri·fĕrəs), *a.* [f. L. *thūrifer* incense-bearing (see prec.) + -ous: see -ferous.] That produces frankincense.

1656 Blount *Glossogr.*, *Thuriferous*, that beareth or brings forth frankincense. 1727–41 Chambers *Cycl.* s. v. *Frankincense*, These thuriferous, or incense-bearing trees. 1863 J. G. Murphy *Comm. Gen.* x. 29 A thuriferous range of hills.

† **Thuri·fic**, *a. Obs. rare*$^{-1}$. [f. L. *thūs, thūr-* incense + *-ficus* making.] = prec. So † **Thuri·ficate** *v. Obs.*, *trans.* = Thurify 2.

1657 Tomlinson *Renou's Disp.* Pref., Inhabiting the Thurifick Groves of Rerum Natura. 1623 Cockeram, *Thurificate*, to perfume.

**Thurification** (þiūᵊ:rifikēⁱ·ʃən). [n. of action f. eccl. L. *thūrificāre* to Thurify: see -fication. Cf. obs. F. *thurificacion* (15–16th c. in Godef.).] The action of thurifying; the burning or offering of, or perfuming with incense.

1496 *Dives & Paup.* (W. de W.) I. xv. 46/2 Thuryfycacyon & encensyng was by olde tyme an hyghe dyvyne worshypp. *a* 1529 Skelton *Ph. Sparowe* 522 With armatycke gummes ..The way of thurifycation To make a fumigation. 1649 Bp. Hall *Cases Consc.* III. iii. (1654) 185 Some semblance of an Idolatrous thurification. 1755 Amory *Mem.* (1766) II. 193 The papal rites of..bowing the body, thurifications, deosculations. 1872 Shipley *Gloss. Eccl. Terms* s. v. *Absolutiones* 5 Prayers, thurifications, and aspersions round the bodies of the dead.

**Thurify** (þiūᵊ·rifəi), *v.* [a. F. *thurifi-er* (15–16th c. in Godef.), ad. eccl. L. *thūrificāre*, f. *thūs, thūr-* incense + *-ficāre*: see Thus *sb.* and -fy.]

†**1.** *intr.* To burn or offer incense; = Cense *v.*[1] 2. *Obs. rare.*

*c* 1440 Capgrave *St. Kath.* v. 350 If ȝe wil consent And thuryfye to Iubiter. *Ibid.* 534 Thanne shul ye now..Thuryfie on-to that mageste Of grete appollo. 1460 — *Chron.* (Rolls) 76 He [Pope Marcellus] wold not obey Maximiane, and thurifie.

**2.** *trans.* To perfume with incense; to burn incense before; to offer incense to; = Cense *v.*[1] 1. Also *transf.* (quot. 1599).

1570 Foxe *A. & M.* (ed. 2) 663/2 By thurifyeng or censing the aultars. 1599 Nashe *Lenten Stuffe* 65 This herring ..was sensed and thurified in the smoake. 1737 G. Smith *Cur. Relat.* I. iii. 417 The while the Corps remains in the House, the Priest comes every Day to thurify it. 1851 Madden *Shrines & Sepulchres* I. 313 Several Priests..came next to thurify the body.

Hence **Thu·rifying** *vbl. sb.*

*a* 1618 Sylvester *Tobacco Battered* 183 The..smoak of Thurifying Of Images.

**Thurindale,** obs. dial. f. Thirdendeal.

**Thuringite** (þiuri·ndʒəit, -iŋgəit)). *Min.* [ad. Ger. *Thuringit* (Breithaupt, 1832), f. Thuringia, in Central Germany, where found + -ite[1].] A hydrous silicate of aluminium and iron, occurring as an aggregation of minute dark-green scales.

1844 Dana *Min.* (1868) 508 Thuringite is from Reichmannsdorf.

**Thurl, -ing,** var. Thirl *sb.*[1] and *v.*[1], Thirling.

**Thurlepole, -polle,** var. Thirlepoll, a whale.

† **Thu·rlhead.** *Obs. rare*$^{-1}$. Alteration of *thurlepolle*, Thirlepoll, with *head* for *poll*.

1610 Holland *Camden's Brit.* II. 184 There came to land a mighty multitude of great sea fishes, to wit, Thurlhedis.

**Thurow,** obs. form of Through.

**Thurrock** (þʊ·rək). *Obs.* exc. *dial.* Forms: 1 **þurruc**, 4–5 **thurrok(e, thorrok(e**, 5 **thorrocke**, 8 **thorruck**, 9 *dial.* **thurrock, -uck**. [In sense 1, OE. *þurruc* 'cumba', small ship (?), bottom of a ship, bilge = Du. *durk* bilge (cf. *durck, dorck* 'sentina' in Kilian), of unknown etymology. It is doubtful whether senses 2 and 3 belong to the same word.]

**1.** The bilge of a ship. Also *fig.*

*c* 1050 *Suppl. Ælfric's Voc.* in Wr.-Wülcker 181/35 *Cumba, uel caupolus*, þurruc. *c* 1386 Chaucer *Pars. T.* ¶ 363 The smale dropes of water that entren thurgh a litel creuace in to the thurrok [*v.r.* thorrok] and in the botme of the shipe. *Ibid.* ¶ 715 Ydelnesse is the thurrok [*v.r.* thorroke] of alle wikked and vileyns thoghtes. *c* 1440 *Promp. Parv.* 493/2 Thurrok, of a schyppe, *sentina.* 1450–1530 *Myrr. our Ladye* 109 A place in the bottome of a shyppe wherein ys gatheryd all the fylthe that cometh in to the shyppe...And that place stynketh ryghte fowle and yt ys called in some contre of thys londe a thorrocke. 1855 *Norfolk Words* in *Trans. Philol. Soc.* 37 *Thurruck*, the lower flooring of the stern of a boat. 1866 in Nall *Gt. Yarmouth & Lowestoft* 672. 1904 in *Eng. Dial. Dict.*

**2.** *dial.* A heap, *spec.* of muck or dirt.

1708 Kersey, *Thorruck* (O.), a Heap. 1721 in Bailey. 1881 *Leicester Gloss.*, *Thurrock*, a heap: chiefly applied to dirt or 'muck'.

**3.** *dial.* A covered drain. Cf. Thorough *sb.* 2.

1847–78 Halliwell, *Thurruck*, a drain. *Kent.* 1887 *Kentish Gloss.*, *Thurrock*, a wooden drain under a gate; a small passage or wooden tunnel through a bank.

**Thurrondell:** see Thirdendeal.

**Thurrow:** see Thorough *sb.* 3.

**Thursday** (þɒ·ɹzdeⁱ, -di). Forms: α. 1 **Đunresdæȝ, þunres dæi, þur(r)es-, þursdæȝ**, 2 **ðursdai**, (3 **Thurday**), 3–4 **þures-**, 4 (**thrusdai**), 4–7 **Thursdaye**, 5 **Thurys-**, 6 (**thursdae**), **Thurss-, Thurse-**; 3– **Thursday**. β. 3–4 **þores-**, 3–5 **þ-, thoris-, Thorsday**, 4 **þorus-, Thoursday**; *Sc.* 6 **Thuirs-**, 7 **Thuris-**. γ. *Sc.* 6 **Furis-**, 6–9 **Fuirs-**, 8 **Fursday**. [The α forms represent OE. *þunresdæg*, 'day of Thunor or Thor', perh. in some cases affected by ON. The β forms are mainly from ON. *þórsdagr*, the long *ó* of which would give ME. *ō* and *ou* (*ū*), and mod.Sc. *ui* (*ö*). The γ Sc. forms show the interchange of *th* and *f*, referred to under Th (6). So Sw., Da. *Tors-dag*, MDu., Du. *Donderdag*, OHG. *Donares-tac*, MHG. *Donrestac*, Ger. *Donnerstag*, orig. rendering late L. *dies Jovis*, It. *Giovedì*, F. *Jeudi.* Cf. Thunderday.]

**1.** The fifth day of the week.

α, β. [*c* 1000 Ælfric *Hom.* II. 242 On ðam fiftan dæȝe ðe ȝe Đunres hatað. *c* 1000 *Sax. Leechd.* II. 346 Gang on þunres æfen þonne sunne on retle sie.] *c* 1000 *Ags. Gosp.* John v. 30 Đys sceal on þurs-dæȝ on þære oðre lencten wucan. *Ibid.* vii. 40 rubric, Đys god-spel sceal on þures dæȝ on þære fiftan wucan innen lenctene. *c* 1205 Lay. 13929 Þa þunre heo ȝiuen þunres dæi [*c* 1275 þorisdai]. 1297 R. Glouc. (Rolls) 11210 Þe verste þorsdai in lente. 1377 Langl. *P. Pl.* B. xvi. 140 Þe þorsday [*v. rr.* thoresday, þorusday, þursday] byfore þere he made his maundee. 1426–7 *Rec. St. Mary at Hill* 65 Þe thorisday in þe Whitson weke. 1591 H. Smith *Lord's Supper* ii. (1611) 91 A schollers thursday, which he loves better then all the daies in the weeke, only because it is his play-day. 1637–50 Row *Hist. Kirk* (Wodrow Soc.) 515 To come in to Aberdeen on Thurisday thereafter. 1774 tr. *Helvetius' Child of Nat.* I. 235 Thursday next, I shall send for the answer. 1899 Mrs. H. Fraser in *Book Lover* Apr. 3/1, I think I was born under the star of long journeys, a 'Thursday bairn that has far to go'.

γ. 1566 *Sc. Acts Jas. V*, *1540*, 141 b, Sonday, monounday, and furisday. 1569 *Reg. Privy Council Scot.* I. 673 Upoun fuirsday nix to cum. 1596 in *Analecta Scotica* II. 13 Ther ansuer..suld haue bein giuen in the last Furisday. 1791 A. Wilson *Laurel Disputed* Poet. Wks. (1846) 124 On this same Fursday night. 1861 Ramsay *Remin.* Ser. II. 99 Mrs. So-and-so's funeral would be on Fuirsday. 1905 [Still used in some parts of Scotland: see Wright *Eng. Dial. Gram.* 648].

**2.** With defining words.

*Bounds Thursday*, Ascension Day, on which parish boundaries are traced (see Beat *v.*[1] 41). *Carnival Thursday*, Thursday before Quinquagesima (see note s. v. Carnival 1). *Great*, also *Great and Holy Thursday* (in the Greek Church), *Green Thursday*, the Thursday before Good Friday, Maundy Thursday. See also 3, and Maundy Thursday, Sheer Thursday.

1601–2 in *Archpriest Controv.* (Camden) II. 41 They.. arrived there upon madd thursday, otherwise called Carnivall thursday: wᶜʰ is the thursday imediately before Shrove sonday.

**3. Holy Thursday,** a name that has been applied to various Thursdays.

**a.** Thursday in Rogation Week, Ascension Day. Also † *Hallow Thursday.*

[*a* 901 *Laws Ælfred* c. 5 § 5 Se ðe stalað on Sunnanniht, oððe on Gêhhol, oððe on Eastron, oððe on þone halȝan þunresdæȝ.] *c* 1290 *S. Eng. Leg.* I. 363/48 Men fastez ..a-seint Marcus dai..And þreo dawes a-ȝein halewe-þoresday. *c* 1430 *Deuelis Perlament* 459 in *Hymns Virg.* 55 Oure lord,..In erþe he was..Til hooly þursday comen were þat he stiȝ to heuene. *c* 1489 Caxton *Sonnes of Aymon* ii. 59 The feste of Penthecoste after the holy thursdaye. 1530 Palsgr. 232/1 Holythursday, *le jour de lassention.* 1685 in *Verney Mem.* 28 May (1899) IV. 348 The House [of Commons] sitts not this day being Holy Thursday. 1869 *Chambers' Bk. Days* 5 May I. 595/1 Our..landlady at Matlock reminded us that on the following day, being Holy Thursday, or Ascension Day, there would take place the.. ancient..custom of dressing the wells of Tissington with flowers. 1891 [see b].

**b.** The Thursday immediately preceding Easter; Maundy Thursday, Sheer Thursday.

In OE. and in Caxton prob. not a specific name; in 17th c. and later quots., after continental usage.

[*c* 1000 Ælfric *Saints' Lives* xxiii B. 621 To þam halȝan þurres-dæȝe ær þam drihten-lican easter-dæȝe. 1483 Caxton *G. de la Tour* cxxiii, Vpon the Holy Thursday in the Passion weke.] 1645 Evelyn *Diary* 11 Apr., On Holy Thursday the Pope said masse. 1867 Lady Herbert *Cradle L.* iii. 109 On Holy Thursday, the day of the institution of the Holy Eucharist. 1885 *Cath. Dict.* 404/2 Mediæval writers connect the procession with the Blessed Sacrament on Holy Thursday with our Lord's journey to the Mount of Olives after the Last Supper. 1891 *Ch. Q. Rev.* Jan. 449 *note*, By Holy Thursday an Englishman has hitherto always understood one day in the year, that is, Ascension Day... Some have nowadays..begun to use the term Holy Thursday as a name for the Thursday before Easter, which in old English is called Sherethursday or Maundy Thursday. This..is a mere borrowing from the Romance tongues, and is a cause of much confusion.

† **c.** The Thursday after Trinity Sunday; Corpus Christi day. *Obs.* (? error.)

1789 Anburey *Trav. Amer.* (1791) I. 184 Holy Thursday, which they term *La Fête Dieu.*

**Thurse** (þɒɹs). *Obs.* exc. *Hist.* Forms: 1 **þyrs**, 3 **þurs(e**, 4 **thirs**, 5 **thursse, thyrce, thirse, thrus(se, thrusche, thrwsse, trusse**, (6 **thrust**, 7–9 **thrush**, in Hobthrush), 7– **thurse**. [OE. *þyrs* = OHG. *duris, turs*, str. m. (MHG. *dürse, türse, turse*, wk. m.), OS. *thuris* the rune þ; ON. *þurs*:—**þursa*ᶻ:—OTeut. **þurisoᶻ*. Cf. Finnish *tursa-s* sea-monster, from ON.]

A giant of heathen mythology; in mediæval times, often, the devil, a demon; later, a goblin or hobgoblin of rustic superstition.

*Beowulf* 426 Ond nu wið Gren-del sceal wið þam aglæcan ana ȝe-hegan ðing wið þyrse. *c* 725 *Corpus Gloss.* (O.E.T.) 1457 *Orcus*, ðyrs, heldiobul. *a* 1225 *Leg. Kath.* 1880 Com þe þurs Maxence, þe wed wulf, þe heaĉene hund aȝein to his kineburh. *a* 1225 *Juliana* 42 (R. MS.) Beelzebub þe alde þurs of helle. 1382 Wyclif *Isa.* xxxiv. 15 Ther shal lyn lamya [*Gloss*, that is, a thirs, or a beste hauende the bodi lic a womman and horse feet]. ? *a* 1400 *Morte Arth.* 1100 Thykke theese as a thursse,..Greesse growene as a galte, fulle grylych he lukez! *c* 1440 *Promp. Parv.* 491/2 Thyrce, wykkyd spyryte (*K.* thirse, goste, *S.*, *A.* tyrce). 1468 *Medulla Gram.* (Promp. Parv.) *Dusius, i. demon*, a thrusse, þe powke. *c* 1700 [see b]. [1886 Corbett *Fall of Asgard* (1889) I. 59 Never would land-wight, be he troll, thusse, vœtte, or dwarf, harm you.]

**b.** *Comb.* **thurse-hole, thurse-house**: see quot. *c* 1700; **thurse-louse**, a wood-louse (see also *thrush-louse* and *thurstlaas* in Eng. Dial. Dict.).

*c* 1450 *St. Cuthbert* (Surtees) 2180 A place with oute his cell, Now calde þe thrus house. 1658 J. Rowland *Moufet's Theat. Ins.* 1048 The English from the form call them Sowes. ..They are called also *Thurslows*..from a spirit that was not hurtful, to whom our Ancestors superstitiously imputed the sending of them to us. *c* 1700 Bp. Kennett *Lansd. MS. 1033*, lf. 396 A Thurse, an Apparition, a Goblin. *Lanc...* A Thurs-house or Thurse-hole, a hollow vault in a rock or stony hill...These were lookd on as enchanted holes.

**Thurst, -e,** obs. ff. Thirst, dial. var. Thrust.

**Thurst, -e, thurt(e** (þ-), pa. t. of Tharf *v. Obs.*

**Thurtene, -teyn,** obs. ff. Thirteen.

**Thurte ouer,** variant of Thwart-over *Obs.*

**Thurty,** obs. form of Thirty.

‖ **Thus** (þɒs, þūs), *sb.* [Late L. *thūs, thūr-*, cl. L. *tūs, tūr-*, generally held to be f. Gr. θύος, -εος sacrifice, offering, incense; cf. θύ-ειν to sacrifice.]

**1.** Frankincense. **a.** Olibanum. **b.** Resin obtained from the spruce-fir, and from various species of pine. *American thus*, the resin of the Long-leaved Pine, *Pinus palustris*, and the Frankincense or Loblolly Pine, *P. Tæda*, both of the southern U.S.

[*a* 1387 *Sinon. Barthol.* (Anecd. Oxon.) 42 *Thus album, i. olibanum*, franke ensens.] 1398 Trevisa *Barth. De P. R.* (Bodl. MS.) lf. 232 b/2 *Thus* is þe name of a tre & of þe gomme þat woseþ and comeþ oute þerof. *Ibid.* 233/1 Thus is beste þat is white faste and sounde and euelong. 1706 Phillips (ed. Kersey), *Thus* or *Tus*, Frankincense, Incense. 1712 tr. *Pomet's Hist. Drugs* I. 201 Thus, or Frankincense, is a Kind of white or yellowish Rosin. 1842 Brande *Dict. Sc.*, etc., *Thus*, the resin of the spruce fir. The term frankincense is also applied to it. 1880 C. R. Markham *Peruv. Bark* xvi. 185 A milk-white fragrant resin, of a nature analogous to gum thus or gum elemi.

†**2.** By early writers, taken also as name of the tree yielding olibanum or frankincense. *Obs.*

1398 Trevisa *Barth. De P. R.* (Bodl. MS.) lf. 232 b/2 Thus is a tre of Arabia..And therof comeþ Iuse wiþ good smelle & is white as almaundes. *Ibid.* [see sense 1].

**Thus** (ðɒs), *adv.* Now chiefly *literary* or *formal.* Forms: α. 1–3 **ðus**, 1–5 **þus**, 3 **þuss** (*Orm.*), **ð-, þusse**, 3–4 **þos**, 4 **þous**, *Sc.* **thws**, 6 *Sc.* **thuss**, 4– **thus**. β. 3 (*Orm.*) **tuss**, 3–4 **tus**, 5 **tas**; (also 1, 4 **dus**). [= OS. *thus*, MDu., Du. *dus*, app. f. the demonstrative stem of That or This, but the pre-Teut. history is obscure. OHG. and MHG. have *sus*, MDu., Du. *zus*, which appear to belong to the stem of *so.* Cf. also This *adv.*]

**1.** In this way, like this. **a.** In the way just indicated. † *And thus far forth*, and so forth, 'and the like' (*obs. rare*$^{-1}$). (In quot. *c* 1430 pleonastically before *such.*)

*c* 725 *Corpus Gloss.* 26 *Sicini* [*siccine*], ac ðus. *c* 888 K. Ælfred *Boeth.* xvi. § 4 Đa se Wisdom ða þis [spell] ðus areaht hæfde. 971 *Blickl. Hom.* 7 Hu mæȝ þis þus ȝeweorþan? *c* 1000 *Ags. Gosp.* Luke xxiv. 46 Đus is awriten & þus ȝebyrede crist þolian. *c* 1200 Ormin 235–7, & tuss ȝho seȝȝde inn hire þohht..Þuss hafeþþ Drihhtin don wiþþ me. 1340 *Ayenb.* 52 Þos he lyest al his time, and þe niȝt: and þane day. *Ibid.* 71 Þous geþ al oure lyf. 1375 Barbour *Bruce* II. 508 Thws in the byllis levyt he. *c* 1430 *Life St. Kath.* (1884) 45 By þus suche tormentes þou schalt somtyme se me wyth payntes in blis. 1530 Palsgr. 720/1 You ought to be a shamed to skowlde thus as you do. 1606 Holland *Sueton.* 103 Victualling houses, tavernes and thus farre foorth. 1689 Hickeringill *Wks.* (1716) II. 39 Thus the Hogen-Dutchman got Money. 1796 H. Hunter tr. *St.-Pierre's Stud. Nat.* (1799) I. 459 It is thus that our general maxims become the sources of error. 1840 Lardner *Geom.* 98 The base and altitude of the parallelogram thus formed. 1847 C. Brontë *J. Eyre* iv, When thus gentle, Bessie seemed to me the best, prettiest, kindest being in the world. 1908 [Miss E. Fowler] *Betw. Trent & Ancholme* 249 And thus the music goes on.

**b.** In the following manner; as follows; in these words.

*c* 888 K. Ælfred *Boeth.* xvi. § 4 Đa ong[an he] eft ȝiddian & þus cwæð. *a* 900 *O. E. Martyrol.* 23 Apr. 60 Ond he sanctus Georgius him to dryhtne ȝebæd ond þus cwæd: 'Hælende Crist'. *c* 975 *Rushw. Gosp.* Matt. i. 18 Kristes soþlice kennisse þus wæs. *c* 1200 *Vices & Virt.* 3

Godes awene muðe, ðe ðus seið: 'Vade prius [etc.]'. *a* **1300** *XV Signs bef. Judgm.* 33 in *E. E. P.* (1862) 8 Þe first tokning sal be þusse..þe sterris..sal adun..be cast. *c* **1330** R. BRUNNE *Chron.* (1810) 61 On þe Wissonday..Com bode to þe kyng, & þus gan þei seie, Þat [etc.]. **1418** S. THOMAS in *E. E. Wills* (1883) 38 Knowe alle men þat I..make þus my testament. **1500–20** DUNBAR *Poems* xxv. 28 The dergy [dirige] begynis thuss. **1697** DRYDEN *Æneid* II. 2 From his lofty couch he thus began. **1766** GOLDSM. *Vic. W.* x, After tea..she began thus. **1837** LOCKHART *Scott* xliv, On the 13th [of May 1819] he wrote thus to Captain Ferguson.

**c.** In the manner now being indicated or exemplified.

*c* **1440** *York Myst.* vii. 6 Here vn-to you þus am I sente. **1535** COVERDALE *Jer.* li. 64 When thou hast redde out the boke, bynde a stone to it, and cast it in the myddest of Euphrates, and saye: Euen thus shal Babilon syncke. **1596** SHAKS. *Merch. V.* II. ii. 203 While grace is saying hood mine eyes Thus with my hat. **1605** — *Macb.* II. i. 49 It is the bloody Businesse, which informes Thus to mine Eyes. **1727** W. MATHER *Yng. Man's Comp.* 36 A Period or full Stop, thus mark't (.). **1812** J. WILSON *Isle of Palms* II. 423 But why thus gleams Fitz-Owen's eye? **1850** TENNYSON *In Mem.* xcviii. 1 Risest thou thus, dim dawn?

**d.** Ellipt. for *thus says, said* (referring either to a preceding or subsequent speech). *poet.* or *arch.*

**1568** GRAFTON *Chron.* II. 632 Thus much Hall. **1667** MILTON *P. L.* XII. 79 To whom thus Michael: Justly thou abhorr'st [etc.]. **1757** W. WILKIE *Epigon.* VI. 164 Cassandra thus; and thus the Paphian maid: Your gen'rous love [etc.]. **1847** TENNYSON *Princess* 160 'And yet, to speak the truth, I rate your chance Almost at naked nothing'. Thus the king; And I [etc.].

† **e.** *Thus and thus*, expressing minuteness or detail in the description given. *Obs.*

**13..** *Cursor M.* 26203 (Fairf.) Þus & þus do þi penaunce [*Cott.* For þus, and þus, þou do penance]. **1413** *Pilgr. Sowle* (Caxton) I. xxi. (1859) 21 Suche day and tyme he dyde thus and thus. **1535** COVERDALE *1 Kings* xiv. 5 Speake thou therfore vnto her thus & thus. **1605** SHAKS. *Lear* I. ii. 114 The wisedome of Nature can reason it thus, and thus, yet Nature finds [etc.]. **1662** STILLINGFL. *Orig. Sacr.* III. ii. § 5 One of the same works shall be done thus and thus formed.

**f.** Preceded by redundant *as*. (Cf. AS *conj.* 34.)

**1426** LYDG. *De Guil.'s Pilgr.* 4195, I mene as thus: conceyveth al [etc.]. **1430–40** — *Bochas* (Bodl. MS.) lf. 144, I meane as thus, I ha no fresshe licour. *Ibid.* 150/2, I meane as thus, yeff ther be set a lawe. *c* **1450** — *Secrees* 757, I mene as thus by a dyvisioun Toward hym sylff kepe his Estat Royal. **1847** C. BRONTË *J. Eyre* xxxvii, When I have clasped her once more to my heart, as I do now; and kissed her, as thus. **1865** J. T. WHITE in *Reader* No. 139. 234/1 The article next proceeds as thus.

**2.** In accordance with this; accordingly, and so; consequently; therefore.

*c* **1200** ORMIN Pref. 81, & tuss iss Crist Amminadab Þurrh gastliȝ witt ȝehatenn, Forr þatt he toc o rode daeþ Wiþþ all hiss fulle wille. *c* **1315** *Shoreham* vii. 859 And þos þat chyld to nyȝt y-bore, Þaȝ hyt deyde, hyt were for-lore ȝef crystnynge nere. *c* **1407** H. SCOGAN *Moral Balade* 97 (MS. Ashm.) By avncetrye þus may yee no-thing clayme. **1591** SHAKS. *Two Gent.* III. i. 17 Thus (for my duties sake) I rather chose To crosse my friend..Then [etc.]. **1796** H. HUNTER tr. *St.-Pierre's Stud. Nat.* (1799) II. 34 Thus, for example, the signs of tempest off the Cape of Good-Hope far exceed those on our coasts. **1857** BUCKLE *Civiliz.* I. i. 19 Thus we have man modifying nature, and nature modifying man. **1892** STEVENSON *Across the Plains* 144 In this path he must thus have preceded..all contemporary roundeleers.

**3.** Qualifying an adj. or adv.: To this extent, number, or degree; as .. as this; so; esp. *thus far*, to this point (often used to indicate the end of a quotation); *thus much*, so much, as much as this. In quot. 1393 correlative to *as* = as .. as (*obs.*).

*Beowulf* 336 Ne seah ic elþeodiȝe þus maniȝe men modiȝlicran. *a* **700** *Epinal Gloss.* (O.E.T.) 1037 *Tantisper*, þus suiþae. *c* **725** *Corpus Gloss.* 1982 Ðus suiðe. *a* **800** *Erfurt Gloss.* 1037 Ðus suidae. *c* **1000** ÆLFRIC *Hom.* I. 316 Seȝe me, beceapode ȝe ðus micel landes? *c* **1205** LAY. 29625 Woldest þu þus sone faren aȝein to Rome? *a* **1250** *Owl & Night.* 758 For ic kan craft & ic kan lyste & þarfore ic am þus þriste. *c* **1369** CHAUCER *Dethe Blaunche* 904 But thus moche dar I sayn. **1393** LANGL. *P. Pl.* C. IV. 181 Hue is assoilid þus [*v.r.* as] sone as hure self lykeþ. *a* **1451** FORTESCUE *Wks.* (1869) 550 Thus longe ys the cooste of Englonde on the oon syde of hym by see. **1531** *Dial. on Laws Eng.* II. xlv. Q iij b, There shall not be layde vpon a ded persone but..thus many tapers or candels. **1578** BANISTER *Hist. Man* I. 22, I write thus much for the excuse of Vesalius, because he is so apertly reproved. **1596** SHAKS. *Tam. Shr.* I. ii. 104 Therefore let me be thus bold with you. **1599** — *Hen. V*, Epil., Thus farre..Our bending Author hath pursu'd the Story. **1681** DRYDEN *Abs. & Achit.* 803 Thus far 'tis duty: but here fix the mark. **1746** FRANCIS *Hor., Epist.* I. xvii. 55 Then you confess, That who succeeds, thus difficult his Part, Gives the best Proof of Courage. **1823** SOUTHEY *Hist. Penins. War* I. xii. 617 The happy issue, thus far, of their civil administration. **1884** W. C. SMITH *Kildrostan* 53 Yet you can speak thus calmly of unsaying All we have said. **1888** FREEMAN in Stephens *Life* (1895) II. 374 The legend..has thus much of foundation.

Hence † **Thus** *v.* (*nonce-use*) *intr.*, to do thus.

**1605** SYLVESTER *Du Bartas* II. iii. IV. *Captaines* 212 Six dayes together had the Hebrews thus't About the Town, seven times the Seventh they must.

**Thusand, -sund,** (þ-), obs. ff. THOUSAND.

**Thuscane,** obs. form of TUSCAN.

† **Thu·s-gate,** *adv. Obs.* or *Sc. arch.* [f. THUS *adv.* + GATE *sb.*[2]] In this way; thus.

*a* **1300** *Cursor M.* 13192 (Cott.) Þus-gat was sant Iohan slan. *c* **1300** *Havelok* 2419 Sule ye þus-gate fro me fle? *c* **1330** R. BRUNNE *Chron. Wace* (Rolls) 14351 (Petyt MS.) And whan þe ton þus gate was ded On þat oþer bataille he led. *c* **1475** *Rauf Coilȝear* 169 Ȝit was I neuer in my lyfe thus gait leird. *a* **1550** *Freiris of Berwik* 578 in *Dunbar's Poems* (S.T.S.) 304 He said, 'Ȝone Freir hes maid me thus gait say'. **1819** W. TENNANT *Papistry Storm'd* (1827) 148 But what befel him thus-gate daddit, In the neist sang ye'll find it addit.

† **Thu·s-gates,** *adv. Obs.* [f. prec. + *-s* of adverbial genitive.] = prec.

*c* **1375** *Cursor M.* 1242 (Fairf.) Til seth his sone, þus gates he spake. *c* **1400** *Destr. Troy* 4500 Þus gatis to the gome þen the god saide. *c* **1450** in *Pol. Rel. & L. Poems* 108 If I my saule þusgates wil fede. **1513** DOUGLAS *Æneis* II. xii. (xi.) 17 Anchises..Lift..hands to hevin, and thus gatis said.

**Thu·sly,** *adv. colloq.* [f. THUS + -LY [2].] = THUS.

**1889** *Boston* (Mass.) *Jrnl.* 17 Jan. 2/3 On his way home George mused thusly. **1893** LADY BURTON *Life Sir R. F. Burton* II. 3 Stories never lose anything in the recital, and consequently this one grew thusly.

**Thusness** (ðʊ·snės). *colloq.* [f. THUS + -NESS.] The condition of being thus. Chiefly *humorous*.

**1883** in W. Hamilton *Parodies* (1886) III. 159 Expound me this thusness I pray. **1888** F. HUME *Mme. Midas* I. xv, Why all this thusness? **1888** *Daily News* 27 Dec. 3/4 Why this 'thusness'? as our Transatlantic humourists would say. **1891** *Nature* 12 Mar. 435/1 Force produces motion, but what determines it and gives it its thusness?

**Thussocke,** obs. form of TUSSOCK.

**Thuswise** (ðʊ·swəiz), *adv.* [f. THUS + -WISE.] In this manner; = THUS. Cf. THISWISE.

**13..** *Cursor M.* 11971 (Gött.) 'Sun', scho said, 'wirk noght þus wise' [*Cott., Tr.* þis wise; *Fairf.* suche wise]. **1509** BARCLAY *Shyp of Folys* (1570) 238 Howe longe shall ye mankinde thus wise oppres? **1526** TINDALE *Phil.* iii. 15 As many as be perfect be thus wyse minded. **1594** CAREW *Huarte's Exam. Wits* (1616) 172 This child, whom we goe thus-wise examining. **1843** E. JONES *Sens. & Event* Poems (1879) 8 Long ere the worms had fretted through The clay that thuswise spake. **1849** M. ARNOLD *In Utrumque Paratus* ii, O waking on a world which thuswise springs. **1887** MORRIS *Odyss.* XI. 504, I spake unto him and thuswise answered again.

So † **Thus ways** *adv. phr. Obs. rare*[−1].

**1616** J. HAIG in J. Russell *Haigs* vi. (1881) 139, I was no scholar to sustain ane argument against him, but thus ways leaves him.

**Thute, þuten,** var. THEOTEN *v. Obs.*, to howl.

**Thutie,** obs. form of TUTTY.

**Thutter** (þʊ·təɹ), *v.* [Echoic; cf. *twitter, stutter*; also OE. *þoterian* to howl, wail.] *intr.* To make the sputtering or shaking sound suggested by the word. Hence **Thu·ttering** *ppl. a.*

**1897** KIPLING *Captains Courageous* (ed. Tauchn.) 12 Blowing through a big conch-shell, he must needs stand up ..and send a grinding, thuttering shriek through the fog. **1904** — *Traffics & Discov.* 370 The old mill shook and the heavy stones thuttered on the grist. **1905** J. C. LINCOLN *Partners of Tide* vii. 139 There boomed out of the dark a thuttering, shaking roar, that swelled to a shriek and died away—the voice of the great steam foghorn.

‖ **Thuya** (þiū·yă). *Bot.* [An irregular repr. of Gr. θυΐα, more correctly θύα, name of an African tree (*Thuja articulata* Linn., now *Callitris quadrivalvis*), the source of the THYINE wood (Gr. ξύλον θύϊνον) of Rev. xviii. 12. See also THUJA.

Theophrastus *H. Pl.* 5. 3. 7 has θύον and θύα, rendered by Pliny *N. H.* 13. 16. 30 '*thyon*, ab aliis *thya*'. Med.Gr. MSS. and early printed edd. gave the Gr. as θύϊον, θυΐα, which Theodorus Gaza *tr. Theophrastus* 1483, Latinized as *tyium, thuia*. Camerarius, 1577, has *thya* from Pliny and *thuia* after Gaza; he applies the name to the American *Arbor Vitæ, Thuya occidentalis*. Bauhin, 1671, has the barbarous form *Thuya* for *Thuia* or *Thuja*. Tournefort used *Thya* from Pliny, which was also preferred by Linnæus *Philos. Bot.* (1750) 175 '*Thya*, male *Thuja* et *Thuya*'. L. had himself used *Thuja* (var. of *Thuia*) in 1737, and reverted to it in his definitive *Sp. Pl.* 1753; and this was generally followed by British botanists and horticulturists, and is still in popular English use. But French botanists continued to use Bauhin's *Thuya* (Littré has '*Thuia* ou *Thuya*'), and this has been followed by Bentham and Hooker, and adopted at Kew as the generic name. (Sir W. T. Thiselton-Dyer.) The only defensible form etymologically is of course *Thya*.]

Name of a genus of coniferous trees, consisting of about ten species, of which the North American *T. occidentalis* and the Chinese *T. orientalis* are commonly cultivated under the name Arbor Vitæ. (The tree so called by the ancients is now known as *Callitris*.) Also *attrib.*, as *thuya-wood*.

[**1483** GAZA tr. *Theophr. H. Pl.* F iiij, Tyium quod thuia ab aliis appellatur. **1671** BAUHIN *Pinax* 488 Thuya Theophrasti. *Arbor Vitæ*, Bellonio; *Thuia sive Thya, vulgo.* Cam[erarius].] **1706** PHILLIPS (ed. Kersey), *Thya*, a kind of wild Cypress-Tree, whose Wood is very sweet and lasting; the Life-Tree.] **1707** MORTIMER *Husb.* (1721) II. 60 *Thuya*, or *Arbor vitæ*, grows of Layers or Slips to a tall straight goodly Tree. **1770** J. R. FORSTER tr. *Kalm's Trav. N. Amer.* (1772) II. 315 All the posts which are driven into the ground are made of Thuya wood. **1836** H. MURRAY, etc. *Hist. & Descr. Acc. China* I. i. 19 Richly clothed with trees, particularly the tallow, the camphor, the thuya or arbor vitæ. **1903** F. EDEN *Garden in Venice* iii. 17 A tiny square of garden, closed in with an unshapely hedge of thuya and euonymus.

**Thuyene** (þiū·yīn), etc. *Chem.*: see THUJENE.

**Thwa,** obs. erron. Sc. form of TWO.

**Thwack** (þwæk), *sb.* [f. the verb.] A vigorous stroke with a stick or the like; a whack.

**1587** T. HUGHES, etc. *Misfort. Arthur* IV. ii, Boystrous bangs with thumping thwacks fall thicke. **1654** GAYTON *Pleas. Notes* III. ii. 76 A company of lusty shoulder-thumpers, who discharg'd the mutuall thwacks so stoutly, that they made a noise, as if they were beating of hemp. **1663** BUTLER *Hud.* I. II. 795 But Talgol first with hardy Thwack Twice bruis'd his head, and twice his back. **1704** SWIFT *T. Tub* xi. (1709) 131 Noble Captain, lend a reasonable Thwack ..with that cane of yours. **1832** W. IRVING *Alhambra* (1851) 250 Bestowing a hearty thwack with a cudgel on the flanks of his donkey. **1859** G. MEREDITH *R. Feverel* xxiii, Sounding a thwack on her knee.

**Thwack** (þwæk), *v.* Also 6–7 **thwacke, thwak,** 6, 8 *dial.* **twack.** [app. echoic, from the sound of beating vigorously: see sense 1.

But it may have been altered from the earlier THACK *v.*[2], orig. to pat, to clap, but in 1480 used of showering blows, the initial *thw-* expressing more forcible effort than *th-*; the sense 'clap' might also pass easily into sense 3 here, which does not easily arise out of 1.]

**1.** *trans.* To beat or strike vigorously, as with a stick; to bang, thrash, whack.

*a* **1530** HEYWOOD *Johan & Tyb* (Brandl) 31, I shall bete her and thwak her. *a* **1535** MORE in Wordsw. *Eccl. Biog.* (1818) II. 123 Now I will speak but three words, and I durst jeopard a wager that none here [on the Continent] shall pronounce it after me: 'Thwarts [? *error for* Thwaites] thwackt him with a thwitle'. **1560** INGELEND *Disob. Child* G ij, Beynge full often with the staffe thwacked. *a* **1626** MIDDLETON *Mayor of Queenb.* v. i, Take all my cushions down and thwack them soundly. **1712** ARBUTHNOT *John Bull* IV. vii, To snatch the cudgel..that he might thwack Lewis with it. **1881** BESANT & RICE *Chapl. of Fleet* I. iv, To see two sturdy fellows thwack and belabour each other with quarter-staff, single-stick, or fists.

*absol.* **1573** TUSSER *Husb.* (1878) 43 Flailes lustily thwack, least plough seede lack.

**b.** *fig.* To 'beat' in a contest, to defeat severely.

**1607** SHAKS. *Cor.* IV. v. 189 Here's he that was wont to thwacke our Generall, Caius Martius. **1821** SCOTT *Kenilw.* ii, What adventurous knight ever thought of the lady's terror, when he went to thwack giant, dragon, or magician, ..for her deliverance? **1869** BLACKMORE *Lorna D.* ii, If we count three before the come of thee, thwacked thou art.

**c.** *intr.* To fall with a thwack or sharp knock.

*a* **1851** MOIR *Winter Wild* vii, To the quaking sheet below, Down thwacks he, with a thud like thunder!

**2.** *trans.* To drive or force by or as by thwacking or beating; to knock (*down, in, out*, etc.). Also *fig.*

**1566** DRANT *Wail. Hierim.* K iv, To thwacke downe walles, to even them with the flore. **1611** SHAKS. *Wint. T.* I. ii. 37 Wee'l thwack him hence with Distaffes. **1743** *Lond. & Country Brew.* II. (ed. 2) 126 Beating or Thwacking the Yeast into working Ale or Beer. **1906** *Outlook* 22 Sept. 374/1 If Busby's rhythmic rod thwacked Latin metre into the head of more than one poet.

**3. a.** To clap; to clap *together*, to pack or crowd together (things or persons); to clap *down*.

**1589** FLEMING *Virg. Georg.* II. 24 The bushie thornie fields, Where many grauell stones be thwackt. **1610** BP. HALL *Apol. Brownists* 14 [He] thwacks fourteene Scriptures into the margent. **1641** MILTON *Animadv.* ii. Wks. 1851 III. 208 Who would have thought a man could have thwackt together so many incongruous similitudes? **1674** N. FAIRFAX *Bulk & Selv.* 151 The shruff, moss and hair, that the nest was thwackt together of. **1687** A. LOVELL tr. *Thevenot's Trav.* I. 25 Many of them being thwackt together into one Room, they are not a little straitned. **1760** [see THWACKING *vbl. sb.*]. **1902** *Daily Chron.* 17 Feb. 7/5 [Prisoner in Police Court], I don't care what you say; thwack me down three months' [hard labour] in the book, quick.

† **b.** *intr.* (for *refl.*) To crowd (*to* a place). *rare.*

**1652** BROME *City Wit* II. ii, All the wise wenches i' the Town will thwack to such Sanctuaries, when the times are troublesome.

† **c.** *trans.* To pack or crowd (a thing or place). Const. *with* something. *Obs.*

Much used in this sense from *c* 1585 to 1700.

**1582** STANYHURST *Æneis* III. (Arb.) 85 Weau'd wurcks thwackt with honor. **1588** A. MUNDAY in Farr *S. P. Eliz.* (1845) I. 229 He that had his barnes so thwakt, And bade his soul take rest. **1607** J. CARPENTER *Plaine Mans Plough* 15 The field was thwacked with thornes, tares, and noysome weeds. **1667** WATERHOUSE *Fire Lond.* 103 Its Streets were ..thwack'd with Carts, pester'd with Porters. **1698** FRYER *Acc. E. India & P.* 58 We could discern the River to be thwacked with small Craft.

† **d.** *intr.* (for *passive*) To be packed or filled full.

**1650** HOWELL *Giraffi's Rev. Naples* I. 114 The Church.. was as full as it could thwack in thick multitudes.

**4.** The verb-stem in combination with a sb.: **thwack-coat** *a.*, that thwacks the coat; **thwack-stave,** a quarter-staff, a cudgel.

**1593** G. HARVEY *Pierce's Super.* Wks. (Grosart) II. 126 To be sold at the signe of the Crabbtree Cudgell in Thwackcoate Lane. **1857** SIR F. PALGRAVE *Norm. & Eng.* II. 504 Every bodily exercise...the footrace or the gallop, single-stick or thwackstave, spear or sword.

Hence **Thwacked** (þwækt), *ppl. a.* **a.** beaten; † **b.** packed, crowded (*obs.*).

*a* **1670** HACKET *Serm. Incarnation* vii. Wks. (1675) 64 Let two or three be gathered together in his name..; but if you will multiply those two or three to hundreds..of souls, O then his desire is upon..those thwackt congregations.

**Thwacker** (þwæ·kəɹ). *rare.* [f. prec. + -ER [1].]

**1.** One who or that which thwacks; a beater; *spec.* an implement for beating half-dried pantiles into shape on the thwacking-frame.

**1867** URE *Dict. Arts*, etc. III. 902 When half-dry the tiles are taken out one by one, placed on the thwacking frame, and beaten with the thwacker to produce the required shape. **1877** KNIGHT *Dict. Mech.*, *Thwacking-frame*, the tool by which the upper side [of half-dried pantiles] is beaten has the shape of the segment of a cylinder, and is called the thwacker. **1879** G. MEREDITH *Egoist* Prelude, Like cudgels of carpet-thwackers expelling dust.

† **2.** A thumper, a whacker; in quot., a 'thumping' lie. *Obs. rare*[−1].

1674 N. Fairfax *Bulk & Selv.* 108 It would follow, that our leasting were greater than somewhat else, or greater than it self; Which would be a thwacker.

**Thwacking** (þwæ·kiŋ), *vbl. sb.* [f. Thwack *v.* + -ing [1].] The action of the verb Thwack in various senses. Also *attrib.*: **thwacking-frame**, a stand on which pantiles are beaten into shape; **thwacking-horse, -stool**, a bench on which the thwacking-frame is placed; **thwacking-knife**, a knife for trimming the edges of pantiles.

1736 Ainsworth *Lat. Dict.* I, A thwacking, *verberatio, fustuarium, fustigatio.* 1760 Mair *Tyro's Dict.* (1820) 372 *Stipatio*,..a cramming or thwacking of things together. 1820 W. Irving *Sketch Bk.* II. 107 We heard a distant thwacking sound,..the rolling pin, struck upon the dresser by the cook. 1867 Thwacking frame [see Thwacker 1]. 1895 Zangwill *Master* III. ix, The thwacking of the dancers' feet in the barn.

**Thwacking** (þwæ·kiŋ), *ppl. a.* [f. Thwack *v.* + -ing [2].] That thwacks; that is a thwacker; big, strong, forcible; thumping, whacking.

1567 Drant *Horace, De Arte Poet.* A iij, Put out no puffes, nor thwackyng words, words of to large assyce. 1620 Middleton *Chaste Maid* v. iii, *Sec. Serv.* A bonfire, Sir? *Sir Oliver.* A thwacking one, I charge you. 1671 H. Foulis *Hist. Rom. Treas.* (1681) 42 After all these thwacking Arguments. 1682 H. More *Annot. Glanvill's Lux O.* 191 In vertue of which thwacking expressions he has fancied himself able to play at Scholastick or Philosophick Quarter-Staff. 1890 *Daily News* 17 Dec. 5/7 Then..came a thwacking blow from Dr. Tanner's blackthorn.

Hence **Thwa·ckingly** *adv.*

1660 H. More *Myst. Godl.* vi. xvii. 270 In riveting the Godhead into his own person so thwackingly and substantially, as that he may give the World to understand that he was as much God as that Christ that died at Jerusalem.

**Thwait(e** (þwēⁱt). *dial.* Also 7 twaite. [a. ON. *þveit, þveiti* a piece of land. a paddock, lit. a cutting, cut-piece, f. **þvíta* = OE. *þwítan* to cut, cut off, Thwite.] A piece of ground; *esp.* a piece of ground cleared from forest or reclaimed from waste. Now *rare* or *Obs.* as a separate word. (Hence the surname *Thwaites.*)

Entering into numerous place-names, esp. in Westmorland, Cumberland, and N. Lancashire, as *Applethwaite, Crosthwaite, Dowthwaite, Ormthwaite, Seathwaite*, etc..

1628 Coke *On Litt.* 4 b, *Twaite* signifieth a wood grubbed up and turned to arable. 1670 in Blount *Law Dict.* s.v. 1777 Nicolson & Burn *Hist. Westmld. & Cumbld.* II. 14 Several parts and parcels,..differing in form and quality of soil, or otherwise inclosed by the inhabitants from the barren waste of the fells, such parts and parcels are..called thwaits. 1825 Brockett *N. C. Words, Thwaite*, a level pasture field. 1832 J. Bree *St. Herbert's Isle* 125 A thwaite was a portion of ground cleared of wood for residence or cultivation.

**Thwang, thwang(u)e**, obs. ff. Thong.

† **Thwarl**, *a. Obs. rare*—[1]. ? Twisted; ? tight.

13.. *Gaw. & Gr. Knt.* 194 Syþen þrawen wyth a þwong a þwarle knot alofte.

**Thwart** (þwǭɹt), *sb.*[1] Now *rare.* [f. Thwart *v.*] An act or instance of thwarting; a check, hindrance, obstruction, frustration.

1611 Cotgr. s.v. *Vent, Batu de mauvais vent*, crost by a contrarie, or malignant thwart. 1632 Rowley *New Wonder* I. 11 Full oft, and many have I heard complaine Of discontents, thwarts, and adversities. 1661 Glanvill *Van. Dogm.* 81 Any considerable thwart in the Motion. 1742 H. Walpole *Lett. to Mann* (1834) I. 104 The number of blows and thwarts which the French have received. 1782 Miss Burney *Cecilia* II. iii, A certain discourteous person..in thwart of your fair inclinations, keepeth and detaineth your irradiant frame in hostile thraldom. 1902 *Blackw. Mag.* Apr. 547/1, I distrust that man—He's a thwart—a moral thwart.

**Thwart** (þwǭɹt), *sb.*[2] [app. a sb. use (which came in after 1725) of Thwart *adv.* and *adj.*, having reference to the position of the rowing benches or seats *athwart* or across the boat. Whether its use was partly due to similarity of sound to *thaught, thawt*, or *thought*, previously applied to the same thing, is uncertain. Our latest contemporary instance of '*thaught* or *thought*' is of 1721, of *thoat* 1697, of *thout* 1725, while our first of '*thaughts* or *thwarts*' is of 1736, so that the appellations were continuous in use, as if the one had passed into the other. But, for the full determination of the relations between *thoft, thought* or *thaught*, and *thwart*, fuller evidence between 1500 and 1700 is needed. Cf. Thoft, Thought [2].] A seat across a boat, on which the rower sits; a rower's bench.

[1721 Bailey, *Thoughts*, the Rowers Seats in a Boat.] 1736 — (folio), *Thaughts*, v. *Thwarts. Ibid., Thwarts*, (a Sea Term) the boards or benches laid a-cross boats and gallies, upon which the rowers sit. 1770 Cook *Voy. round World* II. x. (1773) 462 A considerable number of thwarts were laid from gunwale to gunwale. 1776 *Falconer's Dict. Marine, Thwart*, the seat or bench of a boat whereon the rowers sit to manage the oars. 1897 F. T. Bullen *Cruise Cachalot* 41 We drew each man his oar across the boat and lashed it firmly down with a piece of line spliced to each thwart.

**Thwart** (þwǭɹt), *adv., prep.*, and *adj.* Forms: 3 **þuert, ðwert,** (*Orm.*) **þwerrt, 4 thwert, 5 þwerte, twhert, thuart, 5–7 twart, thwarte, twhart, 6–7 thwarth, thawart(e, (qwarte, whart), 7 twarte, 9** *dial.* **thort, thurt, thirt, thert, 5– thwart.** [Early ME. (*c* 1200) *þwert*, a. ON. *þvert* (Norw. *tvert, tvært*, Sw. *tvert, tvärt*, Da. *tvært*) adv., across, athwart, orig. neuter of the ON. adj. *þver-r* (Norw. *tver, tvær*, Sw. *tver, tvär*, Da. *tvær*), transverse, cross. Cf. OHG. *twer*, MHG. *twer, quer*, Ger. *quer*, and (with adv. gen. *-s*), OFris. *þweres, dwers*, Satl. *twars*, WFris. *dwerz, dwers*, EFris. *dwars, dwas*, MLG., MD. *dwers, dwars*, LG., Du. *dwars*, athwart, crossly, peevishly; ON. *þvers* = *þvert*. ON. *þver* was shortened from **þverh* = OE. *þwerh, þweorh* (genitive *þweores*, in comb. *þweor-*) crooked, cross, perverse = OHG. *dwerh, dwerah, twerh*, MHG. *dwerch, twerch*, Ger. *zwerch-* (in composition), Goth. *þwairhs* cross, angry, :—OTeut. **þwerh-* :—**þwerhw-* :—Indo-Eur. **twerkw-*, whence L. *torquēre* to twist, Skr. *tarku'* spindle. In Eng. the adv. is known *c* 1200, first in the combinations *þwert ūt* (Thwert-out) and *þwert-over* (Thwart-over), later (*c* 1300) *over-þwert* (Overthwart). It was used as an adj., with a vb. *þwerten*, both *fig.*, *c* 1250, and as a prep. bef. 1300. In all these *thwert* became *thwart* in the 15th c. *Thwart* sb. is found in the 17th c.

The ME. material is scanty, and the sense development is not illustrated fully by the extant quotations. The senses are therefore here arranged in what appears to be the logical order.]

A. *adv.*

† **1.** Across or transversely to the length, direction, or course of anything; from side to side; crosswise, transversely; = Athwart A. 1. *Obs.*

*a* 1350 *St. Thomas* 85 in Horstm. *Altengl. Leg.* (1881) 21 A grete blak dog..Thwert in his mouth þe hand he broght. 1483 Caxton *Gold. Leg.* 402/2 A man on hors backe which bare a longe tree thwarte and wold entre in to the temple, and he myght not by cause the tree laye thwarte. 1597 A. M. tr. *Guillemeau's Fr. Chirurg.* 24 b/1 An apertione accordinge to the length of that parte, and not thwart or crosseover. 1624 Capt. Smith *Virginia* III. 79 A great tree (that lay thwart as a barricado). 1664 Evelyn *Sylva* (1776) 405 Till you can lay them thwart, that the top of one may rest on the root or stub of the other.

† **b.** *fig.* Across the course of, so as to obstruct or oppose; adversely; = Athwart A. 3. *Obs.*

*a* 1628 Preston *New Covt.* (1634) 146 There are many things in the Creature that are crosse to us, that fall thwart upon us. 1642 R. Carpenter *Experience* II. xi. 214 A work that lyes thwart, and strives against the current of your naturall inclination.

**2.** From one side to the other of anything (with motion implied); across. *arch.*

1511 Guylforde *Pilgr.* (Camden) 6 We trauersed out of that ryuer into an other lytell ryuer, whiche brought us thawarte ayen into Latyze. 1880 Webb *Goethe's Faust* I. i. 31 Up, down and thwart, without repose, To lead my scholars by the nose.

† **3.** *Thwart of.* **a.** *Naut.* Opposite to, over against (a place on the coast): = Off B. II. 6 b.

1556 W. Towrson in Hakluyt *Voy.* (1589) 98 We were thwart of Porto Sancto. 1670 Narborough *Jrnl.* in *Acc. Sev. Late Voy.* I. (1694) 16 Being thwart of the Shoals of Brazil.

† **b.** Transversely to, across the direction of. *Obs.*

1667 Milton *P. L.* x. 703 With adverse blast up-turns them from the South Notus and Afer black with thundrous Clouds..; thwart of these as fierce Forth rush the Levant and the Ponent Windes Eurus and Zephir.

B. *prep.*

**1.** From side to side of, across: **a.** of position or direction; = Athwart B. 1 b. *arch.* or *poet.*

1470–85 Malory *Arthur* v. viii. 173 Lucyus smote Arthur thwart the vysage. 1585 T. Washington tr. *Nicholay's Voy.* II. x. 44 Our patrone..was..caste thwart the nose of our gallie. 1680 *Lond. Gaz.* No. 1550/4 [He] hath a Scar thwart the back of one of his Hands. 1741 in *Descr. Thames* (1758) 87 No Person..shall..bend any Net, by Anchors or otherwise, thwart the Channel, and so as to draw another Net into it. 1870 Morris *Earthly Par.* II. III. 192 A pink-tinged cloud spread thwart the shore.

**b.** of motion: = Athwart B. 1 a. *arch.* or *poet.*

1583 Stocker *Civ. Warres Lowe C.* III. 91 Came three messengers thwart the fieldes in at the wood gate. 1598 Stow *Surv.* iii. (1603) 14 Which ran..through that streete, thwart Grastreete, and downe Lumbard streete. 1738 Gray *Tasso* 7 Thwart the road a River roll'd its flood tempestuous. 1813 T. Busby *Lucretius* II. 131 When shines the God of Day, And thwart the darkened chamber darts his ray. 1898 T. Hardy *Wessex Poems* 2 Thwart my wistful way did a damsel saunter.

**2.** Across the course or direction of; = Athwart B. 3. *Thwart the hawse* († *halse*), across the stem of a ship. Chiefly *Naut.*

1495 *Trevisa's Barth. De P. R.* v. vi. (W. de W.) g v/1 Two holowe synewes whiche ben callyd Optici..come eyther thwart other, and ben Ioyned in a poynte. 1620 in Foster *Eng. Factories Ind.* (1906) 220 Intending with her to laie the Portingall admirall thwart the halse and soe to burne both together. 1622 R. Hawkins *Voy. S. Sea* (1847) 85 For foure leagues into the sea (thwart it), lye banks of sand. 1737 Bracken *Farriery Impr.* (1756) I. 54 Fibres that cross and go thwart one another.

† **3.** Across the course of, so as to obstruct; = Athwart B. 5. *Obs.*

1641 Milton *Reform.* I. Wks. 1851 III. 31 Crosse-jingling periods which..come thwart a setl'd devotion worse then the din of bells and rattles.

C. *adj.*

**1.** Lying, extending, or passing across; transverse, cross; in quots. 1483, 1712, *perh.* oblique. † *Thwart circle*, the zodiac (*obs.*). See also Thwart-saw.

1404 [implied in Thwart-saw]. 1483 Caxton *Gold. Leg.* 121 b/1 It was made lyke a crosse thwart of whyche the two endes were fyxed in therthe. And that hys membres shold theron be broken. 1551 Recorde *Cast. Knowl.* (1556) 30 The Zodiak (whiche many doo call the Thwarte circle). 1658 J. Rowland *Moufet's Theat. Ins.* 971 The last part is whitish, chequered with right and thwart fibres. 1712 J. James tr. *Le Blond's Gardening* 41 The Diagonal or Thwart-walk. 1836 W. Irving *Astoria* (1849) 86 They have thwart pieces from side to side about three inches thick. 1873 Proctor *Expanse Heav.* 282 The determination of the actual rate of any star's thwart motion.

**2.** *fig.* **a.** Of persons or their attributes: Disposed to resist, oppose, or obstruct; cross-grained; perverse froward, obstinate, stubborn, awkward.

*c* 1250 *Gen. & Ex.* 3099 Ðo pharaun saȝ is lond al fre, His herte ðo wurð ðwert and hard. 1602 *2nd Pt. Return fr. Parnass.* III. iv, This old Sir Raderick it shall be thy taske to cudgell with thy thick thwart termes. 1605 Bacon *Adv. Learn.* I. ii. § 8 Ignorance makes them [the minds of men] churlish, thwart, and mutinous. 1656 Baxter *Reformed Pastor* 234, I would not have any to be thwart and contentious with those that govern them. 1819 Shelley *Prometh. Unb.* II. ii. 90 Noontide would come, And thwart Silenus find his goats undrawn. 1892 Stevenson *Across the Plains* 238 The class public or the thwart reviewer.

**b.** Of things: Adverse, unfavourable, untoward, unpropitious; esp. applied (with mixture of literal sense) to a wind or current: cross.

1610 Healey *St. Aug. Citie of God* 129 These thwart effects fell out even then when things were said to be carried ..so justly. 1621 Lady M. Wroth *Urania* 472 Not only neere it in blood, but allyed in thwart fortune. *a* 1660 *Contemp. Hist. Irel.* (Ir. Archæol. Soc.) II. 36 This secret and thwarte dealinge is worse then open and publicke violence. *Ibid.* III. 42 A demonstration of theire reciprocall thwarte dealinge. 1865 Swinburne *Atalanta* 184 A thwart sea-wind full of rain and foam. 1889 Skrine *Mem. E. Thring* 235 In spite of these thwart currents, Thring built up his large school.

† **3.** Opposed, contrary (*to*); in quot. 1614, opposed in sense, antithetical, contrasted. *Obs.*

*a* 1601? Marston *Pasquil & Kath.* I. 304 Why should you runne an Idle counter-course Thwart to the path of fashion? 1614 T. Adams *Fatal Banquet* iv. Wks. 1861 I. 216 A pair of cross and thwart sentences, handled rather by collation than relation, whose conjunction is disjunctive. 1615 Jackson *Creed* IV. II. vi. § 5 A meaning as ridiculous, as thwart and contradictory to his purpose as the devil himself could have devised. 1624 Bp. Mountagu *Gagg* Pref. 23 To be thwart unto, and against the maine of the business negotiated.

**Thwart** (þwǭɹt), *v.* [f. prec. adv.]

I. **1.** *trans.* To pass or extend across from side to side of; to traverse, cross; also, to cross the direction of, to run at an angle to. *Obs.* or *arch.*

1413 *Pilgr. Sowle* (Caxton) v. i. (1859) 70 A Cercle embelyfyng somwhat, and thwartyng the thycknes of the spyere. 1530 Palsgr. 757/2, I thwarte the waye, I go over the waye to stoppe one, *je trenche le chemyn.* 1608 Shaks. *Per.* IV. iv. 10 Pericles Is now againe thwarting thy wayward seas. 1627 Capt. Smith *Seaman's Gram.* ix. 39 You set your sailes so sharp as you can to lie close by a wind, thwarting it a league or two,..first on the one boord then on the other. 1653 R. Sanders *Physiogn.* 50 If the Hepatique line be thwarted by other small lines. 1769 Falconer *Dict. Marine* N iij, The current thwarts the course of a ship. 1805–6 Cary *Dante's Inf.* xxv. 72 The lizard seems A flash of lightning, if he thwart the road. 1863 P. S. Worsley *Poems & Transl.* 10 That white reach Thwarting the blue serene, a belt of fire.

**b.** *intr.* To pass or extend across, to cross. *Obs.* or *arch.*

*a* 1552 Leland *Itin.* (1744) VII. 53 The Towne of Cokermuth stondeth on the Ryver of Coker, the which thwartheth over the Town. 1598 Stow *Surv.* xli. (1603) 436 A close cart, bayled ouer and couered with blacke, hauing a plaine white Crosse thwarting. 1609 Heywood *Brit. Troy* XIV. xciii, Through the mid-throng the nearest way he thwarted. 1627 Hakewill *Apol.* Pref. 10 It led them some other way, thwarting, and upon the by, not directly. 1856 T. Aird *Poet. Wks.* 189 They scream, they mix, they thwart, they eddy round.

† **c.** *trans.* To cross the path of; to meet; to fall in with, come across. *Obs.*

1601 Chester *Love's Mart., K. Arth.* xx, Merlin..Who by great fortunes chance sir Vlfius thwarted, As he went by in beggers base aray. 1674 N. Fairfax *Bulk & Selv.* 146 Motions to be checkt..without the least hit or stop from other bodies that thwart them. 1812 Cary *Dante's Par.* IV. 89 Another question thwarts thee.

† **d.** *Naut.* Of a ship, etc.: To get athwart so as to be foul of. Also *intr. Obs.*

1809 *Naval Chron.* XXIV. 23 The boat having thwarted against the moorings. 1810 *Ibid.* XXIII. 97 The frigate now..thwarted the Lord Keith's hawse. 1813 *Gen. Hist.* in *Ann. Reg.* 107/1 The Amelia twice fell on board the enemy in attempting to thwart his hawse.

† **2.** To lay (a thing) athwart or across; to place crosswise; to set or put (things) across each other.

*Thwart over thumb* (quot. 1522) app. = *to cross* (one) *over the thumbs*: see Thumb *sb.* 5 d.

1522 Skelton *Why not to Court* 197 Thus thwartyng ouer thom, He ruleth all the roste. 1588 Spenser *Virgil's Gnat* 514 The noble sonne of Telamon..thwarting his huge shield, Them battell bad. 1602 Carew *Cornwall* I. 25 b, Their bils were thwarted crossewise at the end, and with these they would cut an Apple in two at one snap. *Ibid.* 26 b, The inhabitants make use of divers his Creekes, for griste-milles, by thwarting a bancke from side to side. 1623 Markham *Cheap Husb.* I. ii. (1631) 14 Carry your rod..in your right hand, the point either directly upright, or thwarted towards your left shoulder. **1632** LITHGOW *Trav.* VII. 309 They make ..the signe of the Crosse.., thwarting their two foremost fingers.

**3.** To cross *with* a line, streak, band, etc. (Only in pa. pple.) *Obs.* or *arch.*

**1610** GUILLIM *Heraldry* III. xiv. (1660) 162 The blacke line on the ridge of all Asses backes, thwarted with the like over both the Shoulders. **1615** G. SANDYS *Trav.* I. 63 Turbants are made like great globes of callico too, and thwarted with roules of the same. **1658** J. ROWLAND *Moufet's Theat. Ins.* 942 The body all over of a yellow colour, except where it is thwarted with cross streaks or lines. **1861** *Temple Bar Mag.* II. 256, I saw Vesuvius..thwarted by a golden cloud.

**b.** To cross-plough; also, to cut crosswise.

**1847** *Jrnl. R. Agric. Soc.* VIII. II. 318 The burnt earth is then spread on the land and thwarted in (that is, ploughed across the direction in which the land is ploughed when laid up in stetches for sowing). **1871** COUCH *Hist. Polperro* vi. 117 Land broken for wheat is thwarted in the Spring. **1888** ELWORTHY *W. Somerset Word-bk.* s.v. *Thurt*, Why, 'tis a wo'th vive shillings to thurt thick there butt. **1898** RIDER HAGGARD in *Longm. Mag.* Nov. 38 All my three ploughs were at work 'thwarting'—that is crossploughing—rootland on the Nunnery Farm.

**4.** To obstruct (a road, course, or passage) with something placed across; to block. *Obs.* exc. *fig.*

*c* **1630** RISDON *Surv. Devon* § 65 (1810) 63 The rebellious commons..thwarted the ways with great trees. *Ibid.* § 269. 278 [A stream] whose course is thwarted with a damm, which we call a wear. **1725** POPE *Odyss.* x. 72 What Dæmon cou'dst thou meet To thwart thy passage and repel thy fleet? **1760–72** H. BROOKE *Fool of Qual.* (1809) IV. 58 They met with a six-barred gate that directly thwarted their passage. **1807** CRABBE *Par. Reg.* II. 72 They sometimes speed, but often thwart our course. **1856** KANE *Arct. Expl.* II. v. 60 If no misadventure thwarted his progress.

**II. 5.** To act or operate in opposition to; to run counter to, to go against; to oppose, hinder. Also *absol.* Now *rare.*

*c* **1250** *Gen. & Ex.* 1324 Quat-so god bad, ðwerted he it neuer a del. *c* **1430, 1530** [implied in THWARTING *vbl. sb.* 2 and *ppl. a.* 2]. **1600** HOLLAND *Livy* XXXV. xxxii. 907 Such as might.. not sticke to speake their minds franckly, yea, & thwart the king his embassadour. **1671** BP. PARKER *Def. Eccl. Pol.* iii. § 15. 298 To what purpose does he so briskly taunt me for thwarting my own Principles. **1676** W. ALLEN *Address Nonconf.* 130 The danger of Schism, and the evil of thwarting publick Laws. **1783** JUSTAMOND tr. *Raynal's Hist. Indies* VII. 379 They had unfortunately been so much thwarted by the winds as to prevent their landing before summer. **1802** PALEY *Nat. Theol.* xxvi. (1819) 436 General laws, however well set and constituted, often thwart and cross one another. **1811** L. M. HAWKINS *C'tess & Gertr.* II. 370 The countess was not always disposed to thwart and vex: a little flattery would soothe her.

**b.** *intr.* To speak or act in contradiction or opposition; to be adverse or at variance, to conflict. Const. *with.* Now *rare* or *Obs.*

**1519** HORMAN *Vulg.* 59 b, I wyll nat multyplie wordes or thwarte with the. **1601** ? MARSTON *Pasquil & Kath.* II. 185 Is't possible that sisters should so thwart In natiue humours? **1656** *Burton's Diary* (1828) I. 15 This clause thwarts with his Highness's ordinances. **1737** BRACKEN *Farriery Impr.* (1757) II. 272 It would thwart with my intended Brevity. **1862** F. HALL *Hindu Philos. Syst.* 42 They also accept..the Smritis, the Purāṇas, &c., the work of Ṛishis, when those books do not thwart with the Veda.

**6.** *trans.* To oppose successfully; to prevent (a person, etc.) from accomplishing a purpose; to prevent the accomplishment of (a purpose); to foil, frustrate, balk, defeat. (The chief current sense.)

**1581** MULCASTER *Positions* iv. (1887) 17 He may either proceede at his owne libertie, if nothing withstand him, or may not proceede, if he be thwarted by circunstance. **1641** EARL MONM. tr. *Biondi's Civil Warres* v. 166 The Earle seeing himselfe twharted, resolved to fight. **1697** J. LEWIS *Mem. Dk. Glocester* (1789) 34 From being sometimes a little thwarted, and thro' dissatisfaction, she grew sick. **1718** *Free-thinker* No. 65 ¶ 6 Perpetual Obstacles..thwarted his Designs. **1803** DK. WELLINGTON in Gurw. *Desp.* (1837) II. 352 Thus are all our best plans thwarted. **1849** MACAULAY *Hist. Eng.* iv. I. 429 The party which had long thwarted him had been beaten down. **1871** FREEMAN *Norm. Conq.* IV. xvii. 15 But all these good intentions were thwarted by the inherent vice of his position.

**Thwa·rted,** *ppl. a.* [f. THWART *v.* + -ED [1].]

†**1.** Placed across; crossed. *Obs. rare*[−1].

**1655** FULLER *Ch. Hist.* III. iii. § 11 All Knights-Templers make such saltire cross with their thwarted leggs upon their monuments.

**2.** Obstructed; frustrated, balked, defeated.

**1828** CARLYLE *Misc., Burns* (1872) II. 13 Ever-thwarted, ever renewed endeavours. **1837** SIR W. HAMILTON *Metaph.* xlv. (1870) II. 504 A thwarted, and therefore a painful energy of thought. **1879** DIXON *Windsor* II. xx. 208 Harry..understood the misery of a thwarted suit.

Hence **Thwa·rtedly** *adv.*

**1870** RUSKIN *Lect. Art* vii. (1875) 179 An atmosphere through which a burning sun shines thwartedly.

**Thwarteous** (þwǭ·ɹtyəs), *a.* [App. a ghost-word due to misreading *thwarteouer* in Clarendon's *Hist. Reb.* (1849) I. § 174.] Perverse, contrary.

**1890** R. BRIDGES *Chr. Capt.* v. 2319 Satan did persuade our thwarteous king To make a godless bargain. **1903** A. SMELLIE *Men of Covt.* i. (1904) 6 If he touched these treasures, he would find her humour 'thwarteous', indeed.

**Thwarter** (þwǭ·ɹtəɹ). [f. THWART *v.* + -ER [1].] One who or that which thwarts.

†**1.** One who traverses or goes across. *Obs. rare*[−1].

*a* **1693** *Urquhart's Rabelais* III. xlix. 394 Xenomanes the great Traveller, and Thwarter of dangerous ways.

**2.** One who or that which obstructs the path or action of another; an opponent, adversary, obstructor, frustrater.

**1633** T. ADAMS *Exp. 2 Peter* i. 2 O happy soul, that can make his thwarters that cross him, become his porters to carry him to the place of his rest. **1687** WOOD *Life* 16 Aug. (O.H.S.) III. 224 Dr. Fell..would never suffer him to beare that office because a thwarter of him in severall public matters. **1738** tr. *Guazzo's Art Conversation* 71 Those whom I call Contentious and Thwarters are, for the most Part, gross, thick-headed Fellows. **1869** HUGHES *Alfred Gt.* xii. 141 The thwarters of the King's will repented.

**Thwarter-ill,** variant of THORTER-ILL.

†**Thwa·rterous,** *a. Obs. nonce-wd.* [irreg. f. THWART: see -OUS, and cf. *boisterous.*] Tortuous, twisted, gnarled.

**1625** J. WODROEPHE *Marrow Fr. Tongue* 336 The yellow wood so thwarterous [Fr. *torteux*], beares Fruit so precious.

**Thwarting** (þwǭ·ɹtiŋ), *vbl. sb.* [f. THWART *v.* + -ING [1].] The action of the verb THWART.

†**1.** Going athwart, crossing. *Obs. rare*[−1].

*c* **1440** *Gesta Rom.* xlvi. 193 (Harl. MS.) By the Ringe we muste vndirstonde feithe, for that owithe to be Rounde like a Ringe, and with oute eny twartynge.

**b.** Cross-ploughing.

**1847** *Jrnl. R. Agric. Soc.* VIII. II. 318 After the first thwarting of the fallow (cross-ploughing),..the clods are worked..into about the size of a hen's egg.

**2.** Opposition; hindrance, impediment; defeating, frustration.

*c* **1430** *Pilgr. Lyf Manhode* IV. lii. (1869) 200 Þe arguynge, ne þe thuartinge is no thing worth ayens us, ne ayens deth neither. **1581** MULCASTER *Positions* xxviii. (1887) 109 A number of lettes and thwartings which art did prescribe. **1609** DOULAND *Ornith. Microl.* 79 A Discord..is the hard and rough thwarting of two sounds not mingled with themselues. **1653** R. SANDERS *Physiogn.* 53 Great thwartings and misfortunes by the means of women. **1825** SCOTT *Jrnl.* 23 Dec., Those thwartings are what men in public life do not like to endure.

**Thwarting** (þwǭ·ɹtiŋ), *ppl. a.* [f. THWART *v.* + -ING [2].] That thwarts, in various senses.

**1.** Lying or passing crosswise; crossing, traversing, transverse; of the eyes: crossed, squinting. *Obs.* or *arch.*

*c* **1430** *Pilgr. Lyf Manhode* IV. iv. (1869) 176 With purblynde eyen and thwartinge may not be hool lookinge. **1625** K. LONG tr. *Barclay's Argenis* I. i. 3, I fled thorow the bushes, where the thwarting bowes loosened the knots of my hayre. **1632** LITHGOW *Trav.* (1906) 278 Slaine and hung up on two standing and a thwarting tree. **1653** R. SANDERS *Physiogn.* 48 If it [middle line of the palm] be right, continued, and without thwarting lines.

**2.** Conflicting, opposing, obstructing; perverse; frustrating, baffling; adverse, untoward.

**1530** PALSGR. 306/2 Brablyng thwartyng or quarellyng, *noyseux. Ibid.* 327/2 Twhartynge or contraryeng, *captieux.* **1593** SHAKS. 3 *Hen. VI*, IV. vi. 22 That the people of this blessed Land May not be punisht with my thwarting starres. **1658** *Whole Duty of Man* iv. § 3 To entangle themselves by taking one oath cross and thwarting to another. **1718** *Free-thinker* No. 61 ¶ 9 A Thwarting, Cavilling Temper only promotes Contention. **1804** J. GRAHAME *Sabbath* (1839) 23/1 The thwarting surge Dash'd, boiling, on the labouring bark. **1878** J. R. SEELEY *Stein* II. 4 The very moment when the thwarting power..visibly intervenes.

Hence **Thwa·rtingly** *adv.*, transversely; perversely; adversely.

**1579** TOMSON *Calvin's Serm. Tim.* 359/1 Fetch no windelesses, nor goe anye by-wayes and as it were thwartingly. **1618** T. ADAMS *Chr. Walk* Wks. 1862 II. 407 The overprecise are so thwartingly cross to the superstitious..that they will scarce do a good work, because a heretic doth it. **1715** tr. *Pancirollus' Rerum Mem.* II. xiii. 359 These Films ..laid one upon another, some in a direct, and others thwartingly and in a transverse Position.

**Thwartle** (þwǭ·ɹt'l), *v. Obs.* exc. *dial.* [dim. or freq. of THWART *v.*: see -LE 3.] *intr.* To speak or act in contradiction.

**1647** TRAPP *Comm. Rom.* ii. 8 That wrangle and thwartle against clearest truths. **1847–78** HALLIWELL, *Thurtle*, to cross in discourse; to contradict. *Somerset. Whartle*, to cross; to tease. *Norf.*

†**Thwa·rtlo·ng,** *adv. Obs. rare*[−1]. [f. THWART *adv.* + -LONG.] Crosswise, transversely.

**1600** F. WALKER *Sp. Mandeville* 8 Some [children at birth] come forth thwartlong and some with their body double.

**Thwa·rtly,** *adv.* Now *rare.* [f. THWART *a.* + -LY [2].] In a thwart manner.

**1.** Transversely, crosswise, obliquely. Also *fig.*

**1541** R. COPLAND *Guydon's Quest. Chirurg.* D iv b, The seconde bone of the heade in the hyndre parte..is enclosed by a commyssure thwartly in maner of a greke lettre called Lampda. **1654** Z. COKE *Logick* 181 Indirect Solution, is when we answer indirectly, and thwartly to the Syllogism proposed.

**2.** In the way of opposition or contrariety; perversely; 'crossly'.

**1554** W. KETHE in Goodman *How Superior Powers*, etc. (1558) 235 Sith man then in iudgeinge, so thwartly is bente To satisfie fansie, and not true intente. **1581** RICH *Farewell* (Shaks. Soc.) 172 She answered hym thawartly. *a* **1646** J. GREGORY *Terrestr. Globe* Posthuma (1650) 266 Som few Spanish Geographers..reckon the Longitudes quite contrarie, from East to West, but which was thwartly in it self, and, in the proof, inconsiderably don.

†**Thwa·rtness.** Now *rare.* [f. as prec. + -NESS.] The condition or quality of being thwart, in various senses; transverseness; opposition, contrariety; perversity.

**1548–77** VICARY *Anat.* ii. (1888) 20 The third [property is] in thwartnes, in whom the vertue that holdeth hath might. **1614** SIR R. DUDLEY in *Fortesc. Papers* (Camden) 11 *note*, The thawartnes [*sic*]..of late the parlement useth towardes him. **1649** BP. HALL *Cases Consc.* IV. ii. (1654) 303 Some unkinde usages, or thwartnesse of disposition.

**Thwa·rt-o·ver,** *prep., adv., adj. Obs.* exc. *dial.* Also 3 þwert-, 5 twarte-, thurte-, thawrt-, *dial.* 8 thurt-, 9 thirtover. See also THORTER. [Originally, and in A and B usually, two words: THWART *adv.* and OVER *prep.* or *adv.* Cf. OVERTHWART.]

†**A.** *prep.* Athwart over; across one side to the other of. (Also in quot. *c* 1450 *in thurte* (= *a-thwart*) *over.*) *Obs.*

*a* **1225** *St. Marher.* 10 Ant [heo] droh þa endelong hire, ant þwertouer þrefter, þe derewurðe taken of þe deore rode. **1387** TREVISA *Higden* (Rolls) II. 45 The secounde chief kynges hiȝe weye hatte Watlynge strete, and streccheþ þwart ouer Fosse [orig. *per transversum prioris viæ*] out of þe souþ est in to þe norþ west. *c* **1400** *Lanfranc's Cirurg.* 143 (Add. MS.) Aftirwarde he [a band] schal be turnyde twarte offere þe forehed, þat..þe nose declyne to neiþere syde. *c* **1450** *Godstow Reg.* 374 The which lieth in the feld that is I-called Brademore, and strecchith hit-self in thurte ouer the feld in length toward the southe and towarde the northe. *Ibid.* 502 All ther tenementes..in the subarbis of Oxenford toward the northe, fro the fore-named diche thurte ouer bewmounte vnto horsemonger-strete.

†**B.** *adv.* Crosswise; across. *Obs.*

**1398** TREVISA *Barth. De P. R.* XVIII. xi. (Bodl. MS.), Þe spiþer..strecheþ vpward wiþ wonder crafte fro þe neþer side to þe ouer and drawiþ and bringeþ ofte aȝen his þrede þwarte ouer fro pointe to pointe. *c* **1430** *Pilgr. Lyf Manhode* IV. iv. 176 Bakward she ran, and thwart ouer. **1502** ARNOLDE *Chron.* (1811) 141 The worlde is.. viii M myle thwarte ouer and iiij M myle to the midel.

**C.** *adj.* †**a.** Crossing, lying athwart, cross. *Obs.*

**b.** That thwarts or obstructs; obstructive; cross, contrary, perverse, self-willed. Now *dial.*

*a* **1225** *Ancr. R.* 82 Attri speche is eresie & þwertouer leasunge. **1387** TREVISA *Higden* (Rolls) II. 149 Þe souþsyde of Scotlonde þat streccheth from þe þwart ouer wal of Romayn werk to þe Scottische see. *Ibid.* VII. 35 Al aboute þe feeldes and þwart over weies. **1422** tr. *Secreta Secret., Priv. Priv.* 188 An harde and a thawrtouer worde raysyth Stryfe and wodnesse. **1630** J. TAYLOR (Water P.) *Pr. Charles* Wks. III. 102/1 For fifteene long dayes and nights, the thwartouer and crosse North and Easterly Winde blew vs nothing but [etc.]. **1647** CLARENDON *Hist. Reb.* I. § 174 That thwartover humour was enough discovered to rule in the breasts of many. **1790** GROSE *Prov. Gloss.* (ed. 2) s. v. *Thurt*, A thurt-over fellow; a cross-grained or ill-tempered fellow. Berksh. **1891** HARDY *Tess* (1900) 107/2, I have been living on in a thirtover, lackaday way, and have not seen what it may lead to! **1894** MAXWELL GRAY *Innocent Impostor* 173 Things is thirtover when anybody's in a hurry.

**Thwa·rt-saw.** Now *dial.* Forms: see THWART. A saw for sawing timber across; a cross-cut saw.

**1404** *Durham Acc. Rolls* (Surtees) 396, iij sawes irined ex officio, et iij twhertsawes, ij handsawes. **1465** *Finchale Invent.* (Surtees) p. ccxcix, In primis,..j twortsaw, j twybyll, j hak, j pyk. **1567** *Wills & Inv. N. C.* (Surtees) I. 268 A whippt sawe, ij hand sawes, a twart sawe. **1577** *Ibid.* 414 In the Ireon Seller. Eighte qwarte sawes xvj[s].—thre whope sawes xx[s]. **1590** *Inv.* in *Midl. Co. Hist. Coll.* II. 31 Item iij wimbles a handsawe one whartsawe. **1611–12** *Knaresborough Wills* (Surtees) II. 34 My thwartsaw. **1888** ELWORTHY *W. Somerset Word-bk.*, *Thurt saw*,..cross-cut saw. ..'Plase to tich up (sharpen) the thurt saw'.

**Thwart-ship, thwartship** (þwǭ·ɹtˌʃip), *a.* and *adv. Naut.* [f. THWART *prep.* + SHIP *sb.*]

**A.** *adj.* Placed or fixed across the ship's length. *Thwartship tiller*, a tiller fixed at right angles to the rudder.

**1829** H. L. MAW *Jrnl. Passage fr. Pacific to Atlantic* 314 Resting on small thwartship timbers. *c* **1850** *Rudim. Navig.* (Weale) 123 The 'thwartship pieces which frame the hatchways. **1897** *Outing* (U.S.) XXX. 228/1 The crew..manœuvres the craft by means of a five-foot thwartship tiller.

**B.** *adv.* (þwǭ·ɹtˌʃi·p). From side to side of the ship; across the length of the ship.

**1882** NARES *Seamanship* (ed. 6) 242 The correctors..are bar magnets in..holders, thwartship,..within the binnacle. **1895** *Outing* (U.S.) XXVI. 481/2 The modern canoeist puts it [ballast] in his own weight, on the end of the plank extended thwart-ship to windward.

**Thwart-ships** (þwǭ·ɹtˌʃips), *adv. Naut.* [f. as prec. + -*s* of adverbial genitive.] = prec. B.

*a* **1625** *Nomenclator Navalis* (Harl. MS. 2301) s.v., Anie thing that is done or lies acrosse y[e] Shipp from one side to thother wee saie that it lies thwart ships. **1718** STEELE *Fish Pool* 175 The depth of the arch of the deck thwartships is 4 inches.

**Thwartways** (þwǭ·ɹtˌwēɪz), *adv. rare.* Also 7 thwartway. [f. THWART *a.* + -WAYS.] = next, A.

**1665** HOOKE *Microgr.* xxii. 139 There were not more seem'd to lie horizontally then perpendicularly and thwartway. **1893** KIPLING *Many Invent.* 11 He lashed the canes together criss-cross and thwartways.

**Thwartwise** (þwǭ·ɹtwəiz), *adv.* and *a.* [f. THWART *a.* + -WISE.]

**A.** *adv.* Crosswise, transversely.

**1589** P. IVE *Fortif.* 16 Lay a trauers of trees in the bottome ..laying them thwart wise in the work. **1661** LOVELL *Hist. Anim. & Min.* 191 Crab, *Cancer*, they goe thwartwise. **1894** CROCKETT *Mad Sir Uchtred* v, The troop passed thwartwise over the mountain steep. **1899** — *Black Douglas* (1900) 468 Margaret..rode thwartwise to intercept her.

**B.** *adj.* Situated or extending transversely; cross, transverse.

**1890** CLERKE *Syst. Stars* 309 The directly measurable, thwartwise part of its motion. **1891** *Dublin Rev.* Jan. 157 Compounded..of thwartwise and end-on speed.

† **Thwerl**, *v. Obs. rare*⁻¹. Origin and meaning obscure. (Some identify it with TWIRL or WHIRL.)

*c* **1489** CAXTON *Sonnes of Aymon* i. 32 Reynawde..thwerled his swerde by grete fyersnesse.

† **Thwert-nay**: see under next.

† **Thwert-out**, *adv. Obs.* In 3 þuertut, (*Orm.*) þwerrt ut. [f. *thwert*, THWART *adv.* + OE. *út* OUT.] Thoroughly, completely, utterly, absolutely: = THROUGHOUT B. 3.

*c* **1200** ORMIN 194 To ȝarrkenn her onnȝæness Crist All þwerrt ut haliȝ leode. *Ibid.* 313–316 Forr þatt all iss þwerrt ut soþ, & all þwerrt ut to trowwenn Þatt stanndeþþ o þe Goddspellboc þatt þwerrt ut nohht ne leȝheþþ. *c* **1200** *Trin. Coll. Hom.* 123 Þat mannisse þe ne understant ne bisecheð god, is þuertut forlore soule and lichame.

Hence † **Thwert-ut nay**, *Early Eng. Law*, a complete or absolute 'Nay', a downright 'No'; a flat denial by the defendant of the plaintiff's charge.

**1277** in Jeaffreson *Index to Leicester MSS.* 74–5 Si le defendant taunt tost cum la parole ly fust issue de la buche ne deist *thwertutnay*, il fut tenu cum non defendu, e ceo apelerent *swareles*. *Ibid.*, Ke le defendaunt ne poeit a la pleinte le pleintif autre chose respundre for tut granter ou tut dire *thwertutnay*. **1895** POLLOCK & MAITLAND *Hist. Eng. Law* II. 606 A defendant was treated as undefended unless, before he said anything else, he met the plaintiff's tale with a *thwertutnay*, that is a downright No. *Ibid. Note*, The idea of a *thwertutnay* is preserved in our *traverse*.

Originally, † **Thwert-nay**, † **Thwert-nik**. [f. *thwert*, THWART *adv.* or *a.*: see NICH and NICK *v.*¹, and cf. ON. *setja þvert nei* to deny flatly.] *lit.* A traversing or directly contradicting 'Nay' or 'Nik'; also the right or liberty to give such a direct denial.

(Under the influence of *Thwert-ut*, this became *Thwert-ut nay*.)

**1218** *Earl Randal's Charter to Cheshire* (D. of Lanc. Misc. Bks. 12 lf. 25), Per twertnik se defendere poterit. **12..** *Leges Quat. Burgorum* c. 31 in *Acts Parl. Scot.* (1844) I. 338 Et est retinendum quod in placitis burgorum utitur Twertnay in defensionibus defendendo wrang and unlawe. [15*th c. transl.*, And it is to wyt þat in borow mutis þar is hantyd and oysyt thuertnay in defendande wrang and unlawe.] **1275** *Close Roll* 3 *Edw. I*, m. 5 Excepta..libertate quam dictus Robertus habuit in terris et tenementis suis in comitatu Cestrie que vocatur Thwertnik. **1296** *Chancery Inq. p. mort.* Edw. I, 79 (8) Quamdam libertatem que vocatur twertnyc. — *Exchequer Inq. p. mort.* 5 (4) Libertatem que vocatur twertnyk.

**Thweten**, obs. pa. pple. of THWITE.

† **Thwick-thwack.** *Obs.* [Redupl. f. THWACK.] The repetition or exchange of thwacks.

**1575** R. B. *Appius & Virg.* B ij b, With thwicke thwack, with thump thump, With bobbing and bum. **1582** STANYHURST *Conceits* in *Æneis*, etc. (Arb.) 138 With peale meale ramping, with thwick thwack sturdelye thundring. **1611** COTGR. s.v. *Torche*, *Torche lorgne*, words, like our thwicke thwacke, expressing a liberall and free dole of blowes. **1670** RAY *Prov.* 53 When a couple are newly married, the first moneth is honey-moon or smick smack: the second is, hither and thither: the third is, thwick thwack. **1783** AINSWORTH *Lat. Dict.* (Morell) I. s.v. *Thwack*, To lay on thwick, thwack, *ictus geminare*.

**Thwite** (þwəit), *v. Obs.* exc. *dial.* Forms: 1 **þwitan, þweoton**; 4–7 **thwyte**, (7– *dial.*) **thwite**, (4–5 **twhyte**, 5 **twyte**, 6 **thwight**, 9 *dial.* **tweet, twet, toight**). *Pa. pple.* 4–5 **thwyten**, 6 **thwytten, thweten**, 6–7 **thwitten**; 5–7 **thwyted**, 6–7 **thwitted**, 5– **thwited**. See also WHITE *v.* [OE. *þwītan* (**þwát, þwiten*) to cut, cut off; not recorded elsewhere; but ON. had derivatives in *þveita* small ax, *þvita* a kind of ax, *þveit*, *þveiti* cut-off piece, parcel of land, THWAIT(E. In mod.Sc. and north. dial. the word has become *quhyte*, *hwite*, WHITE, in Aberdeen *fite*. See also THWITTLE, WHITTLE.]

*trans.* To cut down, whittle, pare, shave; to shape by paring; to cut away. Also *fig.* Phrase, *To thwite a mill-post* (etc.) *to a pudding-prick.*

*a* **900** tr. *Bæda's Hist.* III. xiv. [xvii.] (1890) 204 ȝe[a] eac swylce of þære ilcan styðe sponas þweoton & sceafþan nomon [*v.r.* ðæt ȝeþwit naman]. *c* **1000** *Sax. Leechd.* II. 292 ȝenim þone neowran wyrttruman delf up, þwit niȝon sponas on ða winstran hand. ? *a* **1366** CHAUCER *Rom. Rose* 933 That other bowe..was peynted wel and thwyten [*MS.* twythen, *Thynne* thwitten]. *c* **1384** — *H. Fame* III. 848 Somme [twigs] weren white Whiche as men to these cages thwite [*v.rr.* thwyte, twhyte] Or maken of these panyers. *a* **1500** in Arnolde *Chron.* (1811) 170 The ende of the graff that was vpward next the firmament must be thweten lyke the neder of a comon graffe. **1529** MORE *Dyaloge* III. Wks. 236/2 Here was a gret post wel thwyted to a pudding pricke. **1575** *Brieff Disc. Troub. Franckford* (1846) 157 It nippeth and thwitethe awaie a great deale off that liberalitie, which might come to us. *a* **1601** SIR T. FANSHAWE *Pract. Exch.* (1658) 112 The Cutter of the Tallyes..provideth a..hasell for the Tallies..and doth somewhat thwite every stick thereof into four square sides. **1674** RAY *N. C. Words*, To *Thwite*, to whittle, cut, make white by cutting. **1897** *Shetland News* 24 July (E.D.D.), A placid roadman 'tweetin' the grass in the ditches with a scythe.

**b.** *intr.* To whittle. Now *dial.*

*c* **1475** *Babees Bk.* I. 179 Kutte nouhte youre mete eke as it were Felde men..They ne rekke..how vngoodly they on theyre mete twyte. **1863** *Lanc. Fents, New Shirt* 5 After 'thwiting' at the topmost bar of the gate till he had made it look almost like a new one. **1870** E. WAUGH *Winter Fire* iii. 24 Let these lads thwite at it [beef] a bit.

Hence **Thwi·ting** *vbl. sb.*; *thwiting-knife*, ? a paring or scraping knife used by bowyers.

**1393** LANGL. *P. Pl.* C. IX. 199 In þresshynge, in þecchyng, in thwytynge of pynnes. *c* **1440** *Promp. Parv.* 493/1 Thwytynge, or telwynge, *sectulatus, abscidula, abscindula*. **1659** HOWELL *Vocab.* li, A thwitting knife, nocksaws, a rasp, a riper, a share, a baldock, &c., *gli stromenti dell arciero* [the tools of the bowyer].

**Thwittle** (þwi·t'l), *sb.* Now *dial.* Forms: 4–5 **þw-, thwitel, thwytel**, 5 **-elle**, *Sc.* **thewtill, quhittil**, 6 **thwitle**, 7 **thwittel**, 7– **thwittle**: see also WHITTLE. [f. THWITE *v.* + -EL, -LE.] A knife, a whittle.

[*c* **1325** *Gloss. W. de Bibbesw.* in Wright *Voc.* 168 *Coteus*, thiwilet (?*for* thwitel).] *c* **1386** CHAUCER *Reeve's T.* 13 A Sheffeld thwitel [*v.r.* thwytel] baar he in his hose. *c* **1470** HENRY *Wallace* I. 218 A Scottis thewtill [*ed.* **1570** quhittil] wndyr thi belt to ber. **1664** COTTON *Scarron.* 37 They rise and wipe their greasy thwittles. **1796** PEGGE *Derbicisms* (E.D.S.), With a Lancashire thwittle I thwited a flail-swipple. **1881** *Antiquary* Feb. 87 A bill-hook has been substituted for the thwittle.

**Thwittle** (þwi·t'l), *v.* Now *dial.* [freq. and dim. of THWITE *v.*: see -LE 3.] *trans.* To pare down or away, to whittle (also *intr.*): = THWITE *v.*

**1593** G. HARVEY *Pierce's Super.* Wks. (Grosart) II. 244 He hath thwittled the milpost of his huge conceit to a pudding-pricke. **1874** E. WAUGH *Jannock* ii. 12 He'll not like to dine off o' what we'n bin thwittlin' at.

**Thwndur, -yr**, obs. forms of THUNDER.

**Thy** (ðəi), *poss. adj.* Forms: 2–5 **þi** (**ti**), 4 **þy** (**ty**), 4–6 **thi**, (6 **yi**), 4– **thy**. [Early ME. *þī*, reduced form of *þīn*, THINE, used in ME. bef. consonants exc. *h*, but occurring before vowels in 15th c., and ultimately universal in prose use as the possessive adj. preceding its sb., = Ger. *dein, deine*, F. *ton, ta, tes*.]

Of or belonging to thee, that thou hast.

For restriction of use see note to THOU *pers. pron.* 1.

*a* **1175** *Cott. Hom.* 225 Þe..and ti wif, and þine þreo sunes. *c* **1175** *Pater Noster* in *Lamb. Hom.* 57 Þi nome beo iblecced. *Ibid.* 59 Cume þi riche. *a* **1225** *Ancr. R.* 98 Þi stefne is me swete, & ti hwite schene. **13..** in *Rel. Ant.* I. 145 Wer es ty sire, wer es ty dame? **13..** *E. E. Allit. P.* B. 330 Enter þis ark with þyn aþel barnez & þy wedded wyf. **1388** WYCLIF *Ruth* i. 16 Thi puple is my puple, and thi God is my God. *c* **1450** *Bk. Curtasye* 71 in *Babees Bk.* 301 Let not þi spone stond in þy dysche. **1502** ATKYNSON tr. *De Imitatione* I. xx. 169 Lyft vp thy iyen to heuen. **1513** DOUGLAS *Æneis* IV. iv. 42 Apon thi top, mont Cynthus, walkis he. **1552** LYNDESAY *Monarche* 4131 Perfytlie prent in yi remembrance Off this Inconstante warld the variance. **1552** HULOET, Thy owne selfe, *te ipsum, temet*. **1667** MILTON *P. L.* V. 153 These are thy glorious works, Parent of good. **1852** MRS. STOWE *Uncle Tom's C.* xiii, [The Quaker Settlement] 'Where's thy baby, Ruth?' said Rachel..'Thy Mary caught him as I came in.' **1859** TENNYSON *Enid* 347 Turn, Fortune, turn thy wheel and lower the proud.

† **Thy**, *adv. Obs.* Forms: 1–2 **þy**, 2–3 **þi**. [OE. *ðý, þý*, instrumental case of demonst. and relative pron. *se, séo, þæt*: see THAT, and cf. THE *adv.*]

**1. a.** *orig.* By means or by reason of that, because of that, therefore. **b.** In relative sense: For the reason that, because.

*c* **897** K. ÆLFRED *Gregory's Past. C.* xxviii. 192 Ðy him is micel ðearf, ðonne he tela lærð, ðæt he eac tela do. *c* **1000** *Sax. Leechd.* II. 86 Smire mid huniȝ, þæt þy þe raþor sio hryfing of fealle. *c* **1175** *Lamb. Hom.* 93 Þi bileafden heo heore timbrunge. *c* **1200** *Trin. Coll. Hom.* 205 Wilfulshipe and lichamliche lustes and liðere lahtres, þi ne mai no man gode folȝen. *a* **1250** *Owl & Night.* 860 Ich rede þi þat men beo ware. *c* **1275** *Woman of Samaria* 39 in *O. E. Misc.* 85 Ich wot..Þat þu me hauest soþ iseyd..Þi of one þinge sey me iredynesse.

**c.** Hence in *for thy*, for that reason, therefore: see FOR-THY; also in OE. *mid þý*, with that, seeing that, since, when, while; *to þý*, to that end or purpose, therefore.

**2.** Preceding an adj. or adv. in the comparative degree: see THE *adv.*

**Thy**, obs. f. THIGH. **Thyad**: see THYIAD.

**Thyck**, obs. f. THICK. **Thyder, -ur**, etc., obs. ff. THITHER. **Thye**, obs. f. THEE *v.*¹, THIGH.

**Thyef** (**þ-**), **Thyefthe** (**þ-**), obs. ff. THIEF, THEFT.

**Thyestean** (þəiˌestī·ăn, þəiˌeˑstiăn), *a.* Also 7 **-æan**, 9 **-ian**. [f. L. *Thyestēus*, ad. Gr. Θυέστειος (f. Θυέστης, prop. name) + -AN.] Of or belonging to Thyestes, in ancient Greek legend brother of Atreus, who at a banquet made him eat of the flesh of his own two sons; hence used allusively.

**1667** MILTON *P. L.* X. 688 The Sun, as from Thyestean Banquet, turn'd His course intended. **1667** J. OWEN *Plea Indulgence & Lib. Consc.* 7 Thiestæan Banquets, promiscuous Lusts, and Incests. **1723** R. MILLAR *Hist. Propag. Chr.* II. v. 73 There is an infamous report that we are guilty of Thyestean feasts, that is feeding on murdered infants. **1746** FRANCIS tr. *Horace, Art of Poetry* 129 Nor will the direful Thyestean Feast In comic Phrase and Language be debas'd. *c* **1850** LOWELL *Fable for Critics* (ed. 2) Prelim. Note, I am not queasy-stomached, but such a Thyestean Banquet as that was quite out of the question. **1882** FARRAR *Early Days Chr.* I. iv. I. 65 Did not popular rumour charge them with nocturnal orgies and Thyestæan feasts?

**Thyf(e**, obs. form of THIEF.

**Thyfe-thorn**, variant of THEVE-THORN *Obs.*

**Thyft, -ly**, obs. forms of THEFT, -LY.

**Thyg(g, Thygh(e, thyh(e, Thyght**, obs. ff. THIG, THIGH, THIGHT, THIGHED.

**Thyiad** (þəi·iˌæd), **Thyad** (þəi·æd). *Gr. Antiq.* [a. Gr. θυιάς, stem θυιαδ- (pl. -άδες) a frenzied woman; properly adj. fem. from verbal root θυι-, Æolic form of θυ- to rush, rage.] A Bacchante.

[**1710** W. KING *Heathen Gods & Heroes* xxvii. (1722) 134 The Women who accompany'd him [Bacchus] as his Priestesses, were call'd *Mænades*, from their Madness; *Thyades*, from their Impetuousness and Fury. **1835** T. MITCHELL *Acharn. of Aristoph.* 221 *note*, The older females figured as Thyades or Bacchantes.] **1846** H. G. ROBINSON *Odes of Horace* II. xix, The Thyads ever wantoning. **1871** R. ELLIS *Catullus* lxiv. 390 Often on high Parnassus a roving Liber in hurried Frenzy the Thyiads drave.

**Thyine** (þəi·in), *a.* Also 4 **tyyn, tyne**, **thyn**, 4–6 **thyne**, 6 **thynne**, (**thynen**), 7 **thine**. [ad. L. *thȳin-us*, ad. Gr. θύϊνος of the tree θύα, *thya*, or THUYA. Formerly sometimes miswritten *tyme, thyme*, from reading *in* as *m*.] Epithet of a tree, and its wood, mentioned in Rev. xviii. 12; supposed to be the African coniferous tree *Callitris quadrivalvis*, which yields gum sandarac.

The Vulgate has *ligna thyina* also in 1 Kings x. 11–12, where the Greek is different, and the version of 1611, following the Heb., has *almug trees*.

**1382** WYCLIF 1 *Kings* x. 11 The nauee of Yram,..brouȝte to of Oofer manye tyyn trees [**1388** trees of tyme, Vulg. *ligna thyina*, LXX. ξύλα πελεκητά hewn trees, Heb. אלמגים *almuggim*, COVERD. costly tymber, 1611 almug trees]. **1382** — *Rev.* xviii. 12 The marchaundises of gold, and siluer, and precious stoon,..and ech tre thyine [*erron.* thyme, *Vulg.* et omne lignum thyinum, *Gr.* καὶ πᾶν ξύλον θύϊνον]. [**1398** TREVISA *Barth. De P. R.* XVII. clxv. (Bodl. MS.), Thina beþ certeyne treene moste precious.] **1526** TINDALE *Rev.* xviii. 12 Off pearle, and raynes, and purple, and scarlett, and all thyne wodde [so *Geneva* & *Rhem.*; COVERD. Thynen wod, *Great* thynne wodde, 1611 Thine wood, *mod. edd.* thyine wood]. *a* **1571** JEWEL *On 2 Thess.* ii. 1, 2 All manner of thyine wood. **1763** C. SMART *Song to David* lx, The wealthy crops of whit'ning rice 'Mongst thyine woods and groves of spice.

**Thyisday**, obs. Sc. form of TUESDAY.

**Thyke, þyke**, obs. form of THILK.

† **Thykston(e.** *Obs. rare.* [f. *thik*, var. of THEEK *v.* to roof + STONE *sb.*] Roofing flags; = *thack-stone*: see THACK *sb.* 4.

**1486–7** *Durham Acc. Rolls* (Surtees) 158 Pro adquisicione vj futhrez del thykston, ijs.

**Thylacine** (þəi·lăsəin). [a. F. *thylacine*, in mod. L. *Thȳlacinus* (Temminck *Monogr. de Mammalogie*, 1827, I. 55), f. Gr. θύλακ-ος pouch + (app.) L. suffix *-inus*, -INE¹. (But some think that Temminck meant to include in the name Gr. κύων, κυνός dog, and that it is short for **thȳlaco-cynus* 'pouched dog', which is improbable. It had been previously described by Harris as *Didelphys cynocephalus*.)] The native Tasmanian 'wolf' or 'zebra-wolf', *Thylacinus cynocephalus*, the largest of existing carnivorous marsupials (now very scarce).

**1838** OWEN in *Proc. Geol. Soc.* III. 19 In the number of the grinders the Phascolothere resembles the Opossum and Thylacine. **1841** G. R. WATERHOUSE *Marsupialia* 127 The *Thylacinus* inhabits Van Diemen's Land where it is called the Tiger, Hyæna. **1846** OWEN *Brit. Fossil Mammals* 67. **1891** *Daily News* 5 May 5/5 The Zoological Society have just acquired a pair of thylacines—a somewhat rare, carnivorous marsupial, from Tasmania. **1901** *Pall Mall G.* 27 May 5/3 The thylacine is confined to Tasmania, although its fossil remains have been found in New South Wales.

**Thylacothere** (þəi·lăkoþīəɹ). *Palæont.* [ad. mod.L. *Thȳlacothērium*, f. Gr. θύλακο-ς pouch + θηρίον beast.] An extinct mammal of the genus *Thylacotherium*, also called *Amphitherium* (see AMPHITHERE), variously supposed to have been a marsupial or an insectivorous placental. Hence **Thylacothe·rian** *a.*

**1838** OWEN in *Proc. Geol. Soc.* III. 17 Objections against the mammiferous nature of the Thylacotherian jaws. *Ibid.* III. 19 In the position of the dental foramen, the Phascolothere, like the Thylacothere, differs from all zoophagous marsupials. **1850** BRODERIP *Note-bk. Naturalist* viii. (1852) 165 There cannot have been any very wide zoological interval between the forms of the thylacine and of the thylacothere.

**Thylk(e**, obs. form of THILK.

**Thyll(e**, obs. f. THILL¹, TILL *prep.* and *conj.*

**Thylose, -osis**: see TYLOSE, -OSIS.

**Thymacetin** (þəimæ·sǐtin). *Pharm.* A trade name of acetaminothymol, a colourless crystalline compound, used as a hypnotic.

**1892** *Pharmaceutical Jrnl.* 27 Feb. 692 Thymacetin..bears the same relation to thymol as phenacetin to phenol.

‖ **Thymallus** (þəimæ·lŏs). [mod.L., a. Gr. θύμαλλος name of an unknown fish: see quot. 1706.] The genus of fishes containing the graylings.

[**1706** PHILLIPS (ed. Kersey), *Thymallus*, a Fish of the Trout-kind, that smells like the Herb Thyme.] **1797** *Encycl. Brit.* (ed. 3) XVI. 616/2 The thymallus, or grayling, haunts clear and rapid streams.

**Thymate**, *Chem.*: see THYMIC *a.*¹ 2.

**Thymbel(l, -bil(l, -byl(l**, obs. ff. THIMBLE.

**Thyme** (təim), *sb.* Forms: *α.* 4–8 **tyme**, 6–8 **time**. *β.* 5– **thyme** (5–7 **thime**). [a. F. *thym* (13th c. in Godef. *Compl.*), ad. L. *thymum*, in late med.L. often *timum, -us*, a. Gr. θύμον (θύμος), f. θύειν to burn sacrifice.]

1. A plant of the genus *Thymus*, N.O. *Labiatæ*, comprising shrubby herbs with fragrant aromatic leaves, found chiefly in the Mediterranean region; esp. *T. vulgaris* (Garden Thyme), a native of Spain and Italy, cultivated as a pot-herb, and *T. Serpyllum* (Wild Thyme), occurring on dry banks and pastures in Britain and throughout Europe. (See also b.)

α. c 1420 *Liber Cocorum* (1862) 53 Saveray, mynt and tyme. c 1440 *Promp. Parv.* 494/1 Tyme, flowre, *timus*... Tyme, herbe, *tima*. 1526 *Pilgr. Perf.* (W. de W. 1531) 65 Wo be to you pharisees, whiche tytheth myntes, rewe, tyme, & suche other small herbes. 1563 Hyll *Art Garden*. (1593) 80 The Garden Time is a plant right profitable. 1590 Shaks. *Mids. N.* II. i. 249, I know a banke where the wilde time blowes. 1653 Walton *Angler* ii. 57 Bruise..a little Time, or some other sweet herb. 1713 *Phil. Trans.* XXVIII. 193 Lemon Tyme.

β. 1398 Trevisa *Barth. De P. R.* xvii. lix. (Bodl. MS.) lf. 203 b/2 Epithimum is þe floure of thyme. c 1425 *Voc.* in Wr.-Wülcker 644/6 Nomina Herbarum.. *Hic caulus*, uwle (?) or thyme. 1562 Turner *Herbal* II. 155 b, Thyme hath the poure to driue furth fleme. 1637 Milton *Lycidas* 40 Desert Caves, With wilde Thyme and the Gadding Vine o'regrown. 1657 S. Purchas *Pol. Flying-Ins.* I. xv. 94 Thyme, which onely yeeldeth Nectar. 1855 Kingsley *Heroes, Theseus* I. 199 The hills are sweet with thyme and basil.

b. With qualifying words, denoting various species or varieties: as **creeping thyme, mother of thyme, running t.** = *wild t.* (see 1); **garden thyme** (see 1); **lemon thyme**, †**musk thyme**, a cultivated variety of *T. Serpyllum*, having a scent like that of lemons (often called *T. citriodorus*); **savory thyme**, *T. virginicus* (see Savory 3). Also applied to plants of other genera, chiefly aromatic labiates, as Basil *thyme*, Cat-*thyme*, Horse-*thyme*; also **water-thyme**, a name of *Elodea canadensis* (*Anacharis Alsinastrum*).

1579 Langham *Gard. Health* (1633) 636 Thyme: Running Thyme prouoketh the termes and vrine. 1597 Gerarde *Herbal* II. clxiv. § 6. 457 Called..in English wilde Time, Puliall Mountaine,..running Time, creeping Time, Mother of Time. *Ibid.* clxv. 459 Our English women call it Muske Time. 1676 Beal in *Phil. Trans.* XI. 587 The Thymes, denominated from Mastic, Lemon, Musk, Yellow and White Thyme. 1713 [see 1 a].

2. *Oil of thyme*: a fragrant volatile oil obtained from the common thyme, used as an antiseptic.

1753 Chambers *Cycl. Supp.* s.v. *Oil*, Mr. Geoffroy made a multitude of experiments on the oil of thyme. 1857 [see Thymene 1]. 1876 Harley *Royle's Mat. Med.* 407 An odour resembling oil of thyme. *Ibid.* 474 [see Thymol].

3. *attrib.* and *Comb.*, as *thyme-blossom*, *-leaf*, *-root*; *thyme-capt*, *-fed*, *-flavoured*, *-grown* adjs.; **thyme-camphor** = Thymol; **thyme fish**, a name for the grayling, its smell being held to resemble that of thyme (whence the generic name *Thymallus*); **thyme-leaved** (-līvd) *a.*, having leaves resembling those of thyme (rendering mod.L. *serpyllifolius* in specific names); **thyme-oil**, oil of thyme: see 2; †**thyme wart** (wert), used by Holland to render L. *thymion*, Gr. θύμιον a kind of wart (= Thymus 2).

1821 Clare *Vill. Minstr.* (1823) I. 119 This *thyme-capt hill beneath one's feet. 1900 Ellis *Rom. Rose* I. 19/545 Her breath was sweet as breeze *thyme-fed. 1756–7 tr. *Keysler's Trav.* (1760) I. 62 Very fine trouts, *thyme fish, and others. 1789 Pilkington *View Derby.* I. viii. 395 *Arenaria serpyllifolia*, *Thyme-leaved Sandwort. 1868 Watts *Dict. Chem.* V. 791 On continuing the distillation of the *thyme-oil, there passes over..a mixture of thymene (and cymene) with about 1/3 pt. of thymol. 1601 Holland *Pliny* xxxii. x. 448 For the *thyme werts particularly, they vse them [Cackerell heads] raw.

Hence **Thyme** *v.*, *trans.* to cover or scent with thyme; **Thymed** (təimd) *a.*, covered with thyme.

1628 Feltham *Resolves* II. [I.] xii. 32 Nor does the sedulous Bee thyme all her thighes from one Flowres single vertues. 1885 *St. James' Gaz.* 17 Aug. 6/2 Upon its thymed banks.

**Thymectomy** (þəime·ktŏmi). *Surg.* [f. as Thym-us + Gr. -εκτομια, from ἐκτομή a cutting out.] Excision of the thymus gland. Hence **Thyme·ctomize** *v.*, *trans.* to remove the thymus gland from.

1905 Gould *Dict. Med. Terms* Suppl., Thymectomy. 1909 Dorland *Med. Dict.* (ed. 5), Thymectomize, Thymectomy.

**Thymelæaceous** (þimīliˌēⁱ·ʃəs), *a. Bot.* Also **thymelaceous**. [f. mod.L. *Thymelæāceæ* (or *Thymelāceæ*), f. specific name (*Daphne*) *Thymelæa*, ad. Gr. θυμελαία, f. θύμ-ον Thyme + ἐλαία olive-tree: see -aceous.] Belonging to the N.O. *Thymelæaceæ* or *Thymelaceæ*.

1837 *Penny Cycl.* VIII. 307/2 *Daphne*, a genus of thymelaceous plants. 1848 Smart *Suppl. to Walker*, *Thymelea*,.. which gives the name thymelaceous to a natural order.

‖**Thymele** (þi·mĭlī). *Gr. Antiq.* [a. Gr. θυμέλη altar, f. θύειν to sacrifice.] The altar of Dionysus in the centre of the orchestra in an ancient Greek theatre.

1753 Chambers *Cycl. Supp.*, *Thymele*, in the antient theatre, a kind of pulpit, where the singers called *thymelici* performed. 1827 *Buckham's Theat. Grks.* (ed. 2) 216. 1835 *Penny Cycl.* III. 298/1 Some large blocks..in front of the stage..supposed by Dr. Hunt to be the ruins of the Thymele. 1842 *Smith's Dict. Grk. & Rom. Antiq.* s.v. *Theatrum*, In the centre of the circle of the orchestra was the θυμέλη, that is, the altar of Dionysus...The chorus generally arranged itself..between the thymele and the stage. 1889 Haigh *Attic Theat.* iii. § 6. 132. 1907 H. Trench *New Poems* 24 The sacred oils On the fragrant thin-flamed thymele.

Hence **Thyme·lic**, † **Thyme·lical** *adjs. rare* [Gr. θυμελικός], of or pertaining to the thymele, scenic, theatric.

1656 Blount *Glossogr.*, *Thymelical* (*thymelicus*), belonging to players in interludes and open dance. 1849 Donaldson *Theat. Greeks* I. vii. (ed. 6) 152 There was another entrance to the thymelic platform.

**Thymelle**, obs. form of Thimble.

**Thymene** (þəi·mīn). *Chem.* [f. Thyme + -ene.] 1. A clear oily hydrocarbon, $C_{10}H_{16}$, of the terpene group, contained in the oil of thyme.

1857 Miller *Elem. Chem.* III. 446 *Oil of Thyme*..consists of an oxidized portion, *thymole*, and of a hydrocarbon, *thymene*. The latter constitutes the more volatile portion of the oil. 1868 Watts *Dict. Chem.* V. 792 Thymene is a colourless oil, having an agreeable odour of thyme. 1900 Gildemeister & Hoffmann *Volatile Oils* 625.

2. Commercially applied to a product of the oil of ajowan, used as a soap perfume.

1900 Gildemeister & Hoffmann *Volatile Oils* 558 The remaining part of the oil [of Ajowan], about one half, consists of hydrocarbons, which are sold in commerce under the name of thymene..a mixture of cymene and a terpene boiling at 172°.

‖**Thymia·ma**. *Obs.* [a. Gr. θυμίαμα, f. θυμιᾶν to burn incense. In *thymyame* (Lydgate) a. OF. *thymiame*, *timiame* incense, perfume (12–14th c. in Godef.).] Incense.

[1430–40 Lydg. *Bochas* vii. ix. (MS. Bodl. 263 lf. 361/1), Silk Synamome, franc ensens withal For sacrefise, the purpurate vesture Wᵗ Thymyame, the riche pectoral Which ordeyned wern, .. For the Solempne place of places alle Sancta sanctorum.] 1697 tr. *Rodriguez' Chr. Perfect.* v. i. I. 269 The smell of well compos'd Thymiama is very delicious. 1706 Phillips (ed. Kersey), *Thymiama*, Incense, Perfume; a Sweet-Gum.

**Thymiatechny** (þəimiăte·kni). [f. Gr. θυμιᾶν (see prec.) + -τεχνία from τέχνη art, craft.] The art of employing perfumes in medicine.

1833–46 in Dunglison. Hence in later Dicts.

‖**Thymiaterion** (þəi:miătīə·riρn). Pl. **-ia**. [a. Gr. θυμιατήριον, f. θυμιᾶν to burn incense.] A censer, as used by the ancient Greeks, or in the Greek Church.

1850 Leitch tr. *C. O. Müller's Anc. Art* § 406 (ed. 2) 547 Nike making libation..; another such, a thymiaterion in the other hand. 1857 Birch *Anc. Pottery* (1858) II. 93 The thymiateria or tall censers.

**Thymic** (þəi·mik), *a.*¹ [f. Gr. θύμος (ῠ) Thymus + -ic.]

1. *Anat.* and *Path.* Of, pertaining to, or connected with the thymus gland.

1656 Blount *Glossogr.* s.v. *Vein*, *Thymick veine*.., the first branch of the subclavicular, goes to the fag peece or kernel, which is under the kannel bone. 1831 R. Knox *Cloquet's Anat.* 633 The arteries of the pericardium..arise from the thymic, phrenic, bronchial, and œsophageal arteries. 1849–52 *Todd's Cycl. Anat.* IV. 1102/1 'Thymic asthma' may occur with an unnaturally small thymus. 1899 *Allbutt's Syst. Med.* VI. 90 Spasm of the glottis — the so-called 'thymic asthma'.

2. *Physiol. Chem.* In *thymic acid*, $C_{16}H_{25}N_3P_2O_{12}$, a colourless acid obtained from the thymus gland. Its salts are **Thymates** (þəi·meⁱts).

1894 *Jrnl. Chem. Soc.* LXVI. i. 156 [see Thymin]. 1896 *Ibid.* LXX. i. 658 Nucleic acid is decomposed by hydrolysis into thymic acid, adenine, guanine, and cytosine... *Barium thymate*, $C_{16}H_{23}N_3P_2O_{12}Ba$,..dissolves readily in water, and, when anhydrous, is excessively hygroscopic... Thymic acid differs from the parent nucleic acid by its ready solubility in water. 1898 *Schäfer's Text Bk. Physiol.* I. 67.

**Thymic** (þəi-, təi·mik), *a.*² *Chem.* [f. Gr. θύμον Thyme + -ic.] Of, pertaining to, or derived from thyme; in *thymic acid*, a synonym of *thymylic acid* or Thymol. Hence **Thymi·cic** *a.*, derived from or containing thymol; = Thymotic.

1868 Watts *Dict. Chem.* V. 792 Thymicic acid, synon. with thymotic acid. 1890 Billings *Nat. Med. Dict.*, *Thymic acid*, thymol.

**Thymin** (þəi·min). *Chem.* Also **thymine**. [f. Thym(ic *a.*¹ + -in ¹.] A colourless crystalline alloxur base, $C_5H_6N_2O_2$, obtained by the action of dilute sulphuric acid on thymic acid (Thymic *a.*¹ 2).

1894 *Jrnl. Chem. Soc.* LXVI. i. 156 Thymic acid..on heating with sulphuric acid.., *thymin*..is formed. This substance has neither basic nor acidic properties; it..is deposited from water in quadratic and hexagonal crystals. 1898 *Schäfer's Text Bk. Physiol.* I. 66. 1900 *Jrnl. Chem. Soc.* LXXVIII. i. 319 Thymin was originally described by Kossel as one of the decomposition products of the nucleic acid of the thymus gland. It has since been obtained from nucleic acid from other sources. 1903 *Amer. Chem. Jrnl.* XXIX. 481 On boiling this mercapto derivative with hydrochloric acid we obtained thymine.

Hence **Thyminic** (þəimi·nik), *a. Chem.* in *thyminic acid*, a synonym of *thymic acid* (Thymic *a.*¹ 2).

1898 Mandel tr. *Hammarsten's Physiol. Chem.* 100 From adenylic acid and..other nucleic acids Kossel and Neumann have prepared an acid called by them *thyminic acid*.

**Thymle**, obs. form of Thimble.

**Thymo-**, combining form from Gr. θύμο-ν Thyme, used in some chemical terms: **Thy·moform** *Pharm.*, a yellowish antiseptic powder prepared from formaldehyde and thymol; **Thy·moïl, Thymo·ïlol**, Lallemand's names for *thymoquinone* and *hydrothymoquinone*; thence **Thymoï·lamide, Thymo·ïlate, Thymoï·lic** *a.* **Thy:moquino·ne**, $C_{10}H_{12}O_2$, a product of the oxidation of thymol, obtained in reddish-yellow 4-sided shining crystalline laminæ, having an aromatic odour.

1899 Coblentz *Newer Remedies* (ed. 3) 134 *Thymoform. 1857 Miller *Elem. Chem.*, *Org.* III. vii. § 1. 447 According to Lallemand, when thymole is treated with oxidizing agents such as chromic acid,..it yields a substance termed *thymoile [*ed.* 1862 *thymoil*]. *Ibid.*, If treated with sulphurous acid or other reducing agents, it [thymole] combines with hydrogen and yields *thymoilole [*ed.* 1862 thymoilol] [$C_{10}H_{14}O_2$], the homologue of hydrokinone. 1868 Watts *Dict. Chem.* V. 793 From these relations, thymoil may be regarded as homologous with quinone, thymoilol with colourless hydroquinone. 1871 *Jrnl. Chem. Soc.* XXIV. 351 This body [Lallemand's thymoilol] is hydrothymoquinone. ..Hydrothymoquinone is easily converted into *thymoquinone by ferric chloride, nitric acid, etc.

**Thymol** (þəi·mρl). *Chem.* [f. Gr. θύμον Thyme + -ol.] The phenol of cymene, $C_{10}H_{13}.OH$, obtained from oil of thyme, also from the volatile oil of horse-mint, crystallizing in transparent rhomboidal plates; a powerful antiseptic.

1857 Miller *Elem. Chem.* III. 446 Thymole [*ed.* 1862 thymol], $C_{20}H_{14}O_2$, is isomeric with cuminic alcohol; it..constitutes about one-half of the essence of thyme. 1876 Harley *Royle's Mat. Med.* 474 Oil of Thyme..consists of a fluid portion, separable into cymene.., and thymene.., and of a solid crystalline body called thymol.., which has a very pungent taste, and the aroma of the crude oil. 1911 *Contemp. Rev.* Feb. 231 The destruction of the parasite in its intermediary host [man] by quinine or thymol.

b. *attrib.* and *Comb.*

1883 *Athenæum* 10 Mar. 316/2 When thymolsulphonic acid is treated with nitric acid, paranitrothymol is formed. 1884 *Health Exhib. Catal.* 62/1 'Thymol-Cresol' Disinfecting Powder. 1899 Cagney *Jaksch's Clin. Diagn.* vii. (ed. 4) 344 Thymol appears in the urine as thymol sulphuric, thymol glycuronic..acids. 1911 Dorland *Med. Dict.* (ed. 6) s.v. *Thymol*, *Thymol-camphor*, a compound of thymol and camphor. *Ibid.*, *Thymol-gauze*, gauze impregnated with a 1 per cent. solution of thymol. *Ibid.*, Thymol-inhalation, -solution [etc.].

Hence **Thy·molate**, a compound of thymol, in which the hydrogen of the OH group is replaced by a metal; **Thymo·lic** *a.*, of or pertaining to thymol, chiefly in compounds, as *sulpho-thymolic acid*, $C_{10}H_{14}SO_4$; **Thy·molize** *v.*, *trans.* to treat (a solution) with thymol (as a preservative); **Thymo·loform** = *thymoform*.

1880 *Athenæum* 27 Nov. 713/1 The authors..have thus prepared aluminic methylate, .. cresylate, and thymolate. 1900 Helen Baldwin in *Jrnl. Exper. Med.* 1 Oct. 30 The urine should be thymolized..to prevent fermentation. 1911 Dorland *Med. Dict.* (ed. 6), *Thymoloform*, a yellowish powder, a product of formaldehyd and thymol.

**Thymo-nucleic** (þəi:moˌniuklī·ik), *a. Physiol. Chem.* [f. Gr. θύμο-s Thymus + Nucleic.] Of or pertaining to the nuclein of the thymus gland; in *t. acid*, either of two or more nucleic acids, which can be isolated from the cells of the thymus.

1911 Dorland *Med. Dict.* (ed. 6), *Thymonucleic acid*, any one of a series of acids which split up into thymin, esp. the compound $C_{25}H_{36}N_9O_{20}P_3$.

**Thymopathy**¹ (þəimρ·păþi). *rare*—⁰. [f. Gr. θυμό-s soul, spirit + -pathy.] Any mental disease.

[1857 Dunglison *Med. Lex.*, *Thymopathia*, *psychopathia*, ..a disease of the mind.] 1860 Mayne *Expos. Lex.*, Thymopathy. Hence in later Dicts.

**Thymo·pathy**². *rare*—⁰. [f. Gr. θύμ-os Thymus + -pathy.] A disease of the thymus gland.

1909 *Cent. Dict. Suppl.* 1911 Dorland *Med. Dict.* (ed. 6).

**Thymopri·vous**, *a. Path.* [f. as prec. + L. *prīvāre* to deprive.] (See quot.)

1911 Dorland *Med. Dict.* (ed. 6), *Thymoprivous*, pertaining to or caused by removal of the thymus.

**Thymotic** (þəimρ·tik), *a. Chem.* [Arbitrarily f. Gr. θύμο-ν Thyme, or Thymol + -ic.] Of, pertaining to, or derived from thymol. *Thymotic acid*, $C_{11}H_{14}O_3$, a white, loosely coherent, crystalline solid, having a silky lustre, prepared from thymol. Also *thymotic alcohol*, $C_{11}H_{16}O_2$; *thymotic aldehyde*, $C_{11}H_{14}O_2$. Hence **Thy·motate**, a salt of thymotic acid; **Thy·motide**, $C_{11}H_{12}O_2$.

1868 Watts *Dict. Chem.* V. 796 Thymotic acid heated with caustic baryta is resolved into thymol and carbonic anhydride... The thymotates of the alkali-metals are soluble in water. 1873 — *Fownes' Chem.* (ed. 11) 824 Thymotic and Thymol-carbonic Acids are produced by the action of sodium and carbon-dioxide on thymol.

**Thymous** (þəi·məs), *a. rare*—⁰. [ad. L. *thymōs-us* (Pliny), f. *thymum* Thyme: see -ous.] Abounding in or having the character of thyme; thymy.

1656 Blount *Glossogr.*, *Thymous* (*thymosus*), full of thime, an herb so called. 1860 Mayne *Expos. Lex.*, *Thymodes*, having or full of, or belonging to, thyme; smelling like thyme: thymous.

‖**Thymus** (þəi·mŏs). Pl. **thymi** (þəi·məi). [mod.L., a. Gr. θύμος (θῡ-) a warty excrescence; also the thymus gland (Galen).]

1. *Anat.* A glandular body of obscure function (one of the so-called 'ductless glands') situated near the base of the neck in vertebrate animals; in man usually disappearing after the period of childhood.

In the calf and lamb called by butchers *sweetbread*, or

more precisely *neck* or *throat sweetbread*, for distinction from the pancreas or *stomach sweetbread*.

**1693** tr. *Blancard's Phys. Dict.* (ed. 2), *Thymus*, a Glandule in the Throat, which separates watry Humour, called Lympha from the Blood, and empties it by the Lymphatick Vessels. **1704** J. HARRIS *Lex. Techn.* I, *Thymus*, is a conglobate Glandule in the Throat, growing to the upper part of the Mediastinum, and seated between the Divisions of the Subclavian Veins and Arteries. **1713** CHESELDEN *Anat.* III. xi. (1726) 232 Just within the Thorax is seated another [gland] called Thymus. **1868** OWEN *Vertebr. Anim.* xxxii. III. 567 The thymus in Monotremes lies between the episternum and the beginnings of the vessels from the aortic arch. **1881** MIVART *Cat* 237 The thymus..is of very large size during immaturity. **1888** ROLLESTON & JACKSON *Anim. Life* 350 The thymus atrophies in the higher *Vertebrata* as a rule. **1899** *Allbutt's Syst. Med.* VI. 89 Several instances of enlarged thymus have been reported of late years. **1904** *Brit. Med. Jrnl.* 10 Sept. 603 It is possible..that a similar extract prepared from human thymi would have a depressor action.

**b.** Now usually *thymus gland* (rarely *body*).

**1776** M. FALCONER (*title*) An Account of the Structure and Offices..of the Thymus Glands. **1797** M. BAILLIE *Morb. Anat.* (1807) 111 The thymus gland is subject to few diseases, and is only of temporary existence. **1847** YOUATT *Horse* xi. 231 It is 'the thymus gland', or, in vulgar language, the sweet-bread. **1862** MILLER *Elem. Chem.* III. 722 Hypoxanthine has also been found in the thyroid or thymus glands. **1899** *Allbutt's Syst. Med.* VI. 73 Abscesses beginning in the thymus body.

†**2.** *Path.* A rugose wart resembling a bud of thyme. *Obs.*

**1693** tr. *Blancard's Phys. Dict.* (ed. 2), *Thymus*,..also a fleshy Tumor that hangs upon the Body like a Wart, of a colour like the Flower of Time. **1811** in HOOPER *Med. Dict.*

**Thymy** (tai·mi), *a.* [f. THYME + -Y.]

**1.** Abounding in or overgrown with thyme.

**1727** GAY *Fables* I. xxii. 11 Whene'er a thymy bank he [a goat] found, He roll'd upon the fragrant ground. **1827–35** WILLIS *Flor. Gray* 3 Upon Hymettus, and the thymy isles. **1860** TENNYSON *Sea Dreams* 38 Lingering about the thymy promontories.

**2.** Pertaining to or of the nature of thyme; *esp.* having the scent of thyme.

**1747** P. FRANCIS tr. *Horace, Ep.* I. iii. 26 The thymy Fragrance of the Spring. **1874** J. BROWN *Lett.* (1907) 228 The thymy breath and free air of the braes and hills. **1880** MISS BROUGHTON *Sec. Th.* III. x, The thymy sweetness of the fell breeze.

**Thymyl** (þai·mil). *Chem.* [f. Gr. θύμ-ον THYME + -YL.] The radical $C_{10}H_{13}$ of thymol and its derivatives; also used attrib. and in comb., as *thymyl hydride*, $C_{10}H_{13}.H$, *thymyl sulphuric* (acid), *thymyl phosphate, silicate, sulphate*. Hence **Thy·mylamine,** $C_{10}H_{13}NH_2$; **Thymy·lic** *a.*, in *thymylic acid, alcohol, hydrate*, obs. synonyms of THYMOL.

**1868** WATTS *Dict. Chem.* V. 797 Thymyl. *Ibid.* 793 Thymylic hydrate [etc.].

**Thyn(e,** obs. ff. THIN, THINE, THYINE.

†**Thyne** (ðain), *adv. Sc.* and *north. dial. Obs.* Forms: 4 **þien, þein, þine, 4–6 thine, 4–7 thyne, 5 þeine, þeyn, 5–6 thyn, 6 thin.** [App. reduced from THETHEN; cf. *hyne, syne, whyne*.] = THENCE. (Also prec. by *fra, from*.)

*c* **1330** R. BRUNNE *Chron.* (1810) 190 Þe templers ilk a dele failed & þien fled. **13..** *Cursor M.* 6676 (Gött.) If he to min auter fly, Men sal him þein [*Cott.* þeþen] draw to die. *c* **1375** *Sc. Leg. Saints* ii. (*Paulus*) 419 Fra þine þire banis men has tane. *c* **1400** MAUNDEV. (Roxb.) iv. 12 Fra þeine men wendes to þe ile of Cophos. *c* **1440** *Alphabet of Tales* 179 He..had hur thyne owr a grete watir in-to a noder contreth. *c* **1450** *St. Cuthbert* (Surtees) 4271 As a pilgryme pure.. Forth fra þeyn he fore. **1513** DOUGLAS *Æneis* III. x. 83 And fra thyne The fertile grownd of Helory passit syne. **1589** *Reg. Mag. Sig. Scot.* 573/1 Beginnand..at the fute of the Skitterane burne..and fra thin streikand and ascendand up the said burne. *a* **1600** MONTGOMERIE *Misc. Poems* xlviii. 237 We weyd from thyn, and wald no langer byde. **1609** *Sc. Acts Jas. VI* (1816) IV. 443 Fra thyne doun Irving burne to ask.

Hence †**Thyne-fo·rth** (-furth) *adv.* = THENCEFORTH; †**Thyne-fo·rward** *adv.* = THENCE-FORWARD. Usually preceded by *from* (*fra*).

*c* **1375** *Sc. Leg. Saints* xxxviii. (*Adrian*) 272 Fra *þine furth sal þu nocht me se. *c* **1440** *Alphabet of Tales* 51 And fro thyne furth, evur after..he had more devocion vnto Saynt Andrew þan he had befor. *c* **1440** *Reg. Aberd.* (Maitland) I. 248 Þe burn of Nessoke, swa þat theyn furth is þe meris betwix þe bischape and þe Lord of Marr. *a* **1572** KNOX *Hist. Ref.* Wks. 1846 I. 378 The said Congregatioun..shall in no wayis from thynefurth use ony force or violence, in casting down of kirkis. *c* **1400** MAUNDEV. (Roxb.) xxiv. 110 Þai schuld fra *þeine forward hald þam payd of þat he wald giffe þam.

**Thynn(e, (Þ-),** obs. ff. THEN, THIN, THYINE.

**Thyrce, Thyrd(e,** obs. ff. THURSE, THIRD.

**Thyreal** (þəi^ə·riăl). *Ichth.* [f. Gr. θυρε-ός shield: see THYRO-.] = HYPOBRANCHIAL b.

**18..** STARKS *Synonymy Fish Skel.* 518 (Cent. Supp.).

**Thyreo-,** combining element repr. Gr. θυρεο- in θυρεο-ειδής THYROID, used esp. in forming names of chemical and pharmaceutical substances derived from the thyroid gland; see THYRO-.

‖**Thyridium** (þəiri·diŏm). *Entom.* Pl. **-ia.** [f. Gr. type *θυρίδιον, dim. of θυρίς, θυριδ- window, opening.] A whitish spot on the fore-wing of Trichoptera, marking a break in the cubital vein; also applied to similar spots occurring on the wing veins of some other insects.

**1861** HAGEN *Synopsis Neuropt. N. Amer.* 259 Thyridium and first subapical areole with a whitish spot.

**Thyrke,** variant of THERK *Obs.*, dark.

**Thyrl(e, Thyrlepole:** see THIRL, THIRLEPOLL.

**Thyro-** (þəi^ə·ro), also (more correctly but less commonly) **thyreo-** (þəi^ə·*rio*), used as combining form of THYROID, in reference to the thyroid cartilage or the thyroid gland.

**1.** In reference to the thyroid cartilage.

**Thyro-arytenoid** (-æritī·noid) *a.* (rarely thyreo-), pertaining to or connecting the thyroid and arytenoid cartilages of the larynx; *t. ligaments* or *folds*, the vocal cords; *t. muscles*, a pair of muscles which relax the vocal cords; also as sb. = *t. muscle.* **Thyrochondro·tomy,** surgical incision of the thyroid cartilage. **Thyro-cri·coid** *a.*, pertaining to or connecting the thyroid and cricoid cartilages; also as *sb.* = *thyro-cricoid muscle.* **Thyro-crico·tomy:** see quot. **Thyro-epiglottic** (-epiglǫ·tik) *a.* (also **thyreo-**), connecting the thyroid cartilage and the epiglottis; so **Thyro-epiglottidean** (-epiglǫti·diăn) *a.* **Thyro-hyal** (-həi·ăl) *a.* = next; usually as *sb.*, applied to the greater cornu of the hyoid bone in mammals, or to each of the long horns of the same bone in birds. **Thyro-hyoid** (-həi·oid) *a.*, pertaining to or connecting the thyroid cartilage and the hyoid bone; *sb.* = thyro-hyoid muscle; so **Thy:ro-hyoi·dean** *a.* **Thyropa·latine** *a.* (also **thyreo-**), connecting the thyroid cartilage and the palate: applied to part of the palato-pharyngeus muscle. **Thyropharyngean** (-fări·ndʒiăn) *a.* (also **thyreo-**), connecting the thyroid cartilage and the pharynx (see quot.). **Thyro·tomy** (also **thyreo-**) [Gr. τομή cutting], incision or division of the thyroid cartilage.

[**1693** tr. *Blancard's Phys. Dict.* (ed. 2), **Thyroarytænoides*, a pair of Muscles that proceed from the Cartilage called *Scutiformis*, and extending themselves forward to the Sides of the *Arytænoides*..serve to close the opening of the Larynx]. **1855** BAIN *Senses & Int.* II. iv. § 32 (1864) 314 The ..vocal cords..are two bands..attached in front to..the depression between the wings of the thyroid cartilage, and behind to the arytenoid cartilages; from this connexion they are called thyro-arytenoid ligaments. **1899** *Allbutt's Syst. Med.* VI. 818 The laryngeal muscles chiefly involved have been the internal thyro-arytenoids. **1911** DORLAND *Med. Dict.* (ed. 6), *Thyrochondrotomy. **1901** BENHAM in *Proc. Zool. Soc. Lond.* 2 Apr. 286 This longitudinal muscle is topographically a '*thyro-cricoid'. **1899** *Syd. Soc. Lex.*, **Thyro-cricotomy*, tracheotomy performed through the crico-thyroid membrane alone. **1857** DUNGLISON *Med. Lex.*, **Thyreo-epiglottic*... Sabatier and Santorini have given this name to the outer portion of the thyro-arytenoid muscle; because it passes from the thyroid cartilage to the anterior part of the epiglottis. **1890** BILLINGS *Nat. Med. Dict.*, Thyro-epiglottic ligament...Thyro-epiglottic muscle. **1901** BENHAM in *Proc. Zool. Soc. Lond.* 2 Apr. 286 The *thyro-epiglottidean muscle..is also a conspicuous constituent in the ventral region of the larynx. **1854** OWEN *Skel. & Teeth* in *Orr's Circ. Sc.* I. *Org. Nat.* 209 The basihyal has..coalesced with the *thyrohyals to form a broad cartilaginous plate. **1881** MIVART *Cat* 134 The thyro-hyal muscle. **1831** R. KNOX *Cloquet's Anat.* 82 The digastric and *thyro-hyoid muscles. **1872** COHEN *Dis. Throat* 134 The *thyreo-palatine portion of the muscle. **1899** *Syd. Soc. Lex.*, Thyro-palatine. [**1857** DUNGLISON *Med. Lex.*, *Thyro-pharyngeus, Thyreo-pharyngeus.] **1860** MAYNE *Expos. Lex.*, *Thyreopharyngeus*,..applied to the middle portion of the constrictor pharyngis inferior muscle: *thyreopharyngean. **1880** M. MACKENZIE *Dis. Throat & Nose* I. 331 *Thyrotomy should never be undertaken until removal by the endolaryngeal method has been first attempted. **1890** BILLINGS *Nat. Med. Dict.*, *Thyreotomy*...*Thyrotomy*, section of the thyroid cartilage. **1899** *Syd. Soc. Lex.*, *Thyreotomy*, division of the thyroid cartilage for exploratory purposes.

**2.** In reference to the thyroid gland. (Often thyreo-.)

**Thyro-antito·xin,** an antitoxin developed in thyroid poisoning; trade-name of a thyroid preparation used as a therapeutic. **Thy·rocele,** a tumour of the thyroid gland; goitre. **Thyro-co·lloid,** the colloid matter of the thyroid gland. **Thyroge·nic, Thyro·genous** *adjs.*: see quot. 1909. **Thyro-, thyreoglo·bulin,** the essential albuminous principle of the thyroid gland, an iodized principle, which forms, together with another albuminous substance belonging to the nucleo-proteins, the colloid substance of the gland. **Thyroglo·ssal** *a.*, in *t. duct*, a duct of the embryo extending from the thyroid to the base of the tongue. **Thyro-i·odine,** a substance containing iodine, obtained by decomposition of thyroglobulin, which has been thought to be the active principle of the gland: now more usually called *iodothy·rin*. **Thyroli·ngual** *a.* = *thyroglossal*. **Thyroly·tic** *a.*, destructive of thyroid tissue. †**Thyropro·teid, Thyropro·tein,** the specific protein of the thyroid gland. **Thyrothe·rapy,** treatment of disease by a preparation of the thyroid glands of sheep. **Thyro·toxic** *a.*, **Thyroto·xin:** see quots. 1909, 1911.

**1895** *Pall Mall G.* 16 Dec. 1/3 Dr. Fränkel, of Vienna, ..has named it provisionally *thyreo-antitoxin. [He] states..that it will be possible to administer it clinically without the risk of ptomaine poisoning. **1899** *Allbutt's Syst. Med.* VIII. 57 Fränkel has succeeded in separating a basic product from the thyroid (thyreo-antitoxin). **1909** DORLAND *Med. Dict.* (ed. 5), Thyro-antitoxin. **1886** *Buck's Handbk. Med. Sc.* III. 350/1 Goitre..*Thyreocele (P. Frank). **1909** DORLAND *Med. Dict.* (ed. 5), Thyrocele, *Thyrocolloid. **1887** *Buck's Handbk. Med. Sc.* V. 143 *Thyrogenic. **1909** DORLAND *Med. Dict.* (ed. 5), **Thyrogenous*,..originating in the thyroid gland. **1908** *Allbutt's Syst. Med.* IV. I. 325 Other bodies..have been separated from the gland,..among these may be mentioned Oswald's iodine-free *thyreo-globulin. **1911** MANDEL tr. *Hammarsten's Text-bk. Physiol. Chem.* (ed. 6) 356 It seems proven that the specifically active substance is..a protein substance: Notkin's *thyreoproteid*, Oswald's *thyreoglobulin*. **1909** DORLAND *Med. Dict.* (ed. 5), *Thyroglossal duct. **1896** *Daily News* 30 Apr. 8/7 Professor Baumann and Dr. Roos..find that the active principle [of the thyroid gland] is a substance named '*Thyro-iodin'. **1897** *Allbutt's Syst. Med.* IV. 469 [see THYROID B. 2]. **1903** CUSHING *Text-bk. Pharmacology* 715 Iodothyrin was at first named *thyroiodin*, but this was liable to be confused with thyreoidin, a term used to indicate the simple extract of the gland. **1896** *Allbutt's Syst. Med.* I. 206 The *thyrolingual duct. **1889** *Buck's Handbk. Med. Sc.*, App. 539 *Thyrolytic. **1899** *Allbutt's Syst. Med.* VIII. 57 Notkin isolated a substance from the thyroid (*thyreo-protein). **1911** DORLAND *Med. Dict.* (ed. 6) s. v., It is probably one of the functions of the thyroid to produce a ferment which neutralizes the toxic effect of an accumulation of thyroprotein in the body. **1907** *Med. Record* 5 Oct. 584 He regretted that *thyrotherapy had been neglected in the treatment of skin diseases. **1904** *Nature* 18 Feb. 375 *Thyrotoxic. **1909** *Cent. Dict., Supp.*, Thyreotoxic. **1909** DORLAND *Med. Dict.* (ed. 5), *Thyrotoxic*,..marked by toxic activity of the thyroid gland. **1911** *Ibid.* (ed. 6), **Thyrotoxin*, a cytotoxin specific for thyroid tissue.

**Thyroid** (þəi^ə·roid), *a.* (*sb.*) Also 9 **thyreoid** (in Dicts.). [Etymologically *thyreoid*, ad. Gr. θυρεοειδής shield-shaped (in Galen χόνδρος θυρεοειδής thyroid cartilage), f. θυρεό-ς oblong shield + -ειδής: see -OID. Cf. obs. F. *thyroide* (Paré, 16th c.), mod.F. *thyréoïde*.] Having the form of a shield, shield-shaped: applied to various natural structures (and hence *transf.* to others connected with them).

**1.** *Anat.* **a.** *Thyroid cartilage*: the largest of the cartilages of the larynx, consisting of two broad quadrilateral plates united in front at an angle, forming the projection in front of the throat known (in men) as 'Adam's apple'; within the angle are attached the vocal cords.

[**1693** tr. *Blancard's Phys. Dict.* (ed. 2), *Thyroides*, the Cartilage, called Scutiformis, of the Larynx.] **1726–41** MONRO *Anat.* (ed. 3) 163 Into this Concavity the Thyroid Cartilage is received. **1808** BARCLAY *Muscular Motions* 498 The larynx is partly composed of five cartilages, which are the cricoid, thyroid, the two arytænoid, and the epiglottis. **1854** BUSHNAN in *Orr's Circ. Sc.* I. *Org. Nat.* 121 The thyroid cartilage is wrapped round the essential parts of the larynx. **1857** DUNGLISON *Med. Lex.*, Thyroid, Thyreoid.

**b.** *Thyroid gland* (also called *thyroid body*): one of the so-called 'ductless glands', a very vascular body adjacent to the larynx and upper part of the trachea in vertebrates.

[**1693** tr. *Blancard's Phys. Dict.* (ed. 2), *Thyroideæ Glandulæ*, two, of a viscous..Substance,..situate about the lower seat of the Larynx]. **1726–41** MONRO *Anat.* (ed. 3) 163 The lymphatic Vessel..is..sent from the thyroid Gland. **1727–41** CHAMBERS *Cycl.* s. v. *Thymus*, Mr. Cheselden observes, that where the thymus in men is very small, the thyroid glands increase proportionably. **1830** R. KNOX *Béclard's Anat.* 240 Formless fibro-cartilages occur in some compound tumours of the thyroid body. **1872** HUXLEY *Phys.* v. 126 The thyroid gland..is that organ which when enlarged by disease gives rise to 'Derbyshire neck' or 'goitre'. **1899** L. HILL *Man. Hum. Physiol.* xxvi. 301 If a cretin be fed on thyroid glands taken from sheep his condition is improved. ..It is clear then that the thyroid gland produces a material necessary for the growth of the body.

**c.** Applied to various structures connected with the thyroid cartilage or gland, as the *thyroid arteries, nerves, veins*, etc. *Thyroid axis*, a branch of the subclavian artery, distributed to the thyroid gland and adjacent parts. (See also B. 2 b.)

**1831** R. KNOX *Cloquet's Anat.* 746 Right Inferior Thyroid Vein..similar to the left, with which it constitutes the thyroid venous plexus. **1840** E. WILSON *Anat. Vade M.* (1842) 271 The Superior Thyroid Artery curves downwards to the thyroid gland to which it is distributed. **1878** T. BRYANT *Pract. Surg.* I. 104 Thyroid cysts may be tapped in the same way as the cervical. **1881** MIVART *Cat* 209 The second branch given off from the subclavian..is the thyroid axis.

**d.** *Thyroid foramen, membrane*: names for the obturator foramen and membrane of the hip-bone (see OBTURATOR 1), from their shield-like shape.

**1890** BILLINGS *Nat. Med. Dict.*, *T[hyroid] foramen*, obturator foramen.

**2.** *Zool.* Applied to a shield-shaped colour-marking, or *transf.* to a bird having such a marking, as the thyroid woodpecker, *Sphyropicus thyroideus*.

**1891** in *Cent. Dict.*

**3.** *Bot.* 'Shield-like, peltiform'.

**1900** in B. D. JACKSON *Gloss. Bot. Terms* 270/2.

**B.** as *sb.* **1.** Short for *thyroid cartilage*.

**1840** E. WILSON *Anat. Vade M.* (1842) 492 The Thyroid is the largest cartilage of the larynx. **1854** OWEN *Skel. & Teeth* in *Orr's Circ. Sc.* I. *Org. Nat.* 210 Extending beyond and sustaining the thyroid and other parts of the larynx. **1868** — *Vertebr. Anim.* xxxiii. III. 603 Castration arrests that prominent growth of the thyroid, &c., which accompanies the elongation of the cords.

**2.** Short for *thyroid gland*; also for *thyroid extract* or *product* (see b).

**1849–52** *Todd's Cycl. Anat.* IV. 1102/2 The normal weight of the thyroid is about one ounce. **1897** *Allbutt's Syst. Med.* IV. 469 The sheep's thyroid is relatively rich in thyroiodine. *Ibid.* 476 In cases of..myxœdema the results of treatment by thyroid justify a strong expectation of cure. **1897** *Trans. Amer. Pediatric Soc.* IX. 65 In cretinism we are certain that the prolonged use of thyroids is followed by distinct changes in the blood.

**b.** *attrib.*

**1895** *Pall Mall G.* 16 Dec. 1/3 The use of thyroid extract as a remedy for certain diseases..is looked upon as one of the most brilliant of recent medical discoveries. **1899** *Allbutt's Syst. Med.* VIII. 68 Thyroid treatment of cases of tetany. *Ibid.* 673 The horny growth fell off, while the patient was under thyroid feeding.

Hence **Thyroi·dal, Thyroi·deal, Thyroi·dean** *adjs.*, pertaining to the thyroid cartilage or gland; **Thyroide·ctomize** *v.*, *trans.* to subject to thyroidectomy; **Thyroide·ctomy** [Gr. ἐκτομή a cutting out], excision of the thyroid gland; **Thyroi·din,** trade-name of a whitish powdered extract of the thyroid gland of the sheep, used as an alterative and an anti-fat; **Thy·roidism,** a morbid state consequent on administration of thyroid extract; thyroid poisoning; **Thyroidi·tis,** inflammation of the thyroid gland; **Thyroidiza·tion,** treatment with a preparation of the thyroid (Dorland); **Thy·roidless** *a.*, having no thyroid gland; **Thyroido·tomy** [Gr. τομή cutting], incision of the thyroid gland.

**1860** MAYNE *Expos. Lex.*, *Thyroideus*,..*thyroidal: *thyroidean. **1872** COHEN *Dis. Throat* 51 The anterior portions of the vocal cords attached to the thyroidal junction. **1827** ABERNETHY *Surg. Wks.* II. 127 The superior *thyroideal, lingual, and facial branches of the external carotid. **1854** JONES & SIEVEKING *Pathol. Anat.* (1874) 122 Ligature of the thyroideal arteries has caused considerable diminution of a goitrous tumour. **1899** *Allbutt's Syst. Med.* VIII. 57 The administration of thyroid in some form to *thyroidectomised animals or man. **1889** *Buck's Handbk. Med. Sc.* VIII. 545/2 Until the middle of the eighteenth century no true *thyroidectomy..had been performed. **1891** *Lancet* 18 Apr. 907/1 M. Reverdin..has performed thyroidectomy in this disease in fourteen cases. **1897** *Allbutt's Syst. Med.* III. 314 Thyroid grafts prolong life after complete thyroidectomy. **1896** *Pharmaceutical Jrnl.* 5 Sept. 215 *Thyreoidin, the active principle of thyroid. **1897** *Allbutt's Syst. Med.* III. 315 A non-proteid substance containing a considerable percentage of iodine—the so-called thyroidin. **1897** *Ibid.* II. 78 In most of them the symptoms of *thyroidism were produced. **1889** *Buck's Handbk. Med. Sc.* VII. 96/1 Inflammation of the thyroid gland (*thyroiditis..) is most commonly..the..result of remedial measures employed in the treatment of goitre. **1890** BILLINGS *Nat. Med. Dict.*, *Thyroidotomy.

**Thyrolingual** to **-toxin**: see THYRO- 1, 2.

**Thyrse** (þəɹs). Also 7 thirse. [a. Fr. *thyrse* (*a* 1502 in Hatz.-Darm.), ad. L. *thyrsus*, a. Gr. θύρσος stalk or stem of a plant; the Bacchic staff: see THYRSUS.]

**1.** *Gr.* and *Rom. Antiq.* = THYRSUS 1.

**1603** HOLLAND *Plutarch's Mor.* IV. 712 There is a Thyrse or Javelot with tabours to be seene expresly printed aloft. **1710** W. KING *Heathen Gods* xxvii. (1722) 134 Their [the followers of Bacchus] Cloathing [was] only the Skins of Beasts, with Thyrses in their Hands. **1845** LONGF. *Drinking Song* iv, Fair Bacchantes, Bearing cymbals, flutes, and thyrses.

**2.** †**a.** A stem or shoot of a plant (= Gr. θύρσος, L. *thyrsus*). *Obs.* **b.** *Bot.* = THYRSUS 2.

**1658** PHILLIPS, *Thyrse*, a stalk or stem of any herb. **1744** J. WILSON *Synopsis Brit. Plants, Bot. Dict.* 14 *Thyrsus*, a Thyrse, differs from a spike, in having flowers or fruit set more thinly on it. **1846** DANA *Zooph.* v. § 91 (1848) 93 The thyrse of lilac blossoms. **1848** LINDLEY *Introd. Bot.* (ed. 4) I. 324 The Thyrse is an inflorescence at first centripetal, afterwards centrifugal. **1861** [see THYRSUS 2].

**3.** An ancient vessel resembling a pine-cone.

**1876** R. M. SMITH *Persian Art* 12 From their..resemblance ..to pine cones they have been called thyrses, and are supposed to have been used for holding mercury.

**4.** *Comb.* as *thyrse-bearing* adj.; **thyrse-flower,** Lindley's name for the genus *Thyrsacanthus.*

**1866** *Treas. Bot.* 1150 Thyrseflower, *Thyrsacanthus.* **1869** SWINBURNE *Ess. & Stud.* (1875) 207 No Bacchus..comes Here, nor mænads thyrse-bearing.

**Thyrsi-** (þəˈɹsi), combining form of THYRSUS, used in a few botanical terms. **Thyrsiferous** (-i·fĕrəs) *a.* [-FEROUS], bearing thyrsi or contracted panicles. **Thyrsiflo·rous** *a.* [L. *flōs, flōr-* flower], having the flowers in thyrsi. **Thy·rsiform** *a.*, having the form of a thyrsus, thyrsoid.

**1895** *Funk's Stand. Dict.*, Thyrsiferous. **1860** MAYNE *Expos. Lex.*, Thyrsiflorous. **1866** *Treas. Bot.* 1150 *Thyrse* (adj. *Thyrsiform*). **1880** GRAY *Struct. Bot.* (ed. 6) I. 159 A thyrsus or thyrsiform inflorescence.

**Thyrsill,** obs. Sc. var. of *thrissill*, THISTLE.

**Thyrsoid** (þəˈɹsoid), *a. Bot.* [f. THYRS-US + -OID: cf. Gr. θυρσοειδής thyrsus-like (Dioscorides).] Of the form of, or resembling, a thyrsus or contracted panicle. So **Thyrsoi·dal** *a.*

**1830** LINDLEY *Nat. Syst. Bot.* 61 Flowers terminal, usually thyrsoid. **1864** WEBSTER, *Thyrsoid, Thyrsoidal.* **1870** HOOKER *Stud. Flora* 238 Privet..Flowers in terminal thyrsoid cymes.

**Thyrst(e, -ylle,** obs. ff. THIRST, THROSTLE.

‖ **Thyrsula** (þəˈɹsiŭlă). *Bot.* [mod.L. dim. of THYRSUS.] (See quot. 1900.)

**1832** LINDLEY *Introd. Bot.* I. ii. 112 Link terms this inflorescence a *thyrsula.* **1900** B. D. JACKSON *Gloss. Bot. Terms* 271/1 *Thyrsula*, the little cyme which is borne by most Labiates in the axil of the leaves.

‖ **Thyrsus** (þəˈɹsɒs). Pl. **thyrsi** (þəˈɹsəi). [L., a. Gr. θύρσος: see THYRSE.]

**1.** *Gr.* and *Rom. Antiq.* A staff or spear tipped with an ornament like a pine-cone, and sometimes wreathed with ivy or vine branches; borne by Dionysus (Bacchus) and his votaries.

**1591** L. LLOYD *Tripl. Triumphes* B iij b, Your Bacchus daunce is done,..Your sacred Thyrsus's wonne. *a* **1661** HOLYDAY *Juvenal* (1673) 110/2 The Thyrsus was a dart or javelin wrapt-about with ivy. **1734** tr. *Rollin's Anc. Hist.* (1827) I. 41 [They] carried a thyrsus in their hands, a kind of pike with ivy leaves twisted round it. **1856** MRS. BROWNING *Aur. Leigh* II. 52 Ivy..as good to grow on graves As twist about a thyrsus.

**2.** *Bot.*, etc. A form of inflorescence: † (*a*) a lax spike, as in some orchids (*obs.*); (*b*) a contracted kind of panicle, esp. one in which the primary branching is centripetal (racemose) and the secondary centrifugal (cymose), as in lilac and horse-chestnut.

**1704** J. HARRIS *Lex. Techn.* I, *Thyrsus*, is a Word used by the Botanists, for the upright, and tapering Stalk: And 'tis often used for *Spica*, which is an Ear, or Blade of Corn. **1744** [see THYRSE 2]. **1760** J. LEE *Introd. Bot.* III. iv. (1765) 173 (tr. Linnæus) A *Thyrsus*, is a Panicle contracted into an ovate Form. **1861** BENTLEY *Man. Bot.* (1870) 195 The Thyrsus or Thyrse is a kind of panicle in which the pedicels are generally very short. **1864** LOWELL *Fireside Trav.* 108 Hop-vines..hung their clustering thyrsi over the open windows.

**3.** *Comb.*, as *thyrsus-bearer, -staff.*

**1844** L. SCHMITZ in *Smith's Dict. Grk. & Rom. Biog.* I. 1048/2 Bacchantic women,..carrying in their hands thyrsus-staffs. **1853** TRENCH *Proverbs* vi. 134 The thyrsus-bearers are many, but the bacchants few.

**Thyrtene, Thyrty,** etc.: see THIRTEEN, etc.

**Thysanopter** (þisæ̆·nǫptəɹ). *Entom.* [ad. mod.L. *Thysanoptera* (Haliday, 1836), f. Gr. θύσανο-ς tassel, fringe + πτερόν wing.] An insect of the order *Thysanoptera*, comprising *Thrips* and allied genera, characterized by long fringes on the wings. So **Thysano·pteran** *a.* = *thysanopterous*; *sb.* = *thysanopter*; **Thysano·pterous** *a.*, belonging to the order *Thysanoptera.*

[**1858** BAIRD *Cycl. Nat. Sci.* 549/1 *Thysanoptera*..an order of insects, lately separated from the order Hemiptera, to contain those insects formerly known as the genus *Thrips*.] **1864** WEBSTER, Thysanopter. **1891** *Cent. Dict.*, Thysanopteran, Thysanopterous.

**Thysanuran** (þisănⁱūə·răn), *a.* and *sb. Entom.* [f. mod.L. *Thysanūra* Cuvier (f. Gr. θύσαν-ος tassel, fringe + οὐρά tail) + -AN.] **a.** *adj.* Belonging to the *Thysanura*, a wingless order of insects, comprising springtails, bristletails, etc., having filamentous appendages at the posterior end of the body. **b.** *sb.* An insect of this order. So **Thysanu·rian** *a.*, **Thysanu·rid** *a.* and *sb.* = *thysanuran*; **Thysanu·riform, Thysanurimo·rphous** *adjs.*, having the form of, or resembling, the *Thysanura*; **Thysanu·rous** *a.*, belonging to or having the characters of the *Thysanura.*

**1835** KIRBY *Hab. & Inst. Anim.* II. xiv. 20 The *Thysanuran, or Sugar-louse tribe. *Ibid.* xx. 314 The Thysanurans are remarkable for their anal appendages. **1842** BRANDE *Dict. Sc.*, etc., *Thysanurans, Thysanura*,..in which the abdomen is terminated by filaments, or by a forked tail adapted for leaping. **1891** *Cent. Dict.* cites J. H. COMSTOCK for *Thysanurian.* **1900** *Nature* 13 Dec. 161/2 The occurrence of *Proiapyx stylifer*, a primitive *thysanurid insect, in Liberia and Argentina. **1826** KIRBY & SP. *Entomol.* III. xxx. 166 Larvæ that approach to a true *Thysanuriform type. **1906** J. W. FOLSOM *Entomol.* iii. 162 Two types of larvæ are recognized by Brauer, Packard and other authorities: *thysanuriform* and *eruciform.* **1860** MAYNE *Expos. Lex.* 1277/2 An Order..which have particular organs of motion on the sides of the extremity of the tail, like fringes: *thysanurous. **1910** *Daily News* 30 May 4/2 A 'silver fish',..*Lepisma domestica*, a thysanurous insect occurring in houses and damaging books, wall-papers, etc. Some of its other common names are bristle-tail, fish-tail, shiner, and silvertail.

**Thyself** (ðəise·lf), *pron.* Forms: 1 þe sylf, 1–4 þe self, 3–4 þi self, sulf, silf, 4 þi selue, zelue, self(e (þei-self), 4–5 thiselfe, 5 (thiselph), þy self(e, selffe, 5–7 thy self, thy selfe, 6 thyselfe, (9 *dial.* theeself), 5– thyself. β. (*orig. oblique cases*) 1 þe sylfne, sylfum, 3–4 þe selven, 4–5 þi seluen, 5 the seluen, -in, -un, 6 *Sc.* thy seluyn, selfin. [In OE. *þé* 'thee' followed by the adj. *self*; the latter either in concord with *þé* (dat. *þé selfum*, acc. *þe(c) selfne*), or, in the constr. *þú þé self*, in concord with *þú* (*þé* being dative or instrumental): see SELF 4, and cf. MYSELF. From 13th c., *þi, þy, thy*, poss. adj., took the place of the pers. pron. *thee*; *self* being treated as a sb.]

As to restriction of use see note to THOU; cf. YOURSELF.

**I.** Emphatic uses: = Very thou, very thee.

**1.** Accompanying the subject-pronoun *thou* (or, after a verb in the imperative, without *thou*).

In mod. Eng., in *thou thyself, thyself* is grammatically in apposition to *thou.*

*a* **800** CYNEWULF *Crist* 114 Þæt þu þa beorhtan us sunnan onsende, ond þe sylf cyme. *a* **800** *Cædmon's Gen.* 608 Þu meaht nu þe self ȝeseon. *a* **1300** *Cursor M.* 4604 (Cott.) Lok þi seluen wit resun [*G.* þi selue, *F.* þi-self]. *Ibid.* 5429 Heit me truli þat þou þe seluen [*G.* þu þi selue, *F.* þou þi-self] Sal me wit mine foreldres deluen. **1340–70** *Alex. & Dind.* 511, Y haue sent þe my sonde as þou þei-self bade. *c* **1420** *Sir Amadace* (Camden) xlix, As thou thi seluun hase. **1535** COVERDALE 1 *Kings* xx. 40 It is thine owne iudgment, thou hast geuen it thyselfe. **1597** SHAKS. 2 *Hen. IV*, IV. v. 111 Then get thee gone, and digge my graue thy selfe. **1611** BIBLE *Luke* vi. 42 When thou thy selfe beholdest not the beame that is in thine owne eye. **1759** JOHNSON *Rasselas* xii, Thou art thyself weary of the valley. **1864** R. F. LITTLEDALE *Hymn*, '*O Fire of God, the Comforter*' ad fin., All praise to Thee..Who art Thyself all praise.

**2.** By ellipsis of *thou*, used as simple subject (with verb usually in 2nd person; occasionally in 3rd, *self* being treated as a sb.).

*a* **1300** *Cursor M.* 9568 (Cott.) 'Fader', sco said, 'þi doghter am i, Als þi-self wat witerli'. *c* **1375** *Ibid.* 876 (Trin.) Þi seluen is to wite I wis. *c* **1400** *Destr. Troy* 11982 Þat thyselfe shuld haue socourd. *c* **1475** *Songs & Carols* xxxii. 23 Man, I am thy frend ay; Thy self art thy foo. **1515** BARCLAY *Egloges* iv. (1570) C iv/2, Why is not thy selfe contented with thy part? **1611** BIBLE 1 *Kings* xx. 40 So shall thy iudgement bee, thy selfe hast discided it. **16**.. DRYDEN (J.), These goods thyself can on thyself bestow. **1742** WESLEY *Hymn*, '*Come, O thou traveller unknown*' ii, Thyself hast called me by my name. **1866** J. B. ROSE tr. *Ovid's Met.* 83 The phantom thou behold'st thyself hath made.

**b.** Used as predicate, or after *as* or *than.*

**1535** COVERDALE *Ps.* xlix. [l.] 21 Thou..thinkest me to be euen soch one as thy self. **1590** SHAKS. *Com. Err.* III. ii. 76 Thou art Dromio, thou art my man, thou art thy selfe. **1593** — *Merry W.* III. iv. 3 Thou must be thy selfe. **1611** BIBLE 2 *Chron.* xxi. 13 Thou..hast slaine thy brethren ..which were better then thy selfe. **1667** MILTON *P. L.* IV. 468 What there thou seest fair Creature is thy self. **1880** G. MACDONALD *Diary Old Soul* Aug. 8, It is thyself, and neither this nor that,..told, taught, or dreamed of thee.

**3.** Used instead of *thee* as object of a verb or preposition.

*a* **1400–50** *Alexander* 328 Noȝt as a prophet ne a prest I prays sall þi selfe. *c* **1400** *Destr. Troy* 7920, I am euyn fayn Of þe sight of þi Self. **1610** SHAKS. *Temp.* I. ii. 68 He, whom next thy selfe Of all the world I lou'd. **1671** MILTON *Samson* 789 If severely thou exact not More strength from me, then in thy self was found. **1857** G. B. BUBIER *Hymn*, My God, I love Thee for Thyself.

**II.** Reflexive uses.

**4.** As direct or indirect object of a verb, or in dependence on a preposition. (Orig. only emphatic refl.; later in general use, taking the place of *thee* reflexive, which is more decidedly archaic: see THEE *pron.* 2.)

*c* **975** *Rushw. Gosp.* Matt. xix. 19 Lufiȝe þa nehstum ðinum swa þæc seolfne [*Lindisf.* ðec seolfne; *Ags. Gosp.* þe sylfne]. *a* **1225** *Ancr. R.* 276 Þenc hwat tu hauest of þi sulf. **13**.. *Cursor M.* 12804 (Cott.) O þe-self [*other texts* þi-self] quat wil þou sai? **1362** LANGL. *P. Pl.* A. I. 131 For to loue þi louerd leuere þen þi-seluen. **1382** WYCLIF *John* i. 22 What seist thou of thi silf? **1490** CAXTON *Eneydos* xvi. 64 Wylt enhabyte thiselfe in a strange contrey? **1535** COVERDALE *Isa.* lxiii. 14 To make thy self a glorious name. **1616** R. C. *Times' Whistle* III. 1120 Learn Solons saying, 'Mortall know thy selfe'. **1741** RICHARDSON *Pamela* II. 227 Well, Child,..how dost find thyself? **1819** SHELLEY *Cenci* IV. iv. 40 Be faithful to thyself. **1825** J. NEAL *Bro. Jonathan* II. 158 Take and read it for theeself. **1841** LANE *Arab. Nts.* I. 92 Thou assertest thyself to be the son of the King. **1847** TENNYSON *Princess* VII. 343 Yield thyself up.

† **Thysia·stery.** *Obs. rare*[−1]. [ad. Gr. θυσιαστήριον (LXX. and N.T.), f. θυσιάζειν to sacrifice, f. θυσία a sacrifice.] An altar.

**1657** REEVE *God's Plea* 349 The Altar of Haliæus defended all that fled to it, and so would such a Thysiastery raised up in your City.

**Thystel, -tell e, -tle, -tylle,** obs. ff. THISTLE.

† **Thyvel, thuvel.** *Obs.* Forms: þyfel, -þel, 3 þuuel. [OE. *þyfel* (or ?*þýfel*: see Note below), early ME. *þuvel(ii).*] A bush, a thicket.

*a* **1000** *Ags. Gloss.* in Wr.-Wülcker 244/20, 22 *Frutectum, i. arborum densitas, uel ramus*, þyfel. *Frutex, frutecta*, þyfel. *c* **1000** *Lambeth Ps.* lxxix. 11 His þyþelas *vel* twygu, *arbusta eius.* *c* **1000** ÆLFRIC *Gram.*, *Nom. Arb.* (Z.) 312 *Frutex*, þyfel. *c* **1000** — *Voc.* in Wr.-Wülcker 139/24 *Spina, uel sentrix*, þyfel. *c* **1000** *Sax. Leechd.* I. 98 ȝenim þysse wyrte þe we leon fot nemdon fif ðyfelas butan wyrttruman. *a* **1250** *Owl & Night.* 278 Vor þi ich am loþ smale vowele [*v.r.* foȝ(e)le] þat fleoþ bi grunde & bi þuuele.

[*Note.* The length of the stem-vowel in OE. is disputed; the dictionaries generally have *þýfel*, viewing it as a derivative of *þúf*, tuft of leaves; Sievers thinks that the *y* was certainly short. Whether *þyfel* or *þýfel*, the form agrees remarkably with that of THIVEL a pot-stick; but no connexion of sense has been found, and there is a gap both of time and place between the Dorsetshire *þuvel* of 1250 and the Yorkshire *thyvelle* of 1483.]

**Thyxtill, -yll, thyzle,** variants of THIXEL.

# Ti—Tz.

‖ **Ti** (tī). Also ti-ti. [Native Polynesian: cf. Ki.] Native name of several trees of the genus *Cordyline* (formerly included in *Dracæna*), N.O. *Liliaceæ*, with edible roots; in Polynesia, *C. terminalis*; in New Zealand, *C. australis* and *C. indivisa*; known also as *cabbage-palm*, Cabbage-tree, *club palm*, and *palm-lily* (Palm *sb.*[1] 1 c, 7).

**1839** Darwin *Voy. Nat.* xviii. (1873) 410 A liliaceous plant called Ti. **1845** E. J. Wakefield *Adv. N. Zealand* I. iii. 58 In these natural shrubberies .. a kind of cabbage-tree, called ti by the natives, flourishes. **1896** *Contemp. Rev.* Aug. 240 The *ti* and the *apé* are taken out well cooked. The *apé* prevents the *ti* from getting too dry in the oven.

**b.** *attrib.*, as *ti-leaf*, *-palm*, *-plant*, *-root*, *-tree*, etc.; **ti-oven**, an oven for cooking ti-roots.

**1840** Lundie *Mission. Life Samoa* xiv. (1846) 89 Many women having no dress but the ti leaves round the waist. **1865** Lady Barker *Station Life N. Zealand* viii. (1870) 52 Ti-ti palms are dotted here and there. **1881** Mrs. C. Praed *Policy & P.* I. 109 The tender shoots of the young ti-trees. **1882** T. H. Potts *Out in Open* 297 (Morris) The tough, fibrous leaves of the ti-palm. **1896** *Contemp. Rev.* Aug. 240 The *ti*-ovens are frequently thirty feet in diameter.

**Tial** (təi·äl). *Obs.* exc. *dial.* Forms: 1–2 tiȝel, tiȝl, 4 tiel, 6–7 tiall, tyall (9 tyal), 7– tial. [OE. **tygel*, *tigel* = OHG. *zugil* (G. *zügel*), Du. *teugel*, ON. *tygell* (Da. *töile*):—OTeut. **tug-ilo*ᶻ, f. **tug*, weak grade of **teuh*, **tauh*: see Tee *v.*[1] + *-ilo-*, -el [1]. In later form taken as f. Tie *v.*, and assimilated to *denial*, *trial*.]

**1.** A rope used to pull, draw, or tow anything; a strap, thong, rein (quot. 1387).

*c* **1000** Ælfric *Gram. & Gloss.* (Z.) 314 *Tractorium*, tiȝel. *a* **1100** *Ags. Voc.* in Wr.-Wülcker 327/33 *Tractorium*, tiȝl. **1387** Trevisa *Higden* (Rolls) IV. 77 Þe plowȝmen radde þat some of hem schulde wende home..and fecche þe reynes oþer þe tiels [*redirent pro loris*].

**2.** That with which something is tied; a rope, cord, string, or thread. Now *north. dial.* (see *Eng. Dial. Dict.*).

**1549** Latimer *6th Serm. bef. Edw. VI* (Arb.) 172 The greate belles clapper was fallen doune, the tyall was broken, so that the Byshop coulde not be runge into the toune. **1575** Banister *Chyrurg.* I. (1585) 90 The tiall or band must bee of such a matter, as will not easily putrifie; as thread of silke. **1600** Surflet *Countrie Farme* I. xxviii. 178 He ..shall carrie him [the colt] backe againe vnto his stable.. and put him in his ordinary tiall or headstall. **1808** Jamieson, *Tyal*, any thing used for tying a latchet.

† **b.** *fig.* A bond, lien, tie, obligation. *Obs.*

**1621** Fletcher *Wild Goose Chase* II. i, Nor to contract with such [a woman] can be a Tial. **1623** T. Scot *Highw. God* 21 Religion then being the band or tyall whereby wee are fastned. **1653** Gataker *Vind. Annot. Jer.* 153 No regard had..of relations and tials natural, civil or sacred.

‖ **Tiao** (tyā·o, tyau). Also tiaou. [Chinese.] A string of Chinese 'cash' (perforated copper coins).

Nominally the *tiao* contains 1000 cash; but the actual number of coins varies from 1000 downwards, according to the custom of the locality.

**1883** S. W. Williams *Middle Kingd.* (enlarged ed.) II. xvi. 86 (Banks and Paper Money) Their [the notes'] face value ranges from one to a hundred *tiao*, or strings of cash, but their worth depends on the exchange between silver and cash. **1886** *Rep. of Sec. Treas.* (U.S.) 390 (Cent. D.) Twenty miles from Peking the big cash are no longer in circulation. Small cash are used, [a nominal] 1000 [at Tientsin, really 500] of which make a *tiao*, and 3000 to 3500 of which are equal to a tael of silver. **1908** Morse *Trade Chinese Emp.* v. 130 Cash are strung on strings, in rolls of 100, of which 10 go to the string or *tiao*, or *ch'uan*, formerly called *kuan*. **1910** *Blackw. Mag.* Dec. 763/2, I paid a tiaou for this; but I don't begrudge the money.

**Tiar** (təi·äɹ), *sb.* Chiefly *poet.* Also 6 tyar(e, 7–9 tiare, (7 theare). [Anglicized f. Tiara, prob. after F. *tiare* (14th c. in Godef. *Compl.*).]

**1.** = Tiara *sb.* 1. (In quot. 1513 *attrib.*)

**1513** Douglas *Æneis* VII. v. 126 The triple King Priame.. His ceptre als, and eik his tyar [*ed.* **1553** tyare] hat, Hallowit quhayrwyth at sacrifice he sat. **1614** Selden *Titles Hon.* 24 The King of Bulgarie..had also his Crown of Gold, his Tiar of Silk, and Red Shoes. **1725** Pope *Odyss.* x. 651 A tiar wreath'd her head with many a fold. **1818** Milman *Samor* 226 When the Median's brow the massy tiar Let fall.

**2.** = Tiara *sb.* 2.

**1616** Sheldon *Miracles Antichr.* 165 His triple Tiare and Crowne. **1624** Darcie *Birth of Heresies* xii. 51 The Myter or Theare, and some other decorations. **1841** *Fraser's Mag.* XXIV. 26 His triple tiare Is flung at his feet.

**3.** = Tiara *sb.* 4. Also *fig.* (In early instances perh. confused with Tire *sb.*[1])

**1660** Jer. Taylor *Duct. Dubit.* II. iii. rule ix. § 29 The spirit of humility and wisedome..ought to be the investiture of a Christians heart and the tiar of his head. **1667** Milton *P. L.* III. 625 Of beaming sunnie Raies, a golden tiar Circl'd his [an angel's] head. **1802** in *Spirit Pub. Jrnls.* VI. 204 Head-dress a tiar of diamonds on purple velvet. **1819** Keats *Lamia* 58 Sprinkled with stars, like Ariadne's tiar. **1886** W. Alexander *St. Augustine's Holiday*, etc. 191 With sackcloth cast above the tiar of gold.

Hence **Ti·ar** *v.*, **Ti·ared** (-äɹd) *ppl. a.* = Tiara *v.*, Tiaraed.

**1824** *New Monthly Mag.* X. 334 Where the tiar'd Pharaohs sleep. **1882** J. Walker *Jaunt to Auld Reekie* 172 Red-hatting thy cardinals and tiaring thy popes.

**Tiara** (ti,ā·rä, təi,ēə·rä), *sb.* Also 6–7 tyara. [a. L. *tiāra*, a. Gr. τιάρα, τιάρας, Ionic τιήρης, of unknown origin. So It. *tiara* the papal crown.]

**1.** The raised head-dress or high peaked cap worn by the Persians and some other eastern peoples, varying in shape according to the rank of the wearer; a kind of turban.

**1555** W. Watreman *Fardle of Facions* II. v. 148 The rounde cappe, whiche thei cal Tiara..passed from them [Medes] to the Persians. **1696** Phillips (ed. 5), *Tiara*, a high sharp pointed Cap, worn by Sovereign Princes, and those of the Blood Royal, among the Persians. **1734** tr. *Rollin's Anc. Hist.* (1827) II. 378 The Persians wore no helmets, but only their common caps, which they called tiaras. **1847** Grote *Greece* II. xxxiii. IV. 300 The upright tiara, the privileged head-dress of the Persian kings.

**2.** A high ovate-cylindrical or dome-shaped diadem worn by the pope, surmounted by the orb and cross of sovereignty, and encircled with three crowns symbolic of triple dignity, and usually richly wrought with jewels; often called *the triple tiara* or *triple crown*. Hence *transf.* the position or dignity of pope, the papacy. Also *fig.*

[1616: see Tiar 2.] **1645** Evelyn *Diary* 18 Jan., There were divers of the Pope's pantofles..also his tyara, or triple crown. **1700** Astry tr. *Saavedra-Faxardo* II. 316 This Tiara, or Triple-Crown, is the Touch-stone on which other Crowns are tried. **1845** S. Austin *Ranke's Hist. Ref.* III. v. II. 173 When Pope Clement VII came to the tiara, he revoked all grants of this nature. **1860** Hawthorne *Marb. Faun* xxxiv, A figure of a pope, arrayed in his pontifical robes, and crowned with the tiara.

**b.** *Her.* A bearing supposed to represent the Pope's tiara; also called *triple crown*.

**1780** Edmondson *Heraldry* II. Gloss., *Tiara*, or *Triple Crown*, with clouds in base issuing rays, being part of the arms of the Drapers' Company. **1894** *Parker's Gloss. Her.*, *Tiara*, the pope's triple crown occurs in the arms of one Company.

**3.** The head-dress of the Jewish High Priest.

**1868** Marriott *Vest. Chr.* 80 The Tiara..was at once a covering and an ornament to the head of the High Priest. **1877** C. Geikie *Christ* lviii. (1879) 709 Was not the tiara worn by a fierce Sadducee? **1890** P. H. Hunter *After the Exile* xiii. 250 The tiara might be worn with safety, while the crown was impossible.

**4.** An ornamental frontal, coronet, or headband.

In modern use, a richly jewelled ornament worn by ladies in the hair, above the forehead.

[1660, 1667: see Tiar 3.] **1718** Prior *Pleasure* 507 A bright tiara, round her forehead tied. **1761** H. Walpole *Let. to H. S. Conway* 9 Sept., Her tiara of diamonds was very pretty. **1895** Rider Haggard *Heart of World* xxi, On her head was set a tiara of perfect pearls.

**b.** *fig.* (Cf. *crown*, *diadem*.)

**1818** Byron *Ch. Har.* IV. ii, She [Venice] looks a sea Cybele..with her tiara of proud towers. **1862** Goulburn *Pers. Relig.* I. iv. (1873) 35 The tiara of the rainbow. **1880** Jas. Legge *Mem. J. Legge* iv. 45 Truth and love are the double tiara that should rest on his brow.

**5.** *Zool.* A mitre-shell, or a genus of mitre-shells.

**1835** Swainson *Elem. Mod. Conchol.* 14 Tiara. Sw. Mouth narrowed at the base; with an internal upper groove. **1840** — *Treat. Malacology* I. iv. 112 The real type of the *Mitrinæ* is our genus *Tiara*, and not that of *Mitra*, as formerly supposed. **1842** *Penny Cycl.* XXIV. 420/2 *Tiara*,..Swainson's name for a genus of 'Mitrinæ'..which are termed 'Mitres' by collectors.

**6.** *attrib.* and *Comb.*, as *tiara-crowned*, *-like*, *-shaped* adjs.; **tiara night**, a night on which tiaras (sense 4) are worn at the opera.

**1792** R. Cumberland *Calvary* (1803) II. 123 Round his brows A cypress wreath tiara-like he wore. **1868** J. A. Wylie *Road to Rome* v. 45 Popery—from its tiara-crowned chief to its sandal-shod friars. **1897** *Westm. Gaz.* 3 June 2/1 The guns sat each in its own little tiara-shaped entrenchment. **1900** *Daily Express* 28 June 1/1 The Opera-house presented a brilliant spectacle last night, the ladies in the audience..having made it a 'tiara' night in expectation of the Khedive's presence.

Hence **Tia·ra** *v.*, *trans.* to adorn with or as with a tiara; **Tia·raed, -ra'd**, (-äd) *ppl. a.*, adorned with a tiara.

**1822** Milman *Martyr of Antioch* 128 The high tiara'd Magian. **1837** *New Monthly Mag.* LI. 312 A pyramid of pilauf literally crowns, or rather tiaras the feast. **1840** Carlyle *Heroes* iii. (1872) 79 All the Tiaraed and Diademed of the world.

**Tib** (tib), *sb.* Also 6 tyb, 7 tybb, tibb(e. [Perh. the same as *Tib*, a shortened hypocoristic form of the female name *Isabel*; now rather rude or slighting (exc. playfully); also with dim. *-y* or *-ie*, *Tibbie*, a common female name in the north.

But in quot. *a* 1553 *Tib* is used as short for *Tibet*. A *St. Tibba* is mentioned in O. E. Chron. an. 963 (Laud MS.).]

† **1.** Formerly, a typical name for a woman of the lower classes, as in *Tib and Tom* (cf. *Jack and Gill*). Also, A girl or lass, a sweetheart, a mistress; *dyslogistically*, a young woman of low or loose character, a strumpet. *Obs.*

**1533** J. Heywood (*title*) A Mery Play betwene Johan Johan the husbande, Tyb his wyfe, and syr Johan the preest. *a* **1553** Udall *Royster D.* I. iii. (Arb.) 19 (*Stage direct.*) Tibet Talk apace, sowyng. *Ibid.* II. iii. 36 Who shall then know our Tib Talke apace trow ye? **1582** Stanyhurst *Æneis* IV. (Arb.) 102 A coy tyb, as vagabund in this my segnorye wandring. **1589** R. Robinson *Golden Mirr.* (Chetham Soc.) 54 The brauest tipling tib, that is within the towne. **1618** Hornby *Sco. Dronk.* (1859) 19 Where tinkers and their tibs doe oft repaire. **1681** Robertson *Phraseol. Gen.* (1693) 1226 A Tib, *mulier sordida*. **1689** *Descr. Summer* in *Poor Robin* C v, When Tib and Tom upon a Holyday, Make fair assault on such good things as they. *a* **1700** B. E. *Dict. Cant. Crew*, *Tib*, a young lass.

**2.** Name for the ace of trumps in the game of gleek. *Obs.* exc. *Hist.*

**1655** J. Cotgrave *Wits Interpr.* (1662) 364 The Ace is called Tib, the Knave Tom, and the four of Trumps Tidie. *a* **1658** Cleveland *Hermaphrodite* 64 That Gamester needs must overcome, That can play both with Tib and Tom. **1688** R. Holme *Armoury* III. xvi. (Roxb.) 71/2 The Ace is 15 in hand and 18 in play, which is called Tib. **1822** Scott *Nigel* xvi, Tib, which went for fifteen.

† **3.** *Tib of the buttery* (also simply *Tib*): a goose. *Obs. slang.*

**1622** Fletcher *Beggar's Bush* v. i, Mergery-praters, Rogers, And Tibs o' th' Buttery. **1641** Brome *Jovial Crew* II. Wks. 1873 III. 388 Here's G[r]unter and Bleater, with Tib of the Buttry, And Margery Prater, all drest without suttry. *a* **1700** B. E. *Dict. Cant. Crew*, *Tib of the Buttery*, a Goose. **1725** *New Cant. Dict.* Song xviii, On Redshanks, and Tibs thou shalt ev'ry Day dine.

† **4.** [? Another word.] Name of a kind of vehicle. *Obs. rare.*

**1793** Mar. J. Holroyd in *Girlhood of M. J. H.* (1896) 243 Papa says he will have a Pole put to the Tib, that it may be drawn by the two horses, like a Curricle. **1794** *Ibid.* 27 June 289 The Aunts go out in the Tib, which just suits them.

**5.** *Comb.* **Tib-cat**, *dial.*, also *Tibby-cat*, a female cat (cf. Tom-cat); **Tib's Eve**, *dial.*: see quots.; *on Tib's Eve*, never.

**1828** *Craven Gloss.*, **Tib-cat*, a female cat, a Tabitha. **1785** Grose *Dict. Vulg. T.* s. v., *Saint Tibb's evening, the evening of the last day, or day of judgement; he will pay you on St. Tibb's eve (*Irish*). **1870** Brewer *Dict. Phr. & Fable*, *St. Tib's Eve*, never. **1893** in *N. & Q.* 8th Ser. IV. 507, etc. **1893** *Newcastle Weekly Chron.* Suppl. 23 Dec. 3 There is no such saint in the calendar as St. Tib. [But see note in Etymol.] Similar expressions to 'Tib's Eve' are 'At Latter Lammas', and 'When two Sundays meet', the time in each case being never. **1902** *N. & Q.* 9th Ser. IX. 109/1 'Yes .. it will be on Tib's Eve, neither before nor after Christmas', expressing thus his incredulity as to the event ever coming off.

**Tib** (tib), *v. School slang.* [Origin unascertained.] *intr.* To slip out; to escape unobserved from school or house; to break bounds. Also **Ti·bble** *v.*, in same sense.

**1840** J. T. Hewlett *P. Priggins* iii, A trick acquired from tibbling-out down the lane, i. e. Charterhouse Lane, to the Red Cow. **1855** Thackeray *Newcomes* ii, Tibbing out and receiving the penalty therefor. *Ibid.* lxxix, I used what they call to tib out and run down to a public-house.

**Tiberian** (təibīə·riăn), *a.* [ad. L. *Tiberiānus*, f. *Tiberius* (see def.) + *-ānus*, -an.] Of or pertaining to (*a*) Tiberius, emperor of Rome 14–37 A. D. (also *fig.*), (*b*) the town of Tiberias in Galilee, where the Masoreth or Masora was formed.

**1601** Holland *Pliny* (1634) I. 439 The Tyberian peares beare the name of Tiberius the Emperor, for that of all others he loued that fruit best. **1659** Owen *Integr. Hebrew & Grk. Text* Wks. 1853 XVI. 392 The points and accents were invented by the Tiberian Masoretes. **1742** Young *Nt. Th.* v. 815 Tiberian arts his purposes wrap up In deep dissimulation's darkest night. **1837** R. Wilson *Pleas. Piety* v. 115, I see Him seated on a hill Near the Tiberian lake.

† **Tiber-, Tyber-stone.** *Obs.* [f. L. *Tibur*, a town of ancient Italy: cf. L. *lapis Tīburtīnus*.] A calcareous stone quarried at Tibur, now Tivoli; travertine: cf. Tiburtine.

**1726** Leoni *Alberti's Archit.* I. 58/2 One fourth part of Tyber-Stone, beat to powder.

**Tibert** (ti·bəɹt, təi·bəɹt). *arch.* Also 5 Tybert. [a. Flem. and Du. *Tybert*, *Tibeert*, OFr. *Tibert*.] The name of the cat in the apologue of Reynard the Fox; thence, used as a quasi-proper name for any cat, and (as a common noun), a cat. (By Shakspere identified with *Tibalt*:—OF. *Thibauld, Thibaut*, Eng. *Theobald*, vulgo *Tibbald*.)

1481 CAXTON *Reynard* iii. (Arb.) 6 Wyth this so cam Tybert the catte..and sprang in emonge them. [1592 SHAKS. *Rom. & Jul.* II. iv. 18 Is he a man to encounter Tybalt? *B.* Why what is Tibalt? *M.* More then Prince of Cats. *Ibid.* III. i. 78 Tybalt, you Rat-catcher, will you walke? *Tib.* What woulds thou haue with me? *Mer.* Good King of Cats, nothing but one of your nine liues.] 1616 B. JONSON *Epigr.* ad fin., *The Voyage itself* 135 Cats there lay divers had been flea'd and roasted...But 'mongst these Tiberts, who do you think there was? 1672 DRYDEN *Assignation* I. i, His violin..squeaks so lewdly, that Sir Tibert in the gutter mistakes him for his mistress. 1872 M. COLLINS *Pr. Clarice* II. iv. 61 He'd have killed that tibert, Tybalt, as willingly as he'd have killed a cat.

**Tiberune**, obs. form of TIBURON.

**Tibet, Thibet** (tibe·t). Name of a country in central Asia; used *attrib.* of wool obtained thence, or of cloth or garments made from this or in imitation of it; applied (usually *thibet*) to (*a*) a heavy stuff made wholly or partly of goats' hair; (*b*) a fine stuff used for women's dresses. *absol.* Tibet cloth, or a gown or shawl made of it. Hence **Tibetan** (tibī·tăn) *a.*, belonging to Tibet.

1827 SCOTT *Surg. Dau.* Concl., 'How could you..collect all these hard words about India?'..'Like the imitative operatives of Paisley, I have composed my shawl by incorporating into the woof a little Thibet wool, which..Colonel Mackerris..had the goodness to supply me with'. 1857 PARKHILL *Hist. Paisley* xiii. 97 Shawls of all kinds..such as thibet and cashmere shawls. *Ibid.* 98 Edinburgh had thibet in the manufacture. 1858 SIMMONDS *Dict. Trade*, *Thibet-cloth*, a camlet or fabric made of coarse goats'-hair. 1894 J. MACINTOSH *Ayrshire Nights' Entertainm.* vii. 129 A small production of thibets, coarse woollens, and muslins. 1900 MARY E. WILKINS *Parson Lord* 196 Her black thibet gown. *Ibid.* 197, I don't care about this old thibet.

‖ **Tibia** (ti·biă). Pl. -æ (-ī). [L. *tībia* shin-bone, a pipe or flute.]

1. *Anat.* and *Zool.* The inner and usually larger of the two bones (*tibia* and *fibula*) of the lower leg, from the knee to the ankle; the shin-bone.

In birds the tibia is fused with some of the bones of the tarsus, forming that more strictly called TIBIOTARSUS.

1726–41 MONRO *Anat.* (ed. 3) 282 The superior Extremity of the Tibia is large. 1791 W. BARTRAM *Carolina* 505 A kind of flute, made of..the tibia of the deer's leg. 1845 TODD & BOWMAN *Phys. Anat.* I. 100 The tibia is convex forwards and outwards. 1872 MIVART *Elem. Anat.* 183 The tibia, or shin-bone, is..an elongated bone, more so than any other..except the femur.

b. Applied also to the corresponding part of the leg itself; now esp. to the tibiotarsus of birds.

[1693 tr. *Blancard's Phys. Dict.* (ed. 2), *Tibia*, the Leg, the part betwixt the Knee and the Ancle. So 1704 J. HARRIS *Lex. Techn.* I.] 1826 STEPHENS in Shaw *Gen. Zool.* XIII. 214 These birds differ..in having..the tibiæ divested of feathers. 1869 GILLMORE tr. *Figuier's Rept. & Birds* iv. 339 Woodcocks differ from Snipes in having..the tibiæ feathered at the joint.

c. *Entom.* The fourth of the five joints of the leg of an insect, that between the femur and the tarsus.

1815 KIRBY & SP. *Entomol.* (1828) I. xv. 488 A pincer formed by the posterior metatarsus and tibia. 1868 DUNCAN tr. *Figuier's Insect W.* Introd. 8 When about to jump they bring the tibia into contact with the thigh. 1888 ROLLESTON & JACKSON *Anim. Life* 499 The thoracic limbs [in *Insecta*] consist typically of a coxa, trochanter, femur, tibia, and tarsus...The tibia is often armed with spines or calcaria.

2. *Antiq.* An ancient (single or double) flute or flageolet.

1705 ADDISON *Italy* 322 The same Variety of Strings may be observ'd on their Harps, and of Stops on their Tibiæ. 1834 LYTTON *Pompeii* I. ii, I paid a visit to Pliny; he was sitting in his summer-house writing while an unfortunate slave played on the tibia.

**Tibiad** (ti·biæd), *adv. Anat.* [f. TIBIA + -*ad*: see DEXTRAD.] Towards the tibial aspect.

1803 BARCLAY *New Anat. Nomencl.* 166 In the sacral extremities, Tibiad will signify towards the tibial aspect. 1808 — *Muscular Motions* 306 They allow the femur to roll tibiad or inward, but not fibulad or outward.

**Tibial** (ti·biăl), *a.* (*sb.*) [ad. L. *tībiālis* pertaining to the shin-bone: see TIBIA and -AL.]

1. *Anat.* and *Zool.* Of or pertaining to the tibia. Also as *sb.*, *ellipt.* for *tibial artery*, *muscle*, etc.

1599 A. M. tr. *Gabelhouer's Bk. Physicke* 342/2 If it be a tibialle Fracture, he must continuallye lye on his Backe. 1786 J. PEARSON in *Med. Commun.* II. 99 The course of the anterior tibial artery. 1847 JOHNSTON in *Proc. Berw. Nat. Club* II. 231 The tibial joints..are furnished with long hairs. 1898 J. HUTCHINSON in *Arch. Surg.* IX. No. 36. 338 The anterior and posterior tibials [*sc.* arteries]. 1899 *Allbutt's Syst. Med.* VI. 668 The nerve and its continuation supply the posterior tibial [*sc.* muscle].

2. Of or pertaining to a tibia or ancient flute.

1656 BLOUNT *Glossogr.*, *Tibial*, of, or belonging to pipes; meet to make pipes of. 1658 PHILLIPS, *Tibial*, belonging to a Pipe or Flute.

‖ **Tibicen** (tibəi·sĕn). *Antiq.* [L. *tībīcen* a flute-player, f. *tībia* flute + *can-ĕre* to sing, also to play on an instrument.] A flute-player.

1776 BURNEY *Hist. Mus.* (1789) I. x. 173 When the Lacedaemonians went to battle a Tibicen played soft and soothing music to temper their courage.

**Tibicinate** (tibi·sineit), *v. rare*$^{-0}$. [f. L. *tībīcināt-*, ppl. stem of *tībīcin-āre* to play on the flute: see prec. and -ATE 3.] *intr.* To play on the tibia or flute. So **Tibicina·tion** (*rare*$^{-0}$); **Tibi·cinist** (*rare*$^{-1}$) = prec.

1656 BLOUNT *Glossogr.*, *Tibicinate* (*tibicino*), to sing or pipe. [Hence in later Dicts.] 1658 PHILLIPS, *Tibicination*, a playing on a Pipe. 1846 RIMBAULT in *North's Mem. Music* 37 *note*, An engraving from a manuscript..in which a tibicinist is delineated..blowing on the *tibia pares*, or two equal flutes.

**Tibio-** (tibiŏ), used as combining form of TIBIA, in anatomical terms in the sense 'pertaining to the tibia and (some other part)', as *tibio-femoral*, *-fibular*, *-metatarsal*, *-peroneal*, *-popliteal*, etc., adjs.; **Tibiota·rsal** *a.*, of or pertaining to the tibia and the tarsus; pertaining to the tibiotarsus; **Tibiota·rsus**, *Ornith.*, the tibia of a bird's leg with the condyles formed by its fusion with the proximal bones of the tarsus.

1835–6 *Todd's Cycl. Anat.* I. 152/1 The inferior *tibio-fibular articulation. 1870 ROLLESTON *Anim. Life* 14 The *tibiometatarsal joint. 1803 BARCLAY *New Anat. Nomencl.* 174 In describing the direction of the superficial femoral artery,..at first it is rotulo-tibial, then *tibio-popliteal. 1835–6 *Todd's Cycl. Anat.* I. 151/2 The anterior *tibio-tarsal ligament arises from this margin. 1872 COUES *N. Amer. Birds* 69 The leg is almost always feathered to or beyond the tibio-tarsal joint. 1883 MARTIN & MOALE *Vertebr. Dissect.* II. 124 The *tibio-tarsus..consists not only of the tibia, but of the proximal bone of the tarsus, which becomes fused with it at an early period.

**Tiborne, Tiburn**(e, obs. forms of TYBURN.

**Tiburon** (tibūrō·n). Also 6–7 tiberune, tuberon. [a. F. *tiburon* (Joubert *Hist. Poiss.* 1558), *tibĕron, tiburin* (Littré), Sp. *tiburon* (*tiburónes péces*, in Minsheu) = It. *tiburino* (Florio), Pg. *tubarão*. Origin uncertain; prob. taken into Sp. or Pg. from some W. Indian or E. Indian lang.] A name given by 16–17th c. navigators to one or more large species of shark; applied specifically to the bonnet-headed shark, *Reniceps tiburo*; now, on the Mexican Pacific coast, to *Carcharinus fronto*.

1555 EDEN *Decades* 201 The Tiburon..is a very great fysshe and very quicke and swifte in the water, and a cruell deuourer....The sayde Tuberon [etc.]. 1565 SIR J. HAWKINS *2nd Voy. W. Ind.* (Hakl. Soc.) 22 Many sharks or Tuberons ..came about the ships [Sierra Leone]. [1579 T. STEVENS *Let. fr. Goa* in Hakluyt *Voy.* (1589) 161 There waited on our ship [in the Atlantic within the Tropics] fishes as long as a man, which they cal Tuberones. 1598 W. PHILLIP *Linschoten* I. xlviii. (Hakl. Soc.) II. 12 There is in the rivers, and also in the Sea along the coast of India great store of fishes, which the Portingalls call Tubaron or Hayen.] 1622 R. HAWKINS *Voy. S. Sea* 68 The shark, or tiberune, is a fish like unto those which wee call dogge-fishes, but that he is farre greater. 1796 MORSE *Amer. Geog.* I. 728 Fish common to both oceans..sword fish, saw fish, tiburones, manitis.

**Tiburtine** (təi·bɒɹtəin), *a.* [ad. L. *Tīburtīn-us*, f. *Tībur*s, *Tīburt-em*, adj., of Tibur.] Of or pertaining to the region or district of Tibur (now Tivoli) in ancient Latium. *Tiburtine stone* = TRAVERTINE: cf. TIBER-STONE.

c1440 *Pallad. on Husb.* I. 372 Stone tiburtyne, or floody columbyne, Or spongy rede, lete brenne, or marble stone, For bylding better is the harder myne. 1644 EVELYN *Diary* 14 Nov., It is built of Tiburtine stone. 1840 *Civil Eng. & Arch. Jrnl.* III. 132/2 A bilingual inscription..sculptured on both sides of a Tiburtine stone.

**Tic** (tik). [a. F. *tic*, first known as the name of an equine affection: *ticq*, *tiquet* 'a disease which on a sudden stopping a horse's breath, makes him to stop, and stand still' (Cotgr. 1611). Origin uncertain; Diez compares It. *ticchio* whim, freak, caprice. See also TICK *sb.*[5]]

1. A disease or affection characterized by spasmodic twitching of certain muscles, esp. of the face; nearly always short for *tic douloureux*: see 2.

1822–34 *Good's Study Med.* (ed. 4) III. 219 The word *tic* is commonly supposed to be an onomatopy, or a sound expressive of the action it imports. 1849 CLARIDGE *Cold Water-cure* 106 A person..suffering from Tic in his legs. 1860 DICKENS *Lett.* 5 June, Smith..has been dreadfully ill with tic. 1873 STEVENSON *Lett.* (1901) I. 62, I do not expect any tic to-night. 1899 *Allbutt's Syst. Med.* VII. 868 Both in this country and in America, the term 'tic' has been applied to..facial spasm ('tic non-douloureux'), or to facial neuralgia ('tic douloureux'). *Ibid.* VIII. 40 A phenomenon in the symptomatology of simple tic (habit-spasm).

‖ 2. *Tic douloureux* (dulurö) [F., = painful twitching], severe facial neuralgia with twitching of the facial muscles.

(Often misspelt by English writers *dolo-*, *dolou-*, *douleu-*, and often mispronounced (dǫlərū), etc.)

1800 *Med. Jrnl.* III. 575 The *Dolor Faciei*, or, as the French call it, *Tic Douloreux*, is a disorder which has, in general, frustrated all attempts of the medical art. 1800 HOME in *Phil. Trans.* XCI. 20 The *Tic douleureux* is a remarkable instance. 1822 GOOD *Study Med.* I. 55 The maddening pain of *neuralgia faciei*, or tic douloureux. 1824 LAMB *Lett.*, *To B. Barton* (1838) II. 162, I hope..thy *tick doleru*, or, however you spell it, is vanished. 1861 LYTTON *Str. Story* I. 58 A poor old gentleman, tormented by *tic-doloreux*. 1878 T. BRYANT *Pract. Surg.* I. 289 The disease known as 'tic-douloureux' is an affection of the fifth nerve and its branches, but any nerve in the body is liable to suffer.

3. A whim: see TICK *sb.*[5] 2.

**Tic**, variant of TIG.

‖ **Tical** (*in Siam* tikā·l, *in Burma* ti·k'l). Also 8 tecul(l, tecal(l, teecall, 9 tickal, tycal, takel, tackal(l. [Representing, through Pg. *tical*, the Indian *ṭaṅkā*, also *ṭakā*: see TANGA. Carried in 16th c. to Siam by the Portuguese; later to Burma. (See Sir R. C. Temple in *Indian Antiquary* XXVIII. 235, 253.)] A term long in use by foreign traders in Siam and more recently in Burma, applied to a silver coin and its weight, representing roughly the Indian rupee (orig. the same as the *ṭaṅkā*), which has varied in value according to time and place from 2*s.* 6*d.* to 1*s.* 2*d.*, and in weight from more than to less than half an ounce Troy. (Sir R. C. Temple.) Also *attrib.*

In Siam, according to Crawfurd, a weight = 225½ grs. (according to Simmonds = 236 grs.); also a silver coin of this weight, the value of which has fallen with that of silver. In Burma, a weight = 255·6 grains, the quasi-standard weight of current (uncoined) silver, said to be equivalent in value to about 1¼ rupee.

1662 J. DAVIES tr. *Mandelslo's Trav.* 130 The money of this Country [Siam] is very good..; there are of it three sorts; *Ticals*, *Mases*, and *Foangs*. 1727 A. HAMILTON *New Acc. E. Ind.* II. xlvii. 164 Some were of pure Gold, others of Tecul Silver, which has no Alloy in it. 1800 *Misc. Tracts* in *Asiatic Ann. Reg.* 317/2 The cost of sinking a new well is 2000 tecals flowered silver of the country, or 2500 sicca rupees. 1840 MALCOM *Trav.* 41/1 They sometimes have a gold fuang, equal to eight ticals. The tical, assayed at the mint of Calcutta, yielded about one rupee three and a half annas, equal to 2s. 6d. sterling. 1858 T. DALTON in *Merc. Marine Mag.* V. 337 Last year the same rice sold for 19 ticals (equal to 60 cents each tical, or 2s. 6d. sterling). 1902 *Daily Chron.* 1 Dec. 5/7 A dispatch from Bangkok..says:—'The Siamese Government has issued a decree fixing the gold standard on the basis of seventeen ticals to the pound'. 1907 *Motor Boat* 19 Sept. 179/1 American two-stroke motors..used to arrive in batches valued at 1,200 ticals each (1 tical = 1s. 5⅜d.).

‖ **Ticca** (ti·kă, tī·kă). *East Indian.* Also teeka. [ad. Hindī *ṭhīkā* or *ṭhīkah* hire, fare, fixed price (Yule).] *attrib.* Engaged on contract, hired; esp. in *ticca gharry*, hired carriage.

1827 *Bengal Regulations* 27 June (Y.), A Rule, Ordinance and Regulation..for regulating the number and fare of Teeka Palankeens, and Teeka Bearers in the Town of Calcutta. 1878 *Life in Mofussil* II. 94 (Y.) We got into a 'ticca gharry', 'hired trap'. 1895 MRS. B. M. CROKER *Village Tales* (1896) 48 You..can, no doubt, retire and set up a ticca gharry, or a shop. 1903 *Blackw. Mag.* Dec. 817 Engaged in a..wrangle with a Ticca carriage-driver.

† **Ticchen.** *Obs.* [OE. *ticcen* = OHG. *zicchîn* :—WTeut. **tikk-īn-*, dim. from the stem which also gave OHG. *ziga*, Ger. *ziege* goat. The modern Eng. form would have been *titchen*.] A kid, a young goat.

c950 *Lindisf. Gosp.* Matt. xxv. 32 Sua hiorde to-sceadas scipo from ticcenum [c975 *Rushw. G.* ticnum; c1000 *Ags. G.* tyccenum; c1160 *Hatt.* ticchenan]. c1000 ÆLFRIC *Gen.* xxvii. 9 Bring me twa þa betstan tyccenu. *Ibid.* 16 Heo..befeold his handa mid þæra tyccena fellum. a1225 *Ancr. R.* 100 Þeos fif wittes he cleopeð ticchenes; for..of a ticchen, þet haueð swete vleschs, kumeð a stinkinde got.

**Tice** (təis), *sb.* [f. TICE *v.*] An act of enticing, an enticement; *spec.* a stroke at croquet, or 'ball' (bowled) at cricket (see quots. 1888, 1901), which tempts or entices the opponent to take aim.

1874 J. D. HEATH *Croquet-Player* 55 It is admissible to give a double shot as a 'tice', so as to tempt him to shoot where his missing would give you the dead ball. 1888 STEEL & LYTTELTON *Cricket* (Badm.) iii. 132 In the first over he [the bowler] should try a 'yorker'. This ball, called in days gone by a 'tice', an abbreviation of 'entice', is certainly one of the most deadly balls that can be bowled. 1900 A. LILLIE *Croquet up to Date* 41 The length of the tice should depend on the trueness of the ground. 1901 *N. & Q.* 9th Ser. VIII. 284/2 It might meet the requirements of present-day definition..if one classed a 'tice' as a lob, or to be more precise, an underhand yorker.

b. *Comb.* tice-basket, a decoy basket.

1884 *19th Cent.* Feb. 245 Fish..falling freely to the native net and tice-basket.

**Tice** (təis), *v. Obs.* exc. *dial.* Forms: 3–7 tyce, 4–6 tise, 4–7 tyse, 5–6 *Sc.* tyss, (6 *Sc.* tist, tyst, tyist(e, tyisce), 5–7 (9 *dial.*) tice, 7 (9 *dial.*) 'tice. [Aphetic form of *atise*, ATTICE or ENTICE, but found earlier than either of these, and perhaps taken immediately from OF. *a-tiser*, dropping the prefix.] *trans.* To entice; to induce or attract by the offer of pleasure or advantage. Also *absol.*

c1275 *Moral Ode* (Jesus MS.) 266 Þe þat were gaderares of þisse worldes ayhte And duden þat þe loþe gost heom tycede [*v.rr.* hechte to, tihte] and tahte. 1303 R. BRUNNE *Handl. Synne* 2152 To tyse a chylde swyche synne to do. c1449 PECOCK *Repr.* v. xii. 548 Which schulde rather lette fro glorie than tice into glorie. 1533 BELLENDEN *Livy* I. xviii. (S.T.S.) I. 103 He tyistit þe ȝoung men of his ciete to his purpois. 1593 NASHE *Christ's T.* 48 b, If one tice a Prentise to robbe his Maister, it is Felony. a1835 MRS. HEMANS *Let.* in Chorley *Mem.* (1837) I. 299 An old gardener of ours used to say of me..that Miss Felicia 'ticed him to do whatever she pleased'. 1859 GEO. ELIOT *A. Bede* xxxix, He's been false to me, and 'ticed her away.

Hence **Ti·cing** *vbl. sb.* and *ppl. a.*

a1400 *Hampole's Psalter* liii. 4 Þat þai take me not in þaire wickidnes & liþere eggynge [*v.r.* tisynge]. 1456 SIR G. HAYE *Law Arms* (S.T.S.) 31 For na mede na othir tyssing. 1568 in H. Fleming *Mary Q. of Scots* (1897) 512 Be persuasioun and tyisting. 1582 T. WATSON *Centurie of*

*Loue* lxxii. (Arb.) 108 My Loue, Whose tising face is of more liuely hewe. **1646** H. P. *Medit. Seige* 69 What a ticeing bayt is golden hope!

† **Ticement.** *Obs.* Aphetic f. ENTICEMENT.

**1303** R. BRUNNE *Handl. Synne* 12016 ȝyf þou wylt..withstonde hys [the devil's] tycement. *c* **1400** *Brut* 182 Lewelyn, Prince of Walys, þrouȝ ticement of Dauid his broþer,..þouȝt disherite Kyng Edward.

**Ticer** (təi·səɹ). [f. TICE *v.* + -ER[1].] An enticer.

*a* **1529** SKELTON *Mann. World* 143 So many carders, Revelers and dicers, And so many yl ticers, Sawe I never. **1869** E. FARMER *Scrap Bk.* (ed. 6) 27 All the lame and the old, With a few (just as 'ticers') are sent to be sold.

**Tichorhine** (təi·korəin), *a.* *Palæont.* Also -orrhine, -orine. [ad. mod.L. *tichorrhinus*, f. Gr. τεῖχο-ς wall + ῥίς (ῥῖν-) nose.] Having an ossified nasal septum; the English form of the specific name of the Woolly Rhinoceros.

**1851** D. WILSON *Preh. Ann.* (1863) I. ii. 42 Man was contemporary with the tichorine rhinoceros. **1854** *Zoologist* XII. 4375 Entire carcases of the extinct mammoth and tichorhine rhinoceros have been handed down in Arctic Siberia. **1860** OWEN *Palæontology* 366 The discovery of the carcase of the tichorrine rhinoceros in frozen soil.

**Ticht** (Sc.), obs. pa. pple. of TIE *v.*; var. TIGHT *v.*[2]; Sc. f. TIGHT.

**Tichy**, obs. form of TETCHY.

**Tick** (tik), *sb.*[1] Forms: (1 ticia), 5 teke; 4–7 tyke, 6 tycke, 6–7 tike, ticke, 7 tique, 7– tick. [*Ticia* (assumed to be an error for **tiica* = *tīca*, or **ticca*) appears once, in the Erfurt Gloss. *a* 800, after which the word is known only in 15th c. as *teke*, from 14th to 17th c. as *tȳke*, and from 16th c. as *tycke*, *tick*. *Teke* agrees with MD., MLG. *tēke*, Du. *teek*, also with the LG. forms *teke*, *täke*. *Tȳke*, *tīke* agree with suggested OE. **tīca*, with LG. *tieke*, *tiek*, whence Du. *tiek*, and mod.EFris. *tike*, *tīk*, applied to beetles generally (Dornkaat-Koolman). Thence also prob. F. *tique* (1464 in Godef.). The later *tycke*, *tick* may be shortened from *teke*: cf. *rick*, *sick*, *wick*. If = OE. **ticca* with OTeut. *cc*, it would correspond to Ger. *zecke* (whence It. *zecca*) :—**tikkon* m. or **tikkôn* f.; if = **tīca*, to MHG. *zeche*. The various forms imply WGer. **tîka-*, **tika-*, **tikka-*. Ulterior etymology uncertain: see Kluge and Franck; also Falk and Torp s. v. *Tæge*.]

**1.** The common name for several kinds of mites or acarids, esp. of the genus *Ixōdes* or family *Ixōdidæ*, which infest the hair or fur of various animals, as dogs, cattle, etc., and attach themselves to the skin as temporary parasites; also for the similarly parasitic dipterous insects of the families *Hippoboscidæ* (bird-ticks, horse-ticks, sheep-ticks) and *Nycteribiidæ* (bat-ticks).

*a* **800** *Erfurt Gloss.* (O. E. T.) 1130 *Ricinus*, ticia *sax.* **1300–25** *Song agst. Retainers* 20 in *Pol. Songs* (Camden) 238 To shome he huem shadde, To fles ant to fleye, To tyke ant to tadde. *c* **1440** *Jacob's Well* xxi. 146 A waterleche or a tyke hath neuere ynow, tyl it brestyth. **14..** *Voc.* in Wr.-Wülcker 565/47 *Ascarida*, a Teke. **1523** FITZHERB. *Husb.* § 135 There is ieopardy both for calues, foles and coltes, for tyckes, or for beynge lousye. **1575** TURBERV. *Venerie* 229 A receipt to kill fleas, lice, tykes, and other vermin on dogs. **1603** HOLLAND *Plutarch's Mor.* 393 The foxe in Æsops fables would not suffer the urchin to take off the tiques that were setled upon her bodie. **1658** ROWLAND *Moufet's Theat. Ins.* 934 The Tick or Sheep-fly. **1688** R. HOLME *Armoury* II. 198/2 The Tike is another kind of Louse,..a Companion for Dogs, Sheep, and Cattle. **1748** *Anson's Voy.* III. ii. 314 An insect called a tick, which, though principally attached to the cattle, would yet frequently fasten upon our limbs and bodies. **1839** DARWIN *Voy. Nat.* i. (1879) 10 A tick which must have come here as a parasite on the birds. **1882** *Garden* 14 Jan. 20/1 The horses..were covered with large blue ticks.

† **b.** Applied in contempt or insult to a person.

**1631** A. WILSON *Swisser* II. i, Yee nigling Ticks you.

**2.** Short for *tick-bean*: see 3.

**1765** *Treat. Dom. Pigeons* 28 Horse-beans are the next food...There is a sort which they call French ticks, which are good food. **1850–2** MORTON *Cycl. Agric.* (1855) I. 200/2 There are several other varieties of the Tick bean in cultivation, known locally [as] Harrow Tick, Flat Tick, Essex Tick, and French Tick.

**3.** *attrib.* and *Comb.*, as *tick genus*, *plague*; **tick-bean**, a small-seeded variety of the common bean, *Vicia Faba*, so called from the resemblance of the seed to a dog-tick; **tick-bird**, a bird which feeds on the ticks that infest large quadrupeds, as the African genus *Buphaga* (rhinoceros-bird) and the S. American and W. Indian *Crotophaga ani*; **tick-eater** = *tick-bird*; **tick fever**, a fever (in men or cattle) caused by the bites of ticks; **tick-fly**, any of the dipterous insects called ticks (see 1); **tick-seed**, name for various plants having seeds resembling ticks, as † the castor-oil plant, *Ricinus communis* (obs.), and the genera *Coreopsis* and *Corispermum*; also = *tick-trefoil*; **tick-seeded** *a.*, having seeds resembling ticks; **tick-spider**, name for a jumping spider; † **tick spot**, a marking as if bitten by a tick: cf. TICKED *a.*; **tick-trefoil**, a plant of the genus *Desmodium*, so named from the joints of the pods adhering like ticks to the fur of animals; **tick-weed**, † (*a*) the castor-oil plant (see *tick-seed* above); (*b*) the American pennyroyal, *Hedeoma pulegioides*.

**1763** *Museum Rust.* (ed. 2) I. 187 The methods followed ..in sowing horse beans, or *tick-beans, as we sometimes call them. **1805** *Trans. Soc. Arts* XXIII. 36 One stalk of the tick bean had 70 pods. **1863** W. C. BALDWIN *Afr. Hunting* ix. 389, I was much amused by watching the *tick birds trying to alarm an old white rhinoceros, that we were approaching from under the wind. **1871** KINGSLEY *At Last* v, The black 'tick birds' (Crotophaga Ani), a little larger than our English blackbird. **1896** BADEN-POWELL *Matabele Campaign* xviii. 133 Colenbrander..they have called the 'tick-bird'—a bird which in this country always accompanies a bull, to relieve him of superfluous ticks. **1903** *Daily Chron.* 11 June 3/3 The gulls,..like the small *tick eaters which live on African game, delighted in warning their friends of our approach. **1901** *Lancet* 23 Nov. 1432/1 *Tick fever is widely distributed throughout the world...It is communicated to cattle by insects known as 'ticks'. **1658** ROWLAND *Moufet's Theat. Ins.* 949 Those things that kill and drive away the *Tyke-flies called *Ricini*, for the most part kill and drive away the Dog-flies. **1889** *Cent. Dict.* s.v. *Hippobosca*, *H. equina* is a winged tick-fly of the horse. **1822–34** *Good's Study Med.* (ed. 4) I. 263 Linnæus..laboured..to prove, that dysentery is the effect of a..larva..belonging to the acarus or *tick genus. **1896** *Daily News* 23 Nov. 8/5 The *tick-plague in Queensland..is not so terrible a scourge as the South African rinderpest. **1562** TURNER *Herbal* II. 116 Ricinus is called..in English palma Christi, or *ticke sede...The sede..when the huske is of..looketh very lyke a dogge louse which is called a tyke. **1760** J. LEE *Introd. Bot.* App. 329 Tickseed, *Corispermum*. **1860** WORCESTER, *Tickseed sunflower*, a smooth-branched herb, having golden-yellow, showy rays; *Coreopsis trichosperma*. *Gray*. **1786** ABERCROMBIE *Arrangem.* in *Gard. Assist.* 54/2 *Coreopsis*, *tick-seeded sunflower. **1721** BRADLEY *Philos. Acc. Wks. Nat.* 135 The Jumper or *Tick Spider. **1704** *Lond. Gaz.* No. 4079/4 A..Greyhound..with some white *Tick Spots. **1857** GRAY *First Less. Bot.* (1866) 127 A one-celled ovary sometimes becomes several-celled..by the formation of false partitions,..as in the jointed pod of the Sea-Rocket and the *Tick-Trefoil. **1563** HYLL *Art Garden.* (1593) 32 The hearbe named *Tick-weed, otherwise in Latin *Palma Christi*. **1884** MILLER *Plant-n.*, Tick-weed, *Hedeoma pulegioides*.

**Tick** (tik), *sb.*[2] Forms: α. 5 tikke, tykk(e, 6 tycke, 6–7 ticke, 6– tick; β. 5–6 teke, 7 teike; γ. (chiefly *Sc.*) 5– tyke, 6 tyik, 6– tike (təik). [Known from 15th c., in the forms *tikke*, *tēke*, *tȳke*; the second corresp. to MLG. and MDu. *têke* (mod.EFris. *têk*, Doornkaat-Koolman), cognate with OHG. *ziahha*, *ziecha*, MHG., Ger. *zieche* bed-tick, pillow-case; the third to MDu. *tîke*, *tijcke*, Du. *tijk*. These forms point to an earlier WGer. **tēka*, and later **tīka*, both a. L. *tēca*, *thēca*, a. Gr. θήκη case, whence also F. *teie*, *taie*, obs. Eng. TAY, TEY. The short vowel in *tykke*, *tikke*, *ticke*, *tick*, is prob. as in *rick*, *sick*, *wick*.]

The case or cover containing feathers, flocks, or the like, forming a mattress or pillow; also, from 16th c., applied to the strong hard linen or cotton material used for making such cases.

α. **1466** *Mann. & Househ. Exp.* (Roxb.) 362 For iij. tykkes [*pr.* tylkes] and bolsteres to the same fore federbeddes. **1480** *Wardr. Acc. Edw. IV* (1830) 118 To Lisbet Ketiller for a grete tikke xxxijs. **1530** PALSGR. 281/1 Ticke for a fetherbed, *coite de lit*. **1569** *Wills & Inv. N. C.* (Surtees) I. 311 One fether bed, the tycke therof I dyd by. **1586** *Rates of Custome* E viij b, Ticks called Brussel ticks, the Tick xiij.s. iiij.d. **1636** *Althorp MS.* in Simpkinson *Washingtons* (1860) App. p. lxxvii, For 2 feather bed ticks for Alexander. **1743** *Phil. Trans.* XLII. 367 Those Ticks and Pillow-biers covering the Matresses and Pillows. **1812** W. TENNANT *Anster F.* II. xxviii, Dunfermline, too, so fam'd checks and ticks. **1842** S. LOVER *Handy Andy* vi, The deep pocket of blue striped tick which hung at her side.

β. **1494** FABYAN *Chron.* VII. 414 And of federbeddes [they] rypped the tekys. **1570** LEVINS *Manip.* 54/25 Ye Teke of a bed, *teca culcitaria*. *c* **1615** in Walcott *William of Wykeham* (1852) 167, 3 yeards of teike for a boulster.

γ. **1495** in Pitcairn *Crim. Trials* I. 20*, iij le tykis de feddirbeddis. **1502** *Acc. Ld. High Treas. Scot.* II. 295 For tua tikis of feddir beddis to hir. **1534** *Inv. Wardr. Kath. Arragon* in *Camden Misc.* (1855) 31 A paliotte of Brusells tyke filled with bastardedowne. **1545** *Rates of Custome* C vij, Tikes for beddes the dossen xxxvj.s. Tikes the pece iij.s. **1573–80** BARET *Alv.* T 241 The tike of a bed: a featherbed. **1580** *Aberdeen Regr.* (1848) II. 36 Auchtene codvarris wiht sextene tyikis. **1618** SIR R. BOYLE in *Lismore Papers* (1886) I. 191, I bought 2 fetherbed tykes. **1806** FORSYTH *Beauties Scotl.* III. 146 The children sleep in beds..with tikes filled with straw.

**b.** 'Used for the bed or bolster itself: as, "That's the tyke or tyken o' the bed: a guid feather tyke or tyken [= tyking]"' (*Suppl. to Jamieson*, 1887).

More distinctively *tyke o' bed*, or *tyke-a-bed*.

**Tick** (tik), *sb.*[3] Forms: 5 tek, tekk, 6–7 ticke, 7 tyck, 6– tick. [Not known *a* 1440, the vb. (TICK *v.*[1]) appearing a century later. Parallels to sb. and vb. appear in Du. *tik* a pat, touch, tick, *tikken* to pat, tick, LG. *tikk* a touch, also a moment, instant, with *ticken* or *tikken* vb., Norw. *tikke* to touch lightly, also MHG. *zic* 'a light touch or push', and *zicken* vb. These may indicate a common OTeut. source, or they may be of later onomatopœic formation, the expression in 'vocal gesture' of the act or sound in question.]

**1.** A light but distinct touch; a light quick stroke; a pat, a tap. *Obs.* exc. *dial.*

*c* **1440** *Promp. Parv.* 487/2 Tek, or lytylle towche (*K.* tekk or lytyl strock), *tactulus*. **1580** SIDNEY *Let.* 18 Oct. in Collins *Lett.* (1746) I. 285 When you play at Weapons..play out your Play lustilie, for indeed Tickes and Daliances are nothing in earnest. **1621** S. WARD *Life of Faith* 84 The least ticke befalls the not, without the ouer-ruling eye and hand..of a wise God. **1625** LISLE *Du Bartas, Noe* 13 He makes us only afraid With fingers tyck. **1674** N. FAIRFAX *Bulk & Selv.* 96 If the forestroke give us but a little tick, the backstroke will be sure to give him a knocker. *a* **1825** FORBY *Voc. E. Anglia*, *Tick*, a very gentle touch, by way of hint, or as a token of endearment.

**b.** A children's game in which the object is to overtake and touch; = TIG *sb.* 2.

**1622** DRAYTON *Poly-olb.* xxx. 144 The Mountaine Nymphs ..doe giue each other chase, At Hood-winke, Barley-breake, at Tick, or Prison-base. **1884** BLACK *Jud. Shaks.* iii, The children playing tick round the grave-stones.

**2.** A quick light dry sound, distinct but not loud, as that caused by the sudden impact of a small hard body upon a hard surface; *esp.* the sound produced by the alternate check and release of the train in the escapement of a watch or clock; also the similar sound made by the death-watch beetle.

Also (repeated) adverbially or interjectionally, as an imitation of this sound: see also TICK-TICK.

**1680** AUBREY *Lives* (1898) I. 28 He [Thomas Allen] happened to leave his watch in the chamber windowe...The maydes..hearing a thing in a case cry Tick, Tick, Tick, presently concluded that that was his Devill. **1702** RAY *Rem.* (1780) 324 The leisurely and constant Tick of the Death-Watch. **1861** *Walsall Free Press* 7 Dec., By a simple arrangement of ticks and intervals..the clerk was enabled to copy the [telegraphic] messages with the utmost rapidity. **1871** TYNDALL *Fragm. Sc.* (1879) I. xxii. 496 Ellicott set one clock going by the ticks of another. **1910** *Nation* 8 Jan. 604/2 With just a 'tick' of his [a robin's] alarm note.

**b.** A beat of the heart or of the pulse.

**1823** BYRON *Juan* x. xxxix, Her physician..found the tick Of his fierce pulse betoken a condition Which augured of the dead. **1855** BROWNING *An Epistle* 194 Something, a word, a tick o' the blood within Admonishes.

**3.** A small dot or dash (often formed by two small strokes at an acute angle), made with a pen or pencil, to draw attention to something or to mark a name, figure, etc., in a list as having been noted or checked. In quot. 1860 used in plural for inverted commas.

**1844** *Fraser's Mag.* XXX. 88/1 Neat pencil ticks indicated favourite passages. **1860** MRS. CARLYLE *Lett.* (1883) III. 48 To..interlard his own note with single words or whole lines of yours 'in ticks'. **1863** *Reader* 28 Nov. 638 A tick at the beginning and end of it..shows of what extent the passage is to be. **1865** DICKENS *Mut. Fr.* III. i, Those lots that I'd mark with my pencil—there's a tick there, and a tick there. **1898** SIR E. HAMILTON in *Daily News* 8 Nov. 6/1 Whether the copy was entered in a large letter-book, or made on a separate sheet, depended on his having made one 'tick' or two 'ticks' at the bottom of the first page.

**b.** A small spot or speck of colour on the skin or coat of an animal.

**1873** D. MACLAGAN in *Mod. Scot. Poets* (1881) III. 181 The ticks upon his gawsy side Show him a new-rin saumon.

**4.** *transf.* (from 2). The time between two ticks of the clock; a moment, second, instant. *colloq.*

**1879** BROWNING *Ned Bratts* 193 Waste no tick of moment more. **1904** JEROME *Tommy & Co.* (ed. Tauchn.) 236 It's all right. Can explain in two ticks. **1907** PHYLLIS DARE *Fr. School to Stage* v, At eight o'clock to the tick, the day's regular lesson's began. **1909** HORNUNG *Mr. Justice Raffles* i. 6, I should have been spotted in a tick by a spy.

**Tick,** *sb.*[4] *colloq.* or *slang.* [app. abbreviation of TICKET *sb.*[1] 7 in the phrase *on the ticket*. Chronology forbids derivation from TICK *v.*[1] 3 or *sb.*[3] 3, which has sometimes been conjectured.]

**1.** Phrases. *On* or *upon* († *the*) *tick*, on credit, on trust (cf. *on ticket*, TICKET *sb.*[1] 7); *to go on tick* (also *go tick*), *run on*, *upon* († *in*) *tick*, to buy on credit, run into debt.

**1642** *Brit. Mus. Add. MS.* 37999 lf. 66 They would haue ..run on tick with Piggin for inke and songs, rather than haue lost the show of your presence. **1668** DRYDEN *Evening's Love* III. i, Play on tick, and lose the Indies, I'll discharge it all tomorrow. **1672** WYCHERLEY *Love in Wood* III. i, A poor wretch that goes on tick for the paper he writes his lampoons on! **1849** THACKERAY *Pendennis* ii, When he had no funds he went on tick. **1861** HUGHES *Tom Brown at Oxf.* i, 'Going tick' for everything which could by possibility be booked. **1892** STEVENSON *Across the Plains* ii. 100 This villainous habit of living upon tick.

**2.** Hence, Credit; trust; reputation of solvency and probity.

**1668** SEDLEY *Mulb. Gard.* II. ii, I confess my Tick is not good, and I never desire to Game for more than I have about me. **1718** RAMSAY *Christ's Kirk Gr.* III. xiv, Wasted was baith cash and tick. **1788** *Trifler* No. 2. 26 If you can cure him, Dr. Bolus, you shall have the best cheese in my shop, and tick for another. **1894** BLACKMORE *Perlycross* 105 Giving tick unlimited, or even remission of all charges.

**3.** A debit account; a score, account, reckoning.

**1681** PRIDEAUX *Lett.* 21 May (Camden) 83 The Marmayd Tavern is lately broke, and we Christ Church men bear ye blame of it, our ticks, as ye noise of ye town will have it, amounteing to 1500l. **1712** ARBUTHNOT *John Bull* III. vii, Paying ready Money, that the Maids might not run a Tick at the Market. **1755** *Connoisseur* No. 92 He..had a long tick at the tavern. **1840** J. T. HEWLETT *P. Priggins* xiv, Oh, never mind paying; I've got a tick here. **1862** THACKERAY *Philip* xxxviii, There are some of my college ticks ain't paid now...Tailors' ticks, tavern ticks, livery-stable ticks.

**Tick** (tik), *sb.*5 Rarely tic. [ad. F. *tic* in same senses: cf. TIC (which retains the Fr. spelling).]

**1.** The vice or morbid habit in horses called crib-biting or cribbing. Cf. TICK *v.*3

**1720** W. GIBSON *Diet. Horses* v. (1731) 83 There is another Vice which some Horses are addicted to..called the *Tick*.

**2.** A whim, a fancy; a peculiar habit or notion, an idiosyncrasy.

[**1896** *Daily News* 30 Sept. 6/3 It is mere 'tic' or habit.] **1900** 'SARAH GRAND' *Babs* ix, She's got some tick in her head about being firm with me.

**Tick,** *sb.*6 [Echoic.] A local name of the whinchat.

**1848** *Zoologist* VI. 2137 The whinchat has the nickname 'utick', or, more simply is sometimes merely a 'tick' from its well-known note.

**Tick** (tik), *v.*1 [f. TICK *sb.*3: cf. Du. *tikken* to pat, tick, Norw. *tikke* to touch lightly.]

**1.** *intr.* To touch or tap a thing or person lightly; *esp.* to bestow light touches or pats by way of caressing; to dally; *esp.* in phr. *tick and toy*; *fig.* to trifle. *Obs.* exc. *dial.*

**1546** J. HEYWOOD *Prov.* (1867) 44 Their tickyng might haue tought Any yonge couple their loue tickes to haue wrought. **1550** LATIMER *Last Serm. bef. Edw. VI* 108 Stand not ticking and toying at the braunches..but strike at the roote. **1682** BUNYAN *Holy War* xii. 268 His sons began to play his pranks, and to be ticking and toying with the daughters of their lord. **1684** — *Adv. Sufferers* Wks. (ed. Offor) II. 738 Though they may but tick and toy with thee at first, their sword may reach thy heart-blood at last. *a* **1825** FORBY *Voc. E. Anglia*, *Tick*, *v.* to toy. Indeed the two are often used together;..two fond sweethearts are sometimes seen 'ticking and toying'.

†**b.** *trans. To tick up*: to lift smartly, whip up.

**1586** WARNER *Alb. Eng.* II. xi, Then ticks he vp her tucked Frocke, nor did Calysto blush.

**2.** *intr.* Of a clock, watch, etc.: To make the light quick sound described under TICK *sb.*3 2.

**1721, 1746–7** [see TICKING *ppl. a.*1, *vbl. sb.*1 2]. **1775** ASH, *Tick*, to make a small quick noise like that of a watch. **1806** J. TRAIN *Poet. Reveries* 94 (Jam.) When she heard the Dead-watch tick. **1812** H. & J. SMITH *Rej. Addr.*, *Playhouse Mus.*, I heard a trowel tick against a brick. **1820** W. IRVING *Sketch Bk.* I. 249 An old fashioned clock ticked in one corner. **1864** THACKERAY *D. Duval* iv, The watch is ticking on the table before me as I write.

**b.** *trans.* with various complements: To wear *away* or *out*, bring to an end, in ticking; to throw *off* or deliver by ticking (as a telegraph).

*c* **1870** W. FREELAND in *Whistlebinkie* (1890) II. 322 You [a wagtail] wag and tick the ages out Quicker still and quicker. **1880** MISS BROUGHTON *Sec. Th.* II. iv, More days pass;..none bringing..much change in..Gillian's life. The clocks tick it monotonously away. **1892** *Leisure Hour* Apr. 411/2 Each slow moment as it ticked itself away was a blow to hope. **1902** *Strand Mag.* Jan. 71/1 The young woman laughed at the answer as it was ticked off to her. **1906** *Daily News* 20 Apr. 6 A telegraphist..ticking out tidings of the affair from its scene.

**c.** *transf.* (*intr.*) To beat, pulse, throb.

**1868** BROWNING *Ring & Bk.* I. 37 When hearts beat hard, And brains, high-blooded, ticked two centuries since.

**3.** *trans.* To mark (a name, an item in a list, etc.) with a tick; to mark *off* with a tick, as noted, passed, or done with. Also *fig.*; *colloq.* to identify.

**1861** DICKENS *Gt. Expect.* xxxiv, I compared each with the bill, and ticked it off. **1871** L. STEPHEN *Playgr. Eur.* (1894) xiii. 323 One more task ticked off from their memorandum book. **1874** GREEN *Short Hist.* vi. § 6. 335 Fragments of his [Thos. Cromwell's] papers still show us with what a business-like brevity he ticked off human lives. **1893** G. ALLEN *Scallywag* I. 17 Ticking him off on her list. *Mod.* I ticked him off as soon as I set eyes on him.

**b.** To mark with small ticks or spots of colour. (But cf. TICKED *a.*, TICKING *vbl. sb.*1 3.)

**1910** *19th Cent.* May 915 The white ticked here and there with black.

**Tick** (tik), *v.*2 *colloq.* or *slang.* [f. TICK *sb.*4]

**1.** *intr.* To 'go on tick' (see TICK *sb.*4 1); to deal with a tradesman, etc. on credit, to take credit; to run into debt, leave one's debts unpaid.

**1648** WINYARD *Midsummer-Moon* 6 He must tick with Charon, and have his Epitaph writ in chalk. *a* **1683** OLDHAM *Poet. Wks.* (1686) 90 Who thither flock to Ghostly Confessor, To clear old debts, and tick with Heaven for more. **1742** FIELDING *Miss Lucy in Town* Wks. 1882 X. 310, I gave that sum to my wife..to buy her clothes. I'll take it from her again, and let her tick with the tradesmen.

**b.** *trans.* To leave (an amount) owing to be entered to one's debit.

**1674** S. VINCENT *Y. Gallant's Acad.* 80 He..tick[s] his reckoning, that he may keep half a Crown in his Pocket. **1712** MRS. CENTLIVRE *Perplexed Lovers* I. i, The Devil a bottle can I tick because he has forsworn the tavern.

**2.** *intr.* To give credit; to supply goods, professional aid, etc. on credit.

**1712** ARBUTHNOT *John Bull* III. viii, The money went to the lawyers; counsel won't tick, Sir. **1721** AMHERST *Terræ Fil.* No. 46 (1754) 247 Smarts in Oxford..who cannot afford to be thus fine any longer than their mercers, taylors, shoemakers,..will tick with them. **1840** J. T. HEWLETT *P. Priggins* xiii, Sykes is your man—ticks for ever, and never duns.

**b.** *trans.* To give (a person) credit.

**1842** APPERLEY ('Nimrod') *Life Sportsman* v, He never refused me a tandem, and he ticked me for a terrier at once.

†**Tick,** *v.*3 *Obs. rare.* [f. TICK *sb.*5] *intr.* Of a horse: To practise crib-biting; = CRIB *v.* 9.

**1720** W. GIBSON *Diet. Horses* v. (1731) 84 While they do this, they give a Belch through their throat, which is that which we call *Ticking*. Some Horses Tick upon the Trench, and some..upon any post or rail they can come at ..because it is sometimes communicated by example, a Ticker ought therefore to stand by himself.

**Tick,** variant of TEAK.

**Tick-a-tick.** [f. same source as TICK *v.*1 or *sb.*3] An imitation of the sound of a clock or watch; ticking; in quot. 1805, throbbing of the pulse. So **Tick-a-tack.** (Cf. TICK-TACK, TICK-TICK.)

**1805** in *Spirit Pub. Jrnls.* IX. 243 Munro shall count of pulse his tick-a-tick. **1883** D. R. SELLARS in *Mod. Scot. Poets* VI. 157 Tick-a-tick, tick-a-tick, My old clock's voice I hear. **1898** DOYLE in *Speaker* 5 Mar. 298/1 The clock goes tick-a-tack.

**Ticked** (tikt), *a.* [f. TICK *sb.*1 + -ED 2: see quot. 1688, and cf. *flea-bitten*; in mod. use associated with TICK *sb.*3 3 b.] Of a dog: Having small markings or spots as if bitten by ticks: cf. *tick spot* (TICK *sb.*1 3); hence of birds, etc.: spotted, dotted.

**1688** R. HOLME *Armoury* III. 185/2 Ticked, when a Dog is spotted with black on white, or with white spots on black, and the like of the fallow and white, which proceeds from the biteing of Ticks. **1828** MISS MITFORD *Village* Ser. III. Introd. 6 The puppy..is fawn-coloured with a dash of white, and promises to be ticked. Are you sportswoman sufficient to know that *ticked* means covered all over with white spots about the size of a pea? **1873** *Spectator* 22 Feb. 239/2 Canaries,..the evenly marked Yellows and Buffs, the 'ticked' or unevenly marked Yellows and Buffs. **1897** *Outing* (U.S.) XXIX. 367/2 Dora [a dog] was so closely ticked that when in a brush-heap checkered black and white, it was almost impossible to see her. **1902** *Fur & Feather* 19 Sept. 207/2 Cats...Female..smooth grey ticked.

**Ticked** (tikt), *ppl. a.* [f. TICK *sb.*3 or *v.*1 + -ED.] **a.** Formed or represented by a series of ticks: as 'a ticked line', one formed thus ·······.

**1833** RICHARDSON *Merc. Mar. Arch.* 22 A ticked line through all these spots will form the cant frame. *c* **1850** *Rudim. Navig.* (Weale) 93 A batten..will form the ticked curve A D B.

**b.** Marked or marked *off* with a tick.

**1863** THERRY *Australia* (title-p.) A supplementary chapter on Transportation and the Ticked-off System.

†**Ti·ckel.** *Obs. rare.* [dim. (?) of TICK *sb.*1: see -EL 2.] = TICK *sb.*1 1.

**1577** B. GOOGE *Heresbach's Husb.* (1586) 143 If they [sheep] be lowsie, or full of tickels, they vse to beate the rootes of Maple, and seething them in water, and opening the wooll with their fingers, they powre the licour. **1741** *Compl. Fam.-Piece* III. 492 To destroy Ticks or Tickels in Sheep.

**Tickel, -ell,** obs. forms of TACKLE, TICKLE.

**Ticken** (ti·k'n, ti·kĕn). [A dialectal form of TICKING *sb.*, the ending app. sometimes associated with -EN 4, as in *hempen*, *woollen*, etc.] = TICKING *sb.*, TICK *sb.*2 Also *attrib.*

**1701** *Lond. Gaz.* No. 3739/4 Striped Ticken Breeches. **1707** E. CHAMBERLAYNE *Pres. St. Eng.* I. iii. (ed. 22) 20 The chief Manufactures are Woollen Cloaths, Cottons, and Ticken. **1769** *De Foe's Tour Gt. Brit.* I. 93 Part of a Street of Booths was taken up with Upholsters Ware; such as Tickens, Sackens,..Rugs, Quilts, &c. **1843** BORROW *Bible in Spain* xi. 78 A long loose tunic or slop, seemingly of coarse ticken.

†**Ti·cker** 1. *Obs. rare.* [f. TICK *v.*3 + -ER 1.] A cribbing horse, a crib-biter.

**1720** [see TICK *v.*3]. **1796** LAWRENCE *Treat. Horses* iv. 218 The crib-biter, formerly called a ticker...These horses will stand biting at the rack, or manger, or even at a post, throwing themselves backward, and sucking in the air with greediness.

**Ti·cker** 2. *slang.* ? *Obs.* [? f. TICK *v.*2 + -ER 1.] ? One who obtains goods 'on tick' and never pays for them; a fraudulent debtor.

**1753** (*title*) The Thief-Catcher .. Containing an ample Discovery of the..Frauds now practised by Highwaymen, Tickers, Gypsies, Horse-stealers [etc.].

**Ticker** 3 (ti·kəɹ). [f. TICK *v.*1 + -ER 1.] Something that ticks. **a.** The pendulum or escapement of a clock or watch; also (*slang*) a watch (rarely, as in quot. 1910, a clock).

**1828** [MOIR] *Mansie Wauch* xxv. (1849) 204 Went to and fro like the ticker of a clock. **1829** MAGINN in *Mem. Vidocq* IV. App. 261 Then his ticker I set a-going, With his onions, chain, and key. **1838** DICKENS *O. Twist* xviii, If you don't take fogles and tickers..some other cove will. **1888** RIDER HAGGARD *Col. Quaritch* xxviii, I've sold all my jewels down to my ticker. **1910** *Contemp. Rev.* July 36 Secreting a copy of Keats behind the ticker.

**b.** A telegraphic recording instrument, a tape-machine; a stock-indicator.

**1883** F. M. CRAWFORD *Dr. Claudius* (1892) 173 A couple of wheels that unwound..long strips of white paper..covered with unintelligible signs. 'That is the ticker', said Barker; and he explained how every variation in the market was instantly transmitted to every place of business..in New York. *Ibid.* 174 'It [the ticker] is the pulse of New York', said Barker...'It tells us everything. Nobody can live here without a ticker'. **1889** *Pall Mall G.* 22 Jan. 7/2 In New York..news agency 'tickers', messenger calls, private as well as public telephones, burglar and fire alarms,..are to be found in all well appointed offices. **1896** *Proc. N. Eng. Hist. Genealog. Soc.* 158 With Edison in 1870 he [F. L. Pope] invented the one-wire printing telegraph or 'ticker'. **1902** *Munsey's Mag.* XXVI. 542/2 Stock and general news tickers..reporting bad news.

**Ticket** (ti·kėt), *sb.*1 Also 6 *Sc.* **tikket, -ett, tek-, ticet, tikk-, tykkatt, tik-, tek-, tecat,** 6–7 *Sc.* **tiket,** 6–8 **tickett,** 7 **tik-, tyckett, tiquet,** *Sc.* **tickket.** [In 16th c. (1528) *tiket*, aphetic form of **etiket*, a. obs. F. *etiquet* 'a little note, breuiate, bill, or ticket; especially such a one, as is stucke vp on the gate of a Court, signifying the seisure &c of an inheritance by order of iustice'; or the parallel F. *étiquette* 'a ticket fastened within the mouth of a Lawyers booke bag, and containing the titles of the bookes, [etc.]; any inscription, superscription, title, note, or marke set on th'outside of a thing ..; also, a token, billet, or ticket, deliuered for the benefit, or aduantage of him that receiues it' (Cotgr.):—OF. *estiquet(te* (1387 in Hatz.-Darm.), f. *estiquer*, to stick, fix, from Teutonic; ad. OLG. *stek-an* = OHG. *stehhan*, Ger. *stechen* to stick, fix. The primary sense was 'a little note or notice affixed to anything, a label', whence extended as in Cotgrave, and in the senses below. It is notable that our earliest instances are Irish and Scotch; but English examples in some senses appear *c* 1600. See also ETIQUETTE, repr. a later sense of the Fr. word.]

**1.** A short written notice or document; a memorandum, a note, a billet. †*In ticket*, in writing (*Sc.*). *Obs.* exc. as in b, c.

This general sense is present in nearly all those that follow, which differ mainly in respect of the purpose or use to which the written statement or note is put.

**1528** in *10th Rep. Hist. MSS. Comm.* App. v. 403 The Bailiefe shall not priese no flesh..unlesse he can get a tiket or bill of the merchanndes hand with the boucher to whom he had sold the same. **1589** *Reg. Privy Council Scot* IV. 395 To present thair desiris in tikkatt to the Lordis compositouris. *c* **1600** JAS. VI in *3rd Rep. Hist. MSS. Comm.* 396/2 Sicc soumis as the Duike of Lenox hes in tickket. **1622** MALYNES *Anc. Law-Merch.* 411 The Bankers..haue a meeting, and by certaine tickets in writing euerie man doth deliuer his opinion, what the price of Exchange ought to be. **1627** USSHER *Lett.* (1686) 374 The Bishop of Derry hath left with me his Ticket, wherein he undertakes to pay 50£ unto any one of the Captains to whom your Lordship shall appoint. **1638** BAKER tr. *Balzac's Lett.* (vol. II.) 157 If your ticket had overtaken me at Orleans, I had certainly returned to Paris. **1661** PEPYS *Diary* 12 Apr., While I am now writing, comes one with a tickett to invite me to Captain Robert Blake's buriall. **1755** in *Hist. Rev. Pennsylvania* (1759), Every one votes as he pleases, the election being by written tickets, folded up and put in a box. **1760** HOOPER in *Priv. Lett. Ld. Malmesbury* (1870) I. 82 A page delivered him a ticket, importing that something had happened to the (late) King.

**b.** *spec.* A written tender for ore, made by the smelter. Cf. TICKETING *vbl. sb.* 2. *local.*

**1778** PRYCE *Min. Cornub.* 287 The highest bidder or ticket should be the purchaser. *a* **1856** PARIS in Jago *Cornw. Gloss.* (1882) 291 Those [agents] of various Companies..produce a sealed ticket of the price they will give for ore; and he whose ticket is highest, takes the ore. **1870** J. PERCY *Metall. Lead* 496 Each Mine sends samples of its ore to the Smelters in various localities, along with a notice to the effect that tenders or tickets will be received up to a certain day, on which they will be opened and the highest offer accepted.

**c.** *Stock Exch.*: see quot. 1882–93.

**1882–93** BITHELL *Counting-Ho. Dict.* s. v. *Ticket Day*, The day for the passing of tickets between brokers and jobbers, by means of which they learn the amount of stocks and shares they have respectively to deliver or receive on the day following. **1912** *Stock Exchange Ticket*, All rights in respect of this ticket are hereby claimed. *Ibid.*, If this Ticket be divided, insert Number and name of party dividing it, or New Ticket will not be paid for.

**2.** A written notice for public information; formerly, a notice posted in a public place; a placard; now *esp.* a slip of cardboard, metal, paper, etc., attached to an object, and bearing its name, description, price, or the like; a label, show-card.

(This may have been the original sense.)

**1567** *Reg. Privy Council Scot.* I. 504 At the occasioun of sum tikkettis affixt on the Tolbuyth dur of Edinburgh, be his lettre sent to hir Majestie, [he] had desyrit James Erll Bothwell, and certane specifiit in the saidis tikkettis, to be apprehendit. *a* **1661** FULLER *Worthies, Buckingham.* (1662) I. 137 Giving notice of the time to his Auditours in a ticket on the School-dores. **1691–** [implied in TICKET *v.* 1]. **1766** in *Westm. Gaz.* 22 Apr. (1910) 2/3 The seats in the House of Commons were begun to be taken for the members by pinning down a ticket with their names in such seats as they chose, which were reserved for them till prayers began. **1804** *Aston's Manch. Guide* 162 A ticket is affixed to each patient's bed, mentioning his name, and that of his physician or surgeon; the time of admission, and the diet ordered for him. **1848** THACKERAY *Van. Fair* xl, The ticket in the window which announced 'Apartments to Let'. **1851** MANTELL *Petrifact.* iv. § 1. 365 The same coloured margin as that on the ticket 'Quartz', surrounds every specimen of quartz in that Case.

**3.** (More fully *visiting ticket.*) A visiting-card. Now *Obs.* or *dial.*; also *Anglo-Ind.*

**1673** [R. LEIGH] *Transp. Reh.* 142, I shall only therefore leave a ticket for his assignes. **1773** LADY MARY COKE *Jrnl.* 30 Nov., Sir Horatio Mann..has desired me to leave a ticket with the *Grande Maitresse* to-morrow. **1778** MRS. THRALE *Let. to Johnson* 11 Nov., Your visiting ticket has been left very completely in Wales. Was it the fashion to leave cards in Prior's time? **1782** MISS BURNEY *Cecilia* I. iii, Why, a ticket is only a visiting card, with a name upon it; but we all call them tickets now. **1862** THACKERAY *Philip* xiii, Poor dear Mrs. Jones..still calls on the ladies of your family and slips her husband's ticket upon the hall table. **1900** C. LEE *Cynthia* ii. 20 Mr. Gibbs come in just now..and left his ticket over the chimley.

†**4.** A writing in which something is certified or authorized; a certificate or voucher; a warrant, licence, permit. Also *fig.*

**1529** *Aberdeen Regr.* (1844) I. 126 Conforme to the saidis maisteris of warkis tikatis. **1553** *Exch. Rolls Scot.* XVIII. 377 Pas this rentell to the lard of Rawelloun..and kep this our tecat for your varrand. *a* **1592** GREENE *Jas. IV*, III. ii, I am the king's purveyor..Here's my ticket, deny it if thou darest. **1615** *Nottingham Rec.* (1889) IV. 334 The Schoole Wardens shall not hencefurth pay or doo any reparacions vpon the howse..without a tyckett for the same vnder Maister Maior's hand. **1641** EVELYN *Diary* 28 Aug., He..then deliver'd me a ticket by virtue whereof I was made excise-free. **1675** V. ALSOP *Anti-sozzo* 554 Paul would have past for a Righteous person upon his producing the Ticket of a blameless Conversation.

**b.** = CERTIFICATE *sb.* 3 b. *slang.*

*c* **1900** CUTCLIFFE HYNE *Master of Fortune* i. (Cent. Suppl.), I'm Captain of the whole of this show now,..and I intend to be respected as such, and hold a full captain's ticket.

**5.** A slip, usually of paper or cardboard, bearing the evidence of the holder's title to some service or privilege, to which it admits him; as a *theatre-ticket*, *railway* or *tramway ticket*, *insurance-ticket*, *lottery-ticket*, *lecture-ticket*, *platform-ticket* (at a meeting), *communion-ticket*, *member's ticket*, *luncheon-ticket*, *soup-ticket*, etc.

**1673** *Galston Sess. Rec.* in Edgar *Old Ch. Life Scot.* (1885) 173 *note*, Several hunders of tickets ar distribute. **1682** LUTTRELL *Brief Rel.* (1857) I. 179 The parties were invited by tickets, of which any man might have one for a guiney, it being the price thereof. **1697–8**, **1710** [see LOTTERY 5, 1]. **1710** HEARNE *Collect.* (O.H.S.) III. 40 The Tickett of a 1000 libs per annum for 32 Years. **1741** WESLEY *Wks.* (1872) I. 301 To those who were sufficiently recommended tickets were given. *a* **1845** HOOD *Double Knock* 11 Sure he has brought me tickets for the play. **1878** F. S. WILLIAMS *Midl. Railw.* 626 The printing of tickets is effected by an ingeniously constructed machine. **1898** FLOR. MONTGOMERY *Tony* 17 You have got your ticket quite safe, haven't you? **1906** *Macm. Mag.* June 625 Subscribers may obtain from the Society supplies of food-tickets, each representing two-pennyworth of food. *Mod.* Admission only by ticket.

**b.** *fig.*

**1713** STEELE *Englishman* No. 21. 135 Your Approbation is the Ticket by which they gain Admittance into your Paper. **1784** COWPER *Task* III. 98 Well dressed, well bred, Well equipaged, is ticket good enough, To pass us readily through every door. **1852** THACKERAY *Esmond* II. xi, Within a month after this day, Mr. Addison's ticket had come up a prodigious prize in the lottery of life. **1864** *Soc. Sc. Rev.* I. 409 Men who have robbed employers, or in some other way sullied their fair fame (in cab language 'lost the ticket') but who have not been..prosecuted, easily become cabmen.

**6.** A pay-warrant; *esp.* a discharge warrant in which the amount of pay due to a soldier or sailor is certified.

**1596** SPENSER *State Irel.* Wks. (Globe) 657/2 There should be a pay-master appoynted, of speciall trust, which should paye everye man according to his captaynes tickett, and the accompte of the clarke of his bande. **1665** PEPYS *Diary* 5 Dec., Mr. Stevens, who is..paying of seamen of their tickets at Deptford. **1836** MARRYAT *Midsh. Easy* xl, Gascoigne, having received his discharge-ticket, went on board of the Rebiera. **1849** MACAULAY *Hist. Eng.* iii. I. 299 The sailors were paid with so little punctuality that they were glad to find some usurer who would purchase their tickets at forty per cent discount. **1858** SIMMONDS *Dict. Trade*, *Ticket, Seaman's*, a register ticket given to seamen from the General Register and Record office of Seamen.

**b.** Short for TICKET OF LEAVE.

**1904** A. GRIFFITHS *50 Years Public Service* xii. 169 Blue dress men of exemplary conduct, who were within a year of release on ticket. *Ibid.* xxiii. 354 Then he is on ticket now, and wanted for failing to report himself, no doubt.

†**7.** An acknowledgement of indebtedness, an I O U; a promise to pay; a note or memorandum of money or goods received on credit; a debit account, a score; hence phr. *on*, *upon* (*the*) *ticket*, on credit, on trust. Cf. *on tick* (TICK *sb.*[4] 1).

Prob. the 'ticket' was orig. the 'note of hand' of the borrower, but it might easily be transferred to the statement of the same rendered by the creditor, and thus to 'a tradesman's bill', as suggested by Nares.

*c* **1600** DAY *Begg. Bednall Gr.* I. i, Your poor Vitler, Sir, where your Lordships men went o' th' ticket. **1632** J. HAYWARD tr. *Biondi's Eromena* 25 The Admirall lost some monies..and then playing on ticket, lost twenty thousand crownes. *a* **1634** RANDOLPH *Hey for Honesty* II. vi, I am resolved to build no more Sconces, but to pay my old tickets. **1643** DAVENANT *Unfort. Lovers* v. i, Let 'em not deal on the Ticket. You know ready Mony makes the Pot boil. **1656** HEYLIN *Surv. France* 147 He that hath..his gold ready shall have a sooner dispatch, then the best Scholar upon ticket.

**8.** In U.S. politics, The list of candidates for election nominated or put forward by a party or faction.

*General ticket*, a list of candidates put forward for a state or other large political division, equal in number to the entire representation to which the division is entitled, but not chosen to represent each local subdivision. *Mixed*, *scratch*, *split*, *straight ticket*: see quot. 1859.

**1711** ISAAC NORRIS in *Penn-Logan Corr.* (1872) II. 438 Chester [Pennsylvania] carried their ticket entire. **1764** (Nov. 3) in *Life* etc. *J. Reed* (1847) I. 36 The Dutch Calvinists and the Presbyterians..to a man assisted the new ticket. **1766** SARAH FRANKLIN *Lett. to B. Franklin* (1859) 191 The old ticket forever! We have it by 34 votes! **1789** *Maryland Jrnl.* 2 Jan. (Thornton *Amer. Gloss.*), The Federal Ticket recommends Mr. Daniel Carroll for the Sixth District; and the opposite Ticket..Mr. Abraham Faw. **1859** BARTLETT *Dict. Amer.* s.v., According to circumstances a man is said to vote the *straight ticket*, i.e. the ticket containing the 'regular nomination' of his party without change; a *scratch ticket*, a ticket from which the names of one or more of the candidates are erased; a *split ticket*, a ticket representing different divisions of his party; or a *mixed ticket*, a ticket in which the nominations of different parties are blended into one. **1861** BLAIR in *Century Mag.* (1889) Sept. 687/2 Chase, who never voted a Democratic ticket in his life. **1888** BRYCE *Amer. Commw.* I. v. 54 Each party runs its list or 'ticket' of thirty presidential electors for that State.

**9.** *slang.* **a.** The correct thing; what is wanted, expected, or fashionable; esp. in phr. *that's the ticket.*

Perh. from 8; or, as some have suggested, from the winning ticket in a lottery.

**1838** HALIBURTON *Clockm.* Ser. II. xxi. 323 They ought to be hanged, sir, (that's the ticket, and he'd whop the leader). **1843** E. FITZGERALD *Lett.* (1889) I. 117, I fancy that moderately high hills (like these) are the ticket. **1847** *Ibid.* 179 This [idealizing of portraits] is all wrong. Truth is the ticket. **1854** THACKERAY *Newcomes* vii, Somehow she's not—she's not the ticket. **1866** *Routledge's Ev. Boy's Ann.* 411 That's the ticket! That's the winning game.

**b.** The program or plan of action; that which is to be done; the thing on hand.

**1842** MARRYAT *Perc. Keene* xiii, 'Well', said Bob Cross, 'what's the ticket, youngster—are you to go abroad with me?' **1861** C. J. ANDERSSON *Okavango* x. 127 [The lion] suddenly squatted, evidently intending to spring upon me. 'Nay, old fellow', I muttered to myself, 'if that's the ticket, I will be even with you'.

**10.** *attrib.* and *Comb.* **a.** simple attrib., as *ticket-box*, *-pocket*, *-punch*, *-system*, *-tax*; **b.** 'having to do with the selling, etc. of tickets', as *ticket-agent*, *-clerk*, *-guard*, *-man*, *-money*, *-office*, *-official*, *-room*; **c.** 'to which admission is obtained by ticket', as *ticket-gathering*, *-meeting*; **d.** obj. and objective genitive, as *ticket-buyer*, *-clipper*, *-collector*, *-examiner*, *-receiver*, *-snipper*; *ticket-clipping*, *-collecting*, *-issuing*, *-punching*, *-snatching*, *-writing*.

**1824** T. CHALMERS in *Mem.* (1851) III. iii. 37 The ticket system operates admirably. **1848–9** CALHOUN *Const. U.S.* Wks. 1863 I. 370 The general ticket system; which has become..the universal mode of appointing electors to choose the President and Vice-President. **1858** SIMMONDS *Dict. Trade*, *Ticket-writer*, one who writes or paints showy placards and legible tickets for goods in shop windows. **1872** O. W. HOLMES *Poet Breakf.-t.* vi, Toll-men and ticket-takers. **1878** F. S. WILLIAMS *Midl. Railw.* 628 The walls of the booking office are provided with ticket-boxes or tubes. **1884** *Law Times* 23 Aug. 301/1 He presented a ticket at the barrier..saying to the ticket-clipper, 'I want the train for Canonbury'. **1889** *Spectator* 9 Nov. 634/1 A quasi-public or ticket meeting. **1890** *Daily News* 22 Sept. 2/6 Wire-plyers and pincers, ticket-nippers, wrenches, spanners, &c. **1893** GUNTER *Miss Dividends* 30 The ticket puncher looks astonished for a moment, and then..cries, 'Next!' **1895** *Westm. Gaz.* 10 Oct. 3/1 After the exhausting and exciting struggle in the ticket-room comes the preparation for the settling or pay day. **1897** *Pall Mall Mag.* July 384 He put the coin carefully in the ticket-pocket of his overcoat. **1897** *Daily News* 6 July 7/3 The minutes consumed in the stoppage for ticket-collecting. **1908** *Westm. Gaz.* 9 May 2/3 In full view of that stern and uncompromising ticket-inspector.

**11.** Special Combs.: **ticket benefit**, an entertainment for which special tickets are sold, the proceeds being for the benefit of a particular person or object; **ticket broker** (*U.S.*), a dealer in unexpired or return railway tickets: = *ticket-scalper*; **ticket-chopper** (*U.S.*), (*a*) a machine which mutilates used railway tickets deposited in it by passengers; (*b*) the employee in charge of this machine; **ticket-day**: see quot. 1858; **ticket-holder**, (*a*) one who holds a ticket of admission, etc.; (*b*) a clip or other device for holding or attaching a ticket or label; †**ticket-jobber**, a jobber of lottery-tickets; **ticket-man**, (*a*) a ticket-holder; *spec.* a seaman who held a certificate exempting him from impressment (now *Hist.*); (*b*) a railway employee who collects or punches tickets; †**ticket-monger**, one who trafficked in the pay-warrants of seamen, giving ready money with a large deduction, and then presenting them for payment; **ticket-night**, a benefit performance: see quot. 1812; **ticket-scalper** (*U. S. slang*), one who buys and sells unexpired or return railway tickets at less than the rates at which they are issued; so **ticket-scalping**; **ticket-shop**, a shop displaying ticketed goods in the window. See also TICKET-PORTER.

**1898** *Daily News* 30 July 2/4 The London Trades Council has arranged for a *ticket benefit..in aid of the Welsh Miners' Relief Fund. **1902** FARMER & HENLEY *Slang Dict.* s.v. *Scalp*, *Ticket-scalper*, a *ticket-broker. **1905** *Daily Chron.* 8 Mar. 5/4 One hundred students from Columbia University..volunteered their services to the company as guards and *ticket-choppers. **1858** SIMMONDS *Dict. Trade*, **Ticket-day*, the day before the settling or pay-day on the Stock Exchange, when the names of bona-fide purchasers are rendered in by one stockbroker to another. **1901** *Westm. Gaz.* 12 Dec. 11/1 The business of ticket-days..is entirely clerical, consisting chiefly..of the passing of buyers' names to sellers of stock or shares. **1877** KNIGHT *Dict. Mech.*, **Ticket-holder*, a device to hold a railway ticket in the hat or to the lappel of the coat; or a tag to a bale or package. **1737** *Gentl. Mag.* VII. 368/1 The Subscriptions being filled, whatever Reflections may be made, they can be of no Prejudice to the Lottery, but only affect the Ticket-Jobbers. **1803** NELSON in Nicolas *Disp.* (1845) V. 46 This ship is navigated to Portsmouth by *Ticket-men (men who are protected from the impress by some cause or other). **1893** GUNTER *Miss Dividends* 37 Miss Travenion is conducted..past the ticket man at the gate, and on board the train. **1904** *Westm. Gaz.* 5 Feb. 10/1 Admission is by tickets, available for six nights, and..'ticket men' get the first chance of entrance. **1668** PEPYS *Diary* 5 Mar., To answer only one question, touching our paying tickets to *ticket-mongers. **1812** H. & J. SMITH *Rej. Addr.* xv, Some forth on *ticket-nights from tradesmen break, To mar the actor they design to make. [*Note.*] Ticket-nights are those whereon the inferior actors club for a benefit: each distributes as many tickets of admission as he is able among his friends. **1889** FARMER *Dict. Amer.*, **Ticket scalper*, a speculator in unused railway tickets. **1892** *Pall Mall G.* 1 Nov. 2/1 (Farmer) **Ticket-scalping*..has reference to the transferability or otherwise of tickets rather than to their date of expiry. **1851** MAYHEW *Lond. Labour* I. 380/2 A thoroughfare full of *ticket-shops.

**Ticket** (ti·kėt), *sb.*[2] *dial.* [app. f. TICK *sb.*[3] + -ET [1].] A minute quantity or part.

**1634** *Reg. Privy Council Scot.* V. 414 Seatoun threatned the notar, avowing to take a ticket aff his haffet if he gave out any instrument in this mater. **1731** FIELDING *Lottery* iii, I have not got it as yet—but, upon my shoul, I was within a ticket of it. **1904** in *Eng. Dial. Dict.* s.v., (Somerset) A donkey load would be called 'just a little ticket'.

**Ticket** (ti·kėt), *v.* [f. TICKET *sb.*[1]]

**1.** *trans.* To attach a ticket to; to mark with a ticket indicating the value, contents, description, origin, destination, or the like; to distinguish by means of a ticket; to label. Chiefly in *pa. pple.*

**1611** [see *ticketed* below]. **1691** *Lond. Gaz.* No. 2624/4 There being one of the said Bags missing, Ticketed 68l. 3s. 6d. **1719** LONDON & WISE *Compl. Gard.* 107 Plant these Trees in Baskets, well tickketted, or..set down carefully in our Book. **1770** *Chron.* in *Ann. Reg.* 135/2 The post-boy..was robbed..of the mail..containing two bags, ticketed Newcastle, and Newcastle and York. **1810** *Sporting Mag.* XXXVI. 128 Pictures which are sold during the exhibition will be ticketed as such. **1839** DARWIN *Voy. Nat.* xvii. (1852) 395 Of those [specimens] which were ticketed with their locality, not one was common to any two of the Islands.

**b.** *fig.* To describe or mark as by a ticket; to designate, characterize, set down (*as* so and so): = LABEL *v.* b.

**1654** WHITLOCK *Zootomia* 435, I make no doubt but confident forwardnesse, and undertakings, would Ticket men passable..that could scarce tell which end of their Bibles to hold uppermost. **1713** BENTLEY *Rem. Disc. Free-think.* § 40. II. 16 A few glittering Prizes..among an infinity of Blanks, drew troops of Adventurers; who, if the whole Fund had been equally ticketed, would never have come in. **1856** T. A. TROLLOPE *Girlh. Cath. de Medici* i. 10 We find certain characters ticketed from age to age in history as monsters of atrocity. **1884** *Chr. Commw.* 14 Feb. 424/2 There is a present fashion of ticketing all outspoken religion as sham talk.

**2.** To furnish with a ticket; to issue a railway or other travelling ticket to; to 'book'; also *absol.*, to issue tickets. *U.S.*

**1842** LONGF. in *Life* (1891) I. 415 To borrow the expression of a fellow-traveller, we were 'ticketed through to the depot'. **1852** *Boston* (Mass.) *Traveller* 24 Dec. 3/2 Passengers ticketed through from New York to Cincinnati. **1882** *Kansas City Jrnl.* 19 Feb. Advt., We ticket directly to every place of importance.

**3.** *intr.* To make a tender *for* tin or copper ore by means of a 'ticket' or written tender: see TICKET *sb.*[1] 1 b, TICKETING *vbl. sb.* 2. *local.*

**1778** PRYCE *Min. Cornub.* 287 Three hundred tons of Ore belonging to the same Mine were to be ticketed for on a day appointed.

Hence **Ti·cketed** *ppl. a.*, marked with or bearing a ticket or tickets.

**1611** COTGR., *Tiqueté*, ticketted, or appointed by ticket. **1827** SCOTT *Chron. Canongate* vi, A hackney coach..that obscure vehicle, which was not permitted to degrade with its ticketed presence the dignity of Baliol's Lodging. **1828** DOBIE *Mem. W. Wilson of Crummock* (1896) 100 On the ball night she was my ticketed companion. **1836–9** DICKENS *Sk. Boz, Hor. Sparkins*, A dirty-looking ticketed linen-draper's shop, with goods of all kinds, and labels of all sorts and sizes, in the window.

**Ticketer** (ti·kėtəɹ). [f. TICKET *sb.*[1] or *v.* + -ER [1].] One who tickets; one who has a ticket.

**1778** PRYCE *Min. Cornub.* 288 One of the ticketers present produced his ticket before all the company, whose offer was nine pounds seventeen shillings per ton [cf. TICKETING 2]. **1865** G. MEREDITH *Rhoda Fleming* xii, I paid, and you're a ticketer...These chaps get tickets given 'm.

**Ticketing** (ti·kėtiŋ), *vbl. sb.* [f. TICKET *v.* + -ING [1].] The action of TICKET *v.*

**1.** Marking with or as with a ticket; labelling.

**1844** G. DODD *Textile Manuf.* vii. 228 After a process of rolling, pressing, ticketing, &c., the article is finished. **1866** DK. ARGYLL *Reign Law* i. (ed. 4) 4 The mere ticketing and orderly assortment of external facts.

**2.** Bidding by a 'ticket' or written tender; with *pl.* a sale of ore at which the bids are made in this way. *local.*

**1778** PRYCE *Min. Cornub.* 288 The present mode of ticketing for Copper Ores. **1854** C. S. EDSALL (*title*) Copper Ore Tables,..with the method of conducting the Ticketings. **1912** *Financial Times* 30 Apr., Redruth Tin Ticketing.

**3.** *attrib.* (chiefly in sense 2).

**1778** PRYCE *Min. Cornub.* 288 On this ticketing day a dinner almost equal to a city feast is provided at the expence of the Mines. *Ibid.*, A duplicate of a ticketing paper. **1839** DE LA BECHE *Rep. Geol. Cornwall*, etc. xv. 541 The copper-ore sales, or ticketing-days, as they are termed. **1905**

HOLMAN-HUNT *Pre-Raphaelitism* I. 9 Securing from the 'ticketing room' a print of Britannia.

**Ticketless** (ti·kėtlės), *a.* [f. TICKET *sb.*[1] + -LESS.] Having no ticket; without a ticket of admission, a railway ticket, etc.

1868 *Daily News* 6 July, Regulations which kept the ticketless public at a distance.

**Ticket of leave.** A ticket or document giving leave or permission; an order, a permit (*rare*). Now, in specific use, a licence to be at large after the expiration of part of the sentence, formerly granted to convicts in the Australian colonies; since 1840, the usual colloquial name for an 'order of licence' giving a convict his liberty under certain restrictions before his sentence has expired, the proportion remitted being dependent on his conduct and industry.

1732 *Acc. Workhouses* 17 That no person presume to go out of the street door without a Ticket of Leave, to return in good order. 1828 P. CUNNINGHAM *N. S. Wales* (ed. 3) II. 293 Whether in depriving an individual of a ticket of leave, or sentencing him to a penal gang, the periods should be always limited. 1843 *Act* 6 & 7 *Vict.* c. 7 (*title*) An Act to amend the Law affecting transported Convicts with respect to Pardons and Tickets of Leave. *Ibid.*, Permission to such Felons..to employ themselves for their own Benefit (which Permissions are usually called and known by the Name of Tickets of Leave). 1895 *Times* 16 Jan. 14/5 A long list of former convictions, beginning in 1852, was proved against the prisoner...He was now on 'ticket-of-leave'.

b. *attrib.* or *Comb.* (hyphened), as *ticket-of-leave holder, man, woman.*

1837 J. D. LANG *N. S. Wales* I. 411 The overseer, on well-regulated farms, is generally a ticket-of-leave man or emancipated convict. *Ibid.* II. 19 A ticket-of-leave holder ..is confined to a particular district, and is liable to lose his ticket for various petty misdemeanours. 1862 *Lond. Rev.* 30 Aug. 178 A great proportion of these crimes were committed by 'Ticket-of-leave Men'. 1871 *Daily News* 25 July, In one of the..most fashionable districts of London many hundreds of domestic servants are ticket-of-leave women.

Hence **Ti·cket-of-lea·ver**, a ticket-of-leave man; **Ti·cket-of-lea·vism** (*nonce-wd.*), the system or operation of tickets of leave.

1852 MUNDY *Our Antipodes* v. (1855) 107 The overseer.. may be a hireling convict—emancipist, expirer, or ticket-of-leaver. 1857 *Tait's Mag.* XXIV. 41 The atmosphere itself was redolent of ticket-of-leaveism. 1858 R. S. SURTEES *Ask Mamma* xlv, The oft-disappointed ticket-of-leaver was again installed in a butler's pantry.

**Ti·cket-po:rter.**

1. A member of a body of porters in the City of London who were licensed by the Corporation; orig. called *street-porters*, and distinct from the TACKLE-HOUSE *porters* of the twelve great Merchant Companies; in later times the two classes of porters were united in the *Society of the Tackle-house and Ticket Porters.* Now *Hist.*

1646 [see TACKLE-HOUSE b] The Ticket-Porters, otherwise called the Street-Porters of this City. 1770 *New Guide London* 257 Ticket-porters are all freemen, and their business is to load and ship off goods exported or imported. Also to house merchants' goods, metals, &c. 1800 COLQUHOUN *Comm. Thames* 328 The Ticket-Porters are persons appointed by the City of London...They give Security in 100l. for Fidelity, and have their Names and Numbers on a Metal Badge. 1833 (Dec. 12) *Rep. Court Com. Council* (London) *on Porters* 4 The Ticket Porters..are entitled to the work or labour of unshipping, landing, carrying, loading, and housing all goods, wares and merchandize imported into the port of London from the several places mentioned in the Act of Common Council, 27th March, 1798, and also of shipping all goods, wares, and merchandize; and they are likewise entitled, by custom and usage, to perform the work at the public markets of this City. *Ibid.*, We were..attended ..by the Rulers and Registers of the Society of Tackle-house and Ticket Porters. 1848 DICKENS *Dombey* xiii, The ticket-porter..always ran officiously before to open Mr. Dombey's office-door.

2. A (railway) porter who collects tickets.

1852 *Aquatic Notes, Camb.* 80 A rush of men takes place from every carriage, and past the ticket-porter.

**Tick-hole.** [? f. TICK *sb.*[3] + HOLE *sb.*] A cavity in nodular stone, usually lined with a crystalline incrustation.

1829 *Glover's Hist. Derby* I. 92 At the lime-quarries, Milltown, Ashover, cavities or tick-holes are frequent in the.. limestone rock,..lined with..quartz crystals. 1881 in RAYMOND *Mining Gloss.*

**Tickil**, obs. form of TICKLE *a.* and *v.*

**Ticking** (ti·kiŋ), *sb.* Forms: α. 7 *Sc.* tyking, 7–8 tiking; β. 7–8 tickin, 7– ticking. See also TICKEN. [f. TICK *sb.*[2] + -ING[1].] The material of which bed-ticks are made: see TICK *sb.*[2]

α. 1649 *Caldwell Pap.* (Maitl. Cl.) I. 102 For ane new sheitt of tyking to ye lard's horss 1. 16. 0. 1674 JEAKE *Arith.* (1696) 65 In 1 Hundred of Tiking and Twill of Scotland, 120 Ells. 1726 SWIFT *Gulliver* IV. x, I had beaten hemp,..and made of it a sort of tiking: This I filled with..feathers.

β. *a* 1661 FULLER *Worthies, Lancs.* (1662) II. 106 It will be the safest way to wrap them all together in some Manchester-Tickin. 1815 J. SMITH *Panorama Sc. & Art* II. 735 Oil-paintings are generally executed on canvass...A kind of ticking has lately been much used. 1883 *Blackw. Mag.* Aug. 192 She wore over her gown of ticking a great apron of grey stuff.

b. Rarely applied to the tick or cover itself.

1683 TRYON *Way to Health* 595 You may have Flock-Beds, with Canvas-Tickings. 1833 MARRYAT *P. Simple* xxi, He.. put it..away in the ticking of his bed.

c. *attrib.* Of the nature of or made of ticking.

1676 COVEL in *Early Voy. Levant* (Hakl. Soc.) 164 A bed ..of twilt or ticking sattin. 1682 WHELER *Journ. Greece* I. 16 Course Ticking-Cloth, well quilted with Wool. 1721 MRS. CENTLIVRE *Artifice* III, The dirtiest Trollup..must have her Top-knot and Tickin-shoes. 1756 C. LUCAS *Ess. Waters* I. 229 A sliding seat, with a thin ticking bottom.

**Ticking** (ti·kiŋ), *vbl. sb.*[1] [f. TICK *v.*[1] + -ING[1].]

1. Touching lightly or wantonly; dallying: see TICK *v.*[1] 1. *Obs.* exc. *dial.*

1546 J. HEYWOOD *Prov.* (1867) 58 Leaue lewde tickyng. 1611 COTGR., *Amourettes*, wanton loue-toyes, ticking, ticklings, daliances.

2. The beating sound of a clock or watch, or any similar sound: see TICK *v.*[1] 2, TICK *sb.*[3] 2.

1746–7 HERVEY *Medit.* (1767) II. 23 The Ticking of my Watch is distinctly heard. 1827 F. COOPER *Prairie* i, The ticking of gun-locks was heard. 1848 DICKENS *Dombey* xliii, She could..count the ticking of the clock.

b. *transf.* A telegraphic message: cf. TICKER [3] b.

1888 M. ARNOLD in *19th Cent.* Apr. 490, I opened a Boston newspaper and came upon a column headed 'Tickings'. By tickings we are to understand news conveyed through the tickings of the telegraph.

3. Small spots or points of colour forming the marking of an animal.

This use may have arisen from TICKED *a.* by association with TICK *sb.*[3] 3, 3 b and TICK *v.*[1] 3.

1885 *Bazaar* 30 Mar. 1269/2 Belgian hare buck, good in colour and ticking. 1886 *Field* 20 Mar. 340/2 Interspersed with a profusion of longer black hairs, giving the appearance known as 'ticking'.

**Ti·cking**, *vbl. sb.*[2] *colloq.* or *slang.* [f. TICK *v.*[2] + -ING[1].] The action of TICK *v.*[2]; the taking of goods on 'tick' or credit.

1748 WARTON *Oxford Ale* 49 Hail, Ticking! surest guardian of distress! Beneath thy shelter pennyless I quaff The cheerful cup.

**Ti·cking**, *ppl. a.*[1] [f. TICK *v.*[1] + -ING[2].] That ticks, as a clock, etc.; making or characterized by a succession of ticks.

1566 in Peacock *Eng. Ch. Furniture* (1866) 116 A hammes hudde [= amice hood] and tickynge belle. 1721 BRADLEY *Philos. Acc. Wks. Nat.* 154 That ticking Noise, which is commonly called a Death-Watch.

**Ti·cking**, *ppl. a.*[2] *colloq.* or *slang.* [f. TICK *v.*[2] + -ING[2].] That 'ticks' or 'goes on tick'; that gives 'tick' or credit; dealing on credit, running into debt.

1673 WYCHERLEY *Gentl. Dancing-Master* Prol., Ready to engage Against the flouting, ticking gentry who Citizen, player, poet, would undo.

**Tickle** (ti·k'l), *sb.*[1] [Generally held to be derived from TICKLE *a.* or *v.*, and so to go with TICKLE *sb.*[2] (see quot. 1908); but some would identify it with Eng. dial. *stickle* 'a rapid shallow place in a river'. In Nova Scotia also *tittle*.] A name given on the coasts of Newfoundland and Labrador to a narrow difficult strait or passage.

1770 *Chart S. E. Part Newfoundland*, [A locality at the head of St. Mary's Bay marked] Tickles. 1792 G. CARTWRIGHT *Jrnl. Labrador* Gloss., *Tickle*, a passage between the continent and an island, or between two islands, when it is of no great width. 1837 *New Sailing Direct. Newf.* (ed. 3) 25 *note*, The word *Tickle* is a local name, in common use at Newfoundland, and signifies a passage between islands or rocks. 1861 L. L. NOBLE *Icebergs* 277 No sooner were we clear of the 'tickle', or narrows, than 'Iceberg ahead!'—'Ice on the lee bow!' was cried by the man forward. 1868 *Admiralty Chart* No. 225 (Labrador), Indian Tickle. 1871 *Ibid.* No. 291 (Newf.), Change Island Tickles. ..Stag Harbour Tickle. 1881 *Standard* 15 July 4/8 In many of the 'tickles', 'guts', 'runs', 'sounds',..and inlets there are still to be found tiny villages which date from those old Acadian times. 1905 *Daily Chron.* 28 Apr. 3/3 See him clinging to the bowsprit, conning the vessel through tortuous 'tickles'. 1908 ABP. HOWLEY in *Newfoundld. Quarterly* Mar. 2 The Tickle...It has always been supposed that this name is a plain English word, implying a passage of some danger, so that it is a 'ticklish' matter to get safe through.

**Tickle** (ti·k'l), *sb.*[2] [f. TICKLE *v.*] An act of tickling, in various senses of the vb.; a touch that tickles; a tickling sensation; a tickled or pleasantly excited feeling.

1801 in *Spirit Pub. Jrnls.* IX. 376, I want you to give those dogs yonder a tickle, *en passant.* 1872 BLACKMORE *Maid of Sker* v, I gave her [a child] a little tickle; and verily she began to laugh. 1880 MRS. WHITNEY *Odd or Even* ix, And vibrant with an inward tickle. 1907 *Daily Chron.* 9 Dec. 4/7 The dinner was a tickle of the palate. *Mod.* (*Yorksh. saying*) To have 'tickles in the feet', said of one given to wandering, who will not settle to any useful work.

**Tickle** (ti·k'l), *a.* (*adv.*) Forms: see the verb; also 4–5 tikil, -ul, tekil, 5 tekyl, -el, tykell, 6 tyckyll, 6–7 tickell, 8 *dial.* tikkle. [Goes with TICKLE *v.*: the use of the vb.-stem as adj. is unusual; but cf. KITTLE *a.* beside KITTLE *v.*]

†1. (Sense uncertain: ? Threatening or in danger to fall. Cf. 6.) *Obs.*

*c* 1325 *Body & Soul* in *Map's Poems* (Camden) 346 Þou hauest y-liued to longe, wo wruth the so suykel!..Pynen harde ant stronge to þe bueþ nou ful tykel.

†2. Pleasantly stirred or excited. (Cf. TICKLE *v.* 1.) *Obs.*

*c* 1330 R. BRUNNE *Chron. Wace* (Rolls) 13413 When y byþenke on ȝoure godnesse..Ffor þat ioye myn herte ys tykel.

†3. Easily moved to feeling or action; easily affected in any way; not firm or steadfast; loose; also, susceptible to tickling, easily tickled or tingled. *Tickle credit*, ready or facile trust or belief; credulity. *Obs.*

1377 LANGL. *P. Pl.* B. (Crowley) v. 166 They are ticle of her tonges, & muste al secretes tel. *c* 1530 H. RHODES *Bk. Nurture* 695 Some men be tickle of tongue, and play the blabs by kynde. 1533 T. HEYWOOD *Play of Love* C j, The paps so small And rounde with all The wast not myckyll But it was tyckyll. 1553 T. WILSON *Rhet.* (1580) 3 Euen these auncient Preachers must now and then plaie the fooles in the pulpit, to serue the tickle eares of their fletyng audience. 1563 *Mirr. Mag., Hastings* xlii, Of tyckle credyte ne had ben the mischiefe. *Ibid.* lxxvii, Flye tickle credyte, shonne alyke distrust.

†b. With reference to incontinency. *Obs.*

1362 LANGL. *P. Pl.* A. III. 126 Heo is Tikel of hire Tayl, Talewys of hire tonge, As Comyun as þe Cart-wei to knaues and to alle. *c* 1475 *Songs & Carols 15th C.* (Warton Cl.) 27 Under the tayl they ben ful tekyl. 1604 W. TERILO *Fr. Bacon's Proph.* 228 in Hazl. *E. P. P.* IV. 276 Wickednes was loath'd so much, That no man lov'd the tickle tuch.

†4. Having the quality of tickling, tickly. *Obs.* (Quots. *c* 1440, 1570 perh. belong here.)

[*c* 1440 *Promp. Parv.* 493/2 Tykel, *titillosus.* 1570 LEVINS *Manip.* 129/14 Tickil, *titillenus, -na.*] 1593 B. BARNES *Parthenophil, Madrigal* xvi, Soft things whose touch is tickle to the mind, Give no like touch, all joys in one to wrap.

5. Not to be depended upon; uncertain (in fact, action, duration, etc.); unreliable; changeable, inconstant, capricious, fickle, 'kittle'. Now *dial.*

13.. *E. E. Allit. P.* B. 655 May þou traw for tykel þat þou tonne moȝtez. *c* 1386 CHAUCER *Miller's T.* 242 This world is now ful tikel [*v. rr.* tekyl, -el, tikil, tykell] sikerly. 1537 *St. Papers Hen. VIII*, I. 531, I assure your Lordeship the people be very tykell. 1566 PAINTER *Pal. Pleas.* I. 58 Holde fast thy fortune, for she is tickle and can not be holden against her will. 1670 COTTON *Espernon* III. XII. 368 His sons..were best acquainted with his tickle & impatient humour. 1737 J. BROADHEAD in *N. & Q.* (1895) 8th Ser. VII. 405/1 A pretty deal of Rain in some places westward, Mad[e] Harvest rather Tickle. 1795 *Chester Chron.* 27 Mar. (E. D. D.), So tikkle as times ar. 1888 DOUGHTY *Arabia Deserta* II. 158 He must learn the English tongue..who can foresee the years to come, this world is so tickle.

6. In unstable equilibrium, easily upset or overthrown, insecure, tottering, crazy; also, easily set in motion or action; nicely poised; delicate, sensitive. Now *dial.* † *Tickle of the sear*: see SEAR *sb.*[1] 1 b.

1515 in Foxe *A. & M.* (1583) 809/2 A stoole, which stoole stood vpon a bolster of a bed, so tickle, that any manne or beaste might not touch it so litle, but it was ready to fall. 1555 *Act* 2 & 3 *Phil. & Mary* c. 16 § 2 Boates..so shallowe & tickle that therby greate perill & danger of drowning hathe many tymes ensued. 1583–1602 [see SEAR *sb.*[1] 1 b]. 1612 CHAPMAN *Widowes T.* Plays 1873 III. 29, I haue set her hart vpon as tickle a pin as the needle of a Diall. 1883 *W. Yorks. Gloss.* s. v., A mouse-trap should be set *tickle*, i. e. easy to go off. 1904 in *Eng. Dial. Dict.* s. v., (Lancs.) That wall's very tickle, you'll have it deawn if yo'r not very careful.

b. *transf.* Of a place, condition, etc.: Insecure; precarious, slippery; risky, dangerous. *Obs.* or *arch.*

1579 SPENSER *Sheph. Cal.* July 14 In humble dales is footing fast, The trode is not so tickle. 1589 *Mar Martine* 5 Thilke way & trood whilke thou dost swade, is steepe & also tickle. 1643 BAKER *Chron., Hen. VII* 148 These words ..seemed to expresse a tickle hold of Loyalty. 1665 BRATHWAIT *Comment 2 Tales* 129 Conventicles are Tickle places for Holy Sisters. 1681 COTTON *Wond. Peak* (ed. 4) 43 Footing ..still more tickle, and unsafe. 1834 SIR H. TAYLOR *2nd Pt. Artevelde* III. iii, I oft before have clomb to tickle places, But this will be the last of all my climbing. 1868 BROWNING *Ring & Bk.* IV. 51 The grey innocuous grub, of yore, Had hatched a hornet, tickle to the touch.

7. = TICKLISH *a.* 5. Now *dial.*

1569 STOCKER tr. *Diod. Sic.* I. xix. 28 The matter stoode upon this tickle and dangerous point. 1581 PETTIE *Guazzo's Civ. Conv.* II. (1586) 71 b, The trueth is a thing so tickle, that a man may incurre reprehension, not onely by disguising it in some part couourably, but euen by very reporting of it simply. 1586 FERNE *Blaz. Gentrie* II. 3 So tickle and nyce be the precepts of those writers, that to swarue but one haire from their prescribed rules, hath fordone all thy former worke. 1595 GOODWINE *Blanchardyn* liv. 223 Seeing the tickle state of his fathers kingdome. *a* 1618 RALEIGH *Soul's Errand* viii. Tell wit how much it wrangles In tickle points of niceness. 1681 W. ROBERTSON *Phraseol. Gen.* (1693) 385 A very tickle point or controversie. 1868 E. WAUGH *Sneck-Bant* iv. (E.D.D.), Hoo's nobbut in a tickle state o' health. 1884 *Chester Gloss.* s.v., Au've getten raythet a tickle job here. 1887 BARING-GOULD *Red Spider* ii, The money-spinner is a tickle (touchy) beast, and may take offence at a godless word.

b. Delicate in the feelings or senses; fastidious, dainty, squeamish; easily upset or disordered. Now *dial.*

*c* 1456 PECOCK *Bk. Faith* (1909) 212 Whi schulde ȝe thanne be so tikil and squaymose? 1762 T. BRYDGES *Burlesque Homer* (1797) II. 96 Juno, whose nose was mighty tickle, Soon smelt their most unsavoury pickle. 1855 *Shevvild Chap's Ann.* 23 (E.D.D.) Thah's a varry tickle stomach. 1901 F. E. TAYLOR *Folk Speech S. Lanc.* (ibid.), He's very tickle abeawt what he ates an' sups.

c. Difficult to deal with.

1570 LEVINS *Manip.* 121/46 Tickle, *impatiens, intactilis.* 1582 STANYHURST *Æneis* Ded. (Arb.) 7 Virgil..and Ouid.. are so tickle in soom places, as they rather craue a construction than a translation. 1887 BARING-GOULD *Gaverocks* xxx, There is a tickle (difficult) bit where I cannot plant a foot.

d. Of an animal: Easily scared; shy, wild. *dial.*

[1737 *Gentl. Mag.* VII. 114/2 But if I shoot Not out of

hand, The bird, which doth So tickle stand, May chance to fly away.] **1877** E. Leigh *Chesh. Gloss.* 212 *Tickle* is also applied to game, particularly hares, when wild and ready to move. 'The snow or frost makes the hares very tickle'. **1877** *N.W. Linc. Gloss.* s.v., Fish, when they bite very shyly, are said to be 'strange an' tickle'. **1879** T. Warden *Crossford* I. 22 The birds were excessively tickle, and persistently got up out of shot.

† **8.** quasi-*adv.* (in senses 6 and 7): In a tickle or ticklish manner; insecurely, precariously. *Obs.*

**1606** Daniel *Funeral Poem* Poems (1717) 313 And this Important Piece..did then so tickle stand, As that no Joint-ure of the Government But shook. **1692** R. L'Estrange *Josephus, Wars Jews* iv. i. (1733) 689 The Houses stand so thick and tickle upon the Steep of the Hill..as if they were ready to drop into the Precipice. **1699** J. Woodward in *Phil. Trans.* XXI. 224 Corpuscles..absolutely Spherical, must stand so very tickle and nicely upon each other, as to be susceptible of every impression.

**9.** *Comb.* **a.** in sense 'easily moved or set in motion', as † **tickle-footed** (of a hawk), having an insecure grasp or clutch; † **tickle-headed**, light-minded, easily influenced; † **tickle-heeled**, having nimble or active heels; † **tickle-tongued**, loose of tongue, talkative, garrulous. See also Tickle-tail. **b. tickle-plough** (*dial.*): see quot. 1875.

*a* **1616** Beaum. & Fl. *Scornf. Lady* v. iv, Lady I would not undertake ye, were you again a haggard, for the best cast of four ladys i' th' kingdom: you were ever *tickle-footed, and would not truss round. **1583** Golding *Calvin on Deut.* lxxiv. 455 In al ages men haue bin *tickleheaded: ..euery man would needs be casting of some peece or collup of his own making, to the things that God had commaunded. **1737** Bracken *Farriery Impr.* (1757) II. 35 A Horse may ..shew abundance of Life and Action, while under a *tickle heel'd Jockey-Boy. **1875** *Sussex Gloss.*, **Tickle-plough*, a plough with wooden beam and handles. **1884** *W. Sussex Gaz.* 25 Sept., Dead stock:..three one-horse dung carts, tickle ploughs..and small harrows. **1577** Stanyhurst *Descr. Irel.* Ep. Ded., His historie .. being .. somewhat *tickle toonged,..it twitled more tales out of schoole [etc.].

**Tickle** (ti·k'l), *v.* Forms: 4 tikelle, 4–5 tikl(en, tykel, 4–6 tikel, 4–7 ticle, 5 tykele, tykle, tykyl(l, 5–6 tyckel, 6 tikell, tykell, tickil, tykil, tyckle, tycle, 6–7 tickel, 6– tickle. [Not recorded in OE., which however had *tinclian* to tickle. Known first after 1300 in form *tikelle*, side by side with the adj. *tykel, tikel*: origin and history doubtful. Falk and Torp take it as a freq. deriv. of Tick *v.*[1] to touch lightly, pat. It has also been inferred to be a metathetic form of Kittle *v.*[1], parallel to Alemannic dial. *zicklen*, beside Ger. *kitzeln* to tickle. See Note below.]

**I.** Intransitive senses.

† **1.** To be affected or excited by a pleasantly tingling or thrilling sensation; to be stirred or moved with a thrill of pleasure: said of the heart, lungs, blood, 'spirits', etc., also of the person. *Obs.*

*c* **1330** R. Brunne *Chron.* (1810) 113 Þe folk ferly mykelle ageyn him [Stephen] þei ros, & Dauid herte gan tikelle, þat him wex fele fos. **1577–87** Holinshed *Chron.* (1808) IV. 378 How the spirits and livelie bloud tickle in our arteries and small veines, in beholding you the light of this realme. **1589** *Pasquil's Ret.* 16, I needed no Minstrill to make me merrie, my hart tickled of it selfe. **1591** Spenser *Muiopotmos* 394 Who..with secrete ioy..Did tickle inwardly in euerie vaine. **1624** Heywood *Captives* ii. i, I'l..sett my mind downe in so quaint a strayne Shall make her laugh and tickle. *a* **1625** Fletcher *Nice Valour* v. i, Oh, how my lungs do tickle! ha, ha, ha! **1647** H. More *Poems* 172 This pretty sport doth make my heart to tickle With laughter.

† **b.** Said of the feeling or its cause. *Obs. rare.*

**1579** Tomson *Calvin's Serm. Tim.* 14/2 For so much as.. this curiositie tickleth in many braines.

**2.** To tingle; to itch; also *fig.* to have an uneasy or impatient desire (usually *to do* something); to be eager. Now *rare.*

This sense was prob. in literal use much earlier, though quots. have not been found.

**1542** Udall *Erasm. Apoph.* 344 The fyngers of the Athenians ticleed to aid and succour Harpalus. **1557** N. T. (Genev.) *Acts* xvii. 19 *note*, People whose eares euer tickled to heare newes. **1591** Savile *Tacitus' Hist.* iv. xliii. 202 The Senatour's fingers euen tickled against him. **1906** N. Munro in *Blackw. Mag.* Dec. 802/2, I fairly tickle to take a walk along. *Mod.* My foot tickles.

**II.** Transitive senses (= L. *titillāre*).

**3.** Said of a thing, or impersonally with *it*: To excite agreeably (a person, his heart, ears, palate, etc.); to give pleasure or amusement to; to please, gratify. *To tickle to death*: cf. Death 12 b.

*c* **1386** Chaucer *Wife's Prol.* 471 It tikleth [*v.rr.* tikeleth, tykelith, ticleþ] me aboute myn herte roote. **1406** Hoccleve *Misrule* 204 So tikelid me þat nyce reuerence þat it me made larger of despense. **1495** *Trevisa's Barth. De P. R.* xviii. i. (W. de W.) Y j/1 By gendrynge hete tyklyth and pryckyth: that falleth moost in spryngynge tyme whan the vertue of ye hete of heuen begynnyþ to haue maystry of bodyes of beestys. **1597** J. Payne *Royal Exch.* 7 More for desire of imitation, then of anie intent to tyckle hym with adulation. **1607** Hieron *Wks.* I. 166 Well might they..haue their eares tickled with some pleasing noise. **1734** tr. *Rollin's Anc. Hist.* (1827) I. ii. 210 Eating in Egypt was designed not to tickle the palate but to satisfy the cravings of nature. **1859** Hawthorne *Fr. & It. Note-Bks.* II. 233 Something..that thrilled and tickled my heart with a feeling partly sensuous and partly spiritual. **1863** Geo. Eliot *Romola* xxv, Elements that..tickled gossiping curiosity, and fascinated timorous superstition.

**4.** To touch or stroke lightly with or as with the finger-tips, a straw, a feather, a hair, or the like; to tease, annoy, or irritate lightly, so as to cause a peculiar uneasy sensation. Also said of the thing. Also *absol.*

*c* **1450** *Voc.* in Wr.-Wülcker 571/23 *Catello*, to mewe or to tykele. [Cf. F. *chatouiller*, OF. *catouller* to tickle.] *c* **1532** Du Wes *Introd. Fr.* in *Palsgr.* 940 To tickel, *catouller.* **1566** Blundevil *Horsemanship* iv. lxviii. (1580) 28 b, By eating a feather, or by eating dustie or sharp bearded strawe, and such like things: which tickling his throte causeth him to cough. **1590** Shaks. *Mids. N.* iv. i. 28 If my haire do but tickle me, I must scratch. **1596** — 1 *Hen. IV*, ii. iv. 340 To tickle our Noses with Speargrasse, to make them bleed. **1704** Norris *Ideal World* ii. iii. 239 Who ever thought of anything like pleasure in a feather that tickles his hand? **1710** J. Clarke *Rohault's Nat. Phil.* (1729) I. 174 None of them will be able to prick the Tongue agreeably, but they will only tickle it in a disagreeable manner. **1837** Dickens *Pickw.* xxxvi, First, something tickles your right knee, and then the same sensation irritates your left.

**b.** To touch, or poke (a person) lightly in a sensitive part so as to excite spasmodic laughter. Also *absol.*

**1530** Palsgr. 349 He tykeleth my sydes, *il me catoille les costes. Ibid.* 758/1 And you tykell me thus I muste nedes laughe, *si vous me gattouillez..il mest force de rire.* **1589** Puttenham *Eng. Poesie* iii. xxii. (Arb.) 266 Her Maiestie laughed as she had bene tickled. **1596** Shaks. *Merch. V.* iii. i. 68 If you tickle vs, doe we not laugh? **1675** Wycherley *Country Wife* iv. iii, I am trying if Mr. Horner were ticklish ..I love to torment the confounded toad; let you and I tickle him. **1872** Darwin *Emotions* xiii. 310 We can cause laughing by tickling the skin.

**c.** Applied to a method of catching trout or other fish: see quot. 1884 s.v. Tickling *vbl. sb.* 3 c. Often in allusive use.

**1601** Shaks. *Twel. N.* ii. v. 26 Heere comes the Trowt, that must be caught with tickling. **1706–7** Farquhar *Beaux Strat.* iii. ii, He..tickles the trout, and so whips it into his basket. **1745** Pococke *Descr. East* II. ii. v. viii. 252 Men go into the water, tickle them on the belly, and so get them ashoar. **1823** Scott *Quentin D.* xxx, He spoke of fishing—I have sent him home a trout properly tickled! **1883** G. C. Davies *Norfolk Broads* xxiii. (1884) 177 The mode of tickling tench which at one time was common enough on some of the Broads.

**5.** *fig.* To excite amusement in; to divert; often in the phrase *to tickle the fancy.* Also *absol.*

*a* **1688** Villiers (Dk. Buckhm.) *Chances* Prol., There are Fools that tickle with their Face, Your gay Fool tickles with his Dress and Motions. **1771** Smollett *Humph. Cl.* 26 June, The young squire, tickled by this ironical observation, exclaimed, '*O che burla!*' *a* **1774** Tucker *Lt. Nat.* (1834) II. 129 Whose play had a quality of striking the joyous perception, or, as we vulgarly say, tickling the fancy. **1837** Lockhart *Scott* an. 1816 *note*, Such..was the story that went the round of the newspapers at the time, and highly tickled Scott's fancy. **1858** Doran *Crt. Fools* 10 Poor as the joke was, it..tickled the fancy of the Tirynthians. **1871** Blackie *Four Phases* i. 69 Brilliant oratorical displays to tickle and amuse. **1885** *Manch. Exam.* 16 May 6/1 Lord Hartington's slow, quiet, dry answer, 'No, sir', somewhat tickled the House.

**b.** To puzzle: cf. Sc. *to kittle. Sc. dial.*

**1865** Tester *Poems* 47 (E.D.D.) I've got ye out, but it tickles my brain How the deuce I'm to pitch ye in again.

**6.** To touch (a stringed instrument, etc.) lightly as in tickling a person; to stir (a fire, etc.) slightly.

**1589** Nashe *Anat. Absurd.* Epist., To tickle a Cittern, or have a sweete stroke on the Lute. **1592** Shaks. *Rom. & Jul.* i. iv. 36 Let wantons light of heart Tickle the sencelesse rushes with their heeles. **1740** Somerville *Hobbinol* i. 143 Hark from aloft his tortur'd Cat-gut squeals, He tickles ev'ry String. **1770** *Acc. Bks.* in *Ann. Reg.* 243/2 One of them began to tickle his guittar. **1796** Pegge *Derbicisms* (E.D.S.), Tickle the fire. **18..** in *Daily Chron.* 10 Dec. (1902) 9/1 A country whose soil, it has been well said, only requires to be tickled with a hoe to laugh with a harvest.

**b.** *ironically.* To beat, chastise.

**1592** Warner *Alb. Eng.* viii. xliii. (1612) 207 Whose Knightes, in 2 Richards dayes, so tickeld France and Spaine. **1601** Shaks. *Twel. N.* v. i. 198 If he had not beene in drinke, hee would haue tickel'd you other gates then he did. **1681** T. Flatman *Heraclitus Ridens* No. 35 (1713) I. 225 Our gracious Queen Elizabeth tickled their Tobies for them, for their Reformation. **1698** J. Crull *Muscovy* 175 They soundly tickle his Back, in the same Manner as we beat the Dust out of Cloaths. **1800** C. K. Sharpe *Corr.* (1888) I. 94 These little rogues..should be well tickled with the birch. **1861** *Sat. Rev.* XII. 199 Hogarth tickles the poor bardling with his pencil.

**c.** To touch *up*, trick *up*; to improve or decorate with light touches.

**1845** Thackeray *Crit. Rev.* Wks. 1886 XXIII. 238 The picture is..tickled up with a Chinese minuteness. **1852** — *Let.* in *Esmond* (1900) p. xxxiii, Dolls—painted and tickled up in the most charming way.

† **7.** To excite, affect, move; also, to vex, irritate, provoke. *Obs.*

**1547–64** Bauldwin *Mor. Philos.* (Palfr.) 116 Some men there be, whom bodily lust tickleth not at all. *a* **1548** Hall *Chron., Edw. IV* 204 These newes sodaynly brought to the kynge did not a littell vexe & tykil hym. **1593** Shaks. 2 *Hen. VI*, i. iii. 153 Shee's tickled now, her Fume needs no spurres. **1693** Dryden *Persius' Sat.* i. 28, I cannot rule my Spleen; My Scorn Rebels, and tickles me within. **1698** Fryer *Acc. E. India & P.* 316 What once tickled the Spleen of a Philosopher, might here hourly give him the Diversion.

† **b.** To arouse by or as by tickling; to stir up, incite, provoke; to prompt or impel *to do* something.

**1532** More *Confut. Tindale* Wks. 551/1 Ye pronity & mocions in the fleshe..whereby we be ticled towarde great actuall deadely sinnes. **1581** Marbeck *Bk. of Notes* 603 When our flesh tickleth vs to speake, we must resist it. *a* **1592** Greene *Alphonsus* iii. Wks. (Rtldg.) 237/1 What foolish toy hath tickled you to this?

**c.** With *up*: To stir up, arouse by tickling, excite to action.

**1567** Drant *Horace, Epist.* xiii. E iv, Such geare, As will embaite our Cesars eye, and tickle vp his eare. **1583** Babington *Commandm.* vii. (1637) 67 These things..tickle us up..to the breach of this Commandement. **1642** [Sir J. Spelman] *View Observ. H. M. Late Answ.* 38 They so tickle up the crasie minds of the multitude. **1674** N. Fairfax *Bulk & Selv.* 127 If such a spring as this is, may be tickled and rous'd up again. **1898** *Daily News* 25 Nov. 2/2 Why don't you tickle up Sandys with those spurs?

**d.** To get or move (a thing) *into* or *out of* some place, position, or state, by action likened to tickling.

**1677** Gilpin *Demonol.* (1867) 389 He endeavours..to tickle Him into a humour of affecting the glory and admiration which [etc.]. **1688** R. Holme *Armoury* iii. 315/1 When the Butcher is to Blood them and tickle them out of their Lives. **1702** *Eng. Theophrast.* Pref. 2 Others..have endeavoured to tickle men out of their Follies. **1704** F. Fuller *Med. Gymn.* (1711) 88 This is to Cheat People with the *Bellaria* of Physick, and Tickle Men into the Grave. **1725** Byrom *Let. to R. L.* ix, The cunning old Pug..took Puss's two Foots, And so out o' th' Embers he tickl'd his Nuts. **1904** *Westm. Gaz.* 28 Dec. 2/2 He slipped from the chair, tickled his toes into his slippers, and threw his shoulders back.

† **8.** *To tickle it*: (?) to bring to an agreeable end; to ensure a satisfactory result. *Obs.*

**1599** B. Jonson *Cynthia's Rev.* iv. v, I am sorry the reuels are crost. I should ha' tickled it soone. **1672** Dryden *Assignation* iii. i, Now, I think I have tickled it; this discovery has reinstated me into the Empire of my wit again. **1761** Sterne *Tr. Shandy* III. xx, Bless us!—what noble work we should make!—how should I tickle it off!

**9.** In various figurative phrases and expressions, mostly with reference to the pleasing effects of tickling. *To tickle in the palm*, to gratify with a 'tip'.

**1694** Motteux *Rabelais* v. xiii. (1737) 54 We tickled the Men in the Palm. **1706** E. Ward *Wooden World Diss.* (1708) 31 The Ale-Wives tickle him in the Gills with the Title of Captain. **1742** Young *Nt. Th.* viii. 755 'Tis pride, or emptiness, applies the straw That tickles little minds to mirth effuse. **1807–8** W. Irving *Salmag.* (1824) 224 This straw tickled the noses of all our dignitaries wonderfully. **1843** Carlyle *Past & Pr.* ii. viii, Tickle me, Toby, and I'll tickle thee! **1874** *Siliad* iv. 110 But, tickled by a shilling in his palm, [he] Walked on discreetly blind. **1901** *Scotsman* 4 Mar. 10/5 An officer..when he gets on a palace-car, he can tickle the porter just as much as he desires at the expense of the Government pocket-book.

**10.** In combination with a sb.; as † **tickle-brain**, potent liquor; hence *transf.* one who supplies it; **tickle-grass**, name given in U.S. to various grasses, as the hair-grass, *Agrostis scabra*, the old-witch grass, *Panicum capillare* (*Cent. Dict.*); **tickle-moth**, **tickle-pitcher** (*slang*): see quots.; **tickle-text** (*slang*), a parson; **tickle-toby** [cf. quot. 1681 in 6 b, also Motteux *Rabelais* iv. xiii], a birch, rod, switch; also, the use of this; **tickle-weed**, swamp hellebore, *Veratrum viride.* See also Tickle-tail.

**1596** Shaks. 1 *Hen. IV*, ii. iv. 438 Peace good Pint-pot, peace, good *Tickle-braine. **1639** Davenport *New Tricke* iii. i, A Cup of Nipsitate, briske and neate; The Drawers call it Tickle-Braine. **1833** *Veg. Subst. Materials of Manuf.* ix. 162 A species of grass growing spontaneously in that part of the United States [Connecticut], and popularly known by the name of *tickle-moth. *a* **1700** B. E. *Dict. Cant. Crew*, **Tickle-pitcher*, a Toss-pot, or Pot-companion. **1725** in *New Cant. Dict.* **1785** Grose *Dict. Vulg. T.*, *Tickle pitcher*, a thirsty fellow, a sot. *Ibid.*, **Tickle text*, a parson. **1830** Bentham *Corr.* Wks. 1843 XI. 37 A touch, every now and then, of the *tickle-Toby, which I keep in pickle for you. **1842** Thackeray (*title*) Miss Tickletoby's Lectures. **1909** *Daily Chron.* 24 July 3/2 Miss Aurora, who, to the peril of her neck, practises tickle-toby on Brother Gustavus's bare soles. **1762** Mills *Syst. Pract. Husb.* I. 156 Swamp hellebore (known in different places by the several names of skunk-cabbage, *tickle-weed, bear-root).

Hence **Tickled** (ti·k'ld) *ppl. a.*

*a* **1586** Sidney *Arcadia* iii. (1605) 343 A smiling countenance,..mixt betweene a tickled mirth, and a forced pittie. **1647** H. More *Song Soul* ii. App. lxvi, His silvered sound would touch our tickled ear. **1880** G. Meredith *Tragic Com.* (1881) 11 They encouraged her with the tickled wonder which bids the bold advance yet farther into bogland. **1896** *Blackw. Mag.* May 769 No corn or tickled up seed could get them [wild-fowl] up the pipes.

[*Note.* Derivation from Tick *v.*[1], in sense 'to touch lightly', would, both in form and sense, suit the later use of *tickle*, but is not favoured by the chronology (since *tick* is not known so early as *tickle*), nor by the fact that the earliest recorded sense includes no notion of light touching or of the action of any external agent, but merely expresses a bodily sensation. These considerations partly also affect the theory of metathesis from *kittle*, inasmuch as the latter, exc. in the vbl. sb. *kitelung* (*a* 1100), *kitlyng*, has not been found before 1440, and is from the first trans., = L. *titillare* to tickle (some one). But in ON., *kitla*, like *hungra, þyrsta*, etc., was an impersonal vb. of primary sensation: *mig kitlar* 'it kittles me', like *mig hungrar* 'it hungers me'. Traces of this appear also with 'tickle': see 'it tikleth me' in sense 3. It was natural for an impers. vb. to develop both intrans. and trans. constructions: cf. the senses of Irk *v.*, and the modern *it grieves me* with *I grieve* and *you grieve me.* It seems possible that ONorse *kitla* was adopted at an early date in some parts of England as *kit(e)l-en, kittel-*, and in others, under the influence of *tick*, as *tikl-, tikel-*, and that the latter became the general Eng. form, while the more original *kitl-, kittle*, was used farther north, and was thus later in literary record. Neither form appears in *Cursor Mundi.*]

†**Tickle,** (?) dial. form of TITTLE *v.*[1], to whisper.

1575 *Gammer Gurton* II. ii, Sig. B iiij, But Tib hath tykled in Gammers eare that you shoulde steal the cock.

† **Ti·cklely, tickly,** *adv. Obs. rare.* Also 7 tickely, tickly. [f. TICKLE *a.* + -LY [2].] In an insecure or unstable manner; ticklishly.

1601 SIR W. CORNWALLIS *Disc. Seneca* (1631) 10 It is meet they should stand thus tickly. *a* 1628 F. GREVIL *Alaham* II. ii, So tickely unworthinesse doth stand. 1674 N. FAIRFAX *Bulk & Selv.* 68 A Coach may be so tickly set upon the surface of the earth, as to give it self a trundling, one way or other.

**Ticklenburgs** (ti·klĕnbɒɹgz). Also 7 **Ticklenburs, Ticklingburs.** [For *Tecklenburg*, from a town and county of this name in Westphalia, noted for its manufactures of linen.] A kind of coarse linen cloth; see quots.

1696 J. F. *Merchant's Ware-ho.* 39 Ticklenburs is .. a coarse Linnen, and generally very uneven, ..the right Ticklingburs are almost as strong again as the Ozenbricks [Osnaburgs]... There is not many Cloths sold in England that hath so great Consumption as this. 1812 J. SMYTH *Pract. of Customs* (1821) 133 Linen: Ticklenburgs are known by that word being stamped on the Cloth. 1858 SIMMONDS *Dict. Trade, Ticklenburghs*, a coarse mixed linen fabric made for the West India market.

† **Ti·ckleness.** *Obs.* [f. TICKLE *a.* + -NESS.] The quality or state of being tickle; insecurity, instability; critical situation, precariousness; inconstancy; uncertainty.

*c* 1390 CHAUCER *Truth* 3 Suffise þin owen þing þei it be smal For horde haþe hate & Clymbyng tykelnesse [*v.rr.* tekil-, tikul-]. 1549 in Tytler *Eng. under Edw. VI*, etc. (1839) I. 232 Weighing as well the state of the things above, as also the tickleness of the country. *a* 1625 in Gutch *Coll. Cur.* I. 182, I found such tickleness in the performance of such charges, that..my prayers will be full of fear. 1674 N. FAIRFAX *Bulk & Selv.* 137 According to the tickleness of its lodging in the *machina mundi.*

**Tickler** (ti·kləɹ). [f. TICKLE *v.* + -ER [1].] One who or that which tickles, in various senses.

1. One who tickles by touching or stroking lightly.

1715 tr. *C'tess D'Aunoy's Wks.* 452 One of those ticklers of Cat-guts that march before the Milk-women upon May-day. 1736 CHESTERF. *Fog's Jrnl.* No. 377 ¶ 5, If, by chance, there be some few unhappy enough not to find ticklers, or some ticklers clumsy enough not to find business, they comfort themselves at least with self-titillation.

2. Something that tickles or is used for tickling.

**a.** A thing (or person) difficult to deal with or understand; a teaser; a puzzler (*colloq.*). **b.** A feather brush used to tickle the face of passers, as a diversion at fairs and carnivals. **c.** A birch or rod used in castigation; also, a single-stick. **d.** An instrument used by frame-work knitters for slipping the loops off one needle of the stocking-frame on to another in narrowing or shaping the fabric. **e.** An instrument for extracting bungs from casks. **f.** An implement for stirring a fire, a poker. **g.** In a motor engine, a device by which a small quantity of petrol is pumped into the carburettor to facilitate the starting of the engine. **h.** A small measure (about half a pint) of spirits (*U. S. colloq.*). **i.** A small knife or pistol carried on the person (*U. S. colloq.*). **j.** A memorandum book, or a series of dated cards on which to enter engagements (*U. S.*).

1680 COTTON *Compl. Gamester* (ed. 2) 4 The Knave and Rascal will violate his trust for profit, and lend him..a Tickler shall do his business. 1765 E. THOMPSON *Meretriciad* (ed. 6) 27 The tickler you must use, And as you flog the Vet'rans, flog the Muse. 1808 J. BALLANTYNE *Let.* in Smiles *Mem. J. Murray* (1891) I. v. 108 A review, termed by Mr. Jeffrey a tickler, is to appear. 1825 JAMIESON, *Tickler*, anything puzzling. 1825 *Sporting Mag.* XV. 349 John now practised often with the 'ticklers'; nor was it long before he attained the reputation of a noted hand at single stick. 1839 *Civil Eng. & Arch. Jrnl.* II. 118/1 A new and important manufacture..in the hosiery trade, in making lace caps from the stocking-frame, by the aid of the jack tickler machine. 1839 *Harry Franco* I. 74 (Thornton *Amer. Gloss.*), I don't see that I have got your name down in my tickler. 1840 HALIBURTON *Clockm.* Ser. III. xi. 155, I..have half a mind to give you a tickler in the ribs. 1844 DICKENS *Mart. Chuz.* xxxiii, A sword-stick, which he called his 'Tickler'; and a great knife, which..he called 'Ripper'. 1848 BARTLETT *Dict. Amer., Tickler*, a common name among merchants and bankers for a book in which a register of notes or debts is kept for reference. 1861 DICKENS *Gt. Expect.* ii, Tickler was a wax-ended piece of cane, worn smooth by collision with my tickled frame. 1875 *Sussex Gloss., Tickler*, an iron pin used by brewers to take a bung out of a cask. 1881 MISS JACKSON *Shropsh. Word-bk., Tickler*, a slender steel rod..used for stirring the fire. 1889 *Harper's Mag.* Aug. 388/2 Whiskey..was not usually bought by the drink, but by the tickler..a bottle..holding a half-pint. 1891 T. ANDERTON *Lett. fr. Country Ho.* 237 They poke out the gleeds at the bottom with the tickler, and put them at the top with the tongs. 1892 *Labour Commission* Gloss., *Ticklers*, four small points firmly fixed into a piece of wood which are pressed upon the eyes of the needles and remove the stitches in the hosiery industry. This is the operation of *fashioning*. 1904 *Sat. Rev.* 18 June 784/1 Patriots, who with whisky, rattles, ticklers, Union Jacks and patriotic melody..celebrated the relief [of Mafeking]. 1906 *Daily Chron.* 14 Nov. 9/3 The carburettor can be flooded without lifting the bonnet, by operating a 'tickler' situated outside the bonnet.

3. A large American longicorn beetle, *Monohammus titillator*, with very long antennæ. *U. S.*

1841–52 T. W. HARRIS *Insects Injur. Veget.* ii. (1862) 105 The largest Capricorn-beetle,..found in New England, is.. the tickler, so named probably on account of the habit which it has..of gently touching now and then the surface on which it walks with the tips of its long antennæ.

**Ticklesome** (ti·k'lsə̆m), *a.* [f. TICKLE *v.* + -SOME.]

1. That tends to tickle; difficult, critical, delicate, precarious, ticklish. Now *dial.*

1585 PARSONS *Chr. Exerc.* II. v. 343 Miserable is that man which placeth the ankor of his eternall wealth .. vpon so ticklesome a point as this is. 1604 — *3rd Pt. Three Convers. Eng.* 314 Hauinge moued such a matter..in so dangerous and ticklesome a tyme. 1898 MACMANUS *Bend of Road* 200 Yis, marriage is a ticklesome subject.

2. ? Easily tickled; tickly; ticklish; suitable or fitted for tickling or laughter.

1844 HOOD *Let. to May Elliot* Apr., Wks. 1873 X. 404, I mean to come in my most ticklesome waistcoat, and to laugh till I grow fat. 1898 MACDONAGH *Irish Life & Char.* xvii. 313 The man's so ticklesome that sorra a tailor in the counthry can..take his measure.

**Ti·ckle-tail.** [f. TICKLE *a.* or *v.* + TAIL *sb.*]

1. A loose or wanton woman; cf. TICKLE *a.* 3 b. Now *dial.*

*c* 1430 LYDG. *Min. Poems* (Percy Soc.) 31 Canst thou no better come to holynesse, Than lese thiself al for a tikeltaylle? 1869 J. P. MORRIS *Lancs. Gloss.* (E.D.D.).

2. That which (or one who) tickles the 'tail'; see quots.

1785 GROSE *Dict. Vulg. T., Tickle tail*, a rod, or schoolmaster. 1828 *Craven Gloss., Tickle-tail*, a rod.

3. A game: = THREAD-NEEDLE 1. *dial.*

1821 *Blackw. Mag.* Aug. 36/2 Another game played by a number of children with a hold of one another, or tickle-tails, as it is technically called in Scotland, is, *Through the Needle-e'e.*

**Tickling** (ti·kliŋ), *vbl. sb.* [f. TICKLE *v.* + -ING [1].] The action or condition denoted by the verb TICKLE.

1. An uneasy sensation as of the teasing of some sensitive part of the skin or mucous membrane; slight nervous irritation akin to itching.

1398 TREVISA *Barth. De P. R.* v. xxviii. (Bodl. MS.) lf. 16/1 þe whiche wormes litel & litel wroteþ and eteþ þe skyn & makeþ tikeling and icching. *c* 1425 tr. *Arderne's Treat. Fistula* 61 When-someuer þe pacient feleþ tyklyng or ychyng or prykkyng in þe lure. 1626 BACON *Sylva* § 766 All tickling is a light motion of the spirits, which the thinness of the skin, and suddenness and rareness of the touch do further. 1843 R. J. GRAVES *Syst. Clin. Med.* xx. 242 A sensation of tickling in the mucous membrane of the trachea. 1898 J. HUTCHINSON in *Arch. Surg.* IX. No. 36. 341 He had some tickling in his throat.

2. *fig.* A tingling or 'itching' to do something; uneasy desire, craving, hankering.

1553 *Short Catech.* in *Liturgies*, etc. (Parker Soc.) 521 Our will is commonly by tickling of affections and stirring of lusts, drawn to do those things that God is displeased with. 1558 KNOX *First Blast* (Arb.) 24 Women haue in them selues a tickling and studie of vaine glorie. 1683 BURNET tr. *More's Utopia* (1685) 101 These Things may create some Tickling in the Senses. 1874 GEO. ELIOT *Coll. Breakf. P.* 628 Whose brain..Has feeble ticklings of a vanity.

3. A repeated light touching, stroking, or poking, such as to cause laughter; a state of being tickled; *fig.* pleasing excitation, gratification; also, excitement of the risible faculty, amusement.

1423 JAS. I *Kingis Q.* xxi, With the tiklyng of his hete and light, The tender flouris opnyt thame and sprad. *c* 1440 *Promp. Parv.* 493/2 Tykyllynge, *titillacio.* 1548 UDALL *Erasm. Par.* Pref. 3 The pleasaunt ticleyng or clawyng of adulacion. 1603 HOLLAND *Plutarch's Mor.* 311 They who naturally are enclined and disposed to laughter, are to avoid and decline the ticklings and soft handling in those parts of the body that are most smooth, sleicke and tender. 1662 PLAYFORD *Skill Mus.* I. xi. (1674) 39 A certain tickling of the ears of those who do not well understand what it is to sing Passionately. 1728 YOUNG *Love Fame* II. (1757) 94 Tickling is unsafe, If still 'tis painful while it makes us laugh. 1872 DARWIN *Emotions* viii. 201 This so-called tickling of the mind is curiously analogous with that of the body.

† **b.** Used as a term of endearment. *Obs. rare.*

1605 B. JONSON *Volpone* III. v, Thou art mine honor, Mosca, and my pride, My ioy, my tickling, my delight!

**c.** *spec.* The taking of trout and other fish by the method described in quot. 1884.

*a* 1616 BEAUM. & FL. *Scornf. Lady* III. ii, Leave off your tickling of young heirs like trouts. 1826 SCOTT *Woodst.* vii, Every fisher loves best the trouts that are of his own tickling. 1884 JEFFERIES *Red Deer* ix. 174 Groping for trout (or tickling)—is tracing it to the stone it lies under, then rubbing it gently beneath, which causes the fish to gradually move backwards into the hand, till the fingers suddenly close in the gills.

4. *attrib.*, as **tickling-house**, (*satirical slang*) a place of preaching: cf. *tickle-text* (TICKLE *v.* 12).

1681 T. FLATMAN *Heraclitus Ridens* No. 29 (1713) I. 192 A Boy that has but..carried his Mistress's Bible to the Tickling-house.

**Ti·ckling,** *ppl. a.* [f. as prec. + -ING [2].] That tickles, in various senses of the verb; exciting pleasantly, gratifying, alluring; amusing, diverting; delicate, tingling, itching; ticklish.

1558 PHAER *Æneid* I. B iij b, In her brest the tykling ioye her hart to myrth enclynes. 1595 SHAKS. *John* II. i. 573 That smooth-fac'd Gentleman, tickling commoditie. 1607 TOPSELL *Four-f. Beasts* (1658) 475 The tickling or itching humor, lying betwixt the skin and the flesh, causeth the poor Sheep either to bite the place with his teeth,..or to rub it upon a tree or wall. 1675 CROWNE *Country Wit* I. i, Fie upon this tickling rheum! 1681 (*title*) Some Observations upon the Tickling Querie, viz. Whether the admitting of a Popish Successor be the best way to Preserve the Protestant Religion [etc.]. 1761 PULTENEY in *Phil. Trans.* LII. 346 A little tickling cough which had remained with him. 1863 GEO. ELIOT *Romola* ix, Such vague memories hang about the mind like cobwebs, with tickling importunity. 1887 RUSKIN *Præterita* II. 30 One evening..a short tickling cough surprised me.

Hence **Ti·cklingly** *adv.*, so as to tickle.

1898 J. A. STEUART *Minister of State* I. iv, He smacked his lips and laughed again;..the recollections of his aunt's choler [were] ticklingly comical.

**Ticklish** (ti·kliʃ), *a.* [f. TICKLE *a.* or *v.* + -ISH [1].]

1. Easily tickled; sensitive to tickling.

1598 FLORIO, *Solético*, ticklish. 1615 CROOKE *Body of Man* 72 Some part of the skin is..thin, as in the sides and soales of the feete, which is the reason that there men are ticklish. 1685 BOYLE *Effects of Mot.* v. 53 A ticklish man, by having the pulp of one's finger passed gently along the sole of his foot,..has divers muscles and other parts of his body and face put into..unusual motions. 1833 MARRYAT *P. Simple* xix, As for not standing the charge of bayonets, it was not because they were less brave, but the fact was, that they were most excessively ticklish. 1899 *Allbutt's Syst. Med.* VIII. 128 A peculiar mental affection, locally known as Latah (a word signifying nervous or ticklish).

† **b.** Sensitive, easily affected; of a horse: Sensitive to touch; tender. *Obs.*

1681 *Lond. Gaz.* No. 1589/4 She drags her hinder feet,.. cuts a little behind, she is very ticklish on her Crest. 1684 R. WALLER *Nat. Exper.* 6 After this manner may be had a very ticklish Thermometer. 1716 *Lond. Gaz.* No. 5415/4 [A mare] with a Malender on her near Fore Leg, and very ticklish to be touch'd on that Place.

2. Unstably balanced or poised; easily unbalanced or upset; unsteady; of a boat: easily capsized.

1601 HOLLAND *Pliny* (1634) II. 584 The follie of the blind & bold people of Rome went beyond al; who trusted such a ticklish frame, & durst sit there, in a seat so moueable. 1639 FULLER *Holy War* III. v. (1840) 123 So ticklish are the scales of victory, a very mote will turn them. 1687 A. LOVELL tr. *Thevenot's Trav.* I. 27 Little slight Boats or Wherries, and so tick'lish that by leaning more to one side than another, it is an easie matter to overset them. 1784 COWPER *Task* III. 550 The ticklish balance of suspense. 1861 DU CHAILLU *Equat. Afr.* xiv. 234 They are ticklish craft.

**b.** Of game: Difficult to approach; shy: = TICKLE *a.* 6 c.

1826 COL. HAWKER *Diary* (1893) I. 290 He got four wigeon, but found the birds very ticklish. 1829 *Ibid.* 359 Birds all scattered and ticklish.

3. *fig.* Easily upset in temper; apt to be offended, sensitive, touchy.

1581 MULCASTER *Positions* xxxvii. (1887) 152 Such parentes as be tikelish, and such scholers as be shifting, removing from maisters and renouncing of obedience. 1634 T. JOHNSON *Parey's Wks.* 1173 There is not any man so ticklish, which taketh not in good part what I have said. 1794 GOUV. MORRIS in Sparks *Life & Writ.* (1832) II. 426 Men are very ticklish in such revolutions as the present. 1821 BYRON *Let. to Moore* 16 Nov., You are ticklish on such points.

4. Unstable, unsteady, unsettled, uncertain, fickle.

1606 in Gardiner *Hist. Eng.* I. 408 *note*, Considering.. how ticklish their disposition is towards the State. *a* 1661 FULLER *Worthies* (1840) III. 265 But foreign friendship is ticklish, temporary, and lasteth no longer than it is advantaged with mutual interest. 1693 SOUTH *Serm.* 99 Uncertain ticklish and variable. 1770–4 A. HUNTER *Georg. Ess.* (1803) III. 514 Resisting the effects of bad weather in ticklish hay seasons. 1847 LD. PALMERSTON *Let.* 5 Feb. in Bulwer *Life* (1874) III. 337 A throne whose stability rests on the point of the bayonet has a very ticklish and uncertain basis.

5. Liable to end in disaster unless treated with great care; needing cautious handling or action; delicate, critical, precarious, risky, hazardous.

1591 SAVILE *Tacitus' Hist.* I. lxxxv. 48 To beare a man's selfe euenly in so nice and ticklish a case. 1600 HOLLAND *Livy* III. lxv. 133 So ticklish and dangerous a thing it is to keepe a meane in maintenance of libertie. 1666 W. BOGHURST *Loimographia* (1894) 81 This is a very ticklish disease, and the least error committed turnes a man out of dores. 1674 N. FAIRFAX *Bulk & Selv.* To Rdr., 'Tis a more ticklish thing to pen a Preface, than 'tis to write a Book. 1711 SWIFT *Lett.* (1767) III. 195 'Tis a plaguy ticklish piece of work, and a man hazards losing both sides. 1775 J. JEKYLL *Corr.* 30 May, Her rash, which perhaps was a critical symptom in her ticklish constitution. 1809 MALKIN *Gil Blas* XII. i. (Rtldg.) 423 A very ticklish predicament. 1899 F. T. BULLEN *Log Sea-waif* 27 This is a ticklish evolution to perform successfully in a crowded anchorage.

6. quasi-*adv.* Ticklishly; in a ticklish or easily moved state; unsteadily; delicately. Now *rare.*

1661 R. BAILLIE in *Lauderdale Papers* (Camden) I. 95, I think you stand tiklish. 1771 LUCKOMBE *Hist. Print.* 318 The upper sides of these Ribs must..be somewhat arching ..then the Cramp-Irons run more easily and ticklish over them. 1775 T. HUTCHINSON *Diary* 24 Oct., Mr. Gibbon.. says the Minister who proposed them stands ticklish.

7. *Comb.*, as *ticklish-tempered.*

1897 MARY KINGSLEY *W. Africa* 651 Ticklish-tempered native gentlemen.

**Ticklishly** (ti·kliʃli), *adv.* [f. prec. + -LY [2].] In a ticklish position or fashion; insecurely, critically, delicately.

1640 E. DACRES tr. *Machiavelli's Prince* 147 The forraine matters stand but ticklishly. 1762 KAMES *Elem. Crit.* xxiv. (1774) II. 478 A bare uniform cylinder..without a base, appears too ticklishly placed to stand firm. 1794 WASHINGTON *Let. to T. Lear* 14 Dec., It is to be lamented however, that in plain matters—a little ticklishly circumstanced—such hazards..should be unnecessarily encountered. 1846 D. JERROLD *Chron. Clovernook* Wks. 1864 IV. 424 Paste-board huts, so loosely, so ticklishly put together, that every wind that blows scares the tenants.

**Ticklishness** (ti·kliʃnės). [f. as prec. + -NESS.] The quality of being ticklish: see the adj.

1583 GOLDING *Calvin on Deut.* lxxxii. 503 Besides yt ticklishnes which we haue alreadie of nature it pricketh vs forewarde to say why should not such a thing be good. 1598 FLORIO, *Gattorigole*, ticklings, ticklishness. 1607 MARKHAM *Caval.* v. (1617) 24 His vncomelinesse onely proceedes from ticklishnesse, or delight which he takes in the friction. *a* 1631 DONNE *Lett.* (1651) 355 You know the ticklishnesse of London-Pulpits. 1647 CLARENDON *Hist. Reb.* v. § 116 Such was the ticklishness of the King's condition, that..it was not thought Counsellable at that time ..to commit them to Prison. 1739 CHEYNE *Regimen* 200 (L.) We know by the ticklishness of the soles [of the feet] what a multitude of fine nervous fibres terminate in them. 1790 PALEY *Horæ Paul.* vi. (1849) 389 The difficulty and ticklishness of the times in which we live. 1905 *Longm. Mag.* Feb. 360 The mare..was in high spirits, which demonstrated themselves by an affectation of extreme ticklishness, when a fly alighted on her shining flank.

**Tickly** (ti·kli), *a.* [f. TICKLE *a.* + -Y.] Ticklish; = KITTLY.

1530 PALSGR. 327/2 Tyckely, that can nat abyde tyckelynge. 1661 FELTHAM *Resolves* II. xxxv. 252 Nor did they, like ticklie Italians, pet at this and put another in his room. 1825 JAMIESON, *Tickly*, puzzling, difficult. 1897 FLANDRAU *Harvard Episodes* 223, I was laughing so that my wrists were all sort of tickly on the inside.

**b. Tickly-be·nders**, thin ice which bends under one's weight; = KITTLY-BENDERS.

1853 KANE *Grinnell Exp.* xxii. (1856) 179 The young ice glazing it over, so as to form a viscid sea of sludge and tickly-benders.

**Tickly**: see TICKLELY *adv. Obs.*

**Ti·ckney.** *Obs.* or *dial.* [From *Ticknal*, name of a place near Derby where this earthenware was made.] Epithet of a coarse kind of earthenware (*Tickney ware*); hence, made of this ware (also *fig.*).

1680 V. ALSOP *Mischief of Impos.* viii. 78 Are Churchmen more afraid their Tickney Rules and China-Canons should be preserved than broken? 1688 R. HOLME *Armoury* III. 113/1 Potters [are] sellers of Earthen or Tickney Ware. *Ibid.* xiv. (Roxb.) 7/1 A drinking Jugg or a Tickney Jugge. [1870 CHAFFERS *Porcelain* (ed. 3) 592 There was a Pottery at Ticknal near Derby as early as the 16th century, which produced articles of a coarse hard body, of a dull brown colour, sometimes decorated with yellow slip.] 1881 MISS JACKSON *Shropsh. Word-bk.*, *Tickney*, *Tickney-ware*, *obsols.*, common, coarse earthenware.

**Tick-seed**: see TICK *sb.*[1] 3.

**Tick-tack** (ti·k,tæ·k). Also 6 *Sc.* **tik tak**, 7 **tic-tack**, **tick(e)-tacke**, 7–9 **tic-tac**. [Echoic: so Du., Norw. *tiktak*, Sw., Da., Ger. *tick-tack*, F. *tic-tac*. In sense 2 an adaptation or kind of translation of F. *trictrac*, a similar echoic word: see TRIC-TRAC.]

**1.** An imitation of a reduplicated or alternating ticking sound, esp. that made by a clock (see TICK *sb.*[3] 2); also that of the firing of small artillery. (Used as *adv.* or *interj.*, and hence as *sb.* to denote the sound.)

1549 *Compl. Scot.* vi. 42 Than the smal artailȝe cryit, tik tak, tik tak, tik tak, tik tak. 17.. in *Ritson's Gamm. Gurton's Garl.* (1783) 53 Here a nail, there a nail, Tick, tack, too. 1840 *P. Parley's Ann.* 54, I am quite tired of your [a clock's] tick tack. 1858 O. W. HOLMES *Aut. Breakf.-t.* viii, Our brains are seventy-year clocks...Tic-tac! tic-tac! go the wheels of thought. 1909 *Daily Chron.* 12 June 5/1 A Gatling gun..played upon the infantry..; one heard the 'tick-tack', 'tick-tack' of the spitting fire.

**b.** In auscultation, The sound of the heart-beat. (Usually in Fr. form *tic-tac.*)

1853 MARKHAM *Skoda's Auscult.* 175 The normal sounds of the heart are generally indicated by the expression 'tic-tac'...This tic-tac I call the sounds (*Töne*) of the heart... By murmurs (*Geräusche*) I understand the abnormal sounds ..blowing, sawing, rasping, etc. *Ibid.* 207, I have occasionally heard two sounds..in the place of the proper second sound: thus, instead of the ordinary 'tic-tac', a 'tic-tac-tac'. 1860 J. M. CARNOCHAN *Operat. Surg.* 136 (Cent. Dict.) The normal tick-tack of the heart beat with healthy precision.

†**2.** An old variety of backgammon, played on a board with holes along the edge, in which pegs were placed for scoring. Also *fig. Obs.* (Also called TRIC-TRAC, in F. *trictrac.*)

1558 FORREST *Grysilde Sec.* I. xi. (Roxb.) 28 To pastyme at Tables, Tick-tacke or Gleeke. 1598 B. JONSON *Ev. Man in Hum.* III. iii. *c* 1618 MORYSON *Itin.* IV. IV. vi. (1903) 396 They play much at Tables, Commonly Tick Tack and lurch, but never at Irish. 1740 tr. *De Mouhy's Fort. Country-Maid* (1741) II. 188 Sometimes we plaid at Tick-tack.

**3.** *attrib.* †**a.** Belonging, or addicted, to the game of tick-tack (*obs.*). **b.** *slang.* Applied to a system of 'telegraphy' or signalling used by bookmakers at race-meetings, and hence to the men who practise this (cf. TICKER[3] b).

1583 BABINGTON *Commandm.* ii. (1590) 104 If hee bee a drunken ale-stake, a ticktack tauerner. 1665 in *Boston* (Mass.) *Transcript* 17 Sept. (1910) II. 8/1 Two tick tack tables. *Ibid.*, A tick tack board with the pieces. 1899 *Daily News* 15 Mar. 5/5 Another class who are persecuted most absurdly, as it seems to me, are the 'tick tack' men. 1905 *Daily Chron.* 1 Feb. 3/6 A prisoner puzzled the King-ston Bench by describing himself as 'a racecourse telegraphist'...A detective explained that the man practised what is known as 'tick-tack telegraphy'—signalling by means of the arms to outside bookmakers.

Hence **Tick-tacker**, one who practises tick-tack telegraphy; **Tick-tacking** *ppl. a.*, making an alternating ticking sound; **Tick-tack-toe**, also called *tit-tat-toe*, *tip-tap-toe*, a children's game played on a slate, consisting in trying with the eyes shut to bring the pencil down on one of the numbers of a set, the number hit being scored.

1842 *Father Oswald* xii. 117 The death-watch..is a little tick-tacking noise. *a* 1847 ELIZA COOK *Old Mill-stream* xxi, Thy pouring cascade, and the tic-tac-ing mill. 1884 *Mag. of Art* Feb. 135/2 He saw those children playing tic-tac-toe. 1899 CROCKETT *Anna Mark* xii, Playing at quoits, tops, marbles, tic-tac-toe, jacks, knuckle-bones. 1912 *Daily News* 28 Mar. 4 Bookies, tipsters, tick-tackers, runners, welshers, backers, and all the great army who go racing.

**Tick-tick** (ti·k,ti·k). [Echoic.] An imitation of the ticking of a clock or watch, or a similar sound; hence a child's name for a clock or watch.

1774 FOOTE *Cozeners* III. Wks. 1799 II. 190 Marianne, who opened the window? *Mar.* Little massa, to shew me de tick-tick. *a* 1849 J. C. MANGAN 20 *Gold. Y. Ago* viii, Tick-tick, tick-tick!—Not a sound save Time's. 1864 GLAISHER in *Circ. Sc.* (*c* 1865) I. 1209/2 We heard..the tick-tick of a threshing machine. 1894 H. DRUMMOND *Ascent Man* 214 The child who says..tick-tick for watch, or puff-puff for train, is an authority on the origin of human speech.

So **Tick-tick** *v.*; hence **Tick-ticking** *vbl. sb.*

1755 *B. Bright's New Jrnl.* 6 If..his Mistress..is absent, the Clock tick-ticks very slow. 1897 *Daily News* 17 May 3/3 The tick-ticking of the [telegraph] machines.

**Tick-tock** (ti·k,tǫ·k). Also **tic-toc**. [Echoic.] An imitation of the ticking of a clock, esp. the slow ticking of a large clock; also of the sound of a double knock, or of resounding footsteps.

1848 THACKERAY *Van. Fair* xxiii, They were both so silent that the tick-tock of the..clock on the mantelpiece became quite rudely audible. 1878 BROWNING *Poets Croisic* cxxvii, Bold tic-toc Announces there's a giant at the door. 1906 R. WHITEING *Ring in New* 197 The tic-toc of the high heels was insistent in the passages.

**Tick-trefoil, Tick-weed**: see TICK *sb.*[1] 3.

**Tickwood**, obs. var. *teakwood* (TEAK).

1794 *Trans. Soc. Arts* XII. 314 Tickwood plant or Iattee.

**Ticky** (ti·ki), *sb.* Also **tiki**, **tickie**, **tikkie**, **tickey**. [Origin uncertain; see Note.] The colloquial name in South Africa for a threepenny piece.

[*a* 1860 Remembered in colloquial use at Cape Town.]
1877 J. A. CHALMERS *Tiyo Soga* xxii. 471 Those poured an unusually large quantity of tickies into the plates at the doors. 1895 *Westm. Gaz.* 6 Mar. 8/1 The coin of smallest value in the Transvaal is the 'tickie', or threepenny-bit. 1903 *Ibid.* 25 July 2/1 In purchasing-power the 'tickey' [of Johannesburg] is certainly not more than equal to the penny of London. In many cases its value is less than a halfpenny.

[*Note.* Residents of Cape Colony, whose memory goes back to *c* 1850, state that they have known 'ticky' all their lives. The prevalent notion is that the word was first used by the Caffres or other native labourers; it is at present in Sesuto (the Basuto lang.), *teke* (te·ke). But it is believed to have been a native imitation of some Dutch or Eng. word; e.g. of Cape Dutch *stukje* 'little piece, little bit', pronounced (stüki), and imitated by the natives as (*tüki*, *tiki*); according to others, of Eng. *ticket*, it being explained that on an occasion when a large body of natives were employed on a public work, they were, for want of small silver coin, paid with tickets for 3d., which were taken in payment by the provision stores, and redeemed at that rate by the authorities. Other statements or conjectures (e. g. that *tikki* was an attempt to say 'little') have been offered in the *Cape Times*, etc., April to June 1912, but nothing in the form of evidence has been adduced.]

**Ticky** (ti·ki), *a.* [f. TICK *sb.*[1] + -Y.] Full of or infested by ticks.

1831 *Blackw. Mag.* XXX. 270 He [a turkey] becomes.. craven and crest-fallen, emaciated and ticky.

**Ticle**, obs. form of TICKLE.

‖**Tic-polonga** (tik,pǫlǫ·ŋgä). *Zool.* [According to *Madras Manual of Administration* III. 154, ad. Sinhalese *tit-polongā*, f. *tita*, in comb. *tit-*, speck, freckle, spot, mark + *polongā* viper. The form with *tic-* is app. due to substituting *tik* 'spot, freckle, mark, spot on tiger-deer', for *tit-*.] A venomous snake of India and Ceylon: the chain viper or necklace-snake, *Daboia Russellii.*

[1681 R. KNOX *Hist. Ceylon* 29 There is another venomous Snake called *Polonga*, the most venomous of all.] 1825 MRS. HEBER in *H.'s Narr. Journ.* (1828) II. xxvii. 258 The Cobra de Capello is the most common, but its bite is not so certainly fatal as that of the Tic Polonga. 1834 CAUNTER *Orient. Ann.* vii. 80 A large dog, belonging to a Cingalese who accompanied us, was bitten by a snake, the ticpolonga. 1910 *Times* 13 Sept. 7/4 Three of the most deadly snakes known in India—the cobra, the tic-polonga or Russell's viper, and the banded krait.

**Tic-tac, Tic-toc**: see TICK-TACK, TICK-TOCK.

**Tid** (tid), *sb.*[1] *Sc.* [? unexplained var. of TIDE *sb.*]

**1.** A fit or favourable time or season; an opportunity, occasion.

1721 RAMSAY *Elegy Patie Birnie* xiii. 1728 — *Fables, Fox & Rat* 40 He took the tid when Lowry was away. 1801 MACNEILL *Poet Wks.* (1844) 54 To catch the tids o' life is sage, Some joys to save.

**2.** *spec.* The proper season for some agricultural operation, as harrowing or sowing; hence, suitable condition of the soil for cultivation or cropping.

1799 J. ROBERTSON *Agric. Perth* 147 If it were not for fear of losing the proper opportunity (the *Tid* of sowing, as it is vulgarly called), the longer the wheat-seed is delayed.. the better. 1825 JAMIESON, *Tid*..2. The condition which any soil is in for the purpose of agriculture; as, 'The ground's no in tid'. *c* 1830 in Stephens *Bk. Farm* (1844) I. 537 A tid (or proper condition of the ground for harrowing) cannot be taken advantage of on the drained furrow until the other is dry. 1842 J. AITON *Domest. Econ.* (1857) 79 The 'tids' of seed-time, hay-time, and harvest, are in a great measure lost. 1863 MORTON *Cycl. Agric.* Gloss. (E.D.S.).

**3.** A humour, mood, or fancy to do something.

*a* 1774 FERGUSSON *Farmer's Ingle* Poems (1845) 38 Tak tent, case Crummy tak her wonted tids, And ca' the laiglen's treasure [i. e. the new milk] on the ground. 1825 JAMIESON s.v., *To tak the tid*, to be seized with a perverse or ungovernable humour. 1890 J. SERVICE *Thir Notandums* viii. 48 I'm no i' the tidd the noo.

**Tid**, *sb.*[2] *? local.* [app. an alteration of TIT *sb.*[3], in sense girl, young woman.] A girl or woman.

1888 BARRIE *When a Man's Single* i, Nanny was a terrible tid for cleanness. 1891 — *Little Minister* xv, You're the bonniest tid I ever saw oot o' an almanack.

†**Tid**, *a. Obs.* A word app. deduced by Bailey from *tid-bit*, but also in independent dialect use. From Bailey in Johnson, whence in later dicts.: also in nonce-use from *tid-bit*: see quots.

1727 BAILEY vol. II, *Tid*, nice, delicate, as a *Tid-Bit.* 1755 JOHNSON, *Tid*, adj. (tydder, Saxon), tender; soft; nice ..*Titbit* (properly *tidbit*; *tid*, tender, and *bit*), nice bit; nice food. [See note below.]
1730 *Panegyric on Swift* 13 While Dunces of the coarsest Clay..Devour the Church's tiddest Bits, That only should be shar'd by Wits. 1799 E. DU BOIS *Piece Family Biog.* I. 70 She is too tid a bit for us lubbers aboard the world.

[*Note.* The OE. word meant by J. is *tīdre*, *tyddre* 'weak, fragile, easily broken; frail in health, infirm'; it could not give *tid* 'tender, soft, nice'. The latter does not appear as general Eng. before Bailey. But the *Eng. Dial. Dict.* has from Midl. counties *Tid*, *tidd* = 'fond, attached, careful (of), solicitous (about); (of a child) tender, nice, fanciful; (of a man) cunningly reserved'. J. D. Robertson's *Gloucester Glossary* (1890) has *Tid*, 'playful, frolicsome', and cites from John Smyth's Berkeley MSS. *c* 1640 (ed. 1885, III. 25) 'Tyd, i.e. wanton. Hee is very tyd, i. e. very wanton. A tyd bit, i.e. a speciall morsell reserved to eat at last'. These evidence the limited dial. use of an adj. *tid*, *tidd*, or *tyd*; though the senses given do not very closely agree with that deduced by Bailey from *tid-bit*.]

**Tid**, *v. Sc.* [f. TID *sb.*[1]] *trans.* To choose the right time for; to time: esp. with reference to land or crops: cf. TID *sb.*[1] 2.

1808 JAMIESON, *Tid*, v.a., to time, to choose the proper season. *The aitseed has been weill tiddit*, the proper season for sowing oats has been taken. 1883 J. MARTIN *Remin. Old Haddington* 317 He judiciously 'tidded' the land and manured highly so as to produce heavy crops.

**Tid**, obs. var. *tit*, TITE *adv.*; obs. pa. t. and pple. of TIDE *v.*[1], TITHE *v.*[1]

**Tidal** (təi·dăl), *a.* [f. TIDE *sb.* II. + -AL.]

**1.** Of, pertaining to, or affected by tides; ebbing and flowing periodically.

**Tidal alarm**, an audible signal, as a bell or whistle attached to a buoy, operated by the movement of the tides (*Cassell's Encycl. Dict.* 1888); **tidal crack** = TIDE-*crack* (*Cent. Dict.* 1891); **tidal friction**, frictional resistance to the motion of the tide-wave, tending to retard the earth's rotation; **tidal motor**, a mechanical motor deriving its power from the movement of tidal waters; **tidal river**, a river which is affected by the tides for some distance from its mouth; **tidal valve**, a valve in a sluice, which opens to the pressure of land water and closes under the influence of the incoming tide; **tidal wave**, see b.

1807 VANCOUVER *Agric. Devon* (1813) 300 Had the lots below..the new Custom House..in Dublin, been left open to the tidal waters, the waters of the Liffy would have preserved a deep channel for their discharge. 1830 LYELL *Princ. Geol.* I. 359 Suppose that..the Mediterranean should form a gulf of the great ocean, and that the tidal current should encroach on the shores of Campania. 1853 HERSCHEL *Pop. Lect. Sc.* i. § 57 (1873) 45 The tidal action of the sun and moon on..the earth's crust. 1878 HUXLEY *Physiogr.* i. 2 Up to Teddington..the Thames is a tidal river. 1880 HAUGHTON *Phys. Geog.* i. 9 When the length of the day shall have become equal to the length of the year, tidal friction will cease. 1884 F. J. BRITTEN *Watch & Clockm.* 256 Tidal Clock..designed..for showing the time of high and low water, the state of the tides at any time of the day. 1911 *Encycl. Brit.* XXVI. 945/1 Tidal friction then diminishes planetary rotation, increases the satellite's distance, and diminishes the orbital angular velocity.

**b.** *Tidal wave*: the high water wave caused by the movement of the tide: = *tide-wave* (TIDE *sb.* 16 b); *erron.* an exceptionally large ocean wave caused by an earthquake or other local commotion.

1830 LYELL *Princ. Geol.* I. 293 On mathematical principles, the rise of the tidal wave above the mean level of a particular sea must be greater than the fall below it. 1878 HUXLEY *Physiogr.* 2 The tidal wave occupies about two hours in coming up from the Nore to London. *Ibid.* 188 The terrible devastation wrought by the great tidal wave, which followed the earthquake at Lima. 1899 *Daily News* 13 June 8/2 The tidal wave sweeps round the earth twice in the twenty-four hours; the great wave produced by an earthquake, erroneously described sometimes as a 'tidal wave', has nothing tidal about it, and it is called by scientific men 'a free wave'.

(*b*) *fig.* A great progressive movement or manifestation of feeling, opinion, or the like.

1884 *Boston* (Mass.) *Traveller* Aug., Van Buren was a candidate again in 1840, but the 'log-cabin and hard cider' tidal wave was sweeping over the country. 1888 BRYCE *Amer. Commw.* III. IV. lxxx. 62 Now and then..there comes a rush of feeling so sudden and tremendous, that the name of Tidal Wave has been invented to describe it. 1895 SCULLY *Kafir Stories* 50 The repression which he had to exercise..caused tidal waves of passion to roll back on his soul, fraught with destruction to himself and to others.

(*c*) *Phys.* The main or primary height of flow in a beat of the pulse.

**1896** *Allbutt's Syst. Med.* I. 314 Sphygmographic tracings show a lowering in the height of the tidal and dicrotic wave.

**2.** *transf.* and *fig.* That 'ebbs and flows'; periodic, intermittent; alternating, varying.

**Tidal air** (*Phys.*), the air passing in and out of the lungs at each ordinary respiration; **tidal breathing** (*Path.*), respiration in which there are pauses alternating with shorter periods of respiratory activity; periodic respiration.

**1872** HUXLEY *Phys.* iv. 92 In ordinary breathing 20 to 30 inches of what is conveniently called Tidal air pass in and out. **1876** GEO. ELIOT *Dan. Der.* IV. xxix, This mood of youthful, elated desperation had a tidal recurrence. **1896** *Daily News* 4 May 3/3 Clerkenwell has..become mixed in population and in its political opinions tidal. **1897** *Allbutt's Syst. Med.* IV. 646 Amongst..the results of derangements of the pulmonary circulation must be placed the occurrence of 'periodic', 'tidal', or Cheyne-Stokes breathing.

**3.** Dependent upon or regulated by the state of the tide or time of high water.

**Tidal basin, harbour,** a basin or harbour which is accessible or navigable only at high tide; **tidal boat, steamer,** a vessel the sailings of which depend on the time of the tide; **tidal train,** a train running in connexion with a tidal steamer.

**1858** SIMMONDS *Dict. Trade, Tidal basin*, a dock that is filled upon the rising of the tide. **1859** LEWIN *Invas. Brit.* 27 Boulogne is a tidal harbour,..it can only be entered or quitted at high water. **1859** REEVE *Brittany* ii. 12 The tidal hours of departure of the steam-packet. **1866** W. COLLINS *Armadale* II. 240 The tidal train..was speeding nearer and nearer to Paris. **1888** GUNTER *Mr. Potter* x, The tidal boat'll be 'ere in twenty minutes.

**b.** Elliptical for *tidal boat* or *train*.

**1883** L. OLIPHANT *Altiora Peto* I. 202 He found himself just in time to take the tidal.

Hence **Ti·dally** *adv.*, in a tidal manner; by or in respect of the tides.

**1879** G. H. DARWIN in *Phil. Trans.* CLXXI. 713 On the Secular Changes in the Elements of the Orbit of a Satellite revolving about a Tidally Distorted Planet. **1880** *Ibid.* CLXXII. 513 In considering the effects of tidal friction the theory has been throughout adopted that the tidally-disturbed body is homogeneous and viscous.

**Tidance, tidand**: see TIDING.

**Tid-bit**, an earlier form of TIT-BIT.

† **Tidder**, *v.*[1] *Obs.* Forms: 1 tíedran, týdran, týddr(i)an, 3 tuderen, (*Orm.*) tiddrenn. [OE. *týdran*, related to *tud(d)or* TUDDER, progeny, offspring.] **a.** *intr.* To be productive or prolific. **b.** *trans.* To produce (offspring), to engender.

*a* **1000** *Cædmon's Gen.* 1507 (Gr.) Tymað nu & tiedrað. *c* **1200** *Trin. Coll. Hom.* 177 Þenne men michel tuderið.. and here tuder swiðe wexeð. *c* **1200** ORMIN 18307 Þa þe33re time wass all gan To tiddrenn & to tæmenn. *c* **1250** *Gen. & Ex.* 630 Of hem ben tudered mani3on.

[† **Ti·dder**, *v.*[2] *Obs. rare*—⁰.

**1755** JOHNSON, *Tidder*, v. a. (from *Tid*), to use tenderly; to fondle. (But there is app. some error here: no trace of such a vb. has been found elsewhere: cf. TID *a.*)]

**Tiddivate**, dial. variant of TITIVATE *v.*

**Tiddle** (ti·d'l), *v. Obs.* exc. *dial.* or *slang*. Also 7–9 tittle. [In sense 1 perh. connected with TID *a.* The two senses may be distinct words.]

**1.** *trans.* To fondle or indulge to excess; to pet, pamper; to tend carefully, nurse, cherish.

**1560** *Nice Wanton* in Hazl. *Dodsley* II. 173 My parents did tiddle me: they were to blame. **1653** *Verney Memoirs* (1894) III. 203 To midwife it out, and to tittle it up and to bring it with you in your coach. **1730–6** BAILEY (folio), *To Tiddle*, to indulge, or fondle, to make much of. **1755** JOHNSON, *Tiddle*, v. a. (from *Tid*), to use tenderly; to fondle. **1839** [SIR G. C. LEWIS] *Herefordsh. Gloss.* (E.D.D.). **1881** MISS JACKSON *Shropsh. Word-bk.*, *Tiddle*, to nurse and nurture tenderly. **1893** *S. E. Worc. Gloss.* s. v., You may tiddle a monkey 'till 'e befouls your trenchud.

**2.** *intr.* To potter, trifle, 'fiddle'; to fidget, fuss.

**1747** RICHARDSON *Clarissa* (1811) I. xlii. 322 To leave the family pictures..to you, because you could tiddle about them, and..wipe and clean them with your dainty hands! **1839** HOLLOWAY *Dict. Prov.* s. v., 'Tiddling about' is being busy about trifles. **1904** *Eng. Dial. Dict.* s. v. *Tittle*, (Cumbld.) I could par' [pare] the fut with a buttress while another is tittlin' over it with a draw-knife.

Hence **Ti·ddling** *ppl. a.*, that 'tiddles'; over-indulgent; **Ti·ddlingly** *adv.*, indulgently.

**1580** LUPTON *Sivqila* 37 The most of our youth..are so tydlingly, fondly, wantonly, and idlely brought up, that it is a griefe to the godlye.

**Tiddle**, dial. form of TITTLE *v.* to tickle.

**Ti·ddler**[1]. [? Related to TITTLEBAT and *tiddly* 'little'.] Nursery name for a stickleback. So **Ti·ddling** *vbl. sb.*, fishing for 'tiddlers'.

**1885** B. E. MARTIN in *Harper's Mag.* May 866/1 Them's tiddlers, they is. **1903** *Blackw. Mag.* Aug. 203/2, I used to come and catch tiddlers in it when I was a kid. **1908** *Daily Chron.* 3 Aug. 7/3 Within reach of that most delightful tiddling water in St. James's Park. **1911** *Daily News* 26 July 4 The long row of boys..in St. James's Park fishing for tiddlers with sticks and bent pins.

**Tiddler**[2]. *slang.* [f. *tiddle*, by-form of TITTLE *v.* to tickle.] A feather or feather-brush for tickling; a 'teaser' or 'tormenter'; a tickler.

**1900** *Daily Chron.* 21 May 5 (Cass. Supp.) In Cheapside.. you were titillated by 'penny tiddlers'. Anything, from a peacock's feather downwards, which is a foot long and tickles,is a 'tiddler'. *a* **1904** E. SMITH *MS. Coll. Warwicksh. Wds.* s. v. (E.D.D.), At 'mops' and fairs in the Midlands the favourite tiddler..drawn rapidly down the back,..made a noise resembling that of the extinct 'rattle' of the policeman. Now the tiddler has degenerated into any light weapon of offence, which drawn across the face or neck, irritates the skin.

**Tiddlywink** (ti·dliwiŋk). Also tidley-, tiddley-, tiddle-a-wink. [In sense 1 perh. connected with slang *tiddly* a drink, drunk; in 3 perh. with *tiddly* dial. or baby-talk for 'little'.]

**1.** An unlicensed public-house or pawnshop; a small beershop; also *kiddlywink*. *slang.*

**1844** J. T. HEWLETT *Parsons & W.* xxxiv, Which does more to demoralise..the lower classes than a Tom and Jerry, tidley-wink, or gin-shop. **1887** BEATTY-KINGSTON *Music & Mann.* II. 15 All the tiny tiddlywinks and spacious beer-gardens filled to overflowing.

**2. a.** A game played with dominoes. **b.** *pl.* A game in which small counters are caused to spring from the table into a bell-like or cylindrical receptacle, by pressing upon their edges with larger counters.

**1870** HARDY & WARE *Mod. Hoyle* 104 (*Dominoes*) Tiddle-a-wink game...In this game..he who plays out first cries Tiddle-a-wink, having won. **1870** *Routledge's Ev. Boy's Ann.* Nov. 672 The marked difference between Tidley-wink and other games of dominoes. **1898** *Westm. Gaz.* 4 Jan. 2/1 Cards, tiddley-winks, and ludo are played. **1906** *19th Cent.* Mar. 509 The Empress suggested the game of tiddlywinks for the Emperor's amusement.

**3.** *pl.* Knick-knacks of victuals. *slang.*

**1893** J. A. BARRY *S. Brown's Bunyip*, etc. 34 A drop o' good stuff, now, to wash these 'ere tiddlewinks down with.

Hence (*slang*) **Tiddlywi·nker**, a cheat, a trifler; **Tiddlywi·nking** *sb.* and *a.*, trifling, pottering; **Tiddlywi·nky** *a. dial.*, tiny, insignificant.

**1869** *Routledge's Ev. Boy's Ann.* 589 Performed some 'tiddly-winking' work, that is he had shifted a few spadesful of earth. **1888** 'R. BOLDREWOOD' *Squatter's Dream* vii, I wonder what old Morgan would say to all this here tiddley-winkin', with steam-engine, and wire-fences. **1893** J. A. BARRY *S. Brown's Bunyip*, etc. 143 It was a fair an' square game...There wasn't no tiddleywinkin' in the thing. *Ibid.* 145 They're nothin' but a lot o' tiddleywinkers up there. **1901** 'ZACK' *Tales Dunstable Weir* 23 Over against Martin's cottage there was a tiddliwinkie bit o' a wood.

**Tiddy** (ti·di). [Origin unknown: perh. = TEDDY.] In the game of gleek, the four of trumps.

**1655** [see TIB *sb.* 2]. **1680** COTTON *Compl. Gamester* vi. (ed. 2) 65 (*Gleek*) The turned up Card is the Dealers; and if it be Tiddy turn'd up is four apiece from each to the Dealer. The Ace is called Tib, the Knave Tom, the four of Trumps Tiddy. **1688** R. HOLME *Armoury* III. xvi. (Roxb.) 73/2. **1822** SCOTT *Nigel* xvi, I gained the cards, and lo you! it pleases his lordship to say that we played without tiddy.

**Tide** (təid), *sb.* Forms: 1 tíd (tiid), týd, 2–5 tid, 2–7 tyd, 3–7 tyde, (5 tyyde, tiid), 3– tide. [OE. *tíd* = OS. *tîd* (MLG., LG. *tît*, Du. *tijd*), OHG. *zît* (*zîd*), MHG. *zît* (Ger. *zeit*), ON. *tíð* (Sw., Da. *tid*):—OTeut. **tî-d-iz*, referred by some to a root **tî-* to extend (whence also TIME). See also note under branch II.]

**I.** Time.

† **1.** A portion, extent, or space of time; an age, a season, a time, a while: = TIME *sb.* 1–3. *Obs.* (or ? *dial.*)

*a* **700** *Beowulf* 147 Wæs seo hwil micel, xii wintra tid torn 3eþolode. *a* **900** tr. *Bæda's Hist.* v. xiii. [xii.] (1890) 432 Þa ic sume tid fram ðe 3ewat. *c* **950** *Lindisf. Gosp.* Mark ix. 21 Huu miceles *vel* longes tides. **971** *Blickl. Hom.* 125 Uncuþ bið æ3hwylcum anum men his lifes tid. *c* **1000** *Ags. Gosp.* Mark ix. 21 Hu lang tid is syððan him þis 3ebyrede? *c* **1000** ÆLFRIC *Hom.* I. 312 Þreo tida sind on ðysre worulde: an is seo ðe wæs butan æ;..seo ðridde is nu æfter Cristes to-cyme. [Cf. *c* **1175** *Lamb. Hom.* 89.] *a* **1300** *Cursor M.* 391 (Cott.) Bath ware made sun and mon,..In takening o tides to stand, Dais and yeirs. *c* **1400** *Destr. Troy* 1974 And þou tary in þis towne, or any tide lenge. *c* **1412** HOCCLEVE *De Reg. Princ.* 847, I mote..suffre storm after þe mery tyde. *c* **1450** *Cov. Myst.* v. (Shaks. Soc.) 50, I come a3en withinne a tyde. *a* **1529** SKELTON *Poems agst. Garnesche* iv. 162 Stop a tyd, and be welle ware. **1590** SPENSER *F. Q.* I. ii. 29 There they alight..and rest their weary limbs a tide. **1603** *Philotus* lxxvii, Prouyde Ane Pages claithis in the meine tyde. **1791** J. LEARMONT *Poems* 331 (E.D.D.), I wiss that tide had been a lang lang year. **1871** WADDELL *Ps.* xxxi. 15 My tides are a' i' yer han'.

† **2.** *spec.* = HOUR 1. *Obs.*

*a* **900** *O. E. Chron.* an. 879, Þy ilcan 3eare aþiestrode sio sunne ane tid dæ3es. *a* **900** *O. E. Martyrol.* 30 June 110 Þonne se monoð byð 3eendod þe we nemnað se ærra lyða, þonne byð seo niht six tyda lang ond se dæ3 eahtatyne tyda lang. *c* **1000** ÆLFRIC *Hom.* II. 388 An wæcce hæfð þreo tida; feower wæccan 3efyllað twelf tida. *c* **1050** *Byrhtferth's Handboc* in *Anglia* (1885) VIII. 298 Ðæt 3er byð 3esett on þrim hund da3um & fif & syxti3um da3um & syx tidum. *a* **1200** *Moral Ode* 137 (Lamb. MS.) Hefde he bon þer enne dei oðer twa bare tide nolde he for al middenerd þe þerdde þer abiden. *c* **1290** *S. Eng. Leg.* I. 408/223 Huy stoden and bi-heolden sein Iohan longue, þre tidene and more. *a* **1300** *Cursor M.* 14193 (Cott.) Ten tides [*F.* oures] has þe dai and tua. *c* **1430** *R. Gloucester's Chron.* (Rolls) App. BB. 3 Þe foure & twenti tydes [*v.r.* houres] in day & in þe ny3t..he dy3te folwel & ri3t Mid þreo grete kandlen To berne eite tides [*v.r.* houres].

**3.** A point in the duration of the day, month, or year, of human life, or of other natural (or, later, artificial) period; in reference to an action or repetition = occasion: = TIME *sb.* 13, 14. *arch.* or *poet.*

*c* **897** K. ÆLFRED *Gregory's Past. C.* xvii. 120 Ðonne cymð his hlaford..on ða tiid ðæt he hiene ær nat. *Ibid.* xlvii. 356 Aworpen mon bið a unnyt..& on ælce tid saweð wrohte. **971** *Blickl. Hom.* 21 Þæt leoht on nanre tide ne ablinneþ. *c* **1205** LAY. 14924 Hit ilomp an are tide heo nom hire to ræde. *a* **1300** *Cursor M.* 5733 (Cott.) Þe flok he fedd opon a tid, Bi a wildrin wod side. *c* **1385** CHAUCER *L. G. W.* 783 (*Thisbe*) Ffor to mete in on place at on tyde. *a* **1400** *Pistill of Susan* 149 Such toret and teone takeþ me þis tyde. *a* **1425** *Cursor M.* 5874 (Trin.) To stonde lete 3e hem not bide As 3e han done mony a tyde. *a* **1529** SKELTON *El. Rummyng* 155 Such a lewde sorte To Elynour resorte From tyde to tyde. *c* **1586** C'TESS PEMBROKE *Ps.* (1823) CXLIV. v, My closett where I wont to hide In troublous tyde. *a* **1605** POLWART *Flyting w. Montgomerie* 470 At that tyd [ane after midnight] was na time for trumpers to tarie. **1635** R. JOHNSON *Hist. Tom a Lincolne* (1828) 106 Which ship had beene seven yeares upon the sea..and before this tyde could never see land. **1805** WORDSW. *Elegiac Verses on J. Wordsw.* vi, But we will see it—joyful tide! Some day..The mountain will we cross. **1868** MORRIS *Earthly Par.*, *Man born to be King* 1272 He, who, from ill death Saved me that tide.

**b.** A suitable, favourable, or proper time or occasion; opportune, fit, or due time; season; opportunity: = TIME *sb.* 16. *arch.* Cf. TID *sb.*[1]

*c* **888** K. ÆLFRED *Boeth.* xxix. § 2 Se ðe his ær tide ne tiolað, þonne bið his on tid untilad. *c* **897** — *Gregory's Past. C.* xxxviii. 274 Hwilum sie spræce tiid, hwilum swi3gean. *c* **950** *Lindisf. G.* Matt. xxiv. 45 Þætte he sella him mett in tid. *c* **1060** *Charter of Eadweard* in Kemble *Cod. Dipl.* IV. 212 Alle þingen ða ðar upaspringeð, inne tyd and ut of tid. *c* **1330** R. BRUNNE *Chron.* (1810) 164 Bi Cipres side Isaac to aspie, If he toke any tide out of lond to flie. *c* **1430** *Brut* 439 Whanne tyde of passage come, thei toke the see, and passid ouyr. **1590** SPENSER *F. Q.* III. ix. 32 Then Paridell,..glad of so fitte tide Him to commend to her, thus spake. **1657** M. LAWRENCE *Use & Pract. Faith* 147 The foolish virgins lost their tide: the wise had much ado to gain it. **1887** MORRIS *Odyssey* IX. 131 For the land is nothing evil, but would bear all things in tide.

† **c.** Appointed or fixed time: = TIME *sb.* 15. *Obs.*

*a* **900** tr. *Bæda's Hist.* III. xiv. [xix.] (1890) 210 Waciað 3e, forðon þe 3e ne weoton ne ðone dæ3 ne ða tide. *Ibid.* IV. iii. 262 Þa cwom his tid, þæt he scolde of middan3earde to Drihtne feran. *c* **950** *Lindisf. Gosp.* John ii. 4, & cueð to him se hælend..ne ða3et *vel* cuom tid min. *a* **1300** *Cursor M.* 21511 (Cott.) Þe Iuu him spedd til-ward his tide, Ouer term durst he noght bide. *a* **1436** *Domesday Ipswich* v. in *Blk. Bk. Admiralty* (Rolls) II. 31 Att tide and hour and tyme, that is to wetyn with ynne the xv. day..that he plete to his aduersarye.

† **4.** Any definite time in the course of the day; as EVENTIDE, MORROW-TIDE, NOON-TIDE, q. v.; *spec.* the point at which any hour is completed; as 'at the tenth tide of the day'; = HOUR 3. *Obs.*

*a* **700** *Beowulf* 484 [see MORN-TIDE]. *a* **900** tr. *Bæda's Hist.* III. xix. [xxvii.] (1890) 240 Ymb þa teo3ðan tid dæ3es. **1056–66** *Inscr. on Dial Kirkdale Ch., Yorks.*, Þis is dæ3es sol merca æt ilcum tide. *c* **1160** *Hatton Gosp.* John i. 39 Hyt wæs þa seo teoðe tyd. *a* **1300** *Cursor M.* 19810 (Edin.) Apon a dai at tide of none, An angel come and stode him bi. *c* **1391** CHAUCER *Astrol.* II. § 15 Thanne wol the point of thi label sit[t]en in the bordure, vp-on the verrey tid of the day. **1493** *Festivall* (W. de W. 1515) 7 He hyred people to labour by all the tydes of the day. **1903** *Westm. Gaz.* 10 June 2/3, I go to you at gloaming-tide.

**b.** A more or less definite point or season in the course of the year, of life, etc., usually defined by a prefixed word; as *April-tide*, *June-tide*; *New-Year's tide*, *summer's tide*, *winter's tide*, etc.; also AUTUMN-TIDE, SPRING-TIDE, SUMMER-TIDE, WINTER-TIDE, etc. q. v.: = TIME *sb.* 13 b. *arch.* or *poet.*

*a* **900** tr. *Bæda's Hist.* IV. xxix. [xxviii.] (1890) 366 Þa ne com ðær næni3 grownes up ne wæstm, ne furðum brordes oð sumeres tida. *c* **1000** ÆLFRIC *Hom.* I. 444 Swa swa on lengctenlicere tide, rosena blostman and lilian hi ymtrymedon. *c* **1122** *O. E. Chron.* an. 1006, In þære midde wintres tide. **1541** *Rutland MSS.* (1905) IV. 312 For bryngyng a bore at Newe Yere tide, ij s. iiij d. **1556–1840** New-year's tide [see NEW-YEAR 3 b]. **1870** MORRIS *Earthly Par.* I. I. 307 When April-tide was melting into May. **1872** TENNYSON *Last Tourn.* 241 High over all the yellowing Autumn-tide. **1900** *Westm. Gaz.* 3 July 2/3 The green woods under the Junetide skies Slope and gleam to the Solent strand. **1902** *Ibid.* 20 Mar. 9/1 The profits at Coronation-tide are expected to be heavy.

† **5.** Each of the seven canonical hours; also, the services recited at these; = HOUR 5. *Obs.*

*c* **1000** ÆLFRIC *Colloq.* in Wr.-Wülcker 90/6 Ic sincge ælce dæ3 seofon tida. *c* **1000** — *Saints' Lives* xxxiii. 344 Nu wille ic þæt þu..singe þær þine tida. **1028–60** *Laws Northumbr. Priests* § 36 3if preost on 3esetne timan tida ne ringe oððe tida ne singe, 3ebete þæt. *c* **1200** *Trin. Coll. Hom.* 215 Þane hit time beð to done þe tiden. *a* **1225** *Ancr. R.* 22 Et þreo tiden siggeð Credo mit te Pater Noster, biuoren Uhtsong & efter Prime, & efter Cumpelie. *Ibid.* 44 Toward te preostes tiden herkneð se wel 3e muwen. **1297** R. GLOUC. (Rolls) 7605 Vor him ne ssolde no day abide þat he ne hurde masse & matines & euesong & ech tide. **13..** *Minor Poems fr. Vernon MS.* xxxvii. 767 Atome þou mai3t ful wel abyde Til he haue seid þe laste tyde. *c* **1400** [see HOUR 5]. **1557** in *10th Rep. Hist. MSS. Comm.* App. v. 386 The said Wardayn..shall dayly saye or singe..in the quere the tydes or houres, as tercio, sexto and nono.

**6.** An anniversary or festival of the church: chiefly in the names of holy seasons or saints' days, e.g. † *St. Andrew's tide*, † *Saint Botulf's tide*. See also ALL-HALLOW-TIDE, CHRIST-TIDE, EASTER-TIDE, LAMMAS-TIDE, SHROVETIDE, WHITSUNTIDE, HIGH-TIDE, HOLY TIDE, etc.

*a* **900** *O. E. Chron.* an. 759, Her Bregowine wæs to ercebisc 3ehadod to Sce Michaeles tide. *a* **900** *O. E. Martyrol.* 18 May 84 On þone eahtateo3ðan dæ3 þæs monðes bið sancte Johannes tid. *c* **1050** *Byrhtferth's Handboc* in *Anglia* (1885) VIII. 300 Fram easter tide þæt he eft cume. *c* **1200** *Trin. Coll. Hom.* 3 To dai is cumen ðe holie tid þat me clepeð aduent. *c* **1200** ORMIN 8895 Att þe Passkemessedda33..þe boc hemm tahhte To frellsenn þær þat he3he tid. **1297** R. GLOUC. (Rolls) 10877 Sir edward ibore was A seint botulfes tid. *c* **1400** *Brut* cxxxix. 146 Þe sege endurede fro Michelmasse vnto Seynt Andrewus tyde. *a* **1568** ASCHAM

*Scholem.* I. (Arb.) 36 In a fair garden about S. James tyde. **1595** SHAKS. *John* III. i. 86 What hath this day deseru'd ..That it in golden letters should be set Among the high tides in the Kalendar? **1611, 1615** Michaels-tide, Michael-tide [see MICHAEL 2]. **1817–18** COBBETT *Resid. U.S.* (1822) 121 The country people, in England, go, to this day,..by the tides; and,..in some cases, by the moveable tides. My gardener..very reluctantly obeyed me ..in sowing green Kale..because Whitsuntide was not come, and that, he said, was the proper season. **1839** J. H. NEWMAN *Par. Serm.* IV. xxiii. 385 Feast-day and fast-day, holy tide and other tide. **1903** E. K. CHAMBERS *Mediæv. Stage* I. i. 16 Holy week, and similar solemn tides.

**b.** *dial.* A village 'feast' or fair (taking place on the festival of the patron saint of the parish).

**1824** [see *tide-time* in 15 a]. **1828** *Craven Gloss.*, *Tide*, a feast; as Bingley tide. **1863** MRS. TOOGOOD *Yorks. Dial.* (MS.), Boistall-tide will be next week. **1865** R. HUNT *Pop. Rom. W. Eng.* Ser. I. (1871) 62 The strongest beer, which was intended to have been kept for a tide. **1884** *Let. to Editor*, The Annual General Holiday at Bingley, Yorks., is still called 'Bingley Tide'.

**II.** Tide of the sea.

[This sense corresponds exactly to MLG. *getîde* neut., *tîde tie*, neut. and fem., LG. *tide*, MDu. *ghetîde* neut., early mod.Du. *tijde*, Du. *tij* neut., 'tide of the sea', a particular application of MLG. *getîde*, 'fixed time, time of prayer, proper time, opportunity, space of time'. OE. had no form corresp. to *getîde* (using for 'tide' (of the sea) *flód* or *flód and ebba*); and *tíd* or *tide* in this sense is not known before 1340; it may have been then introduced from or used after the MLG. word; but as ME. *tide* had neither the difference of form nor of gender seen in *de tît* and *dat tîde*, actual formal evidence of the borrowing is wanting. There may have been a transference of sense in Eng. itself, as well as in LG. The following two early examples appear to mean 'the *time* of high water', rather than the flood tide itself, or the phenomenon of the tides:

**1340** HAMPOLE *Pr. Consc.* 1215 For þe se, aftir þe tydes certayn, Ebbes and flowes, and falles agayn. *c* **1386** CHAUCER *Man of Law's T.* 1036 Fro day to nyght it changeth as the tyde.]

**7.** The flowing or swelling of the sea, or its alternate rising and falling, twice in each lunar day, due to the attraction of the moon and, in a less degree, of the sun; the alternate inflow and outflow produced by this on a coast, the flood and ebb.

*c* **1435** *Torr. Portugal* 1430, I Rede, we take down sayle & Rowe, While we haue this tyde. **1530** PALSGR. 281/1 Tyde of the see, *flet, flote.* **1563** GOLDING *Cæsar* III. (1565) 72 There was no comming to theym on foote, by reason of the rysyng of the tydes. **1590** SHAKS. *Com. Err.* IV. i. 46 Both winde and tide stayes for this Gentleman. **1593** — *Lucr.* 1667 As through an Arch the violent roaring tide outruns the eye. **1599** — *Hen. V*, II. iii. 14 Iust betweene Twelue and One, eu'n at the turning o' th' Tyde. **1698** KEILL *Exam. Th. Earth* (1734) 161 It is certain, that a Comet, when it passed by the Earth, would raise a very strong and prodigious Tide in the Seas that were then on the Surface. **1816** PLAYFAIR *Nat. Phil.* II. 326 The alternate rise and fall of the surface of the sea twice in the course of a lunar day, or of $24^{h}\ 50^{m}\ 48^{sec}$ of mean solar time, is the phenomenon known by the name of the Tides. **1831** FR. A. KEMBLE *Let.* in *Rec. Girlhood* II. viii. 237 The tide had not yet come in.

**b.** In phrases (chiefly technical), as **cross tide**, a tide running across the direction of another; **high tide**, (*a*) = HIGH WATER; (*b*) = SPRING TIDE; **low tide** = LOW WATER; **leeward, neap, windward tide**: see the defining words; also FLOOD-TIDE, SPRING TIDE, HALF-TIDE. Also in fig. uses.

**1627** CAPT. SMITH *Seaman's Gram.* x. 47 You say as well tide of ebbe, as tide of flood, or a windward Tide when the Tide runnes against the wind, as a Lee-warde Tide,..when the wind and the Tide goeth both one way. **1675** TEMPLE *Let. to Sir J. Williamson* Wks. 1731 II. 336, I chose this Conveyance by the Captain of the Yacht, as both surer and speedier too, if not hindred by cross Tides in the River. **1745** P. THOMAS *Jrnl. Anson's Voy.* 120 There having been two or three high Tides before we had finished, we found [etc.]. **1867** SMYTH *Sailor's Word-bk.*, *Cross-tide*, the varying directions of the flow amongst shoals that are under water. **1875** BEDFORD *Sailor's Pocket Bk.* v. (ed. 2) 172 In the English Channel..it is ebb tide in the harbours, while the eastern, or flood stream..is still running up, forming what is known to Pilots as 'Tide and half Tide'.

*fig.* **1579** W. WILKINSON *Confut. Familye of Love* 57 b, When..his high tyde of vpright fredome [shall] become to a falling water. *a* **1700** B. E. *Dict. Cant. Crew*, *High Tide*, when the Pocket is full of Money. *Ibid.*, *Low Tide*, when there's no Money in a Man's Pocket. **1856** EMERSON *Eng. Traits, Relig.* Wks. (Bohn) II. 98 Plenitudes of Divine Presence, by which high tides are caused in the human spirit.

**c.** *transf.* A recurrent flow, alternate rise and fall or increase and decrease, other than of the sea. *Acid tide*, a temporary increase of acidity of the urine while fasting; *alkaline tide*, a corresponding decrease of acidity during digestion.

**1604** E. G[RIMSTONE] *D'Acosta's Hist. Indies* II. xiii. 113 The return of the same windes, which otherwise they call the tide or winde of the sea. **1610** HOLLAND *Camden's Brit.* (1637) 558 A wonderfull Well..which ordinarily ebbeth and floweth foure times in the space of one houre or thereabout, keeping his just Tides. **1786–7** BONNYCASTLE *Astron.* viii. 138 The aerial tides must be much more considerable than those of the ocean. **1822–34** *Good's Study Med.* (ed. 4) I. 676 There are two tides or fluxes [of fever] within the twenty-four hours, the one occurs in the morning, the other in the evening. *Ibid.* IV. 304 A fresh tide of water will not unfrequently accumulate, and the head become as much distended as before. **1856** BRYANT *Earth* 14 Swayed by the sweeping of the tides of air. **1897** *Allbutt's Syst. Med.* IV. 293 This increased excretion is most marked during the alkaline tide.

**8.** The space of time between two successive points of high water, or between low water and high water, in the sea; also, that portion of this time during which the height of the water ('state of the tide') allows of work being done, as in *tide's work*: see quot. 1867. So, in *Mining*, a period of twelve hours (*Cassell's Encycl. Dict.* 1888).

**1495** *Act 11 Hen. VII*, c. 22 § 1 A Calker laboring by the tyde, for as longe tyme as he may labour above the Water and beneth the Water, shall not excede for his Wages for every tyde iiij d. **1534** *Acc. Ld. High Treas. Scot.* VI. 234 Payit..to xv men to cast the space of xv tydis about the schip, viij d. the man for ilk tyde. **1724** DE FOE *Mem. Cavalier* (1840) 281 [They] might..come by sea in two tides. **1758** J. BLAKE *Plan Mar. Syst.* 63 A ship going into dock for a tide or two to clean. **1793** SMEATON *Edystone L.* § 175 We ..landed, and got a tide's work of four hours. **1803** R. PERING in *Naval Chron.* XV. 154 (Royal Naval Yards) The extra [work] was divided into nights and tides:—a night consisted of five hours, and a tide of an hour and an half. **1867** SMYTH *Sailor's Word-bk.*, *Tide's work*, the amount of progress a ship has made during a favourable tide. Also, a period of necessary labour on a ship during the ebbing and slack water of a tide.

**9.** *fig.* Applied to that which is like the tide of the sea in some way; as in ebbing or flowing, rising or falling, or 'turning' at a certain time.

**1390** GOWER *Conf.* II. 61 Betre is to wayte upon the tyde Than rowe ayein the stremes stronge. *c* **1430** *Hymns Virg.* 69/368 Þe tyde [of life] is ebbid, & no more wole flowe. **1508** DUNBAR *Flyting* 188 Oft beswakkit with ane ourhie tyd. **1601** SHAKS. *Jul. C.* IV. iii. 218 There is a Tide in the affayres of men, Which taken at the Flood, leades on to Fortune. **1777** PRIESTLEY *Matt. & Spir.* (1782) I. Pref. 10 The tide of popular prejudice may rise still higher. **1849** MACAULAY *Hist. Eng.* vi. II. 54 From that moment the tide of battle turned. **1900** *Daily News* 7 Dec. 8/5 The dramatic tide has its ebb and flow like other tides.

**10.** *spec.* = FLOOD-TIDE. Also *fig.*

**1570** LEVINS *Manip.* 116/47 Ye Tyde, *accessus maris.* **1606** SHAKS. *Tr. & Cr.* v. i. 90, I haue important businesse The tide whereof is now. **1610** HOLLAND *Camden's Brit.* (1637) 633 The River at every tide riseth to a great heigth. **1652** NEEDHAM tr. *Selden's Mare Cl.* 249 By an exquisite observation of the Tides and Ebbings of the Sea they were wont to reckon their months and years. **1826** DISRAELI *Viv. Grey* III. i, There is that at work in England which, taken at the tide, may lead on to fortune [cf. quot. 1601 in 9]. **1893** STEVENSON *Catriona* iii. 27 It seemed the devil was in it, if I was to die in that tide of my fortunes.

**11.** *transf.* A body of flowing water or other liquid; a stream, a current. *poet.* and *rhet.*

[15.. *Sir A. Barton* xxxix. in *Surtees Misc.* (1888) 75 Betwexte Trent tid and Tyne.] **1585** T. WASHINGTON tr. *Nicholay's Voy.* II. xii. 47 b, The fishes being carried by the violence of the floud, and tyde of the Euxine Sea into Propontide. **1728–46** THOMSON *Spring* 563 Stands each attractive plant, and sucks and swells The juicy tide. **1738** WESLEY *Ps.* CXXXVII. i, Fast by the Babylonish Tide (The Tide our Sorrows made o'erflow). **1757** GRAY *Bard* 144 Deep in the roaring tide he plung'd. **1855** MRS. GATTY *Parab. fr. Nat.* Ser. I. (1869) 39 She used to sing to the tide of the river as it swept along. **1872** TENNYSON *Last Tourn.* 685 Feel this arm of mine—the tide within.. Pulsing full man.

**b.** *transf.* and *fig.*

**1601** SHAKS. *Jul. C.* III. i. 257 Thou art the Ruines of the Noblest man That euer liued in the Tide of Times. **1697** DRYDEN *Virg. Georg.* II. 644 A lofty Gate..T' admit the Tydes of early Visitants. **1781** COWPER *Retirement* 453 The tide of life..May run in cities with a brisker force. **1830** SADLER *Law Popul.* I. 430 A tide of emigration has set in from the Old World to the New.

**12.** The water of the sea; the sea (esp. when the tide is flowing). *poet.*

[**1595** SHAKS. *John* II. i. 74 A brauer choyse of dauntlesse spirits.. Did neuer flote vpon the swelling tide.] **1791** COWPER *Odyss.* xx. 74 Whelm me deep in Ocean's restless tide! **1821** BYRON *Two Foscari* I. i, Bounding o'er yon blue tide. *a* **1847** ELIZA COOK *Rover's Song* 1 I'm afloat, I'm afloat on the fierce rolling tide, The ocean's my home and my bark is my bride.

**III.** Phrases.

†**13.** *Tide and* (*or*) *time* (also *time and tide*: see TIME *sb.* 30): an alliterative reduplication, in which the two words were more or less synonyms, or = time and (or) season. *Obs.*

*a* **1225** *St. Marher.* 18 And te tide and te time þat tu iboren were, schal been iblescet. *c* **1425** *Cast. Persev.* 2456 in *Macro Plays* 150 Þer is no dysese nor debate,..tyde nor tyme, erly nor late, but þat Couetyse is þe grounde. *c* **1475** *Rauf Coilȝear* 48, I leid my life in this land with mekle vnrufe, Baith tyde and tyme in all my trauale. **1583** STOCKER *Civ. Warres Lowe C.* I. 26 b, At al tide and tymes whensoeuer they shall be commaunded. **1609** *Mulb. Trees* in *Harl. Misc.* (Malh.) III. 75 If dancers keep not tide and time in their measures.

†**b.** *The tide abides for, tarrieth* (*for*) *no man, stays no man, Tide nor time tarrieth no man*: now superseded by *Time and tide wait for no man*: see TIME *sb.* 30. Here *tide* originally meant 'time', but from the 16th c. has usually meant the tide of the sea. Cf. TIME *and tide*, in both senses. *Obs.*

**1430–40** LYDG. *Bochas* III. xi. (MS. Bodl. 263) 178/2 The tid abit nat for no maner man. **1546** J. HEYWOOD *Prov.* (1867) 6 The sure sea man seeth, the tide tarieth no man. *a* **1553** UDALL *Royster D.* I. ii. (Arb.) 13 Farewell all my good friendes, the tyme away dothe waste, And the tide they say, tarieth for no man. **1579** [see TARRY *v.* 5]. **1592** GREENE *Disput.* 22 Tyde nor time tarrieth no man. *a* **1625** FLETCHER *Woman's Prize* IV. v, The tide stays no man.

**14.** (*In*) *double tides*, ? as if taking advantage of both the tides in one day; esp. *to work double tides*, to work as hard as possible; so *to roar, spin*, etc. *double tides.* Cf. sense 8.

**1788** MME. D'ARBLAY *Diary* July, I was most content to work double tides for the pleasure of his company. **1805** *Naval Chron.* XIII. 243 The.. Caulkers worked extra double tides in gangs. **1832** *Examiner* 745/2 The artisans work double tides, that is, they perform two days' labour in one. **1852** MISS YONGE *Cameos* (1877) II. vii. 95 There is not a spinster in Brittany who will not spin double tides until my purchase-money be raised. **1889** RIDER HAGGARD *Allan's Wife*, etc. 300 The wounded lioness was now roaring double tides.

**V.** Combinations.

**15.** In senses belonging to I, as **tide-beef**, *dial.* beef provided for a 'tide' or feast; **tide-serving**, time-serving; **tide-time** (see 6 b); †**tide-wise** *adv.*, at times, now and then.

**1896** *Yorksh. Weekly Post* 29 Feb. (E.D.D.), He'd made up his mind they s'ould hae some reight *tide-beef. **1818** SCOTT *Br. Lamm.* xxv, The office shall just cost him as much time-serving and *tide-serving, as if [etc.]. **1824** MISS MITFORD *Village* Ser. I. (1863) 201 At *tide-times he loiters in the chimney-corner at the Rose. **1898** T. HARDY *Wessex Poems* 203 To eyes that had seen her in tide-times of weal. **1611** FLORIO, *Interpollatamente*, at certaine seasons, not continually, *tide-wise.

**16.** In senses belonging to II. **a.** (*a*) simple attrib. 'of the tide, tidal', as *tide-bar* (BAR *sb.*[1] 15), *-channel, -flow, -flux, -lead* (LEAD *sb.*[2] 3 b), *-level, -limit, -line, -mud, -race* (RACE *sb.*[1] 6), *-reach, run, rush, -stream, -turn, -wash*; (*b*) 'dependent on or regulated by the state of the tide, tidal', as *tide-coach, harbour*; 'filled, overflowed, or covered by the tide', as *tide-hole, -land, -marsh, -pool, -rock*; in names of instruments for measuring the tides, or the like, as *tide-ball, -dial, -gauge, -meter, -predictor, -staff*; (*c*) objective and obj. genitive, as *tide-generating, -predicting, -producing, -taking* adjs. and sbs.; (*d*) instrumental, etc., as *tide-beat, -beset, -bound, -caught, -covered, -driven, -flooded, -free, -like* (also adv.), *-locked, -ribbed, -tossed, -trapped, -washed, -worn* adjs.

**1867** SMYTH *Sailor's Word-bk.*, **Tide-ball*, a ball hoisted to denote when the depth of water permits vessels to enter a bar-harbour, or to take the bar outside. **1898** J. BUCHAN in *To Day* 5 Nov. 7/2 The river the noo is no three feet deep a' ower, wi' sands and the shift o' the *tide-bar. **1910** *Q. Rev.* July 88 *Tide-bound at midnight in a small boat off ..Deathhole Creek. **1856** KANE *Arct. Expl.* II. xiv. 142 The outside *tide-channel..was now full of squeezed ice. **1748** SMOLLETT *Rod. Rand.* xxiv, He took a place in the *tide-coach for Rochester. **1756** J. FERGUSON *Astron.* § 409. 262 The *Tide Dial...A moving elliptical Plate, painted blue, to represent the rising of the Tides, under, and opposite to, the Moon. *a* **1644** QUARLES *Sol. Recant.* Sol. viii. 82 As *tide-forsaken Rocks along the Main. **1861** J. BROWN *Lett.* (1907) 142 Glengariff is not *tide-free. **1840** *Civil Eng. & Arch. Jrnl.* III. 342/1 A description of a new *Tide Gauge. **1860** MAURY *Phys. Geog. Sea* (Low) i. § 14 The tide-gauges showed that several well-marked..waves had arrived off the coast. **1863** TYNDALL *Heat* iv. § 122 (1870) 106 The *tide generating forces of the sun and moon. **1793** SMEATON *Edystone L.* § 92 The false idea..of its being a *tide harbour, with a Bar at its mouth. **1856** KANE *Arct. Expl.* I. xx. 260 Our *tide-hole freezes every night alongside. **1891** *Cent. Dict.*, *Tide-land. **1895** *Home Missionary* (N. Y.) Sept. 292 Deep alluvial valleys of great fertility, tide-lands similar to those of Holland. **1856** KANE *Arct. Expl.* I. xxvi. 337 The *tide-leads..one year ago had afforded a precarious passage to the vessel. **1865** MRS. L. L. CLARKE *Seaweeds* vi. 113 If the sea-marks change, and *tide level varies. **1878** HUXLEY *Physiogr.* 180 The Ordnance Survey has fixed its datum line, or standard from which all heights are measured, as the mean tide-level at Liverpool. **1848** MRS. GASKELL *M. Barton* Pref., With ever-returning *tide-like flood. **1854** H. MILLER *Sch. & Schm.* iv. (1860) 40 We found the waves chafing among the rocks just where the *tide-line had rested 12 hours before. **1849** DICKENS *Dav. Copp.* xlvi, This low grip when he picked out of the *tide-mud. **1853** *Zoologist* II. 4055 Almost every *tide-pool and hollow that retains the sea-water. **1898** *Academy* 5 Nov. 194/1 Lord Kelvin's *tide-predicting machine. **1891** *Cent. Dict.*, *Tide-predictor. **1898** *Academy* 5 Nov. 194/1 No more marvellous instrument has ever been invented than the mechanical tide-predictor devised by Lord Kelvin. **1883** *Harper's Mag.* Aug. 375/1 These numerous *tide-races often make the St. Lawrence a rough passage for small craft. **1842** FABER *Styrian Lake*, etc. 43 Thus do idle poets stand Lonely on the *tide-ribbed sand. **1844** W. H. MAXWELL *Sports & Adv. Scotl.* xiii. (1855) 118 The *tide-runs are traceable upon the surface of the ocean. **1857** R. TOMES *Amer. in Japan* v. 128 An officer and two men were also stationed on land, near where a *tide-staff had been planted, and were prepared to make observations. **1875** BEDFORD *Sailor's Pocket Bk.* v. (ed. 2) 146 In describing *tide-streams in the offing, caution must be observed in not confusing the 'flood' and 'ebb' streams. **1889** P. H. EMERSON *Eng. Idylls* 42 *Tide-tossed trees..rise upon the face of the waters. **1882** J. GEIKIE in *Nature* XXVI. 44 Tracts now within *tide-wash. **1832** LYELL *Princ. Geol.* II. 181 Almost every *tide-washed rock is carpeted with fuci and studded with corallines, actiniæ, and mollusca. **1858** N. J. GANNON *O'Donoghue* II. 28 The spray That crowns the *tide-worn rock.

**b.** Special combinations: **tide-board**, a board placed to prevent buildings being flooded at high tides; **tide-crack**, in polar regions, an ice-crack near the shore caused by the rise and fall of the tide, which breaks the floating from the shore ice; **tide-current**, the current caused in a tidal channel by the rise or fall of the tide (Ogilvie, 1882); **tide-day** (see quot.); † **tide-duty**, import or export duty levied at a port; **tide-flap**, a tidal valve opening outwardly at the mouth of a drain or small tidal stream; **tide-house**, a (public) house adjacent to a tidal stream; **tide-lock**, a double lock between tidal water and a canal or the like; a guard-lock; **tide-maker**, that which causes the tides; also, a vessel which is compelled to take advantage of the tide; **tide-plate**, a dial on which the state of the tide is indicated; **tide-register**, a record of tide-movements; also, an apparatus that registers tide-movements; **tide-river**, a tidal river; **tide-rode** *a.*, *Naut.* (for *tide-ridden*), swung by the tide, as a ship at anchor; opposed to *wind-rode*; **tide-runner**, a fish which moves with the tide (*U. S.*); **tide-time**, the time at which the tide serves at any place; **tide-wave**, the undulation which passes over the surface of the ocean, and causes high or low tide as its highest or lowest point reaches any place; also *fig.*; **tide-weather** (see quot.); **tide-wheel**, a water-wheel turned by the flowing and ebbing of the tide through a narrow channel; **tide-work**, work which can be carried on only during hours when the tide is low, or that is paid for by the tide (cf. 8); also, part of the mechanism of a tide-gauge. See also TIDE-BOAT to TIDEWAY.

**1904** *Westm. Gaz.* 31 Dec. 7/2 Thousands of tons of water poured over the *tide boards and protecting walls of various warehouses, flooding the wharves and warehouses. **1856** KANE *Arct. Expl.* II. xiii. 131 He has risen by the side of an ice-berg..or through a *tide-crack. **1833** HERSCHEL *Astron.* xi. 337 The *tide-day (i. e. the interval between two successive arrivals at the same place of the same vertex of the tide-wave). **1769** FALCONER *Dict. Marine* (1789), *Compost*, a *tide-duty, or revenue, arising from shipping. **1843** *Civil Eng. & Arch. Jrnl.* VI. 426/1 At the end of the main sewer was placed a cast-iron frame, upon which were hung three *tide-flaps with brass facings. **1764** *Low Life* 100 The Landlords of *Tide-Houses, both up and down the River Thames, looking out sharp for Boats. **1838** *Civil Eng. & Arch. Jrnl.* I. 148/2 The method by which the main or framing piles of the coffer-dam for the *tide-lock.. were fixed to the rock. **1875** [see *guard-lock* (GUARD *sb.* 18)]. **1903** *Westm. Gaz.* 6 Jan. 4/2 The moon is not only a *tide-maker in the marine sense. Its tangential 'pull' affects the earth's atmosphere. **1910** *Chamb. Jrnl.* Jan. 10/2 His hard overworked apprenticeship to the sea in coasting-schooners, in undermanned, under-engined 'tide-makers'. **1756** J. FERGUSON *Astron.* § 409. 263 The Elliptical or *Tide Plate, with the Moon fixt to it, is upon the Axis of the Wheel. **1825** J. NICHOLSON *Operat. Mechanic* 496 An error of three-quarters of an hour in each lunation will place the tide-plate H, three hours wrong in the space of about four months. **1856** KANE *Arct. Expl.* I. xi. 117 Our *tide-register was on board the vessel. **1739** LABELYE *Short Acc. Piers Westm. Br.* 80 So wide a *Tide-River as the Thames. **1823** CRABB *Technol. Dict.*, **Tide-road* (*Mar.*), the situation of a vessel which, being at anchor when the wind and tide are opposed to each other, has her head towards the current. **1882** NARES *Seamanship* (ed. 6) 197 When not tide rode, pick the lee anchor up. **1877** HALLOCK *Sportsman's Gaz.* 244 These big fellows [weak fish] are designated as *tide-runners. **1840** *Civil Eng. & Arch. Jrnl.* III. 182/1 *Tide-time for vessels of 12-feet draft, is denoted by 2 black balls being kept upon its flag-staff until 12-feet ceases upon the straight course. **1833** HERSCHEL *Astron.* xi. 339 The *tide-wave rushing up a narrow channel, is suddenly raised to an extraordinary height. **1861** T. R. BIRKS *Bible & Mod. Th.* Introd. 5 The tidewave of sceptical thought, which threatens..to bury the old landmarks of Christian faith. **1740** LYNN in *Phil. Trans.* XLI. 689 When the Mercury has been a good while high,..there has fallen mistling Rain; especially about the New and Full Moon, with an Easterly Breeze, which the Borderers on the Coast of Lincolnshire and Norfolk call *Tide-weather, and may be occasioned by the Vapours arising from the Tides, which then cover a vast Wash of Sands in their Neighbourhood. **1864** WEBSTER, **Tide-wheel*. **1888** GOODE *Amer. Fishes* 205 A circular basin,..aerated by a powerful fountain of sea water, forced up by a tide-wheel. **1739** LABELYE *Short Acc. Piers Westm. Br.* 33 The Remainder being only common *Tide-work, has nothing worth relating. **1825** J. NICHOLSON *Operat. Mechanic* 493 The wheel-work and tide-work of this clock are represented by fig. 498. **1852** WIGGINS *Embanking* 122 Some allowance is to be made for tide-work and night-work, for bad weather on the coast, loss of materials.

**Tide** (təid), *v.*[1] Forms: 1 tídan, 3–5 tiden (3–4 tyd, 4 tid, 4–5 tyden, 4–7 tyde, 5 tydyn), 3– tide; *pres. t. 3rd sing.* (for *tideth*) 3–4 tit, tyt, tyd, 4 tid, 5 tite, tytte. *Pa. t.* 1–4 tidde, 4 tydde, tyd (6 *Sc.*), 4–5 tid (5 tyde, tide), 8– tided. *Pa. pple.* 3–4 tid (4–5 tyd(d, tidde, 5 tide, 6 tydde), 7– tided. [OE. *tídan* (oftener *ȝetídan*: see I-TIDE) to happen, come about, f. *tíd*, TIDE *sb.* Perfect tenses usually formed with *be*: cf. COME *v.*]

**1.** *intr.* To happen, befall: = BETIDE *v.* 1. Often impersonal. *arch.*

*a* **1131** *O. E. Chron.* an. 1123 Ða tidde hit on an Wodnes dei..þet se king rad in his der fald. **1297** R. GLOUC. (Rolls) 8649 He..nolde no leng abide þat he nolde to is game, tide wat so bitide. **13..** *Cursor M.* 27412 (Cott.) For nakin case þat mai tide. **1375** BARBOUR *Bruce* I. 127 Ȝe traistyt in lawte,.. And wyst nocht quhat suld eftir tyd. ? *a* **1400** *Morte Arth.* 3655 Of theire termys they talke, how þay ware tydd. **14..** *Sir Beues* (MS. M) 663 Tyde what wyll be-tyde The tone of vs shall dede abyde. *c* **1440** *Promp. Parv.* 493/2 Tydyn, *idem quod* happyn. *c* **1460** *Towneley Myst.* vi. 81 May tyde he wille oure giftis take. **1513** DOUGLAS *Æneis* VI. v. 98 How tyde that cais; declair me, I pray the. **1680** A. HAIG in J. Russell *Haigs* xi. (1881) 309 Com what will com, tyde what may tyde, A Haig shall be Laird of Bemersyde. **1808** SCOTT *Marm.* III. xxii, Soothly I swear, that, tide what tide, The demon shall a buffet bide. **1875** JAS. GRANT *One of the 600* ii, You..shall find that, tide what may, you are not forgotten.

†**b.** const. with *dative*: = BETIDE *v.* 1 b. *Obs.*

*c* **1000** *Inst. Polity* c. 10 in Thorpe *Ags. Laws* II. 316 Þæt heora ȝewitan beon on æȝhwylcne timan, weald hwæt heom tide. *c* **1200** *Trin. Coll. Hom.* 29 Witte wel hwat þu hauest, walte hwat þe tide. **13..** *Guy Warw.* (A.) 4977 Al his lond him tit for-go. **1377** LANGL. *P. Pl.* B. xi. 5 (MS. Rawl.) A merueillous meteles me tydde to dreme. *c* **1384** CHAUCER *H. Fame* I. 255 Euery caas That hym was tyd vpon the see. *c* **1430** *R. Gloucester's Chron.* (Rolls) App. G. 213 Þi lyf þe tydeþ luse. *c* **1590** GREENE *Fr. Bacon* xiii. 14 Some deadly act shall 'tide me ere I sleep.

†**2.** To fall as a lot or portion. (Const. *dative*.)

**955** in Birch *Cart. Sax.* III. 75 ȝif þan biscop[e] hwæt tide. *a* **1272** *Luue Ron* 20 in *O. E. Misc.* 93 Her he haueþ seorewen ryue, Ne tyt him neuer Ro ne Rest. *c* **1300** *St. Margarete* 308 Bote þu do þis dede Ne tyt þe no part wiþ me. *c* **1305** *St. Swithin* 48 in *E. E. P.* (1862) 44 Ho so doþ his dede mid bobance, him ne tyt non oþer mede. *c* **1325** *Poem Times Edw. II* 236 in *Pol. Songs* (Camden) 334 He doth the wif sethe a chapoun and piece beof, Ne tit the gode man noht therof. *c* **1386** CHAUCER *Reeve's T.* 255 This lange nyght ther tydes me na reste.

†**3.** To fare; to get on (well or ill). *Obs. rare*—[1].

*c* **1400** *Destr. Troy* 1202 The Troiens were tyde, & tid þere þe bettur.

¶**4.** *trans.* To meet with, experience (good or evil fortune). *Obs.*

This appears to be an erroneous use, originating with copyists who misunderstood the construction.

*a* **1400** *R. Brunne's Chron. Wace* (Rolls) 5495 (Petyt MS.) For chances þat haf ben tyd [*Lamb. MS.* ffor swylke chaunces þat han bytid]. *a* **1400** *Sir Beues* 1844 Go, or þe tit [*v.r.* þou tytyst] an euel diner. *c* **1472** *Chaucer's Compl. Mars* 202 (MS. Arch. Seld. B. 24) In mony a cas thay tiden oft tyme sorowe [*Fairfax and 2 other MSS.* hem tydeth, *ed. Jul. Notary* hem tyden].

**Tide** (təid), *v.*[2] [f. TIDE *sb.* II.]

**1.** *trans.* **a.** To carry, as the tide does. Chiefly *fig.*

**1640** QUARLES *Enchirid.* III. 48 Man's Will is the Streame that Tydes them [our actions] up and downe. **1693** DRYDEN *Persius' Sat.* vi. (1697) 494 The Relicks of the Wrack..are tided back By the wild Waves, and rudely thrown ashore. **1824** LADY GRANVILLE *Lett.* June, A flow of animal spirits and good humour..tided off anything approaching to bore. **1884** *Daily News* 30 Oct. 7/3 So long will each flood continue to tide up the river varying proportions of sewage or other offensive matter.

**b.** † To carry through (an undertaking) (*obs.*); to enable (a person) to surmount (a difficulty, etc.) as on a swelling tide.

**1626** B. JONSON *Staple of N.* IV. iv, I will tyde this affayre for you; giue it freight and passage. *c* **1860** in Holman-Hunt *Pre-Raphaelitism* (1905) II. 196 We should like to tide him over his low-water difficulties. **1869** GOULBURN *Purs. Holiness* viii. 73 As an exuberant mounting flood shall tide us over the difficulties of our career. **1870** J. BRUCE *Life of Gideon* vi. 109 We are to be tided over all our doubts and difficulties by what I would call a swelling flood of evidences or proofs.

**2.** *intr.* (and with *it*). To flow or surge, as the tide; to flow to and fro; sometimes = 'flow' as opposed to 'ebb'. Also *fig.*

**1593—1654** [see TIDING *vbl. sb.* 1]. **1659** W. BROUGH *Schism* 555 When popular favour blows from us, and secular power tydes it against us and storms us. **1661** WEBSTER & ROWLEY *Thracian Wonder* v, The seas, Whose equal valour neither ebbs nor tides. **1833** T. HOOK *Parson's Dau.* II. xii, The muddy stream of domestic correspondence [*i. e.* between the servants] which 'tided' between Binford and Severnstoke. **1843** E. JONES *Sens. & Event* Poems 3 The sounding crowd That far beneath him tides.

**3.** *trans.* To make to flow as a tide or stream.

**1861** DICKENS *Gt. Expect.* xix, Tiding it [a roll of cloth] out in a flowing manner over the counter.

**4.** *intr.* To float or drift on the tide; *spec. Naut.*, to navigate a ship by taking advantage of favouring tides, and anchoring when the tide turns; usually with adv. of direction. Often *to tide it*.

**1627** CAPT. SMITH *Seaman's Gram.* x. 47 To Tide ouer to a place, is to goe ouer with the Tide of ebbe or flood, and stop the contrary by anchoring till the next Tide. **1691** LUTTRELL *Brief Rel.* (1857) II. 244 Our fleet..are now sailed out, and are now tiding it down with the wind directly against them. **1716** LADY M. W. MONTAGU *Let. to C'tess of Mar* 3 Aug., We..set out in a calm, and he pretended there was nothing so easy as to tide it over [from Gravesend to Holland]. **1836** MARRYAT *Olla Podr* xxvi, We tided and warped how we could. **1893** H. M. DOUGHTY *Wherry in Wendish L.* 71 We could in the morning tide it up further with the flood. **1896** A. AUSTIN *Eng. Darling* IV. ii, Hither there tided The loose-limbed Briton.

**b.** *fig.* To pass or be carried as on the tide; to drift.

**1835** MRQ. LONDONDERRY in Dk. Buckhm. *Crt. Will. IV* (1861) II. vii. 186 These questions would certainly tide on till next year. **1842** MANNING *Serm.* (1848) I. 86 He will most surely tide onward..down the broad current of eternal death.

**c.** quasi-*trans.* *To tide one's way*: to make one's way by using the tides; also *fig.*

**1833** SOUTHEY *Lett.* (1856) IV. 332 Ministers are now endeavouring to tide their way through the session. **1854** H. MILLER *Sch. & Schm.* (1858) 361 We tided our slow way north.

**5.** *intr. fig. To tide over*: to get over or surmount (a difficulty, time of stress, etc.) as if by rising on the flowing tide, or by taking advantage of a favourable tide. With *indirect passive*. Also † *to tide it out* (*obs.*).

*a* **1659** OSBORN *Ess.* ii. Wks. (1673) 558 Christianity..is prescribed by her Institutes to Tide it out, although the Stream of its Inconveniencies runs never so strong against the Nature of Man. **1821** EARL OF DUDLEY *Lett.* 21 Apr., I wish we may be able to tide over this difficulty. **1865** SEELEY *Ecce Homo* iv. (ed. 8) 36 The transgressor has but to tide over a few years. **1884** *Manch. Exam.* 12 May 4/7 We..believe that for the moment the difficulty is tided over.

**Tide**, obs. pa. pple. of TIE *v.*; obs. var. TITE *adv.*

**Tide-boat.** A boat or small vessel which travels with or by means of the tide.

**1576** *The tyde taryeth no man* in Collier *Illustr. E. E. Pop. Lit.* (1863) 77 He dyed in a great madnesse, And went with the tyde boat straight into Hell. **1611** COTGR., *L'Anguille*, the name of the tyde-boat which passes betweene Blaye, and Bourdeaux. **1710** *Brit. Apollo* III. No. 25. 3/2, I lately in Tide-Boat to Gravesend did steer. **1840** DICKENS *Barn. Rudge* li, He may get to the Tower Stairs, and away by the Gravesend tide-boat.

**Tided** (təi·dĕd), *ppl. a.* [f. TIDE *sb.* + -ED [2].] **a.** Having tides, tidal. **b.** Seasoned, as in *well-tided*, well-timed, seasonable (*dial.*).

**a. 1852** WHITTIER *Questions Life* 28 The tided oceans ebb and flow. **1858** — *Swan Song* iii, Broad meadows reached out seaward the tided creeks between. **b. 1801** *Farmer's Mag.* Apr. 225 The operations of husbandry..have been carried forward..in that well-tided order and condition, as to induce us to form the most hopeful prognostication.

**Tideful** (təi·dfŭl), *a.* [f. TIDE *sb.* 3 b, 7 + -FUL.]

†**1.** Seasonable, opportune, right, fit, convenient, expedient. *Obs.*

*a* **1300** *E. E. Psalter* xxxi. 7 [xxxii. 6] For þat sal bid to þe with blisse Al halegh in tideful time [WYCLIF nedful time]. *a* **1340** HAMPOLE *Psalter* cxliv. 16 [cxlv. 15] Þou gifis þe mete of þaim in tydefull tyme. **1382** WYCLIF *Jas.* v. 7 An erthe tilyer abijdith precious fruyt of the erthe, paciently suffringe, til he receyue tymeful [*v. r.* tideful] and lateful.

**2.** Having a full tide; filled with the tide.

**1622** DRAYTON *Poly-olb.* xix. 3 Stem vp his tyde-full streame, vpon that side to rise. *Ibid.* xxvi. 248 The lustie Salmon ..stemming my tydeful Streame. **1887** *Blackw. Mag.* Oct. 539 Up fair Bristol's tideful channel.

Hence † **Ti·defully** *adv.*, opportunely; † **Ti·defulness**, a fit or expedient season; time of need.

*a* **1340** HAMPOLE *Psalter* ix. 9 Helpere in tydfulnesses in tribulacioun. *Ibid.* 22 [x. 1] Þou dispises in tydfulnesis in tribulacyon [L. *despicis in oportunitatibus in tribulacione*]. *Ibid.*, Nedfully [*v. r.* tidfully] þou suffirs vs to be angird and tribled.

† **Tide-gate** [1]. *Obs.* [f. TIDE *sb.* 7 + GATE *sb.*[2]] = TIDEWAY.

**1557** W. TOWRSON in Hakluyt *Voy.* (1589) 113 Like vnto a streame or tyde gate. **1599** NASHE *Lenten Stuffe* 8 Now ..graueld vp, and the streame or tyde-gate turned another way. **1678** PHILLIPS (ed. 4), *Tidegate*, in Navigation is where the Tide runs strongest. **1704** J. HARRIS *Lex. Techn.* I. s. v. *Tide*, When the Tide runs very strong, they call it a Tide Gate. **1711** SIBBALD *Descr. Shetland* 3 The Rousts and high tide-gates of the Sea about the Promontories and the Isles. **1867** SMYTH *Sailor's Word-bk.*

**Tide-gate** [2]. [f. as prec. + GATE *sb.*[1]] A gate through which the water passes into a dock or the like at flood-time, and by which it is retained during the ebb.

**1755** JOHNSON, *Tidegate*, a gate through which the tide passes into a bason. **1838** *Civil Eng. & Arch. Jrnl.* I. 410/2 As the embankments rise, the tide-gates will be arranged so as to regulate the quantity of water inside the bays. **1858** SIMMONDS *Dict. Trade*, *Tide-gate*, the entrance gate of a dock.

**Tideless** (təi·dlĕs), *a.* [f. TIDE *sb.* + -LESS.] Having no tide; unaffected by tides; not washed or covered by a tide. Also *fig.*

**1779** SHERIDAN *Critic* II. ii, Can the quick current of a patriot heart Thus..freeze in tideless inactivity? **1816** BYRON *Siege of Cor.* xvi, There shrinks no ebb in that tideless sea. **1865** *Pall Mall G.* 29 Sept. 11/1 In proximity..to some tideless and stinking port. **1886** *Manch. Exam.* 12 Mar. 5/3 The waters of the tideless Mediterranean.

**b.** *Comb.* **Ti·deless-bloo:ded** *a.*, whose blood is unstirred by passion or emotion.

**1785** BURNS *To Jas. Smith* xxvi, Douce folk, that live by rule, Grave, tideless-blooded, calm and cool. **1806** MAR. EDGEWORTH *Leonora* i, Is it possible that Olivia can envy these tideless-blooded souls their happiness?

Hence **Ti·delessness**, tideless state or condition.

**1901** *Westm. Gaz.* 7 Oct. 3/1 What I particularly like about this Mediterranean sea is its beautiful tidelessness.

**Tideling**, obs. form of TIDLING, pet.

† **Ti·dely**, *adv. Obs.* [f. TIDE *sb.* 8 + -LY [2].] At each tide; each time the tide serves.

**1482** in C. Welch *Tower Bridge* (1894) 89 Layers of wylchons, and other fysshers, lieing almost dayly and tydely at the said stadelynges.

**Tidely**, obs. f. TIDILY; var. TITELY *Obs.*

**Tideman**: see TIDESMAN.

**Ti·de-mark.** The mark left or reached by the tide at high or (rarely) low water; by extension, the mark left by a river flood. Also, a post or the like set up to mark the rise and fall of, or the point reached by the tide. Also *fig.*

**1799** *Scot. Described* (ed. 2) 16 Shells have been discovered ..at a considerable distance above the highest tide-mark. **1861** DICKENS *Gt. Expect.* liv, Red landmarks and tidemarks stuck out of the mud. **1861** J. R. GREENE *Man. Anim.*

*Kingd.* II. *Cœlent.* 232 Many..*Actinidæ*, it is well known, are numerous between tide-marks, the common Sea-anemone tending to encroach upon the line of high water. **1907** *Daily Chron.* 27 Dec. 4/4 You may still trace the tidemark of the flood by tufts of dried grass and driftwood sticking in the branches above your head.

† **Ti·dement.** *Obs. rare*—[1]. [f. TIDE *sb.* + -MENT.] Time, tide, season.

**1560** ROLLAND *Crt. Venus* I. 26 Quhilk..That tydement crauis be his operatioun.

**Ti·de-mill.** [f. TIDE *sb.* 7 + MILL *sb.*[1]]

**1.** A mill driven by the flux and reflux of the tide acting on a water-wheel.

**1796** W. H. MARSHALL *W. England* II. 63 A low bank, thrown up across these marshlands,..gives effect to a tide mill, situated near one end of it. **1825** J. NICHOLSON *Operat. Mechanic* 94 Tide-mills,..are such as employ for their first mover the flowing and ebbing tide, either in the sea or a river. **1870** E. L. GARBETT in *Eng. Mech.* 11 Mar. 624/3 Corn has been ground by tide-mills.

**2.** 'A mill for clearing lands from tide-water' (Webster, 1828).

**Tidend(e, Tider(r,** obs. ff. TIDING, THITHER.

**Ti·de-rip.** [f. TIDE *sb.* 7 + RIP *sb.*[5] I.]

**1.** A commotion of the sea caused by opposing currents, or by a rapid current passing over an uneven bottom.

**1830** N. S. WHEATON *Jrnl.* 518 We are now on George's Bank, and surrounded with tide-rips, having precisely the appearance of those at the mouth of a river. **1860** MAURY *Phys. Geog. Sea* § 752 Tide-rips present their most imposing aspect in the equatorial regions. **1875** R. F. BURTON *Gorilla L.* (1876) I. 2 When the current, setting to the north-west, meets a strong sea-breeze from the west, there is a criss-cross, a tide-rip.

**2.** A tidal wave or current.

**1903** *Blackw. Mag.* Mar. 380/1 It was known as Fort Comosun or 'Rush of Waters' after the tide-rip that races up the Victoria arm. **1904** *Westm. Gaz.* 4 Feb. 5/2 A tidal wave—a 'tide rip', as the sailors call it, because they can see it approaching like a ripple on a smooth sea—is a disturbance on the surface of the ocean depending entirely on the influence of the moon.

**Tidesman** (təi·dzmǣn). Also 8–9 **tideman.**

†**1.** = TIDE-WAITER 1. *Obs.*

**1667** *Lond. Gaz.* No. 194/4 Discovered by some of the Customehouse Tydes-men upon the Watch. **1773** EARL CARLISLE in *Selwyn & Contemp.* (1844) III. 46 Thank Charles for the Tideman's place. **1809** R. LANGFORD *Introd. Trade* 135 Tides men or tide waiters, officers appointed to inspect the loading and unloading ships to prevent contraband transactions.

**2.** One whose work depends on the tide.

**1882** OGILVIE, *Tides-man*, one who is employed only during certain states of the tide. **1894** C. WELCH *Tower Bridge* 51 Twenty-one tidemen working at the ram.

**Ti·de-survey:or.** A customs official who supervised the tide-waiters. So **Ti·de-supervi·sor.**

**1684** E. CHAMBERLAYNE *Pres. St. Eng.* II. (ed. 15) 243 Stephen Chuseman, Tide Supervisor of all the Tide Surveyors on the River of Thames. **1725** *Lond. Gaz.* No. 6390/7 John Etheridge, Gent...Tide Surveyor of His Majesty's Customs. **1806** in J. Smyth *Pract. of Customs* (1821) 145 The articles to be guarded from and to the Ships, and an account to be taken of them by the Tide-waiters, under the special superintendence of the Tide-surveyors. **1892** *Pall Mall G.* 24 Mar. 6/3 For many years tide surveyor and harbour-master at Pakhoi.

†**Ti·des-way.** *Obs.* [f. *tide's*, poss. of TIDE *sb.*] The way of the tide; = TIDEWAY.

**1627** CAPT. SMITH *Seaman's Gram.* i. 1 You may hale in a ship..out of the tides way. **1793** SMEATON *Edystone L.* § 157 A vessel lies..at moorings, though in a Tide's-way.

**Ti·de-table.** [f. TIDE *sb.* 7, 8 + TABLE *sb.* 10.] A table, or tabular list, showing the time of high water at a place or places on each day during the year or other period.

**1594** J. DAVIS (*title*) The Seaman's Secrets,..wherein is taught the three kinds of Sayling,..also an Horizontall Tyde Table. **1710** *Brit. Apollo* III. No. 85. 2/1 Mr. Flamstead's Tide-Table..will shew him the Time of High-Water. **1840** *Encycl. Brit.* (ed. 7) XXI. 284/1 Tolerably accurate tide-tables have long been published annually for London, and still better for Liverpool.

**Ti·de-wai:ter.**

**1.** A customs officer who awaited the arrival of ships (formerly coming in with the tide), and boarded them to prevent the evasion of the custom-house regulations. Now *Hist.*

**1699** FARQUHAR *Constant Couple* I. i, These tidewaiters and surveyors plague us more with the French wines, than the war did with the French privateers. **1754** RICHARDSON *Grandison* (1781) I. xxxv. 247 That I shall get employment on the Keys, or as a tide-waiter extraordinary. **1821** J. SMYTH *Pract. of Customs* 3 Upon the receipt of the Warrants, the Landing-waiter is to give an order to the Tide-waiter on board the Ship, without which no Goods can be permitted to be unladen. **1876** SMILES *Sc. Natur.* xiii. 267 He was willing to be a police officer, a tidewaiter, or anything that would bring in a proper maintenance.

**2.** *fig.* One who waits for a favourable season.

**1841** MIALL in *Nonconf.* I. 249 The tide-waiters and time-servers of reform are evidently at a discount. **1901** *Daily News* 15 Feb. 6/5 Political tidewaiters, whose loyalty..may ultimately be reconciled with high salaried posts.

Hence **Ti·de-wai:tership,** the office of a tide-waiter.

**1855** THACKERAY *Newcomes* xi, He would ask the minister for a tide-waitership for him. **1866** LOWELL *Presid. on Stump* Prose Wks. 1890 V. 265 His own chance of reëlection, or that of some fourth cousin to a tidewaitership.

**Ti·de-wa:ter.**

**1.** Water brought by the flood-tide.

**1799** LD. HAWKE in R. Brown *Agric. Surv. W. Riding* xii. § 6. 164 The tide water that has been previously admitted by the flood gate opens the clough again, and discharges itself. **1836** *Hull & Selby Railw. Act* 108 Conveying the tide-water from the river Ouse. **1911** QUILLER-COUCH *Shining Ferry* vii. 75 A mort o' tide-water have runned up an' down since you spoke they words.

**2.** *U.S.* Water affected by the ordinary ebb and flow of the tide; tidal water. Also *attrib.*

**1868** *Rep. U.S. Commissioner Agric.* (1869) 389 Throughout the tide-water district, the whole country is believed to be underlaid by deposits of fossil shells. **1876** BANCROFT *Hist. U.S.* V. ix. 424 The scanty naval stores..had to be transported from tide-water to the lake. **1888** GOODE *Amer. Fishes* 3 A deep hole in the bed of a tide-water creek.

**Ti·deway.** A channel in which a tidal current runs; also the tidal part of a river; *transf.* a strong current running in such a channel; = TIDE-GATE [1].

[1627–1793: see TIDES-WAY.] **1798** *Hull Advertiser* 4 Aug. 2/4 A gunboat..being very manageable in a strong tideway. **1810** J. T. in *Risdon's Surv. Devon* p. xxxii, It..serves to convey shipping from the Tideway. **1856** KANE *Arct. Expl.* I. xxvii. 359 A moment's check would plunge the whole concern into the rapid tide-way. **1875** BEDFORD *Sailor's Pocket Bk.* v. (ed. 2) 153 Sounding in a tide-way it may be necessary to anchor the boat.

*fig.* **1821–30** LD. COCKBURN *Mem.* iii. (1874) 149 His shop, in the very tideway of all our business, made it the natural resort of..all sorts of literary idlers. **1880** G. MEREDITH *Tragic Com.* (1881) 60 A lead that..would roll him on a good tideway strong in his own passion and his lady's up against the last defences. **1883** *Century Mag.* Oct. 823/1 Henry VIII.'s palace has not been forever a barber's shop, or the Strand a tide-way of shop-keeping.

†**Ti·dife, -ive.** *Obs. rare.* Also 4 tydif(e, tydyf, tideue, ti-, tydyue. [Origin and sense obscure: cf. also TYDIE, and TIDIVE = TIDY *a.*] Name of some small bird. (Swainson, after Skinner, suggests the Blue titmouse.)

*c* **1385** CHAUCER *L. G. W.* 154 And thoo [birds] that hadde doon vnkyndenesse As dooth the tydif [*v. rr.* tydyf, tydife] for new fangelnesse Besoghte mercy..And sworen on the blosmes to be trewe. *c* **1386** — *Sqr.'s T.* 640 Alle thise false fowles As beth thise tidyues [*v. rr.* tydyues, tydifs, tideues] tercelettes and Owles. **1671** SKINNER *Etymolog., Voc. Antiq., Tidefes*..avis genus, nescio an illa avis quam nos Titmouse vocamus.

**Tidily** (təi·dĭli), *adv.* Also 4–6 **tidely.** [f. TIDY *a.* + -LY [2].] In a tidy manner; † betimes, seasonably, duly (*obs.*); suitably, in an orderly manner, skilfully, neatly, etc.: see TIDY.

**1340–70** *Alisaunder* 194 Þe fairest feete þat euer freke kende, With ton [= toes] tidily wrought. *c* **1350** *Will. Palerne* 4454 Alphouns..buskes in to þe baþ..& fond it treuli a-tired & tidily warme. *Ibid.* 5482 He..tok to him tidely trewe cunsayl euere. *c* **1400** *Destr. Troy* 6839 Þen the Troiens, with tene, tidely þai faght. **1557–8** LD. WENTWORTH in Hardwicke *St. Papers* (1778) I. 112, I will do what I can tidily to signify unto your Majesty our State. **1593** G. HARVEY *New Let.* Wks. (Grosart) I. 259 You haue lately ..very tidely playde the Bees part. **1771** MRS. HAYWOOD *A New Present* 252 To dress herself tidily and quickly. **1832** R. & J. LANDER *Exped. Niger* I. iii. 112 The inhabitants are..very tidily clad in cotton dresses. **1870** MRS. RIDDELL *Austin Friars* i, The plates are all ranged tidily away.

**Tidiness** (təi·dinės). [f. as prec. + -NESS.] The quality or condition of being tidy (in various senses: see the adj.); † seasonableness; orderliness, neatness.

**1567** MAPLET *Gr. Forest* 9 b, For lacke of their naturall ..growth and tidinesse in ripening. **1800** AMELIA OPIE *Let.* in *Life* v. (1854) 74 He has gotten a fit of tidyness on him. **1860** BOYD *Recreat. Country Parson* vi. 200 Tidiness is a great source of cheerfulness. **1879** SALA in *Daily Tel.* 9 June, One row of houses..admirable in their neatness, tidiness, cheerfulness, and commodiousness.

**Tiding** (təi·diŋ); pl. **tidings** (təi·diŋz), *sb.* Forms: see sense 2 below. [Late OE. *tídung* f., early ME. *tiding*, as if f. OE. *tíd-an* vb. to happen, befall + -ING [1]; but prob. ad. ON. *tíðendi, -indi* neut. pl., 'events, occurrences, the reports of these, news, tidings', f. *tíðr* adj. happening, occurring + *-endi, -indi*, nominal suffix (see Vigfusson *Icel. Dict.* xxxiii/1); thence MSw. *tidhende* event, occurrence, news, Sw. *tidender* m. pl., Norw. and Da. *tidende* n. sing. tidings. In form, late OE. *tídung* (obl. cases **tídunge (-a)*, pl. nom. *-a (-e)*, gen. *-a*, dat. *-um*) might well be a deriv. of *tíd-an*, TIDE *v.*[1]; but the fact that, beside it, early ME. had also *tīðende, -inde, tīthend*, clearly from Norse, also *tīðing(e*, with Norse stem and Eng. suffix, and *tīdende, -inde*, with Eng. stem and Norse suffix, together with the fact that the word is unknown to OE. before the late 11th or early 12th c., and is recorded first in the transferred sense 'tidings', makes it probable that the whole group in Eng. was adopted from ON., in the north in the Norse form, in the south anglicized, in intervening districts with various mixtures of the two forms. It is noticeable that the English or fully anglicized form is that which happens to occur earliest in an extant writing, and also that which survives in mod.Eng., though the Norse type (with Eng. pl. *-s*) *tithand(e)s, tithans*, came down to 15th c. in north. Eng. and to 16–17th c. in Sc.

In ON. *tíðindi* is only plural; so Sw. *tidender*; in Norw. and Da. *tidende* is sing.; in early ME. *tiðende* was sing. or pl., with a tendency to make the sing. *tiðend*; the anglicized *tidung, -ing*, normally had the pl. **tīdunga, tidinge*; but, as in other fem. sbs., the *-e* of the oblique cases of the sing. was often taken by the nom. A single instance of pl. *tiðenden* occurs in the later text of Layamon; but from *c* 1275 the plurals became *tidinges* and *tithand(e)s*. The existing form *tidings* is usually construed as pl., but sometimes as sing.: cf. *news*. Ger. *zeitung*, MHG. *zîtunge* (1321 in Niederrheinisch) = MLG. *tîdinge* (1458 in Bremen Doc.), Du. *tijding*, which agree in form with Eng. *tiding*, are of later appearance, and by some held to be due to Scandinavian influence (Kluge).]

**1.** Something that happens; an event, incident, occurrence. *Obs.* or *arch.*

(This is the etymologically earlier sense; though not exemplified in Eng. quite so early as sense 2, it was no doubt current in the Danelaw district from the first. In the two late quots. a literalism of translation.)

*c* **1205** LAY. 7543 Þa isæh Cesar tiðend þat him wes sær [*c* **1275** tidinge þat was sor]. *c* **1386** CHAUCER *Man of Law's T.* 628 How that this blisful tidyng [*Petw. MS.* tydyngges] is bifalle. **1502** *Ord. Crysten Men* (W. de W. 1506) v. vi. 411 In the delytes of paradyse is neuer founde ony varyacyon, alwayes in loue without tydynges. **1861** DASENT *Story of Burnt Njal* I. 107 It must be told what tidings [Icel. *hvat tíðenda*] happened at home. **1864** — *Jest & Earnest* (1873) II. 192 The tokens that are left of those tidings which happened there.

†**b.** Custom, usage. *Obs. rare.*

(Cf. ON. *tíðr* customary, habitual, that happens, *tíðska* custom, usage, fashion.)

*c* **1205** LAY. 396 After þen heðene tidende [*c* 1275 lawe] þe wes in þan lande. *Ibid.* 2052 [see TIR]. *Ibid.* 14325 Hit beoð tiðende [*c* 1275 þe wone] Inne Sæxe-londe..þat [etc.].

**2.** The announcement of an event or occurrence; a piece of news (now *obs.* or *arch.*); usually in *pl. tidings*, reports, news, intelligence, information.

**a.**[1] *Sing.* 1–2 **tídung,** 3–4 **tidinge,** (3 **tidding),** 3–6 **tydinge,** 3–7 **tyding,** 4–5 **tid-, tydyng(e,** (5 **tytynge),** 2– **tiding.**

**1069–1125** *O. E. Chron.* an. 995 (MS. F.), Ða wearþ se cing swyþe bliðe þissere tidunge. *c* **1250** *Gen. & Ex.* 2907 Moyses told hem ðis tidding. *c* **1275** LAY. 1376 Þe tiding com to Corineum, þat [etc.]. *Ibid.* 22323 Þe tyding com to þan kinge. **13..** *Cursor M.* 5114 (Gött.) Þis tyding his soru slake. *c* **1385** CHAUCER *L. G. W.* 1424 (*Hypsipyle & Medea*) Theere was swich tydyng [*v. rr.* tidynge, tiding] oueral & swich loos. **1390** GOWER *Conf.* II. 238 This tyding Of Jason. *a* **1400** *R. Gloucester's Chron.* (Rolls) 7979 (MS. B) Þer of com to normandie þe tydynge attelaste. *Ibid.* 9178 (MS. B) Tytynge him com þat [etc.]. *c* **1485** *Digby Myst.* (1882) III. 1087 To me þis is a Ioyfull tydyng. **1620** I. V. tr. *P. du Moulin's Serm.* 4 It is a blessed tyding of which Jesus Christ not only is the subject and substance, but also the bearer and proclaimer. **1879** L. SHEPHERD tr. *Guéranger's Liturg. Year* I. vi. 68 At such a tiding as this, what else can I, than cry out,..Lord! I am not worthy.

**a.**[2] *Plural.* 1 ***tídunga** (-e), 2–3 **tid-, tydinge, tidynge,** 3–4 **tiding;** 3–6 **tid-, tydinges, -ynges,** 4–6 **-ingis, -yngys, -yngges,** 5 **tidenggez,** 5–8 **tydings,** 6 **tid-, tydyngs,** *Sc.* **-engs,** 6– **tidings.**

*c* **1200** *Vices & Virt.* 17 Ic scal iheren reuliche tidinge. *c* **1205** LAY. 3601 Þe swein..seide þas tidinge [*c* **1275** þeos tiding]. *c* **1275** *Ibid.* 1038 Þeos tidinge him were loþe. *Ibid.* 8582 Þe tidinges him were lefue. *Ibid.* 24427 Many tidynge Mid Arthur þan kinge. *c* **1350** *Will. Palerne* 4877 Þe murþe..mad for þo tiding whan þei told were. **13** . *Cursor M.* 7798 (Gött.) I cum, to telle þe tydinges lele. **1486** *Plumpton Corr.* (Camden) 54 Sir, as for tydings, here is but few. **1535** COVERDALE *Jonah* iii. 6 The tydinges came vnto ye kinge of Niniue. **1671** MILTON *P. R.* II. 62 Her Son,..left at Jordan, tydings of him none. **1782** COWPER *Gilpin* xlii, What news? what news? your tidings tell. **1852** MISS YONGE *Cameos* I. ii. 13 Further tidings were anxiously awaited. **1869** FREEMAN *Norm. Conq.* (1875) III. xiii. 260 Perplexed for a moment by the suddenness of the tidings.

**β.**[1] *Sing.* 3 **tiðinge,** (3 **tiþingue),** 4 **teþinge,** 4–5 **tiþ-, tyþ-, tyth-, tith-, -ing, -yng(e,** (6 **teytheyng).**

*c* **1290** *S. Eng. Leg.* I. 6/190 He seide þat one tiþingue to him fram is fader he brouȝte. *c* **1305** *St. Lucy* 155 in *E. E. P.* (1862) 105 A ioyful teþinge ic ȝou telle. *c* **1330** R. BRUNNE *Chron.* (1810) 14 Þat Brittrik was dede him com tiþing. **1375** BARBOUR *Bruce* II. 454 He wes blyþ off þat tithing. **1483** *Cath. Angl.* 389/1 To telle Tythynge, *rumificare.* **1596** *King & Barker* 62 in Hazl. *E. P. P.* I. 7, Y know now teytheyng, the thanner seyde.

**β.**[2] *Pl.* 2–3 **tiðinge;** 3–5 **tiþ-, tithinges,** 4 **tethinges,** 4–6 **tyþ-, tyth-, tith-, -inges, -ynges, -yngus, -ingis, -ingys,** 5 **tithyngs, tythings, tithings.**

*c* **1175** *Lamb. Hom.* 93 Ða iwearð þer muchel eie..on alle þam þat þeos tiðinge iherdon. *c* **1200** *Trin. Coll. Hom.* 31 Gode tiðinge and murie to heren. *c* **1290** *Beket* 1493 in *S. Eng. Leg.* I. 149 Þo þeos tiþinges to þe kingue..cam. *c* **1300** *Ibid.* 695 (Percy S.) 34 Tethinges to the kinge come. *c* **1380** WYCLIF *Serm.* Sel. Wks. I. 198 Good tiþingis of þe kyngdom of hevene. *c* **1400** MAUNDEV. (Roxb.) xxv. 119 When any tythinges er herd in þe cuntree. *c* **1440** *Partonope* 2697 Sone after haue they tithings. **1530** RASTELL *Bk. Purgat.* Prol., What tythinges or news. **1567** *Gude & Godlie B.* (S.T.S.) 49 To zow thir tythingis trew I bring.

**γ.**[1] *Sing.* 3 **tiþennde** (*Orm.*), **tiðende, -end, -ind,** 4–5 **tythand(e,** 4–6 **tiþ-, tithand(e,** (4 **tyȝ-, tiȝand),** 5 **tiþond(e,** (9 **tithand).**

*c* **1200** ORMIN Ded. 158 Goddspell onn Ennglissh nemmnedd iss..god tiþennde. *c* **1205** LAY. 1376 Þa tiðind [*c* 1275 tiding] com to Corineum þat [etc.]. *Ibid.* 7543 Þa isæh Cesar tiðend [*c* 1275 tidinge] þat him wes sære. *a* **1300** *Cursor*

*M.* 12785 Þai sent þair messageres..To bring fra iohn certan tiþand [*Fairf.* tiþande, *Trin.* tiþond]. *c* 1430 *Syr Tryam.* 156 They..tolde the kynge hur tythande. 1513 DOUGLAS *Æneis* II. vii. [vi.] 50 How now, Panthus, quhat tithand do ȝe bryng? 1819 W. TENNANT *Papistry Storm'd* (1827) 69 He'd got some tithand from the coast.

γ.[2] *Pl.* 3 **tiðende**; **-en**; 4 **tiþandus**, (**tyȝandes**, **tiþans**), 4–5 **tythandis**, 4–6 **tiþandis**, **-es**, **tythands**, 5 **tythandes**, **-andys**, **-ondys**, **tithands**, **-anndez**, **-aundes**, 6 **-indes**, *Sc.* **tythance**.

*c* 1205 LAY. 1038 Þæs tiðende [*c* 1275 þeos tidinge] him weren læðe. *Ibid.* 13996 Heo sæiden to þan kinge neowe tiðenden. *a* 1352 MINOT *Poems* iii. 58 Þe galay men.. thanked God of þir tiþandes. 13.. *Cursor M.* 15912 (Cott.) For tiþans þat war tald. *Ibid.* 10312 (Gött.) Þis angel.. Broght him tyȝandes sua gode. *Ibid.* 3322 (Fairf.) Þe maydyn ranne hame tiþandus to tel. *c* 1440 *York Myst.* xxiii. 60 Som new tythandys. *c* 1450 *St. Cuthbert* (Surtees) 7802 Þe tithands went to many towns. 1533 GAU *Richt Vay* (S.T.S.) 105/32 This promis is the vangel or ioiful tithandis. 1560 ROLLAND *Seven Sag.* 115 Of ȝour tythance I am richt wonder glaid. *a* 1584 *Satir. Poems Reform.* xx. 26 At me thay speir Quhat tythands in this land?

δ.[1] *Sing.* 3 **tidende**, **tidind**, 4 **tydand**, **-ant**, 4–5 **tydande**, 5 **tydond**, **tydynde**.

*c* 1205 LAY. 17466 Þat tidende com to þan kinge. *c* 1275 *Ibid.* 9936 Come þe tidind [*c* 1205 þa tiðende] to Maurus þan kinge. *c* 1330 R. BRUNNE *Chron. Wace* (Rolls) 5005 Men tolde þe kyng tydant, þat Romayns were aryue on land. *Ibid.* 15936 Til hym cam ful smert tydande [*rime* on lande]. 13.. *Cursor M.* 10417 (Gött.) Quen þat scho herd þis tydand [*Cott.* tiþand, *Laud* tydond, *Trin.* tiþonde]. *c* 1400 *Laud Troy Bk.* 15242 To telle him of her tydande. *c* 1460 *Launfal* 838 Everych man therfore was wo That wyste of that tydynde.

δ.[2] *Pl.* 3 **tidinde**, **-ende**; 5 **tid-**, **tydandes**, **-is**, **-annes**, **tytandis**, 6 *Sc.* **tydinnis**, **tydance**.

*c* 1205 LAY. 3332 For ȝef ferrene kinges Hiherde þa tidinde. *Ibid.* 5139 Selcuðe tidende. 1451 CAPGRAVE *St. Gilbert* 72 Þe grete fere þat he hadde þat he schuld her no euel tytandis of hem. *Ibid.* 115 The archbischop..saide he was glad of þese tydannes. 1513 DOUGLAS *Æneis* XI. xvii. 65 All the maist cruell tydinnis fillis his eris. *a* 1585 MONTGOMERIE *Flyting* 72 Wee will heir tydance..of thy pow.

ε. *Sing.* and *pl.* 3 **þyþingue**, 4 **thiþand**, (**thyȝandez**), 5 **thythyng**, **-es**, **thiþynges**, 6 **-thingis**.

*c* 1290 *St. Lucy* 157 in *S. Eng. Leg.* I. 105 Ane Ioyeful þyþingue ich eou telle. 13.. *Cursor M.* 10994 (Cott.) To þam he moght tell na thiþand [*v.rr.* tiþand, tiþond, tydond]. ? *a* 1400 *Morte Arth.* 1567, I ȝif the for thy thyȝandez To-louse þe riche. *c* 1400 *R. Gloucester's Chron.* (Rolls) 4251 Hom com tydinge [*MS. β.* thiþynges]. *c* 1425 *Seven Sag.* (P.) 1538 When he herde thys thythyng. *c* 1500 *Lancelot* 2279 Whar that al thithingis goith and cumyth son.

**b.** plural const. as singular.

*c* 1375 *Cursor M.* 15912 (Fairf.) Tiþinges þat was talde. 1595 SHAKS. *John* IV. ii. 115 The tydings comes, that they are all arriu'd. 1619 W. SCLATER *Exp.* 1 *Thess.* (1638) 214 When tidings is brought us of Brethrens faultings. 1643 TRAPP *Comm. Gen.* xxxv. 22 Jacob's great amazement at this sad tidings. 1839 CARLYLE *Chartism* (1842) 48 The tidings was world-old, or older.

† **c.** *fig.* Indications, traces. *Obs. rare.*

*a* 1440 *Sir Eglam.* 367 Where the bore had wonte to bee; Tydyngys of hym sone he fonde, Slayne men on every honde.

**3.** *Comb.*, as *tidings-bearer*, *-bringer*, *-bringing*, *-maker*.

*c* 1440 *Promp. Parv.* 493/2 Tydyngys berare, *rumigerulus*. 1483 CAXTON *Cato* g vj b, Thou arte a lyar and a tydynges maker. 1526 TINDALE *Acts* xvii. 18 He semeth to be a tydynges brynger off new devyls [COVERD. goddes]. 1535 COVERDALE 1 *Sam.* iv. 17 Then answered the tydinge bringer, & sayde: Israel is fled before the Philistynes. 1552 HULOET, Tidynges carier, *renuncius, ij.* 1632 SHERWOOD, A Tidings bringing, *nunciation*.

Hence **Ti·dingless** *a.*, without tidings.

1822 *Blackw. Mag.* XI. 398 As tidingless returning as before. 1870 MORRIS *Earthly Par.* III. 430 Tidingless a while day passed by day.

**Ti·ding**, *vbl. sb.* [f. TIDE *v.*[2], or TIDE *sb.* + -ING [1].]

† **1.** The flowing or rising of the tide; also *fig.*

1593 B. BARNES *Parthenophil* Sonn. xli, More than blessed was I, if one tiding Of female favour set mine heart afloat! 1639 G. DANIEL *Ecclus.* xii. 16 The gust of Sin, may Stir a Surly tiding, In Seas pacifique. 1654 WHITLOCK *Zootomia* Pref. a v, Would you know (saith he) my manner of writing? it is a kind of voluntary Tiding of, not Pumping for; Notions flowing, not forced. 1675 E. WILSON *Spadacrene Dunelm.* 21 No more of the River comes back again by tiding than what the Sea forc'd up at the time of its tiding.

**b.** *attrib.* **Tiding time**: in quot. *fig.*

1693 PASCHALL in *Phil. Trans.* XVII. 816 The Fits generally lasted all the Tiding time, and then went off in gentle kindly Sweats in the Ebbs.

**2.** A sailing or drifting with the tide.

1681 T. DUSELEY in *Trans. Kilkenny Archæol. Soc.* Ser. II. IV. 320 They very easily putt to sea.., a very small matter of tideing (if any) serves turne. 1711 W. SUTHERLAND *Ship-build. Assist.* 164 Stream Anchor; which stops the Ship in tiding up a River. 1774 PENNANT *Tour Scot. in* 1772 241 After tiding for three hours anchor in the Sound. 1817 KEATINGE *Trav.* II. 143 Some little advantage in point of position..with convenience of tiding up inland.

**Ti·ding**, *ppl. a.* [f. TIDE *v.*[2] + -ING [2].] That ebbs and flows; tidal.

1622 DRAYTON *Poly-olb.* xxx. 88 There is a Tyding-well, That daily ebbs and flowes. 1654 WHITLOCK *Zootomia* 372 If we fling our Bread upon the Waters, we chuse not Currents that run all one way (and that from us), but tyding waters. 17.. PHILIPS (J.), Wading within the Ouse, he dealt his blows, And sent them, rolling, to the tiding Humber. 1839 STONEHOUSE *Axholme* p. xiv, The Isle of Axholme.. admirably situated on the banks of a tiding river.

† **Ti·dive**, *a. Obs. rare*[−1]. [Alteration of TIDY *a.*, after adjs. in -IVE; perh. by association with HASTIVE, HASTY, *tardife*, TARDY, etc.] Timely, opportune: = TIDY *a.* 1.

? 17.. *Lord Barnett*, etc. xv. in Child *Ballads* III. (1885) 257/1 Being in the tidive hour.

**Tidliche, tidlike, tidly**, var. TITELY *Obs.*

**Tidling** (ti·dliŋ). *Obs.* exc. *dial.* Also 6 **tideling** (**-ynge**), 9 *dial.* **tiddling**. [? deriv. of TIDDLE *v.* 1 or TID *a.*: see -LING [1].] A pampered or spoilt child; a darling, pet; a young, delicate, or puny child or animal, needing special care; a weakling, 'dilling'.

1520 WHITINTON *Vulg.* 37 b, These cokeneis and tidelynges wantonly brought vp. *a* 1553 *Nice Wanton* in Hazl. *Dodsley* II. 164 She for their sake, Being her tender tidlings, will me beat. [Cf. *ibid.* 173 [referring to the same persons] My parents did tiddle me: they were to blame; *ibid.* 174 Yet were we tiddled, and you beaten now and then.] *c* 1580 JEFFERIE *Bugbears* III. i. in *Archiv Stud. Neu. Spr.* (1897), The gray beard daunceth, and fareth as he weare dame venus tideling. 1657 TRAPP *Comm. Ps.* iii. Introd., Absalom his Son, his Darling, his Tidling, his One Eye. 1904 *Eng. Dial. Dict.* s. v. *Tiddle*, *Tiddling*, (*a*) a young animal, esp. a lamb, brought up by hand; a delicate child needing care; (*b*) the smallest pig in a litter.

**Tidology** (təidǫ·lŏdʒi). *rare.* [irreg. f. TIDE *sb.* + -(O)LOGY.] The study or science that treats of the tides. Hence **Tidolo·gical** *a.*, of or pertaining to tidology.

1834 WHEWELL in Todhunter *Acc. Writ.* (1876) II. 194 Do not omit to mention what the Liverpool people..have done for Tidology. 1840 — *Philos. Induct. Sci.* (1847) II. 509, I have ventured to employ the term *Tidology*, having been much engaged in tidological researches. 1843 MILL *Logic* VI. iii. § 1 No one doubts that Tidology (as Dr. Whewell proposes to call it) is really a science.

**Tidy** (təi·di), *a.* (*sb.*, *adv.*) Forms: 3–5 **tidi**, 4–5 **tide**, 4–7, 9 *Sc.* **tydy**, 5 **tyde**, (**tithy**), 6 **tidie**, **tydye**, 6–8 **tydie**, 7 *Sc.* **tyddie**, (9 *dial.* **teydey**), 4, 7– **tidy**. [ME. f. *tīd* time, TIDE + -Y. Cf. OHG., MHG. *zîtig* (Ger. *zeitig*), Du. *tijdig*, Sw., Da. *tidig* timely.]

† **1.** Timely, seasonable, opportune; in season.

*c* 1350 *Will. Palerne* 1339 Gret merþe..meliors þan made for þe tidy tidinges. *Ibid.* 1710 Til she say tidi time hire prey for to take. *c* 1475 *Partenay* 5722 Of nouel thinges.. No-thing I fynd at no tydy stounde. 1594 CAREW *Tasso* (1881) 66 Nor place serues fit, nor season tidie growes. 1660 F. BROOKE tr. *Le Blanc's Trav.* 270 Hearing of this tydie accident, he was cautious to appear. 1721 RAMSAY *Horace to Virg.* 5 King Æol, grant a tydie tirl.

† **b.** *Tidy cow*, a cow giving milk. *Sc. Obs.*

1493 *Act. Dom. Conc.* (1839) 300 Þe mylk of thre tithy ky. 1533 in *Munim. Burgh Irvine* (1890) I. 39 Ane tydy kow. 1670 in *Proc. Soc. Ant. Scot.* (1896) XXX. 20 Too tydie kay & four yeell [i. e. dry] kay. 1678 *Ibid.*, Two tyddie key and a two yeir old kow.

**2.** In good condition, or of good appearance; fair, well-favoured, comely, bonny; fat, plump, healthy. In quot. 1340–70, showy, gorgeous. Now *dial.*

*c* 1250 *Gen. & Ex.* 2105, .vii. eares wexen fette of coren, On an busk ranc and wel tidi. 1340–70 *Alex. & Dind.* 599 We ..no tidi atir in templus araie. 1393 LANGL. *P. Pl.* C. XIII. 187 Seedes þat been sowen and mowe suffre wyntres, Aren tydyour and tower. 1513 DOUGLAS *Æneis* III. iv. 23 Flockis and hirdis of oxin and of fee, Fat and tydye. 1573 TUSSER *Husb.* (1878) 131 If weather be faire, and tidie thy graine, Make speedily carrege, for feare of a raine. 1597 SHAKS. 2 *Hen. IV*, II. iv. 250 Thou whorson little tydie Bartholmew Bore-pigge. 1607 TOPSELL *Four-f. Beasts* (1658) 518 When a Sow is very fat she hath alway but little milk, and therefore is not apt to make any good tidy Pigs. 1714 GAY *Sheph. Week, Friday* 76 Before my Eyes will trip the tidy Lass. 1803 R. ANDERSON *Cumbld. Ball.* 56 Bonny, teydey, blithe was she. 1808 JAMIESON, *A tydy bairn*, a child that is plump and thriving. 1881 GRANT WHITE *Eng. Without & Within* xvi. 387 Among them [the lower middle class] a tidy girl means a pretty girl, and particularly a girl with a good figure.

**3.** As an indefinite epithet of admiration or commendation. † **a.** Good, excellent, satisfactory, useful; of good character or ability; worthy, brave; able, skilful. (Also ironically.) *Obs.*

*c* 1350 *Will. Palerne* 2496 Forto telle what tidde of þat tide werwolf. *Ibid.* 5384 Al þat touched þer to a tidi erldome, To þe kowherd & his wif þe king ȝaf þat time. 1393 LANGL. *P. Pl.* C. XXII. 441 Trauaileþ..for a tretour al-so sore As for a trewe tydy man. *c* 1400 *Destr. Troy* 1035 Soudiours..Of the tidiest of Tessaile, tore men of strenght. 1567 DRANT *Horace, Ep.* II. ii. H j, A seruaunte at his masters beck tydie, prompte, preste and fyne. 1613 BEAUM. & FL. *Coxcomb* II. i, Thou art the tidiest wittol..I think above ground. *a* 1625 FLETCHER *Woman's Prize* IV. ii, What a hap had I, And what a tydie fortune, when my fate Flung me upon this bear-whelp?

**b.** Now in lighter use: Fairly satisfactory, 'pretty good', 'fair' (in quality); decent, of a good sort; nice. (*colloq.*)

1844 DICKENS *Lett.* (ed. 2) I. 116 Which I thought for a coastguardman was rather a tidy question. 1851 MAYHEW *Lond. Labour* I. 133 Parsons and doctors are often 'tidy customers'. 1865 DICKENS *Mut. Fr.* III. i, A tidy shot that, I flatter myself. 1899 E. PHILLPOTTS *Human Boy* iii. 82, I hope he did [succeed], for he was a tidy chap, though queer.

**c.** Considerable (in amount or degree); 'pretty big'. *A tidy penny* = 'a pretty penny' (PRETTY *a.* 5). (*colloq.*)

1838 DICKENS *Nich. Nick.* xxxii, You came along at a tidy pace. 1851 MAYHEW *Lond. Labour* I. 352 If it is just after quarter-day, she generally gets a tidy tip. 1854 *Househ. Words* IX. 69/1, I have a tidy penny in the funds. 1881 BLACKMORE *Christowell* ii, A horse who had been to Exeter and back with a tidy load. 1893 LADY BURTON *Sir R. F. Burton* II. 252 A very large garden..wherein one could take a very tidy walk. 1903 SIR M. G. GERARD *Leaves fr. Diaries* ix. 324 They do swear a tidy bit.

**4.** (The chief current use.) **a.** Of persons: Orderly in habits, or in personal appearance; disposed to keep things (or one's person or dress) neat and in order.

1706 PHILLIPS (ed. Kersey), *Tidy*, handy, neat, clean, as A tidy Servant. *a* 1800 PEGGE *Suppl. Grose*, *Tidy*, neat. North. 1818 SCOTT *Hrt. Midl.* xxxiii, If thou knowest of any tidy lass like thysell, that wanted a place, and could bring a good character. 1831 D. E. WILLIAMS *Life & Corr. Sir T. Lawrence* II. 72 [The child] folds up her things like a tidy lady's maid. 1849 LYTTON *Caxtons* 13 My dear mother was the tidiest woman in the world.

**b.** Of things, esp. of a house, room, receptacle, etc.: Neatly arranged; with nothing in disorder or out of place; orderly, neat, trim.

1828 WEBSTER s. v., The children are tidy; their dress is tidy...The apartments are well furnished and tidy. 1840 DICKENS *Barn. Rudge* iv, There was not a neater, more scrupulously tidy, or more punctiliously ordered house in Clerkenwell. 1859 *Habits Gd. Soc.* viii. 271 Some underbred ladies..put tidy their work-boxes, making you feel that you are secondary. 1880 JEFFERIES *Gt. Estate* 201 He objected to cut and trim them [shrubs, etc.]. 'For', said he, 'God made nothing tidy'.

**5.** *Comb.*, as *tidy-looking*, *-minded* adjs.; **tidy-betty**, an ash-pan (*dial.*).

1825 J. NEAL *Bro. Jonathan* I. 19 He was a small, meagre, ..tidy-looking somebody. 1884 *Health Exhib. Catal.* 71/2 Front Damper acting as a 'Tidy Betty' with Cinder-sifter. 1900 *Leeds Mercury* 9 May, He struck her on the head with a 'tidy-betty', and then kicked her with his clogs. 1900 J. K. JEROME *3 Men on Bummel* vii. 156 Fit for a tidy-minded lover of German nature.

**B.** *sb.* A name for various articles intended to keep persons or things tidy or neat. **a.** A pinafore or overall. *dial.*

*a* 1825 FORBY *Voc. E. Anglia*, *Tidy*, a light outer covering worn by children, to keep their clothes from dirt and grease.

**b.** An ornamental loose covering for the back of a chair or the like, usually of fancy work; an antimacassar.

1850 *Knickerb. Mag.* XXXVI. 255 (Thornton *Amer. Gloss.*) One cane-seated rocking-chair, the back of which is covered with an unapproachable netting of spotless white, called a 'tidy'. 1861 J. PYCROFT *Agony Point* (1862) 126 After a few magic passes—the placing of a screen, the arrangement of a tidy or the folds of a curtain,..—a room..becomes..instinct with life, and grace, and comfort. 1882 MRS. L. C. LILLIE *Prudence* 61 Is that a tidy? Yes...They call them antimacassars and sofa-backs here.

**c.** A bag or other receptacle in which to keep scraps, odds and ends, etc.; a work-bag; a toilet-tidy.

1828 *Craven Gloss.*, *Tidy*, a work bag, &c. 1863 W. B. JERROLD *Signals Distress* 207 It was in the days when.. every scrap of cotton or linen found its way into the 'tidy'.

**C.** *adv.* Tidily; pretty well; nicely, finely; also *ironical. dial.* or *vulgar.*

1824 in *Spirit Pub. Jrnls.* (1825) 347 They've served me pretty tidy going along,..punching at me with their shilaleaghs as they would at a woolsack. 1851 MAYHEW *Lond. Labour* I. 355 Them as could patter tidy did the best. 1904 *Eng. Dial. Dict.* s. v., That there cak's coming out quite tidy.

Hence **Ti·dyism** (*nonce-wd.*), a principle or practice of extreme tidiness.

1856 MISS YONGE *Daisy Chain* I. ix, His funny little old bachelor tidyisms.

**Ti·dy**, *v.* Chiefly *colloq.* [f. TIDY *a.*] *trans.* To make tidy or orderly; to put in order; to arrange neatly; *refl.* to put one's hair, dress, etc. in order; to make oneself neat. Often with *up*.

1821 MISS MITFORD in L'Estrange *Life* (1870) II. 127, I mean to..have it whitened and tidied up this summer. 1847 C. BRONTË *J. Eyre* iv, Bessie..employed me as a sort of under nursery maid, to tidy the room, dust the chairs, &c. 1868 F. E. PAGET *Lucretia* 106 When the cook went up stairs, after tea, to tidy herself. 1897 MARY KINGSLEY *W. Africa* 73 My notes for a day will contain facts relating to the kraw-kraw, price of onions,..genealogies,..law cases,.. &c., &c. And the undertaking of tidying these things up is no small one. 1898 G. B. SHAW *Plays* II. *Candida* 131 The large table has been cleared and tidied.

**b.** To stow *away* or clear *up* for the sake of tidiness.

1867 [see *tidying* below]. 1884 *Nonconformist* 1 May, It was left on the hall table..and had been 'tidied up' by one of those..housemaids who are the bane of every busy man. 1906 *Westm. Gaz.* 5 July 2/1 If anything is broken or tidied away beyond recall.

Hence **Ti·dying** *vbl. sb.* and *ppl. a.*

1867 H. LATHAM *Black & White* 90 After such a war.. there is no small amount of sweeping up, and tidying away, ..to be done. 1884 *Blackw. Mag.* Dec. 734/2 Comte de Rivaulx! echoed Madame, pausing in her tidying. 1899 *Westm. Gaz.* 7 Jan. 3/2 Lovers of nature..view with horror the onslaughts of these tidying gentlemen.

**Tie** (təi), *sb.* Forms: α. 1 **téaȝ**, **téȝ**, **tǽȝ**, 3 **teȝ**, **teiȝ**, 5 **tey**, 6 *Sc.* (*pl.*) **teis**, (5, 9 *dial.* **tee**). β. 5–9 **tye**, 7 **ty**, (*pl.* **tigges**, **tighes**), 6– **tie**. [OE. *teáh*, *téag* fem., Anglian *tǽg*, later *tēg* = ON. *taug* fem., rope:—OTeut. **taug-ā*, *-o* str. fem.,

f. second grade of the verb-stem *teuh-* : *tauh-* : *tuh* : see TEE *v.*$^1$ The β-forms are assimilated to, or formed from, TIE *v.*]

**1.** That with which anything is tied; a cord, band, or the like, used for fastening something; a knot, noose, or ligature; a natural formation of this kind, a ligament (quot. 1659); *esp.* an ornamental knot or bow of ribbon, etc.

α. *a* **800** CYNEWULF *Crist* 733 He..cyning inne ʒebond..fyrnum teaʒum. *a* **1000** *Gloss.* in Wr.-Wülcker 210/36 *Collarium*, sweorclaþ, *uel* teʒ, *uel* sal. *c* **1205** LAY. 20998 Heo wolden..teien heom to-gadere mid guldene teȝen. *c* **1290** *S. Eng. Leg.* I. 308/301 A teiȝ doggue þat is in strongue teiȝe. **1537** *Acc. Ld. High Treas. Scot.* VI. 335 Thre elnis canves to lyne the teis of the mulatis. **1825** BROCKETT *N. C. Words*, *Tee*, or *Tie*, a hair-rope with which to shackle cows in milking.

β. **1601–2** *Shuttleworths' Acc.* (Chetham Soc.) 141, ij tigges for the maydes to mylke the kyne with, ij$^{d}$. **1602** *Ibid.* 142 To a power man for vj tighes for the kyne, iiij$^{d}$. **1615** CROOKE *Body of Man* 406 Intercept an arterie with a tye, and the part below the tye..will not beate. **1659** MACALLO *Can. Physick* 54 The tyes and ligaments of the brain. **1817** J. BRADBURY *Trav. Amer.* 60 The horse..broke his tie, and gallopped off. **1837** DICKENS *Pickw.* xlix, Great formal wigs, with a tie behind. **1857** HUGHES *Tom Brown* I. iii, Putting impossible buttons and ties in the middle of his back.

**2.** *Naut.* **a.** A rope or chain by which a yard is suspended. See quot. 1841.

α. **1465** *Mann. & Househ. Exp.* (Roxb.) 200 For ij. teyis [for the ship] weyinge vij. stone,..xiij.s. ix.d. **1496** *Acc. Ld. High Treas. Scot.* I. 300 Making of a bonat and the lek [leech] to it, with smal takil and a tee. **1511** *Ibid.* IV. 300 Item..for hed towis to the gret schip..tua cordalis, x trosis, iij teis. **1513** DOUGLAS *Æneis* V. xiv. 6 Than all sammyn, ..Did heis thar saill, and trossit doun ther teis.

β. **1485–6** *Naval Accts. Hen. VII* (1896) 13 An hauser for a tye weying D lb. *Ibid.* 36 Halfe tyes short..ij. Bowe Sesynges. **1611** COTGR., *Estails*...tyes; the strings or ropes of sayles. **1627** CAPT. SMITH *Seaman's Gram.* v. 21 The Ties are the ropes by which the yards doe hang, and doe carry up the yards when wee straine the Halyards. **1762–9** FALCONER *Shipwr.* II. 318 While some above the yard o'erhaul the tye. **1829** MARRYAT *F. Mildmay* iv, I..regained my perch by the topsail-tie. **1841** R. H. DANA *Seaman's Man.*, *Tye*, a rope connected with a yard, to the other end of which a tackle is attached for hoisting.

**b.** A mooring-bridle.

**1867** SMYTH *Sailor's Word-bk.*, *Ties*, an old name for mooring bridles. **1883** *Fisheries Exhib. Catal.* 24 White Manilla Boat Tie.

**3.** A knot of hair; a pigtail; also short for TIE-WIG. ? *Obs.*

**1728** YOUNG *Love Fame* II. 225 The well-swoln tyes an equal homage claim. **1742** RICHARDSON *Pamela* IV. 64 So I think, cries the other; and tosses his Tye behind him, with an Air..of Contempt. **1760** FOOTE *Minor* II. Wks. 1799 I. 259 Some recommended a tye, others a bag: one mention'd a bob. **1817** SHELLEY *Rev. Islam* VI. xxxiii, Cythna's glowing arms, and the thick ties Of her soft hair.

**4.** A neck-tie, a cravat.

**1761** CHURCHILL *Rosciad* Poems 1763 I. 5 Thrice he twirl'd his Tye—thrice strok'd his band. **1860** TRISTRAM *Gt. Sahara* xx. 344 Seated in white gloves and ties at the soirée of Madame R—. **1862** 'SHIRLEY' *Nugæ Crit.* i. 6 Here..That badge of servitude, the white tie, is unloosed. **1895** 'F. ANSTEY' *Lyre & Lancet* I. 7 He'll come down to dinner in a flannel shirt and no tie. **1897** LD. TENNYSON *Mem. Tennyson* II. 222 Adorned by his accustomed blue tie.

**5.** A kind of low shoe fastened with a tie or lace.

**1826** MRS. MCNEILL *Let.* in *Mem. Sir J. McNeill* vi. (1910), Two pair black satin slippers,..two pair neat walking ties. **1904** *Westm. Gaz.* 15 Apr. 10/2 What we call Oxford Ties, which is a brogue shoe, is a favourite form..for walking purposes.

**6.** *gen.* Something that connects or unites two or more things in some way; a link. (See also 8.)

**1711** J. GREENWOOD *Eng. Gram.* 152 Called the subjunctive mood because it is added to the first sentence by some Cople or Tye. **1830** HERSCHEL *Stud. Nat. Phil.* II. vii. (1851) 193 Solid substance[s] retained by a force or united by a tie. **1857** MILLER *Elem. Chem.* (1862) III. 52 The tie between the two typical groups being..the dibasic radicle ($C_2O_2$).

**b.** *Mus.* A curved line placed over or under two notes on the same degree, to indicate that the sound is to be sustained (not repeated): = BIND *sb.* 1 c: cf. LIGATURE *sb.* 4.

Also placed over or under two or more notes to be performed *legato*, or to be sung to one syllable; in this case now called a *slur* (SLUR *sb.*$^3$ 4).

**1656** M. LOCKE *Little Consort*, *Treble* Pref., In printing of Tyes, Holds, Slurrs. **1662** PLAYFORD *Skill Mus.* I. xi. (1674) 35 A Tye is of two uses, first, when the Time is broken..in the middle of the Note, it is usual to Tye two Minims, or a Minim and a Crotchet together. The second sort of Tye is, when two or more Notes are to be sung to one Syllable, or two Notes or more are to be plaid with once drawing the bow on the Viol. **1686** *New Method to Learn to Sing* 54 A Tye thus ⌒, over two or more Notes, signifying that they must be sung to one Syllable, or struck with one motion of the Bow upon an Instrument. **1848** [see SLUR *sb.*$^3$ 4].

**7.** *Arch.*, etc. A beam or rod used to 'tie' or bind together two parts of a building or other structure by counteracting a tensile strain which tends to draw them apart.

**1793** W. H. MARSHALL *W. England* (1796) II. 340 The ties, in this case, are large oak floor-beams. **1855** *Act* 18 & 19 *Vict.* c. 122 Sched. i, The height of every topmost story shall be measured from the level of its floor up to the underside of the tie of the roof. **1861** SMILES *Engineers* II. 183 The eight ribs were firmly connected together by braces and ties. **1869** SIR E. J. REED *Shipbuild.* i. 8 Some of the longitudinal ties of this ship were broken at the bulkheads.

**b.** *U. S.* A (transverse) railway sleeper.

(The transverse or 'cross' sleepers serve as ties to keep the rails from spreading under the lateral strain of the wheels.)

**1857** *U. S. Patent Office Rep.* II. 116 The tie and pedestals cast in one piece, the chairs so constructed as to fit in or on said pedestals. **1869** *Daily News* 7 Oct., Fires..fed by piles of old sleepers, or ties as they are called here. **1881** *Times* 9 Sept., Heaps of 'ties' (the sleepers of the old world) piled up by the side of the road. **1891** *Railroad Gaz.* (U. S.), The requirements for ties comprise the largest consumption of wood in this country.

**8.** *fig.* Something that ties or binds in a figurative or abstract sense. **a.** Something that makes fast or secures; a security; something figured as a band or knot with which things are tied. *rare.*

*a* **1555** LATIMER in Foxe *A. & M.* (1563) 1313/1 They haue charitie in such sure tie that they cannot lose it. **1605** SHAKS. *Macb.* III. i. 17 Let your Highnesse Command vpon me, to the which my duties Are with a most indissoluble tye For euer knit. **1670** COTTON *Espernon* III. x. 531 He had concluded the Marriage.., a match that was to be the main tye of this Accommodation. **1810** SCOTT *Lady of L.* II. ix, Confusedly bound in memory's ties.

**b.** Something that restrains or obliges; a restraint, constraint; † something that enables one to restrain another, a hold *upon* a person (*obs.*); an obligation, a bond (of duty or the like).

**1596** DRAYTON *Leg.* iii. 80 Which soone upon Him got so sure a Tye, As no misfortune e'r could it remove. **1621** ELSING *Debates Ho. Lords* (Camden) 45 The agents complained that they wanted a ty uppon the sylkemen. The bonde was advysed by others. **1641** LD. J. DIGBY *Sp. in Ho. Com.* 21 Apr. 6, I was..under tye of Secrecy. **1754** SHERLOCK *Disc.* (1759) I. xiii. 359 Bound..by..the Ties of Moral Duty. **1768** *Woman of Honor* III. 59 Love..flies with disdain from everything that has an air of tie, or constraint. **1835** J. H. NEWMAN *Par. Serm.* (1837) I. xv. 229 They do not like the tie of religion.

**c.** Something that connects or unites; a bond of union; a uniting principle; a link, connexion: usually with implication of mutual obligation (cf. b), in reference to social relations or the like.

*a* **1625** FLETCHER *Bloody Brother* IV. i, Mercy becomes a prince, and guards him best; Awe and affrights are never ties of love. **1629** CARLIELL *Deserv. Favourite* 82 To procure her bondage; For such she did account all ties of marriage Made by the parents without the childs consent. **1733** P. SHAW tr. *Bacon's De Sap. Vet.* III. ii. Expl., Philos. Wks. I. 591 The Bonds of Affinity, which are the Links and Ties of Nature. **1781** GIBBON *Decl. & F.* (1869) III. l. 149 We are bound to each other by the ties of honour and interest. **1874** GREEN *Short Hist.* i. § 1. 1 The ties of a common blood, and a common speech. **1875** WHITNEY *Life Lang.* 271 There is no necessary tie between race and language.

**d.** Obligation of constant attendance; restraint of freedom. ? *dial.* or *colloq.*

*Mod.* She finds the children a great tie on her. The place is easy, but you wouldn't like the tie.

¶ *To ride in tie*: perversion of *to ride and tie* (see RIDE *v.* 22), *tie* being app. taken in sense 'connexion'.

**1908** *Academy* 8 Feb. 434/2 He rode all the way in tie with his black slave.

**9.** The fact or method of tying; the condition of being tied, bound, or united. (In quot. 1865 ? a bargain settled, a sale.)

**1718** *Free-thinker* No. 66 ¶ 7, I understand the decent Tye of a Cravat. **1793** SMEATON *Edystone L.* § 82 The tye was as good at the bottom as at the top. **1865** *Daily Tel.* 22 Aug. 6/5 The market expenses..are little enough: 2d a head toll, and 1½d 'a tie', as the phrase is—3½d, that is, per beast sold in the market.

**b.** *Mining.* = TEE *sb.*$^1$ 3.

**1747** HOOSON *Miner's Dict.* O iij, He that comes first to the Pee, will take it, be he the older or younger, and he will make the other a way out if possible he can, otherwise if he cannot then it is called a Tye. **1851** [see TEE *sb.*$^1$ 3].

**c.** In silk hand-loom weaving: The tying together of a combination of heddle-strings, so as to move a series of warp-strings together.

**1831** G. R. PORTER *Silk Manuf.* 297 Every variation in the order of succession of the harness used in weaving or in the weavers' language, every different tie, produces a different pattern.

**d.** In plastering: = KEY *sb.*$^1$ 10 c.

**1873** E. SPON *Workshop Receipts* Ser. I. 121/2 After the coat is laid on, it is scored in diagonal directions with a scratcher..to give it a key or tie for the coat that is to follow it.

**10.** Equality between two or more competitors or the sides in a match or contest; a match in which this occurs, a drawn match; a dead heat. Hence, *to play off*, *shoot off*, etc. *a tie*, to resolve or determine a tie, by playing another match.

**1680** [see TIE *v.* 7]. **1736** in Waghorn *Cricket Scores* (1899) 16 A great single-wicket match..the country men got but 6, which made it a tie. **1837** T. HOOK *Jack Brag* iii, To see the ties shot off of the great pigeon match. **1844** DISRAELI *Coningsby* VIII. iii, The Government count on the seat, though with the new Registration 'tis nearly a tie. **1881** T. HARDY *Laodicean* II. vi, We are bracketed—it's a tie. The judges say there is no choice between the designs.

Hence, **b.** A deciding match played after a draw; also, a match played between the victors in previous matches or heats. (See also *cup-tie* s.v. CUP *sb.* 13 c.)

**1895** *Westm. Gaz.* 24 Sept., The..boys prefer the cup ties to the Church Catechism. **1904** *Ibid.* 22 Apr. 12/1 There is something impressive even to the unathletic man in these annual Cup-tie figures. **1905** *Daily Chron.* 17 Apr. 3/7 Probably the Cup-'tie' has been evolved from the phrase 'shooting off' or 'playing off a tie' after two competitors have 'tied'. The match between those who stand on a level gradually gets regarded as itself the 'tie'.

**Tie** (təi), *v.* Inflected **tied, tying.** Forms: see below. [In the α-forms, OE. *tíʒan*, for OWS. **tíeʒan* :—**téaʒ-jan* to bind, f. *téaʒ* rope: see TIE *sb.*: cf. ON. *teygja* to draw. The ME. β-forms are commonly held to represent a non-WSax. (Mercian) form **téʒan* (for **tíeʒan*); but cf. ME. *ēi* and *í* forms under EYE, HIGH.]

**A.** Illustration of Forms.

**1.** *Pres. stem.* α. 1 **tíʒ-an,** 3–4 **tiȝ-en,** 4 **tyȝe, tyen,** 4–9 **tye,** 6–7 **ty**; 4– **tie.** *Pr. pple.* **tying.**

*c* **1000** Tiʒan [see B. 1]. *c* **1000** ÆLFRIC *Gram.* xliv. (Z.) 258 Hu þes dæl tiʒð þa word togædere. *c* **1275** LAY. 20997 And tiȝe heom to-gædere. **1377** LANGL. *P. Pl.* B. I. 96 And taken transgressores and tyen hem faste. *Ibid.* III. 139 And tieth hym faste. **1563** GOLDING *Cæsar* v. (1565) 138 He aduised him to tie the letter to the thong of a Iaueling, & so to throw it into his camp. **1570** *Satir. Poems Reform.* xxii. 92 To ty on tre. **1618** RALEGH in *Four C. Eng. Lett.* (1880) 38 Tyenge them back to backe. **1729** G. ADAMS tr. *Sophocl., Antig.* II. iv. II. 32 If Fear did not tye their Tongues.

β. 3 **teȝ-en,** 3–4 **teiȝ-en, tei-e(n,** 4–6 **teye, teie,** 5 **tey-yn, tey, tegh,** 6–7 **taye,** 7 **tay,** 9 *dial.* **tee.**

*c* **1205** LAY. 20997 And teien heom to-gadere. *c* **1250** *Hymn Virg.* 59 in *Trin. Coll. Hom.* 257 Herre teȝen he him nolde. *c* **1330** R. BRUNNE *Chron. Wace* (Rolls) 11187 Many fair palfray & stede..to wype, & to mangers teye. **1362** LANGL. *P. Pl.* A. I. 94 And teiȝen hem faste. **1387** TREVISA *Higden* (Rolls) IV. 79 Reynes..to teie wiþ oþer oxen. *c* **1440** *Promp. Parv.* 487/2 Teyyn wythe bondys. *c* **1440** *Gesta Rom.* xxiii. 81 (Harl. MS.) Tey him to Tailles of hors. **1533** MORE *Answ. Poysoned Bk.* Wks. 1041/2 Sampson tayeng the Foxes together. **1664** EARL OF TYRCONNEL *Let. to Lauderdale* 14 Nov. (in *Daniell's Catal.* July (1904) 37/2) That wee should taye them all bellye to bellye and throwe them in the sea.

**2.** *Pa. t.* α. [1 ***tíʒede,** 3–4 ***tiȝede,** ***tyȝede**], 5–8 **tyed,** (5–6 **-it,** 6 **tight**), 6–7 **ty'd,** 7– **tied.**

*c* **1400, 1513** Tyed [see B 1, 1 b]. *c* **1470** *Golagros & Gaw.* 61 His hors he tyit to ane tre. **1596** SPENSER *F. Q.* VI. xii. 34 Thereunto a great long chaine he tight. **1604** E. G[RIMSTONE] *D'Acosta's Hist. Indies* VI. xiv. 461 The bridges..which they tied to the bankes. **1686** tr. *Chardin's Trav. Persia* 141 Forces, that ty'd his Hands. **1720** OZELL *Vertot's Rom. Rep.* I. v. 296 Grief..tyed his Tongue.

β. 3 **teide,** 5 **teyde, teghit, tayed.**

*c* **1290** *S. Eng. Leg.* I. 29/91 Huy..teiden ane rop a boute is necke. *c* **1400** *Destr. Troy* 3523 The kyng..teghit her in yernes. *c* **1400** *Three Kings Cologne* 26 Byside þat ox Ioseph teyde his asse. **1470–85** MALORY *Arthur* I. iii. 41 Sir Arthur..tayed his hors to the style.

**3.** *Pa. pple.* α. 1 **ʒe-tíʒ(ʒ)ed,** 3–4 **i-tiȝed,** 4 **ityȝed, tyȝed,** 5 *Sc.* **tichit, ticht**; 4–9 **tyed,** 6 **tiede,** 6–7 **tyde, tide,** 7–8 **ty'd,** 4– **tied.**

*c* **1000** ÆLFRIC *Hom.* II. 62 An ramm..ʒetiʒed be ðam hornum. *c* **1000** *Ags. Gosp.* Matt. xxi. 2, & þonne sona finde ʒyt ane assene ʒe-tiʒʒede [*c* **1160** *Hatton Gosp.* ʒe-teiʒʒede [*v. r.* ʒeteʒʒede]]. *c* **1275** I-tiȝed, *c* **1320** I-tyȝed [see B. 1]. **13..** Tyȝed [see B. 4]. **1382** WYCLIF *Mark* xi. 2 A colt tyed [**1388** tied]. *c* **1450** HOLLAND *Howlat* 405 With tuscheis of trast silk tichit to the tre. *c* **1475** *Rauf Coilȝear* 457 Ane Tyger ticht to ane tre. **1590** SPENSER *F. Q.* I. vi. 21 In sacred bonds of wedlock tyde. **1603, 1688** Tyed [see B. 5]. **1699** J. LOWTHORP *Exper.* in *Misc. Cur.* (1708) II. 198 There was a Bladder ty'd below each Joint..and when it was fill'd with Water it was ty'd above it. **1718** Ty'd, **1816** Tyed [see B. 1].

β. 2 **ʒe-teʒʒed, -teiʒʒed,** 3 **i-teied, -et, iteid,** 3–4 **teid,** 4 **yteyd, teiȝed, teied, teyde,** 4–6 **teyed,** 5 **teyghte,** 6 **teyd, tay(e)d,** 9 *dial.* **teed.**

*c* **1160** ʒete[i]ʒʒed [see α]. *c* **1200** *Trin. Coll. Hom.* 181 Iteied [see B. 5]. *Ibid.* 217 Þat me ne sholde none man bitechen bute he were teid to menden chirche. *c* **1230** *Hali Meid.* 27 Him..þat is..to eni eorðliche þing iteiet. *a* **1250** *Owl & Night.* 776 An hors..i-teid at mulne dure. *c* **1350** *Will. Palerne* 3226 Þe sturnest stede in hire stabul teiȝed. *Ibid.* 3232 Teied in þe stabul. *c* **1386** Yteyd, **1387** I-teyed [see B. 1 b]. **1387** TREVISA *Higden* (Rolls) IV. 77 Þe reynes þat þe oxen schulde be teyde by. **1390** Teid [see B. 5 c]. *c* **1400** *Laud Troy Bk.* 518 Eche a man on londe than gos, ..And lefft here schip teyghte fast. **1489** CAXTON *Faytes of A.* I. xvii. 49 Wel teyed with ropys. **1547** BOORDE *Introd. Knowl.* xiii. (1870) 156 Than am I tonge tayd. **1556** *Chron. Gr. Friars* (Camden) 98 Browte thorrow Cheppesyde teyd in ropes xxiiij$^{ti}$ tayd to-getheres as herrytykes. **1828** *Craven Gloss.*, *Teed*, tied.

**B.** Signification. **I.** The simple verb.

**1.** *trans.* To bind, fasten, make fast (one thing to another, or two or more things together) with a cord, rope, band, or the like, drawn together and knotted; to confine (a person or animal) by fastening to something.

*c* **1000** ÆLFRIC *Hom.* I. 432 Ualerianus..het tiʒan [Ypolitus] be ðam fotum to unʒetemedra horsa swuran. *c* **1205** LAY. 25972 Twælf swine iteied [*c* **1275** itiȝed] to-somme. *a* **1225** *Ancr. R.* 254 Sansumes foxes..weren bi þe teiles iteied ueste. *c* **1320** *Cast. Love* 1130 As fisch..Þat whon þe worm he swoleweþ..He is bi þe hok i-tiȝed [*v. r.* i-tyȝed] fast. *c* **1400** *Laud Troy Bk.* 2733 Anker thei caste, And tyed here schippis in that porte And ȝede to londe. *c* **1440** *Pallad. on Husb.* IV. 752 [772] Stakes..To teye hem to. **1590** SPENSER *F. Q.* I. v. 6 Their shining shieldes about their wrestes they tye. **1638** JUNIUS *Paint. Ancients* 154 A great dogge tyed in a chaine. **1718** POPE *Iliad* II. 55 Th' embroider'd sandals on his feet were ty'd. **1816** SINGER *Hist. Cards* I. 52 Such bells were also tyed to Hawks.

**b.** To draw together the parts of (a single thing) with a knotted cord or the like; to fasten (a part of dress, etc.) in this way, esp. with strings already attached to it (as a bonnet, a shoe); also, to draw together (a cord or the like) into a knot, esp. for the purpose of fastening something.

c 1386 CHAUCER *Prol.* 457 Hir hosen were of fyn scarlett reed, Ful streite yteyd. 1387 TREVISA *Higden* (Rolls) V. 369 Hire hosen tilled to the hamme, i-teyed wiþ layners al aboute. 1513 MORE in Hall *Chron., Rich. III* (1548) 27 b, After which tyme, the prince neuer tyed his pointes. 1592 SHAKS. *Rom. & Jul.* III. i. 31 Did'st thou not fall out..with another, for tying his new shoes with old Riband? 1662 J. DAVIES tr. *Mandelslo's Trav.* 80 They tye their Garments about with a Girdle. 1716 ADDISON *Drummer* III. i, He'll tye a wig. 1819 SHELLEY *Cenci* V. iv. 159 Tie My girdle for me. *Mod.* You must tie the string tighter, or the parcel will come undone.

**c.** *Surg.* To bind and constrict (an artery or vein) with a ligature, so as to prevent the flow of blood through it.

1597 [see TIED *ppl. a.* 1]. 1804 ABERNETHY *Surg. Obs.* 195 To tie the more superficial arteries. 1843 R. J. GRAVES *Syst. Clin. Med.* xi. 123 The effects produced by tying the carotid and vertebral arteries.

**d.** To make or form by tying (a knot, etc.).

1647 COWLEY *Mistr., The Tree* v, Go tye the dismal Knot (why shouldst thou live?). 1808 SCOTT *Marm.* I. Introd. 48 The garlands you delight to tie. 1838 THIRLWALL *Greece* II. xiv. 200 He tied sixty knots in a leathern thong. 1867 F. FRANCIS *Angling* x. (1880) 340 One of the most difficult things in tying flies.

**e.** *Tie neck and heels*: see NECK *sb.*[1] 7. *Ride and tie*: see RIDE *v.* 22.

**2.** In figurative phrases. *To tie the hands of*: to deprive of freedom of action. *To tie the knot*: to effect a union between two persons or things; *esp.* to perform the ceremony of marriage. † *To tie with St. Mary's knot*: to hamstring (*obs.*). † *To tie to the stake, fig.* to put into a position from which there is no escape (*obs.*). *To tie* a person's *tongue*: to prevent (him) from speaking, to compel to be silent (see also TONGUE-TIED). *Tied to* a woman's *apron-strings*: see APRON-STRING.

1559 *Bk. Com. Prayer, Prayers Sev. Occasions*, Tyed and bounde with the chayne of oure synnes. 1576 GASCOIGNE *Compl. Philomene* lxx. (Arb.) 99 Hir swelling sobbes, Did tie hir tong from talke. 1579 LYLY *Euphues* (Arb.) 52 Euphues beeing thus tyed to the stake by their importunate intreatie, began as followeth. ? *a* 1600 *Dick o' the Cow* in Child *Ballads* (1861) VI. 72 He has tied them a' wi' St. Mary's knot, A' these horses but barely three. 1642 FULLER *Holy & Prof. St.* v. v. 375 When God intends a Nation shall be beaten, he ties their hands behind them. 1717 PRIOR *Alma* I. 332 So to the priest their case they tell: He ties the knot. 1781 COWPER *Friendship* 62 A fretful temper will divide The closest knot that may be tied. 1828 [see KNOT *sb.*[1] 11 b]. 1866 CRUMP *Banking* ix. 214 It seems very unjust to tie the hands of the directors in so important a particular. 1889 *The County* viii, One would have thought that very shame would have tied her tongue.

**3.** To fasten together, connect, join (material things) in any way; *spec.* in *Arch.* to connect and make fast by a rod or beam (cf. TIE *sb.* 7), or by other means (cf. BOND *sb.*[1] 13 a).

1585 T. WASHINGTON tr. *Nicholay's Voy.* II. xviii. 51 [A] smal habitation,..made of..glasse, ioyned & tyed together with roddes of Tin. 1632 LITHGOW *Trav.* II. 67 Peloponnesus..is tied to the continent by an Istmus. 1793 W. H. MARSHALL *W. England* (1796) II. 340 Firm purchases..for the purpose of tying in the front wall. 1851 RUSKIN *Stones Ven.* (1874) I. xv. 161 Every arch or gable not tied at its base by beams or bars, exercises a lateral pressure upon the walls which sustain it.

**b.** To check or hinder the free movement or working of: see quots.

1597 A. M. tr. *Guillemeau's Fr. Chirurg.* 10/1 *Spasmus* ..with shakinge and quiveringe, with the tonge tiede, and with irremoveable eyes. 1602 CAREW *Cornwall* 11 The.. Axes and Wedges..(not seldome) are so tied by the teeth, as a good workman shall hardly be able to hew three foote, in the space of so many weekes. 1879 JEFFERIES *Wild Life S. C.* 192 When sawing, the wood operated on often 'ties' the saw, as it is called, that is, pinches it—which makes it hard to work. 18.. *Dogs Gt. Brit. & Amer.* 45 (Cent.) There is a want of liberty in the play of the whole shoulder, because the elbow rubs against the ribs...This is called being tied at the elbow.

**c.** *Mus.* To connect (notes) by a tie or ligature: see TIE *sb.* 6 b, LIGATURE *sb.* 4.

1597 [see LIGATURE 4]. 1662 PLAYFORD *Skill Mus.* I. viii. (1674) 28 Four or more Quavers are Tyed together by a long Stroke on the top of their Tails. *Ibid.* [see TIE *sb.* 6 b].

**d.** *U. S.* To furnish (a railway line) with 'ties' or sleepers (cf. TIE *sb.* 7 b).

1883 *W. Chester, Pa. Local News* II. No. 234. 1 Forty miles of road..had to be..graded, tied, rails laid.

**e.** To fasten or fix otherwise (e. g. † with nails).

1500–20 DUNBAR *Poems* lxxii. 69 Syne tyit him on with greit irne takkis, And him all nakit on the tre Thai raisit on loft. *Mod.* The brick facing of the wall is tied into the concrete backing by headers at frequent intervals.

**4.** *fig.* To join closely or firmly; to connect, attach, unite, knit, bind by other than material ties; *esp.* to unite in marriage (now *dial.*).

c 1000 [see A. 1 *a*]. c 1200 *Trin. Coll. Hom.* 183 Hie [the soul]..to þe licame..seið..Aweilewei þu fule hold þat ich auere was to þe iteied. 13.. *E. E. Allit. P.* B. 702 When two true togeder had tyȝed hem seluen. 1571 CAMPION *Hist. Irel.* II. vii. (1633) 100 Richard..exceedingly tyed unto him the hearts of the noblemen. 1586 DAY *Eng. Secretary* I. (1625) 10 Eloquution is annexed vnto the stile, which..is also tyed to the argument. 1684 *Contempl. St. Man* I. ii. (1699) 21 The greatest felicity of the World, was tyed to the greatest Mishap. 1715 DE FOE *Fam. Instruct.* (1841) II. I. i. 16 How could you think of tying yourself to such a family? 1814 WORDSW. *White Doe* VII. 314 At length, thus..faintly tied To earth, she..died. 1890 *Spectator* 24 May 714/1 If Washington could tie gold and silver together in the ratio of sixteen, so could the rest of the world. 1899 J. LUMSDEN *Edin. Poems & Songs* 287 Ma man was kill'd..Before that we'd been foure days tied.

**b.** *intr.* for *refl.* To attach oneself (*to*). Also, *To tie to*: to fix one's confidence in, trust to, hold on to for support. *U. S. colloq.*

1879 TOURGEE *Fool's Err.* x. 43 He won't du tu tie ter. 1884 A. A. PUTNAM *Ten Y. Police Judge* xxiii. 200 The propensities of the thief strikingly tie somehow to the training begotten of ardent spirit. 1892 W. W. FENN *Bible in Theol.* 17 Those who, as they say, 'want something to tie to'.

**5.** *trans.* To bind, oblige, restrain, constrain *to* (also *from*) some course of action, etc.; to limit, confine, restrict. *To be tied to* (or *for*) *time*: to be bound or limited to a certain time for doing something. (See also phrases in 2.)

c 1200 *Trin. Coll. Hom.* 181 Ilch man of his wise noteð his swinhc swilch se he is to iteied. Clerc on his wise. Cniht on his wise...And ilches craftes þeau swo he beð to iteied. 1387–8 T. USK *Test. Love* III. ii. (Skeat) l. 144 If it wer nat in mannes own liberte of fre wil to do good or bad but to the one teied by bonde of goddes preordinaunce. c 1412 HOCCLEVE *De Reg. Princ.* 1474 God for-beede þou þe haddist tyed þer-to, but if þin herte myght han plyed For to obserue it wel. 1577 HANMER *Anc. Eccl. Hist.* (1619) 359, I will..tie myself..onto the truth of the historie. 1608 SHAKS. *Per.* II. v. 8 She hath so strictly Tyed her to her Chamber. 1688 R. HOLME *Armoury* III. 184/1 The White Friers..were tyed to Fasting, Silence, and Canonical hours. 1713 BERKELEY *Guard.* No. 39 ¶ 12, I must tie this gentleman close to the argument. 1860 MRS. CARLYLE *Lett.* (1883) III. 38 Unfortunately I am tied to time. I must be back in London. 1901 *Daily Tel.* 22 Mar. 9/5 The British being to a certain extent tied in South Africa.

**b.** To bind, oblige; usually in *pass.* to be bound or obliged (*to do* something). Now only *dial.*

1596 SHAKS. *Tam. Shr.* I. i. 217, I am tyed to be obedient, For so your father charg'd me at our parting. 1608 WILLET *Hexapla Exod.* 498 The borrower..is tied to make it good. 1625 BURGES *Pers. Tithes* 66 It was their purpose to tie his conscience the more to doe iustly herein. 1722 DE FOE *Plague* (1756) 108 Nor were they tied to carry the Dead to their respective Parishes. 1798 *Trans. Soc. Arts* XVI. 134 Why should the grower tie himself to plant an equal number of different sorts? 1892 M. C. F. MORRIS *Yorks. Folk-Talk* 259 We do not reckon *obliged* in the sense of forced as part of our vocabulary; instead we make use of *tied*.

†**c.** To bring into bondage; to enthrall. *Obs.*

1390 GOWER *Conf.* II. 129 It is impropreliche seid, For good hath him and halt him teid, That he..is unto his good a thral. *a* 1425 *Cursor M.* 23307 (Trin.) Þei euer tyed were In þis lif for synnes sere. 1426 LYDG. *De Guil. Pilgr.* 17513, I teye my sylff..And bynde me to my rychesse. 1594 KYD *Cornelia* I. 68 What helps it that thou ty'dst The former World to thee in vassalage? 1613 SHAKS. *Hen. VIII*, IV. ii. 36 One that by suggestion Ty'de all the Kingdome.

**d.** To bind by favour or service rendered: usually in *pass.*: = OBLIGE *v.* 6, 7.

1576 FLEMING *Panopl. Epist.* 123, I am so streigtly tyed to his courtesie. 1595 tr. *Blanchardine* Ded. A ij, Whose deserts haue tyed me during life the vassaile of..their commaunds. 1611 SHAKS. *Cymb.* I. vi. 23 He is one of the Noblest note, to whose kindnesses I am most infinitely tied. 1864 BURTON *Scot Abr.* II. ii. 137 We are also tied in duty to our comrades that were with us in danger.

**e.** To restrict (a dealer or firm) to a particular source for articles sold; only in *pa. pple.*, usually applied to a public house so restricted as to liquor. Hence *transf.* as in quot. 1899. See also TIED 2 b.

1817 [see 10 b]. 1853 *Rep. Sel. Committee Public Houses, Min. Evid.* 118, I am the owner of a free house, tied to nobody. 1884 *Lincoln*, etc. *Mercury* 22 Feb., The Masons' Arms Hotel...Tied for beer only. 1894 *Westm. Gaz.* 9 Apr. 2/3 The system of 'tied' trade..is not confined to the drink trade...A retail draper was 'tied' to a wholesale house—i.e. ..he was under contract to buy all his goods from the wholesale draper in question. 1899 *Daily News* 7 Dec. 4/1 The farmers dictate the terms of tenancy. The cottages are 'tied'.

**6.** (*fig.* from 1 b or d.) To make sure, confirm, ratify; to 'knit', 'cement'. ? *Obs.*

1613 SHAKS. *Hen. VIII*, III. ii. 250 That Seale..the King ..gaue me..and..Ti'de it by Letters Patents. 1697 DRYDEN *Æneid* XII. 316 When thus in Public view the peace was ty'd With solemn Vows.

**7.** *intr.* To be equal (*with*) in a contest, etc.

1680 COTTON *Compl. Gamester* xv. (ed. 2) 93 If each win a trick and the third tyed, neither win, because it is trick and tye. 1870 *Routledge's Ev. Boy's Ann.* Oct. 600 The cricketers tied when they were so equally matched that neither won. 1882 *Standard* 31 Aug. 6/4 Captain Burridge..scored 117, and tied with Mr. Meyler. 1902 LD. ROSEBERY in *Daily Chron.* 13 Oct. 7/1 We have not received intellectual faculties equal to Mr. Gladstone's, and we cannot hope to tie with him in their exercise.

**b.** *pass.* in same sense.

1868 *U.S. Newspaper*, The two political parties in Councils were tied on joint ballot.

†**c.** In the House of Commons: = PAIR *v.*[1] 4.

1829 O'CONNELL in *Corr.* May (1888) I. 188 To tie with a Government member.

**d.** *trans.* To be equal with (a competitor); to make the same score as.

1888 ELWORTHY *W. Somerset Word-bk.* s. v., My dog tied yours, so they must run again.

**8.** *Hunting. intr.* Of a hound: To linger upon the scent instead of following it swiftly; to loiter, lag.

1781 P. BECKFORD *Hunting* xv. 188 They learn to tye upon the scent; an unpardonable fault in a fox-hound. *Ibid.* 190 If they [the hounds] tie upon the scent, and come hunting after, hang them up immediately..: there is no getting such conceited devils on. 1826 [see TYING *ppl. a.*].

**9.** *intr. Tie into*: to 'buckle to'. *U. S. colloq.*

1904 S. E. WHITE *Forest* xii. 159 The day following we tied into it again.

**II.** With adverbs.

**10. Tie down. a.** *lit.* To fasten down or confine by tying: see sense 1 and DOWN *adv.*

1699 GARTH *Dispens.* I. 11 More had He spoke but sudden Vapours rise, And with their silken Cords tye down his Eyes. 1728 POPE *Dunc.* I. 37 Bards, like Proteus long in vain tied down, Escape in Monsters, and amaze the town. 1823 J. BADCOCK *Dom. Amusem.* 196 Strain it off, and keep it tied down with bladder. 1827 D. JOHNSON *Ind. Field Sports* 52 The dogs were accustomed to be tied down separately every night.

**b.** *fig.* To confine stringently (*to* some thing or action): cf. sense 5, and DOWN *adv.* 17.

1692 LOCKE *Educ.* § 142 Being forced and tied down to their Books in an Age at enmity with all such restraint. 1720 DE FOE *Capt. Singleton* v. (1840) 90 We did not tie ourselves down when to march and when to halt. 1778 *Eng. Gazetteer* (ed. 2) s. v. *Rochester*, For the maintenance of its bridge, certain lands are tied down by parliament. 1817 *1st Rep. Committee Police Metrop.* 11 The..practice.. for brewers to tie their tenants down to the purchase of specific articles from individuals named by them. 1884 W. C. SMITH *Kildrostan* 87 O you dull fellows, Tied down to facts, you lose the half of life.

**11. Tie up. a.** *trans.* To fasten (a thing) with a cord or band tied round it, so as to prevent its moving or falling loose, or to secure it from being lost or injured; to bind up, wrap up.

1530 PALSGR. 758/1, I tye up my heare, as a woman dothe, *je me atourne.* 1608 SHAKS. *Per.* II. ii. 41 Or Tie my treasure vp in silken Bagges. 1706 E. WARD *Wooden World Diss.* (1708) 70 His Bob Wig ty'd up like a Horse-tail. 1833 HT. MARTINEAU *Manch. Strike* ii. 19 He tore my arm one day,..father got an apothecary to tie it up. 1838 DICKENS *Nich. Nick.* xxii, They had tied up the luggage.

**b.** To tie (a person or animal) to some fixed object or in some confined space, so as to prevent from escaping; to fasten up.

c 1560 [see c]. 1579 W. WILKINSON *Confut. Familye of Love* Ep. Ded. *iij, The bloudy bandoges of the Romish Sinagogue be tyed vp. 1611 SHAKS. *Cymb.* IV. i. 24 My Horse is tyed vp safe. 1719 DE FOE *Crusoe* (1840) I. iii. 53 A malefactor..is tied up. 1883 GILMOUR *Mongols* xxiii. 285 He had stolen the horse, and tied it up in the mountains.

**c.** *fig.* To bind, restrain, or confine strictly; to restrict closely; to hinder from acting freely; to oblige to act in a particular way. (Cf. 5.) Also *to tie up one's hands, one's tongue*: cf. phrases in 2.

[c 1435 *Torr. Portugal* 2658 Sith he did make vp-tyed Chirchus and abbeys wyde, For hym and his to praye.] c 1560 GRINDAL in Foxe *A. & M.* (1583) 1390/2 He hath deserued more gentlenesse at your hande, then to be tied vp so shorte. 1592 SHAKS. *Rom. & Jul.* IV. v. 32 Death that hath tane her hence..Ties vp my tongue, and will not let me speake. 1658–9 *Burton's Diary* (1828) IV. 226, I would have you not to tie up your hands from consideration of either. 1768 COL. CHURCHILL in Jesse *Selwyn & Contemp.* (1843) II. 289 Being tied up by my father's will from assisting my younger children during my life. 1879 STAINER *Music of Bible* 173 It is not tied up in a strait-jacket like a modern chant.

**d.** To moor (a ship or boat); also *absol.*, or (usually) *intr.* for *pass.* said of the vessel.

1853 KANE *Grinnell Exp.* xvi. (1856) 122 The ice was closing in every direction; and our master..had no alternative but to tie up and await events. 1886 E. ARNOLD *India Revisited* iii. 33 At night every steamer 'ties up'. 1893 ELIZ. B. CUSTER *Tenting* 34 The great cable was used to tie us up to the bank.

**e.** *fig.* (from a): To invest or place (money or property) in such a way as to prevent it from being spent or alienated.

1822 J. W. CROKER in *C. Papers* 21 June, He has tied up his real estates as tight as he could. 1841 THACKERAY *Gt. Hoggarty Diamond* xiii, She is close of her money;..she has tied up every shilling of it, and only allows me half-a-crown a-week for pocket-money. *a* 1859 MACAULAY *Hist. Eng.* xxiii. (1861) V. 34 To pass a prospective statute tying up in strict entail the little which still remained of the Crown property. 1870 MISS BRIDGMAN *Rob. Lynne* II. v. 111 Her money..had been tied up all tight for her benefit.

**f.** *slang.* To give up, desist from, quit (a practice or course of action); also *absol.*

1760 FOOTE *Minor* I. Wks. 1799 I. 241, I have a great mind to tie up, and ruin the rascals. 1903 FARMER & HENLEY *Slang Dict.* s. v., *To tie up* = to forswear: e. g., *to tie up prigging* = to lead an honest life.

**g.** *slang.* To vanquish or disable in a contest; to finish; to 'knock out'.

1818 [implied in TIE-UP *sb.* 5]. 1903 FARMER & HENLEY *Slang Dict.* s. v., *To tie up*..= to knock out (pugilists'); *tied-up* = (1) finished, settled. 1909 *Westm. Gaz.* 31 July 16/1 Inclined to lay odds that he and Barnes or Rhodes would have 'tied up' the Australian batsmen.

**h.** To join in marriage: cf. 4 (also *tie the knot* in 2). *colloq.* or *slang.*

1894 ASTLEY *Fifty Years Life* I. 158 A comelier couple parson has seldom..tied up.

**Tie**: see TYE *sb.*[1] and [2], and *v.*

**Tie-** in combination. [f. TIE *sb.*[1] or *vb.*]

**1.** Attributive or objective combinations of TIE *sb.* in various senses: **tie-block** *Naut.*, the block on the yard through which the tie passes (see TIE *sb.* 2 a); **tie-maker**, a maker of ties (in quots., in senses 4 and 7 of the sb.); **tie-pin**, a pin, usually ornamental, worn in a man's neck-tie; **tie-shooting**, the shooting off of a tie (TIE *sb.* 10) in rifle practice; so **tie-shoot, -shot.**

1745 P. THOMAS *Jrnl. Anson's Voy.* 145 We reev'd..a new Strap to the Fore-top-sail *Tye-block. *c* 1860 H. STUART *Seaman's Catech.* 76 There are two iron straps round the yard for the tye blocks to shackle to. 1901 *Daily Chron.* 25 July 6/6 The girl..is a *tie-maker. 1904 *Longm. Mag.* Aug. 306 Any moderately good tie-maker can turn out thirty ties a day in good timber. 1780 *Traveller's Guide*, A silver *tie-pin, three silver studs. 1899 *Daily News* 22 June 7/3 His stand-up collar and his tie-pin. 1909 *Daily Chron.* 23 July 7/2 He tied for the 'Daily Telegraph' Cup and finished second in the *tie shoot. 1902 *Ibid.* 23 July 6/3 The *tie-shooting for the first Coronation Prize. 1887 *Daily News* 18 July 2/1 Many men might beat him in the *tie shots.

**2.** Combinations of TIE *v.* with adverbs: **tie-back**, a contrivance for tying something back, esp. in a woman's dress; **tie-on** *a.*, that is fastened on by tying. See also TIE-UP.

1880 *World* 29 Sept. 15 The days of 'tie-backs', either in the dressing of ladies or artificial flies, were not yet. 1891 *Daily News* 27 July 2/1 Even Lady Harberton could scarcely disapprove of the gored skirt with no tie-backs. 1910 *Times* 4 July 6/5 Tie-on labels should not be used.

**3.** Combinations with sbs., in which the first element may be either TIE *sb.* or *v.*: **tie·-bar**, a bar which ties or acts as a tie, in a building or other structure; **tie·-beam**, a horizontal beam which acts as a tie: see *esp.* quot. 1823; **tie-bolt** *sb.*, a bolt which ties together the component parts of a structure; hence **tie-bolt** *v.*, *trans.* to fasten with tie-bolts; **tie-cord**, a cord used for tying something; **tie-knot**, a knot with which something is tied; **tie-line** (*Surveying*), a line measured on the ground after the principal lines of a triangulated survey have been measured, with the object of checking the accuracy of the work; **tie-match**, a subsequent match played to decide a tie; **tie·-periwig** = TIE-WIG; **tie-plate**, (*a*) *Naut.* a narrow iron plate placed longitudinally or diagonally to space and strengthen deck-beams; (*b*) a plate to receive the pull of a tie-rod, and distribute the pressure on a supporting beam or wall; (*c*) a protecting metal plate laid between a sleeper and the rail; **tie-post**, a post to which a horse, etc. may be tied; **tie-rib**, a rib forming a tie in some structure (in quot. *fig.*); **tie-rod**, a long tie-bolt or iron rod which acts as a tie in a building or other structure; **tie-rope**, a rope for tying something; in quot. *c* 1525, ? = TIE *sb.* 2; **tie-stay**, a stay acting as a tie, used to support some part of a building; **tie-strap**, a strap for tying up a horse or other animal; **tie-string**, a string for tying something, e. g. a bonnet or other part of costume; **tie-tie**, one of several cords fastened to a hammock and serving to tie it up in a roll (*Cent. Dict.* 1891); a negro name for any string; **tie-vote**, a vote resulting in a tie, the numbers on each side being equal: see TIE *sb.* 10; **tie-wall**, a wall having the function of tying together the parts of a structure; esp. 'a transverse wall in the hollow spandril of an arch, at right angles to the spandril-wall' (Knight). See also TIE-DOG, TIE-WIG.

1861 FAIRBAIRN *Iron* 91 The reverberatory furnace..consists externally of an oblong casing of iron plates, firmly bound together by iron *tie-bars. 1823 P. NICHOLSON *Pract. Build.* 125 A *tie-beam is a piece of timber, connecting the feet of the principal rafters, in order to prevent them from spreading. 1851 SIR F. PALGRAVE *Norm. & Eng.* I. 436 The open roof and tyebeams of a Roman Basilica. 1853 SIR H. DOUGLAS *Milit. Bridges* (ed. 3) 308 Considered as a tie-beam its longitudinal strength depends upon the key. 1838 *Civil Eng. & Arch. Jrnl.* I. 126/1 Placing the *tie-bolts diagonally, instead of horizontally. 1874 THEARLE *Naval Archit.* 59 Grooved and tongued together at their edges, and nailed to the cants, being also *tie-bolted where necessary. 1907 C. C. BROWN *China in Leg. & Story* xvii. 240 A queue, scarce big enough to carry its black *tie-cord. 1800 COLERIDGE *Wallenst.* I. iii. 64 The *tie-knot here Is off—this hair must not hang so dishevelled. 1877 RANKINE *Man. Civ. Engin.* 24 The accuracy of the measurements in every important triangle should be checked by measuring a '*tie-line', from one of its angles to a known point in the opposite side. 1864 *Daily Tel.* 26 Oct., Third Kent (Lee) v. Eighth Kent (Sydenham).—These two corps fired for a *tie match. 1898 *Westm. Gaz.* 26 Feb. 3/3 In case of ties..the prizes are to be divided, except the first prize, which must be determined by a tie match of four games. 1727 GAY *Begg. Op.* I. iii, Three *tye-perriwigs and a piece of broad cloth. 1771 SMOLLETT *Humph. Cl.* II. 23 June, An old Scotch lawyer, in a tie-periwig. 1874 THEARLE *Naval Archit.* 119 The deck fastenings are not so efficient in iron as in wood beams, and hence both stringer and *tie-plates are of service in opposing the first tendency of the deck to elongate. 1884 *Harper's Mag.* Jan. 328/2 Throwing the reins over a *tie-post. 1896 KIPLING *Seven Seas, Deep Sea Cables* ii, Here on the *tie-ribs of earth Words..flicker and flutter and beat. 1839 *Civil Eng. & Arch. Jrnl.* II. 191/2 Four iron *tye-rods with washers placed transversely through the arch. *c* 1525 in *Archæologia* XLVII. 332, ij. roopes, called *tye ropes, for the *Henry Grace Dieu.* 1886 T. HARDY *Mayor of Casterbr.* iii, The pens for sheep, the tie-ropes for horses. 1892 *Daily News* 20 Feb. 3/4 The Repair of Canterbury Cathedral...A series of *tiestays are being inserted. 1877 KNIGHT *Dict. Mech.*, *Tie-strap. 1901 *Munsey's Mag.* XXV. 737/2 An attendant snapped a tie strap into his halter and led him back to barn or paddock. 1897 *Outing* (U.S.) XXX. 379/1 A rubber blanket..with *tie-strings at the four corners, can be made into a first-rate shelter by tying two corners to poles driven into the ground, and the other corners to pegs. 1883 MOLONEY *W. African Fisheries* 17 (Fish. Exhib. Publ.) The ..occupants .. standing erect, or perched on seats—cross sticks, secured by *tie-tie on gunwale of canoe. 1894 *Daily News* 6 Oct. 6/5 A proposal only lost..by a *tie-vote.

**Tied** (təid), *ppl. a.* Also 7 tide, tyed. [f. TIE *v.* + -ED [1].]

**1.** Bound or fastened with a cord or the like; joined, connected (as letters in printing, quot. 1891): see TIE *v.* B. 1–3. Also TONGUE-TIED.

1591 SHAKS. *Two Gent.* II. iii. 41 *Panth.* What's the vnkindest tide? *Lau.* Why, he that's tide here, Crab my dog. 1597 A. M. tr. *Guillemeau's Fr. Chirurg.* 38 b/2 The tyed Vayne might chaunce to vntye. 1614 GORGES *Lucan* VI. 253 He stonisht was.., His tyed tong no sound could blunder. 1758 J. S. *Le Dran's Observ. Surg.* (1771) 220, I dressed it with tied Dossils. 1864 BOWEN *Logic* xi. 365 The nervous fluid will not travel along a tied nerve. 1891 W. MORRIS in Mackail *Life* (1899) II. 252 We have no contractions, few tied letters. 1904 BUDGE *3rd & 4th Egypt. Rooms Brit. Mus.* 110 Oxen with tied feet.

**b.** *Tied note*: see quots. and TIE *sb.* 6 b, *v.* 3 c.

1716 (*title*) The Dancing-Master...Sixteenth Edition... The whole Work Revised and done on the New-Ty'd-Note. 1801 BUSBY *Dict. of Music, Tied-Notes*, notes, the tails of which are joined together by cross lines, as in united quavers, semiquavers, &c., or over the heads of which a curve is drawn to denote that they are to be slurred.

**2.** *fig.* United, joined; restrained, confined, etc.: see TIE *v.* B. 4, 5.

1876 T. HARDY *Ethelberta* (1890) 140 That's why married men advise others to marry. Were all the world tied up, the pleasantly tied ones would be equivalent to those at present free. 1907 *Daily Chron.* 22 Mar. 7/1 The sight of the Progressives banded together emphasized the fact of their being the tied party of the Chamber of Mines.

**b.** *spec.* Of an inn or public house: Of which the tenant is bound to take his liquor from a particular brewing firm (which usually owns the house), hence *transf.* of a labourer's cottage: of which the tenant is astricted to work on the farm.

1887 *Pall Mall G.* 23 July 16/1 Local breweries have almost entirely depended upon tied houses for the sale of their products. 1890 *Guardian* 17 Sept. 1434/2 The question of renewing licences to 'tied houses' has been considered at some of the licensing sessions. 1899 *Daily News* 7 Dec. 4/1 The labourers hate the 'tied cottage' system. 1901 *Ibid.* 16 Feb. 5/3 Certain brewers are in the habit of turning unsuccessful houses into tied-house clubs.

**3.** *Tied up*, in *lit.* and *fig.* senses: see TIE *v.* B. 11.

1603 SHAKS. *Meas. for M.* I. iii. 32 It rested in your Grace To vnloose this tyde-vp Iustice. 1693 W. BOWLES in *Dryden's Juvenal* v. 13 And with a Matt, and Crutch, and ty'd up Leg, More honestly and honourably Beg. 1711–12 SWIFT *Jrnl. to Stella* 6 Jan., It was not proper to go to Court without a long wig, and his was a tied-up one. 1822 SAVAGE *Hints Decorative Print.* 46 Four or five octavo pages of tied up letter. 1876 [see 2].

**† Tie-dog.** *Obs.* Forms: see TIE and DOG. [See TIE- 3.] A dog kept tied or chained up, either to guard a house, or because fierce; = BANDOG. (In last quot. *fig.*)

*c* 1290 *S. Eng. Leg.* I. 308/301 Þe deuel..ne may no man.. taken a-ȝein is wille, Nonmore þane a teiȝ doggue þat is in strongue teiȝe. *c* 1380 WYCLIF *Wks.* (1880) 252 Þouȝ þei bynden hem not to o synguler place as a tey dogge. 1430–40 LYDG. *Bochas* III. i. (MS. Bodl. 263) 151/1 Cruel Orchus, the teidogge infernall Shal reende thi skyn..fro thi bonys. 1542 UDALL *Erasm. Apoph.* 127 b, Ther are tye doggues or mastifes for keepyng of houses. 1601 CHETTLE & MUNDAY *Death Earl of Huntington* II. i. E iij, I knowe the villaine.., But as a ty-dogge I will muzzle him. *c* 1700 MATHER in *Harper's Mag.* July (1883) 222/1 The Ty-dogs of the Pit are abroad among us.

**† Tiego** (tai·go). *Obs.* Colloq. or vulgar abbreviation of VERTIGO.

1634 MASSINGER *Very Woman* IV. iii, I am shrewdly troubled with a tiego Here in my head, madam, often with this tiego, It takes me very often.

**Tiel, Tield,** variant of TIAL *Obs.*, TELD *Obs.*

**Tieless** (təi·lės), *a.* [f. TIE *sb.* + -LESS.] Without a tie; wearing no neck-tie.

1903 W. CHURCHILL *Crisis* II. ii, Every gentleman..collarless, coatless, tieless and vestless. 1907 *Westm. Gaz.* 21 Mar. 2/1 His head was bare, and he was tieless.

**Tiemannite** (tī·mănəit). *Min.* [ad. Ger. *Tiemannit*, named by Neumann, 1855, from the discoverer, Tiemann: see -ITE [1] 2 b.] Native selenide of mercury, occurring in dark grey masses or granules with a metallic lustre. 1868 DANA *Min.* 56.

**Tien,** obs. f. TINE *v.* **Tiend,** obs. f. TEIND, TIND. **Tienthe,** obs. f. TENTH.

**Tier** (tīᵊr), *sb.*[1] Also 6–9 tire, 6–8 tyre, (6 teare, 7 tere, 7–8 teer, 8 tear). [Orig. *tire*, a. F. *tire*, in OF. (*c* 1210 in Godef.) 'suite, sequence, range, rank, order': cf. *tire à tire* in succession, one after another, f. *tirer* to draw, elongate. The phonetic history of the forms *teare, tere, teer*, is obscure. Pl. after a numeral sometimes *tier.*]

**1.** A row, rank, range, course; usually one of a series of rows placed one above another, or at least rising each above the preceding one; e.g. tiers of galleries, shelves, boxes in a theatre, or seats on a sloping floor; also of banks of oars in ancient ships or boats; see also b, c.

1569 STOCKER tr. *Diod. Sic.* III. viii. 114/2 Ten gallies of fiue tier of ores. *a* 1625 FLETCHER *Bloody Brother* II. ii, I have ballast for their bellies, if they eat a gods name, Let them have ten tire of teeth a piece, I care not. 1627 CAPT. SMITH *Seaman's Gram.* vii. 33 Caske..stowed tier aboue tier. 1686 J. DUNTON *Lett. New-Eng.* (1867) 35 He has three Tere of Teeth in his Chaps. 1720 in *New Eng. Hist. & Gen. Reg.* (1875) XXIX. 288 Eastward of the first tear of lots. 1722 *Conn. Col. Rec.* (1872) VI. 311 The northermost tier of the three tier of lots lying next to Midletown. 1730 A. GORDON *Maffei's Amphith.* 203 The..Stones..which form'd the first Tyre or Belt thereof. 1743 *Lond. & Country Brew.* III. (ed. 2) 182 The Worts now run swiftly into a single Teer of Backs. 1787 M. CUTLER in *Life*, etc. (1888) I. 311 There are two tiers of galleries, and the [meeting-] house was very full. 1796 MORSE *Amer. Geog.* II. 358 It consists of three bridges, or tires of arches one above another. 1844 LD. HOUGHTON *Palm Leaves* I Above the towers of tripple tire. 1867 SMYTH *Sailor's Word-bk.* 346 A round of grape-shot consists of three tiers of cast-iron balls, generally three in a tier. 1873 SYMONDS *Grk. Poets* ix. 280 The new theatre in Athens contained 30,000 spectators seated in semicircular tiers scooped out of the rock.

**b.** A row of guns or gun-ports in a man-of-war or (as in quot. 1573) in a fort.

1573 in *Calr. Scott. Pap.* IV. 475 Davyes towre..a courten with vj cannons..in loopes of stone..behynd the same standes another teare of ordina[nce] lyke xvj foote clym above the other. 1632 LITHGOW *Trav.* II. 54 [A] man of war..carrying two tyre of Ordonance. *a* 1647 PETTE in *Archæologia* XII. 283 The..distance of the lower tire of ports from the water. 1722 DE FOE *Col. Jack* (1840) 322 A good tier of guns kept the rest at a distance. 1813 BYRON *Corsair* III. xv, She bears her down majestically near, Speed on her prow, and terror in her tier.

**c.** A rank of pipes in an organ controlled by one stop (see RANK *sb.*[1] 1, quots. 1811, 1881).

1828–32 in WEBSTER. 1880 E. J. HOPKINS in Grove *Dict. Mus.* II. 580/2 Although the number of pipes to each key thus continued to be added to, no means was devised for silencing or selecting any of the several ranks or tiers.

**d.** *transf.* and *fig.* Rank, grade; stratum.

1590 SPENSER *F. Q.* I. iv. 35 Such one was Wrath, the last of this ungodly tire. 1646 CRASHAW *Sosp. d'Her.* xxxviii, A gen'ral hiss, from the whole tire of snakes. 1710 PALMER *Proverbs* 201 This is a sin of quality for the most part, tho' the lower tier of people are often tainted with it. 1882 W. B. WEEDEN *Soc. Law Labor* 66 The base Fuidirs composed the lower tier of society.

**2.** *Naut.* **a.** A row of ships moored or anchored at a particular place; hence, an anchorage or mooring-place where ships lie in rows or columns.

1732 *Lond. Mag.* I. 152 All the Ships Crews in the Teer gathered together. 1771 *Ann. Reg.* 148 A Dutch vessel.. broke from her mooring, ran foul of a tier of ships. 1774 *Hull Dock Act* 33 No more than three ships..shall lie in the same tier, within the said haven. 1865 DICKENS *Mut. Fr.* I. i, The tiers of shipping lay on either hand. 1907 *Law Rep.*, *Probate* 61 A steamship..which was lying at Greenwich tier.

**b.** (See quot. 1882.)

1797 *Encycl. Brit.* (ed. 3) X. 644/2 He [the mate] is to have a diligent attention to the cables, seeing that they are well coiled and kept clean when laid in the tier. 1800 COLQUHOUN *Comm. Thames* iii. 94 Tea..stowed in the cable tier of a China Ship. 1825 [see TIERER [1]]. 1833, 1860 [see *cable-tier* s.v. CABLE *sb.* 7]. 1882 NARES *Seamanship* (ed. 6) 95 The tiers are large racks, and stow the stream cable, hawsers for the kedge, etc., anchor gear, runners and tackles,..clothes-lines, etc.

**3.** *attrib.* and *Comb.*: **tier-board**, a board belonging to a cable or rope tier: see 2 b; **tier-ranger**, a (Thames) river thief; **tier-saw**: see quot. 1877; **tier-shot**: see quot. 1867.

1887 MATHER *Nor'ard of Dogger* (1889) 81 They spread some o' the trawl-warp *tier-boards along the thwarts, an' a rug on the top of 'em for me to lie on. 1858 DICKENS *Down with Tide* Repr. Pieces (1899) 198 *Tier-rangers, who silently dropped alongside the tiers of shipping in the Pool, by night. *Ibid.* 200 We took no Tier-rangers..nor other evil-disposed person or persons. 1862 MAYHEW *Lond. Labour* IV. 370/2 Tier-rangers or river pirates. 1877 KNIGHT *Dict. Mech.*, *Tier-saw, one for cutting curved faces to bricks for arches and round pillars. 1828 J. M. SPEARMAN *Brit. Gunner* (ed. 2) 35 *Tier Shot.—At 50 rounds per gun. 1867 SMYTH *Sailor's Word-bk.*, *Tier-shot*, that kind of grape-shot which is secured in tiers by parallel iron discs.

**Tier** (təi·əɹ), *sb.*[2] Also tyer. [f. TIE *v.* + -ER [1].]

**1.** One who ties; *spec.* a person employed to tie something. Also *tier up.*

1633 P. FLETCHER *Poet. Misc.* 57 Hymen, the tier of hearts already tied. 1648 HEXHAM II, *Een Hechter*, a Fixer, a Fastner, or a Tyer to. 1848 *Jrnl. R. Agric. Soc.* IX. II. 554 The tiers can take the best to tie to the poles. 1876 PLUMMER tr. *Döllinger's Hippol. & Callistus* iii. 153 The Church.. is the tyer of the marriage bond. 1895 *Daily Tel.* 18 Sept. 4/2 He begins life at the sandpaper works, as a tier up of bundles, at three and sixpence a week.

**2.** One who ties with another in a match or competition.

1810 *Sporting Mag.* XXXV. 97 The tyers to play with one another in the order they become tyers.

**3.** Something that ties or is used for tying; a band; *spec. pl.* = TIE-UP 4.

1844 *Jrnl. R. Agric. Soc.* V. I. 36 The beans are cut..and tied with strong tyers or straw bands. 1882 NARES *Seamanship* (ed. 6) 130 The sail is secured to the yard with tyers. 1895 *Sotheby's Catal.* 25 Apr. 52 (Kelmscott Press) Morris, ..'The Defence of Guenevere', ornamental title and initial letters, vellum, silk tyers, uncut.

**4.** *U. S.* A pinafore or apron covering the whole

front of the dress. (Also spelt *tire*, *tyre*, and referred by some to TIRE *sb.*[1] q. v.)

1846 WORCESTER, *Tier*, one that ties; a child's apron, tidy. See TIRE. 1864 WEBSTER, *Tier*, a child's apron without sleeves, and covering the upper part of the body, [1890] and tied with tape or cord. 1865 MRS. WHITNEY *Gayworthys* I. 106 She took care of Say; put on her long-sleeved tyers when she sent her out to play. 1889 L. LARCOM *A New Engld. Girlhood* 22 We sometimes smirched our clean aprons (high-necked and long-sleeved ones, known as tiers). 1902 *Dialect Notes* (U.S.) II. 254 (*Let. to G. Hempl*) Even among the older people [in New Engl.], 'cricket' has mostly given place to 'footstool', and 'tier' to 'apron'.

**Tier** (tīəɹ), *v.*[1] [f. TIER *sb.*[1]] *trans.* To arrange or pile in tiers.

1888-9 *N. York Produce Exch. Rep.* 301 (Cent.) Lightermen shall not..be required to tier or pile their freight on the docks.

**Tier**, *v.*[2], erron. spelling of TEER.

1837 J. MATLEY in *Civil Eng. & Arch. Jrnl.* I. 54/2 Machinery for the operation of Tiering used in printing Cotton, Linen, &c. 1909 *Dundee Advert.* 25 Dec. 7 He commenced work..as a tier boy to a calico block printer.

**Tier**, obs. form of TEAR *sb.*[1], TIRE.

**Tierce** (tīəɹs), *sb.* Forms: *α.* 4–8 terse, 6 teyrse, teers, 6–7 tearce, 7 tearse, teirce, teirse, ters, 5–9 terce: see also TERCE. *β.* 5 tyerce, tyrse, 5–6 tyerse, 6 tyers, tiersse, tiers, tirce, 6–7 tierse, 4– tierce. [a. OF. *terce*, *tierce*, fem. of *terz*, *tierz* (Roland, 11th c.), later *ters*, *tiers*, mod.F. *tiers*, fem. *tierce* :—L. *tertium*, fem. *tertiam* third.]

†**1.** A third part; = THIRD *sb.* 1. *Obs.*

1491 *Aberdeen Regr.* (1844) I. 326 Twa tercis beand defalkyt of þe sade some. 1555 EDEN *Decades* 351 Two smaule Ilandes standyng in the xxii degrees and a terce. 1624 CAPT. SMITH *Virginia* 16 We came to Hatorask in 36. degrees and a terse. 1651 DAVENANT *Gondibert* I. v. lvi, Four-hundred leaders..And twice the tierce of these consists of those [etc.].

†**b.** = THIRD *sb.* 7. *Obs. rare*⁻¹.

*c* 1420 LYDG. *Thebes* I. 39 The heauenly mansions Clerely searched, by smale fraccions, First by secondes, terces, and eke quartes.

¶ **c.** Abbreviated title of the treatise *Super Tertium Sententiarum* of Alexander Hales. *Obs.*

1502 *Ord. Crysten Men* (W. de W. 1506) IV. xxi. 240 It is sacrylege, after mayster Alexander de halis in his tyers.

**2.** *Eccl.* **a.** The third hour of the canonical day, ending at 9 a.m.; also, the period from 9 a.m. till noon. (Cf. PRIME *sb.*[1] 1.) *Obs.* exc. *Hist.*

*c* 1375 *Sc. Leg. Saints* xi. (*Symon & Iudas*) 197 To-morne, or it terse be,..sal cum to þe Messyngeris. *c* 1450 *Mirour Saluacioun* 3644 It was bot tierce of the daye ouer ayrly than for drynking. 1483 CAXTON *Gold. Leg.* 84/2 He..prayd fro tyerce vnto none. 1661 MORGAN *Sph. Gentry* IV. iii. 37 Upon St. George's Even, at the hour of Tierce. 1706 tr. *Dupin's Eccl. Hist. 16th C.* II. v. 43 The second [part of the 12 hours] which lasted till Noon, was called Tierce, because it began at the Third Hour of the day. 1844 LINGARD *Anglo-Sax. Ch.* (1858) I. vii. 272 *note*, The third of these hours was called undern or terce.

**b.** (Now usually spelt terce.) The office said at this hour.

*c* 1380 WYCLIF *Wks.* (1880) 41 Late lewid freris seie..for prime, tierce, vndren & noon, for eche of hem seuene pater nostris. 1526 *Pilgr. Perf.* (W. de W. 1531) 164 b, The chirche..in..the..houres canonicall entendeth to..worshyp at vij tymes in the daye, that is to saye, in matyns, pryme, tierce, sext, none, euensonge & complyn. 1753 CHALLONER *Cath. Chr. Instr.* 212 Terce, Sext, and None, begin with Pater, Ave, &c. and consist each of them of a proper Hymn, and six Divisions of the 118th Psalm. 1853 DALE tr. *Baldeschi's Ceremonial* 101 The vesting of the Bishop for Terce. 1897 E. BISHOP in *Prymer* (E.E.T.S.) *Introd.* 38 The day hours, prime and terce, and sext and none, said in every secular church.

**3.** *Sc. Law.* See TERCE.

1754 [see *tercer* s. v. TERCE, quot. *c* 1575].

**4.** An old measure of capacity equivalent to one third of a pipe (usually 42 gallons old wine measure, but varying for different commodities: cf. PIPE *sb.*[2] 2); also a cask or vessel holding this quantity, usually of wine, but also of various kinds of provisions or other goods (e. g. beef, pork, salmon, coffee, honey, sugar, tallow, tobacco); also such a cask with its contents.

1531 *Charterparty* in R. G. Marsden *Sel. Pl. Crt. Admir.* 36 Accounttyng..ij pipes for a ton iiij hoggeshedds for a ton and vj tercys for a ton. 1531–2 *Act* 23 *Hen. VIII*, c. 7 § 5 The butte, tonne, pype..teers, barrell or rondlett. 1538 ELYOT Addit., *Hemicadia*, vesselles callyd a tierce, halfe a hoggesheed. 1588 *Wills & Inv. N. C.* (Surtees) II. 180, ix tearces of honeye, at 16*l.* per tonne, 24*l.* 1707 *Lond. Gaz.* No. 4337/4 On Wednesday..will be exposed to Sale..about 400 Hogsheads and 10 Tierces of..French Claret. 1800 COLQUHOUN *Comm. Thames* iii. 136 Beef and Pork..contained in..Tierces and Barrels. 1825 *Gentl. Mag.* XCV. I. 216 [Coffee berries] closely packed in tierces for exportation. 1886 *Pall Mall G.* 19 June 6/1 The tobacco..comes from abroad..in hogsheads..in what are called tierces (a smaller wooden barrel), and in bales.

†**5.** A band or company of soldiers (cf. TERCIO).

1577–87 HOLINSHED *Chron.* III. 1227/1 Foure hundred harquebusiers Spaniards, of the tierse of Sardigna. 1668 *Lond. Gaz.* No. 237/3 The Leavies of a Terse of Italian Infantry.

**6.** One of the positions in fencing; the third of the eight parries in sword-play, or the corresponding thrust: see quots. Also *fig.* (usually in conjunction with *carte* or *quarte*). Cf. CARTE[2], QUART *sb.*[3] 1.

1692 SIR W. HOPE *Fencing-Master* (ed. 2) 4 When a Man holdeth the Nails of his Sword Hand quite downwards, he is said to hold his hand in Terce. 1707–1878 [see CARTE[2]]. 1779 SHERIDAN *Critic* III. i, O cursed parry!—that last thrust in tierce Was fatal. 1809, 1889 [see QUART *sb.*[3] 1]. 1876 TENNYSON *Q. Mary* v. v, To reign is restless fence, Tierce, quart and trickery.

**7.** In piquet and other card games, a sequence of three cards in any suit.

*Tierce major*, the highest three cards of a suit; *tierce minor*, the lowest three, i. e. seven, eight, and nine; *tierce to a king*, *queen*, etc., a tierce of which the king, queen, etc., is the highest. Cf. QUART[3] 2, QUINT[2] 1 b.

1659 *Shuffling, Cutting, & Dealing* 3, I have got a good Tearse. 1688 R. HOLME *Armoury* III. xvi. (Roxb.) 73/2 A Tierce Major, is the sequence of Queen, King and Ace in Picket, and of Knave, Queene and King in other games. 1765 STERNE *Tr. Shandy* VII. ix, That, Sir, is a terce to a nine in your favour. 1860 *Bohn's Hand-bk. Games* I. 14 Many good players, in playing tierce majors, begin with the king and queen. 1904 M. HEWLETT *Queen's Quair* I. xi. 146 I've a terce to my Queen, mistress.

**8.** *Mus.* **a.** The interval of a third (major or minor); the note at this interval above a given note. Now *rare* or *Obs.* **b.** The note two octaves and a major third (= a major 17th) above a fundamental note; hence, a mutation stop in an organ giving tones at this interval above the normal pitch.

*Tierce of Picardy* (usu. in Fr. form *tierce de Picardie*), a major third used instead of a minor in the final chord of a piece in a minor key.

1696 PHILLIPS (ed. 5), *Tierce*,..in Musick, a Concord. 1704 J. HARRIS *Lex. Techn.* I. s. v., If the Terms be as 5 to 4, 'tis called, a Tierce Major, or a Diton; but if the Terms are as 6 to 5, then 'tis called, a Tierce Minor, or Demi-Diton. 1776 BURNEY *Hist. Mus.* I. 138 The two stops of an organ, called the fifteenth and tierce. 1801 BUSBY *Dict. Mus.*, Tierce of Picardy. 1879 tr. *Du Moncel's Telephone* 43 Vibrations..in the relation of a tierce major, that is in the relation of four to five.

**9.** *Her.* **a.** A charge composed of three triangles, usually all of different tinctures, arranged in fesse, also in bend. **b.** The division of a shield by lines into three equal parts: see TIERCÉ, quot. 1883.

[*c* 1828 BERRY *Encycl. Her.* I. Gloss., *Tierces*, or *Tierches*, ..used by French heralds to express three figures which only take up the space of a fesse, but which are sometimes placed in bend.] 1847 WEBSTER, *Tierce*..a field divided into three parts. 1894 *Parker's Gloss. Her.*, *Tierce* (fr.), a charge occurring in some French arms, consisting of three triangles arranged generally in fesse. There may be two tierces in the same shield.

**10.** *attrib.* or as *adj.* in special collocations: **tierce guard, parade**: see sense 6; **tierce point**, *Arch.* [F. *tiers-point*], the vertex of an equilateral triangle, or of a pointed arch; **tierce rime** = TERZA-RIMA; **tierce-song**, the office of terce (= sense 2 b); cf. *undern-song*.

1692 SIR W. HOPE *Fencing-Master* (ed. 2) 116 The *Terce Guard, with the point higher than the Hilt. *Ibid.* 22 The *Terce Parade, or the Parade without the Sword, because you put by the thrust upon that side which is without your Sword. 1727–41 CHAMBERS *Cycl.*, *Third Point*, or **Tierce-point*...Arches or vaults of the *third point*, called by the Italians *di terzo acuto*, are those consisting of two arches of a circle, meeting in an angle a-top. 1842–76 GWILT *Encycl. Archit.* Gloss., *Tierce Point.* 1877 TOMLINSON (*title*) A Vision of Hell: The Inferno of Dante translated into English *Tierce Rhyme. 1852 ROCK *Ch. of Fathers* III. x. 473 St. Bede died a little after undern-time, or *tierce-song hour.

Hence **Tierce** *v.* (in phr. *carte* or *quart and tierce*: cf. QUART *v.*[1]), *intr.* to parry or thrust in tierce (in quot. 1833 *transf.*); in quot. 1765 *trans.* ? to fence with (or ? as a vague threat).

1765 FOOTE *Commissary* III. (1782) 65 John, fetch me the foils; I'll carte and tierce you, you scoundrel. 1833 *New Monthly Mag.* XXXVIII. 343 He quarts and tierces for twenty minutes, slips, drops, and rolls.

‖ **Tiercé** (tyęrse, tīəɹse), *a. Her.* [F. *tiercé*, *-ée*, f. *tiercer* to divide into three parts (13th c. in Godef.).] Said of a field divided *en tierce*, i. e. into three equal parts all of different tinctures: cf. prec. 9. Also anglicized as **Tierced** (tīəɹst).

1725 COATS *Dict. Her.*, *Tiercé*,..a French Term importing that the Shield is divided into three equal Parts, when those Parts are of as many different Colours or Metals. 1864 BOUTELL *Her. Hist. & Pop.* xxxii. (ed. 3) 471. 1883 *Chambers's Encycl.* s. v., A shield may be tiercé in pale, in fess, in bend, in bend sinister, or in pall; all which, with other arrangements in tierce, are common in French heraldry.

**Tiercel, Tiercelet**: see TERCEL, TERCELET.

**Tierceron** (tīəɹsərǫn). *Arch.* [a. F. *tierceron* (1518 in Godef. *Compl.*), f. *tiers*, *tierce* third + suffix *-on* (see -OON), with intercalated *-er-*: see Godef. § 63. 1.] A subordinate arch springing from the point of intersection of two main arches of a vault.

1842–76 *Gwilt's Encycl. Archit.*, *Index*, Tierceron, in vaulting. 1890 C. H. MOORE *Goth. Archit.* i. 18 *note*, The additional ribs, *liernes*, *tiercerons*, etc., which appear in the later forms of vaulting,..are mere surface ribs having no real function. 1905 BOND *Goth. Archit.* 74 Intermediate ribs, or tiercerons, were added in Lincoln nave.

**Tierceroon, Tiercet**, var. TERCEROON, TERCET.

**Tiered** (tīəɹd), *a.* [f. TIER *sb.*[1] + -ED[2].] Having, or arranged in, tiers; chiefly in parasynthetic comb., as *high-tiered*, *three-tiered*, *triple-tiered*.

1807 J. BARLOW *Columb.* VII. 495 Flames, triple tier'd, and tides of smoke, arise. 1877 BLACKIE *Wise Men* 75 High-tiered, palatial dwellings. 1899 MACKAIL *W. Morris* II. 51 The passage of the shuttle through a double- or triple-tiered warp. 1909 *Daily Chron.* 16 Sept. 7/2 The tiered seats of the big 'demonstration' kitchen.

**Tierer**[1] (tīəɹəɹ). [f. TIER *sb.*[1] or *v.*[1] + -ER[1].] **a.** *Naut.* One who stows the cable in the tier: see TIER *sb.*[1] 2 b. **b.** One who arranges anything in tiers.

1825 H. B. GASCOIGNE *Nav. Fame* 48 Hard work the Tierers in the Tier below, The sturdy Cable in true coils to Stow. 1891 *Cent. Dict.*, Tierer.

**Tie·rer**[2], var. or erron. f. *teerer*: see under TEER *v.*

1836 in *Statist. Acc. Scotl.* (1845) VIII. 384 Block-printers, journeymen 16, apprentices 44, Tierers, one to each printer.

So **Tiering**, = TEERING.

1904 *Eng. Dial. Dict.*, *Tiering*, the cieling or rendering of a roof; the plastering under slates.

**Tiering** (tīəriŋ), *a. rare.* [f. TIER *sb.*[1] (or ? TIER *v.*[1] taken in sense 'to form tiers') + -ING[2].] Forming or rising in tiers.

1892 KIPLING *Barrack-r. Ballads* 132 The skipper looked at the tiering guns and the bulwarks tall and cold. 1896 — *Seven Seas* 137 You'll see her tiering canvas in sheeted silver spread.

**Tierme**, obs. form of TERM.

‖ **Tierras** (tye·ras), *sb. pl. Mining. U. S.* [Sp. *tierras* earths, pl. of *tierra* earth :—L. *terra*.] Pulverulent ore, *spec.* of quicksilver, mingled with sand and earthy matter; in Mexico, inferior pulverulent ores generally. Also *attrib.*, as *tierras-furnace*, *-ore*.

1874 RAYMOND *Statist. Mines & Mining* 397 In 1865, the amount of ore worked was 15,974 tons. Of which the Tierras amounted to 1,955 tons...Tierras yielded (estimated) 3 per cent., or 1,533 flasks. 1877 *Ibid.* 9 Number of tons tierras-ore roasted. *Ibid.* 17 A new tierras-furnace will take its place. 1881 — *Mining Gloss.*, *Tierras*,..fine dirt impregnated with quicksilver ore, which must be made into adobes before roasting.

**Tiers, -e, Tierselet**, obs. ff. TIERCE, TERCELET.

‖ **Tiers état** (tyęrzeta). [Fr., = third estate: see TIERCE and ESTATE.] A third estate or class; *esp.* the third estate, the body of commons or their representatives in the French National Assembly before the Revolution; whence sometimes applied to the corresponding body in other countries: see ESTATE *sb.* 6.

1783 J. ADAMS *Diary* 27 Feb., There are..thirty classes in the *Tiers Etat.* 1794 J. GIFFORD *Reign Louis XVI* 260 The three orders united confirmed all those important decrees that had been made by the *Tiers Etat.* 1799 *Monthly Rev.* XXX. 548 Montesquieu mistakes in affirming that the natives of the country [Russia] are all either lords or slaves, and that there was no *tiers-état.* 1837 CARLYLE *Fr. Rev.* I. IV. i, Necker..emits, if any proclamation or regulation, one favouring the Tiers Etat.

**Tiestie**, dial. var. TEISTIE, the black guillemot.

**Tieth**, obs. form of TITHE.

**Tie-up** (təi·ɒp), *sb.* (*a.*) [f. *tie up*: TIE *v.* 11.]

**I.** Something tied up, or used for tying up.

†**1.** = TIE-WIG. *Obs.*

1714 C. JOHNSON *Country Lasses* II. i, The last tye-up I sold you was as light and bright as silver..with a fine flowing large open curl.

**2.** A ribbon with which some part of a child's dress is tied or fastened up.

1896 *Blackw. Mag.* Oct. 520/2 The little ones..rejoice in clean 'bishops' and 'tie-ups' of various hues. 1909 *Daily Chron.* 18 Nov. 7/1 Brief drawing-room appearances in a nurse's arms with robes and tie-ups—blue for a boy, pink for a girl.

**3.** An animal tied up as a bait for a beast of prey.

1895 MRS. B. M. CROKER *Village Tales* (1896) 27 Where's the chap with the buffalo—where is our tie-up? *Ibid.*, It will be an awful sell if there is no tie-up, and the tiger happens to go by.

**4.** *Bookbinding.* *pl.* Tapes or ribbons attached to a portfolio, book-cover, etc., as a fastening.

1896 *D. Reeves' Catal.* Sept. 11/1 Parchment, with silk tie-ups. 1902 *Ibid.* Jan. 10/2, 4 sheets and a plan of London, 1572,..in portfolio with tie ups, 21s.

**II.** Act of tying up, or state of being tied up.

**5.** *slang.* **a.** A finish, conclusion, 'wind-up'. **b.** *Pugilism.* A knock-out blow, a 'finisher': cf. TIE *v.* 11 g.

1818 *Sporting Mag.* II. 211 He knobbed his adversary well, and floored him by a smart tye-up at the fourth button-hole. 1829 *Ibid.* XXIV. 99 By way of a tie up to the concern..the Ladies' Purse of 50£ for the beaten horses was offered.

**6.** A stoppage of work or business, esp. on account of a lock-out or strike.

1889 *Sci. Amer.* 19 Jan. 32/3 In the event of a 'tie-up', or strike. 1894 *Times* 14 July 7/1 [The Great Northern Pacific Railroad] could not..afford to face a tie-up. 1903 *Westm. Gaz.* 30 June 11/3 No such 'tie-up' has ever before been known in the American cotton industry.

**7.** A condition of being 'tied up'; entanglement.

1906 *Statesman* (Calcutta) 30 Sept. 3/7 She had no desire, she said, to 'get into any more domestic tie ups'.

**III. 8.** as *adj.* Constructed by tying up.

1881 *Cheq. Career* 43 Thirty whares [houses] with their usual tie-up fences around them formed the outside Pah.

**Tiew**, variant of TEW *Obs.*

**Tie·-wig.** Also tye-wig. [Cf. TIE- 3.] A wig having the hair gathered together behind and tied with a knot of ribbon.

**1713** GAY *Guard.* No. 149 ₱ 17 The smart tye-wig with the black ribbon. **1816** SCOTT *Antiq.* iii, In tie-wigs and laced coats. **1852** THACKERAY *Esmond* III. v, The gentleman-usher's horror when the Prince of Savoy was introduced to her Majesty in a tie-wig, no man out of a full-bottomed periwig ever having kissed the Royal hand before.

*attrib.* **1887** BROWNING *Parleyings, B. de Mandeville* iv, Addison's tye-wig preachment.

Hence **Tie·-wigged** (-wigd) *a.*, wearing a tie-wig.

**1763** *Brit. Mag.* IV. 605 The powder'd tye-wigged sons of soot Trip to the shovel with a shoeless foot.

† **Tiff**, *sb.*[1] *Obs. rare*[−1]. [f. TIFF *v.*[1]] Manner of dressing or arranging, get-up; the way in which the hair, wig, etc. is dressed.

**1703** *The Levellers* in *Harl. Misc.* (1745) V. 419/2 Did you mark the beau Tiff of his Wig, what a deal of Pains he took to toss it back?

**Tiff** (tif), *sb.*[2] *colloq.* or *slang.* ? *Obs.* Also 9 *Sc.* tift. [Origin obscure; perh. onomatopœic; cf. TIFF *v.*[2], TIFT *v.*[2]]

**1.** Liquor, *esp.* poor, weak, or 'small' liquor, 'tipple'.

*a* **1635** CORBET *Poems, On J. Dawson*, So let your channels flow with single tiff, For John I hope is crown'd. **1661** A. BROME *Answ. Univ. Friend* Poems 165 Your next is money, which I promise, Full fifty pounds alas the summe is, That too shall quickly follow, if It can be rais'd from Strong or Tiffe. **1703** J. PHILIPS *Splendid Shilling* 15 With scanty offals and small acid tiff (Wretched repast !). **1736** AINSWORTH *Lat. Dict.* II, *Vappa*,..palled wine that hath lost its strength, dead drink, poor tiff. **1823** SCOTT *Quentin D.* Introd., Drinking acid tiff, as above mentioned.

**2.** A sip or little drink of punch or other diluted liquor. Cf. WHIFF.

**1727** BAILEY vol. II, *Tiff*, a small Quantity of potable Liquor, as a Tiff of Punch, etc. **1752** FIELDING *Amelia* VIII. x, What say you to..a tiff of punch by way of whet? **1804** STAGG *Misc. Poems* (1807) 3 (E.D.D.) Monnie a tift o' yell. **1815** SCOTT *Guy M.* xi, Sipping his tiff of brandy punch with great solemnity. **1819** *Sporting Mag.* IV. 272 The gentleman can't take a tiff of beer in a morning. **1820** *Blackw. Mag.* VIII. 98 We shall take a tiff of Campbell and Somerville's best black strap.

**Tiff** (tif), *sb.*[3] *colloq.* [Origin obscure; prob. onomatopœic, from the sound of a slight puff of air or gas.]

**1.** A slight outburst or fit of temper, pettishness, or ill-humour. Now *rare* or merged in 2.

**1727** BAILEY vol. II, *Tiff*,..also a small Fit of Anger, etc. **1729** MRS. DELANY in *Life & Corr.* (1861) I. 230 That common compassion (says he in a tiff) would give me but little satisfaction. **1739** 'R. BULL' tr. *Dedekindus' Grobianus* 102 Returning homewards in a furious Tiff. *a* **1825** FORBY *Voc. E. Anglia*, *Tiff*, a pet; slight anger. 'She was in a tiff'. **1871** CARLYLE in *Mrs. C.'s Lett.* (1883) II. 164 Abrupt Captain Anthony being in some tiff of his own.

**2.** A slight or petty quarrel; a temporary ill-humoured disagreement; a 'breeze'; sometimes applied to a more serious quarrel.

**1754** RICHARDSON *Grandison* (1781) IV. xxxviii. 268 My Lord and I have had another little *Tiff*, shall I call it? it came not up to a quarrel. **1755** KIDGELL *Card* II. 150 Your dear Letter fell into Mamma's Hands, and..Madam thought herself entitled to open it.—So, my Dear, we had a violent Tiff upon it. **1868** LOUISA M. ALCOTT *Little Women* ix, More friendly than ever after their small tiff. **1888** BRYCE *Amer. Commw.* I. xi. 145 'Little tiffs' are frequent when the senatorial majority is in opposition to the executive.

**3.** A short outburst (of laughter, etc.). *rare.*

**1858** CARLYLE *Fredk. Gt.* VII. i. II. 149 Wilhelmina.. answered..him with tiffs of laughter, in a prettily fleering manner.

† **Tiff**, *v.*[1] *Obs.* [a. OF. *tifer*, *tiffer* to adorn (12th c. in Godef.), mod.F. *attifer*: see ATIFFE.]

**1.** *trans.* To attire, dress, deck out, trick out, 'tittivate' (one's person, hair, etc.). (In 18th c. like F. *attifer*, usually familiar.)

*a* **1225** [see TIFFING *vbl. sb.*]. **1303** R. BRUNNE *Handl. Synne* 3201 ȝyf þou tyfyst þe ouer proudly. **13..** *K. Alis.* 4109 Theo maydenes lokyn in the glas, For to tyffen [*Laud MS.* atyffen] heore fas. *c* **1350** *Will. Palerne* 3183 Knew þow nouȝt..þat i was tiffed in a-tir when i wend fro þe. **1382** [see TIFFLE 1]. **1729** MRS. DELANY in *Life & Corr.* (1861) I. 225, I am sorry your ladies should tiff anything but their hair. **1768** TUCKER *Lt. Nat.* (1834) I. 40 Her desire of tiffing out her mistress in a killing attire.

**b.** *absol.* or *intr.*

**1700** CONGREVE *Way of World* II. iv, Poor Mincing tift and tift all the morning. **1741** MRS. MONTAGU *Lett.* (1906) I. 65 While Deb is tiffing and tiffing till my hair is so pure and so crisp.

**2.** *trans.* **a.** To put in order, arrange. **b.** To prepare, make, construct.

**13..** *Gaw. & Gr. Knt.* 1129, & þay busken vp bilyue, blonkkez to sadel, Tyffen her takles, trussen her males. *a* **1400-50** *Alexander* 4465 Sum [idols] ere tiffid all of tree, and sum of tyn pured.

**3.** *intr.* To be idly employed, be busy about trifles.

*c* **1440** *Promp. Parv.* 493/2 Tyffyn, werke ydylly, *idem quod* tymeryn.

Hence † **Tiffed** *ppl. a.*, tricked out, adorned (in quot. *fig.*): see also TIFT *ppl. a.*

**1303** R. BRUNNE *Handl. Synne* 11763 Yn tyfed [*v.r.* tyffede] wurdys þat slyked are, Semeþ þy synnes þat þey noȝt were.

**Tiff**, *v.*[2] *colloq.* or *slang.* ? *Obs.* [f. TIFF *sb.*[2] Cf. TIFT *v.*[2]] *trans.* To drink; *esp.* to drink slowly or in small portions, to sip.

**1769** *Trinculo's Trip* 25, I was tiffing a stout cann of flip. **1809-11** COMBE *Syntax* v. 140 He tiff'd his punch, and went to rest.

**Tiff**, *v.*[3] [f. TIFF *sb.*[3]] *intr.* To be in a tiff or pet; to have a tiff, or petty quarrel.

**1727** BAILEY vol. II, To *Tiff*, to be angry, peevish, fretful, or displeased at. **1859** F. FRANCIS *Newton Dogvane* (1888) 59 The Captain was late, and Miss Bowers tiffed.

**Tiff**, *v.*[4] *Anglo-Ind.* [app. abbreviation of or back-formation from *tiff-ing*, TIFFIN.] *intr.* = TIFFIN *v.*, to lunch.

**1803** ELPHINSTONE in Colebrooke *Life* (1884) I. v. 116 We were interrupted by a summons to tiff. at Floyer's. After tiffin Close said he should be glad to go. **1816** 'QUIZ' *Grand Master* VIII. 230 The huntsman now inform'd them all, They were to *tiff* at Bobb'ry Hall. **1825** T. HOOK *Sayings* Ser. II. *Passion & Princ.* iii, 'I'm afraid you won't like our tiffin, Walford'...'I have tiffed', said Walford. **1859** LANG *Wand. India* 16, I will tiff with you to-day at half-past two.

**Tiffany** (ti·făni). Also 7 tiffanie, -enay, -eney, -inie, -iny, tifine, tifnie, tiphany, 7–9 tiffeny, 9 tiffney. [a. OF. *tifinie* (*c* 1200), *tiphanie* (with 40 variants in Godefroy, s. v. *Tifaigne*):—L. *theophania*, THEOPHANY, applied to the Epiphany (see Du Cange). Sense 2 appears to be English only, and to have arisen about 1600; it is usually taken to be short for 'Epiphany silk' or 'muslin'; but as to the reason of the name no evidence has been found. (Perhaps it was a fanciful name, with allusion to the sense 'manifestation': see quots. 1601, 1645 in 2.)]

† **1.** The festival of the Epiphany or Twelfth Day (Jan. 6). *Obs.* (Scarcely an English use.)

[**1292** BRITTON II. xxi. § 2 Del comencement del Advent jekes as utaves de la Tiphanie [*v. rr.* Tiphayne, Epiphanie; *tr.* from the beginning of Advent until the Octaves of the Epiphany]. **1323** in Tate *Househ. Ord. Edw. II* 62 *margin*, Le jour de la Tyffayne.] *a* **1633** AUSTIN *Medit.* (1635) 56 This is Twelfe day...But more anciently and most properly it was called the Epiphany...Our great grand Fathers..as the Legend sayes called it the Tiffany..we must know it signifies Apparition or Manifestation from above.

**2.** A kind of thin transparent silk; also a transparent gauze muslin, cobweb lawn: see also quots. 1882.

**1601** HOLLAND *Pliny* XI. xxii. I. 323 The invention of that fine silke, Tiffanie, Sarcenet, and Cypres, which instead of apparell to cover and hide, shew women naked through them. **1611** COTGR., *Gaze*,..also (the sleight stuffe) Tiffanie. *a* **1625** FLETCHER *Noble Gent.* I. i, Let her haue Veluets, Tiffinies, Jewels, Pearls. **1645** EVELYN *Diary* June, [Venetian ladies], their sleeves.., shewing their naked armes, thro' false sleeves of tiffany. **1671** SKINNER *Etymol.*, *Tiffeny*, Sericum tenuissimum & mollissimum. **1682** WHELER *Journ. Greece* I. 64 Silken Vail, as thin as Tiphany. **1685** *Lond. Gaz.* No. 2001/4, 33 Yards of Black Tiffeney for Mourning Scarves. **1718** LADY M. W. MONTAGU *Let. to C'tess Mar* 10 Mar., The table-cloth and napkins..were all tiffany, embroidered with silk and gold. **1788** MRS. SHERWOOD in *Life* (1847) v. 63 A shepherdess's hat, of pale blue silver tiffany. **1796** MRS. GLASSE *Cookery* xxi. 325 Good clear isinglass.. tied up in a piece of thin tiffany. **1882** BECK *Draper's Dict.*, *Tiffany*..a kind of transparent gauze stiffened with gum, still produced for employment in the production of artificial flowers. **1882** CAULFEILD & SAWARD *Dict. Needlework*, *Tiffany*, a thin description of semi-transparent silk textile, resembling gauze. *Ibid.*, *Tiffeny*, a description of muslin, of open make,..employed for Needle Embroidery.

**b.** An article made of tiffany, as a head-dress, a garment, a sieve, etc.

**1606** WARNER *Alb. Eng.* XVI. ci. (1612) 400 Fannes, Tifnies, Maskes, Bongraces. *c* **1620** T. ROBINSON *Mary Magd.* I. 423 A tiffany shee wore about her head, Hanginge submissely to her shoulders white. **1788** W. MARSHALL *Yorksh.* Gloss., *Tiffany*, a fine gauze sieve, for separating fine flour. **1882** J. LUCAS *Stud. Nidderdale* 15 Flour..separated from the bran by being worked through a hair-sieve tiffany, or temse.

**c.** *fig.*

*a* **1624** BP. M. SMITH *Serm.* (1632) 132 Put on the silke of honesty, the tiffiny (as it were) of sanctimony, and the purple of chastity. **1650** B. *Discolliminium* 36 As a wel-wrought piece of tiffany or sophistry, but not as a sound Logicall or Theologicall Webbe. **1651** BIGGS *New Disp.* ₱ 250 From the Tiffany and thinner dresse of a vapour. **1829** T. HOOK *Bank to Barnes* 86 The trumpery tiffany of drawing-room tittle-tattle.

**d.** *attrib.* or as *adj.* Made of or resembling tiffany; *fig.* 'transparent', flimsy. **e.** *Comb.* as *tiffany-trader.*

**1608** DEKKER *2nd Pt. Honest Wh.* II. i. Wks. 1873 II. 119 As arrant a whore as euer stiffned tiffany neckcloathes in water-starch. **1626** *Faithf. Friends* I. ii, This tiffany-trader wants customers. **1658** R. FRANCK *North. Mem.* (1821) 48 It's a tiffany plot; any man with half an eye may easily see through it. **1664** H. POWER *Exp. Philos.* I. 30 Another pair of filmy Tiffany long wings, like those of Flyes. **1699** EVELYN *Acetaria* (1729) 174 Stamp it as small as to pass thro' a fine Tiffany Sieve. **1703** MRS. CENTLIVRE *Beau's Duel* II. ii, Whose tiffany natures are so easily impos'd upon. **1823** LAMB *Elia* Ser. II. *New-Y.'s coming of age*, Twelfth Day..came in a tiffany suit, white and gold.

† **Ti·ffety-ta·ffety**, *a. nonce-wd.* Reduplicated form of *taffety* adj. = TAFFETA B. 2 (cf. quot. 1621 there); perh. also associated with TIFF *v.*[1]

**1595** *Maroccus Ext.* 13 Tush, she that I talke of can entertaine you with a duzen of tiffite taffetie girles in a morning.

**Tiffin** (ti·fin), *sb. Anglo-Ind.* Also 9 tiffing. [Appears to have originated in the Eng. colloq. or slang *tiffing*, vbl. sb. from TIFF *v.*[2] to take a little drink or sip (cf. quot. 1785), which has been specialized in Anglo-Indian use. **1785** GROSE *Dict. Vulg. Tongue*, *Tiffing*, eating, or drinking out of meal time. **1867** WEDGWOOD *Dict. Eng. Etymol.*, *Tiffin*, now naturalised among Anglo-Indians in the sense of luncheon, is the North country *tiffing* (properly sipping).]

In India and neighbouring eastern countries, A light midday meal; luncheon.

**1800** WARD in *Carey's Life* vi. (1885) 137 Krishna came to eat tiffin (what in England is called luncheon) with us. **1803** [see TIFF *v.*[4]]. **1810** T. WILLIAMSON *E. Ind. Vade M.* I. 352 The [Mahommedan] ladies, like ours, indulge in tiffings (slight repasts). *c* **1816** MRS. SHERWOOD *Stories on Ch. Catech.* xvi. 141 She gave them a good tiffing about one o'clock. **1831** TRELAWNY *Adv. Younger Son* II. 115 When the gong sounds one, you will find tiffin in the hall. **1896** 'H. S. MERRIMAN' *Flotsam* xx, I'll call for you after tiffin. **1906** *Peking & Tientsin Times* 9 May 1/2 Those wishing to have tiffins at the forthcoming spring meeting will please apply at the secretary's office. Price $2. 00 per tiffin.

**b.** *attrib.*, as *tiffin-bell*, *-table*, *-time*.

**1811** MRS. SHERWOOD *Henry & Bearer* 31 The tiffin time was very stupid to the little boy. **1852** *Life in Bombay* 34 The preparation of the tiffin table. **1890** CLARK RUSSELL *Shipmate Louise* vi, The tiffin-bell rang.

Hence **Ti·ffin** *v.*, **a.** *intr.* to take tiffin, to lunch; cf. TIFF *v.*[4]; **b.** *trans.* to provide with tiffin.

**1866** MISS BRADDON *Lady's Mile* xi, I'd tiffin them if they were my visitors. **1880** P. GILLMORE *On Duty* 51 Here I tiffined. **1903** LD. R. GOWER *Rec. & Remin.* 388 We tiffined at a tea-house in the village.

**Tiffing** (ti·fiŋ), *vbl. sb.* [f. TIFF *v.*[1] + -ING[1].] The action of TIFF *v.*[1]; decking or tricking out, personal adornment.

*a* **1225** *Ancr. R.* 420 (MS. C.) Wrihen ha schal hire scheome, as sunfule Eue dohter;..& naut drah þ wriheles to tiffung & te prude. **1303** R. BRUNNE *Handl. Synne* 3243 Moche she loued feyre tyfyng On here hede. **1635** CRANLEY *Amanda* 33 Thus with thy tiffing, trimming, and thy mending, Thou spend'st whole houres together without ending. **1741** MRS. DELANY in *Life & Corr.* (1861) II. 168 Now for curling, tiffing, etc. Our Duchess will be almost as fine as the Nabob's lady.

**Ti·ffish**, *a. colloq. rare*[−0]. [f. TIFF *sb.*[3] + -ISH[1].] Given to tiffs, ready to take offence; pettish, peevish.

**1855** in CLARKE. **1864** in WEBSTER.

**Tiffle** (ti·f'l), *v.*[1] *Obs.* exc. *dial.* Forms: 4 tifle, 5 tiffel, tyffle, 6 tyf(f)ell, 9 tiffle. [Dim. or freq. of TIFF *v.*[1]]

† **1.** *trans.* To dress up, adorn, deck or trick out (in a trifling or time-wasting way). *Obs.*

**1388** WYCLIF *Ecclus.* xxxii. 15 In the our of risyng, tifle [1382 tyff] thee not. *Margin*, That is, make thee no tariyng in araiyng, ether tiflyng of heeris, as wymmen doon.

**2.** *intr.* To busy oneself idly, 'fiddle', trifle; to potter about. Now *dial.*

*c* **1440** *Promp. Parv.* 493/2 Tyfflynge, or vnprofytabylle werkynge (*S.*, *A.*, *P.* tyffynge). **1530** PALSGR. 758/1, I tyfell with my fyngers, or busye my selfe longe aboute a thyng.., *je tiffe.* You have spente two houres to tyffell about this thyng. *a* **1825** FORBY *Voc. E. Anglia*, *Tiffle*, to be mightily busy about little or nothing.

Hence **Ti·ffler**, one who 'tiffles'; in quot. app. one who dresses up; in mod. dial. a trifler, idler.

*c* **1400** *Plowman's T.* 195 But Antichrist they serven clene, Attyred all in tyrannye;..Tiffelers attyred in trecherye.

**Tiffle, tifle** (ti·f'l), *v.*[2] Chiefly *dial.* [app. onomatopœic.] *trans.* To disorder, disarrange, entangle, ravel; *tiffle out*, to ravel out.

**1811** WILLAN *Words W. Riding* in *Archæol.* (1814) XVII. 161 *Tifle*, v. to entangle, to mix and knot threads together. **1815** *Monthly Mag.* I Mar. 125/1 *Essex Dialect*, *Tiffle*, to disarrange. **1825** BROCKETT *N.C. Words*, *Tifle*, *tyfell*, to entangle,..to ruffle. **1880** *Plain Hints Needlework* 121 Tifflings..is used in some parts to describe the ravellings or threads. 'To tiffle out', to ravel out or unweave.

**Tiffoon**, obs. form of TYPHOON.

† **Tiffu·re.** *Obs. rare*[−1]. [a. OF. *tifeure* a headdress (*a* 1200 in Godef.), f. *tifer*, TIFF *v.*[1]: see -URE.] Dressing up, adornment.

**1303** R. BRUNNE *Handl. Synne* 3290, Y suffre þys mysauenture For on my heuede ouer feyre tyfure.

**Tiffy** (ti·fi), *sb. Naut. slang.* [Contraction of ARTIFICER.] An engine-room artificer.

**1899** F. T. BULLEN *Way Navy* 34 My life-long admiration for the blue-jacket proper will be shared by his brothers in arms, the stoker and engine-room artificer ('tiffy' as we call him). **1904** KIPLING *Traffics & Disc.* 57 Those dirty engine-room objects which we call 'tiffies'.

**Tiffy** (ti·fi), *a.* [f. TIFF *sb.*[3] + -Y.] Given to tiffs; in a tiff; pettish, ill-humoured; faddy.

**1810** *Splendid Follies* II. 126 The old lady felt quite tiffy, and mumbled her roll in silence. **1883** *Bread-Winners* (1884) 27 She's too tiffy for poor folks like us.

**Tifle** (təi·f'l), *v.* Chiefly *dial.* Also 8–9 tyfle. [Origin unascertained.] *intr.* Of a horse: To get a strain in the back: chiefly in **Tifled** *ppl. a.*

**1703** THORESBY *Let. to Ray* s.v. (E.D.S.), A tifled horse, when broken above the loins. **1708** J. C. *Compl. Collier* (1845) 33 Least a Horse or two Tyfle, or be out of Order by a Fall. **1828** *Craven Gloss.*, *Tifled*, sprained in the back. **1863** MRS. TOOGOOD *Yorksh. Dial.* (MS.), The horse will never do any more work; he is tyfled in the back.

**Tift** (tift), *sb.*[1] *Sc.* and *north. dial.* [History obscure; ? related to TIFT *ppl. a.* and TIFT *v.*[1]] Condition, order; condition of mind, mood, humour.

**1717** RAMSAY *Elegy on Lucky Wood* vii, Beef, dry fish, or cheese, Which kept our..health in tift. **1722** WODROW *Hist. Ch. Scot.* II. III. iv. § 4. 140 The King's Horse being in good Tift. **1725** RAMSAY *Gentle Sheph.* I. i, I'm in tift to hear you play and sing. **1824** MACTAGGART *Gallovid. Encycl.* 449 A poet's muse is in tift when she sings well; corn also is in tift when it is dry, viz., in tift to lead. **1904** in *Eng. Dial. Dict.* cited Cumberld., to Cheshire, and n.-w. Derbysh.

**Tift,** *sb.*[2] *Sc.* and *dial.* [app. var. of TIFF *sb.*[3]]

**1.** A slight fit of ill-humour or offendedness; a petty quarrel or disagreement: = TIFF *sb.*[3] 1, 2.

**1751** SMOLLETT *Per. Pic.* (1779) IV. xc. 83 It [his intimacy] was now chequered with occasional tifts. **1761** MRS. F. SHERIDAN *Sidney Bidulph* III. 42 She supposed he married in a tifft, upon my refusal of him. **1808** ELEANOR SLEATH *Bristol Heiress* III. 81 My wife and I have often a bit of a tift. **1887** P. McNEILL *Blawearie* 61 The last time we met—Bob and I—we had a 'tift', ye ken what that is.

**2.** A puff, breath, or slight blast (of wind).

*a* **1765** *Ld. Thomas*, etc. xvii. in Child *Ballads* III. (1885) 183/1 Four and twanty siller bells Wer a' tyed till his mane, And yae tift o the norland wind, They tinkled ane by ane.

†**Tift,** *ppl. a.* *Sc.* *Obs.* [Goes with TIFT *v.*[1]] Prepared, ready; set in order; provided, furnished.

**13..** *Cursor M.* 1761 (Cott.) Quen al was tift [*v.rr.* wroȝt, don] was þar na bide, Þe stormes ras on ilka side. *Ibid.* 5089 Mas your gere al redi tift, Your seckes sal i fil o gift. *Ibid.* 24807 Wit trissor son his scipp was tift. *c* **1375** *Sc. Leg. Saints* xviii. (*Egipciane*) 870, I cane fond To þat flume.., And wesche in yᵗ bath handis & face; Syne come agane, & with schryfte And contryt hart mad me tyfte.

**Tift,** *v.*[1] *Obs.* exc. *dial.* [Origin uncertain; in quots. *c* 1425, 1600 it appears to be a var. of TIFF *v.*[1]; but in the rest it may be a different word: cf. TIFT *sb.*[1], TIFT *ppl. a.*] *trans.* To prepare, make ready, put in order; to dress.

**13..** *Cursor M.* 19425 (Cott.) Steuen tifted him al bun [*so Gött.*; *Fairf.* & *Tr.* made him redi bun], And þan bigan a gret sarmun. *c* **1425** *St. Mary of Oignies* I. i. in *Anglia* VIII. 135/34 Tressynge and tifting of here [=hair]. **1600** ABP. ABBOT *Exp. Jonah* 591 Beholding a woman most curiously trimmed, and exquisitely tiffted up. **1641** BEST *Farm. Bks.* (Surtees) 32 There are many thinges belonge to tiftinge of hay; as spreadinge,..turninge, rakinge, and cockinge. *Ibid.* 33 If it [hay] bee eyther wette or greene when yow cocke it, yow are not to lette it stande above three dayes afore yow throwe it out againe and gette it well tifted [*pr.* tifled] in. *Ibid.* 61 For tiftinge of a newe hive. **1790** MORISON *Poems* 25 (Jam.) The fidler tifted ilka string. **1876** *Whitby Gloss.* s.v., 'Tifted up', cleansed and put into order.

**Tift,** *v.*[2] *Sc.* and *dial.* [var. of TIFF *v.*[2]] *trans.* To drink, quaff; = TIFF *v.*[2] (also *intr.*).

**1722** W. HAMILTON *Wallace* III. i. 18 They..tifted canty wine. **1819** W. TENNANT *Papistry Storm'd* (1827) 101 The siller stoups, on heigh upliftit, Were tootit in a whip, and tiftit. **1833** M. SCOTT *Tom Cringle* x. (1859) 203 The Captain was stowing his cargo with great zeal and tifting away at the fluids as became an honest sailor.

**Tift,** *v.*[3] *Obs.* or *dial.* [f. TIFT *sb.*[2]] *intr.* To have a tiff; = TIFF *v.*[3]

**1777** SHERIDAN *Sch. Scand.* I. ii, We tifted a little going to church, and fairly quarrelled before the bells had done ringing.

**Tig** (tig), *sb.*[1] Also 9 tigg, tic. [f. TIG *v.*]

**1.** A touch: usually a light but significant touch, a tap or pat, = TICK *sb.*[3] 1; rarely applied to one that hurts. *Sc.* and *north. dial.*

**1721** KELLY *Sc. Prov.* 243 Many Masters, quoth the Poddock to the Harrow, when every Tin[e] gave her a Tig. **1822** GALT *Sir A. Wylie* I. v. 36 It's bairnly to mak sic a wark for a bit tig on the haffet. **1825** BROCKETT *N. C. Words*, *Tig*, a slight touch; as a mode of salutation. **1897** LD. E. HAMILTON *Outlaws* ii. 21 Just a tig of the cheek, Gavin....There's nothing in that to shame an honest man, surely?

**2.** A children's game, in which one of the players —usually designated *tig* or *it*—pursues the others until he overtakes and touches or 'tigs' one, who in his turn becomes 'tig': the same as TAG *sb.*[2]

Cf. TICK *sb.*[3] 1 b, and Sanders *Wörterb.* (1865) *Der Zeck*, ein Spiel der Kinder, wobei eins dem Andern einen Schlag giebt.

**1816** S. M. TAIT in *Remin. Lady Wake* v. (1909) 62 If it is wet, we play at tigg up and down the stairs. **1854** WARTER *Last of Old Squires* ii. 15 The sons..would have a start with the fleetest youths of the hamlet at prisoner's-base, or the old fashion'd game of tic. **1885** H. O. FORBES *Nat. Wand. E. Archip.* 68 With varieties of chevy, tig, and blind-man's buff. **1894** MRS. H. WARD *Marcella* I. 12 The mad games of 'tig' which she led..in the top playground.

**Tig,** *sb.*[2], variant of TYG, a drinking-cup.

**Tig** (tig), *v.* [History obscure. It may be, as some think, a variant or alteration of TICK *v.*[1], or a parallel formation. Cf. the parallelism of MHG. and Ger. *zecken* to pat, and *der zeck* the game of tig (TIG *sb.*[1] 2).]

**1.** *intr.* To give light or playfully rough touches; esp. *fig.* to trifle, dally *with*; † *to tig and tar* = *to tick and toy*: see TICK *v.*[1] 1. *Sc.* and *north. dial.*

*c* **1470** HENRYSON *Mor. Fab.* v. (*Parl. Beasts*) i, [The fox] That luifit weill with pultrie to tig and tar. **1634** RUTHERFORD *Lett.* (1862) I. 140 He may get up and lend them a blow who are tigging and playing with Christ and His spouse. **1815** G. BEATTIE *John o' Arnha'* (1826) 41 It was nae joke To tig wi' fiends that vomit smoke. **1825** JAMIESON s.v., Young people are said to be tigging, when sporting with gentle touches, or patting each other.

**b.** *fig.* To interfere, meddle, have to do *with*. *Sc.*

**1599** JAS. I Βασιλ. Δωρον (1603) 29 As for the matter of fore-faltures,..it is not good tigging with these things. **1813** W. BEATTIE *Fruits Time Parings* (1871) 30 They that tig wi you Will soon hae cause to claw. **1873** W. ALEXANDER *Johnny Gibb* xix, Nedder you nor Mr. Sleekaboot made yer plack a bawbee by tiggin wi' her.

**2.** *trans.* To touch in the game of tig (TIG *sb.*[1] 2). Also *absol.* (see also b).

**1821** *Blackw. Mag.* Aug. 38 To join the merry ring at ..Tig me if you can. **1828** *Craven Gloss.*, *Tig*, to touch lightly;..to have the last touch when leaving school. **1866** A. W. BUCHAN *Song of Rest* II. 29 Some tig and run, some ride upon the wall. **1893** E. L. WAKEMAN in *Columbus* (Ohio) *Dispatch* 19 Oct., The chief point in this game [French Tig] is always to tig on a portion of the body difficult to hold whilst tigging another.

**b.** *intr. fig.* To 'pluck' or 'dig' *at*, as if playing tig; to annoy one by petty provocations. *dial.*

**1802** R. ANDERSON *Cumberld. Ball.* 54 Now, tiggin at me suin and late, They're cleekin but the yellow bait. **1844** *Songs of Nursery* in *Whistlebinkie* (1890) II. 153 Father, settle Sandy! He's cryin names to me. He's aye tig, tigging, And winna let me be.

**3.** *intr. transf.* To run from place to place, as if chased. *dial.*

**1834** LOVER *Leg. & Stor. Irel.* Ser. II. 297 He run undher a stool, and kept tiggin' about from one place to th' other. **1882** J. WALKER *Jaunt to Auld Reekie* 13 Like cattle tiggin' frae the clegs and flees Awa they scamper.

‖**Tige** (tīʒ). [F. *tige* stalk:—L. *tibia* shank, pipe.] The shaft of a column; also *transf.*, in a fire-arm or cartridge, see quot. 1877; in *Bot.*, see quot. 1900. **Tige-arm**, a fire-arm fitted with a tige (*Cent. Dict.* 1891).

**1664** EVELYN tr. *Freart's Archit.* 126 That round and long Cylinder diversly named by Authors, Scapus, Vivo, Tige, Shaft, Fust, Trunke. **1710** J. HARRIS *Lex. Techn.* II, *Tige*, in Architecture, is the Shaft of a Column from the Astragal to the Capital. **1727–41** CHAMBERS *Cycl.*, *Tige*, in architecture, a French term for the shaft or fust of a column, comprehended between the astragal and the capital. **1877** KNIGHT *Dict. Mech.*, *Tige*...a stem or stalk. A pin at the base of the breech in the Thouvenin system of fire-arms, for expanding the base of the ball; an anvil or support for the cap or primer in a central-fire cartridge. **1900** B. D. JACKSON *Gloss. Bot. Terms* 271/1 *Tige*,..stem.

‖**Tigelle** (tiʒeˑl). *Bot.* Also tigel, and in L. form **tigella** (tidʒeˑlă), (*erron.* **tigeˑllum**, **tigeˑllus**). [F. *tigelle* caulicle, radicle, dim. of *tige*. (*Tibia, tige, tigelle* are fem., hence the correct Latin form is *tigella*.)]

The embryonic axis or primitive stem, which bears the cotyledons; the caulicle or radicle. Sometimes applied to the plumule, which is properly the growing top of the tigelle. Hence **Tigellate** (ti·dʒelĕit) *a.*, having a tigelle; **Tigellule** (tidʒeˑliūl), see quot. 1860; whence **Tigeˑllular** *a.*, pertaining to or of the nature of a tigellule.

**1860** MAYNE *Expos. Lex.*, *Tigella*, term for that part of the vegetable embryo which unites the radicle to the cotyledon. *Ibid.*, *Tigellatus*, applied to the *plumula* when supplied with a visible *tigella*, as in the *Faba*: tigellate. *Ibid.*, Tigellular. *Ibid.*, *Tigellula*, term by Turpin for the short and sterile filaments which are one of the two elementary organs of the mass of the truffle: a tigellule. **1866** *Treas. Bot.*, *Tigellate*, having a short stalk, as the plumule of a bean. **1900** B. D. JACKSON *Gloss. Bot. Terms* 271/1 *Tigelle*, *Tigella*,..a miniature or initial stem, used for (*a*) caulicle or hypocotyl, (*b*) plumule.

**Tiger** (təi·gəɹ), *sb.* Forms: 1 (*pl.*) tigras, (-es); 4–7 tygre, 4–8 tigre, 5 tigir, -yr, tygyr, -ur, 5–9 tyger, 6 tygir, *Sc.* tegir, tegre, 6–7 tigar, 7 tygar, 7– tiger. [ME. a. OF. *tigre* (*c* 1150 in Godef. *Compl.*), ad. L. *tigrem*, nom. *tigris*, whence also rare OE. pl. *tigras*, *-es*; Ger., Da., Sw. *tiger*, Du. *tijger*, Sp., Pg., It. *tigre*. L. *tigris* was a. Gr. τίγρις, a foreign word, evidently oriental, introduced when the beast became known.

(Some have conjectured connexion with Zend *tīghri* arrow, *tighra* sharp, pointed, in reference to the celerity of its spring; but no application of either word, or any derivative, to the tiger is known in Zend.)]

**1.** A large carnivorous feline quadruped, *Felis tigris*, one of the two largest living felines, a cat-like maneless animal, in colour tawny yellow with blackish transverse stripes and white belly; widely distributed in Asia, and proverbial for its ferocity and cunning.

*Bengal tiger, Royal tiger* († *tiger royal*), the tiger of Bengal, where it attains its typical development.

*a* **1000** *De rebus in Oriente* in Cockayne *Narrat.* 38 Ymb þa stowe beoð..fore hundum tigras & leopardos þ hi fedað. *c* **1000** ÆLFRIC *Hom.* II. 492 Twa hreðe deor, þe sind tigres ȝehatene, þær urnon. **13..** *K. Alis.* 5227 (Bodl. MS.) Lyouns, Olyfaunz, Tygres, and dragouns, Vnces grete, and leopardes. *c* **1386** CHAUCER *Sqr.'s T.* 411 Ther nys Tygre [*v.r.* tigre], ne noon so crueel beest..That nolde han wept. **1484** CAXTON *Fables of Auian* xiii, Whan he sawe passe the tygre before the busshe, he shote at hym an arowe. **1581** PETTIE *Guazzo's Civ. Conv.* III. (1586) 124 So monstrous a creature..that it was doubtfull whether she were a woman or a tigar. **1605** SHAKS. *Macb.* III. iv. 101. **1698** FRYER *Acc. E. India & P.* IV. v. 176 A Youth killed a Tigre-Royal...It was a Tigre of the Biggest and Noblest Kind. **1777** ROBERTSON *Hist. Amer.* I. IV. 260 America gives birth to no creature that equals the lion or tyger in strength and ferocity. **1847** EMERSON *Repr. Men, Napoleon* Wks. (Bohn) I. 369 A man of stone and iron..with the speed and spring of a tiger in action. **1882** F. M. CRAWFORD *Mr. Isaacs* x, Crashing through the jungle after tiger with varying success.

**2.** Applied to other animals of the same genus, as in America to the Jaguar, *Felis onca*, and the Puma or Cougar, *F. concolor* (rare); and esp. in South Africa to the Leopard or Panther, *F. pardus*.

**1604** E. G[RIMSTONE] *D'Acosta's Hist. Indies* III. xv. 166 Vpon the sea shoare the Caymant with his taile gaue great blowes vnto the Tygre. **1698** FRYER *Acc. E. India & P.* IV. v. 177 The lesser sort of Tigres spotted like a Leopard. **1748** *Anson's Voy.* II. xii. 267 There were great numbers of tygers in the woods [Pacific coast, Mexico]..they are by no means so fierce as the Asiatic or African tyger. **1785** G. FORSTER tr. *Sparrman's Voy.* (1786) II. 252 The animals which I and the colonists in this part of Africa call tygers, ..represented in..M. de Buffon's work, under the denomination of panthers and leopards. **1832** MACGILLIVRAY tr. *Humboldt's Trav.* xvi. (1836) 215 When the tigers approached the edge of the forest, a dog which the travellers had began to howl. **1894** E. EGGLESTON in *Century Mag.* Apr. 849 The panther was long called a 'tyger' in the Carolinas.

**b.** esp. with qualifications.

†*American t.*, †*Mexican t.*, the jaguar; *black t.*, a dark variety of (*a*) the jaguar, (*b*) the leopard; *clouded t.*, *marbled t.*, *tortoiseshell t.*, species of TIGER-CAT; †*poltroon t.*, †*red t.*, earlier names for the puma; †*spotted t.*, (*a*) the leopard, (*b*) the cheetah (also †*tiger of chase*).

**1774** GOLDSM. *Nat. Hist.* II. xiv. 332 The tyger of Bengal has been seen to measure twelve feet in length,..whereas the American tyger seldom exceeds three. *Ibid.* III. vii. 244 An animal of America, which is usually called the Red Tiger, but Mr. Buffon calls it the Cougar. **1784–5** *Ann. Reg.* II. 20 His tygers of chase likewise pay him a visit... These are the spotted tygers. **1790** BEWICK *Hist. Quad.* (1824) 220 It [the Cougar] is sometimes called the Poltron tiger. **1825** WEDDELL *Voy. S. Pole* 210 The American tiger, called by the Spaniards jaguar, is often seen on the coast. **1826** HONE *Every-Day Bk.* I. 1176 Panther, or spotted tiger of Buenos Ayres. **1827** ROBERTS *Voy. Centr. Amer.* 95 A species of black tiger will also watch the turtle. **1842** *Penny Cycl.* XXIV. 440/2 The Black Tiger, *Felis melas*,..is considered as only a dark variety of the Leopard. *Ibid.* 441/1 The Mexican Tiger of Pennant is said to be a representation of *F. macroura*. **1863** BATES *Nat. Amazon* xi. (1864) 352 The black-tiger appears to be more abundant than the spotted form of jaguar in the neighbourhood of Ega. **1879** E. P. WRIGHT *Anim. Life* 84 The Clouded Tiger (*Felis macrocelis*) seems to be of a less mischievous disposition than many of the other cats. **1896** *List Anim. Zool. Soc.* 56 *Felis nebulosa*, Clouded Tiger. *Hab.* Assam.

**c.** Applied to other than feline beasts.

(*a*) *Tasmanian* or *Native tiger*: names given to the THYLACINE, the striped wolf or zebra-wolf of Tasmania. (*b*) *Sabre-toothed tiger*: see SABRE *sb.* 4 b.

**1832** Ross *Hobart Town Almanack* 85 (Morris) During our stay a native tiger or hyena bounded from its lair beneath the rocks. **1879** E. P. WRIGHT *Anim. Life* 217 The Tiger, or Striped Wolf of the colonists (*Thylacinus cynocephalus*), inhabits Tasmania. **1892** A. SUTHERLAND *Elem. Geog. Brit. Colonies* xiii. 273 The 'Tasmanian Tiger' is of the size of a shepherd's dog, a gaunt yellow creature, with black stripes round the upper part of its body.

†**d.** Applied (in L. form) to fabulous creatures, beasts or birds: see quots. *Obs.*

**1481** CAXTON *Myrr.* II. vi. 73 In ynde ben ther other bestes grete and fyrs whiche ben of blew colowr, and haue clere spottes on the body,..and ben named Tygris. *c* **1511** *1st Eng. Bk. Amer.* (Arb.) p. xxxii/2 Byrdes the whyche ben called Tygris, and they be so stronge that they wyll bere or cary in theyr neste a man sytting vpon an horse all armyd fro the hede to ye fote.

**3.** The figure or representation of a tiger; *esp.* one used as a badge or crest; hence, popularly applied to an organization or society having this badge; also, a member of such a society;

*spec.* (*Tammany Tiger*), the Tammany organization (*U.S.*).

*c* **1475** *Rauf Coilȝear* 457 He bair grauit in Gold and Gowlis in grene, Ane Tyger ticht to ane tre, ane takin of tene. **1725** COATS *Dict. Her.* s.v., The Heads of Tigers are also born in Arms either Couped or Eraz'd. **1871** *Harper's Weekly* 25 Nov. 1099/2 The tiger, symbol of the Americus Club, is used in a manner to produce the effect of a telling retort. **1874** *Chamb. Jrnl.* 801 (Farmer) The 17 ʰ [foot].. the Bengal Tigers, from their badge—a tiger. **1894** *Parker's Gloss. Her.* s.v., This beast, as drawn by ancient painters, is now often called the heraldic tiger, as distinguished from the natural. **1901** *Scotsman* 7 Nov. 4/3 New York..cannot be worse governed in the future than it has been under the rule of the Tammany Tiger. **1910** *Westm. Gaz.* 14 Mar. 14/2 (*Hockey*) The cup-holders were defeated by the Leicestershire Regiment (the Tigers) by 2–1.

**4.** *transf.* and *fig.* Applied to one who or that which in some way resembles or suggests a tiger.

**a.** A person of fierce, cruel, rapacious, or bloodthirsty disposition; also sometimes, a person of very great activity, strength, or courage.

**1500–20** DUNBAR *Poems* xxxviii. 11 The auld kene tegir, with his teith on char, Quhilk in a wait hes lyne for ws so lang. **1581** *Satir. Poems Reform.* xliv. 175 Thou hes Blasphemit our prophet, Preist, and heid; O filthie tegre Babylonical! **1585** *Thanksgiving* in *Liturg. Serv.* (1847) 585 To save her [Queen Elizabeth] from the jaws of the cruel Tigers that then sought to suck her blood. **1649** ROBERTS *Clavis Bibl.* 510 Antiochus Epiphanes that cruellest Tyger and Persecutor of the Church. **1806** FESSENDEN *Democr.* I. 77 *note*, The blood-thirsty tygers of the French revolution. **1893** BARING-GOULD *Cheap Jack Z.* I. 149, I who have lived in the Fens and among the tigers all my days.

**b.** Any animal of savage or vicious temper or of great rapacity.

**1859** *Art of Taming Horses* i. 23 The boasting Mr. —— ..was beaten pale and trembling out of the circus by that equine tiger. **1884** 'R. BOLDREWOOD' *Melbourne Mem.* xxi. 153 Many of the others [horses] were 'regular tigers', requiring any horseman who essayed to ride them habitually to be young, valiant, in hard training. **1885** LADY BRASSEY *The Trades* 211 The right time of the moon for the 'tigers of the sea' [sharks] to be about. **1894** *Outing* (U.S.) Feb. 393/1, I saw one of these sea-tigers [small sharks] glide towards it, and then a sudden splashing struggle began.

**c.** The tigerish spirit or disposition. Cf. DEVIL *sb.* 6 a.

**1825** T. HOOK *Sayings* Ser. II. *Passion & Princ.* ix. III. 139 The incalculable quantity of nonsense which the admiring fools talked, had nearly roused the tiger. **1877** TENNYSON *Harold* I. i, I trust the kingly touch that cures the evil May serve to charm the tiger out of him.

†**5.** A speckled hemipterous insect of the family *Tingitidæ*, which infests the leaves of pear and other trees. Cf. *tiger-babb* in 13. [F. *tigre, punaise tigre*.] *Obs.*

**1706** LONDON & WISE *Retir'd Gard.* I. I. xiv. 68 Pear-trees planted in an Espalier, have upon trial been found so subject to Tigers, which creates a sort of Sickness in the Trees. **1719** LONDON & WISE *Compl. Gard.* VII. x. 181 Another incurable Distemper is Tigers, which stick to the back of the Leaves of Wall-Pear-Trees, and dry them up, by sucking all the green Matter that was in them. **1725** *Bradley's Fam. Dict.* s.v. *Diseases of Trees*, Tigers attack only Wall Pear-trees, and never Dwarfs.

**6.** A smartly-liveried boy acting as groom or footman; formerly often provided with standing-room on a small platform behind the carriage, and a strap to hold on by; less strictly, an outdoor boy-servant. *slang. obsolescent.*

*c* **1817** [see quot. 1880]. **1825** HOOK *Sayings* Ser. II. *Man of Many Fr.* I. 247 'Ah!' said Arden, 'seven hundred pounds a-year, and a tiger!' **1827** LYTTON *Pelham* xliv, I sent my cab boy (*vulgo* Tiger) to inquire [etc.]. **1836–7** DICKENS *Sk. Boz, Gt. Winglebury Duel*, Leaving his tiger and cab behind him. **1842** W. IRVING in *Life & Lett.* (1886) III. 218 The young gentlemen have made a page, or tiger, of a nephew of Lorenzo. **1855** THACKERAY *Newcomes* xxv, He is the valet or tiger, more or less impudent and acute. **1880** W. H. HUSK in Grove *Dict. Mus.* II. 111/2 Lee, Alexander [1802–1851]...When a boy he entered the service of Lord Barrymore as 'tiger', being the first of the class of servants known by that name.

†**7.** A vulgarly or obtrusively overdressed person; also a sponger, hanger-on, parasite; a roué, rake, swell-mobsman. *slang. Obs.*

**1827** SCOTT *Jrnl.* (1890) I. 367 Our young men..have one capital name for a fellow that *outrés* and outroars the fashion...They hold him a vulgarian and call him a tiger. **1837** T. HOOK *Jack Brag* i, Every well dressed woman.. whom he happened to see with the tigers in whose set he mingled. **1849** THACKERAY *Pendennis* xix, 'A man may have a very good coat-of-arms, and be a tiger', the Major said.., 'that man is a tiger, mark my word—a low man'.

**b.** (See quot.) *slang*

**1899** *Westm. Gaz.* 29 Aug. 8/1 The convict wears a dull yellow cap...The thick rough jacket and trousers are of the same yellowish hue...A favourite form of insubordination is to tear to pieces these yellow suits, the punishment for which is that the 'tiger' appears in the quarry next day arrayed in board-like black canvas.

**8.** *U.S. slang.* A shriek or howl (often the word 'tiger') terminating a prolonged and enthusiastic cheer; a prolongation, finishing touch, final burst.

**1856** *Knickerb. Mag.* XLVIII. 258 (Thornton) Terrific cheers and a tiger. **1859** BARTLETT *Dict. Amer.* (ed. 2) s.v., In 1826 the [Boston Light] Infantry visited New York..,and while there the Tigers at a public festival awoke the echoes ..by giving the genuine howl...Gradually it became adopted on all festive and joyous occasions, and now 'three cheers and a tiger' are the inseparable demonstrations of approbation in that city [New York]. **1869** R. F. BURTON *Highl. Brazil* I. 239 When the ceremony ends, the scamp of the party..proposes three cheers and a tiger for Mr. Gordon. **1880** *Daily Tel.* 8 Oct., 'Three cheers' in properly hearty unison, without the hysterical American supplement of 'tigers'. **1892** *Sat. Rev.* 31 Dec. 759/1 The new festival.. introduced as a sort of 'tiger' to these three days of cheer. **1904** *N. China Herald* 27 May 1119/1 All the guests rising and singing.., giving three times three cheers, followed by a vigorous 'Tiger'.

**9. a.** The game of faro. *To buck* or *fight the tiger*, at faro or roulette, to play against the bank; also, less strictly, to gamble, play cards. *U.S. slang.*

**1851** *Adv. Simon Suggs* iv. (Thornton *Amer. Gloss.*) (heading) Simon starts forth to fight the Tiger. **1852** *Knickerb. Mag.* XL. 317 (ibid.) Such is 'the tiger', as the faro-table is called at the Springs: why, I never could learn. **1863** *Rocky Mountain News* 29 Jan. (ibid.), Bucking the tiger, which we wouldn't advise any one to do. **1888** *Daily Inter-Ocean* (Chicago) 14 Feb. (Farmer *Amer.*), More than one unsuspecting wife will have her eyes opened to the fact that the wicked tiger, and not legitimate business has been detaining her husband out so late at night.

**b.** A hand at poker: see quots.

**1889** GUERNDALE *Poker Bk.* 23 *Tiger.* This hand is, fortunately, very seldom played. It consists of the lowest possible combination of five cards; these are two, three, four, five, and seven. **1909** *Cent. Dict. Supp.*, *Tiger*, in poker, a hand which is seven high and deuce low, without a pair, sequence, or flush.

**c.** *Blind tiger*, an establishment at which intoxicating drinks are surreptitiously sold (*U.S.*).

**1892** *Evening Echo* 30 June 1/7 The proprietor of a 'blind tiger' (an illicit drinking place) in Lancaster, a..town of Kentucky, has been fined in 577 cases.

**10.** As a name for various implements: see quots.

**1864** WEBSTER, *Tiger*,.. a pneumatic box or pan used in sugar-refining. **1877** KNIGHT *Dict. Mech.*, *Tiger* (Sugar), a tank having a perforated bottom, through which the molasses escapes. **1881** RAYMOND *Mining Gloss.*, *Tiger.* See *Nipping-fork.* A tool for supporting a column of bore-rods while raising or lowering them.

**11.** Short for *tiger-moth, -shark, -snake, -wolf*, etc.

**1797** *Encycl. Brit.* (ed. 3) XVII. 714/1 *Squalus*, Shark... 5. *Tigrinus*, or tigre, is about 15 feet long; the body is.. black, interspersed with white stripes and spots, irregularly and transversely. **1819** G. SAMOUELLE *Entomol. Comp.* 418 *Arctia Caja.* The Garden Tyger. **1870** *Eng. Mech.* 21 Jan. 449/3 One of the handsomest moths belonging to..the 'Tigers', is that called the wood tiger (*Chelonia plantaginis*). **1895** *Westm. Gaz.* 14 Sept. 2/3 The traveller in the bush often comes across two 'tigers' pegging away at each other for dear life... Sometimes snakes in captivity are trained to fight, and an owner will occasionally be found to 'back his "tiger" to fight any snake of his inches in New South Wales'. **1895** *Chamb. Jrnl.* XII. 645/1 The sharks.. are at certain seasons a serious drawback, the tiger more especially. **1901** *Scribner's Mag.* XXIX. 455/1 Going out into the garden,..stopping beside the tigers [tiger-lilies] and peonies.

**12.** *attrib.* and *Comb.* **a.** simple attrib., as *tiger-cub, -drive, -hunt, -jungle, -pit* (PIT *sb.*[1] 5), *-skin, -spring, -stripe*; objective and obj. genitive, as *tiger-hunting, -shooting* sb. and adj., *-slayer.*

**1800** *Misc. Tr.* in *Asiat. Ann. Reg.* 343/1 Jackets, turbans, and handkerchiefs, marked with the *bubberee*, or tyger stripe...The tyger stripe was the royal mark, and was peculiar to Tippoo and his family. **1815** SCOTT *Guy M.* xxv, He had..ridden a-tiger-hunting upon an elephant with the Nabob of Arcot. **1848** tr. *Hoffmeister's Trav. Ceylon*, etc. vii. 244 We remained for several days, on account of a tiger-hunt. **1859** LANG *Wand. India* 358 He had enough of tiger-shooting in that one tiger. **1865** SIR T. SEATON *Fr. Cadet to Colonel* II. 26 There was no tiger-jungle within thirty miles of the spot. **1886** KIPLING *Departm. Ditties*, etc. (1899) 56 A pet tiger-cub in wreaths of rhubarb leaves, symbolical of India under medical treatment. **1895** *Daily News* 27 Nov. 6/3 At Shrovetide, 1509,..Princess Mary, afterwards Queen, wore a black mask as an Ethiopian queen, and a little jacket of tigerskin. **1906** *Macm. Mag.* Aug. 778 The spears showed that a tiger-drive was contemplated, for across each, some eighteen inches below the point, a little piece of wood was lashed on at right angles to the shaft.

**b.** passing into *adj.* 'tiger-like, tigerish', as *tiger despair, fury, joy, spasm, thirst*; (*b*) 'distinguished by or marked with the figure of a tiger (or tiger's head)', as *tiger gun, soldier.*

**1800** *Chron.* in *Asiat. Ann. Reg.* 150/1 Tippoo's Tiger grenadiers..are met by a party of the 73d regt. *Ibid.*, A severe conflict is maintained with the leader of the Tiger men by a serjeant of the Highlanders. **1827–39** DE QUINCEY *Murder* Wks. 1862 IV. 64 The impression of his natural tiger character. **1842** *Penny Cycl.* XXIV. 440/1 The tiger soldiers of Hyder Ali and Tippoo Saib were among the choicest of their troops. **1845** STOCQUELER *Handbk. Brit. India* (1854) 288 The arsenal, the gate of which is flanked by two of Tippoo's brass tiger guns, the muzzle representing the open mouth of that animal. **1856** MRS. H. O'B. CONANT *Eng. Bible* xix. (1881) 144 To foster..that tiger thirst for blood. **1885** TENNYSON *Anc. Sage* in *Tiresias*, etc. 61 The tiger spasms tear his chest. **1910** *Westm. Gaz.* 22 Mar. 5/2 The ideal Othello, played with a perfect mastery of all the modes of expressing tiger fury and tiger despair.

**c.** parasynthetic, instrumental, similative, etc., as *tiger-footed, -hearted, -looking, -marked, -passioned, -proof, -striped* adjs. See also TIGER-LIKE.

**1597** BEARD *Theatre God's Judgem.* (1612) 220 The poore old man thus cruelly handled..departed comfortlesse from his Tygre-minded sonne. **1607** SHAKS. *Cor.* III. i. 312 This Tiger-footed-rage..will (too late) Tye Leaden pounds too's heeles. **1616** R. NICCOLS *Overbury's Vision* in *Harl. Misc.* (Malh.) III. 350 Such monsters were my tyger-hearted foes. **1752** SIR J. HILL *Hist. Anim.* 153 The tyger-spotted Porcellana. **1796** CHARLOTTE SMITH *Marchmont* I. 205 This tiger-looking man..was..an Attorney. **1820** KEATS *Hyperion* II. 68 Now tiger-passion'd, lion-thoughted, wroth. **1835** J. DUNCAN *Beetles* (Nat. Libr.) 92 The tiger-marked boa, his tail fixed to the trunk of a tree,..lies in ambush on the bank. **1892** *Daily News* 7 June 5/4 Lofty and tiger-proof night shelters for travellers. **1896** *Ibid.* 13 July 7/2 Pansies, bronzed, tiger-striped, and deep purple.

**13.** Special combs.; chiefly names of animals and plants with tiger-like markings: †**tiger-babb** [? BOB *sb.*[1] 9], a parasite infesting the pear tree: = sense 5; **tiger-beetle**, any species of the family *Cicindelidæ*, characterized by variegated colouring, activity, and voracity; **tiger-bird**, (*a*) a South American scansorial barbet: = THICK-HEAD 2 b; (*b*) = *tiger-bittern*; **tiger-bittern**, a South American bittern of the genus *Tigrosoma*, with striped plumage; **tiger-chop**, a species of fig-marigold, *Mesembryanthemum tigrinum*, the toothed leaf of which suggests a 'chop' or jaw: cf. *cat-chop* (CAT *sb.*[1] 18); **tiger-civet**, a name for the LINSANG: see quot.; **tiger-cowrie**, a white cowrie, *Cypræa tigris*, with brown spots; **tiger-dog**, a dog resembling a tiger (cf. sense 2); *spec.* the spotted carriage-dog; **tiger-eye** = *tiger's-eye*: see b; **tiger-finch**, a name of the Amadavat, *Estrilda amandava*; **tiger-fish**, a large fresh-water fish of South-east Africa; **tiger-flower**, any plant or species of *Tigridia*, a genus of tropical American bulbous plants bearing large purple, yellow, or white spotted flowers; esp. *T. Pavonia* (also *Peacock* or *Mexican tiger-flower, tiger-iris, flower of Tigris*) with brilliant orange blooms; **tiger-foot** = *tiger's-foot* (see b); **tiger-frog**, the leopard-frog or shad-frog (*Rana halecina* or *virescens*) of N. America; **tiger-grass** (**palm**), a dwarf fan-palm, *Nannorhops* (*Chamærops*) *Ritchieana*, of Western India and Persia; **tiger-hound**: see quot., and cf. *tiger-dog*; **tiger-hunter**, one who hunts the tiger; also, a gambler (*U. S. slang*: cf. sense 9 a); **tiger-iris**, see *tiger-flower*; **tiger-lily**, a tall garden lily, *Lilium tigrinum*, with bell-like orange flowers marked with black or purplish spots; also called *tiger-spotted lily*; **tiger-mosquito**, any striped or banded mosquito of the genus *Stegomyia*; **tiger-moth**, a moth of the family *Arctiidæ*, esp. the British species *Arctia caja*, a large scarlet and brown moth spotted and streaked with white; **tiger-mouth** (also *tiger's-mouth*), a local name for the Snapdragon, Foxglove, and various species of Toad-flax; **tiger-nut**, the edible rhizome of *Cyperus esculentus*, used locally as food, and also medicinally; the rush-nut; **tiger-owl**, the tawny or brown owl; **tiger-party**, a tiger-shooting party; **tiger-python**, the Indian python; **tiger-salamander**, a name for the large western salamander, *Amblystoma tigrinum* (*Cent. Dict. Supp.* 1909); **tiger-shark**, a name for various voracious sharks, as *Galeocerdo maculatus* of warm seas, *Stegostoma tigrinum* of the Indian Ocean; in New Zealand, the Porbeagle, *Lamna cornubica*; **tiger-shell** = *tiger-cowrie*; **tiger-snake**, a venomous Australian snake, *Hoplocephalus curtus*, so called from its markings; in Tasmania also called *carpet-snake*; **tiger-spider**, a large American burrowing spider, *Lycosa tigrina*, the legs of which are ringed with grey and black; †**tiger-stone**: see quot.; **tiger-swallowtail**, a large North American butterfly, having yellow wings striped with black; the turnus; †**tiger-table**: see quot.; **tiger-ware**, an old English stoneware with a spotted glaze; **tiger-wolf**, (*a*) the Spotted Hyena (*Hyæna crocuta*); (*b*) = sense 2 c (*a*) (Ogilvie, 1882); **tiger-wood**, a streaked black and brown cabinet-maker's wood: = ITAKA-WOOD; also, a variety of citron-wood. See also TIGER-CAT.

**1693** EVELYN *De la Quint. Compl. Gard.* I. 81 The Persecution of the *Tyger-babbs [Fr. *tigres*] keeps the Pears too far off from the Assistance of Wall-trees. **1826** KIRBY & SP. *Entomol.* III. xxx. 152 That beautiful *tiger-beetle, the *Cicindela campestris* L., not uncommon on warm sunny banks. **1835** J. DUNCAN *Beetles* (Nat. Libr.) 115 The majority are variegated with spots and streaks of yellow. Their rapacity and agile movements have procured for them the name of Tiger-beetles. **1869** A. R. WALLACE *Malay Archip.* I. 409 One beautiful group of insects, the tiger-beetles. **1817** WATERTON *Wand. S. Amer.* II. (1825) 136 The small *Tiger-bird...The throat, and part of the head, are a bright red; the breast and belly have black spots on a yellow ground. **1879** J. G. WOOD *Explan. Index* ibid. (1882) 474 The Tiger-Bird utters its cry in the early morning and late in the evening. **1785** LATHAM *Gen. Synopsis* V. 63 *Tiger Bittern..the plumage deep rufous, marked with black, like the skin of a tiger..inhabits Cayenne, Surinam, and other parts of South America. **1894** LYDEKKER *Royal Nat. Hist.* I. 456 On account of their striking and handsome coloration, the name of *tiger-civets has been suggested for these animals [the Linsangs]. **1839** J. PYE SMITH *Script. & Geol.* 408 A well-known species is on almost every mantel-piece, the *tiger-cowry. **1682** CREECH *Lucretius* (1683) 90 The *Tyger-dog will flie pursuing Deer. **1883** R. GROOM *Gt. Dane* 8 The name Tiger Dog, as used in Germany, was applied to those specimens with patches and spots of black upon a white ground. **1891** *Cent. Dict.*, *Tiger-eye. **1896** CHESTER *Dict. Names Min.*, *Tiger-eye*, a popular name for a siliceous pseudomorph after crocidolite, in allusion to its yellow-brown colour and chatoyant lustre. **1900** *Feathered World* 28 Sept. 399 The common Avadavat is the *Tiger-finch... Brown and reddish copper, spotted with white. **1893** SELOUS *Trav. S. E. Africa* 303 Burnett..caught a fine *tiger-fish. **1894** *Sat. Rev.* 24 Nov. 563/1 In fly-fishing..the chief quarry, the 'tiger-fish', ran to 8½ lbs., and afforded nearly as good sport as salmon. **1797** *Encycl. Brit.* (ed. 3) XI. 671/2 A beautiful flower called the *tyger-flower, with three red pointed petals, the middle part mixed with white and yellow. **1845–50** MRS. LINCOLN *Lect. Bot.* 175 The Mexican tiger-flower, genus Tigridia, is a splendid plant of this order [*Iridaceæ*]. **1888** *Nicholson's Dict. Gard.*, *Tigridia*, Mexican Tiger Flower; Tiger Iris. This genus includes about seven species of..bulbous plants, from Mexico, Central America, Peru, and Chili... *T. pavonia*..Flower of Tigris; Peacock Tiger Flower. **1836** SMART, **Tiger-foot* (a plant). **1884** MILLER *Plant-n.*, Palm, *Tiger-grass, *Chamærops Ritchieana.* **1891** *Cent. Dict.*, *Tiger-grass*, a dwarf fan-palm, *Nannorhops Ritchieana*, of western India, extending into Persia. **1880** LEWIS & SHORT, *Tigris* II. 2, The name of the spotted *tiger-hound of Actæon. **1896** LILLARD *Poker Stories* iii. 87 The unsophisticated young *tiger hunter had something on his mind. **1824** MISS MITFORD *Village* Ser. I. (1863) 40 Those fierce and warlike flowers the *tiger-lilies. **1835** MARRYAT *Olla Podr.* v, No one can have an idea how hard the *tiger-musquito can bite. **1816** KIRBY & SP. *Entomol.* xxi. (1818) II. 226 The caterpillar of the great *tiger-moth (*Bombyx Caja*, F.). **1864–5** WOOD *Homes without H.* xiv. (1868) 286 The well known Tiger Moth whose scarlet, white, and brown robes are so familiar. **1886** BRITTEN & HOLLAND *Eng. Plant-n.*, **Tiger*, or *Tiger's Mouth.* **1887** MOLONEY *Forestry W. Afr.* 72 The *tiger nut, the tuber of the *Cyperus esculentus*, is well known in West Africa. **1864** TREVELYAN *Compet. Wallah* (1866) 133 An account of our *tiger-party in Nepaul. **1784–5** *Ann. Reg.* 241 The squalus or true *tyger shark,..well known to our seamen in the West Indies. **1898** MORRIS *Austral Eng.* s.v. *Shark*, Tiger Shark (N.S.W.), *Galeocerdo rayneri*... New Zealand...Tiger Shark, *Scymnus spinosus* (Maori name, *Mako*). **1753** CHAMBERS *Cycl. Supp.*, **Tiger-shell*, the English name of the red voluta, with large white spots. **1874** BEVERIDGE *Loot Life* 50 [He] eyed me as a *tiger snake The bull-frog or the fieldmouse eyes. **1890** *Science Gossip* XXVI. 37/2 The tiger-snake reaches the length of eight, or occasionally even ten feet. **1907** *Westm. Gaz.* 25 Sept. 12/1 The venom of the tiger-snake is fourteen times more deadly than that of the black snake. **1829** *Glover's Hist. Derby* I. 94 Fluor with barytes, commonly called *tiger-stone, being opaque, and full of dirty brown spots. **1601** HOLLAND *Pliny* (1634) I. 395 The wood curleth in and out along the graine, and therefore such bee named Tigrinæ (*i.* *Tigre-tables).

**1731** MEDLEY *Kolben's Cape G. Hope* II. 108 The Lion, Tiger, and Leopard are bitter enemies to the *Tiger-Wolf. **1838** *Penny Cycl.* XII. 369/1 The Spotted Hyæna, or Tiger-Wolf of the [South African] colonists. **1858** SIMMONDS *Dict. Trade*, *Tiger-wood, a valuable wood for cabinet making,.. obtained in Guiana. **1866** [see ITAKA-WOOD].

**b.** Combs. with *tiger's*: **tiger's-claw**, (*a*) a weapon for secret attack used by the Mahrattas, consisting of short sharp curved steel blades fixed to a plate or strap which is secured to the palm of the hand; (*b*) in *Mech.* a boring or rifling rod in which the cutting tool is automatically sheathed as it enters the bore and expands on the cutting stroke; **tiger's-eye**, popular name for (*a*) a yellowish brown quartz with brilliant lustre, used as a gem (also called *tiger-eye*): see CROCIDOLITE; (*b*) a crystalline pottery glaze, with auriferous reflections (*U. S.*); **tiger's-foot**, a convolvulaceous plant, *Ipomœa Pes-tigridis*, common in India, with hairy palmate leaves; **tiger's horn, tiger's tooth**, old names for species of *Strombus* or wing-shell; **tiger's milk**, (*a*) the acrid white juice of *Excœcaria Agallocha*, a small euphorbiaceous East Indian tree; (*b*) gin (*slang*); **tiger's mouth** = *tiger-mouth* (see 13).

**1891** *Cent. Dict.*, *Tiger's claw, *Tiger's-eye. **1896** CHESTER *Dict. Names Min.*, *Tiger's eye*, same as tiger-eye. **1893** E. A. BARBER *Pottery & Porcelain U. S.* xiii. 290 The highest achievements in glazing are the so-called tiger's-eye and gold-stone, which glisten in the light with a beautiful auriferous sheen. **1828–32** WEBSTER, *Tiger's-foot (citing LEE). **1713** PETIVER *Aquat. Anim. Amboinæ* Tab. iv, *Strombus*.. Brown *Tygers Horn. **1850** R. G. CUMMING *Hunter's Life S. Afr.* (1902) 9/1 A fountain of *tiger's milk had started in the stern of the waggon. **1886** *Tiger's Mouth [see *tiger-mouth* in 13]. **1713** PETIVER *Aquat. Anim. Amboinæ* Tab. v, *Strombus*.. Thick *Tygers-tooth.

Hence (*nonce-wds.*) **Ti·ger** *v. intr.*, to act, behave, or walk to and fro, like a tiger; † **Tigera·ntic** *a.* [? after *elephantic*] = TIGERISH 1; **Tigere·tte**, a diminutive she-tiger, a 'cat'; **Ti·gerling**, a young or diminutive tiger; **Tigero·cious** *a.* [*nonce-wd.* after *ferocious*], = TIGERISH 1.

*a* **1704** T. BROWN *Lett. fr. Dead* Wks. 1720 II. 216 In what Sheeps-head Ordinary have you chew'd away the meridian Altitude of your Tygerantick Stomach? **1858** MRS. GORE *Heckington* xxxi, Miss Corbet, on whom the tamed tigerling [a small boy] was now lavishing his endearments. **1874** F. W. NEWMAN in Davies *Heterodox Lond.* II. 311 He is dietetically, neither swinish nor tigerocious. **1898** MÉNIE M. DOWIE *Crook of Bough* 52 He finished his cigar by tigering on the platform, his hands behind him, his head turning from side to side. **1906** *Daily Chron.* 23 Aug. 5/7 Amongst the tigeresses who devour, and the tigerettes who scheme, you will not find a woman who can claim to have passed through a public school and university training.

**Ti·ger-ca:t.** A name for any of the feline beasts of moderate or small size which resemble the tiger in their markings or otherwise; including the Margay, Ocelot, Serval, etc. (In Zool. Society's *List* applied to two species: see quot. 1896.)

**1699** DAMPIER *Voy.* II. II. 62 The Beasts of Prey that are bred in this Country are Tigre-Cats, and .. Lions. The Tigre-Cat is about the bigness of a Bull-Dog. **1774** GOLDSM. *Nat. Hist.* III. vii. 255 Descending to animals .. still smaller, we find the Catamountain, which is the Ocelot of Mr. Buffon, or the Tiger Cat of most of those who exhibit it as a show. **1785** G. FORSTER tr. *Sparrman's Voy. Cape G. H.* (1786) II. 80 An opportunity of seeing an amorous combat between two tiger-cats. **1842** *Penny Cycl.* XXIV. 440/2 Tiger-Cats. Under this title may be classed all those lesser striped and spotted Asiatic, African, and American Cats which do not come under the well-understood denominations of Tigers, Leopards, and Panthers. **1871** KINGSLEY *At Last* xi, No jaguar or tiger-cat .. would care to meddle with anything so exquisitely nasty. **1896** *List Anim. Zool. Soc.* 58 *Felis planiceps*.., Rusty Tiger Cat. *Hab.* Malacca. ..*Felis chrysothrix*.., Red Tiger Cat. *Hab.* Gold Coast, West Africa. **1907** *Daily Chron.* 19 Feb. 7/4 The dusky African tiger cat, a new animal about the size of a leopard.

**b.** In Australasia applied to two carnivorous marsupials, *Dasyurus viverrinus* and *D. maculatus*.

**1832** J. BISCHOFF *Van Diemen's Land* ii. 52 The skins of the .. opossum, tiger-cat, and platypus .. are exported. **1852** R. C. GUNN *Papers & Proc. Roy. Soc. Van Diemen's L.* II. 11 (Morris) *Dasyurus maculatus* .. the Spotted Martin...'Tiger Cat' of the Colonists of Tasmania,.. distinguished from *D. viverrinus*, the 'Native Cat' of the Colonists, by its superior size.

**c.** Applied to a hybrid between the domestic cat and the wild cat (*F. catus*) (*Cent. Dict.* 1891).

**Tigerhood** (təi·gəɹhud). [f. TIGER + -HOOD.] The state or condition of being a tiger (in any sense); in quot. 1846, the post of boy-groom (see TIGER 6).

**1846** MRS. GORE *Eng. Char.* (1852) 118 Advantages attached to the tigerhood of his establishment. **1871** BLACKIE *Four Phases* i. 34 The true humanity of man as distinguished from tigerhood and spiderhood. **1885** HORNADAY *2 Yrs. in Jungle* xiv. 159 A splendid specimen every way, just in the prime of tiger-hood.

**Tigerine**, variant of TIGRINE.

**Tigerish** (təi·gəriʃ), *a.* Also 6–7 **tygrish**, 6, 9 **tigrish.** [f. TIGER *sb.* + -ISH [1].]

**1.** Like, or like that of, a tiger; *esp.* of the nature or having the qualities of the tiger; cruel, bloodthirsty, fierce, relentless.

**1573** L. LLOYD *Marrow of Hist.* (1653) 265 Her cruel and Tigrish heart. *a* **1586** SIDNEY *Arcadia* (1622) 467 Were thy eyes so stonie, thy breast so tygrish? **1604** EARL STIRLING *Aurora* xci, And with my ashes glut thy Tygrish heart. **1846** *Blackw. Mag.* LIX. 406 [Their] craving for possession is treacherous and tigerish. **1887** MISS E. MONEY *Lit. Dutch Maid.* (1888) 95 A wild-cat skin with handsome tigerish stripes. **1909** *Daily Chron.* 18 Feb. 7/4 There are many predatory and tigerish plants, of which the sundew is a notable example.

**b.** Loud, flashy: cf. TIGER *sb.* 7.

**1831** [see 3]. **1836** *New Monthly Mag.* XLVIII. 458 Whatever deviates from the unique standard of gentlemen's dressing is tigerish. **1853** LYTTON *My Novel* VI. xx, Nothing could be more vagrant,..and, to use a slang word, *tigrish*, than his whole air.

**2.** Abounding in or infested with tigers.

**1819** *Sporting Mag.* IV. 175 They had crossed again Firoze's canal, which appeared very tigerish. **1851** *Fraser's Mag.* XLIV. 19 Through the thickest and most tigerish section of the jungle.

**3.** *Comb.*, as *tigerish-looking*.

**1831** *Society* I. 48 A tigerish looking man planted himself where he could very rudely stare at Miss Delamere.

Hence **Ti·gerishly** *adv.*, **Ti·gerishness.**

**1869** *Daily News* 12 June, A well-known plunger, whose attendant tiger is a miracle of tigerishness. **1879** J. TODHUNTER *Alcestis* 125 This sudden flood of fearful rapture, which Tugs my heart tigerishly.

**Tigerism** (təi·gəriz'm). [f. TIGER *sb.* + -ISM.]

**1.** The qualities or characteristics of a 'tiger' (TIGER *sb.* 7); vulgar ostentation or affectation; pretentiousness, 'side', 'swagger'. ? *Obs.*

**1836** *New Monthly Mag.* XLVIII. 455 We have the neologismal appellatives, 'tiger', and 'tigerism',—words of great intensity and signification, without which it would be impossible to get on for 'one calendar day' in genteel society. **1863** R. H. GRONOW *Remin.* II. 144 All his imitators fell between the Scylla and Charybdis of tigerism and charlatanism. **1868** LEVER *Bramleighs* I. x. 137 His lordship now placed his hat on his head, slightly on one side. It was the 'tigerism' of a past period.

**2.** The condition and functions of a 'tiger' or juvenile groom (TIGER *sb.* 6).

**1846** MRS. GORE *Eng. Char.* (1852) 117 The nature and attributes of tigerism, however, as set forth by the gallant captain, were far from unsatisfactory.

**Tigerkin** (təi·gəɹkin). [f. as prec. + -KIN.] A diminutive tiger; a tiger-cub; also, a cat.

**1849** LYTTON *Caxtons* XIV. ii, It is only from the attic that you can appreciate the picturesque which belongs to our domesticated tigerkin! **1867** *Lond. Rev.* 26 Jan. 116/2 The tigerkin whose claws are not grown and whose habits are ..playful.

**Ti·ger-like,** *adj.* and *adv.* [f. as prec. + -LIKE.]

**A.** *adj.* Like, or like that of, a tiger; tigerish.

**1577–87** HOLINSHED *Chron.* I. 126/1 Which is more than tigerlike crueltie. **1828** SEWELL *Oxf. Prize Ess.* 40 Tyger-like thirst for blood. **1905** *Westm. Gaz.* 28 Jan. 4/2 In colour and markings the wild cat is very tiger-like.

**B.** *adv.* In a tigerish manner.

**1576** GASCOIGNE *Philomene* cxxxi. (Arb.) 107 (Tygrelike) she toke The litle boy. **1587** TURBERV. *Trag. T.* (1837) 67 The tyrants mother Calvia, tygreleeke, Procurde her plagues. **1850** R. G. CUMMING *Hunter's Life S. Afr.* (1902) 142/2 My eye fixed tiger-like upon him.

**Tigerly** (tai·gəɹli), *a. rare.* [f. as prec. + -LY [1].] Tiger-like, tigerish.

**1633** D. DYKE in Spurgeon *Treas. Dav.* Ps. xciv. 12 Tigerly and tyrannical persecutors. **1648** *King's Gracious Messages for Peace* 39 They are not ashamed..to appropriate unto him their own Tigerly dispositions. **1855** *Chamb. Jrnl.* IV. 289 You might mollify the heart of the most tigerly disposed of the human race.

So † **Ti·gerness** *Obs.*, tigerishness, ferocity.

**1535** STEWART *Cron. Scot.* (Rolls) I. 91 He changit syne.. To tigirnes and greit tiranitie.

† **Ti·gerous,** *a. Obs. rare.* Also 6 **tigrous.** [f. as prec. + -OUS.] = TIGERISH. Hence † **Ti·gerously** *adv. Obs. rare*$^{-1}$.

**1532** W. WALTER tr. *Guistard & Sisimond* (1597) B ij, Yet thought her not soe tigrous and cruell. **1698** [R. FERGUSSON] *View Eccles.* 117 He hath Tygerously fallen upon the Dead and Endeavoured to Blacken their Memory.

**Tigery** (təi·gəri), *a. rare*$^{-1}$. [f. as prec. + -Y.] Tigerish, tiger-like.

**1859** *All Year Round* No. 36. 218 The Tchirgee..is of a choleric and rather tigery nature.

**Tigger** (ti·gəɹ). [f. TIG *v.*[1] + -ER [1].] One who 'tigs' or touches; the pursuer in the game of 'tig'.

**1893** E. L. WAKEMAN in *Columbus* (Ohio) *Dispatch* 19 Oct., This impedes the tigger's running.

**Tigh, tighe, tiȝe,** obs. forms of TYE, TIE *sb.*

**Tigh-hee, tighie,** obs. forms of TEHEE.

† **Tight, tyht,** *sb.*[1] *Obs.* Forms: 1–4 **tyht** (1 **tiht**), 3 **tuht** (*u*). [OE. *tyht* m. (with change of gender) = OS. *tuht* (MLG., MDu., LG., Du. *tucht*), OHG., MHG. *zuht* (G. *zucht*), Goth. **tauhts* in *ustauhts* completion :—OTeut. **tuhti*[2] fem., f. **tuh*, weak grade of verb-stem **teuh* (see TEE *v.*[1], and -T *suffix* [3] a).]

**1.** The action of drawing, draught; going, marching, march, course, way. Only OE.

*a* **800** CYNEWULF *Elene* 53 Werod wæs on tyhte. *a* **850** *Phœnix* 525 Fyr bið on tihte, æleð uncyste.

**2.** Bringing up, rearing, training, education; (good) breeding; behaviour.

*c* **888** K. ÆLFRED *Boeth.* viii, Ic ðe ȝeongne..me to bearne ȝenom, & to minum tyhtum ȝetyde...Þu me wære..leof.. ær þon þe ðu cuðe minne tyht & mine þeawas. *a* **1240** *Sawles Warde* in *Cott. Hom.* 247 For þat is þeaw in euch stude ant tuht forte halden. *c* **1330** R. BRUNNE *Chron. Wace* (Rolls) 9307 What for laughynge & oþer tyhtes, What for presentes & oþer delites [*v.r.* sightes], Þe Erl perceyued.. Þe kyng [Uther] louede his wyf Igerne.

**Tight,** *sb.*[2]: see TIGHT *a.* 13; also TIGHTS.

**Tight** (təit), *a.* (*adv.*) Forms: 5–6 **tyght**, 6– *Sc.* **ticht, tycht**, 5– **tight** (also *erron.* 7–8 **tite, tyte**). [App. an altered form of THIGHT, with which in its early literal senses it was synonymous. *Tonne-tight* and *tonne-thight* occur together in *Rolls of Parlt.* 1379: see sense 14. The change from *thight* to *tight* was perh. due to the influence of native words from the **teuh-*, **tauh-*, **tuh-* verbal system: see TEE *v.*[1], and cf. TAUT *a.*, TIGHT *v.*[1], and *ticht* pa. pple. of TIE *v.*]

† **1.** Dense, as a wood or thicket; = THIGHT 1; superseded by *thick* (THICK *a.* 4). *Obs. rare*$^{-1}$.

*c* **1435** *Torr. Portugal* 589 Hys squyer Rod all nyght In a wod, that wase full tyght.

† **b.** Close or compact in texture or consistency, as a solid body or substance; dense, solid; = THIGHT 3. *Obs. rare.*

**1513** DOUGLAS *Æneis* IX. ii. 64 The wyld wolf..Abowt the bowght, plet all of wandis tyght, Bayis and gyrnis. **1677** GREW *Anat. Fruits* v. § 18 The Outer Part..is softer and more succulent; the Inner a tite and strong Membrane. *a* **1728** [implied in TIGHTNESS 1]. **1797** *Encycl. Brit.* (ed. 3) XVII. 424/1 Construct a block of as tight wood as possible.

**2.** Of such close texture or construction as to be impervious to a fluid, etc. **a.** as the second element in combinations, as *water-, wind-, air-, gas-, oil-, light-tight*, the first element denoting that which the vessel keeps in or out.

**1507** *Rec. St. Mary at Hill* 23 Yat they .. yᵉ said tenement..shall kepe, repaire and mayntene, wynd tyght, water tyght. **1760** [see AIR-TIGHT]. **1831** Gas-tight [see GAS *sb.* 6]. **1896** *Pop. Sci. Jrnl.* L. 267 The human mind is not built in thought-tight compartments. **1905** *Westm. Gaz.* 11 Mar. 14/2 Untoned prints should be kept under close pressure in a light-tight and air-tight box.

**b.** as simple word.

(See also *tight barrel, cask, cooper*, etc. in C. 3.)

[**1501**: see THIGHT 4.] **1661** [see d]. **1669** BOYLE *Contn. New Exp.* I. xxxvii, The Nose of a pair of Bellows that are Tite enough is well stopt. **1749** BERKELEY *Word to Wise* Wks. III. 443 A tight house, warm apparel, and wholesome food. **1856** OLMSTED *Slave States* 2, I have faith that there is a tight roof above the very much cracked ceiling. **1857** MILLER *Elem. Chem.* (1862) III. 144 A portion of bread was enclosed in a tight case, to prevent loss of water by evaporation.

**c.** *esp.* Of a ship: Water-tight; well caulked and pitched; not leaky. Cf. THIGHT 4.

**1568** *Satir. Poems Reform.* xlvi. 4 Quhat pylett takis my schip in chairge, Mon hald hir clynlie, trym, and ticht. **1596** SHAKS. *Tam. Shr.* II. i. 381 Two Galliasses And twelue tite Gallies. **1615** BP. HALL *Contempl.*, *O. T.* XI. iii, As some tight vessel that holds out against wind and water, so did Ruth against all the powers of a mother's persuasions. **1704** J. HARRIS *Lex. Techn.* I, *Tite*, the Seamen say a Ship is Tight, or Tite, when she is so staunch as to let in but very little Water. **1747** *Gentl. Mag.* 170 The pitch being put in very hot will..make the ship as tight as a bottle. *a* **1826** A. CUNNINGHAM *Wet Sheet & Flowing Sea* ii, The good ship tight and free.

**d.** *transf.* and *fig.* leading to 3.

**1661** FELTHAM *Resolves* II. xxix. 240 They are not tyte enough to trust with a secret. **1730** in J. Copywell *Shrubs Parnassus* (1760) 130 Old Chaucer and Drayton I found in good plight, And Shakespear and Spencer appear pretty tight. **17..** C. DIBDIN *Song, The Island* i, O, 'tis a snug little island! A right little, tight little island! **1809** MALKIN *Gil Blas* VII. i. ¶ 5 He is a tight vessel, well armed and manned. **1817** COBBETT *Wks.* VI. 31 A Sinecure, which you have secured for your Son,..who is (if all remains tight) to enjoy it for his life after your death. **1865** DICKENS *Mut. Fr.* I. viii, Mr. Boffin's notions of a tight will.

**3.** *fig.* of a person, expressing somewhat indefinite commendation: Competent, capable, able, skilful; alert, smart; lively, vigorous, stout; also in ironical use: cf. FINE *a.* 12 c. *Obs.* exc. *dial.*

**1598** [implied in TIGHTLY 1]. **1606** SHAKS. *Ant. & Cl.* IV. iv. 16 Thou fumblest Eros, and my Queenes a Squire More tight at this then thou. **1653** R. BAILLIE *Dissuas. Vind.* (1655) Pref., That reverent, famous, most able, and tight writer. **1735** BRACKEN *Burdon's Pocket Farrier* 81 *note*, The less Physick the better, provided your Judgment's tite. **1822** SCOTT *Pirate* xl, He..swore..that if he had a thousand daughters, so tight a lad, and so true a friend, should have the choice of them. *a* **1825** FORBY *Voc. E. Anglia*, *Tight*,..prompt; active; alert. 'A tight fellow!' **1829** MARRYAT *F. Mildmay* ii, I'll pay you off for this, my tight fellow. **1851** HAWTHORNE *Ho. Sev. Gables* xiii, It will take a tighter workman than I am to keep the spirits out of the seven gables. **1891** WRENCH *Winchester Word-bk.*, *Tight*, fast, hard. A tight bowler, etc.

**4.** Neat in appearance; neatly and carefully dressed; trim, tidy, smart; also, Of a neat compact build, well-made, shapely. *arch.* or *dial.* Cf. TAUT *a.* 2 b.

**1697** DAMPIER *Voy. round World* (1699) 11 They wear good Cloaths, and take delight to go neat and tight. **1706–7** FARQUHAR *Beaux Strat.* I. i, But you look so bright, And are dress'd so tight. **1712** ARBUTHNOT *John Bull* III. ii, Though the girl was a tight clever wench, as any was. **1721** RAMSAY *Bessy Bell*, etc. iii, She blooming, tight, and tall is. **1821** SCOTT *Kenilw.* iii, There thou stand'st in thy velvet waistcoat, as tight a girl as England's sun shines on. *c* **1830** MRS. SHERWOOD *Houlston Tracts* III. No. 81. 2, I was tight and smart in my own person; so that, as the neighbours used to say, every thing looked well upon me. **1886** M. K.

MACMILLAN *Dagonet the Jester* 8 The tightest and cleanliest lads in the village.

**b.** Of things: Neatly arranged or constructed; tidy, neat, snug, compact. Now *dial.*

**1720** RAMSAY *Edinburgh's Salut.* v, Than I, nor Paris, nor Madrid, Nor Rome, I trow's mair able To busk you up a better bed, Or trim a tighter table. **1725** T. THOMAS in *Portland Papers* VI. (Hist. MSS. Comm.) 126 Improved grounds..with tight, low, new farm houses. *c* **1813** MRS. SHERWOOD *Stories Ch. Catech.* xvi. 139 Sarah was contented with the coarsest gown..if it were but clean and tight. **1831** J. OGILVIE in *Aberdeen Mag.* Dec. 638 His wordy wife ..Hauds a' thing tight about the house.

**5.** Firmly fixed or bound in its place; strongly attached or secured; not easily moved; also *fig.* faithful, steadfast, constant.

**1513** DOUGLAS *Æneis* III. viii. 52 Our fallowis fangis in thair salis tycht [*Vela legunt socii*]. **1687** A. LOVELL tr. *Thevenot's Trav.* I. 23 To gird it about with great bars of Iron to keep it tight, and hinder it from falling. **1690** C. NESSE *O. & N. Test.* I. 153 His faith..kept him all along tight, steady and constant. **1715** DESAGULIERS *Fires Impr.* 129 You may fix it without any trouble, and be sure that it is tight. **1902** MABEL BARNES-GRUNDY *Thames Camp* 202, I pulled and strained, but it was as tight as wax.

**6.** Drawn or stretched so as to be tense; not loose or slack: said of a rope, etc., or of a surface; = TAUT *a.* I, 2.

**1576** FLEMING *Panopl. Epist.* 256 (Like vnto a bowe) sometimes bent very tight, and sometimes againe made slack for the nones. **1589** PEELE *Tale Troy* 256 Away they flye, their tackling teft [*ed.* 1604 toft] and tight. **1703** DAMPIER *Voy.* III. 19 When the Rope is hal'd tight. **1800** COLERIDGE *Christabel* II. 49 That (so it seem'd) her girded vests Grew tight beneath her heaving breasts. **1846** BRITTAN tr. *Malgaigne's Man. Oper. Surg.* 39 The knots ought to be tight enough to hold in apposition the edges of the wound; but not so tight as to cut the skin when the inflammation comes on, and the parts swell. **1857** HUGHES *Tom Brown* I. iv, Tom has eaten..and imbibed coffee, till his little skin is as tight as a drum. **1885** *Law Rep.* 15 Q. B. Div. 360 The belt..was passed over the drums..and drawn tight.

**b.** *fig.* Strict, stringent; severe.

**1872** BAGEHOT *Physics & Pol.* (1876) 37 The efficacy of the tight early polity and the strict early law. **1884** STORRS *Div. Orig. Chr.* v. 152 The larger moral power won by woman, by degrees made the tightest legal restrictions loose and elastic. **1887** *Poor Nellie* (1888) 294 Every boy wants a good tight hand over him.

**7.** Drunk; tipsy. Cf. SCREWED *ppl. a.* 6. *slang.*

**1853** *Household Words* 24 Sept. 75/2 For the one word drunk, besides the authorised synonyms tipsy, inebriated, intoxicated, I find of unauthorised or slang equivalents.. thirty-two, viz.: in liquor,.. half-seas-over, far-gone, tight [etc.]. **1860** LEVER *One of Them* II. 151 (Flügel) He was very 'tight', as we call it..far gone in liquor, I mean. **1868** — *Bramleighs* xxiv. II. 46 'No, sir, not a bit tipsy', said Harding, interpreting his glance; 'not even what Mr. Cutbill calls "tight"!' **1882** SALA *Amer. Revis.* (1885) 269 By the time they reached their hotel [they] were quite 'tight'.

**8.** Of a garment, etc.: Fitting closely, tight-fitting; often = *too tight*, closely fitting because not large enough. *A tight fit*, a garment, etc. which fits tightly; hence *transf.* (*colloq.*).

**1779** COOK *Voy. Pacific* VI. vii. (1784) III. 377 A pair of tight trowsers, or long breeches, of leather. **1831** *Examiner* 11/2 It's rather a tight fit. **1840** DICKENS *Barn. Rudge* vi, A very particular gentleman with exceedingly tight boots on. **1867** TROLLOPE *Chron. Barset* xxxv, A wedding-ring growing always tighter as I grow fatter and older. **1872** *Punch* 15 June 250/2 A tight uniform is so bad a thing for the soldier.

**9.** Difficult to deal with or manage; hard, severe, 'tough', 'stiff'; esp. in phr. *a tight place, corner, squeeze*, etc., a position of difficulty. *colloq.*

**1764** FOOTE *Mayor of G.* II. Wks. 1799 I. 180 Is Lady Barbara's work pretty tight? **1772** NUGENT tr. *Hist. Fr. Gerund* I. 10 This question of yours is a tight one. **1852** TOWNSHEND (of Ohio) in *House Repr.* 23 June (Thornton), I felt myself in a tight spot. **1855** HALIBURTON *Nat. & Hum. Nat.* xvi. II. 121 It's a tight squeeze sometimes to scrouge between a lie and a truth in business. **1864** *Daily Tel.* 26 Sept., When they find they are getting into a tight place—to borrow an Americanism—[they] gather up their gold, and run off. **1889** GRETTON *Memory's Harkb.* 80 We were subjected to a very tight examination; for the prize was one of considerable value. **1891** *Daily News* 14 Nov. 2/3 [It] would suffice to drive the Bears of Russian stock into a tight corner.

**10.** *colloq.* or *techn.* **a.** Said of a contest in which the combatants are evenly matched; close; so of a bargain: with little margin of profit. *orig. U. S.*

**1828** WEBSTER s. v., A tight bargain. **1848** BARTLETT *Dict. Amer.*, *Tight match*, a close or even match, as of two persons wrestling or running together. **1903** *Westm. Gaz.* 1 Sept. 3/1 The tighter the match the better he plays.

**b.** Of a person: Unwilling to part with money, close-fisted; **c.** *Finance*, Of money: Difficult to obtain except on high terms; also *transf.* of the money-market when money is scarce.

**1828** WEBSTER s. v., A man tight in his dealings. **1846–7** MRS. WHITCHER *Widow Bedott Papers* 30 (Bartlett) The Deacon was as tight as the skin on his back; begrudged folk their victuals when they came to his house. **1846** *Daily News* 21 Jan. 4/6 In Paris money is 'tight' also, and discounts difficult. **1866** CRUMP *Banking* vii. 152 A tight money market will force sales, and make purchasers.. reluctant to buy. **1868** LEVER *Bramleighs* xvi. I. 219 Money was 'tight' being the text of all he said.

**11. a.** Closely packed. Cf. TIGHTEN *v.* I b.

**1856** KANE *Arct. Expl.* I. xxiv. 313 For thirty-five miles south the straits are absolutely tight [i. e. with ice].

**b.** Of language: Terse, concise, condensed.

**1870** SWINBURNE *Ess. & Stud.* (1875) 85 The highest form of ballad..must condense the large loose fluency of romantic tale-telling into tight and intense brevity.

**c.** *Art slang.* Lacking freedom or breadth of treatment; cramped.

**1891** SPIELMAN in *Contemp. Rev.* July 60 It [Tenniel's art in 1850] is certainly 'tighter': it is younger. **1902** *Encycl. Brit.* XXVII. 252/1 In his first style [Corot] painted traditionally and 'tight'—that is to say, with minute exactness, clear outlines, and with absolute definition of objects throughout. **1905** *Q. Rev.* July 234 His style, if a little what artists call 'tight', has the rare gift of being entirely lucid in the expression of subtleties.

**d.** Of the edge of a saw: Compressed by hammering (*Cent. Dict.* 1891).

**12.** *Billiards. slang.* (*a*) Said of balls when they are in contact: 'fast', 'frozen'. (*b*) Of pockets: Having a small opening compared with the diameter of the balls.

**1909** in *Cent. Dict. Supp.*

**13.** The adjective used absolutely. (See also TIGHTS.) *Rugby Football* = SCRIMMAGE *sb.* 4. *rare.*

**1904** *Westm. Gaz.* 19 Nov. 15/1 The forwards are strong and hard workers in the tight, but in the loose are slow and cumbersome... Both in the tight and loose they must remember to watch and follow the ball. **1905** *Daily Chron.* 1 Nov. 9/5 They have shown little dash in the open and no skill in the tight.

†**14.** Formerly (14th–17th c.) appended to *ton, pipe, hogshead, dolium*, as measures of capacity, originally and especially in stating the number of tons burden (*i. e.* the tonnage) of a ship; also as an equivalent weight of stones, gravel, salt, etc. See also TON, TONNAGE, TUN.

[**1894** C. N. ROBINSON *Brit. Fleet* 217 The unit of ship measurement, both in England and on the continent, at the time [of Henry VII], was, as heretofore, the tun cask of wine, and the stated tons or tuns burthen of a ship meant the number of tuns or butts of wine she could carry. Warships' tonnage was estimated by roughly comparing their bulk with merchant-ships of known carrying capacity.]

**1379** *Rolls of Parlt.* III. 63/2 Pur prendre de chescun nief & craier, de quele portage q'il soit, qe passe par la mier dedeinz le dite Admiralte alant & retournant, par le voiage de chescun tonne-tight vj d... Item, de prendre de chescun vesseau pessoner, qe pessent sur la mier du dit Admiralte entour Harang, de quele portage q'il soit, en un simaigne de chescun tonne-tight, VI d..en troiz simaignes de chescun tonne-thight, VI d. **1410** in *Proc. Privy Council* (1834) I. 327 La somme des gages & regardz des gens darmes archers conestables & marins deinz especifiez, ovesque le tonnetyght samontent par un q^art^..viij^ml^ ccxlj. li. xviij. s. vjd. **1427–9** *Rolls of Parlt.* IV. 365/1 To have Lettres Patentz..for to take and resceyve of every Vessell ladon of..C tonnetite VIII d, and of every Vessell of lesse tite IIII d. *Ibid.* [French version], P[re]ndre & avoir de chacun Nief del portage de.. C tonelx..VIII d., & de chacun autre Vessell de meyndre portage..IIII d. **1428–9** *Rec. St. Mary at Hill* 70 For a tonne tyght of northerin ston for þe new chirche porche.. vijs viijd. *a* **1483** *Liber Niger* in *Househ. Ord.* (1790) 74 The kinge hathe it intytled by his prerogative to have of every shippe from xx dol' tyght before the mast & behynd to have ii dol' wyne; and soe of every shippe tyll he come to the tyght of ccc dol'; then the kinge hath before and behynd of every such shippe iiii dol' wyne. **1495** *Naval Accts Hen. VII* (1896) 154 Payed..for ccccixviij ton tyght of..Stones vij*li.* xvjs. As for c iiij^xx^vj ton tyght of gravell xxiiijs. vj*d.* **1497** *Ibid.* 186 For the hyre of hys bote conteynyng vij Tonne Tight. *Ibid.* 228 A pipe Tyghte yron price xl*s.* &..for a hoggeshed Tyghte yron price—xx*s.* *a* **1500** in Arnolde *Chron.* (1811) 127 A crane sufficient and able to take vp from the water of the Thamis the weight of a tonne tight. **1504** *Sel. Cas. Crt. Star Chamber* (Selden) 212 Of & for eny ton or ton tyght of marchaundis conteigned in the same vesselles..vj d. **1603** OWEN *Pembrokeshire* (1892) 139 In bargayninge by the toone yt requireth that yt be expressed what number of barrells the toonne shalbe of, ffor of late yeares..toonne tight, wh^ch^ comonly is vsed in bargaynes of freight, differreth from the toonne by measure both of corne and salte.

**B.** *adv.* (The adj. used adverbially.)

**1.** Soundly, roundly; = TIGHTLY I. Now *dial.* and *U. S.*

**1790** J. FISHER *Poems* 61, I charg'd them tight, An' gart them pay o' lawing clink, Mair than was right. **1898** *Elizabeth & German Garden* 29 She had been so tight asleep.

**2.** Firmly, closely, securely; so as not to allow any movement: = TIGHTLY 3.

**1680** MOXON *Mech. Exerc.* xii. 208 You may without more ado screw up your Work tight. **1768** TUCKER *Lt. Nat.* (1834) I. 194 The prospect of getting a livelihood holds them tight to their work. **1838** DICKENS *Nich. Nick.* liii, Holding tight on with both hands. **1878** T. L. CUYLER *Pointed Papers* 206 The tighter I clung the safer I felt.

**b.** *To sit tight*, † to apply oneself closely *to* (*obs.*); to maintain one's position firmly in reference to something; also, to sit close, to remain under cover. *colloq.*

**1738** *Lond. Mag.* 131 Andromache and all the great Ladies 3000 Years ago, sat very tight to their Stitching. **1897** VIOLET HUNT *Unkist, Unkind* xiv, 'Sit tight!' she exclaimed, pinching my arm violently. She always talks slang when she is excited. **1898** *Daily News* 10 Feb. 3/2 No money is forthcoming, and banks sit tight. **1909** *Athenæum* 20 Mar. 345/3 Is not 'Sit tight' the watchword of constitutionalism?

**3.** With close constriction or pressure; closely, tensely; = TIGHTLY 2.

**1818** SCOTT *Rob Roy* xxxii, A horse-girth buckled tight behind him. **1853** LANDOR *Imag. Conv., Hare & L.* Wks. 1891 IV. 423 He whose dress sits tight upon him.

**C.** Combinations.

**1.** Adjectival, as *tight-belted* (having a tight belt), *-bodied, -booted, -hosed, -limbed, -lipped, -skinned, -skirted, -sleeved, -waisted* adjs. (Sometimes not clearly distinguishable from next.)

**1767** S. PATERSON *Another Trav.* I. 315 Their habit is entirely white..and being tight-bodied, gives them the appearance of a company of millers in their holiday-cloaths. **1836** T. HOOK *G. Gurney* v, Perhaps a tight-skinned sailor walking his way to town from Portsmouth. **1859** G. MEREDITH *R. Feverel* ii, The boy was..not so tight-limbed and well-set. **1876** MISS BRADDON *J. Haggard's Dau.* II. 47 How would that tight-waisted, tight-lipped damsel get on with a lovely young wife. **1896** HOWELLS *Impressions & Exp.* 73 She wore a tight-skirted black walking-dress. **1896** EDITH THOMPSON in *Monthly Packet* Christmas No. 80 Tight-booted and tight-belted in correct Continental military style.

**2.** Adverbial, as *tight-bound* (= tightly bound), *-closed, -draped, -drawn, -fitting, -looking, -made, -packed, -pressed, -rooted, -shut, -stretched* adjs.; *tight-reining* sb.; *tight-clasp, -tie* verbs. See also TIGHT-LACED, etc.

**1801** MAR. EDGEWORTH *Angelina* ii, She was hospitably received by a tight-looking woman. **1819** KEATS *Ode Melancholy* i, Go not to Lethe, neither twist Wolf's bane, tight-rooted, for its poisonous wine. **1832** *Scoreby Farm Rep.* 8 in *Libr. Usef. Knowl., Husb.* III, A large and tight-bound sheaf will require to stand two days longer than a small one. **1844** DICKENS *Mart. Chuz.* v, I did not think you were half such a tight-made fellow! **1860** READE *Cloister & H.* (1861) I. 20 Clad in a pair of tight-fitting buckskin hose. **1865** DICKENS *Mut. Fr.* IV. vii, With the palms of his hands tight-clasping his hot temples. **1879** BROWNING *Ivan Ivanovitch* 166 I'll..tight-tie you with the strings Here of my heart! **1884** YATES *Recoll.* ii. (Tauchn.) 80 After tight-reining and regular hours. **1896** A. PALMER in *Academy* 25 Jan. 80/3 It is strange how the tight-stretched tambourine can be called *molle*. **1905** *Daily Chron.* 21 Oct. 5/2 Strong men stood with tight-drawn lips.

**3.** Special combs.: **tight barrel** or **cask**, a barrel for liquids; also called *wet barrel* or *cask*; cf. SLACK *a.* 10; so **tight cooper** (see quot.); **tight-corking** (*Angling*), a method of float-fishing in which the line (with the float or cork) is kept taut between the point of the rod and the plummet at the bottom; **tight-fisted** *a.*, parsimonious, close-fisted; **tight-jeff**: see JEFF; **tight-lock** *dial.* (see quot.); **tight shop**, a cooperage where *tight work* is done; **tight work** (see quot.).

**1884** KNIGHT *Dict. Mech.* Suppl., *Slack Barrel*, one for flour, sugar, cement, fruit, and what not, of a dry character. In contradistinction to 'tight barrel. **1759** ELLIS in *Phil. Trans.* LI. 209 This was put into a *tight cask. **1877** *Encycl. Brit.* VI. 338 Tight or wet and dry or slack cask manufacture. **1889** *Cent. Dict.* s. v. *Cooper*, *Wet* or **tight cooper*, a cooper who makes casks for liquids. **1867** F. FRANCIS *Angling* i. (1880) 59 **Tight-corking* is using a heavyish float well shotted and plumbed some two feet two deep. **1844** DICKENS *Christmas Carol* i, He was a *tight-fisted hand at the grindstone. *a* **1825** FORBY *Voc. E. Anglia*, **Tight-lock*, any species of coarse sedge growing in marsh ditches. So called, from its being used to bind the sheaves of beans or oats, growing very luxuriantly on such land. **1892** *Labour Commission Gloss.*, **Tight Shops*, workshops in which tight work is performed. *Ibid.* s. v. *Work*, *Tight work is a term used in the coopering industry to denote the making of casks or any vessels to hold water or liquids.

†**Tight**, *v.*[1] *Obs.* Forms: 1 tyhtan, tihtan, 3 tuhten (*ii*), tuihten, tihhtenn (*Orm.*), 4 tyȝt. *Pa. t.* 1 tyhte, 1–3 tihte, 2–3 tuhte (*u*), 4 tyȝt, tyht, 4–5 tiȝt, tight. *Pa. pple.* 1 ȝetiht, 2–3 ituht, 4 itiȝt, y-tyght, tyght, tyȝt, tiȝt, tight, *Sc.* tycht. [OE. *tyhtan* = OHG. *zuhten* (*zuhtôn*), MHG. *zühten* (G. *züchten* to breed, train):—OTeut. **tuht-jan*, denominative verb f. **tuht-*: see TIGHT *sb.*[1]]

**1.** *trans.* To draw, pull; = TEE *v.*[1] 1; to stretch.

*a* **1000** in *Anglia* XIII. 421/806 Oferbrædels..onbutan ȝetiht, *uelamen..in gyro tensum*. *a* **1240** *Ureisun* in *Cott. Hom.* 203 Þi sune was ituht on rode. **13..** *Sir Beues* (A.) 3215 Þanne was be-fore his bed itiȝt..A couertine on raile tre, For noman scholde on bed ise. **13..** *Gaw. & Gr. Knt.* 568 Fyrst a tule tapit, tyȝt ouer þe flet..Þe styf mon steppez þeron. *Ibid.* 858 Tapytez tyȝt to þe woȝe, of tuly and tars, And vnder fete, on þe flet, of folȝande sute. *c* **1375** *Sc. Leg. Saints* xl. (*Ninian*) 1331 Quhene it [his curtain] vpe ves tycht, Þane wist he he [had] tynt þe sycht.

**2.** *fig.* To draw, attract, entice, allure (*to* some action, or *to do* something); = TEE *v.*[1] 2.

*c* **1000** ÆLFRIC *Hom.* I. 174 On ðreo wisan bið deofles costnung: þæt is on tihtinge, on lustfullunge, on ȝeðafunge. Deofol tiht us to yfele, ac we sceolon hit onscunian. **11..** *Departing Soul's Addr. Body* 423 Þe [deofel] tuhte his hearpe ant tuhte þe to him. *Ibid.* 437 Ac efre he tuhte þe. *c* **1175** *Lamb. Hom.* 121 Þe deofel heom tuhte to þan werke. *c* **1200** ORMIN 7048 Tihhtenn & turrnenn hæþenn follc..To lefenn uppo Criste.

**3.** To train, discipline; = TEE *v.*[1] 3; to chastise.

*a* **1000** *Ags. Ps.* (Th.) xciii[i]. 12 Þe þu hine..ȝetyhtest [*quem tu erudieris*]. *a* **1225** *Ancr. R.* 184 Hwon he haueð inouh ibeaten his child, & haueð ituht hit wel. *Ibid.* 268 Tu ne schuldest nout tuhten, ne chasten þi meiden uor hire gult. *a* **1240** *Sawles Warde* in *Cott. Hom.* 267 Ah efter þat wit wule þat is husebonde tuhten ant teachen þat wit ga euer biuore.

**4.** *refl.* and *intr.* To betake oneself; to go, proceed, advance; = TEE *v.*[1] 6 a, b.

*c* **1205** LAY. 810 His horn he vastliche bleu. Iherden hit Troynisce & tuhten [*c* 1275 toȝe] to þon Gricken. *Ibid.*

27321 Ure drihten heo bi-læueð And to Mahune heo tuhteð. *a* 1300 *Cursor M.* 3157 Quen he þe sted sagh þar he tight, Þe child he dide o þe ass light. *Ibid.* 20506, I sal far þar mi sun has tight. 13.. *K. Alis.* 7164 (Bodl. MS.) Þat neiȝ þe kyng hij ben ytiȝth. *c* 1330 R. Brunne *Chron.* (1810) 93 To hunte þer he had tight in his new forest. 13.. *E. E. Allit. P.* A. 717 Do way, let chylder vnto me tyȝt. *a* 1400–50 *Alexander* 2304 To þe temple he tight tithanndez to herken. *c* 1400 *Destr. Troy* 1358 All tight to þe tempull of þere tore goddes, For drede of the dethe.

Hence †**Ti·ghting** *vbl. sb.*, persuading, enticement.

*c* 1000 [see 2]. *a* 1175 *Cott. Hom.* 229 Þurh diofles tihtinge beswicen. *c* 1200 *Trin. Coll. Hom.* 29 Þat is þe defles tuihting and mislore.

†**Tight**, *v.*² *Obs.* Forms: 4 tyȝt; *pa. t.* 4 tiȝte, tyȝte, tyȝt, tight, 5 tiȝt, tyght; *pa. pple.* 4 y-tiȝt, tiht, tyȝt, tyȝte (thit, tithte), 4–5 tiȝt, tight(e, 5 tiȝte, *Sc.* ticht. [Etymology obscure: see Note below.]

1. *trans.* To appoint, ordain, set, fix (a time, etc.); to devise, contrive; to prepare, get ready. Cf. Dight *v.* 2, 11, 14.

*a* 1300 *Cursor M.* 24344 (Edin.) To ten al tiht [*v.r.* tight] vs was þat tim Quen we na hel moht se on him. *Ibid.* 18323 (Cott.) Þat þou thoru prophet tald and tight Nu es it fulfilled be-for vr sight. *Ibid.* 11050 (Gött.) [Gabriel says to Zacharias] All þat þe is tight [*v.r.* hight] sal be-tyde. *c* 1330 R. Brunne *Chron. Wace* (Rolls) 5488 Atte water Hamon doun lyght, Intil a bot Hamon had tyght. 13.. *E. E. Allit. P.* A. 502 Of tyme of ȝere þe terme watz tyȝt. *Ibid.* B. 1153 Ȝif ȝe wolde tyȝt me a tom telle hit I wolde. *a* 1425 *Cursor M.* 4124 (Trin.) Þe foly þat his breþeren tiȝt. *c* 1470 *Golagros & Gaw.* 744 The renkis of the Round Tabill, That has traistly thame tight to governe that gait.

2. With *inf.* or *absol.* (rarely *refl.*): To fix it in one's mind; to determine, intend, purpose; to set oneself *to do* something.

*a* 1300 *Cursor M.* 1301 (Cott.) Wen þat drightim had him tight To send him þe oile þat he him hight. *c* 1300 *Havelok* 2990 Hwou the swikes haueden tiht [*MS.* thit] Reuen hem that was here riht [*MS.* rith]. 13.. *Sir Beues* (A.) 838 A stiward was wiþ king Ermin, Þat hadde tiȝt to sle þat swin. 13.. *Gaw. & Gr. Knt.* 2483 Mony a-venture..þat I ne tyȝt, at þis tyme, in tale to remene. *c* 1380 *Sir Ferumb.* 729 To slen him had he tiȝte. *a* 1400 *Octouian* 1476 To brewe the Crystene mennys banys Hy hadden tyght. *c* 1475 *Songs, Carols*, etc. 85/64 Alone to be, she hath her tight. ? *a* 1500 *Chester Pl.* xi. 165 Therfore a songe, as I haue tighte,..I will shewe here in thy sighte.

3. To set, set firmly, fix, set up (an edifice), pitch (a tent). Cf. Dight *v.* 5, 8.

1382 Wyclif *Judg.* xx. 33 So alle the sones of Yrael..tiȝten shiltron in the place that is clepid Baalthamar. *c* 1394 *P. Pl. Crede* 168 Wiþ tabernacles y-tiȝt to toten all abouten. *a* 1400–50 *Alexander* 1373 (Ashm.) Quen he had tiȝt vp þis tram and þis tild rerid. *c* 1420 *Anturs of Arth.* 355 Þe tasses were of topas, þat were þere to tiȝte [*v.r.* tyghte]. *c* 1440 *Bone Flor.* 377 They tyght ther pavylons in a stede. *c* 1470 *Golagros & Gaw.* 526 Ane hie toure, that tight wes full trest.

b. ?To set down in writing, to state. Cf. Dight *v.* 6.

13.. *E. E. Allit. P.* A. 1052 Þe hyȝe trone..With alle þe apparaylmente vmbe pyȝte, As Iohan þe apostel in termez tyȝte.

c. To set or deck *with* jewels. Cf. Dight *v.* 10.

*c* 1475 *Rauf Coilȝear* 473 Bricht braissaris of steill..Ticht ouir with Thopas, and trew lufe atanis.

[*Note.* No word answering to ME. *tihtan* appears in OE. or in the cognate langs., and its origin is a puzzle. Sense 1 corresponds closely to that of OE. *stihtan*, ME. Stight, 'to dispose, arrange, regulate, direct, rule'; senses 1 and 3 b correspond also to various senses of OE. *dihtan*, Dight *v.* Formal connexion with the latter seems impossible; derivation from the former by loss of *s*, if not impossible in such constructions as *is (s)tight, was (s)tight*, cannot be assumed without some direct evidence.]

**Tight** (təit), *v.*³ Also *Sc.* 6 teicht, 7 ticht. [f. Tight *a.*] *trans.* To make tight, in various senses. †a. To make (a vessel) water-tight. *Obs.* †b. To stretch, tighten, brace; to draw tight, compress. *Obs.* c. (also *refl.*) To put in order, make tidy or neat. *dial.* Hence **Ti·ghted** *ppl. a.*

1532 *Acc. Ld. High Treas. Scot.* VI. 156 For boyingis and teichtein of the xij barrellis of aill forsaidis. 1581 Mulcaster *Positions* xvii. (1887) 76 Wrastling..tightes the sinews. 1587 J. Melvill *Diary* (Wodrow Soc.) 255 His lessone was a tichted upe abregment of all he haid tetched the yeir bypast. 1611 Cotgr., *Goudronner*..to pitch, trimme, or tight a ship. 1661 *Sc. Acts Chas. II* (1820) VII. 230/2 The said barrells to be well tichted and double girthed before the transporting thairof. 1775 S. J. Pratt *Liberal Opin.* lxxxvi. (1783) III. 138 Mr. Benjamin..had so spruced and tighted himself up, that he really looked quite interesting. 1895 *Gloss. E. Anglia* s.v., 3. = Tidy. 'Tight yourself up'.

**Tight, tiȝt**, obs. ff. Tite; pseudo-arch. pa. t. Tie.

**Tighten** (təi·t'n), *v.* [f. Tight *a.* + -en 5.] 1. *trans.* To draw tight or tighter; to make taut or tense, to draw close; hence, to fix tightly, to make strict or rigid; to secure. Also *fig.*

1727 Bailey vol. II, To *Tighten*, to make straight, as a Line, Cord, etc., also to dress after a tight Manner. 1755 Johnson, To *Tighten*, to straiten, make close. 1774 Goldsm. *Nat. Hist.* VII. 257 The spider only wants to have one end of the line fast, in order to secure and tighten the other. 1810 Scott *Lady of L.* i. vi, What reins were tightened in despair. 1846 Brittan tr. *Malgaigne's Man. Oper. Surg.* 39 The stitches should not be tightened until all the threads are in; and the rule is, that those of the middle, or angles, should be first tightened. 1859 *Handbk. Turning* 59 If it cuts too deep, tighten the screws a little more. 1896 Lady A. Kerr *Life Seb. Valfré* 232 We find him..revising and tightening-up the rules of a community.

b. To press closely together; to pack; to compress. Also *fig.*

1845 Fairbairn *Typol. Script.* (1657) I. i. ii. 49 A type so tightened and compressed as to admit of nothing but what pertained to the tabernacle worship. 1853 Kane *Grinnell Exp.* xvi. (1856) 123 A gradually increasing breeze from the E.S.E...had tightened the floes.

c. *absol.* = Tight-lace *v. colloq.*

1896 *Daily News* 29 Oct. 9/5 A fellow servant..used to ask why 'she didn't tighten a little more'.

2. *intr.* To grow tight or tense; to be stretched tight or drawn close. Also *fig.*

1846 Landor *Imag. Conv., Emp. China & Tsing-Ti* Wks. 1853 II. 118/1 My skin seemed too small for them, it tightened so. 1868 Rogers *Pol. Econ.* xi. (1876) 150 As the market tightens..the rate of discount rises. 1871 L. Stephen *Playgr. Eur.* vii. (1894) 158 The rope once or twice tightened unpleasantly. 1897 *Allbutt's Syst. Med.* II. 788 The radial artery is felt to tighten day by day.

†3. *refl.* To make oneself 'tight' or tidy; cf. Tight *a.* 4. *Obs. rare.*

1786 Mrs. A. M. Bennett *Juvenile Indiscr.* II. 113 Her daughter was run up to tighten herself, fit, as she said, to walk with them.

Hence **Ti·ghtening** *vbl. sb.* and *ppl. a.*

1846 J. Nicholson *Operat. Mechanic* 34 Placing the tightening roller in the position represented by the dotted lines. *Ibid.* 806 Two of the bracing chains, with their tightening shackle. 1836 W. Irving *Astoria* I. 139 The tightening of the padding and the pressing of the head to the board is gradual. 1877 Knight *Dict. Mech.*, *Tightening pulley*, one which rests against the band in order to tighten it. 1902 *Words Eyewitness* 135 Men..who would have met untold sorrow with but a tightening of the lips.

**Tightened** (təi·t'nd), *ppl. a.* [f. prec. + -ed 1.] Made or become tight; drawn tight or close; tense, stretched; firm, rigid; constricted.

1760 Fawkes tr. *Anacreon, Ode* lix. 7 With tighten'd Rein, I'll urge thee round the dusty Plain. 1810 Scott *Lady of L.* ii. xxxvi, Malcolm did..bind..His ample plaid in tightened fold. 1833 Coleridge *Table-t.* 10 Aug., Like a sigh heaved up from the tightened chest of a sick man. 1880 G. Meredith *Tragic Com.* (1881) 291 The tightened grasp of her hand confessed her understanding of the thing she pressed to hear repeated. 1899 *Allbutt's Syst. Med.* VI. 48 The pulse may be but little changed [in angina], yet it is sometimes tightened.

**Tightener** (təi·t'nəɹ). [f. Tighten *v.* + -er 1.] One who or that which tightens.

1829 *Nat. Philos., Prelim. Treat.* 32 (U.K.S.), [In lizards] the two toes or tightners, by which the skin of the foot is pinned down. 1851 Mayhew *Lond. Labour* I. 66 What is elegantly termed a tightner that is to say, a most plentiful repast. 1890 *Illustr. Lond News* 6 Sept. 298/3 A minstrel ..a tightener of the strong sinews of warlike hearts! 1891 *Wheeling* 25 Feb. 402 Wrenches, spoke tighteners, and padlocks and chain; bearings, hubs, and pedals. 1895 *Standard* 21 Nov. 5/2 There is no such tightener of the purse strings as want of confidence.

†**Tighter.** *Obs. rare.* [f. Tight *v.*³ + -er 1.] 1. One who makes tight the seams of ships; a caulker.

1611 Cotgr., *Goildronneur*, a pitcher, trimmer, or tighter of ships. 1653 Urquhart *Rabelais* ii. xxx, Julius Cæsar and Pompey were boatwrights and tighters of ships.

2. 'A ribband or string by which women straiten their clothes' (J.).

**Tightish** (təi·tiʃ), *a.* [f. Tight *a.* + -ish 1.] 1. Rather tight or close-fitting.

1775 S. J. Pratt *Liberal Opin.* xcvi. (1783) III. 202 Are they [the clothes] not a little tightish? 1848 Curzon *Visits Monast.* i. v. 58 It comes up high upon the neck, and has tightish sleeves. 1893 Quiller-Couch *Delectable Duchy* 223 In a tightish uniform.

b. as *adv.* Somewhat tightly.

1767 J. Ferguson *Lect., Suppl.* 31 The top goes on tightish, but must be made to turn round on the cylinder.

2. Somewhat difficult to accomplish, attain to, etc.; rather 'stiff' or difficult.

1786 Mrs. A. M. Bennett *Juvenile Indiscretions* III. 207 Amounted to a pretty tightish sum. 1801 tr. *Gabrielli's Myst. Husb.* II. 96 They have had a tightish day's work. 1832 Wilson in *Blackw. Mag.* XXXI. 859 'Tis a tightish swim across. 1890 'Boldrewood' *Col. Reformer* (1891) 418, I had a tightish ride to get over before I caught the mail.

**Ti·ght-la:ced** (-lēɪst), *a.* That is laced tightly; having the laces drawn tight; wearing stays tightly laced; constricted or compressed by tight-lacing.

1741 [see b]. 1828 *Lights & Shades* II. 132 The tight-laced spark of fashion, with his hat on one side. 1860 W. G. Clark in *Vac. Tour.* 43 We saw..the belles of the island,..with..tight-laced black bodices. 1871 *Figure Training* 106 May I add a little practical information..on the health of tight-laced ladies? 1905 H. D. Rolleston *Dis. Liver* 11 Tight-laced livers are often associated with dyspepsia.

b. *fig.* Strict in the observance of rules or usages of morality or propriety. (Usually dyslogistic.)

1741 Richardson *Pamela* I. Introd. 26 He made a too tight-laced Objection, where he spann'd the Waist of Pamela. 1831 T. L. Peacock *Crotchet Castle* vi, Even in these tight-laced days, the obscurity of a learned language allows a little pleasantry. 1844 Alb. Smith *Adv. Mr. Ledbury* liv. (1886) 164 Etiquette is not over tight-laced upon the mountains. 1881 Larwood *Lond. Parks* xiv. 282 This somewhat tight-laced gentleman was greatly shocked.

**Ti·ght-la·cing**, *vbl. sb.* The action or process of lacing tightly; *spec.* the practice of wearing tightly-laced stays in order to reduce or preserve the form of the waist.

1834 *Tait's Mag.* I. 101/2 The demon of tight-lacing is still in existence. 1871 *Figure Training* 47 My two daughters..can bear me out in my favourable opinion of tight-lacing, and their good health speaks volumes in its praise. 1897 *Allbutt's Syst. Med.* IV. 343 Cruveilhier long ago pointed out the influence of tight lacing as a cause of displacement [of the kidney].

Hence **Ti·ght-la·ce** *v.* (back-formation) *trans.*, to lace tightly, to compress (the waist) by wearing tightly-laced stays; also *refl.* and *absol.*; so **Ti·ght-lace** *attrib. phr.*, affected by tight-lacing; **Ti·ght-la·cer**, one who practises tight-lacing.

1859 *Habits of Gd. Society* 172 It is often difficult to convince the practised tight-lacer; for vanity is generally obstinate. 1880 tr. *Ziemssen's Cycl. Med.* IX. 40 In slight grades of the so called 'tight-lace liver' only a shallow transverse furrow is observable. 1897 *Allbutt's Syst. Med.* IV. 343 The tight-lace line on the liver is on the same level as the upper pole of the kidney. 1898 *Daily News* 19 Jan. 9/2 She told me that she tight-laced herself to present a good figure in the shop. 1907 *Daily Chron.* 14 Sept. 5/7 The majority of tight lacers develop thick unshapely legs sooner or later.

**Tightly** (təi·tli), *adv.* [f. Tight *a.* + -ly 2.] In a tight manner.

1. Soundly, properly, well; effectively; stoutly, vigorously. Cf. Tight *a.* 3. Now *dial.*

1598 Shaks. *Merry W.* i. iii. 88 Hold Sirha, beare you these Letters tightly. *Ibid.* ii. iii. 67 He will Clapper-claw thee tightly. 1598 B. Jonson *Ev. Man in Hum.* ii. ii, He shall heare on't, and that tightly too. *a* 1625 Fletcher, etc. *Fair Maid Inn* ii. ii, When we have cozen'd 'em most tightly, thou shalt steal away the innkeeper's daughter. *a* 1700 B. E. *Dict. Cant. Crew* s.v. *Sock*, I'll Drub ye tightly. 1700 S. L. tr. *Fryke's Voy. E. Ind.* 193 Our eight Boats..pursued them so tightly, that..by Noon our Boats were all got within a quarter of a League of 'em. *a* 1713 Ellwood *Autobiog.* 163 He stood up titely to them. 1786 Burns *Inventory* 41 An' ay on Sundays duly nightly, I on the questions [= catechism] tairge them tightly. *a* 1825 Forby *Voc. E. Anglia*, *Tightly*,..promptly; actively; alertly.

2. With constriction, tension, or compression; closely, tensely; strictly; not loosely. Also *fig.*

1758 Rutty *Spir. Diary* (ed. 2) 104 A busy week; yet kept to all meetings tightly. 1776 *Trial of Nundocomar* 60/1 A paper, wrapped in a wax cloth..bound tightly down with a string. 1816 Scott *Let.* 22 Nov., I have settled Walter tightly to his Greek and Latin. 1859 *Habits of Gd. Society* iii. 145 Anything which binds any part of the body tightly impedes the circulation. 1879 Stevenson *Trav. Cevennes* (1886) 34, I was tightly cross-examined about my journey. 1883 *Harper's Mag.* Nov. 904/2 The contests were..more tightly fought out than by the trotting equines.

3. Firmly, securely.

1866 Mrs. Gaskell *Wives & Dau.* xlviii, Trying to take one of his hands; but he kept them tightly in his pockets. 1898 Flo. Montgomery *Tony* 13 Their hands clasped tightly.

4. Neatly, tidily, smartly.

1825–9 Mrs. Sherwood *Lady of Manor* II. xv. 297 It does me good to see you going about..so tightly dressed in your neat little cap and blue apron.

5. In comb. with ppl. adj. (used attrib.), as *tightly-clenched, -corsetted, -reined, -wrapped*, etc.

1825 T. Hook *Sayings* Ser. ii. *Passion & Princ.* xii. III. 292 The tightly-strained white kid gloves. 1866 Howells *Venet. Life* xi. 154 Her tightly-corsetted waist. 1888 'J. S. Winter' *Bootle's Childr.* iii, Between her tightly-clenched teeth.

**Tightly, tiȝtli**, erroneous spellings of Titely.

**Tightness** (təi·tnės). [f. Tight *a.* + -ness.] The quality or condition of being tight.

1. Closeness of texture; denseness, solidity (*obs.*); compactness of structure, impermeability. Also *fig.*

*a* 1728 Woodward (J.), The bones are inflexible, which arises from the greatness of the number of corpuscles that compose them, and the firmness and tightness of their union. 1759 Ellis in *Phil. Trans.* LI. 207 The tightness of the cask would secure them from the salt water. 1865 Dickens *Mut. Fr.* i. viii, Make me as compact a little will as can be reconciled with tightness.

2. The condition of being drawn tight, stretched, or strained; tenseness, tautness.

1780 *New Newgate Cal.* V. 152 Placing a fife within the cord so as to twist it to a proper tightness. 1793 Beddoes *Scurvy* 63 It was not occasioned by any tightness of dress. 1869 Spurgeon *Treas. David* Ps. iii. 2 Harp-strings..need to be screwed up again to their proper tightness. 1885 *Manchester Exam.* 7 Oct. 5/2 The very tightness with which the screw is being applied renders the probability of a breakdown of the machinery more probable.

b. *transf.* Constriction felt (as in breathing); hardness (of the pulse). Cf. Tightened.

1785 J. Pearson in *Med. Commun.* II. 63 A sense of tightness across the chest. 1898 *Allbutt's Syst. Med.* V. 37 Nothing will relieve the tightness of the chest and the hardness of the cough..better than antimony. 1899 *Ibid.* VI. 49 Diminution in size and increase in tightness of the pulse.

3. The condition of being tipsy. *slang.*

1864 *Daily Tel.* 4 Oct., At the first blush, the Americans strike a foreigner as being an exceedingly drunken people. ..You cannot fail to observe an immense amount of 'tightness' during your walks abroad.

4. *Comm.* Scarcity of money in the market.

1858 R. S. Surtees *Ask Mamma* lxvii, In consequence of the tightness of the money-market, an early settlement would be agreeable. 1901 *Scotsman* 7 Mar. 6/2 The tightness of money is again beginning adversely to affect gilt-edged stocks.

**Tight rope, ti·ght-rope**, *sb.* A tightly stretched rope, wire, or wire cable, on which rope-dancers and acrobats perform feats of equilibristic skill. Also *attrib.* (Contrasted with Slack-rope.)

1801 STRUTT *Sports & Past.* III. iv. (1810) 188 Tumbling and jumping through a hoop..and dancing upon the tight-rope. 1861 THACKERAY *Four Georges* iv. (1876) 105 A charming young Prince who danced deliciously on the tight-rope. 1890 *Spectator* 22 Nov. 729/2 An interview with a tight-rope dancer.

Hence **Ti·ght-rope** *v.*, *intr.* to perform on the tight-rope; *trans.* to walk along as if on a tight-rope.

1858 A. MAYHEW *Paved with Gold* II. vii, A small.. garden, intersected with gravel paths not broader than deal boards, which entailed balancing on those who tight-roped its walks. 1908 *Daily Chron.* 1 Feb. 5/6 He has tumbled and tight-roped, slept under hedges, and accepted presents from reigning potentates.

**Tights** (təits), *sb. pl.* [Elliptical use of TIGHT *a.*] **a.** Tight-fitting breeches, worn by men in the 18th and early 19th centuries, and still forming part of court-dress.

1833 MARRYAT *P. Simple* xxxi, The frill of his shirt, extending from his collar to the waistband of his nankeen tights, which were finished off at his knees with huge bunches of riband. 1857 DICKENS *Lett.* (1880) II. 26 A pair of common nankeen tights, to button below the calf. 1889 W. S. GILBERT *Foggerty's Fairy* 1, If tights and trunks came in again.

**b.** Garments of thin elastic material, fitting tight to the skin, worn by dancers, acrobats, and others to facilitate their movements or display the form; skin-tights. Sometimes covering the whole body, but usually the legs only.

1836–7 DICKENS *Sk. Boz, Mrs. Joseph Porter* (1870) 300 None of the performers could walk in their tights, or move their arms in their jackets. 1845 ALB. SMITH *Fort. Scatterg. Fam.* xlii. (1887) 140 Gentlemen in flesh tights jumped over strips of cloth, coming down on the horse again. 1897 *Times* 4 Oct. 8/1 [She] would be well advised to abandon her tights and resume the garb of her sex.

**Tiglic** (ti·glik), *a. Chem.* [f. mod.L. *Tigl-ium*, specific name of the croton oil plant, *Croton Tiglium* (Linn.), of the Coromandel coast in India, the seeds of which were known in 17th cent. pharmacy as *grana tiglia* and *grana tilli*; according to Wittstein, 1856, f. Gr. τῖλος liquid fæces, as in diarrhœa, from their purgative quality. If so, the spelling *tiglia* or *tiglii* for *tilia, tilli* prob. arose in Italy.] Contained in or derived from croton oil; *tiglic acid*, $C_5H_8O_2$ (Watts) = $CH_3.CH:C(CH_3).CO.OH$, a colourless crystalline compound, crystallizing in triclinic plates or rods, obtained from croton and other oils; stereo-isomeric with angelic acid. Also called *methyl-crotonic acid*. So **Ti·glate,** a salt of this acid; **Ti·gline** (see quot. 1900); **Tigli·nic** *a.*, tiglic.

1875 WATTS *Dict. Chem.* VII. 395 (*Croton oil, acids obtained from*) Geuther and Fröhlich designate this acid provisionally as tiglic acid, and point out that it is, perhaps, identical with Frankland and Duppa's methyl-crotonic acid. .. Barium tiglate, $(C_5H_7O_2)_2Ba + 4H_2O$. 1876 HARLEY *Royle's Mat. Med.* 440 It is composed of the ordinary fatty acids, and volatile, acetic, butyric, and valerianic, tiglinic acid. 1900 B. D. JACKSON *Gloss. Bot. Terms, Tigline*, the acrid principle in the seeds of *Croton Tiglium*, Linn.

**Tigress** (təi·grès). (Also 9 tigeress.) [f. TIGER + -ESS, after F. *tigresse.*]

**1.** A female tiger.

1611 COTGR., *Tigresse*, a Tigresse, a she Tiger. 1624 MASSINGER *Renegado* III. v, If Christians have mothers, sure they share in The tigress' fierceness. 1647 R. STAPYLTON *Juvenal* xv. 278 The Indian tigresses firme peace enjoy. 1891 E. PEACOCK *N. Brendon* II. 117 She turned on him like a tigress at bay.

**2.** *fig.* A fierce, cruel, or tiger-like woman: cf. TIGER *sb.* 4.

1700 MOTTEUX *Quix.* I. IV. iv. II. 400, I never will give any body reason to call me Tigress and Lioness. 1706 PHILLIPS (ed. Kersey), *Tigress*...a ranting Woman, a cruel Mistress. 1871 M. COLLINS *Marq. & Merch.* I. iii. 121 The proper subjugation of the young heiress and tigress.

†**b.** A vulgarly or obtrusively overdressed woman: cf. TIGER 7. *Obs.*

1836 *New Monthly Mag.* XLVIII. 460 Tigresses, too, shone in a near approach to nudity, in Greek draperies and a Brutus' wig.

**3.** *attrib.* and *Comb.*, as *tigress-heart*, *-like* adj.

1844 LOUISA S. COSTELLO *Béarn & Pyrenees* II. 341 Adieu, tigress-heart! Shepherdess without affection. 1910 *Q. Rev.* Jan. 13 Started in tigress-like revenge by lack of quality.

‖**Tigridia** (təigri·diă). *Bot.* [mod.L., named by Ker 1805, f. Gr. τιγριδ-, variant stem of τίγρις TIGER + -IA [2]; so called from the spotted flowers.] Name of a genus of bulbous plants, N.O. *Iridaceæ*, known as *Tiger-iris* or *Tiger-flower*, esp. *T. Pavonia*, the Peacock Tiger-flower, a native of Mexico, Central America, and tropical S. America.

1866 in *Treas. Bot.* 1888 *Pall Mall G.* 10 Nov., I feel bound to say a word in praise of the orchid-like tigridia, a bulbous plant of about a foot in height, and whose blossoms, like those of the cistus, never last longer than a day.

**Tigrine** (təi·grəin), *a.* (Also tigerine.) [ad. L. *tigrin-us* (Pliny) marked like a tiger: see -INE [1].] Of, pertaining to, or resembling a tiger, esp. in marking or colouring; in specific names of animals translating L. *tigrīnus*.

1656 BLOUNT *Glossogr.*, *Tigrine*, of, or like the swift beast called a Tigre. 1800 SHAW *Gen. Zool.* I. 408 Tigerine weesel..of the size of a Cat, and of mild manners. The body ..with a black stripe from head to tail, and spotted on the sides with brown. 1803 *Ibid.* IV. 556 Tigrine Holocentrus ..native of the Indian seas. 1842 *Penny Cycl.* XXIV. 440/1 Two soldiers..habited and shielded so as to exhibit a tigerine aspect. 1861 G. MEREDITH *Evan Harrington* xl, With tigrine claw thou manglest my speech. 1908 *Times* 8 June 6/3 Carpet, diamond, and tigrine snakes.

**Tigrish, Tigrous:** see TIGERISH, TIGEROUS.

**Tigroid** (təi·groid), *a.* [f. Gr. τιγροειδής like a tiger: see -OID.] Resembling a tiger or tiger's skin; marked like a tiger. *Tigroid body* (*Path.*): see quots. Also *absol.* as *sb.*

1901 *Buck's Handbk. Med. Sc.* II. 338 The tigroid in the cell bodies of the nuclei of origin of the motor cerebral nerves. *Ibid.*, A part of the dendrite where tigroid bodies disappear. 1904 TITCHENER tr. *Wundt's Physiol. Psychol.* I. 41 When highly magnified, most nerve-cells show..a fibrillated structure; clusters of granules are set..between the meshes of this fibrillar network...The granular deposits are named, from their discoverer, the corpuscles of Nissl; they are also known as tigroid bodies, or as chromophilous substance. 1909 *Cent. Dict. Suppl.* s. v. *Granule, Nissl granules*, small, deeply staining bodies found by Nissl in the cytoplasm of nerve-cells...Also called *Nissl's bodies* and *tigroid.*

Hence **Tigrolysis** (təigrǫ·lisis) [Gr. λύσις dissolution], the breaking down of the tigroid substance in the nerve-cell; **Tigrolytic** (-oli·tik) *a.*, of or pertaining to tigrolysis.

1903 *Buck's Handbk. Med. Sc.* VI. 264 This disintegration ..of the tigroid has been variously designated...Kohnstamm gives it the name *tigrolysis*,..which I prefer. *Ibid.*, Cells still tigrolytic may be observed.

**Tigro·logy.** *nonce-wd.* [See -O)LOGY.] The branch of zoology which treats of tigers.

1822–56 DE QUINCEY *Confess.* Wks. V. 70 The indignation arose naturally against my three tormentors (guardian, Archididascalus, and the professor of tigrology).

**Tig-tag** (ti·g,tæ·g), *v. Sc.* [Reduplicated formation, suggesting the continuous alternation of the game of TIG or TAG.] **a.** *intr.* To continue in reciprocal action; to bicker; to haggle in bargaining. **b.** *trans.* To drive to and fro, to keep (a person) running to and fro. Hence **Tig-tagging** *vbl. sb.*

1643 BAILLIE *Lett., to W. Spang* 7 Dec., The King came.. with purpose to break up Waller's quarters,..but..Waller is recruited, from Kent, with horse and foot, and minds to stand to it. They may tig tag on this way this twelve month. 1825 JAMIESON, *Tig-taggin*, the act of hagglin; as, We had an awfu' tig-taggin about it, before we coud mak our bargain. 1844 W. CROSS *Disruption* xxxv. (1846) 383 They've .. been tig-tagit for years, waiting on this Bill and the ither Bill.

**Tigurine** (ti·giurəin), *a.* and *sb.* [ad. L. *Tigurīn-us* in *Tigurīnus pāgus* (Cæsar), a district of ancient Helvetia, generally identified with Zürich (*Turicum*).] **a.** *adj.* Of or pertaining to Zürich (cf. *Consensus Tigurinus*, the Zürich Consensus of 1549); hence = ZWINGLIAN. **b.** *sb.* A Zwinglian.

*a* 1651 CALDERWOOD *Hist. Kirk* (1843) II. 331 The interpretatioun of the Confessioun of the Tigurine kirk made by Mr Robert Pont. 1674 HICKMAN *Quinquart. Hist.* (ed. 2) 59 Blessed is the man who hath not gone in the counsel of the Sacramentarians, nor stood in the way of the Zuinglians, nor sate in the seat of the Tigurines. 1675 V. ALSOP *Anti-sozzo* 273 Those low-spirited, phlegmatic Tigurine doctors, who trade all in..unwieldy systems of Divinity. 1697 POTTER *Antiq. Greece* I. i. (1715) 3 Cf. the Tigurine Version with that of Geneva. 1788 G. CAMPBELL *Four Gospels* (1807) I. 143 This has been followed by the Tigurine translator.

**Tigurye,** obs. variant of TUGURY.

**Ti-he, -hee,** obs. ff. TEHEE. **Tiht,** obs. f. TIGHT, TITE *adv.*

**Tikal,** var. TICAL. **Tikat,** obs. f. TICKET.

†**Tike, tyke** [1]. *Obs. rare*⁻¹. [Generally taken as = TYKE, dog, sense 2; but perh. ad. Welsh *taeog* (taiog), in OWelsh *taiawc* villain, churl, Cornish *tioc* or *tiac* husbandman, farmer, ploughman, rustic :—OCeltic **tegācos*, deriv. of **teg-os*, Welsh *ty* a house: cf. for the sense COTTAR, med.L. *cotarius*, from *cota*; VILLEIN, med.L. *villanus*, from *villa.*] One of a class of persons subject to tallage (cf. TALLAGEABILITY, quot. 1888); a churl, villein.

1377 LANGL. *P. Pl.* B. xix. 37 The iuwes, þat were gentil men, ihesu þei dispised, Bothe his lore & his lawe; now are þei lowe cherlis. As wyde as þe worlde is, wonyeth þere none But vnder tribut & taillage as tykes & cherles [1393 C. xxII. 37 tikes and cheorles].

[*Note.* On this word see A. L. Mayhew in *Guardian* 10 Nov. 1909. *Taeog* was in Welsh a technical term (*Anct. Welsh Laws* 216, 266), and may have been known west of the Severn in English counties on the Welsh Border. *Tike* = 'dog', appears later, and then only in the north.]

**Tike** [2], var. TYKE, a low-bred dog.

**Tike, Tikel, -ell(e, -il, Tiket, tikkat, -et,** obs. forms of TICK, TICKLE, TICKET.

‖**Til** [1] (til). *East Ind.* Also teel, teal. [a. Hindi *til* :—Skr. *tilá.*] The Indian name of the plant *Sesamum indicum*; chiefly attrib. or in comb., as *til seed*; **til oil, til-seed oil,** the oil obtained by bruising the seeds. *Black til* = RAMTIL, *Guizotia oleifera* (formerly called *Verbesina sativa*).

1840 *Penny Cycl.* XVI. 417/1 India, whence..sesamum or til seed is..largely imported, as well as from Egypt. 1845 STOCQUELER *Handbk. Brit. India* (1854) 514 It is..inferior.. to the oil of til (*sesamum*). 1849 BALFOUR *Man. Bot.* § 951 Teel seeds, the produce of *Sesamum orientale*, supply a bland oil. *c* 1865 LETHEBY in *Circ. Sc.* I. 101/2 Sessama, gingilie, or teal oil. *a* 1875 *Table Customs-Duties British India* (Yule), Oils, Jinjili or Til. 1905 *Statesman* 23 Aug. 5/4 The Sesamum (Til or Jinjili) crop of the season.

‖**Til** [2]. [Native name in Madeira: perh. a local use of Pg. *til*, TEIL or linden.] A lauraceous tree, *Oreodaphne fetens*, of the Canary Islands and Madeira; also its wood, which has a fetid smell. Chiefly *attrib.*, as *til-tree*, *til-wood*.

1858 HOGG *Veg. Kingd.* 623 *Til-wood*, produced by *G[œppertia] fœtens*, a native of the Canaries, has a most disagreeable odour. 1884 MILLER *Plant-n.*, *Oreodaphne* (*Laurus*) *fœtens*, Fetid Laurel, or Til-tree. 1885 LADY BRASSEY *The Trades* 30 The black Til..or native laurel.

**Til,** obs. form of TEIL, TILE, TILL.

**Tilbury** (ti·lbŏri). [f. proper name *Tilbury*, in sense 1 that of the inventor, in sense 2 of the place: see quot. 1796.]

**1.** A light open two-wheeled carriage, fashionable in the first half of the 19th c.

1814 *Sporting Mag.* XLIII. 240 Fifteen tilburies, drawn by fine blood horses. 1842 DICKENS *Amer. Notes* vi. (1850) 55/2 Gigs, phaetons, large-wheeled tilburies, and private carriages. 1863 'OUIDA' *Held in Bondage* (1870) 44 We stood waiting for his tilbury.

†**2.** A sixpenny piece; sixpence. *slang. Obs.*

1796 GROSE *Dict. Vulg. T.* (ed. 3), *Tilbury*, sixpence; so called from its formerly being the fare for crossing over from Gravesend to Tilbury fort. 1805 in *Brathwait's Barnabees Jrnl.* (1818) Introd. 43 *note*, As if a man..should say 'Arriving at Tilbury-fort, I gave a beggar a Tilbury (sixpence) for the name's sake'. 1812 J. H. VAUX *Flash Dict.*, *Tilbury*, a sixpence.

Hence **Ti·lbury'd** *a.*, of driving gloves, having the finger-palms strengthened with leather to resist the friction of the reins.

1901 *Trade Catalogue*, Knitted tilbury'd gloves.

†**Tild.** *Obs.* Forms: 4 **tyle**, 5 **tyll, tilde, tylde**, 5–6 **tyld.** [In 14–15th c. *tyle, tyll*, app. a. OF. *tille* a piece or portion: cf. *une tille de son bacon* (12th c.), *tille de lart* (14th c. in Godef.).] Each of the four cuts or portions into which a quarter of beef may be divided.

1342–3 *Durh. Acc. Rolls* (Surtees) I. 38 In j quart. carn. Bou' recent. et ij tyles et j carcos. porc. 1417 *Ibid.* 55 In v Carcass. j qart. et j tyld Carn. bov. *c* 1420 *Ibid.* 56 In iiij carcas ij tyll bov. sals. 1514–15 *Earl Northumberland's Househ. Bk.* (1770) 135 There shal be strikkyn of every Carcass of Beef lxiiij Stroks, whiche is..after iiij Tilde in every Quarter and after iiij Stroks in every Tylde.

**Tild, -e,** var. TELD *sb.* and *v. Obs.*; obs. f. TILE.

‖**Tilde** (ti·lde). [Sp. *tilde*, a popular metathetic form of the type **tidlo* for *tit(u)lo*, ad. L. *titulus* TITLE. Diez cites as a parallel instance *cabildo*, L. *capitulum*.] The diacritic mark ˜ placed in Spanish above the letter *n* to indicate the *mouillé* or palatalized sound (nʸ), as in *señor* (senʸor).

Orig. the *mouillé* sound was written *nn*, as in the parallel *ll*; the *tilde* is an abbreviated form of the second *n*.

1864 in WEBSTER. 1889 *Pall Mall G.* 21 Jan., It is not considered [by the authoress] of any importance if the word señor remains without its tilde.

**Tile** (təil), *sb.* [1] Forms: *a.* 1 **tiȝule**, 1–2 **tiȝele**, 3 **tiȝel**, 4 **teȝele, tijl**, 4–5 **tiel**, 4–6 **tyel**, 4–9 **tyle**, 5 **til, tyl, tille, tyell, tyil, tyȝl(l, tele**, 5–6 **teylle, tylle**, 4– **tile.** *β. Sc.* and *north. dial.* 5–6 **tild, tyld(e.** [OE. *tigule, tigele* :—WGer. *tegala*, ad. L. *tēgula* a tile, f. *teg-ĕre* to cover. So OHG. *ziagal* (MHG., G. *ziegel*), Du. *tegel, tichel*, ON. *tigl* (Sw. *tegel*, Da. *tegl*).]

**1.** A thin slab of burnt clay, shaped according to the purpose for which it is required; usually unglazed and flat or curved for covering the roofs of buildings, flat for lining ovens, etc.; flat, usually glazed and sometimes encaustically ornamented when used to pave floors, or line walls, fire-places, etc.; semi-cylindrical or tunnel-shaped when used for purposes of drainage.

**a.** originally and generally as used for roofing purposes; hence also applied to similar coverings of metal, marble, † wood 'shingles', etc.

*a* 725 *Corpus Gloss.* 1992 (O.E.T.) *Tegula*, tiȝule. *c* 825 *Vesp. Ps.* xxi. 16 [xxii. 15] Adruȝade swe swe tiȝule [L. *testa*] meȝen min. *c* 1000 *Sax. Leechd.* II. 156 ȝebærn under tiȝelan to ahsan. *a* 1300 *Cursor M.* 18930 þe fire es god to strengh þe tile. 1340 *Ayenb.* 167 Tribulacion makeþ pacience..ase þet uer makeþ þe teȝele hard. *c* 1400 *Brut* ccxlii. 352 A large hous of tymbir .. couered with tylez ouyr. *c* 1425 *Voc.* in Wr.-Wülcker 667/22 *Hec tegula*, teylle. 1552 HULOET, Tyles of woode called shyngles. 1555 EDEN *Decades* 150 Their houses..are couered eyther with tyles, slates, reades, or stalkes of certeyne herbes. 1613 PURCHAS *Pilgrimage* (1614) 467 The house wherein his Pagode..standeth, is couered with Tiles of siluer. 1617 MORYSON *Itin.* I. 64 The building is very faire, of free stone ..., but covered with tiles of wood for the most part. 1678 CUDWORTH *Intell. Syst.* I. iv. 460 He uncovered another Temple.., and taking off the Marble-Tyles thereof, sent them into Spain to adorn his new erected Temple withal. 1746–7 HERVEY *Medit.* (1818) 27 Even a single tile, dropping from the roof, may be as fatal as the fall of the whole structure. 1840 R. H. DANA *Bef. Mast* xiii. 30 The better houses..have red tiles upon the roofs. 1850 LEITCH tr. *C. O. Müller's Anc. Art* § 53 Byzes of Naxos invented the art of cutting marble tiles about the 50th Olympiad. 1857 BIRCH *Anc. Pottery* (1858) I. 162 Tiles were extensively used in Greece for roofing.

†**b.** As used in building generally, and including thicker slabs of the shape and quality of bricks: cf. TILE-STONE 1. *Obs.*

(Cf. the corresponding use of G. *ziegel*. The word *brick* first appears in E. in the 15th c.)

c893 K. ÆLFRED *Oros.* II. iv. § 7 [Se weall] is ȝeworht of tiȝelan & of eorðtyrewan. [c 1250–1387: see 2.] c 1385 CHAUCER *L.G.W.* 709, & wallis make Ful hye of harde tilis wel I-bake. 1481 CAXTON *Myrr.* III. xi. 158 They made other [pillar]..of tyles all hole wythoute ony Ioyntures.

**c.** As used for paving floors, lining walls, fire-places, etc.

c 1386 CHAUCER *Sompn. T.* 397 Ne of our pauement Nys nat a tyl yet with-Inne oure wones. [c 1394, 1426–7: see 2.] 1611 COTGR., *Quarreau*,..a square tile, or bricke, fit to paue with. 1688 R. HOLME *Armoury* III. 343/2 Roman Tiles.. found in Vaults and Cellars in Chester. 1715 LEONI *Palladio's Archit.* (1742) I. 27 The Floors may be made.. of square Tyles. 1727–41 CHAMBERS *Cycl.*, *Flemish or Dutch Tyles* are of two kinds, antient and modern.—The antient were used for chimney foot-paces...The modern Flemish tyles are commonly used plastered up in the jaumbs of chimneys, instead of chimney-corner-stones. 1735 BERKELEY *Querist* § 117 Whether tiles and plaster may not supply the place of Norway fir for flooring. 1844 DICKENS *Christmas Carol* i, The fireplace.. paved.. with quaint Dutch tiles. 1888 MISS BRADDON *Fatal Three* I. v, The walls were lined with Minton tiles.

**d.** As used for draining land, roads, buildings, etc., or for other purposes. These are either hollow tubes or semicircular and open.

1830, 1844 [see *tile-draining*, *-machine* in 6]. 1869 BOUTELL *Arms & Arm.* iv. (1874) 60 One of these shields is an elongated and convex oblong, somewhat resembling a hollowed water-course tile. 1870 EMERSON *Soc. & Solit.* vi. 122 See what the farmer accomplishes by a cartload of tiles: he alters the climate by letting off water. 1875 W. MCILWRAITH *Guide Wigtownshire* 118 The spring.. has been diverted into tiles, and forms a spout-well. 1883 *Fisheries Exhib. Catal.* 297 Tiles prepared for collecting Spat...Knives for detaching the young oysters from the chalked tile.

**e.** *Metallurgy.* A small flat piece of baked earth or earthenware used to cover vessels in which metals are fused.

1741 CRAMER *Art Assaying Metals* 67 In Fusions, it is often necessary to cover the Vessels with Tiles...These are made of the same Matter as the melting Pots and Crucibles. 1753 CHAMBERS *Cycl. Supp.*, *Tile*, or *Tyle*, in assaying, a small flat piece of dried earth, used to cover vessels in which metals are in fusion...The Tile sits close upon the vessel. 1877 KNIGHT *Dict. Mech.*, *Tile*..2. (*Brass-founding.*) The cover of a brass furnace. Now made of iron, but formerly a flat tile...3. (*Metallurgy.*) A clay cover for a melting-pot.

**f.** The name given to a small flat plate of copper: cf. *tile copper* in 6.

1868 JOYNSON *Metals* 96 The copper..is cast into 'ingots', 'tiles', or 'wire bars'.

**g.** *To have a tile loose* (and similar expressions derived from roofing tiles): to be slightly crazy, or not quite right in the head. *slang.*

1846 W. H. MAXWELL *Brian o' Linn* xvii. (1848) II. 212 'There is not a tile off your upper story', as they say in the north. 1870 G. MACDONALD *Back of North Wind* xix, He's not right in the head, you know. A tile loose. 1877 BESANT & RICE *Harp & Cr.* iv, Is he cracked? Has my cousin dropped a tile?

**2.** The material of which tiles or bricks consist, burnt clay (cf. BRICK *sb.*[1] 1); tiles (or †bricks) collectively (in early use const. as pl.). †*Oil of tile* = brick-oil (BRICK *sb.*[1] 10). *Obs.*

α. c 1250 *Gen. & Ex.* 2552 Ðo sette sundri hem to waken His tiȝel and lim, and walles maken. a 1300 *Cursor M.* 1533 (Cott.) Tua pilers þai mad, o tile þe tan, þe toþer it was o merbul stan. 1387 TREVISA *Higden* (Rolls) IV. 297, I fonde a citee of brend tyle, and now I leve a citee of marbil. c 1394 *P. Pl. Crede* 194 Þat cloister.. was.. y-paued wiþ peynt til, iche poynte after oþer. 1426–7 *Rec. St. Mary at Hill* 64 Payd for xjml pavyng tyle. 1566 in J. Morris *Troubles Cath. Forefathers* (1877) 336 All the residue of tile, timber, and stuff. 1632 LITHGOW *Trav.* IV. 139 The couertures being erected.. after the Italian fashion with gutterd tyle. 1634 J. B[ATE] *Myst. Nat.* 64 Take of oyle of Tile one pound. 1707 MORTIMER *Husb.* (1721) I. 142 To do them with Dutch Tile, such as they set Chimneys with. 1842 DICKENS *Amer. Notes* xi. (1850) 112/1 Cincinnati is a beautiful city..with..its well-paved roads, and foot-ways of bright tile.

β. c 1425 WYNTOUN *Cron.* I. v. 235 He gert twa pilleris sone be maid: Off tild or plaister wes the tane, The toþer wes of merbill stane. c 1450 *Maitl. Club Misc.* III. 205 A litill basyn of payntit tild for the hee alter. 1552 LYNDESAY *Monarche* 1702 All fell to warke, boith man and chylde, Sum holkit claye, sum brynt the tylde. 1553–4 *Burgh Rec. Edinb.* (1871) II. 346 Item, to Maister Johne Prestoun for ane hundreith tylde..xvs.

†**b.** The covering of a roof, roofing. *Obs. rare.*

1611 CORYAT *Crudities* 362 The tyle of most of their houses is made of pieces of wood.

**3.** *slang.* A hat. Cf. TILED *ppl. a.* 1 c.

1823 in *Spirit Pub. Jrnls.* 55 The prompter's boy threw up his tile. 1825 *Sporting Mag.* XVI. 59 The Suffolk Champion took off his tile, and made a silent appeal. 1837 DICKENS *Pickw.* xii, Afore the brim went it was a wery handsome tile. 1873 O. W. HOLMES *Centenn. Dinner Boston Pier* 22 The square-toed boys in the three-cornered tiles.

**4.** Applied to an ancient Greek game: see quot.

1837 B. D. WALSH *Aristoph., Knights* II. iv. 212 *note*, 'The game of tiles' was played [thus]—A tile is provided, ..black on one side, and white on the other. The players are separated into two..parties, the blacks and the whites. A child tosses up the tile in the air,..if it falls with the black side uppermost, the blacks run after the whites [etc.].

**5.** Short for TILE-FISH.

1893 *Worthington's Mag.* (Hartford, Conn.) I. 150 The Tile should be obtainable in numbers equal to the cod..its flesh is more delicate and has a better flavor.

**6.** *attrib.* and *Comb.*, as *tile pavement*, *paving*, *roof*, *roofing*, *sole*; *tile-layer*, *-moulder*, *-scraper*; *tile-clad*, *-covered*, *-floored*, *-like*, *-lined*, *-paved*, *-roofed* adjs.; **tile-burner**, one who burns or bakes clay into tiles, a tile-maker; **tile-clay**, a kind of clay adapted for making tiles; **tile copper**, impure copper or 'bottoms' (BOTTOM *sb.* 8 b) made in flat rectangular plates or 'tiles'; **tile creasing**: see CREASING *vbl. sb.*[2] 2; **tile-drain** *sb.*, a drain constructed of tiles; so **tile-drain** *v. trans.*, to drain (a field, etc.) by means of tiles; **tile-draining** *vbl. sb.*; **tile-earth** = *tile-clay*; **tile-field**, a piece of ground where tiles are made: cf. *brick-field*; **tile-laths**, laths supporting the tiles of a roof; **tile-machine**, a machine for making tiles, esp. drain-tiles; †**tile-oast** = TILE-KILN; **tile-ore**, an earthy variety of cuprite or copper ore, usually of a reddish colour; **tile-oven** = TILE-KILN; **tile-pipe**, a hollow cylindrical tile for drainage; **tile-pit**, a pit in which clay for tiles is dug; **tile-red** *a.* and *sb.*, (of) a red colour like that of tiles; **tile-root**, name for the South African genus *Geissorhiza* of iridaceous plants, from the overlapping scales on the rhizome, the remains of the bases of the leaves; **tile-seed**, name for the Australian genus *Geissois* of saxifragaceous trees, from the flattened seeds; †**tile-stricker**, a workman who formed the clay into a brick or tile; **tile-tea**, an inferior kind of brick-tea: see quots.; †**tile-theeker**, one who covers roofs with tiles, a tiler; **tile-ways** *adv.*, in the manner or form of a tile or tiles; **tile-work**, work consisting of tiles; formerly including brick-work, and pottery in general; **tile-works**, a place in which tiles are made; **tile-wright** [repr. OE. *tigel wyrhta*], a maker of tiles; **tile-yard**, a yard or enclosure where tiles are made. See also TILE-FISH, -KILN, etc.

1563–6 in *Archæologia* XXXVI. 303 To the *tyle burner. 1830 *Cumb. Farm Rep.* 62 in *Lib. U. K.*, *Husb.* III, The engagement with the Staffordshire tile burner. 1849 CLOUGH *Amours de Voyage* III. 233 Looking down on the *tile-clad streets. 1707 MORTIMER *Husb.* (1721) I. 78 A sort of yellow *Tile-Clay. 1825 J. NICHOLSON *Operat. Mechanic* 714 The copper should be tough cake, and not *tile. 1870 ROSKELL in *Eng. Mech.* 18 Feb. 547/3 They are then separated..and worked up to make an inferior quality of copper, known in the trade as 'tile copper'. 1854 H. MILLER *Sch. & Schm.* (1858) 316 Dingy, low-roofed, *tile-covered hovels. 1591 PERCIVAL *Sp. Dict.*, *Tejo*, a *tile couering. 1844 STEPHENS *Bk. Farm* I. 585 The Marquis of Tweeddale..has..*tile-drained extensively. 1830 *Cumb. Farm Rep.* 67 in *Lib. Usef. Kn.*, *Husb.* III, The system of *tile-draining is.. begun in Ayrshire. 1828 WEBSTER, **Tile-earth*, a species of strong clayey earth; stiff and stubborn land. 1882 OGILVIE s. v. *Tile-field*, The palace of the Tuileries is thus named from standing on what was once a *tile-field. 1849 DICKENS *Dav. Copp.* x, The *tile-floored kitchen. 1844 STEPHENS *Bk. Farm* I. 188 A tile roof requires *tile-lath, 1½ inch square, and 11 inches apart. 1851 RICHARDSON *Geol.* (1885) 448 Ancient reptiles..; their.. covering consisted of long, narrow, wedge-shaped, *tile-like, horny scales. 1895 *Jrnl. Roy. Inst. Brit. Archit.* 14 Mar. 348 The *tile-lined walls of the Alhambra. 1844 STEPHENS *Bk. Farm* I. 581 The.. *tile-machine.. makes tiles at the rate of 10,000 tiles a day. 1591 PERCIVAL *Sp. Dict.*, *Tejar*, a *tile ost. 1823 URE *Dict. Chem.* (ed. 2), '*Tile ore*, a sub-species of octohedral red copper ore. 1535 COVERDALE 2 *Sam.* xii. 31 He broughte them forth..and burned them in *tyle ouens. 1891 in *Cent. Dict.* 1715 LEONI *Palladio's Archit.* (1742) I. 27 Square *Tyle-Pavements are more agreeable to the Eye. c 1440 *Pallad. on Husb.* I. 431 And yote on hit *tyl pauyng playn and stronge. 1849 *Ecclesiologist* IX. 356 Cylindrical *tile-pipes. 1656 HEYLIN *Surv. France* 120 Many lime-kils and *Tile-pits. 1805–17 R. JAMESON *Char. Min.* (ed. 3) 71 *Tile-red is hyacinth-red, mixed with greyish-white...Examples, Porcelain-jasper and zeolite. 1600 HOLLAND *Livy* XXXVI. XXXVII. 939 Two tame oxen climed up a ladder in the street Carinæ, to the *tyle-roofe of a certaine house. 1844 STEPHENS *Bk. Farm* I. 199 In *tile-roofing, tiles are made on purpose to hold a pane of glass. 1829 LOUDON *Encycl. Plants* (1836) 40 *Geissorhiza*, *Tile-Root. 1884 MILLER *Plant n.*, *Tile-seed. 1844 STEPHENS *Bk. Farm* I. 530 The bricks..could form either a smooth inclined sole like *tile-soles, or a series of steps. 1585 *Canterbury Marr. Licences* 22 May (MS.), *Tyle-stricker. 1858 SIMMONDS *Dict. Trade*, **Tile-tea*, a kind of flat brick tea, of much solidity, made in China,..sold to the Armenians and Tartars, who distribute it to the Caucasian provinces and Eastern Siberia...It is..stewed with milk, butter, salt, and herbs, constituting rather an article of food than a..beverage. 1882 OGILVIE, *Tile-tea*, a kind of inferior tea prepared by stewing refuse leaves with milk, butter, salt, and herbs, and solidifying the mixture by pressing it into moulds. c 1440 *York Myst.* xiv. (*heading*) The *tille thekers. 1789 MRS. PIOZZI *Journ. France* II. 272 The roofs are all wood cut *tile-ways. 1535 COVERDALE *Isa.* ix. 10 The *tyle worcke is fallen downe, but we will buylde it with harder stones. 1865 ELIZA METEYARD *Jos. Wedgwood* I. 42 The ..term of tilework embraced every article manufactured by the Saxon, and later by the Norman Potter. 1882 OGILVIE, *Tile-work* [? *Tile-works*], a place where tiles are made; a tilery. 1891 *Cent. Dict.*, Tile-works. 1906 A. B. TODD *Autobiog.* vii. 70, I went to labour at the Lanfine tile-works. c 1000 *Ags. Gosp.* Matt. xxvii. 10, & hiȝ sealdon þæt on *tiȝelwyrhtena æcyr. 1865 ELIZA METEYARD *Jos. Wedgwood* I. 93 Every worker in its clays became a tile-wright, whether he moulded tiles, or formed the homely pipkin or porringer, the slab-like dish, or ale-vat for the hall. 1832 *Scoreby Farm Rep.* 24 in *Lib. U. K.*, *Husb.* III. The price..at the *tile-yards is from thirty-five to forty-two shillings per thousand. 1848 DICKENS *Dombey* vi, Some very uncomfortable places, such as brick-fields and tile yards.

†**Tile**, *sb.*[2] *Obs. rare*[−1]. [ME., ? absol. use of OE. *til* adj. serviceable, competent, good, excellent.] ? Gain, profit; wealth, possessions, goods.

c 1250 *Gen. & Ex.* 1519 An hundred so mikel wex his tile, So may god friðe ðor he wile.

**Tile** (təil), *v.* Also 4– tyle. [f. TILE *sb.*[1]; in sense 2, back-formation from TILER 2.]

**1.** *trans.* To cover with tiles; to overlay (a floor or roof) or line (a wall, fire-place, etc.) with tiles; in quot. 1812, to roof.

c 1375 *Sc. Leg. Saints* xl. (*Ninian*) 930 Þar-of eftire, in schort quhile, He gert his quere rycht wele tyle. 1467 in *Eng. Gilds* (1870) 386 That the owners..tyle the thacched houses. 1591 in *Gentl. Mag.* (1779) XLIX. 81 Many offices new builded..all which were tyled. 1605 in Willis & Clark *Cambridge* (1886) II. 494 Thomas Yates to Slate and Tyle ye Kytchen. 1704 N. N. tr. *Boccalini's Advts. fr. Parnass.* III. 272 My Spanish Palace, which I might easily have Tiled with Massie Gold or Silver. 1812 BIGLAND *Beauties Eng. & Wales* XVI. 629 Open hay barns, tiled with slate. 1829 D. CONWAY *Norway* 152 Assisting to tile a house. 1901 *Westm. Gaz.* 10 Jan. 7/3 The tunnels are to be tiled-up.

**b.** *transf.* and *fig.* To cover as with tiles; to cover *over*, cover *up*: *spec.* of overlapping leaves, scales, etc. (= IMBRICATE *v.* 2). †In quot. 1641–2, to place (a thing) upon another so as to cover it.

1512 *Acc. Ld. High Treas. Scot.* IV. 298 To tile the kingis oratour in the Margret schip, xxxv elnis Kendillye. 1641–2 J. SHUTE *Sarah & Hagar* (1649) 62 God.. hath heaped up blessings upon us; yea, tyled one favour upon another. 1719 LONDON & WISE *Compl. Gard.* IX. 322 By tyling up, or wrapping about, or Earthing up, or otherwise covering them. 1776 WITHERING *Brit. Plants* (1796) III. 783 Sphagnum...Leaves..concave, soft, tiling the branches. 1884 W. K. PARKER *Mammalian Desct.* iv. (1885) 95 The Pangolin is tiled over with patches of cemented hair.

**2.** *Freemasonry.* (Usually **tyle.**) To protect (a lodge or meeting) from interruption and intrusion, so as to keep its proceedings secret, by placing a TILER before the door. Also *transf.* to bind (a person) to secrecy; to keep (any meeting or proceeding) strictly secret.

1762 *Key to Free-Masonry* (1776) 4 *Master to the Junior Deacon.* What is the chief Care of a Mason? *Ans.* To see that the Lodge is tyled. 1768 T. WILSON *Master-Mason* (ed. 2) 26 The master asked his brother warden, if he was a mason, if the lodge was tiled from whence he came. 1846 THACKERAY *Bk. Snobs* xxv, Come, come, Snob my boy, we are all tiled, you know. 1859 SALA *Tw. round Clock* (1861) 308 The doors of those mysterious meeting-places are 'tiled' as securely as Freemasons' lodges. 1896 *Law Times* CII. 123/2 A Parliament chamber [at the Inns of Court] is close tiled, except for purposes of discipline affecting character.

**Tile**, obs. form of TEIL, lime-tree, TILL *v.*

**Tiled** (təild), *ppl. a.* [f. TILE *v.* + -ED[1].]

**1.** Covered, roofed, lined, or laid with tiles.

c 1450 *Godstow Reg.* 495 Bitwene the tyled house of Isabell..and the ovyn of the same Isabell. 1546 J. HEYWOOD *Prov.* (1867) 58 A tyeld house. 1609 *Ev. Woman in Hum.* IV. ii, He that has not a tilde house must bee glad of a thatch house. 1849 DICKENS *Dav. Copp.* xxii, She was in the tiled kitchen. 1881 'RITA' *Lady Coquette* iii, A bright wood fire burns in the old tiled fireplace.

**b.** *Nat. Hist.* Covered with or composed of overlapping leaves, scales, or the like (also said of the leaves, etc.); imbricated. ? *Obs.*

1750–1 MRS. DELANY *Life & Corr.* (1862) III. 27 A present..of a tiled cockle, that weighs above a hundred weight. 1776 WITHERING *Brit Plants* (1796) I. 139 Scirpus...Spike tiled on every side, the florets separated by Scales *Ibid.* 364 The tiled leaves at the extremity of the plant. 1805 PRISCILLA WAKEFIELD *Domestic Recr.* (1806) I. 12 The third order have four tiled or feathered wings.

**c.** *slang.* Hatted.

1792 *Misc. Ess.* in *Ann. Reg.* 153/2 Nor were living heads only new tiled in this taste. The statues of their favorite poets were crowned with a red cap.

**2.** Locally applied to fish dried in the sun (? upon tiles).

1808 SCOTT *Autobiog.* in Lockhart, Dined at Prestonpans on tiled haddocks very sumptuously. 1830 — *Diary* 27 June, [At Cockenzie] we had a tiled whiting, a dish unknown elsewhere.

**3.** *Freemasonry.* See TILE *v.* 2.

**Tile-fish.** [Suggested by the termination of the generic name *Lopholatilus*, and by the brilliant colouring resembling ornamental tiles.] Name for the fish *Lopholatilus chamæleonticeps*, found in abundance in 1879 off the coast of New England, and valued as food; supposed to be extinct from the early part of 1882 till 1892, since which year its numbers have again increased.

1881 TANNER in *Rep. U. S. Comm. Fish & Fisheries* (1884) 34 One of the tile-fish taken in the morning was boiled for dinner and served with egg sauce. 1884 GOODE *Fisheries of U. S.* I. 360 The Tile-fish..a form discovered on a hitherto unexplored ground, eighty miles southeast of Noman's Land, Massachusetts, in [May] 1879...Captain Kirby of Gloucester, who was the first to obtain specimens of this fish, caught in a few hours several hundred. 1893 *Worthington's Mag.* (Hartford, Conn.) I. 150 The Tile Fish, with its back of pale violet hue and greenish-yellow spots, is one of the most brilliantly colored fishes in the world. 1902 JORDAN & EVERMANN *Amer. Food Fishes* 504 The famous tilefish, whose discovery only a few years ago, and sudden disappearance a few months later, has interested commercial fishermen and scientists as well...It was not until 1892 that they were found again.

**Ti·le-kiln.** Also 6-7 -kil(l. A kiln in which tiles are baked.

**1531** *Lett. & Pap. Hen. VIII*, V. 180 A longe cart caryng of tylys from the tyle kyll at Newname Brige unto the Kinges storehouse within the towne of Calais. **1675** COVEL in *Early Voy. Levant* (Hakl. Soc.) 185 There is also just by this town a tile kill. **1830** *Cumb. Farm Rep.* 62 in *Lib. Usef. Knowl., Husb.* III, A proper tile-kiln, shed, etc., were erected.

**Ti·le-maker.** A maker of tiles; a workman employed in making tiles.

**1415** *Ordo pagin. ludi Corp. Cr.* in *York Myst.* Introd. p. xxv, Tielmakers, Milners. **1548** *Nottingham Rec.* IV. 4 Robertus Walesby, tylemaker. **1562** [see TILER 1]. **1688** LUTTRELL *Brief Rel.* (1857) I. 453 The princes nurse is..a tilemaker's wife. **1724** *Lond. Gaz.* No. 6251/3 Every Brickmaker and Tylemaker. **1837** PRICHARD *Phys. Hist. Man.* (ed. 3) II. 135 A caste of potters and tile-makers.

So **Ti·le-making.**

**1437** *Coventry Leet-bk.* 188 That the meire with hys Councell haue the ouersight off Tyle-makyng. **1844** STEPHENS *Bk. Farm* I. 581 Clay of excellent quality for tile-making.

†**Ti·leman.** *Obs.* = TILE-MAKER.

**1479-81** *Rec. St. Mary at Hill* 105 Payd to Knyghte, Tyleman, for ij mⁱ tyle, x s viij d. **1609** *MS. Acc. St. John's Hosp., Canterb.*, Payd vnto the tyll mane for a thousand and a haulfe of tylles.

**Tile-pin.** A 'pin' (PIN *sb.*[1] 1) or peg of hard wood used to fasten the tiles to the laths of a roof.

**1338** in Dugdale *Monasticon* (1846) II. 585/2 In latthenayles..*jd.* Item in latthes, j d...Item in tyelpynnes, ob. **1422-3** *Abingdon Rolls* (Camden) 97 In tyʒlpynnes emptis viij d. **1426-7** *Rec. St. Mary at Hill* 65 A buschel tyle pynnes viij d. **1563-4** in Swayne *Sarum Churchw. Acc.* (1896) 109 A peck of tylepyns—3d. **1679** MOXON *Mech. Exerc.* viii. 145 Tile-pins of Oak. **1825** J. NICHOLSON *Operat. Mechanic* 550 A square of plain tiling will require a bundle of laths,..two bushels of lime, one bushel of sand, and a peck of tile-pins.

**Tiler** (tai·ləɹ). Also 3 tyelere, 5 tylare, tyller, tiller, tiellere, teyller, teler, 6 tyloure, tylar, teiler, 7 tylere, 5-9 tyler. [f. TILE *sb.*[1] and *v.* + -ER[1].]

**1.** One who covers the roofs of buildings with tiles, a tile-layer; also formerly, a tile-maker.

?*a* **1300** *Deed* in *Shropsh. Arch. Soc. Trans.* (1878) I. 368 De domo mea..que est inter domum Willi le galeys et domum Martini le Tyelere. **1415** *Ordo pagin. ludi Corp. Cr.* in *York Myst.* Introd. p. xxi, Tylers. **1467** in *Eng. Gilds* (1870) 374 That euery tyler marke his tyle. **1483** *Cath. Angl.* 379/1 A Teler,..*tegulator.* **1562** *Act 5 Eliz.* c. 4 § 30 Tharte or Occupation of a..Bricklayer, Tyler, Slater, Healyer, Tilemaker. **1663** GERBIER *Counsel* 51 The Tiler, who often removes ten Tiles to lay two new ones. **1735** BERKELEY *Querist* § 399 Whether..tilers, plumbers, and glaziers would not find employment if..building prevailed? **1824** LANDOR *Imag. Conv.* xii. Wks. 1846 I. 49 Like tilers, in mending one hole, they make another.

**2.** *Freemasonry.* (Usually **tyler.**) The doorkeeper who keeps the uninitiated from intruding upon the secrecy of the lodge or meeting.

*c* **1742** in Hone *Every-day Bk.* (1827) II. 525 Two Tylers, or Guarders..are to guard the Lodge, with a drawn Sword, from all Cowens and Eves-droppers. **1762** *Key to Free-Masonry* (1776) 39 As soon as you come to the Door of the Lodge, you will find the Tyler on the Outside, with a drawn Sword in his Hand, and a white Apron on. **1888** [see TILING 1 b].

†**3.** (See quot.) *slang. Obs.*

**1659** *Caterpillers of Nation Anat.*, Tilers, or Cloyers, equivalent to shoplifters.

**4.** A tile-kiln.

**1877** in KNIGHT *Dict. Mech.*

**5.** A cat that frequents the tiles or roofs.

**1905** VIOLET HUNT *Autobiog. Cat* ix. 108 A nice tiler and mouser would be more appropriate.

† **6.** ?A pimple. *Obs. rare*[—1].

**1660** HOWELL *Parly of Beasts* 25 [The Ass says] Our very Urine is found to be good against Tilers or Morphews in Ladies faces.

**Tilery** (tai·ləri). [f. TILE, TILER: see -ERY.] A place where tiles are made; a tile-field or -kiln.

**1846** J. BAXTER *Libr. Pract. Agric.* I. 237 From the tilery to his farm. **1856** *Farmer's Mag.* Jan. 75 In cases where estates extensively require draining, tileries and kilns should be erected. **1871** RUSKIN *Fors Clav.* vi. 11 The first rough potter's fields, tileries, as they called them, or Tuileries.

†**Ti·le-sherd.** *Obs.* or *dial.* [f. TILE *sb.*[1] + SHERD, SHARD; cf. *potsherd.*] A broken piece or fragment of tile.

**1527** *Luton Trin. Guild* (1906) 190 For careeg' of a loode of tyle sherdis to vndre pyn wᵗall. **1533** *MS. Rawl. D.* 776 lf. 147 b, A loode of Tyle sherdes ffor the levelyng vppe of the vnderpynnyng of the said wharffe. **1616** CHAMPNEY *Voc. Bps.* To Rdr, Little children that build Castles of Tile-shards. **1777** HOWARD *Prisons Eng.* (1780) 369 Some prisoners were employed in beating or pounding tile-sherds for the bricklayers. *a* **1825** FORBY *Voc. E. Anglia*, *Tile-sherd*,..a fragment of a tile, as potsherd of a pot.

**Tilestone** (tai·lˌstōun). Forms: see TILE and STONE. [OE. *tigelstán*, f. *tigele*, TILE *sb.*[1] + *stán*, STONE *sb.* Cf. MHG. *ziegelstein.*]

†**1.** A brick or tile; the material of bricks or tiles: = TILE *sb.*[1] 1, 2. *Obs.*

*a* **1100** *Gloss.* in *Eng. Studien* XI. 66 *Hec imbrex*, tigelstan. **1382** WYCLIF *Gen.* xi. 3 Cometh, & make we tiel [1388 tiel] stoons, and sethe we hem with fier. **1388** — *Isa.* ix. 10 Tijl stoonys fellen doun, but we schulen bilde with square stoonys. **1432-50** tr. *Higden* (Rolls) II. 233 Oon ston was of marbole,..that other was of tyleston. *c* **1425** tr. *Arderne's Treat. Fistula* 82 Tak a tile stone or a scarþe of a potte, and putte it in þe middez of brynnyng colez. **1573** L. LLOYD *Marrow of Hist.* (16 3) 21 Pyrrhus..was killed by a..woman with a Tile stone. **1600** NASHE *Summer's Last Will* in Hazl. *Dodsley* VIII. 25 For fear of wearing out my lord's tile-stones with your hobnails. **1681** CHETHAM *Angler's Vade-m.* iv. § 20 Dry them on a Fire-Shovel or Tilestone or in an Oven.

**2.** *Geol.* Any laminated flagstone, splitting into layers thicker than *slate*, suitable for roofing-tiles; *spec.* a group of sandstones forming the transition beds between the Silurian and Devonian systems.

**1668** CHARLETON *Onomast.* 242 *Saxum Fissile*..Slate or Tyle-stone. **1719** STRACHEY in *Phil. Trans.* XXX. 971 At Stanton they have..an Iron-Gritt or grey Tile-Stone, which is a Fore-runner of the Coal-Clives. **1778** *Eng. Gazetteer* (ed. 2), Norton under Hambden-Hill, Som...has large quarries of free-stone,..as well as of tile-stone, &c. **1842** SEDGWICK in Hudson *Guide Lakes* (1843) 213 Three groups—the lowest characterized by red flagstone (or 'tilestone'). **1876** A. H. GREEN *Phys. Geol.* ii. § 7 If the layers are thin enough for roofing purposes the rock is called a Tilestone.

†**Tile·tte.** *Obs. rare*[—1]. [f. TILE *sb.*[1] + -ETTE.] A small or minute tile.

*c* **1440** *Pallad. on Husb.* vi. 195 Brode and thynne Tilette [L. *tesellas*] or tabulette of marbul stoon.

†**Tilfoi·r**, *conj. Sc. Obs.* [f. *til-* = To- prefix + *foir*, FORE *adv.* and *prep.*] = TOFORE, BEFORE.

**15..** *Aberd. Reg.* (Jam.), A yeir tilfoir he deceissit.

†**Tilgi·ddire**, *adv. Sc. Obs.* [for TOGETHER, with *til-* = To-.] Together.

*c* **1375** *Sc. Leg. Saints* xl. (*Ninian*) 420 To god þe fadir be lowinge,..To god þe sone ay honoure be,..Til haly gaste als,..& til þame til-giddire richt.

**Tiliaceous** (tiliˌēi·ʃəs), *a. Bot.* [f. L. *tiliāce-us* (f. *tilia* lime-tree) + -OUS: see -ACEOUS.] Belonging to the Natural Order *Tiliaceæ*, typified by the genus *Tilia*, the lime or linden tree.

**1891** in *Cent. Dict.* *Mod.* Jute is obtained from species of the tiliaceous genus *Corchorus.*

†**Tilie.** *Obs.* Also 2 teolie, 4 tilye. [OE. *tilia*, agent-n. f. *tilian* to TILL.] One who tills or cultivates the soil; a husbandman; = TILLER *sb.*[1]

*c* **1000** *Ags. Gosp.* Matt. xxi. 38 Þa ða tylian [*c* **1160** *Hatt. G.* tylien] þone sunu ʒesawun, þa cwædon hiʒ [etc.]. *c* **1175** *Lamb. Hom.* 133 Alse þe wise teolie þenne he wule sawe nimeð ʒeme of twam þingen, an is hweðer þet lond beo bicumelic to þe sede. *c* **1200** *Trin. Coll. Hom.* 155 On tilie ferde ut and sew. *a* **1225** *Ancr. R.* 416 Þeos riche ancren þet beoð eorðe tilien, oðer habbeð rentes i-sette. *c* **1325** *Chron. Eng.* 93 (Ritson) Muche folk..That were erthe tilyes gode.

**Tilie**, obs. form of TEIL, lime-tree, TILL *v.*[1]

**Tilier**, obs. form of TILLER *sb.*[1]

**Tiling** (tai·liŋ), *vbl. sb.* [f. TILE *v.* and *sb.*[1] + -ING[1].]

**1.** The action of the verb TILE; the covering (of a roof, etc.) with or as with tiles.

*c* **1440** *Promp. Parv.* 494/1 Tylynge, of howsys, *tegulacio.* **1591** PERCIVAL *Sp. Dict.*, *Albañeria*, tiling, Tilers art, Masons craft. **1624** CAPT. SMITH *Virginia* vi. 209 Free-stone for building, Slate for tyling. **1726** LEONI *Alberti's Archit.* I. 57/1 Another..convenient way of Tiling.

**b.** *Freemasonry.* (Usually **tyling.**) The proper guarding of a lodge.

**1888** *Pall Mall G.* 31 Oct. 7/2 Brother W—— E——, Acting Past Master..deliberately broke the tyling of the lodge, and placed the tyler inside along with the ladies.

**2.** *concr.* Work consisting of tiles; the tiles forming the covering of a roof, floor, etc., collectively.

**1526** TINDALE *Luke* v. 19 They went vp..and lett hym doune thorowe the tylynge. **1634** SIR T. HERBERT *Trav.* 61 Churches..their outside tyling, pargetted with azure stones. **1694** tr. *Marten's Voy. Spitzbergen* in *Acc. Sev. Late Voy.* II. 135 The Head of the Whale..goeth down sloaping like unto the tyling of an House. **1725** *Bradley's Fam. Dict.* s. v. *Building*, Tiling is measured by ten Foot Square...Three Bushels of Lime will do a Square of Tiling. **1883** MRS. BISHOP *Sk. Malay Pen.* ii, in *Leisure Hour* 21/2 Dutch tiling and Dutch..conceits of all kinds abound.

**3.** *attrib.*

**1703** MOXON *Mech. Exerc.* 248 A Tyling Trowel, to take up the Morter and lay it on the Tiles. **1765** *Museum Rust.* IV. 80 Tiling lath, 2 s. 10 d. per bunch. **1907** *Westm. Gaz.* 1 Oct. 7/3 Two shillingsworth of cement and sand would be ..required for a yard of tiling-work.

**Till** (til), *sb.*[1] Forms: 5-6 tylle, 6 tille, 6-7 tyll, 7 til, 6- till. [Origin obscure.]

†**1.** A small box, casket, or closed compartment, contained within or forming part of a larger box, chest, or cabinet; sometimes one that could be lifted out, sometimes a drawer in a cabinet or chest of drawers; used for keeping valuables, documents, etc., more safely. *Obs.* except as in 2.

**1452** in *Munimenta Academica* (Rolls) II. 653 Prout patet in scriptis indenturis positis in 'le tylle' in studio meo Oxoniæ. **1530** PALSGR. 281/1 Tyll in a chest, *chettron.* **1534** *Inv. Wardr. Kath. Arragon* in *Camden Misc.* (1855) 40 One cofar..having foure tilles therin, the fore fronte of every of them gilte. **1547-53** SIR R. SADLER *List* in *30th Rep. Dep. Kpr. Publ. Rec.* (1869) 224 Bagges of Bokes, Lettres, and other Writenges remayneng in the study at Westminster, and in several tilles within the same. **1549** in Palgrave *Anc. Kal. & Inv. Excheq.* (1836) III. 417 Which lettres patentes do lye in the nethermost tyll under the tyll wheron is written in text hand Acquietauncies. **1561** in Nichols *Progr. Q. Eliz.* (1823) I. 118 By Anthony Anthony a corbonett fall [full] of tylls. **1591** PERCIVAL *Sp. Dict.*, *Caxon de arca*, the till of a chest, *loculus.* **1633** G. HERBERT *Temple, Confess.* i, Within my heart I made Closets; and in them many a chest;..In those chests, boxes; in each box, a till. **1651** DAVENANT *Gondibert* III. I. liv, A spacious cabinet, with all things fraught... she by degrees Lifts every till, does every drawer draw. **1664** PEPYS *Diary* 8 Jan., Going to his secret till in his desk, wherein the key of his cash-chest lay. **1719** DE FOE *Crusoe* I. 229 When I came to the Till in the Chests, I found there three great Bags of Pieces of Eight. **1737** [S. BERINGTON] *G. de Lucca's Mem.* (1738) 13 Two little Cabinets..full of intricate Drawers or Tills.

**2.** Now *spec.* A drawer, money-box, or similar receptacle under and behind the counter of a shop or bank, in which cash for daily transactions is temporarily kept.

**1698** *Lond. Gaz.* No. 3363/4 Lost out of Mr. Wray's Shop in Little-Britain, a Til. **1801** MAR. EDGEWORTH *Contrast* v, James swept some loose money off the counter into the till. **1866** CRUMP *Banking* i. 31 All the money..excepting what must be kept in the 'till' for immediate use. **1908** *Times* 22 Apr. 5/5 Officers..suspected they had contemplated robbing the tills.

*fig.* **1886** *Harper's Mag.* Jan. 242 There is generally a race to see who shall first tap nature's till [i. e. strike oil].

**3.** *Printing.* Each of the spaces or cells between the ribbed projections of the platen of a hand printing-press, in which the pressman keeps various small requisites.

**1888** JACOBI *Printers' Vocab.* 141 *Tills*, the cell-like divisions in the top side of the platen of a hand printing press.

**4.** *attrib.* and *Comb.* (from 2), as *till-lock, -money, -robber, -robbing*; **till-alarm**, a device by which a bell is automatically rung when the till is opened; **till-box** = sense 1; **till-tapping**, pilfering from a till; so **till-tapper.**

**1692** *Lond. Gaz.* No. 2756/4 Stolen..a Till-box with some Money in it. **1737** *Salmon's Country Builder's Estimator* (ed. 2) 110 Cabinet Locks, Till Locks, and Scrutoire Locks. **1862** *Catal. Internat. Exh.*, *Brit.* II. No. 5152 Ticket, receipt, and till protector. **1877** KNIGHT *Dict. Mech.*, *Till- alarm.* **1891** *Daily News* 7 Feb. 2/4 Part of their reserves..being necessary 'till-money' or daily transactions in small change. **1893** *Columbus (Ohio) Disp.* 14 Nov., For some time the firm has been a loser by persistent till-tapping...The camera lens closed automatically with the photographs of the till tappers. **1895** SNAITH *D. Marvin* xxvii, Pete declared it [the money stolen] was a month's till money.

**Till**, *sb.*[2] Orig. and chiefly *Sc.* [Origin unascertained: cf. THILL [2] in similar sense.]

**1.** A term applied to a stiff clay, more or less impervious to water, usually occurring in unstratified deposits, and forming an ungenial subsoil. Originally a term of agriculture in Scotland.

**1765** A. DICKSON *Treat. Agric.* II. (ed. 2) 222 They [plowmen] are so inattentive, as to leave good soil in some places, and turn up till in others. **1799** J. ROBERTSON *Agric. Perth* 19 On the declivities of almost all the hills a strong stiff till abounds. *Ibid.* 477 Like all the land on the south aspect of the Seedlaws being a red till, capable of high cultivation and in most places approaching to the nature of loam. **1805** FORSYTH *Beauties Scotl.* II. 66 *Till*,..is in universal use among farmers,..implying very various mixtures of mineral substances placed under the fertile mould...In general,..a hard clay of any sort, which in a very slight degree admits the passage of water, and is impenetrable by the roots of plants. **1816** SCOTT *Antiq.* iv, Placing paving-stones beneath the tree when first planted..a barrier between his roots and the unkindly till. *Ibid.* xxiii, We're down to the till now,..and the ne'er a coffin or ony thing else is here.

*fig.* **1831** BREWSTER *Nat. Magic* xi. (1833) 287 It may lie long unproductive in the ungenial till of human knowledge.

**b.** In the majority of cases this clay belongs to the Glacial or Drift period, and in geological use 'till' has the specific sense 'boulder clay'.

**1842** DARWIN in *Life & Lett.* (1887) I. 300 A contribution to the Geological Society, on the boulders and 'till' of South America. **1851** *Jrnl. R. Agric. Soc.* XII. I. 281 This clay ..rests upon 'till', or boulder clay. **1863** LYELL *Antiq. Man* xii. (ed. 3) 218 Erratics of Scandinavian origin occur chiefly in the lower portions of the till. **1863** A. C. RAMSAY *Phys. Geog.* xxiv. (1878) 384 Much of the Lower Boulder-clay is known as 'Till' in Scotland.

**2.** Hard or soft shale; app. = THILL [2]. *dial.*

**1672** SINCLAIR *Misc. Observ. Hydrost.* 260 (Jam.) All metals, as stone and tilles (which are seems of black stone, and participat much of the nature of coal), ly one above another, and keep a regular course. **1831** W. PATRICK *Plants Lanark* Pref. 18 The stratum itself lies on a bed of till above the main coal.

**3.** *Comb.* **Till-stone**, a fissile shale, in coal-mines, etc.

*c* **1830** *Glouc. Farm Rep.* 4 in *Lib. Usef. Kn., Husb.* III, A thin wet clay, of a most adhesive nature, covering the thin fissile till-stone.

†**Till**, *sb.*[3] *Obs.* or *dial.* Abbrev. of LENTIL, *quasi* 'Lent-till': see quot. 1640. (Chiefly in *pl.*)

**1388** WYCLIF *Ezek.* iv. 9 Take..wheete, and barli, and beenys, and tillis [1382 lent]. **1398** TREVISA *Barth. De P. R.* XVII. xcvi. (Bodl. MS.), Malice off Tille is temprid ʒif þe skynne is ido aweye & þe piþ sode in fresche water. **14..** *Voc.* in Wr.-Wülcker 594/5 *Lupinus*, Tylles. **1607** *Schol. Disc. agst. Antichr.* I. ii. 95 What maketh the fitches, tylles, tares..which are mingled with the wheate? **1640** PARKINSON *Theatr. Bot.* 1068 Wee in English [call it] Lentills, but the country people in Hampshire, and other countries..call it Tills, leaving out the Lent, as thinking that word agreeth not with the matter. **1669** WORLIDGE *Syst. Agric.* (1681) 42 The least of all Pulses is the Lentil, in some places called Tills. **1760** J. LEE *Introd. Bot.* App. 330 Tills, *Ervum.*

**Till**, *sb.*[4] *Printing.* [Cf. MHG., Ger. *tülle* (LG. *dulle*, Du. *dille*) a socket in which something is fixed, or through which a rod or spindle passes.] In the early forms of hand printing-presses, a horizontal cross-piece extending between and fixed to the two main uprights, through which passes the hose or sleeve, and the shank of the spindle; also called *shelf*.

1611 COTGR., *Planche*,..the Till of a Printers Presse, or the shelfe that compasseth the Hose. 1683 MOXON *Mech. Exerc.*, *Printing* x. ¶6 The Till is a Board about one Inch thick... In its middle it hath a round Hole..for the Shank of the Spindle to pass through. 1771 LUCKOMBE *Hist. Print.* 366 It may..be botched up by putting scabbord between the Hose and the square holes of the Till. 1841 SAVAGE *Dict. Printing* 796 *Till* or *Shelf*, a mahogany shelf that clasps the hose and causes it and the spindle to come down perpendicularly without any play.

**Till,** *sb.*5 *Obs.* or *dial.* [f. TILL *v.*1]

**1.** An act of tilling or ploughing land: see TILL *v.*1 4.

1647 *Husbandman's Plea agst. Tithes* 36 Item for plowing of the fallow for Wheat at 3 tilles at 5 s. the Acre, for every of the three times plowing 60 li. 1760 BROWN *Compl. Farmer* II. 32 In Oxfordshire..they give their sour land a till, according to the..condition of their lands.

**b.** *concr.* (See quots.)

1794–1806 *Rep. Agric., Lanc.* 27 (E.D.S.) *Till*, a compost of earth and lime, mixed. 1828 *Craven Gloss.*, *Till, Tillage*, manure, compost.

**2.** ? Labour, toil: cf. TILL *v.*1 1.

? *a* 1800 *Dame Oliphant* xii. in Child *Ballads* (1886) IV. 409/1 Willie he gaed hame again, To his hard task and till.

† **Till,** *sb.*6 *Obs. rare*−1. [f. TILL *v.*3] Allurement, enticement.

1596 COLSE *Penelope* (1880) 179, I feare me he hath caught some doue, And keepes her tame, with tills of loue.

**Till** (til), *v.*1 Forms: α. 1–2 tilian (1 til(i)ȝan), 2–5 tilie(n, 3 tiliȝen, tillien, 3–5 tylye, 3–6 tile, tyle, 3–7 tille, 4 tilye, tylie, tilly, 4–6 tylle, 4–7 til, 6 tyll, 6– till. β. 1 tiol-, teolian, 2 teolien, 2–3 teliȝen, 4 telie(n, tell, teile, 4–5 (*Sc.* 6) tele, 5 telle, 6–7 *Sc.* teil, teill, 8–9 *dial.* teel. γ. 1–2 tylian, 3–4 tulie(n (*ii*), 4 tulye (*ii*). [OE. *tilian* to strive, acquire = OFris. *tilia* to get, cultivate, OS. *tilian* to obtain (MDu., Du. *telen* to breed, raise, cultivate, cause, etc.), OHG. *zilôn*, *zilên* to strive (G. *zielen* to aim, strive):—OTeut. **tilô-jan*, **tilêjan*, denom. f. **tilo*m: see TILL *prep.* By breaking of *i* before *l*, *tilian* became *tiolian*, *teolian*, later *tele*: cf. PILL *v.*1, PEEL *v.*1 (Sievers *Ags. Gram.* ed. 3, § 105, 3, § 107 Anm. 4, § 416, 14 a.).]

**I.** To labour, work for or at, cultivate.

† **1.** *intr.* To strive, exert oneself, labour, work.

α. *c* 897 K. ÆLFRED *Gregory's Past. C.* xix. 147 He sceal tilian ðæt he licige. *c* 1000 ÆLFRIC *Saints' Lives* xxviii. 168 To þisum swicolum life we swincað and tiliaþ and to þam towerdan life we tiliað hwonlice. *c* 1175 *Lamb. Hom.* 19 Nu sculle we..tilian to þere saule bihofðe. *c* 1200 *Trin. Coll. Hom.* 37 Sume men..tiliȝet[h] michel to oðre mannæs bihofþe. *a* 1225 *Ancr. R.* 404 Ure Louerd..tiled efter hore luue.

β, γ. 971 *Blickl. Hom.* 219 Se deada man cwic eft..& teolode to arisenne. *c* 1000 ÆLFRIC *Hom.* I. 412 Oxa teolað his hlaforde. *Ibid.* II. 76 Þa tyliað..Gode, þa ðe ne secað heora aȝen ȝestreon ðurh ȝytsunge. *c* 1175 *Lamb. Hom.* 133 Þenne heo fundieð to teoliende efter istreone. *c* 1200 *Trin. Coll. Hom.* 155 Þanne hie wilen tulien after strene.

† **2.** *trans.* To labour after, seek after, provide; to get by effort, to obtain, acquire, or earn by labour; also (later) *simply*, to get, obtain. In OE. and Early ME. const. with genitive, later with acc. *Obs.*

*a* 900 *Ags. Psalter* (Th.) xlviii. 7 Full neah ælc mann þæs tiolað..hu he on ecnesse swincan mæȝe. *c* 1000 ÆLFRIC *Hom.* II. 552 Se asolcena ðeowa, þe nolde tilian nan ðing his hlaforde. *c* 1016 *O. E. Chron.* an. 1016 (Laud), Hi..heom metes tilodon. *a* 1175 *Cott. Hom.* 223 Þu scealt mid ærfeðnesse þe metes tylian. *c* 1220 *Bestiary* 80 in *O. E. Misc.* 3 Ne maiȝ he [the eagle] tilen him non fode. 1297 R. GLOUC. (Rolls) 974 Hii..swonke & tylede hor liflode. *c* 1330 R. BRUNNE *Chron.* (1810) 220 His luf to tak & tille. 1377 LANGL. *P. Pl.* B. XIV. 67 Many wyntres men lyueden and no mete ne tulyeden [*v. rr.* teleden, tiliden, tilieden, tylied; C. XVI. 271 no mete telden]. *c* 1380 WYCLIF *Wks.* (1880) 300 Pore men..þat hauen greet neede..to þyng þat freris tillen of hem. *c* 1425 *Cast. Persev.* 2538 in *Macro Pl.* 153 A-forn mele, men mete schul tyle [*rimes* skyl, wyl, hyle]. *c* 1440 *York Myst.* vi. 59 Adam!..tille with-alle þi meete and drynke for euer-more.

† **3.** To take care of or attend to medically; to treat (a patient, or a disease). Const. as in 2. Only *OE.*

*a* 850 *Laws Ecgbert, Poenit.* IV. c. 20 Wifman..ȝif heo tilað hire cilde mid æniȝum wiccecræfte. *c* 897 K. ÆLFRED *Gregory's Past. C.* lxii. 457 Hwæðres..ðara yfela is betere ær to tilianne? *a* 1000 *Life St. Guthlac* xxii. (Goodw.) 96 His læces hine mid sealfum lange teolodon. *c* 1000 *Sax. Leechd.* II. 60 Þonan se micla ȝeoxa cume, oþþe hu hit mon tilian scule.

**4.** *trans.* To bestow labour and attention, such as ploughing, harrowing, manuring, etc., upon (land) so as to fit it for raising crops; to cultivate.

α. *c* 1205 LAY. 2618 Þat lond heo lette tilien [*c* 1275 tilie]. *a* 1300 *Cursor M.* 23851 (Edinb.) Il worþe it es to til [*v. rr.* tile, tille, *Gött.* tell] þe fild, Þat noht ogain þe sed mai yeld. *c* 1400 MAUNDEV. (Roxb.) xxxii. 147 Þe folk nowþer tillez ne sawez na land. *c* 1449 PECOCK *Repr.* III. i. (Rolls) 275 Feeldis..which thei hem silf tilien. 1535 COVERDALE *Gen.* ii. 5 Nether was there eny man to tylle the earth. 1625 CARPENTER *Geog. Delin.* II. i, He began..to till and manure the soyle with all heedfull industrie. 1765 HUTCHINSON *Hist. Mass.* I. 207 Light land being easily tilled. 1835 THIRLWALL *Greece* I. ix. 342 The prisoners were forced to till the enemy's land.

β. *c* 1200 *Vices & Virtues* 75 And land teliȝen and weriȝen. 13.. Tell [see quot. *a* 1300 in α]. *c* 1400 MAUNDEV. (Roxb.) xxii. 103 Men of oure stature, þe whilk telez þe land. *c* 1450 *Godstow Reg.* 33 In londes I-telyd and not I-telyd. 1536 in *Reg. Mag. Sig. Scot.* 1538. 394 Licence..to ryfe, outbreke and teill yeirlie 1000 acris of thair commounlandis. 1569 *Reg. Privy Council Scot.* I. 653 Na Scottisman dwelland in Scotland sall tak or teill ony ground in England. 1882 JAGO *Cornw. Gloss.*, *Teel*, to plant or sow.

**b.** *spec.* To plough (land).

1377 LANGL. *P. Pl.* B. XIX. 256 My plowman Piers shal ben.., And for to tulye [*v. r.* tilie] treuthe a teme shal he haue. 1513 DOUGLAS *Æneis* VI. xiv. 96 Quhair thow thi riggis telis for to saw. 1535 COVERDALE 1 *Sam.* xiv. 14 Halue an aker of londe, which a pare of oxen maye tyll in one daye. 1652 NEEDHAM tr. *Selden's Mare Cl.* 260 An Hide..is so much Land as a Man can till with one Plow for a year. 1863 FAWCETT *Pol. Econ.* I. iv. (1876) 42 The same ploughs till the land for many successive crops.

**c.** *absol.*

1100–21 *O. E. Chron.* an. 1097, On unȝewederan þa man oððe tilian sceolde oððe eft tilða ȝegaderian. 1340–70 *Alex. & Dind.* 854 Whan ȝe mow take no tol to tilien on erþe. *a* 1400–50 *Alexander* 4581 How suld ȝe telle withouten toles? 1596 DALRYMPLE tr. *Leslie's Hist. Scot.* v. (S.T.S.) I. 293 This Haii..was behaldeng in the neist feild how the pluche teilet. 1652 BP. HALL *Invis. World* I. viii, They then must purvey for their own food, and either till, or famish. 1850 MRS. JAMESON *Leg. Monast. Ord.* (1863) 125 They drained, they tilled, they planted.

† **5.** *trans.* To raise, rear (a crop); to tend and cultivate (a plant) so as to promote growth. *Obs.*

*c* 1250 *Gen. & Ex.* 1278 Abraham..tillede corn and sette treen. 1387 TREVISA *Higden* (Rolls) II. 309 To ere and sowe and haue corne i-teled. *c* 1400 MAUNDEV. (1839) v. 50 Men maken all weys þat bawme to ben tyled of the cristen men. 1483 CAXTON *Gold. Leg.* 391 b/1 Of hym that tylyeth the vyne.

**6.** *fig.* To cultivate (something figured as land or as a crop, e.g. the mind, a 'field' of knowledge, a virtue, etc.).

1393 LANGL. *P. Pl.* C. I. 87 Bisshopes..Ben chargid with holy churche charyte to tulie, Þat is, leel loue..a-mong lered and lewed. 1535 COVERDALE *Ezek.* xxxvi. 9 Vnto you will I turne me, that ye maye be tylled and sowen. 1642 GAUDEN *Three Serm.* 132 Hee becomes tild and polished for the best society. *a* 1764 LLOYD *Author's Apol.* Wks. 1774 I. 6 And tills their minds with proper care. 1889 ROSCOE in *Nature* 10 Oct. 579/1 His most important researches have entered upon fields hitherto tilled, with but scanty success, by the biologist.

**II.** To prepare, set, or spread in readiness.

**7.** *trans.* To spread (a net), set (a trap or snare). Also, to set in any position. Now *s. w. dial.* Cf. TELD *v.* 4. Also *absol.*

*a* 1225 *Ancr. R.* 334 (MS. Nero) Þer me sit mid þe greahundes forte kepen þe hearde, oðer tillen [*v. rr. Vern.* tilleþ, *Corpus, Cleop., Caius* tildeð, *Titus* tildes] þe nettes aȝean ham. 1587 TURBERV. *Trag. T.* 33 The wilie witted boy That tiles his trappe to take the subtile foxe. 1613 W. BROWNE *Sheph. Pipe* II. (1614) D j b, Nor knowes a trappe nor snare to till. *c* 1750 MRS. PALMER *Devon. Dial.* (1837) 2 Took a bard out of the springal that little maester had a-teel'd. 1799 in Southey *Comm.-pl. Bk.* (1851) IV. 523 [By Newton Bushel we saw a board] Man Traps and Spring Guns are tilled in this Garden. 1880 CARNEGIE *Trapping* 5 It is ten chances to one that the rabbit will go over or to the place at which you did not (as it is called in the West) 'till' your gin. *Ibid.* 36 In..trapping rooks..there is no difficulty in telling what part of the field to 'till' in. 1882 JAGO *Cornw. Gloss.*, *Teel*, to set or 'teel a trap'. 1890 *Gloucestersh. Gloss.*, *Tile* or *Teel*..to tile a trap, to set a trap; to tile a gate, to set it open. 1895 QUILLER-COUCH *Wand. Heath* 80 He and his mates went out and tilled the trammel.

† **8.** To pitch (a tent): = TELD *v.* 1; to set (a sail). *Obs.*

1362 LANGL. *P. Pl.* A. II. 44 Ten þousend of Tentes I-tilled [*v. rr.* I-teldyde, teldit, teled] be-sydes. 1628 DIGBY *Voy. Medit.* (Camden) 11 We had not men enough to till our sailes untill the other shippes were gone past our discerning.

**III.** † **9.** *Comb.* of verb-stem. **Till-land** (**teleland**), tilled land, land under cultivation; so **tillridge** (**teill ryge**). *Sc. Obs.*

1437 *Registr. Aberdon.* (Maitland) I. 247 Merkand northwest our a moss to þe nerrast teleland of Ardgrane. 1549 *Aberdeen Regr.* (Spald. Cl.) I. 274 That na maner of takismen..ryif out..ony landis..without thair teill ryge of auld.

† **Till,** *v.*2 *Obs.* Forms: 3–4 tille; also *3rd sing. pres.* 3 tilþ, tylþ; *pa. t.* 3 tylde, 3–4 tilde, 5 tilt. [OE. **tillan*, in comb. *getillan* to touch, reach, attain, *atillan* to touch; cf. Goth. *gatilôn* to attain, obtain.] *intr.* To reach, extend (to a specified point or distance; in quot. 1393, to a specified length).

[*a* 1000 *Blickl. Glosses* (E.E.T.S.) 262/2 Weras bloda & facenfulle na healfe ȝetillað.] *c* 1290 *St. Brendan* 616 in *S. Eng. Leg.* 236 His her tilde doun to is fet, of berde and of heued. 1297 R. GLOUC. 174 Fram douere in to chestre tilleþ watelinge stret. 1387 TREVISA *Higden* (Rolls) II. 107 The kyngdom of Deyra tillede and streiȝte from þe ryuer of Humber anon to þe ryuere of Tyne. 1393 LANGL. *P. Pl.* C. VII. 220 Ich puttehem in pressours..Tyl ten ȝerdes oþer twelue tilled [A. v. 128 tolden; B. v. 214 tolled] out þrettyne.

**b.** *trans.* (*a*) To stretch to, attain to, reach, touch. (*b*) To stretch (a thing) out.

[*c* 961 ÆTHELWOLD *Rule St. Benet* vii. (Schröer) 23 ȝif we þone hrof þære healican eaðmodnesse ȝetillan willað.] *c* 1400 *Destr. Troy* 914 As he tilt out his tung with his tethe grym.

† **Till,** *v.*3 *Obs.* Forms: [1 tyllan, *pa. t.* tylde], 3 tulle(n (*ii*), *pa. t.* tulde, 4–5 tille, tylle, 5 tyll, 4–7 till (4 til, 6–7 *pa. t.* and *pple.* tild): see also TOLL *v.*1 [OE. **tyllan* (in comb. *fortyllan* to draw away, seduce), early ME. *tullen* (*ii*), ME. *tylle, tille, till.* Ulterior history obscure.]

**1.** *trans.* To draw, attract, persuade; to entice, allure, coax; to win over.

*a* 1225 *Ancr. R.* 320 Mi liht onswere, oðer mine liht lates, tulde him erest upon me. *Ibid.* 414 Ne tulle ȝe to þe ȝete none unkuðe harloz. *a* 1300 *Cursor M.* 12175 (Cott.) To þe scole him for to till [*v. r.* tille]. *a* 1340 HAMPOLE *Psalter* xxiv. 2 Þof þai waite nyght and daye with ill suggestions to till me til syn. 13.. *Minor Poems fr. Vernon MS.* xxix. II. 38 On of þe Iewes Malicious Tilled þe child in to his hous. *c* 1375 *Sc. Leg. Saints* xxx. (*Theodera*) 159 For eth is a man to til To do it þat is his wil. 1471 RIPLEY *Comp. Alch.* v. xliii. in Ashm. (1652) 158 Lest wyth theyr flatteryng they so the tyll That thou agre unto ther wyll. 1581 A. HALL *Iliad* IV. 71 He tild them for to trye And proue with him the combate. 1600 HOLLAND *Livy* XXI. xi. 399 By tilling them on, and alluring them with hope of great rewards. 1609 C. BUTLER *Fem. Mon.* ii. (1623) D iv, The sunne rising doth oftimes till them forth. 1666 M. M. *Solomon's Prescript.* 83 Devils..labouring to..till thee on.

**b.** *absol.*

13.. *Cursor M.* 27307 (Cott.) He sal him til a-mendes drau,..wit wordes soft and mild, Als moder tilland dos hir child. *a* 1591 H. SMITH *Wks.* (1866–7) I. 299 As though his eyes would draw his heart, as the bait tilleth on the hook.

**2.** To draw (physically).

*a* 1400–50 *Alexander* 5479 Þai [sirens] droȝe þam doun in-to þe depe & drowned þaim..Or els þai tillid þaim to þe trees.

**b.** *intr.* ? To proceed, go. (Cf. 'draw near'.)

1297 R. GLOUC. (Rolls) 2492 Sire graunte me þanne, quaþ hengist, ȝif it is þi wille As moche place as mid a þuong ich may aboute tille. *c* 1330 R. BRUNNE *Chron.* (1810) 128 To gile no to fraude wild he neuer tille. [But this may be 1.]

**Till** (til), *v.*4 [mod. f. TILL *sb.*1] *trans.* To put (money) into a till.

1841 J. T. HEWLETT *Parish Clerk* III. 68 Having tilled the fourpence three farthings. 1891 GOSCHEN in *Standard* 9 July 2/3 Coins..which have been tilled for many years, thereby not being exposed to any friction.

**Till** (til), *prep., conj., adv.* Forms: 1, 3–7 til, 4–5 tille, tylle, 4–6 tyl, tyll; 3 (*Orm.*), 4– till (in 18th c. often printed *'till* as if short for UNTIL). Also 4 tel, 4–5 tell, 5 telle; 5 (9 *dial.*) tul, 6 (8 *dial.*) tull; 5 thyll(e. [ONorthumb. *til*, a. ON. *til* prep. with genitive (e.g. *til Islands*, to Iceland, *til dauða-dags* to the day of death); mod. Icel., Færo., Norw., Da. *til*, Sw. *till*; also OFris. *til* prep. with dative. Prob. originally a sb. **til* = OE. *till* fixed point, station, OHG., MHG. *zil*, Ger. *ziel* neut. end, limit, point aimed at, goal, late MLG. *tel*, *til* aim, (fixed) point of time; cf. ON. *aldrtili* end of life, death; hence the const. with genitive: prop. 'with the limit or goal of (the place or time named)'. In ON. it filled the place of the WGer. prep. *tô*, *ti*, *te*, Ger. *zu*, *zi*, *ze*, OE. *tó*, To. Characteristically northern in reference to place or purpose (though in ME. occasionally midl. or south.); in reference to time, general Eng. from *c* 1300, though now often superseded by the compound UNTIL. To the same root belong OE. *til* adj. 'to the purpose, serviceable, good', and OE. *tilian*, *-tillan*, TILL *v.*1, *v.*2]

**A.** *prep.* **I.** Local and dative. Now only *n. dial.* and *Sc.*, where normally used instead of *to* before a vowel or *h*.

**1.** = To *prep.* **a.** In the ordinary local sense of *to*.

*a* 800 *Inscription, Ruthwell Cross, Dumfries* in *O. E. T.* 126 Hweþræ þer fusæ fearran kwomu æþþilæ til anum. *c* 1200 ORMIN Ded. 170 He..stah þa siþþenn upp till heffne. *a* 1300 *Cursor M.* 10832 (Cott.) Ar he his wijf til hus wald bring. *c* 1330 R. BRUNNE *Chron.* (1810) 3 Þe fled out of Wales away tille Ireland. *c* 1380 WYCLIF *Sel. Wks.* III. 445 Suche gone privyly til helle. *c* 1386 CHAUCER *Knt.'s T.* 2106 They goon Hoom til Atthenes. *c* 1460 *Towneley Myst.* xv. 113 Tyll egyp weynd shall we. 1489 CAXTON *Faytes of A.* II. xiii. 114 He dyde goo from one place tyl another. 1582–8 *Life James VI* (1804) 256 The Earle of Atholl sent aduertisement heirof till Argyll. *a* 1618 J. DAVIES *Eglogues* Poems (1772) 114 Whan we wenden till another place. 1807 J. STAGG *Poems* 36 As king Solomon hath said, The place I'll not turn tilt [= to it]. 1816 SCOTT *Antiq.* ix, Rab..bang'd out o' bed, and till some of his readiest claes.

**b.** As far as; so as to reach. Cf. also C. 3.

1375 BARBOUR *Bruce* x. 682 Swerdis..War till the hyltis all bludy. *c* 1400 MAUNDEV. (1839) ix. 107 The forpartie of the heed til vnder the chyn is at Rome. 1483 CAXTON *Gold. Leg.* 80/2 Nabugodonosor..sente vnto all Regyons aboute..tyl the mountes of ethyope. 1535 COVERDALE *Judg.* xx. 43 They..folowed vpon them..and trode them downe tyll afore Gibea. 1561 HOLLYBUSH *Hom. Apoth.* 38 That it maye reache..from the nauell tyll the priuy membres. 1828 BUCHAN *Ballads* I. 2 He read it till an end.

**2.** In senses of *to* derived from the local. **a.** where the object is not a point in space. Now *Sc.*

*c* 1200 ORMIN Ded. 18 Þu þohhtesst tatt itt mihhte wel Till mikell frame turrnenn. *a* 1340 HAMPOLE *Psalter* xxiv. 2 Ill suggestions to till me til syn. *c* 1400 MAUNDEV. (Roxb.) Pref. 2 What lufe he had til his sugets. *Ibid.* iv. 12 Changed..fra a faire damysell til a dragoun. 1509 BP. FISHER *Funeral Serm. C'tess Richmond* Wks. (E.E.T.S.) I. 294 She restrayned her appetyte tyl one mele & tyl one fysshe on the day. **1513** DOUGLAS *Æneis* VI. Prol. 64 Till vertu thaim to brod. **1582-8** *Life Jas. VI* (1804) 260 He was putt till extreme tortor. **1655** FULLER *Ch. Hist.* IV. iii. § 40 He was..restored till his liberty and archbishoprick. **1826** J. WILSON *Noct. Ambr.* Wks. (1855) I. 125, I venerate the adherence till't. **1858** RAMSAY *Remin.* v. (1870) 104 'They're what we must all come till'.

†**b.** Conformably to, in accordance with, after. *Obs. rare.*

**1340** HAMPOLE *Pr. Consc.* 90 Ilk man..God made til his awen lyknesse. *c* **1400** MAUNDEV. (Roxb.) Pref. 2 How dere he boght man þat he had made til his awen liknes. *c* **1489** CAXTON *Blanchardyn* xix. 59 He was not armed tyl his plesure.

†**c.** To or for the purpose of, in order to be; to become, as. *Obs.*

*a* **1352** MINOT *Poems* xi. 40 Þat he may at his ending haue heuin till his mede. *a* **1450** *Le Morte Arth.* 637 The feyrest lady..Tille his lemman chosen hath he. *c* **1489** CAXTON *Blanchardyn* xxv. 93, I wolde haue gyuen you tyl his wyff.

**3.** Expressing the indirect object or dative relation. After verbs of giving, telling, comparing, hearkening, pertaining, addition, affecting action; adjs. and sbs. of likeness, agreeableness, belonging, relationship, etc. Now *n. dial.* and *Sc.*

*c* **950** *Lindisf. Gosp.* Matt. xxvi. 31 Ða cueð til him ðe hælend. *c* **1200** ORMIN 803 He seʒʒde þuss till himm. **13..** *Cursor M.* 13632 (Cott. & Fairf.) Hald þe til [*Gött. & Trin.* to] him. **1340** HAMPOLE *Pr. Consc.* 1833 Of twa [reasons] byfore I spake, Now wil I other twa til þam take. **1357** *Lay Folks Catech.* 29 (MS. T.) Of the lawe and þe lare þat langes till halikirke. *Ibid.* 89 Iesu crist..Is sothefastly god euen til [= equal to] his fadir. **1375** BARBOUR *Bruce* I. 565 Þe Endentur till him gaf he. *Ibid.* XIII. 511 Till hym neir syb wes he. *c* **1400** MAUNDEV. (Roxb.) Pref. 2 Knawen openly til all men. *Ibid.* iii. 9 Þai schuld be obedient til him. *c* **1460** *Towneley Myst.* XVIII. 239 Whi dos thou tyll vs thus? **1521** FISHER *Serm. agst. Luther* i. Wks. (E.E.T.S.) I. 317 How that shadowe & this thynge agreeth..one tyll another. **1724** RAMSAY *Tea-t. Misc.* (1733) I. 21 Wad ye compare ye'r sell to me, A Docken till a tansie. **1790** MRS. WHEELER *Westmld. Dial.* (1821) 59 He hes dun tull em oa [= all] alike. **1815** SCOTT *Guy M.* xv, The death of the grey mare..was naething till't. **1818** — *Hrt. Midl.* xviii, 'Hear till her', said Madge.

†**4.** In prec. senses, often placed after its object, for metrical reasons. *Obs.*

*a* **1300** *Cursor M.* 3712 (Cott.) And sithen his sun he cald him till. *c* **1350** *Will. Palerne* 2350, I wold wend hem tille wiþ-oute ani stint. *c* **1380** *Sir Ferumb.* 5264 Þus he spak him tille. *c* **1420** *Chron. Vilod.* 1412 Alle his askyng þey grauntede hym tylle. *a* **1562** G. CAVENDISH *Poems* (1825) II. 19, I espied certeyn persons comyng me tyll.

**II.** Of time.

**5.** Onward to (a specified time); up to the time of (an event); during the whole time before; until. (Denoting continuance up to a particular time, and usually implying cessation or change at that time: cf. B. 1.)

*c* **1330** R. BRUNNE *Chron. Wace* (Rolls) 27 Fro Eneas till Brutus tyme. *c* **1375** *Cursor M.* 498 (Fairf.) Sa þai sal tille [*Cott., Gött.* to] domes day. *a* **1400** *Sir Perc.* 25 Fro thethyne tille his lyves ende. *a* **1548** HALL *Chron., Edw. IV* 232 b, He kepte all these thinges secret, tyll his retorne. **1588, 1827** [see MORN 2 b]. **1591** SHAKS. *1 Hen. VI*, I. ii. 127 Fight till the last gaspe. **1611** BIBLE *Exod.* xvi. 19 Let no man leaue of it till the morning. **1632** LE GRYS tr. *Velleius Paterc.* Ded. 7 From the foundation of the city till the ruine of the Macedonian kingdome. **1824** SCOTT *St. Ronan's* xxxviii, She doubted if the woman would live till morning.

**b.** After a negative, denoting the continuance of the negative condition up to the time indicated (and implying its cessation then); thus nearly equivalent to *before*. Cf. B. 1 b.

**1590** SHAKS. *Com. Err.* II. ii. 164, I neuer saw her till this time. **1649** HEYLIN *Relat. & Observ.* II. 155 To give no account for it till Doomes-day in the afternoone. **1671** LADY MARY BERTIE in *12th Rep. Hist. MSS. Comm.* App. v. 22 The grand ballett is not to be danced till Shrove-Munday. **1719** DE FOE *Crusoe* (1790) I. 28 [He] begged of me not to go on shore till day. **1861** M. PATTISON *Ess.* (1889) I. 41 It was not till the fourteenth century that their guild rose into wealth and importance. **1887** MRS. OLIPHANT *Makers Venice* II. ii. 177 The news..did not reach him till long after the event.

**c.** Followed by an adverb (or adv. phr.) of time. Cf. NOW 13, THEN 7.

*c* **1380** WYCLIF *Last Age Church* 30 Fro Crist til now, þrittene hundrid ȝeer and sixe and fyfty. *a* **1518** SKELTON *Magnyf.* 319 Fare you well tyll sone. **1535** COVERDALE *Prov.* xxix. 11 A foole poureth out his sprete alltogether, but a wyse man kepeth it in till afterwarde. **1598** SHAKS. *Merry W.* v. i. 28, I knew not what 'twas to be beaten, till lately. **1667** MILTON *P. L.* II. 744, I know thee not, nor ever saw till now Sight more detestable. **1746** FRANCIS tr. *Horace, Epist.* I. vii. 107 Till then farewel. **1844** KINGLAKE *Eothen* viii, It was not till after midnight that my visit.. came to an end. *Mod.* I stayed till after ten o'clock.

**III.** = *To* with the infinitive. Now only *Sc.*

**6. a.** as prep. introducing the infinitive of purpose.

Not in Norse. Closely akin to 2 c; *þare sorrow til amese* = to or with the aim of, or for the purpose of, amesing their sorrow, to the mitigation of their sorrow.

**13..** *Cursor M.* 5330 (Cott.) He praid þe god men þat þar wer To lith a quil his word til her. *c* **1375** *Sc. Leg. Saints* xxi. (*Clement*) 519 Thane, þare gret sorow til ames, Petyre þame tald how It was Hapnyt. *c* **1425** WYNTOUN *Cron.* IX. xxv. 2838 Tyll ete ore drink, syng ore dance. **1513** DOUGLAS *Æneis* VIII. vii. 31 Sen Nereus douchtir, Thetis, mycht.. Induce the till enarme hir son Achill. **1535** STEWART *Cron. Scot.* (Rolls) III. 323 For till reskew Thair libertie..Beseikand him to tak auctoritie In that mater and afald ay till be. **1599** A. HUME *Epist. to G. Moncrieff* 164 Till execute their office man be hyred.

**b.** as sign of the simple infinitive; esp. after *for*. Now chiefly used before a vowel or *h*.

*c* **1375** *Cursor M.* 12989 (Fairf.) For tille [*v. r.* to] be myne vnderloute. **1375** BARBOUR *Bruce* I. 98 Trawayllyt for to wyn senyhory, And throw hys mycht till occupy Landis. **1424** *Coldstream Chartul.* (1879) 42 Be it mad kend..me Jon of Swynton..till haue fulli grantit to ye priores [etc.]. *c* **1485** *Digby Myst.* (1882) IV. 1252 Now aught I sore till irke! **1513** DOUGLAS *Æneis* VI. xv. 10 For til excers the art of geometrye. **1816** SCOTT *Antiq.* xxv, An ye had wussed till hae been present. *c* **1880** LYTTLE *Paddy McQuillan* 85 (E.D.D.) Get Mickey Mooney till gie me a lift wi' them.

**B.** *conj.* (orig. the prep. governing the demonstrative pron. *that*, in apposition with the following clause.) Cf. UNTIL, similarly used.

(From the earliest ME. times both *till that* (see THAT *conj.* 1 c) and the simple *till* occur; supplanting OE. *ōþ þæt*, early ME. *oþat, a þat* (see O *prep.*[3], A *prep.*[3]), also OE. *ōþ þe* and the simple *ōþ*. *Till that* represented ON. *til þess* (MSw. *til þes (at), til þet*, Sw. *til dess at.*)

**1.** To the time that; up to (the point) when; until. (Denoting the continuance of the action or state expressed by the principal clause up to the time expressed by the dependent clause, and usually implying that at that time such action or state ceases and a different or opposite one begins.)

Formerly often (and still *arch.*) with dependent clause in subjunctive when expressing supposition, contingency, or expectation (in ME. sometimes even when expressing fact); so also in subordinate senses below.

**1154** *O. E. Chron.* (Laud MS.) an. 1137, Þar he nam þe biscop..&..hise neues & dide ælle in prisun til hi iafen up here castles. *c* **1200** ORMIN 126 Swa þeʒʒ leddenn heore lif Till þatt teʒʒ wærenn alde. *Ibid.* 9147 Fra þatt he wass full litell Till þatt he waxenn wass. *a* **1225** *Leg. Kath.* 720 Þeos meiden ..abad baldeliche aðet me [*v. r.* til þet men] come & fatte hire. *c* **1320** *Cast. Love* 44 To wonen and welden to such ende, Til þat he scholde to heuene wende. **13..** *Cursor M.* 8421 (Gött.) Þu sett him to fostering, Tille he be lerid himself to lede. **1420-30** *Prymer* (E.E.T.S.) 64 Alle þe daies in whiche y trauele now, y abide til my chaungyng come. **1526** TINDALE *Luke* xv. 8 What woman..doth not..seke diligently, till she finde it? **1560** INGELEND *Disob. Child* (Percy Soc.) 22, I thought it surely a whole hundred yere, Tyll in this place I sawe you here. **1588** SHAKS. *L. L. L.* I. ii. 131 Forbeare till this company be past. **1610** — *Temp.* I. ii. 465, I will resist such entertainment, till Mine enemy ha's more pow'r. **1611** BIBLE *Dan.* ii. 34 Thou sawest till that a stone was cut out without hands. **1625** MASSINGER *New Way* III. iii, She..sits on thorns, till she be private with him. **1707** E. CHAMBERLAYNE *Pres. St. Eng.* II. xv. (ed. 22) 194 They..forfeited their Places if they did marry, till by Act of Parliament..they were allowed to take Wives. **1796** *Hist. Ned Evans* II. 213, I shall count the hours till I return. **1833** HT. MARTINEAU *Three Ages* iii. 89 To be left at the Blue Lion till called for. **1850** TENNYSON *In Mem.* xiii. 8 Silence, till I be silent too.

**b.** With negative (expressed or implied) in the principal clause, and the dependent clause with *till* denoting the continuance of the negative condition up to the specified time, and usually (as in 1) implying its cessation or reversal (i.e. the commencement of the opposite or positive condition) at that time.

Here *before* can be substituted for *till*, but is not strictly synonymous with it, since in that case the negative qualifies the whole statement including the dependent clause. This may also be the case with *till*, e.g. 'You need not wait till I come back' (sense 1); cf. 'You must not go till I come back' (1 b). Hence some sentences of this form are ambiguous; but usually the context or circumstances make it clear which is meant.

*c* **1220** *Bestiary* 19 Ne stireð he nout of slepe Til ðe sunne haueð sinen ðries him abuten. **13..** *Seuyn Sag.* (W.) 1276 For thef of steling wil nowt blinne Til he honge bi the chinne. *c* **1386** CHAUCER *Prol.* 21 Til we be roten, can we nat be rype. **1463** *Bury Wills* (Camden) 27 This mony not to be delyuerid..tyl the messe of Requiem be endyd. **1526** TINDALE *John* xiii. 38 The cocke shall nott crowe, till thou have [1611 hast] denyed me thryse. **1648** HERRICK *Hesper., Glorie*, Seldome comes Glorie till a man be dead. **1676** LISTER in *Ray's Corr.* (1848) 125, I shall resolve upon nothing till I see you. **1766** GOLDSM. *Vic. W.* xviii, Man little knows what calamities are beyond his patience to bear, till he tries them. **1780** *Mirror* No. 104 ⁋ 8 At length we set out..but not till repeated instructions were given [etc.]. *a* **1814** *Spaniards* IV. i. in *New Brit. Theatre* III. 239 Nor will the flaming sword of war..Be sheath'd again till that the Moorish pride Be humbled. **1832** HT. MARTINEAU *Demerara* i. 15 We shall never prosper..till the system is wholly changed. **1864** LEVER *Men & Women*, etc. Ser. I. 91 'Never imagine', said a wise prelate, 'that you will root Popery out of England till you destroy Oxford'.

**c.** Formerly, and still dial. and in U. S., used after a negative principal clause, where *before* (or *when*) is now substituted in Standard English.

*c* **1420** ? LYDG. *Assembly of Gods* 1130 No man cowde hym let tyll he came there. **1559** *Mirr. Mag., Edw. IV* iii, I could not be ware tyl I was begiled. **1632** LITHGOW *Trav.* v. 231 Scarcely were wee well aduanced in our way, till wee were beset with more then three hundred Arabs. **1725** DE FOE *Voy. round World* (1840) 79, I had not been many hours on board, till I was surprised with the firing of three muskets. **1756** MRS. CALDERWOOD in *Coltness Collect.* (Maitl. Cl.) 186, I was not long set till Margaret came to see me.

**d.** Depending on a principal clause containing an expression of long duration of time or delay before the act or state expressed by the dependent clause begins or takes effect. Now *dial.*

*c* **1330** *Assump. Virg.* (B. M. MS.) 121 Alle him þenkeþ swiþe longe Til þou comest hem amonge. **1450** MARG. PASTON in *P. Lett.* I. 178, I thynk ryth longe tyll I haue some god tydyngys fro yow. *c* **1530** LD. BERNERS *Arth. Lyt. Bryt.* 445, I shal think tyll that season be come as long or longer than ye shal do. *a* **1533** — *Gold. Bk. M. Aurel.* R iv b, The mayden that tarieth long tyll she be maried. **1590** MARLOWE *Edw. II*, II. i. 82 Come, leade the way, I long till I am there. **1602** SHAKS. *Ham.* IV. vii. 182 But long it could not be, Till that her garments..Pul'd the poore wretch..To muddy death. **1640** tr. *Verdere's Rom. of Rom.* III. iv. 13 He..thought it long till hee was in the Citie. **1825** CARLYLE *Schiller* III. (1845) 189 It was not long till.. he set about turning this new knowledge to account. **1866** HOWELLS *Venet. Life* (1880) 122 So at first she seemed, and it was long till we doubted her perfection.

**e.** Indicating the ultimate result or outcome of a continued action expressed by the principal clause: So long or so far that; so that at length.

*c* **1220** *Bestiary* 65 Ðer-ouer he fleʒeð, and up he teð, Til ðat he ðe heuene seð. *a* **1300** *Cursor M.* 10991 (Cott.) Quen þai had beden til þai war irk. **1377** LANGL. *P. Pl.* B. II. 96 And þanne to sitten and soupen til slepe hem assaille. *c* **1430** *Chev. Assigne* 96 He wente þorow a foreste..Thylle he come to a watur. **1508** DUNBAR *Gold. Targe* 239 Thay fyrit gunnis.. Till that the reke raise to the firmament. **1610** SHAKS. *Temp.* I. i. 8 Blow till thou burst thy winde. **1766** GOLDSM. *Vic. W.* xii, He..stands out and higgles, and ..tires them till he gets a bargain. **1895** MRS. H. WARD *Bessie Costrell* ii. 31 Bessie ran till she was out of breath.

†**f.** After *so long, so far*, etc., indicating ultimate result. *Obs.* (Now expressed by *that*, or by *till* with omission of *so long*, etc. as in e.) (Cf. MSw. *swa lange til þes*; Ger. *so lang bis.*)

*c* **1386** CHAUCER *Sompn. T.* 58 So longe he wente hous by hous, til he Cam til an hous ther he was wont to be Refresshed. **1470-85** MALORY *Arthur* XVII. xxiii. 724 He rode so fast tyl he came to Camelot. **1590** SPENSER *F. Q.* II. ii. 12 So long they traveiled..Till that at last they to a Castle came. **1593** SHAKS. *2 Hen. VI*, III. i. 362 [He] fought so long, till that his thighes with Darts Were almost like a sharpe-quill'd Porpentine. **1599** A. M. tr. *Gabelhouer's Bk. Physicke* 44/1 Vse it as long till it return noe more. **1643** TRAPP *Comm. Gen.* xxxii. 26 The importunate widow teacheth us, to press God so far, till we put him to the blush. *a* **1738** J. SKINNER *Christmas Ba'ing* xiii. Poems (1809) 45 Leitch..gae 'im sic a kick, Till they a' thought him slain. [**1800** COLERIDGE *Piccolom.* IV. v, And till we are indemnified, so long Stays Prague in pledge.]

†**2.** During the time that; so long as; while.

*c* **1330** R. BRUNNE *Chron.* (1810) 18 His childre he wild auance tille he o lyue were. *c* **1375** *Sc. Leg. Saints* Prol. 82 Til saule & body togydir ves. *Ibid.* 107 Til þat he ves vith þaim in lyfe. **1558** BP. WATSON *Sev. Sacram.* xvi. 102 Let vs..make haste to amende our lyues tyll we haue tyme. **1604** T. WRIGHT *Passions* (1620) 14 To prosecute pleasures..enjoy the roses til they flourish.

†**C.** *adv.* = To *adv.* *Obs. rare.*

**1.** In conjunction with *fra* (= fro): see FRO *adv.*, and cf. TO AND FRO.

*a* **1300** *Cursor M.* 11937 Þat water moght rin fra and till, Vte of þe flum al atte will. **13..** *Evang. Nicod.* 195 in Herrig's *Archiv* LIII. 395 Sir Pilates wife..Till hir lord þus gan say Deme noght Ihesu tyll ne fra. *c* **1386** CHAUCER *Reeve's T.* 119 How that the hopur wagges til and fra.

**2.** = *to* prep. (see A. 1) with ellipsis of sb.

*c* **1330** R. BRUNNE *Chron.* (1810) 107 Þe gode erle of Aniowe, of Mald herd he say Fulle richely to trowe tille tok his way. *c* **1375** *Cursor M.* 14523 (Fairf.), & þer-to gode couenande þai hiȝt, & iche an tille þaire trauþis pliȝt.

**3.** Used to qualify *to, into, unto*. In Wyclif rendering L. *usque (ad, in)*, even, as far as, on (to).

**1382** WYCLIF *Acts* xxiii. 1, I with al good conscience haue lyued bifore God, til into [*Vulg.* usque in] this dai. *Ibid.* xxviii. 24 Fro the moru til to euentijde. **1388** — *Jer.* li 9 The doom therof cam til to [*Vulg.* usque ad, 1382 vnto] heuenes. *c* **1435** *Torr. Portugal* 992 That thys fynd hym yeld A-non to me tylle [*rime* wylle]. **14..** in *Hist. Coll. Citizen London* (Camden) 90 The sayde Adam was mayre tylle unto the xxj day of Marche. **1577** KNEWSTUB *Confut.* (1579) 70 b, Euen so remember the suffering of Christ..till vnto his comming.

**Tillable** (ti·lăb'l), *a.* [f. TILL *v.*[1] + -ABLE.] Capable of being tilled or cultivated; usually, capable of being ploughed, arable.

**1573** NORTHBROOKE *Poore Mans Gard.* To Rdr., The Earth then remained to man as a thing tillable. **1610** W. FOLKINGHAM *Art of Survey* I. x. 26 Wee found it scarce tillable with a strong Teeme of Oxen. **1784** TWAMLEY *Dairying* 22 The greater number of Dairys are on Tillable or Arable Farms. **1810** G. CHALMERS *Caledonia* II. II. vii. 135 The most common divisions of tillable lands were carucates, or plough lands, and bovates, or oxgangs. **1893** J. W. HOFF 200 *Miles on Delaware River* 125 The cultivated and tillable soil..in this region is formed from decayed rock.

**Tillage** (ti·lėdʒ). Also 6 tilladge, 6–7 tyllage, 7 tilage, tilledge. [f. TILL *v.*[1] + -AGE.]

**1.** The act, operation, or art of tilling or cultivating land so as to fit it for raising crops; cultivation, agriculture, husbandry.

**1538** STARKEY *England* I. iii. 96 Me semyth ther ys a grete faute in tyllage of the ground. **1616** SURFL. & MARKH. *Country Farme* 555 Barley asketh the greatest tillage of all graines. **1707** MORTIMER *Husb.* (1721) I. 137 Pease and Beans belong to Garden-Tillage, as well as that of the Field. **1712** J. JAMES tr. *Le Blond's Gardening* 166 There is no Danger in giving the Trees a good Tillage, that is to say, in breaking up the Ground pretty deep. **1735** BERKELEY *Querist* § 85 If all the land were tilled that is fit for tillage. **1833** HT. MARTINEAU *Briery Creek* iii, The farmer makes his land yield double by good tillage.

**b.** The state or condition of being tilled or cultivated. *In tillage*, in or under cultivation.

**1488-9** *Act 4 Hen. VII*, c. 19, xx. acres of lond..lyeng in tillage or husbondrie. **1523** FITZHERB. *Surv.* 2 It is at the lordes pleasure wheder they shall lye to pasture or to tyllage. **1523** — *Husb.* § 123 As moche land kept in tyllage. **1669** WORLIDGE *Syst. Agric.* (1681) 37 There is much waste Land,..although for the most part..it may be reduced into Tillage, and become very fruitful. **1787** WINTER *Syst. Husb.* 33 When land has been long in tillage. **1897** G. ALLEN *Type-writer Girl* iii, They have bought ten acres of wild land..; they are getting it into tillage.

**c.** *fig.* The culture of the mind or spirit.

**1555** EDEN *Decades* (Arb.) 64 If I shal perceaue the fruites of this my tyllage to be delectable. **1586** T. B. *La Primaud. Fr. Acad.* I. (1594) 47 The true medicine and tillage of the soule whereby all vertue is taught us. **1683** TRYON *Way to Health* 472 We do also esteem that Country most miserable, that doth neglect the proper Tillage, and Education of Children. **1878** T. L. CUYLER *Pointed Papers* 185 He needs the tillage of prayer and Bible-study.

**2.** *concr.* Tilled or ploughed land; land under crops as distinct from pasturage; the crops growing on tilled land.

**1543** *Act* 35 *Hen. VIII*, c. 17 § 3 Noe persons..shall converte or torne into pasture or tillage anye suche Coppies. **1632** LITHGOW *Trav.* v. 191 It is also beautified with all the ornaments of nature, as Herbage, Tillage, Pastorage, Fructiferous Trees. **1649** *Alcoran* 228 Will ye forsake eternall riches ..to put your trust in your gardens, your fountains, your tillages, your dates, and fruits? **1681** WORLIDGE *Syst. Agric.* viii. § 3 (ed. 3) 159 Of Beans, Pease, Melons, Cucumbers, Asparagus, Cabbage, and several other sorts of Garden-Tillage..An Acre of ground will yield far more of Tillage than of Corn. *c* **1710** CELIA FIENNES *Diary* (1888) 108 Lands ..with all sorts of Herbage and tillage. **1894** LD. WOLSELEY *Life Marlborough* I. 334 The fence..which divided the tillage from the moorland.

*fig.* **1582** BENTLEY *Mon. Matrones* 70, I praie God all men ..may haue grace to become meete tillage for the fruits of the Gospell. **1611** BIBLE 1 *Cor.* iii. 9 Ye are Gods husbandry [*marg.* tillage], ye are Gods building.

**3.** *attrib.* and *Comb.*

**1542** in J. H. Glover *Kingsthorpiana* (1883) 73, xxx acres of tyllage land. **1583** *Exec. for Treason* (1675) 5 These.. Jesuits..have as Tillage-men, laboured..to perswade the people. **1585** T. WASHINGTON tr. *Nicholay's Voy.* II. x. 43 b, Gardens.., tillage grounds and pastures. **1712** J. MORTON *Nat. Hist. Northampt.* 7 Tillage-land or Fielden. **1834** *Brit. Husb.* I. 40 Tillage Farms are the most profitable to the community.

Hence **Ti·llaged** (-ėdʒd) *a.*, brought under tillage.

**1854** *Jrnl. R. Agric. Soc.* XV. I. 24 The servitude of day labour upon the newly tillaged Fens.

‖ **Tillandsia** (tilæ·ndziă). *Bot.* [mod.L. (Linnæus), named after Elias Tillands, a Swedish botanist.] A large genus of herbaceous plants of the pine-apple family (*Bromeliaceæ*), found in tropical and subtropical America and the West Indies, chiefly epiphytic on trees.

*T. usneoides*, also called *long-beard, long-moss, hanging moss*, or *Florida moss*, forms long pendent grey tufts, the fibres of which are used for stuffing mattresses, etc.: other species, as *T. utriculata*, have the leaves dilated at the base so as to form a reservoir for water; many others are cultivated for ornament.

**1759** B. STILLINGFL. tr. *Biber's Econ. Nat.* in *Misc. Tracts* (1762) 76 The tillandsia, which..grows on the tops of trees in the desarts of America, has its leaves turned at the base into the shape of a pitcher..; in these the rain is collected, and preserved for thirsty men, birds, and beasts. **1860** GOSSE *Rom. Nat. Hist.* 61 The tillandsias nestle at the ramification of the smaller branches,..where they often grow to an immense size. **1863** RUSSELL *Diary North & South* I. 220 The overlacing arms and intertwined branches of the tillandsia or Spanish moss, a weeping, drooping, plumaceous parasite, which..clings to the tree everlastingly. **1896** *Daily News* 16 Mar. 6/5 A number of species of the so-called air plants—Tillandsias—exhibited.

**Tilled** (tild), *ppl. a.* [f. TILL *v.*[1] + -ED[1].] Of land: see TILL *v.*[1] 4.

**1546** *Reg. Mag. Sig. Scot.* 10 Exceptis terris aratis vulgariter telitland. **1577–95** *Descr. Isles Scotl.* in Skene *Celtic Scotl.* III. App. 435 The teillit earth. **1733** TULL *Horse-Hoeing Husb.* i. 8 When Roots are in a Till'd Soil. *a* **1859** MACAULAY *Hist. Eng.* xxiii. (1861) V. 95 In that thickly peopled and carefully tilled region.

**Tiller** (ti·ləɹ), *sb.*[1] Now *literary* or *arch.* Forms: 3–4 tiliere, 4 teoliare, telier, tylier, tileer, 4–5 tilier, tylyer, tilyer, 5 tylyar, telar, tillour, tylere, tyllare, 5–6 tyllar, 6 tyller, *Sc.* telare, 5– tiller. [ME. *tiliere*, taking the place of OE. *tilia* (TILIE), f. *tilian*, TILL *v.*[1] + *-ere*, -ER[1]; subseq. spelt conformably to the verb.] One who tills the soil, or cultivates any crop or plant; a husbandman, cultivator; a farmer or farm labourer. See also EARTH-TILLER, *land-tiller* (LAND *sb.* 10 b).

*c* **1250** *Gen. & Ex.* 1482 Esau wilde man huntere, And Iacob tame man tiliere. *c* **1300** *Life Jesus* (Horstm.) 589 Ich am, he seide, a riȝt soth vine, and mi fader teoliare is. **1377** LANGL. *P. Pl.* B. XIII. 239 For alle trewe trauaillours and tilieres of þe erthe. *c* **1400** *Plowman's T.* 453 What knoweth a tillour at the plow The popes name? *c* **1412** HOCCLEVE *De Reg. Princ.* 4418 The Tylere [*v.r.* tilyer] with his pore cote and land. **1530** PALSGR. 187 *Uigneron*, a tyller of vygnes. **1661** J. CHILDREY *Brit. Baconica* 11 The tiller can commonly take but two crops of wheat. **1767** A. YOUNG *Farmer's Lett. People* 74 The little farmer is always considered as the chief tiller of his land. **1849** MACAULAY *Hist. Eng.* iii. I. 418 The remuneration of workmen employed in manufactures has always been higher than that of the tillers of the soil.

**Ti·ller**, *sb.*[2] Forms: (4 AF. teiler), 5 telor, tiler, 6 tyller, -our, 6–7 tillar, 6– tiller. [a. OF. *telier* (*a* 1200 in Godef.), *tellier*, in sense 1; orig. a weaver's beam (*telier des tisserands*, Godef.), med.L. *tēlārium*, f. L. *tēla* web: see -ARY[1].]

† **1.** *Archery*, etc. In a cross-bow: The wooden beam which is grooved for reception of the arrow, or drilled for the bolt or quarrel; the stock. *Obs.*

[**1353** *Mag. Rot.* 27 *Edw. III* in *Archæol. Jrnl.* (1862) XIX. 72 In..xl. lignis vocatis cost' pro balistis inde faciendis, xl. lignis pro telar' balistarum..cxx. clavis vocatis somernailes pro telar'. **1361** *Indenture* 35 *Edw. III* ibid. (1854) XI. 385, xxiiij. arc pur arblastes de corn saunz teilers.] **1412–20** LYDG. *Chron. Troy* IV. 1370 He..hent a bowe þat passingly was stronge, And with an arwe to his tiler longe. **14..** *Voc.* in Wr.-Wülcker 615/44 *Tenorcula*, a telor of an arblast. *c* **1532** DU WES *Introd. Fr.* in *Palsgr.* 914 Tyller of a crosbowe, *cormier*. **1544** in *Lett. & Pap. Hen. VIII* (1905) XIX. II. 405 Oon tyllour, oon paire of chekes, and oon bender,..oon crossbowe case and oon dosen di of crossbowe stringes. **1609** HOLLAND *Amm. Marcell.* 221 An expert..workeman..cunningly bestoweth in the hollow passage of the beame or tiller [of a balista] a shaft of wood. **1611** COTGR., *Arbrier*, the Tillar of a Crosse-bow. *a* **1618** SYLVESTER *Woodman's Bear* xliv, Eyes that arme Love's Arches tillar.

† **b.** A stock or shaft fixed to a long-bow to admit of its being used as a cross-bow, for greater convenience or precision of aim. *Obs.*

**1590** BARWICK *Briefe Disc.* 11 Whether a Cros-bowe, or a Long-bowe in a Tyller, shoot more certainly. **1611** BEAUM. & FL. *Philaster* II. ii, Use exercise, and keep a Sparrow-hawk, you can shoot in a Tiller.

† **c.** *transf.* A bow fitted with a tiller. *Obs.*

**1572** J. JONES *Bathes Buckstone* 12 Rather wyth longe Bowe, than wyth Tyller, Stone bowe or Crosse bowe. **1598** FLORIO, *Balista*,..a crosse bow, a stock-bow or tillar. **1616** SURFL. & MARKH. *Country Farme* 508 Neither is the crosse-bow so daungerous, whether it be the tiller, or the bullet. **1688** R. HOLME *Armoury* III. xvi. (Roxb.) 77/1 The Tiller hath the Bow of wood either Ash or Yew whose string is held vp (when..drawne) by a wooden Nutt as it is called, and a handle to let it off.

**d.** (See quot. 1801.)

**1545** [app. presupposed in TILLERING *vbl. sb.*[1]]. **1801** T. ROBERTS *Eng. Bowman* 295 *Tiller*, an instrument made of a straight piece of wood, with a notch at the end, and notches on the upper side; in which a bow is placed and drawn, to try how it bends.

† **e.** A stock or shaft in the earliest forms of hand-gun or cannon. *Obs.*

[**1353** *Mag. Rot.* 27 *Edw. III* in *Archæol. Jrnl.* (1862) XIX. 74 Pro..portagio x. gunn' cum telar'. **1885** DILLON *Fairholt's Costume* II. Gloss., *Telar*, the stock of a hand gun (with above reference).]

**2.** *Naut.* A horizontal bar or beam attached to the rudder-head, acting as a lever by means of which the rudder is moved in the act of steering.

(Not in Fr., where the tiller is 'barre du gouvernail'.)

*a* **1625** *Nomenclator Navalis* s.v. (Harl. MS. 2301), The Helme and Tiller is all one..only the word Tiller is properlie used for that which we steere the Bote by. **1627** CAPT. SMITH *Seaman's Gram.* ii. 12 The Tiller is a strong peece of wood made fast to the Rudder..whereby the Rudder is so turned to and fro as the Helmesman pleaseth. **1704** J. HARRIS *Lex. Techn.* I, *Tiller*, the very same with the Helm of a Ship: It is most properly used in a Boat where that which would be the Helm in a Ship, is called the *Tiller*. **1743** BULKELEY & CUMMINS *Voy. S. Seas* 17 The Ship struck a second Time, which broke the Head of the Tiller. **1836** MARRYAT *Midsh. Easy* xix, Easy wrested the tiller from Gascoigne's hand. **1875** HELPS *Soc. Press.* vi. 76 You are either..a slave at the oar, or a serf at the tiller. **1905** A. C. BENSON *Upton Lett.* (1906) 39 Not fit..to take the tiller.

**b.** Also *loosely*, the steering-gear of a rowing-boat; cf. *tiller-line, -rope* in 4.

**3.** In various technical uses: see quots.

**1630** J. TAYLOR (Water P.) *A Thiefe* Wks. II. 119/2 As once a Windmill (out of breath) lack'd winde A fellow brought foure bushels then to grinde, And hearing neither noyse of knap or tiller, Laid downe his corne, and went to seeke the miller. **1789** BRAND *Hist. Newcastle* I. 687 *note*, A piece of wood, called a tiller, is..applied to one wheel, and pressed thereon. *a* **1825** FORBY *Voc. E. Anglia*, *Tiller*, the handle of a spade. **1877** KNIGHT *Dict. Mech.*, *Tiller*. 1. A transverse handle at the upper end of a pit saw. **1881** RAYMOND *Mining Gloss.*, *Tiller*. See *Brace-head*.

**4.** *attrib.* and *Comb.*: †**tiller-bow** = sense 1 c; **tiller-chain**, a chain answering the same purpose as a tiller-rope; on steamships, used in conjunction with steel-wire to connect the rudder with the steam steering-gear; **tiller-head**, the extremity of the tiller to which are secured the two ends of the tiller-rope or -chain; **tiller-lines**, two lines or ropes fastened each to one arm of the tiller-yoke in a boat; also called *yoke-lines, yoke-, tiller-ropes*; **tiller-post**, the upper part of the rudder-stock; **tiller-rope**, (*a*) the rope (now usually a chain) connecting the tiller-head with the drum or barrel of a ship's steering-gear; (*b*) a rope leading from the tiller-head to each side of the deck, to assist in steering in rough weather; (*c*) *pl.* = *tiller-lines*; **tiller-steerage, -steering**, the arrangement for steering a motor-car by means of a lever (as distinct from wheel-steerage); **tiller-wheel**, a wheel by which a rudder is actuated, a steering-wheel; **tiller-yoke**, a yoke fixed on the rudder-head of a boat and serving as a tiller.

**1583** W. M. *Remembr.* in Roberts *Eng. Bowman* (1801) 261 Every one bearing a *tiller-bow or cross-bow, and broad arrows. **1590** BARWICK *Disc. Weapons* 11 He..then can either loose Long-bowe, Tiller-bowe, or Cros-bowe. **1591** PERCIVAL *Span. Dict.*, *Zebretana*, a tiller bowe, *balistæ genus*. **1841** R. H. DANA *Seaman's Man.* Dict. s.v. *Tiller-ropes*, Ropes leading from the *tiller-head round the barrel of the wheel. **1905** *Westm. Gaz.* 3 Jan. 4/2 With one hand on the *tiller-lever he can perform all the functions of driver and steersman at once. **1889** J. K. JEROME *Three Men in Boat* 76 Harris at the sculls and I at the *tiller-lines. **1890** *Daily News* 9 Jan. 6/3 Her *tiller post had been carried away, and other damage done to the stern. **1745** P. THOMAS *Jrnl. Anson's Voy.* 148 Our old *Tiller-Rope being much worn, we unreev'd it, and reev'd a new one. **1872** BLACK *Adv. Phaeton* v, Bell pulled the white tiller-ropes over her shoulder.

**Ti·ller**, *sb.*[3] Now *dial.* Forms: 1 (see etymol.); 7– tiller, 8–9 tillar, tellar, teller; 9 *dial.* tellow, tillow, telly. [App. repr. OE. *telgor*, *tealgor* str. m., also *telgra* wk. m. (see sense 1), extended forms of *telga* wk. masc., 'branch, bough, twig' = ON. *tjalga* fem., MLG., LG., Du. *telg*, MDu. *telch, telg-*, m. and n., MHG. *zelch, zelge, zilge* m.:—OTeut. **telgo(n)*, *telgôn-* twig, branch, sprout. Not found in Eng. between 1100 and 1660; the phonetic history is obscure. The dial. *tellow*, *tillow* may repr. OE. *telga*.]

† **1.** (In OE.) A plant, a shoot, a twig; *esp.* a shoot or sucker from the root. *Obs.*

*a* **1000** *Blickl. Glosses* (E.E.T.S.) 261/2 Tealgras, *propagines*. *c* **1000** ÆLFRIC *Gen.* ii. 5 And ælcne telgor on eorðan ær ðam þe he uppasprunge on eorðan. *a* **1050** *Herbarium* in *Sax. Leechd.* I. 276 Ðeos wyrt. of anum wyrttruman manega telgran asendeþ. *Ibid.*, Hyperi..on..Of anum stelan manega telgran weaxaþ. *Ibid.* 324 Heo eal..wið þa eorðan hyre telgran tobrædeþ. *a* **1050** *Medicina de Quadrup.* ibid. 332 Do on anne telgran [þæs morbeamæs] ðe sy adune ʒecyrred.

**2.** A young tree, a sapling; *esp.* a stock-shoot, rising from the stock or stool of a felled tree.

**1664** EVELYN *Sylva* III. iv. § 29 (*Charcoal*) This [ladder] they usually make of a curved Tiller fit to apply to the convex shape of the heap. **1706** PHILLIPS (ed. Kersey), *Tillar* (in Husbandry), a small Tree left to grow till it be fellable. **1712** J. JAMES tr. *Le Blond's Gardening* 50 They are obliged to leave sixteen Tillers on an Acre. **1768** TUCKER *Lt. Nat.* (1834) I. 322 First shoots up a tender twig, which then becomes a sapling, a waiver, a tellar, and at last a perfect oak laden with acorns. **1794** W. PEARCE *Agric. Berks* 55 [They] permit their labourers, during the winter months, to take up the old roots, from which no heir or teller is rising. **1832** *Planting* 92 in *Libr. Usef. Knowl.*, *Husb.* III, Tiller or Tellar, a shoot selected..from those produced by a coppice stool to stand for a timber-tree. **1875** *Sussex Gloss.*, *Teller, Tillow*, a young oak tree. **1878** *N. & Q.* 5th Ser. X. 223 The lessee covenants not to cut down tellows and stemners.

**3.** One of the lateral shoots from the base of the stalk of corn or grass or other herbaceous plant.

**1733** TULL *Horse-Hoeing Husb.* xi. 132 The same Plant that when poor sends out but Two or Three Tillers, would if well nourish'd..send up a Multitude of Tillers, as is seen in Ho'd Wheat and Sown Wheat. **1759** tr. *Duhamel's Husb.* I. xiii. (1762) 70 New stalks, or, as some call it, tillers. **1764** *Museum Rust.* III. XII. 46 If the season is lost to encrease the number of tillers, we may enlarge the ears. **1811** W. LESLIE *Agric. Surv. Moray* Gloss., *Tiller*, the rising blade of growing corn shooting out several stems from one seed. [Cf. **1828** *Craven Gloss.*, *Telly*, a single stalk of grass or corn.]

† **Tiller**, *sb.*[4] *Obs. rare*[−1]. [app. f. TILL *sb.*[1] + -ER[1], ? after *drawer*.] = TILL *sb.*[1] 1.

**1693** DRYDEN *Juvenal* vi. 383 Search her Cabinet, and thou shal find Each Tiller there with Love-Epistles lin'd.

**Tiller** (ti·ləɹ), *v.*[1] Also 7 tillar, 9 tillow. [f. TILLER *sb.*[3]] *intr.* Of corn or other plants: To produce 'tillers' or side shoots from the root or base of the stem; also said of the shoots thus arising. Also with *out, forth*.

**1677** PLOT *Oxfordsh.* 245 The Seed in the rich [Land] does tillar, i. e. sprout into several blades and spread on the ground. **1733** TULL *Horse-Hoeing Husb.* xix. 270 More Stalks would have Tillered out. **1743** MAXWELL *Sel. Trans. Soc. Improv. Agric. Scot.* 24 Clover-plants, when they have room to grow, tiller or stool, and employ more Ground than those of Corn. **1805** R. W. DICKSON *Pract. Agric.* I. 463 Oats do not tiller so much as other grains. **1813** VANCOUVER *Surv. Hampshire* 196 The more that the crown of this plant is..divided, the greater disposition it has to stool and tillow forth in additional stems and succours. **1868** *Rep. U.S. Commissioner Agric.* (1869) 406 It [wheat] tillered astonishingly, as many as fifty heads growing from one kernel.

**b.** *trans.* To throw *out* (stalks, etc.) by tillering.

**1787** WINTER *Syst. Husb.* 207 The roots of the drilled [wheat] tillered out from ten or twelve to upwards of thirty stalks on each root.

Hence **Ti·llered** *ppl. a.*, having several shoots or stems springing from one root; **Ti·llering** *vbl. sb.* and *ppl. a.*

**1733** TULL *Horse-Hoeing Husb.* vii. 72 These Tillered Ho'd Stalks, if they were planted sparsim all over the Interval, it might seem well cover'd. **1764** *Museum Rust.* III. XII. 46 There is a particular season for its tillering, or spreading; another for its upright growth. **1833** *Ridgemont Farm Rep.* 137 in *Libr. Usef. Knowl.*, *Husb.* III, By a rapid and early vegetation of the wheat, the tillering branches of the young plant are apt to exhaust themselves. **1885** W. K. PARKER *Mammalian Descent* vi. 158 The multiplied (or tillered) stems of a wheat-plant.

† **Tiller**, *v.*[2]: see TILLERING *vbl. sb.*[1]

**Tiller**, dial. form of THILLER.

† **Tillerate**, *v. Obs. rare*[−1]. = TILLER *v.*[1]

**1759** tr. *Duhamel's Husb.* III. i. (1762) 299 The roots which stood thin in the rows, tillerated out from ten or twelve.

† **Ti·llering**, *vbl. sb.*[1] *Obs. rare.* [Implies a verb *tiller*, from TILLER *sb.*[2] 1 d: see -ING[1].] The

›utting of a bow upon a tiller (TILLER *sb.*[2] 1 d) in ›rder to stretch or bend it.

1545 ASCHAM *Toxoph.* II. (Arb.) 114, I woulde desyre all ›owyers to season theyr staues well, to woorke them and ›ynke them well, to giue them heetes conuenient, and ›ylleryngés plentye. *Ibid.* 115, I suppose that nether ye ›owe can be to good and chefe woode, nor yet to well ›easoned or truly made, wyth hetynges and tilleryngés. 1801 T. ROBERTS *Eng. Bowman* 295 *Tillering*, trying a bow ›y the tiller. Altering a bow by scraping it.

**Tillering**, *vbl. sb.*[2]: see after TILLER *v.*[1]

**Tillerless** (ti·ləɹlės), *a.* [f. TILLER *sb.*[2] + -LESS.] Without or lacking a tiller.

1870 *Routledge's Ev. Boy's Ann.* Feb. 86 The rudder was ›tillerless.

**Tillet**[1] (ti·lėt), **tillot** (ti·lət). Forms: 5 **tyllete, tillette, 6 tyllet, 7 tillett, -it, 6- tillet, 9 -ot.** [app. ad. OF. *tellette* (14th c. in Godef. *Compl.*), collateral form of *teilete, toilete* a wrapper of cloth: see TOILET.]

**1.** A kind of coarse cloth, used for wrapping up textile fabrics and (formerly) garments; also for making awnings.

1466 *Mann. & Household Exp.* (Roxb.) 211 Paid to Iohn Felaw for xij. yerdes of tyllete for the spynas. 1530 PALSGR. 281/1 Tyllet to wrap clothe in, *toyllette*. 1590 *Inv. Sir T. Ramsey* in *Archæologia* XL. 327 A scarlet cloke faced wth gray with the tillet. 1637 *Specif. S. Mason's Patent* No. 106 The sole dying of buckromes and tillits. 1837 WHITTOCK, etc. *Bk. Trades* (1842) 246 The tillet, or little cloth, for encasing glazed stuffs intended for a foreign market, was the first approach towards pattern floor-cloth painting. 1904 *Times* 5 Sept. 1/2 Mr. Justice Farwell.. restrained..the said Defendants..from wrapping up any goods..in lining papers and tillots supplied by the Plaintiffs.

**b.** A bag made of thin glazed muslin, used as a covering for dress-goods.

1871 in MCELRATH *Dict. Commerce* (Funk).

†**2.** A tilt or awning. *Obs.*

1497 *Naval Acc. Hen. VII* (1896) 110 Cartes with tillettes for shott with all apparelle.

Hence **Ti·lloting**, in *tilloting cloth*, a cloth used as a wrapper, esp. for textile fabrics.

1884 *Specif. Tiller's Patent* No. 2357 Improvements in tillotting cloths.

†**Tillet**[2]. *Obs.* Also 7 **tylet.** [a. OF. *tillet, teillet* (14–15th c. in Godef.), dim. of *til, teil*; see TEIL and -ET.] A lime or linden-tree.

1601 HOLLAND *Pliny* (1634) II. 7 The thin barks of the Linden or Tillet tree. *Ibid.* 185. 1686 tr. *Chardin's Trav. Persia* 370 Groves of Poplers and Tylets, which they plant to serve 'em for building their Houses.

‖**Tilleul.** [F. *tilleul* (ti[l]yöl) linden-tree :—L. **tiliolus*, dim. of **tilius* = *tilia* linden.]

**1.** A lime or linden-tree.

1530 PALSGR 281/1 Tylleull, a kynde of frute [error for *tree*], *tilleul*. 1825–9 MRS. SHERWOOD *Lady of Manor* II. xiv. 180 The gardens of orange trees; the avenues of tilleul; the groves of myrtle.

**2.** *attrib.* **a.** Name of a shade of colour: a pale yellowish green like that of the leaves of the lime-tree.

1884 *Cassell's Fam. Mag.* May 371/2 A light tilleul ground, just the tint of lettuce, shot with white. 1909 *Daily Chron.* 26 June 4/5 Lady St. Germans..becomingly dressed in tilleul voile.

**b.** *Tilleul tea*, an infusion of lime-tree flowers, used as a remedy for headache, etc.

1908 *Daily Chron.* 14 Nov. 4/4 Ordinary tea [has been replaced] by the bitter-tasted tilleul variety, which was first on show at an hotel in Paris.

†**Till-hew**, *v. Obs. rare.* [f. *till-* for To- *prefix*[2] + HEW *v.*] *trans.* To hew or cut to pieces.

1375 BARBOUR *Bruce* II. 381 He all till-hewyt þat he ourtuk. *Ibid.* xx. 367 So fast till-hewyn wes all his face.

**Tilli**, in *tilli berries*: see TILLY *sb.*

**Tilling** (ti·liŋ), *vbl. sb.* [f. TILL *v.*[1] + -ING[1].] The action of TILL *v.*[1]; work done upon land for raising crops; cultivation, tillage.

*a* 1225 *Ancr. R.* 296 Þe winȝeardes..þet mot muche tilunge to uorte beren windberien. 1377 LANGL. *P. Pl.* B. XIV. 63 Fourty wynter folke lyued withouten tulyinge. 1387 TREVISA *Higden* (Rolls) II. 281 Konnynge of telienge [*v. rr.* tellynge, tillyng] of feeldes þey cleped Cereres. 1475 *Bk. Noblesse* (Roxb.) 70 In tilieng, ering, and labourage of his londis to bere corne and fruit. *a* 1610 HEALEY *Theophrastus* (1636) 12 The well tilling and husbanding of the ground. 1678 SIR G. MACKENZIE *Crim. Laws Scot.* I. xix. § 9 (1699) 101 The stealers of Pleugh-graith..in the time of Teiling..are to be punished to the death. 1710 *Lond. Gaz.* No. 4703/2 A Bill..for encouraging the Tilling of Land with Bullocks. 1817 W. SELWYN *Law Nisi Prius* (ed. 4) II. 1206 Whether the land is of such a nature as to require an extraordinary expence in manuring or tilling. *fig.* 1483 CAXTON *Gold. Leg.* 271 b/1 Lyke a tylyer of Ihesu cryst he prouffyted in spyrytuel tylyeng. 1640 H. WOODWARD (*title*) A Childes Patrimony laid out upon the good culture or tilling over his whole man.

†**b.** *concr.* The produce of tilling; a crop: = TILLAGE 2 b. *Obs. rare.*

1680 J. GOODYEAR in *Hereford Dioc. Reg.* 4 Oct., Wanting ropes in the time of Harvest to carry in his tilling with.

**c.** *attrib.*, as **tilling land**, land fit for tilling, arable land.

1387 TREVISA *Higden* (Rolls) II. 89 But now wodes beþ i-hewe adoun and newe telynge lond i-made. 1488 *Cal. Anc. Rec. Dublin* (1889) 494 Parte of the tyllyng land.

**Ti·lling**, *ppl. a.* [f. TILL *v.*[1] + -ING[2].] That tills or cultivates land.

*c* 1380 WYCLIF *Serm.* Sel. Wks. I. 319 Þe first was an heerde, and þe toþer a tiliyng man. 1906 *Daily Chron.* 15 Sept. 3/1 Nor spurn my muse because it sings..Of tilling men who plough and reap.

†**Ti·llman.** *Obs.* [f. TILL *v.*[1] + MAN *sb.*] A man employed in tillage; a farmer, husbandman; a ploughman, peasant; a tiller of the soil.

940 *Grant of land in Wilts.* in Birch *Cart. Sax.* II. 483 Lang weȝes þæt ofer tilmannes dene. 13.. *Cursor M.* 4696 (Cott.) Tilmen oueral þe land a-boute..þair sede had saun. *c* 1375 *Sc. Leg. Saints* xl. (*Ninian*) 201, & he þane, as gud tele-man, To wirk in goddis ȝard begane. *c* 1440 *Jacob's Well* 237 Summe feendys komyn as tylmen wyth here hors & carte. 1573 TUSSER *Husb.* (1878) 34 Good shepheard, good tilman, good Jack and good Gil, Makes husband and huswife their cofers to fil. 1620 T. GRANGER *Div. Logike* 56 The till-man plowing in the field, findeth a treasure.

**Tillocrat** (ti·lǫkræt). *nonce-wd.* [f. TILL *v.*[1] 4 + -(O)CRAT.] A ruling member of an agricultural class.

1858 BAILEY *Age* 5 Farmers, bankers, millocrats, Officials, manufacturers, merchants, tillocrats.

**Tillodont** (ti·lǫdǫnt). *Palæont.* [f. mod.L. *Tillodontia*, f. Gr. τίλλ-ειν to pluck + ὀδούς, ὀδοντ-tooth.] A member of the *Tillodontia*, a group of extinct mammals apparently combining the characters of ungulates, rodents, and carnivora, whose remains are found in the Eocene of N. America.

[1875 *Amer. Jrnl. Sci.* Ser. III. IX. 221 At the last meeting of the Connecticut Academy, Feb. 17th, Professor O. C. Marsh made a communication on a new order of Eocene Mammals, for which he proposed the name Tillodontia. 1876 MARSH *ibid.* XI. 249.] 1889 NICHOLSON & LYDEKKER *Palæont.* II. 1408 The characters presented by the Tillodonts harmonise with the view that both the Ungulates and Rodents have been derived from a primitive Carnivorous stock.

**Tillot**: see TILLET[1]. **Tillow**, var. TILLER *sb.*[3], *v.*

†**Ti·llsman.** *Obs.* In 6 *Sc.* telisman, 6–7 tilsman. Alteration of TILLMAN, with inserted *s*, after *huntsman, spokesman, steersman*, etc.

1561–2 in Keith *Hist. Ch. Scot.* (1734) I. App. 179 All and sindrie Parochinaris, Takkismen, Telismen, Fewaris, Rentalaris, Possessouris. 1589 NASHE *Anat. Absurd.* 30 Theyr father was a Tilsman attendant. 1645 WARD *Serm. bef. Ho. Com.* 26 *Mar.* 31 Like a piece of ground that hath beene stirred by the Plough, and the tils-man doth not follow on to give it more earths in due season.

**Tillward**: see TILWARD.

**Tilly** (ti·li), *sb.* Also 8 **tilli, tyle.** [app. a. F. *tilli*, ad. med.L. *tiglium*, in It. *tiglia*: cf. TIGLIC.] In *tilly-seed*, the seed of a species of *Croton* (formerly called *C. Pavana*, now identified with *C. Tiglium*), which yields Croton oil.

1712 tr. *Pomet's Hist. Drugs* I. 144 The smooth Fruit call'd in the Shops, Tyle Seed, or Tilli-Berries [orig. *Ricinus arbre à fruit lisse, nommé grain de Tilli*]. 1858 SIMMONDS *Dict. Trade, Tilly-seed*, a small tree, the *Croton Pavana* of Hamilton,..the seeds of which have the same properties as those of the *Croton Tiglium*.

**Tilly** (ti·li), *a.* [f. TILL *sb.*[2] + -Y.] Abounding in, or of the nature of, till or tenacious clay.

1799 J. ROBERTSON *Agric. Perth* 14 Houses composed of this mortar or tilly clay. 1812 SIR J. SINCLAIR *Syst. Husb. Scot.* I. 227 Stiff stubborn tilly land. 1844 STEPHENS *Bk. Farm* I. 169 Clay, and tilly clay even more than the unctuous, retains a great deal of water.

**Tilly-vally**, *int.* [Obs.] or *arch.* Also 6 **tully valy, 7 tillie vallie, 7, 9 tilly-fally, 9 tilley-valley.** [Origin unknown.] An exclamation of impatience: Nonsense! fiddlesticks!

*a* 1529 SKELTON *Manerly Marg. Mylk & Ale* 5 Tully valy, strawe, let be, I say! 1597 SHAKS. 2 *Hen. IV*, II. v. 90 Tilly-fally (Sir Iohn) neuer tell me, your ancient Swagerer comes not in my doores. 1601 — *Twel. N.* II. iii. 83 Am not I consanguinious? Am I not of her blood? tilly vally. *c* 1630 *Life Sir T. More* iv. 127 Tillie vallie, tillie vallie: will you sitt and make goslings in the ashes? 1816 SCOTT *Antiq.* vi, Tilley-valley, Mr. Lovel—which, by the way, one commentator derives from *tittivillitium*, and another from *talley-ho*—but tilley-valley, I say, a truce with your politeness. 1864 *St. James' Mag.* 334 Tilly-fally, man!—But go on with your evidence, brother Burt.

‖**Ti·lma.** [Mexican Sp., ad. Nahuatl *tilmatli*, in comb. *tilma-*.] A kind of simple cloak or blanket secured with a knot, worn by the Indians of Mexico.

1851 MAYNE REID *Scalp Hunt.* x, We see mangas and tilmas, and men wearing the sandal as in Eastern lands. *Ibid.* xx, There were pueblos clad in their ungraceful tilmas. 1895 *Daily News* 6 Nov. 3/5 The shrine of our Lady of Guadaloupe had its origin in an alleged apparition of the Madonna to an Indian, Juan Diego, in the early days of the Conquest [9 Dec. 1531]...A picture of the Virgin is said to have appeared on the coarse tilma or cloak of the Indian.

**Tilsent**, early perversion of TINSEL *sb.*[3]

**Tilt** (tilt), *sb.*[1] Also 5 **telt(e, 5–7 tylt, 6 tylte, 7 tillte.** [Collateral form of ME. *tild*, TELD *sb.*, perh. influenced by *tent*.]

**1.** A covering of coarse cloth, in early quots. of hair-cloth; an awning; a booth, tent, or tabernacle.

*c* 1440 *Promp. Parv.* 488/1 Telte, or tente, *tentorium*. 1547 *Privy Council Acts* (1890) II. 133 Tyltes of heare to couver the powder. 1556 TOWRSON in Hakluyt *Voy.* (1589) 110 On shoare, wee made a Tilt with our Oares and saile. 1633 T. ADAMS *Exp. 2 Peter* i. 13 The apostle compares his life to a tabernacle; a little shed or tilt, wherin the immortal soul dwells. 1688 R. HOLME *Armoury* IV. xii. (Roxb.) 504/1 The coffin had ouer it a tilt or stately frame of wood couered with black. 1771 SMOLLETT *Humph. Cl.* 1 July, Machines..fitted with tilts, that project from the seaward ends of them,..to screen the bathers from the view.

**2.** *spec.* An awning over a boat.

1611 MIDDLETON & DEKKER *Roaring Girl* IV. ii, A boat, with a tilt over it. 1716 GAY *Trivia* I. 164 The rowing Crew To tempt a Fare, cloath all their Tilts in blue. 1887 BESANT *The World went* ii, A broad canvas tilt or awning rigged up from stem to stern.

**3.** An awning or cover for a cart or wagon, usually of canvas or tarpaulin.

1620 SHELTON *Quix.* (1746) III. xi. 69 The Waggon's Self was opened, without Tilt or Boughs. *a* 1656 USSHER *Ann.* vi. (1658) 228 They covered the Cart with a base dirty tilt made of skins. 1753 *Scots Mag.* Nov. 541/1 The tilt or some other conspicuous place of his waggon. 1834 PRINGLE *Afr. Sk.* ii. 141 Each wagon is provided with a raised canvas tilt to protect the traveller from sun and rain. 1893 SELOUS *Trav. S. E. Africa* 24 My waggon..on the hinder part of which stood a tilt or tent where I slept.

**4.** In Labrador and Newfoundland: A fisherman's or wood-cutter's hut.

1895 R. G. TABER in *Outing* (U.S.) XXVII. 20/1 A score of shoresmen's 'tilts'—rude turf-covered huts, some little cleaner than the Esquimaux' habitations. 1906 *Toilers of Deep* June 150/2 (*Labrador*) A few wooden 'tilts' nestled at the edge of the river...The 'tilts' are all very much alike—the general 'living-room',..and the beds in curtained-off recesses. The little colony..come from their homes at Cape Charles only for the winter's trapping and wood-cutting.

**5.** *attrib.* and *Comb.*, as *tilt-maker, -weaver, -window*; *tilt-like* adj.; also **tilt-bonnet**, a woman's or girl's bonnet in the form of a wagon-tilt, made by bending a piece of pasteboard into a half-cylinder, and covering it with linen or calico, a drawing-string holding it in shape, the material being extended to cover the crown and form a curtain (T. Hardy): cf. *coal-scuttle bonnet*; **tilt-cloth**, = senses 1–3; †**tilt-hair**, ? hair-cloth for tilts; **tilt-roof**, 'a round-topped roof, shaped like a tilt or wagon-cover' (Knight *Dict. Mech.* 1877); †**tilt-sail**, ? a sail made of coarse cloth; **tilt-wherry**, a wherry having a tilt, a TILT-BOAT.

1874 T. HARDY *Far fr. Madding Crowd* xxv, The women ..wore *tilt bonnets covered with nankeen. 1611 in *10th Rep. Hist. MSS. Comm.* App. IV. 432 For a *tylt cloth, 2s. 6d. 1790 LUCKOMBE *Eng. Gazetteer* III, *Witney, Oxf*... Tilt-cloths for bargemen are likewise made here. *c* 1440 *Promp. Parv.* 488/1 *Telte hayyr (*H., A., P.* telt, hayre), *gauda*. 1562 in Rogers *Agric. & Prices* III. 576/1 Tilt hair.. 35½ bolts @ 1/4, 94 pieces @ 11/-. 1834 H. MILLER *Scenes & Leg.* xiii. (1857) 203 The grey ruins, and the mossy, *tilt-like hillocks. 1847 ADDISON *Contracts* II. vii. § 2 (1883) 921 The defendant ordered the plaintiff to make him a waggon, and..employed..a *tiltmaker to put on a tilt. 1620 SHELTON *Quix.* (1746) IV. xxii. 178 The General made all the Gallies strike their *Tilt-sails. 1579 *Transcr. Favershaw Parish Regr.* (MS.), Erosamas Smalwodd, a tylteweuer. 1573 in Feuillerat *Revels Q. Eliz.* (1908) 219, ii *Tylt whirreyes that caryed the Masking geare & Children. 1799 *Hull Advertiser* 3 Aug. 4/1 She..thrust it out at one of the *tilt-windows.

**Tilt** (tilt), *sb.*[2] Also 6 **tylt(e, 6–7 tilte.** [In branch I from TILT *v.*[1] 1; in br. II fr. TILT *v.*[1] II.]

**I. 1.** A combat or encounter (for exercise or sport) between two armed men on horseback, with lances or similar weapons, the aim of each being to throw his opponent from the saddle; = JUST *sb.*[1] 1; also, the exercise of riding with a lance, or the like, at a mark, as the quintain.

1511 in Ellis *Orig. Lett.* Ser. II. I. 181 Thise iiij Knightes shall present themself..in harneys for the Tylte 1553 T. WILSON *Rhet.* (1580) 13, I maie commende hym for plaiyng at weapons, for runnyng vppon a greate horse, for chargyng his staffe at the Tilt. 1656 EARL MONM. tr. *Boccalini's Advts. fr. Parnass.* I. lvii. (1674) 74 [To] spend a hundred thousand Crowns in Tilt and Turney. 1745 SIR C. WILLIAMS in H. Walpole *Mem. Geo. II* (1847) II. App. 396 Low pleasures, such as operas, plays, masquerades, tilts, and tournaments. 1859 TENNYSON *Enid* 52 Forgetful of the tilt and tournament.

**b.** *transf.* and *fig.* An encounter, combat, contest; a debate, public dispute or discussion. In 17–18th c. often applied to a duel.

1567 TURBERV. *Epit. Dame Elyz. Arkundle* 3 Who ran hir race in vertues tylt aright, And neuer had at Fortunes hand the foyle. *a* 1670 HACKET *Abp. Williams* II. (1692) 21 He would not fly the tilt nor start from any colour of accusation. 1693 *Humours Town* 27 A modish Tilt upon a foolish hot-headed Punctilio. 1709 STEELE *Tatler* No. 39 ¶ 6 We..generally conducted our Dispute and Tilt according to the last that had happen'd between Persons of Reputation. 1882 F. M. CRAWFORD *Mr. Isaacs* ii, I trust that our collision in the flesh has had no worse results than our tilts in print. 1906 *Spectator* 3 Feb. 173/2 She enjoys the tilt of rather rough speech.

**c.** A thrust of a weapon, as at a tilt. Now only *fig.*

1716 ADDISON *Freeholder* No. 10 ¶ 5 His Majesty..entertain'd him with the Slaughter of two or three of his Liege Subjects, whom he very dexterously put to Death with the Tilt of his Lance. 1754 RICHARDSON *Grandison* (1781) I. xiv. 82 Miss Barnevelt took a tilt in heroics. 1863 COWDEN CLARKE *Shaks. Char.* viii. 200 She has a tilt at him, jeering, joking, mystifying, obfuscating him.

**2.** A place for holding tilts or justs; a tilting ground or yard; the lists.

*a* 1510 *Justes May & June* 1507. 68 in Hazl. *E. P. P.* II. 116 Two seruauntes of this lady of delyte Sholde bemounted armed and redy dyght At atyltes ende. 1530 PALSGR. 183 *Vnes lices*, a tylte to lerne to juste at. *a* 1548 HALL *Chron., Hen. VIII* 45 b, The kyng..rode about the Tylt. 1564 HAWARD *Eutropius* VII. 75 He fynyshed sondry pieces of work at Rome among which was..the Tilt [L. *forum transitorium*], a place for men to run in. 1586 WARNER *Alb. Eng.*

II. ix. (1589) 35 In beaten Pathes, ore boorded Tylthes [? Tyltes] to breake their staffe-like Reeds.

**3.** Phr. (from 1 or 2). **a.** *To run at* (*the*) *tilt*: to ride in a tilt or just.

**1548** Elyot *Dict.*, *Decurrere in armis*, to renne at the tylte in harneys. **1590** Marlowe *Edw. II*, v. v, When for her sake I ran at tilt in France, And there unhors'd the Duke of Cleremont. **1611** Cotgr., *Courir la lance*, to tilt, or, to run at tilt. **1636** P. Randall in *Ann. Dubrensia* (1877) 19 As they at Tilt, so wee at Quintain runne. **1649** Jer. Taylor *Gt. Exemp.* III. Disc. xx. 143 Henry II was killed running at Tilt.

**b.** So *to run a tilt* (see also A-tilt 2, A *prep.*[1]); also *fig.* Also rarely *to run tilt*.

**1591** Shaks. *1 Hen. VI*, III. ii. 51 Break a Launce, and runne a-Tilt at Death. **1674** N. Fairfax *Bulk & Selv.* 145 If you make two such bodies..to run a tilt upon such a line of odd leastings. **1762–71** H. Walpole *Vertue's Anecd. Paint.* (1786) I. 158 The next..exhibits two knights running a tilt on the foreground. **1831** Carlyle in Froude *Life* (1882) II. viii. 170 With her..I was provoked.., so pert was she, to run tilt, and I fear transfix her. **1871** Miss Mulock *Fair France* i. 3 Like Don Quixote with his windmill..it is running a tilt against perfectly imaginary foes. **1891** *Temple Bar Mag.* Sept. 102 He runs tilt against the hypocrisies of social life.

**c.** *Full tilt* (advb. phr.): at full speed and with direct thrust; with utmost adverse force or impetus.

?*a* **1600** *Hist. Tom Thumb* II. 45 in Hazl. *E. P. P.* II. 213 The cook was running on full tilt, When Tom fell from the air. **1679** *Hist. Jetzer* 24 Drawing out his knife, [he] made at her Ladyship full tilt. **1861** *Temple Bar Mag.* IV. 83 Managers of schools should run full tilt at the whole scheme. **1889** Gretton *Memory's Harkb.* 145 The Earl rode full tilt at him as though he would have unhorsed him.

**II. 4.** The act of tilting, or fact or condition of being tilted (Tilt *v.*[1] 4); a sudden or abrupt divergence from the normal vertical or horizontal position; inclination upward or downward.

[Implied in quots. 1562, 1658, 1706 in b.]

**1837** Babbage *Bridgew. Treat.* App. 246 The variation of pressure, and the infirmity of supports broken by weights or softened by heat, to produce tilts. **1859** *All Year Round* No. 29. 67 The twinkle of his eye, and the saucy tilt of his ragged cap, spoke volumes. **1872** *Routledge's Ev. Boy's Ann.* Apr. 262/1 Until one tilt, stronger than the others, upset the lamp. **1906** *Daily News* 5 Mar. 6 Leaning against the wall ..with his stool at a perilous tilt.

**b.** *On* or *upon the tilt*: in a tilted position, like a cask or vessel raised on one end or side when nearly empty: = A-tilt 1. Also *fig.*

**1562** J. Heywood *Prov. & Epigr.* (1867) 194 Till tubbe stande a tilte. **1658** T. Goodwin *Fair Prospect* Ep. Ded., When her natural strength, and Abilities began to run low, and on Tilt, as it were; Her Spiritual affections seemed as if but fresh broached. **1706** Baynard in Sir J. Floyer *Hot & Cold Bath.* II. 419 When (low drawn) Time's upon the Tilt, Few Sands and Minutes left to run. **1712** *Spect.* No. 292 ⁋ 4 Liberality..performed with such Chearfulness..that may shew Good-nature and Benevolence overflowed, and do not, as in some Men, run upon the Tilt, and taste of the Sediments of a grutching uncommunicative Disposition.

**c.** *Geol.* An abrupt upheaval of strata to a considerable angle from the horizontal. **d.** *gen.* A slope, or sloping portion, of the surface of the ground.

**1859** Page *Geol. Terms*, *Tilted up*, applied to strata that are suddenly or abruptly thrown up at a high angle of inclination. *Tilts* of this nature are usually accompanied by fractures and crushings of the strata. **1903** G. A. Smith in *Expositor* Jan. 7 This tilt towards Olivet does not exhaust the eastern bent and disposition of the city. **1910** *Daily News* 27 Aug. 4 As we crossed a tilt of the torn heath I saw suddenly between myself and the moon a black shapeless pile.

†**5.** The liquor, or sediment, obtained by tilting a vessel; dregs, lees. *Obs.*

*a* **1603** T. Cartwright *Confut. Rhem. N. T.* (1618) 449 The tilt and lees of traditions, dregges of custome, and poyson of Popish decrees.

**6.** A contrivance used in North America in fishing through a hole in the ice, in which a stick or cross-piece is tilted up when the fish takes the hook.

**1891** in *Cent. Dict.*

**7.** In Newfoundland, A pier on which fishermen unload and dress their fish. **1891** in *Cent. Dict.*

**8.** Short for Tilt-hammer.

**1831** J. Holland *Manuf. Metal* I. 241 The annexed figure is the plan of a tilt. **1858** Greener *Gunnery* 167 [By] welding and forging by the heavy hammer, reducing by a tilt and rolling down to the smallest description of rod, a most excellent, tenacious, and dense body of iron is thus obtained. **1896** *Daily News* 27 Jan. 8/5 The activity at the forges, rolling mills, and tilts where large quantities..are prepared.

**III. 9.** The stilt or long-legged plover of North America. (Cf. Tilt-up A. 2.)

**1831** A. Wilson & Bonaparte *Amer. Ornith.* III. 77 The name by which this bird is known on the seacoast is the stilt or tilt, or long-shanks. **1859** Bartlett *Dict. Amer.*, *Lawyer*. 1. (*Himantopus nigricollis*.) The black-necked Stilt..known also by the names of Tilt and Longshanks.

**IV. 10.** *attrib.* and *Comb.*, as *tilt-day*, *-horse*; **tilt-cart**, a cart of which the body can be tilted so as to empty out the contents; **tilt-forge**, a forge in which a tilt-hammer is used; **tilt guard**: see under Tilt-yard; **tilt house** = *tilt-mill* (*b*); **tilt-mill**, (*a*) the machinery for working a tilt-hammer; (*b*) a building in which a tilt-hammer is worked; **tilt-rod**, a curved rod projecting from the rear of a tricycle so as to catch the ground in the event of the machine being tilted backward; **tilt-staff**, a staff used instead of a lance in tilting; **tilt-wheel**, a little wheel at the end of the tilt-rod of a tricycle. See also Tilt-hammer, Tilt-yard.

**1844** Stephens *Bk. Farm* II. 660 If they are *tilt or coup-carts, he elevates the front a few inches. **1605** Camden *Rem.* 174 At the next *Tilte-day following. **1836** *Blackw. Mag.* XXXIX. 339 We passed some *usines*, *tilt-forges, where the makers of nails [etc.] use the power to tilt hammers of small water wheels placed on one of the..streams. **1894** *Times* 28 May 6/1 The 2nd Life Guards, furnishing the *tilt guard, sent a squadron of about 50 of all ranks. **1909** *Daily Chron.* 20 Feb. 5/3 What we call the Horse Guards, which was then called the Tilt Yard (where the guard, I think, is still called the Tilt guard). **1562** J. Heywood *Prov. & Epigr.* (1867) 178 A *Tilt horse, *alias* a beere horse to bee, Which wouldst thou bee? **1864** Strauss, etc. *Eng. Workshops* 90 Two hammer or *tilt houses. **1825** J. Nicholson *Operat. Mechanic* 337 The *tilt-mills employed in the manufacture of steel. **1912** J. T. Fowler *Let. to Editor*, Modern tricycles cannot be tilted backward, and so do not require *tilt-rods. **1650** W. Saunderson *Aulicus Coquin.* 69 He medled not with the *Tilt-staff. **1886** *Cycl. Tour. C. Gaz.* IV. 144 *Tilt wheels loose are very noisy.

† **Tilt**, *sb.*[3] *slang. Obs.* In 7 tylt. A cant name for some species of rogue.

**1620** Dekker *Dreame* (1860) 38 Base heapes tumbled together,..high-way-standers, Foists, nips, and tylts, prinadoes, bawdes, pimpes, panders.

**Tilt** (tilt), *v.*[1] Also 4 tylte, 7 tylt. *Pa. t.* and *pple.* **tilted**; also 4 *pa. t.* tult, *pa. pple.* tylt, 5 *pa. t.* and *pple.* **tilt**. [In I, ME. *tylten*, repr. an OE. **tyltan* for **tiellan*:—**talt-jan*, f. OE. *tealt* unsteady, shaky, Tealt (whence OE. *tealtian*:—**talt-ōjan* to be unsteady). Cf. Norw. *tylten* adj. inclined to fall over, unsteady, Sw. *tulta* to totter. Branch II is from I; but br. III is from Tilt *sb.*[2] 1 (deriv. of 1 here); br. IV from Tilt-hammer: these are thus, strictly, separate vbs. of secondary origin.]

**I.** †**1.** *trans.* To cause to fall; to thrust, push, throw down or over; to overthrow, overturn, upset. *Obs.* (exc. as in 4 c, 6 b).

**13..** *E. E. Allit. P.* B. 832 Þe trestes tylt to þe woȝe & þe table boþe. *Ibid.* 1213 Ouer-tok hem, as tyd, tult hem of sadeles. *a* **1400–50** *Alexander* 1303 Sone þe top of þe toure he tiltis in-to þe watir. **1577–87** Holinshed *Chron.* III. 1063/1 He..said to his wife; Mistrys Alice what milke haue you giuen me here? Wheerewithall she tilted it ouer with her hand, saieng, I weene nothing can please you.

†**2.** *intr.* To fall over, tumble; be overthrown.

**13..** *E. E. Allit. P.* C. 252 With-outen towche of any tothe he [Jonah] tult in his [the whale's] þrote. *Ibid.* 361 Truly þis ilk toun schal tylte to grounde. *a* **1375** *Joseph Arim.* 4 Feole temples þer-inne tulten to þe eorþe, For heore false ymages þat þei on leeueden. ?*a* **1400** *Morte Arth.* 1144 Untenderly fro þe toppe thai tiltin to-gederz.

**3.** *intr.* To move unsteadily up and down; *esp.* of waves or a ship at sea, to pitch.

**1590** Shaks. *Com. Err.* IV. ii. 6 (Fols. 2 & 3) What obseruation mad'st thou in this case Of [*Fol.*[1] Oh,] his hearts Meteors tilting in his face? **1594** Marlowe *Dido* I. i, Phrygian ships ..so wrack'd and welter'd by the waves, As every tide tilts 'twixt their oaken sides. **1667** Milton *P. L.* XI. 747 The floating Vessel..with beaked prow Rode tilting o're the Waves. **1725** Pope *Odyss.* XIV. 289 And tilting o'er the bay the vessels ride. **1822–56** De Quincey *Confess.* (1862) 238 To and fro, up and down, did I tilt upon those mountainous seas. **1826** A. A. Watts *Death Pompey* v, A bark comes tilting through the spray. **1878** Mrs. Stowe *Poganuc P.* xxviii. 238 The..tree..where the bobolink was tilting up and down.

**II. 4.** *trans.* To cause to lean abruptly from the vertical or incline abruptly from the horizontal; to slope, slant; *to tilt up*, to raise one end or side above the other, to tip up.

In *Geol.* used in *passive* of strata inclined abruptly upwards from their horizontal position: cf. Tilt *sb.*[2] 4 c.

**1594** Plat *Jewell-ho.* III. 59 It is also very good to tilt your beere, when the Vessel is little more then halfe drawn off, for so you shall draw your beere good euen to the latter end. **1607** Middleton *Michaelm. Term* IV. iv, Give her more air; tilt up her head. **1807** Herschel in *Phil. Trans.* XCVII. 199 By gently lifting up or tilting the lens. **1833** Lyell *Princ. Geol.* III. 340 Sedimentary beds tilted up, and more or less contorted on the flanks of the mountains. **1868** Joynson *Metals* 19 Where the waggons are tilted and their contents shot out. **1908** *Blackw. Mag.* Sept. 319/2 His helmet tilted well to the rear to screen his neck.

**b.** *intr.* To move into a slanted position or direction; to incline, slope, slant, heel over, tip *up*.

**1626** Bacon *Sylva* § 155 Keeping it even, that it may not tilt on either side. **1683** Moxon *Mech. Exerc.*, *Printing* xxii. ⁋ 2 Letting the hither side of the Board rest upon the hither Ledge of the Rincing-Trough; that the Form may tilt downwards. **1795** Herschel in *Phil. Trans.* LXXXV. 408 The tube..by its great weight..will..tilt backwards. **1861** Smiles *Engineers* II. 274 He accidentally set his foot upon a loose plank, which tilted up, and he fell into the water. **1909** *Daily Chron.* 24 Feb. 1/5 South Africa also tilts to the east in summer and to the west in winter. This is probably traceable to the seasonal rainfall.

**c.** *trans.* To pour or empty out (the contents of a vessel), or cause them to flow to one side, by tilting the vessel.

*a* **1613** [see Tilted *ppl. a.*[2] 2]. **1865** Lewes in *Fortn. Rev.* II. 702 To tumble out their sentences as they would tilt stones from a cart. **1865** Dickens *Mut. Fr.* I. xii, He poured the wine into his mouth, tilted it into his right cheek. **1883** *Hardwich's Photogr. Chem.* xiii. (ed. Taylor) 281 Tilt the developing fluid backwards and forwards upon the film for about thirty seconds. **1899** *Daily News* 20 Nov. 7/5 They object to being tilted out of a truck like potatoes out of a sack.

**III.** [f. Tilt *sb.*[2] 1.]

**5.** *intr.* To engage in a tilt or just; to just or joust.

**1595** T. Edwardes *L'Envoy to Cephalus & Procris* vii, Although he differs much from men Tilting under Frieries. **1611** Cotgr., *Courir la lance*, to tilt, or, to run at tilt. **1622** in *Crt. & Times Jas. I* (1848) II. 305 He ran at the ring, and tilted with the Lord Montjoy. **1697** Collier *Ess. Mor. Subj.* I. (1709) 131 'Tis not yet the Fashion for Women of Quality to Tilt. **1859** Tennyson *Enid* 480 But in this tournament can no man tilt, Except the lady he loves best be there.

†**b.** *transf.* See quots. *Obs.*

*a* **1700** B. E. *Dict. Cant. Crew*, *To tilt*, to fight with a Rapier. **1706** Phillips (ed. Kersey), *To Tilt*, to run at Tilts, to fence or thrust with Swords or Foils.

**c.** *transf.* and *fig.* To engage in a contest; to combat, encounter, contend (*with*); to strike or thrust *at* with a weapon, to charge or impinge *against*.

**1588** Shaks. *L. L. L.* v. ii. 483 Loe, he is tilting straight. **1589** Greene *Menaphon* (Arb.) 74 Her eyes were like the fierie torches tilting against the Moone. **1592** Shaks. *Rom. & Jul.* III. i. 163 He Tilts With Peircing steele at bold Mercutio's breast. **1613–16** W. Browne *Brit. Past.* II. i, Against whose naked brest The surges tilted. *a* **1661** Fuller *Worthies, Lond.* (1662) II. 193 With which Horn he tilteth at his prey. **1733** Pope *Hor. Sat.* II. i. 70 Satire's my weapon, but I'm too discreet To run a muck, and tilt at all I meet. **1809** Pinkney *Trav. France* 25, I resolved..never to tilt with a French lady in compliment. **1908** [Miss E. Fowler] *Betw. Trent & Ancholme* 12 Coifi struck down the idol.., tilting at it with his spear.

**d.** To 'charge' into a place or on some one; to run *against*, rush or burst *in*, *through*, etc.

**1831** T. L. Peacock *Crotchet Castle* xviii, He..seized a long lance, threw open the gates, and tilted out on the rabble. **1854** H. Miller *Sch. & Schm.* ii. (1857) 21 Not at all sure that I might not tilt against old John in the dark. **1873** Howells *Chance Acquaint.* iv, Tilting along through the crowd with a half-staggering run.

**6.** *trans.* (loose uses): **a.** To poise (the lance) for a thrust.

**1708** J. Philips *Cyder* II. 603 Sons against Fathers tilt the fatal Lance. *c* **1870** B. Harte *Twenty Years* Poems (1886) 36 The apple-blooms shook on the hill; And the mullein-stalks tilted each lance.

**b.** To tilt at; to rush at, charge; to drive or thrust by tilting.

**1796** Morse *Amer. Geog.* II. 465 Shooting at a mark or tilting it with darts. **1822** W. Irving *Braceb. Hall* xxiv, Never so happy as when they can tilt a gentleman logician out of his saddle. **1893** *Cornh. Mag.* June 597 The woodcock often disport themselves,.. tilting one another with ruffled plumage.

**c.** To drive or thrust with violence.

**1582** Stanyhurst *Æneis* I. (Arb.) 29 A tempest..Oure ships to Libye land with rough extremitye tilted. **1697** Collier *Ess. Mor. Subj.* I. (1709) 115 If it was the Custom to Tilt your Head against a Post.

**IV.** [f. Tilt-hammer.] **7.** *trans.* To forge or work with a tilt-hammer.

**1825** J. Nicholson *Operat. Mechanic* 770 It is cast into ingots, which by gentle heating and careful hammering, are tilted into bars. **1831** J. Holland *Manuf. Metal* I. 241 All steel, whether cast or skear, which is to be used for the best articles, should be tilted to the strength required. **1889** *Q. Rev.* July 137 When 'piled' and 'tilted'; that is..cut up into short lengths, laid in bundles, reheated, welded, and consolidated into a solid mass under the tilt hammer.

**Tilt** (tilt), *v.*[2] [f. Tilt *sb.*[1]] *trans.* To cover with a tilt or awning. (Chiefly in *pa. pple.*)

**1499** [implied in Tilting *vbl. sb.*[2]]. **1587** M. Grove *Pelops & Hipp.* Poems (1878) 22 Omaus king doth stay Ere this time long in closet tilte To heare what we can say. **1588** Parke tr. *Mendoza's Hist. China* 295 A great barke..very well tilted and dressed. **1625** *Gonsalvio's Sp. Inquis.* 64 To row vpon the riuer in Barges tilted with purple and silke. **1818** W. Taylor in *Monthly Rev.* LXXXVII. 479 Felt, with which they tilted their waggons. **1839** *Sat. Mag.* Supp., June 253/2 The cart is tilted with canes and straw neatly wattled.

**Tilt**, pa. t. of Till *v.*[2] *Obs.*; obs. f. Tilth.

**Ti·lt-boat.** [f. Tilt *sb.*[1] (or short for *tilted*) + Boat *sb.*] A large rowing boat having a tilt or awning, formerly used on the Thames, esp. as a passenger boat between London and Gravesend.

**1463** *Mann. & Househ. Exp.* (Roxb.) 251 For a tylt bote to London..iiij.d. **1576** in Feuillerat *Revels Q. Eliz.* (1908) 268 For the Cariadge of stuff to Hampton Court..by Tilt bote. **1615** G. Sandys *Trav.* 17 A vessel..like in proportion to a Graves-end tilt-boate. **1737** *Act* 10 *Geo. II*, c. 31 § 8 It shall not be lawful for any Person..who shall..navigate any Tilt-boat..to receive..or carry..at one and the same Time, any more than thirty-seven Passengers. **1764** *Low Life* (ed. 3) 3 Waiting..to go in the Tilt-Boat to Gravesend. **1859** Sala *Tw. round Clock* (1861) 11 Now..we go to Gravesend by the steamer, instead of the tilt-boat.

**Tilte**, obs. pa. pple. of Tilt *v.*[2]

**Tilted** (ti·ltėd), *ppl. a.*[1] [f. Tilt *sb.*[1] or *v.*[2] + -ed.] Having, or covered with, a tilt or awning.

*c* **1440** *Promp. Parv.* 488/1 Teltyd, *gaudatus* (A. *caudatus*). **1562** Bulleyn *Bulwark, Sicke Men* 67 b, To be rowed up and doune, in a tilted Boat or Barge. *a* **1656** Ussher *Ann.* vi. (1658) 230 He was in his poor tilted cart. **1819** H. Busk *Vestriad* III. 557 Wheel off, like Tartars in their tilted towns. **1844** Dickens *Mart. Chuz.* xlii, Faces full of consternation in the tilted waggons that came tearing past.

**Ti·lted**, *ppl. a.*[2] [f. Tilt *v.*[1] + -ed[1].]

**1.** Poised or thrust, as a weapon in tilting; (*loosely*) fought or engaged in, as a tilt or tournament.

**1776** MICKLE tr. *Camoens' Lusiad* VIII. 330 At just and tournay with the tilted lance Victors they rode. **1803** VISCT. STRANGFORD *Camoens' Lusiad* VI. xlii, Their own compatriots ..Who erst the tilted fight 'gainst England's Twelve maintain'd. **1861** LYTTON & FANE *Tannhäuser* 23 And from that hour, in court, And chase, and tilted tourney, many a month,..Men miss'd Tannhäuser.

**2.** Abruptly inclined or sloped from the erect or the horizontal position. In quot. *a* 1613, obtained or emptied out by tilting the vessel.

*a* **1613** OVERBURY *Characters, Whore* (1615) E ij, Her body is the tilted Lees of pleasure. **1892** *Pall Mall G.* 4 June 1/3 The steep northern escarpment, the tilted strata of which..suggest..the denudation of the Weald. **1906** *Daily News* 3 July 6 The question of speed..is..of the greatest importance where a train runs round what I may call a tilted curve.

**Tilter** (ti·ltəɹ), *sb.*[1] [f. TILT *v.*[1] + -ER [1].]

**1.** One who tilts or justs; a combatant in a tilt; also *fig.*

**1611** FLORIO, *Fólla*..a course in the field where many horsemen or tilters, after they haue runne single one to one, they runne pell mell altogether. **1612** WEBSTER *White Devil* III. i, None are judges at tilting, but those that have bene old tilters. **1749** SMOLLETT *Gil Blas* V. i. (1782) II. 148, I was shocked at the inequality of the combat, and, as I am naturally a tilter, flew to the assistance of the old man. **1827** SCOTT *Tales Grandfather* Ser. I. xxiii. (1828) II. 216 The best tilter with the spear received from the King a lance with a head of pure gold. **1898** J. HOLLINGSHEAD *Gaiety Chron.* i. 37, I was always a tilter at windmills.

†**b.** A rapier or sword. *slang. Obs.*

**1688** SHADWELL *Sqr. Alsatia* II. Wks. 1720 IV. 47 Let me see your Porker; here's a Porker! here's a Tilter! **1691** *Islington-Wells* 7 A young spruce City Fop,..With a Long-Wig and Tilter on. **1713** STEELE *Guard.* No. 143 ⁋ 5 To.. reduce their tilters to a more reputable, as well as a more portable size.

**2.** One who or that which tilts, inclines, or slopes (something) up or down; *spec.* (*a*) an apparatus for tilting a cask so as to empty it without stirring up the dregs; (*b*) a workman who tilts or empties out the coal into trucks at the pit's mouth.

**1630** *Maldon, Essex, Documents* Bundle 217 No. 22 In the butterye, i beer stalle and i tilter, 8*d.* **1892** J. LUMSDEN *Sheeph. & Trotters* 213 The neatest tilter and emptier of a brandy and water glass I ever saw. **1896** *Daily News* 1 May 2/1 The only persons in the vicinity of the pit mouth were the banksmen, blacksmiths, and tilters.

**3.** One who works with a tilt-hammer.

**1829** E. ELLIOTT *Vill. Patriarch* I. i, Loud thumps the forge; bright burns the cottage fire, From which the tilter's lad is loth to go. **1831** J. HOLLAND *Manuf. Metal* I. 242 During the operation of hammering,..the tilter sits on a seat reaching nearly to the ground.

**Ti·lter,** *sb.*[2] *dial.* [prob. rustic pronunciation of TILTURE: cf. *pictur, picter* for *picture.*] Proper condition; order: perh. *orig.* of cultivated land, and afterwards of things generally.

**1674** N. FAIRFAX *Bulk & Selv.* 75 The single shove or heave of the spring..puts the Watch thus fadg'd together and in tilter into motions round, right on,..forwards, backwards, upwards, downwards, and otherways. *a* **1880** *Kentish Dial.*, This thurruck is out o' tilter all the way along. **1887** *Kent Gloss.* s. v., He's left that farm purty much out o' tilter, I can tell ye.

**Ti·lter,** *v. dial.* [app. freq. of TILT *v.*[1], sense 3; cf. OE. *tealtrian* to be unsteady, shake, totter, extended form of *tealtian* (TILT *v.*[1]): see -ER [5].

Cf. *a* **800** CYNEWULF *Christ* 371 Hu we tealtrigað tydran mode. *a* **1000** *Haupt's Glosses* 529 Tealtrian, *vacillare, titubare.*]

*intr.* To sway up and down.

**1845** S. JUDD *Margaret* I. xiv, A bobolink clung tiltering to the breezy tip of a white birch. **1895** KATE D. WIGGIN *Vill. Watch-Tower* 36 Butterflies..perch on the..stalks and tilter up and down in the sunshine.

**Tilth** (tilþ), *sb.* Forms: 1 **tilð, tilðe**, 1–5 **tilþe**, (3 *erron.* **tilæhðe, tylehþe**), 4 **tulthe** (*ü*), *Sc.* **tiltht**, 4–6 (8–9) **tilthe**, 4–7 **tylth**, (5 **telþe, telth(e)**, 5–6 **tylthe**, (7–9 **tilt**), 4– **tilth.** [OE. *tilþ* str. fem., *tilþe* wk. fem., f. OE. *til-ian*, TILL *v.*[1] + -TH *suffix*[1]; cf. OFris. *tilath* cultivation.]

†**1.** Labour, work, or effort directed to useful or profitable ends. *Rihtlic tilð*, honest labour. (OE.)

*a* **1023** WULFSTAN *Hom.* x. (Napier) 72 Se ðe wære scadjende, weorðe se tilizende on rihtlicre tilðe.

**2.** *esp.* Labour or work in the cultivation of the soil; tillage, agricultural work, husbandry. (In full in OE. *eorþtilþ.*)

*c* **1000** [see EARTH-TILTH]. *a* **1100** *Gerefa* in *Anglia* (1886) IX. 259 Se scadwis ȝerefa sceal witan ælcre tilðan timan ðe to tune belimpð. *a* **1200** *Moral Ode* 57 Vre swinc and ure tilþe is ofte iwoned to swinden. *a* **1300** *Cursor M.* 3504 He delt als wit tilth o corn. *c* **1375** *Sc. Leg. Saints* xxix. (*Placidas*) 450 Telemen left þe tiltht..& folouyt hym. *a* **1380** *Poems fr. Vernon MS.* l. 269 3if þou wolt knowe þe tilþe of eorþe, þat þe fayle corn none, Go and red virgiles bok. **14**.. *Tretyce* in *W. of Henley's Husb.* (1890) 44 Comaunde your bayle straytly to kepe þis maner off gydynge in telthe. **1573** TUSSER *Husb.* iv. (1878) 13 Tilth wele done, in season due. **1660** SHARROCK *Vegetables* 98 After four years tilth, lay down your land. **1799** J. ROBERTSON *Agric. Perth* 12 Clay..when dried by a long tract of weather, without rain..becomes so hard..as to lose the benefit of any tilth formerly given it by frequent ploughings. **1870** FREEMAN *Norm. Conq.* (ed. 2) I. App. 709 To betake himself to the tilth of the ground.

**b.** *fig.* The cultivation of knowledge, morality, religion, the mind, etc.

*a* **1225** *Ancr. R.* 78 'Cultus justiciæ silencium': þe tilðe of rihtwisnesse, þet is silence. **1550** BALE *Apol.* Pref. 11 In the ydell slouthfulnesse of the church whan the profytable tylthe of Christe was not regarded. **1810** CRABBE *Borough* xxi. 260 Numbers there were defiled by mire and filth Whom he recovered by his goodly tilth. **1847** DE QUINCEY *Schlosser's Lit. Hist.* Wks. 1862 VII. 75 What a tilth of intellectual lava must [Burke] have interfused amongst the refuse and scoria of such mouldering party rubbish.

**c.** (with *pl.*) An act of tilling; a ploughing, harrowing, or other agricultural operation.

**1565** COOPER *Thesaurus* s. v. *Nouo, Agrum nouare*, to vse the seconde tilth: to till the seconde time. **1649** BLITHE *Eng. Improv. Impr.* (1652) 103 The nature of the Land [will not be] changed with fewer Tilths. **1707** MORTIMER *Husb.* (1721) I. 76 They give their sowre Land a tilt. **1844** *Jrnl. R. Agric. Soc.* V. i. 5 The tilths being given at intervals of about one month.

**d.** The condition of being under cultivation or tillage; hence, (good or bad) condition (of land under tillage).

**1488–9** *Act* 4 *Hen. VII*, c. 19 Leyeng to pasture londes which custumeably have ben used in tilthe. **1552** HULOET, Brynge lande in due tempre, or tilthe, with dygging, and labour. **1674** N. FAIRFAX *Bulk & Selv.* 132 The ground that was to be sown that year in as good tilt as in the other. **1805** R. W. DICKSON *Pract. Agric.* I. 538 It is..necessary that the soil should be reduced to a considerable degree of fineness, or what by writers on husbandry is termed tilth. **1825** JAMIESON, *Tilt, tilth*, plight, condition, good or bad ..; 'The land's in sae bad a tilth, that we canna saw'. **1884** *Times* 20 June 4 Working ground into a clean tilth.

†**3.** *transf.* The result or produce of tillage; crop, harvest. Also *fig. Obs.*

*a* **1100** *Gerefa* in *Anglia* (1886) IX. 261 Fela tilða ham gæderian. *a* **1300** *Cursor M.* 1068 Vr louerd loked noght þar-till..O þe tilth þat he wit delt. **1377** LANGL. *P. Pl.* B. XIX. 430 God..*Qui pluit super iustos & iniustos*..And sent þe sonne to saue a cursed mannes tilthe [C. XXII. 434 tulthe, *v. rr.* tilþe, telþe], As bry3te as to þe best man & to þe beste woman. **1390** GOWER *Conf.* II. 190 So that the tilthe is nyh forlorn, Which Crist sew ferst his oghne hond. **1612** DRAYTON *Poly-olb.* xiii. 342 That cruell Bore..Whose tusks turn'd vp our Tilths. **1781** COWPER *Hope* 46 Banks clothed with flowers..The yellow tilth, green meads.

**4.** Land under cultivation, as distinguished from pasture, forest, or waste land; tilled or arable land; a piece of tilled land, a ploughed field.

*c* **1375** *Sc. Leg. Saints* xxix. (*Placidas*) 326 Towne & tilth al mad wast. *c* **1460** *Oseney Reg.* 133 Whereof xij. acris of londe lien in the North felde at Radawelle, that is to say, in þe telth þe which is i-called Brerefurlonge. *Ibid.* 134 Vppon Ramme dune, iij. telthis, þe which conteynen xij. acris. *a* **1577** GASCOIGNE *Wks., Hearbes, Weedes*, etc. (1587) 149 As men can clense the worthless weedes from fruitfull fallowed tilth. **1616** SURFL. & MARKH. *Country Farme* 20 Lead forth your dung, compasse, or manure to your tilth or fallow field. **1851** WORDSW. *Prelude* x. 7, I paused, and cast Upon his rich domains, vineyard and tilth, Green meadow-ground, and many-coloured woods..a farewell look. **1881** *Gd. Words* XXII. 44/1 A 'summer tilt' is, or was, a field which was let alone for a season. Now-a-days people want crops off every acre, every year.

**b.** The prepared surface soil; the crumb, or depth of soil dug or cultivated.

**1743** *Lond. & Country Brew.* IV. (ed. 2) 252 Where Turneps have been eaten off, the Barley..is..not esteemed so good, as that from off a pure Tilth. **1846** J. BAXTER *Libr. Pract. Agric.* (ed. 4) I. 372 The surface or tilth should be made as fine and level as possible. **1881** WHITEHEAD *Hops* 45 The ground is kept stirred till the first week in July, by which time there should be a good tilth, or crumb, at least a foot deep.

**5.** *attrib.* and *Comb.*, as *tilth-ground, -land, -man.*

**1638** MARKHAM *Farew. Husb.* (ed. 4) Pref., The third or fourth part of al arable ground is lost in the fallow or tilth ground. **1657** J. WATTS *Dipper Sprinkled* 92 It is called Tilth-land and a Wheat-field. **1657** REEVE *God's Plea* 235 A lamentable tilth-man, which doth plow and sow for others, and hath not..any crop of his own.

**Tilth,** *v. Obs.* or *rare.* [f. prec. sb.] *trans.* To till, cultivate. Hence **Ti·lthed** *ppl. a.*; †**Ti·lthing** *vbl. sb.*, tillage; also †**Ti·lther,** a tiller, cultivator.

**1495** *Trevisa's Barth. De P. R.* XVII. cxiv. (W. de W.) S j/2 The wyld cole growyth wythout tylthyng [*Bodl. MS.* teleinge]. *Ibid.* clxxx, The erthe tylthers [*Bodl. MS.* tiliers] & kepers of vynes. **1496** *Dives & Paup.* (W. de W.) I. xxii. 58/1 They..gyue them to tylthe the londe. **1866** J. B. ROSE tr. *Ovid's Met.* (1899) 113, I cast the viperous teeth in tilthed ground. *Ibid.* 202 The husbandman beholds the unharnessed bull Fall in the tilthed furrow.

**Ti·lt-hammer.** [f. TILT *sb.*[2] or *v.*[1]] A heavy hammer used in forging, fixed on a pivot and acted upon by a cam-wheel or an eccentric, which alternately tilts it up and allows it to drop.

**1773** *Gentl. Mag.* Oct. 513/2 Any plating forge to work with a tilt-hammer. **1825** J. NICHOLSON *Operat. Mechanic* 345 The tilt-hammer used..weighs about 100 pounds, and makes 130 strokes per minute. **1881** RAYMOND *Mining Gloss., Tilt-hammer*, a hammer for shingling or forging iron, arranged as a lever of the first or third order, and 'tilted' or 'tripped' by means of a cam or cog-gearing, and allowed to fall upon the billet, bloom, or bar. **1894** *Harper's Mag.* Jan. 422 Before James Nasmyth's great invention of the steam hammer, trip or tilt and helve hammers had been the forging tools.

**Tilting** (ti·ltiŋ), *vbl. sb.*[1] [f. TILT *v.*[1] + -ING [1].]

**1.** The action of TILT *v.*[1] in sense 5; charging on horseback with a lance against an opponent, or a mark; justing.

**1610** HOLLAND *Camden's Brit.* (1637) 250 Having unhappily slaine his only sonne while he trained him at Tilting. **1617** MORYSON *Itin.* I. 190 On the right hand as you come in..is a place for Tylting, called Tournelles. **1730** A. GORDON *Maffei's Amphith.* 250 The Armour People put on at tilting with Lances. **1893** KATE SANBORN *Truthf. Woman in S. California* 172 The tournament is exciting, where skilful riders try tilting at rings, trying to take as many rings as possible on lance while galloping by.

**b.** With *a* and *pl.* A tilt, a just. Now *rare* or *Obs.*

*c* **1618** MORYSON *Itin.* IV. v. i. (1903) 465 They haue Tiltings, Runnings with lances against a Post Armed like a man at all peeces. **1621** SIR W. ALEXANDER in *Sidney's Arcadia* III. (1629) 337 At a Tilting in Iberia..I ranne in a Pastorall shew against the Corinthian Knights. **1761** HUME *Hist. Eng.* II. xxxi. 197 At a tilting at Greenwich.

**c.** *transf.* and *fig.*

**1668** HOWE *Bless. Righteous* (1825) 175 A perpetual hostility, a very tilting at his cross. **1752** FIELDING *Amelia* v. ix, His Brother and the Lieutenant were gone out with a Design of Tilting. **1878** STEVENSON *Edinburgh* (1889) 2 Perpetual tilting against squalls.

**2.** The action of TILT *v.*[1] in sense 4; inclination from the vertical or horizontal; sloping, slanting.

**1658** OSBORN *Adv. Son* (1673) 70 Though a Vessel may yield the more for tilting or stirring. **1835–6** *Todd's Cycl. Anat.* I. 655/2 This tilting forwards of the apex gives the heart a pulsation against the ribs. **1850** DANA *Geol.* iii. 238 There are no tiltings—no anticlinal and synclinal valleys. **1878** ABNEY *Photogr.* (1881) 245 Tilting should be cautiously and sparingly used.

†**b.** *concr.* (*pl.*) The dregs of the liquor in a cask, collected by tilting it. *Obs.*

**1611** COTGR., *Bessieres*, the tiltings, dregs, or bottomes of low-running wine, &c.

**3.** Working with a tilt-hammer.

**1839** URE *Dict. Arts* 1173 Condensed..by the operation of tilting, under a powerful hammer driven by machinery. **1864** STRAUSS, etc. *Engl. Workshops* 88 The blistered steel is prepared for tilting.

**4.** *attrib.* and *Comb.* (mostly in sense 1), as *tilting armour, bout, encounter, field,* †*furniture, ground, horse, match, sport*; **tilting bucket conveyor,** a means of transporting coal or other substances, constructed of two endless chains between which on trunnions are slung buckets, the contents of which are tilted or tipped at any given spot by a tippling device; **tilting coffer,** a chest carved with representations of tournaments; **tilting-fillet,** a wedge-shaped slip of wood placed under the front edge of the first or lowest course of slates in a roof, to give to that course the same inclination as in the courses above; **tilting-gauntlet,** a form of gauntlet used in tilting, having a hook with which it could be fastened so as to secure the lance in the grasp of the hand; **tilting-helm, -helmet,** a large heavy helmet worn over the ordinary one in tilting, completely covering the head and face, with slits for breathing and vision; **tilting-lance,** a form of lance used in tilting, often ornamental, with a large guard or vamplate, and a blunt point or a coronal; **tilting-mill** = *tilt-mill* (see TILT *sb.*[2] 10); **tilting-shield,** a shield used in tilting, so constructed as to cause the opponent's lance to glance off sideways; **tilting-spear** = *tilting-lance*; **tilting-staff,** a staff used instead of a lance in tilting; **tilting-target** = *tilting-shield*; **tilting-yard** = TILT-YARD.

**1819** SCOTT *Let. to D. Terry* 18 Apr., in *Lockhart*, I see Mr. Bullock..advertises his museum for sale. I wonder if a good set of real *tilting armour could be got cheap there. **1827** — *Chron. Canongate* vi, A suit of tilting armour of bright steel, inlaid with silver. **1754** RICHARDSON *Grandison* (1810) I. ii. 5 We had..a *tilting-bout..but are sworn friends now. **1911** *Encycl. Brit.* VII. 56 The gravity or *tilting bucket conveyor can be used as a combined elevator and conveyor. *Ibid.* VI. 107 There is a whole class of chests known as '*tilting coffers'. **1599** MARSTON *Sco. Villanie* I. ii, To wage *Tilting incounters. **1859** TENNYSON *Guinevere* 329 In open battle or the *tilting-field. **1823** P. NICHOLSON *Pract. Build.* 399 The slater..nails down these *tilting fillets. **1833** LOUDON *Encycl. Archit.* § 83 Tilting fillets are used to give a slight inclination to the verge or border-slates, where they butt against brick-work. **1667** MILTON *P. L.* IX. 34 *Tilting Furniture, emblazon'd Shields,..Caparisons and Steeds. **1850** MARSDEN *Early Purit.* (1853) 77 Cartwright, if dissatisfied, should have..challenged other hearers than his pupils, and upon some other *tilting-ground than the fenced enclosures of a university. **1880** *Academy* 20 Nov. 371/3 A very fine *tilting helm with the wooden crest of Sir John Gostwick, Master of the Horse to Henry VIII. **1846** FAIRHOLT *Costume in Eng.* 119 [The figure] represents [Sir Geoffrey Loutterell]..receiving from the ladies of his family his *tilting-helmet, shield, and *pavon.* **1623** in *Crt. & Times Jas. I* (1848) II. 385 He hath..sent for his arms and *tilting horses. **1863** THORNBURY *True as Steel* III. 318 This iron hand of mine can handle a *tilting lance better than a pen. **1854** MILMAN *Lat. Chr.* VIII. v. III. 359 Abélard became the most powerful combatant in the intellectual *tilting matches of the schools. **1835** URE *Philos. Manuf.* 61 These are..the foundations of kindred works, such as.. *tilting-mills. **1602** MARSTON *Ant. & Mel.* I. Wks. 1856 I. 13 He is made like a *tilting staffe. **1606** DRUMM. OF HAWTH. *Let. fr. Greenwich* Wks. (1711) 232 His lodging.. was in the house of the *tilting yard, where the king bore him company at supper. **1617** MORYSON *Itin.* I. 10 The same Court serves for a Tilting-yard.

**Ti·lting,** *vbl. sb.*[2] [f. TILT *v.*[2] or *sb.*[1] + -ING [1]: cf. *carpeting.*] The action of covering with a tilt or awning; *concr.* a tilt, or material for tilts.

**1499** *Promp. Parv.* 488/1 (Pynson) Teltinge, *gaudacio.* **1720** DE FOE *Capt. Singleton* vi, Our mats..are our beds to lay under us, and our tilting to cover us. **1862** *Catal.*

*Internat. Exhib., Brit.* II. No. 4014 Witney blankets, tiltings, yarns.

**Ti·lting,** *ppl. a.* [f. TILT *v.*[1] + -ING [2].] That tilts, in various senses.

**1.** Moving unsteadily, rising and falling, swaying up and down. (See also 3.)

**1605** SYLVESTER *Du Bartas* II. iii. I. 123 Sea's foaming Course, whose ever-Tilting Tide (Ebbing or flowing) is confin'd to Season. *c* **1630** in Risdon *Surv. Devon* § 225 (1810) 239 Her tilting tides near unto Appledore Have clean swept Hubba's trophy off the shore. **1841** CATLIN *N. Amer. Ind.* (1844) I. vi. 40 He approached..with a slow and tilting step.

**2.** Justing; encountering in, or as in, a tilt.

**1679** CROWNE *Ambitious Statesm.* III, I have seen..their tilting lips meet close, and grapple.

**3.** Causing something to tilt or slant; also, that is or can be tilted.

**1807** HERSCHEL in *Phil. Trans.* XCVII. 190 A tilting motion, given to the lens..will move the two sets of rings from side to side. **1907** *Daily Chron.* 14 May 6/3 The cost of tilting standards and electroliers was shown to be excessive.

**Til-tree**: see TIL [2].

**Tilt-up,** *sb.* and *a.* [Uses of phr. *to tilt up*: see TILT *v.*[1]] **A.** *sb.* Something that tilts up.

**1.** *Fishing.* = TILT *sb.*[2] 6. *U. S.*

**1891** in *Cent. Dict.*

**2.** The American sandpiper. *U. S.*

**1848** [see TEETER *sb.* 2].

**B.** *adj.* That tilts up; = TIP-UP B.

**1891** *Daily News* 13 Nov. 2/1 St. James's Hall will be..reseated, the balcony being supplied with 'tilt up' stalls.

† **Ti·lture.** *Obs. rare.* [irreg. f. TILL *v.*[1], app. after *culture*, etc.: see also TILTER *sb.*[2]] Tilth, tillage, agriculture.

**1573** TUSSER *Husb.* (1878) 92 Good tilth brings seedes, euill tilture, weedes. **1577** B. GOOGE *Heresbach's Husb.* I. (1586) 16 b, Let me here your opinion of the Feeld, and the tilture thereof.

**Tilt-yard** (ti·ltˌyāɹd). Also tylt-. [f. TILT *sb.*[2] + YARD.] A yard or enclosed space for tilts and tournaments; a (permanent) tilting-ground.

**Tilt Yard guard,** the name of the guard mounted on the site of the tilt-yard of the old Royal Palace of Whitehall. Also called later *tilt guard* (see TILT *sb.*[2] 10). Discontinued 15th Nov. 1898.

**1528** Fox in Pocock *Rec. Ref.* I. 141 Who at that time..lay in the gallery in the Tiltyard. **1711** STEELE *Spect.* No. 109 ⁋ 3 He was the last Man that won a Prize in the Tilt-Yard. **1825** SCOTT *Talism.* vi, A fine figure on horseback, and can bear him well in the tilt-yard. **1735** *Regimental Hist. Coldstream Guards* 29 Oct. (MS.), The Officers to mount all guards in their regimentals and gaiters during his Majesty's residence in town, and the serjeants to mount in their regimentals, the Tylt Yard guard as well as the King's.

† **Ti·lward,** *prep. Obs. rare.* Also 4 tillwar(d. [f. TILL *prep.* + -WARD.] In the direction of, toward. (In first quot. = To.)

*a* **1300** *Cursor M.* 938 (Cott.) 'Loo', he said of adam, 'hu Lik es made tilward us nu, Bath þe god and il knauand'. *Ibid.* 15187 'Gas til-ward [*Gött.* till-ward] þe tun', he said. *Ibid.* 17636 (Gött.) Vp tillwar heuen his heued he bedd.

**Til-wood**: see TIL [2].

† **Ti·ly,** *a. Obs. rare*[−1]. [f. TILE *sb.*[1] + -Y.] Consisting of 'tiles' or bricks.

**1382** WYCLIF *Jer.* xliii. 9 In the caue, that is vnder the tily wal [1388 wal of tiil stoon: Vulg. *muro latericio*].

**Tilye, Tilyer,** obs. ff. TILIE *sb.*, TILL *v.*[1], TILLER *sb.*[1]

† **Tim.** *Obs.* A term of personal abuse.

**1610** B. JONSON *Alch.* IV. vii, Then you are an Otter, and a Shad, a Whit, A very Tim. **1673** *S'too him Bayes* 73.

**Timaliine,** variant of TIMELIINE.

‖ **Timar** (tīmā·r). *Obs.* Also 7 -arr. [Persian (and Turkish) تیمار *tīmār* attendance, watching.] Formerly, in the feudal system of Turkey, a fief held by military service: see quots.

**1601** R. JOHNSON *Kingd. & Commw.* (1603) 51 It is the custome of Ottoman princes to sieze vpon al the land which they take from their enimies, and assigning a small parcell..to the auncient Lordes, they deuide the resydue into Timars, to euery gallant seruitor a portion; but vpon condition, to find so and so many seruiceable horse for the war. **1632** LITHGOW *Trav.* IV. 166 These Timars or grounds, entertaine ..two hundreth and fifty thousand horses. **1681** NEVILE *Plato Rediv.* 87 Planting above sixty thousand Souldiers upon Lands in Lombardy; That is, erecting so many *Beneficia*, or Timarr's. **1819** T. HOPE *Anastasius* (1820) II. xiii. 303 The Spahees, or horse soldiers, on the contrary, often only holding their Zeameth or Timar from some grandee as the wages of domestic service.

¶ **b.** *erron.* One holding a timar: = TIMARIOT.

**1598** DALLINGTON *Meth. Trav.* K iij b, They are bound to serue the Great Turke with horse and in person in his warres. These are called his Timars. **1638** SIR T. HERBERT *Trav.* 232 The Timarrs or Turqmars are more despicable [i.e. than the ranks and degrees before mentioned].

**Timarau,** variant of TAMARAU.

**1898** WORCESTER *Philippine Isl.* xvi. 364 We had been tempted to visit the island [Mindoro] by stories of a strange animal called the '*timarau*', which was said to abound in the interior.

**Timarchy** (təi·mɑɹki). *rare.* [ad. Gr. τιμαρχία, f. τιμή honour + -αρχία government.] = TIMOCRACY.

*c* **1643** *Maximes Unfolded* 4 That they all be present.., his Majestie as the heire of the Kingdome, his Peeres by their Birth, and the Commons by the peoples Election. The first sheweth a Monarchie, the second an Aristocracie, and the third a Timarchie. *Ibid.* 5 *Timarchy*, or *Plutarchy*, is when great men of meanes, wanting the honour of Peeres, ..have the dignity of Gravity and discretion to make them reputed, and to be well esteemed amongst the people. *Ibid.* 28 When the best in wealth and estates governe the poore, it is called Plutarchie, the Empire of riches, or Timocracie, the command of honour, which is also named Timarchie. **1852** [see TIMOCRACY 2].

† **Timariot** (timā·riǫt). *Obs.* Also 7 ty-, -ott, *erron.* timorat. [a. F. *timariot*, ad. It. *timariotto* (Florio, 1598), f. Persian *tīmār* TIMAR + -OT [2].] The holder of a TIMAR. Also *attrib.*

**1601** R. JOHNSON *Kingd. & Commw.* (1603) 52 They can no sooner stirre, but as so many falcons these Timorats are presently on their neckes. **1629** MASSINGER *Picture* I. i, Who knows but some party Of his Timariots..May fall upon us? **1690** TEMPLE *Ess.* II. *Heroic Virt.* 120 The Division of all Lands in conquered Countries into Timariots or Soldiers Shares. **1813** BYRON *Br. Abydos* I. vii, First of the bold Timariot bands.

**Timbal, tymbal** (ti·mbăl). Now *Hist.* or *arch.* Also timbul. [= mod.F. *timbale* (1646 in Hatz.-Darm.), It. *timballo*, Sp. *timbal*, Pg. *timbal*, *timbale*, substituted for, and app. altered from, earlier F. *attabale* (Cotgr. 1611), It. *taballo* (Florio 1611), Sp. *atabal*, Pg. *attabale*, see ATABAL. It is not clear in which lang. or under what influence the change was made (perh. in It., which had already dropped initial *a*): cf. the F. alteration of *tabour* to *tambour*. The spelling *tymbal* was app. due to the influence of *cymbal*.] A kettledrum.

**1680** *Lond. Gaz.* No. 1484/1 The Trumpets and Timbals led the way. *c* **1709** PRIOR *Charity* 15 A tymbal's sound were better than my voice. **1713** *Lond. Gaz.* No. 5106/2 Two hundred of their People [Turks] riding..with Timbals and Chalumeaux. **1788** GIBBON *Decl. & F.* l. (1846) V. 15 A chorus of women, striking their tymbals, and displaying the pomp of their nuptials. **1813** *Arabian Nts.* III. 345 [They] danced and skipped about him to the sound of the tymbals.

So † **Ty·mbalon** (arbitrary form of prec.).

**1817** MOORE *Lalla R., Veiled Proph.*, With gong and tymbalon's tremendous chime.

‖ **Timbale** (tæ̃ba·l). [F.: see prec.]

**1.** *Entom.* A membrane (resembling a drum-head) in certain insects, as the cicada, by means of which a shrill chirping sound is produced.

**1854** BUSHNAN in *Circ. Sc.* (*c* 1865) I. 295/1 [In the cicada] the muscles..act upon the *timbales*, stretching them out or bringing them into their natural state, whereby the sounds are produced. **1867** MARSHALL *Physiol., Hum. & Comp.* I. 271 The noises in certain species [of insects] are dependent upon the rapid movements of folded membranes, called the *timbales*,..moved by..special..muscular fibres.

**2.** *Cookery.* A dish made of finely minced meat, fish, or other ingredients, cooked in a crust of paste or in a mould: so called from its shape.

**1880** 'OUIDA' *Moths* I. 25 Eating her last morsel of a truffled timbale. **1899** *Westm. Gaz.* 16 Sept. 1/3 'If I could only have a little sweetbread timbale', she said longingly. **1908** *Daily Chron.* 10 Apr. 7/5 Chicken Timbales with Sauce.

**3.** *Comb.* **timbale-iron,** a cooking utensil with a bulging head used to form a cup-shaped crust.

**1895** in *Funk's Stand. Dict.*

**Timber** (ti·mbəɹ), *sb.*[1] Forms: *α.* 1- timber; 4-5 -bir, 4-7 -bre, 5 -bur (7 -berr), 3-7 tymber, 4-6 -bre, 5 -byr, -bir(e, 5-6 -bur, (tembre). *β. Sc.* and *north. dial.* 4-5 tymyr(e, 5 tymmir, -yr(e, (temir, -yr), 5-9 tymmer, 6 tymer, -ir, (temmer), 8-9 timmer. [OE. *timber* = OFris. *timber*, OS. *timbar* (Du. dial. *timmer*), OHG. *zimbar* (MHG. *zimber*, G. *zimmer* room), ON. *timbr* timber (Sw. *timmer*, Da. *tømmer*), Goth. **timr* (cf. *timr-jan* to build, *timr-ja* builder, etc.) :—OTeut. **tim-ram* :—**tem-rom* :—Indo-Eur. **dem-rom*, f. ablaut series **dem* : **dom* : **dm*, to build: cf. Gr. δέμ-ειν to build, δόμ-ος, L. *dom-us* house.]

† **1.** A building, structure, edifice, house. Also *fig. Obs.* (? only OE.)

*a* **750** *Cædmon's Gen.* 135 Þa seo tid ȝewat ofer timber [*MS.* tiber] sceacan middanȝeardes. *c* **825** *Vesp. Psalter* ci. 8 Swe swe spearwa se anga in timbre [*unicus in aedificio*]. *Ibid.* cxxviii. 6 Sien swe swe heȝ timbra [*faenum aedificiorum*]. *a* **900** tr. *Bæda's Hist.* III. xiv. [xvii.] (1890) 204 Þa næȝlas..þe heo mid þæm to þæm timbre [*ædificio*] ȝefæstnad wæs. *Ibid.* IV. iii. (1890) 262 Þæt..þa lifiȝendan stanas þære cirican of eorðlicum seþlum to þæm heofonlican timbre ȝebær. *c* **950** *Lindisf. Gosp.* Mark xiii. 1 ȝesih hulco stanas & hulic timber [*Ags. Gosp.* hwylce ȝetimbrunga, *Vulg.* quales structuræ]. *c* **1000** *Sax. Leechd.* II. 198 Sio [liver] is blodes timber, & blodes hus & fostor. *c* **1330** R. BRUNNE *Chron. Wace* (Rolls) 3692 Þey logged hem, & tymber teld [*Petyt MS.* timbred teld = constructed tents (which is prob. the correct reading)].

† **b.** The process of building. *Obs.* (only OE.)

*c* **1000** *Sax. Leechd.* III. 178 On .vi. nihtne monan..he is . god circan on to timbrane and eac scipes timber on to anginnanne.

† **2.** Building material generally; material for the construction of houses, ships, etc., or (in extended sense) of any manufactured article; the matter or substance of which anything is built up or composed; matter, material, stuff. *Obs.* Cf. BELLY-TIMBER, *flesh-timber* (FLESH *sb.* 13).

In early use including 3; in later use prob. fig. from it.

*a* **900** tr. *Bæda's Hist.* III. xvi. [xxii.] (1890) 224 Þætte ne meahten godo beon, þa ðe monna hondum ȝeworhte wæron of eorðlicum timbre, oððe of treom, oððe of stanum. *a* **1000** *Laws Ecgbert, Poenit.* in Thorpe *Ags. Laws* Addit. 16 II. 234 Ne sceal cyrcean timber [L. *ligna ecclesiæ*] to æniȝum oðrum weorce. *a* **1300** *Cursor M.* 333-4 (Cott.) Þis wright ..Fra al oþer, sundri and sere, For þai most oþer timber take, Bot he þis self can timber make. **1607-12** BACON *Ess., Goodness* (Arb.) 206 Such disposicions are..the fittest timber to make great Pollitiques of. **1840** M. F. SHEPHERD in *Life of Adam Clarke* viii. 261 There is much sound timber in these sermons.

**3.** *spec.* Wood used for the building of houses, ships, etc., or for the use of the carpenter, joiner, or other artisan; wood in general as a material; esp. after it has been suitably trimmed and squared into logs, or further adapted to constructive uses.

(A restricted use of sense 2, and in early quots. often not distinguishable from it.)

*a* **1100** *Gerefa* in *Anglia* (1886) IX. 261 On wintra erian and in miclum ȝefyrstum timber cleofan. *c* **1200** *Vices & Virtues* 27 And ðe wrihte his timber to keruen after ðare mone. *c* **1205** LAY. 22929 Timber me lete biwinnen and þat beord bi-ginnen. *a* **1300** *Cursor M.* 1724 Now wat sir noe quat wark to do And hent timber þat fel þar-to. **1398** TREVISA *Barth. De P. R.* XIV. ii. (Tollem. MS.), Ararat is þe hyȝest hill of Armenia;..and ȝit to þis day þe tymber of þe schip is sene in þe mounteyne. **1466** *Burgh Rec. Edinb.* (1869) I. 23 Mak the ruiffes of guid tymmer and theik thame with sclaitt. **1562** TURNER *Herbal* II. 29 Y[e] tymmer of y[e] larche tre..is very..profitable for bildyng. *a* **1674** MILTON *Hist. Mosc.* I. Wks. 1851 VIII. 472 Thir Boats of Timber without any Iron in them. **1712** W. ROGERS *Voy.* 338 Vessels..chiefly imploy'd in carrying Timber, Salt,..and other Commodities. **1830** LINDLEY *Nat. Syst. Bot.* 84 The timber of the Beam Tree (*Pyrus Aria*) is invaluable for axletrees. **1832** *Planting* 92 in *Lib. Usef. Kn., Husb.* III, When the wood of a stem or branch of any species of plant attains to the dimensions of 24 inches in circumference, or upwards of eight inches in diameter, it is termed timber.

**b.** Wood as a substance, or as the material of small utensils or parts of them. Now *dial.*

**1530** RASTELL *Bk. Purgatory* II. xii, A cup of tymber or metal. *a* **1631** DRAYTON *Robin Hood & Merry Men* 31 Their arrows finely paired, for timber and for feather. **1663** WOOD *Life* 30 Nov. (O. H. S.) I. 503 For setting up a strip of timber on my window, 6*d.* **1688** R. HOLME *Armoury* II. 84/2 The Wood, or Timberr, is between the Sap and Heart. **1793** T. SCOTT *Poems* 364 (E.D.D.) A breast o' timmer an' a heart o' stane. **1834** SMART *Rhymes* 135 (ibid.) Her wheels were made o' timmer.

**4.** Applied to the wood of growing trees capable of being used for structural purposes; hence collectively to the trees themselves: *standing timber*, trees, woods. Rarely in *pl.*

*c* **893** K. ÆLFRED *Oros.* IV. vi. § 2 Æfter siexteȝum daȝa þæs þe ðæt timber [L. *arbores*] acorfen wæs. **1426** LYDG. *De Guil. Pilgr.* 11808 A kanker..the werm..That ffreteth the herte off a tre, And..Doth to tymber gret damage. **1566** in *Reg. Mag. Sig. Scot.* 1584. 209/1 Habere lie wattillis et lie fallin tymmer de silva de Cleue. **1634** WOOD *New Eng. Prosp.* (1865) 16 The Timber of the Countrey growes straight, and tall. **1718** *Free-thinker* No. 59 ⁋ 11 A naked Ground, blest only with a small Group of Timber. **1787** G. WHITE *Selborne* viii. (1789) 22 A rough estimate of the value of the timbers..growing at that time in the district of The Holt. **1841** W. ROBINSON *Assam* 41 Another large and elegant timber indigenous to the forests of Assam, is the Cedrela Toona. **1880** C. R. MARKHAM *Peruv. Bark* 158 We continued our journey..through a forest of grand timber.

**b.** *spec.* in *English Law*, Trees growing upon land, and forming part of the freehold inheritance: embracing generally the oak, ash, and elm, of the age of twenty years or more; in particular districts, by local custom, including other trees, with various limitations as to age.

As to the legal bearing of this, see quots. 1766, 1818.

**1766** BLACKSTONE *Comm.* II. xviii. § 6. 281 Timber also is part of the inheritance. Such are oak, ash, and elm in all places: and in some particular countries, by local custom, where other trees are generally used for building, they are thereupon considered as timber; and to cut down such trees, or top them, or do any other act whereby the timber may decay, is waste. **1818** CRUISE *Digest* (ed. 2) I. 131 By the custom of some countries, certain trees, not usually considered as timber, are deemed to be such, being there used for building...And all the Justices at Serjeants' Inn were of opinion that in the county of York birch trees were timber, and belonged to the inheritance; therefore they could not be taken by the tenant for life. **1891** *Daily News* 19 Jan. 5/4 By the custom of the county of Buckingham beech trees are timber.

**5.** *transf.* Applied to any object familiar to the speaker, composed wholly or chiefly of wood, as † a spear-shaft; † a bowl; a ship; the stocks (*slang*); wooden gates and fences (*Hunting slang*); a wicket (*Cricket slang*); *small timber*, lucifer matches (*street slang*).

*c* **1400** *Rowland & O.* 455 Theyre Ioynynge was so harde that tyde That theyre timbir in sondire gan ryde. *c* **1435** *Torr. Portugal* 2349, I pray, that thou woldist my son lere, Hys Tymber ffor to asay. *c* **1450** *Merlin* 117 [They] mette to-geder on the sheldis, so that the horse ne myght not passe ferther till the tymbres were broken. **1725** RAMSAY *Gentle Sheph.* III. ii, Come, turn the timmer to laird Patie's health. **1791** 'G. GAMBADO' *Ann. Horsem.* vi. (1809) 90 The leaps large and frequent, and a great deal of timber to get over. **1851-4** D. JERROLD *Men of Char., Chr. Snub* i, The squire ..gives me over to the beadle, who claps me here in the timber. **1857** LAWRENCE *Guy Livingstone* iii. 17 They.. would grind over..the March Gibbon double timber as.. undauntedly as over the accommodating Bullingdon hurdles. **1871** R. ELLIS *Catullus* iv. 3 Nor yet a timber o'er the waves alertly flew. **1876** in Bettesworth *Walkers of Southgate* (1900) 332 Appleby..dislodged Webbe's timbers by his second ball in the first over.

**b.** *spec.* A wooden leg: cf. *timber-toe* in 10; hence *transf.* a leg. *slang.*

1807 RUICKBIE *Wayside Cottager* 9 (E. D. D.). 1821 CLARE *Vill. Minstr.* I. 35 Boys, miss my pegs .. and hit my legs, My timbers well can stand your gentle taps. 1862 WHYTE MELVILLE *Ins. Bar* (ed. 12) I. 230 [The hounds] have a strong family likeness in the depth of their girth.. and the quality of the timber on which they stand.

**6.** A single beam or piece of wood forming or capable of forming part of any structure. Also collectively in *pl.* **a.** *gen.*

c 1555 HARPSFIELD *Divorce Hen. VIII* (Camden) 288 The treasure that was made of the timbers, bells, and leads, and the ornaments of the church. 1623 GOUGE *Serm. Extent God's Provid.* § 15 The massy timber [a summer] shivered in two, as suddenly as the other knapped asunder. 1793 SMEATON *Edystone L.* § 85 To fasten the outside Timbers. 1859 W. S. COLEMAN *Woodlands* (1866) 11 The original timbers after this immense lapse of time are still sound internally. 1893 *Labour Comm. Gloss., Pair of Timber,* two timbers placed against the sides of the tunnels in a mine at acute angles with the bottom. They support not only these sides but also another timber, which upholds the roof.

**b.** *pl. spec. Naut.* The pieces of wood composing the ribs, bends, or frames of a ship's hull: see FRAME *sb.* 11 d, quot. 1769.

Often preceded by a qualifying word, as *cant-, compass-, cross-, filling-, floor-, futtock-, head-, knee-, knuckle-, rising-, side-, square-, stern-, top-timbers*: see these words.

1748 *Anson's Voy.* II. iv. 158 Her spirkiting and timbers were very rotten. 1782 COWPER *Royal George* 29 Her timbers yet are sound. 1809 A. HENRY *Trav.* 185 We dragged our barges over the neck of land, but not without straining their timbers. 1857 COLQUHOUN *Comp. Oarsman's Guide* 29 All the ribs underneath these [floor-boards] are called floor timbers, the rest simply timbers. 1885 SIR J. C. MATHEW in *Law Times Rep.* LII. 265/1 Her timbers, no doubt, held together, but she was no longer a ship.

*fig.* 1751 SMOLLETT *Per. Pic.* xxxvii, My timbers are now a little crazy, d'ye see; and God knows if I shall keep afloat till such time as I see thee again. 1850 B. TAYLOR *Eldorado* xiii. (1862) 132, I, whose timbers were somewhat strained, laboured after him.

**c.** *Naut. slang*, in exclamations, as *my timbers! shiver my timbers!* (see SHIVER *v.*).

1789 DIBDIN *Song, Poor Jack* ii, My timbers! what lingo he'd coil and belay.

**7.** *fig.* Bodily structure, frame, build; also, in later use, the 'stuff' of which a person is made; personal quality or character.

1612 PAULE *Life Abp. Whitgift* § 138. 93 For his small timber, he was of a good quicke strength, straight and well shaped. 1611 BEAUM. & FL. *Knt. Burn. Pest.* II. ii, The twelve Companies of London cannot match him, timber for timber. 1670 MILTON *Hist. Eng.* VI. Wks. 1851 V. 261 Canute ..doubting to adventure his body of small Timber, against a man of Iron sides. 1822 LAMB *Elia* Ser. I. *Some old Actors,* He was not altogether of that timber out of which cathedral seats and sounding-boards are hewed. 1906 *Munsey's Mag.* Jan. 411 His wish to be courteous to men of Cardinal Rampolla's timber.

**8.** *attrib.* or *adj.* Made or consisting of wood; wooden. (See also 9, 10.)

1529 RASTELL *Pastyme* (1811) 291 The said duke, protectour..toke the lorde Hastynges..and..caused his hede to be smytten of upon a tymber log within the Towre. 1535 COVERDALE *Isa.* xxii. 8 Then was sene the sege of the tymbre house. 1560 DAUS tr. *Sleidane's Comm.* 323 b, The Spaniardes with theyr ordenaunce beate doune a timber walle. 1565 COOPER *Thesaurus* s. v. *Cassandra,* The treason of the tymber horse at the siege of Troye. 1663 GERBIER *Counsel* 23 The making of Timber partitions. 1700 R. SINCLAIR in *Leisure Hour* (1883) 205/2 Timber cups and dishes. 1799 J. ROBERTSON *Agric. Perth* 92 A timber mallet wrought by the hand was all they had..to break the clods. 1890 SERVICE *Notandums* viii. 48 The leg will be stiff for mony a day to come, and like a timmer ane for vera thrawnness.

**b.** *Sc. dial.* Unmusical; having no musical ear; dull, 'wooden'; unimpressionable.

1815 SCOTT *Guy M.* iii, He was a good deal diverted with the harsh timber tones which issued from him. 1874 OUTRAM *Annuity* ix. in *Mod. Sc. Poets* (1881) II. 218 The timmer limmer dauts the knife To settle her annuity. 1875 JAS. GRANT *One of the 600* vi. 46, I regretted my own timbre tones. But I must confess to being enchanted while Louisa sang. 1893 STEVENSON *Catriona* vii. 75 You have the finest timber face. 1901 *Blackw. Mag.* July 58/1 If I were not, so far as music goes, as timber as the table there.

**9.** *Comb.* **a.** attrib. (often two words, as in 8), 'of or for timber', as *timber-ash, -bar, -beam, -broker, -butt* (BUTT *sb.*[3]), *-claim, colour, -crib* (CRIB *sb.* 14), *-culture, elm, -factor, forest,* † *-haw* (HAW *sb.*[1]), *-house, -land, -log, -market, -mell* (MELL *sb.*[1]), *-merchant, -mill, -monger, -nail, -oak, -patch, -plank, -post, -raft, -shade, -ship, -sled, -slide, -trade, -wain, -wright.* **b.** obj. and obj. gen., as *timber-borer, -cutter, -devourer, -feller, -floater, -worker; timber-boring, -carrying, -cutting, -devouring, -eating, -floating, -producing* sbs. and adjs. **c.** instrumental and parasynthetic, as *timber-built, -ceilinged, -covered,* † *-heeled, -laden, -lined, -propt, -skeletoned, -strewn* adjs.; also *timber-like* adj.

1707 *Timber Ash [see *timber oak*]. 1685 BOYLE *Effects of Mot.* v. 44 In the striking of a *timber-beam at one end, the motion..may become sensible at the other. 1815 KIRBY & SP. *Entomol.* viii. (1818) I. 235 The most extensive family ..of *timber-borers are the capricorn beetles. 1817 *Ibid.* xxi. (1818) II. 235 A little *timber-boring beetle. 1703 T. S. *Art's Improv.* 23 An Observation of an Experienced *Timber Broker. 1825-9 MRS. SHERWOOD *Lady of Manor* xii, An old *timber-built cottage. 1608 T. COCKS *Diary* (1901) 32 Payde..for bringinge home my two *tymber butts. 1903 LD. R. GOWER *Rec. & Remin.* 226 A handsome *timber-ceiling'd hall. 1890 L. C. D'OYLE *Notches* 124 He took up a 'homestead' and a '*timber-claim' with the..intention of raising cattle and a family. 1663 GERBIER *Counsel* (1664) 84 Frames..gilded, the ground a *Timber colour. 1895 *Outing* (U.S.) XXVII. 44/2 Enclosed between three great peaks—one *timber-covered to its top. 1888 LIGHTHALL *Yng Seigneur* 11 A *timber-crib which was going to run a rapid. 1887 *Daily News* 3 Nov. 5/4 Buying under the homestead and *timber-culture laws. 1775 ROMANS *Florida* App. 30 Fires..occasioned by the hunters and *timber-cutters, who burn the woods to clear them of under-wood. 1826 KIRBY & SP. *Entomol.* III. xxxiv. 430 In the stag-beetle, and some other *timber-devourers. *Ibid.* xxx. 146 A small *timber-devouring beetle. 1815 *Ibid.* viii. (1818) I. 237 *Timber-eating beetles. 1731 *Gentl. Mag.* Nov. 502/2 James Jelly..*Timber-Factor and Wharfinger. c 1611 CHAPMAN *Iliad* XI. 79 When in hill-environ'd vales the *timber-feller takes A sharp set stomach to his meat. 1854 HOOKER *Himal. Jrnls.* I. xvii. 398 The shelter of *timber-floaters. 1887 MOLONEY *Forestry W. Afr.* 205 The Gambia *timber-floating industry. 1442, 1457 *Tembre haw, tymbre hawes [see HAW *sb.*[1]]. 1640-1 *Kirkcudbr. War-Comm. Min. Bk.* (1855) 149 Women's schoes, *tymber heilled, of the best sort. 1535 *Tymbre house [see 8]. 1723 MANDEVILLE *Fab. Bees* (1725) I. 419 If..Ships should always have fine Weather,..Ships would last as long as Timber-Houses. 1871 KINGSLEY *At Last* xii, A roomy timber house, beautifully thatched with palm. 1842 *Penny Cycl.* XXIV. 191/1 The right to timber and *timber-like trees belongs to the landlord. 1897 P. WARUNG *Tales Old Regime* 95 The walls of the shaft were ..*timber-lined. 1529 *Tymber log [see 8]. 1583 GOLDING *Calvin on Deut.* viii. 44 That there is no more zeal in vs than in a timberlogge. 1681 DRYDEN *Spanish Fryar* III. i. 32 What are become of those two Timber-loggs that he us'd to wear for Leggs? 1477 in *Charters, &c. Edinb.* (1871) 141 The wod and *tymmer merket. 1721 RAMSAY *Horace to Virgil* 41 Hercules, wi's *timber-mell, Plays rap upo' the yates of hell. 1679-88 *Secr. Serv. Money Chas. II & Jas. II* (Camden) 206 John Martyr, *timber merchant. 1771 SMOLLETT *Humph. Cl.* 11 June, He lived some time as a clerk to a timber-merchant. 1908 *Chambers's Jrnl.* Nov. 702/2 Tasmania prides itself on its..giant *timber-mills. 1275 *Memoranda, K. R.* 2 & 3 Edw. I, 11 b (P.R.O.), Recognicio Iohannis le *Tymbermongere. 1552 HULOET, *Tymber nayle, *impago.* 1707 MORTIMER *Husb.* (1721) II. 106 In the above Scheme, the first Column is the Names of the Fields, ..the third the number of *Timber Oaks, the fourth the Timber Ash, the fifth the Timber Elms. 1886 EBBUTT *Emigr. Life Kansas* 96 We could not..get down to our *timber patch. 1609 BIBLE (Douay) *Gen.* vi. 14 Make thee an arke of *timber planke. 1622 CALLIS *Stat. Sewers* (1647) 213 Piles and *Timberposts are set in the waters. 1887 MOLONEY *Forestry W. Afr.* 3 The approximate extent of *timber-producing forests. 1785 BURNS *Halloween* xxiii, It chanc'd the stack he faddom't thrice, Was *timmer-propt for thrawin'. 1853 SIR H. DOUGLAS *Milit. Bridges* 236 The large *timber-rafts which descend the St. Lawrence. 1626 BACON *Sylva* § 936 Plaine Champaignes..Or else *Timber-Shades, as in Forrests. 1704 *Lond. Gaz.* No. 4005/2 Her Majesty's Ship the Shoreham, having under her Convoy 4 *Timber Ships. 1852 MUNDY *Our Antipodes* (1857) 198 The snow affords a road..where the *timber-sled, with its ponderous log, runs glibly down to the creek. 1884 S. E. DAWSON *Handbk. Canada* 287 The *timber-slides, by which the lumber from the upper river passes down .. into the navigable water below. 1855 A. MORRIS *Canada* iv. 64 A new branch of the *timber trade has been established during the present year. 1832 HT. MARTINEAU *Homes Abroad* iv. 59 The creaking *timber-wain. 1848 BUCKLEY *Iliad* 239 Some pine which *timber-workers have cut down. c 1450 *Cov. Myst.* xv. 6, I..am a pore *tymbre wryht [*MS.* wryth], born of the blood of Davyd.

**10.** Special combs.: **timber-beetle**, any beetle which, in the larval or the perfect state, is destructive to timber; **timber-brick**, a brick-shaped block of wood, inserted in brickwork; **timber-capricorn**, a kind of timber-beetle (CAPRICORN 3); **timber-cart**, *spec.* a high-wheeled cart for carrying heavy timber, which is slung under the axles; **timber-chain**, an iron chain used in hauling timber; **timber-dog**, a short wrought iron rod with both ends turned down and sharpened, for driving into and holding together timbers in tunneling or the timbering of trenches; **timber-doodle**, *U.S. local*, the American woodcock, *Philohela minor* (*Cent. Dict.* 1891); *slang*, spirituous liquor; **timber-fall**, a mass of fallen trees; **timber-frame**, † (*a*) timber for use in frames (FRAME *sb.* 10); (*b*) see quot. 1877; **timber-framed** *a.*, having a frame of timber, framed in wood; **timber-grouse**, *U.S.*, any species of grouse frequenting woodlands; **timber-head**, *Naut.*, the head or end of any timber; *spec.* such an end rising above the deck and serving as a bollard: see KEVEL *sb.*[2], quot. c 1860; **timber-headed** *a.*, wooden-headed, dense or obtuse in intellect; **timber-hitch** *sb.*, a knot used in attaching a rope to a log or spar for hoisting or towing it: see quot. 1815; hence **timber-hitch** *v.*, *trans.* to make fast with a timber-hitch; **timber-jumper** (*Hunting slang*), a horse good at jumping over gates and fences; **timber-leader**, *Coal Mining* (see quot.); **timber-limit**: see quot.; **timber-line** (chiefly *U. S.*), the altitude above sea-level at which timber-trees cease to grow; **timber-lode**, in *Feudal Law*, a service by which a tenant was bound to carry wood felled in the forests to the lord's house (cf. BORD-LODE); **timber-mare**, a kind of wooden horse on which offending soldiers and others were made to ride as a punishment; **timber-pond**, a recess in a dock or harbour where timber may be floated; **timber-road**, a road laid with timber for wheels to run upon, an early form of railroad; **timber-rot**, (*a*) rotting of wood caused by various hymenomycetous fungi; (*b*) *New Eng.*, a hot-house disease of cucumbers (*Funk's Stand. Dict.*); **timber-scribe** [SCRIBE *sb.*[2]]: see quots.; **timber-sow**, a wood-louse or sow-bug, *Oniscus*; † **timber-stairs** (*slang*), the pillory; † **timber-taster**, a dockyard official formerly employed in testing the measurement, soundness, and quality of timber; **timber-toe** (*slang*), a wooden leg; hence **timber-toe, -toes**, a wooden-legged man; so **timber-toed** *a.*; **timber-topper** = *timber-jumper*; so **timber-topping**; **timber-tower**, a wooden tower on wheels formerly used in sieges; **timber-tug**: see quot.; † **timber-turner**, humorously used for a player at bowls; **timber-wolf**, *Western U. S.*, the grey wolf, *Canis lupus occidentalis*, as distinct from the prairie-wolf; **timber-worm**, a 'worm' or larva injurious to timber. See also TIMBERMAN, -TREE, etc.

1841-52 T. W. HARRIS *Insects injur. Veget.* (1862) 58 The first was obtained by beating the limbs of some forest-tree. It may be called *Lymexylon sericeum*, the silky *timber-beetle. 1802 BINGLEY *Anim. Biog.* (1813) III. 138 The *Timber Capricorn. Both in its perfect and in its larva state..feeds principally on fir timber, which has been felled. 1884 KNIGHT *Dict. Mech., Suppl.,* **Timber Cart*...The timber, after the cart is driven over it, is raised to the axle by crank-gearing and tackle. 1707 MORTIMER *Husb.* (1721) I. 308 The quickest way of pulling them [shrubs and bushes] up, is to inclose in a *Timber-Chain as many of them as you can, and to clap to them a Team of Horses. 1873 *Punch* 17 May 201/2 Any description of beverage possessing the properties of American '*timberdoodle'. 1897 MARY KINGSLEY *W. Africa* 289 We climbed up one hill,..went through our athletic sports over sundry *timber falls, and struck down into the ravine. 1703 T. N. *City & C. Purchaser* 237, 7s. which indeed is the common price for sawing a good large siz'd *Timber-frame ..per Load. 1877 KNIGHT *Dict. Mech., Timber-frame,* a *gang-saw*; the name by which it is known in England. 1843 *Civil Eng. & Arch. Jrnl.* VI. 179/2 Along a whole range of lofty *timber-framed roofs. 1904 *Essex Rev.* XIII. 215 The house is timber-framed in oak, standing on plinth of brick and septaria. 1891 *Cent. Dict.,* *Timber-grouse. 1894 *Outing* (U. S.) XXIV. 305/1 We..had great fun with the timber-grouse and the sage-hens. 1794 *Rigging & Seamanship* II. 287 The head-rail and *timber-head, on the fore side of the cathead. 1840 R. H. DANA *Bef. Mast* x, We went aft and manned the slip-rope which came through the stern port with a turn round the timber-heads. 1666 W. BOGHURST *Loimographia* 74 Such *timber-headed fellows that they could make noe accurate observations. 1815 BURNEY *Falconer's Dict. Marine* s. v. *Hitch,* *Timber Hitch..is made by taking the end of a rope round the spar, or timber head, leading it under and over the standing part, and passing several turns round its own part. c 1860 H. STUART *Seaman's Catech.* 2 What is a timber hitch used for? For bending to a spar, to haul it along, sending it aloft, &c. 1893 F. M. CRAWFORD *Childr. King* II. xii. 214 He slipped the line under the bags of ballast, and made a timber-hitch with the end, hauling it well taut. 1882 NARES *Seamanship* (ed. 6) 87 The standing part is *timber-hitched round the yard. 1847 THACKERAY *Contrib. to Punch* Wks. 1902 VI. 498, I never put my leg over such a *timber-jumper in my life. 1891 *Labour Commission Gloss.,* **Timber-leader*,..a person whose duty is to ensure the sufficiency of props, planks, brattice, and crown trees, supplied to each hewer in northern coal mines. 1876 *Encycl. Brit.* IV. 774/1 The Governments of the different provinces [Canada] grant licences..to cut timber over vast tracts of land, under the name of '*timber limits'. 1874 COUES *Birds N.-W.* 272 The flowers growing far above *timber-line of Mount Lincoln. c 1400 WILL. THORNE *Chron.* an. 1364, Pro schippeshere, *timberlode & bordlode, vel cariare extra waldam per mare. a 1670 SPALDING *Hist. Troub. Scotl.* (1850) I. 290 He causit big wp..ane *tymber meir, quhairvpone runnaget knaves and runaway soldiouris sould ryde. 1755 JOHNSON, *Horse,*..a wooden machine which soldiers ride by way of punishment. It is sometimes called a timber-mare. 1840 *Evid. Hull Docks Comm.* 9 The *timber-pond to which I allude is at this spot. 1803 *Naval Chron.* IX. 279 Four low wheels,..to run..upon a rail-way or *timber-road. 1858 SIMMONDS *Dict. Trade,* **Timber-scribe*, a metal tool or pointed instrument for marking logs and casks. 1877 KNIGHT *Dict. Mech., Timber-scribe,* a scoring-tool for timber; a race-knife. 1626 BACON *Sylva* § 692 Creatures bred of Putrefaction;..as Earth-Wormes, *Timber-Sowes, Snails. c 1750 in Herd *Songs* (1776) II. 181 Up stairs, down stairs, *Timber stairs fears me. 1803 T. NETHERTON in *Naval Chron.* XV. 220 The *timber tasters..have been paid at the same rate..as the labourers. 1806 *3rd Report Revising Commission,* The several Measurers, Timber Tasters, Converters, and Plug Keepers [etc.], are to be called Single-stationed-men. 1785 GROSE *Dict. Vulg. T.,* **Timber toe*, a man with a wooden leg. a 1845 HOOD *Forget-me-nots* iv, Why did he plant his timber toe on my toe. a 1814 *Sailor's Ret.* II. iii. in *New Brit. Theatre* II. 343 The old *timber-toed pensioners. 1883 *Standard* 12 Feb. 2/6 The champion *timber-topper of the day. 1904 *Daily Chron.* 26 Feb. 9/3 An animal who is to be condemned to the drudgery of *timber-topping. 1614 SYLVESTER *Bethulia's Rescue* III. 111 Here, th' Enginer begins his Ram to rear;..Brings here his Fly-Bridge, there his batt'ring Crow: Besides high *Timber-Towers, on rowling Feet Mov'd and remov'd. a 1800 PEGGE *Suppl. Grose,* **Timber-tug* (Kent), the carriage of a waggon for conveying timber, with a long perch, which may be adapted to any length, or shortened. 1599 PORTER *Angry Wom. Abingd.* (Percy Soc.) 20 Com Swonds, where be these *timber turners, these trowle-the-bowles, these greenemen, these ——? 1891 *Century Dict.,* *Timber-wolf. 1904 *Westm. Gaz.* 28 Apr. 12/1

Last year the female timber-wolf in the Zoological Gardens produced eight cubs. **1530** PALSGR. 281/1 Tymbre worme. **1599** T. M[OUFET] *Silkwormes* 23 Before thou wast, were Timber-worms in price? **1658** ROWLAND tr. *Moufet's Theat. Ins.* 1083 The Philosopher saith that *Kis* is a little Creature bred in wood, like Worms bred in Corn; the English call them Timber-worms, because they are seldome in any wood but that which is cut, and prepared for building. **1668** CHARLETON *Onomast.* 55 *Cossi*, Timber-worms.

**Timber** (ti·mbəɹ), *sb.*[2] Forms: α. 4–6 **tymbre, 5, 9 timbre, 6–7 tymber, 6– timber.** β. *Sc.* **5 tymmyr, tymire, 5–6 tymir, 6 tymyr.** [In OF. *timbre* (1350 in Godef.), med.L. *timbrium, timbria* (1207 Rouen, in Du Cange, also 1314 Upsala); MLG. *timber* (13th c.), *timmer*, LG. *timmer*; MHG. *zimber* (13th c.), Ger. *zimmer*; Norse *timbr* (app. 13th c. in Vigf.), Sw. *timmer*, Da. *simmer* (from Ger.). Supposed to be ultimately a special use of TIMBER *sb.*[1], which prob. arose in the fur trade in Low German, whence it spread into other langs. The immediate source of ME. *timbre* appears to have been French. For the reason of the name cf. quot. 1597, and see TAVELIN. But some suppose a sense 'heap, pile': see Schade, and Falk & Torp; others suspect that it was an eastern word.]

A definite quantity of furs, a package containing 40 skins (i.e. half-skins, 20 pair) of ermine, sable, marten, and the like. (After a numeral usually *timber*, less commonly *timbers*.)

*a* **1150** *Assisa Regis David. R. Scott.* in *Acta Parl. Scot.* I. 667 De custuma tymbriarum. De tymbria uulpium cirogrillorum Martinorum Murelegorum Sabinorum Beueriorum uel similium. De vnaquaque timbria ad exitum. iiij. d. [*15th c. transl.*, Of a tymmyr of skynnis of toddis quhytredijs mertrikis cattis beueris sable ferrettis or swylk vthyr; of ilk tymmyr at the outpassing iiij d.]. *c* **1290** FLETA II. xii. § 8 Lunda autem pellium continet triginta duo timbria. **1390–1** *Earl Derby's Exp.* (Camden) 92 Pro j furrura de grys..de vj tymbre, et de ij tymbre de meniuer, xij nobles. *Ibid.* 93 Pro ij furruris de grys,..quolibet de xij tymbre. **1473–4** *Acc. Ld. High Treas. Scot.* I. 31, iiij tymire of grece to purfell that govne, .. the tymire contenand iij dosane iiij bestis. **1480** *Wardr. Acc. Edw. IV* (1830) 133, xxxij tymbres off ermyns. **1503** *Acc. Ld. High Treas. Scot.* II. 201 For xij tymir of gray grece to lyne the samyn, ilk tymir contenand xl bestis. **1566** A. EDWARDS in Hakluyt *Voy.* (1886) III. 392, I have further received two timbers of Sables. **1577** HARRISON *England* II. v. (1877) II. 122 The prince hath fiue yardes of cloth for his gowne and whood.. beside fiue timber of the finest mineuer. [*margin*] A timber conteineth fortie skins. **1597** SKENE *De Verb. Sign.*, *Timbria Pellium*..ane Timmer of skinnes: That is, swa monie as is inclused within twa broddes of Timmer, quhilk commounlie conteinis fourtie skinnes: In the quhilk manner, merchandes vsis to bring hame Martrick, Sable, and vther coastlie skinnes and Furringes. **1707** E. CHAMBERLAYNE *Pres. St. Eng.* III. ii. 256 Of Furrs, Fitches, Grays, Jennets, Martins, Mincks, Sables, 40 Skins is a Timber; other Skins five Score to the Hundred. **1714** *Fr. Bk. Rates* 41 Ermine per Timber of 20 Couple. **1858** SIMMONDS *Dict. Trade* s.v., In some skins, however, the timbre counts to 120. **1901** *Westm. Gaz.* 27 Nov. 8/2 Ten years ago..ermine..cost 28s. to 30s. per timber of forty skins. The price for a timber to-day.. is 176s.

**Timber** (ti·mbəɹ), *v.* Forms: see TIMBER *sb.*[1] [OE. *timbran* and *timbrian* = OS. *timbrian* (MDu., Du. *timmeren*), OHG. *zimberen, zimbarôn* (MHG. *zimber(e)n*, Ger. *zimmern*), ON. *timbra* (Sw. *timbra*, Da. *tömmre*), Goth. and OTeut. *timr-jan*, f. **tim-r-* TIMBER *sb.*[1]]

**1.** *trans.* To build, construct, make (as a house, ship, etc.); *spec.* (in later use) to build or construct of wood. *Obs.* or *arch.*

*a* **750** *Cædmon's Gen.* 1692 Weall stænenne up forð timbran. *a* **900** tr. *Bæda's Eccl. Hist.* III. xvii. [xxiii.] (1890) 232 Neowan stowe mynster to timbrenne odþe ciricean. *c* **1000** *Ags. Gosp.* Matt. xvi. 18 Ofer þisne stan ic timbriȝe mine cyricean. *c* **1200** ORMIN 13368 To timmbrenn himm an haliȝ hus. *c* **1350** *Will. Palerne* 2015 Sche chold sone be bischet..In a ful tristy tour timbred for þe nones. *a* **1400–50** *Alexander* 2110 (MS. Dubl.) Þar fand he tembret on þe topp & tyldit vp a cyte. **1565–73** COOPER *Thesaurus* s.v. *Contabulo*, *Contabulare murum turribus*..to make towers, to tymber plankes euen with the walles. **1857** SIR F. PALGRAVE *Norm. & Eng.* II. 128 Here had Guillaume timbered and thatched a rustic habitation.

**b.** *absol.*; *spec.* of a bird, to build (*scil.* its nest).

*c* **897** K. ÆLFRED *Gregory's Past. C.* lviii. 445 On ðæm botle, ðær ðær we timbran willen. *a* **1100** *Gerefa* in *Anglia* (1886) IX. 261 Me mæig on sumera..tymbrian, wudian, weodian, faldian. *a* **1300** *Cursor M.* 8763 (Cott.) Quils he was timberand to þis thing. **1377** LANGL. *P. Pl.* B. XI. 352 Moche merueilled me..who tauȝte hem [birds] on trees to tymbre so heighe. **1692** R. L'ESTRANGE *Fables* lxxii. 71 There was a Bargain struck up betwixt an Eagle and a Fox. The One Took-up in a Thicket of Brushwood, and the Other Timber'd upon a Tree hard by. **1706** PHILLIPS (ed. Kersey), To *Timber* (in *Falconry*), to nestle, to make a Nest; as Birds of Prey do.

†**c.** with advb. extension: To build *up*. *Obs.*

**1555** W. WATREMAN *Fardle Facions* II. vii. 156 They timbre vp drie stickes together.

†**2.** *fig.* To construct, frame, effect, do, form, cause, bring about, bring into existence or operation (any action, condition, etc.). *Obs.*

*c* **897** K. ÆLFRED *Gregory's Past. C.* xxxiii. 215 Ða godan weorc ðe he..ær..timbrede. *a* **1000** *Ags. Ps.* (Th.) cxxviii[i]. 2 [3] Ofer minum bæce bitere onguunnon þa firenfullan facen timbrian. *c* **1205** LAY. 6620 Hit wes vmbe fif winter..seoððen he þas seorȝe him seolfen hæfde itimbred. *a* **1225** *Ancr. R.* 124 þeos hond..haueð itimbred me þe bliscen of heouene. ? *a* **1400** *Morte Arth.* 3742 That traytoure.. That this tresone has tymbyrde to my trewe lorde. *c* **1450** *Bone Flor.* 560 That hath tymberde all my teene. **1646** SIR T. BROWNE *Pseud. Ep.* I. v. 14 Heads that were never timber'd for it.

†**3.** To make up or add fuel to (a fire). *Obs.*

**1486** *Bk. St. Albans* F vij b, A ffyre Tymbered. **1513** *Bk. Kerving* in *Babees Bk.* (1868) 265 Tymbre that fyre. **1530** PALSGR. 758/2, I tymber a fyre, *je accoustre*, or *je mets a poynt.* **1688** R. HOLME *Armoury* III. 85/1 Timber the Fire, is to mend the Fire, make it burn better, by putting more Fuel or Wood or Coles to it.

**4.** To furnish with timber. (See also TIMBERED *ppl. a.*) †**a.** To supply or arm with spears: cf. TIMBER *sb.*[1] 5. *Obs.*

*a* **1578** LINDESAY (Pitscottie) *Chron. Scot.* (S.T.S.) II. 98 The earle of Angus was weill temmert witht so money sharp speiris and lang.

**b.** To put in or apply timber to support the roof of a mine or working, the sides of a shaft or a trench, the roof and sides of a tunnel, etc.

**1702** SAVERY *Miners Friend* 6 The more Shafts or Pits are sunk, the more Wood-work will be necessarily imployed in Timbering them. **1725** T. THOMAS in *Portland Papers* (Hist. MSS. Comm.) VI. 106 The lining of it [the pit shaft] with wood in order to hinder it from falling in, is timbering of it. **1844** SIMMS *Pract. Tunnelling* xii. 121 The leaving the lower part of the excavation without being timbered was not general throughout the tunnel. **1872** R. B. SMYTH *Mining Statist.* 62 The new shaft..has been sunk, timbered, and centred to a depth of 260 feet. **1904** *Times* 28 Jan. 10/4 The gang had to timber up the roof.

**c.** To cover or frame with timber or wood.

**1850** HAWTHORNE *Scarlet L.* i. (1883) 67 A wooden edifice, the door of which was heavily timbered with oak. **1904** *Westm. Gaz.* 26 Aug. 3/1 If you have the floor of the butt timbered or stoned.

**5.** *intr.* Of a tree: To form timber. ? *Obs.*

**1610** [implied in TIMBERING *vbl. sb.* and *ppl. a.*].

†**6.** *trans. Timber out*, to divide (timber) into beams, planks, etc., suited for building. Also *fig.*

**1628** *MS. Acc. St. John's Hosp., Canterb.*, To appoynte the tymber to be brought home and to be tymbered out for diuerse vses. **1637** *Ibid.*, Payed for timberinge out of our woode j s. **1662** HIBBERT *Body Div.* I. 69 Many men engage in undertakings, for which their heads were never squared or timbred out.

**Timber**, obs. form of TIMBRE.

**Timbered** (ti·mbəɹd), *ppl. a.* [f. TIMBER *sb.*[1] and *v.* + -ED.]

**1.** Constructed of timber; built or made of wood, wooden.

*c* **1412** HOCCLEVE *De Reg. Princ.* 5338 Castels doun bette, and tymbred houses brent. **1552** HULOET, Tymbred, *materiatus*, ..*materior*,..to worke in tymber. **1632** LITHGOW *Trav.* VIII. 351 A great thicket of wood, where their timberd Cabine stood. **1699** DAMPIER *Voy.* II. I. ix. 172 About a hundred yards from the Fort.. there is a low timbered House. **1848** LYTTON *Harold* I. iv, They entered London, a rude, dark city, built mainly of timbered houses. **1905** A. C. BENSON *Upton Lett.* (1906) 139 A little ancient church, with a timbered spire.

**2. a.** Of a thing (concrete or abstract): Having a structure (of a specified kind); constructed, framed, built, made. (In parasynthetic comb., or qualified by an adv.)

**1570** FOXE *A. & M.* (ed. 2) 1333/1 Loe here the mighty reasons, the stronge tymbered argumentes. **1602** SHAKS. *Ham.* IV. vii. 22 My Arrowes Too slightly timbred for so loud a Winde, Would haue reuerted to my Bow againe. **1697** COLLIER *Ess. Mor. Subj.* II. (1709) 80 Let them be as Sleek and well Timber'd as those Atoms Epicurus made his Soul of. **1771** SMOLLETT *Humph. Cl.* 28 Sept., Lord Oxmington was well known to have his brain very ill timbered.

**b.** Of a person or animal: Having (such and such) a bodily structure or constitution; framed, built. (Usually in parasynthetic comb.)

**1581** MULCASTER *Positions* xxxvii. (1887) 144 Your childe is weake tymbred, let scholing alone. **1622** FLETCHER & MASSINGER *Spanish Curate* II. i, A fine straite timber'd man and a brave soldier. **1769** *Stratford Jubilee* II. i, I'm as well timbered about the legs and face, as one can meet. **1861** *Times* 27 Sept., Cart-horses, young, and well-timbered, and quick walkers.

**3.** Furnished with growing trees; wooded.

**1701** *Lond. Gaz.* No. 3724/4 Piggott's Farm.., being well Timbred. **1754** FIELDING *Fathers* II. i, That estate..of yours in Hampshire is a very ill-timbered estate. **1854** BARTLETT *Mex. Boundary* I. ix. 234 So rich a timbered country. **1887** MOLONEY *Forestry W. Afr.* 6 About one half of the timbered land in the island belongs to the Government.

**Ti·mberer.** [f. TIMBER *sb.*[1] + -ER[1].]

**1.** = TIMBERMAN 3. **1891** in *Cent. Dict.*

**2.** A ship engaged in the timber trade.

**1849** CUPPLES *Green Hand* ix. (1856) 81 'I'd say she's—not a cruiser, Captain Williamson—no, nor a Greenock Indyman—nor a—' 'Oh!' said Finch, 'some African timberer or other'.

**Timbering** (ti·mbəriŋ), *vbl. sb.* [f. TIMBER *v.* + -ING[1].]

**1.** The action of the verb TIMBER, in various senses.

*c* **1175** *Lamb. Hom.* 93 Þi bileafden heo heore timbrunge. *a* **1225** *Ancr. R.* 124 Al is to his bliheue, & timbrunge touward his blisse. **1591** PERCIVAL *Sp. Dict.*, *Maderamiento*, timbering, *contignatio*. **1610** FOLKINGHAM *Art of Survey* I. iii. 6 The boaling, spreading, arming, timbring and tapering of Trees. **1844** SIMMS (*title*) Practical Tunnelling..the setting out of the works; Shaft sinking,..Timbering [etc.]. **1893** *Labour Commission Gloss.*, *Timbering*, propping up the roof or sides of a mine by means of planks and cogs, &c.

**2.** *concr.* Building material (esp. of wood); timber-work; *spec.* in *Mining*, the timber used to support the sides of a shaft or the roof of a working.

**1486** *Bk. St. Albans*, *Hawking* a ij, We shall say that hawkys doon draw when they bere tymbering to their nestes. **1791** NEWTE *Tour Eng. & Scot.* 241 Oak..fit for agricultural utensils, and timbering for the roofs of houses. **1844** SIMMS *Pract. Tunnelling* xii. 121 The whole of the timbering of the top of the new length is..complete down to the first sill. **1867** MUSGRAVE *Nooks O. France* II. i. 6 A lofty domicile..exhibiting laths, timbering and slatework.

**Ti·mbering**, *ppl. a.* [f. as prec. + -ING[2].] That timbers; constructing, building; of a tree, producing timber.

**1610** FOLKINGHAM *Art of Survey* I. iii. 6 The high timbring Oake dilating mightie armes in large extent. **1648** EARL OF WESTMORELAND *Otia Sacra* (1879) 155 Thou maist as well make wonder less, By fancying of two Timbering Phœnixes At the same time.

**Timberless** (ti·mbəɹlės), *a.* [f. TIMBER *sb.*[1] + -LESS.] Without timber; devoid of forest-trees.

**1859** R. F. BURTON in *Jrnl. Geog. Soc.* XXIX. 140 Tracts of dense bush and timberless woods. **1870** *Daily News* 15 Feb., Those prairie States..are mostly timberless States.

**Timberling** (ti·mbəɹliŋ). [f. TIMBER *sb.*[1] + -LING.] A young timber-tree; a sapling.

**1787** W. MARSHALL *Norfolk* I. 99 The timbers, pollards, and timberlings should first be inspected. **1796** — *W. England* I. 83 The ancient law..requires that a certain number of Timberlings should be left standing. *Ibid.* II. 156 Train up the young stands, or timberlings, so as to give them length of stem.

**Timberman** (ti·mbəɹmæ̆n). [f. TIMBER *sb.*[1] + MAN *sb.*[1]]

†**1.** A man who supplies or deals in timber. *Obs.*

**1429** *Rec. St. Mary at Hill* 70 Payd to more tymberman for tymbre for gretynges hous. **1625** BACON *Ess.*, *Riches* (Arb.) 235 A Great Sheepe-Master, A Great Timber Man. **1656** [? J. SERGEANT] tr. *T. White's Peripat. Inst.* 420 Trees are thrown by Timber-men into the Water.

**b.** A man employed in handling timber.

**1890** GORDON *Foundry* vi. (*heading*), Among the timbermen. *Ibid.* 114 We turn into Canada Dock, and are at once among the timbermen. **1891** *Labour Commission Gloss.*, *Timbermen*, men who discharge timber cargoes from ships, and stock timber on shore and upon raft on water.

†**2.** One who makes things of timber; a carpenter. [So Du. *timmerman*, G. *zimmermann*.] *Sc. Obs.*

**1466** *Sc. Acts Jas. III* (1814) II. 87 Þe maister of þe schip sal fynd sufficiand stermane, tymmerman, & schipmen conuenient for þe schip. **1496** *Acc. Ld. High Treas. Scot.* I. 282 To Hermyn, tymmyr man, Duchman, for $v^e$ and xij rachteris. **1502** *Ibid.* II. 281 To fee tymirmen to pas to the wod with the said wricht. **1534** *Ibid.* VI. 234 To Thomas Corry, thre tymmermen,..to pas to calfet the Kingis schip. **1643** in Cramond *Ann. Banff* (1891) I. 90 Any wright or other timberman burger or inhabitant.

**3.** A man employed in timbering the shafts or roofs of a mine, the sides of a trench, or any other excavation.

**1849–50** WEALE *Dict. Terms*, *Timber-man*, in mining, the man employed in placing supports of timber in the mine. **1877** FOSTER & GALLOWAY tr. *Callon's Lect. Mining* I. 231 The timberman who sets up the props has usually no special tool except his axe. **1881** *Echo* 14 Jan. 1/6 A timberman ..had seen..one of the men give a light to the manager, both having their lamps open.

**4.** A species of timber-beetle.

**1894** *B'ham Weekly Post* 14 Apr. 4/7 That curious and interesting beetle the Timberman (*Astinomus ædilis*).

**Timbersome**, variant of TIMORSOME.

**Timber-tree.** A tree yielding timber or wood fit for building or construction.

*c* **1505** *Plumpton Corr.* (Camden) 198 Tha will bey none without they have tymmer tres. **1558–9** *Act 1 Eliz.* c. 15 Any Tymber Tree or Tymber Trees of Oke, Beeche, or Ashe. **1601** R. JOHNSON *Kingd. & Commw.* (1603) 15 The noblemen doe make great profit by selling great quantities..for firewood, but greater by sales of timber trees; for..the greatest part of their buildings consist of timber. **1726** SWIFT *Gulliver* I. viii, Cutting down some of the largest timber trees for oars and masts. **1766** *Act 6 Geo. III*, c. 48 All Oak, Beech, Chestnut, Walnut, Ash, Elm, Cedar, Fir, Asp, Lime, Sycamore, and Birch Trees, shall be deemed and taken to be Timber Trees within the true Meaning..of this Act. **1865** *Chambers' Encycl.* s.v. *Poplar*, The cottonwood of North America is valued as a timber-tree.

**Timber-wood.** Now *rare.* Wood suitable for structural purposes; = TIMBER *sb.*[1] 3.

*c* **1483** CAXTON *Dialogues* 40 Alle the tymbre woode, *tous les boys charpentifs.* **1579** E. K. *Gloss* in *Spenser's Sheph. Cal.* Feb. 146 *Trees of state*, taller trees fitte for timber wood. **1602** FULBECKE *2nd Pt. Parall.* 52 He shal not meddle with great timber-woode without the assent of his lessor...But the cutting of dead wood is not waste. **1653** H. MORE *Antid. Ath.* II. iii. (1712) 47 (*heading*) The designed Usefulness of Quarries of Stone, Timber-Wood, Metals, and Minerals. **1899** *Westm. Gaz.* 15 Feb. 7/3 There have..been many substitutes proposed..for breakwaters... Well-knit timber-wood, filled in with stones, does very well.

**Timber-work.**

**1.** Work executed in timber; the wooden part of any structure.

**1390** GOWER *Conf.* II. 200 A wilde fyr..They caste among the timberwerk. *c* **1470** HENRY *Wallace* VIII. 617 The temir werk thai brynt wp all in playn. **1574–5** *Reg. Privy Council Scot.* II. 432 Amendiment of the ruif and tymmer werk of thair..parroche kirk. **1703** T. N. *City & C. Purchaser* 215 Window-frames.. Friezes, and Cornishes, and all other Timber-works that are expos'd to the Weather. **1864** A. McKAY *Hist. Kilmarnock* (1880) 255 The inner roof [is composed] of open, oak-varnished timber-work.

*fig.* 1594 T. B *La Primaud. Fr. Acad.* II. *Seneca*, The bones as it were the frame and timberworke of mans body.

**2.** *pl.* An establishment where timber is prepared or worked up.

1875 W. McIlwraith *Guide Wigtownshire* 94 Here are extensive timber-works.

**Timbery** (ti·mbəri), *a. rare.* [f. Timber *sb.*[1] + -y.] Abounding in or characterized by timber.

1859 Sala *Tw. round Clock* (1861) 354 The bleak, timbery city of Copenhagen.

**Timber-yard.** An open yard or place where timber is stacked or stored.

In cricket slang applied to the place in which the wickets are pitched. Hence *a row in his t.*, in reference to the wickets being struck with force by the ball.

1482–3 *Acc. Exch. K. R.* Bundle 496 No. 25 (P.R.O.) Pro cariagio..de diversis locis..usque dictum castrum, le tymberyard. 1545 *Act 37 Hen. VIII*, c. 12 § 10 Any Mansion-house with a Shop..Timber-yard, Teinter-yard, or Garden belonging to the same. 1768 Earl Carlisle in Jesse *Selwyn & Contemp.* (1843) II. 272 Why did you not set his timber-yard on fire? 1853 'C. Bede' *Verdant Green* I. xi, The wicketkeeper..informed him 'there was a row in his timber-yard'. 1869 *Routledge's Ev. Boy's Ann.* 638 After a desperate lunge he was startled with a 'row in his timber yard'.

† **Ti·mbester.** *Obs.* [app. for *timberster* or *timbrester*, f. Timbre *v.*[1] + -ster: cf. Timbrer.] A female performer on the timbrel.

? *a* 1366 Chaucer *Rom. Rose* 769 Ther was many a timbestere [F. *tymberresses*]...The timbres up ful sotilly They caste, and henten [hem] ful ofte Upon a finger faire and softe. 1721 Bailey, *Timbestores* [later edd. *-ters*], Players on Timbrels. 1843 Lytton *Last Bar.* I. ii, A young maiden was struggling..to extricate herself from a troop of timbrel girls, or *tymbesteres*.

† **Timbre** (ti·mbəɹ), *sb.*[1] *Obs.* Also 4–5 **tymbre, tymber** (5 -yr(e, -ere), 5–6 *Sc.* **tymmer** (8 **timber**). [a. OF. *timbre* (12th c. in Hatz.-Darm.):—**timbne*:—late pop.L. **timbano*, for L. *tympanum*, a. Gr. τύμπανον timbrel, kettledrum. In OF. *timbre* was used in 13th c., and in ME. by Wyclif, to render L. *tympanum* in Ps. 150. This and the next two words all represent senses of the same French word, but having been taken into Eng. at different dates, and without the intervening links by which the senses were connected in French, are here treated as distinct words.] = Timbrel *sb.*[1]

[*a* 1300 *French Ps.* in *Lib. Psalm. Versio Gallica* (F. Michel, Oxford 1860) App., Ps. cl. 4 Loés-l'en timbre en concorde (*Vulg.* Laudate eum in tympano et choro).] 13.. *K. Alis.* 191 Orgles, tymbres [*Laud MS.* chymbes], al maner gleo, Was dryuen ageyn that lady freo. 13.. *E. E. Allit. P.* B. 1414 Tymbres & tabornes, tulket among. ? *a* 1366 [see Timbester]. 1382 Wyclif *Isa.* v. 12 Harpe, and syngende instrument, and tymbre, and trumpe [1388 Harpe and giterne, and tympan, and pipe]. 1390 Gower *Conf.* III. 63 Ther was ful many a tymber bete And many a maide carolende. *c* 1440 *Promp. Parv.* 494/1 Tymbyr, lytyl tabowre, *timpanillum*. 1525 Ld. Berners tr. *Froiss.* II. clxxi. [clxvii.] 499 They sowned tymbres and tabours, accordynge to their vsage. *c* 1560 A. Scott *Poems, Of May* 12 In May gois gallandis bring in symmer, And trymly occupyis thair tymmer With 'Hunts vp', every morning plaid.

**b.** *attrib.* in *timbre weights*, app. = timbrels or tambourines as formerly used in May-day merrymakings.

A *weight* (Sc. *wecht*) is a vessel like a sieve without holes, formed by stretching a skin across a hoop of a few inches depth. In shape it resembles a tambourine, which may therefore be called, as Jamieson points out, a *timbre* or *timbrel weight*. *Wychtis* appears to be erroneous for *wechtis* or *weights*, and *waits* to embody a false etymology.

*c* 1560 A. Scott *Poems, Of May* 9 And now in May to madynnis fawis [*i. e.* falls] With tymmer wechtis to trip in ringis. 1593 in *14th Rep. Hist. MSS. Comm.* App. III. 41 Dischairgeing [*i.e.* forbidding] also pasche playis, tymmer wychtis, banefyris and ringing of baisingis [basins]. [1756 *Gentl. Mag.* Feb. 73/2 After having completed this circuit, they again enter the town [Alnwick] sword in hand, and are generally met by women dressed up with ribbons, bells, and garlands of gum-flowers, who welcome them with dancing and singing, and are called timber-waits. [*Note*] Perhaps a corruption of *timbrel-waits*, players on timbrels, *waits* being an old word for those who play on musical Instruments in the streets.]

**Timbre, tymber** (ti·mbəɹ), *sb.*[2] *Obs.* exc. *Hist.* Also 4–6 **tymbre**, (4 *Sc.* **tymmer**), 5–7 **timber.** [a. F. *timbre* (14th c.), the same word as in prec., which in OF. was transferred to a kind of bell, esp. a hemispherical clock- or table-bell, and thence to a skull-cap of metal, a helmet, and in Heraldry to the crest over the shield in a coat of arms. (Thence also to a crest impressed or stamped upon a legal or official document, a stamp, whence to a postage-stamp: see Timbro-.)]

The crest of a helmet; hence, the crest or exterior additions placed over the shield in heraldic arms: see quot. 1894.

1375 Barbour *Bruce* XIX. 396 Twa novelreis that day [1327–8] thai saw, That forrouth in scotland had beyn nane. Tymbrys [*v.rr.* Tymbres, Tymmeris] for helmys wes the tane, That thame thoucht than of gret bewte, And alsua wounder for to se. 1478 in W. G. D. Fletcher *Shropsh. Grants of Arms* (1909) 12 A shild of azure and pourpull parted in pale, a cross engrayled gold or bythwen foure rosses silver, and to his tymbre a gauntelet sillver sette in a wrethe gold and azure. 1513 Douglas *Æneis* X. v. 136 (ed. 1555) The creist or schynand tymber, that was set Aboue Eneas helme and top on hicht. 1572 Bossewell *Armorie* II. 88 b, The Tymbre, a palme of an hande dexter, d'Ermyne, sette on a Wreath Or, and Sable, manteled Azure. 1586 [see Achievement 3]. 1894 *Parker's Gloss. Her.*, *Timbre*, this French term..comprises the exterior ornaments of the escutcheon, that is (1) the helmet, (2) the mantelling, (3) the crest. By some, however, it is held to include (4) the escroll, (5) the wreath, (6) the motto, (7) the supporters, as well as (8) the cap of dignity and crown.

‖ **Timbre** (tæ̃nbr'), *sb.*[3] [a. mod.F. *timbre*: see Timbre *sb.*[1] and [2]. From the sense 'bell', 'small bell' (see Timbre *sb.*[2]) arose that of 'sound of a bell', 'sonorous quality of any instrument or of a voice', and finally that of 'character or quality of sound' (= Ger. *klangfarbe*), in which the word has passed into English use, retaining its French pronunciation.]

The character or quality of a musical or vocal sound (distinct from its pitch and intensity) depending upon the particular voice or instrument producing it, and distinguishing it from sounds proceeding from other sources; caused by the proportion in which the fundamental tone is combined with the harmonics or overtones (= Ger. *klangfarbe*).

In first quot. only a nonce-use of the Fr. word.

1849 C. Brontë *Shirley* x, Your voice..has another 'timbre' than that hard, deep organ of Miss Mann's. 1853 Markham *Skoda's Auscult.* 53 The voices of individuals, and the sounds of musical instruments, differ, not only in strength, clearness, and pitch, but (and particularly) in that quality also for which there is no common distinctive expression, but which is known as the tone, the character, or timbre of the voice. The timbre of the thoracic, always differs from the timbre of the oral, voice...A strong thoracic voice partakes of the timbre of the speaking-trumpet. 1876 tr. *Blaserna's Sound* viii. 147 There are scarcely any two individuals who have exactly the same timbre of voice. 1890 'R. Boldrewood' *Col. Reformer* (1891) 184 [His] voice ..being mild and small of timbre.

† **Timbre,** *v.*[1] *Obs.* [f. Timbre *sb.*[1]: cf. F. *timbrer*.] *intr.* To play on the timbrel. Hence † **Ti·mbring** *vbl. sb.*

*c* 1400 *Song Roland* 54 Blowinge off bugles.., Trymlinge of tabers And tymbring soft. 1530 Palsgr. 758/1, I tymber, I playe on an instrument or a tymber, *je timbre.* The maydens of London were wonte to tymber more than they do nowe.

**Ti·mbre,** *v.*[2] [f. Timbre *sb.*[2]] *trans.* To furnish or adorn with a crest; to surmount as a crest. Hence **Ti·mbred** *ppl. a.*, crested; **Ti·mbring** *vbl. sb.*

1513 Douglas *Æneis* XII. ii. 100 Eik his tymbret helm wyth crestis two. 1606 Sylvester *Du Bartas* II. iv. III. *Magnificence* 1034 Loe, the Cock..A purple Plume timbers his stately Crest. 1610 Guillim *Heraldry* VI. v. 264 In some Countries,..it is not permitted to persons inferior to the degree of a Knight, to Timber their Armes, that is to say, to adorne them with Helme, Mantle, Crest, &c. *Ibid.* 267 Rodolph Duke of Lorraigne..was the first that bare his Armes Tymbered. 1688 R. Holme *Armoury* IV. vi. (Roxb.) 320/1 Concerning the coate and Tymbreing in the seale thereof. 1894 Woodward *Eccles. Heraldry* 255 The others [helmets] were timbred with the Crest of the See of Mainz.

**Timbre,** obs. form of Timber.

**Timbrel** (ti·mbrĕl), *sb.*[1] Now chiefly *biblical*. Also 6 **tumbrel(le, timbril, -elle, tymbrel(le,** *Sc.* **timberall,** 6–7 **tym-, timbrell,** 7 **timbrill.** [app. a dim. of the earlier Timbre *sb.*[1] in same sense: see -el [2]. So far as appears, it was an Eng. formation; but Sp. has a somewhat parallel dim. form in *tamboril* tabor, tabret, from *tambor* drum (cf. F. *tambourin*). More's spelling appears to be due to confusion with the earlier word Tumbrel *sb.*, which was also sometimes written *timbrel*.]

A musical instrument of percussion; a tambourine or the like that could be held up in the hand.

Chiefly used (to render Heb. *tōph*) in versions of the Bible from Coverdale onward, or in allusions to the biblical use, and in reference to Oriental instruments thought to be the same or similar. Cf. the earlier Timbre *sb.*[1]

1500–20 Dunbar *Poems* lxxvii. 45 Syne come thair four and twentie madinis ȝing,..Playand on timberallis, and syngand rycht sweitlie. 1534 More *Comf. agst. Trib.* III. Wks. 1261/2 If the Turke stode euen here with all his whole army about him, &..fel al at once in a shoute, with trumpets, tabrets, & tumbrels al blowen vp at once. 1535 Coverdale *Exod.* xv. 20 Miriam the prophetisse..toke a tymbrell in hir hande, and all the women folowed out after her with timbrels in a daunse. 1553 Eden *Treat. Newe Ind.* (Arb.) 14 A great noyse of cimbals, drumslades, timbrelles, shames, pipes, flutes,.. and diuerse other musical instrumentes. 1662 J. Davies tr. *Olearius' Voy. Ambass.* 277 The Indian Timbrels are two foot long, but broader in the middle than at the Extremities, much after the fashion of our Barrels. [app. = tom-toms.] 1768 Beattie *Minstr.* I. xxxv, With merriment, and song, and timbrels clear. *c* 1850 *Arab. Nts.* (Rtldg.) 165 A little hunchbacked fellow came..and began playing on a timbrel, which he accompanied with his voice.

**b.** ? A figure of a timbrel. (Cf. *bells*, etc.)

*a* 1548 Hall *Chron., Hen. VIII* 7 Of their hosen..the nether partes were of Scarlet, poudred with tymbrelles of fyne golde.

**c.** *attrib.* and *Comb.*

1552 Huloet, Tymbrell player, *tympanista*,..*tympanistria*. 1757 Dyer *Fleece* II. Poems (1761) 102 O'er all the timbrelsounding squares and streets. 1843 Lytton *Last Bar.* I. ii, The timbrel-girl sprang into the crowd and vanished.

† **Timbrel,** *sb.*[2] *Sc. Obs. rare.* In 5 **tymeral,** 6 **tymbrall, -ell, -ill.** [f. Timbre *sb.*[2] + -el [2].] The crest of a helmet; = Timbre *sb.*[2]

*c* 1450 Holland *Howlat* 613 Four helmes full fair, And in thar tymeralis tryid trewly thai bere The plesand Povne.. provde to repair. 1513 Douglas *Æneis* II. viii. [vii.] 88 The portratour of armes was mysknaw, All war bot Grekis tymbrallis at thai saw.

**Ti·mbrel,** *v.* [f. Timbrel *sb.*[1]] *intr.* To play upon a timbrel; *trans.* to accompany with a timbrel or similar instrument. Hence **Ti·mbrelled** (-brĕld) *ppl. a.*, accompanied by the playing of timbrels; also **Ti·mbreller,** a performer on the timbrel.

1629 Milton *Hymn Nativity* xxiv, In vain with Timbrel'd Anthems dark The sable-stolèd Sorcerers bear his worshipt Ark. 1785 S. Rogers *Ode Superstit.* 68 A timbrelled anthem swells the gale. 1833 Bowles *St. John in Patmos* II. 165 There the timbrelled hymn Rings to Osiris. 18.. L. Hunt *Death & Ruffians* 14 To let their timbrellers and tumblers in. 1854 S. Dobell *Balder* xxiv. 152 A country song..Fit to be timbrelled to the tambourine.

**Timbrel(l,** obs. form of Tumbrel.

† **Timbrer.** *Obs. rare.* In 5 **tymberer, tymbrer.** [f. Timbre *v.*[1] + -er [1].] A timbrel-player.

*c* 1425 *St. Eliz. of Spalbeck* in *Anglia* VIII. 109/29 Þis newe tymbrer settiþ her flesche for an harpe, and hir chekys for a tymber. *c* 1425 *St. Mary of Oignies* II. v. ibid. 166/22 She, þat ȝonge tymberer, hadde strecchyd hir body, and dryed hit as by-twix two trees of þe crosse.

† **Timbro-,** combining form repr. Fr. *timbre* (*-poste*) postage-stamp [see Timbre *sb.*[2]], used for a short period to form terms relating to stamp-collecting; now superseded by Philately and related words. **Timbro·logy** [-logy] = *timbrophily*; **Timbroma·nia** [F. *timbromanie*], a craze or mania for collecting stamps; hence **Timbroma·niac, Timbro·manist**; **Timbro·phily** [F. *timbrophilie*, Gr. φιλία love, friendship], stamp-collecting; = Philately; hence **Timbrophi·lic** *a.*, **Timbro·philist.**

1864 Lewins *Her Majesty's Mails* 265 It only remains to refer for a moment to the timbromanie or stamp mania. 1865 *Routledge's Ev. Boy's Ann.* 722 We hold timbromania to be just as sensible a pursuit as a taste for numismatics... The timbromaniac..studies history. 1867 *Philatelist* I. 2 Timbromania was its first designation. Timbrophily and Timbrology next had a short reign as a technical term, till Philately..has proved to be the right word. *Ibid.* 203 Timbrophilists would be a respectably large array. 1880 *Bric-a-Brac* Oct. 2 A proof of the great profits made by timbromanists. 1891 *Cornh. Mag.* July 36 Which he will dispose of to Western timbromaniacs.

**Timburine,** obs. variant of Tambourine.

**Time** (təim), *sb.* Forms: 1–2 **tíma, tȳma,** 2–8 **tyme,** 4 **tim, teme, teyme,** 4–6 **tym,** 6 **taym,** 2– **time.** [OE. *tíma* = ON. *tími*, wk. masc., time, fit or proper time, (first, etc.) time, good time, prosperity (Da. *time*, Sw. *timme* an hour), :—OTeut. **tī-mon-*, app. f. a root *tī-* to stretch, extend (see Tide *sb.*) + abstr. suffix *-mon, -man* (see Kluge *Stammbildungslehre* § 154).]

**I.** = A space or extent of time.

**1.** A limited stretch or space of continued existence, as the interval between two successive events or acts, or the period through which an action, condition, or state continues; a finite portion of 'time' (in its infinite sense: see 24), as *a long time, a short time, some time, for a time.*

*In no time, in less than no time* (colloq.), immediately, very quickly or soon. *Absolute time*: see quot. 1842.

*c* 893 K. Ælfred *Oros.* IV. v. § 5 Ymbe ðone timan þe þiss wæs. *c* 1000 Ælfric *Hom.* I. 60 Hit wæs ȝewunelic on ðam timan. *a* 1225 *Leg. Kath.* 437 He heold on..long time of þe dei. *c* 1330 R. Brunne *Chron. Wace* (Rolls) 4190 [Caesar] tok his leue..To wende fro þem for longe teymes. 1377 Langl. *P. Pl.* B. XVIII. 63 And tolde whi þat tempest so longe tyme dured. *c* 1386 Chaucer *Clerk's T.* 386 Nat longe tyme after that this Grisild Was wedded, she a doghter hath ybore. *c* 1440 *Promp. Parv.* 494/1 Tyme, *idem quod* tyyde (*P.* tyme, whyle, *tempus*). 1572 Forrest *Theophilus* 263 in *Anglia* VII, By so longe tyme as his busshoppe dyd lyue. 1610 Shaks. *Temp.* III. ii. 93 After a little time Ile beate him too. 1662 Gerbier *Princ.* 28 No New Building could stand any time without Proppings. 1662 Stillingfl. *Orig. Sacr.* III. iv. § 5 The highest mountains in the World..may be ascended in three dayes time. 1670 Sir S. Crow in *12th Rep. Hist. MSS. Comm.* App. v. 15 [Hangings] that—for a time—will look better to the eye. 1711 Addison *Spect.* No. 37 ⁋ 1 It was some time before the Lady came to me. 1762 Kames *Elem. Crit.* (1833) 479 A child perceives an interval, and that interval it learns to call time. 1794 Mrs. Radcliffe *Myst. Udolpho* xxv, Annette..was absent a considerable time. 1843 Borrow *Bible in Spain* xxix. (1901) 417 Follow me.. and I will lead you to Finisterre in no time. 1849 Macaulay *Hist. Eng.* iii. I. 291 The time occupied..was not to exceed fourteen days in one year. 1875 Jowett *Plato* (ed. 2) I. 195 In less than no time you shall hear. 1842 Brande *Dict. Sci.*, etc. s. v., Absolute Time is time considered in itself without reference to that portion of duration to which it belongs, however noted or marked. 1868 Dk. Argyll in *Mem.* (1906) II. xlvi. 540 Have we any link connecting time-relative with time-absolute?

**b.** †(*a*) The space of an hour (for OE. *tíd*, Tide *sb.* 2). *Obs. rare.* (*b*) A space of time, generally understood to mean a year. (A literalism of biblical translation.)

(*a*) *c* 1320 *Cast. Love* 1403 Riht in to helle he eode, Fourti tymen [*v.r.* tymes] þer he wes [*orig.* Quarante ures i demora] Er þat he vp risen ches. (*b*) 1382 Wyclif *Dan.* iv. 13 [16] The herte of wijlde beest be ȝouen to it, and seuen tymes be chaungid vpon hym. *Ibid.* xii. 7. 1382 — *Rev.* xii. 14 She is fed bi tyme, and tymes, and the half of tyme [*v.r.* half a tyme]. **1535** COVERDALE ibid., She is noryszhed for a tyme, two tymes, and halffe a tyme. [So in later versions.] **1827** G. S. FABER *Sacr. Calend. Prophecy* (1844) I. 27 Of such numbers, the three times and a half, the 42 months, and the 1260 days, are mutually equivalent.

**2.** A particular period indicated or characterized in some way. † *That time* (obs.), *at, for the time, for* (*the*) *time being* († *during*), during the period under consideration.

*c* **1000** ÆLFRIC *Hom.* II. 340 Hit is awriten be ðam yfelum timan. *a* **1023** WULFSTAN *Hom.* ii. (Napier) 19 Æfter þisum fæce ȝewurðan sceall swa eȝeslic tima, swa æfre ær næs. *Ibid.* xiii. 81 Wa ðam wifum, þe þonne tymað and on þam earmlican timan heora cild fedað. **1154** *O. E. Chron.* an. 1137 (Laud MS.), On al þis yuele time heold Martin abbot his abbotrice. **1377** LANGL. *P. Pl.* B. x. 72 Sithen þe pestilence tyme. **1474** CAXTON *Chesse* II. iv. (1883) 53 As the Knyghtes shold kepe yᵉ peple in tyme of peas. **1486** *Rec. St. Mary at Hill* 2 That the forsaid tenementes & Rent.. shall hoolly remayn to the parisshens.. for the tyme beyng for euer. *Ibid.* 15 The Mayre or Wardeyn of the Citee of london for the tyme beyng. **1542** UDALL *Erasm. Apoph.* 75 b, He had the best right & title for the tyme duryng, to the shadoe of the Asse. **1680** BUTLER *Rem.* (1759) I. 114 To pass his Times of Recreation In choice and noble Conversation. *a* **1774** TUCKER *Lt. Nat.* (1834) II. 645 Though the time for them be over, yet time itself is not exhausted. ?*a* **1864** (*attributed to Pres. Lincoln*), You can fool all the people some of the time, and some of the people all the time, but you cannot fool all the people all the time. **1875** JOWETT *Plato* (ed. 2) IV. 233 All times of mental progress are times of confusion.

**3.** A period in the existence or history of the world; an age, an era. In later use more indefinite, esp. in *pl.*

*c* **1000** ÆLFRIC *Hom.* II. 190 Þry timan sind on þyssere woruldе: Ante legem, Sub lege, Sub gratia... Se tima is 'ær æ' ȝecweden, þe wæs fram Adam buton æ oð Moysen. *c* **1200** *Trin. Coll. Hom.* 3 [Advent] bitocneð þre time. On þe was bi-fore þe olde laȝe, þe oðer was on þe holde laȝe, and þe þridde was on þe newe laȝe. **1297** R. GLOUC. (Rolls) 192 Fram þe biginning of þe world to þe time þat now is Seuene ages þer habbeþ ibe as seue times iwis. Þe verste age & time was fram our ferste fader adam To noe. **1483** CAXTON *Chron.* (colophon), Here ende the Croniclis of englonde with the frute of timis. **1560** DAUS tr. *Sleidane's Comm.* 471 Tully calleth an history the witnes of tymes, and light of veritie. **1638** WILKINS *New World* xiv. (1707) 125 Rondoletius, to whose Diligence these later Times are much beholden. **1686** W. HOPKINS tr. *Ratramnus* Dissert. iii. (1688) 59 The Southern Parts of France, where the Albigenses and Waldenses.. have abounded in all Times ever since. **1734** tr. *Rollin's Anc. Hist.* (1827) I. 120 Lay aside the prejudice of birth, nations and times. **1861** M. PATTISON *Ess.* (1889) I. 39 With Northern Germany our connexion was, from the earliest times, most intimate. **1884** W. C. SMITH *Kildrostan* 86 It is a folly, man, A superstition of these modern times.

**b.** *Time*(*s past, past time*(*s*; *old, olden*, or *ancient time*(*s*, etc.

*a* **1067** in Kemble *Cod. Dipl.* IV. 202 Swa he on ældum timum ȝelæȝd wæs. **1340** HAMPOLE *Pr. Consc.* 796 He loves men þat in ald tyme has bene. **14..** *Voc.* in Wr.-Wülcker 564/26 *Antiquitus*, yn olde tyme. *c* **1470** HENRY *Wallace* I. 6 It has beyne seyne in thir tymys bywent. **1474** CAXTON *Chesse* III. ii. (1883) 88 In tyme passid the philosophes dyde the same. **1549** *Compl. Scot.* xi. 88 Thai sal intend veir contrar ȝour maister..as there forbears did in alld tymis. **1605** [see OLDEN *a.* 1]. **1610** HOLLAND *Camden's Brit.* (1637) 259 A towne in ancient time of great fame. *Ibid.*, It was fortified in times past with a castle. **1611** COTGR. s. v. *Argent*, In good old times when men were loath to publish their owne goodnesse. **1784** COWPER *Task* VI. 715 Encomium in old time was poet's work. **1845** M. PATTISON *Ess.* (1889) I. 11 The memory of the great and the saintly of ancient time.

**c.** *Time*(*s to come*, († *time coming*), *times to be* (arch.), future time; *esp.* future ages, the future.

*c* **1340** HAMPOLE *Prose Tr.* i. 4 Þay sall joye nowe..and in tym to come. **1376** in *Eng. Gilds* (1870) 53 Hopyng in tyme comyng to haue ben encresyd. *c* **1440** *Alphabet of Tales* 107 Þe paynys þat er ordand..for syn in tyme to com. **1578** *Reg. Privy Council Scot.* III. 36 That na pensionis of victuall be gevin in tyme cuming furth of the said superplus. **1891** LD. COLERIDGE in *Law Times Rep.* LXV. 581/1 It may become necessary to decide this point in time to come; it is not now.

**d.** *The time* (*the times*): the age now or then present. Cf. *the day, the hour, the moment.*

[**1588** SHAKS. *L. L. L.* v. ii. 791 Rated them..As bumbast and as lining to the time.] **1596** — *Merch. V.* II. ix. 48 How much honor Pickt from the chaffe and ruine of the times, To be new varnisht. ? **1640** *New Serm. of Newest Fashion* (1877) 45 Hee is the onelie man of the time, hee is the onelie able man. *a* **1704** T. BROWN *Two Oxf. Scholars* Wks. 1730 I. 3 Cannot I..sigh for the Iniquities of the Times? **1850** TENNYSON *In Mem.* cvi. 18 Ring out the want, the care, the sin, The faithless coldness of the times. **1869** FREEMAN *Norm. Conq.* III. xi. 55 An act which ran counter to the religious feelings of the time.

**4.** With possessive or *of*: The period contemporary with the life, occupancy, or activity of some one; (his) age, era, or generation. Often *pl.* = DAY *sb.* 14.

**962–3** *Laws Edgar* Suppl. B. *Leges sæculares* c. 2, On minum timan, swa..on mines fæder. **1154** *O. E. Chron.* an. 1135 (Laud MS.), On þis kinges time wes al unfrið & yfel. *c* **1200** ORMIN 14429 Fra þatt tatt Adam shapenn was Anan till Nowess time. *a* **1300** *Cursor M.* 10 Non in his tim was like. *c* **1380** WYCLIF *Serm.* Sel. Wks. I. 27 Phariseis..weren religiouse in Cristis tyme. **1484** CAXTON *Fables of Poge* v, Poge of Florence recyteth how in his tyme one named Hugh prynce of the medycyns sawe a catte whiche had two hedes. **1552** *Bk. Com. Prayer, Ordin.* Pref., From the Apostles tyme there hathe bene these orders of Ministers. **1625** BACON *Ess., Riches* (Arb.) 235 A Nobleman..that had the greatest Audits, of any Man in my Time. **1712** STEELE *Spect.* No. 497 ¶ 2 In the time of Don Sebastian of Portugal. **1814** WORDSW. *White Doe* I. 42 In great Eliza's golden time. **1832** TENNYSON *Dream Fair Women* ii, The spacious times of great Elizabeth. **1865** DICKENS *Mut. Fr.* I. i, In these times of ours.

**5.** A period considered with reference to its prevailing conditions; the general state of affairs at a particular period. Chiefly *pl.*

Often in colloq. phrases, as *as times go* (= as things go in these times), *behind the times* (= behind the modes or methods of these times).

**1484** CAXTON *Fables of Æsop* II. viii, Men say comynly that after that the tyme goth, so must folke go. **1602** SHAKS. *Ham.* I. v. 188 The time is out of ioynt. **1712** STEELE *Spect.* No. 298 ¶ 3 Persons, of tolerable Figure too as Times go. **1757** FRANKLIN *Ess.* Wks. 1840 II. 96 We may make these times better, if we bestir ourselves. **1837** J. H. NEWMAN *Par. Serm.* (ed. 2) III. xii. 178 When times grew cold and unbelieving. **1881** FROUDE *Short Stud.* IV. II. i. 163 How times had changed in the last forty years. *Mod.* We live in perilous times.

**b.** *pl.* Used as the name of a newspaper.

**1788** (*title*) The Times. **1801** G. ROSE *Diaries* (1860) I. 439, I found here the *Times* of Saturday. **1829** (*title*) South Wales Times. **1854** HAWTHORNE *Eng. Note-Bks.* (1883) I. 477 Every Englishman runs to 'The Times' with his little grievance. *Mod.* There is an obituary notice in the Oxford Times.

**6.** A period considered with reference to one's personal experience; hence, an experience of a specified nature lasting some time; esp. in (*to have*) *a* (*good, bad*, etc.) *time* (*of it*); *to make a time*, i.e. a demonstration, fuss (*U. S. colloq.*).

*To have a good time* (= a time of enjoyment) was common in Eng. from *c* 1520 to *c* 1688; it was app. retained in America, whence readopted in Britain in 19th c. (See also GOOD *a.* 10 d.) So *to have the time of one's life*, i.e. the best one has ever had.

*a* **1529** SKELTON *Bk.* 3 *Foles* Wks. 1843 I. 200 For to haue good tyme and to lyue meryly. **1647** TRAPP *Comm. Ep.* 59 They would have a fine time of it. *Ibid.* 199 Those poor.. souls..have an ill time of it. **1666** PEPYS *Diary* 7 Mar., I went and had as good a time as heart could wish. **1673** *S'too him Bayes* 26 It seems his servants had a good time on't. **1709** MRS. MANLEY *Secret Mem.* (1736) I. 97 Berintha ..thought she should have a melancholy Time of it. **1836** MRS. STOWE in *Life* (1889) 81, I wish I were a man in your place—if I wouldn't have a grand time! **1856** OLMSTED *Slave States* 82, I was having a very good time with her, when her father came in and told her she was 'troubling the gentleman'. **1886** P. S. ROBINSON *Valley Teet. Trees* iii, We'll have a high old time together. **1902** ELIZ. L. BANKS *Newspaper Girl* i, Think of that when you are tempted to have a good time instead of studying hard.

**7.** Period of duration; prescribed or allotted term. **a.** Period of existence or action; period of one's life, life-time.

*c* **1000** ÆLFRIC *Hom.* I. 4 His tima ne bið na langsum; forþan þe Godes grama hine forded. *c* **1200** *Vices & Virt.* 39 Behoueþ to charite on alle ðines liues time. *c* **1400** *Brut* cxxxv. 142 Þo seisede Kyng Henry al Normandye into his hand, & helde hit al his lifes tyme. **1535** COVERDALE *Ps.* cii[i]. 15 That a man in his tyme is but as is grasse. **1549** *Compl. Scot.* i. 21 Of this sort euere thyng hes ane tyme. **1577** in *Exch. Rolls Scotl.* (1899) XX. 373 In the resyngnatioun, to hymself [and] his wyf, for their tym. **1600** SHAKS. *A. Y. L.* II. vii. 142 One man in his time playes many parts. **1657** THORNLEY tr. *Longus' Daphnis & Chloe* 55, I am older then Saturn, and the whole time of this Universe. **1833** CARLYLE *Ess., Cagliostro* ii, The foul sluggard's comfort: 'It will last my time.'—It will last thy time, thy worthless sham of an existence.

**b.** *spec.* (*a*) The period of gestation. (*b*) The menstrual period; *transf.* menstruation. (*c*) (One's) term of apprenticeship. (*d*) The duration of a term of imprisonment; usually in phrase *to do time* (slang). (*e*) An unexpired period of compulsory service (*U. S.*). (*f*) The prescribed duration of the interval between two rounds in boxing, or of a round or game in athletics, football, etc., or the moment at which this begins or ends; also *ellipt.* as the signal to begin or end a bout, as in *to call time.* (*g*) The periodic time of a heavenly body: see PERIODIC *a.* 1.

(*a*) *c* **1000** ÆLFRIC *Hom.* I. 30 Hire tima wæs ȝefylled, ðæt heo cennan sceolde. **1577** B. GOOGE *Heresbach's Husb.* III. (1586) 127 A cowe and a quene haue both one time. **1809** MALKIN *Gil Blas* XI. i. (Rtldg.) 392 Beatrice's time was up first: she was safely delivered of a daughter. (*b*) **1564–78** BULLEYN *Dial. agst. Pest.* (1888) 41 Certaine people maie not bleede, as women whiche haue their times aboundauntlie. **1704** *Collect. Voy.* (Churchill) III. 582/1 Women, who shall not be subject to the monthly times. **1889** [see MONTHLY *a.* 1 b]. (*c*) *c* **1645** HOWELL *Lett.* (1650) I. 227 To be both of one trade, because when they are out of their time they may join stocks together. **1718** *Free-thinker* No. 21 ¶ 1 The..Indiscretion of Apprentices Marrying Servant-Wenches, before their Time is expired. **1808** BYRON *Eng. Bards* 63 A man must serve his time to every trade, Save censure—critics all are ready made. (*d*) **1865** [see Do *v.* 11 i]. **1888** 'R. BOLDREWOOD' *Robbery under Arms* xli, People can't be expected to associate with men that have 'done time'. **1904** GRIFFITHS 50 *Years Publ. Service* xiii. 185 He did his 'time' without protest. (*e*) **1769** *Boston Gaz.* (U.S.) 20 Nov. (Thornton *Amer. Gloss.*), To be sold for five Years, The Time of a hearty young Man, who is a good Sailor. **1843** *Missouri Reporter* (U.S.) 28 Jan. (ibid.), I have for sale a very likely yellow woman, about 24 years of age...She has between five and six years to serve. The balance of her time will be sold very low. (*f*) **1812** *Sporting Mag.* XXXIX. 102 George was the first to call 'time'. **1821** EGAN *Boxiana* (1829) III. 571 When time was called, the men were to be immediately brought up to the scratch. **1832** MARRYAT *N. Forster* xlvii, It's a finisher—can't come to time. **1840** DICKENS *Barn. Rudge* xxii, In prize-fighting phraseology, [he] always came up to time with a cheerful countenance. **1857** HUGHES *Tom Brown* i, Three whiffs of which would knock any one else out of time [see KNOCK *v.* 12 d].

**8.** The length of time sufficient, necessary, or desired for some purpose; also, time available for employment; leisure or spare time.

*c* **1220** *Bestiary* 256 Ðus ȝe tileð ðar wiles ȝe time haueð. *c* **1470** HENRY *Wallace* VIII. 502 No teyme we haiff off segyng now to bid. **1585** T. WASHINGTON tr. *Nicholay's Voy.* I. xv. 16 b, There was yet time inough to pleasure them. **1689** *Tryal Bps.* 34 These Gentlemen have had time enough to have prepared Precedents. **1723** *Pres. St. Russia* II. 325 In case the Russian Troops should get time of rallying. **1743** BULKELEY & CUMMINS *Voy. S. Seas* 88 He must have Time to consider of it. **1796** MME. D'ARBLAY *Camilla* II. 23 Pray take your own time. I am not in any haste. **1833** T. HOOK *Parson's Dau.* III. ii, Being pressed greatly for time, in order to get back to London. **1865** RUSKIN *Sesame* ii. § 62, I could multiply witness upon witness..if I had time.

**b.** The (shortest) period in which a given course of action is completed.

**1894** *Times* 19 Nov. 7/3 Various new tandem times were made by the winners. **1899** F. V. KIRBY *Sport E. C. Africa* v. 61 One of them [the boys] came in sight, making excellent time towards the nearest tree, with the wounded cow in close pursuit. **1908** *Daily Chron.* 15 Jan. 7/5 The times ..did not compare with those established by the amateurs the day before. Still some wonderful times were put up.

**9.** *spec.* The amount of time worked under a specific contract; hence, in workmen's speech, pay equivalent to the period worked; also an account or certificate showing the days, hours, etc. worked, and wages due: usually called *back time.*

**1795** NELSON in Nicolas *Disp.* (1845) II. 116 This time as Mid is absolutely necessary as a part of the long six years. You had better get out his Time from the Navy Office. **1888** *Times* 29 Sept. 6/6 The men asked to be paid [for overtime] at the rate of time and a half, but the Masters refused a greater rate than time and a quarter. **1908** *Somerset Mag.* Apr. 564 Tim added 'And I'd like my time'. Time, in the cattle idiom, meant back pay up to date. *Mod.* If you can't move a bit quicker, I'll send you to get your back time.

**10.** *Anc. Prosody.* A unit or group of units in metrical measurement. Also *transf.* in *Mus.*

A *single, primary*, or *least time* is the duration of utterance of a short syllable; = MORA[1] 3; a *double* or *compound time* is composed of two or more single times.

[*c* **1050** *Byrhtferth's Handboc* in *Anglia* VIII. 314 Ðæt riht meter vers sceal habban feower and twentiȝ timan. *Ibid.*, Dactilus stent on anum langum timan and twam sceortum and spondeus stent of feowrum langum.] **1589** PUTTENHAM *Eng. Poesie* II. xii. (Arb.) 132 A new inuention of feete and times. **1686** *New Method to Learn to Sing* 50 In this Example, you have two Staves of Lines; in the upper are Semibreves, each of which is a Time, and fills up a Bar. **1727–41** CHAMBERS *Cycl.* s. v., Some call each half of the measure in common time, a time. **1749** J. MASON *Numbers in Poet. Comp.* 8 The Measure of a single Time is the Space in which we commonly pronounce any of the Liquids or Consonants, preceded by a Vowel, e.g. *an, of, it, in.* **1832** *Encycl. Amer.* XI. 591 The short syllable..is considered as the original unit for the measure of time in the rhythm, and is called a *time*, or *mora.*

**11.** *Mil.* The rate of marching, calculated on the number of paces taken per minute. *Double time, slow time*: see the adjs.; see also QUICK TIME.

**1802–1876** [see QUICK TIME]. **1853** STOCQUELER *Milit. Encycl.* s. v. *Pace*, In quick time, 108 paces, or 270 feet, are taken in a minute; and in slow time, seventy-five paces, or 187 feet. In double time, 150 paces of thirty-six inches, making 450 [feet] in a minute. **1859** *Field Exerc. Infantry* 21 The time having been given on a drum, on the word March, the squad will move off.

**12.** *Music.* **a.** † The duration of the breve in relation to the semibreve; cf. MOOD *sb.*[2] 3 a, PROLATION 2 (*obs.*); hence, the rhythm or measure of a piece of music, now marked by division of the music into bars, and usually denoted by a fraction expressing the number of aliquot parts of a semibreve in each bar (*time-signature*). *To beat time*: see BEAT *v.*[1] 32. *In time, out of time*, in or out of correct rhythm. † *Perfect, imperfect time*: see PERFECT *a.* 10, IMPERFECT *a.* 7.

**1531** ELYOT *Gov.* I. xxi, The associatinge of man and woman in daunsing, they bothe obseruinge one nombre and tyme in their meuynges. **1609** C. BUTLER *Fem. Mon.* v. (1623) K iij, Now and then she beginneth in duple time some two or three Semibriefes. **1706** A. BEDFORD *Temple Mus.* iii. 62 'Tis..in the same Time and Tune. **1710** ADDISON *Tatler* No. 153 ¶ 14 To play out of Time. **1854** HELMORE *Pract. Lect. Church Music* 6 It is sometimes said..that in Plain Song 'there is no time'. **1884** ROCKSTRO in Grove *Dict. Mus.* IV. 117/2 In modern Music, the word Time is applied to rhythmic combinations of all kinds, mostly indicated by fractions (¾ etc.) referring to the aliquot parts of a Semibreve—the norm by which the duration of all other notes is and always has been regulated. **1893** STEVENSON *Catriona* i. 4 A..brisk tramp of feet in time and clash of steel.

**b.** The rate at which a piece is performed; the tempo; hence, the characteristic tempo, rhythm, form, and style of a particular class of compositions (usually in combination, as *dance-time, march-time, waltz-time*).

[**1446** LYDG. *Two Nightingale Poems* i. 80 But, doun descendyng, she said in hasti tyme: 'My lyfe be kynde endure shall not longe'. **1602** MIDDLETON *Blurt* III. i. E j, To keep quick time unto the owl.] **1887** BARING-GOULD

*Caverocks* xiii, Little feet beat the dance time on the.. floor. **1903** *Critic* XLIII. 361/1 Rag-time music, which interprets that divine art only for vulgar heels and toes. *Mod.* A movement in slow time.

**c.** The time-value or duration of a note. (Not in technical use.)

**1727–41** CHAMBERS *Cycl.* s. v., Where the time or duration of the notes is equal, the differences of tune alone are capable to entertain us. **1776** BURNEY *Hist. Mus.* (1789) I. vi. 63 The most common application of this term [Rhythm] has been to express the Time or duration of many sounds heard in succession.

**II.** = Time when: a point of time; a space of time treated without reference to its duration.

The 'point' may be an instant (as the time when a star crosses the meridian), or it may have some duration (as the time for sowing), but the question of its length is not considered, only the question *when* it occurs (i. e. *where it is situated* in the period), and its distinctive qualification.

**13.** A point in the course of time or of a period: = TIDE *sb.* 3; spec. in early ME., the hour of the day; = OE. *tīd*: see TIDE *sb.* 4. In mod.Eng. *What is the time?* i. e. the hour and minute as shown by the clock. *What time, at what time*, = when, (at) the time that: see WHAT.

*c* **1200** ORMIN 12745 Þatt time..Wass rihht swa summ itt off þatt daȝȝ þe tende time wære. *a* **1225** *St. Marher.* 8 As þah hit were þe seoueðe time of þe dei. *c* **1391** CHAUCER *Astrol.* II. § 3 To knowe..euery tyme of the nyht by the sterres fixe. **1764** GRAY *Candidate* 10 At our time of life 'twould be silly, my dear. **1823** J. BADCOCK *Dom. Amusem.* 162 By the light you shall catch a few words in the book, or the time on the watch. **1834** *Nat. Philos.* III. *Astron.* i. 35/1 (Usef. Knowl. Soc.) The difference between the actual time of the sun's being on the meridian and the beginning of the mean solar day. **1908** R. BAGOT *A. Cuthbert* viii, Find out what time the marchesa intends to breakfast.

**b.** A point or fixed part of the year, a season, as in *time of year*; in comb. in *spring-time, summer-time, autumn-time, winter-time*; also *term-time, vacation-time, holiday-time*, etc.; also, of a day, as *time of day, time of night, day-time, night-time, morning-time, evening-time*; also *dinner-time, bed-time*, etc.; also, a point in the moon's age.

*c* **1000** ÆLFRIC *Num.* xiii. 21 Hit wæs ða se tima ðæt winberian ripodon. *c* **1050** *Byrhtferth's Handboc* in *Anglia* VIII. 312 Feower timan beoþ...Uer ys lengten tima,..se oðer tima hatte æstas..Se þridda tima ys autumnus on lyden ȝecweden. *c* **1175** *Lamb. Hom.* 119 Vre drihtnes halie passiun..is nu icumen in,..þe ure drihten þolede for us on þisse timan. **1398** TREVISA *Barth. De P. R.* IX. iii. (Bodl. MS.), Þe ȝere of þe sonne..conteyneþ foure tymes, winter, springingtyme, somer, and harueste. *c* **1400** tr. *Secreta Secret., Gov. Lordsh.* 74 Heruest bygynnes..and lastys lxxxviij dayes...In þis tyme ys also þe day and þe nyght euyne. *a* **1529** SKELTON *On Tyme* 23 The rotys tak theyr sap in tyme of vere. **1566** BLUNDEVIL *Horsemanship* IV. xxxii (1580) 16 The horse that hath this disease, is blind at certaine times of the Moone. **1825** T. HOOK *Sayings* Ser. II. *Passion & Princ.* ix. III. 153 Fleeting showers of rain, unseasonable at the time of year.

†**c.** A season or part of the year considered with reference to the weather experienced; weather (of some kind). *Obs. rare.* (Cf. F. *temps* in similar sense.)

*c* **1400** tr. *Secreta Secret., Gov. Lordsh.* 93 Þe right of hym þat reygnyth ys more profitable to subgitz þan plente of good tyme. **1422** *Ibid., Priv. Priv.* 220 The colerike by kynde..sholde haue a stomake good y-nowe, namely in colde tyme.

**14.** A point in duration marking or marked by some event or condition; a point of time at which something happens, an occasion. † *On a time*, on one occasion, once. *At no time*, on no occasion.

*c* **893** K. ÆLFRED *Oros.* IV. v. § 5 Ymbe ðone timan þe þiss wæs. *c* **1000** ÆLFRIC *Hom.* I. 78 Herodes..ȝeornlice hi befran to hwilces timan se steorra him ærst ætеowode. *a* **1050** *O. E. Chron.* an. 1009 (Laud MS.) On þisum ilcan timan oððe litle ær þet [etc.]. *c* **1205** LAY. 2582 Seoððen him a time com mid teonen he wes i-funden. *c* **1275** *Ibid.*, Suþþe him com a time þat he to wode wende. *a* **1225** *Leg. Kath.* 2 Constantin & Maxence weren, on ane time..hehest in Rome. **13..** *Gaw. & Gr. Knt.* 2243 At þis tyme twelmonyth þou toke þat þe falled. *c* **1386** CHAUCER *Frankl. T.* 830 Aurelius.. Curseth the tyme þat euere he was born. **1470–85** MALORY *Arthur* II. i. 75 Soo it befelle on a tyme whanne kyng Arthur was at London. **1538** STARKEY *Let.* in *England* p. lxxiii, Long and much at sundry tymis. **1590** SIR J. SMYTH *Disc. Weapons* 36 From that time forward he would hold the Bowe to be the onelie weapon of the world. **1766** GOLDSM. *Vic. W.* xii, By this time the unfortunate Moses was undeceived. **1837** J. H. NEWMAN *Par. Serm.* (ed. 3) I. vii. 99 Surely man is at all times the same being. **1845** M. PATTISON *Ess.* (1889) I. 27 This..trick escaped detection at the time. **1873** BLACK *Pr. Thule* xxv, It will be nearly two by the time you get down.

**15.** The appointed, due, or proper time.

*c* **897** K. ÆLFRED *Gregory's Past. C.* lxiii. 459 Nu us is tima ðæt we onwæcnen of slæpe. *c* **1000** ÆLFRIC *Colloq.* in Wr.-Wülcker 102/1 Hwænne wylle ȝe syngan?..Þonne hyt tima byþ [*Quando tempus erit*]. **1154** *O. E. Chron.* an. 1011, Mann nolde him to timan [*MS. C.* atiman] gafol bedan. *c* **1175** *Lamb. Hom.* 103 Þeo deð þet mon et er timan and drinceð. **13..** *Cursor M.* 11814 (Cott.) Nu neghes tim to tak his lai. *c* **1400** *26 Pol. Poems* xxv. 539 Tyme ys that men now for me pray, For *Parce michi, domine!* *c* **1412** HOCCLEVE *De Reg. Princ.* 1274 Sires, it is tyme þat we hennes hye. *c* **1489** CAXTON *Blanchardyn* xxiii. 74 It was tyme to go to bed. *a* **1586** SIDNEY *Ps.* XII. i, Lord, helpe, it is hyghe tyme for me to call. **1741–2** GRAY *Agrippina* 158 'Tis time to go, the sun is high advanc'd. **1809** MALKIN *Gil Blas* VIII. i, My business consisted in..dunning the farmers, and keeping them to time in their payments. **1872** *Routledge's Ev. Boy's Ann.* 349/1 See that you are up to time.

**b.** Qualified by poss. pron., as *his, her, its*; often ellipt. for *time of death, of childbirth*, etc.; *before* (*his*, etc.) *time*, prematurely.

*c* **1000** *Ags. Gosp.* Matt. xxvi. 18 Min tima is ȝe-hende. — John v. 4 Drihtenes engel com to his timan [*Hatton* to hys tyme] on þone mere & þæt wæter wæs astyred. **1388** WYCLIF *Prov.* xxv. 11 A goldun pomel in beddis of siluer is he, that spekith a word in his [= its] time. *c* **1440** *Alphab. Tales* 11 Sho wex grete & drew nere hur tyme. **1560** DAUS tr. *Sleidane's Comm.* 451 b, Yᵉ Quene..was with childe, and nere her time. **1689** HICKERINGILL *Ceremony-monger* 126 A young Lady..Excommunicated for breaking her Leg or coming before her time. **1700** DRYDEN *Sigism. & Guiscard.* 26 In the prime Of youth, her lord expired before his time. **1799** WORDSW. *Lucy Gray* viii, The storm came on before its time. **1853** C. BRONTË *Villette* 180 'Ten minutes behind his time', said she. **1890** *Field* 31 May 799/3 The Banksia roses..are bent on coming out before their time.

**16.** A or the favourable, convenient, or fitting point of time for doing something; the right moment or occasion; opportunity. (Often with *his, her*, etc.)

*c* **897** K. ÆLFRED *Gregory's Past. C.* xxxiii. 220 Se wisa hilt his spræce & bitt timan. **1297** R. GLOUC. (Rolls) 7633 Huld hem euere in Scotlond, & poer to hem nome, To worri vpe king willam, wanne god time come. **1382** WYCLIF *Eccles.* iii. 4 Time of weping, and time of laȝhing [**1388** Tyme to wepe, and tyme to leiȝe]. *c* **1386** CHAUCER *Melib.* ¶ 14 Whan she saugh hir tyme, she seyde hym in this wise: 'Allas! my lord'. *a* **1533** LD. BERNERS *Huon* lxvii. 230 When he sawe his tyme, he cryed his worde & token. **1590** NASHE *Pasquil's Apol.* I. Wks. (Grosart) I. 233 There is a time for speech, and a time for silence. *c* **1610** BODLEY in *Reliq.* (1703) 108 A Clock and a Bell will be needful for the Library..: but every thing must have his time. **1709** STEELE *Tatler* No. 36 ¶ 4 When Stocks are lowest, it is the Time to buy. *a* **1722** FOUNTAINHALL *Decis.* (1759) I. 9 They must wait their tour, since the devil bides his time. **1849** MACAULAY *Hist. Eng.* iv. I. 512 An adversary of no common prowess was watching his time. *Mod.* Now's your time!

**17.** Any one of the occasions on which something is done or happens; each occasion of a recurring action. Often qualified by a numeral. (= OE. *sīð*: see SITHE *sb.*[1] 4–5.)

For †*one time*, †*two times* have been substituted *once, twice*. *At a time*, at one time, at once, simultaneously.

*c* **1300** *St. Julian* 108 (Ashm. MS.) Let me go at þis one tyme. I ne schal neuereft derie þe. *c* **1380** WYCLIF *Sel. Wks.* III. 350 How þat men shulde snybbe þer breþeren bi þre tymes. *c* **1400** *Destr. Troy* 8272 The next tym þou noyes me, þou neghis to þe fer. **1454** *Rolls of Parlt.* V. 241/1 At too tymes hath be made requestes to the seid Lieutenaunt. **1526** *Pilgr. Perf.* (W. de W. 1531) 300 b, How he wolde deny the thre tymes that nyght. **1560** DAUS tr. *Sleidane's Comm.* 441 b, The third way..hath bene diuers times assaied. **1611** BIBLE *John* xxi. 16 He saith to him againe the second time, Simon Sonne of Ionas, louest thou me? **1660** R. ELLSWORTH in *Extr. S. P. rel. Friends* II. (1911) 122 Heere they..haue their Meeteings at all Seasons ..sometymes about 1000 or 1200 att a tyme. **1712** STEELE *Spect.* No. 422 ¶ 1 An utter Aversion to speaking to more than one Man at a time. **1829** LANDOR *Imag. Conv., Villèle & Corbière* I. 123 He did it fifty times, at the very least. **1876** TREVELYAN *Macaulay* II. ix. 125 The publishers..are still pouring forth reprints by many thousands at a time.

**b.** *Agric.* (See quots.) *dial.*

**1813** R. KERR *Agric. Surv. Berw.* 198 The completest harrowing is called a double double time; in which the harrow goes four times successively over the same range. **1857** *N. & Q.* 2nd Ser. IV. 80/1 'A time'..in some parts of Scotland is the act of once furrowing between two ploughings. **1894** *Northumbld. Gloss.*, *Time*, the journey once across a field in agriculture. *Time-aboot*, a double journey in field work, extending from heedrig to heedrig and back again.

**18.** *Many a time*, † *many time, many times*, elliptically *times*, also *times and often, times without number, many a time and oft* (*often*): on many occasions, in many instances; often, frequently.

*c* **1250** *Kent. Serm.* in *O. E. Misc.* 30 Ure lord god almichti..habbeþ mani-time maked of watere wyn gostliche. **1375** BARBOUR *Bruce* I. 336 That may mony tyme awaill. *c* **1400** *Rom. Rose* 6974, I am gladly executour And many tymes a procuratour. **1535** COVERDALE *Ps.* lxxvii. 38 Many a tyme turned he his wrath awaye. **1560** INGELEND *Disob. Child* D ij b, Many a tyme and oft, I am fayne To playe the Priest, Clarke, and all. **1590** SIR J. SMYTH *Disc. Weapons* Ded. 6 Which I haue heard manie, and manie times publikelie reported by manie valiant Gentlemen. **1622** R. HAWKINS *Voy. S. Sea* (Hakl. Soc.) 115 Which..many time is cause of dissention. **1701** DE FOE *True-born Eng.* II. 312 Englishmen have done it many a time. **1760–72** H. BROOKE *Fool of Qual.* (1809) IV. 51 Many a time and oft.. you carried me in your arms. **1808** ELEANOR SLEATH *Bristol Heiress* III. 94 The fine handsome young officer, who has been here times and often. **18..** G. MEREDITH *Juggling Jerry* ii, We've travelled times to this old common. **1892** *Law Times* XCII. 147/1 Times without number the courts in bankruptcy have been called upon to decide the question. **1899** TRINE *In Tune with Infinite* (1903) 186 Those who take great pride in speaking of their own practicality are many times the least practical.

**19.** Preceded by a cardinal numeral and followed by a number or expression of quantity: used to express the multiplication of the number, etc.

*c* **1380** WYCLIF *Sel. Wks.* II. 309 As foure tymes sixe maken þis noumbre. *c* **1425** *Crafte Nombrynge* 2 Ten tymes twene is twenty. *Ibid.* 4 If it stonde in the secunde place of þe rewle, he betokens ten tymes hym selfe, as þis figure 2 here. *c* **1440** *Jacob's Well* 45 Thre tymes ten is thretty. **1726** SWIFT *Gulliver* II. iii, An animal of ten times my strength. **1798** COLERIDGE *Anc. Mar.* III. xvi, Four times fifty living men. **1868** G. DUFF *Pol. Surv.* 48 His territories in Asia.. are more than twenty-one times the size of Scotland.

**b.** Also followed by an adj. or adv. in the comparative degree, or in the positive by *as* (formerly *so*) with an adj. or adv., expressing comparison.

**1551** CROWLEY *Pleas. & Pain* 229 This might you reade, and ten tymes more In the Bible. *c* **1567** STOW in *Surv.* (1908) I. p. li, Fabyan..was a very nowghty cronycle, and Copin..was x. tymes worse. **1583** STUBBES *Anat. Abus.* II. (1882) 45 They shall pay tenne times so much as it is worth. **1644** NYE *Gunnery* I. 5 Which composition I will call 6··1··1, meaning six times so much Peter [nitre], as one time Sulpher, and one time Cole. **1712** ADDISON *Spect.* No. 415 ¶ 8 A Gothick Cathedral tho' it be five times larger than the other. **1876** GLADSTONE *Glean.* (1879) II. 289 Men who had ten or twenty times less to remember. *Mod.* We have five times as many as we can use.

†**20.** *Gram.* = TENSE *sb.* 2. *Obs.*

**1530** PALSGR. Introd. 32 In these syxe modes be dyvers tymes. *Ibid.* 84 Tenses or tymes they have in every of these modes. *c* **1620** A. HUME *Brit. Tongue* (1865) 31 Tyme is an affection of the verb noating the differences of tyme, and is either present, past, or to cum.

**21.** *Fencing.* See quots., and cf. *time-attack, time-thrust* in 52.

**1727–41** CHAMBERS *Cycl.* s. v., Time in fencing.—There are three kinds of time; that of the sword, that of the foot, and that of the whole body. All the times that are perceived out of their measure, are only to be considered as appeals, or feints, to deceive and amuse the enemy. **1753** *Ibid., Supp.* s. v. *Binding*, Binding is a method of pursuit more safe and certain..than taking of time. **1809** ROLAND *Fencing* vii. § 1 To take the time, is making your thrust by a judicious discernment on the motion of your adversary.

**22.** *Manège.* (= F. *temps*.) Applied to each completed motion or action.

**1753** CHAMBERS *Cycl. Supp.* s. v., Time, in the manege, is sometimes taken for the motion of a horse, that observes measure and justness in performing a manege. In the manege of a step and a leap, the horse makes by turns a corvet between two caprioles; and in that case the corvet is one Time that prepares the horse for the caprioles. *Ibid.*, A good horseman disposes his horse for the effects of the heel, by beginning with one Time of the legs, and never runs precipitately upon his Times.

**23.** *pl.* Originally (in sense 15), The fixed hours of the day at which an omnibus started from its various stations; hence, the established business enterprise of running an omnibus on a given route at such times, and the 'good-will' thus created by the owners of public service vehicles over particular routes, as a recognized vendible asset.

**1863** E. YATES *Business of Pleasure* (1865) I. 40 They [the London General Omnibus Company] possessed themselves of the 'times' of all the important routes in London and the suburbs. These 'times' are, in fact, the good will of the roads, and were considered so valuable, that in some cases as much as from £200 to £250 were given for the 'times' of one omnibus. **1906** *Westm. Gaz.* 15 May 2/3 Emphasis [is] laid in one of the various motor-'bus prospectuses, just now ..upon the value of the 'times' owned by each member of the associated companies. *Ibid.*, The 'times', which are a special privilege, religiously guarded by the omnibus fraternity,.. were also made over as a part of the bargain.

**III.** In generalized sense.

**24.** Indefinite continuous duration regarded as that in which the sequence of events takes place.

**a.** Attempts to define or explain.

**1398** TREVISA *Barth. De P. R.* IX. ii. (Bodl. MS.), Tyme is mesure of chaungeable þinges, as Aristotel seith. **1597** HOOKER *Eccl. Pol.* v. lxix. § 2 Now as Nature bringeth forth Time with Motion, so wee by Motion haue learned how to diuide Time, and by the smaller parts of Time, both to measure the greater, and to know how long all things else indure. *Ibid.*, Some haue defined time to be the measure of the motion of heauen. **1690** LOCKE *Hum. Und.* II. xiv. § 17 This Consideration of Duration, as set out by certain Periods, and marked by certain Measures or Epochs, is that, I think, which most properly we call Time. **1854** CALDERWOOD *Philos. Infinite* v. 88 Add event to event, still Time is recognised as stretching forth, and still there is room for more. **1862** SPENCER *First Princ.* II. iii. § 47 (1875) 163 The abstract of all sequence is Time.

**b.** Examples of this use of the word.

**1480** *Robt. Devyll* 121 in Hazl. *E. P. P.* I. 224 The tyme drewe so, that nyne monethes was past. **1539** TAVERNER *Erasm. Prov.* (1552) 38 There is no displeasure so greate, no hatred so impotent, no sorow so immoderate, but tyme aswageth it. **1638** JUNIUS *Paint. Ancients* 29 In processe of time. **1651** HOBBES *Leviath.* II. xxx. 176 Time, and Industry, produce every day new Knowledge. **1743** BLAIR *Grave* 479 Think we, or think we not, Time hurries on With a resistless, unremitting Stream. **1748** B. FRANKLIN *Adv. Yng. Tradesman* Wks. 1799 II. 34 Remember that time is money. **1794** MRS. RADCLIFFE *Myst. Udolpho* xxx, The few gray locks which time had spared on his temples. **1821** BYRON *Cain* III. i, The mind then hath capacity of time, And measures it by that which it beholds, Pleasing or painful. **1908** *Programme of Modernism* 169 We have cast the seed in the furrow, Time will do the rest.

**25.** Personified as an aged man, bald, but having a forelock, and carrying a scythe and an hour-glass. Also called *Father Time*. *To take Time by the forelock* († *by the top*), to seize one's opportunity, to act promptly: see also FORELOCK *sb.*[2] 2.

**1509** HAWES *Past. Pleas.* XLIV. (1555) C iv, Sodainly came Time in breuiacion Whose similitude, I shall anone expresse Aged he was, with a bearde doubtles Of swalowes feaders. **1590** SHAKS. *Com. Err.* II. ii. 71 The plaine bald pate of Father time himselfe. **1606** — *Tr. & Cr.* III. iii. 145 Time hath, my Lord, a wallet at his backe, Wherein he puts almes for obliuion. **1594** [see FORELOCK *sb.*[2] 2]. [**1711** ADDISON *Spect.* No. 63 ¶ 4 Equipped (like the figure of Time) with an Hour-glass in one Hand, and a Scythe in the other.] **1820** W. IRVING *Sketch Bk.* II. 24 Time is ever silently turning over his pages. **18..** MARSDEN *What is Time?* 32, I ask'd old Father Time himself at last; But in a moment he flew swiftly past!

**26.** In restricted sense, Duration conceived as beginning and ending with the present life or material universe; finite duration as distinct from eternity.

**1388** WYCLIF *Rev.* x. 6 And the aungel..lifte vp his hond ..and swoor bi hym that lyueth in to worldis of worldis.. that time schal no more be [**1526** TINDALE, that there shulde be no lenger tyme; **1557** *Geneva*, that tyme should be no more; **1611**, that there should be time no longer]. **1573** TUSSER *Husb.* (1878) 65 For time is it selfe but a time for a time, Forgotten ful soone, as the tune of a chime. **1635** SWAN *Spec. M.* i. § 3 (1643) 15 All time compared with eternitie is but short time, yea indeed as no time. **1650** CRASHAW *Death Herrys* 36 Weak time shall be pour'd out Into eternity. **1745** *Scotch Transl. & Paraphr.* xxxv. ix, He lov'd us from the first of Time, And loves us to the last. *a* **1758** RAMSAY *Some of Contents of Evergreen* xi, A monument..Quhilk sall endure quhyle tymis telled out be days. **1803** HEBER *Palestine*, His voice amid the thunder's roar, His dreadful voice, that time should be no more. **1827** POLLOK *Course T.* x, Time gone, the righteous saved, the wicked damned, And God's eternal government approved. **1836** H. ROGERS *J. Howe* i. (1863) 8 Time, with him, derived all its importance from a reference to eternity. *Mod.* Entirely occupied with things of time and sense.

**27.** A system of measuring or reckoning the passage of time.

**1706** PHILLIPS (ed. Kersey) s. v., Relative, Apparent, or Vulgar Time, is the sensible and outward Measure of any Duration or Continuance estimated by Motion; and this is commonly us'd instead of true Time. **1727-41** CHAMBERS *Cycl.* s. v., Astronomical time, is that taken purely from the motion of the heavenly bodies, without any other regard. Civil time, is the former time accommodated to civil uses. **1764** MASKELYNE in *Phil. Trans.* LIV. 344 There are three different kinds of time used by astronomers, sidereal time, apparent solar time, and mean solar time. **1834** *Nat. Philos.* III. *Math. Geog.* v. 16/1 (Useful Knowl. Soc.) A common sun-dial shows the hour of apparent time. Time-keepers or chronometers, common watches and clocks, are made to show the hour of mean time. **1861, 1893** [see GREENWICH].

**b.** *Phrenol.* (See quot.)

**1860** MAYNE *Expos. Lex., Time,..Phrenol.*, a Faculty.. giving the power of judging of time, and of intervals in general.

**IV.** Phrases. (See also sense 18.)

* With another sb.

**28. Time of day. a.** The hour or exact time as shown by the clock; hence, a point or stage in any course or period (somewhat *colloq.*).

**1596** SHAKS. *1 Hen. IV*, I. ii. 1 Now Hal, what time of day is it Lad? **1634** FORD *P. Warbeck* III. i, How runs the time of day? Past ten, my lord. **1699** COLLIER *Answ. Stages Survey'd* (1730) 382 The Favour of a Prince was not ..unreputable at that Time of Day. **1771** SMOLLETT *Humph. Cl.* 17 Apr., I will not begin at this time of day to distress my tenants, because they..cannot make regular payments. **1862** GEN. P. THOMPSON in *Bradford Advertiser* 15 Mar. 6/1 No man at this time of day pretends to maintain, that [etc.]. **1870** JAS. NICHOLSON *Idylls* 25 A watch...At least 'twad ha'e tald him the time o' the day.

**b.** In salutations, as † *Good, fair time of day* (obs.); also, *to give one*, or *pass, the time of day* (now *dial.* and *colloq.*), to greet, salute, exchange salutations.

**1594** SHAKS. *Rich. III*, I. iii. 18 Good time of day vnto your Royall Grace. **1599** — *Hen. V*, V. ii. 3 To our Sister Health and faire time of day. **1608** — *Pericles* IV. iii. 35. **1611** COTGR., *Saluër*, to salute, greet,..giue the time of the day vnto. **1707** J. STEVENS tr. *Quevedo's Com. Wks.* (1709) 300 It shall be always allow'd to give the Time of the Day, but no New-Years-Gifts. **1851** MAYHEW *Lond. Labour* (1861) II. 489/2 The police..they're very friendly, they'll pass the time of day with me. **1864** *Let. to Editor*, In Radnorshire a clergyman told me the other day that 'there was not one in the parish who would not give him the time of day'. He meant, say 'How do' or 'a fine day, Sir'.

**c.** *colloq.* or *slang.* The prevailing aspect of affairs; the state of the case; (to know) 'what's what'; also, the right way of doing anything; the latest dodge or 'wrinkle'; cf. *to know what o'clock it is* (CLOCK *sb.*[1] 3 d).

**1667** POOLE *Dial. betw. Protest. & Papist* (1735) 144 No, Friend, it is not that time of Day. **1682** BUNYAN *Holy War* 11 If that be done, I know, quickly what time of day 'twill be with us. **1837** DICKENS *Pickw.* xxxix, Steady, Sir, steady! That's the time o'day! **1840** — *Barn. Rudge* xxxviii, Hurrah for the Protestant religion! That's the time of day. **1897** 'OUIDA' *Massarenes* xxvii, 'She knows the time o' day', said the other.

**29. Time of memory**: see quot. 1848. **Time out of mind** (also, † *out of memory*), from a time or during a period beyond human memory; so *time*, † *times* (also *for, from time*) *immemorial.*

Also †*without* or †*out of t. of mind*, †*within time of mind*, †*before t. of mind had*, †*during t. of no mind*; †*from t. whereof is no mind*, or *whereof the memory of man is not (to) the contrary*; †*during, from, out of, of t. that no (man's) mind is the contrary.* See also MIND *sb.*[1] 2 f.

**1407** *Waterf. Arch.* in *10th Rep. Hist. MSS. Comm.* App. v. 329 The nonpaying..during time of noo mynde. **1425** *Rolls of Parlt.* IV. 267/2 Beyng Erles, of tyme yat no mynde is ye contrarie. **1480** *Coventry Leet Bk.* 460 Ther haue ben Chirchewardens..tyme out of mynde electyff yerely. **1504** *Sel. Cas. Crt. Star Chamber* (Selden) I. 211 Which all weyes withoute tyme of mynde hath be made. **1511** *Waterf. Arch.* in *10th Rep. Hist. MSS. Comm.* App. v. 325 Noo such custum here..oute of tyme of mynde. **1515** *Sel. Cas. Star Chamb.* (Selden) II. 93 Bying and sellyng frely within tyme of mynd. **1516** *Ibid.* 107 Liberties.. vsed the tyme wherof mannys mynde is not to the contrarie. **1523** FITZHERB. *Surv.* 7 Except it haue ben vsed tyme out of mynde. **1527** *Sel. Cas. Star Chamber* (Selden) II. 16 So hath been oute of tyme of mynd. **1553** in Leadam *Court Requests* (Selden) 196 Whether it grewe first..before tyme of mynde had. **1602** [see IMMEMORIAL]. **1622** CALLIS *Stat. Sewers* (1647) 89 He and his Predecessors had used time out of memory to repair such a Bridge, which was in decay. **1759** GOLDSM. *Bee* No. 1. ¶ 11 This deformity..it had been the custom, time immemorial, to look upon as the greatest ornament of the human visage. **1760** *Impostors Detected* III. x. II. 103 The beavers having been in possession of it [the island] for time immemorial. **1765** BLACKSTONE *Comm.* I. viii. 281 The king's ordinary revenue is such, as has either subsisted time out of mind in the crown; or else has been granted by parliament. **1831-2** *Act 2 & 3 Will. IV*, c. 71 § 1 Time Immemorial, or Time whereof the Memory of Man runneth not to the contrary. **1848** WHARTON *Law Lex.* s. v. *Memory*, By Statute Westminster the First, 3 Edw. I., A. D. 1276, the time of memory was limited to the reign of Richard 1st, July 6th, 1189. **1887** T. A. TROLLOPE *What I remember* II. iii. 37 An ancient..goblet, which has belonged to the Musgraves time out of mind.

**30. Time and tide**, an alliterative reduplication, in various senses of *time*; now only or mainly in proverbial phrases, as *time and tide wait* (*stay*) *for no man*, etc., superseding the earlier *tide* (*tide nor time*) *tarrieth no man*, etc. (see TIDE *sb.* 13 b).

*a* **1300** *Cursor M.* 778 He wat wel wat tim or tide þat ȝee hade eten o þis tre. *c* **1550** R. BIESTON *Bayte Fortune* B j, And founden wast thou fyrst in euyll time and tyde. **1581** MARBECK *Bk. of Notes* 804 For their penaunce, according to the number, manner, time and tide giuen them by their ghostly father. **1602** MARSTON *Antonio's Rev.* II. iv, The divell in his good time and tide forsake thee.

**31. Time after time**, on many occasions, repeatedly.

**1631** GOUGE *God's Arrows* iii. § 6. 192 The like hath been verified time after time. **1881** JOWETT *Thucyd.* I. 42 Time after time we have warned you.

** With a following adv.

**32. Time about**, alternately, in turns. (Formerly with *their*.) Chiefly *Sc.* or *northern.*

**1537** *Registr. Aberdon.* (Maitland) I. 413 Sex of þe foirsaid viccaris þair tyme about ilk Satirdaye..sall syng þe foirsaid anteme. *a* **1670** SPALDING *Troubles Chas. I* (1850) I. 131 Becaus..diuerss of his freindis sould cum .. thair tyme about, and attend his lordschipis seruice. **1756** MRS. CALDERWOOD in *Coltness Collect.* (Maitl.) 272 That a protestant emperor should be chosen time about with a popish. **1816** SCOTT *Antiq.* xxv, Time about's fair play. **1828** *Craven Gloss.* s. v., *Times about*, in turns, in rotation. **1859** G. WILSON *Gateway Knowl.* (ed. 3) 39 Two paviours, driving in stones, bring down their mallets time about.

**33. Time** (also **times**) **and again**, with frequent recurrence; repeatedly, very often.

**1864** D. G. MITCHELL *Seven Stor.* 49 Time and again I looked over the way. **1870** [see AGAIN *adv.* 4 b]. **1878** MRS. H. WOOD *Pomeroy Abb.* I. 85 Times and again she had wondered..who the recreant truant could be. **1897** HALL CAINE *Christian* IV. xiv, Time and again I thought John's love of you was near to madness.

**b.** *Times and often*; *times without number*; *many a time and oft*: see 18.

**34. Time back**, at some past time. *Obs.* or *dial.*

**1834** LANDOR *Exam. Shaks.* Wks. 1846 II. 298/1 The girl's mother, sir, was housemaid and sempstress in your own family, time back. **1887** *S. Chesh. Gloss.*, *Time ago..*, *Time back..*, some time ago.

**35. Time enough**, soon enough, in time, sufficiently early.

**1377** LANGL. *P. Pl.* B. XI. 35 A man may stoupe tymes [C. XII. 197 tyme] ynow whan he shal tyne þe croune. **1470-85** MALORY *Arthur* VII. xi. 228 Thou shalt see hym tyme ynough. **1583** STOCKER *Civ. Warres Lowe C.* III. 117 b. **1669** R. MONTAGU in *Buccleuch MSS.* (Hist. MSS. Comm.) I. 458 That I may prepare time enough to fit my equipage for the journey. **1726** SWIFT *Stella's Birthday* 7 To-morrow will be time enough To hear such mortifying stuff. **1864** MRS. GATTY *Parables fr. Nat.* Ser. IV. 27 Time enough to go into the depths when you have used up what is so much easier got at.

*** With a governing preposition.

**36. Against time**, in competition with the passage of time; so as to finish one's task before the expiry of a certain period.

**1854, 1868** [see AGAINST *prep.* 12 d]. **1872** *Punch* 10 Feb. 57/2 No member shall speak against time or his own convictions. **1883** SWINBURNE in *Encycl. Brit.* XV. 556/2 A man who..was often..compelled to write against time for his living. **1887** RUSKIN *Præterita* II. 171 [To] walk against time up a regular slope of eight feet in the hundred is the most trying foot-work I know.

**37. At time(s**, etc. **a.** *At times*, † *at* (*a*) *time* (obs. rare), at one time and another, at various times, occasionally. Also *at times and again.*

**1529** MORE *Dyaloge* III. Wks. 245/1 Our sauiour at tyme taught his apostles a part. **1604** SHAKS. *Oth.* II. iii. 319 You, or any man liuing, may be drunke at a time, man. **1611** BIBLE *Judg.* xiii. 25 The Spirit of the Lord beganne to mooue him at times. **1779** *Mirror* No. 39 ¶ 9, I believe most men have, at times, wished to be..possessed of the power of moulding the world to their fancy. **1864** *Reader* 634/3 Some blacks, at times and again, hovering over a few coals. **1884** W. C. SMITH *Kildrostan* 46, I blame myself at times.

**b.** (*At*) *one time with* (*and*) *another*, during various detached periods; on various occasions.

**1612** R. FENTON *Usury* 37 If they could with their owne free stocke raise the like gaine one time with another. **1845** COIT *Puritanism* 252 Winthrop..was governor, at one time with another, eleven years. **1884** MRS. OLIPHANT *Sir Tom* II. vi. 84 He had seen a good deal of her one time and another in his life.

**c.** *At the same time*, during the same period, at the same moment, not before or after. (Formerly without *at.*) Also used in introducing a reservation, explanation, or contrast, = 'while saying this, nevertheless, however, yet, still'.

**1526** TINDALE *Matt.* xviii. 1 The same tyme the disciples cam vnto Iesus, sayng [etc.]. — *Acts* xix. 23 The same tyme there arose no litell a do aboute that waye. **1563** PILKINGTON *Burn. Paules Ch.* D ij b, Tertulian who lyued at the same time of this Pope. **1705** STEELE *Tender Husb.* Ded., At the same time I hope I make the Town no ill Compliment..in acknowledging that it has so far rais'd my Opinion [etc.]. **1749** WEST tr. *Pindar, Nem. Ode* xi. Argt., Lest he should be too much puffed up with these Praises, he reminds him at the same Time of his Mortality. **1780** *Mirror* No. 100 ¶ 4 In two of Shakespeare's tragedies are introduced, at the same time, instances of counterfeit madness, and of real distraction. **1891** 'J. S. WINTER' *Lumley* xv, Give them my best wishes. At the same time I must say I do not envy the girl.

**38. Between times**, in the intervals between other actions; at intervals, between-whiles.

[**1580**, *a* **1641** Between-time *sb.*: see BETWEEN B. 4.] **1902** ELIZ. L. BANKS *Newspaper Girl* 159 She served me faithfully till the very last, packing her humble belongings in between times.

† **39. By time, by times. a.** *By time*: in good time, early; = BETIME *adv. Obs.*

*c* **1250**, *a* **1300** [see BETIME *adv.* 1, 2]. **1340-70** *Alex. & Dind.* 368 We ne sain but soþ & sesen by time. *c* **1425** *Cast. Persev.* 413 in *Macro Plays* 89 ȝa, on þi sowle þou schalt þynke al be tyme. **1565** W. ALLEN in Fulke *Confut. Purg.* (1577) 142 Therfore deare brethern let vs turne and amende by time.

† **b.** *By times*: (*a*) in good time, early; = BETIMES *adv.*; (*b*) at various times; from time to time; at times, now and then. *Obs.*

*c* **1314**, *c* **1380** [see BETIMES *adv.* 1, 3]. *c* **1460** FORTESCUE *Abs. & Lim. Mon.* xi. (1885) 135 The kynge..hade be tymes, sithen he reigned vpon vs, livelod..nerehand to the value of þe v[th] parte off is Reaume. **1530** TINDALE *Answ. More* Wks. (1572) 251/1 Let therfore M. More and his company awake be tymes ere euer their sinne be ripe. **1657** *North's Plutarch* (1676) 960 He slept in the day, and by times in the night. **1743** in Egan *Boxiana* (1830) I. 49 Gentlemen are therefore desired to come by times. **1825** KNAPP & BALDW. *Newgate Cal.* IV. 177/1 The prisoner and I were on good terms by times. **1825** SCOTT *Betrothed* xi, His nephew..was despatched by times every morning.

† **c.** *By a time*, at times, occasionally. *Obs.*

**1721** KELLY *Prov.* 26 A Horse with four Feet may snapper, by a time.

† **40. For time**, for the time being. *Obs.*

**1464** *Rolls of Parlt.* V. 510/2 Any persone or persones for tyme dwellyng..within the same Chapell. **1483** *Ibid.* VI. 257/1 The Goodes and Chattells of the seid Provost and Fellawes for tyme founden upon the seid Lande.

**41. From time to time. a.** At more or less regular intervals; now and again, occasionally; in quot. 1382, † at stated times, at definite intervals (*obs.*); in quot. *c* 1412 with ellipsis of *from.*

**1382** WYCLIF *Ezek.* iv. 11 Fro tyme vn to tyme [1388 fro tyme til to tyme] thou shalt drynke it. *c* **1412** HOCCLEVE *De Reg. Princ.* 4189 Tyme to tyme he ȝaf hem Of his goode. **1423** *Acts Privy Council* III. 88 Ye desire to be acertained fro tyme to tyme of oure prosperite and welfare. **1651** HOBBES *Leviathan* III. xl. 255 From thence proceeded from time to time the civill troubles..of the Nation. **1891** *Law Rep., Weekly Notes* 136/1 The passage..was used only from time to time, and not continuously.

† **b.** Denoting succession of periods without intervals: Continuously, constantly, at all times.

**1553** T. WILSON *Rhet.* 14 Heaven is theirs, saieth David, that doe justly from tyme to tyme. **1586** T. B. *La Primaud. Fr. Acad.* (1589) 519 Therefore nothing was more esteemed from time to time among the auncients, than the institution of youth, which Plato calleth Discipline.

**42. In time**, † **in times. a.** *In time.* (*a*) In the course of time, sooner or later. (*b*) Soon or early enough, not too late. † (*c*) At a suitable time; seasonably; opposed to *out of time*, 44 a (*a*). *Obs. rare.* (*d*) *Mus.* In the correct rhythm: see 12 a.

(*a*) *c* **1450** tr. *De Imitatione* III. xxxv. 103 Consolacion shal come to þe in tyme. **1594** WILLOBIE *Avisa* xlvii, I thinke in tyme she may be wonne. **1656** EARL MONM. tr. *Boccalini's Advts. fr. Parnass.* I. xxiii. (1674) 24 Potent men.. would certainly in time work their revenge. **1818** SCOTT *Hrt. Midl.* xvi, The inner turnkey's office to begin wi', and the captainship in time.

(*b*) **1467-8** *Rolls of Parlt.* V. 623/1 Yf it were used in tyme. **1605** SHAKS. *Macb.* II. iii. 6 Come in time, haue Napkins enow about you. **1742** *Observ. Methodists* 4 It will be too late to remedy it if not attended to in Time. **1834** *Picture of Liverpool* 73 Letters put into any of the Receiving Houses before twelve o'clock will be in time for the early mails. **1912** *Eng. Hist. Rev.* Jan. 44 Mansel soon returned..in time to assume the custody of the seal in September 1238.

(*c*) **1377** LANGL. *P. Pl.* B. IX. 184 Whan ȝe haue wyued, bewar and worcheth in tyme. **1583** STUBBES *Anat. Abus.* II. (1882) 78 The worde of God is to be preached night and day, in time, and out of time, in season and out of season.

† **b.** *In times.* (*a*) At various times, on several different occasions. (*b*) *In times . . in times*, sometimes . . sometimes; at one time . . at another.

**1422** tr. *Secreta Secret., Priv. Priv.* 181 He that is a gouernoure in tymes he shall Spare, and in tymes vengeaunse take. **1612** *MS. Acc. St. John's Hosp., Canterb.*, Payd vnto Thomas Williames in times in consederation of a challing of sartayn tythe wood.

**c.** *In good time.* (*a*) After the lapse of a suitable interval; in due course or process of time; at a proper time, when it seems good. (*b*) Soon or early; quickly. †(c) At the right or a seasonable moment; luckily. *Obs.* †(d) As an expression of ironical acquiescence, incredulity, amazement, or the like: To be sure!, indeed!, very well! (Cf. Fr. *à la bonne heure.*) *Obs.*

(a) c1440 Lovelich *Merlin* 9985 Forth on his message he gan to gon, and dyde his message al in good tyme. 1622 in *Crt. & Times Jas. I* (1848) II. 343 But God, in his good time, will amend all that is amiss. 1777 Sheridan *Sch. Scand.* iv. i, I shall be rich and splenetic, all in good time. 1822 Scott *Pirate* ix, 'The devil take him!' said Mordaunt, in impatient surprise. 'A' in gude time', replied the jagger. 1883 Gilmour *Mongols* xvii. 206 Every true-hearted follower shall, in good time, arrive at the desired goal.

(b) 1585 T. Washington tr. *Nicholay's Voy.* ii. xxii. 60 [They] come home againe in good time without the knowledge ..of their husbands. 1872 *Punch* 19 Oct. 158/1 My aunt wants to be back in good time.

(c) 1586 A. Day *Eng. Secretary* ii. (1625) 62 If it please you then to returne by him those parcels.., they will come now in very good time. 1590 Shaks. *Com. Err.* ii. ii. 65 Learne to iest in good time, there's a time for all things. 1639 S. Du Verger tr. *Camus' Admir. Events* 7 This came in good time to keepe this poore family from necessity.

(d) 1610 Shaks. *Temp.* ii. i. 95 Sowing the kernels of it [an island].. bring forth more Islands. ..Why in good time. 1650 Fuller *Pisgah* ii. vi. 149 There..even at this day, are shewed the ruines of those three tabernacles built according to Peters desire. In very good time no doubt! 1789 Mrs. Piozzi *Journ. France* II. 50 Bonducci..calls him emulous of Milton, in good time! *Ibid.* 369 Making fat the objects of his partial tenderness with their best treasures—in good time!

**43. On time**, punctually; also *pred.* punctual. Chiefly *U.S. colloq.* See also 48.

1878 Mrs. Stowe *Poganuc P.* xxiii. 209 His wife had always been on time, and on duty. 1890, 1892 [see On *prep.* 6 d]. 1893 *Scribner's Mag.* June 781/2 My endeavors to get the family out of the house and into our pew on time. 1904 *Daily Chron.* 5 Feb. 3/4 An Americanism here and there out of place (as..when the native dwarf, Cerberus.. speaks of his mistress as being 'on time' in her return from a trance).

†**b.** *On a time*: see 14. *Obs.*

**44. Out of time. a.** *adv. phr.* †(a) At an inappropriate time; unseasonably. *Obs.* (b) After the prescribed period has elapsed; too late. See also 7 b (f). (c) *Mus.* See 12 a.

(a) 1393 Langl. *P. Pl.* C. xi. 291 ȝe þat han wyues, beþ war worcheþ nat out of tyme. c1420 *Avow. Arth.* xxiii, I, Kay, that thou knawes, That owte of tyme bostus and blawus. 1579 Lyly *Euphues* (Arb.) 100 Doth not Tryacle as well poyson as helpe, if it be taken out of time? 1583 [see 42 a (c)]. 1780 Warner in Jesse *Selwyn & Contemp.* (1844) IV. 325, I went like a thing born out of time, and had the door almost shut in my face.

(b) 1884 Graham Hastings in *Law Times Rep.* L. 175/1 On that view of the case also they are out of time, as they took no steps in the matter until Oct. 1883. 1886 *Law Times* LXXX. 241/2 Counsel for the respondent took a preliminary objection that the appeal was out of time.

**b.** *adj. phr.* Unseasonable: see Out-of-time.

**45. To time.** †**a.** For all time, for ever. *Obs.*

c1200 *Trin. Coll. Hom.* 183 For þine gulte ishal nu to pine, rotie mote þu to time. 1607 Shaks. *Cor.* v. iii. 127, I..that brought you forth this boy To keepe your name liuing to time.

†**b.** *conj. phr.* To the time that, until such time as, till. Also *into, unto, till time. Obs.*

a1352 Minot *Poems* (1887) iv. 6 In þat land..Ordanis he still for to dwell, To time he think to fight. c1449 Pecock *Repr.* ii. xvi. (Rolls) 246 Thei [images] wolden not at alle tymes ȝeue answeris..into tyme thei weren myche preied. c1470 Henry *Wallace* iii. 432, I sall do nocht till tyme I tak my leyff. c1500 *Melusine* 170, I shal neuer departe fro this land vnto tyme I be al dyscomfyted, or þat I haue put them to flyght. 1506 Guylforde *Pilgr.* (Camden) 18 A lytell cave, where they shytte him in, to tyme the Jewes had.. determynyd what they wolde do with hym.

**c.** Within certain limits of time; so as to complete something by the end of a certain period.

1874 Ethel de Fonblanque *Life A. Fonblanque* 40 A growing dislike to the act of 'writing to time'.

**46. With time**, with the lapse of time, in the course of time; = *in time* (42 a (a)).

1578–9 *Reg. Privy Council Scot.* III. 82 Your Hienes sal have pruif with tyme of my following thair trew..service to your Grace. 1650 Earl Monm. tr. *Senault's Man bec. Guilty* 104 When with time he is grown greater. *Ibid.* 272 Ambition increasing with time. *Mod.* With time it will come all right.

†**47. Without time**, outside of or independent of time; for ever; eternal(ly). *Obs.*

a1400 *Prymer* 6 Holi modir of god..þat we..moun stie up to þe seete of endeles blis, þere þou dwellist wiþ þi sone wiþ-outen tyme. 1509 Hawes *Past. Pleas.* xliv. (Percy Soc.) 215 Withouten tyme is no erthly thynge, Nature, fortune, or yet dame Sapyence. 1587 Golding *De Mornay* vi. 79 This Minde is without time and onely everlasting.

†**48.** In commercial phraseology, *at, for, on time*, at the rate which may be current on the day appointed for settling; cf. Time-bargain. *Obs.*

1651 Marius *Adv. Conc. Bills Exch.* 74 Goods sold one part for ready Mony, the rest at Time. 1727 Swift *What passed in London* Wks. 1755 III. i. 188 There were many who called themselves Christians, who offered to buy for time. 1766 W. Gordon *Gen. Counting-h.* 10 Debited..to the persons of whom they are bought, if on time.

* * * * With a verb.

**49. (The) time was (hath been, shall be)**, inversion of *there was* (etc.) *a time* (*when*).

1509 Barclay *Shyp of Folys* (1874) I. 35 The tyme hath ben, nat longe before our dayes Whan [etc.]. 1549 Coverdale, etc. *Erasm. Par. Gal.* v. 18 The tyme was, when it was nedefull. 1611 Bible *Transl. Pref.* 5 The same Hierome elsewhere affirmeth, that he, the time was, had set forth the Translation of the Seuenty for his countrymen of Dalmatia. 1791 Cowper *Iliad* i. 300 Time shall be, when Achilles shall be miss'd. 1874 Micklethwaite *Mod. Par. Churches* 251 Time was when we had a national style.

**50. To keep time. a.** *Mus.* To mark the rhythm by movements of the hand or baton; to beat time; also, of a performer, to adhere to the correct rhythm and rate of the music, to keep pace *with* a measure or another performer, etc. Also *fig.*

1599 B. Jonson *Cynthia's Rev.* i. i, Slow, slow, fresh fount, keep time with my salt tears. 1662 Playford *Skill Mus.* i. ix. (1674) 29 In keeping time your hand goes down at one half, and up at the next. 1687 Lovell tr. *Thevenot's Trav.* ii. 85 They beat this Stuff with one hand two and two over against one another,.. keeping time to this tune. 1817 Byron *Beppo* lxiii, I can't well break it, But must keep time and tune like public singers. 1821 Scott *Kenilw.* xviii, Thy reward shall be princely, if thou keep'st time and touch, and exceedest not the due proportion.

**b.** Of a timepiece: To register the passage of time correctly.

1899 P. N. Hasluck *Clock Jobber's Handbk.* 61 The clock is ready..with every probability of going and keeping time for two or three years.

**V. Combinations.**

**51. a.** Simple *attrib.* (a) 'Of or pertaining to time', as *time-basis, -division, -drop, -guide, -integral* (Integral B. 4 a), *-mark, -ocean, -perspective, -reference, -schedule, -sense, -variation*; also, 'of time as distinct from eternity', as *time-element, -pattern, -state, -vesture, -world*; (b) 'relating to, based upon, or indicating the amount of time occupied in some work or process', as *time-allowance, -board, -log* (Log *sb.*¹ 7), *-march, -prize, -race, -record, -ticket*; (c) in names of instruments, machines, or appliances used as time-signals or timed to operate at a given moment, as *time-alarm* (Alarm *sb.* 7), *-bomb, -fuse, -glass* (cf. Hour-glass), *-gun, -measure, -taper.*

1877 Knight *Dict. Mech.*, **Time-alarm*, an audible notice at the expiration of a set time. 1883 D. Kemp in *Fortn. Rev.* 1 Sept. 324 The yachts..were sailed in classes without *time-allowance. 1849 J. A. Carlyle tr. *Dante's Inferno* p. xxxi, The whole *time-basis of his mighty song has become dim and cold. 1890 W. J. Gordon *Foundry* 34 As the men come in past the time-office they take their piece or *time-boards from the rack, where each is placed against its proper number. 1895 *Times* 7 Jan. 3/3 In the case of one large yard the men have come out on strike against the introduction of the 'timeboard' system. 1893 *Daily Tel.* 9 Nov. 5/7 The engine of destruction was not a *time bomb. 1877 E. Caird *Philos. Kant* ii. x. 415 The schematism of the categories, the translation of them into *time-determinations is no mere idle play of the imagination. 1888 J. Prestwich *Geol.* II. 3 The great *time-divisions are of almost universal application. a1711 Ken *Preparatives* Poet. Wks. 1721 IV. 39 Minutes..On these *Time-drops eternal Joys depend. 1831 Carlyle *Sart. Res.* iii. viii, Pierce through the *Time-element, glance into the Eternal. 1862 *Catal. Internat. Exhib.* II. xi. 23 A fuse..placed and used like the ordinary simple *time fuse. 1804–6 Syd. Smith *Mor. Philos.* (1850) 122 If you were to say that man was like a *time-glass,—that both must run out, and both render up their dust. 1875 *Zoologist* X. 4587 He wished it to be a *time-guide to the appearance of butterflies and moths. 1878 Stevenson *Edinburgh* 133 The *time-gun by which people set their watches. 1885 Tait *Rec. Adv. Phys. Sc.* (ed. 3) 359 Momentum is the *Time-Integral of Force because force is the rate of change of Momentum. 1868 *Time-log [see Log *sb.*¹ 7]. 1891 *Labour Commission* Gloss., *Time-Log*, the printed statement of times allowed for making garments in the tailoring trade, agreed upon between employers and employed. 1896 *Daily News* 22 Dec. 6/6 Captain M——.. was thrown from his horse yesterday near Fleet during a *time march. 1901 *Spectator* 20 July 93/2 The continually recurring *time-marks of winter and summer. 1726 Leoni *Alberti's Archit.* Pref. 3 Vehicles, Mills, *Time-measures, and other such minute things. 1864 Lowell *Fireside Trav.* 125 The old *time-ocean throws upon its shores just such rounded and polished results of the eternal turmoil. 1907 *Gentl. Mag.* July 80 The Australian child is deficient not so much in imagination as in what may be called *time-perspective. 1897 *Outing* (U.S.) Aug. 494/1 In 1890 Murphy was on scratch, and won the *time-prize. 1852 Bateman *Aquatic Notes* an. 1844, P. M—— [won the sculls] after a good '*time-race' with R——. 1887 E. Moore (*title*) The *Time-References in the Divina Commedia, and their Bearing on the Assumed Date and Duration of the Vision. 1877 E. Caird *Philos. Kant* ii. xi. 445 So far as sensations are represented as objects, they must be represented as events in time, and thus..considered as the real subjects of *time-relations like any other events. 1904 *Daily Chron.* 31 Dec. 6/7 The reconstruction of an old [line], when the working moments must be snatched in the gaps of the *time-schedule, and the greater part of the work must be carried out during a period of four hours at dead of night. 1899 *Syd. Soc. Lex.*, **Time sense*, the perception of the lapse of time. 1810 Southey *Kehama* viii. vii, Lo! the *time-taper's flame ascending slow. 1903 R. Wallace *Life* iii. 52 This view of the 'Sabbath' as a sacrifice or *time-tax paid to the Deity. 1900 H. Lawson *Over Shiprails* 123 The door opened. Arvie..took his *time-ticket, and hurried in. 1881 Maxwell *Electr. & Magn.* II. 223 The third term..depends on the *time-variation of the magnetic field. 1831 Carlyle *Sart. Res.* iii. viii, Nature, which is the *Time-vesture of God, and reveals Him to the wise, hides Him from the foolish. 1843 — *Past & Pr.* ii. vi, This *Time-world..plays and flickers in the grand still mirror of Eternity.

**b.** Objective and obj. gen., as *time-beater, -giver, -measurer, -observer, -pleaser, -saver, -setter* (1340), *-spender, -waster* (1661), etc.; *time-beguiling* (1592), *-bettering, -breaking, -deluding, -devouring, -economizing, -noting, -setting* (1340), *-spending* (1509), *-wasting*, etc., adjs. and sbs.; **c.** instrumental, as *time-authorized* (a1628), *-battered, -bent, -bewasted* (1593), *-blackened, -blanched, -born, -bound, -cleft, -discoloured, -eaten, -gnawn, -mellowed, -rent, -rusty, -shrouded, -taught, -tried, -wasted, -wearied, -white, -withered*, etc., adjs.; **d.** in various relations with pples. and adjs., as *time-enduring* (†*-during*), *-lasting, -marked, -proof, -served.*

a1628 F. Grevil *Sidney* xv. (1652) 199 Those *time-authorized assemblies. 1729 Savage *Wanderer* v. 44 *Time-batter'd Tow'rs frown awful in Decay. 1881 *Athenæum* 5 Mar. 342/3 To feel at once the important difference between a conductor and a *time-beater. 1592 Shaks. *Ven. & Ad.* 24 A sommers day..wasted in such *time-beguiling sport. 1863 *Pilgr. over Prairies* II. 302 The grey and *timebent grandsire. c1600 Shaks. *Sonn.* lxxxii, Some fresher stampe of the *time bettering dayes. 1593 — *Rich. II*, i. iii. 221 My oyle-dride Lampe, and *time-bewasted light. 1806 Surr *Winter in Lond.* I. 178 *Time-blanched locks. 1628 Gaule *Pract. The. Panegyr.* 59 He *time-borne Sonne, got from eternitie. 1647 Fuller *Good Th. in Worse T.* (1841) 132 When we are *time-bound, place-bound, or person-bound. 1601 Sir W. Cornwallis *Ess.* ii. xxxvi. (1631) 109 After comes the torture of the *time-breaking wheele. 1800 Hurdis *Fav. Village* 182 The *time-cleft arch Of ancient chantry. a1617 Hieron *Wks.* (1620) I. 10 Idle loyterers..or *time-deluding triflers. 1742 Mrs. Delany in *Life & Corr.* (1861) II. 198 Accustomed to the many hurries and *time-devouring accidents of this huge place. 1836 H. Coleridge *North. Worthies* Introd. (1852) 17 To..run his eye along the *time-discoloured pages. 1548 Udall, etc. *Erasm. Par. John* xi. 80 Not..that it is an uncouth or a *time duryng thyng to me. a1849 Poe *City in Sea* i, *Time-eaten towers that tremble not. 1839 Bailey *Festus* xi. (1852) 142 Now go I forth again..Upon my *time-enduring pilgrimage. 1613 Daniel *Coll. Hist. Eng.* (1626) 33 The King..was no *time-giuer vnto growing dangers. 1863 Hawthorne *Our Old Home* (1879) 162 A gray, *time-gnawn, ponderous, shadowy structure. 1674 N. Fairfax *Bulk & Selv.* 40 This *time-lasting World, and every while-being thing in it. 1888 E. Clodd *Story Creation* xi. 217 The rude..chant of the savage, *time-marked by yell and tamtam. 1864 Hawthorne *S. Felton* (1883) 265 The *time-measurer of one whose mortal life he had cut off. 1904 *Edin. Rev.* Jan. 200 The pendulum was..assigned its function as a time-measurer. 1615 Brathwait *Strappado* (1878) 109 My *Time-noting lines ayme not at thee. 1647 Trapp *Comm. Luke* xiv. 7 Ministers, though they may not be time-servers, yet they must be *time-observers. 1601 Shaks. *Twel. N.* ii. iii. 160 The diu'll a Puritane that hee is, or any thing constantly but a *time-pleaser. 1607 — *Cor.* iii. i. 45 Time-pleasers. 1806 J. Grahame *Birds Scot.* 74 In some vacant niche, Or *time-rent crevice. 1639 Fuller *Holy War* v. xxix. 279 How would a Herald sweat with scouring over these *time-rustie titles. 1873 Hamerton *Intell. Life* iv. i. (1876) 135 The best *time-savers. 1900 *Daily Express* 13 June 5/2 All the men ..at the bureaus for *time-served soldiers. 1340 *Ayenb.* 36 Þe *time-zettere ontrewe. .. Vor hire *time-zettinge hi destrueþ and makeþ beggeres þe knyȝtes. 1794 Coleridge *Monody Death Chatterton* ad fin., Sweet Harper of *time-shrouded Minstrelsy. 1670 G. H. *Hist. Cardinals* i. i. 12 Those impertinent *time-spenders, the Priests. 1509 Hawes *Past. Pleas.* xliv. (Percy Soc.) 215 Eyther hell or heaven, wythout lesynge, Alway he getteth in his *tyme spendynge. 1799 Campbell *Pleas. Hope* ii. 224 The *time-taught spirit, pensive not severe. 1870 Ruskin *Lect. Art* i. (1875) 28 Faithful servant of *time-tried principles. 1814 Scott *Ld. of Isles* i. Introd. iv, Through fields *time-wasted, on sad inquest bound. 1661 Baxter *Last Work Believer* Wks. (1846) 253 She was a stranger to pastimes, and no companion for *time-wasters. 1741–2 Gray *Agrippina* 139 The slacken'd sinews of *time-wearied age. c1611 Chapman *Iliad* viii. 454 To warn the youth, yet short of war, and *time-white fathers.

**52.** Special combs.: **time-attack** (*Fencing*) = *time-thrust*; **time-bill**, (a) a time-table of trains, etc.; (b) a record kept by the guard of a train of the time it leaves each station; **time-book**, (a) a book in which an entry is made of the time worked by employees; (b) a chronicle (cf. Ger. *zeitbuch*); (c) = *time-bill* (a); **time-candle** (see quot.); **time-card**, (a) a card on which a record is kept of time worked; (b) a card time-table; **time-catch**, in a photographic camera, a catch which retains the shutter for a fixed time; **time-catcher**, in *Fencing*, one who 'takes the time': see 21; **time-charter** (see quot.); **time-clause** *Gram.*, an adverbial clause of time, a temporal clause; **time-constant** *Electr.* (see quot. 1902); **time-course** *Naut.*, a ship's run, as in a fog, calculated by the vessel's speed, the time occupied, and the direction; **time-curve** (see quot.); **time-detector**, a clock (stationary at a point) or watch (carried by the watchman) having additional mechanism, operated by the watchman, to show the times at which he was at certain points of his round (Knight *Dict. Mech.* 1877): cf. Tell-tale 2 g; also called *time-watch*; **time-disk**, an instrument used in conjunction with the kymograph for investigating the time-sense; **time-expired** *a.*, whose term of engagement has expired; **time-exposure** *Photogr.*, exposure for a regulated time, as distinguished from instantaneous exposure; so **time-exposed** *a.*; †**time-fellow**, a contemporary; **time-globe**, a terrestrial globe rotated once in twenty-four hours by a clock-movement, and encircled at the equator by a stationary graduated zone, showing the local time at any meridian; **time-lag**, the length of time separating two correlated physical phenomena; **time-line**, (*a*) *pl.* a certificate of apprenticeship (see LINE *sb.*[2] 23 f); (*b*) an undulating line indicating small fractions of a second, by which the time or rate of some process may be measured; **time-lock**, a lock with clockwork attachment which prevents its being unlocked until a set time; **time-marker**, (*a*) an automatic device in a cab, etc., which registers the time it is in use, with the fare payable; (*b*) *Electr.* (see quot. 1902); **time-notice**, a notice given a definite time before; **time-payment**, (*a*) payment by instalments; (*b*) payment on the basis of time worked; **time-policy** (see quot. 1848); **time-rate**, (*a*) rate in time; (*b*) rate of payment on the basis of time worked; **time-recorder**, an apparatus which records the time of an act or event; **time-sheet**, a time-table (on a sheet); the paper on which are entered the names of workmen and the hours worked by them; **time-shutter**, in the photographic camera, a shutter for time-exposures; **time-sight** *Naut.*, an observation of the altitude of the sun or a star for the purpose of ascertaining the time and, hence, the longitude (*Cent. Dict.*); **time-signal**, a visible or audible signal made at an observatory, etc., to announce the exact time, e. g. the fall of a time-ball, or firing of a time-gun; **time-signature** *Mus.*, a sign placed at the beginning of a piece of music, or where the time changes, to show the measure or rhythm; rhythmical signature; **time-taker**, † (*a*) = TIME-SERVER 1; (*b*) one who takes a note of the time occupied in any work or course; **time-taking** *a.*, that takes time, leisurely, slow; **time-thrust** (*Fencing*), an offensive-defensive counter-stroke made within the time of the adversary's movement of attack, and preventing its completion; **time-value** *Mus.*, the relative duration of a note; **time-waiter**, one who awaits a favourable turn of events; cf. TIDE-WAITER 2; **time-watch** = *time-detector*; **time-work**, work which is paid for on the basis of the time occupied; distinguished from *piece-work*; so **time-worker**; **time-zone**, any one of the twenty-four divisions of the surface of the globe (each bounded by two meridian lines), within each of which the standard time adopted is the mean solar time of the meridian distant from Greenwich a number of complete hours: an improper designation, for the regions so bounded are not *zones*. See also TIME-BALL, -BARGAIN, -WORN, etc.

**1889** DUNN *Fencing* 62 '*Time' attacks, whereby, having anticipated in what line your opponent's attack will be delivered, you intercept his blade as he gives in his attack. **1847** (July 1) *East. Counties & E. Union Railways* (*Railw. Mag.* Jan. 1910. 46) *Time bills of a prior date are not correct. **1858** SIMMONDS *Dict. Trade*, *Time-bill*, a time-table of the arrivals and departures of trains, omnibuses, steamers, &c. **1878** F. S. WILLIAMS *Midl. Railw.* 658 To ascertain the precise moment that the train clears certain stations, that he [the guard] may..chronicle the same in his time-bill. **1898** *Daily News* 19 Oct. 3/2 She looked down the timebill for a place a long way off, and seeing Blackpool and the distance it was off took a ticket for there. **1854** H. MILLER *Sch. & Schm.* xiii. (1858) 271, I still retained the *time-book in my master's behalf. **1867** tr. *Ewald's Hist. Israel* 92 Like a true time-book (or chronicle) terminated with the description of the most recent great deeds. **1877** KNIGHT *Dict. Mech.*, **Time-candle*, one in which the size and quality of the material and the wick are so regulated that a certain length will burn in a given time. **1891** *Cent. Dict.*, **Time-card*. **1898** *Engineering Mag.* XVI. 41 Each workman perforates a five-minute time-card for each job on which he is employed, simply piercing the card at the five-minute points most nearly representing his times of beginning and ending. **1890** *Anthony's Photogr. Bull.* III. 383 The *time catch is on the other side, and by means of two slots and pins, is arranged so that it cannot fall backwards or forwards when not in use. **1753** CHAMBERS *Cycl. Supp.* s. v. *Binding*, The great objection made by some people, particularly those *time-catchers, against the frequent use of binding, is [etc.]. **1891** *Labour Commission* Gloss., **Time-charter*, an agreement under which the owner hires his vessel for a stipulated monthly payment, generally in advance, in which case the charterer loads and discharges the vessel. **1895** *Funk's Stand. Dict.*, *Time-constant. **1902** SLOANE *Stand. Electr. Dict.*, *Time Constant.* (*a*) If..we divide the inductance in henries by the resistance in ohms, the ratio gives the time-constant of the circuit, or it expresses the time which it will take for the current to reach 0·63 of its final value. (*b*) In a static condenser the time required for the charge to fall to one 2·7183th part of its original value. **1909** *Cent. Dict. Suppl.*, **Time-curve*, a curve so plotted that one of its coördinates represents time, or periods of time. **1901** E. B. TITCHENER *Exper. Psychol.* I. x. 338 The most useful appliance for investigation is, probably, Meumann's 'time-sense' apparatus, consisting of Baltzar kymograph, *time-disc, set of contacts, and sound-hammers. **1885** SIR H. GREEN in *Pall Mall G.* 14 Feb. 2/1 *Time-expired soldiers in India will not, as a rule, re-enter the ranks. **1889** *Anthony's Photogr. Bull.* II. 79 To level your camera when taking *time-exposed pictures and hence get straight lines. **1893** J. A. HODGES *Elem. Photogr.* (1907) 18 A tripod stand will be required..when '*time' exposures are given. **1899** A. B. LLOYD in *Daily News* 9 Jan. 2/3, I couldn't give a time exposure, as the pigmies would not stand still. **1577** HARRISON *England* I. xviii. (1880) 131 My *Synchroni* or *time fellows can reape at this present great commoditie in a little roome. **1638** CHILLINGW. *Relig. Prot.* I. vi. § 23. 340 The disinterested time-fellowes or immediate Successors of Liberius. **1862** *Cat. Internat. Exhib., Brit.* II. No. 5516 *Time globe, planetary clock. **1895** *Daily News* 5 Dec. 2/2 The masters, it is admitted, would be acting quite within their powers if they refuse to grant the apprentices their *time lines. **1898** *Allbutt's Syst. Med.* V. 814 No pulse is regular, as a time line at the foot of a sphygmographic tracing will prove. **1877** KNIGHT *Dict. Mech.*, **Time-lock*, a lock having clock-work attached which..prevents the bolt being withdrawn when locked, until a certain interval of time has elapsed. **1908** *Daily Chron.* 10 June 7/1 The time-lock on the door of a bank's vaults makes it impossible for the bank's officers themselves to enter the strong room after closing-time. **1898** *Westm. Gaz.* 11 Mar. 7/2 Five hundred cabs provided with the *time and fare marker were put on the stands. **1902** SLOANE *Stand. Electr. Dict.* Suppl., *Time-marker*, a light flexible stylus actuated by an electro-magnet in circuit with an electro-magnetic tuning-fork. It is used for recording tuning fork vibrations on a chronograph drum. **1902** *Westm. Gaz.* 7 Feb. 2/2 The Bill..provides for a *time-notice of seven years to the holders of licences to sell liquor for consumption on the premises. **1908** *Ibid.* 23 Mar. 2/3 The Government proposal..gives a fourteen years' time-notice for licences which until 1904 were granted for one year only. **1898** *Daily News* 5 Dec. 6/6 This *time payment system is far too much bother for me, and I look on it as undignified for our trade. **1848** ARNOULD *Mar. Insur.* I. v. (1866) I. 219 A *time policy is one in which the limits of the risk are designated only by certain fixed periods of time. **1895** KENNEDY in *Law Times Rep.* LXXII. 861/1 The policy is a time policy for six months from the 9th Jan. 1894 to the 8th July 1894. **1882** MINCHIN *Unipl. Kinemat.* 60 The *time-rate of description of area round the fixed centre is constant in all positions of the moving point. **1902** ELIZ. L. BANKS *Newspaper Girl* 263 We always pay the expenses and time rates when you go off on a job like that. **1898** *Engin. Mag.* XVI. 41 Workmen use a mechanical *time-recorder requiring the vibration of a lever on entering and leaving the shop. **1893** *Westm. Gaz.* 7 July 5/1 An elegantly printed *time-sheet had been laid on the table for the use of the Duke and Princess. **1907** *Daily Chron.* 3 May 9/2 A light folding quarter-plate camera, with good lens, *time and instantaneous shutter. **1877** KNIGHT *Dict. Mech.* s. v., The electro-magnetic telegraph has been used for operating *time-signals..; thus, the Greenwich time is indicated at Liverpool..by the dropping of a ball. **1875** STAINER & BARRETT *Dict. Mus. Terms* s. v. *Signature*, There are two kinds of signature, the *time signature and the key-signature...It would be more proper to call the time-signature the measure-sign, as it shows the contents of a bar, but not the pace at which the music should be performed. **1630–56** GORDON *Hist. Earld. Sutherld.* (1813) 325 That *tyme-takers wold be now easalie decerned from true freinds. **1867** LIVINGSTONE in Blaikie *Life* xix. (1910) 323 His time-taker had no conscience and could not be trusted. **1838** DICKENS *Nich. Nick.* i, Mr. Nickleby..was a slow and *time-taking speaker. **1809** ROLAND *Fencing* 81 To leave his body exposed to receive, in the interim of his motion, a *time thrust. **1834** *Encycl. Brit.* (ed. 7) IX. 503 Time thrusts are so called because the success of these movements depends entirely upon their being executed at the exact moment of time employed by the adversary in planning or in executing his attack. *Ibid.*, *Passim.* **1889** *Fencing* (Badm. Libr.) 91 The time-thrust is an attack made with opposition on a complicated attack, and intended to intercept the line where such an attack is meant to finish. **1859** SALA *Tw. Round Clock* (1861) 175 You never see these ghostly *time-waiters anywhere but on 'Change, and out of 'Change hours. **1899** *Globe* 30 June, During the debate Mr. Courtney call'd himself first a Liberal Unionist and then a Time-waiter. **1829** BENTHAM *Justice & Cod. Petit., More Abr. Petit. Justice* 3 He is paid according to the time during which he is occupied ..in doing the work: this is called..*time work. **1910** *Edinb. Rev.* Jan. 12 The advantages which piecework has over timework are more completely secured. **1906** *Outlook* 9 June 774/1 To move the Observatory..would involve the adoption of a new starting-point for the meridians of longitude and for the *time-zones into which the world is divided.

**Time** (təim), *v.* Pa. t. and pple. **timed** (təimd). [f. TIME *sb.*: cf. OE. *getímian* to happen, befall. In sense 1, app. substituted for TIDE *v.*[1], when *time* sb. was superseding *tide*.]

**I.** †**1.** *intr.* To befall, to happen; = TIDE *v.*[1] 1. *Impers.* or with subject *it.* (Perf. with *be.*)

*c* **1205** LAY. 27978 Þa wes hit itimed [*c* 1275 ifunde] þere þat Merlin saide while. *c* **1230** *Hali Meid.* 35 Ofte hit timeð þat tat leoueste bearn..sorheð & sweameð meast his ealdren on ende. *c* **1250** *Gen. & Ex.* 3820 Do we us alle in godes red, Vs sal timen ðe betre sped. *c* **1350** *Will. Palerne* 5433 Þe same sey i be þe, so me wel time. ? *a* **1400** *Morte Arth.* 3150 In-to Tuskane he tournez, whene thus wele tymede.

†**b.** *intr.* To fare (well or ill); *spec.* to fare well, prosper. *Obs.*

*c* **1250** *Gen. & Ex.* 1023 Bi ðan sal sarra selðe timen Ðat ȝe [= she] sal of a sune trimen. *Ibid.* 3392 Amalech fleȝ, and israel Hadde heȝere hond, and timede wel. *Ibid.* 4024 Ðis folc..Is vnder god timed wel. *c* **1460** *Towneley Myst.* ii. 26 God gif you ill to tyme!

**II. 2.** *trans.* To appoint or arrange the time of (an action or event); to choose the moment or occasion for. Usually (in context), to do (a thing) at the right time; 'to adapt to the time' (J.).

**13..** *Gaw. & Gr. Knt.* 2241 Þou hatz tymed þi trauayl as true mon schulde. *c* **1440** *Promp. Parv.* 490/1 Tymyn, or make in tyme (and) in seson, *temporo.* **1625** BACON *Ess.*, *Of Delays* (Arb.) 525 There is surely no greater Wisedome, then well to time the Beginnings, and Onsets of Things. *a* **1708** BEVERIDGE *Thes. Theol.* (1710) II. 329 To teach us to submit to His wisdom..in timing all things. **1786** MME. D'ARBLAY *Diary* 6 Oct., This visit was not so timed as to compose me. **1802** MAR. EDGEWORTH *Moral T.*, *Forester* iii, Pray let me go to sleep..and time your explanations a little better. **1821** SCOTT *Kenilw.* xvi, 'Why, how now, Bowyer', said Elizabeth, 'thy courtesy seems strangely timed!' **1865** KINGSLEY *Herew.* v, They had timed their journey by the tides. **1884** COURTHOPE *Addison* v. 113 Nothing could have been better timed than the appearance of the *Spectator*.

**b.** To arrange the time of arrival of (a train, a ship, etc.); hence, to regulate the rate of travelling of; also, to calculate or judge the moment of impact of (a ball or moving body).

**1861** *Times* 22 Aug., The Royal train was timed to reach Leamington at 1.17 p.m. **1866** *Routledge's Ev. Boy's Ann.* 356 Educating, so to speak, his eye to time the ball correctly. **1880** NEWTON *Serm. Boys & Girls* (1881) 167 Not timing himself right..he met him just in the road. **1889** ACWORTH *Railw. Eng.* 198 The best train each way..is timed at over 45 miles an hour. *Ibid.* 202 The Great Northern..timed their trains to Doncaster..in 6 minutes less. **1890** *Punch* 12 July 15 Special trains, timed to take at least half-an-hour longer. **1893** [see TIMING *vbl. sb.* 2].

**c.** To adjust (a clock, etc.) to keep accurate time.

**1825** J. NICHOLSON *Operat. Mech.* 504 The easy Timing of Watches by the Vibrations of the Pendulum. **1884** F. J. BRITTEN *Watch & Clockm.* 264 [A] Timing Box [is] a brass box for the reception of an uncased watch movement while it is being timed. *Mod.* Your watch is finished, but has not been exactly timed yet.

**3.** To mark the rhythm or measure of, as in music; to sing or play (an air or instrument) in (good or bad) time. Also *fig.*

*c* **1500** in Grose, etc. *Antiq. Rep.* (1809) IV. 408 Yet *rationalis lingua expellit* instrumentis all, Wel tymede and tewnede. **1602** MARSTON *Ant. & Mel.* v, If that thou canst not give, goe hang thy selfe: Ile time thee dead, or verse thee to the rope. **1607** SHAKS. *Cor.* II. ii. 114 He was a thing of Blood, whose euery motion Was tim'd with dying Cryes. *a* **1711** [see TIMING *vbl. sb.* 2]. **1837** LOCKHART *Scott* Mar. an. 1815, He then..joined with a stentorian voice in the cheering, which the Prince himself timed.

**b.** To set the time of; to cause to coincide in time with something (const. *to*).

**1655** H. VAUGHAN *Silex Scint.*, *Isaac's Marr.* 67 Others were tym'd and train'd up to 't. *a* **1719** ADDISON tr. *Ovid* III. *Mariners Transf. Dolphins* 52 Old Epopeus..Who overlook'd the oars, and tim'd the stroke. **1725** POPE *Odyss.* VII. 419 How fleet our sail, When justly tim'd with equal sweep they row. **1805** SOUTHEY *Madoc in W.* xvii, Hark! 'tis the mariners with voice attuned Timing their toil! **1808** SCOTT *Marm.* I. ii, Timing his footsteps to a march, The warder kept his guard. **1871** TYNDALL *Fragm. Sc.* (1879) I. vi. 197 Timing the pull to the lurching of the ship.

**c.** *intr.* To keep time *to*; to sound or move in unison or harmony *with*.

**1850** WHITTIER *Elliott* iv, Timing to their stormy sounds, His stormy lays are sung. **1855** TENNYSON *Maud* I. xviii. 8 Beat, happy stars, timing with things below, Beat with my heart more blest than heart can tell. *a* **1892** WHITMAN *Out of Cradle* 8 The savage old mother, incessantly crying, To the boy's soul's questions sullenly timing.

†**4.** *trans.* To 'give' or tell the time to (any one). *Obs. rare.*

**1583** MELBANCKE *Philotimus* C ij, The fyre to warme thee, the scortching of the sunne: thy clocke to time thee, the scritching of yᵉ owle.

**5.** To fix the duration of; to assign the metrical quantity of (a syllable) or the duration of (a note); also, to regulate the operation or action of (a mechanism, etc.) as to duration (see also 7).

**1589** PUTTENHAM *Eng. Poesie* II. xii[i]. (Arb.) 131 It could not possible be by vs perfourmed, because their sillables came to be timed some of them long, some of them short. **1597** [see TIMING *vbl. sb.* 2]. **1835** *Fraser's Mag.* XII. 416 Lamarck has defined nature to be motion, and law, and space, and time, without reference to a being moving or moved, legislating or legislated upon, and timing or spacing, or being timed and spaced. **1885** *Manch. Exam.* 12 Jan. 5/2 The clockwork apparatus, timed to run for two hours. **1893** J. A. HODGES *Elem. Photogr.* (1907) 58 If we have correctly timed our exposure.

†**b.** *To time it out*, to procrastinate, delay, spin out the time. *Obs.*

**1613** DANIEL *Coll. Hist. Eng.* 81 They timed it out all that Spring, and a great part of the next Sommer. *a* **1649** DRUMM. OF HAWTH. *Hist. Jas. II*, Wks. (1711) 32 Others advised him..to time it out a while: in this lingring war a truce might be agreed upon.

**6.** To ascertain or note the time at which (something) is done or happens; to note the time occupied by or the duration of (an action, etc.).

**1670** MILTON *Hist. Eng.* IV. Wks. (1847) 527/2 So different they often are one from another, both in timing and in naming. **1692** NORRIS *Curs. Refl.* 19 The Question will be concerning the Timing of it, whether any of these Impressions be Original Characters or no. **1723–4** DK. WHARTON *True Briton* No. 71 II. 602 The Timing of the subsequent Piece obliges us to insert the following Letter. **1859** LANG *Wand. India* 393 Slowly as he read, it was over in twelve minutes, for I timed him. **1878** BROWNING *La Saisiaz* 193 We who, darkling, timed the day's birth. **1896** *Daily News* 13 Jan. 8/2 Another letter..timed 9 p.m. states that during the night of the 8th and 9th inst. the Shoans made an attack by surprise. **1907** *Academy* 14 Sept. 885/2 He does not believe in what he cannot see, or time, or measure, or weigh.

**7.** *Mech.* To adjust the parts of (a mechanism) so that a succession of movements or operations takes place at the required intervals and in the desired sequence; to arrange the time of (an operation) in a mechanical cycle or series.

**1895** in *Funk's Stand. Dict.* **1898** *Engineering Mag.* XVI. 108/1 When..a timing valve is used, instead of permitting the ignition to be timed by the compression.

**8.** *Fencing.* = *To take the time* (TIME *sb.* 21, quot. 1809).

1809 ROLAND *Fencing* 109 The too frequent practice of timing their adversary, because they will render their modes of play.. very disagreeable to each other. 1889 DUNN *Fencing* 83 There is always a large element of risk in timing.

**9.** *To time out*: to parcel out or apportion (a space of time). Cf. *to space out*.

1902 *Fortn. Rev.* June 1036 When a man is always timing out his day, and dovetailing together the duties which compose his daily life.

**Time**, obs. form of THYME.

**Ti·me-ball.** A ball moving on a vertical rod or pole, placed in some prominent elevated position, for the purpose of indicating mean time, which it does by dropping at a certain moment each day from the top to the bottom of the rod, usually by the closing of an electric circuit.

The time thus indicated is usually 1 p.m., in U.S. noon.

1858 SIMMONDS *Dict. Trade*, *Time-ball*, a ball, moved by electricity, which is dropped from the summit of a pole to indicate the true meridional or mid-day time. 1878 LOCKYER *Stargazing* 279 This [wire] is used for dropping the time-ball at Deal. 1884 BRITTEN *Watch & Clockm.* 263 The time ball at Greenwich Observatory is of very thin copper.

**Ti·me-ba:rgain.** A contract for the sale or purchase of goods or stock at a stipulated price on a certain future day; in Stock Exchange parlance, a transaction in which one accepts the liability to profit or lose by the amount of the difference between the prices of the stock involved on the day of dealing and on the settling-day.

1775 MORTIMER *Ev. Man his Own Broker* 63 *note*, Time-bargains, which have no foundation in real property. 1844 HARVEY *Rep. Sel. Comm. on Gaming* Q. 869 A time-bargain is in the nature of a bet upon what will be the price of stocks on a given day. 1882 BITHELL *Counting-ho. Dict.* (1893) s.v., Time bargains originated in the practice of closing the bank for six weeks in each quarter for the preparation of the dividends. As no transfer could be made during that period, it became a practice to buy and sell for the opening. 1888 J. S. NICHOLSON in *Encycl. Brit.* XXIII. 89/1 A curious example of legal evasion [of taxes on the transfer of stocks and shares] is furnished by time-bargains; and the imposition of the tax directly on the contracts of sale, instead of as at present on the actual transfer, has been strongly urged.

**Timed** (təimd), *ppl. a.* [f. TIME *v.* (and *sb.*) + -ED.] †**a.** Matured by time, seasoned. *Obs. rare*$^{-1}$. **b.** Done, made, or occurring at a (proper or improper) time; †done at the right time, well-timed, timely (*obs.*). **c.** Of music or verse: Written in measure. **d.** Fixed or regulated as to time.

Also, as second element in a compound, as *ill-timed*, *well-timed*, *even-timed*; *two-*, *three-*, *four-timed*.

1628 FELTHAM *Resolves* II. [I.] xliv. 130 There is a flowing noblenesse, that some men be graced with, which farre outshines the notions of a timed Student. *a* 1760 HOGARTH in Cunningham *Brit. Paint.* (1829) I. 167 The stagnation rendered it necessary that I should do some timed thing to recover my lost time and stop a gap in my income. 1888 *Bookseller* 5 Sept. 920 Two-timed metre is identified with the octave or root, three-timed metre with the fifth, and four-timed metre—the last of the uncompounded metres, and including the other two—is identified with the third. 1896 R. G. MOULTON *Lit. Stud. Bible* iv. 117 The oratorio combines recitative with timed music. 1898 G. MEREDITH *Odes Fr. Hist.* 83 A timed artillery speaks full-mouthed. 1901 R. ELLIS tr. *Aetna* 4 These..kilns the Cyclops used, when bending..to their even-timed strokes, they shook the dreadful thunder-bolt with the beat of their ponderous hammers.

**Timeful** (təi·mfŭl), *a.* Now *rare*. [f. TIME *sb.* + -FUL.]

**1.** Seasonable, due; = TIMELY *a.* 2.

*a* 1300 *E. E. Psalter* cxliv. [cxlv.] 16 Þou giues þar mete in time ful tide. 1614 RALEIGH *Hist. World* I. vi. § 9 (1634) 83 Interrupting..all offer of timefull returne towards God. 1825 CARLYLE *Schiller* II. 92 The timeful change of Christendom;..The universal Spring that shall make young The countenance o' th' Earth.

†**2.** Early in season; = TIMELY *a.* 1. *Obs.*

1382 WYCLIF *Jas.* v. 7 Paciently suffringe, til he receyue tymeful and lateful [1388 *adds* fruyt; *Vulg.* temporaneum et serotinum; TINDALE the yerly and the latter rayne]. 1388 — *Jer.* v. 24 Oure Lord God, that ȝiueth to vs reyn tymeful, and lateful in his tyme.

†**3.** Occurring in or consisting of time; temporal, durational. *Obs.*

*a* 1400 HYLTON *Scala Perf.* II. xxiv. (W. de W. 1494), The nyghte as a tymefull space bytwix dayes two.

Hence **Ti·mefully** *adv.*, with timely action.

1837 CARLYLE *Fr. Rev.* I. III. iii, Warned by friend Talleyrand..he timefully flits over the marches. 1845 — *Cromwell* (1871) I. 105 The Five Members, timefully warned, were gone into the City.

**Ti·me-ho:noured,** *a.* Honoured or made honourable by length of time; revered or respected on account of long existence or old establishment.

1593 SHAKS. *Rich. II*, I. i. 1 Old Iohn of Gaunt, time-honoured Lancaster. 1751 MASON *Elfrida* Poems (1774) 90 That old minstrelsy, which breath'd Through each time-honour'd grove of British oak. 1831 WILLIS *Poem Brown University* 57 They have grown time-honoured on their shrines. 1887 SIR R. H. ROBERTS *In the Shires* ix. 141 A time-honoured custom had prevailed for years.

**Ti·me-kee:per, timekeeper.**

**1.** An instrument for registering the passage of time; a timepiece; formerly, a specially constructed timepiece for scientific use, a chronometer.

1686 MOLYNEUX *Scioth. Telesc.* Title-p., For Regulating and Adjusting Curious Pendulum-Watches and other Time-Keepers. 1764 *Chron.* in *Ann. Reg.* 99/2 Mr. Harrison's new invented time-keeper. 1776 COOK *Voy. Pacific Ocean* I. i. (1784) I. 4 The Board, likewise, put into our possession the same watch, or time-keeper, which I had carried out in my last voyage, and had performed its part so well. 1878 HUXLEY *Physiogr.* 7 True noon does not always coincide with 12 o'clock as indicated by an ordinary timekeeper. *transf.* 1868 LOCKYER *Guillemin's Heavens* (ed. 3) 6 According to the happy expression of Humboldt, they make of the Universe an eternal timekeeper.

**b.** Applied to an almanac. *nonce-use*.

1778 MISS BURNEY *Evelina* lxxviii, It would make me quite melancholy to have such a time-keeper in my pocket.

**2.** One who notes, measures, or records time; *spec.* **a.** one who is employed in keeping account of workmen's hours of labour; **b.** one who beats time in music; **c.** one who marks the time occupied by a race, the rounds in a pugilistic encounter, etc.

1795 SOUTHEY *Lett. fr. Spain* (1808) I. 294 The time-keeper..then turned up an hour-glass. 1851 MAYHEW *Lond. Labour* I. 356/1, I went to a firm..at Beckenham, near Croydon, as working time-keeper, or foreman. 1879 'E. GARRETT' *House by Works* II. 185 A post as timekeeper at some great engineering works. 1903 *Daily Chron.* 28 Nov. 5/2 The Duke of Wellington called [Sir Thomas McDougall] Brisbane the 'timekeeper of the Army'.

**3.** With qualifying word: A person or thing that keeps (good or bad) time.

1899 P. W. HASLUCK *Clock Jobber's Handbk.* 2 Being very cheap..and fair time-keepers, American clocks are exceedingly popular. *Mod.* He is a good executant, but a bad time-keeper.

Hence **Ti·mekee:pership,** the position or office of a time-keeper. So **Ti·me-kee:ping** *sb.*, the keeping of time; *adj.* that keeps time (in various senses of the phrase: see TIME *sb.* 50.)

1816 HERVÉ *Beauties Paris* I. 211 No swing of the shoulders from side to side with graceless timekeeping. 1825 J. NICHOLSON *Operat. Mech.* 522 This degree of time-keeping cannot reasonably be expected from any other clock. 1887 *Pall Mall G.* 16 Sept. 11/1 The need existed for a timekeeping watch at a low price. 1891 *Wheeling* 25 Feb. 414/3 The Timekeepership of the London Centre. 1895 *Daily News* 20 Apr. 2/1 The right of the employer to make reasonable regulations for time-keeping.

**Ti·me-ki:ller.** One who or that which 'kills' time (see KILL *v.* 5): said of a person, an amusement, etc. So **Ti·me-killing** *sb.* and *a.*

1751 RICHARDSON in *Johnson's Rambler* No. 97 ⁋ 24 Another seasonable relief to those modern time-killers. 1825 *Blackw. Mag.* XVII. 28 Much resorted to by..antiquity hunters, view-hunters, Time-killers. 1882 W. CORY *Lett. & Jrnls.* (1897) 484 Hard up for time-killing occupation. 1895 *Outing* (U.S.) XXVI. 427/2 Reading it with the idle interest of a time-killer.

**Timeless** (təi·mlės), *a.* (*adv.*) [-LESS.]

**1.** That is out of its proper time; untimely; unseasonable, ill-timed; *esp.* occurring or done prematurely. Chiefly *poet.*, now *arch.* or *Obs.*

*c* 1560 *Trag. Rich. II* (1870) 96 Wert thou aliue to see How Ile reuenge thy tymless tragedye On all ther heads. 1590 MARLOWE *2nd Pt. Tamburl.* v. iii. ad fin., Let earth and heaven his timeless death deplore. *c* 1611 CHAPMAN *Iliad* VI. 349 Wretched man! So timeless is thy spite That 'tis not honest. 1621 LADY M. WROTH *Urania* 40 A timelesse, and vnseasonable birth. 1751 FALCONER *To Pr. of Wales* 78 Well mayst thou mourn thy patriot's timeless end! 1850 DOBELL *Roman* iii, Cease these timeless babblings.

**b.** as *adv.* = TIMELESSLY a.

1586 KYD *Answ. Tychborne's Lament.* iii. Wks. (1901) 341 Thy glorie and thy glasse are timeles runne. 1631 CHAPMAN *Cæsar & Pompey* II. iv. 152 And 'tis their repaire That timelesse darken thus the gloomy ayre. 1876 SWINBURNE *Erechtheus* 256 To slay thee timeless with my proper tongue.

**2.** Not subject to time; not affected by the lapse of time; existing or operating without reference to duration; eternal. Chiefly *poet.* and *rhet.*

*a* 1628 F. GREVIL *Hum. Learn.* xcvi, Curious mystery Of timelesse time. 1678 CUDWORTH *Intell. Syst.* I. v. § 21. 781 The reason why we cannot frame a Conception of such a timeless Eternity. 1742 YOUNG *Nt. Th.* ii. 222 When worlds..headlong rush To timeless night, and chaos, whence they rose. 1819 *Blackw. Mag.* V. 323 There timeless, spaceless, dwells the Eternal One. 1871 R. ELLIS *Catullus* ci. 10 Yea, take, brother, a long Ave, a timeless adieu.

**b.** *absolutely*. Cf. ETERNAL B.

1825 COLERIDGE *Aids Refl.* (1848) I. 22 All the truths, acts, and duties, that have an especial reference to the timeless, the permanent, the eternal. 1892 TENNYSON *Akbar's Dream*, *Hymn* ii, Kneel adoring Him the Timeless in the flame that measures Time!

**3.** †**a.** Of no duration; brief, short-lived. *Obs. rare*$^{-1}$. **b.** Destitute or ignorant of musical time. **c.** Having reference to no particular time.

1657 COKAINE *Obstinate Lady* Poems (1669) 339 Thy timeless inexperience doth deceive thee. 1821 BYRON *Juan* IV. lxxxvii, An ignorant, noteless, timeless, tuneless fellow. 1837 G. PHILLIPS *Syriac Gram.* 112 The participle is timeless; i.e. it has no time of its own; but partakes of every time with which it may be connected.

**Timelessly** (təi·mlėsli), *adv.* [f. prec. + -LY [2].] In a timeless manner. **a.** Unseasonably, out of due time. *arch.* or *Obs.* **b.** Without reference to time, independently of the passage of time.

1625 MILTON *Death Fair Infant* i, Soft silken Primrose fading timelesslie. *c* 1750 SHENSTONE *Ruin'd Abbey* 73 The cruel meed Of virtuous ardour timelessly display'd. 1824 *Blackw. Mag.* XVI. 580 Destined to be severed timelessly and know no fruitage. 1833 J. H. NEWMAN *Arians* II. v. (1876) 210 Brought into existence 'timelessly', independent of that succession of second causes.

So **Ti·melessness,** the quality of being timeless.

1872 *Spectator* 7 Sept. 1138 Even nature almost witnesses to the timelessness of the Divine Being. 1894 SWETE *Apost. Creed* iii. 33 Because Tertullian has not grasped the timelessness of the mutual relations of the Divine Life.

‖ **Timelia** (təimī·liă). *Ornith.* [Altered by Sundevall (1872) from Horsfield's name *Timalia* (1820), said to be from an E. Ind. name.] A genus of East Indian oscine birds, the type of which is *T. pileata*, a small bird found from Nepāl to Cochin China and Java. Hence **Time·lian** *a.*; ‖ **Time·liidæ** *pl.*, a provisional family or group of passerine birds, which have been supposed to be related to *Timelia*; **Timeliine** (təimī·li,əin) *a.*, allied, or assumed to be allied, to *Timelia*.

1896 NEWTON *Dict. Birds* 963 The *Troglodytidæ* (Wren)..were referred to the *Timeliidæ*, whereas if their union were necessary, the Timelias should have been referred to the Wrens. *Ibid.*, *note*, A solution of the Timelian difficulty will indeed be a great feat. 1874 *Ibis* Jan. 89 (Cass. Supp.) Description of a new Timaliine bird from West Africa. 1881 R. B. SHARPE *Catal. Birds Brit. Mus.* VI. 301 Birds which are true Wrens and others which are truly Timeliine. 1898 *Field* 12 Apr. 518 The concave Timeliine shape of the wing..is reckoned of little worth.

†**Ti·melily,** *adv. Obs. rare.* [f. TIMELY *a.* + -LY [2].] = TIMELY *adv.*

1608 H. CLAPHAM *Errour Left Hand* 85 God giue the truth to preuaile timelily with me and all his people.

**Ti·me-li:mit.** A limit in time, or to the duration of some action or condition; e.g. a limit to the length of speeches in parliament, etc.; also, a limit to the duration of a licence or privilege.

1880 PLUMPTRE in *Dict. Chr. Biog.* II. 192/2 He [Origen] taught the perpetual freedom of the will, and therefore set no time-limits to the capacity for restoration. 1891 KIPLING *Light that Failed* x. 199 'What is my time-limit, avoiding all strain and worry?' 'Perhaps one year.' 1894 *Westm. Gaz.* 3 Jan. 1/2 The stronger..the case appears for..time-limit by Standing Orders. 1899 *Ibid.* 6 Feb. 2/2 Should this be effected, there will be a time-limit granted of from three to five years before any public-house is closed.

**Timeliness** (təi·mlinės). [f. TIMELY *a.* + -NESS.] The quality of being timely. †**a.** Early development or maturity. *Obs. rare*. **b.** Seasonableness, suitableness to the time.

1599 SANDYS *Europæ Spec.* (1632) 81 Difficulties..kindle..the generous spirits, and adde that to their diligence which was wanting in their timelinesse. 1612–13 C. BROOKE *Elegy* Poems (1872) 180 His timelinesse did so preuent his date, That ere the floure was look't for came the fruit. 1860 EMERSON *Cond. Life* iii. (1861) 53 The art of getting rich consists not in industry, much less in saving, but in a better order, in timeliness, in being at the right spot. 1868 RUSKIN *Arrows of Chace* (1880) II. 195 All measures of reformation are effective in exact proportion to their timeliness.

†**Ti·meling.** *Obs.* [f. TIME *sb.* + -LING [1].] A time-server.

1563 BECON *Humble Supplic.* Wks. III. 21 Mynisters, whiche are faynteharted, and..but tymelynges, seruing rather the tyme (as the manner of the worldlynges is). 1631 WILSON *Sweiser* II. i. 158 What sayes my Lip-Ladds My little Time-lings?

**Timely** (təi·mli), *a.* Forms: 2–3 **timelich,** 4 **timlich, tymeli,** 5 **-lie,** 5–6 **-ly,** 6–7 **-lye, timelie,** 6– **timely.** [f. TIME *sb.* + -LY [1]: cf. ON. *tímalig-r* temporal. (Not recorded in OE., and rare in ME.; it may have arisen later than the adv. under its influence.)]

**1.** Occurring or appearing in good time; early; † of a plant, fruit, etc., bearing or ripening early. Now *rare* or *Obs.* (exc. as blending with 2).

1382 WYCLIF *Jer.* v. 24 Oure God, that ȝyueth to vs tymeli rein. 1530 PALSGR. 327/2 Tymely, *temprif*. 1563 HYLL *Art Gard.* (1593) 86 To haue timely Roses. 1585 ABP. SANDYS *Serm.* xv. (Parker Soc.) 301 The timeliest fruit often cometh to least proof. 1598 GRENEWEY *Tacitus, Ann.* II. ii. (1622) 34 Short summers, and timely winters. 1612 T. TAYLOR *Comm. Titus* ii. 6 (1619) 405 It filled Paul with ioy to remember Timothies timely faith. *a* 1715 BURNET *Own Time* (1766) II. 8 If a timely stop were not put to the progress.

**2.** Occurring, done, or made at a fitting or suitable time; seasonable, opportune, well-timed.

*c* 1200 *Trin. Coll. Hom.* 13 [He] nutteð timeliche metes, and ȝemeð his muðes meðe. *a* 1541 WYATT *Compl. Love to Reason* 59 Though my timely death hath been so slow. 1580 SIDNEY *Ps.* I. ii, Lyke a freshly planted tree,..Whose braunches faile not timelie fruite to nourish. 1605 SHAKS. *Macb.* III. iii. 7 Now spurres the lated Traueller apace, To gayne the timely Inne. 1738 WESLEY *Psalms* XVIII. iv, He..sent the timely Rescue down. 1782 COWPER *Gilpin* xliii, Now Gilpin had a pleasant wit, And loved a timely joke. 1890 *Spectator* 31 May 763/2 With the general drift of his essay we heartily agree, and think it both wise and timely.

†**3.** Of or in time, as opposed to eternity; temporal, earthly. *Obs. rare*.

1340 *Ayenb.* 209 We habbeþ niede..of gostliche guodes and of timliche guodes. *c* 1400 *Lay Folks Mass Bk.* App. III. 123 Þat he absteyne hym from alle þingis tymely þat myȝtte fylen his soule. *a* 1615 DONNE *Ess.* (1651) 30 Saying that after John's eternal Beginning, and before Moses's timely beginning, Christ had his beginning.

†**4. a.** Of time or duration; pertaining to the time of day. **b.** Keeping time or measure. *Obs.*

1590 SPENSER *F. Q.* I. iv. 4 A Diall told the timely howres. *Ibid.* v. 3 And many Bardes, that to the trembling chord, Can tune their timely voices cunningly.

**Timely** (təi·mli), *adv.* Forms: 1 **tímlíce,** 2–3 **timliche,** 3 **timeliche, -lyche,** 4 **tymliche,** 4–6 **tymely** (5 **tymli, -ly,** 6 *Sc.* **tymlie**), 4– **timely.**

[Late OE. *tīmlīce*, f. *tīma* TIME + -LY[2]: possibly suggested by ON. *tímaliga* adv. timely, early.]

**1.** Early, betimes; in good time; soon, quickly. Now *arch.* or *poet.*

*c* **1000** ÆLFRIC *De Vet. et de Nov. Test.* ad init., Ic þe ne ȝetiðode ealles swa timlīce, ær þam þe þu mid weorcum þæs ȝewilnodost æt me. *c* **1205** LAY. 31369 Penda..seide þat he wolde sahtnesse wurche and timliche him speken wið. *a* **1225** *Leg. Kath.* 2117 ȝef þu þe timluker [*maturius*] do þe i þe ȝeinturn. *a* **1225** *Juliana* 9 Ase timliche as he hefde iherd þis. *a* **1375** *Joseph Arim.* 415 Þe kyng..Comaundes hem to meeten him tymely on þe morwen. **1390** GOWER *Conf.* II. 107 As tymliche as I may, Fulofte whanne it is brod day. **1455** *Paston Lett.* I. 338, I had lever ye were at London a weke the rather and tymelyer then a weke to late. **1578** LYTE *Dodoens* III. i. 314 The Aristolochias do flowre..timelier in hoate Countries. **1596** DALRYMPLE tr. *Leslie's Hist. Scot.* (S.T.S.) I. 26 Gif in a schip, tymlie in the morning ȝe passe by the craig. **1602** CAREW *Cornwall* 4 b, The Spring visiteth not these quarters so timely, as the Eastern parts. **1680** O. HEYWOOD *Diaries*, etc. (1881) II. 299 Came home pretty timely of the day. **1716** S. SEWALL *Diary* 5 Oct., Got up so timely, that the Comissions were read by 11. *mane.* **1827** KEBLE *Chr. Y.*, *Morning* v, Oh! timely happy, timely wise, Hearts that with rising morn arise!

**2.** †Soon enough, in time, not too late (*obs.*); hence, In due season, at the right or a fortunate time; seasonably; opportunely as regards time.

*c* **1175** *Lamb. Hom.* 25 Ȝet ic mei longe libben and alle mine sunne timliche ibeten. **1552** HULOET, Tymely or in dew season, as nother to tymely nor to late. **1621** FLETCHER *Isl. Princess* V. ii, A virtuous point of gratitude, Timely, and nobly taken. **1678** WANLEY *Wonders Lit. World* V. ii. § 8. 469/1 Ruffinus..sought to betray him to the Goths, but was timely discovered to his ruine. **1715** LEONI *Palladio's Archit.* (1742) I. 1 All requisite materials timely provided. **1828** D'ISRAELI *Chas. I*, II. x. 247 Buckingham had timely perished to be saved from the reproach of one more political crime. **1842** ARNOLD *Hist. Rome* II. 208 The attempt of L. Fulvius to surprise Rome..was timely baffled.

**3.** Usually hyphened to an adj. or pple. when used attributively.

**1593** SHAKS. *2 Hen. VI*, III. ii. 161 Oft haue I seene a timely-parted Ghost, Of ashy semblance. **1651** JER. TAYLOR *Holy Dying* v. § 5 (1727) 221 Our timely-repented and often forsaken habits of sin. *Mod.* Your timely-offered help.

†**Timen**, variant of TAMIN *Obs.*, stamin.

**1756** MRS. CALDERWOOD *Jrnl.* (1884) 334 Window-curtains of English stuff..about the substance of a timen or crape.

†**Ti·menoguy·.** *Naut. Obs.* [app. f. F. *timon* TIMON[2] + GUY *sb.*[1]] (See quots.)

**1794** *Rigging & Seamanship* I. 178 *Timenoguy*, a Rope fastened at one end to the fore-shrouds, and nailed at the other end to the anchor-stock, on the bow, to prevent the fore-sheet from entangling. **1841** DANA *Seaman's Man.*, *Timenoguy*, a rope carried taut between different parts of the vessel, to prevent the sheet or tack of a course from getting foul, in working ship. **1867** SMYTH *Sailor's Word-bk.*, *Timenoguy*, formerly [*as in Dana*; *but adds*] specially from the fore-rigging to the anchor-stock, to prevent the fouling of the fore-sheet. *Ibid.*, *Timonogy*, this term properly belongs to steering, and is derived from *timon*, the tiller, and the twiddling-lines, which worked in olden times on a gauge in front of the poop.., by which the position of the helm was easily read even from the forecastle.

**Timeous, timous** (tɔi·məs), *a.* (*adv.*) Chiefly *Sc.* Forms: 5 tymys, 6 tymouse, -ouis, -ose, tymmos, 6–7 tymous, -eous, 7– timeous, timous. [f. TIME *sb.* + -OUS; perh. after *wrongous*, *righteous*. Occasionally pronounced (tɔi·miəs) or (ti·myəs), from the spelling: cf. *righteous*.]

**1.** Early (in the morning, or in the season); sufficiently early; done betimes: = TIMELY *a.* 1.

*c* **1470** [implied in TIMEOUSLY]. *c* **1520** NISBET *N. T. in Scots* Jas. v. 7 Pacientlie suffring, till he resaue tymouse and laatsum fruit. **1564** *Reg. Privy Council Scot.* I. 292 Upoun lauchfull and tymous warning. *a* **1578** LINDESAY (Pitscottie) *Chron. Scot.* XXI. xvii. (S.T.S.) I. 324 Sayand..that thai sould haue goode huntting on the morne and bad him be tymmos. **1637–50** ROW *Hist. Kirk* (Wodrow Soc.) 319 It cannot be a lawfull Assemblie when there is not lawfull and tymous intimation and premonition made. **1687** *Royal Proclam.* 12 Feb., in *Lond. Gaz.* No 2221/5 We do hereby Command, Our Lyon King at Arms,..to make timeous Proclamation thereof at the Mercat-Cross of Edinburgh. **1825** JAMIESON s. v., See that ye keep timeous hours, i.e. that ye be not too late. **1910** *Highland Railw. Time-table* July, Stops to take up for East of Aviemore [Inverness] on timeous notice being given to the Station Master.

**b.** as *adv.* Early, betimes. Now *dial.*

*a* **1578** LINDESAY (Pitscottie) *Chron. Scot.* XXII. xxiv. (S.T.S.) II. 135 Tymose in the morning he departit of the toun. **1679** J. RUSSELL in Kirkton *Hist. Ch. Scot.*, etc. (1817) App. 430 Timous in the morning they went to their prayers. **1892** *Ballymena Obs.* (E.D.D.), A'll be up gye an' timus in the mornin'.

**2.** Coming in due time; suitable or proper in respect of time; well-timed, seasonable, opportune; = TIMELY *a.* 2.

*a* **1626** BACON (J.), By a wise and timous inquisition, the peccant humours and humourists may be discovered, purged, or cut off. **1656** J. FERGUSSON *On Colossians* 136 Those fruits were timeous, and constant. **1729** WODROW *Corr.* (1843) III. 451, I fear his writings do a world of mischief, without a timeous antidote. **1849** AYTOUN *Lays Scot. Cav.* (ed. 2) 96 His retreat was timeous, for General Mackay ..had despatched a strong force..to make him prisoner. **1884** *Athenæum* 1 Mar. 271/1 The book [R. McCormick's 'Voyages'] is timeous.

**3. a.** Temporal; of finite time: = TIMELY *a.* 3. **b.** Keeping time, moving in time or measure. *nonce-uses.*

**1855** BAILEY *Spir. Leg.* in *Mystic*, etc. 103 Duration, timeous and æterne, and space. **1884** D. GRANT *Lays & Leg. North* 112 Never yet to mortal measures Raise and fell sic timous feet.

**Timeously** (tɔi·məsli), *adv.* [f. prec. + -LY[2].] In a timeous manner; †at an early hour or season, in good time (*obs.*); hence, early or soon enough, in time; at the right or a fitting time; seasonably; opportunely.

*c* **1470** HENRY *Wallace* VIII. 1180 To souppar went, and tymysly thai slepe. **1473** *Rental Bk. Cupar-Angus* (1879) I. 188 A chalder of quhet als arly and tymsly sawn as it ma be. **1571–5** *Diurnal of Occurr.* (1833) 259 Certane..horsmen, and fyftie hagbutaris past furth tymouslie in the mornyng. **1637–50** ROW *Hist. Kirk* (Wodrow Soc.) 319 If one presbyterie was not warnit tymeouslie, all the rest conveening cannot justlie make any conclusion whilk may binde that presbyterie. **1708** *Roy. Proclam.* (Scotl.) in *Lond. Gaz.* No. 4456/2 We Ordain Our Solicitor timeously to dispatch Copies of the above Proclamation. **1758** WASHINGTON *Let. Writ.* 1889 II. 34 Differences..which, if not properly, and timously attended to may be productive of the most serious consequences. **1820** SCOTT *Monast.* ix, That fitting preparation may be timeously made. **1824** SYD. SMITH *Amer. Wks.* 1859 II. 52/1 The existence of slavery,..if not timously corrected, will one day entail (and ought to entail) a bloody servile war upon the Americans. **1901** *Scotsman* 13 Mar. 11/3 Undue detention of two vessels occasioned by the defenders failing timeously to deliver coals for loading.

**Ti·mepiece.** [PIECE 17.] An instrument for measuring and registering the passage of time; in a general sense, any kind of chronometer, including clocks and watches; *spec.*: see quot. 1884.

**1765** (*title*) Minutes of the Proceedings of the Commissioners, concerning Mr. Harrison's Time Pieces. **1784** COWPER *Task* II. (*title*) The Time-piece. **1823** *Mechanic's Mag.* No. 17. 269 What kind of time piece is best adapted for the pocket. **1876** G. CHAMBERS *Astron.* 733 An ordinary good parlour time piece..will meet all the requirements of the amateur. **1884** F. J. BRITTEN *Watch & Clockm.* 264 Any timekeeper above the size of a watch which does not strike at the hours is called a timepiece.

**Timer** (tɔi·məɹ). [f. TIME *v.* and *sb.* + -ER[1].]

†**1.** One who is skilled in time or measure; a musician. *Obs. rare*[−1].

*c* **1500** in Grose, etc. *Antiq. Rep.* (1809) IV. 407 How may a mysmovede tymere judge a trew instrument?

**2.** One who appoints or fixes the time for an action, event, etc.

**1841** LOWELL *Ode* II. 3 [The Poet] fits his singing, like a cunning timer, To all men's prides and fancies as they pass.

**3. a.** A watch or clock, with reference to its time-keeping qualities; a (good or bad) time-keeper. **b.** One who times clocks, etc., i. e. who keeps them to exact time. **c.** One who marks the time in athletics, etc.; = TIME-KEEPER 2 c.

**1884** *Graphic* 20 Sept. 303/2 Guaranteed good Timers. **1884** F. J. BRITTEN *Watch & Clockm.* 14 The want of constancy in the force of the balance spring..is one of the chief difficulties of the timer. **1890** *Century Mag.* June 205/2 The English are partial to a single watch in the hands of an experienced timer, but to make a record in this country requires the presence of three timers or measurers. **1891** *Cycling* 21 Feb. 82, I am aware that timers of professional events in the Midlands use the old-fashioned type.

**4.** As the second element in combinations, as FULL-TIMER, HALF-TIMER, OLD-TIMER; **fast timer**, one who or that which completes a race, etc. in fast time.

**1891** *Daily News* 28 Dec. 3/5 The fastest timers ran in the deciding round. **1903** *Motor. Ann.* 163 In the mile race the fastest timers in the different classes were [etc.].

†**Time·rity.** *Obs.* Also 7 *erron.* temerity. [f. *timerous*, TIMOROUS, app. on mistaken analogy of *temerity* from *temerous* 'rash'; it may also sometimes have been a corruption of *timidity*.

As *timerous* and *temerous* ran together in use, so *temerity* was sometimes put for *timerity*, as n. of quality from *timerous*, TIMOROUS, as well as from *temerous* 'rash'.]

Fear, timidness, timidity.

**1582** MUNDAY *Disc. E. Campion* F viij, The great timeritie and unstable opinion of his conscience..would not suffer him to utter it. **1601** CHESTER *Love's Mart.* (1878) 8 Nature was struck with pale temeritie, To see the God of thunders lightning eyes. **1618** LATHAM *2nd Bk. Falconry* (1633) 2 Without much timeritie or fearfulnesse. *a* **1660** *Contemp. Hist. Irel.* (Ir. Archæol. Soc.) I. 248 Such was the timeritie and cowardize and feare of all men there.

**Timerity**, obs. form of TEMERITY.

**Timerosity, Timerous,** obs. ff. TIMOROSITY, TIMOROUS, q. v.

**Ti·me-se:rver.** [agent-n. from the phrase '*to serve the time*' (cited 1560): see SERVE *v.*[1] 11.]

**1.** One who adapts his conduct to the time or season; usually, one who on grounds of self-interest shapes his conduct in conformity to the views that are in favour at the time; a temporizer, a 'trimmer'. (By Fuller used in a neutral or good sense.)

**1584** G. BABINGTON *Frailty & Faith* (1596) 49 Will then a dissembling time-seruer not be vncased? **1638** SIR T. HERBERT *Trav.* (ed. 2) 136 This brave man is a Georgian by discent, a Mussulman by profession, a Time-server for preferment. *a* **1680** BUTLER *Rem.* (1759) II. 219 A Time-server wears his Religion, Reason, and Understanding always in the Mode. **1770** LANGHORNE *Plutarch* (1879) II. 904/2 He was never a timeserver either in word or action. **1849** MACAULAY *Hist. Eng.* ii. I. 188 The Puritan..deserted by all the timeservers who, in his prosperity, had claimed brotherhood with him. **1898** L. STEPHEN *Stud. Biog.* I. v. 148 Every autobiography is interesting, even when it unveils a mere time-server and hypocrite.

**1642** FULLER *Holy & Prof. State* III. xix. 202 He is a good time-server, that complys his manners to the several ages of this life; pleasant in youth, without wantonness; grave in old age, without frowardness..He is a good time-server, that finds out the fittest opportunity for every action.

†**2.** One who serves only for a time, and afterwards deserts or 'falls away'. *Obs. rare.*

Apparently with reference to the parable of the sower, Matt. xiii. 21, Mark iv. 17, Luke viii. 13.

*a* **1575** BP. PILKINGTON *Expos. Neh.* iv. 15 (1585) 65 Such be those time-seruers which the Gospel speaketh of, that for a time make a shew in seruing the Lord, but in the tyme of triall they fall away.

**Ti·me-se:rvice.** [See prec. and SERVICE.]

**1.** = TIME-SERVING *vbl. sb.*

**1883** SYMONDS *Shaks. Predec.* v. (1900) 150 This freedom from time-service..give[s] a dignity to Heywood's character.

**2.** The work done by an observatory staff in daily furnishing the correct time to the community.

**1890** *Smithsonian Rep.* 160 Observations of nebulæ and physical observations of Jupiter and Saturn; time service. **1899** *Athenæum* 29 July 161/3 The time-service has also occupied part of the energy of the observatory.

**Ti·me-se:rving,** *vbl. sb.* [See TIME-SERVER, and SERVE *v.*[1] 11.] The action or conduct of a time-server; 'trimming'.

**1621** BURTON *Anat. Mel.* II. III. vi. 419 Let them goe on, get wealth,..by impudence, and time-seruing, let them..crosse me on every side. **1642** FULLER *Holy & Prof. St.* III. xix. 202 There be foure kinds of Time-serving: first out of Christian discretion, which is commendable; second, out of humane infirmity, which is more pardonable; third and fourth, out of ignorance, or affection, both which are damnable. **1712** ADDISON *Spect.* No. 445 ⁋6, I have been accused by these despicable Wretches of Trimming, Time-serving. **1894** MRS. OLIPHANT *Hist. Sk. Q. Anne* vi. 315 It was all devotion, not time-serving as the vulgar thought.

**Ti·me-se:rving,** *ppl. a.* [f. as prec. with -ING[2].]

†**1.** Serving the time or season; serviceable, seasonable. *Obs. rare*[−1].

**1627** PERROT *Tithes* 70 His ships..full richly stowed with all manner of choice and time-serving commodities.

**2.** Characterized by interested compliance; 'trimming', temporizing.

**1630** PRYNNE *Anti-Armin.* 77 Not by some one or two ambitious, time-seruing, nouellizing Diuines. **1638** SIR T. HERBERT *Trav.* (ed. 2) 99 His owne two sonnes..brought also to Mahobet by tyme-serving Madoffer-chan to abide his mercy. **1809** MALKIN *Gil Blas* XII. iii. (Rtldg.) 428 The school of time-serving morality. **1860–70** STUBBS *Lect. Europ. Hist.* I. viii. (1904) 100 The leading man..was a time-serving rogue.

Hence **Ti·me-se·rvingness.**

*a* **1734** NORTH *Lives* (1826) I. 2, [I] ascribe it chiefly to ignorance, although I think time-servingness and malice hath the greatest share. **1812** SHELLEY in Hogg *Life* (1858) II. 196 The address..so barefaced a piece of time-servingness. **1890** *Lippincott's Mag.* May 763 The cowardice and the time-servingness.

†**Ti·mesome,** *a. Obs. rare.* [f. TIME *sb.* + -SOME.] Of, pertaining to, existing in, or subject to time as opposed to eternity; of finite duration; temporal. Hence †**Ti·mesomeness.**

**1674** N. FAIRFAX *Bulk & Selv.* 33 Everlastingness is no more All at Once, as a Now of Time is,..than it is it self Timesom. *Ibid.* 154 God..may as well be brought down to the timesomness of that which is bounded, as that which is every way bounded, may be lifted up to the alwayness of him who is unbounded. *Ibid.* 181 When we say, the body is dying or timesom, the soul deathless or endless, we do not mean the body should thereby lose its bodyhood, but only its suchness.

**Ti·me-spi:rit.** [transl. of Ger. *Zeitgeist.*] The spirit of the time, the genius of the age.

**1831** CARLYLE *Sart. Res.* II. ix, To me, in this our life.. which is an internecine warfare with the Time-spirit, other warfare seems constituted. **1873** M. ARNOLD *Lit. & Dogma* (1876) p. xxi, To say that the Church dogmas of his time..on which the Time-Spirit had not then turned his light, were false developments. **1880** T. HODGKIN *Italy & Inv.* III. ix. II. 547 One is disposed to look the present Time-Spirit boldly in the face and ask why it..must be infallible and eternal.

**Ti·me-ta·ble.** A tabular list or schedule of the times at which successive things are to be done or happen, or of the times occupied in the parts of some process.

*spec.* **a.** A printed table or book of tables showing the times of arrival and departure of railway trains at and from the stations; also a similar table of times of arrival and departure of steamboats or other public conveyances. **b.** A chart used in railway traffic offices, showing by means of cross lines, in one direction representing hours and minutes and in the other miles, the position of the various trains at any given moment (*Cassell's Encycl. Dict.* 1888). **c.** A time-sheet on which a record is kept of the time worked by each employee. **d.** A table showing how the time of a school or other educational institution, for any day, or for a week, is allotted to the various classes and subjects. **e.** *Mus.* A table of notes showing their relative time-value.

**1838** OSBORNE *Guide to Grand Junction or Birm'ham, Liverpool & Manch. Rail.*, On and after Wednesday May 23rd...Time Table shewing the Hours [etc.]. **1838** *Cornish's Grand Junction* [etc.] *Railway Companion*, ed. 3, Time Table, shewing the hour of each Train [etc.] after 18th June 1838. **1839** (*title*) Bradshaw's Railway Time Tables..10th Mo. 19th. **1844** J. ALLEN *Rept. Schools S. Distr.* in *Min. Comm. of Council on Education* II. 91 For the morning's work, I have sometimes suggested the following time-table. **1844** F. C. COOK *Rept. Schools E. Distr.* ibid. 178 The time-table should contain an exact account [etc.]. **1856** F. E. PAGET *Owlet Owlst.* 194 The time-table of that man's life was a curiosity in its way. **1858** SIMMONDS *Dict. Trade, Time-table*, a register of the time of high-water, and of the departure of steam boats, railway trains, etc.; a check upon the period of labour of workmen. **1861** M. ARNOLD *Pop. Educ. France* 98 The present time-table..of the lay public schools of Paris. **1862** MISS BRADDON *Lady Audley* xxviii, He walked straight back to the hotel, where he called for a time-table. An express for London left Wildernsea at a quarter-past one. **18..** HULLAH in Stainer & Barrett *Dict. Mus. Terms* (1875) s.v. *Nomenclature*, The Germans call these notes .. the *whole note*, the *half note*, the *quarter note*, and so on. These appellations..form of themselves a time-table. **1889** W. S. ROCKSTRO in Grove *Dict. Mus.* s.v., The earliest known indication of a Time Table is to be found in the well-known work on *Cantus mensurabilis*, written by Franco of Cologne about the middle of the 11th century... The modern Time Table, denoting the proportionate value of all these notes, is too well known in our schoolrooms to need a word of description here. **1889** G. FINDLAY *Eng. Railway* 8 It was not until after some time .. that the time-table became a recognised institution. **1907** *Westm. Gaz.* 7 May 2/2 This is the first time that a time-table has been arranged in advance for a whole [parliamentary] Bill, but it seems to us that the procedure was justified.

**Timeward** (tai·mwǭɹd), *a.*, *adv.* [f. TIME *sb.* + -WARD.] Towards what belongs to time; temporal.

**1883** H. DRUMMOND *Nat. Law in Spir. W.* v. (1884) 158 The mind of the flesh,..by its very nature, limited capacity, and time-ward tendency, is..Death.

**Ti·me-worn,** *a.* Worn by process of time; impaired by age.

**1729** SAVAGE *Wanderer* v. 3 By time-worn Steps a steep Ascent we gain. **1813** W. S. WALKER *Poems* 152 On the green margin of the quiet flood,..a time-worn exile stood. **1901** BIRRELL *Misc.* iii. (1902) 82 An ancient, time-worn ritual, which gives dim expression to ghostly ideas.

**Timid** (ti·mid), *a.* [ad. L. *timid-us*, f. *tim-ēre* to fear. Cf. F. *timide* (*a* 1528 in Godef. *Compl.*).] Subject to fear; easily frightened; wanting boldness or courage; fearful, timorous. Rarely const. *of* (cf. TIMOROUS 1 a). Also *fig.*

**1549** *Compl. Scot.* Ep. Ded. 6, I vas lang stupefact ande timide, for falt of ane peremptoir conclusione. **1697** BENTLEY *Phal.* 14 Another sort of Proofs, that will affect the most slow Judgments, and assure the most timid or incredulous. **1730–46** THOMSON *Autumn* 401 Poor is the triumph o'er the timid hare. **1764** *Museum Rust.* II. 270 Lucern..in its infant state..is very tender, and timid of frost. **1841** ELPHINSTONE *Hist. Ind.* II. 545 The troops became more timid than ever. **1865** DICKENS *Mut. Fr.* IV. xii, Bella was so timid of him.

b. Characterized by or indicating fear.

**1741–2** GRAY *Agrippina* 87 Carry to him thy timid counsels. **1812** J. WILSON *Isle of Palms* III. 168 With a timid smile. **1873** BLACK *Pr. Thule* vi, She has given him some timid encouragement.

**Timidity** (timi·dĭti). [ad. L. *timiditās*, f. *timid-us* TIMID: see -ITY. Cf. F. *timidité* (*a* 1429).] The quality of being timid; fearfulness.

**1598** FLORIO, *Timidità*, timiditie, feare, dread [etc.]. **1603** HOLLAND *Plutarch* 285 This proceedeth from .. extreame folly and timiditie of heart. **1658** SIR T. BROWNE *Pseud. Ep.* III. xvii. (ed. 4) 182 [The hare] figured..pusillanimity and timidity from its temper. **1762** SYMMER in Ellis *Orig. Lett.* Ser. II. IV. 450 Lord Weymouth..spoke with grace and dignity, though with the timidity of a young man. **1849** MACAULAY *Hist. Eng.* vii. II. 244 Burnet was well aware of his danger: but timidity was not among his faults.

**Timidly** (ti·midli), *adv.* [f. TIMID *a.* + -LY [2].] In a timid manner; shrinkingly, apprehensively.

**1767** S. PATERSON *Another Trav.* I. 375 To the timidly-superstitious..they would seem a company of necromancers. **1843** BETHUNE *Sc. Fireside Stor.* 137 The lady..glanced timidly at me to ascertain if I observed her. **1885** *L'pool Daily Post* 11 Apr. 4/9 One traveller timidly attempts the fraudulent experiment.

**Ti·midness.** *rare.* [-NESS.] = TIMIDITY.

**1828–32** in WEBSTER. **1889** STEVENSON *Master of B.* ii, He looked up..with a kind of timidness.

† **Ti·midous,** *a. Obs. rare.* [f. L. *timid-us* TIMID + -OUS.] = TIMID.

**1663** BUTLER *Hud.* I. III. 396 Fortune th' audacious doth *juvare*, But lets the timidous miscarry. *a* **1734** NORTH *Lives* (1826) I. 371 His lordship knew him to be..a timidous man. *Ibid.* 421 His timidous manner of creating and judging..points, some on one side, and some on another.

**Timing** (tai·miŋ), *vbl. sb.* [f. TIME *v.* + -ING [1].] The action of TIME *v.* in various senses.

† **1.** Happening, occurrence, hap; (good or ill) fortune; an event, occurrence, case. *Obs.*

*c* **1250** *Gen. & Ex.* 31 Almiȝtin louerd, heȝest kinge ðu giue me seli timinge. *Ibid.* 1194 Swilc timing was hire bi-tid. *Ibid.* 2644 Bissop Eliopoleos Saȝ ðis timing, & up he ros. *c* **1310** *K. Horn* 164 Crist him ȝeue god tymyng. *c* **1400** *Brut* clxviii. 191 Thus staterand Scottes,..Erly in a mornyng in an euel tymyng went ȝe fro Dunbarr.

**2.** The fixing, ascertaining, noting, or recording of time: see TIME *v.*; in *Cricket*, see quot. 1893.

**1597** MORLEY *Introd. Mus.* 9 *Phi.* What is the timing of a note? *Ma.* It is a certayne space or length, wherein a note may be holden in singing. **1656** *Eirenicon* 20 Let thy charity advance To give them timeing of an Ordinance. **1658–9** in *Burton's Diary* (1828) III. 154 There is no exception against the petition, but against the timing of it. **1693** J. EDWARDS *Author. O. & N. Test.* 357 Josephus is often faulty as to the timing of things. *a* **1711** KEN *Psyche* Poet. Wks. 1721 IV. 278 The Voice, the Lute, the Passion sweet and strong, The Timing, the adapting of the Song. **1889** ACWORTH *Railways Eng.* 202 The acceleration over the ordinary timing of the 2 p.m. was no more than 4 minutes. **1893** W. L. MURDOCH *Cricket* 29 Timing is the working in perfect unison of the hands, arms, legs and all the necessary muscles which are subservient to the eye. **1908** *Daily News* 7 Dec. 9 This, considering the heavy state of the roads, was excellent timing.

b. *attrib.* and *Comb.*, as *timing box, nut, screw, valve, -wheel.*

**1884** F. J. BRITTEN *Watch & Clockm.* 264 Timing Box [see TIME *v.* 2 c]. *Ibid.* 265 [The] Timing Screws [are] four screws or nuts placed at equal distances round the rim of a watch compensation balance,..used for getting the watch to mean time. *Ibid.*, In a marine chronometer there are two timing nuts. **1898** Timing valve [see TIME *v.* 7]. **1907** *Westm. Gaz.* 21 Nov. 4/2 All the timing-wheels are made of fibre and brass, and are contained in an oil-tight aluminium case in front of the engine [of a motor-car].

† **Ti·mish,** *a. Obs. rare.* [f. TIME *sb.* + -ISH [1].] **a.** Of the nature of time; temporal, temporary. **b.** Belonging to the time; in the style of the times, modish, fashionable. Hence † **Ti·mishness.**

**1674** N. FAIRFAX *Bulk & Selv.* 20 The reality of time being grafted in its timeishness, not in its boundlesness; so that every little share of time must have a little of this little reality, and every little must make a mickle. **1676** *Life Muggleton* in *Harl. Misc.* I. 612 A timish gentleman, accoutered with sword and peruke, hearing the noise this man caused.., had a great desire to discourse with him.

**Timist** (tai·mist). Also 8–9 **timeist.** [-IST.]

† **1.** One who follows or complies with the humour of the time; a time-server. *Obs.*

*a* **1613** OVERBURY *Charac.*, *Timist* Wks. (1856) 56 A Timist is a noune adjective of the present tense. He hath no more of a conscience then feare, and his religion is not his but the princes. **1620** BRATHWAIT *Five Senses* iii. 33 The dissembling appearances of all obseruing Timists. **1658** J. JONES *Ovid's Ibis* 162 So Timists and Hypocrites change their opinion.

† **2.** A timepiece, clock. *Obs. nonce-use.*

**1711** E. WARD *Vulgus Brit.* v. 61 To bring the poor condemn'd Machine To th' flaming Pile, and cast therein The costly Timist.

**3.** One who keeps correct time in music.

**1765** GOLDSM. *Ess.* Misc. Wks. 1837 I. 203 Neither the one or the other are, by any means, perfect timists. **1774** J. COLLIER, etc. *Mus. Trav.* (1775) 8 She introduced me to Mr. Dilettanti, a most illustrious timeist. **1866** ENGEL *Nat. Mus.* ix. 339 The Chinese are known to be excellent timists, and they have several marks for indicating how the time is to be beaten.

**4.** One who confines his outlook to time, i. e. to the present life. *rare.*

**1801** R. CECIL *Mem. J. Bacon* Wks. 1881 I. 203 Let the whole world be divided into two great sects, viz. Timists and Eternalists.

**5.** A chronologer. *rare.*

**1897** S. J. HUMPHREY in *Chicago Advance* 23 Sept. 422/1 The next day (Tuesday, Apr. 25, A.D. 60, for so the timists calculate) they [Paul and his companions] came to Rhodes.

**6.** One of a sect of Adventists. *U. S.*

**1884** *Independent Almanac* 18 Only a small company [of Adventists], called 'Timists', now venture to fix a definite time for the advent.

**7.** *Cricket.* One who 'times' (well or badly).

**1893** W. L. MURDOCH *Cricket* 30, I think Lord F—— B—— must have had all the attributes of a good timist..for..it is written of him..that he had a greater variety of hits than anyone else and they were all along the ground.

**Timit** (ti·mit). [Native name in Galibi.] A species of palm, *Manicaria saccifera*, var. *Plukenetii*, a native of Trinidad, and of the tidal swamps of the Amazon. Also *attrib.*

**1858** CRUGER *Outl. Flora Trinidad* 5 The timit (Manicaria) grows in light sandy soils. **1871** KINGSLEY *At Last* xi, Rows of posts, probably of palm-stems thatched over.. with the leaves of the Timit palm. *Ibid.* xii, Each Negro.. carried a Timit-leaf, and hooked it on to his head when a gush of rain came down.

**Timmele,** obs. Sc. form of THIMBLE.

† **Timmen,** variant of TAMIN *Obs.*, stamin.

**1824** MISS FERRIER *Inher.* lxxi, Broadcloth and timmen.

**Timmer,** obs. and dial. form of TIMBER.

**Timmersome,** variant of TIMORSOME.

**Timmy whisky**: see TIMWHISKY.

**Timocracy** (taimǫ·krăsi). Also 6 **-cratie.** [a. OF. *tymocracie* (Oresme 14th c.), mod.F. *timocratie*, ad. med.L. *tīmocratia* (in 13th c. transl. Aristotle), a. Gr. τῑμοκρατία, used by Plato and by Aristotle in two distinct senses, f. τῑμή (*a*) honour, (*b*) value or valuation + -κρατία: see -CRACY. The Aristotelian, the later sense in Greek, was the first to appear in Eng. literature.]

**1.** In the Aristotelian sense: A polity with a property qualification for the ruling class.

**1586** T. B. *La Primaud. Fr. Acad.* (1589) 548 The third kind of a good and right common-wealth is of a Greeke word called *Timocratie*, which we may cal the power of meane or indifferent wealth. **1594** *Mirr. Policy* (1599) Diij, Between the two kinds of a depraved Commonweale, to wit, Oligarchie and Democratie, this Commonweale Timocratie is founded. *a* **1647** SIR R. FILMER *Observ. Aristotle's Pol.* (1652) 6 Of all the right kindes of Government Monarchy was the best, and a Timocratie the worst. **1818** T. TAYLOR *Aristotle's Rhet.*, etc. II. 311 The polities indeed are, a kingdom, an aristocracy, and the third is derived from the distribution of honours through the medium of wealth, which as it seems may be appropriately called a timocracy. **1835** THIRLWALL *Greece* I. x. 408 The scale of the timocracy was gradually lowered, until it was wholly abolished. **1847** GROTE *Greece* II. xi. III. 159 Such were the divisions in the political scale established by Solon, called by Aristotle a Timocracy, in which the rights, honours, functions and liabilities of the citizens were measured out according to the assessed property of each.

**2.** In the Platonic sense: A polity (like that of Sparta) in which love of honour is said to be the dominant motive with the rulers.

**1656** STANLEY *Hist. Philos.* v. (1701) 195 Of a Commonwealth he asserteth five kinds, the first, *Aristocracy*, when the best Rule; the second, *Timocracy*, when the Ambitious; the third, *Democracy*, when the People; the fourth, *Olygarchy*, when a few; the last, *Tyranny*, which is the worst of all. **1845** MAURICE *Mor. & Met. Philos.* in *Encycl. Metrop.* II. 620/1 The fraternal type of equality will be preserved in all friendships under a timocracy. **1852** DAVIES & VAUGHAN tr. *Plato's Rep.* (1858) 307 We will begin on the present occasion by examining the ambitious constitution—(I do not know of any other name in use; we must call it Timocracy or Timarchy). **1871** MORLEY *Crit. Misc.* Ser. I. 333 A timocracy in which the energetic ambitious and military type will become dominant.

**Timocratic** (taimǫkræ·tik), *a.* [ad. med.L. *tīmocratic-us*, a. Gr. τῑμοκρατικ-ός, f. τῑμοκρατία: see prec. and -IC. So F. *timocratique*.] Of, belonging to, or characterized by a timocracy.

a. In the Aristotelian sense: see prec. 1.

**1847** GROTE *Greece* II. xxxi. IV. 168 The timocratic classification of Solon..continued to subsist. **1869** A. W. WARD tr. *Curtius' Hist. Greece* II. II. iv. 89 These were the timocratic constitutions, which arrange the citizens in divisions, and determine the measure of their rights according to the standard of property. **1875** POSTE *Gaius* I. (ed. 2) 32 The Comitia Centuriata was a timocratic assembly, or one in which the ascendency belonged to wealth.

b. In the Platonic sense: see prec. 2.

**1852** DAVIES & VAUGHAN tr. *Plato's Rep.* (1858) 312 Such we find to be the character of the timocratic young man, who resembles the timocratic state. **1905** *Contemp. Rev.* Apr. 556 The timocratic man who seeks honour may easily degenerate to the mere money lover.

**Timocra·tical,** *a.* [f. as prec. + -AL: see -ICAL.] = prec.

a. *a* **1647** SIR R. FILMER *Observ. Aristotle's Pol.* (1652) 6 It may very properly be called a timocratical Government, where Magistrates are chosen by their wealth. **1844** THIRLWALL *Greece* VIII. lxi. 85 A timocratical restriction on the exercise of the franchise.

b. **1822** T. MITCHELL *Aristoph.* II. 13 In..Plato's Republic..the author traces out the origin of four different sorts of government (viz. the timocratical or Lacedæmonian [etc.]). **1875** JOWETT *Plato* (ed. 2) III. 99 Beginning with the timocracy, let us go on to the timocratical man.

**Timon** [1] (tai·mǫn). [Gr. Τίμων, personal name.] The name of a noted misanthrope of Athens, the hero of Shakspere's play of the same name; hence, one like Timon, a misanthrope.

**1588** SHAKS. *L. L. L.* IV. iii. 170 And Critticke Tymon laugh at idle toyes. **1711** SHAFTESB. *Charac.* (1737) II. 197 You discover'd so much aversion, as wou'd make one believe you a compleat Timon, or man-hater. **1819** LADY MORGAN *Autobiog.* (1859) 281 She had grown into a sort of female Timon—not of Athens—bitter, and always going over old, past scenes. **1886** *Pall Mall G.* 15 June 6/1 Both Mr. Ruskin and Mr. Froude have long been known as highly cultivated disciples of the latter-day Timon of Cheyne-row.

Hence **Timo·nian** *a.*, of, pertaining to, or like Timon; **Ti·monism,** misanthropy; **Ti·monist,** a misanthrope; **Ti·monize** *v. intr.*, to play the Timon or misanthrope.

**1770** LANGHORNE *Plutarch* (1851) II. 997/1 He left his *Timonian retreat. **1886** *Pall Mall G.* 15 June 6/1 No new Timon arose, for *Timonism had been found out to be a fraud. **1590** GREENE *Mourn. Garm.* (1616) 2 Yet was he not..such a *Timonist, but hee would familiarly conuerse with his friends. **1602** DEKKER *Satirom.* Liij, I did it to retyre me from the world; And turne my Muse into a Timonist. **1713** *Gentl. Instr.* II. viii. (ed. 5) 180, I should be tempted to *Timonize, and clap a Satyr upon our whole Species.

† **Timon** [2], **temon.** *Obs. rare.* [a. F. *timon*, *temon* pole, staff, handle of rudder, helm :—L. *tēmōn-em* beam, pole.] The rudder of a ship.

[**1392–3** *Earl Derby's Expedition* (Camd.) 225 Item pro reparacione j tymon per le scriuen.] **1506** GUYLFORDE *Pylgr.* (Camd.) 76 Tournynge with suche vyolence y[t] with the jumpe and stroke of y[e] falle of y[e] galye to the rok, the sterne called the temon sterte and flewe frome the hokes.

**Timoneer** (taimŏniə·ɹ). *rare.* [a. F. *timonier* (12th c. in Godef. *Compl.*), It. *timoniere*, f. *timon* helm: see prec. and -EER.] A helmsman, steersman.

**1762–9** FALCONER *Shipwr.* II. 178 The helm the attentive timoneer applies. *Ibid.* III. 67, 115 [etc.]. **1806** G. PINCKARD *Notes W. Ind.* I. 183 The timoneer left the helm; and the ship remained immoveable upon the water. **1883** G. C. DAVIES *Norfolk Broads* xxv. (1884) 188 Her timoneer sitting ..with the tiller in one hand and the sheet in the other.

**Timor** (ti·mǫ̆ɹ). *rare.* [a. L. *timor* fear.] Fear.

**1599** A. M. tr. *Gabelhouer's Bk. Physicke* 102/2 For Asthmasye, or shortnes of breath, and timor of the consumptione. **1850** P. CROOK *War of Hats* 43 In slothful timor.

**Timorat,** erron. variant of TIMARIOT. *Obs.*

† **Timorate,** *a. Obs. rare*—[0]. [ad. late L. *timorāt-us* (Vulg.) full of the fear of God, f. *timor* fear: see -ATE [2]. Cf. F. *timoré* (Cotgr.), It. *timorato* (Florio, 1611).] Devout, full of reverence.

**1570** LEVINS *Manip.* 41/24 Timorate, *timoratus.*

† **Ti·morist.** *Obs. rare.* Also **tymor-.** Derivation and sense doubtful: the context appears to require 'Timist, time-server'.

*c* **1620** FELTHAM *Resolves* xx. 60 What would the world think of me, that could thus in one, be hot, and cold? should I not be censured as a Timorist? [*ed.* **1647** Tymorist.]

†**Timoro·sity.** *Obs.* Forms: (5 tymorysite), 6 timerosity, -itie, tymer-, (temer-), timorositie, 6–7 timorosity. [f. as TIMOROUS + -ITY; cf. obs. It. *timorosità* (Florio).] Timorousness, timidity.

1490 CAXTON *Eneydos* iv. 20 For tymorysite..his tonge..clyued to the palate of his mouuth. 1531 ELYOT *Gov.* I. xxi, Audacitie with timerositie maketh Magnanimitie. *Ibid.* III. viii, The surplusage is called Audacitie, the lacke Timorositie or feare. 1538 *St. Papers Hen. VIII*, III 12 In the end, temerositie putt apart, I have determinid playnly to expres to your Lordship suche thinges..as restith in my knowledg. 1547–64 BAULDWIN *Mor. Philos.* (Palfr.) 151 In men we note audacitie, but commonly in women timerosity. 1647 *Sp. Ho. Com.* 23 June 1 The timorosity of Offending, the volubility of Scandal.

**Timorous** (ti·mŏrəs), *a.* Forms: *α.* 5–6 tymerous(e, (5 tumerous), 6–8 timerous, (6 -ouse). (*β.* 6 temerous.) *γ.* 5–6 timorouse, 6 tymorous, 6–8 timourous, (6 -ouse, 7 timrous, 7–8 tim'rous), 6– timorous. [= OF. *temeros, -ous* (14th c. in Godef.), later *timoureus, timoreux*, OSp., Pg. *temeroso*, It. *timoroso*, med.L. *timōrōsus* (11th c. in Du Cange, and prob. in late L.), f. L. *timōr-em* fear.

The existence of the forms *timerous, temerous* brought this word into formal confusion with TEMEROUS rash; whence *temerity*, properly n. of quality from TEMEROUS, was also used as deriv. of *timorous* in sense 'timidity': see TIMERITY.]

**1.** Full of or affected by fear (either for the time or habitually); fearful. **a.** Feeling fear; frightened, apprehensive, afraid. (Sometimes const. *of*, or with inf. or clause.) Now *rare*.

c1450 *Mankind* 805 in *Macro Plays* 30 He ys so tymerouse; me semyth hys vytall spryt doth expyre. c1530 *Crt. Love* 1 With timerous [*ed.* 1561 temerous] herte, and trembling hand of drede. c1555 HARPSFIELD *Divorce Hen. VIII* (Camd.) 185 The King's doings..may seem..to have proceeded from a tymerous fearful conscience to offend God. 1613 W. BROWNE *Brit. Past.* II. v, Timerous of death. a1631 DONNE *Holy Sonnets* xii. 10 You have not sinned nor need be timorous. 1707 *Reflex. upon Ridicule* II. 269 Our Friends are for the most part timerous. 1750 JOHNSON *Rambler* No. 75 ⁋ 15 He is now more timorous lest his freedom should be thought rudeness. 1840 DICKENS *Barn. Rudge* lxxii, He..was rather timorous of venturing on Joe.

**b.** Subject to fear; of a fearing disposition; easily frightened; timid. †In early use sometimes in good sense: Modest, reverential.

1474 CAXTON *Chesse* II. ii. (1883) 32 A Quene ought to be well manerd & amonge alle she ought to be tunerous and shamefast. *Ibid.* III. ii, Maysters and marroners on the see ..yf they be tumerous and ferdful they shold make aferde them that ben in theyr shippis. 1502 ATKYNSON tr. *De Imitatione* II. x. 189 The grace wherby we may be made humble & tymerous to God. 1534 MORE *Comf. agst. Trib.* II. Wks. 1182/1 Thys faute of pusillanimitye and tymorous mynde. a1557 MRS. M. BASSET tr. *More's Treat. Passion* ibid. 1358/1 O temerous & weake sely shepe, thynke yt sufficient for thee, onely to walke after me, an thy shepehearde. 1600 HOLLAND *Livy* II. lv. 81 Their own timerous conceits & imaginations. 1774 GOLDSM. *Nat. Hist.* (1776) IV. 3 Animals of the hare kind..are inoffensive and timorous. 1855 MACAULAY *Hist. Eng.* xvi. III. 636 Conjunctures such as have often inspired timorous and delicate women with heroic courage.

**c.** Indicating or proceeding from fear; characterized by timidity. Also *fig.*

1581 J. BELL *Haddon's Answ. Osor.* 477 b, Tymerous feare of men hath straightened it. 1603 H. CROSSE *Vertues Commw.* (1878) 139 The linke of wofull wretchednes maketh his death timerous and fearfull by his leaud life. 1652 CRASHAW *Carmen Deo Nostro* Wks. (1904) 254 The timerous light of stares. 1701 C. WOLLEY *Jrnl. New York* (1860) 60 There is the timorous objection: the Ship may founder by springing a Leak. 1781 GIBBON *Decl. & F.* xxvi. (1869) II. 48, I shall proceed with doubtful and timorous steps. 1838 PRESCOTT *Ferd. & Is.* (1846) I. iii. 151 His troops murmured at this timorous policy.

†**2.** Causing fear or dread; dreadful, terrible. *Obs.*

1455 *Rolls of Parlt.* V. 281/1 In as rigorous and timorouse manere as the Chirche wol suffre it. 1513 BRADSHAW *St. Werburge* II. 766 They set theyr ordinaunce agaynst the towne..timorous for to se. 1608 R. JOHNSON *Seven Champions* 45, I grant thee..by the law of arms to choose thy death, els hadst thou suffered a timorous torment. 1632 LITHGOW *Trav.* VI. 262 Wee came to the most scurrile and timorous Discent of the whole passage.

**3.** *dial.* (See quots.)

1691 RAY *N. C. Words*, *Timorous*, by the Vulgar is here used for furious or passionate. 1828 *Craven Gloss.*, *Timorous*, difficult to please, fretful; also, nice, particular in dress.

**Timorously** (ti·mŏrəsli), *adv.* [f. prec. + -LY [2].] In a timorous manner; timidly.

1548 UDALL, etc. *Erasm. Par. John* xxi. 117 He aunswereth sincerely..but timerously and very lowlye withal. 1560 DAUS tr. *Sleidane's Comm.* 273 b, Rendryng so lightly and timourously. 1655 STANLEY *Hist. Philos.* III. (1701) 99/1 Timerously shunning all publick Affairs. 1697 JOS. WOODWARD *Relig. Soc. London* i. (1701) 13 You will stand idly or timorously, when the Goliahs of darkness come forth and blaspheme the living God. 1835 LYTTON *Rienzi* I. iii, 'Hush', said a third, timorously looking round. 1885 *Manchester Exam.* 3 June 5/4 Reflections..timorously emphasised by a letter.

**Timorousness** (ti·mŏrəsnės). [f. as prec. + -NESS.] The quality or state of being timorous; fearfulness, timidity.

1494 FABYAN *Chron.* VI. clxxv. 172 Gosselyne and Conrade ..complaynynge theym vnto her of the vnstablenesse of her lorde and tymerousnesse. 1533 ELYOT *Cast. Helthe* (1541) 75 b, In case that either for age or for timourousnesse a man wyll not be lette bloude. 1624 DONNE *Serm.* ii. (1640) 15 Gideon, in a modest timorousnesse askes a signe. 1681 R. KNOX *Ceylon* 168 Whom we perceiving to be free from timerousness at the sight of us. 1748 HARTLEY *Observ. Man* I. iv. 454 The Ridicule cast upon Timorousness by Boys and Men. 1876 BANCROFT *Hist. U.S.* I. viii. 228 Afflicted..with..an overpowering timorousness of nature.

**Timorsome** (ti·məɹsə̆m), *a.* Now *dial.* Also 7–9 timer-, timour-, *erron.* timber-, (8 timbor-, 8–9 timmor-). [app. f. *timor-ous, timer-ous*, with substitution of *-some* suffix for *-ous*; cf. *burthen-ous, burthen-some, quarrel-ous, quarrel-some*, and esp. *humorous, humoursome* (but *humour* was in common English use, which *timor* was not).]

**1.** Subject to or characterized by fear; timorous, timid.

1599–1600 G. RUGGLE *Club Law* I. iv, Impossible for a man to be a..Headsman..that is timbersome or afraid. 1602 SEGAR *Hon. Mil. & Civ.* I. xxx. 39 The second was impotent of his feet, and the third timersome. a1652 BROME *Covent Gard.* v. i, I never saw a man so timoursome. 1749 FIELDING *Tom Jones* VIII. viii, He is a timborsome Man every Body knows. 1818 SCOTT *Let. to D. Terry* 30 Apr., in *Lockhart*, Last night..the very same noise occurred. Mrs. S., as you know, is rather *timbersome*, so up got I, with Beardie's broadsword under my arm...But nothing was out of order. 1840 MARRYAT *Poor Jack* xxii, A mighty timorsome sort of young chap he appeared for to be. 1897 BARING-GOULD *Bladys* xxvi, I'm forced, when feeling timorsome of nights, to bolt my door.

**2.** Inspiring fear, fearful, dreadful; = TIMOROUS 2. *rare.*

1894 BLACKMORE *Perlycross* 191 It looks..so..strange and ungodly, and—and so timoursome.

**Timothy** (ti·mŏþi). [A Christian name, ad. L. *Timotheus*, Gr. Τιμόθεος (= 'honouring God').]

**1.** Short for TIMOTHY GRASS.

1747 B. FRANKLIN *Let.* Wks. 1887 II. 77 You made some mistake when you intended to favor me with some of the new valuable grass seed..for what you gave me..proves mere timothy. 1840 J. BUEL *Farmer's Comp.* 225 *Timothy*, better known in the east as *herds-grass*, and in Europe as meadow cat's-tail..is the general forage grass of the northern States. 1887 *Daily News* 18 Oct. 3/8 Timothy is scarce both in America and Germany, whence our supplies are mainly derived, and is likely to be dear.

**b.** *attrib.*, as *timothy field, hay, seed, sod.*

1784 *Pennsylvania Gaz.* 17 Mar. 3/2 Timothy seed. 1868 *Rep. U.S. Commissioner Agric.* (1869) 420 A timothy sod plowed late in spring. 1884 ROE *Nat. Ser. Story* viii, The mowing machine would be used in the timothy fields. 1902 *Encycl. Brit.* XXVI. 535/2 Clover seed 60 lb.; timothy seed 48 lb.

**2.** 'A brew or jorum of liquor' (*Sc. slang*; *E.D.D.*).

1855 STRANG *Glasgow & its Clubs* (1856) 338 Rum filled the crystal timothies. 1890 J. SERVICE *Thir Notandums* xii. 87 Drink fair, pree and pree aboot, wi' that timothy o' toddy that you've been hirpling aboot to mak.

**Timothy grass.** [See quots. 1765, 1894.] A name (originally American) for Meadow Cat's-tail Grass, *Phleum pratense*, a native British grass, introduced into cultivation under this name in the North American colonies in the eighteenth century.

a1736 J. ELIOT *Ess. Field Husb.* (1760) 57 Herd-Grass (known in Pennsylvania by the name of Timothy-Grass)... It is said that Herd-Grass was first found in a swamp in Piscataqua by one Herd, who propagated the same. 1747 FRANKLIN *Let.* Wks. 1887 II. 83 A bushel of clean chaff of timothy or Salem grass will yield five quarts of seed. 1750 W. ELLIS *Mod. Husbandm.*, St. Timothy Grass. 1763 *Museum Rust.* (ed. 2) I. 233 Timothy grass..delights in a ..moist soil, and has a running root like couch grass. 1765 *Nat. Hist.* in *Ann. Reg.* 143/2 Another artificial grass called Timothy-grass..because it was brought from New York to Carolina by one Timothy Hanson [according to the Century Dict., about 1720]. 1809 KENDALL *Trav.* I. xxiii. 228 Timothy, here called *English* grass, is the grass cultivated. 1894 *Times* 23 Apr. 12/3 Although *Phleum pratense*, long known as meadow catstail, is a native British grass, its cultivation as an agricultural plant was originated last century by Timothy Hanson, an American, after whom the grass got called timothy grass.

**Timous**: see TIMEOUS.

†**Timp, -e.** *Obs. rare*[−1]. [App. shortened from L. *tympanum*, TYMPAN.] A tambourine.

c1205 LAY. 7003 Ne cuðe na mon swa muchel of song, Of harpe & of salteriun,..Of timpe & of lire. [*Timpe* is prob. dative case.]

**Timp**, var. of TYMP. **Timpan(e, -phan, Timpanie**, obs. ff. TYMPAN, TYMPANY. **Timse**, var. TEMSE, a sieve.

†**Timwhi·sky.** *Obs.* Also 8–9 -whiskey, (8 timmy whisky, -whiskee). [A compound of WHISKY, a light one-horse carriage: first element uncertain.] A kind of high light carriage, seated for one or two, drawn by a single horse or by two horses driven 'tandem'; a gig; a whisky.

1764 T. BRYDGES *Homer Travest.* (1797) II. 324 In spite of him these younkers frisky Went out and hir'd a timmy whisky. 1768 H. WALPOLE *Let. to Conway* 9 Aug., The apprentices that flirt to Epsom in a Tim-whisky. 1769 BURKE *Corr.* (1844) I. 182 Lord Chatham passed by my door on Friday morning, in a jimwhiskee [*error for* tim-] drawn by two horses, one before the other. 1769 CHESTERF. *Lett. to Godson* 15 Aug., Many of our young nobility push for it [fame] by driving a Chaise and four, or a Tim Whiskey. 1813 SOUTHEY in *Q. Rev.* X. 126. 1824 SCOTT *St. Ronan's* xiv, That almost forgotten accommodation, a whiskey, or, according to some authorities, a tim-whiskey. 1837 SOUTHEY *Doctor* Interch. xiv. IV. 43 The difference between a Baptist and an Anabaptist, which Sir John Danvers said, is much the same as that between a Whiskey and a Tim-whiskey, that is to say no difference at all.

**Tin** (tin), *sb.* Forms: 1–3 tin, 3–7 tyn, 4–6 tynne, 5 tyne, 5–7 tynn, (6 teene, *Sc.* twne, tun), 6–7 tinne, 7 tinn, 7– tin. [OE. *tin* neut. = MLG., MDu. *tin(n, ten* (LG., EFris., Du. *tin*), OHG., MHG. *zin* (G. *zinn*), ON. *tin* (Da. *tin*, Sw. *tenn*):—OTeut. **tin-oᵐ*; not known outside Teutonic. Ir. *tinne* is from Eng.

The 16th c. Sc. forms *twne, tun* are difficult to account for.]

**1.** One of the well-known metals, nearly approaching silver in whiteness and lustre, highly malleable and taking a high polish; used in the manufacture of articles of block tin, in the formation of alloys, as bronze, pewter, etc., and, on account of its resistance to oxidation, for making tin-plate and lining culinary and other iron vessels.

Tin is rarely if ever found native, but occurs in two ores, the dioxide, $SnO_2$, called *tin-stone* or *cassiterite*, and, less commonly, in tin-pyrites or sulphide of tin, $SnS_2$. Chemically it is a dyad metallic element, symbol Sn (*stannum*), atomic weight (O = 16) 119 (*Internat. Committee* in *Jrnl. Chem. Soc.* Sept. 1912, 1832); sp. gr. about 7·3. In Alchemy represented by the same sign (♃) as the planet Jupiter.

c897 K. ÆLFRED *Gregory's Past. C.* xxxvii. 266 Ðis Israhela folc is ᵹeworden nu me to sindrum & to are & to tine & to iserne & to leade inne on minum ofne. c1200 *Trin. Coll. Hom.* 163 Ðe caliz [in church is] of tin and hire [the priest's concubine's] nap of mazere and ring of golde. 1297 R. GLOUC. (Rolls) 144 Metal, as led and tyn. 1382 WYCLIF *Num.* xxxi. 22 Brasse, and yren, and tynne. a1450 *Voc* in Wr.-Wülcker 613/20 *Stannum*, tyn. *Ibid.* 653/14 *Hoc stagnum*, tyne. 1544 PHAER *Regim. Lyfe* (1560) C iv, Kepe them in a boxe of tinne. 1548 *Aberdeen Regr.* (1844) I. 259, vij platis of twne,..item, iij quartis of twne. 1561 *Ibid.* 336 Ane charger of tun, ane plait of tun, ane dische of tun. 1559 *Will R. Hoope* (Somerset Ho.), Beades of Teene. 1610 HOLLAND *Camden's Brit.* (1637) 184 Rich and plenteous mines of tinne. 1796 KIRWAN *Elem. Min.* (ed. 2) II. 195 The colour of Tin is greyish white...Fracture hackly, crackles..when bent. 1815 J. SMITH *Panorama Sci. & Art* II. 388 Equal parts of tin and bismuth form a brittle alloy. 1863 LYELL *Antiq. Man* ii. 10 Bronze is an alloy of about nine parts of copper and one of tin.

**b.** With defining attribute, as **bar-tin** = *block tin*; **black tin**, tin ore (the dioxide, $SnO_2$) prepared for smelting; **block tin**, metallic tin refined and cast into blocks; **grain tin**, a very pure tin obtained by fusing stream tin in a blast furnace supplied with charcoal, and breaking it into small pieces; **phosphor tin**, an artificial compound of tin and phosphorus; **stream tin**, tin ore washed from the sand or gravel in which it occurs; **white tin**, refined metallic tin.

1870 YEATS *Nat. Hist. Comm.* 361 Stream ores produce the grain tin,..and the others the *bar or block tin. 1873 WATTS *Fownes' Chem.* 443 Two varieties of commercial tin are known, called grain- and bar-tin. 1610 HOLLAND *Camden's Brit.* (1637) 185 *Black tin..is tinne ore broken and washed. 1865 E. BURRITT *Walk Land's End* 320 The mine produces about 430 tons of black tin annually. 1668 CHARLETON *Onomast.* 295 Mundick, and *Block Tin. 1688 LUTTRELL *Brief Rel.* (1857) I. 455 There is a new patent passing empow'ring commissioners for the making of new tinn farthings of block tinn. 1842 *Penny Cycl.* XXIV 472/2 After refining, the tin is cast into blocks of about three cwt each...Tin thus prepared is sold as *block tin*. 1796 KIRWAN *Elem. Min.* (ed. 2) II. 201 *Grain Tin approaches to the silvery white. Common block Tin is bluer. 1877 KNIGHT *Dict. Mech.* 2575/1 Grain-tin is prepared by plunging blocks of tin into a bath of molten tin, and when they have assumed a brittle crystaling texture, they are broken with a hammer; or, after being heated nearly to the fusing-point, they are allowed to fall from a considerable hight; they are thus broken up into elongated grains. 1884 *Ibid.* Suppl., **Phosphor Tin*...Useful in making phosphor bronze. 1796 KIRWAN *Elem. Min.* (ed. 2) II. 201 In Cornwall the best Tin Ores are those that are washed down the hills by torrents, and thence called *Stream Tin Ores. 1842 BRANDE *Dict. Sc.*, etc., s.v. *Tin*, Stream tin,..from it the purest metal is obtained. 1674 RAY *Words, Prepar. Tin* 124 Two pound of black tin..yields a pound of *White or more. 1706 *Lond. Gaz.* No. 4241/2 A new Invention of Smelting..of Black Tin-Ore into White Tin.

**2.** A vessel made of tin, or more usually of tinned iron; *spec.* a vessel in which meat, fish, fruit, etc., is hermetically sealed for preservation (= CAN *sb.*[1] 3); locally, a small cylindrical drinking vessel or mug with a handle.

1821 CLARE *Vill. Minstr.* II. 73 With shining tin to keep his dinner warm Swung at his back. 1851 MAYHEW *Lond. Labour* I. 354 The sellers of tins, who carry them under their arms, or in any way on a round,..are known as hand sellers. 1853 KANE *Grinnell Exp.* xxx. (1856) 258 Now we had to quarry out the blocks [of ice]..and then melt it in tins for our daily drink. 1898 *British Printer* XI. 218 A couple of opened ink tins. 1900 H. G. GRAHAM *Soc. Life Scot. in 18th C.* IV. ii. (1901) 135 They partook of a tin of ale. 1901 *Westm. Gaz.* 29 Nov. 8/2 An action ..that concerns 200,000 tins of strawberry jam for the troops in South Africa. The manufacturers are proceeding against the tin-makers, as the tins leaked. *Mod.* To open a tin of sardines. (*Scotl.*) Each child brought a tin and received her tinful of milk.

**b.** Tin-plate as the material of such vessels.

1879 MRS. A. E. JAMES *Ind. Househ. Managem.* 85 A tin writing case is much more useful..for in tin nothing will mildew as it is liable to do in leather. 1886 RUSKIN *Præterita* I. 283 Meat of their own herds, untainted by American tin.

**3.** *slang.* Money, cash. Cf. BRASS *sb.* 3 b.

Said to have been first applied to the small silver coins of the 18th c., which before their recall in 1817 were often worn quite smooth without trace of any device, so as to resemble pieces of tin. See quot. for *tin-like* in 4 c.

1836 SMITH *Individual, Thieves' Chaunt* 5 (Farmer)

Because she lately nimm'd some tin, They have sent her to lodge at the King's Head Inn. 1840 DICKENS *Old C. Shop* ii, How much better would it be .. to hand over a reasonable amount of tin. 1854 MARION HARLAND *Alone* xxiv, She married a rich old man for his 'tin'.

**4.** *attrib.* and *Comb.* **a.** *attrib.* or as *adj.* Made or consisting of tin (or of tin-plate), as *tin bar, basin, box, bucket, button, can, farthing, filings, flagon, metal, -nail, saucepan, -solder, spoon, thread, -ware, whistle*; of, pertaining or relating to, producing, or concerned with tin, as *tin-amalgam, -dip, -farm, -float* (FLOAT *sb.* 19), *-furnace, -grain, -kiln, -law, -lode, -merchant, -mine, ore, -pit, -shop, trade, vein*; put up or preserved in tins, tinned, as *tin junk, milk*.

1839 URE *Dict. Arts* 593 The glass..with its interior coating of *tin-amalgam. 1487 *Cely Papers* (Camden) 157 A *tyn basson wt oder geyr. 1858 SIMMONDS *Dict. Trade*, **Tin-box, Tin-case*, a strong iron box tinned and japanned, for holding papers, dress articles, etc. 1642 in J. Lister *Autobiog.* (1842) 78 Michael Woodhead was shot upon his *tin-buttons. 1858 SIMMONDS *Dict. Trade*, **Tin-can*, a metal vessel for holding liquids. 1877 KNIGHT *Dict. Mech.*, *Tin Can*, the ordinary name for the cans of tinned iron now so widely used. 1775 ASH, **Tin-canister*, a canister made of tin. 1839 URE *Dict. Arts* 1253 (*Tin-plate*) The final *tin-dip is useful to remove the marks of the brush. 1758 BORLASE *Cornwall* 190 The *tin-farm of Cornwall at this time amounted to..one hundred marks per annum. 1688 *Tinn farthings [see *block tin* in sense 1 b]. 1822-34 *Good's Study Med.* (ed. 4) I. 288 The anthelmintic virtues of *tin-filings 1589 *Exch. Rolls Scotl.* XXII. 73 Aucht *tin flauconis contenand ane point the pece. 1681 GREW *Musæum* III. II. ii. 328 A Slag, remaining in the bottom of the *Tin-Floate. 1695 WOODWARD *Nat. Hist. Earth* IV. (1723) 213 *Tin-Grains, and other Ores of Metalls. 1710 J. HARRIS *Lex. Techn.* II, **Tin-kiln*, is used for the Burning of the Mundick from the Tin-ore. 1611 SPEED *Theat. Gt. Brit.* xi. (1614) 21/1 This Earle made certain *tinne-laws which with liberties and priviledges were confirmed by Earle Edmund his sonne. 1839 DE LA BECHE *Rep. Geol. Cornwall*, etc. x. 301 Wheal Friendship lode differs but a few degrees from east and west, as is also the case with Wheal Jewel *tin-lode on the north of it. 1708 *Lond. Gaz.* No. 4461/4 Richard Balhatchett,..Tinner, or *Tinn-Merchant. 1882 *Three in Norway* v. 35 When we have only *tin milk. 1610 HOLLAND *Camden's Brit.* 185 The incursions of the Mores had stopped up the *tinne mines of Spaine. 1839 URE *Dict. Arts* 1241 The tin-mines of the Malay peninsula. 1381-2 *Durham Acc. Rolls* (Surtees) 389 In CCC *Tinnail et vernys empt. pro ostio parliamenti in claustro. 1610 *Tinne ore [see *black tin* in 1 b]. 1766 WESLEY *Jrnl.* 12 Sept., My horse was just stepping into a *tin-pit. 1834 *Tait's Mag.* I. 181/2, I have known a blacksmith..unaware of the fact that what are called '*tin saucepans' are made of tinned plate iron. 1603 HOLLAND *Plutarch's Mor.* 189 Like as *tin-soder doth knit and rejoyne a crackt peece of brasse. 1669 STURMY *Mariner's Mag.*, *Penalties & Forfeit.* 2 *Tin and Leaden Spoons. 1674 tr. *Scheffer's Lapland* 105 Adorned with needle work of *tin-thred upon diverse colour'd cloth. 1839 DE LA BECHE *Rep. Geol. Cornwall*, etc. xv. 525 The chief emporium of the *tin trade was Bruges. 1610 HOLLAND *Camden's Brit.* 185 The *tynne veines in Germanie..were not as yet knowen. 1860 PIESSE *Lab. Chem. Wonders* 36 It is this substance which constitutes our famous *tin-ware. 1825 J. NEAL *Bro. Jonathan* I. 90 As if he were sounding a charge with..a *tin-whistle.

**b.** *fig.* in reference to tin as a base metal, esp. in comparison with silver: Mean, petty, worthless, counterfeit. (Cf. COPPER *sb.*$^1$ 9 c.)

1886 KIPLING *Departm. Ditties* (1899) 24 The Little Tin Gods harried their little tin souls. 1902 *Daily Chron.* 10 July 3/3 Those funny little tin revolutions affected by the South American States. 1905 H. A. VACHELL *Hill* ix. 187, I hope he's not going to make a sort of tin parson of you.

**c.** objective and obj. genitive, as *tin-beater, -maker, -melter, -miner, -pedler, -stamper*, etc.; *tin-bearing, -dressing, -getting, -mining, -smelting, -stamping*, etc., sbs. and adjs.; instrumental, as *tin-poisoning, -roofing*; *tin-lined, -mailed, -roofed* adjs.; parasynthetic, as *tin-bottomed, -coloured, -handled, -tabled* adjs.; similative, as *tin-white* adj. and sb.; also *tin-like* adj. and adv.

1899 *Daily News* 30 Nov. 2/1 (Prospectus) Two immense deposits of *tin-bearing drift. 1848 W. H. KELLY tr. *L. Blanc's Hist. Ten Y.* II. 272 François Foucret, *tin-beater, ..living in Vaise. 1872 CALVERLEY *Fly-leaves* (1903) 73 Hit a *tinbottom'd tray Hard with the fireshovel, hammer away! c1515 *Cocke Lorelles B.* 10 Balancers, *tynne casters, and skryueners. 1606 SYLVESTER *Du Bartas* II. iv. II. *Magnificence* 926 On his back he wears *Tin-colour'd Tissue. 1896 *Daily News* 17 Nov. 3/5 He was given a *tin-handled knife. 1846 MRS. GORE *Eng. Char.* 6 Many persons.. remember the villanous old coinage of George III. [properly Queen Anne to Geo. II, still current under Geo. III, but gradually withdrawn after 1817], the *tin-like sixpences, which added a word to the slang dictionary, and the button-like shillings, of which the image and superscription might have been Cæsar's. 1868 *Rep. U. S. Commissioner Agric.* (1869) 192 Heated by circulated air..ascending in *tin-lined flues. 1879 MRS. A. E. JAMES *Ind. Househ. Managem.* 21 Articles ..should be securely packed in tin boxes, or else in boxes tin-lined. 1887 RUSKIN *Præterita* II. 401 The delicately *tin-mailed and glittering spires of the village church. 1592 CHETTLE *Kinde-harts Dr.* (1841) 26 The receipte which the *tinne-melters wife ministred. 1899 R. MUNRO *Prehist. Scot.* i. 6 Diodorus Siculus makes mention of the *tin-miners. 1841 EMERSON *Ess.* Ser. I. iv. (1876) 112 He hears and feels what you say of the seraphim, and of the *tin-pedler. 1904 *Westm. Gaz.* 20 Sept. 3/2 These could not have saved him from *tin-poisoning or a touch of ophthalmia. c1886 KIPLING *Railway Folk* 59 Walk into a huge, brick-built, *tin roofed stable. 1839 URE *Dict. Arts* 1253 Paid for brushing and *tin-washing 225 plates. 1800 HENRY *Epit. Chem.* (1808) 252 The colour of this metal [tellurium] is *tin-white, verging to lead-grey. 1855 J. R. LEIFCHILD *Cornwall Mines* 39 Good specimens of tin-white cobalt.

**5.** Special Combs.: **tin-bath** (BATH *sb.*$^1$ 18), the mass of melted tin in a tin-furnace; **tin bill**: see quot.; †**tin-blain**, a blain or inflammatory swelling of the tongue in horses; †**tin-boat**, a pontoon or the like made of tin (or some alloy of tin): cf. PONTOON *sb.* 1, quots. 1710 and 1811; **tin-bound** *sb.* = BOUND *sb.*$^1$ 3 c; hence **tin-bound** *v. trans.*, to mark out the boundaries of (a piece of ground) for tin-mining; whence **tin-bounder, -bounding**; **tin-clad** *a.*, covered with tin; *sb.* [after *iron-clad*], a lightly armoured boat; **tin-field**, a tract of country yielding tin; **tin-floor**, (*a*) a floor made of tin; (*b*) a horizontal course or stratum of tin ore: see FLOOR *sb.* 12; **tin-frame**: see quot.; **tin-glaze**, a glaze for fine pottery, having an oxide of tin as a basis; hence **tin-glazed** *a.*; **tin-gravel**, gravel containing tin ore, which is obtained by streaming; **tin-ground** = *tin-field*; **tin-hammer**, a hammer with a heavy tin head, used to drive home tightly fitting bolts, etc.; **tin-house**, (*a*) a house constructed of tin; (*b*) a building where tin is worked; **tin-liquor**, a solution of tin in strong acid mixed with common salt, used as a mordant in dyeing; **tin-loaf**, a loaf baked in a tin, a pan-loaf; **tin-mordant**, a mordant consisting of a solution of tin in acid, as *tin-liquor*; **tin-mouth**, a sun-fish found in the Mississippi, the crappie; **tin-opener**, an instrument for opening soldered tins; **tin pan** *sb.*, a pan made of tin, also *attrib.* in reference to the noise made by beating such; hence **tin-pan** *v. trans.*, to serenade in derision by beating tin pans; **tin-pulp**, the precipitate from a solution of tin chloride and yellow prussiate of potash, used for dyeing; **tin-putty**, putty-powder; **tin-pyrites**, a sulphide of tin: see PYRITES; **tin-rock**, a variety of rock pigeon; **tin-salt**, the crystalline hydrated chloride of tin, $SnCl_2 2H_2O$, obtained by dissolving tin in hot hydrochloric acid; also, with *pl.*, any salt of tin; **tin-saw**, 'a saw used by bricklayers for cutting kerfs in bricks' (Knight *Dict. Mech.* 1877); **tin-scrap**, the waste tin-plate in the manufacture of tin-ware; **tin-silver**, imitation silver made of tin; **tin-spar** (see quot. 1796); **tin-spirits** = *tin-liquor*; **tin-stuff**, a miner's name for tin ore; **tin-vat**, a vessel in which tin-liquor is kept; **tin wash**, stream tin (see 1 b); **tin-washing** = TIN-STREAMING; *pl.* works where tin-streaming is done; **tin-witts**: see quots.; **tinwoman**, a woman who sells tin (cf. TINMAN); **tin-work**, often *pl.* **-works**, a place where tin is worked or manufactured; so **tin-worker, -working**; **tin-worm**, the 'worm' or spiral tube of a still, made of tin. See also TINFOIL, -GLASS, -KETTLE, -POT, -TACK, etc.

1839 URE *Dict. Arts* 1249 (*Tin-Refining*) Into the *tin-bath, billets of green wood are plunged. 1778 PRYCE *Min. Cornub.* v. iv. 291 The manner of agreeing for or buying the Tin Ore..being to give *Tin bills or promissory notes to the owners thereof. *Ibid.* 292 This makes what they call the Tin bill trade so noted in this county. 1614 MARKHAM *Cheap Husb.* I. vi. (1668) 74 For the Blain on the tongue, of some called the *Tin-blain, it is a blister which groweth at the roots of the tongue. 1677 *Lond. Gaz.* No. 1199/3 Some of the biggest Cannon out of the Magazine at Delft, and the *Tin Boats from the Hague. 1692 *Siege Lymerick* 4 This day there came into our Camp Twenty Nine Tin-Boats. 1865 *Standard* 11 July, The Beam mine had been worked by *tin bounders under the custom of Cornwall. *Ibid.*, Up to 1858 the mine had been worked under the custom of *tin bounding. 1883 POLLOCK *Land Laws* ii. (1887) 50 In Cornwall..called 'tin-bounding', from the setting out of the working by bounds which is the adventurer's first step towards establishing his claim. 1873 HOWELLS *Chance Acquaintance* ii, The slender *tin-clad spire of its church. 1887 *Sci. Amer.* 23 Apr. 263/3 He converted..seven transports into what were called 'tinclads', or musket-proof gunboats. 1898 *Daily News* 26 Apr. 9/4 The tin wash and tailings of the leading tin sluicing mines of the Ringarooma *Tinfield. 1907 *Daily Chron.* 28 Sept. 5/4 Prospectors in the Government tin-fields at Waterberg. 1707 MORTIMER *Husb.* (1721) I. 185 On this *Tin-floor or Bed may the Hops be turned..with less expence of Fuel. 1839 URE *Dict. Arts* 1241 The stanniferous small veins,..interposed between certain rocks,..are commonly called tin-floors. 1881 RAYMOND *Mining Gloss.*, **Tin-frame*, Corn[wall], a sleeping-table used in dressing tin-ore slimes, and discharged by turning it upon an axis..and then dashing water over it. 1904 *Daily Chron.* 7 July 8/4 The *tin-glazed ware of Delft, and the salt-glazed stoneware of Germany. 1874 J. H. COLLINS *Metal Mining* 55 The deposit of *tin gravel at the mouth of the Carnon Valley. 1839 DE LA BECHE *Rep. Geol. Cornwall*, etc. xiii. 401 To fill up the space once occupied by the *tin-ground. 1798 H. M. WILLIAMS *Tour in Switzer.* I. x. 133 This admirable mimick-creation of silver torrents, mossy forests, *tin-houses and glass lakes. 1904 *Daily News* 19 Nov. 12 The mills and tin house were stopped for nearly an hour. 1858 SIMMONDS *Dict. Trade*, *Tin-liquor. *Ibid.* s.v. *Loaf*, The cottage loaf; *tin loaves. 1839 URE *Dict. Arts* 1252 *Tin mordants, for dyeing scarlet. 1888 GOODE *Amer. Fishes* 71 *Pomoxys annularis*..has other names of local application as '*Tin Mouth', 'Bridge Perch'. 1895 *Daily News* 21 June 3/7 Duggan and Farrell struck at her with a *tin opener. 1854 EMERSON *Lett. & Soc. Aims, Poet. & Imag.* Wks. (Bohn) III. 169 What we once admired as poetry has..come to be a sound of *tin pans. 1885 *Daily News* 8 Jan. 6/6 The female portion of the community '*tin-panning' the rev. gentleman, a great uproar being caused by the beating of old trays, kettles, &c. 1874 W. CROOKES *Dyeing & Calico-Print.* II. i. 166 The so-called prussiate of tin, or *tin-pulp, is chiefly used as an ingredient in printing steam-blues on cotton. 1839 URE *Dict. Arts* 801 The last polish is given [to marble] with *tin-putty. 1796 KIRWAN *Elem. Min.* (ed. 2) II. 75 *Tin Pyrites. 1839 URE *Dict. Arts* 1241 There are only two ores of tin; the peroxide, or tin-stone, and tin pyrites. 1892 GREENER *Breech-Loader* 237 The greater portion of the pigeons used for trap shooting are brought over from that port [Antwerp], and sold here as *Tin Rocks. 1849 D. CAMPBELL *Inorg. Chem.* 229 Boiling with phosphorous acid or *tin salt. 1681 GREW *Musæum* III. I. v. 307 A Yellow *Tin-Spar from Ireland. 1796 KIRWAN *Elem. Min.* (ed. 2) II. 198 The yellowish grey [tin stone] is often called Tinspar. 1877 O'NEILL in *Encycl. Brit.* VII. 574/2 The solution of tin used by dyers..commonly called '*tin spirits'. 1778 W. PRYCE *Min. Cornub.* 67 The Tinners or Miners..give it the name of *Tin-stuff. 1865-72 WATTS *Dict. Chem.* III. 252 In the *tin-vat, commonly used for calico-printing, the indigo is reduced by a solution of stannous oxide in caustic potash or soda. 1898 *Tin wash [see *tin-field* above]. 1869 A. R. WALLACE *Malay Archip.* I. 43 Extensive *tin-washings, employing over a thousand Chinese. 1853 URE *Dict Arts* II. 858 '*Tin witts', the ore obtained from the stamp floors. 1881 RAYMOND *Mining Gloss.*, *Tin-witts*, Corn[wall], the product of the first dressing of tin-ores, containing, besides tinstone, other heavy minerals (wolfram and metallic sulphides). 1884 M. E. WILKINS in *Harper's Mag.* June 29/2 Her customers..had grown used to the novelty of a *tin-woman, instead of a tinman. 1475 *Rolls of Parlt.* VI. 134/2 A *Tyn werk within the said Counte of Cornewaill, called the Myne of the Cleker. 1610 HOLLAND *Camden's Brit.* 184 Of these Mines or tinne-workes, there be two kinds. 1839 DE LA BECHE *Rep. Geol. Cornwall*, etc. xiii. 408 An epoch corresponding with that to which the Cornish stream tin-works belong. 1610 HOLLAND *Camden's Brit.* 185 Hee delivered rules and precepts to these *Tinne-workers. 1827 G. HIGGINS *Celtic Druids* Pref. 51 Before this *tin-working nation dived into the bowels of the earth. 1800 tr. *Lagrange's Chem.* II. 53 The *tin-worms of stills.

**Tin** (tin), *v.* Forms: see prec. [f. prec. sb. Cf. Du., LG. *-tinnen*, Ger. *-zinnen*.]

**1.** *trans.* To cover with a thin deposit of tin; to coat or plate with tin.

1398 TREVISA *Barth. De P. R.* XVI. xxxvii. (Tollem. MS.), Brasen vessel ben sone reed and rousti..and haue an yuel sauoure and smel, but þey be tynned. c1440 *Promp. Parv.* 494/1 Tynnyn wythe tynne, *stanno*. 1599 A. M. tr. *Gabelhouer's Bk. Physicke* 54/1 Take a copper basen which is not tinned. 1601 HOLLAND *Pliny* (1634) II. 517 A deuise to tin pots, pans, and other pieces of brasse..with white lead or tinglasse. 1747 MRS. GLASSE *Cookery* v. 68 Take great Care the Pots or Sauce-pans..be well tinned, for fear of giving the Broths or Soops any brassy Taste. 1816 P. CLEAVELAND *Min.* 525 Tin-plate..consists of iron, whose surface is tinned to prevent oxidation. 1832 BABBAGE *Econ. Manuf.* xix. (ed. 3) 182 The man who pickles and tins the pins.

**2.** In soldering iron, brass, etc., To perform the preliminary process of heating the surfaces and covering them with a thin coating of the solder.

1873 E. SPON *Workshop Receipts* Ser. I. (1888) 366/1 First clean the iron and brass well and then tin them before placing them together for soldering...The articles can be tinned by rubbing while hot with rosin; then rubbing them over with solder.

**3.** To put up or seal (provisions) in a tin for preservation; to can. (In quot. 1887 *intr.* for *pass.*)

1887 *Cassell's Mag.* Feb. 148 Some fish 'tin' well, others do not. 1890 *Daily News* 16 Apr. 6/2 The method of tinning milk for use of troops.

**Tin**, obs. form of *þin*, THINE (after a dental).

**Tin**, var. TIND *v. Obs.*, to kindle; var. TINE *sb.*$^2$ *Obs.*, loss. **Tinacle**, obs. form of TUNICLE.

†**Ti·nage.** *Obs.* Also 6 tynage, 7 tynaxe; and in Sp. forms *tinaja, tinaxa, tinaio* (i.e. *tinajo*). [ad. Sp. *tinaja*, †*tinaxa* (tinā·xa) = It. *tinaccio*, augmentatives of *tina* and *tino*, L. *tīna* wine-vessel.] A large earthenware jar.

1574 HELLOWES *Gueuara's Fam. Ep.* (1584) 241 His souldiers..haue drunke out a whole tinage of wine. 1582 N. LICHFIELD tr. *Castanheda's Conq. E. Ind.* I. xlix. 106 Sixe great Tynages of fine Earth, which they doe call Porcelanas. 1598 W. PHILLIP *Linschoten* I. vi. 16/2 The water that they drinke..they keepe in great pots (as the Tinaios in Spaine). 1622 R. HAWKINS *Voy. S. Sea* xii. 25 The Inhabitants doe reserue water..in their Cisterns and Tynaxes. 1676 LADY FANSHAWE *Mem.* (1830) 195 That admirable wine is kept in great tinajas, which are pots holding about 500 gallons each 1845 FORD *Handbk. Spain* I. 231/1 At Coria are made the enormous earthenware jars in which oil and olives are kept: these tinajas are the precise amphoræ of the ancients.

‖**Tinamou** (ti·nămū). [a. F. *tinamou* (Barrère 1741, Buffon 1771), a. *tinamu*, native name in Galibi.] A bird of the genus *Tinamus* (Latham 1790) or family *Tinamidæ*, dromæognathous birds, according to Huxley forming the bond of union between the *Carinatæ* and *Ratitæ*. The species have an external resemblance to partridges or quails, the place of which they fill on the pampas.

1783 LATHAM *Synopsis Birds* II. 724 Genus LII. Tinamou. No. 1. Great T[inamou]...*Tinamou de Cayenne*...This is found in the woods of several parts of South America, particularly of Cayenne and Guiana. 1842 *Penny Cycl.* XXIV 476/2. 1884 G. ALLEN in *Longm. Mag.* Jan. 293 All other modern birds..are linked..to the still earlier toothed ancestral types, by the South American tinamous. 1889 P. L. SCLATER *Argentine Ornith.* II. 207 The Tinamous constitute one of the most singular and characteristic types of the

Neotropical avifauna. **1895** F. W. HEADLEY *Struct. & Life Birds* xiii. 343 The Spotted Tinnamou, or common Partridge of the Pampas. **1896** NEWTON *Dict. Birds* 964 In 1830 Wagler..placed the Tinamous in the same Order as the Ostrich and its allies. **1902** *Q. Rev.* Oct. 427 Another somewhat less distinguished game-bird..is the *tinamu*.

**Tin-bath** to **-bounding**: see TIN *sb.* 5.

**Tincal** (ti·ŋkăl), **tincar** (ti·ŋkāɪ). Forms: *α.* 7 tyncall, 8–9 tinkal, 7– tincal; *β.* 7–8 tinkar, 8– tincar. [In form *tincal*, a. Malay *tingkal* :—Skr. *ṭankaṇa*; in Pers., Arab., Urdū تنكار *tankār*, *tinkār*, whence the *β*-forms and ALTINCAR.] Crude borax, found in lake-deposits in Tibet, Persia, and other Asiatic countries.

*α.* **1635** in Foster *Crt. Min. E. Ind. Co.* (1907) 99 Tyncall [to Mr. Allen]. **1678** *Phil. Trans.* XII. 1050 If any Dross or filth be in the Melting-Pot, they throw in some Tincal, which gathers the dross together. **1762** tr. *Busching's Syst. Geog.* I. 44 Borax...Its species are a bluish kind called Tinkal, and the proper borax, which is a purified Tinkal and appears white. **1811** A. T. THOMSON *Lond. Disp.* II. (1818) 371 The borax is dug in large masses from the edges and shallows of the lake.. In this state it is named tincal, and is brought home packed in chests, in masses of adhering crystals, of a grey yellowish, or greenish white colour. **1873** WATTS *Fownes' Chem.* (ed. 11) 341 It is imported in a crude state from the East Indies under the name of tincal.

*β.* **1678** PHILLIPS (ed. 4), *Tinkar*, a Chymical word for *Borax*. **1706** *Ibid.* (ed. Kersey), *Tincar* (Arab.), a sort of Nitre, or Salt-peter..dug out of the Earth. **1756** P. BROWNE *Jamaica* 38, 6° Borax. 1. Tinkal or Tinkar.

**Tincel**, obs. form of TINSEL *sb.*[3]

**Tinchel** (ti·nχĕl, ti·ŋkĕl). *Sc.* Forms: 6 tinchill, tynchal, teinchell, 6–7 tinchell, 6, 9 tainchel(l, 7 tinckhell, 8–9 tinkell, 9 tinckell, tinkal, tinchal, tinchel. [ad. Gael. *timchioll* (tʃi·mχ[y]ŏl) circuit, compass, round (as prep. = 'around, about').] In Scotland, A wide circle of hunters driving together a number of deer by gradually closing in upon them. Also *attrib.*

**1549** D. MONRO *Descr. West. Isles* § 15 All the Deire of the west pairt of that forrest will be callit [= driven] be tainchels to that narrow entres, and the next day callit west againe be tainchels through the said narrow entres, & infinit Deire slaine ther. *Ibid.* § 100 The Deire will be callit upwart ay be the Teinchell. *a* **1578** LINDESAY (Pitscottie) *Chron. Scot.* (S.T.S.) I. 56 Ilk ane lyand wait for wther as they had ben settand tinchellis for the murther of wyld beistes. **1618** J. TAYLOR (Water P.) *Pennyles Pilgr.* Wks. (1630) 136/1 Those foresaid Scouts which are called the Tinckhell, doe bring downe the Deere. **1814** SCOTT *Wav.* xxiv, These active assistants spread through the country far and near, forming a circle, technically called the *tinchel*, which, gradually closing, drove the deer in herds together towards the glen where the Chiefs and principal sportsmen lay in wait for them. **1820** HOGG *Tales & Sk.*, *Bridal Polmood* xiii, The tinkell was raised at two in the morning. *Ibid.* xvi, Tinckell. **1834** MUDIE *Brit. Birds* (1841) I. 283 He [dipper] gives chase, with all the confidence of one who drives deer into a tinchal, or ducks into a decoy. **1868** *Nat. Encycl.* I. 238 Hunting, which sport they carry on like the Scottish 'tinkal'. **1904** *Blackw. Mag.* June 757/2 A *tainchel* or hunting drive was to meet at Figinthas.

**Tinck(e**, **Tinckle**: see TINK *v.*, TINKLE.

**Tin-clad**: see TIN *sb.* 5.

**Tincle**, obs. form of TINKLE, TINSEL *sb.*[3]

**Tinct** (tiŋkt), *sb.* Now only *poet.* [ad. L. *tinct-us* a dyeing, f. *tingĕre* to dye, stain.]

**1.** Colour, hue, tint; colouring matter, dye: = TINCTURE *sb.* 1, 2.

**1602** SHAKS. *Ham.* III. iv. 91 There I see such blacke and grained spots, As will not leave their tinct. **1611** — *Cymb.* II. ii. 23 White and Azure lac'd With Blew of Heauens owne tinct. **1706** PHILLIPS (ed. Kersey), *Tinct*, or *Teint* (Lat.), a Colouring. **1748** THOMSON *Cast. Indol.* I. xliv, Raising a world of gayer tinct and grace. *a* **1855** MISS MITFORD *Poems*, *A Portrait*, Such brilliant white, such rosy tinct, The apple blossom shows. **1861** WYNTER *Soc. Bees* 500 The difference of colour is entirely owing to the tinct of the fluid which fills the hollow tube in each hair. **1884** BROWNING *Ferishtah*, *Bean-Stripe* 347 There's no single tinct Would satisfy the eye's desire to taste The secret of the diamond.

**b.** *fig.* A touch, trace, tinge (*of* something): = TINCTURE *sb.* 4.

**1752** FOOTE *Taste* I. Wks. 1799 I. 8 If I do now and then add some tincts of antiquity to my pictures. **1794** MRS. PIOZZI *Synon.* II. 195 That lovely season of life gives to every thing a tinct of its own greenness.

†**2.** *Alch.* A transmuting elixir; = TINCTURE *sb.* 6. *Obs.*

**1471** RIPLEY *Comp. Alch.* XII. i. in Ashm. *Theat. Chem. Brit.* (1652) 184 And Tynct in Projeccyon all Fyers to abyde. **1601** SHAKS. *All's Well* v. iii. 102 Platus himselfe, That knowes the tinct and multiplying med'cine. **1606** — *Ant. & Cl.* I. v. 37 Yet comming from him, that great Med'cine hath With his Tinct gilded thee.

**Tinct**, *ppl. a.* *poet.* [ad. L. *tinct-us*, pa. pple. of *tingĕre*: see prec.] Coloured, tinted; dyed, tinged; imbued. Const. as *pa. pple.*

**1579** SPENSER *Sheph. Cal.* Nov. 107 The blew in black, the greene in gray is tinct. **1615** BRATHWAIT *Strappado*, etc. (1878) 284 Her sanguine colour tinct with Lyons iawes. **1819** KEATS *Eve St. Agnes* xxx, Lucent syrops, tinct with cinnamon. **1839** BAILEY *Festus* xxxi. (1852) 530 In robes Of seagreen hue, engirdled with a zone All variously tinct.

†**Tinct**, *v.* *Obs.* Also 6 tinkt. [f. L. *tinct-*, ppl. stem of *tingĕre* to dye, colour. First used in pa. pple. *tincted*: cf. TINCT *ppl. a.*]

**1.** *trans.* To colour; to dye; to tinge, tint.

**1594** PLAT *Jewell-ho.* II. 22 Water deepelie died, or tincted with..colour of the hearbe. **1596** DRAYTON *Leg.* ii. 541 My delicious Cheeke Tinkted with Crimson. **1626** B. JONSON *Masque, Fort. Isles*, I will but touch your Temples,..and tinct the Tip, the very Tip of your Nose. *a* **1648** DIGBY *Chym. Secr.* II. (1682) 174 It will Tinct itself as red as blood. **1650** ASHMOLE *Chym. Collect.* 127 A Dry earthy Body tincts not, unlesse it be tincted. **1686** GOAD *Celest. Bodies* II. xiii. 337 In dry Seasons the Solar Halo's are sometimes tincted with red.

**2.** *transf.* and *fig.* To imbue or impregnate with some substance or quality, esp. in a slight degree; to tinge, tincture, taint. **a.** with a physical substance or quality: = TINCTURE *v.* 2 a.

*a* **1626** BACON *New Atl.* (1650) 27 Artificiall Wells and Fountaines, made in Imitation of the Naturall Sources and Bathes; As tincted upon Vitrioll, Sulphur, Steele, Brasse, Lead, Nitre, and other Mineralls. **1626** — *Sylva* § 882 So the strainer itself is tincted with salt. **1638** RAWLEY tr. *Bacon's Life & Death* (1650) 48 That towards the Morning, there be used some Anointing, or Shirt tincted with Oyle. **1644** DIGBY *Nat. Bodies* xxiv. (1658) 280 Although the heart should be tincted from its first origine with an undue virtue from some part.

**b.** with a mental or moral quality, or with knowledge, etc.: = TINCTURE *v.* 2 b.

**1599** B. JONSON *Ev. Man out of Hum.* Ded., To take it in your hands, perhaps may make some bencher, tincted with humanity, read and not repent him. **1666** SANCROFT *Lex Ignea* 23 Conjectures..so tincted and debaucht with private prejudice. *a* **1734** NORTH *Exam.* I. iii. § 15 (1740) 132 To suppose his Reader..tincted beforehand with what was ordinarily understood by the Plot.

**3.** *Alch.* To subject to a transmuting elixir: see TINCTURE *sb.* 6.

**1599** [see *tincting* below]. **1601** DOLMAN *La Primaud. Fr. Acad.* (1618) III. 844 Iron too much concocted and highly tincted, is easily changed into brasse. **1610** B. JONSON *Alch.* II. iii, I meane to tinct *C* [a retort] in sand-heat to-morrow, And giue him imbibition. **1655** *Fulke's Meteors, Observ.* 163 Cyprus Copper is made of Brasse and Iron.., and high tincted is easily changed into Brass, and rechanged ..into Copper.

Hence **Ti·ncted** *ppl. a.*, **Ti·ncting** *vbl. sb.*

**1599** THYNNE *Animadv.* (1875) 33 Fermentacione ys a peculier terme of Alchemye..whiche is before tinctinge, or gyvinge tincture or cooler. **1626** BACON *Sylva* § 960 Tincted Lanthorns, or Tincted Skreens of Glasse Coloured into Green, Blew, Carnation &c. **1672** BOYLE in *Phil. Trans.* VII. 5110, I applied a seal'd Weather glass, furnished with tincted spirit of wine.

**Tinction** (ti·ŋkʃən). [ad. late L. *tinctiōn-em* a dipping; baptism administered by non-Catholics (Cyprian *a* 258, Ep. 71/1 and 75/8), n. of action f. *tingĕre* to dip, dye.]

†**1.** Dipping (in baptism); cf. TINCTURE *sb.* 8. *Obs.*

**1657** J. WATTS *Dipper Sprinkled* 33, I yeild tinction or dipping, and immersion to be one and the same likewise in this matter. *Ibid.*, Both perfusion and tinction are called baptism.

**2.** The action of imbuing with colour; colouring, tinging, tinting.

**1888** BILLINGS in *Amer. Nat.* Feb. 118 These micro-organisms..color more diffusely with the same degree of exposure to the tinction.

**Tinctorial** (tiŋktō°·riăl), *a.* [f. L. *tinctōri-us* (Pliny) (f. *tinctōr-em* dyer) + -AL.] Of, pertaining to, or used in dyeing; yielding or using dye or colouring matter.

**1655** How *Let. to Sir T. Browne* 20 Sept., in *B.'s Wks.* (Bohn) III. 517 After wee have thus circumscribed the plant wee shall adde our experiments; ..hortensiall,..medicinall, ..tinctoriall. **1811** W. TAYLOR in *Monthly Mag.* 1 Oct. 258/2 Plants, oleaginous, tinctorial, textile, medical, and culinary. **1837** *Penny Cycl.* IX. 227/1 Tinctorial colours are either simple or compound. **1887** *Pall Mall G.* 5 Sept. 7/2 Mr. C. O'Neill..discoursed on the change of fashion in colour, in a paper on 'The extent to which calico printing and the tinctorial arts are affected by the introduction of modern colours'.

Hence **Tincto·rially** *adv.*

**1898** *Allbutt's Syst. Med.* V. 412 The stain acts tinctorially as a free acid.

**Tincto·rious**, *a.* *rare.* [f. as prec. + -OUS.] = TINCTORIAL.

**1786** ABERCROMBIE *Arr.* in *Gard. Assist.* 66 Tinctorious yellow Virginian. **1900** in B. D. JACKSON *Gloss. Bot. Terms.*

**Tinctumutant** (tiŋktiu,miū·tănt). *Zool. rare*—[1]. [f. L. *tinctu-s* (see TINCT *sb.*) + *mūtānt-em* changing.] An animal that changes colour. So **Ti:nctumuta·tion**, change of colour.

**1895** J. WEIR in *Pop. Sci. Monthly* Jan. 388 The chameleon is the best known of all the tinctumutants. *Ibid.*, Physiological changes that take place in the act of tinctumutation.

**Tincturation** (tiŋktiŭrē¹·ʃən). [f. TINCTURE *v.* + -ATION: cf. med.L. *tinctūrātio* dyeing.] The preparation of a tincture of some substance.

**1860** *Ure's Dict. Arts* III. 427 Tincturation. Musk,.. ambergris,..vanilla, civet, and a few other odorous substances, yield their odours to spirit by tincturation, that is, by putting the fragrant material into the spirit and allowing it to remain..till the alcohol has extracted all the scent.

**Tincture** (ti·ŋktiŭɹ, -tʃəɪ), *sb.* [ad. L. *tinctūra* a dyeing, tinging, f. *tinct-*, ppl. stem of *tingĕre* to dye: see -URE.]

†**1.** A colouring matter, dye, pigment; *spec.* a dye used as a cosmetic. *Obs.*

*c* **1400** *Lanfranc's Cirurg.* 180 If a man desiriþ for to haue blac heeris.., þanne make þis tincture. **1606** WARNER *Alb. Eng.* XVI. ci. 401 Tinctures, Tiers, Maske, Fardingale, and Fan. **1613** PURCHAS *Pilgrimage* (1614) 646 Some of them..rubbed his skin, to see whether his whitenesse were naturall,..perceiuing it to be no tincture, they were out of measure astonished. **1692** DRYDEN *Juvenal* Ded. (1697) 36 When the Wooll has taken the whole Tincture, and drunk in as much of the Dye as it can receive. **1717** LADY M. W. MONTAGU *Let. to C'tess Mar* 1 Apr., The Greeks and Turks have a custom of putting round their eyes..a black tincture, that..adds very much to the blackness of them. **1825** J. NICHOLSON *Operat. Mechanic* 730 Extract, by infusion, the tincture of the colouring substances.

**2.** Hue, colour: esp. as communicated (naturally or artificially) by a colouring matter or dye, or by something that stains; a tinge, tint. Now *rare.*

**1477** NORTON *Ord. Alch.* Proem in Ashm. *Theat. Chem. Brit.* (1652) 7 All such Men as give Tincture to Glasse. **1555** EDEN *Decades* 328 Certeyne waters..do..shewe.. dyuers tinctures of myneral substaunce. **1594** PLAT *Jewell-ho.* II. 11 If you may not giue a tincture to your creame before you chearne it. **1602** MARSTON *Ant. & Mel.* III. Wks. 1856 I. 30 The shuddering morne that flakes, With silver tincture, the east vierge of heaven. **1713** ADDISON *Cato* I. iv, 'Tis not..The tincture of a skin, that I admire. **1800** HELENA WELLS *Constantia Neville* (ed. 2) I. 254 The heat of the mask had given to her complexion such a tincture of red. **1822–34** *Good's Study Med.* (ed. 4) IV. 374 The matter has a bloody tincture and a bilious smell.

**b.** *Her.* Inclusive term for the metals, colours, and furs used in coats of arms, etc.

**1610** GUILLIM *Heraldry* I. ii. (1611) 7 Tincture is a variable hew of Armes and is common as well to differences of Armes as to the Armes themselues. **1725** COATS *Dict. Her.*, *Tincture*, is no other than the Hue or Colour of any thing in Coat-Armour, and under this Denomination may be also included the two Metals Or and Argent..because they are often represented by Yellow and White, and they themselves bear those Colours. **1842** BRANDE *Dict. Sc.*, etc., *Tinctures*, in Heraldry are of three descriptions: metals, colours, and furs. The former are or, argent; the second gules, azure, sable, vert, purpure, sanguine, and tenny. The chief furs are ermine and vair; but there are several varieties of both, distinguished by different names. **1864** BOUTELL *Her. Hist. & Pop.* iv. 20 The representation of the Tinctures by means of dots and lines was not in use..before..the accession of the Stuarts. **1891** *Scott. N. & Q.* Apr. 210/2 At the foot of the stone there is cut the armorial coat..carved so as to show the tinctures, viz., Sable, a fess between three mascles, two and one, or.

†**3.** The action of dyeing, staining, or colouring.

**1601** HOLLAND *Pliny* (1634) II. 619 This stone [Chrysoprase] is very apt to be counterfeited, and especially by tincture. **1650** BULWER *Anthropomet.* ii. 58 This Tincture of Hair is most shameful and detestable in men. **1681** tr. *Willis' Rem. Med. Wks.* Vocab., *Tincture*, a dying or colouring.

†**b.** *fig.* A stain, blemish. *Obs.*

*a* **1640** J. BALL *Answ. to Canne* ii. (1642) 9 Our service was picked and culled out of the masse booke..so it might, and yet be free from all fault and tincture. *a* **1658** CLEVELAND *Poems*, etc. (1677) 149 To offend against so Gracious a Patron, would add a Tincture to our Disobedience.

†**4.** *fig.* An imparted quality likened to a colour or dye; a specious or 'colourable' appearance; a quality or character with which anything is imbued, esp. a derived quality; a tinge. *Obs.*

**1590** NASHE *Pasquil's Apol.* I. D ij, They that abused thys place,..had a little more tincture from hence to lay uppon theyr opinion, than Penrie can haue. **1640** HARVEY *Synagogue* (1647) 7 Hypocrisie in Church is Alchymie, That casts a golden tincture upon brasse. **1652** L. S. *People's Liberty* vii. 13 His speech..having a tincture from his guilty conscience. **1711** STEELE *Spect.* No. 144 ⁋ 7 A goodness mixed with Fear, gives a Tincture to all her Behaviour. **1757** BURKE *Abridgm. Eng. Hist.* II. i, The Saxon language received little or no tincture from the Welsh. **1806** SURR *Winter in Lond.* I. 242, I attributed this tincture of mind in a great degree to his peculiar destiny.

†**5.** A physical quality (other than colour) communicated to something; *esp.* a taste or flavour, a taint. *Obs.*

**1610** HOLLAND *Camden's Brit.* I. 306 Whether it bee by the nature, or tincture and temper thereof. **1625** N. CARPENTER *Geog. Del.* II. v. (1635) 77 They receiue their tincture of saltnesse from some salt minerals of the Earth. **1697** BP. PATRICK *Comm. Exod.* xiii. 6 Anything..that might give a Tincture of Acidity to the Bread. **1727** *Bradley's Fam. Dict.* s. v. *Distilling*, The Waters..smell of Smoke, and had a Tincture of Adustion.

**b.** A slight infusion (*of* some element or quality; a tinge, a shade, a flavour, a trace; a smattering (*of* knowledge, etc.).

**1612** SELDEN *Illustr. Drayton's Poly-olb.* xi. 184 They had lived here C. L. yeers by the common account without tincture of true religion. **1697** BURGHOPE *Disc. Relig. Assemb.* 107 This irreligious custom..has a tincture of atheism in it. **1711** STEELE *Spect.* No. 38 ⁋ 5 This, perhaps, cannot be called Affectation; but it has some Tincture of it. **1775** TYRWHITT *Chaucer* IV. 26 We may fairly conclude, that the English language must have imbibed a strong tincture of the French, long before the age of Chaucer. **1858** CARLYLE *Fredk. Gt.* I. iv. (1872) I. 31 Ernst August has some tincture of soldiership at this time.

†**6.** *Alchemy.* A supposed spiritual principle or immaterial substance whose character or quality may be infused into material things, which are then said to be tinctured; the quintessence, spirit, or soul of a thing. *Universal tincture*, the Elixir. *Obs.*

**1599** T. M[OUFET] *Silkwormes* 68 A Quintessence? nay wel it may be call'd A deathlesse tincture, sent vs from the skies Whose colour stands, whose glosse is ne'er appall'd. **1649** J. E[LLISTONE] tr. *Behmen's Epist* Pref. 10 This.. conduces to the attainment of the Universall Tincture and Signature; whereby the different secret qualities, and ver-ues, that are hid in all visible and corporeall things.. nay be drawne forth and applyed to their right naturall ıse. *Ibid.* iii. § 34 Operation of the philosopher's stone or universal tincture from me. **1693** tr. *Blancard's Phys. Dict.* (ed. 2), *Tinctura*, a Tincture, or *Elixir*, the Extraction of the Colour, Quality, and Strength of any thing.

† **b.** An active principle, of a physical nature, emanating or derivable from any body or substance; a liquid or volatile principle. *Obs.*

**1602** T. Fitzherb. *Apol.* 48 If by chaunce her Maiestie had layed her hand vpon the poysoned pomel of the Sadle in the moneth of Iuly when the pores and veynes are open she might haue byn poysoned or receaue maligne vapors or tinctures. **1671** Grew *Anat. Plants* ii. § 23 The purest part [of the Sap]..recedes, with its due Tinctures, from the said Cortical Body, to all the parts of the Lignous. *Ibid.* vi. § 4 Precipitation is made by the mixture and reaction of the Tinctures of the Lignous and Cortical Bodies upon each other. *a* **1677** Hale *Prim. Orig. Man.* II. xii. 241 The Fertility of their Soil by the Inundation of Nilus, which at its recess leaves so fruitful a Tincture, that thereby and by the heat of the Sun, Animals have their visible production. *Ibid.* III. iv. 267 The..Dew exhaled from some sorts of Herbs or Weeds,..carries with it the Seminal Tincture of the Herb.

**7.** *Chem.* and *Pharm.* † **a.** In early chemistry, and in derived uses: The (supposed) essential principle of any substance obtained in solution. Also, the extraction of this essential principle. *Obs.*

*Tincture of gold*, Potable gold, aurum potabile. *Tincture of the Moon* (i.e. of silver, Luna): see quot. 1706.

**1610** B. Jonson *Alch.* II. iii, Infuse vinegar, To draw his volatile substance and his tincture. **1626** — *Fort. Isles* Wks. (Rtldg.) 649/1 This little gallipot Of tincture, high rose tincture. **1651** French *Distill.* vi. 179 A way by which the tincture of gold which is the soule thereof,..may be..extracted. **1669** Worlidge *Syst. Agric.* (1681) 39 Many of our best Mechanicks being too much addicted to the tincture of this Grain [barley]. **1675** E. Wilson *Spadacrene Dunelm.* Pref. 12 As to the discovery of Metalline tinctures in waters. **1696** Phillips (ed. 5), *Tincture*..In Chymistry, the Extraction of the Colour, Quality and Strength of any thing. **1706** *Ibid.* (ed. Kersey), *Tincture of the Moon*, is a Dissolution of some of the more rarify'd parts of Silver, made in Spirit of Wine, and whetted by Alkali-Salts. **1707** Mortimer *Husb.* (1721) I. 355 'Tis not unlikely that Grain may afford its Tincture, and that excellent Beer and Ale may be made thereof without Malting.

**b.** *Mod. Pharmacy.* A solution, usually in a menstruum of alcohol, of some principle used in medicine, chiefly vegetable, as tincture of opium (laudanum), but sometimes animal, as tincture of cantharides, or mineral, as tincture of ferric chloride.

More particularly called an *alcoholic tincture.* But the menstruum may also be sulphuric ether or spirit of ammonia (both mainly alcohol), which give *ethereal* and *ammoniated tinctures* respectively; when wine is used they are called *medicated wines.* A tincture is *simple* when it is a solution of one substance only, *compound* when of two or more substances.

*a* **1648** Digby *Chym. Secr.* (1682) 172 An excellent Spirit of Wine, fit to draw Tinctures. **1704** J. Harris *Lex. Techn.* I, *Tincture*, in Chymistry, is a Dissolution of the more fine, and volatile Parts of a mixt Body in Spirit of Wine, or some such proper Menstruum. **1712** tr. *Pomet's Hist. Drugs* I. 184 A Tincture is likewise extracted with Spirit of Wine Tartariz'd. **1789** Buchan *Dom. Med.* (1790) 695 Aromatic Tincture. Infuse two ounces of Jamaica pepper in two pints of brandy, without heat, for a few days; then strain off the tincture. **1800** tr. *Lagrange's Chem.* II. 327 Alcohol dissolves resins and resinous gums: these solutions are called Tinctures, Elixirs, Quintessences, &c. **1813** J. Thomson *Lect. Inflam.* 83 The results were the same when tincture of opium was employed. **1842** Brande *Dict. Sc.* etc., s.v., The term tincture is sometimes applied to alcoholic solutions of resins, of which tincture of myrrh, of assafœtida, &c. furnish instances. **1871** Garrod *Mat. Med.* (ed. 3) 162 Tincture of Aconite. (Aconite root, in coarse powder, two ounces and a half; rectified spirit, twenty fluid ounces. Prepared by maceration and percolation.)

† **8.** Affectedly used for 'baptism'. Cf. late L. use of *tingĕre* (to dip) for 'baptize', and Tinction I.

**1612** Selden *Illustr. Drayton's Poly-olb.* iv. 73 Honoured in holy tincture of Christianity with the name of Robert. *Ibid.* ix. 146 Cadwallader..received of P. P. Sergius, with holy tincture, the name of Peter.

**Ti·ncture,** *v.* [f. prec. sb.]

**1.** *trans.* To impart a tincture or dye to; to dye; to colour, tinge, imbue. (Chiefly in pa. pple.)

**1616** [see *tincturing* below]. **1634** Sir T. Herbert *Trav.* 147 Cheekes tinctured with Vermillion. **1664** H. More *Myst. Iniq.* 310 The River that will run tinctured with bloud three hundred years hence. **1715** tr. *Pancirollus' Rerum Mem.* I. I. i. 2 This Juice..which Wooll and Purple-Silk.. were tinctur'd with. **1814** Wordsw. *Excursion* VII. 188 Homespun wool But tinctured daintily with florid hues. **1822-34** *Good's Study Med.* (ed. 4) I. 325 One of the latest fluids that becomes tinctured is the milk in icteric wet-nurses. **1828** Moore *'Tis sweet to think* ii, It will tincture Love's plume with a different hue.

**2.** *transf.* and *fig.* To imbue or impregnate with a quality; to communicate some quality to; to affect, tinge, taint. (Chiefly in pa. pple., const. *with.*) † **a.** with a physical quality, as smell or taste. *Obs.*

**1668** H. More *Div. Dial.* v. xxxviii. (1713) 515 Innocuous Whirl-winds of sincere Air, tinctured only with a cool refreshing smell. **1671** Grew *Anat. Plants* ii. § 23 The remainder..is in part carried off into the Cortical Body back again, the Sap whereof it now tinctures into good Aliment. **1678** R. Barclay *Apol. Quakers* VII. xii. 237 Water may be capable to be tinctured with uncleanness. **1820** Mair *Tyro's Dict.* (ed. 10), *Aluminosus*,.. tinctured with, smelling or tasting of alum.

**b.** with a mental or moral quality or character; with reference to knowledge (*pass.* with *with*), to have a smattering of. (In early use often with allusion to alchemy: cf. prec. 6.)

**1636** Heywood *Love's Mistr.* Prol., So pure a mind, As if tinctur'd from Heaven. **1651** Wittie tr. *Primrose's Pop. Err.* I. xiii. 47 He professed himselfe to be a Physician (although he was but lightly tinctured with the knowledge of Physick). **1662** Sparrow tr. *Behme's Rem. Wks., Apol. conc. Perfect.* 147, I must be Tinctured or else I cannot be Transmuted; If Christ do not Tincture me with his Bloud, then my Holy Paradise-Life remaineth faded. **1718** *Free-thinker* No. 7 ₱ 2 His Conversation was tinctured throughout with the Ancient Mythology. **1878** Spurgeon *Treas. Dav.* Ps. cxv. 1 The prayer is evidently tinctured with a consciousness of unworthiness.

**c.** *intr.* for *pass.* To take or have a tinge *of* something. *rare*$^{-1}$.

**1787** 'G. Gambado' *Acad. Horsemen* (1809) 15 It [a portrait] is like, but a likeness that tinctures of the prejudice of friendship.

† **3.** To deposit (one metal *upon* another). *rare.*

**1670** *Specif. Pr. Rupert's Patent* 2 A new Invencion or Art of Tincturing Copper vpon Iron. **1679** *Essex Papers* (Camden) I. 235 Of tincturing of Copper upon Iron as to him or them shall seem meet.

Hence **Ti·ncturing** *vbl. sb.*

**1616** T. Tuke (*title*) A Treatise against Painting and Tincturing of Men and Women. **1656** *Artif. Handsom.* 110 Hangings, pictures, carvings, guildings, and tincturings. **1679** [see 3 above]. **1902** W. M. Alexander *Demonic Possession in N. T.* iii. 65 [They] may contain a tincturing of medical lore.

**Tinctured** (ti·ŋktiŭɹd), *ppl. a.* [f. Tincture *v.* (or *sb.*) + -ed.] Imbued with a tincture or colour; having a tincture (esp. of a specified kind); dyed, coloured, stained, tinged.

**1626** Capt. Smith *Virginia* I. 17 Very rocky, and much tinctured stone like Minerall. **1737** M. Green *Spleen* 737 And fancy's telescope applies With tinctur'd glass to cheat his eyes. **1782** Eliz. N. Blower *Geo. Bateman* II. 155 The blood-tinctured weapon. **1908** *Daily Chron.* 17 Aug. 4/7 Zinc and other metallically tinctured ointments.

**Tincy,** variant of Tinsey.

**Tind** (tind), *v. Obs.* exc. *dial.* Forms: α. (1 tendan), 2–3 tenden, 3–5 tende, 4 (*3rd pers. sing.*) tent; *pa. t.* 3–5 tende, 4 tendede; *pa. pple.* 2–4 itend, 2 itent, itende, 3–5 tende, 4 ytend, 4–5 tend. β. 4 teende, 6–7 (9 *dial.*) teend; *pa. pple.* 4 teendid. γ. 3 tiende, 5 tynd, 6 tinde, 6–7 tynde, 5– tind; *pa. pple.* 6 tynded, 6–7 tinded. δ. 6 tīnde, 6–7 ?tynde, 6–9 tīnd. ε. 5 tynne, 6–7 tinne, 7–9 tin; *pa. t.* and *pple.* 7 tinn'd. ζ. 5–6 tyne, 7 tine; *pa. t.* 6 tynde, tind; *pa. pple.* 5 tyned, 6 tynde, tind, 6–7 tined. η. 5–6 teyne, *pa. pple.* y-, iteyned. θ. 7, 9 teen, *pa. t.* and *pple.* teened. [ME. had *tend-e(n* from 1175 to 1425; also, in Wyclif and down to 17th c., with lengthened vowel, *teende(n*, in some mod. dialects *teend* (tīnd). From *c* 1400 onward also *tind* and *tīnd* (see γ, δ forms). Later with loss of final *d* from both forms (perh. arising out of shortened pa. pple. *tind, tīnd, teend*, taken as = *tin-d, tīne-d, teen-d*, hence inf. *tin, tīne, teen*; but reduction of *-nd* to *-n* is found in many other words). In mod. dial. surviving from Scotl. to Cornwall as (tind, təind, tin, təin, tīn): see quots. and *Eng. Dial. Dict.* Early ME. *tenden* corresponded to an OE. **tęndan* (in comp. *ontęndan, atęndan, fortęndan*, to set fire to, kindle, and in vbl. sb. *tęnding*, Napier *Contrib. to OE. Lexic.*), corresp. to Goth. *tandjan*, Da. *tænde*, Sw. *tända*; causal of **tindan* str. vb. (ablaut series *tind-, tand-, tund-*), to be on fire, burn, glow, represented by MHG. *zinden* str. vb., in same sense. The history of early ME. *tiende, tinde*, now *tind, tīnd* (təind), is more difficult: as no other example is known of OE. and ME. *-end* becoming later *-ind*, much less *-īnd*, it is probable that we have here a parallel formation, representing an OE. **tyndan* (from the weak ablaut grade *tund-*), cognate with OHG. *zunten* (from **zuntjan*:—**tundjan*), MHG. and Ger. *zünden* to set on fire, kindle, and OE. *tynder* Tinder. In that case, *tend* (*teend, teen, teyne*) and *tind* (*tynd, tīnd, tin, tīne, tyne*) are two distinct but parallel and synonymous formations from the same root verb.]

**1.** *trans.* To set fire to, ignite, light, kindle (a fire, lamp, torch, flame, etc.).

α. [*a* **901** *Laws K. Ælfred* Prol. c. 27 Gif fyr sie ontended ryt to bærnanne. *a* **1000** tr. *Bæda's De Temporibus* in *Sax. Leechd.* III. 242 Ðonne he [moon] of hyre [sun] ontend byþ.] *a* **1050** *O. E. Chron.* an. 994 (MS. C) Eac hi mid fyre on tendon woldan. *c* **1100** *Charms* in *Sax. Leechd.* III. 286 Ontend þreo candela.] *c* **1175** *Lamb. Hom.* 81 He wule aquikien and al þe brond tenden. **1340-70** *Alex. & Dind.* 233 Of a torche þat is tend, tak an en-sample. **1377** Langl. *P. Pl.* B. XVIII. 238 Þo þat weren in heuene token *stella comata*, And tendeden hir [C. XXI. 250 tenden hit] as a torche. **1387** Trevisa *Higden* (Rolls) II. 17 I-tend in þe fire hit feseþ awey serpentes. *c* **1400** *Laud Troy Bk.* 17978 The Troyens ..tende hire fir more than ten sithe, But it ȝede out. *c* **1425** *Seven Sag.* (P.) 2183 He tende hys torche at a cole.

β. **1382** Wyclif *Isa.* l. 11 Lo! ȝee alle teendende vp [1388 kyndlynge] fyr. — *Ecclus.* viii. 13 Teende thou not colis of synneres..lest thou be tend with the flaume of the fyr of the synnes of hem. **1388** — *Matt.* v. 15 Ne men teendith not [1382 Nether men tendyn] a lanterne, and puttith it vndur a busschel. **1598** Sylvester *Du Bartas* II. i. IV. *Handy-crafts* 707 Teend again Truth's near-extinguisht Taper. **1605** *Ibid.* iii. II. *Fathers* 306 Thou whetst a sword, and thou dost teend a brand. **1648** Herrick *Hesper., Candlem. Day* ii, Kindle the Christmas brand..Part must be kept wherewith to teend The Christmas log next yeare.

γ. *a* **1400-50** *Alexander* 4179 It tinds on tend lowe trappour of stede, And many costious costis consumes in-to askis. **1589** R. Harvey *Pl. Perc.* 20, I see no more Candles tinded then wont to be. **1622** Mabbe tr. *Aleman's Guzman d'Alf.* II. 19 Those coales, that were already throughly tinded. *a* **1663** Sanderson *Serm.* (1689) 56 As one candle tindeth a thousand. **1706** Phillips (ed. Kersey), To *Tind*, to light; as *To tind a Candle.* **1904** *Eng. Dial. Dict., Tind*, to light, kindle. [Generally diffused, Scotl. to Heref., Northamp., Bedford, Berks, Cornwall.] **1910** *Old man at Gorsley, Glo'ster*, Get up and tind (tind) the fire.

δ. *c* **1548** Udall, etc. *Erasm. Par. John* v. 40 Only a burnyng candell tynded at our fyre. **1558** Phaer *Æneid* III. G ij, Altars vp againe we make and fiers on them we tinde [*rime* blind]. [**1590** Spenser *F. Q.* II. viii. 11 Stryful Atin in their stubborne mind Coles of contention and whot vengeaunce tind. **1594** Carew *Tasso* I. (1881) 27 For if one feare to crueltie him tinde [*rime* finde], Another greater doubt bridles no lesse.] (?) **1623** in *10th Rep. Hist. MSS. Comm.* App. IV. 433 Paied for sixe faggottes to tynde the coales, 4*d.* **1834** *Tait's Mag.* I. 341/2 For him it [the heavenly torch] beams not,—can but tind [*rime* blind], And lands and cities turn to dust.

ε. **1497** *Croscombe Churchw. Acc.* (Som. Rec. Soc.) 27 Paid to W. Toyt for tynnyng of the lyght. **1562** Phaer *Æneid* VIII. B b ij b, Her couchyd harth she steeres and sturging sparkes of fire doth tinne. **1638** Farley *Emblems* v. B vj, That learned dogge, at noone-tyde tinn'd his light. **1655** H. Vaughan *Silex Scint.* II. *Cockcrow.* (1858) 142 It seems their candle, howe'er done, Was tinn'd and lighted at the sunne. **1674** Ray *S. & E. C. Words*, To *Tine* or *tin* a Candle, to light it. *Mod. Bedford & Northampt. Dial.*, I get up at six, tin the fire, and then sweep the room up.

ζ. [**1471** Ripley *Comp. Alch.* XI. ii. in Ashm. *Theat. Chem. Brit.* (1652) 181 For yt ys Fyer whych tyned wyll never dye.] *c* **1511** (see *Tinding*), Tynyng. **1591** Spenser *Virg. Gnat* 394 Whose bridale torches foule Erynnis tynde [*rime* unkinde]. *Ibid.* 504 Flames, weapons, wounds, in Greeks fleete to have tynde [*rime* minde]. **1594** T. B. *La Primaud. Fr. Acad.* II. 514 With the same fire wherewith that was first tined. **1612** *Pasquil's Night-Cap* (1877) 26 Though others tine their candles at my light. **1667** Milton *P. L.* x. 1075 As late the Clouds Justling or pusht with Winds rude in thir shock, Tine the slant Lightning. **1700** Dryden *Iliad* I. 635 The priest..was seen to tine The cloven wood, and pour the ruddy wine.

η. **1482** Caxton *Trevisa's Higden* I. xxiv. 30 b, Whan it was ones yteyned [*ed.* **1527** Iteyned] and sette a fyre.

θ. **1847-78** Halliwell, *Teen*, to light a candle. Var. dial. **1864** E. Capern *Devon. Provinc.*, 'Teen the candle' is often used for light the candle. **1895** Quiller-Couch *Wandering Heath* 85 She struck flint over touchwood and teened a fire.

**2.** *intr.* To catch fire, kindle, become ignited, begin to burn.

*c* **1290** *St. Michael* 523 in *S. Eng. Leg.* I. 314 And ȝwane it comez a-mong þe fuyre, sone it bi-gynnez forto tiende [*Harl. MS.* 2277 sone hit gynneþ tende: *rime* ende]. **1382** Wyclif *Ecclus.* xvi. 7 Wrathe shal waxe ful out tend [1388 yre schal brenne]. *c* **1400** *Brut* xcvi. 94 Þe fire biganne to tende and brenne al þe toune. **1648** Herrick *Hesper., To Maids*, Wash your hands, or else the fire Will not teend to your desire.

**3.** *fig. trans.* To inflame, excite, arouse, inspire.

*c* **1175** *Lamb. Hom.* 81 For hwat he scal his sunne uor-saken and bileuen and bon itent of þen hali gast. *Ibid.*, Ho weren itende of þan halie gaste. *a* **1225** *Leg. Kath.* 156 Swa i-tend of wraððe þat wod ha walde wurðen. *a* **1240** *Lofsong* in *Cott. Hom.* 215 Tend mine heorte. **1382** Wyclif *Prov.* xxviii. 4 Who kepen, shul ben tend [1388 kyndlid] vp aȝen hym. *c* **1450** Myrc *Festial* 60 Yn token he was yn hyr wombe þat schuld aftyr tynd mony mannys charite. **1590, 1594** [see 1 δ]. **1622** Mabbe tr. *Aleman's Guzman d'Alf.* I. 234 He was some-what too touchy, and would.. quickly be tinded. **1682** Dryden *Duke of Guise* I. i, Shop-consciences,..Preach'd up, and ready tined for a rebellion.

**b.** *intr.* To become inflamed or excited.

**1297** R. Glouc. (Rolls) 4416 In is wod rage he wende Vor to awreke is vncle deþ, as fur is [= fire his] herte tende.

Hence **Ti·nded** (**tende**) *ppl. a.*, **Ti·nding** *vbl. sb.* and *ppl. a.*

*a* **900** Wærferth *Dial. Gregory* (1900) 101 (MS. H.) He.. hine sylfne nacodne awearp .. on þæra netela tendingum. **1297** R. Glouc. (Rolls) 11022 Þo nome tende taperes þe bissops in hor hond. **1382** Wyclif *Num.* xi. 3 He clepide the name of that place Tendynge [1388 Brennyng, *Vulg.* incensio] for thi that the fier of the Lord was tende [1388 kyndlid, *Vulg.* incensus fuisset] aȝens hem. **1497** Tynnyng [see 1 ε]. *c* **1511** in Swayne *Sarum Churchw. Acc.* (1896) 61 To Ros for tynyng of the rode light xij d. **1591** Sylvester *Du Bartas* I. ii. 654 Incessantly th'apt tinding fume is tost Till it inflame. **1662** Hibbert *Body Div.* I. 30 The Romans divided their night into ten parts,..2 Prima fax, candle-tinning.

**Tind,** obs. form of Tine *sb.*[1], prong.

‖ **Tindal**[1] (ti·ndăl). *E. Ind.* [ad. Malayālam *taṇḍal*, Telugu *taṇḍelu*, also Hindūstānī *taṇḍēl*, chief or head man of a body of men.]

**1.** A native petty officer of lascars, on board ship, or in the ordnance department; also the foreman of a gang of labourers on public works (Yule); a boatswain; a foreman.

**1698** Fryer *Acc. E. India & P.* 107 The Captain is called *Nucquedah*, the Boatswain *Tindal.* **1778** R. Orme *Hist. Milit. Trans.* II. IX. 339 One Tindal, or corporal of the Lascars. **1800** Wellington in Gurw. *Desp.* (1844) I. 93 A detachment of gun lascars, consisting of 1 tindal and 20 lascars. **1803** R. Percival in *Naval Chron.* X. 26 Each of the boats carries..a *tindal*, or chief boat-man, who acts as pilot. **1848** tr. *Hoffmeister's Trav. Ceylon*, etc. x. 343 The '*Tindal*', or superintendent of the coolies, was dismissed. **1849** E. B. EASTWICK *Dry Leaves* 23 Our Tindal jumped out on the bank, on which was not four feet water.

**2.** A personal attendant: see quots.

**1859** LANG *Wand. India* 36 Almost every one who visits the Hills keeps a servant called a *tindal*. His duty is to look after the men who carry your janpan, to go errands, to keep up the fire. *Ibid.* 40 My tindal aroused me at eleven, and informed me that a young man wished to see me.

† **Tindal**[2]. *Obs.* See quots.

**1859** SALA *Tw. round Clock* 22 [At Billingsgate] Sprats are sold on board the ships by the bushel. A 'tindal' is a thousand bushels of sprats. **1863** SIMMONDS *Dict. Trade* Suppl., *Tindal*, a thousand bushels of sprats.

**Tinder** (ti·ndəɹ), *sb.* Forms: *α.* 1 tyndre, tyndir, 1–7 tynder, 5 -yr, 3– tinder (7 -ar). *β.* 3–7 (9 *dial.*) tunder, 4 tonder, tondre, 4–5 tundyr, 5 *Sc.* toundire. *γ.* 3–4, 6 tendre, 5 tendern, tendere. [OE. *tynder* ? m., and *tyndre* wk. fem. (?:—**tundrio-*, **tundriôn-*), from OTeut. **tund-* weak grade of **tind-* to kindle: see TIND *v.* Cognate forms (varying in suffix and gender) are MLG., LG. *tunder*, Du. *tonder*, ON. *tundr* (Sw. *tunder*, Da. *tønder*), OHG. *zuntara* fem. (MHG. *zunder* m. and n., Ger. *zunder* m.). ME. and mod. Eng. *tinder* regularly represent OE. *tynder*; ME. *tunder* (*toundir, tonder*), also mod. dial. (Linc.), may be from ON. *tundr*. The 13–16th c. forms *tendere, -dre, -der* (implied for 13th c. in TINDER *v.*), were prob. assimilated to the *a*-type of TIND *v.*]

Any dry inflammable substance that readily takes fire from a spark and burns or smoulders; esp. that prepared from partially charred linen and from species of *Polyporus* or corkwood fungus (AGARIC 1), formerly in common use to catch the spark struck from a flint with a steel, as the means of kindling a fire or 'striking' a light. *German tinder*: see AMADOU.

*α.* *a* **700** *Epinal Gloss.* (O.E.T.) 562 *Isca*, tyndirin [*a* **800** *Erfurt* tyndrin]. *Ibid.* 685 *Naphtha, genus fomenti, id est* tyndir. *a* **800** *Leiden Gloss.* 179 *Isica*, tyndri. *c* **1000** ÆLFRIC *Gloss.* in Wr.-Wülcker 149/30 *Fomes*, ȝeswælud spoon, *uel* tynder. *a* **1050** *Liber Scintill.* 210 Na elleshwar ȝewilnunge tyndran onælþ. *c* **1205** LAY. 29267 Þa..he.. lette þe curneles ut draȝen & tinder nom And lette i þan scalen don. **1398** TREVISA *Barth. De P. R.* x. viii. (1495) 379 Of a lytill sperkyll in an hepe of towe or of tyndyr cometh sodaynly a grete fyre. **1582** STANYHURST *Æneis* I. (Arb.) 23 In spunck or tinder thee quick fyre he kindly receaued. **1610** B. JONSON *Alch.* I. i. **1664** EVELYN *Sylva* (1679) 27 Nor may we..omit to mention the..fungus's to make Tinder. **1682** N. O. *Boileau's Lutrin* III. 57 The spark in Tinder cherisht, toucht with Metch In Sulphur dip't, kindles with quick dispatch The Torch. **1773** COOK *Voy. round World* I. vii. (1777) I. 113 In one there was the stone they strike fire with, and tinder made of bark. **1812** SIR H. DAVY *Chem. Philos.* 90 A machine for setting fire to tinder of the agaric by the compression of air has been for some time in use. **1837** HOWITT *Rur. Life* II. iii. (1862) 115 He strikes a light with his tinder, for lucifers he never saw. **1867** BAKER *Nile Tribut.* xv. (1872) 263 The grass was as inflammable as tinder. **1879** *Cassell's Techn. Educ.* VIII. 114/2 The internal spongy portion of several species of Polyporus, soaked in a solution of nitre, forms tinder.

*β.* *c* **1220** *Bestiary* 535 Of ston mid stel in ðe tunder Wel to brennen one ðis wunder. **1303** R. BRUNNE *Handl. Synne* 7925 Hyt fareþ wyþ hem as fyre and tundyr [*rime* wundyr]. *c* **1375** *Sc. Leg. Saints* xlix. (*Tecla*) 72 Wod dry as toundire. **1377** LANGL. *P. Pl.* B. XVII. 245 Bot þow haue towe to take it with tondre [*v.r.* tunder; **1393** C. xx. 211 tonder, tendere] or broches. **1483** *Cath. Angl.* 396/1 Tundyr, *Incentinum, .. receptaculum ignis, ignicippium.* **1530** PALSGR. 283/2 Tunder to lyght a matche, *fusil.* **1562** TURNER *Herbal* II. 29 b, Agarik..where of som make tunder bothe in England and Germany. **1612** *Sc. Bk. Rates* in *Halyburton's Ledger* (1867) 291 Boxes called fyre or tunder boxes the groce iiii li.

*γ.* *c* **1380** WYCLIF *Sel. Wks.* III. 102 Þanne maist þou wiþ tendre gete fuyre of þat ston. **1393** Tendere [see quot. 1377 in *β*]. *c* **1400** *R. Gloucester's Chron.* App. S. 7 (MS. δ) Þo let he nime tendern [*other MSS.* tynder, tunder]. **1541** R. COPLAND *Guydon's Quest. Chirurg.* M j, They be made of softe tendre, as of seare olde lynen cloth.

† **b.** *transf.* Fire; a spark; a tinder-box; phr. *to strike* (*on*) *a tinder*. *Obs.*

**1570** LEVINS *Manip.* 77/10 Tynder, *incendium.* **1604** SHAKS. *Oth.* I. i. 141 Strike on the Tinder, hoa: Giue me a Taper. **1607** DEKKER & WEBSTER *Northw. Hoe* III. Wks. 1873 III. 44 Ile goe strike a Tinder. *c* **1626** *Dick of Devon.* I. ii. in Bullen *O. Pl.* (1883) II. 12 So from a tinder at the first kindled Grew this heartburning twixt these two great Nations.

**c.** *fig.*

*c* **888** K. ÆLFRED *Boeth.* v. § 3 We habbað nu ȝiet þone mæstan dæl þære tyndran þinre hæle. *a* **1050** *Liber Scintill.* lxxvii. (1889) 206 Tyndre [*fomentum*] and ceap godes cynnes lærestre mæȝenes deð on criste wunian symle. **1595** *Polimanteia* (1881) 61 They haue strook fire into the tinder of my soft heart. **1643** BAKER *Chron., Hen. II* 73 Finding his hot spirit to be fit tinder for such fire. **1794** WOLCOTT (P. Pindar) *Pindariana* Wks. 1812 IV. 212 Nothing to gild thy solitary tinder Save the rude flint and steel of Peter Pindar.

**d.** *attrib.* and *Comb.*, as *tinder-pouch, -purse*; *tinder-cloaked, -dry, -like* adjs.; **tinder-fungus**, a fungus from which tinder is made, as **tinder-polypore**, *Polyporus fomentarius*; **tinder-ore**, **tinder-water**, see quots.

**1647** CLEVELAND *Char. Diurn. Maker* Wks. (1677) 101 It is like over-reach of Language, when every Thin, *Tinder-cloak'd Quack must be called a Doctor. **1891** KIPLING *Light that Failed* ii. 33 The *tinder-dry clumps of scrub. **1896** CROCKETT *Cleg Kelly* vi, He crossed the marshy end of Duddingstone Loch. It was tinder-dry with the drought. **1895** *Funk's Standard Dict.*, **Tinder-fungus*, a large leathery fungus..growing on trees; the amadou of commerce. **1607** SHAKS. *Cor.* II. i. 55 Said to be..hasty and *Tinder-like vppon to triuiall motion. **1887** RIDER HAGGARD *Jess* xxviii, The tinderlike roof burst into a broad sheet of flame. **1868** DANA *Min.* 91 Zundererz, or Bergzunderz (= *Tinder Ore) of G. Lehmann.., which is soft like tinder and dark dirty red in color,..proves to be jamesonite or feather ore mixed with red silver and arsenopyrite. **1883** R. TURNER in *Gd. Words* Sept. 591/1 The common *tinder-polypore has..been found in the lake-dwelling at Lochlee. **1883** *Fisheries Exhib. Catal.* 236 *Tinder-pouch ..used by Hungarian fishermen. **1662** J. BARGRAVE *Pope Alex. VII* (1867) 122 We had..*tynder purses.., with flint, steel, and match, to lighten our torches and candles when they went out. **1748** SMOLLETT *Rod. Rand.* xlvi, *Tinder-water!.. Water extracted from tinder...An universal specific for all distempers.

Hence **Ti·ndered** *a.*, burnt to tinder; **Ti·nderish, Ti·nderous** *adjs.*, of the nature of tinder, tinder-like; **Ti·nderly** *adv.*, like tinder, in a tinder-like degree.

**1809** T. COWDELL *Poet. Jrnl.* 40 in *Nova Scotia Minstr.* (1811) 47 Her tinder'd garments in my hand. **1825** T. HOOK *Sayings* Ser. II. *Passion & Princ.* xiv. III. 343 Harriet was tinderly tender. **1870** *Daily News* 18 July, The furze is dry and tinderous. **1889** CLARK RUSSELL *Marooned* (1890) 213 So damp and tinderous too was the timber. **1890** — *Ocean Trag.* xii, A sound as of the pressure of a light foot upon tinderish brushwood.

† **Tinder, tender,** *v.* *Obs. rare*[−1]. [ME. *tendren*, f. *tendre*, *γ*-form of TINDER *sb.*] *intr.* To become inflamed, glow, burn.

*c* **1230** *Hali Meid.* 31 Ti neb ute-wið tendreð ut of tene.

**Ti·nder-box.** A box in which tinder was kept (also usually the flint and steel with which the spark was struck, and sometimes the brimstone matches with which the flame was raised).

**1530** PALSGR. 283/2 Tunder boxe, *boytte de fusil.* **1580** HAKLUYT *Voy.* (1599) I. 442 Tinder boxes with Steele, Flint, & Matches and Tinder. **1612** [see TINDER *β*]. **1697** COLLIER *Ess.* II. (1703) 84 One would think we might..with a good flint and steel strike consciousness into a Tinder-box. **1759** DUMARESQUE in *Phil. Trans.* LI. 485 They make use of a wooden machine (instead of a tinder-box), to light fire with. **1836** MARRYAT *Japhet* xlvii, I..found a tinderbox. I struck a light. *c* **1840–5** (*Tunder-box* in use in N. Lincolnsh.). **1893** LELAND *Mem.* I. 47 The use of the tinderbox and brimstone was universal.

**b.** *fig.* A thing or person likened to a tinder-box, esp. as being very 'inflammable' or a source of heated strife.

**1598** SHAKS. *Merry W.* I. iii. 27, I am glad I am so acquit of this Tinderbox. **1608** SYLVESTER *Du Bartas* II. iv. v. *Decay* 12 Huff-pufft Ambition, tinderbox of warre, Downfall of Angels, Adam's murderer. **1839** J. MACDONALD in Tweedie *Life* iv. (1849) 335 The tinder-box of mortality within me may at any moment take fire. **1897** *Current Hist.* (Buffalo, N.Y.) VII. 313 One of the chief dangerpoints in Europe, a veritable tinder-box.

**c.** *attrib.* and *Comb.*

*a* **1704** T. BROWN *Lett. to Gentl. & Ladies* Wks. 1709 III. II. 107 A Couple of Tinderbox-cryers. **1856** KANE *Arct. Expl.* I. xxix. 379 He struck them together after the true tinder-box fashion.

† **Ti·ndern,** *a.* *Obs. rare.* [f. TINDER *sb.* + -*n*, -EN[4]: cf. *leathern, silvern*.] In *tindern iron*: ? a steel used in striking the flint to light tinder.

**1586** FERNE *Blaz. Gentrie* 172 Betweene four tindern irons, or fusils argent. **1688** R. HOLME *Armoury* III. 289/2 Tindern Irons, or Clothiers Bench Hooks.

**Tindery** (ti·ndəri), *a.* [f. TINDER *sb.* + -Y.] Of the nature of or resembling tinder, tinder-like; also *fig.* easily inflamed, 'inflammable', passionate.

**1754** RICHARDSON *Grandison* (1781) IV. xviii. 146 What woman would have herself supposed capable of such a tindery fit? **1795** MME. D'ARBLAY *Lett.* 15 June, I love nobody for nothing; I am not so tindery! **1814** — *Wanderer* I. 100 You were in such a tindery fit as to be kindled by that dowdy. **1886** MISS BRADDON *One Thing Needful* v, Sheets of tindery paper.

**Tindle** (ti·nd'l). *dial.* [app. a deriv. of TIND *v.* to kindle; akin to TANDLE and TENDLE, or a var. of the latter.] In *pl.*, A name given locally to small fires lighted out of doors at the beginning of May and November. (Cf. TANDLE.)

See fuller quot. in E.D.D., and references to N. & Q. and Glossaries there given.

**1784** *Gentl. Mag.* Nov. 836/2 At..Findern, in Derbyshire,.. the boys and girls..in the evening of the second of November ..light up a number of small fires amongst the furze..and call them..*Tindles.* **1872** C. HARDWICK *Traditions Lancs.* 30 In Derbyshire these fires [on 1st May] were called Tindles, and were kindled at the close of the last century.

**Ti·ndling,** misreading of *tuidling*, TWEDDLING = TWILLING.

**1565** *Aberdeen Regr.* (Jam.), Ane new sark of tindling.

**Tine** (təin), *sb.*[1] Forms: *α.* 1, 3–6 tind, 4–6 tynde, 5 tyynde, 6 (9 *dial.*) tynd. *β.* (5 tene), 5–9 tyne, 6– tine. [OE. *tind* = MHG. *zint* sharp point, ON. *tindr* tine (Sw. *tinne*, Da. dial. *tind* tooth of a rake) :—OTeut. **tind-iz*. (To the same root prob. belongs OHG. *zinna* merlon of a wall :—OTeut. **tindjôn-*.) OE. *tind* became in ME. *tīnd*, as in *bind*, etc.; whence, by loss of *d*, *tine*, as in TIND *v.* Cf. WFris. *tine*, tooth of fork, etc.]

**1.** Each of a series of projecting sharp points on some weapon or implement, as a harrow, fork eel-spear, etc.; a prong, spike, tooth.

*α.* *a* **700** *Epinal Gloss.* (O.E.T.) 873 *Rostris*, foraeuuallum *uel* tindum. *c* **725** *Corpus Gloss.* (ibid.) 1753 *Rostri*, tindas ? *a* **1400** *Erasmus* (Bedf. MS. lf. 280) in Horstm. *Altengl. Leg.* (1878) 202 Castyng hym oftyn on þe tyndes of an harow *c* **1400** *Laud Troy Bk.* 15724 Thei..Sclow hem thikkere with her arwes Than tyndes of tre stondis In harwes. *c* **1440** *Promp. Parv.* 494/1 Tyynde, prekyl (*K.* tynde, pryke), *carnica.* **1668** R. B. *Adagia Scot.* 37 Many maisters, quoth the Poddock to the Harrow, when every tind took her a knock.

*β.* **1554** *Lydgate's Bochas* IX. vi. 200 b/2 The fiery tines of his brennyng arow. **1591** GREENE *Art Conny Catch.* II. (1592) 25 A long hooke..that hath at the end a crooke, with three tynes turned contrary. **1642** FULLER *Holy & Prof. St.* III. xxi. 211 That fork needing strong tines wherewith one must thrust away nature. **1644** [WALSINGHAM] *Effigies True Fortitude* 12 An old man..with his Pitchforke ran at Captaine Smith, and twice stroke the tynes thereof against his breast. **1649** BLITHE *Eng. Improv. Impr.* xvi. (1653) 104 Two or three sorts of Harrows, each Harrow having his Teeth or tines thicker than other. **1721** [see TIG *sb.*[1] 1]. *a* **1734** NORTH *Lives* (1826) II. 201 A fork with five tines. **1789** *Trans. Soc. Arts* I. 100 A harrow composed of coulters instead of tines. **1828** *Craven Gloss.*, *Tine*, the prong of a fork..; also the tooth of a harrow.

**2.** Each of the pointed branches of a deer's horn.

*α.* [*a* **1000** *Sal. & Sat.* (Kemble) 150 Anra ȝehwylc deor hæbbe synderlice xii hornas irene, and anra ȝehwylc horn hæbbe xii tindas irene, and anra ȝehwylc tind hæbbe synderlice xii ordas.] *c* **1375** *Sc. Leg. Saints* xxix. (*Placidas*) 105 A gret hart..he saw betwen his tyndis brycht A verray croice schenand lycht. *c* **1430** *Syr Tryam.* 1085 The herte stroke hym wyth hys tyndys. **1513** DOUGLAS *Æneis* VII. ix. 18 This hart..With large heid and tyndis fwrnest fayr. **1593** *Rites of Durham* (1903) 24 Dyd cast backe his handes betwixt yᵉ Tyndes of yᵉ said harte to stay him selfe.

*β.* **1495** *Trevisa's Barth. De P. R.* XVIII. xxx. 792 The aege of hartys is knowe by auntlers and tynes of his hornes, for euery yere it encreacith bi a tyne vnto vii yere. **1616** SURFL. & MARKH. *Country Farme* 684 You may likewise iudge of their age by the tynes of their hornes. **1825** SCOTT *Talism.* xxiv, A stag of ten tynes. **1877** *Encycl. Brit.* VII. 23 The antlers of the Stag are rounded, and bear three 'tines' or branches, and a crown consisting of three or more points...The antlers during the second year consist of a simple unbranched stem, to which a tine or branch is added in each successive year, until the normal development is attained.

† **b.** A small branch or twig of a tree; the stalk of a fruit. *Obs. rare.*

**13..** *E. E. Allit. P.* A. 78 As bornyst syluer þe lef onslydez, Þat þike con trylle on vcha tynde [*rime* schynde]. **13..** *Minor Poems fr. Vernon MS.* lii. 82 His hed nou leoneþ on þornes tynde. *c* **1440** *Pallad. on Husb.* IV. 395 Pomes take, The tenes with, to stonde in cannes saue.

**c.** *transf.* Each of two branches of a stream.

**1875** R. F. BURTON *Gorilla L.* (1876) II. 73 We reached a shallow fork, one tine of which..comes from the Congo Grande.

† **3.** A rung or step of a ladder. *Obs. rare.*

*a* **1225** *Ancr. R.* 354 Scheome and pine, ase Seint Bernard seið, beoð þe two leddre stalen..and bitweonen þeos stalen beoð þe tindes ivestned of alle gode þeawes, bi hwuche me climbeð to þe blisse of heouene.

**4.** [f. TINE *v.*[3]] An act of harrowing.

**1778** [W. MARSHALL] *Minutes Agric.* 12 Dec. an. 1776, Our first tine was with fine harrows, which broke the crum, without tearing-up the sod. **1825** JAMIESON s.v., *A double tynd*, or *teind*, is harrowing the same piece of ground twice at the same yoking. **1854** *Jrnl. R. Agric. Soc.* XV. II. 403 Some sow it after the barley, and give it a tine with the harrows.

† **5.** *attrib.* and *Comb.*: **tine-knife**, see quot.; **tine nail** (*tynd nale*), a large sharp-pointed nail, a spike. *Obs.*

**1555–6** *Burgh Rec. Edinb.* (1871) II. 322 For xixᶻᶻ of grait tynd nalis to the greit yat of the tolbuith. **1888** *Sheffield Gloss.*, *Tine-knife*, a knife whose haft is made from a tine of a stag's antler.

† **Tine,** *sb.*[2] *Obs. rare*[−1]. In 4 tin. [f. TINE *v.*[2]] Loss.

*c* **1320** *Sir Tristr.* 3006 In wining and in tin Trewe to ben ay, In ioie and in pin, In al þing, to say.

† **Tine,** *sb.*[3] *Obs.* Also tyne. [a. F. *tine* large vessel, tub (*c* 1230 in Godef.), Sp., It. *tina* :— L. *tīna* wine-jar.] A vessel for brewing; a tub, vat.

[**1310** *Letter-Bk. D. Lond.* lf. 99 b, Item bona capta..super Aliciam relictam Walteri le Cuuer .j. Cumelina et .j. Tyna, precium vj d.] **1337** *Ibid. F.* lf. 20 Hoi'es bracinas tenentes ..qui mittunt... Braciatores suos cum vasis suis vocatis Tynes ad dictum Conductum. **1388–9** *Abingdon Rolls* (Camden) 57, ij vates et j tyne. *a* **1400** CHAUCER *Balade to Rosemounde* 9 For thogh I wepe of teres ful a tyne [cf. *Fr.* Le jor i ot plore de larmes pleine tine (see Skeat's *Chaucer* I. 549).]

**Tine,** *sb.*[4] *Obs.* exc. *dial.* Also tyne. [Etymology uncertain: see Note below.] A wild vetch or tare; a name for certain leguminous plants growing as weeds in corn, etc., and climbing by their tendrils, esp. the strangle-tare, *Vicia hirsuta*; also locally *V. Cracca*, and *Lathyrus tuberosus*.

*c* **1540** J. HEYWOOD in J. Redford *Mor. Play Wit & Sc.* (Shaks. Soc.) 79 This vice I lyken to a weede That husbondmen have named tyne, The whych in corne doth roote or brede. **1567** GOLDING *Ovid's Met.* V. (1593) 120 The tines and bryars did overgrow the wheate. **1573** TUSSER *Husb.* (1878) 109 The titters or tine makes hop to pine. **1707** MORTIMER *Husb.* (1721) I. 128 The Docks, Tyne, Tares, Mayweed, &c. pull up by hand. **1726** *Dict. Rust.* (ed. 3), *Chalkly-Lands*..naturally produce May-weed, Poppeys, Tine, &c. **1733** W. ELLIS *Chiltern & Vale Farm.* 300

Wild Thetch, Tyne, or Bind-weed, is an ugly Companion amongst the Corn.

**b.** Also called *tine-grass*, *tine-tare* (*tintare*, *tyntare*), *tine-weed*.

*c* **1450** *Alphita* (Anecd. Oxon.) 186 *Trifolium acutum*, *an.* wildetare *uel* tintare. *Ibid.* 189 *Viciola*, *angl.* tintare. **1577** B. GOOGE *Heresbach's Husb.* I. (1586) 35 It groweth halfe a yarde hie, leaued like Tyntare. **1621** G. SANDYS *Ovid's Met.* v. (1626) 101 Tintare [*pr.* kintare], and Darnell [L. *lolium tribulique*] tire The fetter'd Wheat; and weeds that through it spire. **1733** W. ELLIS *Chiltern & Vale Farm.* 302 Cliver or chickweed..twists about the Wheat, like the Tyne-weed. **1744–50** — *Mod. Husbandm.* I. I. 143 The Tyne-grass and the Lady-finger grass are the two best sorts of Natural Meadow Grasses. **1861** MISS PRATT *Flower. Pl.* II. 134 *Vicia hirsuta* (Hairy Tare)..the Tine Tare as it is called in some counties. *c* **1878** *Oxford Bible-Helps* 217 *Lentiles*,..a species of vetch, resembling the tine-tare, grown on poorer soils.

[*Note.* As *tintare*, *tine-tare*, appears to occur nearly a century earlier than the simple form *tine*, it was possibly the original name, its first element being one of the other TINE words. If originally applied to *Vicia hirsuta*, the sense 'small or diminutive tare' (cf. TINE *a.*) would be appropriate enough. But perhaps derivation from TINE *v.*[2], or TINE *sb.*[1] or [2], in reference to the injury or trouble which it causes, is more likely. Cf. the name *strangle-tare*.]

† **Tine**, *sb.*[5] *Obs.* Also 6 **tyne**. (Only in and after Spenser.) [By-form of TEEN *sb.*[1] in various senses. Perh. from Norse: cf. Norw. dial. *týne* injury: cf. TINE *v.*[2] 2.] Affliction, trouble, sorrow.

**1590** SPENSER *F. Q.* I. ix. 15 To seek her out with labor and long tyne. **1591** — *Teares Muses* 3 Those piteous plaints and sorrowfull sad tine [*rime* nine]. **1600** TOURNEUR *Trans. Met.* To his Booke, The more the world doth seeke to work their tine. **1610** FLETCHER *Faithf. Sheph.* I. iii, And far more heavy be thy grief and tine.

† **Tine**, *a.* and *sb.*[6] *Obs.* Also 5 **tyn**, 5–7 **tyne**. [Appears as *adj.* and *sb.* about or soon after 1400; origin unknown: see Note below, and TINY *a.*]

**A.** *adj.* Very small, diminutive: = TINY *a.*

App. always preceded by *little*: cf. Sc. *little wee* (*bairn*).

*a* **1400–50** *Alexander* 507 Scho had layd in his lape a litill tyne egg. ? *c* **1450** *Song* ii. in *Two Cov. Corpus Chr. Plays* (E.E.T.S.) 32 Lully, lulla, thow littell tine child, By by, lully lullay, thow littell tyne child. *c* **1460** *Towneley Myst.* xii. 467 Hayll, lytyll tyn mop, rewarder of mede!..Hayll, lytyll mylk sop! hayll, dauid sede! **1597** SHAKS. 2 *Hen. IV*, v. i. 29 A ioynt of Mutton, and any pretty little tine Kickshawes. *Ibid.* v. iii. 60 Welcome my little tyne theefe. **1605** — *Lear* III. ii. 74 He that has and a little-tyne wit.

**B.** *sb.* or quasi-*sb.* A very little space, time, or amount; a very little; 'a bit'.

App. always prec. by *little*: cf. similar Sc. use of *wee*: BARBOUR *Bruce* VII. 182 The kyng than wynkit a little wee.

*c* **1420** (?) LYDG. *Assembly of Gods* 1063 He was constreynyd ..A lytyll tyne abak to make a bew retret. *Ibid.* 1283 A lyttyll tyne hys ey castyng hym besyde. **1523** SKELTON *Garl. Laurel* 505 Sir, I pray you a lytyll tyne stande backe. **1546** J. HEYWOOD *Prov.* I. xi. Wks. (1562) D ij, For when prouander prickt them a little tyne. **1556** — *Spider & F.* lx. Cc iv b, But stey a litle tine [*rime* fine].

[*Note.* In the absence of evidence, the etymology of *tine*, its accidence, and its relation to TINY, have received a good deal of discussion: see Wedgwood *Dict. Eng. Etym.* (1872) 684, Skeat *Notes on Eng. Etymol.* 300, E. Weekley in *Trans. Philol. Soc.* 1909. Prof. Skeat inclines to take *tine* as a later shortening of **tiné*, afterwards *tiny*, and **tiné* as a sb., possibly a. OF. *tinée* 'tubful'. But though it is possible that *tine* was orig. a sb., in sense 'bit', the evidence is that it was always a monosyllable. Prof. Weekley suggests the possibility of *tine*, *tiné*, *tiny* being aphetic for OF. *un tantin* or *tantinet* 'a little time or quantity', related to L. *tantillus* 'so small, so little'. This would suit the sense, but evidence connecting the forms has not been found (cf. TINY *a.*).]

**Tine, tyne** (təin), *v.*[1] *Obs.* exc. *dial.* Forms: see below. [OE. *týnan* = OFris. *tîna*, OLG., MLG., LG. *tûnen*, EFris. *tûnen*, *tünen*, MDu. *tûnen*, Du. *tuinen*, OHG. *zûnen* (MHG. *ziunen*, G. *zäunen*):—OTeut. **tûn-jan*, f. **tûno-* enclosure: see TOWN. From OE. *týn-an*, ME. had three dialect types, α. southern, *tüin-*, *tuin-*; β. midl. and north. *tyn-*, *tin-*, *tine*; γ. Kentish *tēn-*, *teen-*.]

**A.** Illustration of Forms.

α. *Present.* 1 **týnan**, 3 **tunen** (*ü*), 5 **tuyne**, **tuynde**. *Pa. t.* 1 **týnde**, 3 **tunde**. *Pa. pple.* 1 **ȝetýned**, 4–5 **ytund**.

**688–95** *Laws of Ine* c. 42 Gif..hæbben sume ȝetyned hiora dæl, sume næbben. *a* **900** tr. *Bæda's Hist.* IV. iii. (1890) 268 Þonne tynde he his bec. *c* **950** *Lindisf. Gosp.* Matt. xxiii. 13 ȝie tyndon ric heofna. *a* **1000** in *Anglia* IX. 261 Me mæiȝ..on sumera..tynan. *c* **1200** *Trin. Coll. Hom.* 43 Ne þat þe deuel me swelȝe, ne þat þe pit tune ouer me his muð. *Ibid.* 181 Hie tuneð to hire fif ȝaten, and penneð wel faste. *c* **1205** LAY. 15320 Þa ȝæten heo tunden uaste. *c* **1400** *Trevisa's Higden* (Rolls) VI. 229 Þe ȝates..were i-schette [*MSS.* β. tynde, γ. ytund]. *a* **1450** MYRC *Par. Priest* 63 Tuynde þyn ye þat thow ne se The cursede worldes vanyte.

β. *Present.* 3 **tinen**, 4–5 **tynen**, **tynde**, 5 **tyn-yn**, 5–6, 9 *dial.* **tyne**, 7–9 *dial.* **tine**. *Pa. t.* 4 **tyned**, 5 **tynd**. *Pa. pple.* 3 **tined**, 5 **tynde**, **tynyd**, **tyndyd**, 9 **tined**.

*c* **1200** *Trin. Coll. Hom.* 43 Þe pit tineð his muð ouer þe man, þe lið on fule synnen. *Ibid.* 101 Þe ȝiate of paradis, þe þurh Eue gilte wið hem was er tined. **1382** Tyndynge [see B. 1]. *c* **1400** Tynde [see A]. *a* **1400–50** *Alexander* 2193 Þen tened þe Thebees folke & tynd to þe ȝatis. *c* **1440** *Promp. Parv.* 494/1 Tynyn, or make a tynynge, *sepio*. *c* **1460** *Pol. Rel. & L. Poems* 167 Aȝen þee wole y my ȝatis tyne. **1585** JAS. I *Ess. Poesie* (Arb.) 56 And efter that made Argus for to tyne..all his windois. **1674** RAY *N. C. Words*, To *Tine*, to shut, fence. *Tine* the door; shut the door. **1825** BROCKETT *N. C. Words*, *Tine*, to shut, to inclose. **1874** Tined [see B. 1].

γ. *Present.* 4 **tende**, 6 **tene**, 7 **teene**, 7–9 *dial.* **teen**. *Pa. t.* 4–5 **tende**. *Pa. pple.* 4 **i-tend**, 5 **yteynd**, 7 *dial.* **teened**.

**1387** TREVISA *Higden* (Rolls) IV. 443 ȝif eny dore were i-tend [γ. ytund]. *Ibid.* 453 To tende [see B. 1]. *c* **1420** *Chron. Vilod.* 3725 Bot þe durus of þat chapelle weron þo y-teynde. **1626** in *Archæol. Cant.* (1902) XXV. 40 Peter Denham hath lately teened and fenced up a common footway. **1674** RAY *N. C. Words* 49 To enclose, fence, hedge, or teen. *c* **1700** KENNETT *MS. Lansd. 1033* lf. 389 To *Teen* (Lanc. to *Tine*), to hedge or to enclose a field, in Kent. **1887** *Kentish Gloss.*, *Teener*, *Tener*, a man who teens or keeps in order a raddle-fence.

**B.** Signification.

**1.** *trans.* To close, shut (a door, gate, or window; a house, one's mouth, eyes, etc.). Also with *to* adv. (cf. SHUT *to*), and *absol.*

*a* **900** [see A. α]. *c* **950** *Lindisf. Gosp.* Luke xiii. 25, & tyneð þæt duro. *a* **1225** *Ancr. R.* 62 An ancre nule nout tunen hire eiðurles aȝein deað of helle & of soule. **1382** WYCLIF *Gen.* xix. 6 Loth gon oute to hem..and tyndynge to the dore, seith. **1387** TREVISA *Higden* (Rolls) IV. 453 Þe Est ȝate of þe temple..was so hevy of sound bras þat twenty men were besy i-now for to tende [*MSS.* α. tynde, β. tyne, γ. tuynde] it. *a* **1450** MYRC *Par. Priest* 490 To tuynen and open at heyre byddynge. **1523** FITZHERB. *Husb.* § 141 Yf ony gate..go not lyghtly to open and tyne. **1561** *Child-Marriages* 114 That she did se hym tyne the windowes, and put to the dore with his fote. **1674** [see A. β]. **1874** T. HARDY *Far fr. Madding Crowd* xv, Cainy and I haven't tined our eyes to-night.

**2. a.** To enclose or shut (a thing) up *in* something.

**13..** *E. E. Allit. P.* B. 498 Tyl þay had tyþyng fro þe tolke þat tyned hem þer-inne [*i.e.* in the ark]. **1888** A. S. WILSON *Lyric Hopeless Love* XXVIII. 92 Come, choral voices, ..And in my soul the sweetness tine Which harps of Eden wear.

**b.** To enclose with a hedge or fence; to fence, to hedge in.

**688–95** [see A. α]. *c* **1440** *Promp. Parv.* 494/1 Tynyd, or hedgydde (*P.* tyndyd), *septus*. **1570–6** LAMBARDE *Peramb. Kent* (1826) 376 Their [the Saxons'] woorde (Tynan) to tyne, or inclose with a hedge. **1598** STOW *Surv.* xlix. (1603) 547 To inclose or tyne. **1604** in *Eng. Gilds* (1870) 437 That they leaue to tine and keep so that his neighbor be harmelesse by the cattel. **1864** W. BARNES in *Macm. Mag.* Oct. 477 An' there wer my orcha'd a-tined Wi' a hedge on a steep-zided bank. **1892** BROOKE *Hist. E. Eng. Lit.* ix. 202 The place was tyned or girded with a fence of rods.

**c.** To make or repair (a hedge or fence).

**1522** *MS. Acc. St. John's Hosp.*, *Canterb.*, Paied for tenying of a hedge. **1630** *Ibid.*, For two bundles of bushes to teene our orchard hedges viij d. **1887** *Kentish Gloss.*, *Teen*, to make a hedge with raddles [= green sticks].

† **3.** *fig.* To confine, restrain *to* something. *Obs.*

*c* **1430** *Hymns Virg.* 25 To þat loue y schal me so faste tyne, Þat y in herte it euermore holde.

**Tine, tyne** (təin), *v.*[2] Chiefly (now only) *north. dial.* and *Sc.* Pa. t. and pple. **tint** (tint). Forms: 3– **tine**; also 4 **tin**, 4–6 **tyn**, 4–9 **tyne**, (5 **teyn**, 6 **tyen**). *Pa. t.* 4 **tinte**, 4–6 **tynt**(**e**, 4– **tint**; also 5 **tynit**, 6 (Spenser) **tyned**, 8 **tined**. *Pa. pple.* 4 **itint**, **y-tint**, **y-tent**, 5 **ytynt**; 4–6 **tinte**, **tynt**, 5 **tynte**, **tynde**, 4– **tint**. [a. ON. *týna* (:–**tiunjan*), Norw., older Da. and Sw. dial. *týne*, to destroy, lose, to perish, deriv. of *tjón* loss, damage (cogn. with OE. *téon* injury, etc.: see TEEN *sb.*[1], *v.*[1]).]

**1.** *trans.* To lose; to suffer deprivation of; to cease to have or enjoy.

*a* **1300** *Cursor M.* 5518 (Cott.) Þan has þair will our wiþer-win, And we ma sua our landes tin [*v. rr.* tine, tyne]. *c* **1300** *Havelok* 2023 That he ne tinte no catel. **13..** *Sir Beues* (A.) 4386 Treitour! now is þe lif itint. *c* **1320** *Sir Tristr.* 1911 Þou hast y tent þi pride. *c* **1330** R. BRUNNE *Chron.* (1810) 15 He is now in poynt his regne forto tyne. *a* **1340** HAMPOLE *Psalter* lxi. 10 It is a harmefull winninge to win cattell & tine rightowsnes. **1377** LANGL. *P. Pl.* B. XVIII. 140 Þat was tynt þorw tre, tree shal it wynne. *a* **1400** *Octouian* 1147 Tho both hys armes were y-tent. *c* **1400** *Destr. Troy* 12467 Trees, thurgh tempestes, tynde hade þere leues. *c* **1460** *Towneley Myst.* i. 160 Oure Ioye is tynt. **1549** *Compl. Scot.* x. 83 There can no thing be tynt, bot quhen he that tynis ane thing..knauis nocht quhair it is. **1575** CHURCHYARD *Chippes* (1817) 184 Our greedy mind gaines gold and tyens good name. **1596** DALRYMPLE tr. *Leslie's Hist. Scot.* (S.T.S.) I. 51 The Salmonte..tynes in smal watiris,..the gret fatnes, that thay fand in the braid Sey. **1606** WARNER *Alb. Eng.* XIV. lxxxvii. (1612) 358 Both their Kings in following fight did brauely tyne their liues. **1721** RAMSAY *Prospect of Plenty* 162 To stow them..In barrels tight, that shall nae liquor tine. **1752** J. LOUTHIAN *Form of Process* (ed. 2) 31 The Repledger..tined his Court for Year and Day. **1790** BURNS *Tam o' Shanter* 188 Tam tint his reason a' thegither. **1865** G. MACDONALD *A. Forbes* 51, I dinna think the Lord 'll tyne the grip o' his father's son. **1886** STEVENSON *Kidnapped* xix, James must have tint his wits.

**b.** To fail to gain, attain, or win: = LOSE *v.* 7, 8; *absol.* to lose the battle, be defeated: = LOSE *v.* 8 b.

*c* **1250** *Gen. & Ex.* 3518 For if ðu it ȝernes and ȝisse, ðu tines vn-ended blisce. **1340** HAMPOLE *Pr. Consc.* 2054 Þus sal þai dyghe and heven blis tyne And be putted til endeles pyne. *a* **1400** *Relig. Pieces fr. Thornton MS.* 38 Þou tynes þe mede of þi seruyce. **1549** *Compl. Scot.* ix. 80 He tint threttyne battellis. *c* **1560** A. SCOTT *Poems* (S.T.S.) ii. 48 To se quha tynt or wan The feild. **1681** COLVIL *Whigs Supplic.* (1751) 25 Whether he gain the day or tine, He never misseth to kill nine. **1721** RAMSAY *Prospect of Plenty* 50 She grasps the shadow, but the substance tines. *a* **1810** TANNAHILL *Poems* (1846) 101 I'm fear'd that I may tyne The love that ye hae promised me.

**c.** To spend in vain or to no purpose, to waste: = LOSE *v.* 6.

*c* **1330** R. BRUNNE *Chron.* (1810) 43 Kyng Suane gaf assaut, ..Mykelle folk he les, & tynt his trauaile. **1393** LANGL. *P. Pl.* C. xv. 8 Ich haue..counsailede þe..No tyme to tyne. **1563** DAVIDSON *Confut. Kennedy* in *Wodrow Soc. Misc.* (1844) 216 Thay doctours tynt thare tyme. **1631** A. CRAIG *Pilgr. & Heremite* 9 My true travell shall bee tint. **1827** SCOTT *Two Drovers* Introd., If they had burned the rudas queen for a witch, I am thinking, may be, they would not have tyned their coals.

† **d.** To cause the loss of: = LOSE *v.* 9 a. *Obs.*

*c* **1470** HENRYSON *Mor. Fab.* x. (*Fox & Wolf*) vi, This tarying will tyne the all thy thank. **1588** A. KING tr. *Canisius' Catech.* 223 Receauing trew and Christian iustice..in stead of that whilk Adam by his inobedience tint to him and vs.

**e.** *absol.* or *intr.* To suffer loss: = LOSE *v.* 4.

**1340** HAMPOLE *Pr. Consc.* 1457 Now haf we ioy, now haf we pyn, Now we wyn, now we tyn. *c* **1400** *Destr. Troy* 1208 Þe Troiens..tynte of þere folkes. *c* **1470** HENRY *Wallace* VI. 460 Bot thow be war, thow tynys off thi chaffair. **1862** HISLOP *Prov. Scot.* 27 A tale never tines in the telling.

† **f.** *trans.* To incur (a penalty): cf. LOSE *v.* 3 g.

**1426** *Reg. Mag. Sig. Scot.* 11/1 Wnder the payn off perel that efter folowys, and al that yhe may teyn enent ws. **1478** *Rental Bk. Cupar-Angus* (1879) I. 212 At al thir pwntis forsad be treuly kepit ondyr al peynis tha ma tyne of law.

**g.** To let slip from one's remembrance, to forget: = LOSE *v.* 5 d.

**1513** DOUGLAS *Æneis* IX. v. 76, I hecht forsuith that deid sall nevyr be tynt. **1837** R. NICOLL *Poems* (1843) 123 Thae auld-warld fancies my heart winna tyne. *Ibid.* 188 Your father's dying counsels from Your bosoms never tine.

**h.** To leave far behind, as in a race; to outstrip entirely; to get far ahead of: = LOSE *v.* 5 c. *dial.*

**1871** W. ALEXANDER *Johnny Gibb* vii, Oor 'Liza an' you ees't to be heid-y-peers, but ye're tynin her a'thegither.

**II.** † **2.** To ruin, destroy, bring to nought: = LOSE *v.* 2. (Cf. L. *perdĕre* to destroy, and to lose.)

*a* **1300** *Cursor M.* 2911 Sua tin [*v. r.* tyne] þai þam wit-outen end Þat wil noght þam in time mend. *Ibid.* 4774 For þof he proue his freind wit pine, Þar-for wil he noght him tine. **13..** *E. E. Allit. P.* B. 907 We schal tyne þis toun & trayþely disstrye. *c* **1400** *Apol. Loll.* 43 If God schal tyne alle þoo þat spek lesyng. *c* **1520** NISBET *N. Test. in Scots* Mark xii. 9 He sal cum and he sal tyne the teelars [WYCLIF tilieris], and geue the wyneyarde to vtheris. **1589** R. BRUCE *Serm.* (Wodrow Soc.) 110 He has power only to save and tine.

**3.** *intr.* To be lost, ruined, or destroyed; to perish: = LOSE *v.* 1.

**13..** *Sir Beues* (A.) 652 Tiding com to king Ermyn, Þat Beues hadde mad his men tyn. **13..** *Cursor M.* 13511 (Cott.) Quen þai had eten, þat drightin Bad þam late na crummes tin. *c* **1475** *Rauf Coilȝear* 58 Baith myself and my hors is reddy for to tyne. **1570** *Satir. Poems Reform.* xii. 97 For want of ane I wald nocht all suld tyne. *c* **1575** *Balfour's Practicks*, *Ship Laws* (1754) 623 Gif ony ship tine be storm of wether. **1792** BURNS *Gallant Weaver* ii, I was fear'd my heart would tine, And I gied it to the weaver. *a* **1810** TANNAHILL *Poems* (1846) 97 I'll tend thee..Wi' love that ne'er shall tyne.

**Tine**, *v.*[3] [f. TINE *sb.*[1]]

**1.** *trans.* To furnish with tines or prongs: see also TINED.

*a* **1518** SKELTON *Magnyf.* 728 My tonge is with Fauell forked and tyned. **1760** [see TINING *vbl. sb.*[3]].

**2.** To scratch or work with tines; to harrow.

**1766** [see TINING *vbl. sb.*[3]]. **1854** *Jrnl. R. Agric. Soc.* XV. II. 405 Two drills are tined at a time.

**Tine**, variant of TIND *v. Obs.*, to kindle.

**Tine**, obs. form of THINE (after a dental).

‖ **Tinea** (ti·niă). [L. *tinea* a gnawing worm, a moth, bookworm.]

**1.** *Path.* Technical name of the disease RING-WORM.

**1398** TREVISA *Barth. De P. R.* VII. iii. (Bodl. MS.) Þe heed is ofte dissesed with an yuel þatt children haue ofte..and we clepith þat yuel Tinea a moþþe, for it freteþ and gnawith þe oure parties of þe skynne of þe heed as a moþþe freteþ clooþ. *c* **1400** *Lanfranc's Cirurgie* 181 Cirurgians..clepid tineam þere þat þere is corrupcioun in þe skyn wiþ harde crustis & quytture. **1693** tr. *Blancard's Phys. Dict.* (ed. 2) s.v., If running Sores in the Head..continue long..they grow into Tineas, crusty stinking Ulcers of the Head, which gnaw and consume its Skin. **1804** ABERNETHY *Surg. Obs.* 169 A circle of small sores, like what takes place in tinea. **1862** H. MACMILLAN in *Macm. Mag.* Oct. 466 Yeast..granules may be made to induce the ordinary parasitic skin diseases —a few germs rubbed into the head..producing..tinea.

**2.** *Entom.* Name given by Haworth to a genus of small moths (*Microlepidoptera*), the larvæ of which are very destructive to cloth, feathers, soft paper, decaying wood, stuffed birds, etc., examples of which are the common clothes-moths, *T. tapetzella*, and *T. pellionella*, and the very destructive pest in museums of natural history, *T. destructor*. In earlier times the word was applied to other destructive insects and worms.

**1658** ROWLAND *Moufet's Theat. Ins.* 1100 Pliny saith that Tineæ do destroy the seeds of Figs...Niphus cals that little Scorpion which eats books Tineas, whereof I spake in the history of Scorpions. **1706** PHILLIPS (ed. Kersey), *Tinea*, ..the Moth, an Insect that eats Clothes. *Mod.* The genus Tinea contains about 100 species, of which 15 were recorded as British in Rennie's *Conspectus* 1832.

Hence **Ti·nean**, **Ti·neid** *a.*, of or belonging to

the genus *Tinea* or family *Tineidæ*; *sb.* a member of this genus or family.

1891 *Cent. Dict.*, Tinean, Tineid.

**Tined** (təind), *a.* Also 5–6 **tynyd, 6 tinded, 7 tyned.** [f. TINE *sb.*[1] (or *v.*[3]) + -ED.] Furnished with or having tines. **a.** Of a fork, rake, harrow, or other implement. Chiefly in comb., as *long-tined, three-tined*, etc.

*c* 1440 *Promp. Parv.* 494/1 Tynyd, wythe a tyne. 1523 FITZHERB. *Husb.* § 15 They be lyke sloted and tinded. 1577 HARRISON *England* III. viii. (1878) II. 53 The heads of saffron are raised in Iulie, either with plough, raising, or tined hooke. 1611 SPEED *Hist. Gt. Brit.* VI. v. 58 In his hand for a Scepter, a Mace three-tined, as Neptune or God of the Sea. 1698 G. THOMAS *Pensilvania* 8 Their Ground is harrowed with Wooden Tyned Harrows.

**b.** Of a deer's horns. In quot. 1530 *Her.* having the tines of a specified tincture.

*c* 1410 *Master of Game* (MS. Digby 182) xxiv, An hert þat bereth an hye heede þat is wyde and hye ytyneded with longe beemes. 1530 in *Ancestor* XI. (1904) 182 A hertes hede silver tynyd gold. 1878 S. LANIER *Rev. Hamish* I A ten-tined buck in the bracken lay. 1902 *Times* 13 Nov. 13/6 A goodly proportion of strongly tined heads.

[**Tineman**, a spurious word; being a misreading in Harrison of the word *túnman* in a MS. *c* 1570 of *Cnut's Forest Laws* (*c* 1185), whence app. in Manwood and in Spelman 1664, and thence in later writers, and taken to repr. L. *minūtus homo* (as if f. TINE adj. 'very small' + *man*). (The actual OE. *túnman* is found in an 11th c. Vocab. (Wr.-Wülcker 332/22), rendering L. *villanus* villein.)

*c* 1185 *Cnut's Constit. de Foresta* § 4, Camb. MS. *c* 1570 (Liebermann 621) Sub horum iterum quolibet sint duo minutorum hominum, quos tunman [or ? timman] Angli dicunt; hii nocturnam curam et ueneris et uiridis, tum seruilia opera subibunt. So 1577 HARRISON *England* II. xix. (1877) I. 315 [*the same, with* Tineman *and* hi]. 1592 *transl.* in Manwood *Brefe Collect. Lawes of Forest*, Againe, vnder euery one of these meane men, let there be two of the least men of account of the Forest (which Englishmen do call 'Tynemen'): these persons shall vndertake the seruile labour, and also the night charge of Vert and Venison. 1598 MANWOOD *Laws Forest* (1615) 2 (quoting prec. Latin) *margin*, Tineman. These are they that now are called Foresters or Keepers. 1670 BLOUNT *Law Dict.*, *Tineman* or *Tienman*, was of old a Petty Officer in the Forest, who had the Nocturnal care of Vert and Venison, and other servile employments. 1906 DOYLE *Sir Nigel* x, The tineman and verderers have not forgotten me yet.]

**Tiner** (təi·nəɹ). *Sc. Obs.* or *arch.* In 6 **tyner, -ar.** [f. TINE *v.*[2] + -ER[1].] A loser.

1540 *Sc. Acts Jas. V* (1814) II. 375 It is statute..þat þe tynar of þe cause pay the wynnaris expensis. 1560 ROLLAND *Seven Sages* 81 O subtell schrew,..Tyner of treuth, with toung Intoxicat. 1596 DALRYMPLE tr. *Leslie's Hist. Scot.* v. lxxx. (S.T.S.) I. 292 Victor and Vanquist, tyner and Winner war baith present.

**Tinet**: see TINNET. **Tine-tare, Tine-weed**: see TINE *sb.*[4] **Tinewald**, var. TYNWALD.

† **Ti·ne-worm.** *Obs. rare.* Also 8 **tin-.** An unidentified 'worme', said to be injurious to sheep; ? = TAINT-WORM.

1587 MASCALL *Govt. Cattle* (1596) 15 Against the swelling in a beast by eating of a Tyne-worme. *Ibid.* 250 The tine worme is a small red worme with many legs, much like a hog lowse, and they will creepe in grasse: if sheepe or other cattell do eate one, they will swell and within a day die, if he be not remedied. 1704 *Dict. Rust.*, Tinworm.

**Tin-field, -floor**, etc.: see TIN *sb.* 5.

**Tinfoil** (ti·nfoil), *sb.* Forms: see TIN *sb.* and FOIL *sb.*[1]; also 6 **tynfule.** [f. TIN *sb.* + FOIL *sb.*[1]] Tin hammered or rolled into a thin sheet; also, a sheet of the same rubbed with quicksilver, used for backing mirrors and precious stones; a similar sheet of an alloy of tin and lead, used as a wrapping to protect comfits, etc., from moisture or air.

1467–8 *Durham Acc. Rolls* (Surtees) 92 Pro le Tynfole empt. pro ornacione et pictura del Soteltez erga festum Natal. Domini, xj d. 1477–9 *Acc. Exch. K. R.* Bundle 496 No. 18 (P.R.O.) Pro..Tynnefoile, Canvas [etc.]. 1481–3 *Ibid.* No. 26, vij dos' Tynfoill. 1525–6 *Durham Acc. Rolls* (Surtees) 108 Pro preparacione le borehede et tynfule. 1586 *Rates of Customs* E viij b, Tin foile the groce iiij.s. 1681 GREW *Musæum* III. II. iii. 335 With this the Tin-Foile is made to stick close to the backsides of Looking-Glasses. 1762 FRANKLIN *Lett.*, etc. Wks. 1840 V. 408 It is what they call tinfoil, or leaf-tin, being tin milled between rollers. 1825 J. NICHOLSON *Operat. Mechanic* 715 The tin-foils are only used in the case of colourless stones. 1839 URE *Dict. Arts* 1251 Tin-foil coated with quicksilver makes the reflecting surface of glass mirrors. 1876 HARLEY *Royle's Mat. Med.* 256 Tin-foil, so largely used by druggists to wrap up medicines and form capsules for bottles, is an alloy of tin, and contains from 25 to 75 per cent. of lead.

*attrib.* 1849 NOAD *Electricity* (ed. 3) 146 By a tin-foil communication, a connection is made. 1862 *Catal. Internat. Exhib., Brit.* II. No. 5142 Plain, fancy, and tinfoil papers.

**Ti·nfoil,** *v.* [f. prec. sb.] *trans.* To cover or coat with tinfoil. Hence **Ti·nfoiled** (-foild) *ppl. a.*, esp. *fig.*

1598 B. JONSON *Ev. Man in Hum.* I. ii, This man! so graced, guilded, or to use a more fit metaphor..so tinfoild by nature. 1621 BURTON *Anat. Mel.* II. iii. III. 399 T'is *bracteata fælicitas*, as Seneca termes it, tin-foyl'd happines if it be happines at all. *a* 1658 CLEVELAND *Hecatomb* 9 My Text defeats your Art, ties Nature's tongue, Scorns all her Tinfoyl'd Metaphors of Pelf. 1887 *Sci. Amer.* 1 Oct. 215/3 The glass..after being tinfoiled, is..pushed across the table containing the mercury.

**Tinful** (ti·nful). [f. TIN + -FUL.] As much as a tin will contain.

1896 A. MORRISON *Child of the Jago* 169 Tobacco pillaged from a tin-full his father had bought.

**Ting** (tiŋ), *sb.* [f. TING *v.*: cf. DING *sb.*[2]] The sound emitted by a small bell, or other resonant body, as a thin glass vessel, as the result of a single stroke; a thinner or sharper sound than that expressed by TANG. Also *advb.*, or without grammatical construction, esp. when repeated.

1602 MIDDLETON *Blurt* IV. ii, Midnight's bell goes ting, ting, ting. 1611 COTGR., *Tinton*,..the ting of a bell. 1677 WALLIS in *Phil. Trans.* XII. 842 A thin.. Venice-glass, cracked with the..sound of a Trompet..sounding an Unison or a Consonant note to that of the Tone or Ting of the Glass. 1859 CORNWALLIS *Panorama New World* I. 178 The liquid ting—ting—ting of the bell-bird. 1895 ZANGWILL *The Master* II. ix, His own turn came, announced by the sharp ting of a hand-bell. 1898 G. W. E. RUSSELL *Coll. & Recoll.* xxxiv. 473 The shrill ting-ting of the division-bell. 1906 *Daily Chron.* 14 Feb. 6/7 'Ting' went the bell.

**b.** *Ting-a-ling, ting-a-ring*, the sound of the continued ringing of a small bell, or the like. Also *advb.*

1833 MRS. MARCET *Seasons* II. *Spring* iv. 54 The great dinner-bell went ting a ring a ring a ring. 1862 C. C. ROBINSON *Leeds Gloss.* 436 'Ting-elin, all in'..'Its ommast ting-elin now'. 1879 MACDONALD *Sir Gibbie* xix, I hae naething till acquaint yer honour wi', sir, but the ting-a-ling o' tongues. 1906 *Westm. Gaz.* 20 Jan. 5/1 Ting-a-ling. Telephone again. 'Who's there?'

**Ting** (tiŋ), *v.* [Echoic. Cf. PING; also obs. Du. *tinghe, tanghen* 'tintinare'.]

**1.** *trans.* To cause (a small bell or the like) to emit a ringing note; in quot. 1607, to try (a coin) by ringing in order to test its genuineness.

1495 *Trevisa's Barth. De P. R.* XVIII. xii. (W. de W.), Wyth betynge of basynes, tyngynge & tynkynge of tymbres they [bees] ben comforted & callyd to the hyues. 1552 *Berks. Ch. Goods* (1879) 39 A bell used to be tynged before dede corses. 1607 R. C[AREW] tr. *Estienne's World of Wonders* 131 They sticke not to ting and peize the money. 1611 COTGR., *Tintiner*, to ting, or toll, a bell. *a* 1825 FORBY *Voc. E. Anglia*, *Ting*, to ring a small bell.

**b.** *To ting bees*, to make a ringing sound, as with a key and shovel, when bees swarm, to induce them to settle: cf. quot. 1495 in 1; also TANG *v.*[2] 4, RING *v.*[2] 10 b.

1609 C. BUTLER *Fem. Mon.* i. (1623) 3 Tinging of swarmes to make them come downe. *a* 1825 FORBY *Voc. E. Anglia* s. v., 'To *ting* bees', is to collect them together, when they swarm, by the ancient music of the warming-pan and the key of the kitchen-door.

**2.** *intr.* Of a bell, a metal or glass vessel, or the like: To emit a high-pitched ringing note when struck, to ring.

1562 PHAER *Æneid.* IX. D d j, His helmet tincgling tings. 1607 ROWLANDS *Diog. Lanth.* 21 If we but heare a Bell to ting..Into a hole we straite may skippe. 1653 URQUHART *Rabelais* I. v, Bowls [began] to ting, glasses to ring. 1840 [see TINGING *vbl. sb.*].

**b.** *trans.* To announce (an hour) by tinging; to ring or strike (the hour). Also *ting out.*

1888 F. W. ROBINSON *Youngest Miss Green* III. 78 The clock..then tinged out 'One'.

**3.** *intr.* To make a ringing sound *with* a bell, etc. Also *to ting it.*

1605 ARMIN *Foole vpon F.* (1880) 8 They tinged with a knife at the bottome of a glasse. 1613 PURCHAS *Pilgrimage* (1614) 492 Often tinging with a little Bell of Siluer. *a* 1693 *Urquhart's Rabelais* III. Prol. 6 There did he..ting it, ring it, tingle it, towl it. 1872 T. HARDY *Under Greenwood Tree* v. i. II. 186 So he jist stopped to ting to 'em [bees] and shake 'em.

**Ting**: see THING *sb.*[2]

**Ting-a-ling, ting-a-ring**: see TING *sb.* b.

**Tinge** (tindʒ), *sb.*[1] [f. TINGE *v.*]

**1.** A slight shade of colouring, *esp.* one modifying a tint or colour.

1752 J. HILL *Hist. Anim.* 411 But with more of the reddish tinge. 1796 KIRWAN *Elem. Min.* (ed. 2) II. 290 This blue tinge has sometimes occasioned it to be taken for Cobalt. 1815 J. SMITH *Panorama Sc. & Art* II. 540 In purifying the silks which are to remain white, a tinge is given by the addition of a small quantity of different colouring matters. 1907 *Edin. Rev.* Oct. 510 The blue, instead of being converted into buff, had a tinge of red in it.

**b.** *transf.* A minute quantity of colouring matter or dye.

1770 DUNN in *Phil. Trans.* LX. 71 Dying away like a drop of tinge thrown into water. 1825 J. NICHOLSON *Operat. Mechanic* 716 These colours may be had..from a tinge wholly dissolved in spirit of wine.

**2.** *fig.* A modifying infusion or intermixture; a slight admixture of some qualifying property or characteristic; a touch or flavour of some quality.

1797 SCOTT *Let. to Miss C. Rutherford* Oct., in *Lockhart*, A very slight tinge in her pronunciation is all which marks the foreigner. 1800 HT. LEE *Canterb. T.* (ed. 2) III. 121 [It] had given that slight, and almost imperceptible tinge to her manners. 1840 *C. O. Müller's Hist. Lit. Greece* xv. § 7 The language [of Pindar's Odes] is epic, with a slight Doric tinge. 1849 MACAULAY *Hist. Eng.* viii. II. 275 His political opinions had a tinge of Whiggism.

**3.** *Trade.* (See quot.)

1850 *Chamb. Jrnl.* XIV. 217/1 A trader [draper] who has too much window stock upon his hands at the approach of spring tinges his winter goods, after which they rapidly decrease in amount. The tinge is a cabalistic sign appended to the private mark, by which all the shopmen know that a premium is attached to the sale of the article bearing it.

**Tinge**, *sb.*[2] *? dial.* (See quot.)

1812 SIR J. SINCLAIR *Syst. Husb. Scot.* I. 119 If given raw, to horses especially, they are one great cause of the tinge or gripes.

**Tinge** (tindʒ), *v.* Also 6–7 **ting.** [ad. L. *ting-ĕre* to dye, colour.]

**1.** *trans.* To impart a trace or slight shade of some colour to; to tint; to modify the tint or colour of (const. *with*). Also *absol.*

1477 RIPLEY *Comp. Alch.* XI. vi. in Ashm. *Theat. Chem. Brit.* (1652) 182 Saffron when yt ys pulveryzate, Tyngyth much more of Lycour. 1577 HARRISON *England* III. viii. (1878) II. 55 As their saffron is not so fine as that of Cambridge shire and about Walden, so it will not cake, ting, nor hold colour withall. 1577 HOLINSHED *Chron., Descr. Scot.* vii. 9/2 Theyr fleshe moreouer is redde as it were tynged with Saffron. 1658 A. FOX *Würtz' Surg.* III. xvi. 265 Which will tinge the Aquavitæ to a redness. 1725 *Bradley's Fam. Dict.* s. v. *Oak*, A way of tinging Oak..so as it will resemble coarse Ebony. 1769 N. NICHOLLS *Corr. w. Gray* (1843) 99 Just when Autumn had begun to tinge the woods with a thousand beautiful varieties of colour. 1863 MARY HOWITT *F. Bremer's Greece* II. xvi. 138 The summit of Parnassus was tinged with the red light of morning.

**b.** *transf.* To impart a slight taste or smell to; to affect slightly by admixture.

1690 C. NESSE *O. & N. Test.* I. 236 Fragrant flowers and fruits, the sweet odours whereof had likely ting'd those goodly garments. 1707 MORTIMER *Husb.* (1721) II. 353 Liquors tinged with the spirituous Flavour of other Fruits. *c* 1826 *Lond. Encycl.* s. v. *Barometer*, Common water, tinged with a sixth part of aqua regia. 1863 MRS. OLIPHANT *Salem Chapel* xiii, The sweet atmosphere was tinged with the perfumy breath which always surrounded her.

**2.** *intr.* To become modified in colour; to take a (specified or implied) tinge.

1662 R. MATHEW *Unl. Alch.* § 107. 174 Put on more Vinegar..till thou seest that it will ting no more. 1756 C. LUCAS *Ess. Waters* I. 15 The solution..upon the addition of new spirit of salt, tinges a kind of orange color. 1821 CLARE *Vill. Minstr.* I. 93 He [the oak] tinges slow with sickly hue.

**3.** *fig.* To affect in mind or feeling by intermixture, infusion, or association; to qualify, modify, or slightly vary the tone of.

1674 N. FAIRFAX *Bulk & Selv.* 47 Our souls are indeed so far ting'd with body. 1681 WOOD *Life* 14 Mar. (O.H.S.) II. 526 Fame tells us that he is tinged with presbyterian leven. 1702 C. MATHER *Magn. Chr.* III. I. iii. (1852) 303 His exact education..tinged him with an aversation to vice. 1784 COWPER *Task* IV. 553 The town has ting'd the country. 1856 EMERSON *Eng. Traits, Lit.* Wks. (Bohn) II. 106 The influence of Plato tinges the British genius. 1884 JENNINGS *Croker Papers* I. vi. 182 This grief tinged the whole of Mr. Croker's subsequent life.

†**4.** *trans. Alchemy.* To change by the action of a tincture: cf. TINCTURE *v.* 2 b, TINCT *v.* 3. *Obs.*

1650 FRENCH *Distill.* (1651) Ded. A iv b, As men bring lead to Philosophers to be tinged into gold. 1660 tr. *Paracelsus' Archidoxis* I. v. 75 So likewise doth this Tincture tinge the Hydropical..Body into a sound State.

**5.** *Trade.* To mark with a tinge (TINGE *sb.*[1] 3).

1850 [see TINGE *sb.*[1] 3].

Hence **Tinged** (tindʒd) *ppl. a.*

1658 A. FOX *Würtz' Surg.* III. xvi. 265 This ting'd Aquavitæ is to be extracted per Balneum. 1774 M. MACKENZIE *Maritime Surv.* 110 With a smoked or tinged Glass before your Eye. 1867 DEUTSCH *Rem.* (1874) 23 To be dependent on the possibly tinged version of an interpreter.

**Tingeing**: see TINGING *ppl. a.*[2]

**Tingent** (ti·ndʒĕnt), *a.* Now *rare* or *Obs.* [ad. L. *tingent-em*, pres. pple. of *ting-ĕre* to colour, TINGE.] That tinges or colours, colouring, dyeing.

1650 ASHMOLE *Chym. Collect.* 118 Those two Bodies are shining, in which are tingent splendid Raies. 1667 SPRAT *Hist. R. Soc.* 304 In some Colours and Stuffs the Tingent Liquor must be boyling. 1727–41 CHAMBERS *Cycl.* s. v. *Dying*, Some tingent liquors are fitted for use by long keeping. 1813 E. BANCROFT *Dyeing*, etc. I. 166 *note*, The tingent matter was in union with too great a proportion of the other constituents of the plant.

† **Tinger**[1] (ti·ŋəɹ). *Obs. rare.* [app. from a vb. **ting*, OE. **tengan* = ON. *tengja* to make fast, fasten, tie together.] A workman employed in raising and making fast the body of a cart after it has been emptied by tipping.

1587 FLEMING *Contn. Holinshed* III. 1544/2 There were also eight tingers, whose speciall office was to lift vp the courts [= carts] immediatelie after they were vnloden, and to make fast their tackle...There attended also..men called vntingers, to loose and vndoo the tackle..before the vnloding. *Ibid.* 1545/1 The driuer neuer staied, but went foorth for a new lode: the tinger runneth after and pulleth vp the court, and fasteneth the tackle.

**Tinger**[2] (ti·ndʒəɹ). [f. TINGE *v.* + -ER[1].] One who or that which tinges.

1814 W. TAYLOR in *Monthly Mag.* XXXVII. 146 Girdle of the summer rain, Tinger of the dews of air. 1864 in WEBSTER.

**Ti·ngible,** *a. rare.* [ad. L. type **tingibilis*, f. *tingĕre* to TINGE: see -IBLE.] Capable of being tinged or coloured.

1656 BLOUNT *Glossogr.*, *Tingible* (*tingibilis*), that may be stained, dipped or died. 1901 *Jrnl. Exper. Med.* 29 Nov. 58 The adjacent tingible substances in the nucleus.

**Tinging** (ti·ŋiŋ), *vbl. sb.* [f. TING *v.* + -ING[1].] The action of the verb TING; ringing.

1495 [see TING *v.* 1]. 1528 PAYNEL *Salerne's Regim.* Y iij, Whiche..causeth tyngynge or ryngynge in the eare. 1562

TURNER *Baths* A ij b, The wyndenes or synging or tynging of the eares. **1611** COTGR., *Tintement*, a tinging, ringing, tingling. **1840** *P. Parley's Ann.* I. 54 It goes click clack, tick tack,..ting, ting, ting, ting, and stops between its tinging almost as if it were out of breath.

**Tinging** (ti·ŋiŋ), *ppl. a.*[1] [f. TING *v.* + -ING [2].] That tings; ringing, as metal; that emits a ringing sound, as the *tinging frog.*

**1609** HOLLAND *Amm. Marcell.* XXIV. iv. 250 Neither the tinging sound [L. *tinnitus*] of the yron tooles digging hard by could bee heard. **1611** COTGR., *Charivaris de poelles*, the carting of an infamous person, graced with the harmonie of tinging kettles, and frying-pan Musicke. **1802** SHAW *Gen. Zool.* III. I. 135 Tinging Frog. .. Smaller than the European Tree Frog. Native of South America.

**Tinging, tingeing** (ti·ndʒiŋ), *ppl. a.*[2] [f. TINGE *v.* + -ING [2]. The distinctive spelling *tingeing*, on the analogy of *singeing*, appears in Webster 1864, *Cent. Dict.*, Funk's *Standard Dict.*] That tinges or colours slightly.

**1663** BOYLE *Usef. Exp. Nat. Philos.* I. i. 14 My curiosity leading me to abstract the Menstruum from the tinging Powder. **1758** J. KENNEDY *Curios. Wilton House* (1786) p. xiv, Places, where no tinging or fouling Substances touched them. **1838** T. THOMSON *Chem. Org. Bodies* 400 A Florentine, named Federigo, discovered..the tinging properties of this lichen.

**Tin-glass.** Now *rare.* [f. TIN *sb.* + GLASS.]

**1.** An old name for BISMUTH.

*a* **1558** *Off. Augm., Misc. Bk.* XLI. No. 194 (P. R. O.) Vaynes and Mynes .. of..Antimonia and tyne glas and Sonddrye markasites. **1577** HARRISON *England* III. xi. (1878) II. 72 It [pewter] consisteth of a composition, which hath thirtie pounds of kettle brasse to a thousand pounds of tin, whervnto they ad three or foure pounds of tinglasse. **1682** HARTMAN *Preserv. & Restorer Health* 342 The preparation of Magistery of Bismuth or Tinglass. **1704** J. HARRIS *Lex. Techn.* I, *Bismuth*, or *Tin Glass*, by the Ancients was thought to be a natural Marcasite or Mineral. **1815** J. SMITH *Panorama Sc. & Art* II. 397 Bismuth is known among artisans by the name of tinglass.

†**2.** Tin. *Obs. rare.*

**1601** HOLLAND *Pliny* XXXIV. xvi. II. 517 This white lead or tinglasse [*plumbum album*: see LEAD *sb.*[1] 1 b] hath been of long time in estimation, even since the warre of Troy, as witnesseth the Poet Homer, who calleth it Cassiteron *Ibid.* xvii, A devise to tin pots, pans, and other peeces of brass.. with white lead or tinglasse.

**Tin-glaze, -glazed**: see TIN *sb.* 5.

**Tingle** (ti·ŋg'l), *sb.*[1] *techn.* Also 4–5 **tyngyl, -il, 6 tyngle.** [Cognate with MHG. *zingel* 'little tack, little hook' (Lexer), of which the LG. form would be *tingel*. App. f. the same verbal stem *ting-, teng-* as in TINGER[1] + instrumental suffix *-el*: see -LE *suffix* I. The original sense was thus 'that which fastens', a name susceptible of many applications.]

**1.** A very small kind of nail; the smallest size of tack. Usually **tingle nail** (also **tingle sprig**).

[**1288** *Bosham Acc.* (Sussex) in Rogers *Agric. & Pr.* I. 472/4 Tingle 750 @ /1½.] **1377–8** *Durham Acc. Rolls* (Surtees) 587 In D.C tyngylnaile empt. pro fenestr. in granario, xij d. [**1415** *York Acc.* in Rogers *Agric. & Pr.* III. 447/4 Tingle nail 4 m 3 c @ 1/-.] **1449–50** *Durham Acc. Rolls* (Surtees) 239 CC$^{ma}$ del Tyngilnaill. **1582** *Wills & Inv. N. C.* (Surtees) II. 67, vj hondert hetche naills 3/-, xv hondert latt brods 6/-, xij hondreth tyngle naills 5/-. **1831** J. HOLLAND *Manuf. Metal* I. 194 The smallest tingle nails of about a quarter of an inch. **1886** G. R. SIMS in *Daily News* 4 Dec. 5/6 The smallest [nails], which he calls 'tingles', he can buy a farthing's worth of. **1892** *Labour Commission* Gloss., *Tingles*, also called tacks.

**2.** A strip of metal bent into an *S* shape, forming a clip to support heavy panes of glass on roofs; also, a strip of lead turned up at one end, used in replacing slates; also, a strip of lead bent in the middle, of which the lower half is nailed to the board, while the upper half forms a core on which the edges of two contiguous sheets of lead are folded together, to form a close joint.

**1884** *Spon's Mechanic's own Bk.* (1886) 627 Tingle for fixing Ridge. **1887** *Notes Building Constr.* (Rivingtons) 420 When [the roof panes] are large and heavy, any tendency for them to slip down is prevented by hanging the tail of each on to the head of the pane below by means of a zinc or copper tingle. *Ibid.* (1901) 218 The ends of two adjacent sheets are turned up against one another..; the two are then bent over together to form a roll...Between the ends of the two sheets so treated is a 'clip' or 'tingle'..a narrow strip of lead, of which about 2 inches is nailed to the boards.

**3.** *Bricklaying.* A small loop of string attached at intervals to a bricklayer's line, to keep it horizontal and prevent sag. The *tingles* (Sc. *latchets*) are supported on bricks laid at intervals along the course, and kept in place by laying another brick upon each. (In some handbooks the name *tingle* is erroneously given to the supporting bricks.)

**1886** COL. SEDDON *Builder's Work* 43 To prevent sagging, if the line be long, it must be carefully propped at intervals ..by..tingles.

**Ti·ngle,** *sb.*[2] [f. TINGLE *v.* Cf. WFlem. *tingel* nettle.] An act, instance, or condition of tingling. **a.** A tingling or tinkling sound. Also advb. or without construction, as imitation of the sound. **b.** A tingling sensation in the ears, or in some other part of the body; the tingling action of cold, etc.

*a* **1700** in *O. H. S. Collect.* IV. 183 Tingle, tingle, tingle Says the little bell att 9 To call the beerers home. **1841** HOOD *Tale Trumpet* xxxviii, That like the bell With muffins to sell, Her ear was kept in a constant tingle! **1848** LOWELL *Fable for Critics* 1557 A Leyden-jar always full-charged, from which flit The electrical tingles of hit after hit. **1879** BEERBOHM *Patagonia* iv. 49 The wind was just cold enough to give that exciting tingle to the blood which influences one's spirits like a subtile wine. **1906** *Daily Chron.* 8 Mar. 6/4 A tingle of regret runs through me that I have lost my good manners. **1908** *Blackw. Mag.* Oct. 682/2 One feels the tingle of the morning air.

**Tingle** (ti·ŋg'l), *v.* Also 4–5 **tyngle, 6 tingil, tincgle.** [app. in origin a modification of TINKLE *v.*[1] (in both branches), for which it is substituted in some MSS. of the second Wycliffite version: cf. *crinkle, cringle.* It has the form of a frequentative of TING *v.* and *sb.*, and has prob. in later use (in branch II) been associated with that group, but is found earlier.]

**I. 1.** *intr.* Said of the ears: To be affected with a ringing or thrilling sensation at the hearing of anything. Cf. RING *v.*[2] 5.

Perh. the original notion was 'to ring or resound in response to a loud noise'; but it was very early applied to the result of hearing something mentally shocking or painful, without any reference to sound.

**1388** WYCLIF *2 Kings* xxi. 12 Yuelis..that who euer herith, bothe hise eeris tyngle [1382 tynclyn; 1388 *v.r.* tyncle or ringe]. **1581** MULCASTER *Positions* x. (1887) 57 To much shrilnesse straynes the head [of the speaker], causeth the temples pante,..the eyes to swell, the eares to tingle. **1598** HAKLUYT *Voy.* I. 585, Least I cause good and learned mens eares to tingle at his leud and vnseemely rimes. **1623** GOUGE *Serm. Extent God's Provid.* § 11 A judgement which would make a mans eare to tingle again. **1715** ATTERBURY *Serm.* (1734) I. v. 133 Imprecations, which the Ears of sober Heathens would tingle at. **1847** L. HUNT *Jar Honey* x. (1848) 141 His ears tingled, his head turned giddy. **1850** MERIVALE *Rom. Emp.* (1865) I. ix. 355 Senators and knights returned to Rome, their ears tingling with his compliments.

**b.** Said also of the cheeks under the influence of shame, indignation, or the like.

(Here there is no notion of sound, but only of the sensation caused by the rush of blood to the cheeks.)

**1555** in Strype *Eccl. Mem.* (1721) III. App. I. 163 So that thy swoln cheeks shal even tingle at the hearing. **1779** MME. D'ARBLAY *Diary* 3 Nov, Miss Burney, do not your cheeks tingle? **1828** D'ISRAELI *Chas. I*, I. v. 129 This would have made an English Protestant's cheek tingle with indignation.

**2.** Of other parts of the body: To be thrilled by a peculiar stinging or smarting sensation, physical or emotional; to smart, thrill, vibrate; also *fig.* of inanimate things, companies or bodies of persons, etc.

**1398** TREVISA *Barth. De P. R.* VII. lxvii. (Bodl. MS.), A tokene of venym..ȝif he..dreueleþ and þe lippes..smarten and tinglen. *c* **1530** LD. BERNERS *Arth. Lyt. Bryt.* lvii. (1814) 214 The stroke lyght on a grete rocke soo rudely, that his handes tynger [? tyngel] so sore therwith. **1664** PEPYS *Diary* 3 Sept., My blood tingles and itches .. all over my body. **1742** POPE *Dunc.* IV. 147 The pale Boy-Senator yet tingling stands, And holds his breeches close with both his hands. **1848** THACKERAY *Van. Fair* xxxiii, Wounds tingle most when they are about to heal. **1853** KANE *Grinnell Exp.* xxxi. (1856) 273 Your lungs tingle pleasantly as you draw [the cold air] in. **1878** T. L. CUYLER *Pointed Papers* 124 His conscience begins to tingle. **1884** *Times* 13 Feb. 11/4 All England tingles with the pain of the blow. **1898** W. WATSON *Ode in May* i, And Earth, unto her leaflet tips, Tingles with the Spring.

**b.** Predicated of that which causes the sensation: To thrill, vibrate; to pass with a thrill.

**1819** SHELLEY *Prometh. Unb.* I. i. 133 It tingles through the frame As lightning tingles, hovering ere it strike. **1848** THACKERAY *Van. Fair* xxvi, Every note..tingled through his huge frame. **1865** KINGSLEY *Herew.* vii, Hereward..felt the lust of battle tingling in him from head to heel. **1875** LOWELL *Under Old Elm* I. i. 4 The boy feels deeper meanings thrill his ear, That tingling through his pulse life-long shall run.

**3.** *trans.* To cause to tingle; to affect with a thrilling, smarting, or stinging sensation (physical or mental); to sting, excite, stimulate. (Cf. L. *auriculas tinnīre* to tingle or tickle the ears; also WFlem. *tingelen* to sting as a nettle, or like the cold.)

**1572** MASCALL *Plant. & Graff.* (1592) 49 Small spotts.. which will..tingle & trouble you like Nettles. **1607** DEKKER & WEBSTER *Hist. Sir T. Wyatt* Wks. 1873 III. 106 That picture should haue power to tingle Loue In Royall brests. **1860** EMERSON *Cond. Life, Fate* Wks. (Bohn) II. 310 The cold, inconsiderate of persons, tingles your blood. **1875** LOWELL *Fight Concord Bridge* iii, That I might praise her in rhyme Would tingle your eyelids to tears. **1892** MRS. OLIPHANT *Marr. Elinor* III. xxxvii. 63 It tingled her to her very fingers' ends.

**b.** *absol.* or *intr.*

**1872** BEECHER *Lect. Preach.* ix. 178 Don't whip with a switch that has the leaves on if you want to tingle. **1883** E. INGERSOLL in *Harper's Mag.* Jan. 199 Pepper-woods, whose leaves..tingle upon the tongue like curry.

**II. 4.** *intr.* To make a continued light ringing sound: nearly = TINKLE *v.*[1] 2. Now *rare* or *spec.* as in quots. 1771, 1906.

**1398** TREVISA *Barth. De P. R.* XVIII. xii. (Bodl. MS.), Wiþ betinge of bacyns, trillinge and tingelinge þei [bees] beþ icomforted and icleped to þe huyues. *c* **1450** *Wyclif's Bible, 1 Cor.* xiii. 1 (MS. Arundel 104), Y am maad as bras sownynge, or a cymbal tinglinge [*other MSS.* tynkynge, *once* tynclynge]. *a* **1535** SIR T. MORE in Grose, etc. *Antiq. Rep.* (1809) IV. 654 Clerck he was in Wellis, Where tingle a great many belles. *a* **1652** BROME *Queen's Exch.* II. ii, The great Bells of our Town, they tingle they tangle. **1771** N. NICHOLLS *Corr. w. Gray* (1843) 144 Little bells of different tones perpetually tingling for the elevation of the host. **1806–7** J. BERESFORD *Miseries Hum. Life* (1826) x. lx, A little shrill bell..that..keeps tingling. **1820** MAIR *Tyro's Dict.* (ed. 10) 385 *Tinnio*,..to tinkle or tingle. **1906** 'BARONESS ORCZY' *Son of People* xvi, When the little bell had ceased to tingle, few heads dared as yet to look towards the altar.

**5.** *trans.* To cause (a bell) to ring lightly; to ring (a bell, a chime, etc.). Now *rare.*

**1649** G. DANIEL *Trinarch., Rich. II* ccxlvi, Hee..tingles out A Chime. **1775** S. J. PRATT *Liberal Opin.* ciii. (1783) III. 234 He..gave the usual signal .. by tingling a bell. **1812** H. & J. SMITH *Rej. Addr., Macbeth* i, I'd thank her to tingle her bell. **1843** J. BALLANTINE *Gaberlunzie's Wallet* v. 122 We might as weel get the town-crier and gaur him tingle his bell.

**b.** *To tingle bees*: to charm or influence bees by a tingling or metallic sound: cf. TING *v.* 1 b.

**1649** G. DANIEL *Trinarch., Hen. IV* cccxxviii, As you may tingle Bees Hee charmes the gaddings of opinion.

**Tingler** (ti·ŋglər). [f. prec. + -ER[1].] Something that causes tingling, as a blow; a 'stinger'.

**1831** WILSON in *Blackw. Mag.* Feb. 411/1 But the flogging..is far from being equal to his deserts. So he must get some more—one other stripe—but a tingler. *a* **1836** G. COLMAN in W. Irving *Goldsmith* xxxiv. (1849) 291 Which amiable act I returned with a very smart slap in the face; it must have been a tingler.

**Ti·ngle-ta·ngle.** [Reduplication of TINGLE.] A confused tinkling or ringing, as of a number of bells. (In quot. 1653 *attrib.*) Also *fig.* a disturbance, to-do, fuss.

**1653** URQUHART *Rabelais* I. xl, With a tingle tangle jangling of bells they trouble..all their neighbours. **1670** AUBREY *Introd. Nat. Hist. N. Wilts.* in *Misc.* (1714) 35 The tingle tangle of their Convent Bells, .. like the College Bells at Oxford. **1880** SPURGEON *Serm.* XXVI. 527 There is a great tingle-tangle over nothing.

**Tingling** (ti·ŋgliŋ), *vbl. sb.* [f. TINGLE *v.* + -ING [1].] The action or condition expressed by the verb TINGLE, in its various senses.

**I. 1.** The ringing of the ears; a thrilling or unpleasant tickling of the ear.

**1398** TREVISA *Barth. De P. R.* XVII. xii. (Bodl. MS.), Warmod istamped with boles lyuoure & ido into þe eres destruyeþ ringinge and tingelinge þat is þerein. **1607** TOPSELL *Four-f. Beasts* (1658) 93 For the tingling of the ears, take with this gall the Oyl of Roses. **1611** BP. HALL *Impresse of God* I. Wks. (1624) 442 Ten times..is the same word dually used; for Cymbals; and the Verbe of this root [צלל *tsalal*, to tinkle, tingle, vibrate, quiver] is the same, whereby God would expresse the tingling of the eares.

**2.** A thrilling, stinging, or smarting sensation; an emotion likened to this, a thrill.

**1398** TREVISA *Barth. De P. R.* VII. lvi. (Bodl. MS.), Tyngling and fleting in þe riggebone and aboute þe schuldres. **1584** R. SCOT *Discov. Witchcr.* XI. xiii. (1886) 162 The tingling in the finger, the elbowe, the toe. **1597** SHAKS. *2 Hen. IV*, I. ii. 129. **1653** W. G. *Bacon's Hist. Winds*, etc. 222 Also sharp and violent cold produceth a kinde of tingling, like unto burning. **1658** A. FOX *Würtz' Surg.* III. xxiii. 293 When that member felt a tickling or tingling, it was a sign of healing. **1769** PRIESTLEY in *Phil. Trans.* LIX. 62 The explosion..gave it [my hand] a violent jar, the effect of which remained, in a kind of tingling. **1843** LEVER *J. Hinton* xxxiii, Feeling a kind of tingling of shame. **1847** EMERSON *Repr. Men, Uses Gt. Men* Wks. (Bohn) I. 279 We cannot read Plutarch without a tingling of the blood. **1899** *Allbutt's Syst. Med.* VI. 705 Numbness and tingling in the fingers and toes.

**II. 3.** A continued light ringing sound of a small bell or the like; nearly = TINKLING *vbl. sb.* 2.

**1398** [see TINGLE *v.* 4]. *a* **1533** FRITH *Disput. Purgat.* (1829) 134 St. Dominic's box (which hath such power, that as soon as the tingling is heard in the box, so soon the soul is free in heaven). **1653** GATAKER *Vind. Annot. Jer.* 53 They were wont..to keep a whooping and halowing,..and blowing of horns, and tingling of bels. **1817** LADY MORGAN *France* I. (1818) I. 92 We were awakened..by the noise of hammering, and the tingling of bells. *a* **1828** H. NEELE *Lit. Rem.* (1829) 219 And distant tinglings mingled with the lay.

**Ti·ngling,** *ppl. a.* [f. as prec. + -ING [2].] That tingles: see the verb, in its various senses.

**1.** Thrilling; stinging, smarting (as with cold); quivering, vibrating.

**1716** GAY *Trivia* II. 336 The harness'd Chairman..Swings, around his Waste, his tingling Hands. **1735** SOMERVILLE *Chase* I. 361 Quick Pleasures sting Their tingling Nerves. **1751** CAMBRIDGE *Scribleriad* v. 20 The Scratching-stick with which the Seer subdued The tingling tumults of his boiling blood. **1842** TENNYSON *Morte d'Arth.* 199 A cry that shiver'd to the tingling stars. **1863** GEO. ELIOT *Romola* xxxvi, She felt a tingling shame at the words of ignominy she had cast at Tito.

**2.** Ringing lightly, as a small bell; tinkling; jingling.

*c* **1450** [see TINGLE *v.* 4]. **1581** SIDNEY *Apol. Poetrie* (Arb.) 63 A confused masse of words, with a tingling sound of ryme. **1651** *Burton's Anat. Mel.* II. ii. VI. iii. 300 Bees .. when they hear any tingling [*earlier edd.* tinkling] sound, will tarry behinde. **1700** ASTRY tr. *Saavedra-Faxardo* I. 73 Their tingling shrill sound is like a Voice.

Hence **Ti·nglingly** *adv.*, **a.** in a way that makes some part of the body tingle; **b.** quiveringly, tremulously; ticklishly, delicately.

**1889** *Temple Bar Mag.* Nov. 397 Lest..the sanctity of the Sabbath [should] be impressed tinglingly on me. **1905** *Westm. Gaz.* 13 Apr. 10/1 He [Shaks.'s Rich. II] is so nicely balanced, so tinglingly poised.

**Ti·nglish**, *a.* [f. Tingle *sb.*[2] or *v.* + -ish[1].] Characterized by tingling; quivering.

1855 Browning *Old Pict. in Flor.* xxix, For them the panels may thrill, The tempera grow alive and tinglish.

**Tingly** (ti·ŋgli), *a. rare.* [f. Tingle *sb.*[2] or *v.* + -y.] Characterized by tingling.

1898 J. Hutchinson in *Arch. Surg.* IX. No. 36. 332 His finger-tips became numb and tingly, as if frostbitten.

**Tin-gravel, -ground**: see Tin *sb.* 5.

**Ting-tang** (ti·ŋ,tæ·ŋ), *sb.* Also **ting-tong.** [Echoic.] A succession of two ringing sounds, differing in tone or force.

**1.** The alternating sound made by the ringing of a small bell; hence *transf.* a small bell, esp. the sanctus bell. In quot. 1680 *advb.*

1680 V. Alsop *Mischief of Impos.* Ep. Ded., That [bell] which..goes Ting tang, ting tang, before the Hoste, when carried to the sick. *a* 1800 Pegge *Suppl. Grose, Ting-Tang*, called in the South The Saint's-bell. 1808–18 Jamieson, *Ting-tang*, sound of a bell. *a* 1825 Forby *Voc. E. Anglia, Ting-tang*, a small and shrill bell, to summon the family to dinner, the congregation to prayers, &c. 1848 Noake *Rambler Worc.* I. 308 There is a peal of six bells, besides a 'ting tang'. 1881 Miss Jackson *Shropsh. Word-bk., Ting-tang*, a peal of two bells; a term derived from the sound—the lighter bell being *ting*, the heavier *tang*.

**b.** Jingling repetition of sounds, rime.

1686 F. Spence tr. *St. Euremont's Misc.* Pref., Blank-verse..without the necessity of cursing Arabique customs or Moorish innovations, which forced a man to spoil a good thought by tagging it with Ting-tong.

**2.** *attrib.*, as *ting-tang bell*; **ting-tang clock**, see quot. 1884.

1777 in Picton *L'pool Munic. Rec.* (1886) II. 278 A small or Ting Tang bell. 1862 *Catal. Internat. Exhib., Brit.* II. No. 3302, Ting tong carriage clock. 1875 J. W. Benson *Time & Time-tellers* (1902) 99 St. Paul's Cathedral Clock.. may be described as a ting-tang quarter on the rack principle. 1884 F. J. Britten *Watch & Clockm.* 265 Ting Tang Clock..[is] a clock that sounds the half hours or quarters on two bells only.

Hence **Ting-tang** *v. dial.* [cf. WFris. *tingetangen*].

1881 Miss Jackson *Shropsh. Word-bk., Ting-tang*, to ring into church with two bells. 1888 W. Raymond *Misterton's Mistake* viii, As if Wycherney volk had nothing ..to do but to listen to hear the parish bell ting-tangey.

**Tin-hammer**, etc.: see Tin *sb.* 5.

**Tinily** (tai·nili), *adv.* [f. Tiny *a.* + -ly[2].] In a tiny degree; minutely, diminutively.

1862 *Temple Bar Mag.* IV. 552 Hands so tinily, delicately lovely. 1897 F. Thompson *To Snow-flake* 18 So purely, so palely, Tinily, surely, Mightily, frailly, Insculped and embossed.

**Tininess** (tai·nines). Also 7 **tinyness.** [f. as prec. + -ness.] The quality of being tiny; extreme smallness; minuteness.

1674 N. Fairfax *Bulk & Selv.* 21 'Tis such a kind of somewhatkin, as truckles beneath the very tinyness of an half nothing. 1830 J. G. Strutt *Sylva Brit.* 7 When we consider the tininess of its origin. 1891 *Pall Mall G.* 2 Feb. 6/1 His pictures owe much of their fame to their tininess.

**Ti·ning**, *vbl. sb.*[1] *Obs.* exc. *dial.* [f. Tine *v.*[1] + -ing[1].] **a.** The action of Tine *v.*[1]; enclosing, fencing, hedging; making or repairing of a hedge. **b.** *concr.* A hedge or fence, *esp.* a new one made from dead thorns. **c.** *attrib.*, as **tining-gloves**, gloves worn in repairing hedges, hedging-gloves.

*c* 1440 *Promp. Parv.* 494/2 Tynynge, drye hedge, *sepes.* 1522 *MS. Acc. St. John's Hosp., Canterb.*, Paied for tenyng of a hedge. 1546 in Boys *Sandwich* (1792) 80 Paid for tenyng and mendyng of gapps 10d. 1616 T. Adams *End of Thorns* Wks. 1862 II. 486 Men commonly deal with their sins as hedgers do when they go to plash thorn bushes; they put on tining gloves, that the thorns may not prick them. 1813 T. Davis *Agric. Wilts* Gloss., *Tining*, a new enclosure made with a dead hedge. 1894 Atkinson *Old Whitby* 53 He must do the 'tyning' or fencing-in with stoup or stake, and wattle or brush.

**Tining**, *vbl. sb.*[2] Now only *Sc.* and *north. dial.* [f. Tine *v.*[2] + -ing[1].] The action of losing, loss; † destruction. *Between the tining and the winning*: said of being in a critical position, which may issue either in ruin or in success.

*a* 1300 *Cursor M.* 18261 (Cott.) Ha! sathan..all þat þu wan..thoru þe tinning of paradis, Nu has þou tint on oþer wis. *c* 1375 *Sc. Leg. Saints* v. (*Johannes*) 212 Sa gret besynes He has for to get riches, And besy thocht of þe kepynge, And gret dut of þe tynynge. *c* 1400 *Destr. Troy* 7611 For the tene, þat hom tyde, & tynyng of pepull. *c* 1520 Nisbet *N. Test. in Scots* (S. T. S.) III. 283 (Ecclus. l. 4) The gret preest..that delyuirit thame fra tynyng. 1720 Ramsay *Rise & Fall of Stocks* 146 A' the country is repining, And ilka ane complains of tining. 1825 Scott *Diary* 28 Dec., in *Lockhart*, At present he is between the tyning and the winning.

**Tining** (tai·niŋ), *vbl. sb.*[3] [f. Tine *v.*[3] (or *sb.*[1]) + -ing[1].] **a.** The action of Tine *v.*[3]; harrowing. **b.** *concr.* (*pl.*) The tines or teeth of a harrow, etc. collectively.

1760 Washington *Writ.* (1889) II. 163 A new harrow made of smaller and closer tinings. 1766 *Compl. Farmer* s. v. *Tine*, The common phrase, of giving two or three tinings, signifies to draw the harrows twice or thrice over the same spot of ground.

**Tink** (tiŋk), *int.* and *sb.* [Echoic.] A representation of the abrupt sound made by striking resonant metal with something hard and light: cf. Chink, Clink; often reduplicated in imitation of the repetition of such a sound, also with such variations as *tink-tank, tink-a-tink*, etc. Hence as *sb.* a single sound of this kind; also *fig.* in reference to rime or verse (cf. *jingle*). † *To cry tink*, to make such a sound, to tinkle (*obs.*).

1609 B. Jonson *Sil. Wom.* II. iii, How it [the poem] chimes, and cries tinke i' the close, diuinely! 1840 Dickens *Barn. Rudge* xli, There issued forth a tinkling sound.. Tink, tink, tink—clear as a silver bell. *a* 1847 Eliza Cook *Rory O'More* vii, Mars chiming in with his rude tink-a-ting.. He had turned into cymbals the sword and the shield. 1890 J. H. Stirling *Gifford Lect.* xii. 239 It was in the heroic ten-syllabled tink-a-tink, and read like Pope's Homer. 1901 *Blackw. Mag.* Aug. 251 The metallic clang-clank, tink-tank of chisel and hammer and stone saw.

**Tink** (tiŋk), *v.*[1] ? *Obs.* Forms: 4–6 **tynke**, 6 **tyncke**, 6–7 **tinck, tinke**, 7 **tincke**, 7 **tink.** [Echoic; cf. EFris. *tinken.*]

**1.** *intr.* To emit a metallic sound with very short resonance, e. g. as is done by a cracked bell, but sometimes used as = Tinkle; to chink, clink. In quot. 1655 of rime (cf. *jingle*).

Prov. *As the fool thinketh, the bell tinketh*: i. e. to the fool the bell seems to say what he wants it to say; referring to a superstitious notion that the tinkling of a bell sometimes gives an oracular monition or answer. Cf. Southey *Doctor* xxxii. I, the legend of Dick Whittington, etc.

1382 Wyclif 1 *Cor.* xiii. 1, I am maad as bras sownnynge, or a symbal tynkynge. *c* 1540 J. Heywood *Four P. P.* B ij, Syr after dryngking, while the shot is tinkynge, Som heades be swiming, but mine wilbe sinking. 1627 J. Carter *Plain Expos.* 34 Other folkes must thinke as his bels tinke. 1655 Fuller *Ch. Hist.* II. 167 If the verses do but chime and tinck in the close, it is enough to the purpose.

**b.** *trans.* To utter or express by emitting such a sound (with allusion to the proverb: see 1).

1624 Bp. Mountagu *Gagg* 283 Even as the Bell tinketh whatscever the foole thinketh.

**2.** *intr.* Of a person: To make such a sound by striking upon metal or other resonant substance. **b.** *Tink out* (*trans.*): to express or give out in this way.

1533 More *Debell. Salem* Wks. 955/1 That the tinkar would haue tinked out of his pannes bottome a reason that woulde at the leaste wise ring a little better then this. 1609 Armin *Maids of More-Cl.* C iij b, Toures tincks vpon his pan drinking. 1658 Rowland *Moufet's Theat. Ins.* 894 According as he that tinks on the brazen kettle, pleaseth, so they slack or quicken their flying.

**3.** *trans.* To cause (something) to emit an abrupt metallic sound; sometimes = to tinkle (a bell, etc.).

1495 [see Ting *v.* 1]. 1532 *Henryson's Test. Cres.* 144 (ed. Thynne) Cupyde the kynge tynkyng [*ed. Charteris* (1593) ringand] a syluer bel. *c* 1537 *Thersytes* in *Four O. Pl.* (1848) 80 Mercolfe monyles..Tyncke wyll the tables thoughe he there not tary.

Hence **Ti·nking** *vbl. sb.* and *ppl. a.*

1382 [see sense 1]. 1530 Palsgr. 281/2 Tynkynge, the sowndyng of metalls, whan they be strycken togyder, *tintyn.* 1610 Boys *Expos. Dom. Epist. & Gosp.* Wks. (1622) 205 Wee were but as a sounding brasse, or as a tincking cymball.

**Tink**, *v.*[2] ? *Obs.* Also 5 **tynky.** [Goes with Tinker *sb.*, of which, if its history could be traced farther back, it may be the source; but it may also be a back-formation from *tinker.*] *trans.* To mend, solder, rivet (rarely, to make) pots and pans, as a tinker. Hence **Ti·nking** *vbl. sb.*

14.. *Voc.* in Wr.-Wülcker 576/39 *Crusto*, to tynky. *Crustator*, a tynkere. *c* 1500 *World & Child* (1905) 179 Art thou any craftsman? Yea sir, I can bind a sieve and tink a pan. 1565 Harding in Jewel *Def. Apol.* (1611) 525 Tinkers and Tapsters..what should they doe there [at the General Council]? For there is no tinking, nor tipling. 1825 Jamieson, *To Tink, v.a.*, to rivet, as including the idea of the noise made in the act of rivetting; a Gipsy word, Roxb.

[*Note.* L. *crusto* meant 'to cover with a rind, shell, crust, embossing, plaster-work'. It is not easy to apply this to a tinker's work, unless perh. in the sense of 'to cover with a plate or patch', or ? 'with tin' or 'with solder'. Identity of 'tink' = *crustare*, with Tink *v.*[1] seems unthinkable.]

**Tinkal, -ar**: see Tincal, Tinchel.

**Tinkar's** (also **Tinker's**) **root** or **weed.** See quots. (Also called *fever-root* and *fever-wort.*)

1760 J. Lee *Introd. Bot.* (1788) 333/2 Doctor Tinker's Weed, *Triosteum.* 1882 Ogilvie, *Tinkar's-root.* (From Dr. Tinkar, who first brought the root into notice.) A North American shrub (*Triosteum perfoliatum*), N.O. *Caprifoliaceæ*, whose root is an emetic and mild cathartic.

**Tinker** (ti·ŋkəɹ), *sb.* Forms: (3 **tynekere**), 4 **tinkere**, 4–5 **tynkere, -are**, 4–7 **tynker**, 5 **tenker**, 6 **tinkar, tyncar, tinkard(e, tynkard**, 6–7 **tincker**, 6– **tinker.** [Origin uncertain; goes with Tink *v.*[2], either as source or derivative.

Often taken as agent-noun from Tink *v.*[1], in reference to the noise made in hammering metal: cf. *Promp. Parv.* *c* 1440, and Johnson 'because in their work they make a tinkling noise'. This explanation is not in itself very plausible, and its support by the Sc. form *tinkler*, as an assumed parallel derivative of *tinkle*, is overthrown by the fact that *tinkle* vb. was app. not in Sc. use. Moreover Sc. *tinkler* and Eng. *tynkere* appear as trade names or surnames in 1175 and 1265 respectively, and in many instances before 1300, long before any trace of *tink* or *tinkle* has been found.]

**1.** A craftsman (usually itinerant) who mends pots, kettles, and other metal household utensils.

The low repute in which these, esp. the itinerant sort, were held in former times is shown by the expressions *to swear like a tinker, a tinker's curse* or *damn, as drunk* or *as quarrelsome as a tinker*, etc., and the use of 'tinker' as synonymous with 'vagrant', 'gipsy' (see b).

*c* 1265 in *6th Rep. Hist. MSS. Comm.* 578/2 (Corporation of Wallingford) [The lowest assessment is that of] Editha le Tynekere [at 2 pence]. 1362 Langl. *P. Pl.* A. v. 160 Tomkyn þe Tinkere [1393 C. VII. 364 tynkere] and tweyne of his knaues. 1377 *Ibid.* B. Prol. 220 Taillours and tynkeres & tolleres in marketes. 14.. [see Tink *v.*[2]]. *c* 1440 *Promp. Parv.* 494/2 Tynkare,..*tintinarius*; *et capit nomen a sono artis, ut tintinabulum, sus, et multa alia, per onomotopeiam.* *c* 1510 Barclay *Mirr. Gd. Manners* (1570) C ij, What should a hardie knight be felowe to a knaue, Or with a trifling tinkarde a clarke companion. 1566 *Eng. Ch. Furniture* (Peacock) 33 One crysmatorie sold to a tincker. 1573–80 Baret *Alv.* T 265 A Tincker, or tinkeler, *sarctor aerarius.* 1590 Shaks. *Mids. N.* I. ii. 63. 1597 *Shuttleworths' Acc.* (Chetham Soc.) 108 The tynkard for mendynge of mylkinge vessells vij[d]. 1608 Dekker *2nd Pt. Honest Wh.* Wks. 1873 II. 149 He..swore like a dozen of drunken Tinkers. 1611 Cotgr., *Il iure comme vn Abbé* [etc.], [he swears] like a Tinker, say we. 1674 *Warrant for Arrest* (*Westm. Gaz.* 16 Mar. 1904, 5/1), One John Bunnyon of yor said Towne Tynker hath divers times within one Month last past..preached or teached at a Conventicle Meeteing or assembly under color or pretence of exercise of Religion. 1717 Prior *Alma* III. 577 And, for the metal, The coin may mend a tinker's kettle. 1832 Babbage *Econ. Manuf.* i. 10 Worn-out saucepans and tin ware..beyond the reach of the tinker's art. 1854 Macaulay *Biog., Bunyan* (1867) 27 The tinkers then formed a hereditary caste.

**b.** In Scotland and north of Ireland, the ordinary name for a gipsy: see Tinkler[1]. Also, applied to itinerant beggars, traders, and performers generally; † a vagabond, tramp, or reputed thief (*obs.*).

The chief ostensible business of travelling gipsies in Scotland used to be the sale or mending of pots, pans, kettles, and metal-ware generally; hence *tinkers*, or rather *tinklers*, was their ordinary designation.

1561 Awdelay *Frat. Vacab.* (1869) 5 A Tinkard leaueth his bag a sweating at the Alehouse..and..goeth abrode a begging. 1597 *Act* 39 *Eliz.* c. 4 § 2 All Juglers Tynkers Pedlers and Petty Chapmen wandring abroade. 1609 Armin *Maids of More-Cl.* C iv, *Lady.* Is this the tinker you talke on? *Hum.* I madame of Twitnam, I haue seene him licke out burning fire brands with's tongue, drinke two pense from the bottome of a full pottle of ale [etc.]. 1801 Strutt *Sports & Past.* III. v. § 29 Another itinerant, who seems in some degree to have rivalled the lower classes of the jugglers, was the tinker. 1806 *Gazetteer Scotl.* (ed. 2) 615/2 Yetholm. ..This town has been long inhabited by tinkers or gypsies. 1896 Kath. Tynan in *Westm. Gaz.* 14 Nov. 1/3 The 'tinkers' are the gipsies of the Irish country-side...Tinkering is their ostensible trade, but they are supposed not to be particular about *meum* and *tuum.* They are a wild lawless set, and 'tinker' has come to be an abusive term in Ireland from its association with them.

**c.** A clumsy or inefficient mender; a botcher; also *fig.* In U.S. also applied to a 'jack-of-all-trades' (*Cent. Dict.*).

1644–7 [implied in *tinkerwise* below]. *a* 1704 T. Brown *Praise Pov.* Wks. 1730 I. 89 To cure one hole, like a true tinker, he here makes two. 1905 *Westm. Gaz.* 13 Oct. 3/1 Not so, however, the new Secretary of State proved himself, but a 'tinker' like the rest.

**d.** *Not to care*, or *be worth, a tinker's curse* or *damn*, an intensification of the earlier 'not to care, or be worth, a curse or damn' (see Curse *sb.* 2 ?, Damn *sb.* 2), with reference to the reputed addiction of tinkers to profane swearing: see 1. Cf. also quot. 1884, in which 'not to care a straw' is similarly intensified. (An ingenious but baseless conjecture suggesting another origin appears in quot. 1877.)

[1824 Mactaggart *Sir Balderdash* v. in *Gallovid. Encycl.* s. v. *Balderdash*, A tinkler's curse she did na care What she did think or say.] [1877 Knight *Dict. Mech.*, *Tinker's-dam*, a wall of dough raised around a place which a plumber desires to flood with a coat of solder. The material can be but once used; being consequently thrown away as worthless, it has passed into a proverb, usually involving the wrong spelling of the otherwise innocent word 'dam'.] 1884 *St. James' Gaz.* 24 Apr. 12/1, I don't care two tinkers' straws if you do. *a* 1894 Stevenson *St. Ives* xxv, I care not a Tinker's Damn for his ascension. 1907 *Westm. Gaz.* 28 Oct. 2/3 'A tinker's curse', as used in the two new plays 'Irene Wycherley' and 'The Barrier'. *Ibid.*, The suggestion that the phrase really refers to a 'tinker's dam'.. does credit to the speculative person who earliest associated it with the familiar old saying.

**2.** [f. Tinker *v.*] An act or bout of tinkering; a stroke of tinker's work; *fig.* a bungling or unskilful attempt at mending something.

1857 Hughes *Tom Brown* I. i, They must..spend their time and money in having a tinker at it.

**3.** Local name for various fishes, birds, etc. **a.** The skate. **b.** The stickleback. **c.** *U.S.* A small or young mackerel; also, the chub-mackerel (*Cent. Dict.*). **d.** 'The silversides, a fish' (*ibid.*). **e.** The razor-billed auk. *Newfoundland* and *Labrador.* **f.** The guillemot: = Tinkershere. **g.** 'A kind of seal. *Newfoundland*' (*Cent. Dict.*).

1836 Yarrell *Brit. Fishes* II. 421 The Skate. Blue Skate, and Grey Skate, Scotland. Tinker, Lyme Regis. 1856 E. Newman in *Zoologist* XIV. 5125 We have in the ditches round London myriads of a very minute fresh-water fish, known to every boy..by the name of 'tinker'. *Ibid.*, The Tinker or 9-spined Stickleback (*Gasterosteus lævis*). 1856 Atwood in Goode *Fisheries* (1884) 298 The tinkers, two years old...The mackerel..are denominated as follows: Large ones, second size, tinkers, and blinks. 1861 Coues in *Proc. Acad. Nat. Sci. Philad.* 251 It [the razor-billed auk] is known ..to all fishermen and eggers..by the singular name of 'Tinker'. 1886 *Sci. Amer.* 5 June 352/3 Young mackerel or 'tinkers'. 1896 Newton *Dict. Birds, Tinker*, or *Tinkershire*, one of the many names of the Guillemot.

**4.** *Ordnance.* Name for a small mortar fixed on

the end of a staff, and fired by a trigger and lanyard. *U. S.*

**1877** in KNIGHT *Dict. Mech.*

**5.** *attrib.* and *Comb.*, as *tinker-like* adj. and adv., *-preacher*, *-tool*; **tinker mackerel** = sense 3 c.

**1705** HICKERINGILL *Priest-cr.* II. viii. 90 Lest we make Tinker-like Work, like that of the Presbyterian-Directory, mend one hole, and make two. **1753** T. CIBBER *Let. to Warburton* 53 This unmerciful Editor, who, Tinker-like, makes many Holes for one he mends. **1857** BORROW *Romany Rye* xix. 118 Tinker-tools. **1888** GOODE *Amer. Fishes* 179 A considerable school of these fish..were taken in company with the Tinker Mackerel. **1900** *Westm. Gaz.* 26 May 8/1 Bedford..so intimately associated with the tinker-preacher's life and work.

Hence **Ti·nkerdom**, a realm or domain of tinkers; the condition or practice of a tinker; **Ti·nkerwise** *adv.*, in the manner of a tinker; **Ti·nkery**, the business of a tinker (in quot. *attrib.*).

**1630** *Tinker of Turvey* 12 A budget fastened with a thong, ..wherein are All his tooles and tinkery ware. **1644–7** CLEVELAND *Char. Lond. Diurn.* 8 What did this Parliament ever go about to reforme, but Tinkerwise, in mending one hole they made three? **1834** CARLYLE *Let.* 27 June, in *Life* (1882) II. 439 His [Hunt's] house excels all you have ever read of—a poetical Tinkerdom, without parallel even in literature. *Ibid.* 440 Yet the noble Hunt receives you in his Tinkerdom in the spirit of a king. **1887** *Scott. Leader* 27 Oct. 7 Cis-pontine prejudices fed by poultry-larceny and tinkerdom.

**Tinker** (ti·ŋkəɹ), *v.* [f. prec. sb.]

In all senses usually depreciative.

**1.** *intr.* To work as a tinker; to mend metal utensils (and hence *gen.* any material objects), esp. in a clumsy, bungling, or imperfect way.

**1592–1857** [see TINKERING *vbl. sb.* and *ppl. a.*].

**b.** *fig.* To work at something (immaterial) clumsily or imperfectly, esp. in the way of attempted repair or improvement; also more vaguely, to occupy oneself about something in a trifling or aimless way; to trifle, potter. Const. *at*, *with*.

**1658** GURNALL *Chr. in Arm.* verse 14. xiii. (1669) 53/1 He that will be tinkering with his own heart, and not seek out to Heaven for help, will in the end where he mends one hole, he'll make two worse. **1856** KANE *Arct. Expl.* II. xiii. 134 When in-doors and at rest, tinkering over their ivory harness-rings. **1880** MCCARTHY *Own Times* IV. lviii. 258 The public were tired of government which merely tinkered at legislation. **1894** JESSOPP *Random Roaming* Pref. 5 A work of art does not admit of being tinkered at indefinitely.

**2.** *trans.* To mend as a tinker; to repair or put into shape in an imperfect or makeshift way; to patch *up*. **a.** material objects; also, human beings (in reference to medical or surgical treatment).

**1814** JEFFERSON *Writ.* (1830) IV. 240 However we may tinker them [our machines] up for a while, all will at length surcease motion. **1835** F. B. HEAD in Smiles *Mem. J. Murray* (1891) II. xxxi. 362 The waters will tinker you up in a most extraordinary manner. **1851** MAYHEW *Lond. Labour* I. 325/1 If the old article were of good quality, it was polished and tinkered up for sale in the Saturday evening street-markets, and often 'went off well'. **1885** S. O. JEWETT in *Harper's Mag.* Jan. 209/2 She tinkered the rickety bee-hives. **1892** C. T. DENT *Mountaineer.* ii. 68 An axe that does not come out right at first can rarely be tinkered into a good one by alterations.

**b.** *fig.* (immaterial things).

**1753** [see TINKERING *vbl. sb.*]. **1768** H. WALPOLE *Hist. Doubts* Pref. 6 Chronology and astronomy are forced to tinker up and reconcile, as well as they can, those uncertainties [of ancient history]. **1768** — *Let. to Gray* 18 Feb., I am criticised for the expression *tinker up* in the preface. ..I think such a low expression, placed to ridicule an absurd instance of wise folly, very forcible. **1866** BRIGHT *Sp. Reform* 20 Nov. (1876) 388 The Tory party refused even to have it tinkered. **1879** MCCARTHY *Own Times* II. xxv. 257 Little plans of adjustment were tinkered up and tried. **1887** LOWELL *Democr.* 38 Men are prone to be tinkering the work of their own hands.

**c.** *Pugilistic slang.* To batter, maul.

**1826** *Sporting Mag.* XVIII. 253 Tom completely tinkered his antagonist's upper-crust.

Hence **Ti·nkered** (-kəɹd) *ppl. a.*; also **Ti·nkerer**, one who tinkers or works at mending something in a clumsy or ineffective way.

**1862** LYTTON *Str. Story* xx, I clamped and soldered dogma to dogma in the links of my *tinkered logic. **1867** FROUDE *Short Stud.* I. 40 The reconciliation..is no tinkered-up truce, or convenient Interim. **1906** *Athenæum* 28 Apr. 505/3 He reprints Hayley's tinkered version..instead of the *editio princeps* in John Duncombe's 'Works of Horace in English Verse'. **1894** W. H. HOTCHKISS in *Review of Rev.* June 683/1 An examination of the checks on the charter *tinkerer in other constitutions.

**Tinkering** (ti·ŋkəriŋ), *vbl. sb.* [f. TINKER *v.* + -ING [1].] The work of a tinker; the action of TINKER *v.* (in *lit.* and *fig.* senses).

**1592** R. D. *Hypnerotomachia* 48 b, What a stately porche ..with his stone of Phenicea with all the tinkering and pullishing about it. **1753** H. WALPOLE *Lett.* (1846) II. 478, I left the tinkering of the bill. **1857** BORROW *Romany Rye* (1905) II. App. v. 328 He [the Gipsy] took to tinkering and smithery, because no better employments were at his command. **1885** *Athenæum* 14 Feb. 221 A very good [picture] ..free from any after-meddling and tinkering.

*attrib.* **1813** *Examiner* 1 Feb 72/1 The terrible tinkering work there must be. **1841** HOOD *Tale of Trumpet* xxxviii, Or Trudge and his ass at a tinkering job.

**Ti·nkering,** *ppl. a.* [f. as prec. + -ING [2].] That tinkers (in *lit.* and *fig.* senses): see the vb.

**1598** MARSTON *Sco. Villanie* (1599) 167 Fidlers, scrivueners, pedlers, tynkering knaues. **1818** BYRON *Juan* Ded. xiv, A tinkering slave-maker, who mends old chains. **1880** E. WHITE *Cert. Relig.* 44 A purblind tinkering criticism.

**Tinkerly** (ti·ŋkəɹli), *a.* ? *Obs.* [f. TINKER *sb.* + -LY [1].] Having the character of a tinker or of tinker's work; clumsy, bungling, unskilful; of poor quality; mean, low, disreputable. (*Depreciative.*)

**1586** W. WEBBE *Eng. Poetrie* (Arb.) 31, I meane this tynkerly verse which we call ryme. **1592** LYLY *Midas* IV. i, Thou art Pan and all, all Pan and tinkerly. **1593** G. HARVEY *Pierce's Super.* 183 Shewe me any halfe page without piperly phrases, and tinkerly composition. **1647** TRAPP *Comm. Eph.* iv. 25 A base tinkerly sin, as Plutarch calleth it, shamefull and hatefull. **1681** HICKERINGILL *Sin Man-Catching* Postscr., The wary Hollanders..suffer no Tinkerly Pleading, of mending one hole, and making two.

**Tinkerman**, error for TRINKERMAN, q. v.

**Tinkershere, -shire** (ti·ŋkəɹʃiəɹ). Also (? erron.) **-shue.** [f. TINKER *sb.* (cf. 3 f): the second element is obscure.] A local name for the common guillemot; also for the black guillemot.

**1799** R. PULTENEY *Catal. Birds*, etc. *Dorset* (1813) 17 *Colymbus Troile*...The Foolish Guillemot Diver; called here The Tinkershire. **1802** G. MONTAGU *Ornith. Dict.* Q ij b, Guillemot, Foolish...Provincial. Sea-hen. Scout... Willock. Tinkershire. **1831** RENNIE *Montagu's Ornith. Dict.*, Tinker's-hue. **1864** ATKINSON *Provinc. Names Birds*, Tinkershue, Black Guillemot, *Uria grylle*. **1885** SWAINSON *Provinc. Names Birds* 218 Common Guillemot...Tinkershire, or Tinkershue. From its black head and back. **1889** H. SAUNDERS *Man. Brit. Birds* 684 By fishermen it is known as 'Scout', 'Marrot' or 'Tinkershere'.

**Tin-kettle,** *sb.* A kettle of tinned iron.

Often *fig.* with allusion to its being fastened to a dog's tail to tease and frighten it, or to the noise made by beating it.

**1775** R. CHANDLER *Trav. Asia M.* viii. (1825) I. 28 [Our cook's] tin kettle boiling over a fire in the open air. **1831** CARLYLE *Sart. Res.* II. iii, A Conquering Hero, to whom Fate..has malignantly appended a tin-kettle of Ambition, to chase him on. **1864** TREVELYAN *Compet. Wallah* (1866) 172 A new Montgomery..to whose tail fastidious middle life may attach the tin kettle of hostile criticism. **1895** MRS. CROKER *Village Tales* (1896) 42 Battered old tin kettle as it was, that despised piano had cost one hundred pounds!

Hence **Tin-kettle** *v.*, *trans.* to serenade roughly or opprobriously, also to cause (swarming bees) to settle, by beating a tin-kettle; whence **Tin-kettling** *vbl. sb.*; also **Tin-kettly** *a.*, like a tin-kettle.

**1875** A. J. ELLIS tr. *Helmholtz' Sensations Tone* 119 Their quality of sound is..unmusical, bad, and tin-kettly. **1898** *N. & Q.* 9th Ser. I. 116/2 An inn-keeper was reported to have beaten his wife,..so [his neighbours] 'tin-kettled' him right royally. **1900** H. LAWSON *On Track* 5 The diggers.. gave them a real good tinkettling in the old-fashioned style. *Ibid.* 20 We'd tin-kettle 'em [bees],..and..they'd settle on a branch.

**Tinkle** (ti·ŋk'l), *sb.* [f. TINKLE *v.*[1] (sense 2).] The act or action of tinkling; a sharp light ringing sound, such as that made by a small bell, or by pieces of metal, glass, or the like, struck together, etc.

**1804** J. GRAHAME *Sabbath*, etc. (1808) 66 Its runnel by degrees Diminishing, the murmur turns a tinkle. **1825** SCOTT *Betrothed* ix, The shrill tinkle of a harp. **1847** EMERSON *Merlin* i, No jingling serenader's art, Nor tinkle of piano strings. **1871** R. ELLIS *Catullus* lxiv. 262 Now with a cymbal slim would a sharp shrill tinkle awaken. **1877–8** HENLEY in *Ballades*, etc. (Canterb. Poets) 77 Of ice and glass the tinkle, Pellucid, silver-shrill.

**b.** *fig.* in reference to speech or verse. Cf. TINKLE *v.*[1] 2 c, 3 b.

**1725** P. WALKER *Life A. Peden* To Rdr. (1827) 17 None of their Addresses have had the Tinkle or Sound of the Declarations and Faithful Warnings of the General Assemblies of this Church. **1776** MICKLE tr. *Camoens' Lusiad* Introd. 141 *note*, There are a race of Critics..who would strip poetry of all her ornaments,..who would leave her nothing but the neatness, the cadence, and the tinkle of verse. **1789** BELSHAM *Ess.* I. xii. 226 What Dryden calls the tinkle in the close of the couplet. **1795** MASON *Ch. Mus.* ii. 114 The tinkle of the words is all that strikes the ears.

**c.** Reduplicated, expressing repetition of such sounds; also as *adv.*

**1682** *Bells of Oxford* in *Wit & Drollery* 302 Tincle, tincle, goes the little Bell, To call the Students home. **1879** JEFFERIES *Wild Life in S. Co.* 260 There comes the tinkle-tinkle of a bell. **1888** DOUGHTY *Arabia Deserta* I. 149 They make, as the daughters of Jerusalem, a tinkle-tinkle as they go.

**Tinkle** (ti·ŋk'l), *v.*[1] Forms: 4 tyncle(n, 4–6 tynkle, 5 -kel, -kyll, 6 -ckle, tinkel, 6–7 tincle, 6–8 tinckle, 6– tinkle. [*Tinkle* has the form of a frequentative of TINK *v.* (see -LE 3), which also suits the chronology. In some MSS. of the later Wyclif version, it takes the place of the earlier *tink*, as said of a cymbal; and it is frequent from 1450 of the sound of bells, etc.

In both Wyclif versions *tyncle* is also used of the 'ringing' and 'tingling' of the ears; but in some MSS. of the later version *tingle* is substituted. In the 16th c. *tinckle* is said even of the nose. Here it might be thought to represent OE. *tinclian* 'to tickle', L. *titillare*, if there were any trace of that vb. in ME. But it is to be remembered that L. *tinnīre*, which Wyclif rendered *tynke* and *tyncle*, was used of the ringing both of metals and of the ears, and even in the sense 'tingle'. In mod. use, *tinkle* may be said of the ears in the sense 'ring', implying sound objective or subjective, but the thrilling nervous sensation is expressed by *tingle*; 'my ears tingle', like 'my hands tingle': see TINGLE *v.* Cf. WFlem. *tinkelen*, to tingle (as the fingers with the cold), also said of the sound of a drop falling into water.]

**I. 1.** *intr.* Of the ears: To ring, to tingle: = TINGLE *v.* 1 (now *rare*). † Of the nose or other parts: = TINGLE *v.* 2, TICKLE *v.* 2 (*obs.*).

**1382** WYCLIF 1 *Sam.* iii. 11 Loo, Y doo a word in Yrael, the which who so euere herith, bothe his eeris shulen tynclen [1388 tyncle, rynge]. — *Jer.* xix. 3 Eche that shal heren it, tyncle hys eres [1388 hise eeris tyngle]. **1581** MARBECK *Bk. of Notes* 589 Who so heareth of it his eares shall tinckle. ? *a* **1600** J. CONYBEARE *Lett. & Exerc.* (1905) 40 Nasturtium called cresses being eaten doth make the nose tinckle. **1700** DRYDEN *Theod. & Hon.* 94 His Ears tinckled, and his Colour fled. **1722** RAMSAY *Three Bonnets* III. 44, I ha'e a secret to impart..will set baith your lugs a tinkling. **1871** R. ELLIS *Catullus* li. 11 With inward Sound the full ears tinkle.

**II. 2.** *intr.* To give forth a series of short light sharp ringing sounds. Said of bells, musical instruments, and other resonant objects (cf. TINKLE *sb.*).

*a* **1400–50** *Alexander* 1385 (Dubl. MS.) Now tynkyll vp taburnes þat all þe towne ringes. *c* **1440** *Wyclif's Bible*, 1 *Cor.* xiii. 1, Y am maad as bras sownynge, or a cymbal tynclynge [1382 tynkynge, 1388 (MS. 1420) tynkynge, (MS. 1450) tinglinge]. **1526–1563** [see TINKLING *ppl. a.*[1]]. **1617** MORYSON *Itin.* I. 69 Wee could not sleepe for little bels tinckling all night. **1697** DRYDEN *Æneid* II. 745 [The javelin] faintly tinckl'd on the brasen Shield. **1724** RAMSAY *Tea-t. Misc.* Ded. iii, The spinnet tinkling with her voice. **1819** WIFFEN *Aonian Hours* (1820) 50 A sheepbell tinkles on the heath. **1831** POE *Bells* i, How they tinkle, tinkle, tinkle, In the icy air of night! **1873** T. W. HIGGINSON *Oldport Days* ix. 216 The dry snow tinkled beneath my feet.

*fig.* **1654** JER. TAYLOR *Real Pres.* xii. 281 The bell alwayes must tinkle as they are pleased to think. [Cf. TINK *v.*[1] 1.]

**b.** *fig.* To flow or move with a tinkling sound.

**1822** W. IRVING *Braceb. Hall* xvii, A small rill tinkled along close by. **1851** HAWTHORNE *Snow Image, My Kinsman* (1879) 248 The latch tinkled into its place. **1855** BROWNING *Love among Ruins* i, Our sheep Half-asleep Tinkle homeward through the twilight. **1859** KINGSLEY *Misc.* II. 288 A stream tinkling on from one rock-basin to another. **1871** HOWELLS *Wedd. Journ.* (1892) 29 The street-cars that slowly tinkled up and down.

**c.** *transf.* To rime or jingle.

**1626, 1821** [see TINKLING *ppl. a.*[1] b]. **1684** DRYDEN *Ep. to Earl Roscomon* 14 A kind of hobbling prose, That limped along and tinkled in the close. **1711** E. FENTON *Ep. to Southerne* Poems (1717) 82.

**3.** *intr.* Of a person: To produce such a sound.

**17..** *Bob Norice* ix. in Child *Ballads* IV. (1886) 267/2 But whan he came to Lord Barnet's castel He tinklet at the ring [cf. TIRL *v.*[3] 3 a]. **1809** MALKIN *Gil Blas* v. i. ⁋ 29 Our host ..was tinkling on a cracked guitar. **1860** HAWTHORNE *Marb. Faun* x, The musicians scraped, tinkled, or blew.

**b.** *fig.* To utter empty sounds or senseless words, talk idly, prate.

**1641** R. BAILLIE *Parallel Liturgy w. Mass-bk.*, etc. 54 All the question wee and they have long tinkled on for the worshipping of Saints. **1645** MILTON *Tetrach.* II. i. Wks. 1851 IV. 201 We are but crackt cimbals, we do but tinckle, we know nothing, we do nothing. **1646** R. BAILLIE *Let. to Henderson* 16 May, If that man now go to tinkle on bishops, and delinquents, and such foolish toys, it seems he is mad. **1781** COWPER *Conversat.* 892 The tide of speech..No longer labours merely to produce The pomp of sound, or tinkle without use. **1871** [see TINKLING *ppl. a.*[1] b].

**4.** *trans.* **a.** To make known, call attention to, or express by tinkling (*lit.* or *fig.*).

**1562** in Blomefield *Norfolk* (1806) IV. 355 *note*, A woman for whoredom to ryde on a cart..and tynkled with a bason. **1861** *All Year Round* V. 13 Flattery in the fluent phrase that just Tinkled the tender moral o'er the dust Of greatness. **1862** SALA *Seven Sons* I. iv. 76 The multitude of clocks..were tinkling out the hour of nine.

**b.** To affect, attract, or summon by tinkling. *To tinkle bees*: see TING *v.* 1 b.

**1582** STANYHURST *Æneis* I. (Arb.) 29 Of Troy seat yf hap-lye the rumoure Youre ears hath tinckled. **1639** SALTMARSH *Policy* § 130. 111 Bees are best tinckled together when they rise. **1832** J. WILSON *Noct. Ambr.* in *Blackw. Mag.* Feb. 264 The very kirk..whose small bell tinkled the joyous school-boy to worship.

**c.** = TICKLE *v.* 3. *rare.*

**1883** W. M. ADAMSON in *Evang. Union Worthies* 316 The flimsy sensational preacher, whose desire is to tinkle the ear, more than touch the conscience.

**5.** To cause (something) to tinkle or make a short light ringing sound; † to produce by tinkling.

**1582** STANYHURST *Æneis* III. (Arb.) 74 Moonewise Coribants on brasse their od harmonye tinckling. *Ibid.* 80 Thee place she tinckled [*omnem Implevit clamore locum*]. **1617** MORYSON *Itin.* III. 209 Many drums were beaten and basons tinckled about them. **1798** JANE AUSTEN *Northang. Abb.* i, She was very fond of tinkling the keys of the old forlorn spinnet. **1834** SOUTHEY *Doctor* i, I finished my glass of punch, tinkled the spoon against its side. **1900** H. G. GRAHAM *Soc. Life Scot. in 18th C.* VII. i. (1901) 245 The 'bell pennies'—for tolling or tinkling the 'dead bell' before the coffin at funerals.

Hence **Tinkled** (ti·ŋk'ld) *ppl. a.*, made to tinkle.

**1821** CLARE *Vill. Minstr.* I. 160 The tinkled latch startled her.

† **Tinkle,** *v.*[2] *Obs.* [Back-formation from TINKLER [1].] = TINKER *v.* 1. Hence **Tinkling** *ppl. a.*

**1599** MARSTON *Sco. Villanie* III. ix, I once did know a tinkling Pewterer. **1630** B. JONSON *New Inn* I. i, Who tinkles then, or personates Tom Tinker?

**Tinkler** [1] (ti·ŋkləɹ). *Sc.* and *dial.* [app. f. TINKER, with different suffix: cf. *pedder, peddler, pedlar.*] A tinker, a worker in metal; in Scotland, north of England, and Ireland, usually a gipsy, or other itinerant mender of pots, pans, and metal-work.

*c* **1175** *Carta Willelmi Regis* in *Liber Ecclesie de Scon* (1843) 30 [Terra] que iacet inter terram serlon incisoris et terram Jacobi tinkler. **1484** *Nottingham Rec.* II. 346

Christoferus Tynkeler,.. tynkeler. **1570** LEVINS *Manip.* 77/12 A Tinkler, [*sartor ærarius*]. **1572** *Satir. Poems Reform.* xxxii. 49 We Tinklaris, Tailȝeouris...We wait of nocht bot mekill cair and cummer. **1605** *N. Riding Rec.* (1884) I. 3 Joh. Jackson, tinkler. **1681** O. HEYWOOD *Diaries*, etc. (1881) II. 228 Her mother brought a panne to a tinkler's house. **1785** BURNS *Jolly Beggars* Air vi, My bonnie lass, I work in brass, A tinkler is my station. **1818** SCOTT *Hrt. Midl.* xlix, This fellow had been originally a tinkler, or 'caird', many of whom stroll about these districts. **1825** BROCKETT *N. C. Words* s. v., The celebrated Wull Allen was for many years the king of the tinklers in the North. **1847** C. BRONTË *J. Eyre* xviii, She looks such a tinkler. **1911** *19th Cent.* Sept. 546 These wandering cairds or 'tinklers' had four separate languages at their command.

*attrib.* **1786** BURNS *Twa Dogs* 18 Ev'n wi' a tinkler-gipsey's messan. **1787** — '*When Guilford good*' v, An' Charlie Fox threw by his box, An' lows'd his tinkler jaw, man.

**Ti·nkler**[2]. [f. TINKLE *v.*[1] + -ER[1].] That which tinkles; *esp.* a descriptive name for a small bell, etc. (in *slang* = 'bell'); in quot. 1600, a name for some base coin.

**1600** *Stirling Kirk Sess. Reg.* (Bann. Cl.) 133 Ane great part of the almus gevin to the Pure is fals cunȝie callit Tinklaris. **1767** ANNA SEWARD *Let.* in *Poet. Wks.* (1810) I. 195 A Spinnet.., the little tinkler is a wretched substitute for my dear harpsichord. **1787** WOLCOTT (P. Pindar) *Ode upon Ode* Wks. 1812 I. 419 Thus when the Oxford Bell, baptized Great Tom, Shakes all the city with his iron tongue, The little Tinklers might as well be dumb. **1838** DICKENS *O. Twist* xxv, 'Hark!' cried the Dodger at this moment, 'I heard the tinkler'. **1852** R. S. SURTEES *Sponge's Sp. Tour* iii, Giving the little tinkler of a bell a pull as he spoke. **1901** R. ANDERSON *Hist. Kilsyth* vii. 65 The old 'tinkler' which..had done service in the belfry of the disused church.

**b.** A person who tinkles; a rimester.

**1731** A. HILL *Adv. Poets* xxii, But, ah! far short th' unsolid Tinklers rise; Nor soar, but flutter, in the Muse's Skies.

**Tinklerman**, error for TRINKERMAN, q. v.

**1840** THACKERAY *Catherine* xiv, The ferries..and..the pirates who infest the same—namely tinklermen, petermen, hebbermen, trawlermen. *Ibid.*, A combat..between the crews of a tinklerman's boat and the water-bailiff's.

**Ti·nkle-ta·nkle**, *sb.* (also *attrib.*). [Varied reduplication of TINKLE.] Tinkling with alternation of sound. So **Ti·nkle-ta·nkling** *vbl. sb.* and *ppl. a.*

*a* **1619** FLETCHER *Wit without M.* v. i, Here is such a tinkle-tanklings that we can ne're lie quiet. **1859** SALA *Tw. round Clock* (1861) 186 Plenty of good heavy choruses, tinkle-tankling instrumental music. **1882** J. WALKER *Jaunt to Auld Reekie* 205 Stringed guitars with tinkle-tankle tones. **1901** EL. G. HAYDEN *Trav. round Vill.* 125 A flute or violin whose quaint tinkle-tankle adds to the archaic character of the proceeding.

**Tinkling** (ti·ŋkliŋ), *vbl. sb.* [-ING[1].]

**I.** The action of TINKLE *v.*[1]

**1.** The (subjective) ringing of the ears. Now *rare.*

**1495** *Trevisa's Barth. De P. R.* XVII. clv. (W. de W.) T vij/2 Senuey..dooth awaye tynkelynge [*Bodl. MS.* tingelinge] & ryngynge of the eere. **1544** PHAER *Regim. Lyfe* (1553) C vj, Deafenesse by wynde..in the eare,..causeth tyncklyng in the heade. **1635** BRATHWAIT *Arcad. Pr.* 104, I feele a perpetuall tinckling and sowing [? sowning] in mine eares. **1803** *Med. Jrnl.* IX. 145 Affected..with a difficulty of hearing, and a tinkling in the ears.

**2.** A succession of short light ringing sounds, as of a cymbal or a small bell; jingling. Also *fig.*

**1549** COVERDALE, etc. *Erasm. Par.* 1 *Cor.* xiii. 35 A cymball, that with his vnprofitable tinklyng troubleth the eares. **1617** MORYSON *Itin.* III. 32 The Papists at the tinckling of a little Bell, lift up the consecrated Bread. **1651** DAVENANT *Gondibert* Pref. (1673) 9 Old Men..think it lyes in a kinde of tinkling of words. **1750** GRAY *Elegy* 8 Drowsy tinklings lull the distant folds. **1784** COWPER *Task* VI. 1021 Idle tinkling of a minstrel's lyre. **1800** *Hull Advertiser* 8 Nov. 3/3 Pretended half-guineas.., and nothing but the test of tinkling can lead to detection. **1881** BROADHOUSE *Mus. Acoustics* 197 That peculiar high inharmonious noise which we are accustomed to call 'tinkling'.

**II. 3.** Short for *tinkling grackle*: see next, c.

**Tinkling** (ti·ŋkliŋ), *ppl. a.*[1] [f. TINKLE *v.*[1] + -ING[2].] That tinkles; making a short light ringing sound, or a succession of such; jingling.

*c* **1440** [see TINKLE *v.*[1] 2]. **1526** TINDALE 1 *Cor.* xiii. 1, I were even as soundynge brasse, and as a tynklynge Cymball. **1563** WINȜET *Four Scoir Thre Quest.* vii. Wks. (S.T.S.) I. 75 Lyke soundand metell, or ane tincland cimbal. **1621** BURTON *Anat. Mel.* II. ii. VI. iii. 373 Bees..when they heare any tinkling [*ed.* 1651 tingling] sound, will tarry behind. **1663** COWLEY *Verses & Ess.*, *Complaint* vii, The tinckling strings of thy loose minstrelsie. **1717** POPE *Eloisa* 158 The grots that echo to the tinkling rills. **1829** SCOTT *Anne of G.* xiii, A long train of mules—a jolly tinkling team. **1877** MAR. M. GRANT *Sun-Maid* i, There came the tinkling musical echo of a bell.

**b.** *fig.* of speech (or a speaker), or verse.

**1626** B. JONSON *Fort. Isles* Wks. (Rtldg.) 650/1 In Rhime! fine tinckling Rhime! and flowand Verse! **1692** WASHINGTON tr. *Milton's Def. Pop.* Pref., M.'s Wks. 1851 VII. 10 Them, I say, together with their tinkling Advocate,..we shall e'en let whine on, till they cry their eyes out. **1822** HAZLITT *Table-t.* Ser. II. v. (1869) 120 Keep to your sounding generalities, your tinkling phrases. **1871** B. TAYLOR *Faust* (1875) I. i. 24 Beware, a tinkling fool to be!

**c.** *Tinkling grackle*, also simply *tinkling*: a bird, a species of grackle (*Quiscalus crassirostris*) found in Jamaica; so called from its note.

**1847** GOSSE *Birds Jamaica* 217 Tinkling Grakle. *Ibid.* 219 Like the Ani, the Tinkling feeds on the parasites of cattle. **1890** *Blackw. Mag.* June 787 The tinkling may be seen feeding greedily in the pastures. **1896** NEWTON *Dict. Birds*, *Tinkling* or *Tin-tin*, the name in Jamaica for one of the American Grackles, *Quiscalus crassirostris*.

Hence **Ti·nklingly** *adv.*, in a tinkling way.

**1894** CROCKETT *Mad Sir Uchtred* 25 As she spoke she laughed tinklingly.

**Tinkling**, *ppl. a.*[2]: see TINKLE *v.*[2]

**Tinkly** (ti·ŋkli), *a.* [f. TINKLE *v.*[1] or *sb.* + -Y.] Characterized by tinkling.

**1892** KIPLING *Barrack-r. Ballads* 52 The tinkly temple-bells. **1894** *Outing* (U.S.) XXIV. 71/2 An ex-captain sits at the tinkly piano.

**Tink-tank**: see TINK *int.* and *sb.*

**Tinley**, variant of TINDLE *sb. dial.*

**1788** *Gentl. Mag.* July 602/2 It is a custom with the Papists in some parts of the kingdom, upon the eve of All Souls, to illuminate some of their grounds, by bearing round them straw..kindled into a blaze. The ceremony..is called a *Tinley*; and the account vulgarly given of it..is, that it is meant emblematically to signify the lighting of souls out of Purgatory. **1825** HONE *Every-day Bk.* I. 1414.

**Tin-liquor** to **Tin-mouth**: see TIN *sb.* 5.

**Tinman** (ti·nmæ̆n). [f. TIN *sb.* + MAN *sb.*] A man who works in or with tin; a tinsmith; a dealer in tin-ware. In Cornwall, a man employed in dressing tin ore. Also *transf.* a ship engaged in the carriage of tin ore.

**1611** COTGR., *Estamier*, a Tynner, Tynne-man; Pewterer. **1667** *Lond. Gaz.* No. 154/1 A New England Vessel of 16 Guns..was forced with some Tinmen and Colliers to put into St. Ives. **1704** PRIOR *Simile* 2 Didst thou never pop Thy head into a tin-man's shop? **1840** *Civil Eng. & Arch. Jrnl.* III. 284/2 The common soldering irons used by tinmen and plumbers. **1855** J. R. LEIFCHILD *Cornwall Mines* 228 'Tinmen are not copperers', as the Cornish miners say. **1887** *Contemp. Rev.* Sept. 398 Thirty or forty years ago, the tinman..was recognized as one of the leading and most skilful mechanics.

**Tinne**, variant of TIND *v. Obs.*, to kindle.

**Tinned** (tind), *ppl. a.* [f. TIN *sb.* or *v.* + -ED.]

**1.** Coated or plated with tin.

*c* **1384** CHAUCER *H. Fame* III. 392 A pilere That was of tynned yren clere. **14..** *MS. Sloane* 2463 lf. 159 b, Boile hit eftesones in a tynned panne. **1533** *MS. Rawl. D.* 776 A payer of Jemewes for the same Dore..ffor Tynned naylles ffor the same Jemewes. **1691** *Patent Specif.* (1856) No. 282. 1 Iron plates tinned over comonly called tinned plates. **1831** M. RUSSELL *Egypt* x. (1853) 420 A small chafing dish of tinned copper. **1839** *Civil Eng. & Arch. Jrnl.* II. 361/2 Manufacturer of zinc and of tinned iron.

**2.** Preserved in air-tight tins; canned.

**1879** *Echo* 18 Oct. 1/5 The trade in tinned food is enormous, and is constantly on the increase. **1883** *Fisheries Exhib. Catal.* 371 Cooked and tinned Salmon. **1895** SUFFLING *Land of Broads* 19 Try a tinned pineapple.

**3.** Baked in a tin.

**1890** STROUD *Judicial Dict.* 310 Tinned Loaves, made crusty all round..is not 'French or Fancy Bread'.

**Tinneis**, obs. Sc. form of TENNIS.

†**Ti·nnen**, *a. Obs.* [OE. *tinen*, f. TIN *sb.* + -EN[4]. So WFlem. *tinnen.*] Made or consisting of tin.

*c* **1000** ÆLFRIC *Gram.* vi. (Z.) 15 *Stagnum*, tin, *stagneus*, tinen. *c* **1440** *Pallad. on Husb.* VI. 99 Other with tynnen tounges take her strynges. **1551–2** in Swayne *Sarum Churchw. Acc.* (1896) 278 For a tynnen Bottell to fetch Wyne in. **1631** BP. WEBBE *Quietn.* (1657) 82 A tinnen or earthen vessel. **1653** H. COGAN tr. *Pinto's Trav.* xxiv. 91 The women wore great tinnen Bracelets about..their arms.

**Tinner** (ti·nəɹ). [f. TIN *sb.* or *v.* + -ER[1].]

**1.** One who gets or digs tin ore; a tin-miner.

**1512** *Act 4 Hen. VIII*, c. 8 All other tynners..dyggyng of tyn in the severall soyle of the said Richard. **1602** CAREW *Cornwall* 8 b, Where the finding of these affordeth a tempting likelihood, the Tynners goe to worke. **1670** PETTUS *Fodinæ Reg.* 12 The King for advancement of the Stannaries..frees the Tinners from all pleas of the Natives touching the Court. **1743** WESLEY *Jrnl.* (1903) 147 Nine or ten miles east of St. Ives, where we found two or three hundred tinners. **1883** R. T. DYER in *Leisure Hour* Dec. 733/2 In Cornwall, the second Monday before Christmas is a festival kept by the tinners.

**2.** One who works in tin; a tin-plater, tinman, tinsmith.

**1611** COTGR., *Estaingnier*, a Pewterer, a Tinner. *a* **1817** T. DWIGHT *Trav. New Eng.*, etc. (1821) II. 53 His trade was that of a tinner. **1890** *Anthony's Photogr. Bull.* III. 45 Have made for you at any tinner's, a tin pan about an inch larger all around than your toning tray.

**3.** One who tins meat, fruit, etc.; a canner.

**1906** *Referee* 26 Aug. 9/2 Then down with the kickshaws that all taste alike, And the stock of cold storer and tinner.

**4.** Local name for the pied wagtail: see quot.

**1880** *W. Cornwall Gloss.*, *Tinner*...'A water wagtail'. Bottrell. **1904** *Athenæum* 4 June 274/3 The pied wagtail.. known [at Land's End] as the 'tinner', because it builds its nest in the mouth of old mine-shafts.

**Tinnery** (ti·nəri). [f. TINNER + -Y, or f. TIN + -ERY.] Tin-mining; *pl.* tin-mines or tin-works.

**1769** *De Foe's Tour Gt. Brit.* I 409 There is still a great Resemblance between the Scilly Islands and Cornwall, in their Culture, Plants, and other Produce, their Tinnery, Fishery, &c. *a* **1787** S. JENYNS *Wks.* (1790) II. 238 Miners from tinneries, and coal-pits.

**Ti·nnet.** *Obs.* exc. *dial.* Also 7 tennett, tinet, 8 *dial.* teenet. [repr. OE. type **týnet*, f. *týnan*, TINE *v.*[1] + *-et*, as in *thicket.*] Brushwood for making or repairing hedges or fences. Cf. TINSEL *sb.*[2]

[**1443** *Carta Ric. Moninton* (Blount), Et prædictus Firmarius habebit tinettum sufficiens extra boscum ipsius R. ad clausurandum terras & pasturas supradictas.] **1650** *Parl. Surv. Sussex* in *Sussex Archæol. Coll.* XXIII. 311 The Coppieholdrs of Duddleswell doe claime to have ffrith and tennett out of the said Parke for fencing their lands. **1691** *Blount's Law Dict.* (ed. 2), *Tinet* (*Tinettum*).., Trouse, Brushwood and Thorns to make and repair Hedges. **1701** *Cowell's Interpr.*, *Tinettum*, Trouse..is still in Kent called *Teenet.* **1753** CHAMBERS *Cycl. Supp.*, *Tinet*, *Tinettum.* **1904** *Eng. Dial. Dict.*, *Tinnet* [cited from Heref., Glouc., Suss.].

**Tinnicle**, obs. form of TUNICLE.

†**Ti·nnient**, *a. Obs.* [ad. L. *tinnient-em*, pr. pple. of *tinnīre* to ring, tinkle.] Ringing, resonant.

**1668** H. MORE *Div. Dial.* II. v. (1713) 100 A sportful passage of Nature, to try how tight and tinnient her new workmanship was. **1753** *Ess. on Action for Pulpit* 86 It will make every religious string, so to say, more intense and tinnient.

**Ti·nnified**, *ppl. a. rare.* [f. TIN or TINNY *a.* + -FY + -ED[1].] Made tinny or like tin; impregnated with tin; in quot. 1794 *depreciative.*

**1794** *Manners France* 80 Has Horace or Ovid their fair ladies clad In the tinnify'd charm of cork rumps or a pad? **1855** J. R. LEIFCHILD *Cornwall Mines* 38 Stannified granite ..which the plain reader may call tinnified granite.

**Ti·nnikin.** *Sc. rare.* [f. TIN or TINNY *sb.* + -KIN: cf. *mannikin.*] A very small tin or mug.

**1896** CROCKETT *Cleg Kelly* viii, He brought his mistress a drink in a little tinnikin.

†**Ti·nniment.** *Obs. rare*—[0]. [ad. L. *tinnīment-um* a ringing or tinkling ('tinnīmentum auribus', Plautus), f. *tinnīre* to ring, jingle.]

**1656** BLOUNT *Glossogr.*, *Tinniment*, a ringing or tinckling, as metals do. **1658** PHILLIPS, *Tiniment*, (lat.) a tingling, or sounding of metals.

**Ti·nniness.** [f. TINNY *a.*] Tinny quality.

**1891** KIPLING *Life's Handicap* ii. 37 Tinned beef of surpassing tinniness.

**Tinning** (ti·niŋ), *vbl. sb.* [f. TIN *v.* or *sb.* + -ING[1].] **I.** The action of the verb TIN.

**1.** Coating, lining, or plating with tin; working at tin-ware.

*c* **1440** *Promp. Parv.* 494/2 Tynnynge wythe tynne, *stanacio.* **1487–8** *Rec. St. Mary at Hill* 130 Paide to Westwode, smyth,..for tynnyng of the same boltes. **1537** *Acc. Ld. High Treas. Scot.* VI. 337 Item, for grathing and dichting and tynnyng of ten tua handit suerdis. **1611** COTGR., *Plombement*, a leading, or tinning. **1789** *Trans. Soc. Arts* I. 13 Tinning with pure Tin. **1800** tr. *Lagrange's Chem.* II. 107 The tinning of copper consists in applying a coating of tin to the surface of that metal. **1851** MAYHEW *Lond. Labour* (1864) I. 302/1 As you see, sir, I work at tinning. I put new bottoms into old tin tea-pots, and such like. **1873** E. SPON *Workshop Receipts* Ser. I. 9/1 When the article is prepared for tinning, it may be immersed in the tinning metal.

**b.** *concr.* A tin coating or lining.

**1761** *Chron.* in *Ann. Reg.* 143/1 This accident was..occasioned by using a copper sauce pan, from which the tinning was worn off. **1839** URE *Dict. Arts* s.v. *Alloy*, Tinning, gilding, and silvering may also be reckoned a species of alloys.

**2.** The putting up and sealing of meat, fish, fruit, etc., in tins for preservation; canning.

**1903** *Daily Chron.* 13 Jan. 6/1 The tinning of sprats from Honfleur and other points.

**II. 3.** Tin-mining.

**1855** J. R. LEIFCHILD *Cornwall Mines* 197 For a long period in the early history of tin-mining, the mines of Cornwall appear to have been in the hands of the Jews...When the Jews were hotly persecuted, those engaged in 'tinning' were particularly exempted.

**III. 4.** *attrib.*

**1860** TOMLINSON *Arts & Manuf.* Ser. II. *Pins* 47 Then comes the whitening, or tinning process. **1868** JOYNSON *Metals* 104 The plates are now received one by one from the tinning bath. **1898** *Daily News* 11 Aug. 7/2 Tinning factories have more than they want. **1909** *Eng. Rev.* Mar. 621 [They] put them into patent tinning-pots.

**Tinnis**, obs. form of TENNIS.

**Tinnitate** (ti·nitĕ͡ɪt), *v. nonce-wd.* [f. L. *tinnītāt-*, ppl. stem of *tinnītāre*, freq. of *tinnīre*: see next.] *intr.* To ring, give forth a ringing sound.

**1866** J. B. ROSE tr. *Ovid's Fasti* IV. 231 And high and mighty Ida tinnitates To drown the infant's cries.

‖**Tinnitus** (tinəi·tŏs). *Med.* [L. *tinnītus* (*u*-stem), f. *tinnīre* to ring, tinkle.] A sensation of ringing in the ears.

[**1693** tr. *Blancard's Phys. Dict.* (ed. 2), *Tinnitus Aurium*, a certain Buzzing or tingling in the Ears.] **1843** R. J. GRAVES *Syst. Clin. Med.* xiv. 170 On admission, he complained of headache, tinnitus aurium. **1879** *St. George's Hosp. Rep.* IX. 649 The development of constitutional symptoms, such as tinnitus and slight deafness.

**Tinny, tinnie** (ti·ni), *sb. Sc.* [f. TIN *sb.* + *-ie*, -Y, dim. suff.] A small tin mug, a child's tin.

**1825** JAMIESON, *Tinnie*, the small jug or porringer..used by children. **1864** *Auld Ayr* 86 Let us have a tinny of grog. **1906** *Scott. Chron.* 6 July 482/2 They turned up.. each with his or her 'tinnie' well in evidence.

**Tinny** (ti·ni), *a.* [f. TIN *sb.* + -Y.]

**1.** Consisting of, abounding in, or yielding tin; formerly also, Of tin, made of tin.

**1552** HULOET, Tynny or of tynne, *stanneus.* **1576** BAKER *Jewell of Health* 231 Let this be kept in a Sylver or Tynnie vessel. **1596** SPENSER *F. Q.* IV. xi. 31 Dart, nigh chockt with sands of tinny mines. **1612** DRAYTON *Poly-olb.* i. 157 Those armes of sea that thrust into the tinny strand. **1695** BLACKMORE *Pr. Arth.* VI. 419 Pale Tinny Oar, and Copper's brighter Vein. **1881** *Standard* 28 Oct. 1/2 The lode is six feet wide, and tinny throughout.

**2.** Like or resembling tin or that of tin; characteristic of tin; *esp.* of sounds; in *Painting*, hard, crude, metallic.

**1877** HALLOCK *Sportsman's Gaz.* 379 Long tinny mouth [of a fish]. **1892** *Sat. Rev.* 21 May 597/2 We have accused Mr. Parsons of a hard tinny quality in colour and form.

1904 KATE D. WIGGIN *Affair at Inn* 177 She was sitting at the old tinny-sounding spinet. 1908 *Daily Chron.* 24 Oct. 3/1 How tinny look Claude's landscapes in the room at the National Gallery.

**b.** Tasting or smelling of tin; tinged with tin. 1906 *Blackw. Mag.* Aug. 213/1 One of the pans in the dairy smelt suspiciously 'tinny'.

**3.** *slang.* Having plenty of 'tin'; rich, wealthy. 1871 *Punch* 14 Oct. 160/2 There's heaps of tinny fellows who'll be awful glad to give.

**Tinoceratid** (təinǫse·rătid), *a.* and *sb. Palæont.* [irreg. f. Gr. τείν-ειν to stretch, as if = stretching out + κέρας, κερατ- horn + -ID.] **a.** *adj.* Of, pertaining to, or having the characters of the *Tinoceras*, a very large fossil mammal. **b.** *sb.* A fossil of this genus (*Cent. Dict.* 1891). So **Tinoce·ratine** *a.*, **Tinoce·ratoid** *a.* and *sb.*

1889 NICHOLSON & LYDEKKER *Palæont* lxi. II. 1389 The genus [*Uintatherium*] may be divided into a Dinoceratine and a Tinoceratine group. 1891 *Cent. Dict.*, Tinoceratid, *a.* 1895 *Funk's Stand. Dict.*, Tinoceratid, Tinoceratoid, *a.* and *sb.*

**Tin-opener** to **Tin-pan**: see TIN *sb.* 4, 5.

**Tinpan**, obs. (erron.) form of TYMPAN.

**Ti·n-pla·te.** Sheet-iron or, in recent use, often sheet-steel, coated with tin; a plate of this.

1677 YARRANTON *Eng. Improv.* To Rdr., In order to the establishing of the like [trade] in England, to set the Poor on work, which was the Linen, Thread, Tape, and Tin-plates. 1758 REID tr. *Macquer's Chym.* I. 70 Tin-Plates are no other than thin plates of Iron tinned over. 1812 SIR H. DAVY *Chem. Philos.* 393 Tin plate is formed by dipping thin plates of iron into melted tin. 1839 URE *Dict. Arts*, etc. s. v., The formation of tin-plate, or white-iron.

**b.** *attrib.* and *Comb.*

1720 STRYPE *Stow's Surv.* (1754) II. v. xv. 323/1 The Company of Tin plate workers were incorporated by charter in the 22nd year of King Charles II. 1815 J. SMITH *Panorama Sc. & Art* II. 794 A japanned tin-plate tray is of less value than a paper one. 1860 PIESSE *Lab. Chem. Wonders* 37 England is the tin-plate manufacturer for the whole world. 1906 *Westm. Gaz.* 10 Jan. 2/1 The transformation at Welsh tinplate works has been very great.

So **Ti·n-pla·ted** *ppl. a.*, plated with tin; **Ti·n-pla·ter**, a workman who makes tin-plates.

1890 *Engineer* LXIX. 496 The [search-light] projector barrel is 16 in. diameter, rolled out of steel sheet tinplated and very strong. 1903 *Westm. Gaz.* 1 Sept. 5/1 The unions contend..that..the tin platers so treated have a claim for damages against the masters.

**Tin-pot** (ti·n,pǫ·t, ti·npǫt).

**1.** (as two words) A pot made of tin or tin-plate. 1772 T. SIMPSON *Vermin-Killer* 21 A pound of arsenick.. put into a tin pot or kettle.

**2.** The pot of molten tin into which the sheet of iron is dipped in the manufacture of tin-plate.

1839 URE *Dict. Arts* 1253 The first rectangle in the range is the tin-pot. 1864 STRAUSS, etc. *Eng. Workshops* 78 The first pot, called the *tinman's-pan*...The second pot, called the *tin-pot*. 1880 FLOWER *Hist. Trade Tin* xiii. 170 From the palm-oil bath by means of tongs, the sheets are passed by the tinman..to the tin pot, which is full of molten tin, and here they remain to soak for a period of 20 minutes.

**3.** Short for *tin-pot bell*: see 4.

1895 MISS E. P. THOMPSON *Veil of Liberty* ix. 176 The ..church next door began to clink its miserable tin-pot—it had once had a good set of bells, but it had felt it prudent to give these to the nation.

**4.** *attrib.* Resembling or suggesting a tin pot in quality or sound; hence *contemptuously*, without solid worth, of inferior quality, shabby, poor, cheap.

1865 *Slang Dict.* s. v., 'He plays a tin-pot game', *i. e.*, a low or shabby one. *Billiards.* 1875 W. MORRIS in Mackail *Life* (1899) I. 309 Within sound of those tin-pot bells. 1891 KIPLING *Light that Failed* iii, To the tin-pot music of a Western waltz the naked Zanzibari girls danced furiously. 1897 *Daily News* 23 Mar. 6/7 Made a sacrifice to some miserable tin-pot politicians. 1907 *Ibid.* 4 Oct., Some tin-pot comic opera receives praise from the very same critics.

Hence **Ti·n-po·tter** *Naut. slang*, see quot.; **Ti·n-po·ttery**, tin pots or tin-ware collectively.

1867 SMYTH *Sailor's Word-bk.*, *Tin-potter*, a galley skulker, shamming Abraham. 1850 SCARGILL *Eng. Sketch-Bk.* 7 Dealing in grocery, drapery, and tin-pottery.

**Tin-pulp** to **Tin-scrap**: see TIN *sb.* 5.

**Tinsel** (ti·nsĕl, -s'l), *sb.*[1] Chiefly *north.* and (from *c* 1400 only) *Sc.* Also 3 **tinsil, 4 -ill, -elle, 4-7 -ell, 5-7 -ale, -all, 6 -aill; 4 tynsil, -yll, 4-6 -al(l, 4-7 -ell, 5-7 -el, 6 -ele; 5 tensale, -elle.** [ME. *tinsel*, *tynsel*, etc., prob. ad. ON. **týnsla*, f. *týna* (= ME. *tin-en*, *tyn-en*, TINE *v.*[2]) to lose, perish, destroy, with the Norse suffix *-sla* (as in *geymsla*, *rennsla*, etc.): cf. mod.Norw. *tynsla* destruction, damage, spilling.]

†**1.** The losing of something, or the sustaining of harm, damage, or detriment; loss. *Obs.*

*a* 1300 *Cursor M.* 916 (Cott.), I most couer þis tinsel [*T.* loos] are. *a* 1340 HAMPOLE *Psalter* cxxxvi. 1 Worldis men gretis bot nouȝt for tynsil of þair godes. *a* 1400 *R. Brunne's Chron. Wace* 2352 (Petyt MS.) Hure ouer-þoughte mykel more þe wraþþe of hure fader þe kyng..Þan þe tynsell of oþer thyng. *c* 1400 *Laud Troy Bk.* 9936 What harme that day to the be-felle! Thow may telle of thi tenselle. *c* 1470 HENRY *Wallace* v. 387, I meyn fer mar the tynsell off my men. *c* 1520 M. NISBET *N. Test. in Scots*, *Acts* xxvii. 22, I counsale you to be of good counfort, for tynsele [WYCLIF, los; Gr. ἀποβολὴ] of na persoun of you salbe. 1556 LAUDER *Tractate* 382 In this Consistis, withoutin faill, Boith the wynning and tinsaill. *a* 1600 MONTGOMERIE *Misc. Poems* xxxii. 67 Quhair tentles bairnis may to their tinsall tak The neiv with na thing, and the full refuse. 1728 RAMSAY *Twa Cut-purses* 33 Where'er your tinsel be, Ye canna lay the wyte on me. 1737 — *Scots Prov.* xv. (1750) 42 He that's far frae his gear is near his tinsel.

†**2.** The condition of being 'lost' spiritually; perdition, damnation. *Obs.*

*a* 1300 *Cursor M.* 11946 (Cott.) Þou godds fede, Sun o tinsel and o ded! *a* 1300 *E. E. Psalter* lxxxvii[i]. 12 [11] Wher ani in thrughes sal telle þi milthnes, Ore in tinsel [L. *in perditione*] þi sothnes? *c* 1375 *Sc. Leg. Saints* ii. 828 Als he slew petir and paule, Till eke þe tynsale of his sawle.

**3.** *Sc. Law.* Forfeiture, deprivation; now only in some archaic phrases: see quot. 1838.

1424 *Sc. Acts Jas. I* (1814) II. 5/1 Vnder the payne of tynsal of all gold and siluer that beis fundyn. 1565-75 *Diurn. Occurr.* (Bann. Cl.) 80 Vnder the paynes of tynsall of lyif, landis and goodis. *c* 1575 *Balfour's Practicks* (1754) 17 Under the pane of ten pundis, and tinsell of his office. 1678 SIR G. MACKENZIE *Crim. Laws Scot.* I. xxx. § 6 (1699) 155 Punished with tinsel of Life and Goods. 1838 W. BELL *Dict. Law Scot.*, *Tinsel of the Feu*, is an irritancy incident to every feu-right, by the failure to pay the feu-duty for two years whole and together... *Tinsel of Superiority*, is a remedy..for unentered vassals whose superiors are themselves uninfeft, and therefore cannot effectually enter them.

†**Tinsel**, *sb.*[2] *Obs.* [Known from late 15th c.; f. TINE *v.*[1], OE. *týn-an* to enclose, fence, hedge, with Norse suffix *-sl*, prob. taken over from north. dial. *gar-sell*, GARSIL (= ON. **gerðsl*), meaning the same thing.] Brushwood for hedging or fencing.

1486 *Nottingham Rec.* III. 254, ij. lodes of tynsell' from þe Copy. 1610 W. FOLKINGHAM *Art of Survey* I. vi. 13 For woods..how enterlaced, as Timber with Tinsell, Coppice, or vnderwood. 1620 in *N. & Q.* 1st Ser. (1851) III. 478 A few underwoods..of hasell, alders, withie and thornes ..which the tenants doe take and use for Tinsel as need requires. 1637 in *Chesh. Gloss.* (1885) s.v., To take sufficient trouse and tynsel..for the fencing in and repairing of the hedges. 1793-1813 *Rep. Agric., Derby* 45 (E.D.S.) Having stone provided in the quay, and tinsel crop for fencing.

**Tinsel** (ti·nsĕl, -s'l), *sb.*[3] and *a.* Forms: *α.* **6- tinsel; also 6 tynsel(le, -sil(l, -syll, tincel, tincle, tensell, 6-7 tyn-, tinsell, -sill, 7-8 -sil.** *β.* **6 tylsent, tilsent.** *γ.* **6 tynsyn, tensyn, -sen, tinsin, 7 tynsin.** See also TINSEY. [The etymology, though certain in its main fact, presents difficulties of detail, owing chiefly to the want of early OF. examples. Evidently *tincel*, *tinsel*, arose out of OF. *estincelle*, mod.F. *étincelle* 'a sparke or sparkle of fire, a flash', Cotgr. (:—pop.L. **stincilla* for *scintilla* spark), and OF. *estincelé*, mod.F. *étincelé* 'sparkled, sparked, also powdered or set with sparkles', pa. pple. of OF. *estinceler* 'to sparke, to sparkle as fire; to twinkle as a starre or Dyamond; to set thicke with sparkles' (:—pop.L. **stincillāre* for *scintillāre* to sparkle, glitter). In 14-15th c. Fr., the *s* of *es-* had long been mute, and the pronunciation was actually as in mod.Fr. *étincelle*, *-elé*; of this the initial *e* disappeared (app. in Anglo-F. or Eng.) by aphesis, giving *tincel(le*. Our earliest examples show the word used attrib. or as adj. in *tinselle satin*, app. representing a Fr. *satin étincelé* (with *-e* mute in Eng., as in some other words), or else the Eng. 'tinselled satin' (see TINSELLED) with *d* lost between *l* and *s*. Thence sense 2, *tinsel* alone = *tinsel satin*, *tinsel cloth*, etc. Sense 3, which is later, may represent the Fr. sb. *étincelle*. *Tilsent* and *tinsin*, early popular perversions, scarcely survived the 16th c.; they also were at first attrib. in *tylsent satin*, *tynsyn satten*.]

**1.** *adj.* passing into *sb.* used *attrib.* Of satin, etc.: Made to sparkle or glitter by the interweaving of gold or silver thread, by brocading with such thread, or by overlaying with a thin coating of gold or silver.

*α.* 1502 *Priv. Purse Exp. Eliz. of York* (1830) 9 Blake tynselle saten of the riche making. 1537 in *Reliquary* Jan. (1893) 37 A nother Tynsell Satten with a Crowne ouer the breste of the seid lorde Mounte Egles Armes. 1552 HULOET, Bawdkyn or Tynsel clothe.

*β.* 1510-12 *Wardr. Acc.* 2-3 *Hen. VIII* 52/2 (in *N. & Q.* 8th Ser. I. 129) Tylsent satin. 1547 in Kempe *Losely MSS.* (1836) 67 Twoo baces of clothe of golde reysed wth red sylke, tylsent satten. Twoo baces of clothe of golde, blewe tilsent crymsin and purple vellett in clocks.

*γ.* 1509-10 *Act 1 Hen. VIII*, c. 14 Clothe of Golde or cloth of Sylver or tynsyn Satten. 1530 PALSGR. 281/2 Tynsyn satten, *satyn broché*. 1531 *Rec. St. Mary at Hill* 41 Small schredes of tensyn satten. 1552 in Dillon *Calais & Pale* (1892) 97 One Vestimente of reed Tensen satten without albe. 1603 *Ceremonies Coronat. Jas. I* (1685) 11 The Dean ..arrayeth the King..with the Tynsin Hose.

†**2.** A kind of cloth or tissue; tinselled cloth; a rich material of silk or wool interwoven with gold or silver thread (cf. BAUDEKIN); sometimes apparently, a thin net or gauze thus made, or ornamented with thin plates of metal; later, applied to a cheap imitation in which copper thread was used to obtain the sparkling effect. *Obs.*

*α.* 1526 in *Inv. Goods Dk. Richmond* in *Camden Misc.* (1855) 18 A Testour, panyd with clothe of golde, grene tynsell, and crymsen velwet. 1529 *N. C. Wills* (Surtees 1908) 93 My bedde of grene tynsill and white satteyne embrotherid with blue velvit. *a* 1548 HALL *Chron.*, *Hen. VIII* 3 Richely appareled in Tissues, clothe of Golde, of Siluer, Tynsels and Veluettes Embroudered. 1552 *Inv. Ch. Surrey* (1869) 18 A sute of vestimentes of white tynsell. 1552 HULOET, Tynsell or bawdkyn cloth, *intertextus*. 1583 STUBBES *Anat. Abus.* I. (1879) 47 Euery place was hanged with cloth of gold, cloth of siluer, tinsell, arrace, tapestrie. 1599 B. JONSON *Cynthia's Rev.* v. ix, The fourth, in watchet tinsell, is the kind and truly benefique Evcolos. 1603 KNOLLES *Hist. Turks* (1621) 1203 The Embassador and 16 of his companie, received each of them a robe of tinsell. 1611 COTGR., *Brocatel*, tinsell; or thin cloth of gold, or siluer. 1639 MAYNE *City Match* Ep. Ded., Masquers, who spangle, and glitter for the time, but tis through a tinsell. *c* 1645 HOWELL *Lett.* (1650) III. 3 In that more subtill air of yours tinsell sometimes passes for tissue. 1656 BLOUNT *Glossogr.*, *Tincel*.. signifies with us a stuff or cloth made partly of silk, and partly of copper; so called, because it glisters or sparkles like stars or fire. Hence 1721 BAILEY, *Tinsel*, a glittering Stuff made of Silk and Copper. 1755 JOHNSON, *Tinsel*, a kind of shining cloth.

*β.* 1547 Tilsent [see 1 *β*]. *c* 1547 in H. Ainsworth *Constable Tower* I. v. (1861) I. 71 [The Earl of Surrey..appeared in a doublet of black] tylsent [welted with cloth of silver].

*γ.* 1523 in *Archæologia* XXXVIII. 363 A sparver payned with cremesyn tynsyn, and blake velvet. *a* 1548 HALL *Chron.*, *Hen. VIII* 75 b, Clothe of Golde, Clothe of Siluer, Veluettes, Tinsins, Sattins embroudered.

**3.** Very thin plates or sheets, spangles, strips, or threads, originally of gold or silver, later of copper, brass, or some gold- or silver-coloured alloy, used chiefly for ornament; now esp. for cheap and showy ornamentation, gaudy stage costumes, anglers' flies, and the like: see also quot. 1903.

1593 G. FLETCHER *Licia* (1876) 28 As twinckling starres, the tinsell of the night. 1596 NASHE *Saffron Walden* 49 As day-light [is] beyond candle-light, or tinsell or leafe-gold aboue arsedine. 1732 GRAY in *Phil. Trans.* XXXVII. 228 A Piece of Sheet-Brass, commonly called Tinsel. 1782 V. KNOX *Ess.* I. viii. 38 The character of a man of integrity and benevolence is far more desirable than that of a man of pleasure or of fashion. The one is like solid gold, the other like tinsel. 1809 MALKIN *Gil Blas* IV. viii. ¶ 6 Those who are behind the scenes are not to be dazzled by the tinsel of the property-man. 1839 G. BIRD *Nat. Phil.* 211 These gentlemen fixed one end of a cord covered with tinsel..to the cap of an electrometer, and tying the other to an arrow, they projected it..into the air. 1859 LANG *Wand. India* 66 Beside him his..bride, dressed in garments of red silk, trimmed with yellow and gold tinsel. 1867 F. FRANCIS *Angling* x. (1880) 343 Silver tinsel and twist. 1903 *Electr. World & Engin.* 29 Aug. 341 (Cent. Suppl.) The stranded conductors are universally made of very fine copper or copper bronze wire, or what is technically called tinsel.

**4.** *fig.* Anything showy or attractive with little or no intrinsic worth; something that gives a deceptively fine or glittering appearance.

1660 JER. TAYLOR *Rule of Consc.* I. iv. rule x. § 3 There is more gold now than before, but it is..so hidden in heaps of tinsel, that when men are best pleased, now adays they are most commonly cozened. 1747 RICHARDSON *Clarissa* (1811) I. iii. 14 If Miss Clary were taken with his tinsel. 1751 JOHNSON *Rambler* No. 147 ¶ 7 That poverty of ideas which had been hitherto concealed under the tinsel of politeness. 1825 JEFFERSON *Autobiog.* Wks. 1859 I. 105 Chaste eloquence, disfigured by no gaudy tinsel of rhetoric or declamation. 1863 GEO. ELIOT *Romola* vi, An age worse than that of iron —the age of tinsel and gossamer.

**5.** *attrib.* and *Comb.*, as *tinsel-foil*, *-lace*, *-maker*; *tinsel-clad*, *-covered*, *-paned*, *-slippered* adjs.; **tinsel-embroidery**, see quot. 1882.

1575 *Lanc. Wills* (Chetham Soc.) II. 159 One dublite of crimsine satten and one tynsell paned. 1634 MILTON *Comus* 877 Thetis tinsel-slipper'd feet. 1840 HOOD *Up the Rhine* 207 Waxen tapers, Smartened with tinsel-foil and tinted papers. 1858 SIMMONDS *Dict. Trade*, *Tinsel lace-maker*, a maker of imitation gold or silver lace. 1882 CAULFEILD & SAWARD *Dict. Needlework* 495/1 *Tinsel Embroidery*. This is worked upon net, tulle, and thin muslin materials, and is an imitation of the Turkish Embroideries with gold thread upon crepe. 1897 *Daily News* 24 Feb. 5/2 Naked or tinsel-clad savages. 1906 *Daily Chron.* 27 Jan. 3/2 Description of a tinsel-maker in Delhi.

**6.** *attrib.* passing into *adj.* † Glittering, splendid (*obs.*); chiefly in disparagement: Of deceptively brilliant or valuable appearance; showy with little real worth; cheaply gaudy, tawdry.

1595 *Polimanteia* (1881) 39 Then should not the muses in their tinsell habit be so basely handled. 1633 P. FLETCHER *Purple Isl.* VII. xxvi, Upon his arm a tinsell scarf he wore, ..spangled fair. 1635 QUARLES *Embl.* II. v, False world thou ly'st. Thy tinsill boosome seems a Mint Of new-coynd treasure. 1663 J. SPENCER *Prodigies* Pref., All the tinsil-miracles among the Papists most fatally wound Religion. 1667 MILTON *P. L.* IX. 36 Bases and tinsel trappings, gorgeous knights. 1680 BURNET *Rochester* (1692) 175 Neither their tinsel wit, nor superficial learning will hold them up then. *a* 1704 T. BROWN tr. *Æneas Sylvius* Wks. 1709 III. II. 63 A Good of no Value, a mere tinsel Bauble. 1733 BERKELEY *Th. Vision* § 3 A certain way of writing, whether good or bad, tinsel or sterling, sense or nonsense. 1769 *Junius Lett.* xxi. (1770) 132 You assure me, that my logic is puerile and tinsel. 1783 BLAIR *Lect. Rhet.*, etc. xviii. I. 384 Nothing can be more contemptible than that tinsel splendor of Language, which some writers.. affect. 1844 KEBLE *Lyra Innoc.* IX. xiv. (1846) 299 The ears that hear its murmuring, crave No tinsel melodies of earth.

†**Ti·nsel**, *v.*[1] *Sc. Obs. rare.* [f. TINSEL *sb.*[1]] *trans.* To subject to loss; to impoverish, to endamage; to punish by a fine, to mulct.

1475 *Aberdeen Regr.* (1844) I. 34 He is sa tensalit in gudis, that he is nocht of povar to pay certane dettis and soumes of money awing be him. 1609 SKENE *Reg. Maj.* 114 He that swa is essonzied may be tinselled and skaithed.

**Ti·nsel**, *v.*[2] [f. TINSEL *sb.*[3]]

**1.** *trans.* To make glittering with gold or silver (or imitations thereof) interwoven, brocaded, or laid on. Also *fig.* **b.** To embellish (pictures, letters, etc.) with gold leaf; 'to embellish (ceramic ware) with metallic effects' (*Cent. Dict. Suppl.* 1909). Hence **Ti·nselling** *vbl. sb.*

1594 NASHE *Unfort. Trav.* E iv, Hir daintie lims tinsill hir silke soft sheets, Hir rose-crownd cheekes eclipse my dazeled sight. 1611 COTGR., *Pourfiler d'or*, to purfle, tinsell, or ouercast with gold thread, &c. *Ibid.*, *Pourfileure*,.. purfling;..baudkin-worke; tinselling. 1730–6 BAILEY (folio), *Tinselling*, a border of silver. 1851 MAYHEW *Lond. Labour, Answ. Corr.* xvii, I want to do something in the evening on my own account (tinselling pictures, for instance).

**2.** To give a speciously attractive or showy appearance to; to cover the defects of with or as with tinsel.

1748 WARBURTON *Alliance betw. Ch. & St.* I. v. (ed. 3) 83 The Gloom of Equivocation, which spreads itself thro' the formal Chapters of the one; and the Glare of puerile Declamation, that tinsels over the trite Essays of the other. 17.. — *Unpubl. Papers* (1841) 449 False honour may thus tinsel over the gaudy slaves of an absolute master. *a* 1774 TUCKER *Lt. Nat.* (1834) II. 265 The hopes that tinsel the gay and busy hours of life.

**Tinselled** (ti·nsěld), *ppl. a.* Also 6–7 **tinceld.** [In sense 1, app. representing F. *étincelé*: see TINSEL *sb.*[3]; in sense 2, mostly f. TINSEL *v.*[2] + -ED[1].]

**1.** Made to sparkle or glitter with gold or silver thread, brocade, or embroidery. **b.** Embellished with gold or silver leaf.

1532–3 *Act* 24 *Hen. VIII*, c. 13 No Man, vnder the State of an Erle [shall]..weare..any Clothe of Golde or Syluer, or tynseld Saten. 1545 *Rates of Customs* c iv b, Satten tynseld with gold the yarde XIII. s. IIII. d...Satten of bruges counterfete tynselde the yarde III. s. IIII. d. 1634 SIR T. HERBERT *Trav.* 146 Their out Garment or Vest..of cloth of gold and Tinselled. 1653 URQUHART *Rabelais* I. lvi. 244 Figured sattin tinselled and overcast with golden threads. 1748 RICHARDSON *Clarissa* VI. 3 Tinselled hobby-horses, gilt gingerbread. 1853 KANE *Grinnell Exp.* v. (1856) 40 Some of these huts were garnished with little tinseled pictures. 1871 ROSSETTI *Last Confession* 387 Before some new Madonna gaily decked, Tinselled and gewgawed, a slight German toy, I saw her kneel.

**2.** *transf.* and *fig.*; in later use often depreciative or contemptuous (cf. b).

*c* 1620 *Convert Soule* in Farr *S. P. Jas. I* (1847) 89 Then dream of shadowees, make thy coate Of tinsel'd cobwebs. 1648 EARL OF WESTMORELAND *Otia Sacra* (1879) 6 As the Tincell'd Night gives way At th' opening o' th' true Golden Day. 1738 *Gentl. Mag.* VIII. 521/2 Observe the Gentleman in that gaudy slight French Dress, how he is tinsel'd and pouder'd over. 1741 RICHARDSON *Pamela* (1824) I. 180 Tinselled toy! said I (for he was laced all over). *a* 1774 TUCKER *Lt. Nat.* (1834) II. 126 Clouds..whose tinselled edges glitter in the western sun.

**b.** *fig.* Having a flashy superficial splendour without intrinsic value.

1651 CLEVELAND *Poems* 4 His tinsil'd metaphors of pelf. 1820 HAZLITT *Lect. Dram. Lit.* 144 Beaumont and Fletcher ..laid the foundation of the artificial diction and tinselled pomp of the next generation.

**Tinselly** (ti·nsěli), *a.* [f. TINSEL *sb.*[3] + -Y.] Of the nature of, characterized by, or abounding in tinsel; hence, cheaply splendid or sparkling, gaudy without real worth, 'pinchbeck'.

1811 MISS MITFORD in L'Estrange *Life* (1870) I. v. 148 Sometimes pedantic, and sometimes tinselly, none of her works were ever simple..or natural. 1836 *Backwoods of Canada* 289 These Indians appear less addicted to gay and tinselly ornaments. 1885 *Athenæum* 15 Aug. 205 None of that false ornamentation, that tinselly glitter.

So **Ti·nselly** *adv.* [-LY [2]], showily and cheaply. 1864 in WEBSTER; whence in later Dicts.

**Tinselry** (ti·nsělri). [f. TINSEL *sb.*[3] + -RY.] Showy and tawdry material or ornamentation.

1830 S. WARREN *Diary Physic.* (1838) I. xiii. 258 The ghastly visage of Death, thus leering through the tinselry of passion,..was a horrible mockery of the fooleries of life! 1869 S. BOWLES *New West* xxvii. 518 The poor tinselry of the worship.

**Tinsen, -sin,** obs. corrupt forms of TINSEL *sb.*[3]

**Tinsey** (ti·nsi). Also 7 **tincy**, 8–9 **tinsy.** A popular corruption of TINSEL *sb.*[3]

1685 *Lond. Gaz.* No. 2001/4 A Groce of Gimp Lace mixt with Tincy. 1707 E. WARD *Hud. Rediv.* II. III. 10 Built for imaginary Princes To strut in Buskins and in Tinseys. 1771 SMOLLETT *Humph. Cl.* 15 May, I've shown him how little I minded his tinsy and his long tail. 1831 J. WILSON *Noct. Ambr.* Wks. 1856 III. 301 Ye think the peacock's harl and the tinsy hae slipped frae your jaws. 1889 STODDART *Angling Songs* 254 Awa' wi' yer tinsey sae braw!

**b.** *attrib.* or *adj.*; also in *Comb.*

1699 E. WARD *Lond. Spy* x. (1709) 237 The Quality of the Fair, strutting round their Balconies in their Tinsey Robes. 1704 F. FULLER *Med. Gymn.* (1718) 234 They clap a Saddle upon 'em, cover'd with a Sort of Tinsey Stuff. 1721 RAMSAY *Morning Interview* 162 His head reclin'd upon a tinsy roll. 1753 SMOLLETT *Ct. Fathom* (1784) 81/1 You come over like a walking atomy, with a rat's tail at your wig, and a tinsey jacket. 1828 *Blackw. Mag.* Sept. 298/1 [*Angling*] The yellow-bodied, tinsey-tailed, black-half-heckle.

**Tinsmith** (ti·n₁smiþ). [f. TIN + SMITH: cf. *goldsmith, silversmith*, etc.] A worker in tin; a maker of tin utensils; a whitesmith.

1858 SIMMONDS *Dict. Trade*, *Tinsmith*, a worker in tin. 1865 J. CAMERON *Malayan India* 61 These are..blacksmiths, tinsmiths, gunsmiths. 1892 LE CARON *25 Years Secr. Service* (1893) 303 Burke called at a tinsmith's shop, and asked the smith to solder up a box for him.

Hence **Ti·nsmi:thing** *vbl. sb.* [see -ING [1]], doing tinsmith's work; working in tin.

1897 *Westm. Gaz.* 15 Feb. 10/1 His occupation is that of a tinsmith in Leith, and one of his platform stories deals with the tinsmithing job that he was tackling when elected M.P. 1902 *Times* 14 July 12/5 The various industries.. included tinsmithing, carpentry, engineering.

**Ti·n-stone.** The most commonly occurring form of tin ore; cassiterite, native tin dioxide (peroxide). Also *attrib.*

1602 CAREW *Cornwall* 86 They discouer these workes, by certaine Tynne-stones, lying on the face of the ground. 1671 *Phil. Trans.* VI. 2098 Most Tin-stones are porous, not unlike great bones almost throughly calcined. 1805–17 R. JAMESON *Char. Min.* (ed. 3) 210 Annular tinstone..is a four sided prism, truncated on all the edges and angles. 1839 URE *Dict. Arts* 1241 There are only two ores of tin; the peroxide, or tin-stone, and tin pyrites. 1905 *Times* 11 Aug. 3/4 In the tinstone works of Malacca.

**Ti·n-stream.** Usually in *pl.* See quot. 1891, and cf. *stream tin* s. v. TIN *sb.* 1 b.

1855 J. R. LEIFCHILD *Cornwall Mines* 200 There is no regularity in these tin-streams, as they are of different breadths, though seldom less than a fathom. 1891 *Labour Commission* Gloss., A *tin streams* (not stream) deals either with alluvial deposits or with the refuse of the mines..and separates what is valuable..by washing processes.

So **Ti·n-strea:mer**, one who obtains tin from a deposit of sand or gravel by washing; **Ti·n-strea:ming**, the washing of tin from such a deposit.

1839 DE LA BECHE *Rep. Geol. Cornw.* etc. xiii. 405 Whole ground, as the tin-streamers term the stanniferous gravel and superincumbent beds which have not been previously disturbed by the old men. *Ibid.* xv. 545 Tin-streaming seems to have been conducted in Pryce's time much as it is at present. 1881 H. H. DRAKE in *Athenæum* 1 Oct. 432/3 Tin-streaming was a wealthy and influential industry, that enriched landlords, tenants, and 'bounders', who..set Acts at defiance. 1899 BARING-GOULD *Bk. of West* II. 83 This rubble has been turned over and over by tin-streamers.

**Tint** (tint), *sb.*[1] [app. altered from the earlier TINCT, which may already have been so pronounced; but It. *tinta* tint, hue, may have influenced the technical use in painting.]

**1.** A colour, hue, usually slight or delicate; a tinge; *esp.* one of the several lighter or deeper shades or varieties, or degrees of intensity, of the same colour: see quots. 1848–79 in sense 2.

1717 POPE *Epist. to Mr. Jervas* 5 Whether thy hand strike out some free design,..Or blend in beauteous tint the colour'd mass. 1754 GRAY *Pleasure* 42 Chastised by sabler tints of woe. 1798 WORDSW. *Thorn* v, Ah me! what lovely tints are there Of olive green and scarlet bright. 1834 MRS. SOMERVILLE *Connex. Phys. Sc.* xxxvi. 387 Exhibiting all the variety of tints that indicates the changes of combustion. 1838 T. THOMSON *Chem. Org. Bodies* 516 It is nearly colourless, having only a slight tint of yellow. 1878 DALE *Lect. Preach.* v. 128 Autumn tints of brown and gold.

**b.** *fig.* in various senses; *esp.* Quality, character, kind; a slight imparted or modifying character, a 'tinge' *of* something.

1760 STERNE *Serm.* xix, Each one lends it something of its own complexional tint and character. 1768 — *Sent. Journ.*, *Passport, Hotel at Paris*, Liberty!..No tint of words can spot thy snowy mantle. 1817 BYRON *Manfred* III. ii, Our inborn spirits have a tint of thee. 1825 JEFFERSON *Autobiog.* Wks. 1859 I. 114 His virtue was of the purest tint. 1901 *Empire Rev.* I. 369 In New South Wales..free trade was the dominant tint [at the election].

**2.** *spec.* **a.** *Painting*: see quots. *Middle tint, prime tint*: see MIDDLE *a.* 6, PRIME *a.* 9 a.

1753 HOGARTH *Anal. Beauty* xiii. 179 Light and shades.. become, as it were, our materials, of which 'prime tints' are the principal. By these I mean the fixed and permanent colours of each object, as the green of trees, &c. 1784 J. BARRY in *Lect. Paint.* v. (1848) 183 The middle tint, or intermediate passage between the two masses of light and dark. 1848 WORNUM *ibid.* 211 *note*, Although there are but three primitive colours, painters have nine. These are yellow, red, blue,..orange, purple, green,..russet, olive, citrine... All other gradations of colour are mere tints of the above; dark or light, according as they are mixed with black or white, or according to the proportions in which they are compounded. Thus the variety of tints is infinite. 1859 GULLICK & TIMBS *Paint.* 8 *note*, Tints differ from each other in being simply lighter or darker, but hues differ in colour. *Ibid.*, In ordinary usage, however, by 'tints' we frequently mean colours generally, and the word is often substituted for 'hues'. 1879 POLE in *Nature* 6 Nov. 15/2 *note*, In technical language mixtures of a colour with white are called *tints*, with black, *shades*.

**b.** *Engraving.* The effect produced by a series of fine parallel lines more or less closely drawn so as to produce an even and uniform shading.

*Crossed tint*, one produced by lines crossing at right angles. *Ruled tint*, one produced by a single series of parallel lines. *Safety tint*, that used on bills of exchange, cheques, etc., either as a ground of the whole surface, or specially on the parts which have to be completed in writing, as a security against alterations.

1880 *Print. Trades Jrnl.* XXXI. 6 Worked in black, and light tints, on a stone coloured paper.

**3.** *attrib.* and *Comb.*, as *tint work*; **tint-block**, a block of wood or metal hatched with fine parallel lines suitable for printing tints; **tint-drawing**, drawing in diluted shades of various colours, or in one colour so that the gradations are produced by washes of pigment; **tint-tool**, an implement used for hatching or graving a tint-block.

1869 *Eng. Mech.* 10 Dec. 298/3 Tint-tools. 1873 E. SPON *Workshop Receipts* Ser. I. 147/1 The parallel lines forming an even and uniform tint, as in the representation of a clear sky, are obtained by what is called the tint-tool. 1884 *St. James' Gaz.* 24 Oct. 7/1 Mr. Linton..draws an emphatic distinction between wood-cutting..and wood-engraving, or white-line tint-work. 1897 *Daily News* 23 Apr. 6/5 He..is seen to most advantage in tint works, such as the View over Romney Marsh.

**Tint**, *sb.*[2] *dial.* [Origin uncertain: perh. two different words.

In sense 1 *tint* may be a variant of *tent* dial., lit. 'trial', f. L. *tentare* to try. It is also possible that *tint* in sense 2, quot. 1886, has the same origin (quasi 'not a taste, not a trace'); but it is very doubtful whether this origin can be assumed for quot. *a* 1225.]

**1.** ? A trial, taste, touch; a foretaste; a trace, indication (*of* anything). *Sc.*

1768 ROSS *Helenore* III. 122 Great search for her was made, baith far an' near, But tint nor tryal never cud appear. 1878 W. THOM in *Whistle Binkie* (1890) II. 44 The half-ta'en kiss..Is, heaven kens, fu' sweet amen's, An' tints o' heaven here. 1887 *Suppl. to Jamieson*, *Tint*, proof, evidence, indication; forecast, foretaste; 'The beast's awa, and ye'll ne'er get tint or wittins o't'.

**2.** After negative: (Not) a bit, particle, atom.

[*a* 1225 *Leg. Kath.* 1254 Þæt nefde hare nan tunge to tauelin a tint wið.] 1886 ROSA MULHOLLAND *Marcella Grace* xii, We haven't had a tint o' milk these three days.

**Tint** (tint), *ppl. a.* Now only *Sc.* and *north. dial.* [pa. pple. of TINE *v.*[2]] Lost.

*a* 1340 HAMPOLE *Psalter* xvii. 18 Bot if ȝe lefe ȝoure syn and doe penaunce ȝe be tynt men. *c* 1375 *Sc. Leg. Saints* iii. (*Andreas*) 438 How þe tynt sawlis of al men War brocht to þe restorynge Of þe croice. *c* 1500 KENNEDY *Passion of Christ* 214 Lord and King, Send fra þe hevin the tynt man to recure. *a* 1584 MONTGOMERIE *Cherrie & Slae* 816 Tint tyme we may not get again. 1725 RAMSAY *Gentle Sheph.* III. iii, But we're nae sooner fools to give consent, Than we our daffin, and tint power repent.

**Tint** (tint), *v.* [f. TINT *sb.*[1]] *trans.* To impart a tint to; to colour, esp. slightly or with delicate shades; to tinge. Also *absol.*

1791 MRS. RADCLIFFE *Rom. Forest* i, The sun at length tinted the eastern clouds and the tops of the highest hills. 1833 J. RENNIE *Alph. Angling* 22 Silken or hempen lines may be tinted by a decoction of oak bark. 1860 TYNDALL *Glac.* I. xvi. 106 The sun..still tinted the clouds with red and purple. 1873 BLACK *Pr. Thule* xxvii, The beautiful colours of August tinting the great masses of rock. 1893 *Westm. Gaz.* 28 Feb. 3/1, I can't call him a painter at all. A man of marvellous imagination, a surprising flow of lovely fancies —but a painter, no! He merely tints.

*fig.* 1799 ANNA SEWARD *Sonn.* i. Poet. Wks. 1810 III. 122 No more young Hope tints with her light and bloom The darkening scene. 1861 HOLLAND *Less. Life* v. 72 All truth is tinted by the medium through which it passes.

**b.** *techn.* (See quot.)

1857 YOUMANS *Handbk. Househ. Sc.* § 161 By the addition of black the red is said to be shaded, by the addition of white it is tinted.

**c.** *intr.* for *pass.* To become tinted or coloured.

1892 *Pict. World* 7 May 32/3 The forced leaves..begin to tint in about three hours.

Hence **Ti·nted** *ppl. a.*, coloured, tinged, dyed; *tinted drawing* = tint-drawing: see TINT *sb.*[1] 3.

1821 CRAIG *Lect. Drawing* i. 15 Mr. Sandby..denominated this manner tinted drawing. 1831 WILLIAMS *Life & Corr. Sir T. Lawrence* II. 351 *note*, The tinted drawings of Lawrence are calculated to give the finest feelings to the imagination. 1852 THACKERAY *Esmond* II. xi, A face..like a tinted statue. 1905 *Daily Chron.* 8 May 8/5 Talking of make-up reminds me of what we now call 'tinted' hair.

**Tint**, obs. f. TENT *sb.*[4]; pa. t. of TINE *v.*[2]

**Ti·n-ta·ck.** A tack, or short light iron nail, coated with tin.

1840 DICKENS *Old C. Shop* xxviii, Mrs. Jarley served out the tin tacks from a linen pocket. 1887 G. R. SIMS *Mary Jane's Mem.* vii. 91 He had trodden on a tin-tack on the carpet, point up.

**Ti·ntage.** *rare.* [f. TINT *sb.*[1] + -AGE.] Tints in the mass; tinting.

1859 R. F. BURTON *Centr. Afr.* in *Jrnl. Geog. Soc.* XXIX. 213 The sight wearies with the unvarying tintage—all shining green and vivid blue.

**Tintamarre** (tintămā·r). Now *rare.* Forms: 6 **tyntamar**, 7 **tintamare, -marr, tintimare, -marre**, (**tinamar**), 7–8 **tintamar**, (9 **-mara, -merre, tintimar**), 7– **tintamarre.** [a. F. *tintamarre* (15th c.), of obscure origin: see suggestion in Littré.] A confused noise, uproar, clamour, racket, hubbub, clatter.

1567 FENTON *Trag. Disc.* 418, I leave you to judge what a tyntamar entred the head of therle. 1603 FLORIO *Montaigne* III. xiii. 644 Hee learnd and profited much by that hurly burly or tintimare. 1640 HOWELL *Dodona's Gr.* 64 He preservd Ampelona..without the least tintamarre or noise of commotion. 1705 VANBRUGH *Confed.* v. ii, But amongst all this tintamar, I don't hear a word of my hundred pounds. 1806–7 J. BERESFORD *Miseries Hum. Life, Post. Groans* xxiii, During its intolerable, indomitable, and interminable tintamara. 1834 H. GREVILLE *Diary* 21 Nov. (1883) 40 Such a *tintamarre* I never heard, but the audience were enthusiastic. 1901 *Academy* 28 Dec. 635/1 The just..praise he wishes to utter is forestalled by a tintimar of rash eulogy.

**Tintare**, obs. f. *tine-tare*: see TINE *sb.*[4] b.

**Tint-block, -drawing**, etc.: see TINT *sb.*[1] 3.

**Tinte**, obs. form of TENT *sb.*[4] (wine).

**Tintenaga, tintenagall**, erron. var. TUTENAG.

**Tinter** (ti·ntəɪ). [f. TINT *v.* + -ER [1].] One who or that which tints; now *esp.* an artist or painter skilful in tinting; *spec.* **b.** a tinted glass slide used with plain slides in a magic lantern; **c.** an instrument or machine for tinting or colouring paper or engraving tint-blocks.

**1823** BYRON *Juan* XIII. cxi, Good hours of fair cheeks are the fairest tinters. **1830** CUNNINGHAM *Brit. Painters* II. 181 He was a most splendid tinter, but no colourist. **1862** THORNBURY *Turner* I. 48 The tinters of backgrounds still survive. **1891** LEWIS WRIGHT *Optical Projection* viii. (1906) 122 Tinters may add very much to the pleasing effect of plain photographs, if used with suitable subjects.

† **Tinternel.** *Obs.* Also tyn-. [Origin unascertained. (Cf. F. *tinter* to ring.)] ? Some form of instrumental music. Hence † **Tinternelling** *a.*

**1575** GASCOIGNE *Adv. F. I.* Wks. 210 Calling the musitions [he] caused them softly to sounde the Tynternall. *Ibid.* 218 His Mistres could not be quiet vntill she heard hym repeat the Tinternell which he had vsed ouer night. *Ibid.*, She demanded secretly and in sad earnest, who deuised this Tinternell. **1593** NASHE *Christ's T.* (1613) 69 The Virgins on their loud tinternelling Timbrils .. should haue descanted on my praises. [**1847–78** HALLIWELL, *Tinternell*, the name of an old dance. (Hence in later Dicts. Authority for this statement is not given.)]

† **Tint for tant.** *Obs.* Also tint for taunt. [A reduplicated phrase with antithetic modification of the first member: cf. *tit for tat.* Probably altered from *taunt for* (*pour*) *taunt* (TAUNT *sb.*[1] 1).] Retaliation, retort in kind.

**1620** T. GRANGER *Div. Logike* 124 Regestion is commonly termed like for like, pin driuing out a pin, tint for taunt, &c. **1677** COLES *Eng.-Lat. Dict.* s.v. *Tint*, To give one tint for tant, *par pari referre*. **1710** (*title*) Tint for Taunt. The Manager Managed .. in Remarks .. upon a Sermon .. in .. St. Paul Covent-Garden .. by .. R. L. Lloyd. **1828** *Craven Gloss.* s. v., 'Tint for tant', a requital, similar to *tit for tat.*

**Tintiness**: see after TINTY *a.*

**Tinting** (ti·ntiŋ), *vbl. sb.* [f. TINT *v.* + -ING[1].] The action of TINT *v.*; the result of this; tint or tints; colouring. Also *attrib.*; **tinting-tool** = *tint-tool* (TINT *sb.*[1] 3).

**1853** KANE *Grinnell Exp.* ix. (1856) 64 The water and the sky .. had a pearly or ash-colored tinting. **1856** E. CAPERN *Poems, Gentle Annie*, Scarce fifteen rosy years had left Their tintings on her cheek. **1879** ATCHERLEY *Boërland* 72 In colour it is very pleasing, the ground tinting being a cinnamon brown.

**Tintinnabulant** (tintinæ·biŭlănt), *a.* [f. as next + -ANT[1].] Ringing or tinkling as a small bell; jingling. (This and the allied words all pedantic.)

**1812** H. & J. SMITH *Rej. Addr., Johnson's Ghost*, That ligneous barricado .. decorated with frappant and tintinnabulant appendages. **1865** *Daily Tel.* 12 June, The tintinnabulant fancies of an Edgar Poe.

**Tintinnabular** (tintinæ·biŭlăɹ), *a.* [f. L. *tintinnābul-um* bell + -AR.] = next.

**1767** S. PATERSON *Another Trav.* I. 392 The vulgar tintinnabular art of pulling ropes. **1835** *Fraser's Mag.* XII. 97 He seems .. to sympathise with the bell-ringer in his tintinnabular enthusiasm. **1856** 'C. BEDE' *Tales College Life* 57 He threw down the [morning paper], and immediately responded to the tintinnabular call.

**Tintinnabulary** (tintinæ·biŭlări), *a.* (*sb.*) [f. as prec. + -ARY[1]. Cf. med.L. *tintinnābulārius* 'bell-man' (*Oxford Laudian Statutes*).] Of or pertaining to bells or bell-ringing; of the nature of a bell; characterized by bell-ringing.

**1787** G. COLMAN *Prose Sev. Occas., Let. fr. Lexiphanes* Gloss., *Ding-dong*, Tintinabulary chimes, used metaphorically to signify dispatch and vehemence. **1839** *New Monthly Mag.* LVII. 131 That truly tintinnabulary peculiarity of the British nation, the 'half-hour bell'. **1886** T. FROST *Country Jrnlist.* 101 The boy who responded promptly to the tintinnabulary summons.

**b.** *sb.* A bell-ringer.

**1825** *New Monthly Mag.* XIV. 494 Sacred, but at the same time thoughtless tintinnabularies.

**Tintinnabulate** (tintinæ·biŭlĕt), *a. rare.* [ad. L. *tintinnābulāt-us* furnished with a bell or bells, f. *tintinnābulum* bell: see -ATE[2] 2.] Bell-shaped.

**1874** RUSKIN *Val D'Arno* i. § 22 (1886) 13 How that tintinnabulate roof differs from the dome of the Pantheon.

So **Tintinna·bulate** *v.*, *intr.* to ring, tinkle.

**1906** *Daily Chron.* 4 Sept. 4/4 For some days past .. the ox-bells have clinked and tintinnabulated.

**Tintinnabulation** (tintinæbiŭlē·ʃən). [n. of action f. L. *tintinnābulum* bell: see -ATION.] A ringing of a bell or bells, bell-ringing; the sound or music so produced.

**1831** POE *Bells* i, Keeping time .. To the tintinabulation that so musically swells From the bells. **1883** READE in *Harper's Mag.* Jan. 259/1 All this tintinnabulation .. gratified Vladimir's vanity.

**Tintinnabulatory** (tintinæ·biŭlătəri), *a.* [f. as TINTINNABULATE *a.* + -ORY.] = TINTINNABULARY.

**1827** W. G. S. *Excurs. Vill. Curate* 129 Tapster of the tintinnabulatory *cerevisiarum, vulgo* ale-house. **1880** *Daily Tel.* 10 Dec. 5/3 A clause authorising the tintinnabulatory 'promulgation' of muffins.

**Tintinnabule.** *humorous nonce-wd.* [ad. L. *tintinnābul-um.*] A bell.

**1834** *Fraser's Mag.* IX. 711 The tintinnabule .. brought to my hand the promised jug of bubbling water.

**Tintinna·bulism.** *nonce-wd.* [f. as prec. + -ISM.] The art or practice of bell-ringing. So **Tintinna·bulist**, a professional bell-ringer.

**1826** *New Monthly Mag.* XVI. 474 An Armenian mass, with all its 'tintinabulism', and nasal singing, and 'incondite music'. **1830** *Fraser's Mag.* II. 450 An army of red-coated tintinnabulists are called for to remind the greasy citizens of the time.

**Tintinnabulous** (tintinæ·biŭləs), *a.* [f. L. *tintinnābul-um*: see next and -OUS.] Characterized by or pertaining to bell-ringing.

**1791–3** in *Spirit Pub. Jrnls.* (1799) I. 225 Tintinnabulous Intrepidity, or scenes of bell-ringing. **1822–56** DE QUINCEY *Confess.* (1862) 214, I, with many others who suffered from his tintinnabulous propensities. **1897** F. THOMPSON *Poems, New Year's Chimes*, Tintinnabulous, tuned to ring A multitudinous-single thing, Rung all in rhyme.

‖ **Tintinnabulum** (tintinæ·biŭlɒm). Pl. **-a.** [L., a bell, f. *tintinnā-re* to ring, clink, jingle + *-bulum*, suffix of instrument.] A small tinkling bell. Also *fig.* **b.** See quot. 1877.

[**1398** TREVISA *Barth. De P. R.* XIX. cxxviii. (1495) 935 Tintinabulum is the belle that is often hangyd abowte the neckes of houndes & fete of foules and byrdes.] **1597** *1st Pt. Return fr. Parnass.* v. i. 1465 Thoue whorsonn tintunabulum, thou that art the scorne of all good witts. **1782** COWPER *Table-t.* 529 Beating alternately, in measured time, The clockwork tintinnabulum of rhyme. **1877** KNIGHT *Dict. Mech.*, *Tintinnabulum*, a musical instrument of percussion, consisting of a number of bells suspended in a frame.

† **Ti·ntinnate**, *v. Obs. rare*—°. [f. ppl. stem of L. *tintinnāre* to ring: see -ATE[3] 5.] *intr.* To ring, as a bell; to tinkle. Hence † **Tintinna·tion** *Obs. rare*—°, a ringing, a tinkling.

**1623** COCKERAM, *Tintinate*, to ring like a bell. **1658** PHILLIPS, *Tintinnation*, a ringing like a bell.

**Tintist** (ti·ntist). [f. TINT *sb.*[1] + -IST 4.] One skilled in tinting, a tinter; one who prefers tinting to colouring.

**1890** *Univ. Rev.* May 32 There are the camps of the colourists and the tintists.

**Tintless** (ti·ntlės), *a.* [f. TINT *sb.*[1] + -LESS.] Having no tint or tints; devoid of colour.

**1789** E. DARWIN *Bot. Gard.* I. 491 The Adept .. Shades with pellucid clouds the tintless field. **1813** T. BUSBY *Lucretius* I. II. 811 Tintless themselves, no colours seeds unfold. **1878** *Fraser's Mag.* XVIII. 767 The blue heaven, as we rise into it, is mere tintless air.

† **Tinto** (ti·nto), *sb.*[1] *Obs.* [a. Sp. *tinto* tinted, deep-coloured, in *vino tinto* 'a blackish wine in Spaine' (Minsheu).] Tent wine; = TENT *sb.*[4] Also the name of a French wine: see quot. 1833.

**1599** MINSHEU *Sp. Dict., Dial.* 6 Which will you haue Sir, Sack or Tinto [Sp. *blanco o tinto*]? *Marg.*, Tinto is a wine in Spaine red and blackish. **1833** C. REDDING *Wines* (1851) 138 In the arrondissement of Montelimart [in France] .. there is a vineyard .. in the commune of Rochegude, and the wine produced there, called Tinto, sells for a hundred francs the hectolitre. **1858** SIMMONDS *Dict. Trade, Tinto*, a red Madeira wine, wanting the high aroma of the white sorts; and, when old, resembling tawny port.

† **Tinto** (ti·nto), *a.* and *sb.*[2] *Obs.* [a. It. *tinto* dyed, tinted; a dye.] *adj.* Tinted; *sb.* a tint: see quots.

**1686** AGLIONBY *Painting Illustr.* Explan. Terms, *Tinto*, is, when a thing is done only with one Colour, and that generally Black. **1739** ELIZ. CARTER *Algarotti on 'Newton's Theory'* (1742) I. 203 You will see Colours and half Tintos appear.

**Tintometer** (tintǫ·mĭtəɹ). [f. TINT *sb.*[1] + -OMETER.] An apparatus for the exact determination of colour: see quots., and cf. COLORIMETER.

**1889** *Daily News* 9 May 5/7 Royal Society Soiree ... Mr. J. W. Lovibond, of Salisbury, exhibited an instrument called the Tintometer, an invention which, by means of numberless slips of coloured glasses, measures colour blindness and differences of colour vision between the two eyes. **1895** *Westm. Gaz.* 11 Nov. 3/1 The inventor of a tintometer has told us recently that he can account for 60,000,000 shades of colour. **1898** *Allbutt's Syst. Med.* V. 433 With the tintometer .. three sets of definitely graded glasses are provided.

Hence **Tintome·tric** *a.*, of or pertaining to a tintometer; **Tinto·metry**, the use of a tintometer.

**1901** *Buck's Handbk. Med. Sc.* II. 58 Dark Box for Estimating Percentage of Hæmoglobin by the Tintometric Method. **1909** *Cent. Dict. Suppl.*, Tintometry.

**Tint-tool**: see TINT *sb.*[1]

† **Ti·ntregh.** *Obs.* Forms: 1 tintreȝ, -a, tinterȝ, 3 tintreo, -he, tintreow. [OE. *tintreg* str. neut., *tintrega* wk. masc. The second element is the same as in OE. *trega*, ON. *tregi* wk. masc., Goth. *trigo* wk. fem., grief, woe, affliction, OE. *tregian*, ON. *trega*, OS. *tregan* to grieve, afflict. The first part is uncertain; Sievers, on metrical grounds, holds the vowel to be long, *tīntrega.*] Torment, torture.

*c* **893** K. ÆLFRED *Oros.* I. xii. § 4 Þonne he þara manna tintreȝo oferhierde. *c* **950** *Lindisf. Gosp.* Matt. x. 28 Ða sauel & lic-homa losiȝe *vel* fordoa in tinterȝo *vel* cursung. — Luke xvi. 23 In helle ahof ða eȝo his miððy were in tinterȝum. *c* **1000** *Ags. Gosp.*, *ibid.*, Þa he on þam tintreȝum wæs. *a* **1023** WULFSTAN *Hom.* xl. (Napier) 185 In þa ecan tintreȝu. *a* **1225** *Leg. Kath.* 41 Wið stronge tintreohen & licomliche pinen. *a* **1225** *Juliana* 18 For teone ne for tintreow þat ȝe mahen timbrin. *a* **1240** *Sawles Warde* in *Cott. Hom.* 261 Eorðliche tintreohen.

Hence † **Ti·ntreghe** (in 2 **tintraȝen**) *v. trans.*, to torment, torture.

*c* **1175** *Lamb. Hom.* 13 Swa þet heo eow tintraȝed and heow iswenchet.

**Tinty** (ti·nti), *a.* [f. TINT *sb.*[1] + -Y.] Full of tints; having the tints too prominent or inharmoniously combined. Hence **Ti·ntiness.**

**1883** *Athenæum* 2 June 705/2 The prevalence of tinty colouring, thinness of tone, and lack of solidity .. is still observable among the members' works. **1886** *Ibid.* 18 Sept. 377 What painters call tintiness when they observe that the brilliancy of local tints severally affects their harmony and the tertiaries are weak.

**Tin-type** (ti·nˌtəip). *Photogr.* [f. TIN *sb.* + TYPE.] A photograph taken as a positive on a thin tin plate: cf. FERROTYPE 2. Also *attrib.* Hence **Ti·n-typer**, a photographer who takes tin-types.

**1875** KNIGHT *Dict. Mech.* 1684/2 Ferrotypes, or tintypes, as they are sometimes called. **1889** *Anthony's Photogr. Bull.* II. 173 Having dallied with our very attractive art since the early days of tintypes. **1892** STEVENSON & L. OSBOURNE *Wrecker* iii. 43 The trade of a tin-typer proved too narrow for the lad's ambition. **1894** *Brit. Jrnl. Photogr.* XLI. 68 The tin-type man still continues to employ collodion.

**Tin-vat** to **Tin-work**: see TIN *sb.* 5.

**Tin-worm**: see TIN *sb.* 5 and TINE-WORM.

**Tiny** (təi·ni), *a.* (*sb.*) Compared **tinier, -iest.** Also 6 **tynie**, 7 **tyny, tiney, -ye**, 9 *dial.* **teeny.** [app. f. TINE *a.* and *sb.* + -Y (? after adjs. in -y).

But some would take *tiny* as a later spelling of '*tinē*, assumed as the original form of *tine*: see Note to TINE *a.*]

Very small, little, or slight; wee, minute.

(In early use usually, and still often, preceded by *little*.)

**1598** TOFTE *Alba* (1880) 21 Yet still (me thinkes) mine Ayme, being not base, I should deserue some little tynie Grace. **1599** NASHE *Lenten Stuffe* 4 A patterne or tiny sample [*printed* tiny-sample] what my elaborate performance would bee in this case, had I a ful-sayld gale of prosperity to encourage mee. [**1656** BLOUNT *Glossogr.*, *Tiney* (a word used in Worcestershire and thereabouts, as a *little tiney*).] **1664** COTTON *Scarron.* 97 This Cupid was a little tyny, Cogging, Lying, Peevish Nynny. **1677** *Man of Sin* II. v. 93 In what part of the World are such Tiny Crustlings used for Bread? **1691** RAY *N. C. Words*, *Tiny*, puny, little: it is usually joyned with 'little' as an intensive: so they say, a little tiny thing. **1740–6** MRS. DELANY in *Life & Corr.* (1861) III. 31, I told you I was to have a tiny ball on Monday. **1812** J. WILSON *Isle of Palms* I. 63 The tiniest boat that ever sailed Upon an inland lake. **1858** LYTTON *What will he do* I. vi, On that knee she clasped her tiny hands. **1879** AGNES GIBERNE *Sun, Moon & Stars* II. i. (1880) 115 Examination with the microscope only shows tinier and yet tinier wonders of form and life. **1887** *Poor Nellie* (1888) 168 Adela had of late been one tiny bit exacting towards George.

**B.** as *sb.*

† **1.** A very small amount: = TINE *sb.*[6] (perh. only a copyist's error for this.) *Obs. rare*—[1].

*a* **1650** *Lord of Learne* 272 in Furniv. *Percy Folio* I. 192 Thou hast striken the Lord of learne a litle tinye aboue the knee.

**2.** A tiny one, a very small child, an infant. Usu. in pl. *tinies* (cf. *grown-ups*).

**1863** 'HOLME LEE' *Annie Warleigh* II. 270 The little ones .. marshalled by the infant class mistress, and by Alice who was a clever manager amongst the very tinies. **1883** *Sword & Trowel* Jan. 37 Sure to please the growing tinies. **1883** G. MEREDITH *Love in Valley* xxii, When she was a tiny.

**Tinyness**, obs. form of TININESS.

**-tion**, a compound suffix, representing, often through Fr. *-tion*, OF. *-cion*, ME. *-cio(u)n*, L. *-tio*, *-tiōn-em*, consisting of *-io*, *-ion-em* added to the *-t* of a L. participial stem, as in *rela-t-ion, comple-t-ion, frui-t-ion, muni-t-ion, protec-t-ion, deten-t-ion, op-t-ion*: see -ATION and -ION. Rarer forms are *-sion*, *-xion*, as *suspen-s-ion, infle-x-ion.* The etymological meaning was primarily 'the state or condition of being (what the pa. pple. imports)', e. g. the condition of being *related, completed, protected, detained, suspended, inflected*, etc. But already in L. *-tio* was used for the action or process of *relating, completing, suspending*, etc., and also concretely or quasi-concretely, as in *dictio*, the condition of being said, the saying of something, a saying, a word; so *nātio* birth, a brood, a nation; *ōrātio* mode of speaking, an oration. In Eng. the most usual sense is that of a noun of action, equivalent to the native ending -ING[1], and having also the kindred uses mentioned under that suffix.

**-tious**, compound suffix, repr. L. *-t-iōsus*, consisting of *-iōsus*, -IOUS, appended to the *-t* of a L. participial stem. It thus serves to form adjectives belonging to sbs. in *-tion*, as in *ostentation, -tious, ambition, -tious, caution, -tious, contention, -tious, nutrition, -tious, superstition, -tious*; but its range is much narrower than that of *-tion.*

**Tip** (tip), *sb.*[1] Forms: 5–6 **typpe, typ**, 6–7 **tippe**, 7 **tipp**; 6– **tip.** [In 15th c. *typ, typpe*, the former = MLG., MDu., LG., Du., EFris. *tip*, MHG. *zipf*, Da., Norw. *tip*, Sw. *tipp*, all = 'point, extreme end, very top'. Not known in OE., ON., OS., or OHG.; but perhaps cognate with *tip(p)en*, TIP *v.*[1], though the connexion of sense is not clear. The modern cognate langs. have in the same sense a derivative form:—**tippul*, MDu., Du., MLG., LG. *tippel*, MHG., Ger. *zipfel*.

(So far as is known, *tip* has no etymological connexion with *top*; but the proximity of form and relative quality of sound in the two words have caused *tip* to be felt as denoting a thinner or more delicate *top*; cf. *drip, drop, chip, chop*, also TIP-TOP.)]

**1.** The slender extremity or top of a thing; *esp.* the pointed or rounded end of anything long and slender; the top, summit, apex, very end.

(The earlier existence of the sb. is evidenced by the derivs. *tipping c* 1325, *tipped* or *tipt* and *tip-toe c* 1386.)

*c* 1440 *Promp. Parv.* 494/2 Typpe, or lappe [*MS. S.* typ or lap] of the ere, *pinnula*. *Ibid.*, Typ, of the nese. **1526** TINDALE *Luke* xvi. 24 Sende Lazarus that he maye depe the tippe off his fynger in water and cole my tonge. **1535** COVERDALE 1 *Sam.* xxiv. 4 Dauid stode vp, & cut of the typpe of Sauls garment quyetly. **1568** C. WATSON *Polyb.* 68 This hill..hauing a plain on yͤ very tippe, twelue miles in compasse. **1582** STANYHURST *Æneis* I. (Arb.) 21 In typs of billows soom ships wyth danger ar hanging. **1613-16** W. BROWNE *Brit. Past.* I. ii. 30 Where the Raine-bow in the Horizon Doth pitch her tips. **1634** SIR T. HERBERT *Trav.* 8 The Pole-star..in the tip of the little Beares taile. **1753** FRANKLIN *Lett.*, etc. Wks. 1840 VI. 179 That spout..was an inverted cone, with the tip or apex towards the sea. **1844** STEPHENS *Bk. Farm* II. 175 The tip of the horn is used by the makers of knife-handles. **1875** DARWIN *Insectiv. Pl.* xii. 280 Long narrow leaves gradually widening towards their tips. **1881** — in *Life & Lett.* (1887) I. 98 How many and what admirably well adapted movements the tip of a root possesses.

† **b.** *fig.* Utmost point, extremity; highest point, apex, crown. *Obs.* (Cf. also TIPE *sb.*[1])

*a* **1225** *Ancr. R.* 338 On oðer half, moni mon abit to schriuen him uort þe nede tippe. [But this may be TIP *v.*[1] 1.] **1567** HARMAN *Caveat* (1869) 20 Not one amongst twenty wyll discouer, eyther declare there scelorous secretes: yet with fayre flatteringe wordes, money, and good chere, I haue attained to the typ by such as the meanest of them hath wandred these xiii. yeares. **1581** RICH *Farewell* (Shaks. Soc.) 47 From the tippe and heeght of degnitie, you have not spared..to become a subject of all mishaps. **1581** MULCASTER *Positions* xxxix. (1887) 220 The prince and soueraigne being the tippe of nobilitie. **1626** B. JONSON *Staple of N.* II. v, He is..my Chiefe, the Point, Tip, Top, and Tuft of all our family.

† **c.** Old name for an anther, or summit of a stamen. Cf. APEX 6 a. *Obs.*

**1776** WITHERING *Brit. Plants* (1787) I. 133 *Polycarpon.* Allseed...Chives 3...Tips roundish. **1807** CRABBE *Par. Reg.* I. 619 Esteemed of old but tips and chives.

**2.** A small piece of metal, leather, etc., attached or fitted on to something so as to form a serviceable end; as the buckle of a girdle (*obs.*), a ferrule, the leather pad on the point of a billiard-cue, a protecting cap or plate for the toe of a shoe, etc.

*c* **1440** *Promp. Parv.* 494/2 Typpe, of a gyrdylle, *mordaculum*. **1545** *Rates of Customs* c viij, Typpes for hornes the C. III. d. **1570** LEVINS *Manip.* 140/16 Yͤ Tippe of a staffe, *ferretum*. **1801** SOUTHEY *Thalaba* VI. xvi, There hung a horn beside the gate,..He took the ivory tip, And through the brazen-mouth he breath'd. **1873** BENNETT & CAVENDISH *Billiards* 9 About 1807 the leathern tip [of the cue] was invented. **1877** KNIGHT *Dict. Mech.*, *Tip*...3. (*Shoemaking.*) A protecting cap at the toe end of a shoe. 4. The nozzle of a gas-burner. 5. A ferrule; as the tip of a bayonet scabbard. **1878** JEVONS *Prim. Pol. Econ.* 15 The metal iridium..is wanted for making the tips of gold pens.

**b.** *Costume.* The end of a tail of fur, or of a feather, as used in trimming, etc.

**1681** *Lond. Gaz.* No. 1649/8 A large Muff of Sable Tipps for a Woman. **1886** *Cassell's Encycl. Dict.*, *Tip*...3. *Millinery*: The end of a feather in trimming. **1904** *Daily News* 25 Mar. 7 Her hat was set at an alarming angle, and its nodding 'tips' followed her every movement.

**c.** *Angling.* The topmost joint of a fishing-rod.

**1891** *Cent. Dict.* s. v., A tip made of split bamboo is called a quarter-section tip, and by English makers a rent and glued tip. **1895** *Outing* (U.S.) XXX. 431/1 Putting the bait tip on a ten-ounce split bamboo, I tied a spoon and a flight of swivels to the line.

**d.** *Hat-making.* The upper part of the crown of a hat; a stiff lining pasted in this part.

**1864** WEBSTER, *Tip*,..5. The lining of the top of a hat;—so called among hatters. **1877** KNIGHT *Dict. Mech.*, *Tip*... A circular piece of scale or paste board pasted on the inside of a hat crown to stiffen it.

**3.** A thin flat brush, made of camel's or squirrel's hair (originally the tip of a squirrel's tail) fixed between two pieces of cardboard glued together, used for laying gold-leaf, as in bookbinding; also, a piece of wood covered with flannel, similarly used.

**1815** J. SMITH *Panorama Sc. & Art* II. 801 The instruments used in gilding are the following: A cushion...A knife...The tip, which consists of a squirrel's tail with the hairs cut short. It is used for taking up whole leaves of gold, and applying them to the surface to be gilt. **1837** WHITTOCK *Bk. Trades* (1842) 117 (Carver and Gilder) The brush with which the gold is applied to the work; this is called a tip, and is formed by putting a few fine hairs between two pieces of card. **1888** *Arts & Crafts Catal.* 85 Finally, the gold (gold leaf) is applied by a pad of cotton wool, or a flat thin brush called a 'tip'.

**4. a.** A light horse-shoe, covering only the front half of the hoof. **b.** = FOOTHOLD 2.

**1831** J. HOLLAND *Manuf. Metal* I. 172 On turning horses out to grass, it is common to remove their heavy shoes, and furnish them with light ones, or tips as they are called. **1903** *U.S. Dept. of Agr., Spec. Rep. Dis. Horse* 404 A shoe, called a 'tip', is made by cutting off both branches at the center of the foot and drawing the ends down to an edge. The tapering of the branches should begin at the toe.

**5.** Phrases. **a.** *From tip to toe*: from top to bottom (more usually *from top to toe*: see TOP *sb.*). † **b.** *In the tip of the mode*: in the height of fashion (cf. 1 b). † **c.** *Neither tip nor toe*: not a particle or trace, none at all. **d.** *On* (or *at*) *the tip of one's tongue*: on the point of being, or ready to be, spoken. So (rarely) *at the tips of one's fingers*, ready to be performed or executed.

**1610** HOLLAND *Camden's Brit.* I. 520 There is neither tippe nor toe remaining in it [Leicester] of the name Ratæ. **1709** *Brit. Apollo* II. No. 79. 2/2 She..will always be in the Tip of the Mode. **1722** DE FOE *Moll Flanders* (1840) 184 She had arguments at the tip of her tongue. **1823** LOCKHART *Reg. Dalton* VIII. vii, Out with the word, man—it's on the tip. **1853** KANE *Grinnell Exp.* xxx. (1856) 263, I give in detail my dress...Here it is, from tip to toe. **1859** W. COLLINS *Q. of Hearts* i, All the modern accomplishments at the tips of her delicate fingers.

**6.** *attrib.* and *Comb.*, as *tip-drip*, *-eared* adj., *-end* (also *fig.*: cf. 1 b); **tip-foot**, a form of club-foot in which the heel is drawn up; **tip-paper**, a stiff kind of paper used for lining hat-crowns (cf. 2 d); **tip-stretcher**, an apparatus for stretching hat-crowns; **tip-worm**, the larva of a gall-fly (*Cecidomyia vaccinii*) which infests the buds of the American cranberry (*Cent. Dict.*).

**1895** MRS. PHELPS *Chapters fr. Life* vi. 116 How dainty was the *tip-drip of the icicles from the big elm-bough. **1880** *Mem. J. Legge* 258 Is man..the derivative of tailed and *tip-eared progenitors? **1680** MOXON *Mech. Exerc.* x. 179 The *Tip-end of an Horn with its Tip downwards. **1803** FESSENDEN *Poet. Petition* 6 Discover'd worlds within the pale Of tip end of a tadpole's tail. **1885** *Century Mag.* XXIX. 190/2, I mean to flirt with him to the very tip end of my powers. **1857** DUNGLISON *Med. Lex.* s. v. *Kyllosis*, *Talipes equinus*,..*Tip-foot. **1877** KNIGHT *Dict. Mech.*, **Tip-paper*, a variety of paper of a rigid quality, made for lining the tips or insides of hat-crowns. *Ibid.* s. v., Eickemeyer's power *tip-stretcher is shown in Fig. 6470.

**Tip**, *sb.*[2] Also 5 tippe. [app. f. TIP *v.*[1]] An act of tipping, a light but distinct impact, blow, stroke, or hit; a noiseless tap; a significant touch. † *Tip for tap* = tit for tat: see TIT *sb.*[2], and cf. *tap for tap* in quot. 1597 s. v. TAP *sb.*[2] 1. *Foul tip* (Baseball), a foul hit in which the ball is only grazed: cf. FOUL *a.* 14.

*a* **1466** CHAS. DK. ORLEANS *Poems* (Roxb.) 7 Strokis grete, not tippe nor tapp. **1575** GASCOIGNE *Adv. F. I.* Wks. II. 249 Much greater is the wrong that rewardeth euill for good, than that which requiteth [*pr.* requireth] tip for tap. **1577** tr. *Bullinger's Decades* (1592) 154 Not to bragge of any thing ouer arrogantly, not to answere tip for tap [L. *non responsare*]. **1608** WILLET *Hexapla Exod.* 488 He that abused his parents.., that gaue them but a tip, or a reuiling word. *a* **1825** FORBY *Voc. E. Anglia*, *Tip*,..a smart but light blow. **1844** STEPHENS *Bk. Farm* II. 695 A smart tip of the whip will take the courage out of him. **1889** *Century Mag.* Oct. 837/1 Wont to wear a small piece of rubber in the mouth as a protection to the teeth from foul tips.

**Tip**, *sb.*[3] [f. TIP *v.*[4] sense 2 (which occurs *c* 1700).] A small present of money given to an inferior, esp. to a servant or employee of another for a service rendered or expected; a gratuity, a douceur: see TIP *v.*[4] 2.

**1755** J. BAREBONES in *Connoisseur* No. 70. 417, I assure you I have laid out every farthing..in tips to his servants. **1812** J. H. VAUX *Flash Dict.* s. v., To *take the tip*, is to receive a bribe in any shape; and they say of a person who is known to be corruptible, that he will *stand the tip*. **1818** *Sporting Mag.* II. 165 A handsome tip was demanded at the gate. **1825** T. HOOK *Sayings* Ser. II. *Doubts & F.* i, Sir Harry was liberal in his 'tips', and consequently a great favourite of Phillips [the waiter]. **1855** THACKERAY *Newcomes* xvi, What money is better bestowed than that of a schoolboy's tip? **1877** BLACK *Green Past.* xxx, Two sovereigns was the least tip to be slipped into the hands of the custom-house officer. *Mod.* The porter will expect a tip.

**b.** *attrib.* and *Comb.*

**1813** *Sporting Mag.* XLI. 106 The tip-money, or usual fee to the purchaser's coachman, upon the sale of horses. **1899** MORROW *Bohem. Paris* 149 After the bill is paid, the tip-box is supposed to receive two sous for Marie and Augustine.

**Tip**, *sb.*[4] *colloq.* or *slang.* [perh. from TIP *v.*[1], with the notion of tipping or lightly touching the arm or elbow of a person by way of a private hint, or from TIP *v.*[4] in the phrase *to tip* (any one) *a wink*.]

A piece of useful private or special information communicated by an expert; a friendly hint; *spec.* 'an advice concerning betting or a Stock-Exchange speculation intended to benefit the recipient' (Farmer *Slang*); also, a hint as to special points thought likely to come up in an examination; hence *transf.* a special device, 'wrinkle', 'dodge'. Also *attrib.*

The simple word was prob. in use before 1845.

**1845** *Athenæum* Oct. 964/2 Xenophon's Expedition of Cyrus, Books i. ii. iii. Translated literally...Of such books as this ('tip-books' as school-boys call them,)..we doubt the value. **1865** *Daily Tel.* 4 Dec. 4/4 Dejected prophets who have never yet made a single lucky political 'tip'. **1867** F. FRANCIS *Angling* i. (1880) 44 A tip from a good man on the spot is most useful. **1868** *Morning Star* 10 Mar., The evil of cramming and of 'tips' will be increased by the new scheme, instead of being diminished. **1886** *Q. Rev.* July 175 To keep the Foreign Office promptly supplied with every commercial 'tip' that can be of use to British trade. **1888** ANNIE S. SWAN *Doris Cheyne* i, My father was a stockbroker, and he taught me all the tips he knew. **1899** T. M. ELLIS *Three Cat's-eye Rings* 21 Offering her good tips for sporting events. *Mod.* A successful crammer, clever at giving 'tips' for an examination.

**b.** *The straight tip*: see quots.

**1871** *Punch* 26 Aug. 78/2 Honest advice as to wagering will henceforth be known as the straight tip. **1873** *Slang Dict.* s. v., The 'straight tip' is the tip which comes direct from the owner or trainer of a horse. Of late years a 'straight tip' means a direct hint on any subject. **1879** MISS BRADDON *Clov. Foot* xxxviii, That's a kind of thing we never tell. We got the straight tip; that's all you need know. **1894** DOYLE *S. Holmes* 7 Let me have the straight tip and you won't be a loser.

**c.** *transf.* Something with respect to which a 'tip' is given; e. g. the probable winner in a race.

**1873** BESANT & RICE *Little Girl* II. xxiii, He had on some ..occasions taken a long shot, backed a tip or a fancy. **1886** *St. Stephen's Rev.* 13 Mar. 11/2 Florin [racehorse], who was a great tip, performed most moderately.

**d.** *To miss one's tip*: orig. in circus slang (see quot. 1897); hence, to fail in one's aim or object.

**1854** DICKENS *Hard T.* I. vi, Jupe [a circus clown] has missed his tip very often, lately...Was short in his leaps and bad in his tumbling...In a general way that's missing his tip. **1857** HUGHES *Tom Brown* I. iv, One..runs right at the leaders, as though he'd ketch 'em by the heads, only luck'ly for him he misses his tip, and comes over a heap o' stones first. **1887** W. WESTALL *Two Millions* xx. I. 175 One of those fellows who have missed their tip somehow, and come down in life. **1897** BARRÈRE & LELAND *Dict. Slang*, *To miss the tip*, (circus),..in exhibitions it has a special application to the performer not understanding or catching the tip or word which indicates that he must act.

**e.** *Comb.*, *tip-book*: see quot. 1845 above.

**Tip**, *sb.*[5] [f. TIP *v.*[2], esp. senses 1 b, 2, 3.]

**I.** *Skittles.* (Cf. TIP *v.*[2] 1 b.)

† **1.** The knocking over of a pin by another which falls or rolls against it, as distinct from knocking one down by the immediate impact of the bowl. In some forms of the game applied also to other modes of knocking down, distinct from bowling.

**1673** [R. LEIGH] *Transp. Reh.* 54 Down they [nine-pins] all come at a tip and throw. **1694** S. JOHNSON *Notes Past. Let. Bp. Burnet* I. 39 That is a cleaverer Tip..than taking out the Middle Pin, and throwing down none of the rest. **1773** A. JONES (*title*) The Art of Playing at Skittles... Shewing Both the Old and the New Methods of forming General Goes and Tips. *Ibid.* 20 The greatest go that can be had is 40, or 20 at the bowl and the same at the tip; the least go must be 1.

(*b*) **1801** STRUTT *Sports & Past.* III. vii. § 10 Dutch-pins. The player first stands at a certain distance from the frame, and throws his bowl at the pins..; afterwards he approaches the frame and makes his tipp by casting the bowl among the pins. **1819** *Pantologia* X. s. v. *Skittles*, The bowler must stand to take his tip with one foot upon the spot where the bowl stopped.

**II.** The act of tilting and derived uses.

**2.** An act of tipping up or tilting, or the fact of being tilted; inclination. (Cf. TIP *v.*[2] 2.)

**1849** CUPPLES *Green Hand* viii. (1856) 72 Back again it [a shark] came..towards us, till it sank with a light tip, and a circle or two on the blue water. **1862** GROVE *Corr. Phys. Forces* (ed. 4) 138 The 'tip', or the raising of the weight, is performed by the electrical repulsion and attraction. *Mod.* Give the cask a slight tip.

**3.** A place or erection where wagons or trucks of coal, etc. are tipped and their contents discharged into the hold of a vessel, or into a cart, etc. **b.** A wagon or truck from which coal, etc. is tipped; short for *tip-cart*, *tip-car* (*Cent. Dict.*). (Cf. TIP *v.*[2] 3.)

**1862** *Castlemaine* (Australia) *Daily News* 2 July, A young man..met with an accident whilst working the 'tip' at the railway embankment, behind Bruce's Foundry. **1885** SIR J. PEARSON in *Law Times Rep.* LII. 546/1 There is a spring.. close to the bottom of the tip as it at present stands. **1889** *Daily News* 19 July 2/8 There were seventeen fixed tips in the dock..for coal loading, and foundations had been laid for two more tips. **1891** *Labour Commission* Gloss., *Tip*, a lofty erection of wood and iron placed upon the quay wall at the side of the deck, and under which ships are placed to receive their cargoes of coal... *Tips*[1], screens or other arrangements upon which the mineral is upset from the tub or tram and conveyed into a waggon, cart, or boat. *Tips*[2], 'staiths' or other erections with shoots into which the coal is emptied from waggons and then shot or tipped into the hold of the vessel. **1904** A. GRIFFITHS *50 Years Public Service* xii. 169 Long rows of trucks..were hauled up by steam power and run on to the 'tips'.

**4. a.** The mound or mass of rubbish, etc. that is tipped. **b.** A place or receptacle into which earth or rubbish is tipped or shot; a dumping-ground.

**1863** SIMMONDS *Dict. Trade*, *Tip*,..rubbish thrown from a quarry. **1890** *Lancet* 14 June 1311/2 Near to the affected dwellings is the town 'tip' for refuse. **1891** *Daily News* 5 Jan. 6/5 From the temporary termination of the Goldsworth tip to the western side of Brookwood station the work is as yet one of preparation only. **1910** *Times* 18 Jan. 3/1 The defendant corporation had the use of the tip, and their carts were..crossing the field..to the tip.

**5.** *Comb.*: see TIP- *in comb.*

† **Tip**, *sb.*[6] *slang. Obs.* [Perh. from TIP *v.*[2] sense 4 or 5; but possibly shortened from TIPPLE *sb.*] Intoxicating liquor; a draught of liquor. Also in comb. **tip-merry** *a.*, merry with liquor, slightly intoxicated.

**1612** *Burford Reg.* in *Hist. MSS. Comm.*, *Var. Collect.* I. 85 [One man is described as unfit to keep an alehouse] because he will be tipmerrie himself. *a* **1700** B. E. *Dict. Cant. Crew* s. v. *Bub*, *Rum-bub*, c. very good Tip [in **1725** *New Cant. Dict.*, '*Tipple*']. *Ibid.* s. v., *A Tub of good Tip*, (for Tipple) a Cask of strong Drink. **1717** RAMSAY *Elegy on Lucky Wood* vi, (*Sc.*) She ne'er..kept dow'd tip within her waws. **1738** SWIFT *Pol. Conversat.* 144 *Miss* (with a Glass in her Hand). Hold your Tongue, Mr. Neverout, don't speak in my Tip.

**Tip**, *v.*[1] Forms: 6 tippe, 7– tip. *Pa. t.* and *pple.* tipped, tipt. [ME. (?) and 16th c. *tippe* agrees in form and sense with Du., LG., mod.Ger. *tippen*, Sw. *tippa* to strike, poke or touch smartly or lightly; of obscure origin, but perhaps from the same Teut. root as TIP *sb.*[1], q.v. Of this TIP *sb.*[2] is app. a derivative. It is not certain that senses 2 and 3 belong to the same word; sense 2 might be directly from *tiptoe*; but cf. ON. *tifa-sk* 'to move the feet quickly, to trip', which Falk and Torp incline to refer to the same root.]

**1.** *trans.* To strike or hit smartly but lightly; to give a slight blow, knock, or touch to; to tap noiselessly.

[Quot. *a* 1225, in TIP *sb.*[1] 1 b, may perh. belong here with the sense 'until the need or necessity strikes or hits'.]

**1567** GOLDING *Ovid's Met.* v. 57 b, One Cromis tipped of his head [v. Fab. i. 104 Huic Cromis..Decutit ense caput.]: his head cut off streight way Vpon the Altar fell. **1579** GOSSON *Apol. Sch. Abuse* (Arb.) 64 Libels, which are but clay, and rattle on mine armour, or tippe me on the shinnes. *a* **1607** J. RAYNOLDS *Proph. Haggai* x. (1649) 114 To keep them [their sheep] in by threatning them, and a little tipping them. **1708** *Reply to Bickerstaff Detected* in *Swift's Wks.* (1755) II. I. 166 A third rogue tips me by the elbow, and wonders, how I have the conscience [etc.]. **1840** THACKERAY *Bedford-Row Conspir.* ii, [He] felt himself suddenly tipped on the shoulder.

**b.** *Cricket.* To hit (a ball) lightly. ***Tip-and-run***, cricket in which the batsman must run for every hit.

**1891** GRACE *Cricket* viii. 236 S. M. J. Woods and G. McGregor ..almost played tip-and-run for a few overs.

**2.** *intr.* To step lightly; to trip; to walk mincingly, or on tiptoe; also *fig.*

**1819** *Blackw. Mag.* V. 401/2 The shortened notes more tripsomely tipped over than in the modern airs. **1881** L. B. WALFORD *Dick Netherby* v. 49 The sicht o' her..tippin' up to her chair..garred me lauch sae. **1890** *Harper's Mag.* Aug. 390/2 He stopped breathlessly, and then tipped on cautiously, keeping the encircling line of bushes between him and the carriage.

**3.** *Mus.* (See TIPPING *vbl. sb.*[3] b.)

**4.** 'To toss, as carded hair, so that it will fall in tufts' (*Funk's Stand. Dict.* 1895): see TIPPING *vbl. sb.*[3] c.

**Tip,** *v.*[2] Forms: α. 4–7 **type**, 5–6, 9 *dial.* **tipe** (təip); *infl.* 5 **tipen**, 6 **typed.** β. 6– **tip**; *infl.* 7 **tippeth, tipt,** 7–8 **tip'd,** 7– **tipped,** 8 **tipp'd**; 7–9 **tipping.** [Origin and form-history obscure: known first in form *tȳpe* (14th c.), *tipe*, in literary use as late as 1632 (sense 7), and still dialectal from Cumberland to Shropsh. and E.Anglia. *Tip* with short vowel appears in 1581 (sense 6).

The ME. verb may have been *tīpe, tipte, tipt* (cf. *keep, kept, kept*), and the short *i* of the past have been later taken over into the present (perh. under the influence of TIP *v.*[1], though not necessarily so).]

**I.** Transitive senses.

**1.** To overthrow, knock, or cast down, cause to fall or tumble; to overturn, upset; to throw down (off a support, out of a vehicle, etc.) by effort or accidentally.

α. **13..** *E. E. Allit. P.* C. 506, & if I..type doun ȝonder toun when hit turned were. *a* **1400–50** *Alexander* 1303 (Dubl. MS.) Sone þe toppe of þe toure he typys [*Ashmole MS.* tiltis] in þe water. *Ibid.* 1418 Som..Typed torrettes doune, towres on hepes. **1530** PALSGR. 758/2, I type over, I overthrowe, or overwhelme, *je renuerse.* **1570** LEVINS *Manip.* 141/47 To Type a ball, *profligere.* **1862** C. C. ROBINSON *Leeds Gloss.* 442 Type that box off o' that cart. **1887** *South Chesh. Gloss.* s.v., Nai, sey as yo dunna tipe that can o'er wi' yur foot. **1904** in *Eng. Dial. Dict.* s.v.

β. [**1567** in TIP *v.*[1] 1 may possibly belong here.] *a* **1680** BUTLER *Rem.*, *Panegyric on Sir J. Denham* 26 No China Cupboard rudely overthrown; Nor Lady tip'd, by being accosted, down. *a* **1715** BURNET *Own Time* an. 1677 (1823) II. 107 Here would be a precedent to tip down so many lords at a time. **1741** RICHARDSON *Pamela* (1824) I. 77 They..tipped me into the dam, crying, Lie there, parson, till tomorrow! **1791** 'G. GAMBADO' *Ann. Horsem.* ix. (1809) 106, I tipp'd my nag over a broken place in the wall. **1869** TOZER *Highl. Turkey* II. 268 [She] tipped the pot over. **1880** MARY FITZGIBBON *Trip to Manitoba* xii. 138 A wonder we were not tipped over the horse's back. **1894** *Outing* (U.S.) XXIV. 190/1 It would be far from the truth to state that a canoe cannot be upset. Under certain conditions it is easier tipped than a boat. **1909** *Nation* 6 Mar. 851/2 Caricatures of fat Jews tipped out of motor cars.

**b.** *Skittles.* †(*a*) In the older game, said of a pin: To knock down another by falling or rolling against it, as distinguished from the direct action of the bowl. *Obs.* (*b*) In some forms of the game, applied to other modes of knocking down a pin.

**1679** A. LOVELL *Judic. Univ.* 237, I have carried four and tipped six Pins. **1773** A. JONES *Art Skittle Playing* 16 The next in height and value [to the king or middle pin] were the four corner pins..these were called Dukes, Lords, and Nobles..These four counted for three each when tipped by the King or his consequents, but if by the bowl or any other from it, either of their own height or lower, they only counted for two each. The remaining four were called Common,.. and counted for two each when tipped by the King, but by any other only one each. **1884** *Sat. Rev.* 18 Oct. 494/2 The skill was to hit over the King, and make him 'tip' as many pins as possible over with him, as thus the greatest number of points was scored.

(*b*) **17..** *Rules & Instr. for playing at Skittles* (*Sat. Rev.* 18 Oct. 1884, 498/2), Care should be taken in Tipping not to jump into the Frame immediately after, as in this case he is not allowed any of the Pins he Tips. **1785** GROSE *Dict. Vulg. T.* s.v., Tipping, at these games, is slightly touching the tops of the pins with the bowl. **1801** STRUTT *Sports & Past.* III. vii. § 9 In playing at skittles, there is a double exertion; one by bowling, and the other by tipping: the first is performed at a given distance, and the second standing close to the frame upon which the pins are placed, and throwing the ball through the midst of them. **1819** *Pantologia* X. s.v. *Skittles*, When the learner is to tip for four upon game, he should choose the eighth, seventh, sixth, and fourth pins.

**2.** To cause to assume a slanting or sloping position; to raise, push, or move into such a position; to incline, tilt. Often with *up.*

**1624** HEYWOOD *Gunaik.* v. 233 Shee tipped up the table and flung down all that was upon it. **1840** R. H. DANA *Bef. Mast* vii. 16 We hove in upon our chain, and..tipped our anchor, and stood out to sea. **1856** EMERSON *Eng. Traits, Voy. Eng.*, I waked..with the belief that some one was tipping up my berth. **1868** LOCKYER *Guillemin's Heavens* (ed. 3) 479 How much the south pole will be tipped up—how the axis will exactly lie. **1894** CROCKETT *Raiders* 55 May Mischief seemed to incline her ear, tipping it a little to the side to listen.

**b.** *To tip the scales*: to tilt or depress the scale of a balance by excess of weight; to turn the scale; also *fig.*

**1884** *Harper's Mag.* June 111/2 Single fish often tipping the scales at from five to seven pounds. **1893** *St. Louis Globe-Democrat* Oct., She tips the scales at 150 pounds.

**3.** To empty out (a wagon, cart, truck, or the like, or its contents) by tilting it up; to dump.

**1838** *Civil Eng. & Arch. Jrnl.* I. 354/1 On this stage the waggons are run, and the contents tipped with great rapidity. **1842** *Ibid.* V. 85/2 The sub-contractor..had..to keep the road in repair, and tip or turn the dirt. **1895** *Law Times Rep.* LXXIII. 157/1 The Holyhead breakwater..was constructed by tipping into the harbour some 6,000,000 tons of large stones. **1910** *Times* 18 Jan. 3/1 A piece of land which was used for the purpose of tipping rubbish.

†**4.** *fig.* (from 2). To render unsteady, make drunk, intoxicate. *slang. Obs.* (Cf. TIP *sb.*[6])

**1605** [see TIP *v.*[3]]. **1633** MARMION *Antiquary* IV. i, Your master is almost tipt already. **1708** [see TIPPED *ppl. a.*[2]].

**5.** To drink off, 'toss off'. *slang* and *dial.*

*a* **1700** B. E. *Dict. Cant. Crew*, *Tip it all off*, Drink it all off at a Draught. *c* **1765** FLLOYD *Tartarian T.* (1785) 46/2 A large glassful, which I tipped off. **1784** R. BAGE *Barham Downs* II. 49 As good claret as ever was tip'd. **1850** P. CROOK *War of Hats* 47 Who tip sly drams, while feigning to cry 'Sweep'. **1878** *Cumberland Gloss.* s.v., Tipe 't up, man, we've plenty mair.

**II.** Intransitive senses.

†**6.** To be overthrown, to fall. *Obs.* (exc. as in 7).

*c* **1400** *Death & Life* 194 in *Percy Folio* III. 64 Trees tremble for feare, and tipen to the ground. **1581** A. HALL *Iliad* VIII. 142 He thrild them through with deadly wounds, they downe to ground do tip.

**7.** To fall by overbalancing; to be overturned or upset; to tumble or topple over.

α. **1530** PALSGR. 758/2 His carte typed over [*se renuersa*] agaynst a banke. **1632** SANDERSON *Serm.* 558 When they are ready, with catching at babies in the water, to type over. *a* **1825** FORBY *Voc. E. Anglia*, *Tipe*, to kick up or fall headlong, from being top-heavy. **1904** in *Eng. Dial. Dict.* s.v.

β. **1620** SANDERSON *Serm.* I. 161 Like a ship all sail and no ballast, that tippeth over with every blast. **1890** W. A. WALLACE *Only a Sister* 325 Over tips table, candle, and cloth and all.

**8.** To assume a slanting or sloping position; to incline, tilt; e.g. of a balance; now *esp.* of a cart, a plank, etc. (usu. with *up*), to tilt up at one end and down at the other so that anything supported by it is (or may be) thrown off or emptied out.

**1666** BUNYAN *Grace Ab.* § 175 Still my life hung in doubt before me, not knowing which way I should tip. **1807** VANCOUVER *Agric. Devon* (1813) 125 They are made to tip like tumbrils. **1849** ALB. SMITH *Pottleton Leg.* xxxi, His dog-cart..tipped back last year..and lifted the horse in the air. **1864** BOWEN *Logic* ix. (1870) 301 Perhaps I do not know how the table tips. **1885** *Law Times* LXXVIII. 391/2 As the cart was being unloaded, it unfortunately tipped up, and one of the heavy flagstones fell.

**9.** *To tip off*, also simply *to tip*, or *tip* (*over*) *the perch*: to die. *slang* or *dial.*

β. *a* **1700** B. E. *Dict. Cant. Crew*, *To Tip off*, to Dye. **1727** GAY *Begg. Op.* III. i, If that great man should tip off, 'twould be an irreparable loss. **1735** SAVAGE *Progr. Divine* 294 She, with broken heart, Tips off—poor soul! **1737** [see PERCH *sb.*[2] 3 e]. **1808** BENTHAM *Mem. & Corr.* Wks. 1843 X. 444 What if you should happen to tip the perch before all the children are grown up?

α. **1828** *Craven Gloss.*, *Tipe*, 'to tipe our', to fall down, to swoon. 'To tipe off', to die. **1904** in *Eng. Dial. Dict.*

**Tip,** *v.*[3] Pa. t. and pple. **tipped, tipt** (ti·pėd, tipt). Forms: 5–6 **typpe,** 7– **tip.** *Pa. t.* 5 **typpud,** 5– **tipped,** 7– **tipt** (6 **typte,** 7 **tip'd**). [f. TIP *sb.*[1] But perhaps partly representing ON. *typpa* (Norw. *typpa*) to tip or top, and ON. *typptr* (Norw. *typpt*), tipped, topped.]

*trans.* To furnish with a tip; to put a tip on, or put something on at the tip (const. *with*); to form the tip of, or adorn at the tip.

**1483** *Cath. Angl.* 389/1 To typpe, *cornutare.* **1530** PALSGR. 758/2, I typpe a staffe with yron, *je armoye.* **1605** CAMDEN *Rem.* (1637) 414 He that did tip stone iugges about the brimme, Met with a blacke pot, and that pot tip'd him. **1718** POPE *Iliad* VII. 501 Arose the golden chariot of the day, And tipp'd the mountains with a purple ray. **1728** — *Dunc.* I. 142 [162] Quarto's, octavo's, shape the less'ning pyre; And last, a little Ajax tips the spire. **1821** CLARE *Vill. Minstr.* II. 37 The faint sun tipt the rising ground. **1866** ROGERS *Agric. & Prices* I. xix. 471 Steel..to tip the shares and ploughshoes. **1897** FLANDRAU *Harvard Episodes* 104 Two brilliant spots of pink tipped his high cheek-bones.

**b.** Most freq. in pa. pple. (See also TIPPED *ppl. a.*[1] 2.)

*c* **1386** CHAUCER *Sompn. T.* 32 His felawe hadde a staf tipped [*v.r.* typped] with horn. *c* **1400** *Laud Troy Bk.* 6968 A stalworth spere..With stelen hed that wel was tipped. **14..** *Tundale's Vis.* 870 His snowte was with irne typped. **1555** EDEN *Decades* 21 Arrowes typte with bones. **1610** HOLLAND *Camden's Brit.* (1637) 254 Their Hunters horne ..tipt with silver. **1667** MILTON *P. L.* VI. 580 In his hand a Reed Stood waving, tipt with fire. **1776** WITHERING *Brit. Plants* (1796) II. 342 Flowers..white tipped with green. *Ibid.* III. 284 Scales..fringed, tipt and edged with black. **1821** JOANNA BAILLIE *Metr. Leg.*, *Lady G. B.* 27 With ink-stain tipt. **1905** *United Free Ch. Mag.* Feb. 8 The first arrow was tipped with stone of the neolithic age, and the next..with electric telegraph wire, a theft from the twentieth century.

**c.** *fig.*

**1577** NORTHBROOKE *Dicing* (1843) 17 Their venomous tongs (typped with the mettal of infamy and slander). **1607** BEAUMONT *Woman-Hater* IV. ii, Sir, enter when you please, and all good language tip your tongue. **1635** SIBBES *Soul's Confl.* ii. (1638) 18 Doth not Satan tippe the tongues of the enemies of religion now, to insult over the Church? **1735** WEST *Let.* in *Gray's Poems* (1775) 6 The very thought, you see, tips my pen with poetry. **1860** READE *Cloister & H.* lii, An intelligent smile tipped with pity.

**Tip,** *v.*[4] [Orig. Rogues' Cant, of obscure origin. (Possibly related to TIP *v.*[1], through the notion of touching lightly, but this is very uncertain.)]

**1.** *trans.* (*Rogues' Cant*, and *slang.*) To give; to hand, pass; to let one have; to put on, present, or exhibit the character of: usually with dative of person. **a.** in various connexions and shades of meaning; sometimes little more than 'do'.

**1610** ROWLANDS *Martin Mark-all* E ij, Tip me that Cheate, Giue me that thing. **1676** COLES *Dict.*, *Tip the cole to Adam Tiler*, give the (stoln) money to your (running) Comrade. *a* **1700** B. E. *Dict. Cant. Crew*, *Tip*, to give or lend. **1712** STEELE *Spect.* No. 324 ⁋ 1 Some are celebrated for a happy Dexterity in tipping the Lion upon them; which is performed by squeezing the Nose flat to the Face, and boring out the Eyes with their Fingers. **1742** FIELDING *Jos. Andrews* II. xvii, You must not tip us the traveller; it won't go here. *a* **1743** LD. HERVEY *Mem. Geo. II*, I. 408 The King tipped Horace the 'puppy' once or twice. **1763** *Brit. Mag.* IV. 372 Frank, tip us a chaunt; which he did. **1779** MME. D'ARBLAY *Diary* 28 May, I think you should tip the doctor the same compliment. **1798** WOLCOTT (P. Pindar) *Tales of the Hoy* Wks. 1812 IV. 409 My Lord Carlisle can tip ye a hundred rhymes in half an hour. *a* **1825** LD. TAMWORTH *Let. to Parr* Parr's Wks. 1828 VII. 29 My wife has said she means to tip that excellent fellow a visit in the Autumn. **1842** MRS. GORE *Fascin.* 15 'Tip us your fist, old boy!' cried he. **1884** PAE *Eustace* 129 'Tip me your fin, my heart of oak', said Joe. **1904** HICHENS *Woman w. Fan* ix, You've only got to tip her a note of thanks.

**b.** With a coin or sum of money as obj. (Hence sense 2, in which the person, here the indirect or dative, becomes the direct obj.)

**1610** ROWLANDS *Martin Mark-all* E iv, Tip a make ben Roome Coue, Giue a halfepeny good Gentlemen. **1673** R. HEAD *Canting Acad.* 13 Tip him no Cole, give him no Money. **1719** D'URFEY *Pills* VI. 143 You will tip me a Guinea. **1851** MAYHEW *Lond. Labour* I. 325/2 If I could tip up the 5*s.* the day after I'd paid the last week's 1*s.*, I must [etc.]. **1884** PAE *Eustace* 33 Come, tip me a shilling. *absol.* **1848** THACKERAY *Van. Fair* xiii, I am quite out of cash until my father tips up.

**2.** *colloq.* (orig. *slang*). To give a gratuity to; to bestow a small present of money upon (an inferior), esp. upon a servant or employee of another, nominally in return for a service rendered or in order to obtain an extra service; also upon a child or schoolboy. Const. *with.*

**1706–7** FARQUHAR *Beaux Strat.* II. ii, Then I, Sir, tips me the Verger with half a Crown. **1733** SWIFT *Legion Club* 134 Tipping him with half a crown, Now, said I, we are alone. **1747** *Gentl. Mag.* Mar. 147/1 T'wou'd have paid The reck'ning clean, and tipp'd the maid. **1752** FIELDING *Amelia* XI. v, He advised his friend..to begin with tipping (as it is called) the great man's servant. **1848** THACKERAY *Contrib. to 'Punch'* Wks. 1886 XXIV. 189 You..used to tip me when I was a boy at school. **1883** J. H. INGRAM in *Harper's Mag.* July 231/2 He had..tipped him to the extent of a sixpence.

**b.** *absol.* To give a gratuity or gratuities.

**1727** GAY *Begg. Op.* III. i, Did he tip handsomely? **1825** C. M. WESTMACOTT *Eng. Spy* I. 322 He used to tip pretty freely. **1906** *Sat. Rev.* 22 Sept. 358/2 He always manages to secure attention...It is not because he tips: others tip, and get left.

**3.** Phrase. *To tip the* (or *a*) *wink*, to give a wink to a person as a private signal or warning. Also *to tip a nod.*

**1676** ETHEREDGE *Man of Mode* I. i, I only tip him the wink, he knows an Ale-house from a Hovel. **1698** VANBRUGH *Æsop* v. 71 Tip but the wink, he understands you. **1712** STEELE *Spect.* No. 498 ⁋ 3 The coachmen began..to tip the wink upon each other. **1726** SWIFT *Dog & Thief* iii, The stock-jobber..tips you, the freeman, a wink. **1757** SMOLLETT *Reprisal* II. iii, I came as soon as you tipped me the wink. **1841** MARRYAT *Poacher* xxii, The lad tipped a wink to Joey. **1861** DICKENS *Gt. Expect.* xxv, I tipped him several more [nods], and he was in great spirits.

†**b.** To indicate privately by a wink or the like.

**1749** FIELDING *Tom Jones* VIII. xii, I will tip you the proper person..as you do not know the town.

**Tip,** *v.*[5] *colloq.* [from TIP *sb.*[4]]

**1.** *trans.* To give a 'tip' or piece of private information about; *esp.* to mention or indicate as a probable winner, a profitable speculation, etc.

1883 [see TIPPING *vbl. sb.*[5]]. 1894 *Westm. Gaz.* 24 Feb. 7/2, I am inclined to 'tip' Aston Villa both to head the League and to win the Cup. 1897 *Ibid.* 6 July 9/2 Florio Rubattino..has been 'tipped' by some of the papers for this race. 1902 *Ibid.* 15 Jan. 11/1 At this time when South African shares are being 'tipped'. 1909 *Ibid.* 6 Sept. 10/1 A run up to 90, the price for which the shares are tipped, would be the easiest thing in the world.

**2.** To give a 'tip' to; to furnish (a person) with private information as to the chances of some event.

1891 in *Cent. Dict.* 1895 *Funk's Standard Dict.* s. v., The jockey tipped the bookmaker.

**3.** *intr.* To furnish 'tips'; to carry on the business of a tipster.

1903 FARMER & HENLEY *Slang Dict.*, *Tip*...As *verb* = to impart exclusive information. 1909 *Westm. Gaz.* 8 Apr. 8/3 I'm a racing man, and I've tipped on all the principal racecourses in England.

**Tip,** variant of TUP *sb.* 'a ram', and *v.*

**Tip-,** the stem of TIP *v.*[2] (or TIP *sb.*[5]), in combination: esp. in names of vehicles constructed to tip or tilt (endwise or sideways) for the purpose of emptying out the contents at the end or side of the track, as *tip-car, -cart, -sled, -truck, -van, -wagon*; also **tip-head,** the top of the slope over which material or rubbish is tipped; **tip-horse,** the horse which runs out the wagons to the tip-head; **tip-road,** a road along which tip-cars or -wagons run to a tip-head. See also TIP-CAT, etc.

1891 *Cent. Dict.*, **Tip-car*,..a gravel-car or coal-car pivoted on its truck, so that it can be upset to discharge its load at the side of the track; a dump-car. 1879 WEBSTER, Suppl., *Tip-cart. 1883 J. QUINCY *Figures of Past* (1884) 180 Springless tip-carts, very like those used..for the carting of gravel. 1888 H. E. SCUDDER in *Atlantic Monthly* Aug. 226/2 The idle muses are set at work. Pegasus is harnessed to a tip-cart. 1842 *Civil Eng. & Arch. Jrnl.* V. 85/2 The sub-contractor..had to..take up and relay the road at the gullet and *tip-head. *Ibid.* 336/1 The limitation of the quantity of earth-work capable of being executed in one day, occurs at the battery or tiphead. 1852 WIGGINS *Embanking* 65 The rapidity with which a bank could be built..would be limited by the number of *tip-roads. 1877 KNIGHT *Dict. Mech.*, **Tip-sled*, a dumping-sled. The box is supported on trunnions and on a front post, to which it is connected by a hook. 1899 *Westm. Gaz.* 13 Nov. 9/1, 3 engines and 6 boilers, *tip trucks. 1901 *Daily Tel.* 14 Nov. 4/5 *Tip vans for the vestry. 1852 WIGGINS *Embanking* 61 The best way is thought to be by tram-roads and *tip-waggons. 1878 G. DENMAN in *Law Rep.* 3 Com. Pleas Div. 502, 100 tip-waggons at 18 *l.* each.

**Tip-cat.** [f. TIP *v.*[2] + CAT *sb.*[1]]

**1.** A short piece of wood tapering at both ends, used in the game described in 2: = CAT *sb.*[1] 10 a.

1676 GREW *Disc. Salts Plants* ii. § 6 The Crystals ..were about the bigness of a Rice-Corn. In Figure almost like a Tip-Cat, which Boys play with. 1688 R. HOLME *Armoury* III. xvi. (Roxb.) 82/1 Striker or cat stick and tip cat. 1798 *Sporting Mag.* XII. 194 [He] nearly got his eye knocked out by aboy's tip cat. 1853 *Times* 12 Apr., Persons whose eyes have been hopelessly destroyed by blows from tip-cats.

**2.** A game in which the wooden cat or tip-cat (see 1) is struck or 'tipped' at one end with a stick so as to spring up, and then knocked to a distance by the same player: = CAT *sb.*[1] 10 b.

1801 STRUTT *Sports & Past.* II. iii. § 22 Tip-cat, or perhaps more properly the game of cat, is a rustic pastime well known in many parts of the kingdom. 1854 MACAULAY *Biog., Bunyan* (1860) 30 The..chief sins..were dancing, ringing the bells of the parish church, playing at tipcat. 1876 *World* VI. No. 106. 11 The game of tip-cat is also..in full swing. 1907 *Sat. Rev.* 30 Mar. 390/1 Playing tip-cat..requires a good deal of neatness and quickness to tip the cat smartly.

[**Tip-cheese,** ? a mistake for prec.

1837 DICKENS *Pickw.* xxxiv, He forgets the long familiar cry of 'knuckle down', and at tip-cheese, or odd and even, his hand is out.]

† **Tipe, type,** *sb.*[1] *Obs.* [Origin and history obscure. Sense 2 seems to be synonymous with TIP *sb.*[1] 1 b.]

**1.** A small cupola or dome.

1532 in Low *Hampton Court* (1885) I. xxvii. 347 Takyng downe of the iiij types upon the great White Tower, and casting and chasyng of the same iiij types. *a* 1548 HALL *Chron., Hen. VIII* 157 A porche with a tipe and crokettes gilt. 1577–87 HOLINSHED *Chron.* III. 932/1 To Leaden hall, where was a goodlie pageant with a type and a heauenlie roofe, and vnder the type was a roote of gold set on a little mounteine. 1607–8 in Willis and Clark *Cambridge* (1886) II. 493 Half ynch bord to cover yᵉ type of yᵉ Lover [= Louver]. 1613 CHAPMAN *Inns of Court* Plays 1873 III. 95 Aboue all, was a *Coupolo*, or Type. 1708 *New View Lond.* I. 98/2 A Marble Font, whose Tipe or Cover has the Enrichments of Cupids, Fruit Leaves.

**2.** *fig.* The summit, acme, or highest point (*of* honour, dignity, or other state). Cf. TIP *sb.*[1] 1 b.

*a* 1548 HALL *Chron., Edw. IV* 199 How muche more ought a noble man to fume..when the high tipe of his honor is touched. 1579–80 NORTH *Plutarch* (1676) 917 Some of them ..attained to the tipe of royal dignity. 1591 *Troub. Raigne K. John* II. (1611) 106 As if your highnes were now in the highest tipe of dignitie. 1603 KNOLLES *Hist. Turks* (1621) 506 You shall through your rashnesse..tumble downe headlong from the type of so great majestie.

**Tipe** (təip), *sb.*[2] *dial.* [f. *tipe*, variant and earlier form of TIP *v.*[2]] A kind of trap for catching mice, rabbits, etc., in which a board balanced on a pivot is tipped or tilted by the weight of the animal passing over it. Also *tipe-trap*. (See *Eng. Dial. Dict.*)

1788 W. MARSHALL *E. Yorks.* II. Gloss., *Tipe*, a trap or devise for catching rabbits. Also for taking mice, rats, or other vermin. The general principle is that of a balance [etc.]. 1828 *Craven Gloss.*, *Tipe*, a mouse trap, consisting of a board suspended over a vessel of water, and nicely balanced on a pivot. 1846 *J. Baxter's Libr. Pract. Agric.* (ed. 4) I. 335 The usual methods adopted in catching rabbits are by fold-nets, spring-nets, and tipes, a species of trap, being a pit or cistern covered with a floor, with a small trapdoor, nicely balanced near the centre, into which the rabbits pass by a narrow passage.

**Tipe** (təip), *v.* Obs. or dial. form of TIP *v.*[2]

**Tipet,** obs. f. TIPPET. **Tip-foot**: see TIP *sb.*[1]

**Tiphany,** obs. form of TIFFANY.

† **Tiphe.** *Obs.* Also 6–7 typhe, 7 typh. [a. L. *tiphē* = Gr. τίφη 'acc. to Sprengel, Peter's-corn, one-grained wheat, *Triticum monococcum*, Linn.'] A species of wheat having the ripe ear laterally compressed, the spikelets in two very compact rows, each containing, as a rule, one grain. Also *attrib.*

1578 LYTE *Dodoens* IV. iv. 456 Of Typhewheate, called in Latine Triticum Romanorum. *Ibid.* 457 Typhe wheate or Bearded wheate. 1598 FLORIO, *Pane di tritello*, rie or typhe-bread. 1611 COTGR., *Meteil*,..typhe wheat, bearded wheat, flat wheat, Roman wheat. 1688 R. HOLME *Armoury* II. 56/1 Typh Wheat..is very like to our Rye..and doth make very black Bread. 1790 J. BRUCE *Trav. Source Nile* V. 79 (*Teff*) There is one [cereal] which he [Pliny] calls Tiphe, but says not whence it came.

**Tipi,** var. TEPEE. **Tipioca,** obs. f. TAPIOCA.

**Tip-it, tippit.** Also *dial.* -et, -ut, tibbets. [From the phrase *tip it* = give or hand it out.] A game of chance, played by two parties of two or three a side; in one of the hands on one side a button or the like is hidden, and a player on the opposite side has to guess in which hand it is, touching the hand and saying *tip it*. (When played for money or drinks it is reckoned a form of gambling.)

1889 T. A. GUTHRIE *Pariah* IV. vi, A lively..pastime known as 'Tibbets', which consisted in passing a paper-weight from hand to hand under a table-cover, and guessing at a given moment in whose hand it was concealed. 1897 *B'ham Daily Gaz.* 28 Aug. (E.D.D.), Playing tip it for drinks. 1902 *Westm. Gaz.* 8 May 7/3 The offence..was that a servant allowed some miners to play at the game of tippit for beer. 1908 *Daily Chron.* 5 Mar. 5/6 The skill of members at such games as tippit, darts, rings, and dominoes.

**Tiplage, Tiple,** etc., obs. ff. TIPPLAGE, TIPPLE.

**Tipless** (ti·plės), *a.*[1] [f. TIP *sb.*[1] + -LESS.] Without a tip; that has lost its tip or point.

1904 E. F. BENSON *Challoners* vi, A bagatelle board with torn cloth and tipless cues.

**Ti·pless,** *a.*[2] [f. TIP *sb.*[3] + -LESS.] Characterized by absence of 'tips' or gratuities.

1903 *Daily Chron.* 10 Feb. 5/1 Must tipless guard Look stern and hard With nought but thanks to gain? 1909 *Westm. Gaz.* 30 Aug. 5/4 This will be the first hotel in the world to adopt a tipless system.

**Tiplet** (ti·plėt). [f. TIP *sb.*[1] + -LET.] A small or minute tip or point.

1890 C. L. MORGAN *Anim. Life & Intell.* (1891) 106 The feathers composing their tiplets..are of so beautiful a colour that they beggar description. 1899 *Blackw. Mag.* Apr. 671/2 Pale heads of meadow-rue dusted with ruddy tiplets.

**Tipmost** (ti·pmǫust), *a. nonce-wd.* [f. TIP *sb.*[1] after *topmost*.] Situated at the extreme tip. In quot. = 'very tip of the (lance)'.

1871 TENNYSON *Last Tourn.* 441 The Red Knight..Even to tipmost lance and topmost helm, In blood-red armour sallying.

**Tip-paper**: see TIP *sb.*[1] 6.

**Tipped, tipt** (tipt), *ppl. a.*[1] [f. TIP *sb.*[1] or *v.*[3] But perh. a. ON. *typptr* tipped, from *typpa* to tip.]

† **1.** (Meaning uncertain.)

Quot. *c* 1300 may belong to sense 2; but it looks rather like 'having the tips cut off, clipt'. Quot. 13.. is glossed by editor 'extreme', which seems improbable.

*c* 1300 [see TIPPET 1 a]. 13.. *E. E. Allit. P.* C. 77 He telles me þose traytoures arn typped schrewes.

**2.** Having a tip, pointed; furnished or adorned with a tip, or with something at the tip.

*c* 1386 CHAUCER *Nun's Pr. T.* 83 Tipped was his tayl, and bothe hise eeris With blak. *c* 1470 HENRYSON *Mor. Fab.* IX. (*Wolf & Fox*) vi, My tippit twa eiris, and my twa gray Ene. 1483 *Cath. Angl.* 389/1 Typped, *cornutatus*. 1888 *Berks. Gloss.*, *Tipped an' naailed*. Boots for field wear have the soles thus furnished.

† **3. Tipped staff.** A staff tipped with metal: = TIPSTAFF 1. Also *tipped mace, stick, wand.*

*c* 1386 CHAUCER *Sompn. T.* 29 With scrippe and tipped [*v.r.* typped] staf ytukked hye. 1485 *Rutland Papers* (Camden) 9 That the Marshall of England be well accompanyed with men having long tipped staves. 1574 *Reg. Privy Council Scot.* II. 365 Nane suld tak upoun hand to execute ony chargeis without his blason, blawing horne and tippet wand. 1598 MARSTON *Pygmal.* III. 148 Some spirit with a tippet Mace. 1617 MINSHEU *Voc. Hisp. Lat.*, *Vergnēro*, a Vergier, one that carrieth a tipped stick before the Iustices..or the Deane.

† **b.** An officer bearing such a staff: = TIPSTAFF 2.

1494 FABYAN *Chron.* VII. 565 The Erle of Westmerlande, than newely made marshall, rode about the halle wᵗ many typped staues about hym. *c* 1500 *God Speed the Plough* 77 in *P. Pl. Crede*, etc. 71 Then commeth the tipped-staves for the Marshalse, And saye they haue prisoners mo than Inough. *a* 1548 HALL *Chron., Hen. VIII* 3 b, To Westminster hall.. where by the Lord Marshall and his tipped staues, was made rome.

**Tipped, tipt,** *ppl. a.*[2] [f. TIP *v.*[2] + -ED[1].] Inclined, tilted; overturned, upset; † drunken (*obs. slang*).

1708 T. WARD *Eng. Ref.* (1716) 174 In Songs Obscene and Tipt discourse. 1907 KATE D. WIGGIN *New Chron. Rebecca* iii, The good deacon sat..in his tipped-back chair.

**Tippee** (tipī·). [f. TIP *v.*[4] 2 + -EE.] One who is 'tipped'; the receiver of a 'tip' or gratuity.

1897 *Daily News* 23 Sept. 5/1 The working of economic law frustrates the..intention of both tipper and tippee. 1907 LADY GROVE *Soc. Fetich* v, The system of 'tips' is ..at times humiliating to both 'tipper' and 'tippee'.

**Tippence, -penny,** Sc. ff. TWOPENCE, -PENNY.

**Tipper**[1] (ti·pəɹ). [f. TIP *v.*[2], [3], [4], [5] + -ER[1].] One who or that which tips, in various senses of the verbs. *spec.*

† **1.** in *Skittles*: see TIP *v.*[2] 1 b. *Obs.*

1819 *Pantologia* X. s.v. *Skittles*, If the tipper give a sweep round with his hand and bring down any pins by means of his hand or coat-sleeve, that is deemed unfair, and he must lose one pin.

**2. a.** A workman employed in tipping or emptying out coal-wagons, trucks, etc.

1872 *Daily News* 8 Oct. 3 Mr. Pickard contended that engine-men, bankers, tippers, blacksmiths, &c., ought not to be admitted, as their interests were no more identical with those of the miner than the shopkeepers who are the friends of the pitman. 1890 *Ibid.* 29 July 6/5 The s.s. Tasso..was placed under the tips yesterday afternoon; but when it was discovered that the seamen..were non-Union men, the tippers and trimmers refused to load, and left work in protest. 1891 *Labour Commission* Gloss., *Tippers* (1) Those who empty coal waggons or trucks by tipping up one end. (2) The men at the docks who tip the coal into the hold of a vessel by means of the hydraulic lifts..called 'tips'.

**b.** A device or apparatus for tipping or tilting; *spec.* for tipping and emptying coal-wagons.

1870 ATKINSON tr. *Ganot's Physics* ii. § 69 a (ed. 4) 54 The top of this mass [of iron] is provided with a tipper which catches against the end of a bent lever. 1884 *Health Exhib. Catal.* 59/2 Shrewsbury Tipper Flushing Water Closet. 1901 *Scotsman* 15 Oct. 4/8 The coals..in hutches of 10 cwts. ..are..pushed on to the revolving power-driven tippers, which land the coal on to three distributing jiggers.

**c.** A wagon or truck constructed to tip earth, etc., distinguished according to its action as an *end-tipper* or a *side-tipper*: cf. TIP- in comb.

**3.** [TIP *v.*[3]] A person employed in fitting on tips to umbrellas or other articles.

*Mod. Newsp. Advt.*, Umbrella tippers wanted, indoors.

**4.** [TIP *v.*[4]] One who gives a 'tip' or gratuity.

1877 CRAUF. TAIT *Let.* 1 Aug., in W. Benham *Cath. & C. Tait*, This is better both for the class of tippers and tipped than our system. 1894 *Daily News* 18 Dec. 5/3 There are no tippers so hardened and profuse as Anglo-Indian tippers. 1900 *N. & Q.* 9th Ser. V. 526/2 Thackeray, the unfailing tipper of schoolboys, slipped a sovereign into my hand.

**5.** [TIP *v.*[5]] One who gives 'tips' or private information; a tipster. 1891 in *Cent. Dict.*

**Ti·pper**[2]. [Named from one Thomas Tipper (d. 1785), who first brewed it.] A kind of ale brewed in Sussex.

[1785 *Tipper's Tombstone* (Newhaven Churchyard), The best old stingo he both brewed and sold.] 1844 DICKENS *Mart. Chuz.* xix, A pint of the celebrated staggering ale or Real Old Brighton Tipper at supper.

**Tippet** (ti·pėt), *sb.* Forms: 4–6 tipet, 4–7 typet, (4 typeth, 4–5 tepet), 5 typett, -itte; 5–6 typ-, 6 tipp-, typpett(e, 6–7 typpet, tippit, 7 tipit; 4– tippet; also *Sc.* 5 tipat (tuppat), 5–6 tipp-, typp-, typat, tepat, -e. [Origin uncertain; some suggest identity with OE. *tæpped*, *tæppet*, **tęped* (pl. *tæppedu*, *tepedu*) carpet, hanging, etc. = OHG. *teppid, -ith, -it, tepid, -it*: both ad. L. *tapēte* (*-a, -um*) a carpet, tapestry hanging, bedcover, table-cover. But there are great difficulties both of phonology and of sense. Others suggest a derivative of TIP *sb.*[1] See *Note* below.]

**1. a.** A long narrow slip of cloth or hanging part of dress, formerly worn, either attached to and forming part of the hood, head-dress, or sleeve, or loose, as a scarf or the like. *Obs.* exc. *Hist.*

*c* 1300 in *Langtoft's Chron.* in *Pol. Songs* (Camden) 303 For he haves ovirhipped, Hise tipet [*v.r.* typeth] is typped, Hise tabard es tome. [1342 *Concilium Lond.* c. 2 Et caputiis cum tipettis miræ longitudinis.] *c* 1386 CHAUCER *Reeve's T.* 33 On haly dayes biforn hir [his wife] wolde hee [Symkyn] go With his tipet y-bounde about his heed. 1401 *Pol. Poems* (Rolls) II. 69 What meenith thi tipet, Jakke, as longe as a stremer, that hangith longe bihinde, and kepith thee not hoot? 14.. *Beryn* 662 He wissh a-wey the blood, And bond the sorys to his hede with the typet of his hood. *c* 1440 *Promp. Parv.* 494/2 Typett, *liripipium* [a long band or scarf (Du Cange)]. 1463 *Bury Wills* (Camden) 41 My tepet of blak sarsenet. 1473–4 *Acc. Ld. High Treas. Scot.* I. 16, j½ elne of vellous for ij tuppatis to the King. *Ibid.* 17 A typpat to the King. 1502 *Ibid.* II. 197 For ane tepat and ane belt to the King. 1532–3 *Act* 24 *Hen. VIII*, c. 13 § 2 It shalbe lefull to all..Doctors of the one Lawe or the other..to weare..blacke saten, in their tipittes. *a* 1548 HALL *Chron., Hen. VIII* 7 Their heades rouled in pleasauntes and typpets lyke the Egipcians. *a* 1626 BACON *New Atl.* (1650) 6 His Turban was white with a small red Crosse on the Topp. He had also a Tippet of fine Linnen. 1688 R. HOLME *Armoury* III. 12/1 The Tippet [of a Hood] hangs from the hinder part of the Crown, and reacheth backwards to the ground. *Ibid.*, A French Hood..having the Flap or Tippet hanging down the wearers Back, may be termed a Mourning-hood. 1756 NUGENT *Gr. Tour, France* IV. 81 The students [of the Sorbonne]..are qualified for the degree of batchelors, and wear lambskins and tippets two years. **1834** PLANCHÉ *Brit. Costume* 128 From the sleeves of this cote..depended long slips of cloth, ..which were called tippets.

**b.** A garment, usually of fur or wool, covering the shoulders, or the neck and shoulders; a cape or short cloak, often with hanging ends. Now worn chiefly by women and girls, or by men as a part of certain official costumes.

In many early quots. (omitted here), **a** and **b** are not distinguishable.

**1481** CAXTON *Myrr.* III. xvi. 172 They be not alle clerkes that haue short typettis. **1554** Turner *Sel. Rec. Oxford* 219 [He] shall weare..a typpet of velvett as other Aldermen have accustomyd yn thoffyce of Mayraltie to do. **1684–5** WOOD *Life* 11 Feb. (O.H.S.) III. 128 The mayor with his scarlet, and stole or tippet over it. **1686** *Lond. Gaz.* No. 2115/4 Lost a Sable Tippet with scarlet and silver strings to it. **1709–10** ADDISON *Tatler* No. 116 ⁋ 9 The Lynx shall cast its Skin at her Feet to make her a Tippet. **1848** DICKENS *Dombey* i, She had furry articles for winter wear, as tippets, boas, and muffs. **1880** MISS BRADDON *Just as I am* iii, She gave the village children smart hats and tippets for summer.

**c.** *Eccl.* A band of silk or other material worn round the neck, with the two ends pendent from the shoulders in front; = SCARF *sb.*$^1$ 2.

**1530** PALSGR. 281/2 Typpet for a preest, *cornette*. *a* **1555** BRADFORD in Coverdale *Lett. Mart.* (1564) 441 If God's word had place..Priestes should be otherwise knowen then by their shauen crownes and typets. **1588** *Marprel. Epist.* (Arb.) 9 Your corner caps and tippets will do nothing in this poynt. **1604** *Const. & Canons Eccles.* § 58 It shall be lawful for such Ministers as are not Graduates to wear upon their Surplices, instead of Hoods, some decent Tippet of black, so it be not silk. **1617** MINSHEU *Ductor, Tippet*, or habit which Vniuersitie men and Clergie men weare ouer their gownes L. *Epitogium*. **1678** PHILLIPS (ed. 4), *Tippet*, a certain long Scarf which Doctors of Divinity wear when they go abroad in their Gowns. *a* **1750** T. GORDON *Cordial for Low Spirits* (1751) II. 78, I cannot for my heart think, that a Piece of Lawn, or a red Tippet, can make men holier than their neighbours. **1870** DISRAELI *Lothair* vi, He.. wore..over his cassock a purple tippet. **1903** P. DEARMER *Parson's Handbk.* (new ed.) 128 There are many clergymen in Ireland..who can still remember the ecclesiastical scarf called a tippet..The Canons on the subject must be misunderstood when the modern foreign idea of a short cape [see 1 b] is read into the word tippet. **1903** *Church Times* 11 Dec. 784/2 A deacon is entitled, like any other clergyman, to wear the broad black tippet, or scarf, over his surplice.

**d.** Applied to a part of ancient or mediæval armour: = CAMAIL 1. *rare.*

*c* **1400** *Melayne* 960 The Bischoppe gart hym with a spere Appon his tepet lighte. **1845** C. H. SMITH in *Kitto's Cycl. Bibl. Lit.* I. 226/2 In Egypt..a more ancient national form was a kind of thorax, tippet,..or square, with an opening in it for the head, the four points covering the breast, back, and both upper arms. **1869** BOUTELL *Arms & Arm.* viii. (1874) 127 The *camail*..is the lower part of a mail coif, a hood, or a tippet of mail, which was fixed to the basinet, and hung gracefully over the shoulders, covering the upper part of the body-armour.

†**e.** Phr. *To turn (one's) tippet*: to change one's course or behaviour completely; in bad sense, to act the turncoat or renegade. *Obs.*

**1546** J. HEYWOOD *Prov.* (1867) 44 So turned they their typpets by way of exchaunge, From laughyng to lowryng. **1563** FOXE *A. & M.* 1049/2 He changed his typpette, and played the Apostata. *a* **1577** GASCOIGNE *Flowers* (1587) 18 Those trifling bookes from whose lewde lore my tippet here I turne. **1598–9** B. JONSON *Case is Altered* III. iii, You, to turn tippet! fie, fie! **1650** TRAPP *Comm. Exod.* xii. 38 Strangers, that took hold of the skirts of these Jews ..but afterwards turned tippet.

†**2.** A jocular name for a hangman's rope: usually *Tyburn tippet* (also Sc. *St. Johnston's tippet*: cf. RIBAND *sb.* 3 a). *Obs.*

?**1462** *Paston Lett.* II. 86 The seide Perys tyed by an halter...This is a presoner, ye may knowe by his tepet and steff. **1549** LATIMER *2nd Serm. bef. Edw. VI* (Arb.) 63 He should haue had a Tiburne tippet, a halpeny halter, and all suche proude prelates. *c* **1592** MARLOWE *Jew of Malta* IV. iv, When the hangman had put on his hempen tippet, he made such haste to his prayers. **1680** C. NESSE *Church Hist.* 143 The cart at Tyburn drives away when the tippet is fast about the necks of the condemned. **1814** SCOTT *Wav.* xxxix, As I hae dealt a' my life in halters, I think nae mickle o' putting my craig in peril of a St. Johnstone's tippet. **1823** — *Quentin D.* vi, Were I to be hanged myself, no other should tie tippet about my craig.

**3.** An organ or formation in animals resembling or suggesting a tippet; in birds, dogs, etc. = RUFF *sb.*$^2$ 3; in insects = PATAGIUM c.

**1815** [implied in *tippet cuckoo*, in 5]. **1826** KIRBY & SP. *Entomol.* III. xxxv. 539 The *tegulæ* that cover the base of the primary wings of insects of this Order..are what.. I have called in the table *patagia*, or tippets. **18..** MRS. CAMERON *Little Dog Flora* 8 A very small dog..covered with long brown hair, with its tippet and feet quite white. **1866** DK. ARGYLL *Reign of Law* v. (1871) 236 A species of Lophorius with a tippet of emerald spangles. **1872** COUES *N. Amer. Birds* 18 Conspicuous among these are the ruffs, or tippets, of some birds.

**4.** *Angling.* **a.** A length of twisted hair or gut forming part of a fishing-line. *Sc.* **b.** Part of an artificial fly: see quot. 1867, and cf. 3.

**1825** JAMIESON, *Tippet.* 1. One length of twisted hair or gut in a fishing-line. **1867** F. FRANCIS *Angling* x. (1880) 343 The wing is composed of a white ribbed snipe's feather, with longish tippets on either side. **1908** *Dundee Advertiser* 26 Oct. 8 We came upon a young fisherman 'makin' tippits', as he explained. The tippit is of horse-hair, woven in thin strands, knotted at either end.

**5.** *attrib.* and *Comb.*, as *tippet armour* (cf. 1 d), *-box*; *tippet-like* adj.; †**tippet-captain, knight, man**, contemptuous nicknames for a priest or ecclesiastic (cf. 1 c); so †**tippet-scuffle** *nonce-wd.*, an ecclesiastical wrangle; **tippet cuckoo, grouse**, names for species of these birds having a 'tippet' or ruff (cf. 3); **tippet-grebe**, a species of grebe, of which the skin, with the feathers on, is used for tippets.

**1845** C. H. SMITH in *Kitto's Cycl. Bibl. Lit.* I. 226/2 The late Roman legionaries..again wear the *tippet armour, like that of the Egyptians. **1694** *Lond. Gaz.* No. 2980/4 Left in a Hackney-Coach.., a Wainscot *Tippet-Box with 2 Tippets, one Sable,..the other black Ribbond. **1550** BALE *Apol.* 104 Thys *typpet captayne, in bringing fourth here S. Augustynes authoryte..is like to be pearced through wyth hys owne weapon. **1815** STEPHENS in *Shaw's Gen. Zool.* IX. I. 112 *Tippet Cuckow. **1776** PENNANT *Brit. Zool.* II. 418 *Tippet Grebe...The under side of them being drest with the feathers on, are made into muffs and tippets; each bird sells for about fourteen shillings. **1829** COL. HAWKER *Diary* (1893) I. 352, I knocked down a tippet grebe. **1550** BALE *Eng. Votaries* II. L iij, The order of portasse men, *tippet knyghtes, or new shauen Syr Ihons. **1839** *Penny Cycl.* XIII. 439/2 A small *tippet-like appendage..on each side..at the base of the wings. **1550** BALE *Eng. Votaries* II. L iij, The first order of *tippet men, or secular priests. **1641** MILTON *Reform.* II. Wks. 1851 III. 54 To make a Nationall Warre of a Surplice Brabble, a *Tippet-scuffle.

Hence **Ti·ppet** *v., intr.* to wear a tippet; *trans.* to furnish or adorn with a tippet; †**Ti·ppeter**, a member of New College, Oxford, who wore a tippet: see quot. and context.

**1563** BECON *Acts Christ & Antichr.* § 22 Wks. III. 398 b, Antichrist hath his Chaplens knowen by docking & doucking, .. by *tippeting and gowning. **1889** DOYLE *Micah Clarke* xvii. 155 Sweeping gowns of black silk trimmed and tippeted with costly furs. *a* **1677** in Rashdall & Rait *New College* vi. (1901) 156 We call it a Habit, such as New College *Tippiters alwaies wore above their gownes. **1901** *Ibid.*, Who constituted this class of tippeters we are unable to explain.

[*Note.* The normal and regular repr. of OE. *tæppet* down to 1600 was TAPET; and phonetic development of *i* out of *a* would be abnormal; the rare ME. *tepet* and Sc. *tepat* are prob. from *tipet*. The ordinary meaning of the OE. and ME. word, and of the OHG., was 'carpet', as in Latin, but in *Ælfric's Vocabulary*, *tæppet* occurs under the heading *Vestium Nomina*, as if a name of a garment. Yet the gloss '*Sipla* an healfhruh tæppet', seems to come from the same source as one in the 15th c. *Nominale*, under the heading *De Lectis et Ornamentis eorum*, 'Hec amphicapa est tapeta ex utraque parte villosa. Hec sipha idem est' (Wr.-W. 744/5), where the *sipha* or *tapeta* is evidently a bedcover; so that the Ælfric entry is prob. placed under the wrong heading. A change of meaning from 'carpet' or 'bedcover' to the senses above, is very improbable. Derivation of *tippet* from *tip* is favoured by the fact that Ger. *zipfel*, orig. diminutive of *zipf* 'tip', has the senses 'tip, point, end, lappet, tail', etc.]

**Tippet**, obs. form of TIPPED, TIPT.

**Ti·pping**, *vbl. sb.*$^1$ [f. TIP *v.*$^3$ (or *sb.*$^1$) + -ING$^1$.]

**1.** The action of furnishing or fitting with a tip.

**1559** *Dunmow Churchw. MS.* lf. 44 Payed to John Hootte for typpinge of a spade. **1905** *Longm. Mag.* Feb. 355 There is no tipping of split sticks with sulphur to make matches.

**2.** *concr.* A piece fashioned or fitted on to form a tip, esp. of a different material or colour.

*c* **1325** *Gloss. W. de Bibbesw.* in Wright *Voc.* 150 De la ceynture le pendaunt, *gl.* the girdilis ende tipping. **1483** *Cath. Angl.* 389/1 A Typpynge of A bollt. **1647** H. MORE *Poems* 7 Crudled clouds, with silver tippings dight. **1785** *Phil. Trans.* LXXV. 399 Reckoning from the extremities of the bell-metal tippings.

**3.** *Hort.* A method of grafting, also called *tonguing*: see quot.

**1763** MILLS *Pract. Husb.* IV. 217 The third method [of whipgrafting], which is an improvement of the last, is properly named *tipping* or *tonguing*.

**Ti·pping**, *vbl. sb.*$^2$ [f. TIP *v.*$^2$ + -ING$^1$.] The action of TIP *v.*$^2$ in various senses: *spec.*

**1.** Tilting, inclination, upsetting.

**1863** HOLLAND *Lett. Joneses* vii. 105 Scraping of fiddles, and the tipping of tables. **1866** *Lond. Rev.* 25 Aug. 206/2 Whether this tipping of the mental balance was not a physical rather than a mental mishap. **1901** *Essex Weekly News* 8 Mar. 3/3 Owing to the frequent tipping of the tumbril.

**2.** *Skittles.*

**1801** [see TIP *v.*$^2$ 1 b (*b*)]. **1819** *Pantologia* X. s.v. *Skittles*, If in tipping the bowl is caught or stopped by one of the opposite party, who, in so doing, stops or impedes a live pin, the party who stops loses one from his own score.

**3.** The tilting up of a truck so as to discharge its contents; the emptying out of the contents of a truck, etc., by tilting; dumping.

**1838** *Civil Eng. & Arch. Jrnl.* I. 354/1 A contrivance to facilitate the tipping of the earth-waggons. **1842** *Ibid.* V. 85/2 The price he paid for tipping was 13s. 6d. per hundred wagons. **1878** F. S. WILLIAMS *Midl. Railw.* 51 The Oakenshard cutting and embankment..required the quarrying and tipping of some 600,000 yards of rock.

**b.** *pl.* (*concr.*) Material tipped or emptied out from a quarry, etc. **c.** A railway embankment. *local.*

**1884** *Chesh. Gloss.*, *Tipping*, a railway embankment formed by tipping wagons full of soil or stone. **1888** *Pall Mall G.* 3 Aug. 5/1 The quarries at Llanberis, whose tippings are gradually filling up the once beautiful Llyn Peris.

**d.** *attrib.*, as *tipping platform*, *wagon*: cf. TIP-.

**1885** DUCANE *Punishm. & Prevent. Crime* 180 Removing the earth .. by means of .. tipping waggons. **1891** *Daily News* 6 Feb. 6/3, 200 clerks have intimated their readiness to do the tipping work till other arrangements have been made. **1901** *Feilden's Mag.* IV. 436/2 A 'tipping platform' for the storage of the refuse and for the feeding of the furnaces.

**Ti·pping**, *vbl. sb.*$^3$ [f. TIP *v.*$^1$ + -ING$^1$.] The action of TIP *v.*$^1$; in quot., in sense 2 of the vb.

**1819** *Blackw. Mag.* V. 402/1 Leaving out compass, emphasis, shakes, holds, cadences, and tippings.

*spec.* **b.** *Mus.* The action of striking the tongue against the palate so as to produce a *staccato* effect in playing certain wind-instruments; also called TONGUING, q.v.

**1898** STAINER & BARRETT *Dict. Mus. Terms, Tipping.* (Double tongueing.) *Ibid.*, *Double-tongueing*, a peculiar action .. to ensure a brilliant and spirited articulation of staccato notes.

**c.** (See quot.)

**1891** *Cent. Dict.*, *Tipping*$^2$, *n.*..2. In the preparation of curled hair, the operation of tossing the carded hair about with a stick so that it will fall in tufts, to be afterwards consolidated by rapid blows.

**Ti·pping**, *vbl. sb.*$^4$ [f. TIP *v.*$^4$ + -ING$^1$.] The action of TIP *v.*$^4$; the bestowing of gratuities: see TIP *v.*$^4$ 2.

**1761** R. LLOYD *To G. Colman* Poet. Wks. 1774 I. 113 And walking gravely thro' the croud, Which stood obsequiously, and bow'd, To keep the fashion up of tipping, Dropt in each hand a golden pippin. **1869** in *Daily News* 24 July, A system of tipping had prevailed at Somerset-house and in the dockyards..which he would endeavour to uproot. **1893** G. E. MATHESON *About Holland* 30 A good deal of tipping ..has to be done in Holland.

**Ti·pping**, *vbl. sb.*$^5$ [f. TIP *v.*$^5$ + -ING$^1$.] The giving of 'tips' or private information as to the chances of sporting events, etc. Also *attrib.*

**1883** *Pall Mall G.* 24 Oct. 4/1 The 'glorious uncertainties' of turf 'tipping'.

**Ti·pping**, *ppl. a. dial.* and *slang.* [f. TIP *v.*$^3$ + -ING$^2$, after *topping*: cf. *tip-top.*] First-rate, excellent, = TOPPING. (Cf. *ripping.*)

**1887** *South Chesh. Gloss.* s.v., They bin tippin' cheers; they'n do well for go i' ahr parlour. **1903** FARMER & HENLEY *Slang Dict.*, *Tipping* .. (schools'), first-rate; jolly. **1903** ROSA N. CAREY *Passage Perilous* (Tauchn.) 119 It is tipping, Chriss, and suits you down to the ground.

†**Ti·pplage.** *nonce-wd.* In 7 **tiplage.** [f. TIPPLE *v.*$^1$ + -AGE.] Intoxicating drink generally, tipple.

**1653** URQUHART *Rabelais* II. i. 3 The Vine, from whence we have that..liquor which they call the *piot* or *tiplage*.

**Tipple** (ti·p'l), *sb.*$^1$ *colloq.* or *slang.* [f. TIPPLE *v.*$^1$] Drink, liquor for drinking; *esp.* strong drink. Also *attrib.* (quot. 1617; or perh. there the verb-stem in combination).

**1581** A. HALL *Iliad* IX. 165 Of pleasant wine their tipple in they take. **1617** in *Essex Rev.* (1907) XVI. 205, vj cushions, 3 tiple pottes, 8 spoones. **1655** tr. *Com. Hist. Francion* I. 8 Where hast thou got tipple to make thy selfe drunke this night? **1706** E. WARD *Wooden World Diss.* (1708) 47 To lay in a Cargo of fresh Peck and Tipple. *a* **1763** SHENSTONE *Ode Dr. Brettle* 3 Come let's be merry; stir the tipple. **1832** MARRYAT *N. Forster* xxxvi, Champagne is very pretty *tipple*. **1861** HUGHES *Tom Brown at Oxf.* xli, Ah! that's not bad tipple after such a ducking as we've had. **1893** FORBES-MITCHELL *Remin. Gt. Mutiny* 67 Something more potent than blue-ribbon tipple. **1893** SELOUS *Trav. S. E. Africa* 121 A cup of tea, the usual tipple of South African hunters and travellers.

**Ti·pple**, *sb.*$^2$ *dial.* [?f. TIP *sb.*$^1$] A bundle of hay tied near the top so that it tapers to a point.

**1799** *Trans. Soc. Arts* XVII. 226 A truss of Clover Hay, and a few tipples of Lucerne Hay. **1812** SIR J. SINCLAIR *Syst. Husb. Scot.* I. 401 It is proper to make the tipple as soon as the grass is mown, if dry.

**Ti·pple**, *sb.*$^3$ *U.S. local.* [f. TIPPLE *v.*$^3$] = TIP *sb.*$^5$ 3.

**1886** *N. Amer. Rev.* Aug. 181 The law allows a check weighmaster on each tipple. **1894** *Current Hist.* (U.S.) IV. 138 The excited mob [near Bridgeville, Pa.] burned coal cars and coal tipples, and destroyed some mining machinery.

**Tipple** (ti·p'l), *v.*$^1$ Forms: 6– **tipple.** Also 6 **typle, typple, typpel(l, typpil, 6–8 tiple, 7 tippel.** [Known (in simple tenses) from 1544, in pres. pple. *tippling* (as *ppl. a.*), app. before 1500; in vbl. sb. *tippling* from 1531. But the agent-noun TIPPLER occurs as an established and app. legal term in 1396, and frequently in the 15th c.; so that either the verb must have existed before 1400, though not yet in evidence, or *tippler* must have originated otherwise, and *tipple* have arisen from it as a back-formation: cf. PEDLAR, PEDDLE *v.*

The ulterior history is uncertain; *tipple* or *tippler* cannot, from the date, be a freq. deriv. of TIP *v.*$^2$ in any sense; nor is it easy to connect it with LG. and Du. *tippel* 'tip, extreme point' (TIP *sb.*$^1$). But according to Aasen, Norw. dial. *tipla* 'to drip slowly', which Falk and Torp derive from *tippa* to project, to drip, from *tip* 'point', has also the sense 'to drink in small quantities', 'tipple', evidently related to the Eng. word, though the mode of relationship is not clear. An ultimate connexion with TAP *sb.*$^1$, *v.*$^1$ has also been thought possible, but connecting links are wanting.]

†**1. a.** *trans.* To sell (ale or other strong drink) by retail (see TIPPLER$^1$ 1). **b.** *absol.* or *intr.* To carry on the trade of a 'tippler'; to draw and retail liquor, sell from the tap. *Obs.*

?*a* **1500** [see TIPPLING *ppl.a.* 1]. **1531** [see TIPPLING *vbl. sb.*$^1$ 1]. **1544** *Coventry Leet Bk.* 771 That noon inhabitaunt of this Citie shall..brewe or tiple eny ale within this Citie to sell but onelie suche..persones as shal-be therunto appoynted. **1594** in J. Morris *Troub. Cath. Forefathers* (1877) 281 Dorothy Browne,..who by reason she is an obstinate recusant, was heretofore discharged in open sessions from brewing and tippling,..doth not give over the same, but continually since hath brewed and tippled. **1611** in *N. Riding Rec.* (1884) I. 215 John Pearson..for tunning of ale from Yorke with a lycence..and tipling and selling it in his house. **1662** J. Davies tr. *Olearius' Voy. Ambass.* 294 The Taverns where they Tiple, and sell all sorts of Provisions.

**2.** *intr.* To drink of intoxicating liquor: in earlier use, to drink freely or hard; to booze; now *esp.*, to indulge habitually to some excess in taking strong drink.

**1560** Daus tr. *Sleidane's Comm.* 265 b, In this conflict was hurt Albert Brunswick, the sonne of Duke Philip, going vnaduisedly after he had wel tippled. **1570** Levins *Manip.* 128/18 To Typpil, *potitare.* **1603** Florio *Montaigne* II. ii. 198 By making an Ambassador to tipple square..he wrested all his secrets out of him. **1661** Pepys *Diary* 23 Apr., I wondered to see how the ladies did tipple. **1706** Phillips (ed. Kersey), To *Tipple*, to drink hard. **1749** Gray *Let. to Wharton* 25 Apr., We shall smoke, we shall tipple, we shall doze together. **1861** Tulloch *Eng. Purit.* ii. 289 They taught school, and tippled on the week-days.

**b.** *trans.* To drink (intoxicating liquor), esp. to take (drink) constantly in small quantities.

**1581** A. Hall *Iliad* II. 31 Tipling the plesaunt wine they downe to table sit. **1591** Greene *Disc. Coosnage* Pref. (1592) 3 He..had tipled so much malmsey, that he had neuer a readie word in his mouth. **1681** W. Robertson *Phraseol. Gen.* (1693) 1327 How the slut tipples off the wine. **1698** Fryer *Acc. E. India & P.* 93 Sack and Brandy out of the Bottle they will Tipple, till they are well warmed. **1749** Fielding *Tom Jones* VII. xi, The beer, of which having tippled a very large quantity. **1849** Clough *Dipsychus* II. ii. 168 We sit at our tables and tipple champagne.

**c.** *transf.* and *poetic.* To drink, sip. *intr.* and *trans.* Now *rare* or *Obs.*

**1648** Herrick *Hesper., Captiv'd Bee* 4 It chanc't a bee did flie that way,..To tipple freely in a flower. **1649** Lovelace *To Althea fr. Prison* ii, Fishes that tipple in the deep Know no such liberty. **1781** Crabbe *Library* 578 No more the midnight fairy tribe I view, All in the merry moonshine tippling dew.

**d.** *trans.* with *away*, + *up*: To spend, squander, lose, or get rid of by tippling.

*a* **1619** Fletcher *Wit without M.* II. iv, That annuity You have tippled up in taverns. **1687** J. Renwick in *Biogr. Presbyt.* (1827) II. 251 Ve must not be Lovers..of Strong Drink, nor tipple away Time in Alehouses. **1824** W. Irving *T. Trav.* II. x. 42, I took to the bottle, and tried to tipple away my cares.

†**3.** *trans.* To intoxicate, make drunk. See also Tippled *ppl. a.* below. *Obs.*

**1566** Painter *Pal. Pleas.* (1890) II. 13 When they had well whitled and tippled themselues. **1625** Purchas *Pilgrims* IX. xix. § 4. 1660 The most part eate Opium,..which tipples, intoxicates and duls them. **1648** Gage *West Ind.* xix. (1655) 144 By thus cheating and tipling poor Indians.

†**4.** *advb. phr. Tipple square*: cf. 1603 in 2.

**1605** Armin *Foole upon F.* (1880) 41 But he..got downe into the Seller, and fell to it tipple square.

Hence † **Ti·ppled** *ppl. a.*, intoxicated, drunk.

Orig. pa. pple. active, 'that has tippled'; cf. *well read, well spoken*, etc.

**1564** J. Rastell *Confut. Jewell's Serm.* 66 b, Whether God be..forgetfull, or well tipled. **1581** A. Hall *Iliad* I. 7 Thou tipled Knight, a snarring curre, to sight and shew thou art. **1611** Cotgr., *Enyvré*..drunke..mellow, tipled. **1660** Mrq. of Dorchester *Lett. to Ld. Roos* 2 A Tippl'd Fool, and a Bragging Coward. **1669** Dryden *Tyrannic Love* IV. i, Merry, merry, merry, we sail from the East, Half tippled at a rainbow feast.

**Ti·pple,** *v.*2 *dial.* [f. Tipple *sb.*2] *trans.* To bind (hay) in tipples (see Tipple *sb.*2). Also *absol.*

**1799** *Trans. Soc. Arts* XVII. 228, I tippled upwards of eighty acres. *Ibid.* 230 A husbandman..who..tippled some clover for me. **1812** Sir J. Sinclair *Syst. Husb. Scot.* I. 402 In a moderate crop, one woman will tipple to one mower, and a woman will rake to two tipplers or two swathes.

**Ti·pple,** *v.*3 *dial.* [freq. from Tip *v.*2 Cf. *topple.*]

**1.** *intr.* To tumble or topple over.

**1847–78** Halliwell, *Tipple*, to tumble; to turn over, as is done in tumbling. **1850** F. W. Newman *Phases of Faith* iii. 98 To tipple over irrecoverably. **1866** Hallam *Wadsley Jack* iv. (E.D.D.), I scream'd an tippled back into 't midden.

**2.** *trans.* To throw, pitch.

**1887** Hartley *Clock Alm.* 11 in *Leeds Merc. Suppl.* 15 Apr. (1899), Others..started o' tipplin' th' furnitur aght.

**Tippler**1 (ti·plər). Forms: 4–5 **tipeler**, 5 **-ar, tippelar, -ilar, typuler,** 5–8 **tipler,** 6 **typpler, typlar,** 6–7 **-er,** 6– **tippler.** [In form and in sense the agent-noun in -er from Tipple *v.*1, but actually known 150 years earlier than the vb., and prob. a century earlier than Tippling *ppl. a.*, so that the exact nature of the relationship of these words is uncertain: see Tipple *v.*1]

†**1.** A retailer of ale and other intoxicating liquor; a tapster; a tavern-keeper. *Obs.*

**1396** *Nottingham Rec.* I. 314 Johannes Jolivet et Johannes Smyth sunt communes tipelers, et vendunt infra domos suas cum discis et ciphis, contra Assisum. *c* **1420** *Durham Acc. Rolls* (Surtees) 359 Adam Sharp bras' tipelar, Alicia Mut tipelar, Joh'es Hunter tipelar. [So many instances 1424–5, etc.] **1478** *Nottingham Rec.* II. 298 Fines pro licentia merchandizandi Alicia Bult, tipler..iiij d. **1530** in W. H. Turner *Select. Rec. Oxford* (1880) 80 In-holders, and typlers wtin the Towne of Oxford. **1552** Huloet, Typpler or vitayler, *stabularius.* **1564** in *Rep. Hist. MSS. Comm., Var. Coll.* IV. 224 That the bruers or typlars shall not sell any bere or ale above the prices above set. **1642** *Ord. & Declar. Lords & Com. Lords Day* 6 That expresse charge be given to every keeper of any Taverne, Inne, Cooks shop, Tobacco-house, Ale-house, or any other Tipler or Victualler.

**2.** One who tipples; a habitual drinker of intoxicating liquor (implying more or less excess, but usually short of positive drunkenness).

**1580** Hollyband *Treas. Fr. Tong, Vn bon Biberon*, a bibber, a tippler. **1622** Massinger & Dekker *Virg. Martyr* II. i, Bacchus,..grand patron of rob-pots, upsie-freesie tiplers, and super-naculum takers. **1738** *Gentl. Mag.* VIII. 527/1 Which might be apply'd to much higher People, than poor Ale-house Tiplers. **1829** Lytton *Devereux* II. v, The women love not an early tippler. **1899** *Allbutt's Syst. Med.* VIII. 724 The moist palm of the habitual tippler is familiar to every one.

**Ti·ppler**2. *dial.* [f. Tipple *v.*2 + -er1.] One who binds up hay in tipples: see Tipple *sb.*2

**1812** [see Tipple *v.*2].

**Ti·ppler**3. [f. Tipple *v.*3 + -er1.] One who or that which tips or turns over: *spec.*

**1.** A frame or cage into which a wagon, truck, or tub is run, and which is then revolved so as to invert the wagon and discharge its contents.

**1831** J. Holland *Manuf. Metal* I. 46 Instead of the old corve and water bucket, an iron box, mounted on wheels, and called a tippler, and somewhat resembling in shape a common coal skip is made to travel completely round. **1891** Kipling *City Dreadf. Nt.* 83 The tub is run out into a 'tippler' and discharges itself into a coal-truck. **1911** *Encycl. Brit.* VI. 591 The tub..is run into a 'tippler', a cage turning about a horizontal axis, which discharges the load..and brings the tub back to the original position.

**2.** A variety of tumbler pigeon: see quot. 1879.

**1847–78** Halliwell, *Tippler*, a tumbler; hence, when they talk of a tumbler pigeon, you hear them say, 'What a tippler he is!' **1879** L. Wright *Pigeon Keeper* x. 128 [*Tipplers* throw only one such] backward somersault in the air at a time... *Tumblers* often make two, three, or more backward revolutions without stopping. **1885** *Bazaar* 30 Mar. 1265/1 Tipplers.—4 pairs of Macclesfield tipplers. Price 4/- per pair.

**Tippling** (ti·pliŋ), *vbl. sb.*1 [In form and sense, the ordinary vbl. sb. in -ing1 from Tipple *v.*1; as to date, etc., see the latter.] The action of Tipple *v.*1

†**1.** The retailing of ale or other strong drink; the business of a 'tippler' (Tippler1 1). *Obs.*

**1531** in W. H. Turner *Select. Rec. Oxford* (1880) 106 Persons that occupye any typpellyng or coblers crafte. **1579** *Ibid.* 400 To be discharged from keepinge of any tipplinge. **1550–1** in W. Hudson *Leet Jurisd. Norwich* (1892) 87 Amercyd for typplyng of ale and bere with unlawfull metts & measures. **1594** in J. Morris *Troub. Cath. Forefathers* (1877) 280 Also Dorothy Browne, widow who..was heretofore discharged in open sessions from brewing and tippling.

**2.** The drinking of intoxicating drink, esp. in small quantities and often; habitual indulgence in liquor (to some degree of excess, but usually not amounting to positive drunkenness).

**1567** *Let.* in *A. Jenkinson's Voy. & Trav.* (Hakl. Soc.) II. 214 If this typling be not left we will sende no more wyne. **1665** Needham *Med. Medicinæ* 406 Perpetual Tiplings and large drinking Bouts. **1771** Wesley *Wks.* (1872) VI. 152 Preventing tippling on the Lord's day, spending the time in alehouses. **1868** *Regul. & Ord. Army* ¶ 942 No tippling or gambling is to be allowed in any of the barrack rooms.

**3.** *attrib.* and *Comb.* (See also Tippling-house.)

*Tippling Act*, Act 24 Geo. II, c. 40.

**1579–80** North *Plutarch* (1595) 135 But in the ende..this bribing wretch was forced for to hold a typling booth, most like a clowne or snuch. **1616** Sylvester *Tobacco Battered* 215 'Tis vented most in Taverns, Tippling-cots, To Ruffians, Roarers, Tipsie-Tostie-pots. **1621** Burton *Anat. Mel.* Democr. to Rdr. (1628) 55 We liue wholly by Tippling-Innes and Ale-Houses. **1755** W. Duncan *Cicero's Sel. Orat.* xvi. (1816) 623 Under his roofs are..tippling-shops instead of dining rooms. **1784** Cowper *Task* VI. 695 The rabble all alive From tipling-benches..Swarm in the streets.

**Ti·ppling,** *vbl. sb.*2 *dial.* [f. Tipple *v.*2 + -ing1.] The binding of hay in tipples.

**1770–4** A. Hunter *Georg. Ess.* (1803) III. 194 The expense of tipling did not exceed five shillings a statute acre. **1812** Sir J. Sinclair *Syst. Husb. Scot.* I. 401 Tippling..he considers..to be not only a cheap, but a superior mode of making hay.

**Ti·ppling,** *ppl. a.* [f. Tipple *v.*1 + -ing2.] That tipples.

†**1.** That carries on the business of a 'tippler' (Tippler1 1); that sells liquor by retail. *Obs.*

? *a* **1500** *Chester Pl., Harrow. Hell* (Shaks. Soc.) II. 82 With all tiplinge tapsters that are cuninge, Mysspendinge moche maulte, brewinge so theyne. **1552** Huloet, Typplyng wyfe, *stabularia mulier.*

**2.** That habitually indulges (to some excess) in strong drink; given to drinking.

**1567** Harman *Caveat* 59 One of these tipling Tinckers.. robbed by the high way iiij Pallyards. **1693** J. Edwards *Author. O. & N. Test.* 210 Bacchus..the poets tippling deity. **1818** Scott *Hrt. Midl.* xlviii, That tippling body, the Captain. **1872** J. Timbs *Clubs & Club Life* I. 146 A merry company of tippling citizens and jocular change-brokers.

**Ti·ppling-house.** *Obs.* exc. *Hist.* [f. Tippling *vbl. sb.*1 + House *sb.*] A house where intoxicating liquor is sold and drunk; an ale-house, a tavern.

**1547** Boorde *Introd. Knowl.* xxxi. (1870) 200 The best fare is in prestes houses, for they do kepe typlynge houses. **1551–2** *Act* 5 & 6 *Edw. VI*, c. 25 *Preamble*, Comen Ale-houses and other houses called Tiplinge houses. **1639** Laud *Wks.* (1853) V. 239 Our university of Oxford had heretofore the government and correction of all manner of ale-house-keepers, ale-houses, and other tippling-houses. **1757** Washington *Let. Writ.* 1889 I. 502 Instances of the villainous Behavior of those Tippling-House-keepers. **1817** Scott *Let. to Morritt* 11 Aug., in *Lockhart*, There is a terrible evil in England to which we are strangers,—the number, to-wit, of tippling houses, where the labourer.. spends the overplus of his earnings. **1877** Burroughs *Taxation* 393 'To regulate and restrain tippling houses', confers no power to tax them.

**Tipply** (ti·pli), *a. colloq.* [f. Tipple *v.*3 + -y.] Apt to 'tipple' or tip over; unsteady; = Tippy *a.*2

**1906** *Westm. Gaz.* 11 June 8/2 A narrow river crowded.. with pleasure-craft—launches and 'party-boats', safe tubs and tipply canoes.

**Tippy** (ti·pi), *a.*1 (*sb.*) [f. Tip *sb.*1 + -y.]

**I.** *colloq.* or *slang.* **1.** In the height of fashion; smart, fine, fashionable, 'swell', 'tip-top'. ? *Obs.*

**1810** *Splendid Follies* I. 31 'My curricle has..never yet carried a bear', 'Except its Master', thought Seraphina, as she gazed on this tippy-bob. **1825** Jamieson, *Tippy*, adj., dressed in the highest fashion, modish. **1826** *Sporting Mag.* XVII. 177 With his hosen so tight, and his castor so white, and his caxon in tippy curl. **1847** *Blackw. Mag.* LXII. 47 His horse was the swiftest, his coat the tippiest, his cigar the longest. **1871** P. Cartwright *50 Years Presiding Elder* 216 It was not one of your tippy, fashionable, silver-slippered kind of conversions, but it was a backwoods conversion.

†**b.** *absol. The tippy*: the height of fashion; the 'swell' or fashionable thing. *Obs.*

**1794** *Sporting Mag.* III. 104 Being estimated..as quite the Tippy. **1803** *Ibid.* XXI. 145 The two-shilling gallery is now quite the tippy for the boxes. **1804** Charlotte Smith *Conversations*, etc. I. 25 Germain says, I shall be quite the thing, the tippy. **1811** *Ora & Juliet* III. 133 Do you see that handsome young man there?..he at the bottom, ..that's so dressed in the tippy.

**2.** Highly ingenious or clever; neat, smart. [perh. associated with Tip *sb.*4]

**1863** M. Dods *Early Lett.* (1910) 344 A tippy little bit of criticism by Pressensé. **1906** *Daily Chron.* 11 Oct. 3/5 All we think of is the 'tippy' way in which he is got rid of.

**II. 3.** Of tea: Containing a large proportion of the 'tips' or leaf-buds of the shoot.

**1892** Walsh *Tea* (Philad.) 87 The dried leaf [of Paklum] is also very black, fairly made and often 'tippy' in the hand. *Ibid.* 107 The leaf [of Neilgherry] is black, coarse, 'tippy' and unsightly in the hand. **1895** *Times* 21 Jan. 13/5 For the finest qualities: for handsome tippy teas, which are becoming scarce; and for good Darjeelings, the tendency is to higher quotations.

**Ti·ppy,** *a.*2 *colloq.* [f. Tip *v.*2 + -y.] Characterized by tipping or tilting; unsteady.

**1886** *Philadelphia Times* 16 Jan. (Cent.), The tippy sea.

**Tipsify** (ti·psifəi), *v.* [f. Tipsy + -fy.] *trans.* To make tipsy; to intoxicate (in quot. 1837 slightly or partially). Hence **Tipsifica·tion,** intoxication; **Ti·psifica:tor, Ti·psifier,** one who tipsifies (in quots., one who gets drunk, a tippler or toper); **Ti·psified** *ppl. a.*, made tipsy, (slightly) intoxicated. (All more or less *nonce-wds.*)

**1830** *Fraser's Mag.* I. 740 In all matters of coenic revelry and tipsified jollification. **1837** Carlyle *Misc., Mirabeau* (1857) IV. 95 The man was but tipsified when he went; happily, when he returned, which was very late, he was drunk. **1848** Thackeray *Bk. Snobs* xxiii, Poor Raff is tipsifying himself with spirits. **1864** Sala in *Daily Tel.* 27 July, The sharp New England mind..has long since endorsed the locution 'as tight as a peep' to express an utter state of tipsification. **1873** Leland *Egyptian Sketch-Bk.* 288 The last thing attended to by the tipsificators. **1873** Mrs. Whitney *Other Girls* iv, Our first man was a tipsifier, and the last was a rogue. **1888** Stevenson *Black Arrow* 169 A certain air of tipsified simplicity and good-fellowship.

**Tipsily** (ti·psili), *adv.* [f. as prec. + -ly2.] In a tipsy manner; unsteadily as from intoxication.

**1818** Keats *Endym.* IV. 217 Near him rode Silenus on his ass, Pelted with flowers as he on did pass, Tipsily quaffing. **1824** in *Spirit Pub. Jrnls.* (1825) 203 Tom Moore to Lord Lansdown is tipsily speeching. **1864** Lowell *Fireside Trav.* 89 Knocked down by a tipsily-driven sleigh.

**Tipsiness** (ti·psinės). [f. as prec. + -ness.] The state or condition of being tipsy; a partial degree of intoxication; also *fig.*

**1598** Florio, *Ebbriachezza*, dronkennes, tipsines. **1681** H. More *Exp. Dan.* Pref. 7 Partly out of tipsiness, and partly out of consternation of mind. **1840** Dickens *Barn. Rudge* iii, Firmly set upon his legs on that neutral ground which lies between the confines of perfect sobriety and slight tipsiness. **1855** Geo. Eliot *Ess.* (1884) 290 No tipsiness can be more dead to all appeals than that which comes from fitful draughts of sleep on a railway journey by night.

**Tip-sled**: see Tip- *vb. stem.*

**Tipstaff** (ti·pˌstɑf). Pl. **-staffs** (-stɑfs), or **-staves** (-stēivz). [Contraction of *tipped* or *tipt staff*: see Tipped *ppl. a.*1 3.]

†**1.** A staff with a tip or cap of metal, carried as a badge by certain officials: see 2. *Obs.*

**1541–2** *Act* 33 *Hen. VIII*, c. 12 § 26 Anye of the Kinges.. officers, that..shall strike any person..withe anye staffe commonlye called a Tipp staffe. **1579–80** North *Plutarch* (1676) 219 Sergeants and other Officers holding Tipstaves in their hands. **1695** Congreve *Love for L.* I. iv, Two suspicious Fellows like lawful Pads, that would knock a Man down with Pocket Tipstaves.

†**b.** *pl.* Used for 'stilts'. *Obs. nonce-use.*

**1582** Stanyhurst *Craking Cutter* in *Æneis*, etc. (Arb.) 143 Linckt was in wedlock a loftye Thrasonical huf snuffe: In gate al on typstau's stalcking, in phisnomye daring.

**2.** An official carrying a tipped staff; *spec.* **a.** A sheriff's officer, bailiff, constable; **b.** An officer appointed to wait upon a court in session; a court crier or usher. *arch.*

**1570** Foxe *A. & M.* (ed. 2) 1365/1 The knight Marshall

with all hys tippe staues. 1600 HOLLAND *Livy* XLV. xxix. 1220 When they saw the tipstaves and huishers to keepe the doores and places of entrie. 1687 *Magd. Coll. & Jas. II* (O.H.S.) 148 Then their Lordships..commissioned Atterbury the Tipstaff to fetch a Smith to force them open. 1710 J. HARRIS *Lex. Techn.* II, *Tip-staves*, are the Warden of the Fleets Officers attending the Queen's Courts with a Painted Staff, for taking into Custody such Persons [etc.]. 1831 CARLYLE *Sart. Res.* I. ix, Those ministering Sheriffs and Lord-Lieutenants and Hangmen and Tipstaves. 1882 SERJT. BALLANTINE *Exper.* xli. 387 They were tipstaves, prepared to take [him]..into custody. 1888 GOW *Comp. School Classics* 290 Order was maintained by tip-staffs, ῥαβδοῦχοι.

Hence **Ti·psta:very** (*nonce-wd.*), a body of tipstaffs.

1911 B. CAPES *Loaves & Fishes* 224 Cracking their inevitable chestnuts for the benefit of an obsequious tipstavery.

**Tipster** (ti·pstəɹ). [f. TIP *sb.*⁴ + -STER. (In sense 2 erron. f. TIP *sb.*³)]

**1.** A man who makes a business of furnishing 'tips' or confidential information as to the probable chances of an event on which betting depends, esp. in horse-racing.

1862 *Times* 31 Dec., Prophets, tipsters, and welshers—the parasites of the ring—are flourishing upon the infatuation or the ignorance of society. 1865 *Ibid.* 23 Sept., His Lordship asked the meaning of the word 'tipster'. Mr. Soper said it was one who prophesied, or pretended to tell the winners—who 'tipped' the word. 1897 *Daily News* 20 Oct. 3 To stop solicitations from tipsters and bookmakers to persons under the age of twenty-one.

**b.** *transf.* One who furnishes 'tips' in general.

1884 *Manch. Exam.* 17 Nov. 5/2 If it is ever of great consequence to follow the rôle of the political tipster. 1900 *Westm. Gaz.* 11 May 9/1 No wonder the price of..shares has given way...The fall is due entirely to the overthrow of the tipsters, who led us to expect so much, only to plunge us into the deepest disappointment.

**2.** One who systematically gives 'tips' or gratuities: see TIPPER¹ 4.

1889 *Pall Mall G.* 18 Feb. 7/3 It is not uncommon for the 'tipster' to pay to the employé of the purchaser a fixed commission of so much per pound or ton on all goods purchased by the master. It then becomes the interest of the servant to make his master buy as much as possible of any article from the 'tipster'.

**Ti·p-stock.** [f. TIP *sb.*¹ or *v.*² + STOCK *sb.*] A form of gun-stock: see quots.

1891 *Cent. Dict.*, *Tip-stock*, the movable tip or fore end of a gunstock, situated under the barrel or barrels, especially when it is a separate piece, in front of the breech or trigger-guard. A hinged or detachable tip-stock is required for breech-loaders which break in the vertical plane. 1895 *Funk's Standard Dict.* s. v. *Tip¹*, *v.*, *Tip-stock*, a gunstock arranged to hinge or tip, as for convenience in loading.

**Tip-stretcher**: see TIP *sb.*¹ 6.

**Tipsy** (ti·psi), *a.* Also 6–8 **tipsie**, 7–9 **tipsey.** [app. f. TIP *v.*² sense 7 (or ? 4, 5): cf. *tricksy*: see F. Hall *Mod. Eng.* 272.]

Affected with liquor so as to be unable to walk or stand steadily; partly intoxicated: often *euphemistic* for Intoxicated, inebriated, drunk.

1577 HANMER *Anc. Eccl. Hist.* (1663) 117 About ten of the clock, whenas they were somewhat tipsie, and well crammed with victuals. 1590 SHAKS. *Mids. N.* v. i. 48 The riot of the tipsie Bachanals. 1623 MIDDLETON *More Dissemblers* IV. i, He that's a gipsy may be drunk or tipsy. *a* 1668 DAVENANT *Play-house to Let* v. i, Sure Tony and you have drunk till y'are tipsey. *a* 1700 B. E. *Dict. Cant. Crew*, *Tipsy*, a'most Drunk. 1706 PHILLIPS (ed. Kersey), *Tipsy*, that is a little in Drink, fuddled. 1777 MME. D'ARBLAY *Early Diary* 7 Apr., She forced wine and water..down her throat, till she was almost tipsey. 1889 STEVENSON *Master of B.* viii, I have seen them flee from him when he was tipsy, and stone him when he was drunk.

**b.** *transf.* Characterized or accompanied by intoxication; arising from or causing tipsiness.

1634 MILTON *Comus* 104 Tipsie dance, and Jollity. 1760 FAWKES tr. *Anacreon, Ode* xli. 24 Then let me, warm with Wine, advance, And revel in the Tipsy Dance. 1851 THACKERAY *Eng. Hum.*, *Swift* (1858) 32 He was not bred up in a tipsy guard-room.

**c.** *fig.* Affected as if by intoxicating liquor; unsteady as if from drink; inclined to tip or tilt.

1754 RICHARDSON *Grandison* VI. ix. 31 Lord G. could not keep his seat: He was tipsy poor man with his joy. 1852 H. ROGERS *Ess.* I. vii. 339 He was..intellectually as tipsy as ever nitrous oxide could have made him. 1895 *Funk's Standard Dict.*, *Tipsy*..3. Bobbing and swaying; tipping about; also, liable to tip;..as, a tipsy boat. 1905 *Daily News* 26 Aug. 6 They ['To Let' boards] lean into the street at all sorts of tipsy angles.

**d.** *Tipsy key*: a kind of watch-key invented by Bréguet: see quot.

1884 F. J. BRITTEN *Watch and Clockm.* 36 [A] Tipsy key [is] a watch key in which the upper and lower portions are connected by means of a ratchet clutch kept in gear by a spring, so that the upper part will turn the lower part in the proper direction for winding.

**e.** *Comb.* **Ti·psy-to·psy** *a.* (*nonce-wd.*) [cf. *topsy-turvy*], upset or in disorder as if tipsy.

*a* 1845 HOOD *She is far fr. the Land* 59 Trunks tipsy-topsy, The ship in a dropsy.

Hence **Ti·psy** *v.*, *trans.* to make tipsy, tipsify.

1673 SHADWELL *Epsom Wells* I, Why, I..got a little tipsy'd, as they say, and forgot it. 1691 — *Scowrers* v, I was tipsied last night. 1849 JAMES *Woodman* iv, A butt of it would not have tipsied a sucking lamb.

**Ti·psy-ca:ke.** A cake saturated with wine or spirit, stuck with almonds, and served with custard.

1806 MISS MITFORD in L'Estrange *Friendships Mary R. Mitford* (1882) I. 10 We had..tipsey cake on one side, and grape tart on the other. 1845 J. C. ATKINSON in *Proc. Berw. Nat. Club* II. No. 13. 134 Red gypsum, externally set as full of..dog's-tooth crystals as a tipsy-cake with almonds. 1859 *Habits of Gd. Society* xiii. 338 As indispensable an element of the ball-supper as trifle, tipsy-cake, and mayonnaise.

**Tipsy-turvy**, obs. var. TOPSY-TURVY. **Tipt**, pa. t. and pple. of TIP *v.*; now less used than TIPPED.

**Tip-tail.** [f. TIP *sb.*¹ + TAIL *sb.*¹, after *tiptoe.*] The tip of the tail: only in phr. *on* or *upon tip-tail.*

1836–48 B. D. WALSH *Aristoph.*, *Acharnians* II. vi, You sat all the time upon tip-tail [Gr. ἐπ' ἄκρων πυγιδίων on the tips of their rumps]. 1876 MISS BRADDON *J. Haggard's Dau.* xxv, A curly serpent standing on tip tail between them. 1900 A. B. COOK in *Jrnl. Hellenic Stud.* XX. 2 Straightway struck by the crown you sat there on tip-tail.

**Tip-tap** (ti·p,tæp), *sb.* (*a.*), *v.* [f. TIP *sb.*² or *v.*¹ + TAP *sb.*² or *v.*²; or reduplication of TAP *sb.*² or *v.*², with alternation of vowel (cf. *zig-zag*, *pit-a-pat*).] A repeated tapping or light knocking of alternating character, or the sound made by it. **b.** *attrib.* or *adj.* That taps repeatedly. **c.** *vb.* To tap repeatedly or in alternation; hence **Tip-ta·pping** *ppl. a.* Also **Tip-tap-toe** = TICK-TACK-TOE.

1604 MARSTON *Malcontent* III. v, Liues not more faith in a home thrusting tongue, Then in these fencing tip tap Courtiers? *a* 1847 ELIZA COOK *Winter is here* i, The old robin has come To remind us with tip-tapping bill. 1849 [DINSDALE] *Durham Gloss.* (E. D. D.), Tip-tap-toe. 1892 BARRETT *Essex Highways*, etc. 56 The tip-tap of the flail may yet be heard. 1905 *Westm. Gaz.* 29 Nov. 1/3 Many a time and oft have I sat in the sun and hearkened to the tip-tap, tip-tap of his tiny hammer.

**Ti·p-ti:lted,** *a.* [f. TIP *sb.*¹ + TILTED *ppl. a.*²] Having the tip 'tilted', i. e. turned up. Hence **Tip-ti·lt** *v.*, *trans.* to turn up at the tip.

1872 TENNYSON *Gareth* 576 And lightly was her slender nose Tip-tilted like the petal of a flower. 1877 MRS. FORRESTER *Mignon* II. 51 Mignon 'tiptilts' her nose. 1882 ANNIE EDWARDES *Ballroom Repent.* I. 12 A Diana with..a tip-tilted nose. 1884 SIR C. W. WILSON in *Q. Statem. Palestine Explor. Fund* Jan. 48 The tip-tilted shoes are the ordinary sandals of the country.

**Tiptoe, tip-toe** (ti·p,tōᵘ), *sb.* (*adv.*, *a.*) Forms: *pl.* 4–5 **tiptoon**, 5 **typtoon, -ton, -toos, tiptos,** 6 **typtoes, tippetoes,** *Sc.* **typtays, typtaes,** 6– **tiptoes,** 7– **tip-toes**; *sing.* 5 **typto, tiptoo,** 6 **tipto, typtoe,** 6– **tiptoe,** 7– **tip-toe.** [f. TIP *sb.*¹ + TOE *sb.*, pl. in ME. *toon*, mod.E. *toes.*]

**1.** *pl.* The tips of the toes; almost always in phr. *on* or *upon* (one's) *tiptoes*, denoting a posture (in standing or walking) with the heels raised so that the body is supported upon the tips or balls of the toes. (Now more usually *on tiptoe*: see 2.)

*c* 1386 CHAUCER *Nun's Pr. T.* 487 He moste wynke..And stonden on his tiptoon [*v. rr.* typton, typtoon, typtoos, tiptos] ther-with-al, And strecche forth his nekke long and smal. ? *c* 1400 LYDG. *Æsop's Fab.* i. 44 [The cock] On his typton disposyd for to syng. 1513 DOUGLAS *Æneis* IX. xii. 53 Standand on his typtays. 1573–80 BARET *Alv.* G 368 To go soft and faire on his tippetoes. 1591 SPENSER *M. Hubberd* 1009 Vpon his tiptoes nicely he vp went. 1642 FULLER *Holy & Prof. St.* III. ix. 171 He needs to stand on tiptoes that hopes to touch the moon. 1712 *Spect.* No. 460 ¶ 7 Gallantry strutting upon his Tip-toes. *a* 1845 HOOD *As it fell upon a Day* ii, And then upon her tiptoes jumping

*transf.* 1848 TENNYSON in Ld. Tennyson *Mem.* (1897) I. xiii. 281 We arrived at the banks of the loch, and made acquaintance with the extremest tiptoes of the hills.

**b.** *fig.*: usually in reference to expectation or eagerness (formerly to pretension or haughtiness).

1579 TOMSON *Calvin's Serm. Tim.* 550/1 Because men stand willingly vppon their tiptoes, and thinke no man worthie to haue preheminence aboue his fellowes. 1639 FULLER *Holy War* II. ix. (1840) 60 All stood on the tiptoes of expectation. 1651 N. BACON *Disc. Govt. Eng.* II. xxvii. (1739) 125 The minds of men are at a gaze; their Affections and Passions are on their Tiptoes. 1682 N. O. *Boileau's Lutrin* I. 333 Their fligg'ring Souls do now on Tiptoes stand.

**2.** *sing.* The tips of the toes collectively; almost always in phr. *on* or *upon tiptoe* (cf. 1).

*c* 1440 [see b]. 1525 W. SMITH *Wido Edyth* in *Laneham's Let.* (1871) p. xlv, Than Wa[l]ter stode on tipto, and gan him self avance. 1607 DAVIES *Summa Totalis* B ij b, But when we stand on Tip-toe, or. a Ball, (Though sliding still) we finally must fall. 1760–72 H. BROOKE *Fool of Qual.* (1809) IV. 124 [He] entered my chamber on tip-toe. 1833 L. RITCHIE *Wand. by Loire* 164 Standing on tiptoe, [he] looked into one of the windows. 1861 HUGHES *Tom Brown at Oxf.* xxxii, He followed his cousin on tip-toe.

**b.** *transf.* and *fig.*: cf. 1 b. (Often *the tiptoe.*)

*c* 1440 *Pallad. on Husb.* XI. 46 And right so on the typto [*v. r.* tiptoo] lete hem [vines] gey. 1602 MARSTON *Antonio's Rev.* IV. iii, Your eyes should sparkle joy, Your bosome rise on tiptoe at this news. 1642 MILTON *Apol. Smect.* iv. Wks. 1738 I. 118 What with putting his fancy to the tiptoe in this description of himself. 1799 NELSON in Nicolas *Disp.* (1845) III. 374 We are on the tip-toe of expectation. 1860–1 FLOR. NIGHTINGALE *Nursing* 38 Do not keep his expectation on the tip-toe.

**c.** *A-tiptoe* = on tiptoe: see A-TIPTOE.

**B.** *adv.* Short for *on* or *a-tiptoe*: see 2 above.

1592 SHAKS. *Rom. & Jul.* III. v. 10 Nights Candles are burnt out, and Iocond day Stands tipto on the mistie Mountaines tops. 1612 *Two Noble K.* I. ii. 57 To go tip-toe Before the streete be foule. 1821 CLARE *Vill. Minstr.* I. 186 Then tiptoe round the maidens bound, All sorrow lags behind. 1854 EMERSON *Soc. Aims* Wks. (Bohn) III. 182 It is not that they wish you to stand tiptoe, and pump your brains.

**C.** *adj.* Standing or walking, or characterized by standing or walking, on tiptoe.

1593 [see b]. 1744 H. BROOKE *Love & Van.* 120 Why, what unfashion'd stuff you tell us Of buckram dames and tiptoe fellows! 1781 COWPER *Expost.* 84 With tip-toe step Vice silently succeeds. 1801 MAR. EDGEWORTH *Gd. French Gov.* (1831) 146 Grace..made her tiptoe approaches. 1848 MRS. GASKELL *M. Barton* ii, He, with habitual tip-toe step, approached the poor frail body.

**b.** *transf.* and *fig.* in various senses: e. g. straining upwards, ambitious; eagerly expectant; tripping, dancing; silent, stealthy.

1593 NASHE *Christ's T.* Wks. (Grosart) IV. 122 Hath no chyld of Pryde so many Disciples as thys tiptoe Ambition. 1789 E. DARWIN *Bot. Gard.* I. 386 You..Bade his bold arm invade the lowering sky, And seize the tiptoe lightnings, ere they fly. 1818 KEATS *Endymion* I. 831 How tiptoe Night holds back her dark-grey hood. 1823 SCOTT *Peveril* iv, The Cavaliers..were filling the principal avenue to the Castle with tiptoe mirth and revelry. 1879 G. MEREDITH *Egoist* xii, Man or maid sleeping in the open air provokes your tip-toe curiosity.

**D.** *Comb.* of the *adv.*, as † *tiptoe-nice* (so nice or particular as to walk on tiptoe), † *-strouting*, *-tripping* adjs.

1593 NASHE *Christ's T.* Wks. (Grosart) IV. 218 So typtoe-nyce in treading on the earth, as though they walkt vpon Snakes. 1600 S. NICHOLSON *Acolastus* (1876) 39 Their tipto-tripping pace bred double mazing. 1602 *2nd Pt. Return fr. Parnass.* III. iv. 1386 To honour me: For my high tiptoe strouting poesye.

**Ti·ptoe,** *v.* [f. prec.]

**1.** *intr.* To raise oneself or stand on tiptoe.

*a* 1661 HOLYDAY *Juvenal* vi. (1673) 101 Then a girle-pygmie she's more dwarf..and tiptoes for a kisse and flout. 1851 J. H. NEWMAN *Cath. in Eng.* 243 They crowd up together, ..tiptoeing and staring, and making strange faces. 1888 *Century Mag.* Nov. 90/1 The..girls..left their seats to tiptoe and look over each other's shoulders.

**2.** To go or walk on tiptoe; to step or trip lightly. Also *to tiptoe it.*

1748 RICHARDSON *Clarissa* (1811) VI. xxv. 104 Mabell tiptoed it to her door. 1883 MRS. ROLLINS *New Eng. Bygones* 62, I tiptoe across the fragile floor and look out. 1897 HOWELLS *Landl. Lion's Head* 68 Ladies..lifting their skirts and tiptoeing through the dew.

Hence **Ti·ptoed** *ppl. a.*, (*a*) raised on tiptoe; also *fig.*, rising aloft; (*b*) performed on tiptoe; **Ti·ptoeing** *ppl. a.*, standing or going on tiptoe.

1632 LITHGOW *Trav.* X. 499 Meandring Forth from tiptoed Snadoun, the prospicuous mirrour for matchlesse Maiesty. 1682 D'URFEY *Butler's Ghost* 92 To please the tiptoed Girl of Ten. 1819 *Metropolis* III. 164 Eagle-eyed curiosity staring you in the face, tip-toed anxiety standing on either hand. *a* 1847 ELIZA COOK *Rory O'More* viii, His tip-toeing feet seemed inclined for a jig.

**Ti·p-to·p,** *sb.*, *a.*, *adv.* *colloq.* [f. TIP *sb.*¹ + TOP, or reduplicated form of the latter.]

**A.** *sb.* **1.** The very top; the highest point or part; the extreme summit.

1702 [see 2]. 1759 *Compl. Letter-writer* (ed. 6) 219 Upon the tip top of the monument. 1826 S. THOMAS in Hone *Every-day Bk.* II. 186 The tip-top of the plant. 1857 DICKENS *Let.* 15 Apr., On the tip-top of Gad's Hill, between this and Rochester,..I have a pretty little old-fashioned house. *a* 1887 in Frith *Autobiog.* II. ii. 37 You should paint him sitting on the tip-top of the mast of a big ship.

**2.** *fig.* **a.** Highest pitch or degree; extreme height; acme.

1702 S. PARKER tr. *Cicero's De Finibus* IV. 228 When a Wise Man is at the Tip-top of all Felicity, can he wish Things were better with him? 1747 WESLEY *Wks.* (1872) XII. 83 The tip-top of all inconsistencies. 1798 O'KEEFFE *Wild Oats* III. i, All on the tip-top of expectation. 1837 HAWTHORNE *Twice-told T.* (1851) I. x. 171, I cry aloud to all and sundry..at the very tiptop of my voice.

**b.** *sing.* and *pl.* People of the highest quality or rank (collectively); 'grandees', 'swells'. ? *Obs.*

1753 *School of Man* 125 To figure among high company ..this his marriage has done at once, and among the Tip Top. 1797 MRS. A. M. BENNETT *Beggar Girl* (1813) III. 278 The spark was kin to some of the tip-tops of his own kindred. 1849 THACKERAY *Pendennis* lx, We go here to the best houses, the tiptops, I tell you.

**B.** *adj.* Situated at the very top; very highest; almost always *fig.* of the highest quality or excellence; first-rate, prime, superlatively good; of persons, belonging to the highest rank or class.

1722 BYROM *Epil. Hurlothrumbo* Poems 1773 I. 215 Proud of your Smiles, he's mounted many a Story Above the tiptop Pinnacle of Glory. 1732 *Tricks of Town* 8, I have known a tip-top Physician sent for by an Express [etc.]. 1755 SMOLLETT *Quix.* I. II. iv. (1803) I. 93 He made carols for Christmas eve, and plays for the Lord's day;..and every body said, they were tip-top. 1825 *Sporting Mag.* XVI. 272 One hundred guineas, a tip-top price in those days. 1840 THACKERAY *Paris Sk.-bk.* ii, Quite select, and frequented by the tip-top nobility. 1857 HUGHES *Tom Brown* II. v, He is in tip-top training. 1880 DISRAELI *Endym.* xxi, Our friend Ferrars seems in tiptop company.

**C.** *adv.* In the highest degree, superlatively, extremely well.

1888 STOCKTON *Dusantes* III. 120 'That suits us tip-top, ma'am', said the coxswain.

**D.** *Comb.*: **tip-top-castle**, name of some boys' game; **tip-top-gallant** *a.* (*nonce-wd.*) [after *top-gallant*], of superlatively high rank or quality.

1834 KEIGHTLEY *Tales*, etc. i. 12 He was a capital player at *tip-top-castle. 1730 SWIFT *Vind. Ld. Carteret* Wks. 1841 II. 117/1, I do not find how his excellency can be justly censured for favouring none but..*tiptopgallantmen.

Hence **Ti·pto·pness**; **Tip-to·pper**, a 'tip-top' person or thing; in quot. 1822, applied to a glass filled to the very top, a bumper; **Tip-to·pping** [TOPPING *ppl. a.*], **Tipto·ppish** (hence *tipto·ppishness*), **Tipto·psome** *adjs.* = B.

**1891** *Boston Daily Globe* 24 Mar. 5/2 The very topmost *tiptopness of Harvard thought. **1822** *Blackw. Mag.* XI. 89 So I think it but proper to fill a *tip-topper Of Sherry to drink to the King. **1837** THACKERAY *Ravenswing* i, One of the first swells on town ma'am—a regular tip-topper. **1882** ANNIE EDWARDES *Ballroom Repent.* I. 243 Give me your operatic tip-toppers—Patti and Trebelli, or nothing. **1827** S. P. in Hone *Every-day Bk.* II. 54 This is mostly with the *tip-topping part [of people]. **1855** W. K. KELLY tr. *Cervantes' Exemp. Novels* 475 All she had told him of the merits, worth, beauty, modesty, and *tiptoppishness.. of her mistress, he quite believed. **1819** *Blackw. Mag.* V. 717 In the *tiptopsomest degree.

‖ **Tipula** (ti·piŭlă). *Entom.* Pl. **tipulæ** (-lī). [L. *tippula* (incorrectly *tipula*) a water-spider or water-bug; so used also by mediæval and early modern writers. The current use is due to Linnæus.] A genus of dipterous insects, typical of the family *Tipulidæ* or crane-flies, the common British species of which are familiarly known as *daddy-long-legs*.

[**1658** ROWLAND *Moufet's Theat. Ins.* 1023 We shall take Gaza's Tipulæ into our consideration among the Water-worms. **1706** PHILLIPS (ed. Kersey), *Tipula* (Lat.), a Water-spider with six Feet, that runs on the top of the Water without sinking. **1817** KIRBY & SP. *Entomol.* xxiii. (1818) II. 371 Linné, in his Lapland tour, noticed a black Tipula which ran over the water, and turned round like a Gyrinus.] **1752** J. HILL *Hist. Anim.* 36 The great Tipula. This is the largest and the most beautiful of the Tipula kind. **1774** GOLDSM. *Nat. Hist.* (1776) VIII. 152 The tipula is a harmless peaceful insect, that offers injury to nothing; the gnat is sanguinary and predaceous. **1831** *Brit. Farmer's Mag.* VI. 321 The grub of this tipula commits its ravages chiefly in the first crop.

Hence **Tipularian** (-ē·riăn) *a.*, belonging or allied to the genus *Tipula* or family *Tipulidæ*; also as *sb.* (*sc.* insect); **Tipulary** (ti·piŭlări) *a.* = prec. adj.; **Ti·pulid, Tipu·lidan,** *a.* belonging to the family *Tipulidæ*; *sb.* an insect of this family, a crane-fly; **Tipuli·deous** *a.* = prec. adj.

**1828** *Tipularian [see *tipulidan*]. **1832** MACGILLIVRAY tr. *Humboldt's Trav.* xviii. (1836) 248 On the streams..the *tipulary flies do not make their appearance. **1852** TH. ROSS *Humboldt's Trav.* II. xxiv. 438 Perhaps, also, the destruction of forests..will somewhat tend to diminish the torment of the tipulary insects. **1893** *Athenæum* 20 May 641/2 Dicranota, a Carnivorous *Tipulid Larva. **1817** KIRBY & SP. *Entomol.* xxii. (1818) II. 277 The grub of a kind of gnat.., and also another, probably of the *Tipulidan [*ed.* 1828 Tipularian] tribe.., have each a fleshy leg on the underside of the first segment. **1826** *Ibid.* III. xxix. 79 The eggs of..gnats and other Tipulidans [are] set afloat upon, or submerged in, the water. **1840** WESTWOOD *Classif. Insects* II. 170 Checking the over-production of some of the minute *Tipulideous insects.

**Ti·p-up,** *sb.* and *a.* [f. phr. *tip up*: TIP *v.*[2]]

**A.** *sb.* Something that tips or tilts up.

**1.** A name for the American sandpiper.

**1848** [see TEETER *sb.* 2].

**2.** A wagon with wheels set near together.

**1887** LADY BRASSEY *Last Voy.* xiii. (1889) 299 Another conveyance, familiarly known as a 'Tip-up', its narrow wheels making it liable to upset except on good roads.

**3.** = TILT *sb.*[2] 6 (*Cent. Dict.* 1891). (*N. Amer.*)

**B.** *adj.* Constructed to tip or tilt up, as a receptacle, for the purpose of emptying out its contents, or as a seat (in a theatre, etc.) when not occupied, so as to give room for passing.

**1884** *Health Exhib. Catal.* 46/1 Lavatories, fitted complete with Tip-up Basins. **1887** *Times* 25 Aug. 4/5 Turntables, tip-up machines..are provided at distances of 100 ft. apart along the quay. **1904** *Westm. Gaz.* 20 Jan. 10/1 The green upholstery of the comfortable 'tip-up' seats. **1905** *Ibid.* 18 Mar. 10/2 Industrial vehicles, which include.. lorries, tip-up wagons, carts, brewers' drays, and other wagons for heavy traction.

**Tiquet,** obs. Sc. form of TICKET.

† **Tir** (tīr). *Obs.* Also 3 **tyr.** [OE. *tír* glory, honour, cognate with ON. *tírr* str. masc. glory, renown; related to OHG. *zêri, ziari,* MHG. *ziere* adj. costly, splendid, whence OHG. *ziarî* fem., MHG. *ziere,* Ger. *zier* splendour, beauty, adornment, Ger. *zierat* ornament.] Glory, honour, majesty. Hence † **Ti·rful** *a.*, mighty, glorious.

*Beowulf* 1654 Hwæt we þe þas sælac..lustum brohton tires to tacne. *a* **1000** *Sal. & Sat.* 364 (Gr.) Ne bið hira tir ȝelic. *a* **1000** *Ags. Ps.* (Th.) lxxix. 14 Tires Wealdend. *c* **1205** LAY. 2051 Seoððen com oþer tir [*c* **1275** tyr] & neowe tidinde. *Ibid.* 4327 Here tir wes at-fallen. *Ibid.* 2893 Appollones temple þe wes þe tirfulle feond.

**Tirable** (təi°·răb'l), *a. rare.* [f. TIRE *v.*[1] + -ABLE.] That may be (easily) tired.

**1607** TOPSELL *Four-f. Beasts* (1658) 241 A sign of an unskilful Rider, or of a weak and tirable Horse.

† **Tirable,** obs. form of TERRIBLE.

**1562** BULLEYN *Bulwark, Bk. Simples* 37 Doth kepe the minde..from tirable and fearefull dreames.

**Tirade** (ti-, təirē·d), *sb.* [a. mod.F. *tirade* (16th c.) a draught, pull, shot; a long speech, declamation; passage of prose or verse, stanza, paragraph; ad. It. *tirata* a volley, etc., f. pa. pple. of *tirare* to draw, etc. (cf. TIRE *sb.*[3]): see -ADE.]

**1.** A volley of words; a long and vehement speech on some subject; a declamation; a protracted harangue, *esp.* of denunciation, abuse, or invective.

**1801** MAR. EDGEWORTH *Angelina* iv, 'Another cup of tea..', said Miss Hodges, when she had finished her tirade. **1809** HAN. MORE *Cœlebs* II. 236 A fine high-sounding *tirade*, Charles, spoken *con amore*. **1818** COBBETT *Pol. Reg.* XXXIII. 115 Let him hear this debate, these tirades of infamous falsehoods. **1823** SCOTT *Quentin D.* xxiii, She listened with a melancholy smile to her guide's tirade in praise of liberty. **1858** DORAN *Crt. Fools* 27 Tirades of bombastic nonsense. **1874** GREEN *Short Hist.* vi. § 4. 306 The King..had..to impose silence on the tirades which were delivered from the University pulpit. **1899** E. W. GOSSE *Donne* I. 131 The preface is a curious tirade.

**2.** *spec.* A passage or section of verse, of varying length, treating of a single theme or idea.

**1878** HUEFFER *Troubadours* 250 *note*, Tirades or paragraphs of varying lengths, bound together by the same rhyme. **1879** SAINTSBURY in *Encycl. Brit.* IX. 638/1 The lines [in the *chansons de gestes*] are arranged, not in couplets or in stanzas of equal length, but in *laisses* or *tirades*, consisting of any number of lines from half a dozen to some hundreds...Sometimes the tirade is completed by a shorter line. **1900** SANTAYANA *Poetry & Relig.* 257 Euphuism contributes not a little to the poetic effect of the tirades of Keats and Shelley. **1901** J. HALL *K. Horn* p. li, The poem extends to 5,250 alexandrines rhymed in tirades.

**3.** *Mus.* (See quot.)

**1876** STAINER & BARRETT *Dict. Mus. Terms, Tirade*, the filling up of an interval between two notes with a run, in vocal or instrumental music.

Hence **Tira·de** *v., intr.* to utter or write a tirade; to inveigh or declaim vehemently.

**1871** R. B. VAUGHAN *St. Thomas Aquinas* II. 683 *note*, They tirade against the influence of dogma. **1905** *Westm. Gaz.* 15 Jan. 2/1 The papers tirade against England. **1907** J. F. FRASER in *Standard* 13 Mar., A Welsh member tiraded on what the Welsh Church Commission should not do.

‖ **Tirage** (tirā·ʒ). [Fr., action of drawing, bringing out, producing, printing, etc., f. *tirer* to draw, etc. (TIRE *v.*[2]): see -AGE.] A pulling or reprint of a book, from the same type or stereotype (distinguished from an *edition*): cf. IMPRESSION 3 c.

**1873** *Rep. Brit. Assoc.* I. 144 The 1838 edition (or rather *tirage*) has the following notice of errata contained in it. **1888** *Encycl. Brit.* XXIII. 10/1 Babbage, 'Table of the Logarithms of the Natural Numbers from 1 to 108,000' (London, stereotyped in 1827; there are several tirages of later dates), is the best for ordinary use.

‖ **Tirailleur** (tira·lyōr). [Fr. (1740 in Dict. Acad.), f. *tirailler* to shoot in independent firing, f. *tirer* to draw, shoot (TIRE *v.*[2]).] One of a body of skirmishers employed in the wars of the French Revolution (1792); a skirmisher, a sharp-shooter; a soldier (usually of infantry) trained for independent action. Also *attrib.*

**1796** *Campaigns* 1793-4 I. I. vii. 65 The tiralleurs and riflemen could easily..discover and take aim at the Republicans. **1812** *Examiner* 14 Sept. 582/1 Woods, filled with tiraillenrs. **1847** DE QUINCEY *Span. Nun* Wks. 1860 III. 44 Any Spanish tirailleur's bullet. **1898** *Daily News* 17 Oct. 3/7 A column consisting of tirailleurs and irregulars was dispatched to suppress a rising of the Bouboureys.

**Tiralee** (ti·rălī). Also 6 **tireli,** 7 **tirlery.** [Echoic. Cf. OF. *turelu* a comic or burlesque refrain, and see TIRRA-LIRRA.] **a.** The note of the lark; = TIRRA-LIRRA. **b.** A representation of a bugle note or cadence.

**1596** FITZ-GEFFRAY *Sir F. Drake* (1881) 24 Even as the Larke..Mounteth her basinetted head on high,..Quav'ring full quaintlie forth her Tireli. ? *c* **1600** in *E. E. Lyrics* (1907) 255 Tirlery lorpin, the laverock sang. **1847** MARY HOWITT *Ballads* 130 And the bugles blew with a 'tira lee'! As they came by the way.

**Tiran, -ant, -anny,** obs. ff. TYRANT, TYRANNY.

‖ **Tirasse** (tira·s). [Fr., a draw-net, hence, a pedal-coupler, f. *tirasser*, augmentative or pejorative of *tirer* to draw (TIRE *v.*[2]).]

**1.** *Organ-building.* (See quot.)

**1876** STAINER & BARRETT *Dict. Mus. Terms, Tirasse* (Fr.), the pedals of an organ which act on the keys or manuals.

**2.** A draw-net. Hence **Tira·ssing** *vbl. sb.*, the netting of game with the draw-net.

**1897** *Pall Mall Mag.* Dec. 514 The 'tirasse' or drag-net. *Ibid.* 515 In Louis XIV's time 'trassing' pheasants and partridges was sport which the king and his ladies often witnessed.

**Tirdil, tirdle,** obs. ff. TREDDLE, sheep's dung.

**Tire** (təi°ɹ), *sb.*[1] Forms: 4 tyr, 5–9 tyre, 6 tier, 6–7 tyer, 6– tire. [Aphetic f. *atir*, ATTIRE *sb.*]

† **1.** Apparatus, equipment, accoutrement, outfit: = ATTIRE *sb.* 1. *Obs.*

**13..** *Guy Warw.* (A.) 7306 + st. ccli, A swift ernand stede ..His tire it was ful gay. *c* **1330** *Amis & Amil.* 1245 That knight, With helm and plate and brini bright, His tire it was ful gay. *c* **1400** *R. Gloucester's Chron.* 1188 A þousend gode kniȝtes þerinne were adreint & al hor atir [*MSS. a, β* tyr, tire] & tresour was also aseint. **1608** SHAKS. *Per.* III. ii. 22, I much maruaile that your Lordship, Hauing rich tire about you, should at these early howers, Shake off the golden slumber of repose. **1622** F. MARKHAM *Bk. War* III. x. § 5 Ordnance ready mounted with all their cooplements, Ornaments, Tires, and necessaries which belong vnto the same. **1705** J. PHILIPS *Blenheim* 78 Immediate Sieges, and the Tire of War Rowl in thy eager Mind.

**2.** Dress, apparel, raiment; = ATTIRE *sb.* 3. *arch.*

† *Bonnet of tire* (*Sc. Obs.*), a cap of estate, cap of maintenance (see CAP *sb.*[1] 4 f).

**13..** *Coer de L.* 332 In anothir tyre he hym dyght. **1340–70** *Alex. & Dind.* 883 Þat..ȝoure wiuus Ne gon in no gay tyr. *a* **1400** *Siege of Troy* 1190 in *Archiv neu. Spr.* LXXII. 37 His modir..sende him into þeo lond of Parchy In a maydenes tyr [*v. r.* wede]. **1473–4** *Acc. Ld. High Treas. Scot.* I. 32 To covir hire bonatis of tyre. **1536** BELLENDEN *Boece's Cron. Scot.* XIII. viii. (1821) II. 327 This legat als presentit ane bonat of tire, maid in maner of diademe, of purpoure hew; to signify that he was defendar of the faith. *c* **1600** SHAKS. *Sonn.* liii. 8 You in Grecian tires are painted new. **1612** DRAYTON *Poly-olb.* xii. 517 Of all their stately tyres disrobed when they bee. **1719** D'URFEY *Pills* (1872) IV. 81 It is not your flaunting Tires, Are the cause of Men's Desires. **1850** BLACKIE *Æschylus* II. 96 Your tire rich-flaunting with barbaric pride Bespeaks you strangers.

† **b.** *transf.* and *fig.* 'Vesture', 'attire'. *Obs.*

**1594** CAREW *Tasso* (1881) 96 Or she her shamefast and downe clyned eyes With tire and taint of honesty embowres. *a* **1600** M. COSOWARTH in Farr *S. P. Eliz.* (1845) II. 407 If thou disrobe me of th' earthe's tyre I weare. *a* **1660** HAMMOND *Serm.* Wks. 1684 IV. 572 Had not the second person of the Trinity..come down in his tire and personation of flesh. **1695** WOODWARD *Nat. Hist. Earth* VI. (1723) 294 They [plants] display themselves, shewing their whole Tire of Leaves.

**3.** *spec.* A covering, dress, or ornament for a woman's head; a head-dress; = ATTIRE *sb.* 4; in some cases perh. confused with TIAR, tiara. Also *transf.* and *fig. arch.*

*c* **1425** *Cast. Persev.* 223 in *Macro Plays* 84 [Devil says] On Mankynde is my trost, in contre I-knowe, With my tyre & with my tayl, tytly to tene. **1481–90** *Howard Househ. Bks.* (Roxb.) 442 Item..fur a peyer of tyres..and a serclett for my Lady Barnes. *a* **1548** HALL *Chron., Hen. VIII* 7, vi. ladyes..with marueylous ryche & straunge tiers on their heades. **1560** BIBLE (Genev.) *Isa.* iii. 18 In that day shal the Lord take away the ornament of the slippers, & the calles, & the rounde tyres. *Ibid.* 20 The tyres of the head, and the sloppes. **1590** SPENSER *F. Q.* I. x. 31 And on her head she wore a tyre of gold. **1610** *Histrio-m.* II. 117 *Post.* My maisters, what tire wears your lady on her head? *Bel.* Four squirrels tails tied in a true loves knot. **1630** DRAYTON *Muses Elizium* ii. 213 And for thy head Ile haue a Tyer Of netting. **1639** *Bury Wills* (Camden) 183 A mourning tire on their heads, such as gentlewomen weare at the time of ffuneralls. **1653** J. HALL *Paradoxes* 67 What Towers doe the Turkish Tires weare upon their womens heads? **1851** D. WILSON *Preh. Ann.* (1863) II. III. v. 148 The maiden coronet or tire for the hair. **1851** C. L. SMITH tr. *Tasso* I. xlvii, Her forehead lacked its tire. **1887** *Suppl. to Jamieson, Tire, Tyre*, a snood or narrow band for the hair, worn by females.

**4.** Ornamentation of various kinds: see quots. *dial.* or *local.*

**1876** *Whitby Gloss., Tire*, the metallic embellishments of cabinet work. **1887** *Suppl. to Jamieson, Tire, tyre*..an ornamental edging used by cabinet-makers and upholsterers; the metal edging of coffins, which is also called coffin-tyre.

**5.** A pinafore or apron to protect the dress; also (perh. better) written *tier*: see TIER *sb.*[2] 4. *U.S.*

**1846** WORCESTER, *Tire*..attire, a child's apron.. See *Tier*. **1849** LOWELL *Biglow P.* Ser. I. Introd., The humble school-house..Where well-drilled urchins, each behind his tire, Waited in ranks the wished command to fire. **1864** WEBSTER, *Tire*, a child's apron,..a tier. **1867** O. W. HOLMES *Guard. Angel* iii, The child untied her little 'tire', got down from the table. **1883** ROLLINS *New Eng. Bygones* 136 This humble serving woman..in her homespun tyre, filled with wild herbs and roots.

**6.** *attrib.* and *Comb.* (in sense 2; *Obs.* or *arch.*): **tire-glass**, a dressing-glass, toilet-glass; † **tire-house**, the wardrobe of a theatre; also = TIRING-HOUSE; **tire-maid** = TIRE-WOMAN; † **tire-maker**, a head-dress-maker; † **tire-man**, (*a*) a man in charge of the costumes at a theatre; (*b*) a man who assists at the toilet; a dresser or valet; also, a tailor; † **tire-pin**, a pin used in the toilet; **tire-room**, a dressing-room, tiring-room.

**1844** MRS. BROWNING *Duchess May* xxxv, In her *tire-glass gazed she. *c* **1620** *Songs Lond. Prentices* (Percy Soc.) 96 To the *tire-howse broke they in, Which some began to plunder. **1871** ROSSETTI *Dante at Verona* xiv, *Tire-maids hidden among these Drew close their loosened bodices. **1611** RICH *Honest. Age* (Percy Soc.) 18 Shee holdeth on her way ..to the *Tyre makers shoppe. **1611** COTGR., *Perruquiere*, a Tyre-maker, or Attire-maker; a woman that makes Perriwigs, or Attires. **1599** B. JONSON *Cynthia's Rev.* Induct., To have his presence in the tiring-house..[to] curse the poor *tireman. **1711** SHAFTESB. *Charac.* (1737) I. 84 Neither the magistrate, nor the tire-men themselves, cou'd resolve, which of the various modes was the exact true-one. *a* **1450** *Knt. de la Tour* (1906) 63 The settinge of her *tyre pynnes and array. **1681** *Religio Clerici* 52 Strip it naked of its plain English, and send it to be drest in their *Tire-room. **1855** BROWNING *Bp. Blougram's Apol.* 70 Then going in the tire-room afterward, Because the play was done, to shift himself.

**Tire** (təi°ɹ), *sb.*[2] Forms: 5, 7, 9 tyre, (8–9 tier), 7– tire. See also TYRE. [Probably the same word as prec., the *tire* being originally (sense 1) the 'attire', 'clothing', or 'accoutrement' of the wheel. From 15th to 17th c. spelt (like prec.) *tire* and *tyre* indifferently. Before 1700 *tyre* became generally obsolete, and *tire* remained as the regular form, as it still does in America; but in Great Britain *tyre* has been recently revived as the popular term for the rubber rim of bicycle, tricycle, carriage, or motor-car wheels, and is sometimes used for the steel tires of locomotive wheels.]

†1. *collective sing.* The curved pieces of iron plate, called strakes or streaks, placed end to end or overlapping, with which cart and carriage wheels were formerly shod (now rarely used, and only for heavy agricultural vehicles, artillery carriages, etc.).

**1485** in *Ripon Ch. Acts* (Surtees) 373, j tyre pro rota plaustri. **1601** HOLLAND *Pliny* XXXIV. xiv. (1634) II. 514 Yron..such as will not serue one whit for stroke [= strake] and naile to bind cart-wheels withall, which tire indeed would be made of the other that is gentle and pliable. **1624** *Althorp MS.* in Simpkinson *Washingtons* (1860) App. p. lvii, For a new tire for a waine. **1662** *Act* 14 *Chas. II*, c. 6 § 8 Any Waggon Wayne Cart or Carriage..the Wheeles whereof are lesse in breadth then foure Inches in the Tyre. **1753** *Scots Mag.* Nov. 540/1 Unless the wheels and tire of such carriages were made broader. **1769** [see *tire-smith* in 3]. **1803** WELLINGTON in Gurw. *Desp.* (1837) I. 580, I wait only for some iron..to put Tires on some new wheels which I have made. **1827** MEADEN *Patent Specif.* No. 5574, I do not claim..binding them with concave iron tires in streaks or separate plates.

**2.** A rim of metal encompassing the wheel of a vehicle, consisting of a continuous circular hoop of iron or steel.

**1782** NEWCOME *Patent Specif.* No. 1320 The main or outside rim or tire consists of one whole sound ring. **1787** BRODIE *Patent Specif.* No. 1599 The tier is then heated a black red and put on the wheel. **1827** MEADEN *Patent Specif.* No. 5574 My improvements on wheels for carriages consist in binding them with an iron hoop tire having its internal surface concave. **1831** YOUATT *Horse* 436 A strong circular frame of wood..is bound together by a hoop, or several hoops of iron, called tires. **1843** *Penny Cycl.* XXVII. 317/2 The introduction of solid or hoop tires is an immense improvement. **1845** THOMSON *Patent Specif.* No. 10990, I claim..the application of elastic bearings round the tire of carriage wheels. **1858** O. W. HOLMES *Aut. Breakf.-t.* vi, You couldn't pry that out of a Boston man if you had the tire of all creation straightened out for a crowbar. **1860** PIESSE *Lab. Chem. Wonders* 122 The tires of wheels previously to their being fixed are made hot. **1862** *Fraser's Mag.* Nov. 634 Specimens of tires for locomotive engines..made without a weld. **1886** HALL CAINE *Son of Hagar* II. xi, The tires of the wheels were still crusted with unmelted snow.

[*Note.* Thomson's patent (quot. 1845 above) is known as the foundation of the pneumatic tire or tyre (2 b), and was largely cited in the great actions for infringement during the 'tyre boom'. T. did not actually use the expression 'elastic tire' or 'tyre', but spoke of an 'elastic band' around the (iron) tire. This 'band' was however exactly what is now termed a 'pneumatic tyre'—a distended inner tube with an outer cover or jacket. (H. V. Hopwood, Dep. Librarian, Patent Office Lib.)]

**b.** An endless cushion of rubber, solid, hollow, or tubular, fitted (usually in combination with an inner tube filled with compressed air: cf. PNEUMATIC 1 b) on the rim of a bicycle, tricycle, or motor-car; now also often upon the wheels of invalid and baby-carriages, and light horse vehicles. In this sense now commonly spelt *tyre* in Great Britain (see TYRE); *tire* is retained in America.

**1877** KNIGHT *Dict. Mech.* III. 2579 At the same time Mr. Dunlop patented a tire of annealed cast-iron, grooved to receive an india-rubber band. Various other patents followed, embracing india-rubber as a material to be used in constructing tires. **1887** BURY & HILLIER *Cycling* 63 The iron tire was necessarily incompatible with the light iron wheel; rubber tires were introduced. **1905** [see *tire-cover* in 3]. **1910** *Encycl. Brit.* VII. 683/1 Rubber tires, in place of iron ones, appeared in 1868. **1911** WEBSTER, *Tire.* ..4. Commonly spelt *tyre* in British usage...The pneumatic tire for a bicycle or automobile serves primarily to reduce vibration or shock.

**3.** *attrib.* and *Comb.*, as *tire-cover, -cutter, -maker, -smith*; **tire-bender**, a machine in which tires are rolled to a uniform curve (Knight *Dict. Mech.* 1877); **tire-bolt**, a bolt used in securing the tire to the felloes (*Cassell's Encycl. Dict.* 1888); **tire-cement**, cement for fixing or repairing rubber tires; **tire-drill**, a drill adapted to hold and perforate metal tires (Knight); **tire-heater**, a furnace for heating metal tires (*Ibid.*); **tire-iron**, one of the strakes forming the tire of a wheel (see sense 1); **tire-measurer**, a measure for ascertaining the length of the tire required by a wheel (Knight); **tire-press**, a hydraulic press in which the tires of railway wheels are forced on (*Ibid.*); **tire-roller**, a mill in which tires for railway wheels are rolled to develop the flanges, etc. (*Ibid.*); **tire-screw** = *tire-bolt* (*Cent. Dict. Suppl.*); **tire-setter**, a machine for forcing cart and carriage wheel tires into position and compressing them on the wheel (*Cent. Dict.*); **tire-shrinker**, a machine for compressing a heated tire lengthways to decrease the circumference (Knight); **tire-upsetting-machine** (see quot.). See also under TYRE.

**1894** BOTTONE *Electr. Instr. Making* (ed. 6) 33 When quite dry and set firm, the surface..should be painted over with 'bicycle *tire cement'. **1905** *Times* 1 Aug. 14/1 With tire and *tire-cover gone, ten miles away from a garage.. Crœsus..is in as lame a case as the man of modest means. **1897** *Outing* (U.S.) XXX. 213/1 These formidable *tire-cutters [clam-shells] lie along the coastal roads like dead leaves in a windrow. **1852** MUNDY *Our Antipodes* (1857) 32 Our carriages trundled on the nails of their new *tire-irons into Blackheath. **1769** *Public Advertiser* 6 June 3/2 A Coachmaker's or *Tiresmith's Tool for..working the Tire off wheels. **1877** KNIGHT *Dict. Mech.*, **Tire-up-setting Machine*, a machine for shrinking tires without cutting.

† **Tire**, *sb.*3 *Obs.* Also 6–7 **tyre.** [ad. F. *tir* in sense 'shot, volley', verbal sb. from *tirer* to draw, to shoot (*Roland*, 11th c.) = Prov., Sp., Pg. *tirar*, It. *tirare*:—Common Romanic **tīrāre*: see TIRE *v.*2] The simultaneous discharge of a battery of ordnance; a volley or broadside. Also *transf.* of thunder.

(Collective pl., esp. after numeral, *tire.*)

**1575** LD. GREY in *Comm. Serv. & Charges* (Camden) 20 They guave us vij or viij sutche terryble tyres of batterie as tooke cleane awaye from us the top of owre vammure. **1577–87** HOLINSHED *Chron.* (1807) IV. 213 Before that two tires of the artillerie had gone off, they within offered to parlee. **1593** PEELE *Ord. Garter* Wks. (Rtldg.) 586/1 Ordnance pealing in mine ears, As twenty thousand tire had play'd at sea. **1598** FLORIO, *Salua*..a volie or tire off ordinance. **1611** SPEED *Hist. Gt. Brit.* IX. xii. § 92 Discharging sundry tire and peales of Thunder. **1667** MILTON *P. L.* VI. 605 In posture to displode thir second tire Of Thunder. **1687** DRYDEN *Hind & P.* III. 317 The foe discharges every tire around.

† **Tire**, *sb.*4 *Obs. rare.* In 6 tyre. [f. TIRE *v.*2 2.] A tough morsel given to a hawk: see TIRING *vbl. sb.*2

**1589** GREENE *Menaphon* (Arb.) 67 For all she hath let you flie like a Hawke that hath lost hir tyre.

**Tire** (tɔiᵊɹ), *sb.*5 *dial.* and *colloq.* [From TIRE *v.*1] **1.** Tiredness, fatigue.

**1859** F. E. PAGET *Curate of Cumberworth* 86 The settee which was adding discomfort to his tire. **1891** A. MATTHEWS *Poems & Songs* 60, I clean forgot my tire and pain. **1896** KIPLING *Seven Seas, M'Andrew's Hymn*, Sick, sick, wi' doubt an' tire. [**1904** in *Eng. Dial. Dict.* from Scotld. to Devon.]

**2.** pl. *Tires*: see quot.

**1855** DUNGLISON *Med. Lex.* (ed. 12), *Milk Sickness*, Sick stomach, Swamp sickness, Tires, Slows...A disease occasionally observed in..Alabama, Indiana, and Kentucky, which affects both man and cattle, but chiefly the latter... Owing to the tremors that characterize it in animals, it is called the Trembles. **1899** in *Syd. Soc. Lex.*

† **Tire**, *sb.*6 *Obs.* [? a. F. *tire*, from *tirer* to draw, pull: see TIRE *v.*2] In ribbon-weaving: A cord which pulls the high-lisses (LISSE *sb.*2) up.

**1759** *Gentl. Mag.* 517 Description of a new invented machine for drawing the tire in a ribbon loom. *Ibid.*, The tumblers that draw the tire moving with their upper ends in the rake. *Ibid.*, A ribbon that requires tire may be work'd as a plain course, there being no loss of time required in the tire's draught. **1766** CROKER, etc. *Dict. Arts* s.v. *Ribband*, 4. The tires, or the riding cords, which run on the pullies, and pull up the high-lisses...25. The tumblers, or pullies, to which the tires are tied, to clear the course of cords through the high lisses...27. The tire-board.

† **Tire, tyre**, *sb.*7 Variant of TEAR *sb.*3 b, the finest fibre of flax, etc.

**1601** HOLLAND *Pliny* XXXVII. iii. II. 608 They will burne.. more cleare than weekes or matches made of the very tire and best of flax. **1790** *Churchw. Acc. W. Hoathly, Sussex* 27 Feb., Dame Steles wants some tyre—Allowed ½ dozen 7*d.* **1875** *Sussex Gloss.*, *Tire*, flax for spinning. (Probably obsolete, but frequently found in old parochial accounts.)

**Tire** (tɔiᵊɹ), *v.*1 Forms: *α.* 1 **tiorian, teorian, 2 teorien**; 5 **tere.** *β.* 1 (late) (ȝe)**tyrian**; (2–3 (a)**tieren**); 5 **tyere**, *Sc.* **tyr**, 5–8 **tyre**, 6 **tyar**, *Sc.* **tyir**, 6–7 **tyer, tier**, 6– **tire.** [OE. *tíorian*, *téorian* (also with short *io, eo* (Sievers); in comb. *getíorian, getéorian*; with umlaut (late) *getýrian*), also *a-téorian*, with umlaut *a-tíerian, a-térian*; also vbl. sb. *tiurung* 'lassitudo' (Gallée), and *getéorung*. As this vb. does not appear in the cognate langs., it is difficult to determine its original form in OE., and the phonetic relations between the OE. and ME. forms, esp. the origin and history of the current form *tire* († *tyre*), which appears first in Scottish writers in the 15th c.

Prof. Sievers thinks that the various OE. and ME. forms may be explained by the existence of an OE. **tīran* trans., beside *tīorian* (*tiorian*) intr., both formed from an OTeut. verbal root **terh-*; the sound-relations being similar to those between OE. *fīras* and *feorh, fēores* (*feores*), from root **ferhw-*.]

**I.** *intr.* †**1.** To fail, cease (as a supply, etc.); to diminish, give out, come to an end. *Obs.*

*c* **725** *Corpus Gloss.* (O.E.T.) 668 *Desisse*, tiorade [*c* **1050** in Wr.-Wülcker 385/9 teorode]. *a* **1000** *Ord. Dunsætas* c. 4 *heading*, Be ðone ðe lad teorie. *a* **1000** *Ags. Ps.* (Th.) cxviii[i]. 82 Eagan me swylce eac teoredon. **11..** *Soul & Body* in Phillipps *Fragm. Ælfric's Gramm.* etc. (1838) 5 Him trukeþ his iwit, him teoreþ his miht. [*c* **1200** *Trin. Coll. Hom.* 29 Vnwreste þu best ȝef þu wreche ne secst..ȝief mihte þe ne atiereð.]

**2.** To become weak or exhausted from exertion; to have one's strength reduced or worn out by toil or labour; to become fatigued.

*c* **1000** *Sax. Leechd.* II. 16 ȝif mon on langum weȝe teoriȝe. *c* **1470** HENRY *Wallace* IX. 1771 The Scottis hors mony began to tyr [*rime* fyr]. *c* **1470** *Golagros & Gaw.* 34 Tuglit and travalit thus trew men can [= did] tyre. *c* **1480** HENRYSON *Test. Cres.* (ed. 1593) 516 To beir his Scheild his Breist began to tyre. **1587** MASCALL *Govt. Cattle, Horses* (1627) 178 Lap it about his bit,..and then bridle him, and ride him, and he wil not lightly tyer. **1588** SHAKS. *L. L. L.* II. i. 120 Your wit's too hot, it speeds too fast, 'twill tire. **1593** — *Rich. II*, II. i. 36. **1599** PORTER *Angry Woman Abingd.* (Percy Soc.) 41 A swift horse will tier, but he that trottes easilie will indure. **1611** SHAKS. *Wint. T.* IV. iii. 135 A merry heart goes all the day, Your sad tyres in a Mile-a. **1660** F. BROOKE tr. *Le Blanc's Trav.* 230 His horses so tiring, that the servants were fain to carry the baggage themselves. **1716** LADY M. W. MONTAGU *Lett.* 16 Aug., Our horses tired at Stamel, three hours from [Cologne]. **1845** J. COULTER *Adv. Pacific* xiii. 169 They tire—others supply their places.

**3.** To have one's appreciation, power of attention, or patience exhausted by excess; to become or be weary or sick *of*, to 'have enough' *of*.

**1500–20** DUNBAR *Poems* lxvi. 94 Of this fals failȝeand warld I tyre. *a* **1578** LINDESAY (Pitscottie) *Chron. Scot.* XXI. xi. (S. T. S.) I. 307 The quenis grace tyrit of him and pairtit witht him. *a* **1584** MONTGOMERIE *Cherrie & Slae* 99 Quha wald haue tyrit to heir that tune. **1763** GOLDSM. *Misc. Wks.* (1837) II. 484 Unwearied himself, he supposed his readers could never tire. **1803** *Edwin* III. iv. 60 His tongue spoke of nothing but the field, and his ear tired with any other theme. **1819** SCOTT *Bl. Dwarf* xviii, Mareschal..tired of the country, went abroad, served three campaigns, came home. **1857** RUSKIN *Pol. Econ. Art* 54 You will never tire of looking at it. **1897** *Century Mag.* Feb. 623/2 [The squirrel] would grasp one of my fingers with his two paws, and lick it till he tired.

**4.** To become weary with waiting *for* something; to 'weary' or long *for*. *Sc.* ? *Obs.*

**1801** BARBARA MAXWELL in G. Ewing *Mem. B. Ewing* (1829) 41, I really tire for your letters. **1827** ISAB. CAMPBELL in *Mem.* viii. (1829) 247, I tire much for this—I long to be completely conformed to the image of Jesus.

**II.** *trans.* **5.** To wear down or exhaust the strength of by exertion; to fatigue, weary (by either mental or physical exercise). Also *absol.*

*a* **1000** *Ags. Ps.* (Th.) cxli[i]. 3 ȝif mine grame þenceað gast teorian. *a* **1400–50** *Alexander* 1009 All þe ȝeris of oure ȝouthe es ȝare syne passid And we for-traualid & terid [*Dubl. MS.* for-tyred]. *Ibid.* 1404 (Dubl. MS.) It wald tere ony tong hys tournays to reken. **1470–85** MALORY *Arthur* XV. v. 661 The whyte knyghtes helde them nyghe about syr launcelot for to tyere hym and wynde hym. **1500–20** DUNBAR *Poems* lxxix. 7 For rekkyning of my rentis and roumes, ȝe neid nocht for to tyre ȝour thowmes. **1530** PALSGR. 758/1, I tyer a horse, I make him that he can go no farther. **1588** SHAKS. *L. L. L.* IV. iii. 307 Motion and long during action tyres The sinnowy vigour of the trauailer. *c* **1590** MARLOWE *Faust.* I. i. 61 Here, Faustus, tire thy brains to gain a deity. **1621** T. WILLIAMSON tr. *Goulart's Wise Vieillard* 50 Not tyring himselfe, and spending his spirits with much labour and studie. **1698** FRYER *Acc. E. India & P.* 177 The Tigre is.. not long Nimble, Three Leaps Tiring him. **1749** BERKELEY *Word to the Wise* Wks. III. 444 The same work tires, but different works relieve. **1845** J. COULTER *Adv. Pacific* ix. 111 Being well tired by my day's march, and excitement, I lay down..and slept soundly until daylight. **1875** JOWETT *Plato* (ed. 2) III. 338 They would rather not tire themselves by thinking about possibilities.

**6.** To weary or exhaust the patience, interest, or appreciation of (a person, etc.) by long continuance, sameness, or want of interest; to satiate, make sick of something; to bore. Also *absol.*

**1500–20** DUNBAR *Poems* xvi. 17 Sum is for gift sa lang requyrd Quhill that the crevar be so tyrd That, or the gift deliuerit be The thank is frustrat and expyrd. **1599** SHAKS. *Much Ado* I. i. 309 Thou wilt..tire the hearer with a booke of words. **1692** LOCKE *Toleration* ii. Wks. 1727 II. 288, I am tired to follow you so often round the same Circle. **1774** GOLDSM. *Nat. Hist.* (1776) VII. 104, I hope I have not tired your Lordship with my long tale. **1874** L. STEPHEN *Hours in Library* (1892) I. i. 39 He cannot tire us with details, for all the details of such a story are interesting.

**b.** *fig.* To exhaust (another's patience, bounty, efforts, etc.); to wear out, spend (time) (*obs.*).

**1589** GREENE *Menaphon* (Arb.) 46 To trie our wittes, and tire our time. ? *c* **1600** *Distracted Emperor* in Bullen *O. Pl.* III. 169 My constant industry shall tyer the day And outwatche night. **1601** SIR W. CORNWALLIS *Ess.* II. li. (1631) 326 Hee hath tyred his purse before hee can overtake the fashion. **1613** BEAUM. & FL. *Coxcomb* I. i, To tire anothers bounty, And let mine own grow lusty. **1665** SIR T. HERBERT *Trav.* (1677) 181 After he had tyred out a few more minutes with impatience. **1697** DRYDEN *Virg. Georg.* IV. 597 Till tiring all his Arts, he turns agen To his true Shape. **1788** SHERIDAN in *Sheridaniana* (1826) 101 Others tired the chairs in the parlours. **1902** GOSSE in *Daily Chron.* 13 Mar. 3/1 The great artist, who had seemed..to have tired his pen a little.

**7.** With extension. *To tire out, tire to death*, to tire to utter exhaustion. *colloq.* *To tire down*, to exhaust (a hunted animal) by persistent pursuit: cf. *to run down* (RUN *v.* 73 h).

**1563–87** FOXE *A. & M.* (K. O.), Tire him out. **1632** SANDERSON *Serm.* 39 They would quickely tyre out themselues without spurring. **1711** HEARNE *Collect.* (O. H. S.) III. 246 The King being then tired out by factious People. **1740** tr. *De Mouhy's Fort. Country-Maid* (1741) I. 206 He was tired to Death, altho' they used their Endeavours..to amuse him agreeably. **1766** H. WALPOLE in *Lett. C'tess Suffolk* (1824) II. 324, I am tired to death of the place. **1835** W. IRVING *Tour Prairies* xviii, A pack of..wolves..were in full chase of a buck, which they had nearly tired down. **1855** MACAULAY *Hist. Eng.* xvii. IV. 1 William, tired out by the voyage,..determined to land in an open boat.

Hence **Ti·ring** *vbl. sb.* and *ppl. a.*, wearying, fatiguing.

**1588** SHAKS. *Tit. A.* V. ii. 24 Witnesse the tyring day, and heauie night. **1603** KNOLLES *Hist. Turks* (1638) 220 The politicke tyring of the strong forces of Bajazet, was the safegard of his own. *a* **1774** GOLDSM. tr. *Scarron's Com. Romance* (1775) I. 132 This accomplished courtier being tired with tiring of them. **1869** PR. ALICE *Mem.* 1 June (1884) 215 It is always so tiring to see things at Berlin.

**Tire** (tɔiᵊɹ), *v.*2 *arch.* Also 4–7 **tyre**, 6–7 **tyer**, 7 **tier.** [a. F. *tire-r* = Prov., Sp., Pg. *tirar*, It. *tirare*:—Com. Romanic **tīrāre* to draw, etc., of uncertain origin. (Hatz.-Darm. rejects the derivation from Teut. *tairan*, OLG. *teren*, conjectured by Diez.)]

**I.** †**1.** *intr.* and *trans.* To draw, pull, tug. *Obs.*

*a* **1300** *Floriz & Bl.* 736 Floriz forþ his nekke bed And blauncheflur wiþ draȝe him ȝet. Blauncheflur bid forþ hire suere And floriz aȝen hire gan tire. **14..** *Beryn* 2565 Stillith ȝewe..for howe so evir yee tire, More þen my power yee owȝte nat desire. **1580** LYLY *Euphues* To Gentl. Schollers Oxf. (Arb.) 207 Sending me into the Countrie to nurse, where I tyred at a drie breast three yeares, and was at the last inforced to weane my selfe.

II. 2. *Falconry. intr.* Of a hawk: To pull or tear with the beak at a tough morsel given to it that it may exercise itself in this way; also, to tear flesh in feeding, as a hawk or other bird of prey. Const. *on, upon*. (So OF. *tirer*.) ? *arch.* or *Obs.*

*c* **1220** *Bestiary* 438 He billeð one ðe foxes fel..and he tireð on his ket. *c* **1374** CHAUCER *Boeth.* III. met. xii. 84 (Camb. MS.) The fowl þat hihte voltor..is so fulfyld of his song þat it nil etin ne tyren no more. *c* **1450** *Bk. Hawkyng* in *Rel. Ant.* I. 296 Loke that thy hawke tire every other day while she is fleyng, for nothyng..woll clense a hawkes hedde as tyryng. **1486** *Bk. St. Albans* C viij, An hawke.. tyrith vppon Rumppys, she fedith on all maner of flesh. **1558** PHAER *Æneid* VI. R ij, A gastly Gripe, that euermore his growing guttes outdrawes, And tiring tearith furth his euerduring liuer vaines. **1612** DAVIES *Why Ireland*, etc. (1787) 59 An eagle, with three eglets tiring on her breast, and the fourth picking at one of her eyes. **1737** OZELL *Rabelais* I. xli. I. 319 As the Falconers, before they feed their Hawks, do make them tire at a Hen's Leg, to purge their Brains of Phlegm.

b. *transf.* of persons. To feed greedily *upon*.

**1598** DALLINGTON *Meth. Trav.* G ij, The Kitchin Doctor gaue his patient the necke and bones to tyre vpon, and kept the wings himselfe. **1599** NASHE *Lenten Stuffe* (1871) 58 The stall-fed foreman..was grown as fat as an ox with tiring on the sirloins. *Ibid.* 86. *a* **1629** HINDE *J. Bruen* viii. (1641) 29 Rob wife and children of their meanes..and oftentimes tyre upon the carkasses.

† c. *fig.* To prey *upon*. *Obs.*

**1581** T. HOWELL *Deuises* (1879) 208 Your loue the Grype that tyers vpon your harte. **1594** MARLOWE & NASHE *Dido* v. ii, The grief that tires upon thine inward soul. **1610** *Histrio-m.* v. 136 O, how this vulture (vile Ambition) Tyers on the heart of greatnesse. **1624** BP. HALL *True Peacemaker* Wks. 539 Is there any of you..whose heart is daily tyr'd upon by the vultur of his secret guiltinesse?

d. To exercise oneself *upon* (in thought or action).

**1607** SHAKS. *Timon* III. vi. 4 Vpon that were my thoughts tyring when wee encountred. **1611** — *Cymb.* III. iv. 96 When thou shalt be disedg'd by her That now thou tyrest on.

† 3. *trans.* To tear at, tear, pluck. *Obs. rare.*

*c* **1374** CHAUCER *Troylus* I. 787 Whos stomak foughles tiren [*v. r.* tyren] euere mo.

† b. (*causal.*) To cause (a hawk) to 'tire'. In quot. *transf. Obs.*

**1594** ? GREENE *Selimus* Wks. (Grosart) XIV. 217 Like a lion fierce, Tiring his stomacke on a flocke of lambes.

**Tire** (təiəɹ), *v.*$^3$ Also 4–7 **tyre, 6 tyer, tyere, tier.** [Aphetic form of ATTIRE *v.*$^1$; but in sense 1 perh. a. F. *se tirer*.]

† 1. *refl.* To put oneself in order *to do* something; to get ready; also, to get ready to go somewhere; to take one's way, go. Cf. ATTIRE *v.*$^1$ 1, 2; DRESS *v.* 6, 15. *Obs.*

*c* **1330** R. BRUNNE *Chron.* (1810) 274 To Dunbar þei þam drowe, þe sege þer to sette, Þei tirede þam to kest smertly to þe assaute. *c* **1400** *Destr. Troy* 2778 We may tyre vs with truthe to tene hom agayne. *Ibid.* 3625 With a nauy full nobill, naite for þe werre, We shall tyre vs to Troy tomly to gedur.

2. *trans.* † a. To equip; to fit out with arms, accoutrements, etc.; to arm; = ATTIRE *v.*$^1$ 3 a.

*c* **1330** R. BRUNNE *Chron.* (1810) 151 His folk armed & tired, & ay redy to fight. *a* **1400–50** *Alexander* 3603 Thretty tulkis in ilk toure tired in platis. *c* **1400** *Laud Troy Bk.* 984 He toke his armure and tyred him swythe.

† b. To attire, clothe duly, dress, adorn; = ATTIRE *v.*$^1$ 3 b. *Obs.*

*c* **1350** *Will. Palerne* 263 A gret lord þat gayly is tyred. *Ibid.* 4478 To tire him in his wedes. *a* **1400** *Libeaus Desc.* (Kaluza) 891 In a robe of samite Anoon sche gan her tire. **1526** TINDALE 1 *Pet.* iii. 5 After this manner in the olde tyme did the wholy wemen which trusted in god tyre them selves. **1589** GREENE *Menaphon* (Arb.) 76 But am not I a Gentleman, though tirde in a shepheardes skincote? **1602** MARSTON *Antonio's Rev.* v. iii, Slinke to my chamber then, and tyre thee. **1706** PHILLIPS (ed. Kersey), To *Tire*, to dress.

c. To dress (the hair or head), esp. with a tire or head-dress (TIRE *sb.*$^1$ 3); = ATTIRE *v.*$^1$ 3 c. *arch.*

**1539** BIBLE (Great) 2 *Kings* ix. 30 Iezabel..starched her face, and tired her head, and looked out at a window. **1594** CAREW *Tasso* (1881) 74 With lockes of wrythed snakes some tire their pates. **1603** *Eng. Mourning Garment* in *Select. fr. Harl. Misc.* (1793) 208 She never could abide to gaze in a mirror, or looking-glass; no not to behold one, while her head was tyred and adorned. **1907** *Daily Chron.* 8 Aug. 4/4 With her flaxen hair tired in Greek fashion.

3. To plaster or decorate (a building). Now *dial.*

*a* **1400–50** *Alexander* 5644 Off tried topaces & trewe tyrid was þe wawes. *c* **1400** *Destr. Troy* 8751 This tabernacle tristy was tyrit on hegh. **1688** R. HOLME *Armoury* III. xiv. (Roxb.) 19/1 To mixt haire and Lyme together to make plaster, or straw and clay together for the tyreing of the inside of thatched houses. **1904** in *Eng. Dial. Dict.* s. v., (Somerset) I suppose you was all day yesterday tiring the church?

† 4. *spec.* To prepare or dress (an egg) as food.

**1486** *Bk. St. Albans* F vij b, An Egge Tyred. **1513** *Bk. of Keruynge* in *Babees Bk.* (1868) 265 Termes of a Keruer... Tyere that egge. **1530** PALSGR. 758/1, I tyer an egge...Let me se who can best tyer this egge. **1542** BOORDE *Dyetary* xii. (1870) 265 That they [eggs] be tyred with a lytell salte and suger. **1688** R. HOLME *Armoury* III. 78 Tire that Egg.

**Tire** (təiəɹ), *v.*$^4$ [f. TIRE *sb.*$^2$] *trans.* To furnish (a wheel or vehicle) with a tire or tires: see TIRED *ppl. a.*$^2$, TIRING *vbl. sb.*$^4$ See also TYRE *v.*

**1891** *Cent. Dict.*, *Tire*, to put a tire upon, as to tire a wheel or a wagon.

**Tire**, obs. f. TEER *v.*, TIER *sb.*$^1$, TYRE.

**Ti·reball.** In 6 tyreboll, 9 tireballe. [a. F. *tireballe*, in same senses, f. *tire* draw, extract (TIRE *v.*$^2$) + *balle* BALL.] a. An instrument for extracting the charge from a muzzle-loading firearm. b. A bullet-forceps. *Obs.* (exc. as French).

**1591** *Garrard's Art Warre* 4 The carefull souldier may with his Tyreboll pull out hys bullet. [**1611** COTGR., *Tireballe*, an Instrument wherewith Surgeons draw bullets out of the bodie.] **1857** DUNGLISON *Med. Lex.*, *Tire-balle*, forceps (bullet). **1877** KNIGHT *Dict. Mech.*, *Tireballe* (Surgical), the bullet-forceps.

† **Ti·re-brain.** *Obs. rare.* [f. TIRE *v.*$^1$ + BRAIN.] One who (or that which) tires the brain by constant thinking; a 'busy-brain'.

**1589** WARNER *Alb. Eng.* v. xxv. (1597) 124 Not adding or abstracting as conceited Tire-braines will.

**Tired** (təiəɹd), *ppl. a.*$^1$ [f. TIRE *v.*$^1$ + -ED$^1$.]

1. Weakened or exhausted by exertion, etc.; fatigued, wearied; also, sick or weary *of*, impatient *with* (something); *slang*, habitually disinclined to exertion, incorrigibly lazy.

a. in the predicate.

*a* **1400–50** [see TIRE *v.*$^1$ 5]. *c* **1470** HENRY *Wallace* IV. 28 The hors was tyryt, and mycht no forthyr pas. **1523** FITZHERB. *Husb.* § 15 The horses..wyll soone be tyred, and sore beate, that they may not drawe. *a* **1550** *Freiris of Berwik* 257 in *Dunbar's Poems* (S. T. S.) 294, I am verry tyrit, wett and cauld. **1562** TURNER *Herbal* II. 32 b, Medicines which refreshe them that are wery or tyrede. **1573** *Nottingham Rec.* IV. 150 A horse that wase leafte ther tyard. **1590** SHAKS. *Com. Err.* IV. iii. 24 The man, sir, that when gentlemen are tired giues them a sob, and rests them. **1704** F. FULLER *Med. Gymn.* (1711) 29 Thro' the greatness of the Perspiration they grow tyr'd. **1782** COWPER *Gilpin* xxxvii, 'The dinner waits, and we are tired:' Said Gilpin—'So am I!' **1852** MRS. CARLYLE *Lett.* (1883) II. 196, I am very tired; and the tireder I am, the less I sleep. **1888** 'J. S. WINTER' *Bootle's Childr.* vii, I got tired out with him at last. **1897** *Westm. Gaz.* 15 Apr. 2/3 He 'lived nowhere, did nothing, and, in fact, he was born tired', was what he told the inspector when he was arrested, and it was a graphic summary of a worthless life.

b. in attrib. use.

**1508** DUNBAR *Tua Mariit Wemen* 176 Was neuer sugeorne wer set na on that snaill tyrit. **1581** A. HALL *Iliad* VIII. 138 Thy chare, thy driuer, and thy seate, a tiered countenaunce shew. **1672** MARVELL *Reh. Transp.* I. 129 The tyred Magistrates asked them, whether they had not Halters. **1746–7** HERVEY *Medit.* (1818) 211 The tired shepherd has imposed silence on his pipe. **1871** MRS. BROOKFIELD *Influence* II. 74 Nothing is more delicious than the atmosphere of a country house to a tired-out Londoner in the month of August.

2. *transf.* and *fig.* Worked out, exhausted, used up; in quot. *a* 1548, exhausting.

*a* **1548** HALL *Chron.*, *Hen. V* 49 In a long fight and tyred battaile. **1748** RICHARDSON *Clarissa* VI. 64, I must here lay down my tired pen! **1766** *Museum Rust.* VI. 440 When the upper stratum is tired and foul, the owner may..turn down the worn-out soil. **1897** *Daily News* 28 July 8/4 The muslin gowns begin to look more than a little tired. **1899** *Times* 16 June 4/1 The Paris, to use an expressive Americanism, was a tired ship. *Ibid.* 4/2 The fact that the Paris was a tired ship was one result of the continual striving for records and averages. **1909** *Daily Chron.* 3 May 4/7 Colour and shape remind one of a tired cabbage leaf.

3. *Comb.*, as *tired-eyed, -faced, -looking*.

**1841** L. HUNT *Seer* (1864) 85 Happy in their tired-heartiness to get to the first bit of holiday ground they can reach. **1895** CLIVE HOLLAND *Jap. Wife* 91 We leave the terrace, with its lingering crowds of tired-faced holiday-makers. **1905** *Daily Chron.* 30 Aug. 4/7 The tired-eyed conductor took her fare. **1907** *Westm. Gaz.* 3 Dec. 1/3 Vases of somewhat tired-looking pink chrysanthemums.

**Tired** (təiəɹd), *ppl. a.*$^2$ [f. TIRE *sb.*$^2$ or *v.*$^4$ + -ED.] Fitted or furnished with a tire or tires; chiefly as the second element in a combination, as *iron-tired*. See also TYRED.

**1894** [see *pneumatic-tired* (PNEUMATIC *a.* 5)]. **1896** C. ALLEN *Papier Mâché* 118 With a weighty parade of iron-tired Juggernaut justice, they marched in state. **1912** J. MASEFIELD in *Eng. Rev.* Feb. 414 Four newly-tired cartwheels hung to cool.

**Tiredly** (təiəɹdli), *adv.* [f. TIRED *ppl. a.*$^1$ + -LY$^2$.] In a tired manner; wearily.

**1659** TORRIANO, *Alla-strácca*,..wearisomely, tiredly. **1891** MISS DOWIE *Girl in Karp.* xiii, How tiredly she nodded the white-fair, weary head! **1896** MRS. CAFFYN *Quaker Grandmother* 104 Her hands dropped tiredly into her lap.

**Tiredness** (təiəɹdnės). [f. as prec. + -NESS.] The state of being tired; weariness, fatigue.

**1552** ABP. HAMILTON *Catech.* (1884) 175 Hungir and thryst, heit and cald,..tyritnes, service or bondage. **1627** W. SCLATER *Exp.* 2 *Thess.* (1629) 279 Tedious yrkesomenesse, or tirednesse in Gods service. **1644** VICARS *God in Mount* 143 The tyrednes of the Souldiers with their travell. **1804** tr. *W. Heberden's Comm.* lxx. (1806) 369 *note*, At the height of 13 or 1400 toises above the sea, a peculiar tiredness often comes upon those who are ascending. **1889** E. W. BENSON in A. C. Benson *Life* (1900) II. 277 The last fortnight has only driven the London tiredness more over the system.

‖ **Tire-fond** (tīrˌfoṅ). *Surg.* [Fr., f. *tire* draw + *fond* lowest part.] (See quots.)

**1857** DUNGLISON *Med. Lex.*, *Tire-fond*, a surgical instrument formerly used to elevate the piece of bone sawed off by the trephine. **1899** *Syd. Soc. Lex.*, *Tire-fond*, an instrument for penetrating a cavity or tissue, transfixing and withdrawing foreign bodies, usually made in the form of a gimlet.

‖ **Tirela·rigot**, *Obs.*, in *to drink a tirelarigot* = Fr. *boire à tire-larigot* to drink hard, drink like a fish: see Littré s. v. *larigot*.

**1653** URQUHART *Rabelais* I. vii, To quiet the childe they gave him to drink a tirelarigot, that is, till his throat was like to crack with it.

**Tireless** (təiəˑɹlės), *a.*$^1$ [f. TIRE *v.*$^1$ + -LESS.] Untiring, indefatigable. a. Of persons (or their attributes) or other agents.

**1591** SYLVESTER *Du Bartas* I. iv. 597 To sing the swiftness of thy tyer-less Teem. **1827** WILLIS *Healing Daughter Jairus* 13 The same loved, tireless watcher. **1867** H. C. LEA *Sacerdot. Celibacy* 70 The tireless pen of St. Jerome was called into requisition. **1884** R. BRIDGES *Prometh. Firegiver* 195 Attending with tireless ears. **1887** G. HOOPER *Campaign Sedan* 280 Their soldiers..seemed to be tireless, for they never halted.

b. Of qualities, actions, etc.

*a* **1826** HEBER *Transl. Pindar* iv. 1 Oh! urging on the tireless speed Of Thunder's elemental steed. **1859** *Times* 31 Mar. 10/2 Nothing can give our men the tireless elasticity of these Mahrattas. **1889** *Ibid.* 10 Aug. 9/1 With that tireless persistency which they usually display.

**Tireless** (təiəˑɹlės), *a.*$^2$ [f. TIRE *sb.*$^2$ + -LESS.] Of a wheel: Without a tire or tires.

**1862** R. H. PATTERSON *Ess. Hist. & Art* 218 A rough ricketty conveyance, with wooden axletrees and tireless wheels.

**Ti·relessly**, *adv.* [f. TIRELESS *a.*$^1$ + -LY$^2$.] In a tireless manner; without tiring; untiringly.

**1867** AUGUSTA WILSON *Vashti* xxxi, Tirelessly the wife and hired nurse watched the progress of the dreadful disease. **1903** *Times* 25 Feb. 10/2 For 30 years he had been tirelessly active.

So **Ti·relessness**, the quality or condition of being tireless; indefatigableness.

**1887** J. C. FERNALD in *Voice* (N.Y.) 6 Jan. 3 The enthusiasm and energy and tirelessness of youth. **1898** *Daily News* 21 May 2/4 If there was a fault in his strategy it was his tirelessness.

† **Tireling** (təiəˑɹliŋ), *sb.* (*a.*) *Obs.* [app. f. TIRE *v.*$^1$ + -LING: cf. *hireling, shaveling*.] A tired person or animal: in quots. *attrib.* or as *adj.*: cf. *hireling priest*, etc.

**1590** SPENSER *F. Q.* III. i. 17 His tyreling iade he fiercely forth did push. **1596** *Ibid.* VI. vii. 40. **1599** BP. HALL *Sat.* IV. iii. 57 Whiles like a tireling jade he lags half-way. **1613** J. DENNYS *Secr. Angling* I. ix, Neither of Mare nor Gelding let it be; Nor of the tyreling Iade that beares the packe.

† **Ti·rement.** *Obs.* [f. TIRE *v.*$^3$ + -MENT, after OF. *atirement*; ATTIREMENT was later.] Attire; *pl.* articles of attire; garments, or ornaments as a whole.

*a* **1400–50** *Alexander* 4918 With cumly knottis & with koyntis & knopis of perle It ware to tere me to tell þe tirement to-gedire. **1553** BRENDE *Q. Curtius* III. 27 b, As their tirementes were moste precious, the more violently thei plucked them away. **1555** EDEN *Decades* 290 The whyte cappes or other tyrementes they weare on theyr heades.

‖ **Tiremoelle** (tīrˌmwȧl). *Obs.* [Fr., f. *tire* draw, extract + *moelle* marrow.] A marrow-spoon.

**1669** R. MONTAGU in *Buccleuch MSS.* (Hist. MSS. Comm.) I. 448, 2 forks, 2 knives, a toothpick-box, and a tiremoelle.

**Tirer** (təiəˑɹəɹ). *rare.* [f. TIRE *v.*$^3$ + -ER$^1$.] One who attires or dresses.

**1862** MERIVALE *Rom. Emp.* (1865) V. xlv. 355 The tirers of her person.

† **Ti·resol.** *Obs. rare*$^{-1}$. [ad. obs. Sp. and Pg. *tirasol* (= *quitasol*, 'a kinde of hat vsed in China very broad, which the principall men carry ouer their heads, with a short poll or staffe, like a canopie, to keepe the..sunne from them' (Minsheu), f. Pg. *tira-r* to take away, remove, banish + *sol* sun.] A (Chinese) umbrella or parasol.

**1613** PURCHAS *Pilgrimage* v. xvi. 452 Next to whom commeth the King with a Tiresol over his head, to keepe off the Sunne.

**Tiresome** (təiəˑɹsǝ̆m), *a.* [f. TIRE *v.*$^1$ + -SOME; cf. *meddlesome, wearisome*.]

1. Having the property of tiring by continuance, sameness, or lack of interest; wearisome, tedious.

**1500–20** DUNBAR *Poems* lxvi. 82, I wait [it] is for me provydit, Bot sa done tyrsum [*v.r.* tyresum] it is to byd it. **1603** DANIEL *Def. Ryme* in *Panegyr.*, etc. H vj, Those continuall cadences of couplets..are very tyresome, and vnpleasing. **1697** DRYDEN *Virg., Ess. Georgics* (1721) I. 203 The inculcating Precept upon Precept, will at length prove tiresome to the Reader. **1778** MISS BURNEY *Evelina* (1791) I. xii. 33 London soon grows tiresome. **1854** LEWIS *Lett.* (1870) 279 It is slow, tiresome work. **1875** JOWETT *Plato* (ed. 2) IV. 350 What a tiresome being is a man who is fond of talking.

b. *loosely.* Troublesome, disagreeable, unpleasant; irksome, annoying, vexatious. *colloq.*

**1798** CHARLOTTE SMITH *Yng. Philos.* I. 11 The tiresome custom you have got of never being ready. **1836** *Backwoods of Canada* 237 The tiresome things fell to pieces directly they became dry. **1862** MRS. CARLYLE *Lett.* (1883) III. 99 At the top of the house he is safe enough from tiresome interruptions. **1898** FLOR. MONTGOMERY *Tony* 12 A tiresome fidgety schoolboy as a travelling companion.

† 2. Causing physical fatigue; fatiguing, tiring. *Obs.* (Now merged in sense 1.)

**1598** HAKLUYT *Voy.* I. 612 The way was all of dry deepe slyding sand.., and by that meanes so tiresome and painefull as might be. **1710** PHILIPS *Pastorals* ii. 16 The tiresome Burden doubles its Increase. **1725** SWIFT *Let. to Sheridan* 11 Sept., In an employment precarious and tiresome,..this new weight of party malice had struck you down. **1728** MORGAN *Algiers* I. iii. 40 He led his Enemies a tiresome Dance, often drawing them into Ambuscades.

Hence **Ti·resomely** *adv.*

**1847** C. Brontë *J. Eyre* xxxiv, A tiresomely importunate instinct reminded me that vivacity (at least in me) was distasteful to him. **1902** *Times* 14 Mar. 7/5 Mr. Seddon [is] now regarded..as tiresomely insistent upon Imperial views.

**Ti·resomeness.** [f. prec. + -ness.]

†**1.** The condition of being tired; weariness. *Obs. rare.*

**1646** Trapp *Comm. John* i. 10 For thou hast created all things,..without help, tool, or tiresomeness. **1715** Nelson tr. *T. à Kempis' Chr. Exerc.* iii. xvii. 146 Give me..good occupation..against the Tiresomness and Drowsiness of the Heart.

**2.** The quality of being tiresome; wearisomeness, tediousness.

**1668** H. More *Div. Dial.* ii. xxiii. (1713) 162 The tiresomeness of the Fight makes the Victory more pleasant and sensible. **1817** Mar. Edgeworth *On Bores* ⁋ 11 Others are not endured long enough in society to come to the perfection of tiresomeness.

†**Tiret**, obs. f. Terret; in quot. in sense a.

**1587** Holinshed *Chron.* III. 539/1 About his arme he wore an hounds collar set full of SS of gold, and the tirets likewise being of the same metall.

‖ **Tiretaine** (tīrtęn). [Fr.; 1247 in Godef. *Compl.* (also ? *c* 1400 *tierteine*, 1449 *tirtaine* (1718, Littré), 1487 *tertaine*; 1581 *tritaine*): cf. Tartan.] A cloth woven of wool mixed with linen or cotton, 'worne ordinarily by the French peasants' (Cotgr.); linsey-woolsey.

**1863** Sala *Last Crusader* 213 'Many and many a time', writes the good Sire de Joinville,..'have I seen the good king..vestured in a coat of camlet, a surcoat of tiretaine without sleeves, a mantle above the black sandalette'. [**1866** Rogers *Agric. & Prices* II. xxii. 579 We find kersey, tirretin [*c* 1284–5: cf. I. 536/3], murrey, burell, rosete, keynet, reynes, and taursmaurs.] **1901** tr. *V. Hugo's Notre-Dame* xxiii, The petticoat of tiretaine with red and blue stripes. **1910** *Sat. Westm. Gaz.* 15 Jan. 6/2 Plump dames in tiretaines.

‖ **Tire-tête** (tīrtēt). *Obstetr.* [Fr., f. *tire-r* to draw + *tête* head.] (See quot. 1857.)

**1754–64** Smellie *Midwif.* I. Introd. 56 He also invented a tire-tête, which cannot be used until the skull is opened with a knife. **1771** *Encycl. Brit.* III. 238/2 Let Leverot's tire-tête, with the three sides joined together, be introduced along the accoucheur's hand. **1857** Dunglison *Med. Lex.*, *Tire-tête*, a name given to different instruments used for extracting the head of the child when left in the uterus.

**Ti·re-woman.** Also 7–8 **tyre-.** [f. Tire *sb.*[1] + Woman.] A woman who assists at a lady's toilet; a lady's maid (*arch.*); † also, a woman employed in the making or sale of women's clothing; a dressmaker, costumier (*obs.*).

**1615** Brathwait *Strappado* (1878) 126 T'was some tyre-woman he tooke them fro. *c* **1626** *Dick of Devon* iii. iv. in Bullen *O. Pl.* (1883) II. 58 Have they forsaken the Divell and all his fashions? banishd their Taylors and Tyrewomen? **1667** Pepys *Diary* 20 Feb., To Mrs. Grotier's, the Queen's tire-woman, for a pair of locks for my wife. **1709** Steele *Tatler* No. 79 ⁋ 1 Dressed with all the Art and Care that Mrs. Toilet the Tire-Woman could bestow on her. **1790** Cath. M. Graham *Lett. Educ.* 108 Why should they not..value themselves for this outside fashionableness of the taylor or tire woman, when their parents have so early instructed them to do it? **1847** Marryat *Childr. N. Forest* xxv, They will make very nice tire-women to some lady of quality. **1867** 'Ouida' *C. Castlemaine* (1879) 7 To while time away by scolding her tire-woman.

**Tirful**, *a.*: see Tir. **Tiriac**, obs. f. Theriac.

**Tiring**, *vbl. sb.*[1] and *ppl. a.*[1]: see after Tire *v.*[1]

**Tiring** (təiə·riŋ), *vbl. sb.*[2] ? *arch.* Also 5–7 **tyr-.** [f. Tire *v.*[2] + -ing [1].] The action of Tire *v.*[2]; the pulling or tearing of a hawk at a tough morsel given to it to exercise itself; *concr.* a piece of food given to a hawk for this purpose. Also *fig.*

*c* **1450** *Bk. Hawkyng* in *Rel. Ant.* I. 296 The swetteste tyryng that is to goshawke and sperhawke is a pigge is tayle. **1486** *Bk. St. Albans, Hawking* b viij b, She shall nether at the fedyng ner at the tyryng ne at the lightyng ne at the Rysyng hurtte hir selffe. **1575** Turberv. *Falconrie* 146 Gyve hir tyring of a wing or a foote of the sayde pullet. **1891** Harting *Gloss. Falconry, Tiring*,..any tough piece (as the leg of a fowl with little on) given to a hawk when in training to pull at, in order to prolong the meal, and exercise the muscles of the back and neck.

**Tiring** (təiə·riŋ), *vbl. sb.*[3] Also 6–7 **tyring.** [f. Tire *v.*[3] + -ing [1].] The action of Tire *v.*[3]; attiring, dressing (*arch.*: see b); dressing the hair; † fitting out (*obs.*); also *concr.* attire, apparel, head-dress (*arch.*); † equipment, apparatus, garnishing (*obs.*); *spec.* see quot. 1869 (*dial.*).

**1552** Huloet, Byrlet or tyrynge for women. **1558** in Feuillerat *Revels Q. Eliz.* (1908) 23 Sarcenet..imployed into ..Shertes.., translated into lyninge pullinges oute tuftes tyringes and other garnisshinge. *Ibid.* 82 Sarsenettes.. spent in rowles and wrethes tuftinge tyringe of hedpeces and gyrdells. **1602** Dekker *Satirom.* Wks. 1873 I. 186 Such delayes in rising, in fitting gownes, in tyring [etc.]. **1620** Shelton *Quix.* (1746) IV. xxix. 228 In Hell they are working Tapistry Work, and there are made Tyrings and Net-works. **1656** *Artif. Handsom.* 67 Whose either haire, or complexion, or tiring is not natively their own. **1869** *Lonsdale Gloss., Tiring*, the plastering under slates. **1909** *Daily Chron.* 18 Mar. 3/1 He wears his learning as lightly as the tiring of the hair of Aphrodite, borne upon her swan in a Douris vase.

**b.** *attrib.* and *Comb.*, as *tiring-chamber*, *-closet*, *-glass*, *-man*, *-place*; **tiring-woman**, a lady's maid. Also Tiring-house, -room. *Obs.* or *arch.*

**1645** Evelyn *Diary* 27 Feb., A cart, or *plaustrum*, where the scene or tiring-place is made of boughs in a rural manner. **1732** Fielding *Mod. Husb.* iv. iv, I know several women of fashion I could not support for a tiring woman. **1825** Scott *Betrothed* xxii, The..intercession of the tiring-woman obtained admission for travelling merchants, or pedlars. **1844** Mrs. Browning *Duchess May* lxxii, The smile upon her face, ere she left the tiring-glass Had not time enough to go. **1856** Boker *Francesca da Rimini* i. i, I'll be Your tiring-man, for once. **1860** Ld. Lytton *Lucile* ii. iv. 77 From the dark tiring-chamber behind, straight reissue With new masks the old mummers.

**Tiring** (təiə·riŋ), *vbl. sb.*[4] [f. Tire *sb.*[2] or *v.*[4] + -ing [1].] The fitting of a wheel with a tire; the condition or mode of being fitted with tires.

**1831** Holland *Manuf. in Metal* I. 157 The tiring, the breadth, and the inclination of the wheels.

**Ti·ring-house.** *Obs.* or *arch.* Also 6– **tyring-.** [f. Tiring *vbl. sb.*[3] + House.] A dressing-room; *esp.* the room or place in which the actors dressed for the stage; = Tiring-room.

**1590** Shaks. *Mids. N.* iii. i. 4 This greene plot shall be our stage, this hauthorne brake our tyring house. **1612** Raleigh *Poems* (1870) xviii. 29 Our mothers' wombs the tiring-houses be, Where we are dressed for life's short comedy. **1620** Melton *Astrolog.* 31 While Drummers make Thunder in the Tyring-house. **1639** Fuller *Holy War* iv. vii. (1840) 189 That actor who cometh off with the dislike of the spectators stealeth as invisibly as he may into the tiring-house. **1678** Cudworth *Intell. Syst.* i. v. 877 Dying, to the Rational or Humane Soul, is nothing but a withdrawing into the Tyring-house, and putting off the Cloathing of this terrestrial Body. **1908** *Q. Rev.* Apr. 453 He runs his lateral curtains back to the tyring-house wall.

**Tiring-irons** (təiə·riŋ,əiːəɹnz), *sb. pl.* Also 7–8 **tyring-, tarrying-,** 8 **tarring-.** [In its current form, f. *tiring*, pr. pple. of Tire *v.*[1] + Iron; but *tarrying-iron* (also *tarriour*) appears to occur as early, and to have been the more prevalent in the 17th and 18th c. This belongs to Tarry *v.*, in its transitive sense 'to delay, retard, protract, prolong, hold in check' (if not to *tarry*, Tary *v.*).

The evidence does not decide whether *tiring* or *tarrying* was the original epithet, and as both are descriptive, they may have been independent.]

A popular name of the *puzzling rings* or *ring-puzzle* (esp. when made of iron, and of large size), in which a number of rings, usually seven or ten, are placed on an oblong closed wire loop or bow, each being also fastened to a wire within the bow, which passes through the next ring, and is loosely attached by its other end to a thin flat piece of metal or bone of nearly the same length as the loop. The puzzle is to take all the rings thus fettered off the loop or bow.

'This perplexing invention is of great antiquity, and was treated on by Cardan, the mathematician [1501–1576]' (*Boy's Own Book* (1828) 420, in which there is a figure and detailed explanation of the moves).

**1601** Deacon & Walker *Answ. to Darel* To Rdr. 4 The very frame itselfe of their whole proceeding resembleth fitlie a paire of tarriours, or tyring yrons. **1627** Drayton *Elegies, To W. Jeffreys* 100 A Tarrying-iron for fooles to labour at. **1661** Baxter *Mor. Prognost.* i. xvi. 4 Like a Boy with a pair of Tarrying-Irons. *a* **1675** Lightfoot *Serm. 2 Sam. xix. 29* Wks. 1684 II. 1246 They are not unriddleable riddles, and tyring-irons never to be untied. **1690** C. Nesse *O. & N. Test.* I. 277 He would lay his tarrying-irons upon him, and not permit him to go away. *a* **1763** Shenstone *Upon Riddles* 1. in Dodsl. *Coll. Poems* (1782) V. 63 Have you not known a small machine Which brazen rings environ, In many a country chimney seen, Y-clep'd a tarring-iron? **1828** *Boy's own Bk.* 420 It may be purchased at most of the toy-shops, very lightly and elegantly made. It also exists in various parts of the country, forged in iron,..and aptly named 'The Tiring Irons'. **1879** Louisa Potter *Lanc. Mem.* 115 One was called 'tiring-irons', a set of iron rings and two iron bars fastened together.

**Tiring-room** (təiə·riŋ,rūm). [f. Tiring *vbl. sb.*[3] + Room.] A dressing-room (*arch.*); *spec.* the dressing-room of a theatre. Also *transf.* and *fig.*

**1623** I. M. *Pref. Verse* in *Shaks. Wks.*, From the Worlds-Stage, to the Graues-Tyring-roome. *a* **1639** Wotton *De Morte* 2 in *Reliq.* (1651) 539 Mans life's a Tragedy. His mothers womb (From which he enters) is the tyring room. **16..** Fletcher *Poems* 208 (Nares) The stars are all withdrawn from each glad sphear Within the tyring rooms of heaven. **1666** Pepys *Diary* 19 Mar., But my business here was to see the inside of the stage and all the tiring-rooms and machines. **1749** Smollett *Gil Bl.* xii. i. (1782) IV. 217 After the play I..found her in the tyring-room, talking to some gentlemen. **1848** Dickens *Dombey* vi, Then converting the parlour, for the nonce, into a private tiring room, she dressed her.

**Tirl** (tɔ̄ɹl, *Sc.* terl), *sb.*[1] Chiefly *Sc.* Also 5–8 **tirle,** 6 **tirrill,** 7 **tirrle, turle.** [app. related to Tirl *v.*[3]]

**1.** A round or turn at doing anything; a slight experience or trial of something; a touch, taste.

*c* **1660** J. Guthrie in *Union Mag.* Oct. (1902) 463 Many a man has touched the cross, and it has scalded him; and he has given it a tirl and letten it lie. **1697** Cleland *Poems* 32 She was tyred with his speeches; She would far rather had a tirrle Of an Aquavitae barrel. **1715** Ramsay *Christ's Kirk Gr.* ii. vii, The young swankies on the green Took round a merry tirle. **1721** — *Horace to Virg.* 5 King Æol, grant a tydie tirl. **1742** Forbes *Shop Bill* x. in *Ajax*, etc. (1755) 40, I hae..some for those that tak a tirle amo' the sheets.

**2.** A revolving piece of mechanism like a turnstile; a wheel of some kind. *dial.*

**1691** W. B. *Hist. Roman Conclave* ii. 7 In several parts of the Wall of the Conclave, there are seven *Rote*, or Holes with Turles in them, just as there are in Nunneries, wherein the Victuals are put in from without, and turned round to be Received within. **1793** *Statist. Acc. Scot.* V. 193–4 The tirl occupies the same situation under this mill, as the trundles in the inner part of an ordinary mill; and it performs the same office. The diameter of the tirl is always equal to that of the millstones. **1883** *W. Yorks. Gloss.*, *Tirl*, the wheel of a [wheel] barrow.

**3.** An act of twirling; a twirl, whirl. *dial.*

**1790** D. Morison *Poems* 6 (E.D.D.) The temper pin she gi'es a tirl, An' spins but slow.

†**4.** ? A whirled or circular pattern. *rare*[−1].

*a* **1584** Montgomerie *Cherrie & Slae* 334 With dansing, and glansing, In tirlis [*v. r.* tirle] lik dornik champ.

†**5.** A name of some disease: editors suggest St. Vitus's dance. *Obs. rare.*

*a* **1585** Montgomerie *Flyting* 321 The phtiseik, þe twithȝaik, þe tittis, and þe tirrillis [*v. r.* The tisicke, the toothaike, the tites and tirles].

**6.** *Comb.* † **Tirl-bed**, a trundle- or truckle-bed on low wheels or castors.

**1488** *Coventry MSS.* in *1st Rep. Hist. MSS. Comm.* 101/2, iii. stayndinge beddes iii. tirle beddes well bothomed.

**Tirl**, *sb.*[2] *Sc.* [f. Tirl *v.*[3] II.] An act of tirling (see Tirl *v.*[3] 3); *loosely*, a tap or tapping. Also as *int.*

**1808** Jamieson, *Tirl*,..a sharp tap or stroke. **1818** *Blackw. Mag.* III. 531 The slight tirl on the lozen, or tap at the window. **1819** W. Tennant *Papistry Storm'd* (1827) 19 Whan, hark! upon the gowden door, Tirl! comes a rap.

**Tirl**, *sb.*[3], Sc. var. Thrill *sb.*[3], vibration, tremor.

**1882** Jamieson, *Tirl, Tirle*, a vibration, the act of vibrating. **1894** Haliburton *Furth in Field* iv. 183 A good woman.. with a pathetic 'tirl' in her tone.

**Tirl**, *v.*[1] *Sc.* Also 6 **tyrle.** [Origin uncertain: app. not connected with any sense of Trill; but cf. Thrill *v.*[1] 6.]

†**1.** *intr.* To pluck *at*; *esp.* to pluck at the strings of a harp, or the like, so as to cause them to sound. *Obs.*

*c* **1470** Henryson *Mor. Fab.* vii. (*Lion & Mouse*) xiv, Sum [of the mice] tirlit at the campis of his [the lion's] beird, Sum sparit not to claw him on the face. **1567** *Gude & Godlie B.* (S.T.S.) 93 Tak harpe in hand..Tyrle on the ten stringit Instrument.

**2.** *trans.* To pluck (a tense string, etc.) so as to cause vibration.

**1882** Jamieson s. v., (Clydesdale) He tirled the strings. **1894** R. Reid in *Poets Dumfries.* x. (1910) 305 That queer wild cry frae the gurly sky Can tirl my heart-strings still.

**Tirl**, *v.*[2] *Sc.* and *north. dial.* [Apparently related to Tirve *v.*[1] and Tirr *v.* in same senses; perh. orig. a freq. **tyrflian*: cf. *whirl* from *hwirfl-*.]

**1.** *trans.* To roll or turn back, pull or strip off (a garment or the clothes from a person, his back, etc.; the bed-clothes from a bed; the thatch or roof from a house, stack, etc.).

*a* **1500** *Priests Peblis* 993 Off his coate thay tirlit be the croun. **1810** *Cromek's Rem. Nithsdale Song* 33 The wind blaws loud and tirls our strae. **1819** W. Tennant *Papistry Storm'd* (1827) 211 Nae thing was prosperin' there and thrivin', But tirlin' roofs and rafter-rivin'. **1826** L. Proudlock *Poet. Wks., Cuddie & Crawing Hen* 43 Winds loud blew, wi' fury flew, And threat to tirl its riggin'. **1835** Hogg *Tales & Sk.* (1837) V. 275 He was tied to a tree, and his shirt tirled over his head. **1880** *Antrim & Down Gloss.* s. v. *Tirl, thirl*, The wun' tirled the thatch las' nicht. **1894** *Northumbld. Gloss.* s. v., To 'tirl the bed-claes', to strip off the bed-clothes.

**2.** To uncover by rolling back the covering; to strip (a person) naked; to unroof (a building): often *tirl naked, tirl bare.*

**1721** Ramsay *Lucky Spence* x, Suppose then they should tirle ye bare, And gar ye fike, E'en learn to thole. **1785** Burns *Addr. to Deil* iv, Whyles on the strong-wing'd tempest flyin, Tirlin the kirks. **1816** Scott *Old Mort.* xxiii, Our folk had tirled the dead dragoons as bare as bawbees. **1843** Nicholson *Hist. & Trad. Tales* 120 Wi' hideous yells she filled the air, And tirled Simon's cottage bare.

**b.** To uncover (the peat in a moss, the stone in a quarry, etc.) by removing the surface soil, overlying earth, clay, etc.; to lay bare (anything) by removing its covering.

**1815** *Pennecuik's Wks.* 71 *note*, After removing the surface soil with the roots of the heath, or ling, growing on it (called the tirling of the moss). **1816** Scott *Antiq.* xxiii, 'If your honours are thinking of tirling the floor', said old Edie, '..I would begin below that muckle stane'. *Mod. Sc.* About 1845 a new section of Denholm Hill Freestone Quarry was tirled.

**Tirl**, *v.*[3] Now chiefly *Sc.* and *north. dial.* Forms: 6 **tyrle, (turle),** 7 **tirle,** 8– **tirl.** [Metathetic form of Trill *v.*[1] Cf. EFris. *tirreln, tirlen* to turn about quickly.]

**I. 1.** *trans.* To turn; to cause to rotate or revolve; to twirl, spin, twiddle; to turn over (and over); to move by rolling; = Trill *v.*[1] 1. Also, to turn over rapidly (the leaves of a book).

**1543** Traheron *Vigo's Chirurg.* iv. 137 He muste guyde and tyrle the sayd nedle toward the panicle called cornea, tyl he touche the myddes of the apple of the eye and a lytle more. **1582** T. Watson *Centurie of Loue* lxii. Poems (Arb.) 98 Like Sisyphus I labour still To turle a rowling stoane against the hill. **1593** G. Harvey *Pierce's Super.* Wks. (Grosart) II. 150 That rowling stone of Innouation was neuer so turled and tumbled, as since those busie limmes began to rowse, and besturre them. **1638** H. Adam-

SON *Muse's Threnodie* v. (1774) 133 O how they bend their backs and fingers tirle! **1781** J. HUTTON *Tour to Caves* (ed. 2) Gloss. (E.D.S.), *Tirl, v.*, to turn over, as leaves in a book. **1825** BROCKETT *N. C. Words, Tirl*,..to turn over the leaves of a book quickly. **1844** *Ayrshire Wreath* 155 We had a tough game at tirlin' the trencher. *a*1869 C. SPENCE *Poems* (1898) 72 Soft wind sighing o'er the waste, Tirling the seared leaves. **1894** *Northumbld. Gloss.* s.v., 'Tirled heels up', suddenly overturned or turned inside out.

† **b.** ? To cause to move; to circulate; in phrase *tirl on the berry*, ? pass round the wine. Cf. *troll the bowl. Obs.*

**1519** *Interl. Four Elem.* B ij, Make rome, syrs, and let vs be mery, With huffa galand synge tyrll on the bery, And let the wyde worlde wynde. *c* **1537** *Thersytes* in *Four O. Plays* (1848) 79 And we shall make merye And synge tyrle on the berye. [*a* **1553** UDALL *Royster D.* II. iii. (Arb.) 36 Heigh derie derie, Trill on the berie.]

**2.** *intr.* To turn over; to rotate in moving or falling; to roll, whirl.

**1824** MACTAGGART *Gallovid. Encycl.* s.v. *Cankert*, Afore she tirl'd owre [= died] my prayers war fervant. **1860** BLACKIE *Lyr. Poems, Jenny Geddes* vii, Stool after stool, like rattling hail, came tirling through the air. **1894** *Northumbld. Gloss.* s.v., Slates are said to 'come tirlin doon' when they are stripped off in a gale.

**II. 3.** *intr.* To make a rattling noise by turning or moving something rapidly to and fro or up and down. **a.** In the phr. *to tirl at* († *upon*) *the pin*, to make such a noise on some part of the gate or door, in order to gain admittance; also *to tirl at the latch, at the sneck.*

An old phrase of ballad poetry, which in the 19th c. was taken up and used by Scott, and others after him. Now generally identified by antiquaries with the use of the appendage called the *risp and ring* (RISP *sb.*[3] 2), formerly used for this purpose. (Cf. TINKLE *v.*[1] 3, *Bob Norice* ix, 'When he came to Lord Barnet's castel He tinklet at the ring'.) But in this identification there are difficulties; a *risp* is not a 'pin', nor has it any resemblance to a 'pin', in any known sense of the word; the *pin* of a door was the latch or handle which was 'lifted' or 'turned' to open the door: see quots. under PIN *sb.*[1] 1 b; whereas the 'risp' was a fixed appendage which could neither be lifted nor turned, having no connexion with the latch or door-handle. Hence it would seem that 'to tirl at the pin' was to make a noise by moving the latch up and down rapidly. It is possible that the 'risp and ring' was a later device, which came to be erroneously considered as the apparatus by which the 'tirling at the pin' was performed.

[*c* **1500** *Songs, Carols*, etc. 111 Hogyn cam to bowers dore, He tryld vpon þe pyn for love, Hum, ha, trill go bell..Vp she rose & lett hym yn.] **15..** *Ld. Beichan* in *Ballads & Songs* (Percy Soc.) 90 When she came to Lord Beichan's gate, She tirled softly at the pin. ? **16..** in *Ramsay's Tea-t. Misc.* (1762) 324 Ay he tirled at the pin, But answer made she none. ? **17..** *Pr. Robt.* ix. in *Minstr. Scot. Bord.* (1869) 381 O he has run to Darlinton, And tirled at the pin. **1816** SCOTT *Antiq.* xl, There cam..first Pride, then Malice, then Revenge, then False Witness; and Murder tirl'd at the door-pin, if he camna ben. **1833** M. SCOTT *Tom Cringle* xii. (1859) 270, I hear my next door neighbour Madam Adversity tirling at the door pin. **1843** NICHOLSON *Hist. & Trad. T., Brownie o' Blodnoch* 80 He tirled na lang, but he glided ben Wi' a dreary dreary hum. **1879** *Perthshire in Bygone Days* II. v. 300 My Nannie will smile in her sleep and awake When I tirl at the latch of my door. **1895** CROCKETT *Men of Moss-Hags* xiii, She tirled fretfully at the pin, the servant-maid opened, and we went within.

**b.** *trans.* in *to tirl the sneck. Sc. rare.*

(Cf. the name, Jonnie Tirlsneck, of the beadle in Scott's *St. Ronan's Well.*)

*a* **1794** PICKERING '*Keen blaws the Wind*' in *Burns' Wks.* (1856) IV. 91 The Gaber-lunzie tirls my sneck And shivering tells his waefu' tale. **1892** J. LUMSDEN *Sheep-head & Trotters* 44 They..tirl the neebors' snecks Like ouphes this nicht.

**4.** *intr.* Said of the sound of rain on a roof. *rare.*

**1886** STEVENSON *Kidnapped* xxvi, When the wind gowls in the chimney and the rain tirls on the roof.

Hence **Ti·rling-pin**, the 'pin' or latch on which persons 'tirled' for admittance: see above, sense 3.

**1875** JAS. GRANT *One of the 600* i, The old Scotch tirling-pin—to be found now nowhere save in Fife—in lieu of bells and knockers. **1878** *N. & Q.* 5th Ser. IX. 319, I have seen and tirled at an original tirling-pin on the chief entrance door of the vicarage house at Ovingham-on-Tyne. **1894** *Northumbld. Gloss.* s.v. *Tirl*, Doors were formerly provided with a long, notched, iron handle on which a loose iron ring was hung. Instead of rousing the house with a knock, the caller tirled the ring up and down the notches of the 'tirling pin', or handle. [But this was the *risp and ring*.]

**Tirl(e, tyrl(e**, *v.*[4] *Sc.* Var. of THIRL *v.*[1], 3, THRILL *v.*[1]

**1825–82** JAMIESON, *Tirl, Tirle*,..to quiver, vibrate, thrill. *a* **1870** THOMSON *Musings* (1881) 120 Tyrants will ne'er care a snuff for your word, Till ance they heart' tirl frae the point o' your sword.

**Tirleis, -lies**, obs. Sc. forms of TRELLIS.

† **Ti·rler.** *Obs.* [f. TIRL *v.*[3] + -ER[1].] One who tirls; *tirler of square bones*, a thrower of dice, a dicer.

[Cf. *c* **1550** *Lusty Juventus* D iij, I wyll trill the bones while I haue one grote.] **1609** HOLLAND *Amm. Marcell.* XXVIII. iv. 340 Certaine..who decline the name of *Aleatores, i.* Dice-players, and therefore are desirous to be called *Tesserarij, i.* Tirlers of square bones.

† **Ti·rlery**, *a.* (or ? *sb.*) *Obs.* Also **tyr-, -liry, -lary.** [? Related to TIRL *v.*[3]] ? Whirling, flighty, trifling, trumpery: in a few obs. combs.: see quots., and cf. TERLERIE.

**1546** BALE *Eng. Votaries* I. (1550) 24 b, Bertha the quene ..then beynge a Frenche woman caused kynge Ethelbert to admit them wyth al theyr tyrlery trashe. *c* **1560** *Dr. Doubble Ale* 437 in Hazl. *E. P. P.* III. 321 Farewell and adewe, With a whirlary whewe, And a tirlary typpe; Beware of the whyppe. **1638** FORD *Lady's Trial* III. i, The best..prove themselves but flirts, and tirliry-pufkins [see PUFFKIN].

**Ti·rlie, ti·rly**, *sb.* and *a. Sc.* [f. TIRL *sb.*[1], *v.*[3]]

**A.** *sb.* **1.** (See quot.)

**1882** *Jamieson's Dict., Tirlie, tirly*, sb. applied to a waving or ornamental line in scroll-work or carving; also, to the ornament itself.

**2.** A turnstile.

**1824** MACTAGGART *Gallovid. Encycl., Tirlies*, little circular stoppages in pathways which turn round.

**B.** *adj.* Full of twirls or whirls, as in **Tirly-toy, Ti·rlie-whi·rlie**, a whirled figure, ornament, or pattern; anything having this form; a whirligig; a musical twirl or turn of the voice: also *attrib.*

*a* **1807** SKINNER *Misc. Poet.* (1809) 183 What can ye be that cou'd employ Your pen in sic a *tirly-toy? **17..** *Dainty Davie* ii. in Herd *Coll.* (1776) II. 215 It was in and through the window broads, And a' the *tirlie wirlies o'd; The sweetest kiss that e'er I got. **1742** FORBES *Shop Bill* x. in *Ajax*, etc. (1755) 40, I hae to fit the little girl..Wi' mony a bony tirly wirl about the queets [= ankles]. **1816** SCOTT *Antiq.* xxi, They hae contrived queer tirlie-wirlie holes, that gang out to the open air, and keep the stair as caller as a kail-blade. **1885** 'STRATHESK' *More Bits* xiv. (ed. 2) 274 Matthew Riddell..sang with a great many 'tirlywirlies' and grace-notes the following curling song.

**Tirling, Tirling-pin**: see TIRL *v.*[3]

**Tirlist**, obs. Sc. form of TRELLISED.

**Tiro, tyro** (təi·ro). Pl. **-oes, -os** (-ōz). Forms: α. 7 **tyron, tyrone**, *pl.* 7–9 **tyrones** (-ōu·nīz). β. 7–9 **tyro**, 8–9 **tiro**, *pl.* 7–8 **tyro's**, 7– **tyros, tyroes**, 8– **tiroes.** [a. L. *tīro*, pl. *tīrōnēs* (in med.L. often spelt *tyro, tyrones*: so in Du Cange), a young soldier, a recruit, a beginner; It. *tirone*, Sp. *tiron.* Commonly spelt *tyro*, after med.L., down to the date of Cowper's *Tirocinium*, 1784, and still so spelt by the majority of writers; in the 17th c. *tyrone* was even written for It. *tirone*, and *tyrones* as plural after L. is found down to 1824. But a plural of English form *tyroes* (cf. *heroes, negroes*) is found in 1672, and *tyros* in 1690; Cowper has *tiroes.*]

A beginner or learner in anything; one who is learning or who has mastered the rudiments only of any branch of knowledge; a novice.

**1611** CORYAT *Crudities* 63 Of those punies, those tyrones that are brought up under those threescore, there are no lesse then a thousand and five hundred. **1647** R. STAPYLTON *Juvenal* 109 Exercising and training like the tyrones or young souldiers in Camp Mart. **1656** BLOUNT *Glossogr.*, *Tyrone*.., a fresh water-souldier; a young beginner in any art or science, a novice. **1670** E. MAYNWARING *Physician's Repos.* 92 They do but qualify you as a Tyro. **1672** MANLEY *Cowell's Interpr.* Pref., The Students of the Law be no Tyroes in other Learning; or, at least, ought not to be. **1697** EVELYN *Numism.* vii. 252 For the Ease and Benefit of Tyros. **1699** GARTH *Dispens.* III. 31 There stands a Structure on a rising Hill, Where Tyro's take their Freedom out to kill. **1726** LEONI *Alberti's Archit.* III. 24/1 The Tyroes in the art of Painting. **1784** COWPER *Tiroc.* 220 The management of tiroes of eighteen Is difficult. **1797** *Monthly Mag.* III. 240/1 Dr. Travis..was..on entering into this province of theological polemics, a Tiro, compared with his antagonists. **1810** *Edin. Rev.* XV. 399 The tyro will not complain that it [the word] is obscure. **1824** SCOTT *Redgauntlet* let. xiii, A subject upon whilk all the *tyrones* have been trying their whittles. **1828** WHATELY in *Encycl. Metrop.* (1845) I. 282/1 It will..be advisable for a tiro in composition to look over what he has written. **1851** RUSKIN *Mod. Paint.* (ed. 2) I. Pref. 36 The merest tyro in art knows that [etc.]. **1869** FARRAR *Fam. Speech* ii. (1873) 49 The youngest tiro is hardly surprised to learn that *lieu* and *coucher* both spring from one root. **1875** JOWETT *Plato* (ed. 2) IV. 13 It is difficult to acquit Plato..of being a tyro in dialectics, when he overlooks such a distinction. **1880** SWINBURNE *Stud. Shaks.* 14 Easily recognisable by the veriest tiro in the school of Shakespeare.

*attrib. a* **1660** *Contemp. Hist. Irel.* (Ir. Archæol. Soc.) I. 162 Those tyron souldiers and novices in the arte militarie. **1860** PIESSE *Lab. Chem. Wonders* 142 A tyro-chemist in search of the philosopher's stone. **1903** H. G. HUTCHINSON in Watson *Eng. Sport* 272 Conveying some information to the tiro golfer. **1905** *Daily Chron.* 14 July 5/7 Rifle Clubs' Tyro Competition, open to teams of five tyro members.

**Tiro-**: see also TYRO-.

‖ **Tirocinium** (təirosi·niŏm). Also (less correctly) **tyro-.** [L. *tīrōcinium* first military service or campaign, young troops, f. *tīro*, TIRO + *-cinium*, as in *latrōcinium* robbery, *vāticinium* prophecy.]

**a.** First experience of or training in anything; apprenticeship, pupilage, novitiate; hence, inexperience, rawness. **b.** *concr.* A band of novices or recruits.

**1651** *Life Father Sarpi* (1676) 89 The *Tyrocinium* or the young Militia of state in the Commonwealth. **1654** GAYTON *Pleas. Notes* 37 It is the right discipline of Knight-Errantry, to be rudimented in losses at first, and to have the Tyrocinium somewhat tart. **1711** SHAFTESB. *Charac.* (1737) III. v. ii. 274 There the Tyrocinium of Genius's is annually display'd. **1784** COWPER (*title*) Tirocinium; or, A Review of Schools.

† **Tiro·ciny.** *Obs.* In 7 **tyro-.** [ad. L. *tīrōcinium*: see prec.] = prec.

**1600** TOURNEUR *Transf. Metam., Ded. Sir C. Heydon* 14 Mæcenas, strengthen my Tyrocinie. **1646** G. BUCK *Rich. III*, I. 1 The Linage, Family, Birth, Education, and Tyrociny of King Richard the third. **1663** WATERHOUSE *Fortescutus Illustr.* 138 The King incorporated them into the Tyrociny of Nobility. **1670** W. SIMPSON *Hydrol. Ess.* 30 Your tyrocincy in these abstruse studies plead your excuse.

† **Tiro·logy.** *Obs. nonce-wd.* [f. TIR-O + -OLOGY.] Properly, the science of tiroes; in quots. used for Elementary knowledge.

**1560** BECON *Cast. Comfort* Wks. II. 106 Some of the papistes..where so euer they finde *Ignis*, take it for Purgatory streyghtwayes. O noble doctors of Tyrology, rather than of Theology. **1563** — *Display. Popish Mass* ibid. III. 39 But where learned ye this tyrologye? For theologie is it not.

**Tiron, tirone**, obs. forms of TIRO.

**T-iron**: see T 3.

**Tironian** (təirōu·niăn), *a.* [ad. L. *Tīrōniān-us*, in *notæ Tīrōniānæ* Tironian notes.] Of or pertaining to Tiro, the freedman of Cicero: *Tironian notes*, a system of shorthand in use in ancient Rome, said to have been invented or introduced by Tiro.

**1828** *Edin. Rev.* Dec. 359 Manuscripts written entirely in the Tironian notes are not unfrequent in libraries of the date of the seventh century, as it is supposed. **1887** *Daily News* 6 Oct. 5/3 One of the earliest examples shown is a psalter in Tironian notes—the shorthand characters..invented by Marcus Tullius Tiro, the freedman of Cicero; it is in Latin —written early in the tenth century.

**Tironic, tyronic** (təirǫ·nik), *a. nonce-wd.* [f. L. *tīrōn-*, stem of *tīro*, TIRO + -IC.] Of, pertaining to, or characteristic of a tiro; betraying inexperience; amateurish. So (*nonce-wds.*) **Ti·-, ty·ronism**, inexperience; **Ti·-, ty·ronist** = TIRO; **Ti·-, ty·ronize** *v., intr.* to play the tiro, to be a beginner; hence **Ti·-, ty·ronizing** *ppl. a.*

*a* **1660** *Contemp. Hist. Irel.* (Ir. Archæol. Soc.) I. 29 As ignorant of martiall discipline, as the most tyronizinge of them all. **1716** M. DAVIES *Athen. Brit.* III. 3 They..are fitter for Veterans and Criticks in Closets and Libraries, than for Tyronists and Trivialists in Schools. **1832** *Examiner* 660/1 The critic,..though modest and professing tyronism, is a good moderator. **1909** *Daily Chron.* 23 June 3/1 His handling of form and plot is occasionally tyronic, if one may be permitted a word that ought to exist.

† **Tirpei·l.** *Obs.* Forms: 4 **tirpell, -peile, tyrpeyl, -payl, turpel**, 5 **-pell, -pele.** [Metathetic form of OF. *trepeil* uproar, trouble (12th c. in Godef.); according to Diez from OF. *trepeiller* to run hither and thither, f. *treper* to hop, TRIP, of German origin: cf. MLG. *trippen* to tread; also mod.F. *trépigner* to stamp.] A broil, encounter, tumult.

*c* **1330** R. BRUNNE *Chron. Wace* (Rolls) 1665 Þe Troiens þat had ben yn turpel [*v. r.* tirpell], At midnight tok þey conseil. *Ibid.* 15422 Þey [Britons] gadered þem to consail How to venge þat tyrpayl. *c* **1330** — *Chron.* (1810) 216 Withouten his conseile, or þe kynges wittyng, To maynten þer tirpeile he suore ageyn þe kyng. *c* **1400** *Laud Troy Bk.* 8841 But not-for-thi so it be-fell, That he was hurt at that turpell. *Ibid.* 18020 Foure hundrid of damyseles That lyued afftir that turpeles.

**Tirr** (tir, tə̄r), *v. Sc.* and *n. dial.* Also 6–7 **tyr, tyrr**, 6–9 **tir**, 7 **tirre**, 9 **terr.** [app. a reduced form of TIRVE *v.*[1] in same sense (see quot. 1553 in 1 b), and cf. Sc. *ser'* for *serve, turris* for *turves.*]

**1.** *trans.* To strip or tear off (a covering, esp. the thatch, slates, or roofing of a house).

**1571–5** *Diurnal Occurr.* (Bann. Cl.) 219 Ane commandement gevin..to tir and tak doun all the tymmer werk of all houssis in Leith Wynd and Sanctmarie Wynd. **1584** *Reg. Privy Council Scot.* III. 681 [He] tirrit and reft doun the faill and thak of his barnis. **1635** DICKSON *Pract. Wks.* (1845) I. 83 He shall tirr the visorne off your faces. **1670** R. LAW *Mem.* (1817) 33 It tirred the sclates off it. **1777** in Cramond *Ann. Banff* (1893) II. 97 There is no mending of the slating without tirring the sclates. **1795** A. WILSON *Spouter* 581 Mony a fierce storm had tirred the thack.

**2.** To strip (a person) naked; to uncover, unroof (a house, etc.). Also *fig.*

**1553** *Douglas's Æneis* IX. viii. 78 In quhat land lyis thou manglit and schent, Thy fare body and membris tyrryt [*ed. Small* tyrvit] and rent? **1572–5** *Diurnal Occurr.* (Bann. Cl.) 307 The laird of Collingtonis hous in Forrestaris Wynd wes half tirrit. **1578–9** *Reg. Privy Council Scot.* III. 83 Als meikle to say 'Tyr the kirk and theik the queir'. **1590** *Reg. Privy Council Scot.* IV. 492 Eftir thay wer tirrit to thair sarkis. **1644** *Ibid.* VIII. 101 They causit thair officers and hangman tirre us mother naked. *a* **1670** SPALDING *Troub. Chas. I* (1850) I. 70 Quhilk the said James espying, fallis to shortlie and tirris the houss. *Ibid.* (1851) II. 407 Thir cruell Irishis, seing a man weill cled, wold first tyr him and saif the clothis onspoyllit, syne kill the man. **1763** in *Lauder & Lauderd.* (1902) 86 The west side of the Manse must be tirred and sclated anew. **1808** JAMIESON s.v., Tir one to the skin, i.e. strip him naked. **1894** P. H. HUNTER *J. Inwick* xi. (1900) 153 A man..that cares na wha be tirred gin he be theekit. **1901** *Dundee Advert.* 11 Feb. 6 In a minute or two the whole of the north side of the roof was completely tirred.

**b.** *intr.* (for *refl.*) To take off one's clothes; to strip, undress.

**1787** W. TAYLOR *Scots Poems* 67 Hame I gaed..An' than I tirr'd, an' to my bed. **1825** JAMIESON, *Tirr*,..to undress, to pull off one's clothes. **1891** A. MATTHEWS *Poems & Songs* 52, I quickly tirr'd doon to the sark.

**3.** *trans.* To bare (land) of its surface covering; to pare off (the turf or surface soil) from land; to lay bare (the stone in a quarry) by removing the superincumbent soil and clay. With the thing laid bare, or the covering, as object. Also *absol.*

*c* **1567** *Survey Shilbottle* in *New County Hist. Northumbld.* (1899) V. 425 The ground also, by reason of castyng so great numbre of turves, [is] so tyrred and maide baire, that of a greate parte therof groweth no grasse. **1593** *Aberdeen Regr.* (1848) II. 85 The saidis Inchis ar sa flayne and tirrit, that..thair is na faill to be had thairin. **1808** JAMIESON, *Tirr*,..to pare off the sward by means of a spade..before casting peats. **1867** D. D. BLACK *Hist. Brechin* ii. 18 The earth was tirred from the garden on the top of the bank. **1899** MONTGOMERIE-FLEMING *Notes on Jamieson* 169 *Tirr*, ..to remove the soil and sub-soil from above a bed of sandstone in a quarry.

Hence **Tirr** *sb.*, the soil or sub-soil removed from the bed of a quarry (Montgomerie-Fleming *Notes on Jamieson*, 1899); **Ti·rring** *vbl. sb.*, the stripping off of the incumbent soil, etc.

**1794** *Statist. Acc. Scot.* XIII. 201 These quarries require very little tirring. **1902** *Daily Record & Mail* 11 Sept. 3 A couple of men had agreed to do some quarry tirring... The tirr suddenly collapsed and a man..was killed.

**Tirracke, -ick, -ook,** Sc. dial. ff. TARROCK.

**1792** *Statist. Acc. Scot.* V. 189 Redshanks, herons, tirricks. **1822** SCOTT *Pirate* x, The querulous cry of the tirracke and kittiewake. **1825** JAMIESON, Tirracke, Tirrook.

**Tirra-lirra** (ti·rǎ,li·rǎ). Also 7 teery-larry, -lerry, -leery, tyra-lyra. Cf. TIRALEE. [Echoic. Cf. OF. *turelu, tureluru*, 'a comic or burlesque refrain' (Godefroy), *turelure* a bagpipe, a refrain, F. *turlut* a titlark; and quot. 1889.] A representation of the note of the skylark, or of a similar sound uttered as an exclamation of delight or gaiety.

**1611** SHAKS. *Wint. T.* IV. iii. 9 The Larke, that tirra-Lyra chaunts. **1613** W. BROWNE *Brit. Past.* I. v, The Larke.. With the shrill chanting of her teery-lerry. **1688** R. HOLME *Armoury* II. 310/2 The Lark singeth Tyra Lyra. **1832** TENNYSON *Lady of Shalott* III. iv, 'Tirra lirra', by the river Sang Sir Lancelot. **1889** GROVE *Dict. Mus.* IV. 805/1 *Ture-Lure*, or *Toure-Loure*, a very ancient lyrical burden or refrain, probably of Provençal origin. The old English form is 'tirra-lirra'.

Hence † **Tirrili·rring** *ppl. a.*, that sings tirra-lirra; †**Tiry-tiry-leerer**, a lark.

**1659** TORRIANO, *Tirilirante lòdola*, the Tiriliring lark. **1599** T. M[OUFET] *Silkwormes* 50 Let Tiry-tiry-leerers [*marg.* larkes] vpward flie.

**Tirran, -and, -ane, -ant,** obs. Sc. ff. TYRANT.

**Tirret, Tirrill,** obs. ff. TERRET, -IT, TIRL *sb.*[1]

**Tirrit** (ti·rit). *rare.* [perh. illiterate for *terror* (Nares).] A fit of fear or temper; an 'upset', disturbance of one's equanimity.

**1597** SHAKS. 2 *Hen. IV*, II. iv. 220 Here's a goodly tumult: Ile forsweare keeping house, before Ile be in these tirrits, and frights. **1892** *Harper's Mag.* Feb. 405/2 My lady will have her tirrets.

**Tirrivee·, ti·rrivie.** *Sc.* Also tiri-, tiry-, tirry-, tirrie-, tery-, turry-, tira-, tirravee, -vie. [Origin obscure: some suggest a corruption of TAILYEVEY.] A fit or display of ill temper or passion; an unchecked outburst.

**1813** HOGG *Queen's Wake* 342 *note*, He suspected his spouse had taken some of her tirravies. **1814** SCOTT *Wav.* lxix, A very weel-meaning good-natured man .. when he wasna in ane of his tirrivies. **1898** N. MUNRO in *Blackw. Mag.* Feb. 184/2 I'm willing to make some allowance for a lover's tirravee. **1910** W. FINLAY in *Poets Ayrshire* 273 When a party ends up in a wild tirivee.

**Tirrs,** obs. Sc. form of TRUSS.

‖ **Tirshatha** (tiɹʃā·þa). [Heb. אתשרת *tirshāthā*, a. OPersian *tarsāta* 'his reverence', in LXX ἀθερσαθά (-αθά), Vulg. *athersatha* (i. e. *hat-tirshāthā*).] The title of an ancient Persian viceroy or prefect; applied in O. T. to Nehemiah.

**1382** WYCLIF *Ezra* ii. 63 Athersatha [**1388** Attersatha]. — *Neh.* viii. 9 Athirsata. **1535** COVERDALE *Ezra* ii. 63 Hathirsatha. **1611** *Ibid.*, The Tirshatha. **1890** HUNTER *After Exile* II. ix. 192 He stood forward with all the authority that belonged to him as Tirshatha. **1902** *Hastings' Dict. Bible* IV. 779 The Tirshatha appears to have been a royal commissioner..invested with the full powers of a satrap or viceroy, and employed on a special mission.

† **Tirve,** *v.*[1] *Obs.* Forms: 4-6 tirue, tyrue (= -ve), 4 turue (= -ve), (5 terve), 6 tirve, tyrff. [Not in OE.; known from 1300. Identical in meaning with TIRR *v.* (which seems to be a reduced form of the same word), and TIRL *v.*[2] App. distinct in sense from next; but, formally, **tyrfan* and **tierfan* might both be derived from different grades of a verbal ablaut series **terƀ-, tarƀ-, turƀ-*.

It has also been suggested to represent an OE. **tyrfan*, deriv. of *turf*, TURF, to have originally meant 'to strip the turf off the ground', and to have been extended to stripping the turf or thatch off roofs, the clothes off persons, and the hides off beasts. This is plausible, but is not favoured by the chronology of the senses.]

**1.** *trans.* To roll or pull back, or pluck *off* (the covering, clothes, skin, etc. from a person or animal); to strip off (clothes, armour; the thatch, slates, or roof of a house, stack, etc.).

*c* **1300** *Havelok* (1902) 603 [They] sone..funden, Als he [= they] tirueden of [= off] his serk On his rith shuldre a kyne merk. **13..** *E. E. Allit. P.* B. 630 He [Abraham] cached to his cobhous & a calf bryngez..bed tyrue of þe hyde. **13..** *Gaw. & Gr. Knt.* 1921 Syþen þay tan raynarde & tyruen of his cote. *a* **1400-50** *Alexander* 4114 Tuke out þe tuskis & þe tethe & teruen of þe skinnes. **1513** DOUGLAS *Æneis* v. v. 32 A habirgeoun..Quhilk he,..with his strang handis two, Tirvit and rent of bald Demoleo.

**b.** To strip (a person) of his clothes, etc., (an animal) of its skin, (a house) of its roof; to strip naked or bare; to unroof.

[*c* **1300** *Havelok* 918 Ful wel kan ich cleuen shides, Eles to-turuen of here hides.] *c* **1386** CHAUCER *Can. Yeom. Prol.* & *T.* 721 (Ellesm.) The deuel out of his skyn Hym terve [*other MSS.* torne, turne] I pray to god. **1500-20** DUNBAR *Poems* lxxii. 23 Of his claithis thai tirvit him bair. *Ibid.* 33 In tene, thai tirvit him agane, And till ane pillar thai him band. **1533** BELLENDEN *Livy* v. xi. (S.T.S.) II. 187 He gart tirve [*v.r.* tyrff] þis maister nakit of al his clothis. **1590-1** *Reg. Privy Council Scot.* IV. 587 The said Naper.. and others..come and tirvit the said complenaris houssis, and tuke of the rigging and thak thairof.

† **Tirve, terve,** *v.*[2] *Obs.* Forms: 5 tirue (-ve), tyrve, -we, 5-6 terue (-ve), (9 tirvie). [Known *c* 1330 in the comp. OVER-TERVE: app. representing an OE. **tierfan* = OLG. **terƀan*, OHG. *zerben*, :—**zarƀjan*, refl. to turn, turn over or about: cf. OE. *tearflian* to roll over and over, wallow. If this is right, the better form is *terve*. (Texts of MSS. printed before 1900 have usually *n* for *u* (= *v*), the word being taken as a variant of *turn*.)]

**1.** *intr.* To turn; *esp.* to turn upside down, topple over, fall down; also *fig.* to turn *to* some course or action.

*c* **1400** *Destr. Troy* 430 Erthe dymmed by dene, ded men Roose, The gret tempull top terued to ground. *c* **1425** *Disp. Mary & Cross* xxxvii. in *Leg. Rood* 207 (MS. Roy.) Truyt and treget to helle schal terve. *c* **1440** *Psalmi Penitent.* (1894) 45 To trecherie schulde we noght terve [*rime* kerve]. **1567** GOLDING *Ovid's Met.* v. I v b, Ioues ymage..made with crooked welked hornes that inward still doe terue [*rime* serue]. [**1819** W. TENNANT *Papistry Storm'd* (1827) 206 He made him tirvie down and tapple Head-foremost wi' a bang.]

**2.** *trans.* To turn; *esp.* to overturn, overthrow; also *fig.*

*c* **1400** *Destr. Troy* 1512 How his towne was taken and tiruyt to grounde. *Ibid.* 4763 The grete toures þai toke, tiruyt the pepull. *Ibid.* 10197 To take you with tene & tirue you to ground. *c* **1420** *Brut* 378 Our stakez made hem top ouyr terve, eche on oþer, þat þay lay on hepis. *c* **1422** HOCCLEVE *Min. Poems* xxiv. 573 Shee That had him terued with false deceitis.

**b.** To turn *to* some course or *to do* something.

*c* **1400** *Destr. Troy* 2943 Throgh whiche treason betydes, & teruys vmqwhile Bolde men to batell and biker with hond.

**c.** To turn over, up, or down (the edge or hem of a garment). (Cf. TARF, TURF *sb.*[2])

**1482** CAXTON *Contin. Higden's Polycron.* VIII. xiii, The yemanry hadde theyr hosen teruen [? terued] or bounden bynethe the knee hauynge longe jackys.

Hence † **Tirving** *vbl. sb.*, turning; *concr.* a border turned back or up.

*c* **1440** *Promp. Parv.* 494/2 Tyrf, or tyrvynge [*v.r.* tyrwynge] vp on an hoode or sleue.

**Tirvis,** obs. Sc. pl. of TURF *sb.*

† **Tirwhit, tirwit,** obs. var. TEWHIT, lapwing.

**1671** in SKINNER *Etymolog.* Hence **1706** in PHILLIPS, etc.

† **Tiry** (təiə·ri), *a. Obs.* [f. TIRE *v.*[1] + -Y.] Tired, weary. Hence † **Ti·riness,** tiredness.

**1611** CORYAT *Crudities* 37 My horse began to be so tiry that he would not stirre one foote out of the way. **1697** R. PEIRCE *Bath Mem.* I. ix. 192 Having a great share of this Tyrie Distemper. *Ibid.* II. iii. 295 [She] was not unsensible of her Tyryness and Dispiritedness.

**'Tis** (tiz), abbreviation of *it is*, formerly common in prose, now poetic or archaic; see also IT A. γ.

*c* **1450** *Mankind* 821 in *Macro Plays* 30 Alas! tys pety yt schuld be þus. *a* **1566** R. EDWARDES *Damon & Pithias* (1744) 280 Tis a pestens queen. **1598**- [see IT A. γ].

**Tis,** ME. assimilated form of THIS after dentals, etc.: see T 8.

**Tisan, tisane,** var. PTISAN, barley-water.

**Tisar** (tizā·ɹ). *Glass-manuf. rare.* [ad. F. *tisart* opening of a furnace, f. *tiser* to poke, stir, etc.: see TEASE *v.*[2]] The fireplace or furnace used to heat the annealing arch for plate-glass.

**1839** URE *Dict. Arts* 587 The carquaise is heated by means of a fire-place of a square form called a *tisar*, which extends along its side.

**Tische, -ey,** obs. Sc. ff. TISSUE. **Tischera,** var. TEZKERE. **Tise,** obs. f. TICE *v.* **Tiseday,** obs. Sc. f. TUESDAY. **Tisheldar,** var. TAHSILDAR.

**Tishew, -oo, -ue,** obs. ff. TISSUE.

‖ **Tishri** (ti·ʃri), **Tisri** (ti·zri). [ad. late Heb. תשרי *tishrī*, f. Aramaic שרא *shᵉrā* to begin.] The Babylonian name of the first month of the Jewish civil year, or the seventh of the ecclesiastical, corresponding to parts of September and October: substituted after the captivity for the earlier name ETHANIM.

**1833** [see ABIB]. **1877** C. GEIKIE *Christ* xlix. (1879) 578 The seventh month Tisri, part of our Sep. and Oct. **1904** *Daily Chron.* 9 Sept. 6/7 To-night marks the advent of Tishri, the most important month in the Jewish calendar. **1904** *Jewish Encycl.* VIII. 672 Tishri is characterized as the month of the birth of the Patriarchs.

**Tisick, tisical, (tiss-),** obs. and dial. forms of PHTHISIC, -AL. Hence **Tis(s)icking** *a.* = PHTHISICKY; † **Tisickness,** phthisic or asthmatic quality.

**1533** ELYOT *Cast. Helthe* (1539) 82 Tisiknesse or shortnesse of breth. *a* **1825** FORBY *Voc. E. Anglia*, *Tissick*,..a tickling faint cough; called also a 'tissicky cough'. **1888** DOUGHTY *Arabia Deserta* II. 521 The Sherif visited Beyrût some years ago..for the health of a tisical son. **1890** *Blackw. Mag.* CXLVIII. 463/2 Snipe hummed and bleated out a tissicking music. **1904** in *Eng. Dial. Dict.* s. v. *Tissick*, etc.

† **Tisince,** obs. form of *ptisans*, pl. of PTISAN.

*c* **1623** LODGE *Poore Mans Talentt* (Hunter. Cl.) 9 The patient..must bee content to drink Tisince, balme water, or the Iuleb of roses.

**Tisor,** variant of TEASER[2], fireman.

**Tisri**: see TISHRI.

**Tissane,** obs. var. PTISAN, barley-water, etc.

† **Tissed,** *ppl. a. Obs.* [ad. F. *tissu*, pa. pple. of OF. *tistre*:—L. *texere* to weave (cf. TEXTILE): see -ED[1].] In phr. *gold tissed, cotton tissed*, modelled on F. *or tissu, coton tissu* (cf. *gold of tisshue*, quot. 1501 s.v. TISSUE *sb.* 1 a).

**1585** T. WASHINGTON tr. *Nicholay's Voy.* I. xxi. 27 b, A gowne of cloth of gold tissed [*orig.* vne robbe de drap d'or figuré]. *Ibid.* II. xxii. 60 A fine & long smock of cotton tissed [*orig.* vne fine & longue chamisolle de cotton tissue].

**Tissey,** obs. f. TIZZY. **Tissick,** etc: see PHTHISIC, TISICK. **Tisso,** var. TEESOO.

† **Tissu,** *ppl. a. Obs. rare*[−1]. [a. F. *tissu*, pa. pple.: see TISSUE *sb.*] Woven. (Const. as *pa. pple.*)

**1549** *Compl. Scot.* vii. 69 Ane syde mantil..the quhilk hed bene tissu ande vrocht be thre syndrye fassons of verkmenschips.

**Tissual** (ti·ʃu,ăl, ti·siu,ăl), *a. rare*[−1]. [irreg. f. next + -AL, after *virtual*, etc.] Of or pertaining to (living) tissue: see next, 5.

**1837** P. KEITH *Bot. Lex.* 343 Plants..exhibiting..indications of such tissual and organic susceptibilities as are proper to their rank in the scale of being.

**Tissue** (ti·ʃu, ti·siu), *sb.* Forms: α. 4-5 tyssu, 4-6 tissewe, 5 tyssew, -eu, -ywe, (*pl.* -eux), 5-6 tyssue, 5-7 tissu, tissew, 6 tyssewe, tysswe, 5- tissue. β. 5-6 tisshue, tisshewe, *Sc.* tusche, (tuscha), 5-8 tishew, 6 tyshew, tysshewe, tysshiew, tushwe, *Sc.* tischey, -ay, tische, tysche, 7 tishue, tishoo. [a. OF. *tissu* sb., applied to a kind of rich stuff (*c* 1200 in Godef. *Compl.*), from pa. pple. of obs. F. *tître*, OF. *tistre*:—**tissre*:—L. *tex-ĕre* to weave.]

**1. a.** A rich kind of cloth, often interwoven with gold or silver. *Obs.* exc. *Hist.*

? *a* **1366** CHAUCER *Rom. Rose* 1104 The barres were of gold ful fyne, Upon a tyssu of satyne. **1429** in Dugdale *Monast. Angl.* II. 222 Cum tribus capis choralibus de panno Tyssewys vulgariter nuncupato. **1501** in *Cal. Doc. rel. Scotl.* (1888) 336 A gown of tawny cloth of gold of tisshue. **1509** HAWES *Past. Pleas.* xvi. (Percy Soc.) 61 With cloth of tyssue in the rychest maner The walles were hanged. **1513** BRADSHAW *St. Werburge* I. 1647 Fresshely embrodred in ryche tysshewe and fyne. **1543** GRAFTON *Contn. Harding* 591 The quene ..clothed in a riche mantell of tissue. **1562** in Feuillerat *Revels Q. Eliz.* (1908) 114 Cloth of Silver purple tysshiew. **1585** T. WASHINGTON tr. *Nicholay's Voy.* III. viii. 82 Girded with a large girdle of Tissue, or of silke and golde. **1648** CRASHAW *Delights Muses* Wks. (1904) 160 Something more than Taffata or Tissew can. *c* **1710** CELIA FIENNES *Diary* (1888) 4 Good bed Chambers and well furnished velvet damaske and tissue. **1785** G. A. BELLAMY *Apology* I. 130 A dress for me to play the character of Cl[e]opatra,..the ground of it was silver tissue.

**b.** Now applied to various rich or fine stuffs of delicate or gauzy texture.

**1730** SWIFT *Lady's Dressing-room* Wks. 1755 IV. I. 113 Array'd in lace, brocades and tissues. **1769** *Public Advertiser* 2 June 1/3 Sale of Silks..Brocades, Tissues. **1821** JOANNA BAILLIE *Metr. Leg., Wallace* liv, Tissue of threaded gems is worn. **1910** *Westm. Gaz.* 12 Mar. 15/2 Tissues studded with jewels are lightly draped over satin.

† **2.** A band or girdle of rich stuff. *Obs.*

*c* **1374** CHAUCER *Troylus* II. 590 (639) His helm..That by a tissew heng his bak byhynde. *c* **1430** *Pilgr. Lyf Manhode* I. xciv. (1869) 51 The scrippe was of greene selk, and heeng bi a greene tissu. *c* **1440** *Partonope* 6726 That tyssew and bocle..all to peses brak. *c* **1450** HOLLAND *Howlat* 405 Mony schene scheld With tuscheis of trast silk tichit to the tre. **1488** *Acta Dom. Conc.* (1839) 98/2 A tuscha of silk siluerit price v merkis. **1503** *Acc. Ld. High Treas. Scot.* II. 388, xj½ elne tisches to mend the bordoring of the Kingis sadill bordorit with tischeis. **1508** *Test. Ebor.* (Surtees) IV. 274 A gyrdill wt a golde tushwe. **1513** DOUGLAS *Æneis* I. vii. 136 And quhair hir pap was for the speir cut away Of gold thairon was belt ane riche tischay. *Ibid.* XII. v. 133 Quhar as the wovin gyrdill or tysche Abufe his navill was beltit, as we se. **1603** HOLLAND *Plutarch's Mor.* 629 Venus ..cast aside her daintie jewels..and threw away that tissue and lovely girdle of hers.

**3.** Any woven fabric or stuff. In quot. 1850 *transf.* weaving.

**1565** COOPER *Thesaurus*, *Trilix* .. tissue made of three threads of diuers colours. **1757** GRAY *Bard* I. iii, They.. weave with bloody hands the tissue of thy line. [Cf. II. i, Weave the warp, and weave the woof The winding-sheet of Edward's race.] *a* **1765** SHENSTONE *Progr. Taste* I. 24 Constant wear..turns the tissue into tatters. **1850** GLADSTONE *Homer* II. ii. 129 In the arts of tissue and embroidery. **1879** LUBBOCK *Sci. Lect.* v. 155 Tissues of woven flax have been found in some of the Swiss lake-villages.

**4.** *fig.* Something likened to a woven fabric, as being produced by the intertwining of separate elements; an intricate mass or interwoven series, a 'fabric', 'network', 'web' (*of* things abstract, most usually of a bad kind, as absurdities, errors, falsehoods, etc.). Also, the structure or contexture of such a 'fabric'.

**1711** ADDISON *Spect.* No. 62 ¶ 6 Those little occasional Poems..are nothing else but a Tissue of Epigrams. **1762** GOLDSM. *Cit. W.* xlii, The history of Europe,..a tissue of crimes, follies, and misfortunes. **1793** JEFFERSON *Writ.* (1859) IV. 89 The hasty amendments..had so broken the tissue of the paragraph, as to [etc.]. 1820 W. IRVING *Sketch Bk.* I. 104 The tissue of misrepresentations..woven round us. 1842 WHITTIER *Raphael* xvi, The tissue of the Life to be We weave with colors all our own. 1878 GLADSTONE *Prim. Homer* 107 He works it..into the tissue of the poems.

**5.** *Biol.* The substance, structure, or texture of which an animal or plant body, or any part or organ of it, is composed; *esp.* any one of the various structures, each consisting of an aggregation of similar cells or modifications of cells, which make up the organism. **a.** in animals.

The chief forms of tissue in the higher animals are the *epithelial* (incl. *glandular*), *connective* (incl. *cartilaginous* and *osseous*), *muscular*, and *nervous* tissues. (The term is sometimes extended to include the *blood* as a 'fluid tissue'.)

1831 CARLYLE *Sart. Res.* I. i, Every cellular, vascular, muscular Tissue. 1834 J. FORBES *Laennec's Dis. Chest* (ed. 4) 279 Chronic inflammation..of the pulmonary tissue. 1846 G. E. DAY tr. *Simon's Anim. Chem.* II. 40 Materials ..to supply the place of those that have been removed from the body in consequence of waste of tissue. 1857 BUCKLE *Civiliz.* I. xiv. 818 The tissues of the teeth are..analogous to those of other parts. 1861 HULME tr. *Moquin-Tandon* II. I. 41 The organic Tissues are three in number: 1st, cellular tissue; 2nd, muscular tissue; and 3rd, nervous tissue... Some writers admit other organic tissues. 1869 HUXLEY *Phys.* i. (ed. 3) 11 Every such constituent of the body, as epidermis, cartilage, or muscle, is called a 'tissue'. 1880 BASTIAN *Brain* 28 Nerve tissues are..divided into 'grey' and 'white' matter. 1889 MIVART *Truth* 149 The arteries, veins and heart are full of a fluid 'tissue'—the blood.

**b.** in plants.

The various forms of plant tissue may be generally reduced to two classes, typified by *parenchyma* and *prosenchyma*. In the higher plants there are three systems of tissues, the *epidermal*, *fundamental*, and *fibro-vascular*.

1837 [implied in TISSUAL]. 1845 LINDLEY *Sch. Bot.* x. (1858) 159 Tissue is called Woody Fibre when it is composed of slender tubes placed side by side. 1875 BENNETT & DYER *Sachs' Bot.* 68 Every aggregate of cells which obeys a common law of growth..may be termed a Tissue. *Ibid.* 103 The relationship of the three systems of tissue may be observed.. in..foliage-leaves.

**c.** *generally*; also *fig.*

1856 DOVE *Logic Chr. Faith* II. § 2. 114 The new chart must clothe the world with its living tissues. 1858 LEWES *Sea-side Stud.* 400 Histology is the doctrine of the tissues; and tissues are the webs out of which the organism is fabricated. 1872 BAGEHOT *Physics & Pol.* 178 The germ might be foreign, but the tissue was native. 1878 BELL *Gegenbaur's Comp. Anat.* 16 Conversion of the cells into tissue.

**6.** Short for TISSUE-PAPER, q. v.

1780–1 *Act* 21 *Geo. III*, c. 24 § 2 For every Bundle of Paper made in Great Britain for Printing, called Demy Tissue. For every Bundle of Paper called Crown Tissue. 1797 NEMNICH *Waaren-Lexicon* 30/1 Die Englischen Papiersorten...Crown, single, inferior, double, double inferior, and tissue;..Demy single, inferior, plate, short, tissue, writing [etc.].

(The reference here was prob. to sizes of specially prepared tissue-paper (now spoken of as 'printing paper' and 'printing tissue'), on which designs were printed from copper plates for transference to pottery-ware. This was specially taxed.)

**7.** *Photogr.* Paper made in strips coated with a film of gelatine containing a pigment, used in carbon printing.

1873 E. SPON *Workshop Receipts* Ser. I. 267/1 This carbon tissue consists of a layer of gelatine containing the carbon or other permanent pigment spread on paper. 1878 ABNEY *Photogr.* xxiv. 165 Many improvements in the manufacture of the tissue have been made, and the different substances added to the gelatine are only partially known to the public. 1891 *Anthony's Photogr. Bull.* IV. 80 Tissue can be obtained from London and sensitized as required for use.

**8.** Collector's name for two species of moth, *Scotosia* (*Triphosa*) *dubitata* and *cervinata*.

1832 RENNIE *Butterfl. & Moths* 128 The Tissue (*T[riphosa] dubitata*, Stephens)... Wings.. brown, shining; first pair having a tinge of purple. *Ibid.*, The Scarce Tissue (*T. cervinata*, Stephens).

**9.** *attrib.* and *Comb.* **a.** *attrib.* Made or consisting of tissue (sense 1); in quot. *a* 1625, dressed in tissue.

1480 *Wardr. Acc. Edw. IV* in *Privy Purse Exp. Eliz. York*, etc. (1830) 149 A long gowne of grene velvet upon velvet tisshue cloth of gold. 1570 FOXE *A. & M.* (ed. 2) 2143/2 The Vicechauncellour hauing on a tyshew cope. *a* 1625 FLETCHER *Love's Cure* I. iii, Smooth City fools or tisseu Cavaliers. 1704 *Lond. Gaz.* No. 3981/4 A rich Silver Tishia Gown. 1708 *Brit. Apollo* No. 37. 2/2 Tishew Sleves. 1796 MAR. J. HOLROYD in *Girlhood M. J. H.* (1896) 373 Milady wore..a Gold Tissue..Train.

**b.** *Comb.*, chiefly in sense 5, as *tissue-building* sb. and adj., *-cell*, *-change*, *-death*, *-element*, *-form*, *-former*, *-forming* adj., *-growth*, *-like* adj., *-product*, *-system*, *-transformation*; **tissue-lymph**, lymph derived from the tissues (not directly from the blood); **tissue-secretion**: see quots. 1848, 1861. See also TISSUE-PAPER.

1848 DANA *Zooph.* iv. 51 Secretions formed within the animal which are mostly calcareous..may be called tissue-secretions. ..These secretions take place from the tissues of the sides and the base of the polyp. 1861 GREENE *Man. Anim. Kingd., Cœlent.* 153 The sclerobasic corallum is by Mr. Dana termed 'foot secretion'; the sclerodermic, 'tissue secretion'. 1866 ODLING *Anim. Chem.* I Recent advances in chemistry of tissue-products. 1872 HUXLEY *Phys.* vi. 139 Proteids are tissue-formers. 1873 T. H. GREEN *Introd. Pathol.* (ed. 2) 24 The increased tissue-change which accompanies acute febrile diseases. *Ibid.* 88 The pulmonary pigment..may be seen..within the connective tissue-cells. 1875 BENNETT & DYER tr. *Sachs' Bot.* 78 In this manner arise in the higher plants..systems of tissue-forms, which may be designated simply as Systems of Tissue. 1886 A. WINCHELL *Walks Geol. Field* 308 The processes of digestion,..assimilation, and tissue-building. *c* 1890 A. MURDOCH *Yoshiwara Episode* 26 He..wondered..what the soft, flimsy, tissue-like paper was. 1896 *Allbutt's Syst. Med.* I. 213 It is quite possible that a trace of albumose might thus be formed after tissue-death. 1903 G. OLIVER in *Lancet* 3 Oct. 942/1 Physiologists are divided as to whether tissue lymph is a pressure product..or a secretion.

**Ti·ssue,** *v.* Now *rare.* [f. TISSUE *sb.*] *trans.* To make into a tissue, to weave; *spec.* to weave with gold or silver threads, to work or form in tissue; to adorn or cover with tissue (cf. prec. 1 a).

1483 CAXTON *Gold. Leg.* 237/1 A whyte mantel In whiche there were litil ouches and crosses of gold tissued. 1491 — *Vitas Patr.* (W. de W. 1495) II. 249/2 To tyssue the sayd roddes & palmes to make mattes. 1547 *Harl. MS.* 1419 *B*, lf. 535 b, Clothe of silver tissued with flowres of golde and silver. 1562 in Feuillerat *Revels Q. Eliz.* (1908) 114 Gold tysshewed with silver. *a* 1626 BACON *New Atl.* (1650) 25 The Charriot was covered with cloth of Gold tissued upon Blew. *a* 1851 MOIR *Birth Flowers* vi, Her vesture seem'd as from the blooms Of all the circling seasons wove,..And tissued with the woof of Love.

**b.** *fig.*

1637 WOTTON in *Reliq.* (1672) 104 To Countenance any Great action; and then..to Tissue upon it some Pretence or other. 1800 MOORE *Anacreon* xlvi. 14 Cultured field, and winding stream, Are sweetly tissued by his beam. 1905 *Athenæum* 6 May 558/2 'Dream and Reality' is tissued from a series of such metaphors.

**Tissued** (ti·ʃud, ti·siud), *ppl. a.* [f. prec. vb. (or sb.) + -ED.]

**1.** Woven; *spec.* woven with gold or silver thread: see TISSUE *sb.* 1 a and *v.*

1584 in Feuillerat *Revels Q. Eliz.* (1908) 365 The pages sute of Oringe tawney tissued vellet. 1619 *Rutland MSS.* (1905) IV. 516, 19 yardes ½ of tissued grogram at 48s. the yard. 1790 COWPER *Mother's Picture* 75 Thy vesture's tissu'd flowers. 1879 FARRAR *St. Paul* (1883) 224 He entered the theatre..in an entire robe of tissued silver.

*fig.* 1629 MILTON *Ode Nativity* 146 Mercy..With radiant feet the tissued clouds down stearing. 1789 E. DARWIN *Bot. Gard.* (1791) II. 52 Long threads of silver light Dart on swift shuttles o'er the tissued night! 1790 MERRY *Laurel Lib.* 7 Where starry Night weaves thick her tissued rays.

**2.** Dressed or arrayed in 'tissue': see TISSUE *sb.* I.

?16.. WHARTON (Webster 1864), Crested knights and tissued dames.

**Ti·ssueless,** *a.* [f. TISSUE *sb.* + -LESS.] Destitute of tissue (i. e., in quot., of flesh).

1864 BLACKMORE *Clara Vaughan* lxxxi, It rang among the skeletons, and rattled their tissueless joints.

**Ti·ssue-pa·per.** [See quot. 1880, which may be correct; but earlier authority is wanted.] A very thin soft gauze-like unsized paper, used for wrapping delicate articles, for covering engravings or other illustrations in books, as copying-paper, etc.

Various grades are distinguished, as *silver tissue*, specially prepared for wrapping silver ware; *copying tissue*, for copying letters, etc.; *printing tissue*: see TISSUE *sb.* 6.

1777 HENLY in *Phil. Trans.* LXVII. 114 A number of circular pieces of tissue-paper. 1815 J. SMITH *Panorama Sc. & Art* II. 161 The paper must be of that kind called tissue or silver paper. 1854 *Phemie Millar* 24 Encasing in tissue paper a set of ivory handled knives. 1865 LOWELL *Wks.* (1890) V. 285 Leaping through a hoop with nothing more substantial to resist than tissue-paper. 1880 BIRDWOOD *Ind. Arts* II. 75 The flimsy paper called tissue-paper was originally made to place between the tissue to prevent its fraying or tarnishing when folded.

**Tist, tiste**: see TICE *v.*

**Ti·sty-to·sty,** *int.*, *sb.*, *a. dial.* Forms: 6– tisty-tosty, 6 tistitostie, 9 teesty-tosty. [In sense 1 perh. a mere ejaculation. In sense 3 it has been compared with † *tyte tust*(*e* or † *tussemose* a nosegay: see TUZZY-MUZZY; but current dialect use associates it rather with *toss*, and *tost*, *tossed*.]

† **1.** *int.* as an ejaculation of triumph or exultation.

1568 FULWEL *Like Will to Like* C iij, Hey tisty tosty an owle is a bird. *c* 1570 *Marr. Wit & Science* IV. iv. Ej, Mother must I haue his Cote, now mother must [I]? Chal [= I shall] be a liuely lad, with hey tistye tosty.

† **2.** *sb.* A swaggering or blustering fellow (? one who uses the ejaculation). Also *attrib.* or *adj. Obs.*

1598 FLORIO, *Sbrauo*, a swash-buckler, a swaggrer, a hackster, a cutter, a tistitostie. *Ibid.*, *Squassa pennacchio*,..a tisti-tostie-fellow, a swaggrer.

**3.** *sb.* A bunch of flowers, a nosegay (*obs.*); in *mod. dial.*, a cowslip-ball: also *tisty-tosty ball.*

1825 JENNINGS *W. Country Gloss.*, *Teesty-tosty*, the blossoms of cowslips collected together, tied in a globular form, and used to toss to and fro for an amusement called *teesty-tosty*...Sometimes called simply a tosty. 1865 *Cornh. Mag.* July 41 'Blossom-ball'..is evidently formed after the West-country 'cowslip-ball', the 'tisty-tosty ball' of Dorsetshire and Somersetshire, which children yearly make.

**b.** *attrib.* or *adj.* Round like a cowslip-ball; plump and comely.

1888 T. HARDY *Wessex Tales* (1889) 35 She's a rosy-cheeked, tisty-tosty little body enough.

**Tiswin** (tis-, tizwi·n). *U. S.* Also **tizwin.** [ad. Amer. Sp. *texguino.*] An intoxicating drink made from maize, wheat, or mesquite beans by the American Indians.

1891 J. G. BOURKE in *Cent. Mag.* Mar. 655/1 The Apache intoxicant, 'tizwin'..[is] beer, made from fermented corn. 1911 WEBSTER, Tiswin, tizwin.

**Tit** (tit), *sb.*[1] *dial.* (chiefly *Sc.*) [? f. TIT *v.*[1]] A sharp or sudden pull; a tug, jerk, twitch.

1340 HAMPOLE *Pr. Consc.* 1915 Yf þat tre war tite pulled oute At a titte with al þe rotes oboute. 1581 *Satir. Poems Reform.* xliii. 75 Sa Fortoun mountit neuer man sa hie,.. Bot with ane tit sho turnis the quheill. 1827 KINLOCH *Ballad Bk.* 63 He gied the tow a clever tit That brocht her out at the lum. 1881 PAUL *Aberdeen.* 111 The craetur' gied a tit, an' afore I kent fat I was about, I was lyin' o' the braid o' my back.

**Tit,** *sb.*[2] [Goes with TIT *v.*[2]]

**1.** In phr. **tit for tat** [app. a variation of *tip for tap*, known a century earlier: see TAP *sb.*[2], TIP *sb.*[2], and cf. prec. But perh. wholly or partly onomatopœic.] One blow or stroke in return for another; an equivalent given in return (usually in the way of injury, rarely of benefit); retaliation.

The whole phrase is used sometimes as a *sb.*, sometimes as *adj.* or *adv.*; also, elliptically or as *interj.*

1556 J. HEYWOOD *Spider & F.* xxxvii. 26 That is tit for tat in this altricacion. 1586 J. HOOKER *Hist. Irel.* in *Holinshed* II. 94/1 That they would not sticke to set his seruants at libertie, so he would redeliuer them the youth of the citie, which was nothing else in effect, but tit for tat. 1710 ADDISON *Tatler* No. 229 ¶ 3, I was threatened to be answered Weekly Tit for Tat. 1809 J. QUINCY in *Life* 181, I shall..give..what politicians call a Rowland for their Oliver, and what the ladies term tit for tat. 1881 SAINTSBURY *Dryden* iv. 80 A fair literary tit-for-tat in return for the *Rehearsal.* 1891 *Daily News* 16 July 5/1 Fair Traders, Reciprocity men, or believers in the tit-for-tat plan of dealing with other nations. 1905 H. A. VACHELL *The Hill* viii, Tit for tat. If I do this for you, will you do something for me?

**2.** A light stroke or tap; a slap: cf. TIP *sb.*[2]

1808 JAMIESON, *Tyte, tit*...2. A slight stroke, a tap. 1891 *Hartland Gloss.* s. v., I'll gi'e 'ee a tit under the yur.

**3.** *Comb.*: **tit-tat**, an imitation of the sound of alternating taps or blows; **tit-tat-toe**, the beginning of a formula used in 'picking' or fixing upon a person or thing, hence a children's game; also *tick-tack-toe*, *tip-tap-toe.*

In quot. *a* 1700 imitating the noise made in toddling.

*a* 1700 B. E. *Dict. Cant. Crew*, *Tit-tat*, the aiming of Children to go at first. 1855 ANNE MANNING *O. Chelsea Bun-house* xiii. 211, I played at Tit-tat-to with Joe, and posed him with hard riddles. 1909 *Daily Chron.* 22 July 7/1 Drawing to be diversified by noughts and crosses and 'tit tat toe'.

**Tit,** *sb.*[3] Also 6 **tyt, titte**, 6–8 **titt**, 7 **tytt.** [app. of onomatopœic origin, as a term for a small animal or object; found also to some extent in Scandinavian and Icel.; cf. Norw. dial. *titta* little girl, *tîta* a little fish, trout, sprout, minute growth, little kernel, little ball or marble, Icel. *tittr* a little plug or pin, also, a titmouse (Norw. *tite*): see also TITLING, TITMOUSE, in which *tit* occurs much earlier than by itself.]

**I. 1.** A name for a horse small of kind, or not full grown; in later use often applied in depreciation or meiosis to any horse; a nag. Now *rare.*

1548 PATTEN *Exped. Scotl.* D j, He rode on a trottynge tyt well woorth a coople of shillynges. 1563 GOLDING *Cæsar* IV. (1565) 85 But such [beastes] as are bred among them though they be littel tittes & yll shapen, they make..to be very good of labor. 1598 FLORIO, *Bidetto*, a little horse, a nagge, a tit, a little doing horse. 1616 SURFL. & MARKH. *Country Farme* 538 If you will let them haue anie Tytt or meane Iade to goe before them, and lead the way. 1706 PHILLIPS (ed. Kersey), *Tits*, a Country-word, for small Cattel. 1726 *Dict. Rust.* (ed. 3), *Tit*, a little Horse, and some call a Horse of a middling Size a double Tit. 1797 *Sporting Mag.* IX. 338, I keep a curricle and a brace of tits. 1821 SCOTT *Kenilw.* xi, I have as good a tit as ever yeoman bestrode. 1894 ASTLEY *50 Years Life* II. 186 A very promising tit named Woodstock.

† **b.** *fig.* of a person, etc. See also 2. *Obs.*

1706–7 FARQUHAR *Beaux Strat.* I. i, As to our Hearts, I grant 'ye, they are as willing Tits as any within Twenty Degrees. *a* 1734 NORTH *Exam.* I. iii. § 40 (1740) 145 As the willing Tits of the Party, and weaker Brethren.

**2.** A girl or young woman: often qualified as *little*: cf. *chit.* (*a*) Usually in depreciation or disapproval: esp. one of loose character, a hussy, a minx. (*b*) Sometimes in affection or admiration, or playful meiosis. (Common in 17th and 18th c.; now *low slang.*)

1599 MIDDLETON *Micro-Cynicon* Wks. (Bullen) VIII. 122 He hath his tit, and she likewise her gull; Gull he, trull she. 1606 *Sir G. Goosecappe* IV. ii. in Bullen *O. Pl.* III. 69 Hang am Tytts! ile pommell my selfe into am. 1606 *Choice, Chance*, etc. (1881) 66 His Dad a Tinker, and his Dam a Tit. 1693 *Humours Town* 11 My little Tit..loves the Town, as well as my self. 1787 BECKFORD *Italy* (1834) II. 363 A bevy of young tits dressed out in a fantastic, blowzy style..drew their chairs round us [at an assembly in Madrid]. 1837 T. CREEVEY *Papers*, etc. (1904) II. 324, I am sure from Lady Tavistock that she thinks the Queen a resolute little tit. 1886 FENN *Master Cerem.* vii, She's a pretty little tit.

† **b.** Rarely applied to a lad or young man. *Obs.*

1599 MASSINGER, etc. *Old Law* III. ii, Must young court tits Play tomboys' tricks with her, and he [her husband] live?

**II. 3.** A word used in comb. in the names of various small birds as TITLARK, TITLING, TITMOUSE, TOMTIT, q. v. Used alone, as a shortened form of TITMOUSE, applied to **a.** any bird of the genus *Parus*, and, more widely, any member of the family *Paridæ*; **b.** With qualification: some birds of other families as the *Bearded tit*: see TITMOUSE 2 b; *Hill-tit*: see HILL *sb.* 4 f.

1706 PHILLIPS (ed. Kersey), *Tit*, or *Titmouse*, a little Bird.

1802 Marsh Tit [MARSH 4 b]. 1831 Bearded Tit [see *reed-pheasant*, REED *sb.*[1] 14]. 1843 [see COAL-TIT]. 1845 Blue-tit [BLUE *a.* 12 a]. 1851 Bottle-tit [BOTTLE *sb.*[1] 5]. 1859 TENNYSON *Geraint & Enid* 275 Tits, wrens, and all wing'd nothings peck him dead! 1880 A. R. WALLACE *Isl. Life* ii. 20 These are all the European tits, but there are many others. 1906 *Westm. Gaz.* 14 Apr. 15/2 No longer do bands of tits drift through the woods or along the hedgerows... Strange..that the long tailed tit, the only species of the group that builds its nest in a bush, should be the first to start.

**c.** *attrib.* and *Comb.*, as *tit-like* adj.; **tit-babbler**, one of several species of hill-tits, esp. *Trichostoma rostratum*; **tit-pipit**, a name of the TITLARK or meadow pipit, *Anthus pratensis*; **tit-warbler**, 'a bird of the subfamily *Parinæ*' (Swainson).

1893 NEWTON *Dict. Birds* 26 The..Babblers, often with a prefix such as Bush-Babbler, Shrike-Babbler, *Tit-Babbler, .. belong chiefly to the Ethiopian and Indian Regions. 1907 *Westm. Gaz.* 15 Mar. 4/2 But all the rest are bustling about in their own restless, *tit-like manner. 1819 G. SAMOUELLE *Entomol. Compend.* 303 Inhabits the black grouse and *tit-pippit.

**Tit**, *sb.*[4] *techn.* [Of uncertain and possibly diverse origin; in sense 1 perh. related to TIT *sb.*[1] or [2]; in sense 2 perh. = TEAT.]

**1.** *Nail-making.* A loose piece of steel used to jerk the finished nail out of the bore.

1902 BARING-GOULD *Nebo the Nailer* ii, Working in the bore is the 'tit' that..ejects the finished nail. 1912 *Let. to Editor*, The 'tit' is a small loose plain piece of steel which is placed in the 'bore' for the purpose of ejecting the nail from the bore after the nail is headed.

**2.** A small core of metal accidentally left by the shifting of the drill point in boring a hole.

1884 F. J. BRITTEN *Watch & Clockm.* 129 If the centre is missed a tit is formed which gives trouble.

**Tit**, *sb.*[5] [? Infantile variant of KIT *sb.*[3]] Used as a call to a cat.

1828 *Craven Gloss.*, *Tit*, this, with its adjunct puss, is frequently used for calling a cat. 1837 DICKENS *Pickw.* xvi, 'It must have been the cat, Sarah', said the girl... 'Puss, puss, puss—tit, tit, tit'.

**Tit**, *a.* *Obs.* exc. *dial.* Editors suggest, in quot. *c* 1400, 'Dear, loved'. In *mod. dial.* Fond: cf. TID *a.*, TIT-BIT.

*c* 1400 *Destr. Troy* 7106 Þen vnhappely hys hest he hastid to do, Þat angart hym after angardly sore, Turnyt hym to tene & all the tit Rewme. 1854 MISS BAKER *Northampt. Gloss.* s. v., When a person is particularly attentive to, or indulgent to another, it is said, 'He is very tit of her'.

**Tit**, *v.*[1] *dial.* (chiefly *Sc.*) Also 4–5 tyt, 4–6 titte; *pa. t.* 4 tite, (tyd), 4–5 tit, titt, tyt, 5 tyte, 7– titted (9 -et); *pa. pple.* 4 tytted, 5 tyt, tytt, 6–7 tit, 7– titted. [Etymology obscure: goes with TIT *sb.*[1]; see Note below.]

*trans.* To pull forcibly, to tug; to snatch. Also *intr.* to pull *at*.

13.. *Cursor M.* 15303 (Cott.) His fote ful tite he til him tite [*Gött.* titt], Him schamed it was well sene. *Ibid.* 15837 (Gott.) And als þai fra þe erd him titt [*Trin.* pulde] His bodi was all stund. 1375 BARBOUR *Bruce* v. 603 He tit the bow out of his hand. *c* 1470 HENRY *Wallace* VI. 143 Ane maid a scrip, and tyt at his lang suorde; 'Hald still thi hand', quod he, 'and spek thi word'. *c* 1470 HENRYSON *Mor. Fab.* IX. (*Wolf & Fox*) xxiv, The wecht thairof neir tit my tuskis out. 1873 J. OGG *Willie Waly*, etc. 115 Hoo angry he was when ye tittet his tails. 1896 BARRIE *Tommy* xxiv. 281 She realised that Miss Kitty was titting at her dress.

†**b.** To pull *up*, esp. in a halter; hence, to hang. *Obs.*

*c* 1375 *Sc. Leg. Saints* xl. (*Ninian*) 983 About his nek þai knyt a rape, & tit hym vpe, & lefit hyme þare. *c* 1470 HENRY *Wallace* VII. 212 Be he entrit, hys hed was in the swar; Tytt to the bauk, hangyt to ded rycht thar. 1500-20 DUNBAR *Poems* xvii. 28 Sum..nevir fra taking can hald thair hand, Quhill he be tit vp to ane tre. 1638 BRATHWAIT *Barnabees Jrnl.* III. (1818) 125 A piper being here committed, Guilty found, condemn'd and titted.

†**c.** To lay hold of forcibly, clutch, seize; ? to pull or drag about. *Obs.*

*c* 1425 WYNTOUN *Cron.* IV. vii. 1074 His stewart made on hym a schot And tyt [*v. r.* claucht] hym dourly be þe throte. *c* 1450 HOLLAND *Howlat* 837 The Golk..tit the Tuchet be the tope, ourtirvit his hed. *c* 1475 *Rauf Coilȝear* 123 He tyt the King be the nek. *Ibid.* 432 For to towsill me or tit me, thocht foull be my clais, Or I be dantit on sic wyse, my lyfe salbe lorne.

[*Note.* The sense agrees with that of TIGHT *v.*[1], sense 1, but regular *Sc.* forms of that appear in 14th c. as *ticht*, *tycht*, and the disappearance of the *ch* would be abnormal. It is unlikely that OE. *tyhtan*, *tihtan*, should have become **titte* in the language of the Danes in England, in accordance with the treatment of *ht* in ONorse itself.]

**Tit**, *v.*[2] Now *dial.* [Goes with TIT *sb.*[2]: app. an onomatopœic match to TAT *v.*[1], the lighter vowel expressing lighter action and sound: cf. *tip* and *tap*, *pit-a-pat*, etc.]

**1.** *trans.* and *intr.* To strike or tap lightly, pat, tip.

(Quot. 1589 appears to be a parody of 'Come tit me, come tat me, Come throw a kiss at me', quoted of date 1607 under TAT *v.*[1] This seems to have been a couplet from an old song, current before 1589.)

1589 [? LYLY] *Pappe w. Hatchet* B j b, Elderton swore hee had rimes lying a steepe in ale, which shoulde marre all your reasons: there is an olde hacker that shall take order for to print them...The first begins, Come tit me, come tat me, come throw a halter at me. 1607 [see TAT *v.*[1]]. 1901 G. DOUGLAS *Ho. w. Green Shutters* v. 42 He's a brother o' —eh..(tit-tit-titting on his brow)—oh, just a brother o' Dru'cken Will Goudie.

**2.** † *To tit one in the teeth*: to cast in one's teeth, upbraid one *with* (*obs.*); hence *to tit* (simply), to twit, upbraid; *intr.* to scoff or jeer *at*.

1622 MABBE tr. *Aleman's Guzman d'Alf.* I. 147 Or that it should be tit in my teeth, that I had beene at the Court, and not seene the King. *Ibid.* II. 133 They would vpbraid me therewith..; Titting and flouting at me. 1629 J. M. tr. *Fonseca's Devout Contempl.* 424 Notwithstanding all this Absalon titted him in the teeth, saying, Is this thy loue to thy friend? 1631 *Celestina* XII. 146 Doe not tit mee in the teeth with these thy idle memorialls of my Mother. 1891 *Hartland Gloss.*, *Tit*..to twit or teaze. 1904 *Eng. Dial. Dict.* s. v., To tit a person about anything.

**Tit**, var. TEAT (cf. TITTY [3]); obs. 3rd sing. pres. of TIDE *v.*[1]; var. TITE *adv.*

**Titan** [1] (təi·tăn). [a. L. *Tītan*, *-ānem*, name of the elder brother of Kronos, and ancestor of the Titans; also in poetry his grandson, the Sun-god = Hēlios; a. Gr. Τιτᾱ́ν, in pl. Τιτᾶνες, the Titans, a race of gods expelled by Zeus out of heaven. So F., Sp. *Titan*, Pg. *Titão*, It. *Titano*, Du., Ger. *Titan*.]

**1.** Used (chiefly in poetry) as a name for the Sun-god, Sol, or for the sun personified.

1412-20 LYDG. *Chron. Troy* III. 5416 Þe dede cors to carien in-to toun Of worþi Hector, whan Titan went doun. 1501 DOUGLAS *Pal. Hon.* Prol. 33 The assiltrie and goldin chair of price Of Tytan, quhilk at morrow semis reid. 1606 SHAKS. *Tr. & Cr.* V. x. 25 Let Titan rise as early as he dare. 1638 SIR T. HERBERT *Trav.* (ed. 2) 2 The third of April at Titans first blush [*ed.* 1634 early in the morning] we got sight of Porto Santo. 1708 J. PHILIPS *Cyder* I. 10 Then wo to Mortals! Titan then exerts His Heat intense, and on our Vitals preys. 1911 SIR E. RIDLEY in *19th Cent.* May 870 Till flaming Titan nigh to either Pole Beheld thy empire.

**2. a.** *Gr. Mythol.* In *sing.* The ancestor of the Titans: see etymology above. In *pl.* a family of giants, the children of Uranus (Heaven) and Gæa (Earth), who contended for the sovereignty of heaven and were overthrown by Zeus.

1667 MILTON *P. L.* I. 510 Th' Ionian Gods..Titan Heav'ns first born With his enormous brood, and birthright seis'd By younger Saturn. 1727-41 CHAMBERS *Cycl.* s. v., This war lasted ten years; but at length the Titans were vanquished; Jupiter remained in peaceable possession of heaven, and the Titans were buried under huge mountains thrown on their heads. 1858 BUSHNELL *Serm. New Life* ii. (1869) 19 A race of Titans broken loose from order and warring on God and each other. 1908 G. K. CHESTERTON *Orthodoxy* viii. (1909) 258 The Titans did not scale heaven; but they laid waste the world.

**b.** *transf.* and *allusively*, usually denoting a person (mountain, tree, etc.) of gigantic stature or strength, physical or intellectual, a 'giant'; sometimes, one who belongs to the race of 'giants' as distinct from the *Olympians* or 'gods'.

1828 SCOTT *F. M. Perth* xxvii, The clan of Titans seemed to be commanded by their appropriate chieftains—..Ben Lawers, and..Ben Mohr. 1829 — *Anne of G.* vi, The sun was just about to kiss the top of the most gigantic of that race of Titans [the Swiss mountains]. 1838 EMERSON *Addr., Lit. Ethics* Wks. (Bohn) II. 205 Men looked..that nature ..should reimburse itself by a brood of Titans. 1870 SWINBURNE *Ess. & Stud.* (1875) 260 The ranks of great men are properly divisible, not into thinkers and workers, but into Titans and Olympians. 1903 J. STEWART *Dawn in Dark Cont.* i. 22 The weary Titan need not complain too much.

**c.** Applied descriptively to machines of great size and power; e. g. a dredger, crane, etc.

1876 *Daily News* 30 Oct. 6/4 A novel kind of dredger is in use, consisting of a centrifugal pump, called a 'Titan', which raises the sand together with a certain proportion of water, and discharges it in the barges. 1894 *Times* 29 Jan. 14/2 A titan steam crane will be mounted on deck for moving any of the heavy parts for examination or repair. 1911 *Encycl. Brit.* IV. 479 These sloping blocks are laid by powerful overhanging, block-setting cranes, called Titans, which travel along the completed portion of the breakwater, and lay the blocks in advance.

**3.** *Astron.* Name of the sixth and largest of Saturn's eight satellites.

1868 LOCKYER *Guillemin's Heavens* (ed. 3) 252 The diameter of Titan, the largest satellite,..is..more than half the diameter of the Earth. 1878 NEWCOMB *Pop. Astron.* III. iv. 353 The smallest telescope will show Titan.

**4.** *attrib.* or as *adj.*; *transf.* Titanic, gigantic.

1697 DRYDEN *Æneid* VI. 782 The rivals of the Gods, the Titan race. 1851 MAYNE REID *Scalp Hunt.* i, As though ..hurled from the hands of Titan giants! 1858 N. J. GANNON *O'Donoghue*, etc., *Lines on Late War*, Such hands as theirs have more than Titan strength. 1860 TYNDALL *Glac.* I. xx. 139 The Titan obelisk of the Matterhorn. 1860 C. SANGSTER *Hesperus*, etc. 53 Titan strength and queenly beauty.

**b.** *attrib.* and *Comb.* (chiefly in sense 2), as *Titan-born*, *-like* adjs.; also (from 1) † **Titan beam**, a sunbeam.

*a* 1649 DRUMM. OF HAWTH. *Poems* Wks. (1711) 44 Whilst eagles stare on Titan beams. 1816 BYRON *Ch. Har.* III. cv, Their steep aim Was, Titan-like, on daring doubts to pile Thoughts which should call down thunder and the flame Of Heaven. 1839 BAILEY *Festus* xxvii. (1852) 467 Thoughts which were once my masters, now I hold In retributive bondage, Titanlike. 1847 EMERSON *Poems* (1857) 45 Titan-born, to hardy natures Cold is genial and dear. 1904 *Speaker* 28 May 206/2 The Trip-shake and Tumble-tread of Titan-footed Reels.

† **Ti·tan** [2]. *Obs. rare.* [ad. F. *titane*, ad. mod.L. TITANIUM.] **a.** *Chem.* = TITANIUM. **b.** *Min.* = TITANITE. Also *attrib.*

1803 in *Trans. Roy. Irish Acad.* (1806) X. 17 Rutilite. Calcareo-siliceous titan ore of Kirwan. 1828 WEBSTER, *Titan*, *Titanium*, a metal of modern discovery. 1882 in OGILVIE (Annandale).

**Titanate** (təi·tăněit). *Chem.* [f. TITAN-IC *a.*[2] + -ATE [4].] A salt of titanic acid.

1839 URE *Dict. Arts* 1254 By calcination with nitre, it [titanium]..forms titanate of potassa. 1873 WATTS *Fownes' Chem.* (ed. 11) 429 The titanates have not been much studied.

Hence **Titana·tion**: see quot.

1904 VAN HISE in *U. S. Geol. Surv.*, *Monogr.* XLVII. 205 Titanation is the union of titanic acid with base, or the substitution of titanic acid for another combined acid, in either case producing titanates.

**Titanesque** (təităne·sk), *a.* [f. TITAN [1] + -ESQUE.] Resembling or having the characteristics of the Titans; colossal, gigantic.

1882 FROUDE *Carlyle* xx. I. 383 His extraordinary metaphors and flashes of Titanesque humour. 1906 MARIE CORELLI *Treas. Heaven* xi, Titanesque human figures with threatening arms outstretched.

**Titaness** (təi·tănės). [f. TITAN [1] + -ESS.] A female Titan; a giantess. Also *fig.*

1596 SPENSER *F. Q.* VII. vi. 4 So likewise did this Titanesse [Mutability] aspire Rule and dominion to her selfe to gaine. 1649 T. FORD *Ludus Fort.* 82 We can find no place free from the rule of this Titanesse. 1853 C. BRONTE *Villette* xli, Truth,..O Titaness amongst deities! 1862 B. TAYLOR *Home & Abr.* Ser. II. II. iv. 90 St. Helene..rises grandly above all the neighboring chains...This Titaness is robed in imperial hues. 1904 BRANDES *Main Curr. 19th C. Lit.* V. xii. 168 In that generation of heaven-storming Titans and Titanesses he appears a peculiarly earth-bound creature.

**Titanian** (təitēi·niăn), *a.*[1] [f. L. *Tītāni-us* of or belonging to the Titans + -AN.] Of, pertaining to, or like the Titans; Titanic. Also (quot. 1614) of the sun-god; solar, sunlike.

1614 RALEIGH *Hist. World* I. (1634) 6 The Moone's bright Globe, and Stars Titanian. 1667 MILTON *P. L.* I. 198 As whom the Fables name of monstrous size, Titanian, or Earth-born. 1685 COTTON tr. *Montaigne* (1711) I. iv. 27 The Thracians..fall to shooting against Heaven with Titanian madness. 1776 J. BRYANT *Mythol.* III. 76 All these were of the Giant, or Titanian race. 1820 BYRON *Mar. Fal.* IV. i. 83 Titanian fabrics, Which point in Egypt's plains to times that have No other record.

† **Tita·nian**, *a.*[2] *Chem. Obs.* [f. TITANI-UM + -AN.] Of or pertaining to titanium. (Superseded by TITANIC *a.*[2])

1828 in WEBSTER. 1846 in WORCESTER (citing URE).

**Titanic** (təitæ·nik), *a.*[1] [ad. Gr. τιτανικ-ός, f. Τιτᾶν-ες the Titans: see -IC.]

† **1.** Of or pertaining to the sun. *Obs. rare*[—0].

1656 BLOUNT *Glossogr.*, *Titanic*,..of or belonging to the Sun. 1658 in PHILLIPS.

**2.** Pertaining to, resembling, or characteristic of the Titans of mythology; gigantic, colossal; also, of the nature or character of the Titans.

1709 J. CLARKE tr. *Grotius' Chr. Relig.* v. ix. (1818) 226 *note*, Some wicked Daemons and (as I may call them) Titanic or Gigantic ones who were rebellious against the true God. 1818 BYRON *Ch. Har.* IV. xlvi, We pass The skeleton of her [Rome's] Titanic form. 1852 KELLY tr. *Cambrensis Eversus* III. 483 He has assailed heaven itself with titanic audacity. 1858 CARLYLE *Fredk. Gt.* I. i. (1872) I. 6 The figure of Napoleon was titanic.

**Tita·nic**, *a.*[2] [f. mod.L. TITANI-UM + -IC 1 b.] Of, pertaining to, or derived from titanium; in *Chem.* applied to compounds in which titanium has its higher valence, as *titanic oxide* (*t. acid*), a white tasteless powder, $TiO_2$. In *Min.*, *titanic iron-ore* = ILMENITE; *titanic schorl* = RUTILE.

1826 HENRY *Elem. Chem.* II. 701 Method of separating titanic acid from oxide of iron. 1839 URE *Dict. Arts* 682 All volcanic rocks contain a greater or less quantity of titanic iron-ore. 1842 BRANDE *Dict. Sc.*, etc. s. v. *Titanium*, The peroxide, or titanic acid, exists nearly pure in titanite, or rutilite. 1868 JOYNSON *Metals* 87 Bessemer metal containing phosphorus may be dephosphorised by employing titanic pig-iron, in repeated doses, to eliminate the phosphorus. 1894 BOWKER in *Harper's Mag.* Jan. 410 Ilmenite, or titanic iron $(FeTi)_2O_3$..is an ore in which one of the iron molecules of hematite is replaced by the metal titanium.

† **Titanical** (təitæ·nikăl), *a.* *Obs. rare.* [f. as TITANIC *a.*[1] + -AL: see -ICAL.] = TITANIC *a.*[1] 2.

1642 H. MORE *Song Soul* II. i. I. xxi, Rash labour, a Titanicall assay To pluck down wisdome from her radiant seat. 1678 CUDWORTH *Intell. Syst.* I. ii. § 3. 61 A Gigantical and Titanical Attempt to dethrone the Deity.

Hence **Tita·nically** *adv.*, in a titanic manner.

1816 T. TAYLOR *Pamphleteer* VIII. 57 She is bound in body Prometheically and Titanically. 1891 G. MEREDITH *One of our Conq.* vi, A more than Titanically audacious balloonist.

**Tita·nico-**, *Chem.*, combining form of TITANIC *a.*[2], esp. in names of double salts, resulting from the combination of a titanic with another salt. **Titanico-hydric** *a.*: see quot. (now *hydrotitanic*).

1860 MAYNE *Expos. Lex.*, *Titanico-hydricus*..applied by Berzelius to a titanic haloid salt..combined with the hydracid of the same halogenous body..: titanicohydric.

**Titaniferous** (təităni·fĕrəs), *a.* [f. TITAN-IUM + -I-FEROUS.] Containing or yielding titanium.

1828 in WEBSTER (citing CLEAVELAND). 1829 J. PHILLIPS *Geol. Yorks.* 105 Magnetic sand (oxydulated titaniferous iron). 1836-41 BRANDE *Chem.* (ed. 5) 872 Titaniferous Oxide of Iron, which is more abundant than rutilite, may be used as a source of titanium. 1883 *Encycl. Brit.* XVI. 426/1 Schorlomite (Ferrotitanite)...Perhaps a titaniferous garnet.

**Titanious** (təitēⁱ·niəs), *a. rare.* [f. TITANI-UM + -OUS.] **a.** *Min.* Containing or combined with titanium. †**b.** *Chem.* Obs. f. TITANOUS.

1853 TH. ROSS *Humboldt's Trav.* III. xxix. 169 Rocks.. charged with oxidulated and titanious iron, are probably of similar origin.

**Titanism** (təi·täniz'm). [a. F. *titanisme* (? *a* 1825 in Littré): see -ISM.] The character of a Titan. **a.** Revolt against the order of the universe. **b.** Titanic force or power.

1867 M. ARNOLD *Celtic Lit.* Wks. 1903 V. 126 Titanism as we see it in Byron. 1887 *Athenæum* 29 Oct. 566 Their dignity of expression, their melancholy Titanism of feeling. 1900 *Q. Rev.* July 128 Echoes of Schopenhauer's Pessimism, of Nietzsche's Titanism. 1902 *Ibid.* Oct. 369 He has a good deal that is fanciful to say of the Celtic Titanism with its 'indomitable reaction against the despotism of fact'. 1904 G. S. HALL *Adolescence* xi. II. 123 The soul is filled with a Titanism that would achieve a *vita nuova* upon a higher plateau, where the music of humanity is no longer sad but triumphant.

**Titanite** (təi·tänəit). *Min.* [ad. Ger. *titanit* (Klaproth, 1795), f. TITAN-IUM + *-it*, -ITE[1]; named from its containing the metal titanium.]

**1.** A mineral composed chiefly of calcium titanosilicate, $CaO.TiO_2.SiO_2$; also called *sphene*.

Iron is present in varying amounts, sometimes also manganese and yttrium.

1858 DANA *Min.* (1868) 385 Titanite occurs in imbedded crystals in granite, gneiss, mica, schist, syenite [etc.]. 1879 RUTLEY *Stud. Rocks* x. 140 Sphene (titanite) crystallises in the monoclinic system.

†**2.** Erroneously applied by Kirwan to the mineral now called RUTILE, a form of titanium dioxide, which he took to be an element. *Obs.*

1796 KIRWAN *Elem. Min.* (ed. 2) II. 329. 1799 *Monthly Rev.* XXX. 349 Among the metals, are overlooked the Tellurite..and Titanite. 1812 SIR H. DAVY *Chem. Philos.* 430 Titanium is obtained from a mineral long known by the name of red schorl or titanite.

†**Titani·tic**, *a. Min. Obs. rare.* [f. prec. + -IC.] = TITANIC *a.*[2]

1796 KIRWAN *Elem. Min.* (ed. 2) II. 330 [Titanite] melted ..with 5 times it's weight of mild Tartarin... When dissolved in boiling water, it soon let fall a white substance... This I call Titanitic Calx. *Ibid.* 331 Titanitic Ores.

**Titanium** (təitēⁱ·niŏm). *Chem.* [f. Gr. Τιτᾶν-ες the Titans (see TITAN[1]) + -IUM. Named by Klaproth 1795, on the analogy of URANIUM previously named by him.

Cf. *Beitr. z. Chem. Kenntn. d. Mineralkörper* I. 244 Diesem zufolge will ich den Namen, wie bei dem Uranium geschehen, aus der Mythologie..entlehnen, und benenne also dieses neue Metallgeschlecht : *Titanium.*]

One of the rare metals, never found free in nature, but obtainable as an iron-grey powder with a metallic lustre. It belongs to the same group as zirconium, cerium, and thorium. Symbol Ti; atomic weight 48·1 (O = 16).

Discovered by Klaproth as a constituent of a mineral (now called Rutile) from Boinik in Hungary. The same metal had been previously discovered by M'Gregor in a mineral (now called Ilmenite) found in Manaccan in Cornwall, and had been named by him *Menakanet* (*Crell's Chem. Ann.* 1791, I. 119).

1796 PEARSON in *Phil. Trans.* LXXXVI. 426 *note*, A new metal, named Titanium, lately announced in the German Journals. 1800 tr. *Lagrange's Chem.* I. 393 The substance from which titanium is extracted is a red schorl, found chiefly in Hungary. 1812 SIR H. DAVY *Chem. Philos.* 430 The oxide of titanium was discovered by McGregor in 1781 in an ore found in the valley of Menachan in Cornwal, but metallic titanium was not produced till 1796 by Vanquelin and Hecht. 1868 JOYNSON *Metals* 28 A small quantity of titanium improves the quality of steel.

**b.** attrib. *Titanium green*, ferrocyanide of titanium, a green pigment precipitated by ferrocyanide of potassium from a solution of titanic chloride (Watts *Dict. Chem.* V. 849); *titanium sand*, pulverulent titaniferous iron (*ibid.*).

**Titano-**[1], a. Gr. τιτᾶνο-, combining form of Τιτάν, TITAN[1], in **Titano·later**, an admirer of titanic attributes; so **Titano·latry** [-LATRY]; **Titano·machy** [-MACHY], the warfare of the Titans; **Ti·tanosau·r**, ‖**Titanosau·rus** [Gr. σαῦρος lizard], a gigantic fossil dinosaur from the chalk; ‖**Tita·no-, ti·tano,the·rium** [mod.L., f. Gr. θηρίον beast], also anglicized **ti·tanothe·re** [cf. F. *titanothère*], an extinct genus of ungulates from the Tertiary formation, resembling gigantic rhinoceroses; hence **Titanothe·rian** *a.*, of or pertaining to the genus *Titanotherium*; **Titanothe·rioid** *a.*, resembling or allied to this genus; also as *sb.*

1846 HARE *Mission Comf.* 601 Considered as a higher pitch of heroism by the *Titanolaters. 1867 *Hare's Guesses, Mem.* 47 A protest against what he called the *Titanolatry paraded in them. 1887 GLADSTONE in *Contemp. Rev.* June 760 The great myth of the *Titanomachy. 1892 *Pall Mall G.* 22 Mar. 7/1 In Colorado have been found great deposits of the bones of *titanosaurs, the biggest land animals that ever existed. They grew to be 65 ft. long and stood 40 ft. high when erect upon their hind legs. 1881 LUBBOCK in *Nature* 1 Sept. 406/2 Marsh has made known to us the *Titanosaurus, of the American (Colorado) Jurassic beds. 1862 DANA *Man. Geol.* 515 The *Titanothere..having some relations to the modern Tapir. *Ibid.* 532 White River or *Titanotherian beds. 1890 *Nature* 13 Feb. 347/1 These *Titanotherioids appear to have been most nearly allied to the Rhinoceroses among existing forms. 1865 PAGE *Handbk. Geol. Terms*, **Titanotherium*, .. a large herbivorous mammal occurring in the Lower Miocene beds of the Missouri district.

**Titano-**[2] (təi·tăno), combining form of TITANIUM (and TITANITE), used in the names of chemical and mineral compounds, as *titano-cyanide, -ferrite, -fluoride, -silicate* (= *silico-titanate*); **Titano·livine**, 'a variety of olivine (chrysolite) containing titanic acid' (Chester); **Titanomo·rphite**, 'an uncertain alteration product, near titanite' (Chester); †**Titano·xide**: see quot.

1880 *Nature* XXI. 425 Under the name of *Titanomorphite, A. von Lasaulx describes a new lime-titanite from the gneiss of the Eulengebirge. 1884 *Athenæum* 16 Aug. 212/3 Titanomorphite crystallizing in the oblique system. 1860 MAYNE *Expos. Lex.*, *Titanoxydum*, ..term by Beudant for a combination of titanium with oxygen: a *titanoxide.

‖**Ti·tanos.** *Alch. Obs. rare.* Also -us. [a. Gr. τίτανος gypsum, chalk, white earth.] = MAGNESIA 1.

*c* 1386 CHAUCER *Can. Yeom. Prol. & T.* 901 Take the stoon that Titanos men name. Which is that quod he? Magnasia is the same Seyde Plato. 1477 NORTON *Ord. Alch.* iii. (MS. Harl. 853 No. 4 (1589) lf. 40 b), Chawcer rehearseth how Titanos is the same In the Cannon his tale. 1584 R. SCOT *Discov. Witchcr.* XIV. ii. (1886) 295 The end..is, to atteine unto the composition of the philosophers stone, called Alixer, and to the stone called Titanus.

**Titanous** (təi·tănəs), *a. Chem.* [f. TITAN-IUM + -OUS.] Containing titanium, spec. in its lower valence, as *titanous oxide*, sesquioxide of titanium, $Ti_2O_3$; contrasted with TITANIC *a.*[2]

1866 ROSCOE *Elem. Chem.* 206 The oxides of titanium correspond to those of tin; viz. titanous and titanic oxides. 1868 WATTS *Dict. Chem.* V. 842 Titanous oxide dissolves in acids, forming violet solutions. 1873 — *Fownes' Chem.* (ed. 11) 448 Titanous fluoride is obtained as a violet powder by igniting potassio-titanic fluoride in hydrogen gas.

‖**Titar** (tī·tar). *E. Ind.* [Hindī, etc. *titar, -ur.*] Native name of the Grey Francolin, or 'Grey Partridge' of India, *Francolinus ponticerianus.*

1895 in *Funk's Stand. Dict.* 1898 BLANFORD *Fauna Brit. India, Birds* IV. 139 The Grey Partridge, Titar, Ramtitar, Gora-titar.

**Tit-bit** (ti·t,bi·t), **tid-bit** (ti·d,bi·t). [In 17th c., *tyd bit, tid-bit*, f. TID *a.* + BIT; later also *tit-bit*, perh. after compounds of TIT *sb.*[3]]

A small and delicate or appetizing piece of food; a toothsome morsel, delicacy, *bonne bouche.*

α. *c* 1640 J. SMYTH *Lives Berkeleys* (1885) III. 25 A tyd bit, i. e. a speciall morsell reserved to eat at last. 1701 COLLIER *M. Aurel.* (1726) 13 To be always loading the table, and eating of tid-bits. 1755 *Connoisseur* No. 87. (1774) III. 123 For fear any tid-bit should be snapped up before him, he snatches at it..greedily. 1834 L. RITCHIE *Wand. by Seine* 185 The sturgeons, the finest salmons, and other tid-bits of the fishery. 1895 *Outing* (U.S.) XXVI. 436/2 [The coon] locating many a tid-bit by means of his sharp nose and bright eyes.

β. 1694 MOTTEUX *Rabelais* IV. xlvi, He promis'd double Pay..to any one that should bring him such a Tit-bit piping-hot. 1727 ARBUTHNOT *John Bull* Postscr. ix, How John pamper'd Esquire South with Tit-bits, till he grew wanton. 1861 J. PYCROFT *Agony Point* (1862) 363 To see.. such tarts and tit-bits. 1865 TROLLOPE *Belton Est.* xxv, No more tit-bits of hashed chicken specially picked out for her.

**b.** *fig.*; *spec.* a brief and isolated interesting item of news or information; hence in *pl.*, name of a periodical consisting of such items.

α. 1735 FIELDING *Eurydice* I. i, My farce is an Oglio of tid-bits. 1776 FOOTE *Capuchin* III. Wks. 1799 II. 401 A fine girl, as I live! too nice a tid-bit for an apprentice. 1883 C. READE in *Harper's Mag.* June 94/1 He furnished me ..several tidbits that figure in my printed works.

β. 1708 *Brit. Apollo* No. 40. 2/2 Many of them [women] are Tit Bits. *a* 1814 *Last Act* Prol. in *New Brit. Theatre* II. 361 A new tit bit fresh from some author's brain. 1887–9 T. A. TROLLOPE *What I remember* II. vi. 100 During the singing of the well-known tit-bits of any opera.

**c.** *attrib.*

1767 A. CAMPBELL *Lexiph.* (1774) 56 We expedited ambassadors with plenary powers to procure us buttered buns, ..tart tit-bit tartlets. 1820 T. MITCHELL *Aristoph.* I. 167 Such dainty little schemes—such tit-bit thoughts. 1900 *Jrnl. Sch. Geog.* (U.S.) June 240 The danger..is that it should lead to the application of the tit-bits method to the teaching of geography.

Hence **Tit-bi·tical, Ti·t-bi·tty** *adjs.* (*nonce-wds.*), of the nature of, consisting or full of tit-bits.

1887 GURNEY *Tertium Quid* II. 24 He is really the tit-bittiest of composers. 1890 *Speaker* 5 Apr. 369/1 Those journalistic abortions of the tit-bitical kind..now so common. 1899 J. G. MILLAIS *Life Sir J. E. Millais* I. iii. 81 Every tit-bitty paper..repeated the tale.

†**Tit-bore.** *Sc. Obs.* Also teet-bo (Jam.). [First element perh. Sc. *teet* vb., to peep, sb. a peep, a glance; second perh. = *boh!* interj.: cf. *keek-bo* (KEEK *v.* 3).] The childish game of *bo-peep* or *peep-bo.* Also reduplicated, *titbore tatbore* (cf. *tit tat*).

16.. FORBES *Disc. Pervers Deceit* 4 (Jam.) What is this, but (as children in their sporting, childishly practise and more childishly speak) to play titbore tatbore with vs? 1825 JAMIESON s. v., In Aberdeenshire..the phrase *Titbo tatbo* is still used by some old people.

**Titch**, dial. form of TOUCH.

**Titchie, titchy**, obs. and dial. ff. TETCHY.

**Tite** (təit), **tit** (tit), *adv.* (*a.*) *Obs.* exc. *dial.* Forms: α. 3- tite, 4–5 tyt, tytt(e, 4–8 tyte, 4–9 tit. β. 3–5 tid, tyd, 8 tide. γ. 4 tyȝt, tiȝt, tiht, 5 tyght(e. Compared *titter, tittest*: see TITTER *adv.* [From Scandinavian: cf. ON. *titt* adv., 'frequently, often', neuter of *tíðr* adj., 'frequent, eager', OSw. *tid* 'repeatedly, quickly' (Södervall II. 627), Norw. and Sw. dial. *tidt* 'quickly' (Aasen, Ross, Rietz), the development being 'repeatedly, at short intervals, quickly'. The γ-forms are app. erroneous spellings.] Quickly, soon. *Obs.* exc. as in c.

*a* 1225 [implied in TITELY]. *a* 1300 *E. E. Psalter* xxxvi. 2 Als wortes of grenes tite fal sal þai. *a* 1300 *Cursor M.* 18497 Þai war transfigurd als tite [*Laud* tyȝt] Was neuer i-wis snau sa quite. *c* 1330 R. BRUNNE *Chron. Wace* (Rolls) 13235 Archers..on þe Romayns smyten ful tit. *c* 1350 *Will. Palerne* 133 But truly tiȝt hadde þat quene take hire to rede. *c* 1400 *Destr. Troy* 7126 Full tid in hire tene turnys he þe qwell. *Ibid.* 8002 Ector toke hit full tyd. ? *c* 1410 *Sir Cleges* 291 Goo bake.. Full tyghte without teryyng! *c* 1450 *Mankind* 152 in *Macro Plays* 6 Felouse, go we hens tyght! 1575 *Gamm. Gurton* I. iv. A iv, That chal, gammer, swythe and tyte, and sone be here agayn. ? 16.. in Drake *Eboracum* I. vi. (1736) 192 The serjeants shall bring sufficient distress to the court, such as will most disease him and the tittest will gar him answer.

†**b.** *As, als, also tit, als tid*, etc.: as soon, as quickly, immediately. (Cf. F. *aussitôt*; also ON. *semtíðast* with all speed, at once, immediately.)

[*c* 1320–1450: see ALSTITE, ASTITE.] 13.. *E. E. Allit. P.* B. 1213 Ouer-tok hem, as tyd, tult hem of sadeles. 1377 LANGL. *P. Pl.* B. XVI. 61, I shal telle þe as tite [*v. rr.* tyt, tyte, tid] what þis tree hatte. 14.. *Lybeaus Disc.* 784 Than seyde Lybeaus al so tyte [etc.]. 14.. *Tundale's Vis.* 686 And als tyte [*v.r.* tyd] was he all hale. *c* 1435 *Torr. Portugal* 690 To the grownd he felle ase tyght. *c* 1450 *Cov. Myst.* iii. (Shaks. Soc.) 38 Ha don, and answere me as tyght. *c* 1460 *Towneley Myst.* iii. 219 We shalle assay as tyte.

**c.** *As tite . . as*, as soon . . as, as readily, willingly, or well . . as. *dial.*

1587 *Durham Depos.* (Surtees) 322, I may as tite be a ladye as thou a lord. 1876 *Whitby Gloss.* s. v., 'I had as tite go as stay'. 1878 *Cumberld. Gloss.*, 'I'd as tite dea't as nut'.

†**d.** as *adj.* Quick, swift. (*rare* and *doubtful.*)

*c* 1400 *Destr. Troy* 6738 Menelaus, And Thelamon the tore kyng with theire tite batels. 1535 STEWART *Cron. Scot.* (Rolls) II. 258 Tytest that tyme he wes of ony vther Agane Modred. *Ibid.* 305 Oswald, that tyme tytest of other. 1768 ROSS *Helenore* I. 32 Wi' weet an wind sae tyte into my teeth, That it was like to cut my very breath.

**Tite**, obs. pres. 3rd sing. of TIDE *v.*[1]; obs. erron. f. TIGHT *a.* **Titel**, obs. form of TITLE, TITTLE.

**Ti·tely, ti·tly**, *adv. Obs.* or *dial.* Forms: α. 3 tidlike, 3–4 tidliche, 4 tidly, 5 tydely. β. 4 titli, titliche, 4–5 titly, tytely, 5 tytly, -lye, 5, 8 titely. γ. 4 tiȝtly, -li. [f. TITE, TIT *adv.* + -LY[2].] Quickly, speedily, smartly; soon. *As titely* (cf. F. *aussitôt*), immediately.

α. *a* 1225 *Juliana* 58 Þe reue het..swingen hit swiftliche abuten ant tidliche turnen. *c* 1250 *Gen. & Ex.* 3353 Tidlike hem was ðat water wane, Ðor he grucheden for ðrist hane. 1340–70 *Alisaunder* 974 It betid in a time tidly therafter. 1460 *Paston Lett.* I. 528, I trust to God to com tydely i now. *c* 1460 *Towneley Myst.* iii. 291 Tent hedir tydely, wife, and consider.

β. *c* 1320 *Sir Tristr.* 2518 His swerd he drouȝ titly. 1340–70 *Alisaunder* 7 Tend yee tytely to mee & take goode heede. *c* 1350 *Will. Palerne* 2528 Titliche schuld þei be take. *Ibid.* 2694 Þei titly turned aȝen. *c* 1400 *Destr. Troy* 3006 These tythandes full titely told were to Parys. *a* 1400–50 *Alexander* 888 Heraudes.. Touchis titly [*Dubl. MS.* titely] þar tale. *c* 1425 *Cast. Persev.* 223 in *Macro Plays* 84 With my tyre & with my tayl, tytly to tene. *c* 1746 J. COLLIER (Tim Bobbin) *View Lanc. Dial.* Rdr., Wks. (1862) 37 Otto con tell th' tele, and seyth 'Rimes be rot, titely.

γ. *c* 1350 *Will. Palerne* 2476 Tiȝtli al here tene was turned in-to ioye. *Ibid.* 1706. *Ibid.* 285 Tiȝtly.

**Titengis**, obs. form of TIDINGS.

**Titer**, var. TITRE; obs. f. TITTER *v.*[2]

†**Tith**, *a.*, *adv. Obs.* App. a dial. or colloquial variant of TIGHT *a.* or THIGHT *a.*

1618 FLETCHER *Loyal Subj.* III. iv, This [lass] is not so strongly built; but she's good mettle, Of a good stirring strain too: she goes tith, sir. 1619 — *Mons. Thomas* II. ii, *Thom.* Then take a Widow, A good stanch wench, that's tith. *Ibid.* I. iii. [see TEW *sb.*[2] 1]. *a* 1625 — *Woman's Prize* III. v, A ship—which.. With more continuall labour than a gally To make her tith, either she grows a tumbrel, .. or springs more leaks.

**Tith**, obs. form of TITHE.

**Tithable** (təi·ðăb'l), *a.* (*sb.*) Also 5–8 tythable, 5–9 titheable, 6–8 tytheable. [f. TITHE *v.*[2] + -ABLE.]

**1.** Of produce: Subject to the payment of tithes.

*c* 1440 *Jacob's Well* 56 Of heyȝ, corn, wode, fruyte, wolle, chese,..& of all manere thynges tythable. 1548 *Act 2 & 3 Edw. VI*, c. 13 § 3 Any beastis or other cattell tytheable. 1619 SIR J. SEMPIL *Sacrilege Handled* App. 39 By Tradition from their Fathers, all things growing out of the earth, and fit for mans meat, are Titheable. 1632 *Star Chamb. Cases* (Camden) 100 Mines are not titheable by the lawe because they doe not *renovare.* 1737 *Gentl. Mag.* VII. 344 This Piece of Land is Tythe-free, That Piece is Tytheable. 1834 *Brit. Husb.* I. 77 The young of those, which are titheable, pay at the time of their being weaned.

**2.** Liable to pay tithes. *rare.*

1722 R. BEVERLEY *Virginia* IV. v. § 18. 218 The Levies..are a certain Rate or Proportion of Tobacco charged upon the Head of every tithable Person... They call all Negroes above sixteen Years of age tithable, be they male or female; and all white Men of the same Age. But Children and white Women are exempted from all Manner of Duties.

**B.** *absol.* as *sb.* One who or that which is subject to payment of tithes.

**1680** *Virginia Stat.* (1823) II. 488 It is declared .. that such servants soe unsold ought not to be listed as tythables that yeare. **1775** A. BURNABY *Trav.* 12 There are a hundred and five thousand titheables, under which denomination are included all white males from sixteen to sixty. **1828** *Examiner* 210/1 From various tenants and titheables he [the archbishop] receives some 25,000*l.* a-year. **1893** *Nation* (N.Y.) 27 Apr. 309/2 The population of a Virginian county..was probably considerably more than three times as great as its number of tithables.

**Tithal** (təi·ðăl), *a. rare.* [f. TITHE *sb.*[1] + -AL: cf. *tidal.*] Of or pertaining to tithes.

**1882-3** *Schaff's Encycl. Relig. Knowl.* III. 2365 The principal tithal rules are as follows.

**Tithand(e, -ans,** obs. forms of TIDING, -S.

**Tithe** (təið), *a.*[1] and *sb.*[1] Forms: *α.* 1 teoȝoða, etc. (see TENTH A. 1 *α*), 3 tiȝeðe, tiȝðe, 4 tyþe, 4–5 tiþe, (5–7 tyth, 6 tieth (thiethe), 6–7 tith, 7 tyethe), 4– tithe, tythe. *β.* 1 téoða, etc. (see TENTH A. 1 *β*), 3 teoþe, 3–4 teþe, 5–6 tethe, (5 theth(e, 6 teyth). [Early ME. *tiȝeðe, tiȝðe*, ME. *tiþe, tyþe* = OE. *teogoþa, téoþa*, forms of the numeral TENTH, which as a sb. acquired a specialized sense, in which this form has been retained, while the adj. has become *tenth*. For the general sense- and form-history see TENTH A. 1 *α, β*, B. 1. Cf. also TEIND, the specialized northern form.]

**A.** *adj.* Tenth. †**a.** Of order: see TENTH A. 1 *a. Obs.* **b.** Of a division or part; in ME. esp. in *tithe deal.* In modern use, since 16th c., app. taken anew from the sb., B. 3.

*a.* *c* **1250** *Gen. & Ex.* 895 Habram ȝaf him ðe tiȝðe del Of alle [h]is biȝete. *c* **1330** *Arth. & Merl.* (Kölbing) 5429 Erl Does sone..þe .ix. was..; Grifles so was tiþe, Wiȝt he was & noble swiþe. *c* **1350** *Will. Palerne* 5346 Ne þe tiþedel of hire atir to telle þe riȝt. *c* **1375** Tyþe [see TENTH A. 3]. **1377** LANGL. *P. Pl.* B. xv. 480 Persounes and prestes..þat han her wille here,..þe tithe del þat trewemen biswynkyn. *c* **1440** *Jacob's Well* 24 Alle þo þat ȝeuyn þe tythe scheef to þe reperys for here hyre, in takyng vp here cost for þe repyng, & ȝeuyn þe xj. scheef for þe tythe.

*β.* **854-971** Teoða [see TENTH A. 3]. **1297, 1387** Teþe [see TENTH A. 2].

**1601** SHAKS. *All's Well* I. iii. 89 One good woman in ten Madam..: Weed finde no fault with the tithe woman. **1606** — *Tr. & Cr.* II. ii. 19 Euery tythe soule 'mongst many thousand dismes, Hath bin as deere as Helen. *a* **1814** *He must be married* I. i. in *New Brit. Theatre* IV. 239 Why the veriest shrew..cannot muster a tythe part of the vagaries which abound in my composition. **1872** *Westm. Rev.* July 90 We have not space to follow Dr. Newman through a tithe part of his illustrations.

**B.** *sb.* Absolute use of adj.: cf. TENTH B.

In OE. the ordinal *téoða*, pl. *téoðan*, was so used: see TENTH B. 1 b.

**1.** The tenth part of the annual produce of agriculture, etc., being a due or payment (orig. in kind) for the support of the priesthood, religious establishments, etc.; *spec.* applied to that ordained by the Mosaic law, and to that introduced in conformity therewith in England and other Christian lands. (The latter sense appears first in quots.)

**a.** in *sing.*

*a.* *c* **1200** *Trin. Coll. Hom.* 83 Hie giuen here tiȝeðe noht for to hauen heuene blisse, ac for to hauen here þe hereword of eorðliche richeise. *c* **1330** R. BRUNNE *Chron.* (1810) 19 He [Adelwolf] was first of Inglond, þat gaf God his tiþe. **1362** LANGL. *P. Pl.* A. VII. 85 For of my Corn and Catel heo Craueþ þe Tiþe. *a* **1425** *Cursor M.* 1067 (Trin.) For þis tiþe [*Laud* tythe] þat þei delt, Caym..To his broþere ire bare. **1535** COVERDALE *Mal.* iii. 10 Brynge euery Tythe in to my barne. **1551-2** *Rec. St. Mary at Hill* 394 Iohn Crovcher oweth..The Tyth of his hovs. **1611** BIBLE *Lev.* xxvii. 30 And all the tithe of the land..is the Lords. **1621** BP. MOUNTAGU *Diatribæ* 185 It being vncertaine in it selfe, whether Abraham gaue or receiued Tithe. **1771** FRANKLIN *Autobiog.* Wks. 1840 I. 9 My father intending to devote me, as the tythe of his sons, to the church. **1831** *Lincoln Herald* 1 July 3/3 There were three heifers to be canted [sold by auction] for tithe. **1845** McCULLOCH *Taxation* II. iv. (1852) 180 It will be seen that half the cultivated land of Great Britain is unaffected by tithe. **1884** J. TAIT *Mind in Matter* (1892) 206 The last symptom of restiveness..manifested by the Jews related to the tythe.

*β.* *c* **1450** *Godstow Reg.* 43 He grauntyd & gaf to the holy my[n]chons a-foreseyde tethe of hys too Millis of Seweke-worth [= Seacourt] in corne, money, & fysshes.

**b.** chiefly in *plural*, including the various amounts thus due or received.

*a.* *c* **1200** *Vices & Virt.* 139 Chierche-þinges, tiȝeþes, ne offrendes, ne almesses. *c* **1250** *Gen. & Ex.* 1628 Her ic sal offrendes here don And tiȝðes wel ȝelden her-up-on. *c* **1380** WYCLIF *Sel. Wks.* III. 313 We reden not where he took tyþes as we don. *c* **1386** CHAUCER *Prol.* 539 Hise tithes payde he ful faire and wel Bothe of his propre swynk and his catel. **1388** WYCLIF *Gen.* xiv. 20 And Abram ȝaf tithis of alle thingis to hym [1382 And he ȝaue hym dymes of alle thingis]. **1483** CAXTON *Cato* g j b, The tythes whyche they owen to God and the holy chyrche. **1547** in *Richmond Wills* (Surtees) 64, I give to the hye alter for oblited thiethes a newe altare clothe. **1651** R. CHILD in *Hartlib's Legacy* (1655) 23 The Tythes of wine in Glocestershire, was in divers Parishes considerably great. *a* **1660** *Contemp. Hist. Irel.* (Ir. Archæol. Soc.) II. 36 A donation of all the tyethes and other casualties. **1764** BURN *Poor Laws* 2 The whole tithes of the diocese were then paid to the bishop. **1850** KINGSLEY *Alt. Locke* xi, His own tithes here aren't more than thirty pounds.

*β.* *a* **1100** Teoþan [see TENTH B. 1 b]. *c* **1440** *Eng. Conq. Irel.* 67 Euery crystyn man lawfully pay his thethis. *c* **1450** *Godstow Reg.* 46 Certen possessions, tethys, dewteys & othyr thynges. **1517** in 10*th Rep. Hist. MSS. Comm.* App. v. 397 Every shippe..shall paye half tethes to the Colladge of all suche fishe as they shall take.

**c.** Variously qualified:

*Agistment tithe, t. of agistment*, see AGISTMENT 4; *coarse t.* = *great t.*; *crying t.*, tithe of young live stock; *great t.*, the chief predial tithes, as corn, hay, wood, and fruit; also called *large t.*; *mixed t.*, see MIXED *ppl. a.* 11, and quots. there; *parochial t.*, ? small or vicarial tithes; *personal t.*, tithe of the produce of labour or occupation; *petty t.*, *privy t.* = *small t.*; *predial t.*, see PREDIAL *a.* 2 b, and quots. there; *rectorial t.*, tithes pertaining to the rector of the parish, the great tithes; *small t.*, such predial tithes as are not great tithes, together with the personal and mixed tithes; *vicarial t.*, tithes pertaining to the vicar of the parish, the small tithes.

**1464** [see PREDIAL *a.* 2 b]. **1530, 1765** [see PRIVY *a.* 8]. **1531,** *a* **1634, 1672** [see MIXED *ppl. a.* 11]. **1531** *Dial. on Laws Eng.* II. lv. (1638) 169 Some..say there is no tith but it is either a prediall tith, or a personal tith. **1546** *Yorks. Chantry Surv.* (Surtees) 228 The sayd incumbent hathe..all offerynges and pety tythes. **1589** *Shuttleworths' Acc.* (Chetham Soc.) 51 For the smale or pryve tythes of Hetton iij[li] ij[s] vj[d] ob. **1710** PRIDEAUX *Orig. Tithes* ii. 106 Though it be the practice in setting out of Personal Tithes to separate the Charges from the Profits..yet there was never any such thing in predial Tithes. **1718** in *Shropsh. Parish Doc.* (1903) 19 The Vicar hath also all small Tythes as Hemp, Flax, Geese, Eggs, Piggs, Fruit and the Like. **1793** BLACKSTONE *Comm.* (ed. 12) I. xi. 387 The tithes of many things..are in some parishes rectorial, and in some vicarial tithes. **1813** T. N. PARKER in *Gentl. Mag.* May 449/2 Aftermath (or a second mowing of a meadow in the same year) yields a great tithe, as turnips sown on a stubble yield a small tithe. **1817** W. SELWYN *Law Nisi Prius* (ed. 4) II. 1197 The late vicar..made certain compositions with his parishioners for the vicarial tithes, which were payable on the 29th September. **1861** MIALL *Title Deeds Ch. Eng.* (1862) 4 Parochial tithes constitute..the provision for the pecuniary support of the Church of England. **1862** BURTON *Bk. Hunter* (1863) 294 The Bishop of Lichfield..was Dean of Durham, and owner of the great tithes in the parish. **1889** LIPSCOMB in *Land Agent's Record* 6 Apr. 316 In parishes where the great or rectorial tithes remain devoted to the Church, we find a rector and a rectory.

**2.** In more general sense: Any levy, tax, or tribute of one tenth. *Saladin tithe*: see *Saladine tax* (SALADINE *a.*).

**1600** HOLLAND *Livy* v. xxv. 196 As for the collation and gathering of a smal donative, rather than a tithe, he [Camillus] said nothing of it. **1838** THIRLWALL *Greece* II. xi. 64 To defray the expense of these and his other undertakings, he [Pisistratus] laid a tithe on the produce of the land. **1871** DIXON *Tower* III. xiii. 129 The admirals took tithe on every ship and cargo seized at sea.

**3.** A tenth part (of anything); = TENTH B. 1; now chiefly hyperbolical: a very small part.

**1494** FABYAN *Chron.* VI. ccix. 223 He slewe alway .ix. and saued the .x. and yet..he eft agayne tythed agayne the sayd tythe, & slewe euery tenth knyght of theym. **1552** HULOET, Tythe or tenth part, *decima.* **1589** NASHE in *Greene's Menaphon* Pref. (Arb.) 11 No Colledge in the Towne was able to compare with the tythe of her Students. **1648** MILTON *Observ. Art Peace* Wks. 1851 IV. 576 These illiterate denouncers never parallel'd so much of any Age as would contribute to the tithe of a Century. **1772** WILKES *Corr.* (1805) IV. 107 A little parish church, with about a tythe of the people who frequent our chapel. **1836** SIR W. HAMILTON *Discuss.* (1852) 341 A tythe of the agitation. **1838** ARNOLD *Hist. Rome* I. 45 The tithe of the spoil was forty talents of silver. **1848** RICHTER *Levana* 45 From a woodcut some thousand impressions may easily be taken; but from a copperplate only a tithe of that number. **1872** BLACK *Adv. Phaeton* xix, I cannot tell you a tithe of what he said.

**4.** *attrib.* and *Comb.* **a.** Due or paid as tithe. See also TITHE-PIG.

*c* **1450** *Godstow Reg.* 318 Nicholas Iordan..paid..for the tythe hey, ij d. ob. **1455** *Rolls of Parlt.* V. 307/2 In recompense for the tithe veneson in the Forest of Wyndesore. **1555** W. TURNER *Spir. Physic* 50 b, Wyth muche shame, they come wyth tythe pygges by theyr tayles, wyth tythe egges, and tythe hemp and flaxe. **1609** *Mem. Ripon* (Surtees) III. 334 All the Tythe Grain, Hay, Wooll and Lamb. **1765** *Museum Rust.* III. li. 224 Let him by no means attempt to buy tythe barley, for that he is sure is mixed. **1808** TOLLER *Law of Tithes* v. (1816) 152 Tithe-ore is not due of common right, but by particular custom only.

**b.** Of or pertaining to tithes, as *tithe-bill, -bond, -charge, -claim, -commission, -map, -monger, -proprietor, -publican, -right, -system*; objective, etc., as *tithe-collector, -commutation, -farmer, -gatherer, -giving, -haling, -holder, -owner, -payer, -paying, -redemption, -stealer, -taker*; *tithe-free* adj. See also TITHE-BARN, -MAN, -PROCTOR.

**1736** *Gentl. Mag.* VI. 708 Debate concerning the Quakers *Tithe-Bill. **1666** *Ormonde MSS.* in 10*th Rep. Hist. MSS. Comm.* App. v. 24 The said Henry kept *tyth bonds soe long by him that the debitors became insolvent. **1808** TOLLER *Law of Tithes* ix. (1816) 237 It also appeared by ancient *tithe-books of the parson. **1845** McCULLOCH *Taxation* II. iv. (1852) 185 The limitation of the *tithe-charge. **1858** SIMMONDS *Dict. Trade*, **Tithe-collector*, a receiver of tithes. **Tithe-commissioner*,..one of a board authorized to arrange propositions for commuting or compounding for tithes. **1859** J. W. ROSSE *Index of Dates*, *Tithe Commutation Bill (England), introduced, Feb. 9; passed, Aug. 13, 1836. **1780** A. YOUNG *Tour Irel.* I. 217 These *tythe farmers are a bad set of people. **1720** *Lond. Gaz.* No. 5829/3 An Estate.., well wooded, and *Tythe-free. **1591** *Shuttleworths' Acc.* (Chetham Soc.) 66 Spente by the *tythe getherares, v[d]. **1792** A. YOUNG *Trav. France* 433 When the state..permits the cultivators to become the prey of a tythe-gatherer, or loads them with the support of the poor. *a* **1693** *Urquhart's Rabelais* III. xlviii. 386 The Edecimation and *Tith-haling of their Goods. **1785** PALEY *Mor. Philos.* VI. xi. 636 This commutation..might..secure to the *tithe-holder a complete and perpetual equivalent for his interest. **1910** *Edin. Rev.* Jan. 119 The *tithe-maps constructed on all sorts of scales. **1647** *Husbandm. Plea agst. Tithes* 33 Calves, milk, lambe..and all other things that the *Tithe-mongers will have to be titheable. **1805** DICKSON *Pract. Agric.* I. 468 The *tithe-owner refused three guineas per acre for the tithe of the barley. **1621** BP. MOUNTAGU *Diatribæ* 315 Appointed for the Rendez-vous of Tithe-takers, and *Tithe-payers. *Ibid.* 185 In the matter of *Tithe-paying vnto the Priests of the Gospell. **1863** FAWCETT *Pol. Econ.* IV. iv. (1876) 578 It is quite possible that *tithe-proprietors may be ultimately injured by this commutation. **1657** J. WATTS *Vind. Ch. Eng.* 157 Forced to pay the same unto *Tythe-publicanes and Tol-gatherers. **1549** CHALONER *Erasm. on Folly* P iij, How warlyke..the good vicares can strive for theyr *tytheright. **1711** ADDISON *Spect.* No. 112 ¶ 7 The 'Squire has made all his Tenants Atheists and *Tithe-Stealers. **1890** *Boston* (Mass.) *Jrnl.* 1 Mar. 2/4 The French-Canadians are beginning to rebel against the *tithe system, which, in the interest of the Catholic Church, takes a large portion of the farmers' products.

† **Tithe,** *sb.*[2] *Obs.* [OE. **tigð* fem., contr. *tið* (obl. case *tiðe*):—OTeut. **tigiþā*. Not known outside English.] A granting; a concession, boon. *Bene-tiðe, -tuðe*: see BENE b.

*a* **900** tr. *Bæda's Hist.* III. xii. [xiv.] (1890) 196 Moniȝ oðer uncymre hors..þæt wit meahton þearfum to tiȝðe sellan. *c* **1000** ÆLFRIC *Hom.* I. 384 Fela wundra ȝelumpon..ðurh ðæs Hælendes tiðe. *c* **1200** *Trin. Coll. Hom.* 201 Þat he..ȝife us bene tuðe.

† **Tithe,** *a.*[2] *Obs.* [OE. *tigþa, tiþa, -e*, f. *tigð*, TITHE *sb.*[2]] To whom a concession or grant is made; successful in prayer or beseeching.

*a* **900** tr. *Bæda's Hist.* IV. xxx. [xxix.] (1890) 372 Þæt he wæs from Dryhtne tiȝða þære bene, ðe he bæd. *c* **1000** *Ags. Gosp.* Matt. xxi. 22 Ealles þæs þe ȝe biddað ȝe beoð tiþa ȝyf ȝe ȝelyfað. *c* **1200** *Trin. Coll. Hom.* 27 We muȝen mid one worde þese þrie þing bidden and ben bene tiðe. *Ibid.* 119 Þat þe fewe word þe we on ure bede seien be tuðe alle haleȝen.

† **Tithe,** *v.*[1] *Obs.* Forms: 1 tiȝþian, tyȝþian, 1–2 tiþian, 2 teiþian, 2–3 tiðen, tuþen (*ü*), 3 tythe. Pa. t. and pple. (*north.*) 4 tid(d, tyd(e. [OE. *tigþian* (:—**tigiþōjan*), f. *tigð*, TITHE *sb.*[2]] *trans.* To grant, concede, bestow.

*c* **893** K. ÆLFRED *Oros.* VI. xxxiv. § 3 Þa oferhoȝode he ..þæt he him tiȝþade. *a* **900** tr. *Bæda's Hist.* III. xv. [xxi.] (1890) 220 Ne hine mon on oðre wisan his bene tyȝþian wolde. *c* **1000** ÆLFRIC *Hom.* II. 108 Ic wæs nacod, nolde ȝe me wæda tiðian. *c* **1160** *Hatton Gosp.* Matt. xxi. 22 Eow beoð ȝe-teiþað [*v. r.* ȝetiðad]. *c* **1200** *Trin. Coll. Hom.* 135 God haueð herd þine bede, and tiðed te bene. *c* **1200** ORMIN 5365 Forr all þatt æfre ned uss iss All Godess Gast uss tiþeþþ. *a* **1225** *St. Marher.* 9 Nawt [ha] ne þohte þeron þ hire nu were ituðet hire bone. *a* **1240** *Lofsong* in *Cott. Hom.* 207 Leafdi..tuðe me mine bone to þine eadi sune. **1297** R. GLOUC. (Rolls) 2474 Ac o þing icholde bidde þe ȝif þou me woldest tiþe. *a* **1300** *Cursor M.* 10966 (Cott.) Drightin has þe tid [*Gött.* tidd] þi bon. *c* **1375** *Sc. Leg. Saints* xxxiii. (*George*) 829 Þat god his askine had hyme tyde for þaim þat hyme worchyp dyde.

Hence † **Ti·thing** *vbl. sb.*, thing granted, reward.

*c* **1275** *Fragm. Song* 7 in *O. E. Misc.* 101 Þat..he vs skere of þe tyþing þat sunfule schulle an-vnderfon.

**Tithe** (təið), *v.*[2] Forms: *α.* 1 tio-, teoȝoðian, teȝðeȝian, tæȝþiȝan, teiȝðian, teȝði(ȝ)an, 4 tiþe(n, tyþe(n, 5 tyth, 6 tieth, 6–7 tith, 4– tithe, tythe. *β.* 1 téoði(ȝ)an, 3 teoþeȝen, teþeȝen, theoþe, 4 teoþe, 4–5 teþe, tethe(n, 5 teothe, teith(e, teythe, 6 teethe. [OE. *teogoðian*, etc., f. *teogoða, téoða* tenth, TITHE *sb.*[1]] *gen.* To take the tenth of, to decimate.

**1.** *trans.* To grant or pay one tenth of (one's goods, earnings, etc.), esp. to the support of the church; to pay tithes on (one's goods, lands, etc.).

*To tithe mint* (*and anise*) *and cummin* (Matt. xxiii. 23), to be conspicuously scrupulous in minutiæ while neglecting important matters of duty.

*c* **897** K. ÆLFRED *Gregory's Past. C.* lvii. 439 ȝe tioȝoðiað eowre mintan & eowerne dile & eowerne kymen. *c* **950** *Lindisf. Gosp.* Luke xi. 42 ȝiæ teiȝðas meric & cumela & ælc wyrt. *c* **975** *Rushw. Gosp.* ibid., ȝe teȝðiȝas merece [etc.]. *c* **1000** *Ags. Gosp.* ibid., ȝe teoþiað. *c* **975** *Rushw. Gosp.* Matt. xxiii. 23 ȝe þe tæȝþiȝaþ [*Lindisf.* ȝeteȝðeȝes] mintæ & dile & cymen. *c* **1000** *Ags. Gosp.* ibid., ȝe þe teoðiað [*v. r.* teoðiȝað]. *c* **1000** ÆLFRIC *Hom.* II. 428 Ic teoðie ealle mine æhta. *a* **1225** *Ancr. R.* 28 Hwat se beo of oþer hwat vntreouliche iteoþeȝed. **1297** R. GLOUC. (Rolls) 5263 Þe king þer after..teþeȝede wel al is lond, as hii aȝte, wel ynou. **1303** R. BRUNNE *Handl. Synne* 898 Tyþeth weyl alle ȝoure þynges. **13..** *Min. Poems fr. Vernon MS.* xxxvii. 528 Hose wol not tiþe þat god him haþ I-lent, His lyf and his soule boþe schul be schent. *c* **1410** *Master of Game* (MS. Digby 182) xxxv, Þan shulde þe mayster of þe game begynne at one rowe..and tyth alle þe deere reght as þei ligge, rascayle and oþer, and delyuere it to þe procuratoures. **1562** *Child-Marr.* 138 The maner of tiething pigge and gose is, yf one have vij[th], to pay one. **1570** LEVINS *Manip.* 89/42 To Teethe, *decimare. Ibid.* 152/5 To Tythe. *a* **1641** SPELMAN *Tythes* xvi. (1647) 81 Military spoil, and the prey gotten in war is also tithable, for Abraham tithed it to Melchisedek. **1778** *Eng. Gazetteer* (ed. 2) s. v. *Rye*, A peculiar way of tithing their marsh-lands, whereby they pay only 3d. per acre to the rector, while in pasture, but, if ploughed, 5s. **1782** PRIESTLEY *Corrupt. Chr.* II. x. 265 Ethelwolf tithed the kingdom of England. **1879** FARRAR *St. Paul* I. 63 Serio-comic questions as to whether in tithing the seed it was obligatory also to tithe the stalk. **1901** DAKYNS tr. *Xenophon's Anab.* v. iii. § 9. 141 Here with the sacred money he [Xenophon] built an altar and a temple, and ever after, year by year, tithed the fruits of the land in their season and did sacrifice to the goddess.

† **b.** With the tenth which is paid or delivered as the object: To pay or give as tithe. *Obs.*

854 *Grant by Adulf* in Birch *Cart. Sax.* II. 79 He teoðode ȝynd eall his cyne rice ðone teoðan del ealra his landa. 1393 LANGL. *P. Pl.* C. XIV. 84 None tythes to tythen [*v. r.* tetheȝen]. *c* 1450 *Cov. Myst.* iii. (1841) 35, I tythe it [the lamb] to God of gret mercy. 1539 BIBLE (Great) *Deut.* xxvi. 12 When thou hast made an ende of tythinge all the tythes of thyne encrease. 1630 *R. Johnson's Kingd. & Commw.* 510 These slaves are either the sonnes of Christians, tithed in their childhoods, Captives taken in the warres, or Renegadoes.

†**2.** *intr.* To pay tithe; to pay the tenth, esp. to the church. *Obs.*

*c* 1200 *Trin. Coll. Hom.* 215 Þe prest þe meneȝeð rihtliche teðien. *c* 1275 *Sinners Beware* 149 in *O. E. Misc.* 77 If he ..theoþe ryht vnder his honde, To heouene he cume myhte. 1362 LANGL. *P. Pl.* A. VIII. 65 Laborers..þat treuliche..tiþen. 1375 *Creation* 482 in Horstm. *Altengl. Leg.* (1878) 130 Kaym..tyþede of þe worste þynge, And Abel of his beste. *c* 1450 MYRC *Par. Pr.* 349 They schule teythe welle & trewe. ?*a* 1500 *Chester Pl.* (E. E. T. S.) 439 To holy Church neuer Teithed I, for me thought that was lorne. 1530 PALSGR. 758/2 He must nedes go forwarde for he doth tythe well. 1606 S. GARDINER *Bk. Angling* 93 He was not displeased that the Pharisee..should tythe rightly.

**3.** *trans.* To impose the payment of a tenth upon (a person, etc.); to exact tithe from.

1382 WYCLIF *Heb.* vii. 9 Leeuy, that took tithis, is tithid. 1546 BALE *Eng. Votaries* I. (1560) 94 b, As he and his monkes wer able to geue no more mony they tithed them after this sorte. 1582 N. T. (Rhem.) *Heb.* vii. 9 Leui also, which receiued tithes, was tithed. 1647 TRAPP *Comm. Heb.* vii. 6 Melchisedech did not only take that which Abraham was pleased to give him, but he tithed him, saith the text, he took the tenths, as his due. 1843 MARRYAT *M. Violet* xlii. 348 The cost..has been defrayed by tithing the whole Mormon Church. Those who reside at N... have been obliged to work every tenth day in quarrying stone.

**b.** To exact or collect one tenth from (goods or produce) by way of tithe; to take tithe of (goods).

1591 *Troub. Raigne K. John* (1611) 62 The Monks, the Priors, and holy cloystred Nunnes, Are all in health,..Till I had tithde and tolde their holy hoords. 1641 BEST *Farm. Bks.* (Surtees) 24 When the parson or procter cometh to tythe his woolle. 1807–8 SYD. SMITH *Plymley's Lett.* Wks. 1859 II. 136/2 No man who talks such nonsense, shall ever tithe the product of the earth. 1817 W. SELWYN *Law Nisi Prius* (ed. 4) II. 1050 The subject matter was not in a proper state to be tithed, until it came into grass cocks.

**c.** *intr.* To levy tithe *upon* (in quot. *transf.*).

1822 T. L. PEACOCK *Maid Marian* vi. 210 Those who tithe and toll upon them for their spiritual and temporal benefit.

†**4. a.** *trans.* To take every tenth thing or person from (the whole number); to take one tenth of (the whole); to divide into tenths. *Obs.*

*c* 1000 ÆLFRIC *Hom.* I. 178 ȝif we teoðiað þas ȝearlican daȝas, þonne beoð þær six and ðritiȝ teoðing-daȝas. 1610 HOLLAND *Camden's Brit.* (1637) 705 Keeping alive..two principall persons, that they might be tithed with the souldiers...Every tenth man of the Normans they chose out by lot, to be executed. 1632 MASSINGER & FIELD *Fatal Dowry* v. i, But tithe our gallants,..and you will find, In every ten, one—peradventure two—That smell rank of the dancing-school or fiddle. *a* 1641 SPELMAN *Hist. Sacrilege* (1698) 67 Coming to a Desart of Sand, divers of them were constrained to tithe themselves, and eat the tenth Man.

†**b.** *spec.* To reduce (a multitude) to one tenth of its numbers by keeping only every tenth man alive.

The instances all relate to the sacking of Canterbury by the Danes in 1011, *tithe* rendering *decimare* used with this unusual meaning; Higden's words are 'Grex Christi decimatur, novem scilicet occisis et decimo reservato'.

1387 TREVISA *Higden* (Rolls) VII. 89 Þe folk of Crist was tiþed, þat is to seie, nyne slayn and þe tenþe i-kepte. 1494 FABYAN *Chron.* VI. CXCIX. 206 The monkes of Seynt Augustynes abbey they tythed, that is to meane, they slewe .ix. by cruell turment, and yᵉ tenth they kepte alyue. 1577–87 HOLINSHED *Chron.* I. 170/2 They tithed the people after an inuerted order, slaieng all by nines through the whole multitude, and reserued the tenth. 1670 MILTON *Hist. Eng.* VI. Wks. 1851 V. 251 The multitude are tith'd, and every tenth only spar'd.

†**c.** To reduce the number of (a body of soldiers, etc.) by putting to death one in every ten; also *rhet.* to destroy a large proportion of; = DECIMATE *v.* 3, 4 b. *Obs.*

1597 BEARD *Theatre God's Judgem.* (1612) 292 Then tithing again the said tith, he slue euerie tenth knight, and that by cruell torment. 1609 HOLLAND *Amm. Marcell.* D iij b, The Thebane Legion..was first tithed, that is, every tenth man thereof was executed. 1614 SYLVESTER *Bethulia's Rescue* III. 146 These proud rocks..Which yer you scale undoubtedly will cost Ladders of Bodies; and even Tythe your Hoast. 1650 GENTILIS *Considerations* 185 Whole Armies have bin tithed, putting each tenth man to death, for faults which have bin committed in them.

†**d.** *To tithe out*: to take out by lot every tenth (person or thing). *Obs.*

1608 WILLET *Hexapla Exod.* Ded. 1 Irefull Cambyses.. caused euery tenth man to be tithed out for foode. *Ibid.* 759 The Emperour would tithe them out, and put euerie tenth man..to death. 1613 PURCHAS *Pilgrimage* v. iii. 391 Which Armie..he [the Kyng] tythed out of his people, taking one onely of tenne.

†**e.** To form the tenth part of (anything). *Obs.*

1586 WARNER *Alb. Eng.* I. v. (1612) 18 Her sorrowes did not tith her ioy.

**Titheable**: see TITHABLE.

**Tithe-barn.** A barn for holding the parson's tithe-corn.

1546 *Yorks. Chantry Surv.* (Surtees) 14, j teyth barne and a garth lyeng in Clyfton. 1643 [ANGIER] *Lanc. Vall. Achor* 18 Four or five Priests..and other great Papists, whom they had at hand in a tythe-Barn. 1852 MISS YONGE *Cameos* (1877) II. i. 7 The tenth [sheaf] was..lodged in the rector's tithe-barn. *a* 1878 SIR G. G. SCOTT *Lect. Archit.* (1879) I. 21 The tithe barns of an English village are..as admirable and as appropriate as the minster at Rheims.

**Tithed** (təiðd), *ppl. a.* [f. TITHE *v.*[2] + -ED[1].] Subject to, charged with, or liable for the payment of tithes; taken or paid by way of tithe.

1607 SHAKS. *Timon* v. iv. 31 By decimation and a tythed death..take thou the destin'd tenth. 1845 MCCULLOCH *Taxation* II. ii. It is the common opinion that a farm tithe-free is better worth twenty shillings an acre than a tithed farm.. is worth thirteen shillings. 1882 W. CORY *Mod. Eng. Hist.* II. 410 A league of 'Right men', who bound themselves by oath not to pay a high price to clergymen for tithed chattels.

**Titheless** (təi·ðlès), *a.* [f. TITHE *sb.*[1] + -LESS.] Without tithes, not in receipt of tithes.

1615 SYLVESTER *Job Triumphant* III. 555 Tithe-lesse, Taxe-lesse, Wage-lesse, Right-lesse. 1850 WHIPPLE *Ess. & Rev.* (ed. 3) I. 10 The Edinburgh Review..was projected by two briefless barristers and a titheless parson.

†**Ti·theling.** *Obs. rare.* [f. TITHE *sb.*[1] + -LING.] Tenth part, tithe.

*c* 1320 *Cast. Love* 1180 Kuynde ne may for no þinge Þolen her þe tiþelynge.

**Tithely,** obs. form of TIGHTLY, TITELY.

**Ti·the-man.** [f. TITHE *sb.*[1] + MAN *sb.*[1]]

†**1.** = TITHINGMAN[1] a. *Obs. rare.*

*c* 1450 *Godstow Reg.* 69 At þe lawdai .. william edrich, tetheman, & his felawis I-swore, presentid þat [etc.].

†**2.** *U. S.* = TITHINGMAN[1] c. *Obs. rare.*

1638–9 *Laws Maryland* in *Archives Md.* (1883) I. 54 The Lord of every Mannour .. Shall yearly .. nominate some Inhabitant of the Mannour..to be tithman of that Mannour.

†**3.** One who pays tithes. *Obs. rare.*

1680 C. NESSE *Church Hist.* 186 By their Seventh-year Sabbath they [Israelites] acknowledged that their Land belonged to God, and that they were onely Gods tenants and tythe-men.

**4.** A collector of tithes; = TITHING-MAN[2]. Now *Hist.*

1747 HOOSON *Miner's Dict.* V iv, In my time I have known it taken every twentieth Dish in some Places by the Tythman; in others every tenth. 1772 T. SIMPSON *Vermin-Killer* 19 Crows are worse than tithe-men, as they take their tithes at three different times a year. *c* 1830 *Glouc. Farm Rep.* 22 in *Libr. Usef. Knowl., Husb.* III, Nothing can be more galling to an industrious man, than that..the tithe-man should come and take the tenth of the fruits of his industry, capital and talent. 1898 J. A. GIBBS *Cotswold Vill.* 36 The titheman came with the parson's horses and took the stuff away to the barn.

**Tithend, -s,** obs. forms of TIDING, -S.

**Ti·the-pig.** A pig due or taken as tithe.

1555 [see TITHE *sb.*[1] 4 a]. 1562 *Child-Marr.* 138 He thinkes the tithe pigge withelden, was worthe xxᵈ,—for so they sell. 1592 SHAKS. *Rom. & Jul.* I. iv. 79 Somtime comes she with Tith pigs tale [tail], tickling a Parsons nose as a lies asleepe. 1602 *2nd Pt. Return fr. Parnass.* III. i. 1074 A parson that was neuer in the vniuersity, is a liuing creature that can eate a tithe pigge. 1663 BUTLER *Hud.* I. III. 1206 Where ev'ry Village is a See As well as Rome, and must maintain A Tithe-Pig Metropolitan. 1772 R. GRAVES *Spir. Quixote* (1820) II. 249 Then the rector, In sleek surcingle with good tithe-pig stuff'd. 1826 SCOTT *Woodst.* xvi, The parsons..have lost their tithe-pigs.

**Ti·the-pro:ctor.** An agent employed to collect a parson's tithes, or one who farmed the tithe; = PROCTOR 2 c.

1780 A. YOUNG *Tour Irel.* I. 103 They begun with the tythe-proctors, (who are men that hire tythes of the rectors) and these proctors either screwed the cotters up to the utmost shilling, or re-let the tythes to such as did it. 1807, 1898 [see PROCTOR 2 c]. 1817 LADY MORGAN *France* I. (1818) I. 46 The frugal savings of laborious industry do not go to feed the rapacity of the tythe-proctor. 1879 MORLEY *Burke* ii. 24 A church which tried to spread Christianity by the brotherly agency of the tithe-proctor.

**Tither** (təi·ðəɹ). [f. TITHE *v.*[2] + -ER[1].] One who tithes. **a.** One who pays tithes; usually with qualification, as *false, small, true tither.* Now *rare.*

*c* 1386 CHAUCER *Friar's T.* 14 And smale tytheres [*v. r.* tithers] weren foule yshent. *c* 1400 *York Man.* (Surtees) 223 Ye shule pray specially for trew tythers and devout offerers. *c* 1440 *Jacob's Well* 44 Whann þe euyll tythere seeth or heryth þat þou trewely tythest to god, it greuyth him sore. 1573 TUSSER *Husb.* (1878) 25 Yet we doe see ill tithers ill thriuers most commonlie bee. 1705 STANHOPE *Paraphr.* III. 377 Such distinguishing Titles, as the Punctual Tither, the Constant Faster.

**b.** An exactor or receiver of tithes; also, a supporter of the system of ecclesiastical tithes.

1591 FLORIO *2nd Fruites* 83 You are..not onely Parson or tither, but absolute possessor of whatsoeuer I haue. 1653 MILTON *Hirelings* Wks. 1851 V. 376 Tithers themselves have contributed to thir own confutation, by confessing that the Church liv'd primitively on Alms. 1736 BAILEY (folio), *Tither*, a tithe-gatherer. 1884 J. PAYNE *Tales fr. Arabic* I. 273 A certain tither, who exceeded all his brethren in oppression of the people and foulness of dealing.

**Tither** (ti·ðər), Sc. and dial. form of TOTHER.

Esp. in *the tither = thet other*, that other: see OTHER.

1479–81 *Rec. St. Mary at Hill* 98 And for the tithyr ij quarters euery quarter x s. 1786 BURNS *Twa Dogs* 23 The tither was a ploughman's collie. 1858 M. PORTEOUS *Souter Johnny* 32 On the tither haun.

**Tither,** obs. form of TETHER *sb.*

**Tithinde, -s, tithing(e, -s,** obs. ff. TIDING, -S.

**Tithing** (təi·ðiŋ), *sb.* Forms: α. 1 téoþung, -ing, 3 (theoþinge), toðing(e, teuþing(e, 3–4 teþing, -yng, (thething), 4 tuþing, tueþyng, tethinge, teothinge. β. 1 teiȝðuncg, tiȝeðing, 3–5 tiþing, 5–9 tything, 6– tithing. [OE. *téoðung*, Anglian *tigeðing*, f. *téoða, tigeþe* TITHE *sb.*[1] or *téoðian* TITHE *v.*[2]: see -ING[1], 3.]

**1.** One tenth given to the church; = TITHE *sb.*[1] 1.

α. 925–*c* 936 *Laws of Athelstan* I. Prol., Ic Æðelstan cyningc..eow bidde..þæt ȝe ærest of minum aȝenum gode aȝifan ða teoðunga. *c* 1000 ÆLFRIC *Hom.* I. 178 We sceolon ..of ures ȝeares teolunge Gode þa teoðunge syllan. *c* 1000 *Ags. Gosp.* Luke xviii. 12 Ic sylle teoþunga [*c* 1160 *Hatton Gosp.*, Ic ȝife teondunge]. *c* 1200 *Trin. Coll. Hom.* 215 Þu bitechest þe prest alle þine teðinge. *c* 1275 *Sayings of Bede* 137 in Horstm. *Alteng. Leg.* 141 If he may..stelen Cristes teuþinge [*v. r.* theoþinge]. *a* 1325 *MS. Rawl. B.* 520 lf. 38 Offrendes ore Tuþinges þat habbez ben iȝiuene ant vsed. 1387 TREVISA *Higden* (Rolls) VIII. 257 All teþynge [*MS. γ.* tueþyng] schulde be payde to þe moder chirche. 14.. *Childe of Bristowe* 364 in Hazl. *E. P. P.* I. 124 Tethynges and offrynges, sone, he sayd, for y them never truly payd.

β. *c* 950 *Lindisf. Gosp.* Luke xviii. 12 Teiȝðuncgas [*Rushw.* teȝðunge] ic sello allra ða ðe ic ah. *a* 1040 *Bidding Prayer* in *Eng. Hist. Rev.* (1912) Jan. 10 Mid lihte and mid tiȝeðinge. *c* 1200 *Trin. Coll. Hom.* 129 Þeh we gon to chirche and giuen rihte tiðinge. 1382 WYCLIF *Tobit* i. 7 He mynystrede alle tithing [1388 hise tithis]. *c* 1440 *Gesta Rom.* vi. 16 (Harl. MS.) Þey have not of hire owne to lyve with, but of tythingis. 1538 BALE *Thre Lawes* 1000 If we maye haue the tythynges And profytable offerynges. 1861 BERESF. HOPE *Eng. Cathedr. 19th C.* viii. 280, I plead..for a tithing of wealth and art and mechanical power offered at the altar of the Most High.

**b.** *spec.* A shock or stook of ten sheaves (orig. so set up for the convenience of the tithe-proctor): see quots. *dial.*

1764 *Museum Rust.* II. cvii. 362 Repeating the practice till there be thirty or forty tything brought together. 1794 T. DAVIS *Agric. Wilts.* 76 The general custom..is, to set up the sheafs in double rows, usually ten sheaves together, (provincially a tything) for the convenience of the tything-man. 1813 *Ibid.* Gloss., *Tithings*, ten sheaves of wheat set up together in a double row.

†**2.** A tenth part of anything. *Obs.*

1382 WYCLIF *Isa.* vi. 12 ȝit in it tithing. 1388 *Ibid.*, And ȝit tithing [*gloss* ether tenthe part] schal be ther ynne. *a* 1425 tr. *Higden* (Rolls) VII. App. 520 (MS. β) Hym thouȝt that the tethinge were to many ylefte; and teothed efte the teothinge. 1609 BIBLE (Douay) *Isa.* vi. 13 And yet there shal be tithing in it, and she shal be converted [1611 But yet in it shalbe a tenth, and it shall returne].

**3.** A company (originally) of ten householders in the system of FRANK-PLEDGE; now only as a rural division (originally regarded as one tenth of a hundred) to which this system gave its name.

*c* 930–40 *Laws of Athelstan* VI. c. 8 § 1 Þæt we us ȝegaderian .. þa hyndenmenn and þa þe ða teoþunge bewitan. 1297 R. GLOUC. (Rolls) 5402 He by vond..þat ech man wiþ oute gret lond In þe teþinge were ydo & þat ech man knewe oþer þat in teþinge were. *a* 1400 in *Eng. Gilds* (1870) 361 3ef a foreyne empledy þe teþynge, þe teþynge ne haþ bote þre dayes to shewynge... Whanne þe teþynge empledeþ a foreyn, þe foreyn haþ his delay. 1432 [see TITHINGMAN[1]]. 1538 FITZHERB. *Just. Peas* 129 In Towne, Tithinge, Village, or Hamlet. 1570–6 LAMBARDE *Peramb. Kent* (1826) 18 Some were called..Tithings,..bicause there were in eche of them to the number of ten persons, whereof eche one was suretie and pledge for others good abearing. 1610 HOLLAND *Camden's Brit.* (1637) 158 Hee caused the Counties to be parted into Centuries, that is Hundreds, and Decimes, that is Tithings. 1646 W. HUGHES *Mirr. Justices* I. ii, These divisions in some places are called hundreds..and in some places Tythings or Wapentakes, according to the English. 1754 HUME *Hist. Eng.* (1761) I. ii. 49 The neighbouring householders were formed into one corporation, who, under the name of a tithing, decennary, or fribourg, were answerable for each other's conduct. 1839 KEIGHTLEY *Hist. Eng.* I. 81 The institution of tithings did not prevail all through England, perhaps not to the north of the Trent. 1874 STUBBS *Const. Hist.* I. 86 *note*, Tithings at present exist in Somersetshire and Wiltshire.

**4.** *attrib.* and *Comb.*, as *tithing-barn, -sheaf, table.* See also TITHINGMAN[1], -PENNY.

*c* 1540 *Old Ways* (1892) 45 The said Hayside had sowlde the said tythyng ootys. 1654 VILVAIN *Theol. Treat.* Supp. 238 Not a tithing part of Mankind can possibly find place to stand on a new Earth. 1666 *Lond. Gaz.* No. 66/2 A Bill for abolishing of Oblations and Mortuaries, and appointing a Tything Table throughout the Kingdom. 1865 KINGSLEY *Herew.* i, A palace..beside which King Edward's new Hall at Westminster would show but as a tything-barn. 1907 *Contemp. Rev.* June 796 The farmer was bound to cart his tithing-sheaves to the parson's barn.

**Tithing** (təi·ðiŋ), *vbl. sb.* [f. TITHE *v.*[2] + -ING[1].] The action of TITHE *v.*[2]

**a.** Payment of tithes.

*c* 1305 *St. Swithin* 40 in *E. E. P.* (1862) 44 Ech man wolde þurf þe lond his teoþing wel do. 1548 UDALL *Erasm. Par. Luke* xix. 149 Their colde & feble doctryne..concernyng the true tithyng of myntes & rue. 1573 TUSSER *Husb.* (1878) 25 Though some in their tithing be slack or too bold. 1682 BURNET *Rights Princes* i. 20 That the tything of Mint and Anise should not be left undone.

**b.** Exaction of tithes. Also *transf.*

1630 *R. Johnson's Kingd. & Commw.* 513 The tithing of Springals is made every third yeare. 1768 BLACKSTONE *Comm.* III. 89 If the defendant pleads any custom..or other matter whereby the right of tithing is called in question. 1791 BURKE *App. Whigs* Wks. VI. 289 Taxing and tything. 1843 MARRYAT *M. Violet* xxxix, He is receiving regular pay, derived from the tithing of this warlike people.

†**c.** The killing of every tenth; decimation; sometimes, the killing of all but the tenth. *Obs.*

1586 T. B. *La Primaud. Fr. Acad.* (1589) 716 The tithing of armies..when every tenth man throughout a whole hoste was by lot put to death. 1601 F. GODWIN *Bps. Eng.* 24 In that same terrible tithing of the Danes..all the monks were slaine, except onely fower.

**d.** *attrib.*, as *tithing-time*, *port*, etc.
**1548** *Act* 2 & 3 *Edw. VI*, c. 13 § 2 As often as the saide predyall Tythes shalbe due, and at the tythinge tyme of the same. *a* **1786** COWPER *Yearly Distress* 8 But oh! it cuts him like a scythe, When tithing time draws near. **1850** GROTE *Greece* II. lxiii. (1862) V. 462 This place he..erected ..into a regular tithing port for levying toll on all vessels coming out of the Euxine. **1853** ROCK *Ch. of Fathers* III. II. 65 These days [Lent] are the tithing-days of the year.

**Tithingman**[1] (təi·ðiŋmæn). [f. TITHING *sb.* 3 + MAN *sb.*[1]] **a.** Anciently, The chief man of a TITHING (*sb.* 3), a headborough; in later use, a parish peace-officer, or petty constable (CONSTABLE 5 c). Now *Hist.*
**946–c 961** *Laws of Edgar* c. 2 Cyðe hit man ðam hundredesmen, & he syððan ðam teoðingmannum. **1432** *Rolls of Parlt.* IV. 403/1 The Decennare and Decennes, oder wyse called Thethyngman and Thethyngs. **1441–2** *Act* 20 *Hen. VI*, c. 8 Chescun Conestable, Tythingman, ou chief plegge, de chescun ville ou hamell. **1581** LAMBARDE *Eiren.* I. iii. (1588) 15 For Borowhead, Borsholder, and Tithingman, be three seueral names of one self same thing, and doe signifie, The chiefe man of the free pledges within that Borow, or Tithing. **1626** BERNARD *Isle of Man* (1627) 34 There be foure sorts of Officers which may attach Felons by warrant, The Deputy-constable, the Tything-man, the Petty Constable, and the Head Constable. *c* **1640** J. SMYTH *Lives Berkeleys* (1883) II. 345 The Thirdburrow or Tithingman ought to come to Portbury Leete. **1724** *Lond. Gaz.* No. 6232/2 [They] were by his Mittimus put into the Custody of a Tithingman with a strong Guard. **1857** TOULMIN SMITH *Parish* 15. **1874** STUBBS *Const. Hist.* I. v. 90 *note*, The tithingman is of course an elective officer.

†**b.** A chief or ruler of ten: rendering L. *decānus*, *decurio*. *Obs.*
*c* **1000** ÆLFRIC *Exod.* xviii. 21 ȝesete of him þusendmen and hundrydmen and fifties men and teoðingmen. — *Deut.* i. 15 And ic nam wise menn and sette hiȝ to..teoðingmannum. **1608** WILLET *Hexapla Exod.* 275 A ruler of ten, or tithing man.

**c.** In Maryland and New England: A former elective officer of a township, whose functions were derived from those of the English tithingman (a.) in the 17th c.; in particular he was charged with the prevention of disorderly conduct; in New Eng., in later times, chiefly with enforcing the observance of the Sabbath and of order during divine service. Now *Hist.* See *Johns Hopkins Hist. Studies*, No. I.
**1638** *Laws of Maryland*, A Tything-man in each Manor, a Constable in each Hundred. **1677** *Laws of Massachusetts* 23 May, To prevent..Prophanation of the Sabbath..Tithing man or men shall..have power in the absence of the Constable to apprehend all Sabbath-breakers. [**1727–8** Last tithing-men chosen in Boston.] **1836** *Rev. Stat. Mass.* 180 At the annual meeting, every town shall choose..Tythingmen, unless the towns shall vote that it is not expedient to choose the same. [Repealed in 1860.] **1895** A. B. HART in *Forum* (N.Y.) May 377 The interference with Sunday travel by the tithingmen of the Puritan Connecticut towns.

**Ti·thing-man**[2]. [f. TITHING *vbl. sb.*] A collector of tithes; a tithe-proctor.
**1625** BURGES *Pers. Tithes* 60, I will produce Mr. Selden (none of the best Proctors for vs Tithing-men, but One with whom we poore Vicars are daily nosed). **1693** *Rector's Bk. Clayworth* (1910) 103 Tything men 3 entred yᵉ Fields. **1736** *Gentl. Mag.* VI. 705/2 He may often lose his whole Crop, in waiting for the Incumbent's Tything-man. **1807–8** SYD. SMITH *Plymley's Lett.* Wks. 1859 II. 145/2 Soften some of the most odious powers of the tything-man.

†**Ti·thing-penny.** *Obs.* [f. TITHING *sb.* 3 + PENNY, q.v. for Forms.] A customary duty formerly paid by manorial tenants to the lord, and also a payment by lords of manors at the hundred court.
**1208** in *Calr. Charter Rolls* (1903) I. 29 Libera et quieta de..wardpeny et averpeny et thethingpeny et hengwite. **1297** *Inq. Post Mortem* Edw. I 80 (6) (P.R.O.) De tethyngpeny ad visus de hockday et ad festum Sancti Martini xl.*s.* **1334** *Inq. P. M.* Edw. III 37 (22) (P.R.O.) Est ibidem [West Winterslow] quoddam feodum vocatum tethyngpeny viz ad festum Pasche et ad festum Sancti Michaelis xx.*s.* *a* **1600** *MS. Cott. Vitell. C.* 9 lf. 226 b, *Tythinge-pany*, hoc est quieti de tallagio decenæ sive Tythinge per consuetudinem. **1706** PHILLIPS (ed. Kersey), *Teding-*, *Tething-*, or *Tithing-Penny*, a Tax or Allowance formerly paid to the Sheriff, from every Tithing, towards the Charge of keeping Courts.

**Tithly**, obs. form of TITELY *adv.*

**Tithond(e**, obs. form of TIDING.

†**Tithonic** (təiþ-, tiþǫ·nik), *a. Obs.* [Fancifully f. Gr. Τιθων-ός, spouse of Eos (Aurora) + -IC.] Pertaining to or characterized by 'tithonism'; = ACTINIC. Hence †**Tithoni·city** *Obs.* = ACTINISM 2.
**1842** (Dec.) DRAPER in *Philos. Mag.* XXI. 455 Such words as Tithonoscope, Tithonometer, Tithonography, Tithonic effect, Diatithonescence, are musical in an English ear. In this paper I shall therefore use the term Tithonicity and its derivatives. *Ibid.*, The proof of the physical independence of Tithonicity and Light. *Ibid.*, The existence of dark Tithonic rays, analogous to the rays of dark heat. *Ibid.* 457 To insulate a visible red and yellow ray that are without tithonic power, and an invisible tithonic ray beyond the violet. **1854** J. SCOFFERN in *Orr's Circ. Sc.*, *Chem.* 93 The immediate mode of agency of the power—'actinism', 'tithonicity', 'energia', or whatever we may call it—is..unknown. **1882** *Nature* XXV. 274 The works..from Draper's pen upon the chemical and physical properties of the ultra-violet, or as he styled them, *tithonic* rays.

†**Ti·thonism.** *Obs.* [f. as prec. + -ISM.] = TITHONICITY, ACTINISM 2. So †**Ti·thonize** *v.*, *trans.* to subject to actinic influence (hence †**Tithoniza·tion**, 'tithonic' or actinic action; †**Ti·thonized** *ppl. a.*); †**Titho·nograph**, a photograph produced by the action of 'tithonic' rays on a sensitized surface (so **Tithonogra·phic** *a.*, **-o·graphist**, **-o·graphy**); †**Tithono·meter**, †**Titho·notype**, see quots.
**1854** J. SCOFFERN in *Orr's Circ. Sc.*, *Chem.* 93 That peculiar associate of light which has been termed..actinism, *tithonism, and energia. **1844** (July) DRAPER in *Philos. Mag.* XXV. 7 The indigo ray forms the muriatic acid as well as produces the preliminary *tithonization. *Ibid.*, Before placing the tubes in the prismatic spectrum we *tithonize them in the daylight. *Ibid.* 2, I shall speak of chlorine which has been exposed to the beams of the sun, as **tithonized chlorine*. **1842** (Dec.) *Ibid.* XXI. 456 The comparison of different spectras and their corresponding *tithonographs. *Ibid.* 461 If the *tithonographic compound radiates whilst it is undergoing decomposition. **1878** LOCKYER *Spectr. Anal.* iii. § 2. 82 Draper..in his 'tithonographic representation', had..not succeeded in registering the lines of the yellow, orange, and green parts of the spectrum. **1842** DRAPER in *Philos. Mag.* XXI. 456 A principle..which makes the spectra of different *tithonographists comparable. **1842** *Tithonometer [see TITHONIC]. **1843** (Dec.) DRAPER in *P. M.* XXIII. 401 Description of the Tithonometer, an instrument for measuring the Chemical Force of the Indigo-tithonic Rays. **1843** (May) *Ibid.* XXII. 366 As a name for these processes of copying the surface of a Daguerreotype, I would suggest the word **Tithonotype*.

**Tithy**, var. TETHY *Obs.*; obs. f. TIDY.

†**Tithymal.** *Herb. Obs.* Forms: α. 6–8 **tithi-**, **tithymal**, **-e**, 7 **tithymall**, **-e**, **tythimal**, **-l**, **tythymalle**. β. 5 **tytymal**, **titi-**, **titymalle**, 8 **titimale**. [ad. L. *tithymal(l)us* spurge, *tithymalis* sea-spurge (Pliny), a. Gr. τιθύμαλος, τιθυμαλίς. Cf. F. *tithymale* (13th c. in Godef. *Compl.*).] An old name of the Spurge genus of plants.
*c* **1400** *Lanfranc's Cirurg.* 294 Take þe grete titimalle & þe smale, & boile hem in vinegre & in oile. *c* **1410** *Master of Game* (MS. Digby 182) xi, An erbe þe whiche is cleped tytymal, þe whiche poticaryes knoweth well. **1578** LYTE *Dodoens* III. xxix. 355 There are..seuen sortes of Tithymal. **1601** CHESTER *Love's Martyr* (1878) 84 There Mugwort, Sena and Tithiemailes. *a* **1687** PETTY *Pol. Anat.* xiii, What is said of the herb Mackenbory is fabulous, only that 'tis a tythimal, which will purge furiously. **1712** tr. *Pomet's Hist. Drugs* I. 36 The Esula or Spurge is a kind of Tithymal.

**Titi** (tī·ti). [Native or local name, of various origin.]
**1.** In U.S., a name given to certain trees of N.O. *Cyrillaceæ*, as *Cliftonia monophylla*, Buckwheat tree, the *Black Titi* of Southern U.S., also to species of genus *Cyrilla*, esp. *C. racemiflora*, the Leatherwood of south-eastern U.S., distinguished as *Red* or *White Titi*.
**1860** CHAPMAN *Flora South. U. S.* 273. **1880** *Libr. Univ. Knowl.* (N.Y.) III. 147 Buckwheat Tree..an evergreen shrub in the gulf states...Its local name is *titi*. **1903** BRUTTON & SHAFER *N. Amer. Trees* 618.
**2.** A name of *Oxydendron arboreum*, N.O. *Ericaceæ*. **1903** SMALL *Flora S. E. United States* 890.
**3.** See TI.

**Titi, ti-ti**, variant of TEETEE[1], [2].

**Titian** (ti·ʃăn). [The name Titian, for Tiziano Vecellio, Venetian painter, died 1576.] With capital T. A picture by Titian. Also *attrib.* or *adj.*, denoting a colour of the hair favoured by Titian in his pictures, described as a 'bright golden auburn', and more loosely used as an appreciative word for 'red'.
As examples showing the distinctive colour are given 'Ariadne' and 'The Magdalene' in the National Gallery, London, 'Flora' in the Uffizi Palace, Florence, etc.
**1824** BYRON *Juan* XVI. lvi, A special Titian, warranted original. **1896** J. ASHBY-STERRY *Tale Thames* xix. (1903) 111/1 Three maidens..all with Titian-tinted tresses. **1904** *Dundee Advertiser* 27 June 8/1 Twenty years ago hair with a reddish tinge was called 'carrots'; now 'Titian-coloured' locks are reckoned a definite beauty. **1904** BENSON *Challoners* v, The girl..had Titian hair in golden glorious profusion.
Hence **Titia·nic** *a.*, of or belonging to Titian; **Titiane·sque** *a.* [see -ESQUE], in the style of Titian.
**1842** TENNYSON *Gard. Dau.* 167 You cannot fail but work in hues to dim The *Titianic Flora. **1801** FUSELI in *Lect. Paint.* ii. (1848) 403 The *Titianesque colour of Hans Holbein. **1864** LOWELL *Fireside Trav.* 49 He said, 'Excuse me, sir', in a very Titianesque manner. **1895** TROTTER *Mrq. Dalhousie* iii. 76 A noble handsome Titianesque head.

**Titifill, -fyl**, var. TITIVIL *Obs.*

**Titil, -ile, -ill**, obs. forms of TITLE, TITTLE.

**Titillate** (ti·tilēit), *v.* Also 8 titulate, titilate. [f. L. *titillāt-*, ppl. stem of *titillāre* to tickle.]
**1.** *trans.* To excite or stimulate as by tickling; *esp.* to excite agreeably, gratify (the sense of taste, smell, or touch, the imagination); = TICKLE *v.* 3.
**1620** VENNER *Via Recta* vi. 92 It..exciteth the appetite, by corrugating the mouth of the stomacke, and titillating the pallate. **1706** MRS. CENTLIVRE *Love at Venture* I, The elegance of my Fabric has titulated the imagination of many a fine Lady. **1799** SOUTHEY *Snuff* 2 A delicate pinch! oh how it tingles up The titillated nose. **1829** MACAULAY *Misc. Writ.* (1860) I. 291 Not to titillate his palate but to keep up his character for hospitality. **1882** J. PARKER *Apost. Life* I. 74 Your fancy has been titillated.
**2.** To touch lightly; to irritate slightly; = TICKLE *v.* 4. Also *absol.*
**1837** DICKENS *Pickw.* x, The landlady..proceeded to vinegar the forehead, beat the hands, titillate the nose,..of the spinster aunt. **1872** COHEN *Dis. Throat* 7 If the epiglottis be titillated with the tip of the tongue-depressor. **1879** O. W. HOLMES *Motley* xviii, The feathered end of his shaft titillates harmlessly enough.

**Titillating** (ti·tilēitiŋ), *ppl. a.* [f. prec. + -ING[2].] That titillates; pleasantly exciting, exhilarating, stimulating.
**1712–14** POPE *Rape Lock* v. 84 The pungent grains of titilating dust. **1809–10** COLERIDGE *Friend* (1818) I. 27 A petty titillating sting, from affected point and wilful antithesis. **1902** MISS BROUGHTON in *Times* 11 Nov., An object that has nothing of the..abnormal or the titillating.
¶ **b.** Itching, tingling; craving, hankering.
**1858** *Times* 20 Nov. 8/5 [He] sits down with a titillating palate to his plump dainties.
Hence **Ti·tillatingly** *adv.*
**1876** R. M. JEPHSON *He would be a Soldier* x, The chevaux-de-frise [moustache] wandered titillatingly about the wretched recruit's face. **1900** MISS BROUGHTON *Foes in Law* xxiii, A fashionable preacher, while he titillatingly lashes smart bonnets.

**Titillation** (titilēi·ʃən). Also 5 **tytul-**, 6 **titil-**, 7 **tittul-**, 7–8 **titul-**. [ad. L. *titillātiōn-em*, n. of action f. *titillāre* to TITILLATE. Cf. F. *titillation* (14th c. in Hatz.-Darm.).
The form with *-ul-* occurs in med.Lat. (11th c.: see Du Cange). The OF. also had this spelling (Godef. *Compl.*).]
**1.** Excitation or stimulation of the mind or senses; *esp.* pleasing excitement, gratification.
*c* **1425** *St. Mary of Oignies* II. ii. in *Anglia* VIII. 154/18 Wheþer she felte any titillacione of veynglorye of mennys preisynges. **1491** CAXTON *Vitas Patr.* (W. de W. 1495) I. xxxvi. 37/2 To resyste & wythstonde theyr tytulacyons and cauyllacyons as moche as we maye. **1598** MARSTON *Met. Pygmal.*, *Auth. in Prayse of prec. Poem*, Crowne my head with Bayes, Which..wantonly displayes The Salaminian titilations. **1602** CAMPION *Art Eng. Poesie* ii. 5 The noble Grecians and Romaines..abandoning the childish titillation of riming. **1690** C. NESSE *O. & N. Test.* I. 45 Then arises an inward titillation or contemplative delight. **1762** KAMES *Elem. Crit.* (1763) I. vii. 356 A certain sort of titillation, which is expressed externally by mirthful laughter. **1876** T. HARDY *Ethelberta* II. 29 More or less pervaded by thrills and titillations from games of hazard.
**2.** A sensation of being tickled; a tingling, an itching.
**1621** BURTON *Anat. Mel.* I. i. II. vi, The five senses, of touching, hearing, seeing, smelling, tasting, to which you may add Scaliger's sixth sense of titillation if you please. **1704** J. HARRIS *Lex. Techn.* I, *Titillation*, is that sensation we have in any Part of the Body when tickled. **1816** KIRBY & SP. *Entomol.* xvi. (1818) II. 14 *Thrips Physapus*, the fly that causes us in hot weather such intolerable titillation. **1822–34** *Good's Study Med.* (ed. 4) III. 212 The sense of itching, which may be defined a painful titillation local or general, relieved by rubbing. **1855** BAIN *Senses & Int.* II. iv. § 19 (1864) 287 A titillation of the throat is sometimes perceptible.
**3.** The action of tickling, or touching lightly so as to tickle.
**1623** MASSINGER *Bondman* I. ii, These bristles give the gentlest titillations. **1711** SHAFTESB. *Charac.* (1737) II. II. II. ii. 152 Laughter provok'd by Titillation, grows an excessive Pain. **1872** COHEN *Dis. Throat* 25 If it cannot be retracted by titillation or astringent applications, the exuberant portion must be clipped off.
†**4.** *transf.* A means of titillating. *Obs. rare.*
**1606** *Sir G. Goosecappe* II. i. in Bullen *O. Pl.* (1884) III. 40 Tis a pretty kinde of terme new come up in perfuming, which they call a Titillation. **1610** B. JONSON *Alch.* IV. iv, Your Spanish titillation in a gloue [is] The best perfume.

**Titillative** (ti·tilǣtiv), *a. nonce-wd.* [f. TITILLATE *v.* + -IVE: see -ATIVE.] Tending to tickle, having the power of tickling.
**1736** CHESTERF. in *Fog's Jrnl.* No. 377 One Publick Tickler of great Eminency,..whose Titillative Faculty must be allowed to be singly confined to the Ear.

**Titillator** (ti·tilēitəɹ). [agent-n. in L. form from *titillāre* to tickle: see -OR 2 b.] One who or that which titillates; a tickler.
**1823** *New Monthly Mag.* VII. 36 These Protean combinations are the stimulants of fancy, the titillators of the imagination. **1892** *Blackw. Mag.* Sept. 367 Our lives were made miserable by the titillator.

**Ti·tillatory**, *a.* [f. as prec.: see -ORY[2].] Pertaining to or characterized by titillation.
**1762** J. WILKES *N. Briton* No. 7 Doctor Ticklewrist thinks it more his duty..to acquaint the public, that his Titillatory Elixir is a sovereign remedy for the present epidemical distemper. **1862** *Macm. Mag.* Mar. 426 The titillatory powers of his [the fly's] six feet and extended sucker, would be together too much for the skins of reapers.

**Titimal(e, -malle**, var. TITHYMAL *Obs.*

**Titivate, tittivate** (ti·tiveit), *v. colloq.* Also tidi-, tiddi-. [In early examples *tidi-* or *tiddivate*, perh. from TIDY with a quasi-Latin ending, after *cultivate*.] *trans.* To make small alterations or additions to one's toilet, etc. so as to add to one's attractions; to make smart or spruce; to 'touch up' in the way of adornment, put the finishing touches to. Also with *off*, *up*.
**1805** [implied in TITIVATION]. **1824** in *Spirit Pub. Jrnls.* (1825) 35 Decorated with his white flag in front, and tiddivated up to his elbows in a pair of unblemished..Holland sleeves. **1827** *Sporting Mag.* XIX. 341 The shot manufacturers want titivating too. **1833** MARRYAT *P. Simple* xxxiv, You'd better make yourself scarce, Peter, while I tidivate myself off a little, according to the rules and regulations.. when you are asked to dine with the skipper. **1843** HALIBURTON *Attaché* xxii, I'll arrive in time for dinner, I'll titivate myself up, and down to drawin'-room. **1852** R. S.

SURTEES *Sponge's Sp. Tour* xxv, He..saw him titivating his hair and arranging his collar. **1885** MRS. B. M. CROKER *Proper Pride* ix, Helen was calmly titivating herself at the glass. **1893** COUCH *Delectable Duchy* 60 Come here, and let me tittivate you. **1897** *Daily News* 22 Dec. 8/3 It was drawn through the Fair .. by eight oxen tidivated with ribbons and flowers.

**b.** *intr.* for *refl.*

**1836–9** DICKENS *Sk. Boz, Charac.* vii, Regular as clock-work—breakfast at nine—dress and tittivate a little. **1859** THACKERAY *Virgin.* xlviii, Whilst you call in your black man, and titivate a bit.

Hence **Ti·tivated, ti·tt-** *ppl. a.*, **Ti·tivating, ti·tt-** *vbl. sb.* and *ppl. a.*; **Titi-, tittiva·tion,** the action of titivating; **Ti·ti-, ti·ttivator,** one who titivates.

**1805** *Sporting Mag.* XXV. 187 Affords infinite amusement during the ceremony of titivation. **1831** *Fraser's Mag.* IV. 462 One worthy with a titivated brown wig and a sprigged waistcoat. **1876** E. JENKINS *Blot on Queen's Head* 15 He had a fancy for titivation..and for splendour and display. **1889** W. S. GILBERT *Gondoliers* II, Spend an hour in tittivating. **1895** *Sat. Rev.* 1 June 726/2 People who never..compare the scene-painter's titivated imitations with the..originals. **1902** C. G. HARPER *Cambridge, Ely*, etc. 56 The furbishers and titivators of things ancient and worshipful.

† **Ti·tivil.** *Obs.* Forms: 5 Tyti-, Tyty-, Titi-, Tityuillus, -villus, 5–6 Tutiuillus, -villus, Tytyuyllus; 6 titiuil, -ille, -ylle, (Tom Titiuile), titti-, tytyuell(e, tittifill, tyttyfylle, titifyl, 7 -fill. Also 5 Tytyuylly, Tytiuilly. [ad. med.L. *Tuti-, Titivillus*, in OF. also *Tutiville*: of unknown origin. Connexion has been suggested with L. *titivillitium* used once by Plautus, and inferred to mean 'a mere trifle, a bagatelle'.

But in some of the earliest continental instances of the name, it is written *Titinillus*, or *Tutinillus*, and in many it is impossible to say whether the middle consonant is *n* or *u* (*v*). At an early date English usage settled on *u* (later *v* and *f*). Titivillus was evidently in origin a creation of monastic wit, but in its English form the name passed from the Mystery Plays into popular speech as a term of the vernacular, still in use after 1600.]

**1.** Name for a devil said to collect fragments of words dropped, skipped, or mumbled in the recitation of divine service, and to carry them to hell, to be registered against the offender; hence, a name for a demon or devil in the mystery plays. Also found in France and Germany, 13–15th c.

What generally passes as the earliest mention of the name and function of Titinillus or Titiuillus, occurs in a Latin sermon (Wackernagel *Gesch. der Deut. Litt.* II. 466, note) conjecturally attributed to the Dominican Petrus de Palude, a native of Burgundy and student of Paris, who became Patriarch of Jerusalem, and died in 1342. A very similar and app. equally early account is printed in T. Wright's *Latin Stories* (Percy Soc. 1842), from a Brit. Mus. MS. (Arundel 506, lf. 46) of German origin, of first half of 14th c. Both these stories cite the verse, so often quoted by later writers, 'Fragmina psalmorum Titiuillus colligit horum', the former adding 'Quaque die mille vicibus sarcinat ille' (Every day he fills his bag a thousand times). Titiuillus is also mentioned, 1382–85, by Gower *Vox Clamantis* IV. 864; and in the 15th c., esp. *c* 1450, references become frequent. The earliest Eng. form is app. Lydgate's *Tytyuylly*, or ? *Tytyuyll*, *c* 1420 (sense 2).

*c* **1450** *Mankind* 468 in *Macro Plays* 18 *Titivillus* [enters, drest like a devil, and with a net in his hand]. Ego sum dominancium dominus, and my name ys Titivillus. *Ibid.* 869 Tytiuilly, þat goth invisibele, hynge hys nette before my eye. *c* **1460** *Lansd. MS.* 763 lf. 60 b, Janglers cum japers, nappers, galpers, quoque drawers, Momlers [etc.] Fragmina verborum Tutivillus colligit horum. *c* **1460** *Towneley Myst.* xxx. 249 Mi name is tutiuillus, my horne is blawen; Fragmina verborum tutiullus colligit horum, Belzabub algorum, belial belium doliorum. *c* **1475** *Douce MS. 104* lf. 112 b, Tutiuillus þa deuyl of hell He wryteþ har names soþe to tel. *c* **1475–1530** *Myrr. our Ladye* I. xx. 54, I am a poure dyuel, and my name ys Tytyuyllus... I muste eche day..brynge my master a thousande pokes full of faylynges, and of neglygences in syllables and wordes.

**2.** Hence, a term of reprobation: A bad or vile character, scoundrel, knave, villain. **b.** *esp.* A tattling tell-tale, mischievous tale-bearer.

*c* **1420** ? LYDG. *Assembly of Gods* 694 What pepyll they were that came to that dysport...Ther were..Tytyuyllys, tyrauntes, with turmentoures. **1508** KENNEDIE *Flyting w. Dunbar* 513 Cankrit Caym, tryit trowane, Tutiuillus. *c* **1537** *Thersytes* (1820) 67 All the courte of conscience in cockoldshyres, Tynckers and tabberers, typplers, tauerners: Tyttyfylles, tryfullers, turners and trumpers. **1546** J. HEYWOOD *Prov.* (1867) 19 There is no mo such titifyls in England's ground, To holde with the hare, and run with the hounde. *a* **1553** UDALL *Royster D.* I. i. (Arb.) 11 Somewhyles Watkin Waster maketh vs good cheere..Sometime Tom Titiuile maketh vs a feast.

**b. 1523** SKELTON *Garl. Laurel* 642 Theis titiuyllis with taumpinnis wer towchid and tappid. *a* **1529** — *Col. Cloute* 418 Thus the people telles ..And talkys lyke tytyuelles, Howe ye brake the dedes wylles. *a* **1548** HALL *Chron., Hen. VI* 125 b, The deuill .. did apparell certain catchepoules, and Parasites, commonly called titiuils and tale tellers, to sowe discord and dissencion. *Ibid., Edw. IV* 220 Mistrustyng lest her counsayl should by some titiuille, bee published and opened to her aduersaries. **1561** AWDELAY *Frat. Vacab.* 15 This tittiuell knaue commonly maketh the worst of the best betwene hys Maister and his friende. **1611** COTGR., *Coquette*, a pratling, or proud gossip;..a cocket, or tatling houswife; a titifill, a flebergebit.

† **Titiviller.** *Obs. rare.* Also 6 *Sc.* tutivillar. [Extended form of prec.] = prec.

**1500–20** DUNBAR *Poems* xiv. 67 (S.T.S.) 83 Sa mony rakkettis, sa mony ketche-pillaris, Sic ballis, sic nackettis, and sic tutivillaris. **1581** J. BELL *Haddon's Answ. Osor.* 8 Here our clamorous titiviller taketh occasion to scorne my to to foreward diligence. **1583** STUBBES *Anat. Abus.* K iv b, Such Titivillers, flattering Parasits and glosing Gnatoes.

**Titlark** (ti·tˌlāɹk). [f. TIT *sb.*³ + LARK *sb.*¹] A bird of the genus *Anthus* or some allied genus, resembling a lark; a pipit; *esp.* in England, the meadow pipit, *A. pratensis*, also called *tit-pipit*; in U.S., *A. ludovicianus* (American titlark).

**1668** CHARLETON *Onomast.* 81 *Alauda Pratensis*, the Tit-Lark. **1676** GREW *Musæum, Anat. Stomach & Guts* viii. 37 The House-Sparrow, Linnet, Titlark, and many more. **1773** G. WHITE *Selborne* xxxix, Titlarks not only sing sweetly as they sit on trees, but also as they play and toy about on the wing. **1872** COUES *N. Amer. Birds* 90 Titlarks ..are terrestrial and more or less gregarious birds, migratory and insectivorous.

**b.** *slang.* (See quot.)

**1799** in *Spirit Pub. Jrnls.* III. 352 Found the beaks and titlarks reading the papers. *Ibid.* 355 Glossary of fashionable or cant Phrases...*Titlarks*, spectators at Bow Street.

**Title** (təi·t'l), *sb.* Forms: 1 titul; 4 tytel, -e, 4–5 titel, (5 -ell), tityll, 4–6 titil, -ill, (4 titille), 4–7 tytle, 5 titul, -lle, (tetle), 5–6 tytill, -e, 5–7 tytyl, -el(l, ty-, titile, (6 tetel), 8 titule, 4– title; also 6 tyttel, -yll. [ME. a. OF. *title* (12th c. in Godef. *Compl.*):—L. *titulus* superscription, title; in mod.F. *titre*. OE. *titul* was directly from L., as is the later by-form *titule*.

The *i* in OE. and early ME. was prob. short, after L.: see also TITTLE.]

†**1.** An inscription placed on or over an object, giving its name or describing it; a legend; sometimes, a placard hung up in a theatre giving the name of the piece, etc. *Obs.*

In earliest use repr. L. *titulus*, the inscription on the Cross.

*c* **950** *Lindisf. Gosp.* Mark xv. 26, & wæs titul (*vel* tacon *vel* merca) intinges his on awritten cynig iudea. *a* **1300** *Cursor M.* 16685 Abouen his hefd,..A bord was festen plate, Þar-on was þe titel [*Laud* tytle] writen, Thoru þe rede o sir pilate. **1382** WYCLIF *Mark* xv. 26 And the title of his cause was writun, Jhesus of Nazareth, kyng of Jewis. *a* **1400–50** *Alexander* 5071 Þis titill was of twa tongis tane out & grauen. **1535** COVERDALE *Isa.* xix. 19 An aulter.. with this title ther by: Vnto the Lorde. **1592** KYD *Sp. Trag.* IV. iii, Hang up the Title: Our scene is Rhodes. **1611** BIBLE *John* xix. 20 This title then read many of the Iewes:..and it was written in Hebrewe, and Greeke, and Latine. **1645** EVELYN *Diary* 23 Jan., On the bases of one of whose columns is this odd title: Fl. Eugenius Asellus C.C. Præf. Urbis V.S.I. reparavit.

†**b.** An inscribed pillar, column, tombstone, or the like. (A literalism of transl.) *Obs. rare.*

**1388** WYCLIF *Gen.* xxxv. 14 Iacob reiside a title [*gloss.* ether memorial] of stoonys [1382 a stonen signe of worship], in the place where ynne God spak to hym. *Ibid.* 20 Iacob bildide a title [*v. r.* memorial; 1382 a signe of preysing] on the sepulcre of hir. **1609** BIBLE (Douay) *ibid.*

**2.** The descriptive heading of each section or subdivision of a book (now only in law-books); the formal heading of a legal document; hence, †a part or division of a book, or of a subject (*obs.*).

**13..** *Cursor M.* 29530 (Cott.) Þir pointes of cursing haf i.. scortly samen laid, And þar-for sett in titles sere þat þou may lightloker þam here. **1387** TREVISA *Higden* (Rolls) I. 329 For to come to cleer and ful knowleche of þat lond, þese tyteles þat folweþ oponeþ þe way...*De situ Hiberniæ locali... De ejus quanto et quali* [etc.]. **1494** FABYAN *Chron.* IV. lxviii. 46 In the firste Chapitre of the .ix. tytle of his Werke called Summa Antonini. **1581** MULCASTER *Positions* xl. (1887) 228 The fifth title of the fifth booke, *De Magistris*. **1714** *Fr. Bk. of Rates* 412 His Majesty judged it proper to comprehend all the said Regulations and the Merchandizes therein expressed under one Title. **1781** GIBBON *Decl. & F.* xvii. II. 62 *note*, The first twenty-eight titles of the eleventh book of the Theodosian Code are filled with the circumstantial regulations on the important subject of tributes. **1847** WHARTON *Law Lex.*, *Title*, a general head, comprising particulars, as in a book.

†**b.** app. Subject, matter. *Obs.*

**13..** *Propr. Sanct.* (Vernon MS.) in Herrig's *Archiv* LXXXI. 97/18 Whon Petur saih þat disciple Speke to Ihesu of þat title. *c* **1330** R. BRUNNE *Chron.* (1810) 8 Henry of Huntyngton testimons þis title. Þe kyngdom of Westsex, he sais, it was not litelle.

†**c.** *transf.* A document; a writing, a letter. *Obs.*

*c* **1330** [see 7 d]. *a* **1400–50** *Alexander* 1044 Þare tuke he tribute þat tyme þe titill recordis. *Ibid.* 3566 His tulkis of þis titill quen þai þe tenour herd, Þan ware þai sory of þa sawes.

**3.** The name of a book, a poem, or other (written) composition; an inscription at the beginning of a book, describing or indicating its subject, contents, or nature, and usually also giving the name of the author, compiler, or editor, the name of the publisher, and the place and date of publication; also = TITLE-PAGE. Also, the designation of a picture or statue.

*a* **1340** HAMPOLE *Psalter* cxix. 1 Þe tityll of þese fyfeten psalmys is sange of degres. *c* **1430** LYDG. *Min. Poems* (Percy Soc.) 163 Go litel bille withoute title or date. **1560** DAUS tr. *Sleidane's Comm.* 29 He bad that the titles of the Bokes should be read and shewed. **1651** HOBBES *Leviath.* III. xxxiii. 200 In titles of Books, the subject is marked, as often as the writer. **1737** BRACKEN *Farriery Impr.* (1757) II. 137 Bad Books, which are more beholden for their Sale to the Booksellers than to the Author, by reason the first had a better Knack at tossing up a Title. **1863** DICKENS *Lett.* (1880) II. 194, I have found a first-rate title for your book. **1891** C. CREIGHTON *Epidemics in Brit.* I. Pref. 5 The title and contents-table of this volume will show sufficiently its scope.

**b.** *Bookbinding.* The label or panel on the back of a book giving a brief title (*binder's title*).

**1891** in *Cent. Dict.*

**4.** A descriptive or distinctive appellation; a name, denomination, style.

*c* **1383** in *Eng. Hist. Rev.* Oct. (1911) 741 Clerkis moun haue temporal godis bi title of almese. **1523** LD. BERNERS *Froiss.* I. cxci. 227 Thus in euery parte was the realme of Fraunce warredde in the tytell of the kynge of Nauer. **1549** LATIMER *3rd Serm. bef. Edw. VI* (Arb.) 76 He was taken and naped in the head wyth the title of an heretique. **1560** DAUS tr. *Sleidane's Comm.* 61 b, Ye are farre vnworthy of the name of Christians. Whiche tytle..you doe vsurpe to your selues. **1621** SIR G. CHAWORTH in Kempe *Losely MSS.* (1836) 444, I will..beseech you to accept well of my service, under yᵉ titles of faythfull and obedyent. **1756** C. LUCAS *Ess. Waters* II. 59 Some [are] dignified with the venerable titule of physician. **1774** GOLDSM. *Nat. Hist.* (1862) II. VII. iii. 205 To believe this bird to be the same with that described by Wicquefort, under the title of the Alcatraz. **1840** A. JOLLY *Sunday Serv.* 114 This bears the title of Bethphany or the Manifestation in the house. **1861** PALEY *Æschylus* (ed. 2) *Agam.* 946 *note*, But the title Ζεὺς Τέλειος, the god of marriage.., was perhaps a distinct attribute.

**5.** An appellation attaching to an individual or family in virtue of rank, function, office, or attainment, or the possession of or association with certain lands, etc.; *esp.* an appellation of honour pertaining to a person of high rank; also *transf.* (*colloq.*) a person of title (quot. 1900).

**1590** SPENSER *F. Q.* II. vii. 43 Every pillour decked was full deare With crownes, and Diademes, and titles vaine, Which mortall Princes wore. **1610** HOLLAND *Camden's Brit.* (1637) 570 From the death of this young Earle of Warwicke this title lay asleepe. **1613** SHAKS. *Hen. VIII*, II. i. 140, I dare not make my selfe so guiltie, To giue vp willingly that Noble Title Your Master wed me to. **1709** STEELE *Tatler* No. 73 ¶ 9 A gay young Gentleman, who has lately succeeded to a Title and an Estate. **1761** HUME *Hist. Eng.* xxvii. II. 132 Lord Herbert obtained the title of Earl of Worcester. **1837** LOCKHART *Scott* vii, Alexander Fraser Tytler, afterwards a Judge of the Court of Session by the title of Lord Woodhouselee. **1900** HOWELLS in *Scribner's Mag.* Sept. 375/2 He [Lowell] was sorry that he could not have me meet some titles who..found pleasure in my books.

**6.** That which justifies or substantiates a claim; a ground of right; hence, an alleged or recognized right. Const. with *inf.*, or *to*, *in*, *of* the thing claimed.

*a* **1300** *Cursor M.* 20874 (Cott.) His nam es giuen til him o ded, And titel [*Trin.* titul] of his might o mede. **1377** LANGL. *P. Pl.* B. XVIII. 291 We haue no trewe title to hem for þorwgh tresoun were þei dampned. **1412–20** LYDG. *Chron. Troy* IV. 973 Oure comynge hider,..Had no grounde founded on resoun Nor cause roted on no titel of riȝt. **1502** *Ord. Crysten Men* (W. de W. 1506) III. iii. 144 Vagabondes,..the whiche haue no good tytle for to begge. **1625** BURGES *Pers. Tithes* 36 Hee..would manifestly declare.. his iust Title to Bedlam. **1718** *Free-thinker* No 12 ¶ 7 He can have no farther Title to the Esteem of his Fellow-Subjects. **1822** SCOTT *Nigel* Introd. Epist., The..evidence ..brought forward to prove Sir Philip Francis's title to the Letters of Junius, seemed at first irrefragable. **1827** — *Surg. Dau.* i, All farther title of interference seemed now ended. **1868** GLADSTONE *Juv. Mundi* Pref. (1869) 11, I have not the same title to expect obedience.

**7.** *spec. Law.* Legal right to the possession of property (esp. real property); the evidence of such right; title-deeds.

[**1292** BRITTON II. xvi, Title de fraunc tenement pora hom aver en plusours maneres.] *c* **1420** LYDG. *Siege Thebes* 2005, I shal lette hym,..That he shal not be title of no bond, Reioysse in Thebes half a foot of londe. *c* **1440** *York Myst.* xxxii. 347 What title has þou þer-to? is it þyne awne free? *c* **1460** FORTESCUE *Abs. & Lim. Mon.* ix. (1885) 130 Off mariages, purchasses, and oþer titles. **1481** *Cov. Leet Bk.* 490 The title to be examyned be ij persones there chosen afore þe lordez. **1552** HULOET, Tytle of the eldest chyld in enheritaunce, *primogenia*. **1583** *Exch. Rolls Scot.* XXI. 575 Andro Murray .. demittit and overgaif his heretable rycht and titill of the kyngis park..in the kyngis majesties favouris. **1628** COKE *On Litt.* I. 345 b, Euery right is a title, but euery title is not such a right for which an action lieth. **1672** *Cowell's Interpr.*, *Title of Entry*, is, when one is seised of Land in Fee, makes a Feoffment thereof on condition, and the condition is broken; after which the Feoffor hath title to enter into the Land, and may do so at his pleasure. **1765** BLACKSTONE *Comm.* I. iii. 184 Yet while I assert an hereditary, I by no means intend a *jure divino* title to the throne. **1832** AUSTIN *Jurispr.* (1879) II. 1011 Properly speaking the Vendor's title merely consists of the fact by which his right was acquired. **1858** LD. ST. LEONARDS *Handybk. Prop. Law* v. 29 Where difficulties arise in making out a good title, you should not take possession of the estate until every obstacle is removed.

†**b.** *In title*, of a benefice: (Held) as one's proper cure; opposed to *in commendam* (see COMMENDAM). *Obs.*

**1579** *Reg. Privy Council Scot.* III. 177 Upoun the vacance of ony prelacie the kirkis thairof salbe disponit to qualifiit ministeris in titill. **1658** BRAMHALL *Consecr. Bps.* viii. 186 It may be objected, that he held all these Bishopricks as a Commendatory, not in Title.

†**c.** An assertion of right; a claim. *Obs.*

**1534** WHITINTON *Tullyes Offices* I. (1540) 17 It may be vnderstande that no warre is iust, except that which after iust tytle demaunded is done, or els it be denounced or proclaymed before. **1685** WOOD *Life* 12 Aug. (O.H.S.) III. 157 The King of England hath now an army..raised upon defeat of Monmouth, under pretence to keep him in safety against false titles and fanaticks. **1701** SWIFT *Contests Nobles & Com.* Wks. 1755 II. I. 40 An eagerness after employments in the state was looked upon by wise men, as the worst title a man could set up.

†**d.** A title-deed. *Obs. rare.*

*c* 1330 R. Brunne *Chron.* (1810) 248 Þei brouht..Þe olde chartres and titles, Þat wer in Abbays hand. 1579 Tomson *Calvin's Serm. Tim.* 140/1 If that man should make a stewes of that house..and shuld go and make away the titles and writings to depriue the maister of his house.

**8.** *Eccl.* A certificate of presentment to a benefice, or a guarantee of support, required (in ordinary cases) by the bishop from a candidate for ordination.

1377 Langl. *P. Pl.* B. xi. 281–3 Þe title Þat [ye] take ordres by telleth ȝe ben auaunced;..For he Þat toke ȝow ȝowre tytle shuld take ȝow ȝowre wages. 1530 *Knaresborough Wills* (Surtees) I. 26 He shall have his tytle and singynge geyr boughte at the coste of my sayd wyeffe. 1588 J. Udall *Demonstr. Discipl.* (Arb.) 24 The ordination that is made without a title, let it be voide. 1597 Hooker *Eccl. Pol.* v. lxxx. § 9 Euery man lawfully ordained must bring a Bow which hath two strings, a Title of present Right, and another to prouide for future possibilitie or chance. 1720 White *Monit. Clergy Peterbo.* i. 16 If you retain any Curate, to whom you did not give a Title for Orders. 1845 Stephen *Comm. Laws Eng.* (1874) II. 661 By the canon law no person shall be admitted into holy orders without a title. 1860 J. Gardner *Faiths World* s. v., If a bishop ordain any one without sufficient title, he must keep and maintain the person whom he so ordains with all things necessary until he can prefer him to some ecclesiastical living.

**9.** *Eccl.* Each of the principal or parish churches in Rome, the incumbents of which are cardinal priests; a cardinal church (Cardinal *a.* 6).

In L. *titulus*. Bingham (*Antiq.* vii. i. 10) explains the name from the fact that the churches gave a 'title of cure or denomination' to the presbyters who were set over them. See *Catholic Dict.* s. v.

*c* 1460 *Oseney Reg.* 111 Guale, By the mercy of god, title of Seynte Marteyne preste cardinall, popis legat. 1597 Hooker *Eccl. Pol.* v. lxxx. § 9 The Fathers at the first named oratories and houses of prayer titles. 1642 Jer. Taylor *Episc.* § 43 [He] appointed twenty-five titles or parishes. 1706 tr. *Dupin's Eccl. Hist. 16th C.* II. v. 95 Formerly the Sacraments were administred only in these Titles (i. e. Churches so called) and those that presided in them were called Cardinals (if we believe Paurinius) because they were the chief and the principal of those that resided upon these Titles. 1833 Waddington *Hist. Ch.* xxiii. 509 Even the Titles of the Cardinals, abandoned by those who derived their dignities from them, were left without roof, or gates, or walls. 1854 Cdl. Wiseman *Fabiola* (1855) 186 'He distributed the titles'; that is, he divided Rome into parishes, to the churches of which he gave the name of 'title'.

**10.** *Assaying*, etc. The expression in carats of the degree of purity of gold (= F. *titre*).

1873 E. Spon *Workshop Receipts* Ser. i. 364/1 Jewellers solder with gold of a lower title than the article to be soldered. 1879 F. Vors *Bibelots & Curios* 58 Carat.. is only an imaginary weight; the whole mass is divided into twenty-four equal parts, and as many as there are of these that are of pure gold constitute the *title* of the alloy.

**11.** *attrib.* and *Comb.*, as *title-leaf*, *-plate*, *-scroll*, *-trouble*; *title-mad* adj.; obj. and obj. gen., as *title-holder*, *-hunter*, *-hunting* sb. and adj., *-licenser*, *-seeker*, *-sifter*; **title-banner**, a banner on which a title is inscribed; **title-essay**, an essay, usually the first in a volume, giving name to the whole collection; so **title-poem**, **title-story**; **title letter, type**, type of a size and kind used in printing titles; **title-part, -rôle**, the part in a play, etc., from which the title of the piece is taken; **title-sheet**, the first sheet of a book, one page of which bears the title. See also Title-deed, -page.

1880 J. Ross *Hist. Corea* x. 332 The bearer of the *Title-banner advances forward one step. 1902 *Daily Chron.* 7 Feb. 3/4 'Love's Cradle, and Other Papers'. The *title-essay deals with the age of the troubadours. 1904 *Daily News* 27 May 12 Scotland Yard..has got its eye on some of the bogus *title-holders. 1797 Mrs. M. Robinson *Walsingham* II. 203 She was a perpetual *title-hunter. 1893 Goldw. Smith *Ess. Quest. Day* 156 Anybody can guess what titles and *title-hunting in colonial society must beget. 1597 Shaks. *2 Hen. IV*, i. i. 60 Yea, this mans brow, like to a *Title-leafe, Fore-tels the Nature of a Tragicke Volume. 1771 Luckombe *Hist. Print.* 225 To those..we will give the name of *Title Letters; considering that [they]..are used in Titles of Books. *Ibid.* 279 As for Four Lines Pica, and Five Lines Pica, they best become the name of Title Letters. 1673 [R. Leigh] *Transp. Reh.* 26 The gentleman might be advanced to the office of *title-licenser. 1886 W. J. Tucker *E. Europe* 237 The *title-mad and pocket-filled Jewesses. 1762–71 H. Walpole *Vertue's Anecd. Paint.* (1786) III. 107 The *title-plate to a history of Oxford designed by him, and engraved by White in 1674. 1893 *Dict. Nat. Biog.* XXXIII. 440 The *title-poem..is followed by smaller pieces. 1886 *Boston* (Mass.) *Globe* 15 Aug., A grand production of 'The Gladiator', with that talented young tragedian..in the heroic *title role. 1900 *Westm. Gaz.* 30 July 10/1 Mr. Chatterton revived the play [Byron's 'Manfred'] (in 1863) with Phelps in the title-rôle. 1864 Tennyson *Aylmer's F.* 656 Heaps of living gold that daily grow, And *title-scrolls and gorgeous heraldries. 1771 Luckombe *Hist. Print.* 392 The Signature of the *Title-sheet, viz. great A;..we put Little a to the first sheet after the Title sheet. 1615 J. Stephens *Ess. & Charac., Informer*, Let him be a *tytle-sifter and he will examine lands as if they had committed high treason. 1887 *Lit. World* 23 July 229/2 The *title-story, 'Ivan Ilyitch,' alone could be pronounced repulsive. *a* 1619 Fletcher *Wit without M.* i. i, How bravely now I live, ..how free from *title-troubles!

**Title** (təi·t'l), *v.* Forms: see prec. [f. Title *sb.*, or perh. a. OF. *titler* (now *titrer*), ad. L. *titulāre*; from the latter directly came the rarer form Titule.]

**I.** †**1.** *trans.* To write, set down, or arrange under titles or headings; to make a list of; to set down in writing; to inscribe, record, chronicle. *Obs.*

1340 Hampole *Pr. Consc.* 9535 Now haf I..Fulfilled Þe seven partes of Þis boke Þat er titeld byfor, to have in mynde. *c* 1430 *Brut* 458 There were many iourneyes done in dyuers partyes of Fraunce and Normandy, which be not titled in this boke. 1459 *Test. Ebor.* (Surtees) II. 227 The chapell, in the which ar titled of olde tyme the Obitts of the auncetors. *c* 1552 Thomas *Pilgrim* (1861) 44 Some of the selfsame commissioners found of their own wives titled among the rest.

**2.** To furnish with a title; to give a (specified) title to (a book or other literary composition); also, to inscribe the title on (a book or the like); to write the heading or headings to or in (a manuscript book or account). Cf. Entitle *v.* 1.

1387 Trevisa *Higden* (Rolls) III. 351 Helmand seeÞ Þat Plato usede to title his bookes by names of his maistres. 1387–8 T. Usk *Test. Love* ii. i. (Skeat) l. 99 This worke have I writte; and to thee, tytled of Loves name, I have it avowed in a maner of sacrifyse. 1570 T. Wilson tr. *Demosthenes* (title-p.) His fower Orations titled expressely & by name against king Philip of Macedonie. 1653 W. Ramesey *Astrol. Restored* 37 They had but small reason to title that weak piece, *Judicial Astrology Judicially condemned.* 1721 Wodrow *Corr.* (1843) II. 600, I wrote to Mr. M'Ewen to pack up eight copies for you, and send to Borrowstounness, bound and titled. 1824 Miss Ferrier *Inher.* lvi, It was titled 'Correspondence with Colonel F. Delmour—Private, No. 1'. 1894 R. H. Davis *Eng. Cousins* 167 In the Order of the Day these questions now appear numbered and titled.

†**3.** To dedicate (by name); to assign, ascribe.

*c* 1386 Chaucer *Pars. T.* ¶ 820 Thise ordred folk ben specially titled to god. 1390 Gower *Conf.* II. 84 The gold is titled to the Sonne, The mone of Selver hath his part. 1399 *Rolls of Parlt.* III. 452/1 Reservyng evermore to Hymself that Dignite of his Grace and of his Mercy as it longes to his real Estate, and that no man title that to hym bot atte his owne will. 1584 Peele *Arraignm. Paris* ii. ii, And think queen Juno's name, To whom old shepherds title deeds of fame, Is mighty.

†**4.** **a.** To inscribe as a title. *Obs. rare.* **b.** To attach as a label. *Obs. rare*⁻¹. Cf. Title *sb.* 1.

*a* 1400–50 *Alexander* 5640 And Þar was grauyn in Þos gomes with grekin letteris, And titild in Þe tried names of his twelfe princes. [1588: see Titule *v.*] 1642 Milton *Apol. Smect.* Wks. 1851 III. 251 By the intrapping autority of great names titl'd to false opinions.

†**5.** = Entitle *v.* 4. *Obs.*

13.. *Cursor M.* 22093 (Cott.) Sua sal Þe feind him Þis Chese him stede o birth iwise, Þat best es titeld [*v. rr.* stiglid, stighlid, ordeyned] til his stall. 1633 G. Herbert *Temple, Offering* ii, Yet one, if good, may title to a number; And single things grow fruitfull by deserts.

**II.** **6.** To designate by a certain name, indicative of relationship, character, office, etc.; to speak of or describe as, term, style, name, call. Cf. Entitle *v.* 2.

1590 Greene *Orl. Fur.* (1599) 30, I scorne to title her with daughters name. 1610 Bp. Hall *Apol. Brownists* xxx, The presbyters chose one out of their number in euery citie whom they titled their bishop. *c* 1610 Rowlands *Terrible Battell* 43 One builds a house, and titles that his owne, Giues it his name, to keep his name in sound. 1667 Milton *P. L.* xi. 622 That sober Race of Men, whose lives Religious titl'd them the Sons of God. *a* 1734 North *Lives* (1826) I. 399 These his lordship had..titled..' Impudent Assertions'. 1827 Pollok *Course T.* ii. 19 That little orb..was made for man, And titled Earth. 1864 Bryce *Holy Rom. Emp.* vi. (1890) 86 Their sovereign titled himself king of the Franks.

**b.** To endow or dignify with a title of rank; to speak of by a title of dignity.

1746 [see Titled]. 1760–72 H. Brooke *Fool of Qual.* (1809) IV. 154 He is titled below his merits; it was for an emperor that nature intended him. 1868 Browning *Ring & Bk.* i. 779 How title I the dead, alive once more? 1895 *Outing* (U.S.) XXVI. 362/2 When old Bajee Rao died the British Government refused to title 'Nana Sahib', and decided that the titular dignity had ceased.

**Titled** (təi·t'ld), *ppl. a.* [f. prec. + -ed¹.] Having or furnished with a title, esp. a title of rank.

1746 Francis tr. *Horace, Epist.* i. i. 82 Yet want a little of the Sum, that buys The titled Honour, and you ne'er shall rise Above the Croud. 1790 Mme. D'Arblay *Diary* Aug., The titled part of the females were admitted to the Royal table. 1885 *Civilian* 3 Jan. 141/2 The authorities might conveniently adopt and issue some general form of titled Survey Book suitable for use in distillery stations. 1901 J. E. H. Thomson *Rev. Mod. Crit.*, etc. 19 An untitled Psalm follows a titled one. 1909 *Blackw. Mag.* Jan. 25/2 A younger scion of a titled family.

**Title-deed** (təi·t'l,dīd). A deed or document containing or constituting evidence of ownership. Also *fig.* (Most common in *pl.*)

*a* 1768 Erskine *Inst. Law Scot.* i. vii. § 24 Tutors..ought carefully to preserve the title-deeds of the minor's estate. 1830 Praed *Poems* (1865) I. 185 Your agent steals your title-deeds. 1855 Macaulay *Hist. Eng.* III. 393 It was..desirable that..this titledeed by which the King held his throne and the people their liberties, should be put into a strictly regular form. 1865 Kingsley *Herew.* ii, They..got to themselves lands by the title-deed of the sword. 1889 Jessopp *Coming of Friars* v. 224 He lost all his title deeds, the evidences and charters whereby he held his little estate.

**Titleless** (təi·t'l,lės), *a.* [f. Title *sb.* + -less.] Having no title, destitute of a title (in various senses of Title *sb.*); untitled.

*c* 1386 Chaucer *Manciple's T.* 119 Right so bitwixe a titlelees tirant And an Outlawe or a theef errant The same I seye ther is no difference. 1607 Shaks. *Cor.* v. i. 13 He was a kinde of Nothing, Titlelesse, Till he had forg'd himselfe a name a'th'fire Of burning Rome. 1881 *Blackw. Mag.* May 619/1 The titleless condition of her father. 1888 *Vicary's Anat.* App. ii. 121 In the Cofferer's (titleless) Account, 79/3, 1 Oct. 1560 to 30 Sept. 1561, Vicary's Annuity is on the back of leaf 7 from end.

**Ti·tle-page.** The page at (or near) the beginning of a book which bears the title. Also *fig.*

*a* 1613 Overbury *Charac., Meere Scholer* Wks. (1856) 89 In a word, he is the index of a man, and the title-page of a scholler,..much in profession, nothing in practice. 1630 *R. Johnson's Kingd. & Commw.* A ij b, Our Title page acknowledges him to be that famous Botero, the Italian. 1651 Jer. Taylor *Serm. for Year* II. v. 57 Repentance is a great volume of duty; and Godly sorrow is but the frontispiece or title page. 1703 J. Tipper in *Lett. Lit. Men* (Camden) 307 Upon the Title-page is the Picture of the Queen in copper. 1742 Young *Nt. Th.* viii. 333 The world's all title-page, there's no contents. 1830 D'Israeli *Chas. I*, III. vii. 154 He had insisted..that his name should appear in the title-page.

**Titler** (təi·tləɹ). Also 6–7 tytler, 7 titeler. [app. f. Title *sb.* + -er¹.]

†**1.** One who claims or asserts a legal title. *Obs.*

1594 Parsons *Confer. Success.* ii. Pref. Q iv b, His meaning was..to lay down sincerly what..might iustly be alleaged in fauour or disfauour of euery tytler. 1599 Daniel *Musophilus* xix, Leuell'd with th' earth, left to forgetfulnesse; Whilst titlers their pretended rights decide. 1613 Daniel *Hist. Eng.* (1626) 169 John Comyn his cousen German being a Titeler himself. 1634 *Two Noble Kinsmen* v. iii. 83 The two bold Tytlers, at this instant are Hand to hand at it.

**2.** Trade name for a truncated cone of refined sugar.

1858 Simmonds *Dict. Trade, Titlers*, a description of refined sugar. 1859 *Times* 24 Oct. 9/4 Conical loaves of sugar called titlers. 1891 *Ibid.* 9 Oct. 9/3 Titlers, 18s. 9d.; crushed f.o.b., barrels, 20s.

**Titleship** (təi·t'lʃip). *rare.* [f. Title *sb.* + -ship.] Possession of a title; right of ownership.

1780 S. J. Pratt *Emma Corbett* (ed. 4) I. 154 An impertinent old fellow..who presumes upon a sum of money and a paltry piece of titleship. 1876 G. Meredith *Beauch. Career* ii, The pretensions of the town to read things for themselves, documents, titleships, rights and the rest.

**Titling** (ti·tliŋ), *sb.* [f. Tit *sb.*³ + -ling. Cf. Norw. dial. *titling* a small size of dried stockfish (Aasen), Icel. *titlingr* sparrow: see Biörkman *Indog. Forsch.* XXX. 269.]

†**1.** A small size of stockfish. *Obs.*

1386–7 *Letter Bk. H. Lond.* lf. 212 b, De qualibet centena de alio Stokfissh vocat' Croplyng et Titlyng. 1545 *Rates of Customs* c vj, Stokfish called cropling the last v. li...Stokfysshe called tytling the last l.s. 1660 *Act Chas. II*, c. 4 *Sched. Rates Inwards*, Stockfish *voc.* Cropling, Lubfish, Titling. 1818 Scott *Rob Roy* ii, 'Stockfish—Titling—Cropling—Lubfish. You should have noted that they are all, nevertheless, to be entered as titlings.—How many inches long is a titling?'..' Eighteen inches, sir'. 1858 Simmonds *Dict. Trade, Titling*, an old Customs name for stockfish.

**2.** Name for various small birds. **a.** The hedge-sparrow. (Now only *Sc.* and *north. dial.*) **b.** = Titlark. **c.** (*rarely*) = Titmouse.

1549 *Compl. Scot.* vi. 39 The titlene follouit the goilk, ande gart hyr sing guk guk. 1552 Elyot, *Curruca*.., a litle byrd, which hatcheth and bryngeth vp cuckow byrdes. It is supposed to be an hedge sparowe, or rather a titlyng. 1611 Cotgr., *Argatile*, a kind of titling, or titmouse. 1655 Moufet & Bennet *Health's Impr.* (1746) 191 The Cuckow ever lays her Egg in the Titling's Nest. 1802 G. Montagu *Ornith. Dict.*, Warbler, Hedge,..Provincial. Titling. Dunnock...Commonly called Hedge Sparrow. 1831 *Ibid.* 246 Hedge Chanter...Provincial..Dunnock, Dick-Dunnock, Titling. *Ibid.* 512 Titling. A name for the Meadow Pipit and Hedge Chaunter. 1808 Jamieson s. v. *Titlene*, When two persons are so intimate that the one obsequiously follows the other, it is said, 'They are as grit as the gowk and the titlene'. 1829 E. Elliott *Vill. Patriarch* iv. vii, Hark, how the titling whistles o'er the road! 1852 F. O. Morris *Brit. Birds* II. 166 Rock Pipit. Rock Lark. Sea Lark. Field Lark...Sea Titling. 1882 J. Hardy in *Proc. Berw. Nat. Club* IX. No. 3. 429 He had frequently..watched young cuckoos while being fed by titlings (*Anthus pratensis*). 1885 Swainson *Provinc. Names Birds* 45 Meadow Pipit..also Titling, or Tit

**Titling** (təi·t'liŋ), *vbl. sb.* [f. Title *v.* + -ing¹.] The action of Title *v.* †**a.** A writing down under titles or heads; an abstract. *Obs.* **b.** The giving of a title; a naming.

1465 J. Paston in *P. Lett.* II. 219 He must..see his billes of payment, and take therof a titelyng. 1523 Fitzherb. *Surv.* xix. 34 b, He must begyn at a certayne place..and there to make his tytelynge where he beginneth. 1894 H. Gamlin *Romney* 148 The titling of the engraving came about this way.

**Titly**, variant of Titely *adv.*

**Titmal.** *local.* A titmouse, esp. the blue titmouse (*Eng. Dial. Dict.*).

**Ti·tman.** *local U.S.* [f. Tit *sb.*³] The smallest pig, etc. of a litter; hence, a man who is stunted physically or mentally; a dwarf, a 'croot'.

1849 Thoreau *Week on Concord, Friday* 401 We titmen are only able To catch the fragments from their table. 1854 — *Walden, Reading* (1884) 117 We are a race of tit-men, and soar but little higher in our intellectual flights than the columns of the daily paper.

**Titmouse** (ti·t,maus). Pl. titmice (-məis). Forms: α. 4 titemose, 4–6 titmose, 5 tyte-, tetmose, tytmase, 6 tytmus. β. 6 tytmouse, (6–7 tytti-, tittimous(e, 7–9 titty-), 6– titmouse. [ME. *titmōse*, f. Tit *sb.*³ 3 + Mose *sb.* a titmouse. In the 16th c., when *mose* had long been obsolete as an independent word, and in *titmose* had become stressless (cf. the form *tytmus*), it was interpreted as *mouse*, with pl. *titmice*. The smallness and quick mouse-like movements of the common species probably aided the corruption. *Titty-mouse* was app. a childish or rustic adaptation.]

**1.** A bird of the genus *Parus* or family *Paridæ*, comprising small active birds, of which numerous species are distributed over the northern hemisphere, several being common in Britain: see 2. (Now commonly shortened to *tit*: see TIT *sb.*[3] 3.)

α. *c* 1325 *Gloss. W. de Bibbesw.* in Wright *Voc.* 165 (Fr.) *Musenge*, a titemose. *c* 1400 LYDG. *Flour Curtesye* 57 The sely wrenne, the titmose also. *c* 1425 *Voc.* in Wr.-Wülcker 640/28 *Nomina auium...Hic frondator*, tytmase. *c* 1440 *Promp. Parv.* 494/2 Tytemose, bryd, *frondator*. *c* 1475 *Pict. Voc.* in Wr.-Wülcker 762/32 *Hec agredula*, a tetmose. *c* 1537 *Thersytes* in *Four O. Pl.* (1848) 82 The tothe of the tytmus. 1570 LEVINS *Manip.* 149/3 Titmose.

β. 1530 PALSGR. 281/2 Tytmouse a byrde, *musangere*. 1573–80 BARET *Alv.* T 271 A Tittimous bird, *fringillago*. 1576 GASCOIGNE *Compl. Philomene* 26 Sometimes I wepe To see Tom Tyttimouse, so much set by. 1606 SYLVESTER *Du Bartas* II. iv. III. *Magnif.* 705 Finch, Linot, Tit-mouse, Wag-tail (Cock & Hen). 1655 MOUFET & BENNET *Health's Impr.* (1746) 191 Titmice are of divers Shapes with us in England. 1688 R. HOLME *Armoury* II. 243/1 The Bird Cole-Mouse..we in our Countrey call Tittimous or Mop. 1796 MORSE *Amer. Geog.* II. 259 A little species of titmouse. 1872 COUES *N. Amer. Birds* 80 The Titmice compose a natural and pretty well defined group.

**2.** With qualification, denoting various species of *Parus* or of the family *Paridæ*, as

**Black-cap** or **black-headed titmouse**, any species having black feathers on the head, as the COAL-TIT (*Parus ater*), the American CHICKADEE (*P. atricapillus*), or the *marsh-titmouse*; **blue t.**, *P. cæruleus*, also called BLUE-CAP or NUN; **coal t.**, *P. ater* (see COAL-TIT); **crested t.**, *Parus* (*Lophophanes*) *cristatus*, or any species of the sub-genus *Lophophanes*; **fen t.** = *marsh t.*; **great t.**, *Parus major*, also called OX-EYE; **long-tailed t.**, *Acredula caudata*; **marsh t.**, *Parus palustris*; **penduline t.**, *Ægithalus pendulinus* (see PENDULINE 1).

1609 Great titmouse [see COALMOUSE]. 1611 COTGR., *Mesange à la longue queuë*, the long-tayled Titmouse. 1668 CHARLETON *Onomast.* 90 *Parus Cristatus*, the Crested, or Juniper Titmouse. *Ibid.*, *Parus Palustris*..the Black Cap, or Fen-Titmouse. 1674 RAY *Collect.*, *Eng. Birds* 87 The black-headed Titmouse: *Parus ater*. *Ibid.*, The Marsh Titmouse: *Parus palustris*. *Ibid.* 88 The blew Titmouse: *Parus cæruleus*. 1713 DERHAM *Phys.-Theol.* I. i. (1714) 5 *note*, I made..Experiments in compressed air,..one with the Great Titmouse, the other with a Sparrow. 1774 G. WHITE *Selborne* xl, The titmouse, which early in February begins to make two quaint notes, like the whetting of a saw, is the marsh titmouse. *Ibid.* xli, The blue titmouse or nun is a great frequenter of houses, and a general devourer. *Ibid.*, The blue, marsh, and great titmice will, in very severe weather, carry away barley and oat straws from the sides of ricks. 1858 KINGSLEY *Misc.*, *Winter-gard.* I. 146 That flock of long-tailed titmice, which were twinging and pecking about the fir-cones.

**b. Bearded titmouse**, a small bird (*Panurus biarmicus*), of doubtful affinity, frequenting reed-beds; also called *reed-pheasant*.

1848 [see *reed-pheasant*, REED *sb.*[1] 14]. 1896 NEWTON *Dict. Birds* 969 The so-called 'Bearded Titmouse',..has habits wholly unlike those of any of the foregoing, and certainly does not belong to the Family *Paridæ*.

**3.** *fig.* A small, petty, or insignificant person or thing. Also *attrib.*

1596 NASHE *Saffron-Walden* Wks. (Grosart) III. 197 Noddy Nash,..his Apostrophe Sonnet, and tynie titmouse Lenuoy, like a welt at the edge of a garment. 1623 MIDDLETON *More Dissemblers* III. i, You can keep a little tit-mouse page there. 1680 OTWAY *Caius Marius* v. xi, *Nurse.* Wake her? Poor Titmouse. 1691 WOOD *Ath. Oxon.* II. 446 In.. Sept. 1658..the Titmouse Prince called Richard was inaugurated to the Protectorate.

‖ **Titoki** (*tīˈtōki*). [Native Maori name.] A New Zealand tree, *Alectryon excelsum*, N.O. *Sapindaceæ*, producing tough, crooked timber, and bearing panicles of reddish flowers, with leaves like those of the ash. Also called New Zealand Oak and New Zealand Ash. Also *attrib.*

1845 E. J. WAKEFIELD *Adv. in N. Z.* II. xii. 317 The berry of the titoki tree might also be turned to account. 1872 DOMETT *Ranolf* xvi. 253 The youth, with hands beneath his head, Against a great titoki's base.

**Titrate** (tiˈtreⁱt), *v. Chem.* [f. F. *titre-r* in same sense (f. *titre* title, qualification, fineness of alloyed gold or silver; in *Chem.*, proportioning of the fixed weight of a reagent which a given volume of a liquid contains in solution): see -ATE[3] 6.] *trans.* To ascertain the amount of a constituent in (a mixture, or (less usually) a compound) by volumetric analysis; i. e. by adding to a solution thereof of known proportion, a suitable reagent of known strength, until a point is reached at which reaction occurs or ceases.

1870 G. E. DAVIS in *Eng. Mech.* 4 Mar. 605/2 In titrating iron solutions, the ferrocyanide is not used. 1872 WATTS *Dict. Chem.* VI. 154 It is easy by means of the latter to titrate sulphuric, oxalic, or any other acid with perfect certainty. 1899 CAGNEY *Jaksch's Clin. Diagn.* i. (ed. 4) 4 Tauszk weighs the blood used, and titrates with tropæolin or litmus.

So **Tiˈtrated** *ppl. a.* = F. *titré*: see quot. Also **Tiˈtrate** *a. rare*, titrated.

1863 *Intell. Observ.* III. 457 Titrated solutions are thus named from the French, and signify their having a definite strength, or power, so that the action of precipitation or otherwise exerted by a given quantity is readily capable of arithmetical expression, and thus indicates the quantity of the substance acted upon. 1881 *Nature* 6 Oct. 552/1 Determination of phosphoric acid by titrated liquors, by M. Perrot. 1885 *Athenæum* 11 July 54/1 Dr. R. Dubois's apparatus for applying anæsthetics composed of titrate mixtures of chloroform and air was described on June 22nd..before the Academy of Sciences.

**Titration** (titrēˈʃən). [n. of action f. prec.: see -ATION.] The action or process of titrating; volumetric analysis. Also *attrib.*

1864 WEBSTER, *Titration*, the process of analysis by means of standard solutions. 1868 WATTS *Dict. Chem.* V. 849 *Titration.* See *Analysis*, *volumetric* (I. 254 [dated 1863: word not used there]). 1872 *Ibid.* VI. 154 Titration of Compound Ethers. 1877 W. THOMSON *Voy. Challenger* I. i. 26 The amount of baryta neutralized is then ascertained by titration. 1899 CAGNEY *Jaksch's Clin. Diagn.* vii. (ed. 4) 377, 80 cc. of the titration fluid, i. e. sulpho-cyanide, was used. 1900 *Jrnl. Soc. Dyers* XXI. 4 The formation..as shewn by Bernthsen by titration, has now been proved by gravimetric analysis.

‖ **Titre, titer** (tīˈtəɹ). [a. F. *titre*: see TITRATE.] The fineness of gold or silver; in *Chem.* the strength of a solution as determined by titration.

1839 URE *Dict. Arts* 858 The French rule for finding the par of a foreign gold coin,..is to multiply its weight by its standard or titre. 1903 *Amer. Chem. Jrnl.* Mar. 188 The solution was kept cooled to 15°. One cc. was removed at intervals (5 cc. in all), and the 'immediate' titer was found to gradually decrease from its original value of 6·4 to 1·2 in about one-half hour, the total active oxygen content.. remaining the same.

**Ti-tree.** The cabbage-tree of New Zealand, *Cordyline*: = TI.

(Also confused with TEA-TREE 2 and erroneously used as a name of species of *Melaleuca*.)

1890 W. COLENSO in *Trans. New Zeal. Inst.* XXIII. 486 (Morris) In these plains stand a number of cabbage-trees, the ti-trees of the Maori. 1912 J. H. MAIDEN (Dir. Bot. Gdns., Sydney) *Let.* 20 Aug., The name Ti-tree belongs to New Zealand *Cordyline*. For nearly 30 years I have endeavoured by precept and example to stamp out the name Ti-tree for Australian Tea-trees, but the error is full of vitality.

**Titrimetry** (titriˈmĭtri). *Chem.* [f. F. *titre*: see TITRATE *v.* and -METRY.] = TITRATION. So **Titrimeˈtric** *a.*, of or pertaining to titrimetry.

1891 M'GOWAN tr. *E. von Meyer's Hist. Chem.* vi. 365 The application of permanganate of potash to the estimation of iron by Margueritte in 1846, and, more particularly, Bunsen's process with equivalent solutions of iodine and sulphurous acid..are landmarks in the history of 'titrimetry', which soon after this began to rank alongside of gravimetric analysis. 1902 I. K. PHELPS in *Amer. Jrnl. Sc.* Dec. 440 The Titrimetric Estimation of Nitric Acid. 1904 *Ibid.* Mar. 201 A method for the titrimetric estimation of nitric acid or nitrates. ..It consisted, briefly, in the measurement of the amount of ferrous salt oxidized in the reduction of the nitric acid to nitric oxide by an excess of ferrous sulphate in the presence of hydrochloric acid.

**Tit-tat-toe**: see TIT *sb.*[2] 3. **Titte**, obs. f. TIT.

**Titted**, dial. form of TEATED *a.*, having teats.

† **Tittee**, obs. var. TEETEE[1], a kind of monkey.

1756 P. BROWNE *Jamaica* 489 The Tittee. This creature is very small...The head is bare about the ears and eyes.

† **Tiˈtter**, *sb.*[1] *Obs. rare.* [Derivation unascertained.] Some kind of weed found in cornfields; perh. a wild vetch (strangle-tare, tine).

1573 TUSSER *Husb.* (1878) 109 The titters or tine Makes hop to pine. *Ibid.* 113 From wheat go and rake out the titters or tine, If eare be not foorth, it will rise againe fine.

**Titter** (tiˈtəɹ), *sb.*[2] [f. TITTER *v.*[1]] The act of tittering; a stifled laugh, a giggle.

1728 MORGAN *Algiers* II. v. 314, I do not think I ever can forget it: for it so often sets me on the Titter. 1777 MME. D'ARBLAY *Early Diary* 7 Apr., He kept a continual titter among the young ladies. 1874 BURNAND *My Time* xvii. 144 Irrepressible titters among those of the audience most remote from the stage.

**b.** *transf.* A sound as of tittering; a rustling.

1856 BRYANT *Gladness Nat.* iv, There's a titter of winds in that beechen-tree.

**Titter** (tiˈtəɹ), *v.*[1] [app. echoic: cf. Sw. dial. *tittra* to giggle (Rietz); but perh. related to TITTLE *v.*[1]] *intr.* To laugh in a suppressed or covert way (often as a result of nervousness, or in affectation or ridicule); to giggle.

*a* 1619 FLETCHER *Wit without M.* IV. ii, I could so titter now and laugh. 1657 [see TITTERING *vbl. sb.*]. 1706 PHILLIPS (ed. Kersey), To *Titter*, to giggle, or laugh wantonly. 1748 SMOLLETT *Rod. Rand.* xix, She went away tittering. 1792 A. YOUNG *Trav. France* 117, I observed him several times playing off that small sort of wit, and flippant readiness to titter, which, I suppose, is a part of his character. 1838 DICKENS *Nich. Nick.* xxvii, Upon which Mrs. Nickleby tittered, and Sir Mulberry laughed, and Pyke and Pluck roared. 1864 KNIGHT *Passages Work. Life* I. v. 221 The young women tittered when the old clerk indulged in his established joke.

**b.** *trans.* To utter or say with suppressed laughter.

1787 *Minor* I. viii. 28 No, it shall never be tittered about as at the last races. 1838 DICKENS *Nich. Nick.* ix, 'Never mind me', tittered Miss Squeers.

Hence **Titteraˈtion** *nonce-wd.*, tittering.

1754 RICHARDSON *Grandison* (1781) V. xliii. 276 The holding up of a straw will throw me into a *titteration*.

**Titter** (tiˈtəɹ), *v.*[2] Now *dial.* Forms: 5–7 **titer**, 7 **tyter, tytter, tetter**, 8–9 **titter**. [ME. *titer*, implied in *titering*; = ON. *titra* to shake, shiver, OHG. *zittarôn* (G. *zittern*):—OTeut. **titrôjan*; not found outside Teutonic. Cf. TEETER.]

**1.** *intr.* To move unsteadily, as if about to fall; to totter, reel; to sway to and fro.

*c* 1374 [see *tittering* below]. *a* 1618 RALEIGH *Seat Govt.* (1651) 60 So would the other [*i.e.* Kings' Crowns] easily tytter were they not fastened on their heads, with the strong chains of Civil Justice and Martial Discipline. 1644 G. PLATTES in *Hartlib's Legacy* (1655) 198 Then the floor of the sellar will rise up, and tetter and swim like a bog-mere. 1798 FRERE & CANNING *Loves Triangles* I. 26 in *Anti-Jacobin* 16 Apr. (1852) 107 Fair sylphish forms.. Wave the gay wreath, and titter as they prance. 1904 *Eng. Dial. Dict.* s. v., (Worc.) Take care, the table titters.

**2.** *intr.* To see-saw. See also TITTER-TOTTER.

*a* 1825 FORBY *Voc. E. Anglia*, *Titter*, to ride on each end of a balanced plank. Otherwise '*titter-cum-totter*'. 1854 MISS BAKER *Northpt. Gl.*, *Titter*, to ride on a balanced plank.

Hence **Tiˈttering** *vbl. sb.*, the action of tottering or swaying; unsteady movement; *fig.* hesitation, vacillation; *ppl. a.* that totters or sways about.

*c* 1374 CHAUCER *Troylus* II. 1695 (1744) (Campsall MS.) In titeryng and pursuyte and delayes The folk deuyne at waggynge of a stre. 1661 K. W. *Conf. Charac.*, *Juryman Rustick* (1860) 37 Then he gallops a titering pace home. 1739 J. SPENCE *Let.* 23 Dec., in *Academy* 20 Feb. (1875) 191/3 So full of tittering and uncertainty in his carriage.

**Tiˈtter**, *adv.* Now only *north. dial.* Also 3 **titer**, 4 **tyttar**, 4–5 **-er**, 7–8 **tider**. [Comparative of TITE *adv.*, with shortened vowel; cf. *rather*, *latter*, *elder*, *utter*. Cf. ODa. *tidre* more quickly, sooner, compar. of *tit* (Kalkar IV. 338).]

More quickly; sooner, earlier.

*a* 1300 *Cursor M.* 22481 (Edin.) Titer sal tai rin on grund þan firslauht dos quen it es stund. 13.. *E. E. Allit. P.* C. 231 He [Jonah] watz no tytter out-tulde þat tempest ne sessed. *c* 1460 *Towneley Myst.* viii. 293 Go, say to hym we wyll not grefe, Bot thay shall neuer the tytter gang. 1674 RAY *N. C. Words* s. v. *Astite*, *Tide* in the North signifies soon, and *tider* or *titter* sooner. 'The tider..you come, the tider you'll go'. 1684 G. MERITON *Yorks. Dial.* 287 (E.D.S.) He had come titter..if he had knawn. 1874 WAUGH *Chimney Corner* (1879) 8 It brings 'em down, titter or latter,—as how strung they are.

**b.** More readily, more willingly, sooner, rather.

13.. *Cursor M.* 28120 (Cott.) And titter wald i lesyng make þan man my worde vn-treu to take. 1375 BARBOUR *Bruce* II. 518 Þai chesyt tyttar with þaim to ta Angyr and payn, na be þaim fra. *c* 1440 *Alphabet of Tales* 428 He grauntyd vnto þaim..at he wulde furste tytter take þe charge of þe empyre rather þan þe wurschup þeroff. 1724 in *Ramsay's Tea-t. Misc.* (1733) I. 63, I had titter die than live wi' him a year. 1807 R. ANDERSON *Cumberld. Ball.*, *Aul Hollow Tree* v, Far titter than wear them, She'd burn them or tear them. 1855 ROBINSON *Whitby Gloss.* s. v., 'I would titter go than stay'.

**c.** ellipt. *The titter up*, the one that is up sooner or first of two. *north. dial.*

1787 GROSE *Provinc. Gloss.* s. v., *Tider up caw*, let him that is up first call the others. 1790 MRS. WHEELER *Westmld. Dial.* (1821) 112 We set dawn that titter up sud coe tudder up neisht mornin. 1876 *Whitby Gloss.* s. v., 'T' titter up t' sprunt mun ower [= hover] a bit': the first up the hill must wait awhile.

**Titter**, dial. form of TETTER.

**Titterer**[1] (tiˈtərəɹ). [f. TITTER *v.*[1] + -ER[1].] One who titters or laughs restrainedly; a giggler.

1828 *Craven Gloss.*, *Titterer*, a laugher. 1866 GEO. ELIOT *F. Holt* iv, He was too shortsighted to notice those who tittered at him—too absent from the world of small facts and petty impulses in which titterers live.

† **Titterer**[2], obs. variant of TITTLER[1], a tatler.

1377 LANGL. *P. Pl.* B. xx. 297 And made pees porter to pynne þe ȝates Of alle taletellers and tyterers [*v. rr.* titeleris, tutelers; C. XXIII. 299 titereres, *v. r.* titeris] in ydel.

**Tiˈttering**, *vbl. sb.*[1] [f. TITTER *v.*[1] + -ING[1].] The action of TITTER *v.*[1]; giggling.

1657 THORNLEY tr. *Longus' Daphnis & Chloe* 129 The winking, nodding, laughing and tittering that was between them. 1759 DILWORTH *Pope* 124 This story..was the cause of so much tittering, wherever her ladyship went. 1833 D. MACMILLAN in Hughes *Mem.* iii. (1882) 50 The everlasting tittering and smirking is loathsome.

**Tiˈttering**, *ppl. a.*[1] [f. as prec. + -ING[2].] That titters; giggling, laughing with suppressed mirth; characterized by such laughter.

1748 SMOLLETT *Rod. Rand.* lv, A whisper circulated at our expence..accompanied with many..tittering observations. 1802 MAR. EDGEWORTH *Moral T.* (1816) I. viii. 62 Young tittering ladies. 1879 SALA *Paris herself again* (1880) II. xxiii. 338 A group of tattling and tittering..sight-seers.

Hence **Tiˈtteringly** *adv.*

1831 *Examiner* 355/1 'The naughty man', as he will be titteringly styled. 1892 G. HAKE *Mem. 80 Years* xxvii. 86 They had to smile titteringly as well as to listen.

**Tittering**, *vbl. sb.*[2] and *ppl. a.*[2]: see TITTER *v.*[2]

**Titter-totter** (tiˈtəɹ,tǫˈtəɹ), *sb.* (*adv.*) Now *dial.* Also 9 **titter-a-tauter, titter-cum-totter**, etc.: see *Eng. Dial. Dict.* [Reduplication from stem of TITTER *v.*[2] or TOTTER *v.*]

**1.** The pastime of see-saw. Also, a see-saw.

1530 PALSGR. 282/1 Tytter totter, a play for chyldre, *balenchoeres*. 1607 R. C[AREW] tr. *Estienne's World of Wonders* 266 He played with a little boy at titter-totter. 1611 in COTGR. s. v. *Hausse*. 1801 STRUTT *Sports & Past.* IV. i. § 21 We may add another pastime well known with us by the younger part of the community, and called Titter-Totter. 1846 WORCESTER, Tetter-totter [erroneously referred to Strutt]. 1887 W. RYE *Norfolk Broads* xi. 95 We..tried quoits, and 'tittem-a-tauter', as the natives call the pastime of see-saw.

†**2.** One who totters or reels. *Obs.*

*a* **1700** B. E. *Dict. Cant. Crew, Titter-totter*, who is upon the Reel, at every jog, or Blast of Wind. **1785** GROSE *Dict. Vulg. Tongue, Titter tatter*, one reeling, and ready to fall at the least touch.

**B.** *adv.* In a tottering manner; unsteadily; also *fig.* hesitatingly, waveringly.

**1725** BAILEY *Erasm. Colloq.* 35 Don't stand titter, totter, first standing upon one Foot and then upon another. **1762** CHURCHILL *Ghost* Poems 1767 II. 85 Having, as usual, said his pray'rs, Go titter, totter, to the stairs. **1828** *Craven Gloss.*, *Titter-totter*, in a wavering state, on the balance. **1889** *N. W. Linc. Gloss.* (ed. 2), *Titter-totter*, (1) in a state of unstable equilibrium; (2) in hesitation of mind, or wavering.

Hence **Ti·tter-to·tter,** etc. *v.*, *intr.* to see-saw.

*a* **1825** in FORBY *Voc. E. Anglia.* **1864** in WEBSTER. **1897** *Q. Rev.* Jan. 146 They titter-cum-totter. **1901** *Daily News* 12 Jan. 6/4 How few really know East Anglian dialect... What does 'tittymatauterin' mean?.. It simply means 'see-sawing'. **1907** *Black Cat* June 25 [He] called back to the figure teter-tottering with the bowing of the log it rode.

†**Tittery** (ti·təri). *slang. Obs.* Also 8 **titery,** (**tityre**). [app. f. TITTER *v.*² + -Y, lit. unsteady, unstable, tottering.] A slang name for gin.

**1725** G. SMITH *Compl. Body Distilling* I. 49 Geneva hath more several and different names and titles, than any other liquor that is sold here: as double Geneva, royal Geneva, celestial Geneva, Tittery..and has gain'd..universal applause. **1730** BAILEY (folio), *Tityre* or *Tittery*, a Nickname given to the Liquor..called Geneva.., prob. because it makes the Drinkers merry, laugh, and titter. **1751** GORDON *Another Cordial* II. 14 A Shop where Titery, Quorum, or Gin (call it by what name you will) is sold.

**Tittie,** variant of TITTY¹ and ³.

**Tittifill, Tittivate,** var. TITIVIL, TITIVATE.

**Tittish,** dial. form of TETTISH, TEATISH.

**1808** in JAMIESON.

**Tittle** (ti·t'l), *sb.* Forms: 4 **titil, -el,** 5 **ty-, titylle, -tille, titelle,** 5–9 **title,** 6 **tittil, -yl, tytle, tyttle,** 6– **tittle.** [ME. *titel, -il*, orig. the same word as TITLE, but with a special sense developed in late L. and Romanic (see below), and retaining the short *i* of L. *titulus*. The spelling *tittle* is found 1535; *title* is occasional after 1600.

For the mediæval and Romanic senses of L. *titulus* akin to Eng. *tittle*, cf. *a* **1286** BALBI *Catholicon*, 'Titulus etiam dicitur nota quæ causa brevitatis apponitur dictionibus'; also *a* **800** *Corpus Chr. L. & Ags. Gloss.* (Hessels 1890) E 242 Epigramma, titulum; 243 Epigramma, abreuiata scriptura; *a* **1200** NECKAM *De Utensilibus* (Wright *Vocab.* 1857, 117) Glosa enim per subbrevitatem et compendiosam per apices [*Fr. gloss* titles] scribi debet. Diez also cites Sp. *tilde*, Cat. *titlla*, Pg. *til*, 'little stroke, accent, esp. the mark over ñ', also Wallachian *titlę*, 'the circumflex', and Prov. *titule*, 'the dot over *i*', as representatives of the L. word in the modern Romanic langs. As *apex* was used by the Latin grammarians for the accent or mark over a long vowel, *titulus* and *apex* became to some extent synonymous; hence Wyclif's use of *titil, titel*, to render L. *apex*.]

**1.** A small stroke or point in writing or printing.

**a.** Orig. rendering L. *apex* 'point, tip', applied in classical L. to any minute point or part of a letter, also to the mark over a long vowel, as *á*, later also to a line indicating an abbreviation. More recently applied also to the Spanish *tilde* or circumflex over *ñ*, formerly to the cedilla under *ç*. By extension, any stroke or tick with a pen.

The literal notion of a point of a letter passed over to that of the smallest point of that which was written or prescribed. This took place already in late Heb. with the word קוֹץ *qôṣ*, lit. 'thorn, prick', represented in Greek by κεραία 'horn, projecting point', and in L. by *apex*, in Wyclif translated *titil*: see the quots.

**1382** WYCLIF *Matt.* v. 13 Til heuen and erthe passe, oon i [*gloss* that is leste lettre], or titil [**1388** o lettir or o titel; *Vulg.* apex], shal nat passe fro the lawe, til alle thingis be don. — *Luke* xvi. 17 Forsothe it is liȝter heuene and erthe to passe ouer, than o titil [TINDALE (1526), *Geneva*, 1611 title; TIND. (1534), *Great* tytle; COVERD. tittle (*Matt.* v. 18 tyttle), *Rheims* tittle] falle fro the lawe. *c* **1440** *Promp. Parv.* 494/2 Tytylle, *titulus, apex.* **1483** *Cath. Angl.* 389/2 A Tytille (*A.* Titylle), *titulus, apex, epigrama.* **1570** LEVINS *Manip.* 124/15 A Tittil, *apex.* **1636** JACKSON *Creed* VIII. xxvii. § 3 The words..answered punctually and identically to every apex or title of S. Matthew's quotation or paraphrase. **1648** GAGE *West Ind.* 216 This letter ç, or c with a tittle under it, is pronounced like s. **1712** F. T. *Shorthand* 4, I in the beginning of a Word is express'd by a small Tittle or touch of the Pen. **1911** W. CAVEN in *Fundamentals* IV. 61 'Tittle', literally little horn or apex, designates the little lines or projections by which Hebrew letters, similar in other respects, differ from each other.

**b.** The dot over the letter *i*; a punctuation mark; a diacritic point over a letter; any one of the Hebrew and Arabic vowel-points and accents; also, a pip on dice.

**1538** ELYOT, *Punctus, seu punctum*, a poynte or tytle. **1552** HULOET, Tytle or prycke in letters, *punctus.* **1556** WITHALS *Dict.* (1568) 64 b/1 *Canicula*, is the litle blacke title in the dyse,..as sise, sinke, catre, trey. **1665** HOOKE *Microgr.* 121 The smallest black spot or tittle of Ink. **1666** TILLOTSON *Rule Faith* II. v. Wks. 1742 IV. 648 The transcribing..of such myriads of words, single letters and tittles or stops. **1676** MOXON *Print Lett.* 28 The Stem and Tittle of this j is made like i. **1783** MRS. DELANY in *Life & Corr.* Ser. II. (1862) III. 151 Yᵉ person said, 'yᵉ Dᵏ [of Marlborough] puts no tittles upon the i's'. 'O', says yᵉ Prince [Eugene], 'it saves his Grace's ink'. **1785** TRUSLER *Mod. Times* III. 92 Only take care to put the tittles to your i's, and the crosses to your t's. **1888** DOUGHTY *Arabia Deserta* II. 43 [He knows] his jots and his titles (the vowel points in their skeleton writing), and he knows nothing else.

†**c.** A name for the (usually) three dots (∴), following the letters and contractions, in the alphabet on horn-books, where it is usually followed by *Est Amen*; so that *tittle est Amen* came to be used for 'the end or conclusion'. *Obs.*

(See cuts 166–168 in Tuer *Hist. Horn-book* II.)

*a* **1548** HALL *Chron., Rich. III* 35, I then..began to dispute with my selfe, little considerynge that thus my earnest was turned euen to a tittyl not so good as, estamen. **1594** NASHE *Terrors Night* Wks. (Grosart) III. 251 This is the Tittle est amen of it. **1596** — *Saffron Walden* G iv b, A per se, con per se, tittle, est, Amen!..why he comes vppon thee (man) with a whole Horn-booke. **1602** *How a Man may chuse gd. Wife* III. i. E ij b, In processe of time I came to & [*printed* e] percee, and com perce, and tittle; and then I got to a, e, i, o, u. **1630** T. JOHNSON *New Bk. New Conceits* A v, In old time they vsed three prickes at the latter end of the Crosse row,..which they caused children to call tittle, tittle, tittle: signifying that as there were three pricks, and those three made but one stop, euen so there were three Persons, and yet but one God.

†**d.** A dot-like anther in a flower. *Obs. rare.*

**1578** LYTE *Dodoens* II. xlv. 203 There hange also sixe smal thrommes, or short threds, with litle titles or pointed notes, like as in the Lillies.

**2.** *fig.* The smallest or a very small part of something; a minute amount. Often in phrase *jot or tittle* (from sense 1 a): see JOT *sb.*¹

[Cf. **1382** in 1 a.] *c* **1400** *Apol. Loll.* 34 So is no man worþi to mak a letter or title of his to go by vnfillid. **1555** W. WATREMAN *Fardle Facions* App. 314, I neither wille penne any thyng other wise..ne adde..any title of myne owne. **1581** J. BELL *Haddon's Answ. Osor.* 41 Images crept into the Churche by title and litle. **1610** G. FLETCHER *Christ's Vict.* I. xxxvi, Thy love? he hath no title to a tittle. **1730** T. BOSTON *Mem.* x. (ed. Morrison) 303 This makes me to account the better of these titles of the law, as divine. **1820** SCOTT *Let. to Ld. Montagu* 22 Feb., in *Lockhart*, I owe much more to his father's memory than ever I can pay a tittle of. **1884** F. TEMPLE *Relat. Relig. & Sc.* i. (1885) 9 Every tittle of the evidence is valued.

**b.** *To a tittle*, with minute exactness, to the smallest particular, to a T.

**1607** BEAUMONT *Woman Hater* III. iii, I'll quote him to a tittle. **1700** BP. PATRICK *Comm. Deut.* xxviii. 53 This was fulfilled to a tittle by Vespasian and his son Titus. **1805** FESSENDEN *Democr.* (1806) II. 81 That I might suit them to a tittle, Have stretch'd the truth—and lied a little. **1855** BROWNING *Fra Lippo Lippi* 26 He's Judas to a tittle, that man is!

Hence †**Ti·ttled** *a. Obs. rare*, marked by tittles or vowel-points; having the Semitic vowel-points inserted, pointed: cf. POINT *v.*¹ 3 c.

**1684** N. S. *Crit. Enq. Edit. Bible* iv. 28 There is none of them that make use of Tittl'd Vowels.

**Tittle** (ti·t'l), *v.*¹ Now *dial.* or *colloq.* Forms: 4–7 **title,** 5 **tytyll,** 6 **tytle, tyttle,** 8– **tittle.** [Of obscure origin; hardly known before 1400; app. onomatopœic. In use somewhat earlier than TATTLE, but app. treated as a parallel form of that vb. with lighter vowel expressing lighter sound; cf. the reduplicated TITTLE-TATTLE. Its relation to the earlier TUTEL, TOTEL, in the same sense, is difficult to determine.] *intr.* and *trans.* To speak in a whisper or in a low voice, to whisper; also, to tell or utter by way of tattle or gossip; *esp.* † to whisper in the ear of, to tell (a person) confidentially (*obs.*): cf. TICKLE *v.*²

**1399** [implied in TITTLER¹]. *c* **1450** *Mankind* 550, in *Macro Plays* 21, I xall go to hys ere and tytyll þer in. **1525** LD. BERNERS *Froiss.* II. xxiv. 60 They tytled the prince euer in his eare, and entysed hym to haue made warre. *a* **1548** HALL *Chron., Hen. VII* 22 He caused diuerse to inculcate and put in her hed & tyttle in her eare, that the mariage made with Maximilian was of no strength. *c* **1610** SIR J. MELVIL *Mem.* Pref. (1735) 21, I should have..titled in the Queen's ear that her rebellious subjects should have been exemplarily punished. **1887** J. SERVICE *Dr. Duguid* xii. 77 They were a' tittlin' thegether and talkin' in this form.

Hence **Ti·ttling** *vbl. sb.* and *ppl. a.*

**13..** *S. Eng. Leg.* (MS. Bodl. 779) in Herrig's *Archiv* LXXXII. 339/169 ȝif þis titlyng come al to þe emperour no man ne may don him non help. **1565–73** COOPER *Thesaurus* s. v. *Argutus, Meretrix arguta*, a harlot full of wordes: a titlyng harlot. **1596** DALRYMPLE tr. *Leslie's Hist. Scot.* II. (S.T.S.) I. 134 Ferleg..was steired vpe throuch titling of sum of the courteouris in his eires. **1785** BURNS *Holy Fair* ix, Here sits a raw o' tittlin jades.

**Tittle** (ti·t'l), *v.*² *dial.* Also 9 **tiddle.** [perh. in origin a dial. var. of TICKLE *v.*; also locally confused with TIDDLE *v.* Cf. also L. *titillāre* to tickle; but influence of this is doubtful.] *trans.* and *intr.* = TICKLE *v.* in various senses. Hence **Ti·ttling** *vbl. sb.*, tickling; †**Ti·ttler** (titler), one who or that which tickles, a tickler.

**13..** *Gaw. & Gr. Knt.* 1726 Þer he [the fox] watz þreted, & ofte þef called, & ay þe titleres at his tayl, þat tary he ne myȝt. **1579** HAKE *Newes Powles Churchyard* vii. F viij b, The countrey maides that come from far, as straungers to the towne: Whome still the Trottes doe tittle so, that straight all shame layde downe, They yelde them selues as captiues queanes, vnto some whorish caue. *a* **1825** FORBY *Voc. E. Anglia, Tittle, v.* to tickle. **1866** J. G. NALL *Gt. Yarmouth & Lowestoft* 693 A girl says 'I 'ont be tiddled by you nor no one'. **1877** *N. W. Linc. Gloss., Tittling*, tickling. **1881** *Leicestersh. Gloss., Tittle*, v. a., var. pron. of 'tickle'. **1888** J. HARTLEY *Clock Alm.* 8 (E.D.D.) Her nose end's sewer to tittle like mad. **1900** *Daily News* 6 June 6/3 The..vendors of 'tiddlers' sold them quickly—for the 'tiddled' naturally wanted to 'tiddle' others in turn. [See also TIDDLER².]

**Tittle,** var. TIDDLE *v.*, to fondle; to trifle.

**Tittlebat** (ti·t'lbæt). Also **-back.** A variant of STICKLEBACK, of childish origin. Hence **Tittleba·tian** *a. nonce-wd.*, pertaining to tittlebats.

**1820** KEATS & HUNT *K.'s Wks.* (1889) III. 34 They..follow the fish into cool corners, and say millions of 'My eyes!' at 'tittle-bats'. **1837** DICKENS *Pickw.* i, There sat the man who had..agitated the scientific world with his Theory of Tittlebats. *Ibid.*, He had felt some pride when he presented his Tittlebatian Theory to the world. **1844** THACKERAY *Greenwich Whitebait* Misc. Ess. (1885) 430 A fresh dish of tittlebacks or gudgeons. **1869** H. S. LEIGH *Carols of Cockayne* 120 In this brook that flows lazily by I believe that one tittlebat dwells.

**Tittler**¹ (ti·tləɹ). Now *dial.* Forms: 4–5 **titeler, tituler,** 5 **titler,** (*Sc.* **titlar, tittillar**); 9 *dial.* **tittler.** [f. TITTLE *v.*¹ + -ER¹.] One who 'tittles' or tattles; a whisperer, tell-tale, gossip.

**1399** LANGL. *Rich. Redeles* IV. 57 Somme were tituleris and to þe kyng wente, And fformed him of foos þat good ffrendis weren. **14..** Titeleris [see quot. 1377 s. v. TITTERER²]. **1463** *Paston Lett.* II. 133 Prevy titlers and flaterers. *c* **1470** HENRYSON *Poems* (S.T.S.) III. 139 (*title*) Aganis haisty credence of titlaris. *Ibid.* 21 The tittillaris [*v. r.* tutelar] so in his eir [*MS.* heir] can [= gan] roun. **1904** *Eng. Dial. Dict.* (Warwicks.), *Tittler*, a babbler, a tell-tale.

**Tittler**², a tickler: see TITTLE *v.*²

**Tittle-tattle** (ti·t'lˌtæ·t'l), *sb.* Also 6 **tyttel tattyll,** 6–8 **title(-)tatle,** 7 **tittel tattel.** [A reduplicated compound of TATTLE *sb.*, expressing repeated and alternate action: cf. next.]

**1.** Talk, chatter, prattle; *esp.* empty or trifling talk about trivial matters, petty gossip.

(In quot. *a* 1529 perh. used advb.)

*a* **1529** SKELTON *Phyllyp Sparowe* 357, I played with him tyttel tattyll, And fed him with my spattyl, With his byll betwene my lippes. **1542** UDALL *Erasm. Apoph.* 226 Rhymerales..made muche tittle tattle nor would in no wyse lynne pratyng therof. **1573** G. HARVEY *Letter-bk.* (Camden) 106 'Tis but..fond womens title tatle. **1667** PEPYS *Diary* 28 June, After a great deal of tittle-tattle with this honest man, we to bed. **1768** TUCKER *Lt. Nat.* (1834) I. 176 To..be let into all the scandal and tittle tattle of the town. **1820** *Edin. Rev.* XXXIII. 309 The literary tittle-tattle of the age. **1893** LELAND *Mem.* I. 153 Inordinately given to knowing everything about everybody, and to 'tittle-tattle'.

**b.** with *a* and *pl.* An act or spell of petty talk; an item of small talk or gossip. Now *rare* or *Obs.*

**1570** T. WILSON tr. *Demosth.* 47 Every man devising one tittletattle or other, as his own vaine heade imagines. **1639** N. N. tr. *Du Bosq's Compl. Woman* II. 42, I see many..to give themselves to these tittle tattles of other folks matters. **1699** R. L'ESTRANGE *Erasm. Colloq.* (1711) 127 The Tittle-tattles of the Nuns.

†**2.** A habitual tattler, one given up to gossip; esp. a woman so addicted. *Obs.*

**1580** HOLLYBAND *Treas. Fr. Tong, Languarde*, a tittle tattle, a chatting dame. **1611** COTGR., *Babillarde*, a titletatle; a pratling gossip; a babling houswife; a chatting or chattering Minx. **1710** ADDISON *Tatler* No. 157 ¶ 13 Your Castanets or impertinent Tittle-Tattles, who have no other Variety in their Discourse but that of talking slower or faster.

**3.** *attrib.* or as *adj.* Characterized by or addicted to tattling; gossiping.

**1719** *Freethinker* No. 150 ¶ 6 Would not an English-Man be provoked to hear the same Person cry up the Softness, the Politeness, the Copiousness of that Tittle-Tattle Language, and find Fault with the Roughness and Barrenness of his own. **1768** MME. D'ARBLAY *Early Diary* (1889) I. 14 Such a set of tittle-tattle, prittle-prattle visitants! Oh dear! **1780** — *Diary* May, Bath is as tittle-tattle a town as Lynn. **1866** MRS. GASKELL *Wives & Dau.* xvi, In such a tittle-tattle place as Hollingford.

**Ti·ttle-ta·ttle,** *v.* [A varied reduplication of TATTLE *v.*; cf. prec. and LG. *titel-tateln.*] *intr.* To chatter, prate, talk idly; to gossip.

**1583** BABINGTON *Commandm.* ix. (1637) 92 Any woman, when she hath met with her gossip, to tittle tattle, to the slander of another. **1611** SHAKS. *Wint. T.* IV. iv. 248. **1691** SOUTHERNE *Sir A. Love* v. i, A good-natur'd, old merry fellow,..who can tittle-tattle and gossip in their families upon an ancient privilege. **1765** BICKERSTAFF *Accomplish'd Maid* I. ii, It does not become servants to be tittle tattling of their masters and mistresses affairs. **1848** THACKERAY *Let.* Oct., I should like to take another sheet and go on tittle-tattling, it drops off almost as fast as talking.

Hence **Ti·ttle-ta·ttling** *vbl. sb.* and *ppl. a.*; **Ti·ttle-ta·ttler,** one addicted to tittle-tattle, an idle talker, a gossip.

*a* **1586** SIDNEY *Arcadia* II. (Sommer) 163 You are ful of your tittle tattling of Cupid. **1600** W. WATSON *Decacordon* (1602) 37 But for anie other secret..they seldome or neuer impart it to these tittle tatlers. **1780** MME. D'ARBLAY *Diary* 6 Dec., His lady—tittle-tattling, monotonous, and tiresome. **1887** SMILES *Life & Labour* 343 It is better even to have a useless hobby than to be a tittle-tatler and a busybody.

**Tittup** (ti·tŏp), *sb.*¹ Chiefly *dial.* Also 8–9 **tit-up.** [app. echoic, from the sound of the horse's feet.]

**1.** A horse's canter; a hand-gallop; also, a curvet.

**1703** E. WARD *Lond. Spy* VI. (1706) 145 Citizens in Crowds ..all upon the Tittup, as if he who Rid not a Gallop was to Forfeit his Horse. **1710** — *Poet's Ramble* 6 With Whip and Spur, he might be beat-up, Into a Canterbury Tit-up. **1868** BROWNING *Ring & Bk.* IV. 322, I..Had held his bridle, walked his managed mule Without a tittup the procession through. **1882** *Lanc. Gloss., Titherup*, a hand-gallop. From the sound. Also called *tit-up.*

†**b.** *transf.* A cantering horse. *Obs.*

**1805** in *Essex Herald* 9 Apr. (1901) 8/2 Dianas also of the Chase,..some in riding habit, mounted on titups, others.. in gigs. *c* **1875** [Remembered in use in Westmorland].

**2.** An impudent or forward woman or girl; a hussy, a minx. [Cf. TIT *sb.*3 2.] *dial.*

1762 D. GARRICK *Farmer's Return fr. Lond.* 9 Some Tittups I saw, and they maade me to stare! [1901 F. E. TAYLOR *Folk-Speech S. Lanc.* (E.D.D.), *Titty-ups*, also.. *titty-haups*, a pert, forward girl.]

**3.** As *adv.* With a tittup; at a canter.

*a* 1764 R. LLOYD *Poet. Wks.* (1774) II. 82 Perhaps my muse..Which, slouching in the doggrel lay, Goes tittup all her easy way.

**4.** *On the tittup* (*dial.*), in a state of excitement; mentally upset.

1906 *Westm. Gaz.* 6 Oct. 2/2 He couldn't find it [the wedding ring]...Everything was at a standstill, and we was all on the titup.

†**Tittup**, *sb.*2 *Obs. rare*—1. In 6 titup(p. [f. vbl. phr. *tit up*, pull up, TIT *v.*1] The trigger of a cross-bow.

1536 BELLENDEN *Boece's Cron. Scot.* XI. x. (1541) 163/2 Als sone as ony man maid him to throw this apill out of the hand of the image, the wrying of the samyn drew all the tituppis of the crosbowis [*ed.* 1585 quarrels of the crossebowes] vp at anis, & schot at hym yt threw ye apill. [*orig.* quam primum quispiam pomum manu tractando loco etiam paulum moueret: expeditæ ballistarum chordę, catapultas in tractantem ingenti vi emitterent.]

**Tittup** (ti·tŏp), *v.* Also **titup**. [Goes with TITTUP *sb.*1] *intr.* To walk or go with an up-and-down movement; to walk in an affected manner; to mince or prance in one's gait; of a horse or other animal, to canter, gallop easily; also, to prance; hence of a rider, or one driving a vehicle; of a boat, to toss with abrupt jerky movements.

1785 in *European Mag.* (1786) IX. 176 Then tittup'd along with a light mincing step, Little Yoffer Van-Sploom—a well known demi-rep. 1844 J. T. HEWLETT *Parsons & W.* xxxix, A hare that came tit-upping by me. 1852 R. S. SURTEES *Sponge's Sp. Tour* li, [He] saw the horsemen titt-up-ing across a grass field. 1862 THACKERAY *Philip* viii, A magnificent horse dancing and tittuping. 1878 STEVENSON *Inland Voy.* 234 The Abstract Bagman tittups past in his spring gig. 1881 E. WARREN *Laughing Eyes* (1890) 26 The little dingy [a boat] tittuped over the swell. 1904 A. GRIFFITHS *50 Yrs. Publ. Serv.* 71, I can see him now tittupping over the heather on his fat grey pony.

Hence **Ti·ttuping** *vbl. sb.*

1833 *New Monthly Mag.* XXXVIII. 300 The appropriateness of the harmony itself sinks before the tittuping of an arpeggio bass. 1868 *Morn. Star* 30 Jan., For such poetic cantering, such tit-tupping of Pegasus in a rhythmic Rotten Row.

**Tittuping** (ti·tŏpiŋ), *ppl. a.* [f. prec. + -ING 2.] That tittups; bouncing, cantering, prancing; *transf.*, rollicking, lively; also, unsteady, rickety.

1796 *Campaigns* 1793-4 II. vii. 44 My pen glances off into titupping strains. 1809 THEO. JONES *Hist. Breckn.* II. 542 The poem concludes in such galloping tittuping rhymes as almost compel the reader to forget the merits the author certainly possesses. 1824 SCOTT *St. Ronan's* xiii, The 'Dear me's' and 'O laa's' of the titupping misses, and the oaths of the pantalooned or buckskinned beaux. 1895 MRS. B. M. CROKER *Village Tales* (1896) 76 They kept up a steady tittuping canter, raising a cloud of dust.

**Tittupy** (ti·tŏpi), *a. colloq.* [f. TITTUP *sb.*1 or *v.* + -Y.] Apt to tittup or tip up; unsteady, shaky.

1798 JANE AUSTEN *Northang. Abb.* ix, Did you ever see such a little tituppy thing in your life? There is not a sound piece of iron about it. 1865 MISS A. MANNING *Selvaggio* 189 'Shall we have a little sail?' 'Hum—I think not...I think the Petrel a tituppy little thing'. 1881 *Leicestersh. Gloss., Tittupy*, adj. unsteady; shaky; ricketty: often applied to furniture.

**Titty**1 (ti·ti). *Sc. colloq.* Also **tittie**. [perh. infantile pronunciation of *sissie*, sister; ? associated with TIT *sb.*3] A sister; a young woman or girl. Cf. KITTY 1.

*Tittie and billie*, sister and brother (cf. BILLY 1 3); hence *to be tittie-billie*, to be closely associated as brother and sister, or as brothers or sisters.

1725 RAMSAY *Gentle Sheph.* III. ii, That clattern Madge, my titty. 1790 BURNS *Tam Glen* i, My heart is a-breaking, dear Tittie! Some counsel unto me come len'. 1818 SCOTT *Hrt. Midl.* v, 'Has she not a sister?' 'In troth has she—puir Jeanie Deans..; she was here greeting a wee while syne about her tittie'. 1825 JAMIESON s. v., Tam's a great thief, but Will's tittie-billie wi' him. 1896 J. LUMSDEN *Poems* 18 A band of billies And frisky titties.

**Ti·tty**2. [dial. or infantile var. of KITTY 2.] A kitten, a cat; pussy.

1821 CLARE *Vill. Minstr.*, etc. (1823) I. 165 Now she wails o'er Titty's bones With anguish deep. 1828 *Craven Gloss., Titty-pussy*, a cat. *c* 1880 *Northampt. Dial.*, Oh, mother, mother! titty is drinking the milk.

**Ti·tty**3. Also **tetty, tittie**. A dial. and nursery dim. of TEAT, the breast, esp. the mother's breast.

1746 *Exmoor Courtship* 376 (E.D.S.) Es wont ha' ma Tetties a grabbled zo. 1825 [see TEAT 1 *a*]. 1857 DUNGLISON *Med. Lex., Titty, mamma*, nipple. [See *Eng. Dial. Dict.* s. v.]

**Tittymeg** (ti·timeg). *U.S.* Also 8 **titymagg**, 9 **tittameg, tickomeg; attikimek, attihawmeg.** [From Amer. Indian: in Odjibway *atikameg*, Menominee *attaikummeeg*, Chippeway *adikumaig*: see quot. 1851.] A whitefish of Canadian and North American lakes, *Coregonus clupeiformis.*

1748 H. ELLIS *Hudson's Bay* 185 Called by the French, White Fish, but by the Indians and English, Titymagg. 1768 WALES in *Phil. Trans.* LX. 127 Fishermen up the river..brought us down plenty of pyke, mathoy, and tittymeg: these two last being fish peculiar to this country [Churchill River, Hudson's Bay]. 1851 SIR J. RICHARDSON *Arctic Search Exped.* xiv. II. 51 'White-fish', to which the Chippeways..have given the figurative appellation of 'reindeer of the waters', *Adikumaig.* 1879 D'ANVERS tr. *J. Verne's Fur Country* (1890) 21 Countless legions of tittamegs. 1905 A. HAGGARD *Bond of Sympathy* 120 Even attikimek, the whitefish, this year can no longer be captured in nets.

**Tittyry**: see TITYRE-TU.

**Titubancy** (ti·tiŭbănsi). *rare.* [ad. rare late L. *titubāntia*, f. *titubāre* to TITUBATE.] The condition of being titubant; unsteadiness, tipsiness.

(This and allied words all more or less affected.)

1800 COLERIDGE *Let. to W. Godwin* 3 Mar., Not that ..I felt, after I quitted you, any unpleasantness or titubancy. 1829 T. L. PEACOCK *Misfort. Elphin* xi, That amiable state of semi-intoxication which..sets the tongue ..tripping, in the double sense of nimbleness and titubancy.

**Titubant** (ti·tiŭbănt), *a. rare.* [ad. L. *titubānt-em*, pr. pple. of *titubāre* to TITUBATE.] Staggering, reeling, unsteady; *transf.* and *fig.* stammering; rollicking, tipsy; uncertain, hesitating, wavering.

1817 T. L. PEACOCK *Melincourt* v, Sir Oran's mode of progression being very vacillating, indirect, and titubant. 1836 *Fraser's Mag.* XIV. 204 Dryden's..frequently rollicking and titubant progress through the Æneid. 1875 *Anderida* II. iii. 52 His tongue was as titubant as his gait. 1880 F. HALL *Dr. Indoctus* 61 Not the titubant, perplexed, nerveless, and hide-bound English of half-educated, scruple-mongering, provincial pedantry.

Hence **Ti·tubantly** *adv.*, in a titubant manner, stammeringly.

1861 R. F. BURTON *City of Saints* v. 317 The discourse began slowly, word crept titubantly after word.

**Titubate** (ti·tiŭbeit), *v. rare.* [f. L. *tibubāt-*, ppl. stem of *titubāre* to stagger. (See note to TITUBANCY.)]

**1.** *intr.* To stagger, reel, totter, stumble; to rock, roll.

1575 LANEHAM *Let.* (1871) 24 His mare in hiz manage did a littl so titubate, that mooch a doo had hiz manhod to sit in his sadl, & too scape the foyl of a fall. 1715 tr. *Gregory's Astron.* I. (1726) I. 149 At least it [the Sun] ought to titubate or reel as it were, being sometimes attracted more this way, sometimes more that way, according as more Planets happen to come together on the same side. 1854 BADHAM *Halieut.* 530 As neither servants nor links were allowed, it was unpleasant to go titubating home in the dark. 1879 WEBSTER Suppl., *Titubate*, to rock, or roll, as a curved body on a plane.

**2.** *fig.* To stammer; to falter in speaking.

[Cf. Ovid. *A. A.* I. 598 titubat lingua.]

1623 COCKERAM, *Titubate*, to stammer in speaking. 1656 BLOUNT *Glossogr., Titubate*, .. by metaphor to stutter or stammer in speaking. 1820 L. HUNT *Indicator* No. 53 (1822) II. 6 His voice a little titubating with wine.

Hence **Ti·tubating** *ppl. a.*

1653 WATERHOUSE *Apol. Learn.* 29 But what became of this titubating..mountain of snow? 1899 *Allbutt's Syst. Med.* VII. 87 A titubating gait.

**Titubation** (titiŭbēi·ʃən). *rare.* [ad. L. *titubātiōn-em*, n. of action f. *titubāre* to TITUBATE. So F. *titubation* (16th c. in Godef. *Compl.*).] The action of titubating; staggering, reeling, tottering; unsteadiness in gait or carriage, *spec.* in *Path.*; *fig.* faltering, suspense, perplexity, embarrassment; also, † stammering, stuttering (*obs.*).

1641 R. DEY *Two Looks over Lincolne* 32 Gentle Reader, to avoyd titubations, correct these errors with a pen. 1650 S. CLARKE *Eccl. Hist., Lives Fathers* (1654) 590 He went on [with his Lecture] without the least..hesitation in his voice, or titubation of his tongue. 1710 W. HUME *Sacred Succession* 288 Stretches, or mutterings, or titubations of charity are not to be argued from. 1849 *Blackw. Mag.* LXVI. 106 To follow the titubations of Herr G——'s magic wand, which, in its uncertain route, would skip from Europe to Africa and back again. 1910 *Edin. Rev.* Apr. 442 The aimless and besotted titubations of a drunkard.

‖ **Titulado** (titulā·do), *sb. Obs.* [Sp., pa. pple. of *titular* to title; = L. *titulātus.*]

**1.** A titled Spaniard or Portuguese; a man of title.

1609 TUVILL *Vade-mecum* (1629) 16 Such as the puffe-past Tituladoe's of these our times. 1622 MABBE tr. *Aleman's Guzman d'Alf.* I. II. v. 133 Any Knight or Titulado. 1659 RUSHW. *Hist. Coll.* I. 77 Attended and served with Grandees and Tituladoes. 1751 *Affecting Narr. of Wager* 143 Accompanied by no less than a Brasilian Titulado.

**2.** A thing that has only a nominal existence.

1659 *Ant. Land-Mark betw. Prince & People* 15 Meer Tituladoes, Shaddows, or aiery Notions. 1679 V. ALSOP *Melius Inquir.* II. 310 Whilst they deck his Atchievements with Titulado's, useless and cumbersome Regalities,..for thus it has been ever the way of Church-men to sell shadows for substances.

Hence † **Titula·do** *v. Obs., trans.* to title, entitle; to decorate with a grandiose title.

1663 *Flagellum or O. Cromwell* (1672) 84 Cromwel was.. tituladoed with the Style of Lord Governor of Ireland.

**Titular** (ti·tiŭlăɹ), *a.* and *sb.* [ad. L. type **titulār-is*, f. *titul-us* TITLE: see -AR 1. Cf. F. *titulaire* (16th c.).]

**A.** *adj.* **1.** That exists or is such only in title or name, as distinct from *real* or *actual*; holding or bearing a title without exercising the functions implied by it; nominal, so-styled. (Cf. NOMINAL *a.* 4.)

*Titular bishop*, in R. C. Ch., a bishop deriving his title from an ancient see lost to the control of the Roman pontificate: cf. quot. 1885.

1611 SPEED *Hist. Gt. Brit.* VI. xli. § 2. 145 After hee had enioyed a Titular Soueraignty only eighty dayes. 1612 BREREWOOD *Lang. & Relig.* xvi. (1614) 133 Euer since then.. the Church of Rome, hath, and doth still create successiuely, imaginary or titular Patriarchs (without iurisdiction) of Constantinople, Antiochia, Ierusalem, and Alexandria. 1640 YORKE *Union Hon.* 22 Hee was invested tituler King of Sicile and Apulia. 1762-71 H. WALPOLE *Vertue's Anecd. Paint.* (1786) I. 58 Her mother the titular queen of Naples and Jerusalem. 1856 FROUDE *Hist. Eng.* (1858) II. viii. 247 Nothing remained of Strongbow's conquests save the shadow of a titular sovereignty. 1885 *Catholic Dict.* 797 His Holiness Leo XIII has..by a recent decision substituted the phrase 'Titular Bishop' for 'Bishop in Partibus Infidelium'. 1907 *Q. Rev.* Jan. 100 His titular successors never once visited their confiscated diocese.

**b.** With limiting words, as *but, mere(ly, only*, expressing entire absence of the reality.

1591 G. FLETCHER *Russe Commw.* (Hakl. Soc.) 44 They are but men of a titular dignitie,..of no power, authoritie, nor credit. 1681-6 J. SCOTT *Chr. Life* (1747) III. 36 To convince us that he is not a mere titular Deity. 1868 FREEMAN *Norm. Conq.* (1877) II. vii. 49 Recent events have abolished even the titular position of the city as the see of a Bishop.

**2.** Of, pertaining to, consisting of, or denoted by a title of dignity; also, having a title of rank, titled; bearing, or conferring, the appropriate title.

1611 SPEED *Theat. Gt. Brit.* (1614) Pref., Armes of the titular nobles. 1623 HEXAM *Tongue-Combat* 50 You finde them without traine, or pompe, or titular vanities. 1669 PENN (*title*) No Cross, no Crown; or several sober Reasons against Hat-Honour, Titular Respects, You to a Single Person, with the Apparel and Recreations of the Times. *a* 1704 T. BROWN *Praise Poverty* Wks. 1730 I. 97 A vain pride of birth and titular dignity. 1863 KINGLAKE *Crimea* (1876) I. vii. 103 So far as concerns official and titular rank [he] was one of the chief of the Czar's subjects.

**3.** Of or pertaining to a title or name; of the nature of or constituting a title (in various senses). *Titular character*, title-rôle.

1656 EARL MONM. tr. *Boccalini, Pol. Touchstone* (1674) 269 Upon such a titular occasion as this. 1659 PEARSON *Creed* (1839) 292 By the propriety of the punishment, and the titular inscription, we know what crime was then objected to the immaculate Lamb. 1771 LUCKOMBE *Hist. Print.* 390 They set the first line of a Titular Summary all in Capitals. 1889 *Daily News* 7 June 2/3 Madame Gargano in the titular character appeared to far better advantage than in 'Il Barbiere'.

**4.** From whom or which a title or name is taken; *spec.* noting the parish churches of Rome from which the titles of the cardinals are derived (see TITLE *sb.* 9); hence *transf.* of a cardinal.

1664 FULLER *Triana & Paduana* in *Wounded Consc.* etc. (1867) 185 As for Bondi, in a large oration he expressed his thankfulness before the company to his titular Saint. *a* 1668 LASSELS *Voy. Italy* (1670) II. 162 [The church of St. Lawrence] is one of the five Patriarchal Churches, and therefore not titular of any Cardinal. 1706 tr. *Dupin's Eccl. Hist. 16th C.* II. v. 93 There are five Patriarchal Churches in Rome, Twenty-eight Titular ones, and Eighteen Diaconal ones. 1745 BUTLER *Lives Saints* 11 May (1759) V. 199 He [St. Cataldus] is titular saint of the cathedral [Tarentum]. 1854 CDL. WISEMAN *Fabiola* (1855) 141 The cardinals, or titular priests, received instructions about the administration of sacraments..during the persecution.

**B.** *sb.* **1.** *Sc. Law.* In full *titular of the teinds* (*tithes*): a layman who became possessed of the title to the tithes of an ecclesiastical benefice at or after the Reformation; a lord of erection.

1613 EARL WIGTON *Let.* in Hunter *Biggar & Ho. Fleming* xxvi. (1862) 337 Purchessing the Titular's consent to the samin did stand me at no less rate than ten thousand poundis Scottis. 1630 *Reg. Mag. Sig. Scot.* 1634. 13/2 Johnne lord Halyruidhous, titular of the personage teyndis of the parochin. 1799 J. ROBERTSON *Agric. Perth* 398 Every land-holder may buy up the tiends affecting his estate at a specific price from the titular, who now holds them. 1838 W. BELL *Dict. Law Scot.* s. v. *Teinds*, At the Reformation, the King..created the monasteries and priories into temporal lordships, the grantees to which were styled Lords of Erection, or Titulars of the Tithes. 1845 MCCULLOCH *Taxation* II. iv. (1852) 191 The tithes in possession of the titulars or lay impropriators were more rigorously exacted than they had ever been by the clergy. 1894 J. RUSSELL *Reminisc. Yarrow* ix. 219 The Deans of the Chapel Royal, under the Crown, are the titulars of the tiends.

**2.** One who holds a title to an office, benefice, or possession, irrespective of the functions, duties, or rights attaching to it; *spec.* a cleric who bears a title (TITLE *sb.* 8) whether he performs the duties or not; esp. short for *titular bishop.*

1620 BRENT tr. *Sarpi's Counc. Trent* VI. 560 The Titular of Philadelphia, though a Dutch-man, said, that to deny it.. was dangerous, and pernicious to grant it. 1682 T. FLATMAN *Heraclitus Ridens* No. 66 (1713) II. 159 The whiffling Titular of Nova Scotia pretends to say something against our Veracity. 1826 SOUTHEY *Vind. Eccl. Angl.* 204 The candid and urbane Titular says that the poet ought to be dragged down to the solid ground of authentic documents. 1885 *Pall Mall G.* 31 Dec. (Cassell), The small advocate who has become the titular of a portfolio.

**b.** *transf.* One who has a title or appellation of some kind.

1824 LANDOR *Imag. Conv., Washington & Franklin* Wks. 1846 I. 125/1 Gaming is the vice of those nations..which unite the worst qualities of both conditions [barbarous and civilized]; as for example, the rags and lace of Naples, its lazzaroni and other titulars. 1846 *Ibid., Emp. China & Tsing-Ti* II. 117/1 He employed a humbler observer, known ..by the more ordinary appellation of *Spy*, though the titular is never gazetted. 1828 P. CUNNINGHAM *N. S. Wales* (ed. 3) II. 115 If he inquires his way through Sydney of one of our titulars [a convict with a mark or badge], (even decorated with a C. B. appendage), he runs a risk of having his pocket picked.

**3.** One who bears a title of rank; a titled person.

**1757** *Herald* No. 8 (1758) I. 126 No titular among them will accept..an employment beneath that of ambassador. **1829** LANDOR *Imag. Conv.*, *Penn & Ld. Peterb.* Wks. 1846 I. 521/2 All titulars else must be produced by others; a knight by a knight, a peer by a king, while a gentleman is self-existent.

**4.** *R.C.Ch.* (See quot. 1885.)

**1621** BP. MOUNTAGU *Diatribæ* 496 They now, and the Pagans then, did vse to bestow them vpon the Saint and deity Tutelar and titular of the place. **1885** *Cath. Dict.*, *Patron and Titular of church, place, &c*...The titular is a wider term comprehending the persons of the Trinity, mysteries (*e.g.* Corpus Christi), and saints; the patron of a church can only be a saint or an angel...The feast of the principal titular or patron is a double of the first class with an octave.

**Titularity** (titiŭlæ·rĭti). *rare.* [f. prec. + -ITY.] The quality or state of being titular, or merely titular.

**1646** SIR T. BROWNE *Pseud. Ep.* VII. xvi. 374 Julius Augustus and Tiberius with great humility or popularity refused the name of Imperator; but their Successors have challenged that title, and retaine the same even in its titularity. **1777** H. WALPOLE *Let. to Mann* 15 May, Your new Prince of Nassau is perfectly ridiculous—a real peer of England [Earl Cowper] to tumble down to a tinsel titularity.

**Titularly** (ti·tiŭlărli), *adv.* [f. as prec. + -LY [2].] In respect of title, name, or style; in or by title or name; *esp.* in name only, nominally.

**1625** BP. MOUNTAGU *App. Cæsar* II. ii. 116 A Generall Councell; not titularly so, as the Conventicle of Trent; but plenarily true, generall, and lawfull. **1642** J. EATON *Honey-c. Free Justif.* 309 That we are not imaginarily counted, and titularly called righteous. **1700** ASTRY tr. *Saavedra-Faxardo* I. 20 What else..rendred the Emperour Charles really great, as well as titularly so? **1853** LANDOR *Imag. Conv.* Wks. 1876 VI. 566 England is titularly a kingdom. **1905** *Times, Lit. Supp.* 15 Dec. 440/2 Wilkes was court-martialled for wearing a captain's uniform while titularly only a lieutenant.

**b.** By way of hereditary title (of rank). *rare.*

**1756** C. LUCAS *Ess. Waters* III. Ded., You greatly disdain to rely on honors titularly transmitted.

**Titulary** (ti·tiŭlări), *a.* (*sb.*) Now *rare.* [f. L. *titul-us* TITLE + -ARY [1].]

**1.** = TITULAR *a.* 1, 1 b.

**1606** G. W[OODCOCKE] *Lives Emperors* in *Hist. Ivstine* Ll ij, The first action that Adolphus count of Nassau titularie Emperor vndertooke. **1617** MORYSON *Itin.* II. 93 The titulary Earle of Desmond could never after draw 100 men together. **1797** EARL MALMESBURY *Diaries & Corr.* III. 386 The title of King of France..was merely titulary. **1882–3** *Schaff's Encycl. Relig. Knowl.* I. 157 Stephan Evadi Assemani..was titulary archbishop of Apamaea in Syria.

**2.** = TITULAR *a.* 2.

**1603** H. CROSSE *Vertues Commw.* (1878) 21 What is all this worlds pompe, or titulary preferments, if not atchieued by Vertue? **1721** STRYPE *Eccl. Mem.* I. ii. 35 The King seemed to boast much of this titulary honour bestowed upon him so solemnly by the Pope and Cardinals. **1804** EUGENIA DE ACTON *Tale without Title* II. 129 If any man values a titulary distinction.

†**3.** = TITULAR *a.* 3. *Obs.*

*a* **1618** RALEIGH in Gutch *Coll. Cur.* I. 89 To embrace a vain and titulary conceit of land continuing a name, intimateth Paganism rather then Christianity. **1647** N. BACON *Disc. Govt. Eng.* I. xxxvii. (1739) 56 The trial by Battle.. was in criminal matters with sharp Weapons; but in titulary matters with blunt Weapons.

†**4.** = TITULAR *a.* 4. *Obs.*

**1664** FULLER *Triana* in *Wounded Consc.*, etc. (1867) 189 You..have abused your titulary Saint, by pretending his relics the immediate cause of your restored sight.

**B.** *sb.* **a.** One who holds a title to something; = TITULAR *sb.* 2. **b.** One who bears a title of rank; = TITULAR *sb.* 3.

**1726** AYLIFFE *Parergon* 190 Persons..deputed for the Celebration of these Masses..were neither Titularies, nor perpetual Curates; but Persons entirely conductitious. **1792** *State Papers* in *Ann. Reg.* 257 False titularies destitute of all canonical appointment. **1824** LANDOR *Imag. Conv.*, *Alfieri & Salomon* Wks. 1846 I. 188/2 Their..influence, and..character place them..above the titularies of our country, be the rank what it may.

**Titulate, -ation,** obs. erron. ff. TITILLATE, etc.

**Titulation.** [Cf. TITULE *v.*] = INTITULATION.

**1868** M. PATTISON *Academ. Org.* vi. 238 Those who pass this examination might have any titulation which it might be thought expedient to give them.

**Titule,** *sb.*, rare variant of TITLE *sb.*

**Titule** (ti·tiŭl), *v.* [f. L. *titul-āre* to title: cf. INTITULE.] Occasional variant of TITLE *v.*, esp. in pa. pple. or ppl. adj. **Ti·tuled.**

In quot. 1569 app. To set down in writing: cf. TITLE *v.* 1.

**1569** ABP. PARKER *Let. to Sir W. Cecil* 3 June (Lansd. MS. 11, lf. 128), Onys at the request of my L. of leycestre,..I tituled to hym my phantasie, from the wch I do not moche disagre at this tyme. **1588** PARKE tr. *Mendoza's Hist. China* 277 He asked..what those letters did signifie that were tituled ouer his head. **1591** NASHE *Prognost.* Wks. (Grosart) II. 155 Diuers selfe conceited fooles..tituling themselues by the names of Martinistes. **1635** HEYWOOD *Hierarch.* VII. 463 This is tituled by the name of Principate. **1655** FULLER *Ch. Hist.* II. ii. § 107 A great Council (for so it is tituled) was held at Becanceld by Withred, King of Kent. **1894** *Daily News* 16 June 6/1 The foreign favouritism which was tituled one of the most real and serious grievances of those times.

**Tituler,** obs. f. TITTLER *sb.*[1] **Titup:** see TITTUP.

**Tit-warbler:** see TIT *sb.*[3] 3 c.

†**Tityre-tu** (ti·tĭrei,tū·, -ritiū). *Obs.* Also **Titire-Tu, Tytire tu, Tytere-tu, Tittery tu, tittyry.** [From L. *Tītyre tū*, the first words of Virgil's first eclogue, 'Tityre, tu patulæ recubans sub tegmine fagi', adopted as a designation.]

One of an association of well-to-do 'roughs' who infested London streets in the 17th c.

The name 'meant to imply that these blades were men of leisure and fortune, who "lay at ease under their patrimonial beech trees"' (Brewer *Reader's Handbk.*).

**1623** J. CHAMBERLAIN *Let. to Sir D. Carleton* 6 Dec., in *Crt. & Times Jas. I* (1848) II. 438 There is a crew or knot of such people..who..have made an association, and taken certain oaths and orders devised among them selves;.. having certain nicknames, as Tityre-tu, and such like, for their several fraternities. **1630** J. TAYLOR (Water P.) *Navy Land Ships* Wks. I. 77/2 Roaring boyes, and Rough-hewd Tittery tues. **1648** HERRICK *Hesper.*, *New-Yeares Gift to Sir S. Steward*, No newes of navies burnt at seas; No noise of late spawn'd tittyries. **1693** SOUTHERNE *Maid's Last Prayer* II. ii, I remember your Dammee-Boyes, your Swashes, your Tuquoques and your Titire-Tues. **1849** MACAULAY *Hist. Eng.* iii. I. 361 *note*, It may be suspected that some of the Tityre Tus, like good cavaliers, broke Milton's windows shortly after the Restoration.

**Tityrus** (ti·tĭrŏs). *Myth.* [L. *Tītyrus*, name of a shepherd, a. Gr. Τίτυρος, said to be Doric for σάτυρος satyr.] A fictitious monster supposed to be bred between a sheep and a goat.

**1610** GUILLIM *Heraldry* III. xxv. (1660) 255 Like as the Tytirus is ingendred between a Sheep and a Buck Goat, as Upton noteth. **1710** W. KING *Heathen Gods & Heroes* xxvii. (1722) 134 Several cruel Dæmons, Satyrs, Sileni and Tityri, us'd to accompany him [Bacchus] with Cymbals and huge Exclamations. [**1906** VINYCOMB *Fict. & Symb. Creatures in Art* 217 In Guillim's 'Display',..said to be a bigenerous beast, of unkindly procreation, engendered between a goat and a ram, like the Tityrus, the offspring of a sheep and goat, as noted by Upton.]

**Tiver** (ti·vəɹ), *sb. dial.* [mod., app. repr. OE. *téafor* (*téapor*), glossing 'minium' (red lead); in form = OHG. *zoubur*, Ger. *zauber*, ON. *taufr*, secret or magic writing, charm, talisman, sorcery: see Pauls *Grundrisz* (ed. 2) 251.] A red colouring matter: see quots. Hence **Ti·ver** *v. dial.*, *trans.* to mark or colour with tiver.

[*c* **975** *Sax. Leechd.* II. 56 Do æȝes þ hwite to & meng swa þu dest teapor. *a* **1100** *Ags. Voc.* in Wr.-Wülcker 314/21 *Minium*, teafor. *a* **1200** *Ibid.* 541/11 *Minium*, teapor. **1200–1225** *Peri Didaxeon* in *Sax. Leechd.* III. 88 Eft nim ladsar þ teafur & galpani oþres healfes paniȝe whit.] **1792** *Gentl. Mag.* LXII. 521 Strayed sheep..tivered between the shoulders and across the loins. *a* **1825** FORBY *Voc. E. Anglia*, *Tiver*, a composition of which tar is the principal ingredient, to colour and preserve boards exposed to the air. **1863** MORTON *Cycl. Agric.* Gloss. (E.D.D.), *Teen* or *Tiver* (Suff.), red ochre for marking sheep. **1887** *Kentish Gloss.*, Tiver. **1895** *E. Anglia Gloss.* s. v., The sheep are tivered across the loins.

**Tivoli** (ti·vŏli). [Said to be from *Tivoli*, a town near Rome.] A game resembling bagatelle, played on a sloping board or table set with upright pins and hoops, by which the ball shot from a side alley against the curved top of the table is deflected into numbered compartments at the other end.

**Tivy** (ti·vi), *int.* and *v. rare.* [See TANTIVY.] **a.** *int.* = TANTIVY D. **b.** *vb.* = TANTIVY *v.* 1.

**1669** DRYDEN *Tyrannic Love* IV. i, In the bright moonshine while winds whistle loud, Tivy, tivy, tivy, we mount and we fly. **1719** [see TANTIVY D]. **1842** *Tait's Mag.* IX. 528 Thence tivy'd they all, with speed of a sledge, And buried them deep in the hazel hedge.

**Tiwesday, Tiwill,** obs. ff. TUESDAY, TEWEL.

†**Tixell,** obs. form of THIXEL *dial.*

**1542** *Richmond Wills* (Surtees) 35 Item a tixell and a chysell iiijd.

**Tixt, tixte,** obs. forms of TEXT.

‖ **Tiza** (tī·zä). *Min.* [a. Quichua (Peruvian) *t'isa* to card wool; from its fibrous appearance (Webster, 1911).] Ulexite or hayesine.

**1865** PAGE *Handbk. Geol. Terms* (ed. 2), *Tiza*, the name by which borate of lime (*Hayesine*) is called in southern Peru, where it occurs on the dry plains or *salinas* in the neighbourhood of Iquique in white reniform masses. **1868** DANA *Min.* 599 Ulexite..occurs..in the province of Tarapaca (where it is called *tiza*).

**Tizanne,** obs. var. PTISAN, barley-water, etc.

**Tizwin,** var. TISWIN. **Tizzick,** obs. f. PHTHISIC.

**Tizzy** (ti·zi). *slang.* Also **tizzey, tissey.** [Origin obscure.] A sixpenny-piece.

**1804** J. COLLINS *Scripscrap.* 156 So I gets a Tizzy for to let them alone. **1809** in *Spirit Pub. Jrnls.* XIII. 119 That a tizzey be given out of the corporate funds in support of said Colonel Waddle. **1829** *Sporting Mag.* XXIV. 163 The.. rustics, who had ventured their few tisseys and bobs upon their Squire's famous horse. **1835** HOOD *Dead Robbery* viii, Just show me, if you can, A doctor's—if you want to earn a tizzy! **1901** *Longm. Mag.* Oct. 571 A man reads, at a 'tizzy', what he had not read when priced at twelve times the humble tanner.

‖ **Tjalk** (tyalk). [Du. and LG. *tjalk*, a kind of ship, a. WFris. *tsjalk* (tʃalk), according to Franck, perh. dim. of **tjal* for *kjal* = OE. *céol* KEEL.] A kind of Dutch ship or sailing boat.

**1889** *Blackwood's Mag.* Aug. 183 Half a dozen big tjalks laden with peat. **1907** *Outlook* 16 Mar. 341/2 The quiet ripple under the bows of tjalks—those large, useful, picturesque craft favoured by Dutch designers—sailing across the wide Friesland Meers.

**T-joint:** see T 3.

‖ **Tmema** (tmī·mä). Pl. **-ata.** [a. Gr. τμῆμα a part cut off, a section.] A segment, a section.

**1891** in *Cent. Dict.* **1900** B. D. JACKSON *Gloss. Bot. Terms*, *Tmema*.., a cell ruptured in setting free a Mossgemma (Correns).

‖ **Tmesis** (tmī·sis). *Gram.* and *Rhet.* (Also 6 **timesis.**) [a. Gr. τμῆσις a cutting, from verbal ablaut series τεμ-, τομ-, τμ- to cut.] The separation of the elements of a compound word by the interposition of another word or words.

(Often a reversion to the earlier uncompounded structure.)

**1586** DAY *Eng. Secretary* II. (1625) 83 *Timesis* or *Diacope*, a diuision of a word compound into two parts, as, What might be soeuer vnto a man pleasing,..for, whatsoeuer might be, etc. **1678** PHILLIPS (ed. 4), *Tmesis*,..a figure of Prosody, wherein a compounded word is, as it were, cut asunder, and divided into two parts by some other word which is interposed, as *Septem Subjecta Trioni*, for *Subjecta Septemtrioni*. **1844** *Proc. Philol. Soc.* I. 265 Though the constituent parts of compound terms may be disjoined by tmesis, the elements of truly simple words never are. **1889** *Athenæum* 23 Mar. 373/1 Forgive the quaint tmesis of his opening line:—How bright the chit and chat!

†**Tme·tic,** *a. Med. Obs. rare.* [ad. Gr. τμητικ-ός cutting, f. τμητός cut: cf. prec.] Cutting; loosening, resolving.

**1661** LOVELL *Hist. Anim. & Min.* 87 Antepilepticks, having a tmetick, or inciding faculty.

**To,** *a. Obs.* exc. *dial.* Forms: α. (*Sc.* and *n. dial.*) 4–6 **ta,** 5 **taa,** 5 (8–9 *Sc.*) **tae,** 9 **teae**; 9 *n. dial.* **tea, teea.** β. 4–7 **to,** 5 **too,** 7 **toe.** [ME. *tā*, *tō*, shortened form of *tān*, *tōn* TONE *a.*, when standing before a sb. (orig. only before a consonant). For history see TONE *a.*, and cf. *o*, *oo*, *a*, *ae*, shortened forms of ONE *a.*]

**a.** The collocation *the ta*, *the to*, properly *that a*, *that* (*thet*) *o*, 'the one', as opposed to *the tother* = *that other*, 'the other'.

α. *a* **1340** HAMPOLE *Psalter* lvii. 4 The snake that festis the ta ere til the erth, and the tothere stoppis with hire taile. **1387** *Charters, &c. Edinb.* (1871) 35 Betwene worthy men and nobyl..on the ta half, and..masounys on the tothir half. *a* **1400–50** *Alexander* 3978 Þi semble o þe taa syde & myne on þe tothire. *c* **1440** *Alphabet of Tales* 181 Þer war a hate oven on þe ta side me, & þe shapp of hym on þat other partie. **1513** DOUGLAS *Æneis* X. vii. 175 Pallas on the ta part..Lawsus resistis on that vthir syde. **1721** RAMSAY *Horace to Virgil* 10 Bring hame the tae haff o' my saul. **1826** J. WILSON *Noct. Ambr.* Wks. 1855 I. 128 Up with the tae side, down with the tither.

β. *c* **1330** R. BRUNNE *Chron.* (1810) 176 Þe to kyng & þe toþer assailed it so hard. **1423** *Rolls of Parlt.* IV. 256/2 That the too half be forfet to the..Kyng and the tother half to hym. *c* **1425** *Seven Sag.* (P.) 3270 That to [error for *that o* or *the to*] raven was ful holde. **1495** *Trevisa's Barth. De P. R.* XVIII. ix. (W. de W.), He hath tweyne heedys, one in the to [*Bodl. MS.* þat one] ende and a nother in the tother ende. **1609** W. M. *Man in Moone* (1849) 18 Tradesmen treade on the to side of the way. **1642** ROGERS *Naaman* 193 The Angell gave him a bunch on the to-side.

**b.** Used without *the* after a poss. pron. (or case), as in *his to eye*, his one eye, the one of his eyes.

**1513** DOUGLAS *Æn.* IV. ix. 91 The quene..Hir ta fut bair.

†**c.** In phr. *a to-side*, on one side. *Obs.*

**1601** HOLLAND *Pliny* VIII. xxiv. 208 Turning his head a toside. **1606** *Choice, Chance*, etc. (1881) 70 Lookes a toside, and swears at euery word. **1609** HOLLAND *Amm. Marcell.* 389 Winding atoe side and going crosse. **1678** BUNYAN *Pilgr.* I. 139 Then Christian stept a little a to-side to his Fellow Hopeful. **1684** *Ibid.* II. 67 He called you a to-side.

In part of northern England where *the* regularly becomes *tē*, *tă*, *t'* (as *tă fells*, *t'measter*, *t'itter oop caw t'udder*, *t'aud lad*), *to*, *tone*, *tother* stand for *t'o*, *t'one*, *t'other*, i.e. *the o*, *the one*, *the other*; so in colloq. Eng. more widely, *t'one or t'other*, *t'other man*, *t'other day*; hence it is possible that *a-to-side* represents *on-th'o-side*; the northern ME. was *o þe taa side*, mod. Sc. *o*(*n*) *the tae side*.

† **To,** *v. Obs.* Also 5 **too**; *pa. t.* 4–5 **to,** *pa. pple.* 4–5 **ton,** 6 **tone.** The ME. apocopate northern forms *tā*, *tān* for TAKE, *taken*, with the *ā* rounded in north midland speech, or transliterated by midland or southern writers to *tō*, *tōn*; in the pa. t. *to* was apocopated from the original *tōc*.

All the rimed examples of the pres. and pa. pple. rime with words having *ā* in northern dialect; in earlier instances the change of *a* to *o* was mostly scribal; but in late Sc. it was mostly the work of the author anglicizing his native *ā* to *ō* on the analogy of *sā*, *sō*, *bān*, *bōne*, etc.

**13..** *Cursor M.* 16454 (Cott.) Quen þai þe fine gold for-soke, And to [*v.r.* toke] þam to þe lede. *c* **1320** *Sir Tristr.* 947 Þe truage was com to to [*rimes* so, þo, go] Moraunt, þe noble kniȝt. *Ibid.* 1484 His tong haþ he ton [*rime* nek bon] And schorn of bi þe rote. *Ibid.* 2112 Þen sall þis rewel eft furth be ton [*rime* gon]. *c* **1425** *Seven Sag.* (P.) 1432 To speke fayre he to hede. *c* **1440** *Bone Flor.* 887 And Awdegone hur cowncelde soo Oon of these lordys for to too. **1500–20** DUNBAR *Poems* xlvi. 102 That he..nocht in the feindis net be tone [*rime* allone].

**To** (tŭ, tu, tu, tŭ, tə), *prep.*, *conj.*, *adv.* [OE. *tó*, in form = OFris., OS. *tô* (MDu., Du. *toe*, MLG., LG. *tô*, *to*), OHG. *zô*, *zuo*, *zua*, MHG. *zuo*, Ger. *zu*:—OTeut. **tô* adv.; beside which OTeut. had **ti*, OFris., OS. *ti*, *te* (Fris., MDu., Du., MLG., LG. *te*), OHG. *za*, *ze*, *zi* (MHG. *ze*) prep. OTeut. **tô* and **ti* (? *ta*) unite in a pre-Teut. *dō*, *de*, cognate with OSl. and OIr. *do*, Lith. *da-* prefix, Gr. -δε, L. *-do* suffix. Gothic used only the form *du*, and ON. substituted *til*, TILL. In prehistoric OE. the prep. was already levelled with the adv. in the form *to* (*tó*, *to*), as in Ger. both are now *zu*. But while *tó* adv., retaining its stress, came at last to be written *too* (tū), the prep., being usually stressless, remained as *to* (tŭ, tu, tə), and in dialectal specimens is now often written *ta*, *tae*, *teh*, *ti*, *tu* (meaning tă, tĕ, tə), some of which forms are occasional also in earlier writing. (In some northern dialects (tĕ) develops before a vowel into *tev*, *tiv*.)

Exceptional and dialectal forms. (Chiefly with inf., where also before a vowel it was formerly often reduced to *t* or *t'*, as in *tamend*, *t'enjoy*: see T' [1].)

*a* **1175** Tu [see A. 1]. *c* **1200** *Trin. Coll. Hom.* 5 Þat is te cumen a domes dai. *a* **1225** *St. Marher.* 19 He..demde hire te deaðe. **13..** *Cursor M.* 14913 (Gött.) For fast it draus te þe nede. *c* **1380** WYCLIF *Sel. Wks.* III. 433 To [*v. r.* te] kepe Cristis religioun. *c* **1400** *Rom. Rose* 3156 That comest so slyghly for tespye. **1535** STEWART *Cron. Scot.* (Rolls) I. 541 Mony ratche ta ryn under the ryss. **1585** T. WASHINGTON tr. *Nicholay's Voy.* I. vi, The Ambassadour..returning too his Gallies. **1822** W. TENNANT *Thane of Fife* I. 2 Euterpe, aidant come, t'adorn my song. **1894** 'IAN MACLAREN' *Bonnie Brier Bush* v. (1895) 181 It only 'threatened tae be weet'. **1896** R. REID in *N. York Scot. Amer.* Oct., Aff tae the muirs.]

**A.** *prep.* (in ordinary use, before a sb.)

The OE. prep. *tó* normally 'governed' or was followed by the dative case, sometimes, idiomatically, by the genitive or the instrumental (esp. in *tó þæs* and *to þý*), rarely by the accusative. In later Middle and in mod.Eng., *to* is followed by the ordinary 'objective' case, which in sbs. is formally identical with the nominative, and in pronouns is the dative-accusative, *me*, *him*, etc. In Middle and mod.Eng. *to* not only represents the OE. preposition, but also takes the place of the OE. inflected dative case. Even in OE. the simple dative was often reinforced by *tó*, or (what came to the same thing) was supplanted by *tó* and its case. This was very frequent in late OE., and (helped no doubt by the example of French, which had similarly substituted the construction with *à* (L. *ad*) for the L. dative) became universal in ME., the simple dative remaining only in pronouns and substantives as the indirect or remoter object, known by its position before the direct object (as in 'give me the book', 'tell John the news'). Both with pronouns and sbs., the prepositional construction may, and in some cases must, be used (e.g. 'give the book to me', 'tell it to John'). In OE. many verbs 'governed' or took a dative object; with the loss of the dative inflexion, this case could no longer be distinguished from the accusative, and such verbs are now treated as ordinary transitive vbs. governing the objective (e.g. sio heord folʒað ðæm wordum & ðæm ðeawum ðæs hirdes, 'the herd follows the words and the thews [customs] of the shepherd').

The senses and uses of *to* may be arranged in various ways, every way having its peculiar difficulties owing to cross-currents of history and usage. OE. and the West Germanic Languages had two prepositions with the sense of modern *to*, viz. *tó* and *óð*; the second of these always expressed motion reaching its object; it is therefore probable that *tó* had originally the sense of 'direction towards', without any implication of reaching; and in a truly historical account of the word, it would perh. be necessary to start with the two main divisions of 'toward' and 'actually to'. But even in the earliest written OE. this distinction had, so far as concerns *tó*, faded away, and in the various transferred and later senses it could not be successfully carried out. Even the later distinction between *to* as a preposition implying motion, and *to* representing the dative inflexion, can, from the falling together of these notions, only be partially exhibited. The arrangement here followed is thus largely tentative and practical, and not in every case historical.

**I.** Expressing a spatial or local relation.

**1.** Expressing motion directed towards and reaching: governing a sb. denoting the place, thing, or person approached and reached. The opposite of FROM. Also with adv. prefixed, as *away*, *down*, *out*, *up*, etc.

Sometimes preceding another preposition (of position): see quot. *c* 1300, and cf. FROM 15 b.

*Beowulf* (Z.) 2010 Ic ðær furðum cwom, to ðam hring-sele. *c* **893** K. ÆLFRED *Oros.* v. xi. § 4 Mon lædde Aristobolus to Rome ʒebundenne. **1154** *O. E. Chron.* an. 1132 (Laud MS.) Ðis ʒear com Henri king to þis land. *a* **1175** *Cott. Hom.* 229 He com tu us. *c* **1300** *Cursor M.* 21792 (Edin.) Out of þe bridil he [þe nailis] lachte And to biscide þe croz þaim taʒte. *c* **1386** CHAUCER *C. T. Prol.* 16 And specially from euery shires ende Of Engelond to Caunturbury they wende. *c* **1489** CAXTON *Blanchardyn* liv. 211 The beautifull Queene was royally led to and from the Church. **1583** STUBBES *Anat. Abus.* II. (1882) 27 When the poore man might turne out a cow, or two..to the commons. **1611** BIBLE 2 *Kings* xv. 29 [He] caried them captiue to Assyria. **1802** MAR. EDGEWORTH *Moral T.* (1816) I. i. 2 Forester was sent to Edinburgh. **1904** F. C. KITTON *Dickens Country* 63 Dickens returned to London. *Mod.* He has removed to near Rugby. Take this child to his mother's house. Come here to me.

**b.** In figurative expressions of motion; the following sb. denoting (*a*) a state or condition attained, or (*b*) a thing or person reached by some action figured as movement.

*c* **875** *O.E. Chron.* an. 871, Þa feng Ælfred..to Wesseaxna rice. *c* **897** K. ÆLFRED *Gregory's Past. C.* xiv. 300 Hie ðonne astiʒað to Godes anlicnesse. *c* **1175** *Lamb. Hom.* 27 Hit hine tið to þan bittre deðe. *c* **1200** ORMIN 11219 He biginneþþ..Att Abraham, & reccneþþ aʒʒ Dunnwarrd fra mann to manne. *c* **1449** PECOCK *Repr.* III. iv. (Rolls) 293 If thou wolte entre to lijf, kepe the comaundementis. **1555** J. PROCTOR *Hist. Wyat's Reb.* 64 Nowe to retourne to Wyat. **1625** LAUD *Wks.* (1847) I. 95 When he came to the crown. **1766** GOLDSM. *Vic. W.* xviii, To reclaim a lost child to virtue. **1855** MACAULAY *Hist. Eng.* xii. III. 216 The only debate of which any account has come down to us. **1905** M. HUME *Span. Infl. on Eng. Lit.* 97 To trace how the germ of the stories came to Spain. *Mod.* Do not let it run to seed.

**c.** Elliptical uses. (*a*) with ellipsis of *go* or other verb of motion, esp. in commands, or (*arch.*) after an auxiliary verb. (*b*) = Gone to; in going to, on the way to. (Chiefly *dial.*) (*c*) after a sb. implying or suggesting motion: = That goes, or takes one, or causes one to go, to.

(*a*) *c* **1425** *Cast. Persev.* 3038 in *Macro Plays* 167 Þou muste to helle. **1539** BIBLE (Great) 1 *Kings* xii. 16 To youre tentes, O Israel! **1633** G. HERBERT *Temple, Assurance* iv, I will to my Father. **1663** PEPYS *Diary* 19 Oct., She waked and gargled her mouth, and to sleep again. **1666** *Ibid.* 28 Apr., My wife to her father's, to carry him some ruling work. **1843** *Blackw. Mag.* LIV. 733 I'll to bed. **1884** BROWNING *Ferishtah, Eagle* 35 To Ispahan forthwith!

(*b*) **1451** MARG. PASTON in *P. Lett.* I. 221 The Lady Boys ..is to London to compleyn to the Kyng. *c* **1500** *Melusine* lix. 360 For now the sonne is to his rest. **1908** [MISS E. FOWLER] *Betw. Trent & Ancholme* 45 She wore, to church, a black cottage-bonnet.

(*c*) *a* **900** K. ÆLFRED *Solil.* Pref. (1902) 2 Þæt ic maʒe rihtne weiʒ aredian to þam ecan hame. **971** *Blickl. Hom.* 109, & him tæcean lifes weʒ & rihtne gang to heofonum. **1535** COVERDALE *Gen.* xvi. 7 By the well in the waye to Sur. **1673** [see ROAD *sb.* 4]. **1758** GOLDSM. *Mem. Protestant* (1895) II. 137 He had some Business to Nice. **1849** MACAULAY *Hist. Eng.* iii. I. 371 If he asked his way to St. James's. **1852** TENNYSON *Ode Dk. Wellington* 202 The path of duty was the way to glory. **1862** *Chambers's Encycl.* III. 321/1 The railway to C. was opened in 1856. **1874** KINGSLEY *Lett.* (1877) II. 426 We are promised free passes..to California. *Mod.* The first train to London.

**2.** Expressing direction: In the direction of, towards.

*c* **890** tr. *Bæda's Hist.* I. vii. (1890) 38 His eaʒan ahof upp to heofonum. *c* **1000** *Ags. Ps.* (Th.) lxx[i]. 2 Ahyld me þin eare to [*Vulg.* inclina ad me aurem tuam]. **1388** WYCLIF *Ps.* xxiv. [xxv.] 15 Myn iʒen ben euere to the Lord. **1590** SPENSER *F. Q.* II. vii. 1 As pilot..That to a stedfast starre his course hath bent. **1667** MILTON *P. L.* VI. 558 Vanguard, to Right and Left the Front unfould. **1697** DRYDEN *Virg. Georg.* III. 472 A Cote that opens to the South. **1802** MAR. EDGEWORTH *Moral T.* (1816) I. 232 Standing with his back to me. **1843** *Blackw. Mag.* LIV. 14 He pointed to a clump of trees.

**b.** After *look*, *smell* = mod. *at*; also † *behold to*, †*see to* = look at. *Obs.* or *dial.*

*a* **900** *Ags. Ps.* (Th.) xii. 3 Beseoh to me, Drihten,..and ʒehyr me. *Ibid.* xxiv. 14 [xxv. 16] ʒeloca to me, Drihten, and ʒemiltsa me. **1375–** [see LOOK *v.* 21 a]. **1382** WYCLIF *Gen.* iv. 4 Þe Lord biheld to Abel and to his ʒiftis. **1393** LANGL. *P. Pl.* C. II. 55 The dupe dale and durke vnsemely to see to. *c* **1475** *Stans puer* 55 in *Q. Eliz. Acad.* (E.E.T.S.) 58 When þou spekys..Be-hold to þi souereyn in þe face. **1586** B. YOUNG *Guazzo's Civ. Conv.* IV. 191 b, Manie,..before they had dronke, would smell to their wine. **1611** BIBLE *Josh.* xxii. 10 A great altar to see to. **1852** HAWTHORNE *Blithedale Rom.* ix, A young girl's heart, which he held in his hand, and smelled to, like a rosebud.

**c.** In expressing the position of something lying in a specified direction. (Cf. ON *prep.* 4.)

*c* **890** tr. *Bæda's Hist.* I. ix. [xi.] (1890) 44 Eardædon Bryttas binnan þam dice to suðdæle. **1671** MILTON *P. R.* III. 273 Here thou behold'st Assyria,..And..to south the Persian bay. **1789** G. WHITE *Selborne* i, To the north-west, north and east of the village, is a range of fair enclosures. **1820** SCOTT *Monast.* iii, The extensive range of pasturage..lay to the west. **1855** TENNYSON *Charge Light Brigade* iii, Cannon to right of them, Cannon to left of them. **1861** MRS. CARLYLE *Lett.* (1883) III. 79 The bedrooms to the back are much larger.

**d.** In figurative expressions of direction (inclination, tendency, etc.). Also *fig.* from c, in phr. *to the bad*, *to the good* (= on the wrong, or right, side of the account), *to the fore*; in *to the contrary* with both senses (2 and 2 c).

See BAD B. 1 b, GOOD C. 5 b, FORE *a.* 4.

*c* **1300** *Cursor M.* 19326 (Edin.) Þai durste na uiolence þaim do For þe folc þaim heeldit to. *a* **1400** *Birth Jesus* 4 in Horstm. *Altengl. Leg.* (1875) 65 Icome he is..to wham is al oure hope. **1512–** [see CONTRARY B. 1 b, c]. **1637–** [see FORE *a.* 4]. **1753** CHAMBERS *Cycl. Supp.* s. v. *Lime*, Oblong, with a tendency to a rhomboidal shape. **1815** SCOTT *Guy M.* xxxvi, He..commanded Barnes to have an eye to the Dominie.

**e.** With a sb. or pron. (or sb. phrase) followed by *ward* or *wards* (now commonly written as a suffix, hyphened or joined to the preceding word); e.g. *to God-ward*: see -WARD, -WARDS, and cf. TOWARD. *arch.*

**3.** Indicating the limit of a movement or extension in space: As far as (to); = OE. *oð*.

Sometimes followed by another preposition (of position), as in quot. 1641: cf. FROM 15 b. Often correlative to *from*, indicating the remoter, or the second, of two limits: see FROM 2. See also *up to* s. v. UP.

**971–1884** [see FROM 2]. *a* **1300** *Cursor M.* 2742 Þe smike it reches to þe scki. **13..** *Sir Beues* (A.) 1538 Til þe her on is heued greu to his fet. *c* **1384** CHAUCER *H. Fame* III. 840 So grete a noyse, That..Men myghte hyt han herd..To Rome. *c* **1420** ? LYDG. *Assembly of Gods* 462, I smete hym to the hert. **1599** SHAKS. *Much Ado* II. i. 258 She would infect to the north starre. **1641** J. JACKSON *True Evang. T.* I. 62 If their candle had burned to within the Socket. **1843** *Fraser's Mag.* XXVIII. 652 Protestant to the backbone. **1873** TRISTRAM *Moab* i. 14 Wet to the skin. *Mod.* The thermometer has risen to above 32°.

**b.** After expressions of distance, indicating the remote limit (formerly also the near limit, at which the speaker is actually or in idea): = FROM 5 a, OF 4 b.

*c* **888** K. ÆLFRED *Boeth.* xxxv. § 4 Hi woldon witan hu heah hit wære to ðæm heofone. *c* **893** — *Oros.* I. i. § 17 Hit mihte beon þreora mila brad to þæm more. **1551** *Reg. Privy Council Scot.* I. 115 Dwelland within four mylis to this burch. **1605** SHAKS. *Macb.* I. iii. 39 How farre is't call'd to Soris? *Mod.* It is eleven miles (from Oxford) to Witney.

**4.** Expressing simple position: At, in (a place, also *fig.* a condition, etc.). Cf. Ger. *zu Berlin*, *zu hause*. Now only *dial.* and *U. S. colloq.*

**925–** *c* **935** *Laws of Æthelstan* II. c. 14 § 2 On Cantwarabyriʒ VII myneteras..to Hrofeceastre III..to Lundenbyriʒ VIII [etc.]. *c* **1175** *Lamb. Hom.* 27 Swa dreieð his erme saule in eche pine to helle grunde. **13..** *Guy Warw.* (A.) 384 Þou art y-tauʒt to a liþer scole. *c* **1420** *Chron. Vilod.* 1696 Þat his body to Schaftesbury were leyde. *c* **1500** *Melusine* lvii. 335, I haue herd say that there is to Mountferrat ..a deuoute & holy place. **1658** in Morris *Troub. Cath. Foref.* I. vi. (1872) 314 Sister Cornelia who had lain to bed about thirty years. **1835–40** HALIBURTON *Clockm.* (1862) 57, I guess, said he, they have enough of it to home. **1855** KINGSLEY *Westward Ho* xxvi, Lucy Passmore, the white witch to Welcombe. **1889** JEFFERIES *Field & Hedgerow* 272 In Somerset..it is correct to say 'I bought this to Taunton'. **1901** *Harper's Mag.* CII. 672/1 You can get real handsome cups and saucers to Crosby's.

**5.** Expressing the relation of contact or the like.

**a.** Into (or in) contact with; on, against. Often expressing more than mere position, and so passing into transferred senses. See also ON TO.

*c* **890** tr. *Bæda's Hist.* IV. xxv. [xxiv.] (1890) 348 Ond his heafod onhylde to þam bolstre. **13..** *Guy Warw.* (A.) 4844 'Lordinges', he seyd, 'nimeþ þis bodi, & to þe grounde it lay wel softli'. *c* **1400** MAUNDEV. (Roxb.) iii. 9 [They] held to þaire noses spoungez moisted with water..., for þe aer þare was so drie. *a* **1533** LD. BERNERS *Huon* lxxxi. 250 Huon withdrewe..& lened hym to a pyller. **1536** CROMWELL in Merriman *Life & Lett.* (1902) II. 90 A request..the accomplishement wherof I haue..moche to harte. **1599**, **1626** [see FEEL *v.* 2 a]. *a* **1715** BURNET *Own Time* an. 1669 (1823) I. 469 He stood up to the wall. **1837** DICKENS *Pickw.* xxv, Applying plenty of yellow soap to the towel. **1893** D. HYDE *My Grief on Sea* vi, His breast to my bosom, His mouth to my mouth.

**b.** Expressing contiguity or close proximity: By, beside. Also *fig.* or with additional implication, as in *to one's face*, *teeth*, etc. = 'in presence and defiance of' (Schmidt *Shaks. Lex.*): cf. 25 b, and see FACE *sb.* 5 c, TOOTH *sb.*; *to hand*: see HAND *sb.* 34; *to stand to one's post*, *guns*, etc.: see STAND *v.*

*c* **1000** ÆLFRIC *Saints' Lives* xxxi. 629 He sæt to þam casere. *c* **1400** *Rom. Rose* 6355 To Ioly folk I enhabite. *c* **1449** PECOCK *Repr.* III. i. (Rolls) 279 The suburbis..ligging to the same citees. **1614** BP. J. KING *Vitis Palatina* 30 They that walke side to side, and cheeke to cheeke. **1752** J. LOUTHIAN *Form of Process* (ed. 2) 202 The Clerk bids the Keeper set the Prisoners..to the Bar. **1855** MACAULAY *Hist. Eng.* xvii. IV. 59, I sit down to table; but I cannot eat. **1597** SHAKS. 2 *Hen. IV*, III. i. 64 Euen to the eyes of Richard Gaue him defiance. **1602** — *Ham.* IV. vii. 57, I shall liue and tell him to his teeth, Thus diddest thou. **1739** ELTON in Hanway *Trav.* (1762) I. I. iv. 12 We instantly stood to our arms. **1822** HAZLITT *Table-t.* II. ii. 25 He had taken his part boldly and stood to it manfully. **1843** *Blackw. Mag.* LIV. 219 They will find everything ready to their hands.

**II.** Expressing a relation in time.

**6.** Indicating a final limit in time, or the end of a period: Till, until; often correlative to *from*: see FROM 3. (Formerly sometimes preceding an adv. of time, e.g. *now*, *then*: cf. FROM 15 a, TILL *prep.* 5 b.) † Also *rarely* expressing an extent in time: For, during, till the end of (*obs.*); esp. in phr. *to term of life* (see TERM *sb.* 4 b).

*c* **1000** ÆLFRIC *Hom.* II. 356 He worhte his weorc to seofon nihtum. *c* **1175** *Lamb. Hom.* 87 Fram þan halie hester dei boð italde fifti daʒa to þisse deie. **1297** R. GLOUC. (Rolls) 190 Fram þe biginning of þe world to þe time þat now is. *c* **1375** *Sc. Leg. Saints* xviii. (*Egipciane*) 276 Scho saw hyme neuir to þan. *c* **1380** WYCLIF *Serm.* Sel. Wks. II. 37 To þe daie þat Noie wente into þe ship. *c* **1490** CAXTON *Rule St. Benet* lxx. 139 Children to the xv. yere of age shall stande euer vndir..discipline. **1509** [see THEN 7]. **1582** L. KIRBY in Allen *Martyrd. Campion* (1908) 77 Yours to death, and after death. **1711** ADDISON *Spect.* No. 159 ¶ 4 From the Beginning of the World to its Consummation. **1799** WORDSW. *Lucy Gray* xv, Some maintain that to this day She is a living child. **1849** MACAULAY *Hist. Eng.* vi. II. 36 The parliament was prorogued to the tenth of February. **1855** DICKENS *Dorrit* v, The business hours..were from ten to six.

**b.** (So long) before (a definite future time); *esp.* in stating the time of day: (so many minutes) before (an hour). Opposed to *past*.

*c* **1000** *Soul's Addr. to Body* 37 (Gr.) Þæt hit wære xxx. þusend wintra to þinum deaðdæʒe. **1519** in *Fabric Rolls York Minster* (Surtees) 269 To ryng to matyns at evere daie,..at halfe oure to v. **1596** SHAKS. *Merch. V.* v. i. 303 Or goe to bed, now being two houres to day. **1641** R. CARPENTER *Experience* I. Med. xiv. 102 It wil not be long to this time. **1833** T. HOOK *Parson's Dau.* I. iii, How long is it to dinner, sir? **1843** *Blackw. Mag.* LIV. 733 It was exactly a quarter to four o'clock. **1852** R. S. SURTEES *Sponge's Sp. Tour* (1893) 35 'We shall be late. See, it's only ten *to* now' [i.e. 10 minutes to the hour], continued he, pointing to the timepiece above the fire.

**c.** *from..to*, with repeated sb. of time, denoting regular recurrence; as *from day to day*, *from time to time*, *from month to month*.

**1014** WULFSTAN *Serm. ad Anglos* in *Hom.* (Napier) 156 (MS.E.) For folces synnan fram dæʒe to dæʒe. **1297–1712** [see DAY *sb.* 19]. *c* **1325–1895** [see FROM 3 b]. **1423–1891** [see TIME *sb.* 41 a].

**7.** At (a time), on (a day) (now *dial.*); † in, during (a time) (*obs. rare*). Cf. TO-DAY, TO-MORROW, TO-NIGHT, TO-YEAR.

This use of *to* in *tódæg*, etc., has been explained as originating in sense 6, through phrases like *nu gyt to dæg* 'now still to this day', shortened to *to dæg*; but it is doubtful whether this covers the whole ground. The mod. s.w. use of *to* with expressions of time seems parallel to its use with place in 4.

*c* **890** tr. *Bæda's Hist.* I. ix. [xii.] (1890) 46 (MS. B.) Eorðweall..þone mon nu ȝyt to dæȝe sceawian mæȝ. *Ibid.* I. ix. [xi.] 44 Ceastre & torras..þa we to dæȝ sceawian maȝon. *c* **893** K. ÆLFRED *Oros.* II. iv. § 5 Nu ȝiet todæȝe hit is on leoðum sungen. *c* **1000** *Ags. Gosp.* Luke xi. 5 Hwylc eower hæfð sumne freond, & gæþ to midre nihte to him [etc.]. *c* **1000** ÆLFRIC *Hom.* II. 194 Swa micel..swa he to ðam dæȝe ȝeðicgan mihte. *c* **1300** *Beket* 769 Com to morwe to speche time. **13..** *Guy Warw.* (A.) 4595 Þat to hir comen y schold To on day þat was y-sett. **1551** HOOPER *Injunctions* xix. Wks. (Parker Soc.) II. 136 In no parish.. shall the bells be rung to noon upon the Saturdays. **1886** ELWORTHY *W. Somerset Word-bk.* s.v., I'll be ready to dree o'clock.

**b.** Indicating the precise time at which something is to be done, or at which one is to arrive: At and not after (an appointed time), precisely or punctually at or on.

**1722** DE FOE *Col. Jack* (1840) 230 The duke..pressed earnestly to put it to a day, and come to a battle. *a* **1785** LD. SACKVILLE in *Eng. Hist. Rev.* Apr. (1910) 316, I shan't be to my time. **1849** MACAULAY *Hist. Eng.* iii. I. 287 Unable to pay their hearth money to the day. **1893** *Chamb. Jrnl.* 1 July 406/1 Ainsworth came to his time.

**III.** Expressing the relation of purpose, destination, result, effect, resulting condition or status.

**8.** Indicating aim, purpose, intention, or design: For; for the purpose of; with the view or end of; in order to. (Now often replaced by *for.*)

*Beowulf* (Z.) 3016 Nalles eorl weȝan maððum to ȝe-myndum. *c* **893** K. ÆLFRED *Oros.* I. i. § 15 Hiora hyd bið swiðe god to sciprapum. *c* **1000** ÆLFRIC *Hom.* I. 82 To ði he com þæt he wolde his heofenlice rice..mannum forȝyfan. **1297** R. GLOUC. (Rolls) 10691 In gibet hii were anhonge as to more vilte [disgrace]. *c* **1380** WYCLIF *Sel. Wks.* III. 347 Þei..traveiliden more bisili to growynge and profiting of þe Chirche. *c* **1450** *Godstow Reg.* 365 I-strengthed with the seales of bothe chapiters to more suerte. **1585** J. B. tr. *Viret's School Beastes* A vj b, To the ende that the seedes whiche they hyde in the earth, shoulde not growe. **1683** MOXON *Mech. Exerc., Printing* x, He was bred up to Joynery. *a* **1715** BURNET *Own Time* an. 1661 (1823) I. 318 There were few books set out to sale. **1726** LEONI *Alberti's Archit.* Pref. 3 Waters..employ'd to so many different and useful purposes. **1843** *Fraser's Mag.* XXVIII. 715 The captain..came to our rescue. **1894** C. N. ROBINSON *Brit. Fleet* 50 The indispensable means to our end. **1902** *Times* 21 July 13/6 Land..planted to walnuts.

**b.** Combining the notions of 'purpose' and 'motion so as to reach' (1) or 'contiguity' (5 b).

*c* **897** K. ÆLFRED *Gregory's Past. C.* xliv. 328 Dryhten.. ðonne he cymð to ðæm dome. **1471–** [see GRASS *sb.* 5, 5 b]. *a* **1523** HAWES *His Epitaph*, Though the daye be never so long, At last the bells ringeth to evensong. *a* **1592** GREENE *Orpharion* Wks. (Grosart) XII. 69 They sate downe ..to dinner. **1648** GAGE *West. Ind.* 154 That solemn meeting of the people to Fairs and mirth. **1806** A. HUNTER *Culina* (ed. 3) 133 You sit down to writing at your bureau. **1838** TICKNOR in *Life*, etc. (1876) II. viii. 147 We were out..to breakfast.

**c.** *spec.* Towards or for the making of; as a contributory element or constituent of.

*c* **1450** *St. Cuthbert* (Surtees) 807 Stikkes to a fyre þai gadird fast. *c* **1500** *Demaundes Joyous* in *Rel. Ant.* II. 74 Howe many strawes go to gose nest? R. None, for lacke of fete. **1579** *Ibid.* I. 255, 10 yerds yelow lace that went to my lether dublett. **1621** BURTON *Anat. Mel.* III. iv. I. iii. (1651) 667 To the roof of Apollo Didymeus Temple..a thousand okes did not suffice. **1890** *Harper's Mag.* May 961/2 Whole gardens of roses go to one drop of the attar.

**9.** Indicating destination, or an appointed or expected end or event. (After *ready, prepared*, etc., *for* is now substituted.)

*c* **1205** LAY. 13428 A he seide þat Bruttes Neoren noht to nuttes. **13..** *K. Alis.* 2451 (Bodl. MS.) Ten hundreþ weren to deþ ydiȝth. **1388** WYCLIF *Ps.* xxxvii[i]. 18 [17], Y am redi to betyngis. *c* **1430** *Hymns Virg.* 99 To bie oure soulis to blis. *a* **1540** BARNES *Wks.* (1573) 342/2 Your stockes bee made to the fyer. **1697** DRYDEN *Virg. Georg.* IV. 463 Born to bitter Fate. **1865** KINGSLEY *Herew.* xxviii, He had.. made up his mind to the event. **1887** BESANT *The World went* ii, He was..sentenced to transportation.

**10.** Indicating result, effect, or consequence: So as to produce, cause, or result in.

For *to one's cost* or *charge* see COST *sb.*[2] 5 d, CHARGE *sb.* 10.

*c* **893** K. ÆLFRED *Oros.* I. vii. § 1 Þæt wæs þæt forme, þæt hyra wæter wurdon to blode. *c* **1175** *Lamb. Hom.* 27 Mare hit him deð to herme þenne to gode. *c* **1380** WYCLIF *Sel. Wks.* II. 210 What caas þat fallip to him, it mut nedis falle to his betere [= betterment, advantage]. *c* **1425** WYNTOUN *Cron.* I. v. 206 He dang him with his bow to deid. **1563** *Homilies* II. *Inform. Offence H. Script.* II. (1850) 380 Though the rehearsal of the genealogies..be not to much edification. **1623** GOUGE *Serm. Extent God's Provid.* § 13 Fire brake out to the destruction of many. **1802** MAR. EDGEWORTH *Moral T.* (1816) I. xi. 92 To his..astonishment. **1888** *Times* (weekly ed.) 6 Apr. 16/4 To light those buildings by electricity, to the total exclusion of gas. **1908** R. BAGOT *A. Cuthbert* xxviii, But now, to his despair, he felt that his patient herself was fighting against his skill.

†**b.** *To take* (etc.) *to the best* or *worst*: to put the best, or worst, construction upon; to make the best, or worst, of. *Obs.*

*c* **1440** *Jacob's Well* 286 Euyr-more þou demyst euyll & to þe werste. **1563** BALDWIN in *Mirr. Mag.* X viij b, The good take yll thynges to the best. **1569** J. ROGERS *Gl. Godly Loue* (1876) 183 With a loving patience to take all things to the best. **1629** N. CARPENTER *Achitophel* 43 More honour found Homer in expressing mens manners to the best, than Hegemon to the worst.

**11.** Indicating a state or condition resulting from some process: So as to become: = INTO 6 a. Also *colloq.* (after the vb. *to be*, in *all to pieces* or the like): Reduced to the condition of, having become.

† *All to naught*: see ALL C. 12, NAUGHT *sb.* 1 d.

*c* **893** K. ÆLFRED *Oros.* v. iv. § 4 Ealle ða clifu..forburnan to ascan. *c* **1000** ÆLFRIC *Lev.* i. 6 And hyldon þa offrunga & ceorfon to sticcon. *c* **1175** *Lamb. Hom.* 143 He is þet makeð twa to an. *c* **1205** LAY. 9425 Al þa wunliche burh heo barnden to duste. *c* **1400** MAUNDEV. (Roxb.) v. 14 After a ȝere it turnez to whyte. **1470–85** MALORY *Arthur* IV. xvi. 140 Brente to coles. **1612** CAPT. SMITH *Map Virginia* 31 Tops of Deeres hornes boyled to a ielly. *a* **1720** VANBRUGH *Journ. to London* III. ad fin., The glasses [of the coach] are all to bits. **1802** MAR. EDGEWORTH *Moral T.* (1816) I. iv. 24 Forester..took the flowers..and pulled them to pieces. **1870** *Eng. Mech.* 28 Jan. 477/1 Shaped to an accurate figure.

**b.** Indicating resulting position, status, or capacity: For, as, by way of, in the capacity of. *Obs.* or *arch.* exc. in certain phrases, as *to take to wife, to call to witness*, etc.

*c* **890** tr. *Bæda's Hist.* III. xv. [xxi.] (1890) 222 Se wæs ..his freond [and] hæfde his sweostor to wife. *c* **1000** *Ags. Gosp.* Luke iii. 8 We habbað us to fæder abraham. *c* **1000** ÆLFRIC *Gen.* xx. 12 Ic ȝenam hiȝ þa to wife. — *Deut.* iv. 26 Ic hæbbe todæȝ to ȝewitnisse heofen and eorþan. *c* **1175** *Lamb. Hom.* 117 Ic þe ȝef to scawere mine folke israeles hirede. **13..** *St. Ambrosius* 125 in Horstm. *Altengl. Leg.* (1878) 10/1 Ambrose..To vr bisschop we wol haue. *c* **1386** CHAUCER *Pars. T.* ⁋ 271 He ne hadde no mete but herbes and water to his drynke. *c* **1460** FORTESCUE *Abs. & Lim. Mon.* x. (1885) 131 The qwene off Ffraunce hath but v. Mˡ marke yerely to huyr douer. **1590** SPENSER *F. Q.* I. i. 28 So forward on his way (with God to frend) He passed forth. **1632** MILTON *Penseroso* 113 Who had Canace to wife? **1879** SWINBURNE *Stud. Shaks.* i. (1880) 28 The high-born poem which had Sackville to father and Sidney to sponsor.

**12.** Indicating that to which something tends or points. **a.** Indicating the object of inclination, desire, or need: For. Also (after *to drink*, etc.), As an expression of desire for (one's health, success, or the like): cf. 26 b.

*c* **1200** [see LONGING *vbl. sb.*[1] 1]. *a* **1300** *Sarmun* li. in *E. E. P.* (1862) 6 To met no drink þer nis no nede. **1366** [see APPETITE *sb.* 3]. **1451** CAPGRAVE *Life St. Aug.* 4 Þei herd sey þat her child had a grete corage to lernyng. **1605–** [see MIND *sb.*[1] 13 d]. **1605–** [see DRINK *v.* 13 b]. **1760** *Vcy. W. O. G. Vaughan* I. 38 You'll spoil her Stomach to her dinner. **1827** SCOTT *Highl. Widow* v, 'To your health, mother!' said Hamish. **1865** KINGSLEY *Herew.* xxxii, Instead of marrying Torfrida.., I have more mind to her niece.

**b.** Indicating the object of a right or claim.

*c* **1205** [see RIGHT *sb.*[1] 7]. **1377** LANGL. *P. Pl.* B. XVIII. 291 We haue no trewe title to hem. **1481–** [see PRETEND *v.* 13]. **1600** W. WATSON *Decacordon* (1602) 292 When men receiue the Gospell and are baptized..they receiue thereby an interest to the kingdome of heauen. **1602** [see HEIR *sb.* 2]. **1623** *Dial. Laws Eng.* xlvii. 149 If a man buy a horse in open market of him that in right had no propertie to him. **1752** [see CLAIM *sb.* 2]. **1879** M. J. GUEST *Lect. Hist. Eng.* xxv. 252 Thirteen..came forward as claimants to the crown. **1890** LD. ESHER in *Law Times Rep.* LXIII. 694/1 This lease..is a document of title to land.

**IV.** Followed by a word or phrase expressing a limit in extent, amount, or degree.

**13.** Indicating a limit or point attained in degree or amount, or in division or analysis, and thus expressing degree of completeness or exactitude: As far as; to the point of; down to (an ultimate element or item), as in phr. *to a hair* (HAIR *sb.* 8 c), *to the last man, to a man* (including every man, without exception); within (a limit of variation or error), as *to an inch, to a day*. (See also quots. s.v. DOWN *adv.* 14.)

*c* **1000** ÆLFRIC *Saints' Lives* xx. 42 Heo wel drohtnode to anum mæle fæstende. *a* **1300** *Cursor M.* 21527 Of he kest al to his serk. **1377** LANGL. *P. Pl.* B. v. 173 Þei..do me faste frydayes to bred and to water. **1552** HULOET, To the vttermost peny, *ad assem.* **1606–** [see HAIR *sb.* 8 c]. **1607–** [see TITTLE *sb.* 2 b]. **1618** BOLTON *Florus* (1636) 149 They might have had the killing of all his Army to a man. **1670** MILTON *Hist. Eng.* II. Wks. (1847) 491/1 That he would root them out to the very name. **1766** GOLDSM. *Vic. W.* xi, Sir Tomkyn..swore he was hers to the last drop of his blood. **1779** *Mirror* No. 34 ⁋ 5 He was generally punctual to a minute. **1867** FROUDE *Short Stud., Erasm. & Luther* ii. 99 The bishops were hostile to a man. **1872** YEATS *Techn. Hist. Comm.* 349 Balances are made sensitive to the fraction of a grain.

**b.** Indicating the final point or second limit of a series, or of the extent of a variable quantity or quality; correl. to *from* (expressed or implied).

**1699** [see FROM 2 b]. **1725** DE FOE *Voy. round World* (1840) 111 Here they found eleven to thirteen fathom soft oozy sand. **1823** F. CLISSOLD *Ascent Mt. Blanc* 23 The western arc of the misty circle kindled, from a rosy to a deep reddening glow. **1866** LAWRENCE tr. *Cotta's Rocks Class.* (1878) 141 A granular to compact aggregate. **1891** J. LEYLAND *Peak Derbysh.* i. 15 Every style from early Norman to late perpendicular.

**14.** Indicating the full extent, degree, or amount: So as to reach, complete, or constitute. Chiefly in advb. phrases, as *to a certainty, to a degree, to (that,* etc.) *extent, to a fault, to the full*, etc.: see also the sbs. See also *up to* s.v. UP.

*c* **1000** ÆLFRIC *Lev.* xxvi. 5 ȝe etaþ to fylle. *c* **1407** LYDG. *Reson & Sens.* 220 The beaute of hir face..so bryght, That the goddesse Proserpyne..To hir beaute ne myght appere. **1473** WARKW. *Chron.* (Camden) 15 Knyghtes, squyers, and comons to the nombre of xx. mˡ. **1596** DANETT tr. *Comines* (1614) 140 They should not be able to pay a ransome to the value of the spurs and bridle bits in his campe. **1628** GAULE *Pract. The. Panegyr.* 60 Done, Done to full, whatsoe're he came to doe. **1720** *Lond. Gaz.* No. 5814/2 Bank Bills..to the Value of three hundred and sixty Millions of Livres. **1829** SCOTT *Wav.* Introd., Gallant, courteous, and brave, even to chivalry. *Mod.* He was generous to a fault.

**b.** Combining the notion of 'extent' with 'result' (10): So far or so much as to cause.

[*c* **1000** *Ags. Gosp.* Matt. xxvi. 38 Unrot ys min sawl oþ deað.] *c* **1175** *Lamb. Hom.* 121 Crist..wes ibuhsum þan heuenliche federe to þa deðe. ? *a* **1500** *Wycket* (1828) 1 In greate suffirance of persecution euen to the death. **1625** MASSINGER *New Way* II. ii, Yet he to admiration still increases In wealth. **1749** FIELDING *Tom Jones* v. vi, She was in love with him to distraction. **1834** M. SCOTT *Cruise Midge* vi. (1863) 100 We were laughing at this to our heart's content. **1873** RALFE *Phys. Chem.* 108 The filtrate and washings are ..evaporated..to dryness. **1890** *Harper's Mag.* Mar. 564/2 The schoolroom was hot to suffocation.

**c.** After a verb (or derived sb.) denoting limitation or the like, and before a sb. (or sb. phr.) expressing the amount, extent, space, etc. *to* which something is restricted.

**1518** *Sel. Pl. Star Chamb.* (Selden) II. 128 Without that the seid Inhabitauntes..haue byn lymytted..to eny certen nowmber of Catell. **1649–** [see CONFINE *v.* 7 b]. **1691–** [see CONFINEMENT 2]. **1697** VANBRUGH *Relapse* I. iii, Your honour's side-face is reduced to the tip of your nose. **1701** W. WOTTON *Hist. Rome, Marcus* vi. 106 Marcus..fix'd their Allowance to two Attic Talents a Man. **1885** *Law Times Rep.* LIII. 527/2 There is nothing on the face of this will to cut down the widow's absolute interest to a life estate.

**V.** Indicating addition, attachment, accompaniment, appurtenance, possession.

**15.** In addition to, besides, with.

*c* **897** K. ÆLFRED *Gregory's Past. C.* xli. 303 Se læce, ðonne he bietre wyrta deð to hwelcum drence. *c* **1000** ÆLFRIC *Saints' Lives* xxviii. 19 Candidus and uitalis and fela oþre to him. **1387** TREVISA *Higden* (Rolls) III. 73 He putte [orig. *addidit*] Ianeuer and Feuerrer to þe bygynnynge of þe ȝere. **1495** *Coventry Leet Bk.* 567 ȝe shall haue drynk to your Cake. **1593** SHAKS. *Lucr.* 1589 Foretell new stormes to those alreadie spent. **1653** WALTON *Angler* viii. 171 Mix these together, and put to them either Sugar, or Honey. **1742** RICHARDSON *Pamela* III. 327 To the Charms of Person, [she] should have a humble, teachable Mind. **1876** RUSKIN *Fors Clav.* lxix. § 12 (1906) III. 403 He can't have cream to his tea.

**b.** To the accompaniment of; as an accompaniment to. *To ride to hounds*: see HOUND *sb.*[1] 2.

**1561** T. HOBY tr. *Castiglione's Courtyer* II. (1900) 118 Syngynge to the Lute..is more plesaunte. **1676** tr. *Guillatiere's Voy. Athens* 397 Dancing-Masters, who danced to Two or Three Base-Vials, or Instruments very like them. **1794** MRS. RADCLIFFE *Myst. Udolpho* l, Performing a sprightly dance,..to the sounds of a lute and tamborine. **1825** *Sporting Mag.* XV. 346 We formerly rode after hounds, now we ride to them. **1894** NEWTON *Dict. Birds* 693 The old-fashioned practice of shooting Partridges to dogs.

**16.** After words denoting attachment or adherence; hence, sometimes = Attached, fastened, or joined to. (*lit.* or *fig.*)

*c* **890** tr. *Bæda's Hist.* III. xiv. [xvii.] (1890) 204 Þa næȝlas ..þe heo mid þæm to þæm timbre ȝefæstnad wæs. *c* **1050** *Byrhtferth's Handboc* in *Anglia* VIII. 324 Man..ða ræftras to ðære fyrste ȝefæstnaþ. **1297** R. GLOUC. (Rolls) 277 He wilnede mest of alle þing to him eliance. **1382** WYCLIF *2 Kings* i. 8 A rowȝ man, and with an hery gyrdyl to the reenys. **1583** STUBBES *Anat. Abus.* II. (1882) 109 An old gowne girded to him with a thong. **1596** SHAKS. *Tam. Shr.* IV. i. 7 My very lippes might freeze to my teeth. **1780** COWPER *Progr. Err.* 285 As creeping ivy clings to wood or stone. **1800** ADDISON *Amer. Law Rep.* 1 The infant was found dead in the..river, with a stone to it. **1849** MACAULAY *Hist. Eng.* vi. II. 113 Sincerely attached to the Established Church. **1875** JOWETT *Plato* (ed. 2) I. 176 To that opinion I shall always adhere.

**17.** After *belong* and verbs of similar meaning (q.v.); also after *be* with the sense of *belong*; also after a sb., in the sense 'appertaining or belonging to': sometimes equivalent to 'of' or the possessive case of the sb.

*c* **893** K. ÆLFRED *Oros.* I. i. § 21 Þæt Witland belimpeð to Estum. **972** *Charter* in Birch *Cart. Sax.* III. 589 Ðis sind þa land ȝemæra þæs londes þe lympð to Sture. **1451** *Rolls of Parlt.* V. 226/2 Godes..that were sumtyme to the seid William. *c* **1530** LD. BERNERS *Arth. Lyt. Bryt.* 299, I am doughter to a king. **1605** CAMDEN *Rem.* (1637) 281 Katherine, wife to Charles Brandon, Duke of Suffolke. **1719** DE FOE *Crusoe* (1840) I. i. 2 Lieutenant-colonel to an English regiment of foot. *Ibid.* 5 Clerk to an attorney.

**b.** Combining the notions of 'appurtenance' and 'addition' (15) or 'attachment' (16).

*c* **1420** *Chron. Vilod.* 3510 To delyuer hit to a goldesmyȝt, to make a shrene þat body to. **1538** *Acc. Ld. High Treas. Scot.* VI. 13 Gevin for four roundellis to speris, vj cronis. **1682** N. O. *Boileau's Lutrin* II. 126 This paltrey Jack Had scarce a Shooe to 's foot, a Rag to 's back. **1711** ADDISON *Spect.* No. 108 ⁋ 2 Your Whip wanted a Lash to it. **1832** HT. MARTINEAU *Life in Wilds* iii, One little boy complained..that there was no rim to his plate. **1840** R. H. DANA *Bef. Mast* xix. 53 Without clothing to his back, or shoes to his feet. **1847** HELPS *Friends in C.* I. v. 80 Both will and courage. Courage is the body to will. **1886** C. E. PASCOE *Lond. of To-day* xxx. (ed. 3) 269 The Hall now forms the vestibule to the Houses of Parliament.

**VI.** Expressing relation to a standard or to a stated term or point.

**18.** Expressing comparison: In comparison with,

as compared with. Also †*as to* (obs.). (See also 21.)

*c* **1000** ÆLFRIC *Hom.* II. 13 Ðes is ure God, and nis nan oðer ʒeteald to him. **1470–85** MALORY *Arthur* I. xxii. 69 Your myghte is nothyng to myn. **1523** LD. BERNERS *Froiss.* I. cclxviii. 396 His enemyes weer but a handfull of men, as to the nombre of his. **1546** J. HEYWOOD *Prov.* (1867) 46 There is no foole to the olde foole. **1602** SHAKS. *Ham.* I. ii. 140 So excellent a King, that was, to this, Hiperion to a Satyre. **1666** PEPYS *Diary* 21 Apr., It was so thick to its length. **1742** RICHARDSON *Pamela* III. 351 Now, by.. good Physick,..pretty well, to what they had been. **1863** COWDEN CLARKE *Shaks. Char.* viii. 202 The men are noodles to her.

**19. a.** Connecting the names of two things (usu. numbers or quantities) compared or opposed to each other in respect of amount or value, as the odds in a wager or contest, the terms of a ratio, or the constituents of a compound: Against, as against.

**1530** PALSGR. 712/1 Twenty to one he is ondone for ever. *a* **1548** HALL *Chron., Hen. V* 76 b, Their enemies..wer foure to one. **1596** SHAKS. 1 *Hen. IV*, II. iv. 592 O monstrous, but one halfe penny-worth of Bread to this intollerable deale of Sacke? **1628** HOBBES *Thucyd.* (1822) 127 There is no nation ..that are..able one nation to one to stand against the Scythians. *c* **1790** IMISON *Sch. Art* I. 212 The visible part of an object will be to the lens, as the focal distance of the lens, to the distance of the eye. **1846** *Penny Cycl.* Suppl. II. 432/1 The composition..consists of three-fourths of the putty..to one-fourth of calcined gypsum. **1885** *Manch. Exam.* 16 May 6/2 Mr. Gladstone's motion was carried by 337 to 38.

**b.** Connecting two expressions of number or quantity which correspond to each other, or of which one constitutes the amount or value of the other: In; making up. (*To the* = in every.)

*c* **1000**, **1297** [see c]. **1494** *Act* 11 *Hen. VII*, c. 4 That there be but only viii. Bushels rased and stricken to the Quarter of Corn. **1545** *Rates of Customs* c v, Twelue ounces to the pounde. **1593** SHAKS. 2 *Hen. VI*, IV. vii. 25 He..made vs pay..one shilling to the pound. **1660** JER. TAYLOR *Duct. Dubit.* III. iv. xiii. § 17 Three weeks of five days to the week. **1801** W. HUNTINGTON *Bank of Faith* Ded. 21 Thirteen to the dozen. **1891** S. C. SCRIVENER *Our Fields & Cities* 44 An open country..with solitary houses —a house to about five square miles.

**†c.** Introducing an expression denoting price or cost: For, at. *Obs.* (exc. as coinciding with b).

*c* **893** K. ÆLFRED *Oros.* III. vii. § 5 Þæt hie þa æt nihstan hie selfe to nohte bemætan. *c* **1000** *Ags. Gosp.* Matt. x. 29 Hu ne becypað hiʒ tweʒen spearwan to peninge? **1297** R. GLOUC. (Rolls) 8334 An ey [=egg] to tueie ssillinges..þo hii boʒte, & an hen vor viftene. **1483** in *Eng. Gilds* (1870) 337 Thath all Bakers of the said Cite..make butt ij. horse-lofys to a peny. **1656** H. PHILLIPS *Purch. Patt.* (1676) 12 Profit, at least to the rate of eight in the hundred. **1862** THACKERAY *Philip* ii. (1884) 110 Delicious little Havannahs, ten to the shilling.

**20.** Expressing agreement or adaptation: In accordance with, according to, after, by. (See also 21.)

*c* **897** K. ÆLFRED *Gregory's Past. C.* xxxvi. 249 Se ðe to Godes bisene ʒesceapen is. *a* **1300** *Cursor M.* 12946 Bidd þir stanes be bred to will. **1483** CAXTON *G. de la Tour* k v, I pray yow that ye take ensample to them. **1664** DRYDEN *Rival Ladies* Ep. Ded., Ess. (Ker) I. 9 The greatest part of my design has already succeeded to my wish. **1754** RICHARDSON *Grandison* (1781) I. xxxvi. 256 He dresses to the fashion. **1838** MACAULAY *Ess., Sir W. Temple* (1897) 419 Temple is not a man to our taste. **1878** MORLEY *Diderot*, etc. I. v. III. 203 As the neutral scribe writing to the dictation of an unseen authority.

**b.** Combining the senses 'according to' and 'to the extent of' (14): esp. in phr. *to one's knowledge*, †*power* (obs.), *remembrance*, etc. (= as far as one knows, is able, remembers, etc.), now usually *to the best of..*; *to all appearance*; etc. (See also the sbs.)

*To my knowledge*, qualifying a positive statement='as I actually know'; qualifying a negative statement='as far as I know'.

**1399** *Rolls of Parlt.* III. 452/1 If it were so taken and construed to the hegheste sentence and most rigorouste. *c* **1430** *Syr Gener.* (Roxb.) 1680, I shal help, to my power. **1512** *Act* 4 *Hen. VIII*, c. 20 *Preamble*, Strikyng with..swordes..and oder wepons to the uttermost of their powers. *a* **1548** HALL *Chron., Hen. VII* 3 b, The lyke was neuer harde of, to any mannes remembraunce before that tyme. **1636** MASSINGER *Gt. Dk. Flor.* Ded., It is above my strength..to celebrate to the desert your noble inclination. **1749** FIELDING *Tom Jones* IV. xiv, I will be sworn, to the best of my remembrance, I was in a passion. **1793** To all appearance [see APPEARANCE 8]. **1885** SIR H. COTTON in *Law Rep.* 30 Chanc. Div. 12 They were to all appearances distinct bills.

**1542** N. UDALL in *Lett. Lit. Men* (Camden) 3 To my knowlege I have not eftsons offended. **1828** MARLY *Life Planter Jamaica* 78 To my own knowledge he often tries to dissuade. **1883** SIR W. B. BRETT in *Law Rep.* 11 Q. B. Div. 512 The article was, to the knowledge of the defendant, supplied for the use of the wife. *Mod.* He has not been here to-day to my knowledge.

**21.** After words expressing comparison, proportion, correspondence, agreement or disagreement, and the like: see also these words themselves.

In some cases now replaced by or interchangeable with other prepositions, esp. *with*; after *worthy*, and words denoting precise proportion, as *double*, now replaced by *of*; after *different*, *from* is considered more correct. After *like* adj. and adv., *to* is now usually omitted. See these words.

*c* **1290** *Beket* 324 in *S. Eng. Leg.* I. 116 He nam..þan clerkene Robe, ase to is stat bi-cam. *a* **1300**– [see LIKE *a.* 1 a]. **1382** WYCLIF *Heb.* xi. 38 To which the world was not worthi. **1387** TREVISA *Higden* (Rolls) I. 45 Þe proporcioun of þe roundenesse aboute of a cercle is to þe brede as is þe proporcioun of two and twenty to seuene. **1470–85** MALORY *Arthur* v. viii. 175 Arthur.., to whome none erthely prynce may compare. **1550** CROWLEY *Way to Wealth* Sel. Wks. (E.E.T.S.) 133 The rentes be..some double, some triple, and some four fould to that they were. **1599** SHAKS. *Much Ado* v. ii. 38, I can finde out no rime to Ladie but babie, an innocent rime. **1651** WITTIE *Primrose's Pop. Err.* 432 Those things which are the same [=equal] to one third are the same among themselves. **1737** WHISTON *Josephus' Antiq.* Dissert. i, This..testimony..exactly agrees to him under that character. **1823** F. COOPER *Pioneers* iii, Strangely contrasted to the chill aspect of the lake. **1849** MACAULAY *Hist. Eng.* vi. II. 17 Lewis was not inferior to James in generosity and humanity, and was..far superior to James in all the abilities..of a statesman.

**†b.** After an adj. in the comparative degree: Than. Now *rare* or *Obs.* (Cf. *inferior to*, *superior to*, in prec. sense.)

*c* **1315** SHOREHAM *Poems* i. 590 Nys none of wymman beter ibore To seint Iohan þe baptyste. **14..** *MS. Harl. 2261* lf. 225 An oþer Decius, yonger to hym. **1569** J. SANFORD tr. *Agrippa's Van. Artes* 69 There are..philosophers.. herein no lesse ridiculouse to the poetes, which write [etc.]. **1771** T. HULL *Sir W. Harrington* (1797) IV. 108 The really good are so far less in number to the bad. **1895** P. WHITE *King's Diary* 96 A more formal repast, fashioned on a smaller scale to that provided at Langdale.

**22.** Expressing relation (generally or vaguely): In respect of, concerning, about, of, as to (see AS *adv.* 33). Now only in special collocations.

In *to name* (obs.), *to trade*, etc. (*Sc.* and *north. dial.*), now expressed by 'by'.

*a* **1300** *Cursor M.* 19806 Cornelius to nam he hight. **1450** *Rolls of Parlt.* V. 179/1 Reporte her advise what shuld be doon to the Articles comprised in the said Bille. **1481** CAXTON *Reynard* xxxix. (Arb.) 105 He was lygher to fote than he. **1513** DOUGLAS *Æneis* I. v. 69 The ʒoung child, quhilk now Ascanius hecht, And to suirname clepit Iulus. **1590** SHAKS. *Mids. N.* III. ii. 62 What's this to my Lysander? **1593** — *Rich. II*, I. i. 110 What sayest thou to this? **1656** BURTON *Diary* (1828) I. 136 There was one Mr. Thorne..examined to the seal of the statute, whether the seal wanted not all the wax. **1693** J. EDWARDS *Author. O. & N. Test.* 308 Being conscious to my own inabilities. *a* **1716** BLACKALL *Wks.* (1723) I. 312 In speaking to the first of these Heads. **1724** RAMSAY *Clout the Caldron* i, I am a tinkler to my trade. **1884** W. C. SMITH *Kildrostan* 72 What will Doris say to it? **1892** *Guardian* 6 Jan. 8/3 Asking questions intended to show the untrustworthy character of a witness, or, as it is technically called, 'cross-examining to credit'.

**23.** Expressing relative position: esp. in *Geom.*

In some instances allied to senses 5, 16.

**1570**– [see PERPENDICULAR A. 2]. **1600** HAKLUYT *Voy.* III. 56 Parallel to the equinoctiall. **1660** BARROW *Euclid* III. Prop. xvi. Coroll., A right line drawn from the extremity of the diameter of a circle, and at right angles, is a tangent to the said circle. **1796** [see ASYMPTOTE]. **1813** BAKEWELL *Introd. Geol.* (1815) 58 Inclined to the horizon. **1848** J. H. NEWMAN *Loss & Gain* 147 Unable to see how they lie to each other. **1887** *Encycl. Brit.* XXII. 718/1 Turned round so as to place the micrometer tangentially to the circle. **1892** [see RIGHT ANGLE b].

**VII.** Expressing relations in which the sense of direction tends to blend with that of the dative.

**24.** After words denoting application, attention, or the like, indicating the object of this. Also (*arch.* or *rhet.*) with ellipsis of *go*, *betake oneself*, etc. (in imperative, or after an auxiliary).

*a* **1225** *Leg. Kath.* 115 Hire feder hefde iset hire earliche to lare. *c* **1290**– [see LISTEN *v.* 2 b]. **1426** LYDG. *De Guil. Pilgr.* 10104 How that an Ampte, a best smal ..To nouht elles doth entende, But on thys hylle vp tascende. *c* **1485** *Digby Myst.* III. 758, I synful creature, to grace I woll a-plye. *a* **1553** UDALL *Royster D.* IV. viii, Too it againe, my knightesses! **1616** *Marlowe's Faust.* vi, Let's to it presently. **1653** WALTON *Angler* ii. 47 I'll to my own Art. **1710** PALMER *Proverbs* 254 To it they went with great fury. **1719** DE FOE *Crusoe* (1840) I. xvii. 294 We fell to digging. **1843** *Blackw. Mag.* LIV. 219 Come, lads, all hands to work!

**25.** Expressing impact (cf. 1, 5 a) or attack: At, against, upon.

*a* **1225** *Ancr. R.* 62 Vre vo..scheot..mo cwarreaus to one ancre þen to seouene & seouenti lefdies iðe worlde. **1375** BARBOUR *Bruce* x. 312 [He] set a sege to the castele. *c* **1420** *Avow. Arth.* xxiv, Take thi schild and thi spere, And ride to him a couse on werre. **1569** *St. Papers Eliz., Foreign* XI. 151 He had forces sufficient to make head to his enemies. **1641** BROME *Jov. Crew* IV. i, Heark! they knock to the Dresser. **1749** FIELDING *Tom Jones* XVIII. xii, Western..with his hunting voice and phrase, cried out, 'To her, boy, to her, go to her'. **1832** SIR J. CAMPBELL *Mem.* II. ii. 46, I presented it [the gun] to him without any other idea but that of intimidation. **1882** G. MACDONALD *Weighed & Wanting* III. xviii. 256 His father's unmerciful use of the whip to him. **1888, 1889** [see TAKE *v.* 24 b].

**b.** After words denoting opposition or hostility: Against; towards (*obs.* or *arch.*). †In quot. 1670 *simply*: Against, so as to prevent (*obs.*).

Cf. *to one's face*, *teeth*, etc., in 5 b.

**13..** *E. E. Allit. P.* B. 1230 Hade þe fader..neuer trepast to him in teche of mysseleue. **1388** WYCLIF *Ps.* l. 6 [li. 4], I haue synned to thee aloone. *Ibid.* lxxxiv. 6 Whether thou schalt be wrooth to vs withouten ende? **1526** TINDALE *Col.* iii. 13 If eny man have a quarrel to a nother. **1613** SHAKS. *Hen. VIII*, I. i. 43 To the disposing of it nought rebell'd. **1670** WALTON *Life Herbert* Pref., To embalm and preserve his sacred body to putrefaction. **1741** MIDDLETON *Cicero* (1742) I. iv. 264 Clodius had an old grudge to the King, for refusing to ransom him. **1901** G. DOUGLAS *Ho. w. Green Shutters* 261 He had a triple wrath to his son.

**26.** Indicating the object of speech, address, or the like; sometimes more vaguely: Before, in the presence (sight, hearing) of.

*c* **893** K. ÆLFRED *Oros.* VI. xxxiv. § 2 He cwæð to ðæm folce. *c* **1000** ÆLFRIC *Gen.* vi. 13 God cwæð þa to Noe. **1154** *O. E. Chron.* an. 1135 Durste nan man sei to him naht bute god. *c* **1230**– [see ANSWER *v.* 12 b]. *a* **1300** *Cursor M.* 25312 If þou prais [= prayest] to godd þat he..þi sinnes forgiue to þe. *c* **1386** CHAUCER *Sqr.'s T.* 208 Another rowned to his felawe lowe. **1609** BIBLE (Douay) 1 *Kings* xviii. 6 The wemen came forth..singing and dancing to Saul the King. *a* **1625** FLETCHER *Hum. Lieut.* I. i, Did you not mark a woman, my son rose to? **1711** ADDISON *Spect.* No. 60 ¶ 2 An Hymn in Hexameters to the Virgin Mary. **1820** SHELLEY *Skylark* 1 Hail to thee, blithe Spirit!

**b.** In honour of; for the worship of (as *to build a temple* or *altar to*); in salutation of and expression of good wishes for (as *to drink to*: see also 12 a, and DRINK *v.* 13 b).

**1382** WYCLIF *Acts* xix. 24 Sum man..makinge siluerene housis to Dian. **1388** — *Acts* xvii. 23, Y..foond an auter, in which was writun, To the vnknowun God. **1530**– [see DRINK *v.* 13 b]. **1592**– [see HERE *adv.* 2 b]. **1611** SHAKS. *Wint. T.* IV. iv. 62 Her face o' fire With labour, and the thing she tooke to quench it She would to each one sip. **1616** B. JONSON *Forest, To Celia* 1 Drink to me, only with thine eyes. **1712** STEELE *Spect.* No. 462 ¶ 4 With continual toasting Healths to the Royal Family. **1838** THIRLWALL *Greece* II. xvi. 353 They erected an altar to the father of the gods.

**27.** Expressing response or the like (of a voluntary agent); e.g. reply (*to* a statement, question, etc.), obedience or disobedience (*to* a command, etc.).

**1297**– [see ASSENT *v.* 1, 4]. **1382**, *c* **1400**– [see ANSWER *v.* 12 l, d]. *c* **1420** *Chron. Vilod.* 1123 Wylde bestes & folys of flyʒt To here clepynge wolde come. **1582** ALLEN *Martyrd. Campion* (1908) 68 A proclamation was red..and at the end thereof was said, God save the Queene. To which he said, Amen. **1641** R. CARPENTER *Experience* I. ch. xvii. 116 When the silly Shepheard commeth to his call. **1754** RICHARDSON *Grandison* V. xliv. 283, I will write to your letter. *a* **1766** MRS. F. SHERIDAN *Sidney Bidulph* V. 115 Disobedience to his orders. **1897** *Badminton Mag.* Apr. 451 The next step is to take the pups out..and make them drop to hand.

**b.** Expressing reaction or responsive action (of an involuntary or inanimate agent); the object of *to* denoting the agent causing this.

**1682** OTWAY *Venice Preserved* II. i, My heart beats to this Man as if it knew him. **1768** BEATTIE *Minstr.* I. iii, His harp..Which to the whistling wind responsive rung. **1805** SCOTT *Last Minstr.* II. x, Full many a scutcheon and banner ..Shook to the cold night-wind. **1815** — *Guy M.* iii, Little waves..sparkling to the moonbeams. **1850** TENNYSON *In Mem.* Concl. 64 The dead leaf trembles to the bells.

**28.** Expressing exposure (of a thing *to* some physical agent).

**1460–70** *Bk. Quintessence* 9 Sette it to the strong sunne in somer tyme. *c* **1500** *Melusine* xxx. 226 Mounted vpon a grete hors, his banere to the wynd. **1526** TINDALE *Acts* xxvii. 40 They..hoysed vppe the mayne sayle to the wynde. **1852** TENNYSON *Ode Dk. Wellington* 39 That tower of strength Which stood four-square to all the winds that blew.

**VIII.** Supplying the place of the dative in various other languages and in the earlier stages of English itself.

**29.** Introducing the recipient of anything given, or the person or thing upon whom or which an event acts or operates.

In OE. as in Latin, etc., expressed by the simple dative or indirect object; after *give*, *befall*, and various other verbs, *to* is still often omitted.

[*c* **893** K. ÆLFRED *Oros.* I. i. § 13 Ohthere sæde his hlaforde, Ælfrede cyninge, þæt [etc.]. *Ibid.* IV. vi. § 15 He him ʒeswor on his goda noman þæt [etc.]. *Ibid.* IV. x. § 6 He hit het ðæm folce dælan. *c* **897** — *Gregory's Past. C.* xlviii. 368 Godes æ, þe us forbiet deoflum to offrianne. *a* **900** *Ags. Ps.* (Th.) xxi[i]. 23 [25] Ic ʒylde min ʒehat Drihtne.]

**1297** R. GLOUC. (Rolls) 8183 Tancred & biaumond,..god herte hom nome to. *c* **1385** CHAUCER *L. G. W.* 533 Mars ʒaf to hire corone red parde. **1477–9** *Rec. St. Mary at Hill* 89 Paid to the Skauagers..viijd. *a* **1533** LD. BERNERS *Huon* cxlix. 568 All..were ioyful of that aduenture that was fallen to the emperoure. **1566** PAINTER *Pal. Pleas.* II. 336 Great dishonour would redound to us. **1667** MILTON *P. L.* XII. 138 By promise he receaves Gift to his Progenie of all that Land. **1711** ADDISON *Spect.* No. 123 ¶ 4 Having a Son born to him. **1770** GOLDSM. *Des. Vill.* 51 Ill fares the land, to hastening ills a prey, Where wealth accumulates, and men decay. **1850** R. G. CUMMING *Hunter's Life S. Afr.* (1902) 47/1, I fired two shots at them..during the night, but none fell to my shots. **1887** A. BIRRELL *Obiter Dicta* Ser. II. 156 He lost his heart to Peg Woffington.

**b.** Used esp. after *be*, *become*, *seem*, *appear*, *mean*, to indicate the recipient of an impression, the holder of a view or opinion; *to be* (something) *to*, to be (something) in the eyes, view, apprehension, or opinion of; also, to be of importance or concern to: *What is that to you?* What does that matter to you? How does that concern you? What have you to do with that?

**1362** LANGL. *P. Pl.* A. Prol. 32 As hit semeþ to vre siht. **1565** T. STAPLETON tr. *Staphylus' Apol.* 148 To these men Luther is a papist, and Caluin is the right..prophet. **1590**–**1908** [see SEEM *v.* 7]. **1798** WORDSW. *Peter Bell* I. xii, A primrose by a river's brim A yellow primrose was to him, And it was nothing more. **1850** J. H. NEWMAN *Diffic. Anglic.* I. ii. (1891) I. 46 Faith has one meaning to a Catholic, another to a Protestant. **1856** WHYTE MELVILLE *Kate Cov.* xi, Scarcely big enough for a hunter to my fancy. **1862** [see APPEAR *v.* 2]. *Mod.* To me it is simply absurd.

[*c* **950** *Lindisf. Gosp.* John xxi. 22 Huæd is ðe bi ðy? *vel* huæt is ðec ðæs? *Vulg.* Quid ad te?] *c* **1000** *Ags. Gosp.* ibid., Hwæt is to þe? **1382** WYCLIF ibid., What to thee?

sue thou me. **1526** TINDALE ibid., What is that to the? folowe thou me. **1526** — *Matt.* xxvii. 4 What is that to vs? se thou to that. **1611** BIBLE *Lam.* i. 12 Is it nothing to you, all ye that passe by? **1674** GREW *Anat. Trunks* II. ii. § 3 What the Mouth is, to an Animal; that the Root is to a Plant. **1843** *Fraser's Mag.* XXVIII. 328 What's that to you? *Mod.* It means a great deal to him.

**30.** Indicating the person or thing for whose benefit, use, disposal, or the like, anything is done or exists: For; for the use or benefit of; for (some one) to deal with or dispose of (esp. after *leave* vb.); at the disposal of. *To oneself* (as pred.), to or at one's own disposal, free from the approaches or action of others.

**1297** R. GLOUC. (Rolls) 7136 Vpe holi relikes harald suor to willam bastard Treuliche to wite engelond to him. *c* **1330** R. BRUNNE *Chron. Wace* (Rolls) 1033 To mangeneles he dide make stones. **1382** WYCLIF *Rom.* xiv. 6–8 He that etith, etith to the Lord..No man of vs lyueth to hym silf, and no man deieth to him silf. Sothli where we lyuen, we lyuen to the Lord; where we deien, we deien to the Lord. *c* **1400** *Laud Troy Bk.* 17214 The Gregais wol not hir bodi grauen, But let hit ligge to roke & rauen. *c* **1425** tr. *Arderne's Treat. Fistula* 100 It availeþ to al woundez for to hold þam opne. **1474** *Acc. Ld. High Treas. Scot.* I. 70 Gevin to Johne of Murray..to pay for clathis coft to Rannald gunnare. **1502** *Ibid.* II. 346 For ane gus to the Kingis halkis. **1586** MARLOWE *1st Pt. Tamburl.* II. v, I'll first assay To get the Persian kingdom to myself. **1611** BIBLE *Lev.* xxiii. 22 Neither shalt thou gather any gleaning of thy haruest: thou shalt leaue them vnto the poore, and to the stranger. **1653** WALTON *Angler* viii. 169 That hope and patience which I wish to all Fishers. **1695** DRYDEN *Parallel Poetry & Paint.* Ess. (ed. Ker) II. 153 The rest is left to the imagination. **1700** MARWOOD *Diary* in *Cath. Rec. Soc. Publ.* VII. 77 At 8 in the morn we took a Wagon to Our selves to Dunkerque. **1709–10** STEELE *Tatler* No. 118 ¶ 10 Your petitioner..worked to the Exchange, and to several Aldermens wives. **1801** *Farmer's Mag.* Jan. 109 Topped and tailed [turnips]..which I hope to preserve as food to my ewes at lambing time. **1822** W. IRVING in *Life & Lett.* (1864) II. 84 In the country, where I can be more to myself. **1895** FROUDE *Erasmus* xv. 320 Religious houses were dissolved, their property seized to the State. *Mod.* We had the railway-carriage all to ourselves.

**b.** Indicating the person or thing towards which an action, feeling, etc., is directed; esp. as the object of conduct, behaviour, or demeanour.

*To you*, an elliptical phrase of courtesy or deference, = 'my service to you' or the like (quot. 1855).

*c* **970**–*c* **1060** *Wifmannes Beweddung* c. 7 in Liebermann *Gesetze* 442 Ðæt hire man nan woh to ne do. *c* **1000** ÆLFRIC *Hom.* I. 240 Se is hyra and na hyrde, seðe..næfð inweardlice lufe to Godes sceapum. *c* **1175** *Lamb. Hom.* 31 Nat ic hwer heo beoð þeo men þe ic þene herm to dude. **1297** R. GLOUC. (Rolls) 5824 To þe godnesse of þe holymon þe deuel adde enuye. *c* **1430** *How Gd. Wijf tauȝte hir Douȝtir* 163 in *Babees Bk.* 44 To do to þem as þou woldist be doon to. **1712** STEELE *Spect.* No. 286 ¶ 1 That natural Horror we have to Evil. *a* **1758** DYER *Down Among the Dead Men* iii, Bacchus is a friend to Love. **1855** DICKENS *Holly-Tree* ii, 'I should wish you to find from themselves whether your opinion is correct'. 'Sir, to you', says Cobbs, 'that shall be done directly'.

**31.** Used in the syntactical construction of many intransitive verbs. (See also preceding senses, and the verbs themselves.)

**1583** BABINGTON *Commandm.* viii. (1637) 73 Modesty in this hungry creature must yeeld to necessity. **1697** DRYDEN *Virg. Georg.* III. 817 'Tis in vain..[to] trust to Physick. **1769** GOLDSM. *Hist. Rome* (1786) II. 61 That homage to which they had aspired. **1834** WORDSW. *Yarrow Revisited* viii, While they minister to thee. **1843** *Fraser's Mag.* XXVIII. 654, I have already alluded to the fact. **1875** POSTE *Gaius* I. Comm. (ed. 2) 87 The issue of a Denizen cannot inherit to him.

**b.** After *testify, witness, attest, swear, subscribe, confess, speak*, etc.: In support of; in assertion or acknowledgement of.

For *assent to* see 27; cf. also 21.

**1630** PRYNNE *Anti-Armin.* 75 Conclusions which euery man must subscribe too. **1710** ADDISON *Tatler* No. 259 ¶ 6 The Prisoner brought several Persons of good Credit to witness to her Reputation. **1737** WHISTON *Josephus, Antiq.* IX. xiv. § 2 Menander attests to it. **1771**– [see CONFESS *v.* 6]. **1776** *Trial of Nundocomar* 79/1 That is a fact to which I can speak. **1776** *Trial J. Fowke* c. 28/2, I took his affidavit to the truth of the contents of the Letters. **1802** MAR. EDGEWORTH *Moral T.* (1816) I. xix. 157 He would swear to the person from whom he received the note. **1884** *Manch. Exam.* 7 July 4/6 The hon. gentlemen spoke to a resolution congratulating the Government on the passing of the Franchise Bill.

**c.** In obsolete, archaic, or dialectal use: chiefly representing an OE. dative or French const. with *à*; now omitted, the verb being treated as *trans.*

*a* **1325**–*c* **1450** [see PLEASE *v.* 1, 3 a]. *c* **1380** WYCLIF *Sel. Wks.* III. 362 Who shulde..mor obe[i]she to þe pope þan to Crist? **1382** — *Dan.* iii. 57 (Benedicite) Blesse ȝe, alle the werkis of the Lord, to the Lord. *c* **1449** PECOCK *Repr.* I. xvi. 90 Serue to God. *Ibid.* II. xv. 234 Bileue thou to me. **1692** R. L'ESTRANGE *Josephus, Wars Jews* II. xxvi. (1733) 654 They should renounce to all manner of unlawful Violences. **1800** A. SWANSTON *Serm. & Lect.* (1803) II. 318 Titus and..Timotheus also were present and assisting to the apostle. **1874** SWINBURNE *Bothwell* v. iv, If I did ill to seek to that strong hand.

**32.** In the syntactical const. of many transitive verbs, introducing the indirect or dative object. (See also preceding senses, and the verbs themselves.)

*a* **1300** [see sense 26]. *c* **1385** CHAUCER *L. G. W.* 2128 (*Ariadne*) Now be we duchessis..And sekerede to the regalys of Athenys. *c* **1450** *Cov. Myst.* xiv. (1841) 141 To God in this case my cawse I have betaught. **1581** in Allen *Martyrd. Campion* (1908) 15 Her Maiestie will preferre him to great livings. **1666** PEPYS *Diary* 4 June, We fought them and put them to the run. **1779** *Mirror* No. 21 ¶ 1 This day's paper I devote to Correspondents. **1849** MACAULAY *Hist. Eng.* vi. II. 142 To admit Roman Catholics to municipal advantages.

**b.** In obsolete, archaic, or dialectal use; now replaced by other prepositions, or by different constructions. See under the vbs.

*c* **1500** *Melusine* vi. 32 Many..shall axe to you tydynges of the Erle. **1534** CROMWELL in Merriman *Life & Lett.* I. 387 To answer unto suche thinges as then shalbe leyed and obiected to you. **1537** *Bury Wills* 130, I put them to the dysposycion of myne executo^rs. **1558** in Strype *Ann. Ref.* (1709) I. App. iv. 5 Not to pardon, till they..put themselves wholly to her highness's mercy. **1660** F. BROOKE tr. *Le Blanc's Trav.* 37 We now had associated ourselves to a jolly company of Merchants. **1709** STRYPE *Ann. Ref.* I. xl. 410 The French hostages were put to liberty at Windsor. **1780** *Mirror* No. 87 ¶ 3 To masses and crucifixes, and images, were substituted a precise severity of manner, and long sermons, and a certain mode of sanctifying the Sabbath. **1794** G. ADAMS *Nat. & Exp. Philos.* I. xi. 465 If an alkali be substituted to the turnsole. **1823** F. COOPER *Pioneers* xii, His mild features were confronted to the fierce..looks of the chief.

**33.** Expressing the relation of an adj. (or derived adv. or sb.) to a sb. denoting a person or thing to which its application is directed or limited.

In the construction of such adjs. as *accessible, adverse, agreeable, beneficial, common, complaisant, constant, difficult, due, easy, equal, essential, faithful, false, familiar, favourable, friendly, good, grateful, hostile, hurtful, impossible, incredible, injurious, kind, liable, manifest, natural, near, necessary, obedient, possible, proper, requisite, salutary, similar, subject, suitable, true, useful, visible, welcome*, etc., q.v., with their opposites; also, in a special sense, *alive, dead, deaf, blind, insensible*; also many adj. phrases, as *with child, in calf, of use, of value* (see the sbs.).

[In OE. mostly expressed by the dative: e.g. *c* **888** K. ÆLFRED *Boeth.* xiv. § 3 Þam neatum is ȝecynde. *c* **893** — *Oros.* I. i. § 3 Þa sindon neh þæm garsecge. *Ibid.* I. vii. § 1 Hy..him ȝehyrsume wæron. *c* **897** — *Gregory's Past. C.* xxxvi. 260 Hwa sceal..Gode unðoncfull beon?]

*c* **888** K. ÆLFRED *Boeth.* xxiv. § 2 Forðæm hit bið ofdælre ðærto. *c* **890** tr. *Bæda's Hist.* IV. xxv. [xxiv.] (1890) 348 Hwæþer heo ealle smolt mod &..bliðe to him hæfdon. **971** *Blickl. Hom.* 103 Hi wæron to deaþe ȝearwe. *c* **1000** ÆLFRIC *Hom.* II. 60 Þa wæs Abraham ..ȝearo to Godes hæse. **1303**– [see COMMON *a.* 3]. **1382**– [see NECESSARY *a.*] **1393**– [see DUE *a.* 5 a, 9]. **1393** LANGL. *P. Pl.* C. xx. 226 Beoþ nat vnkynde..to ȝoure emcristene. **1398** TREVISA *Barth. De P. R.* XII. xxviii. (Bodl. MS.), Hire crye is loþe and odios to oþer byrdes. *c* **1450**– [see OPEN *a.* 15]. **1451** CAPGRAVE *Life St. Gilbert* 112 He..was in gret opinion both to þe Pope & þe court. **1576**– [see FAMILIAR *a.* 4]. **1593**– [see LIABLE 3 a]. **1601** SHAKS. *Jul. C.* II. i. 289 As deere to me, as are the ruddy droppes That visit my sad heart. **1607** [see DEAF *a.* 2]. **1610** SHAKS. *Temp.* I. ii. 303 Inuisible To euery eye-ball else. **1612**– [see ESSENTIAL *a.* 4]. **1632** MASSINGER *City Madam* v. iii, You are constant to your purposes. **1667** MILTON *P. L.* XI. 864 Grateful to Heav'n. **1711** [see COLD *a.* 7]. **1726** [see DEAD *a.* 3]. **1727** *Hartlepool Par. Reg.*, Mary Farding..murdered by William Stephenson..to whom she was pregnant. **1759** [see BLIND *a.* 2 b]. **1777** [W. MARSHALL] *Minutes Agric.* 14 Apr., This..is new to me. **1824** SCOTT *St. Ronan's* viii, Induced to form conclusions not very favourable to his character. **1835** J. DUNCAN *Beetles* 151 Pervious to air and moisture. **1843** *Fraser's Mag.* XXVIII. 279 True to nature. **1881** BESANT & RICE *Chapl. of Fleet* II. xii, You are welcome to all my cast-off lovers. **1886** *Manch. Exam.* 3 Nov. 3/1 Comte..lays himself specially open to attack. **1887** A. BIRRELL *Obiter Dicta* Ser. II. 80 He was always alive to the value of his wares. **1897** F. HALL in *Nation* (N. Y.) LXIV. 163/2 What is permissible to a critic is not impermissible to a counter-critic. **1905** *Oswestry & Border Cos. Advert.* 1 June (Advt.), The Cows and Heifers..in-calf to a grand Pedigree Shorthorn Bull.

**b.** After pa. pples. of verbs of perception (now only with *known, unknown*; nearly = by). (Cf. *familiar to, visible to*, etc.) In OE. with dative.

[*c* **893** K. ÆLFRED *Oros.* I. i. § 27 Hit is feawum mannum cuð.] *a* **1225** *Ancr. R.* 204 Heo beoð..to monie al to kuðe. **13**.. *Cursor M.* 10621 (Cott.) Þaa þat þis maiden was to cuth. *c* **1380** WYCLIF *Sel. Wks.* III. 432 It is hyd to us whyche of hem ben seynts. *c* **1450** LOVE *Bonavent. Mirr.* lxi. (Gibbs MS.) lf. 115 Þai weren noȝt seen to hyre. **1539** BIBLE (Great) 1 *Sam.* vi. 3 It shalbe knowen to you, why hys hande departeth not from you. **1548** UDALL, etc. *Erasm. Par. John* 47 God was seene and heard to Moses. **1598** SHAKS. *Merry W.* II. ii. 188 A man long knowne to me. **1770** GOLDSM. *Des. Vill.* 149 His house was known to all the vagrant train. **1855** MACAULAY *Hist. Eng.* xii. III. 157 They acted under no authority known to the law.

**B.** To before an infinitive (or gerund: see 22).

*History*:—Beside the simple infinitive, or verbal substantive in *-an* (ME. *-en, -e*), OE., like the other WGer. languages, had a *dative* form of the same or a closely-related sb., which in OE. ended in *-anne, -enne*, in ME. reduced successively to *-ene, -en, -e*, and was thus at length levelled with the simple infinitive, and with it reduced to the uninflected verb-stem. This dative form was always preceded or 'governed' by the preposition *tó* 'to'. By many German writers it is called the 'gerund', after the Latin verbal sb. in *-ndum*. In mod.Eng. the functions of the Latin gerund are more properly discharged by the vbl. sb. in *-ing*, and it is therefore more convenient to speak of the OE. form in *-anne* as the 'dative infinitive' or 'infinitive with *to*'. Originally, *to* before the dative infinitive had the same meaning and use as before ordinary substantives, i. e. it expressed motion, direction, inclination, purpose, etc., toward the act or condition expressed by the infinitive; as in 'he came *to help* (i. e. to the help of) his friends', 'he went *to stay* there', 'he prepared *to depart* (i. e. for departure)', 'it tends *to melt*', 'he proceeded *to speak*', 'looking *to receive* something'. But in process of time this obvious sense of the prep. became weakened and generalized, so that *tó* became at last the ordinary link expressing any prepositional relation in which an infinitive stands to a preceding verb, adjective, or substantive. Sometimes the relation was so vague as scarcely to differ from that between a transitive verb and its object. This was esp. so when the vb. was construed both transitively and intransitively. There were several verbs in OE. in this position, such as *onginnan* to begin, *ondrǽdan* to dread, *bebéodan* to bid, order, *bewerian* to forbid, prevent, *geliefan* to believe, *þencean* to think, etc.; these are found construed either with the simple (accusative) infinitive, or with *tó* and the dative infinitive. There was also a special idiomatic use (sense 13 a) of the infinitive with *tó* as an indirect nominative, where logically the simple infinitive might be expected. From these beginnings, the use of the infinitive with *to* in place of the simple infinitive, helped by the phonetic decay and loss of the inflexions and the need of some mark to distinguish the infinitive from other parts of the verb and from the cognate sb., increased rapidly during the late OE. and early ME. period, with the result that in mod.Eng. the infinitive with *to* is the ordinary form, the simple infinitive surviving only in particular connexions, where it is very intimately connected with the preceding verb (see below). To a certain extent, therefore, i. e. when the infinitive is the subject or direct object, *to* has lost all its meaning, and become a mere 'sign' or prefix of the infinitive. But after an intrans. vb., or the passive voice, *to* is still the preposition. In appearance, there is no difference between the infinitive in 'he proceeds *to speak*' and 'he chooses *to speak*'; but in the latter *to speak* is the equivalent of *speaking* or *speech*, and in the former of *to speaking* or *to speech*. In form, *to speak* is the descendant of OE. *tó specanne*; in sense, it is partly the representative of this and largely of OE. *specan*.

(The simple infinitive, without *to*, remains: 1. after the auxiliaries of tense, mood, periphrasis, *shall, will*; *may, can*; *do*; and the quasi-auxiliaries, *must*, (and sometimes) *need, dare*: 2. after some vbs. of causing, etc.; *make, bid, let, have*, in sense 15 a; 3. after some vbs. of perception, *see, hear, feel*, and some tenses of *know, observe, notice, perceive*, etc., in sense 15 b; 4. after *had liefer, rather, better, sooner, as lief, as soon, as good, as well*, etc.: see HAVE *v.* 22, RATHER *adv.* 9 d, and the other words.)

The infinitive with *to* may be dependent on an adj., a sb., or a vb., or it may stand independently. To an adj. it stands in adverbial relation: *ready to fight* = ready for fighting; to a sb. it stands in adjectival or sometimes adverbial relation: *a day to remember* = a memorable day; to a vb. it may stand in an adverbial or substantival relation: *to proceed to work* = to proceed to working; *to like to work* = to like working.

**I.** With infinitive in adverbial relation.

**Indicating purpose or intention.*

**1. a.** Dependent on a vb., *to* with inf. = *in order to*; equivalent to *that* or *in order that* with subjunctive, or to *for* or *for the purpose of* with gerund.

For *in order to, on purpose to*, see ORDER *sb.* 28 b (*b*), PURPOSE *sb.* 11 b.

The implied subject of the inf. may be either a subject or an object in the principal clause.

(*a*) Dependent on a verb of motion.

*c* **890** tr. *Bæda's Hist.* II. i. (1890) 96 Moniȝe cwomon to bicgenne þa ðing. *a* **900** *Ags. Ps.* (Th.) xxvi. 4 [xxvii. 3] Þeah hi arisan onȝean me to feohtanne. *c* **950** *Lindisf. Gosp.* Mark iv. 3 Eode ðe sawende..to sawenne. **971** *Blickl. Hom.* 165 To hwon eodan ȝe to westenne..witȝan to secenne. *c* **1205** LAY. 5238 Heo wolden fære to Rome to wreken o þon folke. **1297** R. GLOUC. (Rolls) 3523 Þat he to him wende To helpe him in suche nede. **1388** WYCLIF *Matt.* iv. 1 Thanne Jhesus was led of a spirit in to desert, to be temptid of the feend. *Ibid.* xi. 8 Or what thing wenten ȝe out to see [1382 for to seen]? **1577** B. GOOGE *Heresbach's Husb.* I. (1586) 3, I get me into my Closet to serue God. **1592** [see 10]. **1770** GOLDSM. *Des. Vill.* 180 Fools, who came to scoff, remained to pray. **1890** *Chamb. Jrnl.* 28 June 408/1 We made sail to return to Perim. *Mod.* She ran to meet her father.

(*b*) Dependent on other verbs.

*Beowulf* (Z.) 2562 Ða wæs hring-boȝan heorte ȝefysed sæcce to seceanne. *c* **890** tr. *Bæda's Hist.* IV. xiv. [xi.] (1890) 296 Ða ȝearwodon heo his lichoman to byrȝenne. *a* **901** *Laws of Ælfred* c. 62 § 27 ȝif fyr sie ontended ryht to bærnenne. *c* **950** *Lindisf. Gosp.* Matt. ii. 13 Herodes sæcas ðone cnæbt to fordoanne. *c* **1375** *Sc. Leg. Saints* xxxvi. (*Baptista*) 842 Þan þe basare hewit on hicht His hand, to strik, gif he mycht. *c* **1425** WYNTOUN *Cron.* I. ix. 533 As men may be a roundall se, Merkit to be delt in thre. **1445** in *Anglia* XXVIII. 269 Bothe pore and riche labouryd righte sore, encrese to gete. *a* **1548** HALL *Chron., Hen. VI* 146 b, To have a Rowland to resist an Oliver. **1627** MILTON

*Vac. Exerc.* 24 Thoughts that..loudly knock to have their passage out. 1724 De Foe *Mem. Cavalier* (1840) 70, I gave a soldier five dollars to carry them news. 1787 Cowper *Stanzas Yearly Bill Mort.* 14 Like crowded forest trees we stand, And some are mark'd to fall. 1859 Ruskin *Two Paths* iv. § 110 As our bodies, to be in health, must be generally exercised, so our minds, to be in health, must be generally cultivated.

**b.** Dependent on an adj.; indicating the purpose or function to which the adj. refers.

c 890 tr. *Bæda's Hist.* II. i. (1890) 98 Þæt he selfa ȝeara wære..þæt weorc to fremmenne. a 900 *Ags. Ps.* (Th.) xiii. 6 Heora fet beoð swiðe hraðe blod to ȝeotanne. c 1400 tr. *Secreta Secret., Gov. Lordsh.* v. 51 God..make cleer ȝoure vnderstondynge to persayue þe sacrament of þis science. 1578 Lyte *Dodoens* III. lxviii. 410 The lye..is very good to washe the scurffe of the head. *Mod.* Are they quite good to eat?

**c.** Dependent on a sb.; the inf. expressing the use or function of that which is denoted by the sb.

The advb. use may be explained as qualifying the adj. 'intended, adapted' before *to*.

c 890 tr. *Bæda's Hist.* III. xix. [xxvii.] (1890) 242 Bec on to leornienne [hi] ȝefon. c 893 K. Ælfred *Oros.* III. xi. § 3 Þonne seo leo bringð his hungreȝum hwelpum hwæt to etanne. 13.. *Minor Poems fr. Vernon MS.* xxiii. 771 To syke men made is he Medicyn, hem to mende. 1445 in *Anglia* XXVIII. 277 A plastir to cure þe wounde of Rome. 1526 Tindale *Luke* ii. 32 A light to lighten the gentyls. 1609 Bible (Douay) *Numb.* iv. 16 The oyle to dresse the lampes. 1716 in J. O. Payne *Eng. Cath. Nonjurors of 1715* 348 One ciborium of silver, to preserve the consecrated Host. a 1845 Hood *Lay of Labourer* i, A hook to reap, or a scythe to mow.

(*b*) After *time, room*, and words of similar meaning: equivalent to *for* with gerund (cf. a), or = at or in which (one) can or should.. (cf. 11 b, c).

13.. *Cursor M.* 11814 (Cott.) Nu neghes tim to tak his lai. c 1385 Chaucer *L. G. W.* 2000 (*Ariadne*) Rowm..To welde an axe. 1412-20 Lydg. *Chron. Troy* II. 658 To rekne hem alle I haue as now no tyme. 1597 J. Payne *Royal Exch.* 5 Now ys the tyme..to help one another. 1635 Quarles *Embl.* I. vii. 3 Is this a time to pay thine idle vowes At Morpheus Shrine? 1858 Mill *Liberty* iv. (1873) 57 [There was] no time to warn him of his danger. 1887 'L. Carroll' *Game of Logic* iv. 96 The time to learn is when you're young.

**2.** In absolute or independent construction, usually introductory or parenthetic.

*To be* Sure, *to* Wit: see these words.

c 1305 *St. Kenelm* 266 in *E. E. P.* (1862) 54, & to telle hit wiþoute rym þuse wordes riȝt hit were. c 1386 Chaucer *Knt.'s T.* 1037 And schortly to concluden, swich a place Was noon in erthe. c 1450 *Cov. Myst.* xiii. (1841) 129 Than ferther to oure matere to procede, Mary with Elizabeth abod. 1600 Shaks. *A. Y. L.* I. i. 8 He keepes me rustically at home, or (to speak more properly) staies me heere at home vnkept. 1667 Milton *P. L.* II. 922 Nor was his eare less peal'd With noises loud and ruinous (to compare Great things with small) then when Bellona storms [etc.]. 1711 Addison *Spect.* No 26 ¶ 6 But to return to our Subject. 1858 Mill *Liberty* iv. (1873) 53 The pleasure, not to say the useful recreation, of many, is worth the labour of a few. 1888 Bryce *Amer. Commw.* III. vi. xcix. 387 All their ins and outs (to use an American phrase).

***Indicating objectivity.*

**3.** Dependent on various verbs, chiefly transitive, passive, or reflexive, with weakened sense of purpose: indicating an action, etc. to which that of the principal verb is in some way directed. (See also the verbs themselves; and in particular, for specific uses, Be *v.* 16, Have *v.* B. 7 c, Need *v.*$^2$ 8, Ought *v.* B. 5. Cf. also 14 below.)

The subject of the principal clause is also the implicit subject of the infinitive: so also in other senses below, except where the contrary is stated.

c 897 K. Ælfred *Gregory's Past. C.* xli. 302 Weorðen ȝeniedde hiera unðeawas to herianne & to weorðianne. *Ibid.* lvi. 433 Ða ðe ær ðenceað to syngianne. a 900 — *Soliloquy* (1902) 46 Ǽall þæt þu wilnast to habbenne. c 1000 Ælfric *Gen.* xi. 6 Hiȝ begunnon þis to wircanne. *Ibid.* xxvii. 41 Esau..þohte to ofsleanne Iacob. a 1175 *Cott. Hom.* 227 Hi..begunnon þa to worcen. c 1205 Lay. 18738-9 Þu..þrattest hine to slænne, And his cun to fordonne. *Ibid.* 24722 Þa..þe king gon to spekene. c 1290 *St. Gregory* 50 in *S. Eng. Leg.* I. 357 Þou þencst..with þi conseil al rome to bi-traiȝe. c 1386 Chaucer *Prol.* 12 Thanne longen folk to goon on pilgrimages. c 1400 *Destr. Troy* 312 The Emperour Alexaunder Aunterid to come. 1525 Ld. Berners *Froiss.* II. xxi. 45 They determyned to crowne to their kyng this mayster Denyse. 1694 S. Meade in *Jrnl. Friends' Hist. Soc.* (1912) IX. 182 Her Husband thinks to come downe tomorrow. 1746 P. Francis tr. *Horace, Art Poet.* 36, I strive to be concise.

**b.** In obsolete, archaic, or dialectal uses; now replaced by various prepositions with the gerund, or by other constructions. (See the vbs.)

1525 Ld. Berners *Froiss.* II. 627 Every man fell to make his prayers to God. 1533 Cromwell in Merriman *Life & Lett.* (1902) I. 360, I shall aduyse yow to stay to doo [= refrain from doing] any thing. 1698 Fryer *Acc. E. India & P.* 58 Unless they would..content themselves to winter at the Mauritius. 1749 Lavington *Enthus. Meth. & Papists* II. (1754) 34 Her Spouse insisting to play another Game. 1871 G. Meredith *H. Richmond* III. 109 Abstaining to write to her. 1885 J. Hawthorne *Love or Name* 111 We don't aim to establish a monopoly.

**4.** Dependent on various adjs. (and pples., and adjectival or predicative phrases): usually indicating the application of the adj., etc. For *going to*, used as future participle, see Go *v.* 47 b. (See also senses 1 b, 7–9, and the adjs. themselves.)

c 975 *Rushw. Gosp.* Matt. iii. 11 Æfter me cymeð se is me strængra þæt ic næm wyrþe scoas to beranne. a 1225 *Juliana* 5 (Bodl. MS.) Þes ȝunge mon..wes iwunet ofte to cumen wið him. 1297 R. Glouc. (Rolls) 1431 Gwider..is truage athuld sone Of rome þat is eldore were iwoned to done. 1340 Hampole *Pr. Consc.* 8559 Certayne To have endelos ioy. c 1435 *Torr. Portugal* 1680 He is worthy to haue renown. 1513 Douglas *Æneis* vi. xv. 3 The peple..Bene..moir sle To forge and carve lyflyk staturis of bras. 1651 W. Durham *Maran-atha* (1652) 4 Every man that is able to discipline souldiers. 1770 Goldsm. *Des. Vill.* 161 Careless their merits or their faults to scan. 1832 Tennyson *Love thou thy Land* 31 Not swift nor slow to change, but firm. 1838 Thirlwall *Greece* V. xlii. 229 She was at liberty to enforce her claims. *Mod.* I am ready to go.

**b.** With inf. passive: altered from the active (see 9). *arch.*

c 1460 Fortescue *Abs. & Lim. Mon.* xi. (1885) 136 This was not possible to haue ben done. c 1483 *Vulg. Terent.* 02 b, Whatt is best to be doon now? 1693 Evelyn *De la Quint. Compl. Gard.* I. 5 The fittest to be chosen. 1779 *Mirror* No. 21 ¶ 3 Incidents still more frequent, and less easy to be foreseen. 1870 Burton *Hist. Scot.* V. lxii. 382 She was hard to be entreated.

**5.** Dependent on various abstract sbs. (e. g. nouns of action from the vbs. in 3, or of quality from the adjs. in 4): usually indicating object or application, as in 3 and 4; also (after such words as *favour, honour, pleasure*) indicating an action which is the substance or form of that which is denoted by the sb., i. e. in which it consists: often replaceable by *of* with gerund.

For 'what has he to do, to..' (='what business has he to..') and the like, see Do *v.* 33 c.

c 888 K. Ælfred *Boeth.* xxxviii. § 4 Ðæt hi..habbað leafe yfel to donne. 971 *Blickl. Hom.* 63 Us is mycel þearf to witenne þæt [etc.]. c 1000 *Ags. Gosp.* Mark ii. 10 Þæt mannes sunu hæfð anweald..synna to forgyfanne. c 1200 *Trin. Coll. Hom.* 15 Þat he geue us mihte and strengðe to forletene þesternesse, and to folȝie brictnesse. c 1300 *Harrow. Hell* 179 Ȝef us leve,..To faren of this lothe wyke. 13.. *Minor Poems fr. Vernon MS.* l. 593 Haue non hope to liuen longe. 1470-85 Malory *Arthur* xx. vii. 809 Ye haue no cause to loue sir Launcelot. 1525 Bp. Sampson in Ellis *Orig. Lett.* Ser. III. I. 356 Means might be fownde to change hym. 1582 Allen *Martyrd. Campion* (1908) 113 This resolutnes of minde, and willingnes to die. 1665 Boyle *Occas. Refl.* Introd. Pref. (1848) 13, I..took Pleasure to imagine two or three of my Friends to be present with me. 1737 Swift *Proposal for giving Badges*, etc. Wks. 1751 IX. 301, I had the Honour to be a Member of it. 1842 R. I. Wilberforce *Rutilius & Lucius* 249 As though in act to spring. 1859 Geo. Eliot *A. Bede* xvi, Conscious of increased disinclination to tell his story.

****Indicating appointment or destination.*

**6.** Indicating destiny, or (expected or actual) event or outcome. Dependent on vb., adj., or sb.

See also Come *v.* 23 b, Get *v.* 32, Leave *v.*$^1$ 5 b, Live *v.*$^1$ 9.

a 1380 *St. Augustin* 108 in Horstm. *Altengl. Leg.* (1878) 63/2 Þei [the Manichees] forsok þat alle men Schulde rise in flesch, to lyue aȝen. 1445 in *Anglia* XXVIII. 269 No theef iss suffrid to lyen in weyes there felawes him lyke to make. 1638 G. Sandys *Paraphr. Job* xxvii. 34 Borne to begge their bread. 1725 *Bradley's Fam. Dict.* s. v. *July*, Plant out Colliflowers, to blow in September. 1750 Gray *Elegy* xiv, Full many a flower is born to blush unseen. 1781 Cowper *Charity* 74 We come with joy from our eternal rest, To see the oppressor in his turn oppressed. 1808 Byron *When we two parted* 4 When we two parted..To sever for years.

*****Indicating result or consequence.*

**7.** Expressing result or consequence (potential or actual); esp. after *so* or *such* (now always with *as* before *to* = *that* with finite vb.: see As *adv.* B. 20), or *enough*. For inf. after *than*, see Than 1 c.

With *enough, too* (see b), the subj. of the principal clause may be either the implied subj. or obj. of the inf., or obj. of a following prep. (cf. constructions in sense 11), or the subj. of the inf. may be a sb. or pron. preceded by *for*, or may be unexpressed.

1303 R. Brunne *Handl. Synne* 5158 Ne be nat proude..Yn þyn herte to make a rous. c 1386 Chaucer *Can. Yeom. Prol. & T.* 308, I haue yow toold ynowe To reyse a feend. 1577 Fulke *Answ. True Christian* 95 Be not so impudent, to charge vs with these crimes aboue the Papistes. 1611 Bible *Gen.* iii. 22 The man is become as one of us, to know good & euill. 1742 Fielding *Jos. Andrews* iv. iii, The Laws..are not so vulgar, to permit a mean Fellow to contend with one of your Ladyship's Fortune. 1865 Ruskin *Sesame* i. § 15 He has only to speak a sentence..to be known for an illiterate person. 1877 Spurgeon *Serm.* XXIII. 537 A man who has light enough to know he is wrong but not grace enough to forsake the evil. 1884 *Manch. Exam.* 14 May 5/1 The Government have..done much to excite against them the fiercest antipathies of the Opposition.

**b.** After *too*, with negative implication (*too.. to.. = so.. as not to*, or *so..that..not..*). See also Too 2 b.

Here *for* with the gerund may often be substituted.

a 1300 *A Sarmun* xxxv. in *E. E. P.* (1862) 5 Hit is to late whan þou ert þare To crie ihsu þin ore. ? a 1400 *Morte Arth.* 4031 We are..to fewe to feghte with them all. c 1538 R. Cowley in Ellis *Orig. Lett.* Ser. II. II. 98 Too lamentable to expres. 1560 Daus tr. *Sleidane's Comm.* 113 b, It is nowe to late to examyne the licence. 1655 *Nicholas Papers* (Camden) II. 266 Cromwell hath too good a nose as to hunt vpon a false sent. 1665 [see Too 2 b]. 1712 Budgell *Spect.* No. 401 ¶ 4 My Answer would be too long to trouble you with. 1833 Tennyson *Lady Clara Vere de Vere* ii, Too proud to care from whence I came. *Mod.* This tea is too hot to drink. The weight is too heavy for you to lift.

******Indicating occasion or condition.*

**8.** Indicating occasion (passing into ground, reason, or cause): equivalent to *at, in, on, for, of, by*, etc. with gerund, or *because* with finite vb.

? a 1366 Chaucer *Rom. Rose* 122 Wonder glad I was to see That lusty place. 1380 *Lay Folks Catech.* 220 (MS. L.) And so myȝt pardoun be gotun to sey [=by saying] yche day a lady sawter. 1508 *Colyn Blowbol's Test.* 22 in Hazl. *E. P. P.* I. 93 An hors wold wepe to se the sorow he maide. 1535 Coverdale *Ps.* xlvii[i]. 5 They marveled to se soch thinges. 1596 Shaks. 1 *Hen. IV*, II. iv. 343, I blusht to heare his monstrous deuices. 1596 — *Tam. Shr.* III. ii. 27 Goe girle, I cannot blame thee now to weepe. 1766 Goldsm. *Vic. W.* iii, I could not but smile to hear her talk in this lofty strain. 1833 Tennyson *Lady Clara Vere de Vere* ii, I know you proud to bear your name. 1843 Macaulay *Lays, Horatius* xlix, All Etruria's noblest Felt their hearts sink to see On the earth the bloody corpses, In the path the dauntless Three.

**9.** With inf. after an adj. or (predicate) sb., in passive sense (equivalent to the L. supine in *-u*), the main sb. of the principal clause being the implied object of the inf., or of a preposition following (or in ME. preceding).

c 888 K. Ælfred *Boeth.* xxxiv. § 11 Hi bioð swiðe eðe to tedælenne. c 950 *Lindisf. Gosp.* Mark ii. 9 Hwæt is eaður to coeðanne..? c 1200 *Trin. Coll. Hom.* 31 Gode tiðinge and murie to heren. 13.. *K. Alis.* 6312 Heo buth the lothlokest men on to seon. 1340 Hampole *Pr. Consc.* 705 A flour, þat es fayre to se. c 1400 Maundev. (1839) xxvii. 274 Wylde men that ben hidouse to loken on. c 1435 *Torr. Portugal* 617 Gret Ruthe yt wase to se. 1535 Coverdale *Gen.* xii. 11 Thou art a fayre woman to loke vpon. 1617 Moryson *Itin.* II. 101 Ere it be good to eat. 1736 Thomson *Liberty* v. 456 Oh! shame to think! 1805 Scott *Last Minstr.* I. i, Deadly to hear, and deadly to tell. 1899 W. T. Greene *Cage-Birds* 71 Macaws..very gorgeous creatures to look at.

**10.** With inf. expressing a fact or supposition which forms the ground of the statement in the principal clause, or is considered in connexion with it; equivalent to *in* with gerund, or *that, in that, considering that* (or sometimes *if*) with finite vb.

13.. *Seuyn Sag.* (W.) 2544 Sire, thou art wel nice, To leue [=believe] so mochel thin emperice. c 1489 Caxton *Sonnes of Aymon* xxii. 481 He dothe wronge to leve me here. 1592 Shaks. *Rom. & Jul.* iv. i. 23 *Par.* Come you to make confession to this Father? *Iul.* To answere that, I should confesse to you. 1610 — *Temp.* III. i. 37, I haue broke your hest to say so. 1706 Addison *Rosamund* I. iii, Thou art a rustic to call me so. 1846 W. E. Forster in Reid *Life* (1888) I. vi. 186 What a strange little mortal he is, to be ruler of a mighty nation. 1884 R. W. Church *Bacon* iii. 59 He was no mere idealist or recluse to undervalue..the real grandeur of the world. 1887 'L. Carroll' *Game of Logic* i. § 1. 15 You will do well to work out a lot more for yourself.

† **b.** With inf. equivalent to a conditional clause with indefinite subject (= *if one were to*..). *Obs.*

c 1386 Chaucer *Miller's T.* 66 In al this world to seken vp and doun There nas no man so wys. c 1400 Maundev. (1839) ix. 81 Fro that hospitall, to go toward the Est, is a full fayr chirche. 1591 Shaks. 1 *Hen. VI*, IV. vii. 89 To keepe them here, They would but stinke, and putrifie the ayre. 1611 Beaum. & Fl. *Philaster* III. i, Bulls and Rams will fight, To keep their Females standing in their sight.

**II.** With infinitive in adjectival relation.

**11.** With inf. in adjectival relation to a sb.; either as predicate after the vb. *to be* (see Be 16, 17), or immediately qualifying the sb.

**a.** Expressing intention or appointment (cf. 1, 6), and hence simply futurity (thus equivalent to a future participle). (*a*) with inf. act.: *is to..* = intends or is intended to.., is going to.., will...

c 1000- [see Come *v.* 32]. 1297 R. Glouc. (Rolls) 287 Man þou art iwis To winne ȝut a kinedom. c 1420 *Sir Amadas* (Weber) 569 Yffe thou be a mon to wedde a wyfe, Y voche hyr save..On the. c 1460 *Oseney Reg.* 101 Thoo þat be present and to be. 1590 Shaks. *Mids. N.* IV. ii. 29, I am to discourse wonders...I will tell you euery thing as it fell out. 1596 — *Merch. V.* I. i. 5 Whereof it is borne, I am to learne. 1667 Milton *P. L.* XII. 113 A Nation from one faithful man to spring. 1693 South *Serm.* II. 113 He who is to pray..has more to consider of, than..his Heart can hold. 1779 *Mirror* No. 23 ¶ 3 He was not suffered to play with his equals, because he was to be the king of all sports. 1864 Browning *Rabbi Ben Ezra* i, The best is yet to be.

(*b*) with inf. pass. (equivalent to Lat. gerundive): *to be done* = intended to be done, about to be done.

c 1450 *Cov. Myst.* x. (1841) 96 Here is to be maryde a mayde ȝynge. 1585 in *Cath. Rec. Soc. Publ.* V. 108 Articles to be ministred to Tho. Rowe. 1609 Holland *Amm. Marcell.* xxvi. i, Having a presage..of the businesse to bee performed. 1719 De Foe *Crusoe* (1840) II. xii. 245 The happy minute of our being to be seized by the Dutch..ships. 1843 *Fraser's Mag.* XXVIII. 655 Leopold was to be appointed Viceroy.

(*c*) with inf. act., the sb. being the implicit object of the inf.; thus equivalent to the passive in (*b*).

As predicate, *obs.* in literary Eng. exc. in certain connexions, as *a house to let* (Let *v.*$^1$ 8); when following a sb., the sb. is usu. governed by *have* (see Have *v.* B. 7).

c 1200 Ormin Ded. 8 Witt hafenn takenn ba An reȝhellboc te follȝhenn. 14.. in *Rel. Ant.* I. 62 This poure man had suyn to selle. 1487-8 *Rec. St. Mary at Hill* 134 For a hoke to sett on his dorr. 1595 Shaks. *John* I. i. 259 Were I to get againe,..I would not wish a better father. 1771 Smollett *Humph. Cl.* 26 Oct., He has a son to educate. 1797 Canning *Knife-Grinder* ii, Knives and Scissars to grind O! 1852 M. Arnold *Empedocles* I. ii. 334 The mass..Of volumes yet to read, Of secrets to explore. *Mod. Notice.* This house to let or for sale. *Mod.* I have much to tell.

(*d*) with inf. followed (in ME. sometimes preceded) by a preposition, the sb. being the implicit obj. of the prep.

*c* **897** K. ÆLFRED *Gregory's Past. C.* xvii. 126 ʒif ðær ðonne sie ʒierd mid to ðreaʒeanne, sie ðær eac stæf mid to wreðianne. *c* **1200** *Trin. Coll. Hom.* 89 He .. bed hem bringen a wig one te riden. **1408–17** in *Rec. St. Mary at Hill* Introd. 96 Item, .j. short fourme with a tapete and Quysshynes to knele at. **1577** B. GOOGE *Heresbach's Husb.* I. (1586) 13 These great roomes..be Barnes to laye Corne in. **1611** COTGR. s.v. *Rosette*, Red Inke to rule bookes with. **1707** MORTIMER *Husb.* (1721) II. 366 A Dry Season..is best to sow Barley and White Oats in.

**b.** Expressing duty, obligation, or necessity. (*a*) with inf. act.: *is to* . . = is bound to, has to . ., must . ., ought to . . .

*c* **1450** HOLLAND *Howlat* 216 The Ravyne..Was dene rurale to reid. *a* **1529** SKELTON *Phyllyp Sparow* 401 Robyn red breste He shall be the preest The requiem masse to syng. **1591** SHAKS. *Two Gent.* II. iii. 37 Thy Master is ship'd, and thou art to post after with oares. **1598** — *Merry W.* IV. ii. 128 You are not to goe loose any longer, you must be pinnion'd. **1768** GOLDSM. *Good-n. Man* iii, I'm yet to thank you for choosing my little library. **1885** *Manch. Exam.* 13 July 5/2 The Southerners, with only one wicket to fall, were 259 runs to the bad. **1887** 'L. CARROLL' *Game of Logic* i. § 1. 9 What, then, are you to do?

(*b*) with inf. pass. (= L. gerundive): *is to be* . . = is proper to be, ought to be . ., should be . ., need be . . .

The inf. pass. is also occasionally used as adj. preceding the sb.; now with hyphens, as *to-be-dreaded* = dreadful.

**1382** WYCLIF *John* xxi. 25, I deme neither the world him silf to mowe take tho bookis, that ben to be writun. *c* **1410** LOVE *Bonavent. Mirr.* (1908) 49 That is..most profitable, and rather to be chosen. **1560–78** *Bk. Discipl. Ch. Scot.* (1621) 61 Unprofitable questions are to be avoided. **1611** BEAUM. & FL. *Knt. Burn. Pest.* v. iii, There's no more to be said. **1774** BURKE *Amer. Tax.* 32 If, Sir, the conduct of ministry..had arisen from timidity .., it would have been greatly to be condemned. **1858** MILL *Liberty* v. (1873) 60 The taxation..of stimulants..is not only admissible, but to be approved of.

**1548** UDALL, etc. *Erasm. Par. Matt.* 28* That same moste fortunate and moste to be desyred kyngdome. **1606** SHAKS. *Tr. & Cr.* I. iii. 157 Such to be pittied, and ore-rested seeming He acts thy Greatnesse in. **1779** *Sylph* II. 50 This shall be the last letter that treats on this to-be-forbidden theme. **1871** NAPHEYS *Prev. & Cure Dis.* III. vi. 835 The to-be-dreaded legacies of smallpox.

(*c*) with inf. act., of which the sb. is the implicit obj., as in 11 a (*c*).

As predicate, *obs.* exc. in *to blame* (BLAME *v.* 6); otherwise usu. with *have* before the sb., as in a (*c*); also with ellipsis of sb. in *have to do* (see DO *v.* 33 c, d).

**971** *Blickl. Hom.* 63 Nis þæt no be eallum demum ʒelice to secʒʒenne. *c* **1122** *O. E. Chron.* an. 1083, Þa munecas.. nyston hwet heom to donne wære. *Ibid.* an. 1086, Betwyx oðrum þingum nis na to forgytane þæt gode frið. *a* **1225** *Ancr. R.* 52 [Heo] wot betere þen ich wot, hwat heo haueð to donne. **1297** R. GLOUC. (Rolls) 3271 Hii slowe þere a þousend & mo.., & þat was to rywe sore. *Ibid.* 3318 Wat were to done. *c* **1380** WYCLIF *Sel. Wks.* I. 196 Confessioun of cowardise is to drede of men. **1390** GOWER *Conf.* I. 8 The hevene wot what is to done. *c* **1400** *Laud Troy Bk.* 6821 Ector bretheren weren mechel to prayse. **1503** HAWES *Examp. Virt.* vii. 104 A man without wytte is to dyspyse. **1634** W. TIRWHYT tr. *Balzac's Lett.* (vol. I.) 294 Having a thousand old debates to reconcile, and as many new ones to prevent. **1794** MRS. RADCLIFFE *Myst. Udolpho* l, They had no time to lose. **1870** ROGERS *Hist. Gleanings* Ser. II. 214 Everybody..thought Horne to blame.' **1888** W. S. GILBERT *Yeomen of Guard* I. 12, I have a song to sing, O! *Mod.* You are much to blame.

(*d*) with inf. and prep., as in 11 a (*d*).

**1611** BIBLE *Luke* xii. 50, I haue a baptisme to be baptized with. **1779** *Mirror* No. 48 ⁋ 10 The painter has yet more [difficulties] to struggle with. **1859** GEO. ELIOT *A. Bede* xvi, It was not..a thing to make a fuss about. **1888** RIDER HAGGARD *Mr. Meeson's Will* xvii, Ladies need never wear anything to speak of in the evening.

**c.** Expressing possibility or potential action. (*a*) with inf. act.: = that can or may . . .

*a* **1310** in Wright *Lyric P.* (Percy Soc.) 34 Heo hath a mury mouth to mele [= speak]. *c* **1380** WYCLIF *Wks.* (1880) 288 Men stable in bileue ben a þick walle to turnen aʒen þis þondir. *c* **1400** MAUNDEV. (1839) v. 45 In that contree [Egypt] ben the gode astronomyeres; for thei fynde there no cloudes to letten hem. **1526** TINDALE *Matt.* xi. 15 He that hath eares to heare, let him here. *a* **1533** LD. BERNERS *Huon* cxi. 385 There was no man to saye hym naye. **1625** BACON *Ess., Anger* (Arb.) 566 They haue so many Things to trouble them. **1782** COWPER *Alex. Selkirk* 2 My right there is none to dispute. **1799** WORDSW. *She dwelt among the untrodden ways* i, A maid whom there were none to praise And very few to love. **1890** 'L. FALCONER' *Mlle. Ixe* vi, There is no one to see us.

(*b*) with inf. pass.: = that can or may be . .; often equivalent to an adj. in *-ble*, as *to be heard* = audible.

**1533** ELYOT *Cast. Helthe* (1541) 24 The inner part therof is not to be eaten. **1590** SPENSER *F. Q.* II. vii. 30 In all that rowme was nothing to be seene But huge great yron chests. **1611** SHAKS. *Cymb.* III. i. 68 Looke For fury, not to be resisted. **1631** WEEVER *Anc. Fun. Mon.* 222 This inscription..now hardly to be read. **1818** J. FLINT *Lett. Amer.* iv. 46 Not a sound was to be heard.

(*c*) with inf. act., of which the sb. is the implicit obj., as in 11 a (*c*): = that (one) can or may . .; often nearly equivalent to *for* with gerund, as in 1 a.

Rarely in predicate (quots. 1297, *a* 1849[2]). With *drink, eat*, sometimes as apparent obj. of the vb., with ellipsis of *something* or *anything* (*arch.*).

*c* **950** *Lindisf. Gosp.* Mark x. 40 Sitta..to swiðra minra.. ne is min to sellanne. *c* **1000** ÆLFRIC *Gen.* xxviii. 20 Gif Drihten..sylþ me hlaf to etenne and reaf to werigenne. *c* **1205** LAY. 13578 Nefden we noht to drinken. *Ibid.* 13583 ʒe sculleð habben to drinken. **1297** R. GLOUC. (Rolls) 2747 He seste at is clerkes were it to leue [= to be believed, credible] were. *c* **1400** MAUNDEV. (1839) v. 47 There is no watre to drynke, but ʒif it come be condyt from Nyle. **1582** N. T. (Rhem.) *John* iv. 7 Giue me to drinke [so **1611**: *earlier vv.* Geue me drynke]. **1610** SHAKS. *Temp.* III. ii. 102 Without them [his books] Hee .. hath not One Spirit to command. **1736** *Gentl. Mag.* VI. 744/2 A taking pattern! to propose To our slim race of modern beaus. **1815** W. H. IRELAND *Scribbleomania* 190 The great Grecian youth, Who whimper'd for more worlds to conquer. *a* **1849** BEDDOES *Dream-Pedlary*, If there were dreams to sell. *Ibid.*, Were dreams to have at will. **1858** SEARS *Athan.* III. x. 332 Heathen nations..who have had no truth given them to reject. **1897** KIPLING *5 Nations, Our Lady of Snows*, The gates are mine to open, As the gates are mine to close.

(*d*) with inf. and prep., as in 11 a (*d*).

*c* **1410** LOVE *Bonavent. Mirr.* (1908) 49 A pore wommanes sone, that skarsly hadde clothes to wrappe hym inne. **1423** JAS. I *Kingis Quair* clxxiv, Nor sekernes, my spirit with to glad. **1593** NASHE *Christ's T.* (1613) 54 Nere had you such a subiect to roialize your Muses with. **1593** SHAKS. *3 Hen. VI*, II. i. 68 Sweet Duke of Yorke, our Prop to leane vpon. **1784** BURNS *Ep. to J. Rankine* iv, Tak that, ye lea'e them naething To ken them by.

**d.** Expressing quality or character: = such as to . ., fit to, such as would . . . (With various constructions as in a, b, c, but not used predicatively.)

**14..** *Pol. Rel. & L. Poems* 217, I have herde of an erbe to lyss that peyne. **1610** SHAKS. *Temp.* II. i. 313 'Twas a din to fright a Monsters eare. **1735–6** THOMSON *Liberty* IV. 496 A sight to gladden Heav'n! **1824** SCOTT *Redgauntlet* ch. xix, Father Crackenthorp was not a man to be browbeaten. **1833** T. HOOK *Parson's Dau.* I. ii, Is she a person to like? **1859** GEO. ELIOT *A. Bede* xxxii, She was not the woman to misbehave towards her betters.

**12.** With inf. equivalent to a relative clause with indicative; chiefly after *first, last*, or the like (in this case = *in* with gerund): as *the first to come* = 'the first in coming', 'the first who comes *or* came'.

**1535** COVERDALE *2 Sam.* xix. 11 Why wyl ye be the last to fetch the kynge agayne vnto his house? **1591** SHAKS. *Two Gent.* II. i. 42 Not an eye that sees you, but is a Physician to comment on your Malady. **1667** MILTON *P. L.* x. 109 He came, and with him Eve, more loth, though first To offend. **1766** GOLDSM. *Vicar W.* viii, I have an interest in being first to deliver this message. **1821** F. COOPER *Spy* iii, Harper was the last to appear. **1835** LYTTON *Rienzi* I. v, Mine shall be the first voice to swell the battle-cry of freedom. **1855** KINGSLEY *Westw. Ho* xxv, Why..was I.. among the foremost to urge upon my general the murder of the Inca?

**III.** With infinitive in substantival relation.

Equivalent to a noun or gerund: *to* being ultimately reduced to a mere 'sign' of the infinitive without any meaning of its own.

**13. a.** with inf. as subject, or as object with complement, introduced by *it* or an impersonal verb; in quot. *c* 1205[1] without *it*.

Here the inf. app. originally depended on the adj. or sb. in the *it* clause (as in sense 9), or on the impersonal vb., and was therefore put in the form with *to*. Thus *hwilum ða leohtan scylda bioð beteran to forlætenne*, 'sometimes the slight sins are better to let alone' (K. Ælf. *Pa. C.* 457) might also be expressed *hwilum hit is betre ða leohtan scylda to forlætenne* (cf. *hit is god godne to herianne*, quot. *c* 890) 'sometimes it is better to let alone the slight sins'; and this easily passed into the later 'to let alone the slight sins is sometimes better', where the inf. clause becomes the subject as in b.

*c* **888** K. ÆLFRED *Boeth.* xvii, Nan þara þinga wyrcan þe him beboden is to wyrcenne. *Ibid.* xxxviii. § 5 Þæt men sie alefed yfel to donne. *c* **890** tr. *Bæda's Hist.* Pref. (1890) 2 Forþon hit is god godne to herianne & yfelne to leanne. *a* **1175** *Cott. Hom.* 217 Hit is wel swete of him to specene. *c* **1200**– [see BEHOVE *v.* 4 a]. *c* **1205** LAY. 1848 Þa heo best wende to fleonne. *Ibid.* 31107 Hit is on mine rede To don þat þu bede. *a* **1230** [see BECOME *v.* 8 b]. **13..** *K. Alis.* 7346 (Laud MS.) Good it were to ben kniʒth. **1390** GOWER *Conf.* III. 341 Hem nedeth noght a Riff to slake. *c* **1430**– [see GRIEVE *v.* 5 b]. *a* **1440** *Sir Degrev.* 1498 Hyt was a mervelous thing To se the rydalus hyng. **1602** SHAKS. *Ham.* III. ii. 110 It was a bruite part of him, to kill so Capital a Calfe there. **1667** MILTON *P. L.* IV. 427 God hath pronounc't it death to taste that Tree. **1850** TENNYSON *In Mem.* xxvii. 15 'Tis better to have loved and lost Than never to have loved at all. **1880** SHORTHOUSE *J. Inglesant* xx, Many who will have it in their power to be of great use to you.

**b.** with inf. as direct subject or predicate, or in apposition with a sb. or pron., or after *than*: often replaceable by the gerund or vbl. sb. in *-ing*.

**1303** R. BRUNNE *Handl. Synne* 6044 Ful wykkede ys þat coueytyse Wyþ oþer mennes gode falsly to ryse. **1388** WYCLIF *1 Sam.* xv. 22 To herkene Goddis word is more than to offre the ynnere fatnesse of rammes. **14..** *Chaucer's Pars. T.* ⁋ 670 (Selden & Lansd. MSS.) Auarice is to withholde & kepe suche thinges as thow hast withouten rightful nede. *c* **1450** tr. *De Imitatione* II. viii. 48 To be wiþoute ihesu is a greuous helle, and to be wiþ ihesu is a swete paradise. **1539** BIBLE (Great) *1 Sam.* xv. 22 Behold, to obeye [1388 WYCLIF, 1535 COVERD. obedience], is better then sacrifice, & to herken, is better then yᵉ fatt of rammes. **1557** NORTH *Gueuara's Diall Pr.* 126 A woman in nothing sheweth her sageness more then to dissemble with a foolish husband. **1601** SHAKS. *All's Well* I. i. 148 To speake on the part of virginitie, is to accuse your Mothers. **1667** MILTON *P. L.* I. 157 To be weak is miserable Doing or Suffering. **1709** POPE *Ess. Crit.* 525 To err is human, to forgive, divine. **1781** COWPER *Conversation* 8 Talking is not always to converse. **1865** E. BURRITT *Walk Land's End* 208 The Established Church could not do a better thing..than to peopleise these magnificent edifices. **1878** ABNEY *Photogr.* (1881) 160 The result is to render such organic matter insoluble.

**14.** with inf. as direct object of a transitive verb. (See also GIVE *v.* 29 c.)

OE. normally had the simple inf., like mod.German: *Beowulf* 356 Þa andsware..ðe me se goda agifan þenceð. [Cf. *c* 890 tr. *Bæda's Hist.* IV. xxiii. [xxii.] (1890) 330 Moniʒe men þa ðe þas þing ʒehyrdon secgan.] *c* **893** K. ÆLFRED *Oros.* (Contents) I. ii, Her Ninus ongon monna ærest ricsian. *Ibid.* I. xii. § 4 For ðon þe he him cweman þohte. *a* **900** — *Solil.* (1902) 13 Ic wilneʒe cuman to þe. *a* **900** *Laws of Ælfred* c. 66 § 7 And he bebead þone hlaford lufian swa hine selfne. *a* **900** *Ags. Ps.* (Th.) iii. 4 Þa ongan ic slapan. *c* **1000** *Ags. Gosp.* Luke i. 1 Maneʒa þohton þara þinga race ʒeendebyrdan. [*a* **1132** *O. E. Chron.* an. 1127, Þa muneces herdon ða horn blawen.]

Many of the vbs. which in OE. took the simple inf. could also be followed by *to* with the dative infinitive. But the auxiliary vbs. (see *History* above) have always been followed by the simple inf.; e.g. *Hwæt can ic sprecan?* What can I speak? *We magon ʒehyran*, We may hear.

*c* **888** K. ÆLFRED *Boeth.* xxxvi. § 8 Swa hwa swa wilnað good to donne, he wilnað good to habbanne. *c* **897** — *Gregory's Past. C.* lviii. 441 Ðonne hi leorniað..ða soðan god to secanne. *a* **900** — *Solil.* (1902) 59 Ic wundriʒe hwi ðu swa swiðe ʒeorne..þæt to witanne. *c* **1000** *Ags. Gosp.* Matt. i. 20 Nelle þu ondrædan Marian..to onfonne [*Rushw.* onfoiæ]. *Ibid.* ii. 22 He ondred þyder to faranne [*Lind.* ðider fara *vel* to færenne]. **11..** *O. E. Chron.* MS. F. (12th c.) an. 40, Matheus on Iudea agan his godspell to writen. [Cf. anno 47, Marcus se godspellere in Egipta aginþ writan þæt godspell.] *c* **1200** ORMIN 11805 He forrsoc to don þe laþe gastess wille. *c* **1205** LAY. 4569 He þohte to habben [*c* **1275** he þohte habbe] Delgan to quene of Denemarke. **1377** LANGL. *P. Pl.* B. x. 90 Suche lessounes lordes shulde louie to here. *c* **1386** CHAUCER *Knt.'s T.* 1919 What asketh men to haue? *c* **1400** MAUNDEV. Prol. 2 He ches..there to suffre his passioun. **1579** SPENSER *Sheph. Cal.* Feb. 186 Nought aske I, but onely to hold my right. **1601** B. JONSON *Poetaster* III. i. Wks. (Rtldg.) 114/2, I love not to be idle. **1611** BIBLE *Exod.* ii. 15 He sought to slay Moses. **1645** FULLER *Gd. Th. in Bad T.* xxii. (1841) 17 Give me to guard myself. **1727** DE FOE *Syst. Magic* I. iii. (1840) 74 If he would still refuse to grant their demands. **1754** A. MURPHY *Gray's-Inn Jrnl.* No. 83, I fancied to myself, to see my amiable Countrywomen [etc.]. **1812** CRABBE *Tales* xi. 314 He fear'd to die, yet felt ashamed to live. **1837** DICKENS *Pickw.* xxxii, Please, Mister Sawyer, Missis Raddle wants to speak to you. **1849** MACAULAY *Hist. Eng.* I. i. 62 The queen took upon herself to grant patents of monopoly. **1858** CARLYLE *Fredk. Gt.* II. v. (1872) I. 75 A talent..for fighting..and..a talent for avoiding to fight.

**b.** rarely as object of another preposition, instead of the vbl. sb. or gerund. (Prob. imitating French use.)

For inf. with *about to, for to*, see ABOUT A. 10–12, FOR *prep.* 11.

**1485** CAXTON *Paris & V.* (1868) 32 Vyenne salewed parys wythoute to make [Fr. *sans faire*] ony semblaunte of loue. **1591** SPENSER *Ruines of Time* 429 For not to have been dipt in Lethe lake, Could save the sonne of Thetis from to die. **1611** A. STAFFORD *Niobe* 76 The same difference..that is betwixt to sin and not to sinne. **1868** TENNYSON *Wages* 5 Give her the glory of going on, and still to be. **1879** MALLOCK *Life Worth Liv.* 17 Not to affirm is a very different thing from to deny.

**IV.** With infinitive equivalent to a finite verb or clause.

**15.** With inf. as complement to a sb. or pron., forming a compound object or sb. phrase, corresponding to the 'accusative and infinitive' construction in Latin and Greek.

(But certain vbs. in a. and b. are followed (at least in the active voice) by the simple inf. without *to*: e.g. 'they made him come', 'I felt something move'. See *History* above.)

**a.** after verbs of commanding, teaching, desiring, causing, allowing, or the like; equivalent to a *that*-clause with the sb. or pron. governing a vb. in the subjunctive. Also after the passive of such verbs, the sb. or pron. then becoming the subject.

(Also in early OE. often with simple inf.: e.g. *c* **893** K. ÆLFRED *Oros.* IV. x. § 11 Þa het he ænne mon stiʒan on þone mæst, & locian.)

*c* **888** K. ÆLFRED *Boeth.* Prayer (1899) 149 Tæc me þinne willan to wyrcenne. *c* **890** tr. *Bæda's Hist.* v. xx. [xxii.] (1890) 472 Ðara þinga ðe he oðre lærde to donne. *c* **1000** *Ags. Gosp.* Matt. viii. 21 Alyfe me ærest to faranne & bebyriʒean [L. *permitte me primum ire et sepelire*] minne fæder. *c* **1200** ORMIN 10361 Acc wel itt maʒʒ hemm brinngenn onn To rihhtenn þeʒʒre dede. *c* **1200**– [see MAKE *v.*[1] 53 b]. *c* **1330** *Amis & Amil.* 1577 He was y-hote to go. *c* **1400** MAUNDEV. (1839) iv. 25, I do þe to wytene, þat it is made be enchauntement. **1523** LD. BERNERS *Froiss.* I. cxxxiii. 161 The kyng..suffred them to passe through his host. **1611** CORYAT *Crudities* 268 Shee will..cause thy throate to be cut. **1704** SWIFT *T. Tub* ix. 170, I desire the Reader to attend. **1865** RUSKIN *Sesame* ii. § 94, I know you would like that to be true. **1902** GAIRDNER *Hist. Eng. Ch. 16th C.* viii. (1903) 143 She was compelled to act as lady's-maid to her new-born half-sister.

**b.** after verbs of saying, thinking, knowing, perceiving, or the like; equivalent to a *that*-clause with vb. in the indicative. Also after the passive of such verbs, and after intr. verbs of like meaning, as *seem, happen*, etc.

(Also in early OE. with simple inf.: e.g. *c* **890** tr. *Bæda's Hist.* v. ix. (1890) 408 Ðara cynna moniʒ he wiste in Germanie wesan.)

**13..**– [see SEEM *v.* 4]. **13..**– [see HAPPEN *v.* 3]. *a* **1400**– [see CHANCE *v.* 1 c]. **1432–50** tr. *Higden* (Rolls) I. 167 Wyse men denye Eneas to have seen Cathago. *a* **1450** *Cov. Myst.* xxxii. (1841) 324 We merveylyth..That ʒe wryte hym to be kyng of Jewys. **1566** PAINTER *Pal. Pleas.* I. 154 When hee sawe him to weepe. **1632** MILTON *Penseroso* 137 Where the rude Ax..Was never heard the Nymphs to daunt. **1726** SWIFT *Gulliver* IV. iii, The Houyhnhnms..could hardly believe me to be a right Yahoo. **1805** SCOTT *Last Minstr.* VI. xxiii, O'er Roslin.. A wondrous blaze was seen to gleam. **1891** T. HARDY *Tess* xxxiv, Unlocking the case, they found it to contain a necklace. **1912** H. L. CANNON in

*Eng. Hist. Rev.* Oct. 665 The English appear to have used all the methods [etc.].

†**c.** in other constructions, equivalent to a *that*-clause as subject, in apposition, or after a prep. or *than* (cf. THAT *conj.* 1, 1 b, 1 c). *Obs.* (now sometimes replaced by the const. with *for*: see d).

*c* **1175** *Lamb. Hom.* 117 Þere bið uuel to wunienne eni wise men. **1382** WYCLIF *Matt.* xxiv. 6 It bihoueth thes thingis to be don. *c* **1386** CHAUCER *Prol.* 502 If gold ruste, what shal Iren doo. For if a preest be foul,..No wonder is, a lewed man to ruste. *c* **1460** *Towneley Myst.* xviii. 31 A madyn to bere a chyld,..that were ferly. **1470–85** MALORY *Arthur* I. xvi. 60 It is better that we slee a coward than thorow a coward alle we to be slayne. **1474** *Coventry Leet Bk.* 389 Vppon the peyn, who doth to þe contrarie to lose..vj s. viij d. **1535** COVERDALE *Ps.* cxxxii[i.] 1 Beholde, how good & ioyfull a thinge it is, brethren to dwell together in vnite. **1590** SHAKS. *Com. Err.* I. i. 33 A heauier taske could not haue beene impos'd, Than I to speake my griefes vnspeakeable. **1647** in Picton *L'pool Munic. Rec.* (1883) I. 143 Because of the rumour of sicknes to be begune in Warrington. **1678** CUDWORTH *Intell. Syst.* I. iv. § 34. 534 *Qua pateat Mundum Divino Numine verti*..Whereby it may appear the World to be Governed by a Divine Mind.

**d.** preceded by *for* (with various constructions and shades of meaning): see FOR *prep.* 18.

**16.** With inf. after a dependent interrogative or relative; equivalent to a clause with *may*, *should*, etc. (Sometimes with ellipsis of *whether* before *or* in an alternative dependent question.)

*a* **1300**– [see HOW *adv.* 9]. *c* **1386** CHAUCER *Man of Law's T.* 558 She hath no wight to whom to make hir mone. *c* **1400** *R. Gloucester's Chron.* (Rolls) 9237 (MS. B.) Hii nuste wat to do. *c* **1460** *Towneley Myst.* xxiii. 259 Godys son.. Hase not where apon his hede to rest. **1470–85** MALORY *Arthur* XIII. xix. 639 He..wyst not what to do. **1564** STAPLETON tr. *Staphylus' Apol.* Pref. 3 Looking of him to be directed where, howe, and when to strike. **1602** SHAKS. *Ham.* III. i. 56 To be, or not to be, that is the Question. **1732** POPE *Ess. Man* II. 7 In doubt to act, or rest. **1896** A. AUSTIN *Eng. Darling* I. i, To know the worst Is the one way whereby to better it.

**b.** In absolute or independent construction after an interrogative, forming an elliptical question.

This may be explained as an ellipsis of the principal clause (sense 16), or of 'is one', 'am I', etc. before the inf. (sense 11 b or c).

**1713** ADDISON *Cato* III. vii, But how to gain admission? for Access Is giv'n to none but Juba, and her Brothers. **1821** SHELLEY *Hellas* 659 Whither to fly? **1835** J. H. NEWMAN *Lett.* (1891) II. 87 But..how to hinder vexatious prosecutions? **1841** *Ibid.* 347 Talk carries off a good deal of irritation; but how to make talk innocent? **1875** MORRIS *Æneid* XII. 489 Ah, what to do?

**17.** In absolute or independent construction, with subject expressed (in nom.) or omitted: in exclamations expressing astonishment, indignation, sorrow, or (after *O* or other interj.) longing.

*a* **1450** *Cov. Myst.* viii. 77, I to bere a childe that xal bere alle mannys blyss,..ho mythe have joys more? **1460** CAPGRAVE *Chron.* (Rolls) 141 Seynt Thomas hast thou killid; and now to forsake the proteccion of alle Cristen men! **1588** SHAKS. *L. L. L.* III. i. 202 And I to sigh for her, to watch for her, To pray for her, go to! **1596** — *Merch. V.* III. i. 37 My owne flesh and blood to rebell. **1664** PEPYS *Diary* 27 Mar., But, Lord! to see how the trained bands are raised upon this. **1742** YOUNG *Nt. Th.* III. 93 O to forget her! **1832** R. H. FROUDE *Rem.* (1838) I. 257 Only to think that my stars should let me off so easily! **1842** TENNYSON *Locksley Hall* 175, I, to herd with narrow foreheads..! **1845** BROWNING *Home Thoughts*, Oh, to be in England! **1871** R. ELLIS *Catullus* lxv. 9 Ah! no more to address thee, or hear thy kindly replying, Brother!..Ne'er to behold thee again!

†**18.** With inf. immediately following the subject, in vivid narrative, equivalent to a past tense indic.; almost always with *go* and vbs. of like meaning.

? With ellipsis of *gan* (see GIN *v.*[1] 1), *took*, or the like; but cf. the 'historic infinitive' in Latin.

*c* **1205** LAY. 21655 Ah Arður com sone mid selere strengðe, And Scottes to fleonne feor of þan ærde. *a* **1300** *E. E. Psalter* ii. 2 Ogaine þair laverd þai come on ane, And ogaine his criste to gane. **1375** BARBOUR *Bruce* VIII. 351 He turnit his bridill, and to ga. *c* **1385** CHAUCER *L. G. W.* 653 (*Cleopatra*) Antonye..put hym to the flyght And al his folk to go that best go myght. **1387** TREVISA *Higden* (Rolls) III. 161 Tarquinius..come uppon hire while sche slepte..and to lye by hire maugre hir teeþ. **1566** GASCOIGNE *Supposes* Wks. (1587) 34, I to fuge and away hither as fast as I could. **1668** PEPYS *Diary* 18 Sept., I..away home,..and there to read again and sup with Gibson.

**V.** Peculiar constructions.

†**19.** *To* was formerly often used with the second of two infinitives when the first was without it, esp. after an auxiliary, with words intervening between the infinitives. (See also note s. v. THAN *conj.* I.)

*c* **1205** LAY. 1220 Swa he gon slomnen & þer æfter to slepen. *c* **1440** *Ipomydon* 1246 Bettyr is on huntynge goone, ..Than thus lyghtly to lese a stede. *c* **1486** *Rec. St. Mary at Hill* 16 Euery persone..shall haue one of thise smale candelles brennyng in their handes & so to go on procession. *a* **1533** LD. BERNERS *Gold. Bk. M. Aurel.* (1546) I iij, A good prince that wil..governe wel, and not to be a tyraunt. **1598** SHAKS. *Merry W.* IV. iv. 57 Then let them all encircle him about, And Fairy-like to pinch the vncleane Knight. **1611–1803** [see THAN *conj.* 1 γ, δ].

**20.** Occasionally an adverb or advb. phr. (formerly sometimes an object or predicate) is inserted between *to* and the infinitive, forming the construction now usually (but loosely) called 'split infinitive'. (See Onions *Adv. Eng. Syntax* § 177.)

**13..** *Cursor M.* 8318 (Cott. & Fairf.) To temple make he sal be best. *Ibid.* 12965 (ibid.) He sal þe send Angels for to þe defend. *c* **1400** tr. *Secreta Secret., Gov. Lordsh.* 66 To enserche sciences, and to perfitly knowe alle manere of Naturels þinges. **1606** G. W[OODCOCKE] *Hist. Ivstine* IV. 23 To quite rid himselfe out of thraldome. **1650** R. GENTILIS *Considerations* 137 Anniball was advised..to not go to Rome. **1779–81** JOHNSON *L. P., Milton* Wks. II. 100 Milton was too busy to much miss his wife. **1805** EMILY CLARK *Banks of Douro* III. 114 This answer seemed to seriously offend him. **1839** *Times* 15 Jan., This jack-in-office had taken upon himself..to more than insinuate [etc.]. **1893** J. A. HODGES *Elem. Photogr.* (1907) 114 The only way to successfully overcome it.

**21.** Used absolutely at the end of a clause, with ellipsis of the infinitive, which is to be supplied from the preceding clause. *rare* before 19th c.; now a frequent colloquialism.

**13..** *Minor Poems fr. Vernon MS.* xxxiii. 74 Þe soules of synners,.. Þer to take and resseyue sc As þei on eorþe deserueden to. **1448** J. SHILLINGFORD *Lett.* (Camden) 114 He woll amende hit as sone as God well yeve hym grace and tyme to. *c* **1450** *St. Cuthbert* (Surtees) 3330 Sayntes biddings forto do, Þof all' þare seme na resoun to. **1621** LADY M. WROTH *Urania* 7 She..obserued him, as well as she could bring her spirit to consent to. **1719** DE FOE *Crusoe* (1840) I. iii. 33 Going no oftener into the shore than we were obliged to for fresh water. **1828** R. H. FROUDE *Rem.* (1838) I. 229, I feel quite differently from what I ever used to. **1883** HOWELLS *Register* i, I kept on,..I had to. *a* **1909** F. M. CRAWFORD *Uncanny Tales* (1911) 173, I wanted to turn round and look. It was an effort not to.

†**22.** Instead of the dative infinitive, the gerund in *-ing* was sometimes used after *to*: prob. originating in a phonetic confusion of *-en* and *-in(g)*, but later perh. with the notion of a future action (cf. 11 a); as *to coming* = 'to come', or 'coming': see also COME *v.* 32 β (after c). *Obs.*

**1382** WYCLIF *Num.* xxxii. 7 Thei doren not passe into the place that the Lord is to ȝyuynge to hem. — *Acts* xxii. 29 Thei that weren to turmentinge him. **1382–1490** [see COME *v.* 32 β]. **1387** TREVISA *Higden* (Rolls) I. 73 Hit is not to trowynge. *Ibid.* 103 Damascus is to menynge 'schedynge blood'. *Ibid.* 153 They..taught hem to schetynge. **1393** LANGL. *P. Pl.* C. XVIII. 313 Iuwes..hopen þat he be to comynge þat shal hem releue. *a* **1450** *Knt. de la Tour* xxxiv. (1868) 48 That is to menying that ye shulde loue and doute youre husbonde. **1471** FORTESCUE *Wks.* (1869) 530 Both titles, that is to saynge his auncient title,..and this new title.

†**C. To** *conj. Obs.*

**1.** To the time that; till, until.

*a* **1300** *E. E. Psalter* xvii. 38, I sal filghe mi faas,..And noght ogain torne to þai wane swa. **13..** *K. Alis.* 5902 (Bodl. MS.) Þe kyng þere soiourned to he was hoole. *c* **1400** MAUNDEV. (Roxb.) xx. 89 Þase..þai fede to þai be fatte. *c* **1575** *Durham Depos.* (Surtees) 275 Umphray culd gett no reste of the said Thomas to he had cast hym doon on his bedd.

**b.** followed by *that*: cf. THAT *conj.* 7.

*c* **1460** *Towneley Myst.* xx. 332 We shall hy vs before, To that we com to that cyte. **1509** *Sel. Cases Star Chamb.* (Selden) II. 7 [They] vsed..to haue commens..in the same vj closes to now of late that..thei be interupt. **1626** J. HAIG *Let.* 10 Nov., in J. Russell *Haigs* vii. (1881) 178 And to that I be into fashion, I am ashamed to presume.

**2.** During the time that; while; = TILL *conj.* 2. (Also with *that.*) *rare.*

**1357** *Lay Folk's Catech.* 345 (MS. T.) For to lyve samen Withouten ony lousyng to thair life lastes. *c* **1375** *Sc. Leg. Saints* i. (*Petrus*) 304 Mony..He helyt, to þat he was þare.

**D. To** (tū) *adv.*

†**1.** Expressing motion resulting in arrival (cf. A. 1): To a place, etc. implied or indicated by the context. *Obs.* (Often the separable particle of a compound vb.)

*c* **1000** ÆLFRIC *Hom.* II. 182 Gang to and arær hine. *c* **1175** *Lamb. Hom.* 87 Þa on þere ilke nihte iwende godes engel to, and acwalde on elche huse [etc.]. **13..** *Cursor M.* 5530 (Cott. & Fairf.) Þis godds folk bar to þe clay. *a* **1400–50** *Alexander* 1389 Þare presis to with paues peple withouten.

**2.** Expressing direction (cf. A. 2): Towards a thing or person implied; after *end*, *head*, etc., forming advb. phrases (cf. ON *adv.* 7 b).

**1889** *Amer. Nat.* Jan. 19 Three young owls with their feathers turned wrong end to. **1900** *Everybody's Mag.* III. 533 The Monitor came head-to when the cable brought her up.

**b.** In conjunction with other advbs. of direction: In one direction (as contrasted with the opposite one). Now only in TO AND FRO; see also 7, 9.

**1375** BARBOUR *Bruce* x. 604 Him followit thai, With mekill payne, quhill to, quhill fra. *c* **1421** HOCCLEVE *Complaint* 30 The grefe abowte my harte..bolned evar to and to so sore. **1560** ROLLAND *Crt. Venus* I. 356 Scho alteris ay to euerie kinde and stait: Quhylis to, quhylis fra. **1606** SHAKS. *Ant. & Cl.* I. iv. 46 This common bodie, Like to a Vagabond Flagge vpon the Streame, Goes too, and backe.

†**3.** Up to a time indicated by the context; till then: in phr. *not be long to.* (Cf. A. 6.) *Obs.*

**1468** J. PASTON in *P. Lett.* II. 318 When I come home, whyche, I tryst to God, shal not be long to. **1471** *Ibid.* III. 6 It shall not be longe to or then my wronges..shall be redressyd. **1538** HEN. VIII *Let. to Anne Boleyn* in *Select. fr. Harl. Misc.* (1793) 145 Till you repaire hydder, I keep something in store, trusting it shall not be long to.

**4.** Expressing contact (cf. A. 5): So as to come close against something; *esp.* with vbs. forming phrases denoting shutting or closing: see the vbs. Now *arch.* and *colloq.*

*c* **1200** *Trin. Coll. Hom.* 181 Hie tuneð to hire fif gaten. *a* **1225** *Ancr. R.* 96 Schutteð al þet þurl to. *c* **1386** CHAUCER *Miller's T.* 554 Tehee quod she, and clapte the wyndow to. **1534** TINDALE *Luke* xiii. 25 When the good man of the housse..hath shett to the dore. *a* **1619** FLETCHER *Mad Lover* III. ii, Put to the doors. **1620** J. DYKE in Spurgeon *Treas. Dav.* Ps. lxi. 2 This tower and rock were too high.. and therefore he sets to the scaling ladder. **1855** MRS. GATTY *Parab. fr. Nat.* Ser. I. (1869) 61 The banging of the door, blown to by a current of wind. **1898** G. B. SHAW *Plays* II. *Arms & Man* 6 She goes out..and pulls the outside shutters to.

**5.** Expressing attachment, application, or addition (cf. A. 15, 16): after various verbs, as *put*, *set*, etc. (q. v.); also predicatively, *spec.* of a horse: = harnessed to a vehicle. Now *dial.* or *colloq.*

*c* **1425** tr. *Arderne's Treat. Fistula* 84, I putte to regeneratyuez of flesch. *c* **1450** *Oseney Reg.* 96 To this present writyng my seele I haue i-put to. **1530** PALSGR. Introd. 38 Lyke as we out of our adjectyves forme our adverbes..by adding to of ly. **1534** TINDALE *John* iii. 33 He that hath receaved hys testimonye hath set to his seale that God is true. **1596** SHAKS. 1 *Hen. IV*, v. i. 133 Can Honour set too a legge? **1768** *Woman of Honor* I. 68 The horses are to. **1889** HISSEY *Tour in Phaeton* 97 We ordered the horses to, and resumed our pleasant pilgrimage.

**b.** In the senses 'in addition, besides, also', and 'in excess', now written as a distinct word, TOO, q. v.

**6.** Expressing attention or application (cf. A. 24): after vbs., as *fall*, *go*, *set* (see the vbs.). In quot. 1606 *absol.* (with ellipsis of vb. in imperative).

*c* **1200** ORMIN 6134 Forr þe birrþ don þin hellpe to Aȝȝ affterr þine fere. *c* **1425**– [see *set to*, SET *v.* 152 f]. **1606** SHAKS. *Tr. & Cr.* II. i. 119 To Achilles, to Aiax, to. **1610** — *Temp.* III. iii. 49, I will stand to, and feede. *Ibid.* 52 Stand too, and doe as we. **1844** DISRAELI *Coningsby* VIII. i, It's difficult to turn to with a new thing.

†**7.** Expressing assent or adhesion (cf. A. 31 b): In assent to or favour of something implied (opp. to *fra*, FRO *adv.*). Cf. 9 b, TO AND FRO A. 3.

*c* **1450** HOLLAND *Howlat* 270 Sum said to and sum fra, Sum nay and sum ȝa.

**8.** Used idiomatically with many verbs, as *bring*, *come*, *go*, *lay*, *lie*, etc.: see the verbs.

**9. To and again.**

**a.** To a place and back again; alternately in opposite directions; backwards and forwards: = TO AND FRO A. 1. *Obs.* exc. *dial.*

**1627** CAPT. SMITH *Seaman's Gram.* ii. 6 A ship..hath sailed to and againe ouer the maine Ocean. **1628** DIGBY *Voy. Medit.* (Camden) 86 The wind shifted too and againe very vncertainely. **1628–1719** [see AGAIN A. 1 c]. **1719** DE FOE *Crusoe* (1858) 240 Amazed when he saw me work the boat to-and-again in the sea by the rudder. **1760–72** H. BROOKE *Fool of Qual.* (1809) II. 126 Walking..to and again. **1828** *Craven Gloss.*, *To and again*, backwards and forwards. **1888** ELWORTHY *W. Somerset Word-bk.* 763.

*fig.* **1736** NEAL *Hist. Purit.* III. 240 Such as had shifted their religion to and again.

†**b.** For and against a question: = TO AND FRO A. 3. *Obs.*

**1656** *Burton's Diary* (1828) I. 3 All parties have been heard, too and again, in this last case. **1666** J. LIVINGSTONE in *Sel. Biog.* (1845) I. 181 Much debate too and again had been used.

†**c.** Again and again, repeatedly. *Obs.*

**1659** *Burton's Diary* (1828) IV. 379 Your Committee too and again offered it as an expedient. **1666** PEPYS *Diary* 13 Aug., Sent him to and again to get me 1000*l.*

**To**, obs. spelling of TOO, TWO.

**To-**, *prefix*[1], the prep. and adv. TO used in combination with verbs, sbs., adjs., and advbs. in the sense of motion, direction, or addition to, or as the mark of the infinitive: see in their alphabetical places, TO-COME, TO-DO, TO-DRAUGHT, TO-GAINST, TOGETHER, TO-MIDST, TO-WHEN, TO-WHILE, etc. Also the following obs. verbs:

**To-cast**, to add, make addition: = L. *adicere*; **to-hang**, to append; **to-hear**, to hearken to, listen to; **to-knit**, to knit to, bind up: = L. *alligāre*; **to-lay**, to put forward, allege; **to-neighe**, to approach: = L. *accēdere*; **to-put**, to put to, add, affix: = L. *appōnĕre*; **to-set**, to set to, affix; **to-stand**, to stand to, post oneself, assist: = L. *astāre*, *assistĕre*; **to-step**, to step to, advance: = L. *aggredī*; **to-stick**, to stick to, adhere: = L. *adhærēre*; **to-tach**, to fasten to, attach; **to-yield**, to yield to, cede, give up.

*a* **1340** HAMPOLE *Psalter* cxiii. 23 Lord *tokast [L. *adiciat*] on ȝou, on ȝou & on ȝoure sunnys...Oure lord eke ȝoure noumbire. **1464** in *Acc. Fam. Innes* (1864) 78 To thir my present lettres I haf *to hungyn my sele. **1536** *Reg. Mag. Sig. Scot.* 343 *note*, I have subscrivit thir presentis with my hand, and has to hungin my proper sele of armes. *a* **1225** *Ancr. R.* 84 Þet ȝe þe bet icnowen ham..*to-her hore molden. *a* **1300** *E. E. Psalter* cxlvi. 3 Þat heles forbroken ofe hert for wa, And *toknittes [*alligat*] þar sorwes swa. *c* **1450** *Pol. Poems* (Rolls) II. 240 Auctoryteys for hem they *toleye. **1382** WYCLIF *Judith* xiv. 14 He wente *to-neȝhende to the curtin [*Vulg.* Accessit proximans ad cortinam]. **1420** in Pinkerton *Hist. Scot.* (1797) I. 455 The sealls of the forsaid..to thir indentures interchangablie are *toput. **1445** in *Charters rel. Glasgow* (1906) II. 440, I have procurit.. the secrete sele of the burgh of Lithqw to be toput. *a* **1340** HAMPOLE *Psalter* lxxxviii. 22 Þe sun of wickednes sall not *toset [*apponet*] him to noy. *c* **1375** *Cursor M.* 3498 (Fairf.) Þer-to was he maste *to-sette. **1455** in *Charters, &c. Edinb.* (1871) 81 To the parte of this endentur remanand with the said toune the said Sir James sele is to sett. *a* **1340** HAMPOLE *Psalter* ii. 2 Tostode [L. *astiterunt*] þe kynges of erth,

*c* 1205 LAY. 17406 Þa cnihtes *to-stepen [*c* 1275 to-stapte] Mid muchelere strengðe. 1596 DALRYMPLE tr. *Leslie's Hist. Scot.* VI. (S.T.S.) I. 340 The capsell sa fast *tostack.. that the force of man culde neuir sindir thame. 13.. *Gaw. & Gr. Knt.* 579 Queme quyssewes [cuisses]..with þwonges *to-tached. *c* 1350 *Will. Palerne* 3924 He a-liȝt, & wiȝtli to william his wepun vp *to-ȝelde.

**To-,** *prefix*[2]. *Obs.* exc. in rare *arch.* or *dial.* use. [OE. *to-*, ME. *to-* (*te-*) = OFris. *ti-*, *te-* (*to-*), OS. *ti-* (*te-*), OHG. *zi-*, *za-*, *ze-* and *zir-*, *zar-* (MHG. *ze-*, *zer-*, *zir-*, Ger. *zer-*) :—WGer. **ti-* :—OTeut. **tiz-* = L. *dis-*, a particle expressing separation, 'asunder, apart, in pieces'.

The WGer. *ti-* (= L. *dis-*) in prehistoric times ran together in form with *ti* the unstressed prepositional form of *tó* (see To *prep.*), with which it had no etymological connexion (being indeed almost opposite in sense); and when the latter was levelled in vowel with its stressed adverbial form *tó*, *ti-* (= *dis-*) also followed it, and appears constantly in OE. as *to-*. In most grammars and dictionaries this is written *tó-*, like the stressed form of To *adv.* and *prep.* But as it was the *unstressed* form with which the prefix was formally confounded, and as it was itself always stressless (being sometimes written *te* as in OS. and OFris.), it seems more in accordance with the facts to spell it in OE. *to-* with short *o*, which is therefore done here.

In OE., about 125 compound verbs in *to-* are recorded; many of these did not survive in ME., where however so many new compounds appear (some formed even on vbs. from French) that their number in Early ME. was not less than in OE. In the 15th c. they rapidly disappeared and only a few are found after 1500. Many of the verbs which took the prefix *to-* had themselves the sense of separation or division; such were *break*, *burst*, *deal*, *melt*, *scatter*, *strew*, *tear*, etc.; in these *to-* added little but force to the notion: cf. *burst*, *burst asunder*, *tear*, *tear asunder*, etc. This led to the prefixing of *to-* to verbs which had no sense of partition, merely as a strengthening or emphasizing particle, as in *darken*, *to-darken*, *swink*, *to-swink*, etc. From an early time *to*-verbs were often strengthened by the qualifying adv. *all* (ALL C) in sense 'wholly, completely, altogether'; in later times this became universal. Consequently, the prefix began to be viewed as *all-to-* or *allto-*; and (verbal prefixes being very commonly written separate from the vb.) *all to* or *all-to* began to be treated as itself an adverb with the sense 'altogether, completely': see ALL C. 14, 15. Thus in the Bible of 1611, Judges ix. 53 'and all to brake his scull' was etymologically and historically *all to-brake*, i.e. 'all to-pieces-broke', but may have been understood as *all-to brake*, i.e. 'altogether' or 'completely broke'; Fairfax in 1674 by *all-to-be-deckt* can only have meant *all-to bedeckt*, 'completely bedecked'.]

**1.** With separative force: Asunder, apart, to or in pieces; also, away, about, abroad, here and there. Combined with verbs and derived adjs. and sbs. The more important of these appear in their places as main words: the following are obsolete words of single or rare occurrence. (All vbs. *trans.* unless otherwise stated.)

† **To-bray** *v.*, to bray or beat to atoms; † **to-bust** *v.* [BUST *v.*[1]], to beat or thrash to pieces; † **to-crack** *v.*, to crack to pieces, shatter; † **to-dight** *v.*, to put apart, separate; hence † **to-dighting** *vbl. sb.*; † **to-flap** *v.*, to knock to pieces; † **to-gnide** *v.* [GNIDE *v.*], to crush to fragments; † **to-hale** *v.*, to haul or drag asunder; to pull about; to distend; † **to-heave** *v.*, to 'lift up' (one's eyes), to open; † **to-hene** *v.* [HENE *v.*], to mutilate by stoning; † **to-hurt** *v.*, to dash or knock asunder; † **to-leave** *v.*, to relinquish, to abandon; † **to-lithe** *v.* [LITHE *v.*[2]], to dismember; † **to-liver** *v.*, = DELIVER *v.*; † **to-melt** *v. intr.*, to melt away, dissolve; † **to-part** *v. intr.*, = DEPART *v.*; † **to-set** *v.*, to distribute, divide, arrange; † **to-shider** *v.* [cf. SHIDE *sb.*] *intr.*, to break in pieces, to be shivered; † **to-shred** *v.*, to cut to shreds; † **to-skair** *v.* [SKAIR *v.*[2]], to scatter, disperse; † **to-skill** *v.*, to divide, distinguish; † **to-slent** *v.*[1] [SLENT *v.*[1]] *intr.*, to slip away; † **to-slent** *v.*[2] [SLENT *v.*[3]] *intr.*, to split, burst; † **to-slive** *v.* [SLIVE *v.*[1]], to cleave; † **to-sned** *v.* [SNED *v.*], to cut to pieces; † **to-sparple** *v.*, to scatter abroad; = DISPARPLE; † **to-swinge** *v.*, to disperse by beating; to beat to pieces; † **to-thrust** *v.*, to thrust apart, to push open; † **to-torve** *v.*, to hurl about; to dash to pieces; † **to-tose** *v.* [TOZE], to tear to pieces; † **to-twin** *v.*, to separate, divide; † **to-waver** *v. intr.*, to waver uncertainly; to wander; † **to-wawe** *v.* [OE. *wagian*] *intr.*, to move about; † **to-wowe** *v.* [OE. *wáwan*], to scatter by blowing; † **to-writhe** *v.*, (*a*) *trans.* to twist or wrench apart; (*b*) *intr.*, to twist or writhe about; † **to-wry** *v.*, to turn, twist about.

1382 WYCLIF 2 *Chron.* xxxiv. 7 The mawmete wodus and grauen thingus he hadde *to-brayȝide in to gobetis. *a* 1250 *Owl & Night.* 1610 (Cott.) An euer euch man is wið me wroð..An me *tobusteþ & tobeteþ. 13.. *Sir Beues* 4313+180 (MS. E.) Þere men myȝte seen schafftys schake And mennys crownys al *tocrake. *c* 1450 LOVELICH *Grail* xiv. 196 Helmes and hawberkis to-kraked he then. 1340 *Ayenb.* 72 Þanne þridde dyeaþ þet is þe *todiȝtinge of þe zaule and of þe bodie. 1382 WYCLIF 2 *Sam.* xxii. 43 As cleye of streetis I sal breek hem, and *to-flappe [*confringam*]. *a* 1300 *E. E. Psalter* ci. 11 [cii. 10] For vp-heueand *to-gnodded þou me [*v.r.* for þou to-gnod me vpheuand: *Vulg.* elisisti; WYCLIF hurtledest me (down)]. 1387 TREVISA *Higden* (Rolls) V. 327 So was he al day to drawe and *to haled, i-scorned, and i-buffetted [*tractus et illusus colaphizatur*]. 1398 — *Barth. De P. R.* XIX. liv. (Bodl. MS.), Raw hony not wele clarified..strecccheþ and to haleþ the bodie. *c* 1200 *Trin. Coll. Hom.* 201 Man þe nappeð [h]wile *to-heueð his eȝen, and þenne seð. *a* 1250 *Owl & Night.* 1119 Stones hi doþ in heore slytte [= pocket] & þe totoroueþ & *toheneþ. *a* 1225 *Ancr. R.* 426 Sum nouhtunge hwar þuruh heo *to-hurteð [*v.r.* to hurren] eiðer urommard oðer. 1432–50 tr. *Higden* (Rolls) V. 69 The cardinalles supposede that he hade..*to-lefte his benefice for the luffe of theyme. *c* 1000 ÆLFRIC *Hom.* II. 272 Þa *toliðode se engel þæt cild on ðam disce. *c* 1205 LAY. 4216 Stater heo nom & al hene to-liðeden [*c* 1275 to-limekede]. *Ibid.* 25929 Nu hafeð be..Mine leomen al to-leðed [*c* 1275 a-liþede]. 13.. *Metr. Treat. on Dreams* in *Rel. Ant.* I. 266 Of sunne ant peril *to-lyvred he byth. *c* 1425 *Seven Sag.* (P.) 1976 Ham to-lywryd a man anon, And thider fast thay gone gone. *a* 1240 *Wohunge* in *Lambeth Hom.* 269 Hwat herte is swa hard þat ne mei *to-melte i þe munegunge of þe? *c* 1374 CHAUCER *Troylus* III. 249 (298) His olde wo..Gan tho for Ioye wasten and to-melte. *c* 1275 *Passion our Lord* 702 in *O. E. Misc.* 57 Hwanne hi schullen *to-party vt of lyue þisse. 1387 TREVISA *Higden* (Rolls) V. 265 Forto know rediliche þe meres and þe merkes of þe contrayes where þese men were *to set, loke in the firste book. *Ibid.* VII. 307 Everiche celle is departed in foure, and to sette wiþ ynne for þe oratorie, þe dortour, þe fraytour, and þe werkhous. *c* 1450 *Guy Warw.* (C.) 1468 Faste þey smote þen togedur That þer sperys can *toschyder. *c* 1386 CHAUCER *Knt.'s T.* 1751 The helmes they tohewen and *toshrede. *c* 1200 ORMIN 1498 Till rihhte læfe turrnesst þatt flocc þatt was *toskeȝȝredd ær. *Ibid.* 9462 Þatt Judisskenn follc þa shollde beon toskeȝȝredd..Forr heore depe sinne. *Ibid.* 18652 Illc an had iss oþerr fra *Toskiledd & todæledd. 14.. *Sir Beues* 2539 (MS. M.) Ascopard..Smot Beues a strok gret, That his own fote *toslynt And he fel wiþ is owene dentte. *c* 1380 *Sir Ferumb.* 4940 Þe ymage of Mahoun..Wiþ þe axe smot he oppon þe molde, þat al þat heued *to-slente [*pr.* to-flente]. *c* 1050 *Gloss.* in Wr.-Wülcker 406/29 *Findit*, *toslaf, tocleaf. *c* 1314 *Reinbrun* cv. in *Guy Warw.* (E. E. T. S.) 666 Helm and scheld,..Þai gonne hem al to-schliue. *c* 1205 LAY. 4015 Þe uniselie moder mid sexe hine *to-snæde. *Ibid.* 16148 Hengest..hafde..mid sæxen to-snædðe snelle þe þeines. 1387 TREVISA *Higden* (Rolls) V. 287 Hengistus..brouȝte to gydres his knyȝtes and men of arms þat were *to sparpled and to schad [L. *dispersis*]. *c* 1205 LAY. 1533 Þer wes moni steap mon Mid stele *to-sw[u]ngen. *c* 1175 *Lamb. Hom.* 131 He *to-þruste þa stelene gate..of helle. *c* 1000 *Ags. Gosp.* Matt. xiv. 24 Witodlice wæs þ scyp of þam yþum *totorfod, for-þam þe hyt wæs strang wind. *c* 1175 *Lamb. Hom.* 9 Ac me þe sculde nimen and al to-teon mid horse oðer þe al to-toruion mid stane. *a* 1250 [see *tohene*]. *a* 1250 *Owl & Night.* 70 Þe sulue mose..wolde þe *totose. *c* 1200 ORMIN 19060, & tiss lif unnderr Crisstenndom *Totwinneþþ & toshædeþþ All Cristess follc fra defless follc. *a* 1225 *Ancr. R.* 254 Euerichon to dealed [*Corpus* to twuned] from oðer. 1375 BARBOUR *Bruce* VII. 302 For thai trow we so scalit ar, And fled *to-vauerand her and thar. *c* 1350 *Will. Palerne* 19 Þe child..spakly speke it couþe tho & spedeliche *to-wawe. 13.. in *Anglia* III. 279/89 Þe wind hem wolde *towowen. *c* 1000 ÆLFRIC *Gram.* xxvi. (Z.) 155 *Torqueo*, ic wriðe,..*distorqueo*, ic *towriðe. *c* 1320 *Sir Tristr.* 3179 So wo was ysoude,..Þat alle sche wald to wriþe. ? *a* 1400 *Morte Arth.* 3920 He al to-wrythes for woo. 1423 JAS. I *Kingis Q.* clxiv, So tolter quhilum did sche [Fortune] It *to-wrye.

**2.** Used as a mere intensive: Completely, entirely, soundly, greatly, severely, etc.

(A few of these show traces of the separative sense.)

All vbs. *trans.*, unless otherwise stated.

† **To-bent** *pa. pple.*, quite bent, bent low; † **to-bite** *v.*, to bite severely; † **to-blast** *v.*, to blast utterly; † **to-brain** *v.*, to brain completely; † **to-clout** *v.*, to cover with clouts; † **to-darken** *v.*, to darken greatly (rendering L. *contenebrare*); † **to-deraign** (**-dreyn**) *v.* [DERAIGN *v.*[1]], to maintain, vindicate (a cause, etc.) entirely; † **to-drunk** *pa. pple.*, thoroughly inebriated; † **to-dun** *v.* [DUN *v.*[2]], to strike with resounding blows; † **to-establish** *v.*, to establish perfectly or entirely; † **to-harrow** (**-harwe**) *v.*, to harrow completely; † **to-minish** *v.*, to make small, break up (rendering L. *comminuere*); † **to-pierce** (**-perse**) *v.*, to pierce entirely; † **to-punish** *v.*, to punish soundly; † **to-push** *v.*, to push about, to hustle; † **to-ray** *v.* [RAY *v.*[2] 5], to besmear; † **to-rot** *v. intr.*, to rot utterly (rendering L. *computrescere*); † **to-schrape** *v.* [SHRAPE], to scrape entirely; † **to-shell** *v.*, to peel entirely, to make bare of skin; † **to-smite** *v.*, to smite violently (in quot. *absol.*); † **to-spill** *v.*, to confound, ruin utterly; † **to-spreng** *v.*, to besprinkle completely; † **to-stick** *v.*, to prick all over; † **to-sting** *v.*, to sting severely; † **to-stink** *v. intr.*, to stink greatly; † **to-stir** *v.*, to move violently; † **to-stony** *v.*, to astound; † **to-swelt** *v. intr.*, to perish, die; † **to-swink** *v. intr.*, to toil hard; † **to-tar** *v.* (**-ter(re)** [TAR, TARRE *v.*[2]], to provoke greatly; † **to-teen** *v.* [TEEN *v.*[1]], to injure or annoy greatly: see quot. s. v. *to-tray*; † **to-threat** *v.*, to threaten violently; † **to-tray** *v.*, to torment exceedingly; † **to-trouble** *v.*, to trouble greatly, to afflict severely; † **to-turn** *v.*, to overthrow, upset, subvert; † **to-walt** *v. intr.*, to overflow; † **to-waste** *v.*, to waste greatly.

*c* 1401 LYDG. *Flour of Curtesye* 260 Over this, myn hertes lust *to-bente. 1375 *Creation* 640 in Horstm. *Altengl. Leg.* (1878) 132 An addre..al *to-bot Seth in þe face. 1382 WYCLIF *Job* Prol. 2 The boc shortid, and to-torn and to-bite. 1303 R. BRUNNE *Handl. Synne* 8866 Þe syȝte of here myn herte *to-blaste. *c* 1330 — *Chron. Wace* (Rolls) 9293 Þe sight of hure hym al to-blast. *c* 1489 CAXTON *Blanchardyn* xliii. 164 He..*to brayned ther many one. *c* 1430 *Pilgr. Lyf Manhode* III. xxii. (1869) 148 That is thilke that hath thus to ragged me and *to clowted me as thou seest. 1382 WYCLIF *Lam.* v. 17 Therfore dreri mad is oure herte, therfore *to-dercned ben oure eȝen. *c* 1320 *Cast. Love* 974 For I chulle an ende ouercome þt fiht, And *to-dreynen al þi riht. 1382 WYCLIF *Jer.* xlvi. 10 Deuouren shal the swerd,..and be *to-drunke with the blod of hem. *a* 1240 *Wohunge* in *Cott. Hom.* 281 Siðen ȝette buffetet and *to dunet i þe heaued wið þe red ȝerde. *a* 1562 CAVENDISH *Poems*, etc. (1825) II. 158 Your pryncely powers and hault dygnyties Assured me with suche perfection, *To-establyshed me in the hyest degrees. 1393 LANGL. *P. Pl.* C. XXII. 268 (MS. T.) Al þis hus oxen ereden thei *to harwen [*v.r.* to-harewide] after. 1382 WYCLIF *Isa.* xxviii. 28 Bred forsothe shal be *to-mynusht [1388 maad lesse]. *c* 1470 HENRY *Wallace* IV. 662 The trensand blaid *to persyt euirydeill Throu plaitt and stuff. *a* 1400–50 *Alexander* 4330 *To-ponyscht be-fore Fynd we na faute in na freke þat vs emange duellis. 13.. *Lament. St. Bernard* 198 in *Minor Poems Vernon MS.* 306 Þe Iewes of harm hedde non ende, Mi sone to-beten and *to-pust. 1560 WHITEHORNE *Ord. Souldiours* (1588) 46 b, Putting Toe..peeses of linnen cloth all *to-rayed therewith. 1382 WYCLIF *Jer.* xlvi. 15 Why *to-rotide [*v.r.* to-stank] thi stronge? *a* 1225 *Leg. Kath.* 1185 He..schrenchte þen alde deouel, & *teschrapet his heaued. 1377 LANGL. *P. Pl.* B. XVII. 191 Ac þough my thombe & my fyngres bothe were *to-shullen. 14.. *Beryn* 1456 Yeur wyff woll sikirliche..hir tuskis sharpe whet, And *to smyte with hir tunge. *a* 1300 *E. E. Psalter* xliii. 9 [xliv. 7] Þou *tospilte vs hatand. 1382 WYCLIF *Jer.* vi. 26 Be thou gird with an heire, and *to-sprengd with asken. *c* 1315 SHOREHAM ii. 75 Hy *to-stek hys swete hefed Wyþ one þornene coroune. ? *a* 1300 *XI Pains Hell* 177 in *O. E. Misc.* 152 Olde men..neddren..Heom heo *to-styngeþ vychon. 1382 *To-stank [see *to-rot*]. 1382 WYCLIF *Isa.* xxiv. 20 With to-stering shal be *to-stired the erthe. 1375 BARBOUR *Bruce* XVIII. 547 His frendis..He couth ressawe,..And his fais stoutly *to-stonay. ? *a* 1400 *Morte Arth.* 1436 Alle to-stonayede with þe strokes of þa steryne knyghtez. *c* 1205 LAY. 26810 Halmes to-hælden Hæhȝe men *to-swelten. *c* 1386 CHAUCER *Pard. T.* 191 In Erthe, in Eir, in Water man *to swynke. 1382 WYCLIF 2 *Macc.* xii. 14 These that weren with ynne,..diden slowlicher, *to terynge [1388 to-terrynge] Judas with cursyngis. 1377 *Pol. Poems* (Rolls) I. 218 The Frensche men..with heore scornes us *to-threte. *a* 1250 *Prov. Ælfred* 303 in *O. E. Misc.* 120 Ac heo hine schal steorne *To-trayen and to-teone. 1382 WYCLIF *Ecclus.* xxxv. 22 The strengeste shal not han in hem pacience, that he *to-truble the rigge of hem. — *Isa.* xxviii. 17 The hail shal *to-turne vpsodoun the hope of lesyng. *c* 1470 *Golagros & Gaw.* 704 All to-turnit thair entyre, traistly and tewch. 13.. *E. E. Allit. P.* B. 428 *To-walten alle þyse welle-hedez & þe water flowed. 1382 WYCLIF *Jer.* xiv. 15 In swerd and hunger shul be *to-wastid tho profetus.

**3.** Hence **all to-**, **all to**, **all-to**, † **alto**, employed in middle and early modern Eng. as an intensive to any verb: see ALL C. 14, 15.

‖ **Toa** (tōu·ă). Also **tooa**. [Native name in many Polynesian langs.] A species of *Casuarina* (*C. equisetifolia*) found in the South Sea Islands.

Its wood, known from its colour and hardness as South Sea Ironwood, is used by the natives for their clubs.

1817 MARINER *Acc. Tonga Isl.* I. viii. 244 The whistling of the wind among the branches of the lofty *toa*. *Ibid.* 245 Restrictions respecting cutting down the Toa tree. 1823 BYRON *Island* II. i, We will sit in twilight's face, and see The sweet moon glancing through the tooa tree.

**Toad** (tōud), *sb.* Forms: α. 1 **tádiȝe**, **tádie**. β. 1–5 **tadde**, (*pl.* 1 **-an**, 2–4 **-en**, 3–7 **-es**). γ. ? 3, 4–6 *north.* **tade**, 5– *Sc.* **taid**, 9 *north. dial.* **teäde**; **tead**, **ted**, **tyed**. δ. 4–7 **tode**, 5–6 **toode**, 6 **tood**, 6–7 **toade**, 7– **toad**. [OE. *tádiȝe*, of unknown origin and unusual form, has no cognates in the other langs. (Da. and Norw. *tudse* are not connected.) The relation of *tadde* to *tádiȝe*, *tádie* is not clear: Björkman thinks it a hypocoristic form with shortened vowel and doubled cons.; it survived in s.w. ME. *tadde*; cf. also *tadpole* (see 7 b), *tadpole*. The northern *tade*, *taid*, *teäde*, *ted*, and midl. *tōde*, *tood*, *toad*, with long vowel and single cons., prob. represented *tádiȝe*, *tádie*, with its unusual ending reduced to *-e*.]

**1.** A tailless amphibian of the genus *Bufo*; primarily the common European species *Bufo vulgaris*; thence extended to many foreign species of the genus or of the family *Bufonidæ*. *Running toad*, the natterjack.

α. *c* 1000 ÆLFRIC *Voc.* in Wr.-Wülcker 122/11 *Buffo*, tadiȝe. *a* 1100 *Voc.* ibid. 321/23 *Rubeta*, tadie.

β. 11.. *Voc.* in Wr.-Wülcker 544/7 (*Ru*)*beta*, tadde. *c* 1175 *Lamb. Hom.* 51 Þer wunieð in-ne..Blake tadden. *Ibid.* 53 Ah liggeð þer uppon, alse þe tadde deð in þer eorðe. *a* 1225 *Ancr. R.* 214 Schal ine helle iwurðen to hin tadden & neddren. 1387 TREVISA *Higden* (Rolls) VIII. 18 A womman þat hadde a fende wiþ inne her..caste up twey blake taddes. 1398 — *Barth. De P. R.* XVI. lxxi. (Tollem. MS.), This stone is take oute of a tadde heed.

γ. *a* 1300 *Cursor M.* 23227 Fell dragons and tades [*v.r.* tadis] bath. *a* 1340 HAMPOLE *Psalter* xc. 13 Þe snake werpis and þe tade nuryssis þe eg, and þarof is broght forth þe basilyske. *c* 1440 *York Myst.* xi. 271 For tadys and frosshis we may not flitte. *c* 1440 *Alphabet of Tales* 240 He drew oute a grete whik tade. *c* 1480 HENRYSON *Test. Cres.* 578 Heir I beteiche my Corps and Carioun With Wormis and with Taidis to be rent. 1508 KENNEDIE *Flyting w. Dunbar* 287 Tigris, serpentis, and taidis will remane In Dumbar wallis. 1725 RAMSAY *Gentle Sheph.* II. ii, Mixt wi' the venom of black taids and snakes. 1818 SCOTT *Br. Lamm.* xxxv, A taid may sit on her coffin the day. 1823 GALT *Entail* II. xxix. 277 Ye would as soon think of likening a yird tead to a patrick. 1863 ROBSON *Bards Tyne* 353 Now, Geordy, my lad, sit as mute as a tyed.

δ. 12.. *St. Patrick's Purg.* 274 in Horstm. *Alteng. Leg.* (1875) 188 Eddren furi vpen hem sete, and toden grete al so. *c* 1325 *Song Mercy* 56 in *E. E. P.* (1862) 120 Þou seȝe me a monge todes blake Ful longe in harde prisoun lyng. 1370–80 *XI Pains of Hell* 60 in *O. E. Misc.* 224 As Fissches þei were in þat flod þo, Todus, Neddres, Snakes mony mo. 1422 tr. *Secreta Secret., Priv. Priv.* 152 Thay hym yaue pryuely a lytill toode in a drynke. 1530 PALSGR. 281/2 Tode, *crapault*. 1567 MAPLET *Gr. Forest* 16 Nesorpora is a stone of Pontus..found in a Todes heade. 1568 GRAFTON *Chron.* II. 116 Findyng there a most venemous toade. 1600 SHAKS. *A. Y. L.* II. i. 13 Sweet are the vses of aduersitie, Which like the toad, ougly and venemous, Weares yet a precious Iewell in his head. 1667 MILTON *P. L.* IV. 800 Him there they found Squat like a Toad, close at the eare of Eve. 1763 CHURCHILL *Proph. Famine* Poems I. 112 Marking her noisome road With poison's trail, here crawled the bloated Toad. 1849 T. BELL *Brit. Reptiles* (ed. 2) 115 Few animals have ever suffered more undeserved persecution as the victims of an absurd and ignorant prejudice than the toad. *Ibid.* 126 Natter-jack Toad. 1895 Running Toad [see RUNNING *ppl. a.* 7 c]. 1909 *Blackw. Mag.* Apr. 503/2 She was already on friendly terms with my mice and my toads and my snake.

**b.** As a type of anything hateful or loathsome.

*a* 1548 HALL *Chron., Edw. IV* 231 To whom the Frenche nacion was more odious then a tode. 1586 DAY *Eng. Secretary* II. (1625) 125 It behoueth also that..he doe incline to good..that he abhorre flatterie as a Toad. 1606 SHAKS. *Tr. & Cr.* II. iii. 170, I do hate a proud man, as I hate the ingendring of Toades. 1645 MILTON *Colast.* Wks. 1851 IV. 360 To hate one another like a toad or poison.

**c.** In various figurative and proverbial uses. *To eat* (*any one's*) *toads*, to be a mean dependant, to toady (see TOAD-EATER). *Toad under a harrow*, a simile for a person under constant persecution or oppression.

1649 BP. REYNOLDS *Serm. Hosea* i. 46 [As] impossible..as for a Toad to spit Cordials. 1788 LD. BULKELEY in Dk. Buckhm. *Crt. & Cabinets Geo. III* (1853) I. 364 There is no man who eats Pitt's toads with such zeal, attention, and appetite. 1815 *Hist. J. Decastro*, etc. I. 252 [We] were e'en forced to eat our toads and be silent. 1855 THACKERAY *Newcomes* liii, Don't they follow him to college: and eat his toads through life? 1802–12 BENTHAM *Rat. of Evidence* (1827) I. 385 *note*, Kept like toads under a harrow. 1825 BROCKETT *N. C. Words, Toad-under-a-Harrow*, the comparative situation of a poor fellow, whose wife, not satisfied with the mere hen-pecking of her helpmate, takes care that all the world shall witness the indignities she puts upon him. 1903 *Daily Chron.* 16 May 3/4 The 'toad-under-the-harrow' existence of a plain, middle-aged, but cultivated and fine-natured spinster, whose whole life was subordinated to an invalid and rather malignant old mother.

**2.** † Used erroneously for the frog (*obs.*); applied to other allied animals, as *Surinam toad* = PIPA; *horned toad*: see HORNED 2 b; *midwife, obstetrical toad*, the nurse-frog: see OBSTETRICAL.

*a* 1300 *E. E. Psalter* lxxviii. 50 [lxxviii. 45] And sent in am hundeflegh, and it ete þa; Tade [L. *ranam*], and it for-spilt þam swa. 1602 MARSTON *Antonio's Rev.* III. iii, Now croakes the toad. 1757–1894 [see PIPA]. 1812–29, 1817 Surinam toad [see TOADLET, TOADLING]. 1815 KIRBY & SP. *Entomol.* (1843) I. 305 Like the young of the Surinam Toad (*Rana pipa*) they attach themselves in clusters upon her back, belly, head, and even legs. 1901 P. FOUNTAIN *Deserts N. Amer.* viii. 158 The 'Californian toad' which is really a species of lizard.

**3.** Applied opprobriously to human beings and animals.

*a* 1568 *Bannatyne Poems* (Hunter. Cl.) 396/36 Ane fowle taid cairle. 1594 SHAKS. *Rich. III*, IV. iv. 81 To helpe me curse That bottel'd Spider, that foule bunch-back'd Toad. 1605 *1st Pt. Ieronimo* II. v, *Ier.* Is not this a monstrous courtier? *Hor.* He is the court tode, father. 1634 SIR T. HERBERT *Trav.* 159 All true Persians thinke of them as enemies to Mahomet..and that all their Disciples were Toades, the of-scum of the earth & vile Apostates. 1744 in Ozel *Brantome's Span. Rhodomontades* (ed. 2) Advert., A cursed Toad of a Horse..not only threw me but rolled over me. 1771 FOOTE *Maid of B.* III. Wks. 1799 II. 232 What a miserable poor toad is a husband, whose misfortunes not even death can relieve! 1853 R. CARMICHAEL in *Whistle-binkie* Ser. III. 47 Sic a prideful taid Our Tibbie's grown. 1894 ASTLEY *50 Years Life* II. 87 The silly toad had carelessly forgotten to pull the stirrup-irons up.

**4.** = TOADY *sb.* 2.

1831 [see TOAD *v.*]. 1834 BECKFORD *Italy*, etc. II. 159 Mrs. Guildermeester..we found in a vast but dingy saloon, her toads squatting around her. *Ibid.*, Donna Genuefa, the toad-passive in waiting.. Miss Coster, the toad-active, .. makes tea with decorum.

† **5.** *Alchemy.* = BUFO. *Obs.*

1471 RIPLEY *Comp. Alch.* I. xx. in Ashm. *Theat. Chem. Brit.* (1652) 134 Our Tode of the Erth whych etyth hys fyll. 1610 B. JONSON *Alch.* II. iii, Your toade, your crow, your dragon, and your panther.

**6.** (*Cookery.*) *Toad in a hole*: see quots.

1787 GROSE *Prov. Gloss., Pudding-Pye-Doll*, the dish called toad-in-a-hole, meat boiled in a crust. *Norf.* 1797 MME. D'ARBLAY *Lett.* Dec., Mrs. Siddons and Sadler's Wells ..seems..as illfitted as the dish they call a toad in a hole,.. putting a noble sirloin of beef into a poor paltry batter-pudding. 1836 A. FONBLANQUE *Eng. under Seven Admin.* (1837) III. 314 'Toad-in-the-hole', a piece of meat baked in a pudding, with a pool of gravy round it. 1883 F. B. HARRISON *Little Pretty* iv, I give you hashes, and toad-in-the-hole, and curry, and use up all the odds and ends.

**7.** *attrib.* and *Comb.*: attributive, as *toad-hole, -poison, -pond, -spawn, -venom*; objective, similative, etc., as *toad-bellied, -blind, -green, -housing, -legged, -shaped, -spotted, -swollen* adjs., *toad-like* adj. and adv., *toadwise* adv.

1633 FORD *'Tis Pity* IV. iii, You *toad-bellied bitch! 1850 KELLY tr. *Cambrensis Eversus* II. 217 Giraldus, who was *toad blind (*talpâ cæcior*) to everything creditable to the Irish. 1890 *Daily News* 27 Sept. 2/1 A *toad-green cloth redingote. 1825 J. NEAL *Bro. Jonathan* I. 108 Never seed a wood-chuck in a *toad-hole I guess? 1598 E. GILPIN *Skial.* (1878) 41 How *toad-housing scals, and old swart bones, Are grac'd with painted toombs, and plated stones. 1843 *Jrnl. R. Agric. Soc.* IV. I. 190 The fact of wheat being broken down near the root, or '*toad-legged'. *a* 1586 SIDNEY *Arcadia* (1622) 126 A *tode-like retirednesse, and closenesse of minde. 1812 *Religionism* 43 Then lay thy awkward, toad-like twists aside. 1839 BAILEY *Festus* xxxiv. (1852) 550 My purpose..hath grown in me and lived on, Toad-like within a rock—vital where all Beside was death. 1869 *Zoologist* Sept. 1832 The ignorant of all ages have believed in the existence of this *toad-poison, the men of science have almost universally treated its existence as a fable. 1851 BORROW *Lavengro* iv. (1911) 30 The sludge in the *toad-pond. 1854 BADHAM *Halieut.* 507 These last acquired such celebrity in the knowledge of wheedling, as to be called parasite, or *toad-spawn. 1605 SHAKS. *Lear* V. iii. 138 A most *Toad-spotted Traitor. 1603 H. CROSSE *Vertues Commw.* (1878) 82 So *toade-swolne with pride and ambition, that he is ready to burst in sunder. 1852 *Zoologist* X. 3658 The active principle of *toad-venom is alkaline in its character. 1867 LANIER *Strange Jokes* 17 Give lair and rest To him who *toadwise sits and croaks.

**b.** Special comb.: **toad-back** *a.*, of a stair-rail, etc., having a section of three-lobed shape held to resemble the back of a toad; **toad-bit**, a disease of cattle: see quot.; **toad-bug**, any species of the American genus *Galgulus* of small predaceous Hemiptera; **toad-cheese** († **taddechese**), a poisonous fungus; **toad-flower**, an African plant, *Stapelia bufonia*; **toad-frog**, a book-name for the genus *Pelobates* of tailless amphibians: see quot.; **toad-grass** = *toad-rush*; **toad-head**, the American golden plover (*local U.S.*); **toad-lily**, (*a*) *Fritillaria pyrenaica*; (*b*) the American white water-lily (*local U.S.*); (*c*) the Japanese *Tricyrtis hirta*; **toad-lizard**, (*a*) the horned toad (*Cent. Dict.* 1891); (*b*) the labyrinthodon; **toad-marl**, a dark-coloured variety of marl; **toad-orchis**, a tropical West African orchid, *Megaclinium Bufo*, having purple-spotted flowers; **toad-pipe** († **tadpipe**), any one of various species of *Equisetum*; † **toad-pool**, a mass of corrupt poisonous matter; **toad-rock** = TOADSTONE[2]; **toad-rush**, *Juncus bufonius*; † **toad's bread**, a fungus; **toad's cap**, a toadstool; **toad's eye**, a precious stone; ? = CRAPAUD 2; **toad's eye tin**, a variety of cassiterite; † **toad's-guts**, a term of abuse; † **toad's hat**, a toadstool; **toad's meat**, *dial.*, toadstools; **toad's mouth**, the snapdragon, *Antirrhinum majus*; **toad-snatcher**, the reed-bunting; **toad-spit, -spittle** = CUCKOO-SPIT[2] 1. See also TOAD-EATER, etc.

1825 BROCKETT *N. C. Words*, **Toad-bit*, a disease among cattle..imputed to the poison of toads. 1902 L. O. HOWARD *Insect Book* 281 The *Toad Bugs..[These] odd and ugly little insects..have been appropriately termed the 'toad-shaped bugs'. The short, broad body,..the projecting eyes, ..the dull mottled colors, are toad-like. 14.. *Voc.* in Wr.-Wülcker 585/21 *Fungea*..*i. boletus*..a *taddechese. *Ibid.* 618/4 *Tubera*, taddechese. 1703 J. WHITING in C. Marshal *Sion's Trav.* (1704) b viij b, Several of which persecuting Justices soon after dyed with Eating of Tadcheese (alias Mushrooms). 1882 *Science Gossip* 165/1 'Toad's cheeses', rank fungi. 1884 MILLER *Plant-n.* 137/2 African *Toad-flower. 1896 LYDEKKER *New Nat. Hist.* V. 283 The fifth family..comprises eight genera, which may be collectively termed *toad-frogs, since they come neither under the designation of toads or frogs. 1640 PARKINSON *Theat. Bot.* 1190 The Flemmings generally call [it] Padde grasse, that is, *Tode grasse. 1884 MILLER *Plant-n.* 137/2 *Toad-lily, *Fritillaria nigra*. Japanese Toad-lily, *Tricyrtis hirta*. 1899 *Edin. Rev.* Apr. 317 The Labyrinthodon, or monster *toad-lizard. 1764 *Museum Rust.* II. cx. 377 Called *toad marle, from its resemblance in colour to that animal. 1578 LYTE *Dodoens* I. lxviii. 101 The small [horsetail] is called..in English smal Shauegrasse, and of some *Tadpipes. 1607 CHAPMAN *Bussy d'Ambois* III. ii. 452 Thy gall Turns all thy blood to poison, which is cause Of that *toad-pool that..makes thee..rot as thou livest. 1776 WITHERING *Brit. Plants* (1796) II. 348 [Juncus] bufonius..*Toad Rush. Wet Gravelly or sandy meadows and pastures. 1861 MISS PRATT *Flower. Pl.* V. 297 Toad Rush..sometimes called Toad-grass. 1624 T. SCOTT *Lawfulnesse Netherl. Warre* 17 Therefore Philip gaue him *fungos*, or *Toads-bread to eate. *a* 1825 FORBY *Voc. E. Anglia*, **Toad's-cap*, a fungus. 1747 DINGLEY in *Phil. Trans.* XLIV. 505 The *Toad's-Eye, black. 1850 ANSTED *Elem. Geol., Min.*, etc. § 490 Toad's eye tin is the same variety [as wood tin] on a small scale. 1874 J. H. COLLINS *Metal Mining* 13 [In] Cornwall..valuable lumps of 'wood-tin' and 'toad's-eye' tin have been built into hedges. 1634 S. R. *Noble Soldier* IV. ii. in Bullen *O. P.* (1882) I. 317 *Toads-guts..doe you heare, Monsire? *c* 1440 *Promp. Parv.* 495/2 *Todyshatte (or muscheron),..*tuber*. 1886 P. S. ROBINSON *Valley Teet. Trees* 134 The rustic calls [toadstools] '*toad's meat'. 1839 PHILLIPS in *Sat. Mag.* 18 May 190/1 It has..received various names, as Dog's Mouth,..*Toad's Mouth, and Snap-Dragon. 1848 *Zoologist* VI. 2290 The black-headed bunting..a '*toad snatcher'. 1885 SWAINSON *Provinc. Names Birds* 72 Reed Bunting.. Toad snatcher. 1751 WARBURTON *Pope's Wks.* IV. 24 *note*, Those frothy excretions, called by the people *Toad spits, seen in summer-time hanging upon plants. 1658 J. ROWLAND *Moufet's Theat. Ins.* 909 [Nature] hath infected the Sage with *Toad-spittle.

**Toad** (tōud), *v.* [f. prec., after *toad-eat*, etc.] *trans.* To act as a toady to; to toady. Also *intr.*

1802 G. COLMAN *Poor Gent.* II. ii, How these tabbies love to be toaded! 1826 F. REYNOLDS *Life & T.* II. 303 *note*, He could scarcely ever get anybody but dull toading tuft-hunters to remain there above four days. 1831 LADY GRANVILLE *Lett.* 21 Feb., All her toads toad on because they see that I toad her too. 1849 W. IRVING *Goldsmith* xxxix. 335 Boswell's inveterate disposition to *toad*, was a sore cause of mortification to his father.

**Toad**, var. TODE *sb.*[1] *Obs.*, Dutch fishing-boat.

**Toad-eat** (tōᵘ·dˌīːt), *v. rare.* [Back-formation from TOAD-EATER.] *trans.* To flatter, fawn upon (a person); to toady. Also *intr.* So **Toa·d-ea:ting** *vbl. sb.* and *ppl. a.*

1766 LADY S. LENNOX in *Life & Lett.* (1901) I. 199, I have got Charles into such order, that..he toad eats me beyond all conception. 1767 LADY S. BUNBURY in Jesse *Selwyn & Contemp.* (1843) II. 175, I toad-eat a little cur that is here, only because his name is Raton. 1791 EARL MORNINGTON in *14th Rep. Hist. MSS. Comm.* App. v. 7 Some verses which I took down..as being the excess of toad-eating. 1799 — in Stanhope *Pitt* III. 191 The delight of being toad-eated by all India from Cabul to Assam. 1831 JEKYLL *Corr.* (1894) 273 Puffing himself in newspapers, and toad-eating Princes and Ministers. 1836–7 DICKENS *Sk. Boz, Horatio Sparkins*, 'Decidedly', said the toad-eating Flamwell. 1880 MISS BRADDON *Just as I am* xlv, A real sister has no motive for such toad-eating.

**Toad-eater** (tōᵘ·dˌīːtəɹ).

**1.** One who eats toads; *orig.* the attendant of a charlatan, employed to eat or pretend to eat toads (held to be poisonous) to enable his master to exhibit his skill in expelling poison.

1629 J. ROUS *Diary* 45, I inquired of him if William Utting the toade-eater..did not once keepe at Laxfield; he tould me yes, and said he had seene him eate a toade, nay two. *a* 1704 T. BROWN *Sat. on Quack* Wks. 1730 I. 64 Be the most scorn'd Jack-pudding in the pack, And turn toad-eater to some foreign Quack. 1761 LADY S. LENNOX in *Life & Lett.* (1901) I. 53 Beckford, toad eater to the mountebank, as he has been not unaptly call'd.

**2.** *fig.* A fawning flatterer, parasite, sycophant; = TOADY *sb.* 2.

1742 H. WALPOLE *Let.* 7 July, Lord Edgcumbe's [place] ..is destined to Harry Vane, Pulteney's toad-eater. 1807–8 W. IRVING *Salmag.* (1824) 177 Encouraged by the shouts and acclamations of..toad-eaters. 1859 GREEN *Oxf. Stud.* ii. § 1 (O.H.S.) 33 Shabbily-genteel toadeaters, ready at his call. 1876 GEO. ELIOT *Dan. Der.* III. xxv, The toad-eater the least liable to nausea, must be expected to have his susceptibilities.

**b.** A humble friend or dependant; *spec.* a female companion or attendant. *contemptuous.* Now *rare.*

1744 FIELDING *David Simple* II. vii. I. 212 David begged an Explanation of what she meant by a Toad-Eater...Cynthia replied,.. It is a Metaphor taken from a Mountebank's Boy's eating Toads, in order to show his Master's Skill in expelling Poison. It is built on a Supposition..that People who are.. in a State of Dependance, are forced to do the most nauseous things that can be thought on, to please and humour their Patrons. 1746 H. WALPOLE *Let. to Mann* 21 Aug., I am retired hither like an old summer dowager; only that I have no toad-eater to take the air with me. 1750 COVENTRY *Pompey Lit.* I. v. (1785) 16/2 Such female companions, or more properly toad-eaters. 1808 ELEANOR SLEATH *Bristol Heiress* I. 139 Her..Ladyship's confidential woman, or rather *toad-eater*, which is..the most fashionable phrase of the two. 1853 DE QUINCEY *Autobiog. Sk.* Wks. I. 351.

**Toader** (tōᵘ·dəɹ). *rare.* [f. TOAD *v.* + -ER[1].] A sycophant, parasite; = TOADY *sb.* 2.

1842 R. OASTLER *Fleet Papers* II. 415 The only remedy for any man not a toader, who may fall into difficulties.

**Toa·dery.** [f. TOAD *sb.* + -ERY.] A place where toads are kept or abound.

1763 ELIZ. CARTER in Pennington *Memoirs* (1808) I. 335 The dykes..with a perpendicular descent on each side to the toaderies and frogeries below. 1854 *Tait's Mag.* XXI. 695 He had what he called a Froggery and Toadery at the bottom of his orchard.

**Toa·dess.** *nonce-wd.* A female toad.

1871 SMILES *Charac.* iii. (1876) 80 The toad's highest idea of beauty is his toadess.

**Toad-fish** (tōᵘ·dˌfiʃ). A name applied, from their appearance, to several distinct fishes; *esp.*

**a.** A swell-fish, or puffer, spec. *Tetrodon turgidus*, the common puffer of the Atlantic coast of the United States; also other species of *Tetrodon* of the coasts of Brazil and South Africa. **b.** The sea-devil, fishing-frog, angler, or wide-gab, *Lophius piscatorius*. **c.** *American t.-f.*, the oyster-fish (*Sapo* of the Portuguese), *Batrachus tau*, of the Atlantic coast of U.S.A. **d.** *Brazilian t.-f.*, *Chilomycterus geometricus*. **e.** *Poisonous t.-f.*, *Thalassophryne*, also species of *Tetrodon*. **f.** The mouse-fish, *Antennarius histrio*, or other species of *Antennarius*.

1612 CAPT. SMITH *Map Virginia* 15 The Todefish which will swell till it be like to brust, when it commeth into the aire. *a* 1642 SIR W. MONSON *Naval Tracts* VI. (1704) 534/1 There are many venomous Fishes upon that Coast [Brazil], as namely the Toad-fish, of a small bigness. 1668 CHARLETON *Onomast.* 130 *Rana piscatrix*..the Monk, Toad, Nass, or Devil-Fish, or Fishing-Frog. 1704 PETIVER *Gazophyl.* II. xx, *Piscis Brasilianus cornutus*. The American Toad-Fish. *Ibid.*, The Brasil Toad-Fish..found on the shores of

Brasil, and several other Coasts of the West-Indies. **1736** *Gentl. Mag.* VI. 618/1 At Powderham, Devonshire, a Toad-Fish was thrown ashore; it is 4 Foot long, has a Head like a Toad,..and the Mouth opens 12 Inches wide. **1816** Tuckey *Narr. Exped. R. Zaire* ii. (1818) 61 The only fish taken since we have been in muddy ground were two toad fish (*Diodon*) and several eels. **1845** Gosse *Ocean* vii. (1849) 342 The Toad-fishes, or Anglers (*Antennarius*), whose pectoral and ventral fins have much of the form and also the functions of the feet of a quadruped. **1860** Richardson in *Jrnl. Linn. Soc.* (1861) V. 213 The Toad-fish of the Cape is a *Diodon*. **1860** Jameson *ibid.*, A poisonous fish, known at the Cape by the name of the Toad- or Bladder-fish.

**Toad-flax** (tōu·dˌflæks). [f. Toad *sb.* + Flax, from the flax-like appearance of the foliage.] A popular name of the European plant *Linaria vulgaris*; hence extended as a generic name to other species of *Linaria*, as Ivy-leaved Toad-flax, *L. Cymbalaria*, Purple T., *L. purpurea*. *Bastard Toad-flax*, a name for *Thesium linophyllum*, and the American genus *Comandra*.

**1578** Lyte *Dodoens* i. liv. 79 Stanworte, wilde flaxe, or Tode flax, hath small, slender, blackish stalkes. **1630** Drayton *Muses' Elysium* iii. Wks. (1748) 448/1 By toad-flax which your nose may taste, If you have a mind to cast. **1776** Lee *Bot.* 353/1 Toad Flax, *Antirrhinum*. **1866** *Treas. Bot.*, Toadflax. Bastard, *Thesium linophyllum*; also an American name for *Comandra*. **1868** J. T. Burgess *Eng. Wild Flowers* 211 The 'butter-and-eggs' of the country folk—the Yellow Toadflax. **1879** Geo. Eliot *Theo. Such* ii. 50 A crumbling bit of wall where the delicate ivy-leaved toad-flax hangs its light branches. **1893** Couch *Delect. Duchy* 21 A round stone wall, over which the toad-flax spread in a tangle.

**Toa·dish,** *a. rare.* [f. Toad *sb.* + -ish[1].] Of the nature of a toad; like a toad; † venomous.

**1611** A. Stafford *Niobe* ii. 76 Your toadish tongue would neuer haue sought to haue enuenom'd Vertue. **1665** Sir T. Herbert *Trav.* (1677) 384 A speckl'd toadish or poyson fish as the Seamen from experience named it. **1822** Beddoes *Bride's Trag.* ii. iv, Something hath called me thrice, With a low muttering voice of toadish hisses.

**Toa·dlet.** [f. Toad *sb.* + -let.] = next.

**1817** Coleridge *Satyrane's Lett.* ii. in *Biog. Lit.*, etc. (1882) 252 Pretty little additionals sprouting out from it like young toadlets on the back of a Surinam toad. **1834** — *Table-t.* 14 June, So many toadlets, one after another detaching themselves from their parent brute.

**Toadling** (tōu·dliŋ). [f. as prec. + -ling[1].] A young or little toad.

*c* **1440** *Promp. Parv.* 495/1 Todelynge, *bufonulus*. **1779** Johnson in Mme. D'Arblay *Diary* Feb., I always knew you for a toadling. **1812–29** Coleridge in *Lit. Rem.* (1838) III. 121 A Surinam toad with a swarm of toadlings sprouting out of its back and sides. **1883** *Longm. Mag.* Oct. 643 A young toadling once hibernated within the empty rose of a large watering-pot.

**Toad-pole, -poll,** obs. forms of Tadpole.

**Toa·dship.** *nonce-wd.* The personality of a toad.

**1775** J. Berridge *Wks.* (1864) 387 To hear one toad compliment another, and speak very handsome things of his toadship. **1885** C. F. Holder *Marvels Anim. Life* 89 Several lessons of this kind evidently made his toadship put on his thinking cap.

**Toadstone**[1] (tōu·dstoun). [f. Toad *sb.* + Stone.] A name (rendering Gr. and L. *batrachītes*, or med.L. *bufonītes, crapodīnus*, F. *crapaudine* (13th c.): cf. Ger. *krötenstein*), formerly applied to various stones or stone-like objects, likened to a toad in colour or shape, or supposed to be produced by a toad; often credited with alexipharmic or therapeutic virtues, and worn as jewels or amulets, or set in rings. These, though of various origin, were all considered to be forms or species of the same 'stone', the most valued kind of which was fabled to be found in the head of the toad, a belief to which many allusions occur in literature: cf. Toad *sb.* 1 δ, quot. 1600.

**1558** *Gifts to Q. Eliz.* in Nichols *Progr.* II. 539 A iewell containing a Crapon or Toade stone set in golde. **1605** B. Jonson *Volpone* ii. v, His saffron iewell, with the toade-stone in 't. **1645** Evelyn *Diary* 6 May, A ring..which seemed set with a dull, darke stone, a little swelling out, like what we call (tho' untruly) a toadstone. **1668** Wilkins *Real Char.* 63 As for that..styled a Toadstone; this is properly a tooth of the Fish called *Lupus marinus*, as hath been made evident to the Royal Society by..Dr. Merit. **1677** Plot *Oxfordsh.* 128 By my Bufonites or Toad-stone, I intend not that shining polish'd stone,..but a certain reddish liver-colour'd real stone. **1679** *Lond. Gaz.* No. 1435/4 One gold Ring with a large counterfeited Toad stone. **1696** *Phil. Trans.* XIX. 199 These convex osseous Tubercules..are of the same kind with our English *Bufonites* or Toadstones. **1704** *Collect. Voy.* (Churchill) III. 658/1 The Toad-stone is found in the Head of a certain kind of Toads. **1776** Pennant *Brit. Zool.* III. 15 It was distinguished by the name of the Reptile, and called the Toad-Stone, Bufonites, Crapaudine, Krottenstein; but all its fancied powers vanished on the discovery of its being nothing but the fossil tooth of the sea-wolf. **1812** Scott *Let. to Joanna Baillie* 4 Apr. in *Lockhart*, A toadstone—a celebrated amulet..It was sovereign for protecting new-born children and their mothers from the power of the fairies, and has been repeatedly borrowed from my mother, on account of this virtue. **1870** *Murray's Handbk. E. Counties* 291 At the feet [of an image of the Virgin] was a toadstone, indicating her victory over all evil and uncleanness.

*attrib.* **1855** tr. *Labarte's Arts Mid. Ages* xxvi, Toadstone ring. **1877** W. Jones *Finger-ring* 156 A toadstone ring (the fossil palatal tooth of a species of Ray) was supposed to protect new-born children and their mothers from the power of the fairies.

**Toadstone**[2] (tōu·dstoun). *local.* [Of uncertain origin; thought by some to be so named from the resemblance of its amygdaloidal spots to those on a toad's skin; by others to be a corruption of a Ger. *todtes gestein* 'dead rock', reduced perh. to **todt-stein*. But there appears to be no evidence of this, other than the fact that some Derbyshire mining terms appear to be of German origin.] A name given by the Derbyshire lead-miners to an igneous rock, occurring as irregular sheets of contemporaneous lava, interstratified with, or in connexion with the metalliferous mountain limestone.

**1784** Darwin in *Phil. Trans.* LXXV. 5 The vast beds of toad-stone or lava in many parts of this country. **1796** Kirwan *Elem. Min.* (ed. 2) I. 229 *Toadstone* is of a dark brownish grey colour, abounding with cavities filled with crystallized spar. **1823** G. Chalmers *Caledonia* III. ii. iii. 52 The rock is covered occasionally by toadstone, called in that country coppercraig. **1859** Page *Handbk. Geol. Terms* 355 Some of these toadstone beds are compact and basaltic, others are earthy, vesicular, and amygdaloidal. **1888** *Derbysh. Archæol. Soc. Jrnl.* X. 2 The white patches of calcite give to a freshly fractured surface of the rock a peculiar appearance,..considered so like the marks on the body of a toad that the rock is known as Toadstone.

**Toadstool** (tōu·dstūl). Forms: see Toad and Stool. [f. Toad *sb.* + Stool, a fanciful name; cf. Sc. *paddo' stool*.]

A fungus having a round disk-like top and a slender stalk, a mushroom.

α. **1398** Trevisa *Barth. De P. R.* xvi. xxxi. (Tollem. MS.), It setteþ drye tadstoles a fyre. **1483** *Cath. Angl.* 377/1 A Tade stole, *boletus, fungus*. **1578** Lyte *Dodoens* 261 Them that are sicke with eating of venimous Tadstooles or Mousheroms. **1594** T. B. *La Primaud. Fr. Acad.* ii. 97 Soft & like to the substance of a tad-stoole. **1601** Bp. W. Barlow *Serm. Paules Crosse* 50 Like the growth of a Tadstoole..a night's conceit, but vanished in the morning.

β. **1495** *Trevisa's Barth. De P. R.* xvii. cxxiv. (W. de W.), Yf perys ben sodde wyth tode stoles they take awaye fro them all greyf and malyce. **1519** Horman *Vulg.* 101 b, Todestolys, that be gethered from the tree be good to eate. **1530** Palsgr. 281/2 Tode stole, *eschampignon*. **1562** Turner *Herbal* ii. Pref., Dark doctores..which soddenly lyke todestolles stert vp Phisiciones. *Ibid.* 29 b, A todstcle ..in a birche or a walnut tre, where of som make tunder. **1567** Maplet *Gr. Forest* 52 The Mushrom or Toadstoole.. hath two sundrie kinds,..for the one may be eaten: the other is not to be eaten. **1579** Spenser *Sheph. Cal.* Dec. 69 The grieslie Todestoole growne there mought I se And loathed Paddocks lording on the same. **1601** Holland *Pliny* (1634) II. 133 The nearer that a Mushrome or Toadstoole commeth to the color of a fig hanging vpon the tree, the lesse presumption there is that it is venomous. **1707** Hearne *Collect.* 29 Nov. (O.H.S.) II. 76 The Dorians..us'd to write upon Toad-stools. **1872** Black *Adv. Phaeton* xxii, Moist odour of toadstools and fern. **1904** G. K. Chesterton *Browning* vi. 145 We are akin not only to the stars and flowers, but to the toadstools and the monstrous tropical birds.

b. Popularly restricted to poisonous or inedible fungi, as distinct from edible 'mushrooms'.

**1607** Topsell *Four-f. Beasts* (1658) 204 The rennet is also commendable against Hemlock or Toad-stool. **1805** *Med. Jrnl.* XIV. 573 Toad stools and other species of the fungus kind are frequently eaten for mushrooms. **1859** *All Year Round* No. 19. 437 The delicious mushroom, the poisonous toad-stool.

c. *fig.* (in reference to its rapid growth and short duration: cf. *mushroom*).

**1823** in Cobbett *Rur. Rides* (1885) I. 286 This little toad-stool is a thing created entirely by the gamble: and the means have, hitherto, come out of the wages of labour. **1901** *Daily News* 2 Mar. 3/4 Some of the houses that were too solidly built to burn were blown up. Away off on a flank you would see a huge toadstool of dust, rocks, and rafters rise solemnly into the air and then subside in a heap of débris.

d. *attrib.* and *Comb.*, as *toadstool-eater, -eating, -growth*; *toadstool-like* adj.

**1886** P. S. Robinson *Valley Teet. Trees* 137 Some of these penny-reading toadstool-eaters would even turn a toad off its stool to eat its seat. **1887** W. D. Hay *Elem. Text-Bk. Brit. Fungi* Pref. 6 So far as 'toadstool eating' goes, I believe I have a right to speak with authority, since my own gastronomic experiments have been many, frequent, and varied. **1892** *Antidote* 20 Sept. 303 Wretched sects of toadstool growth, which spring up, fester and die out around us. **1903** *Westm. Gaz.* 30 Jan. 2/1 A writing-table (in the North Room) with numerous toadstool-like projections ..whose ugliness and inconvenience are only too obvious.

**Toady** (tōu·di), *sb.* Also 7 tody, 9 toadey. [f. Toad *sb.*, with dim. or familiar suffix -y, as in *slavey*, etc.; in sense 2 perh. sb. use of Toady *a.*]

†1. A little or young toad. *Obs.*

*c* **1690** *Satire* in Kirkton *Hist. Ch. Scotl.* vi. (1817) 199 *note*, Beastly bodies, senseless nodies, venemous todies.

2. A servile parasite; a sycophant, an interested flatterer; also, a humble dependant; = Toad-eater 2, 2 b.

**1826** Disraeli *Viv. Grey* ii. xv, You know what a Toadey is? That agreeable animal which you meet every day in civilised society. **1834** Lytton *Pompeii* I. Notes 172 The umbra or shadow—who accompanied any invited guest—and who was..usually a poor relative, or a humble friend—in modern cant 'a toady'. **1848** Thackeray *Van. Fair* xi, When I come into the country..I leave my toady, Miss Briggs, at home. My brothers are my toadies here. **1883** W. J. Stillman in *Cent. Mag.* Oct. 827/1 A toady to the superior and a bully to the inferior grades.

**Toady** (tōu·di), *a. rare.* [f. Toad *sb.* + -y.]

1. Resembling a toad; toad-like, repulsive.

**1628** Feltham *Resolves* ii. [i.] xii. 30 Vice is of such a toady complexion, that shee cannot chuse but teach the soule to hate. **1719** Gordon *Cordial Low Spirits* I. 159 Gaffer Pitchfork is murder'd too, with thick same toady Clap of Thunder.

2. Infested with toads.

**1882** Edna Lyall *Donovan* xxiv, The very froggiest and toadiest path in the garden. **1901** Meredith *Reading of Life* 76 A toady cave beside an ague fen.

**Toady** (tōu·di), *v.* [f. Toady *sb.*]

1. *trans.* To play the toady to; to flatter, or attend to with servility from interested motives.

**1827** Lady Granville *Lett.* (1894) I. 406 If her friends would..leave off toadying her. **1857** Hughes *Tom Brown* i. ii, Lots of us of all sorts toady you enough certainly. **1878** J. C. Collins *Tourneur's Plays* I. Introd. 28 That they might, in thus toadying the memory of a dead son, toady the patronage of a living parricide.

2. *intr.* To play the servile dependant; to pay deference from interested motives. Const. *to*.

**1861** Hughes *Tom Brown at Oxf.* vii, Let them toady and cringe to their precious idols. **1873** M. Collins *Miranda* III. 8 She..toadied to her superiors when she really came face to face with them. **1881** C. E. Turner in *Macm. Mag.* Aug. 309/2 We never..toadied for a good place at Moscow, or sneaked into a ministry at Petersburg. **1906** *Times* 29 Aug. 4/2 He was toadying round Williamson like a lackey out of work.

Hence Toa·dying *vbl. sb.* and *ppl. a.*

**1863** W. Phillips *Speeches* vi. 135 The toadying servility of the land. **1866** *Cornh. Mag.* Aug. 239 Needy toadying courtiers come to batten on the fatter south. **1897** H. Black *Friendship* iv. 82 They encouraged toadying.

**Toadyism** (tōu·diˌiz'm). [f. Toady *sb.* + -ism.] The action or behaviour of a parasite or sycophant; mean and interested servility.

**1840** Marryat *Olla Podr.* (Rtldg.) 303 A person of her consequence could never exist without..toadyism. **1857** Hughes *Tom Brown* i. viii, By dint of his command of money,..and his adroit toadyism, he managed to make himself..rather popular. **1898** Bealby & Hearn *Sven Hedin's Through Asia* I. 247 He would lash..everything that savoured of toadyism and servility.

**Toa·dyship.** *rare.* [f. as prec. + -ship.] The action or practice of a toady.

**1839** *Times* 9 Sept., Their vanity flattered by the toadyship of some 1500 ignoramuses.

**Toagh,** obs. f. Tow *sb.* **To-airn:** see Tew-iron. **Toakin,** obs. f. Token. **Toal, toale, toall,** obs. ff. Toll. **Toal-pin,** obs. f. Thole-pin. **Toam,** dial. var. Taum.

**To and fro,** *phr.* (*adv., prep., sb., adj., vb.*). [To *adv.* and *prep.*, Fro *adv.* and *prep.*]

A. *adv.* 1. Successively to and from some place, etc.; hence more vaguely: In opposite or different directions alternately; with alternating movement; from side to side; backwards and forwards; hither and thither; up and down.

**1340** Hampole *Pr. Consc.* 471 For a best when it es born, may ga Als tite aftir, and ryn to and fra. *c* **1412** Hoccleve *De Reg. Princ.* 543 Men passen by hym to and fro. *c* **1450** Lovelich *Grail* xlv. 464 Thus the schippe In the se gan to go On day & Oþer, bothe two & Fro as the wynd it Gan to blowe. **1560** Bible (Genev.) *Job* i. 7 The Lord said vnto Satan, Whence commest thou? And Satan answered.., From compassing the earth to and fro. **1660** F. Brooke tr. *Le Blanc's Trav.* 31 Having travelled to and fro, through very many towns and countries of Persia. **1798** Coleridge *Anc. Mar.* vii. xii, His eyes went to and fro. **1807** Crabbe *Parish Reg.* iii. 617 Idle children, wandering to and fro. **1833** Ht. Martineau *Berkeley the Banker* i. vii, The messenger, who went to and fro between D—— and Haleham bank. **1855** Stanley *Mem. Canterb.* ii. (1857) 44 The pendulum which has been..swung to and fro, is at last about to settle.

b. after a verbal or other sb. denoting or implying movement. (Cf. D.)

*c* **1400** *Rom. Rose* 4134 With many a turnyng to and froo. **1582** N. Lichefield tr. *Castanheda's Conq. E. Ind.* xlvi. 102 They spent three daies with messages to and fro. **1688** S. Penton *Guard. Instr.* 59 Letters to and fro are some kind of Guard upon a Youth. **1840** Macaulay *Ess., Ranke* (1851) II. 131 A history of movement to and fro. **1888** Burgon *Lives 12 Gd. Men* II. xi. 312 His rides to and fro.

†2. In places lying in opposite or different directions; here and there. *Obs.*

*c* **1440** *York Myst.* xx. 255 We haue þe sought both to & froo. **1513** Douglas *Æneis* vii. ix. 96 Bayth to and fro our all the cuntre syne Wemen and moderis..Thair ȝing childryng fast to thair breistis did braice. **1617** Moryson *Itin.* ii. 272 The Northerne Borders, where his Lordship (with his retinue) lay to and fro. **1670–1** Narborough *Jrnl.* in *Acc. Sev. Late Voy.* i. (1711) 119 Many Whales spouting to and fro in these Bays. **1697** Dampier *Voy.* I. xv. 425 Many shoals scattered to and fro among them.

†3. *fig.* To or on opposite sides alternately (esp. in discussion or the like); for and against a question; pro and con. *Obs.*

[*c* **1374** Chaucer *Troylus* v. 1313 Troilus..rolleth in his herte to and fro How he may best discryven hir his wo.] **1568** Grafton *Chron.* II. 71 In multipliyng of wordes to and fro. **1583** Stubbes *Anat. Abus.* ii. (1882) 110, I haue heard great disputation and reasoning pro and contra, to and fro. **1610** Holland *Camden's Brit.* (1637) 803 The victory waved alternately too and fro three or foure times. **1649** Milton *Eikon.* 239 Thus shall they be too and fro, doubtfull and ambiguous in all thir doings. **1690** W. Walker *Idiomat. Anglo-Lat.* 30 When there had been some little Arguing to and fro.

†4. So (in *lit.* and *fig.* senses, as above) **to or fro, to nor (ne) fro.** In quot. 1555[2], *neither*

*to nor fro* = 'neither here nor there', indifferent, immaterial. *Obs.*

13.. *Cursor M.* 16762+123 (Cott.) His sely lyms miȝt he not rest. To put hom to ne fro. **13..** *E. E. Allit. P.* A. 347 When þou no fyrre may, to ne fro, Þou most abyde þat he schal deme. *c* **1530** H. RHODES *Bk. Nurture* 329 Cast not thyne eyes to ne yet fro. **1555** PHILPOT in Foxe *A. & M.* (1583) 1814/2 You stande dalying..and will neither answere to nor fro. **1555** LATIMER *Let. to Morice* ibid. 1741/2 As it is called a fire, so is it called a Worme;..but that is neither to nor fro. **1579** FULKE *Heskins' Parl.* 297 Oecumenius saith little to the purpose, too or fro. **1652** ASHMOLE *Theat. Chem. Brit.* 204 Till thou hearest no manner of noyse rumbling to nor fro.

**B.** *prep.* To and from (a place); alternately to and from each of (two places): the latter now commonly expressed by *between* (BETWEEN *prep.* 9). Now *rare.*

**1574** *Calr. Laing Charters* (1899) 225 Ane gait to cum and gang to and fra the same. **1598** HAKLUYT *Voy.* I. 109 Messengers going and comming to and fro the Court of Baatu. **1860** READE *8th Commandm.* 123 Counsel, who were continually flashing to and fro London and Croydon. **1885** JEFFERIES *Open Air* (1890) 126 The stream of lawyers ..rushing to and fro the Temple and the New Law Courts.

**C.** *sb.* (now with hyphens; but pl. *tos and fros*).

**1.** Alternating or reciprocating movement; the action of walking or passing to and fro.

**1847** TENNYSON *Princ.* II. 282 She, Like some wild creature newly-caged, commenced A to-and-fro. **1855** BROWNING *Lovers' Quarrel* xi, How was earth to know, 'Neath the mute hand's to-and-fro? **1906** *Westm. Gaz.* 14 Sept. 2/3 Watching the to-and-fro of a shuttle.

**2.** *fig.* Alternation generally; vacillation; † discussion for and against a question (*obs.*).

**1553** BALE *Vocacyon* 40 In whose returne there was muche to and fro. For some wolde nedes to London..[and some] into Flaunders. *c* **1627** R. CARY *Mem.* (1905) 96 Many tos and fros there were before it was concluded. **1641** EARL MONM. tr. *Biondi's Civil Warres* II. 90 The incommodities and difficulties.., after many too's and fro's, caused a second peace. **1888** GLADSTONE in *19th Cent.* July 3 From the great national to-and-fro of the sixteenth century.

**D.** *adj.* (usually with hyphens). Executed, as movement, in opposite directions alternately; alternating, reciprocating; characterized by, or characterizing, such movement; passing to and fro.

**1839** DE LA BECHE *Rep. Geol. Cornw.*, etc. xv. 580 This to-and-fro motion. **1856** DOBELL *Lyrics in War Time, Even. Dream*, The to and fro storm of the never done hurrahing. **1878** HUXLEY *Physiogr.* 146 The regular to-and-fro motion of the water in its estuary. **1898** *Allbutt's Syst. Med.* V. 755 As a rule pericardial friction-sound has a double, or to-and-fro rhythm.

**E.** as *vb. phr.* (only in pres. pple. and vbl. sb. *toing and froing*, rarely *to-and-froing*). **a.** *intr.* To pass to and fro, to go hither and thither.

**1847** LE FANU *T. O'Brien* 108 The clatter and bustle, the ..toing and froing of the soldiery. **1872** — *In a Glass Darkly* I. 272 There were clerks to-ing and fro-ing. **1888** MORRIS *King's Lesson* (1890) 137 Unto him the King gave the job of toing and froing up and down the hill with the biggest dung-basket. **1904** *Westm. Gaz.* 28 Nov. 2/2 Why all this secrecy about these to-ings and fro-ings?

**b.** *trans.* To lead to and fro. *rare*—[1].

**1852** R. S. SURTEES *Sponge's Sp. Tour* xxxii, A cockaded servant was 'to and froing' a couple of hunters—a brown and a chestnut.

**Toarcian** (to,ā·ɹsiăn), *a.* (*sb.*) *Geol.* [ad. F. *Toarcien*, f. L. *Toarcium*, F. *Thouars*, in western France.] Applied to a series of strata corresponding in position to the Upper Lias of England, which are extensively developed in Central and Southern France.

[**1859** PAGE *Handbk. Geol. Terms* 49 Upper Lias, Toarcien of d'Orbigny.] **1885** GEIKIE *Geol.* 802 In Normandy, the Toarcian stage is only about 20 feet thick. **1912** *Return Brit. Museum* 172 Crinoids from the Oxfordian of Var.. from the Toarcian of the Balearic Islands. *Ibid.* 182 Seven Crinoid stem-fragments from the Toarcian rocks of Cabrera, Balearic Is.

**Toase, Toaser,** obs. ff. TOZE, TOZER.

**Toast** (tōust), *sb.*[1] Forms: see TOAST *v.*[1] [f. TOAST *v.*[1] Cf. OF. *tostée* (13th c.) toast = Sp. *tostada* (:—pop.L. **tostāta*).]

**1.** (With *a* and *pl.*) A slice or piece of bread browned at the fire: often put in wine, water, or other beverage. Now *rare* or *Obs.* except as in b.

*c* **1430** *Two Cookery-bks.* (E.E.T.S.) 12 *Oyle Soppys*..caste þer-to Safroune, powder Pepyr, Sugre, and Salt, an serue forth alle hote as tostes. *c* **1450** *Cov. Myst.* xix. (1841) 183 Ther is no lord lyke on lyve to me wurthe a toost. **1541** R. COPLAND *Guydon's Quest. Chirurg.* N j, Gyue hym a toste with wyne. **1573** L. LLOYD *Marrow of Hist.* (1653) 94 Alphonsus..took a toast out of his cup, and cast it to the dog. **1598** SHAKS. *Merry W.* III. v. 3 Go, fetch me a quart of Sacke, put a tost in 't. **1617** MORYSON *Itin.* III. 53 All within the sound of Bow-Bell, are in reproch called Cocknies, and eaters of buttered tostes. *c* **1645** HOWELL *Lett.* (1688) IV. 489 This Drink..must be attended with a brown Tost. **1709** STEELE *Tatler* No. 24 ⁋ 8 A Toast in a cold Morning, heightened by Nutmeg, and sweetn'd with Sugar, has for many Ages been given to our Rural Dispensers of Justice, before they enter'd upon Causes. **1735** *Dict. Polygraph.* s. v. *China*, A very dry toast. **1769** MRS. RAFFALD *Eng. Housekpr.* (1778) 291 Amulet... You may serve them up hot on buttered toasts.

**b.** As the type of what is hot or dry.

[*c* **1430**: see above.] **1546** J. HEYWOOD *Prov.* (1867) 44 Loue had apeered in him to hir alway Hotte as a toste. **1694** MOTTEUX *Rabelais* v. *Pantagr. Prognost.* x, Keep your selves as hot as Toasts, d'ye hear? **1842** J. WILSON *Chr. North* I. 83 The small brown Moorland bird, as dry as a toast. **1883** STEVENSON *Silverado Sq.* 21 It keeps this end of the valley as warm as a toast.

**2.** As a substance (without *a* or *pl.*): Bread so browned by fire. (The ordinary current use.)

**1730** SWIFT *Panegyrick on Dean* Wks. 1755 IV. I. 144 Sweeten your tea, and watch your toast. **1786** MACKENZIE *Lounger* No. 89 ⁋ 10 Putting him in mind where the toast stood. **1806** *Med. Jrnl.* XV. 454 The diet..consisted of tea and toast. **1807–26** S. COOPER *First Lines Surg.* (ed. 5) 15 The patient..confining himself to vegetable diet, gruels, slops, tea, acidulated drinks, dry toast, &c. **1886** RUSKIN *Præterita* I. iii. 84 Quarrelling with her which should have the brownest bits of toast.

**b.** Coupled with the liquid in which the toast is immersed, as *ale and toast, toast and ale, toast and water*; whence *toast-and-watered* adj., confined to a diet of toast and water.

[**1586** DAY *Eng. Secretary* II. (1625) 47 How I drunk vp my grandams ale and toste.] **1719** D'URFEY *Pills* (1872) II. 324 Many a Night o'er Toast and Ale. **1778** MME. D'ARBLAY *Diary* (1842) I. 97 Our biscuits and toast-and-water, which make the Streatham supper. **1800** *Med. Jrnl.* IV. 313, I then directed her to live on toast and water exclusively. **1810** BYRON *Let. to Hodgson* 3 Oct., What can a helpless, feverish, toast-and-watered..wretch do? **1888** MRS. H. WARD *R. Elsmere* xliv, Lunch was on the table—the familiar commons, the familiar toast-and-water.

**c.** *On toast*, served up on a slice of toast; *fig. had on toast* (*slang*), done, swindled.

**1842** BARHAM *Ingol. Leg.* Ser. II. *St. Medard*, Delicate Woodcocks served up upon toast. **1886** *St. James's Gaz.* 6 Nov. (Farmer), The High Court..took judicial cognizance of a quaint and pleasing modern phrase..'to be had on toast'. **1889** D. C. MURRAY *Danger. Catspaw* 273 We've got him now on toast. **1895** J. G. MILLAIS *Breath fr. Veldt* (1899) 259 Thinking he had fairly got us on toast, he meant to blackmail us pretty freely.

† **3.** *fig.* (usually *old toast*). One who drinks to excess, a soaker, a boon companion; a brisk old fellow fond of his glass. *slang. Obs.*

**1668** R. L'ESTRANGE *Vis. Quev.* 306 How often must I be put to the Blush too, when every Old Toast shall be calling me Old Acquaintance. *c* **1670** COTTON *Voy. Irel.* III. 128 There comes in my Host, A Catholick, good, and a rare drunken Tost. *a* **1688** VILLIERS (Dk. Buckhm.) *Confer.* (1775) 184. **1694** MOTTEUX *Rabelais* v. xviii, Most of 'em of good Families; among the rest Harry Cottiral, an old Tost. *a* **1700** B. E. *Dict. Cant. Crew, Old-Toast*, a brisk old Fellow. **1709** *Rambling Fuddle-Cups* 14 Bring my father a Quart; I'll be hang'd if 'twill do the old Toast any hurt.

**4.** *attrib.* and *Comb.*, as *toast-burner, -crumb, -fork*; **toast-colour**, a light brown; so *toast-coloured* adj.; † **toast-iron**, a toasting-iron; **toast-stand**, a stand for toast, etc. by the fire: see CAT *sb.*[1] 9, quot. 1806; **toast-water**, water in which toasted bread has been steeped, used as a drink for invalids, etc. Also TOAST-RACK.

**1483** *Cath. Angl.* 390/2 A Toste yren (*A.* Tostyrne), *assatorium.* **1801** NEMNICH *Waaren-Lexicon* 687/1 Toast forks, *Röstgabeln, Tohstgabeln.* **1895** *Q. Rev.* Oct. 283 Cobbed by his fagmaster as an incorrigible toast-burner. **1898** *Daily News* 5 May 2/2 A toast-coloured straw toque trimmed with pink ribbon and roses. **1900** *Ibid.* 20 Jan. 6/5 Toast colour is again included among the fashionable tints. **1905** *Daily Chron.* 18 Dec. 4/6 Why should not toast-water become the temperance beverage for [drinking the health of the King]?

**Toast,** *sb.*[2] [A figurative application of TOAST *sb.*[1], the name of a lady being supposed to flavour a bumper like a spiced toast in the drink.

See the *Tatler*, No. 24, of 2 June, and No. 31, of 18 June, 1709, in both of which *toast* is explained as a new name, upon the origin of which 'the Learned differ very much'. No. 24 says that 'many of the Wits of the last Age will assert' that the term originated in an incident alleged to have occurred at Bath in the reign of Charles II, 1660–1684. No. 31 is silent as to the incident, and gives the account cited below.]

**1.** A lady who is named as the person to whom a company is requested to drink; often one who is the reigning belle of the season. Now only *Hist.*

**1700** CONGREVE *Way World* III. x, More censorious than a decayed Beauty, or a discarded Toast. **1705** CIBBER *Careless Husb.* v. 63 Ay, Madam,..'t has been your Life's whole Pride of late to be the Common Toast of every Publick Table. **1709** STEELE *Tatler* No. 24 ⁋ 9 This Whim gave Foundation to the present Honour..done to the Lady we mention in our Liquors, who has ever since been called a *Toast. Ibid.* No. 31 ⁋ 8 Then, said he, Why do you call live People Toasts? I answered, That was a new Name found out by the Wits to make a Lady have the same Effect as Burridge in the Glass when a Man is drinking. *Ibid.* No. 71 ⁋ 8 A Beauty, whose Health is drank from Heddington to Hinksey, ..has no more the Title of Lady, but reigns an undisputed Toast. **1711** SWIFT *Lett.* (1767) III. 185 Lord Rochester, and his fine daughter, lady Jane, just growing a top toast. **1713** STEELE *Guard.* No. 85 ⁋ 7 Was that the silly thing so much talked of? How did she ever grow into a toast? **1766** [C. ANSTEY] *Bath Guide* xi 34 'Tis she that has long been the Toast of the Town. **1779** MME. D'ARBLAY *Diary* Oct., The present beauty,..a Mrs. Musters,..the reigning toast of the season. **1822** W. IRVING *Braceb. Hall* iv. 35 She will often speak of the toasts of those days as if still reigning. **1888** BURGON 12 *Gd. Men* II. 346 He..described how very lovely she was..when she was a toast at Northampton.

**2.** Any person, male or female, whose health is proposed and drunk to; also any event, institution, or sentiment, in memory or in honour of which a company is requested to drink; also, the call or act of proposing such a health.

**1746** FIELDING *True Patriot* No. 13 A toast, which you know is another word for drinking the health of one's friend..or some person of public eminence. **1780** COWPER *Mod. Patriot* 10 When lawless mobs insult the Court, That man shall be my toast, If breaking windows be the sport, Who bravely breaks the most. **1831** SIR J. SINCLAIR *Corr.* II. 84 (Tour in 1775) He then gave as a toast, 'Success to Scotland, and its worthy inhabitants'. The sentiment was drank with much enthusiasm. *a* **1860** T. KEIGHTLEY cited in WORCESTER, When the toast went out of use, the sentiment took its place, and this I can remember myself. At length *toast* came to signify any person or thing that was to be commemorated: as 'The King', 'The Land we live in', etc. **1866** GEO. ELIOT *F. Holt* ii, You'll rally round the throne—and the King, God bless him, and the usual toasts. **1884** *Marshall's Tennis Cuts* 229 Wine (..for doing honour to the toasts), cigars, etc., amounted to another 14*s.*

**3.** *attrib.* and *Comb.*, as *toast-drinking, -list, -man*; **toast-master**, one who at a public dinner or the like is appointed to propose or announce the toasts.

**1749** FIELDING *Tom Jones* VII. xii, The lieutenant, who was the toast-master, was not contented with Sophia only. He said he must have her sirname. **1768** GOLDSM. *Good-n. Man* III, No man was fitter to be a toast-master to a club. **1814** *Sporting Mag.* XLIV. 45 Oft amid the merry tattle, The toastman's empty cup would rattle. **1818** SCOTT *Let. to Ld. Montagu* 12 Nov. in *Lockhart*, I was at the cattle-show on the 6th, and executed the delegated task of toast-master. **1882** LD. DALHOUSIE in *Daily News* 5 Jan. 2/3 Those gentlemen whose names are down on the toast-list to respond for the House of Commons. **1908** *Westm. Gaz.* 12 Aug. 8/1 The members..were pledged to abstain from toast-drinking.

**Toast** (tōust), *v.*[1] Forms: 5–7 **tost**, 5–6 **toste, tooste**, (6 *Sc.* **toyst**), 6– **toast.** [ad. OF. *toster* (12th c. in Godef.) to roast or grill:—pop.L. **tostāre*, f. *tost-*, supine stem of L. *torrēre* to parch; cf. Sp., Pg. *tostar*, It. *tostare.*]

**1.** *trans.* To burn as the sun does, to parch; to heat thoroughly. *Obs.* exc. as *transf.* from 2.

**1398** TREVISA *Barth. De P. R.* XV. lii. (Bodl. MS.), Ethiopia..þe sonne is nyȝe and rosteþ and tosteþ ham. **1582** N. LICHEFIELD tr. *Castanheda's Conq. E. Ind.* I. ii. 6b, They haue for armes or weapons certaine staues of an Oke tree bathed or toasted with fire. **1626** BACON *Sylva* § 665 The Earth whereof the grasse is soon parched with the Sun and toasted. **1657** R. LIGON *Barbadoes* (1673) 106 Some flowers must be warmed, some toasted, and some almost scalded. **1860–1** FLO. NIGHTINGALE *Nursing* 56 A careful woman will air her whole bedding, at least once a week,..by hanging it out in fine weather in the sun and air, or by toasting it before a hot fire.

**b.** *fig.* To redden (by drinking).

**1701** CIBBER *Love makes Man* v. iii, Now, Charles, we'll e'en toast our Noses over a chirping Bottle.

**c.** *intr.* for *refl.* To warm oneself thoroughly.

**1614** W. BROWNE *Sheph. Pipe* i. B iij b, I will sing what I did leere..Of a skilfull aged Sire, As we tosted by the fire. **1861** HOLLAND *Less. Life* i. 10 Toasting in the sunlight is conducive rather to reverie than thought.

**2.** To brown (bread, cheese, etc.) by exposure to the heat of a fire.

*c* **1420** *Liber Cocorum* (1862) 14 Loke thou tost fyne w[h]ete brede. *c* **1440** *Promp. Parv.* 497/2 Tooste brede, or oþer lyke, *torreo.* **1483** CAXTON *G. de la Tour* cxxi. (1906) 170 Men must..toste and Rost them before the fyre. **1562** TURNER *Herbal* II. 106 If it [Psillium] be perched or tosted at the fyre. **1582** STANYHURST *Æneis* I. (Arb.) 23 Theyre corne in quernstoans thye doe grind and toste yt on embers. **1617** MORYSON *Itin.* III. 130 Toasting of cheese in Wales and seething of Rice in Turkey will enable a man freely to professe the Art of Cookery. **1672** GREW *Anat. Plants, Idea Philos. Hist.* § 42 The Root of Horse-Radish, toasted, tasteth like a Turnep. **1796** MRS. GLASSE *Cookery* xiv. 230 Toast a slice of bread brown on both sides. **1808** *Med. Jrnl.* XIX. 74 The seeds are by some people toasted, so as to be used in the manner of coffee. **1849** DICKENS *Dav. Copp.* xxiv, I'll toast you some bacon in a bachelor's Dutch-oven.

**b.** *transf.* To warm (one's feet or toes) at a fire.

**1860** EMERSON *Cond. Life, Culture* Wks. (Bohn) II. 373 People..who toast their feet on the register. **1869** LOWELL *Under the Willows, Prelude* i, My Elmwood chimneys seem crooning to me..As I sit in my arm-chair, and toast my toes. **1894** CROCKETT *Raiders* 240, I toasted my feet at the fire, setting them on the hot hearthstone to dry.

**c.** *intr.* for *pass.* To undergo toasting; to be toasted.

**1845–51** [implied in TOASTER[1] 2 b]. *Mod.* This cheese toasts well.

† **3.** To destroy or disintegrate with fire. *Obs.*

**1577** tr. *Bullinger's Decades* (1592) 174 Nabuchodonosor whose purpose was to toast with fire and vtterly destroy the martyrs of God. **1578** LYTE *Dodoens* II. xcvi. 279 The onely fume or smoake of Nigella tosted or burnt, drieth away Serpents.

Hence **Toa·sted** *ppl. a.*; **Toa·sting** *vbl. sb.*, also in comb., as *toasting-jack, -pan*; **toasting-fork**, a fork used for toasting bread, etc.; *fig.* a rapier or sword; **toasting-iron** (*arch.*) = prec.

**1584** B. R. tr. *Herodotus* II. 116 For their lyuery fiue pound of *tosted bread, two pounde of Beefe, and a gallon of wyne. **1614** RALEIGH *Hist. World* I. (1634) 178 To draw out a Mouse with a piece of tosted Cheese. **1842** LOUDON *Suburban Hort.* 606 Crumbs of toasted bread. **1541–2** *Acc. Ld. High Treas. Scot.* VIII. 51 For..ane kais to ane *toysting pan, and for ane kais to four ladillis. **1595** SHAKS. *John* IV. iii. 99 Put vp thy sword betime; Or Ile so maule you, and your tosting-Iron. **1836** GEN. P. THOMPSON *Exerc.* (1842) IV. 164 An order ensued, that..the Sir Charles Grandisons of the day should leave their toasting-irons in another room. **1838** DICKENS *O. Twist* xiii, The Dodger snatched up the toasting fork, and made a pass at the merry old gentleman's waistcoat. **1861** HUGHES *Tom Brown at*

*Oxf.* xli, If I had given him time to get at his other pistol, or his toasting fork, it was all up. **1873** HOLLAND *A. Bonnic.* viii, The girl with the toasting-jack dropped her implement to answer the unwelcome summons.

**Toast,** *v.*[2] Also 7 tost. [f. TOAST *sb.*[2]]

**1.** *intr.* To name a person to whose health or in whose honour, or a thing or sentiment to the success of which or in honour of which, the company is requested to drink; to propose or drink a toast. Const. *to.*

*a* **1700** B. E. *Dict. Cant. Crew, Tost,* to name or begin a new Health. Who Tosts now? Who Christens the Health? **1701** F. MANNING *Poems* 73 When ere I Toast..I'll begin No Giant's Health. **1709** PRIOR *Hans Carvel* 111 The Colonel toasted to the best. **1756** TOLDERVY *Hist. 2 Orphans* IV. 207 The sage of the cottage..toasted to the prosperity of his liberal benefactors!

**2.** *trans.* To name when a toast is drunk; to drink in honour of (a person or thing).

**1700** CONGREVE *Way World* IV. v, *Mirabell.* That on no Account you encroach upon the Mens prerogative, and presume to drink Healths, or toast Fellows. *Millamant*...I toast Fellows! odious Men! **1703** ROWE *Fair Penit.* Epil., Ev'ry marry'd Man shall toast his Wife. **1712** STEELE *Spect.* No. 462 ⁋ 4 With continual toasting Healths to the Royal Family. **1775** SHERIDAN *Duenna* I. i, I love dearly to toast her. **1828** MACAULAY *Ess., Hallam* (1851) I. 53 The cause for which Hampden bled on the field and Sidney on the scaffold is..toasted by many an honest radical. **1836** *Random Recoll. Ho. Lords* ix. 192 Times without number did he toast 'The Liberty of the Press'. **1852** THACKERAY *Esmond* I. x, They..toasted past and present heroes and beauties in flagons of college ale.

Hence **Toa·sting** *vbl. sb.* and *ppl. a.*; **toasting glass,** a glass used for drinking toasts, formerly inscribed with the name of a belle or with verses in her honour.

**1703** GARTH (*title*) Verses written for the Toasting-Glasses of the Kit-Cat-Club. *Ibid.* 28 When Jove to Ida did the gods invite, And in immortal toasting pass'd the night. **1821–30** LD. COCKBURN *Mem.* i. (1874) 34 In that toasting and loyal age, the King was never forgotten. **1855** MACAULAY *Hist. Eng.* xx. IV. 455 A few well turned lines inscribed on a set of toasting glasses. **1885** *Manch. Exam.* 14 May 5/1 The institution of dinners with elaborate toasting.

**Toa·stable,** *a. rare.* [f. TOAST *v.*[1] + -ABLE.] Capable of being toasted.

**1570** LEVINS *Manip.* 3/1 Tostable, *tostilis.*

**Toastee** (tōustī·). [f. TOAST *v.*[2] + -EE.] One who is toasted, or whose health is being drunk.

**1840** *New Monthly Mag.* LVIII. 530 He had been eating the toastee's mutton throughout the whole oration. **1852** R. S. SURTEES *Sponge's Sp. Tour* xliv, The various intonations that mark the feelings of the speaker towards the toastee.

**Toaster**[1] (tōu·stəɹ). [f. TOAST *v.*[1] + -ER[1].]

**1.** One who toasts anything by the fire.

**1582** STANYHURST *Conceits* in *Æneis*, etc. (Arb.) 137 Chymneys fyrye be scorching Of Cyclopan tosters. **1861** J. PYCROFT *Agony Point* (1862) 233 Dear Willie should be made a fag..a toaster of muffins, with no time to eat his own.

**2.** A toasting-fork. Humorously, a rapier or similar weapon. Cf. *cheese-toaster*: CHEESE *sb.*[1] 7.

**b.** A kind of cheese, bread, or the like, that toasts (well or otherwise, as expressed).

**1695** in *Verney Mem.* (1907) II. 475 A Silver Toster to toast bread on. **1751** SMOLLETT *Per. Pic.* xxiv, His assailant ..desired he would lay aside his toaster [i. e. rapier] and take a bout with him at equal arms. **1838** MAGINN in *Fraser's Mag.* XVII. 8 Sliced into steaks,..Pierced on the toaster's point. **1845** *Jrnl. R. Agric. Soc.* VI. I. 107, I have tasted some of these cheeses, and find them..fair toasters. **1851** MAYHEW *Lond. Labour* I. II. 9/2 'Here's toasters!' bellows one with a Yarmouth bloater stuck on a toasting-fork.

**Toa·ster**[2]. [f. TOAST *v.*[2] + -ER[1].] One who proposes or joins in a toast; in quot. 1896, = *toast-master* (see TOAST *sb.*[2] 3).

*a* **1704** T. BROWN *Amusem. Ser. & Com.* iv. Wks. 1709 III. I. 42 That Toaster there, is it Possible he can give a Judgment of the Beauties of a Play, while he is wholly taken up in Surveying those of the Ladies? **1720** *Humourist* 182 Chief Toaster at a Drinking-Match. **1896** E. P. POWELL in *Chicago Advance* 5 Nov. 614, I would arrange that..the sophomores occupy the special place of entertainers and toasters.

**Toa·st-rack.** [f. TOAST *sb.*[1] + RACK *sb.*[2] 4.] A contrivance for holding dry toast, keeping each piece on edge and separate. Also *transf.* (quot. 1905).

**1801** NEMNICH *Waaren-Lexicon* 687/1 Toast rack or waggon, *ein Tohstgestell.* **1807** *Specif. of Roberts' Patent* No. 3083 So constructing a toast rack or tray that it may be extended or contracted at pleasure. **1861** N. A. WOODS *Pr. of Wales in Canada* 104 The chief..wore something like a beadwork toastrack on his head. **1905** *Westm. Gaz.* 30 May 4/2 A vehicle of the 'toast-rack' type familiar on the Continent, consisting simply of a platform with seats going transversely.

†**Toa·stree.** *Obs. rare.* [First element obscure; second element TREE.] A name used by Markham and Surflet for the main swingletree of a plough, to the end of which are attached the two smaller swingletrees or whipple-trees, to which the two horses or oxen are harnessed.

In the *Eng. Husbandman* Markham appears to use the term as equivalent to swingletree, calling the main swingletree 'the first' or 'hindmost toastree'.

**1613** MARKHAM *Eng. Husbandman* I. I. v. C iv b, Presenteth the plough-cleiusse, which being ioyned to the plough-beame, extendeth, with a chaine, vnto the first Toastree...The hind-most Toastree..is, a broad piece of Ash-woode..which..hath the Swingletrees fastned vnto it.. Because this Toastree is such a notable Implement both in Plough, Cart, or Waine,..I think it not amisse to shew you the figure thereof. **1616** SURFL. & MARKH. *Country Farme* V. vi. 533 When they draw two and two together..then there is needfull the plow, cleuise, and teame, the toastree, the swingle-trees, the treates, the harnesse, the collars [etc.].

**Toasty** (tōu·sti), *a.* [f. TOAST *sb.*[1] + -Y.] Like toast, esp. in having a slightly burnt flavour. Hence **Toa·stiness,** 'toasty' quality (of tea).

**1892** WALSH *Tea* (Philad.) 100 The infusion is also darker in draw, but very 'toasty', that is 'burnt' in flavor, owing to too high firing. *Ibid.* 72 The finer grades [of Pakeong] yield a rich ripe flavor..but lacking in that 'toastiness' for which the former [kinds of tea] are so much admired.

**Toating,** var. TOTING *Obs.*, prominent.

**Tob,** variant of TOBE, Arab garment.

**Tobaccæan, -chian,** etc.: see under TOBACCO.

**Tobacco** (tǫbæ·ko). Forms: α. 6–8 tabaco, tabacco, (6–7 tabacca), 7 tabaccho. β. 6–7 tobaccho, 6–8 tobaco, tobacca, (6 tobacko, tobackco, 7 tobako, tobaccha, tobbacco, towbaco, tobaccow, 8 *erron.* tobago), 6– tobacco. γ. 7 tabac, toback, 7–9 tobac. [Altered from Sp. *tabaco*, according to Oviedo, the name in the Carib of Hayti of the Y-shaped tube or pipe through which the Indians inhaled the smoke; but according to Las Casas, 1552, applied to a roll of dried leaves which was kindled at the end and used by the Indians like a rude cigar. Even before Oviedo's date the name had been taken by the Spaniards as that of the herb or its leaf, in which sense it passed from Sp. into the other European langs.: Pg. *tabaco*, It. †*tabaco* (1578), *tabacco* (Florio, 1598), F. *tabac*, whence Du., Ger., Boh. *tabak*, Du. (17th c.) *taback*; Pol. *tabaka*, Russ. *tabak*ʺ. The original forms *tabaco, tabacco,* were retained in Eng. to the 18th c., but gradually driven out by *tobacco.* Da. and Sw., and many Ger. dialects, have also *tobak*, Ger. 18th c. *toback.*

**1535** OVIEDO *Hystoria de las Indias* (1851) I. 131 A aquel tal instrumento con que toman el humo, o a las cañuelas que es dicho, llaman los Indios Tabaco: e no a la yerva o sueño que les toma (como pensavan algunos).—IV. 96 En lengua desta isla de Haiti o Española se dice tabaco.

But Dr. A. Ernst of Caracas, in *Amer. Anthropologist* 1889, p. 133, criticizes Oviedo's account, citing from the Guarani Vocabolario of Almeida Nogueira (Rio Janeiro, 1879) *taboca* as the extant Guarani name for such a tube as that described by Oviedo, and used for inhaling through the nostrils not smoke but stimulating powders. He gives some reasons for holding that a Guarani tribe using this may have occupied the northern extremity of Hayti; and suggests that Oviedo, writing 43 years after the event, may have confused the use of this instrument with that of the tubular roll of leaves mentioned by Las Casas as *tabacos.*

The island of *Tobago*, after which the herb has been said by some to be named, according to '*Tobago, a Geogr. Description*' etc. (*c* 1750) p. 74, received the name from its resemblance in shape to the Indian pipe; but other accounts have been given: see quot. 1577 in sense 2.]

**1.** The leaves of the tobacco-plant (see 2) dried and variously prepared, forming a narcotic and sedative substance widely used for smoking, also for chewing, or in the form of SNUFF, and to a slight extent in medicine.

**1588** HARRISON *Chronol.* in *England* (1877) I. App. i. p. lv, In these daies [1573] the taking-in of the smoke of the Indian herbe called Tabaco, by an instrument formed like a litle ladell, wherby it passeth from the mouth into the hed & stomach, is gretlie taken-vp & vsed in England. **1589** HAKLUYT *Voy.* 541 *margin*, Tabacco, & the great vertue thereof. **1597** *1st Pt. Return fr. Parnass.* I. i. 397 What, oulde pipe of Tobacco! why, what's to paye? **1598** B. JONSON *Ev. Man in Hum.* I. iv, He dos take this same filthy roguish tabacco, the finest, and cleanliest! *Ibid.* [see DRINK *v.*[1] 5]. **1600** SIR R. CECIL in *Calr. Carew MSS.* III. 485, I haue sent you tobacco, as good as I could procure any. **1601** *Ibid.* IV. 14 Tabacca. **1601** ? MARSTON *Pasquil & Kath.* I. 276 Ha, ha! Her loue is..just like a whiffe of Tabacco, no sooner in at the mouth, but out at the nose. **1608** A. WILLET *Hexapla in Exod.* 442 Taking with them strong beere..tobaccha. **1612** DEKKER *If it be not good* Wks. 1873 III. 293, I thinke the Diuell is sucking Tabaccho, heeres such a Mist. **1616** SYLVESTER (*title*) Tobacco battered; and the Pipes shattered (About their Eares that idlely Idolize so base and barbarous a Weed). **1622** R. HAWKINS *Voy. S. Sea* xvii. 39 With drinking of Tobacco it is said, that the Roebucke was burned in the range of Dartmouth. **1643** BAKER *Chron., Eliz.* 65 Drake brings home with him Ralph Lane, who was the first that brought Tobacco into England. *a* **1668** LASSELS *Voy. Italy* I. (1670) 235 A little Town, famous for perfumed Tobacco in Powder. **1686** *Rec. Co. Merch. Alnwick* in Gross *Gild Merch.* (1890) I. 131 Not to sell any grosser goods..towbaco or pipes. **1689** W. BULLOCK in *11th Rep. Hist. MSS. Comm.* App. VII. 109, 2 rowles of chawing tobbacco. **1705** BEVERLEY *Virginia* I. iv. (1722) 56 The Duty of two Shillings per Hogshead on all Tobacco's. **1726** MRS. DELANY in *Life & Corr.* (1861) I. 120, I am sure tobacca is there in its full force. **1777** *Account of Island of Tobago* 8 *note*, Columbus gave this island the appellation of Tobago, or Tabago, from a whimsical notion that its form resembled that of a tubical instrument, so called by the Aborigines, with which they inhaled the fumes of tobacco—the Indian name of which plant was kohiba. **1823** BYRON *Island* II. xix, Sublime Tobacco! which from east to west Cheers the tar's labour or the Turkman's rest. **1847** DISRAELI *Tancred* III. ii, The choice tobaccoes of Syria. **1875** H. C. WOOD *Therap.* (1879) 364 Tobacco..has almost passed out of sight as a therapeutic agent.

**2.** The plant whose leaves are so used: Any one of various species of *Nicotiana* (N.O. *Solanaceæ*), esp. *N. Tabacum*, a native of tropical America, or *N. rustica* (*green* or *wild t.*), now widely cultivated.

**1577** FRAMPTON tr. *Monardes' Joyfull Newes* II. (*title*) The Seconde Part,..where is treated of the Tabaco, and of the Sassafras [*orig.* Seqvnda Parte...Do se trata del Tabaco, y dela Sassafras]. *Ibid.* 34 This hearbe which commonly is called Tabaco, is an Hearbe of muche antiquitie, and knowen amongest the Indians...The proper name of it amongest the Indians is *Pieciell*, for the name of Tabaco is geuen to it of our Spaniardes, by reason of an Ilande that is named Tabaco. **1588** HARRIOT in Hakluyt *Voy.* (1600) III. 271 There is an herbe [in Virginia] which is..called by the inhabitants Vppowoc: in the West Indies it hath diuers names...The Spanyards..call it Tabacco. **1590** SPENSER *F. Q.* III. v. 32 There, whether yt divine Tobacco were, Or Panachæa, or Polygony, She fownd. *c* **1595** CAPT. WYATT *R. Dudley's Voy. W. Ind.* (Hakl. Soc.) 48 The high land of Paria, one of the fruitfullest places in the worlde for excellent good tobacco. **1660** *Act 12 Chas. II*, c. 34 § 4 The planting of Tobaccho in any Phisike Garden. **1767** J. ABERCROMBIE *Ev. Man his own Gard.* (1803) 172 Tender kinds of annual flowers such as..French and African marigolds, chrysanthemum, broad-leaved tobacco [etc.]. **1853** ROYLE *Mat. Med.* (ed. 2) 579 Tobacco..is now extensively cultivated in most parts of the world.

**b.** With defining words, applied to plants of other genera, as **Congo tobacco** (*Cannabis sativa*), found wild in the Congo (called by the natives *dei-amba*), the narcotic flowers of which are used for smoking; **English tobacco,** †henbane, *dial.* coltsfoot (also real tobacco grown in England); **Indian tobacco,** (*a*) *Lobelia inflata* of N. America, used medicinally, and having properties similar to those of tobacco; (*b*) Indian hemp, *Cannabis indica* (see HEMP); **mountain tobacco,** *Arnica montana* (see ARNICA); **riverside tobacco,** *Pluchea odorata* (N.O. *Compositæ*) of the West Indies; **wild tobacco** = *Indian tobacco* (*a*), (*Cent. Dict.*); see also TOBACCO-PLANT.

**1597** GERARDE *Herbal* II. lxii. 284 Of yellow Henbane or English Tabacco. **1653** *Sev. Proc. Parlt.* 9–16 Aug. No. 4. 48 (Stanf.) Reports..touching the Planting of English Tobacco in the County of Gloucester. **1678** *Anc. Trades Decayed* 15 (Stanf.) He hath laid the like Impost on our English Tobaccho too. **1846** [see MOUNTAIN 9 d]. **1851** [see INDIAN A. 4 b]. **1851** R. O. CLARKE in *Hooker's Kew Jrnl.* III. 9 (*title*) Short notice of the African Plant Diamba, commonly called Congo Tobacco. **1866** *Treas. Bot.* 1154 Tobacco, Indian, *Lobelia inflata*; also *Cannabis indica*... —, Riverside, *Pluchea odorata.*

**3.** *attrib.* and *Comb.* **a.** simple attrib., as *tobacco-ash, -breath, -cask, -fume, -garden, -jar, -juice, -leaf, -merchant, -monger, -powder, -reek* (Sc.), *-smoke, -stalk, -whiff*; in *Path.* = caused by immoderate use of tobacco, as *tobacco amaurosis, angina, disease, vertigo* (see also *tobacco heart* in d). **b.** objective and obj. gen., as *tobacco-abusing, -chewing,* †*-fuming, -growing, -smoking, -taking* sbs. and adjs.; *tobacco-drier, -seller, -smoker, -taker, -trader, -whiffer.* **c.** similative, instrumental, etc., as *tobacco-breathed* (-breþt), *-stained, -stinking* adjs.; *tobacco-like* adj. and adv. **d.** Special Combs.: †**tobacco bait,** ?a regaling with tobacco, a 'smoke' (cf. BAIT *sb.* 4); **tobacco beetle,** a small beetle, *Lasioderma serricorne*, of the family *Ptinidæ*, which infests stores of tobacco and other pungent substances (*Cent. Dict.* 1891); †**tobacco clay** = *tobacco-pipe clay*, pipe-clay; **tobacco-cutter,** (*a*) a person employed in cutting tobacco; (*b*) a machine or knife for this purpose; †**tobacco-docks,** humorous name for a substitute for tobacco made of dock-leaves; **tobacco-dove,** the small ground-dove of the Bahamas, *Chamæpelia* (*Columbigallina*) *passerina* (*Cent. Dict.*); †**tobacco-fellow,** a companion in tobacco-smoking, a fellow-smoker; **tobacco-grater,** a machine for grinding tobacco for smoking; **tobacco heart,** *Path.*, a heart functionally disordered by excessive use of tobacco, characterized by a rapid and irregular pulse; **tobacco house,** †(*a*) a public resort where tobacco was sold and smoked; (*b*) a building in which tobacco is stored; **tobacco-knife,** 'a knife for cutting plug-tobacco into pieces convenient for the pocket' (Knight *Dict. Mech.*); **tobacco-liquor** = *tobacco-water*; **tobacco-man,** a man who sells tobacco, a tobacconist (now *rare* or *Obs.*); **tobacco paper,** (*a*) paper in which tobacco is wrapped, or in which it is rolled for cigarettes; (*b*) paper impregnated with tobacco, used for fumigating; **tobacco-pouch,** a pouch for carrying tobacco for smoking or chewing; **tobacco press,** an apparatus for pressing tobacco into packages, or into a compact shape (Knight *Dict. Mech.*); **tobacco roll,** a roll of tobacco (see ROLL *sb.*[1] 6 c); **tobacco-roller,** a person employed in making up tobacco in rolls; †**toba·cco-room,** a room for smoking tobacco, a smoking-room; **tobacco-root,** a name for the root of the N.

American plant *Lewisia rediviva*, used as food by the Indians; **tobacco-shop**, a shop in which tobacco is sold; formerly a public resort for smoking; **tobacco-stick**, 'one of a series of sticks on which tobacco-leaves are hung to dry in curing-houses (*Cent. Dict.*); **tobacco-stopper**, a contrivance for pressing down the tobacco in the bowl of a pipe while smoking; **tobacco-stripper**, a person employed in stripping or tearing off the midribs of the leaves of tobacco; **tobacco tongs**, a light pair of tongs formerly used by smokers to pick up tobacco or a live coal for igniting it; **tobacco-twister**, a person employed in making twist tobacco (see TWIST *sb.*); **tobacco-water**, an infusion of tobacco in boiling water, used in veterinary medicine, and for sprinkling on plants to rid them of noxious insects; **tobacco-wheel**, a machine for making twist tobacco (see quot.); **tobacco-worm**, the larva of a sphinx-moth, *Protoparce carolina*, which feeds on the leaves of the tobacco-plant. See also TOBACCO-BOX, etc.

1643 [ANGIER] *Lanc. Vall. Achor* 20 Our..*Tobacco-abusing Commanders and Souldiers. 1879 HARLAN *Eyesight* v. 60 *Tobacco amaurosis is a form of partial paralysis of the optic nerve met with in excessive smokers. 1899 *Allbutt's Syst. Med.* VI. 29 *Tobacco angina is more prevalent amongst men. 1857 HUGHES *Tom Brown* II. ix, Soiled with the marks of toddy-glasses and *tobacco-ashes. 1618 S. WARD *Jethro's Justice* (1627) 18 [They] cannot endure to hold out a forenoon or afternoone sitting without a *Tobacco bayte, or a game at Bowles. 1609 DEKKER *Gull's Horn-bk.* ii. 11 That thicke *tobacco-breath which the rheumaticke night throwes abroad. 1638 DRUMM. OF HAWTH. in *Bk. Scot. Pasquils* (1868) 69 Thesse *tobacco-breathed deuyns. 1878 H. B. BAKER *Our Old Actors* II. 95 Not the transpontine trouser-hitching, *tobacco-chewing monster. 1675 EVELYN *Terra* (1729) 7 Vessels made of *Tobacco-Clay. 1670 *Lond. Gaz.* No. 529/4 A *Tobacco-cutter, lately dwelling in Fryingpan Alley in Petticoat-lane without Bishopsgate-street. 1877 KNIGHT *Dict. Mech.*, *Tobacco-cutter.* 1. A machine for shaving tobacco-leaves into shreds for chewing or smoking...2. A knife for cutting plug-tobacco into smaller pieces. 1899 *Allbutt's Syst. Med.* VI. 845 [We] are most familiar with *tobacco disease among seafaring men. 1599 H. BUTTES *Dyets drie Dinner* Ep. Ded. Aa j b, The Yorkers they will bee content with bald *Tabacodocks. [Cf. 1599 CHAPMAN *Humor. Day's Mirth* E j b, *Ber*...Haue you a pipe of good Tabacco?.. *Boy.* Theres none in the house sir. *Ve.* Drie a docke leafe.] 1662 R. MATHEW *Unl. Alch.* § 101. 170 Have ready a *Tobacco-drier, & put upon it a spungy thin brown paper. 1616 SYLVESTER *Tobacco Battered* 148 These beastly, base *Tobacco-Fellowes. 1807 JANSON *Stranger in Amer.* 339 The devastation produced by the *tobacco-fly which is of the beetle species, black and large enough to be seen committing its depredations. 1609 DEKKER *Gull's Horn-bk.* vi. 28 Libertie to be there in his *Tobacco-Fumes. 1634 WITHER *Emblemes* 5 In sleeping drinking and *tobacco-fuming. 1884 H. M. JONES *Hints Health Senses* 144 A functionally affected heart,..resulting from Tobacco, and known as the '*Tobacco Heart'. 1611 RICH *Honest. Age* (Percy Soc.) 42 For *Tobacco houses and Brothell houses, (I thanke God for it) I doe not vse to frequent them. 1676 T. GLOVER in *Phil. Trans.* XI. 635 The greatest part.. had their Tobacco-houses blown down and their Tobacco spoiled. 1833 MARRYAT *P. Simple* xiv, There were spitting-pans placed..that they might not dirty the planks with the *tobacco-juice. 1598 MARSTON *Sco. Villanie* (1599) 166 That neuer turn'd but browne *Tobacco leaues. 1705 tr. *Bosman's Guinea* xvi. 307 The Tobacco-Leaf here grows on a Plant about two Foot high. 1599 H. BUTTES *Dyets drie Dinner* P iv, Whose stomach..Sucks vp *Tobacco like the vpmost ayr. 1854 [see *tobacco-root*]. 1844 STEPHENS *Bk. Farm* III 875 A solution of corrosive sublimate, or a strong decoction of *tobacco-liquor. 1618 N. FIELD *Amends for Ladies* III. i. in Hazl. *Dodsley* XI. 127 Her fortune, o' my conscience, would be To marry some *tobacco-man. *a* 1680 BUTLER *Rem.* (1759) II. 122 There was a Tobacco-Man, that wrapped Spanish Tobacco in a Paper of Verses. 1599 NASHE *Lenten Stuffe* Ep. Ded., By that time his *Tobacco merchant is made euen with. 1618 J. ROLFE in Capt. Smith *Virginia* IV. 126 There are so many sofisticating *Tobaco-mungers in England. 1877 KNIGHT *Dict. Mech.*, **Tobacco-paper.* 1882 *Garden* 21 Jan. 49/1 Fumigate with Tobacco paper on a calm day. 1687 A. LOVELL tr. *Thevenot's Trav.* I. 30 They carry two Hankerchiefs at their girdle,..their *Tobacco-pouch hangs also at it. 1818 SCOTT *Hrt. Midl.* xlv, He knocked the ashes out of his pipe,..returned the tobacco-pouch or spleuchan to its owner. 1672 *Phil. Trans.* VII. 5021 Washing the Sore..and strewing *Tobacco-powder thereon. 1815 SCOTT *Guy M.* xi, I not the *tobacco-reek disagreeable to your honour? 1679 M. RUSDEN *Further Discov. Bees* 108 Much like to a *Tobacco-roll standing upright. 1856 OLMSTED *Slave States* 361 All quiet housekeepers were kept in a state of excited alarm during the seasons when the *tobacco-rollers were in town. 1656 in *Westm. Gaz.* 17 Oct. (1902) 2/3 Uppon my returne into the Howse..I mett Major-General Desborough in the *tobacco roome. 1864 *Chamb. Encycl.* VI. 109/2 *Lewisia..rediviva*...Its roots are gathered in great quantities by the Indians...It is called *Tobacco Root because, when cooked, it has a tobacco-like smell. *c* 1645 in *Archæologia* LII. 137 Seriaunt Maior William Underwood a *Tobacco seller in Bucklersbury. 1605 CHAPMAN *All Fooles* I. i, Th'art known in Ordinaries, and *Tabacco-shops. 1597–8 BP. HALL *Sat.* IV. iv. 41 Quaffs a whole tunnel of *tobacco smoke. 1848 tr. *Hoffmeister's Trav. Ceylon*, etc. iv. 174 Like our *tobacco-smokers lounging on their sofas. 1897 *Westm. Gaz.* 12 May 2/1 He would look at their *tobacco-stained tongues. 1704 LUTTRELL *Brief Rel.* (1857) V. 435 The officers of the customes burnt publickly in this citty 12 load of *tobacco stalks lately seized. 1616 SYLVESTER *Tobacco Battered* 763 Awefull Justice will..at one blow cut-off this Over-Drinking, And ever Dropsie, of *Tobacco-stinking. 1664 BUTLER *Hud.* II. III. 454 By his proper Figure, that's like *Tobacco-stopper. *a* 1701 CIBBER *Love makes Man* I. i, As inseparable Companions, as a Beau and a Snuff Box, or a Curate and a Tobacco-stopper. 1840 DICKENS *Barn. Rudge* lxxviii, He used the little finger..as a tobacco-stopper. 1725 *Lond. Gaz.* No. 6380/7 Elizabeth Sims,..*Tobacco stripper. 1599 NASHE *Lenten Stuffe* Wks. (Grosart) V. 240 Hee will neede be a man of warre, or a *Tobacco taker. 1666 W. BOGHURST *Loimographia* (1894) 55 *Tobacco-taking, Diemerbrook greatly commends; but how many thousand Tobacco-takers think you, dyed this year? 1669 BOYLE *Contn. New Exp.* I. xl. (1682) 139 We fastened a small pair of *Tobacco-Tongs to the inside of the Receivers Brass Cover. 1808 *Cobbett's Weekly Pol. Reg.* XIII. 134 Thread-spinners and *tobacco-twisters. 1899 *Allbutt's Syst. Med.* VIII. 152 *Tobacco vertigo and the other nervous consequences of the weed. 1808 *Nicholson's Jrnl.* XIX. 298 (*heading*) On the Use of *Tobacco Water, in preserving Fruit Crops, by destroying Insects. 1851 *Birmingham & Midl. Gard. Mag.* Dec. 236 Mix up flour of sulphur,..and tobacco-water,..and dress the trees with the mixture. 1877 KNIGHT *Dict. Mech.*, **Tobacco-wheel*, a machine by which leaves of tobacco are twisted into a cord. 1611 [TARLTON] *Jests* (1628) C iij b, *Tobacco whiffes made them leaue him to pay all. *c* 1614 FLETCHER, etc. *Wit at Sev. Weap.* IV. i, Great *tobacco-whiffers. 1773 *Hist. Brit. Dom. in N. Amer.* XI. iii. 190 The *tobacco-worm is a caterpillar of the size and figure of a silk-worm.

Hence (chiefly *humorous nonce-wds.*) † **Toba·cchian** (taba·ckian, tobaccæ·an), *a.* addicted to tobacco; *sb.* a person addicted to tobacco; † **Toba·ccical** (tabackicall), **Toba·ccoic** (-o,ik) *adjs.*, pertaining to, addicted to, or caused by tobacco; **Toba·ccoed** (-oud), **Toba·ccofied** *adjs.*, characterized by the use of tobacco; **Toba·ccoite** (-o,əit), an advocate of tobacco; **Toba·ccoless** *a.*, without tobacco, not supplied with tobacco; **Toba·ccophil(e** [-PHIL], a lover of tobacco; **Toba·ccose** (-bacch-) *a.*, addicted to, or characterized by addiction to, tobacco; **Toba·ccoy** (-o,i) *a.*, impregnated with or smelling of tobacco-smoke.

1597 GERARDE *Herbal* II. lxiii. § 2. 286 It is not so thought nor receiued of our *Tabackians. 1615 SIR E. HOBY *Curry-Combe* i. 25 Whom he describeth to be one of the Knights fellow tobaccæan Wrighters. 1637 VENNER *Tobacco* in *Via Recta* 359 Such..are no base Tobacchians: for this manner of taking the fume, they suppose to be generous. 1604 *Will W. Woodhall*, Perceiving his *tabackicall humor. 1893 *Granta* 2 Dec. 113 Luxurious and *tobaccoed ease. 1846 THACKERAY *Cornhill to Cairo* xv, A dreamy, hazy, lazy, *tobaccofied life. 1878 *Cope's Tobacco Plant* Jan. 130/1 Three hundred years..have failed to develop any distinct *Tobaccoic disease. 1898 *Daily News* 9 Sept. 5/1 Eventually the *tobaccoites completely routed their opponents. 1840 R. G. LATHAM *Norway* I. 189 It is better to be without a whip than *tobaccoless. 1889 *Sat. Rev.* 4 May 528/1 Left tobaccoless after dinner! 1882 M. HOWIE in *Knowledge* I. 343 The smaller appetite of the inveterate *tobaccophile. 1845 FORD *Handbk. Spain* I. II. 194/2 Many *tobacchose epicures who smoke their regular dozen. *Ibid.* II. 731 Tobaccose. 1840 J. T. HEWLETT *P. Priggins* xx, Taken ..out of the *tobaccoy atmosphere into the open air.

**Toba·cco-box.**

**1.** A box for holding tobacco, *esp.* a small flat box to be carried in the pocket.

1599 B. JONSON *Cynthia's Rev.* I. i, Pray Iove the perfum'd courtiers keep their casting-bottles..from you, or our more ordinary gallants their tobacco-boxes. 1654 GAYTON *Pleas. Notes* III. v. 100 A Tobacco box with a Burning Glasse. 1859 FAIRHOLT *Tobacco* 229 The old brass tobacco-box was generally oblong, and contained all the smoker required...There is a horn tobacco-box preserved in London.

**2.** Local name for two N. American fishes, from their flattened shape: (*a*) a species of skate or ray, *Raia erinacea*; (*b*) the common sunfish, *Pomotis gibbosus*, or other species of *Pomotis* (*Cent. Dict.*).

**Tobaccoed, -ic, -ite,** etc.: see after TOBACCO.

**Tobaccona·lian,** *sb.* and *a.* [f. TOBACCO, app. after *bacchanalian*.] **a.** *sb.* A person addicted to tobacco-smoking. **b.** *a.* Relating to tobacco-smoking.

1855 THACKERAY *Newcomes* xxxv, We get very good cigars..for us cheap tobacconalians. 1889 *Sat. Rev.* 23 Nov. 573/2 A cake of golden-leaf..and other tobacconalian fantasies.

† **Toba·cconer.** *Obs.* [f. as TOBACCON-IST + -ER [1].] = TOBACCONIST (senses 1 and 2). So **Toba·cconian** *a.*, of or pertaining to tobacco; † **Toba·cconing**, *vbl. sb.* tobacco-smoking; *pres. pple.* smoking tobacco.

1616 SYLVESTER *Tobacco Battered* 643 For Dumpier none then the *Tobacconer. 1701 *Reg. St. Andrew's, Canterb.*, Charles Jecks Tobackoner of Wapping. 1835 *Fraser's Mag.* XI. 39 The rattling of the diligence,..and..the *tobacconian flavour within. 1616 SYLVESTER *Tobacco Battered* 204 It shall suffice to say, *Tobacconing is but a smoakie play. 1647 BP. HALL *Hard Measure* Rem. Wks. (1660) 64 The Cathedrall..filled with Muskatiers,..drinking and tobacconing as freely as if it had turn'd Alehouse.

**Tobacconist** (tŏbæ·kŏnist). Also 6 tabbaconist, 7 tabaccanist, -onist, tobackonist, -baconist, -bacchonist, -bacconiste. [f. TOBACCO + -IST, with inserted *-n-*, perh. suggested by such words as *Platonist*, with etymological *n*.]

† **1.** A person addicted to the use of tobacco; *esp.* a habitual tobacco-smoker. *Obs.*

1599 B. JONSON *Ev. Man out of Hum.* III. i, It pleases the world (as I am her excellent Tabacconist) to giue me the style of Signior Whiffe. 1615 H. CROOKE *Body of Man* 587 We see that cunning Tobacconistes..can driue the smoake out of their mouthes thorough their eare. 1686 PLOT *Staffordsh.* 302 Who though a great Tobacconist, never spits in the smoking of ten pipes together. *a* 1700 B. E. *Dict. Cant. Crew*, *Smoker*, a Tobacconist. 1757 MRS. GRIFFITH *Lett. Henry & Frances* (1767) II. 280 As phlegmatic as a Dutch tobacconist.

**2.** A seller of or dealer in tobacco; also, a manufacturer of tobacco.

1657 W. RAND tr. *Gassendi's Life Peiresc* VI. 195 That [the books] might..escape the danger of the Tobacconist and Grocer. 1700 T. BROWN *Amusem. Ser. & Com.* viii. 112 In the Tobacconist's Shops Men were sneezing and spawling. 1840 DICKENS *Old C. Shop* vii, Mr. Richard Swiveller's apartments were..over a tobacconist's shop.

Hence **Tobacconi·stical** *a.*, belonging to or characteristic of a tobacconist. Also **Toba·cconize** *v.*, (*a*) *intr.* to smoke tobacco; (*b*) *trans.* to impregnate with tobacco-smoke.

1839 *New Monthly Mag.* LVII. 118 Submitting this *tobacconistical list to the snuff-taking public. 1876 BLACKMORE *Cripps* III. xiii. 204 In picturesque attitudes of *tobacconizing. 1884 *American* VIII. 73 The necessity of enduring a tobacconized atmosphere.

**Tobaccophil, -e**: see after TOBACCO.

**Toba·cco-pipe.**

**1.** A pipe for smoking tobacco, made of clay, wood, or other material, of various shapes and sizes, consisting of a bowl in which the tobacco is placed and ignited, with a slender tube through which the smoke of it is drawn into the mouth by suction. *King's* (*Queen's*) *tobacco-pipe*: see PIPE *sb.*[1] 10 c.

1596 NASHE *Saffron Walden* Wks. (Grosart) III. 199 The pummell of a scotch saddle, or pan of a Tobacco pipe. 1597–8 BP. HALL *Sat.* V. ii, Nor half that smoke..Which one tobacco-pipe drives thro' his nose. 1632 LITHGOW *Trav.* V. 205 The Turkish Tobacco pipes are more than a yard long. 1861 WRIGHT *Ess. Archæol.* I. ii. 27 Tobacco pipes have been found..in very singular approximations with objects of remote antiquity.

**2.** *U.S.* Local name for a parasitic plant, also called *Indian pipe*: see INDIAN A. 4 b.

1845 S. JUDD *Margaret* I. xvi, She found..the curious mushroom-like tobacco-pipe.

**3.** *attrib.* and *Comb.*, as *tobacco-pipe bowl*, *maker*; **tobacco-pipe clay** = PIPE-CLAY; **tobacco-pipe fish** = PIPE-FISH.

1620–1 *Canterb. Marr. Licences* (MS.), John Lyne of Canterbury, tobacco-pipe-maker. 1667 *Lond. Gaz.* No. 156/4 One [vessel]..laden with Tobacco-pipe Clay, and Fullers-Earth. *a* 1672 WILLUGHBY *Ichthyogr.* (1686) Tab. 6 *Petimbuaba* Bras.: Tobacco pipe Fish. 1804 TINGRY *Paint. & Varnish. Guide* 280 A white earthy matter, commonly known under the name of tobacco-pipe clay. 1876 GOODE *Fishes Bermudas* 17 Petimbuabo Brazil (The Tobaccopipe-Fish) is *Fistularia tabaccaria*.

**Toba·cco-plant.** The plant which yields tobacco; = TOBACCO 2.

1761 J. HILL (*title*) Cautions against the immoderate use of Snuff. Founded on the known qualities of the Tobacco Plant. 1796 STEDMAN *Surinam* II. xxv. 224 The tobacco plant grows here with large downy leaves, full of fibres. 1879 *Cassell's Techn. Educ.* VIII. 65/1 The tobacco plant is an annual, growing six feet high.

**b.** A general name for species of *Nicotiana.*

1884 MILLER *Plant-n.* 137 Tobacco-plant. The genus *Nicotiana*...Latakia, Syrian, or Wild T., *Nicotiana rustica*... Persian or Shiraz T., *N. persica*...Tuberose-flowered T., *N. affinis*...Virginian T., *N. Tabacum.*

**c.** Also applied to other plants.

1884 MILLER *Plant-n.* 137 English Tobacco-plant, an old name for *Hyoscyamus*...Indian T., *Lobelia inflata*...Mountain T., *Arnica montana.*

**Tobaccose, -coy**: see after TOBACCO.

‖ **Tobe** (tōᵘb). Also tob, tope. [a. Arab. ثوب *thaub* (locally pronounced *tōb*, *sōb*) a garment.] A length of cotton cloth (see quot. 1889), worn as an outer garment by natives of Northern and Central Africa, and in some parts used as currency.

1835 *Court Mag.* VI. 34/1 His coat of divers colours, his decorated tobe, the panther skin he bestrode, his uplifted arm and threatening spear were seen throughout the field. 1843 McWILLIAM *Med. Hist. Niger Exped.* 87 The articles exposed for sale were bags of salt..,tobes of various colours, country cloths [etc.]. 1858 SIMMONDS *Dict. Trade*, *Tob*, a piece of Dammour cotton cloth, sufficient to make a shirt, which passes as a currency money in Nubia. 1867 BAKER *Nile Tribut.* xiii. 333 The old Abou Do being resolved upon work, had divested himself of his tope or toga before starting. 1872 W. H. D. ADAMS *Land of Nile* IV. i. 278 They [Nubians] have no currency of their own; glass beads, coral, cotton, tobs or shirts, and samoor or cloth, they receive as money. 1889 *Edin. Rev.* Oct. 391 It consists, for men and women alike, of a 'tobe', or straight piece of cotton cloth,.. two breadths wide, and some twelve feet long, draped..about the body, and fastened on the left shoulder.

**To-be** (tŭ,bī·). [inf. of BE *v.* as *sb.* and *a.*; cf. BE *v.* B. 24.]

**A.** as *sb.* That which is to be; the future. Cf. *to-come*, s. v. COME *v.* 32 c.

1819 BYRON *Venice* ii, The everlasting *to be* which *hath been.* 1838 LYTTON *Alice* VI. ii, The *To Be* is as the shadow of a far land in a mighty and perturbed sea. 1847 TENNYSON *Princess* VII. 273 These twain..Sit side by side,..Dispensing harvest, sowing the To-be. 1900 MARIE CORELLI *Master-Christian* xvi, I work and write for the To-Be, not the Has-Been.

**B.** as *adj. phrase* (often following the *sb.*). That is yet to be or to come; future.

*c* 1600 SHAKS. *Sonn.* lxxxi, Toungues to be, your being shall rehearse. *a* 1804 NELSON in Nicolas *Disp.* II. 457 Marry..speedily, or the to be Mrs. Berry will have very little of your company. 1860 MRS. EDKINS *Chinese Scenes* (1863) 102 The four to-be priests I knew before.

† **To-bea·r**, *v. Obs.* [OE. *toberan*, f. To-[2] + *beran*, BEAR *v.*[1]] *trans.* To carry in different directions; to carry off, take away; also *fig.* to separate (persons) in feeling, etc.; to part, sunder, set at variance. Also *refl.*

**971** *Blickl. Hom.* 95 Þeah þe hie ær eorþe bewriȝen hæfde, ..oþþe wildeor abiton, oþþe fuȝlas tobæron. *c* **1000** ÆLFRIC *Hom.* I. 386 He is me ȝecoren fætels, þæt he tobere minne naman ðeodum. *c* **1250** *Gen. & Ex.* 2146 Ðo was vnder him ðanne putifar, And his wif ðat hem so to-bar. *c* **1320** *Cast. Love* 522 Þe kynges sone al þis con heren, Hou his sustren hem to-beeren.

† **To-bea·t**, *v. Obs.* [OE. *tobéatan*, f. To-[2] + *béatan*, BEAT *v.*[1] So MHG. *ze-, zerbôȝen.*] *trans.* To beat to pieces, to destroy by beating (OE.); to beat severely, belabour, thrash. Often emphasized by *all* (ALL C. 14). Also *absol.* or *intr.*

*c* **893** K. ÆLFRED *Oros.* IV. xiii. § 3, & Scipia het ealle þa burȝ toweorpan, & ælcne hiewestan tobeatan. *a* **1122** *O. E. Chron.* an. 1009 (Laud MS.) Þa com him swilc wind onȝean ..and þa scipo ða ealle to beot. *a* **1250** *Owl & Night.* 1610 An euer euch man..me mid stone and lugge þreteþ, An me to-busteþ and to-beteþ. **1390** GOWER *Conf.* I. 283 Mi wofull harte is so tobete. *a* **1425** *Cursor M.* 1846 (Trin.) Þe wawes to bote bifore & bihynde. **1494** FABYAN *Chron.* v. cxxii. 99 He was all to betyn and arrayed in moost vyle maner.

† **To-be·ll**, *v. Obs.* Also 4 **te-belle.** [f. To-[2] + BELL *v.*[1]] *intr.* To swell exceedingly; also *fig.* to be puffed up with pride or swollen with anger. Chiefly in *pa. pple.* **to-bollen.**

*c* **1200** ORMIN 8080, & all himm wærenn fet & þeos To bollenn & to blawenn. *a* **1225** *Ancr. R.* 282 Heorte tobollen & to-swollen, & ihouen on heih ase hul. **13..** *Sir Beues* (A.) 2832 His flesch gan ranclen & tebelle. **1377** LANGL. *P. Pl.* B. v. 84 His body was to-bolle [*v.rr.* tobollen, to-bolne] for wratthe þat he bote his lippes.

**Tobin bronze.** An alloy invented by John A. Tobin of U.S. navy, composed mainly of copper, zinc, tin, with some iron, and lead; one kind is called *delta-metal* (see DELTA 4).

Used for articles of domestic use, parts of machines, parts of ships exposed to the constant action of salt water, etc.

[**1882** (Dec. 14) J. A. TOBIN *U.S. Patent Specif.* No. 309011 The essential elements of my alloy are copper, zinc, and tin.] **1891** *Jrnl. Franklin Inst.* CXXXII. 55 The Ansonia Brass and Copper Company..are..the sole manufacturers of Tobin bronze. **1893** *Outing* (U.S.) XXII. 147/1 The fin [centre-board of a sailing boat] is of Tobin bronze, one-quarter inch thick, six feet long on upper edge. **1899** *Westm. Gaz.* 12 June 7/2 The quality of the skin material.. has been the subject of much thought and experiment, resulting in the use of Tobin bronze, as contrasted with manganese bronze in *Defender* [a racing yacht].

† **Tobi·ne.** *Obs.* [app. an altered form of TABINE, = Du. *tabijn*, ad. It. *tabino* (Florio), by-form of *tabi* (see TABBY), whence also Ger. *tabin*, of which *tobin* is cited by Heyse *Fremdwörterbuch* as an upper German variant.] = TABINE.

**1755** *The Card* II. xi. 59 With superior lustre shine in simple lutestring or tobine. **1799** G. SMITH *Laboratory* II. 45 There are likewise lutestring tobines, which commonly are striped with flowers in the warp, and sometimes between the tobine stripes, with brocaded sprigs. **1858** SIMMONDS *Dict. Trade, Tobine*, a stout twilled silk.

**Tobin's tube.** Also **Tobin tube.** A device for admitting fresh air into a room in an upward direction, invented by Martin Tobin of Leeds.

[**1873** M. TOBIN *Patent Specif.* No. 1081 In some cases.. I pass a tube..into the apartment, and form or turn the mouth or inlet, so as to give the air..an upward or fountain-like direction.] **1884** BILLINGS *Ventilation*, etc. 102 Another form of inlet consists in what are often spoken of as Tobin's Tubes.

† **To-blow·**, *v. Obs.* Forms: see BLOW *v.*[1] [OE. *tobláwan*, f. To-[2] + *bláwan*, BLOW *v.*[1] So OHG. *zaplâen*, MHG. *ze-, zerblæjen.*] *trans.* **a.** To distend with wind, inflate, puff up; also *fig.* to puff up with an emotion. **b.** To blow in different directions, scatter by blowing, blow away.

*c* **1000** ÆLFRIC *Saints' Lives* vii. 139 On ðam [hell fire] ȝe beoþ toblawene. *c* **1000** *Sax. Leechd.* III. 58 ȝif he bið toblawen se innoð. *c* **1200** [see TO-BELL]. **13..** *Sir Beues* (A.) 2696 For þe venim is on me þrowe, Her I legge al to-blowe. *Ibid.* 6872 Þat he no were anon y-slawe, For-brent, and þat dust to-blowe. *c* **1425** *Seven Sag.* (P.) 1523 Hys body was al to-blaw.

**Toboggan** (tŏbǫ·găn), *sb.* Also **tabagane, ta-, tobognay, tarbog(g)in, treboggin, tobogin, -en, toboggen, tobaugan, tobogan, tabougin, tabogan.** [Adaptation of a Canadian Indian name of a sleigh or sledge; given in French spelling *tabaganne* by Le Clercq *Nouvelle Relation de la Gaspesie*, 1691, p. 70 (J. Platt in *N. & Q.* 9th Ser. XII. 467). The nearest Indian forms cited are Micmac (Lower Canada, New Brunsw., Nova Scotia) *tobâkun* (tobā·kən) (Rand *Micmac Dict.* 1888), and Abnaki (Quebec and Maine) *udâbâgan* (Trumbull). Other allied Algonquian langs. have, Montaignais *utapan*, Cree *otâbânâsk* (Lacombe), Odjibwa *odaban-ak*: cf. PUNG *sb.*[2]]

**1.** Originally, a light sledge consisting of a thin strip of wood turned up in front, used by the Canadian Indians for transport over snow; now, a similar vehicle, sometimes with low runners, used in the sport of coasting (esp. down prepared slopes of snow or ice).

**1829** G. HEAD *Forest Scenes N. Amer.* 64 After leaving Fredericton there was no town nor village at which the required articles could be procured: namely, a couple of tobogins, a tobogin bag, a canteen..two pairs of snow shoes. **1846** G. WARBURTON *Hochelaga* I. 122 One of the great amusements..is, to climb up to the top of this cone, and slide down again on a tarboggin. **1850** S. D. HUYGHUE in *Bentley's Misc.* XXVII. 152 Snow-shoes, mocassins, and tobaugans, for the use of the men. **1861** J. LEECH *Pict. Life & Char.* 78 (Punch Office publ.) Militaire recalls his Canadian experiences, builds a treboggin. **1863** H. Y. HIND *Labrador* I. 280 The tabognay is a little sledge upon which people in winter amuse themselves in descending hills covered with snow. **1865** P. B. ST. JOHN *Snow Ship* xv. 106 These tarbogins, or tabougins, as they are indifferently called, are small sleighs drawn by hand over the snow. **1874** SYMMONDS *Sk. Italy & Greece* (1898) I. i. 26 The little hand-sledge..which the English have christened by the Canadian term 'toboggan'. **1880** *Daily Tel.* 18 Feb., The 'toboggin' is a wooden car..which is curled up at the lower extremity, or prow, so as to constitute a seat holding a couple of sitters. **1885** *New Bk. Sports* 239 The steersman ..gives the tobogan a start, and away they go down the hill. **1891** *Month* LXXIII. 24 Travelling with dogs and toboggans during winter.

**2.** [f. next.] The practice or sport of tobogganing.

**1879** *Birmingham Weekly Post* 8 Feb. 1/4 We have heard of a new sport called toboggen, brought from Canada and adopted here when the ground is hilly enough by country house parties. **1896** R. S. S. BADEN-POWELL *Matabele Campaign* i, Madeira...Scramble up on horses to the convent, up the long, steep, cobbled roads, and the grand toboggan down again in sliding cars.

**3.** *attrib.* and *Comb.*, as *toboggan-bag, -cap, -race, -sleigh*, etc.; **toboggan-slide**, a steep incline for tobogganing, also called **toboggan-chute, -run,** or **-shoot**; also applied to an inclined series of rollers down which toboggans run.

**1829** G. HEAD *Forest Scenes N. Amer.* 64 The tobogin bag [for luggage] when full is..laced tightly on the machine by means of a cord. **1881** *Standard* 22 Jan. 5/1 The Canadian..considers the snowy season the period of enjoyment. It is the sleigh-driving, the 'coasting', and the 'toboggan season'. **1887** O. W. HOLMES *100 Days in Europe* 150 Like what..would be a pretty steep toboggan slide. **1903** *Daily Chron.* 4 Feb. 6/1 He gets ready for the toboggan club's train, which leaves Davos for the village of Wolfgang every morning. **1904** *Times* 25 Aug. 7/5 The Royal party returned at noon in toboggan basket sleighs. **1907** C. HILL-TOUT *Brit. N. Amer., Far West* v. 93 A toboggan-shaped basket with an opening near its curved end.

**Tobo·ggan**, *v.* [f. prec. sb.] *intr.* To ride on a toboggan or sleigh; *esp.* to 'coast' or slide down a snowy (or other) slope on a toboggan. Hence **Tobo·gganing** *vbl. sb.*

**1856** MISS BIRD *Englishwom. in Amer.* 264 With balls, and moose-hunting, and sleigh-driving, and 'tarbogginning'. **1863** H. Y. HIND *Labrador* I. xvii. 280, I didn't want to break the canoe, so I sat down and slid as if I was tabognaying. **1874** SYMONDS *Sk. Italy & Greece* (1898) I. i. 27 On a run selected for convenience..tobogganing is a very Bohemian amusement. **1887** MARCHIONESS DUFFERIN *Viceregal Life India* 15 Sept., The children got three tin baths ..and began to toboggan down the grassy slopes in them.

**Tobogganer** (tŏbǫ·gănəɹ). [f. prec. + -ER[1].] One who toboggans.

**1884** J. A. SYMONDS in *Pall Mall G.* 22 Feb. 1/2 The tobogginner sits rather to the back of his sledge; and when he is once in motion has only to steer. **1907** *Times* 19 Feb. 5/5 Expert tobogganers approach the junction at a speed of nearly 40 miles an hour.

So (in same sense) **Tobogganee·r, Tobo·gganist.**

**1880** *Daily Tel.* 18 Feb., Upon the toboggin..a cushion is placed, upon which the tobogginist either lies flat upon his stomach, or assumes a sitting posture, with stiffened knee-joints, the feet being firmly pressed against the roll of the curved prow. **1887** *Cornh. Mag.* Mar. 273 The costume of the tobogganeer differs in no respect from that of the snowshoer. **1910** *Times* 28 Jan. 10/5 All three tobogganists were hurled violently into the road.

**To-bollen, To-bone:** see TO-BELL, TO-BUNE.

**To-bote**, pa. t. of TO-BEAT.

† **To-brai·d**, *v. Obs.* [OE. *tobregdan*, f. To-[2] + *bregdan*, BRAID *v.*[1]] *trans.* To wrench apart, pull to pieces, rend; also, to tear or snatch away.

*c* **893** K. ÆLFRED *Oros.* IV. ii, Þrie wulfas..brohton anes deades monnes lichoman binnan þa burȝ, & hiene þær siþþan styccemælum tobrudon. *c* **975** *Rushw. Gosp.* Matt. xii. 29 Þonne [he] hus his to-breȝdeþ. *a* **1250** *Owl & Night.* 1008 Suych wolues hit hadde tobroude [*v.r.* tobrode]. **1382** WYCLIF *Mark* ix. 25 He criynge, and moche to-breidynge him, wente out fro him. *c* **1400** *St. Alexius* 396 (Laud MS.) She..of hire bedd þe cloþes doun cast And siþen hem al to breyde.

**To-bread** (tū·bred). *Sc.* [f. To-[1] + BREAD.] Additional bread; = IN-BREAD *sb.* Also *fig.*

**1854** *N. & Q.* 1st Ser. X. 531/2 The Scotch baxter..may at times..give a farthing biscuit—as what is called 'too (or additional) bread'—on the purchase of a shilling's worth. **1868** SALMON *Gowodean* III. vii. 104 You were yoursel' the 'to-bread' to the gift.

† **To-brea·k**, *v. Obs.* Forms: see BREAK *v.* [OE. *tobrecan*, f. To-[2] + *brecan* to BREAK. So OHG. *zaprehhan, zibrechan*, Ger. *zerbrechen.*]

**1.** *trans.* To break to pieces; to shatter, rupture; to break down, destroy, demolish; cf. senses of BREAK *v.*

*c* **888** K. ÆLFRED *Boeth.* xxxv. § 4 Woldon þa [the giants] tobrecan þone heofon under him. *c* **1000** ÆLFRIC *Hom.* I. 180 Tobrec ðinne hlaf. *c* **1000** *Sax. Leechd.* II. 22 ȝenim, wiþ tobrocenum heafde, betonican. **1056–66** *Inscr. Kirkdale Ch., Yorks.*, Hit wes al tobrocan & tofalan. *c* **1175** *Lamb. Hom.* 131 He to-þruste þa stelene gate, & to brec þa irene barren of helle. *c* **1275** *Passion our Lord* 490 in *O. E. Misc.* 51 We biddeþ þat heore þyes beon to-broken a to. **1387** TREVISA *Higden* (Rolls) VII. 257 His hors nekke was to brooke. *c* **1440** *Gesta Rom.* lxxxviii. 410 (Add. MS.) Here is my sone..with his hede all to-broke. **1535** COVERDALE *Prov.* vi. 15 Sodenly shal he be all tobroken, and not be healed. **1611** BIBLE *Judg.* ix. 53 A..woman cast a piece of a milstone..and all to brake his scull. **1623** LISLE *Ælfric on O. & N. Test.* Pref. 18 An old Colosse, All soiled, all to broke. *a* **1688** BUNYAN *Acceptable Sacr.* Wks. (ed. Offor) I. 698 This was it, that all to-brake his heart.

**b.** To rend, to tear (clothes or the like).

*c* **1200** *Trin. Coll. Hom.* 163 Þe chirche cloðes ben to-brokene and ealde. *c* **1275** *Passion our Lord* 315 in *O. E. Misc.* 46 Kayphas his weden he to-brek. **1382** WYCLIF *Matt.* vii. 6 Lest houndis turned to gidre al to-breke ȝou.

**c.** To break (a commandment, promise, etc.).

*a* **1067** *Charter of Eadweard* in Kemble *Cod. Dipl.* IV. 213 Ne ðat any man ðas mundbirdnesse tobreke. *a* **1175** *Cott. Hom.* 221 Gif þu þis litle bebod to-brecst. **1297** R. GLOUC. (Rolls) 9287 Asayli þen false king..þat þe grete oþ þat he suor so villiche [h]aþ to broke. **13..** *Guy Warw.* (A.) 572 Þine hest ichaue to-broke. **1393** LANGL. *P. Pl.* C. I. 69 Asoilie hem alle..of vowes to-broke.

**2.** *intr.* To break into pieces; to burst asunder; to be ruptured, shattered, or fractured.

*c* **1205** LAY. 1467 His hæfd-bon to-brec. *a* **1225** *Ancr. R.* 164 Vor gles ne to-brekeð nout bute sum þinc hit arine. *c* **1386** CHAUCER *Can. Yeom. Prol. & T.* 354 Ofte it happeth so The pot tobreketh, and farwel al is go. **14..** *Sir Beues* (M.) 1613 Me thinkyth, my hert wyll tobreke. *c* **1470** HENRY *Wallace* IV. 452 Wallace straik ane, with his gud sper of steill,..the shafft to brak ilk deyll. **1510–20** *Wedn. Faste* (W. de W.) xxv, He tumbled ouer a clyffe, his body all to brake.

**3.** *intr.* To break away from restraint. *rare*—[1].

*c* **1475** *Partenay* 5731 But non retourned, ne myght thens to-breke.

† **To-bre·de**, *v. Obs.* [OE. *tobrǽdan*, f. To-[2] + *brǽdan*, BREDE *v.*[2] So OHG., MHG. *zebreiten*, Ger. *zer-.*] **a.** *trans.* To spread abroad, extend, make broad. **b.** *intr.* To spread, extend itself; to be diffused.

*c* **888** K. ÆLFRED *Boeth.* vii. § 2 ȝif þu þines scipes seȝl onȝean þone wind tobrædest. *c* **1000** *Ags. Gosp.* Matt. xxiii. 5 Hiȝ to-brædaþ hyra heals-bec. *a* **1023** WULFSTAN *Hom.* x. (Napier) 68 Of ðyson eahta deofles cræftan ealle unþeawas up aspringað and syðþan tobrædað ealles to wide. *a* **1300** *E. E. Psalter* iv. 2 Ife þat drouyng in I ware, Þou tobreddest to me þare.

† **To-bre·nn**, *v. Obs.* Forms: see BURN *v.*[1] [ME., f. To-[2] + *brennen, beornen* to BURN. So late MHG. *zerbrinnen* intr.] **a.** *trans.* To burn up; to consume or destroy by burning. **b.** *intr.* To burn, to be 'burning hot': = BURN *v.*[1] 3.

*a* **1300** *E. E. Psalter* ii. 13 When in schorte his wreth tobrent has he; Þat in him traisted alle seli be. **13..** *Cursor M.* 22921 (Fairf.) If his bodi ware alle tobrint. **1382** WYCLIF *Ps.* xlv. 10 Armys and sheeldis he shal to-brenne with fyr. — *Jer.* xi. 16 To-brend ben alle his busshy places. *c* **1440** *Pallad. on Husb.* IV. 21 Ffor [= against] sonne and wynde hem make a tegument, Lest thai in this be shake, in that tobrent. *a* **1500** *Flower & Leaf* 358 The sonne so fervently Wex hoot, that..the ladies eek to-brent, That they [etc.].

† **To-bri·tten**, *v. Obs.* [ME. *tobritne-n*, f. To-[2] + *britnen* :—OE. *brytnian*, BRITTEN *v.*] *trans.* To cut in pieces.

*c* **1200** ORMIN 9468 Forrþi wass þeȝȝre kinedom Todæledd & tobrittnedd. *c* **1440** *Partonope* 596 Hys swerde..oute draweth he And alle to bryttenyth this wylde best. *a* **1400–50** *Alexander* 3905 Oure kniȝtis .. Alto-bretind þaim on bent & broȝt þaim on fliȝt.

**To-broken:** see TO-BREAK.

† **To-brui·se**, *v. Obs.* Forms: see BRUISE *v.* [OE. *to-brýsan*, f. To-[2] + *brýsan* to BRUISE.] *trans.* To crush to pieces, to smash; to bruise severely.

*c* **1000** *Ags. Gosp.* Matt. xxi. 44 Seþe fylþ uppan þysne stan he byð tobrysed [*c* **1160** to-brised]; & he to-bryső þone ðe he onuppan fylð. *c* **1200** ORMIN 12032 He munnde þær Tobrisenn all himm sellfenn. **1297** R. GLOUC. (Rolls) 6059 Hii..henede him wiþ stones..& tobrusede is smale bones. **1382** WYCLIF *Ecclus.* xxviii. 21 The wounde..of a tunge shal to-broosen boenes. *a* **1400–50** *Alexander* 1274 All bebled & to-brissid [*Dubl.* to-brysed]. *c* **1450** *Merlin* x. 157 He..hym threwe to the erthe so rudely, that he hym all to brosed. **1516** *Life St. Birgette* in *Myrr. our Ladye* p. lviii, There theyr Shyppe was all to Broysyd. **1609** HOLLAND *Amm. Marcell.* XXXI. 418 All to brused and broken.

† **To-bry·t, -bri·t**, *v. Obs. rare.* [OE. *tobrýtan*, f. To-[2] + *brýtan* to break: cf. BRIT *v.*] *trans.* To break in pieces.

*c* **1000** ÆLFRIC *Hom.* I. 568 Forðan ðe hi næron godas, ac..treowene and stænene, and he hi forði tobrytte. *c* **1205** LAY. 1602 Corineus heom to-brutte [*c* **1275** to-brut] ban & heora ribbes.

† **To-bu·ne**, *v. Obs. rare.* Also 4 **to-bone.** [ME., f. To-[2] + **bun-en* (perh. related to ME. *bunsen* BOUNCE *v.*).] *trans.* To beat severely, thrash, thump; to pelt.

*a* **1250** *Owl & Night.* 1166 (Cott. MS.) Heruore hit is þat me þe shuneþ An þe totorueþ & tobuneþ Mid staue & stoone & turf & clute. *c* **1315** SHOREHAM ii. 85 For so tobete and so to-boned, Hyȝt was wel reweleche and drery.

† **To-bu·rst**, *v. Obs.* exc. *dial.* Forms: see BURST *v.* [OE. *toberstan*, f. To-[2] + *berstan* to BURST. So OS. *te-brestan*, OHG. *zibrestan*, MHG. *ze-, zerbresten*, Ger. *zerbersten.*]

**1.** *intr.* To burst asunder, to be shattered.

*c* 893 K. ÆLFRED *Oros.* v. x. § 1 Sco eorþe tobærst. *c* 1000 ÆLFRIC *Hom.* I. 86 He eal innan samod forswæled wæs, and toborsten. *c* 1200 ORMIN 16147 Himm þinkeþþ þatt hiss herrte shall Tobresstenn. *c* 1205 LAY. 1921 Al þe feond tobarst. *a* 1225 *Ancr. R.* 214 Te ueond lauhweð þet he tobersteð. *c* 1375 *Sc. Leg. Saints* xli. (*Agnes*) 60 His hart þane cane to-brist for bale. 14.. *Pol. Rel. & L. Poems* (1866) 246 Al to-broste synwe & veyne. 1513 DOUGLAS *Æneis* x. vi. 37 To bristis scho, and rivis all in sondyr. 1535 COVERDALE 2 *Chron.* xxv. 12 They all to barst in sunder. 1881 MISS JACKSON *Shropsh. Word-bk.* s.v., If it freezes we sha'n 'ave it to-bost like the tother.

**2.** *trans.* To cause to burst asunder, to break or dash to pieces, to shatter.

*c* 1000 ÆLFRIC *Hom.* II. 258 Þæs temples wah-ryft eac wearð toborsten. *c* 1205 LAY. 27520 Þer iwurðen to-bursten eorles swiðe balden. *c* 1275 *Ibid.* 5926 Hii to-borste þe lokes. *a* 1300 *Cursor M.* 6615 (Cott.) Þis golden calf he did to brest to pudre [*Tr.* to peces]. *c* 1374 CHAUCER *Troylus* IV. 1518 (1546) Attropos my thred of lif to-breste, If I be fals! 1470–85 MALORY *Arthur* VIII. xxx. 318 They..alle to braste their speres. *c* 1530 REDFORD *Mor. Play Wit & Sc.* (Shaks. Soc.) 71 The fall wherof downe in the rest My joyntes and sinewes all to-brast!

**Toby** (tōu·bi), *sb.*[1] [The familiar form of the Christian name Tobias, employed in various unconnected senses. (But some of the senses here grouped may have a different origin.)]

**1.** The posteriors, the buttocks: esp. in phrase *to tickle one's toby. slang.*

1681 [see TICKLE *v.* 6 b]. 1842 BARHAM *Ingol. Leg.* Ser. II. *Sir Rupert, Lay Naiads,* Throw us out John Doe and Richard Roe, And sweetly we'll tickle their tobies.

**2.** (With capital T.) A jug or mug (formerly common) in the form of a stout old man wearing a long and full-skirted coat and a three-cornered hat (18th c. costume). Also called *Toby Fill-pot, Toss-pot.* Also *attrib.* as *Toby* (*Fill-pot*) *jug.*

1840 DICKENS *Barn. Rudge* iv, 'Put Toby this way, my dear'. This Toby was the brown jug of which previous mention has been made. *Ibid.* lxxx, When he had dined, comforted himself with a pipe, an extra Toby, a nap. 1852 SEWELL *Exper. Life* xix. (1858) 131 The great earthenware cup, the figure of a stout little man, which usually went by the name of Toby. 1857 HUGHES *Tom Brown* I. i, Pouring out his old ale from a Toby Philpot jug. 1901 *Pall Mall G.* 31 Aug. 3 (Cass. Supp.) The brown Toby jug was filled for him. 1908 *Daily Chron.* 3 Nov. 5/6 The Tobies are relics of the old coaching days.

**3.** The name of the trained dog introduced (in the first half of the 19th c.) into the Punch and Judy show, which wears a frill round its neck: hence *Toby collar, frill,* a turn-down pleated or goffered collar worn by women and children.

1840 DICKENS *Old C. Shop* xviii, Producing a little terrier ..'He was once a Toby of yours, wasn't he?' 1885 *Pall Mall G.* 30 Apr. 6/1 A trailing dress with the Toby frill so favoured by these..reformers. 1909 *19th Century* Mar. 446 A young gentleman in so-called skeleton trousers and a Toby frill. 1909 *Daily Chron.* 30 Aug. 7/5 A turn-down Toby collar of frilled lawn.

**4.** A colour-printing machine for textiles.

1876 *Encycl. Brit.* IV. 684/2 By means of a modern invention several colours may be applied at once on the cloth by means of one block. The machine used for this purpose, which is called a 'toby', consists of [etc.].

**5.** An inferior kind of cigar. *U.S. slang.*

1896 *Columbus* (Ohio) *Dispatch* 18 July 15/3 A large supply of..tobies. 1903 *Westm. Gaz.* 23 May 10/1 The railway ticket office clerk twists and swigs at a 'toby' as he asks you 'Where for, sir?'

**Toby** (tōu·bi), *sb.*[2] *Thieves' slang.* [app. altered (? through *toba', toba*) from *tobar,* the word for 'road' in Shelta, the cant or secret language of the Irish tinkers: see Note below.] *The toby*: the highway as the resort of robbers; 'the road'; also *transf.* highway robbery (called also *the toby concern, toby lay*); hence *to ply* or *ride the toby,* to practise highway robbery; *the high* (or *main*) *toby,* highway robbery by a mounted thief; also, the highway itself; *the low toby,* robbery by footpads.

1811 *Lex. Balatr., Toby Lay,* the highway. 1812 J. H. VAUX *Flash Dict.* s.v., The toby applies exclusively to robbing on horseback; the practice of footpad robbery being properly called the *spice,* though it is common to distinguish the former by the title of *high-toby,* and the latter of *low-toby.* 1824 SCOTT *St. Ronan's* xxxi, Armed, as if he meant to bing folks on the low toby. 1904 *Athenæum* 4 May 648/1 Travellers..looked askance at its long, empty reaches, haunted maybe by gentlemen of the high toby. [1890 J. SAMPSON in *Jrnl. Gypsy Lore Soc.* II. 217 *Tober* or *Toby.* This old word has found acceptance in every branch of cant...*Toba,* ground, is given as strolling-players' cant in the 'Sporting Chronicle'. Borrow in his 'Lavo-Lil' calls Tobbar 'a Rapparee word'.]

Hence **Toby** *v., trans.* to rob on the highway; **To·byman,** a highwayman.

So *toby-gill, high toby gloak, high toby spice* (also *high spice toby*): see quots.

1811 *Lex. Balatr.* s.v. *Toby, High toby man,* a highwayman. *Low toby man,* a footpad. *c* 1812 in Byron *Juan* XI. xix. *note,* On the high toby-spice flash the muzzle, In spite of each gallows old scout. 1812 J. H. VAUX *Flash Dict.* s. v., To *toby* a man, is to rob him on the highway, a person convicted of this offence, is said to be *done* for a *toby. Ibid., Toby-gill* or *Toby-man,* properly signifies a highwayman. *Ibid., High-toby-gloak,* a highwayman. 1834 H. AINSWORTH *Rookwood* III. v, Jack Hall, a celebrated tobyman. 1876 HINDLEY *Adv. Cheap Jack* 4 Halting..during the heat on the 'high spice toby', as we used to call the main road. 1881 *Daily News* 22 Dec. 1/3 When the footpad and 'high-tobymen' of ancient turnpike roads are replaced by male and female brigands armed with pistol and chloroform. 1902 *Illustr. Lond. News* 20 Dec. 951/3, I am a-looking anxiously for a tobyman that has wickedly robbed a lady.

[*Note.* For Shelta see J. Sampson in *Jrnl. Gypsy Lore Soc.* 1890, II. 217, also Kuno Meyer, *ibid.* 257. The latter holds Shelta or 'Sheldhru' to be 'a deliberate and systematic modification' of Irish Gaelic, of considerable antiquity, the words being altered by reversal, metathesis, substitution and addition of letters or elements. Hence *tobar* has been viewed as formed by metathesis from Irish *bothar* 'road'; though, if so, it must either have been formed from the *written* word, or be very ancient, since medial *th* has long been mute.]

**Toc,** obs. f. *took,* pa. t. of TAKE *v.*

† **To-ca·rve, to-kerve,** *v. Obs.* [OE. *toceorfan* (ME. *tokerve*), f. TO-[2] + *ceorfan* to CARVE.] *trans.* To cut to pieces, cut up; to cut off.

*c* 950 *Lindisf. Gosp.* Mark xiv. 47 Sum monn..ofslog esne hehsacerdas & tocearf [*Ags. Gosp.* of acearf] him ða earelippica. *c* 1000 ÆLFRIC *Minster Hom.* in *Leg. Rood* (1871) 105 (Cott. MS.) Þeah þe se beam beo to-coruen. 13.. *Guy Warw.* (A.) 3612 Þer nas no man þat þer neye come, Þat he ne was to-corwen anon. 13.. *E. E. Allit. P.* B. 1700, & cowþe vche kyndam to-kerue & keuer. *c* 1500 *Lancelot* 868 His suerd atwo the helmys al to-kerwith.

‖ **Toccata** (tokkā·tă). *Music.* [It. *toccata,* '*toccáta d'vn musico,* a preludium that cunning musitions vse to play as it were voluntary before any set lesson' (Florio 1611); lit. 'a touching', f. *toccare* to touch.] A composition for a keyboard instrument, intended to exhibit the touch and technique of the performer, and having the air of an improvisation; in later times loosely applied.

1724 *Short Explic. For. Wds. in Mus. Bks., Toccata,* or *Toccato,* is of much the same Signification as the Word *Ricercata.* 1753 CHAMBERS *Cycl. Supp.* s. v., But what distinguishes the *Toccata* from other kinds of symphonies, is, first, its being usually played on instruments that have keys, as organs, spinnets, &c. Secondly, that it is commonly composed to exercise both hands. 1855 BROWNING *A Toccata of Galuppi's* 18 While you sat and played Toccatas, stately at the clavichord. 1875 STAINER & BARRETT *Dict. Mus. Terms* (1898), *Toccata,* (1) a prelude or overture...(2) Compositions written as exercises. (3) A fantasia. (4) A suite.

*fig.* 1903 *Trawl* May 22 A sigh of wind; and through the cool air sprang Toccatas of sharp patterings.

**Toche,** rare obs. form of TOUCH *sb.* and *v.*

**Tocher** (tǫ·χər), *sb. Sc.* and *north. dial.* Forms: 5–6 toquhir, -yr, 6 toquher, -eir, touchquhare, touchar, -er, towcher, (towher), tochar, 6–7 tochir, 7 tochare, tougher, 7–9 *dial.* towgher (9 togher), 6– tocher. [a. Irish and OGael. *tochar* (mod. Gael. *tochradh*) assigned portion, dowry, in OIr. assignment, f. *tochuirim* I put to, I assign, f. *cuirim* I put.] The marriage portion which a wife brings to her husband; dowry, *dot.*

1496 *Acc. Ld. High Treas. Scot.* I. 307 Giffen to Robert Lile, in his toquhyr of the Mertymes terme bipast j[c] markis. 1536 BELLENDEN *Cron. Scot.* (1821) II. 194 And [Rolland] in the name of Touchquhare, sall have all thay landis. 1546 *Reg. Privy Council Scot.* I. 43 The said Lord Governour sall gif in tocher with his said dochter to the said Eirle and his airis the soume of twa thousand, thre hundreith, and threttie thre pundis vis viii d. 1568 *Durham Depos.* (Surtees) 86 The parties went..to hir frends, to demand towher. 1569 *Wills & Inv. N. C.* (Surtees) II. 314 *note,* He shall haue 100*l*..as towcher and mariadge money, whiche I gaue him with my dowghter Anne. *c* 1614 SIR W. MURE *Dido & Æneas* II. 192 Now Dido may be tyed to Trojane mate, And thow receave, in tougher, Carthage great. 1674 RAY *N. C. Words* 50 A *Towgher,* a Dower or Dowry. *Dial. Cumb.* 1692 *Sc. Presbyter. Eloquence* (1738) 149 Ye ken well enough..that Lads do not marry Lasses now, except they have a Tocher. 1796 BURNS *Hey for a Lass* i, Then hey, for a lass wi' a tocher; the nice yellow guineas for me. 1894 CROCKETT *Raiders* 22 He married a lass from the hills who brought him no tocher, but..a strong dower of sense and good health.

**b.** *attrib.* and *Comb.,* as *tocher-fee, -gear*; **tocher-band,** a marriage settlement; **tocher-good,** property given as tocher or dower.

1792 BURNS *Gallant Weaver* iii, My daddie sign'd my *tocher-band, To gie the lad that has the land. 17.. in Kinloch *Anc. Sc. Ballads* (1827) 85 'A clerk! a clerk!' the king cried, 'To sign her *tocher-fee'. 18.. *Cath. Jaffery* iv. in Child *Ballads* VII. (1890) 225/1 For *tocher-gear he did not stand. 1538 *Aberdeen Regr.* (1844) I. 158 To pay me the soume of thretty poundis..and that in *tochir gud for the mareage. 1609 SKENE *Reg. Maj.* I. 25 The mariage being dissolved, the tocher-gude returnes and perteins to the wyfe. 1822 SCOTT *Pirate* v, Though I fall heir to her tocher-good, I am sorry for it.

**Tocher** (tǫ·χər), *v. Sc.* and *n. dial.* [f. prec.] *trans.* To furnish with a tocher; to dower.

*a* 1578 LINDESAY (Pitscottie) *Chron. Scot.* (S.T.S.) I. 125 He..tocharit hir with the Lordschipe of Ballvenie. 1781 BURNS *Tarbolton Lasses* ii, Well he can spare't, Braid Money to tocher them a', man. 1829 HOGG *Sheph. Cal.* I. x. 304 It wad tocher a' our bonny lasses. 1878 *Cumberld. Gloss.* s.v. *Tokker, Togher,* 'He tokker't his dowter wi' twenty pund'.

Hence **Tochered** (tǫ·χəɹd) *ppl. a.* (qualified by adverbs, as *well-tochered*).

1728 RAMSAY *Give me a Lass with a Lump of Land* iii, Well tocher'd lasses or joynter'd widows. 1816 SCOTT *Antiq.* xii, Ye are a bonny young leddy, and a gude ane, and maybe a weel-tochered ane. 1881 *Blackw. Mag.* Apr. 524 The fairly tochered spinster.

**To·cherless,** *a. Sc.* [See -LESS.] Having no tocher or portion, portionless.

1790 SHIRREFS *Poems* 76 Wha bids the maist, is sure to win the prize, While she that's tocherless, neglected dies. 1820 SCOTT *Monast.* iv, I wasna sae tocherless but what I had a bit land at my breast-lace.

† **To-chew·,** *v. Obs.* [OE. *tocéowan,* f. TO-[2] + *céowan* to CHEW. So MHG. *zerkiuwen.*] *trans.* To chew to pieces; to tear with the teeth.

*c* 1000 ÆLFRIC *Hom.* II. 270 Þæt husel is..betwux toðum tocowen. *a* 1225 *Ancr. R.* 202 Þes laste bore hweolp..to-cheoweð & to-uret Godes milde milce. *a* 1240 *Sawles Warde* in *Cott. Hom.* 251 Oðer hwile [devils] torendeð ham & to cheoweð ham euch greot.

† **To-chine,** *v. Obs.* [OE. *tocínan,* f. TO-[2] + *cínan,* CHINE *v.*[1]] *intr.* To split asunder or open; to be burst or cloven.

*c* 725 *Corpus Gloss.* (O.E.T.) 653 *Dehiscat,* tocinit. *c* 1000 *Sax. Leechd.* III. 18 ʒif hit ne tocine, tosleah hwon. *c* 1175 *Lamb. Hom.* 141 Þe stan to-chan. *c* 1200 *Trin. Coll. Hom.* 199 Þe nedre..drinkeð þat hie to-chineð. *a* 1250 *Owl & Night.* 1565 Wel neh min heorte wule to chine. *c* 1380 *Sir Ferumb.* 3001 Þe schild to-chon.

**Tock,** obs. f. TOQUE; obs. pa. t. of TAKE *v.*

**Tockay,** var. TOKAY. **Tocken, -in,** obs. Sc. ff. TOKEN. **Tocksaine,** obs. f. TOCSIN.

† **To-cla·tter,** *v. Obs.* [ME. *toclater,* f. TO-[2] + CLATTER *v.*] *trans.* To knock to pieces with a noise; to shatter.

*c* 1350 *Will. Palerne* 2858 Þe komli kerneles were to-clatered wiþ engines. *c* 1380 *Sir Ferumb.* 897 Ys scheld.. Sone þay had hit al to-clatrid; þe peeces leye on þe grounde. *c* 1440 *Partonope* 1078 Alle to clateryd and broken. *a* 1450 *Tourn. Tottenham* 160 in Hazl. *E. P. P.* III. 89 Ther were scheldis al to claterde, Bolles and disshis al to baterde.

† **To-cleave,** *v. Obs.* Forms: see CLEAVE *v.*[1] [OE. *tocléofan,* f. TO-[2] + *cléofan,* CLEAVE *v.*[1] So OS. *tekliođan,* OHG. *zi-, zeklioban.*]

**1.** *trans.* To cleave asunder; to split open; to divide or separate into two parts.

*c* 888 K. ÆLFRED *Boeth.* xxxiv. § 11 ʒif þu þonne ænne stan toclifst, ne wyrð he næfre ʒegadrod swa he ær wæs. *c* 1000 ÆLFRIC *Saints' Lives* xxv. 55 Þa nytenu sind clæne þe to-cleofað heora clawa. *c* 1200 ORMIN 14798 Drihhtin þær toclæf þe sæ. *a* 1375 *Joseph Arim.* 516 Þer weoren.. harde scheldes to-clouen. 1377 LANGL. *P. Pl.* B. XII. 141 For þe heihe holigoste heuene shal to-cleue.

**2.** *intr.* To split or fall asunder.

*c* 1205 LAY. 1920 Corineus..hine fusde mid mæine..Þat his ban to-cluuen. 1377 LANGL. *P. Pl.* B. XVIII. 246 (MS. B.) The erthe..Quaked..and al to-clief þe roche. 1390 GOWER *Conf.* III. 296 The Schip toclef upon a roche. *c* 1430 *Hymns Virg.* 41 His herte to-cloue, and he for-bleed. 1571 GOLDING *Calvin on Ps.* xlvi. 3 The mountaines to clive from their rotes.

‖ **Toco**[1] (tōu·kǒ). *Ornith.* [Native name in Guiana; also in F. *le toco* (Buffon *Ois.* VII. 185).] The typical species of TOUCAN, *Rhamphastos toco,* a native of Guiana.

1781 LATHAM *Synopsis* I. 325 The Toco. The length of this bird is nine or ten inches from the head to the end of the tail...Inhabits Cayenne. *Ibid.* 323 Genus VI. *Toucan.* No. 1. The Toco. 1902 P. FOUNTAIN *Gt. Mts. & Forests S. Amer.* vi. 159 The native name of these birds is *toco.*

**Toco**[2] (tōu·ko). *slang.* Also toko.

[Has been suggested to be a humorous adaptation of Gr. τόκος in sense 'interest', in Public School slang.]

Chastisement, corporal punishment.

1823 BEE *Dict. Turf* s.v., If..Blackee gets a whip (*toco*) about his back, why 'he has caught toco'. 1857 HUGHES *Tom Brown* I. v, The School leaders come up furious and administer toco to the wretched fags nearest at hand. 1903 J. COLEMAN *C. Reade* II. ii. (1904) 274 They both caught 'Toko' when they went back.

**Toco-** (tǫko), combining form of Gr. τόκο-ς offspring, used as a verbal element in some terms (chiefly biological and obstetrical); as **To·codynamo·meter,** an instrument for measuring uterine contractions during parturition (Webster, 1911); **Tocogene·tic** *a.*: see quot.; **Tocogony** (-ǫ·gǒni), propagation by parents as distinct from spontaneous generation; **Tocolo·gical** *a.,* of or pertaining to tocology; **Toco·logist,** one versed in tocology; an obstetrician; **Toco·logy,** the science of parturition, or of midwifery; obstetrics; **Tocoma·nia,** puerperal mania (*Cent. Dict. Supp.,* 1909).

1903 L. F. WARD *Pure Sociol.* II. v. 96 The genetic succession of cosmic products..is not only genetic but *tocogenetic. The higher terms are generated by the lower through creative synthesis, and are thus affiliated upon them. 1876 E. R. LANKESTER *Haeckel's Hist. Creat.* I. 183 At present we must occupy ourselves with Propagation, or *Tocogony. 1902 *Amer. Anthropologist* Oct.-Dec. 739 This element in the story is not without its *tocological significance. *Ibid.,* This feature in the tale must be suggestive to the *tocologist. 1828 M. RYAN in *Lancet* 28 June 400/1 From much consideration on these deficiencies, I would propose the following nomenclature...Τοκολογια, *Tocology, on parturition. 1890 BILLINGS *Nat. Med. Dict.,* Tocology, ..Tokology. 1895 ALICE B. STOCKHAM (*title*) Tokology: A Book for Every Woman.

† **To·come,** *sb. Obs.* [OE. *tócyme,* f. To *adv.* + COME *sb.*[1], rendering L. *adventus*: cf. OHG. *zōquumi, zōquemi,* 'conventus'.]

**1.** Arrival, advent, coming.

*c* 897 K. ÆLFRED *Gregory's Past. C.* xxxii. 212 For ðæm tocyme Dryhtnes Hælendan Cristes. 971 *Blickl. Hom.* 35 Foran to þon tocyme þæs eʒeslican domes dæʒes. *c* 1000

ÆLFRIC *Hom.* I. 404 Storc and swalewe heoldon ðone timan heora to-cymes. *a* **1175** *Cott. Hom.* 227 Christes to-cyme to þis life. *c* **1175** *Lamb. Hom.* 93 Þurh þes halie gastes to-cume. *Ibid.* 153 For to bodien his tokume. *c* **1325** *Metr. Hom.* 8 Cristes to com mad endinge Of al our soru. *c* **1330** R. BRUNNE *Chron. Wace* (Rolls) 5576 (Petyt MS.) Mirth þei mad at þer tocome. *a* **1340** HAMPOLE *Psalter* cxxiv. 4 He prayes þat he wate is to cum. **1513** DOUGLAS *Æneis* XI. xii. 22 The contyr or first tocome.. Full ardent wolx.

**2.** Means of access. *Sc. rare.*

**1513** DOUGLAS *Æneis* IX. ii. 59 Gyf ony entre or tocom espy He myght, fortill assaill the cite by.

†**To·-come,** *v. Obs.* [f. To *prep.* or *adv.* + COME *v.* Cf. OHG. *zuoqueman*, Ger. *zukommen.*]

**1.** *intr.* To happen, befall; cf. COME *v.* 9.

*c* **1200** *Vices & Virtues* 63 Alle unȝelimpes ðe him for his sennes to-cumeð. **1297** R. GLOUC. (Rolls) 7566 As is wille to com, þe eldore soster of þe tuo, in spoushod he nom. *c* **1300** *Beket* 1088 For him was to cominge sorwe ynouȝ.

**2.** *intr.* To approach, arrive, come *to.*

**1393** LANGL. *P. Pl.* C. XXII. 343 These to-comen to conscience. **1455** *Charter* in *Liber Eccl. de Scon* 185 To all þaim to quhais knawlagis þir present lettres sal to-cum.

**b.** *trans.* To come to.

**1596** DALRYMPLE tr. *Leslie's Hist. Scot.* IV. (S.T.S.) I. 206 He.. wastes, burnes, and slayes al that he tocumis.

Hence †**To·-coming** *vbl. sb.*, coming, advent.

*a* **1300** *Cursor M.* 13676 Mi to-cumming In erth es jugement to bring. **1513** DOUGLAS *Æneis* X. viii. 44 On siclyke wys was Turnus tocummyng. *a* **1578** LINDESAY (Pitscottie) *Chron. Scot.* (S.T.S.) I. 75 [They] maid sa great slaughter at the first tocoming.

**To come, to-come,** *inf.* used as *sb.* That which is to come, the future: see COME *v.* 32 c.

So †**To-coming** *a.*, future: see COME *v.* 32 c *β*; also as *sb.* the future.

**1556** *Aurelio & Isab.* (1608) Pj, Therefore, for the toecomminge I shall have boldnesse to liffe joyfulley.

**Tocornalite** (tǫkǭ·ɹnăləit). *Min.* [f. personal name Tocornal (see quot. 1896) + -ITE[1].] An iodide of silver and mercury occurring in pale-yellow granular masses, in Chili.

**1880** DANA *Min.* App. II, *Tocornalite*.. Amorphous, structure granular. Color a pale-yellow, by the action of the air it grows darker... Soft, easily reduced to a powder... From the mines of Chañarcillo, Chili. **1896** CHESTER *Dict. Names Min.*, *Tocornalite*,.. in honor of A. Tocornal.

**Tocque,** obs. form of TOQUE.

†**To-crush,** *v. Obs.* [ME. f. To-[2] + CRUSH *v.*] **a.** *trans.* To crush to pieces. **b.** *intr.* To be crushed, to break to pieces under pressure.

*c* **1300** *Havelok* 1992 Was non þat hauede þe hern-panne So hard, þat he ne dede alto-cruhsse, And alto-shiuere, and alto-frusshe. *c* **1380** *Sir Ferumb.* 5153 Þe walles to-breke, & al to-crusschede. **1542** UDALL *Erasm. Apoph.* 111 b, I will at one stroke all to crushe thy hedde to powther.

**Tocsin** (tǫ·ksin). Forms: 6 tocksaine, 7 tocquesain, toxin, 8 toczin, 8– tocsin. [a. F. *tocsin*, in OF. *toquassen* (1372 in Godef. *Compl.*), *toquesin, -sain, -saint* (16th c.), etc.; ad. Prov. *tocasenh*, f. *toca-r* (F. *touche-r*) to TOUCH, strike + *senh* 'signe, marque, appel de la cloche, cloche' :—L. *signum* sign, in later Latin also a bell; 'campana, nola, Italis *Segno*' (Du Cange).]

**1.** A signal, esp. an alarm-signal, sounded by ringing a bell or bells: used orig. and esp. in reference to France.

**1586** FULKE *Answ. to P. Frarine* 52 The priests then went vp into the steeple, and rang the bells backward, which they call Tocksaine, whereupon the people of the suburbs flocked together. **1603** DEKKER *Wonderfull Yeare* Wks. (Grosart) I. 110 The Allarum is strucke vp, the Toxin ringes out for life. **1670** COTTON *Espernon* I. II. 89 At the same time that the Assault began, the Tocquesain rung throughout all the Churches in the City. **1795** HEL. M. WILLIAMS *Lett. France* II. 13 The signal for ringing that fatal tocsin, which was the knell of liberty. **1837** CARLYLE *Fr. Rev.* I. v. v, The tocsin.. is pealing madly from all steeples. **1861** STANLEY *East. Ch.* xii. (1869) 409 They rang a tocsin with the great bell of the ancient Novgorod.

**b.** *fig.*

**1794** J. STEWART (*title*) The Tocsin of Britannia. **1802** — (*title*) The Tocsin of Social Life. **1803** FESSENDEN *Terrible Tractoration* IV. ii, Sound Discord's jarring tocsin louder. **1832** A. CLARKE in *Life* xv. (1840) 572 He thought the seizure in my foot would turn to an attack of gout. This was a tocsin to me. **1877** MRS. OLIPHANT *Makers Flor.* Introd. 12 The tocsins of immemorial strife were sounding all about.

**2.** *transf.* A bell used to sound an alarm.

**1842** LONGF. *Belfry of Bruges* xvii, The wild alarum sounded from the tocsin's throat. **1868** MILMAN *St. Paul's* iii. 63 The great bell of St. Paul's was the tocsin which summoned the citizens to arms. **1890** LECKY *Eng. in 18th C.* VIII. xxix. 60 Tocsins or alarm bells were set up in various parts of the town.

**3.** *attrib.*, as *tocsin bell, note, sound.*

**1822** BYRON *Juan* VI. lxxxiv, When all around rang like a tocsin bell. **1878** H. PHILLIPS tr. *Poems fr. Spanish & Germ.* 19 And Baeza's tocsin note Bellows forth from brazen throat. **1900** UPWARD *Eben. Lobb* 178 What meaning has the tocsin sound of liberty for ears like yours?

†**To-cu·t,** *v. Obs.* Forms: see CUT *v.* [f. To-[2] + CUT *v.*] *trans.* To cut to pieces, to hew asunder; to cut greatly.

**1382** WYCLIF 1 *Chron.* xx. 3 Thei weren al to-kut and tobrosed alle. **1482** CAXTON *Trevisa's Higden* III. xxxiv. 161 Lete slee somme of the oxen,.. and to kytte [TREVISA kutte] reynes of the skynnes to teye with other oxen. *c* **1489** — *Blanchardyn* xxxviii. 141 The Cassydonyens.. were slayne and all to-cutte and clouen. **1578** LYTE *Dodoens* II. xcvi. 277 His leaues be ashe colour, and all to cut. **1609** HOLLAND *Amm. Marcell.* xxv. iii. 264 Out went our light armed companies,.. and all to cut and hacked them.

**Tod** (tǫd), *sb.*[1] *Sc.* and *north. dial.* Also 5 tode, 6 todd(e, toad, 7 todd. [A northern word of unknown origin; 'app. not from Norse' (Biörkman).

The suggestion that this word may be identical or connected with TOD *sb.*[2], and have reference to the bushy or tufted tail of the fox, is at variance with chronology and local distribution. TOD *sb.*[2] is essentially southern, while *tod* = fox is exclusively Scotch and Northumbrian, and was in use 400 years before *tod* = ivy-bush appears.]

**1.** A fox. Now only *dial.*

*c* **1170** REGINALD DUNELM. *Libellus* (Surtees) xv. 25 Pro caseo quem furto sustulit Tod agnomen accepit. *Ibid.* 28 Nam anglicæ linguæ.. tota illius familia stirpis, Tod, quod vulpeculam sonat, cognominantur eloquio. **1508** KENNEDIE *Flyting w. Dunbar* 288 Todis, wolffis and beistis wyle. **1535** LYNDESAY *Satyre* 3574 Birdis hes thair nestis and todis hes their den. **1536** BELLENDEN *Cron. Scot.* (1821) I. p. xli, Toddis will eat na flesche that gustis of thair awin kind. **1588** KING tr. *Canisius' Catech.* 113 Eschewed as theewes, murtherars, tods, dogs, and wolues. **1637** B. JONSON *Sad Sheph.* I. iv, Or strew Tods haires, or with their tailes doe sweepe The dewy grasse, to d' off the simpler sheep. **1721** RAMSAY *Richy & Sandy* 49 Had the tod Worry'd my lambs. **1825** SCOTT *Betrothed* Introd., I have a grew-bitch at hame will worry the best tod in Pomoragrains. **1871** E. PEACOCK *Ralf Skirl.* II. 150 I'll trap every tod that comes our way, and all t'other farmers..'ll do th' same.

**b.** in proverbial and allusive expressions; cf. Fox *sb.* 1 b, c. (See also 2.)

*c* **1560** A. SCOTT *Poems* (E.E.T.S.) xxv. 29 Be scho wylie as ane tod, Quhen scho winkis I sall nod. **1583** J. MELVILL *Diary* (1842) 137 Bischope Adamsone keipit his castle, lyk a tod in his holl, seik of a disease of grait fetiditie. **1706** *Let. fr. Country Farmer* 2 (Jam.) This will be very odd, for.. Scotsmen to play their own Country sic a Tod's turn. **1820** SCOTT *Monast.* iv, Fear ye naething frae Christie; tods keep their ain holes clean.

**2.** *fig.* A person likened to a fox; a crafty person. *Tod's birds, tod's bairns*, an evil brood, children or persons of a bad stock.

**1500–20** DUNBAR *Poems* xiii. 37 Sum in ane lamb skin is ane tod. **1581** J. HAMILTON in *Cath. Tractates* (S. T. S.) 74 The vnthankfull dealing of sik tydie [= wily] toddis. **1589** R. BRUCE *Serm.*, 2 *Tim. ii. 22* (1591) Y viij, [The affections] wald ever be handled as Tods birds; for they ar aye the war of ouer great libertie. **1639** BAILLIE *Lett.* (1841) I. 196 To hold the islanders and these tod's-birds of Lochaber in some awe. **1721** KELLY *Scot. Prov.* 329 The Tod's Bairns are ill to tame. **1789** BURNS *Kirk's Alarm* viii, Daddy Auld, Daddy Auld, there's a tod in the fauld, A tod meikle waur than the Clerk. **1886** STEVENSON *Kidnapped* vi, Take care of the old tod; he means mischief.

**b.** *transf.* In the game of *tod and lambs* (in draughts), the piece representing the fox.

**1812** W. TENNANT *Anster F.* II. lxx, Some force, t' inclose the Tod, the wooden Lamb on; Some shake the pelting dice upon the broad backgammon.

†**3.** *ellipt.* Fox-skin. *Obs.*

[**14..** tr. *Assisa David Reg. Scott.* in *Acts Parl. Scot.* I. 667 Of a tymmyr of skynnis of toddis [*12th c. orig.* De tymbria wlpium].] **1503** *Kalender Sheph.* Hvb, Gownys ..furryt wyth toddys for yt ys the most heyt furryng that they may wse. **1506** *Acc. Ld. High Treas. Scot.* III. 249 Item, for bordouring of it [goun to the King] with toddis,.. xxiijs. **1564** *Reg. Privy Council Scot.* I. 308 Ane gown, lynit with toddis of blak, begareit with velvot.

**4.** *attrib.* and *Comb.*, as *tod-hunt, -hunter*, † *-pult* (*-powt*) (sense uncertain), *-skin*; **tod-hole,** a fox's hole or den; *fig.* a secret hiding-place; **tod-lowrie** (also *Laurie Tod*), a familiar name for the fox; cf. *Reynard*; †**tod-stripe,** a strip of woodland in which foxes have their holes; **tod-tails** (also **tods'-tails**), name for the club-moss, *Lycopodium clavatum*; **tod-tike** (-tyke), **-touzing, -track**: see quot. 1824.

*c* **1170** *Newminster Cartul.* (Surtees) 62 Usque ad *Todholes. **1844** W. CROSS *Disruption* vi, We maun.. try to find some tod-hole whaur the Doctor can ne'er get his clauts owre me. **1904** A. THOMSON *Remin.* II. v. 154 To go and have a *tod hunt in the Highlands. **1882** *Standard* 10 Feb. 5/3 The '*Tod-hunter', who last century was kept in the Western Isles for the purpose of exterminating the foxes. **1822** GALT *Sir A. Wylie* II. xv. 144 His *tod-like inclination to other folks' cocks and hens. *c* **1470** HENRYSON *Mor. Fab.* v. (*Parl. Beasts*) xxii, The *tod lowrie luik not to the lam. **1725** RAMSAY *Gentle Sheph.* IV. i, As fast as flaes skip to the tate o woo Whilk slee tod-lowrie hauds without his mow. **1511** *Acc. Ld. High Treas. Scot.* IV. 198 Item, to Lance Ferry for ane lyning of *tod pultis to the samyn gowne.. xviij *li.* **1522** *Ibid.* V. 194 Item, for ane lynying of tod powtis to the Kingis nichtgoun.. viij *l.* v *s.* **1424** *Sc. Acts Jas. I* (1814) II. 6/1 Of ilke x of otter skynnis and *tode skynnis, vj d. *c* **1440** *Regr. Aberdon.* (Maitl. Cl.) I. 250 Robert Innes.. takis.. part fra þe *tode stripe to Edinglasse. **1820** *Blackw. Mag.* June 278/1 That singular and beautiful creeping ornament of the moorlands, called by the peasantry *tod tails. **1824** MACTAGGART *Gallovid. Encycl.*, **Tod-tykes*, dogs half foxes, half common dogs... *Tod-tracks*, the traces of the fox's feet in snow... *Tod-touzing*, the Scottish method of hunting the fox, by shooting, bustling, guarding, halloaing, &c.

**Tod** (tǫd), *sb.*[2] [Known in sense 1 from 15th c.; app. the same word as mod. EFris. (= LG. dial.) *todde* 'bundle, pack, small load (of hay, straw, turf, etc.)': see Doornkaat-Koolman; also in dial. (Groningen, Guelderland, Overyssel) *tod* load. With this cf. Sw. dial. *todd* 'a conglomerated mass, esp. of wool' (Biörkman). Answering in form also (though not very satisfactory in sense) is MHG., Ger. *zotte* 'tuft of hair, matted or shaggy hair', also 'rag', mod.Du. *tod, todde* 'rag'. (The ON. *toddi* does not mean 'tod of wool' as erroneously stated in Vigf., but only 'bit, piece'.

An original sense of 'conglomerated mass', passing on the one hand into 'load', and on the other into 'bushy mass, bush', would perhaps suit the various senses. Sense 1 may have come to England in connexion with the wool trade with the continent; sense 2, on the other hand, which is a century later, seems to approach the sense 'tuft' or 'tufted mass'.]

**I. 1.** A weight used in the wool trade, usually 28 pounds or 2 stone, but varying locally.

**1425** in Kennett *Par. Antiq.* (1818) II. 250 De xxiii todde lanæ puræ.. per le todde ix sol. vi den. **1467** in *Eng. Gilds* (1870) 384 Custom for euery todd j d. **1542** RECORDE *Gr. Artes* (1575) 203 In woolle, 28 pounde is not called a quarterne, but a Todde. **1696** *Phil. Trans.* XIX. 343 Three or four Fleeces usually making a Tod of Twenty eight Pound. **1776** ADAM SMITH *W. N.* I. xi. (1869) I. 242 One-and-twenty shillings the tod may be reckoned a good price for very good English wool. **1833** *Wauldy Farm Rep.* 115 in *Libr. Usef. Knowl., Husb.* III, The agreement is made by the tod, which the dealers have contrived to enlarge to 28½ lbs. **1888** *Daily News* 23 July 2/7 The finest growths of home-grown produce.. changing hands at from 23s to 25s per tod.

**b.** A load, either generally, or of a definite weight.

**1530** PALSGR. 281/2 Tode of chese. **1621** FLETCHER *Pilgrim* III. iv, A hundred crowns for a good Tod of Hay. **17..** *Songs Costume* (Percy Soc.) 248 There's the ladies of fashion you see.. With a great tod of wool on each hip. *a* **1722** LISLE *Husb.* (1757) 311 [They] allow three tod and an half of hay to the wintering of one sheep. **1863** W. BARNES *Poems* 3rd Coll. 73 Zoo all the lot o' stuff a-tied Upon the plow, a tidy tod. **1887** ROGERS *Agric. & Prices* V. 302 Prices of hay and straw... The cwt. and its subdivision, the tod, are the commonest of these exceptional measures. **1889** *Devon farmer* (E.D.D. s.v. *Tad*), I've a-got a middlin' tad [load of hay] here, sure 'nough. *fig.* **1648** HERRICK *Hesper., Conjuration to Electra*, By those soft tods of wooll [clouds] With which the aire is full.

**II. 2.** A bushy mass (esp. of ivy; more fully IVY-TOD, q.v.).

**1553** BECON *Reliques of Rome* (1563) 53 b, Our recluses haue grates of yron in their spelunckes and dennes, out of the which they looke, as owles out of an yuye todde. **1592** WARNER *Alb. Eng.* VII. xxxvii. (1612) 183 Your Ladiship, Dame Owle, Did call me to your Todd. *a* **1619** FLETCHER *Bonduca* I. i, Men of Britain Like boading Owls, creep into tods of Ivie. **1626** BACON *Sylva* § 588 Some [trees] are more in the forme of a Pyramis, and come almost to todd; As the Peare-Tree. **1709** *Brit. Apollo* II. No. 73. 3/1 What Tod of Ivy hath so long conceal'd Thy Corps? **1908** *Outlook* 4 Jan. 4/2 Ivy tods were covered with pollen in Christmas week and the smaller gorse is flowering freely.

**III. 3.** *attrib.* or *Comb.* †**Tod-wool,** clean wool made up into tods.

**1636** *Minute Bk. Exeter City Chamber* 5 Apr. (MS.), The weighing and sale of all toddwooll, rudge-washt wooll, and fleecewooll, and unwashed wooll.

**Tod,** *sb.*[3] *U. S. colloq.* Short for TODDY.

**1862** T. WINTHROP *C. Dreeme* xiv, Selleridge's was full of fire-company boys, taking their tods after a run. **1903** J. LUMSDEN *Toorlo*, etc. 250, I spared nowther grub nor tod.

**Tod** (tǫd), *v. dial.* ? *Obs.* [f. TOD *sb.*[2]] *intr.* Of (so many) sheep or fleeces: To produce a tod of wool; *to tod threes* (etc.), to produce a tod from every three (etc.) sheep; hence, To obtain a tod of wool from a specified number of sheep. In quot. *a* 1797 *trans.* (? erron.) to yield (so much wool).

**1611** SHAKS. *Wint. T.* IV. iii. 34 Let me see, euery eleuen [*pr.* Leauen-]weather toddes, euery tod yeeldes pound and odde shilling: fifteene hundred shorne, what comes the wooll too? *a* **1797** R. FARMER *Note* (L.), Dealers in wool say, twenty sheep ought to tod fifty pounds of wool. **1799** A. YOUNG *Agric. Lincoln.* 311 Them sheap 'll tod threes; that is, the fleeces of three of them will weigh a tod... Of what was called Lincoln sheep, he todded all threes. *Ibid.* 327 His flock tods on an average half threes, half fours.

†**To-da·sh,** *v. Obs.* [ME. *todaschen*, f. To-[2] + *daschen* to DASH.] *trans.* To dash to pieces, to shatter by a violent blow or blows.

*c* **1205** LAY. 1469 His blod & his brain ba weoren to-dascte. **1297** R. GLOUC. (Rolls) 1186, & to dasste & drainte vourti ssipes þere. **13..** *Sir Beues* (A.) 3563 Wiþ his hint fot he him smot And to-dascht al is brain. *c* **1450** *Merlin* xv. 246 Theire sheildes were hewen and to daissht. **1582** BENTLEY *Mon. Matrones* i. 1 Thy right hand, O Lord, hath all to dashed the enimie.

**b.** *intr.* To split or burst asunder.

*c* **1305** *Judas Iscariot* 84 in *E. E. P.* (1862) 109 So þat he smot him wiþ a ston:.. þat al þe sculle to-daschte, þe brayn ful out þerate.

**To-day** (tŭdē·), *adv.* and *sb.* Forms: see DAY. [OE. *tó dæg*, To *prep.* A. 7 + DAY. Cf. the parallel *to-night, to-morrow*, and dial. *to-year*; also Ger. *heut zu Tage, heutzutage*.]

**A.** *adv.* **1.** On this very day.

In Scotland and Border counties of England expressed by *the day*: see THE *dem. adj.* B. 1 c, DAY *sb.* 13 b (*b*).

*c* **897** K. ÆLFRED *Gregory's Past. C.* lviii. 441 Ic hæbbe ðe nu todæȝ ȝesetne ofer rice & ofer ðioda. *c* **1000** ÆLFRIC *Hom.* II. 14 Þu eart min sunu, nu to-dæȝ ic ȝestrynde þe. *c* **1120** *O. E. Chron.* an. 656 (Laud MS.) Ic Wulfere gife to dæi Sce Petre [etc.]. *c* **1175** *Lamb. Hom.* 3 Hit is an heste dei to dei. *c* **1200** *Trin. Coll. Hom.* 27 Gif us to dai ure daihwamliche bred. *c* **1205** LAY. 5442 To daie a seouen nihte. **1382** WYCLIF *Luke* xiii. 32 Loo! I caste out fendis.. to day and to morwe. **1483** *Cath. Angl.* 389/2 To day threday (*A.* Today thryday), *nudius tercius.* **1535** COVERDALE *Josh.* xxii. 18 That he maye be wroth to daye or tomorow. **1535** — *Ps.* xciv. [xcv.] 7 To daye yf ye wil heare his voyce [etc.]. **1598** B. JONSON *Ev. Man in Hum.* IV. viii, And bade mee weare this cursed sute too day. **1680** OTWAY *Orphan*

I. i, To day they chas'd the Boar. **1797** GODWIN *Enquirer* II. v. 225 He will plead for the plaintiff today. **1819** KEATS *Isabella* xxix, To-day thou wilt not see him, nor to-morrow. *Mod.* I have met them twice to-day.

**b.** *To-day . . to-morrow* († *to-morn*) = on one day . . on the next day.

**13..** *Cursor M.* 26769 (Cott.) Þat ar to dai, to moru ar gan. **13..** *Minor Poems fr. Vernon MS.* 727/56 Here to-day, a-wey to-morn. **1510–20** *Compl. too late maryed* (1862) 7 To daye I had peas, rest, and unyte, To morowe I had plete and processe dyvers. **1567** *Gude & Godlie Ball.* (S.T.S.) 30 To day ane man, is fresche and fair, To morne he lyis seik and sair. **1710** PALMER *Proverbs* 273 A wise man will save himself to day for to morrow. **1738** GRAY *Propertius* II. 65 To-day the Lover walks, to-morrow is no more.

**2.** *transf.* At the present time, in the present age; in these times; nowadays.

*a* **1300** *Cursor M.* 2123 (Cott.) Þe thrid part..hatt quar mast to day Regns o þe cristen lay. **1699** GARTH *Dispens.* IV. 47 Five Guinneas make a Criminal to Day. **1874** MORLEY *Compromise* i. (1886) 8 What great political cause ..is England befriending to-day?

**B.** *sb.*

**1.** This day; also, any day considered as present.

**1535** COVERDALE *Exod.* xvi. 25 To daye is yᵉ Sabbath of the Lorde. **1742** YOUNG *Nt. Th.* II. 316 Today is yesterday returned. **1802** MAR. EDGEWORTH *Moral T.* (1816) I. iv. 20 Here, for to day!..but, to morrow, it goes away for ever. **1846** LONGF. *Builders* iii, Our to-days and yesterdays Are the blocks with which we build. **1885** *Manch. Exam.* 22 Sept. 5/6 To-day has been beautifully fine throughout.

**2.** *transf.* This present time or age.

**1848** THACKERAY *Van. Fair* xxx, From the story of Troy down to to-day, poetry has always chosen a soldier for a hero. **1889** *Tablet* 14 Dec. 947 The educated Scotchman of to-day. **1900** *Westm. Gaz.* 27 Sept. 10/1 A..tribute to the English girl of to-day. **1910** *Nation* 28 May 307/2 The fad of today is the orthodoxy of tomorrow.

Hence **To-day·ish** *a.*, of or pertaining to the present time; characteristically modern.

**1864** J. D. CAMPBELL in *Glasgow Herald* 9 Nov., 'Old Boy', as a form of familiar address,..to-dayish as it may sound,..is at least a century old. **1885** BARING-GOULD *Court Royal* xviii, The new plate looks to-dayish; there is not the character about it that our ancestral store possesses.

**Todboat, -bote,** var. *tode-boat*: see TODE *sb.*¹

**Todder** (tǫ·dəɹ). *Obs.* exc. *dial.* Also tother. [Origin obscure.] Spawn of a frog or toad; slimy gelatinous matter.

**1604** DRAYTON *Moyses* II. 116 The soile..Lies now a ley-stall as a common ditch, Where in their Todder loathly Paddocks breed. **1881** *Leicester. Gloss., Tother*,..var. pron. of 'todder', slime; spawn.

**Todder,** variant of TOTTER: cf. DODDER *v.* 3.

**1871** *Daily News* 11 Sept., Enter..next a toddering old man—the feeble father.

**Toddle** (tǫ·d'l), *sb.* [f. TODDLE *v.*]

**1.** An act or the action of toddling, as of a child or infirm person; *transf.* a leisurely walk, a stroll.

**1825** C. M. WESTMACOTT *Eng. Spy* I. 32 After a toddle [*mispr.* toodle] of 3 miles. **1837–48** B. D. WALSH *Aristoph., Knights* I. iii, Now falling and now on the toddle. **1871** BLACKMORE *Maid of Sker* v, The little thing..set off in the bravest toddle for the very bow of the boat. **1891** SARAH J. DUNCAN *Soc. Departure* 123 Her toddle was worth many strides of the female suffragist.

**2.** (Also toddles.) A toddling child.

**1825** JAMIESON, *Toddle*, a designation given to a child, or to a neat person of a small size. *Angus.* **1828** *Craven Gloss. Toddles*, an endearing appellation of a child when just beginning to walk. **1854** THACKERAY *Wolves & Lamb* I, I have two girls—Amelia, quite a little toddles [etc.]. **1882** *Society* 18 Nov. 23/1 A..little pelisse..for a toddle of two-and-a-half.

Hence **To·ddlekins, To·ddleskin** = sense 2.

**1879** SALA *Paris herself again* (1880) I. xvii. 287 There were many little manikins and toddlekins. **1890** *Century Mag.* Aug. 511/2 To return perhaps with a toddleskin or two born at sea. **1904** *Daily Record & Mail* 1 Jan. 4 The plump and laughing little toddlekins who can be seen in every home suburban street.

**Toddle** (tǫ·d'l), *v.* Forms: 6–9 todle, (9 taddle), 8– toddle. [Originally *todle*, Scotch and northern Eng.; origin obscure. Not orig. connected with *tottle*; synonymous with DODDLE. (It is doubtful whether sense 1 belongs here.)]

†**1.** *intr.* To play or toy *with. Obs. rare*⁻¹.

**1500–20** DUNBAR *Poems* xxxii. 11 He..todlit with hir lyk ane quhelp.

**2.** *intr.* To walk or run with short unsteady steps, as a child just beginning to walk, an aged or invalid person; also said of a similar walk or run of any animal.

*c* **1600** *Burel's Pilgr.* in Watson *Coll. Sc. Poems* (1709) II. 22 [The mole] Quhiles dodling, and todling, Vpon fowr prettie feit. **17..** *Allison Gross* x. in Child *Ballads* (1884) II. 315/1 She's turnd me into an ugly worm, And gard me toddle about the tree. **1783** JOHNSON 29 May in *Boswell*, I should like to come and have a cottage in your park, toddle about, live mostly on milk, and be taken care of by Mrs. Boswell. **1785** BURNS *Halloween* v, The vera wee things, todlin, rin Wi' stocks out owre their shouther. **1804** CHARLOTTE SMITH *Conversations*, etc. I. 23 It would be curious..if I was to be tied to my mother's apron string, and taddle about so. **1840** THACKERAY *Catherine* vii, When his strength enabled him to toddle abroad. **1859** HOLLAND *Gold F.* xxiii, The first little lambs of the season toddle by the side of their dams. **1879** H. GEORGE *Progr. & Pov.* IX. iv. (1881) 412 The child just beginning to toddle or to talk will make new efforts.

**b.** Hence, To walk or move with short easy steps; to go leisurely, to saunter, stroll; by playful or familiar meiosis, simply = walk, go.

**1724** RAMSAY *Tea-t. Misc.* (1733) II. 167 Could na my love come todlen hame. **1803** R. ANDERSON *Cumberld. Ball.* 59 Now, wi' twee groats and tuppence, I'll e'en toddle heame. **1812** J. H. VAUX *Flash Dict.* s.v., Come, let us toddle, is a familiar phrase, signifying, let us be going. **1825** BROCKETT *N. C. Words, Todle* or *Toddle*, to walk, to saunter about. **1848** THACKERAY *Bk. Snobs* xlviii, We toddled into the Park for an hour. **1882** G. J. ROMANES *Anim. Intell.* xii. 359 It [the hare or rabbit] merely toddles along with the weasel toddling behind, until tamely allowing itself to be overtaken.

**c.** *fig.* Said of the hurried flow of a shallow stream (compared to the running of a child).

*a* **1774** FERGUSSON *Elegy Death Scots Music* x, Cou'd.. todling burns that smoothly play O'er gowden bed, Compare wi' Birks of Indermay? **1838** J. STRUTHERS *Poet. Tales* 78 (E.D.D.) Owre hagg or hill, Whar Irvine todlin rins alang, A wee bit rill.

**d.** *trans.* To cause to toddle. *rare.*

**1791** MME. D'ARBLAY *Diary* 4 June, Catching me fast by the arm..she safely toddled me back.

¶**3.** *intr.* To bubble gently in boiling. *Sc.* (Improperly for *tottle.*)

**1797** A. DOUGLAS *N. Yr.'s Wish* Poems (1806) 67 A junt o' beef, baith fat and fresh, Aft in your pat be todlin!

Hence **To·ddling** *vbl. sb.* and *ppl. a.*

*a* **1774** [see 2 c]. **1861** *Star & Dial* 4 Nov., The poor little child, the toddling innocent. **1905** SIR F. TREVES *Other Side of Lantern* II. ix. (1906) 83 A toddling princess who was the joy of her father's life. *Mod.* Tired of toddling.

**Toddler** (tǫ·dləɹ). [f. TODDLE *v.* + -ER ¹.] One who toddles; *esp.* a toddling child.

**1793** URE *Hist. Rutherglen* i. 95 She who sits next the fire, towards the east, is called the Todler. **1812** J. H. VAUX *Flash Dict., Toddler*, an infirm elderly person or a child not yet perfect in walking. **1821** *Sporting Mag.* IX. 51 The road..exhibited a variety of toddlers eager to arrive at the destined spot. **1876** BESANT & RICE *Gold. Butterfly* III. 197 Little Phillis—a wee toddler of six or seven.

**Toddy** (tǫ·di), *sb.* Forms: *α.* 7 tarrie, tary, 7–8 terry, 9 tareə, tarea; *β.* 7 tadie, -ee, taddy; *γ.* 7 toddey, toddie, 7– toddy. [ad. Hind. *tāṛī* (with cerebral *r*, approaching English *d*), f. Hind. *tāṛ* palm-tree :—Skr. *tâla* palmyra.]

**1.** The sap obtained from the incised spathes of various species of palm, esp. *Caryota urens*, the wild date, the coco-nut, and the palmyra, used as a beverage in tropical countries; also, the intoxicating liquor produced by its fermentation.

*α.* **1609–10** W. FINCH in Purchas *Pilgrims* (1625) I. 436 A goodly Countrey..abounding with wild Date Trees.. whence they draw a liquor called Tarrie or Sure. **1662** J. DAVIES tr. *Mandelslo's Trav.* 23 In this Village we found some Terry. **1687** A. LOVELL tr. *Thevenot's Trav.* III. i. vi. 16 They make a strong water also of tary which they distil. **1850** *Directions Rev. Off. N. W. Prov.* 225 The Taree or juice of the Palm Tree is liable to duty, in its fermented or unfermented state.

*β.* **1611** N. DOUNTON in Purchas *Pilgrims* (1625) I. III. xii. § 4. 298 Palmita wine, which they call Taddy. **1615** in *Calr. Col. Pap., E. Ind.* (1862) 386 A wine called Tadie, distilled from the Palmetto trees. **1626** PURCHAS *Pilgrimage* V. (ed. 4) 539 Goodly Villages full of trees, yeelding Taddy. **1678** PHILLIPS (ed. 4), *Taddy*, a sort of pleasant juice issuing out of a spungy Tree.

*γ.* **1620** in Foster *Eng. Factories India* (1906) 185 Excessive drincking of toddy. **1622** *Ibid.* (1908) II. 144 All stragglinge libertyes and discontented toddey pott companyons. **1634** SIR T. HERBERT *Trav.* 6 [At Sierra Leone] they were often presented with Flowres, Fruits, Toddy, and like things. **1655** E. TERRY *Voy. E. Indies* 97 A very pleasant and clear liquor, called Toddie. **1732** PIKE in *Phil. Trans.* XXXVII. 235 Instead of Toddy, which is a Sort of Palm-Wine, the Liquor from the Birch-Tree comes near to it. **1770** COOK *Voy. round World* III. xi. (1773) 689 A kind of wine, called toddy, is procured from this tree [fan-palm], by cutting the buds which are to produce flowers, soon after their appearance, and tying under them small baskets, made of the leaves, which are so close as to hold liquids without leaking. **1885** G. S. FORBES *Wild Life in Canara* 253 The Khonds drink a great deal of 'toddy', drawn from the sago palm.

**2.** A beverage composed of whisky or other spirituous liquor with hot water and sugar.

Often distinguished by prefixing the name of the chief ingredient, as *brandy-, gin-, rum-, whisky-toddy.*

**1786** BURNS *Holy Fair* xx, The lads an' lasses, blythely bent, To mind baith saul an' body, Sit round the table, weel content, An' steer about the toddy. [Brit. Mus. MS. copy of 1785 in Burns's own handwriting has lines 2 and 4 'Their lowan thirst an drowth tae quench',..'And steer about the punch'.] **1788** GROSE *Dict. Vulg. T.* (ed. 2), *Toddy*, originally the juice of the cocoa tree, and afterwards rum, water, sugar, and nutmeg. **1798** *Root's Amer. Law Rep.* I. 80 For giving her a dose in some toddy, to intoxicate and inflame her passions. **1808** *Sporting Mag.* XXXII. 215 Punch is certainly wholesomer than..toddy, which is grog with the addition of sugar. **1809** A. WILSON *Poems & Lit. Prose* (1876) I. 158 A tumbler of toddy is usually the morning's beverage of the inhabitants [Paisley]. **1818** TODD *J.'s Dict., Toddy*..3. In low language, a kind of punch, or mixture of spirits and water. **1820** Rum-toddy [see RUM *sb.*¹ 3]. **1859** MRS. CARLYLE *Lett.* III. 7 A stiff tumbler of brandy toddy. **1861** HUGHES *Tom Brown at Oxf.* vi, They took to more toddy and singing Scotch songs. **1896** *Allbutt's Syst. Med.* I. 402 A few spoonfuls of hot brandy or whisky toddy.

**b.** With *a* and *pl.* A glass of this beverage.

**1863** S. L. J. *Life in South fr. Commencement of War* I. xv. 299 Your parents do not encourage toddies. **1894** *Blackw. Mag.* July 75, I drank more than one toddy.

**3.** *attrib.* and *Comb.*, as, **a.** from sense 1, *toddy-fruit, -shop, -wine*; **toddy-bird**, any of various E. Indian birds, as *Ploceus baya*, which feed on the sap of palms; see also *toddy-shrike*; **toddy-cat** = *palm-cat* a. (PALM *sb.*¹); **toddy-cutter**, see quot.; **toddy-drawer** = *toddy-man*; †**toddy-fly**, see quot. *c* 1711; **toddy-man**, a man engaged in the collection or preparation of toddy from palms; **toddy-palm**, any palm that yields toddy; spec. *Caryota urens*, and the wild date-tree of India, *Phœnix sylvestris*; also applied to the coco-nut tree and palmyra; **toddy-shrike**, the palmyra swallow (*Artamus fuscus*); **toddy-tree**, a tree that yields toddy; = *toddy-palm.*

**b.** From sense 2, *toddy-drinker, -drinking, -glass, -jug, -maker, -sap, -stirrer*; **toddy-kettle**, see quot.; **toddy-ladle**, (*a*) see quot.; (*b*), a name for the American aloe (*Cent. Dict.*); **toddy-stick**, a spatula, usually of glass or metal, for stirring toddy.

**a.** **1698** FRYER *Acc. E. India & P.* 76 *margin*, The Ingenuity of the *Toddy Bird. **1864–5** WOOD *Homes without H.* xiii. (1868) 249 This is the nest of the Baya Sparrow, sometimes called the Toddy Bird. **1867** JERDON *Mammals India* 127 It [Tree-cat] is very abundant in the Carnatic and Malabar coast, where it is popularly called the *Toddy-cat, in consequence of its fondness for the juice of the palm. **1839** T. BEALE *Sperm Whale* 339 Persons ..called by the English sailors '*toddy-cutters', are employed..for obtaining the juice of the cocoa nut tree. *Ibid.* 340 The 'Toddy-cutter'..cuts off the end of the fructifying bud... He then places under the wounded part a long empty bamboo. **1839** URE *Dict. Arts* 1257 When the flowering branch is half shot, the *toddy-drawers bind the stock round with a young coco-nut leaf. **1681** GREW *Musæum* I. vii. § 2. 162 The *Toddy-Fly..hath but two Horns. *c* **1711** PETIVER *Gazophyl.* VII. 70 The Toddy Fly,..30 or 40 of them together, sawing thro' the Bark by the Help of their Snout-horn, will make themselves drunk with the Liquor that flows down. **1902** *Blackw. Mag.* May 606/2 An over-ripe *toddy-fruit fell off from a tall palm. **1866** *Treas. Bot.* 157/2 As soon as a spike makes its appearance..a *toddyman..securely binds it with thongs so that it cannot expand. **1900** *Daily News* 9 Mar. 6/2 A talking of the breezes in the tops of the *toddy palms. **1842** W. T. HUMPHREY *Let. to Presbyters in Madras* 10 With as little ceremony as if walking into a *toddy shop. **1632** R. CARTWRIGHT in *St. Papers Col., E. Ind.* 291 Order 2 pago[das] worth of *toddy trees. **1638** SIR T. HERBERT *Trav.* 29 The Toddy Tree is not unlike the Date or Palmeto. **1816** 'QUIZ' *Grand Master* II. 44 *note*, Toddy tree, the Indian name for the cocoa-nut tree. **1672** W. HUGHES *Amer. Physit.* 59 It is called by some the Mamin-Tree, or the Mamee-Tree; by others of the Planters Toddie-Tree: and the liquor or Wine that runneth out is called *Toddie-Wine, or Mamee-Wine.

**b.** **1882** MISS BRADDON *Mt. Royal* vii, In the North he may become a confirmed *toddy-drinker. **1838** *Chambers's Jrnl.* 3 Mar. 48/1 The universal practice of *toddy-drinking among the middle classes in the country towns. **1857** HUGHES *Tom Brown* II. ix, Soiled with the marks of *toddy-glasses and tobacco-ashes. **1865** ALEX. SMITH *Summer in Skye* I. 110 The *toddy-jugs were drained. **1858** SIMMONDS *Dict. Trade*, **Toddy-kettle*, a small hot-water kettle used in Scotland for making toddy. *Ibid.*, **Toddy-ladle*, a small deep spoon or ladle, used in Scotland for conveying whisky-toddy from a rummer or punch-bowl to a wine-glass. **1812** W. TENNANT *Anster F.* II. lxix. 50 By the social fires Sit many, cuddling round their *toddy-sap. **1845** S. JUDD *Margaret* I. vi, A small counter covered with tumblers and *toddy-sticks.

Hence **To·ddy** *v.*, *trans.* to intoxicate with toddy; **To·ddyize** *v.*, *trans.* to cause to drink toddy.

**1836** T. HOOK *G. Gurney* (1850) III. iii. 362, I submitted myself to be toddyised according to his will and pleasure. *a* **1849** POE *W. E. Channing* Wks. 1864 III. 239 Better things than getting toddied are to be expected of Socrates.

†**Tode,** *sb.*¹ *Obs.* Also 7 toad, (tod). [Origin obscure: no similar term is known in Dutch; but cf. Groningsche dialect *todden* to drag, tug, tow, *todde, tod*, as much as one can carry, burden, load (Molema); also Guelderland and Overyssel dial. (Gallée) *todden* to drag.] More fully **tode-boat**: A small Dutch fishing-vessel.

*c* **1600** J. KEYMER *Dutch Fishing* (1664) 2 The Hollanders have above 4100 fishing Ships and Vessels, whereof 100 Doggerbotes, 700 Pinks and Wellbotes, 700 Strandbotes, 400 Evers, and 400 Galliotts, Drivers, and Todbotes, and 1200 Busses. **1614** T. GENTLEMAN *Eng. Way to Wealth* 14 Vessels of diuers fashions..go..onely for Herrings.., Sword-pinks, Flat-bottomes, Holland-toads, Crab-skuits, and Yeuers. **1616** CAPT. SMITH *Descr. New Eng.* 12 The poore Hollanders..hauing 2 or 3000 Busses, Flat bottomes, Sword pinks, Todes, and such like. **1620** — *New Eng. Trials* Wks. (Arb.) 239, 3600 [vessels] are fishermen, whereof 100 are Dogers..700 frand botes, 400 Enaces, 400 Galbotes, Britters and Todebotes, with 1300 Busses.

**Tode** (tōᵘd), *sb.*² *U.S.* [Origin obscure; but cf. LG. *todden* to drag, in prec.] A rude sledge used in hauling logs, consisting of a tree-fork with a cross-piece on which the balk rests. Hence **Tode** *v. tr.* and *intr.* to haul (logs) with a tode.

**1895** in *Funk's Standard Dict.* **1911** in WEBSTER.

**Tode,** obs. form of TOAD.

‖ **Todea** (tōᵘ·diă). *Bot.* [Named in honour of H. J. Tode, German botanist, 1733–97.] A small genus of ferns of the Southern hemisphere, related to *Osmunda*, often cultivated in greenhouses, and known as *crape-ferns.*

**1882** *Garden* 25 Feb. 135/3 Todeas are often spoilt through being syringed overhead. **1892** *19th Cent.* Sept. 407 A carpet of maidenhair, umbrella, and brilliant todea ferns.

† **To-dea·l,** *v. Obs.* [OE. *todǽlan*, f. To-$^2$ + *dǽlan* to Deal; = OS. *te-dêlian*, OHG. *zi-, zateiljan*, Ger. *zerteilen*.]

**1.** *trans.* To divide (into parts); to distribute, deal out; also, to separate, sever.

*c* **888** K. Ælfred *Boeth.* xxxiii. § 4 Þone anne noman þu todældest on feower ȝesceafta. *c* **893** — *Oros.* i. i. § 1 Ure ieldran ealne þisne ymbhwyrft þises middanȝeardes .. on þreo todældon. *c* **1000** Ælfric *Hom.* II. 194 Astrece ðine hand ofer ða sæ, and todæl hi. **1154** *O. E. Chron.* an. 1137, Ac he to-deld it & scatered sotlice. *c* **1200** Ormin 9468 Forrþi wass þeȝȝre kinedom Todæledd & tobrittnedd..O fowwre feorþenn daless. *c* **1205** Lay. 2994 Ich wille mi dirhliche lod a þroe al to-dalen [*c* **1275** a þreo al to-deale]. *a* **1225** *Ancr. R.* Pref. 23 This an Boc is todealet in eahte lesse Boke. **1340** *Ayenb.* 164 Þe filozofes..to-delden þise uirtues ine zix deles. **1387** Trevisa *Higden* (Rolls) I. 185 Þe hil mons Olympus..to deleþ tweie londes.

**2.** *intr.* To divide, separate, part.

*a* **900** *O. E. Chron.* an. 885, Her to dælde se fore-sprecena here on tu, oþer dæl east, oþer dæl to Hrofes ceastre. *a* **1023** Wulfstan *Hom.* xxx. (Napier) 149 Swa todæleð se lichoma and seo sawul. *c* **1175** *Lamb. Hom.* 131 Swa sone swa heore saulen and heore licoma to-delden heo ferden to helle. *c* **1205** Lay. 30833 Sone heo gunen to-delen. *c* **1275** *Passion our Lord* 480 in *O. E. Misc.* 50 Þat huding-cloþ to-delde in þe temple a to.

**3.** *trans.* To decide (a contest). *rare.*

*c* **1205** Lay. 9519 He scal..mit fehten hit to-dælen [*c* **1275** to-deale]. *Ibid.* 22799 We þis comp scullen to-delen wið þas uncuðe kempen.

**Toder,** dial. variant of Tother.

† **To·dly,** *a. Obs. rare*—$^1$. [f. Tod *sb.*$^1$ + -ly$^1$.] Foxy, crafty.

**1571** *Satir. Poems Reform.* xxix. 33 The Ministre, far todlyar, his hure in houshold chereis.

**To do, to-do,** *sb.*: see Do *v.* 33.

† **To-do·,** *v. Obs.* [OE. *to-dón*, f. To-$^2$ + *dón* to Do, to put. Cf. MHG. *zertuon*.] *trans.* **a.** To put asunder, divide, separate. **b.** To undo, open.

*a* **839** *Penit. Laws Ecgbert* ii. c. 11 ȝif hwylc wif tweȝen ȝebroðru nimð hire to ȝemæccan, oþerne æfter oþrum, to-do man hiȝ. *a* **900** *Ags. Ps.* (Th.) xxi. 11 Hi todydon heora muð onȝean me. *a* **1000** *Ags. Hexameron St. Basil* iv. (1849) 8 Ðæt wæter and seo eorðe wæron ȝemengede oð ðone ðriddan dæȝ; ða todyde hi God. *c* **1205** Lay. 2945 Ic wlle mine riche to-don..& twemen mine bearnen. *Ibid.* 6507 And þat deor to-dede [*c* **1275** vndude] his chæfles ..And for-bat hine amidden a twa.

**Todpole,** obs. form of Tadpole.

† **To-draught.** *Obs. rare.* [ME., f. To-$^1$ + *draȝt*, Draught *sb.*] **a.** A following, train, retinue. **b.** A place that people draw to; a resort.

*a* **1300** *Cursor M.* 5961 Þan sent godd þam on a flei, ..On pharaon and his to draght. *Ibid.* 14745 (Cott.) Mi hus..yee mak it, witvten leue, A to-draght o reuer and thefe.

† **To-draw,** *v. Obs.* Forms: see Draw *v.* [Early ME. *to-drawen*, f. To-$^2$ + Draw *v.*; = OHG. *zi-tragan*, MHG. *zertragen*.]

**1.** *trans.* To pull apart, draw or drag asunder; to tear to pieces; to destroy by tearing apart.

*c* **1205** Lay. 2603 Heo..his leomen to-drowen & his hors al swa. *a* **1225** *Ancr. R.* 122 Ne to drauhð me þe eorðe? *c* **1250** *Gen. & Ex.* 191 Leunes and beres him wile to-draȝen. *a* **1300** *K. Horn* 181 Hi sloȝen and todroȝe Cristenemen inoȝe. **13..** *K. Alis.* 4613 (Bodl. MS.) Lete non houndes me to-drawe. *c* **1350** *Will. Palerne* 2086 He schal be honged heie & wiþ horse to-drawe. *c* **1425** *Seven Sag.* (P.) 877 How the naddir was y-slawe, That the grewhond hadde to-drawe.

**b.** *fig.*

*c* **1175** *Lamb. Hom.* 53 Heo..heom to-twiccheð and to-draȝeð mid ufele weordes. **1297** R. Glouc. (Rolls) 8729 Þo men miȝte.. lybbe in Ioye & in riȝte, þat er were al to drawe. **1340** *Ayenb.* 57 Þise ten boȝes .. ydelnesse, yelpinge, blondinge, todraȝinge, lyesynges, vorzueriinges, stryfinge, grochinge, wyþstondinge, blasfemye.

**2.** In various other senses of Draw *v.* (*lit.* and *fig.*); to draw or drag away, about, or out.

*a* **1240** *Ureisun* in *Cott. Hom.* 199 Nis hit ðe no wurðscipe þet þe deouel me to-drawe. ***13..** *Cursor M.* 28289 (Cott.) Þe gode vous..Broken ic haue or lang to-draun. *a* **1400-50** *Alexander* 5364 Þis baratour..Fand caratros & candoile at knyfes to-drawen. **1446** Lydg. *Two Nightingale Poems* i. 256 On euery syde to-togged and to-drawe.

† **To-drese,** *v. Obs.* Pa. pple. **to-drore**(n. [OE. *to-dréosan*, f. To-$^2$ + *dréosan*, Drese *v.*, to fall.] *intr.* To fall apart; to decay, fade.

*a* **900** *O. E. Martyrol.* 21 Dec. 222 Þæt goldȝe-weorc todreas, swa swa weax ȝemylt æt fyre. *c* **1250** *Death* 62 in *O. E. Misc.* 173 (Jesus MS.) Er þe saule and þet body a two beon to-drore [*v.r.* to-drehen]. *c* **1275** Lay. 9245 Portcastre..mid hire bitere reses al he gan to-drese. ?*a* **1300** *XI Pains Hell* 182 in *O. E. Misc.* 152 Sum beoþ fur-brend & summe ifrore & alle þe bones beoþ to-drore.

† **To-dreve,** *v. Obs.* [OE. *todrǽfan*, f. To-$^2$ + *drǽfan*, Dreve *v.*$^2$, to drive, impel.]

**1.** *trans.* To drive asunder or apart; to disperse, separate, scatter.

*a* **900** tr. *Bæda's Hist.* iii. xviii. [xiv.] (1898) 227 (MS. O.) Hiora heriȝes þær wæs micel ofslaȝen .. & eal todræfed. *c* **1000** *Ags. Gosp.* Matt. xxvi. 31 Þurh þæs hyrdes sleȝe byð seo heord to-dræfed. *c* **1175** *Lamb. Hom.* 155 He to-drefeð þe þonk þet erre weren to-gedere. *a* **1225** *Ancr. R.* 298 Schrift schent þene deouel..& to-dreaueð his ferde. **13..** *Guy Warw.* (A.) 1483 On þe erþe lip þi scheld to-dreued, Nouȝt o pece is wiþ oþer bileued. *c* **1400** *St. Alexius* (Laud 622) 326 And he fer from his frendes to dreued.

**2.** *intr.* To disperse, go or fly asunder.

*c* **1175** *Lamb. Hom.* 93 Þi bilenfden heo heore timbrunge and to dreofden ȝeond al middeleard. *c* **1400** *R. Gloucester's Chron.* (Rolls) App. XX. 121 (MS. *a*) His ost to drefde sone her & þer. *c* **1400** *Rowland & O.* 573 Þat bothe þaire bodies wexen bare, Þaire armours all to-dreues.

† **To-drive,** *v. Obs.* [OE. *todrífan*, f. To-$^2$ + *drífan* to Drive; = OHG. *zi-, ze-trîban*, MHG. *ze-, zer-trîben*.]

**1.** *trans.* To drive asunder, disperse, rout, scatter; to drive away, dispel; to dissolve.

*Beowulf* 545 Þa wit ætsomne on sæ wæron fif nihta fyrst oþ þæt unc flod to-draf. *c* **950** *Lindisf. Gosp.* John x. 12 Ðe ulf nimeð &..todrifeð ða scip. *c* **1200** Ormin 16397 Forr þatt hiss stren all shollde ben Todrifenn & toskeȝȝredd. **1297** R. Glouc. (Rolls) 4722 At bedeford come þe saxons & smite an bataylle & to driue [*v.rr.* to droue, to drofe] þe brutons. *c* **1330** R. Brunne *Chron.* (1810) 16 Þe kyng was narow holden, his folk alle to dryuen. **1393** Langl. *P. Pl.* C. xxiii. 174 Lechecraft lette sholde elde And to-dryue away deþ with drogges.

**b.** To dash or break in pieces. *rare*—$^1$.

*c* **1320** *Cast. Love* (Halliw.) 862 That ther shuld come a woman blyve That shuld all his hed to-dryve.

**c.** *intr.* To strike violently; to let drive. *rare*—$^1$.

*c* **1205** Lay. 8152 Euelin wes swiðe wrað & mid þan stæue to-draf And smat Herigal a þon ribben.

**2.** *intr.* To fly in pieces; to be splintered or shattered; to burst.

*c* **1205** Lay. 2895 Þe king feol on þene rof Þat he al to-draf. **13..** *S. Eng. Leg.* (MS. Bodl. 779) in Herrig's *Archiv* LXXXII. 410/96 Wiþ þat ilke word..Þe god of bras al to-drof so hit were of clay. *c* **1430** *Hymns Virg.* 122 Alle the worlle schalle to-dryve; Wo be þey þatt ben on lyve! *c* **1460** *Launfal* 482 Than myghte me se..Speres to-breste and to-dryve.

**Tody** (tōu·di). *Ornith.* [ad. F. *todier* (1764 in Littré), ad. L. *todus*, name of some small bird, adopted by Linnæus as generic name.] Any member or species of the genus *Todus* or family *Todidæ* of small insectivorous birds, resembling and allied to the kingfisher; of which four species are found in the Greater Antilles.

**1773** Pennant *Genera Birds* 17 Tody, bill thin, depressed, broad...Inhabits the hot parts of America...The name first given it by Dr. Brown, I suppose, from Todi, small birds. **1834** tr. *Cuvier's Anim. Kingd.* I. 292. **1847** Gosse *Birds Jamaica* 74, I have never seen the Tody eating vegetable food. **1879** E. P. Wright *Anim. Life* 276 The Little Todies ..are only found in a few of the West Indian Islands.

**Toe** (tōu), *sb.* Forms: α. 1 tá, *pl.* tán; *sing.* 4-5 ta, taa; *Sc.* 6 ta, 9 tae, teae, *north. dial.* teea; *pl.* 3 tan, (4 taan); 4 tas, 4-5 taas, 5 taasse; *Sc.* 6 tais, taiss, tayis, tees, 6- taes, (9 *dial.* teaes, teaase). β. *sing.* 3-5 tô, 4-6 too, 5- toe; *pl.* 3-5 ton, 4-5 tone, toon, 5 toone; 4 tôs, 5 tose, tois, toose, 5-6 toos, 5- toes. [OE. *tá* (contr. f. **táhe*, in OMerc. *táhæ*), pl. *tán*, ME. *tô*, pl. *tôn*, *tôs* = OLG. **têha*, MLG. *tê*, MDu., mod. Flem. *tee*, OHG. *zêha* wk. fem. (MHG. *zêhe*, Ger. *zehe*, *zeh*), ON. *tá*, pl. *tǽr* (Da., Norw. *taa*, Sw. *tå*):—OTeut. **taih(w)ôn*.

Beside the above forms OFris. had *tâne*, mod.WFris. *tean* (dial. *tane, teine*), NFris. *tuan*, EFris. *tône* (*tôn*), also MLG. *tene*, MDu., MFl. *teen*, mod.LG. and Du. *tén*, *teen*, also mod.Du. *toon* from Fris.; the origin of the final *-ne*, *-n* is uncertain: it may be from the pl. On the pre-Germanic relations, see Kluge, Franck, Dornkaat-Koolman, Falk & Torp. The OE. pl. in *-n* survived in s.w. till the 14th c.]

**1.** Each of the five digits of the human foot.

*Big* or *great toe* (†*mickle toe*), the thick inner toe; *little toe*, the short outer toe. (See also d.)

α. *c* **725** *Corpus Gloss.* (O. E. T.) 141 *Allox*, tahae. *a* **901** K. Ælfred *Laws* c. 64 ȝif sio micle ta bið ofasleȝen, ȝeselle him xx scill. to bote..æfterre ta..midleste ta..feorþe ta.. sio lytle ta..v scill. *c* **1000** Ælfric *Voc.* in Wr.-Wülcker 161/8 *Allox*, micele tan. *a* **1225** *Juliana* 59 As þat istelede irn strac hire in..from þe top to þe tan. *a* **1300** *Cursor M.* 12967 Wit-vten hurt o fote or ta. **1340** Hampole *Pr. Consc.* 683 Þe tas and þe fyngers alle. *Ibid.* 1910 In ilka taa and fynger of hand. *c* **1400** Maundev. (Roxb.) xxii. 100 Þai hafe on ayther fote viii. taasse. *c* **1440** Thomble ta [see Thumble-toe]. **1500-20** Dunbar *Poems* lx. 54 With his wawill feitt, and virrok taiss. **1513** Douglas *Æneis* v. vi. 66 His tais [*v.r.* tayis] choppand on his heill. **1583** *Leg. Bp. St. And.* 300 Palme croces, and knottis of strease, The parings of a preistis auld te[a]es. **1816** Scott *Antiq.* xxv, Tak care o' your taes wi' that stane.

β. *c* **1290** *S. Eng. Leg.* I. 268/253 Heo orn and ne watte neuere a to. *c* **1315** Shoreham iii. 133 Ten fyngres and ten þine tone. **1340-70** *Alisaunder* 194 Þe fairest feete..With ton tidily wrought. *c* **1400** *St. Alexius* (Laud 463) 317 Þe teres fellen to his tone. *c* **1400** *Lanfranc's Cirurg.* 177 Þe bonys of þe toos. *Ibid.*, þe grete too..haþ...ij. boones. *a* **1425** *Cursor M.* 6703 (Trin.) Foot for foot, to for to [*Gött.* ta for ta]. *c* **1440** *York Myst.* xxii. 108 Þat þou schall on no stones descende to hurte þi tose. *c* **1450** *Cov. Myst.* xiv. (1841) 139 This olde shrewe may not wele gon,..Lyfte up thi feet, sett forthe thi ton. **1526** *Pilgr. Perf.* (W. de W. 1531) 44 Euery hand and fote hath his fyngers & toos particularly distinct. **1591** Nashe *Pref. Sidney's Astr. & Stella*, Tis as good to goe in cut-fingerd Pumps as corke shooes, if one wore Cornish diamonds on his toes. **1632** Milton *L'Allegro* 34 Com, and trip it as ye go On the light fantastick toe. **1741** Monro *Anat.* (ed. 3) 301 The Flexors of the great Toe. **1878** Gamgee tr. *Hermann's Hum. Physiol.* (ed. 2) 314 The toes..are of use in maintaining the balance, particularly in walking.

† **b.** *To stand upon one's toes*, i. e. on tiptoe.

*a* **1300** *Cursor M.* 24446 (Cott.) Apon mi tas of[t] sith i stod. *a* **1550** *Ane littill Interlud* 45 in *Dunbar's Poems* (S. T. S.) 315 He wald vpoun his tais vp stand, And tak the starnis doun with his hand. *c* **1572** Gascoigne *Fruites Warre* clxvi, Thus met we talkt, and stoode vpon our toes, With great demaundes whome little might content.

† **c.** Put for the foot as a whole, or the point of the foot. *Obs.*

*c* **1290** *Beket* 1444 in *S. Eng. Leg.* I. 147 A-non to is þies þe schuyrte tilde, þe brech riȝt to is to. *a* **1300** *Cursor M.* 5932 Man moght noght þeron sett his ta.

**d.** *fig.*

**1607** Shaks. *Cor.* i. i. 159 What do you thinke? You, the great Toe of this Assembly? **1649** Daniel *Trinarch.*, *Rich. II* ciii, Soe was it here; these Petty toes of State, Who would haue Trod a Galliard of Designe..Fell in a ligge. **1650** Fuller *Pisgah* i. iv. § 9 Mustard, the little Toe of trees.

**2.** Each of the digits of the foot of a beast or bird.

*c* **1386** Chaucer *Nun's Pr. T.* 42 A Cok heet Chauntecleer.. Lyk Asure were hise legges and his toon. *Ibid.* 511 This Chauntecleer stode hye vp on his toos. *c* **1400** Maundev. (1839) xxvii. 274 Psitakes..þat speken..and han v. toos vpon a fote. **1596** Dalrymple tr. *Leslie's Hist. Scot.* (S. T. S.) I. 63 As esie as to ken the lione be his taes. **1668** Wilkins *Real Char.* 161 That which hath two toes behind in each foot, with prominencies upon the head like ears,.. Chamelion. **1713** Derham *Phys.-Theol.* vii. i. (1727) 339 *note*, Two of the Toes are somewhat joined, that they [wading birds] may not easily sink in walking upon boggy Places. **1774** Goldsm. *Nat. Hist.* (1776) IV. 262 The feet [of the elephant]..are divided into five toes, which are covered beneath the skin, and none of which appear to the eye. **1841-71** T. R. Jones *Anim. Kingd.* (ed. 4) 810 The Rhinoceros has only three toes to each foot. **1860** *All Year Round* No. 37. 247 Geckoes..by help of padded toes can run up walls like a fly. **1894** *Nature's Meth. in Evol. Life* ii. 21 The Eocene antecessor of the horse possessed..four separate toes, which subsequently became reduced to three, and at the beginning of the Quaternary Age the horse of the present day appeared with a single toe or hoof.

**b.** The front part of the hoof (or shoe) of a horse.

**1566** Blundevil *Horsemanship* iv. cix. (1580) 50 b, If a Horse..halt..in the heele, as by ouer reach, or otherwise, then he will tread most on the toe. **1831** [Youatt] *Horse* 181 Cutting down..at the union between the crust and the sole at the very toe. *Ibid.* 316 For work a little hard, the shoe shall still be light, with a bit of steel welded into the toe.

**c.** The ultimate joints of the tarsus of insects.

**1826** Kirby & Sp. *Entomol.* III. 386 *Digitus* (the Toe),.. includes the *Allux* and *Ungula*.

**3.** *transf.* The part of a shoe or stocking which covers the toes; the hood or cap for the toe sometimes attached to a stirrup; a toe-piece.

**1600** Rowlands *Lett. Humours Blood* vii. 13 From dish-crown'd Hat, vnto th' Shooes square toe. **1722** *Lond. Gaz.* No. 6119/4 Narrow square Toe Shoes with high Tops. **1828** Scott *F. M. Perth* xi, Place thy foot on the toe of my boot. **1842** J. Aiton *Domest. Econ.* (1857) 262 A stirrup for the misses, with toes to be taken off or on as the boy or girl mounts. **1886** C. Dick *The Model*, etc. 95 Skirts, short and sweet, that deftly swing Round pointed heels and patent toes.

**4.** A part resembling a toe or the toes, in shape or position; (usually) the lower extremity or projection of anything; a point, tip; often identical with *foot* (Foot *sb.* IV). (Cf. Heel *sb.*$^1$ 5-7.)

**a.** Generally. **b.** The lower extremity of a spindle or screw, as in a press; the projection on a lock-bolt or the like, against which the key or a cam presses. **c.** A projection from the base of a wall; the foot or base of a cliff or embankment. **d.** The lower extremity of a gun-stock, rafter, organ-pipe, etc. **e.** The thin end of a hammer-head, the peen; the tip of the 'head' of a golf or hockey club.

**a.** *c* **1440** *Pallad. on Husb.* xi. 49 Of vynes yonge The rootis..kitte hem not to nygh, lest they abounde Thre toon for oon, or feester into a wounde. ?*a* **1643** Sandys tr. *Seneca's Œdipus*, About the mast the youthfull Ivy twines, The lofty toe imbrac'd with clustred vines. **1725** *Bradley's Fam. Dict.* s.v. *Saddle*, If .. the Toes of the Fore-bow be too narrow and streight. **1866** Darwin in *Intell. Observ.* No. 56. 85 The toe of the labellum. **1869** Sir E. J. Reed *Shipbuild.* iv. 71 The aftermost rivets were driven through the thin part of the toe, and knocked down in a countersink as usual. **1894** A. J. Evans in Freeman *Sicily* IV. 234 The coinage of Syracuse had now become the only coinage for the whole of Greek Sicily, and even for the toe of Italy. **1904** Maud S. Rawson *Apprentice* 140 The old man..began to chip at the toes of the monster oak. **b.** **1677** Moxon *Mech. Exerc.* ii. 27 The Toe or Nab of the Bolt, which rises..above the straight on the Top of the Bolt. **1683** *Ibid.*, *Printing* x. ℙ 12 The very bottom of the Spindle..is called the Toe, it is..of an hemispherical form. **1833** J. Holland *Manuf. Metal* II. 216 By the operation of the handle, the toe is made to act upon the inside bolt, and thus force down the piston. **1839** *Civil Eng. & Arch. Jrnl.* II. 242/1 The toe of the screw works in the fixed cross piece. **1877** Knight *Dict. Mech.*, *Toe*, 1. a. The lower end of a vertical shaft, as a mill-spindle, which rests in a step, or ink. b. An arm on the valve-lifting rod of a steam-engine. A cam or lifter strikes the toe and operates the valve; such toes are known respectively as steam-toes and exhaust-toes. **c.** **1838** *Civil Eng. & Arch. Jrnl.* I. 98/2 The mode pursued in blasting down high cliffs, by boring at the toe of the rock. **1839** *Ibid.* II. 433 Sheet piling at the toe of the wing walls. **1895** *Law Times Rep.* LXXIII. 156/2 Two vessels..drifted..on to the toe of a breakwater. **1901** *Daily News* 5 Jan. 6/5 A second chalk wall was built to form a watertight toe for the new bank. **d.** *c* **1860** H. Stuart *Seaman's Catech.* 11 On the stock [of the rifle] is a toe. **1892** Greener *Breech-Loader* 94 It is too straight or has too much toe upon the stock. **e.** **1873** E. Spon *Workshop Receipts* Ser. i. 412/1 Take an ordinary hammer,..place the toe upon a piece of veneer previously glued on the under side. **1909** *Westm. Gaz.* 8 Feb. 12/4 The question of whether the toe of the club should point downwards at the top of the swing or somewhat skywards.

**5.** Phrases (chiefly *colloq.* and *slang*).

† **a.** *On old toes*, in old age. *Obs.* **b.** *The toe's length*, a very short distance. **c.** *Toe and heel*, (*a*) a style of dancing in which the toe and heel tap rhythmically on the

ground; also *attrib.*; (*b*) in walking: see quot. 1865; also *attrib.* Cf. *heel and toe* (HEEL *sb.*[1] 14). **d.** *From the crown to the toes, from head to (the) toe(s*, from head to foot, all over; *from top to toe*: see TOP *sb.* †**e.** *To claw one's toes*, to gratify or indulge oneself. *Obs.* †**f.** *To cool one's toes*, to be kept waiting; cf. *to cool* (COOL *v.* 5) or *kick one's heels* (HEEL *sb.*[1] 17). *Obs.* †**g.** *To have* or *hold by the toe*, to have a secure hold of. *Obs.* **h.** *To kiss the pope's toe*, to kiss the golden cross of the sandal on the pope's right foot, as a mark of respect: the customary salutation of those (excepting sovereigns) to whom audience is granted. **i.** *To step* or *tread on the toes of*; also *fig.* to give offence to, to vex. **j.** *To turn one's toes up*, to die; hence *toes up*, lying dead. †**k.** *To turn* (a person) *on the toe*, ? to turn off the ladder in hanging. *Obs.*

**a.** *a* 1400 *Pistill of Susan* 305 Þou dotest nou on þin olde tos [*v.r.* toes] in þe dismale. *c* 1460 *Towneley Myst.* xxx. 592 He that to that gam gose, Now namely on old tose. **b.** 1824 SCOTT *Redgauntlet* Let. x, No to be fit to walk your tae's-length. **c.** 1840 HOOD *Kilmansegg, Marriage* xxiv, The gaping people..turn'd to gaze at the toe-and-heel Of the Golden Boys beginning a reel. 1842 J. WILSON *Ess., Gymnastics* (1856) 103 A first rate walker,..toe and heel—six miles an hour. 1865 *Routledge's Ev. Boy's Ann.* 434 When the heel of one foot is on the ground, the toe of the other must be upon it. This is called toe-and-heel walking. 1869 *Punch* 10 July 4/2 Hungarians..dancing a toe-and-heel step to polka time. **d.** 1297 R. GLOUC. (Rolls) 11177 Þo stode hii I-armed fram heued to þe ton. *c* 1430 *Syr Gener.* (Roxb.) 3405 Fro the crovn to the toon Blak as cole thei were echoon. *c* 1489 CAXTON *Sonnes of Aymon* x. 274 All armed from hede to too. **e.** *c* 1460 *Towneley Myst.* xiii. 414 Dos noght but lakys and clowse hir toose. **f.** 1665 BRATHWAIT *Comment Two Tales* 28 Cooling his Toes at the Blacksmith's door. **g.** *a* 1548 HALL *Chron., Hen. VIII* 186 The Bishop thinkyng that he had God by the too, when in deede he had..the Deuell by the fiste. 1623 BP. HALL *Serm.* v. 139 While they think they have God by the finger, they hold a devil by the toe. **h.** 1768 EARL CARLISLE in Jesse *Selwyn & Contemp.* (1843) II. 296, I kissed the Pope's toe yesterday morning. 1782 PRIESTLEY *Corrupt. Chr.* II. x. 253 All other persons..must kiss the pope's toe. **i.** *c* 1394 *P. Pl. Crede* 649 For stappyng on a too of a styncande frere. 1868 BROWNING *Ring & Bk.* III. 1032 He could not turn about Nor take a step i' the case and fail to tread On someone's toe. 1879 GEO. ELIOT *Theo. Such* (1880) 119 A man who uses his balmorals to tread on your toes with much frequency. **j.** 1851 MAYHEW *Lond. Labour* II. 95/2, I thought I'd be by this time toes up in Stepney churchyard. 1857 LD. DUFFERIN *Lett. High Lat.* xiii. (ed. 3) 393 Ah, my Lord!—the poor thing!—toes up at last! 1860 READE *Cloister & Hearth* xxiv, 'Several arbalestriers turned their toes up, and I among them'. 'Killed..? come now!' **k.** 1594 NASHE *Unfort. Trav.* Wks. (Grosart) V. 36 He for his trecherie was turnd on the toe.

**6.** *attrib.* and *Comb.*, as *toe-action, -bone, -calk, -dresser, -end, -joint, -turn*; *toe-kissing, -scraping, -stretching, -treading* (lit. and fig.), sbs. and adjs.; *toe-like* adj.; **toe-ball**, the thickened fleshy pad under the toe; with quot. 1826 cf. sense 2 c; **toe-board**, a board for the feet to rest upon; also, a board marking the limit of the thrower's run in putting the weight and similar feats; **toe-boot**, a boot (BOOT *sb.*[3] 5) to protect the hind feet of a trotting horse from injury by the fore feet; **toe-cap**, a cap of leather covering the toe of a boot or shoe; hence **toe-capped** *a.*, furnished with a toe-cap; **toe-clip**, (*a*) an attachment to the pedal of a bicycle in which the toe of the shoe is placed to prevent the foot slipping; (*b*) a tip turned up at the toe of a horse-shoe, to keep the shoe in position (= CLIP *sb.*[1] 2); **toe-crack** (*Farriery*), a sand-crack in the front of the hoof; **toe-dancer**, see quot.; **toe-drop** (*Path.*), see quot. 1899; †**toe-gleek**, some variety of gleek; **toe-hardy**, a half-round hardy or cold-chisel; **toe-hold**, in *Wrestling*, a hold in which the toe is seized and the leg forced backwards; **toe-link**, a bottom end link; **toe-movement**, see quot., and cf. *toe-drop* and *toe-scraping*; **toe-nail** *sb.*, the nail of a toe; **toe-nail** *v.*, to fasten with toed nails: see TOED 2; **toe-narrow** *a.* (*Farriery*), having the fore feet too close when standing; **toe-piece**, a toe-cap; a toe-plate; in armour, the toe of a solleret; also, the lengthened tip of this; see also quot. 1879; **toe-plate**, (*a*) an iron plate under the toe of a boot or shoe; (*b*) a metal plate worn as a remedy for hammer-toe; **toe-ring**, a ring worn on the toe; a stout ferrule on the end of a cant-hook (*U.S.*); **toe-scute** = *toe-plate* (*a*); †**toe-shell**, a species of cirriped, *Pollicipes mitella*; **toe-step** (*Mech.*), the socket in which the end of a spindle works; = FOOTSTEP 5 d; **toe-strap, -string**, a strap or thong which secures the toe of a sandal, skate, or the like; **toe-tights**, tights in which the toes are separated like glove-fingers; **toe-tip**, the extremity of a toe; cf. TIPTOE; also = *toe-plate* (*a*); **toe-tuft**, a tuft of hair covering the toe in some dogs; **toe-walking** *a.*, that walks on the toes, digitigrade; **toe-weight**, a small knob of metal attached to the hoof or shoe of a horse to modify the gait in trotting; **toe-wide** *a.* (*Farriery*), having the fore feet too far apart in standing; **toe-writer**, one who writes with his toes; in quot. *allusively*.

1826 KIRBY & SP. *Entomol.* III. xxxiii. 386 Allux (the *Toe-ball). The last joint but one of the Tarsus, when remarkable, as in Rhyncophorous beetles. 1856 AIRD *Poet. Wks.* 15 The big Toeball just resting on the stirrup. 1907 *Westm. Gaz.* 21 Jan. 2/1 Here had trudged the bloody pirate..about to step the dance of death without a *toe-board under the gallows-tree up harbour. 1898 *Guide Mammalia* 11 The tarsus, or ankle-bones, corresponding to the carpus, and the metatarsals and *toe-bones to the metacarpals and finger-bones. 1898 *Daily News* 11 Nov. 5/1 An ill-formed boot with a foot inside, the toe bones all squeezed out of their natural shape. 1901 *Munsey's Mag.* XXV. 736/1 The hind feet were protected with the *toe boots, while the action of the front feet was stimulated by the weight of the quarter boots, made of soft sheepskin or leather. 1877 KNIGHT *Dict. Mech.*, **Toe-calk*, a prong or barb on the toe of a horse's shoe, to prevent slipping on ice or frozen ground. 1797 WOLCOTT (P. Pindar) *Out at Last* Wks. 1812 III. 494 Come hobbling forth without one blush of shame With heel-taps, *toe-caps, soles for worn-out fame. 1907 *Daily News* 4 June 6 Shoes much the worse for wear, often broken across the toecaps. 1861 J. BROWN *Horæ Subs.* (1863) 378 His heavy shoes,..heel-capt and *toe-capt. 1908 *Daily Chron.* 6 June 8/3 The N.C.U. ..leaves it permissible—not compulsory—for riders to use *toe-clips, blocks on the shoes, or slots in the soles, or any other device for assisting to keep the feet in position. 1903 *U. S. Dept. Agric., Rep. Dis. Horse* 405 The *toe-crack ..extending from the coronary band to the sole. 1911 WEBSTER, *Sand-crack*, a fissure or lesion in the horn of the hoof wall, often causing lameness. When in the front wall it is known as toe crack. 1898 *Pall Mall Mag.* Nov. 419 Mrs. Draper was a *toe-dancer..a young lady..flitting hither and thither on the very tips of her tiny feet. 1725 *Lond. Gaz.* No. 6399/3 James Stubs,..*Toe-Dresser. 1899 *Syd. Soc. Lex.*, **Toe-drop*, inability to lift the toes, or the anterior part of the foot, due to a local paralysis, usually from peripheral neuritis. 1689 SHADWELL *Bury F.* III. i, Women, go pack into the drawing room and play at *Toe-gleek. 1911 WEBSTER, *Toe-hardy, *Toe-hold. 1897 MARY KINGSLEY *W. Africa* 606 He..pointed to his distorted *toe-joints, and informed me that once he always wore boots. 1896 *Daily News* 9 Mar. 6/4 As I had said A—I was going to say B, too—and made up my mind to the *toe kissing. 1849 D. J. BROWNE *Amer. Poultry Yd.* (1855) 30 Their legs are..armed with one or more *toe-like claws. *c* 1850 *Rudim. Navig.* (Weale) 105 They are secured to the ship's side by a bolt through the *toe-link, called the *chain-bolt*. 1867 SMYTH *Sailor's Word-bk.*, *Chain-bolt*, a large bolt to secure the chains of the dead-eyes through the toe-link. 1899 *Allbutt's Syst. Med.* VIII. 103 In some cases [of functional paralysis]..the *toe-movement does not occur. 1856 KANE *Arct. Expl.* I. 132 Bonsall was minus a big *toe nail and plus a scar upon the nose. *Mod.* A chiropodist, attending to a defective toe-nail. 1900 *Yearbk. U. S. Dept. Agric.* 443 The braces are *toe-nailed in place to prevent the possibility of their becoming loosened and dropping down. 1903 *U. S. Dept. Agric., Rep. Dis. Horse* 560 The regular position, the base-wide or toe-wide position, or the base-narrow or *toe-narrow position. 1879 *Cassell's Techn. Educ.* IV. 131/1 The *toe-piece or extreme end of the body and boot [of a coach]. 1894 *Daily News* 4 May 6/4 A very enormous boot would be required to receive the *toe-plate, as well as the foot. 1898 *Ibid.* 19 Aug. 4/5 The camp..contains everything needful down to the toeplates for the soldiers' boots. 1905 C. DAVENPORT *Jewellery* v. 87 *Toe-rings were common in India, but, like all native customs of this sort, their use is practically dying out. 1899 *Allbutt's Syst. Med.* VII. 150 Instead of the *toe-scraping of ordinary spastic disease, the whole foot is shoved forwards in walking. 1899 QUILLER COUCH *Ship of Stars* v, A glint of daylight on the *toe-scutes of two dangling boots. 1753 CHAMBERS *Cycl. Supp., Pollicipes*, the *toe-shell...They are multivalve flat shells, of a triangular figure, each being composed of several laminæ, which end in a sharp point. 1888 *Lockwood's Dict. Mech. Engin. Terms* 147 *Foot step*, or *Footstep Bearing*, a bearing closed at its bottom end, to sustain the end thrust of a vertical shaft or spindle. It is, therefore, a bearing socket, called also a step, and *toe step. 1911 *Blackw. Mag.* Dec. 780/1 The *toe-strap of one of his rope-sandals broke. 1862 *Catal. Internat. Exhib.* II. XXVII. 56 His new instep- and *toe-stretching boot tree. 1882 FLOYER *Unexpl. Baluchistan* 72 They all wore huge knitted list stockings, with a division for the *toe-string of the suâss, or grass sandals. 1839 *Civil Eng. & Arch. Jrnl.* II. 318/2 Machinery for manufacturing shoe-heels, and *toe-tips. 1892 SYMONDS *Life Michel Angelo* (1899) I. iv. 168 His whole frame laboured to the toe-tips. 1842 *P. Parley's Ann.* III. 264 The elbowing, the *toe-treading. 1910 *Daily News* 4 Apr. 12 The practice of gibbeting one's enemies in fiction is not a form of toe-treading that one ought to encourage. *a* 1858 in Youatt *Dog* (N.Y.) iii. 138 The ball pads being well protected by the spaniel *toe-tufts. 1598 MARSTON *Sco. Villanie* III. xi. (1599) 225 He dreames of *toe-turnes: each gallant he doth meete He fronts him with a trauerse in the streete. 1894 *Pop. Sci. Monthly* June 284 All the other cats in the world excepting Australia are digitigrade (*toe-walking). 1901 *Scribner's Mag.* Apr. 422/1 A trotting dandy who sported ankle-boots and *toe-weights, pulled up before him. 1903 *Toe-wide [see *toe-narrow*]. 1845 J. KITTO in Eadie *Life* ix. (1861) 307 The danger of being mixed up with the *toe-writers and learned pigs of literature.

**Toe** (tōu), *v.* [f. prec. sb.]

**1.** *trans.* To furnish with a toe or toes; to make or put a new toe on (a stocking, etc.): cf. HEEL *v.*[1] 2.

1607–8 T. COCKS *Diary* 1 Feb. (1901) 26 Paide for heelinge & toynge a payer of iersy stockings vj d. 1660 HOWELL *Party of Beasts* 39 They all bowed their snaky heads down to their very feet, which were toed with Scorpions.

**2.** To touch or reach with the toes; chiefly in *to toe a* or *the line, mark, scratch, crack*, to stand with the tips of one's toes exactly touching a line; to stand in a row; hence *fig.* to present oneself in readiness for a race, contest, or undertaking; also, to conform to the defined standard or platform of a party.

1833 MARRYAT *P. Simple* ix, He desired us to 'toe a line', which means to stand in a row. 1840 R. H. DANA *Bef. Mast* xxvii, The chief mate..marked a line on the deck, brought the two boys up to it, making them 'toe the mark'. 1853 'C. BEDE' *Verdant Green* II. iv, Toeing the scratch for business. 1862 MACLAREN *Milit. Syst. Gymnastic Exerc.* 37 There should be..a permanent mark to 'toe' at starting. 1895 *Westm. Gaz.* 15 Jan. 8/1 The phrase 'toeing the line' is very much in favour with some Liberals. 1910 *Daily News* 30 Mar. 7 To-day they had decided to toe the line with the progressive workers of the country.

**3. a.** To kick with the toe. **b.** *Golf.* To strike (a ball) with the tip of the club: cf. HEEL *v.*[1] 5 c.

1865 NIXON *P. Perfume* 58 Tom toed them out. 1893 LANG in *Longm. Mag.* Apr. 651 They might toe or heel the ball.

**4.** *intr.* To move the toe, to tap rhythmically with the toe in dancing; *to toe and heel* (*it*), to dance.

1828 *Examiner* 630/1 A Sailor toe-and-heels it, and lock-steps and straddles. 1859 DICKENS *Haunted House* VIII. 48 There ensued such toe-and-heeling, and buckle-covering, and double-shuffling. 1882 *Punch* 27 Dec. 302/2 Fiddler, tune up merrily! Toe and heel it happily.

**5.** *trans. Carpentry.* To secure or join together by nails driven obliquely: see TOED *ppl. a.* 2.

Hence **Toe·ing** *vbl. sb.*

1871 G. MEREDITH *H. Richmond* III. 188 Your French phrases and toeings!

**Toed** (tōud), *ppl. a.* [f. TOE *sb.* and *v.* + -ED.]

**1.** Having a toe or toes; mainly in compounds in which the first element specifies the number or kind of toes, as *three-toed, black-toed*. Of a stocking, Having separate divisions for the toes; of a clog, or the like, Having a (leather) toe-piece.

1611 COTGR., *Guillemot*, a certain three-towed fowle. 1757 JEFFERYS *Collect. Dresses* I. 29 The Slipper resembles a toed Clog. 1772–84 COOK *Voy.* (1790) I. 17 On the 25th this gentleman shot a black-toed gull. 1774 *Trinket* 37 In her little black bonnet, India handkerchief, and toed clogs. 1880 HAUGHTON *Phys. Geog.* vi. 281 They..possessed five-toed fore and hind feet. 1895 *Outing* (U.S.) XXVII. 200/1 That old man, upon his old-fashioned, curly-toed skates. 1910 *Daily Chron.* 15 Mar. 7/4 The stockings were toe-ed.

**2.** *Carpentry.* Secured or joined by nails driven obliquely; also of a nail, driven obliquely.

1877 KNIGHT *Dict. Mech.*, *Toed* (Carpentry), a brace, strut, or stay is said to be toed when it is secured by nails driven in obliquely and attaching it to the beam [etc.].

**Toek**, obs. f. *took*, pa. t. of TAKE *v.*

**To-eke, to-eken**: see TEKE, TEKEN.

**Toeless** (tōu·lės), *a.* [-LESS.] Having no toes.

1891 BULLOCH in *Boston Mission Herald* May 208 His own feet are toeless. 1895 *Chamb. Jrnl.* XII. 628/1 Pity! pity! they cried, as they showed their fingerless hands, and toeless feet or stumps of feet.

**Toer**, obs. variant of TOWER.

‖ **Toe-toe** (tō·ĭ,tō·ĭ). Also **toi-toi, tohi, toi.** [Maori.] The native name for various tall reed-like grasses of the genus *Arundo*, esp. *A. conspicua*, natives of New Zealand.

1843 in A. Domett *Collect. Ord.* (1850) (Morris), Every building constructed wholly or in part of raupo, nikau, toi-toi, wiwi kakaho, straw or thatch of any description. 1867 LADY BARKER *Station Life N. Zealand* xv. (1870) 110 Thatching it with Tohi, or swamp-grass. 1892 *19th Cent.* Sept. 409 The Toe-toe, which closely resembles pampas grass.

**To-fall** (tū·fǫl), *sb.* Also 5 taw-, 5–6 tu-, 6 tuf-, (tul-), toy-, 7–9 too-, 9 two-, tee-, -fa, -fal, -falle. [f. TO *prep.* + FALL *v.* or *sb.* In sense 2 = MHG. *zuoval*, Ger. *zufall*, Du. *toeval*, LG. *tofal.*]

**1.** A supplementary building with its roof sloping up to and leaning on the wall of a main building; a lean-to; a penthouse; a shed. *Sc.* and *north. dial.*

*c* 1425 WYNTOUN *Cron.* IX. v. 568 Þe north ile and þe quere, Þe tofallis ii. war mad but were. 1435 *Nottingham Rec.* II. 359 A tawfall' yat standes on ye comon ground. *c* 1440 *Alphabet of Tales* 254 Þe kyngis nowte-hard..tuke provand ..to his catell, & had it home vnto his tofall at he dwelte in. *Ibid.* 393 The erle..ffled with his wife in-to a wudd, and þer he hid hym in a tufall. *c* 1450 *St. Cuthbert* (Surtees) 7651 Þai made þaim tofalles To duell in vndir þe walles. 1512 *Nottingham Rec.* III. 402 The tofalle that ye chyldern lerne inne. 1518 *Burgh Rec. Edinb.* (1869) I. 178 Na tulfais be biggitt to the said wallis. 1523 in *Visit. Southwell* (Camden) 121 My tuffall of paysen the which standeth over myn oxen. 1642–3 in J. Watson *Jedburgh Abbey* (1894) 86 That ane roofe to-fa-wayis may theik vnder the eising of the body of the kirk. *a* 1670 SPALDING *Troub. Chas. I* (1851) II. 154 He tirrit the too-fallis of the haill office houssis ..and careit rooff and sklait away. 1825 BROCKETT *N. C. Words, Toofall, Twofall*, or *Teefall*,..often pronounced *Touffa*. 1844 STEPHENS *Bk. Farm* II. 12 Piling them against a high wall, and thatching them like a to-fall. 1887 D. H. FLEMING *Tourist's Hand-bk. St. Andrews* 31 The slight raggle..marks the height of some to-fall.

**b.** *fig.* (*a*) A dependant. (*b*) A shelter.

1822 AINSLIE *Land of Burns* 209 He was a sort o' toofa' upon their kindness. 1871 WADDELL *Ps.* xviii. 2 The Lord my rock, my hainin-towir, an' my to-fa'.

†**2.** That which befalls or falls to any one; a chance, accident, casualty: cf. FALL *v.* 46. *Obs.*

1562 TURNER *Baths* 17 These that are rytche..may haue other remedies inough agaynst the forenamed tofalles. 1572 J. JONES *Bathes of Bath* III. 22 Accident is that, which the Greekes call *Symptoma*, and wee properly in English, to fall and with fall.

**3.** The act of falling to; *to-fall of the day* or *night*, the close of day or beginning of night. *Sc.*

1749 COLLINS *Ode Superstit. Highl.* 123 For him in vain at

to-fall of the day, His babes shall linger. *a* **1754** W. Hamilton *Braes of Yarrow* xx, But ere the toofall of the night He lay a corps on the Braes of Yarrow. **1831** J. Wilson *Unimore* x. 165 Who only waits the to-fall of the night To wake the jocund sound of dance and song.

† **To-fa·ll**, *v. Obs.* [OE. *tofeallan*, f. To-[2] + *feallan* to Fall; = OS. *te-fallan*, OHG. *zi-, zarfallan.*] *intr.* To fall asunder or to pieces; to fall down, collapse; also, to fall to decay.

*c* **893** K. Ælfred *Oros.* vi. ii. § 2 Þa hie æt hiora theatrum wæron.., þa hit eall tofeoll, & heora ofsloȝ xx M. **1056–66** *Inscr. Kirkdale Ch. Yorks.*, Hit wes æl tobrocan & tofalan. *c* **1205** Lay. 18867 Scullen stan walles Biuoren him to-fallen. *a* **1300** *Signa ante Judicium* 139 in *E. E. P.* (1862) 11 As heuen and erþe sold to-fal. *c* **1380** *Sir Ferumb.* 5011 Þe walle þat was so broken & to-falle. **1398** Trevisa *Barth. De P. R.* xvi. lxxiv. (Bodl. MS.), Ȝif it [a stone] is not fattye it wolle alle to fall bi maistrye of druynes.

† **To-fa·re**, *v. Obs.* [OE. *tofaran*, f. To-[2] + *faran* to go, Fare; = OS. *to-faran*, OHG. *zi-, ze-, za-faran.*] *intr.* To go asunder, disperse.

*a* **900** *Cædmon's Gen.* 1691 Toforan þa on feower weȝas. *c* **1000** *Sax. Leechd.* I. 122 Drincan on win eal, ꝥ attor tofærð. **14..** in *Anglia* III. 546/146 The folk..Shall tofare on every clyve.

† **To-fe·re**, *v. Obs.* [OE. *toféran*, f. To-[2] + *féran*, Fere *v.*[1]] *intr.* = prec.

*c* **1000** Ælfric *Hom.* I. 22 Hi ða ȝeswicon þære ȝetimbrunge, and toferdon ȝeond ealne middanȝeard. *c* **1175** *Lamb. Hom.* 93 Ða apostoli siððan er þon þet heo to-ferden isetten iacob..on cristes setl [*MS.* selt].

**Tofet**, variant of Tovet, measure of two pecks.

**Toff** (tǫf). *vulgar.* Also *rarely* toft. [Perh. a vulgar perversion of Tuft, as formerly applied to a nobleman or gentleman-commoner at Oxford.] An appellation given by the lower classes to a person who is stylishly dressed or who has a smart appearance; a swell; hence, one of the well-to-do, a 'nob'.

**1851** Mayhew *Lond. Labour* I. 217/2. *Ibid.* (1864) II. 562/1 If it's a lady and gentleman, then we cries, 'A toff and a doll!' **1865** *Slang Dict.*, *Toft*, a showy individual, a swell. **1883** *Fortn. Rev.* Dec. 852 The poets who are here are tremendous proud toffs. **1900** Upward *Eben. Lobb* 130 Nonsense, man,..why, in these days a jockey is no end of a toff. **1901** *Essex Weekly News* 29 Mar. 2/1 She..declared that tramps were treated like toffs at Stanway Workhouse.

**b.** Sometimes applied in compliment to a person who behaves 'handsomely'; a 'brick'.

**1898** *Brit. Weekly* 27 Jan. 306/2 A Paisley bailie let off a man easier than the culprit expected, and was addressed, 'Thank you, sir, you're an old toff'. This was meant for a compliment. **1906** *Daily Chron.* 25 May 4/7 One of the witnesses..spoke of a generous employer as 'a regular toff'. 'Toff' is perhaps the highest compliment, or the bitterest sneer, according to the tone, that a man who does not make any pretence to magnificence can aim at a man who does.

Hence **To·ffish, To·ffy** *adjs.*, like or characteristic of a 'toff', stylish.

**1898** *Westm. Gaz.* 13 Jan. 4/2 He wore a 'toffish' side pocket jacket, which fitted him like a glove. **1901** J. K. Jerome *Obs. Henry* 31 Toffy enough she looked in her diamonds and furs.

**Toffee, toffy** (tǫ·fi). [Of uncertain origin: app. orig. dialectal, and sometimes spelt *tuffy, toughy*, as if named from its toughness; but the earlier form is the northern Taffy, q. v.] A sweetmeat made from sugar or treacle, butter, and sometimes a little flour, boiled together; often mixed with bruised nuts, as *almond* or *walnut toffee*.

*a* **1825** Forby *Voc. E. Anglia*, *Toughy*, a coarse sweetmeat, composed of brown sugar and treacle; named from its toughness, though perhaps it should be spelled *tuffy*, and considered as another form of taffy, described in Wilbraham's *Cheshire Dialect* [1817] as compounded of the same ingredients. **1825** Mrs. Cameron *Seeds Greediness* in *Houlston Tracts* I. No. 22. 2 Some shining sticky stuff, which in some countries children call tuffy. **1828** *Craven Gloss.* s.v., 'To join for toffy', to club for making toffy, a custom still very frequent amongst young persons. **1862** Dickens *Lett.* 28 Jan., I am going to bring the boys some toffee. **1877** Black *Green Past.* ii, Is it sixpence you want to buy toffy with?

**b.** *attrib.* and *Comb.*

**1857** Hughes *Tom Brown* I. iii, It being only a step to the toffy shop. **1896** *Westm. Gaz.* 30 May 2/1 The effect.. that a toffee drop has on a churchwarden when he finds it in the bag.

† **To-fleet**, *v. Obs.* [OE. *tofléotan*, f. To-[2] + *fléotan*, Fleet *v.*[1]; = OHG. *zifliozan* 'defluere', to melt, MHG. *zervliezen.*] *intr.* To float away; to be carried away by or as by water.

*a* **1122** *O. E. Chron.* an. 1097, Þa brycȝe þe forneah eall to flotan wæs. *a* **1225** *Ancr. R.* 72 Forstoppeð ouwer þouhtes.. ꝥ heo climben & hien touward heouene, & nout..to uleoten ȝeond te world. *Ibid.* 74–6 Vor mid te fleotinde word, to fleoteð þe heorte.

† **To·-flight.** *Obs. rare.* [f. To-[1] + Flight *sb.*[2]: so OHG., MHG. *zuofluht*, Ger. *zuflucht*, Du. *toevlucht* refuge, shelter, resource.] A shelter, refuge.

*a* **1300** *E. E. Psalter* xvii[i]. 1 [2] Laverd mi festnes ai in nede, And mi to-flight [*v.r.* tofliht] þat es swa, And mi leser oute of wa.

† **To-fly**, *v. Obs.* Forms: see Fly *v.*[1] [OE. *tofléogan*, f. To-[2] + *fléogan*, Fly *v.*[1]; = OHG. *zefliogan*, MHG. *zevliegen.*] *intr.* To fly in different directions, to be dispersed in flight; also, to fly to pieces, be shattered.

*c* **1000** *Sax. Leechd.* I. 188 Sona hyt toflyð [*v.r.* flihð]. *Ibid.* III. 34 Woden..sloh ða þa næddran þæt heo on viiii to-fleah. *c* **1205** Lay. 28668 Þa cnihtes alle..þa weoren wide to-floȝen. **13..** *Cast. Love* (Halliw.) 1559 The stones woll breke and all to-flyn. **1387** Trevisa *Higden* (Rolls) VII. 35 Þe giestes and þe bemes of þe soler al to fligh, and þe soler fil doun.

† **Tofo·re**, *prep.*, *adv.*, and *conj. Obs.* Forms: α. 1–2 tóforan, (1 -on), 2–3 toforen, 3–5 to foren, 4–6 toforn(e, 4–7 to forn(e. β. 3 to vore, 3–4 tovore, 3–6 to for, (3 te for), 3–7 to fore, 4–6 tofor, 4–7 tofore, (5 toffore), 6 *Sc.* to-foir. γ. *Sc.* 5 to forowe, toforowe, 6 to forrow. [OE *tóforan*, f. To *prep.* + *foran* adv., deriv. of OTeut. **fora* fore, for: see Before, also Afore, Atfore, Heretofore. Cognate with OFris. *tô-fora*, OS. *te foran*, MHG. *zevor, zuovor, -vorn*, Ger. *zuvor.*]

**A.** *prep.*

**1.** Of motion: To before, to the front of; of position: In front of; = Before B. 2.

*a* **900** tr. *Bæda's Hist.* iii. xii. [xiv.] (1890) 196 Se cyning ..stop ofostlice toforan [ðam] biscope, & feoll to his fotum. *c* **1000** *Ags. Gosp.* Luke x. 8 Etað þæt eow toforan aset ys. *c* **1275** Lay. 31548 Þo stot him vp Penda: To-vore þan heȝe kinge. *c* **1300** *Beket* 2001 That bred..that tofore him lay. *a* **1325** *Prose Psalter* liii. [liv.] 3 [Thei] ne sett nouȝt God to-forn her syȝt. *c* **1489** Caxton *Sonnes of Aymon* xiv. 346 He cast hym deed to fore his fete. *a* **1547** Surrey *Æneid* iv. 264 Tofore thaltars, in presence of the Gods.

**b.** Into or in the presence of; in the sight or cognizance of; = Before B. 3.

*c* **1000** *Ags. Gosp.* Matt. xxv. 32 Ealle þeoda beoþ toforan hym ȝegaderude. **10..** *Leg. Rood* (1871) 11/4 Þæt hio rædlice coman toforan þare mære cwenan þa hio beforan hire stodan. *c* **1070** *O. E. Chron.* an. 1070 (Parker MS.), Se arcebiscop.. þæt ylce ȝefæstnode toforan þam papan Alexandre. *c* **1205** Lay. 14071 Þan kinge he eode toforen. **1340** *Ayenb.* 218 Þe ilke comþ to-uore god mid ydele honden. **1387** Trevisa *Higden* (Rolls) V. 347 He knowleched his trespas openliche tofore þe bisshop and al þe peple. **1493** *Festivall* (W. de W. 1515) 14 b, Anone tofore them he made a blynde man to se. **1600** Fairfax *Tasso* i. xxxv, All tofore their chieftaine mustred beene.

**c.** *Tofore God*: in the sight of God; at the tribunal of God; hence as an asseveration (also *God tofore*), by God: cf. Before B. 3 b, 4, 5.

*c* **1374** Chaucer *Troylus* iii. 800 (849) So shal I do to morw I-wis..And god to-forn. **1377** Langl. *P. Pl.* B. v. 457 And made avowe to-fore god for his foule sleuthe. *a* **1450** Myrc *Par. Pr.* 213 That ys feyre to-fore god. *a* **1500** *Chaucer's Dreme* 1281 Madame..god tofore, ye shul be there.

**2.** Of position in motion: In advance of, ahead of: = Before B. 1. (In quot. 1297 with a pursuer as object; cf. Before B. 1 c.)

*c* **1000** *Ags. Gosp.* Luke i. 17 He gæð toforan him on gaste and Elias mihte. *c* **1250** *Old Kentish Serm.* in *O. E. Misc.* 26 Swo kam si sterre þet yede to-for hem in-to ierusalem. **1297** R. Glouc. (Rolls) 2202 Ȝe ne conne bote fle Ase ssep to vore wolues. *a* **1450** *Knt. de la Tour* (1906) 63, .ij. yonge women..wolde haue hasted hem tofore her felawes. **1600** Fairfax *Tasso* i. xxxvii, Their wonted ensigne, they tofore them bring.

**3.** Of time: Previously to, earlier than; = Before B. 7–9.

*a* **1000** in Cockayne *Narrat.* (1861) 16 Hit wæs to foran dæȝes. *c* **1025** *O. E. Chron.* an. 1013, On þam ilcan ȝeare to foran þam monðe Augustus. *c* **1275** *Woman of Samaria* 5 in *O. E. Misc.* 84 A lutel te-for þe tyme. **1387** Trevisa *Higden* (Rolls) I. 165 Carthago was i-buld þre score ȝere and twelue to fore þe citee of Rome. **1440** in *Wars Eng. in France* (1864) II. 455 Not longe tyme tofore his deth. **1577–87** Holinshed *Scott. Chron.* (1805) II. 198 Rather.. than we did tofore his fathers invasion.

**4.** Of rank, order, or preference: In precedence of or preference to; beyond, more than; rather than; = Before B. 10, 11.

*c* **888** K. Ælfred *Boeth.* Prayer (at end), Þæt ic mæȝe þe inweardlice lufian toforon eallum þingum. *c* **1000** Ælfric *Deut.* vii. 14 ȝe beoþ ȝebletsod toforan eallum oþrum mannum. *c* **1000** — *Hom.* I. 208 Assa is stunt nyten..and toforan oðrum nytenum unȝesceadwis. *c* **1175** *Lamb. Hom.* 117 He is on heuene on his kine setle to-foran oðer mennen. *a* **1272** *A Luue Ron* 155 in *O. E. Misc.* 98 Nys non betere vnder heouene grunde. He is to-fore alle oþre i-coren. *a* **1325** *Prose Psalter* xliv. [xlv.] 3 Fair artou..in fourme to-fore mennes sones. **14..** *Chaucer's Pars. T.* ⁋ 677 (Harl. MS.) Thus is he an auerous man þat loueth his tresor toforn god.

**b.** Of serial order: Before, preceding.

**1387** Trevisa *Higden* (Rolls) III. 61 Þe peple putte hir owne names to fore þe names of hir felawes.

**5.** Besides, over and above. *rare.* (Cf. B. 5.)

*c* **1000** Ælfric *Hom.* II. 584 Salomon eac forȝeaf þære cwene swa hwæs swa heo ȝyrnde æt him, toforan ðære cynelican lace ðe he hire ȝeaf.

**B.** *adv.* (not in OE.).

**1.** Of time: Previously, beforehand, earlier; heretofore, in the past; = Before A. 5.

*c* **1175** *Lamb. Hom.* 121 Al swa þet writ seide bi him muchel to-foran. **1258** *Proclam. Hen. III*, Þurȝ þe besiȝte of þan to foren iseide redesmen. **1340** *Ayenb.* 7 He deþ aye þe heste of god to uore yzed. *c* **1350** *Will. Palerne* 142 Ac his witt welt he after, as wel as to fore. *c* **1400** *Lanfranc's Cirurg.* 110 Þat I have told to forn. **1423** Jas. I *Kingis Q.* ii, New partit out of slepe a lyte tofore. *Ibid.* xxiii, The way we tuke, the tyme I tald to-forowe [*rimes* morowe, borowe]. *a* **1425** *Cursor M.* 3010 (Trin.) Ysaac hir son.. Þat was longe bihet to forn [*earlier MSS.* biforn, be-forne]. **1481** Caxton *Reynard* xxxiv. (Arb.) 100, I am more hongry now than I was to fore. **1546** *Supplic. of Poore Commons* (E. E. T. S.) 61 Not many yeres tofore. **1649** G. Daniel *Trinarch.*, *Hen. V* c, Mortimer, Earle of March, in the right Line Discendent, and to fore declared Heire.

**2.** Of position: In front; = Before A. 2.

**13..** *Guy Warw.* (A.) 1871 Sadok toforn haþ him smete Of his scheld a quarter wiþ gret hete. *c* **1400** *Lanfranc's Cirurg.* 105 Þe senewis tofore ben drawe togidere. **14..** *Beryn* 155 It is a spere, yf thowe canst se, with a prik tofore.

**3.** Of motion: In advance, ahead; = Before A. 1.

*c* **1330** *Arth. & Merl.* 1365 Now wendeþ to forn, on of ȝou, & tel anon þe king. **1426** Lydg. *De Guil. Pilgr.* 24570 Send hem toforne, on thy massage. **1470–85** Malory *Arthur* ii. ix. 85, xx of hem rode to fore to warne the lady. **1513** Douglas *Æneis* i. Prol. 419 Saying he followit Virgillis lantern to forne, Quhen Eneas to Dido was forsworne.

**4.** Of rank: In precedence; cf. Before A. 4.

*c* **1440** *Gesta Rom.* xci. 416 (Add. MS.) Þe proude man wil all wey be sette aboue and be-fore oþer, he wil all way be putte tofore in Euery place. **1481** Caxton *Godeffroy* cxci. 280 Without doubte the spyrituel thynges be more digne and worthy than the temporall. Therfore..the moost hye thynges ought to goo to fore.

**5.** Beforehand; in hand for the future; left over. Cf. mod.Sc. *to the fore.*

**1597** *Trials for Witchcraft* in *Spalding Misc.* (1841) I. 95 Hir and hir guidman..suld newir haue frie geir tofoir.

**C.** *conj.* Of time: = Before C. 1. **a.** with *that*: cf. Before C. 1 a.

*a* **1325** *Prose Psalter* lxxxix. [xc.] 2 To-fore þat þe mounteins were made. **1388** Wyclif *Matt.* x. 23 To fore that mannus sone come. **1484** Caxton *Curial* 12 Tofore that thou hast ony offyces.

**b.** *simply*: cf. Before C. 1 b.

**1464** *Rolls of Parlt.* V. 563/2 Tofore it passe out of any of the seid Townes. **1477** Sir J. Paston in *P. Lett.* III. 187 Iff I had hadde it toffore he wente. **1560** Daus tr. *Sleidane's Comm.* 9 So cannot he condemne him for an Heretike tofore he be detected of errour.

**c.** *Tofore or* (= ere): cf. Before C. 1 c.

*c* **1440** Lydg. *Hors, Shepe & G.* 5 (Lamb. MS.) On shreffe thursday toforne or he was dede! **1474** Caxton *Chesse* iii. i, Tofore or Adam synned. **1485** — *Paris & V.* (1868) 30 Alwaye tofore or he wente to hys bedde.

**D.** *Comb.*: **toforegoing** *a.*, foregoing, preceding, antecedent; **toforehand** *adv.*, beforehand, previously; **toforesaid** *a.*, previously mentioned, aforesaid; **toforetime** *adv.*, previously, aforetime.

**1387–8** T. Usk *Test. Love* iii. iii. (Skeat) l. 180 That oon is *toforgoing necessite, whiche maketh thing to be. *Ibid.* viii. 30 Onely through grace toforgoing. **1387** Trevisa *Higden* (Rolls) III. 147 I-wrete of hym an hondred ȝere and twenty ȝere *to forehonde. *Ibid.* VI. 175 Seint Aldelyn was to forehonde abbot of Malteby, þat is Malmesbury. **1387–8** T. Usk *Test. Love* i. vi. (Skeat) l. 154 Of errours coming herafter, men may lightly to forne hande puruaye remedye. *c* **1430** *Syr Gener.* (Roxb.) 3681 As ye haue herd tofore hond. **1258** *To foren iseide [see B. 1]. **1387–8** T. Usk *Test. Love* iii. iv. (Skeat) l. 261 If thou have knowing of these to-fornsaid thinges. **1444** *Rolls of Parlt.* V. 121/2 Founden by an enquerre bi the Baillifs toforeseid. *c* **1400** *Three Kings Cologne* 82 (Cambr. MS.) Þe sterre þat *tofore-tyme ȝede a-fore hem. *c* **1477** Caxton *Jason* 46 Him semed that he hadde seen them tofore tyme.

† **To-fret**, *v. Obs.* [ME. *tofreten*, f. To-[2] + *freten*, Fret *v.*[1]; cf. Ger. *zerfressen.*] *trans.* To gnaw, devour, consume.

*a* **1225** *Ancr. R.* 202 Þes laste bore hweolp..to-cheoweð & to-uret Godes milde milce. *c* **1412** Hoccleve *De Reg. Princ.* 3226 Thy disese is lesse, Ffalle in þe daunger of lambes humblesse, Than he [who is] with cruel wolues al to-frete. *a* **1529** Skelton *Garl. Laurel* 1450 This delycate dasy..With frowarde frostis, alas, was all to-fret.

† **To-frush**, *v. Obs.* [ME. *to-frusche(n*, f. To-[2] + *frusch(e* Frush *v.* (from French).] *trans.* To smash or break to pieces; also, to drive violently *into* something as with a blow or blows.

*c* **1300** *Havelok* 1993 Was non..þat he ne dede alto-cruhsse, And alto-shiuere, and alto-frusshe. *a* **1330** *Syr Degarre* 381 Ac he..with his bat leid up an, And al to frusst him ech a bon. **1375** Barbour *Bruce* viii. 303 Speris þat to-fruschyt war. *c* **1400** tr. *Secreta Secret.*, *Gov. Lordsh.* 106 Here y dwelle all to-ffrushyd, & y haue gret myster of pytee. **1513** Douglas *Æneis* ii. viii. [vii.] 40 Hewit, hackit, smate doun, and all to fruschit. **1532** More *Confut. Tindale* Wks. 717/2 Christ shall come down..and all to frush & to breke those earthlye wretched heretikes like a sort of earthen pottes. **1586** Warner *Alb. Eng.* ii. xii. (1589) 51 Who, lying all to frusshed thus, the sonne of Ioue did bring His cruell lades.

**Toft** (tǫft). Also 5–7 tofte, (7 tuft), 8–9 *Sc. dial.* taft. [Late OE. *toft*, a. ON. *topt, tupt*, later *toft, tuft* (Norw. *toft, tuft, tyft* 'ground attached to a house' (Aasen), early and dial. Swed. *toft*, Da. *toft, tofte*), existing beside and commonly identified with ON. *tomt*, OSwed. *tompt* (Vigfusson), Norw. *tomt* (Aasen), Swed. *tomt*, Da. *tomt* 'toft'; both forms :—OTeut. **tumft-*, **tumf(e)t-*, with which cf. Gr. δά-πεδον :—**dm-pedo-m*, a level surface, lit. 'a site for building'.]

**1.** Originally, a homestead, the site of a house and its out-buildings; a house site. Often in the expression *toft and croft*, denoting the whole holding, consisting of the homestead and attached piece of arable land.

**1001** in Kemble *Cod. Dipl.* III. 317 Healf þæt land æt Suðham, innur and uttur, on tofte and on crofte. *a* **1100** in *Sax. Leechd.* III. 286 And ic aȝnian wille to aȝenre ahte ðæt ðæt ic hæbbe, & næfre ðæt yntan, ne plot ne ploh, ne turf ne toft, ne furh ne fotmæl, ne land ne læse, ne fersc ne mersc, ne ruh ne rum. **12..** (orig. *a* **1100**) *Charter of Siflæd* in Birch *Cart. Sax.* III. 217 And ic [an] mine landsethlen here toftes to owen aihte and alle mine men fre. **1290** *Rolls of Parlt.* I. 62/1 Johanna .. petit dotem .. de viii to Toftis et viii to Bovatis terre. **1348** *Ibid.* II. 205/1 Un toft & cink acres de terre. **14..** *Customs of Malton* in *Surtees*

*Misc.* (1888) 63 For every tofte þt is nott beldydd j d. **1473** *Rental Bk. Cupar-Angus* (1879) I. 165 Ilke man sal kepe his pairt of his malyn and his toft that his nichtbur be nocht injuryt. **1592** West *Symbol.* II. *Fines* § 55 A Toft is the place wherein a mesuage hath stand. **1607** Norden *Surv. Dial.* v. 207, I haue..obserued..that many croftes, toftes, pightes, pingles, and other small quillits of land, about farme houses, and Tenements, are suffred to lie together idle. **1683** *Lond. Gaz.* No. 1800/4 A Tuft of Ground..by Thames-Street, will be disposed of by Lease for 61 years, by the Committee for Letting the City Lands. **1760** Ld. Mansfield in *Burrow's Rep.* (1766) II. 1064 The Owner of a House may, if he pleases, pull it quite down, and convert it into a Toft. **1790** A. Wilson *To Eben. Picken* Poet. Wks. (1846) 107 And scores o' times, in kintra tafts, They've gart the fouk maist rive their chafts. **1809** Bawdwen *Domesday Bk.* 614 But the riding say that he has only 9½ acres and one toft, the soke of which belongs to the King's Manor of Gayton. **1818** Hallam *Mid. Ages* ix. I. (1819) III. 366 A house with its stables and farm-buildings, surrounded by a hedge or inclosure, was called a court, or..a curtilage; the toft or homestead of a more genuine English dialect.

**2** Apparently including the croft, or applied to a field or piece of land larger than the site of a house.

c **1440** *Promp. Parv.* 495/1 Toft, *campus.* c **1450** *Godstow Reg.* 315, iij. mesis liyng to-gedir..with the toftis liyng therto..; also with two toftis I-closed in, of the which one strecchith hit-self in lengthe of the gardeyn of the seid Symond, and another in lengthe of the gardeyn of the said abbesse and Couent, in þe forsaid towne of karsynton. **1549** *Reg. Mag. Sig. Scot.* 82/2 Terras de Drumfyne nuncupatas the Toftis of Drumfyne. **1598** Kitchin *Courts Leet* (1675) 151 One Tenement with a Toft adjoining. **1831** Landor *Fra Rupert* II. i, Though the parks and groves and tofts around,..Open would be to her.

**3.** An eminence, knoll, or hillock in a flat region; esp. one suitable for the site of a house or tower. Cf. quot. 1863. Now *local.*

**1362** Langl. *P. Pl.* A. Prol. 14, I sauh a Tour on A Toft triȝely I-maket; A Deop Dale bi-neoþe. **1387** Trevisa *Higden* (Rolls) VII. 359 In þe myddel of þat playn was a litel toft as it were an hille [*colliculus turgescebat*]. **1558** Phaer *Æneid* VII. U iv, They, from their Fescen hilles, and from Faliscus equall toftes. **1863** Baring-Gould *Iceland* xxii. 368 A farm named Tratharholt, crowning a toft which rises out of green meads and almost impossible swamps. **1887** Fenn *Dick o' Fens* (1888) 23 Right up on a high toft with the river on one side and the fens for miles on the other.

† **4.** 'A small grove of trees' (E.D.D.). *dial.* (or ? error in Kersey's Phillips.) *Obs.*

**1706** Phillips (ed. Kersey), *Toft*..also a Grove of Trees. **1726** *Dict. Rust.* (ed. 3), *Toft*, a Grove of trees.

**5.** *attrib.* and *Comb.*, as *toft field, toftstead*; **toftman**, the owner or occupier of a toft.

**1763** *Museum Rust.* I. 35 The soil of your upper *toft field. **1826** Scott *Jrnl.* 16 Mar., I shall have on the toft field a gallant show of extensive woodland. **12..** *Prior. Lewens.* 18 (Cowell's Interpr. 1684) *Toftmanni similiter operabantur. **1706** Phillips (ed. Kersey), *Toft-man*, the Owner of a Toft. **1524** *Test. Ebor.* (Surtees) V. 180 An other *toftstede which I haue in Lownd. **1773** *Burstwick Inclos. Act* 6 Gardens, orchards, toftsteads, crofts. **1839** Stonehouse *Axholme* 35 To the owners of ancient messuages, cottages, tofts, and toftsteads.

**Toft**, variant of *tought*, obs. form of Taut *a.*

**Tofus**, variant of Tophus.

**Tog** (tǫg), *sb.*[1]; usually *pl.* **togs.** *slang* or *colloq.* [app. a shortening of Togeman(s, togman, used in Vagabonds' Cant as early as the 16th c. Its currency in the 19th c. has no doubt been aided by its obvious connexion with Toga; cf. Toge.]

**1.** *Cant* and *slang.* A coat; any outer garment; see also quot. 1809.

**1798** Tuft *Gloss. Thieves' Jargon* (Cent. D.), *Long tog*, a coat. **1809** G. Andrewes *Dict. Slang & Cant, Tatty togg*, a gaming cloth. **1812** J. H. Vaux *Flash Dict., Tog*, a coat. **1821** *Sporting Mag.* IX. 27 Curtis, in a new white upper tog. **1911** *19th Cent.* Sept. 548 A tog and kicks is synonymous with a coat and breeches.

**2.** *pl.* Clothes. *slang* and *humorously colloq.*

**1809** G. Andrewes *Dict. Slang & Cant, Toggs*, clothes. **1812** J. H. Vaux *Flash Dict., Togs* or *Toggery*, wearing apparel in general. **1838** Dickens *O. Twist* xvi, 'Look at his togs, Fagin!' said Charley...'Look at his togs!—Superfine cloth, and the heavy swell cut!'

**b.** Variously qualified: often humorous or depreciative; *long togs* (*Naut.*), landsmen's clothes.

**1830** Marryat *King's Own* x, I retained a suit of 'long togs', as we call them. **1840** [see Long *a.*[1] 18]. **1850** Smedley *F. Fairlegh* iv. 34, I should have thought he had seen the sporting togs. **1860** *All Year Round* No. 66. 380 Three or four days..employed by us in providing sea-going togs, and other requirements. **1867** Smyth *Sailor's Word-bk.* s.v., Sunday togs.

**3.** *Comb.*, as *tog-maker.*

**1901** *Daily Tel.* 16 Apr. 5/2 Describing himself as a 'tog-maker', with no fixed abode.

**Tog** (tǫg), *sb.*[2] *dial.* Local variant of Teg, perh. influenced by *hog.*

**1851** *Jrnl. R. Agric. Soc.* XII. II. 333 A lamb eight or nine months old, and until his first shearing, is called a 'heder' or 'sheder' 'hog', 'hogget', or 'lamb-hog'. In other counties a 'teg', 'tog', 'gimmer', and 'dinmont', &c.

**Tog,** *v.* [Occurs first and chiefly as *togged* (tǫgd), prob. orig. from Tog *sb.*[1]: cf. *booted, hatted*, etc.] *trans.* To clothe, to dress. Const. *out, up.*

**1793** *European Mag.* XXIII. 466 An old fine lady..Tog'd out in each extravagance of fashion. **1811** *Lex. Balatr.* s. v. *Togs*, The swell is rum-togged, the gentleman is handsomely dressed. **1812** J. H. Vaux *Flash Dict.* s.v., To *tog* is to dress or put on clothes; to *tog* a person, is also to supply them with apparel. **1824** Scott *St. Ronan's* iv, He was tog'd gnostically enough. **1862** *All Year Round* 13 Sept. 12/1 He was togged out in first-rate style. **1894** Henty *Dorothy's Double* I. 202 You had better tog yourself up a bit. **1904** J. A. Riis *Roosevelt* xiv. 344 Mrs. Cleveland when he was Governor, togged out his staff in the most gorgeous clothes.

**b.** *intr.* for *refl.* Also *to tog it.*

**1812** [see above]. **1844** Alb. Smith *Adv. Mr. Ledbury* xvi, My pardner's going to tog it. **1869** J. Greenwood *Curses London* (Farmer), She's a dress-woman..they tog out that they may show off at their best, and make the most of their faces. **1903** 'Marjoribanks' *Fluff-Hunters* 132 It was a new experience—togging up to meet a prospective landlady!

‖ **Toga** (tōᵘ·gă). [L. *toga* = cloak or mantle, f. ablaut-stem of *teg-ĕre* to cover.]

*Rom. Antiq.* The outer garment of a Roman citizen in time of peace.

It consisted of a single piece of stuff of irregular form, long, broad, and flowing, without sleeves or armholes, and covered the whole body with the exception of the right arm. *Toga prætexta*, a toga with a broad purple border worn by children, magistrates, persons engaged in sacred rites, and later by emperors. *Toga virilis*, the toga of manhood, assumed by boys at puberty; hence in *fig.* context.

**1600** Holland *Livy* XXII. lvii. 467 All the younger sort above 17 yeares old, yea and some also under that age, that yet were in their *Pretexta*, and were not come to *Toga virilis.* **1638** Junius *Paint. Ancients* 152 The gowne deserved by them,..that had overcome their enemies, was called Toga palmata. **1690** Locke *Hum. Und.* III. xi. § 25 *Toga, Tunica, Pallium*, are Words easily translated by *Gown, Coat*, and *Cloak*; but we have thereby no more true Ideas of the fashion of those Habits..than we have of the Faces of the Taylors who made them. **1838–42** Arnold *Hist. Rome* II. xxxvii. 478 The white *toga* wrapped round the body like a plaid with its broad scarlet border. **1855** Thackeray *Newcomes* xvii, During this period Mr. Clive assumed the *toga virilis.* **1867** Baker *Nile Tribut.* iii. (1872) 46 There is a uniformity of dress throughout all the Nubian tribes of Arabs, the simple *toga* of the Romans.

**b.** *transf.* and *fig.* A robe of office; a professional gown, a cloak, a 'mantle'; a dress coat.

**1738** *Gentl. Mag.* VIII. 435/2 There were found a Chalice, two Crucifixes, a Toga or Pall, with several Mass-Books Latin and English, and other Popish Relicks. **1828** [C. Swan] tr. *Manzoni's Betrothed Lovers* I. vii. 200 Another ancestor, the dread of litigants; seated on a high stool of red velvet, and wrapped in an ample black *toga*—totally black, but for a white collar with two broad facings and lining of sable. **1855** J. Strang *Glasgow & Clubs* (1856) 207 Lord Braxfield wore the scarlet toga of the Justiciary Court. **1867** J. Macfarlane *Mem. T. Archer* v. 128 Can they be expected to don the togas of the geologist, the geographer, the chemist, the linguist, the political economist?

**c.** *Comb.*: **toga-folded** *a.*, folded like a toga; **toga-like** *a.*, resembling a toga; **toga-wise** *adv.*, in the manner of a toga.

**1887** Rider Haggard *Allan Quaterm.* xii. 132 The toga-like garment of brown cloth. **1902** *Westm. Gaz.* 5 Aug. 3/1, I saw my friend the artillery officer, wrapped in his long, pale blue cloak, one fold thrown over his left shoulder toga-wise. **1911** *Blackw. Mag.* Nov. 680/2 The Kapkoto were noticeable with their toga-folded blankets.

**Togaed** (tōᵘ·găd), *a.* Also toga'd. [-ed [2].] Clad in a toga; wearing the toga; togated.

**1860** Hawthorne *Marb. Faun* xli, The togaed [i. e. Roman] nation. **1897** *Archæologia* Ser. II. V. 310 Fullers, a class in great request among a togaed people.

† **To-gains, -gainst, -yenst,** *prep.* (*conj.*) *Obs.* Forms: *α.* 1 toȝæȝnes (-ȝeæȝnes, -ȝeeȝnes), 1–2 toȝeanes, -ȝenes, to ȝeȝnes, 2–4 toȝeines, 3 toȝenes, -ȝenys, toȝanes, (to janes, teȝenes), 3–4 to ȝeȝnes, to-ȝeynes, 4 to yans, to ayens, to ayans. *β.* 5 to ȝenst, -e. *γ.* 1 toȝeæȝn, 3 toȝæn, to ȝein, 3–5 to ȝen. [OE. *tóȝæȝnes, tóȝéanes*, etc., formed, with advb. genitive *-es*, on the simpler **tóȝæȝn, tóȝeæȝn*, from To *prep.* + *ȝæȝn*:—**gagn-, gegn-* 'against', the second element also of Again, Against. In this word, the simpler *tóȝeæȝn* was nearly superseded by the form in *-es*, and was rare both in OE. and ME.: see the *γ*-forms above. In the 15th c., *to-ȝenes* began to be strengthened by adding *-t*, as in *agains-t, amids-t, amongs-t* (app. after superlatives); if the word had survived into mod.Eng., its form would have been *to-yenst* or *to-yainst*; being entirely southern, it never had hard *g*, as in *again, against.*]

**1.** Towards with hostile intent; in opposition or hostility to, contrary to; = Against A. 11, 12.

*Beowulf* 666 Hæfde kyning wuldor grendle to-ȝeanes ..sele-weard aseted. *a* **1000** *Ags. Ps.* (Spelm.) xl. 8 Toȝeanes me runedon ealle fynd mine. *c* **1005** *O. E. Chron.* an. 1001 (Parker MS.), Him þær toȝeanes com Pallig. *c* **1200** *Trin. Coll. Hom.* 55 Flesliche lustes and fule sinnes flited eure toȝanes þe wreche saule. *c* **1205** Lay. 4536 Scip ærne to-ȝen [*c* **1275** to-ȝein] scip. *Ibid.* 9792 Þer ute wes heom to-ȝæn þe kæisere Uaspasien. *a* **1225** *St. Marher.* 15 Ah þeo þ stalewurðe beoð ant starke to ȝein me. *c* **1275** *Passion* 83 in *O. E. Misc.* 39 If he ouht prechede to-ȝeȝnes þere lawe. *c* **1300** *Vox & Wolf* 95 in Hazl. *E. P. P.* I. 61 Hit wes to-ȝeines his wille. **1340** *Ayenb.* 6 Yef he zuereþ uals be his wytinde, he him uorzuereþ and deþ to ayans þise heste. *a* **1440** *R. Gloucester's Chron.* (Rolls) App. G. 197 Þou to ȝenst kunde..Bringest me in sorewe. *Ibid.* App. EE. 20 Charlemaines spere þat to ȝenste þe saracins he was ywoned to bere.

**b.** In defence or protection from; = Against A. 13.

*a* **1225** *Ancr. R.* 66 God is þ ȝe asken red, & salue þ he teche ou to ȝeines fondunges. *a* **1300** *K. Horn* 56 Þe king hadde al to fewe Toȝenes so vele schrewe. *c* **1380** *Sir Ferumb.* 172 He þat scholde me socoury to ȝen myn enymys. *a* **1440** *R. Gloucester's Chron.* (Rolls) App. XX. 380 Þe castel of ȝipeswich..Þat huwe bigod hadde iholde to ȝen his kinedom.

**2.** Towards, forward to, so as to meet; = Against A. 5.

*c* **950** *Lindisf. Gosp.* Mark xiv. 13 And toȝeæȝn iornað iuh monn. — Matt. xxvii. 32 ȝemoeton monno cyriniscne cymmende toȝeeȝnas him [*L.* venientem obuiam sibi]. *c* **1000** Ælfric *Hom.* I. 136 Se ealda man Symeon eode toȝeanes þam cilde. *a* **1200** *Moral Ode* 347 Þos goð un-ieþe toȝeanes þe cliue aȝean þe heȝe hulle. *c* **1205** Lay. 3626 Aganippus..Ferde him to-ȝenes.

**3.** Of time: Towards, at the approach of; towards the coming, arrival, or convenience of (a person); = Against A. 17, 18.

**971** *Blickl. Hom.* 53 Þonne biþ hit eft him toȝeanes ȝehealden. *c* **1122** *O. E. Chron.* an. 1095 (Laud MS.), Toȝeanes Eastron com ðæs Papan sande. *c* **1200** *Trin. Coll. Hom.* 177 To-ȝenes sumere þis woreld floweð..to-ȝanes wintre heo hebbeð. *c* **1250** *O. Kentish Serm.* in *O. E. Misc.* 26 Tojanes þo sun risindde. *Ibid.* 34 To-ȝenes þan euen.

**b.** as *conj.* = Against B.

*a* **1440** *R. Gloucester's Chron.* (Rolls) App. XX. 376 God him greiþede pes to ȝenst he bere croune.

**4.** Towards; with respect to; in regard to; = Against A. 3.

*c* **1175** *Lamb. Hom.* 145 Þos word he seide et sumtime toȝeines þet he walde þis lif forleten. *c* **1200** *Trin. Coll. Hom.* 9 Ure lif we ledeð richtliche toȝenes ure louerd ihesu crist. *Ibid.*, Teȝenes ure emcristene we sulle laden ure lif edmodeliche.

**5.** Opposite, facing; = Against A. 1. *rare.*

*c* **1450** *Two Cookery-bks.* 112 Bray hit wel in a morter, & drie hit toȝenst ye sonne.

† **To-ga·ng,** *v. Obs.* [OE. *togangan*, f. To-[2] + *gangan*, Gang *v.*[1] So OS. *ti-, te-gangan*, OHG. *za-, zi-gangan.*] *intr.* To go away, pass away.

*a* **900** tr. *Bæda's Hist.* IV. xxx. [xxix.] (1890) 372 Forðon ðe æfter þon ðe wit nu betwih unc nu togangne beoð. *c* **1000** *Riddles* xxiv. 10 (Gr.) Ne togongeð þas gumena hwylcum ænigum eaðe, þat ic þær ymb sprice. **1596** Dalrymple tr. *Leslie's Hist. Scot.* x. (S.T.S.) II. 286 Our folk, about the sone togangeng,..met with thame at the fute of ane hill castne betueine.

**Togate** (tōᵘ·gĕit), *a.* [ad. L. *togāt-us*, f. Toga: see -ate [2].] = Togaed; in quots., belonging to ancient Rome.

**1851** Badham *Halieut.* (1854) 2 The existence of togate and eucnemic proficients in the art of angling is competently attested. **1853** Whewell *Grotius* II. 13 The Togate Provinces (*Provinciæ Togatæ*) [of the Roman Empire].

**Togated** (tōᵘ·gĕitĕd), *a.* [f. as prec. + -ed.]

**1.** Clad in a toga; wearing the toga; hence, associated with the idea of peace, peaceful.

**1634** M. Sandys *Prudence* x. 138 Now, I suppose, my Striplings are formally clad, and togated, newly arrived at the Vniversitie. **1651** Howell *Venice* 186* But touching maritime affaires,..these grave men shake off their togated Habitts, and receave Martiall employment. **1695** Kennett *Par. Antiq.* ix. 686 As he was a valiant Warrier, so was he a togated Senator. **1856** Smyth *Rom. Fam. Coins* 193 A togated figure stands towards the left on rough ground.

**2.** Of words: Latinized; stately, majestic.

**1868** Lowell *Shaks. Once More* Wks. 1890 III. 13 What homebred English could ape the high Roman fashion of such togated words as 'The multitudinous sea incarnadine'?

† **Toge.** *Obs.* [a. F. *toge* (older *togue*), ad. L. *toga.*] A Roman toga; hence, a cloak or loose coat.

? *a* **1400** *Morte Arth.* 3189 In toges of tarsse fulle richelye attyryde. *Ibid.* 178 Alle with taghte mene and towne in toges [*MS.* togers] fulle ryche, Of saunke realle in suyte, sexty at ones. **1607** Shaks. *Cor.* II. iii. 122 Why in this woolvish toge [Steevens' conj. for *tongue* of Fol. 1, *gown* of others] should I stand here To beg of Hob & Dick? *a* **1693** *Urquhart's Rabelais* III. vii. 65 Made after the manner of a *Toge*, which was the ancient fashion of the Romans in time of peace. *a* **1700** B. E. *Dict. Cant. Crew, Toge*, a Coat.

† **To·ged,** *a. Obs.* or *arch.* [f. prec. + -ed [2].] Clad in a toga, toga'd: hence, robed.

**1604** Shaks. *Oth.* I. i. 25 (Qo. 1) Unless the bookish theoric Wherein the toged [*folios* tongued] consuls can propose As masterly as he. **1862** Knight *Pop. Hist. Eng.* VIII. xx. 365 To walk in toged state to church [as members of municipal corporations *a* 1836].

† **To·geman(s, to·gman.** *Vagabonds' Cant. Obs. rare.* [app. f. F. *toge* or L. Toga + the cant suffix *-man(s*, as in *crackmans* hedge, *darkmans* night, *lightmans* day, etc.] A cloak or loose coat.

**1567** Harman *Caveat* (1869) 77 For want of their Casters and Togemans. *Ibid.* 82 A caster, a cloke..a togeman, a cote. *Ibid.* 85, I towre the strummel trine vpon thy nabchet and Togman, I see the strawe hang vpon thy cap and coate. *a* **1700** B. E. *Dict. Cant. Crew, Togemans*, a Gown or Cloak. *Ibid.* s. v. *Nim*, Nim a togeman, to steal a cloak. **1785** Grose *Dict. Vulg. T., Togmans*, a cloak.

**Together** (tǔge·ðəɹ), *adv.* (*prep.*, *sb.*) Forms (in most cases either as one word or two, or in mod. edd. of OE. and ME. with hyphen): *α.* 1 **togædere** (to gædere, to-gædere), **togadore**, 3–4 **togadere, togare**, (3 **to gaddre, to gaderen**, 4 **to gadir**); 7 **togather.** *β.* 2–5 **togedere**, 3 (*Orm.*) **togeddre**, 4 **to gedder**, *Sc.* **to geidir**, 4–5 **togeder, togedre**, 4–6 **togedir**, 5 **togedur, togedyr, to gedire**, (**to geyder, to gheder**); 4–5 **to gethir**, 6 **togeather**, 7 **togeither**, 5– **together.** *γ.* 3–5 **togider** (6 *Sc.*), **togydere**, (3 **to giddre**, 4 **to gidir**), 4–5 **togidere, togidre**, 4–6 **togyder,**

togiddir, (5 -yr), 4, 5-7 *Sc.* togidder, 5 to gidur, to gydre, togyddyr, 6 togydur, to gydder (*Sc.* -ir), toguyder; 4 togiþer, 6 togyther, toguyther, *Sc.* togithir, 6 (9 *dial.*) togither; *Sc.* 6 þe gidder, 8–9 thegither. [OE. *tógædere*, *tógadore*, f. To prep. + *gædre* adv. :—**gaduri*, orig. locative or instr. of **gador*, *-ur*, OE. *geador* 'together', whence also *gaderian*, later *gæderian* to GATHER, q. v. So OFris. *togadera*, *-ere*, MDu. *te gader(e*, Du. *tegader* 'together', MLG. *gader*, MG. *gater* 'together', f. same root as OE. *gæd* companionship, fellowship, union, *gegada* companion, associate, Du. *gade*, MDu. *ghegade* companion, comrade, consort, mate. OE. had, beside *tógædre*, of motion or direction, a parallel compound *ætgædere*, of position. The derivatives of *gad-* appear only in the Saxon-Frisian or LG. group of WGer., OHG. substituting *zi-samane*, Ger. *zusammen*: see SAMEN; and cf. GATHER, GOOD. ME. had forms in *-gader* and *-geder*, which in North. ME. and Sc. became *-gidir*. In the 14th c. the *d* or *dd* began to change to (ð) written *th*: cf. GATHER, FATHER.]

**1.** Into one gathering, company, mass, or body.

*707 Charter of Ine of Wessex* in Birch *Cart. Sax.* I. 149 Andlang Icenan þer Cendefer and Icene cumað to gædere; andlang Cendefer þer hit ær upeode. *c* **1000** *Ags. Gosp.* Matt. xv. 10 And he þa ðam menegum to-gædere ȝeclypedum þus cwæð. *c* **1200** ORMIN 1485, & gaddresst swa þe clene corn All fra þe chaff to geddre. *a* **1300** *Cursor M.* 2515 (Cott.) He did togeder samen his men. *c* **1386** CHAUCER *Prol.* 824 Vp roos oure hoost..And gadrede vs togidre alle in a flok. **1482** *Monk of Evesham* (Arb.) 22 Than all the brethirne came to gedyr in to the chaptur hows. *a* **1547** SURREY *Æneid* II. (1557) D iij, A rout exiled, a wreched multitude, From eche where flockke together. **1552–3** *Inv. Ch. Goods, Staffs.* in *Ann. Lichfield* IV. 6 On other grett bell..to call the parishonars to geather. **1611** BIBLE 1 *Cor.* xiv. 23 If therefore the whole Church be come together into one place. **1766** GOLDSM. *Vic. W.* iii, My next care was to get together the wrecks of my fortune. **1818** SCOTT *Rob Roy* xxxii, Laying a' this thegither.

**b.** Of two persons or things: Into companionship, union, proximity, contact, or collision.

*a* **900** *Andreas* 1437 Heofon & eorðe hreosaþ togadore. **1154** *O. E. Chron.* an. 1135, & hi to gædere comen & wurðe sæhte. **1297** R. GLOUC. (Rolls) 8996 Hii were to gadere icome þis bataile to do. *c* **1380** WYCLIF *Sel. Wks.* III. 442 God and iche membre of his Chirche bene weddid togedre. *c* **1400** *Lanfranc's Cirurg.* 142 Brynge þe parties togidere of þe wounde & sowe hem. **1549** *Compl. Scot.* vi. 66 The rammis raschit there heydis to gyddir. **1600** HOLLAND *Livy* VI. xii. 224 When you see the battailes buckle together pell mell, and come to handstrokes. **1610** SHAKS. *Temp.* I. ii. 461 Ile manacle thy necke and feete together. **1703** MOXON *Mech. Exerc.* 194 To contain..both the Cheeks when they are shut together. *a* **1704** [see ADD *v.* 4]. **1850** *Tait's Mag.* XVII. 498/1 Our last extract tells how Dr. Chalmers and Edward Irving came together. **1894** H. DRUMMOND *Ascent of Man* 251 Two flints struck together yielded fire.

**2.** In one assembly, company, or body; in one place. (Not in OE., which used *æt-gædere*.)

*c* **1220** *Bestiary* 369 in *O. E. Misc.* 12 Ðis wune he hauen hem bi-twen, Ðoȝ he an hundred to giddre ben. *c* **1250** *Gen. & Ex.* 1897 So riche were growen hise sunen, Ðat he ne miȝte to gider wunen. **1382** WYCLIF *John* xxi. 2 Ther weren to gidere Symount Petre, and Thomas, that is seid Didymus, and Nathanael [etc.]. *c* **1400** MAUNDEV. (1839) xxiii. 247 Here wyfes ne dwelle not to gydere, but euery of hem be hire self. **1526** *Pilgr. Perf.* (W. de W. 1531) 1 All christians gooth this pilgrymage all togyder in one company. **1607–12** BACON *Ess., Counsel* (Arb.) 324 If they take the opinions of theire Councell, both seperately, and togither. **1749** FIELDING *Tom Jones* XVIII. v, Shall we take a hackney coach, and all of us together pay a visit to your friend? **1826** J. WILSON *Noct. Ambr.* Wks. 1855 I. 244 We'll a' get fou thegither.

**b.** Of two persons or things: In each other's company; in union or contact.

*c* **1315** SHOREHAM I. 1912–8 Þe sibbe mowe to gadere nauȝt Þe foerþe grees wyþ-inne..And ȝef oþer þe fifte of-takeþ, To-gare moȝe hy dwelle. **1393** LANGL. *P. Pl.* C. XVIII. 22 Loue and leel by-leuye heeld lyf and soule to-gedere. *a* **1425** *Cursor M.* 10571 (Laud) Sone after to-gethir [*Cott.* samen] they lay. **1483** *Rolls of Parlt.* VI. 241/1 The said King Edward,..and the seid Elizabeth, lived together sinfully.. in adultery. **1596** SPENSER *F. Q.* VI. ii. 16 He and I together roade Upon our way. *c* **1645** HOWELL *Lett.* (1650) II. 113 You and I have eaten a great deal of salt together. **1726** in W. Wing *Ann. Steeple Aston* (1875) 54 Two lands lye together at Drywell. **1848** THACKERAY *Van. Fair* xxix, She gave George the queerest, knowingest look, when they were together.

**c.** In ideal combination; considered collectively; added or summed up. (Cf. PUT *v.* 52 e.)

**1796** MACNEILL *Will & Jean* III. i, What this warld is a' thegither, If bereft o' honest fame! **1849** MACAULAY *Hist. Eng.* v. I. 645 Jeffreys boasted that he had hanged more traitors than all his predecessors together since the Conquest.

**d.** *pred.* †(*a*) In agreement, consonant (*obs.*); (*b*) Courting, or mutually engaged, as lovers.

**1502** *Ord. Crysten Men* (W. de W. 1506) I. ii. 11 It behoueth that the wordes & the doynge..be holly in ony wyse togyder. **1749** FIELDING *Tom Jones* vi. ii, She..knew better than anybody who and who were together.

**e.** Used expletively in addressing a number of persons. *dial.* (*E. Anglia*).

*a* **1825** FORBY *Voc. E. Anglia, Together*,..used in familiarly addressing a number of persons collectively. Ex. 'Well, together, how are ye all?' **1850** *N. & Q.* 1st Ser. II. 217/2 Where are you going together? (meaning several persons). What are you doing together? **1866** J. G. NALL *Gt. Yarmouth & Lowestoft* 517 It has been wittily observed, that..'together' is [the] plural [of 'bor'] [a single person, male or female, being addressed as *bor* or '*bo*', two or more persons as 'together'].

**3.** In reference to a single thing. **a.** With union or combination of parts or elements; into or in a condition of unity; so as to form a connected whole.

*To pull, shake oneself together*: see the verbs.

*a* **1300** *Cursor M.* 550 (Cott.) Of þir things..was adam cors to gedir graid. *Ibid.* 582 Now haf i sceud yow til hider, How tua thinges halds man to gider. **1521** FISHER *Serm. agst. Luther* Wks. (1876) 324 Euery vertue that is gadred togyder is more stronger. **1562** TURNER *Herbal* II. 2 As runnynge or chese-lope maketh mylke runne together into cruddes. **1581** LAMBARDE *Eiren.* II. ii. (1588) 109 It standeth not well togither, that he should become bound to the Prince in x or xx pounds. **1652** NEEDHAM tr. *Selden's Mare Cl.* 161 The matter hang's well together, if wee say [etc.]. **1832** *Examiner* 562/1 While society holds together, while life and property are..secure.

**b.** After such verbs as *fold, roll*, etc.: Of different parts (sides, ends, etc.): Into or in contact or junction, so as to form a compact body.

**1480** [see FOLD *v.*[1] 1]. **1526** [see ROLL *v.*[2] 8]. **1578** LYTE *Dodoens* IV. vi. 552 His leaues be..crompled, and drawen togither or curled. **1637** RUTHERFORD *Lett.* I. cxli. (1664) 279 Ye..shall one day see God take the heavens in his hands and fold them together like an old holly garment.

**4.** At the same time, at once, simultaneously. (Usually connoting 'in combination or association'.)

*c* **1200** *Vices & Virt.* 35 Ðe hali apostel namneð ðese þrie haliȝe mihtes to gedere. *c* **1375** *Sc. Leg. Saints* ii. (*Paulus*) 806 Þat he [Nero] mycht stand his towr in, And se all togeidir byrne. **1508** FISHER *Penit. Ps.* xxxii. Wks. (1876) 33, I shall knowlege togyder all my synnes. **1610** HEALEY *Vives' Comm. St. Aug. Citie of God* XI. ix. 416 Basil and Dionysius, and almost all the Latines..hold that God made althings together. **1662** STILLINGFL. *Orig. Sacr.* III. iii. § 4 We cannot believe that and the Scriptures to be true together. **1746** FRANCIS tr. *Horace, Epist.* II. ii. 270 If Death..must mow Down Great and Small together at a Blow. **1849** MACAULAY *Hist. Eng.* iv. I. 469 James found that the two things which he most desired could not be possessed together.

**5.** Without intermission, continuously, consecutively, uninterruptedly, 'running', 'on end'. (In reference to time, less commonly to space.)

*c* **1290** *S. Eng. Leg.* I. 280/73 In þe Cite of tolouse ten ȝer to gadere he was. **1450–1530** *Myrr. our Ladye* 29 Where the soulle was..sore tormented longe tyme togidre. **1580** E. CAMPION in Allen *Martyrd.* (1908) 21 Tarying for wind four daies together. **1615** W. LAWSON *Country Housew. Gard.* (1626) 8 Trees cannot beare fruit plentifully two yeeres together. **1630** *R. Johnson's Kingd. & Commw.* 44 That wall of China,..was continued and fortified for six hundred miles together. **1698** FRYER *Acc. E. India & P.* 124 Forests..on Fire two or three Miles together. **1840** GRESLEY *Siege Lichf.* 242 He..never slept twice together in the same apartment. **1856** F. E. PAGET *Owlet Owlst.* 148 Her back aches..if she sits up for long together.

**6.** In concert or co-operation; with unity of action; unitedly; conjointly.

*a* **1300** *Cursor M.* 17351 (Cott.) Eftir þair sabat þai badd togedir, þat [etc.]. *c* **1330** R. BRUNNE *Chron.* (1810) 7 Þe Scottes & þe Peihtes togider gan þei cheue, To waste alle Northumberland. **1474** CAXTON *Chesse* II. i, Birdes of whom the male and female haue to gyder the charge in kepynge and norisshinge of their yonge fowlis. **1538** STARKEY *England* I. i. 9 Conspyryng togydur in al vertue and honesty. **1807** WORDSW. *Alice Fell* viii, Together we released the Cloak. **1891** *Law Times Rep.* LXIII. 776/1 The contract and the label together constituted a written warranty within the meaning of the..section.

**7.** In the way of, into, or in mutual action (friendly or hostile); with or against each other; mutually, reciprocally.

† In quot. 1523 in reference to distance: = of each other.

*c* **1350** *Will. Palerne* 1011 Þan eiþer hent oþer hastely in armes, & wiþ kene kosses kuþþed hem to gidere. **1377** LANGL. *P. Pl.* B. Prol. 46 Pilgrymes and palmers pliȝted hem togidere. *a* **1400** HYLTON *Scala Perf.* (W. de W. 1494) I. li, This is my biddynge that ye loue you togyder as I loued you. *c* **1400** *Laud Troy Bk.* 9244 With swerdes gode ..Fauȝt thei to-gedur. **1477** EARL RIVERS (Caxton) *Dictes* 68 Why it is that tresour and Science may not accorde to gider. **1523** LD. BERNERS *Froiss.* I. xl. 55 They were within two leages toguyther. **1561** T. HOBY tr. *Castiglione's Courtyer* II. (1577) L vj b, Which..(as you knowe) are enimies togyther. **1686** tr. *Chardin's Coronat. Solyman* 107 He resolv'd to set the King's two Chief Eunuchs..together by the ears. **1766** GOLDSM. *Vic. W.* x, I could perceive.. my wife and daughters in close conference together. **1855** LYNCH *Rivulet* XCVI. i, Yet sometimes, and in the sunniest weather, My work and I have fallen out together.

†**b.** After a trans. verb: = each other. *Obs.*

*c* **1330** R. BRUNNE *Chron. Wace* (Rolls) 4863 [Men] þat syþen han loued to gedre wel. **1483** *Vulgaria abs Terentio* 7 b, Scolers shulde loue to gyder lyke as thei were bredyr. **1525** LD. BERNERS *Froiss.* II. cxxviii. [cxxiv.] 364 When they mete, and haue nat sene toguyder longe before. *a* **1548** HALL *Chron., Hen. VIII* 200 After this day, the kyng and she neuer saw together.

†**c.** *Well* or *ill together*: agreeing well or ill; friendly or unfriendly. *Obs.*

**1741** CHESTERF. *Lett.* 30 May, I believe we are yet well enough together for you to be glad to hear of my safe arrival. **1765** *Ibid.*, Probably that is the Cause of their being so ill together. **1766** *Ibid.* 11 July, From the interview at Torgaw, ..they will be either a great deal better or worse together.

**d.** After *multiply*: By or into one another. Cf. *add together* (1 b).

**1709, 1885** [see MULTIPLY *v.* 5 b]. **1894** *Act* 57 & 58 *Vict.* c. 60 Sch. 2 (3) The contents of the shaft trunk shall be ascertained by multiplying together the mean length, breadth, and depth of the trunk, and dividing the product by 100.

**e.** After *belong*: To one another; hence, to one or the same whole, company, or set. Cf. *to hang together* in 3.

**1897** A. LANG *Bk. Dreams & Ghosts* i. 20 The two fragments, which you have published separately..belong together. **1908** *Expositor* Apr. 335 The whole is too closely connected and must, therefore, belong together.

**8. Together with** (in various senses): Along with; in combination with, in addition to, or with the addition of; in company or co-operation with; at the same time as, simultaneously with.

**1478** *Exch. Rolls Scotl.* VIII. 603 *note*, For his servandis mete, togiddir with his horse luveraye. **1596** DALRYMPLE tr. *Leslie's Hist. Scot.* (S. T. S.) I. 49 With a schip read, or hartsum hauining place, togithir with grene Cnowis upon the seysyde. **1608** TOPSELL *Serpents* (1658) 655 The labouring, that is the male Wasps, together with Autumn, make an end of their days. **1641** J. JACKSON *True Evang. T.* II. 120 Simon..entred Persia, together with Thaddeus. **1664** SOUTH *Serm.* (1697) II. ii. 69 He..never weighs the Sin, but together with it He weighs the force of the Inducement. **1686** tr. *Chardin's Trav. Persia* 21 The Gains and Advantages of a Constantinopolitan Embassie, together with the Splendor and Authority that belongs to it. **1858** *Penny Cycl.* XI. 41/1 The former principality of Haliczia or Galiczia, which, together with a considerable portion of Red Russia, once formed part of Hungary.

†**9.** Together with this; in addition, besides, at the same time, moreover. *Obs. rare.*

*a* **1648** LD. HERBERT *Hen. VIII* (1683) 147 This New invention of printing..as it had brought in and restored Books and Learning, so together it hath been the Occasion of those Sects and Schisms, which daily appeared in the World. *Ibid.* 236 The King understanding this, and together finding that their Numbers and Power did daily increase, advis'd to raise Forces.

†**10.** In nonce-combinations (chiefly with a vbl. sb. or agent-n.), after L. *con-* or *co-*: as *together-binding*, *-healing*, *-speaking* (= colloquy, conversation), *-words* (= context), *-worker* (= co-worker, collaborator). *Obs.*

**1382–8** WYCLIF *Gospels* (K.O. I. 141), The *togidere bindingus. **1597** A. M. tr. *Guillemeau's Fr. Chirurg.* 45 b/2 The combinatione or *together healinge is hindered. *c* **1425** *St. Mary of Oignies* II. iv. in *Anglia* VIII. 163/12 Yuel *togedir-spekynges harmeþ good maners. *Ibid.* viii. 173/22 Homely and often togedir-spekynge of seyntes. *c* **1449** PECOCK *Repr.* III. ii. (Rolls) 283 The ful hool riȝt is expressid in these *to gidere wordis 'ȝeue to the dekenis citees forto dwelle in hem'. **1581** J. BELL *Haddon's Answ. Osor.* 151 That the Apostles were *together workers with God: yet that those same together workemen should be hyred to worke in this Vyneard.

†**B.** *prep.* Along with, in addition to, with the addition of, with. *Obs. rare.*

**1556** *Aurelio & Isab.* (1608) E iv, Withe suttell communications unto their maedens, to gether a thousande written thinges that you fynde. **1583** STOCKER *Civ. Warres Lowe C.* IV. 44 The Lordes Liutenauntes..together all Magistrates and Chief Officers..shall be bounde to promise to obserue..this vnion. **1657** R. LIGON *Barbadoes* 25 You shall finde..the worth and value of it, together the whole process of the great work of Sugar-making.

**C.** as *sb.* Condition of being together, union; togetherness. *nonce-use.*

**1880** G. MEREDITH *Tragic Com.* (1881) 271 In their secrecy: in the close and boundless together of clasped hands.

Hence **Toge·therhood, Toge·therness** (*nonce-wds.*), the state or condition of being together or being united; union, association; †**Toge·therward, -wards** *adv.*, towards each other, together.

**1896** MARY C. CLARKE *Long Life* 194 The most exquisite precision of tune, the most perfect *togetherhood in beginning and ending phrases. **1656** [? J. SERGEANT] tr. *T. White's Peripat. Inst.* 302 This *togetherness must not be referr'd to the time but to the way of knowledge. **1892** *Monist* II. 218 Even if the link is a feeling it cannot be less than a feeling of the togetherness of two other feelings. *c* **1205** LAY. 9868 *To-gædereward heo uusden alswa heo wolden fehten. **1530** PALSGR. Introd. 17 They bryng theyr chawes togetherwardes agayne. *a* **1553** UDALL *Royster D.* IV. ii. (Arb.) 60 Now I shrew their best Christmasse chekes both togetherward. *c* **1630** SANDERSON *Serm.* (1681) II. 253 We shall not now stand so much upon any nice distinguishing of the terms, but take them togetherward.

†**Toge·thers,** *adv. Obs.* Forms (in many cases either as one word or two, or with hyphen: cf. TOGETHER): *α.* 3–4 togaderes, 5 to gadders; 6 togathers. *β.* 2–5 togederes, 4–6 togeders, 5 togederis (-ys), to gedrys, togedres, 6 togedirs; 5–6 togethers, 6 togetheres, togethirs. *γ.* 4–5 togidres, -eres, -ers, (4 -irs, -iris, togyderes), 5 to guyders, togyders, 5–6 to gidders, 6 to gydders, togydres; 5–6 togithers, 6 -gythers. [f. prec. with *-s* of advb. genitive: cf. *besides, betimes, eftsoons, towards*, etc.] = TOGETHER (in its various senses).

*c* **1175** *Lamb. Hom.* 139 Sunne dei blisseð to gederes houeneware and horðeware. *c* **1275** LAY. 1834 Hii drowen alle to gaderes. *c* **1300** *Cursor M.* 21749 (Edin.) Þu do togidiris ten and tua. **1362** LANGL. *P. Pl.* A. Prol. 46 Pilgrimes and Palmers Plihten hem to-gederes For to seche seint Ieme. **1387** TREVISA *Higden* (Rolls) I. 177 Þe clergie and the chiualrie hilde so to giders. *c* **1430** *Two Cookery-bks.* 45 Stere it wel in þe panne tyl it come to-gederys wel. **1440** in *Wars Eng. in France* (1864) II. 590 Whiche of his saide retinue he shalle holde togithers. *c* **1450** *Brut* 427 There they foughten to-gederis. **1491** *Act 7 Hen. VII*, c. 22 To take to your remembraunce the wordes we spake to guyders in Seynt Petir Chirch. 1537 Cromwell in Merriman *Life & Lett.* (1902) II. 87 Loyaltie and treason dwell seldome togethers. 1538 in *Lett. Suppress. Monast.* (Camden) 250 Everich of us severally and also alle togethers. *a* 1540 Barnes *Wks.* (1573) 224/1 So tooke they their counsell togithers. 1581 Marbeck *Bk. of Notes* 900 How releasement and payment cannot stand togethers. 1591 Sylvester *Du Bartas* I. ii. 330 All the Links of th' holy Chain, which tethers The many members of the World togethers. 1594 T. Bedingfield tr. *Machiavelli's Florentine Hist.* (1595) 192 Being togithers..they alwaies talked thereof.

**Togge**, obs. f. Tug. **Toggel**, obs. var. Toggle.

**To·gger.** *slang.* [Oxford undergraduates' perversion of Torpid.] A boat rowing in the Oxford college races called 'Torpids'; in *pl.* the Torpids.

1897 *Westm. Gaz.* 18 Aug. 2/1 He once rowed in his second Togger. 1903 *Oxford Mag.* 11 Feb. 213/1 Brasenose. The River.—Good luck to both Toggers.

**Toggery** (tǫ·gəri). *slang* or *colloq.* [f. Tog *sb.*[1] + -ery: cf. *drapery, foolery.*]

**1.** Garments; clothes collectively.

1812 Col. Hawker *Diary* (1893) I. 44 In spite of all coats, 'toggerys and upper benjamins'. *a* 1845 Barham *Ingol. Leg.* Ser. iii. *Blasphemer's Warn.*, Had a gay cavalier Thought fit to appear In any such 'toggery'. 1894 Fenn *Real Gold* 47 That's as much toggery as I can get in the.. portmanter.

**b.** *esp.* Professional or official dress.

*Long toggery* = long togs: see Tog *sb.*[1] 2 b.

1826 *Sporting Mag.* XVII. 378 These, with the squire's pad-groom (all in the same toggery). 1827 *Blackw. Mag.* XXII. 603 [He] is seen hebdomadally in the pulpit, adorned in clerical toggery. 1837 Marryat *Perc. Keene* xx, Cross had dressed himself in long toggery as a captain of a merchant vessel. 1861 *Court Life at Naples* I. 224 Officers in full toggery with clanging swords.

**2.** The trappings of a horse; harness.

1877 C. D. Warner *Levant* vi. 128 The horse I rode on was not an animal to take advantage of the weakness of his toggery. 1890 'R. Boldrewood' *Col. Reformer* (1891) 104, I never thought of wanting the regular colts' toggery.

**Toggle** (tǫ·g'l), *sb.* Also 8–9 **toggel**. [Said to be orig. in nautical use; of obscure etymology, but app. closely related to Tuggle *v.*, to catch, hold fast, entangle, and to Taggle *v.*, Taigle *v.*, and their nasalized form Tangle. The use of a toggle was originally to catch or hold fast a rope or chain and prevent its slipping.]

**1.** *Naut.* A short pin passed through a loop or the eye of a rope, or a link of a chain, or through a bolt, to keep it in place, or for the attachment of another line.

1769–76 Falconer *Dict. Marine, Toggel, cabillot*, a small wooden pin, about five or six inches in length, and usually tapering from the middle towards the extremities. It is used to fix transversely in the lower part of a tackle, in which it serves as an hook whereby to attach the tackle to a strop, slings, or any body whereon the effort of the tackle is to be employed. There are also toggels of another kind, employed to fasten the top-gallant sheets to the spar, which is knotted round the cap at the top-mast-head. 1775 Ash, 1828 Webster, Toggel. 1829 Marryat *F. Mildmay* viii, The yard-ropes were fixed to the halter by a toggle in the running noose of the latter. 1854 Hooker *Himal. Jrnls.* I. ix. 218 Tethered by halters and toggles to a long rope. 1898 F. T. Bullen *Cruise Cachalot* vi, The strap of the second cutting tackle was inserted and secured by passing a huge toggle of oak through its eye. *fig. phr.* 1835–40 Haliburton *Clockm.* (1862) 348 There's an eend to that; you've put a toggle into that chain.

**2.** *transf.* **a.** A cross-piece attached to the end of a line or chain (e. g. a watch-chain), or fixed in a belt or strap for attaching a weapon, etc. by a loop or ring; also, a cross-piece put through a loop to effect compression by twisting. **b.** A device for fixing an anchor: see quot. 1831. **c.** A movable pivoted cross-piece serving as a barb in a harpoon. **d.** *Mech.* A toggle-joint. **e.** *dial.* Each of the two short handles or 'nibs' of a scythe.

1831 J. Holland *Manuf. Metal* I. vi. 100 In 1821, R. F. Hawkins, a Kentish mariner, obtained a patent for an anchor, the arm and flukes of which turned round in eyeholes at the termination of the shank, until they formed therewith an angle of about sixty degrees, in which position they were detained by a thick piece of iron, called by the inventor a 'toggle'. When this anchor is let go, one of the ends of the toggle comes in contact with the ground, and puts both flukes in a position to enter; and when the strain comes on the cable, the other end of the toggle..sets the anchor in its holding position, not with one fluke only, as in the common anchor, but with both. 1873 E. Spon *Workshop Receipts* Ser. i. 310/2 This straightens the toggles, and causes a sharp impression of the stamp upon the leather. 1875 Bedford *Sailor's Pocket Bk.* x. (ed. 2) 380 A strop round the nose, hove short with a short stick or toggle, will rapidly tame an unmanageable horse. 1880 Clark Russell *Sailor's Sweetheart* viii, Around his waist was a broad leather belt with toggles for the reception of a knife or a pistol. 1881 *Sydney Morn. Herald* 24 Oct., The harpoon was a patent one, with a toggle, and opens when there is any strain on the line. 1885 *Reports Provinc.* (E.D.D.), I can't mow the lawn, sir, till I've got a new snead and toggles to my scythe. 1887 *Q. Rev.* Jan. 97 The exquisite workmanship of the toggles and sword guards. 1905 Miss A. S. Griffith tr. *Capart's Prim. Art Egypt* Index, Studs or toggles for cloaks, pp. 57, 59. 1908 *Installation News* II. 22/2 This is done by connecting a bell and dry cell between the screw D and the toggle of the switch, so that when the piston rises and makes contact with the toggle the bell rings before sufficient pressure is exerted to throw off the switch.

**3.** *attrib.* and *Comb.*, as *toggle action, line, -noose, pattern*; *toggle-like* adj.; also **toggle-bolt**, a bolt having a hole through the head to receive a toggle; **toggle-chain**, a short chain fastened to a timber sledge, having a *toggle-hook* at the end by which the effective length of the binding chain is regulated; **toggle-harpoon**, a harpoon with a pivoted toggle instead of barbs; **toggle-hole**, a hole made, as in blubber, for inserting a toggle (*Cent. Dict.*); **toggle-hook**, a long-shanked hook used on a *toggle-chain* (*Cent. D. Supp.*); **toggle-iron** = *toggle-harpoon*; **toggle-joint**, a joint consisting of two pieces hinged endwise, operated by applying pressure at the elbow; **toggle-lanyard**: see quot.; **toggle-pin** = sense 1; **toggle-press**, a press operated by means of one or more toggle-joints.

1893 *Jrnl. R. Agric. Soc.* Dec. 716 The drawing together of the nave flanges..produces a *toggle action of the spokes. 1794 *Rigging & Seamanship* I. 152 **Toggle-bolt.* *c* 1850 *Rudim. Navig.* (Weale) 99 The Toggle-Bolt has a flat head and a mortise through it, that receives a toggle or pin. 1888 Goode *Amer. Fishes* 249 What is known to whalers as a *toggle-harpoon is a modification of the lily-iron. 1884 Knight *Dict. Mech., Suppl.*, *Toggle iron. 1888 *Encycl. Brit.* XXIV. 526/2 The hand harpoon is a light and efficient weapon..introduced by the Americans, to whom it is known as a 'toggle-iron'. 1847 Webster, **Toggle-joint*, an elbow or knee-joint. 1869 *Routledge's Ev. Boy's Ann.* 412 The cranked knee or toggle joint. 1879 *Cassell's Techn. Educ.* IV. 12/2 A box of wooden soldiers, with a slightly jointed framework on which they can be stuck,..which elongates and contracts..is simply a combination of toggle-joints. 1874 Scammon *Marine Mammals* App. 312 It [the toggle] has a hole near one end, through which a rope is attached, which is termed the *toggle-lanyard. This lanyard is used in handling or confining the toggle. 1904 *Brit. & Col. Printer* 10 Mar. 14/2 Links pivoted to the lever are slotted to engage pins carried by the extension of the hand lever, which thus exerts a *toggle-like action on the lever. 1880 *Harper's Mag.* LX. 851 The engines, by means of the *toggle line, steadily haul the seine to the shore. 1883 *Century Mag.* Sept. 675/2 Attaching a *toggle noose where the trace joins the harness. 1885 C. G. W. Lock *Workshop Receipts* Ser. iv. 210/1 The press employed may be either of the 'hydraulic' or of the '*toggle' pattern. 1877 Knight *Dict. Mech.*, **Toggle-press*, one in which the platen is moved by the flexion or extension of two bars which unite to form a knee-joint.

**Toggle** (tǫ·g'l), *v.*[1] [f. prec. sb.]

**1.** *trans.* To secure or make fast by means of a toggle or toggles.

1853 Kane *Grinnell Exp.* xi. (1856) 83 Each man..has a canvas strap..fastened to the tow-line; or, nautically,.. toggled to the warp. 1899 W. Churchill *R. Carvel* xiii, I..beheld him..toggle it [a flag] to the ensign halyard. 1899 *Outing* (U.S.) XXX. 229/1 In the *Mab* and other canoes employing this device, the stick is toggled at one end to the rudder yoke, and at the other to the collar of the deck tiller.

**2.** To furnish with a toggle or toggles.

1875 Bedford *Sailor's Pocket Bk.* vi. (ed. 2) 216 Toggle the bight with a stretcher. 1905 *Sat. Rev.* 14 Oct. 499/1 A Union Jack made of bunting..roped and toggled.

† **To·ggle**, *v.*[2] *Obs. rare*[−1]. [freq. of *tog*, Tug *v.*: see -le 3.] *intr.* To tug, tussle.

*a* 1225 *Ancr. R.* 424 Heo ne schulen cussen nenne mon,.. ne toggen [*v.r.* toggle] mid him, ne pleien.

† **Toggy, tuggy.** [? Connected with Tog *sb.*[1] or L. Toga.] A kind of overcoat for the arctic regions.

1742 J. L. in *Naval Chron.* XII. 118 Our clothing is a beaver or skin tuggy, above our other clothes. 1768 Wales in *Phil. Trans.* LX. 122 We who stayed at the factory began to put on our winter rigging; the principal part of which was our toggy, made of beaver skins.

**Togh, toghe**, obs. ff. Tough *a.*, Tow, Tug.

**Togider, togither**, etc., obs. ff. Together.

**To·gless**, *a.* [f. Tog *sb.*[1] + -less.] Without togs or clothes; naked; also, without proper dress.

1857 E. M. Whitty *Friends in Bohemia* II. 52 Till you are run down roofless and togless.

† **To-gli·de**, *v. Obs.* [OE. *toglīdan*, f. To-[2] + *glīdan* to Glide; = MHG. *zegliten.*] *intr.* To glide or slip away or off; to pass away.

*Beowulf* 2486 Guð-helm toglad, gomela scylfing hreas blac. *a* 1000 *Boeth. Metr.* vii. 34 Grundweal ȝearone; se toglidan ne þearf. *a* 1046 *O. E. Chron.* an. 979 (MS. C.), Blodiȝ wolcen..wæs swyðost on middeniht oþywed..þonne hit daȝian wolde þonne to glad hit. *a* 1272 *Luue Ron* 43 in *O. E. Misc.* 94 Al so hwenne hit schal to-glide Hit is fals.

† **To-gnaw·**, *v. Obs.* Pa.t. **-gnew.** Pa.pple. **-gnowe(n).** [ME., f. To-[2] + *gnawen, gnaȝen* to Gnaw; = MHG., Ger. *zernagen.*] *trans.* To gnaw to pieces; to gnaw away.

13.. *K. Alis.* 4629 No let none houndes me to-gnawe [*Bodl. MS.* todrawe]. *Ibid.* 6119 And they al day..heore flesch to-gnowe. *c* 1305 *St. Kath.* 248 in *E. E. P.* (1862) 96 Hi nome kene hokes of ire and hire flesche to-gnowe. 1340 Hampole *Pr. Consc.* 863 Wormes þan sal it al to-gnaw. 14.. *Sir Beues* (M.) 2174 Into the caue cam lyons two,.. anone they hym slewe And hym and his hors al to-gnewe.

† **To-go·**, *v. Obs.* [OE. *to-gān*, f. To-[2] + *gān* to Go; = OHG. *za-, zigān*, MHG. *ze-, zergān*, Ger. *zergehen*, MLG. *togān.*] *intr.* To go in different directions, go asunder; to be divided, part, separate; to pass away, disappear.

*c* 1000 *Leg. Rood* 103 Þa toeodon ða stanas, & ȝeopenode ðæt ȝet. *c* 1000 Ælfric *Hom.* II. 194 Seo sæ toeode on twa. *c* 1175 *Lamb. Hom.* 141 Þe see toeode and þet iraelisce folc wende ouer. *c* 1275 Lay. 23980 Arthur..smot Frolle vppe þan helm Þat he atwo toȝeode. *c* 1315 Shoreham i. 790 Ȝet þaȝ þe fourme of brede togo, Þat body by-lefþ ȝet þanne. 13.. *Sir Beues* (A.) 1896 Þow schelt nouȝt, whan we tegoþ, Lauȝande me wende fram. 1560 Rolland *Crt. Venus* iv. 704 My riding geir is all to gane and spent.

† **To-grade**, *v. Obs. rare.* [f. To-[2] + Grade *v.*[1]] *trans.* To degrade, put or bring down.

*a* 1440 *Sir Degrev.* 104 He hade a grete spyt of the knyght..And thoght howe he best myght That dowghty to grade [*MS.* grode; *rimes* brade (*MS.* brode), hade, made].

† **To-grind**, *v. Obs.* [Late ME., f. To-[2] + Grind *v.*] *trans.* To grind to dust.

1393 Langl. *P. Pl.* C. xii. 62 Good men for oure gultes he [God] al to-grynt to deþe. *c* 1440 *Pallad. on Husb.* i. 1135 Eek oister shellis drie and al togrounde.

† **To·-grow**, *v. Obs. rare.* [f. To-[1] + Grow *v.*] *intr.* To grow to or towards (something).

1422 tr. *Secreta Secret., Priv. Priv.* 230 Tho that haue a longe heede, and the eeris to-growynge to the forhede negh to the noose.

Hence †**To-grow·ing**, **a.** *vbl. sb.*, a growth, an excrescence; **b.** *ppl. a.*, growing on, attached.

1562 Turner *Herbal* ii. 31 The iuice..healeth outwaxynges or to growinges in the fleshe. *Ibid.* 70 b, Ornithogalum is a tendre stalk..with ij. or thre togrowyng branches in ye top. [But in these the prefix is perh. To-[2].]

**Togue**[1] (tōug). *rare.* [ad. L. *toga* gown, or a. OF. *togue* (14th c. in Godef. *Compl.*).] = Toga 2.

1862 Thoreau *Yankee in Canada* iv. (1866) 70 He was lucky to have brought his togue, or frock coat with him.

**Togue**[2] (tōug). [Adaptation of Indian name in Maine and New Brunswick.] The great lake trout (*Salvelinus namaycush*) of North America; also called *lunge* or *longe* (Lunge *sb.*[3]) and *namaycush.*

1877 Hallock *Sportsm. Gaz.* 304 The togue or gray trout of Maine and New Brunswick. 1884 L. L. Hubbard *Woods & Lakes of Maine* 204 Lakers or togue, the largest of their lake fish. 1888 Goode *Amer. Fishes* 466 The Togue or Lunge..is held in much higher favor by the angler.

**Tog(u)yder, -ther**, obs. ff. Together.

† **To-hack**, *v. Obs.* [OE. *tohaccian*, f. To-[2] + *haccian*, Hack *v.*[1]; = MHG., Ger. *zerhacken.*] *trans.* To hack to pieces.

*c* 1000 *Leg. Veronica* 166 in Grein *Angelsächs. Prosa* (1889) III. 186 Sume hiȝ wæron on feower dælas tohaccede. 1387 Trevisa *Higden* (Rolls) V. 281 He..was alto hakked [L. *dilaniatus*] of Valentinianus his servauntes. *c* 1425 *Eng. Conq. Irel.* 82, & anoon-ryght the yonge man was al to-hakked to-for hym. 1597 *2nd Pt. Gd. Hus-wives Jewell* E vij, Take..a knuckle of yong Veale..and all to hack it.

† **To-hew**, *v. Obs.* [OE. *to-hēawan*, f. To-[2] + *hēawan* to Hew; = MHG. *zerhouwen*, Ger. *zerhauen.*] *trans.* To hew to pieces.

*c* 1000 Ælfric *Saints' Lives* ii. 360 Þæt basilla sceolde ȝebuȝan..Oþþe hi man to-heowe mid heardum swurde on twa. *c* 1010 *O. E. Chron.* an. 1004 (Laud MS.), Þa seonde he þ man sceolde þa scipu to heawan. *c* 1205 Lay. 178 Þar Turnus feol Mid mechen to-heawen. 13.. *Sir Beues* (A.) 4407 Þar hii were..al to-hewe flesch & bon. *c* 1386 Chaucer *Knt.'s T.* 1751 The helmes they tohewen and toshrede. 1494 Fabyan *Chron.* vi. clxxxviii. 191 The sayd felon..at length was all to hewen and dyed forthwith.

† **To-hield**, *v. Obs.* [OE. **tōhieldan*, f. To-[1] + *hieldan*, Hield *v.* Cf. OE. *tōheald* adj. inclined.] **a.** *trans.* To cause to incline, lean, bend, or fall over; to push or pull down. **b.** *intr.* To incline, heel over, bow down, fall, give way. **c.** *intr.* To bend one's course *to*, turn *to*, to approach.

*c* 1205 Lay. 1135 Ane burh swiðe stronge To-hælde [*c* 1275 to-haled] weoren þe walles. *Ibid.* 7522 Þat þe helm to-hælde [*c* 1275 þat hit in wende]. *Ibid.* 14744 Bruttes heom æfter..& heom to-heolden In æchere hælue. *Ibid.* 26809 Þer me iseon mihte sorȝen inoȝe: sceldes scenen, scalkes fallen, halmes to-hælden.

**To-ho** (to,hōu·), *int. Sport.* A call to a pointer or setter to stop.

1825 *Sporting Mag.* XV. 348 It was no uncommon thing for him to call out 'To-ho', and sometimes, with increased emphasis, 'To-ho you devil', in his sleep. 1855 'Stonehenge' *Brit. Sports* (ed. 4) 32 The breaker should walk up to [the dog] quietly, crying 'Toho! toho! toho!' 1884 Speedy *Sport* 52 Hold up your hand and say 'Toho'.

† **To·-hope.** *Obs.* [OE. *tōhopa*, f. To-[1] + *hopa*, Hope.] Hope, expectation.

*c* 888 K. Ælfred *Boeth.* x. § 1 Seo godcunde lufu & se tohopa. *a* 900 *Ags. Ps.* (Th.) xxxix. 4 Eadiȝ byð se wer, þe his to-hopa byð to swylcum Drihtne. *c* 1175 *Lamb. Hom.* 155 Nimeð gode ileue to burne, to hope to helme. *a* 1240 *Ureisun* in *Cott. Hom.* 191 Mi lif and mi tohope.

‖ **Tohu-bohu** (tō·hū,bō·hū). Forms: 7 **tohu and bohu, tohu-vavohu, -vabohu**, 8–9 **tohu-bohu.** [a. Heb. תֹהוּ וָבֹהוּ *thōhū wa-bhōhū* 'emptiness and desolation', in Gen. i. 2, rendered in Bible of 1611 'without form and void'. So F. *thohu et bohu* (Rabelais 1548), *tohu-bohu* (Voltaire 1776).] That which is empty and formless; chaos; utter confusion.

[1613 Purchas *Pilgrimage* (1614) 219 That Prophecie.. that the world should be two thousand yeares *Tohu*, emptie and without Law.] 1619 — *Microcosm.* xxviii. 275 It is.. not any figure, but a *Chaos*, a *Tohu and Bohu*, a meere confusion. 1643 Trapp *Comm., Gen.* i. 24–5 (1867) I. 8/2 Man's heart is a mere emptiness, a very *Tohu vabohu.* 1645 A. Henderson *Serm. bef. Ho. Lords* in *Life* (1846) 105 That such a Tohu vavohu can be the face of the Kingdom of Christ. 1692 Ray *Disc.* i. ii. (1693) 5 The Earth..which was made *tohu vabohu*, without form and void. 1875 Gladstone *Glean.* (1879) VI. 180 Yet a judge may..be required to dive, at a moment's notice, into the tohu-bohu of inquiries, which have never yet emerged from the stage of chaos. **1883** Browning *Jochanan Hakkadosh* 721 How from this tohu-bohu—hopes which dive, And fears which soar. **1894** L. S. Houghton tr. *Sabatier's St. Francis* iii. 36 That tohu-bohu of mystery and folly.

‖ **Tohunga** (tō·hu̇ŋă). [Maori *tóhunga*, lit. one skilled in signs and marks, f. *tohu* sign, omen.

Cognate with Samoan *tufunga* tattooer, carpenter; in Tongan, artificer, skilled workman; in Horne Is. *tufuga* master workman, architect, etc.]

A Maori priest of the second rank; a native doctor.

**1872** A. Domett *Ranolf* v. x, But he whose grief was most sincere.. Was Kangapo the Tóhunga—a Priest And fell Magician famous far and near. **1893** *Westm. Gaz.* 13 Feb. 10/1 His secret longings and natural tendencies are towards the tohungas, the only visible monuments of his old priestly *régime*. **1904** *Daily Chron.* 23 July 4/6 The methods of the 'tohungas', or Maori native doctors of New Zealand, are remarkable.

‖ **Toi** (tō·i) [Maori], var. form of Ti, q. v.

**1861** Bowen *Poems* 57 High o'er them all the toi waved, To grace that savage ground. **1909** *Auckland Weekly News* 29 May 17/4 A few other species are found, such as ..Toi (Cordyline indivisa)..; but these are few and scattered.

**Toil** (toil), *sb.*[1] Forms: 4–7 **toyle**, **toile**, (7 **toiel**), 7–8 **toyl**, 6– **toil**; see also the Sc. form Tuilyie. [a. AF. *toil*, *toyl* dispute, contention, forensic strife = OF. *tooil*, *toeil*, *toel*, *touil*, *tueil* bloody mêlée, trouble, confusion, etc. (12th c. in Godef.), f. *tooillier*, etc.: see Toil *v.*[1]]

**1.** † Verbal contention, dispute, controversy, argument (*obs.*); also, battle, strife, mêlée, turmoil (*arch.* or merged in 2).

(Quot. *a* 1450 may possibly belong to Toil *sb.*[2] 3, but its date is in favour of this sense.)

[**1292** Britton i. xxvii. § 6 Si soit le toyl entre eux et le viscounte. *Ibid.* ii. xi. § 21. *c* **1325** *Gloss. W. de Bibbesw.* in Wright *Voc.* 147 Entre pledoures sourd le toyl [*gloss* strif].] **13..** *K. Alis.* 2212 (Bodl. MS.) Gret & dedly was þe prees, Among þe toyle Hardapilon On of Alisaunders fon Seiȝ theoloman Alisaunders stiwarde Bryngen darryes folk dounwarde. ? *a* **1400** *Morte Arth.* 1802 The bolde.. Tittez tirauntez doune, and temez theire sadilles, And turnez owte of þe toile, whene hym tyme thynkkez. *c* **1400** *Destr. Troy* 6958 Toax þat tyme þurght the toile rode:.. And myche wo with his weppon wroght at þe tyme. [*c* **1425**–: see Tuilyie.] *a* **1450** *Bone Flor.* 1938 He was so tuggelde in a toyle. **1715** Pope *Iliad* i. 351 With these of old to toils of battle bred, In early youth my hardy days I led. **1746** Francis tr. *Horace, Epist.* ii. ii. 141 Like Gladiators, who with bloodless Toils Prolong the Combat, and engage with Foils. **1825** Longf. *Burial of Minnisink* v, The weapons, made For the hard toils of war.

*fig.* **1642** Rogers *Naaman* 136 Hence it is, that selfe hath so continuall a toile to hold correspondence with grace.

**2.** With *a* and *pl.* A struggle, a 'fight' (with difficulties); hence, a spell of severe bodily or mental labour; a laborious task or operation.

**1576** Gascoigne *Steele Gl.* (Arb.) 74 Since al their toyles, and all their broken sleeps Shal scant suffize, to hold it stil vpright. **1589** Puttenham *Eng. Poesie* iii. xix. (Arb.) 215 To till it is a toyle. **1603** Breton *Dial. Pithe & Pleas.* (Grosart) 7/1, I doo not loue so to make a toyle of a pleasure. **1735** Somerville *Chase* iv. 241 The Hunter-Horse, Once kind Associate of his sylvan Toils. **1832** Ht. Martineau *Life in Wilds* ix. 115 The toils of the day were done. **1855** Kingsley *Heroes* ii. iv. (1868) 127 Many a toil must we bear ere we find it, and bring it home to Greece.

**3.** Without *a* or *pl.* Severe labour; hard and continuous work or exertion which taxes the bodily or mental powers.

**1594** W. Har[bert] *Epicedium* 1 You that to shew your wits, have taken toyle. **1697** Dryden *Virg. Georg.* i. 24 Thou Founder of the Plough and Ploughman's Toyl. **1750** Gray *Elegy* 29 Let not Ambition mock their useful toil. **1774** Goldsm. *Nat. Hist.* (1776) VIII. 81 The toil of man is irksome to him, and he earns his subsistance with pain. **1860** Tyndall *Glac.* i. xxvii. 215 On the steeper slopes especially the toil was great. **1884** A. M. Fairbairn in *Congregationalist* Apr. 276 You are many of you accustomed to toil manual; I a man accustomed to toil mental.

**b.** *transf.* The result of toil; that which is produced or accomplished by toil.

**1713** Addison *Cato* iv. iv. 103 How is the toil of fate, the work of ages, The Roman Empire fallen!

**4.** *attrib.* and *Comb.*, as *toil-assuaging*, *-beaten*, *-bent*, *-hardened*, *-oppressed*, *-stained*, *-stricken*, *-won* adjs.; **toil-drop**, a drop of sweat caused by toil. See also Toil-worn.

**1726** Pope *Odyss.* xx. 452 This poor, tim'rous, toil-detesting drone. **1730–46** Thomson *Autumn* 1223 The toil-strung youth, By the quick sense of musick taught alone. **1748** — *Cast. Indol.* ii. xxiii, The best and sweetest far, are toil-created gains. **1760** Fawkes tr. *Sappho, Epigr.* i. 2 The toil-experienc'd Fisher, Pelagon. **1781** Cowper *Conversat.* 732 The scenes of toil-renewing light. **1786** Burns *Lament* viii, My toil-beat nerves, and tear-worn eye. **1791** Cowper *Odyss.* vii. 410 Ulysses toil-inured his words Exulting heard. **1805** Scott *Last Minstr.* ii. xviii, Till the toil-drops fell from his brows, like rain. **1839** Carlyle *Chartism* x. 176 The toilwon conquest of his own brothers. **1847** Mary Howitt *Ballads*, etc. 316 Toil-stricken, though so young. **1907** G. Parker *Weavers* ix, The slave and the toil-ridden fellah.

**Toil** (toil), *sb.*[2] Forms: 6 **toyll**(**e**, (**tull**, **tole**), 6–7 **toyle**, 6–8 **toyl**, **toile**, 6– **toil**. [a. OF. *teile*, *toile* (11th c. in Godef. *Compl.*), mod.F. *toile* cloth, web, etc. :—L. *tēla* web; F. pl. *toiles* 'large pieces of cloth bordered with thick ropes, stretched round an enclosure, for the purpose of capturing wild beasts; also, large nets stretched to take stags and other deer' (Littré).]

**1.** A net or nets set so as to enclose a space into which the quarry is driven, or within which the game is known to be. In later use usually *pl.*

*sing.* *a* **1529** Skelton *How the douty Dk. of Albany* 269 About hym a parke Of a madde warke, Men call it a toyle. **1530** Palsgr. 281/2 Toyll for a prince to hunt with, *toille*. **1577–87** Holinshed *Chron.* III. 1120/2 A generall hunting with a toile raised of foure or fiue miles in length, so that manie a deere that day was brought to the quarrie. *a* **1667** Cowley *Agric.* Wks. 1710 II. 722 He drives into a Toil the foaming Boar. **1827** D. Johnson *Ind. Field Sports* 18 The sudden jerk occasioned by an animal rushing at speed against the toil.

*pl.* **1530** Palsgr. 711/2, I sette, as a hunter setteth his hayes, or his toylles, or any other thinges to take wylde beestes with. **1554** in Kempe *Losely MSS.* (1836) 97 Yt hathe pleased the Quenes mat[ie]..to take yo[r] Accompt for the Revelles, Tentes, and Toyles. **1611** Cotgr., *Toiles*, toyles; or a Hay to inclose, or intangle, wild beasts in. **1707** *Lond. Gaz.* No. 4358/3 The Toiles are already set round a large Lake. **1726** Arbuthnot *It cannot rain but it pours* Swift's Wks. 1755 III. i. 132 The wonderful Wild Man that was nursed in the woods of Germany by a wild beast, hunted and taken in toyls. **1852** Miss Yonge *Cameos* I. xxv. 200 His men-at-arms may come and catch me like a fox in the toils.

† **2.** A trap or snare for wild beasts. *Obs. rare.*

**1607** Topsell *Four-f. Beasts* (1658) 574 The manner of taking of Wolfs..an Iron toil which they still fasten in the earth with Iron pins. *a* **1629** Hinde *J. Bruen* x. (1641) 34 It is lawfull..to set Toyles for Foxes. **1727** Gay *Fables* i. xxi. 21 Again he sets the poison'd toils.

**3.** *fig.* or in fig. context (*sing.* and *pl.*).

*sing.* *a* **1548** Hall *Chron., Rich. III* 56 Let vs not feare to enter in to the toyle where we may suerly sley hym. **1606** Shaks. *Ant. & Cl.* v. ii. 351 As she would catch another Anthony In her strong toyle of Grace. **1671** Milton *P. R.* ii. 453 Extol not Riches then, the toyl of Fools. **1718** Rowe tr. *Lucan* i. 168 Who hope to share the spoil, And hold the World within on common toil. **1774** Goldsm. *Nat. Hist.* (1776) VIII. 258 The spider's..next care is to seize and secure whatever insect happens to be caught in the toil.

*pl.* *c* **1586** C'tess Pembroke *Ps.* cxlii. i, Lord, thou.. knowst each path where stick the toyls of danger. **1648** Herrick *Hesper., Disswasions fr. Idlenesse*, Armes and hands..Are but toiles or manicles. *a* **1704** T. Brown *On Beauties* Wks. 1730 I. 42 Each fair enchanter sets Toyles for my heart. **1738** Wesley *Ps.* lvii. iii, While in the Toils of Hell I lie. **1810** Scott *Lady of L.* ii. xxviii, Themselves in bloody toils were snared.

**4.** *attrib.* and *Comb.*, as † **toil-house**, a building in which toils and other hunting equipments were housed; so † **toil-yard**.

**1558** in Feuillerat *Revels Q. Eliz.* (1908) 48 One greate house called the Toyle house..with a Toyle yerde.

**Toil** (toil), *v.*[1] Forms: 4–7 **toyle**, 5–7 **toile**, 7 **toyl** (**toiel**), 7– **toil**. See also Toly *v.* and Sc. Tuilyie *v.* [a. AF. *toiler* to strive, dispute, wrangle = OF. *toeillier*, *tooillier*, *toillier*, *touellier*, mod.F. *touillier* (12th c. in Godef.), 'salir, souillier', to soil, stir up, agitate, in mod.F. dial. to mix, stir up; 'filthily to mix or mingle,.. shuffle together, to intangle, trouble, or pester by scuruie medling; also, to bedurt, begrime, besmeare, etc.' (Cotgr. 1611); according to Hatz.-Darm. :—L. *tudiculāre* to stir, stir about, f. *tudicula* a machine for bruising olives. The development of sense was app. 'to stir up, make a stir or agitation, struggle, wrangle'.]

**I.** † **1.** *intr.* To contend in a lawsuit or an argument; to dispute, argue; also, to contend in battle; to fight, struggle. *Obs.*

[**1292** Britton v. x. § 11 En ceo cas quant plusours heirs toillent entour heritage [etc.].] *c* **1330** [see Toiling *vbl. sb.*]. [*c* **1350** *Nominale Gall.-Angl.* (E.E.T.S.), *Homme plede et toile pur glebe*, M. motith and striuyth for rit of kyrke.] *c* **1380** *Anticrist* in Todd *Three Treat. Wyclif* (1851) 150 Crist wiþhelde no men of lawe ne pleders at þe barr for robes & fees..to toyle for worldly cause. *c* **1400** *Laud Troy Bk.* 6957 When Paris hadde with him thus toyled, Off his Armes he him dispoyled. *c* **1400** *Destr. Troy* 10160 The Troiens wiþ tene toiled full hard, Wiþ a Rumour full roide & a roght hate.

† **2.** *trans.* To pull, drag, tug about. *Obs.*

*c* **1325** *Body & Soul* 383 in *Map's Poems* (Camden) 344 Hit was in a deolful pleyt, Reuthliche i-toyled to and fro. *c* **1394** [see Toiling *vbl. sb.*]. *a* **1400** *Leg. Rood* (1871) 143 Þe dispitous Iewes nolde not spare Til trie fruit weore tore and toyled. *c* **1440** *Alphabet of Tales* 54 As Saynt Anton lay in a den in wildernes, a grete multitude of fendis come vnto hym and rafe hym, & toylid hym.

**II. 3.** *intr.* To struggle for some object or for a living; to engage in severe and continuous labour or exertion; to labour arduously. Often in the collocation *toil and moil*: see Moil *v.* 3.

*c* **1394** *P. Pl. Crede* 742 Y miȝt tymen þo troiflardes to toilen wiþ þe erþe, Tylyen & trewliche lyven. *c* **1400** *Langland's P. Pl.* A. xi. 183 (MS. T.) And alle kyne crafty men..toille for here foode. **1530** Palsgr. 758/2, I toyle, I stryve to gette my lyvyng, *je me estriue*...I toyle, I laboure, *je me trauaille*. **1548** Forrest *Pleas. Poesye* 57 The Pooreman to toyle for twoe pense the Daye. **1580**, etc. [see Moil *v.* 3]. **1611** Bible *Luke* v. 5 Wee haue toyled all the night. *Ibid.* xii. 27 They toile not; they spinne not. **1654** Gataker *Disc. Apol.* 17 For worldlie wealth, men can toil and moil all the week long. **1729** Law *Serious C.* iv. (1732) 53 If he labours and toils, not to serve any reasonable ends of life. **1833** Ht. Martineau *Manch. Strike* ix. 101 Thirteen thousand workpeople—who toil for twopence halfpenny a day. **1909** R. Nicoll in *Mem. H. Bonar* 103 He toiled on till he was past eighty.

**b.** *fig.* To struggle mentally.

**1788** V. Knox *Winter Even.* I. ii. 22 Language toils in vain for expressions. **1831** Scott *Ct. Robt.* xxxi, Anna Comnena deeply toiled in spirit for the discovery of some means by which she might assert her sullied dignity.

**c.** *intr.* With adverbial extension: To move or advance toilsomely or with struggling and labour.

**1781** Cowper *Truth* 457 The Soul reposing on assured relief ..Forgets her labour as she toils along. **1836** W. Irving *Astoria* I. 296 Trusting to his overtaking the barges as they toiled up against the stream. **1855** Macaulay *Hist. Eng.* xii. III. 163 The road was deep in mire...the women and children weeping, famished, and toiling through the mud up to their knees. *Mod.* Toiling up the steep.

**4.** *trans.* To bring into some condition or position, or to procure, by toil; *toil out*, to accomplish or effect by toil. Also with cognate obj. *rare.*

**1667** Milton *P. L.* x. 475, I Toild out my uncouth passage. **1796** Coleridge *Introd. to Sonn.* Poems 1877 I. 131 When, at last, the thing is toiled and hammered into fit shape. **1817** — *Biog. Lit.* ix. I. 148 In Schelling..I first found a genial coincidence with much that I had toiled out for myself. **1823** Praed *Troubadour* i. 487 'Toil yet another toil', quoth he.

**5.** To subject to toil, cause to work hard; to weary, tire, fatigue, esp. with work. *Toil out*, to tire out or exhaust with toil. *arch.* and *dial.*

**1549** Coverdale, etc. *Erasm. Par. Jas.* 36 You are vexed in your mynde, and..toyled with sondrye tumultes of cares. **1596** Danett tr. *Comines* (1614) 328 The poore man that trauelleth and toileth his body to get foode. **1607** Markham *Caval.* iv. (1617) 16 The very toyling him vpon the deep lands, will bring him to a weaknesse in his limbs. **1610** Holland *Camden's Brit.* 55 The army was toiled out with cruell tempests. **1760** Dodd *Hymn to Gd. Nat.* Poems (1767) 6 Steeds much toil'd, ill fed. **1825** Scott *Talism.* xvi, Physicians had to toil their wits to invent names for imaginary maladies. **1837** Carlyle *Fr. Rev.* I. vii. ix, A man so tossed and toiled for twenty-four hours and more.

† **b.** *refl.* *Obs.*

**1587** Golding *De Mornay* xi. (1592) 160 [For] the diuine Prouidence..to toyle it selfe in the cark and care of so many particular things. **1596** Danett tr. *Comines* (1614) 220 What needed he thus to haue toiled himselfe? *a* **1677** Hale *Prim. Orig. Man.* iv. vi. 343 Let Men toyl themselves till their Brains be fired,..they will toyl in vain.

† **6.** *trans.* To labour upon; to work at; *esp.* to till (the earth, ground, or soil).

**1552** Huloet, Toyle or labour the earth, *solicito*. **1614** W. B. *Philosopher's Banquet* (ed. 2) A ij, Like Alchemists toyling the Stone. **1616** Surfl. & Markh. *Country Farme* 151 The Mules..are vsed to toile the earth.

**III.** † **7.** *trans. Cookery.* To stir, mix by stirring. *Obs.*

*c* **1430** *Two Cookery-bks.* 24 Toyle hem with Flowre, an frye hem. *Ibid.* 54 Toyle yt with þin hond al þes togederys. *c* **1550** Lacy *Wyl Bucke's Test.* (Halliw.) 59 Sete him [the chine] on the fire, and toyle him with a pot staffe tyl he sethe for quailing and then he shal be browne of his owne kinde.

**Toil** (toil), *v.*[2] [f. Toil *sb.*[2]] *trans.* To trap or enclose in a toil; to drive (game) into a toil; also *fig.* to entrap, entangle; *dial.* to set (a trap); cf. Till *v.*[1] 7.

**1592** Warner *Alb. Eng.* viii. xli. (1612) 199 And hath he toyled vp his game? **1621** Elsing *Debates Ho. Lords* (Camden) App. 139 Seeing these poore mene toyled in this maze of affliccions. **1887** T. Hardy *Woodlanders* xlvii, He laid the trap,..set it, or to use the local and better word 'toiled' it.

Hence **Toiled** *ppl. a.*, netted, trapped, snared.

**1852** Jerdan *Autobiog.* II. 16 The toiled bird had been liberated from its cage. **1854** S. Dobell *Balder* xxiii. 85 Lying close like a toiled bird that with wide eyes Is mute and strange. *Ibid.* xxxvii. 186 Bind him down With the strong bonds of love..Naked and toiled.

**Toilanette**: see Toilinet.

‖ **Toile** (twal). In 6 also **toyl**(**e**. [F. *toile* linen cloth, canvas :—L. *tēla* web.]

† **1.** Cloth; in quot. 1575, cloth or canvas used for painting on. *Obs. rare.*

**1561** *Reg. Privy Council Scot.* I. 172 To persew for ane schip and toylis, quhilk is callit lynnyng clayth in oure language. **1575** Laneham *Let.* 51 By toile and pensill so lyuely exprest.

**2.** A dress material: see quots.

**1858** Simmonds *Dict. Trade*, *Toile* (French), linen cloth. **1899** *Westm. Gaz.* 22 June 3/2 A simple pretty afternoon gown of blue toile, that mixture of silk and linen.

**Toile**, obs. f. Tuille, piece of body armour.

**Toile**, obs. f. Toil; obs. Sc. form of Tool.

**Toiled** (toild), *ppl. a.*[1] [f. Toil *v.*[1] + -ed [1].]

**1.** Exhausted with toil; worn-out, weary. *arch.* and *dial.*

**1592** Wyrley *Armorie, Capitall de Buz* 144 His toyled mates do tend But how from death they may themselues defend. **1614** W. B. *Philosopher's Banquet* (ed. 2) A iij, Tedious howres and toyled braines. **1622** Drayton *Poly-olb.* xxv. 203 When the toyld Cater home them to the Kitchen brings, The Cooke doth cast them out, as most vnsauory things. **1791** Cowper *Iliad* ii. 466 Ev'ry buckler's thong Shall sweat on the toil'd bosom.

*Comb.* **1895** J. L. Maxwell *W. B. Thomson* iv. 41 A pale, toiled-looking young mother.

† **2.** Of plants or soil: Subjected to or improved by cultivation, tilled, cultivated. *Obs.*

**1578** Lyte *Dodoens* iii. lix. 399 There be two sortes of Hoppes, the manured or toyled Hop, and the wilde hedge Hoppe. **1601** Holland *Pliny* (1634) II. 278 Cala..loueth to grow in toiled and ploughed grounds. **1616** Surfl. & Markh. *Country Farme* 181 Sowne in a well toyled ground.

**Toiled**, *ppl. a.*[2]: see Toil *v.*[2]

**Toilenet, -ette**: see Toilinet.

**Toiler** (toi·lǝɹ). [f. Toil *v.*[1] + -er [1].] One who toils, a hard worker.

**1549** Coverdale, etc. *Erasm. Par. Peter* i. 2 Goodes (in getting and heaping together wherof the toylers of the world thinke themselfes fortunate). **1580** Hollyband *Treas. Fr. Tong, Tracasseur*, a busie body, a toyler to little purpose. **1858** Miss Mulock *Th. ab. Wom.* 86 'In all labour there is profit'—ay, and honour too, if the toilers could but recognise it. **1909** *Chr. Express* 1 Mar. 41/2 Any toiler in the field of sociology—black or white.

**Toilet** (toi·lėt), *sb.* Forms: 6 *Sc.* **tulat, tolat,** 7–8 **toylet,** 8 **toylett,** 7–9 **toilette,** (8 **toillette**), 7– **toilet**; also 7 **twil(l)et,** (7–9 **twilight**). (Cf. *twily* in *Eng. Dial. Dict.*, var. *toily*.) [a. F. *toilette* (twalɛ·t), dim. of *toile* cloth: see Toil *sb.*[2] Cf. Tillet [1].

Most, if not all, of the English senses are to be found in Fr. (see Littré), esp. in 17th cent. use.]

†**1.** A piece of stuff used as a wrapper for clothes. *Obs.*

Also, in dictionaries, from Cotgrave, a night-dress bag; app. an error and never in Eng. use.

**1540** in Pitcairn *Crim. Trials* (1830) I. 302 For pointis to þe Cote and brekis, and ane Tulat to þe Cote..iij s. **1541** *Ibid.* 318 For ix elnis blak freis, to lyne þe Cote...Item, for pointis and ane tolat to turs it to Sanct Johnestoune. **1611** Cotgr., *Toilette*, a Toylet; the stuffe which Drapers lap about their clothes; also, a bag to put night-clothes, and buckeram, or other stuffe to wrap any other clothes, in. [**1656** Blount *Glossogr.*, *Toylet* (Fr. *toylette*), a bag or cloth to put night clothes in. **1858** Simmonds *Dict. Trade, Toilet*, a bag or case for night-clothes.]

†**b.** A towel or cloth thrown over the shoulders during hair-dressing; also, a shawl. *Obs. rare.*

**1684** J. Phillips in tr. *Plutarch's Morals* (1874) IV. 238 Pleasant..was the answer of Archelaus to the barber, who, after he had cast the linen toilet about his shoulders, put this question to him, How shall I trim your majesty? In silence, quoth the king. **1687** A. Lovell tr. *Thevenot's Trav.* III. 37 When they go abroad, they wear a Chal which is a kind of toilet of very fine Wool made at Cachmir.

**2.** A cloth cover for a dressing-table (formerly often of rich material and workmanship); now usually called a *toilet-cover*.

**1682** *Lond. Gaz.* No. 1739/4 A gold-coloured Tabby Twilet and Pincushion with Silver Lace. **1683** *Ibid.* No. 1811/4 Stolen the 20th Instant, a Toilet of blew Velvet, with a Gold and Silver Fringe. **1696** Phillips (ed. 5), *Toilet*, a kind of Table-cloth, or Carpet of Silk, Sattins, Velvet or Tissue, spread upon a Table in a Bed-chamber. **1703** *Countrey Farmer's Catech.* (N. s.v. *Knit-knot*), Not to spend their time in knit-knots, patch-work, fine twilights. **1767** Mrs. Delany *Life & Corr.* Ser. II. (1862) I. 104 Your fancy about taking a gimp round the flowers on the toilet would be pretty, but too much work. **1858** Simmonds *Dict. Trade, Toilet*,..a cotton cover for a dressing-table.

**3.** *collective.* The articles required or used in dressing; the furniture of the toilet-table; toilet-service; also, †a case containing these (*obs.*).

**1662** Evelyn *Diary* 9 June, The greate looking-glasse and toilet of beaten and massive gold was given by the Queene Mother. **1718** Lady M. W. Montagu *Let. to C'tess of Mar* 10 Mar., In her bedchamber, her toilet was displayed consisting of two looking-glasses [etc.]. **1727–41** Chambers *Cycl.*, *Toilet*,..the dressing-box, wherein are kept the paints, pomatums, essences, patches, &c.; the pin-cushion, powder-box, brushes, &c. are esteemed parts of the equipage of a lady's toilet. **1815** *Chron.* in *Ann. Reg.* 53/2 A superb toilet of plate. *Ibid.* 55/1 His toilet is of silver. **1853** Kane *Grinnell Exp.* iii. (1856) 26 To one long string was fastened.. my entire toilet, a tooth-brush, a comb, and a hair-brush.

**4.** The table on which these articles are placed; a toilet-table.

*c* **1695** Prior *Ode, 'The merchant'*, etc. 6 My darling lyre, Upon Euphelia's toilet lay. **1709** — *Hans Carvel* 60 An untouch'd Bible grac'd her toilet: No fear that thumb of hers should spoil it. **1789** Gibbon *Autobiog.* (1854) 100 My book was on every table, and almost on every toilette. **1803** Mary Charlton *Wife & Mistress* I. 118, I have made up a twilight in her room, and put my white taffety pin-cushion upon it. **1818** Scott *Br. Lamm.* xxvi, On the toilette beside, stood an old-fashioned mirror, in a fillagree frame. **1838** W. Wallace *Mackintosh's Hist. Eng.* VIII. v. 188 The letter of the princess Anne, said to have been left by her on her toilet, was not delivered.

**5.** The action or process of dressing.

Transf. from the table (sense 4) to the process there performed, app. through the phr. 'at her toilet'.

**1681** tr. *Combes' Versailles*, etc. (1684) 32 She was given to understand, being at her Toilette, of the death of her Husband. **1712–14** Pope *Rape Lock* III. 24 The long labours of the Toilet cease. **1713** Swift *Cadenus & Vanessa* 50 Ev'ry trifle that employs The out or inside of their heads Between their toylets and their beds. **1777** Mme. D'Arblay *Early Diary* (1889) II. 194 We were down before Mrs. Wall, whose toilette is an affair of moment. **1822** W. Irving *Braceb. Hall* (1849) 51 She actually spent an hour longer at her toilette, and made her appearance with her hair uncommonly frizzed and powdered. **1826** in *Sheridaniana* 309 One morning, when finishing his toilet. **1858** Lytton *What will he do* II. iv, Lionel's toilet was soon hurried over.

**b.** The reception of visitors by a lady during the concluding stages of her toilet: very fashionable in the 18th c. Now *Hist.* (Cf. *toilet-call* in 9.)

**1703** Steele *Tend. Husb.* I. i, You shall introduce him to Mrs. Clerimont's Toilet. **1765** Chesterf. *Let. to A. C. Stanhope* 21 Mar., I carried him a little time ago to a lady's toilette, who was delighted with him. **1786** Mme. D'Arblay *Diary* 19 Aug., I am forced to deny all admission to my toilette, as it has never taken place without making me too late.

**6.** Manner or style of dressing; dress, costume, 'get-up'; also, a dress or costume, a gown.

**1821** Scott *Kenilw.* iii, His toilette had apparently cost him some labour, for his clothes..were of the newest fashion, and put on with great attention. **1821** *Sporting Mag.* IX. 32 The lady was beautiful, her *tourneure* distinguished, her toilette elegant. **1849** Thackeray *Pendennis* xxiv, Madame noted every article of toilette which the ladies wore. **1867** Latham *Black & White* 128 We observed some show of evening toilet. **1883** *Truth* 31 May 745/2 Lady Dudley's black toilette was much admired. **1889** Gunter *That Frenchman* x, This toilet is a mass of fleecy muslin.

**7.** A dressing-room; in *U.S. esp.* a dressing-room furnished with bathing facilities; in restricted sense, a bath-room, a lavatory (*Funk's Stand. Dict.*).

**1819** Byron *Juan* I. cliii, There is the closet, there the toilet. **1858** Simmonds *Dict. Trade, Toilette* (French), a dressing-table; an ante-room for dressing. **1909** in *Cent. Dict. Supp.*

**8.** *transf.* from 5. **a.** *Surgery.* The cleansing of a part after an operation. **b.** The cleaning up of a street, a ship, etc. **c.** Preparation for execution (in Fr. form *toilette*: see Littré s. v. *Toilette* 10 a).

**a. 1879** *Brit. Med. Jrnl.* 24 May 790 Spencer Wells, by his careful toilette of the peritoneum. **1890** Billings *Nat. Med. Dict.*, *Toilet of the peritoneum*, cleansing the abdominal cavity after abdominal section.

**b. 1901** *Daily Tel.* 9 Mar. 9/6 The toilet of London—to use the picturesque phrase of an authority consulted yesterday—cannot be satisfactory unless the streets are flushed with water every night. **1907** C. Urban *Cinematograph* 21 The performance of the toilet of an ocean greyhound.

**c. 1885** Du Cane *Punishm. & Prev. Crime* ii. 23 The hangman was not allowed to enter the gaol even to receive his wage, but was paid over the gates, the 'toilette' or pinioning being performed by the 'yeomen of the halter'. **1903** Ld. R. Gower *Rec. & Remin.* 281 The ghastly ceremony of his toilette [for the guillotine], as they call the pinioning and cutting off the hair at the back of his head.

**9.** *attrib.* and *Comb.* **a.** Of or pertaining to the toilet: as *toilet-call* (see 5 b), *-can, -chamber, -pail, -quilt, -service, -set, -soap, -stand*, etc.

**1721** Cibber *Refusal* II. i, Vanity is the only fruit of toilette lucubrations. **1766** *Gentl. Mag.* Dec. 558/1 A beautiful alabaster..intended for..her toilet-stand. **1827** Carlyle *Germ. Rom.* I. 26 Toilette calls were not in fashion. **1839** Ure *Dict. Arts* 1147 Ordinary soft toilet soap...The fat generally preferred is good hog's lard. **1848** Thackeray *Van. Fair* vii, [She] examined the dreary pictures and toilette appointments. *Ibid.* xxxi, He would make a present of the silver essence-bottles and toilet knicknacks to a young lady. **1853** James *Agnes Sorel* (1860) I. 87 When they had entered his toilet-chamber, the Duke cast himself into a chair. **1858** Simmonds *Dict. Trade, Toilet-can*, a tin can for water for a dressing-room...*Toilet-pail*, a tin pail for holding slops in a bedroom. *Toilet-quilt*, a bed-cover or cover for the dressing-table. *Toilet-set, Toilet-service*, earthenware and glass utensils for a dressing-room. **1909** Eliz. Banks *Myst. Frances Farrington* xiv. 162 Toilet odds and ends, such as hair-pins, safety-pins,..thread and needles.

**b.** Special Comb.: **toilet-basket**, a wicker dressing-case; †**toilet-cap**, a cap formerly worn by men of fashion while dressing; **toilet-case**, a dressing-case; **toilet-cloth, toilet-cover**, a cloth for the toilet-table; **toilet-cup**, a cup, vase, or the like used as a receptacle for small articles of the toilet; **toilet-glass**, a looking-glass for dressing, a toilet-table mirror; **toilet-paper**, soft paper prepared for shaving, hair-curling, use in lavatories, etc.; **toilet-room**, a dressing-room; in *U.S. spec.* a lavatory or bath-room (*Funk's Stand. Dict.* 1895); **toilet-sponge**, a sponge of fine texture for washing; **toilet-table**, a dressing-table furnished with the utensils and materials of the toilet; **toilet-vase**, see *toilet-cup*; **toilet-vinegar**, aromatic vinegar used as an emollient; **toilet-water**, perfumed liquid for the toilet.

**1908** *Westm. Gaz.* 23 Jan. 4/2 The new automobile *toilet basket is just the thing to carry when touring...It contains ..everything necessary for the toilet. **1660** Pepys *Diary* 3 Sept., To get [my Lord]..a *toilet cap, and comb case of silk, to make use of in Holland. **1889** H. F. Wood *Englishman of Rue Cain* xi, One of our governesses had a *toilette-case sent her as a present. **1858** Simmonds *Dict. Trade*, **Toilet-cover*. **1904** E. Nesbit *Phœnix & Carpet* xii. 226 He's pulled the toilet-cover off the dressing-table with all the brushes and pots and things. **1848** Thackeray *Van. Fair* lviii, The dreary little *toilet-glass on the dressing-table. **1884** *Stationers' & Booksellers' Jrnl.* 31 Mar. 3/1 An attractively put-up packet of *toilet paper. **1794** Mar. J. Holroyd in *Girlhood of M. J. H.* (1896) 289 We have put a *Toilette Table and a neat Pembroke Table.. in your own Room. **1902** *Daily Chron.* 20 June 10/4 Visitors to London..see her now at her toilet table. **1874** Birch *1st & 2nd Egypt. Rooms Brit. Mus.* 32 The present *toilet-vase is a remarkably fine example of this kind of ware [glazed steatite]. **1867** Lady Herbert *Cradle L.* viii. 218 Even scented soap and *toilette vinegar were ransacked from his stores. **1855** Dickens *Dorrit* II. xiv, A bottle of sweet *toilette water.

Hence **Toi·letry,** (*a*) performance of the toilet; (*b*) the apparatus of the toilet; **Toile·tic** *a.*, of or pertaining to the toilet. (*nonce-wds.*)

**1832** J. P. Kennedy *Swallow B.* iv, Sundry evidences.. of what—to coin a word,—I might call a scrupulous *toiletry. **1892** *Edin. Rev.* Apr. 433 The claim to have dug up Priam's treasure and Helen's toiletry. **1879** Baker *Cyprus* 13 He.. plunged into.. their numerous small packages, rumpling clean linen, and producing a *toilettic chaos.

**Toilet** (toi·lėt), *v.* [f. prec. sb.] **a.** *intr.* To perform one's toilet, to wash and attire oneself. **b.** *trans.* To furnish with a toilet; to dress, attire.

**1840** Haliburton *Letter Bag* i. 7 Rose and toileted, went on deck. **1850** 'Peter Crook' *War of Hats* 52 A Guy Fawkes figure toiletted and chaired. **1893** Leland *Mem.* II. 177 As soon as I had toiletted and gone below.

Hence **Toi·leted** *ppl. a.*, dressed, costumed, garbed. Chiefly as second element.

**1875** Bret Harte *John Oakhurst* Wks. 1880 III. 120 And then the long hotel piazza came in view, efflorescent with the full-toileted fair. **1882** Annie Edwardes *Ballroom Repentance* I. 3 There wasn't a well toiletted woman there.

**Toilful** (toi·lfŭl), *a.* [f. Toil *sb.*[1]] Full of toil.

**1.** Of an agent or his actions: Characterized by toiling; labouring; hard-working.

**1596** Spenser *Hymn Heavenly Love* 227 Betweene the toylefull Oxe and humble Asse. *a* **1789** Mickle *Liberty* xvii, The fruitful lawns confess his toilful care. **1832** W. Irving *Alhambra* I. 70 We behold the patient train of the toilful muleteer, slowly moving along the skirts of the mountain. **1839–40** — *Wolfert's R., Mountjoy* (1855) 33 The wild-flowers were no longer..the resorts of the toilful bee. **1887** Blackie in *Blackw. Mag.* Oct. 536 The toilful monks of Croyland Clave the clod.

**2.** Of an action, condition, etc.: = Toilsome 1.

**1614** Sylvester *Bethulia's Rescue* iv. 432 Hee.. that.. In Toil-full Fears will his own death procure. **1621** T. Williamson tr. *Goulart's Wise Vieillard* 105 Long trauell, tyrings, and toylefull labours. **1847** W. Irving in *Life* IV. 11 This has been a toilful year to me. **1859** Farrar *J. Home* 96 Climbing with toilful progress some steep and rocky hill.

Hence **Toi·lfully** *adv.*, in a toilful manner.

**1832** tr. *Tour Germ. Prince* II. vii. 124 A white footpath winded along toilfully through the brown heather. **1860** Farrar *Orig. Lang.* i. 3 We toilfully examine the unburied monuments of extinct nations. **1882** E. Arnold *Pearls of Faith* (1883) 144 There through toilfully, with steps of pain Went an old Jew.

**Toi·linet, -ette, toilene·tte.** Also 8 **-enet,** 9 **-anette.** [Origin unascertained: perh. a fancy trade-name; app. f. F. *toile* linen, cloth, the rest of the word being modelled on *satinet, -ette, sarsenet, -ette*, or the like (in which the *n* belongs to the root).] A kind of fine woollen cloth: used in the first half of the 19th c. for waistcoats of grooms, huntsmen, etc.; for later application see quot. 1858 [2]. Also *attrib.*

**1799** *Hull Advertiser* 12 Jan. 2/2 Waistcoat of kerseymere or toilenet. **1801** Nemnich *Waaren Lexicon* II. 687 *Toilinet*, ein feines Westenzeug von Wolle, das in Yorkshire verfertigt wird; *Striped*, gestreift; *Checked*, gewürfelt. Es ist dem Swansdown ähnlich. **1810** in *Spirit Pub. Jrnls.* XIV. 47 With the broad-cloth, toilinets, waistcoat and breeches-stuff. **1840** Chalmers *Chr. & Civic Econ.* xxii, The making of shawls and the making of toilinette waistcoats. **1858** R. S. Surtees *Ask Mamma* lxviii, His vest [was] a canary-coloured striped toilanette, with a slightly turned-down collar. **1858** Simmonds *Dict. Trade, Toilinet*, a kind of German quilting; silk and cotton warp with woollen weft.

**Toiling** (toi·liŋ), *sb.* ? *Obs. rare.* [f. Toil *sb.*[2] + -ing [1]; cf. Netting *sb.*[2]] (See quot.)

**1805** R. W. Dickson *Pract. Agric.* II. 675 A sort of network, formed of small cord, called toiling.

**Toi·ling,** *vbl. sb.* [f. Toil *v.*[1] + -ing [1].] The action of Toil *v.*[1] in various senses; struggling; tugging; labouring, working hard.

*c* **1330** *Arth. & Merl.* (Kölbing) 6083 Ac on hors in þis toiling Was brouȝt Sornigrex þe king. *c* **1394** *P. Pl. Crede* 753 His syre a soutere y-suled in grees, His teeþ wiþ toylinge of leþer tered as a sawe. **1549** Coverdale, etc. *Erasm. Par. Phil.* i. 3 b, To be losed frome the troublous toylynges of thys lyfe. **1587** Harrison *England* I. iv. in Holinshed I. 7/2 When their toiling and drudgerie could not please them. **1644** Milton *Areop.* (Arb.) 63 He.. resolvs to give over toyling. **1831** Carlyle *Sart. Res.* II. v, The Day of Man's Existence..with all its sick toilings. **1895** *Athenæum* 9 Mar. 307/3 The traveller..must make up his mind to..slow toiling along miserable..roads.

**Toi·ling,** *ppl. a.* [f. Toil *v.*[1] + -ing [2].] That toils, in various senses of the verb; struggling; labouring, laborious, hard-working.

**1552** Huloet, Toylyng, *tuditans*. *c* **1592** Marlowe *Massacre Paris* III. ii, Sorrow seize upon my toiling soul! **1642** Fuller *Holy & Prof. St.* IV. xix. 338 He..avoids a toyling and laborious industry. **1703** Rowe *Ulyss.* II. i, The Labours of the toiling Hind. **1844** Longf. *Sea-weed* i, Landward in his wrath he [storm-wind] scourges The toiling surges. **1890** 'R. Boldrewood' *Col. Reformer* (1891) 108 A toiling owner of a small station.

Hence **Toi·lingly** *adv.*, in a toiling manner.

**1812** W. Tennant *Anster F.* III. vi, Toilingly each bitter beadle swung..his greasy rope. **1828** *Blackw. Mag.* XXIV. 351 Toilingly he raises his body.

**Toille,** obs. Sc. form of Toll *sb.*[1]

**Toilless** (toi·l,lės), *a.* [f. Toil *sb.*[1] + -less.] Without toil; apart or free from toil. †**a.** Entailing no toil. *Obs.* **b.** That is or acts without labour or exertion.

**1606** Sylvester *Du Bartas* II. iv. *Magnif.* 664 There all grows toylless. **1839** Bailey *Festus* xix. (1848) 207 Earth's luxurious toilless tribes. **1894** *Scott. Leader* 4 Jan. 3 And soar o'er life, and toilless comprehend Of flowers and all things dumb the silent speed.

Hence **Toi·llessness,** freedom from toil.

**1881** J. M. Brown *Student Life* 4 They keep as a stimulus to toil the prospect of future toillessness.

†**Toilous,** *a. Obs. rare.* Also 5 **-ose.** [f. Toil *sb.*[1] + -ous.] **a.** Contentious, disputatious, wrangling. **b.** Full of toil; toilsome.

*c* **1430** *A. B. C. of Aristotle* in *Babees Bk.* (1868) 12, T to toilose, ne to talewijs, for temperaunce is beest. *c* **1520**

*Treat. Galaunt* (W. de W.) 17 As tyrauntes and traytours, toyllous in moote. **1530** Palsgr. 327/2 Toylouse, full of toyle and labour.

**Toilsome** (toi·lsǒm), *a.* [f. Toil *sb.*$^1$ + -some.]
**1.** Of actions, conditions, etc.: Characterized by or involving toil; laborious, tiring.

**1581** J. Bell *Haddon's Answ. Osor.* 23 b, O my ouer tedious and toylesome lucke, that hoped to dispute with a learned and discrete Diuine,..: but now finde all contrary. **1590** Spenser *F. Q.* i. iv. 3 For she is wearie of the toilsom way. **1667** Milton *P. L.* xi. 179 What can be toilsom in these pleasant Walkes? **1707** *Curios. in Husb. & Gard.* 111 The making of Cyder being Toilsom and expensive. **1855** Macaulay *Hist. Eng.* xiii. III. 358 The ascent had been long and toilsome.

**b.** Of concrete things: Entailing toil.

**1609** W. M. *Man in Moone* (Percy Soc.) 44 The toylsomest burden that combreth a man. **1791** Cowper *Odyss.* x. 94 Our force Exhausting ceaseless at the toilsome oar.

**2.** Of an agent: = Toilful 1.

**1655** H. Vaughan *Silex Scint.* ii. *Quickness* v, Thou art a toylsom Mole. *a* **1841** Shepard in *Ess. Chr. Ministry* 66/2 Fervent, heroic, toilsome men. **1845** Longf. *Rain in Summer* vii, In the furrowed land The toilsome and patient oxen stand.

†**3.** Caused by toil. *Obs. rare.*

**1590** Spenser *F. Q.* ii. v. 30 Toylsom sweat. *Ibid.* xii. 29 Ne ever sought to bayt His tyred armes for toylesome wearinesse.

Hence **Toi·lsomely** *adv.*, in a toilsome manner, laboriously; **Toi·lsomeness**, laboriousness.

**1614** Bp. Hall *Contempl., O. T.* viii. v, Their life must be *toilesomely spent in hewing of wood, and drawing of water for all Israel. **1816** Scott *Bl. Dwarf* iv, Slowly and toilsomely labouring to pile the large stones one upon another. **1871** Macmillan *True Vine* ii. (1872) 61 Earning toilsomely his daily bread. **1586** Stanyhurst *Ded. to Sir H. Sidney* in Holinshed (1808) VI. 274 The *toilesomnesse of the paine I refer to my priuat knowledge. **1630** *R. Johnson's Kingd. & Commw.* 89 A Peasant, disparaged in his drudgery and servile toilsomenesse. **1889** *Spectator* 30 Nov., All dwelt on the painful toilsomeness of manual work, and not one on the satisfaction it produces.

**Toil-worn** (toi·lwō͡ɹn), *a.* [f. Toil *sb.*$^1$ + Worn.] Worn by toil; showing marks of toil.

**1751** Mason *Elfrida* Poems (1774) 122 Mean and pilgrim weeds, All like an ancient, toil-worn traveller. **1804** Grahame *Sabbath* 24 The toil-worn horse, set free. **1843** Bethune *Sc. Fireside Stor.* 124 The toil-worn countenance, and the anxious eye. **1898** J. Arch *Story of Life* viii. 183 The farmers looked care-worn and toil-worn.

**Tois**, obs. f. *toes*, pl. of Toe.

**Toise** (toiz), *sb.* In 6 toyse. [a. F. *toise*:—OF. *teise* = It. *tesa*:—Late L. *tēsa, tensa* (sc. *brachia*) 'the outstretched arms', taken as a fem. sing.: see also the ME. Teise, taise.] A French lineal measure of 6 French feet, roughly equal to 1·949 metres, or 6⅜ English feet. Chiefly in military use. *Square toise*, a measure = about 4½ square yards.

**1598** Dallington *Meth. Trav.* B iv b, This great City..is within ten Toyses as large as Paris. **1644** Evelyn *Diary* 7 Mar., The Greate Garden, 180 toises long and 154 wide. **1759** tr. *Duhamel's Husb.* ii. xi. (1762) 150, 1344 square toises of 36 feet. **1823** Byron *Juan* viii. vii, The column order'd on the assault scarce pass'd Beyond the Russian batteries a few toises [*rime* noises]. **1904** Quiller-Couch *Fort Amity* xiii, It was quadrilateral with a frontage of fifty toises.

Hence **Toise** *v. rare* [ad. Fr. *toiser*] *trans.*, to measure with the eye, to eye from head to foot.

**1889** Stevenson *Master of B.* iv, At the same time he had a better look at me, toised me a second time sharply, and then smiled. *a* **1894** — *St. Ives* xix, I am acquainted also with the properties of a pair of pistols, said I, toising him.

‖ **Toisech** (tǭ·ʃeχ). *Sc. Hist.* [Gaelic *tòisech* lord, chief; = Welsh *tywysog* 'dux, princeps': cf. *tòisich* to begin, *tùs, toiseach* beginning, front.] A personage or officer of the third rank (in order *king, mormaer, tòisech*) in ancient Celtic Scotland, corresponding generally to the later chief of a clan.

**1836** Skene *Highlanders Scot.* (1902) I. vii. 114 There can be little doubt that the Gaelic title of Toisich was peculiar to the oldest cadet. **1885** *Edin. Rev.* Apr. 309 The Celtic 'Toisechs' took their corresponding place as Chiefs of Clans. **1900** Watt *Aberdeen & Banff* ii. 49 A few appear to have been descendants of the old toisechs.

‖ **Toison d'or** (twazondōr). Also 7 toyson d'ore. [F., = fleece of gold; *toison*:—L. *tonsiōn-em* shearing (i.e. of a sheep), *or*:—L. *aurum* gold.]

**a.** The golden fleece: see Golden *a.* 1; also *fig.* **b.** *Her.* The figure of this, giving name to an order of knighthood (see Fleece *sb.* 1 c), and afterwards borne by certain families.

**1623** Lisle *Ælfric on O. & N. Test.* Ded. xxii, Yea Weathers furr'd with her owne Toyson d'Ore. **1704** J. Harris *Lex. Techn.* I, *Toison d'Or* (French), the Term in Heraldry for a golden Fleece, which is sometimes born in a Coat of Arms. **1854** Thackeray *Newcomes* xxviii, She had done everything for Jason; she had got him the *toison d'or* from the Queen Mother.

**Toist** (toist). Also toyst. App. a dial. form of Teistie: see quot. 1893 s. v.

*a* **1688** Wallace *Descr. Orkney* (1693) 16 There are likewise many Toists and Lyres, both Sea Fowls, very fat and delicious to eat. **1744** Preston in *Phil. Trans.* XLIII. 61 There are many Sorts of Wild-fowl;..Solan Goose,..Whaps, Toists,..Plovers, Scarfs, &c.

**Toi-toi**, var. Toe-toe, a New Zealand grass.

**Tok**, obs. pa. t. of Take *v.*

**Tokan**, obs. form of Toucan.

**Tokay**$^1$ (tokē$^i$·). Also 8 tockay. [Name of a town in Upper Hungary.] (Also *Tokay wine.*) A rich sweet wine of an aromatic flavour, made near Tokay in Hungary. Also applied in U. S. to a Californian wine made in imitation of this.

**1710** Swift *Jrnl. to Stella* vi, I dined at Stratford's in the City and had Burgundy and Tokay. **1714** Mandeville *Fab. Bees* (1725) I. 260 When he has had a large Company, and thought it Extravagant to treat with Tockay. **1773** Douglass in *Phil. Trans.* LXIII. 295 There are four sorts of wine made from the same grapes, which they distinguish at Tokay by the name of Essence, Ausspruch, Masslasch, and the common wine. — 296 The Ausspruch is the wine commonly exported, and what is known in foreign countries under the name of Tokay. **1857** Miller *Elem. Chem.* (1862) III. 160 Sherry yields from 1 to 5 per cent., port from 3 to 7 per cent., and Tokay as much as 17 per cent. of sugar.

**b.** *Tokay grape*, the variety of grape from which this wine is made.

**1896** *Godey's Mag.* Feb. 222/2 The luscious Tokay grapes, the golden oranges, and purple plums may be placed in separate dishes.

‖ **Tokay**$^2$ (tō$^u$·ke). Also tokee, tockay, tookai. [a. Malay توكي *tōkē*, also written تكق *tōkeq*, *tĕkeq*, with final *q* often silent: see Gecko.]

A species of Gecko, or lizard of the family *Geckonidæ*, app. *G. verticillatus*, of Burma, Siam, and the Malay region.

**1753** Chambers *Cycl. Supp.*, *Tockay*,..the name of a species of Indian lizard distinguished from the other kinds, by being spotted all over. **1774** Goldsm. *Nat. Hist.* VII. 149 Directly descending from the crocodile, we find the Cordyle, the Tockay and the Tejuguacu, all growing less in order, as I have named them. **1899** *Proc. Zool. Soc.* 16 May 631 The Great House-Lizard or Tokay is recorded from Penang, Singapore, and the Malay Peninsula...In Siam, however, it is one of the commonest animals.

**Toke**, obs. pa. t. of Take *v.*; see Toque, Tuck.

**Token** (tō$^u$·kĕn), *sb.* Forms: *α.* 1–3 tác(e)n, 2 takan, 2–3 takenn (*Orm.*), 3–7 taken, 4 takein, 4–6 takin, -yn, 6 taikin, 8 -en, 7 tackyn. *β.* 2–4 tocne, 3 tocken, 3–5 tokne, 4 -ene, -in, -un, 5 toocun, tookne, tokyng, 5–6 -yn, tooken, (6 tukne), 7 toakin, 4– token. [OE. *tácen, tácn*; = OFris. *têken, têkn, teiken* (WFris. *teiken*, †*teeckne*), OS. *têcan* (MLG., MDu., LG. *têken*, Du. *teeken*), OHG. *zeihhan* (MHG., Ger. *zeichen*), ON. *teikn* (*tákn* from OE.), Sw. *tecken*, Da., Norw. *tegn*, all neuter:—OTeut. **taik-nom* (in Goth. *taikns* fem. :—**taiknis*), cognate with **taik-jan*, OE. *tǽcean* to show, Teach.]

**1.** Something that serves to indicate a fact, event, object, feeling, etc.; a sign, a symbol. *In token of*, as a sign, symbol, or evidence of.

*c* **890** tr. *Bæda's Hist.* i. viii. (1890) 42, & heora stowe brǽddon & weorðodon, swa swa sigefæst tacon. *c* **897** K. Ælfred *Gregory's Past. C.* xxviii. 196 To tacne ðæt he his ȝeweald ahte. *c* **1200** *Vices & Virt.* 135 Nis þat non god tocne of ripe manne. *a* **1300** *Cursor M.* 16574 Þe rode þai scop þan as þai wald, Als we þe taken se. *c* **1315** Shoreham vi. 15 In tokne þat pays scholde be By-tuexte god and manne. **1483** Caxton *G. de la Tour* lviii. E vij, [The queen] shewed hym many signes and tokenes of loue. *a* **1533** Ld. Berners *Huon* lxxxiv. 266 Charlemayne .. kyssyd Huon in token of peace. **1585** T. Washington tr. *Nicholay's Voy.* iii. xiii. 95 Bearing..a satchell ful of haye in token of their bondage and seruice. **1686** in *Verney Mem.* (1907) II. 409 Friendly cautions are Tokens of Love. **1778** Miss Burney *Evelina* (1784) II. i. 9 He gave him..a cordial slap on the back, and some other equally gentle tokens of satisfaction. **1833** Ht. Martineau *Briery Creek* iii, The hollow tree, from which the mists had drawn off, leaving a diamond token on every leaf.

†**b.** A sign of the zodiac. *Obs. rare.*

*c* **1000** *Sax. Leechd.* I. 164 Sy þæt ðonne þære sunnan ryne beo on þam tacne þe man uirgo nemneð. *c* **1050** *Byrhtferth's Handboc* in *Anglia* (1885) VIII. 303 Seo sunne wunað on þam twelf tacnum. **1535** Coverdale *2 Kings* xxiii. 5 Them that brent incense..to the Sonne, and the Mone, and the twelue tokens, and to all y$^e$ hoost of heauen.

†**c.** An ensign, a standard. (Only OE.)

*a* **1000** *Gloss. Prudentius* 45 Eal werod ȝehwyrfedum tacnum [*versis signis*]..foron. *a* **1000** *Ags. Ps.* (Spelm.) lxxiii. 6 [lxxiv. 4] Hi asetton tacna heora tacna.

†**d.** The sign of an inn, etc. *Obs. rare*$^{-0}$.

*c* **1440** *Promp. Parv.* 495/2 Tokne, or sygne of ane in, *idem quod* seny, *supra* (*P.* signe of an ostry).

**e.** *Coal-mining* (*S. Wales*). A thin seam of coal indicating the vicinity of a thicker bed.

**1883** in Gresley *Gloss. Coal-mining.*

**2.** A sign or mark indicating some quality, or distinguishing one object from others; a characteristic mark.

*c* **1000** Ælfric *Gen.* iv. 15 God him sealde tacn, þæt nan þæra..hine ne ofsloge. *a* **1300** *Cursor M.* 6124 Bot in þat huse noght he yode þar he fand taken wit þe blode. **1398** Trevisa *Barth. De P. R.* vi. v. (Bodl. MS.), Whanne childrenne voice chaungeþ it is a tokene of Puberte. *c* **1400** Maundev. (1839) xxiii. 247 Þat beren the tokne vpon hire hedes of a mannes foot. **1456** Sir G. Haye *Law Arms* (S. T. S.) 281 A maister armoureur .. in his werkis had a takyn that his werkis war knawin by. **1557** North *Gueuara's Diall Pr.* 95 The tokens of a valyant and renowmed captaine are, his woundes and hurtes. **1577** B. Googe *Heresbach's Husb.* iii. (1586) 115 b, Virgill..doth..describe the tokens of a good Horse. **1814** Scott *Ld. of Isles* vi. xiv, The tokens on his helmet tell The Bruce, my Liege: I know him well. **1822** Lamb *Elia* Ser. i. *Chimney-Sweepers*, One unfortunate wight .. by tokens was discovered to be no chimney-sweeper.

**b.** A spot on the body indicating disease, esp. the plague. Now *rare* or *Obs.*

**1634** T. Johnson *Parey's Chirurg.* xxii. xiii. (1678) 500 [In Plague] spots (vulgarly called Tokens) appear over all the body. **1666** J. H. *Treat. Gt. Antidote* 5 The Tokens are, I am confident, Marks sent from God, and it is as impossible to cure any that have them, as to contradict the Divine Decree. **1722** De Foe *Plague* (1756) 225 Those Spots they call'd the Tokens were really gangreen Spots, or mortified Flesh in small Knobs as broad as a little silver Peny, and hard as a piece of Callus or Horn. **1896** *Allbutt's Syst. Med.* I. 932 In the seventeenth century they [purpuric patches] were known as the 'Tokens'. *Ibid.* 934 Petechial eruptions or 'tokens'.

**3.** Something serving as proof of a fact or statement; an evidence.

*Beowulf* (Z.) 1655 Beowulf maþelode..hwæt we þe þas sælac..brohton tires to tacne. *c* **1000** *Ags. Gosp.* John vi. 30 Hwæt dest þu to tacne þæt we ȝeseon & ȝelyfon? *c* **1200** *Vices & Virt.* 31 And wel ilieue be are tacne ðe he hafð iȝiuen me. *c* **1250** *Gen. & Ex.* 2860 Moyses tolde hem ðat bliðe bode, And let hem sen tockenes fro gode. *c* **1425** tr. *Arderne's Treat. Fistula* 28 Þis schal be to þe þe tokne of perfite curyng when þou seez þe linne cloutez..to be drye. **1517** in *Acts Parlt. Scotl.* (1875) XII. 38/1 And in takin of this oure consent and oblissing hereintill We .. have [affi]xt to thir presentis oure Selis. *a* **1533** Ld. Berners *Huon* lxxxi. 246 He shal shew tokens that my sayenge is trewe. **1692** Washington tr. *Milton's Def. Pop.* iii. M.'s Wks. 1851 VII. 73 Money bears the Prince's Image, not as a token of its being his, but of its being good Metal. **1715** De Foe *Fam. Instruct.* i. i. (1841) I. 6 A token of his being, and of his being God. **1769** Cook *Voy. round World* i. viii. (1773) 79 These .. were brought as tokens of peace and amity. **1843** Mill *Logic* i. iii. § 7 By what token could it manifest its presence?

†**b.** Something remaining as evidence of what formerly existed; a vestige, trace, 'sign'. *Obs.*

**1555** Eden *Decades* To Rdr. (Arb.) 49 There remayneth at this daye no token of the laborious Tabernacle whiche Moises buylded. **1610** Holland *Camden's Brit.* (1637) 518 Yet wee with all our seeking could see no tokens of any such Wall. *Ibid.* 547 There be many tokens remaining of old antiquity.

†**4.** In biblical use, An act serving to demonstrate divine power or authority; = Sign *sb.* 10. *Obs.* or *arch.*

*c* **897** K. Ælfred *Gregory's Past. C.* lviii. 443 Ðone Nazareniscan Hælend ðæt wæs afandon wer..on mæȝenum & tacnum. *c* **1000** *Ags. Gosp.* John x. 41 Witodlice ne worhte iohannes nan tacn [*c* **1160** *Hatton G.* takan]. *c* **1175** *Lamb. Hom.* 91 Þa warhte god feole tacne on þan folke þurh þere apostlan hondan. *c* **1200** Ormin 14068 Þiss takenn wrohhte Jesu Crist. **1382** Wyclif *Acts* ii. 22 Jhesu of Nazareth, a man prouyd of God in ȝou by vertues [*gloss* or myraclis], and wondris, and tokenes. **1535** Coverdale *Josh.* xxiv. 17 The Lorde oure God..did soch greate tokens [**1611** signes] before oure eyes. **1611** Bible *Ps.* cxxxv. 9 Who sent tokens [**1885** (R.V.) signs] and woonders into the midst of thee, O Egypt. *Ibid.* lxv. 8 They also that dwell in the vttermost parts are afraid at thy tokens [so **1885** (R.V.)].

**5.** A sign or presage of something to come; an omen, portent, prodigy. *Obs.* (exc. as included in 1).

**971** *Blickl. Hom.* 117 Ealle þa tacno & þa forebeacno þa þe her ure Drihten ær toweard sæȝde. *c* **1175** *Lamb. Hom.* 91 Ic sende min tacna ȝeond þa eorðe. **1297** R. Glouc. (Rolls) 5927 Þis was as a tokne þat to comene was. **1340** Hampole *Pr. Consc.* 4733 Þe grete day of dome, Agayn whilk alle þir takens sal come. *c* **1400** Maundev. (Roxb.) vii. 27 If it brynne, it es a gude taken. *c* **1440** *Promp. Parv.* 495/2 Tokne, of a thynge to cumme or cummynge, *pronosticum.* **1594** Shaks. *Rich. III*, v. iii. 21 The weary Sunne..by the bright Tract of his fiery Carre, Giues token of a goodly day to morrow. *a* **1628** Sir J. Beaumont *Bosworth F.* 73 Some mark his Words, as Tokens fram'd t' express The sharp Conclusion of a sad Success. **1791** Cowper *Iliad* iv. 455 By unpropitious tokens interfered.

**6.** A signal given; a sign to attract attention or give notice. Now *rare* or *Obs.*

*a* **1000** *Prose Life Guthlac* xi. (Goodwin) 54 Comon þær þry men to þære hyðe, and þær tacn sloȝon. *c* **1440** *Promp. Parv.* 495/2 Tokne, wythe eye or wythe the hand, *nutus.* *c* **1450** *Merlin* xviii. 292 Thei sowned theire hornes and tymbres and trumpes, and that was token that thei wolde haue socoure. **1560** Daus tr. *Sleidane's Comm.* 452 As a token or watche worde, they cried that the Frenchemen were vp in harnesse. **1577–87** Holinshed *Chron.* I. 33/2 He gaue the token to fight vnto his souldiers. **1726** Swift *Gulliver* i. i, I gave tokens to let them know, that they might do with me what they pleased. **1833** Ht. Martineau *Fr. Wines & Pol.* iii. 43 Charles lifted his finger in token of silence.

**7.** A sign arranged or given to indicate a person; a word or material object employed to authenticate a person, message, or communication; a mark giving security to those who possess it; a password.

**1377** Langl. *P. Pl.* B. xvi. 147 And [Judas] tolde hem a tokne how to knowe with ihesus. *c* **1440** *Gesta Rom.* xxiii. 80 (Harl. MS.), & told to hir all the prive tokyns þat were ysaid bytwene hem two. **1561** in *Exch. Rolls Scotl.* XIX. 460 Delyverit to Peter Cokburne, quha come with ane takin fra George Symson, the saidis George lettres. **1716** Hearne *Collect.* (O. H. S.) V. 189 Admitting no one..but one or two, to whom I had given tokens that I might know when they were at the Door. **1827** Roberts *Voy. Centr. Amer.* 270 It is customary for the King to give any person..travelling specially 'on King's business' a token [by which he may be known]. **1840** Dickens *Barn. Rudge* lxxi, You bring..some note or token from my uncle.

†**8.** A badge worn to indicate service or party.

**1472** *Coventry Leet Bk.* 374 Noo Reteindres, lyuerees, signes ne tokenys of clothing, nor othir wyse be taken, had nor vsed. **1516** *Sel. Cas. Star Chamb.* (Selden) II. 115 Sworne..that he shall not be receyued ne were any lyuerey or token of or with any lord Gentilman or..other personne foreyn. 15.. *Battle of Balrinnes* in Maidment *Sc. Ball.* (1868) I. 253 He that thought not for to blyne His mistres' tockin taks; They kist it first, and set it syne Upone their helms and jackes.

†**b.** *pl.* Armorial bearings, heraldic arms. *Obs.*

**1562** LEIGH *Armorie* 28 b, In the first inuention of them, they were not called Armes, but Tokens.

**9.** Something given as an expression of affection, or to be kept as a memorial; a keepsake or present given especially at parting.

*c* **1385** CHAUCER *L. G. W.* 1273 (*Dido*) Send hir letres tokens broches and rynges. **1463** *Bury Wills* (Camden) 36 For a tookne to remembre hire husbond. **1606** SHAKS. *Tr. & Cr.* I. ii. 306 A token from Troylus. **1722** RAMSAY *Three Bonnets* III. 62 Accept o' this love-taiken. **1848** DICKENS *Dombey* v, I must present your friend with some little token.

**10.** Something given as the symbol and evidence of a right or privilege, upon the presentation of which the right or privilege may be exercised.

**1538** ELYOT, *Tessera*,..a token [*ed.* 1548 of leade, leather or other thyng] gyuen to people to receyue corne of the kinges almes. **1548** *Ibid.*, *Tesseræ nummariæ*, tokens geuen to men to receiue a summe of money by. **1552** HULOET, Token geuen vnto people in fayres and markets when they bye cattell..*tessera, tesserula*.

**b.** *spec.* A stamped piece of lead or other metal given (originally after confession) as a voucher of fitness to be admitted to the communion: in recent times used in Scotland in connexion with the Presbyterian Communion service, but now generally represented by a 'communion card'.

**1534** in Kitts *Churchw. Acc. St. Martin in the Fields* 37 Item Receued and gathred for howssellyng tokens in the Churche xiij$^s$ vij$^d$. **1583** *Churchw. Acc. St. James'* in *Bristol past & pres.* (1881) II. 37 Paid for tokens to deliver to the howselynge people at Easter, vid. **1608** (Feb. 24) *Churchw. Acc. St. Martin in the Fields* 585 It is ordered That every Communicant, for the generall Communions at Easter, shall the day before Their Receiving, Repaire to the Minister, or Curate, and then and their pay his dueties and take a token, and Restore his Token, at his Comming the next day to the Communion. **1611** COTGR., *Marreau*, the token of lead, etc., giuen for a remembrance, in Churches, to such as meane to receiue the Communion. **1626** in Swayne *Sarum Churchw. Acc.* (1896) 184 The Clarke shall deliver out a token for euerye persone that will receyve [the Sacrament]. **1645** *Dalgety Sess. Rec.* in W. Rose *Past. Wk. in Covt. Times* vi. (1877) 135 All that wants tokens were forbidden to approoch the table. **1791** BOSWELL *Johnson* 27 Aug. an. 1773, Her husband was in the church distributing tokens. **1888** BARRIE *Auld Licht Idylls* iii, Without a token, which was a metal lozenge, no one could take the sacrament. **1896** 'IAN MACLAREN' *Kate Carnegie, A Moderate*, The women had their tokens wrapt in snowy handkerchiefs. *Ibid.*, Domsie went down one side and Drumsheugh the other, collecting the tokens, whose clink, clink in the silver dish was the only sound.

**11.** A stamped piece of metal, often having the general appearance of a coin, issued as a medium of exchange by a private person or company, who engage to take it back at its nominal value, giving goods or legal currency for it.

From the reign of Queen Elizabeth to 1813, issued by tradesmen, large employers of labour, etc., to remedy the scarcity of small coin, and sometimes in connexion with the truck-shop system. *Bank-tokens*, silver tokens for 5*s.*, 3*s.*, 1*s.* 6*d.*, were issued by the Bank of England in 1811: see quots. 1812, 1832.

**1598–1604** Tauerne token [see TAVERN *sb.* 4]. **1614** B. JONSON *Barth. Fair* III. iv, Buy a tokens worth of great pinnes. **1638** SIR R. COTTON *Abstr. Rec. Tower* 25 Retailers of victuals and small wares..using their owne tokens; in and about London there are above three thousand that one with another cast yearely five pound a peice of leaden tokens. **1757** JOS. HARRIS *Coins* 65 To supply the want of very small silver coins, a kind of Tokens or substitutes have been instituted all made of copper. **1812** *Chron.* in *Ann. Reg.* 150/1 The Silver Tokens issued by the Bank of England..Silver Tokens of 3*s.* each...The weight of the 1*s.* 6*d.* token is 4 dwts. 17½ grains. **1832** BABBAGE *Econ. Manuf.* xiv. (ed. 3) 131 Silver tokens for various sums were issued by the Bank of England.

**12.** *Printing.* A measure or quantity of presswork; a certain number of sheets of paper (usually 250 pulls on a hand-press) passed through the press. *Token-sheet*, the last sheet of each token, turned down to facilitate counting the whole number.

**1683** MOXON *Mech. Exerc.*, *Printing* xxv. ¶ 5 A Token.. for Half a Press, viz. a Single Press-man, is generally but five Quires..: But if it be for a Whole Press, it contains Ten Quires. *Ibid.* xxiv. ¶ 9 Having Wet his first Token, he doubles down a..corner of the upper Sheet of it..: This Sheet is called the Token-Sheet, as being a mark..to know how many Tokens of that Heap is Wrought-off. **1867** BRANDE & COX *Dict. Sc.*, etc., *Token*, in Printing [is] ten quires eighteen sheets of perfect paper, or 258 sheets. It is reckoned an hour's work for a hand press, of ordinary work. **1886** *Encycl. Brit.* XXIII. 707/1 It has been mentioned that 250 sheets or a *token* per hour, printed on one side only, represent the work of two men at the hand-press. **1896** T. L. DE VINNE *Moxon's Mech. Exerc.*, *Printing* 427 It required much activity to pull a token in one hour... The full ream printed on both sides is rated as four tokens.

**13.** In the Isle of Man: A legal summons: see quotations.

**1724** BP. WILSON in Keble *Life* xix. (1863) 638 If he owns it he is to have seven days' imprisonment and three penances in Church. If not he is to have a token to clear himself. **1726–31** WALDRON *Descr. Isle of Man* (1865) 40 When a person has a mind to commence a suit against his neighbour for debt, he has no more to do than to take out a token, which is a piece of slate marked with the governour's name on it; and it is the same thing with an arrest in England.

**14.** *Weaving.* See quot.

**1878** BARLOW *Weaving* xv. 177 Several small bobbins with a little of the various colours of the weft that may be used, that is, when several kinds are employed. They are called tokens, and are raised by the Jacquard hooks attached, so as to remind the weaver which shuttle to use.

**15.** *Phrases* (in which the sense of *token* becomes vague). **a.** *By the same token, by this* (or *that*) *token*: (*a*) in the 15th c. app. On the same ground; for the same reason; in the same way; (*b*) since 1600 (= F. *à telles enseignes que*), 'the proof of this being that'; introducing a corroborating circumstance, often weakened down to a mere associated fact that helps the memory or is recalled to mind by the main fact. *arch.* or *dial.*

**1463** *Paston Lett.* II. 134 And to this [course] Maister Markham prayed you to agre by the same token ye mevyd hym to sette an ende be twyx you and my masters your brethern. **1463** *Will of Sir H. Stafford* in *Somerset Med. Wills* (1901) 200 When ye come to him by the same token that I said to thabbat, Sir, I have a goode quarrell, the which is the cause of my journey, by that token he will deliver the said writinges unto you. **1491** *Act 7 Hen. VII*, c. 22 Preamble, Ye may speke with him by the same token that he and y commyned toguyder of matiers touching your maisters sonne. **1606** SHAKS. *Tr. and Cr.* I. ii. 307 *Pand.* I, a token from Troylus. *Cres.* By the same token, you are a Bawd. **1607** R. C[AREW] tr. *Estienne's World of Wonders* I. xxxviii. 305 At Aix in Germany, they were accustomed to shew his breeches, together with the virgin Maries smocke, by the same token that [*orig.* à telles enseignes que] the smocke was big enough for a giant. **1659–60** PEPYS *Diary* 28 Feb., Up in the morning and had some red herrings to our breakfast, while my boot-heel was a-mending, by the same token the boy left the hole as big as it was before. **1662** *Ibid.* 13 Apr., I went to the Temple Church, and there heard another [sermon]: by the same tokens, a boy, being asleep, fell down a high seat to the ground. **1722** DE FOE *Plague* (1756) 280 Others caused large Fires to be made..; by the same Token, that two or three were pleased to set their Houses on Fire, and so effectually sweetened them by burning them down to the Ground. **1857** DICKENS in *Househ. Words* XVII. 46 Max..was a staunch Roman Catholic. (By this token: Many an argument have I had with him on religion). **1907** PHYLLIS DARE *School to Stage* vii. 126 To receive letters from people whom they do not know, and are, by the same token, never likely to know.

**b.** *More by token*: still more, the more so. *dial.*

**1816** SCOTT *Antiq.* xl, Ane suldna speak ill o' the dead—mair by token, o' ane's cummer and neighbour. **1850** HAWTHORNE *Scarlet L.* xxi, Our only danger will be from drug or pill; more by token, as there is a lot of apothecary's stuff aboard. **1861** GEO. ELIOT *Silas M.* i, All this Jem swore he had seen, more by token that it was the very day he had been mole-catching on Squire Cass's land.

**16.** *attrib.* and *Comb.*: †**token-bell**, ? a signal- or alarm-bell; **token coin, coinage, currency**: see TOKEN-MONEY c; †**token-girdle**, ? a girdle mounted with amulets; **token pledge** = sense 7; **token-proprium**: see TOKEN-MONEY b; **token-ring**, a ring worn in token of an engagement or pledge; **token-sheet**, *Printing* (see 12); †**token-teller**, an indicator; **token value**: see TOKEN-MONEY c; †**tokenworth**, the worth of a token (sense 11), the very least amount.

**1486** in J. R. Boyle *Hedon* (1875) App. 130 Soluti pro undecim les *tokyngbelles hoc anno, iij. s. xj. d. **1897** *Daily News* 30 Nov. 4/6 The shilling..is declared to be..the twentieth part of a pound. No evil results follow from this fiction, because the shilling is a *token coin and because silver is not a legal tender, except for a comparatively trivial amount. **1881** H. H. GIBBS *Double Stand.* 73 It would be necessary to re-coin all our silver *token-coinage. **1883** *Times* 14 July 5 Silver..[is] in this country in the nature of a token coinage. **1893** *Daily News* 27 June 2/3 If so, the silver rupee will become '*token' currency. **1477** *Croscombe Churchw. Acc.* (Som. Rec. Soc.) 5 Sylver ryng gylt and a *token gyrdel of sylver. **1896** A. AUSTIN *Eng. Darling* I. iii, Only a *token pledge to make me free Of Alfred's camp at Athelney. **1716** M. DAVIES *Athen. Brit.* III. 78 The Traders were not oblig'd to take one anothers Penny-coyns or such like *Token-Propriums. **1840** MRS. NORTON *Dream*, etc. 296 By the true *token-ring upon thy hand. **1877** W. JONES *Finger-ring* 350 A pledge or token ring of remarkable interest. **1574** NEWTON *Health Mag.* 29 For smellinge is the discouerer and *token teller of tast. **1898** *Daily News* 30 Mar. 5/1 The closing of the Mints to the free coinage of silver, with the view of giving an artificial *token value to the coinage, was adopted. **1614** B. JONSON *Barth. Fair* I. ii, Why? he makes no loue to her, do's he? *Lit.* Not a *tokenworth that euer I saw.

**Token** (tōᵘ·kĕn), *v.* Forms: *α.* 1 **tácnian**, 2 **tacnien**, 2–3 **tacnen** (*Orm.* **-enn**), 3 **taknen**, 4 **-nyn, takenen**, 4–6 **takin, -yn.** *β.* 3 **toknien, -ny, tocknen**, 3–4 **tokenen**, 3–5 **toknen**, (5 **tooken**), 3– **token.** [OE. *tácnian* (also *ge-*) = MLG. *têkenen*, OHG. *zeihhanôn* (Ger. *zeichnen*) :—OTeut. **taiknôjan*, f. **taikno*$^m$, TOKEN *sb.*]

**1.** *trans.* To be a token or sign of; to signify, represent, denote, mean, betoken.

*c* **888** ÆLFRED *Boeth.* xxxix. § 13 Þon tacnað [se steorra] æfen. **971** *Blickl. Hom.* 19 Smeagean we nu..hwæt þæt tacnode. [*c* **1175** *Lamb. Hom.* 7 Nu we wulleð seggen mare wet þis godspel itacnet.] *c* **1205** LAY. 32115 To wulche þinge hit iteon wolde þat him wes itacned þere [*i.e.* in the dream]. *Ibid.* 32131 Al swa godd him hafde itakned to don. *c* **1350** *Will. Palerne* 2957 What þat it tokeneþ telle wol ich sone. *c* **1425** *Craft of Nombrynge* (E.E.T.S.) 5 A cifre tokens noȝt. *c* **1425** tr. *Arderne's Treat. Fistula* 14 Suche pronosticacions sheweþ and tokneþ to þe pacient þat þe leche is experte in þe knowyng of þe fistule. **1535** STEWART *Cron. Scot.* (Rolls) II. 424 Quhat this takynnit I will nocht tell ȝow heir. **1889** C. C. R. *Up for the Season*, etc. 16 On fair leaves and ladies as yet there no shade is To token their coming decay.

**2.** To be a type, emblem, or symbol of; to typify, symbolize.

**971** *Blickl. Hom.* 35 Þa Easterlican daȝas tacniaþ þa ecean eadiȝnesse. *c* **1000** ÆLFRIC *Hom.* II. 280 Wæter ȝetacnað ..mennisc inȝehyd. *c* **1220** *Bestiary* 763 in *O. E. Misc.* 24 Crist is tokned ðurȝ ðis der. *a* **1300** *Cursor M.* 6341 (Cott.) Þis wandes takens persons thre. *Ibid.* 18644 He [Christ] es takend to leon. **1426** LYDG. *De Guil. Pilgr.* 809 And by thys dowe wych thow dost se,..I am tookenyd. **1552** GRINDAL *Fruitful Dial.* in Foxe *A. & M.* (1570) 1558/2 The token of the body of Christ is [not] the thing tokened; wherfore they are not one. **1863** KINGLAKE *Crimea* II. xiii. 195 The principle of the 'moveable column' would be well enough tokened by that simple skinful of water.

†**3.** To mark with a sign or significant mark.

*c* **1300** *Cursor M.* 21713 (Edin.) Þe signe of taue in alde laiis Bitaknis cros nu in ure daiis. The men that tarwiþ takind ware Oft it helpid fra misfare. *c* **1375** *Sc. Leg. Saints* xli. (*Agnes*) 30 With þe fare blud of his passione [He] taknys þar chekis vpe & done. **1483** CAXTON *Gold. Leg.* 431 b/1 He was marked or tokened on the lyppes of hym with an hote and brennyng yron. **1513** DOUGLAS *Æneis* XI. viii. 23 Quhen thou takynnit hes sa worthely With syng tropheall the feyldis.

†**4.** *intr.* To make a sign or signs. *Obs. rare.*

**1535** COVERDALE *Prov.* vi. 12 He wyncketh with his eyes, he tokeneth with his fete, he poynteth with his fyngers.

**5.** *trans.* To betroth, promise in marriage. *dial.*

**1880** in *W. Cornwall Gloss.* **1910** E. PHILLPOTTS *Thief of Virtue* I. ii. 10 'How can she throw over the man afore they'm tokened?'..'If they are tokened, does it follow they've let all the world know it?'

†**6.** *Token up*, to put up in writing, write out. *Obs. rare.*

**1535** COVERDALE *Dan.* v. 23 Therfore is the palme off this honde sent hither..to token vp this wrytinge. — *Ecclus.* l. 27, I Iesus the sonne of Sirac..haue tokened vp these informacions and documentes of wyszdome and vnderstandinge in this boke.

Hence **To·kened, To·kening** *ppl. adjs.*

**1606** SHAKS. *Ant. & Cl.* III. x. 9 *Eno.* How appeares the Fight? *Scar.* On our side, like the Token'd Pestilence, Where death is sure. **1820** CLARE *Rural Life* (ed. 3) 109 We'll mix our wishes in a tokening tear.

†**Tokener** (tōᵘ·kĕnəɹ). *Obs.* Also 6 *Sc.* **takinar, taknair.** [f. prec. + -ER [1].]

**1.** One who or that which portends or prognosticates; a portent.

**1513** DOUGLAS *Æneis* I. v. 114 The dreidful portis sal be schet,..Of Janus temple, the taknair of battail. *Ibid.* vii. 46 Thai, delvand, fand the takinar of Cartage, Ane mekle hors heid that was, I wene.

**2.** One who signs or marks.

**1648** HEXHAM II, *Een Teeckenaer*, a Marker, a Noter, a Signer, or a Tokener.

**Tokening** (tōᵘ·kĕniŋ), *vbl. sb.* Now *rare.* [OE. *tácnung* (*ge-*), f. *tácn-ian*, TOKEN *v.* + -ING [1]: cf. OHG. *zeihnunga*, MHG. *zeichenunge*, Ger. *zeichnung*, Du. *teekening*, etc.]

**1.** The action of the verb TOKEN; representation, signification, meaning, symbolization, betokening, presaging, etc.: see the verb.

*c* **888** K. ÆLFRED *Boeth.* vii. § 2 To hwæm cumað hi þon elles butan to tacnungesorȝes &..sares? [*c* **1175** *Lamb. Hom.* 99 Þe helende ableu his gast on his apostlas for ðere itacnunge þet heo and alle cristen men scullan lufian heore nehstan.] *c* **1200** *Trin. Coll. Hom.* 91 Chirche haueð þe tocninge of bethfage. *a* **1300** *Cursor M.* 6337 Sum-kin takening suld þar be Loken in þir wandes thre. *c* **1410** *Sir Cleges* 217, I am aferd yt ys tokynnyng Of more harme that ys comynge. **1496** *Dives & Paup.* (W. de W.) I. xv. 48/1 Encensynge done..byfore the ymages in dyuerse sygnyfycacyons or tokenynges.

†**b.** *In tokening*, in token, as a token or evidence (*of*). *Obs.*

*c* **890** tr. *Bæda's Hist.* II. vi. (1890) 114 Þa he me in tacnunge his lufan bebead. **1297** R. GLOUC. *Chron.* (Rolls) 1165 Ibured it was uorþ wiþ him as in tokninge Of is prowesse. **1456** SIR G. HAYE *Law Arms* (S.T.S.) 39 A branch of ane olyve tree in takenyng of pes. ? *a* **1500** *Chester Pl.* xi. 147 A signe I offer..in tockeninge shee has lived oo in full devocion.

**2.** A token, emblem, sign, mark; a portent; a signal; † a zodiacal sign (*obs.*).

*c* **888** K. ÆLFRED *Boeth.* viii. § 1 Hwæt syndon ða woruldsælða oðres buton deaðes tacnung? *a* **1300** *Cursor M.* 11252 Þar es þe king ouer al kinges Born to night wit þir takeninges. *c* **1320** *Sir Tristr.* 506 Hunters, whare be ȝe? Þe tokening schuld ȝe blowe. *c* **1400** tr. *Secreta Secret.*, *Gov. Lordsh.* 73 Whenne þe sonne entrys yn to þe firste tokenynge of þe crabbe. *a* **1450** *Tourn. Tottenham* 85 A broche on hur brest.. With the holy-rode tokenyng, was wrotyn for the nonys. **1553** *Douglas's Æneis* III. vi. 67, I sall the schaw taikynnis [*ed. Small* takins] therof full mete. **1710** *Dict. Feudal Law* 151 *Taiknings*, are Signals given to forwarn people of the approach of the Enemy. **1867** MORRIS *Jason* III. 46 Bid him hearken, by this tokening, That I, who send thee to him, am the same.

**To·kenless**, *a.* [-LESS.] Without a token.

*a* **1763** BYROM *On Church Communion* III. ii, Heartless, and tokenless if it remain, It ought to pass, in Strictness, for profane.

**To·ken-mo·ney.**

**a.** *Eccl.* The payment made or contribution given (by way of Easter Offering) by persons on receiving their token that they were duly prepared to make their Easter communion.

(See TOKEN 10 b, quot. 1608, and *Churchw. Acc. St. Martin in the Fields* 37 *note*.)

**1546** *Churchw. Acc. St. Martin in the Fields* 101 In

primis Receued and gatherd of the Paryshyons ffor the pascall and tokyn money at Easter in the Church xlis. vjd. 1564 *Ibid.* 216 It'm Receyued the ix[th] of Aprile 1564 for the halfe of the token monneye at Easter xxvj[s] viij[d]. 1572 *Ludlow Churchw. Acc.* (Camden) 153 Imprimis receaved of the parishenars for the token money at Easter..xlij s. 1573 *Ibid.* 156 Receavede at Easter of token money.. xlv s. x d. 1611 *Churchw. Acc. St. Margaret's Westm.* (Nichols 1797) 29 Received for the token-money for the whole year, ended the 11th day of May, 1611 £6. 5.

**b.** Private tokens (TOKEN *sb.* 11) issued by a trader or company to serve as a fractional currency and temporary medium of exchange between trader and customer; so *token-proprium* (TOKEN 16).

1890 *Pall Mall G.* 9 Jan. 3/3 He has also grocery and provision stores all along the line, and pays all his employés in token-money which he mints himself—probably the most gigantic truck system which ever existed. 1900 M. PHILLIPS (*title*) The Token-Money of the Bank of England, 1797 to 1816.

**c.** State coinage of money not having the intrinsic value for which it is current, but bearing a fixed value relative to gold coin, for which it is exchangeable.

1889 *Spectator* 9 Nov. 641/2 They [gold and silver] perform different functions, and it is this fact which enables a State to use one of them as token-money, the demand for it practically neither rising nor falling according to its price, nor according to the activity of trade. 1892 *Pall Mall G.* 22 Dec. 2/3 The remedy lies not in increased use of token money, but in providing in gold-using countries a second currency for silver.

† **To·ker.** *Obs.* A large variety of garden bean.

1786 J. ABERCROMBIE *Gard. Assist.* Feb. 32 *Beans.*—Plant ..a full crop of long-pods, Windsors, tokers, Sandwich, or other broad kinds, in rows a yard distance. 1802 *Eng. Encycl.* IV. 473/1 The Toker is the largest garden-bean, and somewhat of an oval shape.

**Toker, Tokke,** obs. ff. TUCKER, fuller, TUCK *v.*

**To-kerve**: see TO-CARVE.

**Toko,** var. TOCO [2]. **Toko-**: see TOCO-.

**Tol,** obs. form of TOLL, TOOL.

‖ **Tola** (tōu·lă). *East Ind.* Also 7 tolla; anglicized tole, toll; 9 tolah. [Hindī *tola* :—Skr. *tulā* balance, scale, weight, f. *tul-* to weigh.] An East Indian weight, chiefly used for gold or silver, varying at different times and places; now (since 1833) in the British dominions fixed at 180 grains (the weight of the rupee). Also, a coin of this weight.

1614 PURCHAS *Pilgrimage* v. xvii. (ed. 2) 544 Euery Tole is a Rupia of siluer, and tenne of those Toles is the value of one of golde. 1618 in Foster *Eng. Factories Ind.* (1906) 47, 52½ tole make a seere of 30 pices. 1683 W. HEDGES *Diary* (Hakl. Soc.) I. 83 They..tooke from them 4 or 5 tolas upon a Seer, over weight, on all their Silk brought into y[e] Warehouse. 1687 A. LOVELL tr. *Thevenot's Trav.* III. 18 All Gold and Silver is weighed by the Tole. 1800 *Misc. Tr.* in *Asiat. Ann. Reg.* 45/1 Each of these persons shall pay a fixed revenue of a tola of gold to the Rajah. 1803 GREVILLE in *Phil. Trans.* XCIII. 203 *note*, A tolah is about 180 grains, Troy weight. 1895 *19th Cent.* Aug. 255, I placed a piece of gold, weighing a tola, on his lap.

**Tolat,** obs. Sc. form of TOILET.

**Tolbooth, toll-booth** (tōu·lbūð, -būþ, tǫ·lbūþ), *sb.* Chiefly *Sc.* Forms: 4 tolboþe, 4–6 tolbothe, tolbuth, 5 tolboythe, tolle buthe, tolbuthe, (towboth, -buthe), 5–7 tolbuith, 6 tolboith, -boith, -buyth, tollboothe, -bouthe, (towbuyth, 7 toole-, towle-, tolebooth), 6– tolbooth, 7– tollbooth. [f. TOLL *sb.*[1] + BOOTH, *lit.* the booth, stall, or shed of the tax-collector. Cf. Ger. *zollbude*, Da. *toldbod*, custom-house.]

†**1.** A booth, stall, or office at which tolls, duties, or customs are collected; a custom-house.

[1314–15 *Rolls of Parlt.* I. 331/1 Mandetur..Ballivis de Tolbotha de Lenne.] 13.. *Propr. Sanct.* (Vernon MS.) in Herrig's *Archiv* LXXXI. 309/4 Matheu cald was his name, In a Tol-boþe sat þe same. *c* 1375 *Sc. Leg. Saints* x. (*Mathou*) 8 Quhare in þe tolbuth set lewy. 1381 *Rolls of Parlt.* III. 108/1 Alerent jeske a Tolbothe du dite ville [Canterbury]. 1382 WYCLIF *Matt.* ix. 9 He seiȝ a man sittynge in a tolbothe, Matheu by name. *c* 1475 *Pict. Voc.* in Wr.-Wülcker 804/8 *Hoc toloneum*, a tolbothe. 1483 *Cath. Angl.* 390/1 A Tolle buthe. 1577–87 HOLINSHED *Chron.* III. 1186/1 The tolboth in the market of Durham all of stone. 1587 *Lanc. Wills* (Chetham Soc.) III. 116 Excepte onelie of the tollboothe the toll and stallages of Manchester. 1633 BP. HALL *Hard Texts, N. T.* 14 Sitting in the Tolebooth of the Publicans to gather up the rents. 1756 NUGENT *Gr. Tour, Germ.* II. 133 There is here a great toll-booth, or custom-house, where toll is paid for..black cattle that pass from Jutland into Germany.

**2.** A town hall or guildhall.

(Often (esp. in Scotland) comprehending senses 1 and 3.)

1440 *Sc. Acts Jas. II* (1814) II. 32/2 The Consale Generale haldyn at Strivilyn in the tolbuthe of that ilk. 1467 *Dunfermline Regr.* (Bann. Cl.) 358 Þis inquisicion made at Berwik vpoun twede in þe tolbuth of þe samyn. 1593 *Reg. Mag. Sig. Scot.* 817/2 Ad edificandum pretorium, carcerem domumque ponderum et telonium (lie tolbuith, prissoun, weyhous and customehous)..ad publicos usus dicti burgi. 1596 DALRYMPLE tr. *Leslie's Hist. Scot.* x. (S. T. S.) II. 400 Publiklie be heraldis..scho [the Queen] commandis, that Johne Knox, Wilok, Douglas, and Paul Meffen, compeiring in the Tolbuith of Striuiling in Judgment to mak ansuer. 1665 J. BUCK in Peacock *Stat. Cambridge* (1841) App. B. 54 Upon Michaelmass day the Vice Chancellor with some of the Heads and Doctors..goe to the Toll Booth in their Scarlet Gowns, there to give the Maior his oath. 1820 LINGARD *Hist. Eng.* IV. ii. 74 Margaret..offered to conduct her son (he was only in his twelfth year) to the tolbooth of Edinburgh, and to announce by proclamation that he had assumed the government. 1828 *Craven Gloss., Toll-booth*... In this district it signifies a Town Hall, where the Court Baron is held, and the rents and amercements due to the Lord are paid. 1900 J. KIRKWOOD *United Presbyterians Ayr.* iii. 29 They had to perform the ceremony in the Tolbooth of Irvine.

**3.** A town prison, a jail.

(Formerly usually consisting of cells under the town hall.)

*c* 1470 HENRY *Wallace* VII. 202 A bauk was knyt all full of rapys keyne; Sic a towboth sen syn was neuir seyne. *c* 1520 NISBET *N. T. in Scots, Acts* xxiii. 35 He comandit him to be kepit in the tolbuth of Herode. 1535 CROMWELL in Merriman *Life & Lett.* (1902) I. 432 The said universitie [Cambridge] hath hertefor had..the use of the kings prisoune there called the Tolbothe. 1581 N. BURNE *Disput.* in *Cath. Tractates* (S. T. S.) 109 Being impresoned first in the Castel of Sanctandrois, and nixt in the tolbuith of Edinburgh. 1655 FULLER *Hist. Camb.* vii. § 25 The Maior refused to give them the keys of the Toll-booth, or Town-prison. 1661 BLOUNT *Glossogr.* (ed. 2), *Tolbuyth*, the name of the chief Prison at Edenburgh. 1738 (*title*) Captain Porteous's Ghost, giving an Account how he was dragged from the Tolbooth of Edinburgh, by the outrageous mob, and hung by the neck like a Dog. 1752 J. LOUTHIAN *Form of Process* (ed. 2) 67, I being incarcerate within the said Tolbooth, by Warrant of the Lord Justice-Clerk, for the Crime of Murder alledged committed by me. 1818 SCOTT *Hrt. Midl.* Note C, Since the year 1640..the Tolbooth was occupied as a prison only. 1855 [BURN] *Autobiog. Beggar Boy* (1859) 6, I am not without some pleasing reminiscences of the *gude toun* of Hawick, having been boarded and lodged in the tolbooth there for the space of seven days.

**4.** *attrib.*

1611 *Acc. Bk. W. Wray* in *Antiquary* XXXII. 214 The crosse of stone standing in the toolebooth garth. *c* 1737 in Scott *Hrt. Midl.* Note D, One Stoddart,..was charged of haveing boasted publickly, in a smith's shop at Leith, that he had assisted in breaking open the Tolbooth door. 1818 *Ibid.* iii[i], 'I would claw down the tolbooth door wi' my nails,' said Miss Grizel, 'but I wad be at him [Porteous]'. 1847 MRS. S. MENTEATH *Lays Kirk & Covt.* 65 A gleam is waking—more faintly now—Her Tolbooth prison-hold.

Hence † **To·lbooth** *v.* (*obs. nonce-wd.*), to imprison in a tolbooth.

*a* 1635 CORBETT *Poems* (1648) 35 (*Jas. I's Visit to Cambridge*) And well bestow'd he thought his hen, That they might Tolebooth Oxford men.

† **To·lbot.** *dial. Obs.* **a.** Local name of some measure of capacity: according to some, a bushel. **b.** The tub or cask for the reception of meal taken in multure. [Cf. TOLL *sb.*[1] 2 a (*b*), and *boat* (*dial.*), a tub for meal or meat, a meal-boat (*Eng. Dial. Dict.*).]

1536 *MS. Acc. St. John's Hosp., Canterb.*, Payd for a tolbot off otemell vij d. 1589 R. HARVEY *Pl. Perc.* 3 Make meale of it, and take large tole to the enriching of the Tolbot.

**Told** (tōuld), *ppl. a. rare.* [pa. pple. of TELL *v.*] Related, narrated, recounted; counted, reckoned; † esteemed: see the verb. Chiefly in comb., as *oft-told* (OFT A. c), *twice-told*, etc. † *By told tales*, as is said, as they say (cf. *by all accounts*).

*c* 1310 in Böddeker *Altengl. Dicht.* 292 Ȝef þou art riche & wel ytold, Ne be þou noht þarefore to bold. *a* 1425 *Cursor M.* 18713 (Trin.) Alle þat wolde leue [= believe] þat tolde And bapteme receyue wolde. 1546 J. HEYWOOD *Prov.* (1867) 22 All is not golde that glisters by tolde tales. 1882 W. B. WEEDEN *Soc. Law Labor* 94 Capital is told wealth.

**b.** *Told out*, counted out; hence, played out, spun out, exhausted (*colloq.*).

1861 WHYTE MELVILLE *Mrkt. Harb.* xi. (1862) 89 He could not disguise from himself that the roan was about 'told out'.

**Tol-de-rol, tol de rol** (tǫ·l dĭ rǫ·l). Also in extended form **tol de rol lol.** A combination of syllables used as the refrain of a song, and hence as an exclamation of jollity, or the like. Also as *sb.*, and *attrib.*

1765 H. TIMBERLAKE *Mem.* 56 Just like the toldederols [*sic*] of many old English songs. 1782 MRS. H. COWLEY *Bold Stroke for Husb.* IV. ii, Tol-de-rol! Ah, that won't do—that won't do! You can't hide it. 1797 F. REYNOLDS *The Will* v. ii, What, Mandeville! Howard! all together! all reconciled!—Tol de rol lol! 1798 WOLCOTT (P. Pindar) *Tales of Hoy* Wks. 1816 IV. 18 Let us have something in the tol-de-roll-loll-way—funny. 1815 W. H. IRELAND *Scribbleomania* 40 Some scribes who write fast, and are flippant at rhymes, Think Genius is center'd in tol-de-rol chimes. 1861 DUTTON COOK *P. Foster's D.* i, The policeman sings a sort of a 'tol de rol'. 1889 *Grove's Dict. Mus.* IV. 805 *Ture-lure..*, or *Toure-loure*, a very ancient lyrical burden or refrain.. still survives in English popular music in the forms 'tooral-looral-looral', and 'tol-de-rol'.

‖ **Toldo** (tǫ·ldo). Also 9 tolda. [Sp. *toldo* awning, canopy, penthouse: cf. F. *taudis* a shelter, a hut, OF. *tauder* to shelter; see Körting 9422, 9519.] **a.** A canopy. **b.** A tent, hut, or hovel of the native Indians of South America.

**a.** 1760–72 tr. *Juan & Ulloa's Voy.* (ed. 3) I. 159 To avoid the tortures of the Moscitos..all persons..have *toldos* or canopies over their beds. 1852 TH. ROSS *Humboldt's Trav.* II. xx. 286 We could not make use of mosquito-curtains (toldos) while on the Orinoco.

**b.** 1845 DARWIN *Voy. Nat.* iv. (1873) 65 The Cacique Lucanee constantly have their Toldos on the outskirts of the town. *Note.* The hovels of the Indians are thus called. 1864 *Reader* 9 Apr. 463/1 These *toldas* (or dwelling-places) are constructed only with branches of sticks, joined overhead at a height of about five feet from the ground. 1910 *Blackw. Mag.* June 850/1 An old revolver may find its way into their guanaco-skin toldos.

† **Tole.** *Obs. rare.* [OE. *tál* (str. fem.), a by-form of *tæl*: see TELE *sb.*] Evil-speaking, calumny; blasphemy; reproach, blame.

*c* 1000 *Ags. Gosp.* Luke iii. 14 Ne tale ne doð. *c* 1000 ÆLFRIC *Hom.* I. 498 Ælc synn and tal bið forgifen. *a* 1023 WULFSTAN *Hom.* lvii. (1883) 299 Þæt man god to tale habbe. *c* 1315 SHOREHAM i. 975 Þer-fore ȝe mote þolyen hyt [pain] Wyþ-oute alle manere tole [*rime* hole = whole].

**Tole,** obs. f. or var. TOLA, TOLL (esp. *v.*[1]), TOOL.

**Toledo** (tolī·do). [Name of a city (tolē·do) in Spain, long famous for its manufacture of finely tempered sword-blades.] Short for *Toledo blade* or *sword*: A sword or sword-blade made at Toledo, or of the kind made there.

1598 B. JONSON *Ev. Man in Hum.* II. ii, *Step.* How will you sell this rapier, friend? *Brai.*..'Tis a most pure Toledo. *c* 1626 *Dick of Devon* III. i. in Bullen *O. Pl.* II. 46 A hundred of the best Toledoes. 1645 MILTON *Colast.* Wks. 1851 IV. 357 What doe these keen Doctors heer but cut him over the sinews with their Toledo's? 1713 ADDISON *Ct. Tariff* ℙ 22 A long Toledo sticking out by his side. 1826 SCOTT *Woodst.* ii, Reach me my Toledo.

**Tolenar,** variant of TOLNER *Obs.*

**Tolene** (tǫlīn). *Chem.* [f. TOL(U + -ENE.] The oily constituent of tolu-balsam, $C_{10}H_{16}$.

1868 WATTS *Dict. Chem.* V. 851 Tolene is a colourless very mobile liquid, having a pungent odour...When exposed to the air, it quickly takes up oxygen, and becomes resinised.

**Toler,** variant of TOLLER [2] 2.

**Tolerabi·lity.** *rare.* [f. TOLERABLE: see -ITY.] The quality or state of being tolerable; tolerableness.

1640 FULLER *Joseph's Coat* ix. (1867) 192 Let them labour also to ingratiate every pastor, who hath tolerability of desert, with his own congregation. 1655 — *Ch. Hist.* IX. i. § 35 Alas; tolerability was eminency in that age. 1810 W. TAYLOR in Robberds *Mem.* II. 294, I might fit up the lives of the German poets,..and so mend each into tolerability.

**Tolerable** (tǫ·lĕrăb'l), *a.* (*adv.*). Also 5–7 toller-. [a. F. *tolérable* (14th c. in Godef. *Compl.*), ad. L. *tolerābilis* that may be borne, that can bear or endure, f. *tolerāre* to bear, endure: see -ABLE.]

**1.** Capable of being borne or endured; supportable (physically or mentally); bearable, endurable.

1422 tr. *Secreta Secret., Priv. Priv.* 132 Suche a kynge is tollerabill, as many men thynkyn, for the more myschefe to Enchu. 1515 BARCLAY *Egloges* iii. (1570) B vj b/2 It were thing tollerable To becke and to bowe to persons honorable. 1582 N. T. (Rhem.) *Matt.* x. 15 It shall be more tolerable for the land of the Sodomites and Gomorrheans in the day of iudgement, then for that city. 1604 E. GRIMSTONE *Hist. Siege Ostend* 157 Nakednesse, by reason of the..colde..is not very tollerable. 1653 BAXTER *Worc. Petit. Def.* 39, I abhor as much as most do..not bearing with each other in tolerable differences. *a* 1704 T. BROWN *Two Oxf. Scholars* Wks. 1730 I. 9 He did not know how to maintain himself and his Family in any tolerable sort. 1834 SOUTHEY *Doctor* lxx. (1862) 149/2 The temperature of a glass-house is not only tolerable but agreeable to those who have their fiery occupation there. 1909 *Westm. Gaz.* 27 Aug. 2/2 Ideas..of making the motor less anti-social and more tolerable by the general public.

**b.** Of drugs: That may be endured, or of which the action may be resisted, by the human system: cf. TOLERANCE 1 b, TOLERANT *a.* c.

**2.** Such as to be tolerated, allowed, or countenanced; sufferable, allowable. Now *rare.*

1531 ELYOT *Gov.* II. ii, That langage that in the chambre is tollerable, in place of iugement or great assembly is nothing commendable. 1597–1602 *W. Riding Sessions Rolls* (Yorks. Rec. Ser.) 27 Misdemeanours not tollerable by the lawes of the Realme. 1598 MANWOOD *Lawes Forest* xii. § 4 (1615) 91 When there is no mast in the woods, then hogges nor swine are not tollerable there. 1619 T. CAMPION *Art of Descant* (1674) 41 If the Bass be sharp in F fa ut, it is not tolerable to rise from a sixth to an eight. 1625 BACON *Ess., Revenge* (Arb.) 502 The most Tolerable Sort of Reuenge is for those wrongs which there is no Law to remedy. 1690 LOCKE *Govt.* II. xiii. § 151 Where..the Executive is vested in a single Person,..that single Person in a very tolerable Sense may also be called Supream.

†**3.** *actively.* Capable of bearing or enduring; tolerant. Const. *of. Obs. rare.*

1555 EDEN *Decades* 99 The owlde souldiours..were..excedyinge tollerable of labour, heate, hunger, and watchynge.

**4.** Moderate in degree, quality, or character; of middling quality, mediocre, passable; now *esp.* moderately good, fairly good or agreeable, not bad.

1548 UDALL, etc. *Erasm. Par. Matt.* v. 38 To the intent ye shoulde be of the meane and tollerable sorte. 1597 HOOKER *Eccl. Pol.* v. lxxxi. § 5 Wee are to descend to a lower step, receiving knowledge in that degree, which is but tolerable. 1658 EVELYN *Diary* 9 June, The new front towards y[e] gardens is tollerable, were it not drown'd by a too massie and clomsie pair of stayres of stone. 1693 DRYDEN *Disc. Orig. & Progr. Satire* Ess. (Ker) II. 110 We have yet no English *prosodia*, not so much as a tolerable dictionary, or a grammar. 1706 PHILLIPS (ed. Kersey), *Tolerable*,..also indifferent, passable. 1790 *Cook's Voy.* V. 1729 Some of it, which had adhered in lumps, was of a tolerable [*ed.* 1784 II. 235 sufficient] whiteness. 1833 L. RITCHIE *Wand. by Loire* 53 The staircase is all that now exists even in tolerable preservation. 1835 SIR J. ROSS *Narr. 2nd Voy.* xl. 538 Found a tolerable road. 1866 MRS. GASKELL *Wives & Dau.* xv, He had eaten a very tolerable lunch. 1868 M. PATTISON *Academ. Org.* v. 209 Leisure and tolerable freedom from the anxieties of straitened means.

**5.** As *adv.* **a.** = TOLERABLY 2.

(After 1750 chiefly in inferior writers and *dial.*)

1673 *Remarques Humours Town* 40 If you can but discourse tollerable of good Wine. 1711 STEELE *Spect.* No. 114 ℙ 1, I observed a Person of a tolerable good Aspect. 1796 MRS. E. PARSONS *Myst. Warning* III. 142 They halted at a tolerable large hamlet. 1823 F. COOPER *Pioneers* xxxviii, They..emerged at once into a tolerable clear atmosphere.

**b.** *pred.* In fair health; moderately or passably well: = TOLERABLY 2 b. *colloq.*

1847 C. BRONTE *J. Eyre* xxvi, We're tolerable, sir, I thank you.

**To·lerableness.** [f. prec. + -NESS.] The quality or fact of being tolerable.

**1.** Allowableness: cf. prec. 2.

1612 J. MASON *Anat. Sorc.* 69 Not so much to confirme the lawfulnesse..as to induce or insinuate a tolerablenesse in regard of the necessity.. thereof. 1644 J. GOODWIN *Innoc. Triumph.* (1645) 33 Questioning the Orthodoxisme, yea, the tolerablenesse of the..Doctrine.

**2.** Capability of being borne or endured; bearableness, endurableness: cf. prec. 1.

*a* 1678 WOODHEAD *Holy Living* (1688) 39 Practising..the inconveniences and sufferings of poverty, to try by the tolerableness of these the unnecessariness of wealth.

**To·lerablish,** *a. rare.* [f. as prec. + -ISH [1].] Somewhat tolerable, pretty fair, just passable.

1798 [Given as a 'Hampshirism' in a letter from J. Jefferson to J. Boucher 23 Feb. (MS.)]. 1899 *Pall Mall Mag.* Jan. 80, I vow the music sounds tolerablish.

**Tolerably** (tǫ·lĕrăbli), *adv.* [f. TOLERABLE + -LY [2].] In a tolerable manner or way.

**1.** In a way that may be borne, endured, or permitted; bearably, supportably; allowably, permissibly.

1580 HOLLYBAND *Treas. Fr. Tong, Passablement,* tollerably, that may be borne withall. 1586 W. WEBBE *Eng. Poetrie* (Arb.) 65 What wordes may tollerably be placed in Ryme, and what not. 1597 HOOKER *Eccl. Pol.* v. lviii. § 4 It may be tollerably giuen without them rather then any man without it should..depart this life. 1643 MILTON *Divorce* II. viii. Wks. 1851 IV. 81 He might dismisse her whom he could not tolerably and so not conscionably retain.

**2.** In a moderate or passable degree; passably, moderately, fairly, pretty well.

1485 CAXTON *Paris & V.* Prol. (1868) 12 The matter is reasonable and tolerably credible. 1602 MARSTON *Ant. & Mel.* Induct., Ha! ha! ha! tolerably good; good faith, sweet wag. 1695 WOODWARD *Nat. Hist. Earth* III. i. (1723) 148 Bodyes that are still tolerably firm. 1712 ADDISON *Spect.* No. 275 ¶ 10 [He] had acquitted himself tolerably at a Ball or an Assembly. 1799 HT. LEE *Canterb. T., Frenchm. T.* (ed. 2) I. 198 She had made rapid strides too in her education; she wrote tolerably. 1815 J. SMITH *Panorama Sc. & Art* II. 708 It will be easy to form a tolerably correct idea of the perspective appearance of any object. 1843 RUSKIN *Mod. Paint.* (1848) I. II. I. vii. § 18. 93 He painted everything tolerably, and nothing excellently. 1894 LD. WATSON in *Law Times Rep.* LXXI. 103/1 Two things appear to their Lordships to be tolerably certain.

**b.** *pred.* Moderately well in health; pretty well. *colloq.* and *dial.*

1778 in *Mme. D'Arblay's Early Diary* (1889) II. 241 He is tolerably to-day.

**Tolerance** (tǫ·lĕrăns). Also 5–6 toll-. [a. F. *tolérance* (14th c. in Hatz.-Darm.), ad. rare L. *tolerāntia,* f. *tolerāre* to TOLERATE: see -ANCE. But from 16th c. prob. directly referred to the L.]

†**1.** The action or practice of enduring or sustaining pain or hardship; the power or capacity of enduring; endurance. *Obs.*

1412–20 LYDG. *Chron. Troy* II. 7014 Riȝt so convenient Is to þe wyse..with suffraunce, In al his port to haue tollerаunce. 1603 HOLLAND *Plutarch's Mor.* 230 Sage counsell and wisdome..in dangers and travels, we tearme tolerance, patience and fortitude. *a* 1626 BACON *Apophthegm.* 138 in *Resuscitatio* (1661) 311 Diogenes, one terrible frosty Morning, came into the Market-place; And stood Naked shaking to shew his Tolerance. 1650–3 tr. *Hales' Dissert. de Pace* in *Phenix* (1708) II. 366 [They] have omitted nothing to the most certain Hope of Salvation, and to all the toil of a pious Life, and to the tolerance of Christ's Cross. 1814 W. TAYLOR in *Monthly Mag.* XXXVII. 527 We do not ascribe superior tolerance to the protestant dissenters for enduring more patiently their privations.

**b.** *Phys.* The power, constitutional or acquired, of enduring large doses of active drugs, or of resisting the action of poison, etc. Cf. TOLERANT c, TOLERATE *v.* 1 b, TOLERATION 1 b.

1875 H. C. WOOD *Therap.* (1879) 153 By the aid of opiates and careful dilution a species of tolerance was often obtained for these heroic doses. 1876 BARTHOLOW *Mat. Med.* (1879) 236 When emetic doses even are continued in some subjects, this effect finally ceases, and the drug is borne without producing any gastric symptoms. To this state has been applied the term *tolerance.* 1890 BILLINGS *Nat. Med. Dict., Tolerance,* power of endurance whereby a dangerous drug can be safely taken in excessive doses.

**c.** *Forestry.* The capacity of a tree to endure shade. Cf. TOLERANT d. *U.S.*

1898 PINCHOT *Adirondack Spruce* 6 A provisional scale of tolerance is as follows, beginning with the species which demand most light: Tamarack, Poplar, Bird Cherry, White and Black Ash [etc.]. *Ibid.* 23 All species..are not equal in their tolerance of shade, their resistance to storm and disease [etc.]. *Ibid.* 30 Black Cherry stands about midway in the scale of tolerance among the trees in the Park.

†**2.** The action of allowing; licence, permission granted by an authority. *Obs.*

1539 *Act* 31 *Hen. VIII,* c. 13 § 19 Without any other licence, dispensacion or tollerance of the kinges highnesse. 1567 *Reg. Privy Council Scot.* I. 571 Na persoun sould intromet thairwith..without his rycht licence and tollerance had thairto. 1580–81 *Ibid.* 357 Be the Kingis Majesties permissioun and tollerance.

**3.** The action or practice of tolerating; toleration; the disposition to be patient with or indulgent to the opinions or practices of others; freedom from bigotry or undue severity in judging the conduct of others; forbearance; catholicity of spirit.

1765 LOWTH *Let. to Warburton* 13 It admits..of no tolerance, no intercommunity of various sentiments, not the least difference of opinion. 1809–10 COLERIDGE *Friend* (1865) 56 The only true spirit of tolerance consists in our conscientious toleration of each other's intolerance. 1841 MYERS *Cath. Th.* III. § 5. 15 It may not accord with the undisciplined instincts of some to associate the tolerance of Imperfection in connection with the instrumentality of Perfection. 1868 HELPS *Realmah* vi. (1876) 89 Tolerance, or to use a more Christian word, charity. 1902 C. LENNOX *J. Chalmers* xiv. (1905) 70/1 With the same large tolerance he satisfied the curiosity of the astonished black.

**4.** Technical uses. **a.** *Coining.* The small margin within which coins, when minted, are allowed to deviate from the standard fineness and weight: also called *allowance.* (Cf. TOLERATION 5, REMEDY *sb.* 4.)

1868 *Rep. Royal Commission on Internat. Coinage* 95 As to the minimum of remedy or tolerance to be allowed on coining, it will be observed that there is a near agreement among the Mints of different countries on this head. *Ibid.* App. xi. 228 Gold coins...The margin allowed for error in coining, known as the remedy or tolerance, is calculated upon the pound troy of coin, and amounts to 15 grains for the fineness, plus or minus, or $^1/_{16}$ of a carat, and 12 grains for the weight.

**b.** *Mech.* An allowable amount of variation in the dimensions of a machine or part.

1909 *Cent. Dict. Supp.* s.v., A tolerance of ·00025 [$=^1/_{4000}$] of an inch is allowed above or below the exact dimension in fine machine parts.

**Tolerancy** (tǫ·lĕrănsi). *rare.* [ad. rare L. *tolerāntia*: see prec. and -ANCY.] The quality or habit of being tolerant: cf. prec. 3.

*a* 1556 UDALL *Let.* in *Royster D.* (Shaks. Soc.) Introd., By their excedyng gret tolerancie brought them to goodnes. 1825 COLERIDGE *Aids Refl.* xxvi. (1848) I. 77, I shall believe our present religious tolerancy to proceed from the abundance of our charity and good sense.

**Tolerant** (tǫ·lĕrănt), *a.* (*sb.*) [a. F. *tolérant* (16th c. in Hatz.-Darm.), pr. pple. of *tolérer* to TOLERATE, ad. L. *tolerānt-em,* pr. pple. of *tolerāre.*] Disposed or inclined to tolerate or bear with something; practising or favouring toleration.

1784 JOS. WHITE *Bampton Lect.* iii. 145 His [Gibbon's] eagerness to throw a veil over the deformities of the Heathen theology, to decorate with all the splendor of panegyric the tolerant spirit of its votaries. 1792 BURKE *Let. to Sir H. Langrishe* Wks. VI. 318 A tolerant government ought not to be too scrupulous in its investigations. 1796 MORSE *Amer. Geog.* I. 429 The religion of this Commonwealth [Massachusetts] is established..on a most liberal and tolerant plan. All persons, of whatever religious profession or sentiments, may worship God agreeably to the dictates of their own consciences, unmolested. 1838 LYTTON *Alice* I. xi, His own early errors made him tolerant to the faults of others. 1841 MACAULAY in *Four C. Eng. Lett.* (1880) 537 You were less tolerant than myself of little mannerisms. 1875 MANNING *Mission H. Ghost* ix. 237 Though we are to be tolerant towards the persons of heretics, we are intolerant of the heresies themselves.

**b.** *transf.* Of a thing: Capable of bearing or sustaining. Const. *of.*

1864 J. H. NEWMAN *Apol.* ii. 169 How far the Articles were tolerant of a Catholic, or even of a Roman interpretation.

**c.** *Phys.* Able to endure the action of a drug, an irritant, etc., without being affected; capable of resisting. Const. *of.* Cf. TOLERANCE 1 b.

1879 *St. George's Hosp. Rep.* IX. 748 Chrysophanic acid having at first given rise to irritation, I diluted it...The skin in two or three weeks became tolerant of it. 1881 *Encycl. Brit.* XIII. 210/2 The amount [of ipecacuanha] required to produce its effect varies considerably, children as a rule being more tolerant than adults. 1899 *Syd. Soc. Lex., Tolerant,* withstanding the use of a drug without injury.

**d.** *Forestry.* Capable of enduring shade. Cf. TOLERANCE 1 c. *U.S.*

1898 PINCHOT *Adirondack Spruce* 5 A selection forest is usually composed of species tolerant of shade. *Ibid.* 6 Spruce, Hemlock, Balsam, the Maples [etc.] are tolerant.

**B.** *sb.* (subst. use of the adj.: so in Fr.) One who tolerates opinions or practices different from his own; one free from bigotry; a tolerationist.

1780 J. BROWN *Lett. on Toleration* i. (1803) 35, I dare defy all the Tolerants on earth, to point out one thing..competent to masters and parents [etc.]. 1872 MORLEY *Voltaire* iii. 144 Henry the Fourth was a hero with Voltaire, for no better reason than that he was the first great tolerant, the earliest historic indifferent.

†**Tolerantial** (tǫlĕræ·nʃăl), *a. Obs. rare.* [f. L. *tolerāntia* TOLERANCE + -AL.] Belonging or pertaining to tolerance.

1681 *Religio Clerici* 121 Till we have tried our Strength and Patience to the quick in sharp Exercises of Vertue's other branch, the Tolerantial part.

†**To·lerantism.** *Obs. rare.* [f. TOLERANT + -ISM.] The principles of a tolerant (see TOLERANT B).

1824 *Hist. Europe* in *Ann. Reg.* 196/1 This sect..professes tolerantism (for thus they call it), or indifference.

**To·lerantly,** *adv.* [f. as prec. + -LY [2].] In a tolerant manner; with tolerance; forbearingly.

1822 BYRON *Vis. Judg.* Pref., I have..treated them more tolerantly. 1883–4 J. G. BUTLER *Bible Work* II. 42 It is wise and right to deal tolerantly with errorists in sentiment.

†**To·lerat,** *ppl. a. Obs.* [ad. L. *tolerāt-us,* pa. pple. of *tolerāre* to TOLERATE.] Tolerated: in quot. as *pa. pple.*

1711 *Countryman's Let. to Curat* 24 He [Bacon] advised that Non-conformity should not meerly be conniv'd at, but even Tolerat by a Law.

**Tolerate** (tǫ·lĕreᶦt), *v.* Also 6–8 toll-. [f. F. *tolérer* (15th c. in Godef. *Compl.*), ad. L. *tolerāre* to bear, endure: see -ATE [3].]

†**1.** *trans.* To endure, sustain (pain or hardship).

1531 ELYOT *Gov.* III. xiv, To tollerate those thinges whiche do seme bytter or greuous (wherof there be many in the lyfe of man). *a* 1548 HALL *Chron., Rich. III* 37 The great dolour and sorowe that you haue suffred and tollerated by the cruel murther of your innocente children. 1599 A. M. tr. *Gabelhouer's Bk. Physicke* 39/1 Applye that same as warme as he may or can tollerate it on and rownde about his heade. 1616 BULLOKAR *Eng. Expos., Tolerate,* to indure or suffer.

**b.** *Phys.* To endure with impunity or comparative impunity the action of (a poison or strong drug). Cf. TOLERANCE 1 b, TOLERANT c.

1895 in *Funk's Standard Dict.* 1899 *Allbutt's Syst. Med.* VIII. 932 [Oil of santal wood has] the advantage of being usually well tolerated in reasonable doses by the stomach. 1911 WEBSTER, *Tolerate,* to endure or resist, esp. without injurious effect, the action of, as a poison.

**c.** *Forestry.* Cf. TOLERANCE 1 c, TOLERANT d.

1898 PINCHOT *Adirondack Spruce* 20 This ability to tolerate heavy shade is common to large numbers of forest trees, among which both the Beech and the Hard Maple excel the Spruce in this regard.

**2.** To allow to exist or to be done or practised without authoritative interference or molestation; also *gen.* to allow, permit.

1533 MORE *Debell. Salem* Wks. 981/2 He can..be none other rekened but a plaine heretike.., whome to tolerate so long doth sometyme lyttle good. 1586 FERNE *Blaz. Gentrie* 149 This King ordained, that no person..within his dominions, should..tollerate the bearing of these signes vpon armes to any man. 1631 GOUGE *God's Arrows* I. § 4. 7 Marke how farre such sinnes are winked at, or tolerated by Magistrates and Ministers. 1647 JER. TAYLOR *Lib. Proph.* xvi. 214 The question whether the Prince may tollerate divers perswasions, is no more then whether he may lawfully persecute any man for not being of his opinion. 1651 BAXTER *Inf. Bapt.* 143 A few of them are in some places tolerated, as Jews and Hereticks are. 1722 WOLLASTON *Relig. Nat.* ix. 217 If the expression may be tolerated. 1856 FROUDE *Hist. Eng.* I. ii. 142 England..was in no humour to tolerate treason. 1884 H. N. OXENHAM *Short Stud.* 142 To tolerate a religion does not mean to treat it as true,..but simply as having a fair claim to exist and enjoy civil rights.

†**b.** To allow, permit, suffer *to do* something.

*c* 1585 R. BROWNE *Answ. Cartwright* 15 Hee alloweth or tolleratеth those officers..to haue the power and authoritie. 1635 QUARLES *Embl.* III. iii. (1718) 137 True Lord; yet tolerate a hungry Whelp To lick their crums. 1660 R. COKE *Power & Subj.* 143 Berta the wife of Ethelbert..was tolerated to observe the rites of Christian religion. 1709 *Lond. Gaz.* No. 4525/3 The Groom-Porter doth hereby declare, that he neither Licenses or Tolerates any Person to Game, or keep Gaming-Houses. 1817 JAS. MILL *Brit. India* I. II. ii. 111 The highest of the other classes are barely tolerated to read the will of God.

**3.** To bear without repugnance; to allow intellectually, or in taste, sentiment, or principle; to put up with.

1646 SIR T. BROWNE *Pseud. Ep.* V. xix. 262 We shall tolerate flying Horses, black Swans, Hydrae's, Centaur's, Harpies, and Satyres. 1822 WORDSW. *Sonn., Old Abbeys,* By discipline of Time made wise, We learn to tolerate the infirmities And faults of others. 1841 BREWSTER *Mart. Sc.* i. (1856) 8 Nor could the Aristotelians tolerate the rebukes of their young instructor. 1875 H. C. WOOD *Therap.* (1879) 412 Children almost always learn to tolerate the taste of the oil. 1910 *Daily News* 9 Apr. 6 He cannot tolerate Buddhism. I use the word 'tolerate', of course, in an intellectual, not a political, sense.

†**4.** To relax. *Obs. rare*$^{-1}$.

1579–80 NORTH *Plutarch* (1656) 45 (*Lycurgus* xxii) In their time of Warre, they did tolerate [F. *ils relaschoyent*] their young men a little of their hard and old accustomed life, and suffered them to trim their haires.

Hence **To·lerated** *ppl. a.*, **To·lerating** *vbl. sb.* and *ppl. a.*; whence **To·lera·tingly** *adv.*

1644 MILTON *Judgm. Bucer* xxiv. Wks. 1738 I. 283 For whatsoever is contrary to these, I shall not persuade the least tolerating therof. 1692 PRIDEAUX *Direct. Ch.-wardens* (ed. 4) 109 Not Members of some of the said tolerated Assemblies. 1700 in *Westm. Gaz.* 9 Aug. (1907) 2/3 Notice is given, That the Tollerated Boats bear a Red Flagg in the Stern of each of them. 1711 SHAFTESB. *Charac.* (1733) I. 29 How barbarous..are we tolerating Englishmen. 1724 A. SHIELDS *J. Renwick* (1827) 146 All this never moved the tolerated Ministers. 1848 R. I. WILBERFORCE *Doctr. Incarnation* xi. (1852) 290 Its permission is the main point expressed in the tolerating edict issued by Galerius. 1893 *Pall Mall Mag.* II. 209 She spoke of his views toleratingly. 1902 C. LENNOX *J. Chalmers* v. (1895) 26/1 Tolerated wickedness inevitably cramps the religious consciousness.

**Toleration** (tǫlĕrēᶦ·ʃən). Also 6–8 toll-. [a. F. *tolération* (15th c. in Godef.), ad. rare L. *tolerātiōn-em,* f. *tolerāre* to TOLERATE.]

†**1.** The action of sustaining or enduring; endurance (of evil, suffering, etc.). *Obs.*

1531 ELYOT *Gov.* III. xxi, There is also moderation in tolleration of fortune of euerye sorte, which of Tulli is called equabilite. 1616 BULLOKAR *Eng. Expos., Toleration,* an induring; a sufferance. 1623 COCKERAM III, *Mutius Sceuola,* saued his life by the patient toleration of the burning of his hand.

**b.** *Phys.* = TOLERANCE 1 b. *rare.*

1877 CARNOCHAN *Operat. Surgery* 328 Military surgery supplies many illustrations of toleration of shock and mildness of collapse after severe injuries to the medullary substance of the hemispheres. 1882 A. WILSON *Facts & Fictions Zool.* 10 Suppose that the toleration of the toad's system to starvation and to a limited supply of air is taken into account. **1905** *Allbutt's Syst. Med.* I. 287 *Toleration.* When, on taking a drug continuously, the first effects decrease until they are no longer noticed, toleration is said to be established.

†**2.** The action of allowing; permission granted by authority, licence. *Obs.*

**1517–18** *Rec. St. Mary at Hill* 296 Paid..for goyng to ffulham to my lorde of london..to haue tolleracion of Nasynges chauntry. **1565** JEWEL *Def. Apol.* VI. xxiii. (1579) 735 The yeerely perquisites that yᵉ Pope made of his Elections, Preuentions, Dispensations,..Tolerations. **1571–2** *Reg. Privy Council Scot.* II. 122 Na licencis or tolleratiounis grantit of befoir to have any strenth. **1612** BEAUM. & FL. *Cupid's Rev.* I. i, Would I had giv'n 100*l.* for a tolleration, That I might but use my conscience in mine Own house. **1660** R. COKE *Power & Subj.* 209 If any person or persons..should procure and obtain at the Court of Rome, or elswhere, any Licence or Licences, Union, Toleration, or Dispensation to receive or take any more Benefices with cure, then was limited by the said Act. **1727** A. HAMILTON *New Acc. E. Ind.* II. l. 224 Ordered the Hapoa or Custom-master to.. take the Emperors customary Dues, and give me a free Toleration to Trade.

**b.** Locally in U.S. applied to a licence to gather oysters or keep oyster-beds.

**1891** *Cent. Dict.* s.v., The fee is a toleration fee.

**3.** The action or practice of tolerating or allowing what is not actually approved; forbearance, sufferance.

**1582** N. T. (Rhem.) *Rom.* iii. 26 The remission of former sinnes in the toleration [WYCLIF in the sustentacioun *or* bering vp, 1611 through the forbearance] of God. **1588** HUNSDON in *Border Papers* (1894) I. 367 His tolloracion of the mase in sondrie places of Scotland. *a* **1610** HEALEY *Epictetus' Man.* (1636) 84 Every thing may bee apprehended two waies, eyther with toleration, or with impatience. **1755** YOUNG *Centaur* v. Wks. 1757 IV. 220 Faults which are the natural growth of these distinct periods of life, may meet with some toleration. **1768** STERNE *Sent. Journ.* (1778) I. 201 (*The Rose*) Mutual toleration..taught us mutual love. **1890** *Hardwicke's Science-Gossip* XXVI. 186/1, I think, also, that a wise toleration might be extended to hawks and owls. **1907** *Verney Mem.* I. 571 A large hopefulness and toleration born of his wide acquaintance with human nature.

**4.** *spec.* Allowance (with or without limitations), by the ruling power, of the exercise of religion otherwise than in the form officially established or recognized.

**1609** (*title*) An Humble Supplication for Toleration and Libertie..by some of the deprived Ministers and People. **1643** *Declar. Com., Reb. Irel.* 3 To bring in a more publique Tolleration of the Popish Religion. **1672** EVELYN *Diary* 12 Mar., To this succeeded the King's declaration for an universal tolleration. **1689** POPPLE tr. *Locke's 1st Let. Toleration* ¶ 1 Since you are pleased to inquire what are my Thoughts about the mutual Toleration of Christians in their different Professions of Religion, I must needs answer you freely, That I esteem that Toleration to be the chief Characteristical Mark of the True Church. **1691** BURNET *Orig. Mem.* an. 1689, I. (1902) 317 At the same time that the toleration was proposed to both houses. **1780** BURKE *Corr.* (1844) II. 369, I have been a steady friend, since I came to the use of reason, to the cause of religious toleration. **1849** MACAULAY *Hist. Eng.* vi. II. 9 Locke..contended that the church which taught men not to keep faith with heretics had no claim to toleration.

**b.** *Act of Toleration, Toleration Act*, an act or statute granting such toleration; so *Bill of Toleration, Toleration Bill*; esp. in *Eng. Hist.* Act 1 Will. & Mary (1689) cap. 18, by which freedom of religious worship was granted, on certain prescribed conditions, to Dissenting Protestants.

**1692** *Ho. Lords MSS.* (Hist. MSS. Comm.) 1 Feb., Moved that the Quakers shall not have the benefit of this Act before they take the Declaration in the Act of Toleration. **1714** BARRINGTON *Let. fr. Lay-man* Title-p., A Postscript, shewing How far the Bill to prevent the Growth of Schism is Inconsistent with the Act of Toleration. *a* **1715** BURNET *Own Time* an. 1689 (1823) IV. 16 The bill of toleration passed easily. It excused dissenters from all penalties,.. for going to their separate meetings. **1769** BLACKSTONE *Comm.* IV. iv. 53 The statute 1 W. & M. st. 2. c. 18, commonly called the toleration act. **1799** DRYSDALE (*title*) Popery Dissected; or, a Speech against the Popish Toleration Bill. **1827** JOS. IVIMEY *Pilgr. 19th C.* iv. 139 'Hand me', said the judge, 'the new Toleration Act' [app. 52 Geo. III, c. 155]. **1855** MACAULAY *Hist. Eng.* xi. III. 81 The Toleration Bill passed both Houses with little debate. *Ibid.* 86 The sound principle..is, that mere theological error ought not to be punished by the civil magistrate. This principle the Toleration Act not only does not recognise, but positively disclaims. **1878** GARDINER in *Encycl. Brit.* VIII. 352/1 The Toleration Act..guaranteed the right of separate assemblies for worship outside the pale of the Church. **1910** A. MENZIES in *Encycl. Brit.* XXIV. 463/1 The Act of Toleration [Scotland] of 1712 allowed Episcopalian dissenters to use the English liturgy.

**5.** *Coining.* = TOLERANCE 4 a.

**1887** *Encycl. Brit.* XXII. 71/1 In Great Britain all silver coins are made of 'standard silver', the fineness of which by legal definition is 925. The toleration is 4 units of pure silver in 1000 of alloy. In Germany and in the United States all silver coins, in France and Austria the major silver coins, are of the fineness 900, with a toleration of three units.

**Tolera·tionism.** [f. prec. + -ISM.] Toleration of religious differences as a principle or system.

**1898** *Cath. News* 24 Dec. 12/6 This was sometimes called.. 'Tolerationism—But they would understand it better as Free Trade [in religion].

**Tolera·tionist.** [f. as prec. + -IST.] One who advocates or supports toleration.

**1830** W. TAYLOR *Hist. Surv. Germ. Poetry* I. 472 There lies The prating tolerationist unmask'd. **1899** S. R. GARDINER *Cromwell* 98 A fanatic might have objected that it was unfitting a tolerationist to support the most intolerant clergy in Protestant Europe.

†**To·leratist.** *Obs. rare.* [f. TOLERATE *v.* + -IST.] = TOLERATIONIST.

**1716** M. DAVIES *Athen. Brit.* II. 395 Amongst our Nationalists and Toleratists, High and Low, or those that are indulg'd and others that are conniv'd at.

**To·lerative,** *a. rare.* [f. as prec. + -IVE.] Tending to toleration; permissive.

**1891** E. L. WAKEMAN in *Columbus* (Ohio) *Dispatch* 29 Oct., It may be said that the English folk..universally make mental defense of the Halloween time and spirit,.. while its recognition by the English is complete, its observance is tolerative rather than active.

**Tolerator** (tǫ·lĕreⁱtəɹ). [f. as prec. + -OR.] One who tolerates.

**1706** A. SHIELDS *Inquiry Ch. Commun.* (1747) 29 By that bargain and confederacy with the tolerator. **1791–1823** DISRAELI *Curios. Lit., Toleration*, To this moment it is far from being clear, either to the tolerators, or the tolerated. **1826** SIR T. F. BUXTON in *Mem.* (1872) 90 If not a lover of the vices of the world, at least a tolerator of its vanities. **1884** *Macm. Mag.* Nov. 22/2 The moderate Conservatives or tolerators of progress.

†**Tolera·torist.** *Obs. rare.* [irreg. f. as prec. + -IST.] = TOLERATIONIST.

**1654** E. JOHNSON *Wond.-wrkg. Provid.* 231 There is no room in his [Christ's] Army for toleratorists. **1845** T. W. COIT *Puritanism* 452.

**Toleress**: see TOLLER *sb.*⁴

†**To·lerism.** *Obs. rare*⁻¹. [irreg. f. L. *toler-āre* to TOLERATE + -ISM.] = TOLERATIONISM.

**1851** BORROW *Lavengro* iii, Thou wouldst be sadly out of place in these days of..universal tolerism. [**1851** *Fraser's Mag.* XLIII. 283 How can this master of words [Borrow] justify such a barbarous bit of patchwork as 'tolerism'?]

**Toletan** (tǫlī·tăn), *a.* Also 4–5 **tolletane, tollitane.** [ad. L. *Tolētān-us*, f. *Tolētum* Toledo.] Pertaining to Toledo; in *Toletan tables*, 'the astronomical tables composed by order of Alphonso X, king of Castile (1252–82), from their being adapted to the city of Toledo' (Tyrwhitt in note to the passage in Chaucer); also called ALPHONSINE *tables*.

*c* **1386** CHAUCER *Frankl. T.* 545 Hise tables tolletanes [*Harl.* tollitanes] forth he brought Ful wel corrected. **1894** SKEAT *Chaucer's Wks.* V. 394 (*Notes Cant. T.*) The longitude of a planet at a given date is the 'root'; and its longitude.. twenty-three years later can be obtained from the Toletan tables by adding (1) its change of longitude in twenty years, ..and (2) its further change in three years.

**Tolfrædic** (tǫᵘlfrī·dik), *a.* [f. Icel. *tólf-rǿðr* adj. only in comb. *tolfrǿtt hundrað*, a hundred of twelve tens (f. *tólf* twelve + *rǿða* (:–*rǿða*) to speak) + -IC.] Duodecimal: applied to the ancient Scandinavian system of reckoning, in which twelve tens were counted as a hundred (cf. HUNDRED 3).

[Cf. **1703** HICKES *Thesaurus* I. III. 43.] **1813** ELLIS *Brand's Pop. Antiq.* II. 325 The Doctor observes that this Tolfrædic mode of computation by the greater decads, or tens which contain twelve units, is still retained amongst us in reckoning certain things by the number twelve. **1905** *Daily Chron.* 16 June 4/6 The tolfraedic ten meant twelve, the tolfraedic hundred meant a hundred and twenty, and so on.

**Tolibant, tolipane, -pant,** obs. ff. TURBAN.

†**Toliduse,** illiterate spelling of TAILLE-DOUCE.

**1715** *Grizel Baillie's Acc.* (MS.), For two pictures of King George in Toliduse 5/–.

†**To-lie·**, *v. Obs.* [OE. *toliczan*, f. TO-² + *liczan*, LIE *v.*¹] *intr.* To lie or extend in different directions.

*c* **893** K. ÆLFRED *Oros.* I. i. § 9 Þonne..west irnende heo toliþ on twa ymb an izland þe mon hæt Meroen. **938** in Birch *Cart. Sax.* II. 431 Þær ða wezas to liczað. *c* **1320** *Cast. Love* 1000 Þeose ne mowen Jhc suwen whiþ from heo dede al to-lyth.

†**To-li·m,** *v. Obs.* In 3–4 to-lime(n. [ME. f. TO-² + *lim* limb: cf. OE. *toliþian*, f. TO-² + *liþ* limb. See also LIMB *v.* in same sense.] *trans.* To tear limb from limb, to dismember.

*a* **1225** *Ancr. R.* 84 Auh [he] lihted upon cwike fleschs, tetereð & tolimeð hit. *a* **1225** *Juliana* 79 (Bodl. MS.) Wilde deor..to limeden euer euch lið from þe line. **13..** *Guy Warw.* 6306 In his court he schal deme þe, & al to-lime.

Hence (*dim.*) †**To-li·meken** *v.*, to dismember.

*c* **1275** LAY. 4227 Stater hii nome And al hine to-limekede Leme fram oþer.

**Tolk,** variant of TULK *Obs.*, man.

**Toll** (tǫᵘl), *sb.*¹ Also 2–7 **tol,** 5–7 **tolle, tole,** (5–6 **towl(e,** 6 **toule, towlle,** *Sc.* **toille,** 7 **toal(l, toale**; 4 **tholle,** 5–6 **tholl,** 5 (7 *Sc.*) **thoill,** 6–7 **thole**); the *th*-forms chiefly in Latin context. [OE. *toll* = OFris., OS. *tol* (MLG., LG., MDu., Du. *tol*), OHG., MHG. *zol* (Ger. *zoll*); ON. *tollr* (Sw. *tull*, Da. *told*), all masc., which with their by-forms, OE. *toln*, OFris. *tol(e)ne*, OS. *tolna*, all fem. (see TOLNE), are generally referred to late pop.L. *tolōneum* (recorded in 3–4th c.) for L. *telōnium*, a. Gr. τελώνιον place of custom, toll-house, f. τελώνης farmer or collector of taxes, τέλος toll, tax, duty.

The form-history is in some points obscure, and some etymologists have sought to derive *toll* from an OTeut. **tulno-*, pa. pple. of **tal-*, root of TELL *v.* and of TALE. The derivation from Latin is supported by French, in which *teloneum*, becoming by metathesis **toneleum*, has given mod.F. *tonlieu*, Prov. *tolieu* 'toll'.]

**1.** Orig., a general term for (*a*) a definite payment exacted by a king, ruler, or lord, or by the state or the local authority, by virtue of sovereignty or lordship, or in return for protection; more especially, (*b*) for permission to pass somewhere, do some act, or perform some function; or (*c*) as a share of the money passing, or profit accruing, in a transaction; a tax, tribute, impost, custom, duty. In (*a*) *obs.* exc. *Hist.*; in (*b*) retained in special senses (see 2); in (*c*) still in vague or rhetorical use: see quots. 1832–1909.

*c* **1000** *Ags. Gosp.* Matt. xvii. 25 Hwæt þincð þe symon, æt hwam nymað cyningas gafol oððe toll? **1050–1100** in Earle *Land Charters* 273 Ælsiz bohte anne wifmann..& hire sunu..mid healfe punde..& sealde Ælsiz portzereua[n] et Maccosse hundredes mann iiii. penzas to tolle. *a* **1100** *Aldhelm Glosses* I. 1455 in Napier *O. E. Glosses* 39 *Fiscale tributum*, cynelic toll. *a* **1100** *O. E. Chron.* an. 1086 (Laud MS.), Hy arerdon unrihte tollas, and manize oðre unrihte hi dydan. *c* **1100** in Earle *Land Ch.* 262 Her kyð on þissere boc þ Leowine..&..his wif zebohton Ælfilde..to feower & sixtuze penezon, & Ælfric Hals nam þ toll..for þæs kynges hand. *a* **1300** *Cursor M.* 28438 (Cott.) Toll and tak, and rent o syse, Wit-halden i haue wit couettise. **13..** *K. Alis.* 1760 (Bodl. MS.) Þat ich shal of olde & ȝonge Of þis midlerde tol afonge. *c* **1375** *Sc. Leg. Saints* x. (*Mathou*) 549 Þis mathow..wes tollar, and toll tuke. **1393** LANGL. *P. Pl.* C. I. 98 Boxes..I-bounden with yre, To vnder-take þe tol [*v. rr.* tolle, tool] of vntrewe sacrifice. *c* **1400** MAUNDEV. (1839) xiii. 149 The tolle & the custom of his [Emperor of Persia's] marchantes is with outen estymacyoun to ben nombred. *c* **1440** *Promp. Parv.* 495/2 Tol, or custome, *guidagia,..petagium, toloneum.* **1483** *Cath. Angl.* 389/2 A Tolle,..*talliagium.* **1485** *Rolls of Parlt.* VI. 345/2 The Graunte of the Tolle of oure Towne of Knyghton. **1535** COVERDALE *Ezra* iv. 13 Then shal not they geue tribute, toll, and yearly custome. **1570** LEVINS *Manip.* 218/17 Toule, *census.* **1577** tr. *Bullinger's Decades* (1592) 276 These Publicanes were such as liued vppon the publique toll and customes which they had farmed at the Romanes hands. **1642** FULLER *Holy & Prof. St.* v. xix. 438 Hereby the same commodity must pay a new tole at every passage into a new trade. **1832** TENNYSON *Œnone* 114 'Honour', she said, 'and homage, tax and toll, From many an inland town and haven large'. **1849** MACAULAY *Hist. Eng.* ix. II. 445 All fines, all forfeitures went to Sunderland. On every grant toll was paid to him. **1895** POLLOCK & MAITLAND *Hist. Eng. Law* I. 648 A large part of the borough's revenue was derived from tolls, if we use that term in its largest sense to include 'passage, pontage, lastage, stallage, bothage, ewage, tronage, scavage' and the like. **1909** *Daily News* 14 Sept. 4/2 Sir William Harcourt wished to establish the rule that property should pay toll once every generation, and he succeeded in establishing it.

†**b.** The taking of toll or tribute; the office of a tax-collector. *Obs.*

*c* **1000** ÆLFRIC *Hom.* II. 288 Oðer [is] þæt man ðurh toll feoh zegadrize. *Ibid.* 468 Matheus aras þærrihte fram his tolle, and filizde ðam Hælende. *Ibid.*, He hine zeseah sittan æt tolle.

**c.** In the obsolete law phrase *sac and sóc, toll and team*, etc. (see SAC, TEAM *sb.* 8 b, c): The right to 'toll' included (among others) in the grant of a manor by the crown; see quot. 1895.

**1017–1118** [see TEAM *sb.* 8 b]. **1130–35** *Laws Edw. Conf.* c. 22 § 2 Tol, quod nos vocamus theloneum, scilicet libertatem emendi et vendendi in terra sua. *c* **1250** *Expos. Vocab.* in *Placita de Quo Warranto* 511 *Tol*..pro voluntate sua tallagium de villanis suis. *a* **1400** *Reg. Maj.* I. c. 2 in *Acts Parl. Scot.* (1844) I. 598/1 Qui habent et tenent terras suas cum soko et sako, furca et fossa, toll et them, et infangandthefe. **1456** [see TEAM *sb.* 8 d]. **1597** SKENE *De Verb. Sign.* s.v., He quha is infeft with Toll, is custome free, and payis na custome. **1607** COWELL *Interpr.*, *Toll*, alias *Tholl*.. hath in our common lawe two significations: First it is vsed for a libertie to buy and sell within the precincts of a maner. ..Bracton..interpreteth [it] to be a libertie as well to take as to be free from Tolle. **1818** HALLAM *Mid. Ages* viii. I. II. 156 A charter of Edred grants to the monastery of Croyland soc, sac, toll, team and infangthef. **1871** [see TEAM *sb.* 8 b]. **1895** POLLOCK & MAITLAND *Hist. Eng. Law* I. 566 *Toll* is sometimes the right to take toll, sometimes the right to be free of toll; but often it is merely the right to tallage one's villeins.

**2.** *spec. uses.* **a.** A charge made for some service rendered: †(*a*) for passage in a ship, fare. *Obs.*

*c* **1000** ÆLFRIC *Saints' Lives* xxx. 168 Þa..þæs scypes hlaford..zyrnde þæs scyp-tolles, ac ða hi nan þincg næfdon to syllanne, þa zyrnde he þæs wifes for þam tolle.

(*b*) A proportion of the grain or flour taken by the miller in payment for grinding. ? *Obs.* or *dial.*

*c* **1386** [implied in TOLL *v.*³ 1]. *c* **1440** *Promp. Parv.* 496/1 Tol, of myllarys, *multa.* **1523** FITZHERB. *Husb.* § 146 Mete it to the myll & fro the myll, & se yᵗ thou haue thy measure agayne besyde the toll. **1589** [see TOLBOT]. **1638** PENKETHMAN *Artach.* G iv, If the Baker buy corne unground by the Quarter..he hath 68 l. Troy to the bushell, and is to pay the Millers tolle. **1888** ELWORTHY *W. Somerset Word-bk.*, *Toll*,..the quantity of meal kept by the miller for grinding another's corn.

†**b.** Rent paid for a house, mill, etc. *Obs.*

*c* **1000** ÆLFRIC *Saints' Lives* xix. 253 Hit ne zedafnað þæt man do godes hus anre mylne zelic for lyðrum tolle.

**c.** A charge for the privilege of bringing goods for sale to a market or fair, or of setting up a stall.

*c* **1205** LAY. 13316 Her beoð chæpmen icumen of oðere londen..Heo habbeoð ibroht to me tol for heore æhte. *c* **1460** *Oseney Regr.* 10 Be quyte in all mercates of tol i-axid of thynges i-bowghte or solde. **1500** *Reg. Privy Seal Scotl.* I. 68/1 That the said erle..have tholl and uther small custumez of the fairis. **1567** *Expos. Termes of Law* (1579) 178 b/2 *Tolle* or *Tolne*, is most properlye a payment vsed in Cities, townes, markets & faires for goods and cattel brought thither to bee bought & solde. **1587** *Shuttleworths' Acc.*

(Chetham Soc.) 41 Foure oxen in Prestone xjli xvs iiijd ; towlle for the said besste, viijd. **1818** Cruise *Digest* (ed. 2) III. 273 Toll is not of right incident to a fair or market, and can only be claimed by special grant from the Crown, or by prescription ; and if the toll be unreasonable, the grant will be void. **1863** Fawcett *Pol. Econ.* II. vii. (1876) 614 A market toll is paid for the accommodation which a market provides.

**d.** A charge for the right of passage along a road (at a turnpike or toll-gate : now abolished in Great Britain), along a river or channel, over a bridge or ferry ; formerly also, through the gate or door of a building.

**1477–8** *Acc. Exch. K. R.* Bundle 496 No. 17 (P.R.O.) Omnes summas monete..vel Toles pro dictis edificacionibus ..solutas pro cariagio petrarum maeremii..per terram vel per aquam. **1498** *Coventry Leet Bk.* 592 Howe the Citezenis of Couentre were trobled be there merchandisez in Bristoll, Gloucestre, & Worcestre & compelled to pay tholl & oþer customez contrarie to their liberteez. **1505** *Reg. Mag. Sig. Scot.* 603 Exceptis theoloneo finis pontis, viz. le tholl de le Brig-and de Are. *a* **1548** Hall *Chron., Hen. VIII* 203 b, In this yere was an olde Tolle demaunded in Flaunders of Englysh men, called the Tolle of the Hounde, which is a Ryuer and a passage. The Tolle is .xii. pence of a Fardell. **1604** Drayton *Owle* 386 At his entrance he must pay them Tole. **1617** Moryson *Itin.* I. 56 Here those which carried any merchandise paid tole. **1634** *Althorp MS.* in Simpkinson *Washingtons* (1860) App. p. xiv, For toale at Thrapston bridge 00 00 02. **1663** *Act* 15 *Chas. II*, c. 1 § 5 Summes of money in the name of Toll or Custome, to be paid for all such Horses, Carts, Coaches, Waggons, Droves, and Gangs of Cattell, as..shall passe, bee ledd, or droven, in or through the said waye. **1838** *Murray's Hand-bk. N. Germ.* 254/1 A toll is here paid by all vessels navigating the Rhine, to the Duke of Nassau, the only chieftain remaining on the river who still exercises this feudal privilege. **1840** Howitt *Visits Remark. Places* Ser. I. 234 The tolls at the doors of St. Paul's and the Tower have been relaxed. **1845** McCulloch *Taxation* Introd. (1852) 33 The statute..imposed tolls, or duties collected at toll gates (called turnpikes), on all travellers along the great north road. **1883** 'Ouida' *Wanda* I. 61 With a right to take toll on the ferry.

**e.** A charge for the right of landing or shipping goods at a port; formerly also, a customs duty. *Obs.* exc. *Hist.*

**1680** Morden *Geog. Rect., Germ.* (1685) 132 The place where Ships pay Tole. **1884** S. Dowell *Taxes in Eng.* I. IV. v. 83 Of wine, a toll in the strictest sense of the term was taken by the king's officer from every ship having in cargo ten casks or more, on the arrival of the ship at a port in England.., unless the toll formed the subject of a composition in the way of a money payment.

**f.** A charge made for transport of goods, esp. by railway or canal. (Arising out of d.)

**1889** *Standard* 21 Mar., Railway projectors were empowered to charge 'tolls', not exceeding a specified sum, for the use of their roads. Out of these 'tolls' rates were, in a manner, evolved, covering every service.

**g.** *fig.* (Cf. *tribute*, similarly used.)

*c* **1375** *Sc. Leg. Saints* xlii. (*Agatha*) 256 Þane bad he.. brynnand cole Straw in þe floure..& nakyt þare-one hire rol, Til scho of ded had quyt þe tol. *a* **1882** Rossetti *Ho. Life, Introd. Sonn.*, [Whether] In Charm's palm it pay the toll to Death. **1909** *Blackw. Mag.* July 19/2 Nott's gallant division..paid its toll of killed and wounded.

**h.** with defining words: **through toll** (also *toll through, thorough*), **toll traverse**, **turn toll** (also *toll turn*) : see quots.

**1567** *Expos. Termes of Law* (1579) 179/1 *Through tolle*, is where a Towne prescribes to haue tol for euery beast that goeth through their Towne. *Ibid., Tolle trauers*, that is where one claimeth to haue a halfepeny, or such like toll of euery beast that is driuen ouer his ground. *Ibid., Turne tolle*..is where toll is paied for beasts that are dryuen to bee solde, although that they bee not solde. **1636** Prynne *Rem. agst. Shipmoney* 8 This Tax..layes a farre greater charge on the Subject then any new office, Murage, Toll-travers, or thorough-toll. **1670** Blount *Law Dict.* s.v., *Toll-through..Toll-travers..*; and *Toll-turn*, which is Toll paid at the return of Beasts from Fair or Market, though they were not sold. **1827** Mackenzie *Hist. Newcastle* II. 649 The claim of toll thorough..is made by the corporation upon all goods ..of non-freemen, brought into or carried out of the town. **1911** G. R. Hill in Halsbury *Laws Eng.* XVI. 62 A toll-thorough is independent of any ownership of the soil by the original grantee, the consideration necessary to support it being usually the liability to repair the particular highway or bridge. *Ibid.*, A toll-traverse is a toll taken in respect of the original ownership of the land crossed by the public.

**3.** *attrib.* and *Comb.*: **toll-bar** [Bar *sb.*1], a barrier (usually a gate) across a road or bridge, where toll is taken; in Scotland formerly often applied to the toll-collector's house; †**toll-bell**, a bell rung at the close of the collection of toll at a market; **toll-bridge**, a bridge at which toll is charged for passage; **toll-clerk**, a clerk who keeps a record of tolls collected, e. g. at a market; **toll-collector**, (*a*) a person who collects toll, esp. the tolls at a turnpike, a market, etc.; (*b*) a device for indicating the number of persons passing a turnstile or gate and paying toll; (*c*) a device in the feeder of a mill for separating the toll of grain; **toll-corn**, corn retained by a miller as toll; †**toll-cote**, a toll-collector's cottage or shed; †**toll-customer** [Customer *sb.* 2], a toll- or tax-gatherer; **toll-farmer**, one who farms the tolls at a certain place; = Farmer 2 1; †**toll-fat**, ? a vessel for toll-corn (in quot. 1222 a measure of capacity); **toll-gate**, a gate across a road at which toll was payable, a turnpike-gate; †**toll-hall**, ? = Tolbooth 2, guildhall, town hall; †**toll-hoop** [Hoop *sb.*1 5] = Toll-dish; **toll-keeper**, the keeper of a toll-gate or toll-house; **toll-lodge** = Toll-house 2; †**toll-master**, the master of a toll-office; †**toll mere** [Mere *sb.*2], the boundary within which a local toll is payable; **toll-office**, an office where toll is taken; **toll penny**, a penny paid or charged as toll; †**toll-pin**, (?) a cylindrical stick used as a strake for the toll-dish; †**toll-reeve**, an officer to whom tolls were payable; **toll-road**, a road maintained by tolls, a turnpike road (*Sc.* and *U.S.*); **toll-room**, a room or apartment where tolls are collected, as at a turnpike; †**toll-shop** = Toll-house 2; †**toll-stock** (tolstok), ? = *toll-pin*; **toll-table**, a table of the toll-dues at a turnpike; **toll-taker**, one who takes tolls; a toll-collector, toll-gatherer; so **toll-taking** sb. and adj. See also Toll-book, -dish, etc.

**1813** *Examiner* 19 Apr. 243/1 The only light..was that shed by the *toll-bar lamp. **1825** Jamieson, *Toll-bar*, a turnpike. [*Toll-bar* in *Calr. Inq. P. M.* V. 389, in a docmt. of 1315 is a misreading.] **1858** Surtees *Ask Mamma* lxxvii, [He] trotted across the bridge,..and was speedily brought up at a toll-bar on the far side. **1736** Drake *Eboracum* I. vi. 219 No corn to be carried out of this market till the toll be gathered, and that the *toll-bell be rung. **1790** Luckombe *Eng. Gaz.* III, *Sheperton*..has a *toll-bridge over the Thames to Walton. **1878** Braithwaite *Life & Lett. W. Pennefather* xi. 245 A young man who had been long employed as *toll-clerk. **1887** *Pall Mall G.* 25 Jan. 6/2 The toll clerk of Billingsgate Market. **1822** *Act* 3 *Geo. IV*, c. 126 § 22 If the Owner or Driver of any Waggon..shall resist any Gate Keeper or *Toll Collector, in weighing the same,..[he]shall forfeit and pay..Five Pounds. **1877** Knight *Dict. Mech., Toll-collector.* 1. A counter at a turnstile or gate to indicate the number of persons passing. 2. A device attached to the feed of a grain-mill to subtract the toll. **1903** H. B. Swete in *Expositor* Aug. 196 The rich and well-hated chief of the Jericho toll-collectors. **12..** *Reading Cartul.* (Harl. MS. 1708, lf. 107), Ego Willelmus babbe dedi..abbati et conuentui de Radinges vnam dimidiam summam bladi, scilicet de *tolcorn de molendino de Homstalle. **1701** *Cowell's Interpr., Tolcorn*, Corn taken for Toll at grinding in a Mill. *c* **1460** *Play Sacram.* 540 Inquyre to þe *Tolkote, for ther ys hys loggyng. *a* **1681** Wharton *Fasts & Fest.* Wks. (1683) 28 Saint Matthew, who being..a Publican or *Toll-customer by Profession, became a Disciple, an Apostle, an Evangelist, and Martyr. **1553** Grimalde *Cicero's Offices* I. (1558) 66 The gayne of *tolfarmers and misers. **1820** W. Tooke tr. *Lucian* I. 469 Murderers, adulterers, toll-farmers,.. and others of the same pack. [**1222** in J. Thorpe *Registrum Roffense* (1769) 369, xvj *tolfata faciunt unum quarterium salis.] **1547** in J. H. Glover *Kingsthorpiana* (1883) 93 That all thos persones that have quernes shall suffer noe body to grynde theirat above a Tolfatt, upon payn for every Tolfatt more then their owne..iii*d*. **1773** *Gentl. Mag.* XLIII. 441/1 They..shall pass upon any turnpike road, through any *toll-gate or bar, for half-toll. **1774** Johnson *Journ. West. Isl.* Wks. 1787 X. 17 It affords a southern stranger a new kind of pleasure to travel so commodiously without the interruption of toll-gates. **1884** Pae *Eustace* 95 The toll-gate was closed, but he vaulted over it. **1395** in *Cart. Abb. Whitby* (Surtees) II. 555 De *tolale de Hakeness v *s.* **1416–17** *Durham Acc. Rolls* 285, viij s. x d. de profect. curiæ et tolhale villæ de Hett. **1577–87** Holinshed *Chron.* II. 23/1 Skinners rew reaching from the pillorie to the tolehall, or to the high crosse. *c* **1270** *Customs Gt. Farringdon* (MS. Barlow 49, lf. 22 b), De consuetudine mercati..pro carectata salis dabitur vnus discus salis, qui continere debet unum *tolhop, uel vnus denarius. **1701** *Cowell's Interpr., Tolhop*, a Toll-dish, or small Measure by which they take Toll for Corn sold in an overt Market. **1822** *Act* 3 *Geo. IV*, c. 126 § 22 *margin*, *Toll keepers permitting Waggons, &c. of greater Weight than allowed, to pass without Toll. Penalty 5 *l.* **1840** Dickens *Barn. Rudge* iii, He..had cried a lusty 'good-night', to the toll-keeper. **1858** Carlyle *Fredk. Gt.* III. i. (1872) I. 139 [They] continued their feuds, *toll-levyings, plunderings, and other contumacies. **1818–19** Leigh *New Pict. Lond.* 313 The four *toll-lodges are neat doric structures. *a* **1649** Drumm. of Hawth. *Hist. Jas. IV*, Wks. (1711) 70 These projectors and new *toll-masters, the king giving way to enrich his exchequer, awakened them [old laws]. **1500** *Nottingham Rec.* III. 450 Every shipp sayling with merchandise within the *toll meres. **1841** Pusey tr. *Aquinas' Comm. Matt.* I. 94 He found a man sitting at the *toll-office. **1520** in W. H. Turner *Select. Rec. Oxford* (1880) 24 No person shall pay toll for his Catell..but only a *toll peny..if any catell be sold. **1623** Fletcher & Rowley *Maid in Mill* III. i, The Miller has a stout heart Tough as his *toal-pin. **1433** *Rolls of Parlt.* IV. 477/2 *Tollereves, to resceyve the Toll and.. Custumes. **1444** *Ibid.* V. 124/1 Tolreves to resceyve and gedre the tolle, and such custumes as longeth to hem to take at the Yates of the seid Toun. **1825** Jamieson, **Toll-road*, a turnpike road. **1883** Stevenson *Silverado Sq.* 70 A dry water-course entered the Toll Road. **1749** in Feret *Fulham* (1900) I. 63 Paid for Whitewashing the offices and *Toll Room 5*s.* **1789** Brand *Hist. Newcastle* I. 53 No houses, except *toll shops, were to be erected on the new bridge. **1316–17** *Chester Plea Roll* 9 & 10 Edw. II. m. 35 None partis cuiusdam proficui prouenientis del *Tolstok. **1806** *Chron.* in *Ann. Reg.* 405/1 The *toll-table, against the turnpike house, at Whalley, in Yorkshire. **1555** *Act* 2 & 3 *Phil. & Mary*, c. 7 § 4 The open Place appointed for the *Toll-Taker. **1647** Trapp *Comm. Luke* iii. 12 These [publicans] were toll-takers, custom-gatherers for the Romans. **1882** Mozley *Remin.* I. iv. 30 A quaint little church..adjoining the toll-taker's shed. **1611** Cotgr., *Peagerie*, *Toll-taking.

**Toll** (tōul), *sb.*2 Also 7 **tole, towle.** [f. Toll *v.*2] The act of tolling a bell, or the sound made by a bell when tolled; (with *pl.*) a single stroke made in tolling or ringing a bell, or the sound made by such stroke.

**1452** *Cal. Anc. Rec. Dublin* (1889) 276 The comone bell shuld toll iii. tollis iiii. tymes to warne the comones to harr semble. **1653** H. Cogan tr. *Pinto's Trav.* lxi. (1663) 250 At the sound of a bell which gave three toles, the Bonzes prostrated themselves all with their faces to the ground. **1775** S. J. Pratt *Liberal Opin.* civ. (1783) III. 253 The sermon-bell was upon the toll when I had not so much as penned a slip of paper. **1822** Scott *Nigel* iv, I should lose my good name for ever within the toll of Paul's were I to grant quittance. **1871** Rossetti *John of Tours* v, As it neared the midnight toll, John of Tours gave up his soul. **1875** *Encycl. Brit.* III. 537/2 At the news of Nelson's triumph and death at Trafalgar, the bells of Chester rang a merry peal alternated with one deep toll.

**b.** A sound resembling the tolling of a bell, as the note of the S. American bell-bird or campanero.

**1825** Waterton *Wand. S. Amer.* II. 118 No sound or song from any of the winged inhabitants of the forest..cause such astonishment, as the toll of the Campanero...You hear his toll, and then a pause for a minute, then another toll, and then a pause again, and then a toll, and again a pause.

†**Toll**, *sb.*3 *Falconry. Obs.* [app. f. Toll *v.*1 to lure.] ? A lure. (Cf. quot. 1653 in Toll *v.*1 1.)

**1486** *Bk. St. Albans, Hawking* d j, An hawke flieth to the vew, to the Beke, or to the Toll. *Ibid.* d j b, A Goshawke or a tercell that shall flee to the vew, to the toll or to the beke.

**Toll**, *sb.*4 Now *dial.* (Kent to Hampsh.) Also 7 **tolle**, 9 **tole.** [Origin not ascertained.] A clump of trees.

**1644** G. Plattes in *Hartlib's Legacy* (1655) 245 Feeding of Cattel in racks under a tolle of trees. **1892** A. J. Butler tr. *Marbot's Mem.* I. ii. 13 My father stopped his carriage by the famous toll [*orig.* devant l'arbre remarquable] under which the Constable Montmorency was made prisoner by the troops of Louis XIII.

**Toll, tole** (tōul), *v.*1 Now *dial.* and *U.S.* Forms: 3–7 **tolle**, (4 **tulle**), 4–6 **tol**, (6 **touII**, 6–7 **toule**, **towle**, 7 **toul**, **toal**), 5–7, 9 **toll**, **tole**. [ME. *tollen*, *tullen*, implying OE. **tollian*, **tullian* :–**toll-*, *tullôjan* ; from same root *tull-* as Till *v.*3 :–OE. (*for*)*tyllan* :–**tulljan*.

Ulterior history and phonology obscure. Relation to stem *till-*, in OFris. *tilla*, MLG., MFlem., LG., Du., WFris. *tillen*, 'to raise, lift up, take up', is phonetically difficult.]

**1.** *trans.* To attract, entice, allure, decoy; † to incite, instigate (*obs.*).

In literary use in England down to 1690; in 18–19th c. in midl. and south. dialects (see *E.D.D.*), and U. S. literary use.

*c* **1220** *Bestiary* 545 in *O. E. Misc.* 17 Ðis deuel..Tolleð men to him wið his onde. *a* **1250** *Owl & Night.* 1627 An swa mai mon tolli him to Lutle briddes & iuo. *c* **1386** Chaucer *Reeve's T.* 214 And we wil payen trewely atte fulle With empty hand men may none haukes tulle [*Camb. MS.* folle..tolle]: Loo heere our siluer redy for to spende. *c* **1440** *Promp. Parv.* 496/1 Tollyn, or mevyn, or steryn to doon..a dede, *incito, provoco, excito.* **1548** Udall, etc. *Erasm. Par. Mark* iv. 33 Which allure and tolle men vnto them. **1570** T. Wilson *Demosth.* Ded. 4 If by this meanes I could towle out some other to do this perfitely. **1593** *Tell-Troth's N. Y. Gift* (1876) 18 To tole in customers. **1594** Carew *Tasso* (1881) 117 She..with sweet sighes them on doth toule. **1601** Holland *Pliny* (1634) I. 261 She..by little and little tilleth and tolleth them so neere, that she can easily sease vpon them. **1611** Cotgr., *Emmiellé*..inticed, inueagled, allured, tolled, or drawne on by sweet meanes. **1653** Milton *Hirelings* (1659) 132 By that lure or loubel [he] may be toald from parish to parish all the town over. **1692** Locke *Educ.* § 115 Whatever you observe him to be more frighted at..be sure to tole him on to by.. Degrees. **1801** Jefferson *Writ.* (1830) III. 467 To tell us back to the times when we burnt witches. **1828** *Craven Gloss., Toll-on*, to entice, to draw on by degrees. **1879** J. D. Long *Æneid* I. 785 Now Dido, she Of Tyre, is toling him with tender words. **1879** T. Hardy *Wessex Tales* (1889) 248 'Tis all done to tole us the wrong way. **1885** Howells *Silas Lapham* (1891) I. 271 I'm not going to have 'em say we.. tolled him on.

**2.** *spec. U. S.* To lure or decoy (wild animals) for the purpose of capture; *esp.* (*a*) to decoy (ducks) by means of a dog trained for the purpose (see Toller 2 2); (*b*) to attract (fish) by means of bait thrown into the water (see Toll-bait, also Tolling *vbl. sb.*1 b, quot. 18..). Also *absol.* or *intr.*

**1858** Lewis in Youatt *Dog* iii. 90 In this simple branch of education, within the comprehension of any dog, consists the almost incredible art of toling the canvass-back. **1885** C. F. Holder *Marvels Anim. Life* 131, I..procured a large rabbit and placed it some way up from the pond, to toll her [a snake] away from the water. **1885** *Blackw. Mag.* July 108/1 Captain Kennedy's Indian attendant had toled: but neither stag paid any attention. **1901** *Ibid.* Nov. 691/2 He [a fox] is 'tolled'..by a noise made like two fighting crows.

**b.** *intr.* for *pass.* To admit of tolling.

**1858** Lewis in Youatt *Dog* iii. 90 The canvass-back toles better than any other duck. **1874** J. W. Long *Amer. Wild-fowl* xxv. 251 The black-heads tole the most readily.

**3.** *trans.* To pull, drag, draw (physically). ? *Obs.*

*a* **1400–50** *Alexander* 3640 Þan preses in þe Persyns & of þe proud Medis..agayn all þe yndis, Tolls of þe tirantis.., Seȝes doun on aithire side a sowme out of nounbre. *c* **1440** *York Myst.* xlvi. 58 As a traytour atteynted þei toled hym and tugged hym [Jesus]. **1542** *Lam. & Piteous Treat.* in *Harl. Misc.* (Malh.) I. 243 Thynkynge that..he woulde with strength of men, tolle forth his shippes..into the depth of the see. **1654** Gayton *Pleas. Notes* I. vi. 20 Mr. Nicholas.. toles downe the books with as little remorse, as a Carman does billets.

†**b.** *Toll out*: (?) To stretch out to (a stated length) by being pulled. *Obs. rare*−1.

**1377** Langl. *P. Pl.* B. v. 214 And put hem in a presse and pyn[n]ed hem þerinne, Tyl ten ȝerdes or twelue hadde tolled out threttene.

**c.** *intr.* for *pass.* To pull (itself), move, drift.

**18..** Scott in Goode *Amer. Fishes* (1888) 89 The boat toles round from the tide toward the feeding-ground.

**Toll** (tōul), *v.*[2] Also 6 tolle, 6–7 towle, toul(e, 6–7 (9 *dial.*) towl, 7 toull, 7–8 tole. [Found in this sense in 15th c.: nothing similar outside Eng. Prob. orig. a particular use of Toll *v.*[1] sense 3, 'to pull'; the sense having passed from 'pull the bell-rope', to 'pull the bell', and so to 'make the bell sound by pulling the rope'. The variant forms are exactly the same as in Toll *v.*[1]; but no distinct evidence of the transfer of sense from 'pull' to 'ring' appears in the quots., although these are compatible with it.]

**1.** *trans.* To cause (a great bell) to sound by pulling the rope, esp. in order to give an alarm or signal; to ring (a great bell). *arch.* or *rhet.*

(Since *to toll* is said of the bell itself (sense 3) in 1452, the transitive sense must have been in use before that date.)

**1494** Fabyan *Chron.* (1811) 352 Sir Hughe le Spenser came ..& desyred assystence of the fore named constables, the which commaunded the said belle to be tolled. **1568** Grafton *Chron.* II. 284 Syr John went into the market place, and there tolled the common Bell, and then incontinent men and women assembled. **1573** G. Harvey *Letter-bk.* (Camden) 48 He accusid me of..præsumption for that I tooke uppon me to bid the butler toul the bel. **1684** *Foxe's A. & M.* III. 920/1 Let the Bell of the Church of S. German be touled. **1703** *Lond. Gaz.* No. 3749/4 The Bells were tolled at Caneto, and the Allarm was given on all sides by firing of Guns. **1849** James *Woodman* viii, You run to the porter and tell him to toll the great bell with all his might. *a* **1873** Deutsch *Rem.* (1874) 255 The bells were tolled in an irregular and funereal fashion.

† **b.** *absol.* or *intr.* To ring. *Obs.*

**1513** Bradshaw *St. Werburge* II. 1592 The same glad tidyng shewed an honest woman Tollyng at the churche-dore the sayd day and hour.

**2.** *spec.* To cause (a large or deep-toned bell) to give forth a sound repeated at regular intervals by pulling the rope so that the bell swings through a short arc (in contrast to *ringing* it in full swing), or by striking it with a hammer or the like, or pulling the clapper; esp. for summoning a congregation to church, and **b.** (now) on the occasion of a death (the passing-bell) or funeral. Also *absol.* or *intr.*

**1552** *Bk. Com. Prayer* Pref., The Curate..shall tolle a bell therto [i.e. to Morning and Evening Prayer] a conuenyente tyme before he begyn, that such as be desposed maye come ..to praye wyth hym. **1600** *Weakest goeth to Wall* G iij, Heere take the key and toll to Euening prayer. *a* **1604** Hanmer *Chron. Irel.* (1633) 103 [They] wayted for divine service, they rung the Bell, they tould, they waited long. **1617** Minsheu *Ductor, To toll* a Bell, which is to make him strike onely of one side. *c* **1618** Moryson *Itin.* IV. v. i. (1903) 480 Some one [bell] (as that of Lincolne Minster) requiring the helpe of many men to toule it, and some dossen or twenty men to ringe it out. **1844** Mrs. Browning *Rhyme Duchess May*, Toll slowly. **1868** Denison *Clocks, Watches, & Bells* (ed. 5) 364 A large bell may be tolled easily by one man, if it is properly hung...I should hang a very large bell for tolling only, on wedge shaped gudgeons, so as to move with very little friction, and put a stop to prevent it from being pulled too far.

**b.** **1526**, *c* **1600** [see Passing-bell]. **1635** Cranley *Amanda* 88 My tongue doth faile, goe toule the passing bell. **1782** Cowper *Loss of Royal George* i, Toll for the brave! The brave that are no more! **1790** — *Mother's Picture* 28, I heard the bell toll'd on thy burial day, I saw the hearse, that bore thee slow away. **1832** Tennyson *Death Old Year* 3 Toll ye the church-bell sad and slow..For the old year lies a-dying. **1901** H. E. Bulwer *Gloss. Techn. Terms Ch. Bells* 37 *Tolling*, causing a bell—generally the 'Tenor', or one of the heavier bells—to sound a number of times in slow succession, sometimes with marked intervals between every two or three 'blows', to announce a death or funeral. **1905** *Harmsworth Encycl.* 660/1 The passing bell was tolled when any one was passing out of life. This custom still survives in many parts of Britain, but the bell is now tolled after the death.

**3.** Said of a bell (also of the ringer): To sound (esp. a knell, etc.) by ringing as in sense 2; also of a clock, to strike (the hour) in a deep tone with slow measured strokes. Cf. Knoll *v.*

**1452** *Cal. Anc. Rec. Dublin* (1889) 276 The comone bell shuld toll iii. tollis iiii. tymes. **1651** T. Barker *Art of Angling* (1653) 1 This man may come home..and cause the clerk to tole his knell. **1682** Dryden *Dk. Guise* IV. ii, Some crowd the Spires, but most the hallow'd Bells, And softly Toll for Souls departing Knells, Each Chime thou hear'st, a future death foretells. **1750** Gray *Elegy* i The Curfew tolls the knell of parting day. **1771** Beattie *Minstrel* I. xxxix, Slow tolls the village-clock the drowsy hour. **1805** Scott *Last Minstr.* VI. xxxi, And bells toll'd out their mighty peal, For the departed spirit's weal. **1818** — *Br. Lamm.* xxii[i], She died just as the clock in the distant village tolled one. **1861** Dutton Cook *P. Foster's D.* i, The clock of St. Paul's Covent Garden has just tolled out the hour of two.

**4.** *intr.* Of a bell: To give forth sounds of this character by being tolled; also quasi-*impers.* (quot. *c* 1729). Also said of a clock striking the hour on a deep-toned bell; in quot. 1826 of the hour.

**1551** Hooper *Injunctions* xxiii. Wks. (Parker Soc.) II. 137 In case..any of their friends will demand to have the bell toll whiles the sick is in extremes. **1592** Kyd *Sp. Trag.* III. xii, The Windes blowing, the Belles towling, the Owle shriking,..and the Clocke striking twelue. **1599** Shaks. *Hen. V*, IV. Prol. 15 The Countrey Cocks doe crow, the Clocks doe towle. **1653** H. Cogan tr. *Pinto's Trav.* lxi. 257 Then the same bell having tolled three times more, the two Priests descended. **1678** Bunyan *Pilgr.* I. 189 If I heard the Bell Toull for some that were dead. *c* **1729** in *Cath. Rec. Soc. Publ.* VIII. 88 After compline the same day it toled to Chapter. **1745** R. Leveson Gower in Jesse *Selwyn & Contemp.* (1843) I. 76 The bells toll for prayers. **1816** J. Wilson *City of Plague* II. ii. 289 By day and night the death-bell tolls, And says, 'Prepare to die'. **1826** Scott *Woodst.* xxxiii, Midnight at length tolled. **1858** Hawthorne *Fr. & It. Note-bks.* I. 231 The great bell of St. Peter's tolled with a deep boom.

**b.** *intr.*, *transf.* and *fig.* To make a sound like the tolling of a bell; to give forth a deep-toned or monotonously repeated note; *spec.* (*Sc.*) said of bees before swarming (see Tolling *vbl. sb.*[2] b).

**1747** [see Tolling *vbl. sb.*[2] b]. **1839** Bailey *Festus* xviii. (1852) 265 A thought comes tolling o'er the darkened soul Which we dare hardly guest. *a* **1849** J. C. Mangan *Poems* (1859) 122 Sullen tolls the far-off river's flow. **1857** Borrow *Romany Rye* ix. (1858) I. 110 Oh, that's the cuckoo tolling. **1912** M. Hewlett in *Eng. Rev.* Apr. 5 Then in clear sky the thunder tolled Sudden.

**5.** *trans.* To announce (a death, etc.) by tolling; to toll for (a dying or dead person).

**1597** Shaks. 2 *Hen. IV*, I. i. 103 (Qo.) His tongue Sounds euer after as a sullen bell, Remembred tolling [*Folios* knolling] a departing friend. **1602** Marston *Ant. & Mel.* IV. Wks. 1856 I. 48 Groning like a bell, That towles departing soules. **1850** Tennyson *In Mem.* lvii. 10 One set slow bell will seem to toll The passing of the sweetest soul That ever look'd with human eyes. **1858** O. W. Holmes *Aut. Breakf.-t.* xii. (1883) 248 My room-mate thought..it was the bell tolling deaths, and people's ages, as they do in the country.

**6.** To summon or dismiss by tolling. Const. *in*, *out*, etc.

**1611** Speed *Hist. Gt. Brit.* IX. xxii. § 21 To ring the Masse into England, and to towle Cardinall Poole from Rome. **1683** Dryden *Vind. Dk. Guise* 17 For Conscience or Heavens fear, religious Rules Are all State-bells to toll in pious Fools. **1697** — *Virg. Georg.* IV. 277 When hollow Murmurs of their Ev'ning Bells, Dismiss the sleepy Swains, and toll 'em to their Cells. **1819** Keats *Ode Nightingale* viii, Forlorn! the very word is like a bell To toll me back from thee to my sole self. **1841** Thackeray *Gt. H. Diamond* iv, As she spoke, the bells were just tolling the people out of church.

**b.** *absol.* or *intr. Toll in*: to summon a congregation to church by tolling (said of a person, or of the bell); *esp.* in reference to the change from ordinary ringing or chiming a few minutes before the commencement of worship.

**1710** J. B. *Let. to Sacheverell* 13 The Bells were Tolling in. **1712** Steele *Spect.* No. 372 ¶ 1, I was tolling in to Prayers at Eleven in the Morning. **1860** Warter *Seaboard* II. 455, I had no time to lose, as the bell was tolling in.

**Toll** (tōul), *v.*[3] Now *rare.* [f. Toll *sb.*[1]]

**1.** *intr.* To take or collect toll; to exact or levy toll.

*a* **1350** [see Tolling *vbl. sb.*[3]]. *c* **1386** Chaucer *Prol.* 562 Wel koude he stelen corn, and tollen thries And yet he hadde a thombe of gold pardee. *c* **1440** *Promp. Parv.* 496/1 Tollyn, or make tolle.., *multo.* **1530** Palsgr. 759/1, I tolle, I take the tolle, as a baylyfe dothe in a fayre or market...I tolle, as a myller doth, *je prens le tollyu.* **1576** Gascoigne *Steele Gl.* (Arb.) 79 When millers toll not with a golden thumbe. **1595** Shaks. *John* III. i. 154 No Italian priest Shall tythe or toll in our dominions. *a* **1658** Cleveland *Sing-Song* xxx, He toll'd for the rest of the Grist. **1886** [see Tolling *vbl. sb.*[3]].

**2.** *trans.* To take toll of (something); to exact a part of by way of toll.

**1399** Langl. *Rich. Redeles* III. 81 And tymed no twynte, but tolled her cornes, And gaderid þe grotus with gyle, as I trowe. **1546** [see Tolling *vbl. sb.*[3]]. **1591** *Troub. Raigne K. John* (1611) 62 Till I had tithde and tolde their holy hoords. **1686** W. Hedges *Diary* (Hakl. Soc.) I. 230 Here we were mett by ye Customer of Diarbekeer, who tolled our loads, and tooke ye custom & dutys of all the 3 places. **1794** M. Wollstonecraft *Hist. View Fr. Rev.* I. 76 The poor husbandman,..afterwards forced to carry the scanty crop to be tolled at the mill of monseigneur. **1894** *Westm. Gaz.* 26 May 5/2 The company-promoting system, whereby the City sharper tolls the savings of the credulous investor.

**b.** To charge (a person, etc.) with a toll, impose a toll upon, exact a toll from.

**1583** Melbancke *Philotimus* Dd ij b, Aegeon..doeth scoure the Seas, and toules the trafficke of trading merchauntes. **1592** tr. *Junius on Rev.* xiii. 1 What time the Empire of Rome..was mightily tolled, hauing euer and an one new heads. **1897** *Daily News* 2 Nov. 6/3 You have only to cross the bridge and you are sure to be tolled. **1912** M. Hewlett in *Eng. Rev.* Apr. 10 All [must] be tolled By Charon in his dark-prowed boat.

**c.** To take or gather (something) as toll.

**1597** Shaks. 2 *Hen. IV*, IV. v. 75 (Qo.) Like the bee toling from euery flower [*Folios* culling from euery flower The vertuous Sweetes]. **1820** W. Irving *Sketch Bk.* I. 189 Writers, like bees, toll their sweets in the wide world.

† **3.** *intr.* To pay toll; *to toll for* (*spec.*), to enter (a horse, etc.) for sale in the toll-book of a market.

**1393** Langl. *P. Pl.* C. XIV. 51 For þe lawe askeþ Marchauns for here merchaundise in meny place to tollen. **1530** Palsgr. 759/1, I tolle..as they that come to the myll, *je paye le tollyu.* You shal tolle, or you go, or I wyll tolle for you. **1537** Boorde *Let.* in *Introd. Knowl.* (1870) Forewords 62 They þat bowght þem dyd neuer toll for them. **1596** Bacon *Use Com. Law* (1636) 63 If hee bee a horse hee must bee ridden two houres in the market or faire, between ten and five a clock, and tolled for in the toll-book. **1601** Shaks. *All's Well* V. iii. 149, I will buy me a sonne in Law in a faire, and toule for this. Ile none of him. **1664** Butler *Hud.* II. I. 698 Where, when, by whom, and what y'were sold for, And in the open Market toll'd for?

**b.** *trans.* (in same sense.)

**1697** *Lond. Gaz.* No. 3310/4 The Person who exposed him to Sale being required to Toll him withdrew himself, by which it was conjectured he was stole.

**Toll** (tōul), *v.*[4] *Law.* [a. AF. *toller, toler, touller*, ad. L. *toll-ĕre* to take away.] *trans.* To take away, bar, defeat, annul. *To toll an entry*, to take away the right of, or bar entry.

[**1292** Britton I. vi. § 2 Ensint qe peyne ne lour toulle nule resoun. *Ibid.* xxvi. § 1 Cum il avera tolet ai pleyntif. Et si..ele avera tolu a homme ses membres.] **1467–8** *Rolls of Parlt.* V. 631/1 That the esson and..other delay of eny persone..by this acte be not prejudiced nor tolled in any wise. **1495** *Act 11 Hen. VII*, c. 63 § 4 Wherof their entres..shall be tolled and taken away by the Course of the Lawe. **1544** tr. *Littleton's Tenures* (1574) 86 b, Suche discente shall not tol the entre of the childe, but he may enter vpon the issue that is in by discent. **1642** J. M[arsh] *Argt. conc. Militia* 18 The King may dissolve a Parliament and so totally toll their power. **1726** Ayliffe *Parergon* 74 It..tolls the Presumption in Favour of a Sentence. **1818** Hallam *Mid. Ages* (1878) III. 166 *note*, In what case this right of entry was taken away, or *tolled*, as it was expressed, by the death or alienation of the disseisor.

**Tollable** (tōu·lăb'l), *a. rare.* [f. Toll *v.*[3] + -able.] Subject to toll; on which toll is payable.

**1611** Cotgr., *Peageau*, tollable; of toll. *Chemin peageau*, wherein toll may be taken. **1912** *Daily News* 12 July 3 To take proceedings against the Clayton-square flower-girls for selling tollable articles.

**Tollage** (tōu·lèdʒ). Also 6 -adge, toullage. [?f. Toll *v.*[3] + -age; confounded with Tallage *sb.*[1]]

**1.** = Toll *sb.*[1]; exaction or payment of toll.

**1494** Fabyan *Chron.* VII. (1516) 27 b/2 That ye Cytezyns shulde enioye the lybertyes of ye Fayre euer after without paying of any Tollage [*some MSS.* tallage] or Tolle. **1579** in Willis & Clark *Cambridge* (1886) I. 312 The tolladge at bottle bridge off the cartes yt shall carrye the sayd slate. **1591** *Rutland MSS.* (1905) IV. 398 Paid for swarfage and toullage, ijs. **1612** Drayton *Poly-olb.* xiii. 270 By Leofrick her Lord..The people from her Marts by tollage who expelld. *a* **1835** *Certificate of Freedom of City of Norwich* (MS.), Know ye, That..the Bearer hereof..is Free, and ought so to be from all kind of Tollage, Pontage, Passage, Murage [etc.] and from all other Customs in all the Sea-Ports throughout England. **1888** *Pall Mall G.* 24 Sept. 5/2 Carrying all at the stereotyped figure of 2*s.* 6*d.* per ton..the River Weaver Trustees charging another 1*s.* per ton tollage.

† **2.** = Tallage *sb.*[1] *Obs.*

**1551** (ed. Berthelet) *Act 23 Hen. VIII*, 1531–2, c. 10 § 6 Taxes and Tollages [*Record ed.* Tallages] hereafter to be assessed and leuyed. **1583** Stocker *Civ. Warres Lowe C.* I. 17 We..will faithfully paye all taxes, tollages, customes, impostes, subsidies, tenthes. **1610** Holland *Camden's Brit.* I. 39 The revenewes comming by tollage and pondage and such like imposts. **1634** *Malory's Arthur* I. lxxxix. 155 They..put this land to great extortions and tollages [1470–85 (v. ii. 161) extorcions & taylles].

† **Tolla·tion.** *Obs. rare*[−1]. [irreg. f. L. *tollĕre* to lift + -ation.] The action of lifting.

**1688** R. Holme *Armoury* II. 387/1 An Ellevation, or Tollation, is the lifting up of a thing, which shews it to be light or heavy.

**To·ll-bait.** *U.S.* [f. Toll *v.*[1] 2 + Bait *sb.*] Chopped bait thrown into the water to 'toll' or attract fish; throw-bait.

**1887** *Fisheries of U.S.* Sect. v. II. 594 In the old style of mackerel fishing, ..clams were chopped up (often with a mixture of menhaden) and sprinkled overboard as 'toll-bait' to attract the mackerel to the surface

† **To·ll-book.** *Obs.* [Toll *sb.*[1]] A book containing a register of beasts or goods to be sold at a market or fair, and the tolls payable for them; *in the toll-book*, in the market, for sale (in quot. 1607 *fig.*); also, a tax-collector's register or assessment-book. Also in comb. *toll-book keeper.*

**1596** Bacon *Use Com. Law* (1636) 63 [see Toll *v.*[3] 3]. *Ibid.*, And the seller must bring one to avouch his sale, knowne to the toll-book-keeper. **1607** Tourneur *Rev. Trag.* II. ii, Some that were Maides..are now perhaps i'th Toale-book. **1655** Fuller *Ch. Hist.* IV. iii. § 36 Nor is it probable he was a Mendicant, who was rated in the Publicans Tole-Book, and paid Tribute unto Cæsar. **1679** *Lond. Gaz.* No. 1446/4 Whoever gives notice of the said Horse to John Warren aforesaid, or to John Davenport, Keeper of the Toll-Book in West Smithfield, shall have 20s. Reward.

**Toll-booth**: see Tolbooth.

**Tollcester**, erron. form of Tolsester *Obs.*

**To·ll-dish.** [Toll *sb.*[1] 2 a (*b*).] A dish or bowl of stated dimensions for measuring the toll of grain at a mill; a multure-dish.

*a* **1550** *Mery Jest of Mylner of Abyngton* 50 in Hazl. *E. P. P.* III. 102 The mylner was so trewe and fele, Of each mannes corne wolde he steale More than his toledish by a deale. *c* **1585** *Faire Em* I. 168 You are too fyne to be a Millers daughter: For if you should but stoope to take vp the tole dish You will haue the crampe in your finger At least ten weekes after. **1623** Fletcher & Rowley *Maid in Mill* III. ii, A Lord, a Miller? Take your toal-dish with ye. **1726** Ayliffe *Parergon* 505 Corn Mills pay Tithes in Kind as Mills, which is the tenth Toll-dish. **1778** *Eng. Gazetteer* (ed. 2) s. v. *Farnham*, The toll-dish here was once reckoned worth 200*l.* a year. **1820** Scott *Ivanhoe* xi, The thieves.. crying to their comrade, 'Miller! beware thy toll-dish'.

**Tolled**, pa. t. of Toll *v.*; also obs. f. Told.

**Tollenar, -er**: see Tolner *Obs.*

**Tollent** (tǫ·lĕnt), *a. Logic. rare.* [ad. L. *tollent-em*, pres. pple. of *tollĕre* to lift, take away.] That 'takes away' or negatives: opp. to Ponent 3.

**1837–8** Sir W. Hamilton *Logic* xviii. (1866) I. 344 A Tollent or Destructive syllogism. [See Destructive A. d.]

**Toller**[1] (tōu·ləɪ). Also 4 -ere, 4–5 -are, 4–6 -ar, 6 towler. [OE. *tollere*, f. Toll *sb.*[1] + -er[1].]

**1.** One who takes toll, a toll-collector (now *rare*); † a tax-gatherer, 'publican' (*obs.*); *toller of the sack*, a miller.

*c* **1000** Ælfric *Hom.* I. 510 Hu ðæs caseres tolleras axodon Petrus. *Ibid.* II. 468 God..hine awende of tollere to apostole. *c* **1050** *Supp. Ælfric's Voc.* in Wr.-Wülcker 171/29 *Teloniarius*, tolnere *vel* tollere. **13..** *Cursor M.* 25804

(Cott.) Matheu was first toller And siþen cristes gospeller. *c* 1375 *Sc. Leg. Saints* x. (*Mathou*) 9 In þe tolbuth set lewy, Þat as a tollare þare wes sate. 1377 LANGL. *P. Pl.* B. Prol. 220 Taillours and tynkeres & tolleres in marketes. 1474 CAXTON *Chesse* III. iv. (1883) 108 The customers, tollers, and resseyuours of rentes & of money. *c* 1510 BARCLAY *Mirr. Gd. Manners* (1570) G iv, No towler, catchpoll nor customer No broker nor botcher, no somner nor sergeaunt. *c* 1550 CHEKE *Matt.* ix. 10 Mani tollers and sinners sat doun also with Jesus and with his discipils. 1591 GREENE *Conny-Catch.* II. Wks. (Grosart) X. 79 The Priggar when he hath stollen a horse..bringeth to the touler..two honest men, eyther apparelled like citizens, or plain country yeomen, and they..offer to depose, that they know the horse to be his. 1724 A. SHIELDS *J. Renwick* (1827) 148 One of the Tollers or Waiters discovered the House. 1831 *Lincoln Herald* 6 May, Surely a tailor or shoemaker is as good as a printer's devil or a toller of the sack.

**2.** An apparatus for separating the toll of grain: = *toll-collector* (*c*) (TOLL *sb.*$^1$ 3).

1884 KNIGHT *Dict. Mech.* Supp., *Toller.* (Grist Mill.) The Tom Thumb toller is an automatic divider of the toll from the grist.

**Toller**$^2$, **toler** (tōu·ləɹ). Also 5 tollare. [f. TOLL, TOLE *v.*$^1$ + -ER$^1$.]

†**1.** One who 'tolls', entices, or instigates. *Obs.*

*c* 1440 *Promp. Parv.* 496/1 Tollare or styrare to do goode or badde, *excitator, instigator.*

**2.** A decoy; *spec.* a dog of a small breed used in decoying ducks: see TOLL *v.*$^1$ 2. Also *attrib. U. S.*

1874 J. W. LONG *Amer. Wild-fowl* iii. 72 For deep-water ducks, three or four decoys as tolers may be set out to leeward. *Ibid.* xxv. 250 Most persons on these waters have a race of small, white or liver-colored dogs, which they familiarly call the toler breed.

**Toller**$^3$ (tōu·ləɹ). [f. TOLL *v.*$^2$ + -ER$^1$.] One who tolls a bell.

1562 J. HEYWOOD *Prov. & Epigr.* (1867) 118 The milner tolth corne, the sexton tolth the bell, In whiche tollyng, tollers thriue not a lyke well.

†**Toller**$^4$. *Law. Obs.* [Agent-n. f. TOLL *v.*$^4$] One who tolls or bars the entry of another. Hence **Tol-**, **tolleress**, a female toller.

1313-4 *Eyre of Kent* (Selden) II. 5 Ele entra com nostre toleresse. 1912 *transl.* She entered but as our toleress. *Note.* A toleress is one who tolls the entry.

**Toller-**: see TOLER-.

**To·llery.** *nonce-wd.* [f. TOLL *sb.*$^1$ or TOLLER$^1$ + -ERY.] A place at which tolls are collected.

1858 CARLYLE *Fredk. Gt.* II. v. (1872) I. 69 *Zollern* is equivalent to *Tollery* or Place of Tolls.

**Tolletane**, obs. form of TOLETAN.

**Toll-free**, *a.* Free from toll; exempt from payment of toll. (Usually in predicative or adverbial construction.)

1052-67 *Charter of Eadweard* in Kemble *Cod. Dipl.* IV. 209 Tolfreo ofer ealle Engleland, wiðinne burhe and wiðutan. 1277 *Brit. Mus. Add. Charter* 51563 [Pannage and other rights are granted] cum hopirfre et tolfre in omnibus molendinis meis. 1494 FABYAN *Chron.* VII. 327 That yᵉ cytezens of London shulde passe toll fre thorough all Englande. 1523 FITZHERB. *Surv.* 10 Some men to be tole free, and some to be hopper fre. 1610 HOLLAND *Camden's Brit.* (1637) 493 He obtained that it might bee every where Toll-free. 1829 SCOTT *Anne of G.* x, Such wares will not pass toll-free where Archibald of Hagenbach hath authority.

**To·ll-ga:therer.** Now *rare.* [f. TOLL *sb.*$^1$ + GATHERER.] One who collects tolls or dues; a tax-gatherer: = PUBLICAN *sb.*$^1$ 1.

1382 WYCLIF *Matt.* Prol., Fro the office of a tol gaderer he was clepid to God. 1474 CAXTON *Chesse* III. vii. (1883) 138 Kepars of townes customers and tolle gaderers. 1555 *Act* 2 & 3 *Phil. & Mary*, c. 7 § 2 Every Toll-gatherer..shall ..take their due and lawful Tolls. *a* 1610 HEALEY *Theophrastus* (1636) 25 Fit to keep an Alehouse or an Inne: to be a Pandar or a Tole-gatherer. 1766 BLACKSTONE *Comm.* II. xxx. 451 The horse shall be brought by both the vendor and vendee to the tollgatherer or bookkeeper of such fair or market. 1820 W. TOOKE tr. *Lucian* I. 365 The toll-gatherer Æacus would take it very ill.

So **To·ll-ga:thering**, collection of tolls or dues.

1577 tr. *Bullinger's Decades* (1592) 277 Hee bad not these Publicanes to leaue off their toll-gathering, but willed them to bee content with their appointed duty.

**To·ll-house.** [f. TOLL *sb.*$^1$ + HOUSE: cf. OHG. *zolhûs*, Ger. *zollhaus.*] A house or building at which tolls or dues are collected.

**1.** = TOLBOOTH 1 (*obs.*) or 2 (now *local*).

*c* 1440 *Promp. Parv.* 496/1 Tolhowse, *teloneum.* 1506 GUYLFORDE *Pilgr.* (Camden) 49 Our Sauyor..sawe the publycan named Leui,..syttynge at the tolhous. 1530 PALSGR. 281/2 Tolle house, *mayson de decrepte.* 1889 *N. & Q.* 7th Ser. VIII. 213/1 The 'tolhouse' or 'tolbooth' (as our town halls were called in the Middle Ages). In this place [Great Yarmouth] the name of 'tolhouse' is still retained.

**2.** A house by a toll-gate or toll-bridge, occupied by the toll-taker; † a railway booking-office (*obs.*).

1763 *Chron.* in *Ann. Reg.* 91/1 Richard Watson, tollman of Marybone turnpike, was..murdered in his toll-house. 1841 *Civil Eng. & Arch. Jrnl.* IV. 322/2 The whole rise of the railway from its toll-house in Plymouth to the Prince-town terminus..is 1350 feet. 1906 T. SINTON *Poetry of Badenoch* 163 Her charms were proclaimed everywhere from the toll house to Castle Gordon.

**Tolliban**, obs. form of TURBAN.

**Tolling, toling** (tōu·liŋ), *vbl. sb.*$^1$ Now *dial.* and *U. S.* [f. TOLL *v.*$^1$ + -ING$^1$.] The action of enticing, allurement; † incitement, instigation (*obs.*).

*a* 1225 *Ancr. R.* 116 Þis is wowunge efter Godes grome, & tollunge of his vuel. *c* 1330 *Arth. & Merl.* (Kölbing) 5304 Bot Wawain, þat bi him cam, & he him of his tolling nam. *c* 1440 *Promp. Parv.* 496/1 Tollynge, styrynge, or mevynge to good or badde, *instigacio, excitacio.* 1496 *Dives & Paup.* I. x. 41/2 Suche richesses of clothynge of the ymages is but a tollynge of more offrynge.

**b.** *spec.* The luring or decoying of wild animals, as ducks or fish (see TOLL *v.*$^1$ 2); also *attrib. U.S.*

1858 LEWIS in Youatt *Dog* iii. 90 The toling season continues about three weeks from the first appearance of the ducks. 18.. ATWOOD in Goode *Amer. Fishes* (1888) 180 The present mode of catching mackerel by drifting and tolling with bait did not come into general use until 1812. 1879 *Dogs Gt. Brit. & Amer.* 271 The system pursued on the Chesapeake Bay and the North Carolina Sounds, and known as 'toling', is the most successful...A small dog..is trained to run up and down on the shore in the sight of the ducks. 1901 *Blackw. Mag.* Nov. 692/2 The judicious 'hough', 'hough' or tolling-call of the hunter.

**To·lling,** *vbl. sb.*$^2$ [f. TOLL *v.*$^2$ + -ING$^1$.] The action of TOLL *v.*$^2$; the sounding of a large bell by slow regularly repeated strokes; esp. that of the passing-bell.

1494 FABYAN *Chron.* VII. 352 [In 1264] by tollyng of the great belle of Paules, all the cytie shuld be redy shortly in harneys, to gyue attendaunce. 1526 [see PASSING-BELL]. 1599 MASSINGER, etc. *Old Law* III. i, I am afraid the tolling of the bell will wake her again. 1628 WITHER *Brit. Rememb.* IV. 69 My Fancy tuned so the Bell, As if her Towlings did the story tell Of my mortality. 1711 STEELE *Spect.* No. 14 ¶ 5, I..have not missed tolling in to Prayers six times in all those Years. 1874 SIR E. BECKETT *Denison's Clocks, Watches, & Bells* (ed. 6) 359 The great superiority of tone of bells ringing in full swing over tolling, and even of tolling over striking by a clock hammer, has been often noticed.

**b.** *transf.* A sound resembling this; *spec.* (*Sc.*) a special humming sound made by the queen bee before swarming (see quots. 1747, 1830).

1747 MAXWELL *Pract. Bee-Master* § 147. 46 This Sound, commonly called Towling, proceeds, I suppose, from the young King, giving Signal to his Company to make ready for a March. 1830 *Edin. Encycl.* s. v. *Bee* II. 414/1 Most observers..affirm, that in the evening before swarming an uncommon humming or buzzing is heard in the hive, and a distinct sound from the queen, called tolling or calling. 1869 SIR V. BROOKE in *Life* (1894) 162 Nearer and nearer came the tolling of the grand old hound.

**c.** *attrib.* as **tolling-lever**, a lever attached to a bell or to the clapper by means of which the bell is tolled: see quot.

1874 SIR E. BECKETT *Denison's Clocks, Watches, & Bells* (ed. 6) 357-8 Tolling-levers...The great Worcester bell is hung on wedge-shaped gudgeons.., to enable it to be tolled, almost without friction, by a long lever; for the tower would not bear it in full swing...But..it answers equally well to toll it by a short lever..projecting from the top of the clapper, and pulled by a slight rope.

**To·lling,** *vbl. sb.*$^3$ Now *rare.* [f. TOLL *v.*$^3$ + -ING$^1$.] The action of TOLL *v.*$^3$; the taking or levying of toll; also payment to hop-pickers at so many bushels a shilling. Also *attrib.*

*a* 1350 *St. Matthew* 416 in Horstm. *Altengl. Leg.* (1881) 136 Saint Mathew..A toller was..With tolling mikell gude he gat. *c* 1440 *Promp. Parv.* 496/1 Tollynge, of myllarys, *multura.* 1509 BARCLAY *Shyp of Folys* (1874) I. 64 Brybours and Baylyes that lyue upon towlynge. 1546 in W. H. Turner *Select. Rec. Oxford* (1880) 179 The untrewe and excessyve tollinge of certayne quarters of wheate meale. 1562 PILKINGTON *Expos. Abdyas* 129 As though he were set to gather up Christs tolling money. 1886 J. CRAIG *Tollman's Lament* in R. Ford *Harp Perthshire* (1893) 346 Whan first my tollin' days began. 1888 *Pall Mall G.* 5 Oct. 5/1 If hops are pretty good, however, and the 'tolling' not too low —say, six bushels a shilling—an average hopper can live like a lord. *Ibid.* 5/2 When the hops are large and plentiful the farmer may commence his 'tolling' at twelve a shilling.

**To·lling, toling,** *ppl. a.*$^1$ Now *dial.* and *U. S.* [f. TOLL *v.*$^1$ + -ING$^2$.] That 'tolls'; enticing, alluring; *spec.* used as a decoy (see TOLL *v.*$^1$ 2).

*a* 1225 *Ancr. R.* 50 Vor nabbe ȝe nout þene nome..of totinde ancres, ne of tollinde lokunges. 1642 MILTON *Apol. Smect.* Wks. 1851 III. 258 His own title; hung out like a toling signe-post to call passengers. 1868 R. B. ROOSEVELT *Florida & Game Water Birds* 336 Red is selected by the Southerners for their tolling dogs, but this is with the purpose of making them attractive.

**To·lling,** *ppl. a.*$^2$ [f. TOLL *v.*$^2$ + -ING$^2$.] That tolls, as a bell.

1728 POPE *Dunc.* II. 228 With horns and trumpets now to madness swell, Now sink in sorrows with a tolling bell.

**To·lling,** *ppl. a.*$^3$ Now *rare.* [f. TOLL *v.*$^3$ + -ING$^2$.] Taking toll; tax-gathering.

1641 J. JACKSON *True Evang. T.* II. 110 A greedy Wolfe, a tolling Publicane.

**Tollman** (tōu·lmæ̆n). Pl. **-men.** [f. TOLL *sb.*$^1$] A man who collects tolls; the keeper of a toll-gate.

1743 in Feret *Fulham* (1900) I. 63 It was agreed to take on Mr. Haines (tollman) again. 1763 [see TOLL-HOUSE 2]. 1782 COWPER *Gilpin* 243 The toll-men thinking as before That Gilpin rode a race. 1816 SCOTT *Tales my Landlord* Introd., The tollman at the well-frequented turnpike on the Wellbrae-head. 1886 W. J. TUCKER *E. Europe* 98 'You must pay toll', said the toll-man, stepping forward.

**Tol-lol** (tǫ·l,lǫ·l), *a. slang.* Also **toll-loll.** [f. the first syllable of TOLERABLE, with riming extension.] Tolerable, pretty good, pretty well, passable, 'middling'. Hence **Tol-lo·l-ish** *a.*

1797 MRS. A. M. BENNETT *Beggar Girl* (1813) V. 137 Our lady did nothing..but stare at you all supper time; and he says you looked very toll-loll. 1809 *Sporting Mag.* XXXIII. 278 Lounged to the theatre..Kemble toll-loll. 1835 MARRYAT *Olla Podr.* iii, 'And how does..Maria find herself?'..At last there was a reply. 'Oh! *tol, lol!*' 1866 *Routledge's Every Boy's Ann.* 296 Two friends, who seemed rather tol-lol-ish. 1911 COUCH *True Tilda* ix, How do my bantlings find themselves this morning? Tol-lollish I trust.

**Tollon**, var. TOYON. **Tollsel**: see TOLSEL.

**Tollutate, tollutation**: see TOLUTATION.

†**To·lmen.** *Obs.* [Given by Borlase, 1754, as a common name in Cornwall, and explained by him as 'hole of stone', f. *tol* hole + *mên* stone; but app. the same word as Breton *taol mean* or *tôl mên* 'table-stone', adopted by French archæologists (from the mutated *an dôl mên*) as DOLMEN, q.v.

Borlase app. interpreted the first element as Cornish *toll, toul, tewl,* = Welsh *twll*, 'hole', and was thus misled as to the meaning. (The three examples mentioned by him are app. all natural formations.) Some later writers have identified the second element as Eng. *man*, and made it sing. *tolman*, pl. *tolmen*. The word is now disused.]

See quots., and cf. DOLMEN, CROMLECH.

1754 BORLASE *Observ. Antiq. Cornw.* III. iii. 166 There is another kind of Stone-deity, which has never been taken notice of by any Author that I have heard of. It's common name in Cornwall and Scilly, is Tolmên; that is, the Hole of Stone. It consists of a large Orbicular Stone, supported by two Stones, betwixt which, there is a passage. *Ibid.* 167 The two Tolmêns at Scilly are Monuments..of the same kind with this. *Ibid.*, These Tolmens rest on supporters, and do not touch the Earth...Underneath these vast stones, there is a hole, or passage, between the Rocks. [*Note.* From this Hole they have the Name of Tolmen.] 1827 G. HIGGINS *Celtic Druids* Pref. 45 In Westphalia and East Friesland are some very curious examples of Tolmen. 1845 KNIGHT *Old Eng.* I. i. 18/2 Such are the remains which have been called Tolmen; a Tolman being explained to be an immense mass of rock placed aloft on two subjacent rocks which admit of a free passage between them.

†**To·l-me-nee·r.** *Obs.* Also (? erron.) **tolmeiner, tol(l)meyner.** [app. = *toll* (= draw or attract) *me near*: see TOLL *v.*$^1$, and cf. COLMENIER.] A name for the Sweet William.

1578 LYTE *Dodoens* II. viii. 157 The floures grow at the toppe of the stalkes, many clustering togither after the manner of Tol-me-neers, or sweete Williams. *Ibid.* xiii. 334 They..are taken for Sweete Williams or Tolmeyners. 1597 GERARDE *Herbal* II. clxxiv. § 4. 480 [The great Sweete William and the narrow leafed Sweete William are called] sweete Williams, Tolmeiners, and London Tuftes. 1629 PARKINSON *Paradisus* 320 *Armerius*, or *Armeria*...In some places they call the broader leafed kindes that are not spotted, Tolmeiners, and London tufts; but the speckled kinde is termed by our English Gentlewomen, for the most part, London pride.

**Tolmond, -mont(h, -mount,** obs. forms of TWELVEMONTH.

†**Tolne.** *Obs.* [OE. *toln* = OFris. *tolne, tolene*, OS. *tolna*, f. late L. *tolonēum*: whence also AF. *tolun*(*e.*)] Tax, custom, duty; = TOLL *sb.*$^1$

1023 in Thorpe *Charters* (1865) 318 Heore is þæt scip.. and se tolne of ealle scipen [L. *eorum est navicula..et theloneum omnium navium*]. 1038 *Ibid.* 339 Se þridda pæniȝ of þære tolne on Sandwic. [1292 BRITTON I. xvi. § 5 De ceo [il] paya tolun as baillifs. *Ibid.* xxii. § 13 Totes torcenouses prises..de travers ou de tolune.] *c* 1447-8 *Shillingford Lett.* (Camden) 93 All maner tolne of all maner marchaundyse. 1473 *Rolls of Parlt.* VI. 73/2 The Issues, Fermes, Tolnes, Revenuez, Amerciamentes and other Profittes.

†**Tolner.** *Obs.* Forms: 1 tolnere, 5 tolenar, 5-6 tollenar, 6 tollener, tolner, 7 toulner. [OE. *tolner* = OFris., MLG. *tolner*, MDu. *tolnâre*, Du. *tollenaar*, OHG. *zol*(*l*)*anâri, zolneri*, MHG. *zolner*, Ger. *zöllner*:—late L. *tolōneāri-us*, for L. *telōniārius*, f. *telōnium* custom-house: see TOLL *sb.*$^1$] A toll-taker, tax-gatherer, publican; = TOLLER$^1$ 1.

*c* 1050 *Suppl. Ælfric's Voc.* in Wr.-Wülcker 171/29 *Telonearius*, tolnere, *uel* tollere. 1481 CAXTON *Chesse* Contents, Receyuers of custum and tollenars [*ed.* 1474 toller]. 1483 — *Gold. Leg.* 125/1 Why wepest yᵘ tolenar? 1546 *St. Papers Hen. VIII*, XI. 199 Somme of the tolleners war comme, and somme war not. 1563-87 FOXE *A. & M.* (1596) 295/2 The pope of them maketh his tolners and bankers to get in his monie. *a* 1603 T. CARTWRIGHT *Confut. Rhem. N. T.* 89 The Toulner..asking tribute house by house.

†**Toloney.** *Obs.* Also *Sc.* 6 **tholoney,** 7 **tholnie.** [ad. late and med.L. *t*(*h*)*olonēum* toll, for L. *telōnium*, a. Gr. τελώνιον toll, tax: see TOLL *sb.*$^1$ (In med.L. also *tholneum*, Du Cange, whence F. *tonlieu.*)] = TOLL *sb.*$^1$

1517 in *Reg. Mag. Sig. Scot.* 1542. 644/2 We..grantis to him and his airis,..that thai..bruke ilk yeir..within the.. Toun of Clakmannane, commoun fairis in the feist of Sanct Bartilmo..with all tholoneis. 1563-87 FOXE *A. & M.* (1596) 297/2 Great taxes and tolonies and tenths were required of his subiects. 1633 *Sc. Acts Chas. I* (1870) V. 97/2 With all.. multurs frie ports or harberies customes tholnies and vthers.

†**To·-look.** *Sc.* Also **to-luyke, -luik.** [f. TO-$^1$ + LOOK *sb.*] A looking to, a prospect.

*a* 1572 KNOX *Hist. Ref.* III. Wks. 1848 II. 174 Thocht scho, the to-luyke of Ingland sall allure mony wowaris to me. *a* 1598 ROLLOCK *Serm.* Wks. 1849 I. 306 It is the to-luik to hevin that makis the saull of Paull to rejoyce. 1678 J. BROWN *Life of Faith* I. i. (1824) 14 The sure expectation and to-look for the better and more engaging substantial thing above.

**Tolo·sa-wood.** [f. *Tolosa*, name of a place near Hobart.] A name in Tasmania of the wood of *Pittosporum bicolor*, also called *Cheese-wood* in Victoria, and in both countries *White-wood.*

1866 *Treas. Bot.*, Tolosa-wood, *Pittosporum bicolor.* 1884 MILLER *Plant-n.*, *Pittosporum bicolor*, Cheese-wood or White-wood of Victoria, Tolosa-wood, White-wood of Tasmania.

† **To-louk, to-luke,** *v. Obs.* [OE. *tolúcan*, f. To-[2] + *lúcan*, Louk *v.*[2] to pull.] *trans.* To pull or tear to pieces; to pull apart, wrench asunder.

*c* 890 tr. *Bæda's Hist.* v. vi. (1890) 402 Forðon mine innoðas..fylle tolocene wæran. *c* 1205 Lay. 2602 Heo..to-luken þene king & his leomen to-drowen. *a* 1225 *Juliana* 12 (Roy. MS.) Ichulle leoten deor to teoren ant to luken þe.

† **Tolowr.** *Obs. rare.* (Suggested to be the Tiller of a cross-bow.)

? *a* 1400 *Morte Arth.* 3619 Tolowris tentyly takelle they ryghttene, Brasene hedys fulle brode buskede one flones.

‖ **To·lpatch.** Also **tolpatz.** [Ger. *tolpatsch*, earlier *tolpatz*: according to Kluyver (Beitr. XXX. 211), Magyar *talpas* foot-soldier, f. *talp* sole of the foot.] A foot-soldier. Hence **To·lpatchery** (*nonce-wd.*) infantry.

1705 *Lond. Gaz.* No. 4151/1 The Hungarian Horse were routed, and their Tolpatzes or Foot escaped. 1864 Carlyle *Fredk. Gt.* xv. ii. IV. 21 Tolpatches, Pandours, Warasdins. *Ibid.* v. 65 The matter..not one of Tolpatchery alone.

**Tolpyn,** obs. form of Thole-pin.

**Tolsel** (tǭ·lsěl), **tolzey** (tǭ·lzi). *local.* Forms: α. 4 tol(l)seld, 5 tollsell, (6 tollsill, towllsill, 7 toll(e)shell, towlsell, towsell, towelshill, towellshell, 7–8 tholsel(l), (7 tolser, towlsher); β. 5– tolsey, 8– tolzey. [ME. *tolseld, tollsell*, f. OE. Toll *sb.*[1] + OE. *seld* seat, or *sæl, sęle* hall: cf. OE. *tollsetl* 'tolbooth, custom-house'.]

The ancient name in some English and Irish towns for the guildhall, tolbooth, or borough court-house; also for the local court of justice (more fully *tolsel* or *tolzey court*) there held.

The original form, long retained in Ireland, has been reduced in some English towns to *tolsey* (tǫ·lsi) (sometimes only the traditional name of the building), or *tolzey*, as in the existing *Tolzey Court* of Bristol: see quots. 1883–4, 1906.

α. [1344 in *Litt. Red Bk. Bristol* (1900) I. 41 Constabularii, ballivi et alii ministri tenentes placita in Tols[eto].] 1373 *Charter Edw. III*, 8 Aug. (Seyer *Charters Bristol*, 1812, 50), Placita, quæ in curia nostra in dicta villa Bristoll' vocata Tollseld coram senescallo et aliis ministris nostris.. teneri consuevere. 1486 *Galway Arch.* in *10th Rep. Hist. MSS. Comm.* App. v. 385 His matter or suite be pledid and tried in the Tollsell or Courte-housse befor the Mayor. 1584 *Ibid.* 435 To appeare in the Towllsill or court howse. 1621 *Ibid.* 469 The Towsell or Courthowse of Galwey. 1632 *Ibid.* 480 The Mayor..and Comonaltie of Galwey..assembled in their Towelshill. 1680 *Ibid.* 505 The concerne of the Corporation formerly acted by Tholsell was vested in the Council by charter. 1701 *Ibid.* 515 Nor doe they enjoy any houses.. except the Tholsell and gaole thereunder. 1701 *Lond. Gaz.* No. 3721/3 *Dublin*...The Lord Mayor, with the Aldermen,..and Commons of the City, assembled at the Tholsell at Four a Clock. 1769 Wesley *Jrnl.* 15 June, I.. preached in the Tholsel [Kilkenny].

β. 1479 in *Eng. Gilds* 421 The Maire and the Shiref of Bristowe..to assemble with all the hole counseill, at the Tolsey. 1656 Blount *Glossogr.*, *Tolsey* or Toldsey is a place in the City of Bristow, answerable to the old Exchange in London, where the Merchants meet. 1697 *Lond. Gaz.* No. 3336/3 *Hereford, October* 26...Being returned to the Tolsey, the Mayor gave the Gentry an Entertainment. 1701 *Ibid.* No. 3709/4 The Fair will be kept [at Westbury]..on the first Friday in Lent, as formerly; and a Tolsey duly kept. 1706 *Ibid.* No. 4289/3 The Tolzey or Benefit of the Fair of Wellow aforesaid. 1883 *Wharton's Law Lex.*, *Tolsey*,..a local tribunal, usually spelt 'Tolzey', for small civil causes held at the Guildhall, Bristol. 1884 *Arrowsmith's Dict. Bristol* 278/1 In this Court of the Tolzey all actions of debt, assumpsit, covenant, trespass, trover, and other civil actions arising within the City [of Bristol] could be prosecuted by action, or by foreign attachment...The trial of the Court is by Jury. 1898 J. A. Gibbs *Cotswold Village* 190 The ancient building in the centre of the town [Burford] is called the 'Tolsey'. 1906 *Daily Chron.* 22 Aug. 4/6 Some quaint local courts which have survived innumerable Judicature Acts, such as the Tolzey Court of Bristol and the Court of Passage at Liverpool: courts which for expedition can put all others to the blush.

† **Tolse·ster.** *Obs.* Also **toll-.** [f. Toll *sb.*[1] + Sester.] A toll or duty of a sester of ale (Sester 2) formerly payable in some manors to the lord of the manor for liberty to brew and sell ale.

1232 *Charter Roll* 16 Hen. III, m. 2 (P. R. O.) De singulis bracinis cerusie venalis vnum sexterium ceruisie quod dici consueuit Tolsester. 1499 *Rot. Plac.* in *Itin. apud Cestriam* 14 H. 7 (Blount 1670), Per Tolsester clamat esse quietum de reddendo unum Sextarium Cervisiæ quod continet xvi Lagenas. *c* 1640 J. Smyth *Lives Berkeleys* (1883) I. 341 In the 13th of Edward the third, 284. tollcesters, which I call brewings. 1679 Blount *Anc. Tenures* 153 If any Alewife brewed Ale to sell, she was bound to satisfy the Lord for Tolsester. 1701 *Cowell's Interpr.*, *Tolcestrum, Tolsaster.* 1706 Phillips, Tolsaster or Tolsester.

**Tolstoyan** (tǫ·lstoi,ǎn), *a.* and *sb.* Also **Tolstoian.** [f. proper name *Tolstoi* + -an.]

**a.** *adj.* Of or pertaining to Count Leo N. Tolstoi, a famous Russian writer and social reformer (1828–1910). **b.** *sb.* A follower of Tolstoi or his teachings. So **To·lstoyism,** the opinions or teachings of Tolstoi; **To·lstoyist** = *Tolstoyan* b.

1894 *Westm. Gaz.* 12 Nov. 5/3 An article by a Russian correspondent on the harrying of Tolstoyists by the police in the Southern and Central provinces...the banishment of a certain Prince Khilkov..a rich landowner who had given up his estates to the poor in his neighbourhood, and was actively engaged in propagating the peculiar tenets known as Tolstoyism. 1898 *Daily News* 6 Oct. 5/4 Anything more distant from the Quaker, or Stundist, or Tolstoian view of military things..it would be difficult to imagine. 1900 *Westm. Gaz.* 22 Mar. 2/2 We are not converted to any Tolstoyan gospel by this book. 1901 *Daily Chron.* 30 May 3/1 Already the Tolstoyans are becoming a sect. 1905 *Contemp. Rev.* May 685 The Tolstoyan gospel of Christian morality apart from faith in the Supernatural.

**Tolt** (tǭlt), *sb. Old Law.* [a. AF. *tolte, toulte* = med.L. *tolta*, f. L. *tollĕre* 'to take up, raise, lift', with the form of a sb. from pa. pple.] A writ by which a cause was removed from a court-baron to the county court.

[1294 *Placita coram rege*, Easter 22 *Edw. I*, 18 *d*, Dicit quod..Alicia numquam toltam predicti placiti per probacionem..ei optulit tanquam vicecomiti. 1337 *Year-bks.* 11–12 *Edw. III* (Rolls) 307 Le vicomte manda qil navoit pas fait la toulte.] 1607 Cowell *Interpr.*, *Tolt* (*tolta*) is a writ whereby a cause depending in a court Baron, is remoued into the county court. 1647 N. Bacon *Disc. Govt. Eng.* i. xlviii. (1739) 83 This Suit was originally begun and had its final determination in the County-Court, and not brought by a Tolt out of the Hundred-Court. 1768 Blackstone *Comm.* III. iv. 34 The proceedings on a writ of right may be removed into the county court by a precept from the sheriff called a *tolt*, '*quia tollit atque eximit causam e curia baronum.*' 1876 Digby *Real Prop.* ii. § 2. 73 *note.* 1912 *Eyre of Kent* (Selden) II. 87 The plea [1313–4] was removed by a tolt into the County Court.

Hence **Tolt** *v.* (*nonce-wd.*), *trans.* to raise, lift up.

1896 *Calendar Inner Temple* I. Introd. 35 These [i. e. the clerks commoners], after certain probation, could be called or 'tolted' to the Masters' Commons table.

**Tolter** (tǫ·ltəɹ), *a.* (*adv.*) *Sc.* and *dial.* Also 6 towter, 9 toolter. [Late ME.; goes with next; exact relation obscure.] Moving unsteadily; unsteady, unstable, tottering; insecure, precarious; in quot. 1430–40, giddy. Also as *adv.* unsteadily.

1423 Jas. I *Kingis Q.* ix, Sothe It is, that, on hir tolter quhele, Euery wight cleuerith In his stage. *Ibid.* clxiv, So tolter quhilum did sche it to-wrye. 1430–40 Lydg. *Bochas* iv. xxiii. (MS. Bodl. 263) 252/1 Tascende the mounteyn, feeble wer ther chynes Ther hedis toltir, & ther brayn gan faille. *c* 1470 Henryson *Orpheus & Eur.* 283 Before his [Tantalus'] face ane apill hang also, Fast at his mouth, apon a tolter threid. 1560 Rolland *Seven Sages* 29 That we may all prouyde Sum help, that may put by this towter tide. 1880 Dennison in *Orcadian Sketch-Bk.* 119 His bowie legs..Wur trumblan' like twa toolter stoops.

**To·lter,** *v. dial.* [Early mod.Eng.: app. the same as MDu., Du. *touteren* to waver, totter, swing, *touter* a swing, representing an earlier OLG. or OS. **taltrôn* (cf. *oud*:—*ald*), which exists in a dial. Du. *talteren* (Franck), = OE. *tealtrian* to totter, stagger, be unsteady.] *intr.* To move unsteadily; to flounder; to turn or toss about; to hobble; to jolt along. Hence **To·ltering** *ppl. a.*

1529 More *Suppl. Soulys* 43 You walter peraduenture and tolter in syknes fro syde to syde. 1533 — *Answ. Poysoned Bk.* Wks. 1039/2 There lyeth he still tumblyng and toltryng in myre. 1821 Clare *Vill. Minstr.* II. 76 From..dusty lane, Where home the cart-horse tolters with the swain.

**Tolu** (tolū·, tǭ·lū). [From *Tolu* (tolū·) (now *Santiago de Tolu*) in the United States of Colombia, whence obtained.] In **Tolu balsam, balsam of Tolu**: A balsam obtained by incision from the bark of the **Tolu-tree**, *Myrospermum* (*Myroxylon*) *toluiferum*, a leguminous tree of tropical S. America; used in medicine and perfumery.

1671 Salmon *Syn. Med.* iii. xxiii. 444 Balsam of Tolu.. hath the same virtue with the former. 1789 W. Buchan *Dom. Med.* App. (1790) 697 Tincture of the Balsam of Tolu. 1855 Bailey *Spir. Leg.* in *Mystic*, etc. (ed. 2) 81 Not less renowned Than lote, nepenthes, moly, or tolu. 1858 Hogg *Veg. Kingd.* 282 Balsam of Tolu is a stimulating tonic, with a peculiar tendency to the pulmonary organs. 1871 Garrod *Mat. Med.* (ed. 3) 210–11 *Balsamum Tolutanum.* Tolu Balsam..or Balsam of Tolu Tree. 1912 J. Terry & Sons *Let.*, We can trace their manufacture as Tolu Lozenges for about 100 years.

**Tolu-,** the prec. word as a formative element in chemical terms (first in Ger. *toluin*, Berzelius 1842, whence in Eng. *toluol* 1845, *toluene* 1871). **To·luate,** a salt of toluic acid, as toluate of calcium, $C_{16}H_{14}Ca''O_4$. **Toluene** (tǭ·liu,īn) [so named because obtained by Deville 1841, by the dry distillation of tolu balsam], $C_7H_8$ = Benzylic hydride, $C_7H_7.H$, a colourless very mobile strongly refracting liquid, with a smell like benzene and a burning taste; discovered by Pelletier and Walter, 1837; the source of many compounds and substitution products, into the names of which it enters, e. g. *chlorotoluene, methyltoluene, toluenesulphuric*, etc.; hence **Tolue·nic** *a.*, as *toluenic sulphydrate.* **Toluic** (tǭliū·ik) *a.* [*tolu*(*ene* + -ic], in *toluic* or *toluylic acid*, $C_8H_8O_2$, an aromatic acid, homologous with benzoic acid, prepared from toluene, cymene, or xylene; so *toluic aldehyde*, $C_8H_7OH$, *toluic chloride*, $C_8H_7OCl$, *toluic ether*, etc. **To·luides,** compounds homologous with the anilides, derived from toluidine salts by abstraction of water, e. g. *aceto-toluide.* **Tolu·idine,** also called *ami·doto·luene*, and formerly *toluylia*, $C_7H_7(NH_2)$, a crystalline base, produced by the action of sulphydric acid on nitrotoluene, solidifying in snow-white crystals, which gradually turn brown on contact with the air; it is the source of numerous compounds, e. g. *a·zotolu·idine, phe nyltolu·idine*, etc. **To·luol,** earlier name of *toluene.* **Toluo·xyl,** $C_8H_7O$, the radical of toluic acid and its derivatives. **Tolu·ric** *a.* [Uric], in *toluric acid*, $C_{10}H_{11}NO_3$, also called *toluglycic acid*, homologous with hippuric acid, produced in the passage of toluic acid through the animal body; its salts are **Tolu·rates. Toluyl** (tǭ·liu,il) [-yl], the radical, $C_8H_9$; hence **Toluy·lic** *a.*, of or belonging to toluyl, as *toluylic alcohol*, $C_8H_9OH$, etc.

1860 Kopp in *Phil. Trans.* CL. 262 *Toluate of Ethyl.. $C_{20}H_{12}O_4$. 1868 Watts *Dict. Chem.* V. 862 A mixture of toluate and formate of calcium yields by distillation toluic aldehyde, $C_8H_8O$. 1871 *Jrnl. Chem. Soc.* XXIV. 680 On the determination of the chemical position in some *Toluene derivatives. 1887 *Standard* 16 Sept. 3/3 The toluene was the root substance from which..saccharine was prepared. 1894 *Daily News* 26 Jan. 5/4 One ton of good cannel coal, when distilled in gas retorts, leaves twelve gallons of coal-tar, from which are produced a pound of benzine, a pound of toluene, a pound and a-half of phenol, six pounds of naphthalene, a small quantity of xylene, and half-a-pound of anthracene for dyeing purposes. 1857 Miller *Elem. Chem.* III. 430 In the benzoic series the existence of three homologous terms,..the benzoic, the *toluic, and the cuminic series. *Ibid.* 475 But the acid.., the *toluic* (or toluylic), is known. 1873 Watts *Fownes' Chem.* (ed. 11) 816 Toluic Acid is derived from dimethylbenzene. 1880 *Nature* XXI. 218/2 A toluic alcohol. 1850 Daubeny *Atom. The.* viii. (ed. 2) 243 Methylaniline being identical with *toluidine, an alkali obtained from the balsam of Tolu. 1857 Miller *Elem. Chem.* III. 467 Benzo-hydrochloric ether when heated in a sealed tube with ammonia furnishes the volatile base toluidine. 1866 Roscoe *Elem. Chem.* 348 A basic substance..analogous to aniline, and called amido-toluol, or Toluidine. 1845–8 Noad in *Mem. & Proc. Chem. Soc.* III. 422 Proposed the more appropriate name of *toluol. 1857 Miller *Elem. Chem.* III. 479 When balsam of tolu is distilled, it yields benzoic ether and a hydrocarbon..termed toluole. 1863 Tyndall *Heat* i. 20 Let us compare in this respect toluol and water. 1866 Roscoe *Elem. Chem.* 335 A series of bodies, isomeric with these toluol compounds, exists. 1891 *Anthony's Photogr. Bull.* IV. 415 Formula for the production of toluol matt varnish. 1868 Watts *Dict. Chem.* V. 869 *Toluric acid crystallises from boiling water in colourless laminæ; from alcohol in trimetric prisms. *Ibid.*, *Toluyl. $C_8H_9$. The radicle of toluylic alcohol and its allied compounds; isomeric with xylyl. 1873 Ralfe *Phys. Chem.* Introd. 19 Benzene $C_6H_6$ and Toluene $C_7H_8$ are the most important members of this series...From them are derived the important monad radicals phenyl $C_6H_5$ and toluyl $C_7H_7$. 1896 *Allbutt's Syst. Med.* I. 196 The action on the blood of certain poisons, such as arseniuretted hydrogen and toluyl-endiamine. 1862 Miller *Elem. Chem.* (ed. 2) III. 462 *Toluylia is a fusible crystalline solid, which boils at 388°. 1857 *Toluylic [see *toluic*].

† **To-lu·g,** *v. Obs.* Also 4–5 to-logg. [f. To-[2] + Lug *v.*] *trans.* To lug or pull about.

1362 Langl. *P. Pl.* A. ii. 192 Liȝtliche Lyȝere leop a-wey þennes, Lurkede [*v.r.* lurkynge] þorw lones, to-logged [*v.r.* to-luggid, B. ii. 216 to-lugged] of Monye.

† **Tolu·tan,** *a. Obs. rare.* [ad. mod.L. *Tolūtānus* of Tolu.] Of Tolu, as *Tolutan balsam.*

1681 tr. *Willis' Rem. Med. Wks.* Vocab., *Tolutan balsom* ..brought from the Indies.

† **Toluta·tion.** *Obs. rare.* Also **toll-.** [f. stem of L. *tolūtim* adv. 'at a trot' + -ation; cf. *tolutārius* adj. trotting.] *prop.* Trotting; but used by Sir T. Browne, Butler, and others, for 'ambling'; in later use only as a humorous pedantry. So † **Tolu·tate** (toll-) *v.* (*humorous*), *intr.* to trot (or amble); † **Toluti·loquence** (*rare*—[0]) [L. *tolūtiloquentia*], talking 'at a trot', voluble speech.

1646 Sir T. Browne *Pseud. Ep.* iv. vi. 193 Whether they move *per latera*, that is, two legs of one side together, which is Tollutation or ambling; or *per diametrum*,..which is Succussation or trotting. 1656 Blount *Glossogr.*, *Tolutation*.., an ambling pace, a going easie...*Tolutiloquence*.., a smooth or nimble kinde of speaking. 1663 Butler *Hud.* i. ii. 47 They rode, but Authors having not Determined whether Pace or Trot (That is to say, whether Tollutation, As they do term 't, or Succussation) We leave it, and go on. 1755 Johnson, *Tolutation*, the act of pacing or ambling. 1796 R. L. Edgeworth in *Life* (1821) II. 153 You compose in your chaise, and I on horseback, which..is the reason why your lines roll so smoothly, and mine partake so much of Tolutation. 1803 Fessenden *Terrible Tractoration* 39 We'll jog along in plain narration; And tollutate o'er turnpike path.

**Tolvet(t,** variant of Tovet, two-peck measure.

† **Toly,** *v. Obs.* [Obs. by-form of Toil *v.*[1] Cf. the similar 'oly or oyl', 'bolyyn or boylyn', 'spoylyn or spolyon', 'spoylyng or spolyynge'; also *assolye* = Assoil, and the Sc. form *tulȝie*, Tuilyie.] = Toil *v.*[1] 1, to dispute, argue, *esp.* to contend or plead in a lawsuit.

*c* 1440 *Promp. Parv.* 345/1 Mootyn, or tolyon (*P.* motyn, or pletyn), *discepto, placito.* Motynge, or tolyynge, or pleytynge, *disceptacio.* *Ibid.* 496/1 Tolyon, or motyn.

**Toly,** variant of Tuly *a. Obs.*

**Tolyl** (tǭ·lil). *Chem.* [f. Tolu + -yl.] A hypothetical monatomic radical, $C_7H_7$, isomeric with cresyl, called also benzyl, which may be supposed to exist in benzylic alcohol, toluene, and other compounds. Entering into the names of many compounds and substitution products, e. g. *tolyl-* or *benzyl-acetamide, tolyl-carbamide, tolyl-sulphurous, tolylene*, $C_7H_6$ = benzylene, *tolylene-diamine*, etc. Hence **Toly·lic** *a.*

1868 Watts *Dict. Chem.* V. 870 The name *benzyl* is the

most convenient for it, as tolyl is too much like toluyl. *Ibid.*, Tolylic or benzylic bromide.

**Tolypeutine** (tǫlipiū·təin), *a.* and *sb. Zool.* [f. mod.L. *Tolypeutes* + -INE[1].] **a.** *adj.* Belonging to the genus *Tolypeutes* of armadillos. **b.** *sb.* An armadillo of this genus.

**1885** *Stand. Nat. Hist.* (1888) V. 50 The Apars, or Tolypeutines, exhibit the extreme of modification in the family.

**Tolypyrin** (tǫlipəiə·rin). *Pharm.* [f. TOLYL, after *antipyrin*.] The compound $C_{12}H_{14}N_2O$ (*tolyl-dimethyl-pyr-azol-on*), the homologue of antipyrin.

**1893** *Brit. Med. Jrnl.* 25 Mar. 47/3 In acute rheumatism tolypyrin produced a similar effect to that observed after antipyrin. *Ibid.*, Tolypyrin is excreted in the urine.

**Tolzey**: see the historical form TOLSEL.

**Tom** (tǫm), *sb.* Forms: 4–6 tomme, (5 thomme, 6 thom), 6– Tom.

**1.** With capital T: A familiar shortening of the Christian name *Thomas*; often a generic name for any male representative of the common people; esp. in *Tom and Tib* (cf. *Jack and Jill*); *Tom, Dick, and Harry*, any men taken at random from the common run; *Blind Tom*, blind-man's-buff.

**1377**– [see 7 c]. **1588** SHAKS. *L. L. L.* v. ii. 924 Dicke the Shepheard blowes his naile; And Tom beares Logges into the hall. **1596** — 1 *Hen. IV*, II. iv. 9, I am sworn brother to a leash of Drawers, and can call them by their names, as Tom, Dicke, and Francis. **1606** *Choice, Chance*, etc. (1881) 72 When Tom and Tib, were in their true delight, And he lou'd her, and she held him full deere. **1749** FIELDING (*title*) Tom Jones. **1790** DIBDIN *Song, Poor Tom* i, Here, a sheer hulk, lies poor Tom Bowling. **1815** *Farmer's Almanack* (Boston, Mass.) in Kittredge *Old Farmer* (1904) 88 So he hired Tom, Dick and Harry, and at it they all went. **1818** in *J. Adams' Wks.* (1856) X. 351 Tom, Dick, and Harry were not to censure them and their Council. **1857** HUGHES (*title*) Tom Brown's School-days. **1865** ALEX. SMITH *Summer in Skye* I. 46 Thereafter Tom, Jack and Harry; for every cab, carriage and omnibus..is now allowed to fall in. **1891** Tom, Dick, and Harry [see DICK *sb.*[1] 1]. **1909** HEALEY *Sp. in Ho. of Comm.* 3 Sept., He never could understand this system of playing Blind Tom with the House of Commons—especially in a taxing statute.

†**b.** = *Tom o' Bedlam*: see 7 c. *Obs.*

**1561** AWDELAY *Frat. Vacab.* 3 An Abraham man is he that ..fayneth hym selfe mad..and nameth himselfe poore Tom. **1605** SHAKS. *Lear* III. iv. 51 Who giues any thing to poore Tom? *Ibid.* 59 Blisse thy fiue Wits, Toms a cold.., Do poore Tom some charitie, whom the foule Fiend vexes. **1682–3** DIXON *Canidia* I. 11, We treat mad-Bedlams, Toms, and Besses, With ceremonies and caresses.

**c.** A clown; cf. TOM-FOOL b.

**1820** *Sporting Mag.* VI. 284 Two or three of the company called toms or clowns.

†**2.** The knave of trumps in the game of gleek.

**1655**, *a* **1659** [see TIB *sb.* 2]. **1680** COTTON *Compl. Gamester* vi. 65 The Ace [of trumps] is called Tib, the Knave Tom.

**3.** As the name of some exceptionally large bells, esp. in *great, mighty Tom, Tom of Lincoln, Tom of Christ Church, of Oxford, Tom of Exeter*, etc.

**1630** WHITE in Rimbault *Rounds, Catches*, etc. 30 (Farmer) Great Tom is cast; And Christ Church bells ring..And Tom is last. **1635** R. JOHNSON *Tom a Lincolne* ii. (1682) B iij, He sent..a thousand pounds..to be bestowed upon a great Bell to be rung at his Funeral, which Bell he caused to be called Tom a Lincoln, after his own Name. **1682** H. ALDRICH *Upon Christ Church Bells Oxf.*, The Devil a man Will leave his can, Till he hears the mighty Tom. **1685** WOOD *Life* 7 July (O. H. S.) III. 151 And another [bonfire] in Ch. Ch. great quadrangle, at which time Great Tom rang out. **1705** HICKERINGILL *Priest-cr.* I. (1721) 63 Whose Tongue was as clamorous and loud almost as Tom a Lincoln. **1787** [see TINKLER 2]. **1839** *Penny Cycl.* XIV. 8/2 The old bell, called the Tom of Lincoln..being exceeded only by 'Mighty Tom' of Oxford..and 'Great Tom' of Exeter. **1886** RUSKIN *Præterita* I. xi. 369, I..amused myself till Tom rang in.

**4. a.** (usually *long tom.*) A long trough formerly used in gold-washing: see quot. 1859. Sometimes applied to the rocker or 'cradle'.

**1855** [see LONG TOM 2]. **1859** CORNWALLIS *Panorama New World* I. 135 The Long Tom..consists of a trough ten or twelve feet in length, by sixteen inches in width, and tilted so that water may flow rapidly down it. **1874** RAYMOND *Statist. Mines & Mining* 20 Inefficient implements having been largely superseded..by the long-tom and the sluice. **1890** 'R. BOLDREWOOD' *Miner's Right* xiv, We drove and raised our wash-dirt.., and afterwards separated it..by the old-fashioned expedient of a 'tom'. **1891** E. ROPER *By Track & Trail* xxii. 326 They have to use quicksilver in their Long Toms and cradles to save it [gold].

**b.** *Long Tom*: a long gun; *esp.* a naval gun mounted amidships, as distinct from the shorter guns of the broadside: see LONG TOM 1.

**1867**– [see LONG TOM 1]. **1888** CHURCHWARD *Blackbirding* 44 The ship was armed with four carronades on each side, and a 'long Tom' trained fore and aft, in the bows.

**5.** *Old Tom*: a name for gin. *slang.*

**1823** 'JON BEE' *Slang Dict.* 130 *Old Tom*, he is of the feminine gender in most other nations than this: 'tis a cask or barrel, containing strong gin, and thence by a natural transition..the liquor itself. **1832** EGAN *Bk. Sports* 268 Tis the 'liquor of life', with 'spirits' to boot—'Old Tom', is better than gold. **1836**– [see OLD D. 4].

**6.** The male of various beasts and birds; perh. first for a male cat: see TOM CAT; cf. also 8 a.

**1791** HUDDESFORD *Salmag.* (1793) 141 Cats..Of titles obsolete, or yet in use, Tom, Tybert, Roger, Rutterkin, or Puss. **1826–8** [see TABBY *sb.* 2 b]. **1884** *Bazaar, Exch. & Mart* 17 Dec. 2205/2 Hamburghs...Redcaps, four hens and tom, prize strain, handsome birds. **1893** G. D. LESLIE *Lett. to Marco* xxxii. 214 The tom [swan] is very gallant in defence of his mate. **1898** *Blackw. Mag.* Nov. 663/2 He be a tom. I've heard him crow. **1905** *Daily News* 24 Jan. 8/1 Tiger, their cat (a beautifully marked tabby tom, aged five).

**7.** Combinations and phrases. **a.** *attrib.* and *Comb.*: **tom-pin**, a very large pin (Halliwell 1847–78); **tom-plough** (*local, E. Anglia*), a double breasted plough; also called *tommy* and **tom-tommy**; †**tom-rig** [RIG *sb.*[4]], a strumpet; a romping girl, a tomboy; **tom-toe**, the great toe; **Tom tower**, a tower in which a great bell hangs; *spec.* at Oxford, the western tower of Christ Church; **Tom-trot** (**Trot, Tom-trod**), home-made toffee stretched or drawn out as it cools (Halliwell).

**1849** RAYNBIRD *Agric. Suff.* 301 The **tom* or *tommy* plough is a plough with a double breast for ridging, or for clearing out furrows. **1668** SHADWELL *Sullen Lovers* Pref. a ij b, An impudent ill bred *tomrig for a Mistress. **1728** DENNIS *On Pope's Rape of Lock* 16 The author represents Belinda a fine, modest, well-bred lady: and yet in the very next canto she appears an arrant ramp and tomrigg. **1823** E. MOOR *Suffolk Words*, **Tom toe*, the great toe of either foot. **1857** in DUNGLISON *Med. Lex.* **1853** 'C. BEDE' *Verdant Green* I. iii, As he looks across Christ Church Meadows and rolls past the *Tom Tower. **1844** DISRAELI *Coningsby* I. ix, I want toffy; I have been eating *Tom Trot all day. **1866** [CHARL. M. TUCKER] *Parlt. in Play-room* x. 93 A plateful of brown, tempting tom-trot, otherwise known by the title of toffy.

**b.** As the first element in a personal name applied allusively, as *Tom Astoner* (*Estenor*), *Tom Brown, Tom Dingle* (see quots.); **Tom Farthing**, a fool, simpleton; **Tom Pepper** (*Naut.*), a liar; **Tom Tailor**, the tailor generically; **Tom Tiler, Tyler**, any ordinary man; also, a henpecked husband; **Tom Towly**, a simpleton; **Tom Tram**, a buffoon, jester.

**1706** E. WARD *Wooden World Diss.* (1708) 80 It's barbarous..to have the Bread thus pick'd from our Mouths by little *Tom Estenors. **1867** SMYTH *Sailor's Word-bk.*, *Tom Astoners*, dashing fellows; from astound or 'astony', to terrify. **1812** J. H. VAUX *Flash Dict.*, **Tom Brown*, twelve in hand, in crib. **1711** *Brit. Apollo* III. No. 144. 3/1 Never yet Woman..had..such a poor wretched *Tom Dingle. **1689** SHADWELL *Bury F.* Prol. 21 For writing..silly Grubstreet Songs worse than *Tom Farthing. **1867** SMYTH *Sailor's Word-bk.*, **Tom Pepper*, a term for a liar. **1820** SCOTT *Monast.* xxv, 'We rend our hearts, and not our garments'. ..'The better..for yourselves, and the worse for Tom Tailor', said the baron. **1582** STANYHURST *Epitaphs* in *Æneis*, etc. (Arb.) 154 An Epitaph..such as oure vnlearned Rythmours ..make vpon thee death of euery *Tom Tyler. **1598** (*title*) Tom Tylere and his Wyfe. *a* **1625** FLETCHER *Woman's Prize* II. vi, She shall, Tom Tilers. **1582** STANYHURST *Æneis* Ded. (Arb.) 9 What *Tom Towly is so simple, that wyl not attempt, too bee a rithmoure? **1689** PRIOR *Ep. to F. Shephard* 172 All your wits, that fleer and sham, Down from don Quixote to *Tom Tram. *c* **1700** (*title*) The Mad Pranks of Tom Tram. **1739** 'R. BULL' tr. *Dedekindus' Grobianus* 39 To a Book..in Dutch, entituled, the Life of Uyle-Spegel, or Owl-glass; a Hero of equal Rank with Tom Tram in English.

**c.** Followed by another word denoting or alluding to something (esp. the action or character) distinguishing the person to whom it is applied, forming a *quasi*-proper name or nickname, and in various phrases with specific sense: as *Tom All-thumbs, Tom-ass, Tom(-a-)doodle, Tom Piper, Tom Tapster, Tom Tawny-coat, Tom Tell-troth* (*-truth*), *Tom Trifler, Tom True-tongue, Tom Truth, Tom Two-tongued*; **Tom-a-Stiles**: see quot. 1785, and cf. JOHN-A-STILES; **Tom Bray's bilk**, at Cribbage: see quot.; **Tom-come-tickle-me**, an old card-game; **Tom Cony** (**Conney**), a simpleton, ninny; **Tom Cox's traverse** (*Naut.*): see quot. 1867; **Tom Double**, a shuffler, an equivocator; **Tom Drum**: see DRUM *sb.*[1] 3 b; **Tom Long**, one who takes a long time in coming, or in finishing his tale; **Tom of all trades**, a Jack of all trades; **Tom o' Bedlam**, a madman, a deranged person discharged from Bedlam (see BEDLAM 5) and licensed to beg; **Tom Pat** (*slang*), a parson, a hedge-priest (cf. PATRICO); also, a shoe; **Tom Poker**, †**Tom Po**, a nursery bugbear, a bogy; **Tom tumbler**, name for an imp or devil. See also TOM AND JERRY, TOM-FOOL, TOM-NODDY, TOM THUMB, TOM TIDDLER'S GROUND.

**1598** I. M. *Health Gent. Profession Servingmen* B iij, The Clowne, the Slouen, and *Tom althummes. **1611** J. FIELD *Panegyr. Verses* in Coryat *Crudities*, '*Tom-Asse may passe, but, for all his long eares, No such rich jewels as our Tom he weares. **1772** G. A. STEVENS *Songs Comic & Satyr.* 246 From John o' Nokes to *Tom o' Stiles, What is it all but Fooling? **1785** GROSE *Dict. Vulg. T.* s.v. *Nokes*, John-a-Nokes and Tom-a-Stiles.., fictitious names commonly used in law proceedings. **1812** J. H. VAUX *Flash Dict.*, **Tom Bray's Bilk*, laying out ace and deuce at cribbage. **1819–20** W. IRVING *Sketch-Bk., Litt. Brit.* (1865) 310 We played at All-Fours, Pope-Joan, *Tom-come-tickle-me, and other choice old games. *a* **1700** B. E. *Dict. Cant. Crew*, **Tom Conney*, a very silly fellow. **1840** R. H. DANA *Bef. Mast* xii, Every man who has been three months at sea knows how to 'work *Tom Cox's traverse'—' three turns round the long-boat, and a pull at the scuttled-butt'. This morning every-thing went in his way. **1867** SMYTH *Sailor's Word-bk.*, *Tom Cox's traverse*, up one hatchway and down another: others say 'three turns round the long boat, and a pull at the scuttle'. It means the work of an artful dodger, all jaw, and no good in him. **1708** E. WARD *Terræ-Fil.* v. 10 That one *Tom-doodle of a Son, who..if he happens to be Decoy'd..to fling away Two Pence in Strong Drink, he Talks of nothing but his Mother. **1710** — *Brit. Hud.* 31 Whether on him who'd ..labour'd like a Tom-a-doodle, To place the Rump above the Noddle. **1705** *Charac. of Sneaker* 4 He's for a single Ministry, that he may play the *Tom Double under it. **1707** *Reflex. upon Ridicule* II. 145 Tom-doubles are to be avoided as Enemies that would betray you. **1577, 1603** *Tom Drum's entertainment [see DRUM *sb.*[1] 3 b]. **1609** C. BUTLER *Fem. Mon.* iv. (1623) I ij, They gently giue them Tom Drum's entertainment. **1631** W. FOSTER *Hoplochrisma-Spongus* 43 Surely this is *Tom Long the carrier, who will never doe his errand. **1785** GROSE *Dict. Vulg. T.*, *Tom Long*, a tiresome story teller; it is coming by Tom Long, the carrier, said of any thing that has been long expected. **1631** T. POWELL (*title*) *Tom of All Trades. *Ibid.* Ep. Ded. 13 Our Tom of all Trades hereupon Askt what was his condition. **1605** SHAKS. *Lear* I. ii. 148 *Tom o' Bedlam. **1671** GLANVILL *Disc. M. Stubbe* 28 [I] am afraid that some will think, that I am not well in my Wits, because I seriously answer such a Tom of Bedlam. *a* **1691** AUBREY *Nat. Hist. Wilts.* II. iv. (1847) 93 Till the breaking out of the civill warres, Tom ô Bedlam's did travell about the countrey. They had been poore distracted men that had been putt into Bedlam, where recovering to some sobernesse they were licentiated to goe a begging. **1880** SHORTHOUSE *J. Inglesant* (1881) I. 72 Wandering beggars and halfwitted people called 'Tom o' Bedlams' who were a recognised order of mendicants. *c* **1700** *Street Robberies Consider'd*, *Tom Pat, a parson. **1579** SPENSER *Sheph. Cal.* Oct. 78 *Tom Piper makes vs better melodie. **1616** W. BROWNE *Brit. Past.* II. ii. 32 So haue I seene Tom Piper stand vpon our village greene. **1744** GREY *Hudibras* II. 207 *note*, You are afraid that you shall meet *Tom Po. *a* **1825** FORBY *Voc. E. Anglia*, *Tom Poker*, ..the great bugbear and terror of naughty children, who inhabits dark closets [etc.]. **1902** *Longm. Mag.* Nov. 41, I tells him them days o' Tom-pokers be gone. **1592** GREENE *Upst. Courtier* Wks. (Grosart) XI. 275 Last to you *Tom tapster, that tap your smale cannes of beere to the poore, and yet fil them half ful of froth. *c* **1600** DAY *Begg. Bednall Gr.* I. iii, I think not but thou and this *Tom Tawny coat here gulls me. **1600** J. LANE *Tom Tel-Troth* 713 But sooth to say, *Tom-teltroth will not lie, We heere haue blaz'd Englands iniquitie. **1622** (*title*) Tom Tell Troath, or a Free Discourse touching the Manners of the Tyme. **1847–78** HALLIWELL, *Tom-tell-trouth*, a true guesser. **1377** LANGL. *P. Pl.* B. IV. 17 And also *tomme trewe-tonge-telle-me-no-tales. **1581** J. BELL *Haddon's Answ. Osor.* 68 b, They will all condemne you for *tomme trifler. **1542** UDALL *Erasm. Apoph.* II. 179 b, For his malaparte toungne called at home..Parrhesiastes, (as ye woulde saye in englyshe), *Thom trouthe, or plain Sarisbuirie. **1550** LATIMER *Serm. at Stamford* I. 94 Maister we know that thou art Tomme truth, and thou tellest the very truth, and sparest no man. **1580** G. HARVEY *Let. to Spenser* iv. Wks. (Grosart) I. 83 Tell me, in Tom Trothes earnest, what [he] sayth. **1393** LANGL. *P. Pl.* C. XXIII. 162 *note*, Here syre was a sysour þat neuere swor treuthe, Or *tomme [*v.r.* thomme] two-tounged ateynt at eche enqueste.

**8. a.** In names of animals, denoting the male; see also TOM CAT.

**1762** T. BRYDGES *Homer Travest.* (1772) 192 And, like Tom puss, o'er pantiles dance. **1859** BARTLETT *Dict. Amer.* (ed. 2), *Tom-Dog*, male dogs, as well as cats, take the prefix 'tom', in some parts of the West. **1871** MRS. STOWE *Old-town Stories* 92, I never heard that a tom-turkey would set on eggs. **1875** *Sussex Gloss.*, *Tom*, any cock bird, as a tom-turkey or a tom-parrot. **1890** *Glouc. Gloss.*, *Tom*, used to denote the male of birds, as 'tom-bird', 'tom-chicken', 'tom-pheasant'. **1893** G. D. LESLIE *Lett. to Marco* xxxii. 214 The tom-swan..landed on a likely spot. **1905** *Daily Chron.* 31 Oct. 4/7 In his part [Hampshire] people spoke of tom-rats, tom-rabbits, tom-mice, tom-hedgehogs [etc.].

**b.** In familiar or local names of species: **Tom-hoop** [cf. HOOP *sb.*[3] 2], **Tom-noup** [cf. NOPE[1]] *dial.*, the great tit (*Parus major*); **Tom-pot, Tompot**, name in Cornwall for the gattorugine, a species of blenny; in Devonshire, for the guinea-fowl, from its cry; in Devon and Somerset, a well-known kind of red-cheeked apple (also called **tom-put**); **Tom-pudding**, the little grebe; **Tom-tailor**, the crane-fly; in East Anglia, the stormy petrel; **Tom Titmouse**, = TOMTIT. See also TOM-COD.

**1847–78** HALLIWELL, **Tom-Noup*, the titmouse. *Salop.* **1837** J. F. PALMER *Gloss. Dialog. in Devon Dial.* (E.D.D.), *Tom-put. **1863** COUCH *Brit. Fishes* II. 219 Gattorugine ..is known to fishermen of the west of England by the homely appellation of Tompot. **1891** *Hartland* (Devon) *Gloss.*, *Tom pot*, a name sometimes given to the guinea-fowl on account of its peculiar cry. **1904** *Longm. Mag.* Apr. 489 Cheeks as rosy as a 'tomput' apple. **1848** *Zoologist* VI. 2290 The little grebe or 'dipper' or 'dobber' or '*Tom pudding'. **1853** HICKIE tr. *Aristoph.* (1887) I. 37 A Bœotian might stick it in a *tom-tailor. **1856** P. THOMPSON *Hist. Boston* List Provinc., *Tom-tailor*, the Daddy-long-legs. **1885** SWAINSON *Provinc. Names Birds* 212 They [Stormy Petrels] are called Tom tailors by the Lowestoft and Yarmouth fishermen. **1576** GASCOIGNE *Philomene* 26 Sometimes I wepe To see *Tom Tyttimouse, so much set by. *c* **1776** *Roxb. Ball.* (1889) VI. 308 Says Tom Tit-Mouse then, 'There be some men That will change nine times a day'.

Hence **Tom** *v.* (*nonce-wd.*), *trans.* to address familiarly as 'Tom'; **To·mling**, a small or young tom cat; **To·mship** (*humorous*), the personality of a 'Tom'.

**1821** SOUTHEY *Let. to C. Bedford* 3 Apr., Moved by compassion (his [a cat's] colour and his tomship also being taken into consideration), I consented to give him an asylum. **1821** *Ibid.* 29 Apr., We are promised to succeed him a black Tomling. **1900** S. J. WEYMAN *Sophia* xxiv, 'You may Tom me, you don't alter it', he answered.

**Tom**, var. TAUM; obs. form of TOOM *sb.*[1]

**Tomahawk** (tǫ·măhǭk), *sb.* Also 7 tamahauk(e, -hawk, tomahauke, 8 tommahauk,

**(tomahaw, tomhog)**, 8–9 **tomohawk**, (9 **tommy-hawk**). [a. Renâpe (N. Amer. Indian of Virginia) *tämähāk* (given by Capt. J. Smith as *tomahack*), apocopated form of *tämähākan*, 'what is used for cutting, cutting utensil', from *tämähāken* 'he uses for cutting', from *tämäham* 'he cuts' (W. R. Gerard in *American Anthropologist* X. 1908, p. 277). Cognate with Pamptico (Carolinian) *tommahick*, and with the full forms, Mohegan *tummahegan*, Delaware *tamoihecan*, Abenaki *tamahigan*, Micmac *tŭmeegŭn* (tămī·găn), Passamaqoddy *tumhigen*.]

**1.** The ax of the North American Indians, used as a weapon of war and the chase, and also as a tool and agricultural implement; in English use the word is usually applied to it as the war-ax.

It consists of a wooden shaft about 2½ feet long, with a head originally formed of a long hard stone sharpened at one end, or of a piece of copper, or of the horn of a deer, but after the advent of white traders usually of iron (*trade tomahawk*). Sometimes the shaft was hollow, and a bowl was fashioned at the back of the head (*pipe-tomahawk*).

[**1612** Capt. Smith *Map Virginia* (Arb.) 44 *Tomahacks*. Axes. *Tockahacks*. Pickaxes.] **1634** W. Wood *New Eng. Prosp.* II. i. 58 [They] beate them downe with their right hand Tamahaukes, and left hand Iavelins. [**1701** C. Wolley *Jrnl. New York* (1860) 36 They dig their ground with a Flint, called in their Language tom-a-hea-kan.] **1705** Beverley *Virginia* I. iii. (1722) 39 Knocking the English unawares on the Head, some with their Hatchets, which they call *Tommahauks*, others with the Hows and Axes of the English themselves. **1715** *Phil. Trans.* XXIX. 308 Targets, Tomahaws, poisoned Daggers. **1716** B. Church *Hist. Philip's War* (1865) I. 82 A great surly look'd fellow took up his Tomhog, or wooden Cutlash, to kill Mr. Church, but some others prevented him. **1756** Washington *Lett.* Writ. 1889 I. 393 The wampum and tomahawks I have purchased. **1780** Edmondson *Heraldry* II. Gloss., *Tomahawk*, an Indian war-ax. **1809** A. Henry *Trav.* 41 They walked in single file, each with his tomahawk in one hand, and scalping-knife in the other. **1851** Mayne Reid *Scalp Hunt.* xxvii, They [Indians] break the shanks [of buffalo] with their tomahawks. **1865** Lubbock *Preh. Times* iv. (1869) 91 The North American stone axe or tomahawk served not merely as an implement, but also as a weapon.

**b.** erron. applied to a war-club or knobkerry.

**1674** Josselyn *Voy. New Eng.* 147 Their other weapons are Tamahawks which are staves two foot and a half long with a knob at the end as round as a bowl. *a* **1817** T. Dwight *Trav. New Eng.*, etc. (1821) I. 118 Another of their principal weapons was the well known Tomahawk, or war-club... Since the arrival of the English, they have used fire-arms. To these they add a long knife: and a small battle-axe, to which they have transferred the name of Tomahawk.

**c.** *transf.* Applied to similar weapons used by savages elsewhere; also *Naut.* a pole-ax used by sailors; in Australia, the usual word for *hatchet*.

**1670** Narborough *Jrnl.* in *Acc. Sev. Late Voy.* I. (1694) 23 An Indian Club..called by the Caribbe-Indians at Surinam a Tomahauke. **1681** Grew *Musæum* IV. ii. 367 A Tamahauke, or Brazilian Fighting-Club. **1802** J. Jones in *Naval Chron.* VII. 348, I saw him chop at him with a.. tomahawk. **1833** Marryat *P. Simple* xxxv, In a moment, pikes, tomahawks, cutlasses, and pistols were seized,..and our men poured into the eighty-gun ship, and in two minutes the decks were cleared, and all the Dons pitched below. **1866** Livingstone *Last Jrnls.* (1873) I. i. 20 For they are accustomed to clearing spaces for gardens,.. using tomahawks well adapted for the work. **1875** Bedford *Sailor's Pocket Bk.* vi. (ed. 2) 229 A couple of tomahawks will be found useful. **1880** Fison & Howitt *Kamilaroi* 206 The [Australian] aborigines have obtained iron tomahawks. **1898** Morris *Austral Eng.* s. v., In Australia the word *hatchet* has practically disappeared, and the word *Tomahawk* to describe it is in every-day use. It is also applied to the stone hatchet of the Aboriginals.

**d.** Applied locally to various kinds of rural tools and agricultural implements: see quots.

**1830** *Q. Jrnl. Agric.* III. 653 Mortises made by a centre-bit leave an intermediate piece between the apertures. This is taken out by the tomahawk, a tool made for the purpose. One end is a sharp stout pointed knife, which cuts each side of the middle piece left in the mortise, and the other end hooks out the piece not dislodged by the knife. **1881** Miss Jackson *Shropsh. Word-bk.*, *Tummy-awk*, a dung-fork, carried at the back of the cart, and used to scrape out the manure, on the land, as it is required. **1893** *Wiltshire Gloss.*, *Tommy-hawk*, a potato hacker.

**e.** *fig.* As the imaginary instrument of a savage attack or vindictive onslaught.

**1805** Surr *Winter in Lond.* (1806) II. 195 His meek nature..would..sink beneath the tomahawk of such a barbarian as the writer of the article in question. **1836** H. Rogers *J. Howe* vii. (1863) 183 Such a temper is rare at any period; but in that age of fierce and savage controversy, of the tomahawk and scalping-knife, it was indeed a phenomenon. **1897** *Daily News* 30 Sept. 8/2 He flourished the rhetorical tomahawk over 'those false teachers who say that the articles of Christian faith are illusions'.

**2.** Phrases. *To blow tomahawks*, of the wind, to blow with cutting violence. *To bury* or *lay aside the tomahawk*: to lay down one's arms, to cease from hostilities. *To dig up*, *raise*, or *take up the tomahawk*: to take up arms in warfare, to commence hostilities. Cf. Hatchet *sb.* 2.

**1775** Adair *Amer. Ind.* 239, I persuaded the Choktah to take up the bloody tomohawk against those perfidious French. **1806** Pike *Sources Mississ.* (1810) 86 Grateful that the two nations had laid aside the tomahawk at my request. **1812** Brackenridge *Views Louisiana* (1814) 123 They may come here in peace, or for the purpose of trade, but it will be far hence that they will dare to raise the tomahawk. **1848** Bartlett *Dict. Amer.* s. v., It was and is the custom of the Indians to go through the ceremony of burying the tomahawk, when they made peace; when they went to war, they dug it up again. Hence the phrases 'to bury the tomahawk', and 'to dig up the tomahawk',..sometimes used by political speakers and writers. **1903** Ld. R. Gower *Rec. & Remin.* 297 The weather is boisterous; it blows tomahawks and tornadoes.

**3.** *attrib.* and *Comb.*, as *tomahawk-blow*, *-critic*, *-dance*, *-pipe* (quot. 1860), *tongue*; **tomahawk improvement**, an 'improvement' of a slight character, made to secure a right of pre-emption (Thornton); so **tomahawk settler**.

**1873** R. Brown *Races Man.* I. 235 Until the *tomahawk-blow puts an end to him. **1886** J. Payn *Heir of Ages* xxxviii, He was not..a *tomahawk critic; he thought less of being smart himself..than of doing justice to a book. **1856** Emerson *Eng. Traits, Ability* Wks. (Bohn) II. 39 They have no Indian taste for a *tomahawk-dance. **1842** L. Munsell in *M. Cutler's Life*, etc. (1888) I. 133 They were determined to hold the lands by what is called '*tomahawk improvements'. **1860** Domenech *Deserts N. Amer.* II. 272 The Comanches, in Texas,..have *tomahawk-pipes (small hatchets, the head of which is made hollow like the bowl of a pipe, and the handle perforated in its whole length to serve for a tube). **1907** *Q. Rev.* July 161 A recipe for *tomahawk punch. **1788** M. Cutler in *Life*, etc. (1888) I. 425 Stopped and breakfasted at a little clump of houses on the Indian side. They were *tomahawk settlers. **1849** C. Bronte *Shirley* x, Of whose observant faculties and *tomahawk tongue Caroline stood in awe.

Hence **To·mahawked** *a.*, provided or armed with a tomahawk.

**1895** K. Grahame *Golden Age* (1904) 3 A prairie studded with herds of buffalo, which it was our delight, moccasined and tomahawked, to ride down.

**Tomahawk** (tǫ·măhǭk), *v.* [f. prec. sb.]

**1.** *trans.* To strike, cut, or kill with a tomahawk.

**1755** *Gentl. Mag.* XXV. 579/2 Mac Swine was ordered by the Indian to make a fire, and upon his not doing it so readily or so nimbly as was expected, he was threatened to be tomohawk'd. **1769** *Middlesex Jrnl.* 14–16 Sept. 1/4 By six Indians, the man and woman were tomahawked and scalped. **1791** J. Long *Voy. Ind. Interpr.* 96 The instant the animal drops they tomahawk it. **1829** Southey *O. Newman* IV. 45 Stragglers tomahawk'd And scalp'd, or dragg'd away that they may die By piecemeal murder. **1889** H. H. Romilly *Verandah in N. Guinea* 74 They.. were treacherously tomahawked.

**b.** *fig.* To attack savagely or mercilessly in speech or (more usually) in writing; to 'cut up' or demolish in a review or criticism.

**1815** 'Agrestis' *Feudal Hall* xlv, [She] tomahawks me with sharp words. **1820** *Blackw. Mag.* VII. 388 He afterwards goes out of his way to tomahawk Dryden, for an allusion to Abraham in a dedication. **1895** *Daily News* 19 June 6/2 Her second daughter, Lady Charlotte,..wrote the book which Thackeray tomahawked.

**2.** To cut (a sheep) in shearing it. *Australia.*

**1859** H. Kingsley *G. Hamlyn* xx, Shearers were very scarce, and the poor sheep got fearfully 'tomahawked' by the new hands. **1872** Eden *My Wife & I in Queensland* iv. 96 Some men never get the better of this habit, but 'tomahawk' as badly after years of practice as when they first began. **1896** Paterson *Man fr. Snowy River* 162 The novice who..had tommyhawked half a score.

Hence **To·mahawking** *vbl. sb.* and *ppl. a.*; also **To·mahawker**, one who tomahawks (*lit.* and *fig.*).

**1819** *Metropolis* III. 69 The tomahawkers of the Edinburgh Review. **1833** *Boston*, etc. *Herald* 9 Apr. 2/1 We have not a tomahawking article in the whole number. **1839–40** W. Irving *Wolfert's R.* i. (1855) 2 They recreated themselves occasionally with a little tomahawking and scalping. **1862** *Times* 8 Apr. 11/4 A large body of scalping and tomahawking Indians. **1886** *Pall Mall G.* 2 Oct. 6/1 My father, ..noticing that the sheep were particularly badly shorn, remarked to the manager that 'it was mere tomahawking'. **1886** *Manch. Exam.* 3 Nov. 3/1 A return to a style of literary tomahawking which we had hoped was for ever extinct. **1897** *Athenæum* 20 Mar. 372 Lest he should find himself tomahawked instead of being the tomahawker.

**Tomal**, variant form of Tamal.

‖ **Tomalley** (tǫmæ·li, tǭmæ·li). Also **tomally**, **taumally**, **tomalline**. [According to J. Davies, 1666, a Carib word (see quot.); in F. *taumalin*, (Littré).] The fat or 'liver' of the North American lobster, which becomes green when cooked, and is then known as *tomalley sauce*.

**1666** J. Davies *Hist. Caribby Islands* II. xvi. 300 They call the inner part of the Crab *Taumaly*. *Ibid.*, *Carrib. Vocab.* Zz iv/1 Sauce, Taomali, or Taumali. **1864** Webster, *Tom-alley*, the liver of the lobster, which becomes green when boiled; called also *tom-alline*. **1882** Ogilvie, Tomalley, Tomalline.

¶ *erron.* A Spanish-American dish made of crushed Indian corn, etc.; properly Tamal.

**1860** Bartlett *Dict. Amer.*, *Tamal*, or *Tamauli*, a peculiar Spanish-American dish made up of a paste of crushed or ground maize, sometimes with minced meat added, when it is wrapped in the husks of maize and baked on the coals. *c* **1900** C. W. Greene *Let. to Editor*, When I was a youngster in Massachusetts, we called the gelatinous part of a baked maize pudding, the *tom-alley*. It somewhat resembles in appearance the *tom-alley* of the lobster; but in meaning it comes very near the Mexican, Cuban, and Southern U.S. use of *tamauli* or *tamalli* as the name of a kind of maize pudding.

‖ **Toman** [1] (tomā·n, tu·măn, tɒ·măn). Forms: 7– **toman**; also 6 **tumen**, **thuman**, 7 **tomana**, **thoman**, **thoma(u)nd**, **tomin**, **tumain**, **tummon**, 7–9 **tomaun**. [a. Pers. تومان, تمان, تمن *tūmān*, *tumān*, *tuman*, according to Devic, a Yuzbeg Tartar word (whence its unsettled form), lit. 'ten thousand'.]

**1.** Formerly among the Mongols, Tartars, etc., and thence in Persia and Turkey: The sum of ten thousand; also, a military division consisting of 10,000 men. Now *rare*.

**1599** Hakluyt *Voy.* II. i. 61 The lord of the same citie hath in yeerely reuenues for salt onely, fiftie Thuman of Balis, and one balis is worth a floren and a halfe of our coyne: insomuch that one Thuman of balis amounteth vnto the value of fifteene thousand florens. **1788** Gibbon *Decl. & F.* lxv. VI. 333 The fruitful territory of Cash, of which his fathers were the hereditary chiefs, as well as of a toman of ten thousand horse. **1877** J. M. Porteous *Turkey* 54 Numbering in Turkish custom was by tomans, ten thousands or myriads.

**2.** A Persian gold coin, nominally worth 10 silver krans or 10,000 dinars; formerly a money of account, which was constantly depreciated in value from £3 13*s.* (or more) *c* 1600 to its present (1912) value of 7*s.* 1*d.*: see quots.

**1566** A. Edwards in Hakluyt *Voy.* (1589) 378, I haue receiued 6. tumens in readie money: 200. shaughes is a tumen, reckoning euery shaugh for 6. pence Russe. **1613** Sherley *Trav. Persia* 72 Marganobeague..brought mee..a thousand Tomanas, which is sixteene thousand Duckets of our Money. **1623** *St. Papers, Col.* 212 Sold the Primrose for 400 tomans, every toman 3*l.* 6*s.* 4*d.* **1629** in Foster *Eng. Factories India* (1909) III. 354 Other men pay one keale or quart uppon every tummon. **1662** J. Davies tr. *Olearius' Voy. Ambass.* 300 When they [the Persians] are to name great Sums, they accompt by Tumains. **1686** W. Hedges *Diary* (Hakl. Soc.) I. 215 They were robbed of all their money, to the sum of 4 Tomauns. **1698** Fryer *Acc. E. India & P.* 222 He pays the King yearly Twenty two thousand Thomands, every Thomand making Three pound and a Noble in our Accompt. **1753** Hanway *Trav.* (1762) I. v. lxiv. 292 The toman, bistie, and denaer are imaginary... A toman is 10 hazardenaers.. Value in denaers, 10000. Weight in muscals, 50. **1811** Pinkerton *Mod. Geog.*, *Persia* ii. (ed. 3) 459 The whole revenue was by some estimated at 700,000 tomans, or about thirty-two millions of French livres. **1815** Elphinstone *Acc. Caubul* (1842) II. 269 The sum to be paid for a substitute.. generally is from five to seven tomauns (from 10*l.* to 14*l.*). **1845** Browning *Flight Duchess* xiv, The band-roll strung with tomans Which proves the veil a Persian woman's. **1858** Simmonds *Dict. Trade*, *Toman*, a conventional money of Persia of a very variable character..; it may be valued at about 12*s.* 6*d.* **1882** Floyer *Unexpl. Baluchistan* 505 Ali Abker engages to hire a saddle horse and three mules to Mr. Floyer..for fifteen days, for the sum of eight tomans (£3 16*s.*),..at the rate of two tomans each.

‖ **Toman** [2] (tǫ·măn). (*erron.* **tomhan.**) [Gaelic *toman* hillock, dim. of *tom* hill.] A hillock; a mound of earth. Often applied to mounds representing ancient glacial moraines, found in the heads of valleys in the Highlands.

**1811** Mrs. Grant *Superstit. Highl. Scot.* I. vii. 282 The children's nursery tales are full of wonders performed by the secret dwellers of these *tomhans*, or fairy hillocks. **1830** J. Wilson *Noct. Ambr.* Nov., Wks. 1856 III. 86 The Queen of the Fairies among the tomans of her ancient woods. **1854** H. Miller *Sch. & Schm.* v. (1858) 99 The western slopes of the valley are mottled by grassy tomhans—the moraines of some ancient glacier. **1876** D. Gorrie *Summ. & Wint. in Orkneys* iii. 121 Those huge boulders and gravel-knolls or tomans continued a mystery till the glacial theory.

**Tom and Jerry.** Names of the two chief characters in Egan's *Life in London*, 1821, and its continuation, 1828; whence in various allusive and attributive uses, esp. as name of a compound alcoholic drink, a kind of highly-spiced punch (U.S.); and *attrib.* in *Tom and Jerry shop* (Engl.), a low beer-house. Hence **Tom-and-Jerry** *v.*, *intr.* to drink and indulge in riotous behaviour, like young bloods of the Regency period; **Tom-and-Jerryism**, drunken roistering, window-breaking, and the like.

The title of Egan's original work (1821) is 'Life in London, or Days and Nights of Jerry Hawthorne and his elegant friend Corinthian Tom'; that of the continuation of 1828 is 'Finish to the Adventures of Tom, Jerry, and Logic', whence app. the order of the names in *Tom and Jerry*.

(*Tom and Jerry shop* was app. an expansion of the earlier *Jerry-shop* 'a low beer-house' (in *Preston Temperance Advocate* Mar. 1834, 18/2), which had no original connexion with Tom and Jerry.)

**1828** *Lights & Shades* I. 124 No drinking and raking. No Tom-and-Jerrying in those days. **1829** W. Irving in *Life & Lett.* (1864) II. 387 We are too apt to take our ideas of English life from such vulgar sources as Tom and Jerry, and we appear to be Tom and Jerrying it to perfection in New York. **1852** Mundy *Our Antipodes* (1857) 207 As the glazier prays for hail-storms, civic riots, and the revival of Tom-and-Jerryism, for his own private ends! **1862** Jerry Thomas *How to mix Drinks* (N.Y.) 69 [Recipe]. *Ibid.*, To deal out Tom and Jerry to Customers. *Ibid.*, Adepts at the bar in serving Tom and Jerry [etc.]. **1865** *Slang Dict.*, *Tom and Jerry* [ed. **1873** adds *shop*], a low drinking shop. **1880** *Barman's Man.* 47 [Recipe for Tom and Jerry]. **1884** S. Dowell *Taxation* II. 277 Free trade in beer in over 31,000 'Tom and Jerry' shops, as the new beer-houses and shops were termed. **1894** *Northumbld. Gloss.*, *Tom-and-Jerry*, a catcall. **1899** Morrow *Bohem. Paris* 305 Sipping Manhattan cocktails with a cherry-brandy-and-soda, Tom-and-Jerry, and the rest. **1903** Farmer & Henley *Slang Dict.*, *Tom-and-Jerry days*, the period of the Regency (1810–20); also, 'when George IV was king'.

**Tomasha, -shaw, -sia**, var. ff. Tamasha.

**1623** in Foster *Eng. Factories Ind.* (1908) II. 274 Nothing done more then a tomashaw. **1698** Fryer *Acc. E. India & P.* 159 Two Englishmen were come to the Tomasia or Sight.

1888 *United Presbyt. Mission. Rec.* Sept. 293 They had appointed pioneers to discover what the tomasha was to be.

**Tomato** (təmā·to, U. S. -ē¹·to). Forms: *α.* 7–9 **tomate**; *β.* 8– **tomato**; *γ.* 8–9 **tomata**; *δ.* 8 **tomatum**, 9 **-us**. *Pl.* 8 **tomatos**, 8– **tomatoes**. [In 17th c. *tomate*, a. F. *tomate* (2 syll.) fem., or Sp. and Pg. *tomate* (3 syll.) masc., ad. Mex. *tomatl*. *Tomato* is an English alteration, app. assumed to be Spanish, or perh. after *potato*; *tomata* a later change, app. assuming a Sp. **tomata* like *patata*; *tomatum*, *-us* are erroneous latinizations.

1572 GUILLANDINUS *De Papyro* 90 Americanorum tumatle. *Ibid.* 91 Tumatle..recentiores fere pomum aureum, et pomum amoris nuncupant.]

The glossy fleshy fruit of a solanaceous plant (*Solanum Lycopersicum* or *Lycopersicum esculentum*), a native of tropical America, now cultivated as a garden vegetable in temperate as well as tropical lands. It varies when ripe from red to yellow in colour, and greatly in size and shape, the common form being irregularly spheroidal, while two smaller forms, considered by some as species, are named from their shape, *L. cerasiforme*, the cherry tomato, and *L. pyriforme*, the pear-shaped tomato. Formerly called *love-apple*, from supposed aphrodisiac qualities. Also the plant, an annual with a weak trailing or climbing stem, irregularly pinnate leaves, and yellow flowers resembling those of the potato.

*α.* 1604 E. G[RIMSTONE] *D'Acosta's Hist. Indies* VII. ix. 519 There was also Indian pepper, beetes, Tomates, which is a great sappy and savourie graine. 1775 R. TWISS *Trav. Portugal & Spain* 256 Its district produces..radishes, endive, cucumbers and tomates. 1796 STEDMAN *Surinam* II. xxv. 224, I found plenty of tomatê, which being produced in many British gardens, I will not attempt to describe. 1846 SOYER *Cookery* 10 Preserved tomates.

*β.* 1753 CHAMBERS *Cycl. Suppl.*, *Tomato*, the Portuguese [*error*] name for the fruit of the lycopersicon or love-apple; a fruit..eaten either stewed or raw by the Spaniards and Italians and by the Jew families in England. 1777 G. FORSTER *Voy. round World* II. 588 The *Solanum Lycopersicon*, the fruit of which they call tomatos. 1846 LINDLEY *Veg. Kingd.* 621 Tomatoes..are a common ingredient in sauces. 1856 EMERSON *Eng. Traits, Voy. Eng.*, I find the sea-life an acquired taste, like that for tomatoes and olives.

*γ.* 1759 MILLER *Gard. Dict.*, *Lycopersicon*...Apple-bearing Nightshade, with a soft, round, striated Fruit, commonly called Tomatas [*error*] by the Spaniards. 1806 [see 3]. 1839 *Mag. Dom. Econ.* IV. 127 Directions for the various preparations of the Tomata. 1887 J. ASHBY STERRY *Lazy Minstrel* (1892) 107 The ruddy ripe tomata, In china bowl of ice.

*δ.* 1796 C. MARSHALL *Garden.* xvi. (1813) 276 *Tomatum*, or love apples, we have red, white, and yellow fruited. 1822 *Lancaster* (Pa.) *Jrnl.* 6 Sept. (Thornton), The pies made of the Tomatus are excellent.

**2.** With qualifying words, applied to varieties of this fruit or plant, as *cherry-*, *currant-tomato*, or to other species resembling it, as *cannibal's tomato*, *strawberry-* or *husk-tomato*: see quots.

1867 BRANDE & COX *Dict. Sc.*, etc. III. 806/1 The *Solanum anthropophagorum*, which the Feejeans eat at their feasts of human flesh, is hence called the Cannibal's Tomato. 1884 MILLER *Plant-n.*, Cherry Tomato-plant, *Solanum Lycopersicum* var. *cerasiforme*. *Ibid.*, *Physalis Alkekengi*,.. Bladder Herb, Red Nightshade, Red Winter-cherry, Straw-berry-Tomato. *P. pubescens*, Barbadoes Cape-Goose-berry, Straw-berry Tomato. 1887 *Nicholson's Dict. Gard.* IV. 53/1 *Cherry and Red Currant Tomatoes*, these are chiefly grown for ornament, as their fruits are borne in great profusion in bunches or clusters. They represent, in general appearance, the Cherry and Red Currant, after which they are popularly called.

**b. Tree Tomato**, the shrub *Cyphomandra betacea*, N.O. *Solanaceæ*, a native of Colombia and Peru, now naturalized in many tropical and subtropical countries; also its fruit.

1880–81 MORRIS *Ann. Rep. Public Gardens Jamaica* 35 Tree Tomato. 1884 *Gard. Chron.* XXI. 510 Tree Tomato. This is the popular name of a fruit naturalized in Jamaica. ..It answers in every respect the purposes for which the ordinary Tomato is esteemed. 1887 *Standard* 16 Sept. 5/2 Here..is the tree tomato,..the Tomato de Paz, or the 'vegetable mercury'.

**3.** *attrib.* and *Comb.*, as *tomato-blight*, *-can*, *-grafting*, *-growing*, *-ketchup*, *-leaf*, *-plant*, *-rot*, *-sauce*, *-scab*, *-seed*, *-top*; *tomato-coloured*, *-red* adjs.; **tomato-gall**: see quot. 1891[2]; **tomato hawk-moth** or **sphinx**, an American sphingid moth, *Protoparce celeus*; **tomato-worm**, the caterpillar of this, which feeds on tomato leaves.

1806 A. HUNTER *Culina* (ed. 3) 233 The only difference between this and the genuine tomata sauce, is the substituting the pulp of apple for the pulp of tomata. 1846 SOYER *Cookery* 9 Four tablespoonfuls of tomate sauce. 1887 *Nicholson's Dict. Gard.* IV. 51/2 It is only in warm situations..that the Tomato crop can be depended upon in the open air. *Ibid.* 52/1 Tomato culture. *Ibid.* 52/2 Tomato-plants are seldom very seriously injured by insects. 1891 MISS DOWIE *Girl in Karp.* 68 Her two tomato-coloured aprons. 1891 *Cent. Dict.*, *Tomato-gall*, a gall made upon the twigs of the grape-vine in the United States by the gall-midge *Lasioptera vitis*: so called on account of its resemblance to the fruit of the tomato. 1892 *Daily News* 3 Sept. 2/1 Another tea jacket is in tomato red velvet. 1896 *Ibid.* 25 Nov. 3/5 An alleged libel on the plaintiffs in their trade as sellers of tomato ketchup. 1897 *Westm. Gaz.* 16 Dec. 12/2 To graft the tomato on the potato stalk...So far from taking from the strength of the tubers, the tomato-grafting, he thinks, improves them. He never grew such fine potatoes as with tomato-tops, nor such fine tomatoes as with potato roots. 1897 *Allbutt's Syst. Med.* III. 885 Readily mistaken for tomato-seeds. 1904 E. NESBIT *Phœnix & Carpet* xi. 206 Tomato-coloured Liberty silk. *Mod. Breakfast Menu Card*, Tomato Omelettes.

**Tomaun**, variant of TOMAN[1].

† **Tom-ax.** *Obs. rare.* [A mixture of TOMAHAWK and AX.] = TOMAHAWK.

1759 JOHNSON *Idler* No. 40 ⁋ 7 With his face and body painted, with his scalping-knife, tom-ax, and all other implements of war.

**Tomb** (tūm), *sb.* Forms: *α.* 3–6 **toumbe**, **tumbe**, 4–5 **toumb**, 4–6 **tumb**, 4–7 **tombe**, 5 **towmbe**, 6–7 **toombe**, 4– **tomb**. *β.* 4–5 **towme**, 4–6 **tome**, 5–6 **toume**, 6 *Sc.* **toim**, 6–7 **toome**. [Early ME. *toumbe*, *tumbe*, a. AF. *tumbe*, OF. *tombe* (12th c. in Godef.) = Sp., Pg. *tumba*, It. *tomba*:—late L. *tumba* (Prudentius), ad. Gr. *τύμβος* sepulchral mound.

The final *b* began to be mute in Eng. (cf. *lamb*, *dumb*) early in 14th c., but the spelling *tomb*, which never exactly represented the spoken word, has survived, and from the 17th c. been the accepted form.]

**1.** A place of burial; an excavation in earth or rock for the reception of a dead body, a grave. Also, a chamber or vault formed wholly or partly in the earth, and, in early times, a tumulus or mound raised over the body.

(In quot. 1275, perhaps a coffin or sarcophagus.)

*c* 1275 LAY. 6080 Hii makede one tumbe [*c* 1205 tunne] of golde and of gimmes. þane kinge hii dude þar ine..and leide hine mid honure heȝe in þan toure. *c* 1290 *Beket* 2341 in *S. Eng. Leg.* I. 173 Riȝt so he wende to þe stude þere seint thomas lai At is toumbe he feol a-doun a-kneo wepinde wel sore. *a* 1300 *Cursor M.* 17798 (Cott.) Yee sal find þair tumbs [*Gött.* tumbes] tome [= toom]. *c* 1400 *Destr. Troy* 12113 Þis burd was broght to þe bare toumb. 1474 CAXTON *Chesse* 93 Thenne they took the body out of the tombe. 1513 DOUGLAS *Æneis* V. vii. 16 At the tumbe [L. *tumulum*] ..Quhair beryit was Hector of maist renoun. 1642 FULLER *Holy & Prof. St.* III. xiv. 187 Tombes are the clothes of the dead. 1756–7 tr. *Keysler's Trav.* (1760) II. 232 The church-yard is so full of tombs. 1838 THIRLWALL *Greece* II. xvi. 389 A tomb..which was generally believed to contain his bones.

**b.** *transf.* Anything that is or may become the last resting-place of a corpse.

1812 J. WILSON *Isle of Palms* I. 646 The sails now serve them for a shroud, And the sea-cave is their tomb.

**c.** *fig.*

1816 SHELLEY *Sunset* 42 The tomb of thy dead self. 1818 — *The Past* 9 Memories that make the heart a tomb. 1907 *Nation* (N. Y.) 12 Sept. 222/2 The office of mayor has been the tomb of many political ambitions.

**2.** A monument erected to enclose or cover the body and preserve the memory of the dead; a sepulchral structure raised above the earth. Hence sometimes a cenotaph. Also formerly, a tomb-stone erected over a grave.

*c* 1290 *S. Eng. Leg.* I. 102/33 Þoruȝ touchingue of seinte Agace toumbe þouȝ schalt beo hol a-non. 1297 R. GLOUC. (Rolls) 2617 He bad þat..me is bodi nome & burede it..In an tumbe suiþe hey, þat hii miȝte hit ver yse. *Ibid.* 4594 At glastinbury..at uore þe heye weued,..As is bones liggeþ, is toumbe wel vair is. *c* 1330 R. BRUNNE *Chron. Wace* (Rolls) 7791 Byrieþ me þere..& doþ make a toumbe þat longe may last. 1470–85 MALORY *Arthur* II. xi. 88 Kyng Arthur lete make the tombe of kynge Lot passyng rychely. 1545 *Test. Ebor.* (Surtees) VI. 234 Fortie poundes..to make a tombe over my grave. 1613 PURCHAS *Pilgrimage* (1614) 304 The common sort haue their Tombes of marble engrauen with letters. 1657 in Swayne *Sarum Churchw. Acc.* (1896) 234 To make a Toombe ouer his wiues Graue. *a* 1717 PARNELL *Night Piece on Death* 39 The Marble Tombs that rise on high, Whose Dead in vaulted Arches lye. 1820 W. IRVING *Sketch Bk.*, *Westm. Abbey*, I paused to contemplate a tomb on which lay the effigy of a knight in complete armour.

**3.** Regarded as the final resting-place of every one; hence sometimes used for the state of death.

1559 *Mirr. Mag.*, *Hen. VI* xv, Would god the rufull toumbe had been my royall trone. 1690 LOCKE *Hum. Und.* II. x. § 5 Our Minds represent to us those Tombs, to which we are approaching. 1769 GRAY *Install. Ode* 50 Charity, that glows beyond the tomb. 1777 J. RYLAND in Palmer *Bk. Praise* (1862) 226 He that formed me in the womb, He shall guide me to the tomb. 1822 BYRON *Heav. & Earth* I. iii, Than to behold the universal tomb.

**4.** *R. C. Ch.* Designating a cavity in an altar, where relics are deposited; an altar-cavity.

1886 *Encycl. Brit.* XX. 357/2 Every altar used for the celebration of mass must, according to Roman Catholic rule, contain some authorized relics. These are inserted into a cavity prepared for their reception, called 'the tomb', by the bishop of the diocese, and sealed up with the episcopal seal.

**5.** *attrib.* and *Comb.* **a.** attrib., as *tomb-board*, *-burglar*, *-burglary*, *-cave*, *-chamber*, *-chapel*, *-dweller*, *-house*, *-painting*, *-palace*, *-relief*, *-slab*, *-temple*, etc. **b.** objective, as *tomb-breaker*, *-maker*, *-robber*. **c.** instrumental, etc., as *tomb-paved*, *-strewn*; *tomb-black*, *-like* adjs. See also TOMB-BAT, -STONE.

1590 SPENSER *F. Q.* II. viii. 16 To decke his herce, and trap his *tomb-blacke steed. 1594 ? GREENE *Selimus* Wks. (Grosart) XIV. 269 When thus they see me with religious pompe, To celebrate his tomb-blacke mortuarie. 1785 T. CUMBER *Diary* in *Home Counties Mag.* (1902) IV. 226 The following inscription on a *tomb board. 1631 WEEVER *Anc. Fun. Mon.* 51 These *Tombe-breakers, these graue-diggers. 1654 WHITLOCK *Zootomia* 408 *Tomb-Burglary in this kind, being so uncouth a Case, as Law never made Provision against it. 1891 G. F. X. GRIFFITH tr. *Fouard's Christ* I. 310 *note*, Numerous *tomb-caves are still to be seen hollowed out of the mountain-side. 1906 PETRIE *Relig. Anc. Egypt* iii. 12 In Upper Egypt at present a hole is left at the top of the *tomb chamber; and I have seen a woman remove the covering of the hole, and talk down to her deceased husband. 1908 *Blackw. Mag.* July 59 Solid *tomb-chapels had to be constructed in honour of the more important dead. 1762–71 H. WALPOLE *Vertue's Anecd. Paint.* (1786) I. 176 Leland says that..Henry VII. pulled it down, and erected the present *tomb-house in it's place. 1845 HIRST *Com. Mammoth*, etc. 18 No murmur broke The silence of that *tomb-like spot. 1906 DK. ARGYLL *Autobiog.* I. ix. 203 The lower church is essentially tomblike. 1580 in *Archæol. Jrnl.* (1851) VIII. 185 Richard Roiley..*Tumbe maker. 1619 *Rutland MSS.* (1905) IV. 517 Paid to Nycholas Johnson, tombmaker, for the finishing of the monument for the late Earle Roger of Rutland, 100li. 1887 MAHAFFY & GILMAN *Alexander's Empire* xxix. (1890) 271 Objects represented in the *tomb-paintings with their names written over them. 1901 *Edin. Rev.* Jan. 33 The *tomb-palaces of long-dead kings. 1804 J. GRAHAME *Sabbath* (1805) 14 Slowly the throng moves o'er the *tomb-paved ground. 1906 *Macm. Mag.* Oct. 896 Such an almost pathetic beauty is the dominant note of the later *tomb-reliefs of Athenian sculpture. 1853 HICKIE tr. *Aristoph.* (1872) II. 592 He would thus be a *tomb-robber. 1908 *Athenæum* 21 Mar. 360/3 A tomb-robber could..remove the jewellery and other valuable objects buried with the corpse. 1889 HISSEY *Tour in Phaeton* 329 Ancient and curious *tomb-slabs. 1906 *Daily Chron.* 20 July 5/5 In a quiet *tomb-strewn graveyard among the winding lanes of Welwyn. 1904 H. SPENCER *Autobiog.* II. XII. lvii. 335 The thing which impressed me was the *tomb-temple in which we picnic'd.

**Tomb** (tūm), *v.* Now *rare.* Forms: see the sb. [f. TOMB *sb.*: cf. It. *tombare* to entomb.]

**1.** *trans.* To deposit (a body) in the tomb; to lay in the grave, bury, inter, entomb.

*c* 1330 R. BRUNNE *Chron.* (1810) 48 He lies a Glastenbire toumbed, as I wene. 14.. *Sir Beues* (M.) 4321 He towmbed ham to geder in ffere, Kyng and quene as they were. 1475 *Bk. Noblesse* (Roxb.) 45 And there made his faire ende at Rone, where he liethe tombid. 1591 GREENE *Maidens Dreame* Wks. (Grosart) XIV. 316 Let that [body] be earthed and tombed in gorgeous wise. *c* 1611 CHAPMAN *Iliad* XXIII. 225 Imagine them some monument, of one long since tomb'd there. 1759 W. MASON *Caractacus* Poems (1773) 256 Ye can tomb me in this sacred place. 1899 J. LUMSDEN *Poems* 16 In the Atlantic's bed Tombed ten leagues deep.

**b.** in *fig.* senses of 'bury'.

1611 HEYWOOD *Gold. Age* I. i. Wks. 1874 III. 13 I'le toombe th' usurper in his Infant bloud. 1613 MARSTON *Insat. Countess* I. i, [I'll bury thee] In the Swans downe, and tombe thee in mine armes. 1813 SCOTT *Rokeby* II. xviii, There dig and tomb your precious heap, And bid the dead your treasure keep.

**2.** To enclose or contain as a tomb; to serve as a tomb for. Hence **To·mbing** *ppl. a.*

*a* 1586 SIDNEY *Arcadia* III. Wks. 1724 II. 512 The Stone that tombs the Two. 1865 TENNYSON *On a Mourner* vi, And when no mortal motion jars The blackness round the tombing sod,..Comes Faith from tract no feet have trod.

**Tombac** (tǫ·mbæk). Forms: 7 **tombaga**, **tambaycke**, **tumbeck**, 8 **tombago**, **tambaqua**, **tumbanck**, **tambac**, 9 **tombec**, **tombak**, 8– **tombac**. [The current form is a. F. *tombac* (1700 in Hatz.-Darm.) = It. *tombacco*, Pg. *tambaca*, Sp. *tumbaga*, a. Malay تمباك *tambâga* copper.]

An alloy, of East Indian origin, of copper and zinc, in various proportions, containing from 82 to 99 per cent. of copper. Used in the east for gongs or bells; in Europe, under various names, as Prince's metal, Mannheim gold, etc., as a material for cheap jewellery.

*Red tombac*, that containing above 92 per cent. of copper. *Yellow tombac*, that containing 82 to 90 per cent. *White tombac*, an alloy of copper and arsenic.

1602 LANCASTER *Voy. India* in Purchas *Pilgrims* (1625) I. III. iii. § 3. 153 All the dishes..were, either of pure Gold, or of another Metall..called Tambaycke, which groweth of Gold and Brasse together. 1602–5 SCOTT *Disc. Java* ibid. iv. § 5. 180 Their drummes are huge pannes made of a metall called Tombaga. 1727–41 CHAMBERS *Cycl.*, *Tambac*, or *Tambaqua*, a mixture of gold and copper which the people of Siam hold more beautiful .. than gold itself. 1760–72 tr. *Juan & Ulloa's Voy.* (ed. 3) I. 121 Round their arms, they [women of Panama] wear bracelets of gold and tombac. *Ibid.* II. 60 Jewels set in gold, or for singularity sake, in tombago. 1815 J. SMITH *Panorama Sc. & Art* I. 43 Tombac has still more copper, and is of a deeper red than pinchbeck. *Ibid.* II. 399 Copper combines with five-sixths of arsenic, forming a white, hard, and brittle alloy;..it is called white tombac, and is much used in the manufacture of buttons. 1825 J. NICHOLSON *Operat. Mechanic* 710 Tombac. 16 lb. of copper, 1 lb. of tin, and 1 lb. of zinc. Red Tombac. 5½ lb. of copper, and ½ lb. of zinc... White Tombac. Copper and Arsenic. 1853 URE *Dict. Arts* I. 243 Tombak, or Red Brass, in the cast state, is an alloy of copper and zinc, containing not more than 20 per cent. of the latter constituent. 1864–72 WATTS *Dict. Chem.* II. 47 The most ductile of all the alloys of copper and zinc are those which contain 84·5 per cent. of copper to 15·5 of zinc (tombac), and 71·5 copper to 28·5 zinc (brass)... Karsten.

† **b.** A musical instrument made of this. *rare.*

1662 J. DAVIES tr. *Mandelslo's Trav.* I. (1669) 30 A Tumbeck, or Timbrel, a Haw-boy, and several Tabours.

**c.** *attrib.*, as *tombac-brown* adj.

1796 KIRWAN *Elem. Min.* (ed. 2) I. 30 (Colours) Tombac brown—metallic yellowish brown. 1811 PINKERTON *Petralogy* I. 194 Granite, with tombac brown mica.

**Tombal** (tū·mbăl, tǫ·mbăl), *a. rare.* [f. TOMB *sb.* + -AL.] Of or pertaining to a tomb.

1900 *Daily News* 3 Aug. 5/1 A beautiful tombal monument, shut in, according to French fashion, by an iron grille.

† **Tombazite** (tǫ·mbăzəit). *Min. Obs.* [Named in Ger. *tombazit* by Breithaupt 1838, in allusion to its tombac colour.] An obsolete synonym of GERSDORFFITE, a sulph-arsenide of nickel.

1850 ANSTED *Elem. Geol., Min.*, etc. § 468 Nickel green, Tombazite, Arsenate of nickel, with 36 per cent. of the oxide.

**To·mb-bat.** A name for bats of the genus *Taphozous*, family *Emballonuridæ*, which frequent tombs as their dwelling-places.

1883–96 *List Anim. Zool. Soc.* (ed. 9) 105 *Taphozous nudiventris.* Naked-bellied Tomb-Bat. Hab. Africa.

**Tombe**, obs. f. TOOM *a.* empty, TOME, TOMBO.

**Tomberel, -ell**, obs. forms of TUMBREL.

**Tombestere**, early form of TUMBESTER.

**Tombic** (tū·mbik, tǫ·mbik), *a.* [f. TOMB *sb.* + -IC.] Of, pertaining to, or connected with tombs, sepulchral: esp. in reference to the view that the Great Pyramid was a tomb.

1874 PIAZZI SMYTH *Inherit. in Gt. Pyramid* (new ed.) vi. 96 Different from either the treasure-theory of the East, or sepulchral, i. e. tombic, theory of Western minds. *Ibid.* 92 The Tombic Theory. 1883 R. A. PROCTOR *Gt. Pyramid* iii. 172 There are the strongest possible objections against the credibility of the merely tombic theory (to use a word coined, I imagine, by Professor Piazzi Smyth, and more convenient perhaps than defensible).

**Tomble, -ed, -er**, obs. forms of TUMBLE, etc.

**Tombless** (tū·mlės), *a.* [f. TOMB *sb.* + -LESS.] Having no tomb or sepulchral monument, destitute of a grave; unburied. Also *fig.*

1594 BARNFIELD *Affect. Sheph.* II. xxxvi, Fame is toombles, Vertue liues for aye. 1599 SHAKS. *Hen. V*, I. ii. 229 Or lay these bones in an vnworthy Vrne, Tomblesse, with no remembrance ouer them. *a* 1814 *Orpheus* III. i. in *New Brit. Theatre* III. 298 Shades of the tombless dead! 1823 PRAED *Australasia* 231 The bleak desert, or the tombless sea. *a* 1849 J. C. MANGAN *Poems* (1859) 373 And scorn shall point at our tombless graves. 1855 O. W. HOLMES *Poems* 188 Shroudless and tombless they sank to their rest.

**Tomblet** (tū·mlėt). *rare.* [f. as prec. + -LET.] A small tomb or burial-mound.

1855 BAILEY *Spir. Leg.* in *Mystic*, etc. 128 Earth heaves with tomblets, as the sea with waves.

‖ **Tombo** (tǫ·mbǫ). Also 8 in F. form **tombe.** [Native name.] General African W. Coast name of the fruit of the wine palm, *Raphia vinifera*; also, the native palm wine obtained from it.

1704 *Barbot's Guinea* in *Churchill's Voy.* V. 144 The fruit produced by the tombe tree, from which they also draw the wine called bourdon or tombe. 1819 REES *Cycl.* s. v. *Ivory*, A species of fruit growing on a sort of palmtree, which the natives call tombo or bourbon. 1908 *Daily Chron.* 7 Dec. 4/4 Considerable evidence..adduced to show that intoxication is more frequent from drinking tombo and other native brews than from drinking imported spirit.

**Tombola** (tǫ·mbǒlă). [a. F. *tombola* (1878 in *Dict. Acad.*), or It. *tombola*, f. *tombolare* to turn a somersault, fall upside down, tumble.] A kind of lottery resembling lotto.

1880 'OUIDA' *Moths* xv, You have a tombola for a famine, you have a dramatic performance for a flood, you have a concert for a fire. 1883 *Daily News* 19 July 5/7 There were various other Chinese articles for sale, and a tombola with all prizes and no blanks. 1883 *World* No. 471. 13 One of the features of the Savage Club, which is not advertised, on account of the Lottery Act, is a tombola. 1907 *Daily Chron.* 7 June 7/3 The law has now stepped in, and forbidden the tombola, on the ground that it would be a contravention of the Gaming Act. The tombola was arranged on the novel principle of no blanks, and a prize for every ticket-holder.

**Tomboy** (tǫ·mboi). [f. TOM *sb.* + BOY *sb.*]

† 1. A rude, boisterous, or forward boy. *Obs.* (Generally so taken in quot. *a* 1553; certainly so in 1599.)

*a* 1553 UDALL *Royster D.* II. iv. (Arb.) 37 Is all your delite and ioy In whiskyng and ramping abroade like a Tom boy? 1599 MASSINGER, etc. *Old Law* III. ii, Must young court tits [= young gentlemen courtiers] Play tomboys' tricks with her, and he live?

† 2. A bold or immodest woman. *Obs.*

1579 TOMSON *Calvin's Serm. Tim.* 203/2 Sainte Paule meaneth that women must not be impudent, they must not be tomboyes, to be shorte, they must not bee vnchast. 1611 SHAKS. *Cymb.* I. vi. 122 To be partner'd With Tomboyes hyr'd with that selfe exhibition Which your owne Coffers yeeld. 1619 FLETCHER, etc. *Knt. Malta* II. i, Ye Filly, Ye Tit, ye Tomboy! *a* 1700 B. E. *Dict. Cant. Crew*, *Tom-boy*, a Ramp, or Tomrig.

3. A girl who behaves like a spirited or boisterous boy; a wild romping girl; a hoyden.

1592 LYLY *Midas* I. ii, If thou shouldest rigge vp and downe in our iackets, thou wouldst be thought a very tomboy. 1622 T. STOUGHTON *Chr. Sacrif.* xii. 169 Of such short-haired Gentlewomen I find not one example either in Scripture or elsewhere. And what shall I say of such poled rigs, ramps and Tomboyes? 1656 BLOUNT *Glossogr.*, *Tomboy*, a girle or wench that leaps up and down like a boy. 1730–6 BAILEY (folio), *Tom-boy*, a ramping, frolicsome, rude girl. 1802 in *Spirit Pub. Jrnls.* VI. 72 The violent exercise of the skipping-rope, which is..only fit for some Miss Tomboy. 1830 MISS MITFORD *Village* Ser. IV. Introd. Let. 7 He had no taste for giantesses, and a particular aversion for hoydens and tomboys and women who trespassed against the delicacy of their sex. 1888 MRS. H. WARD *R. Elsmere* x, As a rough tomboy of fourteen, she had shown Catherine..a good many uncouth signs of affection.

4. *attrib.*

1657 HOWELL *Londinop.* 398 Stool-ball, though that stradling kind of Tomboy sport be not so handsome for Mayds. 1675 HAN. WOOLLEY *Gentlewom. Comp.* 52 To laugh, or express any Tom-boy trick is as bad or worse. 1874 MRS. H. WOOD *Mast. Greylands* iv, He saw a great deal to find fault with in her rude, tomboy ways. 1882 *Atlantic Monthly* LI. 87 Having..practiced them in a mere romping, 'tom-boy' spirit when she was a young girl.

Hence **Tomboya·de** *nonce-wd.*, an escapade in the manner of a tomboy; **Tomboy·ful** *a.*, **To·mboy·ish** *a.*, like or having the character of a tomboy; hence **To·mboy·ishness**; **To·mboyism.**

1886 *Blackw. Mag.* Apr. 516 Reminiscences of scrambles and *tomboyades when they were girls together. 1887 J. ASHBY STERRY *Lazy Minstrel* (1892) 82 Careless and joyful. ..Pet in short petticoats—Truly *tomboyful! 1862 MISS YONGE *C'tess Kate* iv, A child .. certainly *tom-boyish except for a certain timidity. 1887 'EDNA LYALL' *Knt.-Errant* (1889) 227 A rather tomboyish young person of fourteen. 1883 L. WINGFIELD *A. Rowe* III. vii. 130 Under the roughness and *tomboyishness was a heart of real gold. 1876 MISS YONGE *Womankind* ii, What I mean by '*tomboyism' is a wholesome delight in rushing about at full speed, playing at active games, climbing trees, rowing boats, making dirt-pies, and the like.

**Tombrell, -il**, obs. forms of TUMBREL.

**Tombstone, tomb-stone** (tū·mstǫun).

1. A horizontal stone covering a grave; in early use, the cover of a stone coffin, or the stone coffin itself.

1565 STAPLETON tr. *Bede's Hist. Ch. Eng.* 125 The very same tombestone was found to be of a fyt length for the quantitie of the bodie. 1672 WILKINS *Nat. Relig.* 28 Suppose he should dig up a large stone of the shape of an ancient tomb-stone. 1696 PHILLIPS (ed. 5), *Tomb-stone*, a Stone that is laid over a Grave, with an Inscription upon it. 1715–20 POPE *Iliad* XVII. 492 Still as a tombstone, never to be mov'd, On some good man or woman unreprov'd, Lays its eternal weight. 1840 DICKENS *Barn. Rudge* i, Sitting down to take his dinner on cold tombstones. 1898 *Saga-Bk. of Viking Cl.* Jan. 34 Two hog-back or coped tombstones, supposed to be one thousand years old.

b. A stone or monument of any kind placed over the grave of a deceased person to preserve his memory; a gravestone; including a headstone (or the like of wood). (Early quots. may be in sense 1.)

1711 ADDISON *Spect.* No. 26 ⁋ 5 When I meet with the Grief of Parents upon a Tomb-stone, my Heart melts with Compassion. 1712 STEELE *ibid.* No. 518 ⁋ 3 There is not a Gentleman in England better read in Tomb-stones than my self, my Studies having laid very much in Church-yards. 1793 SMEATON *Edystone L.* § 98 A well shaped Tomb-stone of Granite. 1820 W. IRVING *Sketch Bk.* I. 84 (*Rip Van Winkle*) There was a wooden tombstone in the church yard that used to tell all about him. 1843 BETHUNE *Sc. Fireside Stor.* 160 That species of erect tombstone which some one has..designated as spectral. 1870 F. R. WILSON *Ch. Lindisf.* 35 The churchyard is crowded with tombstones.

c. *fig.*

*c* 1611 CHAPMAN *Iliad* III. 60 For which thou well deserv'st A coat of tombstone not of steel in which thou serv'st. 1658 (*title*) Mistris Shawes Tomb-stone,..Beeing a Narrative of Remarkable Passages in the Holy Life and Happy Death of Mrs. Dorothy Shaw, of Brampton. 1755 SMOLLETT *Quix.* II. IV. x. (1803) IV. 212, 'I swear to that condition', answered Don Quixote: 'and, for the greater security, will put a tomb-stone over whatever you shall communicate'. 1819 J. MONTGOMERY *Greenland* v. 186 One frozen plain, The mighty tombstone of the buried main. 1902 *Daily Chron.* 24 May 3/1 It puts tombstones to the reputations of many good officers, and buries the blunders of others under cairns of apologetic explanations.

2. *slang.* **a.** A pawn-ticket. **b.** See quot. 1903.

1883 J. GREENWOOD *Odd People in Odd Pl.* 168 The..bag in which the 'tombstones' or pawn-tickets were deposited. *c* 1889 *Sporting Times* (Farmer), The collection for master amounted to 4½*d.*, and a tombstone for ninepence on a brown Melton overcoat. 1903 FARMER & HENLEY *Slang Dict.*, *Tombstone*, a projecting tooth, a snaggle-tooth.

3. *attrib.* and *Comb.*

*a* 1845 HOOD *Valentine* ii, Just stopped before The tombstone steps that lead us to death's door. 1905 *Daily Chron.* 24 Apr. 4/5 An elderly man was sitting dejectedly on the tombstone-shaded bench.

**Tom cat, tom-cat** (tǫ·m,kæ·t). [See TOM *sb.* 6. In 1760 was published an anonymous work 'The Life and Adventures of a Cat', which became very popular. The hero, a male or 'ram' cat, bore the name of Tom, and is commonly mentioned as 'Tom the Cat', as 'Tybert the Catte' is in Caxton's Reynard the Fox. Thus Tom became a favourite allusive name for a male cat (see quot. 1791 s.v. TOM *sb.* 6); and people said 'this cat is a Tom' or a 'Tom cat'.] A male cat.

[1760 *Life & Adv. of a Cat* 11 Chap. iv. Tom the Cat is born of poor but honest parents. *Ibid.* 31 The single adventures of Tom the Cat only.] 1809 MALKIN *Gil Blas* II. vii. ⁋ 27 The devil fetch that tom cat! 1825 *Univ. Songster* (*title*) The Tortoiseshell Tom-cat. 1838 DICKENS *Nich. Nick.* xii, It's enough to make a Tom cat talk French grammar. 1881 J. HAWTHORNE *Fort. Fool* I. xxvii, A cur..unexpectedly confronted by a large tomcat.

**Tom-cod** (tǫ·m,kǫ·d). Name for several small fishes. In U.S.: **a.** The frost-fish (FROST *sb.* 7 c); also, loosely, one of various small fishes confused with this. **b.** In California, the Jack-fish (*Sebastodes paucispinis*), a rock-fish. **c.** = KING-FISH d. In Great Britain: **d.** A young codfish.

1795 J. SULLIVAN *Hist. Maine* 21 The people have tom cod, or what they call frost fish, smelts, and also alewives in great plenty. 1838 HALIBURTON *Clockm.* Ser. II. v. 65 [They] used to..catch herrin' and tom cods, and such sort o' fish. 1854 LOWELL *Leaves fr. Jrnl.* Wks. 1890 I. 108 An old fisherman, browner than a tomcod. 1883 *Fisheries Exhib. Catal.* (ed. 4) 174 Tom Cods, the young of Cod Fish. 1888 GOODE *Amer. Fishes* 123 The King-Fish,..also known..as the 'Tom-cod' on the coast of Connecticut.

**Tome** (tǫum). (Also 7 tombe.) [app. a. F. *tome* (16th c. in Godef. *Compl.*), ad. L. *tomus*, a. Gr. τόμος volume, section of a book, f. ablaut series τεμ-, τομ-, τμ-, to cut.]

† 1. Each of the separate volumes which compose a literary work or book; rarely, one of the largest parts or sections of a single volume. *Obs.*

1519 HORMAN *Vulg.* 84 A *tome* proprely is but a peace vnperfecte of a boke, neuer the lesse, it is taken for a great quantyte of a whole warke. 1548 UDALL (*title*) The first tome of the Paraphrase of Erasmus vpon the newe Testamente. 1549 *Ibid.*, The second tome or volume of the Paraphrase of Erasmus vpon the newe testament. 1563 *Homilies* (title-p.) The seconde Tome of Homelyes, of such matters as were promysed and Intituled in the former part of Homelyes. 1600 J. PORY tr. *Leo's Africa* II. 53 The said volume is diuided into three tomes. 1659 BAXTER *Key Cath.* xxv. 151 A large volume containing six Tomes. 1672 J. FRASER *Polichron.* (S.H.S.) 503, I read over to him my own Triennial Travells abroad, in 3 tombes. 1731 *Hist. Litteraria* II. 493 To the IVth Tome will be prefixed a Collection of ..Pieces, relating to the Life and Writings of the Author.

2. A book, a volume; now usually suggesting a large, heavy, old-fashioned book.

1573 (*title*) The whole workes of..Tyndall..Frith, and.. Barnes .. collected and compiled in one Tome together. 1621 BURTON *Anat. Mel.* I. ii. IV. vii. (1651) 167 To what end are such great Tomes? 1730 SHENSTONE *Ode to Health* 30 Adieu, Ye midnight lamps! ye curious tomes! 1789 J. WHITE *Earl Strongbow* I. 159 Father Hugh..prayed my acceptance of a little tome, covered with fine vellum. 1849 MISS MULOCK *Ogilvies* iv, Ponderous tomes, in century-old bindings,—dusty piles of newspapers. 1890 HALL CAINE *Bondman* II. ix, 'Bring me the Statute Book', and the great tome was brought.

3. *fig.*

1622 DONNE *Serm., Job xxxvi. 25* (1649) II. xxxi. 273 Who knowes..how many volumes of Spheares involve one another, how many tomes of Gods Creatures there are? 1654 FULLER *Two Serm.* 54 Seventhly, the Booke of men's Afflictions. Some account this onely a distinct Tome, or Volume, of the former Booke [Book of Men's Actions]. 1867 BAILEY *Univ. Hymn* 9 He through your space-spread tome ..His starry rede To man predictive speaks.

4. A papal letter or epistle. *Hist.*

[ad. L. *tomus*, a. Gr. τόμος, applied esp. to synodical and pontifical letters or epistles: see Du Cange.]

1788 GIBBON *Decl. & F.* xlvii. (1836) 827 The tome of Leo was subscribed by the Oriental bishops. 1867 MANNING *Petri Privilegium* (1871) 73 The Council of Chalcedon was directed by S. Leo to condemn Eutyches, whom he had already condemned. The Fathers of the Council would define nothing until they had heard the Tome, or dogmatic letter of the Pontiff.

Hence (*nonce-words*) **To·mecide** (tǫ·mĭ-) [-CIDE 1], a destroyer of books; **To·meful** (tǫu·mful), as much as fills a tome; **To·melet**, a small volume.

1849 CURZON *Visits Monast.* 382, I ought, perhaps, to have slain the *tomecide. 1859 SALA *Tw. round Clock* (1861) 141 How many *tomesful [*error for* tomefuls] of gossiping scandal will be talked! 1846 WORCESTER cites *Q. Rev.* for *Tomelet. 1884 *Irish Monthly* Jan. 52 This dainty tomelet.

**Tome**, obs. f. TAUM, TOOM. **To-melt**: see TO-[2] 1.

**Tomentigerous**, etc.: see under TOMENTUM.

**Tomentose** (tǫume·ntǫus), *a.* [ad. mod.L. *tōmentōs-us*, It. *tomentoso*, f. L. *tōment-um* stuffing for cushions + -OSE.]

1. *Bot.* Closely covered with down or short hairs; pubescent, downy. Also as second element, in *albo-tomentose*, covered with white down, *farinose-tomentose*, covered with mealy down, etc.

1698 FRYER *Acc. E. India & P.* 40 (*Plate*) Nutts..whose tomentose husk taken off, leaves the Areca nut. 1699 SLOANE in *Phil. Trans.* XXI. 116 Pappous and tomentose Seeds of *Hieracium, Lisymachia.* 1785 MARTYN *Rousseau's Bot.* xxix. (1794) 455 The surface..tomentose or nappy underneath. 1872 OLIVER *Elem. Bot.* App. 307 Stem..glabrous or sparsely tomentose. 1887 W. PHILLIPS *Brit. Discomycetes* 61 *Peziza grandis* .. externally olivaceous-umber, with a lacunose albo-tomentose base. *Ibid.* 269 Externally farinose-tomentose, pale red or dilute-cinnamon.

2. *Entom.* and *Anat.* Flocculent, flossy, woolly.

1826 KIRBY & SP. *Entomol.* IV. xlvi. 276 *Tomentose*... Covered with short interwoven inconspicuous hairs. 1852 DANA *Crust.* I. 240 The pubescence or tomentose covering is exceedingly short. 1859 *Todd's Cycl. Anat.* V. 636/1 A tomentose or..villous condition of the surface. 1872 PEASLEE *Ovar. Tumors* 35 If the latter be purulent, it becomes fungous, tomentose, reddish.

**Tome·ntous**, *a.* [ad. mod.L. *tōmentōs-us* or F. *tomenteux*: see -OUS.] = TOMENTOSE.

1806 GALPINE *Brit. Bot.* § 285 Leaves cordate, doubly-serrated, tomentous beneath. 1822 J. PARKINSON *Outl. Oryctol.* 40 Soft, tomentous, very jagged and porous. 1900 B. D. JACKSON *Gloss. Bot. Terms.*

‖ **Tomentum** (tǫme·ntǒm). [L.: see above.]

1. *Bot.* The soft down or pubescence growing on the stems, leaves, or seeds of certain plants.

1699 SLOANE in *Phil. Trans.* XXI. 115 Having very soft hairs, down, or tomentum, much longer in proportion to the Seed, then any tomentum I know. 1793 G. WHITE *Selborne* (1853) 375 (*Observ. Wild Bee*) A sort of wild bee frequenting the garden-campion for the sake of its *tomentum*. 1866 *Treas. Bot.* s.v. *Centaurea*, Leaves clothed on both surfaces with a white silky tomentum.

2. *Anat.* A downy covering or investment; *spec.* the flocculent inner surface of the pia mater, consisting of numerous minute vessels entering the brain and spinal cord (in full *tomentum cerebri*).

1811 in HOOPER *Med. Dict.* 1841 RAMSBOTHAM *Obstetr*

*Med.* (1855) 62 The ovum..is completely surrounded by a thick tomentum of minute filamentous, mossy villi.

Hence **Tomenti·gerous, Tomenti·tious, Tome·ntulose** *adjs.*: see quots.

**1860** MAYNE *Expos. Lex.*, *Tomentiger..*, *Entom.*, having the body hairy or downy: *tomentigerous. **1656** BLOUNT *Glossogr.*, **Tomentitious* (*tomentitius*), made of flocks or wool. **1895** *Funk's Stand. Dict.*, *Tomentulose. **1900** B. D. JACKSON *Gloss. Bot. Terms* 272 *Tomentulose*, slightly tomentose.

**Tomerel**, obs. form of TUMBREL.

**To·m-foo·l**, *sb.* [f. TOM + FOOL *sb.*[1]] †**a.** As quasi-proper name, *Tom Fool*: a man mentally deficient; a half-witted person. *Obs.*

**1356–7** *Durham Acc. Rolls* (Surtees) 719 Pro funeracione Thome Fole [from 1337 frequently mentioned as 'Thomas fatuus']. **1565** CALFHILL *Answ. Treat. Crosse* 103 b, I might byd them tell them, as Tom foole did his geese. **1611** J. FIELD *Panegyr. Verses* in Coryat *Crudities*, Tom-Foole may goe to schoole, but nere be taught. ?**1640** *New Serm. of newest fashion* (1877) 32 A foole reall..such ffooles wee commonlie expresse by the names of Tom ffoole, Dick ffoole, and Jack ffoole. **1865** *Cornh. Mag.* Oct. 391 Now though he didn't know Hannah, Hannah knew him. 'More folks know Tom Fool, than Tom Fool knows', asking Mr. Preston's pardon.

**b.** One who enacts the part of a fool in the drama, etc.; a buffoon; *spec.* a buffoon who accompanies morris-dancers; also, a butt, laughing-stock.

**1650** H. MORE *Observ.* in *Enthus. Tri.*, etc. (1656) 91 Come out Tom-Fool from behinde the hangings,..and put off your vizard, and be apert and intelligible. **1677** W. HUGHES *Man of Sin* II. ix. 139 But poor Thomas is made a Tom-fool of; for they make a bridge of his Nose, for ought I find, and leave him nothing. **1796** MRS. M. ROBINSON *Angelina* II. 131 'So then I am to be the only properly drest person at the wedding? In short, the Tom fool of the company', said he. **1846** THACKERAY *Snob Papers* Wks. 1886 XXIV. 319 A theatre manager..walking backwards in a Tom-Fool's coat. **1894** *S. E. Worc. Gloss.* s. v. *Morris-dance*, In the neighbourhood of Pershore the morris-dancers go out for about ten days at Christmas-tide, accompanied by their musician and a 'tom-fool'.

**c.** A foolish or stupid person; one who behaves foolishly. (More emphatic than *fool*.)

**1721** AMHERST *Terræ Fil.* No. 44. (1754) 233 From this tom-fool proceed we to the second, entitled Joseph. **1835** MARRYAT *Pacha* x, I came with the rest of the tom-fools. **1860** MAYHEW *Upp. Rhine* iv. § 1. 173 A titled tom-fool, that some crowned head has been pleased to nickname noble. **1881** BESANT & RICE *Chapl. of Fleet* I. 78 If they were not clergymen, I should say they were all tom-fools.

**d.** *attrib.* (in senses b and c).

**1819** SCOTT *Fam. Let.* 25 Nov., I had some regret in putting him into that Tom Fool dress, which is so unlike that of a British soldier. **1879** SALA *Paris herself again* (1880) I. x. 151 You may..wear whatever tomfool costume you like to assume. **1903** *Sat. Rev.* 7 Feb. 172/2 The absolute tom-fool nonsense in which Fielding could indulge.

Hence **To·m-fool** *v.*, *intr.* to play the fool; whence **To·m-foo·ling** *vbl. sb.*

**1825** T. HOOK *Sayings* Ser. II. *Man of Many Fr.* I. 181 She began lecturing and tom-fooling with as great a quack as herself. **1836** — *G. Gurney* i, All the lovers and their ladies were to be flirting and tom-fooling about in the costume of the then present day. **1881** *Daily Tel.* 27 Dec., In this scene there is very good tomfooling on the part of King Hoity-Toity..and the Nigger Chamberlain.

**Tomfoo·lery.** [f. prec. after FOOLERY.] The action or behaviour of a tom-fool; foolish or absurd action; silly trifling.

**1812** H. & J. SMITH *Rej. Addr.*, *Punch's Apotheosis*, Round let us bound, for this is Punch's holyday; Glory to Tomfoolery, huzza! huzza! **1899** A. DOBSON *Paladin of Philanth.* iii. 65 That solemn tomfoolery, the Stratford Jubilee of 1769.

**b.** With *a* and *pl.* An instance of this; an action, practice, or thing of a foolish or absurd kind.

**1840** T. A. TROLLOPE *Summ. in Brittany* I. 58 One of those solemn tom-fooleries which so much delighted the middle ages. **1862** MISS YONGE *C'tess Kate* xii, Come, don't make a tomfoolery of it. **1885** HUXLEY in L. Huxley *Life* (1900) II. vi. 91 How grown men can lend themselves to such elaborate tomfooleries.

So **To·m-foo·lish** *a.*, of, pertaining to, or of the nature of a tom-fool; hence **To·m-foo·lishness.**

**1799** SOUTHEY *Nondescripts* viii, A man he is by nature merry, Somewhat Tom-foolish, and comical, very. **1889** J. K. JEROME *Three Men in Boat* v, Of all the irritating silly tomfoolishness by which we are plagued, this 'weather-forecast' fraud is about the most aggravating.

**Tomhog**, obs. form of TOMAHAWK.

**To·mial**, *a. Ornith.* [f. TOMI-UM + -AL.] Of or pertaining to the tomia or to a tomium.

**1872** COUES *N. Amer. Birds* 30 'Commissural edge' of either mandible (equivalent to 'tomial edge'). **1895** *Proc. Zool. Soc.* 7 May 369 The lamella of bone between each nostril and the tomial margin is relatively wider.

‖**Tomice** (tǫ·misī, -kī). *rare.* [f. Gr. type *τομική (sc. τέχνη), f. τομικός that cuts.] The art of carving.

**1662** EVELYN *Chalcogr.* (1769) 16 As to working in wood or ivory, *tomice*. **1710** in J. HARRIS *Lex. Techn.* II.

†**To-mi·d**, *prep. Obs.* [ME. *to myd*, f. To *prep.* + MID.] In or into the midst of, amid.

*c* **1420** *Liber Cocorum* (1862) 19 Be sleȝe and powre in water þenne To myd þo pot, as I the kenne.

†**To-mids**, *adv.* and *prep. Obs.* [OE. *tó-middes*, ME. *to-medis*, f. To *prep.* + *middes*: see MIDS.]

**A.** *adv.* In or into the midst.

*Beowulf* 3141 [Hie] Aleȝdon ða to middes mærne þeoden. *c* **1000** *Sax. Leechd.* III. 56 Sete on feower healfe þæs ceapes, and an to middes. *a* **1400** *Sir Perc.* 1202 He roghte wele the lesse Awther of lyfe or of dede, To-medis that he were in a stede, Thar he myghte riste hym in thede A stownde in sekirnes!

**B.** *prep.* In or into the midst of. (Only OE.)

*c* **1000** *Ags. Gosp.* John i. 26 Tomiddes eow stod þe ȝe ne cunnon. *c* **1000** ÆLFRIC *Saints' Lives* xxiii. 609 Hine þanon ealle atuȝan tomiddes þære cypinge.

‖**Tomin** (tomī·n). Also 6 -yne, 7 -ine. [Sp.] A Spanish measure of weight for silver, equivalent to 9·26 grains; also, **b.** in Spain and Spanish America, the name of various small silver coins.

In Bolivia, a coin equal to one-fifth of the Bolivian dollar, i.e. about eightpence; in Paraguay, a coin worth 2 reales or nearly fivepence (*Cent. Dict., Supp.*).

[**1599** MINSHEU *Span. Dict.*, *Tomin*, a kinde of weight weighing the quantity of a Reall in Spaine, neere sixpence English.] **1600** HAKLUYT *Voy.* III. 454 Fiue Tomynes, that is, fiue Royals of plate, which is iust two shillings and sixe pence. **1604** E. G[RIMSTONE] tr. *D'Acosta's Hist. Indies* IV. xxii. 272 In Potozi it is readily worth foure peeces, and five Tomines.

†**c.** As the name of a weight used by jewellers.

**1658** PHILLIPS, *Tomin*, a certain weight among Jewellers, weighing about three Carrats. **1717** *Blount's Law Dict.*, *Tomin*, a Weight so called amongst Goldsmiths and Jewellers, and is twelve Grains.

**Tominorie**: see TOM-NODDY I.

**Tomiparous** (tomi·pǎrəs), *a. Biol. rare.* [f. mod.L. *tomipar-us* (f. Gr. τομή cutting, section + L. *-par-us* producing) + -OUS.] Multiplying (as a cell or organism) by division; fissiparous.

**1860** MAYNE *Expos. Lex.*, *Tomiparus..*, applied by Bory to plants and animals which are multiplied by cuttings or division, i.e. by separation of parts: tomiparous. **1887** W. PHILLIPS *Brit. Discomycetes* 272 The external papillæ are formed by the ends of short, hair-like, tomiparous cells, which are remarkable from their habit of breaking off at the joints under slight pressure.

**Tomistic**, variant of THOMISTIC.

‖**Tomium** (tōu·miǒm). *Ornith.* Pl. **tomia** (-iă). [mod.L., f. Gr. τομ-ός cutting, sharp + L. *-ium* (cf. Gr. τόμιον a sacrifice cut up, also τομεῖον incision).] Each of the cutting edges of a bird's bill.

**1834** R. MUDIE *Brit. Birds* (1841) I. 349 They..do not peck..or grind hard substances between the oblique *tomia*. **1874** COUES *Birds N. W.* 622 Bill greenish-yellow, chrome along the tomia. **1890** — *Field & Gen. Ornithol.* II. 152 The mandibular *tomium*.

**Tomjohn**, corruption of TONJON.

**Tomkin, -king**, obs. variants of TAMPION, plug.

**Tomling**, a young tom cat: see under TOM.

**Tommahauk**, obs. form of TOMAHAWK.

**Tommy** (tǫ·mi). [dim. or pet form of TOM: cf. *baby*, *dolly*, *Bobby*, *Teddy*, etc.]

**1.** With capital T: Familiar form of *Thomas*.

**b.** A simpleton; also, short for *tommy-noddy* (= TOM-NODDY I). *dial.*

**1829** BOWLES *Days Departed* 44 The tandem-driving Tommy of a town. **1833** P. J. SELBY *Illustr. Brit. Ornithol.* II. 439 Puffin..Tommy-nodie, Tommey. **1847–78** HALLIWELL, *Tommy*..a simple fellow. **1899** *Leeds Mercury*, *Suppl.* 6 May (E.D.D.), He's as big a Tommy as iver I knew.

**c.** Short for *Tommy Atkins*: see 7.

**1893** KIPLING *Many Invent.* 28, I was..with sixty Tommies—private soldiers, that is. **1898** *Westm. Gaz.* 26 Jan. 7/1 An occasional detachment of Tommies with the attendant coolies and sweepers. **1901** *Daily Graphic* 23 Feb. 7/4 A vigorous protest is being made on behalf of the dignity of the British line against the use of the too familiar sobriquet 'Tommy'. **1907** *Blackw. Mag.* Nov. 651/2 A group of Tommies in uniform.

**2.** A soldiers' name for the brown bread formerly supplied as rations (also *brown tommy*); with *a* and *pl.*, a loaf of bread (*dial.*); among workmen, Food, provisions generally, *esp.* those carried with them to work each day. *Soft tommy*, *white tommy*: see quot. 1796. See also TAMMIE.

App. personified as *Tommy Brown*, altered to *brown Tommy* and *tommy*. Similarly a hunk of grey bread distributed at Minto House, as part of a Hogmanay gift to the village children, used to be called *Tam Gray*.

**1783** [see quot. 1830]. **1796** GROSE *Dict. Vulg. T.* s. v., Soft Tommy, or white Tommy; bread is so called by sailors, to distinguish it from biscuit. **1803** in *Spirit Pub. Jrnls.* VII. 352 A high sea,..without a bit of soft Tommy to put into your lantern jaws. **1811** *Lex. Balatr.* s.v., Brown Tommy; ammunition bread for soldiers; or brown bread given to convicts at the hulks. **1825** BROCKETT *N. C. Words*, *Tommy*, a little loaf. 'A soldier's tommy'. **1830** in W. Cobbett *Rur. Rides* (1885) II. 353 When I was a recruit at Chatham barracks, in the year 1783, we had brown bread served out to us twice in the week. And, for what reason God knows, we used to call it *tommy*...Any one that could get white bread called it 'bread', but the brown stuff..was called 'tommy'. **1846** *Camp & Barrack-Room* ii. 16 After I had breakfasted upon tommy and insipid coffee. **1865** *Slang Dict.*, *Tommy*, bread,—generally a penny roll. Sometimes applied by workmen to the supply of food which they carry..as their daily allowance. **1911** H. F. RUTTER *Let. to Editor*, Used in provincial dialects and invariably by English navvies as a synonym for food. 'I was that bad I couldn't eat my tommy'. 'Go into the stable and give that old horse his tommy'.

**b.** Goods; *esp.* provisions supplied to workmen under the truck system; also, short for *tommy-shop*, and for the truck system.

**1830** [implied in *tommy-shop*, *system* in 6]. **1845** DISRAELI *Sybil* III. i, Diggs' tommy is only open once a-week. *Ibid.* III. iii, What are you doing here, little dear?; very young to fetch tommy. **1856** *Househ. Words* 21 June 545/1 The navvy knows that he is a helpless being if he cannot get his tommy; and this word..signifies beef, bacon, cheese, coffee, bread, butter, and tobacco. **1860** *Slang Dict.*, *Tommy*, a truck, barter, the exchange of labour for goods, not money.

**3.** As the name of something small of its kind. **a.** See quot. *a* 1825. **b.** A spanner; a screw-driver.

*a* **1825** FORBY *Voc. E. Anglia*, *Tommy*, a small spade to excavate the narrow bottoms of under-drains [**1895** *Gloss. E. Anglia* adds 'Also a small wrench used by engineers']. **1844** *Civil Eng. & Arch. Jrnl.* VII. 35/1 On giving motion to the screw, which is effected by means of a tommy, or spanner. **1881** HASLUCK *Lathe Work* 179 Hooked tommys are employed to actuate all those capstan headed screws and nuts which from insufficiency in the depth of the holes do not afford a hold for the ordinary straight forward tommy.

**c.** The smallest of the gazelles, Thomson's gazelle, of East Africa. [Here orig. from *Thomson*.]

**1906** *Westm. Gaz.* 2 June 2/2 It is a pretty sight to see a herd of the graceful little Thomson's gazelle (locally called Tommies) mingling with a flock of sheep and goats. **1912** *Contemp. Rev.*, *Lit. Suppl.* Jan. 137 Mr. Barnes came across the gigantic eland..Grant's gazelle, Tommy, oryx [etc.].

**4.** A gold-washing trough; = TOM 4 a.

**1892** *Pall Mall G.* 10 Aug. 2/1 At the end of the tiny creek, where a 'tommy' was..set in motion to wash the alluvial soil and extract the tiny glittering particles of gold.

**5.** (Usually **soft tommy.**) Pewter solder (PEWTER 6) used by jewellers.

**1877** G. E. GEE *Practical Gold-worker* 137 'Soft solder'..commonly called in the jewellery trade 'soft tommy'. **1912** *Let. from Jeweller to Editor*, Tommy or soft tommy means the ordinary lead or pewter solder that is in common use for repairing Britannia metal or lead articles.

**6.** *attrib.* and *Comb.*; chiefly in senses 2, 2 b, as *tommy-box*, *-master*, *system*; **tommy-bag**, a bag in which a workman or school-boy carries his day's food; **tommy-book**, an account book of goods supplied on the truck system; **tommy-cod** = TOM-COD a.; **tommy-day**, a day on which a *tommy-shop* is open; **Tommy Dod**(d, the 'odd man' in odd-man-out (ODD D. 2); **tommy-hole**, one of two or more holes in a nut, into which steel pins can be inserted to turn it; **tommy-long-legs**, the daddy-long-legs; **tommy-noddy, -norie** = TOM-NODDY; **tommy-plough** = *tom-plough* (TOM *sb.* 7 a); **tommy-ro·t**, nonsense, bosh, twaddle; hence **tommyro·tic** *a.* [after *erotic*], nonsensical; **to·mmy-shop**, a store (esp. one run by the employer) at which vouchers given to employees instead of money wages may be exchanged for goods; a truck-shop; also *attrib.*; **Tommy-touch-wood**, the game of 'touch wood'.

**1873** *Slang Dict.* s. v. *Tommy*, *Tommy-Bag is the term for the bag or handkerchief in which the [workman's tommy or] 'daily bread' is carried. **1845** DISRAELI *Sybil* III. i, You know as how Juggins applied for his balance after his *tommy-book was paid up. **1906** *Westm. Gaz.* 2 July 5/2 The rescuers ultimately found the two men alive in the old workings...Without food, their '*tommy' boxes having been washed away by the flood, they subsisted on a few candles. **1879** J. BURROUGHS *Locusts & W. Honey*, *Halcyon* (1884) 310 From Rivière du Loup, where we passed the night and ate our first '*Tommy-cods'. **1845** DISRAELI *Sybil* III. iii, It's grand *tommy-day you know. **1873** *Slang Dict.*, **Tommy-Dodd*, in tossing when the odd man either wins or loses, as per agreement. **1884** *Punch* 16 Feb. 73/2 A gambling game known as 'Tommy Dod' is extensively practised. **1897** PEMBERTON *Compl. Cyclist* 125 The head nut, which could be made with a milled edge, and with *tommy holes to start it if stuck beyond finger power. **1863** ATKINSON *Stanton Grange* (1864) 84 Large flies, may-flies, *tommy-longlegs, and grasshoppers. **1860** *Slang Dict.*, **Tommy-master*, one who pays his workmen in goods, or gives them tickets upon tradesmen, with whom he shares the profit. **1849** W. & H. RAYNBIRD *Agric. Suffolk* 301 The *tom* or **tommy* plough is a plough with a double breast for ridging, or for clearing out furrows. **1884** MOORE *Mummer's Wife* (1887) 25 Bill..said it was all '*Tommy rot'. **1899** MARY KINGSLEY *W. African Stud.* ii. 41 My fellow new-comers..thought nothing of calling some of our instructor's best information 'Tommy Rot'! **1895** *Chicago Advance* 4 July 4/1 A whole school of what has been humorously called erotic and *tommyrotic realists..asserting that progress in art requires the elimination of moral ideas. **1830** in W. Cobbett *Rur. Rides* (1885) II. 354 A *tommy shop: a..place containing every commodity that the workman can want, liquor and house-room excepted. **1833** WADE *Hist. Mid. & Working Classes* (1835) 113 An effort was made by 1 & 2 Wm. IV. c. 37 to put an end to what are termed tommy shops, and the practice so general..of paying wages in goods, in lieu of coin and banknotes. **1845** DISRAELI *Sybil* III. i. *note*, The Butty generally keeps a Tommy or Truck shop, and pays the wages of his labourers in goods. **1882** *Standard* 26 Dec. 2/3 The 'foggers', or 'Tommy shop men, live lives of contentment,..at the expense of the poor nail-workers. **1830** in W. Cobbett *Rur. Rides* (1885) II. 352 In the iron country..the truck or *tommy system generally prevails. **1876** MISS BRADDON *J. Haggard's Dau.* ix, The children playing *Tommy Touchwood under the chestnuts.

**7. Tommy Atkins.** Familiar form of *Thomas Atkins*, as a name for the typical private soldier in the British army: for origin, see THOMAS 3; hence *transf.* a private in any army; also, one of the rank and file in any organization.

**1883** SALA in *Illustr. Lond. News* 7 July 3/3 Private Tommy Atkins, returning from Indian service. **1887** *St-*

*Andrews Citizen* (Dixon), In the privacy of his house Tommy Atkins may..hold his baby in his arms. **1892** KIPLING *Barrack-r. Ballads, Tommy*, God bless you, Tommy Atkins, We're all the world to you. **1893** F. ADAMS *New Egypt* 101 The Egyptian Tommy Atkins inspires one rapidly with feelings of sheer affection. **1898** E. J. HARDY in *United Service Mag.* Mar. 646 Some years ago, Lord Wolseley..said, 'I won't call him Tommy Atkins myself, for I think it is a piece of impertinence to call the private soldier Tommy Atkins'. *Ibid.* 649 From talks with these men, I have learned to know and respect Tommy Atkins.

Hence **To·mmy** *v., trans.* to subject to the tommy system; to enforce the truck system on; **To·mmy-hood**, the condition or state of a Tommy.

**1845** DISRAELI *Sybil* III. i, The fact is we are tommied to death. **1857** J. MILLER *Alcohol* (1858) 66 *note*, The razor is kept from Tommy in his Tommyhood.

**Tom-noddy** (tǫ·mˌnǫ·di). [f. TOM + NODDY *sb.*[1]]

**1.** A local name of the Puffin (*Fratercula arctica*). Also *Tommy Noddy, Tom* or *Tommy norie*, and *Tammie-norie*: see TAMMIE 2.

**1702** Tominories [see TAMMIE 2]. **1771** PENNANT *Tour Scotl. in 1769* 36 Puffins, called here Tom Noddies. **1793** *Statist. Acc. Scot.* V. 189 Tomnorries, lyres, calloos. **1805** BARRY *Orkney* III. i. 305 The Puffin..or tommy noddie of this place, is seen very often. **1822** HIBBERT *Descr. Shetl. Isl.* iii. 401 Numberless flocks of birds, such as gulls and scarfs; and along with these,..the Tomnorry. **1885** SWAINSON *Provinc. Names Birds* 219 Puffin..Tom noddy, or Tommie norie (Farn Islands; Scotland).

**2.** A foolish or stupid person; = NODDY *sb.*[1] 1.

**1828** *Craven Gloss., Tom-noddy*,..a tom-fool. **1833** T. HOOK *Parson's Dau.* II. xiv, Why, what a tom-noddy you have made yourself!..that is, if you care for the Parson's Daughter. **1863** COWDEN CLARKE *Shaks. Char.* vi. 144 Our brother John does at times contrive to make a prodigious Tom-noddy of himself.

**To-morn** (tŭmǭ·ɹn), *adv.* and *sb.* Now *dial.* or *arch.* Forms: *α.* 1 **to morʒ(en)ne, 1–2 to morʒen (to morhʒen), 3 to morʒen, 3–4 to morwen, 4 to morewen, 5 to morowen, to moroun.** *β.* **4–5 tomorne, 4–6 to morne, 4– to-morn; 6, 9 tomorn, 9** *dial.* **to moorn.** *γ.* **1 to merne, to mẹrʒen, 2 to marʒan, 3 to marʒen, marhen, mærʒen, marwen, marewene.** [f. TO *prep.* 7 + OE. *morʒenne*, dative of *morʒen, mẹrʒen*, MORN, which see for ulterior etymology. The syncopated *to morn* appears first in northern dial., and is still the vernacular form in a great part of northern England. (In Sc. *the morn*: see MORN 3 d.)

Beside *tō morʒ(en)ne*, OE. had also *on morʒne* (*Beow.* 2484), *on morne* (*Bæda's Hist.* II. vi) in the sense 'on the morrow'.]

**A.** *adv.* = TO-MORROW *adv.* 1. *Obs.* in literary Eng. *c* 1500. Revived as poetical archaism *c* 1850.

*α.* *c* **897** K. ÆLFRED *Gregory's Past. C.* xliv. 324 Ga, & cum to morʒen [*Hatton MS.* to morʒenne]. *c* **1000** To-morhʒen [see quot. *c* 950 in *γ*]. *c* **1050** *Byrhtferth's Handboc* in *Anglia* VIII. 323 We nyton hwæðer we moton to morʒen. *a* **1225** *Ancr. R.* 278 He to dai, ich to morwen. *c* **1330** R. BRUNNE *Chron. Wace* (Rolls) 9081 To morewen schul þey boþe be schent. **13..** in *Pol. Rel. & L. Poems* (1866) 222 To morwen y mai beon wiþoute. **1413** *Pilgr. Sowle* (Caxton) IV. xxxviii. (1859) 63 Abydeth for to morowen.

*β.* *a* **1300** *Cursor M.* 11248 (Cott.) Yee ga to morn wen it es dai To bethleem. **1375** BARBOUR *Bruce* I. 124 Alss weill to-morn as ȝhisterday. *c* **1420** *Anturs of Arth.* 437 Yet þou shalt be mached be myddai to morne. *c* **1475** *Rauf Coilȝear* 85 To-morne, on the morning, quhen thow sall on leip. **1483** CAXTON *Gold. Leg.* 58 b/1 To morn ye shal see y^e glorye of our lord. *a* **1547** SURREY *Æneid* IV. 150 To morne as soon as Titan shall ascend. **1855** ROBINSON *Whitby Gloss.* s. v., 'I'll see thee to moorn'. **1856** DOBELL *Lyrics in War Time, Tommy's Dead*, Stop the mill to-morn, boys. **1870** MORRIS *Earthly Par.* II. III. 125 Bide thou with us to-morn.

*γ.* *c* **950** *Lindisf. Gosp.* Luke xiii. 32 Hælo ic ðerh-doe.. todæg & tomerne [*c* **1000** *Ags. Gosp.* to-morhʒen; *c* **1160** *Hatton* to-morʒen]. *c* **1000** ÆLFRIC *Gram.* xxxviii. (Z.) 224 *Cras*, to merʒen. *c* **1175** *Lamb. Hom.* 21 To marʒan hit [bote] him is awane. *c* **1205** LAY. 16066 Heo cumeð to-mærʒen. *Ibid.* 23661 Þat scal beon tomarʒen. *a* **1225** *Leg. Kath.* 645 Sete, Iesu, swucche sahen i mi muð to marhen.

**b.** In antithesis to *to-day*: see TO-DAY 1 b.

**c.** Followed by *day, eve* (*obs.*), by *morn, morning, night* (*dial.*). Cf. Sc. *the morn's mornin', the morn's nicht*.

*c* **1205** LAY. 17732 Ær to marwen eue. *a* **1300** *Cursor M.* 15343 (Cott.) To-morn dai sal i be dempt On rode tre to hang. **1801** ANDERSON *Cumberld. Ball.* 18 To mworn-o'mworn, i' this seame pleace, We'll hae the stwory out. **1855** ROBINSON *Whitby Gloss., To Moorn't moorn*, or *To Moorn't moorning*, to-morrow morning. *Ibid., To Moorn't neight*, to-morrow night.

**B.** *sb.* = TO-MORROW *sb.* 1.

Truly substantival uses are late, but they were led up to by uses of the adv. in which it might be taken as sb., e.g. when preceded by *till, from*; cf. *till then, from now*.

*c* **1205** LAY. 26393 Nu to-morʒen is þe dæi. **13..** *Cursor M.* 3758 (Fairf.) In þe deu and gresse of thorne Sal be þi blessinge fra to-morne. **1375** BARBOUR *Bruce* I. 621 Tharwith awysit be, Till to morn, that ȝe be set. *c* **1420** *Avow. Arth.* viii, I may haue my leuynge Her tille to-morne atte day. *c* **1440** *York Myst.* xxxvi. 276 To-morne is our dere sabott daye. *c* **1450** *St. Cuthbert* (Surtees) 2873 To morne haly sonday is. **1870** MORRIS *Earthly Par.* II. III. 161 Eager, bright-eyed, and careless of tomorn.

**To-morrow** (tŭmǫ·rōu), *adv.* and *sb.* Forms: *α.* **3 to moruwe, 3–5 to morewe, 3–6 to morowe, to morwe, 4 to morȝe.** *β.* **4 to moru, 5 to morw, to morow, 5–6 to morrowe, 6 tomorow, 6–8 to morrow, 6–9 tomorrow, 6– to-morrow.** Regularly written as two words till 1500 and usually so till *c* 1750. [ME. from *to morȝen, to morwen* (see TO-MORN), with dropping of final *-n*, and later of *-e*, as in inflexions of nouns and vbs., etc. When the final *e* was lost, *w* was vocalized to *-ow*, as in *arrow, borrow, sorrow*. Cf. MORROW.]

**A.** *adv.* **1.** For or on the day after to-day; for or on the morrow.

*c* **1275** *Passion our Lord* 140 in *O. E. Misc.* 41 Er hit beo day to morewe al oþer hit schal go. *c* **1290** *S. Eng. Leg.* I. 393/29 Þus time to-moruwe cum aȝein. **1297** R. GLOUC. (Rolls) 2838 Hii wolleþ tomorwe ariue at te hauene of toteneys. *c* **1320** *Sir Tristr.* 2089 To morwe y schal hir se. *c* **1380** *Sir Ferumb.* 3513 To-morȝe on þe spryng of þe day ..to þe pauyllouns take þe way. **1382** WYCLIF *Ecclus.* xx. 16 To day leeneth a man, and to moru [**1388** to morewe] he asketh it bi ple. *c* **1386** CHAUCER *Knt.'s T.* 1544 Thanne helpe me lord tomorwe in my bataille. **1426** AUDELAY *Poems* 25 To-morw or hit be day. **1484** CAXTON *Fables of Æsop* V. viii, To morowe on the mornyng..sende me a dyssh ful of mylk. **1568** GRAFTON *Chron.* II. 368 Euery day in the weeke it was sayde, he departeth to morwe. *a* **1628** PRESTON *New Covt.* (1634) 435 This doing of it now, and now, and to morrow, and to morrow, these little distances deceive us, and delude us. **1709** PRIOR *Song 'If wine & music have the power'*, But She to Morrow will return. **1897** *Outing* (U.S.) XXIX. 383/2 'Sometime; not to-day; to-morrow'. This is the stereotyped answer which a Turk has always at his tongue's end.

**b.** in antithesis to *to-day*: see TO-DAY A. 1 b.

†**2.** On the morrow after the day mentioned. *Sc. Obs.*

*a* **1699** KIRKTON *Hist. Ch. Scot.* (1817) 126 After he hade drunk liberally in the Advocate's house that same day, went to bed in health, but was taken up stark dead to-morrow morning. **1717** WODROW *Let. to J. Hart* 8 Oct., A committee for peace was proposed to-morrow, who heard the ministers and Mr. Anderson upon the heads of complaint.

**B.** *sb.*

**1.** The day after this day; the next succeeding day; the morrow. **a.** after *till, unto, from*, where it may be adv. **b.** clearly sb.

**a.** *c* **1386** CHAUCER *Melib.* ⁋ 829 The goodnesse þat thou mayst do this day, do it,..ne delaye it nat til to morwe. **1485** CAXTON *Chas. Gt.* II. II. xi. 121 It is better to abyde tyl to morowe. **1526** *Pilgr. Perf.* (W. de W. 1531) 98 b, Knowest thou whether he shall liue vnto to morowe.

**b.** **1535** COVERDALE *Prov.* xxvii. 1 Make not thy boost of tomorow. **1600** FAIRFAX *Tasso* VI. v, To morrowes sun shall spread his timely raies. *a* **1667** COWLEY *Ess. in Verse & Prose, Danger Procrastination*, Our Yesterdays To morrow now is gone. **1711** ADDISON *Spect.* No. 163 ⁋ 11 A..Story..which I shall relate at length in my To-morrow's Paper. **1758** FRANKLIN *Prel. Addr. Pennsylv. Alm.*, One to-day is worth two to-morrows. **1832** TENNYSON *May Queen* i, To-morrow 'ill be the happiest time of all the glad New-year. **1838** LONGF. *Psalm Life* iii, To act, that each to-morrow Find us farther than to-day.

**2.** *attrib.* with times of the day: *to-morrow morning, forenoon, afternoon, evening, night, dinner-time*; also †*to-morrow day*. The combination is used both as *sb.* and as *adv.*

*c* **1275** LAY. 17732 Are to morewe heue. **1382** WYCLIF *Acts* xxiii. 20 That to morwe day thou bringe forth Poul into the counceil. **1470–85** MALORY *Arthur* I. xxiii. 70 He commaunded that..his best hors and armour..be withoute the cyte or to morowe daye. **1539** BIBLE (Great) *Matt.* vi. 34 Care not then for the morow, for to morowe day shall care for it selfe. **1588** SHAKS. *L. L. L.* III. i. 161, I wil come to your worship to morrow morning. **1596** — 1 *Hen. IV*, II. iv. 564, I will by to morrow Dinner time, Send him to answere thee. **1681** OTWAY *Soldier's Fort.* III. i, He shall be Crews-meats by to-morrow Night. **1782** MISS BURNEY *Cecilia* VIII. iii, To-morrow morning I shall but call to see how she is. *Mod.* Can you spend to-morrow evening with us?

**3.** Phrase. *To-morrow come never*, a day that will never arrive; 'when two Sundays meet together'; 'on the Greek Kalends'.

**1725** BAILEY *Erasm. Colloq.* (1878) I. 70 He shall have it in a very little Time...When? To morrow come never? [orig. *ad Calendas Græcas*]. **1770** COLMAN *Man & Wife* III. 46 *Marc.* Very soon, my dear! to-day, or to-morrow, perhaps. *Sally.* To-morrow come never, I believe. **1825** BROCKETT *N. C. Gloss.* s. v. *Nivver*, To-morrow come nivver—when two Sundays meet together.

Hence (*nonce-wds.*) **To-mo·rrower**, one who puts off till to-morrow; a procrastinator; **To-mo·rrowing** *a.*, that procrastinates; **To-mo·rrowness**, the distinctive quality of being to-morrow.

**1810** COLERIDGE *Lett., to Wife* (1895) 563 He is as great a to-morrower to the full as your poor husband. **1880** G. MEREDITH *Tragic Com.* xiv, The postponer, the deferrer, or, as we might say, the to-morrower. **1824** J. MCCULLOCH *Scotl.* IV. 300 The *Cras hoc fiet* of this tomorrowing country. **1897** *Bookman* Nov. 235 If to-morrow..in its essential to-morrowness, has no objective existence.

**Tomp**, obs. form of TUMP. **Tompeon, -ping, -pion, tompkin**: see TAMPION.

**Tompion** (tǫ·mpiən). ? *Obs.* [From the name of Thomas Tompion, a noted watchmaker in the reign of Queen Anne.] A watch made by Tompion or of the same type. Also *attrib.*, as *Tompion clock, watch*.

**1727** POPE, etc. *Art of Sinking* x. 94 Lac'd in her Cosins new appear'd the bride, A Bubble-bow and Tompion at her side. **1727** SWIFT *Circumcision E. Curll* Wks. 1755 III. I. 164 A Tompion's gold watch (which was given her by Mark Anthony). **1729** *Art of Politicks* 10 Think we that modern words eternal are? Toupet, and Tompion, Cosins, and Colmar Hereafter will be called by some plain man A Wig, a Watch, a Pair of Stays, a Fan. **1837** DICKENS *Pickw.* xxxvi, A spacious saloon ornamented with..a music gallery and a Tompion clock. **1871** MISS BRADDON *R. Ainsleigh* xii, I looked at my watch, a bulky Tompion with a clumsy outer case of leather.

**Tom Piper, Tom Poker**: see TOM *sb.* 7 c.

**Tompon**, variant of TAMPON.

**Tom-pudding, Tom-rig**: see TOM *sb.* 8 b, 7 a.

†**Tom-pung**, original form of PUNG *sb.*[2], q. v.

**Tom Thumb.** [In reference to diminutive stature: cf. THUMB *sb.* 3.]

**1.** A dwarf or pigmy of popular tradition or fable, whose history was common as a chap-book; hence a name for a dwarf or diminutive male person; also contemptuously, a petty or insignificant person, a pigmy holder of a high position. Also *attrib.*

**1579** FULKE *Heskins' Parl.* 235 They feigned him to be a little child like Tom Thumb. **1621** R. JOHNSON (*title*) The History of Tom Thumbe. **1630** (*title*) Tom Thumbe, his Life and Death. **1661** NEEDHAM *Hist. Eng. Reb.* 74 Princes are brav'd by Jack and Jill, Wat Tilers and Tom Thums. **1665** *Surv. Aff. Netherl.* 93, Jan. 20. 1651. they Voted our Tom Thombs a free State forsooth, and Commonwealth. *a* **1700** B. E. *Dict. Cant. Crew, Tom-thumb*, a Dwarf. **1806** *Naval Chron.* XV. 159 The Tom Thumb egotism..of the Corsican Usurper. **1889** *N. W. Linc. Gloss., Tom Thumb*, a small and insignificant person. **1907** *Daily Chron.* 6 Feb. 5/5 'Tom Thumb' is a name generally given by showmen to liliputians. The first holder of this 'title' was Charles Stratton, who was brought to London by Barnum.

**2.** *attrib.* Applied to dwarf varieties or specimens of animals or plants; also, *ellipt.* or *absol.* as *sb.* **a.** A kind of dwarf oyster. **b.** A dwarf variety of cabbage, lettuce, or other vegetable, of antirrhinum, nasturtium, or other flower.

**1876** *Rep. Sel. Committee Oyster Fisheries* 49/2 Those oysters which you call buttons, I believe, or which some people call Tom Thumbs. *Ibid.* 77/2 A sort of dwarf oyster, or Tom Thumb oyster, would pass through the two-inch ring. **1898** *Westm. Gaz.* 29 Oct. 1/3 He had gone on sowing radishes and broccoli—making odd signs with pieces of stick and coloured paper to mark 'tom-thumb' or 'giant', 'early' or 'late' [varieties]. *Mod.* The Tom Thumb nasturtiums are preferable to the long straggling forms. Are the antirrhinums Tom Thumbs?

**3.** A popular name of some British wild flowers.

**1886** BRITTEN & HOLLAND *Eng. Plant-n.*, Tom Thumb, *Lathyrus pratensis*. Berks...Suss. *Ibid.*, Appendix, Tom Thumb,..*Lotus corniculatus*. Oxf.

**Tom Tiddler's ground.** Also *dial.* **Tom Tickler's, Tittler's, Tinker's ground.** Name of a children's game.

One of the players is Tom Tiddler, his territory being marked by a line drawn on the ground; over this the other players run, crying 'We're on Tom Tiddler's ground, picking up gold and silver'. They are chased by Tom Tiddler, the first, or sometimes the last, caught taking his place.

**1823** E. MOOR *Suffolk Wds. & Phr.* 437 *Tom Tickler's ground*, a juvenile sport. **1861** MISS YONGE *Stokesley Secret* ii. 34 She heard the joyous cry behind her—'I'm on Tommy Tittler's ground, Picking up gold and silver'. **1880** MRS. LYNN LINTON *Rebel of Family* II. xvi, Squalid children played about the door and made their Tom Tiddler's ground of the steps and street.

**b.** *transf.* Any place where money or other consideration is 'picked up' or acquired readily; also, a disputed or 'debatable territory, a no man's land between two states' (*Slang Dict.*).

**1848** DICKENS *Dombey* xxxvi, Now, the spacious dining-room with the company seated round the glittering table,.. might have been taken for a grown-up exposition of Tom Tiddler's ground, where children pick up gold and silver. **1861** — *Tom Tiddler's Ground* i, 'And why Tom Tiddler's ground?' said the Traveller. 'Because he scatters halfpence to Tramps and such-like', returned the Landlord, 'and of course they pick 'em up'. **1890** 'R. BOLDREWOOD' *Col. Reformer* (1891) 290 He..had come on to..Tom Tidler's ground,..gold..was sticking out of the soil everywhere. **1910** W. SICHEL *Glenbervie Jrnls.* i. 6 Ireland was then the Tom Tiddler's ground of parliamentary fortune hunters.

**Tom-tit, tomtit** (tǫ·mˌti·t). Also 8 **Tom teet.** [See TIT *sb.*[3] 3.] A common name of the Blue Titmouse (*Parus cæruleus*); also *locally*, of the Coal Titmouse (*P. ater*), and the American *P. atricapillus*; incorrectly of other small birds, as the Wren, and the Tree-creeper.

**1709** STEELE *Tatler* No. 112 ⁋ 2 To spare the Life of a Tom-Tit. **1711** ADDISON *Spect.* No. 5 ⁋ 7 The Singing Birds will be Personated by Tom-tits. **1796** MORSE *Amer. Geog.* I. 211 Tom Teet, *Parus atricapillus*. **1812** COMBE *Picturesque* XXII, I must breathe my dogs a-bit, And try my gun at some tom-tit. *a* **1825** FORBY *Voc. E. Anglia, Tom-tit*,..by us it is applied to the wren.., *tom-tit* seems to belong indiscriminately to both sexes. **1909** *Athenæum* 20 Mar. 347/1 Magee characterized somebody's religion as insufficient for a tomtit.

**b.** *transf.* applied to a little man or boy.

**1741** RICHARDSON *Pamela* (ed. 2) I. Introd., I have told you the History of this Tom-tit of a Prater. **1909** *Daily News* 19 July 11 A veritable little tomtit of a man in his jerky little ways and lively good humour.

**Tom-tom** (tǫ·mˌtǫ·m), *sb.* Also 8–9 **tam-tam, 9 tum-tum, tong-tong.** [a. Hindūstānī or other E. Indian vernacular *tam-tam*: cf. Sinhalese *tamaṭṭama*, Malay *tong-tong*; all imitations of the sound of the instrument.]

**1.** A native East Indian drum; extended also to the drums of barbarous peoples generally.

**1693** in Wheeler *Madras* (1861) I. 268 That to-morrow morning the Choultry Justices do cause the Tom Tom to be beat through all the streets of the Black Town. **1764**

in J. Long *Select. Rec. Govt.* (*Fort William*) (1869) 391 (Y.) You will give strict orders to Zemindars to furnish Oil and Musshauls, and Tom Toms and Pikemen, &c., according to custom. **1782** W. F. Martyn *Geog. Mag.* I. 249 The music is composed of small drums called tamtams. **1804** Wellington in Gurw. *Desp.* (1837) IV. 186 Let the cause of their punishment be published in the Bazaar by beat of tom tom. *c* **1813** Mrs. Sherwood *Stories Ch. Catech.* iv. 20 They were almost deafened by the sound of their tum-tums and trumpets. *Ibid.* (*Explan. Ind. words*), *Tum-tums*, small drums. **1860** Tristram *Gt. Sahara* xi. 184 The chief characteristic of the affair was the noise of drums and tomtoms. **1864** Engel *Mus. Anc. Nat.* 63 The other class of Oriental small drums consists of those which are of a barrel-form, covered at each end with skin, carried obliquely, and beaten with one hand at each end. Such drums are best known by the name tom-tom.

**b.** *erroneously.* A Chinese gong. (*tam-tam.*)

**1839** Ure *Dict. Arts* 333 Cymbals, gongs, and the tamtam of the Chinese are made of an alloy of 100 of copper with about 25 of tin. **1856** Mrs. C. Clarke tr. *Berlioz' Instrument.* 229 The gong, or tam-tam, is employed only in funereal compositions and dramatic scenes where terror is carried to its height. **1859** R. Hunt *Guide Mus. Pract. Geol.* (ed. 2) 210 The tam-tams and cymbals of bronze of the Chinese are forged with the hammer.

**c.** *transf.* Anything beaten like a drum so as to make a loud noise. Chiefly *fig.*

**1885** *Pall Mall G.* 7 Apr. 1/1 Those preparations about which the journalistic tom-tom is being beaten so vigorously. **1891** *Scott. Leader* 2 July 5 Mr. Parnell was greeted with such a vigorous beating of tom-toms that he gave up the attempt to speak.

**2.** The beating of a drum; an imitation of the sound of this.

**1898** Alderson *Mounted Infantry Mashonaland* v. 90 Then 'Tom-tom, tom-tom, tom, tom-a-tom tom', go the war drums; out go the fires. **1912** *Eng. Rev.* Mar. 615 The tom-tom of the watchman could be heard.

**3.** *attrib.* and *Comb.*

**1857** Wilkinson *Egypt Time of Pharaohs* 28 The trumpet was chiefly confined to the military band; to which also belonged, though not exclusively, the tomtom drum, the clappers, and a few others. **1884** J. Colborne *Hicks Pasha* 59 The band consisted of three fiddlers and a tam-tam beater. **1908** Sir H. Johnston *Grenfell & Congo* II. xxv. 719 A drum of the tom-tom form is used.

**To·m-tom,** *v.* [Partly f. prec. sb., partly directly echoic.] **a.** *intr.* To beat a tom-tom or drum; to drum. **b.** *trans.* To give notice of or call attention to by beating a tom-tom. **c.** To perform on a tom-tom or drum; *transf.* to play in a monotonous way, to 'drum', 'strum'. Hence **To·m-tomming** *vbl. sb.*, **To·m-tommer.**

**1857** S. Hislop in G. Smith *Life* v. (1888) 166 It had been tom-tomed in the city that all who are too poor to lay in a supply of provisions should leave. **1859** R. F. Burton in *Jrnl. Geog. Soc.* XXIX. 414 A man tom-toming lustily upon a kettle-drum shaped like an European hourglass. **1860** Tristram *Gt. Sahara* ix. 146 While preparing for the night we heard a loud tomtomming without. **1872** 'Aliph Cheem' *Lays of Ind* (1876) 6 The dancer .. Keeping time to the piper's and tom-tommer's strains. **1884** J. Colborne *Hicks Pasha* 118 My friends..trumpet, bugle, and 'tam-tam' all day long. **1898** Barker *Comic Side School Life* 29 Able to tom-tom easy accompaniments on the piano.

**Tom-trot, Tom-turkey**: see Tom.

**-tomy,** a. Gr. -τομία, often through mod.L. *-tomia*, used to form abstract sbs. from adjs. in -τομος cutting; f. verbal ablaut-series τεμ-, τομ-, τμ-, in τέμ-ν-ειν to cut, τομή, τμῆσις cutting: entering into numerous technical terms, as *anatomy*, lit. 'cutting up', *cystotomy*, *dichotomy*, *lithotomy*, *phlebotomy*, *thymotomy*, *tracheotomy*, *zootomy*, etc.

**Tomyll,** obs. form of Tumble.

**Ton**[1] (tɒn). Forms: **4-6 tonne, 5 toun, 6 toonne, (tune),** *Sc.* **twn, 6-7 tunne, 6-8 tun, 7 tunn, 5- ton.** See also Tun *sb.* [In origin the same word as Tun (OE. *tunne*, OF. *tonne*) a cask. In ME. this was commonly spelt, as in French, *tonne*; in 16–17th c., more often *tun*; from *c* 1688 the two spellings have been differentiated, *tun* being appropriated to the sense 'cask' and the liquid measure, and *ton* to the senses here treated, which, it will be seen, are partly measures, and partly weights.]

†**1.** A large wine-vessel, a cask; hence, a measure of capacity used for wine: now spelt Tun, q. v.

**2.** A unit used in measuring the carrying capacity or burden of a ship, the amount of cargo, freight, etc. Originally, the space occupied by a tun cask of wine (see explanatory quot. 1894 on *ton tight* s. v. Tight *a.* 14, and quot. 1539 here). Now, for the purposes of registered tonnage, the space of 100 cubic feet. For purposes of freight, usually the space of 40 cubic feet, unless that bulk would weigh more than 20 cwt., in which case freight is charged by weight. But the expression 'ton of cargo' is also used with regard to special packages which are conventionally assumed as going so many packages to the ton. Cf. also Tonnage.

**1379–1603** Tonne tight, etc. [see Tight *a.* 14]. **1509** Hawes *Past. Pleas.* xix. xxii. (Percy) 92 The shyp was great, fyve c. tonne to charge. **1530** Palsgr. 460/1 A shyppe of a hundred tonne. [**1539** in R. G. Marsden *Sel. Pl. Crt. Adm.* (Selden) I. 89 Unam naviculam vocatam a shippes boat oneris trium doliorum.] **1544** *Ibid.* 126 Ladyn..35 butts wynes wich goith for fyeftey tons ladinge. **1555** Eden *Dec. New World* 349 (*Second Voyage to Guinea*) (Arb.) 379 A shyppe of the burden of seuen score toonne. **1582** N. Lichefield tr. *Castanheda's Conq. E. Ind.* i. ii. 4 b, The King then bought..a Caruell of fiftie tunne. **1587** Harrison *England* ii. xvii. (1877) i. 285 A ship of ours of six hundred tun. **1657** R. Ligon *Barbadoes* (1673) 2 We..had with us a small ship of about 180 tunns, called the *Nonesuch*. *a* **1687** Petty *Pol. Arith.* iii. (1690) 54 The King of Englands Navy consists of about seventy thousand Tuns of Shipping. *Ibid.* 56 In France..there are not above one hundred and fifty thousand Tun of Trading Vessels, and consequently not above fifteen thousand Seamen, reckoning a Man to every ten Tun. **1769** Falconer *Dict. Marine* (1789) Z j, A ton in measure is generally estimated at 2000 lb. in weight. **1821** J. Q. Adams in C. Davies *Metr. Syst.* (1871) iii. 98 The casks of Bordeaux wine were then [1423] and still are made for stowage in such manner that four hogsheads occupy one ton of shipping. The ton was of thirty-two cubic feet by measure, and of 2,016 English pounds, of fifteen ounces to the pound, in weight; equal to 2,560 of the easterling tower pound. **1858** Simmonds *Dict. Trade* s. v., The ton of freight or merchandise varies with the article and the locality from whence shipped. **1867** Smyth *Sailor's Word-bk.*, *Ton*, or *Tun*...In the cubical contents of a ship it is the weight of water equal to 2000 lbs., by the general standard for liquids. *Ibid.*, 42 cubic feet of articles equal one ton in shipment.

**3.** A measure of capacity: **a.** for timber; usually equivalent to 40 cubic feet (or for hewn timber, 50).

**1521** *MS. Acc. St. John's Hosp., Canterb.*, For hewyng of a tune and xvj fote of tymber. **1707** Mortimer *Husb.* (1721) II. 88 To sell your Timber..by the Ton, Load or Foot, forty Foot being reckoned a Ton, and fifty a Load, and in some places just the contrary. **1774** Pennant *Tour Scotl. in 1769* (ed. 3) 107 The tenant is obliged to work 150 tuns of timber annually, paying eighteen shillings and six-pence per tun. **1813** T. Davis *Agric. Wilts.* Gloss., *Ton* of Rough Timber, 40 feet, the load 50 feet, is only used when timber is hewn for the navy.

**b.** for various solid commodities, as stone, gravel, lime, plaster, wheat, cheese, etc.

**1428–9** *Rec. St. Mary at Hill* 70 A tonne tyght of northerin ston. *a* **1500** *How Plowman lerned Pater-Noster* 110 in Hazl. *E. P. P.* I. 213 Of whete amonge them they gate an hole tunne. **1504** *Acc. Ld. High Treas. Scot.* II. 277 For xx twn of plaistir brocht hame be Dorange, Franchman. **1538** in R. G. Marsden *Sel. Pl. Crt. Adm.* (Selden) I. 82 For the freight of every ton tight of the saide wheate, accompting fyve quarters to every ton. **1667** Primatt *City & C. Build.* 68 Half a Tun of Plaister of Paris will lay fifteen yards of Lath-work. *a* **1674** Clarendon *Hist. Reb.* vii. § 335 Threescore and fifteen Barrels of Butter, and fourteen Tun of Cheese. **1821** J. Q. Adams in C. Davies *Metr. Syst.* (1871) iii. 127 Before the statute of 1496, the London quarter of a ton was the one measure, to which the bushel for corn, the gallon, deduced by measure, for ale, and the gallon, deduced by weight, for wine, were all referred. **1858** Simmonds *Dict. Trade* s. v., A ton of flour, in commerce, is 8 sacks or 10 barrels; a ton of potatoes, 10 bushels.

**4.** A measure of weight, now generally 20 cwt.; in Great Britain legally 2240 lbs.; in the United States and some of the colonies, for most purposes 2000 lbs. 'Tons' of different amounts were formerly in use and are still so locally for some commodities. (Where two weights are so known and used, the heavier is distinguished as the *long* or *gross ton* and the lighter as the *short ton.*) *Metric ton* (Fr. *tonne*) = 1000 kilogrammes (2204·6 lbs. avoirdupois).

**1485** *Cely Papers* (Camden) 183 Item the sam day payd for vj toun of balast, ij s. **1539** in R. G. Marsden *Sel. Pl. Crt. Adm.* (Selden) I. 89, lxxj kintalls of yron in ends 44... And it goes for iij tone and xj kintalls. **1545** *Rates of Custome-ho.* b v, Iron called Lukes Iron the tonne conteynynge .xx. C. pounde iii. li. vi.s. viii.d. **1588** Greene *Pandosto* (1607) 6 A pound of goold is worth a tunne of leade. **1670** Eachard *Cont. Clergy* 115 Unless we had some vent for our learned ones beyond the sea, and could transport so many tunn of divines yearly, as we do other commodities, with which the nation is over-stocked. **1725** *Bradley's Fam. Dict.* II, *Tun*, a Measure in Averdupois, consisting of twenty hundred Weight, each Hundred being a Hundred and twelve Pounds. **1793** Smeaton *Edystone L.* § 154 Every thing stood fast with eight ton weight upon the tackle-blocks. **1829** *Glover's Hist. Derby* I. 100 It [pure white gypsum] sells at 10s. per long ton. (*Note.*—120 lb. to the Cwt.) *Ibid.* 265 It was agreed that weighing-houses should be erected upon the several canals, and that the ton should be fixed at 2,400 lbs. **1858** Simmonds *Dict. Trade* s. v., In Great Britain, the legal ton by weight is usually 20 cwt., or 2240 lbs., but in long weight it is 2400 lbs...In Cornwall, the miner's ton is 21 cwt., or 2352 lbs. **1881** Raymond *Mining Gloss.* s. v., For many things, such as coal and iron, the ton in use [in U. S.] is the long ton of 20 hundred-weight at 112 pounds avoirdupois...In gold and silver mining, and throughout the Western States, the ton is the short ton of 2000 pounds. **1894** *Times* 10 Sept. 6/1 The total quantity which exploded was about 3,700 lb., or not far short of two tons, 2,000 lb. being reckoned as a ton in measuring explosives.

**b.** (*colloq.*) A very large amount: cf. Load *sb.* 6. Mostly in *pl.*

**1895** *Daily News* 25 Apr. 6/3 'Is there any culture at Chicago?' asked a young lady of Boston of a damsel of the former city. 'You bet your sweet life!..Tons of it', was the reply. **1911** Barrie *Peter & Wendy* iv, 'I say! Do you kill many [pirates]?' 'Tons'.

†**5. Ton mascull (tonne maskyll),** app. a tun cask of 252 gallons: = Tun *sb.* 2. *Obs.*

[*Mascull* may represent a Latin or Romanic *masc(u)la* = It. *maschia* 'male, large, big, huge', as a description of the largest *tunna* or *tonna.*]

**1432** *Rolls of Parlt.* IV. 405/2 Wynes..not havyng of lyes overe iiij or v ynches in a tonne maskyll. **1531** in R. G. Marsden *Sel. Pl. Crt. Adm.* (Selden) I. 36 Lade the sayd shypp with wynes to the ffull number of lvij tonnes..accounttyng always a ton mascull for a ton, ij pipes for a ton, iiij hoggeshedds for a ton, and vj tercys for a ton, and twenty hundred Englyshe weyght for a ton. **1541** *Ibid.* 113 So many thowsand orenges as makyth by account and custom of Galizia, all with the forsaid xlvj hogsheds whales grece and oyle, xlvj ton mascull.

**6.** *attrib.* and *Comb.*, as *ton-burden*, *-load*; esp. with measures of distance, forming units measuring the work done in the conveyance of heavy bodies, esp. in reference to its cost; as **ton-fathom**, the equivalent of the work done in raising a ton through the depth of a fathom, as in the shaft of a mine; **ton-mile**, the same in carrying a ton the distance of a mile, as by a railway-train or motor-car; so **ton-mileage**, amount of or reckoning in ton-miles, or charge per ton-mile.

**1805** *Act* 45 *Geo. III*, c. 10 § 3 For every *ton burthen of every such ship or vessel, which shall have so arrived without a clean bill of health, fifteen shillings. **1874** J. H. Collins *Metal Mining* (1875) 77 About 1·50th of a penny per *ton-fathom or less. *a* **1400** *MS. Cott. Vesp. B.* xxii. lf. 97 in *Blk. Bk. Adm.* (Rolls) I. 400 Accustumez de doner pur chascun *tonnelode, que le vesseau purra porter .. douze deniers. **1894** *Outing* (U.S.) 393/1 Were the *ton mileage of each contrasted, the waterways would make much the greater showing. **1900** *Engineering Mag.* XIX. 734 Two horses harnessed to one waggon may achieve 35 nett *ton miles daily in regular work. **1902** *Monthly Rev.* Aug. 35 Obtaining the average per ton-mile from other canals. **1906** *Westm. Gaz.* 28 Aug. 4/2 The 10-h. p. [motor car]..ran..at the rate of 41.7 ton miles per gallon.

**b. Ton tight**: see Tight *a.* 14.

†**Ton**[2]. *Obs.* [a. F. *taon* (pronounced tañ, earlier toñ) gad-fly (12th c. in Littré), later also applied in the environs of Paris to the larva of the cockchafer (Littré):—pop.L. **tabōnem*, for L. *tabānum* (*-us*) gad-fly, whence Prov. *tavan*, Sp. *tábano*, Pg. *tavão*, It. *tafa·no*, *tabano*, †*tavano*, gad-fly.] The larva of the cockchafer, which lives underground and feeds on the roots of plants.

**1693** Evelyn *De la Quint. Compl. Gard.* II. 100 Kitchen-Plants, especially Lettuce, and Succory, &c. constantly have some of those Tons, or other little reddish Worms which gnaw them about the neck, and kill them [*margin* Those usually called by the Name of Cock-Chafers]. *Ibid.* 202 The great Enemies of Straw-berry Plantations are the Ton's which are great White Worms, that in the Months of May and June, gnaw the necks of their Roots. **1712** J. James tr. *Le Blond's Gardening* 173 The great Enemies to Trees, are..Snails, Tons, Turks, and abundance of Worms.

‖**Ton**[3] (toñ, †tɒn). Now *rare.* See also *bon-ton* s. v. Bon. [Fr. *ton* manner in general:—L. *ton-us*, Tone in colouring, etc.] The fashion, the vogue, the mode; fashionable air or style.

**1769** *Lloyd's Evening Post* 18–20 Dec. 589 The present fashionable *Ton* (a word used at present to express every thing that's fashionable) is a set of French puppets. **1775** Sheridan *Rivals* i. i, None of the London whips of any degree of ton wear wigs now. **1778** Miss Burney *Evelina* (1791) II. xxxvii. 244 Don't we all know that you lead the *ton* in the *beau monde*? **1812** H. & J. Smith *Rej. Addr.*, *Beautiful Incend.* ix, And if she were here all alone, Our house might nocturnally boast A bumper of fashion and ton. **1812** Combe *Picturesque* xi, A mantle, too, is all the ton, And therefore I have order'd one. **1881** Besant & Rice *Chapl. of Fleet* ii. i, In everything..make my niece an accomplished woman, a woman of ton.

**b.** *transf.* People of fashion; fashionable society; the fashionable world.

**1815** *Sporting Mag.* XLVI. 93 All the 'Ton's' a stage, And Fashion's motley votaries are but play'rs. **1854** J. S. C. Abbott *Napoleon* (1855) I. xiv. 255 The princess, the nobles, and all the *ton* had disappeared.

†**Ton**[4]. *Obs.* [a. OF. *ton* (14–16th c.), F. *thon*:—L. *thunn-us*, Tunny.] A sea-fish, a tunny.

**1624** Middleton *Game at Chess* v. iii, You may eat kid, cabrito, calf, and tons. **1624** [T. Scott] *Vox Populi* ii. 22 A peece of leane Kid, or Cabrito, a Tripe, Tone's or such like. **1672** Josselyn *New Eng. Rarities* 31. **1768** Boswell *Corsica* i. (ed. 2) 37 There is the greatest variety of all the best kinds, and in particular a sort of ton or sturgeon.

**Ton,** obs. ME. pl. of Toe; var. Tone *pron.*; obs. f. Town, Tun; dial. var. of *tan*, obs. pa. pple. of Take (see Take *v.* 5 γ, To *v. Obs.*).

**Tonacle, -culle, Tonage,** obs. ff. Tunicle, Tonnage.

**Tonal** (tōu·năl), *a.* and *sb.* [ad. med.L. *tonāl-is* (St. Bernard of Cluny), f. *ton-us* Tone: see -al; cf. mod.F. *tonal* (Littré).]

**A.** *adj.* Of or pertaining to tone or tones.

**1.** *Mus.* †**a.** Pertaining to the ecclesiastical modes.

**1776** Hawkins *Hist. Mus.* iii. ix. I. 354 The first [discourse]..is on..Guidonian music.., the one [part] treating of Manual, i. e. elementary music..and the other of Tonal music, containing the doctrine of the ecclesiastical tones.

**b.** Applied to a fugue, or a sequence, in which the repetitions of the subject in different positions are all in the same key, and therefore vary in their intervals: opp. to Real *a.* 3 c.

**1869** Ouseley *Counterp. Canon & Fugue* xix. 160 *note*, In the early days of counterpoint a tonal fugue was one in which the relations of the subject and answer were governed by the old Church modes. **1879** — in Grove *Dict. Mus.* I. 567 In most cases the answer [to the subject of a fugue] has to be modified according to certain rules to avoid modulating out of the key...An answer so treated is called a 'tonal answer', and the fugue is called a 'Tonal fugue'.

1889 PROUT *Harmony* v. § 138 The intervals..differ in quality according to their position in the scale...Such a sequence is termed a *tonal* sequence.

**2.** Of, pertaining, or relating to the tone or tones. Of speech or a language: expressing difference of meaning by variation of tone.

1866 *Athenæum* 24 Mar. 404/1 The multiplicity of tonal divagations. 1867 MACFARREN *Harmony* i. 11 Ambrose.. called the modes he adopted according to their tonal ascent, 1st, 2nd, 3rd, 4th. 1886 C. TROTTER in *Encycl. Brit.* XXI. 774/1 But [Shan] is a tonal language, and the vowel sounds are few, so that some have two or three values assigned them. 1896 F. NIECKS *Paper bef. Congr. Incorp. Soc. Mus.*, The Association of Tonal and Verbal Speech.

†**B.** *sb.* (med.L. *tonāle*). A book containing a summary of the rules governing ecclesiastical music, with examples. Cf. the *tonārius* 'liber de tonis seu cantu' (Du Cange). *Obs. rare*—⁰.

*c* 1475 *Pict. Voc.* in Wr.-Wülcker 755/20 (Nomina ecclesie necessaria) *Hoc tonale*, a tonal.

Hence **To·nally** *adv.*, in respect of tone.

1883 GURNEY *Tertium Quid* (1887) II. 22 Bits that are rhythmically and tonally coherent.

**Tonalite** (tǭ·năləit). *Min.* [See quot. 1879.] A proposed name for a variety of quartz-diorite.

1879 RUTLEY *Stud. Rocks* xii. 244 The rock termed tonalite by Vom Rath, which occurs in the Tonale Pass in the Tyrol, ..formerly regarded as a variety of granite, is a micaceous quartz-diorite. 1885 LYELL *Elem. Geol.* (ed. 4) 571 *Tonalite* ..consists of quartz, oligoclase, and hornblende.

**Tonality** (tonæ·lĭti). [f. TONAL *a.* + -ITY: so mod.F. *tonalité* (1866 in Littré).] Tonal quality.

**1.** *Mus.* The relation, or sum of relations, between the tones or notes of a scale or musical system; *spec.* in modern music, = KEY *sb.* 7 c; hence *transf.* a particular scale or system of tones; in modern music = KEY *sb.* 7 b.

1838 G. F. GRAHAM *Mus. Comp.* App. 68 The peculiar tonalities of many old national airs. 1855 *Fraser's Mag.* LI. 568 Grafting..more elegant melodic forms, improved rhythm, and the modern 'tonality' on the sustained grandeur of the old masters. 1867 BRANDE & COX *Dict. Sc.*, etc., *Tonality*..is used generally to denote that peculiarity which modern music possesses, in consequence of its being written in definite keys, thereby conforming to certain defined arrangements of tones and semitones in the diatonic scale. 1875 OUSELEY *Mus. Form* ii. 5 A Melody, if it is to produce a pleasing effect..must be written in some definite tonality.

**2.** *Painting.* The quality of a painting in respect of tone; the general tone or colour-scheme of a picture: see quots.

1866 *Sat. Rev.* 27 Jan. 117/1 Much of the value of a painting depends on the completeness of its tonality,..The *tonalité* of a picture is the proportionate arrangement, and especially the accurate subdivision of tones, both with regard to colour and to relative lightness and darkness. 1884 *Athenæum* 24 May 668 The tonality of the picture is very good, although the illumination is in a low key. 1890 TALBOT ARCHER in *Anthony's Photogr. Bull.* III. 218 By 'tone' or 'tonality' is here meant the correct rendering, in black and white, of any natural object—as a landscape, a portrait, etc.

**To-name** (tū·nēⁱm), *sb.* Now *dial.* Also 3–4 tuo-, tou-, 4 tow-, 4, 7 too-, 9 *Sc. dial.* tee-name. [OE. *tó-nama*, f. TO-¹ + NAME *sb.* So MLG. *toname*, Du. *toenaam*, MHG. *zuoname*, G. *zuname*.] A name or epithet added to an original name; a cognomen, surname, nickname; now in *Sc.* a name added to distinguish one individual from another or others having the same Christian name and surname, a 'by-name'.

*c* 950 *Lindisf. Gosp.* Mark v. 9 [Hælend] ȝefreȝn hine huætd ðe tonoma is? & cuæð to him here tonoma me is, forðon moniȝ we sindon. *c* 1200 *Trin. Coll. Hom.* 143 Ðes wimman hadde ec on toname magdalene..Nu ȝie habbeð iherd þes wimmanes name & ec hire toname. 1303 R. BRUNNE *Handl. Synne* 4741 Þe bysshope Seynt Roberd; Hys toname ys 'Grostest Of Lynkolne'. 1382 WYCLIF *Ecclus.* xlvii. 19 The name of the Lord, to whom is the toname [1388 surname] God of Irael. 1567 SIR R. MAITLAND *Complaynt* vii, Thay theifis that steillis and tursis hame, Ilk ane o' them has ane to-name; Will of the Lawis, Hab of the Schawis. 1636 in Ld. A. Campbell *Rec. Argyll* (1885) 5 Archibald, Earl of Argyle, his too name was Gillispick Dow. 1823 SCOTT *Quentin D.* iii. 1870 F. BUCKLAND in Bompas *Life* xi. 243 There were no less than seven men every one of whom was a 'David Main', hence the necessity of Tee names, to distinguish one person from the other.

Hence **To·-name** *v. trans.*, to give a to-name to.

1775 BUCHANAN *Inquiry Anc. Scott. Surnames* 49 Brian Kennedy, to-named Boraimh, or Taxer.

†**Tonance** (tōᵘ·năns). *Obs. rare*—¹. [f. as next: see -ANCE.] A loud or echoing sound.

1778 H. BROOKE *Antony & Cl.* III. iii, The emperor's trumpet—I do know it, By the pride of its tonance.

**Tonant** (tōᵘ·nănt), *a.* [ad. L. *tonānt-em*, pr. pple. of *tonāre* to thunder, make a loud noise.] Thundering, loud-sounding.

1891 G. MEREDITH *Reading of Life* (1901) 122 Nay, nor so tonant thunders the stress of the gale in the oak-trees. 1898 — *Napoleon* xiii, The penetrant, the tonant, tower of towers, Striking from black disaster starry showers.

†**Tona·tion.** *Obs. rare*—¹. [f. TONE *sb.* or *v.* + -ATION.] The action of toning or producing musical tones; the tones or notes so produced.

1728 R. NORTH *Mem. Music* (1846) 13 To observe the various tonations, and reduce them to a certain order, or scale.

**Tonca bean**: see TONKA.

‖**Tondino** (tondī·no). *Arch.* [It. *tondino*, dim. f. *tondo* round: see next. In Fr. *tondin*.] (See quot. 1823.)

1704 J. HARRIS *Lex. Techn.* I, *Tondino*, a Term in Architecture. See *Astragal*. 1823 P. NICHOLSON *Pract. Build.* 595 *Tondino*, a round moulding resembling a ring.

‖**Tondo** (to·ndo). Pl. **tondi** (to·ndi). [It. *tondo* 'a round, circle, compass; also a round trencher, plate, or little dish' (Florio); in mod.It. a studio term used in relation to paintings, Della Robbia ware, and other fine art work; shortened from *rotondo* round.] An easel painting of circular form; also a carving in relief within a circular space.

1890 *Blackw. Mag.* Jan. 140 A medal representing the great tondo of Botticelli. 1892 SYMONDS *Michel Angelo* (1899) I. III. v. 111 Michel Angelo found time to carve the two tondi, Madonnas in relief enclosed in circular spaces which we still possess. 1901 *Athenæum* 9 Nov. 635 A catalogue..of the Della Robbia monuments and..tabernacles, tondos, reliefs, medallions, and the like. 1909 *Times, Lit. Suppl.* 7 Oct. 361/2 One of the most beautiful of Michelangelo's works, the tondo in the Bargello.

**Tone** (tōᵘn), *sb.* Forms: 4 ton, 4– tone; (5 toun, toyn, 5–6 toyne; 6 toone). [Partly a. OF. *ton* (of voice, 13th c. in Littré) = Prov. *ton*, Cat. *to*, Sp. *ton*, *tono*, Pg. *tom*, *tono*, It. *tuono*:—L. *ton-um*, acc. of *ton-us*; and partly directly f. L. *tonus* 'stretching, quality of sound, tone, accent, tone in painting', in med.L. esp. as a term of music, a. Gr. τόνος 'stretching, tension, raising of voice, pitch of voice, accent, musical mode or key, exertion of physical or mental energy'; f. strong grade of vbl. ablaut series τεν-, τον-, τα-, in τείν-ειν to stretch. In musical senses, much influenced by med.L. uses of *tonus*, and in more recent uses, largely influenced by Greek.

The early phonology is far from clear, the obscurity being increased by the changing values of the spellings *o*, *oo*, *ou*, *oy*, and their ambiguity at certain periods. The normal course of Fr. *-on* was to become *-oun* (= -ūn) in ME., and diphthongal *-own*, *-own* (as in *soun(d*, *noun*, *renown*, *bounty*) in mod.Eng. An example of this appears *c* 1407 in sense 1, where Lydgate rimes *toun*, *sown*. But earlier than this we find *tōn*, *tone* (perh. a more learned or technical formation) direct from L. *tonus*, so well known in mediæval music, which became the prevalent form, and appears *c* 1325 in sense 2 b, riming with *nōn* 'noon'. The normal fate of this was to become in 15–16th c. *toon* (= tūn); cf. 1570 in sense 1, where Levins rimes *toone* with *boone*, *moone*, *noone*, *soone*, etc. But here again the influence of L. *tonus* appears to have prevailed, so as to make *tone* (tōn) the finally accepted form. The sound of *toyn*, *toyne*, in *c* 1460, 1521, is doubtful: *-oy*, *-oi* in Sc. and north. dial. generally meant long ō. The Sc. examples of *tone* in sense 2 c are also doubtful; they may be precursors of mod.Sc. (tön, tün), and more properly belong to TUNE, a divergent form of *tone* which has finally been differentiated as a distinct word, q.v. *Tone*, *toon*, and *toun*, might thus be viewed as separate words; but as the two latter are obs., and all the forms go back directly or indirectly to L. *tonus*, they are here treated as one, under the current spelling, but with the quotations separated.]

**I. 1.** A musical or vocal sound considered with reference to its quality, as acute or grave, sweet or harsh, loud or soft, clear or dull.

1340 HAMPOLE *Pr. Consc.* 9296 Ilkan þat sal won þar, Sal syng with angels,..In swilk tones þat sal be swete to here. 1667 MILTON *P. L.* v. 626 Harmonie Divine So smooths her charming tones, that Gods own ear Listens delighted. 1797 MRS. RADCLIFFE *Italian* xvii, The deep tone of a bell, rolling on the silence of the night. 1855 BAIN *Senses & Int.* II. ii. § 5 (1864) 213 Instruments and voices are distinguished by the sweetness of their individual tones.

β. *c* 1407 LYDG. *Reson & Sens.* 5211 The wherbles, nor the vnkouth touns, Nor the ravysshinge sowns, Nor the sugryd melodye Of ther soot[e] armonye.

γ. 1521 J. T. in Bradshaw *St. Werburge* Prol. 1 Honour, ioye, and glorie, the toynes organicall.

δ. 1570 LEVINS *Manip.* 168/37 A Toone, *tonus* [*rimes* boone, moone, noone, soone, etc.].

**b.** (Without *a* or *pl.*) Quality of sound.

1663 BUTLER *Hud.* I. I. 459 Though Writers, for more lofty Tone Do call him Ralpho, 'tis all one. 1732 LEDIARD *Sethos* II. VIII. 219 The tone of your voice has become more masculine. 1908 [MISS E. FOWLER] *Betw. Trent & Ancholme* 82 You may get much variation of tone, by change of speed [with a THUNDERER].

γ. *c* 1460 *Towneley Myst.* xv. 13 A! myghtfull god, what euer this ment, so swete of toyn?

**2.** *Mus.* and *Acoustics.* A sound of definite pitch and character produced by regular vibration of a sounding body; a musical note.

*Difference-tone* (or *differential tone*), *summation-tone* (or *summational tone*), the secondary or resultant tones produced when two notes of different pitch are sounded together with sufficient force, having rates of vibration equal respectively to the difference and the sum of those of the primary tones. *Combinational*, *fundamental*, *partial*, *resultant* (etc.) *tone*: see the adjs.

*c* 1400 tr. *Secreta Secret.*, *Gov. Lordsh.* 98 Fyue tones er of Musyke. 1579 E. K. *Gloss. Spenser's Sheph. Cal.* Oct. 27 The Arcadian Melodie..being altogither on the fyft and vij tone, it is of great force to molifie and quench the kindly courage. *a* 1650 CRASHAW *Music's Duel* 23 She Carves out her dainty voice..Into a thousand sweet distinguish'd tones. 1666 PEPYS *Diary* 8 Aug., Mr. Hooke..having come to a certain number of vibrations proper to make any tone, he is able to tell how many strokes a fly makes with her wings ..by the note that it answers to in musique. 1867 TYNDALL *Sound* vii. 282 Helmholtz inferred..that there are also resultant tones formed by the sum of the primaries, as well as by their difference. He thus discovered his summation tones before he had heard them. 1875 *Encycl. Brit.* I. 118/2 These resultant tones..are termed *difference-tones*. 1876 BERNSTEIN *Five Senses* 280 Besides the difference tone, Helmholtz has pointed out a much weaker summational tone. 1878 G. B. PRESCOTT *Sp. Telephone* (1879) 6 A series of vibrations, a definite number of which are produced in a given time, and of which we thus become cognizant, is called a tone. 1881 BROADHOUSE *Mus. Acoustics* 130 By a simple tone is meant a musical sound in which no upper partials are present...By a compound tone is meant a tone where not only the fundamental note is present, but where upper partials are found in addition.

†**b.** (Without *a* or *pl.*) Pitch of a musical note; correct pitch, 'tune'. *Obs.*

*c* 1325 *Song* in *Rel. Ant.* I. 292 Thu holdest nowt a note by God in riht ton [*rime* non, 'noon']. *c* 1440 *Alphabet of Tales* 88 A prowde yong monke began at sett it vp abowne þaim iij notis;..yit som þat was on his syde fell in tone vnto hym and helpyd hym. 1704 J. HARRIS *Lex. Techn.* I, *Tone*, a Term in Musick, signifying a certain Degree of elevation, or depression of the Voice, or some other Sound.

†**c.** *fig.* in phr. *in tone*, 'in tune', in harmony or accordance; also, in good condition (quot. 1500–20); *out of tone*, out of order, in a state of disarrangement. *Obs.* [perh. belongs to TUNE.]

*a* 1400–50 *Alexander* 1343 So ware þai troubild out of tone quen þai þaire tild miste. 1500–20 DUNBAR *Poems* xxix. 16 Quhen men that hes purssis in tone, Passes to drynk or to disione. 1513 DOUGLAS *Æneis* Prol. 159 For Caxtoun puttis in his buik out of tone The storme furth sent be Eolus and Neptone. 1597 *Satir. Poems Reform.* xxix. 15 All is owtte of tone. 1647 WARD *Simp. Cobler* (1843) 84 When things and words in tune and tone doe meet.

γ. *c* 1460 *Towneley Myst.* xiii. 477 Hard I neuer none crak so clere out of toyne.

**3.** *Mus.* In plainsong, any of the nine psalm-tunes (including the *peregrine tone*), each of which has a particular 'intonation' and 'mediation' and a number of different 'endings'; commonly called *Gregorian tones*: see GREGORIAN A. 1.

1776 HAWKINS *Hist. Mus.* I. 358 The essential parts of each of the tones, that is to say, the beginning, the mediation, and the close. 1850 HELMORE *Psalter Noted* Pref., The intonation (beginning), mediation (middle), and cadence (ending) of the Tones. 1872 [see GREGORIAN A. 1]. 1893 *Blackw. Mag.* Aug. 253 The plainsong to which Psalms were sung was the 2nd Tone.

†**b.** Applied to the ecclesiastical modes (in which the Gregorian tones were composed). *Obs.*

1776 HAWKINS *Hist. Mus.* I. 347 The tones, as they stood adjusted by Saint Ambrose, were only four. *Ibid.*, The ecclesiastical tones..answer exactly to the several keys, as they are called by modern musicians. 1782, 1839 [see MODE *sb.* 1 a (*b*)].

**4.** *Mus.* One of the larger intervals between successive notes of the diatonic scale; a major second; sometimes called *whole tone*, as opposed to *semitone*.

1609 DOULAND *Ornith. Microl.* 18 A Tone..is the distance of one Voyce from another by a perfect second,..a Tone is made betwixt all Voyces excepting *mi* and *fa*. 1651 J. F[REAKE] *Agrippa's Occ. Philos.* 191 There are six Tones of all harmony, viz. 5 Tones, and 2 half Tones which make one Tone, which is the sixt. 1752 tr. *Rameau's Treat. Musick* 89 The Sixth may be taken upon the Second of two Notes that ascend a whole Tone, or a Semitone. 1881 MACFARREN *Counterp.* ii. 3 A Tone is the interval of a major semitone and a minor semitone, either of which may be above or below the other.

†**b.** *transf.* Applied to the space between planets: see quots. *Obs.*

1601 HOLLAND *Pliny* (1634) I. 14 Pythagoras otherwhiles vsing the termes of Musicke, calleth the space between the earth and the Moone *Tonus*, saying that from her to Mercurie is halfe a tone and from him to Venus in manner the same space. 1660 STANLEY *Hist. Philos.* IX. (1701) 386/2 Pythagoras by Musical proportion calleth that a Tone, by how much the Moon is distant from the Earth.

**5.** A particular quality, pitch, modulation, or inflexion of the voice expressing or indicating affirmation, interrogation, hesitation, decision, or some feeling or emotion; vocal expression.

*a* 1610 HEALEY *Theophrastus* (1636) 25 To whom they speak in a great broken Tone, rayling on them. *a* 1654 SELDEN *Table-T.*, *Preaching* (Arb.) 92 The tone in Preaching does much in working upon the Peoples Affections. 1697 DRYDEN *Virg. Past.* IX. 6 The grim Captain in a surly Tone Cries out, pack up ye Rascals, and be gone. *a* 1739 JARVIS *Quix.* I. I. iv. (1742) 13 He raised his voice and with an arrogant tone cried out. 1796 MME. D'ARBLAY *Camilla* II. 355 She asked in a tone of displeasure, who was there? 1817 JAS. MILL *Brit. India* II. v. iv. 456 He tried the tone of humility; he tried that of audacity. 1824 L. MURRAY *Eng. Gram.* (ed. 5) I. 368 There is not..an emotion of the heart, which has not its peculiar tone, or note of the voice, by which it is to be expressed. 1834 MACAULAY *Ess.*, *Pitt* (1887) 311 Every tone, from the impassioned cry to the thrilling aside was perfectly at his [Pitt's] command.

**b.** The distinctive quality of voice in the pronunciation of words, peculiar to an individual, locality, or nation; an 'accent'.

*a* 1680 BUTLER *Rem.* (1759) I. 204 Strangers never leave the Tones, They have been us'd as Children to pronounce. 1683 WOOD *Life* 19 May (O.H.S.) III. 50 Dr. Robert Morison..hath no command of the English [tongue], as being much spoyled by his Scottish tone. 1711 ADDISON *Spect.* No. 29 ¶ 4 The Tone, or (as the French call it) the Accent of every Nation in their ordinary Speech is altogether different from that of every other People. 1837 LOCKHART *Scott* I. ii. 88 The tone and accent remained broadly Scotch.

**c.** Intonation; *esp.* a special, affected, or artificial intonation in speaking.

1687 A. LOVELL tr. *Thevenot's Trav.* I. 36 The greatest

part of their Poems and songs are in the Persian Tongue, which they sing, not musically as we do, but with a certain tone, which though at first..not pleasing, yet by custom becomes agreeable enough to the ear. **1720** WATTS *Art of Reading* xiv, Let the Tone and Sound of your Voice in reading be the same as it is in speaking. **1748** J. MASON *Elocut.* 16 There are some Kinds of Tone, which, tho' unnatural, yet, as managed by the Speakers, are not very disagreeable. **1795** MASON *Ch. Mus.* (L.) You hear nobody converse in a tone, unless they have the brogue of some other country, or have got into a habit of altering the natural key of their voice when they are talking of some serious subject in religion. **1891** *19th Cent.* Nov. 828 The 'tones' are a short sermon..in which the principal tones taken by a preacher are given one after another.

**d.** *transf.* A particular style in discourse or writing, which expresses the person's sentiment or reveals his character. (Cf. 9.)

**1765** T. HUTCHINSON *Hist. Mass.* I. 138 At first, the Naragansets gave kind words to the messengers..but they soon changed their tone. **1844** H. WILSON *Brit. India* II. 108 He determined,..to adopt a tone of conciliation. **1866** J. MARTINEAU *Ess.* I. 147 His book..is bright and joyous in tone.

**6.** *Phonetics.* **a.** A word-accent; a rising, falling, or compound inflexion, by which words otherwise of the same sound are distinguished, as in ancient Greek, modern Chinese, and other languages.

**1763** FOSTER *Accent & Quantity* Introd. 20 In Dionysius ..accounts of high and low tones..assigned to certain syllables. **1791–1823** DISRAELI *Cur. Lit.*, *Chinese Lang.*, [The Chinese] can so diversify their monosyllabic words by the different tones which they give them, that the same character differently accented signifies sometimes ten or more different things. **1906** PINCHES *Relig. Babyl. & Assyria* i. 2 [They] ask themselves whether the people who spoke it were able to understand each other without recourse to devices such as the 'tones' to which the Chinese resort. **1909** JESPERSEN *Progress Lang.* 86 In the Danish dialect spoken in Sundeved..two..tones are distinguished, one high and the other low...These tones often serve to keep words.. apart that would be perfect homonyms but for the accent.

**b.** The stress accent (Fr. *accent tonique*) on a syllable of a word; the stressed or accented syllable.

**1874** DAVIDSON *Hebr. Gram.* (1892) 46 *A* in the pretone, or *a* in the tone, or *a* in both places. **1891** *Cent. Dict.*, *Tone.* In *Gram.* A stress of voice on one of the syllables of a word.

**II. 7.** *Physiol.* The degree of firmness or tension proper to the organs or tissues of the body in a strong and healthy condition. Also in reference to a plant (quot. 1671).

This seems to be in part a distinct derivative from Gr. τόνος, with reference to the tension of the muscles or nerves. Cf. the Physiol. use of TONICAL 1 (1586) and TONIC A. 1 (1649). (Matth. Sylvaticus, *a* 1480, has 'tonus, id est vigor'.)

**1669** W. SIMPSON *Hydrol. Chym.* 139 This astringeth and keepeth up the right tone of the membranous parts. **1671** GREW *Anat. Plants* I. ii. § 23 With which Sap, the Cortical Body being dilated as far as its Tone..will bear. **1704** F. FULLER *Med. Gymn.* (1711) 27 Exercise..affects the Solids [by] restoring the true Tone of the Parts. **1780** *Mirror* No. 86 ⁋ 2 Of sovereign efficacy in restoring debilitated stomachs to their proper tone. **1802** MAR. EDGEWORTH *Moral T.* (1826) I. Pref. 8 Thus, by alternate exercise and indulgence, their limbs acquire the firmest tone of health and vigour. **1888** J. PAYN *Myst. Mirbridge* (ed. Tauchn.) II. x. 104 The douche..would restore her tone.

*fig.* **1835** I. TAYLOR *Spir. Despot.* ix. 374 There is little tone in our church and chapel ethics. **1860** MAURY *Phys. Geog. Sea* (Low) xi. § 517 How, by this operation, tone is given to the atmospherical circulation of the world.

**8.** A state or temper of mind; mood, disposition.

*a* **1744** BOLINGBROKE *Let. to Pope* Wks. 1754 III. 316 The strange situation I am in, and the melancholy state of public affairs,..drag the mind down by perpetual interruptions, from a philosophical tone, or temper. **1779** *Mirror* No. 60 ⁋ 3 Acquiring..a tone of mind which will render him incapable of going through the common duties of life. **1820** W. IRVING *Sketch Bk.* I. 127 These hardy exercises produce also a healthful tone of mind and spirits.

**9.** A special or characteristic style or tendency of thought, feeling, behaviour, etc.; spirit, character, tenor; *esp.* the general or prevailing state of morals or manners in a society or community.

Partly from 7; but influenced also by 5.

*a* **1635** NAUNTON *Fragm. Reg.* (Arb.) 57 As the tone of his house, and the ebbe of his fortune then stood. **1747** CHESTERF. *Lett.* 16 Oct., Take the tone of the company that you are in, and do not pretend to give it. **1754** RICHARDSON *Grandison* III. xii. 188, I complained to one, and to another; but all were in a [= one] tone: And so I thought I would be contented. **1850** TENNYSON *In Mem.* lx. 1 A soul of nobler tone. **1884** *Times* 5 Feb. 11/6 The tone of the market is..dull. **1908** *Westm. Gaz.* 26 Sept. 2/1 In our elementary schools..the inculcation of a good moral tone is of the greatest importance.

**III. 10.** The prevailing effect of the combination of light and shade, and of the general scheme of colouring, in a painting, building, etc.

*c* **1816** FUSELI in *Lect. Paint.* viii. (1848) 512 The tone, that comprehensive union of tint and hue spread over the whole. **1843** RUSKIN *Mod. Paint.* I. II. II. i. § 2, I understand two things by the word *Tone*: first, the exact relief and relation of objects against and to each other in substance and darkness, as they are nearer or more distant, and the perfect relation of the shades of all of them to the chief light of the picture..: secondly, the exact relation of the colours of the shadows to the colours of the lights, so that they may be at once felt to be merely different degrees of the same light [etc.]. **1844** DISRAELI *Coningsby* III. iv, The tone of rich and solemn light that pervaded all.

**b.** A quality of colour; a tint; *spec.* the degree of luminosity of a colour; shade.

**1821** CRAIG *Lect. Drawing* iii. 143 Tone, then, is the degree of dark that any object has compared with white, independently of its kind of colour. **1870** F. R. WILSON *Ch. Lindisf.* 69 The tone of the interior is a tender silvery grey. **1874** SYMONDS *Sk. Italy & Greece* 212 (*Athens*) The tones of the marble of Pentelicus have daily grown more golden. **1879** *Cassell's Techn. Educ.* IV. 212 Tones, often called shades, signify colours mixed with varying proportions of white or black. **1893** J. A. HODGES *Elem. Photogr.* (1907) 91 A tone a little darker than the desired colour.

**11.** *attrib.* and *Comb.*, as *tone-production*, *-quality*, *-reinforcer*, *-relationship*, *scheme*, *study*, *-work* (sense 10); *tone-producing* adj.; **tone-colour** (after Ger *tonfarbe*), timbre; hence *tone-coloured* adj., *-colouring*; **tone-deaf** *a.*, deaf to the tones of music; **tone-full** *a.*, full of musical or vocal sound; **tone-long** *a.*, in *Hebrew Grammar*: see quot.; **tone-master**, a master or expert in the use of tones, an experienced musical composer; **tone-measurer**, = MONOCHORD 1; **tone-painting**, the art of composing descriptive music: **tone-picture**, a descriptive piece of music; **tone-poet** [Ger. *tondichter*], a musical composer; **tone-syllable**, the stressed syllable; **tone-tester**, an instrument for determining the differential sensibility for (musical) tones.

**1881** A. J. HIPKINS in Grove *Dict. Mus.* III. 193 The tone of the Ruckers clavecins has never been surpassed for purity and beauty of *tone-colour (timbre). **1895–6** *Cal. Univ. Nebraska* 216 No other instruments require so much patient and unremitting toil in their mastery as [the violin, viola, violoncello]; and none are so well adapted for the expression of all shades of musical feeling or so nearly resemble the human voice with all its possibilities of *tone-coloring. **1894** DU MAURIER *Trilby* I. 169 She was quite *tone-deaf, and didn't know it. **1838** KEIGHTLEY *Grk. Mythol.* 338 (Odyssey XIX. 518) She..poureth forth her voice *Tone-full, lamenting her son Itylos. **1874** DAVIDSON *Hebr. Gram.* (1892) 14 [Vowels] called **Tone-long*, *ā*, *ē*, *ō*, that is vowels not long by nature but from occupying a certain position in relation to the place of tone, and therefore changeable, when their relation to the tone alters. *Ibid.* 15 The final accented short syllable and the pretonic open have tone-long vowels. **1905** *Q. Rev.* July 103 *Tone-painting, he [Wagner] admits, may be used in jest. **1901** *Pall Mall G.* 3 May (Cass. Supp.), What may be called the groundwork of his *tone-picture. **1874** F. J. CROWEST (*title*) The great *Tone-poets. **1901** *Pall Mall G.* 1 Apr. 5 The great English word-poet and the great German tone-poet seemed to meet together on that imminent verge. **1899** *Allbutt's Syst. Med.* VI. 528 A continuous, though variable, stream of *tone-producing energy. **1889** BRINSMEAD *Hist. Pianoforte* 172 The *tone-pulsator, patented 1878,..connects the ring-bridge with the continuous rim. **1884** A. J. HIPKINS in Grove *Dict. Mus.* IV. 143/1 These bars..promote the elasticity of this most important *tone reinforcer. **1893** SIR G. REID in *Westm. Gaz.* 4 Feb. 2/1 My own way of working is to make a *tone study with the utmost rapidity, to seize the impression of the moment, if possible, and then, for the knowledge of form and detail to make a careful and accurate drawing. **1847** WEBSTER (citing STUART), *Tone-syllable. **1905** *Athenæum* 29 July 140/3 One of its main characteristics is that the nature of the metre is determined by the tone-syllable alone. **1893** *Yale Psychol. Studies* 81 The instrument used in making the experiments was composed of an adjustable pitchpipe with an index-arm moving over a large scale. The instrument..may for brevity be called the *tone-tester. **1894** CREIGHTON & TITCHENER *Wundt's Hum. & Anim. Psychol.* v. 76 *note*, The vibration-rate of these new *tone-waves is the sum of the vibration-rates of the original tones. **1894** HERKOMER in *Daily News* 28 Apr. 6/7 To use process work for the reproduction of line alone, leaving *tone-work to express the more complete work of the artist, which must be rendered again by an artist-engraver.

**Tone,** *pron.* and *a.* Now only *dial.* Forms: α. (*north. dial.* and *Sc.*) (3 **þat an**), 4 **þe tan**, 4–5 **þe tane**, 4–6 **the tayne**, 6 **the taine**, 4–9 **the tane**, (9 **the taen**). β. 3–5 **þe ton**, (4 **þe tonn**), 4–5 **þe toon**, **þe tone**, 4–6 **the ton**, 4–7 **the tone**, 5 **the toon**, (6 **the tonn**, 7 **the t'one**). γ. (without *the*) 6–7 **ton**, 6–8 **tone**, 8 **t'on**, 9 **t'one**, (**t'an**). [Early ME. *þe tān*, *þe tôn*, for earlier *þet* or *þat ān*, 'the one' (see THAT *dem. adj.* 5); the *t* of *þet* being attached to *ān*, *ôn*, when *þe* became the general form of the definite article. Normally used in antithesis to *þe toþer*, *the tother*, which had a similar origin: see TOTHER. This usage cannot have arisen until the OE. antithesis of *óðer . . . óðer*, as in L. *alter . . . alter*, gave place to *án . . . oðer*, as in Fr. *l'un . . . l'autre*; nor until *þæt* (*þet*, *þat*) was usable for masc. and fem. as well as neuter, i.e. between 1200 and 1250: see ONE *numeral* 18, OTHER *a.* B. 1, 2. Used absolutely or pronominally, *the tone* is found in literature down to *c* 1600, and in many dialects to the present day; in Sc. *the tane* is in ordinary use. But as an adj., preceding a sb., esp. before a consonant, it was reduced at an early date to *þe tā*, *þe tô*, still in Sc. *the tae* (see TO *a.*); although the full *the tone . . . the tother* was also frequent, until gradually superseded in literary Eng. by *the one . . . the other*, dialectally and colloquially also *tone . . . tother*, later sometimes written *t'one . . t'other*. This, in the northern Eng. dialects in which the definite article regularly appears as *tĕ*, *tă*, *t'*, may really stand for *t'one*, *t'other*; but elsewhere, where the article is not *te*, *t'*, it is perhaps rather *'t one . . . 't other*, due to the dropping of *the* from *the tone . . . the tother*. In both *the tone* and *the tother*, *the* is omitted after a possessive pronoun or case, as *dial. his tone* or *to hand*, Sc. *his tae hand* = 'one of his hands'. For full illustration of existing dialect use, see *Eng. Dial. Dict.* s. v. *Tone.*]

The one (of two): often opposed to *tother*.

**1.** as *pron.*

α. [*a* **1225** *Leg. Kath.* 1373 (MS. C) Þa ȝeide þus ꝥ an, & elnede þe oðre.] **13..** *Cursor M.* 1533 (Cott.) Tua pilers þai mad, o tile þe tan, Þe toþer it was o merbul stan [*Gött.* and *Fairf.* þat an, þe toþer; *Trin.* þat oon, þat oþer]. *c* **1440** *Alphabet of Tales* 167 Me thoght att ij angels led þe tane of you vnto hevyn & þe toder vnto hell. **1513** DOUGLAS *Æneis* v. vi. 25 The tane born of Epiria, And the todir was of Archadia. *a* **1774** FERGUSSON *Drink Ecl.* Poems (1845) 49 Brandy the tane, the tither whiskey. **1816** SCOTT *Old Mort.* xxxviii, They will neither want the tane nor the tother while Lord Evandale lives.

β. **1303** R. BRUNNE *Handl. Synne* 4005 Þe toon men calle Eutycyus, Þe touþer hyght Florentyus. *c* **1380** WYCLIF *Wks.* (1880) 190 Neiþer þe ton ne þe toiþer. [*c* **1386** CHAUCER *Pard. T.* 479 That oon spak thus vn to that oother Thou knowest wel thou art my sworn brother.] *a* **1425** *Cursor M.* 13966 (Trin.) His sistres two, Þe toon was martha to seyn And þat oþere Maudeleyn. **1426** *Rolls of Parlt.* V. 409/1 My said ii Lordes or the toon of hem. **1522** MORE *De quat. Noviss.* Wks. 79/2 Within a litle while die the tone may, the tother muste. **1591** HARINGTON *Orl. Fur.* Pref. ⁋ vj, The tone begins, *Arma virumque cano.* The tother [begins] [etc.]. **1891** MISS JACKSON *Shropsh. Word-bk.* 448 Both the tone an' the tother on 'em.

γ. **1573** TUSSER *Husb.* (1878) 123 Vse ton for thy spinning, leaue Mihel the tother. *c* **1590** MARLOWE *Faust.* ix. 19 Well, tone of you hath this goblet about you. **1632** BROME *Court Beggar* III. i. Wks. 1873 I. 230 I'le jowle your heads together, and so beat ton with tother. *a* **1800** PEGGE *Suppl. Grose*, *T'on T'other*, one another. Derb. **1825** BROCKETT *N. C. Words* s. v. *Tane*, Gi me t'an or tother. **1900** [see *Eng. Dial. Dict.* s. v. TONE].

**2.** as *adj.* preceding a sb.

α, β. *c* **1250** *Gen. & Ex.* 2196 Al but ðe ton broðer symeon. **13..** *Cursor M.* 7074 (Gött.) Bot as þe tonn half a-gayn þat oþer. *c* **1380** WYCLIF *Serm.* Sel. Wks. II. 284 Men speken now of Crist bi þe toon kynde and now by þe toþer. *c* **1400** *Destr. Troy* 13206 The ton Egh in the toile lost tynt he belyue. **1529** MORE *Dyaloge* III. i. Wks. 206 The hole church had neuer taken all the tone sorte and reiected all the tother. **1535** STEWART *Cron. Scot.* (Rolls) I. 254 At the tonn end set Cesar in his trune, And at the tother stude king Caratac. **1552** *Lyndesay's Poems* To Rdrs. (E.E.T.S. p. 318), The quhilkis ar verray fals, And wantis the tane half. **1584** COGAN *Haven Health* ccxli. (1636) 274 That wee lie on the tone side. **1622** MABBE tr. *Aleman's Guzman d'Alf.* II. I. v. 48 The t'one halfe of an old broken great Pitcher.

γ. *a* **1765** *K. Estmere* xxvii. in Child *Ballads* III. (1885) 53/1 Tone day to marrye Kyng Adlands daughter, Tother daye to carrye her home. *a* **1800** PEGGE *Suppl. Grose* s. v. *T'on-End*, It must be set a t'on end.

**Tone** (tōun), *v.* [f. TONE *sb.*]

**I. †1.** *trans. Mus.* To sound with the proper tone or musical quality; to intone. *Obs.*

*c* **1325** in *Rel. Ant.* I. 292 Thu tones nowt the note ilke be his name, Thu bitist a-sonder bequarre, for bemol I the blame. **1570** LEVINS *Manip.* 168/38 To Toone, *modulari*.

**b.** To give a good or proper tone to.

**1891** *Advt.*, Pianos toned and repaired.

**2.** *intr.* To issue forth in musical tones. *rare.*

**1447** BOKENHAM *Seyntys* (Roxb.) 74 Wyth ympnys and psalmys wel tonyng Thousandis of aungells aftyr hym dyd goon. **1850** L. HUNT *Autobiog.* ix. 160 The sounding words came toning out of his dignified utterance like 'sonorous metal'.

**3.** *trans.* To utter with a musical sound, or in a special or affected tone; to intone.

**1660** SOUTH *Serm.*, *Matt.* xiii. 52 (1727) IV. i. 52 Those strange new Postures used by some in the Delivery of the Word. Such as shutting the Eyes,..speaking through the Nose, which I think cannot so properly be called Preaching, as Toning of a Sermon. **1704** SWIFT *Mech. Operat. Spirit* § 2 Misc. (1711) 295 Tuning and toning each Word, and Syllable, and Letter to their due Cadence. **1719** D'URFEY *Pills* (1872) III. 334 With pleasing Twang he tones his Prose,.. And draws John Calvin through the Nose. **1796** SOUTHEY *Lett. fr. Spain* (1799) 399 He sung or toned his verses. **1852** MRS. STOWE *Uncle Tom's C.* i, The boy..commenced toning a psalm-tune through his nose with imperturbable gravity. **1883** W. C. SMITH *N. Country Folk* 185 The Common prayer Was sweetly toned to the fishers there.

**†4.** To lay the accent or stress upon, to accent (a word or syllable). *Obs.*

**1683** MOXON *Mech. Exerc.*, *Printing* xxii. ⁋ 5 If it be Set thus, that that That that that Man would have stand at the beginning of the Line should stand at the end; it will, by toning and laying Emphasis on the middlemost That become good Sense.

**II. 5.** To alter or modify the tone or general colouring of; to give the desired tone to; *spec.* (*a*) To cover (a painting) with oil or varnish so as to soften the colouring; (*b*) To alter the tone or tint of (a photograph) in the process of finishing it. Also *absol.*

**1859** GULLICK & TIMBS *Paint.* 215 It was not unfrequent for the possessors of old pictures to have them toned, as it was called. **1868** M. C. LEA *Man. Photogr.* xiii. 219 This bath tones much like the preceding; gives brown, purple-black, or black tones, and by overtoning, blue. *Ibid.* 220 Landscapes should be toned only with the acetate or benzoate bath. **1893** J. A. HODGES *Elem. Photogr.* (1907) 49 A gold bath will only tone when in a neutral or slightly alkaline condition. **1902** *Westm. Gaz.* 13 Mar. 2/2 One can always send the lace..and get it toned exactly.

**b.** *intr.* To receive or assume a tone, tint, or shade of colour; *esp.* in *Photogr.*

**1868** M. C. LEA *Man. Photogr.* xiii. 218 If a washed print be simply thrown into a dilute solution of chloride of gold, it will tone. **1873** E. SPON *Workshop Receipts* Ser. I. 257/2 If delayed many hours the prints will not tone readily.

**c.** To harmonize *with* in colouring. Also with *in*.

**18..** *St. Louis Spectator* (U.S.) XI. 327 (Cent.) Beaded passementerie, which tones in with the delicate shades of blue, and pink chiffon, and dark velvet. **1904** *Westm. Gaz.* 20 Jan. 3/2 In each case her hat tones with the dress. **1907** *Ibid.* 25 Sept. 2/1 The red- or brown-tiled wooden chalets at once tone in with Nature.

**III. 6.** *trans.* To impart a tone to (in various senses of the sb.); to modify, regulate, or adjust the tone or quality of; to give physical or mental tone to, to brace.

**1811** SHELLEY *St. Irvyne* viii, A degree of solemnity, mixed with concealed fierceness, toned his voice as he spoke. **1859** J. CUMMING *Ruth* ii. 18 The husband tones into a loftier pitch the spiritual and moral character of the wife. **1871** L. STEPHEN *Playgr. Eur.* xiii. (1894) 334 Your mind is properly toned by these influences. **1884** W. C. SMITH *Kildrostan* I. ii. 11 Nor many years had toned his heedlessness.

**b.** *Tone down*, to lower the tone, quality, or character of; to soften, make less emphatic. *Tone up*, to raise or improve the tone of, to give a higher or stronger tone to.

**1860** TYNDALL *Glac.* II. xxvi. 371 These [ice-ridges].. become more and more toned down by the action of sun and air. **1864** *Reader* No. 98. 603/1 By toning up public sentiment. **1884** *Times* (weekly ed.) 29 Aug. 14/1 These rosy impressions were decidedly toned down on closer inspection. **1896** *Chatauqua Mag.* Dec. Advt., Some remedy that will tone-up the nervous system. **1906** F. L. DODD *Municip. Milk* 9 A custom has grown up called 'toning down the milk', which consists in the addition of skimmed milk to such an extent as just to reduce the percentage of fat to the legal minimum.

**c.** *intr.* for *pass. Tone down*, to become lowered, weakened, or softened in tone; *tone up*, to rise or improve in tone.

**1850** KINGSLEY *Alt. Locke* xiii, The ivory and vermilion of the complexion had toned down together into still richer hues. **1865** DICKENS *Mut. Fr.* I. ix, Gradually toning down to a motherly strain. **1881** *Chicago Times* 14 May, Trade toned up considerably under the influence of warm weather. **1885** *L'pool Daily Post* 11 Apr. 5/2 Public excitement with respect to Russia has considerably toned down.

Hence **Toning** (tōu·niŋ), *vbl. sb.* and *ppl. a.*, in various senses.

**1660** [see TONE *v.* 3]. **1708** OZELL tr. *Boileau's Lutrin* IV. (1730) 192 The Toning of the Tenebrae. **1796** SOUTHEY *Lett. fr. Spain* (1799) 399 The defects of metre are disguised by toning. **1843** RUSKIN *Mod. Paint.* I. II. II. ii. § 15 This toning down and connection of the colours actually used. **1861** *Photogr. News Alm.* in *Circ. Sc.* (*c* 1865) I. 155/1 Sufficient water tends .. to secure regular toning. *Ibid.*, Several different forms of the alkaline gold toning bath have been proposed. **1878** ABNEY *Photogr.* (1881) 140 A trace of hypochlorous acid was found in the toning solution. **1891** MEREDITH *One of our Conq.* xxxv, She struck a toneing warmth through his intelligence.

**Tone**, Sc. var. of TUNE; obs. f. DHONEY, TEEN *sb.*[1], TOWN, TUN; obs. pa. pple. of TAKE *v.* (see TO *v. Obs.*); obs. pl. of TOE. **Tonecle**, obs. f. TUNICLE.

**Toned** (tōund), *ppl. a.* and *adj.*

**I.** *ppl. a.* [f. TONE *v.* + -ED [1].]

**1. a.** Sounded with the proper, or a specified, tone.

*c* **1460** *Towneley Myst.* xii. 419 Thay [notes] were gentyll and small, And well tonyd with all. **1533** BELLENDEN *Livy* V. xviii. (S.T.S.) II. 208 The cryis & evill tonyt sangis of þe gaulis.

**b.** Of body or mind: Brought into tone (TONE *sb.* 7); braced, strung. Chiefly with adv., as *well-toned, toned-up*.

**1742** YOUNG *Nt. Th.* VIII. 1285 Juices, thro' the well-ton'd Tubes, well-strain'd. **1855** MACAULAY *Hist. Eng* xiv. III. 432 A human being whose mind was quite as firmly toned at eighty as at forty. **1879** H. SPENCER *Data of Ethics* vi. § 36. 90 Showing by toned-up face and vivacious manner ..greater energy.

**2.** Slightly or finely coloured or shaded; tinted. *Toned paper*, paper which is not quite white, but cream-coloured or slightly buff.

**1864** *N. & Q.* 3rd Ser. VI. 454/1 That yellowish-coloured, or what is now called toned paper, is..more beautiful and pleasant to the eyes than the glaring white paper of modern times. **1869** *Advt.* in *A. Stafford's Fem. Glory*, Toned paper, limp cloth, red edges. **1877** MRS. OLIPHANT *Makers Flor.* iv. 117 Soft shades of those toned marbles which fit so tenderly into each other.

**b.** *Photogr.* Treated with chemicals so as to acquire the desired tone or shade of colour.

**1861** *Photogr. News Alm.* in *Circ. Sc.* (*c* 1865) I. 155/1 Imperfectly-toned patches will be the result. **1892** *Photogr. Ann.* II. 97 The toned and fixed prints are immersed in a strong solution of common salt.

**II.** *adj.* [f. TONE *sb.* + -ED [2].] **3.** In combination: Having a tone (in various senses) of a specified kind or quality; e. g. *deep-, fine-, high-, low-toned.* See also the adjs.

**1790** GOUV. MORRIS in Sparks *Life & Writ.* (1832) I. 350 A higher toned Government than that of England. **1812** W. TENNANT *Anster F.* III. xli, The brass-ton'd clarion gave the air a thump. **1870** ROCK *Text. Fabr.* vi. (1876) 54 A fine toned yellow as a ground. **1896** *Idler* Mar. 291/2 The deep-toned, old-fashioned furniture of the housekeeper's room.

**Tonee**, var. DHONEY, E. Indian sailing vessel.

†**Tonekin.** *Obs. rare.* [? dim. of *ton* or *tun*; ? a. Flem. *tonneken*.] ? A small cask or barrel.

**1546** O. JOHNSON in Ellis *Orig. Lett.* Ser. II. II. 174, ij small tonekins of capers $q^t$ 4½ lb. cost $4^s$ $6^d$.

**Tonel, -ell**, obs. forms of TONNEL, TUNNEL.

**Toneless** (tōu·nlės), *a.* [f. TONE *sb.* + -LESS.] Destitute of tone.

**1.** Soundless, mute; of a body: without resonance.

**1773** KENRICK *Rhet. Gram.* ii. § 3 in *Dict.* 35 This sound ..in oratorial and poetical stile..is contracted and rendered almost toneless in speech. **1899** *Allbutt's Syst. Med.* VI. 129 The side of the chest is completely dull and toneless.

**2.** Having no distinctive quality; (*a*) of sound: without modulation or expression; (*b*) of colour: dull.

(*a*) **1847** *Fraser's Mag.* XXXVI. 105 The harsh roar of his toneless, irritating voice. **1861** S. BROOKS *Silver Cord* viii, 'Mrs. Empson is my aunt..', said Mrs. Berry, in a toneless voice.

(*b*) **1843** RUSKIN *Mod. Paint.* I. II. III. i. § 19 In paintings, they [the skies] are commonly toneless, crude, and wanting in depth and transparency. **1856** *Ibid.* III. IV. xv. § 6 The Apennine limestone is so grey and toneless. **1883** GRANT WHITE *W. Adams* 80 Her hair, a toneless brown.

**3.** Lacking tone in body or mind; void of energy; listless, dull.

**1854** F. L. MACKENZIE in Miles *Mem.* (1856) 263 Must I.. withered, toneless..Trudge on through life. **1899** *Allbutt's Syst. Med.* VI. 39 The fibres of the heart are not primarily diseased, but are merely more or less toneless and atrophied.

Hence **To·nelessly** *adv.*; **To·nelessness.**

**1873** EARLE *Philol. Eng. Tongue* (ed. 2) § 438 When this adverbial *-ly* was superadded to the adjectival the latter shrank into tonelessness. **1888** tr. *Ibsen's Ghosts* (Camelot Classics) 198 Oswald (tonelessly as before) The Sun. **1891** G. MEREDITH *One of our Conq.* II. v. 105 Her present tonelessness of blood and being. **1895** ZANGWILL *Master* III. vii, 'I see he calls you Eleanor', he observed tonelessly.

**Toner** (tōu·nəɹ). [f. TONE *v.* + -ER [1].] One who or that which tones: see the verb.

**1888** *Medical News* LIII. 499 Sulphuric and nitric acids have..some claim to be regarded as toners of the vasomotor nerves. **1904** *Daily Chron.* 25 Mar. 10/7 Pianos.—Experienced tuner and toner wanted in factory.

**Toney**, variant of TONY; obs. f. DHONEY.

**1622** in Foster *Eng. Factories Ind.* (1908) II. 154 One of their toneyes.

**Tong** (tǫŋ), *sb.* [Echoic: cf. *ting, tang, dong*, etc.] A deep ringing sound produced by a stroke on a large bell, deeper than that denoted by TANG *sb.*[2], but sharper than that denoted by *dong*; the stroke producing this.

**1881** MISS JACKSON *Shropsh. Word-bk.*, *Tong*, the sound produced by a slow single stroke on a church-bell; the stroke itself...'The bell gies a tong or two w'en they comen out o' Church'. **1883** C. S. BURNE *Folk-Lore* xxxvii. 604 Giving a few tongs on the bell.

**Tong** (tǫŋ), *v.*[1] [Goes with prec. sb.] **a.** *intr.* To emit a deep ringing sound, as a bell when struck. Also with cognate object. Cf. TANG *v.*[2] 1, 3. **b.** *trans.* To cause (a bell, or other resonant body) to emit such a sound. *Tong out*, to sound forth by tonging. Hence **To·nging** *vbl. sb.*

**1584** R. SCOT *Discov. Witchcr.* XII. xviii. (1886) 218 Trusting rather to the tonging of their belles, than to their own crie unto God. **1881** MISS JACKSON *Shropsh. Word-bk.*, *Tong v.a.* and *v.n.*, to cause to sound,—to sound in one tone, as of a church-bell. **1883** *Hampshire Gloss.* s.v., The bells be tonged', i.e. are being tolled. **1907** *Scribner's Mag.* Feb. 151 The great bell of the cathedral tonged out the vespers.

**Tong** (tǫŋ), *v.*[2] *U.S.* [f. TONGS.] **a.** *trans.* To grasp, gather, or handle with tongs; *spec.* to gather (clams or oysters) with oyster-tongs. **b.** *intr.* To use or work with tongs. **c.** *trans.* To lift or move (a log) with skidding tongs. Hence **Tonger** (tǫ·ŋəɹ), one who gathers oysters with oyster-tongs; **To·nging** (tǫ·ŋiŋ) *vbl. sb.*, the use of tongs; *spec.* the taking of oysters with tongs.

**1868** *Rep. U.S. Commissioner Agric.* (1869) 342 Eleven million bushels [of oysters] taken in the legitimate way of dredging and tonging. **1887** *Fisheries of U.S.* Sect. v. II. 552 As soon as a tonger has caught as many as his small boat will carry he sells out to the runner and returns to work. *Ibid.*, The size of the tonging-canoe ranges from 15 or 16 feet to 30 feet or more. **1891** W. K. BROOKS *Oyster* 2 There were 1000 boats engaged in dredging and 1500 canoes engaged in tonging. **1901** *Munsey's Mag.* XXV. 386/1 Before it reaches the mill..a saw log is moved four times in four different ways. First, it has to be 'tonged' a distance of anywhere from ten to a hundred feet.

**Tong**, var. TANG *sb.*[1]; obs. f. TONGUE; see also TONGS.

‖**Tonga**[1] (tǫ·ŋgă). *E. Indies.* Also **tanga.** [a. Hindī *tāngā*.] A light and small two-wheeled carriage or cart used in India.

**1874** *Settlement Rep. Nasik* (Yule), Driving light tongas drawn by ponies or oxen. **1882** F. M. CRAWFORD *Mr. Isaacs* ix, The Himalayan *tonga* is a thing of delight. **1894** IRENE PETRIE in *Life* vii. (1900) 136 A tonga resembles a squat dog-cart with a hood. **1904** *Times* 6 Jan. 5/2 The Indian tongas used in South Africa were very suitable over even ground.

**b.** *attrib.* and *Comb.*

**1881** *Let. fr. Bombay Govt. to Govt. of India* 17 June (Yule), Gallantly defending the mail tonga cart. **1882** F. M. CRAWFORD *Mr. Isaacs* ix, Every tonga-driver is provided with a post horn. **1886** KIPLING *Departm. Ditties*, etc. (1899) 86 So long as 'neath the Kalka hills The tonga-horn shall ring. **1894** IRENE PETRIE in *Life* vii. (1900) 141 The tonga road was demolished by recent snows.

‖**Tonga**[2] (tǫ·ŋgă). [An arbitrary name, said in *Pharm. Jrnl.* to have been invented by Mr. Ryder, who first sent specimens to Europe.] A drug extracted from the root of the Fijian plant *Epipremnum pinnatum*, Engler, used by the natives of Fiji as a remedy for neuralgia; also known in England and America. Also *attrib.*

(For its introduction into England, see *The Lancet* for March, 1880, 360, 361, also 445, and the *Pharmaceutical Journal* for April, 1880. A full history in *Gardeners' Chron.* 1882, XVII. 180, and *Journal of Bot.* 1882, 332.)

**1880** S. RINGER in *Lancet* 6 Mar. 360/1 On Tonga: a remedy for neuralgia used by the natives of the Fiji Islands. **1880** *Kew Report* 55. **882** N. E. BROWN in *Gard. Chron.* XVII. 180/2 The Tonga plant is an ornamental climber of rapid growth, with bold dark green pinnatisect leaves. **1883** *Science* I. 80/2 The drug tonga is shown..to be the product mainly of a climbing aroid (*Epiprem*[*n*]*um mirabile*).

Hence **Tongine** (tǫ·ŋgəin), *Chem.*: see quot.

**1890** BILLINGS *Nat. Med. Dict.*, *Tongine*, a volatile alkaloid found by Gerrard in tonga.

‖**Tonga**[3] (tǫ·ŋgă). [Native name in Peru.] A beverage inducing stupefaction and delirium, prepared from the seeds of *Datura sanguinea* by the Indians of Peru. Also in *comb.*

**1852** KINGSTON *Manco* iii. (1853) 36 Our brother has but drunk the tonga; his spirit has departed for a season. *Ibid.* 37 The group of Indians..collected round the tonga-drinker. **1857** DUNGLISON *Med. Lex.* s. v. *Datura*, A narcotic drink called *Tonga*.

**Tonga bean**: see TONKA.

**Tonger, Tonging**: see under TONG *v.*[2]

**Tongman**: see TONGS 4.

**Tongrian** (tǫ·ŋgriăn), *a. Geol.* [f. *Tongres*, in Belgium, where developed + -IAN.] Name for marine strata of the Lower Oligocene of Belgium.

**1883** [see RUPELIAN]. **1885** GEIKIE *Text-bk. Geol.* (ed. 2) 864 The Tongrian deposits contain an abundant marine fauna = the Egeln beds of Germany. **1885** LYELL *Elem. Geol.* xv. 202 The lower division [of the Oligocene], or Tongrian, includes the sands in the neighbourhood of Tongres, and..corresponds with the upper part of the Gypseous series of Montmartre, and with the Headon series of England.

**Tongs** (tǫŋz), *sb. pl.* Forms: *α. sing.* 1 tang, 1–5 tange; *pl.* 1 tangan, 2–4 tangen; 4 tangs, (5 tangys,-is, tang(g)es, 6 *Sc.* tang(g)is, taingis, tayngis), 6– *Sc.* tangs, tayngs; 6 *Sc.* double pl. tangisis. *β. sing.* 1 tǫng, 3–5 tonge, (4 toenge, 5 tongge), (9 tong); *pl.* 3 tongen; 4 tunges, 4–5 tongys, 5 toonges, tongges, 5–7 tonges, (6 tonkes, thounges, 7 tungs), 7–8 tongues, 5– tongs. [OE. *tang* (str. f.), *tange* (wk. f.) = OLG. *tanga* (MDu. *tanghe*, Du. *tang*), OFris. *tange*, OHG. *zanga* str. fem. (MHG., Ger. *zange*), ON. *tǫng* str. f.,:—**tangu* (Norw. *tong*, Swed. *tång*, Da. *tang*):—OTeut. **tangō-* (also, with weak inflexion, *tangōn-*):—Indo-Eur. **dankā-*, referred to the root **dak-*, *dank-* to bite (Skr. *damç, daç*, Gr. δάκνειν); cf. OHG. *zangar*, MLG., LG. *tanger*, MDu. *tangher* sharp, biting.]

**1.** An implement consisting of two limbs or 'legs' connected by a hinge, pivot, or spring, by means of which their lower ends are brought together so as to grasp and take up objects which it is impossible or inconvenient to lift with the hand. Examples of different forms are seen in a smith's tongs, domestic fire-tongs, and sugar-tongs.

A particular use or shape is often indicated by a prefixed word, as *blacksmith's t., curling-t., gas-fitter's t., pipe t., sugar-t.* When not otherwise particularized usually applied to *fire-tongs*. In early quots. often not distinguishable in sense from *pincers* or *forceps*.

† **a.** in sing. form tong. *Obs.*

*c* **725** *Corpus Gloss.* (O.E.T.) 905 *Forceps*, tong. *a* **1000** *Ags. Gloss.* in Wr.-Wülcker 218/37 *Delebra*, tang. *Ibid.* 272/34 *Forceps*, tang. *c* **1050** *Byrhtferth's Handboc* in *Anglia* (1885) VIII. 325 Mid his gyldenan tange. *a* **1250** *Owl & Night.* 156 Þu twengest þar mid so doþ a tonge. *c* **1305** *St. Dunstan* 77 in *E. E. P.* (1862) 36 He droȝ forþ his tonge And leide in þe hote fur. *c* **1380** *Sir Ferumb.* 1308, & het to brynge wiþ him anon anuylt, tange, & slegge. **1382** WYCLIF *Isa.* vi. 6 A cole, that with the toenge [**1388** a tonge] he toc fro the auter. *c* **1440** *Promp. Parv.* 496/2 Tongge, fyyr instrument. *c* **1483** CAXTON *Dialogues* 8/9 *Ung estenelle, ung greyl*, a tonge, a gredyron.

**b.** in pl. form with plural construction: the usual current use. *Pair of tongs* is used when qualification by a numeral or an indefinite article is wanted.

*a. c* **890** tr. *Bæda's Hist.* v. xiii. [xii.] (1890) 428 Hæfdon heo fyrene eaȝan..ond fyrene tangan him on handa hæfdon. *c* **1000** ÆLFRIC *Hom.* II. 352 Woldon me ȝelæccan mid heora byrnendum tangum. *c* **1300** Tangen [see quot. *c* 1290 in *β*]. **1384–5** *Durham Acc. Rolls* (Surtees) 265, j par de Tangs. **1412–13** *Ibid.* 610, j pare belowys et tangys empt. *c* **1425** *Voc.* in Wr.-Wülcker 657/11 *Hec forceps*, tangges. **1483** *Cath. Angl.* 378/1 A paire of Tanges, *in plurali numero*, *tenalia*. **1500–20** DUNBAR *Poems* lii. 14 The wyff..That with the taingis wald brack his schinnis. **1547** *Reg. Mag. Sig. Scot.* 20 *note*, Tua pair of tayngis. **1595** DUNCAN *App. Etym.* (E.D.S.), *Forceps*, tayngs. **1718** RAMSAY *Christ's Kirk Gr* III. iv, Her aunt a pair of tangs fush in. **1816** J. BOSWELL, etc. *Justiciary Opera* 5 To seize on anither man's geer (As the tangs ance a Highlandman fand). **1825** JAMIESON s. v. *Tangs*, 'You fand that whar the Highlandman fand the tangs' S. Prov. [Cf. quot. 1721 in *β*.]

β. *c* 1290 *St. Brendan* 480 in *S. Eng. Leg.* I. 233 With tongen [*Harl. MS.* 2277 (*c* 1300) tangen] and with hameres brenninde mani on. 1352-3 *Ely Sacr. Rolls* (1907) II. 155 In j pari de Tongys pro plumbario. 1392-3 *Earl Derby's Exp.* (Camden) 158 Pro tunges et aliis necessariis. 1426 LYDG. *De Guil. Pilgr.* 16144 And with thy Toonges pynche hem so. 1483 *Act 1 Rich. III*, c. 12 § 2 Andyrons, Cobbardes, Tongges, Fireforkes. 1495 *Naval Acc. Hen. VII* (1896) 205 Tongges of yron..j payre. 1530 PALSGR. 251/1 Payre of tonges, *tenailles*. *Ibid.*, Payre of smythes tonges, *gresses*. 1531 *Rec. St. Mary at Hill* 37 A payre of andi[r]onis and a payre of tonkes with a fyer Raike. 1586 *Rates of Custome* E viij b, Tongs for fire the dosen vj. s. 1599 *Acc. Bk. W. Wray* in *Antiquary* XXXII. 243 One pair of thounges. 1605 ROWLANDS *Hell's Broke Loose* 47 Their flesh torne from the bones with fiery tongs. 1614 *Liber Depos. Archidiaconat. Colcestr.* lf. 71 (MS.) To saye he would laye her on the pate with the tungs. 1663 PEPYS *Diary* 7 Sept., Dogs, tongues, and shovells, for my wife's closett. 1697 DRYDEN *Virg. Georg.* IV. 255 With Tongs they turn the Steel. 1721 KELLY *Scot. Prov.* 383 You found it where the Highland Man found the Tongs. 1815 J. SMITH *Panorama Sc. & Art* II. 171 Grasping the tongs with the right hand a little below the middle. 1845 JAMES *Arrah Neil* ii, He was as thin and spare, too, as a pair of tongs.

**c.** In pl. form *tongs* const. as sing.; with rare pl. *tongisis*, *tongses*, pairs of tongs. Chiefly *Sc.*

1489 *Act. Dom. Conc.* (1839) 132/1 Twa axis, a wowmill.. a tangis, price xl d. 1542 *Rec. Elgin* (N. Spald. Cl. 1903) I. 71 The masterfull streking of Ellene Murray with ane tanggis. 1576 *Reg. Mag. Sig. Scot.* 691 *note*, 2 pair of tangisis, 3s. apiece. 1596 DALRYMPLE tr. *Leslie's Hist. Scot.* VII. (S.T.S.) II. 46 The rest of his body..the pynouris raue with an yrne tangs. 1708 *Caldwell Papers* (Maitl. Cl.) I. 216, I must also have a tongs and shovel. 1796 BURNS *On Life* vii, Like a sheep-head on a tangs. 1849 W. IRVING *Crayon Misc.* 254 A relic..which, if I recollect right, he pronounced to have been a tongs.

**d.** in sing. form *tong*: One leg of a pair of tongs. *humorous nonce-use.*

1862 THACKERAY *Philip* xxxii, He keeps a tong to the present day, and speaks very satirically regarding that relic. 1864 *Daily Tel.* 26 Aug., With the half of a pair of tongs, or perhaps I should say with a tong, in his tiny fist. 1897 in *Westm. Gaz.* 7 Dec. 4/1 The beetle trotted down the kitchen tong.

**2. a.** *fig.* and in *phrases*: e. g. *not to touch with a pair of tongs*, expressing repugnance to have anything to do with.

*c* 1386 CHAUCER *Pars. T.* ⁋ 481 Thanne stant Enuye and holdeth the hoote Iren vpon the herte of man with a peire of longe toonges of long rancour. 1579 FULKE *Refut. Rastel* 714 [It] maketh M. Rastel..to gnaw the tonges for anger. 1643 J. CARYL *Expos. Job* ii. 8 A man would scarce touch such an one with a pair of Tongs. *a* 1688 BUNYAN *Jerus. Sinner Saved* (1886) 112 We are scarce for touching of the poor ones.., no not with a pair of tongs. 1828 *Craven Gloss.* s.v. *Tangs*, 'He brades of a pair o' tangs', this is applied to a person with long limbs. 1882 MISS BRADDON *Mt. Royal* III. vii. 136, I wouldn't touch it with a pair of tongs.

**b.** As used in burlesque music.

1590 SHAKS. *Mids. N.* IV. i. 32 *Clowne.* I haue a reasonable good eare in musicke. Let us haue the tongs and the bones. 1678 RYMER *Trag. Last Age* 139 The tintamar and twang of the Tongs and Jewstrumps. 1885 DOBSON *Sign of Lyre* 123 Well, our immortal Shakespear owns The Oaf preferred the 'Tongs and Bones'!

**c.** *Snapping tongs*, a game: see quot.

1844 BARNES *Poems Rural Life* Gloss., *Snappen tongs*, a game of forfeits..[played] in a room in which are seats for all but one,.. when the tongs are snapped all run to sit down, and the one that fails to get a seat pays a forfeit. 1847 in HALLIWELL.

**d.** Short for *sugar-tongs*, *curling-tongs*, *oyster-tongs*: see these words; also LAZY-TONGS.

1713 *Lond. Gaz.* No. 5086/3, 6 gilded Tea Spoons with Forks and Tongs. 1837 THACKERAY *Ravenswing* i, He was twiddling the [curling-]tongs with which he had just operated on Walker. 1870 *Standard* 19 Oct., A party of Maryland oystermen were caught sinking their tongs into the Virginia beds.

**3.** In various transferred and technical applications. †**a.** Name for an ancient surgical forceps: see quot. *Obs.* †**b.** A weeding-tool: see quot. *Obs.* **c.** The pincer-like organs of a scorpion. **d.** In a pile-engine, the forceps which grips the staple in the head of the ram. **e.** In diamond-cutting, a stand having at its upper end a vice-like device for holding the dop in which the diamond is imbedded for cutting. **f.** *Railway.* A pincer-like device for grasping the rail on which a vehicle is standing, thus holding it still (Forney *Car-builder's Dict.* 1884). **g.** 'A name for pantaloons and round-abouts [short jackets] formerly in use in New England' (Bartlett *Dict. Amer.* 1848); a skeleton suit.

**a.** *c* 1425 tr. *Arderne's Treat. Fistula* 35 Whiche y-do, be þe lure y-opned wiþ tonges so y-shape þat when þe vtward endes bene streyned togidre þe inner endes be opned & agaynward. **b.** 1523 FITZHERB. *Husb.* § 21 The chyefe instrument to wede with, is a paire of tonges made of wode, and in the farther ende it is nycked, to holde the wed faster. **c.** 1608 TOPSELL *Serpents* 223 The sixt is like a Crabbe, and this is called by Elianus a flamant Scorpion, it is of a great body, and hath tonges and takers very solide and strong, like the Gramuell or Creuish. **d.** 1776 G. SEMPLE *Building in Water* 36 The Tongs are opened by the two inclined Planes. *Ibid.* 37 The Ram.. with the Staple, that the Tongs take hold of. 1825 J. NICHOLSON *Operat. Mechanic* 310 Forceps or tongs are lowered down speedily, and instantly of themselves again lay hold of the ram and lift it up. **g.** 1845 S. JUDD *Margaret* I. vi, The boys dressed in 'tongs', a name for pantaloons or overalls, that had come into use.

**4.** *Comb.*: **tongs-carriage**, a carriage which supports the tongs used in glass-making, foundry-work, and the like; **to·ngsman**, also **to·ngman**, one who uses the tongs in oyster-fishing (*U. S.*).

1839 URE *Dict. Arts* 590 Glass-making...Two powerful branches of iron united by a bolt, like two scissar blades,.. form the tongs-carriage, which is mounted upon two wheels like a truck. 1887 *Fisheries of U.S.* Sect. v. II. 525 In midwinter, when the heavy planters are busy marketing their crops, the tongmen are idle, or are attending to their own little cove-beds. 1891 W. K. BROOKS *Oyster* 140 They are exposed to the depredations of both tongmen and dredgers. 1891 *Cent. Dict.* (citing DAVIDSON), Tongsman.

**Tong-tong**, variant of TOM-TOM.

**Tongue** (tʌŋ), *sb.* Forms: 1-6 tunge, (3 tunke, tonke), 3-6, 7 *Sc.* tonge, (4 tungge, tongge), 3-8 tounge, 4 *Sc.* towng, -e, 4-6 tung (also 8 *Sc.*), *Sc.* twng, 4-7 toung, tong, (5 tounghe), 5-7 toong, (6 toongue, 6-7 toungue), 5- tongue. [OE. and ME. *tunge* wk. f. = OFris. *tunge*, OS. *tunga* (MLG., LG. *tunge*, MDu. *tonghe*, Du. *tong*), OHG. *zunga*, *zunka* (MHG., Ger. *zunge*), ON. *tunga* (Da., Norw. *tunge*, Sw. *tunga*), Goth. *tuggô*:—OTeut. **tungôn-*, held to be cogn. with L. *lingua* tongue, for older **dingua* (as *lacrima*:—*dacrima*: see TEAR *sb.*[1]).

The natural mod.Eng. repr. of OE. *tunge* would be *tung*, as in *lung*, *rung*, *sung* (and as the word is actually pronounced); but the ME. device of writing *on* for *un* brought in the alternative *tonge* with variants *tounge*, *townge*; app. the effort to show that the pronunciation was not (tundʒ(e) led to the later *tounghe*, *toungue*, *tongue*, although it is true that these hardly appeared before final *e* was becoming mute, so that its simple omission would have been equally effective. The spelling *tongue* is thus neither etymological nor phonetic, and is only in a very small degree historical.]

**I.** The bodily member.

**1.** An organ, possessed by man and by most vertebrates, occupying the floor of the mouth, and attached at its base to the hyoid bone; often protrusible and freely movable. In its development in man and the higher mammals, it is tapering, blunt-tipped, muscular, soft and fleshy, important in taking in and swallowing food, also as the principal organ of taste, and in man of articulate speech.

In some mammals, as the ant-eaters, it is attenuated, long, and worm-like; in most birds it is pointed, hard, and horny; in fishes, hard and immovable; in snakes and many lizards, cylindrical, slender, and forked, and an important tactile organ; in some amphibia, it is fixed at the front and free at the hinder end, and (as also in chameleons) used in licking up their prey.

*c* 897 K. ÆLFRED *Gregory's Past. C.* xliii. 309 Ðætte he ȝewæte his ytemestan finger on wættre, & mid ðæm ȝecele mine tungan. *c* 1000 *Sax. Leechd.* II. 272 Do hwon on þine tungan. *c* 1200 *Trin. Coll. Hom.* 181 Teð hine grindeð, tunge hine swoleȝeð. *c* 1250 *Gen. & Ex.* 372 And atter on is tunge cliuen. *c* 1290 *S. Eng. Leg.* I. 206/206 For Anguische þe eorþe heo freten, and hore tongene gnowen al-so. 13.. *Cursor M.* 16767+15 (Cott.) He tast it with tonge Bot þer-of toke he noght. *c* 1380 WYCLIF *Serm.* Sel. Wks. I. 29 Crist touchide his tonge..and þe bonde of his tonge was opened for to speke. *c* 1380 — *Wks.* (1880) 110 He schal make his tounge cleue faste to þe roof of his mouþ. 1398 TREVISA *Barth. De P. R.* v. xxiii. (Bodl. MS.), Soune ..is yschape with þe wraaste of þe tunge and þanne wise men clepeþ it a voice. 1530 PALSGR. 284/1 Tunge to speke with, *langue*. 1604 SHAKS. *Oth.* II. iii. 221, I had rather haue this tongue cut from my mouth. 1697 DRYDEN *Virg. Georg.* III. 666 A Snake..Erect, and brandishing his forky Tongue. 1828 STARK *Elem. Nat. Hist.* I. 29 The tongue in the Mammalia is always fleshy, and attached to the hyoid bone, which bone is suspended by ligaments to the cranium. 1831 R. KNOX *Cloquet's Anat.* 586 The Tongue, a symmetrical organ,..situated in the interior of the mouth, extending from the hyoid bone and epiglottis to behind the incisive teeth.

**b.** In reference to invertebrate animals, applied to various organs or parts of the mouth having some of the functions of the tongue of vertebrates, or some analogy to it.

1753 CHAMBERS *Cycl. Supp.*, *Tongue of a Mussel*,..an organ by means of which it spins a sort of threads..to fix itself to the rocks by. 1826 KIRBY & SP. *Entomol.* III. 358 *Lingua* (the Tongue). The organ situated within the *Labium* or emerging from it, by which insects in many cases collect their food and pass it down to the *Pharynx*. 1870 ROLLESTON *Anim. Life* Introd. 87 'Odontophorous' Mollusca..possessing the peculiar dentigerous rasping organ known as the tongue.

**c.** Erroneously regarded as the 'stinging organ'.

1581 J. HAMILTON in *Cath. Tractates* (S.T.S.) 78/30 Venemous serpentis to stang thame with the fyrie edge of thair tungis. 1595 SHAKS. *John* III. i. 258. 1599 — *Much Ado* v. i. 90 Villaines, That dare as well answer a man indeede, As I dare take a serpent by the tongue.

**2.** A figure or representation of this organ. **a.** A symbolic figure or appearance as of a tongue, as those that appeared on the day of Pentecost.

[*c* 1000 ÆLFRIC *Hom.* I. 314 And wæs æteowed bufon heora ælcum swylce fyrene tungan.] *c* 1175 *Lamb. Hom.* 89 Biforan heore elche swilc hit were furene tungen. 1382 WYCLIF *Acts* ii. 3 And tungis dyuersely partid as fyer apperiden to hem. 1526 TINDALE *Acts* ii. 3 And there apered vnto them cloven tonges, as they had bene fyre..: and they..began to speake with other tonges. *a* 1740 WATTS *Remnants of Time* xi[i], On that day when the tongues of fire sat on his twelve apostles. 1792 HAWEIS *Hymn*, '*Enthroned on high*' ii, Though on our heads no tongues of fire Their wondrous powers impart.

**b.** A delineated or artificial figure of a tongue.

1488-92 *Acc. Ld. High Treas. Scot.* I. 81 A grete serpent toung set with gold, perle and precious stanes. 1536 *Register of Riches* in *Antiq. Sarisb.* (1771) 199 Having.. two white Leopards and two dragons facing them as going to engage, their tounges are done in curiousest wyse. 1577-87 HOLINSHED *Chron.* III. 849/1 Then entered a person called Report, apparelled in crimsin sattin full of toongs, sitting on a flieng horsse..called Pegasus. 1886 *Edin. Rev.* July 151 The classical 'egg and tongue' and 'tongue and dart' patterns are branches from the same stem.

**3.** The tongue of an animal as an article of food; *esp.* an OX-TONGUE or NEAT'S TONGUE.

*c* 1420 *Liber Cocorum* (1862) 26 Take tho ox tonge and schalle hit wele. 1598 *Epulario* C iv, To seeth Tongues. 1653 WALTON *Angler* viii. 165 The tongues of Carps are noted to be choice and costly meat. 1740 SOMERVILLE *Hobbinol* III. Poems (1749) 158 Black Hams, and Tongues that speechless can persuade To ply the brisk Carouse. 1869 'L. CARROLL' *Phantasm.* 112 Dispense the tongue and chicken.

**II.** In reference to speech.

**4.** Considered as the principal organ of speech; hence, the faculty of speech; the power of articulation or vocal expression or description; voice, speech; words, language. Also *fig.*

In many contexts it is impossible to separate the sense of the organ from that of its work or use.

*c* 890 tr. *Bæda's Hist.* IV. xxv. [xxiv.] (1890) 348 Seo tunge, þe swa moniȝ halwende word in þæs scyppendes lof ȝesette. *c* 1000 ÆLFRIC *Exod.* iv. 10 Þa cwæþ Moises..ic hæfde þe lætran tungan. *c* 1200 ORMIN 4879 Þuss spacc þe Laferrd Jesu Crist Þurrh his prophetess tunge. *a* 1250 *Prov. Ælfred* 282 in *O. E. Misc.* 118 Wymmon is word-woþ & haueþ tunge [*v.r.* tunke] to swift. *c* 1290 *Beket* 645 in *S. Eng. Leg.* I. 125 No tounge telle ne may. 13.. *Cursor M.* 8404 (Gött.) Þou salamon mi sone be ȝong, He es wijs and of redi toung. 1414 *26 Pol. Poems* xiii. 100 He wolde trouþes tonge were tyȝed. 1573 G. HARVEY *Letter-bk.* (Camden) 6 A hie point for them to beat there heds and whet there tungs about. 1587 *Mirr. Mag.*, *Brennus* xxxiv, What tong can tell thy mothers griefe. 1600 SHAKS. *A. Y. L.* II. i. 16 This our life..Findes tongues in trees, bookes in the running brookes. 1888 F. HUME *Mme. Midas* I. Prol., As you have not even a tongue to contradict.

**b.** In many colloquial and proverbial expressions of obvious meaning.

*c* 1375 *Sc. Leg. Saints* l. (*Katerine*) 257 Na man of ws had tuth na towng To conclud hir, þocht scho be ȝounge. *c* 1425 *Eng. Conq. Irel.* 46 Tong breketh bon, thegh hym-self ne hawe none. 1484 CAXTON *Fables of Auian* xxii, The felauship of the man whiche hath two tongues is nought. 1546 J. HEYWOOD *Prov.* (1867) 64 Her tong ronth on patens. 1562 — *Prov. & Epigr.* 163 Thy tounge runth before thy wit. 1607 T. WALKINGTON *Opt. Glass* i. (1664) 2 Pythagoras ..had this golden Poesie ever on his tongues end. 1677 W. HUGHES *Man of Sin* III. iii. 77 For a Tongue to pierce an Inch-Board, commend me to Tursellinus. 1820 SCOTT *Abbot* iv, I would..give him a lick with the rough side of my tongue. 1859 READE *Love me Little* x, Wasn't your tongue a little too long for your teeth just now? 1870 DICKENS *E. Drood* ii, Have you lost your tongue, Jack? 1890 MAJOR-GEN. A. F. BOND in Rogerson *Hist. Rec. 53rd (Shropshire) Regt.* 206 Having..given them a taste of his rough tongue. 1895 *E. Anglia Gloss.* s.v. *Length*, *To give one the length of your tongue*, to slang. 1899 RAYMOND *Two Men o' Mendip* xv. 248 Vather'll..call ee everything he can lay his tongue to.

**c.** *To hold one's tongue*, to refrain from speech, keep silence, say nothing. † *To keep one's tongue*, (*a*) to keep one's word; (*b*) to hold one's tongue.

*c* 897 K. ÆLFRED *Gregory's Past. C.* xxxviii. 276 Se mon se ðe ne mæȝ his tungan ȝehealdan sie ȝelicost openre byriȝ. 1377 LANGL. *P. Pl.* B. XVIII. 146 Hold þi tonge, mercy! It is but a trufle þat þow tellest. 1390 GOWER *Conf.* III. 143 Ther schal a worthi king beginne To kepe his tunge and to be trewe. *c* 1440 *Alphabet of Tales* 83 Þe toder..flate with hym agayn & bad hym hold his tong. 1535 COVERDALE *Matt.* xxvi. 63 Iesus helde his tonge. 1596 SHAKS. *Tam. Shr.* I. i. 214, I will charme him first to keepe his tongue. 1605 — *Macb.* II. iii. 125 Why doe we hold our tongues? 1672 *Mede's Wks.* p. xvii, It was a frequent Proverbial speech of our Author's, He that cannot hold his tongue can hold nothing; and he practis'd accordingly. 1749 LADY LUXBOROUGH *Let. to Shenstone* 28 Nov., Shocked to hear in rough English Hold your tongue. 1833 HT. MARTINEAU *Loom & Lugger* I. vii, Hold your impertinent tongue, Sir. 1884 GEORGIANA M. CRAIK *G. Helstone* 26 Here is your father who knows it is, though he thinks it best to hold his tongue.

**d.** Phr. *To put*, or *speak with*, *one's tongue in one's cheek*, to speak insincerely.

1842 BARHAM *Ingol. Leg.* Ser. II. *Black Mousquetaire* II. xv, He..Cried '*Superbe!—Magnifique!*' (With his tongue in his cheek). 1869 M. ARNOLD *Cult. & An.* Pref. 56 If statesmen, either with their tongue in their cheek or through a generous impulsiveness, tell them [etc.]. *Ibid.* 123 He unquestionably..knows that he is talking clap-trap, and, so to say, puts his tongue in his cheek. 1898 SIR E. W. HAMILTON *Gladstone* 10 There was no speaking 'with his tongue in the cheek'. He spoke straight from the heart.

**5.** The action of speaking; speech, talking, utterance, voice; also, what is spoken or uttered; words, talk, discourse.

*c* 897 K. ÆLFRED *Gregory's Past. C.* i. 27 Ac sio tunge bið ȝescended on ðæm lareowdome ðonne hio oðer læro, oðer hio ȝeleornode. *c* 1020 *Rule St. Benet* (Logeman) 4 Se ðe na deþ facn on his tungan. *a* 1225 *Ancr. R.* 78 Wite ich wel mine tunge, ich mei wel holden þene wei toward heouene. 1362 LANGL. *P. Pl.* A. I. 86 Hose is trewe of his tonge..is a-counted to þe gospel. *c* 1470 HENRY *Wallace* I. 294 He was wondyr fayr, Nocht large of tong. 1520 WHITINTON *Vulg.* (1527) 3 b, He is full of tongue [*linguax*]. 1604 S. HARRISON *Archs of Triumph* Bj, Their lastingnes should liue but in the tongues and memories of men. 1667 DRYDEN *Sir Martin Mar-All* III. iii, Sometimes you have tongue enough; what, are you silent? 1835

Montgomery *Hymn*, '*For ever with the Lord*', The choral harmonies of Heaven Earth's Babel tongues o'erpower.

**b.** Speech as distinguished from or contrasted with thought, action, or fact; mere words.

**1382** Wyclif *1 John* iii. 18 Loue we not in word, nether in tunge, but in werk and treuthe. *c* **1400** *Apol. Loll.* 54 Þe tung a lone is not to be axid, but the lif. *c* **1560** A. Scott *Poems* (S.T.S.) iii. 23 Bot offir thame ȝour daly observance Be tung, tho^t naþir hairt nor mynd consentis. **1853** Lynch *Self-Improv.* iv. 102 If religion begins with your tongue, it is very likely only to end there; but if religion is in your heart, it must needs come to your tongue sometimes. **1866** Carlyle in *Morn. Star* 4 Apr. 5/4 It seems to me the finest nations of the world—the English and the American—are going all away into wind and tongue.

†**c.** Spoken as distinct from written or other communication; *by tongue*, by word of mouth. *Obs.*

**1549** *Compl. Scot.* xi. 94 The messengeir gat nay ansuer be tong fra ald tarquine. **1553** Janet Bethune in *Maitl. Cl. Misc.* (1840) I. 41 *note*, I haif committit sum part of my mynd be toung to my broder.

†**d.** A 'voice', vote, suffrage. *Obs. rare.*

**1607** Shaks. *Cor.* II. iii. 216 Have you, ere now, deny'd the asker: And now againe, [? on] him that did not aske, ..Bestow your su'd-for Tongues?

†**e.** Eulogy, fame. *Obs. rare.*

*c* **1616** Fletcher *Thierry & Theod.* v. (last sp.), And because She was born Noble, let that Title find her A private grave, but neither tongue nor honor.

**6.** Manner of speaking or talking, with regard to the sense or import of what is said, the mode of expression or form of words used, or the sound of the voice.

*c* **1460** *How Gd. Wif thaught hir Doughter* 19 in Hazl. *E. P. P.* I. 181 Be of a good beryngе and of a good tonge. **1595** *Enq. Tripe-wife* (1881) 147 Keepe a good tung in your head, least it hurt your teeth. **1596** Shaks. *Tam. Shr.* Induct. i. 114 With soft lowe tongue, and lowly curtesie. **1596** — *Merch. V.* II. vi. 27 Who are you? tell me for more certainty, Albeit Ile sweare that I do know your tongue. **1664** in *Verney Mem.* (1907) II. 204 She gros very malisas in hur toung to us all. **1724** Ramsay *Tea-t. Misc.* (1733) I. 86 Ye..ha' na learn'd the beggars tongue. **1828** *Trial of W. Dyon at York Assizes* 10, I knew him by his tongue.

**7.** Of a dog. **a.** In phrases: *To move* (*its*) *tongue*, to bark (*arch.*); *to give tongue, to throw* (*its*) *tongue*, properly of a hound: to give forth its voice when on the scent or in sight of the quarry. Also *transf.* of persons.

**1535** Coverdale *Josh.* x. 21 No man durst moue his tunge agaynst the children of Israel. **1539** Bible (Great) *Exod.* xi. 7 But amonge all the children of Isrl' shal not a dogg moue his tonge, nor yet man or beast. **1737** Hervey *Mem.* II. 374 To speak in the sportsman's style, he has not given tongue often. **1742** Fielding *Jos. Andrews* III. vi, Ringwood..never threw his tongue but where the scent was undoubtedly true. **1843** R. Palmer in *Mem.* (1896) I. xxiv. 353, I nearly picked a quarrel with a Repealer, who opened tongue to the people in the market place of Larne. **1857** Geo. Eliot *Scenes Clerical Life, Amos Barton* ii, When Papa opened the door Chubby was giving tongue energetically. **1859** *Art of Taming Horses* xii. 203 When a hound throws his tongue he is said to speak. **1871** Freeman *Norm. Conq.* IV. xx. 518 He was for a moment undisputed lord, without a dog moving his tongue against him, from the Orkneys to the Angevin march. **1893** *Black & White* 15 July 81/1 He has a tendency to throw his tongue too freely, to speak without fair warrant.

**b.** Hence, the hunting-cry or 'music' of a hound in pursuit of game.

**1787** Hunter in *Phil. Trans.* LXXVII. 266 Others, as the Hound, have a peculiar howl, which, by huntsmen, is called the tongue. **1879** *Dogs Gt. Brit. & Amer.* 56 (Cent.) The tongue [of the bloodhound should be] loud, long, deep, and melodious. **1890** *The Tongue of the Hound* in *Sat. Rev.* 1 Feb. 134/2 It is odd that the English hound, alone of hounds, should have this melodious tongue. *Ibid.* 135/1 How the squires of bygone times valued the tongues of their hounds.

**8.** The speech or language of a people or race; also, that of a particular class or locality, a dialect.

*c* **1000** *Ags. Gosp.* Mark xvi. 17 Hi sprecaþ niwum tungum. *a* **1300** *Cursor M.* 233 Þis ilke boke is translate In to Inglis tong to rede. **1423** Jas. I *Kingis Q.* vii, Enditing In his faire latyne tong. **1485** *Rolls of Parlt.* VI. 375/1 Maister Stephen Fryon', our Secretary in Frensh tonge. *a* **1560** Rolland *Seven Sages* (1837) A ij, In vulgar toung he bure the bell that day To mak meter. **1570–6** Lambarde *Peramb. Kent* (1826) 233 Erasmus compareth the English toong to a Dog's barking that soundeth nothing els but Baw waw waw in Monosillable. **1667** Milton *P. L.* xii. 501 To speak all Tongues, and do all Miracles. **1689–90** Temple *Ess. Learning* Wks. 1731 I. 165 The three modern Tongues much esteemed, are Italian, Spanish and French. **1711** Addison *Spect.* No. 1 ⁋ 3 Celebrated Books, either in the learned or the modern Tongues. **1868** Gladstone *Juv. Mundi* iii. (1869) 89 There were many races in Crete, and there was a mixture of tongue. **1908** [Miss E. Fowler] *Betw. Trent & Ancholme* 307 Now the local tongue is becoming too 'correct' to be characteristic and picturesque.

**b.** *The tongues*, foreign languages; often *spec.* the classical or learned languages; † *the three tongues*, Hebrew, Greek, and Latin.

[*c* **1450** Capgrave *Life St. Aug.* 4 The Barbar tonge is euery tonge in þe world whech is fer fro þe iij principall tongis, Hebrew, Grek, & Latyn.] **1535** Joye *Apol. Tindale* (Arb.) 11 A man of grete lerning..both in the scriptures and the tongues. **1560** Daus tr. *Sleidane's Comm.* 37 Excellencie in the knowledge of all three tonges. **1577** Harrison *England* II. iii. (1877) I. 71 In..Cambridge & Oxford..the vse of the tongues..are dailie taught and had. **1591** Shaks. *Two Gent.* IV. i. 33 Haue you the Tongues?..My youthfull trauaile, therein made me happy. **1617** Minsheu *Ductor* Title-p., The Guide into the tongues. With their agreement and consent one with another..in these eleuen Languages, viz. [etc.]. **1691** Ray *Creation* I. (1692) 162 We content ourselves with the knowledge of the Tongues. **1907** A. Lang in *Blackw. Mag.* July 17 He was well-educated, familiar with 'the tongues'. **1912** *Bodleian Library, Man. for Readers* 4/1 The rooms once used for the teaching of..the two Tongues (Greek and Hebrew).

**c.** The knowledge or use of a language; esp. in phrases *gift of tongues, to speak with a tongue* (*tongues*), in reference to the Pentecostal miracle and the miraculous gift in the early Church.

**1526** Tindale [see 2 a]. — *1 Cor.* xii. 30 Do all speake with tonges? *Ibid.* xiii. 8 Though that prophesyinge fayle, other tonges shall cease, or knowledge vanysshe awaye. **1533** Gau *Richt Vay* 48 The halie spreit..gaif to thayme ye gift to speik with al twngis. **1538** Cromwell in Merriman *Life & Lett.* (1902) II. 144 Ioynyng wyth you Maister Mason..to declare your purpose for that having the tongue he may doo..it more fully thenne you could percace easly vtter the same. **1593** R. Harvey *Philad.* 3 Neither can you proue that hee had not wealth enough to serue his vses, or tongue enough in euery place of his trauell. *a* **1637** B. Jonson *Underwoods, Execration upon Vulcan* 75 Their.. bright stone that brings Invisibility, and strength, and tongues. **1879** Farrar *St. Paul* I. 96 The glossolalia or 'speaking with a tongue', is connected with 'prophesying', that is, exalted preaching.

**9.** *transf.* in biblical use: A people or nation having a language of their own. Usually in plural: *all tongues*, people of every tongue.

**1382** Wyclif *Rev.* v. 9 In thi blood, of al lynage, and tunge, and puple, and nacioun. **1526** Tindale *ibid.*, Thou ..haste redemed vs by thy bloud, out of all kynreddes, and tonges, and people, and nacions. **1535** Coverdale *Isa.* lxvi. 18, I wil come to gather all people and tonges. **1587** Golding *De Mornay* xxvii. (1592) 433 All People, Nations, and Toungs shal serue that Kingdome. **1745** *Scot. Paraphr.* xviii. ii, To this the joyful nations round, all tribes and tongues shall flow. **1875** Manning *Mission H. Ghost* ix. 234 Throughout all lands, and people, and tongues.

**III.** Anything that resembles or suggests the human or animal tongue by its shape, position, function, or use; a tapering, projecting, or elongated object or part, esp. when mobile, or attached at one end or side.

**10.** Any tongue-like part or organ of the human or animal body. † *Tongue of the throat*, the uvula.

**1398** Trevisa *Barth. De P. R.* v. xxiv. (Bodl. MS. lf. 13 b/1), [Þis] þe phisicians clepiþ þe tunge of þe throte and Cataracta also. **1483** *Cath. Angl.* 396/2 A Tunge in the throte, *vua*; or ye palase of ye mowthe. **1831** R. Knox *Cloquet's Anat.* 253 The *Trachelo-Mastoideus* (*Complexus Minor*),..arises from the last four transverse processes of the neck, and three or four of the back, by tendinous and fleshy tongues. **1897** *Allbutt's Syst. Med.* IV. 527 A projecting tongue [of splenic tissue] becoming pedunculated.

†**11.** A wedge, an ingot of gold or silver. *Obs.* (In quot. a lit. rendering of Heb. לשון זהב l'shōn zahab.)

**1535** Coverdale *Josh.* vii. 21 And two hundreth Sycles of syluer and a tunge of golde, worth fiftye Sycles in weight.

**12.** (= *tongue-fish.*) A young or small-sized sole. [So, in same sense, early mod.Du. *tonghe* (Kilian), Ger. *zunge*, Da. *tunge*, Sw. *tungfisk*.]

*a* **1825** Forby *Voc. E Anglia*, *Tongue*, a small sole, from its shape. **1881** *Daily News* 4 Mar. 4/6 Large soles are put at the top and bottom of the box, and the 'tongues' stowed cleverly in the middle, so that the sole buyer..has but scant opportunity of fairly judging its contents. **1881** *Daily Tel.* 11 Mar., The fishermen know the ground on which little else than tongues can be caught, and they should be prevented fishing over that ground. **1884** F. Day *Fishes Gt. Brit.* II. 40 Sole..slips, or tongues, the market terms for the young.

**13.** A tongue-like projecting piece of anything. **a.** A narrow strip of land, running into the sea, or between two branches of a river, or two other lands; also a projecting horizontal point or spit of ice in the sea, a narrow inlet of water running into the land, etc. **b.** A narrow and deep part of the current of a river, running smoothly and rapidly between rocks. **c.** A tapering jet of flame.

**a. 1566** in *Reg. Mag. Sig. Scot.* 1577. 735/1 Duas acras vocatas *the kirk-dur-keyis* (..descendendo cum uno *lie tung* inter terras de Erlishall). **1615** G. Sandys *Trav.* 231 There is a double haven devided by a tongue of rocke. **1682** Wheler *Journ. Greece* I. 27 You see the Sea on both sides of this long Tongue of Land. **1693** Luttrell *Brief Rel.* (1857) III. 89 The Windsor Castle run on the tongue of the Goodwin sands. **1766** J. Bartram *Jrnl.* 12 Jan. 33 A long tongue of marsh comes from the N.E. end. **1771** *Chron.* in *Ann. Reg.* 73/1 Whitehaven..the tide..overflowed the quays and tongues, and ran..into the market-place. **1775** Romans *Florida* App. 48 To the westward of Stirrup's Key is a tongue of ocean water shooting into the bank. **1820** Scoresby *Acc. Arctic Reg.* I. 228 A tongue is a point of ice projecting nearly horizontally from a part that is under water. Ships have sometimes run aground upon tongues of ice. **1832** *Act 2 & 3 Will. IV*, c. 64 Sched. O, 16 The tongue of land in the river just above Kingsbury fishpond. **1839** Murchison *Silur. Syst.* I. x. 134 A..smaller tongue of the coal measures passes from the Forest of Wyre to the left bank of the Severn. **1857** Livingstone *Trav.* xx. 404 A tongue of rather high land, formed by the left bank of the Lucalla, and right bank of the Coanza. **1895** Mary Kingsley *W. Africa* 573 Tongues of forest go up the mountain in some places a hundred yards or more above the true line of the belt.

**b. 1891** *Cent. Dict.* s.v., A tongue is well-known to anglers as a favorite resting-place of salmon in their laborious ascent of rapid streams.

**c. 1797** Coleridge *Christabel* I. 159 A tongue of light, a fit of flame. **1849** Mrs. Somerville *Connex. Phys. Sc.* xxxiii. (ed. 8) 370 The flame of a taper..is immediately divided into two tongues by the electric current. **1872** Hanna *Resurrection* ix. 178 That broad strong tongue of flame.

**14.** In many technical applications.

**a.** The pin of a buckle or brooch. **b.** The pointer of a balance; also of a dial. **c.** A thin elastic vibratory strip of metal, covering the aperture of a reed in an organ-pipe: = Reed 8 c; hence *transf.* an analogous device in a seed-sowing machine (*obs.*); also, a reed in the oboe or bassoon: = Reed 8 a; the vibrating fork in the Jew's harp or 'trump'; hence *fig.* the essential or principal person in a company or the like; also, a plectrum or jack in the harpsichord (= Jack *sb.*[1] 14). **d.** The clapper of a bell; hence, the pistil or a stamen of a bell-flower. **e.** The pole of a wagon or other vehicle; † the head of a plough (*obs.*). **f.** A projecting piece of leather or the like forming a tab or flap, or means of fastening; the strip of thin leather or kid closing the opening in a boot which is laced or buttoned; hence, any similar appendage. †**g.** In *Fortification*, a pointed horn-work; see quot. *Obs.* **h.** The movable tapered piece of rail in a railway switch. **i.** The wedge-shaped or tapered end of a scion in grafting. **j.** A projecting tenon along the edge of a board, to be inserted into a groove or mortise in the edge of another board; also, a connecting slip, often of iron or steel, which joins two grooved boards; in *Mech.* a projecting flange, rib, or strip for any purpose (*Cassell's Encycl. Dict.* 1888). **k.** The tapered end of a pole, etc. by which it is fixed in a socket; also, the upper main-piece of a made mast. **l.** A short piece of rope spliced into the upper part of the standing backstays, etc. **m.** Of a sword or knife: see quots. **n.** Of a bevel: see quots.

**a.** *c* **1325** *Gloss. W. de Bibbesw.* in Wright *Voc.* 150 Einsy doyt le hardiloun [*gloss*, the tungge]. Passer par tru de subiloun [*gloss*, a bore of an alsene] [nalkin]. *c* **1440** *Promp. Parv.* 506/1 Tunge of a bocle, *lingula*. **1483** *Cath. Angl.* 396/2 A Tunge of ye belte, *lingula*. **1524** in G. Oliver *Hist. Coll.* (1841) App. 15 A silver bokyll without a tong. **1530** Palsgr. 281/2 Tong of a buckell, *hardillon*. **1608** in *Archæologia* XI. 93 Sixteen gold buckles with pendants and toungs. **1802** *Trans. Soc. Arts* XX. 334 A buckle, with its double tongue received in a groove. **1851** D. Wilson *Preh. Ann.* (1863) II. 258 The acus or tongue is wanting.

**b. 1429** *Rolls of Parlt.* IV. 349/1 So yat ye tunge of ye balance encline not to on party. **1530** Palsgr. 281/2 Tong of a balaunce, *languette*. **1626** Massinger *Roman Actor* v. ii, As I can move this dial's tongue to six. *a* **1691** Boyle *Hist. Air* (1692) 91 The scales being gently stirred, the tongue would play altogether on that side, at which the bubble was hung. **1896** M. Rutherford *Cath. Furze* vi, It was just a tremble of the tongue of the balance.

**c. 1551** Turner *Herbal* I. E ij, Ther are dyuerse kyndes of reedes, some are thicke redes; wherof arrowes are made,.. some serue for to make tonges for pypes. **1727–41** Chambers *Cycl.* s.v. *Organ*, The degree of acuteness and gravity in the sound of a reed pipe, depends on the length of the tongue. **1733** Tull *Horse-Hoeing Husb.* xxii. 319 The Tongue of the Seed-Box..differs from that in the Sound-Board of an Organ..in Shape. **1786** Jefferson *Writ.* (1859) I. 503 The last invented tongue for the harpsichord. **1795** Burns *Election* ii, An' there will be black-lippit Johnnie, The tongue o' the trump to them a'. **1854** Bushnan in *Orr's Circ. Sc.* I. *Org. Nat.* 127 The air throws the tongue..into a state of vibration. **1879** Stainer *Music of Bible* 78 The real difference between an oboe and a clarinet is, that the former has a double tongue which vibrates, the latter a single tongue. **1898** Stainer & Barrett *Dict. Mus. Terms* s.v. *Organ Construction* 345 The *reed* is a brass tube.. having a narrow orifice over which lies the *tongue*, a thin elastic piece of brass large enough to cover the orifice and its edges..The lower end of the tongue is..perfectly free.

**d. 1577** B. Googe *Heresbach's Husb.* II. (1586) 65 By plucking out the little yellowe toongs from the bell. **1578** *Burgh Rec. Glasgow* (Maitl. Club) 104 For ane tong to Sanct Mungowes bell 2/. **1590** Shaks. *Mids. N.* v. i. 370 The iron tongue of midnight hath told twelue. **1595** — *John* III. iii. 38. **1690** *Vestry Bks.* (Surtees) 258 For leather to the bell tongues, 2s. 8d. **1721** Wodrow *Sufferings Ch. Scot.* (1838) I. I. iv. § i. 333/1 The bell's tongue in some places was stolen away, that the parishioners might have an excuse for not coming to church. **1842** *Belfast & Environs* 71 This fine bell, which—except that the tongue is wanting —is in as fine preservation as at the moment it was originally cast.

**e. 1591** Percivall *Sp. Dict.*, *Pertiga de carreta*, the toong of a plowe, (L.) *temo*. **1792** Belknap *Hist. New Hampsh.* III. 106 The oxen which are nearest to the tongue are sometimes suspended. **1827** F. Cooper *Prairie* I. ii. 27 The men..applied their strength to the wagon, pulling it by its projecting tongue. **1858** Lewis in Youatt *Dog* (N.Y.) ii. 54 Constantly by the side or at the heels of the horses, or under the tongue of the vehicle.

**f. 1597** A. M. tr. *Guillemeau's Fr. Chirurg.* 32 b/1 The hornes hauinge internally a little leatherne tunge which stoppeth the hoales. **1643** Sir T. Hope *Diary* 25 June (1843) 191 Quhil I wes pulling on my left buit both the tungis of it brak. **1830** Marryat *King's Own* x, He passed the leathern tongue of the [pocket-] book through the strap. **1840** J. Devlin *Shoemaker* 65 A further closing..beginning at the turn of the.. counter, and going right round, along the range, and up the tongue. **1912** W. H. Stevenson in *Eng. Hist. Rev.* Jan. 7 The writs of Edward the Confessor have pendent seals affixed to a tongue of the parchment.

**g. 1688** R. Holme *Armoury* III. xvi. (Roxb.) 99/1 Tongues..are outworks that differ from Horn-works only in this, that in two halfe Bulworks they haue only an acute angle: and this sort is called the Single Tongue: it is called a double Tongue work, when it hath two outward angles with one inward.

**h. 1841** *Penny Cycl.* XIX. 257/1 Switches are moveable rails placed at the point where two tracks fall into one,..to guide vehicles from the single track into either of the two...In the old railways this was effected by short tongues of iron, moved by hand. **1877** Knight *Dict. Mech.*, *Tongue*..the short movable rail of a switch, by which the wheels are directed to one or the other lines of rail.

**i. 1832** *Planting* 30 in *Libr. Usef. Knowl., Husb.* III, The upper division of the scion made by the slit, termed the tongue or wedge, is then inserted into the cleft of the stock. **1887** *Nicholson's Dict. Gard.* s.v. *Tongue-grafting*, A small, thin tongue is cut in an upward direction in the scion, and also a notch the opposite way in the stock.

**j. 1842** Francis *Dict. Arts*, etc., *Tongue*, a projecting part at the edge of a board, to be inserted into a groove ploughed in the edge of another. **1902** *How to Make Things* 57/1 Then add the other boards, fitting the tongue of one into the groove of the other. **k.** **1815** Burney *Falconer's Dict. Marine* 568/1 *Tongue*, in mast-making, the taper part of the lower end of a spindle, or of a scarph. **l.** **1815** Burney *Falconer's Dict. Marine*, *Tongue*, a short piece of rope spliced into the upper part of standing backstays, &c. to the size of the topmast-head. **m.** **1853** Stocqueler *Milit. Encycl.*, *Tongue of a Sword*, that part of the blade on which the gripe, shell, and pummel, are fixed. **1869** Boutell *Arms & Arm.* ix. (1874) 170 The tongue..is the spike..which is fixed into the hilt in order to join the hilt and the blade together. **n.** **1867** Smyth *Sailor's Word-bk.*, *Tongue of a bevel*,..by which the angles or bevellings are taken. **1877** Knight *Dict. Mech.*, *Tongue*, ..the movable arm of a bevel, the principal member being the stock, which forms the case when the instrument is closed.

**IV.** *attrib.* and *Comb.* (very numerous: the following are examples).

**15. a.** Simple attrib., as *tongue-battery*, *-battle*, *-bolt*, *-bully*, *-combat*, *-compliment*, *-craft*, *-debate*, *-drill*, *-fire*, *-government*, *-grace*, *-itch*, *-metal*, *-part* (of a top-boot), *-plague*, *-play*, *-powder*, *-prayer*, *-root*, *-saw*, *-sin*, *-skirmish*, *-slip*, *-squib*, *-structure*, *-tangle*, *-tattle*, *-tip*, *-toil*, *-valour*, *-vice*, *-war*, *-warrior*, *-weapon*. **b.** objective and obj. genitive, as *tongue-biting*, *-cutting*, *-lolling*, *-paralysing*, *-scraper*, *-taming*, *-wagging* (so *tongue-wag* vb. intr.), sbs. and adjs. **c.** instrumental, as *tongue-bang*, *-hammer*, *-kill*, *-lash*, *-taw* vbs., *tongue-baited*, *-bitten*, *-rent* adjs., *tongue-murdering*, *-scourging*, *-smiting*, *-travailing* sbs. and adjs., *tongue-banger*, *-smiter* sbs. **d.** locative, similative, etc., as *tongue-bound*, *-doughty*, *-dumb*, *-flowered*, *-free*, *-gilt*, *-haltered*, *-leaved*, *-like*, *-proof*, *-puissant*, *-valiant*, *-wanton* adjs.

**1750** *Student* I. 304 Socrates was too much *tongue-baited. **1824** Miss Mitford *Village* Ser. I. (1863) 97 The feminine accomplishment of scolding, (*tongue-banging, it is called in our parts, a compound word which deserves to be Greek). **1881** *Good Wds.* 842/2, I heerd her tonguebanging o' ye as I cum past the house. **1880** Tennyson *North. Cobbler* iv, Sally she turn'd a *tongue-banger, an' räated me. **1671** Milton *Samson* 404 Mustring all her wiles, With blandisht parlies, feminine assaults, *Tongue-batteries. *a* **1743** Ozell tr. *Brantome's Span. Rhodomontades* (1744) 84 He did by no means like Handy-blows, but only your *Tongue-Battles. **1898** J. Hutchinson in *Arch. Surg.* IX. No. 34. 126 It [an epileptic fit] came without warning, and was attended by *tongue-biting. **1615** Day *Festivals* xii. 335 Now for us..who are thus *Tongue-bitten and Reviled in such sort. **1611** Beaum. & Fl. *Philaster* II. ii, Look well about you and you may find a *tongue-bolt. **1856** R. A. Vaughan *Mystics* (1860) II. VIII. iv. 52 The..doctors of Lyons hurled back his tongue-bolts with the dreaded cry of heresy. **1906** E. A. Abbott *Silanus* xxix, I stood silent,.. as it were *tongue-bound. *a* **1834** Coleridge *Notes & Lect.* (1849) I. 283 Such a mouthing Tamburlane, and bombastic *tongue-bully as this Cethegus of his! **1897** *Allbutt's Syst. Med.* III. 354 The most important factors in the *tongue-coating of fever. **1623** Hexham (*title*) A *tongve-combat, lately happening be-tweene two English Souldiers in the Tilt-boat of Grauesend. **1660** Fuller *Mixt Contempl.* (1841) 198 The rent-compleating of the one, and the *tongue-compliments of the other. **1837** C. Lofft *Self-formation* I. 220 Despatch..is a surpassing quality in *tonguecraft. **1697** Dryden *Æneid* XI. 588 Ever foremost in a *tongue-debate. **1671** Milton *Samson* 1181 *Tongue-doubtie Giant, how dost thou prove me these? **1886** Tupper *My Life as Author* 73 That was the sort of *tongue-drill and nerve-quieting recommended and enforced. **1556** *Aurelio & Isab.* (1608) H ij, You thoughte..to rendre me *tonge domme. **1876** Swinburne *Erechtheus* 642 *Tongue-fighters, tough of talk and sinewy speech. **1690** C. Nesse *O. & N. Test.* I. 19 This raging *tongue-fire causeth great confusion. **1890** *Cent. Dict.* s.v. *Serapias*, *S. Lingua* is known as the *tongue-flowered..orchis. **1617** Bp. Hall *Quo Vadis* xxi, Others more capricious, some more *tongue-free; few euer better. **1907** 'J. Halsham' *Lonewood Corner* 116 John Board.. to the last degree tongue-free. **1608** Machin & Markham *Dumb Knight* III. i. F j b, Thus are the pauement stones before the doores Of these great *tongue guilt Orators, worne smoth With clients. **1656** E. Reyner *Rules Govt. Tongue* 97 *Tongue-government is needfull to prevent Miseries from our selves. **1637** Rutherford *Lett.* clxxxi. (1881) 314 O that He would give me more than..*tongue-grace. **1847** *Fr. Oxford to Rome* (ed. 2) 105 The din of word-battles and *tongue-hammers. **1836-48** B. D. Walsh *Aristoph., Knights* II. iii, Handed it o'er To us to be *tongue-hammered loudly. **1540** Cranmer *Pref. to Bible*, Wherof commeth all this *tongue itche, that we haue so moch delight to talke & clatter. **1676** Dryden *Aureng-zebe* II. i, My Ears still ring with Noise, I'm vex'd to Death: *Tongue-kill'd. **1885** H. C. McCook *Tenants Old Farm* 74 You..deserve a little *tongue-lashing. **1887** Baring-Gould *Red Spider* ii, Let yourself be led and *tongue-lashed by your housekeeper. **1822** *Hortus Angl.* II. 374 *C. Myconis*. *Tongue-leaved Chrysanthemum. Leaves tongue-shaped, obtuse, serrate. **1832** *Planting* 31 in *Libr. Usef. Knowl., Husb.* III, The scion [should be] split..so as to form the two divisions into *tongue-like processes. **1826** J. Wilson *Noct. Ambr.* Wks. 1855 I. 256 Smoking, and leering, with *tongue-lolling cheek. **1847** L. Hunt *Men, Women, & B.* I. iii. 44 The yelps and tongue-lollings of the dog. **1611** *Coryat's Crudities, Char. Authour*, He is alwaies *Tongue-major of the company. **1608** *Pennyless Parl.* in *Harl. Misc.* III. 79 A quart or two of fine Trinidado shall arm us against the gun-shot of *tongue-metal. **1599** *Broughton's Let.* v. 18 Such a *tongue-murthering Cain..cannot withhold. **1841** *Penny Cycl.* XXI. 410/2 It..goes twice through the hands of the workman; the first time to do what is called the *tongue part, the closing of the vamp and counter to the leg. **1617** Lane *Cont. Sqr.'s T.* IV. 159 What faleshode (which this witch termes veritie)! what *tonge-plages (cowardlie scurrilitie)! **1872** Swinburne *Ess. & Stud.* (1875) 52 The purblind..policy of sword-play and *tongue-play. **1589** R. Harvey *Pl. Perc.* (1590) 7 He that hath most *toong powder hopes to driue the other out of the field first. **1604** Hieron *Wks.* I. 491 Blind deuotions and *tong-prayers, which the hart doth not conceiue. **1652** Bp. Hall *Invisible World* III. v, Another while he bids him be *tongue-proof. **1566** Drant *Horace, Sat.* vii. D vij, Two *tongue puisante knyghts. **1607** Hieron *Defence* I. 3 b, Miserably slandered & *tongue-rente. *a* **1300** *Cursor M.* 1375 Bot þou sal tak þis pepins thre..And do þam vnder his *tong rote. **1825** Jamieson s.v., *It was juist at my tongue-roots*,..intimating either that a person was just about to catch a term that had caused some degree of hesitation, or that he was on the point of uttering an idea in which he has been anticipated by another. *a* **1711** Ken *Edmund* v. 82 Thus Dipsychus when he most Kindness feigns, With his *Tongue-Saw licks Mortals to their Banes. **1599** A. M. tr. *Gabelhouer's Bk. Physicke* 88/1 Then scrape your tunge with a wooden *tungescraper. **1710** Steele *Tatler* No. 245 ¶ 2 [She] carried off..a Silver Tongue-Scraper. **1897** *Star* 20 Apr. 4/7 A curious instrument possessed by everyone in China above the extremely poor is the tongue-scraper. **1713** M. Henry *Check to Ungoverned Tongue* Wks. 1853 I. 149 Peter resolved against a *tongue-sin in his own strength. **1822** T. Mitchell *Aristoph.* II. 214 What, my friends, if we quit This *tongue-skirmish of wit? **1647** Trapp *Comm. Matt.* v. 11 There are *tongue-smiters, as well as hand-smiters. **1690** C. Nesse *O. & N. Test.* I. 18 *Tongue-smiting is as smart as any hand-smiting. **1628** Feltham *Resolves* II. [I.] ii. 6 As for the crackers of the braine, and *tongue-squibs, they will dye alone, if I shall not reuiue them. **1861** *Proc. Amer. Phil. Soc.* VIII. 281 The *tongue-structure of folded anticlinals. **1901** *Westm. Gaz.* 29 Nov. 2/3 He generally got into a *tongue-tangle over the word. **1592** Lyly *Midas* v. ii, I feare nothing so much as to be *tongue tawde. **1896** A. Morrison *Child of the Jago* 299 His *tongue-tip passed quickly over them. **1900** H. Sutcliffe *Shameless Wayne* ix, Martha had a keen answer on her tongue-tip. **1609** Boys *Expos. Script. Eng. Liturg.* Wks. (1629) 29 He praiseth God but little, who makes it a *tongue-toile and a lip labour only. **1603** Dekker *Wonderfull Yeare* B iv, *Tongue-trauelling Lawyers faint at such a day. **1556** J. Heywood *Spider & F.* lx. Dd j, For the feare, that his *tongtromp (to you did sowne:) By thus manie flies: to thus few spiders seene. *a* **1700** Dryden *Iliad* I. 336 *Tongue-valiant hero, vaunter of thy might, In threats the foremost, but the lag in fight! **1838-42** Arnold *Hist. Rome* II. xxx. 186 The Greeks being a tongue-valiant people returned an insulting refusal. **1629** Maxwell tr. *Herodian* (1635) 383 You wel know what weather-cocks the Roman people are: and how great their *tongue-valour is. **1628** Feltham *Resolves* II. [I.] xxx. 96 For the *tongue-vice, talkatiuenesse, I see not, but..Men may very well vie words with them [women]. **1885** B. Harte *Maruja* vi, No..*tongue-wagging gossip. **1887** *Pall Mall G.* 27 Jan. 1/1 It is not necessary that he should say anything wise or true or new. All that he needs do is to keep on tongue-wagging. **1820** T. Roscoe *Gonzalo* III. i, Being *tongue-wanton of his noble friend, And crying up his many excellences. **1730** B. Martyn *Timoleon* IV. iii, I hate This Female *Tongue-War, and will end it thus. **1820** T. Mitchell *Aristoph.* I. 190 A man in tongue-war His superior by far. **1742** R. Blair *Grave* 297 The *tongue-warrior..cannot tell his ails. **1681** Colvil *Whigs Supplic.* (1751) 131, I..have both will and wit to reckon, And beat thee at thy own *tongue weapon. **1849** Miss Mulock *Ogilvies* xviii, The sharpest tongue-weapons that sarcasm ever forged. **1575** R. B. *Appius & Virg.* B j b, Content, for I shall repent it, for this my *tonge wralling.

**16.** Special combs.: **tongue aloe**, *Aloe linguæformis*; **tongue-bar**, each of the processes separating the gill-slits in *Balanoglossus* and *Amphioxus*, suggesting the tongue of a jews' harp (*Cent. Dict., Suppl.* 1909); **tongue-bird**, local name of the wryneck, from its long retractile tongue (Swainson *Provinc. Names Birds* 1885); **tongue-bit**, a bridle bit having a plate attached so as to prevent the horse from putting his tongue over the mouth-piece (Knight *Dict. Mech.* 1877); † **tongue-blade**, the shrub *Ruscus Hypoglossum*; = Double-tongue 2; **tongue-bleed**, **-bleeder**, the Goose-grass or Cleavers (*Galium Aparine*); **tongue-bone**, the hyoid bone; † **tongue-butt** [Butt *sb.*[6]], a butt or odd corner of land at the end or side of a field; **tongue-case** (*Entom.*), the part of a pupa-case enclosing the 'tongue'; **tongue-chain**, the pole-chain of a vehicle: = Team *sb.*[1]; **tongue-cheek** (*Entom.*), a side-piece of a moth's mouth; **tongue-compressor**, a clamp for retaining the tongue during dental operations; **tongue-curve**, a figure showing position and movement of the tongue in speech, etc.; **tongue-depressor**, a surgical instrument for depressing the tongue during operations on the mouth or throat; † **tongue-evil** [Evil *sb.* 7], a disease of the tongue; in quot. *fig.*; **tongue-fence**, argument, debate; **tongue-fencer**, a debater, skilful disputant; **tongue-fish**, the sole: cf. 12; in southern U.S., *Aphoristia* (*Symphurus*) *plagiusa*, a small sole-like fish; **tongue-flower**: see quot.; **tongue-grafting**, whip or splice grafting, in which a thin wedge-shaped tongue of the scion is fitted into a cleft in the stock; **tongue-grass**, name for garden cress (*Lepidium sativum*); **tongue-hero** (*nonce-wd.*), a braggart (transl. G. *wortheld*); **tongue-holder**, an instrument for holding the tongue during dental operations; **tongue-hound** [Hound *sb.*[2] 2], one of the 'hounds' by which the tongue of a vehicle is braced (*Cassell's Encycl. Dict.* s.v. *tongue-support*); **tongue-joint**, a joint formed in metal by welding a tongue in one piece into a recess in the other; **tongue-key**, in *Exper. Psychol.*, a reaction-key which is opened or closed by movement of the tongue; **tongue-membrane** = *tongue-ribbon*; **tongue-mole** (*Her.*): see quot., and cf. Hurt *sb.*[2]; **tongue-oxen** *sb. pl.*, the pair of oxen harnessed to the tongue of a plough, etc.; **tongue-pipe**, a reed-pipe in an organ or similar instrument; **tongue-ribbon**, the odontophore of a mollusc; † **tongue-ripe** *a.*, garrulous, loquacious, voluble, glib (of a person or his utterance); **tongue-scapular**, a scapular on which tongues of red cloth were fastened, worn by the Cistercians as a punishment for evil-speaking (*Funk's Stand. Dict.* 1895); **tongue-sewer**, one who stitches the tongues into boots; **tongue-shell**, a brachiopod of the family *Lingulidæ*; **tongue-shot**, speaking or talking distance, voice-range; † **tongue-sore**, *fig.* evil-speaking; cf. *tongue-evil*; **tongue-spatula** = *tongue-depressor* (Knight); **tongue-speaking**, (*a*) oral as distinct from written communication; (*b*) speaking with tongues (see sense 8 c); **tongue-tacked**, **-it** *a. Sc.* = Tongue-tied (*lit.* and *fig.*); so **tongue-tack** *v. trans.*, to put to silence; **tongue-test**, a test of the existence or strength of an electric current by applying the tongue to a break in the circuit, **tongue-tooth**, one of the teeth of the odontophore of a mollusc; **tongue-tree**, the pole of a wagon; **tongue-triangle**: see quot.; **tongue-twist** *sb.*, a mispronunciation, a provincialism; **tongue-twist** *v. intr.*, to twist the tongue; in quot. to prevaricate; **tongue-twister**, one or that which is said to twist the tongue; *spec.* a sequence of words, often alliterative, difficult to articulate quickly; **tongue-violet**, name for *Schweiggeria parviflora* (N.O. *Violaceæ*), an erect Brazilian shrub bearing white stalked violet-shaped flowers in the axils; **tongue-walk** *v. trans.*, to scold, abuse; hence **tongue-walking** *vbl. sb.*; **tongue-work**, (*a*) work in 'the tongues', philological labour; (*b*) debate, discussion, dispute; (*c*) chatter, gossip, babble; **tongue-worm**, † (*a*) disease of the tongue (*fig.*); cf. *tongue-evil*; (*b*) a tongue-shaped parasite which becomes adult in the nasal fossæ and frontal sinuses of the dog or wolf; a pentastom; (*c*) the 'worm' of the tongue in dogs; = Lytta. See also Tongueman, -pad, -tie, etc.

**1731** Miller *Gard. Dict.*, *Aloe, Africana flore rubro*, ..The *Tongue Aloe. **1902** *Encycl. Brit.* XXVI. 85/1 The *tongue-bar is the essential organ of the gill-slit in Balanoglossus. **1578** Lyte *Dodoens* VI. xiv. 676 *Tongueblade or double tongue, his nature is to asswage payne. **1611** Cotgr. s.v. *Langue*, Tong-blade, Double-tongue, Horse-tongue. *c* **1450** *Alphita* (Anecd. Oxon.) 157 *Rubea minor*, cliure [= cleavers] uel *tongebledes. **1853** G. Johnston *Bot. E. Bord.* 100 *G. aparine*... Children, with the leaves, practise phlebotomy upon the tongue..hence they call the plant Bluid-tongue or *Tongue-bluiders. **1841** *Penny Cycl.* XX. 456/1 The body of the *tongue-bone is most frequently of a rhomboidal form. **1906** *Westm. Gaz.* 17 Apr. 10/2 These sounds are produced in a bony cavity formed by an enlargement of the hyoid, or tongue-bone. **1220-51** *Cockersand Chartul.* (Chetham Soc.) II. I. 450 Et insuper super Waldemurfeld, duas *Tunge-buttes quæ jacent ex utraque parte terræ. **1826** Kirby & Sp. *Entomol.* III. xxxi. 250 Before from the middle [proceeds] the *tongue-case (*Glosso-theca*) [of pupæ]. **1885** H. C. McCook *Tenants Old Farm* 73 The long, slender object which you mistook for the cord by which a cocoon hangs is a tongue-case. **1890** Jul. P. Ballard *Among Moths & Butterfl.* 108 The deep, rich, velvety side-pieces, or *tongue-cheeks. **1902** E. W. Scripture *Exper. Phonetics* 469 Phonograms, palatograms, breath records, *tongue curves, etc. **1872** Cohen *Dis. Throat* 6 A *tongue-depressor, with a handle which is out of the line of vision, is the proper instrument. **1662** T. I. (*title*) A Cure for the *Tongue-Evill. Or, A Receipt against Vain Oaths. **1644** Milton *Divorce* II. xxi, To have her unpleasingness..bandied up and down and aggravated in open Court by those hir'd masters of *Tongue-fence. **1850** Blackie *Æschylus* I. Pref. 18 Euripides, the great master of tongue-fence. **1675** Crowne *Country Wit* II, The most admirable *tongue-fencer I have heard! **1655** Moufet & Bennet *Health's Impr.* (1746) 260 Soles or *Tongue-fishes are counted the Partridges of the Sea. **1672** Josselyn *New-Eng. Rarities* 30 Soles, or Tonguefish, or Sea Capon, or Sea Partridge. **1884** Miller *Plant-n.*, *Tongue-flower, *Glossula tentacula*; Australian [Tongue-flower], the genus *Glossodia*. **1710** J. Harris *Lex. Techn.* II, **Tongue Grafting*, is a way of Grafting in Roots. **1719** London & Wise *Compl. Gard.* 183 Tongue or Whip Grafting, is proper for small Stocks, of an Inch, half an Inch, or less Diameter. **1844** N. Paterson *Manse Gard.* 118 This is supposed to resemble a tongue, and hence this mode of operation is called tongue grafting. **1726** Threlkeld *Synopsis Stirp. Hibern.* G viij, *Nasturtium Hortense*, the Garden Cresses, is..sold by the silly Name of **Tongue-grass*, and used as a Sallet. **1887** *Nicholson's Dict. Gard.*, *Tongue Grass*, a common name for *Lepidium sativum*. **1800** Coleridge *Piccolom.* IV. vii, I Am no *tongue-hero, no fine virtue-prattler. **1902** *Baldwin's Dict. Philos. & Psychol.* II. 419/2 The most common form of motor response is the act of pressing a telegrapher's key with the finger or hand. Other forms are with the lip key, *tongue key, and mouth or voice key. **1562** Leigh *Armorie* (1597) 87 b, These appeare light blewe, and come by some violent strok on men, they are called hurtes, but on women they are commonly called *Tongue-molles. **1851** *Harper's Mag.* III. 518 It would be impossible for the *tongue-oxen to resist the pressure of the load. **1874** WOOD *Nat. Hist.* 638 Feeding..on little bivalves, which they can assault with their short but strongly armed *tongue-ribbon. **1610** HEALEY *St. Aug. Citie of God* v. xxvii. 234 Their *tongue-ripe Satyrisme may more easily disturbe the truth of this world. **1627** [R. BERNARD] *Guide agst. Witches* II. ii. 93 They [women] are more tongue-ripe, and lesse able to hide what they know from others. **1891** *Cent. Dict.*, *Tongue-shell. **1895** *Edin. Rev.* Oct. 355 Tongue-shells and helmet-shells and lamp-shells. **1905** W. J. SOLLAS *Age Earth* i. 26 The little tongue-shell, *Lingula*, has endured..from the Cambrian down to the present day. **1656** S. HOLLAND *Zara* (1719) 82 Who was no sooner within *Tongue-shot of him, but alighting..she made most humble and lowly obeysance. **1860** READE *Cloister & H.* lii, She would stand timidly aloof out of tongue-shot. **1542** UDALL *Erasm. Apoph.* I. 22 b, Imputyng his *tongsore, not vnto maliciousnesse: but vnto the defaulte of right knowelage. *c* **1545** LD. MORLEY *Hyst. Masscutio* 12 b, Neyther with pen wrytyng nor with *tunge spekynge. **1902** SELWYN in *Expositor* Nov. 391 They continue tongue-speaking, which is such a marked feature of the Holy Apostolic Church. **1685** R. HAMILTON in A. Shields *Faithf. Contendings* (1780) 218 It .. hath *tongue-tacked many a valiant hero for Christ in our day. **1727** P. WALKER *Remark. Passages* (1827) 211 That sharp Challenge, which would strike our Mean-spirited Tongue-tacked Ministers dumb. *Ibid.* 228 If ever he saw such an Occasion, he should not be tongue-tacked. **1814** W. NICHOLSON *Peacock* iv. 44 Till fairly tongue-tack'd wi' a pension. *a* **1877** P. P. CARPENTER cited in *Cent. Dict.* for *Tongue-tooth. **1829** T. MOORE *Hist. Devon* I. iv. i. 510 *Tongtree, the pole of an ox-cart. **1899** *Syd. Soc. Lex.*, **Tongue-triangle*, the triangular or wedge-shaped red arch at the tip of a coated tongue seen in typhoid. **1898** *Tit-Bits* 21 May 150/2 These little *tongue-twists..are of such small import. **1836-48** B. D. WALSH *Aristoph., Clouds* II. i, I shall be lost, unless I learn to *tongue-twist. **1898** *Echo* 1 July 1/5 *Tongue-twisters had..composed a sketch called 'The Race'. **1904** *Speaker* 4 June 229/1 The famous tongue-twister, Miss Smith's fish-sauce shop. **1884** MILLER *Plant-n., Schweiggeria*, *tongue-violet. **1841** HARTSHORNE *Salopia Antiqua* Gloss., **Tongue Walk v.* to abuse or scold. Ex. 'Pretty well tongue-walked him'. **1888** *Illustr. Lond. News* Christmas No. 3/2 Give him a *tongue-walking. I would. **1598** FLORIO *Dict.* To Rdr. 12 His labours..which..he may as iustly stand vpon in this *toong-work, as in Latin Sir Thomas Eliot, Bishop Cooper, and after them Thomas Thomas, and Iohn Rider. *a* **1661** HOLYDAY *Juvenal* (1673) 137 Seek then some other Law-courts..: tongue-work there may fill thy purse. **1866** GEO. ELIOT *F. Holt* xx, If a man takes to tongue-work it's all over with him. *a* **1899** R. WALLACE *Life & Last Leaves* (1903) 6, I have done a considerable amount of penwork and tongue-work. **1645** USSHER *Body Div.* (1647) 359 Those *tongue-wormes of swearing, blasphemy, and unreverent speaking of God. **1896** *Yearbk. U. S. Dept. Agric.* 161 The Tongue worm is found encysted in the viscera of cattle, sheep, and other animals. It is about a quarter of an inch long, and when eaten by dogs grows to be 2 to 5 inches long.

**Tongue** (tɒŋ), *v.* [f. TONGUE *sb.*]

**1.** *trans.* To assail with words; to reproach, scold; to discuss or talk about injuriously. In quot. 1388, to drive *out* by talking against.

**1388** in *Wyclif's Sel. Wks.* III. 493 If ony of þese curatus were trewe aungelis of God,..þai my3tten sone be tongide out of court. **1603** SHAKS. *Measure for M.* IV. iv. 28 But that her tender shame Will not proclaime against her maiden losse, How might she tongue me? **1702** C. MATHER *Magn. Chr.* II. App. (1852) 224 Sir William was very hardly handled (or tongued, at least), in the liberty which people took to make most..injurious reflections upon his conduct. **1872** H. COWLES in Spurgeon *Treas. Dav.* (1877) IV. 413 He that tongueth his neighbour secretly. **1901** *Dundee Advert.* 14 Feb. 2 She met him in Small's Wynd, and 'tongued' him.

**2.** *intr.* To use the tongue, talk, speak; *esp.* to talk volubly, to prate. (Chiefly *tongue it.*)

**1624** *Gd. News fr. N. Eng.* in *Story Pilgr. Fathers* (Arb.) 571 Shewing how base and womanlike he was, in tonguing it, as he did. **1679** DRYDEN *Troil. & Cress.* Pref., He shall tongue it as impetuously, and as loudly as the errantest hero in the play. **1885** FORFAR *Cornish Poems* 19 The more they parley voo'd, the more Our maidens tongue'd away. **1898** *Tit-Bits* 21 May 150/2 [When] they tumble across a person who 'tongues' it different to them, they grimly smile.

**b.** Of a hound: To give tongue.

**1832** [see TONGUING *vbl. sb.*]. **1885** *Househ. Words* 20 June 142/2 'What's thee tonguing like that for, Dick?' ..'What's amiss?' **1888** ELWORTHY *W. Somerset Word-bk.* s.v. *Tongy*, I yeard the hounds tongy, and tho I zeed the fox gwain on under the hedge.

**3.** *trans.* To utter or turn *over* with the tongue; to say; also, to pronounce, articulate (*dial.*).

**1611** SHAKS. *Cymb.* v. iv. 148 'Tis still a Dreame; or else such stuffe as Madmen tongue, and braine not. **1841** GEN. P. THOMPSON *Exerc.* (1842) VI. 12 He took up the phrase, and tongued it over in his damning way. **1860** O. W. HOLMES *Elsie V.* vii, The Colonel raged..and tongued a few anathemas inside of his shut teeth. **1876** *Whitby Gloss.* s.v., 'I can't tongue 't', cannot say the word.

**4.** To touch with the tongue; also, to lick *up*.

**1687** WOOD *Life* (O.H.S.) III. 247. *a* **1700** B. E. *Dict. Cant. Crew* s.v. *Velvet*. **1837** S. B. HARPER in *Fraser's Mag.* XVI. 191 An icy shudder shook me through—it stuck there, As you'd tongued iron on a December morn. **1888** H. S. MERRIMAN *Young Mistley* II. vi. 76 Fairy [a horse] ..gently tongued the bit. **1894** BARING-GOULD *Kitty Alone* II. 149 The fire..was tonguing up the heap, sending the tips of its flames tastingly towards him.

**b.** To push *out* or distend with the tongue. *rare.*

**1768** *Woman of Honor* I. 160 Exposing him..by winking with one eye, and tonguing out his cheek.

**5.** *intr.* To project as a protruding tongue (of ice); to throw out tongues (of flame).

*a* **1814** [see *tonguing* ppl. a. below]. **1856** KANE *Arct. Expl.* I. xxiii. 282 Old ices bulge and tongue out below. **1859** MASSON *Brit. Novelists* iv. 303 Scattered through all, is the fiercer element of Fire, here tonguing over the earth wherever it may be kindled, there flashing through the ether. **1871** G. MEREDITH *H. Richmond* xi, It really did look as if they [the firemen] were engaged in slaying an enormous dragon, that hissed and tongued at them.

**6.** *trans.* To furnish with a tongue (*lit.* or *fig.*).

[In this sense perh. a back-formation from TONGUED *a.*]

**a.** To give a speaking tongue or utterance to.

**1602** DEKKER *Satirom.* K ij, Yes, yes, true chastity is tongu'd so weake, 'Tis overcome, ere it know how to speake. **1807** J. BARLOW *Columb.* VIII. 323 What avails..To tongue mute misery, and re-rack the soul With crimes oft copied from that bloody scroll? **1838** S. BELLAMY *Betrayal* III. 102 This Nazarene..hath tongued With a strange speech this talking world of ours.

**b.** (*a*) To cut a tongue on (a plank, etc.). (*b*) To slit or shape a tongue in (a plant-stem or shoot) for grafting or layering.

**1733** W. ELLIS *Chiltern & Vale Farm.* 101 Make a Groove in each Plank, and put in a Slip of Wood, like a Lath, which the Carpenters call Tongueing it. **1766** *Compl. Farmer* s.v. *Layer*, Cut a slit upwards at a joint, as is practised in laying of carnations, which, by gardeners, is called tonguing the layers. **1825** *Greenhouse Comp.* I. 229 Let neither stock nor scion be tongued, but apply the scion to the stock..so that their barks on both edges and below may join. **1908** *Daily Chron.* 13 Nov. 6/5 Each length of maple..is tongued and grooved both at the side and ends.

**c.** To join or fit together by means of a tongue and groove or tongue and socket.

**1823** P. NICHOLSON *Pract. Build.* 163 The sections of two pieces of stuff, grooved and tongued together. **1835** SIR J. ROSS *Narr. 2nd Voy.* iv. 55 Some convenient anchorage.. where we could fish or tongue the foremast. **1862** *Illustr. Catal. Exhib.* I. 26 The gallery floor..was closely boarded and tongued, to prevent the passage of dust.

**d.** To furnish with a tongue-like projection.

**1900** *Westm. Gaz.* 6 July 5/2 Great curling clouds of black smoke, tongued with red and yellow where the light from the fire struck it.

Hence **To·nguer**, an utterer, a speaker; **To·nguing** *ppl. a.* (in quot., throwing out tongues).

*a* **1814** *Apostate* IV. iv. in *New Brit. Theatre* III. 336 The sense of guilt, With keener agony than tonguing flames Lick to the bone. **1822** *New Monthly Mag.* IV. 297 Ceaseless tonguers of 'words of no tone', they lisp.

**Tongued** (tɒŋd), *a.* (*ppl. a.*) [f. TONGUE *sb.* or *v.* + -ED.] Having or furnished with a tongue or tongues (in various senses). Also *fig.*

Also in numerous parasynthetic combs., as *double-tongued, true-tongued*, etc., for which see the first element.

*c* **1369** CHAUCER *Blaunche* 927 Ne trewer tonged, ne scorned lasse. **1390** GOWER *Conf.* I. 218 This false tunged Perseus. **1413** *Pilgr. Sowle* (Caxton 1483) III. iii. 51 Somme were by the eyen hanged with hookes, and som by the tonges, whiche as me semyd were tonged double. **1611** L. BARRY *Ram Alley* IV. i. G ij, Nosd like a Goose, and toungd like a woman. **1635** A. STAFFORD *Fem. Glory* (1860) 185 Were all..the Starres of Heaven tongued, they could not all expresse thee so well, as a silent Extasie. **1666** J. DAVIES *Hist. Caribby Isles* 55 Two kinds of Tobacco Plants, commonly call'd .. Green-Tobacco and Tongu'd Tobacco, from the figure of its leaf. **1839** URE *Dict. Arts* 966 The boring tools are..16. The tongued chisel. *a* **1847** ELIZA COOK *Silence* 108 The soul..Shall keep an eloquence all, all her own, And mock the tongued interpreter. **1854** BUSHNAN in *Circ. Sc.* (*c* 1865) I. 284/1 Reeded and tongued instruments. **1884** *Northern Echo* 11 Aug. 2/5, 24,000 Feet of Grooved and Tongued Flooring Boards. **1886** *Archæol. Cantiana* XVI. p. xlv, The tongued or leaf-like ornament, so common in the period of Transition between pure Norman and pure Early English.

**Tongueful** (tɒ·ŋful). [See -FUL 2.] As much as the tongue will hold or carry.

**1892** M. DODS *Israel's Iron Age* 43 A dog..snatching mouthfuls or tonguefuls of water.

**Tongueless** (tɒ·ŋlės), *a.* [See -LESS.]

**1.** *lit.* Having no tongue, without a tongue.

**1398** TREVISA *Barth. De P. R.* XVIII. xxxii. (Bodl. MS.), Amonge beestes of þe londe he [the crocodile] is tungles. **1570** LEVINS *Manip.* 91/16 Tonguelesse, *elinguis, e.* **1611** COTGR., *Gouttreuse*, a certain white, long-beaked, and tonglesse bird [a pelican]. **1738** *Gentl. Mag.* VIII. 524/1, I doubt very much, whether a Tongueless Person, or one that is without a Roof to the Mouth, can Taste. **1876** L. STEPHEN *Eng. Th. in 18th C.* I. IV. vi. 267 The miracle of the tongueless confessor is mentioned by Gibbon as resting on remarkably good evidence. **1879** BODDAM-WHETHAM *Roraima & Brit. Guiana* 171 *note*, Herodotus, too, who was a keen observer of the crocodile, repeats the idea that it is tongueless. **1907** *Q. Rev.* July 201 The most revered objects in the *ti* are the bells, usually tongueless.

**2.** Without the faculty of voice or speech, dumb, mute; also, without speaking, speechless, silent.

**1447** BOKENHAM *Seyntys* (Roxb.) 196 Why stonde ye thus stylle, be ye tunglees? **1542** UDALL *Erasm. Apoph.* 287 b, That persone, by whose benefite thou art made of a toungelesse bodye, eloquente. **1630** J. TAYLOR (Water P.) *Anagrams & Sonn.* Wks. II. 256/2 Now chirping birds are all turn'd tonguelesse mutes. **1630** LENNARD tr. *Charron's Wisd.* I. xxxi. (1670) 90 We go with our heads hanging,.. our mouths tongueless. **1824** J. SYMMONS tr. *Æschylus' Agam.* 73 The mighty judges heard the tongueless plea.

**b.** Said of things.

**1593** SHAKS. *Rich. II*, I. i. 105 Euen from the toonglesse cauernes of the earth. **1624** F. WHITE *Repl. Fisher* 92 The consent of the Church alone..ought to be of greater esteeme ..than all mute and tonguelesse Bookes. *a* **1822** SHELLEY *Ess. & Lett.* (1852) I. 138 There is eloquence in the tongueless wind. **1868** J. H. NEWMAN *Verses Var. Occas.* 9, I cannot bear those sullen walls, Those eyeless towers, those tongueless halls.

†**3.** Not spoken of; unmentioned. *Obs. rare.*

**1611** SHAKS. *Wint. T.* I. ii. 92 One good deed, dying tonguelesse, Slaughters a thousand, wayting vpon that.

**Tonguelet** (tɒ·ŋlėt). [f. TONGUE *sb.* + -LET.] A little tongue or tongue-like object; *spec.* **a.** in *Entom.* = LIGULA 1 b; **b.** = *tongue-worm* (*b*): see TONGUE *sb.* 16 (*Cent. Dict.* 1891).

**1840** E. WILSON *Anat. Vade M.* (1842) 384 The Linguetta laminosa is a thin tonguelet of grey substance, marked by transverse furrows, which extend forwards..from the grey substance of the cerebellum. **1840** tr. *Cuvier's Anim. Kingd.* 529 The tonguelet consists of two small hairy setæ, extending beyond the large horny mentum. **1866** J. K. LORD in *Intell. Observ.* No. 48. 431 In this tube is the tonguelet [of a Cicada]. **1878** BROWNING *Poets Croisic* v, I shall not sulk If yonder greenish tonguelet [of flame] licked from brass Its life.

**Tongueman, tongue-man** (tɒ·ŋmæ̆n). ? *Obs.* [f. TONGUE *sb.* + MAN *sb.*[1]] A speaker, an orator.

**1594** NASHE *Unfort. Trav.* Wks. (Grosart) V. 69 Our present incorporation .. by me the tongue-man of their thankfulnes..bid you welcome. **1611** SPEED *Hist. Gt. Brit.* IX. xxiv. (1623) 1175 Poysonous tonguemen and libellous Pen-men. **1627** E. F. *Hist. Edw. II* (1680) 55, I am no tongue-man, nor can move with language; but if we come to act, I'll not be idle.

**Tongue-pad** (tɒ·ŋpæd), *sb. slang* or *dial.* [f. TONGUE *sb.* + PAD *sb.*[2] 3, 4.] A talkative person.

*a* **1700** B. E. *Dict. Cant. Crew, Tongue-pad*, a smooth, Glib-tongued, insinuating Fellow. **1709** O. DYKES *Eng. Prov. & Refl.* (ed. 2) 230 'Twas pleasant enough to hear two Tongue-Pads a-scolding, and giving one another the Lie. **1821** *Joseph the Book-Man* 70 Determin'd every ear t'engage Thus spoke the tonguepad of a sage. **1882** JAGO *Cornw. Gloss., Tongue-pad*,..a chatterer, a very talkative person.

Hence **To·ngue-pad** *v.*, *trans.* to assail with words; to scold; also *intr.* (with *it*) to tattle, chatter; whence **To·ngue-padder** = ? *tongue-pad* (see quot.); **To·ngue-padding** *vbl. sb.*, scolding.

**1707** J. STEVENS tr. *Quevedo's Com. Wks.* (1709) 422 They would all *Tongue-pad him at once. **1825** SCOTT *Betrothed* xxx, My wife Gillian, who will tongue-pad it with any shrew in Christendom. **1676** *Warning for Housekprs.* Title-p., Budg and Snudg, File-lifter, *Tongue-padder, The private Theif. **1876** *Whitby Gloss., Tongue-whaling*, or **Tongue-padding*, a scolding lecture.

**Tongue-shaped** (tɒ·ŋʃēɪpt), *a.* Shaped like a tongue; linguiform.

**1776** J. LEE *Introd. Bot.* Explan. Terms 386 *Lingulatum*, Tongue-shaped, linear, fleshy. **1776** WITHERING *Brit. Pl.* (1796) II. 55 A small tongue-shaped glandular substance. **1837** KEITH *Bot. Lex.* 286 The [Mistletoe] leaves are..tongue-shaped, entire, smooth. **1898** *Allbutt's Syst. Med.* V. 464 At each systole of the ventricles the tongue-shaped valve-flaps pendent..are moved together towards those orifices.

**To·nguesman.** *rare.* [Cf. *swordsman, townsman*, etc.] = TONGUEMAN.

**1596** FITZ-GEFFRAY *Sir F. Drake* (1881) 5 So he, and I his tongues-man, doe require Thy Sanctuarie. **1610** *Chester's Tri., Sp. Fame* 22 (Chetham Soc.), [To Mercury] Descend then Tongue's man of the universe. **1837** C. LOFFT *Self-formation* I. 252 Certain rough and ready tonguesmen.. spoke, if not absolutely well, yet forwardly and fluently.

**Tonguester** (tɒ·ŋstəɹ). [f. TONGUE *sb.* + -STER.] A talkative person; a great talker; a gossip.

**1871** TENNYSON *Last Tourn.* 392 The tonguesters of the court she had not heard. **1877** — *Harold* v. i. 47 The simple, silent, selfless man Is worth a world of tonguesters. **1899** *Q. Rev.* Apr. 478 Two such formidable tonguesters as George Borrow and Thomas Carlyle!

*attrib.* **1885** *Punch* 11 Apr. 169/1 Thee, Great heart, whose silent grandeur seems to shame Our tonguester time. **1889** TENNYSON *To Mary Boyle* ix, Lowly minds were madden'd to the height By tonguester tricks.

**Tongue-tie** (tɒ·ŋtəi), *sb.* [f. TONGUE *sb.* + TIE *sb.*] That which ties the tongue, or restrains speech; also, the condition of being tongue-tied (*lit.* and *fig.*); *spec.* (*Path.*): see quot. 1890.

**1641** BROME *Jovial Crew* II. Wks. 1873 III. 374 And asks a stronger tongue-tie then tearing of Books. **1849-52** *Todd's Cycl. Anat.* IV. 1162/1 Tongue-tie..is a congenital malformation. **1890** BILLINGS *Nat. Med. Dict., Tongue-tie*, abnormal shortness of the frænum linguæ, or adhesion of the tongue to the floor of the mouth.

**Tongue-tie** (tɒ·ŋtəi), *v.* [f. TONGUE *sb.* + TIE *v.*, or more prob. a back-formation from next.] *trans.* To tie or confine the tongue of; to restrain or debar from speaking; to render speechless.

**1555** J. ROGERS in Foxe *A. & M.* (1563) 1032/2 Your wycked lawes can not so tongue tye vs, but we will speake the truth. **1611** HEYWOOD *Gold. Age* I. i. Wks. 1874 III. 14 Let euerlasting silence Tong-tye the world. **1833** LAMB *Elia* Ser. II. Pref., The ligaments, which tongue-tied him, were loosened. **1851** D. JERROLD *St. Giles* xxxii. 335 Her face was livid with agony, that seemed to tongue-tie her.

Hence **To·ngue-ti:er**, that which ties the tongue: see quots.; **To·ngue-ty:ing** *vbl. sb.* (*lit.* and *fig.*).

**1754-64** SMELLIE *Midwif.* I. 428 Tongue-tying is easily remedied by introducing the forefinger into the child's mouth, raising up the tongue, and snipping the bridle with a pair of Scissars. **1869** *Routledge's Ev. Boy's Ann.* 469 This tongue-tying was the severest part of our watch. **1883** *Athenæum* 24 Nov. 675/3 [It] shows a woman wearing a branks, or tongue-tier. **1905** *Daily Chron.* 29 Aug. 4/6 There are names..that demand shortening, tongue-tiers such as Giggleswick, which almost necessarily dwindles into Gilzick.

**Tongue-tied** (tɒ·ŋtəid), *ppl. a.* [Locative comb. f. TONGUE *sb.* + TIED *ppl. a.*; becoming at length pa. pple. of TONGUE-TIE *v.*] Tied as to or in the tongue.

**1.** Having the frænum of the tongue too short, so that its movement is impeded or confined;

incapable of distinct utterance from this cause; also, unable to speak, dumb (*poet.*).

1530 PALSGR. 282/1 Tongetyed, *qui a le filet*. 16.. SWINBURNE *Spousals* (1686) 19 Until that time they are as it were Tongue-tied, being unable to speak. 1707 J. STEVENS tr. *Quevedo's Com. Wks.* (1709) 389 If she were deaf, and Tongue-ty'd. 1849–52 *Todd's Cycl. Anat.* IV. 1153/2 The tongue may be unnaturally fixed..the individual thus circumstanced being *tongue-tied*.

**2.** *fig.* Restrained or debarred from speaking or free expression from any cause; speechless, mute, dumb, silent; also reticent, reserved.

1529 MORE *Dyaloge* I. Wks. 107/2 He is of nature nothing tonge tayed. 1571 GOLDING *Calvin on Ps.* iii. 5 He himselfe was not tungtyde, but rather lifted up his voyce. 1576 GASCOIGNE *Steele Gl.* (Arb.) 57 Nor none serue God, but only tongtide men. 1600 HOLLAND *Livy* x. xix. 364 A dumbe and tongue-tide [*elinguis*] Consull. 1640 YORKE *Union Hon.*, *Commend. Verses*, Criticks be tongue-ti'd, stand, admire. 1734 tr. *Rollin's Anc. Hist.* XVIII. i. (1827) VII. 357 Fear kept them all tongue-tied and dumb. 1886 STEVENSON *Kidnapped* xxvi, I was..sitting tongue-tied between shame and merriment.

Hence **To·ngue-tiedness.**

1597 A. M. tr. *Guillemeau's Fr. Chirurg.* 24/2 When as we would cut the tunge-tyednes in yonge children nuely borne. 1661 LOVELL *Hist. Anim. & Min.* 348 The ancylosis, or tongue-tiednesse, caused, by the vinculum; it's cured, by cutting the same with a paire of cisers or sharp knife. 1894 MRS. H. WARD *Marcella* I. 59.

**Tonguey** (tʊ·ŋi), *a.* Also 4–5 tungy, 7–9 tonguy. [f. TONGUE *sb.* + -Y.]

**1.** Full of 'tongue' or talk; talkative, loquacious (now *U.S.* and *dial.*); of hounds, 'giving tongue'.

1382 WYCLIF *Ecclus.* viii. 4 Striue thou not with a tungy man. *a* 1774 R. FERGUSSON *Sandie & Willie* 55 A tonguey woman's noisy plea. 1836 *Life on the Lakes* I. 54 (Thornton) We had on board a very tonguey Yankee lawyer. 1855 EGERTON-WARBURTON *Hunting Songs* (1877) 102 Your babblers draft, as we our tonguey hounds. 1896 HOWELLS *Impressions & Exp.* 39 There were some men..tongueyer than the rest.

**2.** That is so 'in tongue' or 'in word', not 'in deed' (cf. 1 John iii. 18). *nonce-use.*

1612 W. SCLATER *Chr. Strength* 10 Alas! how many bare, tonguy Christians! Linguists only, in religion.

**3.** Of the nature of the tongue; produced or modified by the tongue; lingual.

1859 F. FRANCIS *Newton Dogvane* (1888) 25 He set that tonguey pendulum of his going. 1885 H. C. DEACON in Grove *Dict. Mus.* IV. 321/1 The quality of the voice..will be tonguey, throaty, palatal, or veiled, according to the part thus unnecessarily brought into play.

Hence **To·nguiness.**

1607 COLLINS *Serm.* (1608) 77 Some mens silence profits the Church of Christ more than all their tonguinesse can doe it hurt. 1910 *Boston* (Mass.) *Transcript* 16 July 2/3 The natural gift of what the old Yankee horse traders would have called tonguiness.

**Tonguing** (tʊ·ŋiŋ), *vbl. sb.* [f. TONGUE *v.* + -ING[1].] The action of the verb TONGUE in various senses (see the verb); *spec.* in playing the flute and other wind instruments: see quot. 1880.

1682 D'URFEY *Injured Princess* II. iv, Tonguing, fingering and fighting, don't please her, The Devil's in her. 1687 WOOD *Life* (O.H.S.) III. 247. 1763 MILLS *Pract. Husb.* IV. 217 The third method [of whip-grafting], which is an improvement of the last, is properly named *tipping* or *tonguing*. 1832 J. P. KENNEDY *Swallow B.* xli, The tonguing of this dog was followed by the quick yelping of four or five others. 1862 *Times* 7 Mar., The tonguing and grooving by which the Warrior's plates are dovetailed together. 1880 W. H. STONE in Grove *Dict. Mus.* I. 459/2 s.v. *Double tongueing*, Single tongueing,..signifies the starting of the reed-vibrations by a sharp touch from the tip of the tongue...Single tongueing is phonetically represented by a succession of the lingual letter T, as in the word 'rat-tat-tat'. Double tongueing aims at alternating the linguo-dental explosive T with another explosive consonant produced differently, such as the linguo-palatals D or K, thus relieving the muscles by alternate instead of repeated action. 1895 H. CALLAN *Fr. Clyde to Jordan* 136 You must give them a right good 'tonguing'.

**b.** The furnishing of boards with tongues (TONGUE *sb.* 14 j); *concr.* the tongues of boards collectively.

1841 *Civil Eng. & Arch. Jrnl.* IV. 22/2 Although the deal tongueing has been destroyed by the worms, the greenheart planking remains untouched and perfectly sound.

**Tonic** (tǫ·nik), *a.* and *sb.* [ad. Gr. τονικ-ός of or for stretching, f. τόν-ος: see TONE *sb.* Cf. mod.L. *tonicus*, F. *tonique* (16th c. in Godef. *Compl.*).]

**A.** *adj.*

**1.** *Phys.* and *Path.* Pertaining to, consisting in, or producing tension: *esp.* in relation to the muscles.

*Tonic contraction*, continuous muscular contraction without relaxation. *Tonic convulsion* or *spasm*, one characterized by such contraction (opp. to CLONIC). †*Tonic motion*, a former term for a state of continuous tension in the muscles such as that which keeps the body erect (cf. quot. 1646 s. v. TONICAL 1).

1649 BULWER *Pathomyot.* II. i. 83 Action without motion of the Muscle, is called a Tonique motion. 1666 J. SMITH *Old Age* (1676) 62 They [muscles] can perform adduction, abduction; flexion, extension; pronation, supination, the Tonick motion, circumgiration. 1756 P. BROWNE *Jamaica* 381 Of worms or insects that have no solid props within themselves, but perform all their weakly motions by a mere tonic or muscular power. 1799 *Med. Jrnl.* II. 340 The increased tonic motion of the vessels which the Stahlians ..considered as the efficient cause of inflammation. 1830 R. KNOX *Béclard's Anat.* 135 Motions of tonic contraction, augmented in many places by the action of the elastic tissue. 1834 J. FORBES *Laennec's Dis. Chest* (ed. 4) 375 We cannot regard the tonic spasm of the bronchi, or even perhaps of the air-cells, as impossible; since every muscle is susceptible of spasm. 1899 *Allbutt's Syst. Med.* VII. 351 Tonic or clonic convulsions sometimes occur [in positive hæmorrhage].

**b.** Pertaining to, or maintaining, the tone or normal healthy condition of the tissues or organs (cf. TONE *sb.* 7). See also 2.

1684 T. BURNET *Th. Earth* I. 207 The tone or tonick disposition of the organs whereby they perform their several functions. 1813 J. THOMSON *Lect. Inflam.* 65 Stahl's ideas respecting the tonic or vital action of the capillary vessels. 1855 H. SPENCER *Princ. Psychol.* (1873) I. I. v. 93 This pervading activity of the muscles is called their tonic state.

**2.** *Med.*, etc. Having the property of increasing or restoring the tone or healthy condition and activity of the system or organs; strengthening, invigorating, bracing. (Of remedies or remedial treatment, and hence of air, climate, etc.)

1756 C. LUCAS *Ess. Waters* III. 205 Their vapor..is found to be more tonic. 1800 *Med. Jrnl.* IV. 160 A long course of steel, in conjunction with tonic bitters. 1867 AUG. J. E. WILSON *Vashti* xxiv, Be sure she takes that tonic mixture three times a day. 1885 G. MEREDITH *Diana* v, She spoke of the weather—frosty, but tonic.

*fig.* 1848 KINGSLEY *Saint's Trag.* II. ix, God brings thee The tonic cup I feared to mix. 1867 H. LATHAM *Black & White* p. viii, One great benefit to be derived from a visit to America is its tonic effect upon the mind.

**3.** *Mus.* Formerly applied to the key-note of a composition (*tonic note*), now called simply *tonic* (see B. 2); now (*attrib.* use of B. 2), Pertaining to or founded upon the tonic or key-note: as *tonic chord*, a chord having the tonic for its root; *tonic pedal*, the key-note sustained as a PEDAL (*sb.* 4).

1760 STILES in *Phil. Trans.* LI. 773 Two modes with the same tonic note, the one neither acuter nor graver than the other, make no part of the old system of modes. 1867 MACFARREN *Harmony* (1892) 56 A tonic pedal..has the effect of confirming the conclusion indicated by a perfect cadence. 1880 STAINER *Composition* § 14 The third degree of the scale can form a portion of a tonic chord, or chord of the relative minor.

**b.** *Tonic Sol-fa*: name of a system of teaching music, esp. vocal music, introduced by the Rev. John Curwen about 1850, in which the seven notes of the ordinary major scale in any key are sung to syllables written *doh*, *ray*, *me*, *fah*, *soh*, *lah*, *te* (modifications of the older *do*, *re*, *mi*, *fa*, *sol*, *la*, *si*: see these words and GAMUT), and indicated in the notation by the initials d, r, m, etc.; *doh* always denoting the tonic or key-note, and the remaining syllables indicating the relation to it of the other notes of the scale. Chiefly *attrib.* Hence **Tonic Sol-faist** (-fā·ist), one who advocates or uses the Tonic Sol-fa system.

1852 J. CURWEN (*title*) Pupils' Manual of the Tonic Sol-Fa Method of teaching to sing; and the Tonic Sol-Fa School Music. 1883 *American* VI. 174 At the annual meeting in London..of the Tonic Sol-Fa College. 1881 BROADHOUSE *Mus. Acoustics* 372 We agree most cordially with our friends the tonic sol-faists. 1895 *Daily News* 30 Dec. 5/2 So many of the Welsh are Tonic Solfaists.

**4. a.** Pertaining to musical tone or quality.

1795 MASON *Ch. Mus.* i. 42 This solemn instrument [the organ]...In point of tonic power, I presume, it will be allowed preferable to all others.

**b.** Pertaining or relating to tone or accent in speech; indicating the tone or accent of spoken words or syllables; characterized by distinctions of tone or accent. *Tonic accent* (= F. *accent tonique*), the stress-accent of a word.

1859 S. W. WILLIAMS (*title*) A Tonic Dictionary of the Chinese language in the Canton dialect. 1867 HOWELLS *Ital. Journ.* 72 In their divine language, and with that ineffable tonic accent which no foreigner perfectly acquires. 1868 MAX MÜLLER *Stratif. Lang.* 42 The Thibetan is.. tonic and monosyllabic. 1894 A. H. KEANE in *Church Mission. Intell.* Oct. 723 Thus the monosyllable *pa* will be toned in six or more different ways to represent so many original dissyllables, *pada*, *pake*, *pana*, *pasa*, *pata*..and some of the Chinese and Shan dialects have..as many as ten or twelve such tones...Hence these languages are now called isolating and tonic rather than isolating and monosyllabic. 1896 — *Ethnol.* xii. 324 A far more important feature than the length of the words is their tonic utterance.

**B.** *sb.*

**1.** *Med.* A tonic medicine, application, or agent.

[1693 tr. *Blancard's Phys. Dict.* (ed. 2), *Tonica*, those things which being externally applied to, and rubb'd into the Limbs, strengthen the Nerves and Tendons.] 1799 *Med. Jrnl.* II. 116 When..the hectic symptoms were subdued, and only weakness remained, tonics completed the cure. 1875 H. C. WOOD *Therap.* (1879) 54 Substances..which, when taken internally, act upon the nutrition of the various tissues so as to restore lost tone...Such substances are known as tonics. 1897 *Badminton Mag.* IV. 380 My hair tonic costs eight-and-sixpence a bottle.

**b.** *fig.* An invigorating or bracing influence.

1840 CLOUGH *Early Poems* i. 8 The tonic of a wholesome pride. 1868 FARRAR *Silence & V.* viii. (1875) 136 It is the strongest of moral tonics.

**2.** *Mus.* = KEY-NOTE 1.

*Tonic major* or *minor*: that key (major or minor) which has the same key-note as a given key (minor or major).

1806 CALLCOTT *Mus. Gram.* II. iv. 131 The Tonic Minor must have in its Signature another flat. 1889 E. PROUT *Harmony* i. § 12 The first note of the scale is called the Tonic, or Key-note. This is the note which gives its name to the scale and key.

Hence **To·nic** *v.*, *trans.* to act as a tonic upon, to invigorate, 'brace up'; to administer a tonic to; whence **To·nicking** *vbl. sb.*

1825 *New Monthly Mag.* XV. 199/1 It tonicked the sedentary stomach into unwonted vigour. 1889 MRS. C. PRAED *Romance Station* 126 She needed..tonicking;..her blood didn't nourish her brain properly.

**†To·nical,** *a. Obs.* [f. as prec.: see -ICAL.]

**1.** = TONIC A. 1, 1 b.

1586 BRIGHT *Melanch.* xxvi. 149 The spirits..are the authors by tonicall motion of erection [of muscles]. 1646 SIR T. BROWNE *Pseud. Ep.* III. i. 105 One kinde of motion, relating unto that which Physitians (from Galen) doe name extensive or tonicall. 1693 J. BEAUMONT *On Burnet's Th. Earth* II. 88 The Tone or tonical Disposition of the Organs, whereby they perform their several Functions. 1733 CHEYNE *Eng. Malady* II. xii. § 2 (1734) 240 A Defect in their [Muscles] innate Power of Contraction and Tonical Nature.

**2.** = TONIC A. 4 a, b.

1656 BLOUNT *Glossogr.*, *Tonical*, pertaining to tone, note, tune, or accent. 1677 PLOT *Oxfordsh.* 7 Tonical [Echoes], such as return the voice but once, nor that neither, except adorned with some peculiar Musical note. 1737 *Gentl. Mag.* VII. 9/1 Whatever Musical or Tonical Notes were expressed in the Accents of the Text.

**Tonically** (tǫ·nikăli), *adv.* [f. TONIC *a.* or TONICAL: see -ICALLY.] In a tonic manner.

**1.** By or in relation to tension; in the way of tonic contraction (see TONIC A. 1).

1885 ROMANES *Jelly-Fish* viii. 209 In..Sarsia the irritability of the tonically contracting manubrium is higher than that of the rhythmically contracting bell. 1904 *Brit. Med. Jrnl.* 17 Dec. 1627 The muscles on the right side are somewhat more tonically contracted than those on the left.

**2.** As a tonic (see TONIC B. 1, 1 b); so as to invigorate or 'brace up'.

1873 CURWEN *Hist. Booksellers* 304 The difficulty..might act tonically. 1889 CROUTER in *Amer. Ann. Deaf* July 182 The agreeable labor of planting and harvest, which tonically would be of service to them.

**Tonicity** (toni·sĭti). *Phys.* and *Path.* [f. TONIC + -ITY. So mod.F. *tonicité* (Roquefort, 1829).] Tonic quality or condition; the property of possessing tone (see TONE *sb.* 7); the normal state of elastic tension of living muscles, arteries, etc., by which the tone of the organs is maintained.

1824 BOSTOCK *Elem. Syst. Physiol.* I. iii. 176 Besides contractility,..the muscular fibre has been supposed to possess another specific..quality, which has been called tone or tonicity. 1834 *Good's Study Med.* (ed. 4) I. 242 Even the tonicity of the skin seems to be quite destroyed. 1851 CARPENTER *Man. Phys.* (ed. 2) 212 These same muscles exhibit a tendency to a moderate and permanent contraction, which is not shown by them when they are dead..; this endowment..is called Tonicity. 1899 *Allbutt's Syst. Med.* VIII. 75 An apparently increased tonicity of the muscles.

**b.** Of spasm: see TONIC *a.* 1.

1897 *Allbutt's Syst. Med.* II. 695 Tetanus..may be distinguished by the shorter incubation period, the tonicity of the spasms [etc.].

**Tonicize** (tǫ·nisəiz), *v.* [f. as prec. + -IZE.] *trans.* **a.** To render tonic, give tone to. **b.** To invigorate as with a tonic. Hence **To·nicizing** *ppl. a.*

1884 *Brachet's Aix-les-Bains* I. 96 Thus more effectually tonicizing the cutaneous covering. 1890 *N. & Q.* 7th Ser. IX. 141/2 This would spread a tonicizing analeptic influence throughout our English world of readers.

**Tonico-,** combining form from Gr. τονικός TONIC, used to form compounds in sense 'combining a tonic and (some other) quality': see quot.

1840 PEREIRA *Mat. Med.* II. 1189 In its remote effects myrrh partakes of both the tonic and stimulant characters, and hence some have denominated it a *tonico-stimulant*; and as its stimulant powers are analogous to those of the balsams, it has also been called a *tonico-balsamic*.

**To·nify,** *v.* [app. f. F. *ton* (TON [3]) or Eng. TONE + -I)FY: in mod.F. *tonifier*.]

**†1.** (tǫ·nifəi.) *trans.* To impart a good 'ton' to; to make fashionable or stylish. *Obs.*

1786 MRS. GRANT *Lett. fr. Mountains* (1807) II. xxiii. 118 You can imagine no set of people more polished, powdered, tonified and englified, than they are.

**2.** (tōu·nifəi.) = TONICIZE a.

1858 J. H. BENNET *Nutrition* vi. 185 The cutaneous circulation is tonified and vitalized. 1892 *Star* 29 Aug. 4/1 Tepid water..tonifies the skin and prevents wrinkles.

**To-night** (tŭnəi·t), *adv.* and *sb.* Forms: see NIGHT. [OE. *tó niht*, TO *prep.* A. 7 + NIGHT. Cf. TO-DAY.] **A.** *adv.*

**1.** On this very night (i. e. the night now present).

*a* 1300 *Cursor M.* 11246 (Cott.), I bring yow word wit ioi and blis, Born to night your sauueour es! 1670 NARBOROUGH *Jrnl.* in *Acc. Sev. Late Voy.* I. (1711) 83 Much Wind to Night at Northwest. 1797 NELSON in Nicolas *Disp.* (1846) VII. p. cxlv, Half past 3 A.M. I was merely a spectator to-night. 1832 TENNYSON *May Queen* II. ii, To-night I saw the sun set. 1842 — *Audley Court* 69, I go to-night: I come to-morrow morn.

**b.** On any night (as contrasted with the next day). Cf. TO-DAY A. 1 b.

1500–20 DUNBAR *Poems* xxiii. 5 And with thy nychtbouris glaidly len and borrow His chance to nycht it may be thyne tomorrow. 1557 NORTH *Gueuara's Diall Pr.* I. xxviii. (1568) 41 For many are layde to nighte into their graue, which the next day following [are] thought to be aliue.

**2.** On the night following this day.

*c* 1000 ÆLFRIC *Numb.* xxii. 19 Ac beoþ her toniht, and abidaþ andsware. *c* 1000 — *Hom.* II. 104 Ðu stunta, nu toniht [Luke xii. 20 on þisse nihte] ðu scealt ðin lif alætan. *c* **1205** Lay. 709 Anacletus leofe freond to-niht þu scalt faren. *c* **1275** *Passion of Our Lord* 104 in *O. E. Misc.* 40 He me schal bitraye to nyht er he slepe. *c* **1470** Henry *Wallace* xi. 495, I sall cum out..to morn, Or ellys to nycht. **1539** Bible (Great) *Ruth* iii. 2 Beholde, he wenoweth barleye to nyght in the thresshyng floure. **1596** Shaks. *Tam. Shr.* iv. i. 201 Last night she slept not, nor to night she shall not. **1605** — *Macb.* i. v. 59 Duncan comes here to Night. **1876** Morris *Sigurd* (1877) 237 Tonight shall be the weaving, and tomorn the web shall ye win.

†**3.** On the night just past; last night. (Perhaps only said in the morning.) *Obs.* exc. *dial.*

*c* **1205** Lay. 28011 Þa axede hine an uær cniht, Lauerd hu hauest þu iuaren to-niht? *c* **1290** *Beket* 1542 in *S. Eng. Leg.* I. 150 To-niȝt ase ich was a-slepe a wonder metinge me com. **1390** Gower *Conf.* I. 73 No mannes myht Mai do that he hath do to nyht. **1592** Shaks. *Rom. & Jul.* i. iv. 50. I dreampt a dreame to night. **1610** B. Jonson *Alch.* i. ii, *Sub*...The Queene of Faerie do's not rise, Till it be noone. *Fac.* Not, if she daunc'd to night. **1641** Brome *Jovial Crew* iii. Wks. 1873 III. 393 Ease call'st thou it? Didst thou sleep to night? **1798** J. Jefferson *Let. to J. Boucher* 23 Feb. (MS.), [Hampshire expressions] *To-night* for *last night*, or *yesternight*.

**B.** *sb.* This night, or the night after this day.

*a* **1300** *Cursor M.* 3543 (Cott.) Þou sal neuer forth fra to night In þi forbirth do claim na right. **1601** Shaks. *Twel. N.* ii. iii. 142 Sweet Sir Toby be patient for to night. **1709** Prior *Thief & Cordelier* ix, He that's hang'd before noon, ought to think of to-night. **1799** Wordsw. *Lucy Gray* iv, To-night will be a stormy night—You to the town must go. **1908** [Miss E. Fowler] *Betw. Trent & Ancholme* 212 To-night is cloudy and dull.

**Toning,** *vbl. sb.* and *ppl.a.*: see Tone *v.*

**Tonish, tonnish** (tǫ·niʃ), *a.* Now *rare.* Also 8 ton-ish. [f. Ton[3] + -ish[1].] Having 'ton'; fashionable, modish, stylish. Hence **To·nishly** *adv.*, **To·nishness.**

**1778** *Crt. of Adultery* 6 The finer features of a Ton-ish face. **1779** Mme. D'Arblay *Diary* 26 May, Lord Mordaunt, ..a pretty, languid, tonnish young man. **1780** *Ibid.* Apr., The young lady..half tonish, and half hoydenish. *Ibid.* May, Mrs. North, who is so famed for tonishness, exhibited herself in a more perfect undress than I ever before saw any lady..appear in. **1802** Coleridge *Lett.* I. 368, I should be a thing in vogue,—the very tonish poet. **1804** Eugenia de Acton *Tale without Title* III. 14 Our elevated, spirited, and tonnish readers. **1825–9** Mrs. Sherwood *Lady of Manor* I. vi. 242 The Dashwood family.. spending their money in the most lavish and tonish style. **1872** C. D. Warner *Saunterings* (1873) 11 A footman.. wore the same colors; and the whole establishment was exceedingly tonnish. **1895** *Funk's Stand. Dict.*, Tonishly.

**Tonist** (tōu·nist). [f. Tone *sb.* + -ist.] An artist skilled in giving the proper tone to pictures.

**1883** *Academy* 17 Mar. 193/1 Wilson was a wonderful tonist, a subtle colourist, a painter of *chiaroscuro*, a master of artificial and elegant composition. **1883** *St. James' Gaz.* 11 Apr., His powers as a draughtsman, modeller and tonist.

**Tonit,** obs. Sc. form of Toned.

**Tonite** (tōu·nəit). [f. L. *ton-āre* to thunder + -ite[1].] A high explosive composed of pulverized gun-cotton impregnated with barium nitrate; cotton powder. Also *attrib.*

**1881** Raymond *Mining Gloss.*, *Tonite*, a nitrated gun-cotton, used in blasting. **1883** V. D. Majendie in *Standard* 19 Apr. 5/6 Explosives (such as dynamite, blasting gelatine, ..tonite, potentite). **1893** *Star* 28 Aug. 2/4 A tonite cartridge with a lighted fuse was thrown into the garden of a farmhouse at Euxton...An explosion occurred which almost wrecked the front of the house.

**Tonitrual** (toni·tru͵ăl), *a. rare*[—1]. [ad. rare late L. *tonitruāl-is* (L. Appuleius), f. *tonitru-s* thunder.] Pertaining to, or loaded with, thunder. So **Toni·truant** *a.*, less regularly **tonitrant** (tǫni·trănt) [ad. late L. *tonitruānt-em*, pres. pple. of *tonitruāre* to thunder (*Vulg.* Ps. lxxvi.)], thundering (*fig.*); **Toni·truate** *v.* (less regularly **to·nitrate**) [late L. *tonitruāre*: see -ate[3]], to thunder (*intr.* and *trans.*); **Tonitrua·tion,** thundering (in quot. 1689, ?explosion, or ? = Fulmination 3); **To·nitruo·ne,** a device for imitating thunder (see quot.); **Toni·truous** *a.* (less regularly **to·nitrous**), full of or characterized by thunder, loud noise, or violent utterance; thundery; thundering.

*a* **1693** *Urquhart's Rabelais* iii. li, They may..charging those *Tonitrual Guns afresh, turn the whole force of that Artillery against ourselves. **1861** M. Collins in *Temple Bar Mag.* I. 576 *Tonitrant writer in leading journal. **1907** *Times* 5 Sept. 8/1 Mr. Asche's robust personality and tonitruant style. **1623** Cockeram, **Tonitrate*, to thunder. **1630** Randolph *Shirley's Gratef. Servant* Pref. Verses, I cannot fulminate nor tonitruate words To puzzle intellects. **1656** S. Holland *Zara* (1719) 60 This potent..Incantation ..was no sooner utter'd by the Inchantress, but it tonitruated horribly. **1666** G. Harvey *Morb. Angl.* iv. 42 Winds and rumblings..whose tonitruating noise might have been heard at a great distance. **1658** Phillips, **Tonitruation* (Lat.), a thundring. **1689** G. Harvey *Curing Dis. by Expect.* xvii. 132 Minerals are to be disrobed of their Venom ..by Tonitruation, Sublimation [etc.]. **1909** *Times* 13 Feb. 8/1 The '*tonitruone',..a piece of iron fastened to a wooden frame and shaken by hand, produces a strange thunderous sound—and is of M. Paderewski's own invention. **1606** Drumm. of Hawth. *Answ. to Challenge* Wks. (1711) 233 Most *tonitruous, astonishing chevaliers, reknow ye, that we..do allow you this for answer. **1646** Sir T. Browne *Pseud. Ep.* ii. v. 88 This tonnitruous and fulminating report of gunnes. *a* **1704** T. Brown *Walk round Lond., Thames* Wks. 1709 III. iii. 64 By whom Billingsgate was much outdone in..tonitrous Verbosity, and malicious Scurrility. **1882** J. Nichol *Amer. Lit.* ii. 51 Increase [Mather] had a tonitruous cogency in his perorations.

‖ **Tonjon** (tǫ·n͵dʒǫn). *E. Indies.* Also tomjohn. [Origin uncertain.] A kind of sedan chair slung on a pole and carried by four bearers.

*c* **1804** Mrs. Sherwood *Autobiog.* xvi. (1854) 300, I had a tonjon, or open palanquin, in which I rode. **1838** *Lett. fr. Madras* (1843) 132 After dinner he took us out to see the town: we in our palanquins, and he in his tonjon. [*Note.* A kind of open sedan-chair.] **1885** G. S. Forbes *Wild Life in Canara* 132 It was not practicable to take a horse, ..and I began the journey in a tonjon.

‖ **Tonka** (tǫ·ŋkă). Also 8–9 **tonquin,** (9 **tonkin**), 9 **tonca, tonqua, tonga,** (**tonkay, tongo**). [*Tonka*, according to Focke, *Neger-Engelsch Woordenboek* 1855, the Negro name in Guiana of the bean (the Arawak Indian name being *cumaru*). So Fr. *tonka* or *tonca*, also *tongo* (Littré). Ulterior origin unknown. From the 18th century erroneously referred to *Tonquin* in Further India, and called *Tonquin bean*, in Du. 1770 *tonquin-boontje* (Hartsinck I. 82).]

**1. Tonka bean** (Pg. *fava de tonca*, F. *fève tonka*, Du. *tonka-boon*): the black, fragrant, almond-shaped seed of a large leguminous tree, *Dipterix odorata* (also, according to Taubert in Engler & Prantl, 1894, of *D. oppositifolia*), of Brazil, Guiana, and adjacent regions, used for scenting snuff, and as an ingredient in perfumes. Also the tree itself.

**1796** Stedman *Surinam* (1813) II. xxix. 388 The tonquin beans are said to grow in a thick pulp, something like a walnut, and on a large tree. **1830** Lindley *Nat Syst. Bot.* 92 The volatile oil of the Coumarouma odorata, or Tonka Bean, has been ascertained to be a peculiar principle called Coumarin. **1832** Macgillivray tr. *Humboldt's Trav.* xvii. (1836) 284 The fruit is known in Europe by the name of tonkay or tongo bean. **1833** *Penny Cycl.* I. 446/2 The fragrant tonga bean, which is..employed for perfuming snuff. **1852** Th. Ross *Humboldt's Trav.* II. xix. 224 This fruit,..under the name of tonca, or Tonquin bean, is regarded as poisonous. **1862** *Contrib. fr. Br. Guiana to London Exhib.*, Cuamara or Tonka..yields the Tonquin bean. **1888** *Encycl. Brit.* XXIII. 443/2 Tonqua beans are used principally for scenting snuff. **1902** *Westm. Gaz.* 29 Oct. 4/2 When first engaged as pilot, Gatiño was gathering tonga beans in the forest.

**2. Tonka-bean** (or *Tonga-bean*) **wood,** the wood of *Alyxia buxifolia*, a Tasmanian evergreen shrub, also called *Tonquin Bean-tree*; scentwood.

**1862** W. Archer *Products Tasmania* 41 Tonga Bean Wood (*Alyxia buxifolia*, Br.). The odor is similar to that of the Tonga Bean. A straggling sea-side shrub, three to five inches in diameter. **1866** *Treas. Bot.*, Tonga-bean wood, *Alyxia buxifolia.*

**Tonnage** (tʊ·nėdʒ), *sb.* Also 5–6 **tonage,** (6 **to(u)ndage, t(o)unage**), 7– **tunnage,** (8 **tunnige**). [In sense 1, a. OF. *tonnage* (1300 in Du Cange), *tonaige* (1374 in Godef.), *tonage* (1477 ibid.), f. *tonne* Tun: see -age, also med.(Anglo-)L. *tonnāgium* (Du Cange); in senses 2–7, f. Ton *sb.*[1] + -age.]

**I.** Charge, duty, or payment of so much per tun or ton.

**1.** *English Hist.* A tax or duty formerly levied upon wine imported in tuns or casks, at the rate of so much for every tun. Commonly in association with *poundage*: see Poundage *sb.*[1] 1.

By some historical writers and in some dictionaries written *tunnage* for distinction's sake, and to emphasize the connexion with Tun *sb.*; but *tonnage* is the more usual form.

Tonnage and poundage were first levied in the 14th c., and were granted for life to several sovereigns, beginning with Edward IV. They were abolished by 27 Geo. III c. 13, in 1787.

**1422** *Rolls of Parlt.* IV. 173/2 A subsidie of Tonage and Poundage.., that is to sey of every Tunne iii s; and xii d of every Pounde. *c* **1460** Fortescue *Abs. & Lim. Mon.* vi. (1885) 123 Pondage and tonnage mey not be rekenned as parcell off the revenues wich the kynge hath ffor the mayntenance off his estate, bi cause it aught to be applied only to þe kepynge off the see. **1568** Grafton *Chron.* II. 509 *margin*, This is the custome whiche we nowe paye, called Tonnage and poundage. **1640** Pym in Rushw. *Hist. Coll.* iii. (1692) I. 22 There is First Tunnage and Poundage, and the late new Book of Rates taken by Prerogative, without Grant of Parliament. **1647** Clarendon *Hist. Reb.* iii. § 215 Great Complaint had been made, 'that Tonnage and Poundage' (which is the duty and subsidy paid by the Merchant upon Trade) 'had been taken by the King without consent of Parliament'. **1765** Blackstone *Comm.* I. viii. 304 Tonnage was a duty upon all wines imported, over and above the prisage and butlerage aforesaid. **1845** McCulloch *Taxation* ii. v. (1852) 235 The duties of tonnage and poundage, of which mention is so frequently made in English history, were customs duties. **1875** Stubbs *Const. Hist.* II. xvi. 424 The custom of tunnage and poundage, two shillings on the tun of wine and sixpence on the pound [i. e. pound's worth] of merchandise which had been granted the year before [1371] for the protection of the merchant navy

†**2.** A charge for the hire of a ship of so much a ton (of her burden) per week or month. *Obs.*

**1512** *French Wars of 1512–13* (Navy Rec. Soc. 1897) 5 (*Charge of the Marie Roose*). Also for toundage, after 3d. a ton a weke, 500 tons: nihil, quia navis regis. *Ibid.* 7 Also for toundage of 400 tons: 60l. *Ibid.* 12 Somme total of the charges of the 22 shippes afore said, as in vitayle, wages, deddeshares and toundage for the first 3 mounthes: 5608*l.* 2*s.* *Ibid.* 34 Toundage after 12d a ton a mounth, for 9 shippes tyght 1790 tons, amountyng for 3 mounthes to 268*l.* 10*s.* *c* **1525** in *Archæologia* (1883) XLVII. 335 To David Miller apon the wages and vitailles and tondage of the *Vyncent*, of Eryth, xxxvij. li. ix. s. iij. d... To Christofer Coo apon wages and vitailles and tonage of diverse shippes, dclxxix. li. vj. s. viij. d. **1587** *Spanish War* (Navy Rec. Soc.) 237 For tonnage of the 6 ships for 3 months 141 0 0.

**3.** A charge or payment per ton on cargo or freight; e.g. that payable at any port or wharf, or on a canal; also, sometimes, that received or earned by a railway (quot. 1838).

**1617** Minsheu *Ductor*, *Tonnage*..I haue heard it also a Dutie due to the Mariners for vnloading their shippe arriued in any Hauen, after the rate of euerie Tonne. **1649** G. Daniel *Trinarch., Hen. IV*, cccxiv, The French..surprised as they stood In harbour, by some English Lords, make out The Tunnage lost, & forfeit stock to boot. **1708** J. C. *Compl. Collier* (1845) 53 What other Additions and Allowances of Tunnige for other Wares and Merchandize as are paid at the Ports aforesaid. **1789** *Constitution U. S.* i. § 10 No state shall, without the consent of the Congress, lay any duty of tonnage. **1806** *Gazetteer Scotl.* 409 [Paisley] to defray the expence by a tonnage of 8d per ton upon all vessels navigating the Cart, except those loaded with coal. **1828** Webster, *Tonnage*.. a duty, toll or rate payable on goods per tun, transported on canals. **1838** *Civil Eng. & Arch. Jrnl.* I. 322/2 It was admitted..that the amount of tonnage received by the Railway Company..was 1,236*l.* 0*s.* 6*d.* per mile. *Ibid.*, They would allow..30*l.* 18*s.* per mile, or 2⅓ per cent. for the collection of the tonnage.

**II.** Carrying capacity, weight, etc., in tons.

**4.** The carrying capacity of a ship expressed in tons of 100 cubic feet (see Ton[1] 2).

Originally the number of tun casks of wine which a merchant ship could carry. Afterwards estimated by measurements and calculations which gave rough approximations to the actual cubic content (*Old Measurement*, or O.M.). Now arrived at by measurement of length, and a series of exact measurements of breadth and depth at determinate distances, from which by a mathematical calculation (see Merchant Shipping Acts from 1854 onward, and esp. that of 1894, § 77–82) the cubic content of the space under the tonnage-deck (*Under-deck tonnage*) is obtained. To this are added the contents of all enclosed spaces above this deck, the result being the *Gross tonnage.* The deduction from the latter of the space occupied by the quarters of the crew, and that taken up in a steamer by the engines, boilers, etc., gives the *Register tonnage*, for which vessels are registered, and on which the assessment of dues and charges on shipping is based. The British system of measurement is now adopted in most important countries, but in some places is ignored, and the ship re-measured according to local rules. The *Suez Canal tonnage* makes a smaller deduction for engine-space, etc., and approximates more closely to the gross tonnage. The expression *Dead-weight tonnage* (or *carrying capacity*) is sometimes applied to the number of tons of 20 cwt. that a ship will carry laden to her load-line. *Displacement tonnage*, the number of tons of water displaced by a ship when thus loaded, used in England in stating the tonnage of men of war since *c* 1870.

**1718** Steele *Acc. Fishpool* 170 There is a great difference between a shipwright's and merchant's way of calculating the tonnage of a ship. *Ibid.*, The shipwright's way is to multiply the length of the keel by the middle-breadth, and that product by half the breadth and then they divide the last product by 94, and the quotient is the tunnage. **1748** *Anson's Voy.* iii. vii. 354 The duty..paid by all ships.. according to their tunnage. **1751** Labelye *Westm. Br.* 86 Of more Tonnage or Capacity than a Man of War of 40 Guns. **1836** W. Irving *Astoria* III. 133 Coasting vessels.. of small tonnage and draft of water, fitted for coasting service. **1838** *Civil Eng. & Arch. Jrnl.* I. 384/2 She is 271 tons old measurement,..and has 99 ft. 9 in. [length] for tonnage. **1858** E. B. Tinling in *Merc. Marine Mag.* V. 306 She had a registered American tonnage of 1035, corresponding with 997 British. **1888** *Encycl. Brit.* XXIII. 442/2 There are three terms used in respect of the tonnage of ships,— namely, tonnage under decks, gross tonnage, and register tonnage...In obtaining the tonnage under tonnage deck, ships are divided in respect of their length into five classes. *Ibid.* 443 This formula is also applicable for finding displacement tonnage of ships, that is, the external displacement measured by taking transverse areas to the height of the load water-line to find the cubic content, which divided by 35 gives the displacement in tons weight. **1894** *Pall Mall Mag.* Nov. 388 Gross tonnage means a vessel's actual burthen; ..registered tonnage is her burthen when the capacity of all the space in which cargo is not carried has been deducted.

**b.** *fig.* (Used of mental capacity or bodily size.)

**1806–7** J. Beresford *Miseries Hum. Life* (1826) i. Introd., To settle the comparative tonnage of their minds. **1869** 'Mark Twain' *Innoc. Abr.* ii, A dignitary of that tonnage. **1897** Flandrau *Harvard Episodes* 323 A person, female, aged—say forty-five; of abundant tonnage and affable manners.

**5.** *transf.* Ships collectively, shipping (in relation to their carrying capacity, or together with the merchandise carried by them).

**1633** T. Stafford *Pac. Hib.* ii. xxiv. (1821) 443 Victuals, and tonnage for the victualling and transporting of three thousand and two hundred men. **1748** in Hanway *Trav.* (1762) I. v. lxxvi. 348 He should not otherwise be able to give us any tonnage. **1808** Wellington in Gurw. *Desp.* (1837) IV. 24 If the additional Tonnage does not arrive tomorrow, I shall settle to leave behind the veteran battalion or the 36th. **1809** *Ibid.* V. 212 To send to Lisbon that part of the coppered tonnage of the country which can be spared from service elsewhere. **1833** Ht. Martineau *Vanderput & S.* i. 16 The tonnage of this country is more than half that of all Europe. **1844** H. H. Wilson *Brit. India* I. i. viii. 515 The amount of tonnage then provided for the private trade had never been fully occupied. **1849** Macaulay *Hist. Eng.* ix. II. 484 The tonnage [of Brixham] exceeds many times the tonnage of the port of Liverpool under the kings of the House of Stuart. **1858** Carlyle *Fredk. Gt.* iii. xviii. (1872) I. 250 The Friedrich-Wilhelm's Canal..still carries tonnage from the Oder to the Spree. **1898** *Daily News* 14 Feb. 9/5 An inadequate supply of tonnage has prevented the shipments coastwise being carried on on the large scale which the demand would undoubtedly warrant. 1909 *Daily Chron.* 22 Jan. 1/3 The tonnage built in German yards amounted to only 201,000, against 311,000 in 1907 and 338,000 in 1906.

**6. a.** Weight in tons. *rare.*

1793 SMEATON *Edystone L.* Contents 7 Tonnage of the Stone. *Ibid.* 8 The Moorstone considered as ballast. Its tonnage.

**b.** Weight of (iron or other heavy merchandise) in the market.

1898 *Daily News* 14 Feb. 9/5 Production has..been curtailed with a view to raising prices, but no impression is made upon the tonnage on offer, the Lancashire and Welsh makers being serious rivals.

**7.** Mode of reckoning the ton of cargo for freightage.

1913 *Handbk. Conference of W. I. Atlantic S.S. Comps., Genl. Regulations*, All goods to be freighted at actual measurement, or at actual gross weight, which ever tonnage be the greater..the measurement to be taken at 40 cubic feet to the ton, and the weight at 2240 pounds or 1000 kilos to the ton.

**8.** *attrib.* and *Comb.*, as *tonnage bounty, capacity, due, duty, length, money, tax*; **tonnage annuity**, a government annuity payable out of the proceeds of tonnage duties: see *Act* 5 *&* 6 *Will. & Mary*, 1694, c. 20 §§ 16–18; **tonnage-cheater**, term applied to a vessel built so as to cheat the rules for tonnage measurement, esp. a yacht with a 'dog's-leg' stern-post, by which its length was diminished; **tonnage-deck**, in a ship, the second deck from below in all vessels of two or more decks; the only deck in a vessel of one deck; **tonnage-displacement** = displacement tonnage, in 4.

1698 *Lond. Gaz.* No. 3374/4 The Purchasers may satisfie the Purchase-Money by Arrears, incurred..on the *Tunnage-Annuities or by Lottery-Tickets, which became due within the same Time on the Salt Act. 1846 McCULLOCH *Acc. Brit. Empire* (1854) I. 631 A high *tonnage bounty was granted upon every buss fitted out for the deep-sea fishery. 1901 *Munsey's Mag.* XXIV. 463/2 Commercial competition demanded that *tonnage capacity should be secondary to speed. 1912 DU BOULAY *Compl. Yachtsman* 474 Many yachtsmen attributed her [a yacht's] success to her evading the rule of length-measurement, and she was [1874] commonly known as a '*tonnage-cheater'. 1888 *Encycl. Brit.* XXIII. 442/2 In obtaining the gross measurement the space under the *tonnage deck is first measured; then the space or spaces, if any, between the tonnage deck and the upper deck. 1888 *Daily News* 8 Sept. 2/1 The smaller of the two ironclads will be named the Texas...Her *tonnage displacement is 6,300, and she will steam about 17 knots. 1834 *Tait's Mag.* I. 71/2 At present the orders in Council fix 2s. for the *tonnage dues [in China], and 7s. per cent. on the export and import cargo. 1846 McCULLOCH *Acc. Brit. Empire* (1854) II. 65 The tonnage dues and other revenues being generally insufficient to defray the ordinary expenditure. 1697–8 *Act* 9 *Will. III*, c. 37 (*title*) Annuities..payable out of *Tunnage Duties. 1801 A. HAMILTON *Wks.* (1886) VII. 217 Rather let the tonnage duty on American vessels be abolished. 1705 SIR C. WREN *Let.* in *N. & Q.* 3rd Ser. IV. 103/2, I am sorry Mr. Wood has pd you the *Tunnage-money, but..I shal endeavor that you be made to refund it. 1882 D. A. WELLS *Our Merchant Marine* vii. 179 *Tonnage-taxes on shipping are not levied by Great Britain, nor, it is believed, by any other of the maritime states of Europe, except Spain. Prior to the war, also, there were no tonnage-taxes in the United States. 1899 *Daily News* 19 Aug. 6/6 The challenging yacht is subject to tonnage tax, and must enter and clear at the Custom House like a regular merchant vessel.

**To·nnage**, *v.* [f. prec. sb.]

**1.** *trans.* To impose tonnage upon (see prec. 1); hence **To·nnaging** *vbl. sb.*: in quot. *fig.*

1644 MILTON *Areop.* (Arb.) 64 Nothing..but what passes through the custom-house of certain Publicans that have the tunaging and the poundaging of all free spok'n truth.

**2.** To have a tonnage of (so much): see prec. 4.

1850 SCORESBY *Cheever's Whalem. Adv.* i. (1858) 8 Six hundred and fifty ships, barks, brigs, and schooners, tonnaging two hundred thousand tons. 1874 SCAMMON *Marine Mammals* 241 Sixteen vessels, which tonnaged in the aggregate 1,871 tons.

**Tonne**, obs. form of TON, TUN.

‖**Tonneau** (tǫ·nōu). [F. *tonneau*, spec. application of *tonneau* cask, tun: see TONNEL.] Name for the rounded rear body of a motor-car (orig. with the door at the back). Also *attrib.* Hence **To·nneaued** *a.*, having a tonneau.

1901 *Daily Record & Mail* 26 Dec. 7 The tonneau, which is of the roomiest and most comfortable description, is designed to hold six passengers. 1904 KIPLING *Traffics & Discov.* 200 It was a big, black, black-dashed, tonneaued twenty-four horse Octopod [motor-car]. *Ibid.* 322 She knelt at the bottom of the tonneau telling her beads without pause. 1907 *Westm. Gaz.* 19 Mar. 4/2 A good tonneau seat is as comfortable as anyone could wish.

†**To·nnel, -ell.** *Obs.* Also 4 tonele, 4–7 tonel, 5 tonell. [Earlier form of TUNNEL, a. OF. *tonel, tonnel*, mod.F. *tonneau*, deriv. of *tonne* cask, med.L. *tonna, tunna*. The corresponding med.L. form was *tonnellus* masc., but the more usual and normal form was *tonnella* fem., dim. of *tonna, tunna*. See further under TUNNEL.]

**1.** A cask or barrel for wine or other commodities.

[*c* 991–*c* 1002 *Laws Æthelred* IV. ii. § 10 Duos caballinos tonellos aceto plenos. 1341–2 *Ely Sacr. Rolls* (1907) II. 117 In xij hopes pro tonelis...In iij staues pro uno tonele. 1390–1 *Earl Derby's Exp.* (Camden) 24 Johanni Clerk pro ij tonnellis, pris de tonello iijs... Willelmo Franch pro j tonella j pipa de Rynen, vjs.] 1483 *Act* 1 *Rich. III*, c. 13. § 1 Every Tonell to hold xijxx xij galons. 1483 CAXTON *Gold. Leg.* 111 b/1 A good woman whyche had but a lytyl wyn in her tonnel or vessel. 1582 N. LICHEFIELD tr. *Castanheda's Conq. E. Ind.* I. xxix. 72 A fish which ye sea did cast a land, yt was greater then any Tonel. 1601 TATE *Househ. Ord. Edw. II* (1876) 61 If any tonel be found to be corrupt..let the botome of the tonel be knocked out, and the wine spilt. 1880 O. CRAWFURD *Portugal Old & New* 256 [The wine] is drawn into tonels [= Pg. *toneles*], huge casks often with a capacity of over thirty pipes. 1884 DOWELL *Hist. Taxation* I. II. ii. 28 The Bishop of Winchester owes a tonell of good wine for not reminding the king (John) about a girdle for the countess of Albemarle.

**b.** *Comb.* **Tonnel-hoop**, a hoop of a cask.

1341–2 *Ely Sacr. Rolls* (1907) II. 117 In iiij staues pro uno tonele et iij tonelhopes. Item pro j tonelhope et ij paylhopes.

†**2.** Early spelling, in various senses, of TUNNEL.

**Tonner** (tɒ·nəɹ). [f. TON[1] + -ER[1]: cf. POUNDER *sb.*[4]] In comb. with prefixed numeral: A vessel of (so many) tons burden; e. g. *forty-tonner*, a vessel of forty tons burden: see TON[1] 2.

1883 *Harper's Mag.* Aug. 443/1 The forty-tonners..carried off most of the prizes. 1891 E. KINGLAKE *Australian at H.* 78 There is generally a race of some description, either for forty tonners, ten tonners, half-deckers, or the plain open sailing boat. 1891 *Lit. World* 20 Nov. 419/2 The Vancouver, one of the splendid 5,000 tonners of the White Star Line.

**Tonnie, tonny**, obs. ff. TUNNY.

**Tonnish**: see TONISH, TUNNISH.

**Tono-**, repr. Gr. τονο-, combining form of τόνος stretching, tension, TONE, combining element in many technical words. **Tonogram** (tǫ·nŏgræm) [-GRAM], the record of a tonograph. **To·nograph** [-GRAPH], a recording tonometer; see also quot. 1890; so **Tonogra·phic** *a.*, **Tono·graphy**. **Tonomi·tter** [L. *mittĕre* to send]: see quot. **To·nophant** [Gr. -φάντης one who shows], a device whereby acoustic vibrations are rendered visible. **To·noplast**, *Bot.* [-PLAST]: see quots. **Tonota·ctic** *a.*, of or pertaining to tonotaxis. **Tonota·xis** [TAXIS]: see quot.: also called *osmotaxis*.

1899 *Syd. Soc. Lex.*, *Tonogram. 1911 WEBSTER, *Tonogram*, a curve showing graphically a muscle's isometric contraction. 1890 *Pall Mall G.* 21 Mar. 5/2 Some specimens of a new photographic process, called '*Tonographs', were exhibited by Messrs. Mayall. 1899 *Syd. Soc. Lex.*, *Tonograph*, a machine for recording the tension of the arterial blood-current. 1867 MACFARREN *Harmony* i. 31 The vibrations of the air inducing musical sounds, by a process which might be called *tonography, imprint their [etc.]. 1899 *Syd. Soc. Lex.*, **Tonomitter*, an instrument to improve the hearing near the opening of the Eustachian tube. 1895 *Funk's Standard Dict.*, **Tonophant*, a device in which two thin pieces of steel welded together are used to exhibit acoustic vibrations to the eye. 1895 *Ibid.*, *Tonoplast. 1903 PORTER tr. *Strasburger's Text-bk.* 57 Since the vacuole wall regulates the pressure exerted by the cell sap contained in the vacuole, Hugo de Vries has applied the name Tonoplast to this layer. 1909 *Cent. Dict. Supp.*, *Tonotactic. 1900 B. D. JACKSON *Gloss. Bot. Terms*, **Tonotaxis*,..sensitiveness to osmotic variation.

**Tonometer** (tonǫ·mĭtəɹ). [f. TONO- + -METER.]

**1.** *Music.* An instrument for determining the pitch of tones; *spec.* a tuning-fork, or a graduated set of tuning-forks, as that made by Scheibler about 1833, for determining the exact number of vibrations per second which produce a given tone.

1725 A. WARREN (*title*) The Tonometer, explaining and demonstrating..all the 32 distinct and different Notes, adjuncts or Supplements contained in each of four Octaves inclusive, of the Gamut. 1840 WHEWELL *Philos. Induct. Sc.* I. I. IV. iv. 312 The monochord is a complete and perfect tonometer. 1876 A. J. ELLIS in *Athenæum* 2 Dec. 731/1 Tonometry was first placed on a scientific basis in a..pamphlet..published at Essen, 1834, and entitled 'The Physical and Musical Tonometer' (*Tonmesser*), which proves by the pendulum, visibly to the eye, the absolute vibrations of tones,..invented and executed by Heinrich Scheibler. 1881 BROADHOUSE *Mus. Acoustics* 104 Appunn's reed tonometer is a mode of measuring the pitch by means of harmonium reeds. 1885 *Athenæum* 18 Apr. 513/3 A class is devoted to..tuning-forks, pitch-pipes, sirens, tonometers, and other appliances for the determination of pitch.

**2.** An instrument for measuring (*a*) tension of the eyeball in glaucoma, (*b*) intravascular blood-pressure, (*c*) strains within a liquid.

(*a*) 1876 *Catal. Sci. App. S. Kens.* § 3674 Tonometer, for Measuring the Hardness and Convexity of the Eye. 1879 P. SMITH *Glaucoma* 14 A distinct indication of a different tension was given by the tonometer. (*b*) 1898 *Allbutt's Syst. Med.* V. 924 If the ventricle of a frog beat in a tonometer under a supply of blood from a pressure bottle, at varying heights, curves may be taken to measure the volume of the ventricle. (*c*) 1909 in *Cent. Dict. Supp.*

Hence **Tonometric** (tǫnǫ,me·trik) *a.*, of or pertaining to tonometry; **Tono·metry**, the using of a tonometer; measurement of vibrations of sound or of tension.

1901 *Nature* 24 Oct. 630/2 He also presents a *tonometric apparatus, consisting of about 670 diapasons or tuning forks. 1902 *Encycl. Brit.* XXX. 61/1 At the Philadelphia Exposition of 1876 great admiration was expressed for a tonometric apparatus of his [König's] manufacture. 1876 *Tonometry [see TONOMETER 1]. 1899 *Syd. Soc. Lex.*, *Tonometry*, measurement of tension, as of the eyeball.

**Tonour**, variant of TUNNER *Obs.*

**Tonous** (tōu·nəs), *a. rare.* [f. L. *tonus* TONE + -OUS.] Having a full tone or sound; sonorous.

1773 KENRICK *Rhet. Gram.* in *Dict.* 39 The last is much clearer and tonous in English than in French. 1846 in WORCESTER, and in later Dicts.

**Tonquin** bean: see TONKA.

**Tonse**, *v. Obs.* or *dial.* [f. L. *tons-*, ppl. stem of *tondēre* to shear, clip.]

†**1.** *trans.* To cut the hair of. *Obs.*

1555 W. WATREMAN *Fardle Facions* App. 333 Before that she (being tonsed, and hauing taken on her mourning wiede) haue bemoned her kinsfolke. 1676 in *Vicary's Anat.* (1888) App. xv. 282 If any Brother of the said Company shall..tonse, barbe, or trim any person on the Lord's day.

**2.** To trim; to dress up. *dial.*

1828 *Craven Gloss.*, *Tonse*, to dress, to deck, to trim. *Tonsed*, dressed up. 'Thou's finely tonsed this morning'.

**Tonsil** (tǫ·nsil), usually in pl. **tonsils** (tǫ·nsilz). Also 7 -ell. [ad. L. *tonsillæ* (pl.); cf. F. *tonsilles* (Paré, 16th c., *les tonsilles ou amygdales*).]

**1.** Each of two oval lymphoid glands situated one on each side of the fauces between the anterior and posterior arches.

1601 HOLLAND *Pliny* XXIII. Proem 146 Ulcers that happen in moist parts, and namely those of the mouth, Tonsils or Almond-kernels on either side of the throat. 1603 — *Plutarch's Mor.* 1022 The glandulous parts or kernelles called tonsells. 1776 CRUIKSHANK in *Phil. Trans.* LXXXV. 183 The tonsils were considerably inflamed. 1840 G. V. ELLIS *Anat.* 238 The tonsil is a collection of mucous follicles, situated between the pillars of the soft palate, above the side of the tongue, and below the velum.

**2.** Each of the two lobes of the cerebellum; also called *amygdala*.

1891 in *Cent. Dict.* 1899 in *Syd. Soc. Lex.*

**3.** *Abdominal tonsil*: a name sometimes applied to the lymphatic tissue of the appendix vermiformis.

**4.** *attrib.* and *Comb.*

1767 GOOCH *Treat. Wounds* I. 425 The operation [was] easily performed, with an instrument a little more curved than a tonsil-needle, having an eye towards the point. 1898 J. HUTCHINSON in *Arch. Surg.* IX. No. 36. 349 There may also..be a difference in proneness to tonsil affections in different races.

†**Tonsile** (tǫ·nsil, -əil), *a. Obs.* Also 8 tonsil. [ad. L. *tonsil-is*, f. *tons-*, ppl. stem of *tondēre* to shear: see -IL, -ILE.] That may be clipped or shorn.

1664 EVELYN *Sylva* (1776) 321 The Shrub [Juniper] is tonsile and may be shorn into any form. 1707 MORTIMER *Husb.* (1721) II. 366 In mild Weather, clip Phillyrea and other tonsil Shrubs. 1791 GILPIN *Forest Scenery* I. 93 The yew is of all other trees the most tonsile. 1847–78 HALLIWELL, *Tonsile-hedge*, a hedge cut neat and smooth. *North.*

**Tonsillar** (tǫ·nsilăɹ), *a.* [ad. med. or mod.L. *tonsillār-is*, f. *tonsillæ*: see TONSIL and -AR.] Of or pertaining to the tonsils; affected by the tonsils, as, a *tonsillar voice.*

1831 R. KNOX *Cloquet's Anat.* 589 The arteries of the tongue are furnished by the lingual branches of the external carotid arteries, and by the palatine and tonsillar twigs of the labial. 1899 *Allbutt's Syst. Med.* VIII. 467 Tonsillar, pharyngeal, or bronchial congestion.

**Tonsillary** (tǫ·nsilări), *a.* [f. as prec. + -ARY[2]. Cf. F. *tonsillaire* (Roquefort 1829).] = prec.

1842 F. H. RAMADGE *Curability Consumption* (1850) 9 Preternatural tonsillary development. 1860 MAYNE *Expos. Lex.*, *Tonsillaris*, of or belonging to the tonsil: tonsillary.

**Tonsillitic** (tǫnsili·tik), *a.* [f. next + -IC.] **a.** (Irregularly used.) Of or pertaining to the tonsils; = TONSILLAR. ? *Obs.* **b.** Affected with tonsillitis.

1839–47 *Todd's Cycl. Anat.* III. 953/1 The tonsillitic branches of the glosso-pharyngeal. 1856 TODD & BOWMAN *Phys. Anat.* II. 116 Tonsillitic branches are numerous. 1879 *St. George's Hosp. Rep.* IX. 162 There was but one tonsillitic patient who possessed a healthy constitution.

‖**Tonsillitis** (tǫnsiləi·tis). *Path.* [f. L. *tonsill-a* TONSIL + -ITIS.] Inflammation of the tonsils; when suppuration takes place, called *quinsy*.

1801 E. DARWIN *Zoon.* III. 361 By tonsillitis, the inflammation of the tonsils is principally to be understood. 1878 T. BRYANT *Pract. Surg.* I. 534 Tonsillitis as an acute affection is known as quinsy, and is characterized by the rapid swelling of the part, acute pain, foul tongue, and fever.

**Tonsi·llolith.** *Path.* [-LITH.] A concretion in the substance of the tonsil.

1903 *Buck's Handbk. Med. Sc.* VI. 599 The same fungi have been found in fœtid bronchitis, tracheal ozæna, pulmonary gangrene, rhinoliths, tonsilloliths, vesical calculi.

**Tonsi·llotome.** [irreg. f. L. *tonsilla* TONSIL + -TOME; cf. F. *tonsillitome* (Littré).] A surgical instrument for excising the tonsil.

1857 in DUNGLISON *Med. Lex.* 1872 COHEN *Dis. Throat* 128 When the organ is not very large, it may be excised by the tonsillotome. 1897 *Allbutt's Syst. Med.* IV. 744 The hypertrophy should be reduced..by the lingual tonsillotome.

So **Tonsillo·tomy**, excision of the tonsils.

1897 *Allbutt's Syst. Med.* IV. 778 No belief is too foolish and groundless to be advanced against tonsillotomy. 1901 *Lancet* 27 Apr. 1211/1 Six minor operations (opening of abscesses and two double tonsillotomies).

**Tonsilly** (tǫ·nsili), *a. rare.* [f. TONSIL + -Y.] Affected by the tonsils. (Cf. *throaty.*)

1894 *Westm. Gaz.* 31 Aug. 7/2 His voice..is..weak and tonsilly to the ear.

**Tonsion**, variant of TUNSION, beating.

**Tonsor** (tǫ·nsǫɹ). [a. L. *tonsor* barber, agent-n. f. *tondēre* to shear, clip.]

1. A barber.

1656 [see TONSORIOUS]. 1721 BAILEY, *Tonsor*, a Barber. 1749 FIELDING *Tom Jones* VIII. vi, 'So, tonsor', says Jones, 'I find you have more trades than one'. 1866 R. CHAMBERS *Ess.* Ser. II. 16 When we sit under the tonsor..we fall into chat.

†2. A clipper of coin. *Obs.*

1697 EVELYN *Numism.* vii. 225 Not our Tonsors only, Clippers and False Monyers.

**Tonsorial** (tǫnsōᵊ·riăl), *a.* [f. L. *tonsōri-us* pertaining to a barber + -AL.] Of or pertaining to a barber or his work; often used humorously, as 'a tonsorial artist'.

1813 MOORE *Post-bag* ii. 22 During that awful hour or two Of grave tonsorial preparation. 1851 THACKERAY *Contrib. to Punch* Nov., Wks. 1894 XIII. 575 Under the roof of a tonsorial practitioner in the Waterloo Road. 1910 *Daily News* 15 Dec. 6 American 'tonsorial artists' are furious at the popularity of the safety razor.

So † **Tonso·rian**, † **Tonso·rious** *adjs.*, tonsorial.

1656 BLOUNT *Glossogr.*, *Tonsorious*.., of or belonging to a barber or tonsor. 1658 in PHILLIPS. 1705 ELSTOB in Hearne *Collect.* 30 Nov. (O.H.S.) I. 107 Worthy a Prince of the Tonsorian Race, The best that er'e with steel mow'd human face.

**To·nsurate.** [ad. med.L. *tonsūrāt-us*, f. L. *tonsūra* TONSURE: see -ATE[1].] The state or quality of being tonsured, esp. in preparation for orders, or while only in the lowest order of Reader.

1897 *Tablet* 8 May 725 Cranmer and his associates abolished the Tonsurate and all the minor orders.

**Tonsure** (tǫ·nsiŭı), *sb.* Also 5 tonsur, -our. [a. F. *tonsure* (14th c. in Godef.), or ad. L. *tonsūra* a shearing or clipping, f. *tondēre, tons-um*: see TONSE.]

1. *gen.* The action or process of clipping the hair or shaving the head; the state of being shorn.

1390 GOWER *Conf.* III. 291 For unlust of that aventure Ther was noman which tok tonsure. 1616 BULLOKAR *Eng. Expos.*, *Tonsure*, a clipping or cutting of the haire. 1650 BULWER *Anthropomet.* ii. 56 We..reduce our Tonsure to a just moderation and decency. 1770 LANGHORNE *Plutarch* (1851) I. 3/1 This kind of tonsure, on his account was called Theseis. 1876 C. M. DAVIES *Unorth. Lond.* 183 The 'county crop'—that species of tonsure which all had undergone.

2. *spec.* The shaving of the head or part of it as a religious practice or rite, esp. as a preparation to entering the priesthood or a monastic order.

In the Eastern Ch. the whole head is shaven (*tonsure of St. Paul*); in the Roman Ch. either a circular patch on the crown, as in secular priests, or the whole upper part of the head so as to leave only a fringe or circle of hair, as in some monastic orders and friars (*t. of St. Peter*); in the ancient Celtic Ch. the tonsure 'consisted in shaving the head in front of a line drawn from ear to ear' (*t. of St. John*). A form of tonsure was also practised by the priests of Isis.

1387 TREVISA *Higden* (Rolls) VI. 167 He took tonsure and habit of clerk, þe 3ere of his age foure and twenty. c 1450 *St. Cuthbert* (Surtees) 1366 And gaf him tonsour and habite. 1530 PALSGR. 183 *Les ordres*..benet the first tonsure. 1655 FULLER *Ch. Hist.* II. ii. § 96 No mention herein of settling the Tonsure of Priests..according to the Roman Rite. 1753 CHALLONER *Cath. Chr. Instr.* 153 The Clerical Tonsure.. is not properly an Order, but only a Preparation for Orders. The Bishop cuts off the Extremities of their Hair, to signify their renouncing the World and its Vanities; and he invests them with a Surplice, and so receives them into the Clergy. 1829 J. DONOVAN tr. *Catech. Counc. Trent* II. vii. § 14 In tonsure the hair of the head is cut in form of a crown, and should always be worn in that form, enlarging the crown as one advances in orders. 1842 HOOK *Ch. Dict.* 558 A clerical tonsure was made necessary about the 5th or 6th century. 1846 SHARPE *Hist. Egypt* xiv. 431 In Rome he was very partial to the Egyptian superstitions, and he had adopted the tonsure, and had his head shaven like a priest of Isis. 1849 ROCK *Ch. of Fathers* I. ii. 186 Of the ecclesiastical tonsure ..the Roman form was perfectly round; the Irish was made by cutting away the hair from the upper part of the forehead in the figure of a half-moon, with the convex side before.

b. The part of a priest's or monk's head left bare by shaving the hair.

[1351–2 *Rolls of Parlt.* II. 244/2 Gentz de Religion portantz tonsure.] 1430–40 LYDG. *Bochas* IX. xiv. (MS. Bodl. 263) lf. 418/2 As a prest she [Joan] had a brod tonsure. a 1625 SIR H. FINCH *Law* (1636) 65 But if he shew cause which our law alloweth not (as because hee hath not his tonsure, or *ornamentum Clericale*, &c.) he shall pay a fine, and yet be driuen to take the felon. 1768 STERNE *Sent. Journ.*, *Monk, Calais* i, The monk, as I judged from the break in his tonsure,..might be about seventy. 1849 JAMES *Woodman* xiii, You must cover the tonsure with this peasant's bonnet.

†3. The clipping (*a*) of coin; (*b*) of shrubs or hedges. *Obs. rare.*

1621 BOLTON *Stat. Irel.* 12 (Act 25 Hen. VI) Ireland is greatly impoverished..by the..carriage..into England of the silver plate, broken silver Bullion and wedges of silver made of the great Tonsure of the money. 1691 in *Archæologia* (1796) XII. 185 His yew hedges with trees of the same ..kept in pretty shapes with tonsure. *Ibid.* 186 A fair gravel walk betwixt two yew hedges with rounds and spires of the same, all under smooth tonsure.

4. *attrib.* and *Comb.*, as *tonsure-cap*, *tonsure-plate* (see quot.).

1889 *Pall Mall G.* 23 July 2/1 His rank..distinguished by the scarlet sash which he wears..and by his tonsure-cap, which is of the same colour. 1891 *Cent. Dict.*, *Tonsure-plate*, a round thin plate slightly convex so as to fit the top of the head, used to mark the line of the tonsure according to the Roman rite.

**To·nsure,** *v.* [f. prec. sb. or ad. F. *tonsurer* (14–15th c. in Hatz.-Darm.) or med.L. *tonsūrāre* (845 in Du Cange).] *trans.* To clip or shave the hair of; to confer the ecclesiastical tonsure upon.

1793 *Minstrel* I. 90, I must tonsure those fine tresses to the due form. 1843 CARLYLE *Past & Pr.* II. xiv, Now tonsured into a mournful penitent Monk. 1872 O. SHIPLEY *Gloss. Eccl. Terms* 459 The Greeks tonsured their whole heads, like St. James and the other Apostles. 1878 MACLEAR *Celts* viii. (1879) 123 They..were tonsured from ear to ear, —that is, the fore part of the head was made bare, and the hair was allowed to grow only on the back part of the head.

b. *fig.* To make bald-headed.

1876 W. B. SCOTT *Sonn.* 9 And now that age hath shriven and tonsured me.

Hence **To·nsuring** *vbl. sb.* and *ppl. a.*

1811 *Henry & Isabella* I. 3 He manifested a sufficient genius at the tonsuring business. 1906 *Reader* 24 Nov. 123/2 He..gladly followed her advice to remedy with a curled scalp the 'tonsuring action of middle age'.

**To·nsured,** *ppl. a.* [f. prec. + -ED[1].]

1. That has received tonsure; hence, in orders.

1706 tr. *Dupin's Eccl. Hist. 16th C.* II. III. xxii. 395 By which, Tonsured Clerks..are exempt from Lay-Jurisdiction. 1827 HALLAM *Const. Hist.* (1876) I. ii. 58 The immunity of all tonsured persons from civil punishment for crimes. 1873 M. ARNOLD *Lit. & Dogma* (1876) 370 The cowled and tonsured Middle Age.

b. *fig.* Bald or partially bald.

1855 TENNYSON *Brook* 110 Bowing o'er the brook A tonsured head in middle age forlorn.

2. Clipped, as a yew or box. *rare.*

1837 HOWITT *Rur. Life* I. vii. (1862) 70 Walpole overturned this ancient fondness for pleached walks and tonsured trees.

†**Tonsword.** *Obs. rare.* (?)

1575 LANEHAM *Let.* (1871) 29 Captin Cox.., very cunning in fens, and hardy az Gawin; for hiz tonsword hangs at his tablz eend. [See Editor's Note.] *Ibid.* 31 Captain Cox cam marching on valiantly before..floorishing with hiz tonsword, and another fensmaster with him.

**Tontine** (tǫntī·n), *sb.* (*a.*) [a. F. *tontine*, from name of Lorenzo Tonti, a Neapolitan banker, who initiated the scheme in France c 1653.]

1. A financial scheme by which the subscribers to a loan or common fund receive each an annuity during his life, which increases as their number is diminished by death, till the last survivor enjoys the whole income; also applied to the share or right of each subscriber.

Introduced first in France as a method of raising government loans. Afterwards tontines were formed for building houses, hotels, baths, etc.

1765 *Chron.* in *Ann. Reg.* 71/2 The house of Commons came to a resolution of raising £300,000..by way of tontine, or annuities upon lives, at 3 per cent. with benefit of survivorship. 1777 SHERIDAN *Sch. Scand.* I. i, I hear he pays as many annuities as the Irish tontine. 1791 *Gentl. Mag.* Jan. 27/2 This gentlewoman had ventured 300 livres in each Tontine; and in the last year of her life she had for her annuity..about 3600*l.* a year. 1827 HONE *Every-day Bk.* II. 1533 During a scarcity of money which prevailed in 1644, Lawrence Tonti came from Naples to Paris, and proposed that kind of life-rents, or annuities, which are named after him *Tontines*: though they were used in Italy long before his time. 1871 *Daily News* 4 Jan., It is proposed to organize a tontine, to purchase the Alexandra Palace, with the park of about 100 acres, and utilise them for public recreation. The sum required is 650,000*l.*, which it is intended to raise in shares of 20s. each.

*fig.* 1796 BURKE *Regic. Peace* iv. Wks. IX. 67 The murderers of Robespierre, besides what they are entitled to by being engaged in the same tontine of Infamy,..have inherited all his murderous qualities.

2. A game of cards played on the tontine principle: see quots.

1798 *Sporting Mag.* XI. 24 Tontine may be played by twelve or fifteen persons; but the more the merrier. *Ibid.*, Tontine..is played with an entire pack of fifty-two cards.. every one is to take a stake. *Ibid.* 25/1 He who outlives all the rest, by having counters left, when theirs are gone, wins the party, and enjoys what the others have deposited.

¶3. Applied to a friendly society which shares out its unexpended funds at the end of the year. (*Erroneous use.*)

1871 *2nd Rep. Comm. Friendly Soc.* II. (1872) 38/1 It is curious..that they [these sharing out clubs] call themselves tontines; I do not know why; of course it is a wrong name. 1898 BRABROOK *Provid. Societies* 69 The Dividing Societies ..exist in great numbers, under a variety of names, as Slate Clubs, Tontines, Birmingham Benefit Societies, &c.

B. *adj.* (or *attrib.* use of the sb.). Of, pertaining to, or of the nature of a tontine.

1824 SCOTT *St. Ronan's* i, At length a tontine subscription was obtained to erect an inn. 1834 HT. MARTINEAU *Farrers* i, Some of the lot of lives with which her father and she were joined in a tontine annuity had failed. 1863 KIRK *Chas. Bold* II. IV. ii. 222 The destined survivor of a tontine partnership. 1876 *Haydn's Dict. Dates* (ed. 15) 719 A Mr. Jennings was an original subscriber for a 100*l.* share in a tontine company; and being the last survivor.., his share produced him 3000*l.* per annum. He died aged 103 years, 19 June, 1798, worth 2,115,244*l.* 1891 *Cent. Dict.*, *Tontine policy*, a policy of insurance, in which the holders agree to receive no dividend for a term of years called the *tontine period*. The money is allowed to accumulate till the end of the period, when it is divided among those who have maintained their insurance in force.

Hence **Tontiner** (tǫntī·nəı), a shareholder in a tontine.

1881 *Times* 1 June 6/2 [Two survivors] claimed the whole fund, in their respective classes, as against the representatives of the deceased tontiners in the same class.

‖**Tonus** (tōu·nǒs). *Physiol.* and *Path.* [L. *tonus*, a. Gr. τόνος TONE.]

1. The condition or state of muscular tone; the proper elasticity of the organs; tonicity.

1876 tr. *Wagner's Gen. Pathol.* (ed. 6) 162 In a reflex manner the arterial tonus is reduced or increased. 1882 BURDON SANDERSON in *Lancet* 29 Apr. 678 The paralysed artery recovers, and sometimes over-recovers its normal state of contraction, or, as we call it, its *tonus*. Tonus.. is one of the independent endowments of arteries. 1899 *Allbutt's Syst. Med.* VII. 109 Whence comes this loss of tonus?

2. A tonic spasm.

1891 in *Cent. Dict.* 1899 *Allbutt's Syst. Med.* VII. 890 The clonic spasm may..pass into slight tonus of very short duration. 1899 *Syd. Soc. Lex.*, *Tonus*, tonic spasm.

3. (See quot.)

1902 *Encycl. Brit.* XXXI. 740/1 A continuous lesser 'change' or stream of changes sets through the neuron, and is distributed by it to other neurons in the same direction and by the same synapses as are its nerve impulses. This gentle continuous activity of the neuron is called its *tonus*.

4. *Comb.*, as *tonus-producing* adj.

1897 *Allbutt's Syst. Med.* III. 317 Any failure of the circulation dependent upon the absence from the blood-stream of this tonus-producing substance.

†**Tony** (tōu·ni), *sb.*[1] *slang. Obs.* Also 8 toney. [A particular application of *Tony*, used as short for *Antony*.] A foolish person; a simpleton.

For possible origin, cf. MIDDLETON *Changeling* (1623) I. ii.

1654 GAYTON *Pleas. Notes* III. x. 141 Their Friends and Wives have took them for Tonies or Mad-men. 1699 R. L'ESTRANGE *Erasm. Colloq.* (1711) 148, I saw once an errant Tony, with a Gown to his Heels. a 1700 B. E. *Dict. Cant. Crew*, *Tony*, a silly Fellow, or Ninny. a 1784 JOHNSON in Piozzi *Anecd.* (1786) 195 Teaching such tonies is like setting a lady's diamonds in lead.

‖**Tony,** *sb.*[2] *Obs.* Early variant of DHONEY, DONEY, a small South Indian sailing vessel.

1582 N. LICHEFIELD tr. *Castanheda's Conq. E. Ind.* I. xxiv. 60 There came towarde him to yᵉ number of lx. Tonys full of Souldiers. 1704 *Collect. Voy.* (Churchill) III. 734/2 Four Fishermen were coming to us in a *Tony* or Fisher-boat.

**Tony** (tōu·ni), *a.* *U.S.* and *Colon. colloq.* [f. TONE *sb.* + -Y.] Having a high or fashionable tone; high-toned, stylish; 'swell'.

1886 *Pall Mall G.* 24 Sept. 5/1 Nevern-square, with its comfortable and, as the Americans have it, 'tony' residences. 1895 S. R. HOLE *Tour Amer.* 270 Well you see, it is so toney. 1901 H. LAWSON in *Blackw. Mag.* Apr. 478/1 The furniture looked as if it had belonged to a tony homestead at one time.

†**To·ny,** *v.* *Obs. rare.* [f. TONY *sb.*[1]] *trans.* To make a fool of; to fool, cheat, swindle.

a 1652 BROME *Damoiselle* I. ii. Wks. 1873 I. 391 You, that had all these once,..To be wrought on, and tonyed out of all.

**Tony,** obs. form of TUNNY, a fish.

**Tonycle, Tonyd,** obs. ff. TUNICLE, TONED.

**Too** (tū), *adv.* Forms: 1 tó, 2–7 to, (3 tu, 6 toe), 6– too. [Stressed form of To *prep.*, which in the 16th c. began to be spelt *too*.]

I. 1. In addition (cf. To *adv.* 5); furthermore, moreover, besides, also. (Rarely, now never, used at the beginning of a clause.)

c 888 K. ÆLFRED *Boeth.* xli. § 5 Þa styriendan netenu.. habbað eall þæt ða unstyriendan habbað, and eac mare to. a 1240 *Ureisun* in *Cott. Hom.* 183 Tu art se softe and se swote 3ette to swa leoflic. c 1330 R. BRUNNE *Chron.* (1810) 229 Þe envenomed knyfe [he] out braid, & gaf Edward a wounde. To, I wene, he lauht. ? 1400 *Arthur* 532 Seyþ a Pater noster more to. 1533 MORE *Debell. Salem* Wks. 997/1 Wold not the iudges..geue them yᵉ hearing; yes yes I dout not, and the iury to. 1590 SHAKS *Com. Err.* III. i. 110 Prettie and wittie; wilde, and yet too gentle. 1627 HAKEWILL *Apol.* (1630) 296 Not the bodie only but the minde to..is sickish & indispos'd. 1641 J. SHUTE *Sarah & Hagar* (1649) 156 Too, we profess our selves the Redeemed of the Lord. 1766 GOLDSM. *Vic. W.* iii, Take..this book too. 1821 SCOTT *Kenilw.* xx, I too have sometimes that dark melancholy. 1891 *Law Times* XC. 315/1 If you sell the mansion-house in which the heirlooms are to be kept, you must sell the heirlooms too.

II. 2. In excess; more than enough; overmuch, superfluously, superabundantly. (Preceding and qualifying an adj. or adv.) a. *gen.* In excess of what ought to be; more than is right or fitting.

a 900 CYNEWULF *Crist* 1567 Ac hy to sið doð gæstum helpe. 971 *Blickl. Hom.* 41 3e eow ondrædaþ þæt 3e onfon to lytlum leanum. a 1200 *Moral Ode* 28 in *Lamb. Hom.* 161 Al to muchel ich habbe ispent, to litel ihud in horde. 13.. *E. E. Allit. P.* B. 182 For mon-sworne, & men-sclaȝt, & to much drynk. 1535 COVERDALE *Num.* xvi. 3 Ye make to moch a doo. 1604 SHAKS. *Oth.* V. ii. 345 One that lou'd not wisely, but too well. 1605 — *Lear* I. iv. 279 Woe, that too late repents. 1766 GOLDSM. *Vic. W.* vi, I delivered this observation with too much acrimony. 1852 MRS. STOWE *Uncle Tom's C.* xvi, A fellow's taking a glass too much, and sitting a little too late over his cards.

b. More than enough for the particular case in question; in excess of what is consistent with or required by something expressed by the context.

Usually const. *for* with sb. (cf. FOR *prep.* 13 b); *to* with inf. (cf. To *prep.* B. 7 b); or *for* with sb. + *to* with inf. (cf. FOR *prep.* 18).

a 1300– [see To B. 7 b]. c 1350 *Will. Palerne* 5024 Of here a-tir for to telle to badde is my witte. c 1489 CAXTON *Blanchardyn* xlvi. 177 Blanchardyn shal neuer come ayen at thys syde; kyng alymodes is to myghty a lorde in his lande. c 1518 SKELTON *Magnyf.* 1892 All worldly Welth for hym to lytell was. 1599 SHAKS. *Much Ado* V. ii. 72 Thou and I are too wise to wooe peaceable. 1653 WALTON *Compl. Angler* vii. 160 This dish of meat is too good for any but Anglers. 1665 MANLEY *Grotius' Low C. Warres* 791 The Castle.. was too mean a prize for so great an Army to look after. 1710 STEELE *Tatler* No. 200 ⁋ 2 Men of Letters know too much to make good Husbands. 1804 WORDSW. *She was a phantom of delight* ii, A Creature not too bright or good For human nature's daily food. **1908** R. BAGOT *A. Cuthbert* xix, Too large an apartment for two people not to feel somewhat lost in it.

**c.** Expressing, sorrowfully or indignantly, regret or disapproval: To a lamentable, reprehensible, painful, or intolerable extent; regrettably, painfully. Cf. 5 c.

*c* **1205** LAY. 5268 To late heom þuȝte are heo þer to comen. **1297** R. GLOUC. (Rolls) 4618 Ac to prout he was & to fals, þat ssende þis lond alas. *c* **1380** WYCLIF *Wks.* (1880) 454, & þus ech siche were herde of ech, but þis abusioun were to straunge. **1447** *Rolls of Parlt.* V. 137/1 It apperith to openly in som persones. **1568** GRAFTON *Chron.* II. 501 The old prouerbes be to true. **1592** CHETTLE *Kinde-harts Dr.* (1841) 24 Either witles, which is too bad, or wilfull, which is worse. **1648** *Petit. Eastern Assoc.* 15 Which is too well pleasing to the adverse partee. **1721** WODROW *Suffer. Ch. Scot.* (1838) I. i. iv. § 1. 333/2 Some of them, alas too many, were heard swearing very rudely. **1839** THACKERAY *Fatal Boots* Aug., This was too cool. **1855** MACAULAY *Hist. Eng.* xvii. IV. 87 At best a blunderer, and too probably a traitor.

**d.** Rarely used to qualify a verb: Too much, to excess. (See also 4 b.)

**1509** BARCLAY *Shyp Folys* 59 Whyle one is ladyd to the others backe is bare. **1833** BROWNING *Pauline* 937–8, I have too trusted my own lawless wants, Too trusted my vain self. **1873** — *Red Cott. Nt.-cap* III. 790 The causes,.. Would too distract, too desperately foil Enquirer.

**3.** As a mere intensive: Excessively, extremely, exceedingly, very. (Now chiefly an emotional feminine colloquialism; but see also 5 c and d.)

**1340** *Ayenb.* 95 The wel greate loue and to moche charite of god þe uader. **1697** tr. *C'tess D'Aunoy's Trav.* (1706) 79 He..had not lost nothing of whatever made me heretofore fancy him too Lovely. **1825** T. HOOK *Sayings* Ser. II. *Man of Many Fr.* I. 273 'We shall see you at dinner, perhaps', said the Colonel..'I shall be too happy', replied Noel. **1868** PR. ALICE *Mem.* 4 Sept. (1884) 203 How too delightful your expeditions must have been.

**4.** Reduplicated for emphasis: *too too* (formerly occas. written as one word, *toto, totoo, tootoo*). **a.** Qualifying an adj. or adv.; chiefly in sense 2 c. (Very common *c* 1540–1660.)

*c* **1489** CAXTON *Blanchardyn* liv. 213 Ah! to to well I suspected..that my captiuitie would bring her callamity. **1542** UDALL *Erasm. Apoph.* 271 It was toto ferre oddes yᵗ a Syrian born should in Roome ouer come a Romain. **1582** in Hakluyt *Voy.* (1904) V. 233 Threed..some tootoo hard spun, some tootoo soft spun. **1586** DAY *Eng. Secretary* I. (1625) 5 Vsed *bona fide*, it was too too bad. **1602** SHAKS. *Ham.* I. ii. 129 Oh that this too too solid Flesh would melt. **1654–66** EARL ORRERY *Parthen.* (1676) 547 Her fears were but too-too well grounded. **1745** *Gentl. Mag.* Oct. 550/1 Not apt to toy, and yet not too too nice. **1821** SCOTT *Kenilw.* xxxvi, It is too, too apparent. **1885** LELAND *Brand-new Ballads* (ed. 2) 109 Perishing to find Something which was not too-too-utter-ish To serve for dinner. **1887** *N. & Q.* 7th Ser. III. 109/2 The too-too painfully ceremonious manners..of the French.

†**b.** Qualifying a verb, as in 2 d; also *absol.*

*c* **1518** SKELTON *Magnyf.* 872 He doth abuse Hym self to to. **1533** J. HEYWOOD *Merry Play* (1903) 183 By my soule I love thee too too. **1534** MORE *Comf. agst. Trib.* III. Wks. 1247/2, I cannot then see, that the feare..shold any thing sticke with vs, & make vs toto shrinke. *c* **1537** *Thersites* (1820) 66 It is to to, mother, the pastyme and good chere That we shall see and haue.

**c.** As *adj.* in predicative or attributive use: Excessive, extreme; extremely good, highly exquisite.

A modern affectation, connected with the 'æsthetic' craze of *c* 1880–90. In first quot. = characterized by the use of 'too too'.

**1891** *N. & Q.* 7th Ser. XI. 30/2 Let the exclusive too-too æsthetes tolerate the remark that music and painting do not exist for them. **1893** MRS. A. KENNARD *Diogenes' Sandals* i. 12 The piece is nowhere; but my frocks are too too!

**5.** In special collocations. †**a.** *Too much* (besides its ordinary use) was formerly sometimes used instead of the simple *too* to qualify an adj. or adv. *Obs.*

*c* **1449** PECOCK *Repr.* I. xi. 53 To miche homeli dele with him. **1530** RASTELL *Bk. Purgat.* III. i, When the bodye is to mych hote or to mych colde, or to mych drye or to mych moyste. **1593** SHAKS. *Rich. II*, II. ii. 1 Your Maiesty is too much sad. **1638** JUNIUS *Paint. Ancients* 230 His minde is kept too much busie.

**b.** *Too much* (as predicate): more than can be endured, intolerable: also *too much of a good thing*. *Too much for*: more than a match for; such as to overcome or subdue: so *too many for* (see MANY A. 5 f), *too hard for*, etc. Chiefly *colloq.*

**1533** J. HEYWOOD *Merry Play* (1830) 30 Shall we alway syt here styll, we two? That were to mych. **1692–1872** [see MANY A. 5 f]. **1777** SHERIDAN *Trip to Scarb.* v. ii, Don't be frightened, we shall be too hard for the rogue. **1796** MME. D'ARBLAY *Camilla* I. 233 O too much! too much! there's no standing it! **1809** SYD. SMITH *Wks.* (1867) I. 175 This (to use a very colloquial phrase) is surely too much of a good thing. **1832** HT. MARTINEAU *Life in Wilds* v, The light had been too much for him. **1861** DICKENS *Gt. Expect.* xlviii, Mr. Jaggers was altogether too many for the Jury, and they gave in.

**c.** *But too .., only too*: Here *too* is app. = 'more than is desirable' (cf. 2 c), or 'more than is or might be expected', while *but* (BUT C. 6) or *only* (ONLY A. 1) = 'nothing but', 'nothing else than', app. emphasizes the exclusion of any different quality or state of things such as might be desired or expected.

**1639** MASSINGER *Unnat. Combat* II. i, I have Discourse and reason, and but too well know I can nor live, nor end a wretched life. **1654–66** [see 4]. **1817** CASS. AUSTEN in *Jane Austen's Lett.* (1884) II. 334, I loved her only too well. **1818** SCOTT *Rob Roy* viii, Stay, then, rash, obstinate girl.. you know but too well to whom you trust. **1849** MACAULAY *Hist. Eng.* v. I. 663 It is indeed but too true that the taste for blood is a taste which..men..may..speedily acquire.

**d.** *Only too* in recent use, is often a mere intensive, = 'extremely'. (Cf. 3.)

**1889** 'J. S. WINTER' *Mrs. Bob* (1891) 245 Mrs. Trafford will only be too glad to come and pay you a visit. *Mod.* I shall be only too pleased.

**e.** *None too ..* is used by meiosis for 'not quite .. enough', 'somewhat insufficiently': see also NONE C. 3.

**1885** *Manch. Exam.* 21 May 5/3 The vast territories of the Dominion have hitherto been none too coherent. *Mod.* Money is none too plentiful with us.

**f.** *Quite too ..*: see QUITE 4 c.

**6.** In combination. **a.** With an adj. or adv., forming a (nonce) sb. phr., as *a too-late, a too-little, a too-much*.

**1602** SHAKS. *Ham.* IV. vii. 119 Goodness, growing to a plurisy, Dies in his own too much. **1637** C. DOW *Answ. to H. Burton* 158 There may be a too-much even in the best things. **1784** R. BAGE *Barham Downs* I. 346 [One] who complains of the Too-much of things he does not value, and of the Too-little of things he does. **1860** PUSEY *Min. Proph.* 542 There will be a 'too late'; not a final 'too late', ..but..a 'too late' to avert that particular judgment. **1905** *Daily Chron.* 14 Apr. 5/4 We have suffered greatly in our national life from the domination of the 'too-lates'; political procrastination is the thief of opportunity.

**b.** With an adj. or adv., forming an adj. phr. preceding and qualifying a sb., or an adv. phr. qualifying an adj., as *too-anxious, -celebrated, -familiar, -fervent, -near, -piercing, -trusting, -willing, -wise* adjs.; *too-early, -late, -long, -much* (in quot. 1620 = too great *obs.*; see also 5 a) adjs. and advs. Hence derivatives (*nonce-wds.*), as *too-bigness, -lateness, -muchness, -soonness*.

**1612** *Two Noble K.* II. ii. 32 Like a too-timely Spring. **1620** VENNER *Via Recta* vi. 100 It..represseth the too-much tenuity..of the bloud. **1624** DONNE *Devot.* 221 Those sentences, from which a too-late Repenter will sucke desperation. **1793** HOLCROFT *Lavater's Physiog.* xxvi. 127 The gentleness of his voice [will] temper thy too-piercing tones. **1838** LYTTON *Alice* II. ii, The good man was quite shocked at the too-familiar manner in which Mrs. Merton spoke. **1842** TENNYSON *Day-dream* Prol. 18 Turn your face, Nor look with that too-earnest eye. **1849** MISS OTTÉ tr. *Humboldt's Cosmos* II. II. v. 596 My lamented and too-early deceased friend. **1855** KINGSLEY *Heroes* II. I. (1868) 82 Only one walked apart..Asclepius, the too-wise child. **1887** *Spectator* 16 Apr. 532/1 A too-fervent patriotism. **1858** DE QUINCEY in 'H. A. Page' *Life* (1877) II. xviii. 142 In midst of too-soonness he shall suffer the killing anxieties of too-lateness. **1875** BLACKIE *Let.* in *Biog.* (1895) II. xviii. 122 An everlasting too-muchness. **1904** S. E. WHITE *Forest* iii. 30 Everything was wrinkled in the folds of too-bigness.

**Too,** variant of TEW *v.*, to bustle round (*U.S.*).

**1866** LOWELL *Biglow Papers* Introd., Poems 1890 II. 199 'Ther's sech a thing ez bein' *tu*'..hence the phrase *tooin' round*, meaning a supererogatory activity like that of flies.

**Too,** obs. f. TOE, TWO; var. of TO *v.*, to take.

**Tooa**: see TOA.

‖ **Tooart** (tū·ăɹt). Also **tewart, tuart.** [Native name in Australia.] A West Australian tree, *Eucalyptus gomphocephala*, which furnishes a very hard heavy durable timber used in ship-building.

**1870** BRAIM *New Homes* iv. 181 Another valuable tree is the tooart, a kind of white gum. **1875** LASLETT *Timber & Timber Trees* xxvi. 187 The Tewart Tree (*Eucalyptus*). A variety of the White Gum...The wood is..hard, heavy, tough, strong, and rigid...It is used in ship-building for ..keelsons,..and for other works below the line of flotation.

**Tooche,** obs. form of TOUGH.

**Toocke, Toocun,** obs. ff. TOQUE, TOKEN.

**Toocker,** variant of TUCKER *Obs.*, a fuller.

**Tood(e,** obs. forms of TOAD.

**Toodle** (tū·d'l), *v.* ? *dial.* [In sense 1 echoic (cf. TEEDLE, TOOTLE).]

**1.** *intr.* To hum or sing in a low tone (as to a baby).

**1865** W. G. WILLS *D. Chantrey* xxxii. III. 140 She shall have the toodling and the cooing and a sequestered spot, and be spared these foolish accessions of nerves.

**2.** See quot 1904. [perh. a different word.]

**1890** A. LANG *Sir S. Northcote* I. i. 11 In winter [at Eton] they 'toodled'. **1904** J. A. THOMSON *Eighty Years' Reminiscences* I. i. 19 [At Eton in 1832] One of our great amusements in winter was toodling—hunting birds in the hedges and chasing them till they were blown, when we captured them.

So **Too·dle-loo·dle**; †**toodle-toodle** [cf. Ger. *dudeldudel*], an imitation of the sound of a pipe or flute; **toodle-pipe**, a pipe making such a sound.

**1542** UDALL *Erasm. Apoph.* 223 b, His instrumente wheron to plaie toodle loodle bagpipe. *a* **1553** — *Royster D.* II. i. (Arb.) 32 Then to our recorder with toodleloodle poope As the howlet out of an yuie bushe should hoope. *a* **1566** R. EDWARDS *Damon & Pithias* (1571) F iv b, Wyll singes, Too nidden, and toodle toodle doo nidden. *Ibid.* G j, Todle todle. **1890** DOYLE *White Company* xviii, A Scotch army, where every man fills himself with girdle-cakes, and sits up all night to blow upon the toodle-pipe.

**Toofan,** variant of TYPHOON. **Toogh,** obs. f. TOUGH. **Too-hoo,** var. of TOO-WHOO, owl's cry.

**Took,** pa. t. of TAKE *v.*; obs. form of TUCK.

**Tooken,** obs. f. TOKEN; obs. pa. pple. of TAKE *v.*

**Tool** (tūl), *sb.* Forms: 1 tól, 2–4 tol, 4–7 tole, toole, (5 tule, toyel, 5–6 toile, 5–7 toyle, 6 toyll, towle, 7 tooell), 4– tool. [OE. *tól* neut., = ON. *tól* n. pl. (cf. Norw. *tøler*):—OTeut. **tôwlom*, *tôlom*, f. **tôw-* to prepare, make (cogn. with Goth *taujan*: see TAW *v.*[1]) + agent-suffix *-lom*, -EL [1].]

**1.** 'Any instrument of manual operation' (J.); a mechanical implement for working upon something, as by cutting, striking, rubbing, or other process, in any manual art or industry; usually, one held in and operated directly by the hand (or fixed in position, as in a lathe), but also including certain simple machines, as the lathe; sometimes extended to simple instruments of other kinds, as in quot. 1893. See also EDGE-TOOL.

*c* **888** K. ÆLFRED *Boeth.* xiv. § 1 Þæt mete and drync & claðas, & tol to swelcum cræfte. *c* **1000** ÆLFRIC *Exod.* xx. 25 Gif þu þin tol ahefst ofer hyt, hit biþ besmiten. *a* **1100** *Gerefa* in *Anglia* (1886) IX. 262 He sceal fela tola to tune tilian. *c* **1205** LAY. 29253 Nettes..and þa tolen þer to. **13..** *E. E. Allit. P.* B. 1342 Formed with handes Wyth tool out of harde tre, & telded on lofte. *a* **1400–50** *Alexander* 4708 A pelare of marble Quare-on a tulke wiþ a toile þis titill vp he wrate. *c* **1440** *York Myst.* xxxiv. 298, I warand all redy Oure tooles bothe lesse and more. **1497** *Naval Acc. Hen. VII* (1896) 89 Carpenters toles..j chest. **1501** *Bury Wills* (Camd.) 84 To..Margarett my wyff all my stuff of houshold..excepte my werkyng toole, weche I wyll that John my sone haue. **1570** LEVINS *Manip.* 214/45 A Toyle, *instrumentum*. **1573** TUSSER *Husb.* (1878) 31 Few lends (but fooles) their working tooles. **1597** *Knaresborough Wills* (Surtees) I. 207 One lowme with the towles yr unto belonginge. *a* **1660** *Contemp. Hist. Irel.* (Ir. Archæol. Soc.) II. 172 All theire bagage, tooells, and instruments. **1667** MILTON *P. L.* XI. 572 Moulds..from which he formd First his own Tooles. **1706** E. WARD *Wooden World Diss.* (1708) 62 His [the Surgeon's] Tools are of various Sorts and Sizes. **1818** BYRON *Juan* I. cci, Good workmen never quarrel with their tools. **1877** KNIGHT *Dict. Mech.* s. v., Of late it has become usual to embrace in the general term *machine tools*, such machines as the lathe, planer, slotting-machine, and others employed in the manufacture of machinery. **1893** HODGES *Elem. Photogr.* (1907) 22 The anastigmat [lens] will..prove the more useful tool.

**b.** A weapon of war, *esp.* a sword. *arch.*

[*c* **1000** *Ags. Gloss.* in *Haupt's Zeitschrift* IX. 424 *Instrumenta bellica*, wiȝlice tol.] *c* **1386** CHAUCER *Nun's Pr. T.* 96 We alle desiren..no fool Ne hym þat is agast of euery tool. ? *a* **1400** *Morte Arth.* 3617 The toppe-castelles he stuffede with toyelys, as hyme lykyde. *c* **1400** *Destr. Troy* 938 Iason..gryppet a grym toole, gyrd of his hede. **1592** SHAKS. *Rom. & Jul.* I. i. 37 Draw thy toole, here comes of the house of Mountagues. **1671** H. FOULIS *Hist. Rom. Treasons* (1681) 228 Pope John xxii..pulls out his tools against Lewes. **1706** E. WARD *Wooden World Diss.* (1708) 63 He's somewhat prouder of that long Tool of his, that hangs without board. **1821** SCOTT *Kenilw.* iv, Draw thy tool, man, and after him.

†**c.** The cutting part of a knife, the blade. *Obs.*

**1653** URQUHART *Rabelais* I. xxvii. 129 Little hulchback't demi-knives, the iron toole whereof is two inches long, and the wooden handle one inch thick.

**d.** *spec.* in technical use: (*a*) *Bookbinding.* A small stamp or roller used for impressing an ornamental design upon leather book-covers: cf. TOOLING 2 b. (*b*) A large kind of chisel. (*c*) A generic name for any kind of paint-brush used by house-painters or decorators; also, a large brush used by picture-painters. (*d*) An abbreviated form of *grafting-tool*, etc.

(*a*) **1727–41** CHAMBERS *Cycl.* s. v. *Book-binding*, These ornaments are made with each its several gilding-tool, engraven in relievo. *Ibid.*, To apply the gold, they glaze those parts of the leather, whereon the tools are to be applied, lightly over [etc.]. **1837** WHITTOCK, etc. *Bk. Trades* (1842) 37 (Bookbinder) The tools that produce the figures or letters are applied hot. **1895** ZAEHNSDORF *Short Hist. Bookbinding* 13 He cut most of these tools himself,..because he could not find a tool cutter of sufficient skill.

(*b*) **1815** [see TOOLING 2]. **1823** P. NICHOLSON *Pract. Build.* 341 Of the two kinds of chisels..the tool is the largest. **1842–76** GWILT *Encycl. Arch.* § 1910 The tools used to work the face of a stone are, successively, the point, the inch tool, the boaster..and the broad tool. *Ibid.*, The broad tool 3½ inches at the cutting edge.

(*c*) **1859** GULLICK & TIMBS *Paint.* 198 The larger brushes ..made of hog-hair..are called 'tools'. **1860** PIESSE *Lab. Chem. Wonders* 153 A painter calls a paint-brush 'a tool'.

**2.** *fig.* Anything used in the manner of a tool; a thing (concrete or abstract) with which some operation is performed; a means of effecting something; an instrument.

*c* **1000** *Eccles. Inst.* c. 21 Þis synt þa lara and þa tol gastlices cræftes. **1555** PHAER *Æneid* II. E j b, At last Those toles for shift at death extreme, to fend them selfs they cast. **1611** SIR W. MURE *Misc. Poems* ii. 46 He [Cupid]..left behind his tort'ring toyle [*rime* spoyle; *cf.* l. 40 Ye bow, ye schafts, ye quaver and ye brace]. **1651** HOBBES *Leviath.* II. xxv. 132 They..make use of Similitudes..and other tooles of Oratory. **1674** GREW *Disc. Mixture* ii. § 5 As the World, taken together, is Natures Shop; so the Principles of Things are her Tools, and her Materials. **1749** SMOLLETT *Gil Bl.* VIII. ix. III. 161 You have (to use the expression of our tennis-court) the universal tool: that is to say, you are qualified for every thing. **1847** L. HUNT *Men, Women, & B.* I. i. 7 Mechanical knowledge is a great and a glorious tool in the hands of man. **1884** B. PRICE in *Contemp. Rev.* Mar. 381 Money..is a pure tool—nothing more.

**b.** A bodily organ; *spec.* the male generative

organ (or *pl.* organs). Now *arch.* or *slang.* [So ON. *tól.*]

1553 BECON *Reliques of Rome* (1563) 18 All his toles that appertayne vnto the court of Venus. 1613 SHAKS. *Hen. VIII*, v. iv. 35 Or haue wee some strange Indian with the great Toole, come to Court? 1687 SHADWELL *Juvenal* 307 What pleasure can the weak Old Doting Fool, Expect from that infirm and Aged Tool? 1885 R. F. BURTON *Arab. Nts.* III. 7, I was become even as a woman, without manly tool like other men.

**3.** *fig.* A person used by another for his own ends; one who is, or allows himself to be, made a mere instrument for some purpose; a cat's-paw.

1663 BUTLER *Hud.* I. i. 35 Which made some take him for a tool, That knaves do work with, call'd a fool. 1688 BP. PARKER in *Magd. Coll.* (O.H.S.) 240 To set me here to make me his tool and his prop! 1711 HEARNE *Collect.* (O.H.S.) III. 133 Charlett and his Tools have got Rogers advanc'd. 1769 *Junius Lett.* xxiv. (1770) 153 If there be any tool of administration daring enough to deny these facts. 1849 MACAULAY *Hist. Eng.* iv. I. 494 The sheriffs were the tools of the government. 1874 GREEN *Short Hist.* vii. § 4. 379 Mary had used Darnley as a tool to effect the ruin of his confederates.

**b.** (esp. qualified by *poor* or the like.) An unskilful workman; a shiftless person. *slang* or *dial.*

*a* 1700 B. E. *Dict. Cant. Crew*, *Slug*, a drone, or dull Tool. 1722 G. VERTUE *Diary* in *N. & Q.* (1861) 2nd Ser. XII. 81/1 The organists are poor tools and very deficient. 1863 MRS. TOOGOOD *Yorks. Dial.* (MS.), You are a poor tool, your work is not done as it ought to be.

**4.** *Bookbinding.* (*transf.* from 1 d (*a*).) A tooled design on a book-cover.

1881 CUNDALL *Bookbindings* 76 He began with a small number of dotted tools, foliage, and the so-called seventeenth-century tools. 1885 C. G. W. LOCK *Workshop Receipts* Ser. IV. 252/1 A book on Natural History should have a bird, insect, shell or other tool indicative of the contents.

**5.** *attrib.* and *Comb.*, as *tool-basket, -box*, † *-budget* (BUDGET 2 b), *-chest, -cutter, -dressing, -extractor, -gauge, -handle, -maker, -making* sb. and adj., *-pouch, -rack, -seller, -shed, -shop, -tray, -user, -using* sb. and adj.; **tool-box,** *spec.* the steel box (BOX *sb.*[2] 15) in which the cutting tool of a planing or other machine is clamped; **tool-car** (*U.S.*), a car used on a railway equipped with tools and appliances for clearing the line after an accident; a break-down car; **tool-coupling,** a screw coupling by which the operating part of a tool is fastened to the handle (Knight); **tool-holder,** (*a*) a handle by which a tool is held in the hand, esp. a detachable handle for various tools; (*b*) a tray with a rack for holding a set of tools; (*c*) a device for holding a tool firmly in place, as in a lathe, or when being ground upon a grindstone; **tool-house,** a building in which tools are kept, a tool-shed; **tool-mark,** the mark of a tool upon any object that has been shaped or worked by it; **tool-marking,** the etching of a mark or lettering upon a steel tool; **tool-post,** an upright piece in the tool-rest of a lathe, with a slot and a screw for holding the cutting-tool; **tool-rest,** a part of a lathe serving to support a hand-tool, or to hold a mechanical tool in place (in the latter case often having various adjustments for different positions of the tool); **toolsmith,** a man who makes steel tools; **tool-stack** = *tool-post, tool-holder* (*c*); **tool-stay,** a tool-holder in a lathe-rest, with a slot for a drill or other tool (Knight); **tool steel,** steel of the quality used for tools; **tool-stock** = *tool-post*; **tool-stone,** name for a palæolithic implement consisting of a natural stone very slightly adapted to be held in the hand, or used as a rude tool.

1858 SIMMONDS *Dict. Trade*, **Tool-basket*, a carpenter's or other workman's basket, for holding tools. 1841–4 EMERSON *Ess.*, *Prudence*, [He] builds a work-bench, or gets his *tool-box set in the corner of the barn-chamber. 1904 *Lineham's Text-bk. Mech. Eng.* 171 The tool box is fixed to a ram, the sliding of which in saddle gives the cut. 1794 W. FELTON *Carriages* (1801) I. 223 *Tool budget is a small convenience made to hang by straps under the hind part of a carriage. 1778 COOK *Voy. Pacific* IV. v. (1784) II. 373 As well and ingeniously made, as if they were furnished with the most complete *tool-chest. 1882 *Rep. to Ho. Repr. Prec. Met. U.S.* 594 It includes tools, *tool-dressing and grinding. 1877 KNIGHT *Dict. Mech.*, **Tool-extractor*, an implement for recovering from drilled holes broken tools or portions of rods. *Ibid.* 2594/1 Nasmyth's *tool-gage, for testing the angularity of the cutting-face of iron-turning tools. 1887 MOLONEY *Forestry W. Afr.* 207 Red wood used for *tool-handles and mallets. 1877 KNIGHT *Dict. Mech.* 2594/1 A *tool-holder for dentists. 1887 D. A. Low *Machine Draw.* (1892) 110 Tool-holders must be drawn in their proper positions in the ram, and not separate as in the diagram. 1905 *Athenæum* 14 Oct. 510/1 The needles used were European, fitted into watchmaker's tool-holders. 1818 SCOTT *Rob Roy* xiv, Before he trundled them off to the *tool-house. 1908 *Betw. Trent & Ancholme* 10 A lattice-gate, into the tool-house. 1858 SIMMONDS *Dict. Trade*, *Tool-maker. 1888 E. CLODD *Story Creation* xi. 217 If he is not the only tool-user, he is the only tool-maker among the Primates. 1785 BOSWELL *Jrnl. Tour Heb.* 25 *n.*, Dr. Franklin said, Man was 'a *tool-making animal', which is very well; for, no animal but man makes a thing, by means of which he can make another thing. 1893 ELIZA R. SUNDERLAND in Barrows *Parl. Relig.* I. 630 Religion is an attribute of humanity, as reason and language and tool-making are. 1865 J. F. CAMPBELL *Frost & Fire* I. x. 94 Before a craftsman can recognise a *tool-mark, he must be familiar with the tool. 1864 WEBSTER, **Tool-post*, the part of a tool-rest that holds a stationary cutting-tool;—called also tool-stock. *Ibid.*, **Tool-rest* (*Machine-tools*), the part that supports a tool-post or a tool. 1878 AYLWARD *Transvaal* ii. (1881) 18 Everywhere one may observe that older houses are being used as waggon shelters, coach-houses, *tool-rooms. 1875 SIR T. SEATON *Fret-Cutting* 71 The *tool-seller has to pay the workman for dressing the wood. 1840 DICKENS *Barn. Rudge* lv, To break open a *tool-shed in the garden. 1875 SIR T. SEATON *Fret-Cutting* 71 Unprepared wood bought at the *tool-shop. 1884 C. G. W. LOCK *Workshop Receipts* Ser. III. 269/2 A *toolsmith usually heats cast steel to what he terms a cherry-red. 1868 JOYNSON *Metals* 90 For *tool-steel, from 1·5 to 1·7 per cent [of charcoal being required]. 1894 BOWKER in *Harper's Mag.* Jan. 419 Too costly..to be in demand except for tool steel. 1864 *Tool-stock [see *tool-post*]. 1865 LUBBOCK *Preh. Times* iv. 76 The oval *tool-stones..are oval or egg-shaped stones, more or less indented on one or both surfaces...Some antiquaries suppose that they were held between the fingers and thumb, and used as hammers or chippers. 1888 *Tool-user [see *tool-maker*]. 1831 CARLYLE *Sart. Res.* I. v, This Definition of the *Tool-using Animal appears to us, of all that Animal-sort, considerably the precisest and best. 1862 D. WILSON *Preh. Man* vi. (1865) 96 Man was created with a tool-using instinct.

**Tool,** *v.* [f. prec. sb.]

**1.** *trans.* To work or shape with a tool; *spec.* to smooth the surface of a building stone with the chisels called 'tools': cf. quot. 1842 in TOOL *sb.* 1 d (*b*).

1815 [see TOOLING 2]. 1828 *Craven Gloss.*, *Tool*, to make a level surface on a stone. 1842 *Civil Eng. & Arch. Jrnl.* V. 211/1 The whole exterior..will be faced with stone from the Summit delphs, which is to be neatly hammer-dressed, except the ashlar dressings, which are to be neatly tooled. 1873 SIR T. SEATON *Fret-Cutting* (1875) 56 The stems and branches look very well when simply rounded and tooled with the V-tool, or tooling-gouge, which is the smallest sized round gouge. 1876 PREECE & SIVEWRIGHT *Telegraphy* 238 Chatterton's compound should be warmed, and a small quantity put on the copper and joint, and properly tooled over, so as to cover the joint equally. Before applying the tooling-iron it should be well wiped. 1895 *Daily Chron.* 15 Jan. 6/7 Aluminium..is ductile, but difficult to tool.

**b.** *Bookbinding.* To impress an ornamental design upon the binding of (a book) with a special tool (see prec. 1 d (*a*)). Most usually in pa. pple.; see also TOOLED.

1836 *J. R. Smith's Catal. Bks.* Feb. 14/1 A remarkable fine copy, russia extra, tooled on sides, gilt. 1881 A. LANG *Library* 65 Leather tooled with geometrical patterns. 1885 C. G. W. LOCK *Workshop Receipts* Ser. IV. 246/1 Another method is to tool the edge before burnishing.

**c.** *intr.* To work with a tool or tools; *spec.* in *Bookbinding*: see prec. sense and TOOLING 2 b.

1890 *Daily News* 2 July 5/1 'The Tasmanians'..the very last people who 'tooled' with rudely chipped flints. 1892 *Sat. Rev.* 16 Jan. 64/2 They are a ferocious people..and 'tool' with spears almost as broad in the head as shovels.

**2.** *slang.* **a.** *trans.* To drive (a team of horses, a vehicle, or a person in a vehicle); of a horse, to draw (a person) in a vehicle.

1812 *Sporting Mag.* Oct. 10/2 She intends to tool the Liverpool expedition to-morrow night. 1840 J. T. HEWLETT *P. Priggins* xv, He would only drive to Benson, and 'tool' the down mail back again. 1849 LYTTON *Caxtons* XIII. iv, He could tool a coach. 1865 DICKENS *Mut. Fr.* I. xi, She was on most days solemnly tooled through the park..in a great tall custard-coloured phaeton. 1881 JESSOPP *Arcady* (1887) i. 13 The high-stepping mare that tools him along through the village street. 1882 H. C. MERIVALE *Faucit of B.* II. II. ii. 158, I tooled the little mare over from Luscombe Abbey—the six miles in the half-hour.

**b.** *intr.* To drive, to travel in a horse-drawn vehicle; also said of the vehicle, or team; also, by extension, of any vehicle: to travel, go *along*.

1839 J. FRAZER in *Haileybury Observer* I. 53 The road was so good..as to enable us to 'tool along' in a well-hung britschka, at the rate of ten miles an hour. 1849 THACKERAY *Pendennis* iii, I thought I'd just tool over, and go to the play. 1877 MAR. M. GRANT *Sun-Maid* xi, The Marquis's frisky chestnuts are tooling rapidly through the town. 1893 W. A. SHEE *My Contemp.* iii. 77 Went to Ascot..and we 'tooled' down in very good style.

**Toold,** obs. f. *told*, pa. pple. of TELL *v.*

**Tooled,** *a.* [f. TOOL *sb.* + -ED[2].] In parasynthetic comb.: Having or furnished with a tool.

1577 GRANGE *Golden Aphrod.* Mij, Priapus the great tooled god.

**Tooled** (tūld), *ppl. a.* [f. TOOL *v.* + -ED[1].] Worked or shaped with a tool; *spec.* in *Bookbinding*: see TOOL *v.* 1 b.

1815 [see TOOLING 2]. 1837 *Civil Eng. & Arch. Jrnl.* I. 72/1 Tooling is also practised upon wall stones, when they cost as much as common hewing or tooled work. 1856 MRS. BROWNING *Aur. Leigh* VIII. 895 A copy bound in scarlet silk, Tooled edges, blazoned with the arms of Leigh. 1893 *Q. Rev.* July 200 Specimens of their handiwork in tooled morocco.

**Tooler** (tū·ləɹ). [f. as prec. + -ER[1].]

**1.** A broad chisel used by stone-masons for random tooling; a drove.

1828 *Craven Gloss.*, *Tooler*, a broad chissel.

**2.** *Bookbinding.* A workman who tools the covers of books: see TOOL *v.* 1 b.

1834 DE QUINCEY in *Tait's Mag.* I. 28/2 The King..coming into the binding-room and minutely inspecting the progress of the binder and his allies—the gilders, toolers, &c. 1865 *Englishm. Mag.* Sept. 220 The most finished specimens of the tooler's art in these days.

**Tooling** (tū·liŋ), *vbl. sb.* [f. TOOL *sb.* and *v.* + -ING[1].]

†**1.** Provision of tools; tools collectively. *Obs.*

1673 KIRKMAN *Unlucky Citizen* 210 By such time as he and his are fitted with Clothing, Teething and Tooling, his money is gone.

**2.** The action of the verb TOOL; workmanship performed with some special tool; *spec.* **a.** The dressing of stone with a broad chisel; also, elaborate ornamental carving in stone or wood.

1815 J. SMITH *Panorama Sc. & Art* I. 218 The larger sizes of chisels obtain the name of tools, the act of using them is called tooling, and the stone to which they have been applied is said to be tooled. 1840–1 DE QUINCEY *Style & Rhet.* Wks. 1858 XI. 31 The fine tooling, and delicate tracery of the cabinet artist. 1891 *Edin. Rev.* July 110 The tooling of the Haram stones is peculiar, and is the same found on the later Carthaginian monuments.

**b.** *Bookbinding.* The impressing of ornamental designs upon the covers of books by means of heated tools or stamps; also applied to the designs so formed: either with gilding (*gold-* or *gilt-tooling*) or without it (*blind-tooling*: BLIND *a.* 16).

1821 G. ORMEROD *Let. to J. G. Nichols* May (in *Pearson's Catal.* (1886) No. 60), I would not have any lettering or tooling on the back. 1847 L. HUNT *Men, Women, & B.* II. vi. 78 The charms of vellums, tall copies, and blind tooling. 1875 KNIGHT *Dict. Mech.*, *Gold-tooling*, ornaments impressed by the hot-tool upon gold-leaf laid on book-covers. 1893 *Q. Rev.* July 187 The tooling in gold introduced at this time ..came originally from the East.

**3.** *Comb.*, as *tooling-gouge, -iron.*

1873 Tooling-gouge, 1876 Tooling-iron [see TOOL *v.* 1].

**Toolless** (tū·l,lės), *a.* [f. TOOL *sb.* + -LESS.] Having no tools; destitute of tools.

1831 *Fraser's Mag.* III. 13 Art thou lonely, idle, friendless, toolless? 1889 H. O. PENTECOST in *20th Cent.* (N. Y.) 30 Mar., So low has the landless and toolless man fallen that work seems to him now the greatest boon in life.

**Toolsee, -si, -sy,** variant forms of TULSI.

**Toolsman** (tū·lzmæn). *rare*[−1]. A man who uses tools, a craftsman.

1821 T. G. WAINWRIGHT *Ess. & Cr.* (1880) 193 *note*, That mannered petty toolsman, Raffaëlle Morghen—the admiration of fallen, immasculate Italy.

**Toolter**: see TOLTER *a.* **Tooly,** obs. f. TEWLY *a.*, sickly. **Tooly, -lye,** var. TUILYIE.

† **Toom,** *sb.*[1] *Obs.* (in later use only *Sc.*) Forms: 3–6 tome, 4 tom, (toume, towme, toym), 5 toom, 6 tume. [a. ON. *tóm* sb. neut. emptiness, vacuity, leisure, OSw. *tōm* leisure, occasion, ODa. *tōm* time, occasion; f. *tómr* adj. empty: see TOOM *a.*] Vacant or unoccupied time; time free or sufficient for doing something, leisure; a space or interval of time, a while.

1297 R. GLOUC. (Rolls) 11656 In hor bed hii founde hom in toune þo hii come..Vor to wel cloþi hom hii ne ȝeue hom no tome. *a* 1300 *Cursor M.* 14595 Haf i na tome at ga þar-to. *c* 1315 SHOREHAM I. 2119 Þaȝ he by hyre ne ligge nouȝt, Oþer halt hys ine hys house, In tome. 13.. *E. E. Allit. P.* A. 134 More..Þen I cowþe telle þaȝ I tom hade. 1375 BARBOUR *Bruce* V. 642 Or þe toþir had toym to tak His suerde, þe king sic swak him gaiff. *c* 1430 *Syr Gener.* (Roxb.) 3126 Of Generides dome To speke had thei nomore tome. 1535 STEWART *Cron. Scot.* (Rolls) II. 18 Ȝit will I tell, for I haif space & tume, How efterwart he set ane seig to Rome.

**b.** Time convenient or proper for doing something; opportunity, occasion.

13.. *E. E. Allit. P.* B. 1153 Ȝif ȝe wolde tith [*MS.* tyȝt] me a tom telle hit I wolde. 1390 GOWER *Conf.* I. 249 His Bacheler, which hadde tome, Whan that his lord be nihte slepte, This Ring,..Out of his Pours awey he dede. *c* 1440 *York Myst.* xl. 18 Atte townes for to tarie take we no tent, But take vs tome at þis tyme to taike of sume tales. *c* 1450 *Bk. Curtasye* 10 in *Babees Bk.* 299 Ther-to the nedys to take the tome.

**Toom,** *sb.*[2] *Sc.* [f. TOOM *v.*] A place where rubbish is or may be emptied out; a 'coup'.

1882 JAMIESON, *Toom*, a place into which rubbish is emptied. 1884 *Blackw. Mag.* June 817/1 The piled-up rubbish of millions of years which has been cast out here as into one vast 'toom'. 1894 CROCKETT *Raiders* 226 Great tails [of stones] that spread down the mountain steep, like rubble from a quarry toom.

**Toom** (tūm: in mod.Sc. tŏm, tüm), *a.* Now only *Sc.* and *north. dial.* Forms: *α.* 1 tóm, 3–6 tōme, (5 tombe, toyme, 6 towme), 5–7 toome, 5– toom. *β.* 4 tum, 4–7 tume, 6 twme, (?) twyme, 9 *Sc.* tume, tuim. *γ.* 8–9 teem, 9 *dial.* teeam. [OE. *tóm* = ON. *tómr* (Norw., Da., Sw. *tom*); also OS. *tômi, tōmig*, OHG. *zuomīg*:—OTeut. **tōm-o*[z] or **tōm-u*[z] (OS. *tōmia-*); ulterior origin unknown. Hence TEEM *v.*[2]]

**1.** Empty, vacant, containing nothing, void of contents; destitute (*of* something).

*a* 900 CYNEWULF *Christ* 1211 Þæt hy mostun man-weorca tome lifȝan. *a* 1300 *Cursor M.* 17798 And yee sal find þair tumbs tome [*Gött.* tume]. *Ibid.* 17815 Þai sagh þaa tumbs, tum war þai. *a* 1340 HAMPOLE *Psalter* cxliii. 16 Ful of riches and tome of goednes. *c* 1400 MAUNDEV. (Roxb.) xxxiii. 149 When þai see þe toome vessellez, þai ga and fillez þam with gold. 1435 MISYN *Fire of Love* II. iv. 76 Certan of godis lufe þat ar toyme. *c* 1440 *Promp. Parv.* 496/2 Toom, or voyde, *vacuus*. *c* 1470 HENRYSON *Mor. Fab.* I. (*Cock & Jasp*) iv, As draf, or corne, to fill my tume Intraill. 1508 KENNEDIE *Flyting w. Dunbar* 365 Thow has a tome purs. 1560 ROLLAND *Seven Sages* (1837) 1 Of all vertew that Ceitie was maid tome. 1727 P. WALKER *R. Cameron* in *Biog. Presbyt.*

(1827) I. 241 There were many toom pulpits in Scotland. **1786** BURNS *Earnest Cry & Prayer* vii, Her mutchkin stoup as toom's a whissle. **1831** CARLYLE *Sart. Res.* III. vi, The man John Baliol being quite gone, and only the 'Toom Tabard' (Empty Gown) remaining. **1855** ROBINSON *Whitby Gloss.* s.v., As toom as an egg-shell.

γ. *a* **1774** FERGUSSON *Hallowfair* Poems (1845) 14 Here, tak a rug, and show your pose Forseeth, my ain's but teem And light the day. **1861** E. WAUGH *Lake Country* 180 He was as helpless as a teeam seck.

**2.** *fig.* Empty, insubstantial, vain, void, futile.

*a* **1250** *Owl & Night.* 1672 Me þuncþ þu ledest ferde tome. **1513** DOUGLAS *Æneis* VI. iv. 120 The tume schaddowis smytyn to haue slane. **1568** *Satir. Poems Ref.* xlvi. 27 Till deif ȝow wᵗ tome clatter. **1721** RAMSAY *Prospect of Plenty* 46 O'er lang, with empty brag, we have been vain Of toom dominion on the plenteous main. **1786** G. FRAZER *Fall of Man* 157 Blown up with the toom wind of a flattering empty sound.

†**b.** Idle, unoccupied. *Obs.*

*a* **1340** HAMPOLE *Psalter* xlix. 21 Sitand tome [*MS. S.* ydel], for it likes þe to speke ill. *c* **1460** *Towneley Myst.* xxx. 125 To stand thus tome thou gars me grete.

**3.** *Comb.*, as *toom-handed*, *-headed*, *-skinned* adjs.

*c* **1400** MAUNDEV. (Roxb.) xxv. 120 Na man comme in my sight tome hand. **1629** Z. BOYD *Balme of Gilead* 21 (Jam.) A man as we say that hath not harnes, or brain, a toome headed man. **1768** ROSS *Helenore* Introd. 4 Ye're nae toom handed gin your heart be free. **1824** MACTAGGART *Gallovid. Encycl.*, *Toom-skin'd*, hungry.

**Toom,** *v. Sc.* and *north. dial.* Forms: see prec. [f. TOOM *a.*, taking the place of the earlier TEEM *v.*²]

**1.** *trans.* To empty (a vessel, receptacle, etc.); *esp.* to empty by drinking, to drink off the contents of.

**1500–20** DUNBAR *Poems* xxvi. 64 Ay as thay tomit thame of schot, Ffeyndis fild thame new vp to the thrott With gold of allkin prent. **1580** *Burgh Rec. Edinb.* (1882) IV. 187 The inhabiteris..maist filthely castes furth and tomes thair closettis and pottis on the hie gaitt. **1583** *Leg. Bp. St. Androis* Pref. 136 Concluding this, we toome a tass of wyne. **1721** RAMSAY *Prospect of Plenty* 106 They'll toom their banks before you reap their crap. **1896** 'IAN MACLAREN' *Kate Carnegie* 71 Toom..yir mooth this meenut and say the twenty-third Psalm to the minister.

**2.** To empty out, discharge, pour out (water, the contents of a vessel, etc.).

**1535** STEWART *Cron. Scot.* (Rolls) II. 630 This ilk Banquho, the quhilk the aill gart brew,..Amang the aill gart tume thame in the fat. **1816** SCOTT *Antiq.* xxxvi, She..was like to hae toomed it a' out into the slap-basin. **1818** — *Hrt. Midl.* xxviii, Our gawsie Scots pint..toomed doun the creature's throat wi' ane whorn.

**Toomatoogooroo,** variant of TUMATA-KURU.

**Toomble,** obs. form of TUMBLE.

†**Too·mhead.** *Obs. rare.* In 3 tomehed(e. [f. TOOM *a.* + -HEAD.] Emptiness, vanity. *Over tomehed*, uselessly, to no purpose.

*a* **1300** *E. E. Psalter* xxiv. 4 Schente be alle are quede doand Ouer tomehed in ani land. *Ibid.* xxxiv. 7 Ouer tomehede vpbraided þai.

**Too·mly,** *adv. Sc.* and *north. dial.* [f. TOOM *sb.*¹ and *a.* + -LY ².]

**1.** In a leisurely way; somewhat slowly; without haste.

*c* **1400** *Destr. Troy* 2447 When he told hade his tale tomly to the ende. *Ibid.* 11488 Antenor his tale tombly began.

**2.** †**a.** Idly, without occupation. *Obs.* **b.** Emptily, vainly, to no purpose.

*c* **1400** *Destr. Troy* 4580 Ye haue tarit ouer tyme tomly at home. **1606** BIRNIE *Kirk-Buriall* (1833) 5 Rather to teach what the kirk should doe nor toomely to talke what hes beene done.

**3.** With empty saddle.

**17..** '*Willie's drowned in Gamery*' xi. in Child *Eng. & Sc. Ball.* VII. (1890) 181/2 And every one on high horse sat, But Willie's horse rade toomly.

**Toompe,** obs. form of TUMP.

†**Too·msome,** *a. Obs. rare*⁻¹. [f. TOOM *sb.*¹ + -SOME.] Leisurely, free from haste.

**13..** *Cursor M.* 26350 (Fairf.) Shrift..þer ar xv pointis to shaw..Clene & reuful..wreiande, tomsome [*Cott.* (*erron.*) turnsum] propre, stedefast [etc.].

‖**Toon, tun** (tūn). *E. Ind.* [a. Hindī *tun*, *tūn*, Skr. *tunna*.] An East Indian tree, *Cedrela Toona*, which yields a timber resembling mahogany but softer and lighter, used for furniture and cabinetwork: the wood of this tree, also called *Indian mahogany*. Also *attrib.*, as *toon-tree*, *-wood*.

**1810** MARIA GRAHAM *Jrnl. Resid. India* (1812) 101 The toon, or country mahogany, which comes from Bengal. **1843** HOLTZAPFFEL *Turning* I. 108 Toon-wood has already been mentioned under the head of Cedar. **1879** MRS. A. E. JAMES *Ind. Househ. Managem.* 28 The wood they use mostly in the Punjaub is toon...It is valuable from its durability, and is reddish in colour.

**Toon,** obs. pl. of TOE; obs. f. TONE, TUN; north. dial. f. TOWN. **Toondra,** var. TUNDRA. **Toopick,** obs. f. TOPIC. **Toor, toore,** var. TOR *a.*, *Obs.*, difficult. **Toord,** obs. f. TURD. **Toorkes,** obs. f. TURQUOISE. **Toos**(e, obs. f. *toes*, pl. of TOE. **Toose,** obs. f. TOZE. **Toosie, toosy,** var. TOSY, TOUSY. **Toost,** obs. pa. pple. of TOSS *v.*

**Toot, tote** (tūt), *sb.*¹ *local.* Also 5–9 tout. [f. TOOT *v.*¹]

**I. 1.** An isolated conspicuous hill suitable as a place of observation; a look-out hill; perh. short for TOOT-HILL, q. v. Chiefly *south-western.*

**1387** TREVISA *Higden* (Rolls) III. 85 Temples þat were on groues vppon hiȝe totes [CAXTON or hilles], to worschippe mawmetes inne. *Ibid.* V. 163 Þe eorþe aroos in þe manere of a tote [so *MSS.* α, β, γ, *and* CAXTON; *Camb. MS.* tufte]. **1884** D. CLAYFIELD IRELAND *Let.*, In the west of England I think 'fairy toot' is a tolerably common topographical expression. And there is a curious jagged and pointed hill a few miles from Bristol known as Cleeve toot. **1904** *Daily News* 15 June 5 In the West of England..'toot' signifies hill. **1905** *Eng. Dial. Dict.*, *Toot*,..a hilly promontory, on which there is a coast-guard watch-station and flag. *Mod.* (South Dorset) There's one of the preventive-men on the tout.

†**2.** An elevated structure, or part of one, used as a look-out. *Obs.*

**1770** GRAY *Jrnl. in Lakes* 12 Oct., I went up a winding stone staircase.., and at the angle is a single hexagon watch-tower rising some feet higher, fitted up in the taste of a modern Toot, with sash-windows in gilt frames, and a stucco cupola. **1785** GROSE *Dict. Vulg. Tongue*, *Tout*, a look out house, or eminence.

**II. 3.** A peep or glance. *dial.*

**1865** E. WAUGH *Lanc. Songs* (1871) 56 Th' cat pricks up her ears at th' sneck, Wi' mony a leetsome toot.

**4.** *Comb.*: †**tote-hole**, a hole for spying: cf. *tooting-hole* (TOOTING *vbl. sb.*¹ b).

**1561–6** *Child-Marriages* 113 Lokid in at a tote hole.

**Toot** (tūt), *sb.*² Also *Sc.* tout (tūt). [f. TOOT *v.*²] An act of tooting; a note or short blast of a horn, trumpet, or other wind instrument. Also *fig.*

**1641** *D. Ferguson's Scot. Prov.* (1785) 7 A new tout in an old horn. **1714** RAMSAY *Elegy on J. Cowper* vi, Fame, Wi' tout of trumpet, Shall tell. **1721** KELLY *Scot. Prov.* 28 An old Tout in a new Horn. Spoken when we hear (perhaps in other words) what we have heard before. **1765** BOSWELL in Ramsay *Scot. & Scotsm.* (1888) I. ii. 172 James has taken a tout on a new horn. **1787** BURNS *Tam Samson's Elegy* 59 Now he proclaims, wi' tout o' trumpet, 'Tam Samson's dead!' **1822** SCOTT *Nigel* xxvii, It is just a new tout on an auld horn. **1874** D. MACRAE *Amer. at Home* xlii. 327 She gave two 'toots' with her steam-pipe.

**b.** Reduplicated *toot-toot*; so *toot-tootling*.

**1883** S. C. HALL *Retrospect* I. 7 How pleasant..the jovial toot-toot of the guard's horn. **1904** MARIE CORELLI *God's Good Man* xx, With a weird toot-tootling of his horn he guided the car at quite a respectable ambling-donkey pace. **1905** *Daily Chron.* 19 May 4/7 Of all the noises of London the 'toot-toot' of the motor-car is the most hideous.

**Toot, tout** (tūt), *sb.*³ *Sc.* and *U.S.* [f. TOOT, TOUT *v.*³ *Tout* is Sc. spelling of (tūt).]

**1.** An act or fit of tooting; a copious draught.

**1787** SHIRREFS *Jamie & Bess* I. ii, Were he ay [sober], he then wad ay be kind, But then, anither tout may change his mind. **1816** G. MUIR *Clydesdale Minstr.* 56 (E.D.D.) To your health I'll drink a tout Frae out the whisky gill. **1902** OGILVIE *J. Ogilvie* 96 (ibid.) Sit doon an' tak a hearty tout.

**2.** A drinking match; a drunken fit, a spree (*U.S. slang*); esp. in the phrase *on the toot*; hence, a tea-party.

**1790** SHIRREFS *Poems* Gloss., *Tout*, a drinking-bout, a drinking match. **1891** *Century Mag.* Nov. 54 Grubbsy's went off on a toot, and they've got nobody to ride. **1897** HOWELLS *Landl. Lion's Head* 228 To-day I found him at Mrs. Bevidge's altruistic toot. **1900** LYNCH *High Stakes* xxxii. (Farmer *Slang*), I'd never 'a' carried 'em..if I 'adn't been on a regular toot for the last week.

**Toot** (tūt), *sb.*⁴ *dial.* and *U.S.* [Origin obscure.]

**1.** An idle or worthless person; a simpleton, fool.

**1888** *Harper's Mag.* Oct. 801/1 Marsh Yates, the 'shiftless toot', and his beautiful, energetic wife. **1889** T. E. BROWN *Manx Witch*, etc. 118 Be off, you brute!..you donkey! you thundh'rin toot! **1894** HALL CAINE *Manxman* 157 Success to the fine girl,..lucky they kept her from the poor toot.

**2.** *dial.* 'The devil, *Linc.*' (Halliw.).

**Toot** (tūt), *sb.*⁵ [Anglicized form of the Maori name *tutu.*] A shrub or small tree, *Coriaria ruscifolia*, of New Zealand. It bears shining pulpy black berries containing poisonous seeds, with an action similar to that of strychnine.

**1857** R. WILKIN in C. Hursthouse *N. Zealand* xiii. 372 The plant called 'tutu' or 'toot'..appears to be universal over New Zealand. **1872** *Routledge's Ev. Boy's Ann.* 40/2 Toot is a poisonous shrub of which cattle are very fond.

‖**Toot,** *sb.*⁶ [Hindī *tut.*] The White Mulberry of India (*Morus alba*).

**1879** MRS. A. E. JAMES *Ind. Househ. Managem.* 59 Nectarines, plums, tamarinds, toots, bairs, are all more or less grown. **1898** *Globe* 15 Jan. 1/4 The 'toot' is a ridiculous-looking Indian fruit, which some hold to be an excellent corrective of overnight intoxication.

**Toot** (tūt), *v.*¹ Now *dial.* Forms: 1 tótian, 3–4 tōten, 4–7 tote, toote, 5– toot. [OE. *tótian*, a word of single occurrence (see quot. *c* 897), of which ME. *tōte*, *toote*, and mod. *toot* are the regular representatives. OE. had also *týtan* (:—*tūtjan*) to peep out, become visible, as a star; and ME. had *tūten*, mod. TOUT *v.*¹ These indicate two synonymous OE. and OTeut. stems, *tôt-* and *tût-*, the relation between which is obscure. See Note below.]

**1.** *intr.* To protrude, stick *out*, 'peep *out*', so as to be seen; in *mod. dial.*, of a plant, to begin to appear above ground.

*c* **897** K. ÆLFRED *Gregory's Past. C.* xvi. 104 Se ceac.. oferhelede ða oxan ealle, butan þa heafdu totodun ut. *c* **1394** *P. Pl. Crede* 425 Wiþ his knopped schon clouted full þykke His ton toteden out as he þe londe treddede. *c* **1400** *Destr. Troy* 9540 He was brochit þurgh the body with a big speire, Þat a trunchyn of þe tre tut out behynd. **1519** *Four Elements* (1905) 38 Now rise up, Master Huddypeke, Your tail toteth out behind. **1593** [see *tooting* below]. *c* **1645** [see TOTING *ppl. a.*]. **1777** *Antiq.* in *Ann. Reg.* 149/2 When pease in Derbyshire first appear they are said to toot. **1808–18** JAMIESON, *Tute*, to jut out, to project. [North of Sc.] *c* **1880** *Northampt. Dial.*, I can just see the taters tooting out of the ground.

**2.** *intr.* To peep, peer, look out; to gaze; = TOUT *v.*¹ 1.

*a* **1225** *Ancr. R.* 52 Is hit nu so ouer vuel uor to toten [*MS. T.* lokin] utward? Auh toten vt wiðuten vuel ne mei nouðer of ou. *c* **1300** *Havelok* 2106 He stod, and totede in at a bord. **1377** LANGL. *P. Pl.* B. XVI. 22 Pieres þe plowman.. bad me toten on þe tree. *c* **1400** *Destr. Troy* 862 Sho went vp..To the toppe of a toure, & tot ouer the water For to loke on hir luffe. **1529** MORE *Dyaloge* III. Wks. 225/1 Into the one [wallet]..he putteth other folkes faultes, and therein he toteth and poreth often. **1553** BRADFORD *Serm. Repent.* (1574) D ij b, Get thee Gods law as a glas to toote in. **1603** SIR C. HEYDON *Jud. Astrol.* iv. 140 While the Astrologer tooteth vpward, and examineth in what signe is the Moone. **1884** DOHERTY *N. Barlow* iv. 27 Let cheeky folk as come wi' stools to toot Sit theer an' stare.

**b.** To look inquisitively; to pry.

**1390** GOWER *Conf.* III. 29 Riht so doth he, whan that he pireth And toteth on hire wommanhiede. **1546** J. HEYWOOD *Prov.* (1867) 57 On my maydes he is euer tootyng. **1550** LATIMER *Serm. Stamford* I. B ij b, Those obseruauntes were spyinge, totynge, and lookynge, watchynge and catchinge what they myghte heare or se against the sea of Rome. **1579** SPENSER *Sheph. Cal.* Mar. 66 With bowe and bolts.. For birds in bushes tooting. **1593** B. RICH *Greenes Newes* E iij b, One..who was walking by himselfe, prying and tooting in every corner. **1597–8** BP. HALL *Sat.* IV. ii. 45 Nor toot in Cheapside baskets earne and late To set the first tooth in some nouell-cate. **1829** in HUNTER *Hallamshire Gloss.* **1888** *Sheffield Gloss.*, *Toot*, to pry into anything.

†**c.** *trans.* To peep or look at; to behold, view.

*c* **1200** *Trin. Coll. Hom.* 211 Ech man þe þerto cumeð pleie to toten, oðer to listen, oðer to bihelden. *c* **1394** *P. Pl. Crede* 142 Whow myȝt-tou in thine broþer eiȝe a bare mote loken, And in þyn owen eiȝe nouȝt a bem toten. *Ibid.* 219 Þanne turned y aȝen, whan y hade all y-toted.

Hence **Tooting** *ppl. a.*, in 3 totinde, looking out, peeping, prying, spying; protruding, sprouting.

*a* **1225** *Ancr. R.* 50 Vor nabbe ȝe nout þene nome..of totinde ancres. **1593** *Tell-troth's N. Y. Gift* (1876) 33 If there be any that hath a tooting head [of 'horns'], and would not haue it sene, let him keepe it secretely to himselfe. *c* **1645–1676** [see TOTING *ppl. a.*].

[*Note.* Words app. connected with OE. *tôtian*, *týtan*, ME. *tôte*, *tûte*, mod. *toot*, *tout*, are Du. *tuit* spout, snout, MDu. *tûte* nipple, pap, early mod.Du. (Kilian) *tote*, *tuyte* horn, apex, cone, also *tote* nipple, teat, LG. *tote* point, teat; also MLG. *tûte* horn, funnel, LG. *tûte*, *tût* spout, EFris. *tûte* pipe, spout, snout. Cf. also ON. *tûta* 'teat-like prominence' (Vigf.), *tota* teat, toe of a shoe, Norw. dial. *tota* something projecting, as a spout; Da. *tud* spout of a cask, Sw. *tut*, mod.Norw. *tût* also snout, horn; with many other derivatives all pointing to an original sense of something projecting or sticking out. Except Norw. *tyte*, 'to trickle or ooze out', the verbs appear only in Eng., where also the special sense of 'look or peep out' has been developed.]

**Toot** (tūt), *v.*² Also 6 tute, 6–7 tote, toote; 6 towt, 6, 7–9 *Sc.* tout. [Known only from *c* 1510. Cf. MLG., LG. *tûten*, also Ger. *tuten*, Du. *tuyten*, *toeten* to blow a horn; perh. originally echoic, imitating the sound of a horn, etc. Not related to ON. *þjóta* to blow a horn, whistle (see THEOTEN, in Ormin *þūtenn*, to howl); the Norw. *tûta*, Sw. *tūta*, Da. *tūde*, in same sense, are perh. influenced by LG., whence also the Eng. may have been taken.]

**I.** *intr.* **1.** Of a person: To sound or blow a horn or similar wind instrument. Also with extensions, *to toot it*, *to toot on*, *along*, *one's way*, etc.

**1549** CHALONER tr. *Erasmus' Moriæ Enc.* H j b, That foule musike, whiche a horne maketh, being tooted in. **1570** LEVINS *Manip.* 196/4 To Tute in a horne, *cornucinere.* **1693** J. H. tr. *Juvenal's Sat.* x. 4 See here a Troop of Horn-pipes toot along. **1698** FRYER *Acc. E. India & P.* 108 Tooting with their Trumpets, and beating with their Drums. **1707** E. WARD *Hud. Rediv.* II. VI. vi. 7 These led the Van, each crown'd with Feather Tooting harmoniously together. **1709** MRS. MANLEY *Secret Mem.* I. 149 A great many of 'em..can toot, toot, toot, it upon a Pipe. **1880** SPURGEON *J. Ploughm. Pict.* 29 We can all toot a little on our own trumpet. **1903** *Daily Chron.* 11 Nov. 4/5 The motor-car ..tooting its way through London.

**2.** Of a wind-instrument: To give forth its characteristic sound; to sound.

*c* **1510** *Kalender of Sheph.* li. M vij b, Take hede of my horne, totynge al alowde. **1595** MORLEY *1st Bk. Ballets* xi. C ij b, While as the Bagpipe tooted it. *a* **1800** *Lord Barnaby* xiii. in Child *Ballads* II. 250/2 O lady, I heard a wee horn toot, And it blew wonder clear. **1894** *Daily News* 12 Mar. 2/1 The guard's long tapering horn never toots more merrily.

**3.** Of an animal: To make a sound likened to that of a horn, etc.; to trumpet as an elephant, bray as an ass; *spec.* of grouse, to 'call'.

**1817** COBBETT *Wks.* XXXII. 10 The trick answered very well 'till the Ass began to bray, or toot. *a* **1835** HOGG *Ringan & May* 39 The storm-cock touts on his towering pine. **1877** HALLOCK *Sportsman's Gazetteer* 119 The 'tooting' is the call of the male bird. *Ibid.* 124 The (pinnated) Grouse in the spring commences about April to 'toot', and can be heard nearly a mile. **1890** *Century Mag.* Feb. 613/1 The elephants..raised their trunks, and tooted as no locomotive could toot.

**b.** Said of a person, esp. a child: see quots.

**1808–18** JAMIESON, *Toot*, to make a plaintive noise, as when a child cries loud or mournfully. **1847–78** HALLIWELL *Toot*, to whine or cry.

**II.** *trans.* **4.** To cause (a horn, etc.) to sound by blowing it. Also *transf.* of an animal.

1682 FOUNTAINHALL *Decis.* (1759) I. 182 Suffering Brown then preaching and praying, to be affronted by boys, who touted horns. 1841 FARADAY in B. Jones *Life* (1870) II. 131 At the call of the goat-herd, who tooted a cow's horn. 1890 *Century Mag.* Feb. 613/2 The elephant..tooting his trumpet as though in great fright. 1899 *Daily Graphic* 19 Aug. 7 The Monmouth's whistle was tooted vigorously, and the passengers crowded her rail.

**5.** To sound (notes, a tune, etc.) on a horn, pipe, or the like.

1614 W. BROWNE *Sheph. Pipe* II. C vij b, He..That sits on yonder hill, And tooteth out his notes of glee. c1662 F. SEMPILL *On Birth Princess Mary*, But let those brosie pack tout on..They'll tout anuther tune I true. 1842 BARHAM *Ingol. Leg.* Ser. II. *St. Aloys*, With eight Trumpeters tooting the Dead March in Saul.

**6.** To call out aloud, to shout (something).

1582 STANYHURST *Æneis* IV. (Arb.) 107, In this eare hee towted thee speeche. 1653 URQUHART *Rabelais* II. xx. 143 They to toote, Draw, give (page) some wine here reach hither. 1756 MRS. CALDERWOOD in *Coltness Collect.* (Maitl. Club) 249 You will see them [beggars] standing at a door, and touting a Pater noster through the key-hole.

**b.** To proclaim loudly; to trumpet abroad. *Sc.*

a1810 TANNAHILL *Poems* (1846) 57 Ilk rising generation toots his fame, And hun'er years to come, 'twill be the same. 1887 SERVICE *Dr. Duguid* III. iv. 258 There were plenty to carry the news...It was tootit owre a' the kintra-side.

Hence **Too·ting** *ppl. a.*, that toots, as a horn, siren, etc.

1652 BENLOWES *Theoph.* XI. xxx, Still to have toting Waits unseal thine eyes. 1668 SHADWELL *Sullen Lovers* I. i, Those rogues that..upon their toting instruments make a more hellish noise than they do at a play-house. 1909 *Daily Chron.* 16 Sept. 1/1 No tooting whistles signalled our departure.

**Toot, tout** (tūt), *v.*3 *Sc.* and *U.S.* [In Sc. *tout* (tūt), in Anglicized spelling *toot*. Of obscure origin, perh. orig. thieves' cant. Cf. Sw. (vulgar or familiar) *tūta* to drink grog; but this is perh. from Eng.]

**1.** *intr.* 'To drink copiously; to take a large draught' (Jam.).

1676, a1700 [see *tooting* below]. a1774 R. FERGUSSON *Drink Ecl.* 64 At thee they toot, an' never spear my price. 1813 A. CUNNINGHAM *Songs* 7 She sat singing..And touting at the rosie wine.

**2.** *trans.* 'To empty the vessel from which one drinks, to drink its whole contents' (Jam.). Const. *off, out, up.*

a1774 R. FERGUSSON *Leith Races* xiii, They'll ban fu' sair the time That e'er they toutit aff the horn. 1788 G. TURNBULL *Poet. Ess.* 199 He leugh and toutit up the liquor Out ilka drap. 1811 C. GRAY in Whitelaw *Bk. Scot. Song* 260 'Tis sweet to tout the glasses out.

**3.** *intr.* To go on a spree; to make a night of it. *U.S.*

1890 GUNTER *Miss Nobody* xvii, Spreeing, gaming, and tooting all night.

Hence **Too·ting, tou·ting** *vbl. sb.*, drinking, toping; in †*touting-ken* (*obs. slang*), a drinking-house.

1676 COLES *Dict.*, *Touting-ken*, tavern-bar. a1700 B. E. *Dict. Cant. Crew*, *Touting-ken*, a Tavern or Ale-house Bar.

**Toot, too't, to't,** coalesced form of *to it.*

1596 SHAKS. *Tam. Shr.* I. ii. 195 Too't a Gods name. 1605 CHAPMAN *All Fooles* Plays 1873 I. 170, I will not set my hand toot. 1607 SHAKS. *Timon* III. vi. 37 We shall too't presently. 1828 in *Craven Gloss.*

**Toot, toots,** Sc. form of TUT, *tuts* interj.

**Tootanag,** obs. form of TUTENAG.

†**Too·ter**1. *Obs.* [f. TOOT *v.*1 + -ER1.]

**1.** One who gazes; a watchman; a prier or peeper.

1382 WYCLIF *Isa.* xxi. 6 Go, and put a tootere [1388 lokere]; and what euere thing he shal see, telle he. *Ibid.* lii. 8 The vois of thi tooteres. 1550 LATIMER *Serm. at Stamford* I. Bij b, Obseruantes, yt is watchers, toters, spies. 1583 STUBBES *Anat. Abus.* II. (1882) 57 As these foolish starre tooters promised. 1598 FLORIO, *Bugigattolo*, a sneaker, a pryer into corners, a tooter.

**2.** Something that projects; in quot., a prominent nose.

1638 SHIRLEY *Duke's Mistr.* IV. i, *Val.* Examine but this nose. *Scol.* I have a toter. *Val.* Which placed with symmetry is like a fountain I' the middle of her face.

**Tooter**2 (tū·təɹ). Also 7 to(a)ter. [f. TOOT *v.*2]

**1.** One who toots, or plays on a wind-instrument; a trumpeter or piper.

1620 THOMAS *Lat. Dict.*, *Vocalis*..a tooter, a piper. 1623 FLETCHER & ROWLEY *Maid in Mill* III. i, Hark hark! these Toaters tell us the King's coming. 1633 B. JONSON *Tale Tub* v. v, Come, Father Rosin, with your fiddle now, As two tall toters; flourish to the masque. 1907 *Daily Chron.* 29 Jan. 4/7 A tutor who tootled a flute Tried to teach two young tooters to toot.

**2.** A horn or other wind-instrument.

1860 O. W. HOLMES *Prof. Breakf.-t.* viii, A boy..loves to ..blow squash 'tooters'. 1896 D. S. MELDRUM *Grey Mantle* 108 The guard's blowing it about like a blast on his tooter. 1897 KIPLING *Captains Courageous* 169 'Gimme the tooter'. Dan took the tin dinner-horn, but paused before he blew.

**Tooth** (tūþ), *sb.* Pl. **teeth** (tīþ). Forms: see below, sense 1. [OE. *tōþ, tōð* (:—**tanþ*), Com. Teut. and Com. Indo-Eur.; OFris. *tôth, tond* (NFris. *tôth*, EFris. *tond*); OS. *tand* (MLG. *tand, tan*, LG. *tan*; MDu. *tant* (*d*), Du. *tand*; OHG. *zana, zan* (MHG. *zant, zan*, Ger. *zahn*); ON. *tǫnn* (:—*tanþuz*; Sw., Da. *tand*, NNorw. *tonn*); beside Gothic *tunþus*; :—OTeut. **tanþ*- and **tunþ*- :—Indo-Eur. *dent, dont, dnt*, whence Skr. *dan, danta*, Gr. ὀ-δούς (ὀ-δόντ-ς), L. *dens* (*dent-s*), OIr. *dét* (**dent*), W. *dant*, Lith. *dantìs*. The termination agrees with that of pr. pples., whence Pott conjectured an original **ed-ont-*, pr. pple. of *ed-* to eat; i.e. 'an eater'. OE. *tōþ* was originally a masculine consonantal stem, with dative sing. *tēþ* (:—*tōþi*), pl. nom. *tēþ* (:—**tōþiz*), gen. *tōþa*, dat. *tōþum* (in early ME. *toþen*). A rare pl. *tōþas* after masc. *-o-* stems also occurs. An umlaut pl. is seen also in OFris. *têth*, MLG. *tene*, LG. *täne*, OHG. *zeni*, MHG. *zene*, Ger. *zähne*. In use the plural is much more frequent than the singular, and in some dialects the latter is sometimes assimilated to it as 'a teeth'.

A double plural *teeths* was formerly (and is still *dial.*) used in speaking of a number of persons; e.g. *in spite of their teeths*, pl. of *in spite of his teeth*: see senses 4 d, 5.]

**1.** In plural, the hard processes within the mouth, attached (usually in sockets) in a row to each jaw in most vertebrates except birds (but also in some extinct birds), having points, edges, or grinding surfaces, and serving primarily for biting, tearing, or trituration of solid food, and secondarily as weapons of attack or defence, and for other purposes; in singular, each of these individually.

In mammals usually consisting of dentine coated with cement around the root and with enamel in the exposed part; but in some cases horny, chitinous, or osseous. In some animals, also occurring on other parts, as the tongue or pharynx. Also, applied to similar or analogous structures occurring in the mouth or alimentary canal in some invertebrates.

*Sing.* 1 **tōð** (*dat.* **tēð**), 1–4 **tóþ** (3 **toþþ** *Orm.*), 4–5 **toþe**, 4–6 **toth, tothe, tuth**; 5 **tooþ** (**thothe, toyth, toeth, tuthe**), 5–6 **toothe**; 5– **tooth.** (Also 6 **touthe**, *Sc.* **twth, twith, twithe**, 6–7 **touth**, 6– *Sc.* **tuith.** The shortened vowel in Ormin's *toþþ* is anomalous: see TOTH.)

a900 K. ÆLFRED *Laws* c. 19 Selle his aȝen fore, toð fore teð. c975 *Rushw. Gosp.* Matt. v. 38 Eȝe for eȝe toð for toþ. c1250 *Gen. & Ex.* 4148 Ðoȝ him lestede hise siȝte briȝt, And euerilc toð bi tale riȝt. a1300 *Cursor M.* 23798 To tell þe soth, Bath me wantes tung and toth [*v.r.* toþe, toþ]. 1382 WYCLIF *Matt.* v. 38 It is said, Eiȝe for eiȝe, toth for toth. a1425 *Cursor M.* 6040 (Trin.) A litil beest Of tooþ is not vnfoulest. 1481 CAXTON *Reynard* viii. (Arb.) 15 Olde wymen that..had not one teeth in her heed. 1483 *Cath. Angl.* 398/1 A Tuthe, *dens*. 1530 PALSGR. 282/1 Tothe, *dent*. 1562 TURNER *Herbal* II. 107 b, Pylletoris is good for the tuth ach if the tuth be wasshed with vinegre. 1620 SHELTON *Quix.* (1746) IV. ii. 11 Meddle not with a hollow Tooth. 1709–10 STEELE *Tatler* No. 127 ¶ 11 She has not a Tooth in her Head. 1852 THACKERAY *Esmond* I. ii, She was lean, and yellow, and long in the tooth.

*Pl.* 1 **tóeþ**, 1–4 **téþ, téð**, (*dat.* 1 **tóþum, -an**, 2–3 **-en**), (3 **tieth**), 4 **teþe** (**teþþe**, *Sc.* **tetht**), 4–5 **teeþ**, 4–6 **teth, tethe**, 5–6 **teethe, teithe**, 6 **teath**, (**tithe**), 5– **teeth** (*Sc.* 6– **teith**); also 1 **tóþas**, 6 **tothes.**

c725 *Corpus Gloss.* (O.E.T.) 1967 *Suaeder*, butan toðum. c825 *Vesp. Psalter* iii. 8 Toeð synfulra ðu forðræstes. c1000 *Life Guthlac* v. (1848) 34 Heora toþas wæron ȝelice horses twuxan. c1000 *Sax. Leechd.* III. 104 Oft man smeaþ hwæþer teþ bænene beon. c1200 *Vices & Virt.* 19 Ðar is chiueringe of toðen. a1225 *Ancr. R.* 288 His teð beoð attrie, ase of ane wode dogge. c1290 *S. Eng. Leg.* I. 206/228 With kene tieth al fuyrie. a1300 *Cursor M.* 19354 For tene þair tethe [*v.rr.* teþþe, teþ, teth, teeþ] to gnast. c1375 *Sc. Leg. Saints* i. 25 Vith his tetht he wald haf refyn sone. 1390 GOWER *Conf.* II. 245 A furgh of lond, in which a-rowe The teth of thaddre he moste sowe. 1483 *Cath. Angl.* 380/2 To drawe oute Tethe, *edentare*. 1486 *Bk. St. Albans* f vij, A Rage of the teethe. 1552 HULOET s.v., *Dentosus*, full of teath, or hauyng many teath. 1577 tr. *Bullinger's Decades* (1592) 54 [They] whet their teeth for anger. 1597 A. M. tr. *Guillemeau's Fr. Chirurg.* biij b/2 These artificialle teethe are sometimes made of Ivorye. 1598 Q. ELIZ. *Plutarch* xv. 3 Whan the think ther handz to slow the ad to ther tithe. 1653 WALTON *Compl. Angler* viii. 166 The Carp is..amongst those..fish which..have their teeth in their throat. 1705 VANBRUGH *Confed.* I. iii, There's the woman ..that sells paint and patches, iron-bodice, false teeth, and all sorts of things, to the ladies. 1812 *Examiner* 23 Nov. 752/2 Mrs. G. Gatehouse, in the 101st year of her age;.. cut her teeth about two years since. 1872 MIVART *Elem. Anat.* vii. (1873) 238 Our teeth are dermal structures.. developed from the deeper layer or enderon. 1888 ROLLESTON & JACKSON *Anim. Life* 115 A..lingual membrane bearing transverse rows of teeth [in the snail]. *Ibid.* 217 The three muscular jaws..bear at their edges in the medicinal Leech about 80–90 fine chitinoid teeth. *Ibid.* 348 New teeth in succession to old teeth are either formed without limit of numbers, as in most *Pisces, Amphibia, Reptilia*, or are restricted to a second set in some *Mammalia*.

**b.** *spec.* An elephant's tusk (projecting upper incisor tooth), as a source of ivory.

c1050 *Gloss.* in Wr.-Wülcker 397/27 *Eburneus dens*, elpend toþ. 1483 CAXTON *Gold. Leg.* 73/3 The nauye.. brouht..teeth of Olyphauntes. 1533 ELYOT *Cast. Helthe* (1539) 70 The olyphantes tothe. 1681 R. KNOX *Hist. Ceylon* 21 But few [elephants] have Teeth, and they males onely. 1720 DE FOE *Capt. Singleton* vi, The ground was scattered with elephants' teeth. 1897 MARY KINGSLEY *W. Africa* 325 Ivory is everywhere an evil thing...A very common way of collecting a tooth is to kill the person who owns one.

**c.** In expressions referring to speech (now esp. biting or angry speech).

a1300 *Cursor M.* 13941 Sal yee na leis here o mi toth. 13.. *Guy Warw.* (A.) 4385 Þou lexst amidward þi teþ, & þer-fore haue þou maugreþ. 1864 TENNYSON *Aylmer's Field* 328 So stammering 'scoundrel' out of teeth that ground As in a dreadful dream. *Mod.* Hissing 'Traitor!' through his clenched teeth.

**2.** *fig.* or in figurative expressions: **a.** referring to eating, esp. to the sense of taste; hence often = taste, liking (cf. *palate*). See also various phrases in 8.

c1386 CHAUCER *Wife's Prol.* 449, I wol kepe it for youre owene tooth. 1435 MISYN *Fire of Love* 36 My toyth continuly to myrth of songe was chaungyd. 1555 LATIMER in Strype *Eccl. Mem.* (1721) III. App. xxxvi. 103 For all theis things make you the meter for Gods tothe. 1579 LODGE *Def. Poetry* (Hunter. Cl.) 8 Will you haue all for yon owne tothe? 1598 LODGE & GREENE *Looking Glasse* G iij, The Smith and the diuel hath a drie tooth in his head. 1615 BP. HALL *Contempl.*, *Old Test.* XI. vii, A wanton tooth is the harbinger to luxurious wantonnesse. 1634 *Ibid.*, *N. T.* IV. iv, Well did Herodias know, how to fit the tooth of her paramour. 1675 COTTON *Scoffer Scoft* 6 And keep the best o' th' meat (forsooth) For your own Worships dainty tooth! 1704 J. PITTS *Acc. Mohammetans* ix. (1738) 210 He had a great Tooth for the Dey-ship. 1851 *Beck's Florist* Sept. 213 What a tooth for fruit has a monkey!

**b.** referring to biting or gnawing; hence denoting a hurtful, hostile, destructive, or devouring agency or quality. See also various phrases in III.

1546 PHAER *Bk. Childr.* (1553) A ij, It is impossible to auoide the teethe of malicious enuy. 1603 SHAKS. *Meas. for M.* v. i. 12 It deserues..A forted residence 'gainst the tooth of time. a1659 OSBORN *Ess.* ii. Wks. (1673) 560 Out of fear of the Iron-teeth of the Law. 1742 GRAY *Eton* 66 Jealousy with rankling tooth. a1765 YOUNG *Statesman's Creed*, Records that defy the tooth of time. 1816 BYRON *Prisoner of Chillon* ii, That iron is a cankering thing, For in these limbs its teeth remain, With marks that will not wear away. 1874 D. GRAY *Poet. Wks.* 89 'Tis April, yet the wind retains its tooth.

**II. 3.** *transf.* A projecting part or point resembling an animal's tooth; esp. one of a row or series of such. **a.** As an artificial structure, in an implement, machine, etc.; e.g. one of the pointed projections of a comb, saw, file, rake, harrow, fork, etc.; a prong, tine; one of the series of projections on the edge of a wheel, pinion, etc., which engage with corresponding ones on another; a cog.

1523 FITZHERB. *Husb.* § 24 If the rake be made of grene woode, .. the tethe wyll fall out, whan he hath mooste nede to them. 1577 B. GOOGE *Heresbach's Husb.* II. (1586) 106 b, [These] doe more fill the teeth of the Sawe. 1591 PERCIVALL *Sp. Dict.*, *Pua*,..the tooth of a combe. 1611 COTGR. s.v. *Allochons*, The teeth, or toothing, of a wheele, in a clocke, &c. 1639 T. BRUGIS tr. *Camus' Mor. Relat.* 169 But iron is never..brighter than when it hath been under the sharp teeth of the file. 1680 MOXON *Mech. Exerc.* x. 189 A great Iron Wheel, having Teeth on its edge. 1793 *Statist. Acc. Scotl.* VIII. 48 The teeth, or wooden pins [of a harrow] must be made long. 1807 ROBINSON *Archæol. Græca* IV. xv. 412 Anchors were made of iron, and furnished with teeth, ..fastening to the bottom of the sea. 1829 *Nat. Philos.* I. *Mechanics* II. vii. 27 (Usef. Knowl. Soc.) The cogs on the surface of the wheel are generally called teeth, and those on the surface of the axle are called leaves.

**b.** As a natural structure, in animals, plants, etc.; e.g. the odontoid process of the axis vertebra; a projecting point in the upper mandible of the bill in certain birds (cf. DENTIROSTER); each of a row of small projections on the edge of one valve of the shell in some bivalve molluscs; each of the pointed processes on the margin of leaves or other parts in many plants (cf. DENTATE), or of those forming the peristome of the capsule in mosses; also, generally, a projecting point of rock, etc.

1694–1815 [see AXIS1 2]. c1711 PETIVER *Gazophyl.* vii. 63 A small rugged Shell...Its Navel small with a Tooth or Knag in the Mouth. 1796 WITHERING *Brit. Plants* I. 253 Cal[yx]. Cup 1 leaf, concave, but expanding, with 5 teeth, permanent. 1847 CARPENTER *Zool.* iv. § 361 Its [the upper mandible of a bird of prey] edge is notched, so as to form a kind of projecting tooth on either side. *Ibid.* xviii. § 932 This hinge [in the shell of a bivalve mollusc] is sometimes formed..by a number of little projections or teeth, which fit into corresponding hollows in the opposite valve. 1861 MISS PRATT *Flower. Plants* IV. 88 (Toad-flax)..capsule swollen,..opening by valves or teeth. 1871 L. STEPHEN *Playgr. Eur.* v. (1894) 125 Great rocky teeth, striking up through their icy covering, like the edge of a saw. 1887 J. BALL *Nat. in S. Amer.* 210 The long stiff leaves, edged with sharp teeth.

**c.** An accidental jag or uneven projection at the edge of something.

1612 BRINSLEY *Lud. Lit.* 29 You may make your pen of the best of the quil, & where you see the cleft to be the cleanest, & without teeth.

**d.** A rough surface on paper, canvas, etc., such as to enable pencil-marks, colours, etc. to adhere; a roughness made by a toothing-plane on surfaces to be glued together, to promote adhesion of the glue. (Only in *sing.*)

1811 *Self Instructor* 525 The tooth or grain of the paper catching the crayons in dots. 1884 *Century Mag.* XXIX. 205/2 The substance worked upon being commonly rough paper, to the 'tooth' or burr of which the color partially adheres. 1894 MASKELYNE *Sharps & Flats* 232 [It] is roughened by rubbing it with coarse glass paper. This gives it a kind of 'tooth'. 1906 R. C. BAYLEY *Compl. Photogr.* 382 A polished sheet of copper..has its surface treated in some way to give it a very fine grain or tooth... Fine bitumen dust is generally employed.

**e.** *pl.* The lower zone of facets in a rose-diamond. **1877** in KNIGHT *Dict. Mech.*

**f.** *pl. fig.* A ship's guns. *Naut. slang.*

**1810** B. SILLIMAN *Jrnl. Trav.* (1820) III. 291 The ship had no teeth, as the sailors say, when they mean great guns. **1833** MARRYAT *P. Simple* xlvi, They were..large schooners, ..showing a very good set of teeth. **1849** W. S. MAYO *Kaloolah* ii, There's at least three rows of teeth beneath that mass of spars.

**III.** Phrases.

**4. In the teeth, in** (one's) **teeth. a.** In direct (local) opposition or attack; *in the teeth of*, in direct opposition to, so as to face or confront, straight against.

**1297** R. GLOUC. (Rolls) 8404 Our lord..þe smoke þat hii made ..Riȝt in hor owe teþ bigan hom euene sende. **1581** A. HALL *Iliad* VIII. 138 A Hector, who no lesse desires to meete them in the teeth. **1669** STURMY *Mariner's Mag.* I. ii. 18 The Wind is right in our teeth. **1737** WHISTON *Josephus, Wars* III. x. § 5 Others..met the enemy in the teeth. **1833** L. RITCHIE *Wand. by Loire* 160 They..had run into the teeth of a heavy barge full of armed men. **1892** EMILY LAWLESS *Grania* II. 7 He..had run across in the teeth of the rising gale.

**b.** *In the teeth of*, in direct and manifest opposition to, in defiance of, in spite of.

**1792** GOUV. MORRIS in Sparks *Life & Writ.* (1832) II. 160 State necessity will be urged in the teeth of policy, humanity, and justice. **1818** SCOTT *Hrt. Midl.* xxii[i], In no civil case would a counsel have been permitted to plead his client's case in the teeth of the law. **1847** L. HUNT *Jar Honey* x. (1848) 128 Why do you continue to live here, in the teeth of these repeated warnings? **1885** *Law Times* 13 June 113/1 A judge has no right to enter judgment in the teeth of the finding of a jury.

**c.** *In the teeth of*, in presence of, in the face of; usually implying hostility or danger; threateningly confronted by.

**1825** LAMB *Elia* Ser. II. *Barbara S.*, They were in fact in the very teeth of starvation. **1867** PARKMAN *Jesuits N. Amer.* xxvii. (1875) 381 His post was in the teeth of danger. **1876** BLACKMORE *Cripps* i, The Carrier scarcely knew what to do in the teeth of so urgent a message.

**d.** *To cast* (one) *in the teeth with* (something), later *to cast* (a thing) *in one's teeth* (see CAST *v.* 65), † *to hit* (one) *in the teeth with* (obs.), *to throw in* (one's) *teeth*: to reproach, upbraid, or censure with; to bring up in reproach against. (In quot. 1596 *to throw in* (one's) *teeth* = to send or direct defiantly against: cf. 4 b, 6 b.) Also in similar phrases expressing reproachful or defiant utterance.

**1535** COVERDALE *Matt.* xxvii. 44 The murtherers also that were crucified with him, cast the same in his tethe. **1548** PATTEN *Exped. Scotl.* Pref. biv b, Take it not that I hit you here in the teeth with oure good turnes. **1581** PETTIE tr. *Guazzo's Civ. Conv.* III. (1586) 147 Some..will not sticke to hit him in the teeth, that he was the sonne of [etc.]. **1596** SHAKS. *1 Hen. IV*, v. ii. 42 To Armes, for I haue thrown A braue defiance in King Henries teeth. **1614** DAY *Dyall* Ep. Ded., Caius of Cambridge did twit us in the teeth with some of our Founders here in Oxford that had been themselves Cambridge Men. **1619** W. WHATELEY *God's Husb.* ii. (1622) 53 He giueth to all liberally, and hitteth no man in the teeth. **1640** SIR W. BOSWELL in *Abp. Ussher's Lett.* (1686) App. 27 The main things that they hit in our teeth are, our Bishops to be called Lords. **1694** F. BRAGGE *Disc. Parables* xiii. 441 This neglect of family-devotions is often thrown in our teeth. **1819** KEATS *Otho* IV. ii. 105 In thy teeth I give thee back the lie! **1850** *Tait's Mag.* XVII. 441/2 Perpetually throwing in the teeth of the second wife the unrivalled virtues..of the first.

**5. In spite of** (*despite, maugre*, etc.) one's **teeth**: notwithstanding one's opposition or resistance; in spite of one, in defiance of one. Now *rare* exc. *dial.*

*c* **1230** *Hali Meid.* 47 He ȝarkeð þe unþonc hise teð þe blisse & te crune of cristes icorene. **13..** *K. Alis.* 5840 (Bodl. MS.) He..maugre þe teeþ of hem alle Sette his rigge to þe walle. *c* **1489** CAXTON *Sonnes of Aymon* iii. 86 He putte theym to flight, magre their teeth. **1549** LATIMER *2nd Serm. bef. Edw. VI* (Arb.) 73 A greate man keepeth certaine landes..and wilbe hyr tenaunte in the spite of hyr tethe. **1551** ROBINSON tr. *More's Utop.* II. viii. (1895) 260 Spyte of there tethes wrestynge owt of theire handes the sure and vndowbted victory. **1586** J. HOOKER *Hist. Irel.* in *Holinshed* II. 115/1 Which perforce and maugre of his teeth compelled him to retire with shame. **1586** T. B. *La Primaud. Fr. Acad.* I. (1594) 414 Compelling him..to be liberall in despite of his teeth. **1596** DANETT tr. *Comines* v. xv. (1614) 169 Constrained them spite of their teeth to depart the towne. **1598** GRENEWEY *Tacitus' Ann.* IV. ix. (1622) 103 Noble men which maugre thy teeth mount to authority. **1689** HICKERINGILL *Ceremony-Monger* iii. Wks. 1716 II. 482 Let the People go whistle, they are their Feeders and Pastors in Spight of their Teeths. **1712** ARBUTHNOT *John Bull* IV. vii, [We] will go on with the Lawsuit in spite of John Bull's teeth. **1835** *Court Mag.* VI. 74/2 Pleasing herself before his very eyes, in spite of his teeth.

**6. To the teeth. a.** So as to be completely equipped; very fully or completely: in *armed to the teeth*; so *entrenched up to their teeth.*

*c* **1380** *Sir Ferumb.* 2707 Þey wern y-armed in-to þe teþ & araid wel for þe fiȝt. **14..** *Lybeaus Disc.* 460 All yarmed to the teth. **1708** LUTTRELL *Brief Rel.* (1857) VI. 328 The French..are intrench't up to their teeth. **1845** FORD *Handbk. Spain* I. xi. 43 Everybody in Spain travels armed to the teeth.

**b.** *To* (one's) *teeth, to the teeth of*: intensive of ..ne's face'; directly and openly; defiantly; ..s directly to face, confront, or oppose.

.. *Erasm. Apoph.* 319 Cicero mocked hir to the .. sembleyng that he graunted hir saiyng [etc.].

**1583** MELBANCKE *Philotimus* L iv b, Though I praise you to your teeth. **1602** SHAKS. *Ham.* IV. vii. 57 That I shall liue and tell him to his teeth; Thus diddest thou. **1677** W. HUGHES *Man of Sin* III. iii. 79 Which..plainly gives them the lye unto their Teeths. **1680** OTWAY *Caius Marius* I. i, Now Romes last Stake of Liberty is set, And must be push'd for to the Teeth of Fortune. **1724** DE FOE *Mem. Cavalier* II. 189 The Foot.., coming close up to the Teeth of one another.., fought with great Resolution.

**7. Tooth and nail** (orig. *with tooth and nail*), advb. phr.: *lit.* with the use of one's teeth and nails as weapons; by biting and scratching: almost always *fig.*, in the way of vigorous attack, defence, or action generally; vigorously, fiercely, with one's utmost efforts, with all one's might.

**1534** MORE *Comf. agst. Trib.* III. xxii. (1573) 193 They would faine kepe them as long as euer they might, euen with tooth and naile. **1562** WINȜET *Cert. Tract.* Wks. (S.T.S.) I. 16 Contending with tuith and naill (as is the prouerb). **1568** V. SKINNER tr. *Montanus' Inquisition* 46 b, To perswade them tooth and naile, not to cleaue vnto that doctrine. **1579** W. WILKINSON *Confut. Familye of Love* 51 M. Harding fighteth for it tooth and naile. **1651** CULPEPPER *Astrol. Judgem. Dis.* (1658) 118 He will helpe it forward with tooth and naile. **1692** L'ESTRANGE *Josephus, Antiq.* xv. xi. (1733) 413 Salome and her Faction were Tooth and Nail for dispatching her out of Hand. **1719** D'URFEY *Pills* IV. 156 She flew in her Face Tooth and Nail. **1827** SCOTT *Jrnl.* 26 July, To-morrow I resume the Chronicles, tooth and nail. **1892** HUXLEY in *Life* (1900) II. xviii. 312, I am ready to oppose any such project tooth and nail.

*attrib.* **1900** *Century Mag.* Feb. 509/1 The tooth-and-nail fight to which they and their children were condemned.

†**b.** So *with teeth and all. Obs.*

*a* **1600** HOOKER *Eccl. Pol.* VIII. vi. § 2 Even with teeth and all they that favour the papal throne must hold the contrary.

**8.** Various phrases.

†**a. To have the teeth cold, to have cold at the teeth,** to suffer hunger, go hungry (*obs.*). **b. From the teeth forward**(s **or outward**(s (also *simply* **from one's teeth,** and *ellipt.* **teeth outward**(s)), formally or feignedly, in profession but not in reality (opp. to *from the heart*). †**c. To hide one's teeth,** *fig.* to conceal malice or hostile intention under a show of friendliness (opp. to *to show one's teeth*) (*obs.*). †**d. To love the tooth,** to be fond of eating, to be an epicure (*obs.*). **e. To set one's teeth,** to press or clench one's teeth firmly together from indignation, or fixed resolution as in facing danger, opposition, or difficulty; hence *fig.* or *allusively*; see also SET *v.* 95. **f. To show one's teeth,** *lit.* to uncover the teeth by withdrawing the lips from them, esp. as a beast in readiness for biting or attack; usu. *fig.* to show hostility or malice, to behave in a threatening way. **g. The teeth water,** a variant of *the mouth waters*: see MOUTH *sb.* 2 c (? *obs.*).

**a. 1484** CAXTON *Fables of Æsop* II. xv, Suche weren fayre gownes and fayr gyrdels of gold that haue theyr teeth cold at home. *Ibid.* IV. xvii, He that werketh not..shal haue ofte at his teeth grete cold. **b. 1570–6** LAMBARDE *Peramb. Kent* (1826) 420 They met..and from the teeth forwarde departed good friends againe. **1588** J. UDALL *Diotrephes* (Arb.) 27 Manye of them like vs but from the teeth outwarde. **1647** LILLY *Chr. Astrol.* lxxxviii. 459 They love not [one another], or but teeth outward. **1815** J. HOGG *Let.* 28 Feb., in Lockhart *Scott* xxxvi, To be friends from the teeth forwards is common enough. **c. 1714** T. ELLWOOD in *Life* 230 The Goaler..hid his Teeth,..putting on a shew of Kindness. **d. 1610** HOLLAND *Camden's Brit.* (1637) 543 Meates.. greatly sought for by these that love the tooth so well. **e. 1599** SHAKS. *Hen. V*, III. i. 15 Now set the Teeth, and stretch the Nosthrill wide. **1672** DRYDEN *Marriage-à-la-Mode* Epil. 28 You..set your teeth when each design fell short. **1823** SCOTT *Quentin D.* xxxii, 'If this should prove truth', said the Duke, setting his teeth, and pressing his heel against the ground. **1859** GEO. ELIOT *A. Bede* xxxvii, She set her teeth when she thought of Arthur: she cursed him. **1870** MORRIS *Earthly Par.* III. 350 Her teeth were set hard, and her brow was knit. **f. 1615** J. CHAMBERLAIN in *Crt. & Times Jas. I* (1848) I. 361 It were to no purpose to show our teeth unless we could bite. **1710** O. SANSOM *Acc. Life* 330 He somewhat appeared at the Sessions at Wantage; shewing his Teeth in what he could; and thereby discovering what lodged in his Heart against us. **1742** YOUNG *Love Fame* I. 17 When the law shews her teeth, but dares not bite. **1837** CARLYLE *Fr. Rev.* II. I. i, Such Patriotism as snarls dangerously and shows teeth. **g. 1600** HOLLAND *Livy* VII. xxx. 269 At it their teeth water, that most goodly and beautifull cittie will they either destroy, or be LL. thereof themselves. **1698** FARQUHAR *Love & Bottle* v. i, Oh, my little green gooseberry, my teeth waters at ye! **1724** LITTLETON *Lat. Dict.* (ed. 5) s.v., It makes my teeth water. *Salivam mihi movet.* [**1879**: see *teeth-watering* in 9 b.]

**h.** For other phrases see the words involved, as *To take the bit in one's teeth* (BIT *sb.*[1] 8 d), *to carry a bone in the teeth* (BONE *sb.* 14 b), *colt's tooth* (COLT *sb.* 8), *to cut one's teeth* (CUT *v.* 38), *to set the teeth on edge* (EDGE *sb.* 4), *to grind one's teeth* (GRIND *v.*[1] 10), *to have the run of one's teeth* (RUN *sb.* 32 b), *by* or *with the skin of one's teeth* (SKIN *sb.* 5 g), *a sweet tooth* (SWEET *a.*). For *to lie in one's teeth*, see 1 c.

**9.** *attrib.* and *Comb.*, as *tooth-dint, -dye, -extraction, -point, -stainer, -stump*; *tooth-bred, -chattering, -extracting, -like, -setting, -shaped, -tempting* adjs.; with many others of obvious meaning. Special combs.: **tooth-ax,** 'a stone-cutters' ax the edges of which are divided into blunt teeth' (*Cent. Dict. Suppl.*); **tooth-back,** a moth of the family *Notodontidæ*, or its larva, which has a tooth-like prominence on the back; so **tooth-backed** *a.*; **tooth-bearer** = ODONTOPHORE; †**tooth-blanch,** a substance for whitening the teeth, a dentifrice; **tooth-block,** a block forming part of a machine for moulding in sand the iron teeth of a gear-wheel; **tooth-bone,** (*a*) = DENTINE; (*b*) the bony substance or 'cement' of the teeth; **tooth-chisel,** a chisel with a toothed or serrated cutting edge, used by stone-masons; **tooth-cleaner,** a machine for dressing and finishing the teeth of cog-wheels (Knight *Dict. Mech.* Suppl. 1884); **tooth-comb,** a small-tooth comb; **tooth-coralline** = SERTULARIA; **tooth-cress** = TOOTHWORT 3; **tooth-doctor,** a dentist; **tooth-edge,** the sensation of having the teeth 'set on edge' (see EDGE *sb.* 4); **tooth-fern,** a rendering of *Odontopteris*, a genus of fossil ferns; **tooth-fever,** fever accompanying teething; **tooth-flower,** a name for *Dentella repens*, a small creeping herb found in Australia, Polynesia, etc., having a tooth-like process on each petal of the flower; **tooth-forceps,** a forceps used by a dentist for extracting teeth; **tooth-germ,** the 'germ' or growth of tissue from which a tooth is developed; †**tooth-iron,** ? an instrument for extracting teeth; **tooth-ivory** = DENTINE; †**tooth-key,** a dentist's instrument, turned like a key, formerly used for extracting teeth; **tooth-mark,** a mark made by a tooth in biting, or *transf.* by an edged tool; so **tooth-marked** *a.*; **tooth-mill,** a dentist's drill-stock or drilling-machine; **tooth ornament,** *Arch.* a kind of ornament or moulding suggesting a tooth or teeth: = DOG-TOOTH 3; †**tooth-pain** = TOOTHACHE; **tooth-paste,** a paste used for cleaning the teeth; **tooth-plane** = TOOTHING-*plane*; **tooth-plate** (*Dentistry*) = PLATE *sb.* 4 f; **tooth-plugger,** an instrument for filling or stopping decayed teeth (Knight 1884); **tooth-powder,** a powder used for cleaning the teeth, a dentifrice; also *attrib.*, as *tooth-powder box*; †**tooth-proof** *a.*, having tried strength or efficiency (cf. PROOF *a.* 1); **tooth-puller,** one who extracts teeth; **tooth-pulling,** extraction of a tooth or teeth; **tooth-pulp,** the soft cellular tissue around which the hard parts of a tooth are developed, and which fills the cavity of the fully formed tooth; **tooth-rail,** a tramway rail having teeth or cogs; **tooth-rake,** †(*a*) a toothpick (*obs.*); (*b*) a rake with teeth; **tooth-rash,** an eruptive disease incident to infants when teething; **tooth-ribbon,** the lingual ribbon or odontophore of certain molluscs; **tooth-root** = TOOTHWORT 1; **tooth-sac,** a sac or hollow structure of connective tissue, within which a tooth is developed; **tooth-saw** (*Dentistry*), a fine frame-saw for sawing off portions of the teeth (Knight 1877); †**tooth-scrape** (*obs.*), **tooth-scraper,** an instrument for scraping the teeth, as a toothpick, or a dentist's instrument; **tooth-set** *a.*, set with teeth, having tooth-like projections; †**tooth-shaken** *a.*, having the teeth loosened, as by age; **tooth-soap,** a preparation for cleaning the teeth; **tooth-stick,** †(*a*) a dentifrice in shape of a stick; (*b*) a stick used for cleaning the teeth; **tooth(ed)-violet** = TOOTHWORT 1; **tooth-wark** (now *dial.*) [cf. HEAD-WARK], toothache (cf. *teeth-work* in 9 b); **tooth-wheel,** a wheel with teeth, a toothed wheel, cog-wheel; **tooth-winged** *a.*, having the wings toothed or notched on the outer margin, as certain butterflies; **tooth-work,** (*a*) ornamental work resembling teeth; (*b*) work done with the teeth, i. e. eating (*nonce-use*); **tooth-wound,** a wound inflicted by the tooth of an animal (cf. *teeth-wound* in 9 b); †**tooth-wrest**: see quot. See also TOOTH-BRUSH, -PICK, -SHELL, etc.

**1872** WOOD *Insects at Home* 470 A family of Moths called Notodontidæ, or *Tooth-backs. **1585** HIGINS *Junius' Nomenclator* 260/2 *Dentifricium*,.. tooth powder: tooth sope, or *tooth blanch. **1857** DUNGLISON *Med. Lex.* s.v. *Tooth*, The ivory of the tooth or Dentine,..proper tooth substance, bone of the tooth, osseous substance of tooth, *tooth bone. **1878** T. BRYANT *Pract. Surg.* I. 557 The portion of the case that forms the root or roots is covered by 'crusta petrosa' or tooth-bone. **1642** A. ROSS *Mel Heliconium* (1643) 68 And then the Dragon, he did wound And all his *toothbread sonnes confound. **1887** RIDER HAGGARD *Allan Quaterm.* 73 A *tooth-chattering cook. **1889** STEVENSON *Master of B.* 80 Alone..in this tooth-chattering desert. **1893** *Westm. Gaz.* 24 Apr. 4/3 The force was a mere *toothcomb in the face of the rioters. **1902** *Sat. Rev.* 1 Nov. 556/1 The rake with which Mr. Nield gathers together his authorities is a very tooth-comb. **1873** DAWSON *Earth & Man* iv. 73 The Sertulariæ or *tooth-corallines. **1863–79** PRIOR *Brit. Pl.*, *Tooth-cress, or Tooth-Violet,..*Dentaria bulbifera.* **1767** S. PATERSON *Another Trav.* I. 300 'Tis the celebrated *tooth-doctor—he takes out your old teeth without any pain. **1884** C. G. W. LOCK *Workshop Receipts* Ser. III. 312/1 Adding to crude or branch lacquer, about 5 per cent. of the *tooth dye (haguro) used by women. **1794** E. DARWIN *Zoon.* I. iii. 22 The disagreeable sensation called the *tooth-edge. **1898** P. MANSON *Trop. Diseases* iv. 89 In such patients..*tooth extraction..may prove a dangerous matter. **1867** W. W. SMYTH *Coal & Coal-mining* 37 The Odontopteris, or *tooth-fern. **1783** CHARLOTTE SMITH *Emmeline* (1816) IV. 179 The child was very ill once with a *tooth-fever. **1884** MILLER *Plant-n.*, *Tooth-flower, Australian, *Dentella repens.* **1844** DUFTON *Deafness* 91 A pair of *tooth-forceps was..employed. **1841** *Penny Cycl.* XX. 460/2 The number of successive *tooth-germs..behind the..functional teeth. **1483** *Cath. Angl.* 398/1 A *Tuthe yren, *dentaria.* **1851** MANTELL *Petrifact.* III. § 5. 255 The central body of dentine or *tooth-ivory. **1827** N. ARNOTT *Physics* I. 247 The *tooth-key is an instrument found in many hands. **1835–6** *Todd's Cycl. Anat.* I. 312/1 A *tooth-like process on either side [of the bill]. **1839** BAILEY *Festus* ix. (1852) 99 The toothlike aching ruin of the body. **1889** C. C. R. *Up for the Season*, etc. 53 A *tooth-mark left me by her black-and-tan. **1831** TRELAWNY *Adv. Younger Son* I. 52 Buttered toast, half eaten, and *tooth-marked. **1879** THOMSON & TAIT *Nat. Phil.* I. I. § 109 The dentist's *tooth-mill is an..illustration of the elastic universal flexure joint. **1840** *Civil Eng. & Arch. Jrnl.* III. 2/1 A narrow lancet opening, having the *tooth ornament in the hollow surrounding the same. **1592** CHETTLE *Kinde-harts Dr.* (1841) 30 The only remedy for the *tooth paine, either to haue patience, or to pull them out. **1857** DUNGLISON *Med. Lex.*, **T[ooth] Paste*, Dentifricium. **1823** P. NICHOLSON *Pract. Build.* 246 The *Tooth-plane is fitted with a blade or iron, on the steel side of it covered with rakes or small grooves. **1880** M. MACKENZIE *Dis. Throat & Nose* I. 411 Teeth, real or artificial, or *toothplates, become loosened during sleep. **1542** *Acc. Ld. High Treas. Scot.* VIII. 89 Ane stoppell to keip the kingis grace *twithe pulder. **1823** J. BADCOCK *Dom. Amusem.* 25 As a tooth-powder, nothing can exceed the virtues of charcoal. **1654** GAYTON *Pleas. Notes* III. v. 101 The..more crusty meats fell to Sancho's share, who was *tooth-proofe. **1839** J. BROWN *Lett.* (1907) 46 A good *tooth-puller can pull with any key or claw. **1850** THACKERAY *Pendennis* lxi, No more than *tooth-pulling, or any other pang, eternal. **1854** R. OWEN *Skel. & Teeth* in *Orr's Circ. Sc.* I. *Org. Nat.* 265 The primary basis of the tooth, called '*tooth-pulp'. **1862** SMILES *Engineers* III. 85 Mr. Blenkinsop of Leeds, in 1811, took out a patent for a racked or *tooth-rail. **1585** HIGINS *Junius' Nomenclator* 260/2 *Dentiscalpium*...Curedent. A tooth scraper, or *tooth-rake. *c* **1830** *Pract. Treat. Roads* 17 in *Libr. Usef. Knowl., Husb.* III, Scratching it [the surface], with a tooth-rake regularly all over, as occasion requires. **1818–20** E. THOMPSON *Cullen's Nosol. Method.* (ed. 3) 321 *Strophulus confertus*, sometimes called the rank red gum and the *tooth rash. **1883** J. G. WOOD in *Gd. Words* Sept. 603/2 The still more curious '*tooth-ribbon' set with its hundreds of hooked toothlets. **1890** BILLINGS *Nat. Med. Dict.*, **Tooth-sac*, connective-tissue structure enclosing the dentine germ and enamel-organ in the fœtal development of the teeth. **1552** HULOET, *Tothscrape instrument, *dentiscalpium.* **1585** *Tooth-scraper [see *tooth-rake*]. **1860** MAYNE *Expos. Lex.*, Tooth-scraper. **1860** *Artist & Craftsman* 125 The *toothset edge of those eternal hills. **1650** BULWER *Anthropomet.* 140 Tooth-drawers and *Tooth-setting Chyrurgions. **1549** CHALONER *Erasm. on Folly* F ij, Wrincled, *totheshaken..so desyrous yet of life. **1674** JOSSELYN *Voy. New Eng.* 185 The Women are pittifully Tooth-shaken. **1837** P. KEITH *Bot. Lex.* 292 Peristomium...consists of a circular and double row of fine and *tooth-shaped substances. **1607** TOPSELL *Four-f. Beasts* (1658) 401 That excellent powder, for the scowring and clensing of the teeth called *Tooth-soap. **1762** GOLDSM. *Cit. W.* iii, Your nose-borers, feet-swathers, *tooth-stainers, eye-brow-pluckers. **1729** *MS. Accounts* in *N. & Q.* 7th Ser. VII. 30/1 Disbursed at London..a silver *tooth-stick, 8*d.* **1859** R. F. BURTON *Centr. Afr.* in *Jrnl. Geog. Soc.* XXIX. 323 Some of the more civilized have learned..to use a toothstick. **1862** *Catal. Internat. Exhib., Brit.* II. No. 3533, Improved *tooth-stump instrument. **1634** FOWLDES *Homer's Batt. Frogs & Mice* B v, No *tooth-tempting fare. **1863–79** *Tooth-Violet [see *tooth-cress*]. *c* **1375** *Sc. Leg. Saints* xxii. (*Laurentius*) 567 A man sa disesyt..Of *tuth-wark. **1862** *Catal. Internat. Exhib.* II. XII. 2 A series of shaftings and *tooth-wheels. **1891** *Cent. Dict.*, *Tooth-winged. **1681** GREW *Musæum* I. VI. i. 133 The ridges also of the rounds are wrought with *Tooth-Work. **1899** *Syd. Soc. Lex.*, **T[ooth] wounds*, wounds inflicted by the teeth of animals which do not owe their gravity to poison, but to the laceration of the tissues. **1706** PHILLIPS (ed. Kersey), **Tooth-wrest*, an Instrument to draw, or pull out Teeth.

**b.** Combs. with the pl. *teeth* (most of which have corresponding forms in *tooth-*: see above), as *teeth-ache* (= TOOTHACHE), *-brush* (= TOOTH-BRUSH), *-chatter*, *-chattering* sb. and adj., *-dints* (double pl. of *tooth-dint*), *-edging a.* (setting the teeth on edge), *-filing*, *-gnashing* sb. and adj., *-grinding* adj., *-like* adj., *-mark*, *-plate*, *-pulps* (double pl. of *tooth-pulp*), *-watering* (cf. phr. *the teeth water* in 8 g), † *-wind* (? a wind meeting one in the teeth), † *-work* (= *tooth-wark*), *-wound.*

**1890** P. H. EMERSON *Wild Life* xxii. 96 For *teeth-ache we rub the inside wi' rum. **1651** *Verney Mem.* (1894) III. 39 A gift of the new Paris luxury—' the *Teeth Brushes and boxes'. **1751** SMOLLETT *Per. Pic.* (1779) III. lxxx. 63 Waiting-women..who clean your teeth-brushes. **1834** *Tait's Mag.* I. 43/2 He has managed to get up a masterly *teeth-chatter. **1796** COLERIDGE *Blossom 1st Feb.* 3 This dark ..*teeth-chattering month. **1887** RIDER HAGGARD *Allan Quaterm.* 91 He nearly aroused the Masai camp with teeth-chattering. **1839** BAILEY *Festus* xviii. (1852) 241 The foul fiend's *teeth-dints may be seen. **1603** FLORIO *Montaigne* II. xii. (1632) 336 That sharp, harsh, and *teethedging noise that Smiths make in filing of brasse. **1897** MARY KINGSLEY *W. Africa* 477 The *teeth-filing I think undoubtedly does arise from this. *a* **1711** KEN *Hymnotheo Poet. Wks.* 1721 III. 90 *Teeth-gnashing Envy at the Saints above. **1642** A. ROSS *Mel Heliconium* (1643) 175 *Teeth-grinding anger, with fierce-glowing eyes. **1884** W. S. B. MCLAREN *Spinning* (ed. 2) 6 Seeing the *teeth-like edges which thus catch the fingers. **1898** R. BLAKEBOROUGH *Wit*, etc. *N. Riding Yorks.* 202 *Teeth-marks were found on..part of their body. **1900** *Edin. Rev.* Apr. 362 Their works bear the teethmark of their own age. **1897** *Allbutt's Syst. Med.* III. 346 A badly fitting artificial *teeth-plate. **1859** J. TOMES *Dental Surg.* (1873) 4 The depth of these bony cells is only sufficient to contain the developing teeth and *teeth-pulps. **1879** CALDERWOOD *Mind & Br.* 273 That result known as '*teeth-watering', which may be described as a reminiscence of taste. *a* **1732** T. BOSTON *Crook in Lot* (1863) 45 What a sad thing must it then be to lose this *teeth-wind for Immanuel's land! *c* **1440** *Thornton MS.* lf. 176 (E.E.T.S.) A charme for þe *tethe worke. **1856** KANE *Arct. Expl.* II. xv. 164 Five were scarred by direct *teeth-wounds of bears.

**Tooth** (tūþ), *v.* Forms: see prec. [f. prec.]

**1.** *intr.* To develop, grow, or 'cut' teeth; to teethe. ? *Obs.*

*c* **1410** *Master of Game* vii. (1904) 32/1 Þei tothen [*pr.* tochen; *MS. Digby 182* teth] ii tymes in þe yere whan þei be whelpes. *c* **1440–1796** [see TOOTHING 1].

**2.** *trans.* To furnish or supply with teeth; to fit or fix teeth into; to cut teeth in or upon, to indent.

**1483** *Cath. Angl.* 398/1 To Tuthe, *dentare.* **1523** FITZHERB. *Husb.* § 24 Than maye he..tothe the rakes with drye wethy wode. **1611** *Shuttleworths' Acc.* (Chetham Soc.) 196 Making thre huckes and toothing nyne sicles, $xv^d$. **1745** ARDERON in *Phil. Trans.* XLIV. 170, I toothed two Pieces of Brass..to fit each other. **1833, 1884** [see TOOTHING 3]. See also TOOTHED.

**3.** To exercise the teeth upon; to bite, gnaw. Also *absol.*

**1579** GOSSON *Sch. Abuse* (Arb.) 19 The Syracusans vsed such varietie of dishes..they were many times in doubt, which they shoulde touth first, or taste last. **1858** H. W. BEECHER *Life Th.* (1859) 32 The pragmatic prophecy-monger and the swinish utilitarian have toothed its fruits and craunched its blossoms. **1871** R. ELLIS *Catullus* xxiii. 4 Each for penury fit to tooth a flint-stone.

**4.** To fit or fix into something by projections like teeth, or in the manner of teeth. **a.** *trans.*

[**1672**: cf. TOOTHING 2 b.] **1703** T. N. *City & C. Purchaser* 51 'Tis common to Tooth in the stretching Course 2 Inches with the Stretcher only. **1793** W. H. MARSHALL *W. England* (1796) II. 341 By toothing the one into the other..the whole settles..into one corporate mass. **1888** *Law Rep., Weekly Notes* 77/1 The defendant..might use it..by putting a lean-to against it, or by toothing a door support into it.

**b.** *intr.* for *pass.* To interlock.

**1703** MOXON *Mech. Exerc.* 260 Whereas if the Header of one side of the Wall, toothed as much as the Stretcher on the other side, it would be a stronger Toothing. **1865** MASSON *Rec. Brit. Philos.* 321 The one [mind] might have a conviction that it toothed at some points into the independent constitution of the other [matter].

**Toothache** (tū·þ,ēˡk). Forms: see TOOTH *sb.* and ACHE *sb.*; also 4–7 -ake, 6 *Sc.* -aike, -ȝaik, 7–9 -ach. An ache or continuous pain in a tooth or the teeth. (As a malady, commonly *the tooth ache* down to 19th c. See THE 8.)

**1377** LANGL. *P. Pl.* B. xx. 81 Coughes, and cardiacles, crampes, and tothaches. *c* **1489** CAXTON *Sonnes of Aymon* ix. 215 The Kyng..sayd he had the tooth ache. *a* **1585** MONTGOMERIE *Flyting* 321 The phtiseik, þe twithȝaik [*v.r.* toothaike], þe tittis, and þe tirrillis. **1599** SHAKS. *Much Ado* III. ii. 21, I haue the tooth-ach. *Ibid.* v. i. 36 There was neuer yet Philosopher, That could endure the tooth-ake patiently. **1649** JER. TAYLOR *Gt. Exemp.* III. Disc. xvi. 56 Some persons used certain verses of the psalter as an antidote against tooth-ach. **1711** ADDISON *Spect.* No. 7 ⁋ 4 She lay ill of the Tooth-ach. *a* **1774** TUCKER *Lt. Nat.* (1834) II. 581 Engaged at home by a violent toothache. **1791** BURKE *App. Whigs* Wks. VI. 221 A charm for the tooth-ach. **1887** *Times* 26 Aug. 7/4 All that is the matter with him is a fit of toothache.

**b.** *attrib.*, usually denoting something used as a remedy for toothache, as *toothache spell, tincture*; **toothache-grass**, a N. American grass (*Ctenium americanum*) having a very pungent taste; **toothache-tree**, (*a*) name for several N. American species of the genus *Xanthoxylon*, having pungent aromatic fruit, esp. *X. fraxineum*, also called *prickly ash*; (*b*) the similar N. American *Aralia spinosa*, also called *angelica-tree.*

**1616** SYLVESTER *Tobacco Battered* 655 It is but like some of our Tooth-ake Spells, Which for the present seem to ease the Pain. **1730** MORTIMER in *Phil. Trans.* XXXVI. 428 *Zanthoxylum spinosum*,..the Pellitory or Tooth-ach Tree. **1860** MAYNE *Expos. Lex.*, *Tooth-ache Tree*, a common name for the tree *Aralia spinosa.* **1860** WORCESTER, *Toothache-grass.*

Hence **Too·tha:chy** *a.* (*colloq.*), affected with toothache. So **Too·th-a:ching**, aching of the teeth, toothache.

**1709** *Brit. Apollo* II. No. 7. 3/2, I was taken With a vi'lent Tooth-aching. **1838** LADY GRANVILLE *Lett.* (1894) II. 269 Toothachy and tired, I have been writing this letter. **1900** EL. GLYN *Visits Elizabeth* (1906) 72 That is how she got the toothachy look.

**Tooth and egg**, obs. corr. of TUTENAG, zinc.

**Toothbill** (tū·þ,bil). The tooth-billed pigeon.

**1862** [see next].

**Tooth-billed** (tū·þ,bild), *a. Ornith.* [See BILLED.] Having one or more tooth-like projections on the edge of the bill; dentirostral or serratirostral.

*Tooth-billed bower-bird*, a rare Australian bower-bird, *Scenopœus dentirostris. Tooth-billed pigeon*, *Didunculus strigirostris*, of the Samoan Islands.

**1862** WOOD *Illustr. Nat. Hist.* II. 593 Tooth-billed Pigeon. ..The whole contour of the Tooth-bill is remarkable. **1872** COUES *N. Amer. Birds* 223 Didunculidæ consists of the only less singular tooth-billed pigeon, *Didunculus strigirostris.* **1905** *Westm. Gaz.* 18 Nov. 7/2 The didunculus, or tooth-billed pigeon,..if native accounts are to be believed, ..has only saved itself from extinction by changing its habits in one of the islands.

**Too·th-brush.** A small brush with a long handle, used for cleansing the teeth.

[**1651, 1751**: see *teeth-brush*, TOOTH *sb.* 9 b.] **1690** WOOD *Life* (O.H.S.) III. 319 [Bought] toothbrush [of] J. Barret. **1807** J. BERESFORD *Miseries Hum. Life* 236 While you are waiting..for a fresh supply of tooth-brushes. **1844** W. H. MAXWELL *Sports & Adv. Scotl.* ii. (1855) 35 My chattels are safe,..even to a tooth-brush.

**b.** *attrib.*, as *tooth-brush handle*; **tooth-brush moustache** (*humorous*), a bristly moustache; **tooth-brush tree**, a name for *Salvadora persica*, from the use of its twigs for cleaning the teeth.

**1886** FENN *Master Cerem.* i, That peg was an old tooth-brush handle. **1891** *Cent. Dict.* s.v. *Salvadora*, *S. Persica* ..in India furnishes *kikuel-oil*, and from the use of its twigs is sometimes called *toothbrush-tree.* **1904** *Daily Chron.* 31 Aug. 4/4 Clothes of outlandish cut, toothbrush moustache.

Hence **Too·thbrushy** *a. nonce-wd.*, resembling a tooth-brush; bristly.

**1904** 'A. HOPE' *Double Harness* xiii, His toothbrushy hair had..more than usual of its suggestion of comical distress.

**Too·th-draw:er.**

**1.** One who 'draws' or extracts teeth; a dentist. Now *contemptuous.*

**1393** LANGL. *P. Pl.* C. VII. 370 Of portours and of pykeporses and pylede toþ-drawers. *c* **1440** *Promp. Parv.* 498/1 Toothe drawere, *edentator.* **1529** MORE *Dyaloge* II. Wks. 194/2 Sainct Apoline we make a toth drawer. **1601** SIR W. CORNWALLIS *Ess.* II. xliii. (1631) 199 To heare Tooth-drawers or Rat-catchers sweare themselves the best in the world. **1654** WHITLOCK *Zootomia* 291 Enough to make a Tooth-drawer, or Corn-cutter passe for a generall Physitian. **1833** L. RITCHIE *Wand. by Loire* 40 The only rumbustious individual in the whole crowd was an itinerant tooth-drawer.

**2.** A dentist's instrument for extracting teeth.

**1597** A. M. tr. *Guillemeau's Fr. Chirurg.* 27/2 We must gently and easyly crushe the tooth-drawer together. **1694** *Acc. Sev. Late Voy.* II. (1711) 123 He hath two Claws before, ..somewhat like the Phangs of a Tooth-drawer.

So **Too·th-draw:ing**, *sb.* extraction of a tooth or teeth; *adj.* that extracts teeth.

**1610** HEALEY *St. Aug. Citie of God* 120 The third, sonne to Arsippus,..first inventor of..tooth-drawing. **1764** FOOTE *Mayor of G.* I, You blood-letting, tooth-drawing,.. glistering ——. **1779** WARNER in Jesse *Selwyn & Contemp.* (1844) IV. 260 The tooth-drawing must have been a curious scene. **1860** THACKERAY *Lovel* vi, My bleeding, bolusing, tooth-drawing rival.

**Toothed** (tūþt, *poet.* tū·þèd), *a.* [f. TOOTH *sb.* or *v.* + -ED.] Furnished with teeth (or a tooth).

**1.** *lit.* of an animal: Having teeth; with defining words, Having teeth of a specified kind.

**13..** *K. Alis.* 5392 (Bodl. MS.) Hij weren toþed als a man. **1413** *Pilgr. Sowle* (Caxton) II. xlv. (1859) 51 Somme of them were tothyd as boores. **1592** SHAKS. *Ven. & Ad.* 1117 Had I been tooth'd like him, I must confesse, With kissing him I should haue kild him first. **1661** LOVELL *Hist. Anim. & Min.* Introd., The teeth are wanting in some, others are toothed. **1860** WRAXALL *Life in Sea* i. 3 The Cetacea are subdivided into the 'toothless' and the 'toothed'.

**b.** *fig.* cf. TOOTH *sb.* 2. *rare.*

**1584** B. R. tr. *Herodotus* I. 63 The basest sorte of yonkers that were not so deyntely toothed.

**c.** *fig.* 'Biting', pungent, corrosive. ? *Obs.*

**1628** FELTHAM *Resolves* II. [I.] lxi. 175 Dab it with aqua fortis, toothed waters, and corroding Minerals. **1675** V. ALSOP *Anti-sozzo* ii. 65 Those Severe and Toothed Satyrs wherewith he has Torn and Lasht poor Honest Men.

**2.** Having natural projections or processes like teeth; dentate; indented; jagged: *esp.* of leaves or other parts of plants; also of the bill of birds, the margin of shells, etc.

*Toothed vertebra*, a name for the axis vertebra, from its tooth or odontoid process (*Syd. Soc. Lex.* s.v. *Vertebra*).

**1387** TREVISA *Higden* (Rolls) II. 383 Perdix..took a plate of iren..and made it i-toþed as a rugge boon of a fische. **1610** SHAKS. *Temp.* IV. i. 180 Through Tooth'd briars, sharpe firzes, pricking gosse, & thorns. **1796** WITHERING *Brit. Plants* (ed. 3) III. 679 Leaves smooth, notched and acutely toothed. **1802** PALEY *Nat. Theol.* xiii. § 3 (1819) 221 The middle claw of the heron and cormorant is toothed and notched like a saw. **1859** W. S. COLEMAN *Woodlands* (1866) 27 The leaves..doubly toothed at the edges. **1895** *Oracle Encycl.* I. 594/2 The wing-margin is denticulated or irregularly toothed.

**3.** Made or fitted artificially with teeth or tooth-like projections: *spec.* of a wheel, cogged.

*Toothed ornament* (*Arch.*) = tooth-ornament: TOOTH *sb.* 9.

**1387** [see 2]. **1573** TUSSER *Husb.* (1878) 37 A barlie rake toothed. **1577** GOOGE *Heresbach's Husb.* 42 They holde their leaft hande full of Corne, and..with toothed Syckles they cut it. **1641** MILTON *Animadv.* i. Wks. 1851 III. 191 A toothlesse Satyr is as improper as a toothed sleekstone, and as bullish. **1797** *Encycl. Brit.* (ed. 3) I. 92/2 The toothed wheel D, fixed on the axis EF. **1815** J. SMITH *Panorama Sc. & Art* I. 163 The ribs were often enriched by the toothed ornament. **1834–6** BARLOW in *Encycl. Metrop.* (1845) VIII. 101/2 A toothed wheel is generally understood to be one in which the teeth are cast or cut on the wheel itself, forming one whole. **1862** RICKMAN *Goth. Archit.* 294 An ornament almost as peculiar to the Decorated style as the toothed ornament [is] to the Early English. **1905** *Westm. Gaz.* 20 June 4/2 The protest..against the use of the spring toothed-trap.

**4.** *Comb.*, as *toothed-billed* (= TOOTH-BILLED); also freq. as the second element in parasynthetic combinations, as *buck-toothed*, *sweet-toothed.*

**1523** FITZHERB. *Husb.* § 136 A graffynge sawe..very thyn and thycke tothed. **1670** NARBOROUGH *Jrnl.* in *Acc. Sev. Late Voy.* I. (1694) 64 They are smooth and even toothed. **1706** S. SEWALL *Diary* 25 Dec., I bought me a great Tooth'd Comb at Dwight's. **1841** *Penny Cycl.* XXI. 416/2 The..tribe of *Dentirostres*, or toothed-billed birds.

**Toothenague, -aque**, obs. ff. TUTENAG, zinc.

**Too·ther.** [f. TOOTH *v.* + -ER [1].] One who makes the teeth of saws; a machine for doing this.

**1881** *Instr. Census Clerks* (1885) 45 Saw Making: Parer. Toother. Backer.

**Too·th-fee.** [Literal rendering of ON. *tann-fé*, f. *tǫnn, tann-* tooth + *fé* money.] A gift to an infant on cutting its first tooth, a custom mentioned in Old Norse, and still observed in Iceland (Vigfusson). Also **too·th-gift, -money, -piece.**

**1851** THORPE *North. Mythol.* I. 25 Alfheim was given to him [Frey] by the gods as tooth-money. **1868** G. STEPHENS *Runic Mon.* II. 538 This fine Gold-bracteate..was probably a Tooth-fee or Birthday gift. *Ibid.* 529 It would seem to have been struck as a Birth-day- or Tooth-piece for some highborn child. **1875** R. B. ANDERSON *Norse Mythol.* 445 Alfheim was given him as a tooth-gift. **1884** YORK POWELL in *Academy* 23 Feb. 128/2 What Sigmund gave his son was a sword, *imon-lauk*, a very fitting tooth-fee, or name-gift, to one who was to live and die in arms.

**Toothful** (tū·þful), *sb.* [f. TOOTH *sb.* + -FUL 2.] *lit.* As much as would fill a tooth; a small mouthful, esp. of liquor.

*a* **1774** FERGUSSON *Drink Ecl.* 69 Tho' lairds tak toothfu's o' my warming sap. **1821** *Joseph the Bk.-Man* 132 When Joseph landed, A potent toothful he commanded. **1839** *Fraser's Mag.* XIX. 474 Wiping each platter, so as not to leave One toothful of the garlic sauce behind. **1882** MRS. RIDDELL *Pr. Wales' Garden-P.* 115 If he would be persuaded to take a toothful of brandy before beginning the evening's duties.

**Toothful** (tū·þfŭl), *a.* [f. TOOTH *sb.* + -FUL 1.] **1.** Full of teeth; having many teeth. *rare.*

**1591** SYLVESTER *Du Bartas* I. iii. 834 Our mealy grain.. being covered by the tooth-full Harrow.

†**2.** Pleasant to the taste: = TOOTHSOME. *Obs.*

**1622** MASSINGER & DEKKER *Virg.-Mart.* v. i, What dainty relish on my tongue This fruit hath left! Some angel hath me fed: If so toothfull, I will be banqueted.

**Tooth-gift**: see TOOTH-FEE.

**Toot-hill** (tū·tˌhil). Also 4 tote-, 4–5 **tute-**, 6–8 **tout-hill.** Preserved in many forms *toot-, tote-, tot-, tut-* in place-names. [ME. *tōte-hill*, f. TOOT *v.*[1] (or *sb.*[1]) + HILL.] A natural or artificial hill or mound used for a look-out place; a prominent hill; = TOOT *sb.*[1] 1. (In quot. 1250 a place-name.)

[**1250** *Pat. Roll* 34 *Hen. III*, m. 1 Concessimus..quod illa feria que consuevit esse in eorum cimeterio apud Westmonasterium..fit singulis annis apud Tothull'.]

**1382** WYCLIF 2 *Sam.* v. 7 Forsothe Dauid took the tote [*v. rr.* toot, tute] hil [1388 tour of] Syon; that is the citee of Dauid. — *Isa.* xxi. 8 Vpon the toothil of the Lord I am stondende. *c* **1440** *Promp. Parv.* 498/1 Tote hylle, or hey place of lokynge, *conspicillum.* **1483** *Cath. Angl.* 398/1 A Tute hylle, *aruisium montarium.* **1532–3** *Durham Househ. Bk.* (Surtees) 181 Pro factura unius muri circa le toythyll 5s. 10d. **1535** *Goodly Prymer* (1834) 163 Sion by interpretation signifieth a tout-hill, or a place where a man may see far about him. **1609** HOLLAND *Amm. Marcell.* XVIII. viii. 118 A certaine high Barbican or Toot-hill [*specula*]. **1827** HODGSON *Northumbld.* II. I. 286 *note*, In a field, a little to the north-east of Hartington, there is a small conical hill, apparently natural, but artificially terraced, which is called the Tote-hill. **1886** *Chester Gloss.*, *Toot Hill*, prop. name, a steep hill near Alvanley. **1894** O. HESLOP *Northumbld. Gloss.*, *Tuthill, Tote-hill*, an eminence. Of frequent occurrence in place-names. The Tuthill-stairs in Newcastle ascend the eminence (called Tout-hill in Bourne's map, 1736) from The Close to Clavering Place... In old formal gardens a tout-hill was an artificial mound formed for the purpose of commanding a prospect.

**Toothing** (tū·þiŋ), *vbl. sb.* [f. TOOTH *sb.* or *v.* + -ING[1].]

**1.** Development or 'cutting' of the teeth, dentition: = TEETHING *vbl. sb.* 1. *Obs.* or *rare.*

*c* **1440** *Pallad. on Husb.* I. 665 As seek ar they [peacocks] as children in tothynge. **1656** RIDGLEY *Pract. Physick* 323 Toothing of Children is about the seventh Moneth. **1796** E. DARWIN *Zoon.* II. 51 The pain of toothing often begins much earlier than is suspected.

**2.** A structure or formation (natural or artificial) consisting of teeth or tooth-like projections; such teeth collectively; dentation, serration.

**1611** COTGR., *Allochons d'un rouët*, the teeth, or toothing, of a wheele, in a clocke. **1753** BAKER in *Phil. Trans.* XLVIII. 122 The toothing in the middle thereof almost proves that part to have been the palate of some animal. **1845** LINDLEY *Sch. Bot.* i. (1858) 9 If the toothings are..like those of a saw, the leaves are serrate. **1872** COUES *N. Amer. Birds* 236 A toothing of the under mandible.

**b.** *spec.* in *Building.* Bricks or stones left projecting from a wall to form a bond for additional work to be built on; the bond or attachment thus formed; the construction of this. Also *fig.*

**1672** *Phil. Trans.* VII. 4081 In the first Wall there are Stones in toothings, from the top to the bottom. **1674** BLOUNT *Glossogr.*, *Toothing*, the working in of Bricks in a party-wall. **1769** H. MALDEN in Willis & Clark *Cambridge* (1886) I. 490 On the outer wall, may be perceived Toothings, where the Building was formerly joined. **1841** *Civil Eng. & Arch. Jrnl.* IV. 395/1 Regular half brick toothings were inserted, at intervals of 2 feet 3 inches apart.

**3.** The process of forming teeth or serrations; the furnishing (of a saw, etc.) with teeth.

**1833** J. HOLLAND *Manuf. Metal* II. 56 The toothing [of a sickle] is effected by a small well tempered chisel and a hammer. **1884** C. G. W. LOCK *Workshop Receipts* Ser. III. 287/1 After toothing comes hardening [of saws].

**4.** *attrib.* and *Comb.*, as *toothing-course, -stone* (see 2 b); **toothing-plane,** a plane having the iron almost upright, with a serrated edge, used to score and roughen a surface; see TOOTH *sb.* 3 d.

**1703** T. N. *City & C. Purchaser* 51 Lay it on the last Toothing Course to bear it. **1847** SMEATON *Builder's Man.* 95 Made somewhat rough with either a rasp or toothing-plane. **1875** BRASH *Eccl. Archit. Irel.* 18 The chancel has disappeared; toothing-stones..show it to have been 12 ft. wide.

**Toothless** (tū·þlės), *a.* Forms: see TOOTH *sb.* [See -LESS.] Having no teeth; destitute of teeth.

**1.** *lit.* **a.** That is naturally without teeth; not developing teeth. **b.** Having the teeth still undeveloped; that has not yet cut its teeth. **c.** Having lost the teeth, as from age.

**1398** TREVISA *Barth. De P. R.* VI. ix. (Bodl. MS.), Þe norise ..chewith mete in hire owne mowþe and makeþ it redie to þe toþeles child. *Ibid.* XVIII. xviii. (ibid.), Bestes þat beþ toþeles in þe ouer iowe. *c* **1440** *Promp. Parv.* 498/1 Tootheles, for age, *edentatus.* *Ibid.*, Tootheles, for ȝungthe. **1581** DERRICKE *Image of Irel.* (1883) 19 Let the toothlesse crabbed queane boyle in her owne despight. **1673** HICKERINGILL *Greg. F. Greyb.* 185 A toothless dog bites not much more than a dead dog. **1784** COWPER *Task* IV. 81 Teeth for the toothless, ringlets for the bald. **1810** SOUTHEY *Kehama* XIII. xii, The Tygress leaves her toothless cubs. **1880** GÜNTHER *Fishes* 170 The toothless buccal cavity is surrounded by a semicircular upper lip.

**2.** *transf.* Destitute of tooth-like formations or projections; not jagged or serrated.

**1812** *New Bot. Gard.* I. 8 Follicles oblong, acuminate, toothless. **1822** J. PARKINSON *Outl. Oryctol.* 153 The aperture [of the shell] long, narrow, toothless. **1883** *Gd. Words* Aug. 505/2 There are grooves of the portcullis still, but it is toothless now.

**3.** *fig.* Destitute of keenness or 'edge'; not biting or corrosive; also *fig.*

**1592** NASHE *Four Lett. Confut.* Wks. (Grosart) II. 203 Poore secular Satirist..that with the toothlesse gums of his Poetry so betuggeth a dead man. **1597** BP. HALL (*title*) Virgidemiarum, Sixe Bookes. First three Bookes, Of Tooth-lesse Satyrs. **1650** BAXTER *Saints' R.* III. ii. § 14. 295 If a drunken..Preacher did..read the Common Prayer, or some toothless Homily, instead of a searching.. Sermon. *a* **1764** LLOYD *Epist. to C. Churchill* Poet. Wks. 1774 I. 86 No toothless spleen, no venom'd critic's aim. **1882** MRS. OLIPHANT *Lit. Hist. Eng.* I. 312 The 'Lyrical ballads', at which every toothless critic sneered.

†**b.** *loosely.* Tasteless; not toothsome. *Obs.*

**1679** JANE *Serm. at St. Margarets* 11 Apr. 17 This.. renders all his most exquisite pleasures toothless and insipid.

Hence **Too·thlessly** *adv.*; **Too·thlessness.**

**1631** *Celestina* IV. 49 That toothlessnesse of the gummes. **1855** H. SPENCER *Princ. Psychol.* (1872) II. VI. vi. 62 In the infant, toothlessness coexists with the power of developing thirty-two teeth at maturity. **1891** *Harper's Mag.* Sept. 537/1 Toothlessly smiling.

**Toothlet** (tū·þlėt). [f. TOOTH *sb.* + -LET.] A small tooth or tooth-like projection; a denticle.

**1800** *Misc. Tr.* in *Asiat. Ann. Reg.* 264/2 Calyx very small, tubular, five toothed; toothlets short. **1884** W. K. PARKER *Mammal. Descent* vii. 177 Notched..into eight or nine toothlets like a comb.

Hence **Too·thleted** *a.*, denticulate.

**1812** *New Bot. Gard.* I. 47 The other [stems] having the bases of the petioles toothleted. **1845** LINDLEY *Sch. Bot.* vi. (1858) 74 Leaves heart-shaped, with 5 angles, toothletted.

**Tooth-money**: see TOOTH-FEE.

**Toothpick** (tū·þpik). Forms: see TOOTH *sb.*; also 5–6 -pike, 6 -picke. [See PICK *sb.*[1] 5.]

**1.** An instrument for picking the teeth: usually a pointed quill or small piece of wood; sometimes of gold, silver, or other material.

**1488** *Acc. Ld. High Treas. Scot.* I. 81 Twa tuthpikis of gold with a chenȝe. **1538** ELYOT, *Nitella*, a toothe pike [1545 tothe pykar]. Sometyme it signifyeth elegancy in speche. **1562** TURNER *Herbal* II. 34 b, Stickes and strawes and other tooth pickes. **1579** *N. C. Wills* (Surtees) II. 93 To Mr Roberte Toutte a tothe pyke of silver. **1635** SWAN *Spec. M.* ix. § 1 (1643) 450 Of these [porcupine] quills men make wholesome tooth-picks. **1775** BLACK in *Phil. Trans.* LXV. 125 Stirring it gently with a quill tooth-pick. **1873** DORAN *Lady of last Cent.* xi. 298 A welcome which extended..from the manufacturer of toothpicks to the writer of an epic poem.

**2.** A name for the umbelliferous plant *Ammi Visnaga*, the hardened rays of the umbel of which are used as toothpicks: also called *Spanish toothpick, toothpick bishop-weed* (see 6 b).

**1598** FLORIO, *Bisacuto*, the hearbe toothpick, or cheruill. **1760** J. LEE *Introd. Bot.* App. 330 Tooth-pick, *Daucus.* **1884** MILLER *Plant-n.*, *Ammi Visnaga*, Spanish Toothpick, Tooth-pick Bishop's-weed.

**3.** *pl.* Splinters, small elongated fragments, 'matchwood': in hyperbolic phr. *smashed* (etc.) *into toothpicks.*

**1839** MARRYAT *Phant. Ship* ix, The..ship will be beaten into toothpicks. **1899** *Daily News* 9 Mar. 5/3 The Pavonia tried to lower a boat, but it was smashed into toothpicks on the ship's side.

**4.** A bowie-knife: also *Arkansas toothpick. U.S. slang.*

**1867** LOWELL *Biglow P.* Ser. II. i. 151, I didn't call but jest on one, an' he drawed toothpick on me, An' reckoned he warn't goin' to stan' no sech doggauned econ'my. **1881** A. B. GREENLEAF *Ten Y. in Texas* 27 With..an Arkansas 'toothpick' suspended to a raw-hide belt buckled around their waists.

**5.** A very narrow pointed boat. *slang.*

**1897** KIPLING *Captains Courageous* iv. 104 'You should see one o' them toothpicks histin' up her anchor on her spike outer fifteen-fathom water'. 'What's a toothpick, Dan?' 'Them new haddockers an' herrin' boats'. **1909** J. DALZIEL *High Life in East* 201 The Magistrate got smartly into his 'toothpick', the attendant boat-boys..gave him carefully the necessary offing, he swung forward on his sculls.

**6.** *attrib.* and *Comb.* **a.** *attrib.* or as *adj.*, †(*a*) in reference to the use of the toothpick as an idle occupation; (*b*) denoting objects of narrow and pointed shape.

**1761** CHURCHILL *Night* 109 Or if in tittle-tattle, tooth-pick way, Our rambling thoughts with easy freedom stray. **1767** S. PATERSON *Another Trav.* II. 168 To enjoy uninterrupted, listless, toothpick ease. **1880** 'MARK TWAIN' *Tramp Abroad* I. 235 A heaped-up confusion of red roofs, quaint gables,..toothpick steeples. **1895** S. B. KENNEDY in *Outing* (U.S.) XXVII. 6/1 [She] gave me the go-by for a patent medicine drummer with tooth-pick shoes.

**b.** *Comb.*, as *toothpick-box, -case*; *toothpick-shaped* adj.; **toothpick bishop-weed** (see 2); † **toothpick chervil** = prec., or allied species.

**1866** *Treas. Bot.* 51 *Tooth-pick Bishop-weed, *A*[*mmi*] *Visnaga*, is so called on account of the use made in Spain of the rays or stalks of the main umbel. These, after flowering, shrink, and become so hard that they form convenient tooth-picks. **1669** R. MONTAGU in *Buccleuch MSS.* (Hist. MSS. Comm.) I. 448, 2 knives, a *toothpick-box, and a tiremoelle. **1684** *Lond. Gaz.* No. 1972/4 A *tooth pick Case of Black wood, tipt on both ends, and at the opening with Silver. **1578** LYTE *Dodoens* v. i. 615 This herbe is called ..in Spayne, Visnaga:..it may be called *Toothpicke Cheruill. **1905** W. E. GEIL *Yankee in Pigmy Land* v. 64 We tramped past many trees armed with long, white *toothpick-shaped thorns.

**Too·th-pi:cker.** †**1.** = prec. 1. *Obs.*

**1545** *Rates Custome House* b j b, Ere pikers or tothe pikers of bone the groce xii d. **1591** FLORIO *2nd Fruites* 61, I praie thee giue me a little stick, or a tooth picker. **1655** CULPEPPER *Riverius* VI. ii. 134 To preserve the Teeth, first clense them with a Tooth-picker of Mastich Wood. **1707** MORTIMER *Husb.* (1721) II. 185 Lentisc is a beautiful evergreen..; it makes the best Tooth-pickers in the World.

**2.** One who picks the teeth; in first quot. used of a bird which was fabled to pick the teeth of the crocodile; in second quot. with allusion to this.

**1612** WEBSTER *White Devil* IV. iii, Away flies the pretty tooth-picker from her cruell patient. *a* **1653** G. DANIEL *Idyll.* iii. 37 The Civetts of an Officer, Whose Tooth-picker, like ye Officious Bird Betrayes him Sleeping.

**Too·th-pi:cking,** *a.* Picking the teeth; *fig.* careless, *nonchalant*: cf. TOOTHPICK 6 a (*a*).

**1814** L. HUNT *Feast of Poets*, etc. (1815) 63 Here we have the plainest, tooth-picking acknowledgements, that Charles was a pensioner of France.

**Tooth-piece**: see TOOTH-FEE.

**Too·th-shell.** The long tubular shell, in shape like a tooth or tusk, of any gastropod mollusc of *Dentalium* or other allied genus; also the mollusc itself. **b.** *False tooth-shell*, the similar shell (or animal) of the molluscous genus *Cæca*, or the family *Cæcidæ*. **c.** 'In Australia, the shell of *Marinula pellucida*, a small marine mollusc used for necklaces' (Morris *Austral Eng.*).

*c* **1711** PETIVER *Gazophyl.* vii. 65 Small English Tooth-shell... It's smooth, white, and somewhat crooked with purplish Tips. **1777** PENNANT *Zool.* IV. 127 *Dentalium*, tooth-shell. **1850** MISS PRATT *Comm. Things Sea-side* v. 314 The old shell of the mollusk, commonly called Tooth-shell (*Dentalium entalis*),..so common on our coasts, shaped like a small horn. **1879** E. P. WRIGHT *Anim. Life* 548 The Tooth-shells are animal feeders, devouring foraminifera and minute bivalves.

**Toothsome** (tū·þsŏm), *a.* [See -SOME[1].]

**1.** Pleasant to the taste, savoury, palatable: cf. TOOTH *sb.* 2 a.

*c* **1565** SPARKE *Sir J. Hawkins' 2nd Voy.* (Hakl. Soc.) 46 We ..found water, which although it were neither so toothsome as running water..yet did we not refuse it. **1584** COGAN *Haven Health* cc. (1636) 189 Vineger, that is not onely toothsome, but wholesome also. **1604** E. G[RIMSTONE] *D'Acosta's Hist. Indies* IV. xviii. 260 The Patattoes, which they eate as a delicate and toothsome meate. **1733** CHEYNE *Eng. Malady* III. iv. (1734) 340, I began to find a Craving.. for more solid and Toothsome Food. **1899** E. CALLOW *Old Lond. Tav.* II. 286 Hard to please if they cannot select something toothsome from the menu.

**b.** *fig.* or in *fig.* context: Pleasant, 'palatable'.

**1551** T. WILSON *Logike* (1580) 83 Speaking thinges nothing tothsome. *a* **1568** COVERDALE *Carrying Christ's Cross* iv. 59 Seeing our phisician..(Iesus Chryst I meane) telleth vs that it is veri wholsome, how so euer it be toothsome. **1648** in Rushw. *Hist. Coll.* IV. (1701) II. 1047 Your only News is not very Toothsom but it may prove wholesom. **1805** J. RAMSAY *Scot. & Scotsm. in 18th C.* (1888) I. 287 Elegant and toothsome sermons were most in request.

**2.** Having a 'dainty tooth'; fond of savoury food.

**1837** R. NICOLL *Poems* (1842) 95 She kent na, douse woman! how toothsome was he. **1848** LYTTON *Harold* VII. i, The Earl is a toothsome man.

†**3.** Resembling a tooth; 'biting', sharp. *Obs.*

**1601** T. MORLEY *Madrigales*, etc. Ded., Whose malice (being as toothsome as the Adders sting).

Hence **Too·thsomely** *adv.*; **Too·thsomeness.**

**1612** T. TAYLOR *Comm. Titus* ii. 1. (1619) 336 Others stand so much vpon toothsomnes of their meate. **1880** MRS. ROLLINS *New Eng. Bygones* 12 Here..apples mellowed toothsomely under the matted grass. **1887** BESANT *The World went* xxxvii, I live sufficiently, and..with toothsomeness.

**Toothwort** (tū·þwɒɹt). [f. TOOTH *sb.* + WORT.] Name given to several different plants.

**1.** *Lathræa squamaria* (N.O. *Orobanchaceæ*), a leafless fleshy herb, parasitic on the roots of hazel and other trees, bearing a double row of flesh-coloured drooping flowers, and having tooth-like scales upon the root-stock.

1597 GERARDE *Herbal* III. clxiii. 1386 Great Toothwoorth, or Clownes Lungwoort..in forme like vnto Orobanche, or the Broome Rape,..hauing a tender, thicke, tuberous..bodie, consisting as it were of scales like teeth (whereof it tooke his name). 1778 G. WHITE *Selborne* 3 July, *Lathræa squamaria*, tooth-wort. 1905 E. STEP *Wild Flowers* I. 23 John Ray died exactly two hundred years ago, but the Toothwort still flourishes in Westhumble Lane [Mickleham].

†**2.** A name for Shepherd's-purse, *Capsella Bursa-pastoris*. *Obs. rare.*

1597 in GERARDE *Herbal* App.

**3.** A plant of the genus *Dentaria* (N.O. *Cruciferæ*), characterized by tooth-like projections upon the creeping root-stock; *esp.* the British species *D. bulbifera*, occurring locally in woods; also called *coralwort*.

1668 WILKINS *Real Char.* II. iv. § 5. 100 Dames Violet, Double Rocket Toothwort. 1678 PHILLIPS (ed 4), *Toothwort*, a sort of Herb, called in Latin, *Dentaria*. 1786 ABERCROMBIE *Arr.* in *Gard. Assist.* 73 *Dentaria*, toothwort. 1866 *Treas. Bot.* 393/2 Closely allied to Cardamine, from which it differs in having broad seed-stalks, and in its creeping roots being singularly toothed; hence the systematic name [*Dentaria*], and the English one of Toothwort.

**4.** A name for *Plumbago europæa* and the Central American and West Indian *P. scandens*, whose pungent leaves and roots are used as a remedy for toothache.

1760 J. LEE *Introd. Bot.* App. 330 Tooth-wort, *Plumbago*. 1884 MILLER *Plant-n.*, *Plumbago scandens*, Devil's-herb, or Tooth-wort, of the W. Indies.

**Toothy** (tū·þi), *a.* [f. TOOTH *sb.* + -Y.]

**1.** Having numerous, large, or prominent teeth (in quot. 1881 connoting 'devouring, ravenous').

1530 PALSGR. 327/2 Toothye as one that hath great tethe or plenty of tethe, *denteux*. 1799 CORSE in *Phil. Trans.* LXXXIX. 208 *note*, *Dauntelah* signifies toothy; having large or fine teeth. 1881 F. G. LEE *Reg. Baront.* II. iv, Toothy wolves in lambswool.

**2.** Furnished with or full of teeth or tooth-like projections; toothed.

1611 COTGR., *Dentelé*, .. toothed, toothie; full of iags resembling little teeth. 1705 J. PETIVER in *Phil. Trans.* XXV. 1960 Its [a shell's] Toothy part is finely variegated with red and black. *a* 1770 SMART *Hop-Gard.* II. Poems (1810) 41/1 Next expand The smoothest surface with the toothy rake.

**3.** *fig.* 'Biting', ill-natured, peevish. (Cf. TEETHY *a.*[1]) *north. dial.* and *Sc.*

1691 RAY *N. C. Words*, *Toothy*, peevish, crabbed. 1787 BURNS *Willie's Awa* vi, Toothy critics by the score, In bloody raw! 1824 MISS FERRIER *Inher.* xxiv, 'I suspect that's your case..', retorted Miss P., in a very toothy manner.

**4.** Toothsome, palatable. *rare.*

1864 *Athenæum* 8 Oct. 456/2 A most toothy meal I had of it! 1889 *Alien. & Neurol.* July 459 Meat or game, which is at first tough, becomes more tender and toothy.

**Too·thy-peg.** [f. *toothy, dim. of TOOTH *sb.* + PEG *sb.*[1]] Nursery word for 'tooth'.

1828 HOOD *Kilmansegg, Childh.* iv, Cutting her first little toothy-peg.

**Tooting** (tū·tiŋ), *vbl. sb.*[1] In 4–6 totyng; 6 towting. Now *dial.* [f. TOOT *v.*[1] + -ING[1].] The action of TOOT *v.*[1]; spying, peeping, looking.

1553 *Respublica* I. iii. 5 Theare was suche tooting, suche looking and suche priinge. 1598 FLORIO, *Osolamento*, a spying, a peeping, a tooting.

**b.** *attrib.* as tooting-glass, looking-glass; tooting-hill = TOOT-HILL; so *tooting-hole*, peep-hole; *tooting-place*, *-tower*, etc.

1382 WYCLIF *Jer.* xxxi. 21 Ordeyne to thee a toting place. 1388 — *Isa.* xxi. 8 Y stonde contynueli bi dai on the totyng place of the Lord. *c* 1460 *Med. Gramm.*, *Speculare*, a totynge hylle and a bekyne. *a* 1548 HALL *Chron.*, *Hen. VI* 105 Thei with in the citee [Orleans] perceiued well this totyng hole, and laied a pece of ordynaunce directly against the wyndowe. 1552 HULOET, Towtynge hoole to loke out at in a wall or wyndowe. 1556 PHAER *Æneid* IV. Lij, As dawning waxed white from tooting towres on hie. *c* 1560 GEST *Serm.* in Dugdale *Life* (1840) 182 Senec..wryteth that tootyng glasses be found to know our selfes and to rule our lyfes by...O that we Christen men and women thus used our tootinge glasses. 1894 O. HESLOP *Northumbld. Gloss.*, *Tooting-hole*, a spyhole or loophole.

**Too·ting,** *vbl. sb.*[2] Also 7–9 *Sc.* touting. [f. TOOT *v.*[2] + -ING[1].] The action of TOOT *v.*[2]; the sound made by blowing a horn or other wind-instrument.

1568 *Hist. Jacob & Esau* I. ii. A iij b, Then maketh he with his Horne such tootyng and blowing. 1603 HOLLAND *Plutarch's Mor.* 665 Another mercenary minstrell..kept a foolish and ridiculous tooting. 1630 J. LEVETT *Order. Bees* (1634) 30 You shall heare a touting in manner like the sounding of a Bewgle horne amongst the Bees. 1712 NEVILL in *Phil. Trans.* XXVIII. 270 Will not admit of any sound by Blast as a Horn doth, but by the articulate Voice of tooting it will. 1880 W. NEWTON *Serm. for Boys & Girls* (1881) 410 Tootings innumerable from the steam whistle.

**b.** *attrib.* and *Comb.*, as *tooting-horn*, *-trumpet*.

1737 RAMSAY *Scots Prov.* xx. 75 It is ill making a silk purse of a sow's lug, or a touting-horn of a tod's tail. 1805 J. NICOL *Poems* I. 2 *note* (Jam.), A touting horn (the horn of an ox perforated at the small end) by blowing on which they made a loud..sound. 1889 W. G. DICKSON *Glean. fr. Japan* xiii. 251 The boy behind is provided with a small tooting-trumpet to warn other travellers on the road.

**Tooting, touting,** *vbl. sb.*[3]: see TOOT, TOUT *v.*[3]

**Tooting**: see TOOT *v.*[1], [2], TOUTING *vbl. sb.*[1]

**Tootle** (tū·t'l), *sb.* [f. TOOTLE *v.*]

**1.** An act or the action of tootling or sounding a horn or similar wind-instrument.

1852 R. S. SURTEES *Sponge's Sp. Tour* xli, Bragg's queer tootle of his horn..now sounded at the low end of the cover. 1889 *Scott. Leader* 6 Dec. 5 The sudden and shrill tootle of a trumpet. 1894 *Daily News* 12 Mar. 2/1 The guard's inspiriting tootle wakes the echoes.

**2.** Speech or writing of more sound than sense; verbiage, twaddle.

1883 *Cornh. Mag.* May 542 Sometimes..the tootle becomes a middle in a weekly paper, sometimes it assumes the guise of an amusing review. 1888 *Scott. Leader* 8 Mar. 7 The good old order of English prose which used to be called at the English Universities 'tootle', and for which there are other names, older and more recent, but hardly any more expressive.

So **Tootle-te-too·tle, Tootle-tootle,** a piece of continuous tootling.

1855 BROWNING *Up at a Villa* ix, *Bang, whang, whang* goes the drum, *tootle-te-tootle* the fife. 1884 *Pall Mall G.* 24 July 4/2 The musical powers of most of the bands, whom no amount of entreaty could divert even for a moment from their prearranged and wholly meaningless tootle-ti-tootle. 1910 *Sat. Rev.* 10 Sept. 322/1 Footle-footle-footle goes the clarinet with a fragment of a theme; tootle-tootle-tootle echoes the flute.

**Tootle** (tū·t'l), *v.* [freq. f. TOOT *v.*[2] + -LE 4.]

**1.** *intr.* To toot continuously; to produce a succession of modulated notes on a wind-instrument.

1842 S. LOVER *Handy Andy* xviii, The fifer..tootled with some difficulty. 1878 STEVENSON *Inland Voy.* 4 Tootling on the sentimental flute. 1879 SALA *Paris herself again* II. iv. 53 The sable minstrel..begins to tootle most sweetly.

**b.** Of birds: To make a similar noise.

1820 CLARE *Rural Life* (ed. 3) 207 When tootling robins carol-welcomes sing. 1827 — *Sheph. Cal.* 25 To hear the robin's note once more, Who tootles while he pecks his meal. 1899 O. SEAMAN *In Cap & Bells* (1900) 21 The lark is tootling in the sky.

**c.** *fig.* To write twaddle or mere verbiage.

1883 [see *tootling* below]. 1894 *Daily News* 28 Feb. 5/1 Mr. Skeat's 'Life of Chaucer' is entirely businesslike. He does not 'tootle' over what Chaucer may have done, and seen, and said.

Hence **Too·tling** *vbl. sb.* and *ppl. a.*; also **Too·tler,** a writer of 'tootle', verbiage, or twaddle.

1821 CLARE *Vill. Minstr.* I. 30 He heard the tootling robin sound her knell. *Ibid.* 36 The tuteling fife, and hoarse rap-tapping drum. 1879 JEFFERIES *Wild Life in S. C.* 105 The tootling of pan-pipes in front of the shows. 1883 *Cornh. Mag.* May 542 The sort of scribblers..whom I am wont to call in my own private dialect the tootlers, that is to say the good folk who write a tootle about nothing in particular. *Ibid.* 543 The consumer who takes a delight in the perusal of tootling.

So **Tootle-too** *v.*, **Tootle-tootle** *v.* = TOOTLE *v.* 1.

1857 HUGHES *Tom Brown* I. v, Here's Rugby,..said the old guard, pulling his horn out of its case, and tootle-tooing away. 1892 *Pall Mall G.* 16 Dec. 3/1 The drumming and the tootle-tooing, even the skirling of the Hallelujah maidens.

**Tootman**: see under TOOT-NET.

**Tootnague**: see TUTENAG.

**Toot-net** (tū·t₁net). *Sc. local.* [f. TOOT *v.*[1] + NET.] 'A large fishing net anchored' (Jam.), which is watched in order to be drawn in when the fish enter it. More fully *toot and haul net*.

1805 *Case Ho. Lords, Gray of Carse* (Jam.), The fishing-tackle..sometimes consisted of a common moveable net or siene; sometimes of a toot-net, much larger and stronger than the former, extending to an indefinite length from the beach into the water, and secured at its extremity by an anchor. 1840 LEIGHTON *Hist. Fife* II. 82 The mode of fishing is now confined..to what is called the toot-net. 1898 *Glasgow Herald* 19 May 4 To fish in..the river and estuary of the Tay for salmon kind with toot and haul nets. 1900 *Law Rep., App. Cas.* 410 The First Division..declared fishing with the nets of the description of toot and haul.. an illegal method.

So **Too·tman, too·tsman,** one who watches a toot-net.

1805 *Case Ho. Lords, Gray of Carse* (E.D.D.), A man stands in a coble, or small fishing-boat; and when he sees the fish enter the net, calls the fishers to haul it. He is designed the Tootsman. 1840 LEIGHTON *Hist. Fife* II. 82 The toot-man is seated to watch the net.

**Too-too** (tū₁tū·), *v.* [Echoic: usually depreciatory.] *intr.* To make an instrumental or vocal sound resembling these syllables. Hence **Too-too·ing** *vbl. sb.*; so also **Too-too** *adv.* and *sb.*, **Too-too·er.**

1812 H. & J. SMITH *Rej. Addr.*, *The Theatre* 25 Tang goes the harpsichord, too-too the flute. 1828 MOIR *Mansie Wauch* xi. (1849) 74 The old flute was for Benjie, poor thing, too-tooing on. 1836–9 DICKENS *Sk. Boz, Public Dinners*, The singers..begin too-tooing most dismally. 1840 THACKERAY *Pict. Rhapsody* Concl., Wks. 1900 XIII. 345 Punchman is tootooing on the pipes, and banging away on the drum. 1843 — *Irish Sk. Bk.* xxviii, An unequal and disagreeable tootooing on a horn. 1862 MISS YONGE *C'tess Kate* ix, Kate..came up too-tooing through her hand with all her might. *a* 1884 CALVERLEY *Verses & Transl.*, *To Mrs. Goodchild* x, Checked by that absurd Too-too [of a person practising on a horn].

**Too-too**: see TOO *adv.* 4.

**Tootsicum,** a whimsical expansion of TOOTSY.

1860 LEECH *Pict. Life & Char.* Ser. III. 18 The brutality of connecting..such words [as 'Beetle-crusher'] with the feminine Tootsicums. 1877 BESANT & RICE *With Harp & Crown* xxxiv, Beer is the real magnet for the male feet. Champagne..draws the feminine tootsicums.

**Tootsman**: see under TOOT-NET.

**Tootsy, tootsy-wootsy.** *colloq.* A playful or endearing name for a child's or a woman's small foot.

1854 THACKERAY *Rose & Ring* xi, As for the shoe, what was she to do with one poor little tootsey sandal? 1865 E. C. CLAYTON *Cruel Fortune* III. 90 His poor little tootsies peeping out from the tips of his boots. 1897 GUNTER *Susan Turnbull* v, Yer [a young lady of 19]..little tootsy-wootsies will be as safe as if they were tucked in yer little cot bed upstairs. 1906 CHARLOTTE MANSFIELD *Girl & Gods* xii, But if you are walking along a muddy road with old shoes on, all the idealistic thought in the world won't keep the damp away from your poor tootsies.

**Tooward, Tooze,** obs. ff. TOWARD, TOZE.

**Too-whit, Too-whoo,** cry of the owl: see TU-.

**Toozle, Toozy,** dial. ff. TOUSLE, TOUSY.

**Top** (tǫp), *sb.*[1] Forms: 1 top, 3–6, (?) 7 toppe, *pl.* toppes, 4–6 tope, 4–7 topp, 6– *Sc.* and *north.* tap, 3– top. [OE. *top* (*topp-*), Com. WGer. and Norse; =OFris. *topp* (WFris. *top*, NFris. *top*, *tup*), OLG. **topp* (MDu., Du. *top*(*p*), MLG., LG. *top*), OHG. (MHG., Ger.) *zopf* top, summit, a crest or tuft of hair; ON. *toppr* top, tuft, Sw. *topp* top, pinnacle, Da. *top* top, point, MDa. also tuft of feathers, plume, mod.Norw. also *tupp*:—OTeut. **tuppoz*; not known in Gothic. Outside Teutonic known only in Romanic derivatives: cf. TOUPET.]

**I.** A tuft, crest, or bush of hair, etc.

**1.** The hair on the summit or crown of the head; the hair of the head. *Obs.* exc. *Sc.*

*Foreward top* = FORETOP. *To take* (†*hent*, †*nim*) *by the top*, to seize by the hair, lay hold of violently (also *fig.*).

*c* 1205 LAY. 684 Bi þone toppe [*c* 1275 bi þe coppe] he hine nome Al swa he hine walde of-slean. 1297 R. GLOUC. (Rolls) 5619 He..hente þis lof bi þe top, & fram þe bord him drou. *c* 1386 CHAUCER *Prol.* 590 His tope [*v.rr.* top, toppe] was doked lyk a preest biforn. *c* 1386 — *Reeve's Prol.* 15 This white tope writeth myne olde yeris. *c* 1440 *Promp. Parv.* 496/2 Top, or fortop (*K.*, *P.* top of the hed), *aqualium*. 1535 COVERDALE *Bel & Dr.* 36 Then the angel..toke him by the toppe, and bare him by the hayre of the heade. 1601 SHAKS. *All's Well* v. iii. 39 Let's take the instant by the forward top: For we are old. *a* 1643 CARTWRIGHT *Ordinary* II. ii. 1884 D. GRANT *Lays & Leg.* 21 Eppie got him by the tap..Quo' Davit then,..'Lat go my puckle hair'.

**b.** The crest or 'topping' of a bird; the forelock of a horse, etc. Now *Sc.* and *north. dial.*

*a* 1225 *St. Marher.* 12 And toc him [the dragon] bi þe ateliche top. 13.. *K. Alis.* 5186 (Bodl. MS.) Ypotame a wonder beest..; Toppe, & rugge, & croupe, & cors, Is semblabel to an hors. *c* 1450 HOLLAND *Howlat* 837 The Golk..Tit the Tuchet be the tope, ourtirvit his hed. 1578 in Feuillerat *Revels Q. Eliz.* (1908) 296, vid for iii hearons toppes which were burnte with Torches. 1585 JAS. I *Ess. Poesie* (Arb.) 43 Euen so, had Nature,..Giuen her [the phœnix] ane tap, for to augment her grace. 1650 EARL MONM. tr. *Senault's Man bec. Guilty* 353 We deck ourselves with birds feathers, the tops of herons. 1756 MRS. CALDERWOOD *Jrnl.* iii. (1884) 66 The horses have..a large top betwixt their ears 1808–25 JAMIESON, *Tap*..3. The tuft on the head of some fowls. Hence the phrase, *tappit hen*.

**2.** A tuft or handful of hair, wool, fibre, etc.; *esp.* the portion of flax or tow put on the distaff (in full, *top of flax*, *lint* († *line*), *tow*). Also *fig.* Now only *Sc.* and *north. dial.* [Cf. med.L. *toppus lini* (top of flax).]

*To tak one's tap in one's lap*: see quot. 1825.

[But some refer this sense to TOP *sb.*[2], as having reference to the shape; cf. quot. 1891 in 34.]

*a* 1250 *Owl & Night.* 428 Ne rouhte þe þeyh flockes were Imeynd bi toppes & bi here. *c* 1325 *Gloss. W. de Bibbesw.* in Wright *Voc.* 144 E serencez du lyn le toup [*gloss*] hekele, a top of flax. 14.. *Nom.* in Wr.-Wülcker 696/3 *Hoc lapsum*, a top of lin. 1558 in Feuillerat *Revels Q. Eliz.* (1908) 25 Into vi nighte cappes & toppes of turkes headdes peces. 1681 COLVIL *Whigs Supplic.* 258 A Top of Lint for his Panash. 1794 BURNS *Weary Pund o' Tow* iv, Gae spin your tap o' tow! 1818 SCOTT *Hrt. Midl.* xxxvii[i], 'And does your honour think', said Jeanie, 'that will do as weel as if I were to take my tap in my lap, and slip my ways hame again?' 1825 JAMIESON s.v. *Tap*, *To tak one's tap in one's lap, and set aff*, to turse up one's baggage, and be gone..from the practice of women accustomed to spin from a rock, who often carried their work with them to the house of some neighbour. 1894 *Northumbld. Gloss.*, *Top*, in spinning, the quantity of flax put on the 'rock' at a time.

**b.** *spec.* A bundle of combed wool prepared for spinning. Chiefly *pl.* (also *collect. sing.*).

1637 *Bury Wills* (Camden) 169, I owe John Brightall for combeing of ten skore poundes and ten of tops. 1759 *Overseers' Acc., Holy Cross, Canterb.*, To 1 Top of wool for worsted deliver'd to Mrs. Hawley..0. 2. 0. 1844 G. DODD *Textile Manuf.* iv. 129 The wool generally comes to the factories in narrow bundles or 'tops', about eighteen inches long, and weighing about a pound and a half or two pounds each. 1882 *Worc. Exhib. Catal.* III. 31 Combing process, separating long wool from short, the long wool being then called combed tops. 1888 ELWORTHY *W. Somerset Word-bk.*, *Top*, a bundle of combed wool as made up by the comber for spinning, usually weighing about 28lbs...At present the word is applied to the bundles of combed wool from the machine—hand combing having been quite superseded.

**II.** The highest or uppermost part.

**3.** The highest point or part of anything; perh. originally a pointed or peaked summit, an apex or peak; but now applied to the uppermost part, whatever its nature or shape; the highest place or limit *of* something.

*To swim at the top* (fig.), to maintain a high social position.

*c* 1000 *Ælfric's Voc.* in Wr.-Wülcker 143/26 *Apex*, *summitas galeæ*, helmes top. *c* 1205 LAY. 1339 He hihte hondlien kablen Teon seiles to toppa [*c* 1275 toppe]. *a* 1250 *Owl & Night.* 1422 Vp to þe toppe from þe more. *c* 1275 LAY. 7781 In þan grunde of þe tur mihte sitte Sixti hundred cnihtes And þe toppe [*c* 1205 þa turres cop] mihte wreie On cniht mid his cope. 13.. *K. Alis.* 1417 (Bodl. MS.) Hii drawen sayl to top of mast. *a* 1400–50 *Alexander* 2110 Þan vp he clame to a cliffe..Þare fand he tildid on þe top & tild vp a cite. 1459 *Paston Lett.* I. 488 Pottis of sylver,..enamelyd on the toppys withe hys armys. 1560 DAUS tr. *Sleidane's Comm.* 54 b, Reaching from Thuringe..vnto the toppe of the Alpes. *c* 1630 RISDON *Surv. Devon* § 215 (1810) 223 Trees..no taller than a man may touch to top with his hand. 1686 tr. *Chardin's Trav. Persia* 74 The Door is made..with an opening at the Top. 1691 HARTCLIFFE *Virtues* 229 This Sentence should be writ on our Houses Tops. 1781 COWPER *Truth* 549 From Sinai's top Jehovah gave the law. 1825 SCOTT *Talism.* i, The flat top of his cumbrous cylindrical helmet was unadorned with any crest. 1873 J. RICHARDS *Wood-working Factories* 116 Everything about the top of a bench must be strong and simple.

**b.** That part of anything portable which, when it is in use, occupies the highest place; e. g. the top of a page, map, etc.

1593 SHAKS. *2 Hen. VI*, IV. ii. 107 They vse to writ it on the top of Letters. 1681 S. FELL in *Jrnl. Friends' Hist. Soc.* July (1912) 136 You may see at the Topp of every leafe, which Meetings testimonies followes. 1817 *Parl. Deb.* 430 Lord Cochrane..knew persons in office had frequently procured signatures to petitions without a top. 1859 LANG *Wand. India* 388 'Order a fresh bottle of our wine for him, Blade', said the Colonel, 'and let him taste the top of it'.

**c.** The higher end of anything on a slope; † the head or source of a river (*obs.*), the head of a lake (*arch.*), of a street, etc.; also that end of anything which is conventionally considered the higher, as of a room or dining-table; the end of a billiard-table opposite the baulk.

1624 CAPT. SMITH *Virginia* II. 23 The third navigable river is called Toppahanock...At the top of it inhabit the people called Mannahoacks amongst the mountaines. 1782 MRS. COWLEY *Which is the Man* v. ii, Coming down from the Top [of the room], addressing the Company. 1811 T. WILSON *Country Dancing* (ed. 2) 129 The top of the Dance or Set..is known thus:—the Ladies will always have the top of the Set on their right hands, and the Gentlemen on their left. 1849 MRS. CARLYLE *Lett.* (1883) II. 41 In the omnibus to the top of Sloane Street. 1906 ALICE WERNER *Natives Brit. Cent. Africa* xii. 282 They..went on to the north, and round the top of the lake.

**4.** The uppermost division of the body; the head; *esp.* the crown of the head. Chiefly, now only, in alliterative expressions: see 24, 25.

*a* 1225 *Juliana* 59 Ouer al & from þe top to þe tan. 1303, *c* 1330 [see 24, 24 d]. 13.. *E. E. Allit. P.* C. 229 Tyd by top & bi to, þay token hym synne. *a* 1400–50 *Alexander* 752* And toton owt of hys top als tyndis of hornes. ? *a* 1500 *Chester Pl.* (Shaks. Soc.) II. 176 Thou take hym by þe toppe and I by þe tayle. ? *a* 1500 *Debate Carpenters Tools* 188 in Hazl. *E. P. P.* I. 86 Methinke gode ale is in ȝour tope. 1611 SHAKS. *Cymb.* IV. ii. 354 Soft hoa, what truncke is heere? Without his top? 1821 SCOTT *Kenilw.* ix, The pains I have bestowed on the top and bottom of..Dickie, whom I have painfully made to travel through the accidence.

**b.** The uppermost branch of a deer's horn: esp. in phr. *on* (*upon*) *top*.

1486 *Bk. St. Albans* e j b, When he hath Awntelere with owt any lett Ryall and Surriall also there Isett, And that in the toppe so. 1801 in C. P. Collyns *Notes Chase Wild Red Deer* (1862) App. 211 The remaining horn had three on top with all his rights. 1886 *Wellington* (Som.) *Weekly News* 19 Aug., A large, heavy deer, with two upon top on each side.

**5.** Usually *pl.* The part of a plant growing above ground as distinct from the root; esp. of a vegetable grown for the 'root', as *turnip-tops*. Also the tender tips of branches or shoots.

[1377 LANGL. *P. Pl.* B. XVI. 22 Pieres..bad me toten on þe tree on toppe and on rote.] 1523 FITZHERB. *Husb.* § 28 Thanne he taketh the barley or otes by the toppes. 1552 HULOET, Toppe of an herbe, *capillamentum*. 1639 O. WOOD *Alph. Bk. Secrets* 10 Then take the young tops of Rosemary, Marigolds [etc.]. 1725 WATTS *Logic* I. vi. § 3 If the buds are made our food, they are called heads, or tops. 1766 *Complete Farmer* s.v. *Radish* 6 I 1/1 They will run up in tops, and not increase in their roots. 1844 H. STEPHENS *Bk. Farm* II. 5 Tops of turnips make good feeding at the beginning of the season. 18.. *U. S. Dispensatory* (ed. 14) 827 (Cent. Dict.) The fruits and tops of juniper are the only officinal parts.

**6.** *pl.* (also *collect. sing.*). The smaller branches and twigs of trees as distinct from the timber.

Often with *lop*, as *top(s and lop(s, lop(s and top(s, lop(s, top(s, and bark* (or *crop(s)*).

1485–6 *Durham Acc. Rolls* (Surtees) 98 Rec. xvjs. pro corticibus et Toppys in silva de Rylley. 1523 FITZHERB. *Husb.* § 154 If thou haue any woode to sell..sell the toppes as they lye. 1669, etc. [see LOP *sb.*[3] 1]. 1858 SIMMONDS *Dict. Trade* s.v. *Lop*, In a sale of standing timber trees they are advertised with their 'lop, top, and bark'.

**7.** The extremity of a growing part (which is often the highest and usually the most slender point); hence the narrower end (of anything tapering), the point, tip. *Top and butt* (Shipbuilding), a method of working long tapering planks together in pairs with the top of one to the butt of another, so as to maintain a constant width.

1538 ELYOT, *Sagitta*, an arow, also the top of a twygge or rodde. 1573–80 BARET *Alv.* T 290 The sharpnesse of the top, or tippe of the nose...The tops, or tips of the fingers. 1754 SHEBBEARE *Matrimony* (1766) I. 76 My Lord stept off lightly, on the Tops of his Toes. 1815 BURNEY *Falconer's Dict. Marine*, *Top and Butt*, in ship-building, a general method of working the English plank (except in the topside) to make good work and conversion, which is done by disposing of the top-end of every plank, within six feet of the butt-end of the plank above or below it. 1866 *Chambers' Encycl.* VIII. 684/2 Top-and-butt.

**8.** In various applications. **a.** In *Gem-cutting*: see quot. **b.** The inside of a roof; a ceiling; *spec.* the roof of a coal-mine or tunnel. **c.** *Tops and bottoms*: the flattish halves of small rolls sliced lengthways, and browned in the oven; rusks. **d.** See quot. 1905, and cf. BOTTOM *sb.* 8 a. **e.** *Mining.* See quot.

**a.** 1877 KNIGHT *Dict. Mech.*, *Top*, that portion of a cut gem which is between the girdle, or extreme margin, and the table or flat face. **b.** 1706 SWIFT *Baucis & Philemon* 58 The kettle to the top was hoist, And there stood fasten'd to a joist. 1830 T. WILSON *Pitman's Pay* (1843) 13 For if maw 'top comes badly down. 1844 F. W. SIMMS *Pract. Tunnelling* ix. 83 This stage of progress, which is technically called 'getting in the top' [of a tunnel]. 1889 *N. W. Linc. Gloss.*, *Top*, the ceiling, as 'th' room top', 'th' kitchen top'. 1894 *Northumbld. Gloss.*, *Top*, in mining, the portion of coal that has been kirved and nicked, and is ready to be blasted or wedged down. **c.** 1765 *Univ. Mag.* XXXVII. 371/2 The biskets called tops and bottoms, or rusks. 1866 *Routledge's Ev. Boy's Ann.* 55 Some nice tops-and-bottoms for its supper. **d.** 1905 *Daily Chron.* 17 July 4/7 The labourers who board the steamers inquire anxiously for 'tops and bottoms'—that is, everything that has been left undrunk in the passengers glasses. **e.** 1894 *Northumbld. Gloss.*, *Top*, the blue flame above a candle or lamp.., whose appearance indicates the presence of fire-damp in the mine.

**III.** A piece or part placed upon or fitted to anything, and forming its upper part or covering.

**9.** A platform near the head of each of the lower masts of a ship. In early fighting ships, a platform at the head of the mast, fenced with a rail (cf. *top-armour*, 33), stored with missiles and occupied by archers, etc., called more fully TOP-CASTLE; later, a similar platform on which musketeers or riflemen were stationed (cf. TOPMAN[1] 3); in a modern warship, an armoured platform on a short mast, for machine-guns, signalling, etc.; more fully *fighting-top*, *military top*. In a sailing ship, a framework and platform serving to extend the rigging of the topmast, and for convenience in making sail.

*c* 1420 ? LYDG. *Assembly of Gods* 342 A shyp with a toppe & seyle was hys crest. *a* 1533 LD. BERNERS *Huon* cvii. 360 He caused one of the maryners to mounte vp into the toppe to se yf he myght se any lond. 1561 EDEN *Arte Navig.* I. vii. 9 If you stande in the toppe of the shyppe. 1697 DAMPIER *Voy. round World* (1699) 208 We saw the light in the Admirals top, which continued about half an hour. 1764 VEITCH in *Phil. Trans.* LIV. 291 The top, or round scaffolding on the mast..in this ship it was 18 feet broad. 1859 *All Year Round* No. 17. 399 We literally raced for the lubber's hole, through which we crept, and then stood in the top to survey the scene. 1867 SMYTH *Sailor's Word-bk.*, *Half-top*, the mode of making ships' tops in two pieces, which are afterwards secured as a whole by what are termed sleepers.

**b.** *Naut.* Short for *topsail*: see quots.

† *To pull* or *take down*, *bow*, or *vail one's top*, to lower one's topsail in token of submission or respect; said of a ship, hence *fig.* of a person. *Obs.*

1513–42 *Hist. Sir W. Wallace* x. (1881) 54 All the shipis.. pulling down ther topis, did obeysance vnto the read Lyon. *a* 1600 HOOKER *Serm. Justif.* § 28 Let the Pope take downe his top and captiuate no more mens soules. 1694 MOTTEUX *Rabelais* IV. lxiv. (1737) 264 A fresh gale..began to fill the ..Tops, and Top-gallants.

**c.** *Top and topgallant*, short for *topsail and topgallant sail*; hence *fig.* (also *attrib.*); as *advb.* with all sail set, in full array or career.

1593 NASHE *Christ's T.* 71 b, Theyr heads, with theyr top and top gallant Lawne-baby caps. 1594 PEELE *Battle of Alcazar* III. iii, He cometh hitherward amain, Top and top-gallant, all in brave array. 1607 *Merry Devil Edmonton* I. i. 34 Heele be here top and top-gallant presently. 1626 BACON *Sylva* § 646, I have seen..one Rose grow out of another, like Honey-suckle, that they call Top and Top-Gallants. 1662 OWEN *Animadv. Fiat Lux* xiii. Wks. (ed. Gould) XIV. 111 They carry their top and top-gallant so high that they will go to heaven without Christ. 1812 SCOTT *Rokeby* II. xi, Top and top-gallant hoisted high,.. The Dæmon-frigate braves the gale. 1819 — *Let.* in *Lockhart* (1837) IV. viii. 239, I did not lose my senses,.. but I thought once or twice they would have gone overboard, top and top-gallant.

**10.** The uppermost part of the leg of a high boot or riding-boot, *spec.* when widened out or turned over (as in 17th c.); now, on hunting-boots and the like, a broad band of material (simulating the turned-over part), white, light-coloured, or brown. Also *pl.* short for TOP-BOOTS.

1629 *Disc. Leather* 13 The manner of cutting Bootes out with huge, slouenly, vnmannerly, and immoderate tops. 1683 *Lond. Gaz.* No. 1869/4 A pair of Boots without Tops. 1835 SIR G. STEPHEN *Adv. Search Horse* xv. 193 Boots, that once had tops, approach within six inches of the knee. 1836–9 DICKENS *Sk. Boz*, *First of May*, Knee-cords and tops superseded nankeen drawers and rosetted shoes. 1837 — *Pickw.* x, Mr. Samuel Weller happened to be..engaged in burnishing a pair of painted tops. 1846–79 EGERTON WARBURTON *Hunting Songs* lix. (1883) 162 Above the boots' jet polish Was a top of tender stain, Nor brown nor white, but a mixture light, Of rose-leaves and champagne. 1904 *Blackw. Mag.* Nov. 675/2 They had red waistcoats, white breeches, white tops, black velvet caps and white gloves.

**b.** The gauntlet part of a glove; the turned-down top part of men's hose.

1819 SCOTT *Leg. Montrose* ii, A pair of gauntlets,..the tops of which reached up to his elbow. 1906 in *Daily Chron.* 20 Aug. 3/3 The Highland regiments introduced complications with five different tartans, and three different pattern of hose-tops.

**11.** In various technical applications:

† **a.** A piece (perh. a socket) fitted to the upper end of a torch-staff. *Obs.* **b.** The terminal joint of a fishing-rod. **c.** A jewel worn in the lobe of the ear, often with a 'drop' or pendant; usually in *tops and drops*. † **d.** A lady's high 'head': see HEAD *sb.* 5. *Obs.* **e.** *pl.* A framing which increases the capacity of a cart; shelvings, cart-ladders, load-trees. **f.** *Spinning.* The top-cards in a carding-engine. **g.** The glass or metal stopper of a scent-bottle or the like; also, an inverted tumbler used as a cap to cover a decanter. **h.** The hood or cover of a carriage. **i.** *Typog.* See quot. **j.** A piece of female dress covering the neck and shoulders, worn with a certain kind of gown made without this part.

**a.** 1453 *Mem. Ripon* (Surtees) III. 162 Pro faccione ij torchearum novarum et pro ij toppes magn. torch. **b.** 1676 WALTON & COTTON *Angler* II. xii. 101 Though I have taken with the Angle..some thousands of Trouts..my top never snapt, though my Line still continued fast. 1706 R. H[OWLETT] *Angler's Sure Guide* 79 The Stock [of the Rod] bored no wider than to carry a Ground-top therein, or a Flie-top. **c.** 1703 *Lond. Gaz.* No. 3942/4 Stolen.., a pair of Diamond Ear-Rings, with 4 large Faucet Diamonds (Tops and Drops). 1761 COLMAN *Genius* No. 3 in *Prose on Sev. Occas.* (1787) I. 34 To humour my wife, little Tubal was ordered to furnish her with a pair of diamond tops. 1825 T. HOOK *Sayings* Ser. II. *Sutherl.* I. 79 In her ears hung pendant diamonds, top and drop. **d.** 1780 MRS. DELANY in *Life & Corr.* Ser. II. (1862) II. 524 Rows upon rows of fine ladies with towering tops. **e.** 1844 STEPHENS *Bk. Farm* III. 1087 The common cart..mounted with a framing called tops, is used in some parts of the country. **f.** 1845 *Statist. Acc. Scot.* VI. 147 In 1815 Mr. Smith constructed a carding-engine, having the flats or tops moveable on hinges. 1851 L. D. B. GORDON *Art Jrnl. Illustr. Catal.* p. iv **/2 The large card-drum is generally surmounted by urchin or squirrel cards instead of tops. **g.** 1862 MISS BRADDON *Lady Audley* xvi, Do you suppose that because people don't wear vinegar tops, or part their hair on the wrong side..by way of proving the vehemence of their passion? 1869 *Anthony's Photogr. Bull.* II. 361 This stopper is of tin, has a top screw with two holes. Whenever this top is a little unscrewed the liquid can come out of the bottle by drops. 1893 *N. & Q.* 8th Ser. III. 233/2 A carafe and 'top' is the shop-name for such a vessel [*i.e.* tumbler] and the bottle ministrant. **h.** 1617 MORYSON *Itin.* III. 54 The top of the Coaches is made with round hoopes. 1884–1898 [implied in *top-buggy*, *-phaeton*, *-wagon*: see 26]. **i.** 1888 JACOBI *Printer's Vocab.* 142 *Tops.* In stacking work as printed off, the warehouseman places a few sheets of each signature on the top, so that they may be at hand if a set of advanced sheets are asked for, thereby obviating the lifting of a quantity of work. **j.** 1902 *Westm. Gaz.* 14 Aug. 3/2 The main thing is to have several well-fitting slips and a selection of tops.. I saw a very pretty creamy chiffon top the other day.

**12.** Short for *top-button*: see 32.

1852 W. HUTTON in *Househ. Words* V. 108/1 The long coats of our grandfathers, covered with half a gross of high-tops. 1860 TOMLINSON *Arts & Manuf.* Ser. II. *Buttons* 38 The buttons [are] stirred about in the solution for all-overs; or brushed on the face for tops. 1874 KNIGHT *Dict. Mech.* 416/1 When the face only is gilt, the buttons are technically known as tops.

**IV.** *fig.* and *transf.* The part of anything which has the first place in time, order, or precedence.

**13.** Of time: The earliest part of a period; the beginning.

For *the top of the morning*, as a greeting, see 17.

*c* 1440 *Pallad. on Husb.* III. 1000 In thende of Octob'r, or in the toppe [*orig.* inicio] Of Novemb'r. 1669 WORLIDGE *Syst. Agric.* (1681) 98 A mellifluous Army of Bees, from the top of the morning, till the cool and dark evening. 1825 HONE *Every-day Bk.* I. 403/1 The dawn is awakened by a cry in the streets of 'Hot-cross-buns; one-a-penny buns..!' This proceeds from some little 'peep-o'-day boy', willing to take the 'top of the morning' before the rest of his compeers.

**14.** The highest, chief, or leading position, place, or rank; the head, forefront; now esp. in *the top of the tree* (fig.).

1627 HAKEWILL *Apol.* Pref. 5 By vertue..being come to the top, they lost it againe by vice. *a* 1677 BARROW *Serm.* Wks. 1716 II. 143 We who are placed in the top of nature. 1699 LOCKE *Educ.* (ed. 4) § 70. 104 Take a Boy from the top of a Grammar-School. 1782 MISS BURNEY *Cecilia* IV. x, I thought to have seen him at the top of the tree, as one may say! 1879 B. TAYLOR *Stud. Germ. Lit.* 136 The medieval passion for song began at the top and worked downwards. 1885 W. S. GILBERT *Mikado* I, I'm right at the top of the school. 1908 *Times* 3 Aug. 11/6 Brilliancy and determination..brought them to the top of the tree.

**b.** One who or that which occupies the highest or chief position; the head (of a clan, family, etc.).

1612 DAY *Festivals* ii. (1615) 27 Adam the Top of our Kin. 1646 J. GREGORY *Notes & Obs.* (1650) 30 Muazzus the Toppe of the Fatimæan family, caused the City of Gran Cairo to be set up. 1695 J. EDWARDS *Perfect. Script.* 332 Lastly man, the top and glory of the creatures. 1741 BETTERTON *Eng. Stage* vi. 116 He looks upon himself as the Top of his Family.. 1856 LEVER *Martins of Cro' M.* xxxviii, They barred out the master to make 'the head usher' top of the school.

**15.** The highest pitch or degree; the height, summit, zenith, pinnacle; now esp. in *the top of one's bent* (see BENT *sb.*[2] 9), *the top of one's voice*.

1552 in *Vicary's Anat.* (1888) App. xvi. 294 What thyng at the first can atteyne to the toppe of perfectnesse. 1602 SHAKS. *Ham.* III. ii. 383 From my lowest Note, to the top of my Compasse. 1602–1875 [see BENT *sb.*[2] 9]. 1671 MILTON *Samson* 167 By how much from the top of wondrous glory, ..To lowest pitch of abject fortune thou art fall'n. 1711 STEELE *Spect.* No. 32 ᴘ 2 High Shoulders, as well as high Noses, were the Top of the Fashion. 1737 BRACKEN *Farriery Impr.* (1757) II. 195 Let him be kept to the Top of his Speed.

**1881** Besant & Rice *Chapl. of Fleet* I. iv, All the drivers were swearing at each other at the top of their voices.

**b.** One who or that which is or represents the highest pitch or degree; the most perfect example or type of something. (The constr. in quot. 1682 is *obs.* and *rare.*)

**1593** Q. Eliz. *Boeth.* 80 All such referd to greatest good, as to the top of Natures best. **1594** T. B. *La Primaud. Fr. Acad.* II. 570 His goodnesse, bountie, grace, and fauour towardes vs, which is the toppe of happinesse. **1603** Shaks. *Meas. for M.* II. ii. 76 If he, which is the top of Iudgement, should But iudge you, as you are. **1682** Dryden *Mac Fl.* 167 But write thy best and top; and in each line Sir Formal's oratory will be thine. **1711** Hickes *Two Treat. Chr. Priesth.* (1847) II. 297 The episcopate is the top of all the honours among men. **1885–6** Spurgeon *Treas. Dav.* Ps. cxxx. 8 Redemption is the top of covenant blessings.

**c.** (absol. use of *top* as adj.: see 27–30). *Motoring slang.* The top or highest gear; usually *on* (*the*) *top.*

**1906** *Westm. Gaz.* 21 Aug. 4/2 It was only found necessary twice during the journey to change to the second speed, most of the run being done on the 'top'. **1909** *Ibid.* 30 Nov. 5/2 In this machine the driving is..always done on top.

**16.** The highest point reached in a progression or series; the culminating point; esp. in *the top of high water, of the tide; top of the market,* the moment at which prices are highest.

*a* **1670** Spalding *Troub. Chas. I* (1850) I. 341 Grevous to the people, now in top of harvest. **1719** De Foe *Crusoe* I. 299 It was just at the Top of High-Water when these People came on Shore. **1759** Dilworth *Pope* 131 The hackney scribblers seizing the top of the market, had quite run down the subject. **1801** *Naval Chron.* VI. 76 At the top of the tide she turned off the stocks. **1899** MacManus *Chimney Corners* 168 They'll insure me the top of the market.

**17.** The best or choicest part; the cream, flower, pick. Now esp. in *the top of the morning,* as an Irish morning greeting (cf. 13).

**1663** Bp. Patrick *Parab. Pilgr.* xiv. (1687) 96 A conjunction of the very top and flower of the mind with the beginning and original of all good. **1668** Bp. Hopkins *Serm., Vanity* (1685) 99 The soul, next to angels, is the very top and cream of the whole creation. **1757** W. Thompson *R. N. Advoc.* 44 Which their.. Friends, the top of the Physical Faculty can verify. **1815** Scott *Guy M.* iv, The top of the morning to you, sir. **1843** Lever *J. Hinton* lviii, Captain, my darling, the top of the morning to you! **1894** *Westm. Gaz.* 10 Apr. 2/3 A 'top of the basket' young lady, like Lady Anne, would have been married long before the curtain rises.

**b.** *spec. pl.* (*a*) The best sheep or lambs in a flock. (*b*) Members of the highest social class. (*c*) The better quality of grain, separated from the *tails* (Tail *sb.*[1] 7 b, q. v.).

**1831** *Sutherland Farm Rep.* 80 in *Libr. Usef. Knowl., Husb.* III, The tops (the most choice and best breed) possess the outskirts of the ewe heiding. **1886** C. Scott *Sheep-Farming* 19 When a lot of sheep are drafted, they are assorted. The best lot are called 'tops'. **1887** *Pall Mall G.* 24 Aug. 11/1 Here..were given the dances when a party of London 'Tops' were invited to spend the Christmas holidays or to enjoy a week's shooting. **1906** J. Patterson *Wamphray* vii. 193 It threshes, separates 'tops from tails', bags each separately, and bundles the straw.

**V.** Applied to actions.

**18.** The action of Top *v.*[1]; the putting of a top on something; *top-up,* a finish or conclusion. *rare.*

**1883** *Three in Norway* 146 He thought this a grand top-up for a successful day.

**19.** Forward spin imparted to a ball by the mode of its impulsion or delivery (in billiards, by striking it above the centre; hence in cricket and tennis). Cf. Topside d, and *top-twist* in 32.

**1901** *Westm. Gaz.* 13 Aug. 2/3 A vertical twist given by friction against the ground analogous with 'top' on a billiard ball. **1903** H. G. Hutchinson *Cricket* iv. 88 A ball ..which..is simply propelled with a large quantity of 'top on'. **1907** C. B. Fry in *Daily Chron.* 18 July 7/2 Schwarz's off-break, being produced by a perversion of leg-break action, contains an inordinate amount of 'top'.

†**20.** *Dice-play.* A cheating trick in which one of the dice was retained at the top of the box.

**1709** *Tatler* No. 68 ¶ 5 There is lately broke loose from the London Pack, a very tall dangerous Biter...His Manner of Biting is new, and called the Top. **1711** Puckle *Club* 22 *note,* Supposing both box and dice fair, gamesters have the top, the peep, eclipse, thumbing.

**VI.** Phrases.

**21. At, on top**: see prec. senses and quots.; *fig.* supreme; dominant; († in), on, upon (*the*) top of, above, upon, close upon, following upon.

**1602** Shaks. *Ham.* II. ii. 355 Little Yases, that crye out on the top of question. *Ibid.* 459 Others, whose iudgement in such matters, cried in the top of mine. **1603** Knolles *Hist. Turks* (1621) 394 Hee was vpon the top of his marriage. **1756** C. Lucas *Ess. Waters* II. 125 With this inscription, at top. **1796** Mme. D'Arblay *Camilla* II. 62 One thing heaped o'top of t'other. **1886** *St. Stephen's Rev.* 13 Mar. 11/2 Two heavy falls in a week, and a bad cold on the top of them. **1898** N. Gould *Landed at Last* iv, This year I fancy I shall be on top with my pair of brothers. **1903** Farmer & Henley *Slang* s.v., *To come out on top,* to be successful. **1911** Marett *Anthropol.* ii. 43 On top of the Wealden dome.

**22.** († In), on, upon one's top, attacking or assailing one, esp. from a superior position; 'coming down upon one', 'about one's ears'. So *never off one's top.* † **In tops with,** in or into conflict or antagonism with. Now chiefly *Sc.*

**1494** Fabyan *Chron.* VII. ccxxiii. 249 He..suffered for a season, leste he hadde brought all in his toppe atones. **1519** Horman *Vulg.* 137 Euery man is in my toppe [*omnibus sum infestus*]. **1560** Daus tr. *Sleidane's Comm.* 125 b, To styre vp cruell warres, and set one in an others toppe. **1570** G. Harvey *Letter-bk.* (Camden) 8 Strait wais M. Nevil was on mi top. *a* **1658** J. Durham *Expos. Rev.* xi. 2 (1680) 416 Fear to come in tops with this Word; it is a sword with two edges. **1680** Archd. Aleson in *Cloud of Witnesses* (1810) 46 Ye have Kirk and State upon your top. **1710** J. Wilson in Calderwood *Dying Test.* (1806) 155 Who would have thought that those builders..would have so soon flown upon one anothers tops? **1825** Jamieson s.v. *Tap, To be on one's tap,* to assault, literally; especially by flying at one's head, or attempting to get hold of the hair. **1888** in *Scott. Leader* 3 May 5/1 It's a most singular thing that Bailie Lawson is always on my top about paltry things of that sort.

**23. Top .. bottom. a.** *Top to bottom* (also *bottom to top*), so that the highest part becomes the lowest; with complete inversion. **b.** *From top to bottom* = *from top to toe* (25). **c.** *Top or bottom* = *top or tail* (24 b). **d.** *Top and bottom,* (*a*) = *top and tail,* 24 a (*a*); (*b*) short for *at top and bottom* (of table).

[*a* **1250** *Owl & Night.* 1328 Of clerkes lore top ne more [= root]. *Ibid.* 1422 [see 3].] **1621** Burton *Anat. Mel.* II. ii. III. (1651) 245 Turned..top to bottom, or bottom to top. **1666** Pepys *Diary* 10 June, The management..was bad from top to bottom. **1887** *S. Cheshire Gloss.* s.v., 'That's the top an' the bottom on it' corresponds to 'that is the long and the short of it'.

**24. Top .. tail. a.** *Top and tail* (also †*tail and top*). (*a*) The whole, everything without exception, every part. (*b*) The long and short of it, the substance, upshot (also *the top, tail, and mane*). (*c*) *advb.* From head to foot, from beginning to end; all over. (*d*) Bottom upwards, topsy-turvy (now *dial.*). **b.** *Top or tail,* also *top, tail, or mane* (*root*), (in negative statements), any part; anything definite or intelligible; head or tail. **c.** *From top to tail* = *top and tail,* a (*c*); also *fig.* wholly, absolutely.

**1303** R. Brunne *Handl. Synne* 5416 Þarfor shul þey..Go to helle, both top and tayle. *c* **1384** Chaucer *H. Fame* II. 371 (Fairf. MS.) Toppe and tayle and euery del..euery word that spoken ys. *c* **1440** *York Myst.* xxxi. 193 Tell hyme fro toppe vnto tayle. **1550** Bale *Apol.* 106 b, It is in the whole, toppe and tayle, length and bredth, begynnynge and endynge. **1558** Phaer *Æneid* v. N j b, Headlong down in dust he ouerturnyd tayle and topp. **1727** P. Walker *Remark. Passages* (1827) 212 His Sermon had neither Top, Tail, nor Mane. **1822** Carlyle *Early Lett.* (1886) II. 32 They will..make neither 'top, tail, nor root out of it'. **1874** T. Hardy *Far fr. Madding Crowd* lvi, The top and tail o't is this. **1888** Elworthy *W. Somerset Word-bk.* s. v., The pony put his foot in a rabbit's hole and proper turned top-on-tail.

**d.** *Top over tail,* app. an inversion of *tail over top* (which also occurs: cf. *head over heels,* Head *sb.* 44): upside down, topsy-turvy. Also *attrib.* Chiefly *north. dial.*

*c* **1330** R. Brunne *Chron.* (1810) 70 Into þe waise þam fro he tombled top ouer taile. *c* **1400** *Laud Troy Bk.* 16727 He bar him tayl ouer top. That he lay ther as a sop. **1535** Lyndesay *Satyre* 3744 Bot this fals world is turnit top ouir taill. **1786** *Pogonologia* 6 The *Culbute* (the flying-top-over-tail hoop). **1819** W. Tennant *Papistry Storm'd* 200 Cam tumblin' tap-owr-tail. **1881** Miss Jackson *Shropsh. Word-bk., Top o'er tail,* head over heels—completely over.

**25. Top .. toe. a.** *From top to* († *into,* † *unto*) *toe,* from head to foot, in every part; also *fig.* from beginning to end, throughout, entirely.

[*a* **1225** *Juliana* 59 Ouer al & from þe top to þe tan.] *c* **1375** *Sc. Leg. Saints* xxiii. (*Steperis*) 121 Malchus..tald þame fra tope to ta Quhow decius þame socht to sla. *c* **1425** *Cast. Persev.* 615 in *Macro Plays* 95, I holde þee trewe ffro top to þe too. **1526** *Pilgr. Perf.* (W. de W. 1531) 241 b, Thou art made abhominable from the toppe of [?to] the too. **1545** Raynold *Byrth Mankynde* Prol. B ij, I..reuisying from top to toe the sayde booke. **1613** Purchas *Pilgrimage* (1614) 267 After this follow fifteene other most faire Camels,..couered from top to toe with Silke. **1718** Mrs. Delany in *Life & Corr.* (1861) I. 45 Top-a-Toe, my dear Niece, Your most affectionate, Faithful, humble servant, Lansdowne. **1887** Lowell *Democr.* 87 English from top to toe.

†**b.** *Neither top nor toe,* no part or vestige; = *top nor tail* (see 24 b). *Obs. rare*$^{-1}$.

**1610** Holland *Camden's Brit.* (1637) 269 There stood in old time a citie, but now neither top nor toe, as they say, remaineth of it.

**VII.** Combinations and collocations.

* *attrib. uses, passing into adjective* in 27–30.

**26.** Having a top, fitted with a top, as *top-buggy, -phaeton, -stocking, -wagon*; *top-ship* (see 33).

**1894** Howells in *Harper's Mag.* Feb. 381 Grocers don't drive round in *top-buggies. **1898** — *Open-eyed Conspir.* 52 Buoyant *top-phaetons and surreys, with their light-limbed horses. **1686** *Lond. Gaz.* No. 2126/4 Light-coloured *Top-Stockings striped with black. **1884** Roe *Nat. Ser. Story* x, He hastened to harness Thunder to his light *top-wagon. (See also Top-boot.)

**27.** Of or pertaining to the top, belonging to the top; situated, placed, or growing at or on the top of something; topmost, upper, uppermost. Now usually written separate as *adj.*

**1593** Shaks. *3 Hen. VI,* v. ii. 14 Whose top-branch ouer-peer'd Ioues spreading Tree. **1610** Healey *St. Aug. Citie of God* 225 Nero..got first of all to the top-turret of all this enormity. *c* **1611** Chapman *Iliad* xx. 211 These twice-six colts had pace so swift, they ran Upon the top-ayles of corn-ears, nor bent them any whit. **1656** Earl Monm. tr. *Boccalini's Advts. fr. Parnass.* I. lxxvii. (1674) 99 If they fall to cut down the top-boughs. **1676** Moxon *Print. Lett.* 6 The Top-line is the line that bounds the top of the Ascending Letters. **1707** Mortimer *Husb.* (1721) II. 139 An Herb whose top Leaves are a Sallet of themselves. **1769** Mrs. Raffald *Eng. Housekpr.* (1778) 91 It is proper for a top dish at night, or a side dish for dinner. **1805** R. W. Dickson *Pract. Agric.* I. 34 Advantages in carrying top-loads. **1827** Steuart *Planter's G.* (1828) 328 The topshoots of the former year will inevitably be cut down. **1833** T. Hook *Parson's Dau.* I. vii, A five pound fish..had snapped off the top-joint of his four guinea rod. **1851** Mrs. Browning *Casa Guidi Wind.* I. 700 How..we may..as we reach Our own grapes, bend the top vines to supply The children's uses. **1865** *Sat. Rev.* 21 Jan. 80/2 The want of protection of the top-shifts against fire. **1875** Knight *Dict. Mech.* 1465/2 A crowning molding is a top member. **1888** H. Morten *Sk. Hosp. Life* 46 There were two doors on the top landing. **1904** J. Sweeney *At Scotl. Yard* v. 110 The carriages..passed..along the top side, passing out at the left hand top corner. **1906** *Athenæum* 15 Dec. 777/3 A top stop was equivalent to a stop..in the upper focal plane of the objective. *Mod.* The top end of the tube is sealed.

**28.** Forming or constituting the top, or the exterior surface or layer; upper, outer.

Now usually separate, as in prec. sense.

**1603** Florio *Montaigne* II. xii. (1632) 275 A light stroke that dooth scarce the top-skin wound. **1634–5** Brereton *Trav.* (Chetham) 96 They cutt and flea top-turves with linge upon them. **1707** Mortimer *Husb.* (1721) II. 384 Take away some of the Top exhausted Earth. **1838** *Civil Eng. & Arch. Jrnl.* I. 97/2 Walls of rubble,..which support a top covering of flat stones. **1868** *Rep. U.S. Commissioner Agric.* (1869) 169 Mild loamy top soil, with a subsoil more tough. **1874** Crookes *Dyeing & Calico-Print* 526 Putting a top bloom on blacks. **1879** B. Taylor *Stud. Germ. Lit.* 38 Hollow spaces cut in the top-slab of his tombstone. **1883** R. Haldane *Workshop Receipts* Ser. II. 236/2 Aniline colours..are now usefully employed as top colours..brushed in very dilute solution over vegetable colours. **1891** *Daily News* 11 July 5/4 Top milk and bottom milk have been proved to be practically the same. **1904** *Archæol. Æliana* XXV. II. 253 A foot-and-a-half of blackish top-soil. **1912** *Nation* 10 Feb. 779/2 Good farming increases the humus or productive 'top spit' of the land.

**29.** First in rank, order, or quality; principal, chief, most eminent, best.

**1647** N. Bacon *Disc. Govt. Eng.* I. vi. 22 Bishops, who are now ..the very top-flowers of wisdom and learning. **1649** Roberts *Clavis Bibl.* 292 The flourishing or Top-glory of Israels Kingdome under K. Solomon. **1657** Austen *Fruit Trees* II. 45 This is the top priviledg of beleivers. **1697** Collier *Immor. Stage* iv. (1698) 242 These Sparks generally marry the Top-ladies. **1712** E. Cooke *Voy. S. Sea* 73 The Top Nation of all that Part of the World for Bravery. **1713** Steele *Englishman* No. 40. 261 When they grow up, Dancing is the top Accomplishment. **1727–41** Chambers *Cycl.* s.v. *Physiognomy,* The top modern authors on physiognomy. **1733** Swift *Let. to Pope* 2 Apr., They are certainly the top wits of the Court. **1750** R. Pococke *Trav.* (Camden) I. 50 One of their top merchants. **1774** J. Hawley in *J. Adams' Wks.* IX. 345 Our top Tories here give out..that he will certainly be taken up before the Congress. **1794** Godwin *Cal. Williams* 291 Regarded as the top gentry of the place. **1819** Keats *Let.* (in *Daily Chron.* 26 Mar. (1904) 9/2) Fine writing is, next to fine doings, the top thing in the world.

**30.** Highest (in degree), greatest (in amount); very high, very great; also in weakened sense, first-rate, tip-top, excellent.

**1714** G. Lockhart *Mem. Scot.* 229 Obliged to go off at a top Gallop. **1736** Duchess Portland in *Mrs. Delany's Life & Corr.* (1861) I. 563 The Speaker was in top good humour. **1769** Lady M. Coke *Jrnl.* 6 Aug., The Duchess ..said she was in a top sweat. *a* **1774** Fergusson *Caller Oysters* xi, The fisher-wives will get top livin. **1806–7** J. Beresford *Miseries Hum. Life* XVIII. xii, His common trot is just a match for your top speed. **1872** Michie *Deeside Tales* v. 49 He reached the house 'in a top sweat'. **1894** *Lit. World* 13 Apr. 341/2 One [who] commands 'top prices' for serial rights. **1902** *Daily Chron.* 20 Dec. 7/5 Half a dozen hounds went at top pace towards Tugby.

** *Locative,* etc., *combinations.*

**31.** In sense 'at or to the top', as *top-draining, -pruning*; *top-dry, -filled, -ironed, -laden, -loose, -shackled, -tempestuous, -turned* adjs. See also Top-dress, Top-full, Top-hamper, Top-heavy, Topknot, etc.

**1860** Worcester, **Top-draining,* the act or the practice of draining the surface of land. *c* **1611** Chapman *Iliad* XVI. 219 From a coffer..*top-fild with vests; warme robes to checke cold wind. **1691** tr. *Emilianne's Observ. Journ. Naples* 104 The Treasuries of their Churches are top fill'd with these kind of precious Relicks. **1910** *Daily Chron.* 12 Jan. 5/7 One with perfect nailing, beautifully executed, *top-ironed, and with exquisitely finished edging. **1831** Carlyle *Sart. Res.* I. iii, There, *topladen,..rolls in the country Baron and his household. **1887** *Pall Mall G.* 28 June 6/1 On each side of the hall are aisles, *top-lighted. **1905** *Daily Chron.* 17 May 8/5 Private offices are arranged along the back and top-lighted. **1747** Hooson *Miner's Dict.* U ij b, This being *Toploose, gives more Liberty for the cutting thereof than the taking of a whole Roof. **1842** Loudon *Suburban Hort.* 343 Ringing..may often serve as a substitute both for root pruning and *top pruning. **1612** N. Field *Woman a Weathercock* III. ii. E iv, Oh good old woman, she is *topshackeld. **1632** Lithgow *Trav.* (1906) 346 Like to a halfe ballast ship tottering on *top-tempestuous waves. **1902** *Westm. Gaz.* 5 July 2/3 Black crowns Of wind-worn pines..*top-turned by gales that weighed Them eastward.

*** *Special combinations and collocations.*

**32.** In general senses of *top.*

(When *top* is adjectival, properly without hyphen.)

**Top-beam** = COLLAR-BEAM 1; **top-binder**, ? a branch serving to bind the upper part of a hedge; **top-block**: see quot. (see also 33 b); **top breadth**, the breadth of the ship at the level of the top-timbers; **top-breadth line**, a line in a plan showing the longitudinal curve of the ship's side at the level of the top-timbers; **top-button**, † (_a_) a metal button of which the top or face is gilt or silvered; (_b_) an ornamental knob on the top of a mast; **top-card** (_Spinning_), a flat strip of wood covered with hooked teeth set over the drum of a carding-engine; **top-cast** [CAST _sb._ 18] = _top-swarm_; **top coal**, an important seam, which in the southern part of the Shropshire coal-field is the topmost; **top-coat**, overcoat, great-coat, outer coat; hence **top-coated** _a._; **top-contact**, contact at the top or upper surface; **top-crop**, (_a_) see _top-fruit_; (_b_) (_Mining_) an outcrop; **top-cross** (_Horse-breeding_), a cross in which one parent is of pure or superior blood (_U.S._); **top dog**, _lit._ the dog uppermost or 'on top' in a fight; _fig._ the victorious or dominant party; **top drawer**, the uppermost drawer in a cabinet or the like; also _fig._; **top-drive** (_Mech._) = _top-gear_ (_b_); **top flask** (_Founding_), the upper part of a moulder's flask when made in two parts; the 'cope' when a 'drag' is used (_Cent. Dict. Suppl._ 1909); **top-flat** (_Spinning_) = _top-card_, FLAT C. 8 d (Knight _Dict. Mech._ 1877); **top-fruit**, fruit growing on trees, as distinct from bush-fruit and ground-fruit (strawberries, etc.); **top-fuller**, a _top-tool_ having a narrow rounded edge (Knight 1877); **top-gear**, (_a_) the rigging, sails, and spars of a ship; (_b_) (without hyphen) in power transmission, the alternative gearing which produces the highest speed in proportion to that of the motor; **top-graft** _v._, _trans._ (_Horticulture_) ? to set new grafts on the stumps of lopped boughs; **top-hard** (coal): see quot. 1834–5, and cf. _top coal_; **top-head** (_Mining_): see quot.; **top-heat** (_Horticulture_), heat generated in a frame or greenhouse; cf. _bottom heat_ s. v. BOTTOM _sb._ 19; **top-hole**, (_a_) (_Mining_) = _top-head_; (_b_) = _top-notch_; _attrib._ first-rate, 'tip-top' (_slang_); †**top-honours** (_nonce-use_), the topsails of a ship, in reference to the custom of lowering them in token of respect; **top-house** (_Naut._), a deck-house; **top iron**, the upper iron in a carpenter's plane, adjusted so as to stiffen the cutter and turn up the shavings; the break-iron; **top-land**, high or elevated land, highland; **top-latch** (_dial._), the strap or thong used to fasten the hames together at the top; **top lift**, (_a_) [LIFT _sb._² 5], the uppermost working in a cutting, etc.; (_b_) the external layer of a boot or shoe heel; see also 33 a; **top-line** (in cattle), the profile line of the back from the centre of the shoulders to the end of the hip-bones; **top-loader** (_Lumbering_), one who works at the top of a load of logs (_N. Amer._); **top notch**, the highest notch; _fig._ the highest point attainable; also _attrib._ first-rate, 'tip-top'; hence **to·p-no·tcher**, a first-rate person or thing, a 'tip-topper'; **top note**, the highest note in a singer's compass; also _fig._; **top-onion**, the Canada or tree onion (_Allium Cepa proliferum_), bearing a cluster of small green bulbs at the top of the stem, instead of flowers and seed; **top plate**, the back plate of a watch-movement; **top-proud** _a._, proud to the highest degree; **top-rail** (_Carpentry_): see quot. 1823 (also 33 b); **top-rider** (_Shipbuilding_): see quot.; †**top-right** _a._ (_nonce-wd._), upright, erect; **top rock** (_Coal-mining_), the uppermost stratum of (hard) rock; **top-roll**, some part of a bridle-bit; **top saw**, the upper of a pair of circular saws, cutting down to meet the kerf of the lower; **topscript** [_nonce-wd._ after _postscript_], something written at the top of a letter; **top-set** _sb._, the top section of a vein of ore, which has sections of different width at different depths; **top-set** _a._, set or deposited at the top, or above something else; in _Mining_ and _Geol._, _spec._ of a bed, layer, or stratum; **top-sew** _v._, _trans._ to hem by oversewing; **top shelf**, the uppermost and least accessible shelf; also _attrib._ in _fig._ expressions: (_a_) as in _top-shelf book_, a book seldom used, or that is to be kept out of the way; (_b_) first-rate; cf. _top-notch_; hence **to·p-she·lfer**, a person or thing of the highest class; **top-soil** _v._, to pare off the top soil (see sense 28); **top story**, the uppermost story of a house; _fig._ the head as the seat of intellect; also _attrib._; **top-string** (_dial._) = _top-latch_; **top-swarm** (_Sc._ and _north. dial._), the first swarm of the season thrown off by a hive of bees; also _fig._; hence **top-swarmer**; **top-tail** _v._, _intr._ to turn the tail up and head down, as a whale in diving (_Cent. Dict._); **top-, tap-thrawn** _a._, _Sc._, perverse, obstinate, wrong-headed; **top-tool**, any smith's tool which is held upon the work while being struck, as distinct from a _bottom-tool_, which is socketed in the anvil; **top-turnip**, the turnip-cabbage, KOHLRABI (_Cent. Dict. Suppl._); **top-twist** = sense 19; **top wall** (_Mining_): see quot.; **top-water** (_Mining_): see quot. 1894; **top-weight**, the heaviest weight carried by a horse in a race; also _transf._ a horse carrying this weight; **top-yeast**, the yeast which forms on the top of fermenting liquor (_Cent. Dict. Suppl._). See also TOP-BOOT, etc.

1679 MOXON _Mech. Exerc._ viii. 147 *Top-beam. 1823 P. NICHOLSON _Pract. Build._ Gloss., _Top-beams_, the collar-beam of a truss;..formerly called _wind-beam_ or _strut-beam_, and now _collar-beam_. 1883 PENNELL-ELMHIRST _Cream of Leicestersh._ 402 A horse..will make short work of an ordinary *topbinder when once the sap of the thorn has gone to the roots. 1877 KNIGHT _Dict. Mech._, *_Top-block_, ..a projecting piece on which the bows of a carriage rest when down. 1846 A. YOUNG _Naut. Dict._ 278 The Top-timber Line, or *top-breadth Line, a curve describing the height of the top-timbers, which gives the sheer of the vessel. 1574 in Feuillerat _Revels Q. Eliz._ (1908) 243 *Topp Buttons and frenge Lace. 1856 EMERSON _Eng. Traits_ ii. 34 The mainmast, from the deck to the top-button, measured 115 feet. 1874 KNIGHT _Dict. Mech._ 470/1 These slats are called card-tops, *top-cards, or top-flats. 1827 G. HIGGINS _Celtic Druids_ ii. § 37. 78 It seems reasonable to expect that from these great *top casts, smaller ones should be found branching off to different countries. 1803 PLYMLEY _Agric. Shropsh._ 56 *Top-coal. 1841 HARTSHORNE _Salop. Antiq._ Gloss. 1879 MISS JACKSON _Shropsh. Word-bk._ 90. 1819 *Top-coat [implied in _top-coated_]. 1821 _Blackw. Mag._ Jan. 406/2 He had twa tap-coats and a plaid on. 1858 RAMSAY _Remin._ vi. (1870) 235 [He] offered the beggar an old top-coat. 1819 R. ANDERSON _Cumberld. Ball._ 63 *Top-cwoatet squire. 1849 D. J. BROWNE _Amer. Poultry Yd._ (1855) 114 Artificial heat most ingeniously applied by '*top contact'. _Ibid._, The difference..between top-contact heat and that received from radiation as applied to hatching. 1889 _Daily News_ 29 June 6/3 He foresees a corresponding depression in what he calls 'the *top crops'. 1895 G. HUNTINGTON in _Chicago Advance_ 19 Dec. 910/3 And it ain't top-crop rock, anyhow. 1890 _Breeder's Gaz._ (Chicago) 28 Mar. (Cent.), A filly with three *top crosses or a horse with four top crosses can be registered [in the stud-book]. 1900 _Speaker_ 28 Apr. 97/1 The most popular argument in favour of the war is that it will make the individual Briton *top dog in South Africa. 1906 P. WHITE _Eight Guests_ (Tauchn.) I. 66 Marcus had never had a tussle yet without coming out 'top dog!' 1906 _Daily Chron._ 26 Mar. 6/4, I recall..many in which I started as under-dog and came out top-dog. 1905 H. A. VACHELL _The Hill_ i, Such boys as a rule don't come out of the *top drawer. 1909 _Westm. Gaz._ 16 Nov. 5/2 The gear ratios are given as: 1st, 15 to 1; 2nd, 8.4 to 1; and on the *top-drive 4.7. 1874 *Top-flats [see _top-card_]. 1884 _Pall Mall G._ 15 Aug. 2/1, (1) *Top fruit, such as apples, pears, plums, cherries, medlars, and quinces; (2) bush fruit..; (3) ground fruit. 1903 _Q. Rev._ Oct. 390 A plantation of top and bottom fruit. 1884 PAE _Eustace_ 100 He's a trim craft as I would not like to damage in the *top-gear. 1909 _Westm. Gaz._ 28 Jan. 4/1 Handcross and Reigate, both of which the Napier can stealthily scale on top-gear and think nothing of it. 1910 _Ibid._ 21 Apr. 5/2 The extraordinary top-gear hill-climbing powers of the Ford. 1897 BAILEY _Princ. Fruit-growing_ 342 It will probably pay to *top-graft them. 1834–5 J. PHILLIPS _Man. Geol._ (1855) 190 The thickest coal in the district, called the '*top hard', is the same bed as that called the thick or ten-foot coal in Yorkshire. 1867 W. W. SMYTH _Coal & Coal-mining_ 56 Cutting the top-hard coal at 510 yards deep. 1883 GRESLEY _Gloss. Coal Mining_, *_Top Heads_ (S.S.), passages driven in the upper part of the Thick coal for draining off the gas. 1842 LOUDON _Suburban Hort._ 501 That lively heat within the frame, which is usually called *top-heat. 1905 _Dundee Advert._ 23 Jan. 5 The victims..at the time of the explosion were engaged widening the '*tophole' between No. 6 and No. 7 levels. 1899 DOYLE _Duet_ vi. 74 We certainly did ourselves up to the top hole last night. 1908 E. V. LUCAS _Over Bemerton's_ ii, 'A top-hole idea', he called it. 1909 _Blackw. Mag._ Sept. 409/1 A piece like the Merry Widow..would be top-hole. 1700 PRIOR _Carmen Seculare_ 478 Let all the naval world due homage pay; With hasty reverence their *top-honours lower. 1803 T. NETHERTON in _Naval Chron._ XV. 220 Shipwrights employed in the capstern and *top house. 1815 J. SMITH _Panorama Sc. & Art_ I. 108 It is always necessary to make the *top-iron fit the blade so correctly that no shaving can get between them. 1877 KINGLAKE _Crimea_ VI. vi. 71 The high..*topland or spine of Mount Inkerman. _Ibid._ 446 The Inkerman toplands. 1842 _Civil Eng. & Arch. Jrnl._ V. 60/1 The '*top lift' was deposited in spoil bank. 1901 _Daily Record & Mail_ 28 Nov. 2 A new machine..will do heel-shaving, rough scouring, fine scouring, heel-edge blacking, top-lift blacking, heel-burnishing, top-lift burnishing, and breasting. 1904 _Amer. Inventor_ 15 Apr. 184 The *toploader is the man who runs the greatest risks. 1848 _N. York Com. Adv._ 16 Oct. (Bartlett), To-day the editor of the _Union_ is cheered to the very *top notch of joyous exultation..; to-morrow he is horrified. 1888 _N. York Herald_ (Dixon), The effect of their [locusts'] blighting touch has not yet reached the top notch. 1910 I. K. BANGS _Pursuit of House-boat_ iii. 51 My seamanship, which was top-notch for my day. 1902 _13th Rep. Kansas State Bd. Agric._ 64 There are not a sufficient number of '*top-notchers' to go around, the result being..the use of many inferior specimens. 1896 _Daily News_ 28 Dec. 3/2 Another even more popular ballad (or whatever he calls it), known as 'Mary Jane's *Top-note'. 1908 A. NOYES _W. Morris_ 54 Never once do we feel that he is exerting himself, or on his top-note. 1884 BRITTEN _Watch & Clockm._ 47 The full cap to full plate watches covers the *top plate. 1885 C. G. W. LOCK _Workshop Receipts_ Ser. IV. 327/1 Push out the pillar pins, and remove the top plate. 1613 SHAKS. _Hen. VIII_, I. i. 151 This *top-proud fellow..I doe know To be corrupt and treasonous. 1679 MOXON _Mech. Exerc._ viii. 147 *Top-rail of the Balcony. 1823 P. NICHOLSON _Pract. Build._ Gloss., _Top-rail_, the upper rail of a piece of framing or wainscotting. 1867 SMYTH _Sailor's Word-bk._, _Upper_ or *_top-rider futtocks_, these timbers stand nearly the same as breadth-riders, and very much strengthen the topside. 1562 PHAER _Æneid_ IX. Ddj, His *topright crest from crown downe battred falles. 1803 PLYMLEY _Agric. Shropsh._ 56 *Top-rock 7 yds. 0 ft. 0 in. _a_ 1879 in Miss Jackson _Shropsh. Word-bk._ 89 Soil,..Clay,..Loose Rock,..Coal,..Blue Clod, ..Red Clunch,..Top Rock,..White Clod,..Brown Clunch. 1728 CHAMBERS _Cycl._ s. v. _Bit_, The several parts of a snaffle or curb bit are..Trench, *Top-roll, Flap, and Jeive. 1877 KNIGHT _Dict. Mech._ 2597/2 The *top-saw is a little in advance or rear of the under one, to make the kerf complete without collision of the teeth of the respective saws. 1731 LADY B. GERMAIN _Let. to Swift_ 4 Nov., So much for your *topscript, not postscript;..I heartily thank you for remembering me so often. 1747 HOOSON _Miner's Dict._ S ij, There are some Veins when once discover'd, carry Ore of a whole Stool-end, twenty or thirty Yards in Depth..; then the Ore cuts off on the Sole, and the Vein becomes hard and streat,..and endures so many Yards in Sinking, and then at last breaks over again, and the Ore proves to be as good and stronge as..before; these Levells are called Sets, as the first is the *Top-Set, the second which is found out by Sinking through the Deadness, is called the Under-Set. 1905 CHAMBERLIN & SALISBURY _Geol._ I. iii. 191 Deposition is also taking place on the top of the delta. These *top-set beds are laid down in a nearly horizontal position. 1876 MISS BRADDON _J. Haggard's Dau._ x, The sheets and table-cloths we *top-sewed when we were children. 1808 G. ELLIS _Let._ in Lockhart _Scott_ (1837) II. iv. 145, I should have ranked it..on the very *top shelf of English poetry. 1882 Top-shelf [implied in _top-shelfer_]. 1891–2 _Lupton Bros. Catal._ Dec. and Jan., Gentlemen requiring scarce and top-shelf books. 1905 HORNUNG _Thief in Nt._ (Tauchn.) 12 'Nice house?' said Raffles..'Top shelf', said I. 1882 _N. York Tribune_ 12 July, The rich tourist, or as the frontiersman calls him, 'the *top-shelfer', who goes about with guides and a luxurious outfit. 1860 WORCESTER, *_Top-soiling_, the act of taking off the top-soil. 1855 MACAULAY _Hist. Eng._ xiii. III. 347 From a window in the *top story of one of the loftiest of those gigantic houses 1903 [LD. W. NEVILLE] _Penal Servitude_ 150 [Prisoners] who are more or less touched in the top story. 1904 _Daily Chron._ 9 May 8/4 In every top-storey window the machinery can be seen working. 1690 J. WODROW in _Life_ (1828) 112 These may be named the *Tap-swarm. _a_ 1905 _Eng. Dial. Dict._ s. v. _Top_, Twea topswarms 'll mak' a strang hive. 1856 AIRD _Poet. Wks._ 404 The unfinished skep For June *top-swarmers. 1808–18 JAMIESON, *_Tapthrawn_, adj.,..having the..top or head distorted; or in allusion to the hair of the head lying in an awkward and unnatural manner. 1819 W. TENNANT _Papistry Storm'd_ (1827) 194 A tap-thrawn monk wi' roundit cap. 1877 KNIGHT _Dict. Mech._, *_Top-tool_, a blacksmith's tool..used above the work, being struck by a hammer. 1881 RAYMOND _Mining Gloss._, *_Top-wall_. See _Hanging-wall_. _Ibid._, _Hanging-side_ or _Hanging-wall_, or _Hanger_ (Cornw.), the wall or side over the vein. 1778 W. PRYCE _Min. Cornub._ 21 A very large proportion of our Mine Water is temporary; and..is denominated *Top Water. 1894 _Northumbld. Gloss._, _Top-watter_, water percolating through the roof of a coal mine. 1892 _Daily News_ 28 Mar. 3/5 It looks as if the *top-weights are in the Grand National precluded from winning...It is time the top-weights had a chance in this event. 1896 _Ibid._ 19 Feb. 2/6 Another top-weight got home safely in the February Hurdle Handicap, Doge, about whom as little as 3 to 1 was taken.

**33.** From senses 9 and 9 b; (_top_ being also short for _topsail_ or _topmast_), as **a.** **top-bowline**, **-lift** (LIFT _sb._² 7; see also 32), **-sheet**, **-shroud**, **-stay**, **-yard**. **b.** † **top-arming**, **top-armour**, † **top-arms** (_pl._): see quots. _a_ 1625, 1867; **top-block**, a large block suspended below the cap of the lower mast, used in hoisting or lowering topmasts (see also 32); **top-brim**: see quot. 1794, and cf. _top-rim_; **top-burton**: see quot. 1867 and BURTON; also _attrib._; **top-chain**, a chain used to sling the yards in action, in case the ropes by which they are hung should be shot away; **top-cloth**: see quot. and cf. _top-armour_; **top-lantern**, **top-light**: see quot. 1867; **top-lining**, topsail-lining: see quots.; also 'a platform of thin board nailed upon the upper part of the cross-trees on a vessel's top' (Smyth); **top-maul**: see quot. 1867; † **top-nail**, ? = FID _sb._²; **top-nettings** _sb. pl._: see _top-armour_ (quot. 1867); **top-pendant**, a pendant used in hoisting and lowering topmasts (_Cent. Dict._ 1891); **top-rail**: see quot. (also 32); **top-rim** = _top-brim_; **top-rope**: see quot. _a_ 1625; _to sway_ (erron. _swing_) (_away_) _on all top-ropes_, to go to great lengths; so _to be on_ (_the_) _top-ropes_; † **top-royal**, short for _top-gallant royal_: see TOPGALLANT; † **top-ship**, a ship having tops; = TOPMAN¹ 1; **top-tackle**, a tackle used in raising or lowering topmasts. See also TOP-CASTLE, TOPGALLANT, TOPMAN¹, TOPMAST, TOPSAIL.

1486 _Naval Acc. Hen. VII_ (1896) 14 A *Top Armyng of say. 1867 SMYTH _Sailor's Word-bk._, _Top-armings_, hammocks stowed inside the rigging for the protection of riflemen. 1485 _Cely Papers_ (Camden) 184 Item ij ȝerdes di rede ..for the *topearmer...Item an ȝerde of wyght for the same. 1514 _Inv. Henri Grace de Dieu_ in Oppenheim _Admin. Roy. Navy_ (1896) I. 377 Top Armours..vii. _a_ 1625 _Nomenclator Navalis_ (Harl. MS. 2301), _Topparmors_ are the clothes which are tied aboute the Tops of the mastes for shewe and also for to hide menn in the Fight which lie there to fling fire-potts [etc.]. 1823 CRABB _Technol. Dict._ s. v. _Top_, This top was formerly fenced on the afterside by a rail about three feet high, between the stanchions of which a netting was usually constructed, and stowed in action with hammocks. This was covered with red baize, or canvas painted red, and called the top-armour. *c* 1599 *MS. Otho E. ix.* in Bree *Cursory Sk. Nav., Mil. & Civ. Estab.* (1791) I. 217 For waste cloaths and *top-arms. 1769 FALCONER *Marine Dict.* (1776) s. v. *Block*, The *top-block is used to hoist up or lower down the top-masts, and is for the purpose hooked in an eye-bolt driven into the cap. 1762 — *Shipwr.* II. 149 The halyards and *top-bow-lines soon are gone. 1730 CAPT. W. WRIGLESWORTH *MS. Log-bk. of the 'Lyell'* 30 Nov., Arm'd the fore Shrouds, Matted the *Top-brims. 1794 *Rigging & Seamanship* I. 90 *Top-brim*, a space in the middle of the foot of a topsail, containing one-fifth of the number of its cloths, ..so called from..being near the fore part of the top,..when the sail is extended. 1797 *Encycl. Brit.* (ed. 3) XVII. 433/2 The holes for marling the clues of sails and the top-brims of topsails have grommets of log-line. *c* 1860 H. STUART *Seaman's Catech.* 46 The topmen will hand out the *top burtons. 1867 SMYTH *Sailor's Word-bk., Burton*, a small tackle..generally used to set up or tighten the shrouds, whence it is frequently termed a top-burton tackle. 1698 in *MSS. Ho. Lords* N.S. (1905) III. 344 Asked if the *top-chains, davits and fishes were made use of to make a boom. 1772–84 COOK *Voy.* (1790) VI. 1989 The boats were moored with top-chains. 1815 BURNEY *Falconer's Dict. Marine*, **Top-Cloth*, a large piece of canvas, used to cover the hammocks which are lashed in the top when prepared for action. 1748 *Anson's Voy.* I. x. 98 The main top-sail shook so strongly in the wind, that it carried away the *top lanthorn. 1867 SMYTH *Sailor's Word-bk., Top-lantern*, or *Top-light*, a large signal lantern placed in the after-part of a top. 1485 *Naval Acc. Hen. VII* (1896) 48 Toppe yerdes..j, *Toppe lyftes..ij. 1809 J. THICKNESSE in *Naval Chron.* XXII. 57, I carried a *top-light. 1794 *Rigging & Seamanship* I. 93 The *toplining of topsails is of canvas, No. 6 or 7. 1882 NARES *Seamanship* (ed. 6) 11 *Top lining.*—Double part on the after side of a topsail, to take the chafe of the top, etc. 1726 SHELVOCKE *Voy. round World* 214 The *top mall, which being made fast to the head of the main-mast, was wash'd ashore. 1867 SMYTH *Sailor's Word-bk., Top-maul*, a large hammer used to start the topmast fid, and to beat down the top, when setting up topmast-rigging. 1352 *Acc. Excheq. Q. R.* Bundle 20 No. 27 (P. R. O.) Pro quadam clav[o] ferri vocato *toppenaill* pro eodem mast. 1769 FALCONER *Dict. Marine* (1789), *Cercles de hune*, the *top rails, which formerly surrounded the tops, when circular. *Ibid.* (1780) s.v. *Out-rigger*, It is then thrust out to it's usual distance beyond the *top-rim, where it is securely fastened. *a* 1625 *Nomenclator Navalis* (Harl. MS. 2301), **Top-Roapes* are those Roapes wherewith wee sett or strike the Top-mastes. 1762 FALCONER *Shipwr.* II. 259 At each mast-head the top-ropes others bend. 1864 BURTON *Scot Abr.* I. iii. 119 Apt to attempt feats..in nautical phrase, 'to swing on all top-ropes'. 1867 SMYTH *Sailor's Word-bk.* s. v., 'Swaying on all top-ropes', figuratively, 'going the whole hog' in joviality or any trickery. 1868 W. PENGELLY in H. Pengelly *Life* xii. (1897) 188 The veteran..was on the top ropes about the meeting. 1500–20 DUNBAR *Poems* lxxxviii. 30 Thy Ryuer..Where many a ship doth rest with *toppe-royall. 1485 *Naval Acc. Hen. VII* (1896) 48 Toppe lyftes..ij, *Toppe shetes..ij. 1562 PHAER *Æneid* VIII. Z iv, His crowne couragious shines with garland wun from *topshipsnout. 1631 WEEVER *Anc. Fun. Mon.* 718 Two and fifty religious structures, as many wind-mils, and as many toppe Ships in Dunwich. 1485 *Naval Acc. Hen. VII* (1896) 48 Toppe mastes..j, *Toppe shrowdes ..vj. 1751 SMOLLETT *Per. Pic.* (1779) IV. xcviii. 275 'Split my *topstay-sail', said he. 1769 FALCONER *Dict. Marine* (1789) B b iij, To the lower end of the top-rope is fixed the *top-tackle. 1485 *Naval Acc. Hen. VII* (1896) 48 Toppe mastes..j, Toppe shrowdes..vj, *Toppe yerdes..j.

**34.** In sense 2 b, as *top-dyeing, -maker, -making, -master,* (*tops-*)*mill*; † **topwork**, wool-combing.

1888 *Daily News* 16 Apr. 2/7 Merino tops are firm in price,..though *top makers are said to have little margin for profit. 1891 *Labour Commission* Gloss. s.v., Some woolstaplers are also 'top-makers', i. e., woolcombers. In woolcombing the long smooth fibres are combed out into 'tops', so called from the form in which the 'ribbon' of wool is coiled upon its spindle being like a spinning top. 1896 *Balme & Co. Wool Brokers Circular* 15 May, Long-stapled parcels which..were largely purchased by the Bradford Topmakers. 1884 W. S. B. McLAREN *Spinning* (ed. 2) 116 Balling or *Top-Making.—One other process follows combing..namely, balling, or making into 'tops'. 1902 *Times* 6 Nov. 10/5 *Top-masters report a fair trade during the week at satisfactory prices. 1909 *Edin. Rev.* Oct. 284 He was building the largest *tops mill in the United States. 1637 *Bury Wills* (Camden) 169 A great deale of *topworke abroad at spynners.

**Top** (tǫp), *sb.*[2] Also 4–6 toppe, 4 topp (toop); (7– *Sc.* tap). [A word of difficult history, found (app.) in late OE. (*c* 1060) as *top*, also *c* 1325 in Walter de Bibbesworth (AFr. and Eng.), and common from late 14th c. onward. There are words coinciding in sense, and app. related in form, both in German and French, but their phonological relations are not normal: see Note below.]

**1.** A toy of various shapes (cylindrical, obconic, etc.), but always of circular section, with a point on which it is made to spin, usually by the sudden pulling of a string wound round it; the common *whip-* or *whipping-top* is kept spinning by lashing it with a whip.

Other tops, as the peg-top, are spun in the same way, but not whipped; some are spun by the action of a spring. *Humming-top*, a hollow top, usually of metal, with perforations, which makes a humming noise in spinning. *Parish top, town top*, a large top kept for public use, which two players or parties whipped in opposite directions. See also quot. 1911.

[*c* 1060 *Apollonius of Tyre* (Thorpe) 13 Mid ȝelæredre handa he swang þone top mid swa micelre swiftnesse, þæt þam cynge wæs ȝeþuht swilce he of ylde to iuȝuðe ȝewænd wære.] *c* 1325 *Gloss. W. de Bibbesw.* l. 39 (Camb. MS.) En la rue iuez au toup [*All Souls MS.* a toop]; *Gloss. All Souls* [In the] strete plaies þe toop, *Camb. MS.* atte toppe, *B.M. Arundel* a top of tre. 13.. *K. Alis.* 1727 (Bodl. MS.) Þere fore, ich habbe þee ysent, A top and scourge to present. *Ibid.* 1756 Þe Top þat is rounde aboute, Signefieþ also saunz doute, Þat þe werlde þat þe rounde is, Shal be myne also I wys. 1398 TREVISA *Barth. De P. R.* III. xvii. (1495) d iiij b/1 All þe lynes þt ben drawe fro all þe partyes of þe thynge þt is seen, make aperaunce, shapen as a toppe, and the poynt therof is in þe black of the eye, and the brode ende in þe thynge þt is seen, as in this fygure & shappe. *c* 1400 *Destr. Troy* 1624 Soche soteltie þai soght to solas hom with; The tables, the top, tregetre also. *c* 1425 *St. Christina* xxiv. in *Anglia* VIII. 128/36 Whirlynge about as a scoprelle or a toppe þat childer pleye with. *c* 1440 *Promp. Parv.* 496/2 Top, of chylderys pley, *trochus*. 1567 DRANT *Horace, Art Poet.* B iv, The stoole ball, top, or camping ball if suche one should assaye. 1581 MULCASTER *Positions* ix. (1887) 54 Fensing, and scourging the Top. 1601 [see PARISH *sb.* 7]. 1616–61 HOLYDAY *Persius* iii. (1673) 311 For the scourg-stick I did strive, That none his top with greater art might drive. 1623 [see TOWN 10]. 1628 WITHER *Brit. Rememb.* Pref. 209 Are no more worthy of my serious hopes, Then Ratles, Pot-guns, or the Schoole-boyes Tops. 1697 R. PEIRCE *Bath Mem.* I. x. 235 To play at Trap, and Top and Scourge, with the Boys. 1838–43 C. KNIGHT *Pict. Shaks., Twel. N.* I. iii. *note*, The *town-top* and the *parish-top* were one and the same. The custom..existed in the time of Elizabeth, and probably long before, of a large top being provided for the amusement of the peasants in frosty weather. 1851 [see HUMMING *ppl. a.* 1 c]. 1868 LOCKYER *Guillemin's Heavens* (ed. 3) 457 The motion of our globe has often been compared..to that of a top. 1911 *Encycl. Brit.* XXVII. 47/2 Other kinds of tops are made as supports for coloured disks which on revolving show a kaleidoscopic variation of patterns. The top is also used in certain games of chance, when it is generally known as a 'teetotum'.

**b.** As the type of a sound sleeper, in reference to the apparent stillness of a spinning top when its axis of rotation is vertical: cf. SLEEP *v.* B. 3 c; esp. in *to sleep like* (*as sound* or *as fast as*) *a top*: cf. SLEEP *v.* B. 1 e. † Rarely *fig.* = sound sleeper.

*c* 1616 FLETCHER & MASSINGER *Thierry & Theod.* v. ii, I will assure you, he can sleep no more Than a hooded Hawk; a centinel to him, Or one of the City Constables are tops. 1693 CONGREVE *Old Bach.* I. 8 'Tis but well lashing him, and he will sleep like a Top. 1711 RAMSAY *On Maggy Johnstoun* x, I took a nap..As sound's a tap. 1763 MRS. F. SHERIDAN *Discov.* I. ii, In two minutes I was as fast as a top. 1909 G. TYRRELL in *Q. Rev.* July 106 Its [a perfect life's] quiet is that of a sleeping top,—the ease of intense well-balanced activity.

**2.** A marine gastropod having a short conical shell; any species of the genus *Trochus* or family *Trochidæ*; a top-shell. In earliest use, *sea top*.

*a* 1682 SIR T. BROWNE *Norf. Fishes* Wks. 1835 IV. 332 Also *trochi, trochili*, or sea tops, finely variegated and pearly. 1856 GOSSE *Mar. Zool.* II. 118 *Trochus* (Linn.), Top. Shell pyramidal, nearly flat at the base. 1857 WOOD *Com. Objects Sea Shore* 25 Little shells, called Tops from their form...One of the most beautiful of these shells, the Livid Top (*Trochus ziziphinus*).

**3.** *Rope-making.* (Also *laying-top.*) See quots.

1794 *Rigging & Seamanship* I. 58 *Tops*, to lay ropes,.. are conical pieces of wood, with three or four grooves..from the butt to the end, for the strands to lie in, and form a triangle. 1797 *Encycl. Brit.* (ed. 3) XVI. 485/1 The top comes away from the swivel..and the line begins to lay. 1841 *Penny Cycl.* XX. 154/2 A piece of wood called a *top*, in the form of a truncated cone, being placed between the strands, and kept during the operation gently forced into the angle formed by the strands, where they are united by the closing or twisting of the rope. 1877 KNIGHT *Dict. Mech.* s. v., The top is forced as far as possible toward the sledge-hook, so as to allow the twist to commence at that end, the top giving way as the twist crowds it forward to the head end of the yarns.

[Some would refer to this word 'top of flax or wool': see TOP *sb.*[1] 2.]

**4.** *attrib.* and *Comb.*, as *top-fashion, -shape, -spinner, -spinning* (sb. and adj.), *-string*; *top-giddy, -like, -shaped* adjs.; **top minor** (*Rope-making*): see quot. 1835–6; **top-shell** = sense 2; **top-wise** *adv.*, like a top, in the manner of a top. See also TOPMAN[2].

1824 J. SYMMONS tr. *Æschylus' Agam.* 60 They vanish'd in deep night, *Top-giddy, whirl'd about, or scatter'd wide. *c* 1711 PETIVER *Gazophyl.* vii. 65 A small Pyramidal or *Toplike Shell. 1895 I. B. RICHMAN *Appenzell* xi. 195 To execute..a series of top-like revolutions about the room. 1793 J. D. BELFOUR *Specif. Patent* No. 1939. 10 To prevent the strand from being twisted too quick, I have introduced an instrument which I call the *top minor. 1835–6 *Encycl. Metrop.* (1845) VIII. 754/2 The yarns were all united..round the notches of an implement which he [J. D. Belfour] called a *top minor*. 1776 J. LEE *Introd. Bot.* Explan. Terms 394 *Turbinatum*, *top-shaped, like an obverse cone. *c* 1711 PETIVER *Gazophyl.* Dec. VII. Tab. 70 The large Barbadoes Magpye *Top-shell. 1885 C. F. HOLDER *Marvels Animal Life* 83 Usually a Top-shell (*Trochus*). 1398 TREVISA *Barth. De P. R.* III. xvii. (Tollem. MS.), Þe syȝte is nouȝt mad but by a piramys schape a *top wise [orig. *per piramidem*; 1535 shapen top wise] þt comeþ to þe ye. *Ibid.* x. v, In the moost ouermest poynt of his shappe that is a topwyse the flamme is moost hote. 1900 F. T. BULLEN *Idylls of Sea* v. 27 The angry currents..whirling us topwise in defiance of wind and helm.

[*Note.* The meaning of *top* in the OE. quot. is only inferential, as the OE. *Apollonius* here diverges from the Latin original, which contains no such terms as *turbo, trochus* or other word meaning 'top'; but it is difficult to see what else the OE. word could mean. In *c* 1325 the sense is clear. On the continent, the name of the toy in Holland generally is now *tol*; but *top* is used in East and West Flanders, Antwerp, and parts of Brabant; also in Friesland, Groningen, and Drente, in the North Netherlands; but this has not been found earlier than 1500. In Brussels, Mechlin, South Brabant generally, and Limburg, the form used is *dop*. *Dop, doppe*, was also the MDu. form, occurring from 13th c., and was the normal LG. equivalent of OHG. *topfo, topf*, MHG. *topfe, topf*, Ger. dial. *topf* (= Ger. *kreisel*) in this sense. Of this comparatively late substitution of *top* for *dop* in Flemish, etc., no explanation appears, and it does not help to account for the use of *top* in English in 1060 or even in 1325. The most that could be suggested would be that the word meaning *turbo* or *trochus* has in both cases run together in form with that meaning *apex* (TOP *sb.*[1]). On the other hand, the use in 1325 of an Anglo-French *toup* (*toop*) in this sense seems to form a link with F. *toupie* (also †*topie*) and its kindred words, OF. *topet* or *toupet*[2], obs. F. *toupin*, and the derivative vbs. OF. *topier* or *toupier, topiner* or *toupiner*, and *toupiller*. But the etymology of *toupie* and its family is beset by as many difficulties as that of *top*; it does not answer in form to either OHG. *topfo* or MLG. *doppe*.]

† **Top**, *sb.*[3] *Obs.* Also 5 toppe. [a. MLG., MFl. *toppe, top* (14–15th c.) basket (as a measure of raisins, figs, etc.): cf. MLG. *top* basket, as a measure of grapes (Walther-Lubben), MDu. *top-kine* (*c* 1334), *toppen* (1486), *top van vijghen* basket of figs (Kilian); OF. (Picard) *toppe* (cf. *trois toppes ou vaisseaulx*). See also TOPPET[2] and cf. TAP *sb.*[3], *topnet*, TAPNET.] A basket, as a measure of grapes or figs.

1440–1 *Durham Acc. Rolls* (Surtees) 78 It. in ij sorttes ficuum et racemorum magnorum cum viij toppes racemorum magnorum. 1530–1 *Durham Househ. Bk.* (Surtees) 44, 7 fraylls ficuum et 1 tope racemorum magnorum.

**Top** (tǫp), *v.*[1] Also (5 toppyn), 6–7 toppe, (7 tope). [f. TOP *sb.*[1], in various senses.]

**I.** † **1.** *intr.* To fight, struggle, strive. *Obs.*

[For the original sense of this and its connexion with that of the sb., cf. obs. Du. '*toppen, tobben* crines pugnando invadere, crinibus apprehendere' (Kilian); Ger. *zupfen*, formerly *zopfen* to pull by the hair, pull, pluck.]

*c* 1305 *Pilate* 15 in *E. E. P.* (1862) 111 Þat child..and pilatus also..to-gadere were ido As hi wexe hi toppede ofte, þer nas bituene hem no loue Ac þat child riȝt biȝute euer was aboue. *c* 1315 SHOREHAM vii. 577 Ac þo hy hedde ine heuene y-topped Wy nedde hy be ine helle y-stopped For evere mo. *c* 1440 *Promp. Parv.* 496/2 Toppyn, or fechte be the nekke (..*P.* feightyn by the nek).

**II.** To deprive of the top.

† **2.** *trans.* To cut *off* (the hair of the head), poll (the head), crop (a person). *Obs.*

*c* 1330 *Arth. & Merl.* (Kölbing) 7715 For diol he topped of his hare And him self tobete and tare. 14.. *Beryn* 2917 Getith a peir sisours, sherith my berd..And aftirward lete top my hede. 1632 *Star Chamb. Cases* (Camden) 112 Lord Privy Seale..found great fault with his long ruffian-like haire, and would have topped him if the vote of the Court had been for it.

**3.** To cut off the top of (a growing tree, a plant, or the like); to poll or pollard (a tree); to lop, prune, or shorten back (branches or shoots); to cut or break off the head, flower, or ear of (a plant), the withered calyx from (a gooseberry or other fruit); often in phr. *to top and lop, top and tail.*

1509 *Brasenose Coll. Doc.* C[2] 40 He shall toppe ne byhede Elme Asshe ne Oke. 1616 *MS. Acc. St. John's Hosp., Canterb.*, Payd for toping of treses. 1637 EARL MONM. tr. *Malvezzi's Romulus & Tarq.* 225 Hee tops off the heads of the highest flowers. 1649 LOVELACE *Grass-hopper* iv, Sharpe frosty fingers all your Flow'rs have topt. 1688 J. CLAYTON in *Phil. Trans.* XVII. 982 They top their Tobacco, that is, take away the little top-bud. 1794 *Rigging & Seamanship* I. 58 *Topping and Tailing* is the clearing both ends of the hemp with the hatchell. 1824 L. M. HAWKINS *Mem.*, etc. II. 52 A gentleman..was topping and tailing gooseberries for wine. 1894 R. H. ELLIOT *Gold, Sport*, etc. *in Mysore* 387 Some planters top [the coffee trees] at from three to three and a half feet.

**b.** *transf.* and *fig.*, or in *fig.* context.

1605 *1st Pt. Ieronimo* III. ii, Ile top thy head for that ambitious word. 1633 P. FLETCHER *Purple Isl.* x. xxii, Topping rank desires which vain exceed. 1690 LOCKE *Govt.* I. vi. (Rtldg.) 60 Just as Procrustes did with his guests, top or stretch them. 1840 DICKENS *Barn. Rudge* vii, Those prejudices of society which lop and top from poor handmaidens all such genteel excrescences.

† **4.** To snuff (a candle). *Obs.*

1594 PLAT *Jewell-ho.* III. 50 The candle..after it is newly topped. 1607 MIDDLETON *Your Five Gallants* I. i, Top the candle, sirrah. 1785 GROSE *Dict. Vulg. T., Top*, the signal among taylors for snuffing the candles. 1840 MARRYAT *Poor Jack* xxii, Let us top this glim a bit.

**5.** To pare off the surface soil of (land).

1638 A. CANT *Serm.* in Kerr *Covenants & Cov.* (1895) 120 The mountain must not be pared or topped.

**6.** To put to death by hanging; perh. originally to behead; cf. TOPSMAN. *slang.*

1811 *Lexicon Balatr.* s.v., The cove was topped for smashing queer screens. 1851 MAYHEW *Lond. Labour* (1861) III. 387/1 Thirty-six were cast for death, and only one was 'topped'. 1904 A. GRIFFITHS *50 Y. Public Service* xxii. 337 [One] hoped the day would be fine when he was to be topped.

**7.** To shorten the teeth of (a toothed or cog-wheel, etc.); cf. TOPPER *sb.*[1] 1.

1874 [implied in TOPPER *sb.*[1] 1]. 1884 F. J. BRITTEN *Watch & Clockm.* 74 Very slightly top the wheel by holding a piece of Arkansas stone against the teeth. *Ibid.* 152 If the lockings are too deep..the wheel is too large and should be topped.

**III.** To put a top on or form a top to.

**8.** To furnish with a top; to put a top on; to cover or surmount, crown, cap (*with*). Also *fig.* Cf. sense 16, with which this sometimes blends.

1581 A. HALL *Iliad* VII. 133 When as their towres they topt aloft, and rampires great did raise. 1583 MELBANCKE

*Philotimus* U iij b, I suppose that..Nanes and Dwarfes muste needes be topped with such heades. **1679** O. Heywood *Diaries*, etc. (1881) II. 188 To Roger Stocks, topping orchard wal. **1705** Addison *Italy*, *Tirol* 527 The little *Notredame*.. topp'd with a Cupola. **1864** Burton *Scot Abr.* I. v. 294 The practice..of topping the flanking round towers with conical roofs.

**9.** To complete by putting the top on, or forming the top of (a stack, etc.): often *to top up*; hence (*colloq.*) to put the finishing touch to (a process); to finish *off*, round *off*, crown.

**1504** [see Topping *vbl. sb.*$^1$ 1 a]. **1641** Best *Farm. Bks.* (Surtees) 35 The other comming behinde with a rake, to correckt, toppe up, and finish the cocke [of hay]. **1787** M. Cutler in *Life*, etc. (1888) I. 231 Her hair in front is craped at least a foot high,..and topped off with a wire skeleton in the same form covered with black gauze. **1837** W. Irving *Capt. Bonneville* I. 162 The chiefs leading the van, the braves following in a long line, painted and decorated, and topped off with fluttering plumes. **1872** O. W. Holmes *Poet Breakf.-t.* ii, He has topped off his home training with a..foreign finish. **1892** *Cornh. Mag.* Oct. 363 One [governess] grounded and another topped. **1903** Morley *Gladstone* III. viii. xii. 217 The sea voyage that was to 'top up' the rest and the treatment.

**b.** *absol.* or *intr.* To finish *up* or *off*, wind *up*, conclude (*with* something). *colloq.*

**1836** J. H. Newman *Lett.* 15 Apr. (1891) II. 189 Before they would venture to top up with such a..startling enunciation. **1840** R. H. Dana *Bef. Mast* xxv, We had the usual southeaster ..and finally topped off with a drenching rain of three or four hours. **1848** Thackeray *Bk. Snobs* xxxix, They absorb pale-ale.., and top-up with glasses of strong waters. **1870** *Daily News* 6 Oct., Then you..find the inmates of another room topping off with chocolate or coffee. **1885** Rider Haggard *K. Solomon's Mines* i, Everything went wrong that trip, and to top up with I got the fever badly.

**c.** *To top* (*up*) *one's fruit*, *punnet*, etc., to put the best fruit on the top of the basket, punnet, etc. *Market slang.*

**1888** [see Topping *vbl. sb.*$^1$ 1 a]. **1891** *Brit. Workman* Aug., I mean..that you're a topper... You've been topping your punnets. **1896** *Jrnl. R. Hortic. Soc.* Nov. 209 A grower who does not top up his fruit deserves to be canonised.

**10.** *trans.* **a.** *Dyeing.* To give a final bath of colour to; to finish *off* (a dyeing process) with a certain dye. **b.** To top-dress land. **c.** To stain the tips of the hair of (fur).

**1856** *Jrnl. R. Agric. Soc.* XVII. i. 188 A friend of mine always tops from 1½ to 2 cwt. [of salt] per acre before ploughing the clover leys. **1874** Crookes *Dyeing & Calico-Print.* 526 Such increase of oxalic acid is not recommended for topping blacks. **1875** F. J. Bird *Dyer's Handbk.* 35 Top-off with serge blue to shade. **1882** Crookes *Dyeing & Tissue-Print.* 118 Lift, and top in a fresh water with magenta and a little alum. **1910** W. Parker in *Encycl. Brit.* XI. 352/2 The paler skins from all districts in Siberia are now cleverly coloured or 'topped', that is, just the tips of the hair are stained dark.

†**11.** To 'cover', copulate with. Cf. Tup *v.* *Obs. rare.*

**1604** Shaks. *Oth.* iii. iii. 396. *Ibid.* v. ii. 136. **1633** Ford *Love's Sacr.* iii. i, Oh, for three Barbary stone-horses to top three Flanders mares!

**IV.** To exceed or come up to in height.

**12.** *trans.* To exceed in height; to overtop; also to exceed in weight, amount, number, etc.

**1582** Stanyhurst *Æneis* ii. (Arb.) 50 Two serpents..charg Laocoon..His neck eke chayning with tayls, hym in quantitye topping. **1686** Plot *Staffordsh.* 380 When they come to top them, [they] will quickly shade, and so kill them. **1747** *Gentl. Mag.* Dec. 589/1 The sea ran so high at Rotterdam, as to top two stories of many houses. **1760** R. Brown *Compl. Farmer* ii. 82 White oats..come up sooner, and top the weeds better than black. **1867** F. Francis *Angling* iii. (1880) 57 Many of them topped two pounds. **1887** Besant *The World went* ix, She was so tall that she topped her father..by a head. **1901** *Daily Express* 21 Mar. 5/4 Thames ..topped the Trinity high water mark by 3½ feet.

**b.** To surpass, excel, outdo; to cap.

**1586** Marlowe *1st Pt. Tamburl.* ii. iii, But, when you see his actions top his speech Your speech will stay. **1607** Shaks. *Cor.* ii. i. 23 Topping all others in boasting. **1787** Burke *Corr.* (1844) III. 55 A measure, if possible, to top the former. **1852** Thackeray *Esmond* iii. v, [One] who for fun and humour seemed to top them all.

**13.** To rise above; to mount beyond the level of.

**1773** *Poetry* in *Ann. Reg.* 233 Another bird, just flushing at the sound, Scarce tops the fence, then tumbles to the ground. **1869** Blackmore *Lorna D.* xviii, My head topped the platform of rock. **1870** Morris *Earthly Par.* III. iv. 159 At last the low sun topped the garden-wall. **1883** *Century Mag.* XXVI. 376 The sun was just topping the maples when [etc.].

**b.** To get or leap over the top of, to surmount.

**1735** Somerville *Chase* ii. 164 With Emulation fir'd They ..top the barr'd Gate, O'er the deep Ditch exulting bound. **1826** *Sporting Mag.* XVII. 242 Topping a high paling, he makes play over the country. **1835** Sir G. Stephen *Adv. Search Horse* xvi. 241 Many a little horse will top a fence that he cannot put his nose over.

**14.** To reach the top of, ascend to the top of.

**1600** W. Watson *Decacordon* (1602) 75 Their harts were inflamed with flashes of conspiracies, how to top the highest place. *a* **1668** Denham *Of Prudence* Poems 157 Wind about, till thou have topp'd the Hill. **1775** Burke *Sp. Conc. Amer.* Wks. III. 63 Already they have topped the Apalachian mountains. **1807** J. Barlow *Columb.* i. 204 The sun's blue ray Topt unknown cliffs and call'd them up to day. **1865** Kingsley *Herew.* vi, A pale yellow line, seen only as they topped a wave. **1886** Corbett *Fall of Asgard* I. 61 As they topped the crags that overhung the tarn.

**15.** *Theatr.* *To top one's part*, to play one's part to its utmost possibilities or to perfection; also, to transcend the character assigned to one; *transf.* to sustain (a character) with success. *To top the officer* (Naut.): see quot. 1867.

**1672** Villiers (Dk. Buckhm.) *Rehearsal* iii. i. (Arb.) 71 He does not hit me in't: he does not top his part. **1697** Dennis *Plot & no Plot* A iij, But are you sure, Daughter, that you can act a fit of the Mother well?.. Ay, and top my part too, Mother. **1761** Churchill *Rosciad* 46 Palmer! Oh! Palmer tops the janty part. **1786** Earl Malmesbury *Diaries & Corr.* II. 219 Warm as I am in wishing to see her [England] once more topping her part on the Continent. **1797** Mrs. A. M. Bennett *Beggar Girl* (1813) IV. 212 Delighted to be queen of the company where she might top the great personage. **1827** Hare *Guesses* Ser. ii. (1848) 72 By diligently performing the part assigned to him, by topping it, as the phrase is. **1831** *Examiner* 177/1 The Opposition ..are acting up to their character—nay, topping their parts. **1833** Marryat *P. Simple* lii, I've been hail-fellow well met with the ship's company so long, that I can't top the officer over them. **1867** Smyth *Sailor's Word-bk.*, *Top the officer, to*, to arrogate superiority.

**16.** To be at the top of, constitute the top of. (In literal sense often running together with 8.) Also *fig.* to be the first, chief, or best of, to be at the head of, to take the lead in.

**1615** G. Sandys *Trav.* 42 Rhodope still topt with snow. **1629** Wadsworth *Pilgr.* iii. 14 A Dormitory, which containes three long Galleries topping the house. **1707** *Reflex. upon Ridicule* 21 They kindle against such as will be Topping and Monopolizing the Conversation. *a* **1734** North *Lives* (1826) I. 46 His youthful habits were never gay, or topping the mode. **1770** Goldsm. *Des. Vill.* 12 The decent church that topt the neighbouring hill. **1802** Mrs. J. West *Infidel Father* xvii. II. 208 It came in two winters ago for very high ladies to stand godmothers to the natural children of all their relations. Lady Random topped the fashion. **1850** Blackie *Æschylus* II. 160 Mount the battlements: Top every tower; crown every parapet. **1861** Dixon *Pers. Hist. Ld. Bacon* xii. § 7 In character as in intellect Bacon tops the list.

**b.** To have the supremacy over; to get the better of.

**1633** Shirley *Gamester* iii. ii, I'll..send my nephew; he shall top and top him, And scourge him like a top too. **1681** Hickeringill *Black Non-Conf.* ii. Wks. 1716 II. 18 Legions of Lordly Priests and Cardinals that topt the whole world. **1832** Austin *Jurispr.* (1879) I. xxii. 462 Our aversion from the sanction tops the conflicting wish.

†**c.** *intr.* To have the supremacy. *Obs. rare*$^{-1}$.

**1718** W. Wright in *Wodrow's Corr.* (1843) II. 353 But.. the magistrates..were in as great danger as ever, for now the Cocceians begin to top.

**V.** Idiomatic uses, and phrases. (Chiefly *slang.*)

†**17. a.** *Dice-play.* *trans.* and *intr.* To retain one of the dice at the top of the box by unfair manipulation, to palm the die: cf. Top *sb.*$^1$ 20; hence, to cheat, trick (a person). *Obs.*

**1663** [see Topping *vbl. sb.*$^1$ 1 c]. **1671** [implied in Topper *sb.*$^1$ 1 b]. **1678** Dryden *Limberham* iv. i, I think in my Conscience he's Palming and Topping..before he comes into the World. *a* **1700** B. E. *Dict. Cant. Crew*, *Top*, to Cheat, or Trick any one; also to Insult. *What do you Top upon me?* do you stick a little Wax to the Dice to keep them together, to get the Chance? *He thought to have Topt upon me*, he design'd to have.. Sharpt me,.. or Affronted me. **1726** [see Topping *vbl. sb.*$^1$ 1 c].

†**b.** *intr.* To practise cheating or trickery; to impose *upon*; in quots. 1697, 1709, with mixture of sense 'to encroach or obtrude upon'. *Obs.*

**1664** Etheredge *Com. Revenge* ii. iii, How neatly I could tope upon him! **1676** Shadwell *Virtuoso* i. i, A Rascal.. that would Slur and top upon our Understandings. **1697** Collier *Ess. Mor. Subj.* i. (1709) 49 When a Man finds his Hopes disappointed, himself unsupported, and topp'd upon by Persons of meaner Pretences and Employments. *a* **1700** B. E. *Dict. Cant. Crew*, *To Passe upon one*, to top upon him, or impose upon him. *Ibid.* [see a above]. **1709** J. Johnson *Clergym. Vade M.* ii. p. lxxxvii, Patriarchs..did, in the latter end of the 4th, and in the 5th century top upon the Metropolitans, and reduced many great Provinces with their Bishops under the direction of one. *Ibid.* 118 They were still growing and topping upon their neighbours.

†**c.** *trans.* To impose (a thing) *upon* a person; to foist, fob *off*, palm *off upon*. *Obs.*

**1672–5** Comber *Comp. Temple* (1702) 558 It is no less than Blasphemy to Top a device of Men upon the People whom they were to lead into all Truth. **1682** T. Flatman *Heraclitus Ridens* No. 73 (1713) II. 199 'Tis but topping upon 'em a Sermon now and then about Mortification. **1712** in Somers *Tracts* (1815) XIII. 211 As to the topping a king upon the throne of Spain, so by the same reason the king of France by his power may top the Pretender on England. **1733** *Revolution Politicks* ii. 63 The Pope and his Jesuits.. were going to top Popery and Slavery upon us in good earnest.

†**d.** To insult. *Obs. slang.*

*a* **1700** [see a above]. **1785** Grose *Dict. Vulg. T.*, *Top*,.. to insult.

†**e.** *trans.* To oppose. Cf. *in tops with* (Top *sb.*$^1$ 22). *Obs. rare*$^{-1}$.

**1641** R. Baillie *Lett.* (1841) I. 390 Whill Argyle topes this nomination, as of a man unmeet, because of irresponsableness to the law for his debts.

**18. a.** *To top a ball* (*Golf*), to hit the ball above its centre; so *to top one's drive, to top*. **b.** *To top a clout* (*Thieves' slang*): see quot. **c.** *To top the deck* (*Card-sharping*): to cause a particular card to fall on the top of the pack. **d.** *To top a saw* (*U.S.*): to fix a stiffening piece or a gauge for limiting the depth of the cut (*Cent. Dict.*).

**a. 1881** Forgan *Golfer's Handbk.* 24 For ball I when struck will be 'topped' with the result of lacerating the turf. **1889** *Scott. Leader* 20 Apr. 6 He who never, or hardly ever, 'tops' a ball does not undergo the temptations to cast all his clubs into the whins. **1893** A. Lang in *Longm. Mag.* Apr. 652 My cleek seems merely made to top. **1894** *Times* 28 Apr. 13/3 Playing to the first hole Mr. L—— topped his drive, and Mr. B—— won the hole in 4 to 5.

**b. 1812** J. H. Vaux *Flash Dict.*, *Top*, to top a clout or other article (among pickpockets) is to draw the corner or end of it to the top of a person's pocket, in readiness for..taking out, when a favourable moment occurs.

**c. 1894** Maskelyne *Sharps & Flats* v. 83 [The cuff holdout] is a neat invention to top the deck. *Ibid.* 86 The cards are simply slipped between the jaws, where they are held until required. The hands being crossed..the lever is pressed and the cards fall upon the top of the pack...This operation is termed technically 'topping the deck'.

**Top** (tǫp), *v.*$^2$ Forms: 5–6 toppe, 6– top; see also Tope *v.*$^1$ [Of uncertain origin: appears doubtfully in 1497, certainly in 1549; in regular nautical use in 1627 and onward. So mod.Du. and Ger. *toppen*. Possibly a special application of Top *v.*$^1$, or an independent deriv. of Top *sb.*$^1$; but the difficulty is increased by the synonymous Tope *v.*$^1$ It is also possible that branch II is a distinct word; but Tope *v.*$^1$ has also both senses.]

**I.** *Naut.* **1.** *trans.* To tip *up* or slant (a yard), by tilting up one arm and depressing the other; sometimes = Peak *v.*$^3$, to tilt up vertically or nearly so; but sometimes more loosely, to alter the position of (a yard), whether by raising, depressing, or levelling it.

The exact meaning in quot. 1497 is not clear; ? to shore the ship up.

[**1497** *Naval Acc. Hen. VII* (1896) 249 To Retourne the seid mastes to Portesmouth where they served to toppe the Regent in the dokke at euery tyde bothe ebbe & flowde.] **1549** *Compl. Scot.* vi. 41 Than the master cryit, top ȝour topinellis. **1627** Capt. Smith *Seaman's Gram.* v. 24 The Lifts are two ropes which belong to all yards armes, to top the yards; that is, to make them hang higher or lower at your pleasure. **1688** R. Holme *Armoury* iii. xv. (Roxb.) 51/1 Top the yards, that is make them hang euen. **1762–9** Falconer *Shipwr.* ii. 261 Topp'd and unrigg'd, they [topgallant yards] down the backstays run. **1769** — *Dict. Marine* (1789), *Apiquer une vergue*, to top a sail-yard, or peek it up. **1802** *Eng. Encycl.* VIII. 431/1 'Top the yard to port!' the order to make the larboard extremity of a yard higher than the other. **1816** Tuckey *Narr. Exped. R. Zaire* ii. (1818) 39 The Portuguese vesels putting themselves in mourning by topping their yards up and down. **1844** *Hull Dock Act* 91 No vessel shall enter..except the same have her yards topped up. **1867** Smyth *Sailor's Word-bk.* s.v. *Boom*, *To top one's boom*, to start off.

**2.** *intr.* To assume a slanting position, tip *up*, tilt *up*; = Tip *v.*$^2$ 8.

*c* **1860** H. Stuart *Seaman's Catech.* 57 A martingale is sometimes used to prevent the davit from topping up.

**II. 3.** *intr.* To fall over, or to one side, by overbalancing; to tumble head foremost; = Topple *v.* 1, Tip *v.*$^2$ 7. *To top over tail* (cf. *to towp tail over end*, dial.), to turn head over heels; cf. *topple up tail* (Topple *v.* 3 b).

**1545** Ascham *Toxoph.* i. (Arb.) 47 To tumble ouer and ouer, to toppe ouer tayle..may be also holesome for the body. **1620** Shelton *Quix.* ii. xxix. 194 Don Quixote and Sancho topted [*ed.* 1746 top'd; (? error for *topled* = *toppled*)] into the Riuer.

**4.** *trans.* To tip or throw over, overturn, upset; = Topple *v.* 3, Tip *v.*$^2$ 1. *Obs.* exc. *dial.*

**1662** Hibbert *Body Div.* i. 135 A little ship without ballast..is soon either dasht against the rocks, or topped over. *c* **1890** W. S. Pasmore *Song of Press Gang* 5 They took'd me up both neck and heels, And topped me into the zay.

† **Top,** *v.*$^3$ *Obs.* [Origin obscure: known 1598. Perhaps identical with prec. vb., with the primary sense 'to tip up into the mouth', whence 'to drink in large draughts': cf. *tip*, *tip off*, Tip *v.*$^2$ 5. See also Tope *v.*$^2$, which is identical in sense, though, as in prec., the phonetic relation is difficult.]

**1.** *trans.* = Tope *v.*$^2$ 1; *to top off*, to drink off, quaff; cf. *tip off* (Tip *v.*$^2$ 5).

**1598** R. Bernard tr. *Terence's Adelphi* i. i, It's no heinous offence for a young man to hunt harlots, to toppe of a canne roundly. **1690** D'Urfey *Collin's Walk thro. London* i. 41 This said, they top'd off t'other quart.

**2.** Only in pa. pple. (topt): Made tipsy, intoxicated, drunk. Cf. Tip *v.*$^2$ 4.

*a* **1632** T. Taylor *God's Judgem.* vi. ii. (1642) 82 When she with her son were together topt with wine. **1637** Heywood *Dial.*, *Vulcan & Jupiter* Wks. 1874 VI. 220 She leaps and capers, topt with rage divine.

**Top,** *v.*$^4$ *rare.* [f. Top *sb.*$^2$ 3.] *trans.* To lay (a rope) with a top: see Top *sb.*$^2$ 3.

**1825** [see Topping *vbl. sb.*$^3$].

†**Top,** *prep.* *Obs. rare.* In 4 toppe. [From Top *sb.*$^1$: app. either aphetic for Atop B., or elliptical for *top of.*] Above, beyond, more than.

**1340** *Ayenb.* 6 Hi ssolden him..toppe alle þinges louie. *Ibid.* 248 Þise uirtue me ssel loky toppe alle þinges.

**Top**, obs. Sc. form of Tap *v.*$^1$

‖ **Topalgia** (tǫpæ·ldʒiă). *Path.* [mod.L., f. Gr. τόπ-ος place + -αλγία, f. ἄλγ-ος pain: cf. *neuralgia*.]

**1896** *Allbutt's Syst. Med.* I. 829 Local pain, allied to local neurasthenia (topalgia of Berequi) is occasionally noticed. **1899** *Syd. Soc. Lex.*, *Topalgia*, pain in a circumscribed area, not referable to the distribution of any particular nerve.

† **To·p-a·nnual.** *Sc. Law.* *Obs.* [f. Top *sb.*$^1$ + Annual.] An annual sum payable out of the rent

of a building or buildings as distinct from the land: cf. GROUND-ANNUAL. So †**Top-a·nnualler.**

(The distinction appears to have disappeared soon after the date of the Act cited; and after 1693 there was no legal way of making such a distinction.)

**1555** *Sc. Acts Mary* (1814) II. 490/2 [Mentions] few annuellaris [and] tope annuellaris. **1597** SKENE *De Verb. Sign.* s.v. *Annuel*, Top-annuel, is ane certaine duty, given and disponed furth of ony bigged tenement or land, of the quhilk tenement the propertie remainis with the disponer, and he is onely oblished to pay the said annuel. **1681** STAIR *Instit.* xv. § 7. 320 The case being there of Tenements within Burgh, the *Feu Annual* is [etc.]; *Ground-annuals* is a distinct several annualrent, Constitute upon the Ground, before the House was built; and the *Top*-annualrent is out of the House.

**Toparch** (tǫ·pɑɹk). [ad. Gr. τοπάρχης ruler of a small district, f. τόπ-ος place + -αρχης ruler. Cf. mod.F. *toparque*.] The ruler or prince of a small district, city, or petty state; a petty 'king'.

**1640** FULLER *Joseph's Coat* 11 By those many Kings mentioned in the old Testament, thirty and one in the little land of Canaan,..is meant onely Toparchs, not great Kings, but Lords of a little Dition, and Dominion. **1646** SIR T. BROWNE *Pseud. Ep.* VII. viii. 353 Toparks, Kings of Cities or narrow territories, such as were the Kings of Sodome and Gomorrah, the Kings of Jericho and Ai. **1737** WHISTON *Josephus, Antiq.* XI. iii. § 2 The toparchs of India and Ethiopia. **1852** MISS YONGE *Cameos* (1877) I. xxii. 162 The top-arch, Turlogh O'Connor, was the friend of O'Rourke.

So **Topa·rchical** *a.* [-ICAL], of, pertaining to, or of the nature of a toparch or toparchy.

**1650** FULLER *Pisgah* II. xiv. 302 Communicating it to the Sons and Nephews of Toparchicall Princes.

**Toparchy** (tǫ·pāɹki). Also in L. form **toparchia.** [ad. L. *toparchia*, a. Gr. τοπαρχία, f. τοπάρχης TOPARCH. So mod.F. *toparchie*.] The small district or territory under the rule of a toparch.

**1601** HOLLAND *Pliny* (1634) I. 100 It is diuided into ten gouernments or territories, called Toparchies..: to wit, that of Hiericho..: Emmaus,..Lydda, Ioppica, Accrabatena, Gophnitica, Thamnitica, Betholene, Tephena, and Orine, wherein stood Jerusalem. **1737** WHISTON *Josephus, Hist.* I. i. § 5 Judas..fled to the toparchy of Gophna. **1848** A. HERBERT in Todd *Irish Nennius* Notes p. lxiii, When the general name is improperly added to *ri* [king], instead of the name of the toparchy. **1883** EDERSHEIM *Life Jesus* I. 87 Judæa proper, to which Galilee, Samaria, and Peræa were joined as Toparchies. These Toparchies consisted of a group of townships under a Metropolis.

†**To-pa·rt,** *v. Obs.* [ME., f. To-[2] + PART *v.*]

**1.** *trans.* To dispart, separate, divide, distribute.

*c* **1325** *Poem Times Edw. II* 202 in *Pol. Songs* 332 And he shal ben to-parted..From his wif. **1340** *Ayenb.* 170 Saynt Ion..toparteþ zeue ouercomeinges and zeue coroues. **1387** *E. E. Wills* (1882) 1 Or my godes be to-partyd.

**2.** *intr.* To depart: see To-[2] 1.

**Topass** (tōu·pǟs). *E. Indies.* Also 7–8 **topaz.** [a. Pg. *topaz* (topa·s), Lucena, 1600; said in *Madras Manual of Administration*, 1893, to be ad. *tōpāshé*, Malayālam form of Hindī *dōbāshī*, man of two languages, interpreter (in which capacity these men of mixed descent were employed): see DUBASH. (A fancied derivation from Hindī *tōpī* hat, making the term = *tōpī-wālā* 'hat-man', European (see TOPI) has been current since the middle of the 18th c.)] A dark-skinned half-breed of Portuguese descent; often applied to a soldier, or a ship's scavenger or bath-attendant, who is of this class.

[**1648** *Van Spielbergen's Voy.* (Dutch) 34 (transl. in Yule) We saw to seaward another Champaigne (Sampan) wherein were 20 men, Mestiços and Toupas.] **1680** in J. T. Wheeler *Madras* (1861) I. 121 It is resolved and ordered to entertain about 100 Topasses or Black Portuguese into pay. **1727** A. HAMILTON *New Acc. E. Ind.* II. xlviii. 199 There are about two hundred Topasses, or Indian Portugueze settled and married in Cambodia. **1758** *Ann. Reg.* 283/2 A Topaz. [*Note*] A black Christian soldier; usually termed subjects of Portugal. **1766** J. H. GROSE *Voy. E. Ind.* (ed. 2) I. xiv. Gloss., *Topasses*, a tawny race of foot-soldiers, descended from Portuguese marrying natives, and called Topasses, because they wear hats. **1865** *Daily Tel.* 24 Oct. 5/1 Thirty 'topasses' on board the deserted ship launched a boat and got to Port Canning as soon as the steamer.

**Topaz** (tōu·pǣz). Forms: 3 **tupace,** 3–7 **topace,** 4–6 **topias,** 5 **thopas, topeus, tapace,** (**topyes**), 5–7 **topas, topaze, topase,** 6– **topaz.** β. 4 **topasie;** (**topazius**), 7 **topasius.** [ME. a. OF. *topaze, topace, -ase* (Roland, 11th c.), mod.F. *topaze* = Prov. *topazi*, Sp. *topacio*, Pg. *topazio*, It. *topazio*, ad. L. *topazus* (also later *topazius, -ion*), a. Gr. τόπαζος, -ιον, a foreign word; according to Pliny named from an island in the Red or Arabian Sea, where it abounded; but thought by some to be connected with Skr. *tapas* heat, fire.]

**1.** The name given (with or without distinguishing adjunct) to several highly valued precious stones. **a.** According to King, *Antique Gems* 26, given by the Greeks and Romans to the *yellow* or *oriental topaz*, a yellow sapphire or corundum; by Pliny, also to the modern chrysolite. **b.** In modern use (*true* or *occidental topaz*), a fluo-silicate of aluminium, usually in prismatic crystals, transparent and lustrous, yellow, white, pale blue, or pale green, found in Brazil, Mexico, Saxony, Scotland, the Ural Mountains, etc.

Also with distinctive adjuncts: **False topaz,** a transparent pale yellow variety of quartz; **Pink t.,** pink or rose-coloured topaz, artificially produced from the yellow Brazilian stone by exposure to strong heat; **Scottish** or **smoky t.,** the smoky variety found in Scotland; **Siberian t.,** a bluish white variety; **Spanish t.,** a golden brown variety of smoky quartz; **Star-topaz,** a yellow asteriated sapphire.

*a* **1272** *Luue Ron* 172 in *O. E. Misc.* 98 Hwat spekstu of eny stone.. Of Amatiste, of calcydone, Of lectorie, and tupace? *a* **1300** *Floriz & Bl.* 287 And suþþe riche cassidoines And Jacinctes and topaces. *c* **1375** *Sc. Leg. Saints* vi. (*Thomas*) 279 With brycht & schenand preciuse stanys, As sardiane, topias fyne, Iaspis. **1382** WYCLIF *Job* xxviii. 19 Topasie of Ethiope. *c* **1400** *Emaré* 91 Of topaze and rubyes, And oþur stones of myche prys. *c* **1407** LYDG. *Reson & Sens.* 6719 Hyr Rokys..Wer makyd of a ryche stoon, Of a Thopas. *c* **1420** *Anturs of Arth.* xxviii, The tassellus were of topeus, that was ther-to tiȝte. *a* **1440** *Sir Degrev.* 635 With topyes and trechoure Overtrasyd that tyde. **1481** CAXTON *Myrr.* II. vii. 79 A stone called Topace whiche is of colour lyke vnto fyn golde. **1567** MAPLET *Gr. Forest* 22 The Topaze..Plinie sayth, is a Gem of grassie colour: although that in Germanie it is found like to Golde. **1584** R. SCOT *Discov. Witchcr.* XIII. vi. (1886) 239 A topase healeth the lunaticke person of his passion of lunacie. **1645** EVELYN *Diary* 21 May, Many pearls, diamonds, amethysts, topazes. **1738** GLOVER *Leonidas* IV. 266 The flaming topaz with its golden beam. **1888** *Encycl. Brit.* XXIII. 446 The topaz of modern mineralogists was unknown to the ancients.

**2.** *Her.* In blazoning by precious stones, the designation of the tincture Or.

**1562** LEIGH *Armorie* 4 b, That precious stone, which y[e] Herhaughts do vse in blason, for, and in y[e] name of this metall [or] and Planett [the sun] that is called a Topace. **1572** BOSSEWELL *Armorie* II. 56 The field is parted per fesse embattyled, Topaze and Emeraude, two Lyciskes passant conterchanged of the fielde. **1766–87** PORNY *Heraldry* Gloss., *Topaz*, the name of a precious Stone used instead of Or, in blazoning the Arms of the English Nobility only.

**3.** *attrib.* and *Comb.*, as *topaz-colour, -fire, -gleam, -seal, -stone*; *topaz-coloured, -tailed, -throated, -tinted* adjs.; also **topaz humming-bird,** two S. American species of humming-bird of brilliant colours, *Topaza pella* and *T. pyra*; **topaz-pycnite** *Min.*, a variety of topaz, occurring in columnar aggregations; **topaz-rock**: see quot. 1796.

**1902** *Westm. Gaz.* 2 Aug. 2/1 The yellow cat lay motionless and supine, its *topaz-coloured eyes rolling from one to the other. **1816** J. SCOTT *Vis. Paris* App. (ed. 5) 321 An infinity of glass lamps..sparkling with green, crimson, and *topaz fires. **1782** LATHAM *Synopsis Birds* I. II. 746 *Topaz Humming-Bird. This bird is not much inferior to a Wren in size. **1839** URE *Dict. Arts* 1243 The rare mineral called *topaz pycnite is found in this mine. **1796** KIRWAN *Elem. Min.* (ed. 2) I. 368 **Topaz rock*..presents a compound of topaz, quartz, shorl, and lithomarga, confusedly compacted together. **1812** SCOTT *Let. to J. B. S. Morritt* 10 Dec. in *Lockhart*, A pretty *topaz seal, with a talisman which secures this letter. *c* **1470** HENRY *Wallace* VII. 77 Off *topastone him thocht the plumat was. **1595** *Locrine* II. i. 24 Enthronized in seates of Topace stones. **1811** SHAW *Gen. Zool.* VIII. 335 *Topaz-tailed Humming-bird...Length four inches: Native of Paraguay. *Ibid.* 274 *Topaz-throated Humming-bird...The throat..is of the most splendid *topaz yellow. **1867** AUG. J. E. WILSON *Vashti* xiv, The glassy stretch of *topaz-tinted sea. **1845** LINDLEY *Veg. Kingd.* (1846) 114 Barley-straw melts into a glass of a topaz yellow colour.

Hence **To·pazy** *a.* (*nonce-wd.*) [see -Y], like topaz.

**1892** STEVENSON *Vailima Lett.* xxii. (1895) 224 The colour ..is a topazy yellow.

**Topazine** (tōu·pǎzin, -ǝin), *a.* [f. TOPAZ + -INE[2], after *amethystine, crystalline*, etc.] That resembles topaz; topaz-coloured.

**1826** KIRBY & SP. *Entomol.* IV. xlvi. 283 Topazine...The yellow splendour of the topaz. **1829** *Glover's Hist. Derby* I. 94 Amethystine and topazine fluors. **1888** *Harper's Mag.* Aug. 338 How the emerald and the topazine eyes glow!

†**Topa·zion.** *Obs.* Also 4 **topasiune,** 4–5 **-ion,** 5 **topazyon,** 6 **topatioun, -ason.** [a. late L. *topazion*, a. Gr. τοπάζιον, dim. of τόπαζος TOPAZ.] An early name for a topaz.

*c* **1305** *Land Cokayne* 92 Þer is saphir and uniune..Beril, onix, topasiune. *c* **1430** LYDG. *Min. Poems* (Percy Soc.) 188 Lyke topasion of colours sonnyssh bright. *c* **1460** *Play Sacram.* 168, I haue..topazyons smaragdis of grete degre. **1560** ROLLAND *Crt. Venus* I. 109 With Iacinth fine, and Topazion sa fair. **1622** PEACHAM *Compl. Gent.* (1661) 169 The first colour is *Or, i.e.* Yellow, and signifieth in Plannets the Sun, in Pretious Stones, Topazion and Chrysolith.

**Topazolite** (topǣ·zolǝit). *Min.* [f. Gr. τόπαζο-s topaz + λίθος stone: see -LITE.] A variety of garnet resembling topaz in colour.

**1819** W. PHILLIPS *Introd. Min.* (1823) 31 Topazolite... This variety of the garnet has been discovered within the last few years. It occurs in remarkably well-defined dodecahedral crystals, of a topaz yellow colour. **1823** URE *Dict. Chem.* (ed. 2) 1 *Topazolite*, a variety of precious garnet, found at Mussa in Piedmont.

**Top-boot** (tǫ·p₁būt). [f. TOP *sb.*[1] 10 + BOOT *sb.*[3] 1.]

**1.** *properly.* A high boot, having a top of white, light-coloured, or brown leather or the like (TOP *sb.*[1] 10), formerly habitually worn by gentlemen, yeomen, and farmers, in riding or country dress; now by hunting men, jockeys, grooms, and coachmen. Usually in *pl.*

**1813** J. F. REES *Art & Myst. Cordwainer* 103 How to take the measure..for a jockey or top boot. **1821** *King in Ireland* in *New Monthly Mag.* II. 407 [The priest] in his black satin breeches and bright top-boots. **1836** E. HOWARD *R. Reefer* ii, He has purchased a pair of *top* boots, a swell *top* coat, and..thinks himself..a topping gentleman. *c* **1868** G. PRYME *Autobiog. Recoll.* xiv. (1870) 220 [In 1782] the County Members went up to the Throne—according to their privilege—in leather breeches and top-boots, instead of Court-dress. **1875** W. S. HAYWARD *Love agst. World* 73 In hunting-dress, buckskin, top-boots and scarlet coat. **1893** VIZETELLY *Glances Back* I. iii. 81 Burdett, in his customary buckskins and top boots. **1910** O. BARRON in *Encycl. Brit.* VII. 243/2 Men of fashion [in late 18th c.] walked the streets in short top-boots of soft black leather. **1911** *Ibid.* XXIV. 993/1 Such forms as jack-boots, top-boots, Hessian boots and Wellington boots. **1912–13** *Civil Serv. Co-op. Soc. Price List* 916 Coachman's Top Boots. Any Colour Top.

**2.** Improperly applied to any long or high boots which partly cover the leg.

**1891** *Cent. Dict.*, *Top-boot*, a boot having a high top; spec. [as in sense 1]. **1906** G. W. CHRYSTAL tr. *Mem. Pr. Chlodwig of Hohenlohe-Schillingsfuerste* II. 260 She appeared in pink stockings, black top-boots. **1906** *Athenæum* 19 May 606/3 The new heresy which, to the horror of makers and wearers of 'top-boots', gives to the military boot of Eastern Europe that time-honoured name. **1907** *Ibid.* 13 Apr. 440/1 We..dislike the practice of writers on Russia of using for the boot of Eastern Europe the classical term 'top-boot', which has in our literature a special meaning. For the British hunting boot there is no other term.

**3.** *attrib.* and *Comb.*

**1854** KNIGHT *Once upon a Time* xxxvii. (1859) 497 The top-boot wearers.

Hence **To·p-boo·ted** *a.*, wearing top-boots.

**1831** CARLYLE *Sart. Res.* II. ii, Topbooted Graziers from the North; Swiss Brokers, Italian Drovers, also topbooted, from the South.

†**Top-castle.** *Obs.* [Cf. TOP *sb.*[1] 9 and CASTLE *sb.* 7.] An embattled platform at the head of a ship's masts, from which missiles were discharged: later called also *top* (TOP *sb.*[1] 9).

**1335** *Exch. Acc., K. R.* 19/14 m. 6 (P.R.O.) In paracione de guerra et arraiamenta cuiusdam magni Navis vocat' la Trinite, vt in Ofcastel, Topcastel et Forcastel...In cordis emptis pro petris tractandis apud Topcastel. xviij d. [Rendered, in Nicolas *Hist. Royal Navy* (1847) II. 170 The 'Trinity', of two hundred tons, was prepared for war with an 'ofcastle, topcastle, and forecastle'; the 'ofcastle' being the aftcastle, and the 'topcastle' the 'top' or stage at the top of the mast; and ropes were bought for pulling stones up to the topcastle.] **13..** *Coer de L.* 2539 Sterne strokes with harde stones Out off the top-castel on hygh. *a* **1400** *Siege of Troy* 695 in *Archiv neu. Spr.* LXXII. 27 Vche maste hade top castel And asayliþ þe cite harde and wel. **1411** *Exch. Acc., K. R.* 44/17 La barge appelle la Marie de la Toure..ove lapparail..une mast, un trief ove iiij. bonetz, un topchastiell, un seilyerde. *c* **1450** *Chron. London* (Kingsford 1905) 145 Beryng the standard of Seynt Jorge in the topcastell lyke Englissh schippes. **1555** EDEN *Decades* 27 The foreshyppe and the sterne, the toppe castel, the maste [etc.].

**b.** *transf.* and *fig.*

**1548** UDALL *Erasm. Par. Luke* xi. 110 To sytte euen in the high topcastell of true seruyng of God. **1556** *Chron. Gr. Friars* (Camden) 84 There was a man made too topecastelles above the crosse of the stepulle, and there stode with a flagge in hys honde and viij. flagges hangynge besyde. **1688** R. HOLME *Armoury* III. xxi. (Roxb.) 252/1 He beareth Vert, the top castle of a Loome, with its pullaces, issueing out of base, Or.

**To·p-dre:ss,** *v.* [f. TOP *sb.*[1] + DRESS *v.* 13 c.] *trans.* To manure on the surface, as land, grass, or any crop. Also *absol.*

**1733** W. ELLIS *Chiltern & Vale Farm.* 15 Much better than top-dressing the Grain after it is in the Ground. **1764** *Museum Rust.* III. xii. 47 The advantages of top-dressing wheat in the spring with soot, or other light manure. **1852** *Beck's Florist* June 117 To enable us to 'top-dress', as it is termed; *i.e.* to clean the surface, and cover it with a mixture of half-rotten manure and loam.

**b.** *transf.* and *fig.*

**1834** *Tait's Mag.* I. 381/2 Before I was sixteen, [I] grinded, and partly top-dressed the Autobiography and Opinions of Men and Things, at home and abroad, of Stephen Fox, Esq. **1849** F. B. HEAD *Stokers & Pokers* i. (1851) 13 The wealth..almost without metaphor top-dressed the greater portion of the old as well as of the new world. **1862** WHYTE MELVILLE *Ins. Bar* 342 Plumtree was a mere boy,..actually shaving for whiskers, top-dressing with balm of Columbia, and raising an abundant crop of pimples as the result.

**To·p-dre:ssing,** *vbl. sb.* [f. as prec. + DRESSING *vbl. sb.* 4 c.] The application of manure to the surface of the soil; *concr.* the manure or fertilizer so applied.

**1764** *Museum Rust.* III. ii. 5, I bestow on it a top-dressing of wood ashes, soot,..or coal ashes. **1770–4** A. HUNTER *Georg. Ess.* (1803) I. 324 Pigeon dung, and rape-dust are considered as top-dressings. **1799** J. ROBERTSON *Agric. Perth* 311 When this powerful top-dressing..with sheep dung and urine has been completed. **1892** *Garden* 27 Aug. 195/2 The top-dressing was put on early in spring before the plants began to grow.

**b.** *transf.* and *fig.*

**1846** MRS. CARLYLE *Let. to Carlyle* 7 Sept., Helen has been most diligent in my absence, and left nothing for me to do but a little 'top-dressing'. **1884** J. PAYN *Lit. Recoll.* 35 Culture is more common, but very little comes of such 'top dressing'. **1906** *Edin. Rev.* Jan. 196 Stimulated..by this top-dressing of the northern energy.

†**Tope,** *sb.*[1] *Obs.* [Origin obscure.] A measure (of hay, corn, etc.).

**1530–1** *Durham Househ. Bk.* (Surtees) 263 [In threshing and winnowing account] Item 4 topez of pyese. **1618** *Inv. F. Banks* in W. F. Irvine *Hist. Rivington, Lanc.* 65 Item, a tope of haye. **1676** *Will of Jas. Kenyon of Middleton, Lanc.* (Prob. Reg. Chester), In the Barne. A tope of Wheate 10s. od. 2 topes of Barley 14s. od. A tope of Oates 3l. 6s. 8d.

**Tope** (tōup), *sb.*[2] [Etymology not ascertained. ? Cornish name.] A small species of shark, *Galeus galeorhinus* or *G. canis*, native to British seas, especially off the coast of Cornwall. Called also *dog-fish, penny-dog, miller's-dog*.

1686 RAY *Willughby's Hist. Pisc.* I. xii. 22 Canis galeus Rondeletii & aliorum. Cornubiensibus, ni fallor, *A Tope* dicitur. 1774 GOLDSM. *Nat. Hist.* (1862) II. II. i. 269 The Dog Fish, the Zygæna, the Tope, the Cat Fish. 1846 OWEN *Compar. Anat. Vertebr.* iii. 56 In the Tope..may be seen the highest stage of vertebral ossification in the Chondropterygian Fishes. 1909 *Daily Chron.* 9 Oct. 7/3 Another kind of shark..is the tope, an ugly and rapacious brute, attaining an average length of about six feet.

**b.** The Australasian species, *Galeus australis*.

1898 MORRIS *Austral English*, *Tope*, an Australasian Shark, *Galeus australis*, Macl...Called also School-Shark.

**Tope** (tōup), *sb.*[3] A local name for the Wren.

1813 G. MONTAGU *Suppl. Ornith. Dict.*, *Tope*. Vide *Wren, common*. 1831 *Ibid.*, *Tope*, a name for the Wren. 1885 SWAINSON *Provinc. Names Birds* 35 Tope (Norfolk, Cornwall).

‖**Tope** (tōup), *sb.*[4] *East Indies.* [ad. Tamil *tōppu*, Telugu *tōpu*.] A clump, grove, or plantation of trees; in Upper India, chiefly of fruit-trees; *esp.* a mango grove or orchard.

1698 FRYER *Acc. E. India & P.* 41 The Country is .. plentiful in Provisions; in all Places Topes of Trees. 1792 Q. CRAUFORD *Sk. Hindoos* (ed. 2) II. 104 *note*, Topes are very frequent, and some..containing perhaps 100 acres of land. 1826 *Soldier's Album* 82 The word 'tope' means clump. .. We encamped nightly in the topes of Mangoe trees. 1834 *Penny Cycl.* II. 233/1 The 'toddy topes', or coco-nut tree orchards, are very extensive in Ceylon.

‖**Tope** (tōup), *sb.*[5] *East Indies.* [a. Hind. (Panjābī) *tōp*, held to be:—Prākrit or Pālī *thūpo* :—Skr. *stūpa*.] An ancient structure, in the form of a dome or tumulus of masonry, for the preservation of relics or in commemoration of some fact; numerous specimens, usually of Buddhist or Jain origin, exist in India and south-eastern Asia.

A tope containing relics is specially called a DAGOBA.

1815 ELPHINSTONE *Caubul* I. 80 *note*, Tope is an expression used for a mound or burrow as far west as Peshawer. 1853 — in *Calcutta Rev.* July–Dec. 266 The famous Tope at Manikhyla. 1882 *Edin. Rev.* Oct. 360 A tope may be described as a domed structure, not unlike the dome of St. Paul's if it were lifted from the cathedral and placed on the ground. 1886 *Guide Galleries Brit. Mus.* 202 A Tope is a shrine peculiar to the Buddhist religion...In the centre is a solid dome-shaped structure, termed a *dagoba*, enclosing one or more small chests, with relics of Buddha or of his principal followers. This is generally surrounded by an elaborately carved rail. 1903 *Athenæum* 26 Sept. 405/2 A notable feature of these towns, the dagabas, or topes, are not themselves especially Buddhist monuments.

**Tope** (tōup), *v.*[1] Also *dial.* towp, toup; cf. TOP *v.*[2] [Known from 1669; of obscure origin. Synonymous with TOP *v.*[2], which occurs much earlier; but the long *o* is difficult to account for.]

†**1.** *Naut. trans.* To tilt, tip (a yard): = TOP *v.*[2] 1.

1669 STURMY *Mariners Mag.* I. ii. 17 Tope your Sprit-sail Yard.

**2.** To tilt over, cause to slope or lean to one side; to overturn, turn upside down; = TOP *v.*[2] 4. *Obs.* exc. *dial.*

1684 *She-Wedding* P 6 in *Harl. Misc.* (1810) VI. 404 When the good wives are together, toping their noses over the brandy-bottle. 1701 FARQUHAR *Sir H. Wildair* IV. i, Here, boy.—No Nants left.—(Topes the Glass.) 1901 F. E. TAYLOR *Folk-sp. S. Lancs.* (E.D.D.), Hoo [= she] tope't her yed o' one soide.

**b.** *intr.* To incline, nod, or fall to one side; to topple or fall over; to fall asleep; to die. *dial.*

1796 W. MARSHALL *Rur. Econ. Yorks.* (ed. 2) Gloss., To *Towp*, to heel; to towp-over; to topple. 1800 *Spec Yorks. Dial.* 24 (E.D.D.) T' ows [the ox] towpt ower hedge intil a lang dyke. 1863 BRIERLEY *Waverlow* 168 If her father would 'just tope o'er' [doze off, fall asleep]..she could steal out. 1876 *Whitby Gloss.*, *Towp*, *Towple*, or *Towple down*, to fall over. c 1900 in *Eng. Dial. Dict.* (E. Yorks.), Old you [ewe] 'z boon te toup ower.

**Tope**, *v.*[2] Now only *literary* or *arch.* [Known 1654; origin obscure. Synonymous with the earlier TOP *v.*[3], but, as in prec., the substitution of long *o* offers difficulties. See Note below, and that to TOPE *int.*]

**1.** *trans.* To drink, *esp.* to drink copiously and habitually.

1654 GAYTON *Pleas. Notes* IV. ix. 230 Tope it about mine Host; the wine bags now Had been as good, as milke of the red Cow. c 1679 *Roxb. Ball.* (1890) VII. 13 They tope the brandy, beer, and ale. 1719 D'URFEY *Pills* (1872) I. 41 And could we tope an ocean His due we hardly give. 1772 MRS. DELANY in *Life & Corr.* Ser. II. (1862) I. 410 Fat John will no more..snore by the great kitchen fire or tope Staffordshire ale! 1876 T. S. EGAN tr. *Heine's Atta Troll*, etc. 250 Our Rhine-wine constantly toping.

**2.** *intr.* To drink largely or in large draughts.

1667 DRYDEN *Maiden Queen* V. i, I'll Tope with you, I'll Sing with you, I'll Dance with you. 1671 CROWNE *Juliana* I, I can go into the Cardinal's cellar and tie my nose to one barrel, and my horse to an' ..er, and tope who shall tope most for a wager. a 1701 SEDLEY *Toper* Wks. (1766) 27 Let's tope and be merry, Be jolly and cheery. 1754 *Connoisseur* No. 9 P 4 On Sundays, while the husbands are toping at the alehouse,..their wives..go to church. 1827 HOOD *Don't you Smell Fire* 7 Now where can the turncock be drinking?..But he still may tope on, for I'm thinking That the plugs are as dry as himself.

Hence **Toping** *vbl. sb.* (also *attrib.*) and *ppl. a.* (The word in first quot. may be for TOPPING.)

1667 DRYDEN & DK. NEWCASTLE *Sir Martin Mar-all* V. iii. (1668) 68 A rare toping health this. a 1680 BUTLER *Epigr. on Club of Sots*, The jolly Members of a toping Club. 1690 DRYDEN *Don Sebast.* I. i, This Mufty..is some English Renegade, he talks so savourly of toping. a 1701 SEDLEY *To Phillis* Wks. (1766) 20 A club of witty, toping boys. 1709 O. DYKES *Eng. Prov. & Refl.* (ed. 2) 298 Tipling, and Toping, and Bouzing above measure is as bad as Bouncing in our Liquor. 1753 *Scots Mag.* Oct. 491/2, I had..got by heart several toping..songs. 1855 KINGSLEY *Westw. Ho!* ii, To amuse themselves in something more intellectual than mere toping in pot-houses. 1884 *Edin. Rev.* Oct. 314 The country squires who sang Durfey's songs at their 'toping-tables'.

[*Note.* One theory would identify this with TOP *v.*[2], TOPE *v.*[1], with the primary sense 'to tilt a bottle or vessel in drinking', hence 'to drink with great draughts, or copiously'; another would connect this vb. with TOPE *int.*, for which there is something to be said; only that TOP *v.*[2] occurs a good deal earlier.]

†**Tope**, *int. Obs.* [See Note below.] An exclamation used in drinking; app. = I pledge you.

1651 STANLEY *Excit. Anacreon* Poems 94 By thy tall Majestic Flaggons; By Mas, Tope, and thy Flap-dragons.. To thy frolick Order call us, Knights of the deep Bowle install us. 1659 SHIRLEY *Hon. & Mammon* V. i, *2nd Sol.* To my Colonel, honest Squanderbag. (*Drinks.*) *1st Sol.* Who wants my colonel? *2nd Sol.* I want it, tope: give me 't. 1663 COWLEY *Cutter of Coleman St.* II. viii, Fill us t'other Quart, That we may drink the Colonel's Health.. Why dost thou frown, thou arrant Clown? Hey Boys—Tope. 1664 ETHEREDGE *Love in Tub* II. iii, Lend me your hand, Sir..; here's a good health To all that are so: Tope ..here pledg me.

[*Note.* Generally held to be a. F. *top, tope, tôpe*, according to Littré ellipt. for *je tope*, from *toper, tôper, tauper*, 'to accept a stake or wager', orig. a word of dice-play (cf. Littré s.v. L'un des joueurs ayant dit: mâsse dix pistoles, l'autre a dit, tôpe); hence, to accept an offer or proposal; = It. *toppa* 'done!', a word said to signify acceptance of a bet, *toppare* 'to say "done" when another offers to lay a wager'; orig. to strike against, 'give a counter-shock' (Florio), Sp. *topar* to meet, to run or strike against. Its use in drinking is cited in It. 1659 (see quot. below), and in F. in 1671 (see Littré). The Fr. *tope* has passed into Du. *top*, Ger. *topp*, Sw. *topp*, in sense 'done!', 'agreed', and for the acceptance of a pledge in drinking. Hence some would derive TOPE *v.*[2] to drink deeply.

1659 TORRIANO *Ital. Dict.*, *Topa*, a word among Dicers, as much to say, 'I hold it, done, throw', or 'I see the By'; also by good fellows, when they are drinking: 'I'll pledge you'.]

**Tope**, obs. Sc. f. TAP *v.*[1]; var. TOBE. **Topee**, var. TOPI. **Topen**, var. TO-UP *Obs.*, above. **To-pens**, obs. f. TWOPENCE.

**Toper** (tōu·pəɹ). Now chiefly *literary*. [f. TOPE *v.*[2] + -ER[1].] One who topes or drinks a great deal; a hard drinker; a drunkard.

1673 *S' too him Bayes* 56 Your right topers now, when a friend begins to flag..use to rouse him up again. 1675 COTTON *Scoffer Scofft* 60 A sturdy piece of flesh, and proper, A merry Grig, and a true Toper. 1768 TUCKER *Lt. Nat.* (1834) I. 41 The cobbler..sits among his fellow topers at the two-penny club. 1816 J. WILSON *City of Plague* I. iv. 153 Bacchanalian song By toper chaunted o'er the flowing bowl. 1844 DICKENS *Mart. Chuz.* xxxvi. 1898 *Allbutt's Syst. Med.* V. 162 Topers are prone to tuberculous affections.

Hence **To·perdom**, **To·perism** (*nonce-wds.*).

1891 *Scott. Leader* 30 Dec. 4 Much rejoicing has..been caused in London toperdom by the issue by certain enterprising publicans of 'free insurances'. 1896 *Speaker* 6 June 618 The besotted toperism of so many of his companions.

**Topet, Topeus**, obs. ff. TOPPET, TOPAZ.

†**To·pful**, *a. Obs. rare.* [f. TOP *sb.*[1] + -FUL.] High, lofty, towering.

c 1611 CHAPMAN *Iliad* V. 761 Soone they wonne The top of all the topfull heauens. *Ibid.* VIII. 4 In top of all the topfull heights, that crowne th' Olympian hill.

**Top-full** (tǫ·pfu·l), *a.* Now *rare*. Also *erron.* topful. [f. TOP *sb.*[1] + FULL *a.*] Full to the top; brim-full.

1553 BALE *Gardiner's De vera Obed.* G vj b, As it were a vessell being toppe full of water. 1617 MORYSON *Itin.* III. 49 A huge great purse top full of gold. 1762 STERNE *Tr. Shandy* V. xxxviii, My father drew in his lungs topfull of air. 1827 G. DARLEY in *Q. Rev.* July (1902) 186 Both go tottering, tattling home Topful of wine as well as glee.

†**b.** *transf.* Said of that which fills (to the top): brimming. *Obs. rare.*

1602 DOLMAN *La Primaud. Fr. Acad.* (1618) III. 769 If one cast into the same so toppefull water, some heavy thing, the water..will swell onely. 1608 SYLVESTER *Du Bartas* II. iv. IV. *Decay* 52 Achab's House, whose cursed wickednesse Was now top-full.

**c.** *fig.*

1579 TOMSON *Calvin's Serm. Tim.* 944/1 We shall haue the measure of our perfection and of all good workes toppefull. 1648 DARNELL in *I. Basire's Corr.* (1831) 74 Topfull of busines as I am. 1751 R. PALTOCK *P. Wilkins* xiv. (1883) 46/1 Top-full of these thoughts, I re-entered my grotto. 1881 FAIRBAIRN *Stud. Life Christ* v. 86 She, unsexed, filled from crown to toe, topfull of direst cruelty.

**Topgallant** (tǫpgæ·lănt, təgæ·lănt), *sb.* and *a.* Also 6 **-galand**. [f. TOP *sb.*[1] 9 + GALLANT *a.*, as making a brave or gallant show in comparison with the lower tops. The guess that the name was orig. *top-garland* (from GARLAND *sb.* 8) is disproved by the early evidence, and does not suit the sense.]

**A.** *sb.*

†**1.** *Naut.* A top (TOP *sb.*[1] 9) at the head of the topmast, and thus in a loftier position than the original top-castle or top. *Obs.*

The thing was in use before the name: see quot. 1497, where it is described without a name. The name was prob. *obs.* by 1600, when sense 2 came in.

[1497 *Naval Accts. Henry VII* 278 *The Regent*, Also a Toppe maste aboue the mayne Toppe maste, Rotteyn perused & consumyd to noght. A sayle to the same..Also viij Shrowdes belongyng to the same.] 1514 *Inv. Henri Grace de Dieu* in Oppenheim *Admin. Roy. Navy* I. 374 Toppe Galant apon the foretopmast..j. *Ibid.* 375 The top Galant apon the mayne topmast..j. 1514 *Inv.* in *United Serv. Mag.* (1910) Mar. 581 The top galant. The mast to the same .j. The sayle yerd. 1569 SPARKE *Sir J. Hawkins' 2nd Voy.* (Hakl. Soc.) 50 The *Jesus* also bare a light in her toppegallant. 1590 SPENSER *Vis. World's Van.* ix, A goodly ship with banners bravely dight, And flag in her top-gallant, I espide.

**2.** *pl.* Short for *topgallant sails*, the sails above the topsail and topgallant.

This use appears to have come in as sense 1 became obs.

1599 DALLAM in *Early Voy. Levant* (Hakl. Soc.) 9 They ..made away with all the sayle they had, drablings and topgalands, but..we came nearer and nearer unto them. 1647 WARD *Simp. Cobler* (1843) 49 When Kings are hailing up their top-gallants, Subjects lay hold on their slablines. 1694 MOTTEUX *Rabelais* IV. lxiv, A fresh gale..began to fill the..Top-gallants. 1833 MARRYAT *P. Simple* xlix, She had..got up..jury-masts, with topgallants for topsails.

**3. a.** *transf.* (from 1 and 2) The most elevated (*lit.* or *fig.*) part or member *of* anything; see quots., and also *top and topgallant* (TOP *sb.*[1] 9 c).

1581 J. BELL *Haddon's Answ. Osor.* 388 If these two gallaunt Gyaunts apply no stronger pillers..to vphold the Majesticall State of theyr toppegallaunt of Rome. 1618 G. STRODE *Anat. Mortalitie* 83 The Peacocke..when he.. seeth his black feete,..vaileth his top-gallant, and seemeth to sorrow. 1656 I. BOURNE *Def. Script.* 15 A faith in Christ ..was the top gallant of a Christian. 1878 STEVENSON *Edinburgh* (1889) 29 A few spires, the stone top-gallants of the city.

**b.** *fig.* The highest point or pitch; summit.

1592 SHAKS. *Rom. & Jul.* II. iv. 202 Which to the high top gallant of my ioy, Must be my conuoy in the secret night. 1666 SANCROFT *Lex Ignea* 17 The very Top-gallant of all our Glory. 1679 C. NESSE *Antichrist* 149 From..the top-gallant of his Luciferian pride. 1862 CARLYLE *Fredk Gt.* XIII. ix. (1872) V. 92 He seems to himself a man at the topgallant of his wishes.

†**c.** Used for the nonce as an intensive of *gallant*.

1701 FARQUHAR *Sir H. Wildair* IV. ii, And such as he are all those topgallants that daily haunt my house, ruin your honour, and disturb my quiet.

**B.** *attrib.* or *adj.*

**1.** Of, pertaining to, or having the position of topgallant: *topgallant mast, sail, yard*, the mast, sail, or yard above the topmast and topsail; the third mast, sail, or yard above the deck; †**topgallant royals**, early name for *royals* (ROYAL B. 5).

Often forming with the sb. an attrib. phrase, as *topgallant-mast head, topgallant-sail yard, topgallant-yard man*.

1514 *Inv. Henri Grace de Dieu* in Oppenheim *Admin. Roy. Navy* I. 374 Bowlynes to the topgalant yerd...Lyftes to the foretopgallant yerd with iiij single polies. *Ibid.* 377 Topgalant Sayle. 1514 *Inv. Kateryn Forteleza* in *United Serv. Mag.* Mar. (1910) 581 Top galant, top galant mast, shrowdes to the same .vj. 1588 *State Papers Dom. Eliz.* CCXX. lf. 54 (P.R.O.), The Revendge .. A mayne topgallant saile made of an olde myzon. *Ibid.* lf. 71 The Dreadnoughte .. one mayne topgallant saile, servic[eable]. 1626 CAPT. SMITH *Accid. Yng. Seamen* 12 The top gallant mast, the maine top gallant sayle yard, the trucke or flagge staffe. 1627 — *Seaman's Gram.* vii. 31 There is also your maine top-saile, and fore top-saile, with their top-gallant sailes. 1634 SIR T. HERBERT *Trav.* 7 Sometimes the surges or sea-flashes doe rebound top-gallant height. 1671 *Lond. Gaz.* No. 544/3 He caused his Top-gallant Masts and Yards to be taken down, and his Galleries and Quarter Decks to be covered with Canvas made for that purpose, to the end they might take him for a Merchant man. 1692 in *Capt. Smith's Seaman's Gram.* I. xiv. 64, 7 Main Topsail Lifts, 8 Topgallant Lifts. 1704 J. HARRIS *Lex. Techn.* I, *Top-Gallant-Masts* of a Ship, are two, viz. *Maintop-gallant-Mast*, and *Foretop-gallant-Mast*; And these two are small round Pices of Timber, set on to their respective Top-Masts; on the Top of which Masts are set the Flagg-staffs. 1756 *Gentl. Mag.* XXVI. 506/1 Making all the sail they possibly could set to get from us, with top gallant ryalls, lower top-mast, and top-gallant steering sails, keeping a good full. 1835 SIR J. ROSS *Narr. 2nd Voy.* iii. 32 There were two seamen on the topgallant yard. 1840 R. H. DANA *Bef. Mast* iv, We sprang aloft immediately, and furled the royals and topgallant-sails. c 1860 H. STUART *Seaman's Catech.* 45 The topgallant yard men..will go aloft. 1891 *Times* 21 Oct. 7/4 The *Hoffnung*,..having..foretopmast and topgallant, with yards and sails attached, carried away; also main topgallant mast with yards.

**b.** See quotations.

1839 MARRYAT *Phant. Ship* viii, On her forecastle another small deck ran from the knight-heads, which was called the top-gallant forecastle. 1869 SIR E. J. REED *Shipbuild.* xii. 238 It is customary to complete the topsides above this gunwale by, what is termed, a top-gallant bulwark formed of wooden berthing and stanchions.

**2.** Allowing topgallant sails to be used, as *topgallant gale, breeze, weather*.

1697 DAMPIER *Voy. round World* (1699) 79 We had it [wind] at E.S.E. where it stood a considerable time and blew a fresh Top-gallant gale. 1769 FALCONER *Dict. Marine* (1789), *Tems à perroquet*, a top-gallant gale; top-gallant weather. 1806 A. DUNCAN *Nelson* 68 The wind.. blew what seamen call a top-gallant breeze. It was necessary to take in the royals when the squadron hauled upon a wind. 1873 *Routledge's Yng. Gent. Mag.* July 494/1 A good 'topgallant breeze' sprung up.

**3.** *fig.* Lofty, grand, fine, topping: cf. A. 3.

1613 SYLVESTER *Lachr. Lachr.* B iv, Stript..Of guiddie-Gaudes, Top-gallant Tires and Towers. 1650 FULLER *Pisgah* IV. vi. 108 Sure I am, the Babylonians were more top-gallant then the Jews, and quite put them down with bravery. 1735 POPE *Donne's Sat.* IV. 230 Top-gallant he, and she in all her trim. 1849 CUPPLES *Green Hand* ix, Here he [the sailor] came out with a regular string of top-gallant oaths.

**Toph**[1], **tophe** (tōᵘf). Now *rare.* [ad. L. *tōph-us*, more correctly *tōf-us*: see TOPHUS.]

**1.** Usually *toph stone*: Travertin, or other soft stone: = TOPHUS 1.

*a* 1552 LELAND *Itin.* VI. 72 A Quarre of Tophe Stone by Driselege, wherof much of the Castelle was buildid. 1577 HARRISON *England* III. xv. (1878) II. 61 For Tophe stone, not a few allow of the quarrie that is at Drisley, diuerse mislike not of the veine of hard stone that is at Oxford, and Burford. 1811 J. MILNER *Eccles. Archit. Eng. Mid. Ages* 95 Arched with hard stone for the ribs and light toph stone for the interstices.

**2.** *Path.* A calcareous deposit or calculus formed within the human or animal body: = TOPHUS 2.

1584 T. BASTARD *Chrestoleros* (1880) 10 Phisition Mirus talkes of saliuation, Of Tophes and Pustules, and Febrication. 1651 BIGGS *New Disp.* § 141 A neutrall nature of a tophe, between a Cartilage and a Stone. 1694 SALMON *Bate's Dispens.* (1713) 64/2 It softens, dissipates, yea, and dissolves the chalky Concretions..pocky Nodes, Tophs, Gums, and Swellings. *Ibid.* 682/1 It cleanses the Skin,.. takes away Gouty Tophs, cures the Leprosie. 1706 PHILLIPS (ed. Kersey), *Toph*, a word us'd by some Chirurgical Writers for a kind of Swelling in the Bones. 1822–7 GOOD *Study Med.* (1829) IV. 532 Some structural irritation within the cavity of the skull, such as a node or toph. 1843 R. J. GRAVES *Syst. Clin. Med.* xxviii. 355 Exanthemata..nodes, tophes, syphilitic gout and rheumatism.

‖ **Toph**[2] (tōf). [Heb. תֹּף *tōph*, f. תָּפַף *tāphaph* to sound or beat the timbrel; app. echoic.] A Hebrew instrument of music, of the nature of a timbrel or tabret.

[1749 Thoph: see TOPHET 1.] 1864 ENGEL *Mus. Anc. Nat.* 222 This deff may have been the *toph* of the Hebrews, as well as the square tambourine of the ancient Egyptians. 1879 STAINER *Music of Bible* 155 Among the instruments which the company of prophets bare..was a toph.

**Tophaceous** (tofēi·ʃəs), *a.* [ad. L. *tōf-*, *tōphāce-us*, f. TOPHUS: see -ACEOUS.]

**1.** Of the nature of tophus or toph; sandy, gritty; rough, stony.

1672 *Phil. Trans.* VII. 4064 It is scabrous or rough, sand-like, although the substance is Tophaceous. 1692 RAY *Disc.* II. iv. (1732) 128 The Tophaceous Hills and Cliffs about Andria in Apulia. 1749 *Phil. Trans.* XLVI. 221 The Waters of these hot Springs..are so replete with tophaceous Matter, that where ever they run, Masses of Tophus are formed. 1777 LIGHTFOOT *Flora Scot.* II. 535 *Chara.* Incrusted with a kind of tophaceous coat, which is like sand between the teeth. 1819 H. BUSK *Vestriad* IV. 698 Sapphire brooks on beds tophaceous play.

**2.** *Path.* Gritty or calcareous, as the matter deposited in gout.

1687 *Phil. Trans.* XVI. 553 The Generation of the Tophaceous Matter in the nodose Gout. 1728 *Ibid.* XXXV. 493 That tophaceous gouty Substance commonly found about the Joints. 1879 *St. George's Hosp. Rep.* IX. 643 Gouty, or so-called tophaceous, deposits.

‖ **Tophaike** (tofēi·k). [ad. vulgar Turkish تفك *tüfek* (literary تفنگ *tufeng*) musket: cf. Pers. *tufak* blow-pipe.] A (Turkish) musket.

1813 BYRON *Giaour* viii, Though too remote for sound to wake In echoes of the far tophaike (*note* 'Tophaike', musquet). 1816 *Sporting Mag.* XLVII. 285 Their coming was announced by the firing of their tophaikes. 1882 ARMSTRONG *Garl. Greece, Last Sortie* 268 At my new-found foe I sprung, And clutched with both my hands the raised tophaike.

**To·p-ha·mper.** [f. TOP *sb.*[1] + HAMPER *sb.*[2] 2.] *Naut.* Weight or encumbrance aloft: orig. said of the upper masts, sails, and rigging of a ship; later, also, weight or encumbrance on the deck, as in a steamer, ironclad, etc.

1791 *Jrnl. Barth. James* (Navy Rec. Soc.) 207 The ship being very uneasy from the loss of so much top hamper. 1800 *Naval Chron.* IV. 52 The objects of this invention are: ..The great reduction in top-hamper, height, and size of masts. 1829 MARRYAT *F. Mildmay* xiv, To disengage this enormous top hamper, was to us an object more to be desired than expected. 1840 R. H. DANA *Bef. Mast* xxxi. 114 To see our noble ship dismantled of all her top-hamper of long tapering masts and yards. 1857 MAURY in Corbin *Life* (1888) 135 She was a side-wheel steamer, with not a little top hamper, and therefore an ugly thing to manage in such a situation. 1870 *Daily News* 16 Sept., One cannot but suspect that the enormous top hamper, consisting of 4 25-ton guns with her immense turrets, had something to do with her heeling over.

**b.** *transf.* and *fig.* An encumbrance on the top or upper part of anything; something that makes it 'top-heavy'; the 'head-piece'.

1861 SMILES *Engineers* II. 269 Though the top-hamper of houses had long been removed, and the piers patched and strengthened at various times, the [London] bridge was becoming every year less and less adapted for accommodating the increasing traffic to and from the City. 1881 G. W. CABLE *Mme. Delphine* viii, The returned rover was a trifle snarled in his top-hamper. 1894 SALA *Things I have seen* I. iv. 147 The luggage..was piled..on the roof of the machine; and the whole tophamper was covered with a thick tarpaulin. 1905 W. P. KER *Ess. Mediæval Lit.* i. 11 Many of Hakluyt's men..carry more rhetorical top-hamper than Ohthere.

**To·p-ha·t.** *colloq.* A man's silk or beaver hat with high cylindrical crown; a tall or high hat.

1881 MISS BRADDON *Asph.* xvi, She liked to have her son well-dressed and in a top-hat. 1883 E. F. KNIGHT *Cruise of Falcon* (1887) 222 Black men in coats and top-hats. 1886 J. K. JEROME *Idle Thoughts* xiii, How I do hate a top hat! 1905 A. R. WALLACE *My Life* I. 17 He always wore a top-hat—a beaver hat as it was then called, before silk hats were invented.

*attrib.* 1902 R. HICHENS *Londoners* 159 Another top-hat Ascot! I wish the Prince would set the fashion of billycocks.

Hence **To·p-ha·tted** *a.*, wearing a top-hat; **To·p-ha·tter**, one who wears a top-hat.

1892 *Spectator* 27 Feb. 305/1 To wonder at pig-tailed China and top-hatted Japan. 1892 R. BUCHANAN in *Pall Mall G.* 19 July 3/2 Far from the realms of hansoms and top-hatters all. 1900 *Westm. Gaz.* 21 Aug. 8/1 Of every social standing, from the top-hatted City man to the picturesque newspaper urchin.

**Tophe**, variant of TOPH[1].

**Top-heavy** (tǫ·pˌhe·vi), *a.* Disproportionately heavy at the top; having the upper part so heavy as to overbalance the lower; hence, unstable and inclined to topple. Also *transf.* and *fig.*

*a* 1533 FRITH *Answ. More* (1829) 184 They have made it so top-heavy, that it is surely like to have a fall. 1641 BEST *Farm. Bks.* (Surtees) 36 That they make theire loades broade, and large, but not over high and toppe-heavy, for feare of throwinge over..the waine. 1647 H. MORE *Song Soul* I. II. lxxvii, Top heavy was his head with earthly policy. 1707 MORTIMER *Husb.* (1721) II. 81 If your Trees grow too top heavy, you must abate the Head to lighten them. 1862 T. A. TROLLOPE *Lenten Journ.* xvi. 259 We were top-heavy with eight or nine great sacks of letters on the roof [of the vehicle]. 1889 *Anthony's Photogr. Bull.* II. 118 Do not make your picture topheavy with clouds. 1895 K. GRAHAME *Gold. Age* (1904) 20 Harold,..top-heavy with eagerness of possession, had fallen into the pond.

**b.** Said of an intoxicated person: tipsy.

1687 in *Dk. Buckhm.'s Wks.* (1705) II. 120 Jack was too top-heavy to escape undiscovered. *a* 1700 B. E. *Dict. Cant. Crew*, *Top-heavy*, Drunk. 1823 T. W. L. in Hone *Every-day Bk.* (1827) II. 859 Being top-heavy with liquor, he..lost his balance.

Hence **To·p-hea·viness; To·p-hea·vyish** *a.*

1853 G. J. CAYLEY *Las Alforjas* II. 204 A noble top-heavyish Gothic tower. 1869 SIR E. J. REED *Iron-Clad Ships* vii. 137 To the unprofessional eye there does appear to be a 'top-heaviness' in armoured ships. 1889 WELCH *Text Bk. Naval Archit.* iii. 63 The mistaken view..that 'top-heaviness' was the cause of the excessive rolling.

**Tophet** (tōᵘ·fĕt). Also 4 tofeth, 4–9 topheth. [a. Heb. תֹּפֶת *topheth* pr. name, of uncertain etymol.

For conjectures, see references in *Oxford Heb. & Eng. Lex.* s.v., One of the most ancient sought to connect it with TOPH[2], or its vb.: see quots. 1388, 1749, 1865.]

**1.** *orig.* Proper name of a place near Gehenna or the Valley of the Son or Children of Hinnom, south of Jerusalem, where, according to Jer. xix. 4, etc., the Jews made human sacrifices to strange gods. Later it was used as a place for the deposit of refuse, and became symbolic of the torments of hell.

1382 WYCLIF 2 *Kings* xxiii. 10 Forsothe he defoulide Topheth, that is in the valeye of the sone of Ennon, that no man schuld sacryn his sone or his douȝtre thorȝ fyr to Moloch [1388 has *marg. note*..Tophet signefieth tympan.. for the prestis of this idol, maden noyse with timpans, lest fadres and modris schulden here the cry of her sones, diynge bi fier in the hondis of the idol]. 1535 COVERDALE *ibid.*, He suspended Tophet also in the valley of the children of Ennon [etc.]. 1611 BIBLE *ibid.*, He defiled Topheth. 1667 MILTON *P. L.* I. 404 [Moloch] made his Grove The pleasant valley of Hinnom, Tophet thence And black Gehenna call'd, the Type of Hell. 1749 STACKHOUSE *Hist. Bible* VI. iv. II. 911 *note*, It is the general Opinion of the Jews, that the Word *Tophet* comes from *Thoph*, which, in their Language, signifies a Drum. 1865 GROSART *Lambs all Safe* 117 (tr. Pintus 1582) That the parents of the child might not hear its wailing, the priests beat drums, from which cause the place was called Tophet, or a drum.

**2.** The place of punishment for the wicked after death; the place of eternal fire; hell, Gehenna.

1388 WYCLIF *Isa.* xxx. 33 For whi Tophet [1382 Tofeth], *that is, helle*, deep and alargid, is maad redi of the kyng fro ȝistirdai. 1611 BIBLE *ibid.*, For Tophet [1885 *R. V.* a Topheth] is ordained of olde..the breath of the Lord, like a streame of brimstone doeth kindle it. 1678 BUNYAN *Pilgr.* I. 2, I fear that this burden..will sinck me lower then the Grave; and I shall fall into Tophet. *a* 1708 BEVERIDGE *Priv. Th.* I. (1816) 95, I never did see..the flaming tophet that is below. 1825 SCOTT *Talism.* xviii, Whose ashes, when this earthly fuel is burnt out, must yet be flung into Tophet.

**3.** *fig.* A place, state, condition, or company likened to hell. **a.** A 'hell upon earth'.

1618 J. TAYLOR (Water P.) *Pennyles Pilgr.* E ij b, Yet all I saw was pleasure mixt with profit, which prou'd it to be no tormenting Tophet. 1849 MACAULAY *Hist. Eng.* iv. I. 498 The chief of this Tophet [Claverhouse], a soldier of distinguished courage and professional skill, but rapacious and profane. 1883 MISS BRADDON *Gold. Calf* xxv, If she could ..lead her husband's footsteps out of this Tophet into which he had sunk himself.

**b.** A place or state of wild chaos and warring elements; a roaring furnace; a raging whirlpool, a maelstrom.

1837 HAWTHORNE *Twice-told T.* (1851) I. x. 172 Converted quite to steam, in the miniature tophet, which you mistake for a stomach. 1856 MRS. BROWNING *Aur. Leigh* I. 418 Shuffling off The hearer's soul through hurricanes of notes To a noisy Tophet. 1912 *Daily News* 4 July 1 The officer barked out the short order, 'Load twelve-inch gun'.. Instantly tophet was let loose in the turret.

**4.** *Comb.*, as *tophet-black*, *-red* adjs.

1837 CARLYLE *Fr. Rev.* III. v. iv, Simultaneously with this Tophet-black aspect, there unfolds itself another aspect, which one may call a Tophet-red aspect, the Destruction of the Catholic Religion; and indeed, for the time being, of Religion itself.

Hence (*nonce-wds.*) **Tophe·tic, -ical** *adjs.*, of, pertaining to, or of the nature of Tophet; **To·phetize** *v.*, *trans.* to make a Tophet or hell of; **To·phetism**, hellishness.

1684 N. S. tr. *Crit. Enq. Edit. Bible* xxv. 226 All the stratagems of Popery, all the tophetical Tyranny of the School-men. 1698 C. MATHER *Magn. Chr.* VII. (1702) 105 A Room Tophetized with Smoke, and Rhume, and Spittle, and Malice, and Lies. 1859 M. NAPIER *Mem. Visct. Dundee* I. 20 It is brutality rendered dangerous and Tophetical by excessive bumptuousness. [Cf. quot. 1849 in 3 a.] *Ibid.* 38 The idealized Tophetism of a trooper's 'damning'.

**Tophic** (tōᵘ·fik), *a.* [f. TOPH-US + -IC.] Of the nature of toph or tophus; tophaceous.

1789 J. WILLIAMS *Min. Kingd.* II. 383 There are great quantities of the concreted substance called *tufa* in many parts of Scotland...The process of nature, in the formation of this tophic substance, is to be explained upon the same principles as the stallactites.

† **Topho·se**, *a.* [f. as next: see -OSE.] = next.

1752 J. HILL *Hist. Anim.* 581 The Capra, with a tophose bunch on the head.

† **To·phous**, *a. Obs.* [ad. rare L. *tōph-*, *tōfōsus*, f. TOPHUS, *tōfus*: see -OUS.] Of the nature of a stony or calcareous concretion: **a.** in the body, **b.** in deposits from springs, etc. (cf. next).

1634 T. JOHNSON *Parey's Chirurg.* XIX. iii. (1678) 432 You shall find them [pustules] stuffed with a certain plaister-like and tophous matter. 1692 RAY *Disc.* 110 Now these Teeth being burnt, pass presently into a Coal, but the tophous substance adhering to them, doth not so. 1699 MISAURUS *Hon. Gout* (1720) 8 And threw off the tophous Injury. 1754–64 SMELLIE *Midwif.* II. 79 Bones..perfectly sound with a few spots of tophous concretions on them. 1756 C. LUCAS *Ess. Waters* II. 141 A..petrifying incrusting or tophous water, which rises in several large springs.

**Tophus** (tōᵘ·fɒ̆s). Also 6–7 tofus, 7 tophis, -as. *Pl.* ‖ **tophi**; also 7 tophy, tophoes. tophuses, tofusses. [a. L. *tōphus*, better *tōfus*, a general name for loose porous stones of various kinds, whence It. *tufo* (also *tofo* in Florio, 'a kind of soft, crumbling, or mouldring stone, to build withall'), Fr. *tuf* (16th c. in Hatz.-Darm.), 'generic name of porous stones, produced in the form of sediment or incrustation, as calcareous, siliceous, volcanic *tuf*' (Littré): see also TUFF, TUFA.]

**1.** A soft porous stone, arenaceous, calcareous, or volcanic; *esp.* a stony substance deposited by calcareous springs.

1555 EDEN *Decades* 19 The stone cauled *Tofus* whiche is soone resolued into sande. 1615 G. SANDYS *Trav.* 161 (tr. Juvenal) How much more venerable had it beene, If grasse had cloth'd the circling banks in greene, Nor marble had the natiue tophis marr'd. *Ibid.* 272 The artificiall rocks, shells, mosse and tophas, seeme euen to excell that which they imitate. 1621 — *Ovid's Met.* III. (1632) 84 A natiue Arch she drew, With Pumice and light Tofusses, that grew [III. 160 nam pumice vivo, Et levibus tophis nativum duxerat arcem]. 1692 RAY *Disc.* III Among Tophi and Stones in those dry places. 1696 *Phil. Trans.* XIX. 194 He produces one Echinus, bruised in the Tophus in which it lay. 1789 PILKINGTON *View Derby.* I. vii. 316, I have seen a stag's head..which was found in the tophus at Alport. 1842 BRANDE *Dict. Sc.*, etc., *Tophus*, the term has been applied to porous deposits of calcareous matter from water.

**2.** *Path.* A concretion which forms on the surface of the joints, the teeth, the pinna of the ear, etc. in gout; a gouty deposit; also gravel, or a stone or calculus, formed within the body.

1607 TOPSELL *Four-f. Beasts* (1658) 65 In the second venter of a cow there is a round black tophus found, being of no weight. 1612 WOODALL *Surg. Mate* Wks. (1653) 71 *Amoniacum*..dissolveth Tophoes or hard stones grown in the flesh. 1663 BOYLE *Usef. Exp. Nat. Philos.* II. iii. 77 With a very few Doses..the Merchant was quickly free'd, not onely from his Pains, but from his Gouty Tophy. 1698 TYSON in *Phil. Trans.* XX. 132 These Hairy Tophi are frequently to be met with in the Stomachs of Bruits. 1860 MAYNE *Expos. Lex.*, *Tophus*...*Med.* A name for the matter concreted in the joints of the gouty; also the calculous matter concreted in the kidneys and urinary bladder; also the tartar on the teeth. *Surg.* Term for a swelling particularly affecting a bone, or the periosteum: a toph. 1866 A. FLINT *Princ. Med.* (1880) 1103 These gouty concretions are called tophi or chalk-stones.

**3.** *Comb.* tophus-stone = TRAVERTIN.

1830 LYELL *Princ. Geol.* I. 211 Pallas..enumerates a great many hot springs, which have deposited monticules of travertin precisely analogous in composition and structure to those of the baths of San Filippo, and other localities in Italy... Speaking of the tophus-stone, as he terms these limestones, he often observes that it is snow-white.

‖ **Topī, topee** (tōᵘpī·). *East Ind.* [a. Hindī *topī* hat; prob. the word mentioned in the Vocab. of *Linguagem de Calicut* in the *Roteiro de Vasco da Gama* 1497, 'barrete: *tupy*', related to Hindī '*top* helmet or hat' (Yule). (But some think the latter is an adaptation of Pg. *topo* top.)] Originally applied by Indian natives to the European hat; now specialized in Anglo-Indian, as a name for the *sola topī*, sola hat or helmet: see SOLA *sb.*

1835 *Court Mag.* VI. 207/2 The white *sombrero* solah topee, was supplanted by a raking cocked hat. 1845- Sola topi [see SOLA *sb.* (*b*)]. 1849 E. B. EASTWICK *Dry Leaves* 2 And there is need of many a fold of twisted muslin round the white topí to keep off his [the sun's] importunacy. 1872 'ALIPH CHEEM' *Lays of Ind* (1876) 41 The boat came back in a little space, With Grant and the topee blue. 1889 *Blackw. Mag.* Aug. 245 You wear a pith topee. 1904 *Daily Record & Mail* 1 Jan. 4 The white topee, green-lined, is a favourite hat.

*Comb.* 1880 A. M. RUTHQUIST in *Life* xi. (1893) 201 A rather lengthy lesson in topee-making was given.

Hence ‖ **Topī-, topee-wallah** (topīˌwā·lā), also **-wala** [a. Hindī *topīwālā*, one who wears a hat, f. *topī* + WALLAH fellow], the Indian name for a European, because he wears a hat.

The term is used 'by the natives with a shade of disparagement', while 'all persons claiming European blood' take pride 'in wearing a hat' (Yule s.v. *topaz*). R. Drummond says that in his time (before 1808), *Topeewala* and *Puggry-wala* were used in Guzerat and the Mahratta country for 'European' and 'Native'. So 'the author of the Persian *Life of Hydur Naik* calls Europeans *Kalāh-posh* hat-wearers' (*Ibid.* s. v.).

1826 HOCKLEY *Pandurang Hari* vi. I. 88 It was now evident we should have to encounter the *Topee Wallas.* 1834 A. PRINSEP *Baboo* I. viii. 126 The Topee-walas are within matchlock shot of this grove! 1864 TREVELYAN *Compet. Wallah* (1866) 44 The idea got about that they were to be forcibly turned into topee-wallahs, hat-fellows, a synonym for the hated name of Frank or Christian.

‖ **Topia** (tōu·piă). *Rom. Antiq.* [L. *topia*, a. Gr. τόπια, pl. of τόπιον, diminutive of τόπος a place.

But others (e. g. Casaubon) suppose it to be the pl. of τοπεῖον, a 'rope' or 'cord' (used of the cordage of a ship).]

Interior wall-decorations in the style of those found at Pompeii, consisting usually of landscapes or figures of trees and bowers; fanciful mural fresco.

1891 in *Cent. Dict.*; and in other mod. Dicts.

‖ **Topiaria** (tōupiˌēᵊ·riă). [L. *topiāria*, fem. sing. (sc. *ars*) of TOPIARIUS.] The art of cutting trees and shrubs into quaint devices.

1599 R. LINCHE *Fount. Anc. Fict.* K iv, This Statue was ..supported by foure Images of Victoria, hewen out..with inimitable skill of the art Topiaria. 1706 PHILLIPS (ed. Kersey), *Topiaria*, the Art of making Arbours with Trees or Twigs cut and plaited. 1900 B. D. JACKSON *Gloss. Bot. Terms* 272/1 *Topiaria*,..ornamental gardening.

**Topiarian** (tōupiˌēᵊ·riăn), *a.* [f. L. *topiāri-us*: see below and -AN.] = TOPIARY.

1694 MOTTEUX *Rabelais* IV. i. 3 A small Vine of large Indian Pearl, of Topiarian work. 1816 SCOTT *Antiq.* iii, Tall clipped hedges of yew and holly, some of which still exhibited the skill of the topiarian artist, and presented curious arm-chairs, towers, and the figures of St. George and the dragon. 1880 *Q. Rev.* Apr. 334 The most famous specimen of Topiarian work in England is probably that at Levens Hall in Westmoreland.

So **To·piarist** = next.

1910 *Athenæum* 15 Jan. 65/3 To the ordinary tourist, however, the place is noteworthy for the art of the topiarist.

‖ **Topiarius** (tōupiˌēᵊ·riŏs). [L. adj. 'of or belonging to ornamental gardening'; sb. 'an ornamental gardener': see TOPIA and -ARY [1].] One skilled in fanciful landscape-gardening.

1706 PHILLIPS (ed. Kersey), *Topiarius*, a Gardener that orders Arbours or Bowers; or that makes divers Kinds of Knots and Devices in Plants, as they grow. 1895 *Edin. Rev.* July 162 The zeal of the *topiarius*..tortured the bushes into extravagant forms. 1907 *Ibid.* Jan. 150 The shrubs clipped and pruned by the 'topiarius'.

**Topiary** (tōu·piări), *a.* (*sb.*) *Gardening.* Also 6–7 -arie. [ad. rare L. *topiāri-us*: see prec. Cf. F. *topiaire* adj. and sb. (Rabelais, 1548).] Consisting in clipping and trimming shrubs, etc. into ornamental or fantastic shapes.

1592 R. D. *Hypnerotomachia* 51 By a turnyng downe the transomes, did joyne decently one with the other with a Topiarie woorke. [Cf. F. *ouvrage topiaire.*] 1644 EVELYN *Diary* 22 Oct., There was much topiary worke, and columns in architecture about the hedges. *a* 1680 BUTLER *Rem.* (1759) I. 184 No topiary Hedge of Quickset Was e're so neatly cut. 1838-9 HALLAM *Hist. Lit.* IV. IV. v. § 52 Rapin was a great admirer of box and all topiary works, or trees cut into artificial forms. 1902 *Lond. Mag.* June 474 A topiary garden is by no means an inexpensive hobby to indulge in.

**b.** *sb.* The topiary art; the training and clipping of trees into artificial shapes.

1908 *Sphere* 10 Oct. 30/1 Topiary is essentially the art of a leisurely age, for it takes a long time to develop a tree into the acquired shape.

**Topias**, obs. variant of TOPAZ.

**Topic** (tǫ·pik), *a.* and *sb.* Also 6 topicke, (toopick), 7 topike, -ique, -yc, 7–8 -ick. [As adj., ad. Gr. τοπικ-ός of or pertaining to τόπ-ος a place (see -IC); local, or concerning τόποι commonplaces. As sb., ad. L. *topica*, a. Gr. τοπικά adj. neuter pl., in τὰ τοπικά, title of a work of Aristotle, lit. matters concerning τόποι commonplaces.

The use of τόπος 'place' for a class of considerations which would serve as a 'place' in which a rhetorician might look for suggestions in treating his theme, goes back to Isocrates. By Aristotle τόπος was especially appropriated to classes of considerations of a general character, *common* to many kinds of subjects, the use of which was open to any one dealing with his subject as a rhetorician or dialectician, not with special knowledge with a view to scientific demonstration. Such were more fully described as κοινοὶ τόποι, *loci communes*, COMMONPLACES. Aristotle's treatise on *probable* (as distinguished from *demonstrative*) reasoning, which started from such general considerations and dispensed with special knowledge, was referred to as τὰ τοπικά; and such general considerations and arguments based thereon as were treated of in that work were called *topic axioms*, *rules*, or *maxims*, *topic arguments*, or simply *topics*; sometimes with less, sometimes with more emphasis on the general character of such arguments. (C. C. J. Webb.)]

**A.** *adj.*

**I.** †**1.** Pertaining to or of the nature of a 'commonplace' (COMMONPLACE A. 1) or general maxim. *Rule topic*, a general rule, which may fail to apply in a particular case, so that its application is only probable and not certain: see above. *Obs.*

1581 J. BELL *Haddon's Answ. Osor.* 117 b, You fayle in the rule Topicke: whereby we are taught to apply true proper Causes, to true effectes. And therefore your consequent is faultie. 1589 *Marprel. Epit.* (1843) 18, I marveile upon what topike place this reason is grounded. 1627 WREN *Serm. bef. King* 17 Feb. 26 That's the first, and it is a Topick rule that; particularly applied by him upon this ground, because of the generall Image of God, which is upon a mans brother. 1645 HOWELL *Twelve Treat.* (1661) 360 The Topique Axiome tells us, that *Dolus versatur in universalibus*, there is double dealing in universals. 1645 RUTHERFORD *Tryal & Tri. Faith* xxi. 231 Uncertain and topick arguments to conclude a God-head and a golden heaven in the creature. 1650 *Vind. Dr. Hammond's Addr.* § 58. 23 Would it not be a strange reply, to say, That this consequence depended on the Authority of a Topick Maxime? The word (Topicke) I suppose to be here prefixt by him upon a designe of diminution, as Topicall is equivalent with probable, and oppos'd to demonstrative. 1653 R. BAILLIE *Dissuas. Vind.* (1655) 3 Such aerious and Topick arguments can give no strength to a cause.

†**b.** Containing 'commonplaces'; *topic folio*, a commonplace-book. *Obs.*

1644 MILTON *Areop.* (Arb.) 64 To finish his circuit in an English concordance and a topic folio, the gatherings and savings of a sober graduatship, a Harmony and a Catena.

**II.** †**2.** Of or pertaining to a particular place or locality; local. *Obs.*

1610 HOLLAND *Camden's Brit.* I. 691 These Locall or Topick Gods doe never passe unto other Countries. 1683 E. HOOKER *Pref. Pordage's Mystic Div.* 79 That Topic Proverb among the Spaniards, There are two Magicians in Segura, the one Experience, the other Wisdom. 1793 HELY tr. *O'Flaherty's Ogygia* II. 195 Solemn conventions .. to appease the topic deities.

†**b.** *Med.* Of or pertaining to a particular part of the body; designed for external local application.

1601 HOLLAND *Pliny* XXIX. vi. II. 364 The places ought before the application of those topicke medicines, to be well prepared with the razour. 1671 SALMON *Syn. Med.* III. xxvii. 474 *Linimentum* is a fat topick Medicine.

**B.** *sb.*

**I.** Representing Gr. τοπικά. (See note in etymol.)

**1.** *pl.* As title of the treatise of Aristotle, or as name for a work of the same nature, or for a set of general rules or maxims.

*a* 1568 ASCHAM *Scholem.* II. (Arb.) 131 Aristotle..when he had written that goodlie booke of the Topickes, did gather out of stories and Orators, so many examples as filled xv. bookes, onelie to expresse the rules of his Topickes. 1599 NASHE *Lenten Stuffe* D iv, Had I my topickes by me in stead of my learned counsell to assist me, I might haps marshall my termes in better aray. 1603 HOLLAND *Plutarch* Explan. Words, *Topicks*, That part of logicke which treateth of the invention of arguments, which are called *Topi*, as if they were places, out of which a man might redily have sufficient reasons to argue and dispute with *Pro & contra.* 1783 BLAIR *Lect.* xxxii. II. 180 These Topics or Loci, were no other than general ideas applicable to a great many different subjects, which the Orator was directed to consult, in order to find out materials for his Speech.

*fig.* 1644 BULWER *Chiron.* 9 For the Hands are those common places and Topiques of nature.

†**2.** A kind or class of considerations suitable to the purpose of a rhetorician or disputant: passing into the sense 'consideration', 'argument'. *Obs.*

1634 JACKSON *Creed* XI. xxvii. § 4 A new topic or frame of arguments which they draw from this. 1652 HEYLIN *Cosmogr.* II. 137 Acts of Violence and Force..justified onely by the false Topick of successe. 1662 BOYLE *Seraph. Love* (ed. 4) *Refl. on Let.* 170 When we have employed the loftiest hyperboles, and exhausted all the celebrating Topicks and Figures of Rhetorick. 1669-96 AUBREY *Brief Lives* (1898) I. 170 Judge Richardson harangued against him long, and like an orator, had topiques from the Druides, etc. 1692 BENTLEY *Boyle Lect.* vi. 179 This first Topic was very fitly made use of by our Apostle. 1719 W. WOOD *Surv. Trade* 96 The most general Topick made use of by the Advocates for it, was, That by prohibiting the French Trade, we only hurt our selves. 1756 HUME *Hist. Eng.* II. xxi. 29 These strong topics, in favour of the house of Lancaster, were opposed by arguments no less convincing on the side of the house of York. 1825 SCOTT *Betrothed* xxviii, Interrupting those tears to suggest topics of hope and comfort, which carried no consolation to her own bosom. 1840 J. H. NEWMAN *Par. Serm.* (1842) V. xxiii. 351 How cold and dreary do all such topics prove, when a man comes into trouble?

†**b.** A head under which arguments or subjects may be arranged. (This passes imperceptibly into 3.) *Obs.*

*a* 1661 FULLER *Worthies, Linc.* (1662) II. 150 What remaineth concerning Mastiffes is referred to the same Topick in Somerset-shire. *a* 1677 HALE *Prim. Orig. Man.* II. i. 131 These are the Heads of those Evidences of Fact which I shall use in this Argument.., whereunto possibly other occasional Topicks of the like nature may be added. 1705 ADDISON *Italy* Pref., There are still several of these Topicks that are far from being exhausted. *a* 1806 HORSLEY *Serm.* (1811) 375 It is a new kind of argument against the truth of a proposition..that it hath been asserted and maintained by wise and good and learned men...This is a new way of managing the topic of authorities.

**3.** The subject of a discourse, argument, or literary composition; a matter treated in speech or writing; a theme; also, a subject of admiration, animadversion, satire, mockery, or other treatment.

1720 SWIFT *Intelligencer* No. 3 Wks. 1761 III. 363 It is allowed that Corruptions in religion, politics, and law, may be proper topics for this kind of satire. *a* 1768 SECKER *Serm.* (1771) VII. xvi. 364 We are much to blame, that we banish religious Topics from our Discourse. 1770 *Junius Lett.* xxxvi. (1820) 172 The sovereign should..not..make them a topic of jest and mockery. 1797 MRS. RADCLIFFE *Italian* i, He had exhausted every topic of conversation. 1874 GREEN *Short Hist.* vi. § 4. 308 The New Testament of Erasmus became the topic of the day.

**II.** †**4.** *Med.* An external remedy locally applied, as a plaster or blister. *Obs.*

1587 *Burgh Rec. Edin.* 12 Apr. (1882) IV. 489 Ane vlcer ..applying thairto toopickis and vtheris emplasteres. 1621 BURTON *Anat. Mel.* II. v. III. i, Amongst topics or outward medicines none are more precious than baths. 1668 CULPEPPER & COLE *Barthol. Anat.* man. III. i. 323 To which part of the Back-bone Topicks are to be applied. 1758 J. S. *Le Dran's Observ. Surg.* (1771) 241 Phlebotomy, and emollient Topicks, are our principal Resources.

†**5.** App. used as = Gr. τόπος 'place'. *Obs.*

1650 FULLER *Pisgah* IV. iii. 60 Their Cities being one of David's Topicks or place where he haunted.

**Topical** (tǫ·pikăl), *a.* (*sb.*) [f. as TOPIC + -AL.]

**1.** Of or pertaining to a place or locality; local.

1588 J. HARVEY *Disc. Probl.* 121 Is it..to be supposed, that the Verticall, Perpendicular, or Topicall stars haue now conspired together to desolate, or oppresse the seuerall regions which they aspect? 1610 HEALEY *St. Aug. City of God, Vives' Comm.* II. xxiii. (1620) 89 The Topicall gods, that is, the locall gods of such and such places. 1624 BP. MOUNTAGU *Gagg* 44 Particular and topical churches have erred. 1664 H. MORE *Myst. Iniq.* 473 Rites or Opinions that are but Temporary or Topical. 1722 WOLLASTON *Relig. Nat.* v. 92 If [the flood] was only topical, affecting some one tract of the globe. 1870 LOWELL *Among my Bks.* Ser. I. (1873) 177 Their truth is not topical and transitory, but of universal acceptation.

**b.** *Med.* That belongs or is applied to a particular part of the body.

1608 TOPSELL *Serpents* (1658) 621 First I will speak of such means as are topical, or such as are outwardly applyed. *c* 1645 HOWELL *Lett.* (1688) IV. 503 This..Powder heals at a distance without topical Applications to the place affected. 1733 G. CHEYNE *Eng. Malady* I. vii. § 4. 65 Small and Topical Disorders of the Nervous Kind. 1800 *Med. Jrnl.* IV. 173 The symptoms..may be divided into topical and general. 1871 GARROD *Mat. Med.* (ed. 3) 157 It [creasote] is..used as a topical styptic in hæmorrhages.

*fig.* 1673 O. WALKER *Educ.* (1677) 98 In Religion lies the universal and never failing remedy of all the evils of the Soul. But many times particular and topical ones are also to be applied.

**c.** *Topical colour, colouring*: see quot. 1877.

1839 URE *Dict. Arts* 234 After printing-on the topical colour, the goods must be dried at a gentle heat. 1877 KNIGHT *Dict. Mech.*, *Topical coloring*, a term used in calico-printing to indicate that the color or mordant is applied to specific portions of the cloth forming the pattern.

†**2.** Pertaining to a topic or general maxim; hence, not demonstrative but merely probable.

1594 CAREW *Huarte's Exam. Wits* iii. 24 Aristotle.. with a purpose of crossing Plato..turned to reuiue the former opinion, and with topical places to make it probable. 1624 BEDELL *Lett.* v. 86 This Argument is..but Topicall and probable. *a* 1677 HALE *Prim. Orig. Man.* II. i. 132 It cannot be expected in an Argument of this nature,..that Evidences of Fact can be no more than topical and probable. 1697 tr. *Burgersdicius his Logic* II. xv. 65 A Syllogism Dialectical is also..called Topical,..because its Propositions tho' true, are yet Contingent. 1710 NORRIS *Chr. Prud.* viii. 385, I am now upon the larger and more topical part of my Subject.

**3.** Of or pertaining to a general heading, a topic or subject of discourse, composition, etc.

1856 MASSON *Ess., Milton's Youth* 40 He passes, by a very slight topical connexion, into an account of himself, his education, his designs, and his relations to the matter in question. 1879 MORLEY *Burke* vi. 122 Conversation..was ..ever taking new turns, branching into topical surprises. 1890 *Nature* 2 Jan. 196/2 The writer expects that the topical skeleton furnished by him will be clothed upon by the lessons of the intelligent teacher.

**b.** Of or pertaining to the topics of the day; containing local or temporary allusions.

1873 *Punch* 15 Mar. 111/1 The popular 'topical' song which delights music-hall politicians. 1881 *Daily News* 8 Nov. 5/2 A great many 'topical' allusions to events of the hour, and rough political hits. 1899 *Month* Apr. 410 A review accustomed to bestow articles on topical subjects as they came up. 1905 *Westm. Gaz.* 18 Jan. 12/1 M. Combes, whose resignation makes him topical, is a man with few recreations.

†**B.** as *sb.* = TOPIC B. 4. *Obs. rare*⁻¹.

1656 RIDGLEY *Pract. Physick* 98 Apply purgative Topicals.

Hence **Topica·lity**, the quality of being topical (see 3 b); an instance of this, a topical allusion.

1904 *Longm. Mag.* Nov. 93 The Beck case gives the subject a curious topicality. 1905 *Westm. Gaz.* 10 June 2/2 Fair actresses recite, and Pantomimes Rattle with Fiscal topicalities.

**Topically** (tǫ·pikăli), *adv.* [f. prec. + -LY [2].] In a topical manner.

**1. a.** In respect to place; locally. *rare.* **b.** *Med.* In respect to some particular part of the body.

1646 SIR T. BROWNE *Pseud. Ep.* III. iii. 109 Their dung and intestinall excretions..Topically applyed become a..Rubifying medecine. **1648** Evelyn *Let. to Sir R. Browne* 15 June, And now for the news. The scene is Essex, more topically Colchester. **1741** *Compl. Fam.-Piece* I. i. 73 An excellent Medicine to be used topically in Gleetings. **1803** *Med. Jrnl.* IX. 100 Bleeding, either generally or topically, I never had recourse to. **1845** Garrod *Mat. Med.* (1855) 23 It acts topically on the mucous membrane of the respiratory passages.

**2.** In reference to topics.

**1881** *Gentl. Mag.* Feb. 252 These letters are arranged topically not chronologically. **1896** W. D. Mackenzie in *Chicago Advance* 26 Mar. 445/1 A man who has only preached topically for five years.

‖ **Topinambou** (tǫpinæ·mbu). Also 9 -bour, -bar. [a. F. *topinambou* (16th c.), now *topinambour*, from the name of a people of Brazil.] A name for the Jerusalem Artichoke, *Helianthus tuberosus*, a native of tropical America.

**1666** J. Davies *Hist. Caribby Isles* 56 Topinambous or artichokes which are now not only very common in most parts but cheap. **1698** Osborne tr. *Froger's Voy. Straits Magellan* 60 The potato and ighname are roots very like the toupinanbous. **1858** Simmonds *Dict. Trade, Topinambar*, a name for the Jerusalem artichoke. **1866** *Treas. Bot.*, Topinambour, (Fr.) *Helianthus tuberosus*.

[**Topinch**, a spurious word, founded on an erroneous emendation of *to pinch*, in Shaks. *Merry W.* iv. iv. 57. See To *prep.* B. 19, quot. 1598.]

† **Topinel.** *Obs. rare*⁻¹. app. = *Topping-lift*: see Topping *vbl. sb.*²

**1549** *Compl. Scot.* vi. 41 Than the master cryit, top ȝour topinellis, hail on ȝour top sail scheitis.

**Toping,** *vbl. sb.* and *ppl. a.*: see Tope *v.*²

**Topit** (tǫ·pit). [app. f. phrase *top it* (Top *v.*¹).] An attachment at the top of a boring rod by means of which it is withdrawn.

**1839** Ure *Dict. Arts* 966 The boring tools..13. The topit, or top-piece. *Ibid.*, The runner, for taking hold of the topit. **1883** Gresley *Gloss. Coal Mining, Topit*, a kind of bracehead, but much smaller, which is screwed on to the top of boring rods when withdrawing them from the hole. It is attached to a rope worked from a jack-roll.

**Topknot** (tǫ·pnǫt). [f. Top *sb.*¹ + Knot *sb.*¹]

**1. a.** A knot or bow of ribbon worn on the top of the head by ladies towards the end of the 17th and in the 18th century; later, a bow of ribbon worn in a lace cap; ? also of flowers, feathers, etc.

*c* **1686–8** *Roxb. Ball.* (1890) VII. 21 The lofty Top-knots on her crown,..Makes me with care, alas! look down. **1688** R. Holme *Armoury* iii. xiv. (Roxb.) 12/1 Glasses.. used by Lady's..to see how to dress their heads, and set their top knotts on their fore heads vpright. **1716–20** *Lett. fr. Mist's Jrnl.* (1722) I. 51 Let me beg thee..to insert a polite History of Hoop-Petticoats, Top-Knots,..and all that. **1831** Scott *Nigel* Introd., Obliged to compel..a fellow-knight or squire to restore the top-knot of ribbon which he had stolen from a fair damsel. **1910** O. Barron in *Encycl. Brit.* VII. 242/2 A cap [late 17th c.] whose top-knot or commode stood up stiff and fan-shaped.

**b.** A tuft of hair on the top or crown of the head of a person or animal; a knob of hair worn on the crown of the head in some styles of hair-dressing; also, a plume or crest of feathers or filaments on the head of a bird.

**1700** T. Brown *Amusem. Ser. & Com.* 22 A..Trumpeter calling in the Rabble to see a Calf with Six Legs and a Top-knot. **1849** D. J. Browne *Amer. Poultry Yd.* (1855) 12 Unacquainted with fowls with topknots. **1867** Baker *Nile Trib.* iii. (1872) 41 A Bishareen Arab wears his hair in hundreds of minute plaits..surmounted by a circular bushy topknot upon the crown. **1894** Gladstone *Odes of Horace* ii. xi. 24 Her hair be dressed like Spartan maid, With comely top-knot upwards tied. **1902** O. Wister *Virginian* i, Have you ever seen a cockatoo—the white kind with the top-knot—enraged by insult?

**c.** The head. *slang.*

**1869** E. Waugh *Hermit Cobbler* iii, I doubt it's unsattle't his top-knot a bit. **1889** 'J. S. Winter' *Mrs. Bob* (1891) 63 The little tip-tilted nose and curly top-knot.

**2.** *transf.* **a.** One who wears a topknot.

**1697** Isobel Wright in *Collect. Dying Test* (1806) 42 Like gowkhorns, topeknots and I know not what to call them. **1909** *Bible in World* Feb. 60/1 Dirty children, and everywhere dreamy 'Top-knots', as the Korean men are called because they wear their hair in a top-knot.

**b.** One of several species of small European flat-fish, with a tapering filament on the head.

**1832** Johnston in *Proc. Berw. Nat. Club* I. No. i. 7 The most remarkable [fishes]..were..the top-knot, the toothed gilt-head. **1843** *Zoologist* I. 106 Description of Muller's Top-knot..taken from a fresh specimen. **1880** Günther *Stud. Fishes* 555 'Bloch's Top-knot', *Rh*[*ombus*] *punctatus*. *Ibid.*, The 'Top-knot' (*Ph*[*rynorhombus*] *unimaculatus*) occurs occasionally on the south coast of England.

**3.** *attrib.*, as **topknot duck**: see quot.; **topknot pigeon**, an Australian crested fruit-pigeon, *Lopholaimus antarcticus*.

**1849** D. J. Browne *Amer. Poultry Yd.* (1855) 197 Also the 'crested', or 'topknot duck', a beautiful ornamental tame variety. **1891** F. Adams *J. Webb's End* i. ii. 33 Flying for a moment by a lovely, melodious top-knot pigeon.

Hence **To·pknotted** *a.*, having a topknot.

**1859** Geo. Eliot *A. Bede* vi, The old top-knotted hens, scratching with their chicks among the straw. **1868** Darwin *Anim. & Pl.* I. viii. 295 There are topknotted canaries, and it is a singular fact, that, if two topknotted birds are matched, the young, instead of having very fine topknots, are generally bald, or even have a wound on their heads.

**Topless** (tǫ·plės), *a.* [f. Top *sb.*¹ + -less.]

**1.** Having no top; without a top or summit.

**1596** *Edw. III*, iv. v. 114 There is a loftie hill, Whose top seems toplesse. **1614** C. Brooke *Trag. Rich. III*, ii, Thou toplesse builder of great Babel's Spyre, (Damnéd Ambition!). **1859** G. Meredith *R. Feverel* xliii, Gray topless ruins. **1910** *Daily Chron.* 14 Jan. 6/7 Statues to well-known Parsees wearing their topless hats.

**2.** *fig.* Seeming to have no top or summit; immensely or immeasurably high; unbounded.

**1589** Greene *Menaphon* (Arb.) 39 The glister of the Sunne vpon the toplesse Promontorie of Sicilia. **1602** Marston *Antonio's Rev.* i. i, And even adore my toplesse villany. *a* **1656** Bp. Hall in Spurgeon *Treas. Dav.* Ps. lxviii. 19 Oh the boundless, topless, bottomless, load of divine benefits. **1707** Watts *Hymn*, '*Lord, we are blind*' ii, Where neither wings nor souls can fly, Nor angels climb the topless throne. **1863** *Pilgr. Prairies* II. 134 Where topless cliffs frown down on the intruder, forbidding further passage.

† **b.** Than which there is nothing higher; having no superior; supreme, paramount. *Obs. rare*⁻¹.

**1606** Shaks. *Tr. & Cr.* i. iii. 152 Sometime great Agamemnon, Thy toplesse deputation he puts on.

† **Topliffe.** *Obs. rare*⁻¹. (See quot.)

**1602** Carew *Cornwall* i. 13 b, They measure their black Tynne, by the Gill, the Topliffe, the Dish,.. which containeth a pint, a pottell, a gallon.

**Toploftical** (tǫplǫ·ftikăl), *a. humorous colloq.* [app. f. *top loft*, topmost gallery or story + -ical, after words like *magnifical*, *tyrannical*, etc.] High-flown, 'high and mighty', 'highfalutin', 'stuck-up'; also *lit.* lofty, elevated.

**1823** *Blackw. Mag.* XIV. 104 Very toploftical to be sure. *c* **1824** Mrs. Carlyle *Early Lett.* (1889) 84 At the first she was quite intolerable with her fine-lady airs, and toploftical notions. **1884** J. Burroughs *Birds & Poets* 74 Our toploftical brilliancy and cleverness. **1892** *Century Mag.* Apr. 837/2 Whose turban handkerchief towered in a toploftical structure. **1894** *Harper's Mag.* May 940/2 A few days of toploftical strutting around town. **1898** *Speaker* 22 Jan. 100/2 Eaten up by pride and a toploftical sense of independence.

**Toplofty** (tǫ·plǫ·fti), *a. humorous colloq.* [app. f. Top *sb.*¹ + Lofty *a.*, or f. *top loft*: see prec.; said in Farmer *Slang* to be of American origin.] Lofty in manner or character; elevated; haughty, 'high and mighty'. Hence **Toplo·ftiness**.

**1859** F. Francis *Newton Dogvane* (1888) 218 Everything was very toplofty in the landlord and waiters' parts. **1889** *Pall Mall G.* 13 July 6/1 Lord F—— is dignity itself... There is a 'toploftiness' about him which is meant to be very impressive. **1896** *Chicago Advance* 25 June 941/2 The council sermon... A little top-lofty perhaps for children. **1898** *Contemp. Rev.* Jan. 17 They were snubbed with rather toplofty denials.

**Top-maker, -making**: see Top *sb.*¹ 34.

**Topman**¹ (tǫ·pmæn). [f. Top *sb.*¹ + Man *sb.*¹]

† **1.** A ship (Man *sb.*¹ 14) with a top on its mast; = *top-ship* (Top *sb.*¹ 33). *Obs.*

**1513** N. West in Ellis *Orig. Lett.* Ser. i. I. 67, I found none but ix. or x. small topmen,..and other small balyngiers and crayers,..one little topman of the burdon of threescore tonne. **1577** Harrison *England* ii. xvii. (1877) i. 290 There are 135 ships that exceed 500 tun; topmen vnder 100, and aboue fortie, 656.

† **2.** A hangman: = Topsman 2. *slang. Obs.*

**1607** W. N. *Barley-Breake* D iv b, A nimble Ape his topman strait will be And hangs vp Streton.

**3.** *Naut.* A seaman stationed in one of the tops, to attend to the upper sails, or in a fighting ship as a marksman.

**1748** *Anson's Voy.* iii. viii. 379 Her topmen..made prodigious havock with their small arms, killing or wounding every officer..on the quarter-deck. **1825** H. B. Gascoigne *Nav. Fame* 74 The Topmen now the Backstays well attend, To lesser duties all attention lend. **1830** Marryat *King's Own* xvi, Topmen, aloft! loose top-gallant sails. **1898** Newbolt *Isl. Race* 8 One morning the topmen reported below The old Agamemnon escaped from the foe.

**4. a.** The upper man in a saw-pit: = Top-sawyer a; cf. Pitman 3. **b.** A miner or pitman working at the top of the shaft.

**a. 1678** Moxon *Mech. Exerc.* v. 98 With the Pit-Saw they enter the one end of the Stuff, the Top-man at the Top, and the Pit-man under him. *Ibid.* vi. 113 Of the two Sawyers, the uppermost is called the Top-man. **1881** *Lumber World* Mar., The frame or sash saw is operated in the same manner by a top-man and a pit-man.

**b. 1890** 'R. Boldrewood' *Miner's Right* iii, The bucket appeared slightly above the brace at the shaft, and was taken by the topman. **1912** *Scotsman* 5 Apr. 5/2 There was..no settlement of the banksmen's or topmen's question.

**To·pman**². *rare.* [f. Top *sb.*² 3 + Man *sb.*¹] A man who is engaged in laying rope.

**1851–4** Tomlinson *Cycl. Arts* (1866) II. 465/2 The motion of the top requires to be regulated so as to ensure equal hardness in the rope: the topman, therefore, before putting in the top, makes a mark across the strands of every beam: if, when the top reaches a beam the mark be above the bearer, the topman knows that the turning at the foretop has been too fast.

**Topmast** (tǫ·pmast, -məst). A smaller mast fixed on the top of a lower mast; *spec.* the second section of a mast above the deck, which was formerly the uppermost mast, but is now surmounted by the topgallant mast.

**1485** *Naval Acc. Hen. VII* (1896) 48 Toppe mastes..j, Toppe shrowdes..vj. **1497** *Ibid.* [see Topgallant A. 1]. **1556** W. Towrson in Hakluyt *Voy.* (1599) II. ii. 43 Perceiuing the Admirall to be farre a sterne of his company, because his maine top-mast was spent. **1610** Shaks. *Temp.* i. i. 37 Downe with the top-Mast: yare, lower, lower, bring her to Try with Maine-course. *a* **1625** *Nomenclator Navalis* (Harl. MS. 2301) s.v., The Top-mastes are ouer halfe soe long as the Mastes vnto which theie belong. **1764** Veitch in *Phil. Trans.* LIV. 287 In great ships the masts are composed of three parts,..the lowermost part is called by its proper name, the middlemost part is called the top-mast, and the uppermost part the top-gallant-mast. **1795** Nelson in Nicolas *Disp.* (1845) II. 21 The Ça Ira lost her topmasts, which enabled the Agamemnon and Inconstant to close in with her. **1873** C. Robinson *N. S. Wales* 98 Every ship in port, from whatever clime, is decorated with flags of all colours, from stem to stern, from top-mast to hull.

**b.** *attrib.*, as *topmast-block*, *-head*, etc.

**1672** *Lond. Gaz.* No. 690/1 Who carried the Union Flags on their Topmast-head, and each a White Flag in their Poupe. **1709** Dampier *Voy.* III. ii. 37 This Island..may be seen from a Ship's Topmast-head about ten Leagues. **1840** R. H. Dana *Bef. Mast* xi, The topmast-studding-sail boom..broke off at the boom-iron. **1897** *Daily News* 7 June 2/3 Through the thinner veil overhead..the gilded topmast-blocks could be seen gleaming in sunshine.

**Topmost** (tǫ·pmǫ̆st), *a.* [f. Top *sb.*¹ + -most.] Uppermost, highest. Also *absol.*, highest part.

**1697** Dryden *Æneid* vii. 99 A swarm of bees..Upon the topmost branch in clouds alight. **1768** Tucker *Lt. Nat.* (1834) I. 668 An ambition of..gaining the topmost summit of it. **1807** Crabbe *Par. Reg.* i. 442 Susan..had some pride Among our topmost people to preside. **1827–35** Willis *Scholar of Thebet Ben Khorat* 228 Wisdom sits alone, Topmost in heaven. **1875** Morris *Æn.* xii. 493 The eager-driven spear Smote on his helm, and shore away the topmost of his crest. **1899** E. J. Chapman *Drama of Two Lives* 17 The topmost peaks were still aflame With the red sunset's dying glow.

**Topnet**, obs. form of Tapnet.

**Topo-**, before a vowel **top-**, a. Gr. τοπο-, combining form of τόπος place, as in τοπο-γράφος topographer; a formative element in various words.

**Topo·latry** [-latry], excessive reverence for a place. **To·pomorph** [Gr. μορφή form]: see quot. **Toponarco·sis**, local narcosis. **Toponeu·ral** *a.*, having separate marginal sense-organs; as in the *Toponeura*, a proposed division of *Hydrozoa*. **Topopho·bia**, a morbid dread of certain places. **Topopo·litan** *a.* [Gr. πολίτ-ης citizen: cf. *cosmopolitan*], that inhabits a definite or restricted locality. **To·potype**, a specimen from the locality where the original type-specimen was obtained; hence **Topoty·pic, -ical** *adjs.*, of or pertaining to a topotype.

**18..** *Macm. Mag.* (Ogilvie), This little land [Palestine] became the object of a special adoration, a kind of *topolatry, when the Church mounted with Constantine the throne of the Cæsars. **1897** Sclater in *Geog. Jrnl.* June 673 Various areas [of the earth] are characterized by the presence of certain forms of animal life which do not occur elsewhere. These forms it is proposed to call '**Topomorphs*'. Thus the giraffe is a 'Topomorph' of the Æthiopian region. **1860** Mayne *Expos. Lex.*, **Toponarcosis*. **1890** Billings *Med. Dict.*, *Toponarcosis*, local anæsthesia. **1899** *Syd. Soc. Lex.*, **Topophobia*. **1897** Sclater in *Geog. Jrnl.* June 673 The sloths and anteaters are confined to tropical America, and the polar bear to the North Polar lands. Such animals may be called '**topo-politan*'..in contradistinction to those that are universally distributed, or '*cosmo-politan*'. **1893** O. Thomas in *Proc. Zool. Soc.* 14 Mar. 242 The word *topo-type (or place-type)..should.. be restricted to specimens collected within, say, a few miles of the original typical locality. **1900** *Ibid.* 3 Apr. 405 The Mice of Hillerød, in Zealand (an almost *topotypical locality for the former name), belong to the latter form.

**Topograph** (tǫ·pǫgraf). *rare.* [f. Gr. τόπ-ος place + -(ό)γραφος and -γράφος: see -graph 1.] **a.** A representation or description of localities. **b.** Name given to a surveying instrument. **c.** (See quot. 1911.)

**1833** Carrington (*title*) The Topograph, or the bye-ways within 9 miles of Devonport and Plymouth. **1865** *Athenæum* 7 Oct. 472/2 On the Topograph, a New Surveying Instrument, by Capt. Lendy. **1865** *Reader* 7 Oct. 409/2 A useful little instrument, called by the inventor a 'Topograph'..combines a plane table, prismatic compass, level, and clinometer. **1911** Webster, *Topograph*, a model or draft of a place.

**Topographer** (tǫpǫ·grăfəɹ). [f. Gr. τοπογράφ-ος topographer + -er¹. Cf. F. *topographe* (16th c. in Godef. *Compl.*).] One who is skilled in topography; one who describes or delineates a particular locality.

**1603** Florio *Montaigne* i. xxx. (1632) 101 We had need of Topographers to make us particular narrations of the places they have beene in. **1625** N. Carpenter *Geog. Del.* ii. i. (1635) 2 Topographers, who spend their stocke in the description of some particular place or Region. **1774** Warton *Hist. Eng. Poetry* Diss. ii. (1840) I. p. cxxiv, Giraldus Cambrensis..was an historian, an antiquarian, a topographer,..and a poet. **1884** *Manch. Exam.* 18 July 4/6 The Russian topographers are..correcting the existing maps.

**Topographic** (tǫpǫgræ·fik), *a.* (*sb.*) [ad. Gr. τοπογραφικ-ός studious of topography, f. stem of τοπογραφ-ία Topography: see -ic. Cf. F. *topographique* (16th c. in Godef. *Compl.*).] Of or pertaining to topography; = Topographical 1.

**1632** E. Robertson in Lithgow *Trav.* B iv, Townes Topographick view, and Riuers courses. **1638** Sir T. Herbert *Trav.* (ed. 2) 1 If I have made no Topographic mistakes. **1730–6** Bailey (folio), *Topographic, topographick*, pertaining to the art of topography. **1803** W. Taylor in *Ann. Rev.* I. 437 Some displays of topographic knowledge. **1883** *Daily News* 1 Sept. 5/3 A lieutenant employed in the topographic service..perished by the eruption of the 27th inst. **1898** *Jrnl. Sch. Geog.* (U.S.) Oct. 289 The lines followed by pioneer settlement..are greatly influenced by topographic configuration.

**b.** = TOPOGRAPHICAL 2.

1899 *Syd. Soc. Lex.*, *Topographic anatomy*, descriptive anatomy; or, used in the restricted sense, surface anatomy.

**B.** *sb. pl.* **Topogra·phics,** the science of topography. *rare.*

1831 CARLYLE *Sart. Res.* II. viii, Statistics, Geographics, Topographics came..almost of their own accord.

**Topographical** (tǫpǫgræ·fikăl), *a.* [f. as prec. + -AL: see -ICAL.]

**1.** Of, pertaining to, or dealing with topography.

1570–6 LAMBARDE *Peramb. Kent* Introd. (1826) 6 Which collection (bicause it was digested into Titles by order of Alphabet, and concerned the description of places) I called a Topographicall Dictionarie. *a* 1586 SIDNEY *Lett.* Misc. Wks. (1829) 280 The topographical description of each country. *a* 1646 J. GREGORY *Maps & Charts* Posth. (1650) 323 A particular Description and Topographical Table of Middlesex. 1710 *Stillingfleet's Wks.*, *Life* 56 An unusual variety of..topographical observations. 1803 WELLINGTON in Gurw. *Desp.* (1837) II. 104, I am also desirous of having..any general topographical account of the country. 1860 MAURY *Phys. Geog. Sea* (Low) xxi. § 871 The topographical features and the climates of the antarctic regions.

† **b.** *Topographical instrument*, the name given by Digges to a combined surveying instrument, such as is now called a THEODOLITE. *Obs.*

1571 DIGGES *Pantom.* I. xxxiv. K iij b, Set vp your Instrument Topographicall on his staffe. 1611 A. HOPTON *Topogr. Glass* vi. 27 To work as the Theodelitus, and Topographicall Instrument...If you make this instrument like to that which Maister Digges called the Topographical Instrument, then is there a Boxe and a Needle..in the center of the Planisphere, over which there doth stand a perpendicular, whereon is placed a Semicircle..to move about with the Alhidada.

**2.** Pertaining to the description of the parts or regions of the body: cf. TOPOGRAPHY 3.

1857 DUNGLISON *Med. Lex.* s.v. *Anatomy*, Topographical anatomy. 1890 BILLINGS *Med. Dict.* s.v. *Anatomy*, Topographical anatomy, describing them [the organs] by regions.

**Topogra·phically,** *adv.* [f. prec. + -LY [2].] In a topographical way; in relation to topography.

1625 N. CARPENTER *Geog Del.* II. i. (1635) 3 To the constitution of a place (as it is here Topographically taken). 1797 DALLAWAY *Constantinople* xxi. 341 That it is topographically [exact], an examination of the present face of the country will amply prove. 1893 W. CHOATE in *Home Mission.* (N. Y.) Sept. 264 Topographically, it [New Mexico] is composed of lofty plateaus, crossed by mountain ranges. 1899 *Allbutt's Syst. Med.* VII. 414 No actual proof..that the centre for writing-movements is topographically distinct.

**Topogra·phico-,** combining form of TOPOGRAPHIC, as in *topogra·phico-mythical*, of or pertaining to a topographical or local myth.

1892 A. NUTT in *Folk Lore* III. 41 The 'Dindseuchas', a topographico-mythical poem of the 10th..century.

**Topo·graphist.** *rare.* [f. as TOPOGRAPH-ER + -IST.] One versed in topography; a professional topographer.

1776 DA COSTA *Conchol.* II. 46 This author is a topographist, or describer of a particular country, *viz.* Senegal. 1870 *Daily News* 18 Oct., The most accurate and rapid military topographist I have ever known.

**Topo·graphize,** *v.* [f. as prec. + -IZE.] **a.** *trans.* To describe or treat topographically. **b.** *intr.* To make topographical researches.

1810 BYRON *Let. to H. Drury* 3 May, We had topographised Attica. 1837 SOUTHEY *Doctor* Interch. xiv. IV. 44 Leaving..Sir William Gell to genealogise, if he pleases, as elaborately as he has topographized,..I proceed with my promised explanation. 1876 (*title*) Cuninghame, Topographized by Timothy Pont, A.M., 1604–1608.

**Topo·grapho,me·tric,** *a.* [f. as TOPOGRAPH + METRIC.] Of or pertaining to topographical measuring or surveying.

1911 WEBSTER, *Topographometric*, connected with, or devised for, the measurement of heights, angles, and distances, as for topographical maps.

**Topography** (tǫpǫ·grăfi). [ad. late L. *topographia* (in Servius and Jerome), ad. Gr. τοπογραφία, f. τοπογράφ-ος (see TOPOGRAPHER) + -ια, -Y. Cf. F. *topographie* (16th c.).]

**1.** The science or practice of describing a particular place, city, town, manor, parish, or tract of land; the accurate and detailed delineation and description of any locality.

1549 *Compl. Scot.* vi. 46 Al them that hes studeit in cosmographie, geographie, and in topographie. 1570–6 LAMBARDE *Peramb. Kent* (1826) 474 We might at the last by the union of many partes and papers compact one whole and perfect bodie and booke of our English Topographie. 1621 HEYLIN *Microcosmus* Introd. 10 Topographie which is the description of a particular place, be it Towne, Citie or Village. 1642 FULLER *Holy & Prof. St.* II. vii. 75 Acquainted with Cosmography, treating of the world in whole joynts; with Chorography, shredding it into countries; and with Topography, mincing it into particular places. *a* 1646 J. GREGORY *Maps & Charts* Posth. (1650) 323 The late Geographers..call these Kind of Descriptions (of small Parcels of the Earth ..) *Topographie.* 1864 BURTON *Scot Abr.* I. iv. 164 *note*, He..explains how lifeless all history is without topography.

**b.** A detailed description or delineation of the features of a locality.

1432–50 tr. *Higden* (Rolls) I. 329 Irlonde..whom Giraldus describenge in his Topographye, extollethe hit with mony laudes. 1586 J. HOOKER *Hist. Irel.* Pref. A iv b, in *Holinshed*, In our Topographie we haue at large set foorth and described the site of the land of Ireland. 1659 R. KILBURNE (*title*) A Topographie, or Survey of the County of Kent. 1665–6 *Phil. Trans.* I. 121 A Map of the Moon..with a Topography as it were..of all the considerable places therein.

**c.** Localization, local distribution; the study of this.

1658 SIR T. BROWNE *Hydriot.* ii. (1736) 31 If according to Learned Conjecture, the Bodies of Men shall rise where their greatest Relics remaine, many are not like to err in the Topography of their Resurrection. 1658 — *Gard. Cyrus* i, Of deeper doubt is its Topography, and locall designation. 1835 URE *Phil. Manuf.* iii. 67 The topography of the textile manufactures is a most interesting subject of philosophical research. It investigates the causes why one district is occupied chiefly with cotton fabrics, a second with flax, a third with wool, and a fourth with silk.

**2.** The features of a region or locality collectively.

1847 LYTTON *Lucretia* II. xxvi, Towards that [staircase] used by the servants, and which his researches into the topography of the mansion had..made known to him. 1858 GLADSTONE *Homer* III. 519 [Virgil] is not less neglectful of the actual topography; for he implies that Ilium is among the hills. 1873 G. C. DAVIES *Mount. & Mere* xxv. 224 The water is often very clear, and the frost has cut the weeds down so that one learns the topography of the river bed and the exact locale of the 'homes' of the fish.

*fig.* 1642 MILTON *Apol. Smect.* Wks. 1851 III. 262 Having rambl'd over the huge topography of his own vain thoughts. 1764 REID *Inquiry* vi. § 11. 155, I confess I am not so well acquainted with the topography of the mind.

**3.** *transf.* **a.** *Anat.* The determination of the position of the various parts and organs of the body; regional anatomy. **b.** *Zool.* The determination and naming of the different regions or parts of the surface of an animal.

1847 LEWES *Hist. Philos.* (1867) II. vi. 408 The organs are definitely indicated both as to position and size, by the topography of the skull. 1891 *Cent. Dict.* s.v., The topography of a bird, a crab, an insect.

**Topology** (tǫpǫ·lŏdʒi). [f. TOPO- + -LOGY. Cf. F. *topologique* adj., Littré, related to sense 1 b.] A term meaning 'science of place', which has been tentatively proposed or used in various senses.

**1.** † **a.** The department of botany which treats of the localities where plants are found. *Obs.*

1659 LOVELL *Compl. Herball* Pref., The Topologie or place of gathering them. Thus, Herbes, are to be gathered in mountaines, hills and plain places.

† **b.** The art of assisting the memory by associating the thing to be remembered with some place or building, the parts of which are well known. *Obs.*

1860 WORCESTER cites FLEMING. Hence in later Dicts.

**c.** *Geom.*: see quots.

1883 *Nature* 1 Feb. 316/2 The term Topology was introduced by Listing to distinguish what may be called qualitative geometry from the ordinary geometry in which quantitative relations chiefly are treated. 1895 *Funk's Standard Dict.*, *Topology*..2. *Geom.* The geometrical theory of situation without respect to size or shape, including the theory of knots in a closed curve and the relations of the bounding parts of a solid.

**d.** *Anat.*: see quot.

1899 *Syd. Soc. Lex.*, *Topology*, topographic anatomy. The relation of the presenting part of the fœtus to the pelvic canal.

**2.** The scientific study of a particular locality: see quot. 1905 [1].

1850 S. TYMMS *Bury Wills* (Camden) Introd. 12 The selection of wills..has been made more with a view to illustrate the peculiar customs and language of the period than the topology or genealogy of the district. 1902 *Cassell's Encycl. Dict. Suppl.*, *Topology*, the study of the places or localities in a given district. 1903 *Cornh. Mag.* Feb. 251 The fact that topology is not synonymous with topography, but bears the same relation to topography as geology does to geography. 1905 *Q. Rev.* Apr. 346 The comparatively new study of topology, the science by which, from the consideration of geographical facts about a locality, one can draw deductions as to its history. 1905 *Spectator* 10 June 856/1 We need a knowledge not only of topography, but..of that ..sister science which has been christened 'topology'.

So **Topolo·gic, -ical** *adjs.*, of or pertaining to topology, chiefly in sense 2 (hence **Topolo·gically** *adv.*); **Topo·logist**, one versed in topology.

1872 M. COLLINS in *Lett. & Friendships* I. 113, I might go on with *topologic lore, Until you voted me an awful bore. 1903 *Cornh. Mag.* Feb. 259 The topologic compass keeps his prow true. 1715 M. DAVIES *Athen. Brit.* I. 183 Another noted Historian..publish'd two *Topological Pamphlets, containing the Description of Britanny and Ireland. 1716 *Ibid.* III. *Diss. Physick* 37 Ancient Chiron..the most direct Predecessor, at least in the topological Line, of the Great Hippocrates. 1836 *For. Q. Rev.* XVII. 286 Except the following somewhat ingenious topological (not phrenological) explanation of Richter's genius. 1903 *Times* 4 Apr. 7/2 The Azores..have a topological importance. 1716 M. DAVIES *Athen. Brit.* III. *Diss. Physick* 12 They were distinguish'd *topologically or Geographically. 1903 *Cornh. Mag.* Feb. 258 The French *topologist has shown that the Odyssey is subsequent to a vanished Phœnician sea power. 1905 *Spectator* 10 June 856/1 To the topographist ..the site..is a mystery; to the topologist..it is full of meaning.

**Toponymy** (tǫpǫ·nimi). Also *erron.* toponomy. [f. TOPO- + Gr. -ωνυμία, f. ὄνομα name: cf. *homonymy*, *synonymy*.]

**1.** The place-names of a country or district as a subject of study.

1876 W. K. SULLIVAN in *Encycl. Brit.* V. 306/2 The substitution of vague descriptions of dress and arms, and a vague toponomy, for the full and definite descriptions and precise toponomy of the primitive poems. 1887 *Athenæum* 20 Aug. 240/3 This book..does not deal at all with topography in the proper sense, but merely (if the word may be tolerated as English) with 'toponymy'. 1893 *Academy* 22 July 72/3 These papers are of interest for Basque toponymy and language. 1900 DENNIKER *Races of Man* xiii. 557 The pre-Columbian aborigines of Porto Rico, Haiti, Jamaica, and Cuba were Arawaks, to judge from the toponymy of these islands.

**2.** *Anat.* (See quot.)

1882 WILDER & GAGE *Anat. Techn.* 20 Terms of Position and Direction—Toponymy. *Ibid.* 23 The Intrinsic Toponymy. ..We..shall designate the aspects and regions of the body by terms derived from names which have been applied to the parts themselves. 1899 in *Syd. Soc. Lex.*

So **To·ponym**: see quot.; **Topo·nymal** *a.*, of or pertaining to toponymy; **Topony·mic,** *a.* = prec.; *sb.*: see quot. 1906: cf. *patronymic*; **Topony·mical** *a.* = prec. adj.; **Topo·nymist,** one who deals with place-names.

1891 *Cent. Dict.*, **Toponym*,..the technical designation of any region of an animal, as distinguished from any organ. *Ibid.*, **Toponymal*,..**Toponymic*. 1896 *Nat. Geog. Mag.* (U.S.) VII. 222 We miss in the works of a government board of names all evidence of acquaintance with toponymic literature. 1906 *Cornish N. & Q.* 142 Toponymics, i.e. personal names derived from the place where a particular ancestor lived. 1882 WILDER & GAGE *Anat. Techn.* 20 Such terms constitute a *Toponymical Vocabulary which is based upon intrinsic instead of purely extrinsic and accidental relations. *a* 1852 MACGILLIVRAY *Nat. Hist. Dee Side* (1855) 235 Appropriately named by the Celts—who were famous *toponymists,..*Na claisean*—The Furrows.

**Topophone** (tǫ·pŏfoᵘn). [f. TOPO- + Gr. -φωνος sounding, φωνή voice, sound.] (See quots.)

1880 *Patent Specif.* No. 495, A topophone, or instrument for locating sounds, applicable more especially to the navigation of a vessel in a fog. 1881 *Standard* 1 Jan., The topophone of Professor Mayer..is intended to determine the direction and approximately the distance of a fog-horn. 1902 *Harper's Mag.* Feb. 498 Another wireless telephone for maritime use is known as the topophone. *Ibid.* 499 By the use of the topophone,..sounds can be heard which are inaudible to the unassisted ear.

† **To-pou·ne,** *v. Obs.* Also 4 to-powne, (-pone, -poyne). [f. TO- [2] + ME. *pounen*, POUND *v.*[1]] *trans.* To pound to pieces.

*c* 1290 *S. Eng. Leg.* I. 39/181 Þis desciples forthe wende And to-pouneden it [the dragon] al to deþe. 1382 WYCLIF *Ps.* civ. [cv.] 16 Alle fastnesse of bred he to-ponede [1388 wastide; Vulg *contrivit*]. 1382 — *Matt.* xxi. 44 Vpon whom it shal falle, it shal togidre poune [*v.r.* al to-powne] hym.

† **Top over terve,** *vb. phr.* [Cf. TOPSY-TURVY.] *intr.* To topple over, fall topsy-turvy.

*a* 1450 *Brut* ccxliv. 378 Our stakez made hem top ouyr terve, eche on oþer, þat þay lay on hepis.

**Topped** (tǫpt), *ppl. a.*[1] Also 5–6 *Sc.* toppit, 7–9 topt. [f. TOP *sb.*[1] and *v.*[1] + -ED.]

**1.** Having or furnished with a top or tops (see the senses of TOP *sb.*[1]). Also in parasynthetic comb., as *large-topped*, *sharp-topped*, etc.

*c* 1450 HOLLAND *Howlat* 186 Heronnis contemplatif..With toppit hudis on hed. 1513 DOUGLAS *Æneis* IV. x. 86 The seis large, All wmbeset with toppit schip and barge. 1567 MAPLET *Gr. Forest* 35 The other is rather Spearelike and sharpe topped. 1632 LITHGOW *Trav.* II. 44 Taking their directions from the topped hills of the maine continent. 1675 HAN. WOOLLEY *Gentlew. Comp.* 58 The large-topt stockings with supporters to bear them up. 1681 W. ROBERTSON *Phraseol. Gen.* (1693) 1240 To make topped, or sharp at the top. 1826 HOGG *C. Dinmont* in *Lit. Souvenir* 257 He had huge topped boots, all of one colour. 1852 R. S. SURTEES *Sponge's Sp. Tour* ix. 38 A pair of..brown topped boots.

**2.** Having the top removed; of a tree: polled, pollarded; of hemp: see TOP *v.*[1] 3, quot. 1794.

1712 J. JAMES tr. *Le Blond's Gardening* 169 Some topped Elms..in five or six Years time have form'd a handsome.. Head. 1794 *Rigging & Seamanship* I. 62 Ropes made from topt hemp will not stretch so much. 1844 STEPHENS *Bk. Farm* II. 8 The topped and tailed turnips. 1890 W. A. WALLACE *Only a Sister* 322 Under that topped willow.

**Topped** (tǫpt), *ppl. a.*[2] *Golf.* [pa. pple. of TOP *v.*[1] 18 a.] Struck, as a ball, in the upper half; in which the ball is so struck.

1901 *Westm. Gaz.* 16 Aug. 2/2 If you put forward that plea for the foundered drive, the topped approach, or the putt that 'gangs agee', your partner must accept it. 1902 *Ibid.* 17 Oct. 4/2 The topped stroke with an iron, that sent the ball no great distance when gutta-percha was employed, answers nearly as well as a perfectly aimed shot when the 'Haskell' or 'Kempshall' is in use. 1907 *Ibid* 13 Sept. 3/1 The natural penalty of an errant shot or a topped shot.

**Topper** (tǫ·pəɪ), *sb.*[1] [f. TOP *v.*[1] + -ER [1].]

**1.** A person or thing that tops; one who cuts off the top of a tree; an instrument for topping (TOP *v.*[1] 4, 7); a candle-snuffer; a comb-maker's equilateral single-cut file or float.

1688 R. HOLME *Armoury* III. 381/2 A pair of Snuffers, or a pair of Toppers. 1874 KNIGHT *Dict. Mech.* s.v. *Float*, A single-cut file, or one in which the teeth are parallel and unbroken by a second row of crossing teeth...The floats of comb-makers and ivory-carvers..are known by specific names, as graille, found, carlet, topper. 1883 H. WALKER in *Leisure Hour* 505/1 Beeches unscathed by topper and lopper. 1895 *Oracle Encycl.* II. 125/1 Finished off with wedge-shaped files, called the graille, carlet, topper, &c.

† **b.** One who 'tops' (TOP *v.*[1] 17 a) at dice; a cheating gamester. *Obs. rare.*

1671 SHADWELL *Humourist* III. Wks. 1720 I. 174 Nor is it five months, since I saw you..by help of a dozen men, chastise one poor Topper or Palmer.

**c.** A horse or rider that tops a fence.

1854 WARTER *Last of Old Squires* xii. 133 A fence that would have baulked a Leicestershire topper.

**2.** One who makes or adds the top to something; one who works at the upper part of a garment.

1884 E. SIMCOX in *19th Cent.* June 1041 A shirtmaker proper, otherwise called a 'topper'. 1905 *Daily Chron.* 23 June 8/7 Shirt Hands.—Wanted a few good buttonholers and toppers.

**Topper** (tǫ·pəɹ), *sb.*[2] Chiefly *slang* or *low colloq.* [f. TOP *sb.*[1] + -ER[1]; in some uses perh. f. senses of TOP *v.*[1]]

**1.** A 'top' thing or person; a person or thing surpassingly or exceptionally good or excellent; the best or one of the best of the kind. *colloq.*

1709 *Brit. Apollo* II. No. 2. 3/2 A Bowl that is full of Punch, of all these is the Topper. 1802 R. ANDERSON *Bards of Tyne* 22 The king's meade a bit of a speech, And gentlefwok say it's a topper. 1825 BROCKETT *N. C. Words, Topper*, any thing superior—a clever, or extraordinary person. 1828 *Craven Gloss.* s. v., This coat's a topper for turning rain. 1891 A. LANG *Angling Sk.* 115 He gets flurried with a big fish...And this one is a topper. 1894 ASTLEY *50 Years Life* I. 59 He was a real good fellow then, and..he is a topper now.

**2.** A top-hat, a tall hat. *slang* and *colloq.*

1820 *Sporting Mag.* VI. 269 The wind blew his white topper out of the ring. 1885 JESSOPP in *19th Cent.* July 48 We all wear black coats and dark trousers and 'toppers', at least in London. 1905 H. A. VACHELL *The Hill* v, The 'topper' you wear on Sunday.

**3.** A blow on the 'top' or head. *slang.*

1834 H. AINSWORTH *Rookwood* IV. ii, Vile Jem..Straight threatened Tommy with a topper. 1887 FENN *Dick o' Fens* xvi, How I should have liked to give him a topper with the pole.

**4.** *pl.* The largest and finest fruit (esp. strawberries) displayed at the top of a punnet or package; cf. *to top one's fruit* (TOP *v.*[1] 9 c). *slang.*

1839 MOGRIDGE *Old Humphrey's Observ.* 252 There are toppers in dress,..and toppers in religion, as well as toppers in strawberries. 1891 *Brit. Workman* Aug., The punnet was a very bad case of what is generally bad enough at the best—of 'toppers'. The few good berries at the top were the only good ones. 1898 *Daily Tel.* 2 Mar. 5/4 Has a keen eye for 'toppers'..the attractive oranges which are displayed in the first row in order to entice buyers.

**5.** A large wave with curling or breaking summit.

1863 N. MACLEOD *Remin. Highl. Parish* iii, Quick as lightning the little craft, having again gathered way,..is spinning over the third topper, not a drop of water having come over the lee gunwale.

**6.** A cigar-stump or cigarette-end; also, the remains of tobacco in a pipe-bowl. *slang.*

1888 in *Cassell's Encycl. Dict.* 1902 *Westm. Gaz.* 13 Nov. 5/1 It was his custom to rise before daybreak every morning and search the streets of the West End,..picking up the ends of cigarettes and cigars commonly known as 'toppers'.

Hence **To·pper** *v., trans.* to knock on the head; to kill by a 'topper' or blow on the head. *slang.*

1869 E. FARMER *Scrap Bk.* (ed. 6) 128 Full ninety [rats] had died, Without counting seven they'd topper'd outside.

**Topper,** obs. dial. form of TAPPER[1].

† **Toppet**[1]. *Obs.* [ME. *topet*, app. a. OF. *topet*, *toupet* (12–13th c.) tuft, dim. of *top*, *toup* top, crest: in Eng. perh. eventually taken as dim. of TOP *sb.*[1]] Top, summit, tip.

1439 in *Archæologia* XXI. 37, ij Salers of Gold, whereof yᵗ oon ys a man..garnysshed wᵗ vij rubees and vij troches, every troche of iij perles, and upon yᵉ topet is a saphur. 1561 HOLLYBUSH *Hom. Apoth.* 8 Take..the parynge of the toppet of hertes horne. *Ibid.* 23 Lyke vertue..hath Fenell, Penyreal, the floures of Hoppes. Branck vrsyne the toppets of the floure. *Ibid.* 38 Take the toppet of an onyon.

† **Toppet**[2]. *Obs.* Also 5 topet, 6 tappet. [Late ME., dim. of *toppe*, TOP *sb.*[3] basket (of fruit); analogous to MFl. *topkin* ('viij topkine rosinen' 1334), OF. (Picard) *toppequin* (15th c. in Godef.). Cf. also TAP *sb.*[3], TAPNET.] = TOP *sb.*[3], TAPNET.

1481–90 *Howard Househ. Bks.* (Roxb.) 22 There cam from London x. lb. coton & a toppet figges. *Ibid.* 351 A topet of fygge dodes [see FIG-DOTE]. 1510–11 *Durham Acc. Rolls* (Surtees) 290 Et in quinque lez toppettis Racemorum parvorum ad ij s. viij d. 1511–12 *Ibid.* 291 In 4or le tapettes racemorum magnorum ad 2 s. 8 d., 10s. 8 d. 1516 in Rogers *Agric. & Prices* III. 535/1 [Figs] Toppet.

**Top-piece,** *sb.* The piece that forms or is at the top of anything; *spec.* † **a.** The best or finest piece; the *chef-d'œuvre*, masterpiece. *Obs. rare.* **b.** The head. *colloq.* **c.** = TOPIT. **d.** *Shoe-making*: see quots.

**a.** 1682 BUNYAN *Greatness of Soul* Wks. (ed. Offor) I. 122 The soul is the..top-piece that He hath made in all the visible world. 1682 — *Holy War* i. 3 The Top-piece beyond any thing else that he did in that country. **b.** 1838 in *Eng. Dial. Dict.* 1864 LOWELL *Fireside Trav.* 180 The Acephali, with whom Herodotus..wound up his climax of men with abnormal top-pieces. **c.** 1839 URE *Dict. Arts* 966 The topit, or top-piece. **d.** 1911 *Encycl. Brit.* XXIV. 993/1 Lifts and top-pieces for the heels. *Ibid.* 993/2 The top-pieces, similar to the outsoles, are put on and nailed down to the lifts.

**Top-piece,** *v. trans.* To put a top-piece on.

1830 GALT *Lawrie T.* IV. iv, In less time than Dick the Cobbler takes to top-piece an old shoe.

**To·pping,** *vbl. sb.*[1] [f. TOP *v.*[1] + -ING[1]. In some concrete senses associated with TOP *sb.*[1]]

**1.** The action of TOP *v.*[1] in various senses.

**a.** The making, formation, putting on, or adding of a top or tops (see TOP *v.*[1] III). **b.** The cutting off of the top (of a tree or plant). † **c.** A method of cheating at dice (TOP *v.*[1] 17 a). **d.** Levelling the teeth of a wheel or a saw. **e.** *Topping up*, completing, bringing to perfection.

**a.** 1504 *Acc. Ld. High Treas. Scot.* II. 279 His task of the ending and topping of the chimnais of Halyrudhous. 1883 R. HALDANE *Workshop Receipts* Ser. II. 228/1 This colour may be modified by topping with small quantities of magenta, &c. 1888 *Times* 8 Sept. 9/2 The practice of what is known..as topping, that is of putting good fruit at the top, and of filling the rest of the hamper with rubbish. 1896 *Jrnl. R. Horticult. Soc.* Nov. 209, I believe the old system of..'topping-up' is not quite as prevalent as it was some years ago. 1908 *Toilers of Deep* Sept. 185/2 The herrings have also shrunk and settled down—'pined', as it is called—and several more layers have now to be added in order to fill the barrel again. This is called 'topping'. 1909 *Daily Chron.* 18 Jan. 9/5 Trousers.—A smart girl wanted for topping and seams. **b.** 1513 *MS. Acc. St. John's Hosp., Canterb.*, For toppyng of xij treys & broshyng. 1550 CRANMER *Def. Sacrament* Pref. *iij b, The cuttyng away wherof is but like toppyng and loppyng of a tree. 1657 W. MORICE *Coena quasi Κοινή* ii. 37 Those that could not be satisfied with the topping, but wished the cutting down of the..Tree. 1797 A. YOUNG *Agric. Suffolk* 109 Take up [carrots] at 14d. to 16d. a load, topping included. 1807 J. HALL *Trav. Scot.* II. 445 Hedges frequently require topping. **c.** 1663 *Proposal to use no Conscience* 3 Holding one or two Dice at the top of a Dice-Box, which we Gamesters call Topping. 1680 KIRKMAN *Eng. Rogue* IV. xvi. 226 You must sometimes use Topping; that is, by pretending to put both Dice into the Box, whereas you have dropt but one, holding the other between your fore-fingers. 1680 COTTON *Compl. Gamester* (ed. 2) II. [Fully described.] 1726 *Art & Myst. Mod. Gaming* (title-p.), Working with a grate Box, Eclipsing, Sighting, Waxing, and Topping. **d.** 1884 BRITTEN *Watch & Clockm.* 152 The wheel is so fragile that care is required in topping. **e.** 1890 'R. BOLDREWOOD' *Col. Reformer* (1891) 403 It was not thought advisable to wait longer for the ultimate 'topping up' of the beeves. They were good enough.

**f.** *Topping of the land*, the sighting of the land from a ship's top; the limit or distance at which this is possible.

1666 *Lond. Gaz.* No. 77/1 Whitby, August 3. Several of our Fisherboats inform us that the Dutch Busses, and Doggers are fishing, a little off the Topping of the Land.

**2.** A distinct part or appendage which forms a top to anything, a crest; the top-lock or forelock of the hair of the head; the forelock of a horse or other beast; the crest of a bird. Also the erect tassel of a Scotch cap, and *humorously* the head (*dial.* usually *toppin*).

13.. *Gaw. & Gr. Knt.* 191 Þe tayl & his [a horse's] toppyng twynnen of a sute, & bounden boþe wyth a bande of a bryȝt grene. *c* 1400 *Rule St. Benet* 146 Þen sal þe prelete with a payr of schers be-gyn forto kut hir hair befor at þe toppyng. 1483 *Cath. Angl.* 390/1 A Toppynge, *cirrus, cirritus, crista, coma.* 1593 *Bacchus' Bountie* in *Harl. Misc.* (1809) II. 268 Shee..tooke him roundly by the topping. 1688 J. CLAYTON in *Phil. Trans.* XVII. 997 [In Virginia] The Tewits are smaller than the English, and have no long Toppins. *a* 1720 SHEFFIELD (Dk. Buckhm.) *Wks.* (1753) II. 140 A little Indian Bird is call'd a Pope, only because there grows a high Topping upon his head. 1751 MRS. DELANY in *Life & Corr.* (1861) III. 39 A black cock and hen with white toppings. 1814 W. NICHOLSON *Peacock* II. Poet. Wks. 91 Wi' frills an' feathers on his tappin'. 1817 *Lintoun Green* II. xvi. Notes 154 His bonnet..Has tappin [1685 button] either nane. 1828 *Craven Gloss., Topping*, a crest, a plume or tuft of feathers on the head of birds; also, the hair on a person's forehead. 1872 J. HARTLEY *Yorks. Ditties* Ser. II. 66 Thi toppin's grown whiter nor once.

† **b.** *Typog.* The fine line or serif at the top of a letter. *Obs.*

1676 MOXON *Print Lett.* 7 The Topping is the small Arch above the Letter, as the Arches in the Tops of the Letter V are the Toppings of that Letter. 1683 — *Mech. Exerc., Printing* xiv. ₱ 2 The Topping, is the straight fine Stroak or Stroaks that lie in the Top-line of Ascending Letters.

**c.** Local term in Yorkshire for a hill.

1876 *Whitby Gloss., Topping*, a high hill. 'Roseberry topping'. 'Blakey topping'. *a* 1904 *Summer Holidays in N. E. Eng.* p. xi, Hills and mountains..are anything and everything, from hopes, laws, fells and nabs, to howes..and toppings.

**3.** † **a.** Arming for the tips of bows and arrows. *Obs. rare.* † **b.** A high head-dress or coiffure; cf. TOP *sb.*[1] 11 d. *Obs.* **c.** That which is put on the top of anything to complete it; a top layer; cf. TOP *v.*[1] 9. **d.** *Angling*: see quots. 1856, 1877.

1495 *Trevisa's Barth. De P. R.* XVIII. xiii. (W. de W.) 773 Of oxe hornes ben made tappynge [*Bodl. MS.* tippinges] and nockes to boowes..and arowes to shete ayenst enmyes. *c* 1690 *Roxb. Ball.* (1891) VII. 481, I wear my Topping, Lace, and Fan, and am on daintys feeding. 1700 T. BROWN *Amusem. Ser. & Com.* 57 They..touch the Clouds with their proud Toppings. *a* 1704 — *Walk round Lond., Quaker's Meet.* (1709) 23 High Topping and Lace in a Woman, they abominate, as Ensigns of Vanity. 1839 URE *Dict. Arts* 580 The pot is now ready for receiving the topping of cullet, which is broken pieces of window glass. 1856 'STONEHENGE' *Brit. Sports* I. v. ii. § 4. 247/1 Tail of two slips of brown mallard's feather, with a thin topping of golden-pheasant's crest. 1877 HALLOCK *Sportsman's Gaz.* 599 The tail [of a salmon fly] is what is usually called a 'topping', *i.e.* feather from the crest of the golden pheasant. 1895 *Westm. Gaz.* 23 Nov. 7/2 From five to twelve score of whiting, with a topping of codling, form average baskets.

**4.** *pl.* **a.** Cuttings from the tops of trees: cf. TOP *sb.*[1] 6; also, the tops of hemp removed in hatchelling. **b.** The second skimmings of milk. *dial.* **c.** The best bran. *dial.*

1668 ROLLE *Abridgm., Tit. Action sur Case* (N.) pl. 22. 108 Les toppings del arbers cresent sur son Copihold. 1774 FOOTE *Cozeners* I, You are to have all the loppings and toppings. 1794 *Rigging & Seamanship* I. 62 The toppings of all hemp..is made into spun-yarn. 1801 *Farmer's Mag.* Apr. 231 Many individuals have used heath and toppings of whins for their cattle. *a* 1825 FORBY *Voc. E. Anglia, Toppings*, the second skimming of milk; the first being properly called cream. 1880 JEFFERIES *Hodge & M.* I. vi. 122 Old Hodson..would not even fatten a pig, because it cost a trifle of ready money for 'toppings', or meal.

**To·pping,** *vbl. sb.*[2] [f. TOP *v.*[2] + -ING[1].] The action of TOP *v.*[2] *Topping-lift* (*Naut.*), each of a pair of lifts (LIFT *sb.*[2] 7) by which a yard may be topped; in quot. 1841 *transf.*

1743 BULKELEY & CUMMINS *Voy. S. Seas* 117 We made the Signal for her, by hoisting an Ensign at the Topping-Lift. 1769 FALCONER *Shipwr.* II. 261 *note*, To raise one yard-arm higher than the other..is..called *topping*. 1841 *Civil Eng. & Arch. Jrnl.* IV. 56/2 The shaft rotates in a bearing, and can be raised or lowered by means of a topping lift. 1882 NARES *Seamanship* (ed. 6) 51 The sprit-sail-gaff topping lift [is] fitted with an eye splice.

**To·pping,** *vbl. sb.*[3] [f. TOP *v.*[4] + -ING[1].] The twisting of the strands over a top (TOP *sb.*[2] 3) in laying a rope. *Topping sledge*, the loaded sledge or carriage to which one end of the strands is attached in laying, which advances as they are shortened by twisting.

1825 J. NICHOLSON *Operat. Mechanic* 438 The forward movement of the stranding, topping, and dragging sledges, is that slow progressive movement necessarily required..by the shortening or shrinking up of the strands in twisting,..and of the strands and cordage, either common or patent, whilst hardening and topping.

**To·pping,** *ppl. a.* [f. TOP *v.*[1] + -ING[2].] That tops, in various senses of TOP *v.*[1]

**1.** *lit.* That exceeds in height; very high. *Obs.*

1681 HICKERINGILL *Vind. Naked Truth* II. 4, I never heard of a King shut out even from the Topping-Pulpit, if he had a mind to climb so high. 1691 RAY *Creation* I. (1692) 205 Chains of lofty and topping Mountains. 1705 HICKERINGILL *Priest-cr.* II. v. 48 Every little Domine (when mounted over our heads in the topping Pulpit) is as positive..and pragmatical, as any Woman.

**2.** *fig.* Very high or superior in position, rank, degree, amount, or estimation; chief, principal; pre-eminent, distinguished; overhanging; 'towering'.

*c* 1685 DK. BUCKHM. *Conference* Wks. 1705 II. 51 She was able to buy out her Lease, and is now the Topping Dame of the Parish. 1690 LOCKE *Hum. Und.* II. xxi. § 38 All the thoughts of the mind..are uninterruptedly employed that way,..influenced by that topping uneasiness. 1698 J. CRULL *Muscovy* 306 The topping Saint of all Muscovy for Miracles, is one Sergius. 1703 E. WARD *Lond. Spy* V. (1706) 119 More Money..than the Topping'st Taylor in Town ever got by a Young Heir. *a* 1716 SOUTH *Serm.* (1720) II. iv. 48 Some of the topping Sinners of the World. *Ibid.* xxii. 319 Wheresoever in any topping degree it finds them. 1722 WOLLASTON *Relig. Nat.* iii. 46 Just as men learn rules in arithmetic..and grow very ready and topping in the use of them. 1840 MRS. F. TROLLOPE *Widow Married* v, Taking her to court, and to a few other topping places. 1893 *Daily News* 6 June 7/3 Some prime animals which took the topping rates of the day's trade. 1893 KATE D. WIGGIN *Cathedral Courtship* 3 Fondness for the very toppingest High Church ritual.

**b.** Ironically used; cf. 'fine', 'pretty'.

1693 SIR T. P. BLOUNT *Nat. Hist.* Pref. 5 Let these high-flown Topping Sparks, swell and strut as much as they please. 1706 E. WARD *Wooden World Diss.* (1708) A vj, Some..topping Dawber of Sign-Posts. 1847 ALB. SMITH *Chr. Tadpole* xix, One of those topping gents you see in the slips of the play-houses at half price.

**3.** Of high quality; very fine, excellent; tip-top, first-rate. *colloq.* and *slang.*

1822 GALT *Provost* xlvi, Instead of being drowned..in debt, it might have been in the most topping way. 1841 LEVER *C. O'Malley* lxix, We came on at a topping pace. 1861 HUGHES *Tom Brown at Oxf.* xxiii, He may have made topping averages in first-rate matches of cricket.

**4.** Domineering; confident, boastful. *U.S.*

1885 M. E. WILKINS in *Harper's Mag.* Mar. 595/1 He was awful toppin' at first. 1890 *Harper's Mag.* Apr. 769/1, 'I never saw such nerve. It was superb.' 'Perhaps a little topping', I suggested. 'Yes, perhaps a little topping...But still, it was a toppingness that could have consisted only with the most perfect conscience.'

**5.** Swelling into crested billows; crested.

1857 W. COOK in *Merc. Marine Mag.* (1858) V. 42 The sea..changed to a kind of boil, or topping sea, as if surged up from beneath.

**6.** quasi-*adv.* = next.

1683 *Lond. Gaz.* No. 1860/8 [He] rides very topping, and hath all his paces. 1694 *Ibid.* No. 2959/4 A Bay Nag,..carries his head very topping. 1706 *Ibid.* No. 4209/4 A very dark bay Gelding.., lean, but rides bold and topping.

**To·ppingly,** *adv.* [f. prec. + -LY[2].] In a topping manner; gallantly, splendidly; in excellent condition or health. ? *Obs.* or *dial.*

*a* 1739 JARVIS *Quix.* II. III. xviii, I mean to marry her toppingly when she least thinks of it. 1828 *Craven Gloss., Toppingly*, excellently. 1829 BROCKETT *N. C. Words, Toppenly*, in good health. 'He's toppenly to day'.

So **To·ppingness.** 1890 [see TOPPING *ppl. a.* 4].

† **To·ppingly,** *a. Obs. rare*[−1]. [app. f. TOPPING *vbl. sb.*[1] 4 b + -LY[1].] ? Pertaining to 'toppings', skimmings of milk; hence, pertaining to cheese-making or cheese.

1573 TUSSER *Husb.* (1878) 107 A lesson for dairie maid Cisley, of ten toppings gests...These toppingly gests be in number but ten, As welcome in dairie as Beares among men.

† **To·pple,** *sb.*[1] *Obs.* In 5 topylle. [f. TOP *sb.*[1] + -LE I.] ? A crest, tuft: cf. TOPPING *vbl. sb.*[1] 2.

14.. *Nom.* in Wr.-Wülcker 675/29 *Hic cirrus*, a topylle.

**Topple** (tǫ·p'l), *sb.*² *rare.* [f. next.] An act of toppling or overbalancing and falling.

**1907** *Blackw. Mag.* Aug. 272/2 This ain't the topple over of the Coll building yet.

**Topple** (tǫ·p'l), *v.* [f. Top *v.*¹ + -le 3.]

**1.** *intr.* To fall top foremost, or as if top-heavy; to fall headlong, tumble or pitch over. Also *fig.*

**1590** Shaks. *Mids. N.* ii. i. 53 The wisest Aunt..Sometime for three-foot stoole, mistaketh me, Then slip I from her bum, downe topples she. **1605** — *Macb.* iv. i. 56 Though castles topple on their Warders heads. **1621** T. Williamson tr. *Goulart's Wise Vieillard* 200 Although you bee ready to topple into your grave, and haue not much longer to liue. **1786** tr. *Beckford's Vathek* (1868) 108 The watch-towers were ready to topple headlong upon them. **1853** Kane *Grinnell Exp.* xxvi. (1856) 211 When these [bergs] attain their utmost height, still pressed on by others, they topple over. **1884** *Pall Mall G.* 16 Feb. 5/2 Water stocks toppled all round yesterday.

†**b.** ? To roll or tumble about; in quot. 1568, ? to wrestle, to 'try a fall' *with. Obs.*

**1542** Udall *Erasm. Apoph.* i. 146 b, When ye must lye toppleyng in the dust. **1568** *Jacob & Esau* ii. ii. C j b, *Esau*...I will not eate thee Ragau...*Ragau.* No...Being in your best lust I woulde topple with ye, And plucke a good crowe, ere ye brake your fast with me.

**c.** To turn somersaults. *dial.*

**1801** Bloomfield *Rural T., Rich. & Kate* xxx, The Children toppled on the green. **1802** W. Taylor in Robberds *Mem.* I. 411 A boy about eleven .. was toppling beside the Diligence in hope of halfpence. *a* **1825** Forby *Voc. E. Anglia, Topple*, to tumble; to bring the head to the ground and throw the heels over.

**2.** *intr.* To lean over unsteadily, as if on the point of falling; to overhang threateningly.

**1827** Pollok *Course T.* v. 585 Toppling upon the perilous edge of Hell. **1850** Tennyson *In Mem.* xv. 19 Yonder cloud That..topples round the dreary west, A looming bastion fringed with fire. **1860** Tyndall *Glac.* i. vii. 47 Masses of granite..toppling above the terminal face of the glacier.

**3.** *trans.* To cause to tumble over or fall headlong; to thrust over, overturn, throw down. Also *fig.*

*To topple one's heels*, to die: see Heel *sb.*¹ 23.

**1596** Shaks. 1 *Hen. IV*, iii. i. 32 (Qos.) Vnruly wind.. which..Shakes the old Beldame earth, and topples [*Fol.* tumbles] down Steeples and mossegrown towers. **1599** Nashe *Lenten Stuffe* 13 In one year, seauen thousand and fifty people toppled vp their heeles there. **1809** W. Irving *Knickerb.* vii. xi. 434 At the moment when the victorious legions of Titus had toppled down their bulwarks. **1856** Miss Mulock *J. Halifax* ix, Don't..topple us at once down the slope. **1907** C. Hill-Tout *Brit. N. Amer., Far West* vii. 136 They topple over the biggest trees in this way.

**b.** *Topple* (*tapple*) *up tail, topple tail*: in phr. † *to play tapple up tail*, ? to die (cf. *topple up one's heels* in 3); *to turn topple-tail*, to turn a somersault (cf. 1 c).

**1573** Tusser *Husb.* (1878) 57 Take heede..To thresher for hurting of cow with his flaile, Or making thy hen to plaie tapple vp taile. **1828** *Craven Gloss.*, *Topple*, 'to turn topple tail ower', to turn topsy turvy. **1884** *Pall Mall G.* 6 Mar. 11/2 How many..have you..who can turn topple-tail accurately?

**4.** To cause to tip or tilt so as to be in danger of being upset. *rare.*

*a* **1656** Bp. Hall *Breathings Devout Soul* (1851) 187 Like some little cock-boat in a rough sea, which every billow topples up and down, and threats to sink.

Hence **To·ppled** *ppl. a.*, overturned, thrown down; **To·ppler**, one who topples; *dial.* a tumbler, acrobat.

**1871** J. Miller *Songs Italy* (1878) 23 *Toppled old columns that tumble across. **1897** *Daily News* 30 Sept. 5/4 Toppled cartloads of..bricks. *a* **1825** Forby *Voc. E. Anglia*, **Toppler*, a tumbler, who, among various antic postures, throws his heels over his head.

**To·ppling,** *ppl. a.* [f. Topple *v.* + -ing ².] That topples.

**1.** Overhanging or leaning as if about to fall.

**1804** J. Grahame *Sabbath* 259 Back from the toppling edge his fancy shrinks. **1817** Byron *Manfred* i. ii. 74 Ye toppling crags of ice! Ye avalanches, whom a breath draws down. **1883** Symonds *Ital. Byways* v. 83 The storm-clouds ..climbing the heavens with toppling castle towers.

**2.** Falling headlong (*lit.* and *fig.*).

**1812** H. & J. Smith *Rej. Addr.*, *Archit. Atoms* xvi, Jill ..Head over heels begins his toppling track. **1884** Browning *Ferishtah, Pillar at Sebzevar* 14 Gain, to-day, Was toppling loss to-morrow.

**Toppy** (tǫ·pi), *a.* Now *low colloq.* [f. Top *sb.*¹ + -y.] †**a.** Having or characterized by a top or tops; peaked. *Obs.* **b.** Top-heavy, inclined to tip over; in quot., tipsy. **c.** Showy, stylish.

*c* **1557** Abp. Parker *Ps.* lxviii. 185 Why leape ye so: to spyte thys mounte, ye toppy hillockes gay? **1885** *Times* 6 Aug. 3 The lady gave her some whisky..and it made her 'toppy'. **1893** *Columbus* (Ohio) *Dispatch* 8 Apr., On military or civic parades the horse has been conspicuous for several years for its toppy appearance. *a* **1905** H. S. H. in *Eng. Dia.. Dict.* s.v., She looks toppier to-day.

† **Top-root,** obs. var. of Tap-root; hence † **Top-rooted** *a.*, = *tap-rooted.*

**1651** N. Bacon *Disc. Govt. Eng.* ii. xxxvii. 283 Edward the sixth came in like a storm that tore up Episcopacy by the Roots, yet a Top-Root remained intire with the stock. **1669** Worlidge *Syst. Agric.* vi. § 9 (1681) 105 Leave as much of the Root on as you can, abating only the top-Root, or downright Roots. **1765** A. Dickson *Treat. Agric.* (ed. 2) 278 The top-rooted plants, that is, such as push one principal root perpendicularly downwards.

**Topsail** (tǫ·psĕl, tǫ·ps'l). *Naut.* [f. Top *sb.*¹ 9 + Sail *sb.* So LG. *toppsegel.*] A sail set above the lower course, orig. the uppermost sail (cf. Topgallant A. 1). In a square-rigged vessel, orig. a single square sail set next above the lower sail or yard; now, in larger ships, divided for convenience in handling into an *upper* and a *lower topsail* (*double topsails*). In a fore-and-aft rig, a square or triangular sail set above the gaff.

**1390** [see d]. [**1399** Langl. *Rich. Redeles* iv. 72 They bente on a bonet, and bare a topte saile Affor þe wynde ffresshely to make a good ffare.] *c* **1420** ? Lydg. *Assembly of Gods* 129 [Eolus] With hys boystous blast,..other whyle he brak top seyle and mast. **15..** *Sir A. Barton* in *Surtees Misc.* (1888) 67 Full soone he let his toppe-saill fall. **1622** R. Hawkins *Voy. S. Sea* (1847) 126 Bearing up before the winde wee put out our topsayles and spritsayles. **1674** *Lond. Gaz.* No. 891/4 He met..with part of the Dutch Fleet,..having with them a Vice-Admiral, who upon sight of the Fregat lowred his Flag and Topsails, and saluted. **1762** Falconer *Shipwr.* i. 361 The topsails low'r and form a single reef. **1820** Scoresby *Acc. Arctic Reg.* I. 402 The ship could only bear close-reefed topsails and courses. **1860** Maury *Phys. Geog. Sea* (Low) xix. § 807 At 8 p.m. took in fore and mizen top-sails.

**b.** *fig.* esp. in *to hoist, lower, strike the topsail.*

*a* **1629** Hinde *J. Bruen* xli. (1641) 128 For the practice and power of Religion, the very Topsaile of all England. **1745** J. Mason *Self Knowl.* i. vii. (1853) 53 The Sin, to which not our Vertues only, but Vices too, lower their Topsail, and submit. **1805** Southey *Madoc in W.* xx. 114 You may tell Your Pope, that..I shall not strike a topsail for the breath Of all his maledictions!

†**c.** Phrases, etc. (*a*) *Topsails over* (also simply *topsail*), head over heels, topsy-turvy. *Topsail walten*, upside down. (*b*) *With topsail*, with top-sails set; under all sail, in full career. *Obs.*

Those in (*a*) may have some bearing upon Topsy-turvy.

(*a*) *c* **1400** *Destr. Troy* 1219 Mony turnyt with tene top-sayles ouer, þat hurlet to þe hard vrthe, & þere horse leuyt. *c* **1400** *Sege Jerus.* 706 Þe lered men of þe lawe a litel bynyþe Weren tourmented on a tre, topsail walten. *c* **1430** *Chev. Assigne* 320 And eyther of hem so smerlye smote other,.. And eyther of hem topseyle tumbledde to yᵉ erthe. (*b*) *c* **1400** *Sc. Trojan War* ii. 1963 Tharfor with topsall all & sum Vpon þe craggis suld cum.

**d.** *attrib.* and *Comb.*, of or pertaining to the topsail, as *topsail halyard, sheet, truss, yard*; carrying a topsail or topsails, as *topsail barge, schooner, vessel*; allowing a vessel to carry topsails, as *topsail breeze*, † *cole, topsail gale.*

(With *topsail cole* cf. quots. under Cool *sb.*¹ 2.)

**1390** Gower *Conf.* II. 231 The wynd stod thanne noght amis Bot evene topseilcole it blew. *Ibid.* III. 338 Thei hadden wynd at wille tho, With topseilcole and forth they go. **1549** *Compl. Scot.* vi. 41 Hail on ȝour top sail scheitis, vir..ȝour top sail trossis,..hail out the top sail boulene. **1673** *Lond. Gaz.* No. 807/4 The Wind has been all this day between the South and the South-West, a fine Topsail Gale. **1711** W. Sutherland *Shipbuild. Assist.* 109 Top-sail Yards [are] ⁵/₉ of the Main-yards.., the Top-gallant Yards ½ the Top-sail Yards. **1796** Morse *Amer. Geog.* I. 766 The number of top-sail vessels..is about 150. **1840** R. H. Dana *Bef. Mast* ii, The topsail halyards had been let go. **1867** Smyth *Sailor's Word-bk.*, *Topsail-schooner*, is full schooner-rigged, but carries a square-topsail on the foremast.

**To·p-saw·yer.** **a.** The sawyer who works the upper handle of a pit-saw; cf. Topman ¹ 4 a, *pit-sawyer* (Pit *sb.*¹ 14), and Saw-pit. Hence, **b.** *fig.* One who holds a superior position; the best man. **c.** *loosely.* A first-rate hand at something; a distinguished person.

**a.** **1823** *Grose's Dict. Vulgar T.*, *Top-sawyer*, signifies a man that is a master genius in any profession. It is a piece of Norfolk slang, and took its rise from Norfolk being a great timber country, where the top sawyers get double the wages of those beneath them. **1836** E. Howard *R. Reefer* ii, The top-sawyer had been..pleased to toss his arms up and down over the pit.

**b.** **1826** *Sporting Mag.* XVIII. 215 To ascertain which of two competitors is top-sawyer. **1869** Blackmore *Lorna D.* xxxvi, 'See-saw is the fashion of England always, and the Whigs will soon be the top-sawyers'. 'But', said I,..'the King is the top-sawyer, according to our proverb; how then can the Whigs be?'

**c.** **1823** [see a]. **1829** *Sporting Mag.* XXIII. 412 Many a top-sawyer will speedily give me 'the go by'. **1854** Thackeray *Newcomes* xv, How he had paid the post-boys, and travelled with a servant like a top-sawyer. **1880** Disraeli *Endym.* xxxiii, There are some top-sawyers here to-day, Ferrars!

So **To·p-saw·ing** *vbl. sb.*, top-sawyer's work.

**1894** *Times* 11 Sept. 16/7 A decayed wheelwright who had done top-sawing in his young days.

†**Topset downe,** *adv. Obs.* = *topside down* (Topside e); upside down.

**1569** J. Sanford tr. *Agrippa's Van. Artes* xlvii. 62 A certaine Greekishe Cabala, turninge topset downe all the misteries of the Christian faith.

**Topset turvie,** etc., obs. var. Topsy-turvy.

**Topsey,** *adv.*: see Topsy-turn, quot. 1664.

**Topside** (tǫ·psəid), *sb.* (*adv.*) [f. Top *sb.*¹ + Side *sb.*¹] **a.** *gen.* The upper side of anything.

**1677** Moxon *Mech. Exerc.* i. 27 This Bolt must be wrought straight on all its sides, except the Topside.

**b.** *Shipbuilding.* The upper part of a ship's side: cf. Top-timber. Also *attrib.*

**1815** [see Top *sb.*¹ 7]. **1836** Marryat *Pirate* iv, She is.. taking it in at the topsides. **1874** Thearle *Naval Archit.* 49 At the present day we hear only of topside planking, wales, bottom plank, and garboards. **1877** Knight *Dict. Mech.*, *Topside-line*,.. a sheer line drawn above the top timber at the upper side of the gunwale. **1889** Welch *Text Bk. Naval Archit.* vi. 96 The transverse frames..are continuous from topside to topside across the keel. **1903** *Daily Chron.* 21 Feb. 9/4 With nickel-steel top-sides and a bronze under-body, the boat will be the first composition yacht since the Defender.

**c.** *Butchering.* The outer side of a round of beef, cut from the haunch between the 'leg' and the 'aitch-bone'; the bottom of this is the 'silver-side'.

**1898** *Westm. Gaz.* 25 Feb. 5/2 In schools, where topsides and legs of mutton are the chief supply, the price would be proportionately less.

**d.** *Billiards.* = Top *sb.*¹ 19.

**1904** Mannock *Billiards Expounded* I. 163 'Top side' is, as its title would suggest, gained by hitting the cue-ball as high up as possible.

**e.** Phr. *Topside down, topsides under*, upside down. *rare.*

**1725** *Bradley's Fam. Dict.* s.v. *Miroton*, Let it be well clear'd from the Fat, and laid Topside-down in the Dish. **1872** W. Morris in Mackail *Life* (1899) I. 288 Unless the world turns topsides under, some day.

**B.** *adv.* On the top. Also *fig. colloq.*

**1873** Leland *Egypt. Sketch Bk.* 89 Will the big nigger sit ..top-side of the carriage, or on the locomotive? **1898** *Westm. Gaz.* 29 Sept. 2/3 Straining every nerve to keep 'top-side' in China. **1899** F. T. Bullen *Way Navy* 85 All the privileges attaching to those who work 'topside' in a ship of war.

**Topside-turn**: see Topsy-turn. **Topside turvy,** etc.: see Topsy-turvy *adv.* ¶ γ, δ.

**To·psman.** *dial.* and *slang.* Also *Sc.* taps-. [f. *top's*, genitive of Top *sb.*¹ + Man *sb.*¹]

**1.** *Sc.* and *north. dial.* A head man, bailiff, principal servant; *esp.* the chief drover in charge of a herd of cattle on the road.

**1825** Brockett *N. C. Words, Topsman*, the head man or manager, the chief hind or bailiff. **1827** Scott *Two Drovers* i, Many large droves were about to set off for England, under the protection of their owners, or of the topsmen whom they employed. **1844** Stephens *Bk. Farm* II. 92 Some dealers' top's-men, that is, the men who take charge of their master's lots after delivery.

**2.** *slang.* A hangman. Cf. Top *v.*¹ 6, Headsman.

**1825** *Celebrated Trials* IV. 171 R. Turpin..after speaking half an hour to the topsman, threw himself off the ladder, and expired in about five minutes. **1836** Milner *Turpin's Ride to York* i. iii. (1885) 5/2, I shall never come to the scragging-post, unless you turn topsman. **1883** A. Dobson *Old World Idylls* 29 Waved to the crowd with his gold-laced hat; Talked to the Chaplain after that; Turned to the Topsman undismayed.

**Topsoltiria, tops o're tiria**: see Topsy-turvy A. ¶ ι. **Topstar, -er,** obs. ff. Tapster.

**To·p-stone.** A stone which is placed upon or forms the top of something; a cap-stone: chiefly *fig.* Also, the upper end-stone or jewel in a chronometer.

**1658–9** in *Burton's Diary* (1828) III. 222 Our kings: those that know history, know they were kings before the Parliament declared them so, their top-stone. **1662** Jer. Taylor *Serm. to Univ. Dublin* 51 Humane learning is an excellent Foundation; but the top-stone is laid by Love and Conformity to the will of God. **1707** Mortimer *Husb.* (1721) I. 3 Where are abundance of flat Stones, they make Fences of them by laying of them one upon another like a Wall, and only lay the Top-stones in Clay to keep them together, the weight of which secures the under ones. **1871** *Routledge's Ev. Boy's Ann.* Sept. 513 Religion, that indispensable top-stone of every social edifice. **1901** *N. Amer. Rev.* Feb. 292 The strict observance of the rules of Caste, with the Brâhman as the top-stone of the social pyramid, was everything.

**To·psy-tu·rn,** *v.* Also 7 topside-turn. Now *rare.* [f. *topsy* as in Topsy-turvy + Turn *v.*: cf. the form *topsiturnie* s. v. Topsy-turvy *adv.* ¶ θ. Sometimes hyphened; also used analytically, *to turn topsy.*] *trans.* To turn topsy-turvy, turn upside down; *fig.* to throw into confusion. Hence **To·psy-tu·rning** *vbl. sb.*

**1573** Twyne *Æneid* x. Dd iv b, Than graue Auletes went, and with his hundred beating ores, He topsy turnes vp streames [L. *centenaque arbore fluctus Verberat assurgens*]. **1605** Sylvester *Du Bartas* ii. iii. i. *Vocation* 744 He.. by his travell topsi-turneth then The live and dead, and half-dead horse and men. **1608** *Ibid.* ii. iv. iii. *Schisme* 919 Now the furious waues All topsie-turned by th' Æolian slaues Do mount & roule. **1632** Heywood *Iron Age* v. i. Wks. 1874 III. 341 This obiect..Which topsiturnes my braine. **1637** — *Dialogues* ix. ibid. VI. 214 All things are topside-turn'd. **1664** Cotton *Scarron.* 108 Then turning't [a mug] Topsey on her Thumb Says look, here's *Supernaculum.* **1870** S. Bowles in Merriam *Life* xxxviii. (1885) II. 159 In the presence of such wickedness, of such suffering, of such topsy-turning of right and wrong.

† **Topsy-turve,** *v. Obs. rare*⁻¹. In 7 topsie-. [Back-formation from next: cf. Tirve *v.*²] = prec.

**1603** Florio *Montaigne* ii. xii. 337 Confounding and topsie-turving the visage of all things.

**Topsy-turvy** (tǫ·psi,tɝ·ɹvi), *adv.* (*a.*, *sb.*, and *v.*) Forms: *α.* 6 topsy tervy, tyrvy, turuie, turvy; 6– topsy-turvy, (8–9 -turvey). Also 6 topsituruie, -turuy, 7 -turvy, -turvie, topsi-turvi, top-si-turvy; 6 topsie turuie, -vie, -vey, 6–7 -turuy, 7 -turvie, -turvy; 7 topse-turvie. See also the inverted Turvy-topsy. (Now almost always hyphened; in early use more usually two words; sometimes (in every century) as one word.) *β–ι*: see below. [A kind of alliterative or assonant combination, known in print from 1528, but prob. in popular use from an earlier period. The early spelling was *topsy-tervy* or *-tirvy*, from *c* 1540 written *-turvy*, *-turvie*. (Cf. the pronunciation of *nerve*, *curve*.) As to the actual components no external evidence has been found, and numerous conjectures and suggestions (many of them absurd and impossible) have been offered. Some of the more plausible of these, taking *topsy* as representing *top-set* or *top-side*, have been introduced (by those who favoured them) into the spelling; but amid all these aberrations, the typical form, with mere spelling variants, as *topsy*, *topsie*, *topsi-*, and *tervy*, *tirvy*, *turvy*, *turvie*, has remained practically constant. It seems certain that the first element contains *top* (or *tops*) and probable that the second is related to *terve* or TIRVE *v.* to turn, turn over, overturn; but the *-sy* of the first and *-y* of the second still want explanation: the former is viewed by some as representing an earlier *so*, as in *up-so-down*, now *upside-down*, *so* becoming *sy* under the influence of *turvy*, the *y* of which is apparently as in *hitty-missy*, *hurly-burly*, *arsy-versy*. A suggestion that *turvy* was connected with *turf* or *turve*, and referred to the laying of cut turfs or turves face downward, to keep them fresh, is now discarded, as is the earlier notion that *turvy* might have been altered from *t'other way*.

(There is a certain parallelism between the series *up-so-down*, later *upset-down*, *upside-down*, and **top-so-tervy*, *topsy-tervy*, *topset-tervy*, *topside-tervy*; but the former has not become *upsy-down*, nor has any trace of **top-so-tervy* been yet found, so that the analogy is incomplete.)]

With the top where the bottom should be; in or into an inverted position; upside down, bottom upwards; also less definitely, In or into the position of being toppled over, overturned, overthrown, or upset; right over. (Most commonly qualifying the vb. *turn*, or used predicatively after *be*, *lie*, etc.)

**1530** PALSGR. 843/1 Topsy tyrvy, *ceu dessus dessoubz*. **1555** EDEN *Decades* 46 They say that..they see the houses turne topsy turuye, and men to walke with theyr heeles vpwarde. **1615** G. SANDYS *Trav.* III. 205 The huge wals and arches turned topsie turuey. and lying like rockes vpon the foundation. **1747** MRS. DELANY in *Life & Corr.* (1861) II. 450 As soon as I got into my chair, the chairmen fairly overturned it:.. Lord Westmoreland .. found me topsy turvy. **1847** ALB. SMITH *Chr. Tadpole* ix, Wondering how the flies could walk topsy-turvy on the ceiling. **1848** DICKENS *Dombey* vi, A chaos of carts, overthrown and jumbled together, lay topsy-turvy at the bottom of a..hill. **1871** R. ELLIS *Catullus* xvii. 9 Catullus adjures thee Headlong into the mire below topsy-turvy to drown him. **1907** *Verney Mem.* I. 297 He writes topsy-turvy in sympathetic ink, between the lines of a letter ostensibly full of public news.

**b.** *fig.* With the higher where the lower should be; in or into a reversed condition; with inversion of the natural or proper order; less definitely, With things all in wrong places or positions; in or into utter confusion, dislocation, or disorder.

**1528** ROY *Rede me* (Arb.) 51 He tourneth all thynge topsy tervy. *c* **1540** tr. *Pol. Verg. Eng. Hist.* (Camden) I. 283 The deathe of Canutus didd noe lesse turne all thinges topsie-turvie in Denmarcke. **1579** FULKE *Heskins' Parl.* 215 This comparison is topsituruie. *a* **1623** FLETCHER *Love's Cure* II. ii, Custom hath turn'd Nature topsy-turvy in you. **1670** G. H. *Hist. Cardinals* II. I. 128 Turning all Europe as it were top-si-turvy. **1713** ADDISON *Guard.* No. 154 ¶ 2, I found nature turned topsy-turvey, women changed into men, and men into women. **1833** HT. MARTINEAU *Fr. Wines & Pol.* viii. 125 How strangely the values of things are turned topsy-turvy! **1866** R. M. BALLANTYNE *Shift. Winds* xxvii, A world of inconsistencies, where things are all topsy-turvy, so to speak.

¶ Also in various altered or corrupt forms, mostly indicating popular or conjectural etymologies: see above.

*β*. **6 topset tourvie, toruie, turvie, -tirvi.**

**1549** CHALONER *Erasm. on Folly* A iij, Bothe holy and vnholy thyngs be tourned topset touruie. **1553** GRIMALDE *Cicero's Offices* I. (1558) 12 Who tourned topset toruie all the lawes of God. **1573** G. HARVEY *Letter-bk.* (Camden) 53 Thus within a few years al shuld be turnid topset tirvi.

*γ*. **6 top syd turuye, (topside turfway), 6–8 topside turvy, 6–9 -vey.**

**1582** STANYHURST *Æneis* II. (Arb.) 59 Top syd turuye be turned Al thee Princelye thrasholds. *c* **1586** C'TESS PEMBROKE *Ps.* LVIII. vii, With whirlwinds topside turfway blown. **1596** SPENSER *F. Q.* v. viii. 42 At last they have all overthrowne to ground Quite topside turvey. **1686** GOAD *Celest. Bodies* III. iv. 499 Dreadful Tempest, turned several Villages.. Topside-turvy. **1761** STERNE *Tr. Shandy* IV. xix, How was my system turned topside turvy! **1815** MRS. PILKINGTON *Celebrity* III. i. 25 The world must be turned topside-turvey.

*δ*. **6 topside thother-way, 7 topside t'other way, 8 topside the other way.**

**1577** HOLINSHED *Chron.* I. *Descr. Irel.* 14 b/1 The estate of that flourishing towne was tourned arsye versye, topside thother-way. **1654** H. L'ESTRANGE *Chas. I* (1655) 75 Thus were all things strangely turned in a trice topside t'other way. **1768** TUCKER *Lt. Nat.* (1834) I. 456 His [Socrates'] words are to be turned topside the other way to understand them.

*ε*. **6 typsiturvy, typsy tyrvye, 8 tipsy-turvy.**

**1581** J. BELL *Haddon's Answ. Osor.* 324 b, The generall fraylty of nature will violently carry you away typsiturvy. *Ibid.* 569 Typsy tyrvye. **1766** [C. ANSTEY] *Bath Guide* ii. 35 Their Systems..all turn'd tipsy-turvy [*later edd.* topsy-].

*ζ*. **7 tupsiturvie.**

**1640** HOWELL *Dodona's Gr.* 50 They would have turned up tupsiturvie the very kingdome of Satan.

*η*. **6 top turuye.**

**1582** STANYHURST *Æneis* (Arb.) 33 His launce staffe thee dust top turuye doth harrow.

*θ*. **7 topsiturnie, topsie turnie.**

**1617** MINSHEU *Duct. Ling.*, *Topsiturnie*, the topside turned .. Arsiuersie. **1655** in *Clarendon Papers* No. 1753, [They] would assuredly turne all that hath been ajusted topsie turnie.

*ι*. *Sc.* (? associated with *topsail*: see TOPSAIL c.) **7 topsoltiria, tops o're tiria, 8–9 tapsalteerie, 9 tapsal-, tapsil-, tapsul-teerie, -teery, tapseeteerie, topsieteerie.**

**1623** LITHGOW *Trav.* 202 Let all the misticall drifts and ambiguous designes..turne topsoltiria, or upside downe, I care not. **1684** in Maidment *Bk. Scott. Pasquils* (1868) 326 There was a duke so full of pryde There durst no man come neeria Till cam a monkey out of Fife And dang him tops o're tiria. **1784** BURNS '*Green grow the Rashes*' iv, An' warly cares, an' warly men, May a' gae tapsalteerie, O! **1801** MACNEILL *Poet. Wks.* (1844) 90 And dealing round strong punch and joke, Good-humoured mad, near twa o'clock, Turns a' things tapsilteery! **1805** A. SCOTT *Poems* (1808) 100 For tapsee-teerie lie the sheaves. **1827** J. WILSON *Noct. Ambr.* July, Wks. 1855 II. 10 Wi' ae desperate wallop we baith gaed tapsalteerie.

**B.** *adj.* Turned upside down; inverted, reversed; *fig.* utterly confused or disorderly.

**1618** BP. W. BARLOW *Breife Disc.* 8 With those topsituruy motions. **1710** SWIFT *On a Broomstick* ¶ 2 Wks. 1755 II. I. 181 What is man, but a topsy-turvey creature..his head where his heels should be? **1748** RICHARDSON *Clarissa* (1811) II. xxxiv. 248 Dear! what a topsy-turvy house is this! **1856** F. E. PAGET *Owlet Owlst.* 1 This queer topsy-turvy world. **1873** MISS BRADDON *L. Davoren* I. i, It was the topsy-turviest kind of thing I ever heard in my life. **1887** *Spectator* 6 Aug. 1050/2 A very topsy-turvy way of reasoning. **1904** *Westm. Gaz.* 3 June 8/1 Inventor and engineer of the topsy-turvy railway.

**C.** *sb.* The act of turning or fact of being turned upside down; inversion of the proper order; state of utter confusion or disorder.

**1655** tr. *De Parc's Francion* IV. 10 They played topsy turvy excellently well, for there was not a book in all the Study which..they had not thrown on the ground. **1683** E. HOOKER *Pref. Pordage's Mystic Div.* 24 The whol frame of the world seemeth to me..to circumgyrate, to wheel, whirl. and turn round about in a Topsi-Turvi. **1692** tr. *Sallust* 3 Nor should we see such Topsy-Turvies in the World. **1823** MOORE *Fables, Holy Alliance* iv. 2 Of all that, to the sage's survey, This world presents of topsy-turvey. **1879** GEO. ELIOT *Theo. Such* x. 181 Finds matter for screaming laughter in mere topsy-turvy.

**D.** as *vb. trans.* To turn topsy-turvy or upside down; to invert; *fig.* to reverse; to throw into utter confusion, upset or disorder greatly. Hence **To·psy-tu·rvied** *ppl. a.*, **To·psy-tu·rvying** *vbl. sb.* and *ppl. a.*

**1626** T. H[AWKINS] *Caussin's Holy Crt.* 163 They had ..one sole action in this life, which is to topsy-turuy all things, and to do nothing. **1741** RICHARDSON *Pamela* (1824) I. 119 My poor mind is all topsy-turvied. **1807** SOUTHEY *Let. to J. May* 30 Mar., In this topsey-turveying of ministers. **1834** — *Doctor* xxxix. II. 59 In the topsy-turveying course of time. **1863** SALA *Capt. Dangerous* II. iv. 148 He.. Topsy-turvies his goblet.

Hence (chiefly *nonce-wds.*) **Topsy-tu·rvical** *a.*, of a topsy-turvy character; **Topsy-turvifica·tion,** a making or turning topsy-turvy, reversal of the natural order; **Topsy-tu·rvify** *v.*, *trans.* to make or turn topsy-turvy; **Topsy-tu·rvily** *adv.*, in a topsy-turvy manner; **Topsy-tu·rviment,** act of turning or condition of being turned topsy-turvy; **Topsy-tu·rviness,** topsy-turvy quality or condition; † **Topsy-tu·rvyan,** an inhabitant of an imaginary 'Topsy-turvy Island'; **Topsy-tu·rvydom,** the realm of topsy-turvy, inversion, or confusion; also, topsy-turvy condition or state; **Topsy-tu·rvyhood** = *topsy-turviness*; **Topsy-tu·rvyism,** topsy-turvy system or method; **Topsy-tu·rvyist,** an advocate of something (considered to be) topsy-turvy; **Topsy-tu·rvyize** *v.*, *trans.* to turn topsy-turvy, throw into confusion, upset.

**1882** *Pall Mall G.* 10 Oct. 6 Its *topsy-turvical fun is characteristic of the author. **1840** THACKERAY *Paris Sk.-Bk.* xvii. Wks. 1900 V 191 A regular *topsyturvyfication of morality. **1879** G. SAINTSBURY in *Fortn. Rev.* No. 151. 55 One of the oddest topsyturvifications of a noble sentiment to be anywhere found. **1886** *Sat. Rev.* 27 Feb. 286/1 We have *topsyturvified the whole theory of politics. **1887** SAINTSBURY *Hist. Elizab. Lit.* iv. (1894) 146 The topsy-turvified conceits which came to a climax in Crashaw. **1886** *Daily Tel.* 5 Feb. (Cassell), [He] might well be employed for Faust viewed *topsyturvily. **1908** *Athenæum* 29 Aug. 233/1 All the MSS. topsy-turvily give με . . . γε σοῦ, with the exception of one, which has σε . . . γε σοῦ, whence Brunck restored σε . . . γέ μου. **1884** *Daily News* 28 Mar. 5 The *topsy-turvyment of the house. **1842** *Fraser's Mag.* XXVI. 544 Full of sport and fun, frolic and '*topsy-turvyness'. **1892** *Times* 22 Dec. 9/3 They lost all perception of the topsy-turvyness of the situation. **1745** ELIZA HEYWOOD *Female Spect.* No. 19 (1755) IV. 11 The present race of the *Topsy-Turvyans are..too indolent to reflect on their misfortunes. **1878** L. WINGFIELD *Lady Grizel* III. v. 107 A faint hope that *topsy-turvydom might bring with it the glorious bygone days. **1904** *Edin. Rev.* Apr. 469 The most absurd instance of Japanese topseyturveydom. **1791** H. WALPOLE *Let. to Miss M. Berry* 19 May, That *topsy-turvy-hood which characterizes the present age. **1855** DICKENS *Lett.* (1880) I. 408 In that state of topsy-turvyhood. **1880** F. G. LEE *Church under Q. Eliz.* I. p. xv, Disorder and *topsy-turvyism must certainly have risen to a perfect climax. **1890** *Illustr. Lond. News* 9 Aug. 166/2 The new school of *topsy-turvyists. **1893** *Daily News* 24 July 6/2 Something like an unusual *topsy-turvyising of this great throughfare might be looked for.

**Topt,** var. TOPPED; obs. var. TAP *v.*[1]

† **Topteler.** *Obs.* *rare*$^{-1}$. (Derivation and meaning uncertain.)

*a* **1440** *Sir Degrev.* 1182 Greyþ myn hors on hore gere, And lok þat þei be gay; Þat þey be trapped a get In topteler and in mauntolet.

**To·p-ti:mber.** *Shipbuilding.* One of the uppermost timbers in the side of a ship: see quot. *c* 1850. Also *attrib.*

**1626** CAPT. SMITH *Accid. Yng. Seamen* 8 Then plancke your out-side and inside vp, with your Top timbers. **1664** E. BUSHNELL *Compl. Shipwright* 20 Marke it on the foot of the Toptimber Mould. **1769** FALCONER *Dict. Marine* (1789) C iv b, The top-timbers, which are .. united to the floor-timbers. **1797** *Encycl. Brit.* (ed. 3) XVII. 378/1 The top-timber line, is a curve [drawn along the top of the ribs] limiting the height of the ship at each timber. *c* **1850** *Rudim. Navig.* (Weale) 156 *Top-timbers*, the timbers which form the topside: those which reach the tops are called the long top-timbers, and those below..the short top-timbers.

† **Topty·re.** *Obs.* *rare*$^{-1}$. (Derivation and meaning uncertain.)

*c* **1400** *Laud Troy Bk.* 5740 Thei sclow ther many a gret sire, When thei were comen In that toptyre.

† **To-pu·ll,** *v.* *Obs.* [f. TO-[2] + ME. *pullen*, PULL *v.*] *trans.* To pull to pieces. Also *fig.*

*c* **1330** R. BRUNNE *Chron. Wace* (Rolls) 10210 [The eagles] feighte to-gydere..& al to-pulle þe feþeres, & ryue. **1382** WYCLIF *Isa.* xviii. 7 Fro the puple to-pullid and to-torn, fro the ferful puple. **1390** GOWER *Conf.* I. 61, I am to-pulled in my thoght, So that of reson leveth noght. *c* **1430** *Pilgr. Lyf Manhode* III. xvi. (1869) 143 Whan the poore ben skorched thus and topulled. **1565** CALFHILL *Answ. Treat. Crosse* 37 Silvester..was killed, all to pulled, of the promoter of his, the Diuel.

**To-punish, To-put:** see TO- *pref.*[1], [2] 2.

† **To·p-u·p,** *adv.* *Obs.* *rare.* [f. TOP *sb.*[1] + UP *adv.*] Up to the top, to the brim.

**1581** A. HALL *Iliad* III. 52 With good wine..of Goate a ful great hide They fild top vp.

**Topwork:** see TOP *sb.*[1] 34.

**Topyc, Topylle,** obs. forms of TOPIC, TOPPLE.

† **Topynett,** obs. variant of *topnet*, TAPNET.

**1530–1** *Durham Househ. Bk.* (Surtees) 44, 1 topynett ficuum. **1532–3** *Ibid.* 227, 2 topynetts feggs 5s.

† **To-qua·ke,** *v.* *Obs.* [f. TO-[2] + ME. *cwacien*, OE. *cwacian*, to QUAKE.] *intr.* To quake violently.

*c* **1275** LAY. 15946 Þe eorþe gan to-cwakie. *c* **1400** *Rom. Rose* 2527 And eke thy blode shal al to-quake. *c* **1410** *Sir Cleges* 353 Ar wyth a staffe I schall the wake, That thy rebys schall all to-quake.

† **To-qua·sh,** *v.* *Obs.* Also 4 to-quassen. [f. TO-[2] + ME. *quaschen*, QUASH *v.*] *trans.* To crush or squash to pieces.

*c* **1375** *Sc. Leg. Saints* xlviii. (*Juliana*) 160, & syne hir banys sa to-quassyt, Þat þe self merch out passyt. **1494** FABYAN *Chron.* VII. 598 A gunne was leuellyd out of the cytie .. whiche brake y[e] tymber or stone of the wyndowe with suche vyolence, that the pecys therof all to quasshed y[e] face of the noble erle. **1583** STUBBES *Anat. Abus.* (ed. 2) 126 Some had their braines dasht out, some their headés all to quasht.

**Toque** (tōuk, ‖ tok). Forms: 6 toocke, tock, *Sc.* towk, 7, 9 tocque, 9 toque, (toke). [a. F. *toque* (15th c. in Godef.), app. the same word as It. *tocca* cap, 'tinzell cloath of Gold or siluer' (Florio), Sp. *toca* a female head-dress, '*toca* or *tocado*, a womans kerchiefe or coife' (Minsheu), Pg. *touca* a woman's coif. Ulterior origin uncertain.]

**1. a.** A kind of small cap or bonnet worn by men and women in various countries. (In quot. 1505, a large tippet.)

**1505** *Acc. Ld. High Treas. Scot.* III. 42 Item, for vij quartaris taffetj to be ane gret tepat to the King, callit ane towk. **1582** N. LICHEFIELD tr. *Castanheda's Conq. E. Ind.* I. ii. 29 The hayre of their heades is long lyke vnto womens, and pleited vnder theyr toockes, which they weare on theyr heades. **1599** HAKLUYT *Voy.* II. I. 244 On their heads they weare a small tock of three braces, made in guize of a myter, and some goe without tocks, and cary (as it were) a hiue on their heades. **1644** EVELYN *Diary* 23 Nov., The Knight Gonfalonier and Prior of the R. R. in velvet tocques. **1823** SCOTT *Quentin D.* vii, To confound our Scottish bonnets with these pilfering vagabonds' *tocques* and *turbands*, as they call them. **1864** BABBAGE *Passages Life Philos.* 366 A kind of head-dress called a toke.

**b.** † A cushion or pad worn by women to raise up the hair (*obs.*, quot. 1817); also, a kind of head-dress (quot. 1835); now, since *c* 1880, a kind of bonnet, cap, or small hat without a projecting brim, or with a very small or closely turned-up brim.

**1817** MAR. EDGEWORTH *Harrington* xiii, A sort of triangular cushion, or edifice of horse hair..called I believe a *toque* or a *system*, was fastened on the female head.., and upon and over this system the hair was erected, and crisped, and frizzed [etc.]. **1835** *Ladies' Cabinet* Jan. 68 Ball Dress. ..Head-dress a white satin toque, profusely trimmed with white ostrich feathers. *Ibid.* Mar. 202 The head-dress is a *toque* of pink terry velvet,..the brim very deep. **1837**

THACKERAY *Ravenswing* iv, Her hats, toques,..marabouts, and other fallals. **1881** MISS BRADDON *Asph.* xxvii, Her neat travelling-gown of darkest olive cashmere, and coquettish little olive-green toque. **1903** *N. & Q.* 9th Ser. XI. 366/1 The term 'bonnet', as applied to the costume of ladies, may be taken to mean either bonnets or tocques, but not hats.

*attrib.* **1884** *West. Daily Press* 29 May 3/7 The toque hat is too comfortable, too convenient, and too becoming to be lightly laid aside.

**2.** *Toque monkey*, also simply *toque*: the bonnet-monkey or bonnet-macaque, *Macacus pileatus*, a native of Ceylon (see BONNET *sb.* 10).

**1840** *Cuvier's Anim. Kingd.* 59 The Bonneted Macaque (*Macacus sinicus*) and the Toque (*M. radiatus*) have the hairs on the top of the head disposed as radii. **1882** OGILVIE (Annandale), *Toque*..2. A name given to the bonnet-macaque. **1883** *List Anim. Zool. Soc.* 16 *Macacus pileatus* (Shaw), Toque Monkey. **1892** *Pall Mall G.* 28 Sept. 3/1 The Guinea baboons and the toque monkeys.

**To-queme, Toquher**: see QUEME *sb.*, TOCHER.

**Tor** (tǭɹ), *sb.* Forms: 1, 6– torr, 4–7 torre, 4– tor. [Occurs as an element in topographical names in early West Saxon charters; also, as a local term for a topographical feature from OE. onward. Generally held to be Celtic; but, though frequent in place-names in Cornwall, Devon, etc., not recorded as a 'common noun' in Cornish or Breton. In Welsh the nearest word is app. *twr* (= *tŭr*), OW. *twrr* 'heap, pile' (rare in place-names, but cf. *Mynydd Twrr*, old name of Holyhead Mountain, Rhŷs). Prob. cognate with Gaelic *tòrr* 'hill of an abrupt or conical form, lofty hill, eminence, mound, grave, heap of ruins' (Macleod and Dewar), primarily 'heap, pile', cf. *tòrr* vb. 'to heap up, pile up, bury', Ir. *torraim* 'I heap up', and the deriv. Gael. *torran* 'little hill, knoll, hillock', Ir. *torrán* 'heap, pile, hillock'. Cf. also quot. 1905.]

**1.** A high rock; a pile of rocks, *gen.* on the top of a hill; a rocky peak; a hill. In proper names of eminences or rocks in Cornwall, Devon, Peak of Derbyshire; also sporadically in some other counties, e.g. *Glastonbury Tor*, in Somerset.

**847** *Grant by K. Æthelwulf* in Birch *Cart. Sax.* II. 34 Ærest on merce cumb [in Dorset], ðonne on grenan pytt, ðonne on ðone torr æt merce cumbes æwielme. *a* **1000** *Boeth. Metr.* v. 17 Oð him [a brook] oninnan felð muntes mæȝenstan..atrendlod of ðæm torre [in *Prose* vi, Micel stan wealwiende of þam heohan munte]. *a* **1400–50** *Alexander* 4863 So hedous & so hoge hillis þam beforn, Cloȝes at was cloude he [cloud-high] clynterand torres, Rochis & rogh stanes, rokkis vnfaire. **1539** POLLARD in *Lett. Suppress. Monast.* (Camden) 261 The late abbott of Glastonberye..was drawyn thorowe the towne apon a hurdyll to the hyll callyd the Torre, wheare he was putto execucion. *a* **1552** LELAND *Itin.* (1711) II. 38 Camallate, sumtyme a famose Toun or Castelle, apon a very Torre or Hille, wunderfully enstrengthenid of nature. **1610** NORDEN *Spec. Brit., Cornw.* (1728) 38 Mount St. Michaells, a steepe and most craggie torr. *c* **1630** RISDON *Surv. Devon* (1810) 6 A chain of hills..whose tops and torrs are in the winter often covered with a white cap. **1681** COTTON *Wond. Peake* (1702) 42 Tor in that Country-Jargons uncouth sense, Expressing any Craggy Eminence. **1806** GOUGH *Camden's Brit.* II. 423/2 Matlock great Torr is 140 yards perpendicular. **1894** BARING-GOULD *Kitty Alone* II. 160 Tors rise to the height of from twelve to fifteen hundred feet. **1905** *Eng. Dial. Dict.* s. v. *Torr*, In E. Cornw. 'Tor' means a pile of rocks, and is never used for a hill, or the top of a hill, unless the hill or top is so very rocky that the whole may be considered one pile of rocks. **1913** *Let. to Editor*, A high hill in Haslingden, Lancashire, is simply called 'The Tor'.

**b.** Locally in Scotland, applied to an artificial mound; a burial mound.

**1794** BUCHANAN *Def. Scott. Highl.* 142 What are the Torrs ..but burrying hills? **1845** *Statist. Acc. Scot.* VI. 887 Its name [Torrance] was taken from an artificial mound of earth, still known by the name of the Tor, which is situated a quarter of a mile from the present house of Torrance.

†**2.** ? A heavy mass of cloud. *Obs.*

(But the sense 'rock mass' seems also possible.)

**13..** *E. E. Allit. P.* A. 874 A hue fro heuen I herde þoo, Lyk flodez fele laden, runnen on resse, & as þunder þrowez in torrez blo. *Ibid.* B. 951 Torres, þat þe þik þunder þrast þirled hem ofte.

**3.** *attrib.* **Tor ouzel**, local name of a bird, the ring ouzel, *Turdus torquatus*.

**1770** G. WHITE *Selborne* xxxi. (1789) 84 [The ring ousels] breed in great abundance all over the Peak of Derby, and are called there *Tor-ousels*. **1885** SWAINSON *Provinc. Names Birds* 8 Ring Ouzel (*Turdus torquatus*)..Tor ouzel (Devon). Rock, or crag ouzel (Craven).

†**Tor**, *a.* *Obs.* Forms: 3–5 tor, 4 toor, 4–5 toore, 5 tore, toure. See also TERE *a.* [The Old Norse and OE. adverbial particle *tor-* 'hardly, with difficulty, ill-', used esp. with verbal adjs. as in ON. *tor-fengr* hard to get, *tor-næmr* hard to learn, *tor-sýnn* hard to see, *tor-talinn* pple., counted with difficulty, *tor-tryggr* hard of belief; also OE. *tor-cyrre* hard to turn or convert, *tor-begête* hard to get. In ME., esp. in those parts in which the Norse influence was strong, this particle was treated as a separate word, in the sense 'hard, difficult, ill', and was used esp. with the infinitive, as *tor* (*for*) *to tell*, *tor for to ken*; the former of these was a favourite phrase of the alliterative poets. In some instances, as already in Ormin, *tor* alone was used attributively. ON. and OE. *tor-* were cognate with OHG. *zur-*, Gothic *tuz-*, Gr. δυς-, Skr. *dus-*, hard, evil, ill-: with the ON. and OE. words cf. Gr. δυσαής ill-blowing, δύσβρωτος hard to eat, δυσμαθής difficult to learn. Senses 2 and 3 appear to be the same word, but the change of sense is remarkable.]

**1.** Difficult, hard, toilsome; irksome, tedious; = TERE *a.*

*c* **1200** ORMIN 6350 Harrd & strang & tor & hefiȝ lif to ledenn. *a* **1225** *Ancr. R.* 108 (MS. T.) Ho is grucchere, & ful itohen: dangeruse & tor for to paien. *Ibid.* 254 An honful ȝerden arn tor to breken [*v. r.* beoð erueð forte breken]. **13..** *Cursor M.* 14085 (Cott.) O þair gladnes war tor to tell. *c* **1350** *Will. Palerne* 5066 It were toor forto telle treuli al þe soþe. *c* **1400** *Destr. Troy* 644 But this tyme is so tore & we no tome haue.

**2.** Strong, sturdy. (? Hard to conquer.)

*a* **1400–50** *Alexander* 5500 Ser Tarbyn, a tulke with many toore thousandis. *c* **1400** *Destr. Troy* 320 Grete toures full toure all þe toune vmbe. *Ibid.* 1035 Of the tidiest of Tessaile, tore men of strenght. *Ibid.* 1131 Telamon, þat is a tore kyng. *Ibid.* 6156 Dissyrus..Of all the Troiens to tell torest in armys.

**3.** In vague or loose uses: **a.** Full, replete; **b.** Great, violent, excessive.

*c* **1400** *Destr. Troy* 3348 Trowe ye not Troy is tore of all godis, As plaintiouse in yche place as þe prouynse of Achaia? *Ibid.* 13723 Þis proud in hir yre..Bad hym turne vnto tessail in a tore hast.

**Tor**, erron. spelling of TAW *sb.*², a marble; obs. pa. t. of TEAR *v.*¹

†**To-ra·ce, to-ra·nce, to-ra·se**, *v.* *Obs.* Forms: 3–4 to-rauncen, -rancen, -rassen; 3–5 -racen, -rasen. [ME. *to-racen*, etc., f. TO-² + RACE *v.*³, RANCH *v.*², RASE *v.*¹] *trans.* To hack, slash, cut, or tear to pieces.

**1297** R. GLOUC. (Rolls) 524 He was al to ranced pecemele in a stounde, Ech lime fram oþer, among þe rockes, ar he com to gronde. *Ibid.* 4412 Hor king..Wiþ woundes to Raunced so þat he moste nede deye. **13..** *Gaw. & Gr. Knt.* 1168 What wylde so at-waped wyȝes þat schotten Watz al to-raced & rent, at þe resayt. *c* **1386** CHAUCER *Clerk's T.* 516 Burieth this litel body in som place, That beestes ne no briddes it to-race. *a* **1400–50** *Alexander* 2088 Þai haue hedid of oure hathils..Bet doun oure bachelers, my banir to-rased. *c* **1450** *Mirour Saluacioun* 4370 With breres and with sharpe thornes thaire bodyes alto racyng.

†**To-ra·g**, *v.* *Obs.* [ME., f. TO-² + RAG *v.*¹] *trans.* To tear the clothes of, to make very ragged.

*c* **1430** *Pilgr. Lyf Manhode* III. xxii. (1869) 148 That is thilke that hath thus to ragged me and to clowted me. *a* **1550** *Friar & Boy* 266 in Hazl. *E. P. P.* III. 72 All to ragged and to rente, And torne on euery syde.

‖**Torah** (tōᵊ·rā). Forms: 6, 9 thora, 7 tora, 7, 9 thorah, 9 torah. [Heb. תּוֹרָה *tōrāh* 'direction, instruction, doctrine, law', f. ירה *yārāh* 'to throw', in Hiphil 'to show, direct, instruct'.] The teaching or instruction, and judicial decisions, given by the ancient Hebrew priests as a revelation of the divine will; the Mosaic or Jewish law; hence, a name for the five books of the law, the Pentateuch.

**1577** tr. *Bullinger's Decades* I. (1592) 9 The lawe of Moses, which is in deede the lawe of God, and is most properly called Thora, as it were the guide and rule of faith. **1842** BONAR & M'CHEYNE *Narr. Mission to Jews* iv. (1843) 215 The [Samaritan] priest agreed to shew us the copy of the Torah, or five books of Moses..so famed for its antiquity. **1875** M. ARNOLD *God & Bible* iv. 188 Thus the Pentateuch, or five books of Moses, stood alone as the 'Thora'. **1890** P. H. HUNTER *After the Exile* xiv. 273 The word Torah.. signifies doctrine, instruction. This wider sense is lost in the usual translation by νόμος or law.

‖**Toran** (tōᵊ·răn). [Hindī *tōran*:—Skr. *toraṇa* arched portal.] A sacred Buddhist gateway, of wood or stone, consisting of a pair of uprights with one or more (often three) cross-pieces; sometimes elaborately carved.

**1886** E. C. ROBINS *Temple of Solomon* (1887) 27 A design ..based on the Japanese and Indian *toran*, like those forming gateways to the Great Tope at Sanchi.

**To-rance, to-rase**, by-forms of TO-RACE *v.*

†**To-ra·t**, *v.* *Obs. rare*—¹. [f. TO-² + RAT *v.*³] *trans.* To break up, scatter.

? *a* **1400** *Morte Arth.* 2235 Thane þe Romayns..alle torattys oure mene with theire riste horsses.

**Torbanite** (tǭ·ɹbănəit). *Min.* [f. *Torbane Hill* in Linlithgowshire, where found: see -ITE¹ 2 b.] A deep brown shale, allied to cannel coal: also called **Torbane Hill mineral** or *Boghead coal*; valuable for the production of petroleum and gas, and famous as the subject of a great lawsuit hinging upon the dispute whether or not it was legally 'coal'.

**1858** GREG & LETTSOM *Man. Mineral.* 16 Torbanite... Boghead mineral. Boghead coal. *c* **1865** LETHEBY in *Circ. Sc.* I. 139/2 Mr. James Young..has..been engaged in producing an oil..from a shale known as the Torbanehill mineral. **1867** W. W. SMYTH *Coal & Coal-mining* 18 It is by no means easy..to draw a distinct line of demarcation between cannel and the black basses, bats, or crisp shales, which occur in the coal measures...And between all these and the torbanite, or 'Boghead mineral', there exists a relationship which makes the difference only one of degree.

**Torbant**, obs. form of TURBAN.

**Torbel, torble**, obs. ff. TROUBLE *sb.* and *v.*

**Torbernite** (tǭ·ɹbəɹnəit). *Min.* Also torberite. [ad. Ger. *torbernit* (Werner 1792), orig. *torberit*, f. *Torbernus*, latinized form of the name of the chemist Torber Bergmann: see -ITE¹.] A native phosphate of uranium and copper, found in bright green tabular crystals; also called *copper-uranite*, and (erroneously) *chalcolite*.

**1852** BROOKE & MILLER *Phillips' Introd. Min.* 517 Torberite.—Uranite (in part)..is found in attached crystals, massive, and investing other minerals, in veins in slate and in granite. **1868** DANA *Min.* 585 Torbernite.

**Torbith**, obs. form of TURBIT.

**Torc**: see TORQUE¹.

**Torcas**, obs. f. TURQUOISE. **Torcasse**, var. TURKIS, -E *v.* *Obs.*, to distort, transform.

**Torce**, variant of TORSE¹, *Her.*, wreath.

†**To·rcenous**, *a.* *Obs. rare*—¹. *erron.* torcencious. [a. AF. *torcenous*, OF. *torçonos* (also *torçonereus*), f. *torçon*, *torcion* extortion, *torçoneor* extortioner.] Extortionate, exacting.

[**1292** BRITTON I. xxii. § 13 Et ausi de totes torcenouses prises fetes par nos ministres. **1314–15** *Rolls of Parlt.* I. 292/2 Dont il prient qe tiel torcenouse demaunde soit oste.] **1387–8** T. USK *Test. Love* I. vi. (Skeat) l. 131 The gouernementes..of your citee, left in the handes of torcencious citezins, shal bring in pestilence and distrucion to you.

**Torch** (tǭɹtʃ), *sb.* Forms: 3–6 torche, (4 torge, thorche, 5 tourche, 6 tortche, towrge, *pl.* torchesse), 6– torch. [ME. a. OF. *torche* = Pr. *torcha*, according to Diez:—late pop.L. **torca*, from stem **tork-* of *torquēre* to twist; cf. also It. *torcia* (Veronese, and Venetian *torzo*), Sp. *antorcha*, earlier *entorcha*, Pg. *tocha* 'torch'. The primary sense is taken to have been 'a twist', 'something twisted', torches having been made of twisted tow dipped in pitch, or the like. Cf. also TORTIS.

(The derivation of the Eng. from F. *torche* is certain, but the etymology of the latter, and of the Romanic forms as a whole, is still in dispute: see Diez s. v. *Torciare*, Gröber *Archiv f. Lat. Lexicog.* VI. 128, Körting *Lat. Rom. Wbch.* 1901 s. v. *Tortica* 9616.)]

**1.** A light to be carried in the hand, consisting of a stick of resinous wood, or of twisted hemp or similar material soaked with tallow, resin, or other inflammable substance. Also applied to a lamp carried on a pole or similar appliance.

*c* **1290** *S. Eng. Leg.* I. 467/187 With-oute liȝht of torche. *c* **1330** *Assump. Virg.* 598 (B.M. MS.) Loke þat ȝe haue candele Torches boþe faire & fele. **13..** *Sir Beues* (A.) 1659 Þar inne he seȝ torges [*v. r.* torches] i-liȝt. **1377** LANGL. *P. Pl.* B. XVII. 203 To a torche or a tapre þe trinitee is lykned; As wex and a weke were twyned togideres, And þanne a fyre flaumende forth oute of bothe. **1483** *Cath. Angl.* 390/1 A Torche, *torticius, torchia*. **1546–7** in Swayne *Sarum Churchw. Acc.* (1896) 274, viij lb. of waxe to make twoo torches agaynst Alholoutyde. **1555** in *Shropsh. Par. Documents* (1903) 56 Peyde towrd byying of ii towrges. **1606** SHAKS. *Tr. & Cr.* v. i. 92 Follow his Torch, he goes to Chalcas Tent. **1721** BAILEY, A *Torch*..a Staff of Deal on which Wax-Candles are stuck, to be lighted on several Occasions. **1821** SCOTT *Kenilw.* xxx, Onward came the cavalcade, illuminated by two hundred thick waxen torches. **1906** *Daily Chron.* 14 July 5 The ordinary tarred-rope torch.

**b.** *fig.* or *allusively*. Something figured as a source of illumination, enlightenment, or guidance, or of heat or 'conflagration'.

**1621** BURTON *Anat. Mel.* III. ii. VI. i. (1651) 545, I light my Candle from their Torches. **1664** JASZ-BERENYI (*title*) A new Torch to the Latine Tongue. **1775** SHERIDAN *Rivals* Epil., The torch of love. **1878** BOSW. SMITH *Carthage* 19 The torch of Greek learning and civilisation was to be extinguished.

**2.** *transf.* **a.** A spike composed of spikelets; also *fig.* said of a red or flame-coloured flower.

**1578** LYTE *Dodoens* I. lxiii. 91 Of this kinde, there is founde an other, the Spikes, eares, or torches wherof, are very dubble,..in steede of the little knappes or heades, it bringeth forth a number of other smal torches, wherof eche one is lyke to the spike or torch of great Plantayne. **1862** B. TAYLOR *Poet's Jrnl.* II. *Lost May*, And burns in meadow-grass the phlox His torch of purple fire.

**b.** (Usually in *pl.* **Torches.**) The Great Mullein, *Verbascum Thapsus* (or other species): from its tall spike of yellow flowers (or, according to some, from the use of its thick woolly leaves and stalks as material for torches).

**1552** COOPER *Elyot's Dict.*, *Blattaria*, an herbe called Moleyne, or a kinde of Moleine called Torche. **1578** LYTE *Dodoens* I. lxxxi. 120 Mulleyn is called..in English also.. Hig[h]taper, Torches, and Longworte. [Cf. 118 The whole top with his pleasant yellow floures sheweth like to a waxe Candell or taper cunningly wrought.] **1657** W. COLES *Adam in Eden* cxii, Called of the Latines *Candela Regia* and *Candelaria*, because the elder age used the stalks dipped in Suet to burn...In English also some call it Torches. **1861** MISS PRATT *Flower. Pl.* IV. 135 Its tall tapering spike of light yellow flowers..suggested..the old names of High Taper..and Torches.

†**c.** Applied to a species of cactus or cactaceous plant: prob. = TORCH-THISTLE. *Obs.*

**1597** GERARDE *Herbal* 1015 The torch or thornie Euphorbium..called of the Indians *Vragua*..a torch, taper, or waxe candle, whereupon..in Latine of those that understoode the Indian toong, *Cereus*, or a torch. **1666** J. DAVIES *Hist. Caribby Isles* 62 The Plant..some of the European Inhabitants of these Islands call the Torch: it is a kind of great Thistle.

3. *attrib.* and *Comb.*, as *torch-blaze, -brand, -carrier, -flame, -glare, -stick, -waving, -wick*; *torch-like* adj. and adv., *-lit* adj.; also, **torch-blade**, the Great Mullein (= 2 b); **torch-course** = *torch-race*; **torch-dance**, a dance in which some of the performers carry lighted torches; **torch-fish**, a deep-sea fish, *Linophryne lucifer*, having a luminous bulb upon the first dorsal spine, above the eye; **torch-fishing**, fishing by torch-light at night (also called *torching*: see TORCH *v.*[1] 3); **torch-flower**, any bright red or yellow flower resembling or suggesting a torch, e. g. the *torch-lily*; † **torch-herb**, the great mullein; **torch-holder**, one who or that which holds a torch; *spec.* a device for supporting a torch; also, a gas-bracket or the like imitating this; **torch-lily**, the liliaceous genus *Tritoma*, having spikes of bright scarlet flowers; also called 'red-hot poker'; **torch-man**, a man who carries a torch, a torch-bearer; also *fig.*; **torch-pine**, *Pinus rigida* of N. America; = *pitch-pine*; **torch-plant** = TORCH-THISTLE; **torch-race**, in *Gr. Antiq.*, a race held at certain festivals, in which the runners carried lighted torches, and (in some cases) passed them on to other runners posted at certain points: = LAMPADEDROMY; **torch-staff** (*pl.* -staves), a staff upon which a torch is carried; † **torch-tree**, rendering L. *tæda*, a resinous species of pine, the wood of which was used for torches; also *Ixora parviflora*, an East Indian shrub with showy flowers. See also TORCH-BEARER, etc.

1861 MRS. LANKESTER *Wild Flowers* 102 Great Mullein, ..'*Torch-blade', or 'King's Taper'. 1818 MILMAN *Samor* 317 A *torchblaze, meet to search Earth's utmost. 1825 SCOTT *Talism.* iii, I am Theodorick of Engaddi—I am the *torch-brand of the desert—I am the flail of the infidels. 1864 TREVELYAN *Compet. Wallah* (1866) 220 The other half are ..listening to a disquisition of the *torch-carrier. 1839 T. MITCHELL *Aristoph., Frogs* 124 *note*, From .. Pausanias we learn that three *torch-courses were held in the Ceramicus. 1907 *Discovery* Oct. 122 The *Torch-fish... On the upper jaw..there is a larger ovate bulb supported on a tentacle...It possesses powerful phosphorescent properties, the light being under the control of the fish. This is the 'torch'. 1840 BROWNING *Sordello* I. 80 Like a *torch-flame turned By the wind. 1849 [W. M. CALL] *Reverberations* I. 59 The *Torch-flower burning by the river. 1905 in *Daily Chron.* 28 Dec. 3/2 It is now ablaze with the red torch flowers of an aloe. 1908 L. BINYON in *Academy* 14 Mar. 553/1 He stands on high in the *torch-glare. 1598 FLORIO, *Lunaria*, the herbe called *torch herbe or woollblade. 1874 tr. *Hugo's Ninety-Three* III. I. xix, They stuck an iron *torch-holder into the wall. 1579 J. JONES *Preserv. Bodie & Soule* I. xl. 87 [Comets] Swordlike, hornelike, *torchlike. 1897 *Daily News* 25 June 2/6 Meanwhile our [Jubilee] bonfires [on Skiddaw]..burned torch-like downwards with a grand head of flame. 1884 MILLER *Plant-n.*, *Torch-lily, the genus *Tritoma.* 1842 SIR A. DE VERE *Song Faith* 186 The *torch-lit gloom of Auchen's aisle. *a* 1618 SYLVESTER *Mayden's Blush* 364 The sacred *Torch-man (to that end imploy'd). 1856 J. M. KAYE *Sir J. Malcolm* I. vii. 162 The bearers or torchmen who ran by his side. *a* 1845 HOOD *Incendiary Song* xviii, Burn all *torch-parading elves! 1890 *Cent. Dict.* s. v. *Pine, Pitch-pine, (a)* in America, *Pinus rigida*...Also called *torch-pine.* 1696 *Phil. Trans.* XIX. 296 The Dildoe-tree is the same with the Cereus or *Torch-Plant. 1812 C. DUNSTER tr. *Aristoph., Frogs* I. ii. *note*, In [Ceramicus] was situated the academy, where the *torch-race was held. 1875 JOWETT *Plato* (ed. 2) III. 12 The promise of an equestrian torch-race in the evening. 1599 SHAKS. *Hen. V*, IV. ii. 46 The Horsemen sit like fixed Candlesticks, With *Torch-staues in their hands. 1601 HOLLAND *Pliny* XVI. x. I. 462 A sixt sort..of these trees..is properly called Teda (i. the *Torch-tree): the same yeeldeth more plentie of moisture and liquor than the rest. 1862 BALFOUR *Timber Trees Asia* (ed. 2) 135 *Ixora parviflora*:..Torch Tree..A small tree..more used for torches than for any other purpose, as it burns very readily and clearly. 1706 PHILLIPS (ed. Kersey), *Torch-weed*, a kind of Herb. 1444 *Compota Domest.* (Abbotsf. 1836) 18 In vij petris di...huiusmodi *torchweke emptis.

**Torch** (tǭɹtʃ), *v.*[1] [f. TORCH *sb.*]

1. *trans.* To furnish, or light, with a torch or torches. (See TORCHED, and cf. TORCHER[1] 1.)

2. *intr.* To flare like a torch; to rise like smoke from a torch. *dial.*

1847–78 HALLIWELL s.v., Recently heard at Boyton,.. 'Law! how them clouds torch up, we shall ha rain'.

3. To catch fish, etc., by torch-light. *U.S.*

1887 *Fisheries of U.S.* Sect. v. II. 502 Another method, known as 'torching',..is practiced principally by negroes. Having provided themselves with torches they visit the sandy shores at night and catch the terrapins as they come upon the beach to spawn.

**Torch** (tǭɹtʃ), *v.*[2] [a. F. *torcher* to wipe, daub, rough-cast, build or plaster with clay mixed with chopped straw, etc., f. *torche* twisted straw, etc. (the same word originally as *torche* TORCH *sb.*).] *trans.* In *plastering*, To point the inside joints of slating laid on lath with lime hair mortar.

*a* 1850 [Remembered in use by workmen in Oxford]. 1851 [implied in TORCHER[2]]. 1882 in OGILVIE (Annandale). 1895 *Jrnl. R. Inst. Brit. Archit.* 14 Mar. 351 The roof should be torched—not bedded.

Hence **To·rching** *vbl. sb.*, pointing or daubing of this kind: see also TORCHER[2].

**Torch**, var. of TROCH, -E, tine of stag's horn.

**Torch-bearer** (tǭɹtʃ,bēəːrəɹ). One who carries a torch. Also *fig.*

1538 ELYOT, *Facularii*, torche bearers. 1596 SHAKS. *Merch. V.* II. vi. 40 Descend, for you must be my torch-bearer. 1624 BEDELL *Lett.* xi. 140 As if all that are made Priests among you were Psalmists, Sextons, Readers, Exorcists, Torch-bearers, Subdeacons, and Deacons before. 1814 SCOTT *Ld. of Isles* II. xxii, Twelve sandall'd monks, who reliques bore, With many a torch-bearer before. 1847 GROTE *Greece* II. xxxii. IV. 272 The enterprising mariners who inhabited it had been the torch-bearers of Grecian geographical discovery in the west. 1853 DALE tr. *Baldeschi's Ceremonial* 189 The Torch-bearers having genuflected, consign their torches to the first they meet in choir.

So **To·rch-bea:ring** *sb.* and *a.*

1721 STRYPE *Eccl. Mem.* III. xxi. 175 There he saw torch-bearing in day-light, at mass. 1881 RUSKIN *Bible of Amiens* ii. 88 No torch-bearing maid of battle, like Clotilde.

**Torched** (tǭɹtʃt, *poet.* tǭɹtʃèd), *a.* [f. TORCH *sb.* or *v.*[1] + -ED.] Furnished with a torch or torches; lighted with torches.

1819 KEATS *Isabella* xiv, In torched mines and noisy factories. 1901 *Harper's Mag.* CII. 774/1 Whirling six-foot sticks, torched at each end, in circles of fire.

**Torcher**[1] (tǭɹtʃəɹ). [f. TORCH *v.*[1] + -ER[1].]

† 1. One who gives light, as by carrying a torch. *Obs. rare*$^{-1}$.

1601 SHAKS. *All's Well* II. i. 165 Ere twice the horses of the sunne shall bring Their fiery torcher his diurnall ring.

2. One who fishes by torch-light: see TORCH *v.*[1] 3. *U.S.* 1891 in *Cent. Dict.*

**To·rcher**[2]. [f. TORCH *v.*[2] + -ER[1].] A workman employed in torching.

1851 TURNER *Dom. Archit.* I. 25 The wages of workmen.., as..mud-plasterers, torchers, excavators, and barrow-men.

‖ **Torchère** (torʃēr). [Fr., f. *torche* TORCH.] A tall ornamental candlestick or lamp-stand.

1910 *Sale Catal.*, Boudoir and Bed-room Furniture, Louis XVI. carved console table,..pair Adam torchères.

† **To·rchet.** *Obs.* Also 5–6 -ett(e. [= OF. *torchete*, dim. of *torche*: in med.L. *torchetta* (1420 in Du Cange).] A small torch; also *fig.*

1470–1 *Mem. Ripon* (Surtees) III. 214 Nec r. de aliquo proficuo proveniente de torcheis sive torchettis consimili modo oblatis ad corpora mortuorum. 1497 in W. M. Williams *Ann. Founders' Co.* (1867) 48 Paid to the Waxchandler for ij torchets weynt iij quarters, vj d. 1535 in *Rep. Hist. MSS. Comm., Var. Coll.* IV. 218 That then the said torches and torchettes to be in a redynes, light with convenyent berers. 1604 in *Househ. Ord.* (1790) 305 Mortores, Torchetts, Torches, Quarrioures, Waxelights, Sizes, and Pricketts. 1614 GORGES *Lucan* VI. 429 Where Leos sparkling torchets are In enterchange with Cancers starre.

**Torchless** (tǭɹtʃlès), *a.* [f. TORCH *sb.* + -LESS.] Without a torch; not lighted by a torch.

1814 BYRON *Lara* II. xii, Consenting Night Guides with her star their dim and torchless flight. 1901 tr. *Hugo's Notre-Dame* (ed. Nelson) 388 Showing the interior of the Church..torchless and voiceless.

**To·rch-li:ght.** The light of a torch; illumination by a torch or torches.

*c* 1425 *Brut* ccxliii. 367 He was brouȝt to London on an hors beere, with myche torche lyghte. 1470–85 MALORY *Arthur* XVII. ii. 691 The mayde..armed hym by torche lyght. 1555 *Coventry Leet Bk.* 813 Euery of them to haue a man weytinge vppon hym with torche-light. 1619 MIDDLETON *Love & Antiq.* Wks. (Bullen) VII. 329 His lordship returns by torchlight to his own house. 1726 POPE *Odyss.* XVIII. 401 The shining baldness of his head survey, It aids our torch-light. 1855 MACAULAY *Hist. Eng.* xvi. III. 629 He made a final inspection of his forces by torchlight. *fig.* 1847 WHITTIER *Lost Statesman* 25 Yet firmer hands shall Freedom's torchlights trim.

b. The time when torches are lighted; dusk.

*a* 1656 BP. HALL *Hard Meas.* Rem. Wks. (1660) 47 It now grew to be Torch-light. 1798 SOPH. LEE *Canterb. T., Yng. Lady's T.* II. 323, I faintly recollect, that it was torch-light.

c. *attrib.* Performed or carried on by torch-light.

1876 BANCROFT *Hist. U. S.* III. xix. 521 In the evening, a torch-light procession. 1884 *West. Morn. News* 15 Sept. 5/4 Lord Fife gave a torchlight ball at Mar Lodge.

‖ **Torchon** (torʃoǹ). [F., f. *torcher* to wipe.] The French word for a duster or dish-cloth: used *attrib.* in **torchon board**, a board covered with *torchon paper*, used in water-colour drawing; **torchon lace** (also abbreviated *torchon*, pl. *-ons*), a coarse bobbin lace, of loose texture; **torchon mat**, a picture-frame mat (MAT *sb.*[2] 3) made of torchon paper; **torchon paper**, a kind of paper with a rough surface, used for water-colour drawing and for picture-frame mats.

1879 MRS. A. E. JAMES *Ind. Househ. Managem.* 10 But laces certainly would not, not even the 'Torchon' now so much in vogue: the very first wash they are torn, look ragged and unsightly. 1891 *Times* 1 Oct. 9/3 Operations in torchon and cheap Maltese laces are still on a small scale. 1908 *Athenæum* 16 Feb. 198/3 From Russian lace to torchon is not a wide step, but the latter is superior, shading off..into Maltese.

**Torch-thistle** (tǭɹtʃ,þiːs'l). A name for a columnar cactus of the genus *Cereus*.

1731–3 MILLER *Gard. Dict.* s.v. *Cereus*, The Torch-Thistle. Call'd Cereus, because it is, as it were, a kind of taper or torch..because when these plants have been cut down and dry'd upon the ground, they dip them into oil, and burn them as torches. *Ibid.* s. v. *Greenhouse*, Euphorbiums, Torch-Thistles, and other tender succulent Plants. 1753 HOGARTH *Anal. Beauty* viii. 44 The indian-fig or torch-thistle,..as well as all that tribe of uncouth shaped exotics. 1884 MILLER *Plant-n.* 177 *Cereus*, Torch-thistle.

**Torchwood, torch-wood** (tǭɹtʃ,wud).

1. (*torch-wood*) Resinous wood of which torches are made.

1601 HOLLAND *Pliny* XXIV. vii. II. 184 As for Tæda or Torch-wood, if it be sodden in vinegre, it maketh a singular collution for to wash the teeth withall when they ake. 1603 — *Plutarch's Mor.* 685 Trees that yeeld torch-wood and pitch, as pines, cone trees, and such like. 1842 BONAR & M'CHEYNE *Narr. Miss. to Jews* vi. (1843) 343 The Jews [there] are much employed in gathering and selling torch-wood.

2. (*Torchwood*) Name for several plants. a. A tree of the genus *Amyris*, N.O. *Rutaceæ*, having resinous wood, as *A. sylvatica* and *A. balsamifera*, of West Indies and Florida. b. A West Indian shrub, *Casearia* (*Thiodia*) *serrata*, N.O. *Samydaceæ*. c. A species of cactus, *Cereus heptagonus*.

1866 *Treas. Bot.*, Torchwood, *Cereus heptagonus*: also *Thiodia serrata*. Torchwood, Mountain, *Amyris balsamifera.* 1880 *Libr. Univ. Knowl.* (N.Y.) VI. 65 There are [in Florida] splendid flowering magnolias,..palmette, mangrove, torchwood.

**Torchwort** (tǭɹtʃwɒɹt). [f. TORCH *sb.* + WORT.] The Mullein: = TORCH *sb.* 2 b, *torch-herb.*

1642 H. MORE *Song of Soul* I. II. lix, At either end of this well raised sod A stately stalk shot up of Torchwort high.

**Torchy** (tǭɹtʃi), *a. rare.* [f. TORCH *sb.* + -Y.] Full of torches; in which torches are used.

1629 F. LENTON *Gallant's Whirligigg* 16 All his spangled rare perfum'd attires, Which once so glistred in the Torchy Fryers, Must to the Broakers to compound his debt.

**Torcion, Torcious**: see TORSION, TORTIOUS.

‖ **Torcular** (tǭɹkiulăɹ), *sb.* [L., a press for wine or oil; also an oil-cellar.]

1. *Anat.* (in full *torcular Herophili*) = *Press of Herophilus*: see PRESS *sb.*[1] 11 b.

1657 *Physical Dict.*, *Torcular*, a press. 1693 tr. *Blancard's Phys. Dict.* (ed. 2), *Torcular Herophili*, that place where the four Cavities of the thick Skin of the Brain [*Dura Mater*] are joyned. 1840 G. V. ELLIS *Anat.* 56 Its opening into the torcular Herophili is sometimes double. 1879 *St. George's Hosp. Rep.* IX. 152 A pus-laden clot extending to the neighbourhood of the torcular.

2. *Surg.* A TOURNIQUET.

1727–41 CHAMBERS *Cycl.*, *Torcular*, among chirurgions, a contrivance for stopping bleedings in amputations. 1860 MAYNE *Expos. Lex.*, *Torcular*..applied to the tourniquet.

**To·rcular,** *a.* [ad. L. *torculārius*, f. *torcular*: see prec. (In 2 arbitrary f. *torques*: see TORQUE[1].)]

1. *Anat.* Pertaining to or connected with the *torcular Herophili*: see prec. 1.

1656 BLOUNT *Glossogr.* s.v. *Vein*, *Torcular vein* (*vena torcularia*), the second branch of the outward throat vein. 1899 *Allbutt's Syst. Med.* VII. 602 Never plug the torcular end of the sinus if it can possibly be helped.

† 2. Twisted, spiral, torqued. *Obs. rare*$^{-1}$.

1661 LOVELL *Hist. Anim. & Min.* Introd., The Turbinate have a torcular shell, out of the middest whereof commeth the head with two hornes.

So † **Torcula·rious**, *a. Obs. rare*$^{-0}$. (See quots.)

1656 BLOUNT *Glossogr.*, *Torcularious*.., of, or belonging to a Presse that squieseth grapes. 1658 PHILLIPS, *Torcularious*, belonging to a Vine presse.

**Tord, torde,** obs. ff. TOWARD, TURD.

**Tore** (tōr), *sb.*[1] *Sc.* Also 6, 9 tor, 7 torre, 8 torr. [Origin uncertain: Welsh *torr* belly, bulge, boss, knob, has been compared.]

† 1. An ornamental knob upon a piece of furniture, as a chair or a cradle. *Obs.*

1560 ROLLAND *Seven Sages* 55 Betuix thame twa, the Creddill ouir thay cast, With boddum vp, and on the Toris it stude ..That the four Toris sauit the Childis face. *a* 1572 KNOX *Hist. Ref.* IV. Wks. 1848 II. 404 The Quene..wes placeit in the chyre, haifing twa faithfull supportis, the Maister of Maxwell upoun the ane tor, and Secretour Lethingtoun on the uther tor of the chyre. *a* 1825 *Balankin* xi. in Child *Ballads* IV. (1886) 323/2 Till all the tores of the cradle wi the red blood down ran.

2. The pommel of a saddle. *rare* or *Obs.*

*a* 1671 SIR A. BALFOUR *Lett.* ii. (1700) 33 To Carry one.. in a Carpet Bag..tyed to the Tore of my Saddle. 1751 in Burton *Crim. Trials Scot.* (1852) I. 62 Placing her body across the horse upon the torr or forepart of the saddle. 1828 *Thomas o' Yonderdale* in Whitelaw *Scot. Ball.* (1874) 147/1 On the tor o' her saddle A courtly bird did sweetly sing.

**Tore** (tōəɹ), *sb.*[2] [a. F. *tore*, ad. L. *torus.*]

1. *Arch.* See quot. 1704; = TORUS 1.

1664 EVELYN tr. *Freart's Archit.*, etc. I. vii. 24 He thinks fit to deck the Tore's with I know not what delicate foliages. 1704 J. HARRIS *Lex. Techn.* I, *Tore*, and *Torus*..is that round Ring which encompasses in the Column, between the Plinth, and the List. This is the third Member of the Base of a Column. 1723 CHAMBERS tr. *Le Clerc's Treat. Archit.* I. 66 The preceding Orders..have two Tores. 1850 INKERSLEY *Roman. & Pointed Archit. in France* 182 A central tore flanked by a smaller parallel one.

2. *Geom.* = TORUS 4.

1867 TAIT *Quaternions* ix. § 322 An immediate proof of the very singular property of the ring (or tore) discovered by Villarceau. 1890 EAGLES *Descript. Geom.* 248 This surface is known as a tore or anchor ring.

**Tore** (tōəɹ), *sb.*[3] *local.* Also toar (*Eng. Dial. Dict.*). [Origin unascertained.] Long coarse grass remaining in the field in winter or spring. Also *attrib.*

1707 MORTIMER *Husb.* (1721) I. 234 Which you must proportion according to the quantity of Rowen or Tore that you have upon the Ground; The more Tore you have, the less quantity of Hay will do. *Ibid.*, When your Tore is quite eaten up, which it will commonly be about February, you must house your Milch-Cows, that you give Hay to in your Cow-house all Night. 1766 *Compl. Farmer*, *Tore*, rowen, or winter-grass. 1836 Sir G. Head *Home Tour* 253, I found fields over-run with coarse tore grass, in many parts blotchy and covered with thistles. 1904 in *Eng. Dial. Dict.* from Kent, Sussex, Surrey, Hampshire.

**Tore**, pa. t. and obs. and dial. pa. pple. of Tear *v.*[1]

**Tore**, *a. Obs.*: see Tor *a.*

‖ **Toreador** (tǫrĭădǭ·ɹ). Also 8 tauridore, tawridore, 8–9 torreadore, 9 torreador, tauridor, (tauréador). [Sp. *toreador* 'a bull-baiter' (Minsheu), mod.Sp. 'a bull-fighter on horseback'; so in Fr. The forms in *taur-* agree with earlier Fr. *tauréador* and with L. *taurus*.] One who engages in a (Spanish) bull-fight, esp. on horseback; a bull-fighter.

1618 T. Lorkin in *Crt. & Times Jas. I* (1848) II. 82 The Conde de Cantilliana, that excellent Toreador, hath stolen away the wife of a Procurador de Corte. 1797 *Encycl. Brit.* (ed. 3) III. 771/1 When the price of the horses and bulls, and the wages of the Torreadores, have been paid. 1823 Byron *Age of Bronze* vii, Up! up again! undaunted Tauridor! 1825 T. Hook *Sayings* Ser. ii. *Passion & Princ.* xii. III. 263 As the Matador puts the finishing stroke to the ..victim of the lighter efforts of the Picadores and Torreadores who have preceded him. 1884 *Pall Mall G.* 3 June 3/2 The entertainment commenced with a flourish of trumpets as the tauréadors, five in number, marched in, bowed to the public, and ranged themselves.

¶ **b.** Erroneously used for 'bull-fight'. *Obs.*

1728 ? De Foe *Capt. Carleton's Mem.* 304 A Diversion less to be complained of than their Tauridores; because attended with less Cruelty to the Beast, as well as Danger to the Spectator.

**c.** *attrib.*: esp. in fancy names of styles of women's hats or dresses.

1892 *Daily News* 14 Nov. 6/3 The Zouave is as great a favourite as it has been for some seasons, and though it varies in form—being sometimes a bolero, sometimes a toreador, and sometimes a cross between an Eton jacket and a Zouave. 1899 *Westm. Gaz.* 5 Oct. 3/2 The toreador toque is another very popular species just now—a toque, or really a hat, of rounded crown and rounded brim that is always much tilted to one side by a broad bandeau.

† **To-rea·ve**, *v.*[1] *Obs.* [f. To-[2] + ME. *reve*, Reave *v.*[1]] **a.** *intr.* To commit robbery or plunder. **b.** *trans.* To rob, plunder, deprive by violence *of*.

13.. *Minor Poems fr. Vernon MS.* xxxvii. 515 Wel wynnen he may, But Robbe ne to-reue Nouþer niht ne day. 1393 Langl. *P. Pl.* C. iv. 203 Religion hue [Law] al to-reueþ. 1563 *Mirr. Mag.* ii. Induct. R j b, We sawe.. pale death..to reve her of her breath.

† **To-reave**, *v.*[2] *Obs. rare.* Also 5 torafe. [f. To-[2] + Reave *v.*[2]] *trans.* To break, shiver, or tear in pieces.

*a* 1400 *Sir Beues* (E.) 2753+87 Hys helme, was al toreuyd, To gedere he ffastnyd on hys heuyd. *c* 1400 *Destr. Troy* 7629 Þe grym windes..al to rafet & rent all the riche clothes.

**Torel, -elle**, obs. forms of Tourelle.

† **To·rely**, *adv. Obs.* [f. *tore*, Tor *a.* + -ly [2].] Stoutly, sturdily.

*c* 1400 *Destr. Troy* 8015 The Troiens, on the tothir syde torely withstode.

**Toren**, obs. f. *torn*, pa. pple. of Tear *v.*[1]

† **To-re·nd**, *v. Obs.* [OE. *torendan*, f. To-[2] + *rendan* to Rend. So OFris. *to-, te-renda*.] *trans.* To rend in pieces.

*c*950 *Lindisf. Gosp.* Mark xiv. 63 Se heh ðonne sacerd torende woedo his. *a* 1000 *Ags. Ps.* (Th.) cxxiii[i]. 7 Grin bið on sadan grame torænded. *a* 1225 *Ancr. R.* 362 He.. þet to-tereð his olde kurtel, & to-rendeþ þe olde pilche of his deadliche uelle. *c* 1330 R. Brunne *Chron. Wace* (Rolls) 2145 Lym fro lym hym al to-rent. 1388 Wyclif *Matt.* xxvii. 51 The veil of the temple was to-rent in twey parties. — *Acts* xiv. 13 Whanne the apostlis .. herden this, thei to-renten her cootis. 1430–40 Lydg. *Bochas* viii. xiii, Hir clothes to rent, bedewed with weepyng. 1596 Danett tr. *Comines* (1614) 266 Their nauie all to rent and torne. 1631 Weever *Anc. Fun. Mon.* 306 He..plucked the other out of his place, and all to rent his casule, Chimer, and Rochet.

Hence † **To-re·nt** *ppl. a.*, † **To-re·nding** *vbl. sb.*

1388 Wyclif *Isa.* xxxvi. 22 Eliachym..and Sobna..entriden with to-rent clothis to Ezechie. — *Nahum* iii. 1 Wo to the citee of bloodis, al of leesyng, ful of to-reendyng [*dilaceratione*].

† **To-rent**, *v. Obs.* [f. To-[2] + Rent *v.*[2]] = To-rend.

*c* 1410 *Master of Game* (MS. Digby 182) x, She altorenteth hem with hyr tethe. 1526 Tindale *Matt.* vii. 6 Lest..the other tourne agayne and all to rent you. 1608 Dod & Cleaver *Expos. Prov.* ix–x. 21 Christ saith, that hogs will all to rent them that so offer to feede them.

† **To-reo·se**, *v. Obs.* [OE. *to-hréosan*, f. To-[2] + *hréosan*, Reose (where see Forms).] *intr.* To fall to pieces, fall into ruins; to decay.

*a* 900 tr. *Bæda's Hist.* i. xi. [xiii.] (1890) 48 Monize oðre ceastre tohrorene wæron. *a* 1023 Wulfstan *Hom.* xlix. (Napier) 263 Þonne bið..þa lichaman tohrorene and to duste zewordene. *c* 1205 Lay. 9245 Al heo gunnen to-reosen. *Ibid.* 9426 Þus Port-chæstre to-ræs [*c* 1275 to-reos].

‖ **Torero** (torē·ro). Also 8 tauriro. [Sp.] A (Spanish) bull-fighter (on foot). Cf. Toreador.

1728 ? De Foe *Capt. Carleton's Mem.* 264 So that the poor Creature may be said to fight, not only with the Tauriro (or Bull-hunter..) but with the whole Multitude in the lower Class at least. *Ibid.* 267 The Taurirоes are very well paid. 1832 Macgillivray tr. *Humboldt's Trav.* xix. 287 They observe the manners of the crocodile as the torero studies those of the bull.

† **To-re·se**, *v.*[1] *Obs.* [ME. *to-ræsen, -reasen, -resen*, f. To-[2] + *ræsen*, OE. *rǽsan* to rush, Rese *v.*[1]] *intr.* To make a violent assault or attack.

*c* 1205 Lay. 18682 Ofte heo to-ræsden [*c* 1275 hii to-resde]. *Ibid.* 26813 Bruttes heom to-ræsden. *Ibid.* 26964 Romleoden ræsden to [*c* 1275 to-reasde].

† **To-re·se**, *v.*[2] *Obs.* [ME. *to-rusien, to-rese*, f. To-[2] + Rese *v.*[2]] *intr.* To shake, to quake; to be shaken to pieces.

*c* 1205 Lay. 15946 Þe eorðe gon to rusien & þi wal toreosen. *c* 1275 *Ibid.*, Þe eorþe gan to-cwakie and þin wal to-rese. *a* 1225 *Juliana* 58 Swa þat hit al to resde [*v.r.* to reasde].

† **Toret**, ? *pa. pple. Obs.* Of doubtful meaning.

13.. *Gaw. & Gr. Knt.* 960 Hir frount folden in sylk.. Toret & treieted with tryflez aboute.

**Toret, -ett(e**, obs. forms of Torret, Turret.

**Toreumatography** (torūmătǫ·grăfi). *rare*—0. [ad. med.L. *toreumatographia*, f. Gr. τόρευμα(τ-, embossed work, etc. (f. τορεύειν: see Toreutic) + -graphy.] Description of the toreutic art, or of works done in it: see Toreutic. So **Toreumato·logy**, *rare*, the science or study of toreutics.

1727–41 Chambers *Cycl.*, *Toreumatography*, a Greek term, signifying the knowledge, or rather description, of ancient sculptures, and basso-relievo's... The invention of *toreumatographia* is owing to Phidias, and its perfection to Polycletes. 1842 Brande *Dict. Sc.* etc., *Toreumatology*..signifies either the science or art of sculpture, or a description of ancient and modern sculpture and bas-relief. 1846 Worcester, *Toreumatography, Toreumatology* [cites *Brande*].

‖ **Toreutes** (torū·tīz). [a. Gr. τορευτής, f. τορεύειν: see next.] A worker in toreutics; an artist in metal or ivory.

1840 tr. *C. O. Müller's Hist. Lit. Greece* xiii. § 15 *note*, Anacreon's advice to the toreutes, who is to make him a cup. 1847 Leitch tr. *C. O. Müller's Anc. Art* § 85 *note*, The designation of toreutes hovers between caelator or enchaser and artist in gold and ivory. *Ibid.* § 173 The work of the toreutes..was especially prized in Etruria.

**Toreutic** (torū·tik), *a.* and *sb.* [ad. Gr. τορευτικός, f. τορεύειν to work in relief, etc.]

**A.** *adj.* Of or pertaining to toreutics (see B.); chiefly in phr. *toreutic art* = toreutics; also, of figures, etc., executed according to the toreutic art; of an artist, working in toreutics.

1837 *Antiq. Athens* 38 The Minerva of the Parthenon, also by Phidias, wrought in ivory and gold, the noblest example of the *toreutic* art. 1854 Gantillon tr. *Propertius, Elegies* 87 *note*, *Mys.*—A toreutic artist who lived B.C. 444. 1874 *Edin. Rev.* July 187 The best toreutic representations of children are those of the Flemish artist du Quesnoy. 1910 D. G. Hogarth in *Encycl. Brit.* I. 248/2 The..free sculpture and toreutic handiwork of Crete.

**B.** *sb.* [rendering Gr. τορευτική (sc. τέχνη) toreutic art: the Romanized form *toreuticē* occurs in 17th c. Eng. use]. Chiefly in pl. **Toreutics**: The art, esp. the ancient art, of working in metal or ivory, including embossing, work in relief, chasing, etc.

[1662 Evelyn *Chalcogr.* (1769) 16 Then the *toreutice*..for I can only name them briefly.] 1847 Leitch tr. *C. O. Müller's Anc. Art* § 85 This species of work..is reckoned as a branch of toreutics, by which is meant sculpture in metals..and also this combination of metal with other materials. 1900 *Year's Work Class. Stud.* 45 Pernice continues his notes on toreutic.

**Torey** (tōᵊ·ri), *a. nonce-wd.* [for *tory*, f. Tore *sb.*[3] + -y.] Of the nature of or consisting of 'tore' or coarse grass.

1893 *Blackw. Mag.* Mar. 392 The bleached torey grass of a sheltered hillside suits him.

**Torf**, obs. form of Turf.

**Torfaceous** (tǫɹfē·ʃəs), *a. Bot. rare.* [f. assumed mod.L. *torfa* Turf + -aceous.] 'Growing in bogs or mosses' (*Treas. Bot.* 1866).

† **Torfer.** *Obs.* Forms: 4 torfere, (-phere), -fir, 4–5 -fer, -fare, 5 torfor, tourfer, torfoyr, *Sc.* torfeir. [Northern ME., a. ON. *tor-fǿra* fem., or *torfǿri* neut. (mod.Norw. *torføre*), a difficult or dangerous passage, f. *torfǿrr* adj. hard or difficult to pass, f. *tor-* Tor *a.* + *fǿr*, pret. stem of *fara* to go.] Hardship, trouble, distress; harm, mischief, injury.

13.. *Cursor M.* 6498 (Cott.) Þat he sal hald vs hale and fere, And warn vs fra ilkin tor-fere [*Fairf.* alkin torfere]. *Ibid.* 20002 Ful mani torfer [*Trin.* mony turment] sufferd þai. *c* 1325 *Metr. Hom.* (1862) 158 For than pin we our bodye, With torfir and with martyrye. ? *a* 1400 *Morte Arth.* 1956 That schalle turne the to tene and torfere for ever. *a* 1400–50 *Alexander* 3729 Quat tene & torfare may tide & tent to þine ende. *c* 1440 *York Myst.* xl. 174 Suche torfoyr and torment of-telle herde I neuere. *c* 1470 *Golagros & Gaw.* 876 Ye sall nane torfeir betyde, I tak vpone hand.

**Torfle** (tǫ·ɹf'l), *v. dial.* Also 7–9 -fell, 9 -fil. [Origin unascertained. Cf. Torple.] *intr.* To founder, go lame (? *obs.*); to decline in health, pine away, languish; *fig.* to lose interest in or draw back from an undertaking.

(Hogg's use of the word is vague.)

1575–6 *Durham Depos.* (Surtees) 285 This deponent..had an ox that torfled. 1818 Hogg *Brownie of B.*, etc. II. 149 It was reportit, that there was to be seen every morning at two a clock, a naked woman torfelling on the Alemoor loch, wi' her hands tied behind her back, and a heavy stane at her neck. 1820 — *Bridal of Polmood* viii, I..fleechyt Eleesabett noore to let us torfell in the waretyme of owir raik [in the springtime of our life's journey]. 1825 — *Q. Hynde* i. 439 She saw him swathed in bloody red, And torfell'd on the monster's head. 1876 [see Torple 2].

**To·rgant**, *a. Her.* Also **targant**. [app. an erroneous form of *torquent*, L. *torquent-em*, or for Torqued.] = Torqued 2.

*c* 1828 Berry *Encycl. Her.* I. Gloss., *Targant, Torgant*, or *Torqued*, bending and rebending, like the letter S. 1890 Elvin *Dict. Her.*, *Targant*, see Torqued.

‖ **Torgoch** (tǫ·ɹgǫχ). Also 7 torcoch; (*erron.*) 7 torcoth, 8 torgotch. [Welsh *torgoch*, f. *tor* belly + *coch* red.] The red-bellied char, a variety of the common char, found in the Welsh lakes.

1611 Speed *Theat. Gt. Brit.* (1614) 123/2 In the poole Lin-Peris, there is a kinde of fish called there Torcoch, having a red belly, no where else seene. 1756 in *Gentl. Mag.* XXVI. 616/2 Torgotch, or Red-belly, which distinguishes the female. 1787 Best *Angling* (ed. 2) 4 The English fishes that we have in our ponds, rivers, &c. are as follow: Umbla minor, Gesn. The Red Charr, or Welch Torgoch.

† **Torht**, *a. Obs.* [OE. *torht* bright, splendid, illustrious.] Bright, clear.

*a* 1000 *Phœnix* 96 Æþelast tungla...Torht tacen godes. 12.. *Prayer to our Lady* 20 *O E. Misc.* 193 Mi brune her is hwit bicume..& mi to[r]hte rude iturnd al in-to oðre dehe.

**Tori**, pl. of Torus.

**Toric** (tōᵊ·rik), *a.* [f. Tor-us + -ic.] Of or pertaining to a torus (see Torus 4); having the form of a torus or a portion of one.

1900 *Buck's Handbk. Med. Sc.* I. 595 A concave spherical combined with a convex toric surface.

**Torify**: see Toryfy.

**Toriness, toryness** (tōᵊ·rinės). *nonce-wd.* [f. Tory *a.* + -ness.] Tory quality or condition.

1890 *Sat. Rev.* 12 Apr. 425/1 Mr. Gladstone deplored the Toriness of Hertfordshire.

**Torism**, obs. form of Toryism.

† **To-ri·t**, *v. Obs.* [ME., f. To-[2] + *ritten*, Rit *v.*[1]] *trans.* To cut or tear asunder.

13.. *Orfeo* (Auchinleck MS.) 43 Hir riche robe hye al to rett [*Ashm. MS.* to-ryte] And was remeyd out of hir witt.

† **To-ri·ve**, *v. Obs.* [ME., f. To-[2] + Rive *v.*[1]]

**1.** *trans.* To rive or tear asunder; to split open, cleave. Also *fig.*

*c* 1300 *Havelok* 1953 Hwo haues the thus ille maked, Thus to-riuen, and al mad naked? 13.. *K. Alis.* 6216 (Bodl. MS.) Schippes..Ful ycharged of her clay, Þat men clepeþ Butumay, Þat water non ne may to Ryue Ne irne ne steel ne metal to dryue. 13.. *E. E. Allit. P.* A. 1196 Þer-for my ioye watz sone to-riuen. *Ibid.* C. 379 His ryche robe he to rof of his rigge naked. 13.. *Sir Beues* (A.) 2159 Þat hors.. His rakenteis he al te-rof. *c* 1400 *Destr. Troy* 1234 The king..the rod all-to roofe right to his honde. 1470–85 Malory *Arthur* i. xxviii. 75 The shyp..was al to ryuen.

**2.** *intr.* To burst asunder; to split, cleave, splinter, shiver.

*c* 1275 Lay. 7844 Mani sip al to-rof. *c* 1330 R. Brunne *Chron.* (1810) 170 Þat schip salle alle toryue. 1390 Gower *Conf.* III. 296 The mast tobrak, the Seil torof. *c* 1440 *York Myst.* xiii. 153 Was neuer wight sa wa, for ruthe I all to ryff. *c* 1470 Henry *Wallace* ii. 52 The tre to raiff & fruschit euiredeille. 1470–85 Malory *Arthur* viii. xxxviii. 330 A wynde drofe hem..vpon this yle of seruage..and there the Barget all to rofe.

**Tork**, variant of Torque [1].

**Torkes**, var. Turkis *v. Obs.*, to distort, alter.

**Tormaline, Tormarith**, obs. ff. Tourmaline, Turmeric.

**Torment** (tǫ·ɹment), *sb.* Forms: 3–6 turment, (4 -te), tourment, (5–6 -te), 3– torment, (*pl.* 3–4 -menz, -mens). (Also β. 5 torna-, tourne-, turna-, turnement, 6 tornement.) [ME. a. OF. *tor-, tourment*, ONF. *turment* (11th c.) = It., Sp., Pg. *tormento*:—L. *torment-um* (:—**torqu(e)mentum* something operated by twisting, f. *torquēre* to twist). In sense 5, a. F. *tourmente* fem. from L. *tormenta* neut. pl., which became fem. sing. in Romanic, sometimes with final *-e* in ME. The β-forms show confusion with Tournament.]

† **1.** An engine of war worked by torsion, for hurling stones, darts, or other missiles. *Obs.*

1382 Wyclif 1 *Macc.* vi. 51 And ordeynede there balistis, and engynes, and dartis, or castyngis, of fyr, and tourmentis for to cast stoons and dartis. 1398 Trevisa *Barth. De P. R.* xviii. ix. (Bodl. MS.), Regulus þe Emperoure slowe an addre..þat was xx. fote longe wiþ alblastes and tormentes. 1531 Elyot *Gov.* i. viii, All turmentes of warre, which we cal ordinance. [1866 J. B. Rose tr. *Ovid's Met.* 229 Like the bolt from the tormentum cast, Smiting the wall.]

**2.** An instrument of torture, as the rack, wheel, or strappado (*rare* or *doubtful*); hence, the infliction of torture by such an instrument as a form of punishment, a means of extracting information, etc.; torture inflicted or suffered.

*c* 1290 *S. Eng. Leg.* I. 84/33 Heo bad ore louerd..þat he ire ȝeue þere Studefaste bi-leue..And in hire tormenz treowe heorte. *c* 1300 *Seyn Julian* 49 Þe more turment þat hi hire dude þe bet hi hire paide. 1340 *Ayenb.* 166 We redeþ of zaynte Agase, þet mid greate blisse hi yede to torment alsuo ase hi yede to feste. *c* 1384 Chaucer *H. Fame* i. 445 And euery turment eke in helle Saugh he. 1413 *Sat. agst. Lollards* 113 in *Pol. Poems* (Rolls) II. 246 And namly James among hem alle, For he twyes had turnement. 1483 Caxton *Gold. Leg.* 289/2 He dyde doo strayne and payne them in the torment of Eculee. 1494 Fabyan *Chron.* iv. lxviii. 46 [Mexencius] pursued ye Christen with all kynde of turment. 1550–1 *Acts Privy Counc.* (1891) III. 230 Order shalbe given that he may be sent up hither to be put to torment. 1610 Shaks. *Temp.* i. ii. 289 It was a torment To lay upon the damn'd. 1668 Culpepper & Cole *Barthol. Anat.* iv. ii. 161 That torment which the Italians call *Tratta de corda*, the Strappado. 1709 J. Johnson *Clergym. Vade M.* ii. 169 Those who had done sacrifice thro' the violence of torment in time of persecution. 1725 Pope *Odyss.* ix. 454 They swift let fall The pointed torment on his visual ball.

b. *spec.* The punishment of hell.

1852 Mrs. Stowe *Uncle Tom's C.* xviii, 'I knows I'm gwine to torment', said the woman, sullenly.

3. A state of great suffering, bodily or mental; agony; severe pain felt or endured.

c 1290 *Beket* 434 in *S. Eng. Leg.* I. 119 So þat þe preost was i-brouȝt In tormenz bi þe meste. 13.. *Guy Warw.* (A.) 325 Thus he lay in grete turment, Til þat þe fest was al to-went. c 1386 Chaucer *Knt.'s T.* 440 That doubleth al my torment [*v.r.* turment] and my wo. c 1489 Caxton *Sonnes of Aymon* i. 34 Ye haue broughte me in grete sorowe and tournement irrecouerable. 1500–20 Dunbar *Poems* lxxvi. 6 A schoirt torment for infineit glaidnes. 1590 Spenser *F. Q.* i. x. 28 In which his torment often was so great, That like a Lyon he would cry and rore. 1732 Pope *Let. to Swift* 5 Dec., In acute torment by the inflammation in his bowels and breast. 1861 Kingsley *Lett.* (1878) II. 134 The feeling of being always behind-hand ..is second only in torment to that of debt.

†b. *spec.* A griping or wringing pain in the bowels: = Tormina. *Obs.*

1578 Lyte *Dodoens* ii. xcii. 273 The seede of Ameos is very good against the griping payne and torment of the belly. c 1610 *Women Saints* 112 She..endured moste sharpe payne and torment of stomacke. 1688 R. Holme *Armoury* ii. 172/1 Swelling and Torment in the Belly [of Cows] ..if not speedily helped, is Death to the Beast.

4. An action, circumstance, or condition which causes extreme pain or suffering of body or mind; a source of pain, trouble, or anguish, or in weakened sense, of worry or annoyance.

1599 Shaks. *Much Ado* ii. iii. 130 No, and sweares she neuer will, that's her torment. 1611 B. Jonson *Catiline* v. vi, Why, death's the end of evils, and a rest Rather than torment. 1789 Mrs. Piozzi *Journ. France* II. 364 Want of language, our still recurring torment. 1825 T. Hook *Sayings* Ser. ii. *Passion & Princ.* vii. III. 102 The conviction that he had made himself absurd..was his torment. 1841 Helps *Ess., Aids Contentm.* (1842) 13 A habit of mistrust is the torment of some people.

b. Applied to a person who causes trouble. Cf. Plague *sb.* 2 c.

1784 Cowper *Task* iv. 632 That instant he [a recruit] becomes the serjeant's care, His pupil, and his torment, and his jest. 1873 'Ouida' *Pascarèl* I. 32 They were the pride and torment of Mariuccia's life. 1881 'Rita' *Lady Coquette* i, Will you be quiet, you torment.

c. In jocular use: An instrument of irritation or annoyance: = Tormentor 3 f. (In quot. *attrib.*)

1882 *Daily News* 30 May 2/1 The Vale of Health was.. the most frequented spot of all,..the 'torment' and squirt fun rather too buoyant.

5. A violent storm; a tempest, tornado. *Obs.* (exc. in Fr. form *tourmente*).

a 1300 *Fragm. Pop. Sc.* (Wright) 184 For þeras the weder is, þer is turment strong Of wynd, of water, and of fur. c 1330 R. Brunne *Chron.* (1810) 148 In to þe se of Spayn wer dryuen in a torment. 1471 Caxton *Recuyell* (Sommer) 540 Ther roose so a grete torment in the see [*orig.* si grant tormente leva de vent]. 1530 Palsgr. 282/1 Torment a storme on the see, *tourmente, tempeste*. 1604 E. G[rimstone] *D'Acosta's Hist. Indies* iii. xxvi. 199 Vpon the coast of Peru, there be no torments from heauen, as thunder and lightning. [1847 G. B. Cheever *Wand. Pilgr.* xii. 90 The fury of these tourmentes is inconceivable. 1909 *Blackw. Mag.* Sept. 341/1, I reached it..in a more than usually objectionable tourmente of snow.]

6. *attrib.* and *Comb.*, as *torment-house, robe.*

1649 J. E[lliston] tr. *Behmen's Epist.* v. 62 Being in the torment-house of the stars. 1846 T. Aird *Poet. Wks.* (1856) 240 With torment-pointed threatenings. 1890 E. Hatch *Fields of Light* 55 Saints who were wafted to the skies In the torment robe of flame.

**Torment** (tǫɹme·nt), *v.* Forms: see prec. sb.; also 5 *pa. pple.* (*contr.*) tor-, turment. [a. OF. *tor-, turmenter* (12th c.), *tourmenter*, f. *tor-, turment* sb.: cf. med.L. *tormentāre*, f. *tormentum*, Pr. *turmentar*, Sp. *tormentar*, It. *tormentare*.]

1. *trans.* To put to torment or torture; to inflict torture upon.

c 1290 *St. Edmund* 181 in *S. Eng. Leg.* I. 436 Fiet and hondene þat neren nouȝt i-tormentede with þat here Necke and face and al is heued. c 1300 *St. Brandan* 595 Oure maister ous hath i-turmented so grisliche allonge niȝt. 1382 Wyclif *Rev.* xiv. 10 This..shal be tourmentid [1388 turmentid] with fijr and brunston. c 1440 *Alphabet of Tales* 177 When a devull had turment horrebly a man þat he was in. 1475 *Bk. Noblesse* (Roxb.) 66 They turmentid hym in prison in the most cruelle wise to dethe. 1560 Daus tr. *Sleidane's Comm.* 168 To moue the Frenche kynge, that innocente persones be not tormented, for Religion. 1651 Hobbes *Leviath.* iii. xxxviii. 238 For what offences..men are to be Eternally tormented.

2. To afflict or vex with great suffering or misery, physical or mental; to pain, distress, plague.

1297 R. Glouc. (Rolls) 4920+36 Seynt Petur to hym come, as þe slep hym toke, & tormented hym sore ynou. 1382 Wyclif *Acts* v. 33 Whanne thei herden thes thingis, thei weren turmentid, and thouȝten for to sle hem. c 1420 *Chron. Vilod.* 2902 Þo whyche was wᵗ sekenesse so tourmentyd. a 1450 *Knt. de la Tour* (1906) 41 The pepille that were.. oute of her mynde and turmented. 1514 Barclay *Cyt. & Uplondyshm.* (Percy Soc.) 6 Whan the northe wynde.. Hath brought cold wynter pore wretches to turment. a 1548 Hall *Chron., Rich. III* 28 b, What ys he..that wil not..be moued & tormented with pitie and mercie? 1713 Steele *Englishm.* No. 48. 308 Great Evils..torment the Life of Man. 1804 *Med. Jrnl.* XII. 143 A disease which had tormented me for sixteen years. 1856 [see Tormenting *ppl. a.*].

b. In lighter sense: To tease or worry excessively; to trouble, 'plague'.

1718 Lady M. W. Montagu *Let. to Abbé Conti* 19 May, We are tormenting our brains with some scheme of politics. 1862 Maurice *Mor. & Met. Philos.* IV. vii. § 44. 373 He tormented the Rabbins with questions.

†3. To throw into agitation; to toss, disturb, shake up, or stir physically. *Obs.* (exc. as a Gallicism).

1491 Caxton *Vitas Patr.* (W. de W. 1495) ii. 246 Lyke.. raymentes when the foller fulleth them & tourmenteth them often vnder his fete. a 1533 Ld. Berners *Huon* xlvi. 156 The shyppe was so sore tormentyd, that the shyppe brast all to peces. 1667 Milton *P. L.* vi. 243 That warr..then soaring on main wing Tormented all the Air; all Air seemed then Conflicting Fire. 1784 Cowper *Task* ii. 101 The fixed and rooted earth, Tormented into billows, heaves and swells. 1822 [see Tormented *ppl. a.*]. 1908 *Academy* 27 June 927/2 After madame had 'tormented' the ingredients—the salad was a dish from fairyland.

b. *fig.* To twist, distort (sense, style, etc.).

1647 Hammond *Power of Keys* iii. 26 Sure this is to peruert and torment the sense. a 1680 Butler *Rem.* (1759) I. 230 And pay 'em for tormenting Texts. 1895 *Daily News* 18 Oct. 4/7 In Mr. Pater we had a writer of singular natural gifts, who..ended by embroiling and tormenting his style.

Hence **Tormented** *ppl. a.* (whence **Tormentedly** *adv.*); also **Tormentable** *a.*, capable of being tormented, susceptible of torment; †**Tormentation** *Obs.*, tormenting, torment; †**Tormentative**, †**Tormentive** *adjs. Obs.*, that torments, tormenting.

1876 Emerson *Ess., Circles* Wks. (Bohn) II. 263 The great man is not convulsible or *tormentable. 1789 A. C. Bower *Diaries & Corr.* (1903) 53, I shall have no more *Tormentations. 1654 Gayton *Pleas. Notes* iii. viii. 124 From Furies, and things worse *tormentative. 1552 Huloet, *Tourmented, *cruciatus, excruciatus.* 1686 Horneck *Crucif. Jesus* v. 72 A fiery serpent..a symbol of God's presence and power to heal the tormented Israelites. 1808 G. Edwards *Pract. Plan* iii. 16 Evils, which our tormented imaginations apprehend. 1822 Scott *Pirate* vii, More than once, large fragments..gave way before him, and thundered down into the tormented ocean. 1891 *Longm. Mag.* Mar. 531 She was going to break out *tormentedly, pleadingly: 'For God's sake tell me!' 1653 F. G. tr. *Scudery's Artamenes* viii. i. (1655) IV. 3 His presence is so *tormentive unto me.

†**Tormentful**, *a. Obs.* [f. Torment *sb.* + -ful.] Full of, or fraught with torment.

1596 R. L[inche] *Diella* (1877) 30 My most tormentfull case. 1647 Trapp *Comm. Matt.* vi. 31 Carefulness is a tormentful plodding upon businesses. a 1694 Tillotson *Wks.* (1717) II. 199 In what Nature soever they [malice, envy, revenge] are, they are as vexatious and tormentful to it self, as they are troublesome and mischievous to others.

**Tormentil** (tǭ·ɹmĕntil). Forms: 5 tormentille, -ylle, 6 -yll, 6–8 -ill, -ile, (8 tormentle), 6– tormentil; 5 turmentylle, 5–6 -ill, 6 -yll. [= F. *tormentille* (1314 in Hatz.-Darm.), ad. med.L. *tormentilla*, in form dim. of *tormentum*: see Torment *sb.* Reason of name obscure: cf. quot. 1616; according to others from its being used to relieve the gripes, L. *tormina*.] A low-growing herb, *Potentilla Tormentilla* (*Tormentilla repens*), N.O. *Rosaceæ*, of trailing habit, common on heaths and dry pastures, bearing small four-petalled yellow flowers, and having strongly astringent roots; in use from early times in medicine, and in tanning. Also called *septfoil*.

[a 1387 *Sinon. Barthol.* (Anecd. Oxon.) 42/1 Tormentilla pilos, pentafilon non habet ullos.] a 1400–50 *Stockh. Med. MS.* 6 Water of turmentill. 1530 Palsgr. 284/1 Turmentyll an herbe, *tourmentine.* 1578 Lyte *Dodoens* i. lvii. 83 Tormentill is much like vnto Sinckefoyle. 1610 Fletcher *Faithf. Sheph.* ii. i, This Tormentil, whose vertue is to part All deadly killing poyson from the heart. 1616 Surfl. & Markh. *Country Farme* 204 Called Tormentill, because the powder or decoction of the root doth appease the rage and torment of the teeth. 1698 M. Martin *Voy. St. Kilda* (1749) 56 Their Leather is tanned with the roots of Tormentil. 1906 *Daily Chron.* 4 May 6/7 Tormentil and potentil, names fulfilled of pleasure, Set the world in tune again with the May Day measure.

b. *attrib.*, as *tormentil-root.*

1712 tr. *Pomet's Hist. Drugs* I. 43 The best Tormentil Roots come from grassy, wet Places about the Alps and Pyrenees. 1811 A. T. Thomson *Lond. Disp.* (1818) 400 Tormentil root is a powerful astringent.

So † **Tormentine** [from F.] in same sense.

14.. *Nom.* in Wr.-Wülcker 713/6 *Hec tormentilla*, tormentyne [cf. 1530 Palsgr. above].

**Tormenting**, *vbl. sb.* [f. Torment *v.* + -ing[1].] The action of the verb Torment; torturing, vexing; an instance of this.

c 1290 *S. Eng. Leg.* I. 12/389 His soule wende to þe Joye of heouene After is tormentingue. 1382 Wyclif *Isa.* xiii. 8 Tormentingus and sorewes thei shul holde. 1535 Coverdale *Wisd.* ii. 19 Let vs examen him with despitefull rebuke and tormentinge, that we maye knowe his dignite & proue his pacience. 1633 P. Fletcher *Elisa* ii. iv, So sat she, as when speechlesse griefs tormenting Locks up the heart. 1884 *Athenæum* 6 Dec. 732/2 [They] suffer from no fancied ills and self-conscious tormentings.

**Tormenting**, *ppl. a.* [f. as prec. + -ing[2].] That torments, in various senses of the verb.

1575 [implied in Tormentingly]. 1594 Shaks. *Rich. III*, i. iii. 226 While some tormenting Dreame Affrights thee. 1637 Prynne *Passages Star Chamb.* in *Harl. Misc.* (1809) IV. 234 Let me be put to the tormentingest death they can devise. 1667 Milton *P. L.* iv. 505 Sight hateful, sight tormenting! 1780 *Mirror* No. 74 ¶ 9 Haunted with the most tormenting thoughts. 1856 Kane *Arct. Expl.* II. viii. 87 The eruption, a tormenting and anomalous symptom.

Hence **Tormentingly** *adv.*; **Tormentingness.**

1575 Gascoigne *Dan Barthol. of Bathe* Wks. 1907 I. 105 He bounst and bet his head tormentingly. 1727 Bailey vol. II, *Tormentingness*, tormenting Quality or Faculty. 1857 *Chamb. Jrnl.* VII. 397 Visits were tormentingly delayed.

†**Tormentise**. *Obs.* Torment, torture.

c 1386 Chaucer *Monk's T.* 527 But nathelees this Seneca the wise Chees in a Bath to dye in this manere Rather than han any oother tormentise.

**Tormentor** (tǫɹme·ntəɹ). Also 5–9 -er. [ME. and AF. *tormentour* = OF. *tor-, tourmenteur*, earlier *-teour, -teor* (c 1150 in Godef.):—L. type **tormentātōr-em*, agent-n. from *tormentāre* to Torment.] One who or that which torments.

1. An officer who inflicts torture or cruelty; an official torturer; an executioner. Also *transf.*

c 1290 *St. Edmund* 43 in *S. Eng. Leg.* I. 298 His luþere tormentores þat beoten him so sore. a 1350 *St. Andrew* 171 in Horstm. *Altengl. Leg.* (1881) 6 Þe turmentours.. Toke his bodi with bitter brayde, Vnto þe cros þai gun it bend. 1382 Wyclif *Matt.* xviii. 34 His lord wroth, tok hym to tourmentours [1388 turmentouris; 1582 (Rhem.) tormenters; 1611 tormentors], til that he paiede al the dette. 1483 Caxton *Gold. Leg.* 185 b/2 The tormentour as he had smyten of his heed both his eyen sterte out of his heed. 1513 More *Rich. III* (1883) 79 He that playeth the sowdayne is percase a sowter. Yet if one should..calle him by his owne name.., one of his tormentors might hap to breake his [= one's] head. 1581 Pettie *Guazzo's Civ. Conv.* i. (1586) 25 Such, who..are holden for infamous, as Sergeants, Hangmen, Tormentours. 1895 Rider Haggard *Hrt. of World* xxv, That your souls be handed over to the tormentors of the under-world.

2. One who or that which persistently inflicts intense pain, suffering, vexation, or annoyance.

In quot. 1642 *humorously*: = Teaser[1] 2.

1553 Becon *Reliques of Rome* (1563) 199 They dissent both in the tormentours and in the tormentes of the soules. 1593 Shaks. *Rich. II*, ii. i. 136 These words heereafter, thy tormentors bee. 1642 Milton *Apol. Smect.* Pref., Wks. 1851 III. 274 Certainly this tormentor of Semicolons is as good at dismembring and slitting sentences. 1712 Addison *Spect.* No. 447 ¶ 10 They will naturally become their own Tormentors. 1751 *Affecting Narr. of Wager* 84 The Prospect of that horridest Tormenter, Famine, [was] continually before our Eyes. 1846 J. Baxter *Libr. Pract. Agric.* (ed. 4) I. 419 A host of tormentors, in the shape of flies,..persecuting the poor animal. 1897 'Ouida' *Massarenes* viii, The person whose instructress and tormentor she was.

3. An instrument that torments in some way.

†a. Some device for catching fleas. *Obs.* b. *pl.* A long-handled fork used for taking the meat from the coppers on board ship; also, *Sc.* 'an implement on which to toast bannocks, etc.' (*E.D.D.*); in quot. 1866 (*sing.*), a piercing implement carried by excise officers. c. A wheel-harrow of which each tine is a small share or hoe, for breaking up stiff soil. d. *pl.* A slang name for riding-spurs. e. *Theatre.* (See quots.) f. A device used to annoy at pleasure-fairs: cf. Tickler 2 b, Scratch-back 2. *colloq.*

a. 1609 Heywood *Rape of Lucrece, Cries of Rome* Wks. 1874 V. 254 Buy a very fine Mouse-trap, or a tormentor for your Fleaes. 1614 B. Jonson *Barth. Fair* ii. iv. a 1619 Fletcher *Bonduca* ii. iii, *Daughter.* Are they not our Tormentors? *Car.* Tormentors? flea-traps! 1622 J. Taylor (Water P.) *Trav. Twelve-pence* (1635) B vij b, Of MowseTraps, and tormentors to kill Fleas. b. 1706 E. Ward *Wooden World Diss.* (1708) 84 He [a sea-cook] is never without a Pair of Tormentors in his Hand. 1823 Galt *Gilhaize* I. ii. 22 Toasting an oaten bannock on a pair of tormentors. 1866 Fitzpatrick *Sham Sqr.* 18 Sham made a violent pass at Peck with his tormentor. 1898 F. T. Bullen *Cruise Cachalot* 186 The cook uncovered his coppers, plunged his tormentors therein, and produced such a succession of ugly corpses of fowls as I had never seen before. c. 1807 Vancouver *Agric. Devon* (1813) 121 Scarifiers, scufflers, shims, and broad-shares of various constructions,..called under the general name of tormentors. 1882 Jago *Cornw. Gloss.*, *Tormentor*, an agricultural implement for breaking up the clods of a ploughed field. d. 1875 Whyte Melville *Riding Recoll.* iv. (1879) 59 Fordham..wholly repudiates 'the tormentors', arguing that they only make a horse shorten his stride, and 'shut up'. e. 1886 *Stage Gossip* 70 The 'tormentor' is the name for a door, placed in the R. I. E. and L. I. E., and which prevents anybody from obtaining a view of the performance from either of the entrances named, and also prevents the actor being seen by the 'house'—these doors are annoying at times. 1893 *N. York Herald* 25 Dec. 26/2 (Funk) The first wing has been known to the stage as 'tormentor' wing from time whereof memory of man runneth not to the contrary. 1898 *Westm. Gaz.* 12 Jan. 9/3 A strip of white bunting is waved by a master of the ceremonies from a wooden hutch in the 'tormentor' wing. f. 1891 in *Cent. Dict.* 1903 Farmer & Henley *Slang Dict.*, *Tormentor*..3 (common), a back-scratcher.

†**Tormentous**, *a. Obs. rare.* [f. L. *torment-um* Torment + -ous: cf. OF. *tormentos*.] Of tormenting nature; torturing. Hence †**Tormentously** *adv.*

1583 Stocker *Civ. Warres Lowe C.* ii. 47 His body being trysed vp into the ayre with a tormentous [*printed* tormentrous] Engine, they bynd to his feete instruments of Yron. 1657 Thornley tr. *Longus' Daphnis & Chloe* 195 Astylus was not to learn that Love was a tormentous fire. 1669 *Address Hopeful Yng. Gentry Eng.* 87 Why so tormentously [do they] rend their weary throats?

So † **Tormentuous** *a.* [ad. late L. *tormentuōsus*.]

1597 J. PAYNE *Royal Exch.* 44 So ys yt a moste bitter and tormentuouse estate to such as love not to gethers. 1860 MAYNE *Expos. Lex.*, *Tormentuosus*, having or full of racking pains: tormentuous.

**Tormentress** (tǭɹme·ntrės). [a. AF. *tormenteresse*, fem. of *tormentour* TORMENTOR.] A female tormentor.

1426 LYDG. *De Guil. Pilgr.* 11691 A gret turmenteresse Wych doth to ffolk fful gret dystresse. 1601 HOLLAND *Pliny* XXVIII. iv. II. 301 Fortune..ordinarily commeth after ..as the scourge and tormentresse of glorie and honour. 1895 R. Y. TYRRELL *Latin Poetry* 103 He [Catullus].. breaks down in a wild burst of rage against his tormentress.

**To·rmentry.** Now *rare.* [a. OF. *tourmenterie* (1427 in Godef.), office of a tormentor or executioner, f. *tormenteur* TORMENTOR: see -RY.]

†**1.** A company or body of tormentors or executioners. *Obs.* [Cf. *Jewry*, *yeomanry*.]

*a* 1350 *St. Andrew* 108 in Horstm. *Altengl. Leg.* (1881) 5 Egeas þan..Sent efter al his turmentry, And bad þam.. ordan a cros. *Ibid.* 208 Both he and al his turmentri.

†**2.** The infliction or suffering of torture or torment, as by executioners or fiends. *Obs.*

1375 *XI Pains of Hell* 159 in *O. E. Misc.* 215 A sorouful syȝt, a hore hold mon, Be-twene iiij fyndis in turmentre. *c* 1412 HOCCLEVE *De Reg. Princ.* 2825 He snybbed is, and put to tormentrie. 1534 MORE *Comf. agst. Trib.* III. xvii. (1847) 253 All the tormentry that the devil..could devise.

**3.** Tormenting feeling; severe suffering, pain, or vexation. Now *rare.*

*c* 1386 CHAUCER *Wife's Prol.* 251 Thanne seistow it is a tormentrie To soffren hire pride and hire malencolie. 1434 MISYN *Mending of Life* I. 106 Ioy or turmentry we sal resayfe. 1509 FISHER *Serm. Funeral Hen. VII*, Wks. (1876) 279, I founde in them all but vanyte & turmentry of soule. 1885 R. F. BURTON *Arab. Nts.* III. 19 O joy of Hell and Heaven! whose tormentry enquickens frame and soul.

**Tormeryke, Tormican,** obs. ff. TURMERIC, PTARMIGAN.

‖**Tormina** (tǭ·ɹmină), *sb. pl. Path.* [L. *tormina* gripes, griping of the bowels, pl. of **tormen*, for **torqmen*, f. *torquēre* to twist.] Acute griping or wringing pains in the bowels; gripes. Also *fig.*

1656 R. ROBINSON *Christ All* 106 They have not those tormina and gripings in their consciences which other Sinners have. 1658 PHILLIPS, *Torminous*, troubled with Tormina, i. gripings of the Belly. 1843 R. J. GRAVES *Syst. Clin. Med.* vi. 75 They have costive or irregular bowels, diarrhœa, tormina. 1866 A. FLINT *Princ. Med.* (1880) 413 Griping or colic pains which are called *tormina*.

Hence **To·rminal,** †**To·rminous** *adjs.*, of the nature of or characterized by tormina; †affected with tormina.

1656 BLOUNT *Glossogr.*, *Torminous*,..that frets the guts, or that hath torments and frettings in the guts. 1666 G. HARVEY *Morb. Angl.* x. 85 A torminous diarrhé. 1822–34 *Good's Study Med.* I. 198 A few slight torminal pains.

**Tormit,** dial. form of TURNIP.

**Tormodont** (tǭ·ɹmǒdǫnt), *a. Ornith.* [f. Gr. τόρμο-ς hole, socket + ὀδούς, ὀδοντ- tooth.] Of a tooth or teeth: Set each in a separate socket or alveolus, as in certain fossil birds; of a bird: having socketed teeth.

1888 GADOW in *Nature* 20 Dec. 178/2 Ichthyornis and Apatornis..differ from recent Carinate birds in degree only, viz. by their tormodont teeth and amphicœlous vertebræ.

**Tormoyl, -e,** obs. forms of TURMOIL.

**Torn** (tǭɹn), *ppl. a.* [pa. pple. of TEAR *v.*[1], q. v. for Forms.] Rent or riven by being pulled violently asunder; wearing torn garments.

1362 LANGL. *P. Pl.* A. v. 111 In A toren Tabart of twelue Wynter Age. *c* 1425 *Cast. Persev.* 109 in *Macro Plays* 80 Þer schal com a lythyr ladde with a torne hod. 1552 HULOET, Torne garmentes, *lacides.* *a* 1631 DONNE *Hymn to Christ* 1 In what torne shipp soever I embark. 1693 DRYDEN *Juvenal* I. 159 Tho born a Slave, tho my torn Ears are bor'd. ?*a* 1750 *Nursery Rime*, '*House that Jack Built*' viii, This is the man all tattered and torn, That kissed the maiden all forlorn. 1818 SCOTT *Rob Roy* xxxiii, A rent and torn ravine resembling a deserted watercourse. 1839 DARWIN *Voy. Nat.* x. (1873) 210 Masses of rock and torn-up trees. 1860 READE *Cloister & H.* lxxi, The poor torn, worn creature wept. 1861 J. BARR *Poems* 119 (E.D.D.) Like some torn-doun play actor, That had sung for his bread thro' a fair.

**b.** *spec. Bot.*: see quots.; also in comb.

[1760 J. LEE *Introd. Bot.* (1776) 384 *Lacerum*, lacerate, where the Margin is variously divided, as if torn.] 1888 *Cassell's Encycl. Dict.*, *Torn*,..*Bot.*, irregularly divided by deep incisions. 1895 *Funk's Standard Dict.*, *Torn-crenate*, *Bot.*, crenate by a torn margin.

**c.** In combination with adverbs, as *torn-off*, *-out*, *-up*; also torn-down, rough, riotous, boisterous, disorderly (*dial.* and *U.S.*); reduced in circumstances (*Sc.* and *dial.*). Also *sb.*, a rough riotous person.

1870 W. M. BAKER *New Timothy* xxxii. (U.S.) 1877–88 in *N. W. Linc. Gloss.* 1886 in *S. W. Linc. Gloss.*

**Torn,** obs. f. TOURN (sheriff's court), TURN.

‖**Tornada** (tǫɹnā·dă). [Prov., from pa. pple. of *tornar* to turn.] An envoy of three lines, in which the verse-endings of all the preceding stanzas recur.

[Cf. Littré, *Tornade*, se dit, dans les chansons provençales, de la ritournelle.]

1823 ROSCOE *Sismondi's Lit. Eur.* (1846) I. vi. 173 The songs are usually in seven stanzas, followed by an envoy, which he calls a tornada. 1874 BREYMANN in *Ess. Owens Coll. Manch.* xi. 384 The Troubadours borrowed from the Saracens several of their poetical forms as, for instance, the Tornada. 1880 [see ENVOY *sb.*[1] 1].

†**Torna·de.** *Obs. rare.* Also 7 tornathe. Anglicized form of TORNADO.

1638 Tornathe [see TORNADO 1]. 1727 BAILEY vol. II, *Tornade*, a sudden and violent Gust of Wind or Storm. 1813 SCOTT *Rokeby* I. viii, Inured to danger's direst form, Tornade and earthquake, flood and storm.

**Tornadic** (tǫɹnæ·dik), *a.* [f. next + -IC.] Of, pertaining to, or of the nature of a tornado.

1884 *Amer. Meteorol. Jrnl.* I. 7 Four series of storms of tornadic character have passed over the states east of the Mississippi River since the beginning of the year. 1890 *Columbus* (Ohio) *Dispatch* 13 June, These are tornadic conditions. 1898 H. W. LUCY in *Daily News* 18 Feb. 2/2 Mr. Orchardson's portrait..presenting the ex-Speaker in one of his not unfamiliar tornadic moods.

**Tornado** (tǫɹnē¹·do). Forms: (6–7 ternado), 7– tornado; also 7–8 turnado, (7 tornatho, tornada, 8 tournado). See also TORNADE. [In Hakluyt and his contemporaries, *ternado*; from Purchas 1625 onward, *turnado*, *tournado*, *tornado*. In none of these forms does the word exist in Spanish or Portuguese. But the early sense makes it probable that *ternado* was a bad adaptation (perh. orig. a blundered spelling) of Sp. *tronada* 'thunderstorm' (f. *tronar* to thunder), and that *tornado* was an attempt to improve it by treating it as a derivative of Sp. *tornar* to turn, return; cf. *tornado* pple., returned. It is notable that this spelling is identified with explanations in which, not the thunder, but the turning, shifting, or whirling winds are the main feature. This is emphasized in the variants *turnado*, *tournado*. Mod.F. *tornado* is from Eng. (not Portuguese, as in Littré).]

**1.** A term applied by 16th c. navigators to violent thunderstorms of the tropical Atlantic, with torrential rain, and often with sudden and violent gusts of wind. Now *rare* or passing into 2.

1556 W. TOWERSON in Hakluyt *Voy.* (1589) 100 The 4. day we had terrible thunder and lightning, with exceeding great gusts of raine, called Ternados. 1599 HAKLUYT *Voy.* II. II. 103 We had nothing but Ternados, with such thunder, lightning, and raine, that we could not keep our men drie. 1600 *Ibid.* III. 719 The ternados, that is thundrings and lightnings. 1634 SIR T. HERBERT *Trav.* 216 We crost the Æquator, where we had too many Tornathoes [*ed.* 1638, 355 wee were pesterd with continuall Tornathes; a variable weather compos'd of lowd blasts, stinking showers, and terrible thunders; *ed.* 1677, 393 Tornado's]. 1697 DAMPIER *Voy. round World* (1699) 31 We had fine weather while we lay here [an. 1681], only some Tornadoes or Thunder-showers. 1727 A. HAMILTON *New Acc. E. Ind.* II. xliv. 140 The Coast is subject to frequent Tornadoes, or Squalls of Wind and Rain, introduced with much Thunder and Lightning. 1788 J. MATTHEWS *Voy.* iii. (1791) 30 Had at least one tornado every twenty-four hours, which are always attended with violent gusts of wind, thunder, lightning, and excessive rain; but which greatly purify the air. 1832 G. DOWNES *Lett. Cont. Countries* I. 71 The return of the storm, swooping down in its various elements of thunder, lightning, and rain, with all the fierce grandeur of an Alpine tornado.

†**b.** *transf.* Chiefly in *pl.* The season at which such storms are prevalent. *Obs. rare.*

In quot. 1657 perh. associated with the 'turning' of the sun at the tropic.

1634 SIR T. HERBERT *Trav.* 5 Nor is this weather rare about the Æquinoctiall; by Mariners termed the Tornadoes: and tis so vncertaine, that now you shall haue a quiet breath and gale, and suddenly an vnexpected violent gust. 1657 R. LIGON *Barbadoes* (1673) 9 The time of our stay there, being the Turnado, when the Sun..became Zenith to the Inhabitants. 1698 FRYER *Acc. E. India & P.* 10 These Seasons the Seamen term the *Tornados.*

**2.** A very violent storm (now without implication of thunder), affecting a limited area, in which the wind is constantly changing its direction or rotating; a whirling wind, whirlwind; loosely, any very violent storm of wind, a hurricane. *spec.* **a.** On the west coast of Africa, a rotatory storm in which the wind revolves violently under a moving arch of clouds; **b.** In the Mississippi region of U.S., a destructive rotatory storm under a funnel-shaped cloud like a water-spout, which advances in a narrow path over the land for many miles.

(Quot. 1625 shows the transition from 1 to 2.)

[1625 PURCHAS *Pilgrims* II. IX. vi. § 1. 1463 We met with winds which the Mariners call The Turnadoes, so variable and vncertaine, that sometime within the space of one houre, all the two and thirtie seuerall winds will blow. These winds were accompanied with much thunder and lightning, and with extreme rayne.] 1626 CAPT. SMITH *Accid. Yng. Seamen* 17 A gust, a storme, a spoute, a loume gaile, an eddy wind, a flake of wind, a Turnado. 1656 BLOUNT *Glossogr.*, *Tornado*, (from the Span. *Tornada*, *i.* a returne, or turning about) is a sudden, violent and forcible storme of raine and ill weather at sea, so termed by the Mariners; and does most usually happen about the Æquator. 1688 R. HOLME *Armoury* II. 23/1 A Turnado [is] a fierce Wind. 1693 SIR T. P. BLOUNT *Nat. Hist.* 434 The Tornados are variable Winds, call'd in the Portugal Language Travados. 1710 J. HARRIS *Lex. Techn.* II, *Tornado*, is the Name given by the Seamen for a violent Storm of Wind, and sometimes followed by Rain; it usually swifts or turns about to almost all Points of the Compass, whence I suppose its name. 1719 DE FOE *Crusoe* I. 47 When a violent Tournado or Hurricane took us quite out of our Knowledge. 1727 [DORRINGTON] *Philip Quarll* 51 Several Storms and Turnadoes. 1755 JOHNSON, *Tornado*, a hurricane, a whirlwind. 1760–72 tr. *Juan & Ulloa's Voy.* (ed. 3) I. 13 From what quarter these tornadoes or squalls proceed, I cannot positively affirm. 1770 GOLDSM. *Des. Vill.* 357 While oft in whirls the mad tornado flies. 1788 COWPER *Negro's Compl.* 33 Hark! He answers—Wild tornadoes..Wasting towns, plantations, meadows. 1815 J. SMITH *Panorama Sc. & Art* II. 45 This tract is subject to frequent calms, and to sudden gusts of winds called tornadoes which blow from all points of the horizon. 1849 COL. HAWKER *Diary* (1893) II. 296 The gale increased to an absolute tornado. **b.** 1849 LYELL *2nd Visit U.S.* (1850) II. 199 This tornado checked the progress of Natchez, as did the removal of the seat of Legislature to Jackson. 1883 *Encycl. Brit.* XVI. 130/1 The region of most frequent occurrence of tornadoes is the region where a large number of the cyclones of the United States appear to originate. *Ibid.* 130/2 The wind of the tornado reaches a velocity probably never equalled in cyclones.

**c.** *fig.*; cf. *tempest*, *storm*, *whirlwind.*

1818 LADY MORGAN *Autobiog.* (1859) 28 We live in a sort of tornado between business and pleasure, and my head literally turns round. 1840 THACKERAY *Pict. Rhapsody* Wks. 1900 XIII. 334 Beneath one of Turner's magnificent tornadoes of colour. 1849 CLOUGH *Bothie* I. 156 On this passage followed a great tornado of cheering. 1863 COWDEN CLARKE *Shaks. Char.* xvii. 416 The tornado of the north—Harry Percy, most commonly surnamed 'Hotspur'.

**3.** *attrib.* and *Comb.*, as *tornado cloud*, *mood*, *night*, *oath*, *pitch*, *rain*, *spirit*, *wind*; *tornado-breeding*, *-haunted* adjs.; **tornado-cellar, -pit,** an underground place of refuge from tornadoes (in sense 2 b); a cyclone-pit; **tornado-funnel**: see 2 b; **tornado-lamp, tornado-lantern,** a hurricane-lamp, storm-lantern.

1861 H. ANGUS *Serm.* 150 The death-distilling, *tornado-breeding atmospheric stagnation of the tropics. 1899 MARY KINGSLEY *W. Afr. Stud.* ii. 48 If..you see that well-known *tornado-cloud arch coming..the sooner you get her [the ship] ready to run, the better. 1896 *Westm. Gaz.* 28 Dec. 7/1 Her ascent..to the bleak summit of a *tornado-haunted volcano. 1897 *Dublin Rev.* Oct. 299 Saner counsels prevailed over Gordon's *tornado mood. 1897 MARY KINGSLEY *W. Africa* 312 Particularly vigilant has he got to be on *tornado nights. *Ibid.* 396 When the wet season's *tornado rain comes down on it. 1863 COWDEN CLARKE *Shaks. Char.* xiii. 330 His *tornado spirit hurries him at once into a quarrel with the Duke of Austria. 1669 *Phil. Trans.* IV. 1003 These North-East-Winds hold most commonly to 8 degrees North-Latitude, and then begin the *Tornado Winds. 1671 R. BOHUN *Wind* 236 So variable and unsteady are the Tornado-winds, so little obliged to any certain law.

Hence **Torna·do,ish** *a.* [-ISH[1]]. (*nonce-wd.*)

1889 *Columbus* (Ohio) *Dispatch* 16 Jan., Its [a storm's] powerful warm, wet, tornadoish right, and cold, snowy, blizzardy left hand.

**Tornal:** see TORNUS.

**Tornament,** obs. f. TOURNAMENT, TORMENT.

‖**Tornaria** (tǫɹnē³·riă). *Zool.* [mod.L., f. Gr. τόρν-ος or L. *torn-us* a turner's wheel, in reference to the shape of the larva.] The larval form of species of the Sea-acorn, *Balanoglossus.* Hence **Torna·rian** *a.*, of or pertaining to a tornaria.

1888 ROLLESTON & JACKSON *Anim. Life* 592 Tornaria requires a fresh examination...Balfour regarded Tornaria as intermediate in structure between the Echinoderm larva and the Trochosphere. 1891 *Cent. Dict.*, Tornarian. 1892 THOMSON *Outl. Zool.* xvi. 355 The Tornaria becomes pelagic, acquires a proboscis, loses its special bands of cilia, and becomes diffusely ciliated, but has not yet a mouth or anus.

†**To·rnatil,** *a. Obs. rare*—⁰. [ad. L. *tornātil-is* turned in a lathe.] (See quot.)

1661 BLOUNT *Glossogr.* (ed. 2), *Tornatil* (*tornatilis*), that is turned, or made with a wheel.

**Tornay,** obs. form of TOURNEY.

‖**Torne** (tǫɹn). *Obs.* [MLG., LG. *torn* = MDu., Du. *tōren*, MHG. *turn*, Ger. *turm.*] A tower.

1637 R. MONRO *Exped.* II. 80 Their Leaders..pursued the enemy so hard, till they had beaten them out of a *Torne*, they had fled unto. [1871 WADDELL *Isa.* xxix. 4 (*pseudo-arch.*) Tornes I sal bigg fornenst yo.]

**Torne,** obs. f. TORN, TOURN, TURN.

**Torneament, Tornebroche,** obs. ff. TOURNAMENT, TURNBROACH. **Tornel, -elle,** var. TOURNELLE *Obs.* **Tornement(e,** obs. ff. TOURNAMENT, TORMENT. **Tornepyke, Torner,** obs. ff. TURNPIKE, TURNER.

‖**Tornese** (tǫrnē·zĕ). Pl. **tornesi** (-ē·zi). [It., = F. *tournois*, L. *turonens-is*, lit. (money) of Tours. Cf. TOURNOIS.] An obsolete subsidiary coin of the Two Sicilies, $\frac{1}{300}$ of a ducat.

**Torne-seke, Tornesol(e, -solt,** obs. forms of TURN-SICK, TURNSOLE.

†**Torney.** *Obs.* exc. *dial.* Aphetic f. ATTORNEY.

1490 *Acc. St. Dunstan's, Canterb.* (1885) 13 Payde for one torneys labor ij s...the recorde of the torney ij d.

**Torney,** obs. form of TOURNEY.

**Tornhexactine** (tǭɹnheksæ·ktəin, -in). *Zool.* [f. Gr. τόρν-ος turner's wheel + HEXACTINE.] A six-rayed sponge-spicule in which the rays are abruptly pointed. 1909 in *Cent. Dict. Suppl.*

**Tornil,** obs. form of TURNEL.

‖**Torni·llo, torni·lla.** *U.S.* [Sp. *tornillo* screw, dim. of *torno* turn.] A tree, the screw-pod mesquite (*Prosopis pubescens*) of Texas, New Mexico, and California.

1866 *Treas. Bot.* 930 The Tornillo of the Sonora Mexicans. 1891 in *Cent. Dict.*

**Tornit,** obs. Sc. f. *turned*, pa. pple. of TURN *v.*

**Tornly** (tǭ·ɹnli), *adv. rare*—$^{0}$. [f. TORN *ppl. a.* + -LY [2].] In a torn condition, raggedly, in pieces.
1548–67 THOMAS *Ital. Dict.*, *Squarsiatamente*, toarnely, or peacemeale.

**To·rnote**, *sb.* (*a.*) *Zool.* [ad. Gr. τορνωτ-ός adj. rounded with the τόρνος (see TORNUS).] A form of sponge-spicule: see quot.
1888 SOLLAS in *Challenger Rep.* XXV. p. lv, When the rhabdas is very abruptly pointed at each end a *rhabdus amphitornota* results, which we shall call a 'tornote'.

**Tornour, Tornoye**, obs. ff. TURNER, TOURNEY.

**Tornsell, -sole**, obs. forms of TURNSOLE.

‖ **Tornus** (tǭ·ɹnɒs). Pl. **-i** (-əi). *Entom.* [L. *tornus* turner's wheel or lathe, a. Gr. τόρνος a tool for rounding.] The inner or anal angle of the wing of an insect, esp. of the secondary wing of a tineid moth. Hence **To·rnal** *a.*, of or pertaining to the tornus.
1897 LD. WALSINGHAM in *Proc. Zool. Soc.* 19 Jan. 76 A creamy-ochreous dorsal streak..runs from the base through the tornal cilia. *Ibid.* 96 The apical and tornal angles of the cell;..cilia with a slight ochreous tinge about the tornus. 1904 SIR G. F. HAMPSON in *Annals & Mag. Nat. Hist.* Sept. 176 Hind wing..a fiery red stigma on termen near tornus.

**Toroi·dal**, *a. Geom.* [f. L. TOR-US + -OIDAL.] Resembling or pertaining to a torus (TORUS 4).
1889 *Cent. Dict.* s. v. *Function*, *Toroidal function*, a function serving to express the potential of an anchor-ring. 1895 *Scotsman* 3 Dec. 4/6 Professor Tait made a communication on, 'The application of net-work to a surface, in particular to a toroidal surface'.

**Torope**: see TERRAPIN.

‖ **Torosaurus** (tǫrosǭ·rɒs). *Palæont.* [mod.L., f. stem of Gr. τορός adj. piercing, τόρος borer (f. τείρειν to pierce) + σαῦρος lizard.] A genus of horned dinosaurs, occurring in the Laramie formation in U.S.
1891 MARSH in *Amer. Jrnl. Sc.* XLII. 266. 1892 *Ibid.* XLIII. 82 The open perforations in the parietal which have suggested the name *Torosaurus*. 1908 *Daily Chron.* 20 Feb. 4/6 The largest skull of any known land animal,..is the skull of a new horned dinosaur, the torosaurus, and is 8 ft. 6 in. long and 5 ft. 8 in. across.

**Torose** (torōu·s), *a. Nat. Hist.* [ad. L. *torōs-us*, f. *torus* bulge, brawn: see -OSE.] Bulging, swollen, protuberant: said of an approximately cylindrical body swollen here and there.
1760 J. LEE *Introd. Bot.* III. xxii. (1765) 229 The *Pericarpium* is..torose. 1785 MARTYN *Rousseau's Bot.* xxiii. (1794) 322 Radish has a cylindric, jointed, torose or swelling silique. 1829 LOUDON *Encycl. Plants* (1836) 461 Caps[ules] subglobose torose hispid.
So † **Toro·sity** *Obs. rare*—$^{0}$, torose condition.
1656 BLOUNT *Glossogr.*, *Torosity* (*torositas*), fleshiness, fatnesse, brawninesse. 1727 BAILEY vol. II, *Torosity*, Fatness, Grossness.

**Torous** (tōᵊ·rəs), *a.* [ad. L. *torōs-us* TOROSE, as if through a F. **toreux*: see -OUS.] = TOROSE.
1657 R. CARPENTER *Astrol.* 35 The solid and succous body of Divinity still grows more and more torous and quadrangular. 1684 tr. *Bonet's Merc. Compit.* v. 139 Whole torous Muscles, and long tendons. 1828 WEBSTER, *Torous*, in botany, protuberant; swelling in knobs, like the veins and muscles; as, a torous pericarp.

**Tor-ouzel**: see TOR *sb.* 3.

† **Torpedinal** (tǫɹpī·dinăl), *a. Obs. rare.* [f. L. *torpēdin-em*, TORPEDO + -AL.] Of or pertaining to the torpedo or electric ray.
1772 WALSH in *Phil. Trans.* LXIII. 465 The vigour of the fresh taken Torpedos at the Isle of Ré, was not able to force the torpedinal fluid across the minutest tract of air. *Ibid.*, Notwithstanding the weak spring of the torpedinal electricity, I was able..to convey it through a circuit, formed from one surface of the animal to the other, by two long brass wires, and four persons. 1800 *Med. Jrnl.* IV. 118 He..offers his own new and striking apparatus as more nearly resembling the torpedinal organ.

**Torpedineer** (tǫɹpīdiniᵊ·ɹ). *rare.* [f. as prec. + -EER: cf. *engineer*.] One who is engaged in the management of marine torpedoes.
1881 *Times* 18 Jan. 4/1 The young Prince of Naples, in the sailor's dress of his rank as corporal of Torpedineers..was on the bridge.

**Torpedinoid** (tǫɹpī·dinoid), *a. Zool.* [f. as prec. + -OID.] Of the form or kind of the torpedo or electric ray; belonging to the *Torpedinoidea* or *Torpedinidæ* considered as a group distinct from the true rays and the saw-fishes.

**Torpedinous** (tǫɹpī·dinəs), *a. rare.* ? *Obs.* [f. as prec. + -OUS.] Having the quality of a torpedo; benumbing, paralysing; also = TORPEDINAL.
1774 PRINGLE *Torpedo* 23 Nor in this circumstance only did the similitude between the electric and torpedinous fluids appear. 1845 DE QUINCEY *Coleridge & Opium-eat.* Wks. 1859 XII. 92 First came Dr. Andrew Bell..Fishy were his eyes; torpedinous was his manner.

**Torpedism, -ist**: see after TORPEDO *sb.*

**Torpedo** (tǫɹpī·do), *sb.* Also 6 -ido. Pl. -oes. [a. L. *torpēdo* stiffness, numbness, also the cramp-fish or electric ray, f. *torpēre* to be stiff or numb; = Sp., Pg. *torpedo*, It. *torpedine*. Cf. F. *torpille*, It. *torpiglia* from the same verb.]

**1.** A flat fish of the genus *Torpedo* or family *Torpedinidæ*, having an almost circular body with tapering tail, and characterized by the faculty of emitting electric discharges; the electric ray; also called *cramp-fish*, *cramp-ray*, *numb-fish*.
*c* 1520 L. ANDREWE *Noble Lyfe* xcii. in *Babees Bk.* (1868) 239 Torpido is a fisshe, but who-so handeleth hym shalbe lame & defe of lymmes that he shall fele no thyng. 1589 R. HARVEY *Pl. Perc.* (1860) 13 Like the fish Torpedo, which being towchd sends her venime alongst line and angle rod, till it cease on the finger, and so mar a fisher for euer. 1603 SIR C. HEYDON *Jud. Astrol.* xxiii. 547 Neither doth the Torpedo benumme other things, though it benummeth the fishers hand. 1646 SIR T. BROWNE *Pseud. Ep.* III. vii. 119 Torpedoes deliver their opium at a distance, and stupifie beyond themselves. 1772 *Chron.* in *Ann. Reg.* Nov. 136/1 Mr. Walsh touched the back of the torpedo; when all the five persons ..felt a shock at the same instant, which differed in nothing from the Leyden experiment. 1815 J. SMITH *Panorama Sc. & Art* II. 253 The torpedo is a flat fish, of the ray tribe, very seldom exceeding twenty inches in length, and twenty pounds in weight...It inhabits the Mediterranean and the North Seas. 1879 E. P. WRIGHT *Anim. Life* 465 The Torpedo (*T. vulgaris*), is found occasionally on the south coasts of England and Ireland.

**b.** *fig.* One who or that which has a benumbing influence.
1590 MARLOWE *Edw. II*, I. iv, Fair queen, forbear to angle for the fish..I mean that vile torpedo, Gaveston. 1762 GOLDSM. *Nash* 34 He used to call a pen his torpedo whenever he grasped it, it numbed all his faculties. *c* 1855 B. S. HOLLIS *Hymn-bk. C'tess Huntingdon's Conn.* Pref., The torpedo of formality had benumbed the churches.

**2.** orig. A case charged with gunpowder designed to explode under water after a given interval so as to destroy any vessel in its immediate vicinity; later also, a self-propelled submarine missile, usually cigar-shaped, carrying an explosive which is fired by impact with its objective.

The original torpedo was a towed or drifting submarine mine, still used to defend channels, harbours, and the like (*drifting* or *moored torpedo*); it was towed at an angle by means of a spar extending at right angles (*otter* or *towing torpedo*), or carried on a ram or projecting pole (*boom-*, *outrigger-*, *spar-torpedo*).

1807 (Aug. 14) W. IRVING *Salmag.* xiii. (1855) 135 A torpedo; by which the stoutest line-of-battle ship..may be..decomposed [i.e. blown up] in a twinkling. 1807 (Sept. 6) *Admiralty Secretary In-Lett.* No. 4353 (P.R.O.) A description of the machine invented by Mr. Robert Fulton for exploding under ships' bottoms and by him called the torpedo. 1810 FULTON *Torpedo War* (N. Y.) 4. 1868 *Daily News* 3 Nov., The particular kind of torpedo used on this occasion is an American invention, which was found very effective in the defence of the harbour of Charleston. 1877 KNIGHT *Dict. Mech.* s.v., The drifting torpedo..is carried against the enemy's works or vessels by the current,..the tide, or..the wind...Anchored torpedoes are attached to mooring piles or anchors. 1880 *Standard* 29 Dec. 6/1 In 1777 a schooner was destroyed in the harbour of New London, Connecticut, by a drifting percussion torpedo.

**3. a.** *Milit.* A shell furnished with a percussion or friction device buried in the ground, which explodes when the ground is trodden upon; a petard. *U.S.* **b.** A toy consisting of fulminating powder and fine gravel wrapped in thin paper, which explodes when thrown on a hard surface. **c.** A cartridge exploded in an oil-well to cause a renewal or increase of the flow. *U.S.* (In use 1873: see *torpedoed* s.v. TORPEDO *v.*) **d.** A detonator placed on a railway line, as a fog-signal, etc. *U.S.*
1786 tr. *Beckford's Vathek* (1883) 127, I will spring mines of serpents and torpedos from beneath them, and we shall soon see the stand they will make against such an explosion. 1831 T. P. JONES *Convers. Chem.* xix. 197 Those dangerous playthings called torpedoes, which explode when thrown upon the floor, derive this property from some preparation of silver. 1877 KNIGHT *Dict. Mech.* s.v., Torpedoes for opening the fissures of oil-wells...4. (*Railway.*) A cartridge placed on a rail to be exploded by a passing train. 1909 *Westm. Gaz.* 28 July 2/1 The use or abuse of Roman candles, paper-caps, display pieces, small crackers, or..torpedoes.

**4.** *attrib.* and *Comb.*; in sense 1, as *torpedo-fish*, *-ray*; esp. *fig.* in allusion to its benumbing power, as *torpedo history*, *narrative*, *quality*, *touch*; *torpedo-like* adv.; in sense 2, as *torpedo armament*, *craft*, *department*, *flat* (FLAT C. 10 b), *-fuse* (Knight *Dict. Mech.* 1877), *-instructor*, *-launch*, *room*, *school*, *-vessel*, *-works*; *torpedo-launching*, *-shaped* adjs.; also **torpedo-anchor**, an anchor for mooring a stationary torpedo (Knight, 1877); **torpedo beard**, a pointed beard; **torpedo-body**, a motor-car body tapered at the ends; **torpedo-boom**, 'a spar bearing a torpedo on its upper end, the lower end swiveled and anchored to the bottom of the channel' (Knight, 1877); **torpedo-catcher**, (*a*) see quot. 1877; (*b*) a torpedo-boat catcher; **torpedo-cruiser**, a cruiser which serves also as a torpedo-boat; **torpedo destroyer**, a torpedo-boat destroyer (officially called simply 'a destroyer'); **torpedo director**, an instrument by which the direction for aiming a locomotive torpedo is determined; **torpedo-drag**, a cable with a grapple or drag for clearing a channel of torpedoes (Knight, 1877); **torpedo gun** = *torpedo-tube*; **torpedo-lieutenant**, a naval officer in charge of torpedoes; **torpedo man**, in the British navy, a man who has passed certain courses of training in torpedo-work, to whom a non-substantive rating is granted; (*U.S.*), one whose business is the clearing of oil-wells by means of torpedoes (see 3 c); **torpedo-net**, a steel-wire netting suspended round a ship on projecting booms as a protection against torpedoes; **torpedo-ram**, a ram (RAM *sb.*[1] 3 c) provided with torpedo-tubes; **torpedo-spar**, a spar rigged to a torpedo boat, to which a torpedo is attached; **torpedo-tube**, a kind of gun from which torpedoes are discharged by compressed air or gunpowder. See also TORPEDO BOAT.
1896 *Daily News* 4 Nov. 7/2 As to the *torpedo armament, it is instructive to quote Commander Bacon's words. 1899 SOMERVILLE & ROSS *Irish R. M.* 29 A saturnine young man with a black *torpedo beard. 1877 KNIGHT *Dict. Mech.*, **Torpedo-catcher*, a forked spar or boom extending under water, ahead of a vessel, to displace or explode torpedoes. 1888 *Encycl. Brit.* XXIII. 451/2 Special vessels, called 'torpedo catchers', are being built by most nations. 1885 *Times* 30 Apr. 10/6 The four first-class *torpedo craft which have hoisted the white ensign are being fitted with Nordenfelt guns. 1901 *Daily Graphic* 12 July 6 The *torpedo-cruiser Kapitan Sacken. 1899 *Westm. Gaz.* 8 Mar. 9/2 The *torpedo destroyer instructional flotilla. 1825 J. NEAL *Bro. Jonathan* I. 29 Lying in wait like a *torpedo-fish. 1885 *Times* 30 Apr. 10/6 Each boat will have five *torpedo guns or tubes. 1845 CARLYLE *Cromwell* (1871) I. 3 Dryasdust, who wishes merely to compile *torpedo Histories. 1878 *N. Amer. Rev.* CXXVII. 384 Dispatched their *torpedo-launches against their intended victim. 1895 *Daily News* 29 May 6/4 She still has..quick-firing guns, and two *torpedo-launching tubes. 1718 *Entertainer* No. 12. 74 'Tis the way to lay waste the Fences of Virtue,..and *Torpedo-like, petrify and benum us. 1839 BAILEY *Festus* xix. (1852) 307 As though to touch but on that topic had, Torpedo-like, numbed thought. 1883 *Century Mag.* July 330/2 The '*torpedo man'..travels about in a light vehicle with his tubes and his nitro-glycerine can. 1885 *Times* 30 Apr. 10/6 The Colossus is coaled and has been fitted with *torpedo nets. 1828 CARLYLE *Misc.* (1857) I. 82 The old man has a *torpedo quality in him. 1877 KNIGHT *Dict. Mech.*, **Torpedo-ram*. 1900 *Daily News* 4 May 2/5 The Polyphemus, torpedo-ram, arrived at Sheerness yesterday from the Mediterranean. 1804 SHAW *Gen. Zool.* V. 297 *Torpedo Ray. 1822–34 *Good's Study Med.* (ed. 4) IV. 214 The torpedo-ray was well known by the Romans to possess this extraordinary power. 1889 WELCH *Text Bk. Naval Archit.* xii. 133 The air finally reaches the under-water *torpedo room. 1899 *Westm. Gaz.* 29 June 1/3 A telephone chamber communicating with the *torpedo-school ship and also with the target. 1903 *Ibid.* 2 July 7/3 The *torpedo-shaped blue Mors cars. 1792 S. ROGERS *Pleas. Mem.* I. 278 What tho' the fiend's *torpedo-touch arrest Each gentler, finer impulse of the breast. 1809–10 COLERIDGE *Friend* I. xvi. (1865) 220 Benumbed into selfishness by the torpedo touch of extreme want. 1898 KIPLING in *Morn. News* 10 Nov. 5/1 We are blessed with a pair of deck *torpedo-tubes, which weigh about ten tons, and are the bane of our lives. 1878 *N. Amer. Rev.* CXXVII. 230 The *torpedo-vessel has been successfully developed.

Hence **Torpe·doic** *a.* (*nonce-wd.*), of a torpedo, like that of a torpedo; **Torpe·doism** (**torpe·dism**), (*a*) action or quality like that of a torpedo or electric ray; (*b*) the use of the torpedo (sense 2) in warfare; **Torpe·doist** (**torpe·dist**), one who is employed or skilled in, or advocates, the use of torpedoes; **Torpe·do-less** *a.*, having no torpedoes.
1893 H. W. LUCY in *Strand Mag.* Feb. 201 Mr. Gladstone leaped to his feet with *torpedoic action and energy. 1845 CARLYLE *Cromwell* (1871) I. 68 Dilettantisms, Dryasdust *Torpedoisms. 1880 *Athenæum* 21 Aug. 242/2 Readers must not expect to find..an elaborate treatise on torpedism, nor..the so-called secret of the Whitehead torpedo. *Ibid.* 242/1 During..1877, the Russian *torpedists made a night attack upon the Ottoman squadron lying off Batoum. 1883 *19th Cent.* May 796 The naval officer should be a perfect navigator, a good artilleryman, torpedoist, and electrician, a steam engineer, &c. 1886 *Pall Mall G.* 29 Dec. 6/2 The command of a small *torpedo-less cruiser in the Indian Ocean.

**Torpe·do**, *v.* [f. prec. sb.]

† **1.** *trans.* To benumb, deaden; = TORPEFY. *Obs.*
1771–2 *Ess. fr. Batchelor* (1773) I. 269 The faculties of that consummate orator..may be torpedoed by that wicked weed, before he has half delivered the following abstract of his sentiments.

**2.** To destroy or damage by means of a torpedo; to attack with a torpedo.
1879 in WEBSTER *Suppl.* 1881 P. ROBINSON *Under the Punkah* 221 If..an ironclad were to be run down, accidentally torpedoed, or suffer from an explosion. 1898 *Westm. Gaz.* 1 Apr. 7/2 In action the battleship would have been torpedoed before she could have fired a gun.

**b.** *fig.* To paralyse, destroy: cf. *to explode*.
1895 SIR W. HARCOURT *Sp. Ho. Comm.* 18 Feb., The consummate speech..might be described as having torpedoed the amendment. 1899 *Folk-Lore* Mar. 105 It seems effectually to have torpedoed the enemies' arguments.

**c.** *intr.* To discharge torpedoes.
1896 *Westm. Gaz.* 15 Jan. 2/1 In four hours they'd be inside the Isle of Wight, torpedoing away right and left.

**d.** *trans.* To lay (a channel, etc.) with torpedoes or submarine mines; to defend with torpedoes.
1877 *Daily News* 16 Nov. 5/7 The Russians are supposed to have immediately torpedoed the river in his front and rear. 1890 *Sat. Rev.* 11 Jan. 29/1 The *canard* that German officers have been torpedoing the Tagus.

**3.** To explode a 'torpedo' at the bottom of (an oil-well) to increase the output by shattering the rock or clearing the passage. Also *intr.* *U.S.*

**1873** [see *torpedoed* below]. **1883** *Century Mag.* July 330/1 When a well fails it is usually 'torpedoed' to start the flow afresh. A long tin tube containing six or eight quarts of nitro-glycerine, is lowered into the hole and exploded by dropping a weight upon it. *Ibid.* 330/2 Sometimes well-owners 'torpedo' their wells..by night to avoid paying the ..price charged by the company.

Hence **Torpe·doed** (-oʊd) *ppl. a.*, **Torpe·doing** *vbl. sb.*; **Torpe·doer** (-oˌəɹ), one who operates torpedoes.

**1873** HOWELLS *Chance Acquaint.* vi, As if I were..an inflammable naiad from a torpedoed well. **1884** *Pall Mall G.* 1 Sept. 8/1 It may be said torpedoing is a game at which two can play. **1903** *Contemp. Rev.* Aug. 186 Captain Sigsbee, formerly commander of the torpedoed 'Maine'. **1905** *Edin. Rev.* Oct. 322 Our torpedoers, operating in the open sea, were at no small disadvantage.

**Torpe·do boat.** A vessel carrying one or more torpedoes; now a small, fast war-ship from which torpedoes are discharged. Hence **Torpedo-boat** *v.* (*nonce-wd.*), *trans.* to furnish or arm with torpedo boats.

**1810** FULTON *Torpedo War* (N. Y.) 44 It would be difficult for a Torpedo boat to depart from any port of America, and return without being detected. **1865** in *Morn. Star* 2 Feb., They took advantage of the storm and darkness to send down a fleet of eight vessels of war and three torpedo boats. **1880** *Standard* 29 Dec. 6/1 The first [torpedo boat] ever known being a very primitive model, invented by Captain David Bushnell, of the Engineer Corps, United States Army, and launched in New York harbour in 1776. **1898** *Harper's Mag.* XCVI. 830 She is building twelve new first-class torpedo-boats and four destroyers. **1884** *Pall Mall G.* 8 Dec. 5/2 To torpedo boat our coast on the German, Russian, or Austrian scale we should require not 100 torpedo boats, but 1,000.

**b.** *attrib.* and *Comb.*, as *torpedo-boat engagement*, *workshop*; **torpedo-boat catcher, torpedo-boat destroyer**, two types of small, fast warships, originally designed to prevent torpedo boats from operating against a fleet.

(The *torpedo-catcher*, officially termed *torpedo-gunboat*, was superseded in 1893 by the *torpedo boat destroyer*, a larger, faster, and more powerful torpedo boat, designed for offensive purposes; the *torpedo boat* being appropriated to coast and harbour defence.)

**1893** *Daily News* 14 Feb. 8/7 They are to be termed Torpedo-boat Destroyers, and in size will be between a torpedo catcher of the sharpshooter class and a first-class torpedo boat. **1899** F. T. BULLEN *Way Navy* 59 But torpedo-boat people are accustomed to put up with many things of which landsmen have little idea. **1901** F. T. JANE in *New Penny Mag.* 30 Nov. 205/1 We had..a number of torpedo-boat catchers, which..were unable to catch the craft they were intended to chase.

**Torpedoic, -ism, -ist**: see after TORPEDO *sb.*

**Torpefy** (tǭ·ɹpĭfəi), *v.* (erron. **torpify**). [ad. L. *torpefacĕre*, f. *torpē-re* to be numb + *facĕre* to make.] *trans.* To render torpid, benumb, deaden, paralyse. Also *fig.* Hence **To·rpefying** *ppl. a.*

**1808** *Nat. Hist.* in *Ann. Reg.* 117/2 The common eel, when equally frozen and torpefied, is capable of being conveyed a thousand miles up the country. **1822–34** *Good's Study Med.* (ed. 4) III. 203 Sternutatories, which exhaust, weaken and torpefy the nerves of smell. *Ibid.* 432 Carbonic acid,..chiefly found in the guise of a torpefying vapour, in close rooms where charcoal has been burnt. **1829** SOUTHEY *Sir T. More* II. 117 To stablish, and to quicken his belief, not to shake, or torpify it. **1875** JOWETT *Plato* (ed. 2) I. 280 Like the flat torpedo fish, who torpifies those who come near him with the touch.

† **To·rpel.** *Obs. rare*⁻¹. [var. of TIRPEIL, *-pell.*] Turmoil, throng of battle, mêlée.

*c* **1400** *Laud Troy Bk.* 16736 Thei put hem certes In gret perel To saue her lord In that torpel. But al was not that thei coude do, For thei no-wyse myght come him to.

† **Torpelness.** *Obs. rare*⁻¹. [app. f. prec. + -NESS.] ? State of turmoil.

*a* **1225** *Ancr. R.* 322 Ure Louerd sulf seid to his deciples ..'Go we eft..into Iudee'. Judee speleð schrift...Galilee speleð hweol, uorte to leren us þet we of þe worldes torpelnesse, & of sunne [= sin's] hweol, ofte gon to schrifte.

**Torpent** (tǭ·ɹpĕnt), *a.* and *sb. rare.* [ad. L. *torpĕnt-em*, pr. pple. of *torpēre* to be torpid.] **a.** *adj.* = TORPID *a.* **b.** *sb. Med.* See quots.

**1647** H. MORE *Song of Soul* Notes 342 Let..anon an universall soul flow into this torpent masse. **1699** EVELYN *Acetaria* (1729) 126 Cresses..quicken the torpent Spirits, and purge the Brain. **1882** OGILVIE (Annandale), *Torpent*, *n.*, a medicine that diminishes the exertion of the irritative motions. **1899** *Syd. Soc. Lex.*, *Torpent*, incapable of the active performance of a function. A medicine or agent that reduces or subdues any irritative action.

† **Torpe·scent,** *a. Obs. rare.* [ad. pr. pple. of L. *torpēscĕre* to become torpid.] That grows torpid; becoming numb. Hence † **Torpe·scence** [see -ENCE], the process of becoming torpid.

*c* **1750** SHENSTONE *Economy* I. 139 Their torpescent soul Clenches their coin. **1784** JOHNSON in *W. Windham's Diary* (1866) 19 Torpescence, much of the faculties of mankind lost in them.

**Torpid** (tǭ·ɹpid), *a.* (*sb.*) Also 7 **torpide**. [ad. L. *torpid-us* benumbed, f. *torpē-re* to be numb.]

**1.** Benumbed; deprived or devoid of the power of motion or feeling; in which activity, animation, or development is suspended; dormant.

**1613** PURCHAS *Pilgrimage* I. v. 22 If he descend not lower, to become torpide and lifelesse. **1621** BURTON *Anat. Mel.* I. iii. III. i, Drinesse, which makes the nerues of the tongue torpid. **1784** COWPER *Task* III. 468 When..November dark Checks vegetation in the torpid plant Expos'd to his cold breath. **1860** EMERSON *Cond. Life, Fate* Wks. (Bohn) II. 323 Some animals became torpid in winter, others were torpid in summer.

**b.** *Path.* Sluggish in action or function.

**1807** *Med. Jrnl.* XVII. 72 Complaints of phlegmatic and torpid constitutions. **1843** SIR C. SCUDAMORE *Med. Visit Gräfenberg* 41 Digestive functions torpid. **1899** *Allbutt's Syst. Med.* VIII. 477 Gout and tendency to torpid liver.

**2.** *fig.* Wanting in animation or vigour; inactive; slow, sluggish; dull; stupefied; apathetic.

**1656** BLOUNT *Glossogr.*, *Torpid*, slow, dull, drowzy, astonied. *a* **1677** HALE *Prim. Orig. Man.* I. ii. 63 They [connatural principles] lye more torpid, and inactive, and inevident. **1703** T. N. *City & C. Purchaser* 92 The Workmen are taken to be torpid Operators. **1764** GOLDSM. *Trav.* 171 No vernal blooms their torpid rocks array. **1778** JOHNSON 9 Apr., in *Boswell*, It is a man's own fault..if his mind grows torpid in old age. **1834** MACAULAY *Ess.*, *Pitt* (1865) I. 293/2 To a small, a torpid, and an unfriendly audience. **1885** DUNCKLEY in *Manch. Weekly Times* 7 Feb. 5/5 In the counties..the population is comparatively torpid and inert.

**3.** Causing torpidity; torporific. *rare.*

**1830** WHITTIER *Frost Spirit* iv, The Frost Spirit comes! and the quiet lake shall feel The torpid touch of his glazing breath, and ring to the skater's heel.

**B.** *sb.* **1.** At Oxford: (*pl.*) The races rowed in Lent term in eight-oared clinker-built open boats: originally designating the boats; later also the crews.

'The "Torpid boats" were originally the second boats of a college, which until 1837 rowed with the "Eights". They are understood to have started *c* 1827, when Christ Church put a second boat on the river; but no record of the name has been found till 1838, when it was app. well established. In that year, the Torpids were made a class by themselves, and raced in the days between the Eight-oared Races (which were not then continuous). In 1852 they were moved to the Lent Term, and reorganized on their present basis.' (W. E. Sherwood.)

**1838** *Trin. Coll. Boat Club Bk.*, It was determined at a meeting of Strokes that no Torpid should put on with the racing boats. **1839** *Oxford Herald* 31 May, A race between the Torpids, or second crews, took place on Thursday Evening. **1839** *O.U.B.C. President's Bk.*, [After the Chart of] The Eights [is one of] The Torpid Races. **1853** 'C. BEDE' *Verdant Green* II. vi, The little gentleman..did not join with the 'Torpids' (as the second boats of a college are called). **1861** HUGHES *Tom Brown at Oxf.* xxvii, The torpids being filled with the refuse of the rowing-men—generally awkward or very young oarsmen. **18..** *Inscr. on picture of Exeter White Boat in O.U.B.C. barge*, 'Presented..by the Honourable John Joclyn, late of Exeter College, and stroke oar of the Torpid in 1827'. **1866** *Oxf. Undergraduates' Jrnl.* 20 Brasenose went head in Torpids as well as Eights. **1869** BRADWOOD *O. V. H.* (1870) 4 He had..done two years hard duty in the college torpid. **1910** *Westm. Gaz.* 24 Feb. 4/1 Oxford 'Torpids'..were so named about 1827, when Christ Church staggered humanity by putting a second crew on the river.

**2.** At Harrow: see quots.

**1903** FARMER & HENLEY *Slang Dict.*, *Torpid* (Harrow), a boy who has not been two years in the school. **1905** H. A. VACHELL *The Hill* ii. 39 Scaife expects us to be Torpids. [*Note*] Boys [at Harrow] who have not been more than two years in the school are eligible as 'torpids'; out of each house a Torpid football eleven is chosen.

**C.** *Comb.* **a.** of the adj., as *torpid-minded*; **b.** of the sb., as *Torpid eight*, *-race.*

**1884** *Pall Mall G.* 19 Feb. (Farmer), Twenty-six *Torpid eights were out at Oxford in training for the races. **1909** *Nation* 18 Sept. 878/2 The average man..may be..less ignorant and *torpid-minded than in the older countries. **1858** 'M. SPLENE' *Almæ Matres* 49, I see myself now..pulling for very life in the *torpid-race.

Hence **To·rpidly** *adv.*, in a torpid manner; **To·rpidness**, torpidity, torpor.

*a* **1677** HALE *Prim. Orig. Man.* I. i. 3 It keeps it from rust and torpidness. **1820** C. R. MATURIN *Melmoth* (1892) III. xxvii. 107 The aged father and mother, retreating torpidly to their seats. **1831** TRELAWNY *Adv. Younger Son* xii, A death-like torpidness came over me. **1845** DAY tr. *Simon's Anim. Chem.* I. 227 The torpidly circulating blood.

**Torpidity** (tɒɹpi·dĭti). [f. prec. + -ITY.] The condition or quality of being torpid; torpor, sluggishness, numbness.

**1614** PURCHAS *Pilgrimage* VII. xi. (ed. 2) 710 You see one Retrograde..vnto a stonie torpiditie they obserued in the same plant. **1772** BARRINGTON in *Phil. Trans.* LXII. 298 As the swallows were found in the winter, they must have been in a state of torpidity. **1843** R. J. GRAVES *Syst. Clin. Med.* xxx. 388 A torpidity of the kidneys supervened. **1887** A. BIRRELL *C. Brontë* ix. 100 In a world of torpidities any rapid moving thing is hailed somewhat extravagantly.

**Torpitude** (tǭ·ɹpitiūd). Now *rare.* [Irregularly for **torpetude*, f. L. *torpē-re* + -TUDE: the L. form, if existent, would be **torpetūdo*: cf. *consuētūdo*, *hebetūdo*. (Perh. by false analogy with *turpitude*, f. L. *turpi-s*.)] = TORPIDITY.

**1713** DERHAM *Phys.-Theol.* IV. vii. 158 In a Torpitude, or sort of Sleep, or middle state between Life and Death. **1788** JEFFERSON *Writ.* (1859) II. 396 The Russians seem not yet thawed from the winter's torpitude. **1817** J. GILCHRIST *Intell. Patrimony* 24 His Elysian torpitude of many weeks duration. **1822–34** *Good's Study Med.* (ed. 4) IV. 105 In some cases there is great torpitude or sluggishness in the growth..of the ovaries.

**Torple, turple,** *v. Obs.* exc. *dial.* [Early ME.: origin obscure. Cf. TOPPLE *v.* and TORFLE.]

† **1.** *intr.* To fall, tumble; = TOPPLE *v.* I. *Obs.*

*a* **1225** *Ancr. R.* 266 Ant, ȝif a miracle nere..heo hefde iturpled [*v.r.* torplet] mid him, boðe hors & lode, adun into helle grunde. *Ibid.* 322 Mid al þet schendlac, þu schalt trussen & al torplen into helle. *Ibid.* 324.

**2.** Of an animal: To die; = TORFLE. *dial.*

**1876** *Mid-Yorksh. Gloss.*, *Torple*,..*Turple*,..*Torfle*,..or *Turfle*, *v.n.*, to die. The term is only used in connection with animals.

**Torpor** (tǭ·ɹpǫɹ). [a. L. *torpor*, *-ōrem*, f. *torpēre* to be numb.] Torpid condition or quality; torpidity. **a.** Absence or suspension of motive power, activity, or feeling; † inertia (*obs.*); suspended animation or development; in *Path.* morbid inertia or insensibility, stupor.

**1626** BACON *Sylva* § 763 Motion doth discusse the Torpour of Solide Bodies Which..have in them a Natural Appetite, not to move at all. **1681** tr. *Willis' Rem. Med. Wks.* Vocab., *Torpor*, a numness, heaviness,..and unaptness for any motion. **1774** GOLDSM. *Nat. Hist.* (1862) I. v. 443 Strictly speaking.., these animals cannot be said to sleep during the winter; it may be called rather a *torpor*, a stagnation of all the faculties. *a* **1854** H. REED *Lect. Brit. Poets* ii. (1857) 63 Why does the earth break forth from its winter's torpor in all the luxuriance of Spring?

**b.** *transf.* Intellectual or spiritual lethargy; apathy, listlessness; dullness; indifference.

[*a* **1225** *Ancr. R.* 202 Þe Bore of heui Slouhðe haueð þeos hweolpes: Torpor is þe uorme þet is wlech heorte..þe oðer is Pusillinimitas.] **1607** *Schol. Disc. agst. Antichr.* I. i. 38 What meaneth our torpor? what our frozen coldnesse in zeal? **1789** BELSHAM *Ess.* I. xvii. 333 A universal torpor of the mental faculties must take place. **1878** LECKY *Eng. in 18th C.* I. i. 62 That intellectual torpor which we are accustomed to associate with ecclesiastical domination.

**c.** Comb., as *torpor-shedding* adj.

**1806** J. GRAHAME *Birds Scot.*, etc. 140 Till noon-tide pour the torpor-shedding ray.

**Torporific** (tǭɹpŏri·fik), *a.* (*sb.*) [ad. L. type **torpōrific-us*, f. *torpōr-em* TORPOR + *-ficus* making: see -FIC.] Causing torpor; producing numbness; paralysing; also *fig.* stupefying, deadening. † *Torporific eel*, the gymnotus or electric eel (*obs.*).

**1769** E. BANCROFT *Guiana* 190 There is one of the Eel tribe,..which I shall beg leave to call the Torporific Eel. **1825** *New Monthly Mag.* XV. 77/2 The torporific sway of Austria. **1852** *Fraser's Mag.* XLV. 632 Galen..tells the Torpedo affects by a torporific action peculiar to itself.

**b.** *absol.* as *sb.* Something causing torpor.

**1840** MANNING *Let.* in Purcell *Life* (1895) I. ix. 169, I find the want of such opportunities of conversation a great torporific.

**Torporize** (tǭ·ɹpŏrəiz), *v.* [f. TORPOR + -IZE.] *intr.* To cause torpor. Hence **To·rporizing** *ppl. a.*

**1822** *New Monthly Mag.* VI. 223/2 The..torporizing effects of the Lancastrian system of education.

† **To·rpulent,** *a. Obs. rare*⁻¹. [irreg. f. TORPOR, after *corpulent*, etc.: see -ULENT.] Torpid. So † **To·rpulency** *Obs. rare*⁻¹, torpidity, torpor.

**1657** REEVE *God's Plea* 350 Lay aside neglect, awake from torpulency. *Ibid.* 142 Our prayers do show, what an oscitant and torpulent people we are.

**Torquate** (tǭ·ɹkweit), *a. Zool.* [ad. L. *torquāt-us* adorned with or wearing a *torques*: see TORQUES and -ATE [2].] Having a ring-like marking, formed by hairs or feathers of special colour or texture, round the neck; collared.

**1661** LOVELL *Hist. Anim. & Min.* Introd., The pigeon, ring-dove,..wild, torquate, juglandine.

**To·rquated,** *a.* [f. as prec. + -ED [1].]

**1.** Wearing a torque: see TORQUE [1].

**1623** COCKERAM, *Torquated*, one wearing a chaine. **1656** BLOUNT, *Torquated*.., that weares a collar or chain.

**2.** Formed as or like a torque; twisted from a narrow strip or band.

**1851** D. WILSON *Preh. Ann.* (1863) I. 113 The parish of Shapinsay..in which was found a beautiful torquated ring. *Ibid.* II. vi. 470 The discovery of..torquated neck and arm rings. *Ibid.* II. IV. iii. 258 The torquated hoop.

**3.** *Zool.* = TORQUATE. **1891** in *Cent. Dict.*

**Torque** [1], **torc** (tǭɹk). Also **tork**. [ad. L. *torquēs*, *-is* (see TORQUES); so mod.F. *torque*.] A collar, necklace, bracelet, or similar ornament consisting of a twisted narrow band or strip, usually of precious metal, worn especially by the ancient Gauls and Britons.

**1834** PLANCHÉ *Brit. Costume* 10 The Britons..who could not procure them of the precious metals wore torques of iron. **1851** D. WILSON *Preh. Ann.* (1863) II. IV. vi. 472 The torc may be regarded as the most characteristic relic of primitive Celtic and Teutonic art. **1877** LL. JEWITT *Half-hrs. among Eng. Antiq.* 226 Having torn a torque of gold from the neck of a vanquished Gaul.

*attrib.* **1877** W. JONES *Finger-ring* 66 This might be denominated a torque ring.

**Torque** [2]. *Physics.* [f. L. *torquēre* to twist.] The twisting or rotary force in a piece of mechanism (as a measurable quantity); the moment of a system of forces producing rotation.

**1884** (Apr.) JAS. THOMSON in *Sci. Papers* (1912) p. civ. **1884** S. P. THOMPSON *Dynamo-electric Mach.* xvii. 308 The torque or turning-moment is, in a series dynamo, both when used as a generator and when used as a motor, very nearly proportional to the current. **1906** *Daily Chron.* 21 Apr. 3/7 Torque is the amount of force in a rotary direction—the power of the twist. If you hold one end of a rod and I hold the other, and I twist it round in your hands, that is because I am giving it a torque greater than you can resist. **1907** *Installation News* Oct. 9/1 This small boss takes up the torque due to screwing up the tube.

**b.** A proposed unit of this: see quot.

**1899** JUDE *Physics, Exper. & Theor.* I. I. i. § 46. 33 In the French system, the absolute unit of moment would be the moment of a force of one dyne, about a point at one centimetre perpendicular distance from its line of action; this unit we shall call one *torque*.

**c.** *attrib.* and *Comb.*

**1907** *Westm. Gaz.* 9 Nov. 16/2 The propeller shaft casing ..fitted with a massive hinged bracket to form its own torque rod. **1909** *Ibid.* 30 Nov. 5/1 Intended as a torque-increasing mechanism to propel motor-cars within reasonable limits without the intervention of change-speed gears.

**Torqued** (tǭɹkt), *a.* Also 6 **torquet.** [after obs. F. *torqué*, pa. pple. of *torquer*, ad. L. *torquēre* to twist: see -ED [1].]

**1.** Twisted, convoluted; formed like a torque.

**1577** D. SETTLE *M. Frobisher's Voy.* II. in Hakluyt *Voy.* (1589) 625 We found a dead fishe..which had in his nose a horne streight and torquet, of length two yardes lacking two ynches. **1857** *Archæologia* XXXVII. 102 A pair of ear-rings of base silver, the large torqued circles of which were closed by a sort of hook and eye.

**2.** *Her.* Twisted or bent into a double curve like the letter S: said of a serpent or dolphin used as a bearing. (In quot. 1572 app. Bent into a coiled form.)

**1572** BOSSEWELL *Armorie* II. 63 b, The fielde is of the Saphyre, a Serpente torqued, Topace. **1688** R. HOLME *Armoury* III. xvii. (Roxb.) 119/1 A Fasce, or fiue arrowes in fasce, with a serpent Torqued about the same. *c* **1828** [see TORGANT]. **1894** *Parker's Gloss. Her.*, *Torqued*, bowed-embowed, especially of a serpent's tail; also *wreathed.*

‖**Torques** (tǭɹkwīz), *sb.* and *a.* Also 6 **torquess,** 7, 9 **torquis.** [L. *torquēs*, *torquis* a twisted neck-chain or collar, f. *torquēre* to twist.]

**A.** *sb.* **1.** = TORQUE [1].

**1693** PEPYS in *Lett. Lit. Men* (Camden) 211 Your account of the *Torquis* spoken of in your..Letter. **1695** GIBSON *Add. to Camden* 658 In..1692 an ancient golden Torques was dug up..near this castle of Harlech. **1778** *Eng.Gazetteer* (ed. 2) s. v. *Pattingham*, Where, in 1700, was found a large torques of fine gold, 2 feet long, 3 pounds 2 ounces weight. ..These torqueses were worn by the ancient Britons. **1865** *Pall Mall G.* 24 Oct. 5 There is no torques, no finger ring ..nothing but 'the seal of Tirhaka, King of Æthiopians'.

**2.** *Zool.* A collar or ring-like marking round the neck of an animal, formed by hair, feathers, etc. of special colour or texture. **1891** in *Cent. Dict.*

† **B.** *adj.* Twisted, bent. *Obs. rare*$^{-1}$.

*a* **1568** WEDDERBURN in *Bannatyne Poems* 695/27 With ane bow torquess diuerss Greikis did scho kill.

**Torr(e,** obs. form of TOR *sb.*

† **Torrefa·cted,** *ppl. a. Obs. rare.* (*irreg.* **torri-.**) [f. L. *torrefact-us*, pa. pple. of *torrefacĕre* to TORREFY + -ED [1].] Torrefied, roasted.

**1601** HOLLAND *Pliny* XXX. viii. II. 385 Sheepes tallow incorporat with salt torrifacted.

**Torrefaction** (tǭrĭfæ·kʃən). [n. of action f. L. *torrefacĕre* to TORREFY: see -TION and cf. F. *torréfaction.*] The process of drying or roasting by fire; the state or condition of being roasted.

**1612** WOODALL *Surg. Mate* Wks. (1653) 274 Torrefaction like siccation, but more violent. **1648** BP. HALL *Serm. at Higham* Rem. Wks. (1660) 196 Here was not a scorching and blistering but a vehement and full torrefaction. **1758** REID tr. *Macquer's Chym.* I. 155 The term calcination is generally used to express this torrefaction of antimony. **1829** TOGNO & DURAND *Man. Mat. Med.* 189 The torrefaction to which coffee is subjected..gives it a light brown colour. **1839** DE QUINCEY *Casuistry Rom. Meals* Wks. 1859 III. 252 Ping..now for the first time tasted it [pig] in a state of torrefaction.

**Torrefica·tion** (torri-), erron. form for prec.

**1763** HORNE in *Phil. Trans.* LIII. 53, I gave it a very powerful torrification (or roasting). **1853** SOYER *Pantroph.* 314 The Italians extract from cocoa more exalted qualities by torrefication.

**Torrefied** (tǭ·rĭfəid), *ppl. a.* [f. TORREFY *v.* + -ED [1].] Roasted; dried or parched by the action of fire; scorched.

**1612** WOODALL *Surg. Mate* Wks. (1653) 21* Any torrified or dry powdred medicaments. **1670** CAPT. J. SMITH *Eng. Improv. Reviv'd* 290 Some torrefied Rhubarb. **1796** KIRWAN *Elem. Min.* (ed. 2) II. 373 He also extracted Copper from the torrefied Ore. **1829** TOGNO & DURAND *Man. Mat. Med.* 189 The stimulating influence of torrefied coffee. **1857** MILLER *Elem. Chem.* (1862) III. 99 This soluble torrefied starch is known under the name of British gum.

**Torrefy** (tǭ·rĭfəi), *v.* Also *irreg.* **torrify.** [a. F. *torréfi-er* (1566 in Hatz.-Darm.), ad. L. *torrefacĕre* to dry by heat, f. *torrēre* to dry, parch, roast + *facĕre* to make: see -FY. (The spelling *torrify* follows *terrify, horrify.*)]

**1.** *trans.* To roast, scorch, or dry by fire.

**1601** HOLLAND *Pliny* XXIII. Proem II. 147 To bring it into ashes, it must bee torrified in an oven. **1661** LOVELL *Hist. Anim. & Min.* Introd., It's hardly concocted..and torrifieth the bloud. **1819** H. BUSK *Banquet* I. 234 The housewives..on the embers torrify their cake. **1883** R. HALDANE *Workshop Receipts* II. 159/2 Taking care not to torrefy them too much.

**b.** To deprive of all moisture by heating, as a chemical or drug.

**1601** HOLLAND *Pliny* XXVII. iv. II. 272 It [Aloe] ought to be torrefied in an earthen vessell. *Ibid.* XXXI. x. 422 Torrifie nitre untill it begin to looke blacke. **1713** *Phil. Trans.* XXVIII. 230 They torrify a Spoonful of white Cummin-seed.

**c.** *Metallurgy.* To roast, as ores, in order to deprive of sulphur, arsenic, or other volatile substance.

**1686** PLOT *Staffordsh.* 188 *Pyrites aureus* (which if torrefy'd..prove all Iron Ores). **1806** FORSYTH *Beauties Scotl.* III. 100 To prepare iron-stone for the furnace, it must be roasted, or torrified, to expell all volatile matters. **1840** *Civil Eng. & Arch. Jrnl.* III. 415/1 It contains carbonaceous matter enough to torrify the stone and make it fit for the furnace.

**2.** *intr.* To become reduced to a cinder or ash; to become calcined.

**1615** CROOKE *Body of Man* 89 This Fat..is not melted by fire, but rather torrifieth.

† **Torrelite** (tǫ·rĕləit). *Min.* [Named after Dr. J. Torrey: see -LITE.] Obs. syn. of COLUMBITE.

**1836** T. THOMSON in *R. D. & T. Thomson's Rec. Gen. Sc.* IV. 408 Torrelite. I give this name to the new species, which I have just received from New York, by the liberality and kindness of Dr. Torrey.

**Torrent** (tǫ·rĕnt), *sb.* (*a.*) [a. F. *torrent* (*a* 1200 in Godef. *Compl.*), ad. L. *torrĕnt-em* burning, boiling, rushing, impetuous, pr. pple. of *torrēre* to scorch, burn; also as sb. a torrent. Cf. the sense-transition of L. *æstus* fire, fierce heat, the surging or flowing of the sea, the tide.]

**1.** A stream of water flowing with great swiftness and impetuosity, whether from the steepness of its course, or from being temporarily flooded; more esp. applied (as in Fr.) to a mountain stream which at times is full of rushing water and at other times is more or less dry: cf. WINTER-BOURN.

[**1398** TREVISA *Barth. De P. R.* XIII. iii. (Bodl. MS.), Of ryuers beþ twei manere kindes..one is icleped a lyuynge ryuer; þat oþer manere ryuer hatte Torreens and is a water þat comeþ wiþ swifte rees and passeþ; and hatte torrens for it creseþ in grete rayne and fordruyeþ in druye wedeir. **1506** GUYLFORDE *Pilgr.* (Camden) 31 So firste we come to Torrens Cedron, which in somer tyme is drye. [Cf. Vulgate *John* xviii. 1, trans torrentem Cedron, in *Lindisf. gl.* ꝥ uinterburna cedron.]] **1601** SHAKS. *Jul. C.* I. ii. 107 The Torrent roar'd, and we did buffet it With lusty Sinewes. **1609** BIBLE (Douay) *Gen.* xxvi. Comm., *Torrent*, the chanel where sometimes a vehement streame runneth, sometimes none at al. **1697** DRYDEN *Virg. Georg.* I. 160 The wary Ploughman, on the Mountain's Brow, Undams his watry Stores, huge Torrents flow. **1760** JOHNSON *Idler* No. 97 ⁋ 5 He observed among the hills many hollows worn by torrents. **1835** THIRLWALL *Greece* I. i. 14 The *Ilissus*..is a mere brook, which is sometimes swollen into a torrent. **1856** STANLEY *Sinai & Pal.* vii. 299 This green thread is the course of the torrent now called Kelt, possibly the ancient Cherith. **1858** HAWTHORNE *Fr. & It. Note-Bks.* I. 247 We discerned the dry beds of mountain torrents, which had lived too fierce a life to let it be a long one.

**2. a.** *fig.* A violent or tumultuous flow, onrush, or 'stream', e.g. of words, feelings, opposition, etc.; a 'flood'.

**1647** CLARENDON *Hist. Reb.* I. § 1 Those, who out of Duty and Conscience have opposed..that Torrent which did overwhelm them. *Ibid.* § 70 The torrent of his Impetuous Passions. **1784** MME. D'ARBLAY *Let.* 14 Nov., She poured forth again a torrent of abuse. **1826** MARGRAVINE OF ANSPACH *Mem.* I. viii. 304 He was forced to follow the torrent of his notes [in music]. **1845** S. AUSTIN *Ranke's Hist. Ref.* I. 249 The near approach of the resistless torrent of Turkish power.

**b.** *transf.* A forcible stream or rushing body (of various physical things, as lava, loose stones, wind, light); also, a violent downpour of rain.

**1781** MORE in *Phil. Trans.* LXXII. 52 The force of those violent torrents of wind. **1806–7** J. BERESFORD *Miseries Hum. Life* (1826) II. xiv, A soaking torrent of rain. **1821** R. TURNER *Arts & Sc.* (ed. 18) 37 Torrents of smoke and of flames, rivers of melted metals. **1839** DE QUINCEY *Recoll. Lakes* Wks. 1862 II. 11 The moon arose, and shed a torrent of light upon the Langdale fells. **1840** R. H. DANA *Bef. Mast* x. 23 The rain coming down in torrents. **1858** LARDNER *Hand-bk. Nat. Phil.* 360 The torrents of liquid lava which flow from volcanos. **1860** TYNDALL *Glac.* I. viii. 58 A torrent of what appeared to me to be stones and mud.

**c.** A mass of hanging foliage, drapery, etc. resembling in appearance a descending stream.

**1864** LOWELL *Fireside Trav.* 284 A cliff over which the ivy pours in torrents. **1880** 'OUIDA' *Moths* II. 271 A loose white gown that was all torrents and cascades of lace.

**3.** *attrib.* and *Comb.* **a.** Simple attrib., as *torrent-action, -bed, -flood, -line, -scar, -sound, -stream, -voice, -water*; *torrent-wise* adv.; **b.** objective, as *torrent-braving* adj.; **c.** instrumental, as *torrent-bitten, -borne* adjs.; **d.** similative, etc., as *torrent-like, -mad* adjs. **e.** Special combs.: **torrent-bow**, a rainbow formed in the spray of a torrent; **torrent-duck**, any species of duck of the South American genus *Merganetta.*

**1856** KANE *Arct. Expl.* II. xiv. 150 The evidences of *torrent-action were unequivocal. **1867** LADY HERBERT *Cradle L.* vii. 203 We rode through this same *torrent-bed, at this time of the year, dry. **1863** ATKINSON *Stanton Grange* (1864) 258 The huge sweeping wave whirling the *torrent-borne sticks and boughs. **1832** TENNYSON *Pal. of Art* ix, In misty folds, that, floating as they fell, Lit up a *torrent-bow. **1777** WARTON *Odes* VIII. vi, The foam-beat pier, and *torrent-braving mound. **1899** *Camb. Nat. Hist.* IX. 116 This peculiar and tame *torrent-duck is rarely seen on the sea, though it can fly from one gorge to another. **1825** J. WILSON *Poems* II. 209 Each misty cataract, and *torrent-flood. **1769** PENNANT *Zool.* III. 241 Salmon..gain the sources of the Lapland rivers in spite of their *torrent-like currents. **1865** ALEX. SMITH *Summ. Skye* I. 287 They stand with all their scars and *torrent-lines bare to the blue heavens. **1728** D. MALLET *Excurs.* Wks. 1759 I. 92 A hundred *torrent-streams, Each ploughing up its bed. **1898** *Westm. Gaz.* 1 Nov. 7/2 The feeding torrents might be diverted or blocked, and the Abyssinian *torrent-water might be so interfered with as largely to deprive the river of the fertilising matter which it carries in suspension. **1862** CARLYLE *Fredk. Gt.* XII. xii. III. 379 These..fly *torrent-wise along the winds.

**B.** *adj.* Rushing like a torrent.

**1667** MILTON *P. L.* II. 581 Fierce Phlegeton, Whose waves of torrent fire inflame with rage. **1859** TENNYSON *Enid* 1020 As one That listens near a torrent mountain-brook.

Hence **To·rrentful** *a.*, full of torrent or rush of words (whence **To·rrentfulness**); **To·rrentless** *a.*, void of torrents.

**1873** SYMONDS *Grk. Poets* Ser. I. vi. 162 The *torrent-fulness, the intoxicating charm of Pindar. **1911** B. W. BACON in *Expositor* Mar. 205 The rainless, *torrentless, alluvial valley of the Nile.

**Torrential** (tǫre·nʃăl), *a.* [f. L. *torrĕnt-em* TORRENT + -IAL: cf. *tangential.*]

**1.** Of, pertaining to, or of the nature of a torrent; produced by the action of a torrent.

*Torrential months*, months characterized by torrents.

**1861** J. H. BENNET *Winter Medit.* I. i. (1875) 11 A series of hills..rent by numerous ravines and torrential valleys. **1873** J. GEIKIE *Gt. Ice Age* xxvi. 362 The denuded and partially rearranged portions of old torrential gravel and sand. **1880** V. BALL *Jungle Life in India* ii. 57 These rivers are..fed by thousands of torrential streams which, when there is no rain, completely dry up. **1892** *Daily Graphic* 8 Jan. 7/3 The torrential months of January and February.

**2.** Like a torrent in rapidity or violence; torrent-like; rushing; falling in torrents, as rain.

**1849** *Fraser's Mag.* XL. 605 No eddying groups; no torrential processions. **1863** TYNDALL *Heat* 388 The condensation of the vapour, and its torrential descent to the earth. **1865** *Morn. Star* 21 July, To the intense heat,..has succeeded torrential rain. **1894** *Scotsman* 27 Aug. 7 A rainstorm which the newfangled appellation 'torrential' only feebly describes.

**b.** *fig.* As copious or impetuous as a torrent.

**1877** D. M. WALLACE *Russia* xxv. 396 The poetasters poured forth their feelings with torrential recklessness. **1879** G. MEREDITH *Egoist* III. xiv. 293 He could woo, he was a torrential wooer. **1897** in *Academy* 13 Mar. 308/2 A man of torrential eloquence. **1909** *Blackw. Mag.* Aug. 232/1 They broke and fled with the British in torrential pursuit.

Hence **Torrentiality** (tǫrenʃiˌæ·lĭti), torrential character or condition; **Torre·ntially** *adv.*, in a torrential way; in torrents, or like a torrent.

**1882** PROCTOR in *Nat. Stud.* (N. Y.) 52 Since the woods were cleared the rain falls more torrentially than before. **1891** *Cent. Dict.*, Torrentiality. **1901** *Daily Chron.* 4 Nov. 5/7 To the stern, where sailors and marines rushed torrentially, called for 'three cheers, and one cheer more'.

† **Torrentille.** *Obs. rare*$^{-1}$. App. var. of next.

*c* **1460** J. RUSSELL *Bk. Nurture* 548 ȝiff ye haue salt purpose, ȝele, torrentille, deynteithus fulle dere, Ye must do afture þe forme of frumenty, as y said while ere.

† **To·rrentine,** *sb. Obs. rare*$^{-1}$. [In note to passage quoted, said to corresp. to an Ital. *torrentina*, a fish so called because it abounds in mountain streams.] A kind of fish; perh. trout.

*c* **1460** J. RUSSELL *Bk. Nurture* 835 in *Babees Bk.* (1868) 173 Vynegur is good to salt purpose & torrentyne, Salt sturgeon, salt swyrd-fysche savery & fyne.

† **To·rrentine,** *a. Obs. rare.* [f. L. *torrĕnt-em* TORRENT + -INE [1].] (See quot.)

**1656** BLOUNT *Glossogr.*, *Torrentine*, belonging to, or abiding in torrents, or swift and violent streames. **1864** in WEBSTER; and in later Dicts.

**Torrentuous** (tǫre·ntiuˌəs), *a.* [= mod.F. *torrentueux* (neologism in Littré), f. L. *torrĕnt-em* TORRENT: see -UOUS, and cf. *tempestuous.*] Torrent-like, impetuous.

**1840** THACKERAY *Paris Sk.-bk.* vii. *Fr. Fash. Novels*, Wks. 1900 V. 84 My affairs whirl onwards together in such a torrentuous [orig. *torrentueux*] galopade. **1897** F. THOMPSON in *Academy* 6 Feb. 180/2 Womanly and unstayed of nature, torrentuous of golden talk.

**Torrepine**: see TERRAPIN.

**Torret, turret.** *Obs.* or *dial.* Forms: 4–5 **toret,** 5 **torett, touret,** 5–6 **torrett, turet(t,** **turrett,** 5–8 **torret,** 6 (9) **turret.** [ME. *toret*, *touret*, a. OF. *toret*, dim. of *tor* (12th c.), *tour* a round, circuit, circle, ring: see TOUR. From the 15th c. this word is also found as *ter(r)et, tyret, tyrret*, which in senses b and d are the ordinary forms: see TERRET.] **a.** A swivel ring on a dog's collar by which a string can be attached.

*c* **1386** CHAUCER *Knt.'s T.* 1294 Aboute his Chaar ther wenten white Alauntz..with mosel faste ybounde Colored of gold, and tourettes [*v.rr.* turrettes, torettys, torettes, torretes, turettes, toretz] fyled rounde. **1552** HULOET, Turret of a dogges collare, *vertibulum.*

**b.** Each of the two rings by which the leash is attached to the jesses of a hawk. See TERRET b.

[Cf. *c* **1247** *Emperor Fredk. II's* '*De arte venandi cum avibus*' (1596) II. xl. (*heading*) De tornetto, qualiter factum sit, et ad quid sit utile.]

**c.** A ring or the like, often moving on a swivel, whereby an object can be attached to a chain.

*c* **1391** CHAUCER *Astrol.* I. § 2 Thyn Astrelabie hath a ring to putten on the t[h]owmbe of thy ryht hand in takyng the heyhte of thynges...This ring rennyth in A Maner turet, fast to the Moder of thyn Astrelabie. **1463** *Bury Wills* (Camden) 16 My lityll bagge of blakke ledyr with a cheyne and toret of siluyr. **1554** in *Shropsh. Par. Doc.* (1903) 55 For three cheynes and two turettes for the sensor viij[d]. **1900** *N. & Q.* 9th Ser. VI. 235/2 Turettes, tirrets, tirets, or tyrritts, swivels (of metal), a term also used in heraldry. In the trickings of arms in many early heraldic MSS. these are represented as a ring at the end of a chain. **1910** *Let. to Editor*, The term 'turret' (pronounced 'torret') is still in use at Winterton, North Lincolnsh., though obsolescent, to indicate the bow and pendant of a watch case. The word is used principally by farm men.

It is the local name for the swivel with which all plough traces are furnished to prevent them from becoming twisted.

**d.** In horse-harness, A ring on the harness of a horse through which a rein passes: see TERRET d.

*1429–30 Durham Acc. Rolls* (Surtees) 230 In iiij Renes, ij colers de coreo novis cum Turettes emptis. 1849 DE QUINCEY *Eng. Mail Coach* Wks. 1863 IV. 306 Inspecting professionally the buckles, the straps, and the silvery turrets of his harness. [*Note*] The little devices through which the reins are made to pass.. This same word.. I heard uniformly used by many scores of illustrious mail-coachmen.

**Torret**, obs. form of TURRET.

**Torricellian** (tǫritʃe·liăn, tǫrise·liăn), *a.* [f. the name of *Torricelli*, an Italian physicist (1608–1647) + -AN.] Of or belonging to Torricelli.

*Torricellian experiment*, that by which, in 1643, Torricelli proved that the column of mercury in an inverted closed tube is supported by the pressure of the atmosphere on the mercury in the vessel, and that the height of the column corresponds exactly to the atmospheric pressure. *Torricellian tube*, early name for the tube of the mercurial barometer. *Torricellian vacuum*, the vacuum above the mercurial column in the barometer, produced by filling the tube with mercury and then inverting it in a cup of mercury.

1660 BOYLE *New Exp. Phys. Mech.* xvii. 123 We are unwilling to examine any further the Inferences wont to be made from the Torricellian Experiment. 1663 — *Usef. Exp. Nat. Philos.* I. iv. 69 Nor did it appear that by repeated Suctions.. it could at all be rais'd above the seven and twenty Digits at which it us'd to subsist in the Torrecellian Experiment *De Vacuo*. *a* 1680 BUTLER *Rem.* (1759) I. 162 Or measuring of Air upon Parnassus With Cylinders of Torricellian Glasses. 1682 H. MORE *Annot. Glanvill's Lux O.* 130 The Quicksilver in a Torricellian Tube will sink deeper in an higher or clearer Air. 1812 SIR H. DAVY *Chem. Philos.* 97 Even the best Torricellian vacuum must contain elastic matter. 1812–16 PLAYFAIR *Nat. Phil.* (1819) I. 243 The weight of air is known from the Torricellian experiment, or that of the barometer. 1835 *Penny Cycl.* III. 483/2 It is a Torricellian barometer.

**Torrid** (tǫ·rid), *a.* Also 7 *erron.* **torred.** [ad. L. *torrid-us*, f. *torrēre* to dry with heat: see -ID. Cf. F. *torride* (Rabelais 1546), Sp., Pg. *tórrido, -a*, It. *torrido, -a.*]

**1.** Scorched, burned, exposed to great heat; also, intensely hot, burning, scorching.

1611 COTGR., *Torride*, torride, scorched, burned, parched; also,..dried by the extremitie of heat. 1613 PURCHAS *Pilgrimage* VIII. i. 603 A torrid and scorched earth. 1658 J. ROBINSON *Endoxa* ix. 48 Exotick simples..corrupted by the long and torrid space of the Voyage. 1667 MILTON *P. L.* XII. 634 Fierce as a Comet; which with torrid heat ..Began to parch that temperate Clime. 1798 CANNING in *Anti-Jacobin* No. 27. 146 All in the town of Tunis, In Africa the torrid. 1809 BYRON *Ch. Har.* I. xxviii. *note*, Such torrid weather. 1876 MERIVALE *Rom. Triumvirates* vii. (1877) 146 The march through this torrid and trackless region occupied seven days.

**b.** *esp.* in *torrid zone*, the region of the earth between the tropics. (Orig. in L. form, *torrida zona* or *zona torrida*; cf. Virg. *Georg.* I. 234.)

[1398 TREVISA *Barth. De P. R.* XI. iii. (Bodl. MS.), Þe cercle þat hatte Torrida zona [L. orig. *a* 1350] vnder þe whiche þe sonne meueþ alwei. 1553 EDEN *Treat. Newe Ind.* (Arb.) 33 The burning lyne called *Zona Torrida.*] 1586 MARLOWE *1st Pt. Tamburl.* IV. iv, Thence by land unto the torrid zone. 1794 SULLIVAN *View Nat.* I. 156 Why, under the torrid zone, have the little islands a temperature always supportable..? 1834 MRS. SOMERVILLE *Connex. Phys. Sc.* xxvii. 272 In the valleys of the torrid zone, where the mean annual temperature is very high.

**c.** *transf.* Inhabiting the torrid zone.

1771 PENNANT *Syn. Quadr.* 297 Torrid jerboa.

†**d.** Of colour: Burned, blackened with burning.

1634 SIR T. HERBERT *Trav.* 24 Their colour is (answerable to the Zone they breathe in) blacke and Torrid. 1650 CHARLETON *Paradoxes* 18 It grows not black and torrid.. by the affriction of the Saphire.

**2.** *fig.* **a.** In reference to the 'heat' of persecution, or sometimes to the burning of heretics.

*a* 1635 CORBET *Poems* (1807) 48 Had shee bin then In Maryes torrid dayes engend'red, when Cruelty was witty. 1702 C. MATHER *Magn. Chr.* III. I. iii. (1852) 316 The countries which the bloody Popish inquisition has made a clime too torrid for a Protestant.

**b.** Hot in temper or passion; ardent, zealous, enthusiastic.

1646 CRASHAW *Steps to Temple* 84 Temper'd 'twixt cold despair and torrid joy. 1685 in Maidment *Bk. Scott. Pasquils* (1868) 287 But I was ne'er in love so torrid As to miscarry with my mate. 1909 *Nation* 16 Oct. 129/2 Mr. Finck is about as torrid a hot gospeller as one could meet with.

Hence **To·rridly** *adv.*; **To·rridness.**

1657 R. LIGON *Barbadoes* (1673) 9 Finding the Air so *torridly hot, I thought good to make tryal of the water. 1638 SIR T. HERBERT *Trav.* (ed. 2) 36 The [ayre] inflamed by the *torriddnesse of the Zone. *a* 1656 USSHER *Ann.* vi. (1658) 271 Their horses being all spent.. with the length and torridnesse of the way.

**Torridity** (tǫri·dĭti). [f. prec. + -ITY, corresp. to a L. type *torriditās.] The state, condition, or quality of being torrid; intense heat.

1846 in WORCESTER. 1890 *Columbus* (Ohio) *Dispatch* 23 June *heading*, Torridity likely to continue for the coming 24 hours. 1901 *Wide World Mag.* VIII. 131/1 There is no relief by night from the torridity of the daylight hours.

**Torrify**, erron. form of TORREFY.

†**To·rrion.** *Obs.* [a. obs. F. *torrion*, ad. It. *torrione* 'any great towre, or strong keepe' (Florio), augm. of *torre* tower.] A large tower (in Italy).

1652 HOWELL *Giraffi's Rev. Naples* II. 144 Hereupon there went off from the Torrion of Carmine, twenty six shot of Ordinance. *Ibid.* 191 That the said Torrion or Bastion should be put into his hands.

**Torrit**, obs. form of TOWERED *a.*

**Torrock**, local form of TARROCK, a gull.

1752 J. HILL *Hist. Anim.* 449 The Larus, with a white head, with a spot of black on each side..; Our common people in Cornwall call it the Torrock.

‖**Torru·bia.** *Bot.* [mod.L., named after Joseph Torrubia (d. 1768).] A genus of ascomycetous fungi, parasitic on living insects: a synonym of *Cordyceps*, but frequent in Eng. use.

1883 R. TURNER in *Gd. Words* Nov. 731/2 The Red Torrubia, growing from the pupa of a moth.

**Torsade** (tǫɹsē·d). [a. F. *torsade* a twisted fringe, f. L. stem *tors-* twisted: see TORSE[1] and -ADE.] A twisted fringe, cord, or ribbon, used as an adornment in head-dresses, curtains, etc.

1882 *Society* 14 Oct. 24/1 Another..hat was composed of cream white felt,..trimmed with..torsades of cream velvet. 1889 *Harper's Mag.* Apr. 753/1 Little children,.. with their heads shaven, and on the crown a tuft of hair bound up and lengthened out with torsades of red wool. 1894 *Season* X. 35/2 A velvet and silk torsade.

**Torsal** (tǭ·ɹsăl), *a.* *Geom.* [f. TORSE[3] + -AL.] Of or pertaining to a torse: see quot.

1869 CAYLEY *Math. Papers* VI. 334 If there is at each point of the line one and the same tangent plane, then the section of the surface by the tangent plane contains the line at least twice; if it contain it twice only, the line is *torsal*; if three times the line is *oscular*, and the tangent plane containing the torsal or oscular line may in like manner be termed a torsal, or an oscular tangent plane.

**Torse**[1] (tǭɹs). *Her.* Also 6–9 **torce.** [a. obs. F. *torse, torce*, fem. a wreath:—Romanic type *torsa, f. stem *tors-* for L. *tort-* from *torquēre* to twist.] An occasional term for the twisted band or wreath by which the crest is joined to the helmet.

1572 BOSSEWELL *Armorie* II. 60 b, For the Creaste uppon the Helme an Hiricion passante, of the Diamonde, charged with Grapes propre, sett on a torce, Pearle and Emeraude. 1652 J. WRIGHT tr. *Camus' Nat. Paradox* x. 265 A Milk-white Plume shadowed the Torse of his glittering Helmet. *a* 1700 B. E. *Dict. Cant. Crew, Wreath*,..a Torce between the Mantle and the Crest. 1892 E. CASTLE *Eng. Bk.-plates* 92 The crest is supported by a plain torce. 1910 E. R. SUFFLING *Eng. Ch. Brasses* 124 A torse, or wreath of two bands of coloured silk.

Hence **Torsed** (tǭɹst) *a.*, also **torced**, furnished with a torse.

1892 EGERTON CASTLE *Eng. Book-plates* 51 The crested, torced, and mantletted helm.

**Torse**[2] (tǭɹs). [a. F. *torse* masc. (16th c.), ad. It. *torso.*] = TORSO.

1622 PEACHAM *Compl. Gent.* xii. (1634) 110 To Painters for the picturing of some excellent arme, leg, torse or wreathing of the body, or any other rare posture. 1762 GOLDSM. *Cit. W.* xxxiv, The torse..is at last discovered to be a Hercules spinning, and not a Cleopatra bathing. 1892 LD. LYTTON *King Poppy* v. 78 The necessary quantity of heads To suit the growing torse.

**Torse**[3] (tǭɹs). *Geom.* [f. med.L. *tors-us, -um*, for L. *tort-us* twisted.] A developable surface; a surface generated by a moving straight line which at every instant is turning, in some plane or other through it, about some point or other in its length.

1863 CAYLEY *Math. Papers* (1892) V. 182 By Torse (*m, n*) I denote the developable surface or 'Torse' generated by a line which meets each of the curves *m* and *n*. 1879 — in *Encycl. Brit.* X. 417 If the system be such that a line does not intersect the consecutive line, then the surface is a skew surface, or scroll; but if it be such that each line intersects the consecutive line, then it is a developable, or torse.

**Torsel**: see TASSEL *sb.*[2]

**Torsibi·lity.** [f. *torsible (f. *tors-*, ppl. stem (see prec.) + -IBLE) + -ITY.] Capability of being twisted; esp. in reference to degree or amount.

1864 WEBSTER s.v., The torsibility of a rope. 1884 A. DANIELL *Princ. of Physics* x. 234 Torsibility of a body is measured in the simplest case—that of a rod or wire—in terms of the angle through which a unit of force, applied at the distance of one cm. from the axis..can twist it.

**Torsile** (tǭ·ɹsil, -əil), *a.* [f. L. *tors-*, ppl. stem (see prec.) + -IL, -ILE.] Of the nature of torsion.

1882 *Athenæum* 25 Mar. 385/1 A process for increasing the resistance of iron to tensile, torsile, and transverse strains.

**Torsio·meter.** *Ophthalm.* [f. late L. *torsio* (see next) + -METER.] An instrument for investigation of the declination of the meridians of the eye.

1904 in *Dunglison's Med. Lex.* (ed. 23).

**Torsion** (tǭ·ɹʃən). Also 5 **torcion**, 6 **-syon**, 7 **tortion.** [a. F. *torsion* (1314 in Littré, in sense 2 below), ad. late L. *torsiōn-em* (Vulg.), by-form of *tortiōn-em*, n. of action from L. *torquēre*, *tort-um* to twist, wring. Cf. Pr. *torsio*, Sp. *torsion*, Pg. *torsão*; also It. *torzione*, ad. L. *tortiōnem.*]

**1.** The action of twisting, or turning a body spirally by the operation of contrary forces acting at right angles to its axis; also the twisted condition produced by this action; twist.

*Angle of torsion*, (*a*) the angle through which one end of a rod or other body is twisted while the other end is held fast; (*b*) *Geom.* the infinitesimal angle between two consecutive osculating planes of a tortuous curve. *Balance of torsion* = torsion-balance: see 3.

1543 TRAHERON *Vigo's Chirurg.* VI. i. 180 Yf the dislocation be lytle, so that the bone be not out all togyther, it is called dislocation not complete, and it is it which commonly is called torsion, or wresting. 1658 PHILLIPS, *Torsion*, a wresting, or wringing of any thing. 1807 T. YOUNG *Lect. Nat. Phil.* I. 140 Torsion, or twisting, consists in the lateral displacement, or detrusion, of the opposite parts of a solid, in opposite directions, the central particles only remaining in their natural state. *Ibid.* 141 The force of torsion, as it is determined by experiment, varies simply as the angle of torsion. 1814 R. BUCHANAN *Shafts Mills* 24 *note*, Journals, or journeys, are gudgeons subject to torsion. 1834 *Nat. Philos.* III. *Hist. Astron.* xxi. 105/2 (Usef. Knowl. Soc.) By means of a delicate instrument, called the balance of torsion, the attraction of a leaden sphere, eight inches in diameter, was made sensible. 1835 URE *Philos. Manuf.* 106 With very short filaments like those of wool, cotton, and cachemire, a thread of the greatest length may be formed by torsion. 1859 J. TOMES *Dental Surg.* 163 Torsion, or twisting of the central incisors upon their axis, is far from rare. 1867 THOMSON & TAIT *Nat. Phil.* I. I. § 608 The fundamental principle that spiral springs act chiefly by torsion seems to have been first discovered by Binet in 1814.

**b.** A twisting of the body or a part of it; contortion, distortion. *rare.*

1660 F. BROOKE tr. *Le Blanc's Trav.* 89 They ejulate, weep, and lament with exotick gestures, and tortions. 1899 *Allbutt's Syst. Med.* VII. 242 During the flexions and torsions of the vertebral column.

**c.** *Surg.* The twisting of the cut end of an artery to stop hæmorrhage.

1835–6 *Todd's Cycl. Anat.* I. 224/2 The successful employment of torsion of the arteries as a means of suppressing hæmorrhage. 1878 T. BRYANT *Pract. Surg.* (1879) II. 5 Any bleeding taking place can usually be checked by cold styptics, or torsion.

**d.** *Bot.* The condition of being twisted spirally.

1875 BENNETT & DYER *Sachs' Bot.* 772 A distinction must be drawn between two kinds of torsion; firstly, that of erect organs; and secondly, that of organs..in a horizontal or oblique position. In the former case the torsion results from internal conditions of growth, and especially from the outer layers growing more rapidly than the inner ones.

†**2.** *Path.* A wringing or griping of the bowels; tormina. *Obs.* (The earliest sense in Eng.)

*c* 1425 tr. *Arderne's Treat. Fistula* 78 It availeþ..to euery inflacion of þe wombe, and to ventosite of it, and torcions, i.[e.] gryndyng. 1543 TRAHERON *Vigo's Chirurg.* III. *Wounds* I. ii. 100 Knowen by the greate payne, and torsyon or grypynge of the bellie. 1626 BACON *Sylva* § 39 All Purgers have in them a raw Spirit, or Winde; which is the principall Cause of Tortion in the Stomach, & Belly. 1689 MOYLE *Sea Chyrurg.* III. vii. 109 Sometimes there is..intolerable tortion of the Bowels.

**3.** *attrib.* and *Comb.*, as *torsion arm, axis, circle, pendulum, screw, spring*; **torsion-balance**, an instrument for measuring minute horizontal forces, consisting of a wire or filament having a horizontal arm to the end of which the force is applied so as to make it revolve and twist the wire, etc., through an angle proportional to the twisting moment of the force; **torsion-basin** *Geol.*, a basin formed by torsion of the earth's crust in any region; **torsion-curve**, a curve caused by torsion; **torsion electrometer**, an electrometer that measures by means of a torsion-balance.

1831 HOLLAND *Manuf. Metal* I. 199 It does not appear that these torsion nails have ever found much favour. 1837 BREWSTER *Magnet.* 15 The torsion balance, for measuring small forces. 1873 MAXWELL *Electr. & Magn.* § 38 The torsion-balance was devised by Michell for the determination of the force of gravitation between small bodies, and was used by Cavendish for this purpose. *Ibid.* § 215 The angle through which the electrical force twisted the torsion-arm. *Ibid.* § 725 The torsion-screw, which turns the torsion-head round a vertical axis. 1884 F. J. BRITTEN *Watch & Clockm.* 265 Small clocks..are made with torsion pendulums. 1899 MAR. M. OGILVIE-GORDON in *Nature* 7 Sept. 445/1 Two great internal torsion-basins, within the Alpine systems of southern Europe, are the Hungarian and the west Mediterranean. 1901 — *Ibid.* 24 Jan. 294/1, I wrote my paper on the 'Torsion-structure of the Dolomites' in 1898. *Ibid.* 295 The torsion-curves round the northern periphery of the Adriatic crust-basin.

Hence **To·rsionless** *a.*, not subject to torsion.

1858 HERSCHEL *Outl. Astron.* I. iv. (ed. 5) 160 A metallic arc..supported from its middle..by a torsionless suspension.

**Torsional** (tǭ·ɹʃənăl), *a.* [f. prec. + -AL.] Of, pertaining or relating to, or caused by or resulting from torsion.

1861 FAIRBAIRN *Iron* 195 Experiments..on the torsional strength of iron cast in various forms. 1873 MAXWELL *Electr. & Magn.* § 215 The torsional elasticity of a glass fibre or metal wire. 1879 THOMSON & TAIT *Nat. Phil.* I. I. § 435 The torsional rigidity of iron, copper, and brass wires is diminished about ⅛ per cent. with 10° elevation of temperature. 1882 *Rep. to Ho. Repr. Prec. Met. U. S.* 583 There is..considerable torsional strain upon the shaft, depending on its length. 1909 *Athenæum* 6 Mar. 292/1 Interesting experiments are described on the energy dissipated through torsional hysteresis.

Hence **To·rsionally** *adv.*, in respect of torsion.

1890 *Nature* 2 Jan. 198 The internal friction of a torsionally oscillating iron wire.

**Torsive** (tǭ·ɹsiv), *a.* *Bot.* [f. med.L. *tors-us* twisted + -IVE.] Twisted spirally; = CONTORTED 2: see quot.

1866 *Treas. Bot.*, *Torsive*, twisted spirally. The same as Contorted, except that there is no obliquity in the form or insertion of the pieces as in the petals of *Oxalis*.

**Torsk** (tǭɹsk). Also locally **tursk, tosk, tusk** (tɒsk). [a. Norw. *torsk, tosk*, Sw., Da. *torsk*:—ON. *þorskr, þoskr*; prob. f. root of ON. *þurr*, Sw. *torr*, Gothic *þaurs-us* dry. Cf. LG. (and Ger.) *dorsch.*]

A gadoid fish, *Brosmius brosme*, abundant in the northern seas, especially about the Shetland Islands, and much used for food in the dried form of *stockfish*. Also *attrib.*

1707 MIEGE *St. Gt. Brit.* ii. 14 They have abundance of Fish on that Coast call'd Tusk, as big as Ling. 1776 PENNANT *Zool.* III. 179 The Torsk, or as it is called in the Shetlands, Tusk and Brismak is a northern fish; and as yet undiscovered lower than about the Orknies. 1822 SCOTT *Pirate* xxii, There is torsk for the gentle, and skate for the carle, And there's wealth for bold Magnus, the son of the earl. 1837 M. DONOVAN *Dom. Econ.* II. 179 The Torsk is not so slender as the ling, and is altogether a smaller fish. As food it is considered more delicate than ling. 1864 COUCH *Brit. Fishes* III. 96. 1875 W. A. SMITH *Lewsiana* 237 The tursk or tosk..is perhaps the finest of the *Gadidæ* when fresh. 1883 *Fisheries Exhib. Catal.* 72 Dried Salted Tusk-fish,..mostly consumed in Scotch Markets.

**Torso** (tǭ·ɹso). *Pl.* **torsos.** [a. It. *torso* stalk, stump (e. g. of a cabbage), core (of apple or pear), trunk of a statue:—L. *thyrsus* stalk, stem (of a plant), a. Gr. θύρσος the THYRSUS (q. v.) or Bacchic wand. The common Romanic form was **turso-*, whence also OF. *tors, tros, trous,* Pr. *tros,* Sp. *trozo* stem, stump.]

**1.** *Sculpture.* The trunk of a statue, without or considered independently of head and limbs; also, the trunk of the human body. Also *attrib.*

1797 HOLCROFT *Stolberg's Trav.* (ed. 2) II. xlvii. 144 The thigh, and *torso*, or body, from the neck to the hip, are inimitable. 1805 W. TAYLOR in *Monthly Mag.* XX. 43 An antique female statue, or rather the torso of a statue, had formerly stood in the library at Wolfenbüttel. 1833 ELLIS *Elgin Marbles* II. 29 The torso of Apteral Victory is 4 ft. 9 in. in height. 1860 HAWTHORNE *Marb. Faun* v, Headless and legless torsos. 1865 DICKENS *Mut. Fr.* I. ii, With..too much torso in his waistcoat. 1875 F. WEY *Rome* xxiii. 300 The Torso of the Belvedere, a colossal fragment of Herculean stature... Michelangelo studied it to such a degree that he was wont to call himself pupil of the Torso. 1899 F. T. BULLEN *Log Sea-waif* 296 Clad only in a waist-cloth, his torso was fully revealed.

**2.** *fig.* Something left mutilated or unfinished.

1852 LONGFELLOW in *Life* (1891) II. 240 We have seen only the brief and mutilated torso of your speech. 1892 STEVENSON *Across the Plains* 132 Headless epics, glorious torsos of dramas. 1906 H. BLACK *Edin. Serm.* 56 Without Christ the Old Testament is only a torso.

**Torsocclusion** (tǭɹsǫklū·ʒən). *Surg.* [f. med.L. *tors-us* twisted + OCCLUSION.] Treatment by acupressure combined with torsion.

1899 *Syd. Soc. Lex.*, *Torsoclusion*, a form of acupressure in which the point of the pin is pushed through a portion of tissue parallel to the course of the vessel to be secured, then carried over its anterior surface, and..swept round until it is brought to a right angle to the course of the artery, when its point is thrust into the soft parts beyond.

**Tort** (tǭɹt), *sb.* Also 6–7 **torte.** [a. OF. *tort* (11th c. in Hatz.-Darm.) = Pr. *tort*, Sp. *tuerto*, It. *torto*, med.L. *tortum*, wrong, injustice (cf. *tortum facere*, 864, in *Capitul. Caroli II*), sbst. use of L. *tortus, -um* twisted, wrung, pa. pple. of *torquēre* to twist, wring.]

†**1.** Injury, wrong. *Obs.* [see TORTIOUS *a.* 1].

1387–8 T. USK *Test. Love* II. ii. (Skeat) l. 71 Than wer tort & forthe [? force] nought worthe an haw about. 1585 JAS. I *Ess. Poesie* (Arb.) 33 So Iob and Ieremie, preast with woes and wrongs, Did right descryue their ioyes, their woes and torts. 1590 SPENSER *F. Q.* II. v. 17 It was complaint that thou hadst done great tort Unto an aged woman, poore and bare. 1591 — *M. Hubberd* 1078 No wild beasts should do them any torte. 1632 LITHGOW *Trav.* x. 425 To show King Iames, my torments, pangs, and tort. 1748 MELMOTH *Fitzosb. Lett.* lxxii. (1749) II. 215 Deem not, ye plaintive crew, that suffer wrong, Ne thou, O man! who deal'st the tort, misween The equal gods.

†**b.** Physical injury or pain; torment. **c.** A false or wrong statement. *Obs. rare.*

1632 LITHGOW *Trav.* v. 193 Good t'expell all sorts Of burning Feauers, in their violent torts. *Ibid.* x. 488 No Tort I introduct,..I Organize the Truth.

**2.** *Eng. Law.* The breach of a duty imposed by law, whereby some person acquires a right of action for damages.

1586 FERNE *Blaz. Gentrie* 214 Ministers of the Gospell, to whome the keyes of right do apperteine (for the others did by dissesin and tort, hold the possession of them). 1609 SKENE *Reg. Maj., Stat. Robt. I*, 23 Saifeand the Law and consuetude of Burghis, quhilk is, to defend preciselie torte and non reason, that is wrang and vnlaw. 1622 CALLIS *Stat. Sewers* (1647) 184 If two be admitted to a Copyhold by Tort, or to an Office in a Court of Justice unlawfully. 1647 N. BACON *Disc. Govt. Eng.* I. lxvii. (1739) 162 In case it concerned only a Tort done to the party, he was amerced. 1714 SCROGGS *Courts-leet* (ed. 3) 59 This is a private Tort to the particular Inhabitants of this Vill. 1768 BLACKSTONE *Comm.* III. viii. 117 Personal actions are such whereby a man claims a debt, or personal duty, or damages in lieu thereof; and, likewise whereby a man claims a satisfaction in damages for some injury done to his person or property. The former are said to be founded on contracts, the latter upon *torts* or wrongs. 1887 SIR F. POLLOCK (*title*) The Law of Torts. 1895 POLLOCK & MAITLAND *Hist. Eng. Law* II. 510 *note*, *Tort* again is [in 13th c. A.-Fr.] a large, loose word. Britton, I. 77, heads a chapter on some of the smaller offences present in the eyres by the title *De plusours tortz.* 1909 SIR F. POLLOCK in *Encycl. Laws of Eng.* (ed. 2) XIV. 134 What we now understand by a tort is a breach of some duty between citizens, defined by the general law, which creates a civil cause of action. The duty must be founded in common right...It must be a duty assigned by law, not dependent on the will of the parties...There must be a private right of action.

†**Tort,** *ppl. a. Obs.* [ad. L. *tort-us*, pa. pple. of *torquēre* to twist.] Twisted; in quot. 1513, ? tortured (const. as *pa. pple.*).

1513 DOUGLAS *Æneis* x. xi. 30 Now sall he perisch,..be Troianis tort and rent. 1568 GRAFTON *Chron.* II. 210 Henry Erle of Lancaster with ye wrie neck, called Tort coll. 1765 J. LEE *Introd. Bot.* I. xii. 28 *Tort*, twisted, as in *Nerium.*

**Tort,** erroneous variant of TAUT *a.*

‖**Torta** (tǭ·ɹtă). *Mining.* [Sp. *torta*: see next.] One of the large flat circular heaps or 'cakes' of ore spread upon the floor or *patio* (PATIO 2) in the Mexican amalgamation process.

1839 URE *Dict. Arts* 1119 The *patio*, or amalgamation floor..is capable of containing 24 *tortas*, or flat circular collections of *lama*, of about 50 feet diameter, and 7 inches deep. 1881 RAYMOND *Mining Gloss.*, *Torta*, a flat heap of silver ore (slime or pulp) prepared for the patio process.

**Tortayes, tortays:** see TORTIS.

†**Torte.** *Obs.* [ad. F. *tourte*, dial. *torte* = Sp. and It. *torta*:—late L. *tōrta* (Vulg. 1 Chron. xvi. 3 *tortam panis*, Wyclif 'a kake of brede'). A different word from L. *torta* twisted: see also TOURTE and TART.] A round cake (of bread).

1555 EDEN *Decades* 194 They drawe a mylke thereof [i. e. of the coco-nut]..The which the Christian men of those regions put in the tortes or cakes which they make of the grayne of *Maizium*..by reason of the sayde mylke of *Cocus*, the tortes are more excellent to be eaten withowt offence to the stomake.

‖**Torteau** (tortō). *Pl.* **torteaux** (tortōz). Also *pl.* 5 **tortellis**, 6 **tourteaulx, torteaulxes**, 6–8 **torteauxes**, 7 **tortauxes**, 8 **torteaux's, tourteaux, tourteauxes.** [a. F. *tourteau* 'a large round cake or flat bannock of bread', a mass of oilcake, a wooden disk used as a crusher, and in heraldry as below; in OFr. *tortel* (12th c. in Hatz.-Darm.), in Guernsey *tourtel* (= Pr. *tortelh*, Cat. *tortell*), deriv. of *tourte* (TOURTE, TORTE).]

**1.** *Her.* A roundle gules; the specific name of a small red circular figure charged upon a shield, supposed to represent a cake of bread.

1486 *Bk. St. Albans, Her.* e vj, Ther be also tortellis yt be litill Cakys the wich be grettir then ballys & [=if] tharmys be truly made as here it is opyn...*Portat tres tortellas rubias in campo aureo*... He berith golde & iij. Cakys of gowles. 1530 in *Ancestor* XI. (1904) 180 A lymmers hede rased sable with a coller siluer full of tourteaulx. 1562 LEIGH *Armorie* 151 b, He beareth or, x torteauxes...These haue been called of olde blazoures, wastelles, and are cakes of breade. 1725 COATS *Dict. Her.*, *Tourteaux*, according to the French, and *Tourteauxes*, as we make the Plural Number in English, are small Rounds..in England,..they are always Red; but the French give the same Name to such as are of any other Colour, expressing the same...The *Tourteaux* in Latin are call'd *Tortellæ.* 1825 *Gentl. Mag.* XCV. I. 305/1 Sir Thomas Dacre..used these arms: Argent, a chevron Sable between three Torteaux, on each an escallop Argent. 1894 *Parker's Gloss. Her.*, *Torteau*..: the name now always applied to a *roundle gules*...The figure is said to have been intended to represent the sacred Host.

†**2.** A flat cake, a pancake. *Obs.*
(Cf. quot. 1562 in 1.)

1625 PURCHAS *Pilgrims* II. IX. xix. § 3. 1652 Torteaux and Bignets, and many other sorts of food...They make pottage, and Torteaux and Galletus.

**Torteaux, torteise, tortesse,** obs. ff. TORTOISE. **Tortel,** early f. TORTEAU; obs. f. TURTLE.

**Tortes:** see TORTIS.

†**Tortey.** *Obs.* Variant of TORTEAU 1.

1688 R. HOLME *Armoury* I. 103/3 Our old English terms were..Torteys for Torteauxes.

**Tortfeasor** (tǭ·ɹtˌfīːzǫɹ). *Law.* [a. OF. *tort-fesor, tort-faiseur, torfesor*, f. *tort* wrong, evil + *-fesor, faiseur* doer. (In OF. *tortfesor*, *tort* is an adj. qualifying *fesor*; hence pl. *torzfesors*.)] One who is guilty of a tort; a wrong-doer, trespasser.

1659 CROKE *Reports* II. (1669) 383 He is meerly a *Tort feasor*, and that Trespass liable against him to recover damages. 1670 BLOUNT *Law Dict.*, *Tortfeasor*, a Doer of wrong, a Trespasser. Hence in later Law Dicts. 1883 *Law Times Rep.* XLIX. 11/2 Waiving the tort and bringing an action of *indebitatus assumpsit* for work and labour done against the tort feasor. 1886 *Times* 27 Jan. 4 The father and son were here being sued by the plaintiff as joint tortfeasors.

‖**Torticollis** (tǭɹtikǫ·lis). *Path.* [mod.L., f. L. *tort-us* crooked, twisted + *collum* neck. Cf. obs. F. *torticolis.*] A rheumatic or other affection of the muscles of the neck, in which it is so twisted as to keep the head turned to one side; wry-neck.

1811 HOOPER *Med. Dict.*, *Torticollis*, the wry neck. 1857 DUNGLISON *Med. Lex.*, *Torticollis*..*Stiffneck, Wryneck*.., a variety of rheumatism, seated in the muscles of the neck. 1859 SEMPLE *Diphtheria* 347 There was also painful torticollis. 1897 *Allbutt's Syst. Med.* III. 63 In cases of rheumatic torticollis there is conspicuous muscular spasm.

**Tortile** (tǭ·ɹtil, -əil), *a. rare.* [ad. L. *tortilis*, f. *tort-*, ppl. stem of *torquēre* to twist: see -IL, -ILE.] Twisted, coiled; winding; capable of being twisted.

1658 SIR T. BROWNE *Gard. Cyrus* iii. 59 He..may observe it in the Tortile and tiring stroaks of Gnatworms. 1760 J. LEE *Introd. Bot.* III. xxii. (1765) 227 The Arista is tortile, twisted, when it has a twisted Joint in the Middle. 1819 H. BUSK *Vestriad* IV. 116 Each in her arms two fiery dragons holds, With slender limbs restrains the tortile folds. 1835 URE *Philos. Manuf.* 62 Tortile fabrics used for making webs of various kinds.

Hence **Torti·lity**, the quality of being tortile.

1835 URE *Philos. Manuf.* 62 Under tortility must likewise be considered..fulling, felting, and the manufacture of hats. 1846 WORCESTER cites *Monthly Review.*

‖**Tortilla** (tortī·lya). Also 9 **tortillia.** [Sp. dim. of *torta* cake: see TORTA.] In Mexico, A thin round cake made of maize-flour, baked on a flat plate of iron, earthenware, etc. and eaten hot.

1699 DAMPIER *Voy.* II. II. 43 Tartilloes are small Cakes made of the Flower of Indian Corn. 1828 LYON *Mexico* x. II. 142 Obliged to seek..for some woman, who will make a few tortillas or a dish of black beans. 1842 *New World* 11 June 373/3 Maiz..is chiefly used in the Tortillia cakes, of which we hear so much in Mexico..a tortillia is indispensable at least once a day for all classes. 1854 J. LL. STEPHENS *Centr. Amer.* 29 The people live exclusively upon tortillas, flat cakes made of crushed Indian Corn, and baked on a clay griddle. 1888 LEES & CLUTTERBUCK *Brit. Columbia 1887* xxii. (1892) 239 One of our favourite luxuries is the tortilla (pronounced torteea).

**Tortilly** (tǭ·ɹtili), *a. Her.* [ad. F. *tortillé* twisted, (in heraldry) wreathed, pa. pple. of *tortiller* to twist closely, f. *tort*, pa. pple. of *tordre* to twist.] (See quots.)

[c 1828 BERRY *Encycl. Her.* I. Gloss., *Tortillé*, a French term for nowed, twisted, or wreathed. 1889 ELVIN *Dict. Her.*, *Tortille*, nowed, twisted, or wreathed.] 1894 *Parker's Gloss. Her.*, *Tortilly*,..a term applied to Ordinaries which are wreathed,..the term *wreathy* is also found...Or, a lion rampant gules, a chief tortilly gules and vert..Macritchie.

†**Torti·loquy.** *Obs. rare*–0. [ad. late or med. L. *tortiloquium* (Du Cange), f. *tortus* crooked + *loqui* to speak.] (See quot.)

1656 BLOUNT *Glossogr.*, *Tortiloquy*,..crooked talk.

**Tortion,** obs. form of TORSION.

†**To·rtionary,** *a. Obs. rare*–1. [ad. med.L. *tortiōnāri-us* unjust, injurious (1394 in Du Cange), F. *tortionnaire*, f. L. *tortiōn-em* 'torment, torture', in med.L. 'exercise of violence': see -ARY.] Wrongful, illegal.

1694 FALLE *Jersey* vii. 215 A Prize made by one Pointy, ..was..pronounced Tortionary, and Illegal, and Pointy adjudged to make Restitution.

**Tortious** (tǭ·ɹʃəs), *a.* Also 4–6 **torcious**, 6 **torteouse.** [a. Anglo-Fr. *torcious* (14th c.), f. stem of *torcion, tortion*: see prec. and -IOUS. In use associated with TORT *sb.*, as if from *tort* + *-eous*: cf. *righteous, wrongous*, etc.]

†**1.** Wrongful, injurious, hurtful; illegal. *Obs.*

1387–8 T. USK *Test. Love* II. ii. (Skeat) l. 73 Than wer tort & forthe [? force] nought worthe an haw about, and pleasen no men, but thilke greuous and torcious been in might and in doinge. a 1548 HALL *Chron., Edw. IV* 217 b, A cruell man and a torcious vsurper. 1583 STUBBES *Anat. Abus.* I. (1879) 36 The deuil..inticed him (oh, torteouse serpent!) to eat of the forbidden fruite. 1590 SPENSER *F. Q.* II. ii. 18 Ne ought he car'd whom he endamaged By tortious wrong, or whom bereav'd of right. 1742 SHENSTONE *Schoolmistress* xv, When..tortious death was true Devotion's meed.

**2.** *Law.* Pertaining to or of the nature of a tort. (Early quots. show the gradual development of sense.)

1544 tr. *Littleton's Tenures* 90 The more..that he came to the dede by a lawfull meane, than by a torcyous meane. 1619 DALTON *Country Just.* xciii. (1630) 237 Where the arrest is tortious,..there the killing of him that maketh such an unlawful arrest, is..manslaughter onely. 1671 F. PHILLIPS *Reg. Necess.* 259 The parties..endeavouring such breaches of Priviledge, should not take advantage *de son tort*, of their own wrongs or tortious doings. 1766 BLACKSTONE *Comm.* II. ix. 150 Unless the owner..will declare his continuance to be tortious, or, in common language, wrongful. 1863 H. COX *Instit.* II. viii. 500 To restrain threatened irremediable injuries to property by acts of a tortious kind. 1907 *Law Rep.* in *Cycl. Tour. Club Gaz.* June 220 The animal..would have done no harm but for the tortious act of a third person.

†**3.** Wrong, incorrect, improper. *Obs. rare.*

1644 [H. PARKER] *Jus Pop.* 66 A tortious, unnatural sense of the words. 1657 W. MORICE *Coena quasi Κοινὴ* I. ii. 106 It seemes a very Tortious and improper answer.

¶**4.** Misused for TORTUOUS.

1682 in R. Burthogge *Argt. Infants Bapt.* iv. (1684) 170 The most involved, tortious, intricate, that ever you heard of, except Origens Allegorical and Mystical Commentaries.

**To·rtiously,** *adv.* [f. prec. + -LY 2: cf. AF. *torciousement* (Godef.).] Wrongfully, illegally; by tort.

a 1812 LD. THURLOW in G. D. Collinson *Idiots & Lunaticks* (1812) I. 577 (Jod.) An application, where timber was cut by a stranger tortiously, to have the produce restored to the estate. 1818 CRUISE *Digest* (ed. 2) IV. 461 If a purchaser is tortiously evicted..he has his remedy at law. 1882 *Times* 22 Feb. 9/5 Not because the House had tortiously debarred Mr. Bradlaugh from taking his seat, but because Mr. Bradlaugh was disqualified by law from so doing.

†**To·rtis.** *Obs.* Forms: 4 ?*pl.* **tortyse**, 4–5 *sing.* and *pl.* **torteys**, 5 *sing.* and *pl.* **tortes**, *sing.* **tortays**, *pl.* **tortayes, torteies**, 5–6 *sing.* and *pl.* **tortys**, 6 *pl.* **tortaysez**, 7 *sing.* and *pl.* **tortis**, *pl.* **tortiz.** [a. OF. *tortis*, *-iz* masc. (a 1200), also perh. *tortise, -isse* (a 1377), *-ice, -iche* fem., twisted thing, torch, in med.L. *tortīcius* (? 11th c. in Du Cange), *-īsius, -ītius* masc., also *tortīcia* fem. (a 1400) a torch, f. L. *tort-us* twisted, or med.L. *tortia* TORCH + *-īcius, -īcia*: see -ITIOUS. The forms in *-eys, -ays* are from OF. *torteis*, alteration of *tortis*

after such words as *semeis*, for *semeïs* :—**seminātīcius*.]

**1.** A kind of very large wax candle. (Usually distinguished from a *torch*: cf. quot. 1611.)

A note to Way's ed. of *Promp. Parv.* s. v. *Percher*, mentions *torticios*, 2 ells long and weighing 5 lb. each.

c **1375** *Sc. Leg. Saints* x. (*Mathou*) 250 Vith incense & lampis lycht And tortyse al brynnand brycht. **1404–5** *Abingdon Rolls* (Camden) 68 In j torteys empto xxij d. **1413** *Pilgr. Sowle* (Caxton) II. lx. (1859) 58 This wycked sauour, and smoke of the torteys when the fyre is oute. **1421–2** *Durham Acc. Rolls* (Surtees) 141 In candelis cerijs et albis..cum ij torchis, ij tortys, iiij prikettys & factura eorundem. c **1450** *Bk. Curtasye* 492 in *Babees Bk.* 315 Fyrst to þe chaundeler he schalle go, To take a tortes lyȝt hym fro. a **1483** *Liber Niger* in *Househ. Ord.* (1790) 22 iii torches, one tortays, and iii prickettes. *Ibid.* 41 And he [a Grome of Chambyr] setteth nyghtly, after the seasons of the yere, torchys, tortays, candylles of wax, morters. **1506–7** *Burgh Rec. Edinb.* (1869) I. 111 That they have ilk ane ane new tortys reddy. **1533–4** *Durham Househ. Bk.* (Surtees) 249 Pro factura 4 le torchez et 4 tortaysez 16 d. **1601** F. TATE *Househ. Ord. Edw. II* (1876) 6 This stewarde..shall take everi night for his chamber, one sextier of wine, xij candels, two tortis, one tortis for wine, and one torche. [**1611** COTGR., *Tortis de cire*, a wreathed Linke or great candle of wax; most in vse about Candlemas.]

**2.** A twisted chain; a wreath. [mod.F. *tortis.*]

**1688** R. HOLME *Armoury* IV. ix. (Roxb.) 390/2 A tortis or double chaine of gold.

**Tortive** (tǭ·ɹtiv), *a. rare.* [ad. L. *tortīv-us*, f. *tort-*, ppl. stem of *torquēre* to twist: see -IVE.] Twisting, twisted, tortuous.

**1606** SHAKS. *Tr. & Cr.* I. iii. 9 Tortiue and errant from his course of growth. **1656** BLOUNT *Glossogr.*, *Tortive* (*tortivus*), that is wrung or pressed out. *Br.* **1880** SWINBURNE *On Cliffs* 12 Between the tortive serpent-shapen roots.

So † **Tortivous** *a. Obs.*, in same sense.

**14..** LYDG. *Temple of Glas* (E.E.T.S.) p. 14 Ielusye, The vile serpent, the snake tortyvous.

**Tortle**, obs. form of TURTLE.

† **To·rtlet.** *Her. Obs.* [dim. of *tortel* TORTEAU.] A little cake of bread.

**1486** *Bk. St. Albans, Her.* b iv b, Tortlettis be calde in armys wastell.

† **To·rtness**, obs. f. TAUTNESS: cf. TAUT *a.* 2 γ.

**1727** BAILEY vol. II, *Tortness* (spoken of a Rope, etc.) Straightness, Tightness, by being hard pulled.

**Tortoise** (tǭ·ɹtəs, -tĭs). Forms: see below. [Found in 15th c. in forms *tortuca, tortuce, tortuge, tortu, tortuse, tortose*. *Tortūca* (c 1255 in Albertus Magnus *Animal.* 24 § 126, 25 § 59) was the late popular L. name (see below), which later regularly became, as still in Prov. and Sp., *tortuga*, and in F. *tortue*. (Diefenbach cites also med.L. *turtus, tortus*.) Of the Eng. forms, *tortuce* evidently represented the Latin, *tortue* and *tortu* the French, and the 16th c. *tortuga* the Sp. form. *Tortuse* was prob. a mere variant of *tortuce* (cf. *lettuce, letuse* below); *tortose* and the later forms in *-esse, -ise, -oise*, being further variants, partly at least due to shifting of stress and obscuration of the vowel. The forms in final *-s* may have arisen simply from dropping *-e* mute; but some of them may have come from taking the possessive *tortu's, tortou's*, in *tortou's skin, tortue's shell*, as the nominative. The form *tortoise* appears c 1569, preceded by *tortoyse*, 1552.

The late popular L. or Romanic *tortūca* is commonly held to be a derivative of L. *tortus* twisted, with the formative suffix seen in L. *carrūca, festūca, lactūca, verrūca*, and to refer to the crooked feet of the south European species (Diez). With L. *tortūca*, F. *tortue*, Eng. *tortuce, tortuse*, cf. L. *lactūca*, F. *laitue*, Eng. *lettuce, letuse*, and the variant forms of the last. The classical L. name was *testūdo*, from *testa* shell, whence It. *testudine, testuggine*.]

**1.** A four-footed reptile of the order *Chelonia*, in which the trunk is enclosed between a carapace and plastron, formed by the dorsal vertebræ, ribs, and sternum; the skin being covered with large horny plates, commonly called the shell.

The *Chelonia* are usually divided into Land-tortoises (*Testudinidæ*), Marsh-tortoises (*Emydæ*), River-tortoises (*Trionycidæ*), and Marine tortoises (*Chelonidæ*), in which the feet are compressed into flippers or paddles. The last are now commonly distinguished as *turtles*; but this name is sometimes extended to species of the *Emydæ* and *Trionycidæ*. By some zoologists the name 'tortoise' is confined to the terrestrial genus *Testudo* and its immediate congeners; see also TERRAPIN.

α. 5 **tortuce, tortuge,** (**tortuca,** 6 **tortuga**).

**1398** TREVISA *Barth. De P. R.* XVIII. cviii. (Bodl. MS. c 1450) lf. 287 b/1 The tortuge [*ed.* 1495 tortuse] is acounted amonge snailles for he is closed bitwene twey hard schellis ..and of tortuca is double kinde þat one woneþ in ryuers & þat oþer in londe. c **1440** *Promp. Parv.* 497/2 Tortuce, beest.., *tortuca*. **1577** FRAMPTON *Joyfull Newes* II. 73 b, [Lagartos] take out their yonglynges, as the Tortugas of the sea doeth. **1596** RALEIGH *Discov. Guiana* 54 We found thousands of Tortugas egs, which are very wholesome meate. [**1832** MACGILLIVRAY tr. *Humboldt's Trav.* xvii. 223 The arraw or tortuga is a large fresh water tortoise.]

β. 5 **tortu, turtu, tortou**; 6–7 **tortue.**

c **1440** *Pallad. on Husb.* I. 874 The sedis in a tortous skyn [*testudinis coreo*] thou drie. a **1450** *Knt. de la Tour* (1906) 15 In sayeng youre praiers..be not like the crane or the tortu;..thei are like the crane and the turtu that turnithe her hede and fases bacward, and lokithe ouer the shuldre. **1587** MASCALL *Govt. Cattle, Horses* (1627) 184 If Sinews or Nerues bee broken or bruised,..Yee shall lay thereon the flesh of a Tortue,..beaten with the powder of Mullenherbe.

γ. 5 **tortose,** 5–7 **tortuse,** 6 **-tuous, -tueis,** 7 **-tuis, -tus.**

**1484** CAXTON *Fables of Auian* ii, The..fable..of the tortose and of the other byrdes. **1495** *Trevisa's Barth. De P. R.* XVIII. cviii. (W. de W.) gg iv b/1 The londe Tortuse [*Bodl. MS.* tortuge] dwellyth in houses and in wodes and is clene and good to etynge. **1565** COOPER *Thesaurus* s. v. *Tegimen*, The Tortuous, when she is shronke into hir shelle. **1590** TARLTON *News Purgat.* (1844) 76 She that.. hath the tortueis under her feet, and gads not abroad. **1598** YONG *Diana* 49 Their shields ..were broad shels of monstrous Tortuses. **1630** LENNARD tr. *Charron's Wisd.* (1658) 39 In the sense of Hearing, the Hart excelleth all others..; of Feeling the Tortuis. **1651** Tortus [see TORTOISE-SHELL 4].

δ. 6 **torteyse, torteaux,** 6–7 **tortesse, -teise,** 7 **tortise,** (**-ties**).

**1545** ELYOT, *Chelys*, a torteyse. **1567** MAPLET *Gr. Forest* 106 The Tortesse is reckned one amongst the Snaile or Wormes. **1581** PETTIE *Guazzo's Civ. Conv.* I. (1586) 3, I goe to it as the Torteise to the inchantment. **1600** *E. de Jonghe's True Declar. Army by Sea* 22 There they saw verie great Torteauxes. *Ibid.*, The same day they took a Torteaux. **1615** G. SANDYS *Trav.* 205 The brooke it selfe abounding with Tortesses. **1661** LOVELL *Hist. Anim. & Min.* Introd., Having shells, as the Torteise. *Ibid.* 124 Tortise. In the deserts of Africa, Lybia, and Mauritania.

ε. 6–7 **tortoyse,** 6–8 **-tois,** (6 **-toys,** 7 **-toisse, turtois**), 6– **tortoise.**

**1552** HULOET, Tortoyse fyshe, *chelys*. **1555** EDEN *Decades* 200 In..Cuba, are founde great Tortoyses (which are certeyne shell fysshes) of such byggenesse that tenne or fyfteene men are scarsely able to lyfte one of them owt of the water. **1569** Tortoises [see 2]. **1589** GREENE *Menaphon* (Arb.) 39 Venus standeth on the Tortoys, as shewing that Loue creepeth on by degrees. **1601** HOLLAND *Pliny* VI. xxii. I. 131 Tortoisses..so great..that one of their shels will serve to cover an house. **1611** BIBLE *Lev.* xi. 29 The Weasell, and the Mouse, and the Tortois, after his kinde. **1617** KEYMIS in *Raleigh's Apol.* 34, I have sent..one roule of Tobacco, one Tortoyse. **1648** Turtoises [see b]. **1666** J. DAVIES *Hist. Caribby Isles* 133 There are Land-Tortoises, Sea-Tortoises, and Fresh-water Tortoises, which are of different figures. **1699** GARTH *Dispens.* II. 19 And there, the Tortois hung her Coat o' Mail. **1719** DE FOE *Crusoe* I. 102 Going down to the Sea-side, I found a large Tortoise or Turtle. **1841–71** T. R. JONES *Anim. Kingd.* (ed. 4) 737 The perfect and typical Reptile, as the Lizard, the Tortoise, and the Serpent, breathes air, and air only.

**b.** A figure or image of a tortoise.

**1648** J. RAYMOND *Il Merc. Italico* 42 Two Marble Pyramids that stand on brasse Turtoises. **1853** HUMPHREYS *Coin-Coll. Man.* iii. (1876) 21 The coins of Ægina are easily recognized by the tortoise which is their invariable type. **1897** *Westm. Gaz.* 22 Apr. 3/3 Two metal tortoises—probably tobacco-jars?..were lying at hand on the table.

**c.** Taken as a type of slowness of motion; hence, applied to a very slow person or thing.

[**1670** G. H. *Hist. Cardinals* II. III. 198 He is slow in his Negotiations, advancing like a Tortoise.] **1825** SCOTT *Talism.* xxii, The speediest horse he had ever mounted was a tortoise in comparison to those of the Arabian sage. **1842** I. WILLIAMS *Baptistery* II. xvii. (1874) 6 One is travelling with a tortoise by his side, How slowly doth he wend.

**2. a.** A sort of penthouse, under which besiegers were protected as a tortoise by its shell; = TESTUDO 3.

**1569** STOCKER tr. *Diod. Sic.* III. viii. 113/2 He had also many other Engines..and two great and puissant Tortoises to helpe them. **1610** W. FOLKINGHAM *Art of Survey* I. xiii. 45 Battering-Rams, Sowes, Horses, Tortuses. **1795** SOUTHEY *Joan of Arc* VIII. 159 Tortoises, beneath whose roofing safe, They, filling the deep moat, might for the towers Make fit foundation. **1856** GROTE *Greece* II. xcii. XII. 129 His soldiers, protected from missiles by moveable penthouses (called Tortoises).

**b.** = TESTUDO 3 b.

**1697** DRYDEN *Æneid* II. 601 Their Targets in a Tortoise cast, the Foes Secure advancing, to the Turrets rose. **1734** tr. *Rollin's Anc. Hist.* XIX. iv. (1827) VIII. 139 They came forward in the form of the testudo, or tortoise. **1863** WHYTE MELVILLE *Gladiators* 408 He bade them form with their shields the figure that was called 'the Tortoise'.

**3.** Short for TORTOISE-SHELL. Usually *attrib.* or as *adj.*

**1654** DOROTHY OSBORNE *Lett. to Sir W. Temple* (1888) 240 The ring..is very well, only a little of the biggest. Send me a tortoise one that is a little less. **1702** *Lond. Gaz.* No. 3833/4 A Gold Snuff-Box,..the bottom Tortoise. **1902** *Fur & Feather* 19 Sept. 232/2 The Young Brindle or Tortoise class [of Cavies].

**4.** *attrib.* (sometimes = adj.) and *Comb.*, as *tortoise broth, -feeder, god, -heart, -myth, pond*; *tortoise-headed, -shaped* adjs., *-like* adj. and adv.; esp. with reference to the slow gait of the tortoise, as *tortoise-hours, -pace, race*; *tortoise-footed, -paced* adjs.; also **tortoise-beetle**, a leaf-beetle of the family *Cassididæ*, from the resemblance of the wing-cases and prothorax to the carapace of a tortoise; † **tortoise encrinite**, a fossil crinoid of the genus *Marsupites*; **tortoise-flower**, a plant of the genus *Chelone*, from the resemblance of the corolla to the head of a tortoise (also called *turtle-head*); † **tortoise-iron**, ? a peg for tethering captured tortoises; **tortoise-lyre**, a lyre made of a tortoise-shell; **tortoise-plant**, a South African plant, *Testudinaria elephantipes*, allied to the yam, having a large fleshy root-stock growing above ground, the surface of which becomes deeply cracked so as to suggest the carapace of a tortoise; also called *elephant's foot* and *Hottentot's bread*; **tortoise-roof** = sense 2; **tortoise-roofed** *a.*, having a roof resembling a tortoise-shell; **tortoise rotifer**, a rotifer or wheel-animalcule of the family *Brachionidæ*, having a broad shield-shaped body; **tortoise tent**, a kind of tent with a roof shaped like the shell of a tortoise; **tortoise-wood**: see quot.

c **1711** PETIVER *Gazophyl.* VI. lix, Brasil *Tortoise Beetle ..Its Legs and Body of a golden green, with Copper Edges, it creeps softly, and is slow to fly. **1826** KIRBY & SP. *Entomol.* III. xxix. 74 *Cassida viridis*, a tortoise beetle,.. covers her group of eggs with a partially transparent membrane. **1861** HULME tr. *Moquin-Tandon* II. III. 178 *Tortoise broth is prepared from the flesh of the Testudo Græca. ..Some of the fresh-water tortoises may be substituted. **1808** PARKINSON *Org. Rem. Former World* II. xxii. 225 The extraordinary fossil, which, from the disposition of the plates of which it is formed, may be termed the *Tortoise Encrinite. **1855** KINGSLEY *Heroes, Theseus* II. 213 Holla, thou *tortoise-feeder. **1818** MILMAN *Samor* 83 Thou *tortoise-footed sluggard! **1750** PARSONS in *Phil. Trans.* (1753) XLVII. 120 The *tortoise-headed seal. On the shores of many parts of Europe. **1865** J. H. INGRAHAM *Pillar of Fire* (1872) 223 A tortoise-headed god. **1873** E. BRENNAN *Witch of Nemi*, etc. 163 Fain would I beguile the *tortoise-hours. **1697** DAMPIER *Voy. round World* (1699) 37 The Moskito-men make their own striking Instruments as Harpoons, Fish-hooks, and *Tortoise-Iron or Pegs. c **1630** DRUMM. OF HAWTH. *Poems* Wks. (1711) 36 Stone-rolling Tay, Tine *tortoise-like that flows. **1645** BP. HALL *Remedy Discontents* 141 What is this, but Tortoise-like to be clogg'd with a weighty shel? **1804** [see TORTOISE-SHELL 4 b]. **1820** SHELLEY *Hymn to Mercury* xxv, With his left hand about his knees—the right Held his belovèd *tortoise-lyre tight. **1865** TYLOR *Early Hist. Man.* xii. 334 The *Tortoise-myths of North America and India. **1690** DRYDEN *Don Sebast.* III. i, Thou mov'st a *tortoise-pace to my relief. a **1649** DRUMM. OF HAWTH. *Cypress Grove* Wks. (1711) 122 Swift and active pilgrims come to the end of it in the morning or at noon, which *tortoise-paced wretches..scarce..crawl unto at midnight. **1866** *Treas. Bot.*, *Tortoise-plant. **1855** SINGLETON *Virgil* I. 288 Leaguered by the *tortoise-roof. **1886** *Pall Mall G.* 12 Oct. 4/1 They [Mormons] convene within that hideously ugly, *tortoise-roofed building called the Tabernacle. **1826** KIRBY & SP. *Entomol.* III. xxix. 77 Those singular immovable *tortoise-shaped insects. **1890** *Daily News* 8 Apr. 3/2 The patients found every care bestowed upon them in the *tortoise tent. **1901** *Daily Chron.* 23 July 3/2 A good case made out for the 'tortoise' tent as used by the Portland Hospital. **1866** *Treas. Bot.*, **Tortoise-wood*, a variety of Zebra-wood.

**Tortoise-shell** (tǭ·ɹtəs,ʃe·l, *colloq.* tǭ·ɹtəʃel).

**1.** The shell, esp. the upper shell or carapace, of a tortoise, consisting of horny scales covering the dermal skeleton. **a.** with *a* and *pl.*

**1601** HOLLAND *Pliny* IX. x. I. 241 Among the Islands principally in the red sea, they use Tortoise shells..for boats and wherries. **1644** EVELYN *Diary* 21 Mar., Curiosities of ivory and tortoise-shells. a **1843** SOUTHEY *Common-pl. Bk.* Ser. II. (1849) 570 In Yucatan they made a musical instrument of the tortoise-shell, preserved whole. **1863** W. C. BALDWIN *Afr. Hunting* 388 A drink of muddy water..out of a dirty tortoise-shell.

**b.** As a material (without *a* or *pl.*): The shell of certain tortoises, esp. that of the hawk's-bill turtle, *Chelone imbricata*, which is semi-transparent, with a mottled or clouded coloration, and is extensively used in ornamental work, as inlaying, etc.

**1632** EARL OF CORK *Diary* in *Lismore Papers* Ser. I. (1886) III. 132 A cabbonett of Torties shell. **1688** R. HOLME *Armoury* II. 206/1 The Turks have a kind of Tortois-shell..of which they make hafts for Knives. **1703** DAMPIER *Voy.* III. I. 81 The Hawksbill-Turtle..of Brazil is most sought after..for its Shell, which..is the clearest and best-clouded Tortoise-shell in the World. **1756** MRS. CALDERWOOD in *Coltness Collect.* (Maitl. Club) 199 A bit of horn or tortyshell. **1768** HOLDSWORTH *On Virgil* 131 Some of the Romans were so extravagant as to cover their doors and door-cases with Indian tortoise-shell. **1779** FORREST *Voy. N. Guinea* 112 At Krudo, and the islands near it, may be got much tortoiseshell. **1838** DICKENS *Nich. Nick.* xv, The tortershell would have affected the brain. **1841** LANE *Arab. Nts.* I. 123 Made of wood,..inlaid with mother-of-pearl, tortoise-shell, etc.

† **2.** = TORTOISE 2 a and b. *Obs.*

a **1661** HOLYDAY *Juvenal* ii. (1673) 29/2 Like souldiers,.. when..they cast themselves..into the military figure of the testudo, or the torteise-shell. **1726** LEONI *Alberti's Archit.* I. 68 The ditch..will hinder the moveable Tortoise-shell.. from approaching the wall.

**3.** Short for (*a*) *tortoise-shell cat*, (*b*) *tortoise-shell butterfly*: see 4 b.

**1840** *P. Parley's Ann.* 113 Oh, what a pretty little kitten! what a beautiful little dear tortoiseshell! **1884** *Pall Mall G.* 12 Aug. 3/2 A splendid specimen of the large tortoise-shell was fluttering about Westminster Bridge. **1903** *Westm. Gaz.* 11 Aug. 10/2 Of all flowers..that which the Red Admirals, Peacocks, and Tortoiseshells seem to like best is peppermint. **1903** F. SIMPSON *Bk. Cat* xvii. 208 Real tortoiseshells may be called tricolour cats, for they should bear three colours.., namely black, red, and yellow, in distinct patches or blotches.

**4.** *attrib.* or as *adj.* **a.** Made of tortoise-shell.

**1651** in *Verney Mem.* (1904) I. 480 His toilet equipment includes..12 Tortus shell Agendas, 2 gold picktooths. **1652** in *10th Rep. Hist. MSS. Comm.* App. I. 38 Fyue torter shell spoones. **1683** *Lond. Gaz.* No. 1809/4 A great Tortoise-shell Comb, in a Case of the same. **1689** *Ibid.* No. 2416/4 A very large Tortoise-shell Tobacco Box. **1836–9** DICKENS *Sk. Boz, Doctors' Commons*, A very fat and red-faced gentleman, in tortoise-shell spectacles.

**b.** Having the colouring or appearance of tortoise-shell; mottled or variegated with black, red, and yellow, or similar colours; *spec.* **tortoise-shell butterfly**, one of several butterflies, esp. the European *Vanessa urticæ* and *V. polychloros*, and the American *Aglais milberti*; **tortoise-shell cat**, a domestic cat of this colour; **tortoise-shell goose** (see quot. 1885); **tortoise-shell palm** (see quot. 1902); **tortoise-shell tiger** (see TIGER *sb.* 1 b); **tortoise-shell ware**, a fine kind of pottery coloured with oxide of copper and manganese.

1782 W. CURTIS *Brown-tail Moth* 6 The *Papilio Urticæ*, and *Iō*, small Tortoise-shell and Peacock Butterflies. 1791 HUDDESFORD *Salmag., Monody death Dick* 141 Cats..sable, sandy, grey, and tortoiseshell. 1803 SHAW *Gen. Zool.* IV. 471 Tortoise-shell Sparus..: colour brown, with a strong suffusion of pale yellow. 1804 *Ibid.* V. 444 Tortoise-shell Tetrodon...The Linnæan name [*Tetrodon testudineus*] of this fish is supposed to have been given from its tortoise-like beak, but perhaps, with more propriety, from its variegated skin. 1858 LYTTON *What will he do* I. xiv, They kept a tortoise-shell cat and a canary. 1885 SWAINSON *Provinc. Names Birds* 148 White-fronted Goose (*Anser albifrons*)... Tortoise-shell goose (Ireland). From the mottled markings on the abdomen. 1902 P. FOUNTAIN *Mounts. & Forests S. Amer.* x. 270 The tortoise-shell palm ..the leaves of which are so hard, and withal flexible, that combs, spoons, and ornamental articles are made of it. 1903 F. SIMPSON *Bk. Cat* xxv. 284 The tortoiseshell tom is a most rare and uncommon animal.

**c.** Producing tortoise-shell: **tortoise-shell turtle**, the hawk's-bill turtle, or other species from which tortoise-shell is obtained.

1886 MIVART in *Encycl. Brit.* XX. 446/2 In the other Chelonians there are large epidermal shields, which may overlap, as in the Tortoise-shell Turtle (*C[helonia] imbricata*) and others.

**5.** *Comb.*, as *tortoiseshell-producing* adj.

1883 W. S. KENT in A. J. Adderley *Fisheries Bahamas* 31 (Fish. Exhib. Publ.) The edible turtle (*Chelone midas*) and the tortoiseshell-producing variety (*Caretta imbricata*) ..among the marine products of the Bahamas.

† **To·rtor.** *Obs.* Also 6–7 -our(e. [L., agent-n. from *torquēre*, *tort-um* to twist, torture.] A torturer, tormentor; an executioner.

1570 FOXE *A. & M.* (ed. 2) 125/2 The boucherlye tortoure pluckte the skynne from the crowne of hys head. 1606 tr. *Rollock's Lect. on 1 Thess.* 305 The conscience..as a tortor within thee to torment thee. 1610 HOLLAND *Camden's Brit.* I. 410 The Tortor proudly did the feat, but cleere he went not quit; That holy Martyr lost his head, this cruell wretch his sight. 1619 PURCHAS *Microcosmus* xlii. 401 Tortures and Tortours, Deuills and Deuillish Plagues.

**Tortor, Tortou**, obs. ff. TORTURE, TORTOISE.

**Tortour**, var. TORTOR *Obs.*; obs. f. TORTURE.

**Tortricid** (tǭ·ɹtrisid), *a.* and *sb.* [f. mod.L. *Tortrīcidæ* pl., f. TORTRIX: see -ID [3].] **a.** *Entom. adj.* Belonging to the family *Tortricidæ* of *Lepidoptera*, comprising the leaf-roller moths, typified by the genus *Tortrix*; *sb.* a moth of this family. **b.** *Zool. adj.* Belonging to the family *Tortricidæ* of snakes, typified by the genus *Tortrix* or *Ilysia*; *sb.* a snake of this family. So **To·rtricine** (-səin), *a.* and *sb.* = tortricid; **To·rtricoid** (-koid) *a.*, belonging to the suborder *Tortricoidea* of *Ophidia*, including the family *Tortricidæ* (see b above).

1889 MARY E. BAMFORD *Up & Down Brooks* 113 The small tortricid moths that, as caterpillars, curl the leaves of rose-bushes.

‖ **Tortrix** (tǭ·ɹtriks). Pl. **tortrices** (-əi·sīz). [mod.L. *tortrix*, *-īcem*, fem. of TORTOR, but taken in the literal sense 'twister', in reference to the leaf-rolling habits of the larvæ.]

**1.** *Entom.* A genus of moths, typical of the family *Tortricidæ* (see prec. a); a moth of this genus or family, a leaf-roller moth.

1797 *Encycl. Brit.* (ed. 3) XIV. 263/2 (Families of Moths) 5. The tortrices. The wings are exceeding obtuse, their exterior margin is curve, and declines towards the sides of the body. 1819 G. SAMOUELLE *Entomol. Compend.* 425 *Tortrix Avellana.* The hazel Tortrix. 1834 R. MUDIE *Brit. Birds* (1841) I. 347 The eggs and larvæ of the tortrices and other insects which they [tits] pick up. 1909 *Daily News* 31 Mar. 5 The rook..preys largely on the larvæ and pupæ of the oak tortrix, a most destructive insect.

**2.** *Zool.* A genus of snakes, also called *Ilysia*, including the coral-snake of Guiana, *T.* (*I.*) *scytale*.

1843 *Penny Cycl.* XXV. 79/2 *Tortrix*, Oppel's name for a genus of serpents. 1864 in WEBSTER.

**Tortu, tortuce, tortue**, obs. ff. TORTOISE.

† **Tortue**, *a. Obs. rare*—[1]. [a. F. *tortu*, *-ue* (1314 in Hatz.-Darm.), f. L. *tortus*, F. *tort* twisted.] = TORTUOUS 1.

c 1450 *Merlin* xiv. 206 He bar [on a banner] a dragon.. and the taile was a fadome and an half of lengthe tortue.

**Tortueis, tortuga, tortuis**: see TORTOISE.

[**Tortulous**, erron. form of TORULOUS.

1864 in WEBSTER.]

**Tortuose** (tǭ·ɹtiu,ōus), *a. rare*—[1]. [ad. L. *tortuōs-us*: see TORTUOUS.] = TORTUOUS 1.

1829 LOUDON *Encycl. Plants* (1836) 471 Stem tortuose.

**Tortuosity** (tǭɹtiu,ǫ·sĭti). [ad. L. *tortuōsitās*, from *tortuōs-us* TORTUOUS: see -ITY. Cf. F. *tortuosité*, Pr. *tortuositat*, It. *tortuosità*.] The quality or condition of being tortuous; twistedness, crookedness, sinuosity; an instance of this.

**1.** *lit.*: cf. next, 1.

1603 HOLLAND *Plutarch's Mor.* III. 686 The tortuositie of the bodie and branches. 1658 PHILLIPS, *Tortuosity*,.. a winding, or crooking in and out. 1793 R. MYLNE *Rep. Thames* 40 The crookedness or tortuosity of its course. 1851 LANDOR *Popery* xiv. 42 A thread which has long been twisted carries with it when untwisted the tortuosity of its entanglement. 1887 *Proc. R. Geog. Soc.* Apr. 253 The extreme tortuosity of the river Yang-tsze.

**b.** *Geom.*: see quot. 1867, and cf. next, 1 c.

1867 THOMSON & TAIT *Nat. Phil.* I. I. § 7 There are not two curvatures, but only a curvature..of which the plane is continuously changing...The course of such a curve is, in common language, well called 'tortuous'; and the measure of the corresponding property is conveniently called Tortuosity. 1898 A. N. WHITEHEAD *Univ. Algebra* I. 131 A curve locus of any order of tortuosity.

**2.** *fig.* Mental or moral crookedness: cf. next, 2.

1621 T. GRANGER *Comm. on Eccl.* ii. 14. 63 Hee discerneth the vprightnesse of godlinesse, and the tortuosity of wickednesse. 1767 A. CAMPBELL *Lexiph.* (1774) 62 To convict him of the tortuosity of his imaginary rectitude. 1818 BYRON *Juan* I. ccviii, Led by some tortuosity of mind. 1851 *Fraser's Mag.* XLIV. 336 The charge of deliberate tortuosity of action and double-dealing.

**3.** with *a* and *pl.* An instance of this, or something that exemplifies it; a twisted or crooked object, a twist, turn, winding. **a.** *lit.*: cf. 1.

1646 SIR T. BROWNE *Pseud. Ep.* v. v. 239 That tortuosity or complicated nodosity we usually call the Navell. 1853 KANE *Grinnell Exp.* xvii. (1856) 131 The linear distance, including tortuosities, is but three hundred miles.

**b.** *fig.*: cf. 2.

1677 GALE *Crt. Gentiles* II. IV. 109 Sin is said to be a Tortuositie or wresting of the Law. 1751 JOHNSON *Rambler* No. 122 ℙ 3 The tortuosities of imaginary rectitude. 1837 CARLYLE *Misc., Mirabeau* (1840) V. 139 The strangest of styles..distracted into tortuosities, dislocations. 1856 DORAN *Knts. & their Days* viii. 126 In tracing the tortuosities of this chivalric romance.

**Tortuous** (tǭ·ɹtiu,əs), *a.* [a. AF. *tortuous* (12–13th c. in Hatz.-Darm.) = 14th c. F. *tortueux*, ad. L. *tortuōs-us*, 'full of crooks or turns or twists', f. *tortu-s* a twisting, f. *tort-*, ppl. stem of *torquēre* to twist.]

**1.** Full of twists, turns, or bends; twisted, winding, crooked, sinuous.

1426 LYDG. *De Guil. Pilgr.* 18320 A camell..is so encomerous Off bak corvyd and tortuous. c 1450 *Merlin* xxii. 393 The dragon..be-tokened the kynge Arthur and his power;..and the taile that was so tortuouse be-tokened the grete treson of the peple. 1551 RECORDE *Pathw. Knowl.* I. Defin., Paralleles tortuouse, whiche bowe contrarie waies with their two endes. 1667 MILTON *P. L.* IX. 516 Hee..of his tortuous Traine Curld many a wanton wreath in sight of Eve. 1768 STERNE *Sent. Journ., Riddle Explained*, The most difficult and tortuous passages of the heart! 1811 A. T. THOMSON *Lond. Disp.* II. (1818) 317 The root is perennial, woody, and tortuous. 1839 DARWIN *Voy. Nat.* ix. (1879) 186 We found the river-course very tortuous.

† **b.** *Astron.* Applied to the six signs of the zodiac from Capricornus to Gemini, which (in northern latitudes) rise more obliquely than the other six. *Obs. rare*—[1].

c 1391 CHAUCER *Astrol.* ii. § 28 Thise same signes, fro the heued of capricorne vnto the ende of geminis, ben cleped tortuos signes or kroked signes, for they arisen embelif on owre Orisonte.

**c.** *Geom.* Applied to a curve of which no two successive portions are in the same plane; also called a *non-plane curve*, *curve in space*, or *curve of double curvature* (see CURVATURE 1 b).

1867 [see TORTUOSITY 1 b].

**2.** *fig.* Not direct or straightforward; indirect, irregular, devious, circuitous, crooked: esp. in a moral sense. (In quot. 1801 app. Dealing in quaint 'turns' of speech or expression.)

[1682: see TORTIOUS 4.] 1801 LD. CALTHORPE *Let.* in *Wilberforce's Priv. Papers* (1897) 104 Sir W. Scott..was very tortuous and amusing. 1823 SCOTT *Quentin D.* viii, The unscrupulous cunning with which he assisted in the execution of the schemes of his master's tortuous policy. 1858 SEARS *Athan.* III. vii. 319 A narrow and tortuous criticism. 1865 MILL *Exam. Hamilton* 415 The tortuous phraseology by which our author evades recognising the ideas of truth and falsity. 1911 *Times* 2 Nov. 3/4 A more tortuous way of trying to get possession of goods he had never heard of.

¶ **3.** Malign (*obs.*); wrongful. (Misused for or confused with TORTIOUS.)

1594 GREENE & LODGE *Looking Glasse* (1598) E iv b, What tortuous planets..Hath made the concaue of the earth vnclose? 1839 *Times* 13 May, Keeping tortuous possession of premises after their several gentlemen had departed. 1839 *Morn. Herald* 3 June, The first action ever brought against a returning officer for the tortuous refusal of a vote for members of parliament.

Hence **To·rtuously** *adv.*, in a tortuous manner (*lit.* and *fig.*; in quot. 1839 misused for TORTIOUSLY); **To·rtuousness**, the quality or condition of being tortuous, tortuosity.

1824 *New Monthly Mag.* X. 175 Musty precedents.. which an ingenious tortuousness may call in. 1839 *Morn. Herald* 3 June, Any person, whose vote has been..tortuously refused at an election. 1853 KANE *Grinnell Exp.* xlv. (1856) 413 We wound our way tortuously among them. 1862 H. SPENCER *First Princ.* II. ix. § 80 (1875) 245 In proportion to the complexity of social forces is the tortuousness of social movements. 1884 *Pall Mall G.* 8 Aug. 5/1 Puget Sound..runs southward tortuously from Vancouver Island far into the rugged heart of the Washington territory.

**Torturable** (tǭ·ɹtiŭrăb'l), *a. rare.* [f. TORTURE *v.* + -ABLE.] Capable of being tortured. Hence **To·rturableness** (*rare*).

1655–87 H. MORE *App. Antid.* v. § 4. 193, I..assert that a torturable being is a Spirit incorporate. 1727 BAILEY vol. II, *Torturableness*, capableness of Torture. 1852 BURTON *Crim. Trials Scot.* I. 229 Long confinement having reduced the extent of his torturable strength.

**Torture** (tǭ·ɹtiŭɹ, -tʃəɹ), *sb.* Also 6–7 **tortour, tortor.** [a. F. *torture* (12th c. in Hatz.-Darm.), ad. L. *tortūra* twisting, wreathing; torment, torture; f. *torquēre*, *tort-* to twist, torment.]

**1.** The infliction of excruciating pain, as practised by cruel tyrants, savages, brigands, etc., from a delight in watching the agony of a victim, in hatred or revenge, or as a means of extortion; spec. *judicial torture*, inflicted by a judicial or quasi-judicial authority, for the purpose of forcing an accused or suspected person to confess, or an unwilling witness to give evidence or information; a form of this (often in *pl.*). *To put to* (*the*) *torture*, to inflict torture upon, to torture.

1551 *Acts Privy Counc.* (1891) III. 407 Assisting to the sayd Commissioners for the putting the prisoners..to suche tortours as they shall think expedient. 1593 SHAKS. 2 *Hen. VI*, III. i. 131 You did deuise Strange Tortures for Offendors. 1608 D. PRICE *Chr. Warre* 21 To punish the bad, and to prouide some sharpe and fearful tortors for them. 1653 H. COGAN tr. *Pinto's Trav.* iv. 10 We put the Captain and Pilot to torture, who instantly confessed. 1708 *Act 7 Anne* c. 21 § 5 After [1 July 1709] no Person accused of any Capital Offence or other Crime in Scotland, shall suffer, or be subject or liable to any Torture. 1769 BLACKSTONE *Comm.* (1830) IV. xxv. 326 They erected a rack for torture. 1838 THIRLWALL *Greece* III. xxv. 393 Pisander moved that the persons ..should be put to the torture, that all their accomplices might be known. 1849 MACAULAY *Hist. Eng.* i. (1871) I. 16 According to law, torture..could not..be inflicted on an English subject. 1882 GARDINER *Hist. Eng.* (1884) VI. lxv. 359 *note* 2 Torture had been allowed [in England] by custom as inflicted by the prerogative, but not by law...Torture was inflicted as late as 1640 by prerogative.

† **b.** *transf.* An instrument or means of torture.

1601 SHAKS. *All's Well* IV. iii. 135 He calles for the tortures, what will you say without em? 1621 G. SANDYS *Ovid's Met.* IX. (1626) 178 To teare the torture [*letiferam vestem*] off, he striues. 1721–2 R. WODROW *Suffer. Ch. Scot.* II. xiii. § 5 (1837) II. 458/2 His leg being in the torture [i.e. the boot].

**2.** Severe or excruciating pain or suffering (of body or mind); anguish, agony, torment; the infliction of such.

c 1540 tr. *Pol. Verg. Eng. Hist.* (Camden) I. 269 Doe you preferre the horrible tortures of warre beefore tranquillitee? 1593 SHAKS. *Lucr.* 1287 And that deepe torture may be cal'd a Hell, When more is felt than one hath power to tell. 1612 WOODALL *Surg. Mate* Wks. (1653) 185 Pain and torture of the intestines. 1659 H. MORE *Immort. Soul* II. x. § 6. 220 Who would bear the tortures of Fears and Jealousies, if he could avoid it? 1734 BP. PETRE *Let.* in E. H. Burton *Life Challoner* (1909) I. 93 He wasted away by degrees under the torture of the Strangury. 1744 M. BISHOP *Life & Adv.* 52 They were in such great Torture, wishing they had never come to Sea. 1797 MRS. RADCLIFFE *Italian* ii, He determined to relieve himself from the tortures of suspense. 1878 BROWNING *La Saisiaz* 353 As in one or other stage Of a torture writhe they.

**b.** *transf.* A cause of severe pain or anguish. (In quot. 1859 *humorous*.)

1612 BRINSLEY *Ludus Lit.* viii. (1627) 106 The labour of learning..Authours without booke..is one of the greatest tortures to the poore schollers. 1859 *Habits Gd. Society* xi. 300 Never was a more solemn torture created for mankind than these odious dinner-parties. 1873 HAMERTON *Intell. Life* II. i. (1875) 52 An ugly picture was torture to his cultivated eye. 1908 R. BAGOT *A. Cuthbert* xxvii, Do not make me put it into words, it is torture!

**3.** *transf.* and *fig.* with various allusions: Severe pressure; violent perversion or 'wresting'; violent action or operation; severe testing or examination.

1605 BACON *Adv. Learn.* II. xvii. § 9 All the kernell [is] forced out and expulsed with the torture and presse of the Methode. c 1670 HOBBES *Dial. Com. Laws* (1681) 147 This Statute cannot by Sir Edw. Cokes Torture be made to say it. 1691 RAY *Creation* I. (1692) 87 All the Tortures of Vulcan or corrosive Waters. 1818 BYRON *Ch. Har.* IV. lxix, The hell of waters! where they howl and hiss, And boil in endless torture. 1855 BREWSTER *Newton* I. iv. 91 Experimental results, that may put his own views to the torture. 1887 *Spectator* No. 3067. 491/2 Much so-called wit of the present day is nothing more than the systematic torture of words.

**4.** *attrib.* and *Comb.*, as *torture-chamber*, *-house*, *-monger*, *-rack*, *-room*, *-wheel*; *torture-scored* adj.

1615 J. STEPHENS *Ess. & Char.* (1857) 133 An Impudent Censurer—Is the torture-monger of Wit, ready for execution before Judgement. 1829 SCOTT *Anne of G.* x, Building castles with dungeons and folter-kammers, or torture-chambers. 1837 CARLYLE *Fr. Rev.* I. I. ii, Torture-wheels and conical *oubliettes*. a 1847 ELIZA COOK *Silence* 2 Poverty has a sharp and goading power To wring the torture cry. 1898 S. COLERIDGE *Step by Step* 4 The guardian of the secret of the torture-house. 1899 *Westm. Gaz.* 9 Feb. 2/1 The torture-instinct (common alone to human and feline).

**To·rture**, *v.* Also 6 -or, 7 -er. [f. prec. sb.: cf. F. *torturer* (1480 in Hatz.-Darm.).]

**1.** *trans.* To inflict torture upon, subject to torture; *spec.* to subject to judicial torture; put to the torture. Also *absol.*

1593 SHAKS. 2 *Hen. VI*, III. i. 376 Say he be taken, rackt, and tortured; I know, no paine they can inflict vpon him, Will make him say, I mou'd him to those Armes. 1594

*First Pt. Contention* (1843) 35 A murtherer or foule felonous theefe..I tortord above the rate of common law. **1611** BIBLE *Heb.* xi. 35 Others were tortured [*16th c. versions* racked], not accepting deliuerance. **1632** LITHGOW *Trav.* x. 480 Hee thought hee saw a man Torturing [*i. e.* being tortured]. **1651** HOBBES *Leviath.* I. xiv. 70 What is in that case confessed, tendeth to the ease of him that is Tortured. **1847** MRS. A. KERR tr. *Ranke's Hist. Servia* x. 203 Shall I live to see thee slowly tortured to death by the Turks? **1896** 'M. FIELD' *Attila* II. 48 You will not torture? *Placidia.* We use that to extort confession, not As punishment.

**2.** To inflict severe pain or suffering upon; to torment; to distress or afflict grievously; also, to exercise the mind severely, to puzzle or perplex greatly. Also *absol.* to cause extreme pain.

**1588** SHAKS. *L. L. L.* v. ii. 60 That same Berowne Ile torture ere I goe. **1611** SPEED *Hist. Gt. Brit.* IX. xvi. (1623) 842 To consider how Writers torter us with the diuersities of reports. **1715–20** POPE *Iliad* XI. 985 The closing flesh.. ceas'd to glow, The wound to torture, and the blood to flow. **1769** *Junius Lett.* xxix. (1797) I. 203 When the mind is tortured, it is not at the command of any outward power. It is the sense of guilt which constitutes the punishment, and creates that torture. **1849** MACAULAY *Hist. Eng.* vi. II. 67 Jeffreys was..tortured by a cruel internal malady. **1855** *Ibid.* xii. III. 167 It was rumoured..that he was tortured by painful emotions.

**3.** *fig.* **a.** To act upon violently in some way, so as to strain, twist, wrench, distort, pull or knock about, etc.

**1626** BACON *Sylva* § 137 The Bow tortureth the String continually, and thereby holdeth it in a Continuall Trepidation. **1743** DAVIDSON *Æneid* VII. 198 A top whirling under the twisted lash, which boys.. exercise and torture in a large circuit. **1822** SHELLEY *To Jane—the Recollection*, Pines..Tortured by storms to shapes as rude As serpents interlaced. **186**. B. HARTE *My Other Self* in *Fiddletown*, etc. (1873) 120, I stood at the glass in the desperate attempt to torture my hair after the fashion of young Wobbles.

**b.** To 'twist' (language, etc.) from the proper or natural meaning or form; to distort, pervert.

**1648** JENKYN *Blind Guide* i. 8 To torture Scripture for the defending of his errors. **1682** DRYDEN *Mac Fl.* 208 There thou mayst.. torture one poor word ten thousand ways. **1803** VISCT. STRANGFORD *Camoens' Poems* Notes (1810) 127 It is surprising that this idea has not been more ramified and tortured by the English metaphysical poets of that school. **1869** BALDW. BROWN *Chr. Policy Life* (1880) 281 There might be a sentence here and there which might be tortured to bear that meaning.

**4.** To extract by torture; to extort. *rare.*

**1687** tr. *Sallust's Wks.* (1692) 29 They..by all manner of extortions hale and torture money to themselves. **1818** KEATS *Endym.* III. 256 Like a wretch from whom the rack Tortures hot breath, and speech of agony.

**Tortured** (tǭ·ɹtiŭɹd, -tʃəɹd), *ppl. a.* [f. prec. + -ED[1].] Subjected or put to torture (*lit.* and *fig.*); tormented; wrested, etc.: see the verb.

**1603** DRAYTON *Bar. Wars* IV. xxxix, Eu'ry cadence as a torturde cry. **1687** DRYDEN *Hind & P.* II. 119 The tortur'd Text. **1743** FRANCIS tr. *Hor., Odes* II. xiii. 44 Charm'd by the melodious Strain The tortur'd Ghosts forget their Pain. **1814** SCOTT *Ld. of Isles* IV. xi, Scarba's isle, whose tortured shore Still rings to Corrievreken's roar. **1838** LYTTON *Leila* I. vi, Thy father filled his treasuries from the gold of many a tortured Hebrew.

**To·rturer.** Also 6–7 -or. [f. TORTURE *v.* + -ER[1].] One who or that which inflicts or causes torture; a tormentor; *spec.* one who executes judicial torture.

**1593** SHAKS. *Rich. II*, III. ii. 198, I play the Torturer, by small and small To lengthen out the worst, that must be spoken. **1597** A. M. tr. *Guillemeau's Fr. Chirurg.* 52 b/2 Two torturors will deprive a man of life..the torturer of greefe and sorrowe is the most cruellest. **1611** SHAKS. *Cymb.* v. v. 215 Thou King, send out For Torturors ingenious. **1780** BECKFORD *Italy* (1834) I. 69 That respectable corps, the torturers of butterflies. **1805** SOUTHEY *Madoc in Azt.* II. 114 Thou know'st how manfully These tribes..in bonds Defy their torturers. **1830** SCOTT *Ayrshire Trag.* III. i, A torturer of phrases into sonnets.

**To·rturesome** (-sǝ̆m), *a. rare.* [f. TORTURE *sb.* + -SOME.] Characterized by, or causing torture; extremely painful or distressing.

**1889** E. SALTUS *Tristrem Varick* 146 The enforced inactivity was torturesome as suspense. **1906** CHARL. MANSFIELD *Girl & Gods* viii, Your life in every way must be one of exquisite or torturesome emotion.

**To·rturing,** *vbl. sb.* [f. TORTURE *v.* + -ING[1].] The action of the verb TORTURE; infliction of torture; tormenting; *fig.* wresting, perversion.

**1633** P. FLETCHER *Purple Isl.* XII. lxv, He soon was led Unto a thousand thousand torturings. **1638** DRUMM. OF HAWTH. *Irene* Wks. (1711) 170 Ruines of noble houses,.. confiscation of estates, torturing of bodies. **1753** W. STEWART in *Scots Mag.* Mar. 135/2 What strange..torturing of.. upright actions must there be, to make this criminal? **1765** BLACKSTONE *Comm.* (1830) I. i. 133 Prohibition not only of killing and maiming, but also of torturing (to which our laws are strangers). **1855** MAURICE *Patriarchs & Lawg.* xii. (1882) 223 These are not inferences drawn from the story by an unnatural torturing.

**b.** *attrib.* **To·rturing-stock** (*nonce-wd.*), one upon whom torture is inflicted.

**1622** BP. HALL *Serm. bef. Jas. I* 15 Sept., Wks. (1624) 493 Yet..were these poor torturing-stocks higher..than their persecutors.

**To·rturing,** *ppl. a.* [f. as prec. + -ING[2].] That tortures; inflicting or causing torture; tormenting, excruciating.

**1611** SIR W. MURE *Misc. Poems* ii. 46 He [Cupid]..fled away..; But, (woes me,) left behind his tort'ring toyle. **1669** A. THOROLD in *St. Papers, Dom.* 505 An eminent French Protestant..put to a torturing death. **1794** MRS. RADCLIFFE *Myst. Udolpho* xxxiii, This state of torturing suspense. **1817** SHELLEY *Rev. Islam* x. viii, [He] bade the torturing wheel Be brought. **1867** AUG. J. E. WILSON *Vashti* xvii, Her past.., of which the bare memory was so torturing.

Hence **To·rturingly** *adv.*

*a* **1625** FLETCHER & MASSINGER *Laws of Candy* III. ii, An host of furies Could not have baited me more torturingly. **1882** T. HARDY *Two on a Tower* ix, He was there a torturingly long time.

**Torturous** (tǭ·ɹtiŭrəs), *a.* Also 5, 7 torterous. [a. AF. *torturous* = OF. *tortureus, -eux*, f. L. *tortūra* TORTURE: see -OUS.] Full of, involving, or causing torture; tormenting, excruciating; in first quot., given to inflicting torture.

*c* **1495** *Epitaffe*, etc. in *Skelton's Wks.* (1843) II. 392 O turmentoure, traytoure, torterous tyraunte. **1600** ABP. ABBOT *Exp. Jonah* 199 Dying he must live and living he must dy in a torturous execution. **1618** M. BARET *Horsemanship, Cures*, They follow the torterous inventions of hard snaffles. **1711** SHAFTESB. *Charac.* II. II. ii. (1737) II. 146 The assuaging of the most torturous Pain. **1871** R. ELLIS *Catullus* lxv. 1 Outworn with sorrow, with hours of torturous anguish.

**b.** *fig.* Involving perversion or violent dislocation (of words, etc.): cf. TORTURE *sb.* 3, *v.* 3 b.

**1841** D'ISRAELI *Amen. Lit.* (1859) II. 27 Their torturous arrangement of words without rhythm or cadence. **1890** *Standard* 23 Aug. 3/2 Tortuous, as well as torturous, renderings of Psalms, Te Deums, Canticles, and responses.

Hence **To·rturously** *adv.*, very painfully.

**1857** W. ARNOT *Let.* in Mrs. A. Fleming *Life* vi. (1877) 320 They make the carriages torturously hard. *c* **1873** J. ADDIS *Eliz. Echoes* (1879) 77 A fate Through all thy Future torturously throbbing.

**Tortus, -use,** obs. forms of TORTOISE.

**Tortys, tortyse**: see TORTIS.

‖ **Torula** (tǫ·riulă). *Biol.* Pl. **-æ** (-ī). [mod.L. dim. (with change of gender) of TORUS (sense 3): cf. F. *torule* masc.] *lit.* A small rounded swelling or bulge. **a.** Each of the minute rounded cells of various fungi or microbes, as the yeast-plant and certain endoparasitic organisms; also, a chain of such cells. **b.** (With capital.) A genus of fungi, chiefly fermentative. (Introd. by Persoon, 1796.)

**1833** HOOKER *Brit. Flora* II. II. 359 (Genus) *Tórula.* Pers. *Sporidia* chained together into moniliform erect flocci. **1860** BERKELEY *Brit. Fungology* 326 Torula, P. Spores tomiparous, simple. **1861** H. MACMILLAN *Footn. Page of Nat.* 243 In all saccharine fluids undergoing the alcoholic and even the acetous fermentation these minute torulæ or yeast-cells make their appearance. **1875** HUXLEY & MARTIN *Elem. Biol.* i. 2 Each granule [of yeast] (which is termed a *Torula*) is..a round, or oval, transparent body...The *Torulæ* are either single, or associated in heaps or strings. *Ibid.* iv. 26 *Bacteria*, like *Torulæ* and *Protococci*, are not killed by drying up, and from their excessive minuteness they must be carried about still more easily than *Torulæ* are.

Hence **Torulaceous** (-ēi·ʃəs) *a.*, consisting of torulæ; belonging to the order *Torulacei* of fungi; **To·rulifo·rm** *a.* (erron. torulaform: see -FORM), having the form of a torula or chain of rounded cells, moniliform; **To·ruloid** *a.*, resembling a torula; belonging or allied to the genus *Torula.*

**1876** tr. *Schützenberger's Ferment.* 205 The *torulaceous growth is developed with difficulty, and the transformation is very slow. **1876** tr. *Wagner's Gen. Pathol.* (ed. 6) 92 The filaments are not constricted at the joints, like the moniliform chains (*torulaform) of the globular bacteria. **1874** COOKE *Fungi* 120 Formation of networks of mycelium, or masses of *toruloid cells.

**Torulose** (tǫ·riulōus), *a. Nat. Hist.* [f. TORULA + -OSE (after L. type **torulōsus*): cf. mod.F. *toruleux.*] Having at intervals small rounded swollen parts, as a stem, pod, tube, antenna.

**1806** J. GALPINE *Brit. Bot.* § 309 Arabis...Silique linear, torulose. **1826** KIRBY & SP. *Entomol.* IV. xlvi. 325 Torulose...When they [joints of the antennæ] are a little tumid. **1835** LINDLEY *Introd. Bot.* (1848) I. 154 Thickened slightly at the articulations (torulose). **1887** W. PHILLIPS *Brit. Discomycetes* 103 The paraphyses were septate, and nearly torulose at the upper part.

So **To·rulous** *a.*, in same sense.

**1752** J. HILL *Hist. Anim.* 11 The Brachionus, with a conic torulous body. **1860** MAYNE *Expos. Lex.*, *Torulosus*, ..swelled, or bulged out in a slight degree here and there, like knotted cord: torulous.

‖ **Torulus** (tǫ·riulǝ̆s). *Entom.* Pl. **toruli** (-əi). [mod.L. dim. of *torus* in sense 'couch, bed, seat'.] A cavity or orifice in the head of an insect, forming the socket of the antenna.

**1826** KIRBY & SP. *Entomol.* III. xxxiv. 511 In considering the insertion of antennæ..we must advert first to the orifice (*Torulus*) that receives them. This is a perforation of the crust of the head; commonly..circular...In..*Rhipicera*.. it is a long process..: in another Coleopterous genus, *Priocera*, it has somewhat of the shape of a trumpet. *Ibid.* 512 A membranous ligament is attached by which it is affixed to the torulus.

‖ **Torus** (tōə·rǝ̆s). Pl. **tori** (tōə·rəi). [L. *torus* a swelling, bulge, knot; muscle, brawn; bolster, cushion, couch, etc.: in *Arch.* a round moulding.]

**1.** *Arch.* A large convex moulding, of semicircular or similar section, used especially at the base of a column: resembling the astragal, but much larger.

**1563** SHUTE *Archit.* 11 The Torus, beneth shalbe y^e forth part greater then the Torus aboue. **1768** SPENCE in Holdsworth *Remarks Virgil* 16 The plant which we see sometimes carved on the Torus of Pillars. **1854** H. MILLER *Sch. & Schm.* xiii. (1858) 271 Stairs of polished stone, ornamented in front and at the outer edge by the common fillet and torus. **1873** *Proc. Amer. Phil. Soc.* XIII. 210 The tori were rudely cross-barred.

**2.** *Bot.* The swollen summit of the flower-stalk, which supports the floral organs: = RECEPTACLE 3 b, THALAMUS 2 a.

**1829** LOUDON *Encycl. Plants* (1836) 537 *Sisymbrium.* Silique roundish, sessile upon the torus. **1880** GRAY *Struct. Bot.* vi. § 1. 167 The Torus or Receptacle of the flower, also named Thalamus, is the axis which bears all the other parts.

**3. a.** *Zool.* A protuberant part or organ, as the ventral parapodia in some annelids. *Torus angularis*, a single ossicle which articulates with a pair of interambulacral plates in some starfishes. **b.** *Anat.* 'A smooth rounded ridge or elongated protuberance, as of a muscle; *spec.* the *tuber cinereum* of the brain' (*Syd. Soc. Lex.*).

**1877** HUXLEY *Anat. Inv. Anim.* ix. 564 The free surface of the torus angularis lies in the walls of a sort of vestibule in front of the mouth.

**4.** *Geom.* A surface or solid generated by the revolution of a circle or other conic about any axis; e. g. a solid ring of circular or elliptic section.

**1870** CAYLEY *Math. Papers* VII. 246 The 'Conic Torus', or surface generated by the rotation of a conic about a line whether not in or in the plane of the conic. **1871** *Ibid.* VIII. 25 The general Torus, or surface generated by the rotation of a conic about a fixed axis anywise situate.

**5.** *attrib.* and *Comb.* (chiefly in sense 1).

**1697** EVELYN *Archit.* Misc. Writ. (1825) 378, I take a fillet to be more flat and torus-like. **1789** *Gentl. Mag.* Dec. 1101/2 The torus cap that bears the plinth of the balustrade. **1842** GWILT *Archit.* § 2129 The distinction between torus mouldings and beads in joinery is, that the outer edge of the former always terminates with a fillet, whether the torus be single or double. **1877** KNIGHT *Dict. Mech.*, *Torus Bead-plane*, a certain form of plane for making the semicircular convex molding known as a torus.

† **To-ru·sh,** *v. Obs.* [ME. *to-ruschen*, f. TO-[2] + *ruschen*, RUSH *v.*[2]] *trans.* To dash in pieces; to disperse with force; to rout.

**1387** TREVISA *Higden* (Rolls) IV. 399 Al þis was by Goddis ordinaunce so sodeynliche destroyed, so to russhed and to broke. ? *a* **1400** *Morte Arth.* 1428 The Romaynes..arrayez þame better, And al to-ruscheez oure mene withe theire ryste horsez. **1470–85** MALORY *Arthur* v. x. 176 He..al to russhed and brake the precious stones.

**Torve** (tǫɹv), *a. rare.* [ad. L. *torv-us* grim, frowning: cf. obs. F. *torve* (Cotgr.), Sp., Pg., It. *torvo.*] Stern in aspect; grim, fierce-looking.

**1650** BULWER *Anthropomet.* 72 [They] become thereby dim-sighted, and of a torve or crooked aspect. *a* **1661** FULLER *Worthies, Linc.* (1662) II. 153 He [the devil] is supposed to have overlook'd this Church..with a torve and tetrick countenance, as maligning mens costly devotion. **1862** J. BROWN *Horæ Subs.* Ser. IV. *Our Dogs* 144 Toby made straight at him with a roar too, and an eye more torve than Scrymgeour's. **1894** BLACKMORE *Perlycross* 405 A man,.. torve of aspect.

So **To·rvid** (also 7 *erron.* -ed) [ad. late L. *torvidus*], **To·rvous** *adjs.*, in same sense; **To·rvity** [ad. L. *torvitās*], grimness, fierceness of aspect.

*a* **1639** WEBSTER *Appius & Virg.* v. iii, But yesterday his breath Aw'd Rome, and his least *torved frown was death. **1656** BLOUNT *Glossogr.*, *Torvid*, cruel and spightful in looks, stern, grim, sowre, unpleasant. **1706** E. WARD *Hud. Rediv.* I. XII. 19 Whose torvid Aspect made him show so Like some revengeful Furioso. **1866** J. B. ROSE tr. *Ovid's Met.* iv. 110 With torvid brow Saturnia gazed upon Ixion. **1620** FELTHAM *Resolves* lxxxix. 290 To shew us the inticing spots of this Panther, concealing the *torvitie of her countenance. **1787** *Minor* IV. i. 204 This..increased my governor's natural torvity. **1825** W. TENNANT in Conolly *Mem.* iii. (1861) 75 Terrible John, with his countenance of Sabine torvity. **1694** R. BURTHOGGE *Reason & Nat. Spir.* 162 Some Ludicrous, some *Torvous. **1713** DERHAM *Phys.-Theol.* IV. xiv. 242 It is natural for many Quadrupeds, Birds and Serpents..to put on a torvous angry Aspect, when in Danger. **1833** PALMERSTON *Let.* 7 May, in Bulwer *Life* II. x. 160 Sefton looks torvous when I meet him, that I have not appointed Molyneux.

† **Torve,** *v. Obs.* [OE. *torfian* to throw, cast.] *trans.* To throw, cast.

*c* **1000** *Ags. Gosp.* Mark xii. 41 Ða sæt se hælend..& ʒeseah hu þæt folc hyra feoh torfude on þone toll-sceamul, & maneʒa weliʒe torfudon fela. *c* **1122** *O. E. Chron.* an. 1083, Þa Frencisce men bræcen þone chor & torfedon to wærd þam weofode þær ða munecas wæron. *c* **1175** To-toruion [see TO-[2] 1]. *c* **1205** LAY. 16703 Samuel ꝥ sweord an-hof..& al to-swadde þene king..& þa stucchen tarueden [*c* **1275** toruede] Wide ʒeond þa straten. *a* **1250** *Owl & Night.* 1119 Stones hi doþ in heore slytte & þe to-toruеþ.

**Torves,** obs. pl. of TURF.

**Torvid, Torvity, Torvous**: see after TORVE *a.*

**Tory** (tōə·ri), *sb.* and *a.* [Anglicized spelling of Irish **tóraidhe, -aighe* (tōrĭye) 'pursuer', implied in the derivative *tóraigheachd, tóraidheachd* pursuit: cf. the syncopated Sc. Gaelic *tòrachd* pursuit, pursuing with hostile intent, f. Ir. *tóir* to pursue, *tóirighim* I pursue.

The OIr. agent-nouns in *-(a)id* and *-(a)ige* fall together in mod.Irish in *-(a)idhe* or *-(a)ighe*, whence the uncertainty of the spelling; the native form has not been found in writing, outside of dictionaries. In some Irish Dictionaries, the meaning is given as 'a pursued or persecuted person', hence an 'outlaw', which is not without historical suitability: but the best Irish etymologists agree that the form of the word is that of an agent-noun.

The following passage has what at first sight appears to be the same word, but the date makes this impossible. The writer is treating of the diversity of North American Indian languages, and *Torries* was possibly an Indian word:—

**1634** W. WOOD *New Eng. Prosp.* II. xviii. 92 When any ships come neare the shore, they [Tarrenteens, Indians of Maine] demand whether they be King Charles his Torries, with such a rumbling sound [of *r*], as if one were beating an unbrac't Drumme.]

**A.** *sb.* **1.** In the 17th c., one of the dispossessed Irish, who became outlaws, subsisting by plundering and killing the English settlers and soldiers; a bog-trotter, a rapparee; later, often applied to any Irish Papist or Royalist in arms. *Obs.* exc. *Hist.*

**1646** (Jan. 22) *Exam. P. Congan* in *Cal. Ormonde MSS.* N.S. (1902) I. 105 Some others of the Irish called Tories. **1646** (May 17) MAJ. W. CADOGAN in *Calr. Ormonde MSS.* (1899) II. 39 Divers that had served under Finglas, Rowen and Welsh and such as had been Tories. **1647** *Proclamation* 2 Nov. (MS. Trinity Coll. Dublin, F. 3. 18. No. 22) Roberies ..comitted by the Tories and Rebells upon the Protestants and others adhering to the Protestant partie. **1650** WHITELOCK *Mem.* 12 July (1732) 464/1 That eight Officers..riding upon the Highway [in Ireland], were murder'd by those bloody Highway Rogues called the Tories. **1652** (Dec. 18) *Cal. St. Papers, Dom.* 41, I took the little island in Waterford river, and beat off Sturlock, the great Tory. **1656** BLOUNT *Glossogr.*, *Banditi*, .. in the north of England, Moss-Troopers; in Ireland Tories. **1657** BURTON *Diary* 10 June, *Major Morgan*...We have three beasts to destroy, that lay burdens upon us,—1st, is a public Tory, on whose head we lay 200*l.*, and 40*l.* upon a private Tory's..2d. beast, is a priest, on whose head we lay 10*l.*, if he be eminent, more. 3d. beast, the wolf, on whom we lay 5*l.* a head if a dog; 10*l.* if a bitch. **1675** *Essex Papers* (Camden) I. 307 Wee, the undernamed parrish priests in the County of Kyery,..doe undertake and faithfully promise..That in our respective congregations wee shall publike and solemnly declare, and denounce, all toreys, murtherers, thieves & Robors. **1676** COLES *Dict.*, *Tories*, Irish Out-laws. **1681** E. MURPHY *State Ireland* § 1 Being a cruel Murderer, Rebel and Tory. **1693** G. STORY *Contn. Hist. Wars Irel.* 50 They [Rapparees] never can be reputed other than Tories, Robbers, Thieves, and Boggtrotters. **1707** *Irish Act* 6 *Anne*, c. 11 An Act for the more effectual suppression of tories, robbers, and rapparees. **1769** *Dublin Merc.* 16–19 Sept. 3/2, 24 heifers..were.. driven..into a bog by tories, robbers and rapparees out in arms. **1849** MACAULAY *Hist. Eng.* ii. I. 257 The bogs of Ireland..afforded a refuge to Popish outlaws, much resembling those who were afterwards known as Whiteboys. These men were then [*temp.* Chas. II] called Tories.

†**b.** Extended to (*a*) robbers or bandits of other races, as Border moss-troopers, Scottish Highlanders, (*b*) Rajpoot marauders or outlaws. Also (*c*) *fig.* *Obs.*

(*a*) [**1651** *Mercurius Scoticus* 28 Oct., The Highlanders under Marquesse Huntley and Lord Balcarras..are now betaking themselves to the High-wayes to play the Tories and Robbers.] **1653** COL. LILBURNE *Let. to Cromwell* 16 Oct. (Clarke MSS. LXXXVI. lf. 109 b), Argyll tells mee hee cannott advise mee to advance further, though hee suffer never soe much by those Tories. **1654** R. BAILLIE *Lett. & Jrnls.* (1841) III. 255 The discussing of the Northern Tories would cost him bot a few weeks labour. *a* **1661** FULLER *Worthies, Cumbld.* (1662) I. 216 The..Earl of Carlisle, who routed these English-Tories [*i. e.* moss-troopers] with his Regiment. **1680** KIRKTON *Hist. Ch. Scot.* ii. (1817) 67 Among the tories in the Highlands. **1690** *Ibid.* v. 158 Middleton had undertaken to command the tories on the hills in Cromwell's time.

(*b*) **1662** J. DAVIES tr. *Mandelslo's Trav.* I. 25 These Racboutes are a sort of High-way men or Tories. *Ibid.* 237 The distractions which then shook the State wherein there were eight Armies of Tories, or common Rogues.

(*c*) **1687** KIRBY & BISHOP *Marrow of Astrol.* I. 43 And now I must..drop down a little lower to the Sphere of Mars, who is termed a Tory amongst the Stars.

**2.** With capital T: A nickname given 1679–80 by the Exclusioners (q. v.) to those who opposed the exclusion of James, Duke of York (a Roman Catholic) from the succession to the Crown.

According to Roger North *Examen* (1740) II. v. ¶ 9 The Bill of Exclusion 'led to a common Use of slighting and opprobrious Words; such as *Yorkist*. That..did not scandalise or reflect enough. Then they came to *Tantivy*, which implied Riding Post to Rome...Then, observing that the Duke favoured Irish Men, all his Friends, or those accounted such by appearing against the Exclusion, were straight become *Irish*, and so *wild Irish*, thence *Bogtrotters*, and in the *Copia* of the factious Language, the Word *Tory* was entertained, which signified the most despicable Savages among the Wild Irish'. See also WHIG.

**1681** [see TANTIVY B. 2]. **1681** O. HEYWOOD *Diaries*, etc. 24 Oct. (1881) II. 285 A new name lately come into fashion for Ranters calling themselves by the name of Torys...A gentleman..had a red Ribband in his hat,..he said it signifyed that he was a Tory, whats that sd. she? he ans. an Irish Rebel...I hear further since that..instead of Cavalier and Roundhead, now they are called Torys and Wiggs. **1681** DRYDEN *Abs. & Achit.* To Rdr., Wit and fool are consequents of Whig and Tory; and every man is a knave or an ass to the contrary side. *a* **1685** EARL OF DORSET *Whigs & Tories* in *Coll. Poems* 15 The Fools might be *Whigs*, none but Knaves shou'd be *Toryes*. *a* **1734** NORTH *Exam.* II. v. (1740) 321 Thus the Anti-exclusioners [*c* 1679] were stigmatised with Execration and Contempt, as a Parcel of damn'd *Tories*, for diverse Months together. *Ibid.* 324 The Faction..had found a sarcasmous Name to fling upon the Loyallists,..that of *Tory*, the same as savage Brute and Idiot.

**3.** Hence, from 1689, the name of one of the two great parliamentary and political parties in England, and (at length) in Great Britain.

The party sprang from the 17th century Royalists or Cavaliers, and its members at first were more or less identical with the Anti-Exclusionists or 'Tories' in sense 2. For some years after 1689 the Tories leant more or less decidedly towards the dethroned House of Stuart; but upon the accession of George III they, as a party, abandoned this attitude, retaining the principle of strenuously upholding the constituted authority and order in Church and State, and of opposing concessions in the direction of greater religious liberty. In opposition to the growing demands of Liberalism (see LIBERAL 5), a consistent antagonism to measures for widening the basis of parliamentary representation, or tending to impair the exclusive privileges of the Church as by law established, became their most marked characteristic; but this has in course of time undergone many modifications. As a formal name, 'Tory' was superseded *c* 1830 by CONSERVATIVE, merged after 1886 (when the Conservatives were joined by many who had previously belonged to the Liberal party, in opposing Home Rule for Ireland) in that of UNIONIST. But 'Tory' is still retained (1) colloquially; (2) as expressing attachment to a policy either more old-fashioned (cf. *Old* or *High Tory* in b), or more positive and constructive than that of ordinary Conservatism (cf. *Tory democracy*, C. 3); (3) in hostile usage, identifying the party with the bigotry and opposition to reform and progress charged upon earlier Toryism. Opposed originally and during the 18th c. to WHIG; later to LIBERAL, and (still more) to RADICAL.

**1705** G. LOCKHART *Let. to Dk. Athole* 15 Oct. in 12*th Rep. Hist. MSS. Comm.* App. VIII. 62 Her Majesty having now, more than ever before, devoted herself and interest to the Whigs, the Torys have no hopes of being succesfull in allmost anything..during this parliament. **1710** SWIFT *Jrnl. to Stella* 7 Nov., The Queen passed by us with all Tories about her; not one Whig:..and I have seen her without one Tory. **1711** ADDISON *Spect.* No. 126 ¶ 8 The Knight is a much stronger Tory in the Country than in Town, which..is absolutely necessary for the keeping up his Interest. **1718** [see HIGH-FLYER 3]. **1735–8** BOLINGBROKE *Parties* viii. Wks. 1809 III. 132 The real essences of Whig and Tory were thus [in 1689] destroyed, but the nominal were preserved. **1741** HUME *Ess., Parties Gt. Brit.* (1758) 45 A Tory, therefore, since the revolution, may be defined in a few words, to be a lover of monarchy, tho' without abandoning liberty; and a partizan of the family of Stuart. **1755** JOHNSON, *Tory.* (A cant term, derived, I suppose, from an Irish word signifying a savage.) One who adheres to the ancient constitution of the state, and the apostolical hierarchy of the church of England: opposed to a whig. **1781** — in *Boswell* (1906) II. 396 The prejudice of the Tory is for establishment; The prejudice of the Whig is for innovation. A Tory does not wish to give more real power to Government; but that Government should have more reverence. **1806** T. W. COKE *Let.* 23 Sept. in *Parr's Wks.* (1828) VII. 246 It was..a glorious victory of the Whigs over the Tories. **1827** HALLAM *Const. Hist.* III. xvi, To a tory the constitution, inasmuch as it was the constitution, was an ultimate point,..from which he thought it altogether impossible to swerve; whereas a whig deemed all forms of government subordinate to the public good. **1830** MACAULAY *Ess., Southey's Coll.* (1865) I. 115/2 A Tory of the Tories..won and wore that noblest wreath, 'Ob cives servatos'. **1831** ARNOLD Apr., in *Life & Corr.* (1845) I. vi. 303 The old state of things is gone past recall, and all the efforts of all the Tories cannot save it. *c* **1832** BORROW in Knapp *Life* (1899) I. xiv. 144 As the question is, or will shortly be, Tory or Radical, we say Tory! and advise every honest man to say so too. **1833** GEN. P. THOMPSON *Exerc.* (1842) II. 329 The Tories in Great Britain are defunct;.. they are all vaccinated into 'Conservatives'. **1839** Q. VICTORIA *Jrnl.* 9 May, I said..that I never talked politics with them [the Ladies], and that they were related, many of them, to Tories. **1843** *Penny Cycl.* XXV. 82/2 From the Revolution down to the present time the struggle between the two parties..has been a struggle by the Tories on behalf of the Church, to invest it with political power and privileges, and against the increase of the power of the people in the state, through the House of Commons. **1844** MACAULAY *Ess., Chatham* (1865) II. 361/2 If..we look at the essential characteristics of the Whig and the Tory, we may consider each of them as the representative of a great principle...One is, in an especial manner, the guardian of liberty, and the other of order. One is the moving power, and the other the steadying power of the state. **1882** M. ARNOLD *Irish Ess.*, etc. 164 The Conservatives, or, as they are now beginning to be called again, the Tories. **1886** T. E. KEBBEL *Hist. Toryism* viii. 364 The Tories are for administrative reform: the Radicals for social revolution. **1892** SAINTSBURY *Earl of Derby* Pref. 5, I define a Tory as a person who would, at the respective times and in the respective circumstances, have opposed Catholic Emancipation, Reform, the Repeal of the Corn Laws, and the whole Irish Legislation of Mr. Gladstone. **1895** OMAN *Hist. Eng.* xxxix. 636 The generation of Tories who had grown up during the great French war, had forgotten the old liberal doctrines of their great leader Pitt. *Ibid.* xlii. 700 Down to 1865, the Liberals and the Conservatives alike retained in a great measure the characteristics of their forefathers the Whigs and Tories.

**b.** With various qualifications, as

*High*, *High-flying T.*, a Tory of 'high' principles; in 17–18th c. a High-Church Tory, a 'Church and King' man; cf. HIGH-FLYER 3 a; later, a thorough, old-fashioned, or reactionary Tory; *Jacobite T.*, a Tory of Jacobite principles, or tending to Jacobitism; *Old T.*, a Tory of a non-modern type; in quot. 1827, a Jacobite Tory; *ultra T.*, a Tory of extreme principles or opinions.

**1713** SWIFT *Jrnl. to Stella* 9 Apr., The Bishop of Chester, a *high Tory, was against the Court. **1827** SCOTT *Jrnl.* 3 Sept., The King..probably looks with no greater [favour] on the return of the High Tories. **1842** *Mem. M. T. Sadler* x. 335 One..whom it is customary..to hold up to popular abhorrence as a 'bigot', a 'borough-monger', and a 'high Tory'. **1863** G. PRYME *Autobiog. Recoll.* 12 Nov., I have been told by at least two high Tories that they could not discover by my lectures what political sentiments I held. **1738** BOLINGBROKE *Lett.* ii. *Patriot King* (1856) 165 What gives obstinacy without strength..to the *Jacobite-tories at this time? **1827** HALLAM *Const. Hist.* (1876) III. xv. 125 *note*, The thorough-paced royalists, or *old Tories [*c* 1690]. **1850** HT. MARTINEAU *Hist. Peace* I. III. xi. 555 We have, what the old Tories have not and cannot conceive of. **1886** T. E. KEBBEL *Hist. Toryism* viii. 366 The first Factory Bill ..was introduced by the typical old Tory, Mr. Sadler. **1895** OMAN *Hist. Eng.* xxxix. 646 When O'Connell's agitation grew formidable, and the old Tories urged him to repress it by force, he [Wellington] refused. **1833** CROKER 25 Mar., in Kebbel *Hist. Toryism* v. (1886) 254 [Sir R. Peel] foresaw that Radicals and *ultra-Tories would unite against him. **1862** KNIGHT *Pop. Hist. Eng.* VIII. vi. 109 The measures..hardly came up to the expectation of the ultra-Tories of that day [1819].

**4.** *U.S. Hist.* A member of the British party during the Revolutionary period; a loyal colonist.

(These were orig. 'Tories' in the English political sense, who naturally continued loyal to the King.)

[**1774** J. ADAMS in *Fam. Lett.* (1876) 7 Dr. Gardiner, arrived..from Boston, brings news of a battle at the town meeting, between Whigs and Tories. **1774** — *Wks.* (1854) IX. 336 The tories were never, since I was born, in such a state of humiliation as at this moment.] **1775** *Pennsylvania Even. Post* 1 July 278/1 The Whigs and Tories at Georgia are disputing with each other, and Governor Wright is much alarmed for his safety. *Ibid.* 18 July 309/2 The Tories in Georgia are now no more, the province is.. about to choose Delegates to send to the Congress. **1776** M. CUTLER in *Life*, etc. (1888) I. 54 The ships lay down below the castle with the soldiers and tories and their families on board. **1776** *Ann. Reg.* 29 Many of the well-affected (or Tories, which was the appellation now given to them throughout America) thought it prudent..to seek the same asylum. **1777** [implied in *Toryess* below]. **1821** J. F. COOPER *Spy* xxix, Washington will not trust us with the keeping of a suspected Tory, if we let this rascal trifle in this manner with the corps.

**5.** *transf.* Applied to any one in foreign countries or former ages holding views analogous to those of the English Tories; also, one who is by temperament or sentiment inclined to conservative principles.

**1797** J. BOUCHER *View Amer. Rev.* Pref. 22 Every man capable of forming an opinion..is, in some degree, either a Whig or a Tory. Now the American revolution was clearly a struggle for pre-eminence between Whigs and Tories. **1827** HALLAM *Const. Hist.* (1876) III. xvi. 201 The names whig and tory are often well applied to individuals. **1836** ARNOLD *Let.* 28 Nov., in *Life & Corr.* (1845) II. 65 Men are all Tories by nature, when they are tolerably well off. **1841** *Ibid.* 26 June *ibid.* I. ix. 267 After all, those differences in men's minds which we express, when exemplified in English politics, by the terms Whig and Tory, are very deep and comprehensive,..they seem to be the great fundamental difference between thinking men. **1860** RUSSELL *Diary India* II. x. 191 Purrus Ram and Khoom Dass ..fear greatly..that the Tories of Bussahir will triumph.

**B.** *adj.* **1.** That is a Tory; of, pertaining to, or characteristic of a Tory or Tories; consisting of or constituted by Tories; also, having the principles or aims of a Tory; supported or recognized by the Tory party; Conservative.

**1682** DRYDEN *Loyal Brother* Epil. 3 He's neither yet a Whigg nor Tory-Boy. **1682** — *Dk. Guise* Epil. 44 A kind of Bat..With Tory Wings, but Whiggish Teeth and Claws. **1689** EVELYN *Diary* 15 Jan., There was a Tory party (as then so call'd) who were for inviting his Majesty [Jas. II] againe upon conditions. **1693** ROKEBY *Diary* 15 Aug., It is a Tory complaint agt a Whigg. **1694** *Ibid.* 2 Apr., A Tory Bigot. **1710** SWIFT *Jrnl. to Stella* 5 Dec., [They] drank Mr. Harley's, Lord Rochester's, and other Tory healths. **1711** ADDISON *Spect.* No. 81 ¶ 2 [She] has most unfortunately a very beautiful Mole on the Tory Part of her Forehead. *a* **1734** NORTH *Exam.* II. v. (1740) 322 He has split the former Church of England into two Churches, the Tory Church, and the Whig Church of England. **1735–8** BOLINGBROKE *On Parties* viii. Wks. 1809 III. 136 This inconsiderable faction could not be deemed the tory party, but received the name of jacobite with more propriety. **1738** — *Lett.* ii. *Patriot King* (1750) 165 Men who had sense,.. before that moment, thought of nothing, after it, but of setting up a tory King against a whig King. **1776** *Pennsylvania Even. Post* 18 July 356/1 Yesterday several Tory prisoners were sent to Halifax jail. **1791** BOSWELL *Johnson* 11 June an. 1784, We drank 'Church and King' after dinner, with true Tory cordiality. **1826** SCOTT *Jrnl.* 15 Dec., The Tory interest was weak among the old stagers, where I remember it so strong. **1830** GEN. P. THOMPSON *Exerc.* (1842) I. 306 The advice of the English High Church and Tory party has been taken; and the Bourbons are driven from France. **1886** T. E. KEBBEL *Hist. Toryism* viii. 398 The Tory revival was but the twin sister of the Anglican revival. *Ibid.* ix. 468 In its defence of the Monarchy, the Church, and the territorial Constitution of the country, the Tory party has never faltered.

**b.** With various qualifications: see A. 3 b.

**1791** BOSWELL *Johnson* 11 June an. 1784, A sermon (1772) .., full of high Tory sentiments. **1827** SCOTT *Jrnl.* 11 Aug., A High Tory Administration would be a great evil at this time. **1850** HT. MARTINEAU *Hist. Peace* II. v. xvii. 445 It was cheering to see..high tory and deep radical chemists helping out one another's information about soils and manures. **1854** EARL ABERDEEN 6 Jan. in *Lett. Q. Victoria* (1908) III. xxiii. 2 The base and infamous attacks made upon the Prince..chiefly..in those papers which represent ultra-Tory or extreme Radical opinions. **1862** KNIGHT *Pop. Hist. Eng.* VIII. xviii. 320 The expectations of the ultra-Tory party that the Reform Bill [1832] would be repealed. **1895** OMAN *Hist. Eng.* xl. 667 Benjamin Disraeli, ..who combined high Tory notions on Church and State with extreme Radical views on certain social questions. **1908** *Lett. Q. Victoria* I. i. 6 The ultra-Tory party, who had opposed to the last the Emancipation of the Catholics and the Reform Bill.

**2.** In extended or transferred senses: see A. 5.

**1832** GEN. P. THOMPSON *Exerc.* (1842) II. 7 The Catilinarian conspiracy..was manifestly a plot in a green bag, and Cicero a Tory Secretary for the Home Department. **1837** *Ibid.* IV. 367 To pick holes in the history of the Greek republics, on the strength of the remains of the Tory poets of that time. **1899** R. H. CHARLES *Eschatology* v. 162 It

[Ecclesiasticus] is uncompromisingly tory, and refuses to admit the possibility of the new views as to the future life. *Ibid.* vi. 204 The still orthodox and tory view found in the Old Testament.

**C.** Phrases and combinations.

**1.** Used advb. in phr. *to talk, vote Tory.*

**1827** SCOTT *Jrnl.* 21 July, Nobody talks Whig or Tory just now. **1913** *Ch. Q. Rev.* Jan. 452 He had the manhood to stand by his chapel and refuse to vote Tory.

**2.** *Comb.*, as *Tory-Radical* sb. and adj.; *Tory-Irish, -leaning, -ridden, -voiced* adjs.; **Tory-Williamite**, a Tory who supported or adhered to William III.

**1696–7** ROKEBY *Diary* (Surtees) 51 Mr. Ratcliff, sheriff of Devonshire, is a Tory-Williamite. **1834** *Tait's Mag.* I. 387/2 The Governor, save on the question of slavery, the black niggers, and the Church, latterly became a sort of Tory-Radical. **1836** K. OF BELGIANS 18 Nov., in *Lett. Q. Victoria* (1908) I. v. 53 An infamous Radical or Tory-Radical paper, the *Constitutional*, which seems determined to run down the Coburg family. **1894** *Westm. Gaz.* 21 Sept. 2/3 Cases like mine, where in Tory-ridden villages the overseers resent both Liberal and women voters. **1898** *Ibid.* 24 Mar. 2/2 It must in the long run be a new Tory-Irish understanding. **1908** W. CHURCHILL in *Nation* 7 Mar. 812/2 The pressure of Tory-voiced discontent.

**3. Tory Democracy**, combination of Toryism with democracy; democracy under Tory leadership; new or democratic Toryism; progressive Conservatism.

**1879** *Spectator* 21 June 776 Tory democracy—Jingoism is its proper name. **1884** *Pall Mall G.* 29 Nov. 3/2 We would venture to lay very long odds that Tory Democracy is much more likely to come in with a boom than to go out with a fiz. **1885** GLADSTONE *Let. to Ld. Acton* 11 Feb. in Morley *Life* (1903) III. VIII. x. 173 'Tory democracy'..is no more like the conservative party in which I was bred, than it is like liberalism. In fact less. It is demagogism, only a demagogism..living upon the fomentation of angry passions, and still in secret as obstinately attached as ever to the evil principle of class interests. **1910** S. J. LOW in *Encycl. Brit.* VI. 346/2 (Lord Randolph Churchill) By this time [1882] he had definitely formulated the policy of progressive Conservatism which was known as 'Tory democracy'. He declared that the Conservatives ought to adopt, rather than oppose, reforms of a popular character, and to challenge the claims of the Liberals to pose as the champions of the masses.

**b.** So **Tory Democrat**, one who professes or supports Tory democracy. Also **Tory Democratic** *a.*

**1868** *Daily News* 2 Dec., Constitutionalist, tory, and tory democrat, are the names between which their choice wavers. **1902** *Daily Chron.* 29 Aug. 4/5 The policy of the advanced Tory Democratic section. **1903** *Westm. Gaz.* 14 Jan. 2/2 Recommended..to the electors..on the ground that he is a 'Tory Democrat', in which hybrid political creature it is roundly declared 'there is really more of true, old-fashioned Liberalism than in the Liberal Party to-day'. **1910** *Encycl. Brit.* VI. 976/2 Lord Randolph Churchill called himself a 'Tory democrat'.

Hence (chiefly *nonce-wds.*) † **To·rycal** *a.* [after *historical*] = *Tory* adj.; **To·rydom**, the realm or rule of Tories; **To·ryess**, a female Tory (in quot. in sense 4); **Toryi·stic** *a.*, inclined to Toryism; **To·ryize** *v.*, *trans.* = TORYFY; **To·ryship** (*humorous*), the personality of a Tory.

**1682** THORESBY *Diary* 14 July, Had some ineffectual discourses..with the *Torycal Papists. **1859** W. CHADWICK *Life De Foe* ii. 104 The bill passed; and, thanks to *Torydom, there it remains! **1908** M. BARING *Russian Ess.*, etc. Ded. 11 Here, they thought, was the voice of officialdom, Torydom, and hypocrisy speaking. **1777** FRANKLIN *Let.* Wks. 1889 VI. 67 You must know she is a *Toryess as well as you, and can as flippantly call *rebel.* **1899** HOWELLS in *Literature* 1 July 692 By a curious irony of fate he came to stand in later years for something *toryistic to men who were fighting other anti-slavery battles. **1887** *L'pool Mercury* 5 Jan., He was the first to show that London might be *Toryised. **1890** *Pall Mall G.* 22 Aug. 2/1 A narrow little clique—fossilized and Toryized to an almost incredible degree. **1793** PARR *Let. to Routh* 12 June, Wks. 1828 VII. 652 Farewell, and believe me..your *Toryship's friend and servant.

† **Tory**, *v. Obs.* [f. TORY *sb.*]

**1.** *intr.* To live as an Irish Tory or outlaw.

**1651** G. RAWDON *Let.* 24 Dec. in *St.Pap., Irel.* CCLXXXII. 104 (P.R.O.) Sir Phill and Cormack Mulhallon Torye about Braintree woodes; soe that they cannot stirr out of Charlemount but with a considerable strengthe. **1655** [V. GOOKIN] *Gt. Case Transpl. Irel.* 21 Many Inhabitants, who are able to subsist on their Gardens in their present Habitations,.. will rather choose the hazard of Torying, than the apparent danger of starving [in Connaught].

**2.** *trans.* To becall or nickname *Tory.*

**1681** T. FLATMAN *Heraclitus Ridens* No. 34 (1713) I. 218 [They] shall pass for white Boys, and have never a word said to them for Torying, Tantivying and Masquerading his Majesty's most loyal and dutiful Subjects.

**Toryfy, torify** (tōə·rifəi), *v. humorous.* [f. TORY + -FY.] *trans.* To make a Tory of, convert to Toryism (*generally dyslogistic*). Hence **To·ryfied, To·ryfying** *ppl. adjs.*; also **To·ryfica·tion**, conversion to Toryism.

**1763** WILKES *N. Brit.* No. 37 (1766) 212 The strict harmony subsisting between the whiggified Tories, the torified Whigs, and the amphibious North Britons. **1834** LADY GRANVILLE *Lett.* (1894) II. 177 Neither of the Clanricardes seems pleased, or Tory-fied at the news. **1853** SIR G. C. LEWES *Lett.* 262 Most of his [Gladstone's] High church supporters stick to him, and..he is Liberalizing them, instead of their Torifying him. **1876** G. MEREDITH *Beauch. Career* xxviii, Mr. Tuckham was..prophesying the Torification of mankind. **1901** A. BIRRELL in *N. Amer. Rev.* Feb. 251 The Toryfication..of London and of so many of our great towns ..is one of the most striking political facts of recent times. **1902** *Academy* 11 Jan. 667/1 Lowell was born and bred in a Toryfied old country seat at Elmwood, Cambridge, New England.

**Toryish** (tōə·riˌiʃ), *a.* [f. TORY *sb.* or *a.* + -ISH [1].] Somewhat Tory; inclined to Toryism. So **To·ryishly** *adv.*

**1681** T. FLATMAN *Heraclitus Ridens* No. 41 (1713) II. 17 The Mistress of the House being, it seems, Toryishly affected, would have two Pence the Dish for true Protestant Coffee. **1684** (Mar. 26) *Let. fr. Irel.* in T. Hutchinson *Hist. Mass.* (1764) I. ii. 343 *note*, I suspect you of the Massachusets, are more whiggish, and your neighbours more toryish, to express it in the language of late in use. **1794** PARR *Let. to Routh* 22 July, Wks. 1828 VII. 658 Manners which you would call Toryish, because they were at once correct, elegant, and dignified. **1826** *New Monthly Mag.* Jan. 20 He must not be too whiggish for his Tory customers, nor too toryish for his Whigs. **1876** G. MEREDITH *Beauch. Career* xiv, I fancy he is Toryish.

**Toryism** (tōə·riˌiz'm). Also 7–8 **Torism.** [f. as prec. + -ISM.] The principles, practices, and methods of Tories: *spec.* **a.** those of the British Tory party; Conservatism.

**1682** in *Westm. Gaz.* 22 Jan. (1909) 2/3 [The *Loyal London Mercury* declared that it would not go with either] Whigism or Torism. **1711** *Medley* No. 24. 279 Put Torism instead of it, and it sits exactly in all its Parts. **1713** (*title*) Torism and Trade can never agree. **1735–8** BOLINGBROKE *On Parties* ii. Wks. 1809 III. 47 An inquiry into the rise and progress of our late parties; or a short history of toryism and whiggism from their cradle to their grave. **1786** MRS. PIOZZI *Anecd. Johnson* 40 Of Mr. Johnson's toryism the world has long been witness. **1791** BOSWELL *Johnson* 22 Mar. an. 1776, I felt all my Toryism glow in this old capital of Staffordshire. *Ibid.* 3 June an. 1784, Oxford, that magnificent and venerable seat of Learning, Orthodoxy, and Toryism. *c* **1832** BORROW in Knapp *Life*, etc. (1899) I. xiv. 144 The chief reason for Toryism, a reason sufficient by itself, is that within it are comprised love of country and pride of country. **1862** KNIGHT *Pop. Hist. Eng.* VIII. xxix. 528 The principle of ultra-Toryism. **1886** T. E. KEBBEL *Hist. Toryism* viii. 335 Lord Beaconsfield carried Toryism into the next stage. *Ibid.* 337 The Toryism of the future must be popular Toryism or nothing. **1895** OMAN *Hist. Eng.* xlii. 709 Disraeli, seated firmly in power, was able to display the characteristics of the 'New Toryism'. **1910** S. J. LOW in *Encycl. Brit.* VI. 346/2 He was actively spreading the gospel of democratic Toryism in a series of platform campaigns. *Ibid.*, In 1884 the struggle between stationary and progressive Toryism came to a head, and terminated in favour of the latter. **1913** F. E. SMITH in *Daily Express* 12 Feb. 2/4 Not the least potent method of preserving it [the State] is to link the conception of State Toryism with the practice of Social Reform.

**b.** of the American Tories or Loyalists at the War of Independence: see TORY *sb.* 4.

**1777** J. ADAMS *Diary* 18 Sept., We are yet in Philadelphia, that mass of cowardice and Toryism. **1888** BRYCE *Amer. Commw.* III. ciii. 468 Because the Anglican Clergy were prone to Toryism (as attachment to the British connection was called).

**c.** Applied generally to principles analogous to those of English Toryism: cf. TORY *sb.* 5.

**1832** GEN. P. THOMPSON *Exerc.* (1842) II. 7 Why will nobody re-write the Greek and Roman histories, and give us an insight into the Toryism of antiquity? **1837** *Ibid.* IV. 367 Toryism..is not a thing of modern date, but goes back to the earliest histories. **1837** ARNOLD *Let.* 3 Mar., in *Life & Corr.* (1845) II. 79 If I dared, I would put in a word for 'As in præsenti', perhaps even for 'Propria quæ maribus'. Is not this a laudable specimen of Toryism?

**Torymid** (tǫ·rimid), *a.* and *sb. Entom.* [f. mod.L. *Torymidæ* pl., f. *Torymus*, name of the typical genus: see -ID [3].] **a.** *adj.* Of or pertaining to the *Torymidæ*, a group of chalcididan parasitic hymenoptera. **b.** *sb.* An insect of this group.

**1895** *Camb. Nat. Hist.* V. 547 Some of these Torymid fig-Insects have winged males, as is normal in the family.

**Toryn**, obs. f. *torn*, pa. pple. of TEAR *v.*[1]

† **To·ry-ro·ry**, *a.* (*adv.*) *Obs.* [Origin obscure: perhaps orig. a reduplication or riming expansion of *rory*, ROARY, f. ROAR *sb.* or *v.* The Eng. Dial. Dict. cites it from S. Lancash. as meaning 'a state of hurry or excitement'. After 1680 it was sometimes abusively associated with TORY *sb.*; but there can hardly have been any original connexion. Reference to the Irish *tories* or outlaws and marauders is chronologically possible, but not evidenced.]

**1.** Roaring, uproarious, roistering, boisterous; in quots. 1694, 1716 with allusion to TORY A. 2, 3.

**1678** DRYDEN *Limberham* I. i, And, before George, I grew tory rory, as they say. *Ibid.* IV. i, Sing like nightingales, you tory-rory jades. **1678** OTWAY *Friendship in F.* II. i, Methinks you look like two as roring, ranting tory rory Sparks as one would wish to meet withal. [**1681** O. HEYWOOD *Diaries*, etc. 24 Oct., Theres a book called the character of a Tory wherin it runs, A Tory, a Whory, a Roary, a Scory, a Sory.] **1694** MOTTEUX *Rabelais* v. *Pantagr. Progn.* v. 237 Swaggering Huffsnuffs,.. Tory-rory Rakes and Tantivy-boys. **1716** M. DAVIES *Athen. Brit.* II. 337 From a Tory-Rory-Boy, he is become a cool-temper'd Wig.

**2.** Ruffianly (like the Irish tories, or Judge Jeffreys).

**1682** MRS. BEHN *City Heiress* 52 Some damn'd Tory-rory Rogues, to rob a man at his Prayers! **1822** PARR *Let. to Hill* 25 Jan., Wks. 1828 VII. 605 Servile and corrupt judges, prejudiced and perjured juries, merciless jailors and a tory-rory hangman.

**B.** *adv.* In a roaring or uproarious manner; boisterously, rantingly, roisteringly.

It may have been the name of a rowdy song or tune.

**1664** COTTON *Scarron.* IV. (1715) 97 Roaring and drinking tory-rory. [**1667** DRYDEN & DAVENANT *Tempest* IV. iii, I found her an hour ago under an elder tree,..singing Tory Rory, and Rantum Scantum, with her own natural brother.] **1673** SHADWELL *Epsom Wells* II. i, We were at it Tory Rory, and Sung old Rose, the Song that you love so.

Hence † **To·ry-ro·ry** *v. Obs., intr.* to behave uproariously.

**1685** CROWNE *Sir C. Nice* IV. 43 Well the house is our own, and the Night our own,..we'l Tory-rory, and 'tis—a fine Night, we'l Revel in the Garden.

† **To-sa·me, to-sa·men**, *adv. Obs.* Forms: 1 tosǫmne, tosamne, 2–3 to somne, (*Orm.*) tosamenn, 2–4 to same, 3 to somnen, 3–4 to samen, 4 to samyn. [OE. *tósamne, tósǫmne*, f. *tó*, To *prep.* + SAMEN together. Cf. OFris. *to samene*, OS. *tô samane, te samne* (MDu. *te-zamen*, Du. *samen*), OHG. *saman, zi samane* (MHG. *ze-samene*, Ger. *zusammen*); also ON. *til-samans.*

The element *samen* represents an orig. sb., of which *saman, samane, samans* were case-forms: cf. Skr. *samana* concourse, assembly, *samana* adv. together; also OIr. *samain* assembly, the Tara-festival.]

Together; into or in one body or company.

*c* **893** K. ÆLFRED *Oros.* IV. xi. § 9 Raðe þæs þe hie tosomne comon. **971** *Blickl. Hom.* 191 Þa coman þær tosamne unarimedlico menȝeo. *c* **1000** ÆLFRIC *Hom.* II. 100 Moyses fæste feowertiȝ daȝa and feowertiȝ nihta tosamne. *c* **1200** *Trin. Coll. Hom.* 23 Boðe to same þe sowle and þe lichame. *c* **1200** ORMIN 649 Forrþi shulenn alle þa..Tosamenn stanndenn att te dom. *c* **1205** LAY. 8597 To-somnen we scullen gliden. *c* **1315** SHOREHAM i. 116 Crist is mid ous to-same. **13..** *Cursor M.* 11461 (Cott.) And did he suith to samen call þe maisters of his kingrik all. *c* **1375** *Ibid.* 3073 (Fairf.) To-samyn dwelled þai þare.

‖ **Tosaphoth** (tǭu·săfǭuþ). Also **tosafoth.** [Heb. תּוֹסָפוֹת *tōsāphōth*, pl. of תּוֹסָפָה *tōsāphāh* addition, f. יָסַף *yāsaph* to add.] Critical and explanatory notes on the Talmud. Hence **To·saphist** (-fist), a writer of tosaphoth.

**1887** H. ADLER in *Papers Anglo-Jewish Hist. Exhib.* 272 The marvellously exhaustive list of Tosafists (authors of comments on the Talmud) contained in Zunz's 'Zur Geschichte und Literatur'.

† **To·sard.** *Obs.* Some kind of fire-wood, or a form in which it was sold in 14th to 16th c.

**1336** in Rogers *Agric. & Prices* (1866) II. 396 (Farley, Surrey) Tosards 1250 at 2/- [*Ibid.* 393 *note*, Tosards..are sold by the hundred]. **1339** *Ibid.*, Tosards 50 at 2/-. **1341** *Ibid.*, Tosards 1000 at 2/-. **1429** *Ibid.* III. 257 (Charles & Rowhill) Tosards 15^c at 2/-. **1550** in Strype *Stow's Surv.* (1755) II. v. xxii. 422/2 If any Freeman of this City use to resort into the Countries near to this City, and there to ingross and buy up much Billet, tall Wood, Faggot, Tosard, or other Fire-wood.

‖ **Tosca** (tǫ·skă). Also **tosco, toska.** [Sp. *tosca*, fem. of *tosco* coarse.] A soft dark-brown limestone occurring embedded and sometimes stratified in the surface formation of the Pampas.

Also applied to various lavas in southern Italy and Sicily; and in Colombia, S. America, to a surface rock of supposed volcanic origin (*Cent. Dict.*).

**1818** *Amer. St. Papers, For. Relat.* (1834) IV. 277 This concretion, as it projects along the water's edge of the Rio de la Plata at the city of Buenos Ayres, is called *tosco*, or rough earth. **1846** DARWIN *Geol. Observ. S. Amer.* iv. 77 For convenience sake, I will call the marly rock by the name given to it by the inhabitants, namely, Tosca-rock. **1859** PAGE *Handbk. Geol. Terms, Tosca-Rock*, a name given by the inhabitants of Buenos-Ayres to a marly arenaceous rock found imbedded in layers and nodular masses among the argillaceous earth or mud of the Pampas.

**Toscan**, obs. or alien form of TUSCAN.

† **To-sca·tter**, *v. Obs.* [ME. *to-scater-en*, f. To- [2] + *scateren*, SCATTER *v.*] *trans.* To scatter abroad, disperse.

**1382** WYCLIF 2 *Chron.* xxxiv. 7 Whanne the auters he hadde to-scaterede..he is turnede aȝein in to Jerusalem. — *Jer.* vi. 5 To-scatere wee ther houses. *c* **1386** CHAUCER *Sompn. T.* 261 Lo ech thyng that is oned in it selue Is moore strong than whan it is toscatered. **1494** FABYAN *Chron.* VI. CCXVII. 236 Lastely Harolde was wounded in the iye with an arowe..& was slayne, and his people to scatered.

**b.** *intr.* To part asunder, go to pieces. *rare.*

**13..** *Cast. Love* (Halliw.) 1556 Castell, toure, boure ne halle, But thei shulle to-skatur and downfalle.

**Toschach, Tosche**: see TOSHACH, TUSH.

**To-schrape, To-set**: see To- *pref.*[1], [2].

**Tose, Toser**, etc.: see TOZE *v.*[1], TOZER.

**Tose**, obs. f. *toes*, pl. of TOE.

**Tosh** (tǫʃ), *sb.*[1] *School slang.* A bath; a foot-pan. Also *tosh-can, -pan.*

**1881** LEATHES in Pascoe *Life Publ. Sch.* ii. 20 A 'tosh' pan ..is also provided. **1883** Tosh-can [see TOSH *v.*[2]]. **1905** H. A. VACHELL *The Hill* i, We call a tub a tosh. *Ibid.* iii, His feet were thrust into a 'tosh' filled with steaming water.

**Tosh** (tǫʃ), *sb.*[2] *slang.* Bosh, trash; nonsense, rubbish, twaddle; in *Cricket*, see quot. 1898.

**1892** *Oxf. Univ. Mag.* 26 Oct. 26/1 To think what I've gone through to hear that man! Frightful tosh it'll be, too. **1898** *Tit-Bits* 25 June 252/3 Among the recent neologisms of the cricket field is 'tosh', which means bowling of contemptible easiness. **1906** E. V. LUCAS *Listener's Lure* (1909) 36 This London business seems to me the most awful tosh.

Hence **Toshy** (tǫ·ʃi) *a. slang*, trashy, rubbishy.
1902 Belloc *Path to Rome* 163 The poor public..is driven back to toshy novels about problems, written by cooks.

**Tosh**, *a.* (*adv.*) *Sc.* [Origin not ascertained.]
**1.** Neat, clean, tidy, trim.
1776 D. Herd *Coll. Songs* Gloss., *Tosh*, tight, neat. 1794 Ritson *Scot. Songs* I. 99, I gang ay fou clean and fou tosh, As a' the neighbours can tell. 1823 J. Wilson *Trials Marg. Lyndsay* xxxiii. 271 The hedges will do—I clipped them wi' my ain hands..and, nae doubt, they make the avenue look a hantle tosher.
**2.** Agreeable, comfortable; friendly, intimate.
1821 *Blackw. Mag.* X. 4 We were a very tosh and agreeable company. 1887 *Suppl. to Jamieson*, s. v., 'They're unco tosh wi' ither'.
**B.** as *adv.* = *Toshly* (see below).
1780 Mayne *Siller Gun* I. xxiii, Shouther your arms; o! ha'd them tosh on, And not athraw! 1828 Moir *Mansie Wauch* vi, Matters were..settled full tosh between us.
Hence **To·shly** *adv.*, neatly, tidily, trimly; snugly; **To·shy** *a.*, neat, tidy, pretty.
1788 Picken *Poems* 176 Row't toshly up, an' franket. 1827 J. Wilson *Noct. Ambr.* Wks. 1855 II. 21 Phrenologists ..hae nae slicht o' haun in curlin their hair toshly. 1856 J. Ballantine *Poems* 47 And see how it's keepit sae toshy and clean. 1881 Jessie Simpson in *Mod. Sc. Poets* III. 263 Nae mair wee toshie feet to bath, nor gowden locks to kaim.

**Tosh** (tǫʃ), *v.*[1] *Sc.* [f. Tosh *a.*] *trans.* To make 'tosh'; to tidy, trim.
1826 J. Wilson *Noct. Ambr.* Wks. 1855 I. 266 Hoo she wad try to tosh up..her breest. 1886 A. Wardrop *Mid Cauther Fair* 9 Let's tosh yer plaid a wee.

**Tosh**, *v.*[2] *School slang.* [f. Tosh *sb.*[1]] **a.** *trans.* To splash, souse. **b.** *intr.* To bath, 'tub'.
1883 J. P. Groves *Fr. Cadet to Capt.* iii. 227 'Toshing' was the name given to a punishment inflicted by the cadets on any one of their number who made himself obnoxious. The victim, dressed in full uniform, was forced to run the gauntlet of his brother cadets, who, as he passed, emptied the contents of their 'tosh-cans' (small baths holding about three gallons of water) over the wretched lad's head. 1903 Farmer & Henley *Slang* s.v., He toshed his house beak by mistake, and got three hundred. 1905 H. A. Vachell *The Hill* i, I believe he toshes now—once a month or so.

**Tosh**, obs. and dial. form of Tush, tusk.

**Toshach, -och, toschach**, phonetized forms of Toisech.
1836 W. F. Skene *Highl. Scot.* (1902) II. vi. 289 Toshoch being unquestionably the title anciently applied to the oldest cadets of the different clans. 1861 C. Innes *Sk. Early Scot. Hist.* 396 The magistrate and head man of a little district known among his Celtic neighbours as the Toshach. 1872 — *Lect. Scot. Legal Antiq.* iii. 97 Some of the inferior executors of the law had Celtic names long preserved as Maor and Toschach.

† **To-sha·ke**, *v. Obs.* Forms: see Shake *v.* [OE. *tosceacan*, f. To-[2] + *sceacan*, Shake *v.*]
**1.** *trans.* To shake to pieces, shake asunder; to disperse or destroy by shaking.
a 1000 *Gloss.* in Wr.-Wülcker 214/34 *Concutit*, i. *turbat, terreat*, toscæcþ. c 1000 Ælfric *Hom.* I. 570 He ða tosceoc þone liȝ of ðam ofne. a 1250 *Owl & Night.* 1647 Þu seyst þat gromes þe ivoþ..& þe to twiccheþ & to schakeþ. 13.. *Sir Beues* (A.) 742 Man and houndes, þat he tok wiþ his toskes he al to-schok. 1382 Wyclif *Isa.* xxiv. 20 With shaking shal be to-shaken the erthe. c 1440 *Pallad. on Husb.* ii. 240 The plauntis bigge a depper delf desireth And larger space, as wynd may hem to shake. 1584 R. Scot *Disc. Witchcr.* xii. xviii. (1886) 222 In the bloud of Adam death was taken, In the bloud of Christ it was all to shaken.
**2.** *intr.* To tremble, quiver, shiver violently.
a 1300 *Cursor M.* 22552 All þe erth it sal toscak. 1303 R. Brunne *Handl. Synne* 2528 He broghte on þat brynnyng croke, A brennyng soule þat al to-shoke. 14.. *Gosp. Nicodemus* 797 Þe erth trembled and al toschoke. 1508 Dunbar *Gold. Targe* 231 With the blast the leuis all to-schuke.

† **To-sha·tter**, *v. Obs.* [ME. f. To-[2] + Shatter *v.*] *trans.* To break into small pieces.
1494 Fabyan *Chron.* vi. clxiii. 156 Whan ye shote was spent and the sperys to shateryd, than bothe hoostis ran to gyther with Rowlandys songe, so yt in shorte whyle the grene feelde was dyed into a parfyte redde.

† **To-she·d**, *v. Obs.* Forms: see Shed *v.*[1] [OE. *tosceádan*, f. To-[2] + *sceádan*, Shed *v.*[1]: = OHG. *za-, zisceidan.*] *trans.* To separate, divide, diffuse, scatter, part; in OE. also, to discriminate, discern, distinguish.
c 888 K. Ælfred *Boeth.* xxxiv. § 3 Ælc þing þe tosceaden bið from oðrum bið oðer, oþer þæt þing. *Ibid.* xl. § 7 Se þe ȝesceadwisnisse hæfð, se mæȝ deman & tosceadan hwæs he wilniȝan sceal. c 1000 Ælfric *Hom.* II. 106 He toscæt hi on twa, swa swa scephyrde toscæt scep fram gatum. c 1200 Ormin 19862 Forr þatt he wollde hire & te king Todælenn & toshædenn. c 1205 Lay. 30262 He nom his lauerdes hefd..& his lockes he to-scædde. 1387 Trevisa *Higden* (Rolls) III. 241 Leonida..fil vppon the oþer deel anyȝt..and to schad hem euerich oon from oþer. 1398 — *Barth. De P. R.* xix. xiv. (Bodl. MS.) lf. 295 b/2 Depe rede toschedeþ þe siȝt as liȝt doþe.
**b.** *intr.* To divide, separate, fall apart.
c 1330 R. Brunne *Chron. Wace* (Rolls) 6276 So þat þe Romayns route to-schadde, & dide hem to þe hauene fle. 1387 Trevisa *Higden* (Rolls) I. 133 Þe hepes of grauel to schedeþ and to falleþ.

† **To-she·nd**, *v. Obs.* [f. To-[2] + Shend *v.*] *trans.* To ruin or destroy utterly.
1382 Wyclif *Ps.* lvi. [lvii.] 1 In to the ende, ne destroȝe thou or shend [*v.r.* to-sheende] Dauid. c 1425 *Cast. Persev.* 794 in *Macro Plays* 101 Now schal careful Couetyse, Mankende trewly al to-schende. c 1500 *Lancelot* 1221 His face was al to-hurt and al to-schent.

† **To-she·ne**, *v. Obs.* Forms: 1 to-scǽnan, 3 to-scænen, to-scenen, to-schenen. [OE. *to-scǽnan*, f. To-[2] + *scǽnan* to break: see Shene.] *trans.* To break or dash to pieces; also, to disperse, break up (an army).
c 950 *Lindisf. Gosp.* Mark v. 4 Ða fattro [he] forbræc *vel* tosceænde [c 975 *Rushw.* feoturo..toscænde]. — John xix. 36 Ban ne to-scænas *vel* ni ȝebræcȝað ȝe from him. c 1000 Ælfric *Saints' Lives* xxiii. 496 Ne furðon an ban næfde he mid oþrum, ac toscænede ofer eall laȝon. a 1250 *Owl & Night.* 1120 Stones hi doþ in heore slytte..& þine fule bon toscheneþ.
**b.** *intr.* To come or break in pieces.
c 1205 Lay. 2309 Al þu scalt to-scæne Mid scearpe mire eaxe. *Ibid.* 2315 Þe stan al to-sceande. c 1275 *Ibid.* 4537 Sip orn to-ȝein sip þat hit al to-scende.

**Tosher**[1] (tǫ·ʃəɹ). *Thieves' Cant.* A Thames thief who purloins copper sheathing from the bottoms of vessels in the river or from the docks. So **To·shing**, the practice of a 'tosher'.
1859 *Slang Dict.*, *Toshers*, men who steal copper from ships' bottoms in the Thames. 1867 Smyth *Sailor's Word-bk.*, *Toshing*, a cant word for stealing copper sheathing from vessels' bottoms, or from dock-yard stores.

**To·sher**[2]. [Origin uncertain; ? from Tosh *v.*[2]] A small fishing smack.
1885 *Daily Tel.* 26 Nov. (Farmer), A tosher is not a longshore driver, though both little vessels are employed in catching what they can close into the land. 1911 *Daily News* 10 Oct. 4 Time after time her stout-hearted skipper thrashed the smaller craft (she is but a 'tosher' of 23 tons, carrying only three hands), to windward.

**Tosher**[3] (tǫ·ʃəɹ). *Undergraduates' slang.* [A humorous deformation from *unattached*: cf. Footer *sb.*[1] 3 b, Rugger[2], Socker, etc.] An 'unattached' or non-collegiate student at a university having residential colleges.
1889 *Durham Univ. Jrnl.* 9 Nov. 216 The 'toshers' as they are called in 'Varsity slang—the term is a corruption of the word 'unattached'—have been looked down upon in the past. 1891 Duncan *Amer. Girl in Lond.* 254 The man ..being an unattached student, a 'tosher'. 1897 *Blackw. Mag.* May 724 A third deemed that the millennium had arrived with the advent to Oxford of the humble 'tosher'.

† **To-shi·ft**, *v. Obs.* Forms: see Shift *v.* [OE. *tosciftan*, f. To-[2] + *sciftan* to divide, Shift.] *trans.* To divide, separate, distribute.
c 1122 *O. E. Chron.* an. 1085, Ac se cyng let to scyfton þone here ȝeond eall þis land to his mannon. *Ibid.* an. 1095, He.. into Wealan ferde & his fyrde to scyfte. c 1315 Shoreham i. 721 For þer he hys, he hys al y-hol Ne mey me hym to-schifte. 1387 Trevisa *Higden* (Rolls) I. 59 Noþer water noþer fire myȝte ham to schifte noþer to dele. *Ibid.* II. 251 Þere..þe longages and tonges of þe bulders were i-schad and to schift. c 1400 tr. *Higden* (Rolls) VII. 528 (MS. β) So thei beth departed and to schufte [γ scheft] atweyne.

† **To-shi·ver**, *v. Obs.* Also to-shever. [f. To-[2] + Shiver *v.* So MHG. *ze-, zer-schiveren.*]
**1.** *trans.* To break into shivers, shatter, splinter.
c 1200 *Trin. Coll. Hom.* 113 Ure helende..alto shiurede þe ȝiaten and in wende. c 1300 [see To-crush]. c 1435 *Torr. Portugal* 1172 Hors and man down he bore, And alle to-sheverd his sheld. 1470–85 Malory *Arthur* ii. x. 87 They..smoten to gyders and al to sheuered their speres.
**2.** *intr.* To fly to shivers, break into splinters.
13.. *K. Alis.* 2728 The scharpe spere gynneth al to-schivere. c 1381 Chaucer *Parl. Foules* 493 The noyse of ffoules..So loude ronge..Þat wele y went þe wode had Al to-sheuered [*v.r.* Alto-shyuered]. c 1430 *Syr Gener.* (Roxb.) 5156 His sheld to-sheuered euen in twoo. c 1530 Ld. Berners *Arth. Lyt. Bryt.* (1814) 270 Bothe theyr speres all to sheuered to theyr fystes.

† **To-shoo·t, to-she·te**, *v. Obs.* [OE. *to-scéotan*, f. To-[2] + *scéotan*, Shoot *v.* Cf. MHG. *zeschieȝen*, Ger. *zerschiessen* to destroy by shooting.] *intr.* To spring apart; to burst asunder.
c 1000 Ælfric *Hom.* II. 352 Þa toscuton ða deoflu sona þe me mid heora tangum ȝelæccan woldon. c 1122 *O. E. Chron.* an. 1083, Þa munecas..to scuton, sume urnon in to cyrcean. 1340–70 *Alisaunder* 1008 Þe ai [=egg] fell on þe flore..And þe shell to-shett on þe schire grounde.

**To-shred, To-skair, To-skill**: see To- *pref.*[2] 1.

**Toshy**, *a.*[1], [2]: see under Tosh *sb.*[2], *a.*

**Tosie, Tosily, Tosiness**: see Tosy.

**Tosk**, dial. var. Torsk. **Toske**, obs. f. Tusk.

† **To-slay·**, *v. Obs.* Forms: see Slay. [OE. *tosléan*, f. To-[2] + *sléan* to strike, Slay. So OS. *te-slahan*; OFris. *to-slâ*, OHG. *za-, zi-slahan*, MHG. *zerslahen, zerslân*, Ger. *zerschlagen.*]
*trans.* To strike or knock to pieces; to strike down violently; also, to kill outright.
a 700 *Epinal Gloss.* (O. E. T.) 195 *Concidit*, tisloȝ. c 725 *Corpus Gloss.* 516 Tosloȝ. c 893 K. Ælfred *Oros.* iv. ii. § 1 Þunor tosloȝ heora hiehstan godes hus Iofeses. c 1000 Ælfric *Hom.* II. 450 Swiðlic wind..tosloh þæt hus. c 1430 *Syr Tryam.* 372 Why dyd he the to-slon? 14.. *Sir Beues* (C.) 2712 And had caste on hym venome, And the knyght all to-sloon.

† **To-sli·ft**, *v. Obs. rare*[—1]. [ME. *toslyfte(n*, deriv. vb. f. OE. *to-slífan* to split, cleave, cut to pieces: cf. Slive *v.*[1]] *trans.* To break to pieces.
c 1315 Shoreham i. 726 To-slyfte A myrour þou myȝt fol wel, Bote nauȝt þe ymage schifte.

† **To-sli·t**, *v. Obs.* [ME. *to-slitte(n*, f. To-[2] + *slitte(n*, Slit *v.*] *trans.* To slit open, split.
a 1250 *Owl & Night.* 694 Ac ȝif þat he forlost his wit, Þonne is his red purs al toslit. c 1300 *Seyn Julian* (Ashm.) 146 Þe bones hi to slitte & þe marw out drowe. c 1400 *Laud Troy Bk.* 16808 Many a baly scho ther rittes And many a scheld sche al to-sclittes. 14.. *Sir Beues* (M.) 520 There was no sarzin, that hym hitte, But he is body all to-slitt.

**To-slive, To-smite, To-sparple**, etc.: see To- *pref.*[2] **To-souse** (*all to souse*): see All C. 15, and Souse *v.*[1]

† **To-sprea·d**, *v. Obs.* Forms: see Spread *v.* [OE. *tosprǽdan*, f. To-[2] + *sprǽdan*, Spread *v.* So OHG. *za-, zi-, zarspreitan*, MHG. *ze-, zerspreiten.*] *trans.* To spread abroad, spread open; to expand, stretch out; also, to disperse, scatter.
a 1000 in *Techmer's Zeitschr.* II. 122 (B.–T.) Tospræd ðine fingras. c 1200 *Trin. Coll. Hom.* 21 His holie lichame was tospred on þe holie rode. *Ibid.* 205 Was to sprad. a 1225 *Ancr. R.* 402 To luuien þene king of blisse þet tospret so touward ou his ermes. 1297 R. Glouc. (Rolls) 4317 Þo þe romeyns..to spradde hom her & þer. 1390 Gower *Conf.* II. 260 With..fot al bare, Hir her tosprad sche gan to fare.

† **To-spri·ng**, *v. Obs.* [OE. *tospringan*, f. To-[2] + *springan*, Spring *v.* So OHG. *zispringan*, MHG. *ze-, zerspringen*; Ger. *zerspringen.*] *intr.* To spring apart; to burst asunder.
c 1000 Ælfric *Hom.* II. 156 Se niðfulla deofol..wearp ða ænne stan to ðære bellan, þæt heo eall tosprang. *Ibid.* 382 Þæt [isene ȝeat] tosprang þærrihte him toȝeanes. 1303 R. Brunne *Handl. Synne* 10672 Þe bondes to-braste, and alle to-sprunge. c 1320 *Cast. Love* 593 Er him ouȝte þe herte to springe Þen he scholde him wraþþe for eny þinge. c 1400 *St. Alexius* 1020 Myne herte wil to-sprynge.

† **To-squa·t**, *v. Obs.* [ME. f. To-[2] + Squat *v.*] *trans.* To flatten, crush, squash.
c 1325 *Poem Times Edw. II* (Percy) lxxii, Trechery is imeynteynd And trewth is al tosqwat. a 1380 *St. Ambrose* 544 in Horstm. *Altengl. Leg.* (1878) 16 Wiþ seknes he was al to squat. c 1380 Wyclif *Wks.* (1880) 461 She shal al to-squatte þyn heed. 14.. *Sir Beues* (N.) 3563 Arondel..Wiþ his hinder fot him smot þat he al tosquat is brain.

**Toss** (tǫs), *sb.*[1] [f. Toss *v.*] An act of tossing.
**1.** A pitching up and down or to and fro.
1634 Sir T. Herbert *Trav.* Ded., This poore Barque.. hath endurde many tosses at Sea, and is now tost on Land. 1801 Southey *Thalaba* xi. xl, The little boat rides rapidly, And pitches now with shorter toss Upon the narrower swell. a 1849 Sir R. Wilson in *Life* (1862) I. iii. 139 The continual toss almost made me mad. 1859 *Habits Gd. Soc.* ix. 286 The man who gives your hand one toss, as if he were ringing the dinner-bell.
† **2.** A state of agitation or commotion. *Obs.*
1666 Pepys *Diary* 2 June, This put us at the Board into a tosse. 1667 *Ibid.* 10 Oct., Lord! what a tosse I was for some time in. a 1734 North *Lives* (1826) II. 319 You can easily imagine what a toss I was in, to lie about a week aboard the ship for want of pratique. 1837 Longf. in *Life* (1891) I. 278 The Little-Pedlington community of Boston is in a great toss,..first about the college, and then about Dr. Channing and the abolitionists.
**3.** An act of casting, pitching, throwing, or hurling; a throw, a pitch. *Full toss*, in *Cricket*, the delivery of a ball which does not touch the ground in its flight between the wickets.
1660 F. Brooke tr. *Le Blanc's Trav.* 119 The Criminal.. expected death, a tosse or two at the least. 1833 Nyren *Yng. Cricketer's Tutor* 81 By one stroke from a toss that he hit behind him, we got ten runs. 1862 Pycroft *Cricket Tutor* 52 Some balls of a loose sort—Volleys, Long-hops, and Tosses.
**4.** A sudden jerk; *esp.* a quick upward or backward movement of the head.
1676 Dryden *Man of Mode* Epil. 22 His various modes from various fathers follow; One taught the toss, and one the new French wallow. 1718 *Free-thinker* No. 17 ¶ 8 She throws up her Head with a scornful Toss. 1836 J. Gilbert *Chr. Atonem.* viii. (1852) 242 The question is dismissed from the minds of some with an indignant toss. 1848 Thackeray *Van. Fair* xlviii, She walked in..with a toss of the head which would have befitted an empress.
† **5.** A bout, an encounter. *Sc. Obs.*
1730 T. Boston *Mem.* x. (1899) 316, I had a toss with Mr. Murray, he affirming and I denying that I had given them ground by word or deed. 1730 — *View of this & other World* (1799) 399 You may get enough ado even to die through a vehement toss of sickness.
**6.** An act of tossing a coin: see Toss *v.* 9, 14; a decision arrived at by this means: see *toss-up* in 10, and cf. Pitch and toss.
1798 T. Jefferson *Writ.* IV. 227 The question of war and peace depends now on a toss of cross and pile. 1838 De Morgan *Probabilities* 75 Let us find the probability that, out of 200 tosses with a halfpenny, there shall be exactly 100 heads and 100 tails. 1859 *All Year Round* No. 13. 305 The town won the toss for innings. 1876 Geo. Eliot *Dan. Der.* xxviii, I don't care a toss where you are. 1887 L. Stephen in *Dict. Nat. Biog.* XI. 467/2 They..decided by the toss of a halfpenny that Concanen should defend the ministry.
**7.** The throwing off of homing pigeons in a trial of their flight and homing powers.
1897 *Westm. Gaz.* 1 June 9/2 As some of the 'tosses' numbered 6,000 birds at one time, the sight was a remarkable one. 1899 G. J. Larner in *19th Cent.* XLV. 819 The first of these two experimental tosses took place on the 17th of December last year.
† **8.** (?) A payment. *Obs.*
1630 Massinger *Picture* ii. ii, Yet, not to take From the magnificence of the King, I will Dispense his bounty too, but as a page To wait on mine: for other tosses, take A hundred-thousand crowns.
**9.** A measure for sprats: see quot.
1851 Mayhew *Lond. Labour* I. 69/2 They [sprats] are sold at Billingsgate by the 'toss' or 'chuck', which is about half a bushel, and weighs from 40 lbs. to 50 lbs.
**10.** Toss-up. The throwing up of a coin to arrive at a decision: see Toss *v.* 14.

17.. *Laws of Cricket* in Grace *Cricket* (1891) 14 The party that wins the toss-up shall go in first at his option. 1802–12 BENTHAM *Ration. Judic. Evid.* (1827) V. 64 What charity-boy..was ever at a loss to know that the toss-up of a halfpenny was worth a farthing. 1868 'S. DARYL' *Quoits & Bowls* 48 A toss-up decides which party is to play first.

b. *fig.* A chance where the probability either way is equal; an even chance. *colloq.*

1809 MALKIN *Gil Blas* XI. vii. (Rtldg.) 407 It is a toss up who fails and who succeeds. 1844 DICKENS *Mart. Chuz.* xii, It was a toss-up with Tom Pinch whether he should laugh or cry. 1862 J. SKELTON *Nugæ Crit.* vi. 257 It is generally the merest 'toss-up' what verdict the..critic pronounces on any work. 1888 *Times* (weekly ed.) 14 Sept. 15/1 It was a toss up whether Lord Salisbury was going to offer them an Irish Government or a Coercion Act.

**Toss**, *sb.*² *dial.* [A variant of TASS¹.] A heap, stack; = TASS¹.

1695 KENNETT *Par. Antiq.* II. Gloss. s.v. *Thassare*, To lay up hay or corn into a tass, toss, stack or mow. *Ibid.*, A mow of corn in a barn is called in Kent the toss. 1847–78 HALLIWELL, *Toss*, the mow or bay of a barn into which the corn is put preparatory to its being threshed.

†**Toss**, *sb.*³, var. of or misprint for TASS².

1698 FRYER *Acc. E. India & P.* 231 A Silver Toss, or Cup. *Ibid.* 399 Bowls of Wine,..most of Silver, some of Gold, which we call a *Toss*, and is made like a Wooden Dish.

**Toss** (tǫs), *v.* Pa. t. and pple. **tossed** (tǫst), also 6– **tost.** [In use soon after 1500, and current in nearly all its senses by 1550. Origin uncertain: the only cognate word appears to be the Norw. and Sw. dialect *tossa* to spread, strew (Aasen); Welsh *tosio* is from Eng.]

**I.** *trans.* **1.** To throw, pitch, or fling about, here and there, or to and fro: expressing the action of wind or wave, or the light, careless, or disdainful action of a person, on something easily moved.

1506 GUYLFORDE *Pilgr.* (Camden) 73 Howbeit the wroughte sees tossyd and rolled vs ryght greuously. 1526 TINDALE *Matt.* xiv. 24 The shippe was in the myddes of the see, and was toost with waves. — *Jas.* i. 6 Lyke the waves off the see, tost off the wynde. 1526 *Pilgr. Perf.* (W. de W. 1531) 301 Not restynge, they dyd cary the & tosse the from place to place. 1603 *Miracles Our Saviour* in Farr *S. P. Jas. I* (1848) 356 The Shaking ships amid the seas ytost. 1634 SIR T. HERBERT *Trav.* 19 The shippes are tossed they know not where. 1782 COWPER *Parrot* i, A native of the gorgeous east, By many a billow tost. 1852 THACKERAY *Esmond* II. vii, Mistress Beatrix,..tossing her rustling flowing draperies about her, and quitting the room, followed by her mother. 1887 BOWEN *Virg. Æneid* I. 524 We Troy's ill-starred sons, long tossed by the winds on the deep.

**b.** *fig.* or in fig. context.

1545 BRINKLOW *Compl.* 21 b, How men be tossed from one court to another. *Ibid.* 59 b, He that denyeth them but one grote..how will thei tosse hym in the lawe. 1569 W. SAMUEL *vii Chapter of Job* ii, Both night and day they haue their toyl With work and dreames itost. 1592 G. HARVEY *Four Lett.* iii. Wks. (Grosart) I. 195 He tost his imagination a thousand waies. 1611 BIBLE *Eph.* iv. 14 That we..be no more children, tossed to and fro, and caried about with euery winde of doctrine. 1633 P. FLETCHER *Purple Isl.* XII. lii, Though I poore changeling rove, Tost up and down in waves of worldly floud. 1727 GAY *Fables* I. xvi. 17 Here, there, by various fortune tost. 1823 CHALMERS *Serm.* I. 245 This unhappy man thus tost and bewildered and thrown into a general unceasing Frenzy. 1862 MRS. H. WOOD *Mrs. Hallib. Troub.* I. i, I have been tossed about a good deal of late years.

†**2.** To turn over and over, to turn the leaves of (a book, etc.). *Obs.*

1555 W. WATREMAN *Fardle Facions* Ded. 2 The searche of wisedome and vertue, for whose sake either we tosse, or oughte to tosse so many papers and tongues. 1579 LYLY *Euphues* (Arb.) 99, I will to Athens, there to tosse my books. 1581 PETTIE *Guazzo's Civ. Conv.* III. (1586) 159 Whether in tossing ouer your bookes, you haue light vpon that place where Cicero giueth a nip to his daughter. 1597 MORLEY *Introd. Mus.* Pref., What labour it was to tomble, tosse, and search so manie bookes. 1730 T. BOSTON *Mem.* xi. (1899) 373 The huge toil in tossing lexicons and the Hebrew concordance.

**3.** To shake, shake up, stir up.

1557 N. T. (Genev.) *Matt.* xxiv. 29 The powers of heauen shall be tossed. 1610 HOLLAND *Camden's Brit.* (1637) 208 Thomas..was much tossed and shaken. 1811 *Ora & Juliet* I. 205 She tossed the cup after breakfast, and read the fortunes of the maid-servants. 1834 M. SCOTT *Cruise Midge* (1859) 391 A tall solitary palm shot up and tossed its wide spreading fan like leaves in the night wind.

†**b.** To fling (hay, wool, etc.) abroad, so as to loosen the mass. *Obs.* exc. as in I.

1557 TUSSER *100 Points Husb.* xci, With tossing and raking, and setting on cox: The grasse that was grene, is now hay for an ox. 1573 — *Husb.* (1878) 131 No turning of peason till carrege ye make,..By turning and tossing they shed as they lie. 1581 A. HALL *Iliad* VI. 118 Of some Greeke thou shalt become the slaue Who to his country shal thee leade to tease and tosse his wul.

**c.** *Tin-refining.* (See quot.)

1884 C. G. W. LOCK *Workshop Receipts* Ser. III. 452/1 The refining [of tin] may be divided into two stages, liquation and tossing...The same effect is sometimes produced by 'tossing', or raising the metal in ladles, and pouring, from some height through the air, back again into the pan.

¶**d.** *Tin-mining.* Erron. used for TOZE *v.*², q.v.

**4.** *fig.* To disturb or agitate socially or politically.

1552 ASCHAM *Germany* 36 Cæsar..also tossed the whole world with battle & slaughter, even almost from the sun setting unto the sun rising. 1618 BOLTON *Florus* (1636) 250 Hee tossed both Sea, and Land with mixture of his miseries. 1796 BURKE *Regic. Peace* ii. Wks. VIII. 256 The..speculator Harrington, who has tossed about society into all forms.

**b.** To disquiet or agitate in mind; to set in commotion, as by shifting opinions, feelings, circumstances, or influences; to disturb, disorder.

1526 *Pilgr. Perf.* (W. de W. 1531) 172 b, To be exercised and tossed in dyuerse temptacyons. 1561 T. NORTON *Calvin's Inst.* I. 53 Contrary motions do tosse and diuersly draw his soule. 1590 SPENSER *F. Q.* I. i. 55 That troublous dreame gan freshly tosse his braine. 1632 LITHGOW *Trav.* v. 199 Thus was I tost..With strugling doubts. 1833 HT. MARTINEAU *Tale of Tyne* iv, The seamen were tossed in spirit through fear of the press gang. 1834 J. MACDONALD in Tweedie *Life* iii. (1849) 238 My mind is tossed by various considerations.

**II.** *intr.* (Related to I.)

†**5.** To be in mental agitation or distraction; to be disquieted in mind or circumstances. *Obs.*

1509 HAWES *Past. Pleas.* ii. (Percy Soc.) 14 So forthe I went, tossynge on my brayne. 1513 MORE *Rich. III*, Wks. 35/1 Katheryne whiche longe tyme tossed in either fortune sommetime in wealth, ofte in aduersitye. 1582 N. LICHEFIELD tr. *Castanheda's Conq. E. Ind.* I. viii. 20 b, The Captaine generall and the other Captaines thus tossing vp and downe, to and fro, as well with their ships, as also in their mindes, determined to beare towards the Ilande of Mombassa.

**6. a.** for *refl.* To fling or jerk oneself about; to move about restlessly.

1560 BIBLE (Genev.) *Job* vii. 4, I am euen ful with tossing to and fro vnto the dawning of the day. 1575 *Gamm. Gurton* I. v. 11 See how Hodg lieth tomblynge and tossing amids the floure. 1638 JUNIUS *Paint. Ancients* 151 Burning fevers shall leave you never a whit sooner,..if you tosse in woven imagerie,..than if you lie under..ordinarie coverings. 1754 GRAY *Pleasure* 45 Wretch, that long has tost On the thorny bed of Pain. 1886 *Tip Cat* xix, The child was tossing and turning and talking in her sleep.

**b.** for *pass.* To be flung or rocked about; to be kept in motion; to be agitated.

1582 [see 5]. 1596 SHAKS. *Merch. V.* I. i. 8 Your minde is tossing on the Ocean. 1809 JAS. MOORE *Camp. Spain* 2 The soldiers..remained tossing on board the crowded transports. 1827 POLLOK *Course T.* x. 471 The unfathomable lake, Tossing with tides of dark, tempestuous wrath. 1855 MACAULAY *Hist. Eng.* xviii. IV. 131 A fleet of merchantmen tossing on the waves. 1884 W. C. SMITH *Kildrostan* I. i. 20 Roots that cling as the branches toss.

**III.** *trans.* *To throw in a specified direction.

**7.** To throw, cast, pitch, fling, hurl (without any notion of agitation).

1570 GOOGE *Pop. Kingd.* IV. (1880) 47 b, The Dice are shakte and tost, and Cardes apace they teare. 1611 BIBLE *Isa.* xxii. 18 He will surely violently turne and tosse thee, like a ball into a large countrey. 1670 COTTON *Espernon* II. VI. 283 Had he known his temerity, he would have caus'd Marsillac to have been tost out of the Windows. 1700 S. L. tr. *Fryke's Voy. E. Ind.* 139 We lost one Man, who was Tossed off the Maintop Mast into the Sea. 1718 LADY M. W. MONTAGU *Let. to Abbé Conti* 31 July, The governor's daughter..tossed a note to him over the wall. 1810 SCOTT *Lady of L.* III. xiv, The falc'ner tossed his hawk away. 1830 in Cobbett *Rur. Rides* (1885) II. 308 Two or three, or even one man, may, if not tossed out at once, disturb and interrupt every thing. 1853 KINGSLEY *Hypatia* xvi, He tossed his purse among the crowd. 1857 *G. Bird's Urin. Deposits* (ed. 5) 217 It seems now to run some risk of being tossed aside as a thing of no consequence.

**b.** *absol.* To fling oneself (like a body tossed).

1728 YOUNG *Love Fame* v. 477 They throw their persons with a hoydon-air Across the room, and toss into the chair. 1852 THACKERAY *Esmond* I. xiii, She tossed out of the room, being in one of her flighty humours then.

**8.** *esp.* Of two players: To throw, or impel by hitting (a ball, etc.) to and fro between them: cf. *to toss from pillar to post* (PILLAR *sb.* 11). Often *fig.* or in fig. context.

1514 BARCLAY *Cyt. & Uplondyshm.* (Percy) 67 From poste unto piller tossed shalt thou be. *a* 1533 FRITH *Another Bk. agst. Rastell* Pref. A v, It is not Inoughe for a man playinge at tennes to tosse the ball agayn, but he must so tosse it that the tother take it not. 1550 CROWLEY *Last Trump.* 562 To play tenise, or tosse the ball. 1570–6 LAMBARDE *Peramb. Kent* (1826) 248 This Ball was busily tossed betweene the King and the Pope. 1879 STAINER *Music of Bible* 83 Shrill echoes ever and anon tossed from side to side.

**b.** *fig. spec.* To bandy (a subject or question) from one side to the other in debate; to discuss; to make the subject of talk.

*c* 1540 tr. *Pol. Verg. Eng. Hist.* (Camden) II. 8 The Frenche, somewhat appalled,..tossed the matter amongst themselves what best were to do. 1637 GILLESPIE *Eng. Pop. Cerem.* III. viii. 177 When questions and controversies of Faith, are tossed in the Church. 1700 BLAIR in W. S. Perry *Hist. Coll. Amer. Col. Ch.* I. 68 There is nothing more usual among schollars..than to toss an argument, and that sometimes to too great a height of heat and animosity. 1795 BURKE *Corr.* (1844) IV. 325 If we were to toss the matter about..for twenty days, we could only end as we began. 1859 TENNYSON *Lanc. & El.* 233 Then she, who..heard her name so tost about, Flush'd slightly at the slight disparagement.

***spec.* To throw up.

**9.** To throw up, throw into the air; *esp.* to throw (a coin, etc.) up to see how it falls; = *toss up*, 14 a.

*To toss in a blanket*, to throw (a person) upward repeatedly from a blanket held slackly at each corner: see BLANKET *sb.* 2. *To toss a pancake*, to throw it up so that it falls back into the pan with the other side up.

1526 *Pilgr. Perf.* (1531) 166 As a ball, whiche yf it be tossed and cast vp streyght, it falleth down directly..in the hande of hym that cast it vp. 1597, 1682 [see BLANKET *sb.* 2]. 1598 FLORIO, *Zombata*, a tossing in a blanket. 1619 [see PANCAKE I]. 1687 A. LOVELL tr. *Thevenot's Trav.* I. 45 He that has a minde to be tossed in the Air, sits down on a good seat of Wood, that is fastened to the end of the Ropes. 1688 in Ellis *Orig. Lett.* Ser. II. IV. 125 Capt. Ouseley is said to be come to town to give his reasons for tossing the Mayor of Scarborough in a blanket. *a* 1711 KEN *Blondina* Poet. Wks. 1721 IV. 526 A mad furious Bull..Who gor'd and toss'd her to the Sky. 1713 YOUNG *Last Day* I. 250 The foaming surges, tost on high. *a* 1756 MRS. HAYWOOD *New Present* (1771) 206 Turn it [a pancake] or, if you can, toss it, which is much better. 1841 CATLIN *N. Amer. Ind.* I. iv. 25 Mons. Chardon 'tossed the feather' (a custom always observed to try the course of the wind). 1863 KINGSLEY *Water Bab.* i, He was tossing halfpennies with the other boys. 1900 G. C. BRODRICK *Mem. & Impress.* 4 The newly-elected members were bound to undergo the ceremony of 'chairing', and were regularly 'tossed' at a particular spot.

*fig.* 1791 BOSWELL *Johnson* 8 May an. 1778, I don't care how often, or how high, he tosses me, when only friends are present. 1843 LYTTON *Last Bar.* IV. ii, He thinks he tosseth all London on his own horns.

**b.** *absol.* = *toss up*, 14 b. (Cf. TOSS *sb.*¹ 9.)

1833 NYREN *Yng. Cricketer's Tutor* 20 The parties shall toss for the choice of innings. 1893 D. J. RANKIN *Zambesi Basin* iv. 66 We tossed who should have first shot. My friend won.

**10.** To throw or jerk up suddenly without letting go; †*spec.* to brandish (arms) (*obs.*). *To toss oars*, 'to throw them up out of the rowlocks, and raise them perpendicularly an-end' (Adm. Smyth).

1590 SPENSER *F. Q.* I. vii. 48 Sword,..speare,..Where haue yee left your lord, that could so well you tosse? 1598 BARRET *Theor. Warres* III. i. 37 The good Picquier ought to learne to tosse his pike well. 1626 GOUGE *Serm. Dignity Chivalry* § 11 More fit..to lift a pitchforke then to tosse a pike. 1697 DRYDEN *Alexander's Feast* vi, Behold how they toss their torches on high. 1718 POPE *Iliad* III. 323 Paris thy son, and Sparta's King advance, In measur'd lists to toss the weighty lance. 1830 MARRYAT *King's Own* xxx, The boats' crews tossed their oars while the cheers were given. 1894 C. N. ROBINSON *Brit. Fleet* 181 The junior salutes the senior, if the latter be royalty, or a flag-officer, by tossing oars.

†**b.** To drink out of (a cup, etc.), tilting it up; hence, to empty by drinking; = *toss off*, 12 a. *Obs.*

1568 FULWEL *Like will to Like* B iv, From morning til night I sit tossing the black bole. 1695 CONGREVE *Love for L.* III. xv, For my Part, I mean to toss a Can, and remember my Sweet-Heart, a-fore I turn in. 1708 HUDSON in Hearne *Collect.* 3 Aug. (O. H. S.) II. 123 Who wth our merry Greek tosst a bottle.

**11.** To lift, jerk, or throw up (the head, etc.) with a sudden, impatient, or spirited movement.

1591 SYLVESTER *Ivry* 119 Some Savage Bull..tosses his head on high. 1678 DRYDEN *All for Love* I. i, Sea-horses..Toss'd up their heads, and dash'd the ooze about 'em. 1756 C. SMART tr. *Horace, Sat.* I. vi. (1826) II. 55 Do you..toss up your nose at obscure people. 1822 SCOTT *Nigel* i, Tossing his head as one who valued not the raillery to which he had been exposed. 1849 MISS MULOCK *Ogilvies* i, The first speaker tossed her head.

**IV.** With adverbs.

**12. Toss off. a.** To drink off with energetic action. **b.** To dispose of in an off-hand manner.

*c* 1590 GREENE *Fr. Bacon* i. 15 Tossing off ale and milk in country cans. 1816 T. L. PEACOCK *Headlong Hall* xi, Having..insisted on every gentleman tossing off a half-pint bumper. 1840 DICKENS *Old C. Shop* lxii, Drink that...Toss it off, don't leave any heel-tap. 1845 JUDD *Margaret* II. i, Have you read Cynthia?..It is a delightful thing to toss off a dull hour with. 1884 G. ALLEN *Philistia* II. 32 Herbert, having tossed off his coffee.

**13. Toss out.** See prec. senses and OUT; in quot., to dress smartly, 'trick out'.

1759 GOLDSM. *Bee* 13 Oct. (*On Dress*), A damsel, tossed out in all the gaiety of fifteen.

**14. Toss up. a.** See also prec. senses and UP.

1588 DELONEY *Q. Eliz. at Tilbury* Poems (1912) 476 Tossing up her plume of feathers to them all as they did stand. 1802 MARSTON *Ant. & Mel.* III. Wks. 1856 I. 36 Rubbing my quiet bosome, tossing up A gratefull spirit to Omnipotence! 1719 DE FOE *Crusoe* I. 59 The Boat..lay as the Wind and the Sea had toss'd her up upon the Land. 1743 in Howell *St. Trials* (1813) XVII. 1179 One's hair is now tossed up in such a manner that its hard to distinguish between a person's own hair and a wig. 1840 MARRYAT *Poor Jack* vi, We tossed up our oars, and laid by. 1859 *Habits Gd. Society* vii. 249 The head should..not [be] tossed up nor jerked on one side with that air of pertness.

**b.** *absol.* To toss a coin or some object in the air to wager on which side it will fall, or to determine a question by this: see HEAD *sb.* 3 b.

1704 *Hymn Vict.* lviii, Victoria Tosses-up for Cross or Pile. 1762 WILKES *Let. to Earl Temple* (1769) I. 31 They tossed up, and it fell to my adjutant to give the word. 1809 MALKIN *Gil Blas* I. v. ¶ 9 Tossing up for heads or tails was not my ruling passion. 1861 DICKENS *Gt. Expect.* xxxi, Some inclining to both opinions said 'toss up for it'.

†**c.** To cook or dress (food, a meal) hastily; to prepare, to serve up. Also *fig. Obs.*

*c* 1685 VILLIERS (Dk. Buckhm.) *Confer.* Wks. 1705 II. 54 Our ancient Matron had tossed up a nice Breakfast, out of the remainders of the Capons. 1710 *Tatler* No. 258 ¶ 1 To toss up the Fragments of a Feast into a Ragoust. 1737 BRACKEN *Farriery Impr.* (1757) II. 137 The Booksellers..had a better Knack at tossing up a Title [for a Book]. 1818 SCOTT *Rob Roy* viii, But you have not dined—we'll have something nice and ladylike, sweet and pretty like yourself, tossed up in a trice.

**Toss-**, the vb.-stem and sb. in Comb.: **toss-about** *a.*, that tosses about; **toss-ball**, a ball that is tossed; **toss-blade**, one who 'tosses' a blade or sword; **toss-cup**, one who tosses off drink; **toss-halfpenny, -penny**, the tossing of money in gambling, pitch and toss; **toss-loser**, the loser of a toss; so *toss-winner*; **toss-pan**, a pan used for tossing in cooking. See also TOSSPOT.

1844 J. T. HEWLETT *Parsons & W.* lv, That dreamy, *toss-about sort of slumber. 1681 W. ROBERTSON *Phraseol. Gen.* (1693) 1078 Fortunes *toss-ball. 1659 TORRIANO, *Accoltellatore*, a fighter, a *tosse-blade, a swash-buckler. 1883 G. H. BOUGHTON in *Harper's Mag.* Apr. 684/2 The merry, liquid-eyed *toss-cup of Ostade. 1849 THACKERAY *Pendennis* v, A little scamp of a choir-boy, who played *toss-halfpenny. 1906 *Daily Chron.* 8 Sept. 3/2 When that has been the case the writer cannot remember the *toss-losers failing to win the event. 1796 MRS. GLASSE *Cookery* v. 57 Put half a pint of gravy into a *toss-pan. 1874 SYMONDS *Sk. Italy & Gr.* (1898) I. v. 96 Men and boys play for the most part at bowls or *toss-penny.

**Toss, Tosser,** etc., erron. ff. TOZE, TOZER, etc.

† **To·ssant,** *a. Obs. rare*—[1]. (*pseudo-arch.*) [irreg. f. TOSS *v.* + -ANT [1] of F. pr. pple.] Tossing.

1616 LANE *Cont. Sqr.'s T.* xi. 267 His tossant plume, which sublimeth his head, All colors wore, save white, that mote bee read.

**Tossed** (tǫst), *ppl. a.* Also tost. [f. TOSS *v.* + -ED [1].] Thrown about, hurled this way and that; disordered; disturbed, troubled: see the vb.

1621 BP. HALL *Heaven upon Earth* § 4 The galled soule ..after many tossed and turned sides, complaines of remedilesse and vnabated torment. 1659 R. CROMWELL in *Clarke Papers* (Camden) IV. 297 Oh,..that poore tossed Ingland might at laste finde a quiet harbour! 1780 A. YOUNG *Tour Irel.* I. 265 Wild tossed-about ground. 1807 CRABBE *Village* I. 116 On the tost vessel bend their eager eye. 1825 SCOTT *Talism.* vi, His tossed couch and impatient gestures showed..the energy and the reckless impatience of a disposition, whose natural sphere was [etc.]. 1844 H. G. ROBINSON *Odes of Horace* I. xxxii, His toss'd bark made fast to the watery shore.

**Tossel, -ell,** obs. ff. TASSEL *sb.*[1], [2], TERCEL.

**Tosser** (tǫ·səɹ). [f. TOSS *v.* + -ER [1].]

**1.** One who or that which tosses. Also with *adv.*

1612 T. TAYLOR *Comm. Titus* ii. 12 (1619) 475 Scoffers of such as walke in these straite waies of God, tossers of reproaches against them. 1623 FLETCHER & ROWLEY *Maid in Mill* II. ii, As satisfaction to the blustring god, To send his tossers forth. 1837 *New Monthly Mag.* LI. 195 Ticket-porters are..such..tossers-off of beer. 1846 MRS. GORE *Eng. Char.* (1852) 109 The hapless tosser-up of omelets. 1896 A. MORRISON *Child of the Jago* 130 The last of the tossers stuffed away his coppers. 1905 *Daily Chron.* 7 Sept. 4/4 As a caber tosser he has never been equalled.

**2.** A cooking-vessel, a tossing-pan.

1884 *Hand & Heart* Oct. 123/2 Cut the other parts in small bits, put them in a small tosser with a grate of nutmeg, the least white pepper and salt,..simmer a few minutes before you fill.

**Tossicate,** variant of TOSTICATE.

**Tossily,** *adv.*: see TOSSY *a.*

**To·ssing,** *vbl. sb.* [-ING [1].] The action of TOSS *v.* in various senses. Also with *adv.*

1557 [see TOSS *v.* 3 b]. 1578 LYTE *Dodoens* 367 The other ..stirreth vp tossinges, wamlings, windinesse, and vomiting. *a* 1586 SIDNEY *Arcadia* II. (Sommer) 173 When Basilius after long tossing was gotten a sleepe. 1642 FULLER *Holy & Prof. St.* III. x. 174 Like the tossing of a pike, which is.. to shew the strength and nimblenesse of the arm. 1711 ADDISON *Spect.* No. 63 ℙ 1 The Tossings and Fluctuations of the Sea. 1801 *Sporting Mag.* XIX. 115 No cards, dice, odd-horse or tossing-up to be permitted.

**b.** *attrib.*: †**tossing iron,** some cooking utensil; **tossing-pan,** a pan for tossing food in cooking.

*a* 1625 FLETCHER *Woman's Prize* II. v, They heave ye stool on stool, and fling main pot-lids Like massy rocks, dart ladles, tossing irons And tongs like thunder-bolts. 1769 MRS. RAFFALD *Eng. Housekpr.* (1778) 75 Put them all in your tossing-pan, and shake it over the fire till it boils, then put in your woodcock. 1796 MRS. GLASSE *Cookery* v. 47 Put it into a tossing-pan with a tea-spoonful of lemon-pickle.

**To·ssing,** *ppl. a.* [f. TOSS *v.* + -ING [2].] That tosses: see the vb.

1575 *Gamm. Gurton* II. iv, My goodly tossing sporyars neele, chaue lost ich wot not where. 1742 YOUNG *Nt. Th.* I. 167 How I dreamt..Of stable pleasures on the tossing wave! 1816 J. WILSON *City of Plague* II. iv. 106 Beside the couch of tossing agony. 1896 'H. S. MERRIMAN' *Flotsam* iv, A fine boy with tossing fair curls.

Hence **To·ssingly** *adv.*

1620 THOMAS *Lat. Dict.*, *Volutatim*..rollingly, tumblingly, tossingly.

† **To·ssment.** *Obs.* [f. TOSS *v.* + -MENT.] The action of tossing or fact of being tossed.

1650 T. B. *Worcester's Apoph.* lix. 108 After so long a voyage as threescore and sixteen years tossement upon the waves of this troublesome world.

**Tosspot** (tǫ·spǫt). [f. phr. *to toss a pot*, TOSS *v.* 10 b.] One accustomed to toss off his pot of drink; a heavy drinker; a toper, drunkard.

1568 FULWEL *Like Will to Like* D j b, I wil pledge Tom tospot, til I be as drunk as a mouse a. 1577 tr. *Bullinger's Decades* (1592) 153 Come not in companie of blasphemous tossepots. 1674 JOSSELYN *Voy. New Eng.* (1675) 76 The eggs of an owl put into the liquor that a tospot useth to be drunk with, will make him loathe drunkenness. 1809 W. IRVING *Knickerb.* VI. v. (1861) 204 They were sturdy toss-pots of yore. 1890 BESANT *Demoniac* iv, He is .. a brother tosspot.

**b.** *Comb.*, as **To·sspotlike** adv.

1580 H. GIFFORD *Gilloflowers* (1875) 150 Doste thinke that such as tospotlike Set all at sixe and seuen, Are in a ready way to bring Their sinfull soules to heauen?

**To·ssy,** *a. rare.* [f. TOSS *sb.*[1] or *v.* + -Y.] Contemptuous, pert. Hence **To·ssily** *adv.*

1851 KINGSLEY *Yeast* vii, Argemone answered by some tossy commonplace. *Ibid.*, She answered tossily enough.

† **Tost,** *v.* Corruption of TOSS *v.*

1606 tr. *Rollock's Comm. on 2 Thess.* 138 (Jam.) Thou shalt be beatten and tosted here and there. 1632 LITHGOW *Trav.* v. 215 The Whirlwind of Time, still so speedy posts, That like it selfe, all things therein, it tosts.

**Tost,** var. TOSSED, pa. t. and pple. of TOSS *v.*, also *ppl. a.* Still frequent in poetry, and as second element in compounds, as *tempest-tost*.

**Tost,** obs. form of TOAST.

**To-stand, To-step:** see TO- *pref.*[1]

**Tosticate** (tǫ·stikeɪt), *v.* Also 9 *dial.* tossicate. Usually in pa. pple. *tosticated*, app. originally a mispronunciation of *intoxicated* and so used, but later also associated with *tossed, tost*, and used as = tossed about, distracted, perplexed. So **Tostica·tion.** Common dialectally; cited in E.D.D. for many counties from W. Yorksh. to Somerset.

1650 J. REYNOLDS *Flower of Fidelity* 3 His tosticated conceits fixt upon renowned travel. *Ibid.* 42 Being tosticated with the beauty. 1691 MRS. D'ANVERS *Academia* 8 Madam's most sadly tosticated, Knowing her Boy but empty-pated, Lest the soft Squire might starv'd be, When e're he's sent to th' 'Versity. 1712 SWIFT *Jrnl. to Stella* xlviii, I have been so tosticated about since my last. 1748 RICHARDSON *Clarissa* xvii. (1810) V. 181, I want these tostications (thou seest how women and women's words fill my mind) to be over. 1811 *Ora & Juliet* I. 32 Get thee to bed..and sleep off that odious strong liquor that has tosticated thy senses. 1828 *Craven Gloss.*, *Tossicated*, tossed, perplexed. Also, drunk. 1881 MISS JACKSON *Shropsh. Word-bk.*, *Tossicated*, harassed; worried,—'upset', as by vexation or trouble.

**To-stick, To-sting, To-stink,** etc.: see TO- *pref.*[1], [2].

† **Tostock(e, -stok(e,** shortening of TAVISTOCK, q. v. *Obs.*

1511–12 *Act* 3 *Hen. VIII*, c. 6 § 3 Wollen Clothes called Tostokes made in the Countie of Devonshire. 1523 *Act* 14 & 15 *Hen. VIII*, c. 11 Any Clothes callyd Tostokkes.

† **To-swe·ll,** *v. Obs.* [OE. *toswellan*, f. TO-[2] + *swellan*, SWELL *v.* So OHG. *ziswellan*, MHG. *ze-, zerswellen*.] *intr.* To swell out; also *fig.* to be puffed up, as with an emotion. Chiefly in pa. pple. to-swolle(n.

*c* 1000 ÆLFRIC *Saints' Lives* iii. 481 He hæfde ænne licðrowere..Eʒeslice to-swollen. *c* 1205 LAY. 17815 Al ic æm to-swollen..Nu nan ich wurðe dæd. *a* 1250 *Owl & Night.* 145 Þeos vle..Sat toswolle & tobolewe So heo hedde one frogge iswolwe. *c* 1330 R. BRUNNE *Chron. Wace* (Rolls) 10876 Þem þoughte for wo þey al to-swal. 1382 WYCLIF *Jer.* v. 22 To-swelle shul his flodis. *c* 1400 *Lanfranc's Cirurg.* 311 Humouris fel so myche þerto þat his leggis & his hipis to-swollen al greet.

**To-swelt, To-swinge, To-swink:** see TO- *pref.*[2]

**Tosy, tosie** (tōˑzi), *a. Sc.* Also tozie, -y. [Origin uncertain: it can hardly be the same as TOZY *a.*]

**1.** Warm; comforting or comfortable, snug, cosy. Sometimes app. = 'fresh, refreshing'.

1720 RAMSAY *Patie & Rodger* I. i, How tosie is't tae snuff the cauller air. 1722 HAMILTON *Wallace* III. i. (1774) 58 He..brought them wealth of meat and tosie drink. 1890 J. SERVICE *Notandums* x. 71 As tozie a howff as you would fin' in a' Glesco.

**2.** Slightly intoxicated; tipsy. Also *tosy-mosy*.

1727 P. WALKER *R. Cameron* in *Biogr. Presbyt.* (1827) I. 278 The Magistrates gave him Drink and kept him tozy. 1794 *Poems Eng., Sc., & Lat.* 95 (Jam.) What puir man, whan he's tozy, But spends as he ware bein and cozy? 1828 MOIR *Mansie Wauch* xvii. (1849) 111 We had another jug, after which we were both a wee tozy-mozy.

Hence **Tosily, -lie,** *adv.*; **To·siness.**

1825 in JAMIESON.

† **Tot,** *sb.*[1] *Obs. rare.* In 5 totte, 7 toute. [Origin unascertained.] A person of disordered brain, a simpleton, a fool.

*c* 1425 *Cast. Persev.* 2880 in *Macro Plays* 162 Werldlys good þou hast for-gon, & with tottys þou schalt be torn. *c* 1440 *Promp. Parv.* 497/2 Totte, *supra* in folte. *Ibid.* (MS. Winch.), Totte, fowle, supra in ff. [*Ffolt* idem quod *folet*, *ffolette*, ffatuellus]. *a* 1660 *Contemp. Hist. Irel.* (Ir. Archæol. Soc.) I. 278 Whoe answeared like a toute, or a maddman, as he was, that he was for the Kinge.

† **Tot** (tǫt), *sb.*[2] *Obs.* Also 6–7 tott(e. [f. TOT *v.*[1] (or its source).] The word *tot* or letter T written against an item in an account to indicate that the amount specified has been received; hence, an item in an account; also generally, a note, jotting, or comment written down.

1529 GARDINER *Let. to Wolsey* in *St. Papers Hen. VIII* I. 345 The copy..I sende unto Your Grace,..adding in the margyne tottes, wherby Your Grace may perceyve omne consilium rei gestæ. *a* 1601 SIR T. FANSHAWE *Pract. Exch.* (1658) 71 After his said Secondary hath made up the Sheriffs second summ upon his *De debitis plurimum*, which be his Tots and upon his *De pluribus debitis* charge which be his greene wax, and his whole as before, or so many of them as he is charged with, hee causeth the Sheriffs forraigne accounts to be cast up. *Ibid.* 80 He maketh speciall *tot* against the same summe thus [etc.]. 1642 C. VERNON *Consid. Exch.* 32 The greatest part of the Sheriffes totts and summes of money by him taken in charge at his apposals, would be set off and discharged. 1798 T. FARRER in Manning *Exch. of Pleas* (1819) II. App. 267 Such fines, recognizances and amerciaments, as each sheriff has received he answers by saying *Tot*, whereupon I [deputy clerk] mak that answer upon the roll of the estreat. When the sheriff receives part and not the whole, he answers Tot as to part, and Nil as to the rest.

**Tot** (tǫt), *sb.*[3] *colloq.* [Short for *total* or L. *totum*: see also TOTE *sb.*[1]] The total of an addition, sometimes having *tot.* written against it; hence, an addition sum; also (*tot-up*) the action of TOT *v.*[2]; adding up, totalling.

[1690 PEPYS *Mem. Royal Navy* 36 Repaires, *l.* 132000, Sea-stores, *l.* 88000. Tot, 220,000.] 1871 *Standard* 13 Feb., The task of going over the cards..and comparing the lists, and doing the general tot-up, is very arduous. 1879 C. MARVIN *Our Public Offices* 11, I fell upon the row of 'tots' with the same vigour. 1894 *Daily News* 14 July 5/1 He has seen children in Standards IV and V using their fingers freely during the examination, and even trying to do 'tots' by this cumbrous method.

**Tot,** *sb.*[4] *colloq.* or *local.* [app. a recent word; recorded 1725. Origin uncertain. *Tottr* occurs in Icel. as the nickname of a dwarfish person, and *tommel-tot* as Danish for Tom Thumb; but no connexion has been traced.]

**1.** A very small or tiny child.

1725 RAMSAY *Gentle Sheph.* I. ii, Wow! Jenny, can there greater pleasure be Than see sic wee tots toolying at your knee? 1865 *Cornh. Mag.* Mar. 355 Her tiny trembling tot with yellow hair. 1896 'IAN MACLAREN' *Kate Carnegie* 25 I've had it since I was a little tot and could remember anything.

**b.** *Tot-o'er-seas*, a local name of the Goldcrest.

1885 SWAINSON *Provinc. Names Birds* 25 Goldcrest... From its tiny size. *Tot o'er seas.* 1895 NEWTON *Dict. Birds*, *Tot-o'er-seas*, a name by which *Regulus cristatus* is said to be known on some parts of the east coast.

**2.** A very small drinking-vessel; a child's mug. (See also quot. 1845.) Chiefly *dial.*

1828 *Craven Gloss.*, *Tot*, a cup or glass. 1845 SIR H. B. EDWARDES in *Mem.* (1886) I. 33 That half-mad camel, who is overladen with tents and tots. [*Note.* Tin pots, out of which the European soldiers drink.] 1872 *Daily News* 5 Sept., Dark figures [soldiers]..throw themselves down on the straw, and investigate into the contents of the mug or of the tot. 1890 'R. BOLDREWOOD' *Miner's Right* xxvii, Give me that 'tot' that I see tied to your saddle. 1891 *Sale Catal. Glass Wks. Stourbridge*, Twenty-seven tots. Two flower bowls.

**3.** A minute quantity of anything, esp. of drink; a dram; also, anything very small.

1828 in *Craven Gloss* 1847–78 HALLIWELL, *Tot*, anything very small. *East.* 1856 KANE *Arctic Explor.* II. vii. 78 We jabbed the stopper down the whiskey-tin and gave you a tot of it. 1878 F. S. WILLIAMS *Midl. Railw.* 527 The hole is charged with gunpowder,—about a pint—or two 'tots'..being usually enough. 1908 *Times* 30 July 8/3 The issue of 'tots of rum' on cold nights was not only not desirable, but absolutely pernicious.

**Tot,** *sb.*[5] *slang.* [Origin unascertained: cf. TAT *sb.*[5], *v.*[3]] A dust-heap picker's name for a bone; whence by extension, anything worth picking from a refuse-heap or elsewhere. Hence **To·tter,** a rag-and-bone collector; **To·tting,** dust-heap picking.

1873 *Slang Dict.* s. v., 'Tot' is a bone, but chiffoniers and cinder-hunters generally are called *Tot-pickers* nowadays. *Totting* also has its votaries on the banks of the Thames, where all kinds of flotsam and jetsam, from coals to carrion, are known as *tots*. 1880 *Law Rep.*, 5 *Q. B. D.* 369 The contents of the dust-bins consisted chiefly of cinders and ashes and the sweepings of the houses, but they also contained a number of articles thrown into them as refuse by the occupiers of the houses, and known as 'tots'. 1891 *Daily News* 11 Mar. 3/3 Costermongers, wood-cutters, and 'totters', men who lounged about areas in the hope of getting old bottles and things from servants. 1910 *Lond. City Mission Mag.* May 85/2 The Totters. Up betimes, these queer people set out by the dozen, with sack or barrow, in quest of rags and bones, rubber, and bottles, scrap iron and cast-off clothing. *Ibid.*, When all else fails, and one can stoop so low, a day's totting is bound to yield the cost of a night's lodging.

† **Tot,** *v.*[1] *Obs.* [f. L. *tot* so much, so many; acc. to Blount, short for *tot pecuniæ Regi debentur* 'so many sums of money are due to the king'.]

**1.** *trans.* To mark (an item in the sheriff's list) with the word *tot* or the letter T, showing that the amount had been levied, and was to be accounted for, by him. Cf. NICHIL, O.NI. Also used in certain accounts between the Exchequer and other persons: see quot. 1785. Hence **Totting** *vbl. sb.*

[1368 *Act* 42 *Edw. III*, c. 9 Est ordene..qe homme veie les dites estretes ensealees, & qe ce qest paie soit tottee, et meismes les estretes mandez as Viscontes sur la receite. *transl.* a Man shall see the same Estreats sealed, and that the same which is paid, be totted, and the same Estreats sent to the Sheriffs upon the Receipt.] 1530–1 *Act* 22 *Hen. VIII*, c. 15 All other yssues and amercyamentes.. whether they be totted or not totted, taken to the charge of the Shyryff or not taken to his charge. 1620 J. WILKINSON *Coroners & Sherifes* 75 An ignorant Undersherif may both undoe his high Sherife and himselfe, both in this world and in the world to come by totting and nichiling. *Ibid.*, If it bee totted, that is charged, though it can never be levied, it will now hardly be avoided, but it must be paid. *a* 1726 SIR G. GILBERT *Treat. Crt. Exchequer* vii. (1758) 115 If the Sheriff has levied any Part of these Debts he Totts it, and the Letter T is set upon such Sum. 1785 *MS. Dean's Bk. Canterb. Cathedr.* lf. 129 Agreed that the process called Totting, in the Exchequer, for a share of the Post Fines, attended with great expence, and little or no advantage, be in future discontinued. 1798 T. FARRER in Manning *Exch. of Pleas* (1819) II. App. 267 As to such sums as are totted by the sheriff.

**2.** *transf.* To note or distinguish (a name in a list) by some mark or a prick, e. g. to prick the sheriffs; also to make a note against a name in a list or a sum or item in an account; also, to write down by way of note, to jot down in writing.

**1444** *Paston Lett.* I. 55 Sir, ther arn xv. jurores abowe to certifie ye, as many as ye will: but lete these men that be tottid be certified, for thei be the rewleris. **1522** Wolsey *Let. to Hen. VIII* in *St. Papers* I. 115 The Judges procedyd to election of your Schreffes..for thys yere; whos namys be comprisid in a byll of parchement herin closid; desyring Your Grace to tot and marcke suche oon of thre namyd for every schire, as may stand with your gracious pleasure. **1524** *Ibid.* 150 The copy.., with my poore opinion upon the same, totted in the margyne. **1587** Fleming *Contn. Holinshed* III. 1545/1 Such as were absent, had no allowance that daie: if they came late, their wages was totted at the expenditors good discretion. **1612** *Manch. Crt. Leet Rec.* (1885) II. 270 Those ffreeholders..whose names are not totted in the Courtbooke.

**Tot** (tɒt), *v.*[2] *colloq.* [f. Tot *sb.*[3]] *trans.* To add *together* and bring out the total of; to sum *up*.

**1760–72** H. Brooke *Fool of Qual.* (1809) IV. 82 These, totted together, will make a pretty beginning of my little project. **1839** T. Hook *Gurney Married* 403 Now, ma'am, if you will just tot up your account for schooling and that, I'll arrange the whole matter. **1876** Farjeon *Love's Vict.* xiv, When he totted up the figures, he was rather serious. **1895** Stuart & Park *Variety Stage* ii. 31 A waiter totting up the account as you passed through.

**b.** *intr. To tot up*: to amount, 'come' (*to*).

**1882** Besant *All Sorts* iv, I..wondered how much it would tot up to. Something, I thought, in four figures. **1892** *Idler* July 719 Three stalls a week tot up frightfully in a year.

Hence **To·tting** *vbl. sb.*

**1823** *Monthly Mag.* LV. 237 All the items were tenaciously preserved in the toting up. **1863** Cowden Clarke *Shaks. Char.* vi. 152 The very 'totting up' of his qualifications creates a 'real presence' of the man. **1865** *Standard* 31 July, The totting [of the votes] was not concluded by Mr. Dames until half-past two.

**Tot** (tɒt), *v.*[3] *Sc.* [Not recorded before 19th c.; ? playful shortening of *totter* or *tottle*. Connexion with Tot *sb.*[4] 1 'tiny child' uncertain.] *intr.* 'To move with short steps as a child does' (Jamieson 1825); to totter; to toddle; also playfully, to walk, go, move.

**1824** W. Jameson in *Mem. & Lett.* (1845) 46 My little Benoni is gathering strength and totting about. **1844** A. McKay in *Mod. Sc. Poets* II. 377 When ye were wee bairnies, tot, totting about. *c* **1850** *Whistle-binkie* (1890) II. *Songs Nursery* 81 Awa they tot wi' ane anither.

**Tot**, in phr. *tot and quot*: see Tot-quot.

†**To-tag.** *Obs.* In 3 to tagge, (to tage). [app. f. To-[1] + *tagge*, Tag *sb.* pendant or addition, or *v.* to append. But the simple sb. and vb. are not known bef. *c* 1400, and then not in abstract sense.

It is to be remembered however that *tag* was prob. a word not likely to occur in literature; and that there are other words in which the compound with *to-* is known much earlier than the simple word, e. g. *to-crush, to-touse*.]

Something 'tagged' or attached to a fact; a circumstance.

*c* **12..** *Ancr. R.* 316 (Corpus MS.) Six þinges O Latin circumstances: On Englisch to tagges mahe beon icleopede [*MS. Cott. Nero* On Englisch heo muwen beon ihoten totagges: persone, stude, time, manere, tale, cause]. *Ibid.* 346 Þurh sum uuel to tagge þe lið þer biseden. *Ibid.*, Efter þe to tagges [*Nero* circumstances] þe beoð iwriten þruppe. [So in 8 instances in Corpus, in 2 of which Cott. Nero has *circumstances* without a gloss.]

**Total** (tōu·tăl), *a.* and *sb.* [a. F. *total* (14th c. in Hatz.-Darm.) = Sp., Pg. *total*, It. *totale*, ad. Schol.L. *tōtāl-is* (in St. Bernard 1150), f. L. *tōt-us* entire: see -al.]

**A.** *adj.* **1.** Of, pertaining, or relating to the whole of something. Now *rare*, exc. in

*Total eclipse*, an eclipse of the sun or moon in which the whole of the disk is obscured. (Often taken as sense 3.)

*c* **1386** Chaucer *Pars. T.* ⁋ 218 His contricion..shal be vniuersal and total. **1594** Blundevil *Exerc.* ii. (1636) 105 The total Sine, which is the whole Semidiameter, and greatest right Sine. **1627** W. Sclater *Exp. 2 Thess.* (1629) 172 There are two kindes or degrees of it [faith]. 1. Totall respecting the whole word of God...2. Partiall. *a* **1653** Gouge *Comm. Heb.* ii. 9 (1655) 170 He was a totall Saviour. He saveth soul and body. **1671** Milton *Samson* 81 Irrecoverably dark, total Eclipse Without all hope of day. **1683** *Phil. Trans., Abr.* II. 604 Total Eclipse of the Moon, Feb. 11–21, 1682, observed at Paris and Copenhagen. **1697** tr. *Burgersdicius his Logic* i. xv. 51 That Cause is total, which in its Species wholly causes the Whole Caused. **1715** Halley in *Phil. Trans.* XXIX. 245 Observations on the..Total Eclipse of the Sun..22nd of April. **1857** Whewell *Hist. Induct. Sc.* (ed. 3) I. 362 The eclipse must have been one decidedly total.

**2.** Constituting or comprising a whole; whole, entire.

*c* **1400** *Plowm. T.* 418 Goodes frendship hem makes, They toteth on hir somme totall. **1474** *Acc. Ld. High Treas. Scot.* I. 72 Sum totale of bath thir sidis, lix li. xv d. *c* **1477** Caxton *Jason* 7 b, The veray and sewre foundement vpon which my total espayr and hope resteth. *c* **1586** C'tess Pembroke *Ps.* xcviii. iii, Thou totall globe and all that thee enjoy. **1610** Donne *Pseudo-martyr* 201 The whole totall body..of the points of their profession. **1709** Lady M. W. Montagu *Let. to Mrs. Hewet* 12 Nov., This is the sum total of all the news I know. **1807** J. Barlow *Columb.* iii. 174 The flaming deluge..Sweeps total nations from the staggering world. **1810** in Sir W. Napier *Penins. War* (1878) II. App. 418 Total number of bayonets..4924. **1833** Ht. Martineau *Cinnamon & P.* vi, Its total revenue does not pay its expenses. **1903** *Daily Chron.* 25 Mar. 8/7 The percentage of total rainfall which reaches the river is diminishing, as well as the total rainfall itself.

**3.** Complete in extent or degree; absolute, utter.

**1647** Clarendon *Hist. Reb.* i. § 1 Nothing less..could have produced such a total and prodigious Alteration and Confusion over the whole kingdom. **1769** *Def. Locke's Opin. Pers. Identity* 31 After a total interruption of thought ..during sound sleep. **1770** *Aberdeen Burgh Rec.* in Bulloch *Pynours* (1887) 76 To put a total stop to the rolling of all sorts of Casks. **1816** Coleridge *Human Life* 1 If total gloom Swallow up life's brief flash for aye, we fare As summer-gusts, of sudden birth and doom. **1837** Lockhart *Scott* I. iv. 127 Notwithstanding all that Scott says about the total failure of his attempts in the art of the pencil,.. they proved very useful to him afterwards. **1838–9** Fr. A. Kemble *Resid. in Georgia* (1863) 24 A total absence of self-respect.

**b.** *Total abstinence*: *spec.* entire abstinence from the use of alcoholic drinks. So *total abstainer*; also (rare) *total abstinent, total abstention*.

**1831** J. Tuckerman *Let. respecting a City Temperance Soc., Boston, Mass.* 5 A total abstinence from intoxicating stimulants, except for medicinal purposes. **1856** Vaughan *Mystics* (1860) II. 219 How much easier is total abstinence from scenes of amusement than temperance in money-getting. **1862** Total-abstainers [see Abstainer]. **1880** Richardson in *Med. Temp. Jrnl.* 71 In their allegiance to 'total abstention'. **1882** (in a *Magazine*), Very few public men..care to order a bottle of wine at a public table. It is not because they are total abstinents.

†**4.** Summary, concise, brief. *Obs. rare*[−1].

*a* **1586** Sidney *Astr. & Stella* xcii, Or do you meane my tender eares to spare, That to my questions you so totall are? When I demaund of Phœnix-Stellas state, You say, forsooth, you left her well of late: O God, thinke you that satisfies my care?

**B.** *sb.* (the adj. used absolutely). The aggregate, the whole sum or amount; a whole.

**1557** Recorde *Whetst.* Cc ij b, The totalle will bee (as here in worke appeareth) 335,016. **1621** Bp. Mountagu *Diatribæ* 65 To cast vp these particulars into one totall. **1656** Earl Monm. tr. *Boccalini's Advts. fr. Parnass.* ii. xi. 224 Here.. is a business in which consists the total of our safety. **1772** Burke *Corr.* (1844) I. 380 But I must say with as great, as just suspicions of him and his, as with attachment to you, on the total. **1841** Marryat *Poacher* xxii, You can..sum up totals. **1849** Grote *Greece* ii. xlii. V. 218 The grand total was not less than 110,000 men.

Hence **To·talness**, totality. *rare*[−0].

**1727** Bailey vol. II, *Totalness*, the Wholeness, or whole Sum. Hence **1818** in Todd; and in later Dicts.

**Total** (tōu·tăl), *v.* [f. Total *a.* and *sb.*]

**1. a.** *trans.* To reach the total of, amount to.

**1859** *All Year Round* No. 13. 305 One of our adversaries scored 70 off his own bat: they totalled 138. **1884** *Pall Mall G.* 22 Aug. 2/2 The proofs actually issued in neither case totalled 1,000. **1901** *Cycl. Tour. Cl. Gaz.* Oct. 389 A list [of accidents]..totals no less than twenty.

**b.** *intr.* To amount *to*, mount *up to*.

**1880** *Scotsman* 24 Jan., For the whole of 1879 they probably totalled up to between 16 and 17 millions. **1896** *Daily News* 23 Jan. 7/5 Even the 5s. or 10s. required as deposit on each ticket must total to a large amount.

**2.** *trans.* To bring to a total, add up, complete.

**1716** M. Davies *Athen. Brit.* III. 99 One, if not both of those Collectors dy'd..before those Collections were total'd. **1863** P. Barry *Dockyard Econ.* 23 The rating, valuing, totalling, and proving of workmanship notes in the Accountant's department. **1894** *Cath. News* 16 June 4/5 The heavy legal costs..if totalled up, would strike our readers with surprise.

**Totality** (totæ·lĭti). [ad. Schol.L. *tōtālitās* (*a* 1141 in Hugo de S. Victor, also in Albertus Magnus, Aquinas, Duns Scotus), f. *tōtālis* Total: cf. F. *totalité* (14th c. in Hatz.-Darm.).]

**1.** The quality of being total; entirety.

**1627** Donne *Serm.* xliv. (1640) 443 God the Father, God the Son, and God the Holy Ghost, whom this day we celebrate, in the Ingenuity, and in the Assiduity, and in the Totality, recommended in this text. **1684** Baxter *Answ. Theol. Dial.* 4 We will not be cheated by it to believe that it causeth any more than Totality or Integrality. *c* **1819** Coleridge in *Rem.* (1836) II. 149 Instead of unity of action I should greatly prefer the more appropriate, though scholastic and uncouth, words homogeneity, proportionateness, and totality of interest. **1869** Ingleby *Introd. Metaph.* ii. ii. 171, I remark, *obiter*, that Totality is plurality in unity.

**b.** *Astron.* Total obscuration of the sun or moon in an eclipse; the moment of occurrence or time of duration of this.

**1842** G. B. Airy in *Mem. R. Astron. Soc.* (1846) XV. 12 About six minutes before the totality. *Ibid.* Plate ii. Fig. 1 Appearance of the sun a short time before totality. **1860** F. Galton in *Vac. Tour.* 439 About twenty-five minutes before totality they gave place to our wishes. **1871** Tyndall *Fragm. Sc.* (1879) I. vi. 208 The appearance of the corona and prominences at the moment of totality.

**2.** That which is total; a whole; the total number or amount, the aggregate.

**1598** Florio, *Totalita*, a totalitie or whole sum. **1602** Warner *Alb. Eng.* xiii. lxxix. (1612) 327 Whence, and to which Totalitie begins and ends alone. **1654** Jer. Taylor *Real Pres.* xi. 224 There is a new heap of impossibilities, if we should reckon that which flowes from the multiplication of totalities. **1660** R. Coke *Justice Vind.* 35 The will of the major part cannot be the will of the totality, but plurality. **1789** Gouv. Morris in Sparks *Life & Writ.* (1832) I. 336 The totality of the public debt here is about 4,700,000,000 livres. **1864** Bowen *Logic* iv. (1870) 76 'The universe'..means only the totality of that class of objects which we are thinking of. **1884** H. Spencer in *Contemp. Rev.* XLVI. 33 The totality of all powers and rights originally existed as an undivided whole in the sovereign people.

**Totaliza·tion.** [f. Totalize *v.*: see -ation. Cf. F. *totalisation* (neologism in Littré).] The action or process of totalizing, or the condition of being totalized; calculation of the total.

**1888** *Sci. Amer.* 29 Dec. 404/1 The totalization of the slight liftings due to the repetition of this maneuver on each of the cables finally effected a general lifting of four inches. *Mod.* The totalization of the returns from different parts.

**Totalizator** (tōu·tăləizĕⁱtəɹ). [f. as if from a L. **totalizāre* to totalize: prob. ad. mod.F. *totalisateur* (1869 in Littré, in scientific use).] A machine or apparatus for registering and showing the total of operations, measurements, etc.; *spec.* an apparatus for registering and indicating the number of tickets sold to betters on each horse in a race.

**1879** *S. Australian Independ. & Presbyt.* Nov., The passing through Parliament of the Totalizator Bill—a measure to legalise a certain form of betting. **1881** *Standard* 7 Sept. 5/2 'Paris mutuals'..would perhaps be better understood by English people under their other appellation of 'totalisators', instruments much in vogue upon the race-courses of Australia. **1885** *Q. Rev.* Oct. 455 A board is exhibited, containing the names of the horses starting. A person who wishes to back a horse pays in a pound, or as many pounds as he likes, to the officer in charge of the totalisator. When the race is over, all the money staked is divided between the backers of the winning horse, less ten per cent, which is the profit of the management. **1890** *Times* 26 Feb. 5/3 The Lower House of the Reichsrath to-day adopted a resolution in favour of increasing the tax on the totalisator, or *pari-mutuel*, used on Austrian race-courses, from 3 to 5 per cent.

**Totalize** (tōu·tăləiz), *v.* [f. Total *a.* + -ize: cf. F. *totaliser* (neologism in Littré).] *trans.* To make total; to combine into a total or aggregate. Hence **To·talized** *ppl. a.*; **To·talizing** *vbl. sb.* and *ppl. a.*; *totalizing machine*, a totalizator.

**1818** Coleridge in *Rem.* (1836) I. 223 To place these images totalized and fitted to the limits of the human mind so as to elicit from..the forms themselves the moral reflexions to which they approximate. **1855** Bain *Senses & Int.* iii. ii. § 33 (1864) 525 This force, or impulse, of mind that resists the totalizing influence of a complex object, and isolates for study and comparison its individual effects. **1865** Grote *Treat. Mor. Ideas* iv. (1876) 43 A number of partial views which we cannot harmonize and totalize or bring into a whole. **1888** *Daily News* 27 Aug. 3/5 [At Baden] Betting is now strictly prohibited, except by the medium of the totalising machine, which is worked under State supervision. **1888** *Sci. Amer.* 29 Dec. 404/1 The cables..constituted a totalizing apparatus that permitted of moving million-pound masses by means of..successive stresses never exceeding 15 tons.

**To·talizer.** [f. prec. + -er[1].] That which totalizes; in quot. = Totalizator.

**1887** *Daily News* 18 Apr. 3/6 The Jockey Club and the National Steeplechase Society have applied for permission to make use of the betting-machines known as 'totalisers', which are in use throughout the Continent.

**Totally** (tōu·tăli), *adv.* [f. Total *a.* + -ly[2]: cf. Schol.L. *tōtāliter*, OF. *totalement* (Oresme, 14th c.).] In a total manner or degree; wholly, completely, entirely, altogether.

**1509** Hawes *Past. Pleas.* xliv. (Percy Soc.) 216 Lyke as the worlde was distroyed totally By the virgins sone, so it semed well A virgins sone to redeme it pyteously. **1647** Clarendon *Hist. Reb.* i. § 32 The Imprudence and Presumption..of carrying the Prince into Spain, was totally Forgotten. **1660** Blount *Boscobel* 23 Thus was the Royal Army totally subdued, thus dispersed. **1711** Addison *Spect.* No. 121 ⁋ 6 Tho' the Mole be not totally blind (as it is commonly thought). **1815** W. H. Ireland *Scribbleomania* 30 *note*, He seems to be at present totally eclipsed by Walter Scott. **1882** Mrs. Pitman *Mission L. Greece & Pal.* 155 It is totally beyond human effort to control the memory.

†**b.** In a body, collectively, in one lot. *Obs. rare.*

**1676** *Lond. Gaz.* No. 1073/4 Divers Watches and Pocket Clocks..are to be Sold, either totally or severally, at his late shop,..on the back-side of the Royal Exchange, London.

†**Totangle.** *Obs. nonce-wd.* [f. L. *tōt-us* whole, entire + *angulus*, Angle *sb.*[2]] A figure that is 'all angle': applied to a circle as the limit of regular polygonal figures when the number of angles is infinite.

**1628** Jackson *Creed* vi. xxi. § 3 The circle likewise is as truly ἰσόπλευρος and ἰσογώνιος, of equal sides and equal angles, as ὁλόπλευρος and ὁλογώνιος, a totangle or totilater.

**Totanine** (tǫ·tănəin), *a. Ornith.* [f. mod.L. *Totaninæ*, f. *Totan-us*, name of a genus of birds, including the redshanks: see -ine[1].] Of or pertaining to the *Totaninæ*, a subfamily of the *Scolopacidæ*; called by some the tattlers (Tattler 3).

‖ **Totara** (tōu·tără, tǫtā·ră). Also *erron.* totarra. [Maori *to'tāra* (Morris).] A large New Zealand coniferous tree, *Podocarpus Totara*, producing light, durable, tough timber of a dark red colour, highly valued for building, piles, cabinet work, etc.

**1832** G. Bennett in Lambert *Genus Pinus* II. 190 (Morris) This is an unpublished species of *Podocarpus*, called Totara by the natives. **1840** J. S. Polack *Mann. & Cust. N. Zealanders* I. xx. 227 The *totarra* or red-pine. **1860** Donaldson *Bush Lays* 38 A ponderous totara down on them doth bear. **1872** A. Domett *Ranolf* vi. i. 107 One lone totára-tree that grew Beneath the hill-side. **1892** E. Reeves *Homeward Bound* 73 Totara piles immersed in salt water for forty years have been taken up at Wellington sound as the day they were put down.

**Tote** (tōut), *sb.*[1] Now *dial.* Also *Sc.* tot (tot, tǫt). [Short for *total*: cf. Tot *sb.*[3]]

**1.** The total amount, number, or sum. Mostly in pleonastic phrase *the whole tote*.

**1771–2** *Ess. fr. Batchelor* (1773) II. 40 That this was the whole tote of his case is notoriously known. **1774** FOOTE *Cozeners* III. Wks. 1799 II. 180 My bill?..what is the tote? *a* **1801** R. GALL *Poems, Tint Quey* (1819) 37 Where the hale tot, for fear o' skaith, Were fley'd to speak aboon their breath. **1810** BENTHAM *Mem. & Corr.* Wks. 1843 X. 460 Let me have the whole tote. **1825** J. NEAL *Bro. Jonathan* III. 384 Our gals—the whole tote of them. **1830** GALT *Lawrie T.* I. iv, Only myself of the whole tot was accustomed to the handling of iron. **1905** in *Eng. Dial. Dict.* (from Northumbld. to E. Anglia and Cornwall, with long *ō*).

**2.** Also *dial.* or *low colloq.*, abbreviation of *total abstainer* (also *tot*); and in *Australian colloq.* of TOTALIZATOR; hence *tote-man, tote-shop*.

*c* **1870** *Music Hall Song* (Farmer), By all of his mates called the Tote. **1887** MATHER *Nor'ard of the Dogger* 239 The fishermen are all 'totes'. **1891** E. KINGLAKE *Australian at H.* 74 Altogether, bookmakers, 'tote' proprietors, sweep promotors, in spite of occasional fines of £50 and £100..drive a roaring trade in Australia. **1901** *Westm. Gaz.* 8 Mar. 5/1 One of his audience called out: 'Are you a 'tot.'? 'Yes', the Bishop replied. 'All right, go on, then; if you wasn't I wouldn't listen to you'. **1902** *Ibid.* 25 July 1/3 You..walk into the money order department and deposit the amount you would have invested on the Tote. **1906** *Daily Chron.* 3 Aug 4/7 Nearly 2,000..entering the gambling dens or 'tote-shops'.

**Tote** (tōut), *sb.*[2] Also 9 toat. [app. f. *tote*, obs. and dial. form of TOOT *v.*[1] to project, stick out. (R. Holme belonged to Cheshire, where the vb. is still *tote*.)] The handle of a carpenter's plane.

**1678** MOXON *Mech. Exerc.* iv. 61 A Fore Plain. *a* The Tote. **1688** R. HOLME *Armoury* III. 352/2 All the difference is in the Tote or Handle, which every Workman maketh according to his own Fancy. **1823** P. NICHOLSON *Pract. Build.* 243. **1873** *Routledge's Yng. Gentl. Mag.* July 503/1 The handle [of a jack plane] is called a toat or horn. **1901** *J. Black's Illustr. Carp. & Build., Home Handicr.* 10 The jack plane is used by grasping the 'tote', or handle, firmly with the right hand, placing the left hand on the fore part of the plane [etc.].

†**Tote**, *sb.*[3] *Obs. rare*[−1]. Of doubtful origin and meaning; recorded only in the passage quoted. Prob. = MDu. *tote*, pl. *toten*, 'the point or toe of a shoe'; from the same root as prec.

The suggestion has also been made that *totez* is a verb (viz. *tote*, TOOT *v.*[1]), and that *toez* or *totz* 'toes' has been omitted before it, the reading being *his toez totez oute* 'his toes peep out': cf. *his ton toteden out* 'his toes peeped out' (*P. Pl. Crede* 425).

**13..** *E. E. Allit. P.* B. 41 His tabarde to-torne and his totez oute.

**Tote** (tōut), *v. U.S. colloq.* Also toat. [In current use 1676–7; origin unascertained.

For an alleged Negro origin there is no foundation; the quot. 1676–7 from Virginia does not refer to negroes; later the word is found well-established in the New England States; evidence for an Indian origin is also wanting.]

*trans.* To carry as a burden or load; also, to transport, esp. supplies to, or timber, etc. from, a logging-camp or the like. *To tote fair*, to carry one's fair share; *fig.* to act or deal fairly or honestly.

For catena of quots. see Mr. A. Matthews in *N. and Q.* 10th Ser. II. 161, and Thornton *Amer. Gloss.* s. v.

**1676–7** (Feb.) *Grievances of Glouc. Co.* (Va.), (Col. Office Rec., P.R.O. 5/1371, p. 326), They [Governor's out-guard] were by Beverly comanded to goe to work, fall trees and mawle and toat rails, which many..refusing to doe, he presently disarm'd them. **1769** *Boston Gaz.* 7 Aug. 3/2 The next Morning he was toated on board the Rippon, in a Canoe.. or some other small boat. **1781** J. WITHERSPOON *Wks.* (1802) IV. 470 *Tot* is used for *carry*, in some of the southern states. **1803** J. DAVIS *Trav. U.S.* 389, I..cart all the wood, tote the wheat to the mill. *Note*, Tote is the American for to carry. **1807** W. IRVING *Life & Lett.* (1864) I. 189 At Baltimore I made a stay of two days, during which I was toted about town. **1809** *Monthly Anthology* VII. 264 *Tote* is marked by Mr. Webster 'Virg.' But we believe it a native vulgarism of Massachusetts. **1812** J. J. HENRY *Camp. agst. Quebec* 38 (Arnold's Exped. 1775) We slided glibly along, over passages where a few days previously, we had toted our canoes. **1852** MRS. STOWE *Uncle Tom's C.* vii, Is that ar man going to tote them bar'ls over to-night? **1883** A. FORBES in *Contemp. Rev.* Oct. 605 His lordship and the lady had toted the trunk on to a cart. **1892** KIPLING *Barrack-r. Ballads* 117 The Government Bullock Train toted its load. **1896** *Current Hist.* (Buffalo, N.Y.) VI. 865 The trust maintained a regular force of inspectors to keep all the members of the pool 'toting fair'.

**b.** The verb-stem in combination with a sb.; as *tote-pole, -team, -wagon*; **tote-load** (see quot. 1859); **tote-road**, a rough temporary road for conveying goods to or from a settlement, camp, etc.

**1857** THOREAU *Maine W.* (1894) 296–7 The Indian was greatly surprised that we should have taken what he called a 'tow' (i. e., tote or toting or supply) road, instead of a carry path. **1859** BARTLETT *Dict. Americanisms, Tote-load*, as much as one can carry. *Southern*. **1887** M. ROBERTS *West. Avernus* 71 On this 'toat' or freight-road the wagons went east during one part of the day and west during the other. **1895** F. A. C. EMERSON in *Century Mag.* July 478/2 One might visit every one of the hundreds of logging camps [in Maine]..and he would find each one furnished with its separate 'tote road', 'tote team' and 'toter'.

Hence **To·ting** *vbl. sb.*; also **Tote** *sb.*, an act of carrying or transporting (Webster, 1911); **To·ter**, one engaged in toting, a carrier, teamster, etc.

**1857** Toting [see b. above]. **1860** OLMSTED *Journ. Back Country* i. 48 Each gang was attended by a 'water-toter'. **1895** Toter [see b. above]. **1911** *Blackw. Mag.* Sept. 362/2 So accustomed are some of them to this 'toting' of loads.

**Tote**, var. TOOT *sb.*[1]; obs. or dial. f. TOOT *v.*[1]

†**To-tea·r**, *v. Obs.* Forms: see TEAR *v.*[1]



[OE. *to-teran*, f. TO-[2] + *teran*, TEAR *v.*[1] So MHG. *zerzern*.] *trans.* To tear to pieces.

*c* **893** [see TO-TEE]. *a* **900** *Ags. Ps.* (Th.) xxix. 11 Þu totære min hwite hræȝl. *c* **1000** ÆLFRIC *Hom.* II. 238 Ða næddran hi totæron. *c* **1205** LAY. 4994 Heo nom hire on anne curtel þe wes swiðe to-toren [*c* **1275** al to-tore]. *a* **1225** *Ancr. R.* 84 Ȝet wolde he teteren & pileken, mid his bile, roted stinkinde fleshs. **13..** *K. Alis.* 4658 Alisaundre his clothes to-tare. *c* **1380** WYCLIF *Serm.* Sel. Wks. II. 204 Þis spirit..al to-teerynge him, wente oute from him. *c* **1440** *Partonope* 4452 Why be your clothes thus to tore? *c* **1485** *Digby Myst.* (1882) IV. 305 The tormentours..With sharp scowrges te-terre his fleshe. **1520** *Treat. Galaunt* (W. de W.) xiv, In our wanton werynge of clothes to-torne. **1605** SYLVESTER *Du Bartas* II. iii. III. *Law* 784 Their shields, and staves, and chariots (all-to-tore).

†**To-tee·**, *v. Obs.* [OE. *to-téon*, f. TO-[2] + *teon*, TEE *v.*[1] to draw, pull. So OHG. *ziziohan*, MHG. *zerziehen*.] *trans.* To pull to pieces.

*c* **893** K. ÆLFRED *Oros.* III. xi. § 3, & his æfterfolȝeras feowertiene ȝear hit siþþan totuȝon & totæron. *a* **1000** *Ags. Ps.* (Th.) cxxiii. 5 Þam þe us mid toðum toteon woldan. *c* **1175** *Lamb. Hom.* 9 Ac me þe sculde nimen and al toteon mid horse. **13..** *Guy Warw.* (A.) 517 Al mine limes it wil to-te. **13..** in *Rowland & V.* (1836) p. xxiii, Ther men might reuthe y-sen, Mani baroun her here to ten.

**Totel, -er**, var. TUTEL, -ER *Obs.*, to whisper.

**Totem** (tōu·tĕm), *sb.* Also 8 totam, 9 otem. [From Odjibewa, or some kindred Algonkin dialect. Mentioned (apparently) in 1609 by Lescarbot as *aoutem* (in Acadia); by Long 1791 as *totam*, by Henry *a* 1776, Cooper 1826, Catlin 1841, as *totem*, by Rev. P. Jones (a native Odjibewa) 1861, as *toodaim*, by Francis Assikinak (an Ottawa Indian) as *Ododam*, while the Abbé Thavenel gives the simple form as *ote*, 'the possessive of which is *otem*'. The initial *t* is explained by some as the final letter of a prec. possessive pronoun. The meaning given by most of these is 'mark'; by the younger Henry 'tribe'; Thavenel gives 'mark' and 'family or tribe', app. meaning 'that which marks the family or tribe'. Lescarbot and Long explain it as applied to a familiar spirit.]

**1.** Among the American Indians: The hereditary mark, emblem, or badge of a tribe, clan, or group of Indians, consisting of a figure or representation of some animal, less commonly a plant or other natural object, after which the group is named; thus sometimes used to denote the tribe, clan, or division of a 'nation', having such a mark; also applied to the animal or natural object itself, sometimes considered to be ancestrally or fraternally related to the clan, being spoken of as a brother or sister, and treated as an object of friendly regard, or sometimes even as incarnating a guardian spirit who may be appealed to or worshipped.

[**1609** LESCARBOT *Hist. Nouvelle France* vi. 683 Son dæmon appellé Aoutem, lequel ceux de Canada nomment Cudonagni.] **1760–76** A. HENRY (the elder) *Travels* (1809) 305 To these are added his badge, called, in the Algonquin tongue, a totem, and which is in the nature of an armorial bearing. **1791** J. LONG *Voy. Indian Interpr.* 86 One part of the religious superstition of the Savages, consists in each of them having his *totam*, or favourite spirit, which he believes watches over him. This *totam* they conceive assumes the shape of some beast or other, and therefore they never kill, hunt, or eat the animal whose form they think this totam bears. *Ibid.*, One of the animal, whose totam was a bear. **1799–1808** A. HENRY (the younger) *Journals* (1897) I. 106 Should he not belong to the clan (totem). **1826** F. COOPER *Mohicans* (1829) II. x. 162 There was one chief of his party who carried the beaver as his peculiar symbol, or 'totem'. **1841** CATLIN *N. Amer. Ind.* II. liv. 168 Here are to be seen (and will continue to be seen for ages to come), the totems and arms of the different tribes, who have visited this place for ages past. *Ibid.* 170 We [a Mandan chief and his tribe] left our *totems* as marks on the rocks. We cut them deep in the stones, they are there now. **1851** SCHOOLCRAFT *Indian Tribes* 294 A single element in the system attracted early notice. I allude to the institution of the Totem, which has been well known among the Algonquin tribes from the settlement of Canada. **1855** LONGF. *Hiaw., Picture Writing* 23 From what old, ancestral Totem, Be it Eagle, Bear, or Beaver, They descended, this we know not. **1865** J. G. HODGINS *Hist. Canada* 101 The *totem*, or outline of some animal, (from *do-daim*, a family mark,) was always the chief's signature to a treaty. **1861** P. JONES *Hist. Ojebways* 138 Each 'nation' is subdivided into a number of tribes or clans called 'toodaims', and each tribe is distinguished by certain animals or things, as for instance: the Ojebway nations have the following toodaims:—the Eagle, Reindeer, Otter, Bear, Buffalo, Beaver, Catfish, Pike, Birchbark, White Oak Tree, Bear's liver, etc., etc. The Mohawk nation have only three divisions or tribes—the Turtle, the Bear, and the Wolf. **1865** TYLOR *Early Hist. Man.* x. 281 The Indian tribes are usually divided into clans, each distinguished by a *totem* (Algonquin *do-daim*, that is 'townmark') which is commonly some animal, as a bear, wolf, deer, etc., and may be compared on the one hand to a crest, and on the other to a surname. **1885** CLODD *Myths & Dr.* I. vi. 106 The Dacotahs would neither kill nor eat their totems. **1887** L. OLIPHANT *Episodes* 72 Twelve of these placed their totems opposite my signature; each totem consisting of the rude representation of a bear, a deer, an otter, a rat, or some other wild animal. **1893** A. LANG *Custom & Myth* 105 Prof. Max Müller (Academy, Jan., 1884) says the word should be, not Totem, but Ote or Otem. Mr. Tylor's enquiries among the Red Men support this.

**b.** By anthropologists the name has been extended to refer to other savage peoples and tribes, which (though they may not use totem marks) are similarly divided into groups or clans named after animals, etc.; such animals, animal-names, or animal-named groups, being spoken or written of as their totems, and their organization, their complex system of mutual and marriage relations and religious usages, being styled TOTEMISM, q. v.

There are also said to be among certain races (as the Australians) *sex-totems*, peculiar to men or to women, and *personal totems*, pertaining to the individual and not hereditary.

[**1851–9** PRICHARD in *Man. Sci. Enq.* 263 The institution of the *Totem* as it was termed among the North American nations has its counterpart among the nations of Australia.] **1874** LUBBOCK in *Manch. Sci. Lect.* Ser. v. & vi. 248 In Australia we seem to find the Totem, or, as it is there called, the 'kobong', in the very process of deification. **1879** A. LANG in *Academy* 11 Jan. 24/3 A man or woman is born of such or such a totem, and choice has nothing whatever to do with the matter. **1883** — in *Contemp. Rev.* Sept. 415 The totem was but a badge worn by all the persons who found themselves existing in close relations. **1887** J. G. FRAZER *Totemism* 52–3 Clearly these sex totems are not to be confounded with clan totems...The sex totem seems to be still more sacred than the clan totem; for men who do not object to other people killing their clan totem will fiercely defend their sex totem against any attempt of the opposite sex to injure it. **1888** — in *Encycl. Brit.* XXIII. 467/1 A totem is a class of material objects which a savage regards with superstitious respect, believing that there exists between him and every member of the class an intimate and altogether special relation. **1905** *Athenæum* 21 Jan. 87/1 They have no special word answering to 'totem' for such animals. *Ibid.*, M. van Gennep..uses 'totem' only in the sense of the hereditary name-giving animal or other object of the kin. **1909** tr. *Hopf's Hum. Species* 300 The necessity for setting up sub-totems first arose from the great extension of the totem in a single tribe, and it was convenient to take the sub-totem from the father who transferred his totem-name to his son.

**c.** *fig.*

**1890** *Pall Mall G.* 30 June 7/2 The vulgar embroidered smoking-cap, which used to be the distinctive totem of the bazaar debauchee. **1893** *Times* 11 May 9/5 Mr. Bryce, whose totem is very different, threatened the Unionists that their vote against a bogus second chamber would be remembered against them.

**2.** *attrib.* and *Comb.*, as *totem ancestor, animal, clan, figure, god, group, kin, name, people, plant, soul, stage, system, tree, worship*, etc.; **totem exogamy**, the custom of marrying only one of a different totem or totem-clan; **totem-pole, totem-post**, a post carved and painted with totem figures, erected by the Indians of the north-west of North America in front of their houses; **totem-stone**, a stone with markings supposed to be prehistoric totemic figures.

**1869** M'LENNAN in *Fortn. Rev.* Oct. 408 Men in, what we may call, the Totem stage of developement. **1870** *Ibid.* Feb. 213 The tribesmen..esteem themselves as of the species of the Totem-god. **1871** TYLOR *Prim. Cult.* II. xv. 213 Some accounts describing the totem-animal as being actually regarded as the sacred object. *Ibid.* 214 Considering it [animal-worship] as inherited from an early totem-stage of society. *Ibid.* 215 The systematic division of a whole people into a number of totem-clans. **1872** MORLEY *Voltaire* v. 241 The needs and aspirations..of the developed polytheist [would not be satisfied] by totem-worship. **1882** *Athenæum* 22 Apr. 501/3 Even ethnologists..will maintain that the totem-kin became the *gens*. **1888** J. G. FRAZER in *Encycl. Brit.* XXIII. 468/1 The Bechuanas in South Africa..have a well-developed totem system. *Ibid.* 470/1 The fundamental rules of totem societies. *Ibid.* 470/2 The Australian ceremony at initiation of pretending to recall a dead man to life by the utterance of his totem name. **1889** W. ROBERTSON SMITH *Relig. Semites* viii. 276 Among totem peoples..the sacred animal is forbidden food, it is akin to the men who acknowledge its sanctity. **1891** *Cent. Dict.* s.v., Totem Posts, Canadian Pacific Coast. **1896** F. B. JEVONS *Introd. Hist Relig.* xx. 294 The sacramental eating first of totem-animals and then of totem-plants. **1901** *Athenæum* 7 Dec. 779/1 Mr. N. W. Thomas exhibited a collection of 'totem-stones'. **1902** *Folk-Lore* Dec. 363 To savage reasoners, the totem-soul may perhaps seem to tenant each plant or animal of its species. **1907** C. HILL-TOUT *Brit. N. Amer., Far West* ix. 177 The family or kin totem-figures which are customarily carved on the beams or painted on the sides of their houses. **1910** SELIGMANN *Melanesians of Brit. N. Guinea* Introd. 10 Totem exogamy is still generally observed. **1910** A. F. CHAMBERLAIN in *Encycl. Brit.* XIV. 470/1 The wood art of the Indians of the North Pacific coast (masks, utensils, houses, totem-poles, furniture, &c.).

Hence **To·tem** *v., trans.* to draw, paint, or tattoo (a totem mark).

**1894** S. JACKSON *Educ. in Alaska* in *Educ. Rep.* (U. S.) 1891–2, 890 Some [Tchuktchi men] have a small mark or figure totemed on their cheek.

**Totemic** (tote·mik), *a.* [f. prec. + -IC.] Of, pertaining to, or of the nature of a totem or totems; characterized by or having totems.

**1865** LUBBOCK *Preh. Times* xiv. (1878) 528 The totemic tie that binds relationships together. **1867** PARKMAN *Jesuits N. Amer.* Introd. (1875) 68 The names of the totemic clans, borrowed in nearly every case from animals. **1885** CLODD *Myths & Dr.* I. vi. 99 The belief of the Moquis of Arizona, that after death they live in the form of their totemic animal. **1905** *Athenæum* 21 Jan. 87/1 Mr. Haddon derives totemic names from such surnames as 'Eaters of Turtle'. **1906** *Ibid.* 17 Mar. 332 There are many tabous on food which are certainly not totemic in origin.

Hence **Tote·mically** *adv.*, in reference to totems or totemism; after the manner of a totem.

**1902** *Folk-Lore* Dec. 373 Two cases in which Australian

totem-groups averred that they were named totemically after a small species of opossum. **1910** *Athenæum* 11 June 707/3 We may regard Africa, totemically speaking, as an unexplored continent.

**Totemism** (tōu·tĕmiz'm). [f. TOTEM + -ISM.] The use of totems, with the clan division, and the social, marriage, and religious customs connected with it.

**1791** J. LONG *Voy. Indian Interpr.* 87 This idea of destiny, or, if I may be allowed the phrase, 'totamism',..is not confined to the Savages. **1870** LUBBOCK *Orig. Civiliz.* v. (1875) 199 Nature-worship or Totemism, in which natural objects are worshipped. **1883** A. LANG in *Contemp. Rev.* Sept. 414 Totemism is the name for the custom by which a stock (scattered through many local tribes) claims descent from some plant, animal, or other natural object. *Ibid.*, Totemism..is a widespread institution prevailing all over the north of the American continent. **1905** *Westm. Gaz.* 13 Dec. 3/1 Here is the beginning of totemism—'the bearing of the name of an object by a human group', as Mr. Howitt says. 'Naming' is the 'original germ', says Mr. Lang, 'of totemism'.

**To·temist.** [f. TOTEM + -IST.]

**1.** One who belongs to a totem clan, or has a totem.

**1881** *Cornh. Mag.* Sept. 332 Our Aryan ancestor in person was a most undoubted totemist. **1883** F. SEEBOHM *Eng. Vill. Community* 362 The hasty conclusion that the Saxons were 'totemists'. **1887** A. LANG *Myth, Ritual & Relig.* I. 73 Totemists..spare the beasts that are their own..kin. **1905** *Athenæum* 21 Jan. 87/1 If the people were once true totemists, the traces thereof are indistinct.

**2.** One who is versed in the history of totemism.

**1897** *Edin. Rev.* July 239 Some of the highest authorities on the myths and customs of savage races are by no means on the side of the thoroughgoing totemist. **1902** *Folk-Lore* Dec. 361, I am not aware that any totemists do make this assertion.

So **Totemi·stic** *a.*, of, pertaining to, or characterized by totemism.

**1881** *Sat. Rev.* 12 Feb. 216/2 Why were the 'primary divisions', as Mr. Fison says they were, totemistic? **1882** *Athenæum* 22 Apr. 502/1 While Huitzilopochtli had many features of the magician, he had also elemental and totemistic sides to his complex nature. **1884** *Pall Mall G.* 18 Oct. 5/1 Their society is Totemistic; that is to say, they are divided into stocks of kin (real or assumed), each designated by the name of its Totem plant, animal, or what not. **1905** C. SQUIRE *Mythol. Brit. Isl.* 20 An agricultural.. people, still in the Stone Age, dwelling in totemistic tribes on hills.

**Totemite** (tōu·tĕməit). [f. TOTEM + -ITE [1].] = TOTEMIST 1.

**1904** HOWITT *Native Tribes S.E. Australia* iii. 145 To dream about his own totem means that some one has done something to it for the purpose of harming the sleeper or one of his totemites. **1911** MARETT *Anthropol.* vi. 167 Sometimes the totem is thought of as an ancestor, or as the common fund of life out of which the totemites are born and into which they go back when they die.

† **Toth.** *Obs. rare.* [Only in Ormin, *toþþ*. Origin unknown: the short *o* makes connexion with OE. *tóþ*, TOOTH, highly improbable.] Exact meaning uncertain: the context implies some kind of wrongdoing.

*c* **1200** ORMIN 7186 Alle þa þatt lufenn toþþ & woh & unnsahhtnesse. *Ibid.* 9317 ȝiff þatt ȝe wel ȝuw lokenn Fra clake & sake, & fra þat toþþ Þat follȝheþþ ȝifernesse.

**Tother** (tʊ·ðəɹ), *pron.* and *a.* Now *dial.* Forms: α. (3 **þet oþer**), 3–5 **þe toþer**, 4–6 **the tothir, the toder**, etc. (see OTHER), 4–7, 9 **the tother**, 7–8 **the t'other**, 8–9 *Sc.* **the tither**. β. 4 **þat toþer, þat toiþer**. γ. (without *the*) 6 **tothir**, (*dial.* **toore**), 6–7, 9 **tother**, 7–9 **t'other**. [ME. *þe toþer*, for earlier *þet oþer*, *þat oþer* 'the other'; formed in the same way as *þe tone* from *þet* or *þat one*: see TONE *pron.* and *a.* *The tother* is still used in Sc. and in north. Eng. dialects, but in general Eng. is replaced by *the other*, and often in familiar use by the simple *tother*, also written *t'other*. Cf. the similar use of *tone*, *t'one*. When a possessive pronoun or case took the place of *the*, *tother* remained, e. g. *his tother hand*, in literary Eng. 'his other hand'.]

**A.** *pron.*, or *adj.* used absolutely.

**1.** The other (of two): often opposed to *tone* (see TONE *pron.*).

α. [*a* **1225** *Leg. Kath.* 101 Ane dale ha etheold..& spende al þ oðer. **1340** *Ayenb.* 16 Þet uerste heaued of þe beste of helle ys prede, þet oþer is enuie.] *c* **1250** *Gen. & Ex.* 2724 Ðis on wulde don ðe toðer wrong. *a* **1300** *Cursor M.* 11056 Þe tan was leuedi maiden ying, Þe toþer [*Gött.* toder] hir hand-wornman kerling. *c* **1380** WYCLIF *Sel. Wks.* III. 248 Þe toon pope fallip þe toþurs bullis. **1382** — *Isa.* vi. 3 Thei crieden the tother to the tother. **1388** *Ibid.*, Thei crieden the toon to the tother. *c* **1440** *Anc. Cookery* in *Househ. Ord.* (1790) 435 Dresse up the tone with the tother. **1533** J. HEYWOOD *Play Wether* (1903) 1200 Nother wyll we do the tone nor the tother. **1613** FLETCHER, etc. *Captain* II. ii, *Fran.* What's the tother? *Clor.* What tother? *Fran.* He that lyes along there. **1715** M. DAVIES *Athen. Brit.* I. 7 Two small Dissertations, the one upon Noe's arrival..the t'other was about the Origin of the Druids. *a* **1774** FERGUSSON *Drink Ecl.* Poems (1845) 49 Brandy the tane, the tither whiskey. **1816** SCOTT *Antiq.* xxvii, My lord cares as little about the tane as the tother.

β. **13..** *Cursor M.* 84 (Cott.) And in þat toþer [*v. rr.* þe toþer, þat oþer] scho lastes ever. *Ibid.* 2032 'Þi fader slepand', said þat toiþer [*other MSS.* þe toþer], 'Liggus here-oute'. *Ibid.* 3494 His moder him luued mare þan þat toþer [*other MSS.* þe toþer].

γ. **1587** FLEMING *Contn. Holinshed* III. 1339/1 Tone gone to God,..still reigning tother. **1632** BROME *North. Lasse* I. iv, Here's one, there's tother. **1688** PRIOR *On Exod. III* vi, He on t'other's Ruin rears his Throne. **1710** PALMER *Proverbs* 129 Securing the vogue on one side and t'other. **1800** MAR. EDGEWORTH *Lame Jervas* i, I saw the ghost.. with the light in one hand, and a chain dragging after him in t'other. **1870** LOWELL *Study Wind.* 259 You cannot tell one from tother.

† **2.** The second (of two or more): cf. OTHER B. 3. (Cf. Ger. *der andere.*) *Obs.*

*a* **1300** *Cursor M.* 1629 (Cott.) Þe first was sem, cham was the toþeir [*other MSS.* þe toþer], And Iaphet hight þat yongest broþer. **1380** *Lay Folks Catech.* 332 (Lamb. MS.) Þe fyrst ys syȝt of eye, þe toþer heryng of Ere. *c* **1450** *Merlin* ii. 24 Thre sones, the first hight Moyne, and the tother Pendragon, and the thirde Vter.

**3.** *pl.* (*the tother* obs., *tothers* rare): The others, the rest: cf. OTHER B. 4.

*c* **1330** R. BRUNNE *Chron. Wace* (Rolls) 45 Þat were Maysters of alle þe toþire, Hengist he hight, & Hors his broþire. **13..** *Cursor M.* 4948 (Gött.) Þan spac ruben þe eldest broder Stille menand til þe toder. **1494** FABYAN *Chron.* VII. 339, xviii. were conuycte and hangyd, & the tother remayned longe after in pryson. **1691** J. WILSON *Belphegor* v. iii, When t'others shall..break themselves, on what they fall.

**B.** as *adj.* preceding a sb.

**1.** The other (of two). In early use often opposed to To, TONE *a.*: see these.

α. *a* **1300** *Cursor M.* 6305 (Cott.) In sirie apon þe toiþer side. *Ibid.* 16721 Þe toþer [*Laud MS.* the todir] theif him gaf ansuer. **1303** R. BRUNNE *Handl. Synne* 3993 Yn þe toþer worlde þer þey shul be, Þey are nat wurþy any ioye to se. *c* **1385** CHAUCER *L. G. W.* 325 (*Balade*) Or he haue herd the tothyr partye speke. **1419** *Munim. de Melros* (Bann. Cl.) 502 Betwix..Dauid abbot..and hys Conuent on þe ta part and Nychole of Wedale on þe toþer part. **1465** *Cal. Anc. Rec. Dublin* (1889) 320 The tothyr half to the cowrte. **1482** *Monk of Evesham* (Arb.) 71 He..brought certen worde to the todyr man that tolde me. **1522** MORE *De Quat. Noviss.* Wks. 75/1 On the tother syde wher as one doth such spirituall busines with a dulnes of spirite & werines. *a* **1578** LINDESAY (Pitscottie) *Chron. Scot.* (S.T.S.) I. 149 He dissaweit baith the tuddar twa. **1681** DRYDEN *Span. Friar* v. ii, No! the t'other old gentleman in black shall take me if I do. **1716** M. DAVIES *Athen. Brit.* II. 172 In requital to the t'other Prelate's Urias's Letter. **1816** SCOTT *Antiq.* xxxix, I heard Puggie Orrock, and the tother thief of a sheriff-officer..speaking about it.

γ. **1627** W. SCLATER *Exp. 2 Thess.* (1629) 299 Wee, Britans of t'other race. **1720** WHITE *Monit. Clergy Peterbo.* I. 27 This, that, and t'other invented Order of their Church. **1727** GAY *Begg. Op.* II. xiii, How happy could I be with either, Were t'other dear Charmer away!

† **b.** After a possessive: Other. *Obs.*

**1482** *Cely Papers* (Camden) 108 Accordyng as hit specyfyeth in my toder letter. **1549** *Compl. Scot.* 6 The grit armye of enemeis valkand on ther tothir syde. **1613** HEYWOOD *Silver Age* II. i. Wks. 1874 III. 113 Vnlesse it were my tother selfe, I haue no hand in it. **1721** D'URFEY *Two Queens Brentford* v. i, Now you shall have my t'other Walk.

† **2.** The second (of two or more): cf. OTHER A. 3. *Obs.*

*a* **1300** *Cursor M.* 1627 *heading* (Cott.) Her bigins at noe þe lede Þe toþer werld right for to del. *c* **1400** MAUNDEV. (1839) xxi. 225 The first statute was, that [etc.]..The tother Statute was, that [etc.]. *a* **1400** *Relig. Pieces fr. Thornton MS.* (1867) 3 The toþer artecle es þat we sall trowe. **1456** SIR G. HAYE *Law Arms* (S.T.S.) 2 The ferde is of the first angel..The fyft is of the tothir angel.

**b.** The second, another, one more. *Obs.* exc. *Sc.*

**1600** ROWLANDS *Lett. Humours Blood* xix. 25 He calleth: Boy, fill vs the tother quart. **1653** WALTON *Angler* xi. 218 Then each man drink the tother cup and to bed. **1733** RAMSAY *Tea-t. Misc.* (ed. 9) I. 9 The lover he ga'e her the tither kiss, Syne ran to her dady and tell'd him this. **1785** BURNS *Jolly Beggars* ii, And aye he gies the tozie drab The tither skelpin' kiss.

**3.** (*The*) *tother* (*day*, etc.). † **a.** The second; the following, the next (day, etc.): cf. OTHER A. 3 b (*a*). *Obs.* † **b.** The preceding (day, etc.): cf. OTHER A. 3 b (*b*). *Obs.* **c.** The other (day, night, etc.); a few (days, etc.) ago: cf. OTHER A. 3 b (*c*).

**a.** *a* **1300** *Cursor M.* 7619 (Cott.) Þe toþer morn [*Gött.* day] her after-ward Þe warlau trauail saul ful hard. *Ibid.* 13249 In aueril þe toþer dai. *c* **1330** R. BRUNNE *Chron.* (1810) 38 Þe toþer ȝere next of his coronment. **13..** *Cursor M.* 5993 (Gött.) Moyses praid þe toder day, All þe flijs wair quit a-way. *c* **1430** *Syr Tryam.* 508 The tother day, on the same wyse, As the kynge fro the borde can ryse. *a* **1765** *K. Estmere* xxvii. in Child *Ballads* III. (1885) 53/1 Tone day to marrye Kyng Adlands daughter, Tother daye to carrye her home.

**b.** *c* **1470** HENRY *Wallace* v. 908 Schir Jhone the Grayme,..To the Corhed come on the tothir nycht.

**c.** **1575** *Gamm. Gurton* III. iv, Did not Tom Tankard rake his Curtal toore day standing in the stable? **1680** SIR C. LYTTELTON in *Hatton Corr.* (Camden) 232 Tother day, in shifting of a cabinet. **1711** STEELE *Spect.* No. 153 ¶ 1 An old Gentleman t'other Day in Discourse with a Friend. **1779** *Mirror* No. 12 ¶ 8, I confess, I could not help being in a passion t'other day. **1863** *Tyneside Songs* 31 Tuther Seturday neet aw saw a grand foot race Alang at the Victoria grund.

**C.** *Comb.* (*nonce-wds.*): **tother-day** *a.* (see B. 3 c), that happened or existed a few days ago, very recent; **to·thersi:der**, one from the other side.

**1662** OWEN *Animadv. Fiat Lux* Wks. 1851 XIV. 65 Do we talk of t'other-day things? **1900** H. LAWSON *Over Sliprails* 72 We were all T'othersiders, and old mates, and we worked things together. It was in Westralia—the Land of T'othersiders.

**Tothing**(e, obs. form of TITHING *sb.*

**To-threat, To-thrust**: see To- *pref.*[2]

† **To-throw,** *v. Obs.* Forms: see THROW *v.*[1] [ME. f. To-[2] + *thrawe*(*n*, *throwe*(*n*, OE. *þrāwan*, to twist, THROW *v.*[1] Cf. MHG. *gedræjen*, *gedræn*.] *trans.* To wrench asunder; to separate, part.

*c* **1315** SHOREHAM i. 1740 Þe tyme is, wane aþer can Oþer fleschlyche y-knowe; For wanne hy habbeþ þet y-do, Ne mowe hi be to-þrowe. **1340** *Ayenb.* 256 Þe norþene wynd to-þrauþ þe raynes.

**Totient** (tōu·ʃĕnt). *Math.* [irreg. f. L. *totiēs*, *totiens*, f. *tot* so many, after QUOTIENT.] The number of numbers (including unity) less than and prime to a given number. So **Totitive** (tǫ·titiv) [irreg. f. L. *tot* + *-itive* in such words as *primitive*, *unitive*], any one of such numbers in relation to the given number.

**1879** SYLVESTER *Math. Papers* (1909) III. 337 Understanding by the 'totitives' of *k* the numbers less than *k* and prime to it, these totitives may be arranged in (among others) the natural groups hereunder written. **1883** *Ibid.* (1912) IV. 102 The sum of the totients of all the natural numbers up to *j* inclusive—a totient to *x* (which I denote by *τx*) meaning the number of numbers less than *x* and prime to it. **1891** *Athenæum* 21 Mar. 383/1 'Some Theorems concerning Groups of Totitives of *n*', by Prof. L. Tanner.

‖ **Toties quoties** (tōu·ʃiīz kwōu·ʃiīz), *adv.* Also **totiens quotiens** (tōu·ʃienz kwōu·ʃienz). Also 6 **tociens quociens, tossyens quossyens.** [L., 'so often as often'.] As often as something happens or occasion demands; repeatedly.

In quot. 1845 applied to a jubilee of the Latin Church, at which a general pardon was granted.

**1525** *Order Com. Counc. Lond.* in *Vicary's Anat.* (1888) App. viii. 214 Commaundyd & compelled vppon the payne of imprisonament of xx days, tociens quociens, that they shall no more occupie phisike till they be examyned. **1555** MACHYN *Diary* (Camden) 94 He declaryd..clen remyssyon of all ther synes *tossyens quossyens* of all that ever they dyd. **1569** *Reg. Privy Council Scot.* I. 685 He sall na wyis.. troubill Alexander Quhitlaw..under the pane of V[c] li. toties quoties. **1698–9** *Act* 11 *Will. III*, c. 2 § 141 And such Assignee may in like manner assigne again and soe toties quoties. *a* **1734** NORTH *Exam.* I. ii. § 165 Grand Juries may enquire *toties quoties* of the same Offence. **1845** FORD *Handbk. Spain* II. 771/1 Hence the jubilee was called 'toties quoties', for it was an annual benefit.

† **To-ti·ght,** *v. Obs.* [ME. *to-tuhten*, f. To-[2] + *tuhten*, OE. *tyhtan*, TIGHT *v.*[1] to draw.]

**1.** *trans.* To stretch or spread out; to extend.

*c* **1200** *Trin. Coll. Hom.* 205 His lichame beð to-spred and to-tiht on þe rode. *Ibid.*, Þeh his lichame..ne beo to-spred ne to-tuht on lichamliche rode.

**2.** To pull or draw asunder.

**13..** *Guy Warw.* (A.) 511 Mi sorwe is euer cominge,..al mi limes it hath to-tiȝt; Swiche liif y lede day & niȝt. *Ibid.* 3711 Her armes & legges he to-tiȝt, [*C.* to-twighte = twitched] & cleped hem wreches [*MS.* wroches] anon riȝt.

† **Totila·ter.** *Obs. nonce-wd.* [f. L. *tōt-us* whole, entire + *latus*, *later-* side: cf. QUADRILATER.] A figure that is 'all side', or consists of an infinite number of sides: applied to a circle as the limit of regular multilateral figures when the number of sides is infinite.

**1628** [see TOTANGLE].

† **To·tilde,** ? *sb.* (? *a.*). *Obs.* [f. ME. *tot-en*, TOOT *v.*[1], to peep out, pry, + (perh.) *-ild*, fem. suffix, as in *beggild*, *begenild*, *cheapild*, *fostrild*, etc.] ? A peeping, peering, or prying woman.

*a* **1225** *Ancr. R.* 102 Hweðer eni totilde [so also *Corpus*] ancre uondede euer þis, þet bekeð [*C.* breakeð] euer utward ase untowe brid ine cage?

[But the attrib. or adj. use, and the final *-e*, suggest that *totilde* here is perh. a scribal error for *totinde*, pr. pple. of *toten*, TOOT *v.*[1]: cf *totinde ancres*, ibid. 50 and 100.]

† **To·ting,** *ppl. a. Obs.* [pr. pple. of *tote*, earlier form of TOOT *v.*[1]; see also *tooting* under the verb.] Protruding, projecting, sticking out.

*c* **1645** HOWELL *Lett.* (1650) I. III. xxxi. 91 Though perhaps he had never a shirt to his back, yet would he have a toting huge swelling ruff about his neck. *Ibid.* (1655) IV. vii. 19 A poor shallow-brain'd puppy, who..would have men to have a priviledg to change their Wives,..deserves of all other to wear a toting horn. **1648–60** HEXHAM, *Geneust*, Nosed, or he that hath a great Nose, or a toting Nose. **1650** HOWELL *Giraffi's Rev. Naples* I. 87 With a toting plume of feathers in his hat all white. **1676** WISEMAN *Chirurg. Treat.* I. xxvi. 141 Rendring the Visage fiery, and in progress of time make those toting Copper-noses, as we generally express them.

**Totipalmate** (tǫtipæ·lmĕt), *a.* (*sb.*) *Ornith.* [f. L. *tōti-*, from *tōt-us* whole + PALMATE.] Wholly webbed; having all the toes connected by membrane which reaches to the extremities; steganopodous. **b.** *sb.* A totipalmate bird. Hence **Totipalma·tion**, the condition of being totipalmate.

**1872** COUES *N. Amer. Birds* 48 Goatsuckers, some Western swifts, loons, and all the totipalmate swimmers. *Ibid.* 296 Feet totipalmate, with three full webs; hind toe semi-lateral,.. connected with the inner toe by a complete web reaching from tip to tip. **1884** *Ibid.* (ed. 2) Index, Totipalmation.

**Totipotent** (toti·pŏtĕnt), *a. Biol.* [f. L. *tōti-* (see prec.) + POTENT: cf. *omnipotent*.] Capable of developing into or generating a complete organism: said of a cell. So **Toti·potence, To·tipotentia·lity**, the quality of being totipotent.

**1901** T. H. MORGAN *Regeneration* xii. 243 If we substitute the term 'totipotence', meaning that any meridian of the egg has the possibility of becoming the median plane of the embryo. **1904** *Amer. Nat.* July–Aug. 504 While in this species also the material is totipotent, yet when the determining influence of polarity is removed the stronger tendency is to produce a tail. **1909** J. W. JENKINSON *Experim. Embryol.* 281 In very many, though not in all, instances the parts of the ovum—blastomeres or egg fragments—are totipotent...The totipotence is, however, sooner or later lost. *Ibid.* 76 From other sources also there is evidence of a progressive loss of totipotentiality of the parts. **1911** — *Sea Urchin* 292.

† **Totipre·sent,** *a. Obs. nonce-wd.* [f. as prec. + PRESENT: cf. *omnipresent.*] Present throughout the whole of a space. So † **Totipre·sence,** the fact of being totipresent.

**1768** TUCKER *Lt. Nat.* (1834) I. 337 Our own manner of existence in a sphere or portion of space sufficient to receive the action of many corporeal particles, we may term a *totipresence* throughout the contents of that sphere...A totipresence throughout all immensity amounts to the same as omnipresence. *Ibid.* 409 There is a certain portion of space throughout which we are totipresent, because we can receive the action of many corporeal particles at once which cannot be brought into contact with a mathematical point.

**Totitive**: see TOTIENT.

**Totive** (tōu·tiv), *a. nonce-wd.* [f. L. *tōt-us* whole + -IVE.] Denoting a whole: see quot.

**1874** KEY *Language* xviii. 225 A leading use of the genitive is that called 'partitive', but might more fitly be called 'totive', for the genitive here denotes the whole whence a part is taken.

**Totle, Totnam**: see TOTTLE *v.*[1], TOTTENHAM.

‖ **Toto** (tōu·to), abl. sing. masc. and neut. of L. *tōtus* all, whole, entire: occurring in a few phrases in literary use, as **Toto cælo** (tōu·to sī·lo), 'by the whole heaven', by as much as the distance between the poles, diametrically; in quot. 1844 *attrib.* entire, absolute; **Toto genere** (dʒe·nĕrī), in the whole nature or character; **Toto orbe** (ǭ·ıbī), 'by the whole world'; = *toto cælo.*

**1727** POPE *Art of Sinking* i. Wks. 1751 VI. 167 In their others [pieces] they differ'd *toto cælo from us. **1844** W. G. WARD *Ideal Chr. Ch.* (ed. 2) 272 The toto-coelo difference in kind between [etc.]. *a* **1878** SIR G. G. SCOTT *Lect. Archit.* xvi. (1879) II. 234 The dome [of the Pantheon]..differs *toto cælo* from the normal mode of construction. **1672** BOYLE *Orig. & Virt. Gems* I. 49 Bodies, that differ *toto genere*, as Metals and Stones. *a* **1834** COLERIDGE in *Lit. Rem.* (1839) IV. 232 Here I differ *toto orbe* from Waterland.

**Toto, totoo** (16th c.), i. e. *too too*: see TOO.

**Toto-,** used as combining form of L. *tōtus* whole, in certain cases, instead of the normal form *toti-* (see -O), forming compound adjs., **a.** in sense 'entirely, wholly, utterly' (see -O 1), as **to·to-conge·nital, to·to-mu·te, to·to-offi·cious**; **b.** in sense 'total and ..' (see -O 2), as **To·to-pa·rtial** *Logic*, applied to a proposition in which one term is universal and the other particular; so **To·to-to·tal,** having both terms universal.

**1890** *Q. Rev.* Jan. 68 The marriage of *toto-congenital deaf mutes. **1893** F. W. BOOTH *World's Congr. Instruct. Deaf* 59 The German semi-mute brought to a study of English has a decided advantage over his *toto-mute brother. **1586** in J. Morris *Troub. Cath. Forefathers* (1877) 69 Condemned as rude, troublesome, and *toto-officious. **1833** SIR W. HAMILTON *Discuss.* (1852) 162 *Toto-total—all is all. ..*Toto-partial—all is some.

**To-tog,** variant of TO-TUG *v. Obs.*

† **To-to·ll,** *v. Obs.* [ME. f. TO-[2] + TOLL *v.*[1] to draw.] *trans.* To pull or drag hither and thither.

*c* **1325** *Poem times Edw. II* (Percy) lix, Hit schal be totolled, hit schal be totwyȝt [*v.r.* Hit shal be forpinched, totoilled & totwiht]. *Ibid.* lxi, Hit is so to-tolled, bothe heder & theder Hit is halfendel istole, ar hit be brout togeder. *c* **1330** *Arth. & Merl.* (Kölbing) 8531 Þe heþen me tok & totoiled, Tobeten, todrawe & defoiled.

**To-torve, To-tose, To-tray,** etc.: see TO-[2].

† **Tot-quot.** *Obs.* [L. *tot quot* as much or as many as (there may be).]

**1.** *Eccl.* A dispensation or licence to hold as many ecclesiastical benefices as the holder pleases or can get; hence, the holding of such benefices, unlimited pluralism; *pl.* benefices so held.

**1509** BARCLAY *Shyp Folys* (1570) 60 He hath hope To haue another benefyce of greater dignitie, And so maketh a false suggestion to the pope, For a tot quot or els a pluralitie. **1522** SKELTON *Why not to Court?* 125 We shall haue a tot quot From the Pope of Rome. *a* **1550** *Image Ipocr.* I. in *Skelton's Wks.* (1843) II. 420/2 Ye drawe and cast lottes, In hattes and in pottes, For tottes and for quottes. **1583** STUBBES *Anat. Abus.* II. (1882) 79 They purchase a dispensation, a licence,..by vertue whereof they may hold totquots so manie, how manie soeuer. **1637** BASTWICK *Litany* II. 9 The Pope selleth nonresidences, pluralityes, trialityes, totquots, the Prelats doe the same.

**b.** *transf.* One who holds tot-quots; an unlimited pluralist.

**1628** P. SMART *Serm. Durh. Cath.* 7 July 21 The same will be also a notorious Non-resident, a very Tot-quot. **1677** W. HUGHES *Man of Sin* II. iv. 82 S. Wereburga,..being Governess of three Nunneries (being no more, she was no Tot-quot then).

**2.** An indefinite or infinite number; as many as you like.

**1565** JEWEL *Repl. Harding* xiii. (1611) 360 He pleadeth his toties, quoties, and thereby would erect a whole totquot of Masses, sans number... By these words, M. Hardings Totquot is much abridged.

**3.** A rate or tax assessed in proportion to income.

**1611** COTGR., *Quottité*, an euen assessement, a rate or totquot imposed; the laying on euerie one his share.

† **To-trea·d,** *v. Obs.* [OE. *totredan*, f. TO-[2] + *tredan*, TREAD *v.* So OS. *te-tredan*, OHG. **zatretan*, MHG. *ze-, zertreten*, Ger. *zertreten.*] *trans.* To trample down, trample upon. Hence † **To-treading** *vbl. sb.*

[*c* **725** *Corpus Gloss.* (Hessels) D 77 *Desicit* [? *Deficit*], tetridit.] *c* **1175** *Lamb. Hom.* 133 Sum [feol] bi þe weie and werð to-treden and fuȝeles hit freten. **13..** *K. Alis.* 3946 (Bodl. MS.) Horses totraden alle þe Boukes Of noble Barouns & of Dukes. **1382** WYCLIF *Prov.* xxvii. 7 The soule fulfild shal to-trede the hony comb. **1535** COVERDALE *Isa.* xxviii. 18 The greate destruction..shal all to treade you.

**Totsane, Tott(e,** obs. ff. TUTSAN, TOT.

† **To·tted,** *ppl. a. Obs. rare*[−1]. [? related to TOT *sb.*[1]] ? Muddle-headed; or = TOTTY *a.*[2]

*c* **1480** *Kyng & Hermyt* 348 in Hazl. *E. P. P.* I. 26 And you schall here a totted frere Say *Stryke pantnere*; And in yᵉ cope leve ryȝt nouȝt.

**Tottenham** (tǫ·t'năm). In 6 **Totnam.** Name of a northern suburb of London. † *Tottenham is turned French*, a proverb used in reference to any unlikely or remarkable change.

**1546** J. HEYWOOD *Prov.* (1867) 14 Their faces told toies, that Totnam was tournd frenche. **1581** A. HALL *Iliad* IV. 60 Do what thou canst, the time wil come that Totnam French shal turn; The Gods and I will so prouide. *a* **1661** FULLER *Worthies, Middlesex* (1662) II. 178.

**Totter** (tǫ·təɹ), *sb.*[1] Forms: 4–5 **totre,** 5 **totyr, totoure,** 6– **totter.** [f. TOTTER *v.* Cf. Flem., Du. (and WFris.) *touter* in sense 1.]

†**1.** A swing; a board suspended by two ropes, on which a person sits and is swung to and fro.

**1387** TREVISA *Higden* (Rolls) II. 387 Whan men [fel] of þe totres and were i-herte sore, it was ordeyned among hem þat images i-liche to þe bodies schulde be sette in þe totros, and meue and totery in stede of hem þat were a-falle. Þat game is cleped ocillum in Latyn. *c* **1440** *Promp. Parv.* 498/1 Totyr, or myry totyr, chylderys game.., *oscillum.* **1468** *Medulla Gram., Oscillum*, genus ludi, cum funis suspenditur a trabe in quo pueri et puelle sedentes impelluntur huc et illuc,—a totoure. *Petaurus*, quidam ludus, a totre. **1483** *Cath. Angl.* 390/2 A mery Totyr (*A.* A Totyr), *petaurus, & cetera.* **1552** HULOET, Totter playe, betwene two bell ropes to tottre to and fro, *petaurum.*

**2.** The action, or an act, of tottering; wavering, oscillation; an unsteady or shaky movement or gait as of one ready to fall.

**1747** E. POSTON *Pratler* I. 1 My Mind is so on the Totter between For and Against. **1751** JOHNSON *Rambler* No. 109 ⁋ 8, I..had his bend in my shoulders, and his totter in my gait. **1830** *Chron.* in *Ann. Reg.* 35/2 He seemed all of a totter and tremble. **1898** WATTS-DUNTON *Aylwin* II. iv, Without raising an arm to balance her body, without a totter or a slip.

**3.** *attrib.* and *Comb.* (or from the verb-stem), as **totter-arse,** † (*a*) the game of see-saw; = TITTER-TOTTER 1; (*b*) one who totters (*dial.*); **totter-grass,** quaking-grass, *Briza media*, or sometimes another grass with slender stalk; **to·tter-hea·ded** *a.*, light-headed, frivolous, changeful; **totter-kneed** *a.*, yielding, 'weak-kneed'.

**1611** COTGR., *Baccoler*, to play at titter-totter, or at *totter-arse; to ride the wild Mare; as children who sitting vpon both ends of a long Pole, or Timber-log (supported only in the middle) lift one another vp and downe. **1888** ELWORTHY *W. Somerset Word-bk.* s. v., I ant a-zeed no such two double totterarse 's longful time. **1821** CLARE *Vill. Minstr.* II. 198 And *totter-grass, in many a trembling knot. **1909** *Spectator* 10 July 48/2 The ox-eye daisies white among the totter-grass and sorrel. **1662** PETTY *Taxes* ii. § 14 The things which cause animosities among the *totter-headed multitude. **1887** G. MEREDITH *Ballads & P., Whimper of Sympathy*, The feelings of the *totterknee'd.

**Totter,** *sb.*[2]: see TOT *sb.*[5]

† **Totter,** *a. Obs. rare*[−1]. In 4 **totyre.**

[If genuine, goes with TOTTER *v.* (but it may be a copyist's error for TOLTER).]

Tottering, shaky, unstable, insecure.

*c* **1375** *Sc. Leg. Saints* xxviii. (*Margaret*) 42 Þe wikit warld scho ourcom als, Þat ay is totyre, fekil, & fals.

**Totter** (tǫ·təɹ), *v.* Also 3–5 **toter,** 6 **tottre.** [Appears first *c* 1200; has the form of a frequentative from a stem *tot-*, expressing instability or unstable movement. Perh. from Norse: cf. Norw. dial. *tutra, totra* to quiver, shake (Ross), Sw. dial. *tuttra* (Rietz). The sense is found in Flem. & Du. *touteren* to swing, though it is difficult to connect this phonologically: cf. TOLTER *v.*]

†**1.** *intr.* To swing to and fro, esp. at the end of a rope; *fig.* to waver, vacillate. *Obs.*

*c* **1200** *Vices & Virtues* 135 Ne mid fote sitten toterinde. **1387** TREVISA *Higden* (Rolls) II. 387 Men of Athene heng vp ropes in þe ayer and men totrede þeron and meued hider and þider [*orig.* huc et illuc agitabantur]. *Ibid.* [see TOTTER *sb.*[1] 1]. *c* **1440** *Promp. Parv.* 498/1 Toteron, or waveron, *vacillo.* **1552** [see TOTTER *sb.*[1] 1]. **1594** PLAT *Jewell-ho.* III. 47 It should seeme that before the breaking of the yolke, that the yolke did hang playing or tottering within the white. **1601** SHAKS. *All's Well* I. iii. 129 Manie likelihoods..which hung so tottring in the ballance.

†**b.** *spec.* To swing from the gallows, to be hanged. *Obs.*

*c* **1530** *Hickscorner* B ij b, That is a knauysshe sight to se them totter on a beme. **1542** UDALL *Erasm. Apoph.* 122 Diogenes..had a greate zele..to see theim euery one swyngyng & tottreyng in halters. **1556** J. HEYWOOD *Spider & F.* xv. 13 If they be had, they shall hang therupone, And yet if they totter twenty togyther, Still do theeues rob there. **1623–33** FLETCHER & SHIRLEY *Night-Walker* III. v, I would lose a limb, to see their rogueships totter.

†**c.** To play at see-saw. Cf. TITTER-TOTTER.

**1530** PALSGR. 760/1, I totter to and fro, as chylder do whan they play.., *je ballance*...Totter nat to moche leste you fall.

†**2.** To move up and down or to and fro, as a ship on the waves; to toss, to pitch. *Obs.*

**13..** *E. E. Allit. P.* C. 233 Þenne þaȝ her takel were torne, þat totered on yþez. *c* **1400** *Laud Troy Bk.* 4294 Other.. In the water swam and flotered, And there schippis a-boute tótered. **1596** *Edward III*, III. i. 170 Then might ye see the reeling vessels split, And tottering sink into the ruthlesse floud.

**3.** To rock or shake to and fro on its base, as if about to overbalance or collapse; † in quot. *c* 1400, to tremble.

*c* **1400** *Laud Troy Bk.* 9717 Thei sat toterynge as it were gece—What for the strokes & the hete. **1522** MORE *De Quat. Noviss.* Wks. 99 The hands trimbling..and the feete totteryng. **1576** PETTIE *Petite Pallace* 33 As a tree hewen downe with axes, redy to fal.., tottereth euery way, being vncertayne which way to fal. **1697** DRYDEN *Æneid* II. 384 Troy nods from high, and totters to her fall. **1775** SHERIDAN *St. Patr. Day* II. ii, I was..taken with a sudden giddiness, and Humphrey seeing me beginning to totter, ran to my assistance. **1836** MARRYAT *Midsh. Easy* xxx, Her mainmast was seen to totter, and then to fall over the side.

**b.** *fig.* or in fig. context.

**1610** SHAKS. *Temp.* III. ii. 8 If th'other two be brain'd like vs, the State totters. **1641** MILTON *Ch. Govt.* i. Wks. 1851 III. 100 So long as the Church is mounted upon the Prelaticall Cart..it will but shake and totter. **1719** YOUNG *Revenge* IV. i, O forbear! You totter on the very brink of ruin. *a* **1774** TUCKER *Lt. Nat.* (1834) II 173 Their faith..will be apt to shake and totter grievously in the storms of opposition. **1874** GREEN *Short Hist.* v. § 1. 221 From the day of Cressy feudalism tottered slowly but surely to its grave.

†**c.** To oscillate, vibrate, rock (without any notion of falling). *Obs. rare.*

**1668** CULPEPPER & COLE *Barthol. Anat.* I. xi. 27 The use of which bones, is to hinder that the valve do not easily totter. **1678** MOXON *Mech. Exerc.* iv. 64 Not letting the Plain totter to or from you-wards.

**4.** To walk or move with unsteady steps; to go shakily or feebly; to toddle; also, to walk with difficulty; to reel, stagger.

**1602** MARSTON *Ant. & Mel.* I. Wks. 1856 I. 17 He totterd from the reeling decke. **1796** MORSE *Amer. Geog.* II. 489 Chinese women..may be said to totter rather than to walk. **1797** DOWNING *Disorders Horned Cattle*, etc. 106 When the staggers and convulsive symptoms arise, the horse..is feeble, reels and totters about as he moves. **1818** SCOTT *Br. Lamm.* xix, The old blind woman arose, assumed her staff, ..tottering to her hut. **1863** W. C. BALDWIN *Afr. Hunting* vii. 280 Three niggers staggering after us with as much as ever they could totter under.

**b.** *trans.* (*nonce-uses.*) (*a*) To make (one's way) totteringly. (*b*) To carry with tottering steps.

**1846** MRS. GORE *Eng. Char.* (1852) 57 Poor Corney tottered his way from the miserable cellar of St. Giles's..towards the fashionable quarter of the town. **1864** LOWELL *Fireside Trav.* 280 After our little bearers [mules] had tottered us up and down the dusky steeps.

†**5.** *trans.* To cause to shake to and fro, to rock; to render unstable. Also *fig. Obs.*

**1615** T. ADAMS *White Devill* 45 There is some disobedient and fugitive Jonasses that thus totter our ship. *a* **1625** FLETCHER *Hum. Lieut.* I. i, Earthquakes To shake and totter my designs. *a* **1693** *Urquhart's Rabelais* III. Prol. 7 He..totter'd it, lifted it,..transpos'd it, transplaced it.

**Totterdemal(l)ion,** obs. f. TATTERDEMALION.

† **Tottered** (tǫ·təɹd), *ppl. a. Obs.* [Orig. a variant of TATTERED, and used in that sense (cf. Norw. dial. *totra* rag); subsequently associated with TOTTER *v.*, and more or less assimilated in sense.]

**1.** = TATTERED 2, 3.

**1570** FOXE *A. & M.* (ed. 2) 1357/1 He..was not so disguised in hys tottered attyre, but that hys countenaunce gaue signification [etc.]. **1596** SHAKS. 1 *Hen. IV*, IV. ii. 37 A hundred and fiftie totter'd Prodigalls, lately come from Swine-keeping. **1657** S. PURCHAS *Pol. Flying-Ins.* 118 [They] have their wings tottered and torn. *a* **1693** *Urquhart's Rabelais* III. xvii, The ragged and tottered Equipage of her Person.

**2.** Of a building or a ship: Battered and shaken, rendered ruinous and liable to fall; in a tottering condition.

**1615** G. SANDYS *Trav.* 178 A tottered Tower doth challenge regard for the waste receiued in that places protection. **1649–50** in Swayne *Sarum Churchw. Acc.* (1896) 221 Carpenter pulling down yᵉ tottered seiling over yᵉ East end of the Chancell. **1689** SHERLOCK *Disc. Death* (1715) 26 Merciless waves even overwhelm his tottered and decayed vessel. **1808** SCOTT *Marm.* IV. xi, Thy turrets rude, and tottered Keep, Have been the minstrel's loved resort.

**3.** Made to totter, shaken, reeling. *rare.*

**1621** G. SANDYS *Ovid's Met.* XV. (1626) 317 The hot horses ..O'r ragged rocks the totterd charriot driue: While I to curb their furie vainly striue.

**Totterer** (tǫ·tərəɹ). [f. TOTTER *v.* + -ER [1].] One who totters, or walks with tottering steps.

**1711** SWIFT *Jrnl. to Stella* 21 Apr., I am much better than I was, though something of a totterer. **1827** *Blackw. Mag.* XXII. 702 He snatched the little totterers..up in his arms. **1890** [see next].

**To·ttering,** *vbl. sb.* [f. TOTTER *v.* + -ING [1].] The action of the verb TOTTER; oscillation, wavering, shaking as if about to fall.

1387 TREVISA *Higden* (Rolls) II. 387 That game is cleped ocillum in Latyn, . . of cilleo cilles þat is forto mene toterynge. *c* 1440 *Promp. Parv.* 498/1 Toterynge, or waverynge, *vacillacio.* 1577 B. GOOGE *Heresbach's Husb.* 40 The Wayne or Cart must be lyned with sheets, lest with iogging and tottring of the carriage, the seede fall thorowe. 1672 CLARENDON *Contempl. Ps.* Tracts (1727) 280 The prodigious tottering and instability of that [church] they are about to enter. 1890 J. H. STIRLING *Gifford Lect.* xii. 262 If you totter already, the tottering against you of ever so many totterers will only floor you.

**To·ttering,** *ppl. a.* [f. TOTTER *v.* + -ING [2].] That totters, in various senses of the verb.

1534 MORE *Comf. agst. Trib.* IV. xxiv. (1847) 298 The three feet of this tottering stool. 1585 ABP. SANDYS *Serm.* xiv. 232 Our tottering boate is tossed in the stormie seas. 1610 HOLLAND *Camden's Brit.* (1637) 642 The tottering walles of Caer-philli Castle. 1700 T. BROWN *Amusem. Ser. & Com.* ii. 12 The tottering Earth made them Giddy and Stumble. 1801 SOUTHEY *Thalaba* IX. xvii, She leans on her staff With a tottering step. 1877 BLACK *Green Past.* xxxv, A tottering white-headed old man.

*fig.* 1554 LATIMER *Disput. Oxford* in Foxe *A. & M.* (1563) 980/1 That thys world hath bene, and yet is, a tottering world. 1649 MILTON *Eikon.* v. Wks. 1851 III. 375 A tottring and giddy Act rather then a settling. 1796 BURKE *Regic. Peace* i. Wks. VIII. 158 The tottering imbecility of a new government. 1870 'H. SMART' *Race for Wife* iii, Tottering coronets must be propped by wealthy alliances.

Hence **To·tteringly** *adv.*

1660 INGELO *Bentiv. & Ur.* I. (1682) 82 It seem'd to stand totteringly upon a pitiful foundation. 1891 L. KEITH *Lost Illusion* II. xii. 41 An old man totteringly and feebly cleaning a little vegetable-bed.

**Totterish** (tǫ·tәriʃ), *a. rare.* [f. TOTTER *a.* or *v.* + -ISH [1].] Inclined to totter; somewhat tottery.

1817 SCOTT *Let. to Mrs. M. Clephane* 23 Mar., in *Lockhart*, I am still very totterish and very giddy. 1819 — *Let. to Southey* 4 Apr. *ibid.*, My health is at present very totterish.

**Tottery** (tǫ·tәri), *a.* [f. TOTTER *v.* + -Y.] Given to tottering; shaky; unsteady.

1861 HUGHES *Tom Brown at Oxf.* vi, When I looked up and saw what a tottery performance it was, I concluded to give them a wide berth. 1880 MISS BRADDON *Just as I am* xviii, Frances felt very faint and tottery. 1907 *Speaker* 19 Jan. 484/2 Stocks have been distinctly 'tottery' this week.

**Tottie** (tǫ·ti). Also **Totty.** With capital T: Familiar diminutive of HOTTENTOT.

1849 E. E. NAPIER *Excurs. S. Africa* I. 55 To portray. . the Hottentot of the time of Van Riebeck, and the 'Totty' of the present day. 1863 W. C. BALDWIN *Afr. Hunting* ix. 366, I have. . five horses, six Kaffirs, and one Tottie, and have every comfort in my wagons. 1883 *Gd. News in Africa* viii. 110 The Hottentots are a miserable little race, sometimes called 'Totties' in contempt.

**Tottie,** variant of TOTTY.

**Totting:** see TOT *sb.*[5], *v.*[1] and [2].

**Tottle** (tǫ·t'l), *a. dial.* [? f. *tot-* in TOTTER *v.* + -LE I, as in *brittle.*] Weak-headed, silly, dazed.

1894 BARING-GOULD *Kitty Alone* II. 94 Wi' the death of her little maid, gone almost tottle (silly). 1897 — *Furze-Bloom* (1899) 13, I reckon, Genefer, the old lady be gone quite tottle (dazed).

**Tottle** (tǫ·t'l), *v.*[1] Also 8–9 totle. Chiefly *dial.* [In sense 1 app. onomatopœic, representing the motion and sound involved. In senses 2 and 3 perh. by-form of TODDLE or TOTTER, and TOPPLE.]

**1.** *intr.* To move and bubble, as a boiling liquid; also said of the vessel; and applied to the somewhat similar motion and sound of a rivulet over a stony bed. *Sc.* Hence **To·ttling** *vbl. sb.*

1717 *Lament for Ld. Maxwell* in *Jacob. Songs & Ball.* (1887) 103 'Side the sang o' the birds, where some burn tottles owre. 1739 A. NICOL *Nat. without Art* 100 In Winter-time a Piece fat Beef to tottle. 1835 MONTEATH *Dunblane* (1887) 32 The woman. . cast a longing eye at the kail-pot 'tottling on the fire'. 1864 A. LEIGHTON *Myst. Leg. Edinb.* (1886) 68 They heard the sound of. . the sweltering and tottling of the pot.

**b.** *trans.* To cause to simmer or boil. *Sc.*

*a* 1774 FERGUSSON *To Principal, etc. St. Andrews* 40 Imprimis, then, a haggis fat, Weel tottl'd in a seything pat. 1776 HERD *Collect. Scot. Songs* II. 182 Ye's get a cock well totled i' the pat, An ye'll come hame, an ye'll come hame.

**2.** *intr.* To move unsteadily and with short tottering steps; to toddle.

1821 GALT *Sir A. Wylie* III. xxxiii. 287 Their bairns. . when they begin to tottle about the house. 1824 — *Rothelan* VI. iii, The tidy grand-dame. . is seen with a pitcher slowly tottling across the fields to the dairy. 1873 HALE *In His Name* i. 4 The twin babies who could hardly tottle along the road.

**3.** *intr.* = TOPPLE *v.* 1. *dial.*

1830 HOGG in *Blackw. Mag.* XXVIII. 895 Off flew the English warder's head, And tottled into Foxton burn. *a* 1905 in *Eng. Dial. Dict.* s.v., (N. Yorks.) T'oad fella nearly tottled of t' steul 'at he was set on wi' laughing.

Hence **To·ttledom,** *nonce-wd.* (for *toddledom*), the sphere of toddlers or toddling; babyhood, infancy; **Tottlish** (tǫ·tliʃ) *a.*, unsteady, totterish.

1889 *Anthony's Photogr. Bull.* II. 354 There not being the least fear of its. . ever exceeding the limits of cameraic *tottledom. 1853 MRS. MOODIE *Life in Clearings* 16 This was the first time he had ever ventured upon the water in such a *tottleish machine [as a birch-bark canoe]. 1889 C. F. WOOLSON *Jupiter Lights* xxviii, She'll soon fill it full of tottlish little tables and dimity.

**To·ttle,** *v.*[2], altered form of TOTAL *v.*, with shortened vowel. (Common *dialectally.*)

1891 GOSSE *Gossip in Library* xiii. 164 She did not tottle up her milk-scores on the bastard-title [of a book].

**To·ttling,** *ppl. a.* [f. TOTTLE *v.*[1] + -ING [2].] That tottles; moving unsteadily; apt to tip or topple; shaky; crazy; also *fig.* feeble or shaky in intellect. Cf. TOTTY *a.*[2]

1746 *Exmoor Scolding* (E.D.S.) 53 A toteling, wambling, zlottering, zart-and-vair yheat-stool. 1849 DANA *Geol.* ii. (1850) 31 Safe navigation for the tottling canoe. 1873 E. H. CLARKE *Sex in Educ.* 35 The girl. . will caress a doll, that her tottling brother looks coldly upon. 1880 MRS. PARR *Adam & Eve* xxxvi, Th' ole chap was gone reg'lar totlin' like, and can't tell thickee fra that.

**Totty** (tǫ·ti), *sb.* (*a.*[1]) Also **tottie, totie.** Affectionate diminutive of TOT *sb.*[4]; a tiny tot or little child. Also as *adj.* Tiny, wee. Hence **To·ttykins** = TODDLEKINS.

1821 GALT *Sir A. Wylie* III. xxxiii. 287, I would be blithe to see the wee totties spinning about the floor like peeries. 1849 J. MILNE *Let.* in Bonar *Life* ix. (1868) 129 There is not a day that I don't think of our poor little totty. *Ibid.* 128 Bonnie wee totikins, Bricht as a bee. 1906 A. MCCORMICK *Tinkler Gipsies Galloway* ii. 89 The fairies,—totie wee bodies a' cled in red.

**Totty** (tǫ·ti), *a.*[2] Now *dial.* Forms: 4–6 toty, 6 tottye, -ie, 6– totty. [app. f. *tot-*, as in *totter* and *tottle* + -Y.] Unsteady, shaky, tottery (physically or mentally); dizzy, dazed; tipsy, fuddled.

*c* 1386 CHAUCER *Reeve's T.* 333 Myn heed is toty of my swynk to nyght. 1412–20 LYDG. *Chron. Troy* II. 5752 Somme also so toty in her hede þat þei. . haue no foot for to stonde vp-riȝt. 1522 MORE *De Quat. Noviss.* Wks. 97 What good can the great gluton do w[t]. . his noll toty with drink? 1570 LEVINS *Manip.* 112/11 Totty, *vacillans, ebriolus, a.* 1594 O. B. *Quest. Profit. Concern.* 23 b, I thought his head was but tottie. 1652 *Season. Exp. Netherl.* 10 Who proving totty, They thought to ballast him. 1819 SCOTT *Ivanhoe* xxxiii, I was somewhat totty when I received the good knight's blow, or I had kept my ground. 1828 *Craven Gloss.*, *Totty*, half drunk, tipsy. 1890 DOYLE *White Company* xvii, Nay, nay, your head I can see is still totty.

**b.** *Comb.*: **totty-grass**, totter-grass, quaking-grass; **totty-head**, an imbecile; **totty-headed** *a.*, light-headed, silly, frivolous; dizzy, giddy.

1901 *Speaker* 20 Apr. 86/2 Who ever saw a child that did not love to gather primroses, horse daisies, or *totty-grass? 1680 *Honest Hodge & Ralph* 28 Not such *Totty-heads yet, as to be led by the Nose by him. *a* 1700 B. E. *Dict. Cant. Crew*, *Totty-headed, Giddy-headed, Hare-brain'd. *a* 1825 FORBY *Voc. E. Anglia*, *Totty, totty-headed*, dizzy. Particularly from the effect of too much drink.

**Totty,** variant of TOTTIE.

† **To-tu·g,** *v. Obs.* Also 3 te-, 5 to-togge. [ME. f. TO- [2] + *toggen, tugge*, TUG *v.*] *trans.* To pull to pieces.

*c* 1220 *Bestiary* 420 in *O. E. Misc.* 13 [He] tetoggeð and tetireð hem mid hire teð sarpe. *c* 1400 *Destr. Troy* 8042 All fadit that faire of hir fyn coloure, . . All to tugget hir tresses of hir triet here. 1446 LYDG. *Two Nightingale Poems* i. 256 On euery syde to-togged and to-drawe.

**Totum** [1] (tōu·tǝm). Now *dial.* [a. L. *tōtum* all, the whole, the initial T of which was one of the four letters inscribed on the teetotum: cf. F. *toton*, in Cotgr. and *Dict. Acad.* 1694–1740 *totum*, pronounced (totoṅ).] = TEETOTUM, q. v.

[1500–20 DUNBAR *Poems* xxii. 74 He playis with *totum* and I with *nichell.*] 1706 PHILLIPS (ed. Kersey), *Totum*, a Whirl-bone, a kind of Die that is turned about. 1734 CHESTERF. in *Lett. C'tess Suffolk* (1824) II. 116 A couple of totums set a spinning. 1825 JAMIESON, *Totum* sb. 1, the game of *Te-totum*. [See *Eng. Dial. Dict.*, TOTUM [2].]

**To·tum** [2]. *Sc.* [perh. a humorous extension of TOT *sb.*[4]; but generally associated with prec.] A little child, a wee tot.

17.. *Cauld Kail in Aberdeen* in Aitken *Scott. Song* (1874) 146 Whene'er the totums cry for meat She curses aye his cogie. 1844 A. COCHRANE in Whitelaw *Bk. Scott. Song* (1875) 73/1 Our twa bits o' totums are toddlin their lane. 1898 *Westm. Gaz.* 6 Oct. 3/2 The fact. . that had generated so critical an eyesight in this 'totum' of three.

‖ **To·tum** [3]. [L.: see TOTUM [1].] A whole.

1657 J. SMITH *Myst. Rhet.* A viij b, *Totum*, is whatsoever hath parts: . . and so parts are such as make up the whole. *a* 1658 CLEVELAND *On little Gentleman* 22 How comes it that she thus converts So small a *Totum*, and great Parts? 1678 CUDWORTH *Intell. Syst.* I. i. § 31 The *totum* or *compositum* of a man or animal may be said to be generated and corrupted, in regard of the union and disunion, conjunction and separation of those two parts, the soul and body.

† **To·tuple,** *a. Obs.* [f. L. *tot* so many, after QUADRUPLE, etc.] So many-fold: = TANTUPLE.

1656 HOBBES *Six Less.* iii. Wks. 1845 VII. 240 The antecedents are of their consequents totuple or tantuple, that is, equimultiple. *a* 1696 SCARBURGH *Euclid* (1705) 201 Therefore. . Totuple shall AB, CD together, be of E, F together.

**To-turn, To-twin:** see TO- *pref.*[2]

† **To-tu·se,** *v. Obs. rare*[—1]. [ME. f. TO- [2] + **tūsen*, TOUSE *v.* (The later ME. form would have been *to-touse.*)] *trans.* To pull asunder; to dishevel.

*c* 1300 *Havelok* 1948 Al to-tused and al to-torn.

† **To-twee·n,** *prep. Obs. rare.* [f. TO- [1] + *-twen* in BETWEEN.] Between.

*c* 1440 *Partonope* 4170 And cleuyd hys forhed to twene þe yen.

† **To-twe·me,** *v. Obs.* Forms: see TWEME. [OE. *totwǣman*, f. TO- [2] + *twǣman*, TWEME *v.* to separate, part.] **a.** *trans.* To separate, divide; also to distinguish, discriminate.

*c* 893 K. ÆLFRED *Oros.* III. vii. § 6 Hie eft totwæmde wæron. *a* 1225 *Ancr. R.* 396 Auh ure Louerd willeliche totweamede [*v. r.* to-twinnede] his soule urom his bodie.

**b.** *intr.* To separate, part asunder.

*c* 1205 LAY. 26593 Ær heo to twemden [*pr.* to-tweinden] þe wurse wes Rom-leoden. *a* 1225 *St. Marher.* 17 Wið þe ilke þe eorðe to twemde ant bitunde him.

† **To-twi·tch,** *v. Obs.* [ME. *to-twicchen*, f. TO- [2] + TWITCH *v.*] *trans.* To pull apart or away with a sudden jerk or twitch. Also *fig.*

*c* 1175 *Lamb. Hom.* 53 Swa sone se hi beoð iturned awey from heom, [hi] heom to-twiccheð & to-draȝeð mid ufele weordes. *a* 1250 *Owl & Night.* 1647 Gromes þe ivoþ. . & þe to twicceþ & to schakeþ. *c* 1350 *Will. Palerne* 2097 His berde & his briȝt fax for bale he to-twiȝt.

‖ **To·ty.** *Anglo-Ind.* [Tamil and Canarese *toṭi.*] A man of a low caste employed as messenger and odd man of a South Indian village. Also **totyman.**

1800 in Gurw. *Wellington's Suppl. Desp.* (1858) I. 452 Washerman, barber, and totyman. 1886 YULE & BURNELL *Hobson-Jobson*, Toty.

**Toty, Totyr,** obs. ff. TOTTY *a.*[2], TOTTER.

**Tou, Toual**(l, obs. forms of TOUGH, TOWEL.

**Touart, Toubbe,** obs. forms of TOWARD, TUB.

**Toucan** (tukā·n, tū·kǎn). Also 8 **tokan**, 9 **toukan.** [= F. *toucan*, Sp. *tucan*, Pg., It. *tucano*, a. Brazilian, Tupi *tucana*, Guarani *tucà, tucãn* (*a* nasal), the native name, prob. from its cry or call; but other suggestions have been offered.

The statement of Buffon that the name means 'feather' arose from his misunderstanding a statement of Léry *c* 1558: see J. Platt in *N. & Q.* 9th s. VII. 486–VIII. 250.]

**1.** A Neotropical bird of the genus *Rhamphastos*, or, in a wider use, of the family *Rhamphastidæ*, inhabiting the tropical parts of South America, a few species being also found in Central America and Mexico. They are noted for the enormous size of the beak and their striking colouring. The species originally so named was app. *R. toco.*

[1558 THEVET *Sing. France Antarctique*, D'un oyseau qu'ils appellent en leur langue Toucan.] 1568 tr. *Thevet's New-found World* 73 Of a birde named toucan. 1634 T. JOHNSON *Parey's Chirurg.* xxv. xxii. (1678) 621 He saw a Bird in America, which in that Countrey Speech is called Touca, . . that the beak in length and thickness exceeds the bigness of the rest of the body. 1668 CHARLETON *Onomast.* 115 *Tucana*. . Toucan. 1677 PLOT *Oxfordsh.* 178 In. . 1644 the *Pica Brasiliensis*, or Toucan, whose beak is near as big as its whole body, was found within two miles of Oxford. 1681 GREW *Musæum* I. IV. i. 59 The Head of the Toucan, so called by the Indians. 1796 STEDMAN *Surinam* I. vi. 117 The toucan is not larger than a tame pigeon, and yet its beak is no less than six inches in length. 1863 BATES *Nat. Amazon* xii. (1864) 404 Toucans. . . Two of them are often heard yelping alternately, and in different notes. These cries have a vague resemblance to the syllables Tocáno, Tocáno, and hence the Indian name of this genus of birds. 1875 WHITNEY *Life Lang.* vii. 120 The cuckoo and the peewee and the toucan were named from their notes.

**b.** Sometimes applied or misapplied to other birds with large or curious beaks; esp. in the East Indies to species of Hornbill (*Buceros*).

But the word in the latter case is said to be the Malay *tukang* 'workman' or 'artificer', and entirely distinct from the Brazilian: see Yule & Burnell *Hobson-Jobson.*

1816 TUCKEY *Narr. Exped. R. Zaire* iii. (1818) 82 Several varieties of the king fisher, a toukan, and many small birds. 1862 JERDON *Birds of India* I. 242 They [the hornbills] are, indeed, popularly called *Toucans* throughout India; and this appears to be their name in some of the Malayan isles; the word signifying 'worker', from the noise they make.

**2.** *Astron.* Name of a southern constellation.

1669 STURMY *Mariner's Mag.* VI. iii. 128 The Bird Toucan [*pr.* Taican], or Brasilian Pye, in which Constellation is 7 Stars. 1868 LOCKYER *Guillemin's Heavens* xii. (1872) 319 The splendid cluster in Toucan, quite visible to the naked eye.

**3.** *Comb.*, as *toucan skin*, etc.; **toucan-beak**, the beak of the toucan, or the substance of this used as a decorative material.

1862 *List Contrib. fr. Brit. Guiana to Lond. Exhib.* in Veness *El Dorado* (1866) App. 145 Tassel of Toucan Skins, worn by the Accawai Indians. . hanging down the back. 1886 *Art Jrnl., Exh. Suppl.* 26/2 Some clever and minute carvings in toucan-beak set with alternate links in gold.

Hence **Toucanet** (tū·kǎne:t), any of the smaller kinds of toucan, as those of the genera *Pteroglossus* and *Selenidera*; **Toucanity** (tukæ·nīti), *nonce-wd.*, the character of a toucan.

1825 WATERTON *Wand. S. Amer.* II. 118 There are three species of Toucans in Demerara, and three diminutives, which may be called Toucanets. 1892 *Cornh. Mag.* May 525 A large bill. . a mark of perfect and advanced toucanity.

**Touch** (tɒtʃ), *sb.* Forms: see TOUCH *v.* [Originally a. OF. *touche*, f. *toucher* to TOUCH: cf. Pr., It. *tocca* stroke, blow, touch; also Prov. *toc*, It. *tocco* knock, stroke; f. *toccare* to hit, strike. In some later uses, directly from TOUCH *v.*]

**I.** Literal and directly connected senses.

**1.** The action or an act of touching (with the hand, finger, or other part of the body); exercise of the faculty of feeling upon a material object. † In quot. 1340, ? a tactile organ (*obs.*). In quot. 1591, Hold, grasp, embrace (*nonce-use*).

1340 HAMPOLE *Pr. Consc.* 779 Fyngers and taes, fote and hande, Alle his touches [*MS. Lansd.* lymmes] er tremblande. 1390 GOWER *Conf.* II. 136 For he. . preide, That wherupon his hond he leide, It scholde thurgh his touche anon Become gold. 1398 TREVISA *Barth. De P. R.* XVI. vii. (Bodl. MS.),

Quyke siluer..semeþ ful colde in touche. **1513** DOUGLAS *Æneis* III. iv. 36 The Harpyes..with thair laithlie tuiche all thing file thai. **1591** SHAKS. *Two Gent.* V. iv. 60 Ruffian: let goe that rude vnciuill touch. **1614** PURCHAS *Pilgrimage* IX. vii. (ed. 2) 864 He toucheth the face and breast with cold touches. **1681** H. MORE *Exp. Dan.* iv. Notes 120 He healed the Blind and the Lame with Spittle and touch. **1705** *Lond. Gaz.* No. 4126/3 They never had before received the Royal Touch. **1841–71** T. R. JONES *Anim. Kingd.* (ed. 4) 464 The antennæ..may be regarded as special instruments of touch. **1842** TENNYSON '*Break, break, break*' iii, But O for the touch of a vanish'd hand! **1898** G. B. SHAW *Widowers' Houses* I. 6 The porter..receives it with a submissive touch to his cap.

**b.** *euphem.* Sexual contact.

*a* **1300** *Cursor M.* 2985 (Cott.) Fra toche of hir i saued þe. **1412–20** LYDG. *Chron. Troy* I. 2860 Sche Ay kepte hir clene from touche of any man. **1603** SHAKS. *Meas. for M.* V. i. 141 Who is as free from touch or soyle with her As she from one vngot.

**c.** *Med.* Examination by feeling, esp. of a cavity of the body; palpation.

**1805** *Med. Jrnl.* XIV. 245 Had we..trusted to the touch, it might have been said we were deceived. **1860** MAYNE *Expos. Lex.*, *Touch..Obstet.* Term for the examination of the womb, or mouth and neck of the womb.

**d.** *Milit.* Contact between the elbows of a rank of soldiers; see quots. and cf. TOUCH *v.* 2 g.

**1877** *Man. Field Artillery Exerc.* 23 The right-hand or left-hand man being first placed, the remainder will fall in in line one after the other, closing lightly towards him, turning the elbow slightly outwards. Soldiers must be carefully instructed in the 'Touch', as, in this formation, it is the principal guide when marching. *Ibid.* 25 During the march..the dressing is kept by the touch.

**e.** *Within* or *in touch*, near enough to touch or be touched; within reach (*of*); accessible; also *fig.*

**1854** S. DOBELL *Balder* v. 29 Tottering..In touch of the inestimable prize. **1858** HAWTHORNE *Fr. & It. Note-Bks.* I. 119 The rough-hewn roof was within touch. **1896** *Times* 16 Dec. 5/3 [He] is not yet within touch of the telegraph.

†**f.** The act of touching at a port (TOUCH *v.* 11); a passing call during a voyage. *Obs. rare*⁻¹.

**1603** KNOLLES *Hist. Turks* (1621) 1331 His first touch was upon the Island of Cerigo.

**g.** A boys' game in which one player touches another, who then chases and tries to catch him; in full *touch-and-run*; also allusively (cf. TOUCH AND GO). Cf. TIG.

**1815** LADY GRANVILLE *Lett.* (1894) I. 80 His favourite has hit the line between good-humoured frankness and vulgarity, just touch and run. **1912** *Daily News* 4 Nov. 2/2 The lad was playing 'touch-and-run' with a number of others.

**2.** The act, fact, or state of touching or being touched (of inanimate objects, or as an involuntary act: see TOUCH *v.* 3); contact.

**13..** *E. E. Allit. P.* C. 252 With-outen towche of any tothe he tult in his þrote. *a* **1586** SIDNEY *Arcadia* II. (1590) 149 b, The touch of the cold water made a prettie kinde of shrugging come ouer her bodie. **1596** SHAKS. *Merch. V.* III. ii. 273 And not one vessell scape the dreadfull touch Of merchant-marring rocks? **1667** MILTON *P. L.* VI. 520 Part incentive reed Provide, pernicious with one touch to fire. **1784** COWPER *Task* II. 11 The flax That falls asunder at the touch of fire. **1874** O'SHAUGHNESSY *Music & Moonlight* 40 Her passing touch was death to all, Her passing look a blight.

†**b.** *Geom.* Contact; point of contact. *Obs.*

*a* **1400** in Halliwell *Rara Mathem.* (1841) 62 Counte þe poyntes fro þe begynnyng of þe side of þe vmbre to þe touche of þe perpendicle. **1551** RECORDE *Pathw. Knowl.* I. xxix, In the very poynte of the touche muste I make an angle. **1570** BILLINGSLEY *Euclid* III. def. iii, Such a touch of circles is euer in one poynt onely.

**c.** A small quantity of some substance brought into contact with a surface so as to leave its mark or effect; a dash, as of paint; a mark or stain so produced. See also 10.

In quot. 1581 with figurative allusion: cf. PITCH *sb.*¹ 4, and quot. 1382 s.v. TOUCH *v.* 1. So *a touch of the tar-brush*: see TAR-BRUSH b, quot. 1864.

**1581** PETTIE *Guazzo's Civ. Conv.* I. (1586) 24 Of one selfe pitch, we all haue a touch. **1664** POWER *Exp. Philos.* I. 31, I..glew'd them to the object-plate, as I do stronger Insects with a touch of Turpentine. **1818** SCOTT *Hrt. Midl.* xvii, Maybe a touch o' a blackit cork, or a slake o' paint.

**d.** A very close approach, a 'shave': cf. TOUCH *v.* 14, TOUCHER 4.

**18..** DICKENS (Ogilvie), The hind coach passed my engine by a shave. It was the nearest touch I ever saw.

**e.** *No touch to* (*U. S. colloq.*): 'nowhere near', nothing approaching to.

**1838** HALIBURTON *Clockm.* Ser. II. vi. (1862) 206 Our sea sarpant was no touch to it. **1840** — *Letter Bag* ii. 18 You ab seen fourth July day,..well he [is] no touch to it.

**3.** That sense by which a material object is perceived by means of the contact with it of some part of the body; the most general of the bodily senses, diffused through all parts of the skin, but (in man) specially developed in the tips of the fingers and the lips.

*c* **1394** *P. Pl. Crede* 537 Þanne haue y tynt all my tast, touche and assaie! **1599** DAVIES *Immort. Soul* ccxxii, By touch the first pure qualities we learn Which quicken all things, hot, cold, moist, and dry. *a* **1704** LOCKE *Elem. Nat. Philos.* xi. (1754) 50 The fifth and last of our senses is touch; a sense spread over the whole body, tho' it be most eminently placed in the ends of the fingers. **1764** REID *Inquiry* vi. § 8. 213 That figure and that extension which are objects of touch have been tortured ten thousand ways for twenty centuries. **1851** CARPENTER *Man. Phys.* (ed. 2) 551 There is strong reason to regard the sense of Taste as only a refined kind of Touch, combined with the sense of Smell.

**b.** The sensation caused by touching something (considered as an attribute of the thing); tactile quality, feel.

**1674** DRYDEN *Epil. opening of New House* 4 A Country Lip may have the Velvet touch. **1804** J. GRAHAME *Sabbath* (1805) 37 The smooth birch With rind of silken touch. **1839** URE *Dict. Arts* 1202 Most decide by 'the touch', that is, the feel and appearance of a drop of the syrup..drawn into a thread between the thumb and fore-finger. **1844** *Jrnl. R. Agric. Soc.* V. I. 259 The first token..for the purpose of ascertaining the feeding properties of an ox, is technically called the touch.

**4.** A hit, knock, stroke, blow; *esp.* a very slight blow or stroke.

[Quot. 1297 here appears to be the earliest example of the word in Eng., and perh. shows the original sense, as 'hit, stroke, blow'.]

In quot. *c* 1375, ? a slight wound or abrasion such as might be produced by a blow or scratch.

**1297** R. GLOUC. (Rolls) 12020 So þat þe erl of wareine slou atte verste touche Biuore þe iustises atte bench sir alein de la souche. *c* **1375** *Cursor M.* 14012 (Fairf.) Þer ho fande any touche of sare [*Cott.* ani breck or sare; *Trin.* chyn or soore] Wiþ hir þingus anoynt hit þare. *c* **1420** *Anturs of Arth.* 605 (Thornton MS.) Swylke a touche at þat tyme he taughte hym in tene. **1581** T. HOWELL *Deuises* (1879) 216 For some perchance will byde a toutch or two, And will not seeme to flye when you shall fall. **1879** F. W. ROBINSON *Coward Consc.* II. xvii, 'It requires the finest touch', said Mr. Slitherwick, shutting one eye to admire the position of the balls, 'one of your very best touches, Mr. Oliver'.

**b.** *fig.* A 'hit', stroke (of wit, satire, etc.); a 'knock'; a 'blow'.

**1522** *World & Child* (1817) C j, How sayeste thou now folye hast thou not a touche? **1667** MILTON *P. L.* IX. 1144 To whom soon mov'd with touch of blame thus Eve. *c* **1720** PRIOR *Paulo Purganti* 29 It yet may feel the nicer touch Of Wycherley's or Congreve's wit. **1852** THACKERAY *Esmond* II. v, There was a hard touch for his Grace,..in the concluding sentence of the Don.

**II.** Technical and allied senses.

* *Relating to the touchstone.*

**5.** The action or process of testing the quality of gold or silver by rubbing it upon a touchstone. [So OF. *touche*, It. *tocco*.]

**1436** *Pol. Poems* (Rolls) II. 187 Whereof was fyned metalle gode and clene, At the touche, no bettere coude be sene. **1587** *Mirr. Mag.*, *Runa* ii, Good metall bides the touch that trieth out the gold. **1686** W. DE BRITAINE *Hum. Prud.* xx. 94 He is like Gold, which hath too much Allay, that feareth the Touch. **1837** WHITTOCK, etc. *Bk. Trades* (1842) 279 This test, by the touch, is performed at the present day. ..Touch needles are small bars made of compound metals, the proportions whereof are accurately marked on each.

**b.** An official mark or stamp upon gold or silver indicating that it has been tested, and is of standard fineness; also, a die, punch, or stamp for impressing this. Also, an official mark stamped upon pewter.

**1423** [see TOUCH *v.* 8 b]. **1443** *Test. Ebor.* (Surtees) II. 132 A quart pot of silver with the touche of Parys. **1522** *Will J. Surdevall* (Somerset Ho.), Which spones hath the toche of the Goldesmythes. **1526–7** in Welch *Hist. Pewterers' Co.* (1902) I. 118 A fyn for delieryng vessell vn-markyt wᵗ his towch..v s. [**1564–1750** *ibid. passim.*] *a* **1553** UDALL *Royster D.* II. ii. (Arb.) 34 If he haue not one Lumbardes touche, my lucke is bad. **1594** PLAT *Jewell-h.* III. 79 Plate as either carieth no touch, or so old a touch as the buier shall not bee acquainted withall. **1697** *View Penal Laws* 142 If the Keeper of the Touch mark such harness with the Leopards head. **1852** A. RYLAND *Assay of Gold & Silver* 38 The *Touch* is used in the old Statutes to denote in some places the Standard, in some the punch used in marking the wares, and in others the mark impressed upon the plate. **1860** J. SCARTH *12 Yrs. China* 116 Of the enormous amounts of gold..the greater part is guaranteed by a certain touch.

**c.** The quality or fineness of gold or silver (or other metal) as tested with the touchstone and indicated by the official mark. [Cf. OF. *touche de Paris*, etc.]

*a* **1325** *MS. Rawl. B.* 520 lf. 53 b, Þat is to witen golde of certein touche. *Ibid.*, Ant þat non ne wurche worse gold þan þe touche of paris. **1465** *Paston Lett.* I. 134, j. herneyse complete of the touche of Milleyn. **1601** HOLLAND *Pliny* XXXIII. ix. II. 479 An act..for the proofe and allowance of silver deniers, what touch and what poise they should have. **1697** *Observ. on Money & Coin* 9 Gold shall be of the fineness of the Touch of Paris. **1766** T. BROOKS *Coins E. Indies* 6, 1 Madrass Rupee..is Country Touch 9⅞. China Touch 98⅝. **1908** H. B. MORSE *Trade Chinese Emp.* 149 'Pure silver' of the Kuping tael touch is actually 987 fine when reduced to the Western standard of chemically pure silver.

**d.** *fig.* Quality, kind, sort, 'stamp'. In quot. 1878 *transf.* Quality or degree of purity (of opium).

**1388** *Pol. Poems* (Rolls) I. 274 Fresch of the newe towch, *incedunt ridiculose*, Lityl or noght in her powch, *pascuntur deliciose.* **1579** J. STUBBES *Gaping Gulf* A vij, To be of one assaie or touche with the idolatrous and trayterous Israelits. **1607** SHAKS. *Cor.* IV. i. 49 Come my sweet wife, my deerest Mother, and My Friends of Noble touch. **1821** LAMB *Elia* Ser. I. *Imperfect Sympathies*, He never stoops to catch a glittering something..before he quite knows whether it be true touch or not. **1878** BABER *Rep. Chinese Opium* (Parl. Paper Eng. C. 3378, 1882, 29) The advantage of 'touch', or percentage of extract, possessed by the Indian drug.

†**6.** Short for *touchstone* (see TOUCHSTONE 2); *esp.* applied to black marble or some similar black stone used in monumental work. *Obs.* [So OF. *touche* for *pierre de touche* (Godef.).]

*a* **1509** *Will. of Hen. VII* (Parker *Gloss. Archit.* 1845), In which place we wol, that..be made a Towmbe of Stone called Touche, sufficient in largieur for us booth. *a* **1548** HALL *Chron.*, *Hen. VIII* 96 b, Gates all like Masonrie, of White and Blacke, like Touche and White Merbell. **1577** STANYHURST *Descr. Irel.* in *Holinshed* (1808) VI. 41 Such notable quarries of greie marble and touch. *c* **1625** BACON *Will* Wks. 1874 XIX. 541 Also the armour, and also all tables of marble and towch. *a* **1661** FULLER *Worthies, York* (1662) II. 186 Vulgar eyes confound the inlayings made of black Marble..with Touch, Geat, and Ebony. **1665** SIR T. HERBERT *Trav.* (1677) 143 Several parts of it were as bright and splendent as Touch or Steel-mirrour.

**7.** *fig.* (from 5). An act of, or thing that serves for, testing; a test, trial, proof; a criterion, 'touchstone'. Now chiefly in phr. *to put to the touch.*

**1581** MULCASTER *Positions* iii. (1887) 12, I will binde vpon proofe, and let triall be the tuche. **1594** SHAKS. *Rich. III*, IV. ii. 8 Ah Buckingham, now doe I play the Touch, To trie if thou be currant Gold indeed. **1624** QUARLES *Job* VII. med. xiii, Affliction is the Touch, whereby we proove, Whether 't be Gold, or guilt. **1688** R. HOLME *Armoury* III. 206/1 Verity is not ashamed of the Light, nor afraid to come to the touch. **1706** KENNETT *Compl. Hist. Eng.* III. 561/1 That when it came to the Touch, they wou'd never bear the Brunt of a Battle. **1886** STEVENSON *Kidnapped* 10 Till I had put the matter to the touch of proof.

** *In instrumental music.*

**8.** *Mus.* The act or manner of touching or handling a musical instrument, so as to bring out its tones; now *esp.* the manner of striking or pressing the keys of a keyboard instrument so as to produce special varieties of tone or effect. Hence *transf.* (chiefly *poet.*) a single sound produced by touching an instrument; a note or brief strain of instrumental music.

**13..** *Gaw. & Gr. Knt.* 120 Nwe nakryn noyse with þe noble pipes, Wylde werbles & wyȝt wakned lote, Þat mony hert ful hiȝe hef at her towches. **1591** SHAKS. *Two Gent.* III. ii. 79 Orpheus Lute,..Whose golden touch could soften steele and stones. **1596** — *Merch. V.* V. i. 67 With sweetest tutches pearce your Mistresse eare, And draw her home with musicke. **1628** MILTON *Vac. Exerc.* 38 Listening to what unshorn Apollo sings To th' touch of golden wires. **1667** — *P. L.* IV. 686 With Heav'nly touch of instrumental sounds. **1828** SCOTT *F. M. Perth* x, I hear no unpleasing touch of minstrelsy. **1879** A. J. HIPKINS in Grove *Dict. Mus.* I. 647 A sensitive instrument of touch, instead of one of mere percussion. **1884** F. TAYLOR *ibid.* IV. 152 Pianoforte music demands two distinct kinds of touch, the one adapted for..brilliant passages, the other for sustained melodies.

**b.** As an attribute of the performer: Capacity, skill, or style of playing; now esp. on a keyboard instrument, in relation to the action of the fingers upon the keys (see above).

**1601** ? MARSTON *Pasquil & Kath.* I. 15, I had the best stroke, the sweetest touch, but now..I am falne from the Fiddle. **1613** FLETCHER, etc. *Captain* I. iii, You had a pleasant touch o' th' cittern once, If idleness have not bereft you of it. *Mod.* He has a remarkably delicate touch, and excels in *pianissimo.*

**c.** As an attribute of a keyboard instrument, referring to the manner in which its keys and action respond to the touch of the player.

**1884** W. PARRATT in Grove *Dict. Mus.* IV. 153 It is rare to find any two [organ] manuals with a similar touch, and the amount of force required to press down the key varies within wide limits. Even on the same keyboard the touch is appreciably heavier in the bass. **1885** C. G. W. LOCK *Workshop Receipts* Ser. IV. 279/2 The next item, and one claiming serious attention, is the 'touch', for on this depends in a great measure the pleasure and comfort of the performer. **1906** *Edin. Rev.* Apr. 412 It has a flexibility, what musicians call a sense of touch. *Mod.* This piano (or organ) has a very stiff (or, a very light) touch.

†**d.** app. = TOCCATA. *Obs.*

*a* **1623** in Grove *Dict. Mus.* IV. 154 (*title of MS. in Brit. Mus.*) A touche by Mr. Byrd. *a* **1782** *Ibid.* (*title of MS. in Lib. Roy. Coll. Music*), Mr. Kelway's touches.

**9.** *Bell-ringing.* Any series of changes less than a peal.

**1872** ELLACOMBE *Ch. Bells Devon*, etc. ix. 471 A peal.. means the performance of the full number of changes which may be rung on a given number of bells; any less number of changes would be called 'a touch'. **1898** G. S. TYACK *Bk. about Bells* viii. 141 Five thousand changes..is the smallest number to which the name of a peal is technically allowed, less than that number merely constitutes a 'touch'.

*** *In artistic work.*

**10.** An act of touching a surface with the proper tool in painting, drawing, writing, carving, etc.; a stroke or dash of a brush, pencil, pen, chisel, or the like; hence, a stroke or dash of colour in a picture, etc., or a detail of any artistic work, as in literary description; a slight act or effort added in doing or completing a piece of work of any kind.

**1607** SHAKS. *Timon* I. i. 38 It [a picture] tutors Nature, Artificiall strife Liues in these toutches, liuelier then life. **1693** DRYDEN *Juvenal* Ded. (1697) 5 Some few Touches of your Lordship, some secret Graces which I have endeavour'd to express after your manner. **1712** ADDISON *Spect.* No. 357 ⁋ 8 Milton never fails of..bestowing the last finishing Touches to every Incident. **1768** W. GILPIN *Ess. Prints* 39 Unless the pencil add those high-blown touches, which mark the passion. **1847** L. HUNT *Men, Women, & B.* II. x. 212 She might be suspected of having given it some after touches. **1894** J. T. FOWLER *Adamnan* Introd. 74 Eddius's graphic touch about St. Wilfrid..some life-like touches in Colgan's *Vita Secunda.*

**b.** Capacity of using the brush, pencil, pen, or other instrument; artistic skill or faculty; style or quality of artistic work; method of handling, execution. (Cf. 8 b, 18.)

1815 J. SMITH *Panorama Sc. & Art* II. 748 Painting in crayons..may serve to teach him a masterly freedom of touch. 1880 WARREN *Book-plates* iv. 35 In Mountaine's early Chippendale style, and with that engraver's touch.

* * * * *In Magnetism.*

**11.** The action or process of magnetizing a steel bar or needle by contact with one or more magnets; different methods are known as *single, double*, and *separate touch*.

1705 DERHAM in *Phil. Trans.* XXV. 2143 This gave so vigorous a Touch, that I am almost of opinion, It is the best way of Touching. 1837 BREWSTER *Magnet.* 15 The science of magnetism is..indebted to Mr. Michell for his invention of the method of double touch. 1849 NOAD *Electricity* 308 Mr. Michell states that two magnets will, by his process of double touch, communicate as strong a magnetic virtue to a steel bar, as a single magnet of five times the strength, when used in the process of single touch.

* * * * * *In Football.*

**12.** The act (in the Rugby game) of touching the ground with the ball behind the goal, usually the opponents' goal (see TOUCH *v.* 30, also *touch-back, -down* s.v. TOUCH- 2); *transf.* (esp. in phr. *in* or *into touch*), that part of the ground outside the bounding lines of the field of play (*touch-lines* and *goal-lines*); *touch-in-goal*, that part of this behind the goal-line.

1864 *Field* 5 Nov. 331/1 The School..managed to keep the ball close to their opponents' goal, till at length a long drop of Poole's took the ball into touch-in-goal. *Ibid.* 19 Nov. 354/2 [see TOUCH *v.* 2 f]. 1877 *Ibid.* 24 Feb. 220/2 Clifton scored a touch in goal. 1886 *Ibid.* 9 Oct. 535/2 An easy victory..by eight goals, three tries, and six touches to one goal. 1889 H. VASSALL *Rugby Football* 18 Our full-back..should always bear in mind that he must send it [the ball] into touch at all costs, as that means so much ground gained for his side for the next line out. 1895 *Outing* (U.S.) XXVII. 250/1 The ball is thrown out from touch by the side that carried it in, or by the opposite team to that which kicked it in.

**III.** Various figurative senses. (See also 1 e, 2 e, 4 b, 5 d, 7.)

**13.** *fig.* The act of touching or fact of being touched (in *fig.* senses of the vb.). **a.** A stroke, action, or influence (esp. slight, or momentary); a slight or instantaneous act producing some effect.

*c* 1586 C'TESS PEMBROKE *Ps.* XC. i, Free From all touch of age and yeare. 1602 MARSTON *Ant. & Mel.* III. Wks. 1856 I. 35, I will..strike her thoughts with the pleasing touch of my voice. *c* 1742 GRAY *Ignorance* 21 With damp, cold touch forbid it [spark of wit] to aspire. 1780 BURKE *Sp. Econ. Reform* Wks. III. 261 That their ancient..castles should moulder into decay, under the silent touches of time. 1799 *Monthly Rev.* XXX. 490 The Cartesian hypothesis melted away under the touch of geometry. 1819 SCOTT *Leg. Montrose* xvi, Curing me, in respect that I had got a touch of the wars in my retreat. 1878 BROWNING *La Saisiaz* 329 Death's kindly touch..gave Soul and body both release. 1884 H. JAMES *Little Tour France* xxvii. 173 Vineyards red with the touch of October.

**b.** *spec.* An impression upon the mind or soul; a feeling, sense (*of* some emotion, etc.); †a feeling of interest or concern *in* something (cf. TOUCH *v.* 20, 21).

*c* 1586 C'TESS PEMBROKE *Ps.* CIII. viii, And looke how much The neerly touching touch The father feeles towards his sonne most deare. 1591 SHAKS. *Two Gent.* II. vii. 18 Didst thou but know the inly touch of Loue. 1690 C. NESSE *O. & N. Test.* I. 210 If the Holy Spirit doth not touch us with his divine touches, the unclean spirit will with his deadly touches. 1866 B. TAYLOR *Over Possession* Poems 270, I wait the touch of song. 1869 TOZER *Highl. Turkey* II. 232 One occurrence, or idea, or touch of feeling, is selected, and..seldom treated at any great length. 1873 BLACK *Pr. Thule* xii, Some touch of compunction smote him.

**c.** The condition of being mentally 'touched' or affected (TOUCH *v.* 23 b); slight derangement. *rare*⁻¹.

1710 STEELE *Tatler* No. 178 ⁋ 2 My Friend the Upholsterer, whose Crack towards Politicks I have heretofore mention'd. This Touch in the Brain of the British Subject is..owing to the reading News-Papers.

**d.** A close relation of communication, agreement, sympathy, or interest; chiefly in phr. *in* or *out of touch with*, also *to keep* or *lose touch with* (rarely *of*). [Perh. orig. in literal use, in military drill; cf. 1 d.]

1884 CHURCH *Bacon* vi. 153 The Kingship of the Tudors..always seeking..to be in touch and sympathy with popular feeling. 1884 *Pall Mall G.* 25 Jan. 4/2 Sir Henry Parkes has always kept himself in touch with English public opinion. 1884 *Christian World* 15 May 369/2 He had never lost touch with his brethren. 1887 A. FLEMING in *Libr. Mag.* 29 Jan. 325 To bring religion into touch with conduct. 1901 EARL SPENCER in *Parl. Deb.* 5 July 948 But they are not in touch..with all the best information which the Board of Admiralty have at their command.

**14.** (*fig.* from 3.) A faculty or capacity of the mind analogous or likened to the sense of touch; mental or moral perception or feeling.

1656 STANLEY *Hist. Philos.* IV. (1701) 134/1 They held that..those things only can be perceived which are felt by inward touch as grief and pleasure. 1872 LIDDON *Elem. Relig.* v. 179 An accuracy and delicacy of intellectual touch. 1904 H. BLACK *Pract. Self Cult.* vii. 168 You will develop tact, which is just the faculty of touch, fineness of sensation.

**15.** A stroke of action, an act; a brief turn or 'go' *at* some occupation; † in early use, a sly, mean, or deceitful act, a trick (*obs.*). Now *rare.*

1481 CAXTON *Reynard* xxv. (Arb.) 56 O what false touches can he, how can he stuffe the sleue wyth flockes. *a* 1521 J. HEYWOOD *Pard. & Friar* Plays (1905) 21 If thou play me such another touch I sh' knock thee on the costard. 1530 PALSGR. 640 It is no good felowes touche to stande mouching in a cornar. 1572 GASCOIGNE *Counc. to B. Withipoll* 7 Beleeue me now it is a friendly touch, To vse fewe words where friendship doth remaine. *a* 1591 H. SMITH *Wks.* (1867) II. 406 Mahomet..went and first took part with the Romans, but afterwards served them a sly touch, and forsook them. 1598 T. BASTARD *Chrestoleros* (1880) 36 Some will giue sixe pence for a witty touch, And some to see an Ape will giue as much. 1681 T. FLATMAN *Heraclitus Ridens* No. 37 (1713) I. 246 We'll have a Touch with him for it one of these Days. 1791 O'KEEFFE *Wild Oats* II. ii, I'll take a touch at the London theatre. 1833 HT. MARTINEAU *Loom & Lug.* II. i, She might not only clean her husband's loom in peace but have a touch at the old man's.

**16.** An act of touching upon or mentioning something; a mention, reference, allusion, slight notice, hint; a brief statement or narration. Now *rare* or *Obs.*

13.. *Gaw. & Gr. Knt.* 1301 Bot he had craued a cosse, bi his courtaysye, Bi sum towch of summe tryfle, at sum talez ende. 1460 CAPGRAVE *Chron.* Ded. (Rolls) 1 Whanne I loke upon hem, and have a schort touch of the writing, I can sone dilate the circumstaunses. 1600 O. E. *Repl. Libel* I. vii. 169 He passeth this ouer without touch, and onely telleth vs [etc.]. 1628 COKE *On Litt.* (1629) 289 Two ancient Records..whereof to my remembrance, I neuer read any touch in our Bookes. 1653 H. MORE *Antid. Ath.* II. ii. § 7 (1712) 43 First I shall recurr and give a touch upon the nature of gravity. 1685 BAXTER *Paraphr. N. T.* Mark xvi. 14 Mark doth but give us a brief touch of some of Christ's appearances, and leaves much, recorded by others. 1706 J. LOGAN in *Pa. Hist. Soc. Mem.* X. 120, I cannot think it becomes me when I write about thy business to give it by hints and touches. 1855 W. ARNOT *Let.* in Mrs. A. Fleming *Life* vi. (1877) 295, I can on short warning give you a little touch, with a moral in it like the two papers I have sent you.

†**b.** The fact or quality of touching, affecting, concerning, or relating to something; relation, reference, concern. *Obs. rare.*

1612 BACON *Ess., Discourse* (Arb.) 21 Speech of touch toward others, should bee sparingly vsed; for discourse ought to bee as a field, without comming home to any man. 1625 *Ibid., Anger* 566 Opinion of the Touch of a Mans Reputation, doth multiply and sharpen Anger.

†**17.** The quality or fact of affecting injuriously; reproach, blemish, stain, taint. *Obs.*

1567 Q. ELIZ. *Let. to Throgmorton* in Robertson *Hist. Scot.* (1759) II. App. 47 We..cannot but think them to have therein gone so far beyond the duty of subjects, as must needs remain to their perpetual touche for ever. *c* 1580 WALSINGHAM in Digges *Compl. Ambass.* (1655) 366 They did not see how their Monsieurs honour..could be salved, without great touch to both. 1588 *Copy of Let.* in *Harl. Misc.* (Malh.) II. 71 Reported, to the dishonour of the Duke of Medina..and to a great touch to the commanders of the Spanish navy. 1616 SIR R. DUDLEY in *Fortescue Papers* (Camden) 16 That I have lived these nine yeares abroade, without all tutche of disloyalty.

**18.** A distinguishing quality, characteristic, trait. (Cf. 5 d; but app. partly *fig.* from 10.) In later use often passing into 'trace': see next sense.

1539 TAVERNER *Erasm. Prov.* (1552) 38 It is theyr owne maners, theyr owne qualities, touches, condicions, & procedynges that shape them this fortune. 1603 B. JONSON *Sejanus* I. i, But he had other touches of late Romans, That more did speak him: Pompey's dignity, The innocence of Cato, Cæsar's spirit. 1606 SHAKS. *Tr. & Cr.* III. iii. 175 One touch of nature makes the whole world kin [=One natural trait proves the kinship of all mankind]: That all with one consent praise new borne gaudes. 1679 J. GOODMAN *Penit. Pard.* II. i. (1713) 144 As if men had forgone all touches of humanity and were become a kind of walking-ghosts. 1856 EMERSON *Eng. Traits, Ability* Wks. (Bohn) II. 35 You shall trace those Gothic touches at school, at country fairs, at the hustings, and in Parliament. 1897 H. NEWBOLT *Admirals All* 30 But cared greatly to serve God and the king, And keep the Nelson touch.

**19.** A slight amount or trace *of* some quality, attribute, or ingredient; 'a small quantity intermingled' (J.); a trace, spice, smack.

1594 SHAKS. *Rich. III*, IV. iv. 157 Madam, I haue a touch of your condition, That cannot brooke the accent of reproofe. 1643 J. M. *Soveraigne Salve* 21 Hath not even the Lord Chancellour a little touch of such a power? 1707 NORRIS *Treat. Humility* vi. 282 The bashful and blushing speaker must have a touch of vanity in his constitution. 1821 SCOTT *Kenilw.* vii, She hath in her a touch of her father Henry. 1835 LINDLEY *Introd. Bot.* (1839) 477 Grey with a touch of red.

**b.** *spec.* A slight affection or attack *of* illness or disease; a twinge. (Cf. 4.)

1662 J. DAVIES tr. *Olearius' Voy. Ambass.* 259 Monsieur Mandelslo was the onely person who had no touch of sicknesse all along our Travels. 1687 A. LOVELL tr. *Thevenot's Trav.* I. 260 Every one threatned me with that Distemper, and yet..I never had the least touch of it. 1791 'G. GAMBADO' *Ann. Horsem.* viii. (1809) 102, I have a touch of the gout in my knees. 1890 BESANT *Demoniac* ii, He said he had had a touch of sore throat.

**c.** Without *of*: A very little, a slight amount; in advb. const. = slightly, somewhat, 'a little bit'.

1786 BURNS *Twa Dogs* 81 Ye maist wad think, a wee touch langer, An' they maun starve o' cauld and hunger. 1827 SCOTT *Surg. Dau.* vii, Still this story..seems a touch even beyond Tom Hillary. 1868 FREEMAN in Stephens *Life & Lett.* (1895) I. 405, I really think that the Great Unpaid are a touch more sensible.

**20. a.** *slang* or *colloq.* An article or 'affair' that will touch or move purchasers to the extent of a certain price.

1712 SWIFT *Pref. to Burnet's Hist. Ref.* Wks. 1738 VI. 53, I desire you to print in such a form, as in the Bookseller's phrase will make a Sixpenny touch. 1720 SIR E. PHILIPPS *Diary* 22 Sept., At night went to the Ball at the Angel. A guinea touch. 1815 SCOTT *Let. to J. B. S. Morritt* 2 Oct., in *Lockhart*, I think..the Poems of David [Hume] would make a decent twelve-shilling touch. 1865 *Slang Dict., Touch*, a slang expression in common use in phrases which express the extent to which a person is interested or affected, as 'a fourpenny touch', i. e. costing that amount.

**b.** *slang.* An act of stealing or theft, esp. of pocket-picking; also, the act of getting money from a person; *transf.* a sum of money gained or got at once, esp. by theft. (Cf. TOUCH *v.* 15, 16 b.)

1888 'R. BOLDREWOOD' *Robbery under Arms* xliv, A thousand ounces of gold was no foolish touch. 1900 *Westm. Gaz.* 13 Dec. 12/2 Returns of pocket-picking. He estimates twenty-five dollars a 'touch' as a fair record if there is much money in the crowd, and five or six touches a day as a good average. 1912 *Nation* 7 Dec. 428/2 No two thefts are ever absolutely alike, and no 'touch' of any merit is brought off but with study and preparation.

**IV.** Concrete senses. (See also 2 c, 6, 10, 20.)

**21.** Short for TOUCH-POWDER, TOUCHWOOD, or the like. *Obs.* exc. *dial.*

1541–2 *Act* 33 *Hen. VIII*, c. 6 § 1 Little handguns, ready furnished with..Gunpouder, fyer, & touche. 1619 H. HUTTON *Follies Anat.* (Percy Soc.) 18 Where's your tobacco box, your steele and touch? 1649 G. DANIEL *Trinarch., Hen. IV* cclviii, The fangle which Fires the drye touch of Constitution. 1887 *Suppl. to Jamieson, Touch, touche*, short for *touch-wood*, but applied to amadou and other materials used as tinder: 'as sharp as touch', as quick [to 'fire up'] as touch-wood, quick-tempered.

†**22.** = TOUCH-PIECE 2. *Obs.*

1659 LEAK *Waterwks.* 26 When the Barrel turns the pins Q and R, they may make the said conveiances open..according to..the disposition of the Pins and Touches Q and R.

**23.** *Shipbuilding.* In a plank tapering both ways, the projecting angle at the broadest part (near one end if worked top-and-butt, in the middle if worked anchor-stock fashion); also, each of the angles of the stern-timbers at the counters.

1711 W. SUTHERLAND *Shipbuild. Assist.* 25 Set off the exact Length forward and aftward from the Observation of the rising of the Keel, by Shipwrights called the Touch, or Place where the Keel's upper Part ends to be streight. 1797 *Encycl. Brit.* (ed. 3) XVII. 392/1 On the pencil line set off the distance the touch of the lower counter is abaft the aft side of the wing transom. *c* 1850 *Rudim. Navig.* (Weale) 128 This work is the best when the touch or knuckle is at the planksheer.

**V.** Phrases.

†**24.** *To keep touch.* **a.** To keep covenant, keep faith, keep one's promise, or engagement, act faithfully. Also *to hold touch.* (? From the practice of striking hands, or of touching something sacred (cf. TOUCH *v.* 1, quot. 1491), in making a covenant.) So *to break touch. Obs.*

13.. *Gaw. & Gr. Knt.* 1677, I schal..halde þe towchez. *a* 1529 SKELTON *Mann. World* 90 Amonge them that are riche, No frendshyp is to kepe tuche. 1540–1 ELYOT *Image Gov.* (1556) 159 By kepyng his promise and touche. *c* 1557 ABP. PARKER *Ps.* lxxviii. 219 They kept not true tutch wyth God hys pact they overyed. 1594 *Death of Usurie* 4 If a shop-keeper lend mony..to his neighbour .., if he breake touch the shop-keeper may lawfully take so much as he sustained losse. 1663 BUTLER *Hud.* I. I. 847 Quoth Hudibras, Thou offer'st much, But art not able to keep touch. 1706 *Reflex. upon Ridicule* 47 To promise every body and keep touch with no body. 1825 LAMB *Elia* Ser. II. *Superannuated Man*, When the week came round did the glittering phantom..keep touch with me?

**b.** To keep up communication, keep in touch *with*: so *to lose touch*: see 13 d.

†**25.** *To flee touch*, to make off, to escape; also = *break touch* (see 24 a). *Obs.*

*c* 1530 *Hickscorner* B j b, A strype he gaue me, I fledde my touche, And frome my gyrdle he plucked my pouche. *a* 1569 KINGESMYLL *Man's Est.* x. (1580) 56 He was fain to flee touche and avoide from Bethlehem into Egypt. 1583 GOLDING *Calvin on Deut.* xxvi. 153 They were vnconstant and fled touch anon after.

†**26.** *True* (*good, sure*) *as touch*: perfectly or absolutely true, etc. (? from sense 5.) *Obs.*

1590 SPENSER *F. Q.* I. iii. 2 To thinke how she through guyleful handeling, Though true as touch,..Is from her knight divorced. 1620 SHELTON *Quix.* (1746) IV. x. 77 Of Sancho's Proceeding in his Government, with other Successes as good as Touch. *a* 1670 HACKET *Abp. Williams* I. (1692) 187 And that was sure as touch, because the House was to be past by Act of Parliament to the King's Majesty.

†**27.** *Rum touch*: an odd or queer fellow. *Obs. slang.*

1804 T. CREEVEY in *C. Papers*, etc. (1904) I. 22 To meet Brogden and Col. Porter, two cursed rum touches that he has persuaded to vote with him and to desert Fox. 1806 S. GRILDRIG *Miniature* (ed. 2) II. 9 The last whom I shall mention is an Odd Fellow, or according to the language of the day, 'a rum touch'. *Ibid.* 10 Whereas many young fellows ..have..attempted to sustain the character of a Rum Touch, and have..failed most miserably, notice is hereby given [etc.].

**28.** *In* or *out of touch with*: see 13 d. *In* or *within touch*: see 1 e. *To put to the touch*: see 7.

**VI.** Combinations: see TOUCH- in comb.

**Touch** (tʌtʃ), *v.* Forms: *α.* 3–6 **touche**, 3–7 **towche**, (4 **tuoche**), 4–6 **toche**, **tuche**, (**tuouche**), 4–7 **tuch**, 5–7 **towch**, (6 **twoche**, 6–7 **toutch**, **tutch(e**, 7 **towtch**), 6– **touch**. *β.* (chiefly *Sc.*) 4–6 **twech(e**, 5–6 **twich(e**, **twych**, **tuiche**, **tuech(e**, 5–7 **tuich**, 6 **tweich**, **tueiche**, **tuitch**, 6–7 **twitch**; 7–9 *dial.* **titch**. [ME. a. OFr. *tochier*, *tuchier* (11th c. in *Chanson Roland*), mod.F. *toucher* 'to touch' = ONF. *toquer*, Pr. *toquar*, *tocar*, *tochar*, Sp. and Pg. *tocar*, It. *toccare* 'to strike, to smite, to hit, to touch' (Florio), Roumanian *tocà* to knock.

The passage of the sense 'knock, strike' into that of 'touch' (in Fr., etc.), is like that of Eng. 'thrust, push' into 'put': a stroke at its lightest is a mere touch. The Romanic *toccare* has been held, after Diez, to be from an OLG. **tokkôn*, **tukken*, MLG. *tocken*, *tucken*, = OHG. *zocchôn*, *zucchen*, 'to draw or pull with force, pluck'; but a change of sense from 'pull' to 'knock' is inexplicable, and it is a more probable view that *toccare* was not from German, but an onomatopœic formation of the Romanic langs. from the syllable *toc* imitating a knock. *Tocken*, in its own sense 'draw', is still in use in LG. and in parts of Holland on the German frontier, but not in Dutch itself. But the South Netherlands (Flanders, Antwerp, etc.) use now, as in Kilian's time, a vb. *tokken* in the same sense as the *toquer*, *touker* of Old Northern French and its modern dialects, whence this has prob. been taken over. There is thus a gap in local continuity, as well as in sense, between the German and Romanic words. (Cf. Diez s.v. *Toccare*, Scheler s.v. *Toucher*, Körting 9802 *Tukkôn*; Gaston Paris in *Romania* XXVII. 626.)]

**I.** The simple verb. * *Physical senses.*

**1.** *trans.* To put the hand or finger, or some other part of the body, upon, or into contact with (something) so as to feel it; 'to exercise the sense of feeling upon' (Phillips, 1696). Also with the hand, etc., as subject of the verb.

Usually denoting a momentary and slight act: cf. TOUCH *sb.*

*c* **1300** *Beket* 2229 And ho miȝte him enes tuochi, he was glad ynouȝ. **13..** *Cursor M.* 24498 (Cott.) Þat i moght toche him hand and fote. **1382** WYCLIF *Ecclus.* xiii. 1 Who shal touche pich, shal be defoulid of it. **1382** — *Matt.* viii. 3 And Jhesus holdynge forthe the hond, touchide hym, sayinge, I wole, be thou maad clene. **1491** *Regr. Aberdon.* (Maitl. Cl.) I. 328 Þe parteis..ar oblist..be þe haly ewangell tuechet befor þir vytnes. **1526** TINDALE *John* xx. 17 Jesus sayde vnto her: touche me not. **1528** LYNDESAY *Dreme* 1088 All that he twychit, but delatioun, Turnit in gold. **1570** LEVINS *Manip.* 182/30 To Tutche, *tangere.* **1599** DAVIES *Immort. Soul* cxcvi, And in those fiue All things their Formes expresse, Which we can touch, tast, feele, or heare, or see. *a* **1657** SIR W. MURE *Misc. Poems* xi. 5 Hands, forbeare to tuich Oght ȝor tuiching can bewitch! **1764** REID *Inquiry* v. vi. 127 My two hands touch the extremities of a body. **1800** tr. *Lagrange's Chem.* I. 22 When I touch a warm body, the caloric passes from the body into my hand. **1847** KINGLAKE *Eothen* xvi, With tremulous boldness she touches—then grasps your hand.

*Constructions.* **b.** To touch (a thing) *with* the hand or other part, or *with* some instrument.

*c* **1375** *Cursor M.* 20759 (Fairf.) Ga to þa men..& touche ham he saide wiþ hit. **1598** SHAKS. *Merry W.* v. v. 88 With Triall-fire touch me his finger end. **1643**– [see TONGS 2 a]. **1667** MILTON *P. L.* IV. 811 Him thus intent Ithuriel with his Spear Touch'd lightly. **1704** POPE *Messiah* 6 O thou my voice inspire, Who touched Isaiah's hallow'd lips with fire. **1839** URE *Dict. Arts* 582 (Glass-making) The ..workman..touching its tubular neck with an iron chisel dipped in cold water. **1847** KINGLAKE *Eothen* xviii, She has touched the poor Levantine with the hem of her sleeve.

**c.** To touch (the hand or other part, or something held) *to* (†*till*) something, = to bring it into contact with something; with *pl. obj.* to bring (two things) into mutual contact.

*a* **1300** *Cursor M.* 21549 (Cott.) Þe thred [third cross] þai toched til his hide, And up he ras wit-vten bide. *c* **1460** *Play Sacram.* 775 And towche thyn hand to thy saluacon. **1715** PRIOR *Down-Hall* 173 Now let us touch thumbs, and be friends ere we part. **1760–72** H. BROOKE *Fool of Qual.* (1809) IV. 141 He then touched his white wand to the neck of his steed. **1897** *Outing* (U.S.) XXX. 378/2 Touch a match to it, and you will presently have a fire.

**d.** *absol.* or *intr.* (in general sense).

**1388** WYCLIF *Isa.* lix. 10 We as with outen iȝen touchiden. *a* **1648** DIGBY *Chym. Secr.* II. (1682) 232 Dip a Straw or Feather in it, and touch all round about the borders of the Sore with it. *a* **1897** G. MEREDITH *Marian* i, She can talk the talk of men, And touch with thrilling fingers.

**2.** Specific applications of sense 1.

**a.** To have sexual contact with. *trans.*, or (obs.) *intr.* with *to* (*till*). *Obs.* exc. as merged in 12.

**13..** *Cursor M.* 10877 (Gött.) Þe womman þat neuer touchid man, How sal scho conceyue? tel me þan. *Ibid.* 11139 (Cott.) Als quen he fand wit barn his wijf, Þat he neuer had toched till. *c* **1375** *Ibid.* 2422 (Fairf.) Þat muȝt na mon of lecchery hir body touche wiþ velany. **1512** *Helyas* in Thoms *Prose Rom.* (1828) III. 40 Your noble person hath touched often times to hers after the constitucion of the sacrament of mariage. **1762** BRYDGES *Burlesque Homer* (1772) 361 May I for cats and dogs turn butcher, If ever yet she'd let me touch her.

**b.** To lay the hand upon (a diseased person) for the cure of the 'king's evil' or scrofula, as formerly practised by French and English sovereigns. Also *absol.*

**1606** J. MELVILL *Diary* (Wodrow Soc.) 657 The Royall ceremonie of tuiching of some diseased childrein for hailling off sume of the escrolles. **1660** EVELYN *Diary* 6 July, His Majestie began first to touch for the evil, according to costome. **1705** *Lond. Gaz.* No. 4126/3 All Persons who shall..apply to be Touched, shall bring a Certificate. **1716** HEARNE *Collect.* (O.H.S.) V. 359 He said the King touched many for yᵉ Evil..and that they recovered. **1791** BOSWELL *Johnson* (1906) I. 17 His mother..carried him to London, where he was actually touched by Queen Anne. **1880** DIXON *Windsor* IV. xxxi. 298 The King began to touch for scrofula.

**c.** *Sc. Hist.* referring to the touching of an Act of Parliament with the sceptre in token of the royal assent.

**1694** FOUNTAINHALL in M. P. Brown *Suppl. Decis.* (1826) IV. 179 This act was not touched; and so the Lords thought they could not supply the royal assent, nor make it an act. **1855** MACAULAY *Hist. Eng.* xviii. IV. 186 He [William] had ..suffered the law which abolished patronage to be touched with his sceptre. **1907** A. LANG *Hist. Scot.* IV. i. 3 Of the Acts passed by the Estates at this time, hardly one was 'touched' with the sceptre by the Commissioner. *Ibid.* ii. 29 He was to 'touch' and pass the Acts of 1689 for restoring Presbyterian preachers.

**d.** *Med.* To examine by touch or feeling: see TOUCH *sb.* 1 c. Also *absol.*

**1734** E. HODY *W. Giffard's Cases Midwif.* lxxxi. 192, I thought it proper to touch her. **1754–64** SMELLIE *Midwif.* III. 424 Upon touching I found the os uteri a little more dilated.

**e.** To bring by touching *into* some condition.

**1813** MONTGOMERY *World bef. Flood* II. 207 Time had but touch'd her form to finer grace. **1892** TENNYSON *Making of Man* 4 Shall not æon after æon pass and touch him into shape?

**f.** *Football*: = Touch down: see 30.

**1864** *Field* 19 Nov. 354/2 When the ball is touched inside goal-line, must it be touched down dead? that is, is it fair touch if the ball move or roll afterwards? **1877** *Ibid.* 24 Feb. 220/1 Hutchinson..safely touched the ball behind the home team's line.

**g.** *absol.* or *intr.* Of soldiers in the rank: To close up until the elbows are in contact.

**1803** DICKINSON *Instr. Infantry* 79 The leading man of the Front Rank..marks Time, the Rest wheel up to him, dressing by the Left, and touching lightly to the Right. **1877** *Man. Field Artillery Exerc.* 26 During the wheel, each man must touch lightly..towards the pivot flank.

**h.** *intr.* for *pass.* (with descriptive extension): To 'feel' to the touch; to cause a specified sensation when touched.

**1770–4** A. HUNTER *Georg. Ess.* (1803) IV. 575 We say this beast touches nicely upon its ribs. **1885** JEFFERIES *Open Air* (1890) 104 They touch rough—dusty rough, as books touch that have been lying unused.

**3.** *trans.* To come into, or be in, contact with. (Expressing an involuntary act or state of a person or part of the body, or of an inanimate thing.)

*c* **1330** R. BRUNNE *Chron.* (1810) 190 He smote him in þe helm, bakward he bare his stroupe. Þe body he did ouerwhelm, his hede touched þe croupe. **1382** WYCLIF *Numb.* xxxi. 19 Who sleeth a man, or a man sleyn touchith. **1398** TREVISA *Barth. De P. R.* XVI. vii. (Bodl. MS.), Quike siluer ..cleueþ nouȝt to þinge þat it toucheþ. **1506** GUYLFORDE *Pilgr.* (Camden) 65 If the galye had ones towched the rok, we had ben all perysshed. **1653** H. COGAN tr. *Pinto's Trav.* iv. 10 The ends of their sailyards, whereof some were so long that they touched even the very water. **1771** LUCKOMBE *Hist. Print.* 385 Its touching the letters underneath may be prevented. **1860** TYNDALL *Glac.* I. viii. 263 Loose shingle..falls upon the ice where it touches the rocks.

**b.** *intr.* or *absol.*: usually of two things, in reciprocal sense.

**1615** W. LAWSON *Country Housew. Gard.* (1626) 23 That no tree..drop vpon, or touch his fellowes...If they touch, the winde will cause a forcible rub. **1821** SHELLEY *Epipsych.* 578 Those spheres..Touch, mingle, are transfigured. **1832** TENNYSON *Dream Fair Wom.* 116 The bright death quiver'd at the victim's throat; Touch'd; and I knew no more. **1842** — *Talking Oak* 131 So fleetly did she stir, The flower, she touch'd on, dipt and rose. *Mod.* Place them close together, but do not let them touch.

**4.** *trans.* To be in contact with, or immediately adjacent to; to adjoin, border on; to skirt.

*c* **1391** CHAUCER *Astrol.* II. § 5 Waite wel wher as thin Almury towcheth the bordure, & set ther a prikke of ynke. **1630** *R. Johnson's Kingd. & Commw.* 361 This State, touching the Apenine mountaines on the South, and the Adriatike Sea upon the North. **1865** DICKENS *Mut. Fr.* III. viii, A part of the road where it touched the river. **1896** BADEN-POWELL *Matabele Campaign* x, The Transvaal border touches ours near Tuli.

**b.** *intr.* †To be contiguous *to* (obs.); *fig.* to have mutual contact; (with *upon*) to succeed continuously.

*c* **1400** MAUNDEV. (1839) vii. 80 The vale of Josaphathe, þat touchethe to the walles, as thoughe it were a large dyche. **1669** FLAVEL *Husb. Spir.* III. iii. (1674) 211 There are several particulars in which this .. design..and the pains of Husbandmen..do meet and touch. **1794** PALEY *Evid.* I. ix. § 4 (1817) 238 A series of writers touching upon one another.

**c.** *Geom.* (*trans.*) Of a line (straight or curved) or a surface: To meet (another line or surface) at a point so that when produced it does not (ordinarily) intersect or 'cut' it at that point; to be tangent to. Also *absol.* or *intr.* in reciprocal sense.

(A straight line may exceptionally both *touch* and *cut* a curve or curved surface at the same point, viz. at a point of inflexion, where the curvature changes from convex to concave or *vice versa.* In some cases also two surfaces (e. g. a cylinder and a plane, or two cylinders) may touch *along a line* instead of at a single point. See TANGENT A. 1, B. 1 b.)

**1570** BILLINGSLEY *Euclid* III. def. ii. 81 A right line is sayd to touch a circle, which touching the circle and being produced cutteth it not. **1840** LARDNER *Geom.* 52 The straight line joining the centres of circles which touch externally, must pass through their point of contact. **1885** EAGLES *Constr. Geom. Plane Curves* 136 To describe an ellipse to touch five given lines. **1885** LEUDESDORF *Cremona's Proj. Geom.* 147 An infinite number of conics can be drawn to touch a given straight line at a given point, and to touch two other given straight lines.

**5.** To strike or hit lightly (esp. with the spur, or in *Fencing*); in quot. *c* 1550, to hit, beat.

*a* **1330** *Otuel* 84 Wiþ þat word þe kinges a non Touchede here stedes & made hem gon. *c* **1550** R. WEVER *Lusty Juventus* D iij b, If thou tel not truth, I wil not be behind, To touch you as wel agayne. **1596** DALRYMPLE tr. *Leslie's Hist. Scot.* IX. (S.T.S.) II. 181 As a noble horss tuechte with the spur is mair quik. **1809** ROLAND *Fencing* 124 At no time should you endeavour to touch your adversary while thrusting carte and tierce. **1831** SCOTT *Ct. Robt.* iii, Achilles ..touched the door with a rap, distinct at once and modest.

**6.** To affect physically in some way by contact. **a.** To make an impression upon; to stain, scratch, abrade, corrode, decompose, etc.

*Touched with the tar-brush* (fig.): see TAR-BRUSH b.

*c* **1440** *Gesta Rom.* xii. 40 (Harl. MS.) If ȝe hadde on your cloke, the reyne shuld not haue y-towchid your clothing. **1677** MOXON *Mech. Exerc.* i. 3 So hard that a File will not touch it (as Smiths say when a File will not cut or race it). **1725** *Bradley's Fam. Dict.* s. v. *Silver*, The Aqua Regalis, which dissolves Gold, will not touch Silver. **1881** YOUNG *Every Man his own Mechanic* § 1438 No file or cutting tool will 'touch' it.

†**b.** *intr.* with *upon*, in same sense. *Obs.*

*a* **1626** BACON *Phys. Rem.* Wks. 1879 I. 245/1 For dissolution into liquor, we are to inquire..what will touch upon the one [metal] and not upon the other.

**c.** *trans.* To magnetize by contact or rubbing with a magnet. ? *Obs.* (Cf. TOUCH *sb.* 11.)

**1627** CAPT. SMITH *Seaman's Gram.* ii. 12 The darke Compasse hath the points blacke and white, and the other onely touched for the true North and South. **1698** BALLARD in *Phil. Trans.* XX. 418, I took my Knife, which had been formerly toucht..and profering it to the Needle, it drew the North Pole. **1706** E. WARD *Wooden World Diss.* (1708) 13 The Loadstone,..tho' never so well touch'd, will often point from its true Pole. **1769** FALCONER *Dict. Marine* (1789), *Toucher un compas*, to touch the needle of a compass with a magnet. **1795** HUTTON *Math. Dict.* s. v. *Magnet*, This vertical way of touching a bar will not give it quite so much of the magnetic virtue.

**d.** To apply some substance lightly to (a part of the body, etc.) by contact, esp. for medicinal purposes (const. *with* the substance); *spec.* (*Med.*) *to touch the gums*, to induce salivation, as by the use of mercury.

**1602** SHAKS. *Ham.* IV. vii. 147 Ile touch my point, With this contagion, that if I gall him slightly, It may be death. **1843** R. J. GRAVES *Syst. Clin. Med.* xxvi. 332 The raw surface itself..touched with zinc ointment. **1893** W. R. GOWERS *Man. Dis. Nerv. Syst.* (ed. 2) II. 358 The patient should be brought slightly..under its [i. e. mercury's] influence, so as just 'to touch the gums' as the phrase is.

**7.** To affect injuriously in some physical way (e. g. by fire or frost), esp. in a slight degree; to communicate disease to by contagion, to infect, taint; also *spec.* in reference to a horse's 'wind' or breathing. (Usually in *pa. pple.*)

**1595** SHAKS. *John* v. vii. 2 It is too late, the life of all his blood Is touch'd corruptibly. **1601** W. LEIGH *Soules Solace* (1617) 7 When..he [Job] was toucht in his own person, so as his bone claue to his flesh. **1681** *Lond. Gaz.* No. 1584/4 Lost.., A bright Bay Gelding,..all his Paces,..his Wind touch'd. **1772** R. GRAVES *Spir. Quix.* (1820) I. 82 A horse which was touched in the wind. **1794** MRS. RADCLIFFE *Myst. Udolpho* xxviii, An icy coldness touched her cheeks, and her fears for awhile overcame her judgment. **1884** ROE *Nat. Ser. Story* ii, The plants that were touched with frost.

**8.** To test the fineness of (gold or silver) by rubbing it upon a touchstone (see TOUCHSTONE 1); †*fig.* to test, try, make trial or proof of (*obs.*).

*a* **1548** HALL *Chron., Hen. VIII* 193 There the crounes were wayed and touched. **1595** SHAKS. *John* III. i. 100 A counterfeit Resembling Maiesty, which being touch'd and tride, Proues valuelesse. **1607** — *Timon* III. iii. 6 They haue all bin touch'd, and found Base-Mettle. **1745** P. THOMAS *Jrnl. Anson's Voy.* 136 They..then carry [the bars of Silver] to be touch'd and mark'd. **1908** H. B. MORSE *Trade Chinese Emp.* 160 It is then 'touched' and the difference..from a certain standard, as indicated by the colour on the touchstone, is written on the other side.

**b.** To mark (metal) as of standard purity, etc., with an official stamp, after it has been tested.

**1423** *Rolls of Parlt.* IV. 257/1 That no..Man that werketh Selver Hernois, put noon therof to the sale..or [=ere] that it be touched wyth the touche of the Liberdisheed, that that may resonabli bere the touche. **1697** *View Penal Laws* 142 None shall put to sale any Silver Harness in London before it is touched. **1746–7** in Welch *Hist. Pewterers' Co.* (1902) II. 193 That all..wares capable of a large Touch shall be touched with a large Touch. **1772–3** *Act 13 Geo. III*, c. 52 § 6, I will touch no silver but what shall be of the goodness of and according to the standard of this kingdom. **1852** A. RYLAND *Assay Gold & S.* 72 The silversmiths..were under great difficulties..for want of assayers in convenient places to assay and touch their plate.

**c.** *intr.* for *pass.* To appear or prove to be of standard fineness on testing; to undergo or stand the test. *lit.* and *fig.* ? *Obs.*

**1618** FLETCHER *Loyal Subject* I. v, And now you are brought to th' test; touch right now, soldier, Now shew the manly pureness of thy mettle. **1701** COLLIER *M. Aurel.* 31 His honesty is right sterling, and touches as well as it looks. **1705** tr. *Bosman's Guinea* 81 These Lumps or Pieces are called Mountain-Gold; which being melted, touch better than Dust-Gold.

**9.** *trans.* To strike the strings, keys, etc. of (a musical instrument) so as to make it sound; to play on, esp. to play a few notes on; to sound (a horn, a bell). [Cf. Fr. *toucher la lyre*, Sp. *tocar la lira.*] †Also *intr.* with *on* (quot. *c* 1470).

*c* **1470** HENRYSON *Orpheus & Eurydice* 611 Than Orpheus our ressoun is full wo, And twichis on his harp. **1484** CAXTON *Fables of Æsop* VI. vii, A fyssher .. somtyme touched his bagpype nyhe the Ryuer for to make the fysshe to daunce. **1580** LYLY *Euphues* (Arb.) 473 Instruments sound sweetest when they be touched softest. **1633** MASSINGER *Guardian* II. iv, I'll touch my horn (Severino blows his horn): they know my call. **1697** DRYDEN *Alex. Feast* 22 Timotheus.. With flying fingers touched the lyre. **1779** *Mirror* No. 43 ¶ 6 The organ was touched with a hand less firm. **1818** PEACOCK *Melincourt* xxi, Touch the bell for the waiter. **1830** SIR J. BARRINGTON *Pers. Sk. own Times* (ed. 2) II. 164, I recollect Moore one night..touching the piano-forte in his own unique way. **1888** BURGON *Lives 12 Gd. Men* II. ix. 214 Having touched the piano, [he] was requested to sing.

**b.** *transf.* To produce (musical sounds) by 'touching' an instrument; to play (an air).

**1823** SCOTT *Peveril* xxx, A person in the royal retinue touched a light and lively air on the flageolet. **1848** THACKERAY *Van. Fair* lix, Touching, to the best of her simple art, melancholy harmonies on the keys. **1848** DICKENS *Dombey* xviii, Her low voice in the twilight, slowly and stopping sometimes, touched the old air to which he had so often listened.

**10.** In drawing, painting, etc.: To mark, draw, delineate (a detail of the work) by touching the surface with the pencil, brush, etc.; also, to modify or alter by such touches. Hence *transf.* in literary composition. (See also *touch in*, 31, *touch up*, 34.)

**1675** A. BROWNE *App. Art of Limning* 10 The next you touch the Tips of the Ears with the forementioned Temperature. **1709** POPE *Ess. Crit.* 22 The lines, tho' touch'd but faintly, are drawn right. **1780** COWPER *Let.* 2 July, To touch and retouch is .. the secret of almost all good writing especially in verse. **1890** *N. & Q.* 7th Ser. X. 118/2 My impression [of the engraving] is unequal, being faint in some parts, very dark in others. If the plate was worn, it has been 'touched' afterwards.

†**b.** *intr.* with *upon*: To add touches to, modify by touching, touch up. *Obs.*

**1675** BENTLEY in *Dryden's Mistaken Husb.* To Rdr., If a great Master have but touch'd upon an ordinary Piece, he makes it of Value. **1762–71** H. WALPOLE *Vertue's Anecd. Paint.* (1786) III. 219 A French painter who was suffered to alter and touch upon his pictures.

**c.** *fig.* (*trans.*) To mark slightly or superficially *with* some colour or aspect: chiefly in *pa. pple.* Also said of the colour, etc.

*c* **1600** SHAKS. *Sonn.* xvii, Such heauenly touches nere toucht earthly faces. **1829** SCOTT *Anne of G.* xiii, The dawn had scarce begun to touch the distant horizon. **1847** L. HUNT *Jar Honey* xii. (1848) 158 The rock on the woody promontory .. is touched with rose-colour. **1883** F. M. PEARD *Contrad.* xix, A faint smile touched her lips as she wondered.

**11.** *intr.* Of a ship, or those on board: To arrive and make a short stay in passing at a port or place on the way; to call in passing. Also *transf.* (of a traveller), and *fig.* Usually with *at*.

**1517** TORKINGTON *Pilgr.* (1884) 16 Many Shippys and galyes towche ther rather thanne at Parence. **1582** N. LICHEFIELD tr. *Castanheda's Conq. E. Ind.* I. xlii. 96 That in his way he should touch at the Ilande of S. Blaze. **1697** DRYDEN *Æneid* VII. 29 Lest the Trojan's pious host Should bear, or touch upon th' inchanted coast. **1725** DE FOE *Voy. round World* (1840) 58 Whenever any ship touched at that port. **1745** P. THOMAS *Jrnl. Anson's Voy.* 59 For the Ships who frequently touch here. **1828** DUPPA *Trav. Italy*, etc. 206 We touched at Panaria..on account of its warm baths of which there are numerous vestiges. **1870** KINGSLEY in *Gd. Words* 203/1 Our own mail steamers..could as easily touch at Terceira now, as they did a few years since.

**b.** *trans.* with the port or place as obj.: To land upon; to visit in passing; also *transf.* and *fig.*

**1593** SHAKS. *Rich. II*, II. i. 288 All these..With eight tall ships..meane to touch our Northerne shore. **1632** J. HAYWARD tr. *Biondi's Eromena* 7 Supposing that they could not touch land in Sardegna. **1774** JOHNSON *Let. to Boswell* 26 Nov., Shall we touch the continent? **1850** TENNYSON *In Mem.* xiv. 2 If one should bring me this report, That thou hadst touch'd the land to-day.

** *Physical, passing into non-physical.*

**12.** To handle or have to do with in any or the slightest degree; to meddle or interfere with however slightly; to 'lay a finger on'. (Usually with negative expressed or implied.)

**1377** LANGL. *P. Pl.* B. XVIII. 192 Þat Adam & Eue..Shulde deye doune riȝte..If þat þei touched a tre, and þe fruite eten. *c* **1400** *Destr. Troy* 1337 All loste þe lyfe þat þe lede touchet. **1591** SPENSER *M. Hubberd* 702 He so light was at legierdemaine, That what he toucht came not to light againe. **1655** FULLER *Ch. Hist.* I. ii. § 1 Being conscientiously scrupulous, not to take or touch a thread which is none of our own. **1711** HEARNE *Collect.* (O.H.S.) III. 103 Five hundred Pounds..wch he said he never did or would touch. **1886** RUSKIN *Præterita* I. xi. 345, I had never touched a card.

**b.** *spec.* To lay hands on or meddle with so as to harm; to injure, hurt, in any or the least degree.

**1297** R. GLOUC. (Rolls) 10369 In þe popes half he sede, ich uorbede..Þat no man ne touchi þulke clerc. *c* **1400** MAUNDEV. (1839) ix. 76 The Soudan hath do make a wall aboute the sepulcre, þat noman may towche it. **1596** SHAKS. *1 Hen. IV*, II. iv. 300 The Lion will not touch the true Prince. **1716** HEARNE *Collect.* V. 271 He stood [in the Pillory]..on Wednesday, and was not touch'd; but yesterday ..he was pelted miserably. **1812** LD. WELLINGTON in *Examiner* 23 Nov. 742/2 No officer was touched. **1836** J. GILBERT *Chr. Atonem.* vii. (1852) 204 The hand of violence must not touch them. **1888** *Times* (weekly ed.) 21 Dec. 4/2 Enemy in full retreat...No English officers touched.

**c.** To take (food or drink); to 'taste': usually (with negative), not to take any at all. (Cf. L. *tangĕre* to touch, in this sense.)

*c* **1400** *Destr. Troy* 466 That euyn full was þat fre and no fode touchet. *c* **1450** *St. Cuthbert* (Surtees) 3346 Þe forsaide gose þai touched noȝt. **1600** SHAKS. *A. Y. L.* II. vii. 98 He dies that touches any of this fruite, Till I, and my affaires are answered. **1766** GOLDSM. *Vic. W.* xxi, If a spoonful of liquor were to cure me of a fever, I never touch a drop. **1886** W. J. TUCKER *E. Europe* 191, I could not touch another drop, unless more of the gentlemen join me.

†**d.** *intr.* with *with*, *at*, *on*: To meddle with, have to do with (slightly or at all); to deal with cursorily (quot. 1693); to come into contact with.

*a* **1656** BP. HALL *Revelation Unrev.* viii, That they ever offered to touch with any either secular or sacred business, we never find. **1693** LOCKE *Educ.* § 175 Studies which a Gentleman should not barely touch at, but constantly dwell upon. **1697** COLLIER *Ess. Mor. Subj.* II. (1709) 29 He will never touch at a great Proposal; nor run any generous Hazards for his Friends or Country. **1701** *Col. Rec. Pennsylv.* II. 63 But they refused to touch with it unless it was intirely surrendered to ym [them]. **1746–7** HERVEY *Medit.* (1818) 214 Our purity is of so delicate a complexion, that it scarce touches on the world without contracting a stain.

**13.** *trans.* To get or go as far as; to reach, attain (*lit.* and *fig.*).

*c* **1384** CHAUCER *H. Fame* III. 285 And with hir hed she touched hevene. **1613** SHAKS. *Hen. VIII*, III. ii. 223, I haue touch'd the highest point of all my Greatnesse. **1713** STEELE *Guard.* No. 82 ¶ 1 Mr. William Peer [an actor] distinguished himself particularly in two characters, which no man ever could touch but himself. **1842** TENNYSON *Vis. Sin* 23 The music touch'd the gates and died. **1864** — *En. Ard.* 57 Ere he touch'd his one-and-twentieth May. **1883** *Manch. Exam.* 3 Dec. 4/1 The price, after touching 88, fell back on French sales to 86.

**b.** *fig.* To attain equality with, 'come up to', rival, compare with. *colloq.*

**1838** DICKENS *O. Twist* xliii, Is there one of you that could touch him or come near him on any scent? **1902** VIOLET JACOB *Sheep-Stealers* viii, I thought there was nothing that could touch that mare of mine.

†**c.** *intr.* with *to*, in same sense. *Obs.*

**1450–1530** *Myrr. our Ladye* 198 Tyl there were rysen a starre..that myght with hys heate touche to the heate of the sonne.

**14.** *intr.* with *at*, *to*, *on*, *upon* (also *absol.*): To approach closely, draw very near; to verge upon; † in quot. 1615, to resemble closely (*obs.*).

**1451** CAPGRAVE *Life St. Gilbert* 75 Thus seknes growyng, and age of an hundred ȝere touching, he was in party compelled for to passe fro þis lif. **1615** CHAPMAN *Odyss.* I. 326 Thy forehead and fair eyes at his form touch. **1791** BURKE *App. Whigs* Wks. VI. 116 During the course of a political life just touching to its close. **1801** *Lusignan* IV. 224 Brother Ambrose touches at that dreadful hour, which delivers us to the sentence of an incorruptible judge! **1819** LADY MORGAN *Autobiog.* (1859) 315 He sometimes touched on the very verge of meanness. **1832** LYTTON *Eugene A.* IV. iii, At length the time touched upon dinner.

**b.** *Naut.* (*trans.*) To keep as close to (the wind) as the vessel will sail. Also *absol.*

**1568** *Satir. Poems Reform.* xlvi. 54 Syne treveiss still, and lay abowt, And gar hir top twiche wind and waw. **1627** CAPT. SMITH *Seaman's Gram.* ix. 37 Touch the wind, and warre no more, is..to bid him at the Helme to keepe her so neere the wind as may be. **1692** *Ibid.* I. xvi. 76 In keeping the Ship near the Wind, these terms are used,.. *Veer no more,..touch the Wind.* *c* **1860** H. STUART *Seaman's Catech.* 85 Keep your eye on the weather leech of the sails, and just keep them touching.

**15.** *trans.* To take in the hand, take, receive, draw (money) [cf. F. *toucher de l'argent* (16th c. in Littré)]; sometimes, to get by underhand means; hence (*Thieves' cant*), to steal. Also *absol.* Now chiefly *slang* or *colloq.*

**1654** in *Nicholas Papers* (Camden) II. 153 He will give you a good account of Mr. Lovell and that he hath touched ..over £1000 sterling to his owne use. **1691** WOOD *Ath. Oxon.* I. *Fasti* 859 Out of which, he had, I think, 1000l., which, with 200l. more, was all he touched in the said 19 years. **1720** SWIFT *Elegy on Demar* 27 He touch'd the pence when others touch'd the pot. **1758** SMOLLETT *Hist. Eng.* III. II. vii. 82 For secret service money during the last ten years the Earl of Orford had touched £1,453,400 of public money. **1833** MARRYAT *P. Simple* xxxii, I proved the [will]..at Doctors' Commons, and touched the whole of her money. **1855** THACKERAY *Newcomes* xxxi, The..matrimonial arrangement is concluded (the agent touching his percentage). [**1898** BODLEY *France* II. III. v. 238 The average annual ministerial salaries touched by French legislators.]

**16.** To fee, 'tip', bribe, tamper with. ? *Obs.*

**1752** FIELDING *Amelia* XI. iv, He had heard that the great man must be touched; for he never did anything without touching. **1754** J. SHEBBEARE *Matrimony* (1766) I. 95 Mr. N——..having 'scaped the Servants..without touching one of them. **1770** FOOTE *Lame Lover* III. Wks. 1799 II. 84 The court may proceed...But..I hope no gentleman has been touch'd on both sides.

**b.** To 'come down upon', 'get at', or 'tap' (a person) *for* money, to succeed in getting money from (*colloq.*); also, to rob (*thieves' cant*); in *Australian slang*, to swindle, cheat.

**1760** C. JOHNSTON *Chrysal* (1822) II. 43, I am quite broke up; his grace has touched me for five hundred. **1809** E. S. BARRETT *Setting Sun* III. 105 If you could get me a commission, I could touch Dad for a few hundreds. **1898** *Tit-Bits* 21 May 139/3 Well, old boy, I've just touched Reggy for another tenner. **1898** *Westm. Gaz.* 14 Nov. 8/1 L.'s going to touch the public to a pretty tune for this.

**c.** To lay hold upon, to arrest.

**1791** O'KEEFFE *Wild Oats* II. i, Knock [at his door], and when he comes out touch him.

*** *Non-physical senses.*

**17.** *trans.* To apprehend, succeed in getting at, 'hit', hit upon; to guess or state correctly. ? *Obs.*

*c* **1325** in *Rel. Ant.* I. 292 Thu tuchest nowt the notes [in singing], thu bites hem on sonder. **13..** *Cursor M.* 18940 (Cott.) Als gaf to þaim þe haligast Alkin wiit to tuche and tast. **1606** SHAKS. *Tr. & Cr.* II. ii. 194 There you toucht the life of our designe. **1715** DE FOE *Fam. Instruct.* I. iii. (1841) I. 58 O you have touched it! there it lies. **1797** HT. LEE *Canterb. T.*, *Old Wom. T.* (1799) I. 380 He had at length, then, touched the point of truth.

†**b.** *intr.* with *at*: To succeed in hearing, to 'catch'. *Obs.*

*c* **1611** CHAPMAN *Iliad* XIX. 77 Hard it is, in such a great concourse (Though hearers' ears be ne'er so sharp) to touch at all things spoke.

**18.** *trans.* To speak or write of, treat of, mention, tell, relate; now always, to mention briefly, casually, or in passing; to refer to, allude to. Now *rare* or *arch.*

**13..** *E. E. Allit. P.* B. 1437 Þenne towched to þe tresour [= treasurer] þis tale watz sone. **1380** *Lay Folks Catech.* (Lamb. MS.) 266 The secunde part of þis Crede..towchis xiiij artyculis. *c* **1440** *Gesta Rom.* i. 1 (Harl. MS.) And shortly for to touche þis mater; he tooke his leve. **1585** T. WASHINGTON tr. *Nicholay's Voy.* III. xi. 91 b, I will not forgette to touch the manner of the apparrell. **1669** STURMY *Mariner's Mag.* V. xii. 67, I shall come to touch how to make a good Shot. *a* **1704** T. BROWN *Sat. agst. Wom.* 120 Nor shall I touch their secret murders. **1895** GLADSTONE *Psalter* 170 Subjects specially touched in particular passages of the Psalms. *a* **1903** 'H. S. MERRIMAN' *Last Hope* v, She gave a curt laugh, as if he had touched a topic upon which they would disagree.

**b.** *intr.*, usually with †*of*, †*at* (obs.), *on*, *upon*, in same sense. Now the more usual construction.

*c* **1320** *Cast. Love* 1309 Sumwhat touchen Ichulle fonde Of þat Ich may vnderstonde. *c* **1400** MAUNDEV. (1839) xxx. 303 The roundenesse of the erthe, of the whiche I haue towched to ȝou of before. **1549** [see 26]. **1573** L. LLOYD *Marrow of Hist.* (1653) 39 To omit..to touch any more of women. **1610** HEALEY *St. Aug. Citie of God* 139, I thought good to touch at this Asian luxurie. **1638** R. BAKER tr. *Balzac's Lett.* (vol. II) 39 One cannot touch upon any point where he is not ready for you. **1665** J. SERGEANT *Sure Footing* 85 We will briefly touch at some of the Advantages which those Assistances .. give the Church. **1746** WESLEY *Answ. Ch.*, *Princ. Methodist* 8 To touch only on what seems of the most Importance. **1875** JOWETT *Plato* (ed. 2) IV. 5 He touches on the same difficulties and he gives no answer to them. **1883** *Manch. Guard.* 22 Oct. 5/2 The matter was touched upon in a general way at the Leeds Conference.

†**19.** *trans.* (? *fig.* from 5.) To take to task, rebuke, reprove, censure; to charge, accuse. *Obs.*

**1526** *Pilgr. Perf.* (W. de W. 1531) 142 Yf we be touched with a sharpe worde, we shal yelde a benigne & gentyll answere. **1570** *Darrell Papers* in H. Hall *Soc. Eliz. Age* (1886) App. 248 Sur Water Hungerfo, and his brother hathe touched me in iij thinges. **1596** DALRYMPLE tr. *Leslie's Hist. Scot.* x. (S.T.S.) II. 474 Gif tha tuouche ouer scharplie, tha be suspected of Jnuious persounis. **1643** *5 Years K. James I* in *Select. fr. Harl. Misc.* (1793) 306 He is stung with fear to be touched with Overbury's death. *a* **1677** BARROW *Serm.* (1687) I. xxii. 307 Our Saviour..touched Martha for being troubled about many things.

**b.** With mixture of senses: To say something apt or telling about, esp. in censure; to 'hit' by some apt or smart saying. Also *to touch to the quick* (cf. 25 b).

*a* **1529** SKELTON *Agst. Scottes* 86 Thalia, my Muse, for you also call I, To touche them with tauntes of your armony. **1548** UDALL *Erasm. Par. Luke* x. 92 b, The Pharisee beeyng somewhat touched with ye aunswer of our Lorde,.. woulde not acknowelage his owne faulte. *a* **1566** R. EDWARDES *Damon & Pithias* Prol., In commedies the greatest skill is this, rightly to touche All thinges to the quick. **1693** *Humours Town* A vj, If, therefore any find themselves touch'd, they ought to make a Right Use of it. **1733** POPE *Hor. Sat.* II. i. 41 Ev'n those you touch not, hate you. **1831** SCOTT *Ct. Robt.* xxxiii, 'Marry, you touch me there', said the centurion.

**20.** *trans.* To pertain or relate to; to have bearing upon; to be the business of; to concern. *Obs.* or *arch.* (passing into next sense).

*a* **1325** *MS. Rawl. B. 520* lf. 52 b, That þer ne passe no writ..vnder þe kinges lutele seal þat tuchi þe commune lawe. *c* **1350** in *Eng. Gilds* (1870) 349 Þinges þat toucheþ the rewle of þe town. **1428** *Surtees Misc.* (1888) 7 Yis mater touched all ye gude men of ye consell. **1535** COVERDALE *Eccl.* xii. 14 Feare God, and kepe his comaundementes, for that toucheth all men. **1697** BENTLEY *Phal.* (1699) 128 [These] Arguments touch only those particular Epistles. **1883** *Manch. Guard.* 22 Oct. 5/3 This..touches us not as Liberals or Conservatives, but as citizens.

†**b.** *intr.* with *to*, *unto*, *upon*, in same sense.

*c* **1325** *Poem times Edw. II* (Percy Soc.) xxxix, Ȝut ther is another craft That towcheth to clergy. **1390** GOWER *Conf.* I. 225 That oght unto my ladi toucheth. **1456** SIR G. HAYE *Law Arms* (S.T.S.) 220 The offence touchis to the realme, and to the citee anerly of thair propre burges. **1523** LD. BERNERS *Froiss.* I. cccxcv. 682 [It was] the duke of Lancastre, to whome the matere moost touched. **1673** *Essex Papers* (Camden) 104 This may a litle touch upon his Father in Law, my Lord Chancellr. **1816** SCOTT *Antiq.* xxxiv, Ne'er a man should steer a hair touching to Monkbarns while Steenie and I could wag a finger.

**c.** To have affinity with. †*intr.* with *at* (*obs.*), or *trans.* (*obs.* or *arch.* exc. as directly *fig.* from 3 or 4).

*c* **1611** CHAPMAN *Iliad* XXI. 103 None now of all the brood of Troy..shall any breath enjoy.., specially that touch at Priam's race. **1774** BURKE *Corr.* (1844) I. 505 To secure the attendance of those whom they touched the most nearly. 1888 Burgon *Lives 12 Gd. Men* II. v. 6 He never identified himself with any school of religious thought, though he touched them all.

**21.** *trans.* To be felt as the concern of or important to; to be a matter of moment to; to affect, make a difference to.

c1470 *Golagros & Gaw.* 1177 It tuichis myne honour sa neir. 1491 *Act 7 Hen. VII*, c. 16 § 8 That this Acte..in no wise extend to ne touche the warde ne mariage of Henry Erle of Essex. 1523 Ld. Berners *Froiss.* I. cxv. 136 A thynge..which herafter may sore touche the Countrey of Flaunders. 1613 Shaks. *Hen. VIII*, II. ii. 54 His Curses and his blessings Touch me alike: th' are breath I not beleeue in. 1882 Pebody *Eng. Journalism* xxi. 156 Till the publication of penny newspapers a few years ago the position of the Provincial Press was hardly touched.

†**22.** To produce an impression on, strike, impress (the senses, or organs of sense). *Obs.*

c1400 *Destr. Troy* 1668 Bright Aumbur, þat..smellis full swete, With taste for to touche the tabull aboute. 1596 Shaks. *Merch. V.* v. i. 76 If..any ayre of musicke touch their eares. 1607 — *Cor.* II. i. 61 If the drinke you giue me, touch my Palat aduersly, I make a crooked face at it. 1629 Milton *Morn. Christ's Nativity, Hymn* xiii, Ring out ye Crystall sphears, Once bless our human ears, (If ye have power to touch our senses so). 1667 — *P. L.* IX. 987.

**23.** To affect mentally or morally, to imbue *with* some quality; in bad sense, to infect, taint (cf. 7). Also predicated of the quality. Usually in *pa. pple.*

13.. *Cursor M.* 11328 (Cott.) Þis symeon þat had his tast Toched o þe hali gast. 13.. *E. E. Allit. P.* A. 897 For neuer lesyng ne tale vntrwe Ne towched her tonge for no dysstresse. a1568 *So Fremmit is my Fortoun* 14 in *Bannatyne Poems* (Hunter. Cl.) 717 Hairtles I am, for slewth twichis me so. 1600 Shaks. *A. Y. L.* III. ii. 366, I thanke God, I am not a Woman to be touch'd with so many giddie offences as hee [my uncle] hath generally tax'd their whole sex withal. 1640–1 Sir B. Rudyard *Sp.* in Rushw. *Hist. Coll.* (1721) IV. 167 The Scots being truly touched with Religion, according to their Profession. 1850 Tennyson *In Mem.* cix. 10 High nature amorous of the good, But touch'd with no ascetic gloom. 1871 Morley *Crit. Misc.* Ser. I. *Byron* (1878) 211 Byron was touched by the same fire.

**b.** *pass.* To be deranged mentally in a slight degree; in *pa. pple.* slightly insane or crazy, 'cracked'.

[1603 Shaks. *Meas. for M.* v. i. 51 With that opinion That I am touch'd with madnesse.] 1704 Steele *Lying Lover* v. iii, Pray mind him not, his Brain is touch'd. 1705 Vanbrugh *Confed.* v. ii, You see master's a little—touched, that's all. 1810 *Sporting Mag.* XXXV. 292 He thought he was a little touched, or insane. 1873 Miss Thackeray *Old Kensington* xxviii, What an extraordinary creature poor Sarah is! touched, certainly.

**24.** To affect with some feeling or emotion; to move or stir the feelings of; to produce an emotion in; *spec.* to affect with tender feeling, as pity or gratitude. Const. *with.*

c1340 Hampole *Prose Tr.* 2 Þe mynd towchede with þe souerayne swettnes. c1500 *Three Kings Sons* 188 He thought it touchid hir hert somwhat. 1603 H. Crosse *Vertues Commw.* (1878) 119 [He] heareth a buzzing sound in his eares, but is neuer truly toucht in his heart. 1631 Gouge *God's Arrows* III. § 50. 277 It is inhumanity not to be touched with others needs. 1711 Steele *Spect.* No. 11 ⁋ 7, I was so touch'd with this Story..that I left the Room with Tears in my Eyes. 1833 Tennyson *Poems* 133 That man, of all the men I ever knew, Most touched my fancy. 1860 Thackeray *Round. Papers, Nil nisi bonum* 227, I can't say how much the thought of that fidelity has touched me.

**b.** With the feeling as subject; in *passive* const. *with* the feeling.

1560 Daus tr. *Sleidane's Comm.* 371 They are neither touched with the gilt of conscience, nor haue given none any occasion of displeasure. 1663 Bp. Patrick *Parab. Pilgr.* xii. 70, I know this touches you with a strong inclination to it. 1718 Pope *Iliad* XXI. 105 If ever yet soft pity touch'd thy mind. 1810 Scott *Lady of L.* I. ix, Then, touched with pity and remorse, He sorrowed o'er the expiring horse.

**c.** To influence, move (in mind or will).

1570 T. Wilson *Demosth. Orat., Life* 127 As for corrupting him wyth giftes or rewardes, he is no more to be touched that way, than was Aristides. 1667 Milton *P. L.* x. 45 No Decree of mine Concurring to necessitate his Fall, Or touch with lightest moment of impulse His free Will.

**25. a.** To grieve, vex; to injure, harm: esp. in a slight degree. ? *Obs.* (or merged in 23). Cf. 5.

1535 Stewart *Cron. Scot.* (Rolls) II. 262 As ressone wald, it tuechit him full soir. 1581 *Reg. Privy Council Scot.* III. 401 Be the violatioun and brek of the same his Hienes is sumquhat twitchit and offendit unto. 1608 *Yorks. Trag.* I. ii, Shall I stand idle And see my reputation touch'd to death?

**b.** To hurt or wound in mind or feelings, as if by touching a sore or tender part; to irritate, sting, nettle. Often in *fig.* phrases, as *touch to the quick.* (Cf. 5, 19 b.)

1589 *Love & Fort.* A ij b, He hath been lately rubde and toucht perhaps too neere. 1600 E. Blount tr. *Conestaggio* 85 They touched the ministers of iustice to the quicke. 1711 Addison *Spect.* No. 99 ⁋ 7 Telling a Man he lyes, is touching him in the most sensible Part of Honour. 1820 Hogg *Tales & Sk., Bridal of P.* II. 66 He feared it would be.. touching the king upon the sore heel. 1898 J. Arch *Story of Life* xi. 257 It touched scores and scores of labourers on the raw.

**II.** Phrases.

**26.** Phrases with other verbs or sbs. **Touch and go**: to touch for an instant and immediately go away or pass on; to deal with momentarily or slightly. (See also Touch and go *sb.* and *a.*)

1549 Latimer *1st Serm. bef. Edw. VI* (Arb.) 26 As the text doeth ryse, I wyl touche and go a lyttle in euery place, vntyl I come vnto to much. 1600 Abp. Abbot *Exp. Jonah* 446 Therefore it shall be enough for me, now to touch and go. c1670 in *Roxb. Ball.* (1891) VII. 486 A Taylor in the Strand ..Most finely was Trappan'd, touch and go.

**b.** *Touch and run*: see Touch *sb.* 1 g.

**27. Touch and take**: in various senses (see above and Take *v.*); in quot. 1793, to take fire at a touch.

1670 Narborough *Jrnl.* in *Acc. Sev. Late Voy.* I. (1694) 14 One blinded with a Cloth serv'd every Man as they were called to touch and take. 1793 *Regal Rambler* 40 Our hero laid in a large cargo of fresh fuel, ready to touch and take like phosphorus. 1805 Nelson *Let. to J. D. Thomson* 5 Sept., The Enemy have a shoal of frigates with their fleet and other Small Vessels, which will take their Crippled Ships in Tow. My Motto shall be Touch and Take.

**28.** In comb. with *sb.* *To touch one's hat*: to raise the hand to the hat and touch it in token of salutation (an abbreviated form of the act of taking off or raising the hat). Const. *to* (the person saluted).

1782 Miss Burney *Cecilia* VII. ix, And, touching his hat, he was riding away. 1820 W. Irving *Sketch Bk.* II. 149 Not a stage coach-man..but touches his hat as he passes. 1840 Haliburton *Letter Bag* iv. 54 We bow and touch our hats with much formality. 1863 Kingsley *Water-Bab.* i, So Mr. Grimes touched his hat to him.

**29.** In *To touch wood.* **a.** In a children's game: see quots. 1849, 1888. **b.** In folk-lore, or *quasi*-superstitious use: To touch wood as a charm to avert apprehended misfortune, esp. that apt to follow untimely boasting or self-gratulation: cf. L. *absit omen!* (Omen *sb.*, quot. 1637).

1849 *Boy's Own Bk.* 37 This..game [Touch *sb.* 1 g] is sometimes called 'Touch-iron' or 'Touch-wood'; in these cases the players are safe only while they touch iron or wood, as may be previously agreed. They are liable to be *touched* only when running from one piece of wood or iron to another. 1888 *Berksh. Gloss., Touch 'ood.* Boys have games called 'touch 'ood' and 'touch-iron', where anyone not touching either of the substances named is liable to be caught by the one standing out and has to stand out accordingly. 1908 *Westm. Gaz.* 30 Dec. 2/3 On the next occasion when we read of Christmas with spring weather or of the changing seasons we shall 'touch wood'.

**III.** In combination with adverbs.

**30. Touch down.** *Rugby Football. trans.* To touch the ground with (the ball) behind the goal, usually that of the opposing side; also *absol.* See also *touch-down* sb. (Touch- 2).

1864 *Field* 5 Nov. 331/1 The Old Rugbeians..soon touched the ball down in the School goal. *Ibid.* 19 Nov. 354/2 [see Touch *v.* 2 f]. 1882 *Standard* 20 Nov. 2/8 The Military had..to touch-down several times in self-defence. 1891 *Football*: *Rugby Union Laws* § 19 A Maul in Goal is when the ball is held inside the goal line and one of the opposing sides endeavours to touch it down. 1897 *Sportsman* 16 Dec., [B.] took a shot at goal..but the ball went wide and J. touched down.

**31. Touch in.** *trans.* In drawing, painting, etc.: To insert (a detail) by touching with the pencil, brush, etc.

1871 *Routledge's Ev. Boy's Ann.* Oct. 615 The dry leaves in the hedges..may be touched in with burnt sienna. 1892 *Photogr. Ann.* II. 262 Touching in as small a portion of top edge as possible.

**32. Touch off.** *trans.* **a.** To represent exactly, to 'hit off' (cf. 17); also *to touch it off*, to do exactly right, hit the mark exactly; in quot. 1766, to 'take the measure of' correctly, 'size up'; hence to be a match for (*obs.*).

1758–65 Goldsm. *Ess.* i. ⁋ 5, I was [told]..that I should now see something touched off to a nicety, for Mr. Spriggins was going to give us 'Mad Tom' in all its glory. 1766 Goldsm. *Vic. W.* xii, I knew you would touch them off. 1821 Galt *Ayrshire Legatees* viii, He's such a funny man! and touches off the Londoners to the nines.

**b.** To fire off (a cannon, etc.), orig. by putting a match to the touch-hole.

1907 *Daily Chron.* 6 Dec. 7/3 The only delay..is due to a fear that a dispatch of the troops will touch off the magazine.

**33. Touch out.** *trans.* To clean out (corners) by touches or light strokes, as in wood-carving.

1879 *Cassell's Techn. Educ.* IV. 71/2 Tools..for fancy work, and for touching out corners difficult of access.

**34. Touch up. a.** *trans.* To improve, finish, or modify by adding touches or light strokes.

1715 Addison *Freeholder* No. 44 ⁋ 3 What he saw was.. her natural Countenance, touched up with the usual Improvements of an aged Coquette. 1748 *Phil. Trans.* XLV. 173 All the illuminated Sets were..touch'd up and finish'd by his own Hand. 1860 Thackeray *Round. Papers, Screens,* Suppose the Editor..never 'touched up' one single line of the contribution. 1863 Baring-Gould *Iceland* 277 It is touched up, but it is for the most part quite trustworthy.

**b.** To stimulate by striking lightly or sharply, as with a whip; hence *fig.* to remind, 'to gently jog the memory' (Farmer *Slang*).

1810 *Sporting Mag.* XXXV. 34 (*Single Stick*) Maslen set to with great confidence, sharply touching up the right arm of his antagonist. 1838 Dickens *Nich. Nick.* xxxii, He let out his whip-lash and touched up a little boy on the calves of his legs. 1902 'Mrs. Alexander' *Stronger than Love* viii, She touched up the ponies, and brought them over the bridge..at a great pace.

**Touch-** *sb.* or *vb.* in combination.

**1. a.** Simple attrib. combinations of the sb., as *touch-feeling, -knowledge, -pleasure, -sensation.*

**b.** Special combinations of the sb. (or in some cases directly from the vb.-stem): **touch-bodies, -corpuscles** *Anat.*, minute bodies of connective and nervous tissue occurring in the skin of the hands, feet, lips, and other parts, supposed to be connected with the sense of touch; also called *tactile corpuscles*; **touch-cell** *Anat.*, a nerve-cell at the end of a sensory nerve in a touch-corpuscle; **touch judge**, in *Rugby Football*, an umpire who marks when and where the ball goes 'into touch' (Touch *sb.* 12), corresponding to a *linesman* in the Association game; **touch-key**, name given to an instrument for scientific experiments on the sense of touch; **touch-needle**, a slender bar or rod of gold or silver, one of a set of different standards of fineness, used in conjunction with a touchstone for testing the fineness of gold or silver; **touch-plate**, one of a set of plates bearing the 'touches' or official marks of the company of pewterers (Touch *sb.* 5 b); †**touch-point** *Geom.*, point of contact; **touch-proof**, in *Sugar Manuf.* a method of testing the degree of crystallization of the syrup by touching a drop of it, laid on the thumb, with the forefinger, and drawing it out to a thin thread; †**touch-warden**: see quot. 1676 (cf. Touch *sb.* 5, *v.* 8); also *fig.*; **touch watch**, a watch so contrived that the time by it can be ascertained by touch, e. g. in the dark; **touch-weight**, one of a set of weights used in experiments on the sense of touch. **c.** Connected with the notion of ready ignition: see Touch-powder; **touch-pan**, the pan of an old-fashioned gun, into which the touch-powder was put; **touch-paper**, paper steeped in nitre so as to burn slowly on being touched by a spark, used for firing gunpowder, etc.; **touch-plate**, the metal plate in which was the touch-hole of a culverin; **touch-string**, string steeped in nitre used as a fuse (cf. *touch-paper*). See also Touch-box, Touch-hole, Touchwood.

1889 *Cent. Dict.* s.v. *Corpuscle*, Tactile corpuscles..Also called..touch-corpuscles, *touch-bodies, palpation-corpuscles. 1897 Parker & Haswell *Zool.* II. 100 Touch-corpuscles are formed of an ovoidal mass of connective tissue containing a ramified nerve, the terminal branches of which end in *touch-cells. 1876 Duhring *Dis. Skin* 26 Tactile corpuscles are also called *touch corpuscles. 1899 *Allbutt's Syst. Med.* VI. 641 A trophic centre in a touch corpuscle. 1884 tr. *Lotze's Metaph.* IV. 507 *heading*, How can *Touch-feelings form a series? 1893 *Daily News* 14 Dec. 2/6 Messrs. Temple Gordon and Percy Christopherson were *touch judges. 1894 *Westm. Gaz.* 11 Jan. 5/3 Altogether 14 players were injured, the touch-judge was threatened, and the referee reported that it had never been his lot to witness such a shameful exhibition. 1905 Titchener *Exper. Psychol.* II. I. 159 Fig. 60. Scripture's *touch key. 1884 *St. James' Gaz.* 13 June 4/2 The true dealer's *touch-knowledge of Oriental antiquities. 1763–6 W. Lewis *Comm. Phil.-Techn.* 124 Accustoming himself to compare the colours of a good set of *Touch needles. 1884 F. J. Britten *Watch & Clockm.* 266 Touch needles are small bars of gold, one each of all the different standards likely to be tested. 1591 Sylvester *Du Bartas* I. vii. 36 Down falls the Cock, up from the *Touch-pan flies A ruddy flash. 1750 *Phil. Trans.* XLVI. 449 Neither these, nor those of Cheltenham, will deflagrate or flash in *Touch-Paper. 1832 Miss Mitford *Village* Ser. v. 113 Why dost thou not fire?.. So please your worship, the wind hath extinguished the touch-paper. 1873 E. Spon *Workshop Receipts* Ser. I. 131/2 Touchpaper..placed..round the mouth of the firework, and twisted into a point. 1778 Pryce *Min. Cornub.* 178 [The miners] have a *touch-pipe, that is, rest..half an hour to smoke a pipe. 1508 *Acc. Ld. High Treas. Scot.* IV. 122 For vernesing of ane lang culveryn and gilting of the end of it and the *twich plaith. 1902 Welch *Hist. Pewterers' Co.* I. Introd. 1 The..inventories of the Company's goods show that touch-plates existed at an early date. a1618 Sylvester *Spectacles* xii, How soon doe Odours from thy Nostrils fly! How short, *touch-Pleasures (tipt with pain and fear)! 1602 Blundevil *Theoriques Seuen Planets* 29 The *Touch-point, otherwise called the point of concauitie. *Ibid.* 73 The right line BHP sheweth the Touch-point. 1899 *Allbutt's Syst. Med.* VII. 35 The transmission of ordinary *touch sensations being unimpaired. a1860 Alb. Smith *Lond. Med. Stud.* (1861) 61 Crackers..contrived to explode at any period..by attaching graduated pieces of *touch-string to them. 1644 Bulwer *Chirol.* 172 The grape of the Index [finger]..is..chiefe *Touch-warden to the King of the five senses. 1676 B. W[illis] *Man. Goldsm.* 30 The Wardens that are to make the Assays and mark the Silver, are now called the Touch-Wardens. 1862 *Catal. Internat. Exhib., Brit.* II. No. 3324 *Touch watches, regulators, and railway clocks. 1884 F. J. Britten *Watch & Clockm.* 33 *Blind Man's Watch*...A watch in which the progress of the hands may be ascertained by touch...The objection to this form of touch watch is that if the pointer is pressed hard against the finger it is apt to advance the hands of the watch. 1905 Titchener *Exper. Psychol.* II. II. 46 The *Touch-Weights. Sets of these weights were made, a few years ago, by Willyoung.

**2.** Substantival phrases consisting **a.** of the vb. in combination with an advb.: **touch-back** (*Rugby Football*), the act of touching the ground with the ball on or behind the player's own goal-line after it has been driven there by the opposing side; **touch-down** (*Rugby Football*), the act of touching the ground with the ball behind the goal-line, usually that of the opposing side; *safety touch-*

*down*, the same done behind the player's own goal-line after it has been driven there by his own side, in order to prevent the opposing side from making a touch-down; **touch-up**, an act of touching up (see TOUCH *v.* 34 a); a stroke added by way of improvement or finish; also a slight incitement or reminder; **b.** of the vb. with object; **touch-no-wall, -s**, *Tennis*: see quots.

**a.** 1864 *Field* 29 Oct. 315/1 The School.. obtaining two '*touches down', which Poole..was unable to turn into a goal. 1895 *Outing* (U.S.) XXVII. 249/2 Canadian system of scoring...A 'touch-down' or 'try' consists of four points with the privilege of trying a kick at the goal, which, if successful, nets the team which scored two points more. 1885 *Athenæum* 1 Aug. 144/3 Tom Moore did not..give the great novelist a retrospective *touch-up with his poetic pencil. 1907 *Times* 3 May 4/1, I ask your lordship to give a sort of a kind of 'touch-up' to these people.

**b.** 1777 [T. SWIFT] *Gamblers* I. 221 Now sounds the Grill; 'tis Setts, and Touch-no-wall, And Chaces echo thro' the lattic'd Hall. 18.. *Laws Tennis* § 33 in J. Marshall *Ann. Tennis* (1878) 166 When the odds of touch-no-walls, or touch-no-side-walls, are given, a ball returned by the giver of the odds, which makes a nick, is counted for the striker. 1878 J. MARSHALL *Ann. Tennis* 160 Touch-no-walls, or All-the-walls: a point of cramped-odds, by which the giver of the odds loses a stroke whenever a ball, returned by him, touches a wall or a gallery-post, or enters an opening, before falling on the floor.

**Touchable** (tʊ·tʃăb'l), *a.* [f. TOUCH *v.* + -ABLE.] Capable of being touched.

**1.** Affecting the sense of touch; tangible.

*c* 1400 *Wyclif's Bible* Heb. xii. 18 ȝe han not come to the tretable fyer, or able for to touche [*v.r.* or toucheable]. 1572 J. JONES *Bathes of Bath* II. 18 The truest touchestone, of all properties, trying both toucheable and tasteable qualities. 1656 W. D. tr. *Comenius' Gate Lat. Unl.* § 469. 135 To the end that things touchable may in lying down gently affect us. 1829 JAS. MILL *Hum. Mind* (1869) I. 13 In that case, we should have no idea of objects as seeable, as hearable, as touchable, or tasteable.

**b.** Fit to be touched or tasted. *nonce-use.*

1751 SMOLLETT *Per. Pic.* lxxxvii. 1881 BLACK *Beautiful Wretch*, etc. III. 177 The butter was not touchable.

**2.** Capable of being affected in mind or feeling.

1822 *Examiner* 154/2 Every mind touchable by musical sounds. 1890 *Church Union* (N.Y.) May, Such of our readers as are touchable by the appeal of this writer.

Hence **Tou·chableness.**

1620 T. GRANGER *Div. Logike* 66 Also visiblenesse, touchablenesse, which are inseparable both in state of mortalitie, and in the state of glory. 1674 BLOUNT *Glossogr., Tangibility*, touchableness.

**Tou·ch and go·**, *sb.* and *adj. phr.* (Also with hyphens.) [The vbl. phrase *touch and go* (TOUCH *v.* 26) used as sb. or adj.]

**A.** *sb.* **1.** The act of touching for an instant and quitting immediately; something done quickly or instantaneously.

1655 MOUFET & BENNET *Health's Impr.* (1746) 59 Howsoever we may taste of it to bring on Appetite, let it be but a touch and go.

**2.** Applied to a person of hasty temper or disposition. *nonce-use.*

1675 DUFFETT *Mock Temp.* III. i, Old touch and go, why so hasty?

**3.** A risky, precarious, delicate, or ticklish case or state of things (such that a mere touch may cause disaster); a narrow escape, 'near shave'.

1815 R. WARDLAW *Let.* in Alexander *Life* vi. (1856) 166 'Twas touch and go—but I got my seat. 1831 MISS FERRIER *Destiny* iv, So it was with Glenroy and his lady. It had been touch-and-go with them for many a day; and now ..ended in a threatened separation. 1858 C. HUNT in *Merc. Marine Mag.* V. 84 Passing so close, that it is often a 'touch and go'. 1867 SMYTH *Sailor's Word-bk., Touch-and-go*, said of anything within an ace of ruin; as in rounding a ship very narrowly to escape rocks, &c., or when, under sail, she rubs against the ground with her keel, without much diminution of her velocity. 1887 'H. SMART' *Cleverly Won* iii, She caught [the horse]..by the mane, and though it was touch and go she managed to retain her seat.

**B.** *adj.* **1.** Involving or characterized by rapid, slight, or superficial execution; sketchy; casual, careless; instantaneous; expeditious.

1812 H. & J. SMITH *Rej. Addr.* Pref. 11 There is an art of writing for the Theatre, technically called *touch and go*,.. indispensable when we consider the small quantum of patience which..a London audience can be expected to afford. 1832 MOORE *Mem.* (1854) VI. 247 Free to introduce anecdotes, quotations, and all such touch-and-go things as the formality of an essay would not admit of. 1832 J. P. KENNEDY *Swallow B.* xii, It was a touch-and-go manner which spoke volumes. 1879 STEVENSON *Trav. Cevennes* (1886) 98 In the neighbourhood of women, it is but a touch-and-go association that can be formed amongst defenceless men. 1885 MISS BRADDON *Wyllard's Weird* iv, A murder of that kind must be touch and go—no sooner thought of than done. 1891 *Spectator* 14 Feb. 246/2 They are 'touch-and-go' sketches, and impressions such as a clever man may throw off at will.

**2.** Risky, of the nature of a narrow escape: cf. A. 3.

1856 ALEXANDER *R. Wardlaw* vi. 168 His getting off at all was generally a 'touch and go' matter. 1897 BLACKMORE in *Blackw. Mag.* Sept. 361 Some touch and go adventure he has been through.

† **Tou·changle.** *Obs. rare.* ? = ANGLE-TWITCH, worm used as bait in angling.

1581 J. BELL *Haddon's Answ. Osor.* 291 With this touch-angle he may fishe a good while, and catch a foole at the last.

† **Tou·chant,** *prep. Obs. rare.* [a. F. *touchant* prep. use of pr. pple. of *toucher* to TOUCH.] = TOUCHING *prep.*

*c* 1375 *Cursor M.* 26439 (Fairf.) Touchant dedeli synne say we. 1425 *Paston Lett.* I. 21, I send yow..the copie of unfrendly lettre..sent to me late, touchant the same matier. ? 1430 *Ibid.* 30 My clerke, to wham I prey yow to gyve feith and credence touchant this matier. 1457 HARDING *Chron.* in *Eng. Hist. Rev.* Oct. (1912) 751 His greuance..touchant the Euydence of the souereynte of Scotlonde.

**Touchar**, obs. form of TOCHER.

† **Tou·ch-box.** *Obs.* exc. *Hist.* [for *touch-powder box*: see TOUCH-POWDER.] A box for 'touch-powder' or priming-powder, formerly forming part of a musketeer's equipment.

1549 *Acts Privy Council* (1890) II. 348 Flaskes, cviij; touche boxes, c. 1564 *Wills & Inv. N. C.* (Surtees) I. 226 One dagg wth flask and tutchbockes vs. 1590 SIR J. SMYTH *Disc. Weapons* 21 The touchpowder in the touch-boxes also. 1591 *Garrard's Art Warre* 3 Hys Flaske and Tutchboxe must keepe hys Pouder. 1598 BARRET *Theor. Warres* III. i. 34 To haue his touchboxe fastened by the string..and to prime his peece with touch-powder. 1627 CAPT. SMITH *Seaman's Gram.* xiv. 68 A Horne is his touch-box. 1660 *Act 12 Chas. II*, c. 4 Sched. s. v. *Boxes*, Touch-boxes of iron or other mettal, guilt, the dozen..j. l. 1902 FIRTH *Cromwell's Army* iv. 81 A fine powder for priming..in what was termed a touch-box or primer, and a coarser powder for loading..in his flask.

**Touched** (tʊtʃt), *ppl. a.* Also 7–8 toucht. [f. TOUCH *v.* + -ED 1.] In various senses corresponding to those of TOUCH *v.*

In quot. *a* 1625, tried, proved (sense 8); in quot. 1667, magnetized (sense 6 c); in quot. 1660 *absol.* from sense 2 b.

**Touched gold**, the touch-piece given by the sovereign when he touched for the 'king's evil', supposed to retain a healing virtue. **Touched proof**, a 'proof' from an engraved or etched plate approaching completion, submitted to the artist of the picture copied, for his approval or criticism.

*a* 1400 HYLTON *Scala Perf.* (W. de W. 1494) II. ii, It was impossyble goddis sone to be borne of towchyd woman. *a* 1586 SIDNEY *Arcadia* (1622) 461 To repay the touched honour of her house. *a* 1625 FLETCHER *Women Pleased* II. i, Ye shall be sure I am a touch'd friend. 1660 EVELYN *Diary* 6 July, The other Chaplaine.., having Angel gold strung on white ribbon on his arme, delivers them one by one to his Majestie, who puts them about the necks of the touched as they passe. 1667 H. OLDENBURG in *Phil. Trans.* II. 423 Whether touched Needles move otherwise, when the Veins of Iron do not lie North and South. 1715 E. BETTS 1 Mar. in *The Betts of Wortham* xvi. (1912) 167 My mother lent Coz Mary Betts ye piece of toucht gold with ye Britaine and this motto [etc.]. 1861 THORNBURY *Turner* I. 408 Turner was always quarrelling with the engravers about his touched proofs. He wanted every proof on which he had written directions to be returned.

**b.** With adv., as *touched-up*: see TOUCH *v.* 34.

1875 tr. *Vogel's Chem. Light* vi. 48 A single touched-up negative gave hundreds of unexceptionable impressions.

Hence **Tou·chedness** (in quot., state of being mentally 'touched', slight insanity).

1883 F. W. ROBINSON *Hands of Justice* II. v, Clambering out of the window in the middle of the night was a striking example of his 'touchedness'.

**Toucher** (tʊ·tʃəɹ). [f. TOUCH *v.* + -ER 1.] One who or that which touches, in senses of the verb.

**1.** *gen.* **a.** *lit.* or in physical sense.

1435 MISYN *Fire of Love* I. xxv. 54 Qwhils þe hart of þe toucher in dyuers desires is takyn. 1495 *Trevisa's Barth. De P. R.* VII. lxvi. (W. de W.) S iij, Yf he [torpedo] be touchyd with a spere, the towcher shall fele the vyolence of the venym. 1548 UDALL, etc. *Erasm. Par. Matt.* ix. 59 [Jesus] loked about hym as seking for the priuy toucher. 1680 C. NESSE *Church Hist.* 340 Touch a great man upon the sore..he fumes and casts the toucher into prison. 1763 *Life Swift* in *Wks.* XI. 265 A thistle is the Scotish arms Which to the Toucher threatens harms. 1904 *Times, Lit. Suppl.* 1 Apr. 97/2 That high sort..means death to the profane toucher.

**b.** *fig.*

1601 DEACON & WALKER *Spirits & Divels* 121 This argument..is a toucher. 1709 MRS. MANLEY *Secret Mem.* (1720) III. 323 A Heart truly touch'd, values nothing in comparison with the Toucher. 1846 HAYDON in Gullick & Timbs *Paint.* (1859) 235 The touchers..are the great men who had discovered the optical principles of imitating nature to convey thought.

**c.** With adv., as *toucher-up.*

1908 *Westm. Gaz.* 28 Jan. 4/1 Taken..advantage of by the wily dealer and his ally, the 'toucher-up'.

**2.** *Bowls.* A bowl which touches the jack.

1600 NASHE *Summer's Last Will* 1178 Ho, wel shot, a tutcher, a tutcher! 1659 FULLER *App. Inj. Innoc.* (1840) 552, I expected when the Animadvertor had knocked away my bowl, he would have laid a toucher in the room thereof. 1868 'S. DARYL' *Quoits & Bowls* 51 A bowl which touches the Jack at any time during its course..is called a 'toucher'.

**3.** An instrument for touching: see quot.

1885 C. G. W. LOCK *Workshop Receipts* Ser. IV. 327/2 By means of a little strip of brass—called a 'toucher'—the crossings are found [in examining a watch].

**4.** *colloq.* or *slang.* **a.** A case of close contact, an exact fit. **b.** A very near approach, a 'near go'; in phr. *as near as a toucher*, very nearly, all but.

1828 *Craven Gloss.* s.v., An exact fit. 'It hits to a toucher', i.e. so exactly that the joints touch each other. 1840 J. T. HEWLETT *P. Priggins* ix, 'So Dick and Tripes were nearly being rusticated this morning'...'As near as a toucher'. 1860 SALA *Baddington Peerage* I. xvii. 298 It was a near toucher, though! 1894 ASTLEY *50 Years Life* II. 199, I was as near as a toucher turning too short, through mistaking the post.

**Toucher**, obs. form of TOCHER.

**Tou·ch-hole.** [f. TOUCH- in *touch-powder* + HOLE.] A small tubular hole in the breech of a fire-arm, through which the charge is ignited; the vent.

1501 *Acc. Ld. High Treas. Scot.* II. 25 Item, for casting of the erd fra Mons [Meg], and to turne hir and lay the twych hole vp,..iij s. ij d. 1560 WHITEHORNE *Ord. Souldiours* 33 Putting sum poulder in the touchehole and aboute the touchhole, the Gunne is then charged. 1618 in Foster *Eng. Factories Ind.* (1906) 31 The fire out of hir toutchole (as yt is most likely) tooke hold of the bandeleros. 1709 DAMPIER *Voy.* III. II. 81 Six bad Guns..whose Touch-holes..are so enlarg'd..that a great part of the strength of the Powder flies away there. 1837 W. IRVING *Capt. Bonneville* (1849) 193 Some of the more knowing..contrived to stop the touch-holes of the field-pieces with dirt.

**b.** *fig.* or *allusively.*

1602 MARSTON *Ant. & Mel.* II. Wks. 1856 I. 19 The match ..will presently set fire to the touch-hole of intemperance. 1617 MIDDLETON & ROWLEY *Fair Quarrel* II. ii. *a* 1625 FLETCHER & MASS. *Cust. Country* III. iii. 1664 BUTLER *Hud.* II. II. 830 Like linstock, to the horse's touch-hole.

**Touchily** (tʊ·tʃĭli), *adv.* [f. TOUCHY + -LY 2.] In a touchy manner; irritably, testily; † saucily.

1653 WATERHOUSE *Apol. Learn.* 251 The King answered only, Say what I can do acceptable to the Athenians; the Varlet Democrates replyed touchily, Nothing better then to hang thy selfe. 1844 WARDLAW *Prov.* II. xxxix. 47 The hasty spirit..startles touchily at every word. 1888 MRS. H. WARD *R. Elsmere* xlv, Rose..had grown so touchily sensitive.

**Touchiness** (tʊ·tʃinės). [f. as prec. + -NESS.] The quality of being touchy.

**1.** Sensitiveness of temper, irritability, testiness.

1653 GAUDEN *Hierasp.* To Rdr. 26 Nor is he ignorant of the touchinesse, and roughnesse..of many mens spirits in these times. 1660 HICKERINGILL *Jamaica* (1661) 96 Their discontents had heated them to so (tinder-like) a Touchinesse, that they were ready to take fire on all occasions. 1828 *Lights & Shades* II. 52 She is known only by her one absorbing quality of touchiness, and is dreaded and hated accordingly.

**2.** Ticklishness, precariousness.

1648 *Eikon Bas.* iii. 14 My friends resented it as a motion ..not guided with such discretion, as the touchinesse of those times required.

**3.** *Painting*, etc.: see TOUCHY 4.

1813 *Examiner* 8 Feb. 90/2 The heads and hands have.. a rich touchiness of pencil. *Ibid.* 1 Mar. 141/1 The trees.. have perhaps too minute a touchiness of foliage. 1821 *New Monthly Mag.* III. 391 It is too much limited to the outline of the body: it wants a good filling up, a breaking and touchiness in the intermediate spaces.

**Touching** (tʊ·tʃiŋ), *vbl. sb.* [f. TOUCH *v.* + -ING 1.] The action of the verb TOUCH.

**1.** The action, or an act, of feeling something with the hand, etc.; the fact or state of being contiguous; touch, contact; a touch; *spec.* for the 'king's evil' (quot. 1704).

*c* 1290 *St. Lucy* 33 in *S. Eng. Leg.* I. 102 Þoruȝ touchingue of seinte Agace toumbe þouȝ schalt beo hol a-non. *a* 1450 *Knt. de la Tour* (1906) 58 Leude touchinge and handelyng sterithe and chafithe the flesshe. 1561 T. NORTON *Calvin's Inst.* IV. xix. (1634) 723 Some he healed with touchings, other some with his word. *a* 1657 SIR W. MURE *Misc. Poems* xi. 6 Hands, forbeare to tuich Oght 30r tuiching can bewitch! 1704 *Lond. Gaz.* No. 4020/4 Her Majesty thinking it necessary to discontinue Touching for this Season. 1842 TENNYSON *Locksley Hall* 38 Our spirits rush'd together at the touching of the lips.

† **b.** The sense of touch. *Obs.*

*c* 1460 *Wisdom* 1105 in *Macro Plays* 72 By towchynge, I felte peyne smerte. 1500–20 DUNBAR *Poems* IX. 12 My wittis fyve,—In hering, seing, gusting, twiching, and smelling. 1656 STANLEY *Hist. Philos.* V. (1701) 189/1 The sense of Touching. 1774 GOLDSM. *Nat. Hist.* (1776) II. 179 The closer senses, if I may so call them, such as smelling, tasting, and touching, are..as simple as they are limited.

**c.** In various *spec.* senses: see the verb.

1671 MILTON *P. R.* II. 370 No interdict Defends the touching of these viands pure. 1705 DERHAM in *Phil. Trans.* XXV. 2143 This way of Touching [with a magnet]. 1833 T. HOOK *Parson's Dau.* III. xii, The only difference between the passages is the frequency of touching in the one case. 1908 H. B. MORSE *Trade Chinese Emp.* 148 A lot of sixty [silver ingots] of which I saw the weighing and touching.

**d.** In reference to painting, or artistic or other work; also with *up*: see TOUCH *v.* 10, 34 a.

1781 SIR J. REYNOLDS *Journ. Flanders*, etc. Wks. 1797 II. 87 [Tenier's] manner of touching, or what we call handling, has perhaps never been equalled. 1825 J. NICHOLSON *Operat. Mechanic* 465 The several touchings and retouchings requisite. 1902 *Athenæum* 26 Apr. 538/3 The touchings-up of the Gavotte were in the worst possible taste.

**e.** *slang.* Getting hold of money, as by theft, or pocket-picking; also bribery (? *obs.*): see TOUCH *v.* 15, 16.

1726 C. D'ANVERS *Craftsman* No. 32 (ed. 3) 299 If once he gives himself up to touching..I give him over as incurable. 1896 A. MORRISON *Child of the Jago* 231 It would never do to go home without touching.

**2.** In various *fig.* senses: Mention, treatment or discussion; affecting or injuring; † charging, accusation, etc.

*a* 1400 HYLTON *Scala Perf.* (W. de W. 1494) I. ii, Made bi the presence and the touchyng of a good angell. 1410 in *Proc. Privy Council* (1834) I. 326 And yf by that mocioun and touchyngge the forseide Emonde may fele the forseide Duc be ther of righte desirous. 1590 SIR J. SMYTH *Disc. Weapons* Ded. 13 Is no other but a blaspheming and offending of God in the highest degree, a touching of the honour of the Princes. *a* 1625 SIR H. FINCH *Law* (1636) 185 The touching of him with some hainous crime. 1711 ADDISON

*Spect.* No. 34 ⁋ 6 To commend my Prudence in not touching upon the Army.

†3. *Building.* (*pl.*) Projections from the foundations of a building, from which those of the adjoining building are begun. *Obs.*

1663 GERBIER *Counsel* 50 To cause the foundation of the intended building to be generally laid, without leaving any toutchings.

4. *attrib.*, as *touching-distance*; **touching-stuff**, in engraving, a composition of cork ashes, ivory-black, gall, and treacle, used for touching up the dark parts of a plate (*Cent. Dict.*).

1884 J. TAIT *Mind in Matter* (1892) 314 'Criticism' has never reached nearer than touching-distance to the extreme outworks of divine truth.

**Tou·ching**, *ppl. a.* Forms: see TOUCH *v.* [f. as prec. + -ING [2].] That touches: in various senses of the verb.

1. *lit.*: chiefly of things: Coming into, or being in contact.

1674 N. FAIRFAX *Bulk & Selv.* 113 Because this touching draught is more broken in some, and more tight in others. 1875 KNIGHT *Dict. Mech.* s.v. *Riding-part*, The joint part of a scissors-blade which forms the touching portion back of the rivet.

2. *fig.* That touches the feelings or emotions; such as to excite tender feeling or sympathy; affecting, pathetic. (The usual sense.)

In quot. 1508, ? 'sharp', satirical or reproachful.

1508 DUNBAR *Tua Mariit Wemen* 303, I wald ryght tuichand in talk be. 1601 SHAKS. *Jul. C.* IV. iii. 151 O insupportable, and touching losse! 1742 YOUNG *Nt. Th.* III. 240 If not forgot my touching tale. 1823 SCOTT *Peveril* xiii, So touching, also, in her simplicity and purity of thought. 1870 HUXLEY *Lay Serm.* iii. (1874) 30 A touching faith in the efficacy of acts of parliament.

**Tou·ching**, *prep.* Now somewhat *arch.* Forms: see TOUCH *v.*; also 4 -end(e, 4, 5 *Sc.* -and(e. [The pres. pple. of TOUCH *v.* used prepositionally; cf. CONCERNING *prep.* Prob. after F. *touchant*, used in the same way: see also TOUCHANT.]

1. (*introd.*) Where *touching* is in concord with a prec. sb. or pron., and may be rendered 'that refers or relates to' (TOUCH *v.* 18, 20). In later use passing into 2. (Cf. CONCERNING *prep.* 1.)

*c* 1350 *Will. Palerne* 1383 For þe tyding þat þei told touchend hire fader. 1456 SIR G. HAYE *Law Arms* (S.T.S.) 10 The visioun touchand the first tyme of the sorouful persecucioun. 1542 HEN. VIII in *Buccleuch MSS.* (Hist. MSS. Comm.) I. 221 Certeine thinges..towching vs and.. our Realme. 1621 ELSING *Debates Ho. Lords* (Camden) 129 There was debate touching Sir Gyles Mompesson. 1709–10 STEELE *Tatler* No. 145 ⁋ 1 A late Request..touching the Care of a young Daughter. 1867 FREEMAN *Norm. Conq.* I. iv. 196 *note*, The dealings of the Assembly touching the abdication of Rolf.

2. Without concord, becoming entirely prepositional: In reference or relation to; as to, respecting, regarding; in the way of mentioning or treating of; concerning, about. (Cf. CONCERNING *prep.* 2.)

*c* 1375 *Cursor M.* 23011 (Fairf.) Saint austin sais touchand [*C., G.* enent, *T.* of] þat day Is nane can goddis consail say. *c* 1400 MAUNDEV. (Roxb.) xxiii. 107 Wonder sutell of witte towchand any thing þat þai will do. 1513 DOUGLAS *Æneis* XII. Prol. 271 Twichand the lattyr buke of Dan Virgill. 1594 T. B. *La Primaud. Fr. Acad.* II. 49 The composition of the head touching the bones thereof. 1611 BIBLE *Transl. Pref.* 5 This may suffice touching the Greeke translations of the old Testament. 1771 SMOLLETT *Humph. Cl.* 17 Apr., The master of the company being sent for, and examined touching the said Wilson. 1855 DICKENS *Dorrit* II. xxviii, Touching the bargain, your..mother was a little too calm.

3. Preceded by *as*. (Cf. CONCERNING *prep.* 3.)

*c* 1386 CHAUCER *Frankl. T.* 685 Mo than a thousand stories ..Koude I now telle as touchynge this mateere. 1428 *Munim. de Melros* (Bann. Cl.) 521 As twichand þe plew of land in þe husbandry..þe assis saide it nedit na departisoun. *a* 1533 LD. BERNERS *Huon* lix. 203 What counsell wyl ye geue me as touchyng yᵉ admyrall? 1601 HOLLAND *Pliny* x. xxxii. I. 287 As touching the Guls or Sea-cobs, they build in rockes. 1780 M. MADAN *Thelyphthora* (1781) I. 105 The exceeding ignorance of mankind as touching the acts and dispensations of that infinitely wise Being. 1890 FREEMAN in W. R. W. Stephens *Life & Lett.* (1895) II. 420 Your facts are very valuable, specially as touching your own stay in Crete.

†4. Followed by *of* or *to* (and mostly preceded by *as* as in 3), forming a prepositional phr. *Obs.*

*As touching for* in *Paston Lett.* is app. a confusion between *as touching* and *as for*.

1390 GOWER *Conf.* I. 307 Now tell me forth if ther be more As touchende unto Wraththes lore. *Ibid.* III. 174 And as touchende of this bataille, Thou schalt noght of the sothe faile. 1417–19 *Paston Lett.* I. 10 As towchyng to the derth of vytayles withyn thys..Cytee. ? 1450 *Ibid.* 161 As towchyng for tydynges, I can none. 1523 [COVERDALE] *Old God & New* (1534) P j, Speake as towchyng to yᵉ workes of theym selues.

**Touchingly** (tʊ·tʃiŋli), *adv.* [f. TOUCHING *ppl. a.* + -LY [2].] In a touching manner; so as to touch the feelings; affectingly, pathetically.

1717 GARTH *Ovid's Met.* Pref., This last fable shows how touchingly the poet argues in love affairs, as well as those of Medea and Scylla. 1824 *Examiner* 246/2 Sympathy.. makes the scene tell more touchingly. 1884 Q. VICTORIA *More Leaves* 210 He prayed most touchingly for me.

So **Tou·chingness**, touching or affecting quality, pathos.

*a* 1750 A. HILL *Wks.* (1753) II. 355 He..charm'd me infinitely..by a peculiar touchingness, in cadency of voice. 1823 *Examiner* 411/1 Her medium notes have a touchingness about them which is not common. 1841 *Fraser's Mag.* XXIII. 315 To..prove The simple touchingness of Morn. 1876 G. MEREDITH *Beauch. Career* II. v. 79 Beauchamp had the history..recounted to him, with a mixture of Gallic irony, innuendo, openness, touchingness, ridicule, and charity novel to his ears.

**Touchit**, Sc. obs. var. TEWHIT, the lapwing.

**Touchless** (tʊ·tʃ,lės), *a.* [f. TOUCH *sb.* + -LESS.] **a.** Devoid of the sense of touch. **b.** Incapable of being touched, intangible: cf. *viewless*.

1813 T. BUSBY *Lucretius* I. III. 936 As the touchless space, they're free from blow. 1871 HUXLEY *Crit. & Addr.* xiii. (1873) 343 Of course our touchless man would be devoid of any notion of resistance. 1888 B. W. RICHARDSON *Son of Star* xii, Touchless with human hands, Sightless with human eyes.

**Tou·ch-line.** [f. TOUCH *sb.* or *v.* + LINE *sb.*[2]]

†1. *Geom.* A straight line that touches a curve; a tangent. *Obs.* (Orig. two words.)

1551 RECORDE *Pathw. Knowl.* I. Defin., A touche lyne, is a line that runneth a long by the edge of a circle, onely touching it, but doth not crosse the circumference of it. 1593 FALE *Dialling* 7 Which shall be called the touch line or line of Contingence. 1675 COLLINS in Rigaud *Corr. Sci. Men* (1841) I. 217 If you conceive a chord line to join R, T, and a touch-line to be drawn at either of those.

2. (*touch line.*) A line in a diagram representing the touch of the counter of a ship: see TOUCH *sb.* 23.

1797 *Encycl. Brit.* (ed. 3) XVII. 392/1 Take the round up of the upper counter from the dimensions, and set it below the touch at the middle, and with a pencil draw a level line; take also the round aft, and set it forward from the touch on the touch line, and square it down to the pencil line.

3. *Football.* The boundary line on each side of the field of play, extending from goal-line to goal-line: cf. TOUCH *sb.* 12.

1868 *Boy's Own Bk.* 132 [Diagram of football ground]. The goals at either end;..the goal lines;..touch, the touch lines. 1889 *Pauline* VIII. 38 The kick, which was very near the touch-line, was not successful. 1895 *Outing* (U. S.) XXVII. 247/2 The Canadian football field...Along the edges, from one end to another, run the 'touch lines', and when the ball goes over these it is not in play.

**Tou·ch-me-no·t**, *sb.* [phrase used as *sb.*]

1. Name for two different kinds of plants with seed-vessels which burst at a touch. †**a.** The Squirting Cucumber: see CUCUMBER 3. *Obs.*

1597 GERARDE *Herbal* II. ccCxxvii. 766 *Cucumis asininus.* Wilde Cucumber...Called..wilde Cucumber..and Touch me not. 1611 in COTGR. s.v. *Coucombre.* 1760 J. LEE *Introd. Bot.* App. 330 Touch me not, *Momordica.*

**b.** The Yellow Balsam (*Impatiens Noli-tangere*), or other species of *Impatiens*, the ripe capsules of which split open with a jerk on being touched.

1659 GAUDEN *Tears Ch.* ***ij, Presbytery seeming like the plant called Touch me not, which flies in the face, and breaks in the fingers of those that presse it. 1760 J. LEE *Introd. Bot.* App. 330 Touch me not, *Impatiens.* 1885 HORNADAY *2 Yrs. in Jungle* xxv. 300 A bed of touch-me-nots took me back like a flash to the terrace flower-beds at college. 1888 *Harper's Mag.* Dec. 153/2 The 'touch-me-not' or 'snapweed' of the loitering school-boy, with its touchy, jumping pods, popping even at a hard look or breath.

2. A name for the disease Lupus.

1860 MAYNE *Expos. Lex.*, *Touch-me-not*, common name for the disease *Noli me tangere*.

3. *gen.* A person or thing that must not be touched; in quot., a forbidden topic.

1893 *Daily News* 8 May 5/5 Military matters..are a 'touch-me-not' here.

**b.** *attrib.* or as *adj.*

1852 THACKERAY *Esmond* III. iv, The saucy little beauty carried her head with a toss..and assumed a touch-me-not air, which all her friends very good-humouredly bowed to. 1880 'OUIDA' *Moths* 43 Just the old-fashioned, prudish, open-air, touch-me-not Englishwoman.

Hence **Tou·ch-me-no·t-ish** *a.* [-ISH [1]], having a 'touch-me-not' character; whence **Tou·ch-me-no·t-ishness** (*nonce-wd.*). Cf. *stand-off-ish.*

1837 DICKENS *Pickw.* viii, There was a dignity in the air, a touch-me-not-ishness in the walk, a majesty in the eye of the spinster aunt.

**Touch-no-wall, -s**: see TOUCH- 2 b.

**Tou·ch-piece.** [f. TOUCH *v.* or *sb.* + PIECE *sb.*]

1. A coin or medal (originally a gold angel, in later times specially struck for the purpose in gold or silver) given by the sovereign to each person touched for the 'king's evil' (TOUCH *v.* 2 b).

1844 *Chron. Seasons* II. 26 Touch-pieces were a sort of coins, of which the king, when he touched a person in order to cure the evil, used to hang one round the neck of the patient. 1855 SMEDLEY, etc. *Occult Sc.* 341 The touch-pieces were generally preserved with great care, and worn as amulets. 1908 *Athenæum* 20 June 769/1 There are varieties of gold and silver touch-pieces of the time of James II.

2. A piece of mechanism operated by a touch.

1897 *Daily News* 7 June 6/4 The observer taps a little touch-piece by the side of the instrument, and this movement is conveyed by galvanic wire to the chronograph.

3. A piece of music designed to exhibit the touch of the performer, a toccata. (*nonce-use.*)

1900 *New Cent. Rev.* VII. 394 A Toccata (or touch-piece).

†**Tou·ch-powder.** *Obs.* [This appears to be the earliest of the series of compounds mentioned in TOUCH- 1 c, in which *touch-* signifies the ready kindling or setting fire to something; app. from OF. *tochier* (*le feu*), *touchier* to set fire. *Touch-powder* prob. represented an OF. **poudre-à-toucher* (*le feu*). Thence *touch-box*, *-hole*, *-pan*, etc., and the parallel *touch-wood*, etc.] A fine kind of gunpowder placed in the pan over the touch-hole in an old-fashioned fire-arm; priming-powder. Also *attrib.*

1497 *Naval Acc. Hen. VII* (1896) 88 Towchepoudre.. j barell. 1508 *Acc. Ld. High Treas. Scot.* IV. 137 Item, for double gilting of the Kingis twich powdir horn, xxvj s. 1591 *Garrard's Art Warre* 6 Let him make hys Tutch Pouder. 1598 [see TOUCH-BOX].

**Touchquhare**, obs. form of TOCHER.

**Touchstone** (tʊ·tʃ,stoun). Forms: see TOUCH *v.* [f. TOUCH- 1 + STONE: cf. OF. *touchepierre*, F. *pierre de touche*, Sp. *piedra de toque*.]

1. A very smooth, fine-grained, black or dark-coloured variety of quartz or jasper (also called BASANITE), used for testing the quality of gold and silver alloys by the colour of the streak produced by rubbing them upon it; a piece of such stone used for this purpose.

1530 PALSGR. 282/1 Touch stone to prove golde with. 1754 *Phil. Trans.* XLVIII. 664 The difference in colour of these compositions was much less conspicuous on the touchstone. 1812 J. SMYTH *Pract. of Customs* (1821) 262 Touchstone is the Basaltes, a heavy hard stone, of a very fine texture, of a deep glossy black, resembling that of polished steel. 1908 H. B. MORSE *Trade Chinese Emp.* 149 A silver commercially pure, as shown by the crude methods of the touchstone.

**b.** *fig.* That which serves to test or try the genuineness or value of anything; a test, criterion.

*a* 1533 FRITH *Another Bk. agst. Rastell* (1829) 216 Lay them to the touchstone, and try them with God's word. 1535 COVERDALE *Ecclus.* vi. 21 Vnto soch she is as it were a twichstone, & he casteth her from him in all the haist. 1677 *Govt. Venice* 106 Therefore it is that Venice is called the School and Touchstone of Embassadors. *a* 1720 SHEFFIELD (Dk. Buckhm.) *Wks.* (1753) II. 207 Time..in all matters of writing, is the only true touchstone of merit. 1822 HAZLITT *Table-t.* I. xi. 253 Well-digested schemes will stand the touchstone of experience. 1871 BLACKIE *Four Phases* i. 42 The touchstone..to distinguish the true man..from the false pretender.

2. Applied to other stones of similar texture and colour, as black marble or basalt. (Cf. TOUCH *sb.* 6.)

1481–3 *Acc. Exch. K. R.* Bd. 496. No. 26 (MS.), Ultra lv dolijs lapidum de Cane,..et xxxiij doliis de Touchestone. 1509 HAWES *Past. Pleas.* xxxv. (Percy Soc.) 184 Into the castell of olde foundacion, Walled about with the blacke touche stone. 1584 in Willis & Clark *Cambridge* (1886) I. 294 The pece of tutch stone wᶜʰ my Ladye Bacon hath gyven vnto this woorke. 1607 TOPSELL *Four-f. Beasts* (1658) 377 Upon the steps of the Capitol of Rome, there were two Lions of black Marble touch-stone. *a* 1647 HABINGTON *Surv. Worc.* in *Worcs. Hist. Soc. Proc.* I. 102 All..wrytten in Tuchstone with letters of goulde. 1670 PETTUS *Fodinæ Reg.* 1 If common Stones onely are found (as Marble, Touchstone, Freestone, etc.) we call them Quarries, and not Mines. 1845 PARKER *Gloss. Archit.*, *Touch-stone* [is] a name sometimes applied to compact dark-coloured stones, such as Purbeck and Petworth marble ..frequently used for fine work in Gothic architecture.

**Touchwood** (tʊ·tʃ,wud). [f. TOUCH- 1 c + WOOD *sb.*] Wood or anything of woody nature, in such a state as to catch fire readily, and which can be used as tinder. **a.** The soft white substance into which wood is converted by the action of certain fungi, especially of *Polyporus squamosus*, and which has the property of burning for many hours when once ignited, and is occasionally self-luminous.

By confusion the name is sometimes applied to the powdery snuff-coloured mass into which wood is sometimes converted without the agency of fungi, by a process of slow chemical combustion (*eremacausis*), which is not distinguishable from the effects of dry rot, except by the absence of fungous spawn. (M. J. Berkeley in *Treas. Bot.* 1866.)

1579 LYLY *Euphues* (Arb.) 62, I, but Euphues, hath she not hard also that the dry touchewoode is kindled with lyme..that the fire quickly burneth the flaxe? 1621 BURTON *Anat. Mel.* III. ii. II. i. (1651) 450 As match or touchwood takes fire, so doth an idle person love. 1646 SIR T. BROWNE *Pseud. Ep.* II. v. 89 To make white powder...The best I know is by the powder of rotten willowes; spunck, or touchwood prepared, might perhaps make it russet. 1706 E. WARD *Wooden World Diss.* (1708) 14 He had rather see the whole Fleet parch'd up like Touchwood, for want of Water. 1799 *Med. Jrnl.* II. 298 Observations..on the luminous property of touchwood. 1809 MALKIN *Gil Blas* IV. vii. ⁋ 13 Gonzales, dry as touchwood, with all its inflammability. 1887 T. HARDY *Woodlanders* III. ix. 183 The rain had imparted a phosphorescence to the pieces of touchwood. 1898 WATTS-DUNTON *Aylwin* XV. vi, A fallen willow tree, the inside of which was all touchwood.

**b.** A name given to various fungi, esp. two species of *Polyporus* (*P.* or *Fomes fomentarius* and *P.* or *F. igniarius*), also called *Touchwood Boletus*, or to the tinder called 'amadou' made from them. Cf. TINDER.

The former of these is found on oak, beech, birch, lime, etc., the latter (which requires a process of preparation) on ash, poplar, willow, plane, fir, etc.

1598 FLORIO, *Pano*..touchwood, or a spungie swelling on trees like a mushrume. 1666 PEPYS *Diary* 12 Nov., His skeleton [is here seen], with the flesh on; but all tough and dry like a spongy dry leather, or touchwood all upon his bones. 1688 R. HOLME *Armoury* II. 85/2 Touchwood [is] a kind of hard, dry, spungy Mushroom. 1778 LIGHTFOOT *Flora Scot.* (1789) II. 1034 *Boletus igniarius.* Touchwood Boletus. ..An excellent touchwood is made from this Fungus by..

pounding and boiling it up with saltpetre. **1845–50** Mrs. Lincoln *Lect. Bot.* 199 The genus Boletus contains the touchwood, or spunk, which is sometimes used as tinder.

**c.** *fig.* Said of a thing or person that easily 'takes fire', or which, like tinder, 'kindles' something else (quot. 1601); *esp.* an irascible or passionate person, one easily incensed. Now *rare.*

[**1601** Dent *Pathw. Heaven* 204 Sins of oppression..be the very fire-brands of Gods wrath, and as it were touch-wood, to kindle his anger.] **1617** Middleton & Rowley *Fair Quarrel* II. i, The Colonel, soon enrag'd, as he's all touch-wood. *c* **1620** Fletcher & Massinger *Lit. French Lawyer* II. iii, Peace touchwood. **1761** G. Colman *Jealous Wife* I. i, She is all Impetuosity and Fire.—A very Magazine of Touchwood and Gunpowder. **1840** *Life of Origen* vii. 66 Wood, hay, stubble, and that which soonest burns of anything, the touchwood of denial.

**d.** *attrib.* and *Comb.*

**1784** Cowper *Task* VI. 688 From his touchwood trunk the mulberry-tree Supplied such relics as devotion holds Still sacred. **1864** Tennyson *Aylmer's F.* 514 There the manorial lord too curiously Raking in that millennial touchwood-dust Found for himself a bitter treasure-trove.

**Touchy** (tʊ·tʃi), *a.* Also 7 tutchie. [f. Touch *sb.* or *v.* + -y; but in sense 1 perh. an alteration of Tetchy.]

**1.** Easily moved to anger; apt to take offence on slight cause; highly sensitive in temper or disposition; irascible, irritable, testy, tetchy.

**1605** *King Leir & Daughters* D j, She breeds yong bones, And that is it makes her so tutchy sure. **1619** Beaum. & Fl. *Maid's Trag.* III. ii, Y'are touchie without all cause. *a* **1652** Brome *Queen* I. iv, Ther's the old tutchie testie Lord. **1656** H. Jeanes *Fuln. Christ* 79 If earthly Potentates be so tender, and touchy in the point of their Embassadours honour and safety. **1702** C. Mather *Magn. Chr.* I. ii. (1852) 50 Avoid all discoveries of a touchy humour. **1843** Le Fevre *Life Trav. Phys.* I. I. viii. 170 She was most touchy upon the subject of age. **1903** G. H. Birch *Lond. on Thames* ii. 18 The citizens wanted no foreigners—they were always very touchy on that subject.

**2.** Sensitive to touch; physically irritable.

Quot. 1618 perh. belongs rather to 1.

**1618** Latham *2nd Bk. Falconry* xiv. 57, I perceiued her to bee very tutchie and coy to bee handled. **1658** A. Fox *Würtz' Surg.* I. vi. 25 As often as a vein or sinew is toucht ..is a new pain caused; for they are very touchy and full of sense. **1710** T. Fuller *Pharm. Extemp.* 209 Those whose Guts being wove up of fine-spun Fibrillæ, are touchy and irritable. **1806–7** J. Beresford *Miseries Hum. Life* (1826) XI. xv, Jarring the touchy part of your elbow against the edge of the table. **1888** [see Touch-me-not 1 b].

**b.** Taking fire when touched with a spark; easily ignited.

In quots. 1660 and 1766 combining this sense and 1.

**1660** [implied in Touchiness 1]. **1679** *Phil. Collect.* XII. 7 Our Colliers assure me that those touchy Works which are continually apt to take Fire, do it most..in the Winter. **1766** *Goody Two-Shoes* iv. (1882) 111 You are both as touchy as Tinder, and very often make your own House too hot to hold you.

**3.** Ticklish, risky, precarious; not to be touched without danger. (Cf. 2 b.)

**1620** Wotton in *Reliq.* (1672) 500 In such a touchy time as this, I had almost had my share. **1651** N. Bacon *Disc. Govt. Eng.* II. vi. (1739) 36 It is a touchy thing to have to do with fire, lest it get too high. **1697** Collier *Ess. Mor. Subj.* I. (1709) 53 You are upon a touchy Point, and therefore I hope you will treat so nice a Subject..with proportionable Caution. **1884** *Graphic* 15 Nov. 518/2 These were, of course, very touchy subjects to ask of courtiers.

**4.** *Painting, Drawing*, etc. Characterized by or composed of distinct touches or light strokes.

**1820** *Examiner* No. 651. 634/1 One of the prime beauties ..is its extensiveness of touchy marking, whereby in all the parts the eye is most satisfactorily entertained. **1826** *Ibid.* 342/1 Indifferent anatomical drawing and a want of touchy pencilling. **1839** Chatto & Jackson *Wood Engraving* viii. 649 The drawing, which originally may have been clear and touchy, loses its brightness, and becomes indistinct from its frequent contact with the soft pliable paper.

**5.** Involving a mere light touch. *nonce-use.*

**1879** G. Macdonald *Sir Gibbie* xiv, As if some gentle hand had..dipped them—just a tiny touchy dip, in a molten ruby.

†**6.** 'Touched' or slightly affected in the head; slightly crazed or crack-brained, 'cranky': in comb. *touchy-headed.*

**1666** J. Smith *Old Age* To Rdr. A iij b, The Author..is himself as willing, as any touchy-headed Decryers of Anatomy and Anatomists..that all the shame..should return upon his own pate. **1675** E. Wilson *Spadacrene Dunelmensis* Pref. 17 Those touchy headed Chymists, who pretend to Panacæa's, Universal Medicines, Secrets, and such like whimsical Remedies.

**Touck, -e, Toucker,** obs. ff. Tuck *sb.* and *v.*, Tucker. **Touel, Touele,** obs. ff. Towel, Tewel. **Touffan, -on,** obs. forms of Typhoon.

‖**Toug** (tūg). [a. F. *toug*, ad. Turk. توغ *tūgh* tail of a horse.] The Turkish standard, consisting of a horse's tail fixed at the end of a short pike.

**1687** A. Lovell tr. *Thevenot's Trav.* I. 81 The *Toug* is a Horses Tail fastened to the head of a Pike: It is neuer put out but in extreme necessity, and then all the Militia must take the Field. **1902** R. W. Chambers *Maids of Paradise* v, I could still hear..the tinkle of the silver chimes on their *toug.*

**Tough** (tʊf), *a.* (*adv.*, *sb.*) Forms: *α.* 1 tóh, tóch, 3 tou, 3–5 touȝ, toȝ, 3–6 tow, 4 touh, towh, towȝ, toȝe, 4–5 togh, towe, 5 touȝe, towȝe, toghe, towghe, toogh, touhe, (towhhe), 5–6 towgh, toughe, 4– tough. *β. Sc.* 5–9 teuch, teugh, (5–6 tewch, 6 tuich, tewgh, teoch, twch, -e, twich). *γ.* (with inorganic *-t*) 3 toht, 3–4 toȝt, 3–5 touȝt, *Sc.* 4 tucht, 5 touȝte, tout; 6 *Sc.* tewcht. *δ.* 4–5 tuf, 7 tuffe, 7–8 tuff. [OE. *tôh* :—**tǫnh* :—**tanh*, OTeut. **taŋχu-z*; NFris. *toch, tuch.* From an OTeut. stem **taŋχ-, taŋg-*, whence OE. *ge-tęnge.* Cf. (with ending of *-ja* decl.) OS. **tâhi* (MLG. *tâ, tei*, LG. *taa, tage, tau*, Du. *taai*); OHG. *zâhi* (MLG. *zâhe, zæhe, zæch*, Ger. *zähe, zäh*).]

**1.** Of close tenacious substance or texture; strongly cohesive, so as to be pliable or ductile; not easily broken, divided, or disintegrated; not fragile, brittle, or tender; of food, difficult to masticate.

*α.* *a* **700** *Epinal Gloss.* (O.E.T.) 581 *Lenta, tarda vel* toch. *Ibid.* 614 *Lentum vimen*, toch ȝerd. *c* **725** *Corpus Gloss.* 1207 *Lentum vimen*, toh ȝerd. *c* **1275** Lay. 5865 Kereþ ȝoure speres lang and makeþ heom toȝe an strang. **1340–70** *Alex. & Dind.* 691 Hue tilede in hur time on þe touh erþe, & whete soþliche sew. **13..** *E. E. Allit. P.* B. 630 [Abraham] a calf bryngez þat watz tender & not toȝe; bed ..þat he hit seþe faste. **1387** Trevisa *Higden* (Rolls) IV. 317 Temperynge of glas to make þe glas tough i-now to bende. *c* **1400** *Laud Troy Bk.* 10877 The spere was tow & long. *c* **1400** *Destr. Troy* 7495 Telamon, the tore kyng, with a togh speire. *c* **1440** *Promp. Parv.* 498/1 Towhhe, not tendyr (*A.* tow, *P.* tough). **1552** Huloet, Towgh, *tenax.* **1612** *Two Noble K.* II. v. 2, I have not seene..a man of tougher synewes. **1697** Dryden *Virg. Georg.* II. 628 The tougher Yeugh Receives the bending Figure of a Bow. **1769** E. Bancroft *Guiana* 209 Its body is tough and fibrous. **1827** Faraday *Chem. Manip.* v. (1842) 151 A wrought-iron mortar ..would be too tough. **1843** Mrs. Carlyle *Lett.* (1883) I. 219 The 'cold fowl' was..as tough as leather.

*β.* *c* **1470** Henry *Wallace* XI. 1061 With seuir cordys..Bath scharp and tewch. **1513** Douglas *Æneis* VII. xiii. 65 Knyt wyth a teuch string. *a* **1584** Montgomerie *Cherrie & Slae* 328 The Cherries..grewe On trimbling twistis tewch. *a* **1758** Ramsay *Address of Thanks* xii, That setting-dog his man, May..use a teugh St. Johnston ribbon.

*γ.* **1297** Touȝt [see 8]. *c* **1586** *Dunbar's Poems* xxxii. 24 Na ȝowis auld, twch [*Maitl. MS.* tewcht] and sklender.

*δ.* *a* **1400–50** *Alexander* 319 Tachid in his for-top—twa tufe hornes. *a* **1602** Tuffe [see sense 4]. **1653** Walton *Angler* xii. 223 Gentles..is a good bait..being lively and tuffe. **1665** Hooke *Microgr.* 51 The pure parts of metals are of themselves very flexible and tuff. *a* **1679** R. Boyle *Guzman* II. Dram. Wks. 1739 II. 267 Let his Skin be tuff as Wall. **1683** Pettus *Fleta Min.* I. (1686) 3 Silver which is tuff or hard. **1733** W. Ellis *Chiltern & Vale Farm.* 8 Being tuffer, and more tenacious than any other.

**2.** Of viscous consistence or nature; sticky, adhesive, tenacious; glutinous.

*c* **1000** *Sax. Leechd.* III. 16 Gnid ða buteran on ðæm hwetstane mid copore þæt heo beo wel toh. **1382** Wyclif *Gen.* xi. 3 Thei hadden..towȝ cley for syment. *c* **1440** *Pallad. on Husb.* I. 66 Tough to glue ayein though thowe it delve. **1460** Capgrave *Chron.* (Rolls) 30 Tow erde, cleped bitumen. **1530** Tindale *Answ. More* IV. xii. Wks. (1573) 338/1 A carte that is ouer laden..in a tough mire maketh them [the horses] stand still. **1658** A. Fox *Würtz' Surg.* III. iv. 228 Clear water, somewhat tuff and slimie. **1789** W. Buchan *Dom. Med.* (1790) 675 Tough viscid saliva. **1800** *Med. Jrnl.* III. 154 The first class possess tough, glutinous juices.

**3.** *fig.* Stiff; severe, violent; †(sometimes) grievous, painful; of a contest, etc.: stoutly maintained, strenuous, vigorous and stubborn.

*α.* *c* **1205** Lay. 9319, & Hamun him to strac Mid toȝen [*c* 1275 luþer] his mæine. **1297** R. Glouc. (Rolls) 10605 Wan tueye stronge comeþ to gadere, it is somdel tou [*rime* slou]. ? *a* **1300** *Cursor M.* 24439 (Cott.), I sagh him dei, i sorud ai, ..mi tening es sa togh. *c* **1430** *Hymns Virg.* 120 With wawys grete, & stormys towe. **1539** Taverner *Erasm. Prov.* (1552) 3 They wil giue much tougher and more ernest strokes. *a* **1661** Fuller *Worthies, Warwick* (1662) II. 122 There was a tough contest betwixt the South and Northern-men in that university. **1865** Gosse *Land & Sea* (1874) 4 A tough breeze from the westward. **1891** C. Roberts *Adrift Amer.* 153 In spite of the tough racket I had had.

*γ.* **13..** *R. Gloucester's Chron.* (Rolls) 517 Þe wrastlinge bitvene hom was somdel toȝt [*rime* ibroȝt]. **1400–40** *Ibid.* App. H. 41 Þat bataile was wel towȝt [*rime* nouȝt]. *Ibid.* App. XX. 150 Sumdel þat was tout [*rime* nout].

**4.** Capable of great physical endurance; strongly resisting force, injury, fatigue, etc.; not easily overcome, tired, or impaired; hardy, stout, sturdy.

*c* **1330** R. Brunne *Chron. Wace* (Rolls) 13038 Petron had go, nad Beofs be tow. **1393** Langl. *P. Pl.* C. XIII. 187 Ac seedes þat been sowen and mowe suffre wyntres, Aren tydyour and tower to mannes by-hofthes. **1451** Capgrave *Life St. Gilbert* 73 His witte as fresch,..his mynde as tow, ..as euyr þei were. **1571** *Satir. Poems Reform.* xxv. 100 They know I am ane tuilȝeour teoch. **1576** Fleming *Panopl. Epist.* 258 A painefull and laborious fellowe, and such a one as is hard and toughe, and able to indure toile. *a* **1602** in Campion *Art Eng. Poesie* v. 18 All the glebe His tuffe hands manur'd. **1697** Dryden *Virg. Georg.* II. 322 A Glebe that asks Tough Teams of Oxen, and laborious Tasks. **1775** Sheridan *Rivals* I. i, There is an old tough aunt in the way. **1818** Scott *Br. Lamm.* xxi, That was what tough old Sir Evan Dhu used to say. **1856** Emerson *Eng. Traits, Ability*, Even the..sots of England are of a tougher texture.

**5.** Having great intellectual or moral endurance; difficult to influence, affect, or impress; steadfast, firm, persistent; also, stubborn, obstinate, hardened.

*c* **1400** *26 Pol. Poems* xxv. 521 Yef myn hert be styf and towe, To thanke the in wele and woo. **1411** *Ibid.* x. 35 My loue to man it was so tow. **1519** Horman *Vulg.* 142 b, The stewarde of the house is harde and toughe. **1603** Knolles *Hist. Turks* (1621) 965 A man of ripe yeares, but yet fierce of courage, tough in opinion. **1780** Cowper *Table-Talk* 458 Obduracy takes place; callous and tough, The reprobated race grows judgment proof. **1848** Dickens *Dombey* x, You'll find him tough, Ma'am. Tough, Sir, tough is Joseph. **1898** *Daily News* 25 Jan. 6/2 As a witness before Parliamentary Committees he was what is called 'a tough customer'.

**6.** Difficult to do, accomplish, perform, or deal with; hard, trying, laborious, troublesome.

**1619** Visct. Doncaster *Let.* in *Eng. & Germ.* (Camden) 133 To perswade them to hearken to a treaty would prove a tough piece of worke. *c* **1645** Howell *Lett.* (1650) I. IV. xv. 117 [The town of Breda] hath yeelded.., after a tough siege of thirteen months. **1797** Mrs. Radcliffe *Italian* xiii, They should find tough work of it. **1828** Scott *F. M. Perth* xv, 'It will be a tough job', growled the assassin. **1853** Kingsley *Hypatia* xxv, [He] comforted his troubled soul with a tough problem of astronomy.

**b.** Hard to believe or understand; taxing credulity or comprehension.

**1820** W. Irving in *Life & Lett.* (1864) I. xxvii. 459 When your boy grows large enough to understand tough stories. **1840** Barham *Ingol. Leg.* Ser. I. *Acc. New Play*, Tell us tough yarns, and then swear they are true. **1861** Du Chaillu *Equat. Afr.* xii. 155 This seemed to them the toughest yarn of all.

**7.** *U.S.* Of criminal or vicious proclivities. Cf. B.

**1884** J. Miller *Mem. & Rime* i. 9 And oh! but this is a tough town! **1894** Stead *If Christ Came to Chicago* 35 An oasis of cleanliness and light in the midst of a district which was decidedly tough. *Ibid.* 36 One of the toughest of the toughs in the slums.

†**8.** Phrase. *To make it tough.* **a.** To make it difficult; to make difficulties about doing something; to show reluctance. *Obs.*

**1297** R. Glouc. (Rolls) 10498 Þe king glosede her & þer & made it somdel touȝt, Ac þo it com to þe strengþe he nolde it graunti nouȝt. *c* **1369** Chaucer *Dethe Blaunche* 531 Lo howe goodly spake this knyght..And made it neyther tough ne queynt. *c* **1400** *Rowland & O.* 118 Þou may Iangill & make it toughe. *c* **1412** Hoccleve *De Reg. Princ.* 3516 'Iulius', quod he, 'make it noght so tow [*v.r.* tough]'. *c* **1470** *Golagros & Gaw.* 1069 It may nocht mend the ane myte to mak it so teugh. **1530** Palsgr. 624/2, I make it tough, I make it coye, as maydens do, or persons that be strange if they be asked a questyon...Mary, you make it toughe, *Marie, vous faitez le dangereux.*

†**b.** To be persistent or obstinate. *Obs.*

*a* **1549** in *Laneham's Let.* (1871) Pref. 151 Albeit ye mak it never sa tewch, To me your labour is in vane. *c* **1560** A. Scott *Poems* (S.T.S.) ii. 154 Quhen thai saw Sym sic curage ta, And Will mak it sa twche.

†**9.** quasi-*adv.* Vigorously, stoutly; persistently.

**1398** Trevisa *Barth. De P. R.* XI. xviii. (Tollem. MS.), Yf it be touȝe [*ed.* 1535 strongly] blowe, and þanne broke. *c* **1470** *Golagros & Gaw.* 704 The wyis..All to-turnit thair entyre, traistly and tewch. **1581** *Satir. Poems Reform.* xliv. 125 Quhen as he draue and Knox held steue the pleuch, And Methuen seu adulterie so teuch. **1805** A. Douglas *Poems* (1806) 12 At Luncarty they fought fu' teuch. **1827** W. Taylor *Poems* (ed. 2) 98 (E.D.D.) The carle he did play sae teugh.

**10. a.** In special collocations, as **tough-cake**: see quots. 1881, 1896; **tough-iron**: see quot. 1686; **tough-pitch** = *tough-cake*; **tough-stone** = *puff-stone* (Puff *sb.* 9 b).

*c* **1640** J. Smyth *Hundred of Berkeley* (1885) 175 In this toune [Dursley] is a rocke of a strange stone called a Puffe stone or as some pronounce it a tough stone. **1686** Plot *Staffordsh.* 161 The fourth and best sorts of Iron they call tough-Iron of which they make all sorts of the best wares. **1881** Raymond *Mining Gloss.*, *Tough-cake*, refined or commercial copper. *Ibid.*, *Tough-pitch*, see *Tough-cake*. **1896** *E. Durham Gloss.*, *Toughcake*, a water-cake, or white-cake, baked on the girdle. No currants used.

**b.** In comb. (chiefly parasynthetic) with other adjs., as *tough-backed, -looking, -metalled, -shelled, -skinned, -strung.*

*a* **1625** Fletcher & Massinger *Elder Brother* v. i, A true tough-metall'd blade. **1682** N. O. *Boileau's Lutrin* II. 14 A tough-back't Knave. **1768** Tucker *Lt. Nat.* (1834) I. 644 Their solid bones, their tough-strung muscles, their strong-bounding blood. **1825** Coleridge *Lett.*, to *J. Gillman* (1895) 743 Nature is..tough-lived as a turtle. **1826** Miss Mitford *Village* Ser. II. 132 A tall, spare, tough-looking woman, with a long bony face. **1872** Browning *Fifine* xxxi, Unsensitive, tough-thonged In lieu of our fine nerve.

**B.** *sb.* *U.S.* A street ruffian; cf. Rough *sb.*[1] 7.

**1866** Howells *Venet. Life* ii, The toughs of the distant alleys. **1884** J. Miller *Mem. & Rime* i. 9 Another 'tough' ..helped them hustle me in. **1897** *Outing* (U. S.) XXX. 429/1 It has spoiled our football, ruined our baseball, except for the 'tough'. **1903** C. Lumholtz *Unknown Mexico* I. 3 A raid on the camp by some toughs in the neighbourhood.

**Tough,** obs. variant of Tow *v.*[1]

†**Toughe, towghe.** *Irish Hist. Obs.* Also 6 toghe. [repr. Ir. *tuath* (*-th* = *-h*) territory, district. Joyce *Irish Names of Places* ser. 2 (1875) 212, cites *Tuoghnafall* and *Tuogh of the Fall* from early 17th c. grants, as name of a district south of Belfast, now known as 'The Falls'; the orig. Irish being *Tuath-na-bhfál*, district of the *fáls*, i.e. hedges or enclosures.]

A territory or district in Ireland.

[.. Old Ir. doct., cited in G. Hill *Plantation in Ulster* (1877) 102 This is the number of Tuaths [districts] that are in Tirconnell.] **1584** *Calr. Carew MSS.* II. 391 The towghe of the two towghes, called the barony of Clonballykernan **1586** *Ibid.* 428 The three toughes of Donseverige, Loghgill, and Toghe Ballamonyn. **1906** *Proc. R. Irish Acad.* XXVI. 58 Ancient Castles of Co. Limerick...These baronies were divided into Toghes, 'tuaths', or cantreds.

**Toughe,** variant of Tow *sb.*[3] *Obs.*

**Toughen** (tʊ·f'n), *v.* [f. Tough *a.* + -en 5.]

**1.** *trans.* To make tough.

1582 Stanyhurst *Æneis* iii. (Arb.) 76 O my son Æneas, with Troian destenye toughned. 1703 T. N. *City & C. Purchaser* 213 To toughen his Nails that were brittle. 1739 G. Smith *Laboratory* (1799) I. ii. 69 *heading*, Method of testing, refining, separating, allaying, and toughening [gold and silver]. 1901 F. W. Maitland *Rede Lect.* 27 Any scheme better suited to harden and toughen a traditional body of law. 1906 *Mem. Abp. Temple* I. 471 The experience of life had toughened the fibre of thought.

**2.** *intr.* To become tough.

1707 Mortimer *Husb.* (1721) I. 185 Lay them in some Room three or four Weeks or more, that they may cool, give and toughen. 1801 Southey *Thalaba* ix. xxx, Ere the green beauty of their brittle youth Grows brown, and toughens in the summer sun.

Hence **Toughened** (tʊ·f'nd) *ppl. a.*, **Toughening** (tʊ·f'niŋ) *vbl. sb.* and *ppl. a.*; **Toughener** (tʊ·f'nəɹ), one who or that which toughens.

1876 *Encycl. Brit.* V. 754/2 *Toughened glass invented. 1894 *Chicago Advance* 25 Oct. 118/1 [They] went away.. with a toughened propensity to be bad. 1895 C. W. Lyman in *Voice* (N. Y.) 5 Dec. 7/2 Recommended as a *toughener of the constitution. 1868 Joynson *Metals* 45 The *toughening of cast-iron. 1869 Sir E. J. Reed *Shipbuild.* xxi. 317 The toughening effect produced on a mass of Steel when it is heated, and plunged into a bath of oil. 1881 Raymond *Mining Gloss.*, *Toughening*, refining, as of copper or gold.

**Tougher**, obs. form of Tocher.

**Toughish** (tʊ·fiʃ), *a.* [f. Tough *a.* + -ish 1.] Somewhat tough.

1776 Da Costa *Conchol.* v. 121 A kind of toughish coriaceous or leather-like substance. 1840 Darwin in *Life & Lett.* (1887) I. 271 A toughish argument. 1882 *Standard* 26 Sept. 2/1 The limpet is..a toughish comestible.

**Toughly** (tʊ·fli), *adv.* [f. Tough *a.* + -ly 2.] In a tough manner (in various senses of Tough); strenuously; persistently; stoutly; vigorously.

*c* 1400 *Apol. Loll.* 68 [Þei] þat he knawiþ to stond touȝly in þer synnis þat þei han don. *c* 1450 tr. *De Imitatione* iii. viii. 74 Not to cleue ouer touȝly to þis affeccion. 1589 Greene *Menaphon* (Arb.) 83 They fell toughly to blowes. 1635 Shirley *Coronat.* i, Cassander,..oppos'd him toughly with his faction. 1728 Ramsay *Fables* xi. 32 He..laid till 't teughly tooth and nail. 1821 Joanna Baillie *Metr. Leg.*, *Lady G. B.* liii, Strong and toughly nerved. 1883 Stevenson *Silverado Sq.* iii. (1886) 20 We struggled toughly upward.

**Toughness** (tʊ·fnės). Forms: see Tough *a.* [f. Tough *a.* + -ness.] The state or quality of being tough, in various senses of the adjective.

*c* 1440 *Promp. Parv.* 498/2 Towghenesse (*K.*, *A.* townesse, *P.* toughnes), *tenacitas*. 1573–80 Baret *Alv.* T 307 *Lentor*, toughnesse: a clammie, or gluish humour. 1597 A. M. tr. *Guillemeau's Fr. Chirurg.* 48 b/2 The great toughenes of the.. Pituita. 1613 Fletcher, etc. *Honest Man's Fort.* v. ii, Stock fish.., If it be well drest, for the tuffness sake. 1674 Grew *Veget. Trunks* vii. § 12 Hence likewise we may understand the Cause of the Toughness of Flax. 1732 Arbuthnot *Aliments*, etc. (1736) 422 The Viscosity or Toughness of the Fluids. 1733 W. Ellis *Chiltern & Vale Farm.* 9 Red Clays..stand in the front..for..Tuffness, Coldness, and Moistness. 1830 Herschel *Stud. Nat. Phil.* iii. i. (1851) 238 The toughness of a solid, or that quality by which it will endure heavy blows without breaking. 1845 J. Coulter *Adv. in Pacific* xi. 141 From its extreme toughness, we could not eat it. 1895 R. P. Herrick in *Boston* (U. S.) *Pilgr. Missionary* June 11/1 You have gained a very good idea of the toughness of these mining towns.

**Tought.** Now *dial.* Also 7 **towght**, 9 *dial.* **towt** (taut). [Origin obscure. It answers in form, but barely in sense, to OFris. *tocht*, EFris. *tocht*, *togt*, MDu. *tocht*, *togt*, Du. *togt*, draught, drawing.] A length or section of an angler's hair-line, a link, a trace; also a piece of spun yarn (*E.D.D.*).

1676 Cotton *Angler* ii. v. 39 Take a strong small silk..and then whip it twice or thrice about the bare hook..both to prevent slipping, and also that the shanck of the hook may not cut the hairs of your Towght. 1681 Chetham *Angler's Vade-m.* ii. § 6 (1689) 10 When you make lines, especially 4 or 5 of the lowermost links, Gildards or toughts. 1905 *Eng. Dial. Dict.*, *Towt*, *tout*, *towght*, old rope, a piece of spun yarn, or a single strand of tarred rope used as a lashing.

**Tought, -e**, obs. ff. Taut, Tough. **Toughy**, dial. var. Toffee. **Touh, -e**, obs. ff. Tough.

**Touit(t**: see Tovet, two-peck measure.

**Touk(e**, obs. form of Tuck (of drum).

**Toul, toule, toull**, obs. forms of Toll.

**Tould(e**, obs. f. *told*, pa. t. and pple. of Tell *v.*

**Toulner, Toulsell**: see Tolner, Tolsell.

† **Toum**, obs. variant of Taum, fishing-line, etc.

1670 *Bk. Barony of Urie* (1892) 90 Showe them wher they ar to cast in ther severall toumes.

† **Toumbe**, *v.* *Obs.* *rare*—1. [ad. F. *tomber* to fall. Cf. Tumb *v.*] *intr.* To fall.

1297 R. Glouc. (Rolls) 10830 Þe king..bigan nei vor pite isuowe vpriȝt toumbe.

**Toun(e**, obs. f. Ton 1, Tone, Town, Tun, Tune.

**Tounder, -ire**, obs. Sc. forms of Tinder.

**Toundra**, var. Tundra. **Toung**, obs. f. Tongue.

† **Toup, to-u·p**, *prep.* *Obs.* *rare.* Also 4 **topen.** [f. To- 1 + Up, *uppan*: cf. OE. *on-uppan.*] Above, beyond, in addition to.

*c* 1315 Shoreham v. 284 Ac toup alle oþren ys y-blessed, Soþe wyf and mayde. 13.. *Guy of Warw.* (A.) 2735, & topen al þis, ȝif Gij wer ded, We miȝten haue þe lesse dred.

**Toup, toupe**, obs. forms of Tup.

**Toupee** (tupī·, tū·pi). Now *rare.* Also 8 **toupé, tupee, toppee**, 9 **towpee.** [app. ad. F. *toupet*: see next.] A curl or artificial lock of hair on the top of the head, esp. as a crowning feature of a periwig; a periwig in which the front hair was combed up, over a pad, into such a top-knot, worn by both sexes in the 18th c.; also the natural hair dressed in this mode; a patch of false hair or small wig to cover a bald place.

1731 Fielding *Grubstreet Op.* iii. xv, Love in his lac'd coat lies, And peeps from his toupee. 1742 Pope *Dunc.* iv. 88 Whate'er of dunce in College or in Town Sneers at another, in toupee or gown. 1753 in Fairholt *Costume in Eng.* (1885) I. 376 A tye-wig is banished for a pigeon-winged toupée. 1770 Barretti *Journ. fr. Lond. to Genoa* I. 137, I hate to see a little girl with a tupee. 1778 F. Marion in *Harper's Mag.* Sept. (1883) 546/1 The Lt. Col. recomends to every Soldier to have.. the fore top short without toppee & short at the sides. 1843 Macaulay *Ess.*, *Mme. D'Arblay* (1887) 740 He stalked about the small parlour, brushing the ceiling with his toupee. 1862 *Catal. Internat. Exhib.*, *Brit.* II. No. 4586 Fronts, partings, and toupées on the same novel principle.

*attrib.* 1817 Coleridge *Satyrane's Lett.* iii. 241 In the portrait of Lessing there was a toupee perriwig.

† **b.** One who wears a toupee; a person of fashion; a beau, a spark, a buck. *Obs.*

1727 Pope, etc. *Art of Sinking* x. 94 Then oh! she cries, what slaves I round me see? Here a bright Redcoat, there a smart Toupee. 1747 *Gentl. Mag.* Nov. 537/2 Here swiftly move toupee's, in spruce undress.

Hence **Toupee·d** *a.*, wearing a toupee.

1847 R. Chambers *Traditions of Edinburgh* 45 Their toupeed and deep-skirted beaux.

‖ **Toupet** (tupę, tū·pe, tū·pėt). [a. F. *toupet* (*tupę*) tuft of hair, esp. over the forehead, deriv. (in form dim.) of OF. *toup*, *top*, *tup*, tuft of hair, foliage, etc.; ad. *LG. *topp-* = OHG. *zopf* top, tuft, summit; cf. OFris. *top* tuft, top, ONorse *toppr* top, tuft, lock of hair: see Top *sb.*1]

**1.** = Toupee.

1729 *Art of Politicks* 10 Think we that modern words eternal are? Toupet, and Tompion, Cosins, and Colmar Hereafter will be called by some plain man A Wig, a Watch, a Pair of Stays, a Fan. 1818 Scott *Rob Roy* vi, These *fadeurs*, which every gentleman with a toupet thinks himself obliged to recite to an unfortunate girl. 1863 *Cornh. Mag.* VII. 395 Wigs are dangerous unless frankly avowed. A toupet may easily escape detection.

† **b.** *transf.* = Toupee b. *Obs.*

1728 Fielding *Love in Sev. Masques* Epil., From you then—ye toupets—he hopes defence. 1748 Richardson *Clarissa* Wks. 1883 VII. 495 A couple of brocaded or laced-waistcoated toupets..with sour screwed up half-cocked faces.

**2.** † The forelock of a horse or other animal (*obs.*); a thick head of hair (in quot., of a negro).

1797 *Sporting Mag.* X. 295 The *Tuft* or *Toupet*, that part of the mane which lies between the two ears. 1834 Southey *Doctor* iii. (1862) 5 Some of the inhabitants of Congo make a secret fob in their woolly toupet.

**3.** *attrib.*, as *toupet-coxcomb*, *-man*, *-wig*; **toupet-titmouse**, the Crested Titmouse.

1731 Fielding *Mod. Husb.* i. ix, I meet with nothing but a parcel of toupet coxcombs, who plaster up their brains upon their periwigs. 1748 Richardson *Clarissa* (1811) VII. vi. 35 No mere toupet-man; but all manly. *a* 1784 Pennant *Arct. Zool.* (1785) II. 423 Titmous. Toupet.. feathers on the head long, which it erects occasionally into a pointed crest, like a toupet. 1884 E. Yates *Rec. & Exper.* II. 238 A carefully arranged toupet-wig.

Hence **Toupeted** *nonce-wd.* (tū·pėtėd, tū·pęd) *a.*, wearing a toupet.

1903 *Smart Set* IX. 53/2 We go in to dinner with the toupeted colonels.

**Toupinambou**, obs. form of Topinambou.

**Tour** (tūəɹ), *sb.* Also 7 **toure, tower**: see also sense 4. [ME. a. F. *tour*, in OF. and Prov. *tor*, back-formation from nom. *tors*:—L. *tornus*, a. Gr. τόρνος a tool for describing a circle, a turner's wheel, a circle. The orig. acc. form was *torn*, *tourn*:—L. *tornum*; cf. Prov., Cat. *torn*, Sp., Pg., It. *torno*. In some of the Fr. and English senses, perh. n. of action f. *tourner* to turn.]

**I. 1.** One's turn or order (to do something); also, a spell of work or duty; a shift: see Turn *sb.* † *By tour*, *by tours*, by turns (*obs.*). Now mainly *Mil.*

[1292 Britton iv. ii, Si soen tourn soit a cele foiz de presenter ou noun.] *c* 1320 *Cast. Love* 1334 He was a-bated of his tour [Fr. *Il est de son torn abatuz*]. 1546 *Reg. Privy Council Scot.* I. 57 To cum and remane at the assege of the Castell.., ilk quarter in his tour. 1640 *Sc. Acts Chas. I* (1817) V. 311/1 If any of these whose toure fallis to be present shalbe absent. 1781 in Simes *Mil. Guide* (ed. 3) 9 That..each [may] march in their tour. 1868 *Regul. & Ord. Army* ¶ 837 When an Officer is in the performance of a duty, and his tour for another duty occurs, he is not to make good that other duty, but his tour is to pass him. 1887 *Harper's Mag.* June 129/2 The 'machine-tenders'..work in 'tours' or 'shifts' twelve hours each.

† **2.** A turning round, circular movement, revolution (in quot. 1688 *fig.*). *Obs.* *rare.*

1477 Caxton *Jason* 95 b, They go to the masse..for to make their tours and signes thenne for ony deuocion. 1688 Burnet *Lett. conc. St. Italy* 175 After the many tours, that the matter made in the many Ballotings, it came to the fixing of the last three out of whom the Doge was to be chosen. 1712 Blackmore *Creation* ii. 77 The Tours by Heav'nly Bodies made. 1719 De Foe *Crusoe* xix. (1840) I. 349 He made so many Tours..and led us by such winding Ways.

**3.** A going or travelling round from place to place, a round; an excursion or journey including the visiting of a number of places in a circuit or sequence; often qualified, as *cycling*, *walking*, *wedding tour*; *esp.* a circuitous journey embracing the principal places of the country or region mentioned. *On tour*, touring: see Tour *v.* 2.

*The* (*grand*) *tour*, a journey through France, Germany, Switzerland, and Italy, formerly fashionable, esp. as a finishing course in the education of young men of rank: see Grand tour.

1643 Denham *Cooper's H.* 183 Visits the World, and in his flying towers Brings home to us, and makes both Indies ours. 1652 Evelyn *St. France* Misc. Writ. (1805) 46 A traveller..making the tour as they call it. 1688 Burnet *Lett. conc. St. Italy* 155 He made the Tower of Italy with him this year. 1697 Dampier *Voy. round World* (1699) 104 Having made a Tour, or Semi-circular March they return to the Sea again. 1748–1869 [see Grand tour]. 1779 *Mirror* No. 57 ¶ 15 Manly and I..had set out together to make the tour of Europe. 1812 Combe (*title*) Dr. Syntax's Tour in Search of the Picturesque. *Ibid.* i, I'll make a tour—and then I'll write it. 1815 Scott *Guy M.* xiv, He.. resolved..to make a short tour of a fortnight. 1887 *Graphic* 15 Jan. 62/1 An actor..' on tour' in the *Vetah* company. 1888 *Spectator* 28 Apr. 561/1 President Carnot is on tour in the Gironde. *Mod.* We made the tour of the town and saw all the places of interest.

**b.** *transf.* and *fig.* A round.

1704 Swift *T. Tub* Pref., Thrice have I forced my imagination to make the tour of my invention. 1718 Lady M. W. Montagu *Lett.* (1887) I. 238 After having made their tour, the bride was again led..round the rooms. 1746 Coetlogon (*title*) A Tour through the Animal World; or an historical and accurate Account of near 400 Animals, Birds, Fishes, Serpents, Insects, &c. 1857 Jas. Hamilton *Less. Gt. Biogr.* (1859) 152 Making another tour of the company, each disciple filled his basket.

† **c.** A short outing taken for exercise, recreation, as a social function, or the like; also, the route taken on such occasions; in 17th c., in London, the drive round Hyde Park. *Obs.*

1656 Duchess of Newcastle *True Relation* in *Life* (1886) 309, I go sometimes abroad..in my coach..about some of the streets, which we call here a tour, where all the chief of the town go to see and to be seen. 1665 Pepys *Diary* 19 Mar., Mr. Povy and I in his coach to Hyde Parke, being the first day of the tour there. 1667 Duchess of Newcastle *Life Dk. of N.* (1886) ii. 99 Whereas at first there were no more but four coaches that went the Tour,.. all those that had sufficient means, and could go to the price, kept coaches, and went the Tour for their own pleasure. 1725 De Foe *Voy. round World* (1840) 250 Now and then making a little tour about the fields, and towards the mountains. 1773 *Life N. Frowde* 46 Whilst the Ship staied at Cork we were perpetually diverted with Visits,..Tours into the adjacent Country, and Entertainments at Home.

**d.** The circuit *of* an island, etc.; a round.

1719 De Foe *Crusoe* (1840) I. x. 162 My next design was to make a tour round the island. 1748 *Anson's Voy.* iii. v, He one day, attended by some of his officers, endeavoured to make the tour of the Island. 1756–7 tr. *Keysler's Trav.* (1760) II. 124 The tour is something above fifteen Italian, or three German miles.

† **4.** A crescent front of false hair (F. *tour de cheveux*). *Obs.* exc. *Hist.*

Cf. also Taure. Also, in this sense, by confusion with Tower *sb.*1, spelt 7 **towr**, 7–8 **tower.**

1674 *Lond. Gaz.* No. 900/4 Lost.., a Red Russia leather Trunk about two foot long..; a very light curled Tower and Locks,..with..other wearing apparel in it for Women. 1676 Etheredge *Man of Mode* ii. i, Her Tour wou'd Keep in Curl no longer. *a* 1700 B. E. *Dict. Cant. Crew*, *Tower*, a Woman's false Hair on their Fore-heads. 1727–41 Chambers *Cycl.*, *Tour of hair*, a tress or border of hair, going round the head, which mingled dextrously with the natural hair, lengthens and thickens it. *a* 1732 Gay *Toilette* Poems 1737 II. 81 Ancient matrons with their frizled tow'rs. 1837 Thackeray *Ravensw.* vii, People in tours and pig-tails.

**b.** See also Tower *sb.*1 6 b.

**II.** Figurative uses (mostly from French).

† **5.** A course to turn to; a shift, device, expedient.

1555 Phaer *Æneid* ii. D iij b, What shift? what tour is best we take? 1699 Vanbrugh *False Friend* iii. iii, We are still in the dark. I have one tour yet. Impudence be my aid!

† **6.** A mode of phraseology; a 'turn' given to a phrase or sentence, etc. *Obs.*

1685 Boyle *Eng. Notion Nat.* ii. 39 A dextrous Writer may oftentimes be able to give such a Form (or, as the Modern Frenchmen speak), such a Tour to his many-ways variable Expressions, as to avoid the necessity of making use of the Word Nature. 1751 J. Brown *Shaftesb. Charac.* 32 With regard to the oratory of the bar,..it is easy to observe, what a different tour the learned council takes, in addressing himself to the judge or jury.

† **7.** Manner of presenting or exhibiting anything; an aspect given to a matter. *Obs.*

1687 Burnet *Reply to Varillas* 28 Yet Mr. Varillas has a sublime tour in every thing, so that instead of setting before us the reasons which led him to depend upon such an Author,..he gives one, which indeed no man beside himself would ever have thought on. *Ibid.* 119, I find I judged too well of his Invention, in ascribing to him those Romantick Tours that he gave matters. *a* 1734 North *Exam.* iii. vi. § 22 (1740) 438 The next Tour of the Author..is to demonstrate, that although there were very good Reasons for the King to indulge the Fanatics.., yet he did it for none of those, but for other Reasons that were abominably bad.

† **8.** The course or compass of anything; what it amounts to; range, scope. *Obs.*

1697 Bentley *Phal.* (1699) 81 The latter part of his Life was the whole Tour and Compass that the Sophist designed to write of. 1713 — *Free-thinking* xviii. 36 The whole Tour of the Passage is this: A man given to Superstition can have no security, day or night, waking or sleeping.

**1737** WATERLAND *Eucharist* vii. 232 Such is the Tour of the Argument, such the Chain of Ideas that forms it.

†**9.** Manner or mode of being. *Obs.*

**1702** FARQUHAR *Inconstant* v. ii, Something I saw of a well-furnished, careless, agreeable tour about you. **1736** MRS. MANLEY *Secret Mem.* III. 204 The new-fashion Tour of Religion and Politicks.

†**10.** A round, a course (of engagements, etc.).

**1711** STEELE *Spect.* No. 156 ⁋ 4 Scarce one of all the Women who are in the Tour of Gallantries ever hear any thing of what is the common Sense of sober Minds.

**11.** One of the several trills, variations, or changes in the song of a trained canary.

**1906** *Daily Chron.* 20 Oct. 6/7 There are..in all, some twenty known trills or 'tours' in the song of a really accomplished roller canary.

**III. 12.** *attrib.* and *Comb.*, as *tour-book*, *-making*, *-writer*, *-writing*; **tour-money**, money paid for travelling fare and accommodation on a tour.

**1767** BUSH *Hibernia Cur.* (1769) p. vi, Neglected by the.. tour-writers. **1793** W. ROBERTS *Looker-On* No. 74 (1794) III. 171 The rage for tour-writing, which prevails in the female world. **1824** MCCULLOCH *Highl.*, etc. *Scot.* I. 41, I shall be obliged to write a tour book myself. **1869** P. LANDRETH *Life & Min. A. Thomson* i. 1 This occasional tour-making did not break up the continuity of his energetic life. **1909** *Daily Chron.* 5 Aug. 4/4 A third member of the party took fright..and requested the return of the tour-money.

**Tour** (tūᵊɹ), *v.* [f. TOUR *sb.*]

†**1.** *intr.* To 'take a turn' in or about a place, esp. riding or driving. *Obs.*

**1746** MRS. DELANY in *Life & Corr.* (1861) II. 443 The coach is ready for D. D. and me to tour in the park, and to see my lord's improvements. **1760** *Ibid.* III. 619 The Duchess has carried us to tour about the park and to see her hot-house.

**b.** To turn, direct one's steps. *dial.*

**1768** ROSS *Helenore* I. 33 Aff I scours Blessing my lucky stars, an' hame I tours.

**2.** *intr.* To make a tour or circuitous journey, in which many places are visited, usually without retracing one's steps; to make a prolonged excursion for recreation or business; *spec.* of an actor, a theatrical company, or the like: to go 'on tour', to travel from town to town fulfilling engagements.

**1789** A. C. BOWER *Diaries & Corr.* (1903) 97 We are all got thus far touring for Health. **1799** COLERIDGE *Lett.*, *to T. Poole* (1895) 306 The man who toured with me in Wales and afterwards published his 'Tour'. **1858** CARLYLE *Fredk. Gt.* x. vii. (1872) III. 276 Algarotti..has been touring about as a celebrity these four years past. **1886** *Cyclist's Tour. Club Gaz.* IV. 126 A word of advice to those about to tour at Easter. **1897** *Literature* 13 Nov. 123/2 [He] has made up his mind to take up once again lecturing work, and he will tour in several of the large American towns. **1907** H. WYNDHAM *Flare of Footlights* xii, Godfrey Deane has decided not to tour,..so I shall ask Antony for the part.

**3.** *trans.* To make the tour or round of, to tour in (a country or district).

**1885** J. COLEMAN in *Longm. Mag.* VII. 67 Barrett organised a company with which..he toured the provinces. **1887** *Bicycling News* 8 Oct. 3/2 He landed at Melbourne, and toured the colonies with great success. **1898** *Westm. Gaz.* 25 Jan. 5/3 Mr. R. is this week touring his constituency. **1899** *Ibid.* 2 Feb. 9/1 To tour India..with an English amateur cricket team.

**b.** To cover (a distance) in touring.

**1891** in *Pall Mall Gaz.* 12 Feb. 1/2 One good performance on the path does more to arouse attention than 20,000 miles quietly toured.

**4.** *spec.* (*Theatr.*) To take (a play or entertainment) on tour; to tour with.

**1897** *Westm. Gaz.* 22 May 8/1 'The County Fair', the American drama..now being toured in the provinces by Mr. Neil Burgess's Company. **1904** *Ibid.* 12 Feb. 5/2 It is the intention of the lecturer to tour his illustrated entertainment in the provinces. **1910** *Stage Year Bk.* 52 This production [Peter Pan] was magnificently staged in Sydney, but the business was poor, and it was never toured.

⁋ *Touring* in Capt. Smith *Virginia* (1624) VI. *New Eng.* 212 is an error for *turning* in the earlier *Descr. New Eng.* (1616) 17.

Hence **Tou·ring** *ppl. a.*, that tours.

**1870** *Athenæum* 15 Oct. 506 A touring troupe of singers from this country. **1883** *Pall Mall Gaz.* 27 Oct. 4/1 Town-abiding and touring Americans. **1888** J. PENNELL *ibid.* 25 Oct. 5 From the standpoint of a touring cycler.

**Tour**, obs. form of TOWER, TWIRE.

‖**Touraco** (tūᵊrăko). Also touracou, -caw, turaco, -ko, -koo. [= F. *touraco*, Du. *toerako*: native name in W. Africa of *Turacus persa*.

Buffon, *Hist. Nat. Oiseaux* (1783), calls it *tourocco*, which name he claims to have invented from the first part of *tourterelle* turtle-dove + *hocco*, Fr. name of the curassow; but the bird was known to G. Edwards 40 years earlier as *touraco*.]

Any bird of the family *Musophagidæ* (plantain-eaters), natives of southern, west, and central Africa, and esp. of the genus *Turacus* (or *Corythaix*), large birds with brilliant purple, green, and crimson plumage and prominent crest (hence formerly called *crown-birds*); also of the genus *Schizorrhis*, with plumage of a plainer character.

**1743** G. EDWARDS *Hist. Birds* I. 7 The Touraco. This Bird is about the Bigness of a Magpye or Jay; the Make of its Body is rather long than round; the Head of a moderate Size. **1840** *Penny Cycl.* XVI. 29/2 The Touracos ..feed principally on soft fruits. **1861** DU CHAILLU *Equat. Afr.* vii. 77 (*Among the Fans*) His head was..decorated with the red feathers of a touracaw. **1863** R. F. BURTON *Abeokuta* I. 38 The gay crested touraco (*Corythaix*), with its jay-like manner, beautiful and harsh-voiced as the Maids of Athens, aired its gorgeous coat in the sunbeams upon the tree-top. **1896** *List Anim. Zool. Soc.* 321 *Turacus persa*.. Senegal Touracou...West Africa...*T. livingstonii*..Livingstone's Touracou...British Central Africa...*T. corythaix*.. White-crested Touracou...South Africa. *Ibid.* 322 *Gallirex chlorochlamys*..Green-necked Touracou...*Schizorhis africana*..Variegated Touracou.

**Tourbe**, var. TURB *Obs.*, a troop.

**Tourbillion** (tuəɹbi·lyən), ‖ **tourbillon** (*tur*-bi*l*yoṅ). Also 5 turbilloun, 8 -billion. [a. F. *tourbillon* whirlwind, in OF. *torbeillon* (12th c. in Hatz.-Darm.), *torbillon*, app., from the sense, an irregular derivative of L. *turbo*, *-inem* 'whirlwind'; though the form seems to connect it with vulgar L. *turbēla*, *turbella* 'bustle, stir', deriv. of *turba* crowd. See Hatz.-Darm., Littré, and Scheler.]

**1.** A whirlwind; a whirling storm. Also *fig.* *rare.* ? *Obs.*

*c* **1477** CAXTON *Jason* 57 A meruaillous turbilloun of winde roose in the see. **1585** T. WASHINGTON tr. *Nicholay's Voy.* I. xi. 13 A wind called..vulgarly Tourbillon or whirlewinde. **1751** ELIZA HEYWOOD *Betsy Thoughtless* III. 138 With the more violence those tourbillions of the mind rage for a while, the sooner they subside. **1819** W. TENNANT *Papistry Storm'd* (1827) 57 A scharp-ee'd man, whase sicht was clear, Beneath the stowry tourbillon Micht see [etc.].

**2.** *transf.* A whirling mass or system; a vortex; a whirl. Also *fig.* *Obs.* exc. as French.

**1712** STEELE *Spect.* No. 472 ⁋ 4 Each of them [the fixed stars] is a Sun moving on its own Axis in the Centre of its own Vortex or Turbillion. **1753** CHESTERF. *Lett.* 26 Nov., I am very glad, that you are whirled in that *tourbillion* of pleasures. **1779** H. WALPOLE *Let. to C'tess Ossory* 27 Oct., The *tourbillon* of Ranelagh surrounds you. **1824** SCOTT *St. Ronan's* iii, All things were engaged in the *tourbillon*, of which she formed the pivot and centre.

**3.** A kind of firework which spins as it rises, describing a spiral.

**1765** R. JONES *Fireworks* IV. 121 When you fire tourbillons, lay them on a smooth table, with their sticks downwards. **1842** G. FRANCIS *Dict. Arts*, etc., s. v., Fire will issue from four holes; that from the two lower holes will drive the tourbillion into the air, and that from the side holes will spin it round. **1873** E. SPON *Workshop Receipts* Ser. I. 135/1 The tourbillon is a species of firework very ingeniously contrived to represent a spiral column of fire.

**4.** (See quot.)

**1884** F. J. BRITTEN *Watch & Clockm.* 266 *Tourbillon*..a carriage in which the escapement of a watch is fitted so that it revolves round the fourth wheel. The idea of the tourbillon..is to get rid of position errors.

**Tourbine, Tourche, Tourcheman, Tourd(e**: see TURBINE, TORCH, TRUCHMAN, TURD.

‖ **Tour de force** (tūrdəfors). [F. *tour* turn, feat, *de* of, *force* force, strength.] A feat of strength, power, or skill.

**1805** G. ELLIS *Let.* in Lockhart *Scott* (1837) II. ii. 80 Leyden's breakfast was only a *tour de force* to astonish Ritson. **1818** LADY MORGAN *Fl. Macarthy* II. v. 234 Each should try a tour de force with the other. **1870** RUSKIN *Lect. Art* i. (1875) 15 The execution of the best Artists is always a splendid tour-de-force. **1895** SALMOND *Chr. Doctr. Immort.* VI. iii. 640 It is only by a tour de force that they can be driven that length.

**Toure**, variant of TOR *a. Obs.*, difficult, tedious; obs. form of TOWER, TWIRE *v.* (to peep).

**Tourelle** (‖ *tu*-, ture·l). Also 4 torel, -elle, tourel, towrelle, turel, -eile. [a. F. *tourelle*, dim. of *tour* TOWER.] A turret.

**13..** *Cursor M.* 10005 (Cott.) Þe four torels [*v. rr.* turret, trettis, turrettes] on hei er sett. *c* **1330** R. BRUNNE *Chron.* (1810) 178 A darte..com fro þat tureile, þat R[ichard] had doun smyten. **13..** *K. Alis.* 7173 (Bodl. MS.) He haþ taken myne castels, He haþ afelled myne Tourels [*v. r.* torellis]. **13..** *Coer de L.* 1841 A castel..With six stages ful of towrelles, Wel flourished with cornelles. **1840** LOUISA S. COSTELLO *Summer amongst Bocages* II. 218 Two beautiful and exquisitely carved tourelles. **1895** CROCKETT *Men of Moss-Hags* 391 In the little sunlit tourelle at Earlstoun.

**Touret, -ette**, obs. forms of TORRET, TURRET.

**Tourette** (tūre·t). [f. TOUR *sb.* + -ETTE.] A little or short tour; an excursion.

**1881** HARE *Story of Life* (1900) V. xxii. 332, I made a tourette into Norfolk. **1906** BUMPUS *Cathedr. Eng. & Wales* II. 197 Charming tourettes may be made in one direction to Rushden..in another to Chelveston.

**Tourify** (tūᵊrifəi), *v. colloq.* [f. TOUR *sb.* + -(I)FY.] *intr.* To make a tour; to tour. Hence **Tou·rifying** *ppl. a.* So **Tourifica·tion**, a touring.

**1802** R. COUPER (*title*) The Tourifications of Malachi Meldrum, Esq. **1819** MISS MITFORD in L'Estrange *Life* (1870) II. iii. 71 Mr. Hofland is just now setting out on a tourification along the banks of the Seine. **1820** *Ibid.* 116 Dr. Nott..has been tourifying about Normandy. **1825** W. TAYLOR in *Monthly Rev.* CVI. 14 In this tourifying age.

**Tou·ring**, *vbl. sb.* [f. TOUR *v.* + -ING [1].] The action of the verb TOUR.

**1818** *Sporting Mag.* II. 225 Some persons call this touring. **1827** SOUTHEY *Lett.* (1856) IV. 76 It was in the summer season of touring and visiting. **1874** BLACKIE *Self-Cult.* 44 The modern habits of travelling and touring can be made to subserve the double end of health and culture.

**b.** *attrib.*, as *touring club*, *ground*; **touring-car**, a motor car designed for touring purposes, with accommodation for passengers and luggage.

**1858** CARLYLE *Fredk. Gt.* VII. iii. II. 181 Touring expeditions; which are now..done by steam, without even eyesight, not to say intelligence. *c* **1878** *Prospectus*, The Bicycle Touring Club, founded at the North of England Meet held at Harrogate on the 5th August, 1878. **1885** *Manch. Exam.* 11 Nov. 3/2 Norway has become such a.. popular touring ground. **1908** *Westm. Gaz.* 23 July 4/1 The Grand Prix was in no sense a touring-car race.

**Tourism** (tūᵊriz'm). [f. TOUR *sb.* + -ISM.] The theory and practice of touring; travelling for pleasure. Usually depreciatory.

**1811** *Sporting Mag.* XXXVIII. 251 Sublime Cockey Tourism. **1843** THACKERAY *Irish Sk.-bk.* xvii, No doubt, ere long..the rush of London tourism will come this way [West of Ireland]. **1872** JERNINGHAM tr. *Hübner's Sixtus the Fifth* I. vi. I. 87 Tourism was born in the seventeenth century, and Englishmen were the first to practise it. **1903** C. WHIBLEY *Thackeray* iii. 44 The literature of 'tourism' is ever increasing.

**Tourist** (tūᵊrist). [f. TOUR *sb.* + -IST.] One who makes a tour or tours; *esp.* one who does this for recreation; one who travels for pleasure or culture, visiting a number of places for their objects of interest, scenery, or the like.

*c* **1800** PEGGE *Anecd. Eng. Lang.* (1814) 313 A Traveller is now-a-days called a Tour-*ist*. **1803** SYD. SMITH *Wks.* (1850) 34 An agricultural tourist will faithfully detail the average crop per acre. **1824** SCOTT *St. Ronan's* i, It provoked the pencil of every passing tourist. **1855** H. SPENCER *Princ. Psychol.* § 66. 246 The Swiss tourist whose inquiries respecting distances are answered in '*stunden*', or hours. **1873** SMILES *Huguenots Fr.* III. i. (1881) 383 Dauphiny..lying completely out of the track of ordinary tourists.

**b.** *attrib.* and *Comb.*, as *tourist agency*, *country*, *rendezvous*, *ticket*; *tourist-crammed*, *-haunted*, *-laden*, *-mobbed*, *-ridden*, *-trodden* adjs.; **tourist-car**, a railway carriage with special accommodation for tourists.

**1867** J. G. FENNELL (*title*) The Rail and the Rod; or, Tourist-Angler's Guide to Waters and Quarters around London. **1881** I. E. B. COX (*title*) The Angler's Diary and Tourist Fisherman's Gazetteer of the Rivers and Lakes of the World. **1887** RUSKIN *Præterita* II. 379 Ruin was inevitable in the valley after it became a tourist rendezvous. **1892** *Pall Mall G.* 16 July 2/1 A tourist country like Switzerland. **1895** P. HEMINGWAY *Out of Egypt* I. ii. 22 It was no good applying to the hotels or tourist agencies. **1897** MRS. E. L. VOYNICH *Gadfly* ii, The glaring white streets and dusty, tourist-crammed promenades. **1898** *Edin. Rev.* Oct. 521 The beautiful but now..hackneyed and tourist-mobbed route to Chamonix. **1905** E. CANDLER *Unveiling of Lhasa* xiii. 242 Just as one is dragged into a church in some tourist-ridden land. **1908** *Westm. Gaz.* 9 May 3/1 His [ticket] had the tourist-car ticket appended as a portion of the fare.

Hence (*nonce-wds.*) **Tou·ristdom**, the realm or collective body of tourists; **Tou·risting**, the practice or habit of touring; **Tou·ristry** = *touristdom* or *touristing*; **Tou·ristship**, the quality or position of a tourist; **Tou·risty** *a.*, *colloq.*, characteristic of the tourist.

**1888** *Pall Mall G.* 28 Aug. 13/2 Ere those Circe's sties, the Club-huts, harboured *touristdom in flocks. **1883** A. STEWART *Nether Lochaber* xxxviii. 233 Never before were all the conveniences for '*touristing' so perfect. **1878** STEVENSON *Inland Voy.* 32 All the ruck and rabble of British *touristry. **1883**—*Silverado Sq.* 27 It was a pure little isle of touristry among these solitary hills. **1894** *Speaker* 7 Apr. 390/2 A Venice vulgarised by Cook's touristry. **1849** *Fraser's Mag.* XL. 375 He was rather a tourist than a traveller, and this *touristship was the worse for his scientific crotchets. **1906** *Athenæum* 8 Sept. 278/3 The letterpress ..is..slight, sketchy, '*touristy', but genial.

**Touristic** (turi·stik), *a.* [f. TOURIST + -IC.] Of or pertaining to tourists or touring.

**1848** *Blackw. Mag.* LXIV. 373 The touristic hordes, who paddled up and down the well-known old banks. **1865** LD. STRANGFORD in *Lett. & Papers* (1878) 98 (There is no such thing as a record of touristic journeying in Crete. **1894** *Athenæum* 26 May 672 It has importance from another than the touristic point of view.

So **Touri·stical** *a.*, in same sense.

**1863** W. CORY *Lett. & Jrnls.* (1897) 98 A long quiet walk, only one touristical carriage all the way. **1893** *Sat. Rev.* 18 Feb. 189/3 His discursive record is chiefly 'touristical'.

**Tourize** (tūᵊraiz), *v.* [f. TOUR *sb.* + -IZE.] *intr.* To make a tour, to go touring.

**1837** SIR J. PAGET *Let.* 22 Mar., in *Mem.* v. 102, I think, if we are spared to tourize together, our first trip shall be to Fontainebleau. **1864** *Macm. Mag.* Apr. 521 Let him tourise out of the beaten track.

**Tourmaline** (tūᵊɹmălin, -*i*n). *Min.* Also tour-, turmalin, -ine, (tormaline). [= F. *tourmaline* (1771 in *Dict. Trev.*), Ger. *turmalin* (1707, Garmann), Du. *toermalijn* (1778), It., Sp. *turmalina*; all ultimately f. Sinhalese *tōramalli*, according to Clough 'a general name for the cornelian'. The origin of the European final *-n(e* is obscure: cf. *mandarin*, *talapoin*, etc. The better (18th c.) English spelling was *tour-*, *turmalin*; the spelling *-ine* is in imitation of French, in which the *e* merely supports the *n*.] A brittle pyro-electric mineral, occurring in crystals, also massive, compact, and columnar, originally obtained from Ceylon; a complex silicoborate with a vitreous lustre, usually black or blackish and opaque (SCHORL), but also blue (INDICOLITE), red (RUBELLITE), green, or colourless, and in various rich transparent or semi-transparent shades, known as *precious tourmaline*, and much used as a gem. Also formerly called, from its electrical properties, *ash-drawer*, Du. *aschentrecker*, Ger. *aschenzieher*, F. *tire-cendre*.

**1759** B. WILSON in *Phil. Trans.* LI. I. 308, I have the

pleasure to communicate to you some experiments made upon the Tourmalin, or Ashstone. **1794** SULLIVAN *View Nat.* I. 440 The tourmaline is a variety of the schoerl. **1798** EDGEWORTH *Pract. Educ.* (1811) II. 294 A small electrical stone called tourmalin. **1799** KIRWAN *Geol. Ess.* 121 All..lose some part of their weight when exposed to a strong heat..; turmaline loses 15 per cent. **1812** SIR H. DAVY *Chem. Philos.* 131 There is a stone..called tourmaline, which is sometimes crystallized as a nine-sided prism, terminated by a three-sided and a six-sided pyramid. **1825** HEBER *Jrnl.* xxvii. (ed. 2) 189 The topaz, ruby, tormaline, diamond, and various others. **1853** TH. ROSS *Humboldt's Trav.* III. xxxii. 382 The granite is traversed by..veins..abounding with rock-crystal, black tourmalin, and pyrites. **1866** RUSKIN *Eth. Dust* ix. 179 This black thing,..one of the prettiest of the very few pretty black things in the world, is called 'Tourmaline'. **1888** RUTLEY *Rock-Forming Min.* 38 A plate of tourmaline cut parallel to the principal axis.

**b.** With *a* and *pl.* A specimen or gem of this mineral; also a transparent plate of tourmaline cut parallel to the vertical crystal axis, used in polariscopes, etc.

**1816** P. CLEAVELAND *Min.* 261 When a Tourmaline is viewed perpendicularly to the sides of the prism, it is more or less transparent, but, if observed in the direction of the axis, it is opaque. **1843–54** PEREIRA *Pol. Light* (ed. 2) 211 If the two tourmalines be crossed the rays are suppressed—if they coincide the rays are transmitted. **1890** *Academy* 12 Apr. 252/1 It [a bracelet] consists of a broad and heavy band of Californian gold, set with two large tourmalines.

**c.** *attrib.* and *Comb.*, as *tourmaline crystal, granite, pendant*; **tourmaline pincette, tongs**, a simple polariscope, consisting of tongs having a plate of tourmaline mounted in each grasping jaw; **tourmaline-rock, -schist**: see quots. 1882.

**1843–54** PEREIRA *Pol. Light* (ed. 2) 213 The two sets of rays..successively pass through the tourmaline analyzing plate. **1879** RUTLEY *Stud. Rocks* x. 138 The terminations of tourmaline crystals are frequently composed of a great number of faces. **1882** GEIKIE *Text-bk. Geol.* (1885) 73 Tourmaline..with quartz forms tourmaline-rock. *Ibid.* 131 Tourmaline-schist..,a blackish, finely granular, quartzose rock with abundant granules and needles of black tourmaline. **1888** RUTLEY *Rock-Forming Min.* 59 The tourmaline pincette, or tongs.

Hence **Tourmali·nic** *a.*, pertaining to, of the nature of, or consisting of tourmaline; **Tou·rmalinite** *Min.*, tourmaline; **Tou·rmalinize** *v.*, *trans.* to impregnate or charge with tourmaline.

**1879** DANA *Man. Geol.* (ed. 3) 70 *Tourmalinic*, containing tourmaline. **1896** CHESTER *Dict. Names Min.*, *Tourmalinite*, variant of tourmaline. **1908** *Amer. Jrnl. Sc.* Apr. 323 Along the margin..the granite is often strongly tourmalinized.

**Tourment**, etc., obs. form of TORMENT, etc.

**Tourn** (tūᵊɹn). *Eng. Hist.* Also 6–7 tourne, turne, 6–8 torn, 6–9 turn, 7–8 torne. [a. Anglo-Fr. *tourn*, TURN, n. of action f. *tourner* to turn, go round; in med.L. *turnus*. In the ordinary senses the sb. and vb. have become *turn*; but in this historical sense the Anglo-French spelling is usually retained, though Pollock and Maitland prefer to call it 'the sheriff's *turn*'.]

The tour, turn, or circuit formerly made by the sheriff of a county twice in the year, in which he presided at the hundred-court in each hundred of the county; the great court leet of the county, held by him on these occasions; it was a court of record.

[**1217** *Magna Carta, 2nd Reissue* c. 42 Nec aliquis vicecomes vel baillivus suus faciat turnum suum per hundretum nisi bis in anno,..semel post Pascha et iterum post festum Sancti Michaelis. **1292** BRITTON I. xix. § 3 Sutes dues a noster Counté, et a nos hundrez, et a nos maners, et a tourns de noster viscounte. *Ibid.* xxx. § 1 Les..pletz sount apelez tourns de viscounte; qi deus foiz par an les deit tener par mi chescun hundred de soen counté.] **1432** *Rolls of Parlt.* IV. 403/1 By cause the Decennare and Decennes..comen noght hole and full unto the Sherrefes tourn. **1531** *Dial. on Laws Eng.* I. vii. 16 In euery shyre..there is a courte ..that is called the Shyryffes torne. **1542–6** in *14th Rep. Hist. MSS. Comm.* App. IX. 272 Bobbingworth Village come to the Turne aforesaid by iiii men, Tennants by coppie, and the Reeve of the village there. **1608** BACON *Office Constables* etc., *Sheriffs*, [The sheriff] hath authority to hold two several courts of distinct natures; the one called the tourne, because he keepeth his turn and circuit about the shire. **1765** BLACKSTONE *Comm.* I. 368 The sheriff's tourn, which is the court-leet of the county. **1875** STUBBS *Const. Hist.* II. xiv. 27 The 42nd article orders..the sheriff's tourn, which now first appears in the charters, [to be held] twice a year. **1895** POLLOCK & MAITLAND *Hist. Eng. Law* I. 515 Twice a year the sheriff makes a tour or turn (*turnus vicecomitis*) through all the hundreds of the country. He holds each of the hundred courts, and on these occasions many persons besides the ordinary suitors ought to be present.

**Tourn, Tournado**, obs. ff. TURN, TORNADO.

**Tournament** (tūᵊ·ɹnămĕnt), *sb.* Forms: *α.* 3 tornei-, 3–5 torne-, 4–7 tornea-, 5–7 tornament. *β.* 3–5 turne-, 4–8 turna-, 5–6 turnei-, turney-, 7 turneament. *γ.* (5 tournoy-), 5–7 tourne-, 7 tournea-, 6– tournament. (Also 4–6 -mente, *pl.* 3–5 -mens.) [a. OF. *torneiement* (*Enéas*, c 1150), *torney-, tornee-, torniement*; central and later OF. *tornoiement, tournoiement, tournoie-, tournoyement*; also *turnoie-, turneie-, turneement*, f. *tourneier, -oier*, etc., TOURNEY *v.*: see -MENT. Cf. Pr. *torneiament*, It. *tornia-*, †*torneamento*; the later Eng. spellings *tornea-, tourna-* were app. due to the influence of med.L.

Cf. med.L. *torneamentum* (fr. Fr.), 1157 in Reims Synod, Canon iv, and 1179 in Lateran Council, Can. xx 'detestabiles illas nundinas vel ferias, quas vulgo torneamenta vocant'.]

**1.** Originally, A martial sport or exercise of the middle ages, in which a number of combatants, mounted and in armour, and divided into two parties, fought with blunted weapons and under certain restrictions, for the prize of valour; later, A meeting at an appointed time and place for knightly sports and exercises.

According to Roger of Hoveden III. 268, first introduced into England by Richard I.

*α.* **1297** R. GLOUC. (Rolls) 2896 In ioustes & in tornemens. *Ibid.* 11041 Sir edward..hauntede torneimens [*v.r.* (C.) turnemens] with wel noble route. **13..** *Sir Beues* (A.) 3766 Þai ben come for a tornement Þat is cride for a maide faire. *c* **1440** *Promp. Parv.* 497/1 Torneament, *torneamentum.* **1612** SELDEN *Illustr. Drayton's Poly-olb.* iv. 70 Torneaments and jousts were their exercises.

*β.* *a* **1225** *Ancr. R.* 390 He dude him ine turnement, & hefde uor his leofmonnes luue, his schelde ine uihte. **13..** *Guy Warw.* (A.) 821 He schal bring to þe turment [*v.r.* turnement] þat day (Wele is him þat it winne may) A gerfauk þat is milke white. *Ibid.* 829 Who so winneþ þe turnament al Bi aiþer half, þe priis have schal. *c* **1450** *Merlin* ix. 133 After they be-gonne a turnemente, and departed hem in two partyes. **1590** SPENSER *F. Q.* I. v. 1 That doughtie turnament. **1596** *Ibid.* IV. iv. 12 Against the Turneiment. *Ibid.* 13 Unto the place of Turneyment. *a* **1700** DRYDEN *Theodore & Hon.* 18 He..At tilts and turnaments obtained the prize, But found no favour in his lady's eyes.

*γ.* **1470–85** MALORY *Arthur* I. v. 41 Vpon newe yeersday the barons lete maake a Iustes and a tournement. *c* **1483** CAXTON *Dialogues* 25/1 For suche ladies Ben the tournemens. **1485** — *Paris & V.* 11 Ioustes and tournoyment doon in his cyte of vyenne. **1552** HULOET, Tournamente or iuste. **1656** BLOUNT *Glossogr.* (1674), *Tournement*, or *Tourneament.* **1756–7** tr. *Keysler's Trav.* (1760) IV. 291 A cuirass used by the elector Augustus in tournaments. **1801** STRUTT *Sports & Past.* III. i. 103 Every kind of military combat made in conformity to certain rules..was anciently called a tournament. **1818** HALLAM *Mid. Ages* ix. II. (1819) III. 502 Tournaments..may be considered to have arisen about the middle of the eleventh century; for..the name of tournaments, and the laws that regulated them, cannot be traced any higher. **1841** JAMES *Brigand* i, Henry the Second [of France]..closed his career in the last tournament [1559] which Europe was destined to witness. **1888** *Encycl. Brit.* XXIII. 489/1 Tournaments and jousts differed from one another principally in the circumstance that in the first several combatants on each side were engaged.., and in the second the contention was between two combatants only.

**b.** A modern imitation of the mediæval pastime.

**1701** *Lond. Gaz.* No. 3734/2 The Imperial Court continues at the Palace at Favorita, where they were entertained yesterday with a Turnament. **1839** LD. COCKBURN *Jrnl.* (1874) I. 239 In August last the display called the *Tournament* took place at Eglinton Castle.

**c.** Applied to the Olympic and other ancient games or contests.

**1387** TREVISA *Higden* (Rolls) I. 11 After þe strif, ioustes, and turnementis of Olympy. *Ibid.* II. 381 Theseus..slowȝ Minotaurus in þe tornemente [*in agone interemit*]. **1610** HOLLAND *Camden's Brit.* (1637) 703 Severus..His body was ..committed to the flames, honoured with Justs and Turneaments of his souldiers and his owne sonnes. **1866** FELTON *Anc. & Mod. Gr.* II. v. 358 They..utterly disappeared from the face of Hellas, with their language, their manners, their jousts and tournaments.

**2.** *fig.* An encounter or trial of strength.

**1638** BP. REYNOLDS *Peace Ch.* 31 Happy..the Church of God, when curious novelties, and as it were Tourneaments in sacred things are esteemed prophane. **1659** *Gentl. Calling* (1696) 118 They keep, as it were, solemn Justs and Turnaments of Debauchery. **1901** *Empire Rev.* I. 370 When this dogmatic tournament has spent its force. **1902** R. BAGOT *Donna Diana* xx, In the rose-gardens below, the nightingales were holding a tournament of song.

**3.** *transf.* A contest in any game of skill in which a number of competitors play a series of selective games, e. g. a *chess* or *lawn tennis tournament.*

*Military* or *naval tournament*, an athletic meeting at which there are a large proportion of contests especially adapted for soldiers or sailors.

**1761** *Ann. Reg.* 152 A naval tournament, or race upon the waters, resembling those practised at Venice in the carnival season. **1852** H. STAUNTON (*title*) The Chess Tournament. A collection of the games played at this celebrated assemblage. **1869** in J. D. Heath *Croquet-Player* (1874) 95 N.C.C. Open tournament at Highgate (6 inch hoops). **1872** R. C. A. PRIOR *Croquet* 55 The Gardener's Chronicle announced last year a 'Potato Tournament'. **1885** *Sat. Rev.* 24 Jan. 113 If..the old Counties Chess Association..holds its tournaments in the provinces. **1888** *Daily News* 15 Sept. 3/5 Lawn Tennis. The Essex Open Tournament was resumed yesterday at the Connaught Grounds.

**4.** *attrib.*

**1848** THACKERAY *Van. Fair* lii, It had been a Cistercian Convent in old days, when the Smithfield, which is contiguous to it, was a tournament ground. **1902** *Munsey's Mag.* XXVI. 476/2 When the skater has become proficient in all of them, he is ready to proceed to the simpler combinations of the tournament figures.

Hence **Tou·rnament** *v.* (*nonce-wd.*), *intr.* to ride as in a tournament, to tilt; **Tourname·ntal** *a.*, of or pertaining to a tournament; †**Tou·rnamentee·r**, *Obs. rare*, a combatant at tournaments.

**1884** J. SHARMAN *Hist. Swearing* i. 10 They bestrode chairs and benches,..and *tournamented about the room. **1801** STRUTT *Sports & Past.* III. i. 127 When the grand *tournamental conflict was finished. **1896** *Daily News* 28 May 3/1 The rumour..that there was tournamental antagonism between the Navy and Army. **1737** OZELL *Rabelais* II. 221 Great Tilters and *Turnamenteers.

**Tournasin** (tūᵊ·ɹnăsin). [a. F. *tournasin, tournassin* (Littré), f. *tournaser, -nasser* to turn (pottery) on the wheel, derivative of *tourner* to TURN.] A knife or spatula used to remove excess of slip from decorated pottery when partially dried.

**1839** URE *Dict. Arts*, etc. 1017 The excess of the paste is removed by an instrument called a *tournasin*, till the ornamental figure produced by the stamp be laid bare. **1874** KNIGHT *Dict. Mech.* 308/1 Excess of slip is removed, after a certain amount of drying, by a spatula or knife, known as a *tournasin*.

**Tournay** (tūᵊ·ɹneⁱ). [a. F. *Tournai, Tournay* (Flem. *Doornik*), name of a town in Belgium. Cf. DORNICK.] See quot.

**1858** SIMMONDS *Dict. Trade*, *Tournay*, a printed worsted material used for furniture. Hence in mod. Dicts.

**Tournay**, obs. form of TOURNEY.

**Tourne**, obs. form of TOURN, TURN.

‖**Tourné** (turne), *a. Her.* [Fr., pa. pple. of *tourner* to turn.] = REGARDANT A. 2.

**1725** COATS *Dict. Her.*, *Tourné* is used by French Heralds for what we call Regardant, that is, looking back, or behind. **1882** in OGILVIE; and in later Dicts.

**Tournell**, var. TURNEL *Obs.*, ring, terret.

‖**Tournelle** (turne·l). *Obs.* Forms: 4, 6 tornel, 6 tornelle, 6–7 tournel, 7 tornil, tournell, 6–8 tournelle; also 5 turnelle. [a. OF. *tornele*, F. *tournelle*, according to Hatz.-Darm. deriv. of *tour* TOWER, influenced by *tourner* to turn.] A small tower; a turret. With capital T, name in the 16–18th c. of the building in Paris in which the criminal court sat; hence applied to this court, its prison, and other courts.

*a* **1400** *Siege of Troy* 1015 in *Archiv neu. Spr.* LXXII. 33 Vche tornel of þe toun þey gonne assaile. **1532** *Yatton Churchw. Acc.* (Som. Rec. Soc.) 147 Payd to R. Grenefelde for poyntyng a tornelle of yᵉ cherche ijˢ. viijᵈ. **1586** T. B. *La Primaud. Fr. Acad.* (1589) 646 There also is the Tournel, or place where criminall actions are judged, and the Treasure-Chamber for causes touching the Kings revenues. **1611** SPEED *Hist. Gt. Brit.* IX. xvi. § 29 All runne to the Bastile. The Tournels are presently seized, and all approaches vnto the Bastile are soone wonne. **1689** tr. *Jurieu's Past. Lett.* ii. 43, I was carried to the Tournel, where they put the persons condemned to the Gallies. **1771** *Ann. Reg.* 102 Eleven members of the great council, who composed part of the great chamber and the Tournelle of the new parliament, have resigned their places.

**Tournement, Tourner, -erie, Tournesoll, -soule, tournsol**, obs. ff. TOURNAMENT, TORMENT, TURNER, -ERY, TURNSOLE.

**Tourney** (tūᵊ·ɹni, tʊ̄·ɹni), *sb.*[1] Forms: *α.* 4 torneie, -aie, 5 -eye, -oye, 5–6 -ey, -oy, 6 -ay. *β.* 4–7 turnay, 4–8 -ey, -y, 6 -ei(e, -oye, -oi. *γ.* 4 tourneie, 4–9 -ay, 5 -eye, -oy, 6 -ai, 6–7 -oi, 4– tourney. [ME. a. OF. *tornei* (*Enéas*, c 1150), *turnei, tornai, tournay*, F. *tournoi*, vbl. sb. f. *tornei-er*, TOURNEY *v.* So Prov. *tornei*, It., Sp., Pg. *torneo*.]

**1.** = TOURNAMENT 1.

*α.* *c* **1374** CHAUCER *Troylus* IV. 1641 (1669) In werre or torney [*v.r.* tournay] Marcial. *c* **1440** LOVELICH *Merlin* 9614 There departed the Torneye anon. *c* **1483** CAXTON *Dialogues* 45/27 Reyner the squyer Is atte Justes At the tornoye. *a* **1533** LD. BERNERS *Huon* xxi. 62, I..hauntyd the iustes & tornoys. *a* **1548** HALL *Chron., Edw. IV* 197 b, These ij valeant persones coped together in the tornay. **1579** FENTON *Guicciard.* III. (1599) 107 The King..amused the time about iustes, torneys, and other pleasures of Court.

*β.* **13..** *K. Alis.* 141 Ladies loven solas, and play; Swaynes, justes; knyghtis, turnay [*Bodl. MS.* tournay]. **1516** *St. Bridget* in *Myrr. our Ladye* p. lv, In turneys and in vanytes of the worlde. **1550** J. COKE *Eng. & Fr. Heralds* § 125 (1877) 95 Assaultes, turnois, scremuses and syeges. **1556** *Chron. Gr. Friars* 27 The kynge helde ryall justes, turnayes, & bankettes six dayes after. **1558** in Feuillerat *Revels Q. Eliz.* (1908) 70 The appareil & Trappers..appointed..for his Justes & Turneis. **1585** T. WASHINGTON tr. *Nicholay's Voy.* IV. xxvii. 146 All sortes of turnoyes and cumbates. **1632** MILTON *Penseroso* 118 Great Bards..have sung, Of Turneys and of Trophies hung. **1742** COLLINS *Ode Poet. Char.* 7 The magic Girdle..At solemn Turney hung on high.

*γ.* **13..** *Seuyn Sag.* 719 In a mede was this tourney Of men that were of gret noblai. **1523** LD. BERNERS *Froiss.* I. xix. 27 There was also great iustes, tourneys, daunsyng, carolyng, and great feastis euery day. **1552** HULOET, Tournay, *vide in* turnay. **1556** *Aurelio & Isab.* (1608) E iv, She can not keape hir from the danses, jostes, tournois. **1569** STOCKER tr. *Diod. Sic.* III. xviii. 134 For the sportes, tournais, and diuerse other pastimes. **1625** BACON *Ess.*, *Masques & Triumphs* (Arb.) 540 For Iusts, and Tourneys. **1820** W. IRVING *Sketch Bk.* I. 193 The suit of armour..embellished as if to figure in the tournay. **1868** FREEMAN *Norm. Conq.* (1877) II. viii. 265 Not justing with his lance as in a mimic tourney.

*fig.* **1878** E. JENKINS *Haverholme* 33 A few days' trial, a tourney of keen lawyers..and the poor man walked out of court beat.

†**b.** Applied to ancient games; = TOURNAMENT 1 c. *Obs.*

**1485** CAXTON *Trevisa's Higden* II. xxxii. (1527) 87 b, There the Iliens haue theyr tornamentes from iiij yere to iiij yere, so that iiij yere was bytwene the tornoyes. **1586** T. B. *La Primaud. Fr. Acad.* I. (1594) 103 Cæsar the first Romane emperor..not sparing any cost upon plaies, turneies, feastes, largesses, and other baits to curry favour. **1600** HOLLAND *Livy* XXIX. xxii. 726 The land souldiours, running and charging one another at turney. **1601** — *Pliny* VIII. ii. I. 192 In the late solemnitie of tournois & sword-fight at the sharpe, which Germanicus Cæsar exhibited to gratifie the people.

**2.** *attrib.* and *Comb.*, as *tourney-day*, *-fall*, *-field*, *-fight*, *-prize*; †**tourney-head**, ? a blunt spear-head used in a tournament; **tourney-helm**, a helmet worn in tournaments, with light open bars across the face; distinguished from a *tilting-helm*; **tourney-queen**, the 'queen of beauty' at a tournament.

1813 SCOTT *Trierm.* III. xxxvii, Forgot was that fell *tourney-day. 1886 J. RICHMOND *Pref. Notice to Chatterton's Poet. Wks.* 25 The gay crowd of the *tourney-field. 1872 TENNYSON *Gareth & Lyn.* 88 In those brain-stunning shocks and *tourney-falls. 1814 SCOTT *Ld. of Isles* IV. xxv, Victor in Woodstock's *tourney-fight. 1506–7 *Acc. Ld. High Treas. Scot.* III. 364 Tua tournay suordis, four *tournay hedis to the tournay. 1872 TENNYSON *Last Tourn.* 32 Take thou the jewels of this dead innocence, And make them..a *tourney-prize. 1848 KINGSLEY *Saint's Trag.* IV. iii. 97 Now ruffling up like any *tourney queen.

†**Tourney, -ay**, *sb.*[2] *Obs.* Also 5–6 turn-. [a. OF. *tornee* (13th c. in Hatz.-Darm.), F. *tournée*, It. *tornata*, ppl. sb. from *tourner*, *tornare* to TURN; lit. a turning, going round, circuit.]

†**1.** The sheriff's tourn: see TOURN. *Obs. rare.*

*a* 1500 in *Arnolde's Chron.* (1811) 181 All maner preuylegis frauncheses hundredis wapentakes leetis rapis vyew of frankpledge sherefs turnays sherefgyldes amerciamentis.

†**2.** One's turn in order or rotation. *Obs. rare.*

1523 FITZHERB. *Surv.* 29 b, Also what lordes or Gentylmen haue their tourneyse [1539 turneys] with them in the same benifyce..who shall haue next.

**Tourney** (tūə·ɹni, tɜ̄·ɹni), *v.* Forms: see TOURNEY *sb.*[1] [ME. a. OF. *tornei-er*, *-ey-er*, *tornai-er*, *-ay-er* (later *tornoi-ier*, *-oy-er*, *tournoy-er*, etc. = Pr. *torneiar*, *-ejar*, *torniar*, Cat. *tornejar*, Sp., Pg. *tornear*, It. *torneggiare*:—Romanic type **tornizāre*, **tornidiāre*, f. *torno*, L. *torn-us* sb. or *torn-āre* vb.: see TURN *sb.* and *v.* *Tornizāre* was a secondary formation, with a specific sense, referring to wheeling or evolutions.] *intr.* To take part in a tourney; to contend or engage in a tournament.

α. 13.. *Sir Beues* (A.) 611 Mani a gentil kniȝt Torneande riȝt in þe feld. *Ibid.* 3774 Þanne seide Beues vnto Terry: 'Wile we tornaie for þat leuedy?' 1390 GOWER *Conf.* I. 126 On jousteth wel, an other bet, And otherwhile thei torneie. *c* 1440 LOVELICH *Merlin* 7177 Þere eche man torneyed with oþer. 1470–85 MALORY *Arthur* VII. xi. 228 His custome is ..to lye in this medowe to Iuste and torneye.

β. *c* 1435 *Torr. Portugal* 2591 They justyd and turneyd there. 1513 DOUGLAS *Æneis* V. x. 10 Bid hym bring hiddir his rowtis to turnay. 1567 DRANT *Horace, De Arte Poet.* B iv, He dare not turney, nor yet tilte which neuer knew the play. 1600 HOLLAND *Livy* XXVI. li. 624 He conversed among the legions, and turnoied with them.

γ. 13.. *K. Alis.* 195 (Bodl. MS.) Þer was kniȝttes tourneyying [*v.r.* turnyng]. 1470–85 MALORY *Arthur* I. v. 41 Alle knyȝtes that wold Iuste or tourneye. *a* 1533 LD. BERNERS *Gold. Bk. M. Aurel.* (1546) Diij, Yf he vse armes, all wil tourney. 1570 LEVINS *Manip.* 197/15 To Tournay, *hastis concurrere.* 1577–87 HOLINSHED *Chron.* III. 803/1 So presented themselues..readie to tourneie. 1622 MABBE tr. *Aleman's Guzman d'Alf.* I. 86 Because he might not Tourney. 1715 tr. *Pancirollus' Rerum Mem.* I. IV. xviii. 227 There were .. tourneying together with coursing Chariots. 1855 SINGLETON *Virgil* I. 189 They tourney; in high heaven a din is raised.

**b.** *transf.*

*a* 1400–50 *Alexander* 5429 Ilka twelmonth a turne þai [snakes] turnay to-gedire.

**Tou·rneyer.** Also 4 tourn(e)our, 8 turnier. [ME. a. OF. *tornoieor*, *tournoieur*, *-ieur*, f. *torneier*: see prec.] One who engages in a tourney.

1303 R. BRUNNE *Handl. Synne* 4615 For wymmen sake knyghteys tournaments make..loke now whedyr swyche tournours [*v.r.* tourneours] Mow be kalled turmentours? 1738 [G. SMITH] *Curious Relations* II. 358 Forty-eight Turniers, dress'd after the ancient German manner, in yellow Liveries, trim'd with black Velvet, and small Gold Lace. *Ibid.* 359 Twenty-eight Turniers on Horse-back, after the ancient Manner. 1846 H. W. TORRENS *Rem. Milit. Hist.* 191 Mere fantastic tourneyers breaking a lance for the bright eyes of their lady.

**Tou·rneying,** *vbl. sb.* [f. TOURNEY *v.* + -ING[1].] The action of the verb TOURNEY. Also *attrib.*

13.. *K. Alis.* 1045 (Bodl. MS.) Carolyng & turneieyng And wrestlyng & skirmyng. *c* 1386 CHAUCER *Knt.'s T.* 1699 No lenger shal the turneiynge [*v.rr.* torneyenge, turnyinge, tourneying] laste. 1483 CAXTON *G. de la Tour* g viij b, The Ioustynge and the tornoyeng was fayre to see. 1503 *Acc. Ld. High Treas. Scot.* II. 202 To the turnaying at Fasteringis evin. 1548 UDALL, etc. *Erasm. Par. Mark* Pref., To proue masteries with wagoners in the listes or turneiyng place called Circus. *a* 1631 DONNE *Paradoxes* (1652) 75 No way ..to win a Lady but by Tylting, Turnying, and riding in Forrests. 1657 C. BECK *Univ. Char.* L vij b, Tournaying or tilting. 1843 CARLYLE *Past & Pr.* II. xv, A liberty of tourneying.

**Tourniquet** (tūə·ɹniket, ‖ turnīke). Also 7 turneke, 8 turniket, tournequet. [a. F. *tourniquet*, dial. *torniquai*, deriv. of *tourn-er* to TURN.]

**1.** A surgical instrument, consisting essentially of a bandage, a pad, and a screw, for stopping or checking the flow of blood through an artery by compression; also, a bandage tightened by twisting a rigid bar put through it.

1695 W. W. *New Lt. Chirurg. put out* 53 His..slacking the Turneke..caused such an additional Expence of Blood. 1721 NAISH in *Phil. Trans.* XXXI. 227 Upon slackening the Turniket. 1756 *Gentl. Mag.* XXVI. 381 The offender is..strangled by putting a cord twice round his neck, and twisting it tight with a piece of stick behind, like a tournequet. 1806 *Med. Jrnl.* XV. 149 Remarks..on the screw tourniquet. 1869 *Latest News* 10 Oct. 7 He strangled himself in bed with a tourniquet made of a handkerchief and a piece of stick. 1877 ERICHSEN *Surg.* I. 34.

*attrib.* 1767 GOOCH *Treat. Wounds* I. 443 When such a wound happens in a limb, the leaving a tourniquet ligature loose about it,..till the Surgeon can be called, is a precaution. 1820 *Sporting Mag.* VII. 108 The tourniquet [hand] shake is the next in importance.

**2. a.** A turnstile. *rare.* **b.** = BARKER'S MILL (Ogilvie, 1882).

1706 PHILLIPS (ed. Kersey), *Tourniquet*, a Turn-Still. 1768 STERNE *Sent. Journ.* (1775) I. 56 Seek some winding alley, with a *tourniquet* at the end of it, where chariot never rolled or flambeau shot its rays. 1876 RUSKIN *Fors Clav.* lxiv. VI. 113 We..are to work outside, here, for your dinners, and hand them through the wall to you at a tourniquet.

**Tournit, -yt,** obs. Sc. forms of TURNED.

‖**Tournois** (turnwā), *a.* (*sb.*) *Hist.* Forms: 4–5 **Tourneys**, 5 **Turneis**, 6 **Tornois**, 7 **Tor-**, **Turnoys**, 7– **Tournois.** [Fr. *Tournois* adj. :—L. *Turonēnsis*, of Tours, *Turonēs*, a city of France.] Of or pertaining to Tours: esp. said of the money coined at Tours, one-fifth less in value than that struck at Paris.

1475 *Bk. Noblesse* (Roxb.) 32 To the yerely valeu of .x. Mˡ. marcs yerely, whiche was .lx. Mˡ. li. Turneis. 1523 LD. BERNERS *Froiss.* I. cliv. 184 The french kyng shall delyuer to the kyng of Nauer, xxxviii .M. li. tornois of lande. 1625 in Rushw. *Hist. Coll.* (1659) I. 331 The sum of Two hundred and thirteen thousand Livres Turnoys. 1769 *Chron.* in *Ann. Reg.* 85 The ship of war..has on board..about an hundred thousand crowns tournois in piastres. 1852 MISS YONGE *Cameos* (1877) III. iii. 27 Sufficient to pay nine thousand soldiers at the rate of ten livres tournois per month.

**b.** *sb.* Money or a coin of Tours: see quots.

13.. *Coer de L.* 2856 They myghte have none othir thyng For whyt tourneys, ne for sterlyng. 1426 LYDG. *De Guil. Pilgr.* 17664 To tourne, by hys sotylte, A Tourneys to A parysee. 1656 BLOUNT *Glossogr.*, *Tournois*.., a French penny, the tenth part of a penny sterling...In France they say so much money *Tournois*, as we say *sterling*. 1893 *Antiquary* Mar. 105 Coins found in St. Queran's Well, 1869. ..Double Tournois.

‖**Tournure** (turnüˑr). [F. *tournure*, earlier *tourneüre*:—late pop.L. *tornātūra*, f. *tornāre* to TURN; in Fr. (1) rounded form given to anything; (2) manner in which anything is fashioned.]

**1.** (Graceful) manner or bearing; cultivated address.

1748 CHESTERF. *Let.* 12 Oct., The easy manners and *tournure* of the world. 1816 *Sporting Mag.* XLVII. 118 That ease and *tournure* so indispensable in the composition of a gentleman. 1832 MRS. F. TROLLOPE *Domest. Mann. Amer.* ii. (1839) 7 Her manner was easy and graceful, with a good deal of French *tournure*. 1878 *Cornh. Mag.* June 687 She had the tournure of a princess.

**2.** The turning of language or of a phrase; mode of expression. *rare.*

1816 J. SCOTT *Vis. Paris* (ed. 5) 194 The *tournure* of the phrase, when a woman is spoken to, cannot be mistaken.

**3.** Contour, outline, shape (of a limb, etc.).

1841 LADY BLESSINGTON *Idler in France* I. xv. 354 There was the same classic *tournure* of heads and profiles. 1848 CLOUGH *Bothie* v. 112 The tournure of the elbow is shapely. 1864 *Daily Tel.* 5 Nov., You have..the exquisite tournure of a figure, the subtle trick of a ridiculous expression.

**4.** A pad worn round the waist or hips to give shapeliness to a woman's figure; also = BUSTLE *sb.*[2]

1874 *Echo* 30 Dec. (Stanf.), The tournure..is still worn. 1882 *Daily News* 3 June 3/1 The tournure is a small horse-hair pad, worn under the dress at the waist. It throws out the skirt from the figure.

**Tourrette,** obs. form of TURRET.

†**Tours** (tūrz). *Obs.* Also 6 **Towres**, 6–7 **Towers.** [Name of a city in France.] Used *attrib.* in names of things made at or associated with Tours; as *Tours taffeta* (also *taffeta Tours*).

1558 in Feuillerat *Revels Q. Eliz.* (1908) 31 Taffita Towers white xix yardes. *Ibid.* 38 The gownes lyned with white towres taffita. 1572 *Ibid.* 187 Of Taffata crimsin thirtie two yardes, of Taffata Tawnie Towers thirtie and sixe yardes. 1586 *Rates of Custome* E vij b, Taffata, called Towers Taffata the yarde iii. s. iiij. d. 1640 in Entick *London* (1766) II. 169 Tabbies of silk, towers taffaty, the dozen yards, 2*d.*

**b.** *Tours sorrel*, buckler-shaped or French sorrel, *Rumex scutata.*

1578 LYTE *Dodoens* v. ix. 558 *Oxalis Romana*, Tours Sorrel or Romayne Sorrel. [*Ibid.* 559 Romayne Sorrel..in Frenche *Ozeille Romaine*, and *Ozeille de Tours*.] 1611 COTGR., *Ozeille Romaine*, Roman Sorrell,..Tours Sorrell.

‖**Tourte** (turt). Also **tourt.** [mod.F. *tourte*, now, a piece of pastry containing meat, fish, etc., eaten hot, a pie; *dial.* bread in the form of a disk, a round flat cake, also in transferred senses; in dial. F. *torte*, Sp. and It. *torta*:—late L. *tōrta* a cake of bread, of uncertain origin. Cf. also TORTA.] (See quots.)

1706 PHILLIPS (ed Kersey), *Tourte*, (in *Cookery*) a kind of Pastry-work bak'd in a Pan; a Pie. 1725 *Bradley's Fam. Dict.*, *Tourte* or *Pan-pie*, in general a Pie bak'd in a Pan, of which there are several Sorts. *Ibid.*, To make a Tourte of Veal Sweet-Breads. 1762 *Char.* in *Ann. Reg.* II. 34 The pheasant tourt was a discovery he made in Spain. 1895 *Funk's Stand. Dict.*, Tourte.

**Tourteaux:** see TORTEAU.

**Touse** (tauz, taus), *sb. dial.* [f. TOUSE *v.*]

**1.** Rough pulling about, horse-play; a 'row', commotion, uproar; an outcry, a fuss.

1795 WOLCOTT (P. Pindar) *Lousiad* IV. 173 Let's have no more touse. 1802 — *Middlesex Elect.* II. vi, Amongst the derty, lowzy crew, There's zich a touse and hallibulloo. 1835–40 HALIBURTON *Clockm.* (1862) 28 Marm Lecain makes such an eternal touss about her carpets. 1882 JAGO *Cornwall Gloss.*, *Touse*, fuss, row, uproar, hurry. 'Making such a touse'.

**2.** A tousled mass: in quot. of hair.

1894 CROCKETT *Lilac Sunbonnet* v. 43 With a touse of lint-white locks blowing out in the gusts.

**Touse** (tauz), *v.* Now *rare.* Forms: (3 to-tuse, 4–5 be-touse), 6–7 towse, 6–8 touze, towze, 6– touse, 8–9 *Sc.* and *north. dial.* toose (*tūz*). [The simple vb. is known only from *c* 1509; but the compounds with *be-* and *to-* are found in ME. from *c* 1300, pointing to an unrecorded OE. **tūsian*, ME. *tūsen*, *tousen*, cognate with OHG. *-zūsōn* in *zir-zūsōn* to pull to pieces, MHG. *er-zūsen*, *er-zousen*, Ger. *zausen*; also LG. (EFris.) *tūsen* to pull or shake about, tease, treat roughly, NFris. *tuuse* to pull by the hair:—OTeut. vb. stem **tūs-*, closely allied in sense to **tais-*, whence TEASE and TOZE.]

**1.** *trans.* To pull roughly about; to drag or push about; to handle roughly; of a dog: to tear at, worry.

[*c* 1300 *Havelok* 1948 Bernard sone ageyn [him] nam Al to-tused and al to-torn. *c* 1400 *Laud Troy Bk.* 12944 Thei were alle thorow wet...Al be-rayned and be-toused.] 1509 HAWES *Conv. Swearers* xii, Beholde my body with blody proppes endewed..Towsed and tugged with othes cruelly. 1567 MAPLET *Gr. Forest* 83 b, There was a Dog..which at the first dash or onset..daunted and toused the Lyon. 1590 SPENSER *F. Q.* II. xi. 33 As a Beare, whom angry curres have touzd. 1633 HEYWOOD *Eng. Trav.* II. Wks. 1874 IV. 26 The Cooke..did so Towse them and Tosse them, so Plucke them and Pull them. 1736 MRS. DELANY in *Life & Corr.* (1861) I. 556 To Court, where we were touz'd and hunched about to make room for citizens in their fur gowns. 1869 PEACOCK *Lonsdale Gloss.*, *Touze*, to tug or pull about. 1898 T. HARDY *Wessex Poems* 66 When she used to sing and pirouette And touse the tambourine.

†**b.** To pull out of joint, to rack. *Obs. rare.*

1603 SHAKS. *Meas. for M.* V. i. 313 To th' racke with him: we'll towze you Ioynt by ioynt, but we will know his purpose.

†**c.** To pull (a woman) about rudely, indelicately, or in horse-play; to tousle. *Obs.*

1623 MASSINGER *Bondman* I. iii, They are rough, Boisterous, and saucy, and at the first sight Ruffle and touze us. 1638 FORD *Fancies* III. iii, He towzes the lady-sisters as a tumbling dog does young rabbits. 1675 HOBBES *Odyssey* XVI. 105 Maids tous'd ill-favouredly. 1719 D'URFEY *Pills* (1872) I. 93 And she..Still gave him leave to towze her. 1751 ELIZA HEYWOOD *Betsy Thoughtless* I. 71 He..began to kiss and touze me so, that..I was frighted almost out of my wits.

**2.** To disorder, dishevel (the hair, dress, etc.); to tumble, rumple (bed-clothes, sheets, etc.).

1598 FLORIO, *Sparpagliare*, to desheuell, to vnkembe, to touze a womans haire. 1647 STAPYLTON *Juvenal* 215 Though her..hair be tows'd, her face and eares do glow. 1682 D'URFEY *Butler's Ghost* 149 A Rampant shaver,..with licentious hands does touze The Bridal Vesture of your Spouse. 1693 CONGREVE *Old Bach.* IV. viii, Oh the most inhumane barbarous Hackney-Coach! I am jolted to a Jelly! —Am I not horribly touzed? 1912 R. MACDONALD *First of Ebb* xi, Upon the lap of Clothilde..lay the toused, sleeping poll of the little Antoinette.

**3.** *fig.* To abuse or maltreat in some way compared to the literal senses. Now *rare* or *Obs.*

1530 TINDALE *Answ. More* III. xiii. Wks. (1573) 311/1 There he biteth, sucketh, gnaweth, towseth, and mowseth Tyndall. 1593 DRAYTON *Eclogues* i. 59 Fortune, the World that towzes to and fro. 1609 BP. W. BARLOW *Answ. Nameless Cath.* 86 Hee hath rowsed her in her Death-bed; now hee runnes backe 70. yeeres, to towse her in her Cradle. *c* 1680 HICKERINGILL *Hist. Whiggism* I. Wks. 1716 I. 37 If they get a piece of a Text by the end..they do so tear it, and towze it, and towzer it..that they lose themselves. 1844 *Blackw. Mag.* LVI. 212 Invite especially those that have hitherto tightly toused, mocked, and scorned thee.

†**4.** To tease (wool); = TOZE *v.*[1] 1. *Obs.*

1599 T. M[OUFET] *Silkwormes* 4 Deuising beetles, hackels, wheeles, and frame, Wherwith to bruse, touse, spin, and weaue the same. 1601 HOLLAND *Pliny* IX. xxxviii. I. 259 They let the wooll lie to take the liquor..: then they have it forth, touse, and card it. 1706 PHILLIPS (ed. Kersey), To *Towz* or *Toze Wooll*, is to Card or dress it.

†**5.** *intr.* To touse each other, tussle; also *fig.*; in quot. 1607, to pull things about in disorder, rummage. *Obs.*

1542 UDALL *Erasm. Apoph.* 25 While she & I be touzyng & topplyng together. 1606 FORD *Hon. Tri.* (1843) 16, I touze to gaine me fame and reputation. 1607 DEKKER & WEBSTER *Northw. Hoe* III. Wks. 1873 III. 41 Sondry times shee..opend her chests, touz'd among her linnen. 1681 OTWAY *Soldier's Fort.* I. i, To see a pretty Wench and a young Fellow touze and rouze and frouze and mouze.

Hence **Toused** (tauzd) *ppl. a.*, **Tou·sing** *vbl. sb.* and *ppl. a.*

*a* 1550 *Jack Juggler* (1873) 66, I haue forgotten with tousing by the here, What I deuised to say a lytle ere. 1582 STANYHURST *Æneis* I. (Arb.) 21 Hee noted Aeneas his touzdtost nauye to wander. 1682 MRS. BEHN *City Heiress* 21 Be sawcy, forward, bold, towzing, and lewd. 18.. MOORE *Moral Positions* 111, To guard the frail package from tousing and routing. 1912 Toused [see sense 2].

**Tou·sle, tou·zle** (see next), *sb.* [f. next.]

**1.** A struggle, a tussle; a rough romping with a woman. *Sc.*

1788 R. GALLOWAY *Poems* 214 For tho' I be baith blyth and canty, I ne'er get a touzle at a'. 1814 J. BOSWELL *Justiciary Op.* (1816) 11 A child had taen a glass, and had A towzle wi' a gauger. 1830 GALT *Lawrie T.* VII. vi, Ye're no' a pin the worse of all the bit touzle.

**2.** A tousled mass or mop (of hair).

1880 *Daily Tel.* 26 Nov., The eyes peeping out from under the overshadowing touzle, like young birds through a hedge. 1887 FLO. WARDEN *Scheherazade* ii, The thick tousle of hair..was entirely innocent of curling tongs.

**3.** *attrib.* and *Comb.*, as *tousle-haired*, *-headed* adjs.

1880 *Cornh. Mag.* Feb. 136 A couple of bare-armed touzle-headed viragoes. 1898 *Westm. Gaz.* 8 Dec. 2/1 Cattle of all kinds... Touzle-haired, tawny Highlanders with great sweeping horns, polled Galloways with coats like black astrachan.

**Tousle, touzle** (tau·z'l, *Sc.* tū·z'l), *v.* Forms: 5, 8 tousel, (5 *Sc.* towsill, 7 -ell, 9 towsel), 6– tousle; 7– touzle, (8–9 towzle, 9 -zel, *Sc.* and *north.* toozle). [Iterative of TOUSE *v.*: see -LE 3. Cf. LG. *tūseln* (*Brem. Wbch.*); Oberd. *zusseln*, *züsseln* (Doornkaat-Koolman).]

**1.** *trans.* To pull about roughly; to handle (esp. a woman) rudely or indelicately; to disorder, dishevel (the hair, clothes, etc.); = TOUSE *v.* 1, 1 c, 2.

*a* 1440 *Sir Degrev.* 1492 Fayre schetus of sylk..Quyltus poyned of that ylk Touseled they ware. *c* 1475 *Rauf Coilȝear* 432 For to towsill me or tit me, thocht foull be my clais, Or I be dantit on sic wyse, my lyfe salbe lorne. *a* 1585 MONTGOMERIE *Flyting* 362 Tousled and tuggled with towne tykes. 1642 H. MORE *Song of Soul* II. i. I. xiv, His rugg'd flowing mane, Which the fierce winds do tosse and tousell sore. 1725 RAMSAY *Gentle Sheph.* IV. i, I have towzled his harigalds a wee! 1764 FOOTE *Mayor of G.* I. i, Come, Jane, give me my wig; you slut, how you have touzled the curls. 1839–40 W. IRVING *Wolfert's R.* xiii. (1855) 181 [He] kissed and tousled the young vrouws. 1884 *Harper's Mag.* Aug. 464/1 Romping with the dogs, tousling a big St. Bernard.

**b.** With *about*, *out*, *up*.

1816 SCOTT *Antiq.* ix, After they had touzled out mony a leather poke-full o' papers. 1822 W. IRVING *Braceb. Hall* xxxviii, Mrs. Hannah..being tossed and tousled about by the crowd. 1883 *Mem. S. Miller* Pref. 20 [She] requested us ..if she should be drowsy to be sure and 'touzle' her up.

**c.** *fig.* = TOUSE *v.* 3.

1826 J. WILSON *Noct. Ambr.* Wks. 1855 I. 260 Hoo your een sparkle as you touzle the clergy. 1900 HARE *Story my Life* VI. xxv. 188 Religion worried and touzled by a thousand million vagaries of personality.

**2.** *intr.* To toss oneself about; also, to rout, rummage (cf. TOUSE *v.* 5).

1852 MRS. STOWE *Uncle Tom's C.* xxxvii, Tom Loker we left groaning and touzling in a..clean Quaker bed. 1880 BARING-GOULD *Mehalah* xxiv, Do you think she is to come here toozling about among the wittles in her best gown?

Hence **Tou·sling, tou·zling** *vbl. sb.*

1749 FIELDING *Tom Jones* XVIII. xii, Damn me, if he shan't ha the tousling her. 1771 E. LONG *Trial Dog 'Porter'* in Hone *Every-day Bk.* (1827) II. 202 Tearings, woundings, pullings, .. touzleings, .. maliciously inflicted. 1865 E. BURRITT *Walk Land's End* 284 What tugging and touzling, and pinching and pulling at the tail he [a dog] will take.

**Tousled, touzled** (tau·-, *Sc.* tū·z'ld), *ppl. a.* [f. TOUSLE *v.* + -ED [1].] Disarranged, dishevelled, tumbled; also shaggy, matted.

1848 DICKENS *Dombey* xxv, Rob the Grinder..stood then, panting at the captain, with a flushed and touzled air of bed about him. 1852 MRS. STOWE *Uncle Tom's C.* ix, A very heavy mat of sandy hair, in a decidedly tousled condition. 1861 *Crt. Life at Naples* II. 1 Prudent mammas carried off reluctant daughters, whose touzled dresses, disordered hair, and heavy eyelids bore witness..to the wisdom of the measure. 1890 W. BOOTH *Darkest Eng.* 104 A grimy footsore tramp..with filthy shirt and towselled hair.

**b.** *Comb.*, as *tousled-headed*, *-looking* adjs.

1860 DICKENS *Uncomm. Trav.* xiii, The touzled-headed man..hadn't got his coat on yet. 1883 CLELAND *Inchbracken* xiii. 105 A damp and tousselled-looking youth, who grasped his dripping 'Tam o' Shanter' tightly in both hands.

‖ **Tous-les-mois** (tulemwā). [F., = 'all the months, every month'; but probably a popular perversion of *toloman*, according to Duss and Jumelle the name in the French Antilles, prob. of native S. American origin.] The name in St. Kitts, etc., of species of *Canna*, esp. *C. edulis*, and of the starch obtained from its root-stocks, also called *tous-les-mois starch*.

*Canna coccinea* was introduced into W. Indies from S. America in 1731; *C. edulis* from Peru in 1820 (A. W. Hill, Kew). Samples of the farina were sent to England from St. Kitts in 1835–6: see Ryan's *Med. & Surg. Jrnl.* Aug. 1836, and *Morning Chron.* 4 Aug. 1837.

1839 OLPHERS *Let.* cited in *Pharm. Jrnl.* VII. 56 (On the *Canna Achira* or Tous les Mois). 1858 HOGG *Veg. Kingd.* 787 The article known as *Tous-les-mois* is obtained from the root-stocks of some species of *Canna*...The substance is prepared in the island of St. Kitts. 1861 BENTLEY *Man. Bot.* 669 One or more species of this genus [*Canna*] yield 'Tous les mois', a very pure and useful starch, now largely consumed in this country and elsewhere. 1867 J. HOGG *Microsc.* I. ii. 153 The larger-grained starches form splendid objects; tous-les-mois being the largest may be taken as a type of all the others.

**Tously** (tau·zli), *a.* Also touzley, towsly. [f. TOUSLE *sb.* or *v.* + -Y.] Characterized by being tousled or dishevelled; having tousled hair or dress.

1891 *Pall Mall G.* 14 Feb. 6/2 Hither came the women, a blowsy, touzley crew, with mouth agape. 1905 *Daily News* 2 Aug. 6 One [humble-bee] with a tously yellow head and thorax and dark brown abdomen. 1911 *Ibid.* 7 Mar. 4 Why should a man send many men and teams of horses..to fetch towsly brown grass to clothe his town lawn?

† **Toust**, *sb. Sc. Old Law.* Also 6–7 towst, 6 towist. [a. AF. *toste*, *touste* (13–14th c. in Godef.), var. spelling of *tōte*, *toute*, *toulte*, *tolte*, 'enlèvement' = med.L. *tolta*, f. OF. *toldre*, L. *tollĕre* to lift, take away, raise: see TOLT.] An impost, rate levied, tax.

1574 *Reg. Privy Council Scot.* II. 408 Gif ony towst sould be takin of thair gudis. *Ibid.*, The said towist and impositioun. 1596 in *Munim. Burgh Irvine* (1890) I. 85 Grant to the provost, bailies, council and community of Irwing..the toust, exactioun and impoist of all the following sorts of merchandise. 1598 in *Reg. Mag. Sig. Scot.* 1603. 513/1 Pro receptione cujusdam taxationis lie toust and taxatioun. 1620 *Ibid.* 777/2 Cum potestate..recipiendi parvas custumas ..*lie towst* aliasque devorias nundinarum et portus.

Hence † **Toust** *v.*, *Sc. Obs. rare*, *trans.* to tax; whence † **Tou·sting** *vbl. sb.*

1565 in Calderwood *Hist. Kirk* (1843) II. 574 The taxing and tousting of her Majestie's barons and other lieges,which are tousted for repairing of that which was so indiscreitlie of the patrimonie forsaid dilapidated.

**Tousy, towsy** (tau·zi, tū·zi), *a.* Chiefly *Sc.* and *north. dial.* Also 8 touzie, 9 touzy, towzy, -sie, toosy. [f. TOUSE *v.* + -Y.] Dishevelled, unkempt, tousled; shaggy, rough. Also in *comb.*

[1500–20 DUNBAR *Poems* xviii. 32 And be I ornat in my speiche, Than Towsy sayis, I am sa streiche.] 1786 BURNS *Twa Dogs* 33 His breast was white, his touzie back Weel clad wi' coat o' glossy black. 1820 *Blackw. Mag.* May 159/1 Like yere ain towsie hassock o' hair, that has nae been kamed since Kate Kimmer kamed it with the three-footed stool. 1826 J. WILSON *Noct. Ambr.* Wks. 1855 I. 180 What an outlandish, toosy-headed, wee sun-brunt deevil o' a lassie that. 1871 C. GIBBON *Lack of Gold* xiv, His hair was long and 'touzy'.

**Tout** (taut), *sb.*[1] Also 8 toute. [f. TOUT *v.*[1]]

**1.** A thieves' scout or watchman. *slang.*

1718 C. HIGDEN *True Disc.* 13 (Farmer) He is a pushing toute, alias thieves' watchman, that lies scouting in and about the City to get and bring intelligence to the thieves.

**2.** One who solicits custom; = TOUTER 1.

1853 *Household Words* VII. 26/1 Touts and spungers to foreign hotels and on foreign visitors. 1879 SALA *Paris herself again* (1880) II. xi. 163 A regular house to house visitation was made..by touts or agents of the insurers. 1881 BESANT & RICE *Chapl. of Fleet* I. vi, Ludgate Hill, where the touts of the Fleet parsons ran up and down. 1881 HUGHES *Rugby, Tennessee* 34 The hotel touts rush on you.

**3.** (More fully *racing tout*.) One who surreptitiously watches the trials of race-horses, so as to gain information for betting purposes: = TOUTER 2.

1865 *Slang Dict.*, *Tout*, in sporting phraseology..signifies an agent in the training districts, on the look-out for information as to the condition and capabilities of those horses entering for a coming race. 1887 BLACK *Sabina Zembra* I. vi. 86, I..don't object to seeing the touts coming about; it shows they think we have some horses worth watching.

**4.** The action of TOUT *v.*[1]; in phrase *to keep* (*the*) *tout*, to watch. *slang.*

1812 J. H. VAUX *Flash Dict.* s. v., *To keep tout*, is to look out or watch, while your pall is effecting any private purpose. *A strong tout*, is strict observation, or eye, upon any proceedings, or persons. 1834 H. AINSWORTH *Rookwood* IV. ii, [They] on each other kept the tout.

**Tout** (taut), *sb.*[2] *Sc.* Also towt. [Origin obscure: cf. TOUT *v.*[2]]

**1.** A fit of ill humour; a transient displeasure; a pet.

1787 SHIRREFS *Jamie & Bess* I. ii, Were he ay sae, he then wad ay be kind, But then, anither tout may change his mind. 1818 SCOTT *Br. Lamm.* xi[i], He taks the tout at every bit lippening word. 1835 CARRICK *Laird of Logan* (1841) 76 Leezie was..discontented, and subject to bits o' touts now and then.

**2.** A fit or slight bout of illness.

1808–18 JAMIESON, *Tout*, *towt*, an ailment of a transient kind. 1823 GALT *Entail* II. ii. 12 It's neither the t'ane nor the t'ither, but just..a bit towt that's no worth the talking o'. 1831 MISS FERRIER *Destiny* lxxvi, The baby had a sad towt with its teeth. 1855 MUCKLEBACKIT *Rhymes* 219 (E.D.D.) She teuk the tout, near Galashiels,..She dee'd that vera nicht.

**Tout**, *sb.*[3] [? Fr. *tout* all.] A term for a specially successful result in certain games: see quots. and cf. Littré s. v. *Tout* 47.

1678 DRYDEN *Limberham* IV. ii, Well, I have won the Party and Revenge however: A Minute longer, and I had won the Tout. 1687 SEDLEY *Bellamira* IV. i, I lost three sets at back-gammon, and a tout at trick-track, all ready money. 1891 *Cent. Dict.*, *Tout*[1] 3. In the game of solo, a play when one person takes or proposes to take all the tricks.

**Tout** (taut), *v.*[1] Forms: 4–5 tute(n, 7– tout. [ME. *tūte-n*, pointing to an OE. **tūtian*, synonymous with OE. *tōtian*, TOOT *v.*[1], and OE. *tȳtan* :—**tūtjan*. (For etymological relations, and cognate words in the other Germanic langs., see under TOOT *v.*[1]) As used in ME., *tūte-n* was identical in sense with *tōten*, TOOT *v.*[1], sense 2; the two forms occur even as textual variants: see the first quotation in sense 1. The mod.Eng. form *tout* was in use before 1700 as a cant or slang word, whence the later sense-development, which has differentiated the word from TOOT.]

† **1.** *intr.* To peep, peer, look out; to gaze; = TOOT *v.*[1] 2. *Obs.*

*a* 1400–50 *Alexander* 694 (Ashmole) Anec[tanabus] .. treyned doune fra þe toure to tute in þe sternes [*Dubl. MS.*, to tote on þe sternes]. *Ibid.* 4776 (Ashm.) Þe kyng in his caban with his kniȝtis he ligis, Tutand out of his tents. *a* 1603 T. CARTWRIGHT *Confut. Rhem. N. T.* (1618) 192 Dare you also affirme, that the soules in hell haue the same knowledge, by touting into the diuell? 1676 COLES *Dict.*, *Tout*, to look out or upon.

**b.** To keep a sharp look-out or watch; to take heed; to be on the look-out. *Thieves' cant.*

*a* 1700 B. E. *Dict. Cant. Crew*, *Tout*, to look out Sharp, to be upon one's Guard. 1728 [DE FOE] *Street Robberies Consider'd*, *Tout*, take heed.

**2.** *trans.* To watch, spy on. *slang.*

*a* 1700 B. E. *Dict. Cant. Crew*, *Tout the Culls*, Eye those folks which way they take. 1812 J. H. VAUX *Flash Dict.*, *Tout*, to tout a person, is to watch his motions. 1832 *Examiner* 67/1 Two of them were sent forward..in disguise, to tout (watch) the door of the house. 1870 *Sat. Rev.* 2 Apr. 445 But..the Prince of Wales is touted, Mr. Gladstone is touted, their minutest actions are eagerly watched and regularly reported; why should not we be allowed to procure similar information about race-horses?

**b.** To watch furtively or spy upon (a race-horse or his trainer) with a view to using or disposing of the information for betting purposes.

1812 *Sporting Mag.* XXXIX. 283 He made it his business to be at the Wheat Sheaf public-house..to tout Mr. Prince, who had the mare under his training. 1870 *Sat. Rev.* 2 Apr. 445 The touting of race-horses is practised, not to gratify curiosity, but as an aid to gambling. 1894 M. H. HAYES *Men & Horses* vi. (ed. 2) 94 With the fear of being touted ever on them, the Newmarket trainers are..shy of strangers. 1895 *Westm. Gaz.* 2 Oct. 7/3 One of the most assiduously 'touted' animals at Newmarket during the last fortnight has been M. Aumont's Dormeuse.

**3.** *intr.* To look out busily for customers; to solicit custom, employment, etc. importunately; also, *Colonial* and *U.S.*, to canvass for votes.

1731–54 [see TOUTING, TOUTER 1]. 1837 DICKENS *Pickw.* x, Doctors' Commons... Two porters..as touts for licences... Two coves in vhite aprons—touches their hats ven you walk in—'Licence, sir, licence?' 1847 ALB. SMITH *Chr. Tadpole* xix, He used to go backwards and forwards..to tout for customers. 1857 KINGSLEY *Two Y. Ago* x, I am to tout for introductions for you? 1869 ROGERS *Hist. Gleanings* (1870) II. 200 Before Lord Hardwicke's Marriage Act, a particular class of clergymen, not..in very good repute, touted for marriage-fees. 1881 *Nation* (N. Y.) XXXII. 397 It has never occurred to him that people would be shocked by seeing him 'tout' at Albany. 1891 *Melbourne Argus* 28 Sept., He should have gone round cap in hand and touted for votes. 1898 J. HOLLINGSHEAD *Gaiety Chron.* ii. 119 The same way as postmen tout for Christmas boxes.

Hence **Tou·ted**, **Tou·ting** *ppl. adjs.*

1812 *Sporting Mag.* XXXIX. 283 An object worthy the consideration of the touting firm. 1895 [see 2 b].

**Tout** (taut, tūt), *v.*[2] *Sc.* Also towt. [Origin of sense 1 obscure. Sense 2 evidently goes with TOUT *sb.*[2], and may be a different word from 1.]

**1.** *trans.* To toss or throw about in disorder. Also *fig.* to canvass, discuss.

*a* 1568 *Bannatyne Poems* (Hunter. Cl.) 408/18 To spill the bed it war a pane, Quoth he, the laird will nocht be fane, To fynd it towtit and ourtred. 1596–7 J. MELVIL *Diary* (Wodrow Soc.) 410 We perceave the purpose is bot to canves and towt our maters heir a whyll, that thairefter men of lytle skill and les conscience may decern in to tham as they pleis. 1812 P. FORBES *Poems* 38 (E.D.D.) [He] lang an' sair the claise did tout, Dreaming o' an invasion An' fights yon night. 1899 J. LUMSDEN *Edin. Poems & Songs* 250 Their waters mountain high Uprear in never-ending wars And tout the ships an' flout the sky As if they'd quench the eternal stars.

**2.** To irritate, vex, tease. Cf. TOUT *sb.*[2]

1725 *Ramsay's Gentle Sheph.* 718 (E.D.D.) Losh preserve us, Bess! At thys tym; and swa towtit! 1832 CARRICK in *Whistle-Binkie* Ser. II. (1853) 124 Weel, weel, Janet, dinna be sae toutit about it—I was awa' at a burial. 1887 P. M'NEILL *Blawearie* 61 If Bob toutit you, very likely ye hae been toutin' him too.

**b.** *intr.* (See quot.)

1825 JAMIESON, *Tout*, to be seized with a sudden fit of sickness [or] ill humour.

**Tout**, obs. f. TAUT, TAUGHT; var. TOOT.

**Toutch**, obs. form of TOUCH.

† **Toute.** *Obs.* Also 5–6 towte. [Derivation obscure: ME. *toute* answers to an OE. **tūte*, belonging to the root **tūt-*, to stick out, project: see Note to TOOT *v.*[1]] The buttocks, fundament, posteriors, rump.

*c* 1305 *Land Cokayne* 136 He [the abbot] takeþ maidin of þe route And turniþ vp her white toute And betiþ þe taburs wiþ is hond To make is monkes liȝt to lond. *c* 1386 CHAUCER *Miller's T.* 626 Of gooth the skyn an hande brede aboute, The hoote kultour brende so his toute. *c* 1450 *Cokwolds Daunce* 120 in Hazl. *E. P. P.* I. 43 To vse we[l]e the lechers craft, With rubyng of ther toute. *c* 1460 *Towneley Myst.* ii. 63 Com nar, & other drife or hald, and kys the dwillis toute.

**Toute**, var. TOT *sb.*[1] *Obs.*, fool; obs. f. TOUT *sb.*[1]

**Touteaul**, obs. erron. form of TORTEAU.

**Tout ensemble**: see ENSEMBLE B.

**Touter** (tau·təɹ). [f. TOUT *v.*[1] + -ER [1].]

**1.** One who touts or canvasses for customers or clients; = TOUT *sb.*[1] 2.

*a* 1754 RICHARDSON *Corr.* (1804) III. 316 Here [Tunbridge Wells] are a parcel of fellows, mean traders, whom they call touters, and their business touting..riding out miles to meet coaches and company coming hither, to beg their custom while here. **1762** DERRICK *Lett.* (1767) II. 49 The tradesmen of Tunbridge Wells, who use this silly practice [of waylaying visitors to solicit their custom] are called Touters or Touters. **1844** THACKERAY *Wand. Fat Contrib.* i, Touters were about seizing upon the passengers and recommending their hotels. **1881** *Nation* (N. Y.) XXXII. 397 His performances at Albany as a touter for votes.

**2.** A spy upon race-horses; = TOUT *sb.*[1] 3.

**1812** *Sporting Mag.* XL. 200 A touter, that is, a person who hides up between the furzes on the heath to see the trials of horses.

**3.** A thief's scout; = TOUT *sb.*[1] 1.

**1844** DICKENS *Mart. Chuz.* xxxvii, Thimble-riggers, duffers, touters, or any of those..sharpers,..known to the Police.

†**4.** One who or that which watches: see quot. and cf. TOOTER[1] 1. *Obs.*

**1867** SMYTH *Sailor's Word-bk.*, *Tout*, an old term for looking out, or keeping a prying watch; whence the revenue cruisers and the customs officers were called touters.

**Touting** (tau·tiŋ), *vbl. sb.*[1] [f. TOUT *v.*[1] + -ING[1].] The action of TOUT *v.*[1]

**1731** *Gentl. Mag.* Sept. 399/1 Soon as they set Eyes on you, off flies the Hat, Does your Honour want this, does your Honour want that?..Now this, please your Honour, is what we call *Tooting*, A Trick in your Custom to get the first footing. **1777** *Antiq.* in *Ann. Reg.* II. 149/2 Tooting at Tunbridge-wells means..inviting and bringing guests to their master's house. **1820** W. C. OULTON *Pict. Margate* 47 This practice, called by the inhabitants touting, is exceedingly troublesome to strangers upon their first landing at Margate. **1883** *Manch. Exam.* 26 Nov. 5/1 If there was any touting for the Irish vote at York. **1894** M. H. HAYES *Men & Horses* vi. (ed. 2) 93 The disease of touting is endemic in Newmarket.

**Touting,** *vbl. sb.*[2], in *touting-ken*: see TOOT, TOUT *v.*[3] **Toutsayne,** early form of TUTSAN.

**Touward, Touzle**: see TOWARD, TOUSLE.

†**Tovet.** *Obs. local.* Forms: 6 tolvet, -vett, 7 talvett, tovit(t, 7–8 tof(f)et, 7–9 tovet; also 9 tavort, tobit, tofet, tofiet (*Eng. Dial. Dict.*). [A local word of Kent; evidently the same as *tollfat* (see TOLL *sb.*[1] 3).] A measure of two pecks or half a bushel.

[**1222** [see *tollfat* s. v. TOLL *sb.*[1] 3].] **1520** *MS. Acc. St. John's Hosp., Canterb.*, Paied..for a tolvet of malt in drynk vj d. **1527** *Ibid.*, For iij tolvettis of otemele xviij d. **1547** [see *tollfat*, as above]. **1618** *MS. Acc. St. John's Hosp., Canterb.*, When he brought the iij tovitis of wheat, ij d. **1629** *Ibid.*, For a taluett of wheate ij s ij d. **1639** *Ibid.*, Payed for mending of a touitt ij d. **1674** JEAKE *Arith.* (1696) 81, 1 Bushel 2 Tovits or Half Bushels, 1 Tovit 2 Pecks. **1674** RAY *S. & E. C. Words* 77 A *Tovet* or *Tofet*, half a bushel: Kent. **1695** *Birchington Par. Acc.* in *Archæol. Cant.* XII. 407 For three tovets of hair. **1777** *Ann. Reg.* II. 149 Tovet..in Kent means two pecks.

**Tovore,** variant of TOFORE *Obs.*, before.

**Tow** (tōu, *Sc.* tɒu, tou), *sb.*[1] Forms: 4–7 towe, (5 toow, 6 toa, 7–8 toe), 5–6 tawe, 5– tow. [Known only from last quarter of 14th c. Origin doubtful: perh. related to ON. *tó* n. uncleansed wool or flax, unworked fibre of thread; which is doubtfully connected with OE. **tow-* spinning, weaving, in *towcræft*, *towhūs*, and *towlīc* fit for spinning, textile, and obs. MDu. *touwen* to knit, to weave (Kilian). The original sense may have been 'textile fibre' generally.

Kilian has '*Touw* Fris. Ang. j. *werck*, Stupa'; and '*Tauw* j. *touw*'; also, '*Werck*, Stupa, lini stupa, linum vile, lini purgamentum, lana crassior & recrementitia'; which evidently agrees with our word; but *touw* has not been found in Fris., and the value of Kilian's entry is uncertain.]

†**1.** *app.* The unworked stem or fibre of flax, before it is heckled. *Obs. rare*—[1].

*c* **1400** MAUNDEV. (Roxb.) xi. 49 Raab..þat ressayued þe messangers of Israel..and seled [*pr.* feled] þam in hir hous amang towe of lyne [cf. *Vulgate* Josh. ii. 6 operuitque eos stipula lini; WYCLIF, couerd hem with stuble of flaxe].

**2.** The fibre of flax, hemp, or jute prepared for spinning by some process of scutching.

**1377** LANGL. *P. Pl.* B. XVII. 245 Ac hewe fyre at a flynte fowre hundreth wyntre But þow haue towe to take it with tondre or broches Al þi laboure is loste. *c* **1385** CHAUCER *L. G. W.* 2004 (*Ariadne*) Ballis ek also Of wex & tow [*v. r.* towe]..To slake his hungir & encombre his teth. *c* **1440** *Promp. Parv.* 498/2 Toow, of a rok, or a roket (..*K.* towe of hempe, or flax, or othyr lyke), *pensum*. **1545** *Rates of Customs* c vij b, Towe fyne the C. pounde v. s. Towe the .c. pounde iij s. iiij. d. **1599** A. M. tr. *Gabelhouer's Bk. Physicke* 38/2 Madefye heerin hempen toa, and applye.. rownde about his heade. **1616** SURFL. & MARKH. *Country Farme* 568 To the end that..in beating it with beetles, heckling and spinning of it, such filth may not remaine among the tow. **1674** GREW *Anat. Trunks* II. vii. § 13 The Qualities of the best Tow,..are that the Staple be long, small, tough, and white. **1725** RAMSAY *Gentle Sheph.* II. i, Gae break your wheel, and burn your tow, And set the meiklest peat-stack in a low. **178**. BURNS (*title*) The weary pund o' tow. *Ibid.* i, I think my wife will end her life Before she spin her tow. **1825** JAMIESON, *Tow*, hemp in a prepared state. **1839** *Cumbld. & Westmorld. Dial.* 13 Tae..spin tow for bord claiths en sheets.

**b.** *fig.*; esp. in phrase *to have tow on one's rock* (*distaff*), to have business to attend to.

*c* **1386** CHAUCER *Miller's T.* 588 This Absolon..hadde moore tow [*v. r.* towe] on his distaf Than Gerueys knew. *c* **1460** *Towneley Myst.* xiii. 389, I haue tow on my rok more then euer I had. **1756** MRS. CALDERWOOD in *Coltness Collect.* (Maitl. Club) 155 'In good faith', says John,..'the Dutch has some other tow in their rock'. **1890** DOYLE *White Company* v, They may find they have more tow on their distaff than they know how to spin.

**3.** More strictly, the shorter fibres of flax or hemp, which are separated by heckling from the fine and long-stapled, called *line*; = HARDS, *hurds*.

**1530** PALSGR. 183 *Unes estovpes*, a locke of towe or hurdes. *Ibid.* 282/1 Towe, *estouppes*. **1552** HULOET, Tow, *stipa, æ, stupa, æ*. **1601** HOLLAND *Pliny* XIX. i. II. 4 That part..which is utmost and next to the pill or rind, is called Tow or Hurds, and it is..good for little or nothing but to make lampe-match or candle-wicke. **1844** G. DODD *Textile Manuf.* v. 165 The flax ceases to be called by that name after it has passed through the heckling-machines; the good portion is then called '*line*', and the inferior '*tow*'. **1893** *Daily News* 14 July 3/7 Prices of lines and tows unchanged. **1896** *Ibid.* 12 Dec. 8/6 Flax, tow, and codilla quiet.

**4.** *attrib.* and *Comb.* **a.** *attrib.* 'Of or for tow', as *tow-beetle* (BEETLE *sb.*[1]), *-card* (CARD *sb.*[1] 2 a), *-quality*, *-waste*; 'consisting or made of tow', as *tow cloth*, *goods*, *hards*, *rope*, *sheeting*, *string*, *thong*, *weft*, *yarn*. **b.** Comb., as *tow-heckler*; *tow-coloured*, *-haired*, *-like*, *-made* adjs. **c.** Special combs.: **tow-head**, a light-coloured head of hair; also an unkempt or tousled head; a person having such hair; *spec.* a local name in southern U.S. for *Mergus cucullatus*, the Hooded Merganser of North America, the male of which has a semicircular crest with a white patch; hence **tow-headed** *a.*, having whitish or tousled hair; **tow-wheel**, a large spinning-wheel for making coarse tow yarn.

**1601** HOLLAND *Pliny* XIX. i. II. 4 To be beaten and punned ..with an hurden mallet or *tow-beetle made for the purpose. **1801** JAS. THOMSON *Willy Weir's Legacy* xxv, A pair o' gude *tow-cards. **1775** COOKE in Sparks *Corr. Amer. Rev.* (1853) I. 27 Such a demand for *tow-cloth for family use. **1822** J. FLINT *Lett. Amer.* 232 A tent was dismantled of its tow cloth covering. **1887** J. ASHBY-STERRY *Cucumber Chron.* 5 There are six *tow-haired children playing beneath a guide-post. **1617** J. BARBIER *Jan. Ling.* 98 The remnants of *tow-hards..are turned into smoke, or burned in the chimney. **1884** G. H. BOUGHTON in *Harper's Mag.* Sept. 530/2 The *tow-headed children rolling about in the orchards. *a* **1800** PEGGE *Suppl. Grose*, **Tow-Heckler*, a dresser of tow for spinning. North. **1907** *19th Cent.* Apr. 584 Her *tow-like hair was tied up with white tape. **1896** *Daily News* 12 Dec. 8/6 *Tow-made goods are selling freely in heavy makes for unions. **1336** *Acc. Exch., K. R.* 19/31 m. 4 (P.R.O.) In x. petris cordis de canabo..pro vno *towerope inde faciendo. **1902** CROCKETT *Dark o' Moon* xxxix, Saunders Lennox's tow rape will break mony a promise on Monday mornin' by nine o' Kirkcudbright clock. **1776** *Pennsylv. Even. Post* 25 May 264/2 A pair of *tow trowsers. **1837** *Civil Eng. & Arch. Jrnl.* I. 79/2 Bags filled with clay and *tow-waste. **1900** MARY E. WILKINS *Parson Lord* (ed. Tauchn.) 26 The great arc of an old *tow-wheel. **1780** A. YOUNG *Tour Irel.* I. 262 The warp of *tow-yarn.

**Tow** (tōu, *Sc.* tɒu, tou), *sb.*[2] Also 5–7 towe. [Known in Sc. use *c* 1470: not in OE. (exc. perh. in '*tōh-line* remulcus', tow-line, in Wr.-Wülcker 182/32). Corresponds to OFris. *tow* (from 15th c.), WFris. *tou*, NFris. *tau*, *tāw*, mod.Du. *touw*, early mod.Du. *touwe* (Kilian), MLG. *touwe*, *touw*, LG. and EFris. *tau*, whence mod.Ger. *tau* (1663 in Kluge); generally identified (at least the monosyll. forms) with ON. *tog*, Norw. *tog*, Sw. *tåg*, Da. *toug*, *tov*, all meaning 'rope, cable, cord': akin also to ON. *taug* f., OE. *tēag*, *tēah* string, rope, TIE *sb.* The fundamental meaning was app. 'means for drawing', f. ablaut stem *teuh-*, *tauh-*, *tug-* (*tog-*) to draw: see TEE *v.*[1]] A rope. Chiefly *Sc.*

*c* **1470** HENRYSON *Mor. Fab.* v. (*Parl. Beasts*) xii, With towis proud ane palȝeoun can thay picht. **1513** DOUGLAS *Æneis* v. xii. 163 Thair cabillis new, and thar heid towis reparis. **1534** *Acc. Ld. High Treas. Scot.* VI. 234 Cabillis and towis brocht hame to the Kingis schip. *a* **1578** LINDESAY (Pitscottie) *Chron. Scot.* (S.T.S.) I. 175 His handis bund witht sic ane tow of hempt. **1646** *Alloa Kirk Session Rec.* in *North. N. & Q.* 18 For towes to the bell. *a* **1670** SPALDING *Troub. Chas. I* (1829) 12 Upon Monday..at night, he came down over the castle wall, upon tows brought to him secretly by his wife, and clearly wan away. **1785** BURNS *Holy Fair* xxvi, Now Clinkumbell, wi' rattlin tow [= bell-rope] Begins to jow and croon. **1888** J. M. E. SAXBY *Lads of Lunda* 117 She was scudding out the Voe, Erik steering, Bill at the tows.

**b.** *spec.* A hangman's rope, a halter.

**1596** DALRYMPLE tr. *Leslie's Hist. Scot.* VIII. cii. (S.T.S.) II. 66 The tow, quhilke he maid to hang vtheris in, him selfe was first caught in. **1822** SCOTT *Pirate* xviii, It can end in naething but trees and tows [= gallows]. **1886** STEVENSON *Kidnapped* 50 There's many would like to see him girning in a tow.

**c.** In various specific or contextual uses (*Sc.* or *Eng. dial.*): e.g.

The rope or chain by which the weights of a clock are suspended (*Sc.*); a line or rope for sea-fishing (*Orkney & Shetl.*); the winding-cable for raising and lowering the cage, etc. in a coal-pit (*Sc.* and *north. Eng.*); a rope or chain for hauling timber (*Eng. dial.*); a line attached to the horns of the leading oxen in a South African team (also *fore-tow*).

**1834** A. SMART *Rhymes* 136 Just pou' the tow up when ye beddit. **1844** W. H. MAXWELL *Sports & Adv. Scot.* xv. (1855) 136 They prepare to set their *tows*, or lines, provided with ling hooks...The whole of the *packies* a boat carries is a head of *tows*. **1850** R. G. CUMMING *Hunter's Life S. Afr.* (1902) 8/1 The twelve oxen are soon all securely yoked in their proper places; the leader has made up his 'fore-tow', which is a long spare rheim attached round the horns of each of the fore or front oxen. **1863** W. C. BALDWIN *Afr. Hunting* viii. 357 When the front oxen had reached the boys, I shouted, 'Let go the tow, and get out of the road'. **1883** GRESLEY *Gloss. Coal-mining*, *Tow*,..2. A winding rope of hemp. **1884** *W. Worc. Gloss.* (Upton-on-Severn), *Tow*, a chain for hauling timber. **1893** HESLOP *Northumbld. Gloss.*, *Tow*, a small rope or painter. **1898** *Daily News* 25 Feb. 3/1 He went down with the first tow and found the fireman there.

†**Tow,** *sb.*[3] *Obs. local.* Forms: 5 toughe, 7 tawe, 8 tow. [Agrees in form and sense with Norw. *toge* (for *togje*), Aasen.] Orig. an iron chain, later, a large iron link, attached to the heel of the turn-wrest plough, and by which this is drawn. Also called **tow-chain.**

**1407** in Kennett *Par. Ant.* (1818) II. 213 (Oxf. & Bucks.) Pro uno vomere et una cultura et dimid. Toughe cum uno Plowsho emptis, xxiii[d]. **1607** J. CARPENTER *Plaine Mans Plough* 160 The Tawe, or that yron Rope which embracing the Beame, assureth it to the Tractory or Lambe. **1733** TULL *Horse-Hoeing Husb.* xxi. 301 The Tow-Chain which fastens the Plow-Tail to the Plow-Head. **1796** J. BOYS *Agric. Kent* (1813) 52 The plough there being drawn by a long large iron link, called a tow, which comes from the axle of the carriage round the heel of the plough.

**Tow** (tōu), *sb.*[4] Also 7 tawe. [f. TOW *v.*[1]]

**1.** A rope used for towing, a tow-line.

**1600** HAKLUYT *Voy.* III. 585 [The Phenix] kept her company vntil the next morning, then taking in a small cable from her for a towe: but by 9..she spent her maine mast and split her foreyard, breaking also her tow. **1625** J. GLANVILL *Voy. Cadiz* 61 Wee could not thus have fastned a towe unto her. **1669** STURMY *Mariner's Mag.* I. ii. 16 Those that be on Shore may have a Towe, and be blest with a Ruther; for we will stay for no man.

**2.** The action of towing or fact of being towed; chiefly in *in tow*, in the condition of being towed (*of* or *by* the towing vessel); esp. *to take in tow* (said of a ship, etc.): to begin and continue to tow, to tow.

**1622** R. HAWKINS *Voy. S. Sea* (1847) 226 The *Daintie* sayled badly,..and with the advantage which all the South-sea shippes have of all those built in our North-sea, the admirall gave her a tawe. **1704** J. HARRIS *Lex. Techn.* I. s. v., Whatever is drawn after a Ship, or Boat with a Rope, &c. is said to be Towed after a Ship, or to be in her Tow. **1720** DE FOE *Capt. Singleton* i. (1840) 4 As they were sailing away with our ship in tow as a prize. **1793** SMEATON *Edystone L.* § 109 One of these blocks..is by a strong chain attached to the carriage,..which is then drawn forward with the block in tow. **1865** LIVINGSTONE *Zambesi* xvi. 324 We took the hippopotamus in tow. **1900** F. T. BULLEN *With Christ at Sea* viii. 151 The long upward tow was nearly at an end. **1902** *Westm. Gaz.* 11 Apr. 5/2 The worst weather experienced during the tow was a fresh gale and lumpy sea.

**b.** *fig.*, esp. *to take in tow*, to take under one's guidance or patronage; to take charge of.

**1789** DIBDIN *Poor Jack* ii, Providence takes us in tow. **1790** WOLCOTT (P. Pindar) *Advice to Future Laureat* II. xxiii, Too proud for bards to take in tow my name. **1804** FESSENDEN *Democr.* (1806) II. 30 Till he will condescend, I trow Our commonwealth to take in tow. **1883** GILMOUR *Mongols* (1884) 226 A young lama..took me in tow, and conducted me to all the tents. **1896** MRS. CAFFYN *Quaker Grandmother* 28 She set off..to explore the world, with a one-eyed old aunt in tow, and a prize bull-dog.

**3.** A vessel taken in tow; also, a string of boats, barges, etc., being towed.

**1805** in Nicolas *Disp. Nelson* (1846) VII. 189 *note*, Trinidada in tow. Employed knitting fore and mizen rigging, and securing the masts and tow. **1883** *Fisheries Exhib. Catal.* (ed. 4) 175 Methods of Crossing a Channel with Tows of Seals. **1883** *Law Times* 24 Nov. 62/1 The *R. R.*, by reason of the inefficiency of the *V. S.* to command the seven tows, stranded and became a total wreck. **1885** *Law Times Rep.* LIII. 53/2 The schooner..having come into collision with a tug and her tow. **1897** *Outing* (U.S.) XXX. 120/1 The tow consisted of thirty-four boats towing four abreast, a floating village with its houses and families and small children. **1906** *Roy. Comm. Canals, Min. Evid.* 59, I have seen a tow of as many as 23 boats in the Blisworth tunnel on the Grand Junction.

**b.** A vessel that tows; a tug.

**1874** BEDFORD *Sailor's Pocket Bk.* vi. 172 The heaviest boats should be nearest the tow. Weighted boats tow best.

**4.** *attrib.* and *Comb.* (or perh. from TOW *v.*[1]), as *tow-barge*, *-horse*, *-man*, *-vessel*; **tow-boat**, a boat used in towing; *spec.* a small vessel built for towing others, a tug; **tow-car**, on street-railways in *U.S.*, a car which is towed by another, a trailer (*Funk's Stand. Dict.* 1895); **tow-iron**, in *Whaling*, the toggle-iron or harpoon to which the tow-line is attached (*Cent. Dict.* 1891); **tow-post**, a towing-post; **tow-rail**: see quot. See also TOW-LINE, -NET, -PATH, -ROPE.

**1681** W. ROBERTSON *Phraseol. Gen.* (1693) 1085 A *tow-barge. **1815** *Massachusetts Statute* 7 Feb., His patent steam *tow-boats..said patent bearing date the 2 day of April 1814. **1860** *Merc. Marine Mag.* VII. 99 Two powerful tow boats..are stationed at the bar. **1864** CARLYLE *Fredk. Gt.* XVII. vii. IV. 590 New boatmen, forty new *towmen. **1908** *Daily News* 29 July 4 He braced his back against the *tow-post as he flicked the cleanings overboard. **1894** *Pall Mall Mag.* Nov. 380 A stout arched timber, reaching from bulwark to bulwark [of a tug], termed a *tow-rail. **1698** T. SAVERY *Navig. Impr.* 10 The *Tow Vessel in [16]82 drew but four and a half Water the Outside.

†**Tow,** *sb.*[5] *Obs. rare. local.* Forms: 5 togh, 6 tow, towe, tawe. [Origin obscure: it cannot easily be connected with TYE, *tie* in same sense.] A pillow-case; cf. TYE *sb.*[1] 4.

*a* **1490** BOTONER *Itin.* (Nasmith 1778) 268 Unam cimbam cum una togh de raycloth. **1535** in Weaver *Wells Wills* (1890) 95 A coffer, ij pelowtowes, a salte, a gyrdell. **1542–3** (Jan. 29) *Will J. Dowdynge, widow* (Wells Prob. Reg.),

A syller, price of 7s; a pelow with a tawe. **1543** (Sept. 8) *Will R. Antell* (Ibid.), A pillow with the tow.

**Tow** (tōu), *v.*[1] Forms: 1 toȝian, 3 toȝen, 4 towen, 4–6 tou(e, 4–8 towe, (6 toagh, tough, tough, 6–7 togh, toe; 6 taw, 6–7 tawe), 6– tow. [OE. *toȝian* to draw or pull by force, to drag, ME. *toȝen, towen* = OFris. *toga* to pull roughly, pull about, MLG. *togen* (early mod.Du. *togen* (Kilian)), OHG. *zogôn* to draw, tug, drag (MHG. *zogen*), ON. and Norw. *toga* to draw, pull:—OTeut. **togōjan*, deriv. vb. from *tog-*, weak grade of ablaut-series *teuh-, tauh-, tug-* (*tog-*) to draw: see TEE *v.*[1]]

†**1.** *trans.* To draw by force; to pull, drag.

*c* **1000** *Passio St. Margaret* in Assmann *Ags. Hom.* 178 And þa godes wiðerwinnan þa fæmnan ȝenamon, ut of þære byriȝ unȝerædelice hi toȝoden. *c* **1275** LAY. 7536 Julius þat sweord heold; and Nennius þane sceald and longe þus i toȝede. ? *a* **1400** *Morte Arth.* 3655 The marynerse..Towyne trvsselle one trete, trvssene vpe sailes. **1494** *Acc. Ld. High Treas. Scot.* I. 248 Item, for a rape..quhilk was brokyne wyth towen of the tymmyr..ijs. iiijd. **1581** STUDLEY *Agamemnon* III, They tough their oars and with their toyle they helpe the wynd and weather.

*fig.* **1583** STUBBES *Anat. Abus.* II. (1882) 50 What tricking & toying, and al to tawe out mony, you may be sure.

†**b.** To convey, carry. *Obs. rare.*

**13..** *E. E. Allit. P.* C. 100 Jonas..Maches hym with þe marynneres, makes her paye, For to towe hym in-to Tarce, as tyd as þay myȝt. *a* **1375** *Joseph Arim.* 374 Þenne þei taken þis mon and towen him to þe temple.

**c.** To draw *up* or let *down* with a tow or rope. *Sc.* In this sense perh. directly from Tow *sb.*[2]

**1596** DALRYMPLE tr. *Leslie's Hist. Scot.* (S.T.S.) I. 27 With lang towis and Lathiris lattin doune thay ar towit vpe. **1755** *Edom o' Gordon* xxii. in *Percy Reliques* (1765) I. 104 O row me in a pair o' sheits, And tow me owre the wa.

**2.** *spec.* To draw or drag (a vessel, persons in a boat, etc.) on the water by a rope.

*To tow* (a boat) *under water*, to swamp by towing.

[**1290**: ? implied in TOWAGE 1.] **1391** *Earl Derby's Exp.* (Camden) 23 Pro touyng navem domini de la hauen apud Boston. *a* **1500** in *Arnolde's Chron.* (1811) 133 After tyme she was weyed and toued to the hauyn at Caleis. **1553** in Hakluyt *Voy.* (1904) V. 92 The boat (which we toed asterne from Jaffa). **1557** W. TOWRSON *ibid.* (1589) 117 Her rudder was broken, so that the *Hart* was glad to towe her. **1562** J. SHUTE tr. *Cambini's Turk. Wars* 34 b, They tawed the palandre after them. **1589** WARNER *Alb. Eng.* VI. xxix. (1612) 144, I will..tough the Pinnesse of my thoughts to kenning of your eyes. **1591** SYLVESTER *Du Bartas* I. i. 578 He that..toghes against the tide His laden barge. **1597** J. KING *On Jonas* (1618) 56 They..labored..to toagh their ships to land. **1620** R. COCKS *Diary* (Hakl. Soc.) II. 113, I sent out 4 barkes to helpe to toe her. **1630** DRAYTON *Muses Elizium* II. 343 Swans vpon the Streame to tawe me, Stags vpon the Land to draw me. **1644** Z. BOYD *Gard. Zion* in *Zion's Flowers* (1855) App. 7/1 In thy great Barge me togh against the tide. **1743** BULKELEY & CUMMINS *Voy. S. Seas* 143 We took from the Indians a Canoe, made of the Bark of Trees, but soon towed her under Water. **1769** *De Foe's Tour Gt. Brit.* (ed. 7) I. 153 King's Ferry, where a long Cable of about 140 Fathom,..fastened at each End across the Water, serves to get over the Boat by Hand... The Ferry-keeper..is obliged to tow all Travellers over free. **1877** A. B. EDWARDS *Up Nile* vii. 174 Barges towed by government steam-tugs.

**b.** *intr.* To pull or tug as in trying to move.

1884 *Law Times* 10 May 26/2 A tug towed at her for an hour and a half before she was got off.

**3.** *trans.* To drag by or as by a line. (*humorous.*)

**1663** BUTLER *Hud.* I. II. 1125 The Knight himself did after ride Leading Crowdero by his side, And tow'd him, if he lagg'd behind. **1767** LADY MARY COKE *Jrnl.* 29 July (1889) II. 68 Monsieur Wangenheim was towing up Lady Sarah, and complain'd it was hard work. **1803** SCOTT *Let. to Ellis* 14 Oct., in *Lockhart*, A rosy lass..entered our cottage, towing in a monstrous sort of bulldog. **1883** W. H. BISHOP in *Harper's Mag.* Mar. 503/1 A mounted Mexican towing a bull. **1884** *Nonconf. & Indep.* 12 June 578/1 Mr. Cumberland, blindfolded, towed another dignified gentleman through the streets by a silken cord.

**4.** *intr.* or *absol.* To advance or proceed by towing or being towed.

**1612** DRAYTON *Poly-olb.* ii. 451 When toghing vp that streame..shee yet conceales her name. **1624** CAPT. SMITH *Virginia* III. vi. 61 He would..cause..divers of his Country-men helpe vs towe against winde or tyde. **1667** *Lond. Gaz.* No. 186/4 One of them endeavoured to tow after him. **1695** BLACKMORE *Pr. Arth.* VI. 371 At last King Octa.. Commanding all to follow, tows away. **1720** DE FOE *Capt. Singleton* v. (1840) 90 We towed up as far as..our boats would swim. **1813** SOUTHEY *Nelson* I. iii. 143 The French vessels were allowed to tow out of the port of Genoa. **1874** [see Tow *sb.*[4] 3 b].

Hence **Towed** (tōud), **Towing** (tōu·iŋ) *ppl. adjs.*

**1898** *Daily News* 4 Aug. 5/3 The river journey in *towed barges from Shellal to Wady Halfa. **1901** *Westm. Gaz.* 8 July 9/3 One tug, and one towed raft, two self-propelled rafts. **1795** *Act* 35 *Geo. III*, c. 106 § 23 For the making..a Way or Road for the *Towing Horses. **1842** BRANDE *Dict. Sc.*, etc. s. v. *Tow*, As the vessel towed affects the motions of the other, much attention is required on her part to second the intentions of the towing vessel. *transf.* **1909** *Westm. Gaz.* 2 Feb. 4/1 To couple up a towing machine to a fully equipped [motor-] car by means of a strap.

**Tow** (tōu), *int.* and *v.*[2] **a.** *int.* A word used in calling a hawk, and in urging on greyhounds. **b.** *vb. trans.* To urge (greyhounds) *on* with this call.

**1575** TURBERV. *Falconrie* 182 Make them come from it to your fist..with calling and chirping to them, saying: *Towe, Tewe*, or *Stowe, Stowe*, as Falconers vse. **1793** F. GROSE *Olio* (1796) 178 Towing on two greyhounds, the constant attendants on his steps, pursued the game. *Note.* Tow, Tow, used in setting on greyhounds in Gloucestershire.

**Tow** (tōu), *v.*[3] [f. Tow *sb.*[1]] *trans.* To comb or card flax; also, to reduce to the state of tow or fibre. Hence **Tow·ing** *vbl. sb.*, *spec.*: see quot. 1891; †**towing-mill**, a carding-machine: see quot. 1789.

**1615** MARKHAM *Eng. Housew.* II. v. (1668) 134 That which comes from the flaxe being a little towed again in a pair of Wooll Cards, will make a course harding. **1789** *Trans. Soc. Arts* VII. 195 Mills..in Yorkshire..called Towing-Mills..worked by men turning them backward and forward, till the wool is sufficiently opened for use. **1891** *Cent. Dict.*, *Towing*, in *curled-hair manuf.*, the operation of picking to pieces the ropes of hair after they have been steeped in water and then subjected to slow heat [to give a permanent curl to the hair].

**Tow,** *v.*[4] *Pottery manuf.* [f. Tow *sb.*[1]] *trans.* To smooth the surface of (earthenware or china) when in the dry clay state before firing, by rubbing it with tow, sand-paper, or flannel. Hence **Tow·er, Tow·ing** *vbl. sb.*

**1892** *Daily News* 23 July 5/4 Mr. Brewer, a factory inspector in the Derby district, calls attention to the probable extension of the method of putting a finer surface on earthenware, which is known as 'towing'. **1894** *Labour Commission Gloss., Towers*,..pottery workers, who, when plates that are still unfired are dried till nearly all the moisture is out of them, pass over the surface while they..are rotating on a wheel a piece of 'tow', or sandpaper, to make them smooth.

**Tow,** obs. form of TOUGH, TWO.

**Towage** (tōu·ėdʒ). [Used in 13th c. in med.L. form *towāgium*, in 13th or 14th c. in F. form *touage*, implying verbs med.L. *towāre*, F. *touer*. These verbs, however, have not yet been found at that date, and Hatz.-Darm. consider Fr. *touer* to be a deriv. of ON. *toga* to draw, pull; it might also be from MLG. *togen*: see Tow *v.*[1] The Eng. form *towage* appears in L. context *a* 1327. In mod. use it is felt as a direct derivative of Tow *v.*[1]]

**1.** The charge or payment for towing a vessel (in quot. 1670, for permission to tow along the bank). Also *attrib.*

[**1286** Towagium (Du Cange). **1290** *Rolls of Parlt.* I. 27/1 Cum Dominus Rex habeat & habere debeat Towagium navium & batellorum majorum & minorum in Aqua de Tyne, ascendendo versus Novum Castrum.] **1562** in R. G. Marsden *Sel. Pl. Crt. Adm.* (Selden) II. 64 Towage, sownage, and petye lodemanshippe with all other accustomed averages. **1670** BLOUNT *Law Dict.*, *Towage*..is the towing or drawing a Ship...Also, that Money or other recompence, which is given by Bargemen to the owner of the Ground, next a River where they tow a Barge, or other Vessel. *a* **1688** DALLAS *Stiles* (1697) 414 Merchant of the said Towage, Rowage, Anchorage,..and other dues. **1755** MAGENS *Insurances* I. 72 To the petty, or accustomary Average..belong Lodemanage, Towage, and Pilotage.

**2.** The action or process of towing or being towed.

[**1297** *Boston Customs Acc. Customs, K.R.* Bd. 5 No. 5 *dorso* (P.R.O.), In frectagio pro .lij. saccis et .xx. petris lane..et in touwagio dictarum lanarum et in loadesmanagio .lxxj.s... Item in primagio .ij.s.] *a* **1327** *Acc. Exch. K. R.* 17/34 m. 3 (P.R.O.) In towage eorundem [xl doleorum vini] per aquam ..de lostwithiel vsque Fawe ad nauem .xiij.s. .iiij.d. **1611** COTGR., *Toüaige*, Towage, the towing of a ship by boats, or at the sterne of another ship. *a* **1640** JACKSON *Creed* XI. xliv. § 1 There is no possibility for two to go on breast, nor any room for steerage, but only towage. **1670** [see sense 1]. **1827** *Blackw. Mag.* XXI. 244 Under his towage we made way at a tolerably rapid rate. **1894** *Times* 12 Feb. 4/2 The Mosquito proceeded to tow the Cathay towards the Humber. The Cathay continued to labour heavily, and the towage required great care.

‖ **Towai** (tō·wai). Also **towhai.** [Native Maori name. (Not to be confused with TAWHAI.)] A large New Zealand timber tree, *Weinmannia racemosa*, N.O. *Saxifragaceæ*, also called by colonists *Black Birch.*

**1845** WAKEFIELD *Adv. N. Zealand* II. 95 (Morris) Its banks..are covered almost wholly with the towai. This tree has very small dark leaves. It is used for ship-building, and is called by Englishmen the 'black birch'. **1851** MRS. WILSON *N. Zealand* 43 The ake..and towai (*Leiospermum racemosum*) are almost equal, in point of colour, to rosewood. **1883** J. HECTOR *Handbk. N. Zealand* 132 (Morris) Towhai, Kamahi. A large tree; trunk two to four feet in diameter, and fifty feet high.

**Towail**(e, **-aille, -ale, -all,** obs. ff. TOWEL.

**Towan** (tau·ăn). *Cornw.* Also towin, tewen, tuan, tûyn. [Cornish *towan*, Welsh *tywyn* in same sense.] A coast sand-hill.

**1803** POLWHELE *Hist. Cornw.* I. v. 161 The green hillocks or levels of our downs in the vicinity of the sea. We call them *towans.* **1859** M. WALCOTT *Guide Devon & Cornw.* 529 The neighbourhood of Hayle is remarkable for sands composed of shells, the towans. **1882** JAGO *Cornw. Gloss.*, *Towan, towin, tewen, tuan*, or *tûyn*..are Celtic Cornish words for a dune or heap of sand. **1899** QUILLER COUCH *Ship of Stars* iv, He heard a horn blown somewhere high on the towans behind him.

†**Towanite** (tau·ănəit). *Min.* [Named 1852, from Huel Towan in Cornwall: see -ITE [1].] An obsolete synonym of CHALCOPYRITE.

**1852** BROOKE & MILLER *Phillips' Introd. Min.* 182 Bornite..occurs in beds and veins in the older rocks with towanite [etc.]. **1878** GURNEY *Crystallogr.* 79 Towanite or Copper Pyrites is a double sulphide of copper and iron.

**Towar,** obs. Sc. form of TOWER *sb.*[2], 3.

**Toward** (tōu·(w)əɹd, tō·əɹd), *a.* and *adv.* Forms: see next. [OE. *tóweard* adj., f. *tó*, To *prep.* + *-weard*, -WARD. So OS. *tóward, -werd*, OHG. *zuowart, -wert*, adjs. In OE., when used attributively, inflected like other adjs.; when in the predicate, uninflected exc. with pl. *-e*. The advb. use appears to arise out of the predicative use of the adj., or from the neuter adj.]

**A.** *adj.* †**1.** That is to come, coming, future. *Obs.*

*c* **888** K. ÆLFRED *Boeth.* xxxix. § 11 Tacn þæs toweardan welan. **971** *Blickl. Hom.* 15 Be þisse ondweardan tide, ȝe eac be þære toweardan. *c* **1000** *Ags. Gosp.* Mark x. 30 On toweardre [*Hatt. G.* towearde] worulde ece lif. **11..** *12th Cent. Hom.* xiv. 136 Næfð he næfre þærof forȝyfenesse, ne on þisse weorlde, ne on þa towearden. **1590** SPENSER *F. Q.* II. iv. 22 He, either envying my toward good, Or of him selfe to treason ill disposd. **1613** CHAPMAN *Rev. Bussy D'Ambois* I. i, The toward victor of the whole low Countryes.

†**b.** *predicatively.* Coming or going (to be), about to be, future. *Obs.*

*c* **888** K. ÆLFRED *Boeth.* xi. § 1 He nat hwæt him toweard bið, hwæðer þe god þe yfel. *c* **1000** ÆLFRIC *Gen.* xviii. 18 He ys toweard on micelre mæȝðe. *Ibid.* xlix. 1 Ic eow cyðe þa þing þe eow towearde synd. — *Deut.* xxix. 15 Eallum mannum, þam þe nu sint and þam þe towearde sint. *c* **1530** LD. BERNERS *Arth. Lyt. Bryt.* (1814) 48 And she grew and amended dayly, so that she was towarde to be fayrest creature of yͤ worlde.

†**2.** Approaching, imminent, impending. *Obs.*

*c* **890** tr. *Bæda's Eccl. Hist.* IV. i. (1890) 256 Hy nedde se towearda winter, þæt heo stille wunedon. **971** *Blickl. Hom.* 195 Forþon þe he ær nolde onȝytan þone towerdon deaþ. **1586** J. HOOKER *Hist. Irel.* in Holinshed II. 154/2 Dispatching also a messenger to hir maiestie of these toward broiles and rebellion.

**b.** *pred.* Now *rare* or *Obs.*

*c* **890** tr. *Bæda's Eccl. Hist.* IV. xiv. [xi.] (1890) 294 Mid þy he..onȝet þæt him deaðes dæȝ toweard wæs. *a* **1000** *Læceboc* II. xlvi. in *Sax. Leechd.* II. 256 Tacn hu sio adl toweard sie. **1387** TREVISA *Higden* (Rolls) V. 101 Also for werre and batailles þat were toward [L. *propter imminentia bella*]. **1462** J. PASTON in *P. Lett.* II. 121 Mak as merry as ye can, for ther is no joperte toward not yet. **1494** FABYAN *Chron.* VII. 387 For so moche as wynter was towarde. **1582** N. T. (Rhem.) *Acts* xxvii. 20 No smal storme being toward [*imminente*] al hope was now taken away. **1600** SHAKS. *A. Y. L.* V. iv. 35 There is sure another flood toward, and these couples are comming to the Arke. **1795** *Montford Castle* II. 50 There was a trifling banquet toward, at which they would be glad of his company. **1877** MACQUOID *Doris Barugh* xviii. (E.D.D.), Ah knawed fower weeks sin' at ther war a wedding toward.

**c.** In progress, going on; being done.

**1838** CAROLINE FOX *Old Friends* (1882) 229 Louis Buonaparte has reached France from London to see what is toward. **1892** A. MURDOCH *Yoshiwara Episode* 60 News of the encounter that was toward had spread.., and all the inmates ..had pushed into the ante-room where the contest was in progress. **1893** RIDER HAGGARD *Montezuma's Dau.* xxi, A fierce hope smote me..when I saw what was toward.

**d.** 'Getting on', forward, advanced.

**1893** *Cornh. Mag.* Nov. 522 Glidders's operations were well toward.

**3.** Of young persons: Promising, 'hopeful', forward; making good progress in learning or practice; disposed, apt, or willing to learn; docile. = TOWARDLY *a.* 2. *Obs.* or *arch.*

*c* **1290** *S. Eng. Leg.* I. 42/278 Swuch a child touward as þou art i-loked. **1538** CROMWELL in Merriman *Life & Lett.* (1902) II. 163 On the behalfe of a ryght towarde yonge man, Edwarde Bashe, this Berer. **1598** B. JONSON *Ev. Man in Hum.* II. i, Where proving A toward Imp. **1600** HEYWOOD *1st Pt. Edw. IV*, Wks. 1874 I. 5 There was neuer mother had a towarder son. **1625** B. JONSON *Staple of N.* II. i, Vouchsafe my toward kinsman, gracious madam, The favour of your hand.

†**4.** Disposed to do what is asked or required; willing, compliant, obliging, docile. (The opposite of FROWARD *a.* 1.) *Obs.* or *arch.*

*c* **1440** *York Myst.* xxvi. 159 Goode sir, be toward þis tyme, And tarie noght my trace, For I haue tythandis to telle. **1472–3** *Rolls of Parlt.* VI. 6/1 Of their fre wille, toward, herty and lovyng dispositions. **1532** CROMWELL in Merriman *Life & Lett.* (1902) I. 350 What shalbe your towarde mynde herin I pray you to Aduertise me. **1592** SHAKS. *Ven. & Ad.* 1157 Peruerse it shall be, where it showes most toward, Put feare to valour, courage to the coward. **1713** STEELE *Guard.* No. 142 ¶ 3 Miss hath hitherto been very tractable and toward. **1738** tr. *Guazzo's Art Conversation* 233 A Child of a toward Disposition.

**b.** Of things: Favourable, propitious: the opposite of *untoward. rare.*

**1850** GLADSTONE *Homer* II. 100 She can order out a rattling zephyr..or simply a toward breeze. **1868** — *Juv. Mundi* viii. (1870) 281 He too sends for the Greek ship a toward breeze. **1902** *Daily Chron.* 29 May 3/2 There are plenty of what we may call toward coincidences in Mr. Yoxall's book.

**5.** Left, as opposed to right. *dial.*

[From the fact that the left side of a horse, etc., is toward the person who mounts or leads it. Cf. NEAR *a.* 3.]

**1866** BLACKMORE *Cradock Nowell* xxii, 'Mark, does Mr. Cradock Nowell generally shoot with cartridges?' 'He laiketh mostways to be with a curtreege in his toard barryel, sir'. 'Oh, keeps a cartridge in his left barrel, does he; and fires first the right, I suppose?' **1879** MISS JACKSON *Shropsh. Word-bk.* s.v. *Frommet*, A harvest-field term. *Toërt* is left hand...'Theer, now yo'n chucked it down toërt way'.

†**6.** ? Forthcoming, ready at hand; in existence, 'going'. *Obs.* (Quotations obscure.)

*c* **1350** *Will. Palerne* 1101 Of proude princes sones, douȝti men toward, Fulle foure schore. *Ibid.* 1443 He has a sone dere, On þe triest man to-ward of alle douȝti dedes, Þat any man vpon molde may of here. **1393** LANGL. *P. Pl.* C. I. 214 And ȝe, route of ratons of rest men a-wake, Ne were þe cat of þe court And ȝonge Kytones to-warde. *c* **1530** LD. BERNERS *Arth. Lyt. Bryt.* cxiv. (1814) 540 And this chyld was the most fair chyld toward of the world, and wel fourmed, byg and myghty. [*orig.* & si estoit l'enfant le plus beau qu'oncques fut veu grand & gros & bien forme.] **1559** AYLMER *Harborowe* 12, I shewed you the lyke towarde in a man of late.

**B.** *adv.* [Cf. MHG. *zuowart* adv.]

**1.** In a direction toward oneself, or toward something aimed at. *Obs.* or *arch.* † *Toward and froward* (dial. *fromward*), to and fro.

*a* **1300** *E. E. Psalter* cxviii[i]. 8 To-ward, fra-ward, forlete me noght. *a* **1400** in Halliwell *Rara Mathem.* (1841) 58 Come toward and go froward til þe perpendicle..falle vpon þe mydel lyne of þe quadrant. *Ibid.* 66 Go toward and froward til þou se þe toppe of þat thing in þe mydel of þat myrure. **1470–85** MALORY *Arthur* XIII. xvi. 634 He rode many Iourneyes bothe toward and froward. **1858** BUSHNELL *Serm. New Life* xi. (1869) 148 The motion is outward and not toward, as we conceive it to be in happiness.

**b.** To the left or near side (of a horse, etc.). *dial.*

**1711** *Lond. Gaz.* No. 4917/4 The forepart of his Mane longest, the one part being short, lies toward, the other fromward. [Gloucester, Hampsh., Wilts, in *Eng. Dial Dict.*]

**2.** Onward (in a course), forward (*lit.* and *fig.*).

**1426** LYDG. *De Guil. Pilgr.* 12159 Al that thow wendyst ha be toward, Ys but a passage that goth bakward. **1509** HAWES *Past. Pleas.* xxx. (Percy Soc.) 148 The time renneth toward right fast. **1529** MORE *Dyaloge* Wks. 110/1 By that way, yͤ faith went well toward, and one heritique so tourned did turne many other. **1888** *Berksh. Gloss., Towart,* towards; forward. When a come a little tow-art I could zee as 'twas a pawle cat.

**Toward** (tōu·əɹd, tō·əɹd, tōᵊɹd; tŭwǭ·ɹd), *prep.* Forms: 1–2 **toweard,** 2 **towaard,** 2–3 **touward,** 2–4 **to-ward,** 2, 4–6 *Sc.* **towart,** (4 **tawart,** 6 *Sc.* **touart**), 3 (*Orm.*) **towarrd,** (3–4 **to(-)war**), 4–5 **taward(e,** 4–6 **towarde,** 5 **tooward, to-warde, to ward, to warde,** (**towor,** 6 **towerde, towrd, tward, torde**), 3– **toward,** (8–9 **tow'rd,** 9 *dial.* **toard**). [OE. *tóweard*, f. *tó*, To *prep.* + *-weard*, -WARD; orig. the uninflected form or singular neuter of TOWARD *a.* In OE., originally followed by a genitive; later by a dative like the simple *to.*

The first pronunciation figured above is now chiefly northern and (app.) American; the fourth is not recognized in any modern dictionary, British or American, nor app. by any orthoepist; but it appears to be the prevailing one in London and the south of England. See Walker on the word. It was app. referred to in 1749 by Chesterfield *Lett.* 27 Sept.: 'The vulgar man goes *to wards* and not *towards* such a place'. It may have arisen from the analytical form in *to us ward, to heaven ward,* in which *to* has its ordinary stressless pronunciation as a preposition; and, if so, may have existed locally or as an alternative form, esp. in verse, from the 16th c. So with TOWARDS.]

**1.** Of motion (or action figured as motion): In the direction of; so as to approach (but not necessarily reach: thus differing from To *prep.* 1).

*c* **893** K. ÆLFRED *Oros.* I. i. § 22 Þonne ærnað hy ealle toweard þæm feo. *c* **897** — *Gregory's Past. C.* ix. 59 Ða ðe gað on ryhtne weȝ toweard ðæs hefonrices. *c* **1175** *Lamb. Hom.* 3 Þe helend nehlechede to-ward ierusalem þare burh. *c* **1290** *S. Eng. Leg.* I. 18/589 Þo þe deuelene comen toward him, huy ne miȝten come him neiȝ. *c* **1375** *Cursor M.* 3356 (Fairf.) Quat mon ys he þat comande tawarde [*v.r.* tilward] vs I se. *c* **1375** *Sc. Leg. Saints* xxxiii. (*George*) 844 Dacyane .. towart his palace went. *c* **1400** *Destr. Troy* 6112 Þo ledys..gon tooward þe grekis. *c* **1470** HENRY *Wallace* I. 98 Towart Dunbar without restyng thai raid. **1552** HULOET, Torde, *vide* in toward. **1611** BIBLE *Phil.* iii. 14, I presse toward the marke. **1715–20** POPE *Iliad* XI. 641 The steeds with sounding feet Shake the dry field, and thunder tow'rd the fleet. **1807** J. BARLOW *Columb.* I. 504 Tow'rd the Northern sky..the Hero cast his eye. **1870** MORRIS *Earthly Par.* (1890) 233/2 The company of maidens drew Toward where they stood.

†**b.** *pred.* after *to be*: On the way to. *Obs.*

**1297** R. GLOUC. (Rolls) 3569 Þe king was toward scottlond. *c* **1425** *Seven Sag.* (P.) 660 Toward the deth as he was..He mette with myster Baucillas.

†**c.** With implication of reaching; to. *Obs.*

*c* **1386** CHAUCER *Prol.* 27 Pilgrimes were they alle That toward Caunterbury wolden ryde. *c* **1425** *XI Pains of Hell* 238 in *O. E. Misc.* 218 Vp taward heuen þai con him bryng. **1440** *Paston Lett.* I. 40 This same weke shall he to ward Fraunce. *c* **1500** *Melusine* 102 They departed fro Lusynen and camme to Poytiers toward the Erle. **1596** SHAKS. *Merch. V.* IV. i. 403, I must away this night toward Padua. **1611** — *Wint. T.* V. i. 232 Vpon which Errand I now goe toward him.

**2.** Of position: In the direction of; on the side next to; turned or directed to, facing.

**13..** *Cursor M.* 2474 (Cott.) Abram chese him toward þe est. **1387** TREVISA *Higden* (Rolls) I. 235 Alway his face was toward þe sonne. *c* **1400** MAUNDEV. (Roxb.) xxxii. 147 Þat tyme occupied Cristen men many cuntreez toward þase partiez. *c* **1482** J. KAY tr. *Caoursin's Siege of Rhodes* (1870) ꝑ 10 Atte fote of a hylle toward the Weste. *a* **1548** HALL *Chron., Hen. V* 55 When he entred into the chambre the dukes backe was towarde him. **1610** HOLLAND *Camden's Brit.* (1637) 306 Under Suth-rey toward the South lieth.. Suth-sex. **1760–72** H. BROOKE *Fool of Qual.* (1809) I. 75 This needle..[was] three-square toward the point. **1853** M. ARNOLD *Scholar Gypsy* xii, Have I not passed thee on the wooden bridge..Thy face toward Hinksey and its wintry ridge?

†**b.** Beside, near; about, in attendance upon; in the possession of; with. *Obs.*

*c* **1400** tr. *Secreta Secret., Gov. Lordsh.* 110 And þe gretteste with-holde toward þe. *c* **1400** *Brut* cxxxii. 136 Harolde..wolde nouȝt departe with his peple of þing þat he hade gete, but helde it al toward [*v.r.* towards] him-self. **1433** *Rolls of Parlt.* IV. 423/1 Makyng þo þat beth toward hym to do the same. **1469** in *Archæologia* XV. 170 The oon key shall abyde toward the wardeyn, and the second toward the maister aboveseid. **1601** BP. ANDREWES *Serm., Matt.* xxii. *21* (1631) II. 88 Herod and they that were toward him, being all that they were by Cæsar.

**3.** In the direction of (in *fig.* senses). **a.** *gen.*: esp. with words expressing tendency or aim, and followed by an abstract noun expressing state, condition, etc. (In quots. 13.. and 1553 'on the way to': cf. 1 b; in quot. 1600, 'to': cf. 1 c.)

[*a* **1225** *Ancr. R.* 120 Tu schalt demen þi suluen wod, þo þu þer touward þouhtest.] **13..** *Cursor M.* App. ii. 790 (B. M. Add. MS.) What þinges þat I say may To myn felawis.., That I was toward þi buriynge. **1426** LYDG. *De Guil. Pilgr.* 75 That folk may the Ryhte weye se Best assuryd to-warde ther passage. **1553** *Respublica* IV. iv. 1126 So ye though oppressed with longe aduersitee, Yet doubte not, are towarde wealth & prospiritee. **1600** SHAKS. *A. Y. L.* II. vii. 162 His bigge manly voice, Turning againe toward childish trebble, pipes And whistles in his sound. *a* **1677** BARROW *Serm. Eccl.* ix. *10* Wks. 1686 III. 224 Incessantly working toward the end for which it was designed. **1818** SOUTHEY *Ess.* (1832) II. 135 There is no danger of our tending toward the same extreme. **1875** WHITNEY *Life Lang.* ii. 18 Tracing the history of words toward their origin. **1891** MRS. MAUDE *Pyrography* i. 7 An immense advance has been made toward perfection.

**b.** With a noun or pronoun denoting the object of action or feeling: To; against.

*c* **1175** *Lamb. Hom.* 17 Gif we suneȝieð towaard him˜we sculen gan to bote. *c* **1200** ORMIN 2601 Forr ȝho wass..milde & meoc & bliþe, ȝa towarrd Godd, ȝa towarrd mann. **1390** GOWER *Conf.* I. 122 Bot wolde god that grace sende, That toward me my lady wende, As I towardes hire wene. *c* **1400** *Laud Troy Bk.* 10049 He is wel wroth toward his wiff. *c* **1460** *Oseney Reg.* 123 The seruice..that þe saide chanons schall aquite towarde the Chefe lordes. *c* **1500** *Melusine* xxxvii. 297 Now haue I betrayed you..and haue forsworne my self toward you. **1601** SHAKS. *Twel. N.* III. ii. 13 This was a great argument of loue in her toward you. **1785** *Liberal Amer.* II. 226 To explain the real motives of his conduct toward me in America. **1813** SOUTHEY *Nelson* II. vi. 84 The policy which ought to be pursued toward the French in Egypt. **1867** R. COLLYER *Nat. & Life* xiii. 247 This is the way in which I act toward my own children.

†**c.** With regard to, in reference to, respecting, concerning, about. Also *as toward* (cf. *as to*). *Obs.*

*a* **1240** *Lofsong* in *Cott. Hom.* 211 Opene ham [my wits] heouenliche king touward heouenliche þinges. *c* **1300** *Beket* 765 If thu wolt owȝt toward me, thu wost wel y ne mai noȝt fiȝte. **1390** GOWER *Conf.* II. 34 Wel me qwemeth, That thou thiself hast thus aquit Toward this vice, in which no wit Abide mai. **1433** *Rolls of Parlt.* IV. 423/2 As toward his abode here..he saide þat he knoweth [etc.]. *a* **1548** HALL *Chron., Hen. VI* 96 b, And as towarde the letter sent..vnto my lorde of Bedford of the whiche the tenor is before rehersed. **1564** *Reg. Privy Council Scot.* I. 285 Swa that na complaint salbe..maid to the Quenis Majestie towart the saidis contraversiis and debattis. **1670–1** MARVELL *Corr.* Wks. (Grosart) II. 360 On Munday next, when the House will probably proceed severely toward their penaltyes.

**d.** In comparison with: = To 18. Now *dial.*

**1527–8** in Strype *Eccl. Mem.* (1721) I. App. xvii. 38 Which bookes..be not to be regarded toward the new printed Testament in Englishe. **1887** *S. Chesh. Gloss., To'art as,* in comparison with.

**4.** Of time: So as to approach; at the approach of, nearly as late or as far on as, shortly before, near.

**14..** *Torr. Portugal* (E. E. T. S.) Fragm. ii. 511 It drewe towarde the nyght. ? *a* **1500** *Wycket* (1828) p. ii, Towarde the laste dayes the kynge of the northe shall come. **1797** HOLCROFT tr. *Stolberg's Trav.* (ed. 2) III. lxxx. 240 Toward the conclusion of their independence. **1802** M. CUTLER in *Life*, etc. (1888) II. 89 Gentlemen most accustomed to speaking..were principally to wait till toward the close of the debate. **1844** SOUTHEY *Life A. Bell* I. 54 Toward the close of October letters..had reached him by way of Glasgow. **1876** STEDMAN *Victorian Poets* 103 At dates well toward the middle of this century.

**5.** †**a.** Of condition or quality: Verging upon, near; somewhat like, nearly, as if; *toward blackness*, somewhat or nearly black. *Obs.*

**1533** ELYOT *Cast. Helthe* (1541) N iij, Whan the bladder is towarde any syckenes. **1562** TURNER *Herbal* II. 153 The Thlaspi yͭ cometh out of Cappadocia is toward blacknes, and the sede is not fully rounde. **1566** BLUNDEVIL *Horsemanship* IV. iv. (1580) 3 It is best knowne, whether a Horse be sicke or not, or toward sicknesse, by these signes.

**b.** Of quantity: Nearly as much as, nearly.

*c* **1449** PECOCK *Repr.* I. iv. (Rolls) 20 Welnyȝ or weel toward the al hool lawe with which Cristen men ben chargid. **1879** S. C. BARTLETT *Egypt to Pal.* xxi. 453 They rise..toward a hundred feet above the plain.

**6.** In prospect of; in the imminence of; (as predicate) in preparation for. *Obs.* or *arch.*

**1542** UDALL *Erasm. Apoph.* 327 b, When Crassus was towarde a iourney into Syria. **1576** GASCOIGNE *Steele Gl.* (Arb.) 79 Towarde shipwracke, many men can pray. **1865** SWINBURNE *Atalanta* 877, [I] stand, girt as they toward hunting.

†**b.** Coming upon, 'in store for'; usually of evil: ready to fall upon, threatening. *Obs.*

**1375** BARBOUR *Bruce* I. 82 Þai couth nocht persawe þe skaith þat towart þaim wes apperand. **1606** G. W[OODCOCKE] *Hist. Ivstine* XXVI. 94 By the inwardes of those beasts, perceiuing..that there was toward them a great slaughter. **1609** HOLLAND *Amm. Marcell.* 399 All which.. plainely shewed, that this kind of death was toward him.

**7.** In the way of contribution to; as a help to; for the purpose of making up, promoting, assisting, or the like; for.

**1468** in Blades *Caxton* (1882) 151 Hit is accorded that [they] shall haue in honde xl li sterling towarde thoire costs & charges. **1483** *Cely Papers* (Camden) 144 To pay thys hallff ȝerys wages..here ys nothyng toward hytt. *c* **1530** H. RHODES *Bk. Nurture* 655 in *Babees Bk.* 100 Giue the pore of thy good; Part thou therof toward their want. **1662–3** MARVELL *Corr.* Wks. (Gros.) II. 83, I have writ this same..to prepare our correspondence toward your service. **1710** SWIFT *Jrnl. to Stella* 5 Oct., Here is two and eightpence halfpenny toward your loss. **1828** SOUTHEY *Ess.* (1832) II. 273 Raising a fund..toward the expenses of removing paupers by emigration.

**8.** For *to . . . -ward*, separated by the sb. or pron., as in *to us-ward, to God-ward*, see -WARD, and cf. To *prep.* 2 e.

**To·wardliness** (see next). Now *dial.* or *arch.* [f. TOWARDLY *a.* + -NESS.] The quality or character of being 'towardly'.

**1.** Good disposition towards something, willingness; *spec.* aptness to learn, docility, tractableness; forwardness in learning, 'promise'; ingenuity, proficiency: = TOWARDNESS 1, 2.

*a* **1569** KINGESMYLL *Confl. Satan* (1578) 25 Such as haue no towardlinesse nor framing of their hearts..to do the will of God. **1603** KNOLLES *Hist. Turks* (1621) 360 [He] appointed eight hundred of the Christian children, in whom appeared most towardlinesse, to be brought up for Ianezaries. **1612** BRINSLEY *Lud. Lit.* p. xxv, All schollars of any towardlinesse and diligence may be made absolute Grammarians, and euery way fit for the Vniuersitie, by fifteen yeares of age. **1735–6** CARTE *Ormonde* I. Introd. 65 The loss of his only son, a noble young gentleman and of great towardliness. **1830** GODWIN *Cloudesley* III. i. 3, I had children that improved every day in towardliness and beauty.

**2.** Favourableness, friendliness, affability.

**1566** Q. MARY *Let.* in *Sir J. Melvil's Mem.* (1735) 144 Touching our Towardliness to them of the Religion. **1603** KNOLLES *Hist. Turks* (1621) 573 The great towardlinesse and courteous nature of the Turkish emperour.

**3.** Furtherance, advancement, promotion.

**1553** S. CABOT *Ordinances* in Hakluyt *Voy.* (1589) 262 In towardlinesse of beneficiall traffike. **1653** MANTON *Exp. James* iv. 16 Wks. 1871 IV. 394 If God suspend his concurrence, the creatures cannot act, at least not with any towardliness and success.

†**4.** Likelihood, likely condition or position, prospect; in such phrases as *in great towardliness*, very likely. (Cf. TOWARDNESS 3.) *Obs.*

**1579–80** NORTH *Plutarch* (1676) 297 Cato put out of the Senate also, one Manlius, who was in great towardliness to have been made Consull. **1655** OWEN *Vind. Evang.* Wks. 1853 XII. 192 The signs..that he would be exalted to a Kingdom. He was by them in a good towardliness for it.

**Towardly** (tōu·(w)əɹdli, tō·əɹdli), *a.* [f. TOWARD *a.* + -LY[1]: cf. OE. *tóweardlíc* that is to come, future (which did not survive into ME.).]

**1.** Likely to lead to a desired result; promising success, propitious; helpful, favourable, advantageous; seasonable, befitting. (Cf. TOWARD *a.* 4 b.)

**1520** *St. Papers Hen. VIII*, II. 34 After ye shall have atteyned..any towardly comfourte, this yere, to bring our rebellious subjecttes there to summe obedience. **1644** MILTON *Areop.* (Arb.) 69 What wants there to such a towardly and pregnant soile, but wise and faithfull labourers? **1704** SWIFT *T. Tub* Concl. ꝑ6, I have observed many a towardly word to be wholly neglected. **1825** MRS. CARLYLE in Froude *Life Carlyle* (1882) I. 322 Your circumstances..may be in the process of time rendered more towardly. **1884** *Athenæum* 15 Mar. 340 He must choose a towardly hour.

**2.** Promising, 'hopeful', forward; apt to learn, docile: chiefly of young persons or their dispositions.

**1528** J. LONDON *Let. to Bp. Lincoln* 25 Feb., in *Lett. & Papers Hen. VIII*, XLVII. 90 (P.R.O.) Neuer..to calle hym nor any other cambridge manne vnto hys most towardely colledge [Christ Church, Oxford]. **1561** T. HOBY tr. *Castiglione's Courtyer* I. (1577) C ij b, One of the best fauoured, and towardlyest personages in the worlde, deformed and marred in his greene age. **1587** FLEMING *Contn. Holinshed* III. 959/1 They..rode to Enfield to see the prince,..greatlie reioising..to behold so proper and towardlie an impe. **1627** ABP. ABBOT *Narr.* II. in Rushw. *Hist. Coll.* (1659) I. 451 He was my Pupil at Oxford, and a very towardly one. **1670** MILTON *Hist. Eng.* V. Wks. 1738 II. 90 Them also I wish..mistaken, who write that Athelstan, jealous of his younger Brother Edwin's towardly Virtues,.. caus'd him to be drown'd in the Sea. **1712** STEELE *Spect.* No. 263 ꝑ1, I am the happy Father of a very towardly Son. **1863** *Sat. Rev.* 21 Mar. 368/2 He will be a towardly scholar under a willing teacher.

**b.** Of plants: Promising, forward. ? *Obs.*

**1580** LYLY *Euphues* (Arb.) 451 Easterly windes blasteth towardly blossoms. **1664** EVELYN *Sylva* (1776) 303 Purge them of all superfluous shoots and cions, reserving only the most towardly for the future stem. **1676** HALE *Contempl.* II. 98 Towardly Plants, are by Death Transplanted into another Region, a Garden of Happiness and Comfort.

**3.** Well-disposed, dutiful, tractable.

**1513** DOUGLAS *Æneis* III. viii. 70 Sen the sammyn four futtit beistis eik Bene oft vsit, full towartlie and meik, To draw the cart, and thoill bridill and renȝe. **1601** R. JOHNSON *Kingd. & Commw.* (1603) 234 [A slave's] faithfulnesse and towardly disposition. *a* **1629** HINDE *J. Bruen* xx. (1641) 64 If hee saw them any more towardly, in duties of Religion. **1672** EACHARD *Hobbs' State Nat.* (1705) 13 I'le promise you to be very towardly for the future.

**b.** Favourably disposed, friendly, affable. (Cf. TOWARD *a.* 4.)

**15..** in Maton *W. Counties* (1797) I. 55 The ladi Elizabeth so towardli with the kinges honorable counselers. **1649** DAVENANT *Love & Hon.* III. iii, Good heart, it is As towardly an old thing! *a* **1674** CLARENDON *Hist. Reb.* XIV. § 41 England proved not yet so towardly as he expected. **1893**

*Nat. Observ.* 18 Feb. 340/2 The men..were very courteous, and the women very towardly.

**To·wardly** (see prec.), *adv.* Now *dial.* or *arch.* [f. TOWARD *a.* + -LY 2. Cf. OE. *tóweardlice*, in time to come, in the future (which did not survive in ME.).] In a 'toward' or 'towardly' manner; with favourable disposition; willingly, compliantly, obligingly; docilely, tractably, submissively; with promise of good progress, promisingly: see the adj.

**1481** *Coventry Leet Bk.* 484 Wherin ye shewed yewe ryght benyvolent and towardly disposed. **1523** HEN. VIII in Ellis *Orig. Lett.* Ser. I. I. 238 Thanks unto all the lords, capitains, and other whiche..have right towardly, benivolently, and conformably served as under you in this Jorney. **1562** J. HEYWOOD *Prov. & Epigr.* (1867) 195 Wyll you reedes shrinke still to all windes towardly? **1597** MORLEY *Introd. Mus.* 55 To see my schollers go towardlie forward in their studies. **1704** PENN in *Pa. Hist. Soc. Mem.* IX. 342 If our friends will not behave towardly, I shall be constrained to break it. **1819** R. ANDERSON *Cumbld. Ball.* 43 How tow'rtly she com heame! **1874** *Daily News* 12 Aug., Postmaster-General Lord John Manners hands in the Twentieth Annual Report of his office as towardly as if he had done nothing but deliver letters all his life.

**Towardness** (tōᵘ·(w)ǝɹdnės, tō·ǝɹdnės). Now *Obs.* or *arch.* [f. as prec. + -NESS.] The quality or condition of being 'toward'.

†**1.** Disposition, inclination towards or to do something; readiness, willingness. *Obs.*

**1461** *Coventry Leet Bk.* 316 Trustyng..that ye in so doyng shall thynke your true hertis and towardnesse right welle be-sette. **1530** TINDALE *Answ. More* IV. xi. Wks. (1573) 337/2 What good towardnes can we haue vnto the will of God while we hate it and be ignoraunt therof? **1563** RANDOLPH in Robertson *Hist. Scot.* II. App. vii. (1759) 14 This queen being before advertized of his towardness, by many means, hath sought..to know my lord of Murray's mind herein. **1610** E. SKORY *Extr. Hist. Hen. IV of France* 2 His qualitie drewe him into the knowledge of the world, where his royall towardnesse begot him estimation. **1692** BURNET *Past. Care* viii. 101 [This] may put some of them in a greater towardness to hear Reason.

**2.** *spec.* Willingness and aptness to learn; natural aptitude and good disposition; docility, tractableness; forwardness in learning or practice, 'promise', proficiency.

**1509** FISHER *Funeral Serm. C'tess Richmond* Wks. 1876 I. 292 In her tendre aege she beynge endued with so grete towardnes of nature, & lyklyhode of enherytaunce. **1564** HAWARD *Eutropius* IX. 98 A yonge man of a wonderful towardnesse. **1601** FULBECKE *1st Pt. Parall.* 24 Knighthoode is bestowed in regard of precedent merite, or of some eminent prowesse and towardnesse. **1671** F. PHILLIPS *Reg. Necess.* 222 That none should be admitted into any place within his House..but such as be of good towardness, likelihood, behaviour, demeanour and conversation.

†**3.** Condition or appearance of approaching in time, coming on or impending; imminence; likelihood, prospect. *Obs.*

**1549** in Strype *Eccl. Mem.* (1721) II. 310 If there should be any towardness of a meeting..likely to take any good effect, they would certify him of it. *a* **1586** SIDNEY *Arcadia* IV. (1598) 392 O Mopsa,..here am I thine owne father Dametas, neuer in such a towardnesse of hanging, if thou canst not helpe mee. **1660** SHARROCK *Vegetables* 12 When the great frosts breake, at the first towardnesse to spring. **1721** STRYPE *Eccl. Mem.* II. 310 If there appeared any towardness of a good conclusion, he should be certified of it.

†**4.** State of advancement or forwardness; *in (a) good* (etc.) *towardness*, making good progress, getting on well. *Obs.*

**1475** SIR J. PASTON in *P. Lett.* III. 122 All suche coumfforte as ye ffynde or heer off the towardnesse theroff. **1577** VAUTROUILLIER *Luther on Ep. Gal.* 107 All things were in a happie course and great towardnes with you. **1579–80** NORTH *Plutarch* (1676) 225 All his doings, which were now so far onwards in good towardness.

**Towards** (tōᵘ·ǝɹdz, tō·ǝɹdz, tōᵊɹdz; tǝwǭ·ɹdz), *prep.* and *adv.* Forms: 1 toweardes, 1, 6 to wardes, 3–7 towardes, (5 -is, -ys, tawardes, 6 towerdys, *Sc.* towartis, 7 towardst), 5– towards, (7–8 tow'rds). [OE. *tóweardes*, f. *tóweard*, TOWARD *a.*, with *-es*, *-s* of adverbial genitive: see -WARDS.

(As to varieties of pronunciation see TOWARD *prep.*)]

**A.** *prep.*

**1.** Of motion, etc.: In the direction of, on the way to: = TOWARD *prep.* 1.

*c* **888** K. ÆLFRED *Boeth.* xxxix. § 1 Hwy ne maᵹon ᵹe ᵹebidan ᵹecyndelices deaðes, nu he eow ælce dæᵹ toweardes onet? *c* **1122** *O. E. Chron.* an. 1094, Se eorl innon Normandiᵹ..mid þam cynge of France..ferdon to wardes Ou þær se cyng Willelm inne wæs. *c* **1205** LAY. 515 Brutus iherde seggen..þat Pandrasus þe king him towardes com Mid muchelere ferde. **1442** T. BECKINGTON *Corr.* (Rolls) II. 190 Maister John de Batute departed hens on Saturday at noon towards his cuntrey. **1538** in R. G. Marsden *Sel. Pleas Crt. Admiralty* (1894) I. 73 They made saile towards their owne countrey. **1552** HULOET, Towardes and toward. ..Yet marke the maner of phrase as you dyd in amonge & amongest. **1766** GOLDSM. *Vic. W.* x, The procession marching slowly forward towards the church. **1816** J. WILSON *City of Plague* I. i, Every step I take Towards the city. **1860** TYNDALL *Glac.* I. viii. 59, I turned towards home.

†**b.** *pred.* after *to be*: On the way to: = TOWARD *prep.* 1 b. *Obs.*

**1601** SHAKS. *All's Well* III. ii. 71 Towards Florence is he?

†**c.** To (with implication of reaching): = TOWARD *prep.* 1 c. *Obs.*

**1467** *Coventry Leet Bk.* 335 Also þat [they] sufficiently amende þe fotewey towardes Crab-tre-feld. **1585** T. WASHINGTON tr. *Nicholay's Voy.* I. xxii. 29 Too dispatche and sende away the knight..towardes the court, too aduertise the king. **1611** SHAKS. *Wint. T.* IV. iii. 121, I will..pace softly towards my Kinsmans. **1613** T. MILLES tr. *Mexia's*, etc. *Treas. Anc. & Mod. T.* 698/1 Pope Innocent ..sent verie Learned and Religious men towards Baty.

**2.** Of position: In the direction of; on the side next to; directed to, facing: = TOWARD *prep.* 2.

**1423** JAS. I *Kingis Q.* civ, Benignely sche turnyt has hir face Towardis me. **1503** in *Lett. Rich. III & Hen. VII* (Rolls) I. 202 The said bishop as he stode..towardes the quere. **1555** BRADFORD in Strype *Eccl. Mem.* (1721) III. App. xlv. 129 To make all our Haven-Townes mor stronger towardes the Land, than they be towardes the Sea. **1611** BIBLE *Ps.* xxv. 15 Mine eyes are euer towards the Lord. **1662** J. DAVIES tr. *Olearius' Voy. Ambass.* 58 Canon, with the mouths towards that street. **1726** LEONI *Alberti's Archit.* I. 99/2 Hills towards the North..encrease the heat. **1727** SWIFT *Let. Eng. Tongue* Wks. 1755 II. I. 186 The Northern parts lying towards the Euxine. **1851** HELPS *Comp. Solit.* vi. 85, I sat upon a garden seat in a sheltered nook towards the south.

†**b.** Beside, near; in attendance on, about; in the possession of; with: = TOWARD *prep.* 2 b. *Obs.*

? **1447** *Lett. Marg. Anjou & Bp. Beckington* (Camden) 94 We..praye yow hertely, that..ye wil have oure said secretary towards yow. **1459** *Rolls of Parlt.* V. 367 Persones of grete myght, havyng towardes theym of their lyverey.. such multitude of Robbers, Rioters, and myschevous persones. **1614–15** *Archdeaconry of Essex Minutes* lf. 103 b (MS.), The prince his landresse and a man towards the prince were by the harbenger placed to lodge in his house. **1664** MARVELL *Corr.* Wks. (Grosart) II. 166 Had chosen his Excellence the Earle of Carlisle..for his Ambassador Extraordinary towards him.

**3.** In the direction of (*fig.*). **a.** *gen.* = TOWARD *prep.* 3 a.

**1634** SIR T. HERBERT *Trav.* 49 Their beauties are..such as preuaile in my iudgement, towards chastitie, more then Ouids Remedy of Loue. **1692** E. WALKER *Epictetus' Mor.* lxxi, He that labours on Towards Perfection. **1763** J. BROWN *Poetry & Mus.* xiv. 241 In all polished States, these Arts have a natural Tendency towards Corruption. **1849** MACAULAY *Hist. Eng.* ii. I. 231 The king was suspected by many of a leaning towards Rome. **1871** R. H. HUTTON *Ess.* v. (1888) 118 The absolute will towards right.

**b.** Introducing the object of action or feeling: = TOWARD *prep.* 3 b.

**1390** GOWER *Conf.* II. 32, I mai wel..Excuse me of negligence Towardes love in alle wise. **1483** in *Lett. Rich. III & Hen. VII* (Rolls) I. 48 Good will towardes hir housband. *c* **1495** *Ibid.* II. 57 To ordre that matier towardis hym as he shalbe right well contented. **1536** *Cal. Anc. Rec. Dublin* (1889) I. 498 Thankes off hys grett goodnes towerdys me. **1536** in *Lett. Suppress. Monasteries* (Camden) 99 How I shal use me self towardes thaim. **1596** SPENSER *F. Q.* VI. ii. 11 To blame him for such cruelty Towards a Ladie. **1682** NORRIS *Hierocles* 32 Friendship ought to be exercised towards all, but especially toward good men. **1713** BERKELEY *Guard.* No. 3 ¶ 1 A sense of piety towards heaven. **1802–12** BENTHAM *Ration. Judic. Evid.* (1827) IV. 53 He has as good a pretence and (as towards the public) a justification, as heart can wish. **1885** *Manch. Exam.* 10 July 5/2 The sentiments of the Thibetans towards us.

†**c.** In favour of; favourable to: = FOR *prep.* 7. *Obs. rare.*

**1472** *Paston Lett.* III. 52 To have thys Parlement as for one of the burgeys of the towne of Maldon, syche a man of worchep and of wytt as wer towardys my seyd Lady. **1477** *Ibid.* 171 And [= if] ye come and fynde the mater no more towards you then ye dyd afortyme.

**d.** Compared to, in comparison with: = TO *prep.* 18, TOWARD *prep.* 3 d. Now *dial.*

*a* **1568** COVERDALE *Bk. Death* xxv. (1579) 113 In comparison whereof..myrthe and cheere vpon earth is scarce to be esteemed as castinge counters towardes the finest coynes of Golde. **1685** TRAVESTIN *Siege Newheusel* 27 They fought with such desperation and courage towards what they had done before. **1887** *S. Cheshire Gloss.*, To'arts as, in comparison with.

**e.** In expression of good wishes for (a person, or his health): = TO *prep.* 12 a, 26 b. *dial.*

**1766** GOLDSM. *Vic. W.* xxi, Drinking towards my good health. **1855** THACKERAY *Newcomes* xi, Here's towards you, my buck.

**4.** Of time or succession: = TOWARD *prep.* 4.

**1594** SHAKS. *Rich. III*, III. v. 101, I goe, and towards three or foure a Clocke Looke for the Newes. **1661** LOVELL *Hist. Anim. & Min.* Introd., Snailes, which some count most dainty sweet and nourishing meat, and are best towards winter. **1754** SHERLOCK *Disc.* (1759) I. ix. 251 These Words stand towards the Close of St. John's Gospel. **1836** *Backwoods of Canada* 208 The skins are very thick and glossy towards winter. **1886** C. E. PASCOE *Lond. of To-day* xxxi. (ed. 3) 282 In Whitehall Gardens..Beaconsfield lived for a short time towards the latter part of his life.

**5.** 'Getting on for', verging upon, nearly as much as; tending to: = TOWARD *prep.* 5.

**1570** FOXE *A. & M.* (ed. 2) 2276/2 Being iudged by the common people, more then an hundreth yeare of age, and by her own estimation well towardes a c. **1619** HALES *Gold. Rem.* II. (1673) 84 When Gomarus had spoken towards an hour and a half. **1626** BACON *Sylva* § 77 Water, thicker, and more towards Ice, than Common Water. **1712** STEELE *Spect.* No. 437 ¶ 1 She was gay, airy, and a little towards Libertine in her Carriage. **1777** BURKE *Corr.* (1844) II. 195 Where there are towards six hundred persons. **1845** J. H. NEWMAN *Ess. Developm.* 41 When he is towards fifty, Mr. Wesley marries.

†**6.** In prospect of, approaching: = TOWARD *prep.* 6. *Obs.*

**1523** LD. BERNERS *Froiss.* I. cccxxvii. 512 He was towardes a treaty for a maryage for him with the doughter of yᵉ kyng of Castell. **1541** *St. Papers Hen. VIII*, VIII. 599 As towching ony maryage that she was towardes, I harde of non. **1611** TOURNEUR *Ath. Trag.* II. v, What, is not thy mistresse towards a husband yet? *a* **1624** BP. M. SMITH *Serm.* (1632) 141, I did not know that thou hadst a cause towards hearing. **1661** in *Verney Mem.* (1907) II. 175, I here your son is towardes a good fortewen. **1688** SHADWELL *Sqr. Alsatia* v, Your brother has heard of this great match you are towards.

†**b.** Coming upon, in store for: = TOWARD *prep.* 6 b. *Obs.*

**1560** DAUS tr. *Sleidane's Comm.* 14 b, There was muche trouble towardes him, what by the Turkes, and what by the Frenche men. **1633** BP. HALL *Hard Texts, N. T.* 123 Jesus..well knew what evill was towards him. **1719** YOUNG *Busiris* v. i, I fear some ill is tow'rds me. **1749** FIELDING *Tom Jones* VIII. vi, I dreamed..that I stumbled over a stool without hurting myself; which plainly showed me something good was towards me.

**7.** In contribution to; for making up, promoting, etc.: = TOWARD *prep.* 7.

**1474** *Coventry Leet Bk.* 412 Such benivolence as his louyng subgettes there schall shewe vnto hym towardes his grete viage in-to ffraunce. **1521** in *Essex Rev.* XIII. 221 Item I bequeth to Bryghtlyngsey Church towards lengthing of our Lady Chapell..iii. quarters of the ship called the Trinitie. **1639** S. DU VERGER tr. *Camus' Admir. Events* 77 Nothing could have prevailed towards the saving of his life. **1729** LAW *Serious C.* viii, She pays their rent, and gives them something yearly towards their clothing. **1806** *Act* 46 *Geo. III*, c. 132 (*title*) To advance a certain sum..towards that purpose. **1908** *Month* Mar. 317 This is a contribution towards what is now denominated 'Methodology'.

**8.** For *to..-wards*, separated by the sb. or pron., see -WARDS. Cf. TO *prep.* 2 e, TOWARD *prep.* 8.

**B.** *adv.* or predicative *adj.*

**I.** Predicative, or following a sb.: cf. predicative uses of TOWARD *a.*

†**1.** In preparation, at hand, coming on, imminent: cf. TOWARD *a.* 2 b. *Obs.*

**1468** SIR J. PASTON in *P. Lett.* II. 328 If ye undrestond that any assawte schold be towardys. **1585** T. WASHINGTON tr. *Nicholay's Voy.* I. xxii. 28 There was no danger towards. **1592** SHAKS. *Rom. & Jul.* I. v. 124 We haue a trifling foolish Banquet towards. **1637** SUCKLING *Aglaura* II. i, If there be not some great storme towards, Ne'er trust me. **1652** DOROTHY OSBORNE *Lett.* (1888) 30 His marriage, which I hear is towards, with a daughter of [etc.]. **1697** VANBRUGH *Relapse* III. ii, Take heed my heart, for there are dangers towards.

†**2.** Favourable, compliant, forward, ready. *Obs.*

*c* **1525** ABP. WARHAM in Ellis *Orig. Lett.* Ser. III. I. 366 Seing men grudgeth to be towardes in graunting, it is to be feared they will make more murmur and busynes in the tyme of payment.

†**3.** At hand, ready, present: cf. TOWARD *a.* 6.

**1548** UDALL, etc. *Erasm. Par. John* 71 b, Being redy and towardes at his call. **1564** HAWARD *Eutropius* VI. K vij b, Hys Sonne also, a valyaunte and worthye yonge man towardes.

**II. 4.** In the direction of some person or thing indicated by the context (cf. TOWARD *adv.* 1, *forwards*, *onwards*). *Obs.* or *arch.*

**1590** SPENSER *F. Q.* I. ii. 15 The knight.., when him he spide,..Gan fairely couch his speare, and towards ride. *Ibid.* II. iv. 37 A varlet ronning towards hastily. **1592** *Arden of Feversham* III. vi, At your dags discharge Make towards. **1818** KEATS *Endym.* III. 494 This fire, like the eye of gordian snake, Bewitched me towards; and I soon was near A sight too fearful for the feel of fear.

†**b.** ? Towards some end or purpose; (as a contribution) towards something. *Obs.*

**1473** SIR J. PASTON in *P. Lett.* III. 104, I pray yow sende me worde..iff I have Caster ageyn, whethyr she [my modre] wolle dwelle ther or nott, and I wyll fynde hyr a prest towardes at my charge.

†**5.** Onwards, on (in quot., of time): cf. TOWARD *adv.* 2. *Obs. rare*—¹.

**1586** J. HOOKER *Hist. Irel.* in Holinshed II. 158/1 The daie being spent to small purpose, and the night drawne towards, he incamped.

†**To-wa·rp**, *v. Obs.* Forms: see WARP. [OE. *toweorpan*, f. TO-² + *weorpan* to throw, WARP *v.* = OFris. *to-*, *tiwerpa*, OS. *tewerpan* (LG. *tewerpan*), OHG. *za-*, *ziwerphan*, *-werfan*, MHG. *ze-*, *zerwerfen*, Ger. *zerwerfen*.] *trans.* To throw about, throw down, overthrow, destroy; also *fig.*

*c* **888** K. ÆLFRED *Boeth.* xxxv. § 4 Þa sceolde he sendan þunras & liᵹeta & windas, & toweorpan eall hira ᵹeweorc mid. *c* **1000** *Ags. Gosp.* Matt. xxiv. 2 Ne bið her læfed stan uppan stane þe ne beo to-worpen. *c* **1000** ÆLFRIC *Hom.* II. 510 Mennisce handa hit ne mihton towurpan. *c* **1200** ORMIN 14861 Þe sæ wass þærr Dun till þe grund toworrpenn. *c* **1200** *Trin. Coll. Hom.* 161 Storemes falleð in þe sæ and toworpeð hit.

**To-waste, To-waver, To-wawe**: see TO- *pref.*²

**Towayl(e, -aylle**, obs. ff. TOWEL.

**Towch(e, Towe**, obs. ff. TOUCH, TOUGH, TWO.

**Towcher**, obs. form of TOCHER.

‖**Towcok** (tau·kǫk). [ad. Cantonese *tau-kok* string beans, peas in the pod, f. *tau* bean, pea + *kok* horn, pod.] The Cow-pea, *Vigna* (*Dolichos*) *sinensis*; in India called *chowlee*.

**1866** *Treas. Bot.* s.v. *Vigna*, The Chinese..call the plant Tow-Cok, cook and eat the green pods as we do kidney-beans. When ripe the pods are frequently..a yard long.

**Towee**, var. TOWHEE, N. Amer. bird.

**Towel** (tau·ĕl), *sb.* Forms: see below. [ME. *towaille*, *-aile*, etc., a. OF. *toaille* (Wace 12th c.), *toaile*, mod.F. *touaille* = Pr. *toalha*, Cat. *tovalla*, Sp. *toalla*, Pg. *toalha*, It. *tovaglia* (whence F., in spec. sense, *tavaïolle*); in med.L. *toacula, toailla, tovalia, toualia*, etc., from the mod. langs.: f. WGer. **þwahljô* (Kluge), OHG. *dwahilla, -ila*, cloth for washing or wiping (MHG. *dwähele, twähele, dwêle*, Ger. dial. *zwehle* napkin), f. OHG. *dwahan, twahan* (OS. *thwahan*, Goth. *þwahan*, OE. *þwéan* to wash, *þwéal* (Goth. *þwahl* washing).]

**1.** A cloth, usually of linen or hemp, for wiping something dry, esp. for wiping the hands, face, or person after washing or bathing. Also formerly more widely, including a table-napkin or other cloth used at meals.

Often with prefix indicating its particular use, as *bath-, dish-, face-, glass-towel*.

α. 3–5 **towaille**, 4 **touwayle**, (**thoayle**, **thoyale**), 4–5 **towaile**, **-ayle**, 5 **tow-**, **touaylle**, **towail**, **-ayl**, **-ayle** (**tavayle**).

*a* **1300** *Floriz & Bl.* 563 Þat oþer bringe towaille and bacin For to wasse his honden in. **13..** *Sir Beues* (A.) 3220 On a towaile ȝhe [= she] made knotte riding. **13..** SHOREHAM i. 1387 Þo hym wyþ a schete [*marg.* touwayle] ihesus After soper bygerte. *c* **1386** CHAUCER *Monk's T.* 755 And Phebus eek a fair towaille [*v.rr.* towayle, towail, towale, towel] hym broughte To dryen hym with. **1395** *Will of Thornholm* (Comm. Crt. London), Thoayle wt a blak lyst, borthcloth cum vna thoyale accordyngg. *c* **1400** MAUNDEV. (1839) xxiii. 250 Whan þei han eten, þei wypen hire hondes vpon hire skirtes, for þei vse non naperye, ne towaylles. *c* **1435** *Chron. London* (Kingsford 1905) 18 The goode Duk off Gloucetre.. was ffoule mordred at Caleys with ij Tovaylles..putte aboute his nekke. *c* **1440** *Promp. Parv.* 498/2 Towayl (*H.* towayle or tavayle)..*manitergium.* *c* **1450** *Merlin* 225 The maiden her-silf wosh his visage..and dried it full softely with a towaile. **1480** *Wardr. Acc. Edw. IV* (1830) 131 Towails playne vj.

β. 3 **towele**, 4–5 **touel**, 4–6 **towelle**, **-all**, 4–7 **towell**, (5 **toual**, **towale**, **towylle**, 6 **touall**, **towle**); 4– **towel**.

? **1284** Toweles [see 2]. **13..** *Seuyn Sag.* (W.) 3877 Thai set forth water and towell, Herkens now, how if befell! **13..** Touel [see quot. *a* 1300 in γ]. **1378** in *Test. Karl.* (1893) 118, ij lectos, ij dorclaes, ij towels. **1387–8** T. USK *Test. Love* II. ii. (Skeat) l. 62 On his meate borde there shall been borde clothes and towelles many paire. **1407–8** *Durham Acc. Rolls* (Surtees) 607, liiij uln. panni linei emp. ..pro towales. **1466** *Maldon, Essex, Crt.-Rolls* (Bundle 42, No. 6), Towylles. **1542** Towle [see 2]. **1557** *Lanc. Wills* (Chetham Soc.) I. 71 The best bason and ewer and also the best towall. **15..** in *Laneham's Let.* (1871) Pref. 31 Ane touall off Alifyne. **1609** B. JONSON *Sil. Wom.* IV. v, I will strangle him in this towell. *a* **1658** CLEVELAND *Mary's Spikenard* 31 For a Towel he shall have My hair, such flax as nature gave. **1718** LADY M. W. MONTAGU *Let. to C'tess of Mar* 10 Mar., After dinner, water was brought in a gold basin, and towels of the same kind of the napkins. **1808** *Med. Jrnl.* XIX. 112 His body to be well rubbed by two persons with coarse towels. **1897** MARY KINGSLEY *W. Africa* 563 Wading across to the bank, I wring out my skirts, but what is life without a towel?

γ. 4 **tueil**, 4–5 **tuel**, **-ell**, 5 **tuayl(e**, **-ale**, **tewelle**, 5–6 **tewell**, (8–9 *Sc.* and *north. dial.* **tooel**, **tool**).

*a* **1300** *Cursor M.* 15285 (Cott.) Wit a tuell he belted him [*G.* tuel, *F.* touel, *T.* twaile]. *Ibid.* 15299 Wit his tueil efterward Þair fete he weped clene. *c* **1450** *Brut* ccxli. 352 Þai..caste þe tewellys aboute þe Dukis nek..and þan þei drowen her towellis eche wayez. **1494** in *Somerset Medieval Wills* (1901) 323 A Mete cloth and iij tuels. **1496** Tuell, **1504** Tewell [see 2]. **1727** P. WALKER *Life R. Cameron* in *Biog. Presbyt.* (1827) I. 202 He dried his face and hands with a Tool. **1905** *Eng. Dial. Dict.* s. v., *Westmld.* Tooel.

δ. 3–4 **twayle**, 5 **twaylle**, **twaile**, 6 **twell**.

*a* **1300** Twayle [see 2]. *a* **1375** *Joseph Arim.* 285 Þenne comen two Angeles wiþ twayles white. *a* **1425** Twaile [see quot. *a* 1300 in γ]. **1507** Twell [see 2].

ε. 5 **towaly**, **twaly**, **tualy**.

*c* **1440** *Promp. Parv.* 498/2 Towayl, or towaly (*S.* twaly... *A.* tuayl or tualy). *manitergium.*

**2.** Applied to cloths for various other purposes.

**a.** *Eccl.* A cloth, either of linen for use at communion, or of silk or other rich material for covering the altar at other times; also, a communion-cloth (see quot. 1737, and quot. 1866 s. v. COMMUNION 8). Cf. F. *tavaïolle*. ? *Obs.*

? **1284** in *Shropsh. Archæol. Soc. Trans.* (1878) I. 358 Item ij. Toweles pro ij. altariis cum apparatu precii xij s. iiij d. *a* **1300** in Hearne *Collect.* 18 Apr. II. 187 Tham that this Cherche, honour with book, with bell, with vestiments, with twayle. **1387** TREVISA *Higden* (Rolls) V. 11 No womman schulde handle þe towayles of þe auȝter. **1474** *Will of Selly* (Somerset Ho.), Howseling towell. **1496** *Croscombe Churchw. Acc.* (Som. Rec. Soc.) 21 A tuell of dyapper. **1504** *Ibid.* 27, ij tewells. **1507** *Ibid.* 29 A twell of dyaper. **1542** in *Archæologia* XLVI. 217 Paid for a new dextclothe & a towle xj d. *c* **1550** in *Labarte's Arts Mid. Ages* ii. (1855) 91 A blest towell for the high altar, of black silk. **1623** *Primer* in *Month* Oct. (1911) 340 If any be to communicate at Mass, the Servitour after the Priest hath taken the Chalice and before he purifieth it, spreadeth a towel or a white vele before them and then sayeth *Confiteor Deo* in their name. **1737** CHALLONER *Cath. Chr. Instr.* (1753) 66 Such of the people as are to communicate,..taking the Towel, hold it before their Breasts, in such Manner, that, if in communicating, it should happen that any Particle should fall, it may..be received upon the Towel.

†**b.** A cloth used as a part of dress, e. g. as a head-dress, a girdle, etc. *Obs.*

? *a* **1366** CHAUCER *Rom. Rose* 161 Hir heed y-writhen was, y-wis, Ful grymly with a greet towayle. **1485** CAXTON *Paris & V.* (1868) 80 Mantellys and towellys. **1582** N. LICHEFIELD tr. *Castanheda's Conq. E. Ind.* I. xii. 29 b, The King of Mylynde came..to our Fleete, apparelled in a Cassocke of Crimson Damaske, lined with greene satten, hauing vpon his head a rich towell. **1615** G. SANDYS *Trav.* 63 Shashes are long towels of Callico wound about their heads. **1634** SIR T. HERBERT *Trav.* 146 The coat..ingirted with a towell of silke and gold eight or nine yards long.

**3.** *slang. Oaken towel*, also simply *towel*, a stick, cudgel (cf. next, 2); *lead towel*, a bullet.

**1739** *Joe Miller's Jests* (1745) 73 The Farmer..rear'd his Oaken Towel, and..gave him two..Drubs on the Shoulder. **1748** SMOLLETT *Rod. Rand.* ii, I shall rub you down with an oaken towel. **1756** TOLDERVY *Hist. 2 Orphans* II. 128 Brandishing his stick [he] cried aloud, 'this towel..should bastinado the bones of that rascal Tom Throw'. **1812** H. & J. SMITH *Rej. Addr., G. Barnwell* vi, Make Nunky surrender his dibs, Rub his pate with a pair of lead towels. **1815** *Hist. Jn. Decastro* I. 24 Old Crab..raising his oaken towel gave the door three bangs that shook the garrets.

**4.** *attrib.* and *Comb.*, as *towel-coffer, friction, -maker, -room, -warmer*; **towel-gourd**, a name for *Luffa ægyptiaca* and *L. acutangula*, also called *sponge-gourd* or *washing-gourd*, the fibrous inner layer of the fruit being used in washing like a towel or sponge (cf. LOOFAH); **towel-horse**, a wooden frame or stand on which towels are hung; **towel-pattern** (*Wood-carving*) = *linen-scroll*: see LINEN B. 5; **towel-rack** (see quot.); **towel-roller**, a horizontal roller on which an 'endless' towel (*roller-* or *round-towel*) is hung.

*c* **1400** *Sc. Troy-bk.* I. 375 Cowpis out brought of golde sa clere, One *towalle burdys arayit & drest. **1891** G. MEREDITH *One of our Conq.* ix, The oaken *towel-coffer. **1898** *Allbutt's Syst. Med.* V. 1031 Spongings..followed by dry *towel friction. **1872** OLIVER *Elem. Bot.* II. 176 The fibrous inner layer of the pericarp of the *Towel-Gourd..is used as sponge and gun-wadding. **1860** H. F. TOZER in *Vac. Tour.* 386 Hay hanging to dry on large hurdles strongly resembling a gigantic *towel-horse. (Cf. **1541** *Aberdeen Regr.* XVII. (Jam.), Ane towall ross of aik worcht v ss.) **1878** HUXLEY *Physiogr.* 67 The damp towel on which you have just wiped your wet hands does not stand long on the towel-horse before it becomes dry again. **1591** PERCIVALL *Sp. Dict.*, *Mantelero*, a *towel maker. **1877** KNIGHT *Dict. Mech.*, **Towel-rack*, a frame or rod on which to hang towels to dry. **1833** LOUDON *Encycl. Archit.* § 609 A *Towel Roller ought to be placed on the back of the kitchen-door of every cottage. *a* **1619** FLETCHER *Wit without M.* IV. v, Allow you but a *towel-room to tipple in. **1884** *Health Exhib. Catal.* 94/2 Hot linen closet, and *towel warmer.

**Tow·el**, *v.* [f. prec. sb.]

**1.** *trans.* To apply a towel to; to rub or dry with a towel.

**1836–9** DICKENS *Sk. Boz, Ladies' Societies*, The children were yellow-soaped and flannelled, and towelled, till their faces shone again. **1886** D. C. MURRAY *1st Pers. Singular* xix, Zeno..was towelling himself before the mirror. **1894** A. MORRISON *Mean Streets* 15 Solemn little faces towelled to a polish.

**b.** *intr.* (with *at*).

**1861** DICKENS *Gt. Expect.* xxvi, Letting his head drop into a festoon of towel, and towelling away at his two ears. **1865** — *Mut. Fr.* I. vi.

**2.** *slang.* To beat, cudgel, thrash. (Cf. prec. 3.)

**1705** J. DUNTON *Life & Errors* (1818) I. ix. 356, I would towel him myself..if I did not think him an honest man. **1824** in *Spirit Pub. Jrnls.* (1825) 164, I shouldn't have towelled her if she hadn't tempted me to it! **1903** SIR M. G. GERARD *Leaves fr. Diaries* vi. 182 He caught him by the collar and towelled him down with a cutting whip.

**3.** To cover with a towel or towels.

**1865** DICKENS *Mut. Fr.* III. iv, I mean to apron it and towel it all over the front.

**Towel**, obs. form of TEWEL.

**Towelling, toweling** (tau·ĕliŋ). [f. TOWEL *sb.* and *v.* + -ING [1].]

**I. 1.** Linen cloth to be made into towels; material for or of towels.

**1583** *Rates of Custome ho.* B vj b, Diaper toweling the peece XXX. s. **1640** in Entick *London* (1766) II. 167 Damask for towelling and napkenning. **1862** *Catal. Internat. Exhib., Brit.* II. No. 3742 Sheetings, towellings, huckabacks. **1880** 'OUIDA' *Moths* II. 19 A dozen yards of bath towelling.

**b.** A piece of this material, a towel. *nonce-use.*

**1845** BROWNING *Flight of Duchess* xi. 15 To wash the hands of her liege In a clean ewer with a fair toweling.

**II. 2.** Rubbing with, or application of, a towel.

**1859** DICKENS *T. Two Cities* II. xi, A correspondingly extra quantity of wine had preceded the [wet] towelling. **1865** — *Mut. Fr.* I. vi, His head was soon in a basin of water, and out of it again, and staring at her through a storm of towelling. **1911** QUILLER COUCH *Shining Ferry* iv, Her cheeks glowed after a vigorous towelling.

**3.** *slang.* A beating, drubbing, thrashing.

**1851** MAYHEW *Lond. Labour* I. 421/1, I got a towelling, but it did not do me much good. **1906** *Blackw. Mag.* Apr. 446/2 The towelling administered to a dog..was not pleasant to behold.

**Towellshell, towelshill**, obs. ff. TOLSEL.

**Tow·elry.** *nonce-wd.* [f. TOWEL *sb.* + -RY: cf. JEWELRY.] Articles of the towel kind; towels collectively.

**1885** R. F. BURTON *Arab. Nts.* I. 201 Then the Wazir.. sent him a suit of the best of his own especial raiment, and napkins and towelry.

† **Tow·en**, *a. Obs.* [f. TOW *sb.*[1] + -EN [4].] Made of tow, i. e. coarse flax or hemp.

**1686** in *Essex Rev.* (1906) XV. 173 Tenn payer of flaxen sheets, fourteen payer of Towen sheets.

† **To-we·nd**, *v. Obs.* [OE. *towendan*, f. To-[2] + *wendan* to turn, WEND.]

**1.** *trans.* To turn over; to overthrow, demolish; to turn upside down, disturb greatly.

*c* **893** K. ÆLFRED *Oros.* VI. x. § 1 Hi woldon towendon ealle þa ȝesetnessa & ealle þa ȝebodu þe Domitianus hæfde ær ȝeset. *c* **1000** ÆLFRIC *Hom.* I. 46 We ȝehyrdon..þæt Crist towyrpð þas stowe, and towent ða ȝesetnysse ðe us Moyses tæhte. *c* **1200** *Trin. Coll. Hom.* 191 Mid þusendfeld wrenches þe deuel to-wendeð þe herte. *c* **1205** LAY. 27062 Þæ astalden þer flem..Þa rugges to-wenden [*c* 1275 Þo torne..hii þe rugges]. *a* **1225** *Ancr. R.* 324 A wummon þet haueð forloren hir nelde [= needle] oðer a sutare his el, he secheð hine anonriht, & to-went euerich strea uort he beo ifunden.

**2.** *intr.* **a.** To turn in different directions, disperse, separate. **b.** To go to pieces, break asunder; also *fig.*

*c* **1175** *Lamb. Hom.* 75 Þe twelue apostles..er heo towenden in to al þis middelerd. *c* **1205** LAY. 30235 Duglas þa water wes ihaten þer heo tou-wenden. *c* **1374** CHAUCER *Compl. Mars* 102 His myghty spere as he was wont to fyght He shaketh so that almost it to-wonde Ful hevy was he to walken ouer londe. *c* **1380** *Sir Ferumb.* 2568 Ogier Denys..smot to sire Mahound Þat al to pieces he to-wond & ful doun on þe ground. *a* **1400** *Sir Beues* (E.) 1645 + 27 He smoot þe dore vp wiþ hys ffoot, Þat þe dore al towond.

**Tower** (tau·əɹ, tau·əɹ), *sb.*[1] Forms: α. 1–2, 5–6 **torr**, 3–4 **tor**; β. 2–4 **tur**, 4 **ture**, (6 *Sc.* **tuire**); γ. 3–8 **tour**, 4–7 **toure**, 9 *Sc.* **toor** (tūr); δ. 3–4 **towr**, 4–7 **towre**, (4 **towyr**, 6 **touuer**), 6– **tower**, (8–9 **tow'r**). [In OE. *torr* masc., ad. L. *turr-is*; in late OE. and early ME. *tūr*, *a* 1300 written *tour*, a. OF. *tor, tur* (11th c.), F. *tour* (12th c.) = Pr. *tor*, Sp., Pg., It. *torre* :—L. *turr-em* (*-im*), acc. of *turris* fem. 'tower'. It is doubtful whether the ME. *tor(r* was a survival of the OE. form, since OF. had also *tor*.

(But the Sc. examples in 1 α may perhaps belong to TORE *sb.*[1], and quot. *c* 1400 in 4 to TOR *sb.* 2.)]

**I. 1.** A building lofty in proportion to the size of its base, either isolated, or forming part of a castle, church, or other edifice, or of the walls of a town.

Often with prefixed word expressing its nature or use, as *bell-tower, church-tower, gong-tower, Martello tower, sea-tower, watch-tower, water-tower*: see the first element. *Round tower*: see ROUND *a.* 15. *Tower of silence*, the structure on which the Parsees expose their dead.

In the Border counties of England and Scotland, 'tower' is often the name of a solitary high fenced house, a tower-house or 'peel-house' (PEEL *sb.*[1] 4, 6), too small to be called a 'castle', e.g. Gilnockie, Goldilands, Smailholm Tower.

α. *c* **897** K. ÆLFRED *Gregory's Past. C.* xi. 64 Ðin nosu is swelc swelce se torr on Libano ðæm munte. *c* **950** *Lindisf. Gosp.* Matt. xxi. 33 Faeder hiorodes seðe..dalf in ðær wintroȝ & ȝetimberde torr [*Ags. Gosp.* stypel]. [*c* **1470** *Golagros & Gaw.* 42 Ane ciete thai se, With torris and turatis, teirfull to tell. **1501** DOUGLAS *Pal. Hon.* III. xvii, Gilt birneist torris, quhilk like to Phebus schone.]

β. *c* **1100–1154** Tur [see 2]. *c* **1200** *Trin. Coll. Hom.* 143 On ure ledene tur, quod interpretatur turris. *c* **1250** *Gen. & Ex.* 661 To make a tur, wel heȝ & strong.

γ. *c* **1290** *S. Eng. Leg.* I. 13/406 A suyþe heiȝ tour of gold and seluer. **1297** R. GLOUC. (Rolls) 8303 He ȝeld him vp.. Þre toures of þe cite, þat in is warde were. *a* **1300** *Cursor M.* 2230 (Cott.), I rede we bigin a laboure And do we wel and make a toure. *c* **1400** MAUNDEV. (Roxb.) vi. 21 Þe toure of Babilon. *Ibid.* ix. 35 A faire kirke with many kirnelles and toures. **1530** LYNDESAY *Test. Papyngo* 633 Adew, fair Snawdoun, with thy touris hie. **1590** SPENSER *F. Q.* III. ix. 35 Which they far off beheld from Trojan toures.

δ. **1375** BARBOUR *Bruce* IX. 451 And syne þe towris eueril-kane And vallis gert he tummyll doune. **1382** WYCLIF *Gen.* xi. 4 Comeþ, and make we to vs a citee and a towr, whose heiȝt fulli ateyne vnto heuene. *c* **1440** *Promp. Parv.* 498/2 Towre, *turris.* **1526** TINDALE *Matt.* xxi. 33 Bilt a tower, and lett it out to husbandmen. **1625** BACON *Ess., Building* (Arb.) 550 Those Towers, are not to be of the Height of the Front. **1667** MILTON *P. L.* XII. 44 They cast to build A Citie & Towre, whose top may reach to Heav'n. **1742** GRAY *Eton* 1 Ye distant spires, ye antique towers. **1750** — *Elegy* 9 From yonder ivy-mantled tow'r The mopeing owl does to the moon complain. **1815** J. SMITH *Panorama Sc. & Art* I. 131 If it be square-topt, it is called a tower. **1849** PARKER *Goth. Archit.* I. iii. (1874) 47 Early in the twelfth century occurred the fall of the tower of Winchester Cathedral. **1853** M. ARNOLD *Scholar Gypsy* iii, And the eye travels down to Oxford's towers. **1910** MRS. YOUNGHUSBAND *Africa & Zanzibar* xxii. 262 Vultures, within one hour of a body being placed in the tower of silence, tear off all flesh from the bones, then the hot tropical sun soon dries and bleaches the bones.

**2.** Such a structure used as a stronghold, fortress, or prison, or built primarily for purposes of defence. (In this sense the name is sometimes extended to include the whole fortress or stronghold of which a 'tower' in sense 1 was the original nucleus.)

Thus the *Tower of London*, in official designation *His Majesty's Tower*, and in English History or contextually often simply *The Tower*, is the entire fortress surrounding the original *White Tower* of William Rufus.

*c* **1100** *O.E. Chron.* an. 1097, Þurh þone weall þe hi worhton on butan þone tur [on Lundenne]. *c* **1122** *Ibid.* an. 1101, Se b[iscop] Rannulf..ut of þam ture on Lunden nihtes oðbærst. **1154** *Ibid.* an. 1140, Me læt hire dun on niht of þe tur [at Oxford] mid rapes. *a* **1225** *Ancr. R.* 228 Þe tur nis nout asailed, ne þe castel. *c* **1330** R. BRUNNE *Chron.* (1810) 50 Edrik was hanged on þe toure, for his trispas. **1387** TREVISA *Higden* (Rolls) VII. 449 Men myȝte wade bytwene Temse-brugge and þe toure of Londoun. *a* **1400–50** *Alexander* 1296 With trawynns and trebgetes þe towre to assaylle. **1503** WRIOTHESLEY *Chron.* (Camden) I. 5 In Februarie, died Queene Elizabeth at the Towre of London. **1557–75** *Diurn. Occurr.* (Bann. Cl.) 84 Thay war commandit to remayne in waird within the auld tuire quhairin my lord of Murray lugeit. 1613 Shaks. *Hen. VIII*, v. iii. 89 That forthwith, You be conuaid to th' Tower a Prisoner. 1625 *Crt. & Times Chas. I* (1848) I. 36 A lioness hath whelped in the Tower. 1768 Sterne *Sent. Journ., Hotel at Paris*, The Bastile is but another word for a tower. 1813 Scott *Trierm.* ii. xvii, She has fair Strath-Clyde and Reged wide, And Carlisle tower and town. *Ibid.* xvi, Carlisle town and tower. 1849 Macaulay *Hist. Eng.* viii. II. 357 A warrant..directing the Lieutenant of the Tower to keep them [seven Bishops] in safe custody.

**b.** In early religious use, often applied to heaven.

a 1240 *Lofsong* in *Cott. Hom.* 207 In syon þe heie tur of heouene. a 1300 *Cursor M.* 418 (Cott.) He fordestend tuin creature To serue him in þat hali ture. 13.. *E. E. Allit. P.* A. 965 Þou may not enter with-inne hys tor.

**3.** *fig.* (Cf. 'stronghold', etc.)

13.. *St. Ambrosius* 793 in Horstm. *Altengl. Leg.* (1878) 20/2 Ambrose..him self was wal and tour, To kepe holi-chirches honour. c 1374 Chaucer *Boeth.* iv. Met. iii. 96 (Camb. MS.) For with inne is Ihydd the strengthe and vigor of men in the secre toure of hir hertes. 1483 Caxton *Gold. Leg.* 407/1 Thenne she began strongely to assayle the toure of hys conscience. 1560 Bible (Genev.) *Ps.* cxliv. 2 He is my goodnes and my fortres, my tower and my deliuerer. 1605 Bacon *Adv. Learn.* i. v. § 11 As if there were sought in knowledge..a tower of state for a proud mind to raise itself upon. 1909 G. K. Chesterton *Orthodoxy* iii. 55 The whole modern world is at war with reason, and the tower already reels.

**4.** *transf.* A lofty pile or material mass.

a 1340 Hampole *Psalter* cl. 4 Orgyns þat is made as a toure of sere whistils. [c 1400 *Destr. Troy* 1983 A tempest hom toke on þe torres hegh [of waves].] 1604 E. G[rimstone] *D'Acosta's Hist. Indies* iii. xxvii. 202 There is a place.. where are seene as it were two towers or pikes of a very high elevated rocke, rising out of the middest of the sea. 1840 Dickens *Barn. Rudge* iv, Sundry towers of buttered Yorkshire cake. 1843 Marryat *M. Violet* xli, The Grand Tower, one of the wonders of the Mississippi. It is a stupendous pile of rocks, of a conical form. 1852 Thackeray *Esmond* i. iii, She had a tower of lace on her head, under which was a bush of black curls. (Cf. 6 b.)

**5.** In other transferred uses:

**a.** In ancient and mediæval warfare, a tall movable structure, used in storming a fortified place. Cf. *summer castle.*

c 1440 *Promp. Parv.* 498/2 Towre, made oonly of tymbyr, *fala.* 1483 *Cath. Angl.* 391/1 A Towre of a tree, *fala.* 1552 Huloet, Towre made of tymbre, *fala.* 1665 Manley *Grotius's Low C. Warres* 287 The Besiegers erected a great Tower of Wood, after the manner of Antiquity.

†**b.** The 'castle' borne on the back of an elephant. *Obs.*

1553 Eden *Treat. Newe Ind.* (Arb.) 15 Vpon the pack-saddels, they haue on euery side a little house or towre. [*margin*] The Elephants towre. 1701 W. Wotton *Hist. Rome, Alexander* ii. 489 They had 700 Elephants, all loaden with Towers. 1762 [see *tower-backed* in 10]. c 1820 [implied in Towered 1].

**c.** The gun-turret on an ironclad.

1889 Welch *Text Bk. Naval Archit.* xiv. 143 The plan of placing the guns in revolving towers or turrets.

**6.** Applied to various things having the form, figure, or appearance of a tower, or likened to one.

† **a.** *Chess.* The Castle or Rook. *Obs.*

1562 Rowbothum *Play Cheasts* A v, Of the Rooke or Towre. The Towre is named amongest the Spaniards, Portingales, and Italians, *Rocho.* a 1649 Drumm. of Hawth. *Fam. Ep.* Wks. (1711) 146 For the towers or castles named rooks, these are the walled towns, which serve for a refuge for the conservation of the kingdom.

**b.** A very high head-dress worn by women in the reigns of William III and Anne. It was built up in the form of a tower of pasteboard, muslin, lace, and ribbons. Cf. Tour *sb.* 4. *Hist.*

c 1612 Sylvester *Lacrymae Lacrym.* 159 Stript, from Top to Toe, Of giddie Gaudes, Top-gallant Tires and Towers. 1693 Dryden *Juvenal* vi. 646 With Curls on Curls, they build her Head before, And mount it with a Formidable Tow'r. [*Note*] This dressing up the Head so high, which we call a Tow'r, was an Ancient way amongst the Romans. 1706, 1894 [? implied in Towered 1, Towering *vbl. sb.*]. [1852 Thackeray *Esmond* ii. xv, My Lady of Chelsea in her highest tour, my Lady Viscountess out of black.]

**c.** Applied to various technical structures and contrivances, now only descriptively: see quots. and cf. *shot-tower.*

1662 Merrett tr. *Neri's Art of Glass* 243 The Leer (made by Agricola, the third furnace, to anneal and cool the vessels..) comprehends two parts, the tower and leer. *Ibid.* 365 *Tower* is the Iron on which they rest their Pontee when they scald the Glass. 1688 R. Holme *Armoury* iii. xx. (Roxb.) 228 The Philosophers Tower..is a kind of Tower furnace...The Maner of the Tower is four square. 1727-41 Chambers *Cycl.* s.v. *Furnace.* 1857 Miller *Elem. Chem.* (1862) III. 649 In many works the process of washing with acid is superseded by..a *scrubber*, consisting of a tower, the interior of which is filled with small coke resting upon perforated shelves. 1885 *Athenæum* 21 Feb. 252/1 A concise account of the treatment of iron ores for the blast furnace, a careful examination of the peculiar action of that vast metallurgical tower in all its modified forms.

**7.** *Astrol.* = House *sb.*1 8, Mansion *sb.* 5 a.

c 1374 Chaucer *Compl. Mars* 113 Now fleeth Venus in to cilenios toure. 1911 Ramsay in *Expositor* Mar. 224 The twelve zodiacal stations of the sun were called towers by the Greek astrologers.

**II. 8. a.** Lofty flight; soaring. (Cf. Tower *v.* 3.)

1486 *Bk. St. Albans* D iv, Ther is an Hoby. And that hauke is for a yong man. And theys be hawkes of the toure: and ben both Ilurid to be calde and reclaymed. c1518 Skelton *Magnyf.* ii. xv. 926 Torde! man, it is an hawke of the towre. 1575 Turberv. *Falconrie* 53 She [the hobby] is of the number of those hawkes that are hye fleeing and towre hawkes. 1667 Milton *P. L.* xi. 185 Nigh in her sight The Bird of Jove, stoopt from his aerie tour, Two Birds of gayest plume before him drove.

**b.** The vertical ascent of a wounded bird.

1890 *Pall Mall G.* 18 Jan. 2/3 A single goose..bravely struggles onwards, and finally, after a perfectly executed 'tower', falls dead not far from the boat. 1895 J. G. Millais *Breath fr. Veldt* (1899) 82 The outlined figures are intended to represent the tower and drop of a single bird.

**III. 9.** Phrases. **a.** *Tower and town* (also *town and tower*), an alliterative phrase for the inhabited places of a country or region generally. †**b.** *Towers in the air*, visionary projects, 'castles in the air' (see Castle *sb.* 11).

a 1300 *Cursor M.* 12983 (Cott.) Al þis werld, bath tur and tun. c 1420 *Sir Amadace* (Camden) lxxii, Thenne was he lord of toure and towne. 1599 *Broughton's Let.* ii. 9 Your humours building towers in the ayre,..faine a sounding in your eares. 1813 [see 2]. 1842 Wordsw. *Poet's Dream* viii, O'er town and tower we flew, and fields in May's fresh verdure drest. 1870 Tennyson *Flower* iv, Thieves..Sow'd it far and wide By every town and tower.

**IV. 10.** *attrib.* and *Comb.* **a.** Simple attrib. 'of or belonging to a or the tower', as *tower-bell, -clock, -gate, -gun, -head, -pier, -room, -stair, -top, -ward, -wharf*; 'that is, consists of, has, or contains a tower', as *tower-distillatory, -furnace, -gateway, -house, -keep, -porch, -steeple*; **b.** objective, as *tower-keeper, -transporter*; *tower-bearing, -razing, -supporting, -tearing* adjs.; **c.** instrumental, locative, etc., as *tower-backed, -capped, -crested, -crowned, -encircled, -flanked, -full, -studded* adjs.; **d.** similative, etc., as *tower-high, -like, -shaped* adjs.; *tower-wise* adv. **e.** Special Combs.: **tower-ball**, a game for children; **tower-cress**, the cruciferous plant *Arabis Turrita*; sometimes applied to Tower mustard, *Turritis glabra*; †**tower-fellow**, a fellow prisoner in the Tower; **tower-fellowship**, a political division of citizens in the states of ancient Greece; **tower hill**, a hill near or on which a tower is built; *spec.* (with caps.) the rising ground by the Tower of London; **tower-light**, a window or hole in a tower; **tower-proof** *a.*, proved or tested in the arsenal at the Tower of London; also *allusively*; **tower-ring**, a finger-ring bearing an image of a tower; **tower-stamp**, the official stamp or mark on gold and silver articles; ball-mark; †**towers treacle** = Tower mustard; **tower-wagon**, a wagon with a structure which can be raised and lowered to serve as a platform for repairing overhead wires, etc.; †**tower-window**, each of the turreted lights at the head of a late Gothic or Perpendicular window; **tower-work**, masonry built in the form of towers. Also Tower mustard, pound, weight, -wort.

1608 Sylvester *Du Bartas* ii. iv. iii. *Schisme* 437 The *Towr-back't Camel, that..on his bunch could have transported yerst Neer a whole Household. 1762 *Judas Macc.* iii. 18 The huge Tow'r-back'd Elephants. 1555 Eden *Decades* 189 The *towrebearynge shoulders of Elephantes. 1592 R. D. *Hypnerotomachia* 7 b, A sound, as if the *tower bell of Saint Iohns Colledge in the famous Vniuersitie of Cambridge had beene rung. 1816 Byron *Siege of Cor.* i, Yon *tower-capt Acropolis. 1895 A. J. Evans in *Folk-Lore* Mar. 44 As soon as the *tower-clock strikes twelve. a 1835 Mrs. Hemans *Abencerrage* ii. 39 *Tower-crested rocks. 1771 *Gentl. Mag.* Nov. 490/1 At the sight Of distant Bremen's *tower-crown'd height. 1688 R. Holme *Armoury* iii. xx. (Roxb.) 229 This is the form of another *Tower distillatory, but four square in the foundation with a round tower in the midst. 1896 *Spectator* 31 Oct. 586/1 There are other tribes of *tower-dwelling birds. 1730-46 Thomson *Autumn* 114 Nurse of art, the city reared..her *tower-encircled head. 1709 Strype *Ann. Ref.* I. xlv. 457 He and his *Tower-fellows, hearing the bill..should pass. 1847 Grote *Greece* ii. xiii. III. 247 The symmories or *tower-fellowships of Teôs seem to be analogous to the phratries of ancient Athens. 1799 H. Gurney *Cupid & Psyche* viii. (1800) 18 A vast and *tower-flank'd palace stood. 1598 Sylvester *Du Bartas* ii. ii. iii. *Colonies* 424 Th' ingenious, *Towr-full, and Law-loving Soil. 1688 *Tower furnace [see sense 6 c]. a 1832 Scott *Eve St. John* xxxii, He oped the *tower-gate And he mounted the narrow stair. 1886 Willis & Clark *Cambridge* III. 285 Wykeham's *tower-gateway at New College is in three floors. 1719 D'Urfey *Pills* III. 2 It seiz'd on the *Tow'r Guns. 1767 Wesley *Jrnl.* 5 Nov., I was surprised..to hear the Tower-guns so plain at above fifty miles distance. 1539 in *Archæologia* XI. 437 Uppon the same *towre hed a saker of brasse of Scottyshe makinge. c 1480 Warkw. *Chron.* (Camden) 5 To the *Towre Hylle. 1485 *Rolls of Parlt.* VI. 372/2 The Gardyns upon the Towre hill. 1843 *Penny Cycl.* XXV. 98/1 The chief place of execution was outside the walls [of the Tower of London] on the neighbouring Tower Hill. 1687 A. Lovell tr. *Thevenot's Trav.* i. 100 A little *Tower-house, with two or three Rooms. 1797 *Statist. Acc. Scot.* XIX. 602 Tower houses are met with in a ruinous condition. 1897 Windle *Life in Early Brit.* ix. 176 The erection of the rectangular *tower keep, which the Norman used when he was building on a perfectly new site. 1885 McCook *Tenants Old Farm* 135 Easy victims to the vigilant *tower-keeper. 1848 Rickman *Archit.* (ed. 5) 220 'Sound-holes'..seems not so appropriate as air-holes or *tower-lights. 1552 Huloet, *Towrelyke, *turreus.* 1625 K. Long tr. *Barclay's Argenis* iv. xix. 309 Elephants..brought into the Battell with their tower-like carriages. 1729 Savage *Wanderer* iv. 119 He sees yon Tow'r-like Ship the Waves divide. 1893 *Scribner's Mag.* June 718/1 The tower-like building of stone and stucco, octagonal in form, had a forbidding air. 1880 *Archæol. Cantiana* XIII. 26 Lanfranc's *tower-piers, and a few feet of his crypt walls undoubtedly remain. 1886 Willis & Clark *Cambridge* III. 356 Access to the hall is provided through a *tower-porch. 1673 *Phil. Trans.* VIII. 6072 Powder proved *Tower-proof is a fifth part stronger than any Dutch powder. 1805 T. Lindley *Voy. Brazil* 252 Brasil being supplied by the mother country with British tower-proof musquets. 1858 Hogg *Life Shelley* II. 365 Blessed amongst women,..a tower-proof, fire-proof, bomb-proof blue. 1606 Sylvester *Du Bartas* ii. iv. i. *Tropheis* 401 'Twas the Breach of a *Tower-razing Ram. 1877 W. Jones *Finger-ring* 298 In the same collection is a Jewish '*tower' betrothal ring. *Ibid.*, Another betrothal ring..called 'temple' or 'tower' from the figure of the sacred temple placed on the summit. 1886 Willis & Clark *Cambridge* III. 331 The President is to have certain *tower-rooms. 1897 *Jacob Primmer in Rome* (1903) 319 In this *tower-shaped tomb. 1800 *Hull Advertiser* 17 May 3/3 A pamphlet, just published, price a good *Tower Shilling. 1848 Thackeray *Van. Fair* lxii, The Batavier steamboat left the *Tower stairs laden with a goodly company of English fugitives. 1642 Fuller *Holy & Prof. St.* ii. xix. 120 He knows if he sets his mark, (the *Tower-stamp of his credit) on any bad wares, he sets a deeper brand on his own conscience. 1845 Clough *Silver Wedding* xii, That wariest glance would here Faith, Hope and Love, the true Tower-stamp discern. 1610 Holland *Camden's Brit.* (1637) 216 A new Church with..an high spire besides the *Toure steeple. *Ibid.* 468, I saw the towre steeple of a small suppressed Friery. *Ibid.* 290 The *tour-supporting bankes, at Windsore. 1614 Sylvester *Bethulia's Rescue* iii. 125 *Tower-tearing Mars, Bellona thirsting-bloud. 1840 Dickens *Old C. Shop* lv, One of these..climbed with her to the *tower-top. 1903 *Daily Chron.* 25 June 4/5 An opportunity of witnessing the coaling of the flagship Majestic by the new Temperley *tower transporter. 1597 Gerarde *Herbal* ii. xxii. § 3. 213 (*heading*) Towers Mustarde..*Towers Treacle groweth in the west part of Englande vpon dunghils and such like places. 1911 *Daily News* 20 Apr. 1 A collapsible structure similar to a *tower wagon, was blown over by the wind. c 1450 *Brut* 423 The persone of the Toure and this ffrere Randulf fillen in debate and stryffe withynne the *Toure ward. *Ibid.* 431 Iohn Mortymere, knyght, brake pryson oute of the Toure of London, and was take ayen vpon the *Toure-wharf. 1593 *Rites of Durham* (Surtees) 43 In this wyndowe, above all, are six little glasened *towre wyndowes. 1581 A. Hall *Iliad* vii. 127 His huge and waightie targe, Which *towerwise so stoode aloft. 1634-5 Brereton *Trav.* (Chetham Soc.) 94 A little fort..built towerwise. 1653 H. Cogan tr. *Pinto's Trav.* xxv. (1663) 93 The top of the Platform was bordered with the same stone, cut into great *Tower-work.

**Tower** (tōu·əɹ), *sb.*2 Also 5 *Sc.* towar. [f. Tow *v.*1 + -er 1.] One who tows or draws with a rope; *esp.* one who tows a boat on a river or canal.

(In quots. 1494 the sense is uncertain; cf. quot. 1494 in Tow *v.*1 1, which refers to the same transaction.)

[1494 *Acc. Ld. High Treas. Scot.* I. 248 For the drawyne of viij treis fra the Sallache to the bote, and to a towar to gid thame,..vs. iiij d. *Ibid.*, Item, gyffyne tyll a towar, for to helpe to bryng doune the cariour fra Lochlomond,..ij s.] 1611 Cotgr., *Tireur*, a drawer..tugger, tower. 1795 Anderson *Brit. Emb. China* vi. 80 These pieces of wood..rest upon their breasts, and by leaning against them the towers increase the power of their exertions. 1883 M. H. Hayes *Ind. Racing Remin.* 231 The broken ground over which these native towers have to travel. 1887 J. Ashby Sterry *Lazy Minstrel* (1892) 155 My tow-ers are young and my tow-ers are fair: The one is Eleven, the other Nineteen, The merriest maidens that ever were seen. 1889 J. K. Jerome *Three Men in Boat* ix, A couple of towers walking briskly along.

**Tow·er**, *sb.*3 *Sc.* [f. Tow *sb.*2 + -er 1.] A rope-maker, a roper.

15.. *Aberdeen Regr.* (MS.) XXVIII. (Jam.), Towar.

**Tower**, *sb.*4: see Tow *v.*4

**Tower** (tauəɹ, tau·əɹ), *v.* Forms: see the sb. [f. Tower *sb.*1]

**I. 1.** *intr.* To rise or extend to a great height like a tower; to rise aloft, stand high.

(In quot. c 1400 the sense of *torret* is very uncertain.)

[c 1400 *Destr. Troy* 1637 Toures full tore torret aboue, Þat were of heght so hoge, as I here fynde.] 1582 Stanyhurst *Æneis* i. (Arb.) 31 O wights most blessed, whose wals be thus happelye touring. 1590 Spenser *F. Q.* ii. xii. 30 On th' other side an high rocke toured still. 1610 Holland *Camden's Brit.* (1637) 581 Dudley Castle towreth up upon an hill. 1690 C. Nesse *O. & N. Test.* I. 268 Like pillars of smoke towering upward. 1715-20 Pope *Iliad* ii. 565 The king of kings, majestically tall, Tow'rs o'er his armies, and outshines them all. 1834 Mrs. Somerville *Connex. Phys. Sc.* xxvii. (1849) 300 Magnificent trees tower to the height of 150 or 200 feet above the banana, the bamboo. 1863 Geo. Eliot *Romola* vi, Over every fastness .. there towers some huge Frankish fortress. 1885-94 R. Bridges *Eros & Psyche, March* xxiv, She saw the evening light In shifting colour to the zenith tower.

**b.** *fig.* Usually const. *above.*

1776 Boswell 11 Apr., in *Johnson*, Does not Gray's poetry, sir, tower above the common mark? 1820 Hazlitt *Lect. Dram. Lit.* 12 He [Shakspeare] towered above his fellows. 1822 — *Table-t.* Ser. ii. iii. (1869) 66 Her voice towered above the whole confused noise of the orchestra. 1869 Trollope *He knew he was Right* xxviii, When she first read the letter ..she towered in her passion.

**2.** *trans.* To raise or uplift to a height; to exalt.

1596 Warner *Alb. Eng.* xii. lxx. (1612) 295 English Poets Many, Of which are some..that towre their wits too hie. 1645 Rutherford *Trial & Tri. Faith* (1845) 299 The Soul is lifted up and towered like a high building. 1821 Clare *Vill. Minstr.* I. 75 Where hills tower'd high their crowns. 1849 W. S. Mayo *Kaloolah* vi. (1851) 26 Gigantic trees, which towered their lofty heads to the clouds.

**3.** *intr.* **a.** *Hawking.* To mount up, as a hawk, so as to be able to swoop down on the quarry: cf. Tower *sb.*1 8. Also *fig.*

1593 SHAKS. 2 *Hen. VI*, II. i. 10 My Lord Protectours Hawkes do towre so well. 1605 — *Macb.* II. iv. 12 A Faulcon towring in her pride of place. 1616 B. JONSON *Epigr.* I. lxxxv, Shee doth instruct men by her gallant flight, That they to knowledge so should toure upright And never stoope, but to strike ignorance. 1878 M. A. BROWN *Nadeschda* 27 Loose thy hawk and let it tower.

**b.** To soar aloft, as a bird.

1647 N. BACON *Disc. Govt. Eng.* I. xlvii. (1739) 77 The Eagle had cast its Feathers, and could towre no more. *a* 1682 H. BLUNT *Poem addr. to Garth* 14 in *Dispens.* (1709) Pref., So the Young Eagle that his Force would try, Faces the Sun, and tow'rs it to the Sky. 1728 RAMSAY *Lure* 93 See, see! he like a lavrock tours. 1817–18 COBBETT *Resid. U.S.* (1822) 211 The pheasant does not tower, but darts through the trees. 1885–94 R. BRIDGES *Eros & Psyche, Sept.* xvi, He flasht his pens, and sweeping widely round Tower'd to air.

**c.** To rise vertically, as a bird when wounded.

1812 COL. HAWKER *Diary* (1893) I. 39 With the exception of one which towered, all my birds fell dead to the gun. 1887 [see TOWERING *vbl. sb.*].

†**4.** *fig.* To rise on high, to soar. *Obs.*

1597 DELONEY *Canaans Calam.* (1912) 422 Their mounting minds that towred past their strength. 1641 J. JACKSON *True Evang. T.* II. 113 S. John..towred aloft into the highest mysteries of Divinity. 1643 SIR T. BROWNE *Relig. Med.* II. § 8, I have seen a Grammarian towr and plume himself over a single line in Horace. 1748 JOHNSON *Van. Hum. Wishes* 103 Still to new heights his restless wishes tower.

†**5.** *trans.* To soar aloft in or into; to rise to.

1604 DRAYTON *Owle* 149 By Night I towre the Heauen, deuoy'd of feare. *a* 1649 DRUMM. OF HAWTH. *Poems* (1790) 283 He towers those golden bounds He did to sun bequeath. 1667 MILTON *P. L.* VII. 441 Yet oft they quit The Dank, and rising on stiff Pennons, towre The mid Aereal Skie.

†**II. 6.** *trans.* To furnish with a tower or towers.

*c* 1440 [see TOWERING *vbl. sb.*]. 1450 in *Charters*, etc. *Edinb.* (1871) 71 To..wall, toure, turate, and uther wais to strengthen oure foresaid Burgh. *a* 1548 HALL *Chron.*, *Hen. VIII* 59 This Gardeyn was towred at euery corner.

**Towerde, -dys**, obs. ff. TOWARD, TOWARDS.

**Towered** (tau·əɹd, *poet.* tau·ə·rĕd), *a.* [f. TOWER *sb.*[1] and *v.* + -ED.]

**1.** Having a tower or towers; adorned or defended by towers; bearing or surmounted by a tower; raised or rising on high like a tower.

*c* 1400 *Sege Jerus.* 868 Þis toured toun is tenful to wynne. *c* 1430 *Seven Sag.* (P.) 2842 Who hys thys castel, That hys touryde and kernelde wel? *a* 1552 LELAND *Itin.* II. 67 The Tourrid Steple of the Paroche Chirch. 1632 MILTON *L'Allegro* 117 Towred Cities please us then. 1706 HEARNE *Collect.* 19 Jan. (O.H.S.) I. 165 Cybele..is represented with a Tower'd Head. 1796 W. H. MARSHALL *W. England* II. 208 The towered height of Stourton forms a prominent feature. *c* 1820 S. ROGERS *Italy, Alps* 24 The towered elephant Upheld his trunk. 1832 TENNYSON *Lady of Shalott* I. iv, From the river winding clearly Down to tower'd Camelot. 1909 RIDER HAGGARD *Yellow God* 42 The towered gateway of red brick.

†**2.** Immured in a tower; committed to the Tower of London. (Cf. *prisoned.*) *Obs.*

1716 M. DAVIES *Athen. Brit.* II. 409 The two that turn'd Non-jurors with the t'other five tower'd Bishops. 1750 *Student* (1751) II. 22 The noble Septemvirate of tower'd Prelates.

**3.** Of a wounded bird: That has 'towered'.

1827 COL. HAWKER *Diary* (1893) I. 320 Besides 4 towered and lost birds.

[**Toweret**, 'a little tower', in mod. Dicts., deduced from *towret*: see TURRET.]

**Towering** (tau·əriŋ), *vbl. sb.* [f. TOWER *v.* + -ING [1].] The action of the verb TOWER in various senses: *spec.* †**a.** The building of a tower. *Obs. rare*—°. **b.** Rising, soaring; raising. **c.** See quot. 1887 and TOWER *sb.*[1] 8 b, *v.* 3 c. **d.** *Photog.* See quot. 1891.

*c* 1440 *Promp. Parv.* 498/2 Towrynge, *turrificacio.* 1646 J. HALL *Poems* (1906) 224 Ambition's towerings do some gallants keep From calmer sleep. 1750 JOHNSON *Rambler* No. 72 ⁋ 5 The hearers either strain their faculties to accompany its towerings, or are left behind in envy and despair. 1887 COUES in *Science* X. 322 The convulsive muscular action which..results in the well-known 'towering' of hard-hit birds. 1891 *Anthony's Photogr. Bull.* IV. 38 How often is it that an otherwise good picture is spoiled by what we might call towering. The top of the building being much narrower than the bottom [etc.]. 1894 *Yellow Bk.* I. 66 Women..gave the best hours of the day to the towering of their coiffures.

**Tow·ering**, *ppl. a.* [f. TOWER *v.* + -ING [2].] That towers, in various senses.

**1.** Rising to a height; standing high; lofty.

1638 SIR T. HERBERT *Trav.* (ed. 2) 193 A spatious Garden, succinct with a great Towring wall of mud. 1697 DRYDEN *Virg. Past.* VII. 91 The towring Ash is fairest in the Woods. *c* 1743 FRANCIS tr. *Hor., Sec. Poem* 46 The cypress, when by storms impell'd,..Low bends the towering head. 1793 *Statist. Acc. Scotl.* VII. 501 The hills are steep and towering. 1833 L. RITCHIE *Wand. by Loire* 21 The girls..with their towering caps of the snowiest muslin. 1859 J. R. GREEN *Lett.* I. (1901) 33 My eye wanders..to the towering dome of the Radcliffe.

**b.** Of lofty stature; very tall.

1756 JOHNSON *K. of Prussia* Wks. IV. 532 To review this towering regiment was his daily pleasure. 1835 LYTTON *Rienzi* I. iii, The towering form of the smith. 1894 HALL CAINE *Manxman* III. xii, Kate saw him come, a towering dark figure between her and the door.

**2.** Rising high in flight, as a bird, etc. Also *fig.*

1598 MERES *Pallad. Tamia* II. 285 b, Yong Charles Fitz-Ieffrey, that high touring Falcon, hath..penned the honourable life and death of worthy sir Francis Drake. 1598 DRAYTON *Heroic. Ep.* xix. 179 Vnder thy towring blade haue coucht in fight. *c* 1673 *Roxb. Ball.* (1887) VI. 271 Where towering Larks do soar on high, In consort, making Melody. 1709 PRIOR *To C. Montague* vi, Our Hopes, like tow'ring Falcons, aim At Objects in an airy height. 1765 R. JONES *Fireworks* IV. 128 One rocket on the top of another. When..thus managed, they are called towering rockets. 1892 GREENER *Breech-Loader* 228 If beaters or keepers are not occupied in picking up, and can look after wounded and towering birds.

**3.** Rising to a height (*fig.*); exalted; aiming high; ambitious.

1663 BP. PATRICK *Parab. Pilgr.* v. (1687) 18 Others..teach me to fly aloft in towring speculations. 1702 *Eng. Theophrast.* 4 Nothing less than the writing of a Play can satisfie his towring Ambition. 1781 COWPER *Charity* 536 A bold remark, but which, if well applied, Would humble many a towering poet's pride. 1840 THIRLWALL *Greece* VII. lvi. 179 A man..of towering ambition. 1894 J. KNIGHT *Garrick* iv. 59 No man of towering ability was on the stage.

**4.** Rising to a high pitch of violence or intensity.

1602 SHAKS. *Ham.* v. ii. 80 The brauery of his griefe did put me Into a Towring passion. 1818 SCOTT *Rob Roy* xviii, I was in a towering passion. 1848 DICKENS *Dombey* liv, The towering fury and intense abhorrence. 1877 BLACK *Green Past.* xxxiii, He came down in a towering rage.

Hence **Tow·eringly** *adv.*, in a towering manner.

1822 E. IRVING *Let.* in Oliphant *Life* (1862) I. vi. 135, I should rise toweringly aloft into the regions of a very noble and sublime character. 1830 *Fraser's Mag.* I. 38 Tall palmtrees, that on the plain stood toweringly. 1885 G. MEREDITH *Diana of Crossways* xiii, The Hercules of dogs..toweringly big.

**Tow·erless**, *a.* [f. TOWER *sb.*[1] + -LESS.] Without a tower; devoid of towers.

*c* 1820 S. ROGERS *Italy, Campagna Florence* 201 Towerless, and left long since, but to the last Braving assault. 1886 STOKES *Irel. & Celtic Ch.* xii. (1888) 238 The earliest Christian churches..were utterly towerless.

**Tow·erlet.** [f. as prec. + -LET.] A little tower.

18.. JOANNA BAILLIE (Ogilvie), Our guiding star Now from its towerlet streameth far.

**Tow·er mu·stard.** *Herb.* [So named, according to Britten and Holland, from its habit of growth. According to Linnæus, called *Turritis* (Tournefort) as being 'alta et stricta'.] Popular name of a cruciferous plant, *Turritis glabra*, found on banks and cliffs. Called also *Towers treacle*, *Towerwort*, and sometimes *Tower Cress.*

1597 GERARDE *Herbal* II. xxii. 212 Towers Mustarde, of some hath beene taken for a kinde of Cresses. 1731 MILLER *Gard. Dict.*, *Turritis*, Tower-Mustard. 1842 C. W. JOHNSON *Farmer's Cycl.* s.v., *Turritis*, from *turris*, a tower; the foliage is so disposed on the stems as to give them a pyramidal form, and for the same reason the plants are called tower-mustard.

**b.** Sometimes applied to *Arabis Turrita* (see TOWER-*cress*); also called Bastard Tower mustard.

1760 J. LEE *Introd. Bot.* App. 320 Mustard, Bastard Tower, *Arabis.* 1866 *Treas. Bot.* s. v. *Mustard*, Mustard, Tower..also *Arabis Turrita.* 1874 GRAY *Man. Bot.* (ed. 5) 69 *A[rabis] perfoliata*, Lam. (Tower Mustard).

**Tower pound.** Also 6–8 **pound Tower.** [So called from the standard pound which was kept in the Tower of London.] A pound weight of 5400 grains (= 11¼ Troy ounces), which was the legal mint pound of England prior to the adoption of the Troy pound of 5760 grains in 1526. So **Tower weight**, weight expressed in terms of the Tower pound.

[1343 *Close Roll* 17 Edw. III. m. 4 d (P.R.O.), Vne liure de pois de la Tour de Loundres.] 1469 in *Archæologia* XV. 166 For coynage of every lb. of Tour weght of sylver..iiii s. vi d. 1526 *Proclam.* 5 Nov. (Pat. Roll 18 Hen. VIII. II. m. 2 d. P.R.O.), It is..determyned..that the said pounde Towre shalbe no more vsed nor occupied. 1545 *Rates of Customs* d v b, A pounde of Tower wayght wayeth of the Troy .xi. ounces .i. quarter. 1622 MALYNES *Anc. Law-Merch.* 292 There hath beene vsed from the beginning (in the Mint) both Troy and Tower weight, each of them containing twelue ounces in the pound weight, sauing that the Troy weight is heauier by sixteen penie weight vpon the pound weight: by which Troy weight the merchants bought their gold and siluer abroad, and by the same did deliuer it to the Kings mint, receiuing in counterpeaze but tower weight for Troy, which was the Princes Prerogatiue. 1789 WALTER MERREY *Remarks Coinage* 8 The silver penny was about twenty-two grains and a half of Troy-weight, but called a penny-weight Tower. The shilling was twelve of these pennies, and the pound Tower was twenty of these shillings. 1821 J. Q. ADAMS in C. Davies *Metr. Syst.* (1871) 94 This [silver] penny was the two hundred and fortieth part of the tower pound. 1844 LINGARD *Anglo-Sax. Ch.* (1858) II. App. O. 388 The Anglo-Saxon pound is believed to have been that known by the name of the Tower pound; the Norman was the Troy pound, heavier by three-quarters of an ounce than the former.

**Towers**, obs. form of TOURS.

**Tower weight**: see TOWER POUND.

**Towerwort**: see TOWER MUSTARD.

**Towery** (tau·əri), *a.* [f. TOWER *sb.*[1] + -Y.]

**1.** Characterized by or having towers; adorned or defended with towers.

1611 COTGR., *Tourrelé*, Towerie, tower-like, begirt or incompassed with towers. 1672 DRYDEN *2nd Pt. Conq. Granada* III. iii. 114 The Genius of the place its Lord will meet; And bend its tow'ry forehead to your feet. 17.. POPE *Imit. Spenser* 54 Meandring streams, and Windsor's tow'ry pride. 1834 J. WILSON in *Blackw. Mag.* XXXVI. 842 Crowned with her towery diadem—Queen of the Sea. 1870 BRYANT *Iliad* VII. I. 214 Till ye possess the towery city of Troy.

**2.** Rising to a lofty height; tower-like; towering; also *fig.* aspiring; exalted.

1731 A. HILL *Adv. Poets* xvi. 9 Hence, have all towery Minds, sublimely fir'd, With in-born Strength, to their own Heav'n aspir'd. 1738 H. BROOKE tr. *Tasso's Jerus. Del.* II. Poems (1810) 376/1 One step alone 'twixt triumph and defeat, The gulfy ruin and the tow'ry height. 1825 J. WILSON *Poems* II. 114 Long ensigns brightening on the towery mast. 1870 R. R. COVERDALE *Poems* 39 'Neath towery trees that lowly bent.

**3.** *Comb.* **towery-topped** *a.*, having a towery top; topped or crowned with towers.

1602 CAREW *Cornwall* II. 121 A towry-topped Castle heere, wide blazeth ouer all.

**Towgh, -e, towȝ, towh, -he**, obs. ff. TOUGH.

**Towghe, Towgher**: see TOUGHE, TOCHER.

**Towght**, obs. form of TOUGHT.

**Towhee** (tau·hī, tau·ī). *U.S.* Also 8 towee, 8–9 towhe. ['From one of its notes' (Newton).] The ground-robin or CHEEWINK of North America, *Pipilo erythrophthalmus*; also *towhee bird*, *-finch*, *-bunting*, *-goldfinch*. Also any species of *Pipilo.*

1730 MORTIMER in *Phil. Trans.* XXXVI. 430 The Towhe Bird. 1791 W. BARTRAM *Carolina* 172 The towee birds..are very numerous. 1859 BARTLETT *Dict. Amer.* (ed. 2), *Chewink*, the ground robin...On Long Island it is called the Towhee Goldfinch. 1893 *Scribner's Mag.* June 762/2 He utters his loud 'Towhee', a note so characteristic that it has become one of his names.

†**To-whe·n**, *interrog. adv. Obs.* [f. TO *prep.* + WHEN.] Until what time? How long?

*a* 1300 *E. E. Psalter* iv. 3 Mennes sones, towhen ofe herte vn-meke? Whi loue yhe fantom, and lighinge seke? *Ibid.* lxxxviii. 45 Towhen, laverd, turnes tou in ende, at laste? Als fire sal bren þi wreth laste?

**Towher**, obs. form of TOCHER.

†**To-whi·le**, *conj. adv. Obs.* [f. TO *prep.* 7 + WHILE *sb.*, q.v. 2 c.] During the time that, while.

*c* 950, *c* 1000, *c* 1250, 13.. [see WHILE *sb.* 2 c.] *c* 1330 R. BRUNNE *Chron. Wace* (Rolls) 4141 To whyle þe kyng & his cosyns In loue loken ar þer lynes.

†**To-whi·les**, *conj. adv. Obs.* Also 4 toquil(i)s, to whils. [f. prec. + *-es* of adverbial genitive: see WHILES, WHILST.] = prec.; whilst.

13.. *Cursor M.* 4269 (Cott.) Hir luue..Sco miþed [*Gött.* kithid] it, to-quils [*Gött.* ay quilis] sco moght. *Ibid.* 6264 (Gött.) Þe se on ayder side him stod As wallis to quilis þai forth ȝode. 1357 *Lay Folks Catech.* (MS. T.) 139 To whiles that his bodi lai in þe graue The saule with the godhede went untill hell. *a* 1400 *R. Brunne's Chron. Wace* (Rolls) 2645 Þe while [*Petyt MS.* Towhils] þer fader was on lyue For þe royalme gon þey to stryue.

**To-whit, To-who(o**: see TUWHIT, TUWHOO.

†**To-whi·ther**, *v. Obs.* [ME. *to-hwiðeren*, f. TO-[2] + **hwiðeren* (?).] *trans.* To 'whirl in pieces' (Stratm.).

*a* 1225 *Leg. Kath.* 1964 Ha schal beon tohwiðeret Wið þe hweoles. *Ibid.* 2018 Smit se smertliche herto, þet alle þeos fowr hweoles Tohwiðerin to stucchen. *a* 1225 *Ancr. R.* 362 Loðlease meidenes þe tittes ikoruen of, and to-hwiðered o hweoles, & hefdes bikoruen.

**Tow-hook.** ? *U.S.* See quot.

1877 KNIGHT *Dict. Mech.*, *Tow-hook*, an artilleryman's hook, used in unpacking ammunition-chests. [Unknown in British military service.]

**Towi·llee.** *dial.* [See quot. 1758.] A local name for the Sanderling: cf. CURWILLET; also, for the Ringed Plover: cf. DULWILLY.

1758 BORLASE *Hist. Cornw.* 247 Here we have coots, sanderlings, (which, from the noise they make when flying, we call Towillees), sea-larks, sea-pies. 1804 BEWICK *Brit. Birds* II. 1 Sanderling, Towillee, or Curwillet. 1880 RODD *Birds Cornw.* 315/2 *Towillees*, and *Turwillie*, Ringed Plover.

**Towing** (tōu·iŋ), *vbl. sb.*[1] [f. TOW *v.*[1] + -ING [1].] The action of TOW *v.*[1]; *esp.* the dragging of a boat or ship by a tow-line; also, the drawing of a fine net behind a boat or other vessel for the capture of marine zoological specimens, and in *pl.* the proceeds of this, the specimens captured.

1494 [see TOW *v.*[1] 1]. 1611 [see TOWAGE 2]. 1617 MORYSON *Itin.* II. 168 Sir Richard Levison,..with towing, got out the Warspite, the Defiance, the Swiftsure, the Marline. 1725 DE FOE *Voy. round World* (1840) 325 By the help of towing and setting as well as they could, they came to a flatter shore. 1857 C. GRIBBLE in *Merc. Marine Mag.* (1858) V. 7 They monopolize the towing in and out. 1887 *Smithsonian Rep.* II. 135 The surface towings he obtained are very rich in interesting forms.

**b.** *attrib.*, as *towing-banquette*, *barge*, *-bitts*, *bollard*, *-boom*, *-gear*, *-vessel*; **towing-bridle** (BRIDLE *sb.* 5 a), a stout chain, cable, or iron rail secured at the ends, with a *towing-hook* to which the tow-line is attached; **towing-lights** *sb. pl.*, white lights carried one above another by a vessel which has another or others in tow (*Funk's Stand. Dict.* 1895); **towing-net** = TOW-NET; **towing-path** = TOW-PATH; **towing-post**: see quot.; **towing-rope** = TOW-ROPE; **towing-timber** = *towing-post.*

1791 *Rep. Navig. Thames & Isis, Estimate* 4 A Loop of the River cut through, a *Towing-Banquette formed, and Water deepened, £90. 1889 WELCH *Text Bk. Naval Archit.* xii. 132 Advantage is taken of the hollow *towing bollards..and the mast..to utilise these also as uptakes. 1897 G. GRENFELL in Sir H. Johnston *Life* (1908) I. xii. 258

[It] had been firmly secured to the after bollards, as well as to the *towing-boom forward. **1867** SMYTH *Sailor's Word-bk.*, **Towing-bridle*, a stout chain, with a hook at each end, for attaching a tow-rope to; also, a large *towing-hook* in the bight of the chain. **1857** DUFFERIN *Lett. High Lat.* viii. (ed. 3) 205, I began to be afraid that something must have gone wrong with the *towing-gear. **1816** TUCKEY *Narr. Exped. R. Zaire* i. (1818) 11 The *towing-net was now .. tolerably successful, taking up from time to time various species of mollusca. **1726** *Lond. Gaz.* No. 6447/7 Using for *Towing or Haleing-Paths. **1795** J. PHILLIPS *Hist. Inland Navig.* Add. 100 The towing path of this canal may be used by occupiers of lands as a bridle-way. **1867** TROLLOPE *Chron. Barset* I. xii. 102 A cottage which stood alone, close to the towing-path of the canal. **1867** SMYTH *Sailor's Word-bk.*, **Towing-post*, a substantial timber fixed through the deck of a steam-tug for making the tow-rope fast to. Also, a similar post in canal barges to keep the tow-line up clear of the path. **1838** *Civil Eng. & Arch. Jrnl.* I. 322/1 Whether it was feasible without a *towing-rope to get the barge through the water-way. **1882** E. O'DONOVAN *Merv Oasis* I. 315 A towing rope was fastened to the top of the mast. **1834** *Oxf. Univ. Mag.* I. 308 The recent introduction of steam *towing-vessels.

**Towing,** *vbl. sb.*², ³: see TOW *v.*³, ⁴.

† **Tow-iren, towyrene,** obs. ff. TEW-IRON.

**1399** *Will W. West* (Comm. Crt. Lond.), Towiren. **1408** *Durham Acc. Roll* in *Eng. Hist. Rev.* XIV. 520 In portagio unius towyrene de forgeo praedicto usque Westaukeland pro emendatione ejusdem, *id.*

**Towist,** variant of TOUST *Obs.*

**Towk(e, Towker(e:** see TOQUE, TUCK, TUCKER.

**Towl, towle, towlle,** obs. forms of TOLL.

**Tow-line** (tō^u·lǝin). [f. TOW *v.*¹ or *sb.*⁴ + LINE *sb.*²] A line, rope, or hawser by which anything is towed; *spec.* in *Whaling*, the whale-line.

**1719** DE FOE *Crusoe* (1840) II. ix. 204 Taking the end of a tow-line in his hand. **1725** — *Voy. round World* (1840) 347 The greatest difficulty was for tow-lines to draw the boats by. **1839** MARRYAT *Phant. Ship* xvii, The boats had cast off the tow-lines. **1881** *Times* 20 June 6/5 The tow-lines of the tugs were made fast to the barque.

**Towlsell,** obs. form of TOLSEL.

**Towm(e,** var. TAUM, fishing-line; obs. f. TOOM.

**Towmond, towmont,** Sc. ff. TWELVEMONTH.

**Town** (taun), *sb.* Forms: 1 tuun, 1–4 tūn, (4–5 tounne), 4–5, *Sc.* 6– toun, (4–5 ton, tone), 5–6 toune, (5 townne, 6 toen), 5–7 towne, 5– town, (8–9 *Sc.* toon (= tūn)). [OE. *tuun, tún* m. = OFris., OS., MLG. *tûn* (MDu. *tuun*, Da. *tuin*, LG. *tuun, tûn*), OHG., MHG. *zûn* (Ger. *zaun*); ON. *tûn* neut. (Norw. dial. *tūn* farm-yard, older Da. *tūn*, Sw. dial. *tūn, tōn* hedge, fence):—OTeut. **tūno*ᶻ, *-o*ᵐ, cogn. with Celtic *dūn* in *-dūnum*, OIr. *dūn*, W. *dīn* fortified place, castle, camp. The sense in OHG. was 'fence, hedge', as in Ger. *zaun*; in mod.Du. and LG. it has both the senses 'fence or hedge' and 'enclosed place, garden'. In OE. the sense 'fence, hedge' does not occur, only that of 'enclosed place', as in sense 1, and its developments in senses 2 and 3, in which it was frequently used to render L. *villa*. The modern sense 4 is later than the Norman Conquest, and corresponds to F. *ville* 'town, city', as similarly developed from L. *villa* 'farm, country-house'.]

† **1.** An enclosed place or piece of ground, an enclosure; a field, garden, yard, court. *Obs.*

*c* **725** *Corpus Gloss.* (O. E. T.) 546 *Co[ho]rs*, tuun. *a* **800** *Erfurt Gloss.* 281 *Cors*, tuun. *c* **870** *O. E. Chron.* an. 867, His lic lið þær on tune. *c* **950** *Lindisf. Gosp.* Matt. xxvi. 36 Ða cuomon ðe hælend mið him in tun ðe hata gezemani [*Lat.* villam; *Gr.* χωρίον; WYCL. toun; TIND., *Geneva*, 1611, place; COVERD. felde; CRANMER farme place; *Rheims* village]. *c* **1000** *Ags. Gosp.* Mark xv. 21 Simonem cireneum cumende of þam tune [*Lind.* cummende of lond; *Rushw.* cymende of londe; *Lat.* de villa; *Gr.* ἀπ' ἀγροῦ; WYCL. fro the toun; TIND. oute of the felde; COVERD. from the felde; *Gen.*, *Rheims*, 1611, out of the countrey]. — Luke xiv. 18 Ic bohte æne tun [*Lind.*, *Rushw.* lond ic bohte; *Lat.* villam emi; *Gr.* ἀγρὸν ἠγόρασα; WYCL. a toun; TIND., COVERD. a ferme; 1611 a piece of ground]. *Ibid.* xv. 15 Ða sende he hine to his tune þæt he heolde his swyn [*Lind.* on lond his; *Lat.* in villam suam; *Gr.* εἰς τοὺς ἀγροὺς αὐτοῦ; WYCL. in to his toun; TIND. to the felde; COVERD. into his felde]. — John iv. 5 Neah þam tune [*Lat.* juxta prædium; *Gr.* πλησίον τοῦ χωρίου; WYCL. the manere, *gloss* or feeld, *later vers.* the place; TIND. the possession; COVERD. yᵉ pece of londe; *Rheims* the maner; 1611 the parcell of ground]. *c* **1000** *Sax. Leechd.* II. 132 Harewyrt lytelu oftost weaxeþ on tune. *a* **1123** *O. E. Chron.* an. 1114, And þæt ʒehwær on wudan and on tunan ʒecydde. **1388** WYCLIF *Matt.* xxii. 5 But thei..wenten forth, oon in to his toun [1382 vyneʒerd; *Lat.* villam; *Gr.* ἀγρὸν; *Ags. G.* tune; TIND. ferme place; COVERD. huszbandrye; 1611 farme], anothir to his marchaundise.

(Cf. also the OE. compounds *tún-cressa* garden cress, *tún-melde*, *Atriplex hortensis*; *æppel-tún* apple orchard, *cyric-tún* churchyard, *déor-tún* deer-park, *gærs-tún* meadow, *líc-tún* graveyard, *wyrt-tún* vegetable garden.)

† **b.** *spec.* The enclosed land surrounding or belonging to a single dwelling; a farm with its farmhouse (still *Sc. dial.*); a manor, 'an estate with a village community in villenage upon it under a lord's jurisdiction'; the enclosed land of a village community; sometimes also = parish, when this was coextensive with a manor. *Obs.*

**601–4** *Laws Ethelbert* c. 17 ʒif man in mannes tun ærest ʒeirneþ, vi scillingum ʒebete; se þe æfter irneþ, iii scillingas. **972** *Charter Eadgar* in Birch *Cart. Sax.* III. 586 Þis sind þara feower tuna lond ʒemæra. *a* **1100** *Gerefa* in *Anglia* (1886) IX. 259 And ælcre tilðan timan ðe to tune belimpð. *c* **1200** *Vices & Virt.* 77 Uppe ða chirch-landes, oðer uppe tunes. *c* **1220** *Bestiary* 391 Fox is hire to name..Ðe coc & te capun ʒe fecched ofte in ðe tun. *c* **1375** *Sc. Leg. Saints* xxvii. (*Machor*) 93 He gaf of heritable rycht to godis seruice al þat ton In-to fre possessione. *c* **1380** WYCLIF *Serm.* Sel. Wks. I. 22 A man hadde a fermour, as keper of a toun. **1628** COKE *On Litt.* § 1. 5 By the name of a towne, *Villa*, a mannor may passe. *Ibid.* § 193. 125 b, If a matter be alledged *in Parochia*, it shall be intended in Law that it containeth no more Townes then one, vnlesse the party doth shew the contrary. **1785** J. MILL *Diary* (1889) 75 Some hill towns [= farms] had a good deal of corn on the ground to shear.

**2.** The house or group of houses or buildings upon this enclosed land; the farmstead or homestead on a farm or holding. Now esp. *Sc.*

*c* **890** tr. *Bæda's Hist.* II. xi. [xiv.] (1890) 140 Þes tun [*villa*] wæs forlæten..& oðer wæs fore þæm ʒetimbred. *Ibid.* III. xiv. [xvi.] 202 Aslat þa þa tunas ealle ymb þa burʒ onwæʒ. *a* **900** *O. E. Martyrol.* 9 June 92 Þa ongan se tun bernan ..þa forburnon ealle þara monna hus þa on þæm tune wæron. **1362** LANGL. *P. Pl.* A. x. 134 Barouns and Burgeis and Bonde men of tounes [*MS. U.* towne]. *c* **1400** *Plowman's Tale* III. 1043 Threshing and dyking fro town to town. **1551** ROBINSON tr. *More's Utopia* I. (1895) 57 They whyche plucked downe fermes and townes of husbandrye. *c* **1689** *Depred. Clan Campbell* (1816) 42 Taken out of Achingoul..be Lochaber men, ten coues...Item, be them out of that toun, 30 sheep and goats. **1814** SCOTT *Wav.* ix, Waverley learned..from this colloquy that in Scotland a single house was called a *town*. **1815** — *Guy M.* xxiii, Two or three low thatched houses, placed with their angles to each other, with a great contempt of regularity. This was the farm-steading of Charlie's Hope, or, in the language of the country, 'the town'. **1888** BRYCE *Amer. Commw.* II. xlviii. 226 *note*, In Scotland (where it is pronounced 'toon') it still denotes the farmhouse and buildings.

**3.** A (small) group or cluster of dwellings or buildings; a village or hamlet with little or no local organization. (Often = L. *vicus.*) Now *dial.*

In var. Eng. dials., *the town* is spec. applied to the hamlet or cluster of houses contiguous to the church; more fully *the church-town*.

*c* **725** *Corpus Gloss.* (O.E.T.) 557 *Conpetum*, tuun, þrop. *a* **800** *Erfurt Gloss.* 307 *Conpetum*, tuun vel ðrop. *c* **950** *Lindisf. Gosp.* John xxi. 2 Se ðeʒn seðe uæs of Cana ðæm tuune on galilees meʒð. *c* **1000** ÆLFRIC *Hom.* II. 54 ʒifta wæron ʒeworden on anum tune ðe is ʒeciʒed Chana. *a* **1067** *Charter of Eadweard* in Kemble *Cod. Dipl.* IV. 203, .x. hyden lond on Waltham, and ðe cherche of ðan seluen tune. *c* **1200** ORMIN 7016 Þatt tun wass nemmnedd Beþþleæm. *a* **1300** *Cursor M.* 14790 (Cott.) Þat es þe tun of bethleem. *c* **1386** CHAUCER *Prol.* 478 A poure Person of a toun [*v.r.* toune]..Wyd was his parisshe and houses fer a sonder..With hym ther was a Plowman was his brother. **1387** TREVISA *Higden* (Rolls) II. 39 In Mon [Anglesey] beeþ þre hondred townes [*villas*] þre score and þre, and beeþ acounted for þre candredes, þat beeþ þre hundredes. **1483** *Cath. Angl.* 391/1 A Towne, *pagus*, *pagulus*, *pagos grece*, *villa*, *villula*. **1508** DUNBAR *Poems* vii. 55 In euery cete, village, and in toune. **1526** TINDALE *John* xi. 1 Lazarus of Bethania the toune of Mary and her sister Martha. **1576** E. WORSELY *Surv. Mannor of Felsted, Essex* 129 (MS.) The highway leading from Felsted towards the town of Leighes. **1731** T. BOSTON *Mem.* vii. (1899) 112 The circumstances of my charge, all in one little town [i. e. the hamlet of Simprin], within a few paces from one end to the other. **1809** MAR. EDGEWORTH *Absentee* ix, He arrived at a village, or, as it was called, a town, which bore the name of Colambre. **1812** BRACKENRIDGE *Views Louisiana* (1814) 119 Amongst the Americans, every assemblage of houses, no matter of how small a number, is denominated a town. **1887** *Pall Mall G.* 19 Aug. 11/1 Wretched villages, misnamed towns, scattered throughout Ireland. **1887** I. R. *Lady's Ranche Life in Montana* 12 We are only a mile from the town (eight houses and an hôtel); but only think, in this barbarous region, being only a mile from railway station, telegraph, and post-office! **1888** BRYCE *Amer. Commw.* II. xlviii. 226 *note*, In parts of eastern England the chief cluster of houses in a parish is still often called 'the town'. **1888** ELWORTHY *W. Somerset Gloss.*, *Town*, a collection of houses. ..In all parts of the district the villages are called *towns* when the collection of houses is specially referred to.

**4.** Now, in general English use, commonly designating an inhabited place larger and more regularly built than a village, and having more complete and independent local government; applied not only to a 'borough', i.e. a corporate town, and a 'city', which is a town of higher rank, but also to an 'urban district', i.e. a non-corporate town having an 'urban district council' with powers of rating, paving, and sanitation more extensive than those possessed by a parish council or the administrative body (where such exists) of a village. Sometimes also applied to small inhabited places below the rank of an 'urban district', which are not distinguishable from villages otherwise, perhaps, than by having a periodical market or fair ('market town'), or by being historically 'towns'.

The distinction between a small town which is not a municipal borough, and a village, is somewhat indefinite; there are also decayed towns, even municipal boroughs, which are surpassed in population by many villages.

**1154** *O. E. Chron.* an. 1137. § 3 (Laud MS.) Hi læiden ʒæildes o þe tunes æure um wile...Þa þe uurecce men ne hadden nan more to gyuen, þa ræueden hi & brendon alle the tunes. *c* **1200** ORMIN 8511 Fra land to land, fra tun to tun, Fra wic to wic i tune. *c* **1205** LAY. 14246 Ane burh he arerde muchele & mare ..& for swulche gomen Þa tun [Lancaster] hafde þas þreo nomen. *a* **1225** *Juliana* 8, & tuhen him ʒont te tun from strete to strete. *c* **1275** *Passion* 70 in *O. E. Misc.* 39 As he com in-to þe bureh so rydinde Þe children of þe tune [Jerusalem] comen syngynde. **1297** R. GLOUC. (Rolls) 5249 Hii come, & londone, & kaunterbury, & oþer tounes nome. **1375** BARBOUR *Bruce* XI. 138 Sum lugit without the townys In tentis and in palʒeownys. *c* **1400** *Laud Troy Bk.* 7429 Thei dyed thikkere then men dryues gece To chepyng-toun for to selle. *c* **1400** MAUNDEV. (1839) iv. 30 Joppa..is on of the oldest townes of the world. **1419** *Munim. de Melros* (Bann. Cl.) 502 All þe landis Tenementis and byggynnis..in þe said Towne of Edynburghe. **1472–3** *Rolls of Parlt.* VI. 33/2 The Chaunceler and Scolers of the Universite in your Toune of Oxonford. **1512** *Act* 4 *Hen. VIII*, c. 7 § 2 And that in all other Cities, Borowes, and Townes .. the Maires, Bailiffes, or hede Officers, and Wardeyns to haue like Authoritie. And wher noo Wardeyns be, then the hede Officers or Governours of the same Cities, Borowes and Townes to appoynt certeyn persones .. to make serche. *Ibid.* c. 19 § 10 In Hundredes, Townes Corporate & nott corporate, parisshes & all other places. **1552** HULOET, Towne beynge walled, *oppidum*. *Ibid.*, Towne incorporate, *municipium*. **1555** W. WATREMAN *Fardle Facions* 10 Of Tounes, thei made cities, and of villages, Tounes. **1597** in *Maitl. Cl. Misc.* I. 89 Within the toune and citie of Glasgw. *a* **1600** MONTGOMERIE *Misc. Poems* xlviii. 39 Constantinopil..Eftir his name he callit the citie syn, Becaus he lovit it best of tounis all. **1610** HOLLAND *Camden's Brit.* (1637) 497 This is the chiefe Towne of all this Shire. **1628** COKE *On Litt.* § 171. 115 b, If a Towne be decayed so as no houses remayne, yet it is a Towne in Lawe...It cannot bee a Towne in Law, vnlesse it hath, or in time past hath had a Church and celebration of Diuine Seruice...It appeareth by Littleton, that a Towne is the genus, and a Borough is the species, for .. euery Borough is a Towne, but euery Towne is not a Borough. **1649** BP. GUTHRIE *Mem.* (1702) 80 A Wonder lasts but nine Nights in a Town (as we use to say). **1765** BLACKSTONE *Comm.* I. Introd. iv. 114 The word *town* or *vill* is indeed.. now become a generical term, comprehending under it the several species of cities, boroughs, and common towns. **1809** KENDALL *Trav.* I. ii. 12 A collection of houses joining, or nearly joining each other, is the first requisite in the definition of *town*, though the word be taken in the loosest sense. **1861** M. PATTISON *Ess.* (1889) I. 44 The free towns of Lübeck, Bremen, and Hamburg.

**b.** Without article, after prepositions and verbs, as *in*, *out of*, *to town*, *to leave town*, etc.: i.e. the particular town under consideration, or that in or near which the speaker is at the moment; the town with which one has to do, the market-town, the chief town of the district or province, the capital; in England since *c* 1700 *spec.* said of London.

There are earlier uses referring to London, but only as said by persons living there.

*c* **1250** *Gen. & Ex.* 2311 And quuan he weren ut tune went, Iosep haueð hem after sent. **13..** *Cursor M.* 3346 (Cott.) On morn wit godds beniscon Was mai rebecca lede o ton [*Gött.* of þe tun]. **1377** LANGL. *P. Pl.* B. XIII. 266 Alle Londoun..likeþ wel my wafres...Þere was a carful comune whan no carte come to toune With bake bred fro stretforth. **1389** in *Eng. Gilds* (1870) 5 Be he in toun [London] oþer out of toun. **1431** *Ibid.* 275 If he be in towne [Cambridge] and comyth not. **1450** *Rolls of Parlt.* V. 182/2 The kyng sent for all his Lordes..thenne beyng in Towne [London]. **1618** BOLTON *Florus* IV. i. (1636) 260 The ambassadours of the Allobroges (at that time, as it hapned, in town [Rome]) were dealt with. **1638** JUNIUS *Paint. Ancients* 122 Strangers ..as soone as they come to Towne [London], enquire for him first of all. **1645** EVELYN *Diary* 31 Oct., We invited all the English and Scotts in towne [Padua] to a feast. **1648** *Commons' Jrnls.* V. 545/1 That a Letter be directed to the Vice Admiral, to desire him to suffer Prince Philip, Brother to the Prince Elector, to come to Town. **1689** in *Acts Parlt. Scotl.* (1875) XII. 60/2 Þat the macers advertise such as are in towne [Edinburgh] That they be present accordingly. **1711** STEELE *Spect.* No. 2 ⁋ 1 When he is in Town, he lives in Soho-Square. **1711** HEARNE *Collect.* (O. H. S.) III. 127 Dr. Charlett went out of Town [Oxford] on purpose that he might not be present. **1739** CHESTERF. *Lett.* (1792) I. 122, I shall come to town next Saturday. **1770** FOOTE *Lame Lover* I. Wks. 1799 II. 60 Well known about town. **1791** *Gentl. Mag.* Jan. 1/1 A friend of mine, who was lately in town, saw many of them in the shop-windows. **1815** SIMOND *Tour Gt. Brit.* I. 17 At Richmond..I set out by myself for town, as London is called *par excellence*. **1825** T. COSNETT *Footman's Direct.* 217 So necessary is it for footmen to know town. **1848** DICKENS *Dombey* xxx, A stately relative..who was out of town. **1902** R. HICHENS *Londoners* 17, I shall leave town at least by the first of July.

**c.** *spec.* as distinct from or contrasted with *the country* (COUNTRY 5).

*c* **1386** CHAUCER *Miller's T.* 194 And for she was of toune [*v.rr.* towne, tounne, town] he profreth meede, For some folk wol ben wonnen for richesse. **1712** LADY M. W. MONTAGU *Let. to W. Montagu* 9 Dec., You say I love the town. **1715** POPE *2nd Ep. Miss Blount* 2 As some fond Virgin, whom her mother's care Drags from the Town to wholesome Country air. **1780** *Mirror* No. 105 ⁋ 2, I would beg of those who migrate from the city, not to carry too much of the town with them into the country. **1784** [see COUNTRY 5]. **1909** LLOYD GEORGE in *Daily News* 30 Apr. 8 Land in the town seems to be let by the grain as if it was radium.

**d.** In ME., and later in ballad poetry, etc., often added after the name of a town, in apposition. *arch.* (Cf. OE. *Rome-burh, Lunden-burh*, etc.)

**13..** *Seuyn Sag.* (W.) 551 Whilom a riche burgeis was, And woned her in Rome toun. *? a* **1700** *Sir Patrick Spence* i. in *Percy Reliques* (1845) 20/1 The king sits in Dumferling toune. *? a* **1700** *K. John & Abbot* ii. ibid. 167/2 They rode poste..to fair London toune. **1703** ROWE *Ulysses* Prol. 8 Her husband..Left her..., to..battle for a harlot at Troy toun. **1782** COWPER *John Gilpin* i, A trainband captain eke was he Of famous London town. **18..** ROSSETTI (*title*) Troy Town.

**5.** As a collective sing. **a.** The community of a town in its corporate capacity; the corporation; **b.** The inhabitants of a town, the townspeople; **c.** *spec.* the fashionable society of London (or other leading city thought of); 'society'. *arch.*

*c* 1330 R. Brunne *Chron.* (1810) 334 Þe toþer day on þe morn com þe Brus Roberd, þe toun wist it beforn, þorgh spies þat þei herd. *c* 1470 Henry *Wallace* ii. 19 So he desirit the toune of Air to se His child with him. 1582 Allen *Martyrd. Campion* (1908) 96 All the towne loved him exceedingly. *a* 1616 Beaumont *Let. to B. Jonson* 50 Wit able enough to justify the Town For three days past! 1632 Massinger & Field *Fatal Dowry* iv. i, 'Tis all the town talks. 1665 Pepys *Diary* 21 June, I find all the town almost going out of town. 1693 Dryden *Persius' Sat.* i. 5 That this vast universal Fool, the Town, Shou'd cry up Labeo's Stuff, and cry me down. 1713 Swift *Frenzy J. Denny* Wks. 1755 III. i. 144 That vile piece, that's foisted upon the town for a dramatick poem! 1742 Pope *Dunc.* iv. 292 [He], all at once let down, Stunn'd with his giddy Larum half the town. 1849 Macaulay *Hist. Eng.* iii. I. 405 His Absalom and Achitophel, the greatest satire of modern times, had amazed the town, had made its way.. even into rural districts.

**d.** *absol.* At Oxford and Cambridge: The civic community or body of citizens or townsmen as distinct from members of the university; esp. in phr. *town and gown* (often *attrib.*); cf. Gown *sb.* 5.

*a* 1647 Pette in *Archæologia* XII. 218, I was forced,..my graces for Bachelor of Arts being passed both in house and town, to abandon the university. 1828 *Sporting Mag.* XXI. 428 Parties of five or six, both 'gown' and 'town', were parading abreast. *a* 1845 Hood *Lament Toby* xv, Farewell to 'Town!' farewell to 'Gown!' I've quite outgrown the latter. 1853 'C. Bede' *Verdant Green* ii. iv, The battle of Town and Gown was over. 1861 Hughes *Tom Brown at Oxf.* xi, I wish..to disclaim..all sympathy with town and gown rows. 1912–13 *Kelly's Oxford Directory* 2/2 In 1354 a desperate Gown and Town riot began on St. Scholastica's day, February 10th, and lasted three days, during which 40 students and 60 townsmen lost their lives.

**6.** *U.S.* A geographical division for local or state government. **a.** A division of a county, which may contain one or more villages or towns (in sense 4); a township; also, the inhabitants of such a division as a corporate body. (Esp. in the New England states.) **b.** A municipal corporation, having its own geographical boundaries (as distinct from a.), considered either in reference to its area or as a body politic.

1808 A. Wilson *Poems & Lit. Prose* (1876) I. 148 The people here make no distinction between town and township, and travellers frequently asked the driver..'What town are we now in?' when perhaps we were on the top of a miserable barren mountain. 1809 Kendall *Trav.* I. ii. 12 In New England..a town is very commonly described as containing two or three villages. *Ibid.* 13 A town..in Connecticut, and the other parts of New England, is first a district, or geographical subdivision..; secondly, it is a body politic and corporate. *Ibid.* x. 113 The constitution of the towns appears to be..a mixture of those of the shire, hundred and parish. 1819 *Boston Centinel* 31 July (Thornton), The crops of hay in the lower towns were in all parts heavy. 1822 Z. Hawley *Tour [in Ohio]* 33 (ibid.) The timber of these towns is beech..and black walnut. 1882 W. D. Howells in *Longm. Mag.* I. 42 In New England the 'town' is the township, and there are some 'towns' in which there is no village at all. 1888 Bryce *Amer. Commw.* II. ii. xlviii. 226 The Town is..a rural, not an urban community. ..Its population is usually small. *Ibid., note,* In New England the word 'town' is the legal and usual one; in the rest of the country 'township'. *Ibid.* 240 The words 'town' and 'township' signify [in Illinois, etc.] a territorial division of the county, incorporated for purposes of local government. 1890 Hosmer *Anglo-Sax. Freed.* 192 Each Massachusetts town sent a representative to a central assembly at Boston. 1906 W. Churchill *Coniston* i. v, The town of Coniston..was a tract of country about ten miles by ten, the most thickly settled portion of which was the village of Coniston, consisting of twelve houses.

**7.** *fig.* and *transf.* (from 4). **a.** Something analogous to a town as being the home of many people.

1890 W. J. Gordon *Foundry* 75 The ship is a flying town, self-contained and independent of outside aid. 1898 Kipling in *Daily News* 7 Nov. 5/2 That which was a line has suddenly become a town on the waters.

**b.** An assemblage of burrows of prairie-dogs, nests of penguins, etc.

1808 Pike *Sources Mississ.* ii. (1810) 156 *note*, The Wishtonwish of the Indians, prairie dogs of some travellers.. reside on the prairies of Louisiana in towns or villages. 1812 Brackenridge *Views Louisiana* (1814) 58 The Prairie dog ..lives in burrows, or as they are commonly called towns. 1839 Marryat *Phant. Ship* xviii, These [penguins] were in myriads on some parts of the island, which, from the propinquity of their nests..went by the name of *towns*. 1890 W. P. Lett in *Big Game N. Amer.* 470 Danger occasioned by badger-holes and prairie-dog towns.

**8.** Phrases. (See also 4 b.) **a.** *To come* († *go*) *to town*, to make one's appearance, arrive, come in; † to 'come to stay', to become common (*obs.*). Cf. *to come to land* (Land *sb.*[2] d).

Prob. the original notion was 'come to our village, come to dwell with us, come to the dwellings of men'. In later times associated with the later sense of *town* (4 b).

*a* 1000 *Menologium* (Gr.) 8 Se kalendus cymeð..on þam ylcan dæȝe us to tune. *c* 1050 *Byrhtferth's Handboc* in *Anglia* VIII. 312/19 Lengten tima..gæð to tune on vii. id'. febr'. *c* 1200 Ormin 9160 Allse bidell birrþ beon sennd To ȝarrkenn & to greȝȝþenn Onnȝæn hiss Laferrd þær þær he Shall cumenn sket to tune. *a* 1275 *Prov. Ælfred* 534 in *O. E. Misc.* 133 Elde cumið to tune mid fele unkeþe costes. *a* 1300 *Cursor M.* 14277 'Crist', sco said, 'es cummen to tun'. *c* 1475 *Rauf Coilȝear* 349 Folkis..Thankand God.. Thair Lord was gane to toun. 1600 *Newe Metamorphosis* (MS.) (Farmer), This first was court-like, now 'tis come to towne; 'Tis common growne with every country clowne. 1851 D. Jerrold *St. Giles* ii. 11 I've been quite in the way of babies to-night,..young master's come to town. 1905 *Daily Chron.* 11 Mar. 4/6 This Thrums sketch proved to delighted Londoners that J. M. Barrie had 'come to town'.

**b.** *Man about town* (also formerly *young fellow, youth, girl about town*), one who is constantly seen at public and private assemblies in 'town'; one who is in the round of social functions, fashionable dissipations, etc. (cf. d. (*a*)).

*c* 1645 Howell *Lett.* (1650) II. 94, I was a youth about the Town when he undertook that expedition. 1749 Lady Luxborough *Let. to Shenstone* 28 Nov., Miss Jenny Hamilton, a pretty girl about town. 1766 Goldsm. *Vic. W.* xx, I'll show you forty very dull fellows about town that live by it [authorship] in opulence. 1769 Chesterf. *Let. to Godson* 6 Sept., There are now two sorts of young fellows about Town, who call themselves Bucks and Bloods. 1844 Dickens *Mart. Chuz.* xxvi, He was quite the man-about-town of the conversation. 1889 W. Roberts *Hist. Eng. Bookselling* 121 Wits, men-about-town, and fashionable notabilities.

**c.** *Man* or *woman* (*girl*) *of the town*: one belonging to the shady or 'fast' side of town life.

*a* 1700 B. E. *Dict. Cant. Crew, Man o' th' Town*, a Lew'd Spark, or very Debaushe. *a* 1704 T. Brown *Dial. Dead* Wks. 1730 II. 313, I have been a man of the town..and admitted into the family of the rakehellonians. 1766 Goldsm. *Vic. W.* xx, The lady was only a woman of the town. 1785 Grose *Dict. Vulg. T., Man of the town*, a rake, a debauchee. *Ibid., Woman of the town, or..of pleasure*, a prostitute. 1817–18 Cobbett *Resid. U. S.* (1822) 239 Never is there seen in the streets what is called in England, a girl of the town.

**d.** *On the town*: (*a*) in the swing of fashionable life, pleasure, or dissipation; (*b*) getting a living by prostitution, thieving, or the like; cf. *on the streets*; (*c*) chargeable to the parish (*dial.*). So *to come upon the town*.

1712 Steele *Spect.* No. 266 ⁋ 2 This Creature is what they call newly come upon the Town. 1727 Gay *Begg. Op.* ii. iv, I han't been so long upon the Town. 1819 *Metropolis* I. 213 She had got with her a listening novice on town. *Ibid.* II. 167 We have a man looked up to-day..in the Gazette in three months, and on the town again, brighter than ever. 1842 Egan *Capt. Macheath, J. Flashman* (Farmer), Jack long was on the town, a teazer; Could turn his fives to anything, Nap a reader, or filch a ring. 1843 R. J. Graves *Syst. Clin. Med.* xxvi. 333 Prostitutes who had been a long time on the town. 1855 Thackeray *Newcomes* x, Five-and-twenty years ago the young Earl of Kew came upon the town, which speedily rang with the feats of his Lordship.

**e.** *Town and tower, tower and town*: see Tower *sb.*[1] 9 a.

**9.** *attrib.* and *Comb.* **a.** Simple attrib. passing into adj. use (now usually without hyphen): Of, pertaining to, or characteristic of the town (as distinct from some other place or community, esp. the country); that is or lives in towns or the town; urban.

1468 *Medulla Gram., Comedia*, a toun song. 1560 Daus tr. *Sleidane's Comm.* 160 The towne wiues, whan they go to here Masse, cary with them bokes of Latin prayers. 1594 Hooker *Eccl. Pol.* Pref. ii. § 3 One of the Towne-Ministers, that saw in what manner the people were bent for the reuocation of Caluine. 1673 *Charac. Coffee-house* (title-p.) The Symptomes of a Town-wit. 1693 J. Dunton *Athenian Merc.* 14 Nov., The ridiculous Folly of our Town-Sparks who make an Oath their Argument. 1702 Steele *Funeral* iii. i. 44 She has of a sudden left her Dayry, and sets up for a fine Town-Lady. 1710–11 *Examiner* No. 30 Lewdness and intemperance are not of so bad consequences in a town-rake as in a divine. 1753 *World* No. 3 ⁋ 2 According to the town-acceptation of the term. 1794 W. Felton *Carriages* (1801) II. iii. § 2. 35 A neat ornamented, or town coach. 1844 Wardlaw *Lect. Prov.* (1869) II. 16 Town missions and country missions. 1848 Mill *Pol. Econ.* Prel. Rem. (1876) 9 These [agricultural communities of ancient Europe]..were mostly small town-communities. 1848 Thackeray *Van. Fair* v, He fought the town-boys. 1855 Macaulay *Hist. Eng.* xiv. III. 493 The difference.. between a town divine and a country divine. 1867 H. Latham *Black & White* 100 Houses which look like the town-residences of well-to-do gentry. 1887 A. Jenks in *Lippincott's Mag.* Aug. 295 These performances were very attractive to old graduates and town-people. 1897 *Allbutt's Syst. Med.* II. 842 It is safer to take a lower standard for the average town inhabitant.

**b.** attrib. in sense 'of or belonging to a town as a community or place', as *town armoury, back, bell, charge, church, clock, close, dike, drummer, father, field, folk, green, herd, loan* (Loan *sb.*[2] 2), *mead, moor, mote* (Moot *sb.*[1] 2), *piper, plate* (Plate *sb.* 17), *pump, relief, seal, stocks, swineherd, wait, watch, wharf.*

1596 Shaks. *Tam. Shr.* iii. ii. 47 An olde rusty sword tane out of the *Towne Armory. 1577 Holinshed *Chron.* II. 475/2 All their horsemen issued out of the *towne backe with certayne footemen. 1483 *Cely Papers* (Camden) 137 To be redy in harnesse as sone as the *towne bell ryngygth. 1877 Green *Hist. Eng. People* I. 298 Its citizens mustered at the call of the town-bell at Saint Paul's. 1619 *Min. Archdeaconry of Colchester* lf. 104 b (MS.), The some of viij d. toward a rate for *towne charge which the Churchwardens of Alresford haue layd out. [1045 *Will of Thurstan* in Thorpe *Charters* 572 þat [lond]..after here bothere day into þe *tunkirke, and þo men fre.] 1888 P. Schaff *Hist. Chr. Ch.* VI. xxvii. 136 He preached both in the Convent and in the town-church. 1779 *Mirror* No. 41 ⁋ 1 He..had been regulating his watch by our *town-clock. 1716 Addison *Drummer* i. i, I verily believe I saw him last night in the *Town-close. 1801 *Farmer's Mag.* Jan. 10 The horses, cattle, sheep, and swine..are not to be suffered to go loose within *town-dikes. 1872 C. Gibbon *For the King* i, Bauldy Dodholm, the *town-drummer, at their head. 1892 *Pall Mall G.* 15 June 6/1 At the station the *town-fathers [cf. Father *sb.* 10] offered her some refreshments. 1297 R. Glouc. (Rolls) 1582 Þo wende vorþ þe *toun folc. 1902 'J. Halsham' *Lonewood Corner* 33 Town-folk foundered in these drenched wood-paths. 1641 *N. Riding Rec.* 212 A yeoman presented for an encroachment on the *towne-greene by building a barn to the damage of the inhabitants. 1822 Galt *Provost* xxxvii, Tammy Tout, the *town-herd. 1812 W. Tennant *Anster F.* i. lv, Hobbling in each *town-loan in awkward guise. 1822 Galt *Provost* xlvi, A considerable portion of the *town moor. 1879 Green *Read. Eng. Hist.* xiv. 67 The burgesses gathered in *town-mote when the bell swung out from St. Paul's. 1701 *Lond. Gaz.* No. 3729/4 A *Town-plate of about 15l. value will be Run for at the same Place. 1810 Crabbe *Borough* xxi. 171 For *town-relief the grieving man applied, And begg'd with tears, what some with scorn denied. 1594 Hooker *Eccl. Pol.* Pref. ii. § 5 By common consent of their whole Senate, and that under their *Towne-Seale. 1821 Scott *Kenilw.* ii, To get your legs made acquainted with the *town-stocks. 1825 — *Betrothed* vii, He blows like a *town swineherd. *a* 1805 A. Carlyle *Autobiog.* (1860) 75 His band..consisted of two dancing-school fiddlers and the *town-waits. 1560 Rolland *Seven Sag.* 73 Gif I be heir now with the *toun watche found. 1531 *Lett. & Pap. Hen. VIII*, V. 184 Caryng of rubys out of the towne to the *towne wharffis.

**c.** objective and obj. genitive, as *town-builder, -taker; -destroying, -frequenting, -going, -keeping, -loving, -taking* sbs. and adjs.; see also Town-planning; instrumental, etc., as *town-dotted, -flanked, -girdled, -sick, -stained* adjs.; locative, similative, etc., as *town-bred, -cured, -imprisoned, -killed, -like, -looking, -pent, -spent, -tied, -trained* adjs.; see also Town-born, Town-dweller.

1685 Bowles *Theocritus' Idyllium* xx. 43 in *Dryden's Misc.* ii. 390 How nice these *Town-bred Women are, how vain! 1869 *Routledge's Ev. Boy's Ann.* 396 Smart, active fellows, but thoroughly town-bred. 1905 *Daily News* 14 Jan. 4 Painter of sea and shore and *town-flanked river. 1895 *Athenæum* 27 Apr. 530/2 The Danes were a *town-frequenting people. 1812 W. Tennant *Anster F.* iii. xxiv, Fife's *town-girdled shire. 1838 Mary Howitt *Birds & Fl., Sunshine* i, *Town-imprisoned men. 1899 *Daily News* 23 May 4/6 For *town-keeping people the cart-horse parade was one of the prettiest sights of the day. 1899 *Q. Rev.* Oct. 480 *Town-killed meat is a diminishing element. *c* 1000 *Ælfric's Voc.* in Wr.-Wülcker 127/15 *Comedia*, racu, *tunlic spæc. 1876 A. Plummer tr. *Döllinger's Hippolytus* ii. 73 All that has any townlike appearance relates to Ostia. 1849 J. Forbes *Physic. Holiday* v. (1850) 47 Waldshut is a neater and more *town-looking place than we had yet passed through. 1649 G. Daniel *Trinarch., Hen. V* cli, The *Towne-pent Rutters, willingly enlarge Their Quarters. 1840 T. A. Trollope *Summ. Brittany* I. 71 As enchanting a cottage..as *town-sick mortal ever dreamed of. 1654 tr. *Scudery's Curia Pol.* 5 That antient Captaine, which the Greekes stiled the *Towntaker. 1849 J. Forbes *Physic. Holiday* i. (1850) 5 That..I may induce some of my *town-tied friends to do as I have done.

**10.** Special combs.: † **town-adjutant**, formerly, a garrison officer, ranking as lieutenant, charged with certain routine duties; cf. Town-major; **town-bound** *a.*, (*a*) bound or confined to town; (*b*) townward bound; **town-box**, the town chest; the public funds of a town; **town-bull**, a bull formerly kept in turn by the cow-keepers of a village; hence *fig.* of a man; **town-bushel**, a local standard bushel measure; cf. Bushel *sb.*[1] 1; † **town-child**, a child born in the town (where a school is founded, and thus sometimes entitled to be a free scholar); **town-council**, the elective deliberative and administrative body of a town: cf. Council 10; hence **town-councillor**, a member of a town-council; **town-crier**, a public crier; = Crier 2 b; **town-cross**, the market cross of a town; **town-dab** (*local*), the lemon-sole; **town-foot**, the lower end of a town or village; **town-guard**, (*a*) *Sc. Hist.*, the military or quasi-military guard of a town; (*b*) the guard policing a garrison-town; also *attrib.*; **town-head**, the upper end of a town or village; † **town-husband** (*local*): see quot.; **town-life**, life in a town; *spec.* the social life of a town; **town-liver**, one who lives in a town; **town-living**, town-life; also an ecclesiastical benefice in a town (Living *vbl. sb.* 5); **town-mouse**, *fig.* a dweller in a town, esp. as unfamiliar with country life (in allusion to Æsop's fable); **town-officer**, (*a*) an officer (of excise) posted in a town; (*b*) in New England, a selectman; (*c*) *Sc.* an officer charged with keeping public order (cf. Town-major, *town-guard*); **town-park**: see Park *sb.* 3 a; also *attrib.*; **town-piece** [Piece *sb.* 13], a token issued by or current in a town; **town-place** (*dial.*): see quots.; **town-plat, town-plot** (*U.S.*), a plan of a township: cf. Plat *sb.*[3] 2, Plot *sb.* 3; **town-reeve** (now *Hist.*), the bailiff or steward of a *tún*; **town-row**, the sequence of houses in a town, or of homesteads in a parish or manor; also *fig.* the roll of townsmen: see quots. and cf. House-row; † **town-side**, the land close beside a town; **town-site**, the site of a town; *spec.* in U. S. and Canada, a tract of land set apart by legal authority to be occupied by a town, and (usually) surveyed and laid out with streets, etc.; **town-skip**, a jocular name for a city urchin; **town-taking**, the taking of a town; hence *town-taking day* at Hull, the anniversary of the day on which that city was secured for William of Orange; **town-tallow**, English, as distinct from continental tallow; †**town-top**, a whipping-top kept for public use: = *parish-top* (PARISH *sb.* 7); **town-way**, the way to the town; **town-weed**, a name for Dog's Mercury; †**town-widow**, ? a widow supported by public charity; **town-woman**, a woman of the town, a prostitute. See also TOWN BOOK, -CLERK, -GATE, HALL, etc.

**1737** *Town-Adjutant [see TOWN-MAJOR]. **1801** *Brit. Mil. Libr.* II. s. v., The Town-Adjutant is an assistant to the Town-Major. **1858** A. MACMILLAN *Lett.* (1908) 3 Poor *town-bound mechanics and shopmen. **1905** *Westm. Gaz.* 17 Oct. 7/1 There was a breakdown in the Town-bound trams at Balham. **1659** GAUDEN *Tears Ch.* **ij, Upon the confiscation of them to their *Town-box or Exchequer. **1597** SHAKS. *2 Hen. IV*, II. ii. 172 A Kinswoman of my Masters...Euen such Kin, as the Parish Heyfors are to the *Towne-Bull? **1611** COTGR. s. v. *Bannier*, *Taureau bannier*, a common, or town, bull. **1709** *Brit. Apollo* II. No. 55. 2/2 As dull as a Dormouse at hom, but a vary toun Bull abroad. **1647** FULLER *Gd. Th. in Worse T.* (1841) 136 As the *town-bushel is the standard both to measure corn and other bushels by. **1886** *Dict. Nat. Biog.* VIII. 277/1 Entered at Christ's Hospital, probably as a '*town child' or 'free scholar'. **1681** *Acts Parlt. Scotl.* VIII. 411/2 Ane Act of the *Town Council of the Burgh of Dumbartan in favors of the trades therof. **1775** A. BURNABY *Trav.* 75 *note*, Each township is managed by a town-council. **1851**, **1863** [see COUNCIL 10]. **1874** GREEN *Short Hist.* iv. § 4. 188 Their merchant-gild..acted, in fact, pretty much the same part as a town-council of to-day. **1850** J. WILSON *Annals of Hawick* an. 1727, Walter Scott, *town councillor, is degraded as such by the council..in respect of his twice breaking prison, after being convict by the bailies of a riot. **1602** SHAKS. *Ham.* III. ii. 4, I had as liue the *Town-Cryer had spoke my Lines. **1867** TROLLOPE *Chron. Barset* II. lix. 166 Her secret had been published, as it were, by the town-crier. **1836** YARRELL *Brit. Fishes* II. 222 [Lemon, or Smooth Dab] is taken on the Sussex coast, where it is known by the name of *Town-Dab. **1805** FORSYTH *Beauties Scotl.* I. 107 To raise, for the defence of the city [Edinburgh], a corps of no fewer than 126 men, .. which is called the *town-guard. **1811** *Gen. Regul. & Ord. Army* 101 An Adjutant of the Day is to be furnished from the Regiment which gives the Town Guard, or the Commander in Chief's Guard. **1818** SCOTT *Hrt. Midl.* v[i], There was a sentinel upon guard, who, that one town-guard soldier might do his duty.., presented his piece, and desired the foremost of the rioters to stand off. **1905** *Blackw. Mag.* July 100 Not far from the Tolbooth stood the Town Guard House. **1847–78** HALLIWELL, **Town-husband*, an officer of a parish who collects the moneys from the parents of illegitimate children for the maintenance of the latter. *East.* **1693** *Humours Town* 103 You have none of these in your *Town-life. **1779** *Mirror* No. 58 ¶ 5 Emilia had acquired a stronger attachment to the pleasures of a town life, than was..right in itself. **1620** E. BLOUNT *Horæ Subs.* 153 Riding, Shooting,..some *towne-liuers, sometimes make hard shift to practise. **1832** J. J. BLUNT *Sk. Reform. Eng.* iv. 65 Thus it came to pass that *town livings (contrary to all reason) are at present, of all others, the poorest. **1863** E. FITZGERALD *Lett.* (1889) I. 290, I suppose Town-living makes one alive to such a Change. **1857** HUGHES *Tom Brown* II. iii, Here's Arthur, a regular young *town-mouse with a natural taste for the woods. **1887** LD. CHURCHILL in *Times* (weekly ed.) 24 June 9/1 What I shall call a town mouse like myself. **1737** J. CHAMBERLAYNE *St. Gt. Brit.* II. (ed. 33) 84 Chief Examiner of *Town-Officers Books for London Brewery. *a* **1817** T. DWIGHT *Trav. New Eng.* (1821) I. 243 On the refusal, death, or removal, of a Town-Officer, a meeting is to be holden for..choosing another. **1864** A. MCKAY *Hist. Kilmarnock* (1880) 235 The procession was headed by Mr. Paton, town-officer, on a gallant charger. **1870** *Act* 33–4 *Vict.* c. 46 § 15 Any demesne land, or any holding ordinarily termed '*townparks' adjoining or near to any city or town. **1887** *Act* 50–1 *Vict.* c. 33 § 9 A holding shall not be deemed to constitute a town park, though within the definition of the expression 'Town parks',..if it is let and used as an ordinary agricultural farm. **1887** in *Pall Mall G.* 24 Mar. 13/2 To secure the just rights of the town park holders. **1805** *Brathwait's Barnabees Jrnl.* Introd. (1818) 42 A Harrington was a *town piece, tradesman's token, or other small coin current in the early part of the seventeenth century. **1787** GROSE *Provinc. Gloss.*, **Town-place*, a farm-yard. *Cornw.* **1867** R. S. HAWKER *Prose Wks.* (1893) 109 There dwelt in scattered villages, or town-places.., the bold and hardy Keltic people. **1880** COUCH *E. Cornw. Words*, *Town*, *Town-place*, applied to the smallest hamlet, and even to a farm-yard. *a* **1817** T. DWIGHT *Trav. New Eng.*, etc. (1821) II. 335 The *town-plat is originally distributed into lots, containing from two to ten acres. **1714** in *Hist. Northfield, Mass.* (1875) 134 That the *Town-Plot be stated in the old place, in such form and measure as the Committee can allow it, according to the Court's order. *c* **890** tr. *Bæda's Hist.* v. xi. [x.] (1890) 416 Þa onfoeng hio se *tunȝerefa. *c* **1000** *Ags. Gosp.* Luke xvi. 18 Ða herede se hlaford þære unrihtwisness tunȝerefan. **1861** PEARSON *Early & Mid. Ages Eng.* 100 A few adventurers even sailed to Dorchester, 787 A.D., and slew the town-reeve when he sought to call them to account. **1610** BP. HALL *Apol. Brownists* § 52 To bee ranged in the same *Towne-rowes, with Iewes, Arrians, Anabaptists. **1825** JAMIESON, *Toun-raw*, used to denote the privileges of a Town-ship. *To thraw one's self out o' a toun-raw*, to forfeit the privileges enjoyed in a small community. **1886** *S. W. Linc. Gloss.* s. v. *Town-row*, *By Town-row*, or *by House-row*, was the term for the old plan for keeping men off the parish when work was scarce, by finding them so many days' work at each farm in turn. **1523** FITZHERB. *Husb.* § 10 If it be veray ranke grounde, as is moche at euery *towne syde, where catel doth resort. **1657** W. COLES *Adam in Eden* cxxxi, The fifth groweth..by hedge sides and path wayes, in fields and town-sides. **1872** RAYMOND *Statist. Mines & Mining* 170 The Silver State Mining Company..have located a *town-site—Crystal City ..—on the old Salt Lake route. **1878** *N. Amer. Rev.* CXXVII. 445 The improvement of town-sites. **1896** WRENN in *Critic* (U. S.) 31 Oct. 270/1 We have made a plan of Trilby Townsite, Pasco Co., Fl[orid]a. **1837** DICKENS *Pickw.* xxvi, 'Well, young *townskip', said Sam, 'how's mother?' **1788** G. HADLEY *Hist. Kingston-upon-Hull* xxi. 277 Thus by the spirited conduct of the Protestant officers, was Hull preserved, on the 4th of December, 1688; which is still observed as a holiday, under the appellation of *Towns Taking Day. **1866** J. J. SLEAHAN *Hist. Hull* (ed. 2) 188. **1912** *Times* 19 Dec. 20/4 To-day's 'Market Letter' quotes—*town tallow, 33s. 6d. per cwt. **1623–33** FLETCHER & SHIRLEY *Night-Walker* I. iii, He..dances like a *town-top, and reels and hobbles. **1670** EVELYN *Sylva* xx. 92 For the Turner, Kyele-pins, great Town-Topps. *a* **1780** BLACKSTONE *Note on Shaks.'s Twel. N.* I. iii. 44 To sleep like a town-top. **1598** SHAKS. *Merry W.* III. i. 7 *Euans.* Which way haue you look'd..? *Sim.*..Euery way but the *Towne-way. **1861** MISS PRATT *Flower. Pl.* V. 3 Perennial or Dog's Mercury...From the growth of the plant in towns and town gardens, it is sometimes called *Town-weed. **1632** BROME *North. Lasse* I. i, [She] has been the *Town-widow these Three years. **1675** WYCHERLEY *Country Wife* II. i, What! you would have her as impudent as yourself?..a mere notorious *town-woman? **1710** ADDISON *Tatler* No. 260 ¶ 11 To regard every Town-Woman as a particular Kind of Siren.

II. Combinations with *town's*, as *townschildren*, *townsfolk*, *town's-hall*, *town's-piper*; **town's-bairn**, a native of the (or one's own) town (*Sc.*); so **town's-boy**, **town's-fellow**, in similar sense; †**town's husband**, obs. title of a borough official having charge of the accounts, etc.: cf. HUSBAND *sb.* 4; †**town's-like** (†**towneslike**) *a.*, townish, townly; **town's-money**, the public funds of a town; **townswoman**, a woman inhabitant of a town; with possessive, a woman of the same town. See also *town's-book* (Sc. *townis buk*) s. v. TOWN BOOK, *town's-end* s. v. TOWN-END, TOWNSMAN, TOWNSPEOPLE.

**1808** J. MAYNE *Siller Gun* III. xvi, M'Ghee, our ain *town's-bairn. **1822** SCOTT *Nigel* iii, He was a kindly Scot himsell, and, what is more, a town's-bairn o' the gude town. **1764** *Mem. G. Psalmanazar* 90 Having acquainted four or five of our clan that were my *townsboys with my design. **1857** GLADSTONE in *Westm. Gaz.* 20 May (1898) 3/3 [Mr. Gladstone gave an address to the assembled pupils in the large lecture-hall, and invented a new phrase by addressing us as] 'fellow townsboys'. **1837** SIR F. PALGRAVE *Merch. & Friar* i. (1844) 23 He found them in the yard, where they were absolutely beset by townsmen, townswomen, and *townschildren. **1906** *Academy* 7 Apr. 328/1 Townschildren and nurses are often woefully ignorant on the subject of edible berries. **1850** ALLINGHAM *Poems, Dream* ii, On they passed, .. *Townsfellows all from first to last. **1737** SWIFT *Let. to Richardson* 30 Apr., That the *townsfolks and tenants of the estate round Colrane would be content to double the rent. **1833** HT. MARTINEAU *Berkeley the Banker* I. i, The new banker..could not know so much of the characters of the townsfolks as he who had lived among them. **1866** ROGERS *Agric. & Prices* I. xxvii. 653 Some common market in which the agent for the townsfolk purchased country produce. **1812** J. BIGLAND *Beauties Eng. & Wales* XVI. 412 A large room, now used as a *town's hall. **1757** in *N. & Q.* 7th Ser. VIII. 447/2 James Mihill, *Town's Husband [buried at Beverley]. **1795** *Hull Advertiser* 8 Aug. ibid. 496/1 Wanted by the Corporation of this Town, a proper person for the office of Town's Husband, or Common Officer. **1833** [see HUSBAND *sb.* 4]. **1574** HELLOWES *Gueuara's Fam. Ep.* 296 The good *towneslike craftsman, needes no daughter in lawe that can fril and paint hirselfe. *c* **1600** *Maldon MS. Records* in *Essex Herald* 9 May (1905) 7/5 [One of Cade's charges against the authorities was] spending of *townes's-money against their lawful preacher. **1819** W. TENNANT *Papistry Storm'd* I. (1827) 7 The *town's piper, wi' a blatter. **1684** BUNYAN *Pilgr.* II. 73 And this..is one of my *Towns-Women. **1834** H. MILLER *Scenes & Leg.* xx. (1857) 292 Well-known resorts of his townswomen. **1837** [see *townschildren* above].

Hence (*nonce-wds.*) **Tow·neen** [with Irish dim. suffix], **Towne·tte**, **Tow·nikin** [after G. *städtchen*], diminutives of *town*; **Tow·nhood**, the condition or status of a town.

**1893** J. A. BARRY *S. Brown's Bunyip*, etc. 120 An' thin.. Jillibeejee is as ructious a *towneen as is on God's earth. **1839** LADY LYTTON *Cheveley* (ed. 2) II. i. 5 Though not quite a town, it was something more than a village: the French call those mule-like domiciles, between a house and a bandbox, *maisonnettes*, and I don't see why Blichingly should not be called a **townette*. **1880** J. B. HARWOOD *Yng. Ld. Penrith* xiii, It would be unreasonable to expect a tiny townette such as Ireport to engage as the chief of its police a man of tact as well as energy. **1865** E. BURRITT *Walk Land's End* 203 The first centuries of its *townhood..mellow off under the horizon of the past. **1891** KATE FIELD *Washington* IV. 383/1 At the time of my visit, L—— had just attained the dignity of townhood. **1863** H. MAYHEW *Germ. Life & Mann.* (1864) I. 5 The little village..lying far away on the moors..from which the *townikin..is said to derive its name.

**Town**, *v. rare.* (Only in *pa. pple.* Towned.) [f. prec. sb.] *trans.* **a.** To furnish with towns. **b.** To make into or constitute (a community) a town.

**1585** R. LANE *Let.* in Hakluyt *Voy.* (1600) III. 254 The continent is of an huge and vnknowen greatnesse, and very well peopled and towned. **1633** P. FLETCHER *Purple Isl.* II. xv, With many a citie grac't, and fairly town'd. **1897** I. O. REICHEL in *Trans. Devon. Assoc.* XXIX. 458 There were reeves of various kinds..the town-reeve in a 'towned' village.

**Town**, obs. form of TUN.

**Town-adjutant** to **-bell**: see TOWN 9, 10.

**Townage**, obs. Sc. var. of TOWNISH.

**Town book.** Also 6 *Sc.* townis buk. A book in which the records of a town are kept.

*a* **1547** in J. R. Boyle *Hedon* (1875) App. 72 All suche re[n]talles, presidences, or towne bookes as they had in theire kepinge. **1567** *Reg. Privy Council Scot.* I. 506 The townis bukis, court bukis, and scrollis. **1641** *Rhode Isl. Col. Rec.* (1856) I. 114 Ordered, that each Towne shall provide a Towne Book, wherein they shall Record the Evidences of the Lands by them impropriated. **1765** *Univ. Mag.* XXXVII. 377/1 That this vote be recorded in the town book. **1816** SINGER *Hist. Cards* 41 The Old Town Books of the Suabian and Franconian cities.

**Tow·n-born**, *a.* Born in a or the town.

**1579** LYLY *Euphues* (Arb.) 50 Philautus being a towne borne childe..crept into credit with Don Ferardo one of the chiefe gouernours of the citie. **1674** in *N. & Q.* 9th Ser. IX. 463/1 A free School to teach 20 poor town-born children born in Westminster. **1821** LAMB *Elia* Ser. I. *Old & New Schoolm.*, From the circumstance of my being town-born.

**Town-bound** to **-church**: see TOWN 9, 10.

**Tow·n-cle·rk.** The clerk or secretary to the corporation of a town, who has charge of the records, correspondence, and legal business, the conduct of municipal elections, etc.

**1343** *Inq. ad q. d.* 268/18 in *List* (1904) 399 [Si concedamus Thome de Legh de Oxonia] tounclerk. **13..** *S. Eng. Leg.* (MS. Bodl. 779) in Herrig's *Archiv* LXXXII. 419/17 Þey him made toun-clerke..Alle aȝen his wille. **1433** *Rolls of Parlt.* IV. 476/1 Charged bi the Toun Clerk for the tyme beyng. **1526** TINDALE *Acts* xix. 35 When the toune clarcke [Gr. γραμματεύς] had cessed the people he sayd: Ye men of Ephesus [etc.]. **1631** *High Commission Cases* (Camden) 198 This cause was prosecuted by some of the towne of Stamford, of which the towne clarke was one. **1835** *Act* 5 & 6 *Will. IV*, c. 76 § 58 That the Council of every Borough.. shall appoint a fit Person..to be the Town Clerk of such Borough, who shall hold his Office during Pleasure.

**b.** = PARISH CLERK. *dial. rare.* Cf. TOWN *sb.* 3.

**1597** *Min. Archdeaconry of Essex* lf. 237 (MS.), He willfully deniethe the paiment of the vsuall clerk's wages to father God our towne clerk. **1597–8** *Min. Archdeaconry of Colchester* lf. 186 b (MS.), Great Chishill..Richard Watson..allegavit that he is towneclerk there. **1879** D. J. HILL *Bryant* 55 [Bryant] being himself at the time, the town-clerk, he was placed in the embarrassing position of having to proclaim his own nuptials.

Hence **Tow·n-cle·rkship**, the office of town-clerk.

**1439** *Coventry Leet Bk.* 192 They ordeyne that Symkyn Birches enjoy and haue off the office off Toun-clerkship terme of hys lyffe. **1521** *Maldon, Essex, Liber B.* lf. 57 b (MS.), The office of towneclerkshipp for this yere followynge. **1817** W. TAYLOR in *Monthly Rev.* LXXXIII. 496 The town-clerk-ship having become vacant.

**Town-clock** to **-councillor**: see TOWN 9, 10.

†**Town-cress.** *Obs.* Forms: see TOWN and CRESS. [OE. *túncressa*, f. *tún* garden, TOWN + CRESS.] Garden Cress (*Lepidium sativum*).

*a* **700** *Epinal Gloss.* (O.E.T.) 676 *Nasturcium*.., tuuncressa. *c* **725** *Corpus Gloss.* 1359 Tuuncressa. *c* **1000** *Sax. Leechd.* II. 22 ȝenim..tun cersan, sio þe self weaxeð, & mon ne sæwð. *c* **1420** *Liber Cocorum* (1862) 42 Take therto Town cresses, and cresses that growene in flode. **1533** ELYOT *Cast. Helth* (1541) 90 Let him eate hartyly small radysshe rootes, townkersis,..or purslane. **1578** LYTE *Dodoens* I. lxiv. 96 The Swines Cresses..is hoate and dry, like to garden or towne Cressis. *Ibid.* v. lix. 623. **1615** MARKHAM *Eng. Housew.* II. i. (1668) 30 Take the powder of Town cress dried. **1620** VENNER *Via Recta* vii. 158 Towne-Cresses, or as the vulgar sort doe pronounce, Town-karsse, is more byting in taste then Rocket.

**Town-crier** to **-dike**: see TOWN 9, 10.

**Towndir, -dire**, obs. Sc. forms of TINDER.

**Town-ditch.** Now *Hist.* The ditch or moat surrounding a walled town.

**1423** *Coventry Leet Bk.* 48 Poody-Crofte, þe wich lieth from Crow-lane vnto a diche, þat is callyd the town diche in breid. **1568** GRAFTON *Chron.* II. 1349 Ridley and Latimer ..were sone condempned, and after burned in the towne Diche at Oxforde. **1603** HOLLAND *Plutarch's Mor.* 466 At the verie instant there was espied an hare, running crosse over the towne ditch. **1680** C. NESSE *Church-Hist.* 213 Oh that our reformers had cast all Romish reliques into the town-ditch!

**Town-drummer**: see TOWN 9 b.

**Tow·n-dwe·ller.** One who dwells in a town; a townsman.

**1483** *Cely Papers* (Camden) 146 Sarten Town dwellers of Callez hath ben at Bruges. **1550** in Strype *Eccl. Mem.* (1721) II. App. QQ. 142 To take their answers, and the proofs of the said town-dwellers. **1623** MIDDLETON *More Dissemb. Besides Wom.* IV. i, Th' unhous'd race of fortune-tellers May never fail to cheat town-dwellers. **1891** C. JAMES *Rom. Rigmarole* 2 No jaded town-dweller..would grudge the few shillings. **1912** *Times* 19 Oct. 7/3 The ignorance of town-dwellers about the elementary facts of rural economy is astounding.

So **Tow·n-dwe·lling** *a.*

**1899** *Westm. Gaz.* 27 Feb. 2/3 The town-dwelling Westminsterians have beaten the rural Carthusians twice running at football.

**Towne**, obs. form of TOWN, TUN.

**Townee** (taunī·). [f. TOWN *sb.* + -EE.] A townsman, esp. as distinguished from a member of the university: cf. TOWNY *sb.* 2.

**1897** *Westm. Gaz.* 13 May 6/3 The 'townees' [at Oxford] had notified their intention of breaking all undecorated windows. **1900** G. SWIFT *Somerley* 69 Mr. Bobber, a Cambridge grocer,..considered that there was one law for the collegian and another for the 'townee'. **1902** *Daily Chron.* 16 Aug. 8/3 Just of as much importance is comfortable footgear to the townee as to the dweller in the country.

**Towneen, Townette**: see under TOWN *sb.*

**Town-end.** Now *dial.* Also town's end. The end of the main street of a town or village; one of the extremities of a town.

*c* 1440 *Alphabet of Tales* 330 Þe fflawme at had burnyd all þe town-end..sesid. **1591** *Reg. Privy Council Scot.* IV. 625 Quha..raid away with him oute at the toun end of Sanctandrois. **1818** Scott *Hrt. Midl.* xxxi[i], She's fast in the stocks at Barkston town-end. **1886** *S. W. Linc. Gloss.* s. v., There's a pinfold at the town-end.

**1421** *Coventry Leet Bk.* 30 Ne þat no man..lay no dong at the townsend in no placys, but without the stakes..beyond the Frer gate. **1472** *Paston Lett.* III. 71, I have begonne to felle asshe at the townes ende. **1621** Sanderson *Serm. 1 Cor. vii. 24* § 21 Our idle sturdy rogues, and vagrant towns-end beggars. **1760–72** H. Brooke *Fool of Qual.* (1809) IV. 55 Yonder church-yard below the town's end.

**Tow-net** (tōu·net), *sb.* [f. Tow *sb.*[4] or *v.*[1] + Net *sb.*[1]] A drag-net or dredge used for the collection of natural specimens. Hence **Tow-ne·t** *v., trans.* to drag with a tow-net; *intr.* to use a tow-net; whence **Tow·-netter, Tow·-netting** *vbl. sb.*

**1816** Tuckey *Narr. Exped. R. Zaire* i. (1818) 9 The townet was put overboard, and collected some of these animals. **1883** C. F. Holder in *Harper's Mag.* Jan. 186/2 Dr. Bennet..captured a specimen in a tow-net. **1891** Herdman in *Nature* 23 July 274/1 While townetting during the last few days about the North Cape, we have had some large hauls of Copepoda. **1894** *Q. Rev.* Apr. 367 The direct evidence of tow-netting the upper layers of water with fine silk nets. **1899** *Geogr. Jrnl.* Feb. 153 There are two schools of townetters: the old-fashioned method..by which the nets are towed horizontally; and the new method, by which an opening and closing net is let down as vertically as may be, and hauled in open through a given vertical area and then closed. **1902** R. Valentin in *Jrnl. R. Inst. Cornw.* XV. 84 No ephyræ were obtained in any of the tow-nettings made in the spring.

**Town-father** to **-foot**: see Town 9, 10.

**Townful** (tau·nful). [f. Town *sb.* + -ful.] As many as a town contains or will contain.

**1855** Motley *Dutch Rep.* iv. iv. (1866) 617 Had they not slaughtered unarmed human beings by townfuls, at the word of command? **1894** *Westm. Gaz.* 18 June 7/2 There were in the country not only junkers but big townfuls of poorly-paid working people, whose lives depended on a cheap loaf.

**Tow·n-ga:te**[1]. The gate of a walled town.

**1433** *Rolls of Parlt.* IV. 477/1 The kepyng of the Town Yate called the Castell Yate. **1588** Shaks. *L. L. L.* I. ii. 75 Sampson..carried the Towne-gates on his backe like a Porter. **1799** *Hull Advertiser* 21 Sept. 4/1 Mr. Bray..protected the town-gate efficaciously with grape.

**Tow·n-ga:te**[2]. *Sc.* and *north. dial.* Also 6–7 gait(e. [Gate *sb.*[2] 4.] The main street of a town or village.

**1587** *Durham Wills* (Surtees) III. 129 Frome the particione of the said barene northward, unto the toune-gaite. **1607** in *N. Riding Rec.* (1883) I. 99 Will. Kidd of Kirby Moorside presented for keeping disorder in the Towne-gate. **1817** *Blackw. Mag.* May 155/1 The straggled houses..with their gable-ends, backs, or corners, turned to the street or town-gate. **1867** *Crim. Chronol. York Castle* 207 The towngate in Mirfield.

**Town-green** to **-guard**: see Town 9, 10.

**Tow·n ha·ll.** A large hall used for the transaction of the public business of a town, the holding of a court of justice, assemblies, entertainments, etc.; the great hall of the town-house or municipal building; now very commonly applied to the whole building. Also *attrib.*

**1481–90** *Howard Househ. Bks.* (Roxb.) 460 Item, for pottes that ware brokyn in the towne hall. **1538** London in *Lett. Suppress. Monast.* (Camden) 223 [At Reading] Ther towne hall ys a very small howse, and stondith upon the ryver. **1697** *Lond. Gaz.* No. 3336/3 Colchester, Oct. 28. Yesterday the Mayor..proclaimed the Peace before the Town-Hall and Dutch Bay Hall. **1701** in *Gentl. Mag.* LXXXVIII. ii. (1818) 601/2 We inned here at the town-house, the town-hall being over part of it. **1897** R. N. Bain tr. *Jókai's Pretty Michal* xxii. 172 The clock in the town-hall tower struck eight.

**Town-head, -herd**: see Town 10, 9 b.

†**Town-ho.** *Obs.* Also 8 townor. (See quots.)

**1791** in *Coll. Mass. Hist. Soc.* (1810) III. 154 The boys, as soon as they can talk, will make use of the common phrases, as *townor*, which is an Indian word, and signifies that they have seen the whale twice. **1851** H. Melville *Whale* II. 78 *Town-ho*,..the ancient whale-cry upon first sighting a whale from the mast-head, still used by whalemen in hunting the famous Gallipagos terrapin.

**Tow·n-house, town house.**

**1.** A municipal building containing the public offices, court-house, and Town hall, and in some continental towns the official residence of the chief magistrate. Cf. F. *hôtel de ville*; Ger. *stadthaus.* In England now commonly called Town hall.

**1530** Palsgr. 282/1 Towne house, *pretoire.* **1550** Bp. Hooper *Serm. Jonas* v. 106 Certeyne pictures in the towne house at Basyll. **1579** in W. H. Turner *Sel. Rec. Oxford* (1880) 403 Suche arrowes as the towne howsse nowe hathe. **1610** Holland *Camden's Brit.* (1637) 396 The greater part of the Towne [Buckingham] beareth North, wherein standeth the Towne-house. **1678** *Lond. Gaz.* No. 1287/3 The Burghers of Ghent have been commanded to bring in their Arms to the Town-House. **1701** [see Town hall]. **1756–7** tr. *Keysler's Trav.* (1760) III. 333 Placentia. On the area before the town-house are two bronze equestrian statues. **1765** T. Hutchinson *Hist. Mass.* I. iii. 381 A long declaration was read from the balcony..of the town-house. **1773** *Hist. Brit. Dom. in N. Amer.* iii. ii. 71 The city-hall, or town-house, is a strong brick building, two stories in heighth. **1857** Whittier *Last Walk Autumn* xxi, The painted, shingly town-house where The freeman's vote for Freedom falls. **1896** Barrie *Sent. Tommy* : If you jest see'd the Thrums townhouse!

**b.** *U.S.* (*a*) An almshouse, a workhouse. (*b*) A town prison (*Cent. Dict.* 1891).

**1889** Farmer *Americanisms* s.v. *Town, Townhouse*,..in Connecticut, an almshouse.

**2.** (Town house.) A house in a town; a residence in town, as distinguished from a country house.

**1825** T. Hook *Sayings* Ser. ii. *Man of Many Fr.* I. 284, I have no other town house to offer. **1862** H. Marryat *Year in Sweden* II. 393 The monks possessed a town-house in Söfde. **1886** C. E. Pascoe *London of To-day* xxii. (ed. 3) 211 Where now the maze of little courts and side streets extends to the Thames Embankment, there stood, centuries ago, the town-houses of the bishops, the ambassadors, and the powerful nobles. **1888** Saintsbury *Marlborough* x. 203 Tradition..assigns the fine Georgian house now used as the judge's lodgings [Oxford] as having been built by the Duke for a town house.

**Town-husband**: see Town 10.

**Townify** (tau·nifəi), *v. colloq.* [f. Town + -(i)fy.] *trans.* To render town-like, or characteristic of the town. Hence **Tow·nified** *ppl. a.*

**1777** Mrs. Grant *Lett. fr. Mount.* (1813) II. ii. 10 You have no notion how townified folks are, in all these little garrisons. **1881** A. Strettell in *Macm. Mag.* XLV. 120 This encircling grandeur will prevent it from ever getting a townified air. **1906** *Academy* 15 Dec. 602/1 Besides writing curious little townified poems about green fields, it builds curious little townified cottages in them.

**Townikin**: see under Town *sb.*

**Tow·niness.** *colloq.* [f. Towny *a.* + -ness.] Towny quality or condition.

**1881** Miss Braddon *Asph.* II. 153 Mrs. Turchill was so delighted with Torquay in its increased towniness and shoppiness. **1901** F. W. Lawrence *Heart of Empire* ii. 73 There are thus two ideas of towniness: one represented by the number of persons to the acre, and the other by the distance in time and space of the centre from the outer limits of the suburbs.

**Townish** (tau·niʃ), *a.* [f. Town *sb.* + -ish[1].]

†**1.** Of or pertaining to a town; living, situated, or existing in a town; urban. *Obs.*

**1412–20** Lydg. *Chron. Troy* I. 1339 To gape & loke, as it wer on a mase; Þis townysche folk do so comownly On euery þing þat falleth sodeinly. *a* **1542** Wyatt *Sat. J. Poins* 4 A song made of the feldishe mouse: That..Would nedes go se her townish sisters house. **1587** Turberv. *Trag. T.* (1837) 53 Leave off to leade thy life in lawndes, imbrace thy townish good. **1674** Jeake *Arith.* (1696) 74 Bakers that dwell in Cities and Towns were allowed 6*s.*.. which.. is still generally allowed to Townish Bakers.

**2.** Pertaining to or characteristic of the town or town life, esp. as distinguished from the country (in quot. 1500–20, from the court); having the manners or habits of town-dwellers.

**1500–20** Dunbar *Poems* xlii. 39 Ȝe be to townage, be this buke, To be my ladeis presoneir. *Ibid.* lxxv. 247 He wes townysche, peirt, and gukit. **1530** Palsgr. 464 To bringe up an uplandysshe person in better maners or more townysshe condycions. **1600** *Maides Metam.* iv. in Bullen *Old Pl.* (1882) I. 149 As townish damzels lend the hand But send the heart to him aloofe doth stand. **1820** *Blackw. Mag.* VIII. 16 There is a certain townish something about the inhabitants in general.

Hence **Tow·nishly** *adv.*, **Tow·nishness.**

**1645** J. Bond *Occasus Occid.* 33 Another Place, Person, or Town-ship, (peradventure) have stood too Townishly upon their Priviledges and Liberties. *a* **1859** De Quincey *Posth. Wks.* (1891) I. 222 A peculiar style of gossip, of babble, and of miniature intriguing, invests the atmosphere of little 'townishness'.

**Tow·n-land.** †**a.** OE. *tún-land.* The land forming a *tún* or manor. **b.** In Ireland, A division of land of varying extent; also, a territorial division, a township. **c.** In Scotland, The enclosed or infield land of a farm.

**a.** **972** in Earle *Land Charters* (1888) 445 Ðis sindon ða lond ȝemæra þæra tun londa ðe into perscoran belimpað. **b.** **1658** Petty in *Calr. S. P., Irel.* (*Advent.*) 362 The survey of every particular townland. **1662** *Ir. Act* 14 & 15 *Chas. II*, c. 2 (iii). § 3 The..number of acres..in each town-land, village, balybo or quarter of land. **1804** Mar. Edgeworth *Ennui* v, Two or three cabins gathered together were sufficient to constitute a town, and the land adjoining therto is called a townland. **1842** S. C. Hall *Ireland* II. 354 The origin of townlands..is of great antiquity. **1846** McCulloch *Acc. Brit. Empire* (1854) I. 365 Townlands are sometimes attached to one parish for the assessment of the county taxes, while, with respect to tithes and other ecclesiastical contributions, they are considered as forming part of another. **1873** W. K. Sullivan in O'Curry *Anc. Irish* Introd. 98 The modern townland may be looked upon as the representative of all the parcels of land of whatever denomination from the *Baile Biatach* down, which had separate designations. **1892** Emily Lawless *Grania* iv. i. 166 Inishmaan possesses but two townlands, containing six quarters each, with sixteen croggeries to every quarter, and sixteen acres to every croggery. **1903** *Times* 17 Jan. 8/1 Ballycotsey is a townland in the county Tipperary. **c.** **1801** *Farmer's Mag.* Nov. 420 The infield, or town-land..looked to be good.

**Tow·nless,** *a.* [f. Town *sb.* + -less.] Having no town or towns; devoid of towns.

*a* **1400–50** *Alexander* 2288 How tidis it þe [þ]at tounles þi toname is callid? **1601** Holland *Pliny* iv. xii. I. 80 Townlesse, and therfore obscure and of no reckoning. **1846** Ford *Gatherings fr. Spain* 15 This space..appears one townless level. **1884** *Athenæum* 1 Mar. 273/2 The inhabitants of these townless steppes live in carts, each cart containing a family.

**Townlet** (tau·nlĕt). [f. as prec. + -let.] A tiny or diminutive town.

*a* **1552** Leland *Itin.* V. 94 Oglesfeld and Bradfeld, ij townelettes or villages, long to one paroche chirche. **1610** Holland *Camden's Brit.* ii. 32 The coasts are well bespred with prety townlets. **1658** Phillips, *Paston*, a Townlet in Northfolk, giving sirname and residence to an honourable family of this County. **1807** Southey *Espriella's Lett.* II. 244 One of those townlets in which every thing reminds us of the distance from a metropolis. **1890** *Times* 14 Oct. 4/1 [In Russia] Many townlets are changed by virtue of a local order into villages, and Jews resident in them are expelled.

**Town-life, -living,** etc.: see Town 9, 10.

**Tow·nling.** [f. Town *sb.* + -ling[1].]

**1.** A small town; a townlet.

**1887** M. Betham-Edwards in *Temple Bar Mag.* Apr. 557 So dead-alive this townling of two or three thousand souls. **1892** E. Reeves *Homeward Bound* vi. 165 The rugged, bare mountains that look down on the Gulf of Salerno, and whereon nestle the townlings of Salerno and Amalfi.

**2.** A town-bred person. Also *attrib.*

**1888** Doughty *Arabia Deserta* I. 128 Turns and terms of the herdsmen poets of the desert, which are dark or unknown in any form to the townling Syrians. *Ibid.* 214 He watched to see if the townling were discouraged, in viewing only their empty desert before him.

**Townly** (tau·nli), *a.* [f. Town + -ly[1].] Pertaining to or characteristic of a town; having the manners or habits of town-dwellers; = Townish 2.

**1749** Fielding *Tom Jones* xii. vii, I suppose she is one of your quality folks, one of your townly ladies that we saw last night in the puppet-show. **1822** Galt *Sir A. Wylie* xxiii, I intend to settle my townly affairs. **1895** *Pall Mall G.* 26 Jan. 3/2 Our country manners have grown townly.

Hence **Tow·nliness.**

**1832** Mrs. F. Trollope *Dom. Mann. Amer.* xxxiii. (1839) 321 They throw off..their airs, and their 'townliness'.

**Tow·n-made,** *a.* Made or manufactured in a town; spec. in the town of the district. Also as *sb.*

**1809** *Edin. Rev.* XIII. 253 This is the very slang of..the lowest of our town-made novels. **1837** Dickens *Sk. Boz, Dancing Acad.*, [He] bought a pair of the regular seven-and-sixpenny, long-quartered town-mades. **1840** Hood *Kilmansegg, Marriage* xxv, Town-made joys how dearly they cost. **1853** Perkins *Haberdashery* (ed. 8) 90 Kid is valuable in proportion to its elasticity. When this quality is united with closeness of texture, the gloves called 'Town made' are so superior to most others of our own manufacture, as to rival the French. **1861** Wynter *Soc. Bees* 163 Adulteration to which all town-made bread is obnoxious.

**Tow·n-ma·jor.** *Obs.* or *Hist.* **a.** The major of a town-guard, as formerly in Edinburgh. **b.** The chief executive officer in a garrison-town or fortress. **c.** Applied vaguely to the chief magistrate or administrative officer of a foreign town.

**a.** **1676** W. Row *Contn. Blair's Autobiog.* (1848) 554 Several meetings in Edinburgh were dispersed by Robert Johnston town-major. **1693** *Apol. Clergy Scot.* 29 Town Major of Edenburgh, living in the Parish of Leswade, Major Will. Murray. **b.** **1702** *Milit. Dict., Town-Major*, the third Officer in order in a Garrison, and next to the Deputy Governor. He ought to understand the Fortification, and has a particular Charge of the Guards, Rounds, Patrouilles, and Sentinels. **1715** *Lond. Gaz.* No. 5300/5 Robert Dalzell, Esq., to be Town Major thereof [of Portsmouth]. **1737** J. Chamberlayne *St. Gt. Brit.* ii. (ed. 33) 115 (Gibraltar) John Preston, Esq., Town-Major, Mr. Anthony Robinson, Town-Adjutant. **1856** Kaye *Life Sir J. Malcolm* I. iv. 62 The change was beneficial to Malcolm, who was nominated Town-Major of Fort St. George. **1876** Voyle *Milit. Dict.* (ed. 3) 436/1 *Town-Major*, an officer who regulates the duties of a garrison, such as the detail and supervision of garrison guards, the disposal of prisoners in the garrison guard-room, the roster of officers for garrison duties [etc.]. **c.** **1748** *Earthquake of Peru* ii. 168 The Town-Major of Callao would not. **1784** T. Hutchins *Descr. Louisiana*, etc. 17 The people..sending three deputies to General O'Riley, viz. Messieurs Grandmaison town-major, La Friniere attorney-general, and De Mazant. **1809** A. Henry *Trav.* 12 After some further delay, in obtaining a passport from the town-major, I dispatched my canoes to Lachine, there to take in their lading. **1864** Burton *Scot Abr.* II. ii. 159 The town-major, finding them without credentials, or passports, ordered them to be carried to prison.

Hence **Town-ma·jorship.**

**1856** Kaye *Life Sir J. Malcolm* I. iv. 62 New arrangements were made for the Town-Majorship of the Fort.

**Tow·nman.** Forms: see Town *sb.*

†**1.** In OE. *túnman* and ME. A villein; a tenant in villenage. *Obs.*

*c* **1000** Ælfric *Hom.* II. 344 Furseus oncneow sona ða sawle; se wæs his tun-man ær on life. *c* **1000** *Ags. Voc.* in Wr.-Wülcker 333/22 *Uillanus*, tunman. **11..** *Voc.* ibid. 550/14 *Uillanus*, tunmon. **14..** *Metr. Voc.* ibid. 630/3 *Uillicus*, towneman. *c* **1450** *Godstow Reg.* 204, iij. acres liyng in longefurlange vttermost toward the lond of the towne men.

**2.** A man who lives in a or the town: as contrasted with a countryman, or formerly with a courtier.

**1399** Langl. *Rich. Redeles* ii. 41 So trouthe to telle as toune men said, Ffor on þat ȝe merkyd ȝe myssed ten schore. *c* **1475** *Rauf Coilȝear* 523 Thair is mony toun man, to tuggill is full teuch. **1896** N. Munro *Lost Pibroch* (1902) 37 A townman would think the world slept, so great was the booming quietness. **1896** *Westm. Gaz.* 17 Apr. 1/3 You are calling upon the townman, the doctor, the lawyer, the shopkeeper, and the artizan, who has his own Local Government to pay for, to pay also for the police, the highways, and the sanitation of his country neighbours.

**Tow·n-mee·ting.** A general assembly of the inhabitants of a town; *spec.* in *U.S.* a legal meeting of the qualified voters of a 'town' for the transaction of public business, having certain powers of local government.

**1636** *Salem, Mass., Town Recds.* 16 At a generall Court or towne meeting of Salem held the second of.. May aº 1636.

1639 *Boston Town Recds.* 2 July, At the next townes meeting. 1747 SHIRLEY in *Eng. Hist. Rev.* Oct. (1912) 786 The principal cause of the mobbish turn of this town [Boston] is its constitution, by which the management of it is devolved upon the populace, assembled in their town meetings. 1819 JEFFERSON *Autobiog.* Wks. 1859 I. App. 116 The resolutions ..were probably those you mention of the town-meeting of Boston. 1876 BANCROFT *Hist. U. S.* I. xiii. 426 Each town-meeting was a legislative body. 1878 STUBBS *Const. Hist.* III. xx. 414 Those whom their townsmen had chosen in their own town-meeting.

**Town-moor** to **-place**: see TOWN 9, 10.

**Towne**, obs. form of TUN.

**Tow·n-pla·nning,** *sb.* The preparation and construction of plans in accordance with which the growth and extension of a town is to be regulated, so as to make use of the natural advantages of the site, and to secure the most advantageous conditions of housing and traffic, the convenient situation of public buildings, open spaces, etc. Also *attrib.* So **Tow·n-plan** *sb.*, a ground-plan showing the positions of the streets and buildings in the proposed development of a town; **Tow·n-plan** *v.*, *intr.* to prepare a plan for the development of a town (whence **Tow·n-planned** *ppl. a.*); **Tow·n-pla·nner.**

[1904 T. C. HORSFALL *Improv. Dwellings People* 43 In preparing a rational town-building plan our task will be to avoid these faults. *Ibid.* 56 The preparation of building and town-extension plans.] 1906 (Nov. 6) *Official Rep. Housing Deput. to Prime Minister* 8 Notes on Speeches. [Subject heading.] Town Planning and Village Development Commission. 1907 *Daily Chron.* 3 May 8/4 'The Hampstead Tenants, Limited', began their work of town-planning in earnest yesterday, when the first sod of 'Temple Fortune Farm' (Finchley-road) was cut. 1908 *Westm. Gaz.* 18 Apr. 4/3 Some points of experience..to future town-planners. 1909 *Act 9 Edw. VII*, c. 44 (*title*) An Act to amend the Law relating to the Housing of the Working Classes, to provide for the making of Town Planning schemes [etc.]. *Ibid.* § 76 This Act may be cited as the Housing, Town Planning, &c. Act, 1909. 1909 H. I. TRIGGS (*title*) Town Planning, Past, Present, and Possible. 1909 *Daily Chron.* 14 Apr. 6/1 It seems incredible that any town should allow a new suburb to be made without a preliminary 'town plan'. 1909 *Westm. Gaz.* 16 Apr. 12/4 We must learn..at least two lessons before we can hope to 'town plan' successfully. 1909 *Daily Chron.* 14 Sept. 3/3 The town-planned communities of the Continent. 1912 *Daily News* 3 Jan. 4/7 Birmingham will be able to submit to the Local Government Board for approval its first town planning scheme in a completed form. At present the city has secured permission to 'town plan' two or three sites.

**Town-plat** to **-pump**: see TOWN 9, 10.

†**Tow·nred.** *Obs. rare.* In 7 townredd, town reed. [f. TOWN *sb.* + -RED.] A township, a cluster of homesteads.

1603 OWEN *Pembrokeshire* (1892) 4 To make a Mappe for that sheere alone, and then he gaue a lardge space to that shere, and placed euerye Townredd farre of from other in distance. *Ibid.* 33 Theire buildinges are Englishe like, in Townreddes and villages, and not in seuerall and lone houses. 1617 *Calr. S. P., Irel.* 153 A late proclamation.. from the Lord Deputy for composing scattered houses into town reeds, and to be so planted..that two or three towns may build together upon the meares and meeting of their several town reeds. 1618 *Ibid.* 231 Every undertaker and native to build in town reedes.

**Town-reeve** to **-row**: see TOWN 9 b, 10.

**Towns-** in comb., **Townsfolk**: see TOWN 11.

**Tow·nscape.** *nonce-wd.* [f. TOWN *sb.*, after *landscape.*] A picture or view of a town.

1880 LD. R. GOWER *Figure Painters Holland* 66 It is a landscape, or rather a townscape. 1889 HISSEY *Tour in Phaeton* 263 Some of the quaint townscapes (to invent another word) of our romantic, unspoilt English towns.

**Township** (tau·nʃip). [OE. *túnscipe*, f. *tún* (see TOWN) + *-scipe*, -SHIP. Cf., for sense, *landscipe*, and Ger. *dorfschaft*. After the OE. period the word was app. disused till 15th c: see sense 2.]

†**1.** In OE., The inhabitants or population of a *tún* or village collectively; the community dwelling in and occupying a *tún* (TOWN *sb.* 1). *Obs.*

*c* 890 tr. *Bæda's Hist.* v. xi. [x.] (1890) 416 Þa wæs he swiðe eorre; sende þa weord þider & heht ðone tunscipe ealne ofslean, & þone tun forbernan [*orig.* mittens occidit vicanos illos omnes, vicumque incendio consumpsit]. 962-3 *Laws K. Edgar* IV. c. 8 Cyðe hit þonne he ham cyme, and ..mid his tunscipes ʒewitnysse on ʒemænre læse ʒebringe. ʒif he swa ne deð ær fif nihtum, cyðan hit þæs tunes men þam hundrodes ealdre. 1154 *O. E. Chron.* an. 1137 § 4, ʒif twa men oþer iii coman ridend to an tun, al þe tunscipe fluʒæn fer heom. 1155-8 in *Calr. Charter Rolls* (1912) IV. 183 Homines suos liberos et quietos de..placitis et querelis et portmannesmot et tuncipesmot.

**2.** The inhabitants of a particular manor, parish, or division of a hundred, as a community, or in their corporate capacity. Now chiefly *Hist.*

1444 *Rolls of Parlt.* V. 111/1 [To] assesse well and duly every Tounship withinne the seid Hundredes. 1494 FABYAN *Chron.* VII. 575 (anno 1410) With prouycion yt euery towneshyp shuld kepe all poore people of theyr owne dwellers, whiche myght nat labour for theyr lyuynge. 1547 in *E. Anglian* May (1885) 69 Itm solde Ao primo Ed. sexti Regis &c. by the Towneshippe and Churchewardens [of Beccles] so moche plate as amounteth to the Summe of xl *li.* 1593 SHAKS. 2 *Hen. VI*, I. iii. 27 Alas Sir, I am but a poore Petitioner of our whole Towneship. 1628 WITHER *Brit. Rememb.* IV. 203 When halfe the Towneship, and the Hamlets nigh Are met to revell, at some Parish, by. 1817 W. SELWYN *Law Nisi Prius* (ed. 4) II. 773 The court held, that all the subjects of England, of common right, might fish in the sea,..and that therefore a prescription for it as appurtenant to a particular township was void.

**b.** Applied to the manor, parish, etc. itself, as a territorial division. Now chiefly *Hist.*

1414 *Rolls of Parlt.* IV. 571 The maner and Tounshipe of Chestreton. 1422 tr. *Secreta Secret., Priv. Priv.* 172 He desyrith more grete lordshuppe, othyr lytill rente, than a townshup of londe othyr a grete Some of catele to charlys appertenynge. 1491 *Act 7 Hen. VII*, c. 16 § 1 Honours lordshippes townshippes maners londes..and all other hereditamentes. 1523 FITZHERB. *Husb.* § 57 That there be no maner of sycknes amonge the cattell in that towneshyp or pasture that thou byest thy catel oute of. 1527 *Plumpton Corr.* (Camden) 227 For the right and intrest of one spring liing within the tewinship of Litle Ribston. 1610 HOLLAND *Camden's Brit.* (1637) 807 Hexham..a manour or Township belonging to the Archbishops of Yorke. 1670 PETTUS *Fodinæ Reg.* 33 All which are in the Township of Skibery Coed. *a* 1677 HALE *Prim. Orig. Man.* II. x. 234 In this Book are entred the Names of the Mannors or inhabited Townships, Boroughs and Cities,..the Number of Plough-Lands that each contains, and the Number of the Inhabitants upon them. 1819 SCOTT *Ivanhoe* xxv, A less orderly and a worse armed force, consisting of the Saxon inhabitants of the neighbouring township.

**c.** *spec.* Each of the local divisions of, or districts comprised in, a large original parish, each containing a village or small town, usually having its own church (formerly a chapel of the mother church of the original parish, whence such divisions were also known ecclesiastically as *chapelries*).

*Township* in this sense is chiefly retained in the north of England for the ancient divisions of such original parishes as Crosthwaite, Grasmere, Windermere, and Kendal, e.g. the townships of Borrowdale, Langdale, Rydal, and Ambleside; but it is applied in the Ordnance maps also to the ancient divisions of such original parishes as Cumnor and St. Giles', Camberwell, which for most purposes are now distinct parishes and are usually so called.

1540 *Test. Ebor.* (Surtees) VI. 117 Beinge of the towneshipe of Witley. 1662 *Act 14 Chas. II*, c. 12 § 21 That all and every the poore..persons within every Township or Village within the severall Counties aforesaid shall from and after the passing of this Act be maintained..and sett on worke within the several and respective Towneship and Village.. and that there shall be yearely chosen and appointed..twoe or more Overseers of the Poore within every of the said Townships or Villages. 1764 BURN *Poor Laws* 111 The head of a township or village is the constable; and there are many townships in a parish wherein there is no churchwarden. 1846 MᶜCULLOCH *Acc. Brit. Empire* (1854) I. 141 In the northern counties, where the parishes sometimes embrace 30 or 40 square miles, the poor laws, the due administration of which must always depend on an intimate knowledge of the situation and character of every one applying for relief, could not be properly carried into effect. To remedy this inconvenience, an act was passed in the 13th of Charles II, permitting townships and villages, though not entire parishes, severally and distinctly to maintain their own poor. Hence townships in the north of England may be regarded as divisions subordinate to parishes; and are, in practice, as distinctly limited as if they were separate parishes. 1891 J. P. EARWAKER *Manch. Constables' Accts.* I. Introd. 17 The two constables whose proceedings are recorded in the following pages, were appointed for the Township of Manchester alone; but, as that then embraced the whole of the town, they had entire charge of the town. 1906 S. & B. WEBB *Eng. Local Govt.* I. ii. 70 The great parish of Manchester, which extended over an area of quite 54 square miles, included no fewer than thirty semi-independent townships—one of them having, like the whole parish, the name of Manchester.

**3.** *transf.* Often rendering L. *pagus*, Gr. δῆμος (DEME), and thus applied to independent or self-governing towns or villages of ancient Greece, Italy, and other lands, and sometimes to foreign towns or villages of mediæval or modern times.

1602 FULBECKE *Pandectes* 57 So likewise *Pagi*, towneships, are deriued of the Doricke word πάγα, which signifieth a fountaine, and in the Atticall dialect is πηγη. 1681 NEVILE *Plato Rediv.* 74 The Swisses consist of Thirteen Soveraignties; some Cities..and some Provinces which have but a Village for their head Township. 1798 W. TAYLOR in *Monthly Mag.* V. 3 Now, the land of Cush (Genesis x. 7.) comprehended the five subdivisions or townships of Seba, Havilah, Sabtha, Raamah, and Sabthechah. 1838 THIRLWALL *Greece* II. xi. 11 The incorporation of several scattered townships in one city, such as took place in Attica. 1841 ELPHINSTONE *Hist. India* I. 39 His internal administration is to be conducted by a chain of civil officers, consisting of lords of single townships or villages, lords of ten towns, lords of 100, and lords of 1000 towns. 1846 GROTE *Greece* II. viii. II. 587 Rescuing the Arcadian townships from their dependence on Sparta. 1872 YEATS *Growth Comm.* 301 An insignificant township named Calcutta. 1905 *Expositor* Feb. 81 A Jebusite township existed around or beside the stronghold Zion. 1908 S. A. COOK *Relig. Anc. Palestine* i. 8 The small townships of Palestine and Syria—the average city was a small fortified site surrounded by dwellings, sometimes with an outer wall.

**4.** *Sc.* A farm held in joint tenancy.

1813 J. HEADRICK *Agric. Surv. Forfar.* 561 A township is a farm occupied by two or more farmers, in common, or in separate lots, who reside in a straggling hamlet, or village. 1884 MARQ. OF LORNE in *Pall Mall G.* 10 May 1/2 Recommending that the State should prop the fast vanishing feudal tenure of the 'township' of the crofter. 1886 SIR K. MACKENZIE *ibid.* 3 Mar. 11/2 Its Gaelic equivalent 'Baile'..designates a farm held by a number of joint tenants, but it also designates a farm held by an individual tenant...To the Gaelic language, the distinction between farm and township is unknown; and the illusions which seem to hang round this word township would be dispelled if it were realized that it merely means a farm held in joint tenancy by a greater or less number of persons. 1901 *Scotsman* 4 Mar. 7/2 They found..about forty men from the township of Lemreway [in Lewis] outside ready to resist.

**5.** *U.S.* and *Canada.* A division of a county having certain corporate powers of local administration; the same that in New England is called a town (TOWN *sb.* 6 a).

In the newer states, in which the divisions were laid off by government survey, a township is a division six miles square, and is so called even when still unsettled. The name is similarly used in the western provinces of Canada, from Ontario to British Columbia, and in Eastern Quebec and Prince Edward Island.

1685 PENN *Further Acc. Pennsylv.* 5 We do settle in the way of *Townships* or *Villages*, each of which contains 5000 Acres in square, and at least Ten Families. 1714 S. SEWALL *Diary* 23 Feb., This Court a large Township, of 12 miles square, is granted near Wadchuset. 1775 J. ADAMS in *Fam. Lett.* (1876) 120 The division of our.. counties into townships..gives every man an opportunity of showing and improving that education which he received at college or at school. 1779 *Hist. Europe* in *Ann. Reg.* 91 The settlement of Wyoming consisted of eight townships, each containing a square of five miles. 1801 *Farmer's Mag.* Apr. 164 Method of clearing New Land,..as practised in several parts of New Hampshire, particularly in the Township of Dartmouth. 1824 SYD. SMITH *Wks.* (1859) II. 45/2 All the public lands..are divided into townships of six miles square, by lines running with the cardinal points, and consequently crossing each other at right angles. 1866 J. E. H. SKINNER *After the Storm* I. 85 A 'township' is here a territorial division like a parish with us, and need not necessarily contain any houses. 1871 *Athenæum* 27 May 660 From 20 to 30 feet of pure graphite are stated to exist on the Ottawa river, in the township of Buckingham. 1888 BRYCE *Amer. Commw.* II. II. xl. 91 *note*, A town or township means..generally in the United States, a small rural district, as opposed to a city. It is a community which has not received representative municipal government. 1899 CROSSKILL *Prince Edward Isl.* (1904) 16 The parish lines are but little recognized, the more general sub-division being by lots or townships, of which there are 67 running numerically from west to east. 1912 *Province of Quebec for Brit. Emigr.* 13 The Eastern townships have also a well deserved reputation as a grazing country.

**6.** In Australia, A site laid out prospectively for a town, meanwhile often consisting of a few 'shanties' grouped around a railway station, store, hotel, post office, or the like; a village or hamlet. (Cf. the *town-site* (TOWN *sb.* 10) of U. S. and Canada.)

1802 BARRINGTON *Hist. N. S. Wales* x. 419 The timber of 120 acres was cut down..a township marked out, and some few huts built. 1861 MRS. MEREDITH *Over the Straits* II. 40 It used to seem to me a strange colonial anomaly to call a very small village a 'township', and a much larger one a 'town'. But the former is the term applied to the lands reserved in various places for future towns. 1890 *Melbourne Argus* 14 June 4/2 Will you come into the township to-night? 1892 A. SUTHERLAND *Elem. Geog. Brit. Col.* xiii. 276 Villages, which are always called 'townships', spring up suddenly round a railway station or beside some country inn.

†**7.** The state or condition of a town; also, a jocular title for a town. *Obs. rare.*

1665 SIR T. HERBERT *Trav.* (1677) 193 They..have little or no civility save in Zagathai, where they associate in Township. 1780 *Mirror* No. 105 ¶ 2 Such people are apt to assume in conversation [a consequence], which, I think, goes beyond the just prerogative of township, and is a very unfair encroachment on the natural rights of their friends ..in the country. 1809 MALKIN *Gil Blas* II. ix. ¶ 1 Olmédo looks like a..town. I beg its township's pardon, replied the barber.

**8.** By some 19th c. historical writers, adopted to designate what they consider to have been the simplest form of local or social organization in primitive Old English times.

This modern use of the term does not agree with the OE.; it appears to be founded on a confusion of OE. *tún* and *túnscipe* (sense 1), and the carrying back into early Anglo-Saxon or Teutonic times of the ME. sense 2, 2 b. (See W. J. Ashley *The Anglo-Saxon 'Township'* in *Q. Jrnl. Economics* (Harvard) VIII. Apr. 1894.)

1832 SIR F. PALGRAVE *Eng. Commw.* I. iii. 65 (*marg.* Anglo-Saxon state composed of Townships.) Ascending in the analysis of the Anglo-Saxon State, the first and primary element appears to be the community, which, in England, during the Saxon period, was denominated the Town, or Township. 1853 CREASY *Eng. Const.* iv. 45. 1867 PEARSON *Hist. Eng.* I. 16 The stronger and more warlike tribes secured themselves from surprise in townships or camps,.. fortified with felled timber and a ditch. 1874 STUBBS *Const. Hist.* I. v. § 39 The unit of the constitutional machinery, the simplest form of social organisation, is the township, the *villata* or *vicus*. It may represent the original allotment of the smallest subdivision of the free community, or the settlement of the kindred colonising on their own account, or the estate of the great proprietor who has a tribe of dependents. 1881 GREEN *Making of Eng.* iv. 180. 1889 G. E. HOWARD *Local Instit. Hist. U. S.* I. i. 18 In the early records of English history the *tunscipe* or township, appears as the lowest form of self government and the primary division of the state. 1910 J. W. HARPER *Soc. Ideal* xxi. 243 The township is older than the manor.. English feudalism destroyed the territorial organisation and reared itself on the ruins of the townships.

**9.** *attrib.* and *Comb.*, esp. in senses 5, 6: **township bridge, drain, road,** a bridge, etc. made and kept up by the township; **township farm** = sense 4; **township trustee** (*U.S.*), a member of a committee elected to administer the affairs of a township.

1868 *Rep. U. S. Commissioner Agric.* (1869) 43 Harrison County, Ind.—The township trustee of Corydon has paid out to farmers, for loss of sheep by dogs..three hundred and ninety-eight dollars. **1888** BRYCE *Amer. Commw.* II. II. xlviii. 235 *note*, Any county desiring to forsake township organization may do so by a vote of the electors. **1904** *Daily Chron.* 19 Oct. 8/3 A simple and traditional dramatisation of some scene in early English township life. **1910** W. L. MATHIESON *Awakening Scot.* vi. 276 The type of agriculture..is still that of the township farm.

**Town-side, -site,** etc.: see TOWN 10.

**Townsman** (tau·nzmæ̆n). Forms: see TOWN. [f. *town's*, genitive of TOWN + MAN *sb.*[1]]

†**1.** OE. (*túnesman*). One who lives in a *tún*; a villager, a villein. *Obs.*

**962–3** *Laws of Edgar* IV. c. 13 And ic wille, þæt tunesmen and heora hyrdas habban þas ylcan smeaȝunge on minum cucum orfe and on minra þeȝena, ealswa hy habbað on heora aȝenum. **1028–60** *Laws Northumbld. Priests* c. 59 ȝif hwilc tunesman æniȝne pæniȝ forhele oððe forhæbbe, ȝildese landrica þone pæniȝ and nime ænne oxan æt ðam men.

**2.** A man who lives in a town or city; a citizen: esp. as distinguished from a countryman, a stranger, a soldier of the garrison, or other such.

**1433** in *Hist. Sudbury* (1896) 125 A Supplicacon of the Maior and Tonsmen of Sudbury to the B. of Norwich. **1519** *Coventry Leet Bk.* 666 Iff eny fforener or Townesman fforstall eny Corne within the libertie of this Cetie of Couentre or it com into the markett. **1577** tr. *Bullinger's Decades* (1592) 144 Of the countrie men as well as of the townesmen. **1615** G. SANDYS *Trav.* 6 Here a garrison is kept; supplyed by the townesmen. **1745** *De Foe's Eng. Tradesman* xxvi. (1841) I. 265 She being a good honest townsman's daughter. **1749** *Little Cornard (Suff.) Overseers' Acc.* (MS.), Paid to Sarah Flower by the order of the Townes men that She Laid out. **1863** H. COX *Instit.* III. ix. 727 The whole body of resident trading townsmen.

**b.** A man of one's own or the same town; a fellow-townsman. Usually after *possessive*. Cf. COUNTRYMAN 2.

**1601** A. DENT *Pathway to Heaven* (1617) 18 For me thinks you go too far, you goe beyond your learning in this, that you condemne good neighbours, and good Townesmen. **1715–20** POPE *Iliad* XVIII. 578 There, in the forum swarm a numerous train, The subject of debate, a townsman slain. **1838** THIRLWALL *Greece* II. xv. 258 A citizen of Abdera advised his townsmen to offer a solemn thanksgiving to the gods.

**c.** An ordinary citizen or resident of a university town as distinguished from a *gownsman* or member of the university; cf. TOWN *sb.* 5 d.

**1768** WILKES *Corr.* (1805) III. 254 Only another proof that the townsmen of Oxford have always hated the university. **1823** LAMB *Elia* Ser. II. *Poor Relations*, The distance between the gownsmen and the townsmen, as they are called ..is carried to an excess that [etc.]. **1889** JESSOPP *Coming of Friars* vi. 273 The townsmen under great provocation had seized three of the gownsmen.

**3.** *New England.* = SELECTMAN.

**1656** in T. Dwight *Trav. New Eng.* (1821) I. 343 [In 1656] town's-men [(or select-men) were chosen]. **1696–1715** *Maryland Laws* iv. (1723) 11 Any Action..arising between the Townsmen or Freemen of the said Town. *a* **1817** T. DWIGHT *Trav. New Eng.* (1821) I. 243 At this meeting the inhabitants choose, not exceeding seven men, inhabitants, able, discreet and of good conversation, to be Select-men, or Townsmen, to take care of the order, and prudential affairs of the town.

**Townspeople** (tau·nz,pīːp'l). Also 7 townes people. [f. as prec. + PEOPLE. Orig. two words; now written as one.] People or inhabitants of a town or towns; townsmen and townswomen; townsfolk. (Usually const. as *pl.*)

**1648** CROMWELL *Let.* 25 Nov., And without money the stubborn towns-people will not trust them for the worth of a penny. **1691** in *Somerset & Dorset N. & Q.* June (1905) 263 Many died as also many Townes people of yᵉ same distemper. **1833** MARRYAT *P. Simple* xxi, We had no parole, and but little communication with the townspeople. **1849** MACAULAY *Hist. Eng.* v. I. 573 The town's people repaired to the cliffs and gazed long and anxiously. **1872** BAGEHOT *Physics & Pol.* iv. 132 The place was crowded and a whole townspeople looking on.

**b.** People inhabiting the same town; fellow-townsmen. (Usually after *possessive.*)

**1823** *Examiner* 761/1 They are townspeople, we believe, the native place of both being..Edinburgh. **1870** EMERSON *Soc. & Solit.* iii. 45 Not by his friends or his townspeople or his contemporaries.

**Town-stocks, Townswoman**: see TOWN 9, 11.

**Tow·n-ta·lk.** The common talk or gossip of the people of a town; the subject or matter of such talk or gossip.

**1654–5** CROMWELL *Speech to Parl.* 22 *Jan.* 23 If it be not folly in Me to listen to Town-talk, such things have been proposed. **1667** PEPYS *Diary* 26 Apr., All the town-talk is now-a-days of her extravagancies. **1694** CONGREVE *Double-Dealer* III. i, You'll ruin me if you take such public Notice of it, it will be a Town-Talk. **1712** SWIFT *Jrnl. to Stella* 26 Mar., The news of the French desiring a cessation of arms..was but town talk. **1848** THACKERAY *Van. Fair* lv, It was town-talk for at least three days. **1867** AUG. J. E. WILSON *Vashti* xii, Why should she taboo society, and make herself the town-talk?

**Town-tallow** to **-wait**: see TOWN 9, 10.

**Tow·n-wa·ll.** The wall of a fortified town.

*c* **1400** *Destr. Troy* 10746 The troiens in toures, & on toun walles, Laidon spies specially. **1480** *Coventry Leet Bk.* 447 Enploye hit to oder reparacions of þe seid town wall. **1548** UDALL, etc. *Erasm. Par. Acts* ix. 36 They..by nyght let hym downe by a corde of the towne walles, in a basket. **1649** MILTON *Eikon.* viii. Wks. (1847) 294/1 The king much incensed proclaims him traitor before the town walls. **1843** *Penny Cycl.* XXVII. 456/1 The town-wall of Worms.

**Townward** (tau·nwǫ̈ɹd), *adv.* (*a.*) [f. TOWN *sb.* + -WARD.] Towards or in the direction of the town. (Originally *to the townward.*)

**1434** *Indenture Fotheringhey* in Dugdale *Monast.* (1846) VI. 1414/2 A dore yn the west side..to the town-ward. **1633** T. STAFFORD *Pac. Hib.* II. xii. (1821) 362 The Irish.. beat the Spaniards from their ground to the Towneward. **1808** SCOTT *Marm.* III. xxxi, He heard..The foot-tramp of a flying steed, Come town-ward rushing on. **1846** LONGF. in *Life* (1891) II. 52 A beautiful pile of granite.. looking townward and seaward.

**b.** *adj.* Going or directed toward the town.

**1806** J. GRAHAME *Birds Scot.* 35 Follow his townward steps. **1833** L. RITCHIE *Wand. by Loire* 184 Ditches..still remain on the townward side. **1864** LONGF. in *Life* (1891) III. 34 Walking..along the accustomed townward walk,.. I met the East Wind. **1893** *Chicago Advance* 27 July, Evidence of the townward drift of the people.

**c.** *Comb.*

**1870** MORRIS *Earthly Par.* III. IV. 288 In a fair-hung townward-looking bower.

**Tow·nwards,** *adv.* [-WARDS.] = prec.

**1895** P. HEMINGWAY *Out of Egypt* II. 175, I stood watching a vessel in the harbour, that stared townwards with a hundred unblinking eyes. **1908** *Daily Chron.* 15 Feb. 7/5 A West London [cycling] club, recently returning..townwards, through Brentford.

**Town-watch** to **-woman**: see TOWN 9, 10.

**Towny** (tau·ni), *a.* and *sb.* *colloq.* Also -ey, -ie. [f. TOWN *sb.* + -Y.]

**A.** *adj.* Of, pertaining to, or characteristic of the town; townish.

**1837** *New Monthly Mag.* L. 248 His acquired habits were of the town, towny. **1857** E. M. WHITTY *Friends in Bohemia* I. 211 Are you not weary of this towney life? **1908** *Treasury* Feb. 507 A house so towny and stylish, compared with our farm homesteads.

**B.** *sb.* **1.** A town-bred man; *spec.* a Londoner.

**1828** P. CUNNINGHAM *N. S. Wales* (ed. 3) II. 223 If we could not say we had committed as many [robberies] as these townies, they would look upon us with contempt. *Ibid.* 230 Many surgeons find that by putting all the old townies into double irons whenever robberies begin to prevail, a cessation soon takes place.

**2.** *U.S. university slang.* A townsman as distinct from a member of the university; cf. TOWNEE.

**1853** *Yale Lit. Mag.* XIX. 2 (Thornton) The genus by the German students denominated 'Philistines', by the Cantabs ignominiously called 'Snobs', and which custom here has named 'Townies'. **1869** W. T. WASHBURNE *Fair Harvard* 54 (ibid.) One beholds the conscious 'towney' on his evening promenade.

**3.** A fellow-townsman or townswoman. *slang.*

**1865** *Morn. Star* 18 July, She is a 'towny' (of the same town) of mine, and I want to see her safe home. **1869** *Routledge's Ev. Boy's Ann.* 347 Then you and me's 'towneys' it seems. **1892** STEVENSON & OSBOURNE *Wrecker* xii, A townie of mine was lost down this way, in a coal-ship.

**To-wond(e**, pa. t. of TO-WEND *v.* *Obs.*

†**To-worth,** *v.* *Obs. rare.* [ME. *to-wurðen*, f. TO-[2] + *wurðen*:—OE. *weorðan* to become.] *intr.* To come to nought; to perish.

*c* **1205** LAY. 20744 For betere us is on londe Mid monscipe to liggen þene we þus here For hungere to-wurðen.

**To-wowe, -writhe, -wry**: see TO- *pref.*[2] 1.

**Tow-path** (tōᵘ·paþ). [f. TOW *v.*[1] + PATH.] A path by the side of a canal or navigable river for use in towing; = *towing-path* (TOWING *vbl. sb.*[1] b).

**1846** WORCESTER, *Tow-path*, a narrow path travelled by horses in dragging boats along a canal. *Baldwin.* **1882** R. MACKENZIE *America* 305 He had begun life on the tow-path as a driver of mules. **1910** *Blackw. Mag.* May 634/1 The towpath was knee-deep in water.

**Tow-pung,** ? error or misprint for *tom-pung*, orig. form of PUNG *sb.*[2], q. v., quot. 1851.

**Towrd, Towres, Towret, -ette,** obs. forms of TOWARD, TOURS, TURRET.

**Tow-rope** (tōᵘ·rōᵘp). [f. TOW *v.*[1] + ROPE *sb.*[1]] A rope (hawser, cable, or the like) used in towing.

**1743** BULKELEY & CUMMINS *Voy. S. Seas* 119 We called to them to take hold of a Towe-Rope, but they refused. **1801** JEFFERSON *Writ.* (ed. Ford) VIII. 75 You will follow the bark of liberty only by the help of a tow-rope. **1865** DICKENS *Mut. Fr.* III. viii, The tow-rope was slackened by a turn of the stream.

Hence **Tow·-ro:ping,** in railway-shunting, the drawing of a vehicle by an engine on a parallel line of rails by means of a rope connecting the two. An illegal practice. See PROPPING *vbl. sb.* 3 for quots.

**Tow-row** (tau·rau·), *sb.* and *a.* [Reduplicated or extended form of ROW *sb.*[3]; orig. *dial.*]

**A.** *sb.* An uproar, hubbub, noisy disturbance, din.

**1877** *Holderness Gloss.*, *Tow-row*, a confusion, or noisy disturbance. **1886** STEVENSON *Kidnapped* iv, A blinding flash,..and hard upon the heels of it, a great tow-row of thunder. **1894** CROCKETT *Raiders* (ed. 3) 15 Then..came a great towrow of laughter. **1894** MAX PEMBERTON *Sea-Wolves* xxii, For a long space they kept up the tow-row and the din.

†**B.** *adj.* Intoxicated (? 'drunk and disorderly'). *slang. Obs.*

**1709** STEELE & SWIFT *Tatler* No. 71 ⁋ 8 He that drinks till he stares, is no more Tow-Row, but Honest.

So **Tow-row** *v.*, *intr.* **a.** to make a tow-row; **b.** *dial.* (see quot. 1854). Hence **Tow-rowing** *vbl. sb.*

**1840** THACKERAY *Barber Cox* Mar., Directly the tow-rowing began, off went Trumpeter like a thunder-bolt. **1854** MISS BAKER *Northampt. Gloss.*, *Tow-rowing*, cleaning out dirty and disorderly places. 'I've been tow-rowing about all day among the dust'. **1899** MRS. E. KENNARD *Morals Midlands* xxvii. 240 The hounds were tow-rowing all round the covert.

**Towrpyke**, a winding stair: see TURNPIKE.

†**Tow·ry-low·ry.** *dial.* (Cf. TIRRA-LIRRA.)

**1632** BROME *North. Lasse* I. ii, And then towry, lowry, faith, my noble Governor, and I. **1878** *Cumberld. Gloss.*, *Towry lowry*, all in disorder.

**Towsell,** obs. form of TOLSEL, TOLZEY.

**Towser** (tau·zəɹ), *sb.* Also 7 towzer, touzer, 9 touser. [f. TOUSE *v.* + -ER[1]; with senses c, d, e cf. *thumper*, *whopper*, etc.] One who or that which touses. **a.** (with capital T). A common name for a large dog, such as was used to bait bears or bulls; also *transf.* of a person.

**1678** OTWAY *Friendship in F.* IV. i, Fresh Game; that great Towser has started it already. **1681** *Trial S. Colledge* 59 Mr. Char...it was the Pictures of the Tantivies and the Towzer [Roger L'Estrange]. **1681** T. FLATMAN *Heraclitus Ridens* No. 30 (1713) I. 197 *Earn.* What Papers? Did he mean the Towzers, and the Gallows, and the Broom, for which he was so famous? **1682** N. N. (*title*) The Heu and Cry: or, a Relation of the Travels of the Devil and Towzer, Through all the Earthly Territorys, and the Infernal Region. **1684** OTWAY *Atheist* III. i, Never was seen so termagant a Towzer. **1696** tr. *Du Mont's Voy. Levant* 257 Poor Towzer was condemn'd to be Cudgel'd to Death. **1881** A. MᶜLACHLAN in *Mod. Sc. Poets* II. 261 Ahint him Towser wags his tail.

†**b.** The five of trumps in the game of gleek. *Obs.*

**1680** COTTON *Compl. Gamester* vi. (ed. 2) 65 The fifth [is called] Towser, the sixth Tumbler, which if in hand Towser is five and Tumbler six, and so double if turn'd up. **1688** R. HOLME *Armoury* III. xvi. (Roxb.) 73/2 Towser, is the fifth of the trumps.

†**c.** A large ship. *Obs.* **d.** A large coarse apron. *dial.* **e.** A rough or energetic person. *dial.*

**c.** **1690** *Pagan Prince* xxix. 81 Now the Belgians, having lost..some three or four more of their biggest Towzers, made all the Sail they could to their own Coasts. **d.** **1865** R. HUNT *Pop. Rom. W. Eng.* Ser. II. 244 The Touser is a large apron or wrapper to come quite round and keep the under-garments clean. **1882** JAGO *Cornw. Gloss.*, *Touser*, a large coarse apron for kitchen use. **e.** **1901** E. PHILLPOTTS *Striking Hours* 222 A wonnerful bowerly maid her was, an' a towser for work, an' 'mazin' even-tempered tu. **1901** R. M. F. WATSON *Closeburn* xiii. 221 A certain big, uncouth, unhallowed 'towser' named Tibbie Murdoch.

Hence **Tow·ser, -zer** *v.* (*nonce-wd.*), *trans.* to worry as a dog does.

*c* **1680** HICKERINGILL *Hist. Whiggism* I. Wks. 1716 I. 37 If they get a piece of a Text by the end..they do so tear it, and towze it, and towzer it..that they lose themselves.

**Towst, Towsy**: see TOUST, TOUSY.

**Towster** (tōᵘ·stəɹ). *nonce-wd.* [f. TOW *v.*[1] + -STER.] = TOWER *sb.*[2]

**1885** WARREN & CLEVERLY *Wand. 'Beetle'* 24 The towsters came to a halt.

†**Towtaw·,** *v.* *Obs. rare*⁻¹. [f. TOW *sb.*[1] + TAW *v.*[1]] *trans.* To scutch (flax). Cf. TOW *v.*[3]

**1649** BLITHE *Eng. Improv. Impr.* (1653) 260 Kilne-drying it, then breaking and towtawing it, then hetchelling and dressing it up.

**Towtch,** obs. form of TOUCH.

**Towy** (tōᵘ·i), *a.* [f. TOW *sb.*[1] + -Y.] Like or of the nature of tow.

**1601** HOLLAND *Pliny* XIX. i. II. 4 You shall know by the skin or rind thereof if it be loose and readie to depart from the towie substance of the stem. **1673** GREW *Anat. Trunks* I. ii. § 30 The Lignous and Towy Parts of all Plants are Tubulary. **1858** *Sat. Rev.* 21 Aug. 184/2 Painted..with bullet eyes, vermilion cheeks, towy locks, and pudgy limbs. **1881** *Gard. Chron.* XVI. 654/3 Its leaves .. produce a soft towy herbage.

**Towylle,** obs. form of TOWEL.

†**Towyth,** obs. erroneous form of THOUGHT.

*c* **1430** *Hymns Virg.* 121 We be sorry þatt we dede agayn þi wille Or with towyth or with dede.

**Towze, Towzer**: see TOUSE, TOWSER.

†**Towze-match.** *Obs. rare.* [?f. TOUSE *v.* 4 + MATCH *sb.*[2] 2 b.] 'Match' made of 'toused' or teased hemp or other fibrous material.

**1627** CAPT. SMITH *Seaman's Gram.* ii. 13 Okum is old Ropes torne in peeces like Towze Match, or Hurds of Flax. **1630** — *Trav. & Adv.* v. 8 Over that a strong Searcloth, then over all a good thicknesse of Towze-match well tempered with oyle of Linseed.

**Tox** (tǫks), *sb.* *Zool.* [ad. Gr. τόξον TOXON [1].] A sponge-spicule having the form of a double curved rod, like a Cupid's bow; = TOXASPIRE.

**1909** in *Cent. Dict. Supp.*

†**Tox,** *v.* *Obs.* ? *slang.* Short for *intoxicate*. Hence †**Toxed, toxt,** †**To·xing** *ppl. adjs.*

**1635** HEYWOOD *Philocothon.* i. 3 When their more sober consciences can Iustifie against their toxed Insolence. *Ibid.* iv. 29 Addicted to strong and toxing drinkes. **1637** — *Dial.* iv. Wks. 1874 VI. 191 Braines well toxt with wine.

**Tox-**[1], combining form, repr. TOXI- or TOXO-[2] before a vowel. ‖ **Toxæmia** (tǫksī·miă), also anglicized **toxemy** [Gr. αἷμα blood, after *anæmia*, etc.], a morbid condition of the blood caused by a toxin; blood-poisoning; hence **Toxæmic** (-ī·mik) *a.*, pertaining to or affected with toxæmia. **Tox-albumin** (-ælbiū·min), also -en, a poisonous or pathogenic albumin or protein produced by bacteria; a protein toxin; hence **Toxalbu·mic** *a.*, pertaining to or caused by a toxalbumin; so

**Toxa·lbumose**, a poisonous albumose. **To·xamine** (-āmǝin), a poisonous amine. **Toxanæmia** (-ănī·miă), anæmia caused by the action of a poison, usually a ptomaine.

1860 MAYNE *Expos. Lex.*, *Toxæmia, .. a contaminated state of the blood, as in syphilis; poisoned blood; toxemy. 1881 *Trans. Obstet. Soc. Lond.* XXII. 283 There was a dangerous state of toxæmia. 1876 BRISTOWE *The. & Pract. Med.* (1878) 124 Which so often..cause *toxæmic symptoms. 1899 *Allbutt's Syst. Med.* VIII. 418 The post-febrile insanities are divisible into two classes—the purely anæmic, and the toxæmic. 1902 *Buck's Handbk. Med. Sc.* V. 33 As the effects of other chemical or *toxalbumic poisons manifest themselves as a psychosis. 1890 *Pall Mall G.* 26 Apr. 6/3 *Toxalbumen is said to be the excretion of a bacillus of diphtheria. 1892 *Pop. Sc. Monthly* XLI. 633 It neutralizes the potent toxalbumin of tetanus in test-tube cultures. 1896 *Allbutt's Syst. Med.* I. 767 Brieger and Fränkel then described a proteid poison which they obtained from cultures of the tetanus bacilli and named tox-albumin. 1902 R. MUIR in *Encycl. Brit.* XXVI. 64/2 Such a powder gives a proteid reaction, and is no doubt largely composed of albumoses, hence the name *toxalbumoses has been applied. 1897 *Allbutt's Syst. Med.* III. 735 Certain specimens of cheese contain a *toxamine, termed by its discoverer, Professor Vaughan, 'tyrotoxicon'. 1891 *Cent. Dict.*, *Toxanemia, *Toxanæmia*. 1899 *Syd. Soc. Lex.*, *Toxanæmia, Toxanemia*, anæmia caused by the actions of ptomaines.

**Tox-** [2]: see Toxo- [1].

**Toxarch** (tǫ·ksaɹk). *Anc. Gr. Hist.* [ad. Gr. τόξαρχος 'lord of the bow', captain of the archers, f. τόξον bow + -αρχος ruler.] The title of the captain of the city-guard of mercenaries at Athens.

1828 [G. C. LEWIS] tr. *Böckh's Publ. Econ. Athens* I. 278 The public slaves who composed the city-guard..are generally called bow-men (τοξόται), or, from the native country of the majority, Scythians... Their officers had the name of Toxarchs (τόξαρχοι).

**Toxaspire** (tǫ·ksăspəiǝɹ). *Zool.* [irreg. (for **toxospire*) f. Gr. τόξο-ν bow + σπεῖρα coil, SPIRE.] In sponges, a form of microsclere or flesh-spicule: see quots. Hence **Toxaspi·ral** *a.*, pertaining to or of the form of a toxaspire.

1887 SOLLAS in *Encycl. Brit.* XXII. 417/2 A turn and a part of a turn of a spiral of somewhat higher pitch than that of a sigmaspire gives the *toxaspire*. 1888 — in *Challenger Rep.* XXV. p. lxii, *Toxaspire*.—A spiral rod in which the twist a little exceeds a single revolution. The pitch of the spiral is usually great and the spicule consequently appears bow-shaped when viewed laterally.

**Toxi-** (tǫksi), combining form arbitrarily repr. TOXIC or TOXIN, in recent scientific words, chiefly pathological. **Toxidermic** (-dǭ·ɹmik) *a.* [Gr. δέρμα skin], pertaining to skin-disease produced by a poison: cf. *toxicodermitis* in TOXICO-. **Toxi·ferous** *a.* = *toxophorous* in TOXO- [2]. **Toxignomic** (-gnǫ·mik) *a.* [Gr. γνώμη judgement, opinion], enabling one to diagnose the action of a toxin. ‖ **Toxihæ·mia** [Gr. αἷμα blood] = *toxæmia*: see TOX- [1]. **Toxi-infe·ctious, -infe·ctive** *adjs.*, involving or characterized by infection due to a toxin. ‖ **Toxiphagus** (-i·făgǫ̆s), pl. **-phagi** (-fădʒəi) [Gr. -φάγος eating], one who eats poisons: cf. *toxicophagous* in TOXICO-. ‖ **Toxipho·bia** [-PHOBIA], fear of being poisoned, as a form of insanity or monomania; hence **Toxipho·biac**, one affected with toxiphobia. **Toxiphoric** (-fǫ·rik) *a.* = *toxophoric*: see TOXO- [2]. **Toxiresin** (-re·zin), name of a poisonous substance obtained from digitalis by the action of acids.

1899 *Allbutt's Syst. Med.* VIII. 587 A pilo-sebaceous folliculitis of..microbic or *toxidermic character. 1899 *Syd. Soc. Lex.*, **Toxiferous*, carrying or conveying poison. 1890 BILLINGS *Med. Dict.*, **Toxihæmia*, Toxæmia. 1907 *Jrnl. Med. Research* Dec. 352 The statement of Dide, who asserts that there is a diminution in alexin in patients suffering from the '*toxi-infectious' forms of insanity. 1897 *Allbutt's Syst. Med.* III. 749 Microbic agency which sets up *toxi-infective processes. 1875 H. C. WOOD *Therap.* (1879) 377 The *toxiphagi are asserted to be remarkably long-lived people. 1876 C. A. CAMERON in *Dublin Jrnl. Med. Sc.* Feb. 98, I propose to apply the term *toxiphobia to a species of monomania..those labouring under which believe that persistent attempts are being made to poison them. Of the sixty-three *toxiphobiacs, only two were obviously insane. 1902 G. M. STERNBERG in *Science* 24 Oct. 665/1 The atom-groups which..Ehrlich calls the '*toxiphoric side chain'. 1890 BILLINGS *Med. Dict.*, **Toxiresin*, a product of the action of acids upon digitoxin; a powerful cardiac poison. 1899 *Syd. Soc. Lex.*, Toxiresin.

**Toxic** (tǫ·ksik), *a.* (*sb.*) [f. med.L. *toxic-us* poisoned, imbued with poison, f. TOXIC-UM. So F. *toxique* 'poison' (1762 in *Dict. Trévoux*).]

1. Of the nature of a poison; poisonous.

1664 EVELYN *Sylva* 65 The toxic quality was certainly in the liquor.., not in the nature of the wood; which yet he [Pliny] affirms is cur'd of that Venenous quality by driving a brazen wedge into the body of it. 1674 BLOUNT *Glossogr.*, *Toxic*, venemous, poisonous. 1876 T. BRYANT *Pract. Surg.* I. ii. 53 Poisoning..due to the introduction into the torrent of the circulation of toxic substances. 1899 *Allbutt's Syst. Med.* VII. 815 The urine is normally toxic, and incessantly takes from the blood its toxicity.

2. Caused or produced by a poison; due to poisoning.

1872 *Contemp. Rev.* XX. 751 Whether it be the toxic condition of the blood. 1874 MAUDSLEY *Respons. in Ment. Dis.* iii. 79 The peculiar disorders of the physical and mental functions..to which he gave the name of Toxic Insanity. 1899 *Allbutt's Syst. Med.* VIII. 310 Toxic insanity depends on poisons either derived from without or generated within the body.

b. Of intoxication, intoxicated, tipsy. *humorous.*

1899 MARY KINGSLEY *W. Afr. Stud.* i. 2 A toxic state where a man can't see the holes through a ladder.

B. *sb.* A toxic substance, a poison.

1890 *Spectator* 6 Dec., M. Pasteur..pointing out..that the lymph is really a 'toxic' or poison, of terrible energy and unknown effects. 1904 *Westm. Gaz.* 15 June 2/1 Alkaloids and toxics, such as chloral, emit the N-rays freely.

**Toxical** (tǫ·ksikăl), *a.* [f. as prec. + -AL: see -ICAL.] Of toxic nature or character.

1607 TOPSELL *Four-f. Beasts* (1658) 199 Goats bloud sod with marrow may be taken against all toxical poison. 1650 CHARLETON *Paradoxes* 65 Why the blood of a Bull is toxicall and poysonous. 1855 WHARTON & STILLÉ *Med. Jurispr.* § 496. 378 The production of toxical effects. 1863 *N. Syd. Soc. Year-bk. Med.* 444 Symptoms of the toxical action of the drug. 1884 *Manch. Exam.* 29 Dec. 6/5 Tobacco smoke ..contains a second toxical principle called colidine.

Hence **To·xically** *adv.*, poisonously; in quot., in relation to toxicology.

1887 A. M. BROWN *Anim. Alkal.* 39 This base is toxically interesting.

**Toxicant** (tǫ·ksikănt), *a.* and *sb. rare.* [f. pr. pple. of med.L. *toxicāre* to poison: see -ANT.] a. *adj.* Acting as a poison; poisonous, toxic. b. *sb.* A poisonous substance, a poison.

1882 OGILVIE (Annandale), *Toxicant*, ..a poison of a stimulating, narcotic, anæsthetic nature, especially such as seriously affects the health when habitually indulged in. *Dr. Richardson.* 1891 *Cent. Dict.*, *Toxicant* adj. 1892 *Illustr. Lond. News* 13 Aug. 211/3 Coffee (that favourite vehicle of the deadlier toxicants in the East).

† **To·xicate**, *ppl. a. Obs.* Also 5 toxicat, 6 tocksicate. [f. med.L. *toxicāt-us*, pa. pple. of L. *toxicāre* to smear with poison: see next.] Charged or infected with poison; poisoned; poisonous.

*c* 1470 HENRYSON *Mor. Fab.* III. (*Cock & Fox*) xxx, Flatteraris..With fals mening, and mynd maist toxicate. *c* 1475 *Partenay* 1429 The king..With toxicat uenym replete was certain. 1581 J. STUDLEY *Seneca's Hercules Œtæus* 199 b, So yet my wits be tocksicate, although my feare be gone.

† **To·xicate**, *v. Obs.* [f. ppl. stem of med.L. *toxicāre* to poison (in John of Salisbury, *c* 1150), f. L. *toxic-um* poison: see TOXICUM.] *trans.* To poison. Hence † **To·xicating** *vbl. sb.*

1635 HEYWOOD *Hierarch.* VIII. 518 Which Feuer shakes him,.. And a strange Megrim toxicates his head. 1653 CHISENHALE *Cath. Hist.* 12 Each morning to bite on Rue, which..secures her against the toxicating of that venomous Basilisk.

**Toxication** (tǫksikē̆i·ʃən). [n. of action f. med.L. *toxicāre*: see prec.] Poisoning: esp. by toxic substances produced by disease-germs.

1821 COLERIDGE in *Blackw. Mag.* X. 243, I..know of no reason, why to these *toxications*, (especially when taken through the skin, and to the cataleptic state produced by them,) we should not attribute the poor wretches' own belief of their guilt. 1860 in MAYNE *Expos. Lex.* 1887 A. M. BROWN *Anim. Alkal.* 127 The patients so affected have all the appearance of toxication, and by the poisonous alkaloids—that is, the vital alkaloids or leucomaines.

**Toxicity** (tǫksi·sĭti). [f. TOXIC + -ITY.] Toxic or poisonous quality, esp. in relation to its degree or strength.

1881 *Nature* 3 Nov. 24/2 On the comparative toxicity of different metals, by M. Richet... He named the limit of toxicity the quantity of poison per litre of water, allowing a fish to live more than forty-eight hours. 1881 *Pharmaceut. Jrnl.* 26 Nov. 439/2 Neither would there appear to be any relation between toxicity and chemical function, for although potassium and sodium are nearly allied.., the former is—at least in respect to fish—twenty-four times more poisonous than sodium. 1898 P. MANSON *Trop. Diseases* xvii. 283 The microbes were increased in toxicity to a definite point.

**Toxico-** (tǫ·ksiko), before a vowel **toxic-**, repr. Gr. τοξικόν in sense 'poison' (see TOXICUM), but chiefly used as combining form of TOXIC, in scientific terms, mostly pathological. ‖ **Toxicæ·mia, -e·mia** [Gr. αἷμα blood] = *toxæmia*: see TOX-. ‖ **Toxicoderma** (-dǭ·ɹmă), **-dermati·tis, -dermi·tis** [Gr. δέρμα skin: see -ITIS], inflammation of the skin caused by an irritant poison. **Toxicogenic** (-dʒe·nik) *a.* [-*genic*: cf. -GEN, -GENY], producing or generating poison. ‖ **Toxicohæ·mia**, also anglicized **-hemy** [Gr. αἷμα blood] = *toxæmia*: see TOX-. ‖ **Toxicoma·nia** [MANIA], a morbid craving for poisons. **Toxicophagous** (-ǫ·făgəs) *a.* [Gr. -φάγος eating], addicted to eating poisonous substances; so **Toxicophagy** (-ǫ·fădʒi), the habit of eating poisonous substances. **Toxicophobia** (-fōu·biă) = *toxiphobia*: see TOXI-. **To:xicotrauma·tic** (-trǭmæ·tik) *a.* [Gr. τραυματικός, f. τραῦμα wound], pertaining to a poisoned wound. See also TOXICODENDRON, TOXICOLOGY, etc.

1857 DUNGLISON *Med. Lex.*, **Toxicæmia*, Toxicohæmia. 1890 BILLINGS *Med. Dict.*, **Toxicoderma* or **Toxicodermatitis*... **Toxicodermitis*, dermatitis caused by a poison. 1899 *Syd. Soc. Lex.*, **Toxicogenic*, ..as a toxicogenic micro-organism. 1902 *Buck's Handbk. Med. Sc.* IV. 184 A relatively small number of bacteria are capable of making poisonous products, and to these..the term *toxicogenic* may be applied. 1871 YULE *Marco Polo* III. xxv. (1903) II. 392 *note*, The famous *toxicophagous Sultan Mahmúd Begara (1459–1511). 1899 *Allbutt's Syst. Med.* VI. 657 Oppenheim attributes the latter..to a *toxico-traumatic cause.

‖ **Toxicodendron** (tǫ:ksikoᵢde·ndrǫn). *Bot.* [mod.L. (Tournefort, 1700, in sense a), f. Gr. τοξικόν (see TOXICUM) + δένδρον tree.]

a. A former genus, now reckoned as a species of *Rhus* or sumac (*R. Toxicodendron*), a N. American shrub, also called *poison-ivy* (see POISON *sb.* 5 b). b. A synonym of *Hyænanche*, a S. African genus of euphorbiaceous trees or shrubs with poisonous fruit, used for killing noxious animals, whence the local names *Wolveboon* (i. e. Wolf's-bane) and Hyena-poison.

1721 W. SHERARD in *Phil. Trans.* XXXI. 147 The Poyson-Tree...Tis a species of Toxicodendron, tho' not nam'd by Dr. Tournefort in his Institutions. 1755 *Gentl. Mag.* Sept. 395/1 Experiments made on staining of linen with the juice of Toxicodendron. 1758 ELLIS in *Phil. Trans.* L. 445 He still insists on it, that these two Toxicodendrons are the same. 1801 MASON *Suppl. to Johnson*, *Toxicodendron*, a North-American plant. 1888 *Nicholson's Dict. Gard.* IV. 63 *Toxicodendron* Syn. *Hyænanche.*

Hence **To:xicode·ndric** *a.*, *Chem.* applied to an acid derived from *Rhus Toxicodendron* and other species, subsequently found to be identical with acetic acid; **To:xicode·ndrol** [-OL 3], *Chem.* a non-volatile oil constituting the poisonous principle of *Rhus Toxicodendron* and other species.

1865 J. M. MAISCH in *Proc. Amer. Pharm. Assoc.* 172 A new organic acid, for which I propose the name of *Toxicodendric acid.* 1876 DUHRING *Dis. Skin* 325 The poison is an exceedingly volatile acid,—toxicodendric acid. 1898 *U. S. Dept. Agric., Bot.* Bulletin No. 20. 37 The poison is in reality a non-volatile oil. In January, 1895, Dr. Franz Pfaff ..announced this discovery. The oil has since been purified and named toxicodendrol.

**To·xicoid**, *a.* [f. Gr. τοξικόν (TOXICUM) + -OID.] Resembling poison.

1891 *Cent. Dict.* cites DUNGLISON. 1899 in *Syd. Soc. Lex.*

**Toxicology** (tǫksikǫ·lŏdʒi). [= F. *toxicologie* (1812 in Hatz.-Darm.), f. Gr. τοξικόν taken in sense 'poison' (see TOXICUM) and -LOGY.] The science of poisons; that department of pathology or medicine which deals with the nature and effects of poisons. So **To:xicolo·gical** *a.*, belonging or relating to toxicology (sometimes erron. used for *toxical*). Thence **To:xicolo·gically** *adv.*, in relation to toxicology; **Toxico·logist**, a person versed in toxicology, one who studies poisons.

1839 *Blackw. Mag.* XLV. 59 To guess whether the *toxicological agent..was a mineral, a vegetable, or an animal poison. 1842 BRANDE *Dict. Sc.*, etc. s. v. *Toxicology*, We have elsewhere..referred to their toxicological history. *c* 1865 J. WYLDE in *Circ. Sc.* I. 320/2 In toxicological analyses. 1882 SPRINGMUHL in *Standard* 23 Mar. 2/2 It differs *toxicologically and constitutionally from pure Aconitine. 1829–32 R. CHRISTISON *Treat. Poison* xiii. (ed. 2) 387 The rule laid down by almost all modern *toxicologists. 1897 *Allbutt's Syst. Med.* II. 876. 1799 HOOPER *Med. Dict.*, **Toxicology*,..a dissertation on poisons. 1853 W. GREGORY *Inorg. Chem.* (ed. 3) 230 The reader is referred to the works on toxicology and legal medicine.

‖ **Toxicosis** (tǫksikōu·sis). *Path.* Pl. **-oses** (-ōu·sīz). [mod.L., f. as prec. + -OSIS.] A disease or morbid condition produced by the action of a poison.

1857 DUNGLISON *Med. Lex.*, *Toxicoses*, a family of diseases ..caused by the reception of poisons into the system.

‖ **To·xicum.** Pl. **-a.** [L. *toxicum* 'poison', orig. 'poison for arrows', ad. Gr. τοξικὸν φάρμακον poison (φάρμακον) for smearing arrows (τοξικός, -όν, f. τόξα pl. arrows, transf. fr. τόξον bow). Τοξικόν = 'of or pertaining to the bow', and had originally nothing to do with poison. But the effect of using τοξικόν, *toxicum* as short for the Gr. phrase was to transfer the sense 'poison' from φάρμακον to *toxicum*, first as 'poison for arrows' and at length as 'poison' generally, = L. *venēnum*.] Poison: cf. TOXIC *sb.*

1601 HOLLAND *Pliny* XXIX. iv. II. 355 It is generally thought, that for the venome called Toxicum, there is not a better counterpoyson than dogs bloud. 1657 *Physical Dict.*, *Toxicum*, a venom or poyson wherewith arrows are poysoned. 1669 W. SIMPSON *Hydrol. Chym.* 78 The vital spirits stand amazed as if smitten with a thunder-clap from the uterine toxicum. 1693 tr. *Blancard's Phys. Dict.* (ed. 2), *Toxica*, poysonous Medicaments, wherewith Barbarians use to anoint their Arrows. 1704 in J. HARRIS *Lex. Techn.* I.

**Toxidermic** to **Toxi-infective**: see TOXI-.

**To·xifer.** *Zool.* [ad. mod.L. *Toxifera* (Gray), f. Gr. τόξα arrows (or τόξευμα arrow, dart) + L. *-fer* bearing.] A mollusc of the sub-order *Toxifera.* (Cf. TOXOGLOSSATE.)

1853 J. E. GRAY in *Ann. & Mag. Nat. Hist.* Ser. II. XII. 177 The subulate barbed teeth are implanted by a distinct root into the substance of the tube... The structure and organization of the mouth are so unlike that of the other *Proboscidifera* and *Rostrifera*, where the teeth are placed on a lingual ribbon and used to rasp the food..that I am inclined to form the *Cones* into a third sub-order, which may be called *Toxifera*. 1861 P. P. CARPENTER in *Rep. Smithsonian Instit.* 1860, 193 So far as known, the teeth and proboscis are like those of other Toxifers. 1863 — in *Proc. Zool. Soc.* 23 June 347 Species belonging to different families of Proboscidifers and Toxifers.

**Toxin** (tǫ·ksin). Also *erron.* **-ine.** [f. TOX-IC + -IN [1].] A specific poison, usually of an albuminous nature, esp. one produced by a microbe, which causes a particular disease when present in the system of a human or animal body.

**1886** E. R. LANKESTER *Advancem. Science* (1890) 168 In other cases the toxin and the vaccin seem almost certainly to be distinct. **1891** *Lancet* 3 Oct. 792 In a few cases..the introduction of the toxines secreted by the bacilli sufficed to set up a commencement of the process in the joints characteristic of rheumatism. **1904** *Brit. Med. Jrnl.* 10 Sept. 557 The union of toxin and antitoxin is dissociable. **1905** G. A. REID *Princ. Heredity* ii. 21 Toxins, extremely complex chemical compounds, are defensive weapons which protect the organisms producing them from their enemies, the phagocytes of the blood and tissues.

**b.** *attrib.* and *Comb.*

**1896** *Allbutt's Syst. Med.* I. 893 In order to produce an immunity all that is required is to render the body toxin-proof. **1902** *Encycl. Brit.* XXVI. 66/2 In the development of toxin-immunity the doses, small at first, are gradually increased. **1903** *Brit. Med. Jrnl.* 4 Apr. 784 No proof is afforded..of a separate toxophore group in the toxin molecule. **1904** *Ibid.* 10 Sept. 576 The chemical interpretation of toxin-antitoxin antagonism.

Hence ‖ **Toxinæmia** (-ī·miă) [Gr. αἷμα blood], the presence of a toxin in the blood: cf. *toxæmia* (TOX-¹), *toxicæmia* (TOXICO-).

**1900** *Buck's Handbk. Med. Sc.* I. 284 Various toxæmic conditions..and the different toxinæmias induced by the infectious diseases—diphtheria and typhoid or typhus fever.

**Toxin**, rare obs. spelling of TOCSIN.

**Toxiphagus** to **Toxiresin**: see TOXI-.

**To·xity**, abbreviated form of TOXICITY.

**1887** A. M. BROWN *Anim. Alkal.* 103 Previous alkaline saturation of the material did not revive its toxity. **1894** *Westm. Gaz.* 11 Oct. 2/1 By multiplying the intensity of the toxity of the bacillus.

‖ **Toxius** (tǫ·ksiŭs). *Zool.* Pl. **toxii** (-i,əi). [mod.L., f. Gr. τόξον bow.] A form of sponge-spicule: see quot.

**1886** *Proc. Zool. Soc.* 21 Dec. 562 Sponges..Flesh-Spicules..6. Toxius. Curved in the centre, the two ends in a straight line, thus ⌒.

**Toxo-¹** (tǫkso), before a vowel **tox-**, combining form repr. Gr. τόξον bow, in TOXOCAMPID, TOXODON, TOXOLOGY, TOXOPHILITE, etc., q. v.

**Toxo-²**, used as combining form of TOXIN (cf. TOXI-) or instead of TOXICO-, in recent scientific terms, chiefly of pathology or physiological chemistry. **Toxo-infe·ctious** *a.*, involving infection by a toxin: = *toxi-infectious* (TOXI-). **Toxope·ptone,** (*a*) a poisonous substance, of the nature of a peptone, found in cultures of cholera bacillus (*Cent. Dict. Suppl.*); (*b*) = PEPTOTOXIN. **To·xophil** (-fil) *a.* [Gr. -φιλος loving], having affinity for a toxin. **To·xophore** (-fōᵊɹ), **Toxophoric** (-fǫ·rik), **Toxophorous** (-ǫ·fŏrəs) *adjs.* [Gr. -φορος bearing, carrying], poison-bearing; applied to a particular group of atoms in the molecule of a toxin to which its toxic properties are due. **Toxophylaxin** (-filæ·ksin) [Gr. φύλαξ guard, protector], **Toxosozin** (-sōᵘ·zin) [Gr. σώζειν to save], names for defensive proteins or antitoxins (see quots.). **Toxoprotein** (-prōᵘ·tī,in), a toxic protein, or mixture of a toxin and a protein.

**1907** *Med. Record* 17 Aug. 279 The original cause of the lack of coagulation may be *toxoinfectious, or due to marked congestion. **1896** *Allbutt's Syst. Med.* I. 526 Scholl, growing the vibrio, in eggs, obtained a *toxo-peptone. **1902** VAUGHAN & NOVY *Cellular Toxins* (ed. 4) 182 The body cells must possess *toxophil side chains. By this we mean that..there are groups of atoms which may combine with bacterial toxins. **1900** *Lancet* 18 Aug. 528/1 The *toxophore group of the toxin molecule being much less stable than the haptophore group was much more easily destroyed. **1903** *Brit. Med. Jrnl.* 21 Mar. 654 The other atomic group is toxophore, namely, is the cause of the specific toxic action. **1902** *Ibid.* 29 Mar. 785 The toxin molecule..must possess a second group which he [Ehrlich] calls the *toxophoric group. **1904** *Ibid.* 10 Sept. 574 Although the toxophoric group may be similar, the haptophor is dissimilar. **1902** *Encycl. Brit.* XXVI. 65/1 In the molecule of toxin there are at least two chief atom groups—one, the 'haptophorous', by which the toxin molecule is attached to the cell protoplasm; and the other the '*toxophorous', which has a ferment-like action on the living molecule, producing a disturbance which results in the toxic symptoms. **1899** *Syd. Soc. Lex.*, **Toxophylaxin*, a defensive proteid produced in the body of an animal which has acquired immunity for a given infectious disease, and which has the power of rendering inert the toxic products of the pathogenic micro-organisms to which the condition was due. **1896** *Allbutt's Syst. Med.* I. 523 The *toxo-proteins in reality are mixtures of albuminous, proteid, or albuminoid bodies with the true toxins. **1899** *Syd. Soc. Lex.*, **Toxosozin*, a defensive proteid found in the body of a normal animal which has the power of protecting itself to a greater or less degree against micro-organisms and their products.

**Toxocampid** (tǫ·ksokæ·mpid), *sb.* and *a. Entom.* [ad. mod.L. *Toxocampidæ*, f. *Toxocampa*, f. Gr. τόξον bow + κάμπη caterpillar.] **a.** *sb.* A Noctuine moth of the family *Toxocampidæ*, typified by the genus *Toxocampa*, having bow-shaped marks on the fore wings, e. g. *Toxocampa Pastinum*, the black-neck. **b.** *adj.* Belonging to or having the characters of the family *Toxocampidæ*.

**Toxodon** (tǫ·ksŏdǫn). *Palæont.* [mod.L. (Owen, 1837), f. Gr. τόξον bow + ὀδούς, ὀδοντ- tooth: see quot. 1849.] A genus of large extinct quadrupeds, having strongly curved molar teeth, whose remains are found in Pleistocene deposits in S. America. Hence **To·xodont,** *adj.* belonging to or having the characters of the order *Toxodonta*, typified by this genus; *sb.* a quadruped of this order.

**1837** OWEN in *Proc. Geol. Soc.* II. 542 So far as dental characters have weight, the *Toxodon* must be referred to the rodent order. **1839** G. ROBERTS *Dict. Geol.*, *Toxodon*, ..a gigantic quadruped, approaching, in character, to the pachydermata. **1849** *Sk. Nat. Hist.*, *Mammalia* III. 115 The molar teeth also were rootless, and curved, whence the name toxodon. **1859** DARWIN *Orig. Spec.* xi. (1878) 294 Remains of Mastodon, Megatherium, Toxodon and other extinct monsters.

**To:xoglo·ssate,** *a. Zool.* [f. mod.L. *Toxoglossa* (Troschel, 1848), f. Gr. τόξα arrows, darts + γλῶσσα tongue (not from τοξικόν poison): see -ATE² 2.] Having the characters of the *Toxoglossa* of Troschel, a group of gastropod molluscs; the same as Gray's *Toxifera*.

[**1848** TROSCHEL in Wilfmann & Ruthe's *Handbch. d. Zoologie* (ed. 3).] **1853** J. E. GRAY in *Ann. & Mag. Nat. Hist.* Ser. II. XI. 230 [following Troschel] Sub-order *Rostrifera*...Section 2. *Toxoglossa*, lingual membrane with two series of subulate, elongate, often barbed lateral teeth. **1891** *Cent. Dict.* s. v., A toxoglossate gastropod. [**1913** PROF. G. C. BOURNE in *Let.*, I am pretty sure that Troschel compared the teeth to arrows..when he described and classified 3 families as *Toxoglossa*...As a matter of fact all the *Toxoglossa* have a poison-gland, but this was a later discovery.]

**Toxoid** (tǫ·ksoid). [f. TOX(IN (cf. TOX-¹) + -OID.] A modification or transformation product of a toxin, in which the toxophoric group of atoms is lost, and which has therefore no toxic effect, but retains affinity for the antitoxin. Also *attrib.*

**1900** *Lancet* 18 Aug. 528/1 Very sensitive animals such as mice and guinea-pigs might..be easily and rapidly immunised against tetanus by means of toxoids only. **1902** *Brit. Med. Jrnl.* 29 Mar. 785 The modified toxin consists of a molecule with a haptophoric but no toxophoric group and is called 'toxoid'. **1903** *Ibid.* 21 Mar. 654 The toxoids may again be subdivided into three groups, according to their affinity for the antitoxin, which may obviously be either greater (protoxoid), equal (syntoxoid), or less than (epitoxoid) that of the toxin. **1904** *Ibid.* 10 Sept. 577 They were however able to produce toxoid formation in this constituent.

**Toxology** (tǫksǫ·lŏdʒi). *nonce-wd.* [f. Gr. τόξον bow + -LOGY.] *prop.* The study of the bow, i. e. archery; in quot. humorously used for 'archery'.

**1843** *Fraser's Mag.* XXVII. 401 He is reluctant to..run the risk of exposing his well-varnished cab as a pleasing target for the poles of the loitering omnibuses, the drivers of which latter have obtained a well-earned fame for their dexterity in this..department of toxology.

**Toxon¹** (tǫ·ksǫn). *Zool.* [a. Gr. τόξον bow.] A bow-shaped sponge spicule. Cf. Tox *sb.*

**1894** *Jrnl. Marine Zool.* Feb. 40 A second and slender form of spicule, bow-shaped (toxon) can also be made out.

**To·xon²**. *Path. Chem.* [f. TOX(IN + *-on*, -ONE.] (See quotation.)

**1900** *Lancet* 18 Aug. 528/1 Löffler's diphtheria bacillus produced substances of two kinds—toxins and toxons...The action of the toxons was different from, and weaker than, that of the toxins. **1904** *Brit. Med. Jrnl.* 10 Sept. 567 The diphtheria poison is not a single substance, but consists of two chief components, toxin and toxon.

Hence **To·xonoid**, a modification of a toxon, in which the toxic properties are lost. (Cf. TOXOID.)

**1904** *Brit. Med. Jrnl.* 10 Sept. 573 Ehrlich explained the peculiarity that the 'toxon' has acute killing properties, by the assumption of two different kinds of toxon, thus introducing the conception of a new body—the toxonoid.

**Toxopeptone, Toxophil**: see TOXO-².

**Toxophilite** (tǫksǫ·filəit). [app. f. *Toxophil-us* (imaginary proper name invented by Ascham, and hence title of his book (1545), intended to mean 'lover of the bow' (f. Gr. τόξον bow + φίλος lover), for which the regular Gr. formation would have been *φιλότοξος: see -PHIL, PHILO-) + -ITE¹: *quasi* 'a follower of Toxophilus'.] A lover or devotee of archery, an archer.

**1813** J. C. HOBHOUSE *Journey* (ed. 2) 929 Memorials of the distance to which some of the Sultans, and other distinguished Toxophilites, have shot their arrows. **1845** THACKERAY *Leg. Rhine* viii, His Grace..gives an archery meeting once a year, and prizes for which we toxophilites muster strong. **1868** MISS BRADDON *Dead Sea Fr.* xxi, A triumphant display of his genius as a toxophilite.

**b.** *attrib.* Of or pertaining to archers or archery.

**1794** *Sporting Mag.* III. 206 That the Toxophilite Society shall not exceed the number of one hundred and sixty subscribing members. **1845** THACKERAY *Leg. Rhine* viii, All his new toxophilite friends. **1848** — *Van. Fair* iii, To wear Lincoln Green toxophilite hats and feathers.

Hence (*nonce-wds.*) **Toxophilitic** (-i·tik) *a.*, pertaining or relating to archers or archery; **Toxo·philitism, Toxo·philism, Toxo·phily,** the practice of, or addiction to, archery.

**1887** *All Year Round* 29 Sept. 185 The spirit of *toxophilism is essentially different from..the spirit of the age. **1857** *Chamb. Jrnl.* VII. 141 The *toxophilitic proficiency of William Tell. **1840** T. HOOK in *New Monthly Mag.* LX. 152 Dressed in green, with hats, and feathers, and quivers, and all the paraphernalia of *toxophilitism. **1887** *Field* 16 July 103/1 Amongst the votaries of *toxophily.

**Toxophore** to **Toxosozin**: see TOXO-².

**Toxt**: see TOX *v.*

**Toy** (toi), *sb.* Forms: ? 4, 6–7 **toye**, 6– **toy**; *Pl.* 6–7 **toyes, toies,** 6– **toys.** [*Toy* sb. and vb. (formerly *toye*) have been in common use since *c* 1530, when both are given by Palsgr., and used by Skelton and Tindale. But a single instance of *toye* sb., apparently the same word, occurs in Robert of Brunne. It is difficult to conceive how such a word in use *c* 1300 should thus disappear for two centuries, and then should all at once burst into view with a wide sense-development. The etymology is equally problematic, and, in spite of current conjectures, must still be considered unascertained: see Note below.]

**I.** Abstract senses, meaning action, act, notion, feeling.

†**1.** Amorous sport, dallying, toying; with *pl.*, an act or piece of amorous sport, a light caress.

[**1303** R. BRUNNE *Handl. Synne* 7891 Whedyr hyt be yn a womman handlyng, Or yn any oþer lusty þyng;..Amendeþ ȝow, þur charyte, And makeþ nat a-mys þe toye [*so all MSS.*], Þat þe fende of ȝou haue Ioye.] **1565** COOPER *Thesaurus* s. v. *Amo*: *Amatoriæ leuitates*, Louers toyes. **1590** SPENSER *F. Q.* II. vi. 37 A foe of folly and immodest toy. **1594** — *Epithal.* 365 For greedy pleasure, carelesse of your toyes, Thinks more upon her paradise of joyes, Then what ye do. **1594** WILLOBIE *Avisa* XLVII. iii, These toyes in tyme will make her yielde. **1667** MILTON *P. L.* IX. 1034 So said he, and forbore not glance or toy, Of amorous intent, well understood Of Eve. **1668** ETHEREDGE *She Would if She Could* II. ii, Her toy was such, that every touch Would make a lover madder. **1707** WARD *Hud. Rediv.* II. ii. 8 (Farmer) Kisses, Love-Toys, and am'rous Prattle.

†**2.** A sportive or frisky movement; a piece of fun, amusement, or entertainment; a fantastic act or practice; an antic, a trick. *Obs.*

*a* **1500** MEDWALL *Nature* I. 786 (Brandl), Though I say yt a praty boy..He maketh me laugh wyth many a toy, The vrchyn ys so mad. *Ibid.* 1001 He that wold lordshyp enioy And playe euer styll the old boy Me semeth he doth but make a toy. **1530** TINDALE *Answ. More* Wks. (1572) 249/1 We heare but voyces with out signification,..& wonder at disguisings & toyes wherof we know no meanyng. *c* **1555** HARPSFIELD *Divorce Hen. VIII* (Camden) 291 Neither was there ever any bearwards Jackanapes that made more pastime and toys to the people, than this. **1561** HOLLYBUSH *Hom. Apoth.* 9 Somtyme croweth he like a cocke, somtyme barketh he like a dogge, and many such foolish toyes vseth he. *c* **1575** *Perfect Bk. Kepinge Sparhawkes* (1886) 15 Lest she get a toye of flinginge her head. **1616** R. C. *Times' Whistle* v. 1948 Are apish tricks and toies, which vse to bring Men in dirision, sportes to breed delight? **1777** *Horæ Subsec.* 437 (E.D.D.) He hath taken a toy to scratch his head, when he is speaking to a gentleman.

**3.** A fantastic or trifling speech or piece of writing; a frivolous or mocking speech; a foolish or idle tale; a funny story or remark, a jest, joke, pun; a light or facetious composition. *arch.*

**1542** UDALL *Erasm. Apoph.* I. *Diogenes* § 79 Nothyng but a toye, in daliyng with the affinitee and similitude of woordes. **1553** T. WILSON *Rhet.* (1580) A iv, Suche as seeke the greatest praise for writyng of Bookes, should doe beste.. to write foolishe toyes, for then the moste parte would best esteme them. **1577** BRETON *Flourish on Fancie* (Grosart) 11/2 Toyes of straung deuise, With stories of olde Robin Hood. **1590** SHAKS. *Mids. N.* V. i. 3, I neuer may beleeue These anticke fables, nor these Fairy toyes. **1621** MOLLE *Camerar. Liv. Libr.* III. xx. 215 They gaue credit to all these foolish toies. **1719** D'URFEY *Pills* (1872) I. 126 Fye George, she crys, these Words are but Toys.

*arch.* **1821** SCOTT *Kenilw.* xvi, Think of what that arch-knave Shakspeare says—a plague on him, his toys come into my head when I should think of other matters. **1905** R. GARNETT *Shakespeare* 104 She hath heard A little toy of thine, a comedy ('Tis called, I think, The Taming of a Shrew).

**b.** † (*a*) A light, frivolous, or lively tune. *Obs.* (*b*) A particular turn or phrase of melody in a bird's song: see quot. 1851.

**1591** GREENE *Art Conny Catch.* III. (1592) 19 In the time of ceissing betweene the seuerall toyes and fancies hee plaied. **1641** SANDERSON *Serm.*, *Ad Aulam* xiii. (1660) II. 267 One would have a grave Pavane, another a nimbler Galliard, a third some striking toy or Jigg. **1851** MAYHEW *Lond. Labour* (1861) III. 14 There are four-and-twenty changes in a linnet's song...It sings 'toys', as we call them.

†**4.** A foolish or idle fancy; a fantastic notion, odd conceit; a whim, crotchet, caprice. *Obs.*

*c* **1530** H. RHODES *Bk. Nurture* 330 in *Babees Bk.* (1868) 80 Cast not thyne eyes to ne yet fro, as thou werte full of toyes. **1555** W. WATREMAN *Fardle Facions* II. x. 225 This people [Tartarres] hath many supersticious toyes. **1563** B. GOOGE *Eglogs* vii. (Arb.) 59 But yf a toye com in your Brayne, your mynde is altered quyght. **1591** FLORIO *2nd Fruites* 161 Euen as the toy takes me in the head. **1642** ROGERS *Naaman* 98 So deadly doth this conceit and toy of his owne braine worke with him. **1668** R. L'ESTRANGE *Vis. Quev.* (1708) 101 Yet when the Toy took them, they'd make now and then a Sally. **1699** — *Fables* II. vii. (1715) II. 5 A New Marry'd Couple had a Toy took them in their Heads, so soon as ever the Office was over, to Shrift one another before they came together.

†**b.** *spec.* A foolish or unreasoning dislike or aversion: esp. in phr. *to take* (*a*) *toy* (in quot. 1612 = to take fright, start, shy) *at* something. *Obs.*

*a* **1593** MARLOWE *Hero & Leander* v. Wks. (Rtldg.) 304/2 [To hear this] Made the well-spoken nymph take such a toy, That down she sunk. **1612** *Two Noble K.* v. iv. 79 The hot horse, hot as fire, Took Toy at this. **1647** SANDERSON *Serm.*, *Ad Aulam* xiv. (1660) II. 277 Common friends many times ..take toy at a trifle,..and pick quarrels to desert us. **1697** J. SERGEANT *Solid Philos.* 308 Thence they take a Toy at Metaphysics, and pretend it insuperably hard and mysterious

**II.** Concrete senses.

(Sense 5 is also often *abstract*, connecting I and II; the connexion of 10 with the other senses is doubtful.)

**5.** *gen.* A thing of little or no value or importance, a trifle; a foolish or senseless affair, a piece of nonsense; *pl.* trumpery, rubbish. (In mod. use regarded as *fig.* from next sense.)

**1530** PALSGR. 281/2 Toy a tryfell, *truffe, friuolle.* **1538** ELYOT, *Abydena*, trifles, thinges of smalle estimation, wanton toyes, thynges vnseemely for menne to vse. **1587** HARRISON *England* II. vi. (1877) I. 166 To stand vpon such toies would spend much time. **1605** SHAKS. *Macb.* II. iii. 91 From this instant, There's nothing serious in Mortalitie: All is but Toyes. **1631** GOUGE *God's Arrows* I. § 29. 44 Of Popish toyes to pacifie God. **1664** H. MORE *Myst. Iniq.*, *Apol.* 554 If they leave not off their animosities and asperities of mind about toys and trifles. **1719** WATTS *Hymn*, '*Come, holy Spirit, Heavenly Dove*' ii, Look, how we grovel here below, Fond of these earthly Toys. **1848** THACKERAY *Van. Fair* ix, But a title and a coach and four are toys more precious than happiness in Vanity Fair.

**6.** A material object for children or others to play with (often an imitation of some familiar object); a plaything; also, something contrived for amusement rather than for practical use (esp. in phrase *a mere toy*). In quot. *a*1586 *playing toy.* Now the leading sense, to which the others are referred.

*a* **1586** SIDNEY *Arcadia* IV. Wks. 1725 II. 771 There was never poor scholar, that having instead of his book some playing toy about him, did more suddenly cast it from him. **1598** BARCKLEY *Felic. Man* (1631) 152 The rattles and toyes which children use to play with. *a* **1656** BP. HALL *Occas. Medit.* (1851) 111 We cry for every toy, even that which may most hurt us. **1672** R. WILD *Poet. Licent.* 29 We all know Popes-head-Alley trades in Toyes, Our Merchants come not thither, but our Boys. **1781** COWPER *Hope* 128 Men deal with life as children with their play, Who first misuse, then cast their toys away. **1881** STEVENSON *Virg. Puerisque, Child's Play* (1905) 157 Lead soldiers, dolls, all toys, in short, are in the same category. **1893** J. A. HODGES *Elem. Photogr.* (1907) 14 The very low-priced sets [of photographic apparatus]..are generally mere toys.

*fig.* **1893** LIDDON, etc. *Life Pusey* I. xvi. 363 He handles it with the delight that a new mental toy inspires in most men at a certain time of life.

**7.** A small article of little intrinsic value, but prized as an ornament or curiosity; 'a petty commodity' (J.), a knick-knack, trinket, gewgaw; hence (often in allusion to 6) applied to anything small, flimsy, or inferior of its kind (now chiefly *attrib.*: see 11 b).

**1596** SHAKS. *Tam. Shr.* IV. iii. 67 Heere is the cap... Why 'tis a cockle or a walnut-shell, A knacke, a toy, a tricke, a babies cap. **1624** CAPT. SMITH *Virginia* I. 3 We presented him with diuers toyes, which he kindly accepted. *c* **1630** HALES *Serm. John xviii. 36* Rem. (1673) 154 So like one another, that one of them must wear a toy in his cap, that so the spectators may distinguish them. **1711** in *10th Rep. Hist. MSS. Comm.* App. v. 139 A weak town, haveing noe outward works, but a toy of a pallisade before a litle part of the wall. **1712** ARBUTHNOT *John Bull* III. i, Ladies, hung about with toys and trinkets. **1768** *Tom Thumb's Folio* i. 4 His Father was greatly disconcerted at having such a little tiney Toy of a Child. **1888** BLACK *Houseboat* xi, Perched on the top of a hill was a conspicuous toy of a church.

**b.** Applied technically to small steel articles, as hammers, pincers, buckles, button-hooks, nails, etc. More fully 'steel toys' (? i.e. steel petty things).

**1833** J. HOLLAND *Manuf. Metal* II. 319 Heavy Steel Toys. By this not very appropriate description the Birmingham manufacturers refer to a class of articles... To enumerate all the 'toys' of this class would be to transcribe a large list of miscellaneous cheap and useful wares, from a joiner's hammer to a shoemaker's tack. The pincers of the last-named workman, and the edged nippers.. in use for breaking up loaf-sugar, are both of them well-known specimens.

**c.** *Thieves' slang.* A watch; *toy and tackle*, a watch and chain. Cf. *toy-getter* (see 11 d).

**1877** HORSLEY *Jottings fr. Jail* i. (1887) 17 He was very tricky at getting a poge or a toy, but he would not touch toys because we was afraid of being turned over.

**8.** *fig.* Applied to a person: **a.** (from 5) slightingly or contemptuously; in quot. 1822 affectionately = pet, darling (cf. 7); **b.** (from 6) as being used as a plaything or for sport.

**1598** SHAKS. *Merry W.* v. v. 46 Elues, list your names: Silence, you aiery toyes. **1616** B. JONSON *Devil an Ass* IV. vii, I ha' sworne to ha' him by the eares: I feare The toy, wi' not do me right. **1681** DRYDEN *Span. Friar* IV. ii, O, Vertue! Vertue!.. That men should leave thee for that Toy, a Woman? **1821** BYRON *Mar. Fal.* I. ii, Thou idle, gilded, and degraded toy. **1822** T. MITCHELL *Aristoph.* II. 171 Why, Xanthias, my toy, Why, what ails the poor boy! **1883** STEPNIAK in *Contemp. Rev.* Sept. 317 A Russian.. being a mere toy in the hands of the commonest policeman. **1888** STEVENSON *Black Arrow* 46 This toy.. that's not fit for wounds or warfare.

**9.** Applied to a diminutive breed or variety of animals. **a.** Short for *toy dog*: see 11 c.

**1877** *Field* 24 Feb. 214/2 In toys no great change has taken place, except that..pugs, Italian greyhounds, and toy terriers are on the decline. **1899** *Pall Mall G.* 3 Oct. 9/1 Ladies' toys were in strong force... Sporting dogs were not numerous. **1903** *Daily Chron.* 25 May 5/2 The 'chiens de luxe', or Toys, are in a roomy and well-warmed 'pavillon' by themselves.

**b.** Any dwarf variety of tame pigeon.

**1909** *Cent. Dict. Suppl.* s.v., The toys resemble the tumblers in general build and are among pigeons what bantams are among fowl.

**10.** *Sc.* A close cap or head-dress, of linen or wool, with flaps coming down to the shoulders, formerly worn by women of the lower classes in Scotland. ? *Obs.* Also *toy-mutch* (11 d). [In this sense perh. = Du. *tooi* attire, dress: see Note below.]

(The *English* quots. 1611, 1612, are placed here as perh. suggesting the origin; but they may belong to 7.)

[**1611** SHAKS. *Wint. T.* IV. iv. 326 Any Silke, any Thred, any Toyes for your head? **1612** *Two Noble K.* I. iii, On my head no toy But was her pattern.] **1724** RAMSAY *Tea-t. Misc.* (1762) 2 Their toys and mutches were sae clean, They glanced in our ladses' een. **1793** *Statist. Acc. Scot.* IX. 325 The tenants wives wore toys of linen of the coarsest kind, upon their heads, when they went to church, fairs or market. **1816** SCOTT *Old Mort.* xxxix, The face of Alison ..now presented itself, enveloped in a 'toy'. **1824** — *Redgauntlet* Let. iv, An elderly woman, in a grey stuff gown, with a check apron and 'toy'. **1900** H. G. GRAHAM *Soc. Life Scot. in 18th C.* v. vi. (1901) 181 Farmers' wives and daughters with 'toys' or head-covering of coarse linen.

**III. 11.** *attrib.* and *Comb.* **a.** *attrib.* That is a toy (in sense 6): applied to small models or imitations of ordinary objects used as playthings, as *toy boat, cannon, dog, engine, horse, house, man, train, trumpet, woman*, etc.

**1836** [MISS MAITLAND] *Lett. fr. Madras* iv. (1843) 25 Cape Town is just like the Dutch toy-towns. *a* **1860** ALB. SMITH *Lond. Med. Stud.* (1861) 13 A stethescope—a curious instrument, something like a sixpenny toy-trumpet with its top knocked off. **1880** MRS. F. D. BRIDGES *Jrnl. Lady's Trav. round World* xviii. (1883) 298 One never quite gets over the impression of being amongst dolls and living in a toy-house.. in Japan. **1888** HASLUCK *Model Engin. Handybk.* iii. (1900) 24 The most simple form of toy-engine is that illustrated below. **1897** *Edin. Rev.* Oct. 480 The babies had toy-animals on wheels.

**b.** *transf.* and *fig.* Applied to things of diminutive size, flimsy construction, or petty character, as if intended for sport or diversion rather than serious use.

**1821** SCOTT *Kenilw.* xli, You go not to your gew-gaw toy-house yonder; you will sleep to-night in better security. **1855** HT. MARTINEAU *Autobiog.* I. 437 My surprise at the smallness and toy-character of Abbotsford was extreme. **1895** MISS BRADDON in *Westm. Gaz.* 6 Nov. 1/3 A very popular writer may launch three of these toy-pinnaces in a year. **1897** GLADSTONE *E. Crisis* 5 The Concert of Europe included toy-demonstrations, which might be made under the condition that they should not pass into reality. **1909** *Daily Chron.* 19 Feb. 3/2 Ruritania was something more than the first toy-kingdom of our modern stage.

**c.** Applied to an animal, esp. a dog of a diminutive breed or variety, kept as a pet, e.g. a *toy spaniel* or *terrier*.

**1863** *Sat. Rev.* 28 Mar. 408/1 These very large dogs are not much more useful than the very small ones which are called, with perfect aptness, toy dogs. **1872** B. CLAYTON *Dogs* 20 A Toy Terrier was exhibited which weighed only six ounces. **1889** G. STABLES *Dog Owners' Kennel Comp.* vi. § 10. 66 There are several other kinds of Toy Terriers.. but I need only mention..the Toy Black and Tan and the Toy Blue or Slate colour.

**d.** *Comb.*: attrib. (of or for toys), as *toy-box, -cupboard, -fair, -land, -manufacture, -trade*; objective and obj. gen., as *toy-maker, -making, -turner*; instrumental, similative, etc., as *toy-bewitched, -like, -sized* adjs.; also **toy-block**, one of a set of wooden or papier-mâché blocks, usually with letters or designs, for children to play with; **toy-getter** (*Thieves' slang*), a watch-stealer; so *toy-getting*; † **toy-headed** *a.*, having 'toys' or odd fancies in the head, crotchety; **toy-line** = *toy-railway*; **toy-mutch**, *Sc.* = sense 10; † **toy-pate**, a head full of 'toys', crotchets, or frivolities (cf. *toy-headed*); **toy-railway**, (*a*) a model of a railway, with its engine, train, etc.; (*b*) *pop.*, a small narrow-gauge railway, often orig. constructed for the use of slate-works or the like, but subseq. carrying tourists or other passengers; also *toy-line*; **toy-service**, a church-service at which toys are brought as an offering for sick or poor children; **toy-woman**, a woman who keeps a toy-shop. See also TOYMAN, -SHOP, -WORT.

**1794** COLERIDGE *Relig. Musings* vii, We become An anarchy of Spirits. *Toy-bewitched. **1891** *Cent. Dict.*, **Toy-block*, one of a set of small blocks,..forming a plaything for children. **1865** (*title*) Aunt Louisa's *Toy Books. **1831** CARLYLE *Sart. Res.* II. vi, He descries lying far below, embosomed among its groves and green natural bulwarks, and all diminished to a *toybox, the fair Town. **1900** *Westm. Gaz.* 11 Dec. 12/1 The season for the ransacking of *toy-cupboards. **1908** *Westm. Gaz.* 29 Oct. 1/2 The order.. that there shall be no *toy-fairs in London this Christmas-tide deprives the City of..one of its sights. **1896** A. MORRISON *Child of the Jago* 102 Dicky knew the small man for a good *toy-getter. **1633** T. ADAMS *Exp. 2 Peter* ii. 1 It sticks upon the stomach of some *toy-headed professors. **1908** *Daily Chron.* 5 Nov. 7/5 No one realises unless he penetrates into *Toyland how much whimsical humour, how much scientific skill and craftsman's ingenuity are devoted to the invention of the playthings for the festive season. **1818** SCOTT *Hrt. Midl.* i, The gay glancing of the equipage, its diminished and *toy-like appearance at a distance. **1883** *Manch. Exam.* 26 Nov. 5/3 The Swiss lake steamers are..too toy-like to ensure their passengers against reasonably probable risks. **1878** JENKINSON *Guide N. Wales* 271 Leaving the Cambrian train at Mynffordd Junction, the traveller walks up a path to the *toy line, and enters one of the little carriages. **1859** *Habits of Gd. Society* v. (new ed.) 194 Worth all the amusements which a *toy-maker could dream of. **1858** CARLYLE *Fredk. Gt.* IX. iii. (1872) III. 87 *Toy-manufactures of those simple people. **1742** FORBES *Dominie Depos'd* II. i, The *toy-mutch maun then gae on, Nae mair bare-hair'd. **1693** PENN *Maxims* lx. Wks. 1726 I. 847 He never deals but in substantial Ware, and leaves the rest for the *Toy-Pates (or Shops) of the World. **1892** BADDELEY *Guide N. Wales* (ed. 4) 165 *heading*, Portmadoc to Ffestiniog by the '*Toy' Railway. *Ibid.*, No orthodox tourist visits Wales without taking a turn..on the 'Toy' railway. **190**. *Guide to Lynton, Lynmouth*, etc. Introd. 19 *heading*, Barnstaple to Lynton by the Toy Railway. **1889** *Standard* 1 Feb., '*Toy Services' which are becoming very popular in some of our churches. **1895** CLIVE HOLLAND *Jap. Wife* (ed. 11) 27 *Toy-sized cups of tea. **1757** W. THOMPSON *R. N. Advoc.* 41 Our Sons of War are to be served after our Sons of *Toy-Trade. **1893** A. N. PALMER *Hist. Wrexham* IV. 11, I find mentioned..one *toy-turner. **1827** SCOTT *Diary* 2 Oct., in *Lockhart*, An old lady, who proved a *toy woman in Edinburgh.

[*Note.* Eduard Müller suggested the identity of *toy* with Du. *tooi*, late MDu. *tôi*, 16th c., 'attire, ornament, finery, dress', which suits the form, but hardly the sense (exc.? in 10 or 7). Others have thought of Du. *tuig* 'harness, horse-trappings', in pl. 'sails, rigging, implements, tools; stuff, lumber, refuse, trash'; in Kilian 1599 *tuygh*, dial. *tuych*, *tugh*, 'arms, implements, armaments, impedimenta, ornaments', = Ger. *zeug* 'apparatus, tools, gear, furniture, stuff, trash, etc.', LG. *tüg, tüüg*, MLG. *tûch, tûg*. But, if the sense-development shown above is historically correct, it is difficult to see in either of these suggestions the origin of the English word. It is indeed true that Du. *speeltuig*, Ger. *spielzeug*, and Da. *legetoi*, mean 'play-tool or implement, plaything, toy', and that Sidney in 1586 used 'playing toy', which might conceivably be a rendering of one of these compounds; but this would still leave the earlier English history unexplained.]

**Toy**, *v.* [Goes with TOY *sb.*, q. v.]

**1.** *intr.* To act idly or without seriousness; to trifle, 'play', deal carelessly (*with* a person or thing); also † to make sport, mock (*obs.*).

*a* **1529** SKELTON *Bowge of Courte* 290 It was no tyme with him to jape nor toye. **1530** PALSGR. 758/2, I toye, or tryfell with one, I deale nat substancyally with hym, *je me truffe.* **1549–62** STERNHOLD & H. *Ps.* xxxv. 16 Yea abject slaves at me did toy with mocks and cheekes ful stout. **1563** *Homilies* II. *Inform. H. Script.* I. (1859) 373 It is a shame that christian men should be so light headed, to toy as ruffians do with such manner of speeches. **1576** DERING *Expos. Heb.* v. 4–6. Cc iij, They must haue oyle, candels.. wine and water,..trifled and toyed with all. **1653** W. RAMESEY *Astrol. Restored* 19, I fear I do toy in recording these vain Objections. **1868** DIXON *Spir. Wives* I. vii. 75 He toyed with astrology, and had fitful dreams of enjoying the elixir of life. **1888** BRYCE *Amer. Commw.* II. lxxxi. 296 [Class issues] are usually toyed with by both parties alike.

**b.** So *to toy it.*

**1657** J. SERGEANT *Schism Dispach't* 379 Thus Dr. H. toyes it with his Readers. *Ibid.* 574 Let them not toy it now.

**2.** To sport amorously; to dally, flirt. Usually const. *with*. (Cf. TOY *sb.* 1.)

**15..** *Song Bachelor's Life* 7 (Ritson) If he [the married man] be merie and toy with any, His wife will frowne, and words geve manye. **1566** in *Daily News* 10 Sept. (1897) 6/7 That none toy with the maids, on paine of 4d. **1592** SHAKS. *Ven. & Ad.* 106 And for my sake [he] hath learnd to sport, and daunce, To toy, to wanton, dallie, smile, and iest. *c* **1613** MIDDLETON *No Wit like Woman's* v. i, Not toy, nor bill, and imitate house-pigeons. **1727** GAY *Begg. Op.* I. viii, O Polly you might have toy'd and kist. **1811** W. R. SPENCER *Poems* 73 Whilst he and Psyche toy'd together.

*fig.* **1793** WORDSW. *Descr. Sketches* 52 To where the Alps, ascending white in air, Toy with the Sun, and glitter from afar. **1842** H. ROGERS *Ess.* I. i. 4 He had in early life toyed a little with the muses.

**3.** To play, sport, amuse oneself; to move sportively, play or frisk about.

**1530** PALSGR. 758/2, I toye, I playe with one, *je me joue.* **1590** SPENSER *F. Q.* II. ix. 35 But other some could not abide to toy; All pleasaunce was to them griefe and annoy. **1678** CUDWORTH *Intell. Syst.* I. v. § 44. 674 The senseless atoms, playing and toying up and down without any care or thought. **1827** POLLOK *Course T.* v. 1007 The hare, unscared Sported and toyed familiar with his dog. **1836** O. W. HOLMES *Poetry* ii. 18 Pale dreamers, whose fantastic lay Toys with smooth trifles like a child at play. **1848** KINGSLEY *Saint's Trag.* II. iv. 63, I have toyed too long..down the stream of life.

**b.** *Toy with*: to play with (a material object), to handle or finger idly; hence, to work idly or carelessly with or at.

**1822** W. IRVING *Braceb. Hall* xxvi. (1845) 121 The gallant general took his station..at her side, and toyed with her elegantly ornamented work-bag. **1840** DICKENS *Barn. Rudge* lxiv, The fire was seen sporting and toying with the door. **1879** E. GARRETT *House by Works* I. 115 Mrs. Pendlebury looked down, and toyed with her rings.

**4.** *trans.* (with adv.) To spend or waste in toying; to bring by toying (into or out of some condition).

**1575** ABP. PARKER *Corr.* (Parker Soc.) 474, I toy out my time, partly with copying books. **1685** J. SCOTT *Chr. Life* II. 134 So fools and fleers on, till he hath toyed and laughed himself out of all sense of Religion. **1749** JOHNSON *Irene* I. i, He toys his hours away.

**To-yans, to-ȝanes**: see TO-GAINS.

**Toydom** (toi·dəm). *nonce-wd.* [f. TOY *sb.* + -DOM.] **a.** The condition of being or resembling a toy. **b.** The realm or domain of toys.

**1882** M. A. BARKER in *Macm. Mag.* XLVI. 68/1 The tan sail of a canoe or whiter sheet of a fishing boat..dwarfed into toydom whenever they come near the great war ship. **1905** *Times* 7 Jan. 11/2 At the Crystal Palace..side-shows are numerous, and toydom there is most attractive.

**To-year** (tŭ͡yīə·ɪ), *adv.* Now *dial.* Forms: see YEAR. [f. TO *prep.* A. 7 + YEAR: cf. *to-day, to-night.*] This year.

*c* **1205** LAY. 8039 Her ligged to-ȝere Ten þusend of his iferen. *c* **1290** *St. Brendan* 240 in *S. Eng. Leg.* I. 226 Ȝoure ester ȝe schulle holde þer as ȝe dude to-ȝere. *c* **1386** CHAUCER *Wife's Prol.* 168 Yet hadde I leuere wedde no wyf to yeere. *c* **1400** *Gosp. Nicodemus* 966 Of Iosepħ..þat ȝe presond to ȝere. **1483** *Cath. Angl.* 391/1 To ȝere, *horno*; *hornus, hornotinus.* *a* **1575** R. B. *Appius & Virg.* B j, Man, be mery to yeere. **1623** WEBSTER *Duchess of Malfi* II. i, I have heard of none to year. **1727** GAY *Begg. Op.* I. ii, Betty hath brought more Goods into our Lock to-year than any five of the Gang. **1828** *Craven Gloss.* s. v. *To*, 'We've a famous clip to year', that is, this year. **1882** TENNYSON *Promise of May* I. Poems (1889) 781/2, I reckons they'll hev' a fine cider-crop to-year. **1886** T. HARDY *Mayor of Casterbr.* I. 64 Not but what he's been shook a little to-year about this.

**Toyel**, obs. form of TOOL.

**To-ȝe(i)n, to-ȝe(i)nes**: see TO-GAINS.

**Toyer** (toi·əɹ). [f. TOY *v.* + -ER [1].] One who toys; a trifler.

*a* **1713** W. HARRISON *Passion of Sappho* 5 in Nichols *Coll.* (1780) IV. 183 Wanton Cupid, idle toyer. **1814** L. HUNT *Notes Feast Poets* (1815) 51 These toyers in versification.

**Toyful** (toi·fŭl), *a.* Now *rare* or *Obs.* [f. TOY *sb.* + -FUL.] Full of sport or fun; sportive, playful; funny, amusing.

**1580** SIDNEY *Let. to Robert S.* 18 Oct., My toyfull Books I will send..by February. *a* **1631** DONNE *Progr. Soul* xlvi, It quickned next a toyfull Ape. **1744** ARMSTRONG *Preserv. Health* II. 290 When Favonius, flush'd with love Toyful and young, in ev'ry breeze descends.

Hence **To·yfulness.**

*a* **1859** DE QUINCEY *Posth. Wks.* (1893) II. 24 The playfulness and..the toyfulness (if we may invent that word) of childhood.

**Toy-getter, -headed**, etc.: see TOY *sb.* 11 d.

**Toying** (toi·iŋ), *vbl. sb.* [f. TOY *v.* + -ING [1].] The action of the verb TOY; playing, sporting; trifling, idle or careless dealing (*with* anything), amorous dalliance.

**1565–73** COOPER *Thesaurus* s. v. *Arguo, Digitorum argutiæ*, toyinges or gesturinges of the fingers: often mouyng. **1580** HOLLYBAND *Treas. Fr. Tong, Ragement*, wantonnesse, or toying. **1726** *Adv. Capt. R. Boyle* (1768) 236 After our Toying was over, she told me she was afraid of losing me. **1840** CARLYLE *Heroes* ii. (1872) 67 Toying and coquetting with Truth: this is the sorest sin. **1865** DICKENS *Mut. Fr.* I. xi, Slightly in contrast with this brief airy toying. **1911** W. W. PEYTON in *Contemp. Rev.* Sept. 374 Evil is in toying with imperfection.

**Toy·ing**, *ppl. a.* [f. as prec. + -ING [2].] That toys; playful, sportive; *esp.* amorously sportive.

*a* **1566** R. EDWARDES *Damon & Pythias* Prol. 6 Frustrate quite of toying plaies. **1711** STEELE *Spect.* No. 155 ⁋ 4 None of these toying Fools will do any more..to preserve her from Infamy. **1769** G. WHITE *Selborne* xxii. (1853) 93 When the cock has been pursuing the hen in a toying way through the boughs of a tree.

Hence **Toy·ingly** *adv.*

**1731** BAILEY, *Toyingly*, triflingly, wantonly.

**Toyish** (toi·iʃ), *a.* Now *rare.* [f. TOY *sb.* + -ISH [1].] Having the character of a toy, or addicted to toys (in various senses of the sb.).

**1.** Trifling, trivial, of no importance, worthless; foolish, senseless, nonsensical.

**1574** *Life 70th Abp. Canterb.* Pref. E vj b, The thinges therin described being in part not all so true and in greatest part to to toyishe. **1583** CROWLEY *Delib. Answ.* 48 b, Your ringing of Belles, your burning of lightes in the open day-light, with..many other toyishe diuises. **1653** S. FISHER *Baby Baptism* 7 It's a most Pedantick, toyish and boyish piece of business. **1711** in *10th Rep. Hist. MSS. Comm.* App. v. 119 Mallice..is apt to make any toyish pretence to be her warrant for evil actions. **1850** C. WORDSWORTH *Occas. Serm.* Ser. I. 162 By it we have been secured from the hollow mockery of tedious and toyish ceremonies.

†**b.** Wanting in gravity of style; light, frivolous. ? *Obs.*

**1603** G. JOHNSON *Disc. Troub. Eng. Ch. Amsterdam* 135 A copple crowned hatt with a twined band,..Immodest and toyish in a Pastors wife. **1615** MARKHAM *Eng. Housew.* II. i. (1668) 3 Adorn the person, altogether without toyish garnishes, or the gloss of light colours. **1676** MACE *Musick's Mon.* 129 Serabands are of the Shortest Triple-Time: but are more Toyish, and Light.

**2.** Sportive, playful, frisky, skittish. ? *Obs.*

**1577** HARRISON *England* III. vii. (1878) II. 49 The last kind of toiesh curs are named dansers, and those being of a mongrell sort also, are taught & exercised to danse in measure. *c* **1613** ROWLANDS *Paire of Spy-Knaves* 5 From merry drunk, and toyish as an Ape. **1680** O. HEYWOOD *Diaries*, etc. (1883) III. 306 Oh this dodging, toyish, frisking heart kills me.

†**b.** Amorously sportive, wanton, licentious.

**1563** *Homilies* II. *Place & Time of Prayer* I. (1859) 341 They rest in wantonness, in toyish talking, in filthy fleshliness.

†**3.** Fantastic, odd, whimsical, queer. *Obs.*

**1598** FLORIO, *Humorista*, humorous, fantasticall, toish. **1599** HARSNET *Agst. Darell* 98 Somers had counterfeyted certaine fits and toyish behaviour at M. Brakenburie. **1638** SANDERSON *Serm., Ad Aulam* viii. (1660) II. 158 Some peevish and obstinate, some toyish, fickle, and humorous.

**4.** Of the nature of, or fit for, a plaything; of a humorous or sportive character, as a writing.

**1699** POMFRET *Dies Noviss.* Rem. (1724) 8 Adieu, ye toyish Reeds that once could please My softer lips. **1830** SCOTT *Demonol.* v. 163 They have many light toyish books.

**5.** Resembling a toy, toy-like; diminutive or flimsy; *spec.* like, or like that of, a 'toy' dog.

**1886** *Field* 23 Jan. 113/2 Richmond Puzzle, fourth prize, is at present small and toyish. **1890** *Ibid.* 8 Mar. 355/2 His [a Fox Terrier's] head is now toyish and effeminate.

Hence **Toy·ishly** *adv.*; **Toy·ishness.**

**1607** MARKHAM *Caval.* II. (1617) 150 He will exercise his lesson with such wantonnesse and apish toyishnesse. **1624** BP. MOUNTAGU *Immed. Addr.* 116 See how toyishly these great Masters play with their owne fancies. **1665** GLANVILL *Scepsis Sci.* Addr. 23 Your Society..will discredit that toyishness of wanton fancy.

**Toyl**, obs. form of TOIL, TOILE, TWILL.

**Toyle, toyll**, obs. forms of TOIL, TOOL.

**Toyless** (toi·lės), *a.* [f. TOY *sb.* + -LESS.] Destitute of toys; not having any toys.

**1898** G. TAYLOR in *Chicago Advance* 13 Jan. 43/3 Telling us of the children's gifts to their toyless little down-town neighbors. **1906** *Blackw. Mag.* Apr. 647/1 My toyless condition was due to anatomical longings.

**Toym, toyme**, obs. forms of TOOM *sb.*[1] and *a.*

**Toyman** (toi·mæn). [f. TOY *sb.* + MAN *sb.*[1]] A man who sells toys, or who keeps a toy-shop: formerly, one who sold requisites for sports, trinkets, and fancy goods; now, one who makes or sells playthings for children (cf. TOY-SHOP 1, 2).

**1707** *Lond. Gaz.* No. 4328/8 Ralph Ayscough, of St. James's Westminster, Toyman. **1710–11** SWIFT *Jrnl.* 7 Jan., I will go to the toyman's here just in Pall Mall, and he sells great hugeous batoons. **1749** FIELDING *Tom Jones* XII. iv, The pocket-book..had cost five and twenty shillings, having been bought of a celebrated toyman. **1758** JOHNSON *Idler* No. 6 ⁋ 5 The toyman will not give his jewels. **1813** SHELLEY *Q. Mab* Notes, Poet. Wks. (1891) 41/1 The jeweller, the toyman, the actor gains fame and wealth by the exercise of his useless and ridiculous art. **1886** C. E. PASCOE *Lond. of To-day* xl. (ed. 3) 347 Those admirable examples of the toyman's craft—whole garrisons of miniature soldiers, artillery, cavalry, and infantry.

**Toy-mutch**, etc.: see TOY *sb.* 11.

**Toyn, toyne**, obs. forms of TONE *sb.*

‖ **Toyon** (toi·ǫn). Also tollon. [a. Mexican Sp. *tollon* (tolˈ*y*ǫn), the native name.] The Californian Holly, *Heteromeles* (*Photinia*) *arbutifolia*, N.O. *Rosaceæ.*

[**1848** BENTHAM *Plantæ Hartweg.* 307 Photinia arbutifolia, *Toyon* incolarum.] **1876** BREWER, etc. *Bot. California* I. 188 *Heteromeles arbutifolia*, Toyon or Tollon. **1884** MILLER *Plant-n.*, Tollon, or Toyon.

†**Toy·ous**, *a. Obs. rare.* [f. TOY *sb.* + -OUS.] **a.** Trifling, ornamental, unessential. **b.** Inclined to toy or flirt, coquettish. Hence **Toy·ousness.**

**1581** MULCASTER *Positions* xxxviii. (1887) 178 Those ouerraught qualities for the toyousnesse therof being misplaced in her, do cause the young woman rather to be toyed withall..then to be thought verie well of. **1592** WARNER *Alb. Eng.* VII. xxxvi. 157 The faire sweet wittie wench grew toyous in the end.

**Toy-pate, -railway**, etc.: see TOY *sb.* 11.

**Toy·-shop.**

**1.** A shop for the sale of trinkets, knick-knacks, or small ornamental articles; a fancy shop. *arch.*

**1693** W. FREKE *Sel. Ess.* xxxii. 201 Are not these..fitter for a Toy-shop, than a Wise Man's Head? **1711** ADDISON *Spect.* No. 10 ⁋ 6 If they [women] make an Excursion to a Mercer's or a Toy-shop. **1712** *Ibid.* No. 499 ⁋ 5 Ribbons, brocades, embroidery,..sufficient to have furnished a whole street of toy-shops. **1791** BOSWELL *Johnson* 28 Apr. an. 1778, We stopped again at Wirgman's, the well-known *toy-shop*,..he sent for me to..help him to choose a pair of silver buckles. **1852** [see 3].

**2.** A shop for the sale of toys or playthings.

**1818** SCOTT *Hrt. Midl.* vi, These booths have degenerated into mere toy-shops, where the little loiterers..are..enchanted by the rich display of hobby-horses, babies, and Dutch toys. **1858** LYTTON *What will he do* I. xvi, Lionel could not find in the toyshops of the village a doll good enough. **1886** C. E. PASCOE *Lond. of To-day* xl. (ed. 3) 347 A toy shop, crowded with all sorts of interesting playthings.

**3.** *attrib.*

**1840** DICKENS *Old C. Shop* xxii, Such..as was never before seen or heard of out of a toy-shop window. **1852** THACKERAY *Esmond* III. vi, Esmond found the antechamber crowded with milliners and toyshop women..mercers' men with hangings, and velvets, and brocades.

†**Toysome** (toi·sŏm), *a. Obs. rare.* [f. TOY *sb.* + -SOME.] Full of 'toys', or having the character of a 'toy'; fantastic, whimsical; inclined to toy, sportive, playful; amorously sportive.

**1638** FORD *Fancies* II. i, I have an excellent humour to be pettish, A little toysome. **1659** HOOLE *Comenius' Vis. World* (1777) 178 The fool causeth laughter by his toysome actions. **1719** D'URFEY *Pills* (1872) III. 113 Tom was toysome, Will was sad. **1754** RICHARDSON *Grandison* (1783) VI. 192 As we sat at breakfast, two or three toysome things were said by my Lord (no ape was ever so fond !).

Hence **Toy·someness.**

**1697** CREECH tr. *Manilius* Pref. 46 There are so many boldnesses scatter'd thro' his Poem, and so much of Toysomness just by them, that a man may read his Youth in his Writings.

†**Toy·son, -e**, obs. ff. *toison*: in quots. short for TOISON D'OR.

*a* **1505** in Kingsford *Chron. Lond.* (1905) 230 Other honourable personages in Ambassade, as his second Chamberlayn and Knyght of the Toyson. *a* **1548** HALL *Chron., Hen. VIII* 13 b, The lord Bresley, knight of the Toyson. **1601** R. JOHNSON *Kingd. & Commw.* (1603) 244 There is also the order of the Toysone, of which his maiestie is chiefe.

**Toyte, toit** (toit), *v. Sc.* and *north. dial. intr.* To totter, walk feebly or unsteadily.

**1787** BURNS *To Auld Mare* xviii, We'll toyte about wi' ane anither. **1871** W. ALEXANDER *Johnny Gibb* xliv, I've toitit aboot wi' you upo' this place naar foorty year noo.

†**Toy·wort.** *Obs.* [f. TOY *sb.* + WORT.] A local name for the herb Shepherd's purse (*Capsella Bursa-pastoris*), from the resemblance of the capsule to a toy purse.

**1597** GERARDE *Herbal* II. xxiii. § 2. 215 Shepheardes purse is called..in the North part of England Toywoort, Pickepurse, and Caseweede. **1657** W. COLES *Adam in Eden* 71.

†**Toze, tose** (tōuz), *v.*[1] *Obs.* exc. *dial.* Forms: 3–7 tose, 4–7 toose, 6 tooze (toese), 7–8 toase, (7 toaze), 6– toze. [ME. *tosen* (*a* 1250 in compound *to-tosen*); not recorded in OE.; but the later forms *toase*, etc. indicate an OE. **tásian*, f. verbal root *tás-* :—OTeut. *tais-*, whence also OE. *tǽsan* (:—**taisjan*) to TEASE (q. v. for further relations).] *trans.* To pull asunder; to separate or unravel the fibres of; to comb or card (wool, etc.); = TEASE *v.*[1] 1.

*a* **1250** [see *To-tose*, To-[2] 1]. **1346** *Litt. Red Bk. Bristol* (1900) II. 2 Item si fila deficiant in panno vel quod nimis distent quod textores appellant *tosed.* **1390** GOWER *Conf.* I. 17 And what Schep that is full of wulle Upon his back, thei toose and pulle, Whil ther is eny thing to pile. *c* **1400** *Lanfranc's Cirurg.* 41 A good quantite of tow I-tosid. *c* **1440** *Promp. Parv.* 497/2 Toson wulle or other lyke [*v.r.* tosyn or tose wul], *carpo.* **1530** PALSGR. 760/1, I toose wolle, or cotton, or suche lyke, *je force de la laine*, and *je charpis de la laine.* **1567** GOLDING *Ovid's Met.* XIV. 305 What toozing wooll did meene. **1577** NORTHBROOKE *Dicing* (1843) 81 Many ..may pick wool, and sow garments, or tose okam. **1615** MARKHAM *Eng. Housew.* II. v. (1668) 123 Toase it every lock by lock. **1622** R. HAWKINS *Voy. S. Sea* (1847) 155 Peeces of a junke or rope, chopped very small,..and after tozed all as oacombe. **1665** HOOKE *Microgr.* 42 The Internal parts ..were..as it were, tos'd open like a Lock of Wool. **1725** *Bradley's Fam. Dict.* s. v. *Mixing Colours*, Wool..must be taken out and toas'd over-again; for the first Toasing was to make it receive the Colour or Die; but the second is to..make it fit for Spinning. **1881** MISS JACKSON *Shropsh. Word-bk.* s. v. *Tag*, Snip the end off the tag, an' toze it well as the grace can get among it.

**b.** *transf.* To pull, pull about. (Cf. TOUSE.)

**14..** *Sir Beues* 1952+2 (MS. M) That they were in the grene wose, And I shold hem well tose. **1573** TUSSER *Husb.* (1878) 206 For euerie crime, What toesed eares, like baited beares!

**c.** *fig.* To separate, search out; to analyse; to elicit, 'tease out'.

*c* **1450** *Cov. Myst.* xlii. (1841) 401 The trewthe fful trewlye he wyl tose, And send ȝow to hevyn or helle. **1611** SHAKS. *Wint. T.* IV. iv. 760 For that I insinuate, or [*printed* at] toaze from thee thy Businesse. **1633** D. R[OGERS] *Treat. Sacram.* II. 44 Doe it more fully, toze your consciences. **1648** JENKYN *Blind Guide* i. 8 The spurious expositions.. upon the Scriptures in his tedious tozing of them.

Hence † **Tozed, tosed** *ppl. a.*, †**To·zing** *vbl. sb.*; † **To·zer**, a comber or carder (of wool, etc.).

**1346** Tosed [see above]. *c* **1440** *Promp. Parv.* 497/2 Tosare, of wulle or other lyke, *carptrix.* Tosynge, of wulle or oþer thyngys, *carptura.* **14..** *Noble Bk. Cookry* (1882) 103 Charge it with the tosed flesshe. **1563–87** FOXE *A. & M.* (1596) 321/1 For euerie sacke of tosed wool, seuen marks. **1632** tr. *Bruel's Praxis Med.* 22 Dippe toosed Wooll herein. **1648** Tozing[see c above]. **1725** Toasing [see above].

**Toze** (tōuz), *v.*[2] *Tin-mining.* Also 9 toas (*erron.* toss). [Possibly the same word as prec.; but connexion of sense is not certain.

(The spelling *toss* seems due to a bad etymological guess (see quot. 1839) which has passed into dictionaries.)]

*trans.* To separate tin ore from the gangue or rough ore by stirring the slimes in a kieve, and allowing the heavier particles to settle.

**1758** BORLASE *Nat. Hist. Cornw.* 180 The coffer is then emptied the second time, the tin carried again to the keeve, there tozed, skimmed, and packed. **1839** DE LA BECHE *Rep. Geol. Cornw.*, etc. xv. 577 Another let the tin ore fall into it [*sc.* the water] by degrees at the side of the keeve, where it was tozed (tossed), or stirred by the other until the vat was almost full. **1882** JAGO *Cornw. Gloss.*, *Toas*, or *Toze*, to shake or toss the wet tin to and fro in a kieve or vat, with water, to cleanse and dress it.

Hence **To·zing** *vbl. sb.*, the action of thus cleaning the ore; also in comb., as **tozing-tub**, the tub or kieve in which tin ore is tozed. Also **To·zer**: see quot. 1885; (also a Cornish surname).

[**1758** BORLASE *Nat. Hist. Cornw.* 179 The tin-ore is then sifted in a sieve purposely constructed, and if it needs must be sent to be buddled again, then returned to the keeve and worked as before with a shovel, which they call *tozing* the tin.] **1789** J. WILLIAMS *Min. Kingd.* II. 210 They are obliged to take another method to clean it, which is called turloobing, or tozing. *Ibid.* 212 The tozing operation. **1839** URE *Dict. Arts* 1244 The rough is washed in buddles, and in tossing tubs. **1877** KNIGHT *Dict. Mech.* 2603/2 *Tossing*, or *Tozing*, the operation of agitating ore in a kieve; a tub in which it is rotated in water by a stirrer on a vertical axis. **1885** *Black's Guide to Cornw.* (ed. 13) 54 Tozer, the man who tozes, stirs, or washes the crop-tin.

**Tozie**, variant of TOSY.

†**Tozy** (tōu·zi), *a. Obs.* [app. f. TOZE *v.*[1] + -Y. But cf. TOSY.] Soft like teased wool. Hence †**To·ziness**, softness.

**1706** PHILLIPS (ed. Kersey), *Tozy*, soft like Wooll. **1727** BAILEY vol. II, *Tozyness*, softness, like tozed Wooll. *absol.* **1824** SCOTT *St. Ronan's* xx, I can tell it [a shawl] to be a real *tozie. Ibid.*, That tozie now will keep its colour while there is a rag of it left.

†**Tphrowh**, *int. Obs. nonce-wd.* An exclamation to arrest or call attention: cf. PROO.

**1575** *Gamm. Gurton* I. ii. A iij, And chad not cryed tphrowh, hoore, shead lept cut of his Lees.

† **Tprot.** *Obs.* An expression of contempt.
13..in *Pol. Songs* (Camden) 223 Tprot, Scot, for thi strif! Hang up thyn hachet ant thy knyf.

† **Tprw.** *Obs.* Imitation of the sound of a horn.
c 1430 *Pilgr. Lyf Manhode* II. cxv. (1869) 118 Tprw tprw, j sey, tprw tprw.

**Tra,** Sc. variant of TRAY *sb. Obs.*, affliction.

**Traas, Traass,** obs. ff. of TRACE *sb.*[1], TRASS.

‖ **Traba·colo.** Also trabaccolo. [It. *trabacolo, -accolo* :—med.L. **trabāculum*, f. L. *trab-em* beam, timber (cf. *tabernāculum*).] An Italian ship of medium size; a small coasting vessel.
1809 CAPT. HOSTE in *Naval Chron.* XXII. 506 A convoy of merchant trabaccolos. 1812 *Examiner* 12 Oct. 648/1 Twelve sail of the enemy's trabaccoloes. 1846 RAIKES *Life Sir J. Brenton* 360 Accompanied by three trabacolos for the purpose of landing the troops. [1866 HOWELLS *Venet. Life* vii, Small coasting vessels (*trabaccoli* at Venice).]

**Trabal** (trēⁱ·băl, træ·băl), *a.* [ad. L. *trabāl-is*, f. *trab-s*, *trab-em* beam: see -AL.] † **a.** Pertaining to or of the nature of a beam; trabeal. *Obs. rare*⁻⁰. **b.** *Anat.* Pertaining to the *trabs cerebri* or *corpus callosum* of the brain.
1656 BLOUNT *Glossogr.*, *Trabal*, of, or belonging to a beame; great or big like a beame. 1889 *Buck's Handbk. Med. Sc.* VIII. 517 *Trabal*..would merely recall the obsolete name for the callosum, *trabs cerebri*. 1899 *Syd. Soc. Lex.*, *Trabal*, pertaining to the *Trabs*; callosal.

‖ **Trabant** (traba·nt). Now chiefly *Hist.* Also 7 **trabanto, travant,** 7–8 **traband.** [a. Ger. *trabant* a life-guard, an armed attendant, a satellite (also in Astron.), in It. *trabante*, F. *traban*, Boh. *drabanti*; of Turkish (orig. Pers.) origin: see DRABANT.] In some European countries, a life-guard, an armed attendant, a satellite.
1617 MORYSON *Itin.* III. 188 He [the Emperor] had one hundred for his Guard, (called Trabantoes)...Ten Hascheres and twelue Trabantoes attended each day. a 1634 CHAPMAN *Alphonsus* III. F iv b, Six travants well arm'd. 1693 *Lond. Gaz.* No. 2845/2 Thus they went through several stately Rooms, having the Trabands on each side of them. 1762 tr. *Busching's Syst. Geog.* V. 317 The fifty halberdeers and the fifty trabands or horse-guards here being rather instituted for the splendor of the court than the military establishment. 1904 *Daily Chron.* 15 Dec. 1/7 It was announced that the President [of the Hungarian Chamber]..would not appear, and that the guard of 'Trabants' had been removed.

‖ **Trabea** (trēⁱ·biă). Pl. **-eæ** (-iˌī). *Rom. Antiq.* [Latin *trabea.*] A toga ornamented with horizontal purple stripes, worn as a state robe by kings, consuls, and other men of rank in ancient Rome.
1600 HOLLAND *Livy* I. 30 Then came Servius abroad in his roiall robe, called *Trabea*. 1702 ADDISON *Dial. Medals* iii. (1726) 160 Our modern Medals are full of Toga's and Tunica's, Trabea's and Paludamentums. a 1746 HOLDSWORTH *Rem. Virgil* (1768) 291 The Lituus and Trabea of Romulus and the Ancilia were kept in the Sacrarium of the Salii. 1842 W. SMITH *Dict. Gr. & Rom. Antiq.* s.v. *Toga*, Servius..mentions three kinds of trabeae; one wholly of purple, which was sacred to the gods, another of purple and white, and another of purple and saffron which belonged to augurs. The purple and white trabea was a royal robe.

**Trabeal** (trēⁱ·biăl), *a. Arch.* [irreg. f. L. *trab-em* beam, instead of the regular form TRABAL.] Of the nature of a horizontal beam, beam-like.
1862 SIR H. ACLAND in *Macm. Mag.* V. 527 (*Descr. Oxford Museum*) Extending laterally..arise two slender spanners to the [iron] trabeal beam before referred to as sustaining the rafters. 1866 *Athenæum* 18 Aug. 214/2 Trabeal forms prevail.

**Trabeate** (trēⁱ·biˌeⁱt), *a. Arch.* [irreg. (for **trabate*), f. L. *trab-s*, *trab-em* beam + -ATE [2], on analogy of TRABEATION, q. v. (L. *trabeātus* meant 'clad in the trabea'.)] = next.
1890 C. H. MOORE *Gothic Archit.* i. 6 *note*, It is not until we scrutinise the joints of masonry that the trabeate principle of its construction is perceived. 1905 *Athenæum* Apr. 441/2 The ordinary house [in Syrian architecture, 85 B. C. to 609 A. D.] was a purely trabeate building...The construction was in cut stone blocks laid without mortar; but the arch ..was gradually evolved.

**Trabeated** (trēⁱ·biˌeⁱtėd), *a. Arch.* Also **trabiated.** [f. as prec. + -ED [1].] Constructed with beams; having beams or long squared stones as lintels and entablatures, instead of using the arch; covered with a beam or entablature, as a doorway.
*Trabeated architecture* is opposed to *arcuated*, *arched*, or *vaulted*. *Trabeated ceiling*, a flat ceiling sustained by beams, by which it is divided into compartments, as distinguished from a vaulted ceiling.
1843 *Civil Eng. & Arch. Jrnl.* VI. 96/1 The happy union of the arch and the trabeated systems. 1857 G. J. WIGLEY *Borromeo's Instr. Eccl. Build.* v. 13 Ceiling..(either vaulted or trabiated, according to the proportion of the edifice). 1863 *Sat. Rev.* 21 Mar. 367/1 Strictly it was a propylæum, not an arch, for the opening was trabeated.

**Trabeation** (trēⁱbiˌēⁱ·ʃən). *Arch.* Also 6 **trabiacion.** [irreg. for **trabation*, f. L. *trab-s*, *trab-em* beam: see -ATION.] † **a.** A member resembling a horizontal beam; an entablature. *Obs.* **b.** Construction with horizontal beams or the like, as opposed to arches or vaults; trabeated structure.
1563 SHUTE *Archit.* C j b, This pillor..supported no other ..but his owne Trabiacions. 1704 J. HARRIS *Lex. Techn.* I, *Trabeation*, or *Entablature*,..comprehends the Architrave, Frize, and Cornice. 1831 *Fraser's Mag.* IV. 283 To apply to an entire cornice, or even to a whole 'trabeation', those curved forms which have hitherto been exclusively confined to mouldings and lesser details. a 1878 SIR G. G. SCOTT *Lect. Archit.* (1879) I. 19 Arcuation plastered over to look like trabeation.

‖ **Trabecula** (trăbe·kiulă). Pl. **-æ** (-ī). Also **trabe·culum** (-ŏm), pl. **-a** (-ă); **trabe·culus** (-ŏs), pl. **-i** (-əi); and in anglicized forms **trabecle** (træ·bėk'l), **tra·becule** (-kiul). [L. *trabecula*, *trabicula*, dim. of *trabs* beam; the forms in *-um* and *-us* are mod.L. variants.] A structure in an animal or plant resembling a small beam or bar.
*spec.* **a.** *Anat.* and *Zool.* Each of the plates of bony substance forming the cancellated tissue of a bone; any slender band of tissue extending like a cross-bar across a cavity, as of the heart (*trabeculæ carneæ*), or through the substance of a soft organ, as the spleen or kidney; each of two cartilaginous bars (*trabeculæ cranii*) in front of the pituitary body in the embryo, which coalesce and develop into part of the cranium; each of the calcareous plates connecting the dorsal and ventral walls in echinoderms; each of a pair of appendages on the head in front of the antennæ in certain bird-lice. **b.** *Bot.* A projection extending across the cell-cavity in the ducts of some plants, or across the cavity of the sporangium in mosses and other cryptogams.
1866 *Treas. Bot.*, *Trabecula* (adj. *Trabeculate*), a cross-bar; as in the teeth of many mosses. 1873 T. H. GREEN *Introd. Pathol.* (ed. 2) 137 This tissue, like bone, is made up of trabeculæ and medullary spaces. 1874 COUES *Birds N. W.* 611 Divided..by a cartilaginous trabeculum, which is thrown across from the posterior side to the anterior apex of the base of the pyramid. 1875 SIR W. TURNER in *Encycl. Brit.* I. 853/2 The interior of a bone..is made up of thin delicate plates or bars, or trabecles, which intersect each other at various angles, and form..the spongy or cancellated tissue. 1875 BENNETT & DYER *Sachs' Bot.* II. iv. 413 Both kinds of sporangia [in Isoëtes] are imperfectly segmented by threads of tissue (*Trabeculæ*) which cross from the ventral to the dorsal side. 1890 BILLINGS *Med. Dict.*, *Trabecula cinerea*, soft commissure of the brain.

Hence **Trabe·cular** *a.*, pertaining to or of the nature of a trabecula; composed of or furnished with trabeculæ; **Trabe·cularism,** trabecular condition, trabeculation; **Trabe·culate, -ated** *adjs.*, furnished with or having trabeculæ; **Trabecula·tion,** formation of trabeculæ, trabeculated condition.
1822–34 *Good's Study Med.* (ed. 4) III. 164 A cystic form [of cataract] without pus,..a siliquose and a *trabecular. 1847–9 *Todd's Cycl. Anat.* IV. 773/1 The trabecular tissue consists of..cylindrical fibres. 1891 *Cent. Dict.*, **Trabecularism*, in *anat.*, a coarse reticulation, or cross-barred condition, of any tissue. 1866 *Trabeculate [see TRABECULA]. 1876 tr. *Wagner's Gen. Pathol.* (ed. 6) 359 They..unite by opposite processes into networks, form *trabeculated membranes. 1898 *Allbutt's Syst. Med.* V. 182 Cavities..traversed by tough septa and bridles..are..described as trabeculated. 1900 *Lancet* 5 May 1275/2 *Trabeculation of the bladder. 1904 *Jrnl. R. Microsc. Soc.* Dec. 636.

† **Trabo·ccant,** *a. Obs. rare.* [ad. It. *traboccante*, pres. pple. of *traboccare* to overflow, superabound.] Superabundant, excessive; preponderant.
1651 HOWELL *Venice* 208 The power of one might not so out-poize and be trabocant that the rest shold be in danger to be blown up. 1654 — *Parthenop.* Pref. A j b, One could hardly discern which Scale would be traboccant and overpoising.

**Trabuch** (trăbu·k). *Obs.* or *arch.* Also 7 **trabucche, trabuck.** [a. OF. *trabuc* (Sp. *trabuco*), f. *tra-*, *très-* (:—L. *trans-*, expressing displacement) + OF. *buc* trunk (of the body), bulk, a. WGer. *būh*, Ger. *bauch* belly.] A mediæval engine of war for throwing great stones against walls, etc.: cf. TREBUCHET.
1610 HOLLAND *Camden's Brit.* I. 400 Of these Mangonells, Patraries, Trabucks..by which..they discharged volies of mighty huge stones..much might heere be said. 1614 CAMDEN *Rem.* 238 Our nation had the practise of most of these, and moreouer of Mangonels, Trabucches, and Bricolles, wherewith they vsed to cast mil-stones. 1890 DOYLE *White Company* xv, The Norman hath a mangonel or a trabuch upon the forecastle.

**Trabuschette,** obs. form of TREBUCHET.

‖ **Tracas** (trăka). *Obs.* [Fr., f. *tracasser*: see next.] Bustle, hurry, fuss; embarrassment.
[1611 COTGR., *Tracas*, much trotting, or hurrying vp and downe; hence also, toyle, trouble, turmoile.] 1656 BLOUNT *Glossogr.* [from Cotgr.], *Tracas*, or *Tracasserie*. 1673 O. WALKER *Educ.* iv. 35 He then desired of the Emperor to be dismissed into his own Countrey, where he might dye in quiet out of the tracas and noise of the World.

‖ **Tracasserie** (trăkasəri). [Fr., f. *tracasser* to bustle, worry oneself: see -ERY.] A state of disturbance or annoyance; a turmoil, bother, fuss; an embroilment, petty quarrel. (Chiefly in *pl.*)
1656 [see prec.]. 1658 PHILLIPS, *Tracasserie* (French), a needlesse hurrying, or restlesse travelling up and down. 1715 in P. M. Thornton *Stuart Dynasty* (1890) App. I. 353, I am of your opinion that to avoid tracassaries one should let the different correspondences take their course. 1812 SCOTT *Let. to Miss J. Baillie* 17 Jan., in *Lockhart*, A wonderful man..acquainted with all the intrigues and tracasseries of the cabinets. 1833 T. HOOK *Parson's Dau.* I. vii, Adept as she was in all the tracasseries of flirtation. 1879 MRS. LYNN LINTON in *Life* xvi. (1901) 219 Life seems to me empty of all but tracasseries.

**Trace** (trēⁱs), *sb.*[1] Forms: 3– **trace**; also 4–5 **tras,** 4–7 **trase,** (4 **traze,** *Sc.* **trass, traiss,** 4–5 **trays,** *Sc.* **traise,** 5 **traas, trayse,** (**trasche**), 6 *Sc.* **trais**). [a. F. *trace* (12th c. in Godef.) = Pr. *trassa*, It. *traccia* (Sp. *traza* draught, first sketch), vbl. sb. f. OF. *tracier*, F. *tracer*: see TRACE *v.*[1]]

† **1.** The way or path which anything takes; course, road; esp. in *to take one's trace*, to make one's way, take one's course, proceed. *Obs.*
a 1300 [see b]. 13.. *K. Alis.* 7759 (Bodl. MS.) Alisaunder & Candace To Chaumber token her trace. 13.. *E. E. Allit. P.* A. 1112 To-warde þe þrone þay trone a tras. c 1425 *Cast. Persev.* 1923 in *Macro Plays* 131 Haue don, felaus! & take ȝoure trasche. c 1440 *Promp. Parv.* 498/2 Trace, of a wey over a felde, *trames*. c 1450 *St. Cuthbert* (Surtees) 3394 To farne agayne he takes his trace. c 1470 HENRYSON *Mor. Fab.* IX. (*Wolf & Fox*) xvi, All the trace he [the Cadger] trippit on his tais. 1530 PALSGR. 282/2 Trace, a streyght way, *trace*. 1596 SPENSER *F. Q.* VI. i. 6 Now I begin To tread an endlesse trace, withouten guyde. 1678 CUDWORTH *Intell. Syst.* I. v. § 25. 684 The striate particles finding no fit pores or traces for their passage through it. 1768 STERNE *Sent. Journ.* (1778) I. 69, I wanted the traces through which my wishes might find their way to her.

† **b.** *fig.* A course of action or conduct; way of proceeding; 'path', 'way', 'road'; esp. in phrases *to follow, take, tread the trace*. *Obs.*
a 1300 *Cursor M.* 25528 Until us þat al to mikel has ben vnbuxs Vnto þi suet trace [*Fairf.* for to folow þi trace]. c 1375 *Cato's Mor.* 374 *ibid.* p. 1674 (Fairf. MS.) Gode grante vs grace To folow catouns trace In his teyching. c 1375 *Sc. Leg. Saints* xxvi. (*Nycholas*) 43 þus he be-gane to god seke, & held furth ay in þat trace. c 1430 *Hymns Virg.* 35, Y took to þe world, & wente from þee, Y folewide þe feend al in his traas. c 1586 C'TESS PEMBROKE *Ps.* CXIX. D. iii, From the lyers trace, From falshoods wreathed way, O save me, Lord. 1631 WEEVER *Anc. Fun. Mon.* 67 The rest of the Nobilitie..trode also the same trace. 1652 J. WRIGHT tr. *Camus' Nat. Paradox* VIII. 163 To reduce him into the trace of his Duty and Reason. a 1716 SOUTH *Serm.* (1823) III. 252 God, by a secret, unobserved trace of his providence, may cast men under a..seducing ministry.

† **2.** A line, file, or train of persons. *Obs.*
c 1385 CHAUCER *L. G. W.* Prol. 285, I saugh comyng of ladyes Nientene..And after hem coome of wymen swich a traas. 1598 BARRET *Theor. Warres* IV. i. 102 The Sergeant Maiors..haue conducted these Regiments very disorderly, making a long trace, file, or lyne (as it were) of them.

† **3.** A series of steps in dancing; a measure; a dance. *Obs.*
c 1450 *Mankind* ii. 521 in *Macro Plays* 20, I xall make hym to dawnce a-noþer trace! c 1460 SIR R. ROS *Belle Dame* 190 Whan he thought tyme to daunce with her a trace. 1500–20 DUNBAR *Poems* lxxxi. 26 Thane com the ladyis, danceing in ane trace. 1519 *Interl. Four Elements* (Percy Soc.) 48 Folow all! I wyll lede a trace. 1577 [see TRACING *vbl. sb.*[1] 2].

† **4.** *pl.* The series or line of footprints left by an animal; hence in *sing.* a footprint. *Obs.*
13.. *Guy Warw.* (A.) 4732 Of hors traces hy þer seye. c 1374 CHAUCER *Boeth.* v. Met. v. 133 (Camb. MS.) Other bestis gladen hemself to diggen hir traas or hir steppis in the Erthe with hir goyngz or with hir feet. 1484 CAXTON *Fables of Æsop* IV. xii, We knowe wel by thy traces that all the beestes whiche haue entryd in to thy hows came not oute ageyne. 1552 HULOET, Trace or steppe, *vestigium*. 1575 TURBERV. *Venerie* 114 In Beasts of pray and rauine as Beare and Bore &c. they are called traces. 1616 SURFL. & MARKH. *Country Farme* 694 There is more regard to bee taken vnto her traces: for the print of the hares foot is sharpe, and fashioned like vnto the point of a knife. 1706 PHILLIPS (ed. Kersey), *Trace* (among *Hunters*), the Footprint of wild Beasts.
*fig.* 1610 *Crt. & Times Jas. I* (1849) I. 114 One who hath left so good traces and steps wherein to walk.

† **b.** *pl. loosely.* Footsteps. *Obs.*
1613 W. BROWNE *Brit. Past.* I. iv. 294 Till at the last.. Ye bend your traces up some shady hill.

**5.** The track made by the passage of any person or thing, whether beaten by feet or indicated in any other way: = TRACK *sb.* I. *On one's trace(s*, in pursuit of one; *to keep trace of*, to follow the movements of, keep sight of in going.
1375 BARBOUR *Bruce* VI. 553 In his traiss þe hund he set. *Ibid.* 583 þe hund..ay followit þe kyngis trass. c 1420 *Anturs of Arth.* v, The king blowe rechas, And folowed fast on þe tras. c 1489 CAXTON *Sonnes of Aymon* ix. 238 Men myghte well folow hym bi the trase, by cause of the blode that cam out of his body. 1556 W. TYMMES in Foxe *A. & M.* (1583) 2142/1 A sheepe [= ship] that passeth ouer the waues.., when it is gone by, the trace thereof cannot be found. 1810 SCOTT *Lady of L.* I. vii, Two dogs of black Saint Hubert's breed..Fast on his [the stag's] flying traces came. 1887 BOWEN *Æneid* II. 528 On his traces aflame with murderous stroke, Pyrrhus—behind—the pursuer!

**b.** *spec.* A beaten path through a wild or unenclosed region, made by the passage of men or beasts; a track, a trail. *U.S.*
1807 WILKINSON in Pike *Sources Mississ.* II. (1810) App. 24 We..took the large Spanish trace for the Arkansaw river. 1808 PIKE *Sources Mississ.* II. (1810) 134 We marched, leaving the Osage trace, which we had hitherto followed. 1817 J. BRADBURY *Trav. Amer.* 65 We..soon fell in with the trace from the Maha village to the monument. 1837 R. M. BIRD *Nick of the Woods* xxiv. II. 247 Leaving the broad buffalo-trace by which he descended the banks. 1904 W. CHURCHILL *Crossing* vii, They were going ahead up the trace towards his mother's.

**c.** In the West Indies, A grass drive, a lane.
1871 KINGSLEY *At Last* vii, The heat of a cane-field trace is utterly stifling. *Ibid.* xiii, A grass drive, as we should call it in England—a 'trace', as it is called in the West Indies—some sixty feet in width.

**6.** *pl.* Vestiges or marks remaining and indicating the former presence, existence, or action of something; *sing.* a vestige, an indication.
c 1400 MAUNDEV. (1839) vi. 71 Sche mylked hem on the rede stones of marble; so þat the traces may ȝit be sene in the stones alle whyte. 1814 MRS. J. WEST *Alicia de Lacy*

III. 2 No trace of inhabitation but the fortified castle or the sacred monastery. **1816** SCOTT *Antiq.* iv, My niece..saw the traces of the ditch at once. **1865** LUBBOCK *Preh. Times* ii. 29 At the end of the coffin were found traces of leather, doubtless the remains of boots. *Mod.* Of the fortifications no trace now remains.

**b.** A mark or impression left on the face, the mind, etc.

**1809** MALKIN *Gil Blas* III. v. ᴾ 12 My brain full of joyous traces. **1844** A. B. WELBY *Poems* (1867) 45 Where beauty left so soft a trace. **1848** LYTTON *Harold* I. i, It was on that forehead that time had set its trace.

**c.** An indication of the presence of a minute amount of some constituent in a compound; a quantity so minute as to be inferred but not actually measured; esp. in *Chem.*; *transf.* a very little.

**1827** FARADAY *Chem. Manip.* iv. (1842) 99 It burns away completely in a blast-furnace, leaving scarcely a trace of slag. **1838** T. THOMSON *Chem. Org. Bodies* 578 Traces of oxalic acid can be detected. **1859** R. HUNT *Guide Mus. Pract. Geol.* (ed. 2) 209 Its composition is: Gold 48·67, Silver 51·33, Copper, a trace. **1875** DARWIN *Insectiv. Pl.* xvi. 375 The distance was a trace less. **1876** GLADSTONE in *Contemp. Rev.* June 22 Like a chemist who, in a testing analysis,.. if he finds something behind so minute as to refuse any quantitative estimate, calls it by the name of 'trace'.

**7.** *fig.* A non-material indication or evidence of the presence or existence of something, or of a former event or condition; a sign, mark.

**1656** COWLEY *Pind. Odes* I. iii, With Oblivions silent stroke deface Of foregone Ills the very trace. **1696** WHISTON *Th. Earth* II. (1722) 186 There are Traces..of a Tradition that a Comet did appear at the very Beginning of the Deluge. **1710** POPE *Windsor For.* 372 The shady empire shall retain no trace Of war or blood, but in the sylvan chase. **1849** MACAULAY *Hist. Eng.* x. II. 661 In countries where all trace of the limited monarchy of the middle ages had long been effaced. **1850** MᶜCOSH *Div. Govt.* I. ii. (1874) 36 We discover everywhere in this world traces of design and wisdom. **1909** H. M. GWATKIN *Early Ch. Hist.* xi. 188 There is no trace of any veneration of pictures or images before the fourth century.

**8.** A line or figure drawn; a tracing, drawing, or sketch of an object or of a piece of work; the traced record of a self-recording instrument; in *Fortif.* the ground-plan of a work. (In quot. 1861 app. a tracing-instrument.)

**1744** AKENSIDE *Pleas. Imagination* III. 362 Not the sculptur'd gold More faithful keeps the graver's lively trace. **1861** SMILES *Engineers* II. 76 Picked out from the heap were also found his drill,..his trace, his T square,..and his engraving tools. **1879** *Cassell's Techn. Educ.* I. 21 The trace of a work is the plan of its guiding or magistral line. **1895** COL. MAURICE in *United Service Mag.* July 430 He made out both a trace of the work including the interior retrenchment and an exact profile of the ditched parapet. **1898** *Allbutt's Syst. Med.* V. 847 The respiration is an important factor in the blood-pressure, and in the run of the circulation is apparent to everyone who has watched the traces of the kymograph. **1899** BALDOCK *Cromwell* 293 The rampart..was strong and high, and of regular trace.

**9.** *Geom.* **a.** The track described by a moving point, line, or surface. **b.** The intersection of a line or surface with a surface; *spec.* the intersection of a plane with one of the co-ordinate planes, or with one of the planes of projection. **c.** The projection of a line upon a surface (*Funk's Stand. Dict.* 1895).

**1834–47** J. S. MACAULAY *Field Fortif.* (1851) 287 Let AB, Fig. 71, be the horizontal trace of a vertical plane. **1840** LARDNER *Geom.* i. 11 The notion of a mathematical surface may be formed by imagining a mathematical line to move in any manner in space, leaving behind it, as it moves, a trace or track. This trace or track will be a mathematical surface. **1867** THOMSON & TAIT *Nat. Phil.* I. I. § 111 When a body rolls and spins on another body, the trace of either on the other is the curved or straight line along which it is successively touched.

†**10.** *Her.* = TRACT *sb.*³ 6 (*a*), TRESSURE. *Obs.*

**1486** *Bk. St. Albans, Her.* e vij, He berith golde a dowble trace florishyt contrari and a Lyon rampyng of gowles. *Ibid.*, He berith golde a trace triplatit of Siluer.

**Trace** (trēⁱs), *sb.*² Forms: see below. [ME. *trays*, a. OF. *traiz*, *trais*, pl. of *trait* (12th c. in Littré) action of drawing, rope or leather strap by which a draught-beast is harnessed; = It. *tratto*, L. *tractus* draught (*u*-stem), f. *trahĕre* to draw. In Eng. written also *trayse*, *trayce*, *trace*, and treated as collect. pl. and at length (*c* 1400) as a sing. with a new pl. *trasys*, *traces*: cf. TRUCE.]

†**1.** as *pl.* The pair of ropes, chains, or (now usually) leather straps by which the collar of a draught-animal is connected with the splinter-bar or swingletree. *Obs.*

Usually *collective* like *tongs*, *scissors*, *shears*, *pincers*, etc.; but sometimes a numerical pl., as in quots. 1458, 1481.

4–5 **trais, trays,** 5 **trayse, treyse, trayce,** 5–8 **trace,** 6 **treas,** 7 **tress, traise, traits,** 9 *dial.* **traice.**

**13..** *Seuyn Sag.* (W.) 1327 He let him drawe out of the pit..With trais an two stronge hors. *c* **1350** *Nom. Gall.-Angl.* 884 *Esteles, trays et valuere* [glossed] Hamys, trays, taylerope. *c* **1365–6** *Durham Acc. Rolls* (Surtees) 568 Pro ij paribus de Trays et ij cartrapes; in trays, cartrapes, capistris, et reynes, xviij s. *c* **1386** CHAUCER *Knt.'s T.* 1283 With foure white boles in the trays. **1412–20** LYDG. *Chron. Troy* I. 2209 Ryȝt as an hors out of þe traise at large. **1458** *Nottingham Rec.* II. 368 For treyse and oder ropes. **1480** *Wardr. Acc. Edw. IV* (1830) 123 For v pair trays garnyssht. **1481–90** *Howard Househ. Bks.* (Roxb.) 150 Paid to John Wygge, Ropper, for iij. thrays ij.s. ix.d. **1557** *Lanc. & Chesh. Wills* (1884) 61, iiij payre of treas. *c* **1611** CHAPMAN *Iliad* XXIII. 412 His reins lost, or seat, or with the tress His chariot fail'd him. **1616** SURFL. & MARKH. *Country Farme* 16 Collars, Cart-saddles, Traits, thicke clothes, and other furniture for Horses. *Ibid.* 123 Be carefull that their traise, cart-saddles, collars, bridles, or other parts of their geares, and harnesse, be not torne. **1725** POPE *Odyss.* IV. 861 Twelve young mules, a strong laborious race, New to the plough, unpractis'd in the trace. **1807** A. YOUNG *Agric. Essex* I. 107, 5 pair of plough chain traice.

**2.** as *sing.* Each of the individual ropes or leather straps mentioned above; in *pl.* = sense 1.

*α.* *sing.* 5 **trays, -e, trayce, trahys,** 7 **traise, tress,** 9 **traice,** 6– **trace.**

**14..** *Voc.* in Wr.-Wülcker 566/26 *Attractorium*, a trayne, *sed melius*, a trays. *Ibid.* 617/7 *Tractorium*, a trays. *c* **1440** *Promp. Parv.* 499/1 Trayce, horsys ha(r)neys, *tenda*. *c* **1475** *Pict. Voc.* in Wr.-Wülcker 811/33 *Hoc retinaculum*, a trayse. **1570** LEVINS *Manip.* 6/44 A Trace for drawing, *traha, æ.* **1794** W. FELTON *Carriages* (1801) II. x. 134 A square, bent ring is sewed in the end [of each trace], which, with the trace, forms a loop to hitch round the splinter-bar rolls.

*β.* *pl.* 5 **tracez, traices,** 5–6 **trasys, -is,** 6 **trasseis,** 6–7 **tresses,** 6– **traces.**

**1404** *Durham Acc. Rolls* (Surtees) 397, iiij trasys ij trysyns rapis. **1405–6** *Ibid.* 400 Rec. pro lez tracez del char. **1497** *Naval Acc. Hen. VII* (1896) 95, iij chestes, Anfeld..j, Traices..cxx pair. **1523** FITZHERB. *Husb.* § 5 If he go with a hors ploughe, than muste he haue .. his hombers or collers, holmes whyted, tresses, swyngletrees, and togwith. **1529** *Act 21 Hen. VIII*, c. 12 § 1 Thereof make Cables, Ropes, Halsers, Traces, Halters, and other Tackle. **1569** in *Richmond Wills* (Surtees) 218, vj pair trasis with girthes. **1577** B. GOOGE *Heresbach's Husb.* II The smaller sort be these.. Traces. **1582** *Shuttleworths' Acc.* (Chetham Soc.) 6 A pare of trasseis vjᵈ. **1607** J. CARPENTER *Plaine Mans Plough* 192 Thirdly, the foure Traces or Tresses. **1718** POPE *Iliad* V. 398 His panting steeds.. He fix'd with straiten'd traces to the car. **1762** WESLEY *Jrnl.* 30 Mar., The horses pulled till the traces broke. **1841** MISS MITFORD in L'Estrange *Life* (1870) III. viii. 117 About four miles from home one of the traces came undone.

**3.** *fig.* (from 1 and 2), esp. in phrases; cf. COLLAR *sb.* 8. † *Out of trace*, out of proper connexion, out of order. *Into the traces*, into regular work. *To kick over the traces*: see KICK *v.*¹ 1 c.

*c* **1518** SKELTON *Magnyf.* 914 All is out of harre And out of trace. **1824** W. IRVING *T. Trav.* I. 203 He was too fond of my genius to force it into the traces. **1843** LYTTON *Last Bar.* I. iii, Cut thy trace from the cloister, and take thy road to the shop.

**4.** †**a.** (?) The tug or end-piece of a bell-rope. *Obs.* **b.** *Angling.* A length of gimp or gut of varying fineness attached to the end of the reel line. **c.** *Organ-building.* In the draw-stop action, a rod which connects the draw-stop rod with the trundle, or the trundle with the lever moving the slider; also called *trace-rod*. **d.** *Bot.* The fibro-vascular tissue of a stem, of which the *leaf-trace* is a continuation.

**a. 1663** in *Archæol. Æliana* XVII. 126 For two traces for yᵉ bellroops 6*d*. **b. 1839** [see MINNOW 3]. **1867** F. FRANCIS *Angling* iv. (1880) 105 A tackle called a trace is used. **1883** *Fisheries Exhib. Catal.* 56 Flights and Traces, Floats for various kinds of fishing. **c. 1852** SEIDEL *Organ* 59 The upper end of the roller..is connected..with the end of a short pole called the *trace*. **1876–98** STAINER & BARRETT *Dict. Mus. Terms* s. v. *Organ*, When the stop is pulled out, the arms *aa* draw the trace *b* from right to left. **1881** C. A. EDWARDS *Organs* 90 Another arm communicates with the trace by means of a mortise and pin. **d. 1875, 1877** [see *leaf-trace*, LEAF *sb.* 17]. **1884** BOWER & SCOTT *De Bary's Phaner.* 239 The median bundle of the leaf-trace..as it reaches the four bundles of the leaf-trace of the second node curves to one side, and unites with the lateral bundle of the next lower trace. *Ibid.* 257 Each leaf has three bundles of the trace, one median and two lateral.

**5.** *attrib.* and *Comb.*: **trace-beaten** *a.*, (of a horse) marked by the beating or friction of the traces; **trace-block**, the splinter-bar or draught-bar; formerly called the *fore-block* or *fore-bar*; **trace-boy**, a trace-horse boy; **trace-buckle**, a large buckle by which the trace is attached to the tug (Knight, 1877); **trace-bundle**, *Bot.*: cf. 4 d above; **trace-chain**, (*a*) a trace of chain, a chain trace; † (*b*) a long chain by which a team is yoked to the plough; = TEAM *sb.* 9; **trace-fastener**, one of a pair of hooks or catches by which the traces are hitched to the draught-bar (Knight, 1877); **trace-galled** *a.*, (of a horse) galled by the friction of the traces; **trace-harness**, harness of trace-horses; **trace-high** *adv.*, to the level of the traces; **trace-hook**, one of the hooks on the draught-bar for attaching the traces (Knight, 1877); **trace-horse**, a horse which draws in traces, as distinct from a shaft-horse; *attrib.* **trace-horse boy**, a boy in charge of a trace-horse; **trace-iron**, one of the upright iron studs round which the traces are looped; **trace-loop** = *trace-ring*; **trace-mate**: see quot.; **trace-ring**, an iron ring fastened to the end of the trace, by which it is attached to the trace-hook; **trace-rod** (*Organ*) = 4 c; **trace-rope**, a trace made of rope; **trace-tug**, a strap supporting the trace; † **trace-wheel** = PULLEY *sb.*¹ 2.

**1687** *Lond. Gaz.* No. 2287/8 Stolen.., a brown Mare above 14 hands,..*Traise-beaten on her Ribs. **1707** *Ibid.* No. 4295/4 A brown Gelding.., trace-beaten, most on the further Side. **1900** *Daily News* 12 Nov. 3/4 The firemen..having attached drag ropes to the *trace blocks, proceeded to drag the carriage to Government House. **1897** *Ibid.* 31 Mar. 7/1 Daily wages..for *trace-boys 2*s.* 6*d.* **1884** BOWER & SCOTT *De Bary's Phaner.* 293 The rapid longitudinal divisions of the bundle-ring always begin..in a young internode, in the position of the single, or of the median *trace-bundle going to the next leaf above. **1844** STEPHENS *Bk. Farm* I. 618 The horse is yoked to the swing-trees by light chains, called *trace-chains. **1896** *Cosmopolitan* XX. 398/1 The jangling of trace-chains in the quiet, darkening air, as the workmen return from the fields to the barn. **1673** *Lond. Gaz.* No. 783/4 One Iron Grey Nag..a little *trace Galled. **1885** *Wellington Weekly News* 15 Oct. (E. D. D.) Nine sets of breeching and *trace harness. **1899** SOMERVILLE & ROSS *Irish R.M.* ix, Horses that ranged from the cart mare, clipped *trace high, to shaggy and leggy three-year-olds. **1844** STEPHENS *Bk. Farm* III. 1087 In Forfarshire the *trace-horse is harnessed in a different manner. **1907** *Nation* 19 Oct. 79/1 Awaiting the chance of a trace-horse to give our caravan a pull. **1902** *Daily Chron.* 1 July 6/1 One of the horses attached to the fire engine was caught by the *trace-iron on the off side of the cattle-float. **1880** L. WALLACE *Ben-Hur* 208 They termed the two [horses] next the pole yoke-steeds, and those on the right and left outside *trace-mates. **1794** W. FELTON *Carriages* (1801) II. x. § 2. 144 The *Trace-Rings are iron square loops sewed in the ends of the traces, a part of which they receive, and loops round the splinter-bar. **1880** E. J. HOPKINS in Grove *Dict. Mus.* (1880) II. 606/1 A *trace-rod, which spans the distance from the trundle to the end of the soundboard...The trundle partly revolves and moves the trace-rod. **1900** *Daily News* 24 Feb. 6/3 The struggling, terrified horses inextricably mixed the *trace ropes, and the position looked serious. **1794** W. FELTON *Carriages* (1801) II. x. § 1. 135 The *trace-tugs are loops for the trace to run through and hang by. **1519** HORMAN *Vulg.* 241 b, There must be made a *trace whele [*tympanum*] to wynd vp stone.

**Trace** (trēⁱs), *sb.*³ *Obs.* or *dial.* Forms: 4 **trace,** 5 *pl.* **trasses,** 6 *Sc.* **trase, trais, traiss,** 6 (*Sc.*) 7– *dial.* **trace.** [Possibly an altered form of TRESS *sb.*, with which this largely coincides in sense; but no explanation of the alteration of form presents itself. See also the cognate TRACE *v.*³

(The different senses are cited from widely separate localities, so that they can scarcely be considered as a verbal unity, except in their apparent relation to TRESS.)]

†**1.** A tress or plait of hair; = TRESS *sb.* 1. (*s.w. Eng.*) *Obs.* (but cf. TRACE *v.*³).

*c* **1380** *Sir Ferumb.* 5882 Wyþ eȝene graye, and browes bent, And ȝealwe traces, & fayre y-trent. *a* **1400** *Trevisa's Higden* (Rolls) VIII. VII. 63 Þe ȝelew heere of þe womman trasses [*MS.* γ. ȝelou tresses; HIGDEN *trica comæ mulieris flava*] was i-founde hoole and sounde.

†**2.** A flat plait or braid of gold or silver thread, or other material, for trimming a robe, etc. *Sc. Obs.*

**1539** *Inv. Roy. Wardr.* (1815) 32 Item, ane nycht gowne of gray dammes with ane walting trais of gold. *Ibid.* 35. [*Ibid.* p. 42 has *tress* of silver; 82 *tres* of gold.] **1543** *Acc. Ld. High Treas. Scot.* VIII. 181 For xx tracis of gold to the cote, weyand thre unce..vli. ijs. **1548** *Ibid.* IX. 149, xxx elnis of trasis to eik ane goun of hirris [= hers] of blak welwote...Item, thre elnis blak welwote to eik this goun. **1549** *Ibid.* 334 Tua unce and ane quarter unce Parice silk to sew the pasmentis and traiss of the said coit.

**3.** A string of ears of Indian corn plaited together so as to be hung up. (*N. America.*)

**1678** *Phil. Trans.* XII. 1066 After 'tis gather'd, it [maize] must, except laid very thin, be presently stripped from the Husks...The common way (which they call Tracing) is to weave the Ears together in long Traces by some parts of the Husk left thereon. **1753** CHAMBERS *Cycl. Supp.* s.v. *Tracing*, These traces of [Indian] corn they hang up within doors,..and they will..keep good the whole winter.

**b.** A 'rope' or string of onions. *dial.*

**1891** *Hartland* (*Devon*) *Gloss.*, *Trace*, a rope of onions. [Cf. *Trecces de cepis* in same sense, in *Tabularia Portus Regii* (Du Cange).] (Cf also RACE *sb.*¹ 9 b.)

**Trace** (trēⁱs), *v.*¹ Forms: 4 **trais(e,** 4–7 **trase,** 4– **trace.** [ME. *trace-n*, a. OF. *tracier*, 12th c. (*trasser*, *traser*, *traicier*, etc.), F. *trace-r* = Sp. *trazar*, It. *tracciare* to follow by foot, to trace, indicating a pop.L. or Com. Romanic **tractiāre*, f. L. *tractus* a drawing, dragging, trailing, crawling; a train, track, course. The primary meaning of the verb was app. 'to proceed in a line, course, or track'. The early sense-development in OF. and ME. is not very clear, and some of the senses attach themselves immediately to TRACE *sb.*¹ in its sense of 'mark left by anything moving, footprint', itself a derivative of the vb. in its earlier senses.]

**I.** †**1.** *intr.* To take one's course, make one's way; to proceed, pass, go, travel, tread. Also *fig.*

*c* **1400** *Rom. Rose* 6745 Yit may he go his breed begging; Fro dore to dore he may go trace, Til he the remenaunt may purchace. ?*a* **1400** *Morte Arth.* 1629 Traise to-warde Troys þe tresone to wyrke. **1503** HAWES *Examp. Virt.* x. viii, No man by yonde this marke may trace. **1513** DOUGLAS *Æneis* VIII. v. 5 The prestis..Gan trasing furth. *a* **1518** SKELTON *Magnyf.* 692 As good to be occupyed as vp and downe to trace And do nothynge. **1598** *Mucedorus* IV. iii. 52 The wood lanes..strawed With violets, cowslips, and swete marigolds For thee to trampel and to trace vpon. **1603** H. CROSSE *Vertues Commw.* (1878) 23 Induce them .. to trace in the wholsome path that leadeth to the house of honour. *a* **1688** VILLIERS (Dk. Buckhm.) *Restoration* Wks. (1775) 104 Fall off again,..and every man trace to his house again. **1793** *Minstrel* II. 126 The forest, which she did not chuse to enter, but traced along its edge.

† **2.** *intr.* To pace or step in dancing; to tread a measure; to dance. Also *trans.* (*rare*). *Obs.*

*c* 1425 LYDG. *Dance of Macabre* in *Bochas*, etc. (1554) 220 b, Death I may not flee, On this daunce with other for to trace. 1445 in *Anglia* XXVIII. 273 Orpheus harpe which trees made trace. 1509 BARCLAY *Shyp of Folys* (1874) II. 290 To hunt to chace: to daunce: to trace: what one is he That beryth face. 1602 HEYWOOD *Woman Killed* Wks. 1874 II. 96 Come, Nick, take you Ioane Miniuer to trace withall. 1697 DAMPIER *Voy.* (1729) I. 541 They traced too and fro promiscuously, often clapping their Hands and singing aloud. 1808 SCOTT *Marm.* v. vii, The king loved well The merry dance, traced fast and light.

† **3.** *trans.* To pass along or over, tread (a path, way, street, etc.). Also *fig. Obs.*

*c* 1381 CHAUCER *Parl. Foules* 54 Oure present wor[l]dis lyuys space Nys but a maner deth what weye we trace. 1580 SIDNEY *Ps.* VIII. viii, The fish,..And what thing els of waters traceth The unworn paths. 1621 J. REYNOLDS *God's Rev. agst. Murder* I. i. 5 Tracing the street in a neate perfumed boote with iangling spurres. 1650 FULLER *Pisgah* III. xii. 343 The passage.. commonly called the dolorous way,.. traced with the blessed feet of our Saviour. 1794 BLAKE *Songs Exper., Lit. Girl Found* 8 Arm in arm seven days They traced the desert ways. *fig.* 1508 FISHER 7 *Penit. Ps.* Prol., Wks. (E. E. T. S.) I. 2 That al tho persones that ententyfely rede or here them may be styred the better to trace the way of eternall salvacion.

† **4.** *trans.* To travel or range over; to go or pass about, around, or through; to tread, traverse.

1430–40 LYDG. *Bochas* VI. iv. (Bodl. MS. 263) lf. 314/2 Fond no loggyng, tracing the contres Saue in kauernys, & in holwe trees. 1577 GRANGE *Golden Aphrod.* G j b, My harte it dothe bothe skippe and ioye to see hir trace the grounde. 1594 MARLOWE & NASHE *Dido* I. i, But hapless I.. Do trace these Lybian deserts, all despis'd. 1598 HAKLUYT *Voy.* I. 235 We sayled.. with diuers other courses, trauersing and tracing the seas, by reason of sundry and manifolde contrary windes. 1632 LITHGOW *Trav.* IX. 412, I traced the fertile soyles of Carindia. 1807 CRABBE *Par. Reg.* I. 306 He soon arrived, he traced the village green.

**II. 5.** To follow the footprints or traces of; *esp.* to track by the footprints; also with the traces as object; hence, to pursue, to dog.

*c* 1420 *Pallad. on Husb.* Tab. 39 Been forto trace vnto their dwellyng. 1530 PALSGR. 760/2 It is forbydden to trace hares in snowe tyme. 1559 *Mirr. Mag., Owen Glendour* xxxi, So traste they me among the mountaynes wide. 1605 SHAKS. *Macb.* IV. i. 153 His Wife, his Babes, and all vnfortunate Soules That trace him in his Line. 1632 LITHGOW *Trav.* I. 17 Still left vntold, something there must be seene For them, who trace our feete, with Argus eyne. 1677 W. HUBBARD *Narrative* (1865) II. 124 By the help of the Snow that fell about that Time, [they] were traced till they were overtaken. 1841 ELPHINSTONE *Hist. India* I. 123 Bound to find out the possessor of any stolen property within the township, or to trace him till he has passed the boundary. 1886 C. E. PASCOE *London of To-day* XXI. (ed. 3) 207 We might have traced Thackeray through his wanderings from street to street. *Mod.* Note the number of the postal order, so that it may be traced if lost.

**b.** *fig.* To follow, pursue (instructions, example, etc.).

1649 BLITHE *Eng. Improv. Impr.* (1653) 100 Observe my Method, and strictly trace my Instructions. 1745 *Transl. & Paraphr. Sc. Ch.* LII. i, You who the Name of Jesus bear, His holy Footsteps trace.

**6.** *fig.* To follow the course, development, or history of. Also with the course, etc. as object.

1654 BRAMHALL *Just Vind.* v. (1661) 90 If we trace on this argument a little further, to search out how the Bishop of Rome comes to be Saint Peters heire. 1729 BUTLER *Serm.* Wks. 1874 II. 168 The common virtues, and the common vices of mankind, may be traced up to benevolence, or the want of it. 1766 BLACKSTONE *Comm.* II. xiv. 236 The tracing the inheritance back through the male line of ancestors. 1849 MACAULAY *Hist. Eng.* iv. I. 503 No libel on the government had ever been traced to a Quaker. 1887 *Westm. Rev.* June 309 We have traced the history of Lower Canada down to the year 1839.

**b.** *intr.* for *pass.* To trace its origin or history; to go *back* in time, to date *back*.

1886 *Field* 4 Sept. 346/1 The Belvoir Senator and the Brocklesby Harbinger traced directly to the Fitzwilliam. 1889 JACOBS & LANG *Æsop's Fables* 53 The earliest form ..cannot trace back earlier than the third..century. 1907 *Daily Chron.* 9 Sept. 3/2 The scare of invasion traces to the Armada of 1583.

**7.** *trans.* To make out and follow (with the eye or mind) the course or line of; to ascertain (the course or line of something).

1703 MAUNDRELL *Journ. Jerus., Euphrates*, etc. (1732) 2 Its Walls, which may be traced all round. 1779 *Mirror* No. 9 ℙ 3, I..amused myself with tracing in the daughters, those features which, in the mothers and grandmothers, had charmed me so often. 1818 in Tuckey *Narr. Exped. R. Zaire* Introd. 8 The stream of this mysterious river [the Niger] being now traced with certainty from west to east as far as Tombuctoo. 1839 MURCHISON *Silur. Syst.* I. xxxvii. 572 In situations where the boulders may be traced..to their parent rocks. 1856 STANLEY *Sinai & Pal.* i. 19 Often their course can be traced, not by visible water, but a track of moss here, a fringe of rushes there. 1907 *Verney Mem.* I. 2 The form of the ancient manor house may still be traced.

**b.** To make out (worn or obscure writing); to discern, decipher.

1761 GRAY *Odin* 22 Thrice he traced the runic rhyme. 1792 S. ROGERS *Pleas. Mem.* I. 137 It calls me..to trace The few fond lines that Time may soon efface. 1859 JEPHSON *Brittany* ii. 17 The characters may still be traced on a block of granite.

**8.** To discover, find out, or ascertain by investigation; to find out step by step; to search out.

1642 FULLER *Holy & Prof. St.* v. i. 359 God..varieth his ways of dealing with wantons, that they may be at a losse in tracing him. 1697 DRYDEN *Virg. Georg.* II. 699 Happy the Man, who, studying Nature's Laws, Thro' known Effects can trace the secret Cause. 1745 *Transl. & Paraphr. Sc. Ch.* XXII. iv, Tho' him thou can'st not see, nor trace the working of his hands. 1869 TOZER *Highl. Turkey* II. 306 Tracing a connection..where in reality none exists.

**b.** To discover evidence of the existence or occurrence of; to find traces of.

1697 DRYDEN *Æneid* Ded. (1721) 350 He observes no Method that I can trace, whatever Scaliger the Father, or Heinsius, may have seen. 1782 MISS BURNEY *Cecilia* VIII. ix, The earliest circumstances she could trace were kindnesses received from her. 1856 RUSKIN *Mod. Paint.* III. IV. x. § 8 There is a great deal more in your heart, of evil and good, than you ever can trace. *a* 1862 BUCKLE *Civiliz.* (1871) III. v. 367 Black..called it latent heat, because though we conceive it as an idea, we cannot trace it as a fact.

**III. 9.** *trans.* To mark, make marks upon; *esp.* to mark or ornament with lines, figures, or characters: cf. TRACERY.

*a* 1400–50 *Alexander* 4914 Þe testre trased full of trones with trimballand wingis Þe silloure full of Seraphens. 1523 SKELTON *Garl. Laurel* 395 With diamauntes and rubis there tabers were trasid. 1582 D. INGRAM in Hakluyt *Voy.* (1589) 558 The haire of their heads is shauen in sundry spots, and the rest of their head is traced [? tattooed]. 1832 TENNYSON *Pal. Art* xiii, The deep-set windows, stain'd and traced, Would seem slow-flaming crimson fires From shadow'd grots of arches interlaced. 1858 WHITTIER *Palm-Tree* 24 He holds a palm-leaf scroll in his hands, Traced with the Prophet's wise commands. 1890 *Daily News* 6 Jan. 5/2 Stockings and buckles were richly traced; the pocket was often a blaze of the richest embroidery.

**10.** To make a plan, diagram, or chart of (something existing or to be constructed); to mark out the course of (a road, etc.) on, or by means of, a plan or map; to mark or set out (the lines of a work or road) on the ground itself. Also *fig.* to devise (a plan of action), map out (a policy).

1374–5, 1399 [implied in *tracing-house, -board*: see TRACING *vbl. sb.*$^1$ 5]. 1599 PORTER *Angry Wom. Abingd.* (Percy Soc.) 60 When I had doubled my poynt, traste my ground. 1624 LD. KENSINGTON in Ellis *Orig. Lett.* Ser. I. III. 173 What they traced out for the breaking of the match, you follow, pretending to conclude it. *c* 1645 HOWELL *Lett.* (1650) I. 66 The castle [in Milan], by which the citadel of Antwerp was traced. 1669 STAYNRED *Fortification* 6 Tables..Whereby you may trace out any Fort by help of a Line of Equal Parts. 1696 PHILLIPS (ed. 5), To *Trace*, to draw upon Paper the plane of a Building or Fortification. 1834 L. RITCHIE *Wand. Seine* 120 Rollo's..path, like that of other conquerors, was traced in blood and ashes. 1871 FREEMAN *Norm. Conq.* IV. xviii. 212 The Ermine Street, notwithstanding all the centuries which have passed since it was first traced out and paved, is still distinguished from a yet older track.

**11.** To draw; to draw an outline or figure of; also, to put down in writing, to pen. [So OF. *tracier.*]

1390 GOWER *Conf.* III. 46 Babilla with hire Sones sevene ..With Cernes bothe square and rounde He traceth ofte upon the grounde. *c* 1440 *Promp. Parv.* 499/1 Tracyn, or draw strykys, *protraho.* 1665 BOYLE *Occas. Refl.* v. iii. *heading*, Killing a Crow.., and immediately tracing the ensuing Reflection with a Pen made of one of his Quills. 1712 J. JAMES tr. *Le Blond's Gardening* 96 Then trace upon the Ground the Triangle CDE. 1859 GULLICK & TIMBS *Paint.* 8 The mode of commencing a picture by tracing the outline was followed by the early oil painters. 1888 BURGON *Lives 12 Gd. Men* I. i. 26 These last [annotations] were evidently traced by fingers rendered tremulous by age.

**b.** To copy (a drawing, plan, etc.) by following the lines of the original drawing on a transparent sheet placed upon it; to make a tracing of.

1762–71 H. WALPOLE *Vertue's Anecd. Paint.* (1786) V. 211 There were an hundred and four heads, hands and feet, traced off from the Cartoons. 1885 'MRS. ALEXANDER' *At Bay* iii, They practiced duets together, and traced patterns.

**IV.** † **12.** In phr. *trace and traverse, trace and rase*, in reference to combatants: sense uncertain: cf. RACE *v.*$^3$, RASE *v.*$^1$, and TRAVERSE *v. Obs.*

1470–85 MALORY *Arthur* VI. viii. 194 Thus they ferd two houres or mo trasyng and rasyng eyther other where they myght hytte ony bare place. *Ibid.* VII. iv. 217 They rasshyd to gyders lyke borys tracynge, rasynge and foynynge to the mountenaunce of an houre. *Ibid.* x. xxx. 463 Thus they tracyd and trauercyd and hewe on helmes and hawberkes... And euer sire Tristram tracyd and trauercyd and wente forward hym here and there. 1596 SPENSER *F. Q.* v. viii. 37 Thus long they trast, and trauerst to and fro.

Hence **Traced** (trēɪst) *ppl. a.*, †(*a*) travelled, journeyed: with adverbial qualification (*obs.*); (*b*) outlined, drawn, written; **Tracing** *ppl. a.*, that traces or draws lines.

1632 LITHGOW *Trav.* vii. (1906) 293 My life and liberty being deare to me, my long traced feete became more nimble in twelve score paces, then they could follow in eighteene. 1712 J. JAMES tr. *Le Blond's Gardening* 92 The traced Line AB. 1875 SIR T. SEATON *Fret-Cutting* 146 Place the edge of the tool on the traced line. 1884 *Mil. Engineering* (ed. 3) I. II. 21 A sapper should be stationed..to await the arrival of the tracing party. 1907 *Daily Chron.* 24 Jan. 8/1 The spiral..must be skated boldly,..the knee of the tracing leg rather strongly bent.

† **Trace**, *v.*$^2$ *Obs. rare.* [f. TRACE *sb.*$^2$] *trans.* To attach by traces, to harness in traces.

1605 STOW *Ann.* 1432 They [Bayliffs of the Town] presented him with three-score and ten Teeme of horse, all traced to faire new Ploughes. 1656 COWLEY *Pind. Odes, Muse* i, Go, the rich Chariot instantly prepare;.. Unruly Phansie with strong Judgment trace, Put in nimble-footed Wit. 1786 BURNS *Inventory* 20 My furr-ahin's a wordy beast, As e'er in tug or tow was trac'd.

**Trace**, *v.*$^3$ *Obs.* exc. *local.* Forms: 4–5 trase, (pa. pple. **trased, trast**), 7– **trace.** [Belongs to TRACE *sb.*$^3$; possibly an altered form of TRESS *v.*]

**1.** *trans.* To plait, twine, interweave, braid.

13.. *Gaw. & Gr. Knt.* 1739 Þe hazer stones Trased aboute hir tressour, be twenty in clusteres. *c* 1450 HOLLAND *Howlat* 405 Mony schene scheld With tuscheis of trast silk tichit to the tre. 1613–16 W. BROWNE *Brit. Past.* II. iv. 320 A little lad..Tracing greene rushes for a winter chayre. *Ibid.* 358 As oft as I..Trace the sharpe rushes ends. 1678 [see TRACE *sb.*$^3$ 3]. 1753 CHAMBERS *Cycl. Supp., Tracing*,..a term used by our planters for the method of preserving the maize... [They] trace it, that is, they leave it in the ear, and weave, or fasten together a great number of ears by the ends of the husks. 1888 ELWORTHY *W. Somerset Word-bk., Trace*, to plait (always) 'I can't only trace dree, but our Jim can trace zix' [plait six strands together].

**2.** To plait or braid the hair of the head in tresses; = TRESS *v.* I.

1832 R. & J. LANDER *Exped. Niger* I. i. 41 Her hair was traced with such extraordinary neatness, that we expressed a wish to examine it more minutely. 1905 *Eng. Dial. Dict.* s. v. (W. Cornwall), She traces her hair every day.

Hence **Traced** *ppl. a.*; **Tra·cing** *vbl. sb.*, interweaving, embroidering, braiding; also *attrib.*

*c* 1450 Trast [see sense 1]. 1549 *Acc. Ld. High Treas. Scot.* IX. 334 Thre score thre elnis trasing silk to the samyn coit. 1681 *Scot. Proclam.* 1 Mar., Silver and gold threde, silver and gold lace, fringes or tracing. 1808–25 JAMIESON s. v., A *traced hat* is a hat bound with gold lace.

**Trace**, obs. erron. form of TRICE *sb.* and *v.*

**Traceable** (trēɪ·săb'l), *a.* [f. TRACE *v.*$^1$ + -ABLE.] Capable of being traced (in various senses of the vb.).

1748 RICHARDSON *Clarissa* (1811) III. ix. 65 Lest we should be traceable by her direction. 1793 RENNELL in *Phil. Trans.* LXXXIII. 184 The gulf stream..is discharged with such velocity, through the Straits of Bahama, that its motion is traceable through the Atlantic, to the Bank of Newfoundland. 1802 PALEY *Nat. Theol.* xxii. (ed. 2) 423 If attraction be..a primordial property of matter, not dependent upon, or traceable to, any other material cause. 1854 W. OSBURN *Mon. Hist. Egypt* II. ii. 55 Fragments on which the remains of hieroglyphics were yet traceable. 1874 CARPENTER *Ment. Phys.* I. viii. (1879) 372 In her family a very characteristic type of handwriting is traceable through five generations.

Hence **Traceabi·lity, Tra·ceableness,** the quality of being traceable; **Tra·ceably** *adv.*, in a manner or degree that can be traced.

1847 WEBSTER, Traceableness. 1855 *Tait's Mag.* XXII. 97 Slightly monotonous, and traceably imitative too, this young melodist yet runs his fingers over the strings with a ..power that instantly make[s] him a marked man. 1875 WHITNEY *Life Lang.* ii. 16 There is, recognizably and traceably, a time when..many of our words came into use. 1891 *Cent. Dict.*, Traceability. 1896 *Law Times* C. 436/2 The doctrine of following trust money depends upon its traceability.

**Traceless** (trēɪ·slės), *a.* [f. TRACE *sb.*$^1$ + -LESS.] Leaving no trace or track; that cannot be traced; of a surface, that shows no traces or lines.

1651 DAVENANT *Gondibert* II. I. xxiii, Traceless and Swift, and Changing as the Winde. 1789 WOLCOTT (P. Pindar) *Subjects for Painters* xxxv, On traceless copper sees imperial heads. 1889 F. L. OSWALD in *Voice* (N. Y.) 31 Oct., The strangest case of traceless disappearance is perhaps that of the Hungarian poet Petoefi. 1892 J. MATHER *Poems* 68 To traceless nothingness its course has run.

Hence **Tra·celessly** *adv.*, in a traceless manner; without leaving a trace.

1839 BAILEY *Festus* xxix. (1852) 472 May they pass quick and perish tracelessly. 1894 ILLINGWORTH *Personality Hum. & Div.* (1895) Notes 234 Vanishing tracelessly to give place to its successor.

† **Tra·cent.** *Sc. Obs.* Corruption of F. *treizain* (f. *treize* thirteen), popular name in France for certain heavy *douzains* (silver pieces of 12 deniers tournois) or *grands blancs au soleil* of Louis XI.

These had been issued at 78 to the *marc* instead of 86, and were thus about $^1/_{12}$ heavier than the ordinary *douzains*, and passed as worth 13 deniers. (M. Dieudonné, Cabinet de Medailles, Paris, through Mr. G. F. Hill, Brit. Mus.)

1524 *Acts Parlt. Scot.* (1875) XII. 40/2 Forsamekle as sowsis tracentis & karolusis franche monye beand layit w$^t$ coper has passage in þis Ralme.

**Tracer**$^1$ (trēɪ·səɹ). [f. TRACE *v.*$^1$ + -ER$^1$.] One who or that which traces.

**1.** One who follows the footprints or track of anything; one who tracks, investigates, or searches out; *spec.* one whose business is the tracing of missing persons, property, parcels, letters, etc.

1552 HULOET, Tracer, *uestigiator.* 1611 FLORIO, *Rintracciatore*, a tracer. Also a sifter out of secrets, a narrow searcher. 1627 HAKEWILL *Apol.* III. i. § 5. 152 Plyny..a diligent and curious tracer of the prints of Natures footsteps. 1629 H. BURTON *Truth's Triumph* 210 The timorous..hare.. to deceiue her pursuers or tracers, makes many doubles. 1724 MOFFET *Hesperi-neso-gr.* (1755) 4 To be performed by Some tracer of antiquity. 1866 *Intell. Observ.* No. 56. 99 Some deep-thinking tracer of structural relations. 1888 *Sci. Amer.* 6 Oct. 217/1 Nearly all the great [rail] roads employ a corps of what are known as 'lost car searchers' or 'tracers'. 1902 *Daily Chron.* 18 June 10/7 Furniture (Hire).—Wanted immediately smart man as collector and tracer; must have good knowledge of the hire trade. 1904 *Ibid.* 22 Aug. 4/5 The various postal organisations of sorters, telegraphists, postmen, linemen, tracers, &c.

**2.** A thing used in tracing; *spec.* **a.** *Anat.* A slender probe used in tracing the course of a nerve or vessel. **b.** In *U. S. railway* or *postal* usage, An inquiry form forwarded from point to point on which the successive movements of a missing car, parcel, or article have to be recorded.

1882 WILDER & GAGE *Anat. Technol.* 72 The tracer is apparently similar to the 'seeker' of the English anatomists. 1899 *Syd. Soc. Lex.*, *Tracer*, an instrument used in dissection for isolating nerves or vessels by teasing. 1899 *Westm. Gaz.* 17 June 7/2 The 'tracer' had chased the ore into the master-mechanic's possession.

**3.** *gen.* One who or that which traces lines or makes tracings; *spec.*

**a.** *Mil.* At a siege, one who traces parallels; a member of a tracing party. **b.** One whose work it is to trace copies of drawings or plans. **c.** One whose business is the tracing of patterns for embroidery. **d.** A tool for marking out designs or patterns; also, a chasing or engraving tool. **e.** A stylus for tracing on copying paper; also, the writing instrument of a pantograph or of a self-recording machine. **f.** A mechanical contrivance for making tracings on a larger or smaller scale. **g.** *Ice-cutting*: see quot. 1884.

[1541 *Aberdeen Regr.* (1844) I. 176 Item, ane traschor, ane stuffin sclyise.] c 1790 IMISON *Sch. Art* II. 29 With a little pointed tracer or burnisher go over your strokes which you drew upon the oiled paper, and you shall have the same very neatly and exactly drawn upon the white paper. 1799 G. SMITH *Laboratory* II. 37 Trace the out-line with a brass bodkin, or a tracer, made on purpose, of a piece of wire, of iron or brass. 1812 SHELLEY in Hogg *Life* (1858) II. 150 The tracers of a circle. 1825 J. NICHOLSON *Operat. Mechanic* 317 The frame carrying the dividing-point or tracer, is made to slide on the frame which carries the endless-screw to any distance. 1844 *Civil Eng. & Arch. Jrnl.* VII. 187/1 A solid cone revolving on its axis, during the perpendicular descent of a tracer. 1852 *Trans. Soc. Arts* LVI. 134 The cutters and tracers used together should be of the same size. 1859 F. A. GRIFFITHS *Artill. Man.* (1862) 250 Tracers [of a siege-battery]—1 non-commissioned officer, and 2 privates. 1878 G. B. PRESCOTT *Sp. Telephone* (1879) 297 The lower diagram is what the tracer wrote when the stanza was repeated. 1884 *Cassell's Fam. Mag.* Feb. 188/1 There are..tracers, or hand-ploughs, to mark out the areas to be cut by grooves [in ice]. 1890 W. J. GORDON *Foundry* 174 At last the film of putty with which the flat plate was spread to show the tracer's progress is scored along every line. The roller is finished. 1908 *Daily Chron.* 12 June 9/6 Tracer for embroidery, female; also cutters wanted. 1911 WEBSTER, *Tracer*,..any of several chasing tools for ornamenting in metal, esp. for making and finishing corners, borders, and the like.

**Tracer** [2] (trēⁱ·səɹ). [f. TRACE *sb.*[2] + -ER [1].] A trace-horse; also, a trace-horse boy.

1839 BLACK *Hist. Brechin* ix. 212 He loosed the tracer, leaped on its back..and..went off. 1843 BETHUNE *Sc. Fireside Stor.* 134 The sudden jerk..brought the shaft horse, who was a powerful animal, still nearer to that side of the road, while it made both him and the tracer lower their heads. 1899 J. LUMSDEN *Edin. Poems & Songs* 110 Boot-blackers, news-boys—the smartest we ken! An' their billies, the tracers—Dickie an' Ben.

**Traceried** (trēⁱ·sərid), *a.* [f. TRACERY + -ED [2].] Ornamented with or characterized by tracery.

1843 *Civil Eng. & Arch. Jrnl.* VI. 10** Over this traceried wall is a series of clerestory windows of large dimensions. 1849 FREEMAN *Archit.* II. iii. 337 France was the first to produce..traceried windows. 1856 RUSKIN *Mod. Paint.* IV. v. xvi. § 26 The narrow meadows and traceried cloisters of the Convent of the Réposoir. 1861 BERESF. HOPE *Eng. Cathedr. 19th C.* ii. 51 In England we are first introduced to complete traceried Gothic in Westminster Abbey.

**Tracery** (trēⁱ·səri). [app. an English formation f. TRACE *v.*[1], or TRACER [1]: see -ERY.]

†**1.** A place for tracing or drawing: cf. *tracing-house* s.v. TRACING *vbl. sb.*[1] 5. *Obs. rare*—[1].

1464 *Rolls of Parlt.* V. 530/1 For the Mansions, Storehouses, Traceries, Voide places for framyng, longyng unto the said Office, within oure Palice of Westm'.

**2.** *Arch.* The term given to the intersecting rib-work in the upper part of a Gothic window, formed by the elaboration of the mullion, and to the interlaced work of a vault, and that on walls, in panels, and in tabernacle work or screens. (In Fr. *réseau*, *remplissage*.)

In this sense, app. short for *tracery work*, as according to S. Wren 'they (i. e. the masons) called it'; this was perh. connected with sense 1 as work designed in the *tracery* or *tracing-house*, or executed according to tracings thence furnished; but it may have been formed directly from TRACER[1] or from TRACE *v.*[1] senses 9–11; cf. TRACING *vbl. sb.*[1] 3. *Tracery-work* and *tracery* were constantly used by Sir Christopher Wren, and taken from him by Plot and Randle Holme, under whose influence it became generally accepted as the recognized name for this work.

*Bar-, fan-, flamboyant, geometrical, plate-, wall tracery*: see these words.

1669 WREN *Surv. Salisbury Cath.* in *Parentalia* (1750) 304 The whole Church is vaulted with Chalk between Arches and Cross-springers only,..without Orbs and Tracery, excepting under the Tower, where the Springers divide, and represent a wider Sort of Tracery. *Ibid.*, The Windows are not made too great, nor yet the Light obstructed with many Mullions and Transomes of Tracery-work. 1686 PLOT *Staffordsh.* 360 The tracery in the Stone-work of the West-window..is a curious piece of Art. 1688 R. HOLME *Armoury* III. 112 Trasery is the working of the top part of a Window into several forms and fashions. 1713 WREN in *Parentalia* (1750) 302 The two West-towers.. ought certainly to be carried to an equal Height, one Story above the Ridge of the Roof, still continuing the Gothick Manner in the Stone-work, and Tracery. 1750 S. WREN *ibid.* 307 Thus they made their Pillars of a Bundle of little Torus's,..these Torus's split into many small ones, and traversing one another, gave Occasion to the Tracery-work (as they called it) of which this Society were the Inventors. *Ibid.*, A great part of the Outside-ornament of Churches consisted in the Tracery Works of disposing the Mullions of the Windows, for the better fixing in of the Glass. 1820 W. IRVING *Sketch Bk.* II. 5 (Westm. Abb.) The sharp touches of the chisel are gone from the rich tracery of the arches. 1849 MACAULAY *Hist. Eng.* viii. II. 277 Ancient buildings rich with the tracery of the middle ages. 1850 PARKER *Gloss. Archit.* 485 The tympanum..always retains the character of a flat surface or plate of stone pierced with openings. Hence this kind of tracery has been termed plate tracery by Professor Willis. a 1878 SIR G. G. SCOTT *Lect. Archit.* (1879) I. 127 The eastern chapels at Winchester, built about 1204..show suggestions of tracery. 1911 R. P. SPIERS in *Encycl. Brit.* XXVII. 115/1 The tracery in windows is usually divided into two sections, plate tracery and rib or bar tracery. *Ibid.* 116/1 The walls and buttresses were all panelled with blank tracery.

**3.** *transf.* and *fig.* Any delicate interweaving of lines or threads, as in embroidery, carving, etc.; also, an interlacing of boughs or foliage; network, open-work.

1827 HOOD *Mids. Fairies* lix, An elf..Whose coat..was quaintly wrought and overrun With spangled traceries. 1827 KEBLE *Chr. Y.*, *Monday Whitsun Week*, Wild-flower wreaths from side to side Their waving tracery hang. 1841 LEVER *C. O'Malley* lxvii, The thin tracery of the leafless twigs was finely marked.

**4.** *attrib.* and *Comb.*, as *tracery bar, glass, head* (of a window), *light, -window, -work* (see 2 above).

1835 R. WILLIS *Archit. Mid. Ages* vi. 53 *note*, The vertical portions below the imposts of the small arches of the lights, are termed *mullions*; the bending and ramifying parts above, I have called *tracery bars*. *Ibid.* 62 Tracery windows of the lancet proportion are great favorites with the Italians. 1886 *Pall Mall G.* 29 Sept. 11/2 The apse has four single-light windows high up in the wall with tracery heads. 1913 EDEN *Anc. Glass* 56 The task of the glass-painter was to fill tracery lights in a way that would harmonise with the glass of the main lights. This he did by making his tracery-glass white and yellow when the lower lights were wholly of that kind.

‖ **Trachea** (trăkī·ă, *often less regularly* trēⁱ·kiă). Pl. **-eæ**. [med.L. *trāchēa* (Albertus Magnus, c 1255) = late L. *trāchīa* (Macrobius, c 400), a. Gr. τραχεῖα (fem. of τραχύς rough); short for ἀρτηρία τραχεῖα 'rough artery': see ARTERY 1.]

**1.** *Anat.* and *Zool.* **a.** The musculo-membranous tube extending from the larynx to the bronchi, and surrounded by gristly (or in birds often bony) rings, which conveys the air to and from the lungs in air-breathing vertebrates; the windpipe.

In early use also in full form (L.) *trachēa artēria*, occas. anglicized as *trache arterie* or *arter trache*, or in one word *trachearteria*, and (from Fr.) *trachiartere*.

c 1400 *Lanfranc's Cirurg.* 153 Þou3 þat trache arterie be peersid..3itt he may be heelid wiþ gode medicyns. 1495 *Trevisa's Barth. De P. R.* v. xxiv. (W. de W.) h viij/2 The waye of the brethe, that is callyd Trachearteria. 1525 tr. *Brunswyke's Surg.* B ij/2 The throte bolle or trachea, ysophagus or meri. 1541 R. COPLAND *Galyen's Terap.* 2 H ij, The vlcere yͭ is in the sharpe artere called tracheia. 1543 TRAHERON *Vigo's Chirurg.* 5 b/2 The Trachea Arteria or wesaunde compouned of gristellye rynges. 1547 BOORDE *Brev. Health* ccxxvi. 77 The longes, the midryffe, the arter trache, the Epigloote. 1548–77 VICARY *Anat.* v. (1888) 44 *Trachia arteria*, that is, the way of the ayre. 1653 URQUHART *Rabelais* II. xviii, Trachiartere or pipe of the lungs. 1693 tr. *Blancard's Phys. Dict.* (ed. 2), *Aspera Arteria*, or *Trachea*, is an Oblong Pipe, consisting of various Cartilages and Membranes. 1713 DERHAM *Phys.-Theol.* IV. vii. 147 Blowing Wind into the Lungs, through the Trachea. 1808 BARCLAY *Muscular Motions* 499 Trachea..should always be pronounced with the *e* long, and not short, as is usually the practice. 1888 ROLLESTON & JACKSON *Anim. Life* 350 The organ of voice..in *Aves* is developed at the junction of the trachea and bronchi, and is known as the syrinx.

*attrib.* 1878 T. BRYANT *Pract. Surg.* (1879) II. 17 The cartilages and trachea rings. 1898 *Allbutt's Syst. Med* V. 4 Trachea-bronchitis, or bronchitis of the larger tubes.

**b.** Each of the tubes, usually opening by stigmata on the surface of the body, which constitute a special form of respiratory organ in insects and other arthropods, conveying air to the blood and tissues generally.

1826 GOOD *Bk. Nat.* (1834) II. 22 The tracheæ, or respiratory organs, are singularly placed at the verge of the tail. 1843 OWEN *Invertebr. Anim.* xix. 251 The smaller Arachnidans breathe by tracheæ exclusively. 1877 HUXLEY *Anat. Inv. Anim.* i. 59 In Arachnida, tracheæ may exist alone, or be accompanied by folded pulmonary sacs.

**2.** *Bot.* One of the ducts or vessels in the woody tissue of plants, formed from the coalescence of series of cells by disappearance of the partitions between them, formerly supposed to serve for the passage of air; a wood-vessel.

1744 BERKELEY *Siris* § 32 By means of air expanded and contracted in the tracheæ or vessels made up of elastic fibres, the sap is propelled through the arterial tubes of a plant. 1753 CHAMBERS *Cycl. Supp.* s. v., Tracheæ, in vegetables, are certain air-vessels. 1813 SIR H. DAVY *Agric. Chem.* (1814) 60 The tracheæ contain fluid matter, which is always thin, watery, and pellucid. 1885 GOODALE *Physiol. Bot.* § 271. 84 Ducts, or Tracheæ, are variously marked by pits. 1895 OLIVER tr. *Kerner's Nat. Hist. Plants* I. 276 Formerly the idea was held that these structures [wood-cells and wood-vessels] served for the passage of air, and it was believed that they were analogous to the respiratory organs—the so-called tracheæ—of insects; therefore these wood-vessels were also called 'tracheæ', and the wood-cells 'tracheides'.

**Tracheal** (trēⁱ·kiăl, trăkī·ăl), *a.* [ad. mod.L. *trāchēālis*, f. prec.: see -AL.]

**1.** *Anat.* and *Zool.* **a.** Of, pertaining to, or connected with the trachea or windpipe.

*Tracheal artery*: †(*a*) = TRACHEA 1 a (*obs.*); (*b*) each of the small arteries, branches of the inferior thyroid, which supply the trachea.

1710 T. FULLER *Pharm. Extemp.* 271 The Remedy..is convey'd..into the Tracheal Ducts. 1725 *Bradley's Fam. Dict.* s. v. *Spitting of blood*, If it [the Blood] proceeds from the Oesophagum,..or from the Stomach, Lungs, Tracheal Artery, or the Breast. 1849 LYTTON *Caxtons* II. iii, Coughing is either a tracheal, bronchial, pulmonary, or ganglionic affection. 1857 DUNGLISON *Med. Lex.*, *Tracheal Glands*, mucous follicles on the posterior surface of the trachea. 1881 MIVART *Cat* 227 The tracheal cartilages.

**b.** Pertaining to or of the nature of the tracheæ of insects and other arthropods; connected with tracheæ, as *tracheal gills*; performed by means of tracheæ, as *tracheal respiration*. (In quot. 1899 = TRACHEATE *a.*)

1826 KIRBY & SP. *Entomol.* IV. xxxviii. 64 The ramifications of the tracheal tree may be seen without dissection. 1888 ROLLESTON & JACKSON *Anim. Life* 505 (*Insecta*) Respiration is tracheal...Each stigma leads into a single tracheal stem, rarely into several. 1899 *Allbutt's Syst. Med.* VIII. 865 The tracheal order of the Arachnidæ.

**2.** *Bot.* Of the nature of, or composed of, tracheæ: see prec. 2.

1828 STARK *Elem. Nat. Hist.* II. 454 The Monocotyledonous vegetables have, besides this cellular tissue, porous and tracheal vessels. 1885 GOODALE *Physiol. Bot.* § 265. 81 To this class of elements it is difficult to give any satisfactory name...The name Tracheal (or Tracheary),..while it is a significant term when applied to trachea-like bodies (ducts) is a misnomer when applied to an elongated cell wholly free from annular or spiral markings.

**Trachean** (trēⁱ·kiăn, trăkī·ăn), *a.* (*sb.*) *Zool.* [f. TRACHEA + -AN.] Pertaining to or of the nature of a trachea, tracheal; having tracheæ, tracheate. **b.** *sb.* A tracheate arachnid.

1826 KIRBY & SP. *Entomol.* III. xxviii. 21 He has also considered the Trachean and Pulmonary Arachnida as forming one class. *Ibid.* 24 This appears to have had great weight with Lamarck, inducing him to include in his *Arachnida*, not only the Tracheans and Myriapods, but even the apterous Hexapods. 1891 *Cent. Dict.* s. v., Trachean respiration..trachean branchiæ.

**Trachearian** (trēⁱkiˌēə·riăn), *a.* (*sb.*) *Zool.* [f. mod.L. *Trăchēāri-a*, neut. pl. + -AN.] Belonging to the order *Trachearia* of arachnids: see TRACHEATE *a.* **b.** *sb.* A tracheate arachnid.

1854 BUSHNAN in *Circ. Sc.* I. *Org. Nat.* 77 The Trachearean Arachnidians..breathe..by means of air-tubes opening upon the surface of the body, by which the air is conveyed to every part of the system.

**Tracheary** (trēⁱ·kiări), *a.* (*sb.*) [ad. mod.L. *trăchēāri-us*, neut. pl. *-a*: see above.]

**1.** *Zool.* = prec. **b.** as *sb.* = prec. b.

1835 KIRBY *Hab. & Inst. Anim.* II. xix. 281 Trachearies, or those [Arachnidans] that breathe by spiracles in connection with tracheæ. 1872 LATHAM, *Tracheary*, adj., breathing by means of tracheæ, rather than lungs.

**2.** *Bot.* = TRACHEAL 2; esp. applied to tissue containing both tracheæ and tracheides.

1885 [see TRACHEAL 2]. 1900 in B. D. JACKSON *Gloss. Bot. Terms.*

**Tracheate** (trēⁱ·kiˌeⁱt), *a.* (*sb.*) *Zool.* [ad. mod.L. *Trăchēāta*, f. *trăchēa*: see above and -ATE[2] 2.] Furnished with or having tracheæ, as an arthropod; belonging to the group *Tracheata*, in some classifications comprising the insects, myriapods, arachnids, and the genus *Peripatus*, or *spec.* to the order *Tracheata* or *Trachearia* of arachnids, which breathe by tracheæ alone. In quot. 1888[1] = TRACHEAL 1 b. **b.** *sb.* A tracheate arthropod. So **Tra·cheated** *a.*

1877 WOODWARD in *Encycl. Brit.* VI. 654/2 The terrestrial tracheated air-breathing *Scorpionidæ*. 1878 BELL *Gegenbaur's Comp. Anat.* 288 None of these rudiments are retained in any living Tracheate. 1888 ROLLESTON & JACKSON *Anim. Life* 494 (*Arthropoda*) Respiration may be cutaneous..; or branchiate..; or tracheate, and carrying air to all the tissues. *Ibid.* 496 The majority of *Arachnida* are tracheate.

**Tracheide** (trēⁱ·ki-, trăkī·ˌəid). *Bot.* Also **-id.** [a. Ger. *tracheïde*, introduced 1863 by Sanio *Bot. Zeitung* 113 'cellulae sive fibrae ligneae tracheïdeae, kurzweg Tracheïdzellen oder Tracheïden': f. TRACHEA + *-ide*, -ID [2].] A vascular cell, with pitted lignified wall, which serves for the conduction of water; a vascular wood-cell.

The wood of the vascular tissue of Gymnosperms and Vascular Cryptogams consists wholly of tracheides.

1875 BENNETT & DYER *Sachs' Bot.* 98 To the Vascular forms belong the ducts and the vascular wood-cells or Tracheïdes. *Ibid.* 99 Vessels with prosenchymatous constituents now form the immediate passage to the vascular wood-cells (Tracheïdes). 1885 GOODALE *Physiol. Bot.* § 266. 82 Cells..which are closed throughout..are known as *Tracheids.* 1895 OLIVER tr. *Kerner's Nat. Hist. Plants* I. 276 The walls of the wood-vessels exhibit similar thickenings to those of the wood-cells or tracheides.

Hence **Tracheidal** (trēⁱkiˌəi·dăl, trăkī·ˌidăl) *a.*, pertaining to or of the nature of a tracheide.

1891 in *Cent. Dict.*

‖ **Tracheitis** (trēⁱkiˌəi·tis). *Path.* Also *erron.* **trachi·tis.** [mod.L., f. TRACHEA + -ITIS.] Inflammation of the trachea.

[1842 BRANDE *Dict. Sci.*, etc., *Trachitis*, inflammation of the trachea.] 1859 SEMPLE *Diphtheria* 40 A simple tracheitis or even a very mild sporadic affection. 1880 M. MACKENZIE *Dis. Throat & Nose* I. 521 The majority of cases of simple tracheitis scarcely call for any therapeutic measures. 1898 *Allbutt's Syst. Med.* V. 27 The tubular casts of diphtheria and of membranous tracheitis.

**Trachelate** (træ·kĭleᶦt), *a. Entom.* [ad. mod.L. *trachēlāt-us*, f. Gr. τράχηλος neck: see -ATE [2].] Having a neck, or a constriction like a neck: said of the prosternum in certain hymenopterous insects. So **Tracheliate** (trăkī·li,eᶦt) *a.*, belonging to the division *Trachelia* or *Trachelida* of beetles, which have a neck-like constriction behind the eyes; also **Trachelidan** (trăke·lidăn), *a.* = *tracheliate*; *sb.* a member of the *Trachelida*.

1826 KIRBY & SP. *Entomol.* IV. xlvi. 328 Trachelate... When of itself it forms a neck, the prothorax being represented only by membrane. 1842 BRANDE *Dict. Sci.*, etc., *Trachelidans*, the name of a family of Coleopterous insects, comprising those which have the head supported on a kind of pedicle or neck. 1891 *Cent. Dict.*, Trachelate..Trecheliate..Trachelidan.

† **Trachelipod** (trăke·lipǫd), *sb.* and *a. Zool. Obs.* [ad. mod.L. *Trachēlipod-a*, neut. pl. (Lamarck), irreg. (for **Trachēlopoda*) f. Gr. τράχηλος neck + πούς, ποδ- foot.] **a.** *sb.* A univalve mollusc of the order *Trachelipoda* in Lamarck's classification, having the foot or locomotive organ attached to the neck. **b.** *adj.* Belonging to or having the characters of this order. Also † **Trachelipodan** (trækĭli·pǫdăn), † **Tracheli·podous** *adjs. Obs.*

1835 KIRBY *Hab. & Inst. Anim.* I. ix. 276 The Trachelipods, constituting Lamarck's Third Order of Molluscans. *Ibid.*, The carnivorous,trachelipod Molluscans. 1841 JOHNSTON in *Proc. Berw. Nat. Club* I. No. 9. 263 *Animal* shelled, trachelipode, rarely gasteropode. 1847 ANSTED *Anc. World* xii. 271 The absence of the whole group of Ammonites, and their replacement by a newly introduced genus of carnivorous Trachelipods, animals of lower organization. 1860 MAYNE *Expos. Lex.* 1285 Trachelipodous. 1891 *Cent. Dict.*, Trachelipodan.

**Trachelo-** (trăkī·lo), combining form representing Gr. τράχηλος neck, occurring in modern scientific terms, chiefly of anatomy. **Trache·lo-acro·mial** *a.* and *sb.*, name of a muscle connecting the acromion or extremity of the shoulder-blade with the vertebræ of the neck. **Trache·lo-branchiate** (-bræ·ŋki,eᶦt) *a.*, *Zool.* having branchia or gills on the neck, as the division *Trachelobranchia* of gastropod molluscs. **Trache·lo-bregma·tic** *a.* [BREGMA], denoting a diameter of the head: see quot. **Trache·loclavi·cular** *a.*, denoting a small muscle occasionally connecting one of the vertebræ of the neck with the clavicle or collar-bone. **Trache·loma·stoid** *a.* and *sb.*, name of a muscle at the back of the neck, connecting it with the mastoid process of the temporal bone. **Trache·lo-occi·pital** *a.*, connecting the neck and the occiput: applied to the muscle usually called *complexus* (COMPLEXUS [2]). **Trache·loplasty** [-PLASTY], **Trachelo·rrhaphy** [Gr. ῥαφή sewing], *Surg.*, repair or suture of a laceration of the neck of the womb. **Trache·losca·pular** *a.*, common to the neck and scapular region or shoulder, as the branches of the external jugular vein. **Trachelotomy** (trækĭlǫ·tŏmi) *Surg.* [Gr. τομή cutting], amputation of the neck of the womb.

1891 *Cent. Dict.*, *Trachelo-acromial. 1899 in *Syd. Soc. Lex.* 1891 *Cent. Dict.*, *Trachelobranchiate. 1857 BULLOCK *Cazeaux' Midwif.* 221 The vertical diameter, properly so called, or the *trachelo-bregmatic, traverses the head perpendicularly, passing from the most elevated point of the vertex to the anterior part of the occipital foramen. 1891 *Cent. Dict.*, *Tracheloclavicular. 1899 in *Syd. Soc. Lex.* 1840 G. V. ELLIS *Anat.* 136 The *trachelo-mastoid, the other muscle of prolongation to the longissimus, is situated internal to the transversalis colli. 1891 *Cent. Dict.*, *Trachelo-occipital. 1899 in *Syd. Soc. Lex.* 1890 BILLINGS *Med. Dict.*, **Tracheloplasty*, operation for closure of a laceration of the cervix uteri. 1886 *Brit. Med. Jrnl.* 2 Jan. 1/1 The deep laceration was repaired by *trachelorraphy, five stitches being used. 1891 *Cent. Dict.*, *Trachelo-scapular. 1899 in *Syd. Soc. Lex.* 1890 BILLINGS *Med. Dict.*, **Trachelotomy*, amputation of the cervix uteri.

‖ **Trachenchyma** (trăke·ŋkimă). *Bot.* Also anglicized as **trache·nchym.** [f. TRACHEA + Gr. ἔγχυμα infusion, after PARENCHYMA.] Tracheary tissue: see TRACHEARY 2.

1848 LINDLEY *Introd. Bot.* (ed. 4) I. 21 Vascular tissue, or Trachenchym. 1861 BENTLEY *Man. Bot.* 34 Spiral vessels are sometimes called *Tracheæ* or *Trachenchyma*, from their resemblance to the tracheæ or air-tubes of insects.

**Tracheo-** (trăkī·o, treᶦ·kio), used as combining form of TRACHEA, in modern terms of anatomy, zoology, pathology, and surgery. ‖ **Tracheo-branchia** (-bræ·ŋkiă), pl. **-æ**, a respiratory organ in certain insect larvæ, combining the characters of a trachea and a branchia or gill. **Tracheo-bronchial** (-brǫ·ŋkiăl) *a.*, pertaining to the trachea and the bronchi; also as *sb.* a tracheobronchial muscle (in birds). ‖ **Tracheobronchi·tis**, 'inflammation of the trachea and bronchia' (Dunglison, 1857). **Trache·ocele** (-sīl) [Gr. κήλη tumour], a tumour in or upon the trachea; also loosely applied to goitre or enlargement of the thyroid gland (also called *bronchocele*). **Tracheolaryng-o·tomy** [LARYNGOTOMY], incision of the trachea and larynx, laryngotracheotomy (see LARYNGO-). **Tracheo-œsophageal** (-īsǫfæ·dʒiăl) *a.*, pertaining or common to the trachea and the œsophagus. **Trache·ophone** (-fōun) [Gr. φωνή voice], *sb.* a member of the *Tracheophonæ* or *Tracheophones*, a group of S. American passerine birds, having the syrinx or vocal organ situated wholly or chiefly in the trachea (cf. *tracheobronchial* above); *adj.* belonging to this group; so **Tracheo·phonine, Tracheo·phonous** *adjs.* **Tracheophony** (-ǫ·fŏni), 'the sound heard over the trachea on auscultation' (*Syd. Soc. Lex.* 1899). **Tracheo·scopy** [Gr. -σκοπία, f. σκοπεῖν to view], inspection or examination of the trachea, as with a laryngoscope; so **Tracheosco·pic** *a.*, pertaining to tracheoscopy; **Tracheo·scopist**, one who practises tracheoscopy. See also TRACHEOTOMY, etc.

1877 HUXLEY *Anat. Inv. Anim.* vi. 252 The so-called **Tracheo-branchiæ*..are in no sense branchiæ, but simply take the place of stigmata. 1896 NEWTON *Dict. Birds* 939 One pair of *tracheo-bronchial muscles, arising mostly from the Trachea and attached to one or more of the bronchial semi-rings. *Ibid.*, Two dorsal and one ventral tracheo-bronchials. *Ibid.* 940 According to the position of the sound-producing membranes, three types of Syrinx are distinguishable:—Tracheal, Bronchial and Tracheo-Bronchial. 1828 WEBSTER, **Tracheocele*, an enlargement of the thyroid gland; bronchocele or goiter. *Cyc.* 1880 M. MACKENZIE *Dis. Throat & Nose* I. 561 Tracheocele does not, as a rule, appear to be attended with much danger. 1890 BILLINGS *Med. Dict.*, *Tra'cheocele*, a tumor of the neck containing air and communicating with the trachea. 1909 *Cent. Dict. Suppl.*, *Tracheolaryngotomy. 1897 *Allbutt's Syst. Med.* III. 365 This may lead to a *tracheo-œsophageal or broncho-œsophageal fistula. 1884 *Ibis* July 241 This at once removes it from the *Tracheophones, in which a tenth primary is always present. 1906 *Athenæum* 10 Mar. 304/2 Mr. W. P. Pycraft read a paper on the 'Tracheophone Passeres', which he described as a group differing from all the remaining Passeres in the formation of the syrinx. 1888 NEWTON in *Encycl. Brit.* XXIV. 689 *note*, The *Furnariidæ* of Garrod, consisting of about 8 genera of *Tracheophonine Birds, some of whom build marvellous nests of mud spherical in form. 1896 NEWTON *Dict. Birds* 940 Indications of such a *tracheophonous Syrinx exist in various *Cotingidæ* and *Pittidæ*. 1857 DUNGLISON *Med. Lex.*, **Tracheophony*, Laryngophony. 1880 M. MACKENZIE *Dis. Throat & Nose* I. 519 A *tracheoscopic examination. 1899 *Syd. Soc. Lex.*, *Tracheoscopist. 1880 M. MACKENZIE *Dis. Throat & Nose* I. 502 (*title of section*) *Tracheoscopy. 1904 *Brit. Med. Jrnl.* 10 Sept. 605 Instructions for the practice of laryngoscopy and tracheoscopy.

**Tracheole** (treᶦ·ki,ōul). *Entom.* [ad. mod.L. type **trāchēola*, dim. of TRACHEA: see -OLE.] A small or minute trachea or branch of a trachea (in insects). Hence **Trache·olar** *a.*, pertaining to a tracheole, or consisting of tracheoles.

1904 *Amer. Nat.* Feb. 134 The tracheæ..pass over into the tracheolar network...The term tracheoles..is used elsewhere in insect histology to designate fine tracheal branches not possessing spiral thickening.

**Tracheome** (treᶦ·ki,ōum). *Bot. rare.* [f. TRACHEA + *-ome* as in *rhizome*, *caulome*, etc.] General term for a wood-vessel (*trachea*), wood-cell (*tracheide*), or other structure of the same class.

1900 B. D. JACKSON *Gloss. Bot. Terms* 273/1 *Tracheome*, stated by Potonié not to be the tracheal, but the hydral system of the bundle, he therefore names it Hydrome.

**Tracheotomy** (treᶦki,ǫ·tŏmi). *Surg.* Also *erron.* **tracho·tomy.** [f. TRACHEO- + -TOMY.] Incision of the trachea or windpipe.

1726 QUINCY *Lex. Phys.-Med.*, *Trachotomy*, the same as *Bronchotomy*. 1805 *Med. Jrnl.* XIV. 151 Bronchotomy, or (speaking more correctly) tracheotomy, was now thought of. 1878 T. BRYANT *Pract. Surg.* I. 75 Tracheotomy is one of these means, and deserves trial.

**b.** *attrib.*, *tracheotomy instrument*, etc.; **tracheotomy tube**, a tube inserted into the opening made by tracheotomy, to facilitate breathing.

1880 M. MACKENZIE *Dis. Throat & Nose* I. 514 *note*, I returned home for my *tracheotomy instruments. 1884 *Health Exhib. Catal.* 104/1 Bronchitis or *Tracheotomy Kettle. 1897 *Allbutt's Syst. Med.* IV. 822 The intubation tube is more comfortably worn than the *tracheotomy tube.

Hence **Tracheotome** (treᶦ·kiotōum), a surgical instrument for performing tracheotomy; **Tracheo·tomist**, one who performs tracheotomy; **Tracheo·tomize** *v.*, *trans.* to perform tracheotomy upon.

1857 DUNGLISON, **Tracheotome*, an instrument of the trocar kind, for opening the trachea. 1890 in BILLINGS *Med. Dict.* 1891 *Cent. Dict.*, *Tracheotomist. 1885 *Science* 27 Feb. 173/2 He [Leo] worked with rabbits, which were *tracheotomized and supplied with pure oxygen.

**Trachiartere**: see TRACHEA.

**Trachinoid** (træ·kinoid), *a.* and *sb. Ichth.* [f. mod.L. *Trachin-us* (Linnæus, 1758), name of the typical genus + -OID; f. med.L. *trachina*, said in Acts of S. Francis of Paula (1416–1507) to be a local name of a fish (Du Cange).] **a.** *adj.* Resembling, allied to, or having the characters of, the *Trachinidæ* or weevers, a family of spiny-finned fishes. **b.** *sb.* A fish of this family.

[1774 GOLDSM. *Nat. Hist.* (1862) II. III. i. 295 The Trachinus or Weever.]

**Trachitis**, incorrect form for TRACHEITIS.

**Trachle, trauchle** (trā·χ'l, trāu·χ'l), *sb. Sc.* [f. next.]

**1.** A fatiguing or exhausting journey or effort; exhausting struggle or toil.

1823 W. TENNANT *Cdl. Beaton* v. vii. 174 It's een a lang trachle frae the Kirk Wynd in Anster, to the Castle Wynd in St. Andrews. 1840 A. LAING *Wayside Flowers* (1878) 33 A' broken and pined Wi' trachle o' body and trouble o' mind. 1881 P. DUNCAN in *Mod. Scott. Poets* III. 171 Life's trachle's near a close.

**2.** A person who 'trachles' or gets 'trachled'.

1887 J. SERVICE *Dr. Duguid* xxiii. 157, I have had to ding some useless trauchle out of my gate. 1901 G. DOUGLAS *House w. Green Shutters* 39, I would have thocht the thowless trauchle hadna the smeddum left to interfere. [*Note*] *Trauchle*, a poor trollop who trails about.

**Trachle, trauchle** (trā·χ'l, trāu·χ'l), *v. Sc.* [Known from 16th c. Of obscure origin; but bearing a striking resemblance in sense to West Flemish *tragelen*, given by De Bo as a variant of *trakelen*, to go with difficulty, to walk laboriously and heavily; also trans. to drag or trail, as a canal-boat: cf. *tragel* or *trakel* a tow-path. Cf. also Du. *traag*, MDu. *traech* slow, heavy, sluggish; also Sw. dial. *traggel* sb., *traggla* v., worry, bother (Rietz).]

**1.** *trans.* To bedraggle, dishevel; to disorder, injure, or befoul by trampling. (Chiefly in *pa. pple.*)

1549 *Compl. Scot.* vii. 68 Hyr hayr..vas feltrit & trachlit out of ordour, hingand ouer hyr schuldirs. 1825 JAMIESON s. v., A person is said to trauchle corn or grass, when he injures it by treading on it. 1871 W. ALEXANDER *Johnny Gibb* i, We canna hae the beast's maet trachel't amo' their feet.

**2.** To tire out or fatigue greatly by long walking; to exhaust by over-exertion; *fig.* to distress. (Chiefly in *pa. pple.*)

*a* 1578 LINDESAY (Pitscottie) *Chron. Scot.* (S.T.S.) I. 274 Thay war vondrous tyrd and foirgeine and trachled gretlie in travell. 1588 J. MELVILL *Diary* (Wodrow Soc.) 263 That night, the Lard..sufferit the [Spanish] souldiours to com a-land..for the maist part young berdles men, sillie, trauchled, and houngered. 1776 C. KEITH *Farmer's Ha'* xxxvi, Quo' they, 'We're trachled unco sair, We've gane twal mile o' yerd and mair'. 1889 BARRIE *Window in Thrums* xx. 189 Ye mauna trachle yersel', mother.

**b.** *intr.* for *refl.* To tire oneself out; to drudge.

1823 W. TENNANT *Cdl. Beaton* v. vii. 171 I'm a wee forjeskit though, wi' trachlin' sae lang. 1840 A. LAING *Wayside Flowers* (1878) 37 Then why need ye toil on an' trachle sae sair?

Hence **Tra·chled** (tra·chlet), **trau·chled** *ppl. a.*; **Tra·chling, trau·chling** *vbl. sb.* and *ppl. a.*

1902 *Blackw. Mag.* Sept. 364/2 It's a trauchling game [golf] and I wish I'd never seen it. 1910 *Dundee Advert.* 25 Nov., A scheme..whereby a 'trauchled' working class mother could be relieved of part of her domestic toil.

**Tra·chly**, *a. Sc.* [f. prec. sb. or vb. + -Y.]

1825 JAMIESON, *Trachlie*, adj. 1. Always drudging, dirty, and slovenly, *Clydes.* 2. Fatiguing, exhausting, *ibid.*

‖ **Trachoma** (trăkōu·mă). *Path.* [mod.L., a. Gr. τράχωμα roughness (Dioscorides), f. τραχύς rough.] An infectious disease of the eyes, characterized by roughness or granulation of the inner surface of the eyelids, often supervening upon purulent ophthalmia; also called *granular lids*. **b.** Also, an affection of the larynx characterized by nodular swellings on the vocal cords (quot. 1880).

1693 tr. *Blancard's Phys. Dict.* (ed. 2), *Trachoma*, a Scab, or Asperity of the inner part of the Eye-lid. 1857 DUNGLISON *Med. Lex.*, *Trachoma*...A roughness of the inner surface of the eyelids. A variety of ophthalmia, of which three kinds have been designated. 1880 M. MACKENZIE *Dis. Throat & Nose* I. 293 This condition has been called *chorditis tuberosa* or *trachoma*. 1904 *Daily Chron.* 18 Oct. 3/4 So prevalent is the disease in Egypt..that a travelling hospital..has been for some months at work in that country, confining its attention solely to trachoma.

**b.** *attrib.* **Trachoma glands**, a name for the lymph-follicles of the conjunctiva, which increase in number in trachoma.

1873 T. H. GREEN *Introd. Pathol.* (ed. 2) 142 The trachoma glands of the conjunctiva. 1890 BILLINGS *Med. Dict.*, *Bruch, follicles of*, conjunctival lymph-follicles, trachoma glands of Henle.

Hence **Tracho·matous** *a.*, pertaining to, of the nature of, or affected with trachoma.

1891 in *Cent. Dict.* 1900 *Brit. Med. Jrnl.* 12 May *Epit. Curr. Lit.* 74 Trachomatous Pannus cured by intercurrent Erysipelas.

**Trachomedusan** (treᶦ:kǫmĭdiū·săn), *a.* and *sb. Zool.* [f. mod.L. *Trachomedusæ*, pl., f. *tracho-*, var. of TRACHY- + MEDUSA: see -AN.] **a.** *adj.* Belonging to the sub-order *Trachomedusæ* of the order *Trachymedusæ* of Craspedote Hydrozoa. **b.** *sb.* A hydrozoan of this sub-order.

[1888 ROLLESTON & JACKSON *Anim. Life* 749 The order *Trachymedusæ*..contains Medusæ which possess tentacles with a solid axis...There are two sub-orders, the *Narcomedusæ* and *Trachomedusæ*.] 1907 *Gentl. Mag.* July 97/2 No other known Trachomedusan had gourds on the manubrium.

**Trachotomy**, bad form for TRACHEOTOMY.

**Trachour**, variant of TREACHER *Obs.*, traitor.

**Trachtscoot**, obs. form of TREKSCHUIT.

**Trachy-** (treᶦki), combining form, repr. Gr. τραχύ-ς rough, in a few modern scientific terms. **Trachyca·rpous** *a. Bot.* [Gr. καρπός fruit], rough-fruited. **Tra·chychroma·tic** *a.* [Gr. χρῶμα colour], applied to certain cells in bone-marrow which take a deep stain. **Trachyglo·ssate**, *Zool.* [Gr. γλῶσσα tongue], *a.* belonging to the division *Trachyglossa* of octopod molluscs, having radular teeth upon the tongue; *sb.* a trachyglossate octopod. **Tra·chymedu·san**, *Zool.*, *a.* belonging to the order *Trachymedusæ* of Craspedote Hydrozoa; *sb.* a hydrozoan of this order. **Trachynemid** (-nī·mid), *Zool.* [Gr. νῆμα thread], *a.* belonging to the family *Trachynemidæ* of Craspedote Hydrozoa; *sb.* a hydrozoan of this family. **Tra·chynote**, a fish of the extinct genus *Trachynōtus*. ‖ **Trachypho·nia**, *Path.* [mod.L. f. Gr. φωνή voice], roughness or hoarseness of voice. **Trachypteroid** (trǎki·ptĕroid), *Ichth.* [Gr. πτερόν wing, taken as = fin: see -OID], *a.* resembling or allied to the genus *Trachypterus* or family *Trachypteridæ* of spiny-finned fishes, including the 'king of the salmon', *T. altivelis*; *sb.* a fish of this family. **Trachyspe·rmous** *a.*, *Bot.* [Gr. σπέρμα seed], rough-seeded.

**1860** MAYNE *Expos. Lex.*, *Trachycarpus*, having rough fruit,..*trachycarpous. **1900** in B. D. JACKSON *Gloss. Bot. Terms.* **1909** *Cent. Dict. Suppl.*, *Trachychromatic. **1891** *Cent. Dict.*, *Trachyglossate. **1890** *Q. Jrnl. Microsc. Sc.* Feb. 511 No *Trachymedusan has been observed to pass through a hydroid phase. **1888** ROLLESTON & JACKSON *Anim. Life* 751 In the family *Aglauridæ*, the Petasid sub-family *Petachnidæ*, and the *Trachynemid *Pectyllidæ*. **1848** SMART, **Trachynotes*, rough-backed creatures—the generic name of a division of fossil fishes. **1860** MAYNE *Expos. Lex.*, **Trachyphonia*, term for a rough voice. **1891** *Cent. Dict.*, *Trachypteroid. *Ibid.*, *Trachyspermous. **1900** in B. D. JACKSON *Gloss. Bot. Terms.*

**b.** *Min.* In names of rocks, taken as combining form of TRACHYTE, and denoting an igneous rock or lava intermediate between trachyte and that denoted by the second element, as **trachya·ndesite, trachyba·salt, trachydo·lerite, trachyrhy·olite.**

**1888** *Cassell's Encycl. Dict.*, Trachybasalt, Trachydolerite. **1897** H. S. WASHINGTON *Jrnl. Geol.* (U.S.) May–June 351 For those intermediate effusive rocks in which the plagioclase occurring along with orthoclase is acid..the name *trachyandesite*, which is in use in France, will be reserved. *Ibid.*, The intermediate potash-rich rocks..carry basic plagioclase-labradorite to anorthite—along with orthoclase, and such rocks will be called collectively in this paper by the name of *trachydolerite*,..proposed by Abich as far back as 1841. **1909** *Cent. Dict. Suppl.*, Trachyrhyolite.

**Trachyte** (trē¹·kəit, træ·kəit). *Geol.* and *Min.* [a. F. *trachyte* (Haüy); f. Gr. τρᾱχύς rough, or perh. τρᾱχύτης roughness.] A group of volcanic rocks, having a characteristically rough or gritty surface. The name was given by Haüy to certain volcanic rocks from Auvergne, and at first used in a wide sense; now confined to rocks consisting mainly of sanidine (or glassy orthoclase) felspar, as distinguished from oligoclase- and quartz-trachytes, and intermediate forms: see TRACHY- b.

**1821** R. JAMESON *Man. Min.* 427 Rocks of extinct and ancient volcanoes...1. Trachyte. This rock which is of the nature of felspar, is generally porphyritic, the imbedded crystals being most frequently of the glassy kind. **1830** LYELL *Princ. Geol.* I. 386 These isles are formed of brown trachyte..full of crystals of glassy felspar. **1854** MURCHISON *Siluria* xviii. 425 These were, in ancient times, penetrated by granites, porphyries, trachytes, and other eruptive matters. **1876** PAGE *Adv. Text-bk. Geol.* v. 105 The trachytes are rough-grained subcrystalline varieties of felspathic lava. **1911** *Encycl. Brit.* XXVII. 116/2 *Trachyte* ..was long used in a much wider sense..in fact it included quartz-trachytes (now known as liparites and rhyolites) and oligoclase-trachytes, more properly assigned to Andesites.

**b.** *attrib.*, as *trachyte rock*, *porphyry*; **trachyte tuff**, a tuff having the composition and structure of trachyte.

**1872** C. KING *Mountain. Sierra Nev.* ix. 188 Rounded domes of trachyte rock. **1877** TYLOR in *Nature* 5 July 191/1 In a still larger chulpa [*i.e.* Peruvian burial-tower] there are hewn trachyte blocks as large as twelve feet long [etc.]. **1885** GEIKIE *Text-bk. Geol.* II. II. vii. (ed. 2) 166 Thus we have felsite-tuffs, trachyte-tuffs, basalt-tuffs, pumice-tuffs, porphyrite-tuffs, etc.

**Trachytic** (trăki·tik), *a.* [f. prec. + -IC: cf. F. *trachytique*.] Consisting, or of the nature, of trachyte; containing, or abounding in, trachyte.

**1827** *Edin. Rev.* XLV. 320 Those hills consist of a trachytic formation. **1830** LYELL *Princ. Geol.* I. 396 Where it [felspar] is in great excess lavas are called trachytic; where augite (or pyroxene) predominates, they are called basaltic. **1833–4** J. PHILLIPS in *Encycl. Metrop.* (1845) VI. 767/1 Trachytic porphyry..occurs on the Western shore of the Island of Arran. **1869** PHILLIPS *Vesuv.* viii. 211 Slopes of crumbling tufaceous, pumiceous and trachytic rocks.

**Trachytoid** (træ·kitoid, trē¹·ki-), *a.* [f. as prec. + -OID, after F. *trachytoïde*.] Resembling or allied to trachyte.

**1885** GEIKIE *Text-bk. Geol.* II. II. v. (ed. 2) 110 *note*, For this [semi-crystalline] structure the term 'mixed' has been proposed, as being a mixture of the crystalline and amorphous (glassy) structures. It has been designated by Fouqué and Michel-Lévy 'trachytoid', as being typically developed among the trachytes. *Ibid.* vii. 137 Two leading types of structure are recognised by these authors among the eruptive rocks. 1. Granitoid...2. Trachytoid, distinguished by a more marked contrast between the crystals of the first and second consolidation, the usual presence of an amorphous magma, and the fluxion structure.

**Tracing** (trē¹·siŋ), *vbl. sb.*[1] [f. TRACE *v.*[1] + -ING [1].] The action of TRACE *v.*[1], or its result.

**1.** The following of traces, tracking; also †*concr. pl.* traces left, tracks (*obs.*).

**1523** *Act* 14 & 15 *Hen. VIII*, c. 10 Diuers persons..by reason of the trasinge in snow, haue killed and destroied.. the same Hares, by .x. xii. or .xvi. vpon a daye. **1657** THORNLEY tr. *Longus' Daphnis & Chloe* 116 A Wolf pursued me: where are the tracings of a Wolf? **1753** CHAMBERS *Cycl. Supp.*, *Training*, or *Tracing*,.. used by our miners to express the tracing up the mineral appearances on the surface of the earth to their head.., and there finding a mine. **1910** M. GASTER in *Encycl. Brit.* XII. 40/1 In various parts of Germany and Austria a special register is kept for the tracing of the genealogy of vagrant and sedentary Gipsy families.

†**2.** The treading of a measure; dancing. *Obs.*

**1577** GRANGE *Golden Aphrod.* F iij b, It fell by course N.O. shoulde leade this trace, bycause he knewe it beste, the tracyng of this rounde requyred in the middle thereof a conge. **1596** DAVIES *Orchestra* xiii, No..sight more pleasing to behold, With all their turnes and tracings manifold. **1643** TRAPP *Comm. Gen.* xxix. 22 Of dancing and dalliance, of tracing, and tripping on the toe, we read not.

**3.** Drawing, delineating, marking out; the copying of a drawing, etc., by means of a transparent sheet placed over it.

*c* **1440** *Promp. Parv.* 499/1 Tracynge, or drawynge for to make an ymage or an other thynge (*K.* to make a pycture or gravynge). **1573** (*title*) A..treatise, wherein is..sett forthe the arte of Limming, which teacheth the order in drawing & tracing of letters, vinets, flowers, armes and Imagery. **1712** J. JAMES tr. *Le Blond's Gardening* 87 The Manner of Tracing, reduced to Twenty Practices. **1815** J. SMITH *Panorama Sc. & Art* II. 728 Tracing against the Light. **1843** *Civil Eng. & Arch. Jrnl.* VI. 236/1 The slow progress of a fresco-painting, from the 'tracing' to the last touch. **1884** *Mil. Engineering* (ed. 3) I. II. 21 The tracing of parallels and approaches is commenced in the dusk of the evening, when sufficiently dark to conceal men from the view of the besieged.

**b.** *concr.* That which is produced by tracing or drawing; a drawing; *spec.* a copy made by tracing; also, the record of a self-registering instrument.

**1811** WELLINGTON in Gurw. *Desp.* (1838) VII. 142 Murray ..tells me that he sent after you..a tracing of a large part of Alemtejo. **1857** RUSKIN *Pol. Econ. Art* ii. (1868) 127 Tracings from frescos and other large works are also of great value. **1864** *Lond. Rev.* 27 Aug. 247/2 The Psychonomy of the Hand..is illustrated by tracings from living hands of various endowments. **1866** ROGERS *Agric. & Prices* I. xxvi. 644 A collection of such tracings will be found in the Bodleian Library. **1874** H. H. COLE *Catal. Ind. Art S. Kens. Mus.* 251 The centre [of the embroidered pattern] is occupied by a circular disc of beautiful floral tracing. **1899** *Allbutt's Syst. Med.* VIII. 373 The sphygmographic tracing [in melancholia] usually indicates a feeble systole.

†**4.** A timber used in building; ? a framing timber. *Obs.*

**1601** DEACON & WALKER *Answ. to Darel, Catal. D.'s Contradict.* No. 50 The groundsels, the studs, the raysing peeces, the iouystes, the tracings, and all the rest of the timber belonging thereto. **1616** *Nottingham Rec.* (1889) IV. 348 For ouer liggers and trasinges for yᵉ same bridge x s.

**5.** *attrib.* and *Comb.*: **tracing-board**, a board on which a plan, as of a building, is traced; **tracing-braid**, ? narrow braid used in an interlacing design; **tracing-cloth**, smooth transparent linen sized on one side, used for making tracings; **tracing-house**, a house in which the plans of a building are traced; **tracing-instrument**, an instrument for copying any outline or plan on the same or a larger or smaller scale; **tracing-lace**, narrow lace used in an open design; cf. *tracing-braid*; **tracing-linen** = *tracing-cloth*; **tracing-machine** = *tracing-instrument* (*Cent. Dict.* 1891); **tracing-paper**, (*a*) transparent paper for copying drawings, etc. by tracing; (*b*) lithographic transfer paper; **tracing-picket**, a picket used in siege work to mark lines and angles; **tracing-pin**, a peg or pin used to mark out lines on the ground in setting out work; **tracing-point**, (*a*) a point that traces or draws lines; (*b*) in *Fretwork*, a sharp tool used to mark out a design; **tracing-staff**: see quot.; **tracing-thread**, in *Lace-making*, a heavy thread or fillet of fine threads used to form the outline of the pattern; **tracing-wheel**, a toothed wheel or roulette for marking out patterns.

**1399** in *York Fabric Rolls* (Surtees) 17 In le loge [mason's work-shop] apud Ebor, in cimiterio, lxix stanexes, j magna kevell, xcvj chisielles ferri.., ij *tracyngbordes. **1906** *Daily Chron.* 4 Oct. 3/4 The jacket was..elaborately braided with silk *tracing-braid. *Ibid.*, The skirt..with a girdle, braided with tracing-braid to match the jacket. **1842–76** GWILT *Encycl. Archit.* Gloss., **Tracing cloth*, a fine white cloth, prepared in a similar way to paper for rendering it transparent. **1873** E. SPON *Workshop Receipts* Ser. I. 6/2 If ink or colour does not run freely on tracing cloth, mix both with a little ox-gall. **1374–5** in Oliver *Exeter Cath.* (1861) 385 Custus nove domus in Calendarhay vocate '*Trasyng hous'. **1581–2** *York Fabric Rolls* (Surtees) 118 For xj daies worke on the leades over the tracinge hows, etc., 10s. 8d. [**1859** *Ibid.* Gloss. 358 *Tracinge-hous*, the place or room used by the draughtsman.] **1877** KNIGHT *Dict. Mech.*, **Tracing-instrument*, an instrument for copying figures on an enlarged or reduced scale. **1901** *Daily News* 13 Feb. 5/1 A very long robe..trimmed with gold lace, some of it what is technically called '*tracing-lace', i.e., arranged in small loops placed alternately hither and thither. **1824** *Mech. Mag.* 31 Jan. 365/2 An excellent method to make *tracing-paper. **1834** *Penny Cycl.* II. 203/2 The design is..copied on very thin transparent paper, called tracing-paper. **1862** *Catal. Internat. Exhib.* II. XIII. 17 To the horizontal arm is fixed the *tracing pencil. **1870** WESSELY *Germ.-Eng. Dict.*, *Absteckpfahl*.. *tracing-picket. **1712** J. JAMES tr. *Le Blond's Gardening* 89 Tracing two Portions of a Circle..by means of a small *Tracing-Pin fixed at the End of the Cord. **1815** J. SMITH *Panorama Sc. & Art* II. 728 Where long, straight, or parallel lines occur, the *tracing point may be guided by a ruler. **1712** J. JAMES tr. *Le Blond's Gardening* 84 A **Tracing-Staff*..is a long strait Stick tipt with Iron at the lower End, having the Point triangular..; with this Tracing-Staff you strike out and design all the Figures of a Garden.

**Tracing**, *vbl. sb.*[2]: see TRACE *v.*[3]

(Here perhaps belong quot. 1874 in prec. 3 b, and *tracing-braid*, *-lace* in sense 5 above.)

**Track** (træk), *sb.* Forms: 5–6 **trak**, 6 **tracke**, 6– **track**. [a. OF. *trac* (1440 in Hatz.-Darm.), *traq*, F. *trac*: ulterior derivation uncertain, but generally thought to be from Teutonic. Diez and Scheler would connect it with MLG. and Du. *treck*, *trek* draught, drawing, pull, line drawn, etc., f. *trecken*, *trekken* to draw, pull, tug, drag, haul (in MDu. rarely *tracken*): see TRACK *v.*[2]

If this be the source, the original sense would appear to have been the line or mark made on the ground by anything hauled or dragged, whence also the mark made or path beaten by the feet of man or beast; the sense-development being parallel to that of TRACE from L. **tractiāre*. It is noticeable that the senses of the verbs *trace* and *track* are sometimes identical; also that *track* and *tract* were often identified in pronunciation and use.]

**I. 1.** The mark, or series of marks, left by the passage of anything; a trail; a wheel-rut; the wake of a ship; a series of footprints; the scent followed by hounds; *spec.* in *Geol.* a series of fossilized footprints of an animal.

**1470–85** MALORY *Arthur* x. xiv. 435 Myght I fynde the trak of his hors I shold not fayle to fynde that Knyghte. *c* **1500** *3 Kings' Sons* 30 They came on the trakkys of there enmyes. *c* **1595** CAPT. WYATT *R. Dudley's Voy. W. Ind.* (Hakl. Soc.) 27 Wee discried the track of theire feet in the woodes by the impression of the sandes. **1685** COTTON tr. *Montaigne* (1711) I. xxxviii. 349 Like the Beasts of Chace, who put out the Track at the Entrance into their Den. **1706** PHILLIPS (ed. Kersey), *Track*, a Foot-print, or Foot-step, the rut of a Coach-wheel, the run of a Ship, a Mark that remains of any thing. **1840** DICKENS *Barn. Rudge* viii, The walls and roof..tapestried with the tracks of snails and slugs. **1842** *Act* 5 & 6 *Vict.* c. 79 § 17 Any stage carriage.. the bearing of which on the ground shall be less than 4 ft. 6 in. from the centre of the track of the right or off wheel to the centre of the track of the left or near wheel. **1912** *Return Brit. Museum* 174 A large slab of tracks from the Palaeozoic rocks of the Alleghany Mts.

†**b.** The pacing of a horse. *Obs. rare*—[1].

**1653** URQUHART *Rabelais* I. xliii, I hear the track [F. *trac*] and beating of the enemies horse feet.

**c.** *Zool.* The sole of the foot, esp. in birds.

**1891** in *Cent. Dict.* **1911** in WEBSTER.

†**2.** *fig.* = TRACE *sb.*[1] 6, 7. *Obs.*

**1652–62** HEYLIN *Cosmogr.* Introd. (1674) 11/2 Of Sabteca ..I can find no track in any of the Ancient Authors. **1662** J. DAVIES tr. *Olearius' Voy. Ambass.* 219 Now there is no track to be seen of any such thing. *Ibid.* 223 In all this Citie, I found not the least track of Antiquity. **1692** BENTLEY *Boyle Lect.* viii. § 8 To consider the Atmosphere and the exterior Frame and Face of the Globe; if we may find any tracks and footsteps of Wisdom in the Constitution of Them. **1694** ADDISON *Story of Calisto* 9 No tracks of heaven's destructive fire remain.

**3.** A way made or beaten by the feet of men or animals; a path; a rough unmade road.

**1643** CROMWELL *Let.* 31 July, We..came to the bottom of a steep hill: we could not well get up but by some tracks. **1675** N. THOMAS in I. Mather *K. Philip's War* (1862) 231 We took notice that an Indian track, newly made, wheeled about from west to South. **1791** MRS. RADCLIFFE *Rom. Forest* i, The road was only a slight track upon the grass. **1832** *Act* 2 & 3 *Will. IV*, c. 64 Sched. O. 48 The point at which the same [road] meets the mountain track from Dowlais to Quakers Yard. **1883** W. GARDNER in *Science Gossip* May 97 The southern corner is crossed by a mountain track running from Trefriw to Capel Curig.

*fig.* **1656** COWLEY *To Sir W. Davenant* 36 Thy Fancy like a Flame its way does make, And leave bright Tracks for following Pens to take.

**4.** A line of travel, passage, or motion; the actual course or route followed (which need not be any beaten or visible path, or leave any traces, as the path of a ship, a bird in the air, a comet).

**1570–6** LAMBARDE *Peramb. Kent* 287 This place..as also the whole track of their journey (remaining euer after a greene pathe) the Towne dwellers were wont to shew. **1671** MILTON *P. R.* I. 189 The better to converse With solitude, till far from track of men. **1681** NEVILE *Plato Rediv.* 79 Like Horses who know their Track well enough, without considering East or West, or what business they go about. **1748** *Anson's Voy.* II. x. 240 To give a better idea of the track which they hold in this navigation, I have..laid down the particular route..in..this chart. **1840** R. H. DANA *Bef. Mast* xxxiv. 131 We were just in the track of the tremendous hurricane of 1830. **1853** KANE *Grinnell Exp.* iii. (1856) 24 The ferry-boats and steamers came out of their track to salute us in the bay. *fig.* **1565** T. STAPLETON *Fortr. Faith* 126 After the tracke of Caluins trace.

**b.** The course of a nerve or blood-vessel, or the like; the course of a wound.

**1807–26** S. COOPER *First Lines Surg.* (ed. 5) 444 All the surfaces, in contact with each other, and surrounding the track of the wound, become generally so intimately connected together. **1841–71** T. R. JONES *Anim. Kingd.* (ed. 4) 668 The whole track of the intestinal tube, as well as the (so-called) hepatic viscus, is covered internally with vibratile cilia.

**c.** (?) A long narrow stretch (of light). (But both examples may belong properly to TRACT *sb.*[3]: cf. branch II.)

**1693** CONGREVE *To Dryden* in *D.'s Persius* 400 In their room bright Tracks of Light are seen. **1757** GRAY *Bard* 103 In yon bright track, that fires the western skies, They melt, they vanish from my eyes.

**5.** *fig.* **a.** A course of action or conduct; a method of proceeding; 'way', 'path'. *The beaten track*, the ordinary (*quasi* well-worn) way.

**1638** JUNIUS *Paint. Ancients* 242 They..propound unto us the right way, and not one usually beaten track onely. **1658–9** in *Burton's Diary* (1828) IV. 54 You are in a track, and cannot go back or forwards. **1714** LADY M. W. MONTAGU *Lett.* (1887) I. 96 The world never believes it possible for people to act out of the common track. **1742** YOUNG *Nt. Th.* III. 332 To..Pace the Round Eternal?.. To beat and beat The beaten Track? **1785** G. A. BELLAMY *Apology* II. 166 You see me now entered into a new track of life. **1864** SKEAT *Uhland's Poems* 56 Would ye have me wish to wander From the tracks of daily care? **1906** KROPOTKIN *Mem. Rev.* (1908) IV. viii. 254 Austria and Hungary followed in the same track.

**b.** A train or sequence of events, thoughts, etc.

**1681** J. OWEN *Spiritual Mindedness* Wks. 1852 VII. 307 A continual track of fruitless impertinent thoughts about their own concerns. **1693** DRYDEN *Disc. Orig. & Progr. Sat.* Ess. (ed. Ker) II. 29 When he is got into a track of Scripture. **1725** WATTS *Logic* IV. i. § 2 In writing the Lives of Men, which is called Biography, some Authors follow the Track of their Years. **1793** BURKE *Corr.* (1844) IV. 199 My pen goes in the track of my thoughts. **1827** R. POLLOK *Course T.* x. *ad fin.*, Thus have I sung beyond thy first request, Rolling my numbers o'er the track of man, The world at dawn, at mid-day, and decline.

**6.** A path made or laid down for a special purpose; *spec.* **a.** (now *U.S.*) A continuous line of a pair of rails and the space between them, on which railway vehicles travel: commonly called in Great Britain *a* or *the line*, and in some connexions *the rails*. (Cf. TRACKAGE [2].) Also, an iron path or pair of rails which a carriage in a machine or a gun-chassis traverses. *Off the track*, off the line or rails, derailed; also *fig.*

**1805** REES *Cycl.* VI. s. v. *Canal*, Surrey Iron Rail-Way... The width of each track is about 5½ feet, the waggons carry about 3¼ tons each...Crossing rails are used at every passing-place or point where waggons are to pass out of one track of rails into another. *a* **1824** [see RAILWAY 3]. **1860** BARTLETT *Dict. Amer.* (ed. 3), *Track*, the line of a railroad, or rather between the rails. 'A man walking on the track was run over and killed'. **1875** LOWELL *Spenser* Prose Wks. 1890 IV. 277 A series of jolts and jars, proving that the language had run off the track. **1894** *Times* 14 July 7/1 The switchmen [in U.S.]..control the yards, the making up of the trains, and the freedom of the tracks.

**b.** A course prepared or laid out for racing, or the like: often in comb., as *cinder-*, *race-*, *racing-*, *running-track*.

**1887** *Field* 20 Aug. 328/2 The six-lap grass track on which the above sports were held. **1912** *Throne* 7 Aug. 228/1 The..Italian sprinter Giongo..should..be seen frequently on the track at Metropolitan meetings.

**7.** *Her.* A longitudinal division of an ordinary or sub-ordinary, or in the representation of certain furs.

**1868** CUSSANS *Her.* iii. 53 The Furs Vair, Countervair, Potent, and Counterpotent...They are usually represented as of four rows, heraldically termed Tracks. *Ibid.* iv. (1882) 67 A Bordure or other Ordinary composed of Metal and Colour alternately, is termed Company...If there be two *Tracks*, it is then said to be Counter-Company.

**8.** [from TRACK *v.*[1]] The action of tracking; the pursuit of a criminal or fugitive.

[**1542–3**: see TRACT *sb.*[3] 10 b.] **1617** *Carte Papers* LXII. 438 The Track shalbee vndertaken within foure and twenty howres, after the goodes have bin stolne,..that the Inhabitants of that place, may have time to put the track forwardes.

**9.** Phrases. *In one's tracks* (*U.S.*), on the spot where one is at the moment; instantly, immediately. *On the track* (*of*), in pursuit of; also, having a trace of or clue to. *To cover* (*up*) *a person's tracks*, to conceal or screen his motions or measures. *To keep track*, to follow or grasp the course, progress, or sequence *of*; to keep account *of*; so *to lose track of*. *To make* (*take*) *tracks* (*for*), to make off, to make *for*; to go off quickly (orig. *U.S.*).

**1835–40** HALIBURTON *Clockm.* (1862) 30 I'd a made him make tracks, I guess. **1843** R. CARLTON *New Purchase* xvii. I. 130 The rifle was fired..and he fell dead in his tracks. **1866** LOWELL *Biglow P.* II. Introd., Poems 1890 II. 189 *In his tracks* for *immediately* has acquired an American accent, and passes where he can for a native. **1871** FARRAR *Witn. Hist.* ii. 49 Not on the false track of myths, artificially elaborated. **1878** *Masque Poets* 244 Whatever else he lacks, He has the art of covering up his tracks. **1883** GILMOUR *Mongols* (1884) 251 The noise of the two crowds.. made it difficult to keep track of what was going on. **1886** EMMA MARSHALL *Tower on Cliff* xii, The men are on the track. **1894** *Outing* (U. S.) XXIII. 387/1 Day after day passes in precisely the same manner.., until one loses all track of the days of the week. **1902** *Munsey's Mag.* XXVI. 569/1 Theater-goers who have kept close track of the dramatic tastes of New York and London.

**II.** Used by confusion in senses of TRACT *sb.*[3] (*Tract* is very commonly pronounced dial. (træk), and some of the senses are identical with those of *track*.)

†**10.** A feature, lineament, trait; = TRACT *sb.*[3] 7. *Sc. Obs. rare.*

**1513** DOUGLAS *Æneis* XII. xiii. 135 And all elike wympillit and cled thir trakis With eddris thrawin, and haris full of snakis. **1808–18** JAMIESON, *Track*, feature, lineament.

**11.** An extent of land; also, a space of time, a period; also, † a sequence or succession of actions or events (*obs.*); cf. TRACT *sb.*[3] 1 c, 2, 3.

**1687** BURNET *Trav.* iii. (1750) 166 All the Way to Florence this Track of Hills continues, tho' there are several Bottoms. **1760–72** H. BROOKE *Fool of Qual.* (1809) III. 43 Their conquest or seizure of any track of country. **1765** *Museum Rust.* IV. lxii. 268 Very large tracks, of two or three thousand acres. **1796** H. H. HUNTER tr. *St.-Pierre's Stud. Nat.* (1799) I. 132 The track of land inundated was lower than the Ocean. **1835** I. TAYLOR *Spir. Despot.* iii. 91 During a much longer track of time. **1851** *Jrnl. R. Agric. Soc.* XII. I. 127 If a track of dry weather sets in. **1893, 1901** in *Eng. Dial. Dict.* (of weather). **1896** W. B. WILDMAN *Hist. Sherborne* i. 1 A track of country won for England from the West-Welsh.

†**12.** An attraction, enticement; = TRACT *sb.*[3] 4. *Obs. rare*[−1].

**1673** O. WALKER *Educ.* i. 6 Since we find great tracks and encouragements in the way of pleasure.

**III. 13.** *attrib.* and *Comb.*, as *track-chart*, *-cutting*, *-side*; in sense 6 a (mainly *U.S.*), *track-cleaner*, *construction*, *elevation*, *material*; in 6 b, *track athlete*, *athletics*, *event*, *-measuring*, *meeting*, *-racing* sb. and adj., *record*; **track-brake**, a railway brake which acts by pressure directly against the rail; also, a device consisting of rails with curved ends, kept in position alongside the ordinary rails by springs, which by friction automatically retards a vehicle passing over them by compressing the flanges of the wheels; **track-channeler**, in quarrying, a groove-cutting tool mounted on a rail truck (*Cent. Dict. Suppl.* 1909); **track-chisel**, a plate-layer's hammer with a flat cutting peen (*ibid.*); **track-clearer**, a cross-bar carried immediately in front of the wheels of a locomotive or tram-car to push obstructions off the rails; also, a cow-catcher or snow-sweeper fixed in front of a locomotive; also, a wedge-shaped board fixed at the outer end of the cutter-bar of a reaping machine, which directs the swath to the cutters and leaves a clear track for the next passage of the machine; **track-edge**, the abrupt edge of a mill-stone furrow; **track-harness** (*U.S.*), light harness for trotting-races (Knight *Dict. Mech.* 1877); **track-hound**, a hound capable of following a track, a sleuth-hound; **track-iron**, *Golf*; see quot. 1908 and IRON *sb.* 4 e; **track-layer**, a man employed in laying or repairing a railway track, a plate-layer; also, a railway truck equipped with machinery for laying rails; so **track-laying** *sb.* and *adj.*; **track-leveller**, a railway truck having heavy projecting wings or shares which can be raised or lowered so as to level the ballast on a railway line as it is drawn along (*Cent. Dict. Suppl.* 1909); **track-lifter**, a wheeled frame or truck with powerful jaws for grasping the rails, and mechanism for getting a lifting purchase against the ground; used in levelling a railway line (Knight *Dict. Mech.* 1877); **track-line**, the line of a (former) track or path: see quot. 1889; **track-man**, a workman employed in the construction or maintenance of a railway or tramway; **track-master**, one who is responsible for the inspection and repair of a section of railway track (*Cent. Dict.* 1891); **track-mile**, a mile of 'track' or single line; hence **track-mileage**; **track-rail**, the rail on which the wheels run, as distinct from a guide-rail or the like; **track-raiser**, a jack for lifting sunken rails, a *track-lifter*; **track-scale**, a weigh-bridge for railway vehicles (Knight *Dict. Mech.* 1877); **track-scraper**, a snow-scraper attached to a railway car for clearing the line (*Cent. Dict. Suppl.* 1909); **track-shoe**, a track-brake shoe; **track-sprinkler**: see quot.; **track-walker**, a man employed to walk along and examine a certain length of railway track regularly; so **track-walking**; **track-work**, (*a*) the construction of a railway track or line; (*b*) action or use on a racing track. Also TRACKWAY.

**1888** *Pall Mall G.* 27 Aug. 14/1 The baseball and *track athletes graduated 34 per cent. of their number...In physical development..the crew men coming first, the base-ball players next, and track athletes last. **1890** W. CAMP in *Century Mag.* June 204/2 The..games..generally classed under the term '*track athletics' are walking, running, jumping, bicycling, pole vaulting, throwing of weights, and tug-of-war contests. **1903** *Science Abstracts* VI. § B. 57 The Westinghouse-Newell *track brake...In this an electro-magnet..grips the rail with a pressure which may reach two tons. **1906** *Westm. Gaz.* 29 Oct. 7/2 It seems to Colonel Yorke that the track brake can at its best only be regarded as a supplementary to the wheel brakes. **1900** *Daily News* 12 Nov. 8/5 With a view to minimising the amount of water used a large number of *track cleaners were employed [on the tramways]. **1877** KNIGHT *Dict. Mech.*, **Track-clearer*, (1) (*Railway.*) (*a*) A cow-catcher..(*b*) A track-sweeper to remove snow. (2) (*Harvesting.*) A triangular frame on the outer end of the cutter-bar of a mowing or reaping machine [etc.]. **1890** *Goldfields of Victoria* 27 *Track-cutting..enables parties to proceed into the jungle country, which would otherwise be unknown. **1874** KNIGHT *Dict. Mech.* s. v. *Furrow*, The steep edge of the furrow [in a millstone] is called the *track-edge; the more inclined edge is called the feather-edge. **1888** *Century Mag.* May 42/2 Intending to return on the morrow with a good *track hound. **1883** *Standard* 16 Nov. 5/2 He..is ready with..the *track-iron [at golf]. **1908** *Daily Chron.* 3 Aug. 2/4 A collection of 'track' irons, round-headed with concave face, used fifty or sixty years ago to get the ball out of the cart tracks. **1877** KNIGHT *Dict. Mech.*, **Track-layer*, a carriage provided with apparatus for placing the rails in their proper positions..as the machine advances. **1888** *Pall Mall G.* 2 Nov. 7/2 The Provincial tracklayers by a ruse have got a locomotive across the Canadian Pacific Company's line, and are now carrying rails across and laying a new track to the north of that line. **1909** *Lightkeeper* June 14/2 The track-layer..is useful in making 'skid-roads', over which the heavy logs are hauled. **1884** KNIGHT *Dict. Mech.* Suppl., *Track-laying machine. **1900** *Engineering Mag.* XIX. 797/2 Tracklaying by Machinery on the Canadian Pacific Ry. **1848** S. ROWE *Peramb. Dartmoor* 47 Greatly similar..are the *Tracklines, or Boundary Banks, which are invariably observed in connexion with aboriginal dwellings and sepulchral remains. **1889** PAGE *Explor. Dartmoor* iii. 43 Oftentimes low banks of earth and stone are observed among the traces of ancient settlements. These are tracklines. **1881** *Chicago Times* 30 Apr., *Track men and mechanics now in employment on the road. **1893** *Labour Commission Gloss.*, *Trackmen*, men who clean the groove of tramway rails with scoops, and when necessary sand or salt the track between the metals. **1901** *Westm. Gaz.* 18 June 8/3 The engineers will ..refuse to run trains over a system not properly examined by trackmen. **1880** P. L. SCLATER *Jacamars & Puff-birds* 75 In 1861 Mr. James M'Leannan, then *track-master of Lion-hill station on the Panama Railway, began to explore the dense tropical forests surrounding his abode. **1909** *Q. Rev.* Oct. 354 The actual *track-mileage of British railways is approximately 53,000 miles. **1896** *Daily News* 28 Dec. 5/2 One of the earliest and most notable of *track-racing cyclists. **1877** KNIGHT *Dict. Mech.*, *Track-rail. **1902** *Daily Chron.* 18 Oct. 6/7 The tender for the supply of track rails and other accessories. **1908** *Daily Chron.* 6 May 5/2 Witness admitted that one of the magnetic *track shoes was useless. **1886** STEVENSON *Kidnapped* i, He..lighted on a big boulder under a birch by the *trackside. **1860** BARTLETT *Dict. Amer.* (ed. 3), **Track-sprinkler*, a contrivance for sprinkling railroad tracks, in order to lay the dust. **1890** GILDERSLEEVE *Ess. & Stud.* 127 The solitary *track-walker, who turns his lantern on every inch of the road. **1905** *Westm. Gaz.* 14 Apr. 6/3 The usual precautions were taken.., including a track-walker at every mile on the line. **1907** *Daily Chron.* 15 July 6/6 The total cost of the *track work from Aldgate to Bow is estimated at about £66,000, which works out at about £11,000 a mile of single track. **1909** *Westm. Gaz.* 23 Feb. 4/2 To encourage young riders to come..and learn the use of their machines for track-work.

**Track**, *v.*[1] [f. TRACK *sb.*: cf. F. *traquer* (*c* 1440) f. *trac.*]

**I. 1.** *trans.* To follow up the track or footsteps of; to trace the course or movements of; to pursue by or as by the track left; with *down*, *out*, *up*, to follow up or trace until found or caught. Also *fig.*

**1565** CALFHILL *Answ. Treat. Crosse* 89 Ye may tracke hym by yᵉ foote. **1582** STANYHURST *Æneis* II. (Arb.) 67 Soon fle, they doe track vs. *Ibid.* III. 73 Track owt youre moother. **1590** R. PAYNE *Descr. Irel.* (1841) 8 If you track any stolne goodes into any mans land, he must tracke them from him, or answer them within xl. daies. **1600** HOLLAND *Livy* XXVII. xii. 636 Marcellus tracked him still, and followed him hard at heeles. **1662** J. DAVIES tr. *Olearius' Voy. Ambass.* A iij b, Without which [Maps], it were impossible to track the Travellors through all those remote Countries. **1716** B. CHURCH *Hist. Philip's War* (1867) II. 104 An Indian Souldier..track'd them by the bloud about half a Mile. **1814** WORDSW. *White Doe* VII. 136 The White Doe tracked..The Lady to her dwelling-place. **1819** SCOTT *Ivanhoe* xxviii, The misfortunes which track my footsteps like slot-hounds. **1834** PRINGLE *Afr. Sk.* viii. 258 The first point was to track the lion to his covert. **1871** R. ELLIS *Catullus* xi. 10 Whether o'er high Alps he afoot ascending Track the long records of a mighty Cæsar. **1874** SYMONDS *Sk. Italy & Gr.* (1898) I. xv. 315 The murderer..was at last tracked down and put to death.

**b.** To find out and follow (a track, course, etc.).

**1681** HICKERINGILL *Vind. Naked Truth* II. 1, I am obleiged to Track his Methods. **1799** WORDSW. *Lucy Gray* xii, Then downwards from the steep hill's edge They tracked the footmarks small. **1888** MRS. McCANN *Poet. Wks.* 70 Through the lonely wilderness brave Howitt tracked his way.

**c.** *intr.* To follow up a track or trail.

**1805** PIKE *Sources Mississ.* (1810) 38 Not knowing how to track, we lost her. **1898** R. POCOCK in *Westm. Gaz.* 12 Sept. 8/2 Henceforth no offer of reward could induce the Indians to continue the hopeless search, and white men cannot track.

**d.** *intr.* Of the wheels of a vehicle: To run in the same track; hence of a gear-wheel, To be in alinement (*with* another wheel, etc.).

**1826** *Sporting Mag.* XVIII. 390 The wheels had not tracked as they ought. **1838** [see *tracking* vbl. sb. below]. **1879** in *Eng. Dial. Dict.* s. v., The machine does not track nicely. **1898** H. GRAVES, etc. *Cycling* 10 Next inspect the frame for twists, and see that the wheels 'track'.

**2.** *trans.* To mark out, trace (a path); to indicate the path or course of; *esp.* to mark out (a path) by repeatedly traversing it; to mark (a way) with tracks; to tread, beat.

**1589** [see *tracked* ppl. adj. below]. **1603** DRAYTON *Bar.*

*Wars* I. xxxii, When the straight Course to her Desire was tract [*rimes* act, backt]. *a* 1713 Ellwood *Autobiog.* Pref. (1765) 4 But also gain some Direction from the Path so fairly tract out. 1815 Anne Plumtre tr. *Lichtenstein's S. Africa* II. 76 The way was smooth and well tracked. 1869 Tozer *Highl. Turkey* I. 36 The Mendere..tracked through all its ..windings by the willow-trees on its banks.

**b.** To make one's way through; to traverse.

*To track the dancers*, to go upstairs (*slang*); cf. quots. 1671, 1785 in 3.

1823 Scott *Peveril* xxx, His surprise..was increased by the rapidity and ease with which she seemed to track the dusky and decayed mazes of the dilapidated Savoy. 1858 Lytton *What will he do* III. xvi, Come, my Hebe; track the dancers, that is, go up the stairs. 1871 Macduff *Mem. Patmos* xx. 275 When white-winged commerce is tracking.. the highway of the nations.

**c.** To leave a track or trail of footprints upon (a floor); to make a track with (dirt or snow) carried on one's feet. *U.S.*

1869 Mrs. Stowe *Oldtown Folks* iii, 'Stand still there!' she called to me..' and don't come in to track my floor'. 1878 — *Poganuc P.* i, Sweep out that snow you've tracked in.

**d.** To lay a track on or for (a railway); to furnish with a line of rails. Only in compounds, as *to double-track, four-track, single-track. U.S.*

1874 *Bay State Transp. League, Bill* (Boston, U.S.) 8 It will cost to single track the Massachusetts Central.. $3,000,000. It will cost to double track the same an additional $2,000,000.

**3.** *intr.* To follow a track or path; to make one's way, pass, go, travel. Now *U.S. slang.*

1590 Greene *Never too late* (1600) 1 Downe the valley gan he tracke, Bagge and bottle at his backe. 1671 [see Dancer 4]. 1676 Coles *Dict.*, *Track*, to go. 1785 Grose *Dict. Vulg. T.*, *Track*, to go; *track up the dancers*, go up stairs (*cant*). 1897 Kipling *Captains Courageous* i, 'The West don't suit her. She just tracks around with the boy and her nerves, trying to find out what'll amuse him, I guess'.

**b.** *Path.* To make a track or path for itself; to find its way.

1903 *Lancet* 18 Apr. 1102/2 The effused blood had tracked down between the coats of the œsophagus into the wall of the stomach. 1905 H. D. Rolleston *Dis. Liver* 20 The resulting peritonitis unfortunately is rarely localized, and may then contain gas as well as pus, or track [*mispr.* tract] up from perforation of an inflamed appendix.

**II.** Erroneously used for Tract *v.*[2]

†**4.** *trans.* To put off, delay; = Tract *v.*[2] 2.

1524 Hen. VIII in Strype *Eccl. Mem.* (1721) I. App. xiii. 28 By delaies the matier was alwaies tracked, and put over without any fruteful determination.

Hence **Tracked** (also 6 **tract**, 7 **trackt**) *ppl. a.*, **Tra·cking** *vbl. sb.* (also *attrib.*): in various senses of the vb.

1524 in Strype *Eccl. Mem.* (1721) I. App. xiii. 30 The delaying and tracking of this matier may do moche harme. 1589 Nashe *Anat. Absurd.* Wks. (Grosart) I. 32 The tract path of theyr treacherie. 1653 R. Robinson *Christ all* II. (1656) 28 It's a trackt way. Prophets, Apostles..have by their walking made this way smooth and even. 1838 *Arcana of Science* 49 The friction arising from the unequal tracking of ordinary carriages is avoided. 1888 in *Times* 13 Oct. 7/6 Testing their [bloodhounds'] tracking powers. 1894 H. Nisbet *Bush Girl's Rom.* 49 The tracking down of escaped convicts and bushrangers. 1895 Wood-Martin *Pagan Irel.* 400 Oval pebbles of quartzite, with a score..in the North of Ireland..are styled 'tracked-stones'. 1902 *Daily Record & Mail* 7 Oct. 4 Tracked pathways have long ago given place to good roads. 1904 *Westm. Gaz.* 30 Sept. 10/2 The double tracking of the line from coast to coast will be completed in a few years. 1908 *Daily Chron.* 28 Aug. 7/4 Tracking dogs are kept in readiness at certain centres.

**Track,** *v.*[2] [app. ad. Du. *trekken* to draw, pull, tug, drag, tow (see Trek), assimilated in form to Track *v.*[1]] *trans.* To tow (a vessel), esp. from the bank or tow-path. Also *absol.* Cf. Tract *v.*[2] 1.

1727 Hamilton *New Acc. E. Indies* II. xxxiv. 21 They [vessels] come down..before the Stream of the River, but [they] are obliged to track them up again, with Strength of Hand, about 1000 Miles. 1769 Falconer *Dict. Marine* (1789), *Chemin de halage*, a path on the side of a river, or canal, for horses to track..vessels along the stream. 1817 *Chron.* in *Ann. Reg.* 101/2 The Tug..tracks these vessels between Leith and Grangemouth. 1856 Kane *Arct. Expl.* I. iv. 41 They can generally find room to track their vessels along its solid margin. 1887 J. Gibson *Gt. Waterfalls* 165 They made their way..through miles of rapids, over which they were tracked, poled, rowed, and portaged.

**b.** *intr.* To proceed by towing. Said of a boat or of those in it.

1854 Milman *Lat. Chr.* IV. v. (1864) II. 304 They tracked in their boats along some of the rivers. 1880 A. E. Moule *Chinese Stor.* v. 74 Our boat tracked slowly against the stream. 1888 C. D. Bell *Winter on Nile* viii. (1889) 83 You may have to 'track' at a slow pace.

Hence **Tra·cking** *vbl. sb.* (also *attrib.*) and *ppl. a.*; also **Tra·ckable** *a.*, such as to admit of tracking or towing.

1839 Darwin *Voy. Nat.* ix. (1879) 178 The party .. was divided into two spells, each of which hauled at the tracking line alternately. 1849 E. B. Eastwick *Dry Leaves* 24 Boats are got up against the stream chiefly by tracking, being towed by the crew. 1853 Kane *Grinnell Exp.* xii. (1856) 88 Enlarging it [a crevice] into a 'trackable' canal. 1873 *Routledge's Yng. Gentl. Mag.* Aug. 524 The channel was too wide to permit of 'tracking', as it is called in Arctic language—that is, towing with ropes along a margin of ice.

**Track-,** stem of Track *v.*[2], in comb. (after Du. *trek-* 'draw-, drag-, tow-', similarly used in *trek-koord, -lijn, -schuit*, etc.), as *track-barge, -line, -path, -road, -rope*; see also Track-boat.

1795 *Track-barge [see Track-boat]. 1856 Kane *Arctic Expl.* I. x. 112 Each man had..his own *track-line. 1839 *Civil Eng. & Arch. Jrnl.* II. 221/1 A *track-path to be formed upon the slope of the deep cutting at Laggon. 1828 Webster, **Track-road*, a towing-path. *Cyc.* 1816 Tuckey *Narr. Exped. R. Zaire* iv. (1818) 143 With the aid of oars, and a *track rope at times, [we] got the boats up. 1864 Carlyle *Fredk. Gt.* xvii. vii. IV. 589 By oar and track-rope.

**Trackage**[1] (træ·kėdʒ). [f. Track *v.*[2] + -age.] The action or process of tracking or towing, or fact of being tracked; towage, haulage.

1820 *Blackw. Mag.* VII. 436 In the Caledonian Canal,.. much animal or steam power will be saved, in trackage. 1826 J. Adamson *Sk. Inform. Railroads* 39 With such prodigious powers of locomotion and trackage.

**Tra·ckage**[2]. *U.S.* [f. Track *sb.*[1] 6 a + -age.] The tracks or lines of a railway system collectively. Also *attrib.* **trackage charge**, charge made for the use of a railway line by another company.

1884 *Morning Herald* (Reading, Pa.) 17 Apr., Our general agent has, therefore, advanced this trackage charge. 1888 *Science* 27 July 46/2 The total trackage is twelve miles, the equipment is forty cars. 1894 *Times* 14 July 7/1 Our railroads have about 170,000 miles of trackage and 1,000,000 of *employés.*

**Tra·ck-boat.** [f. Track- vb.-stem + Boat.] A boat which is tracked or towed; a tow-boat. (Originally *Sc.*, rendering Du. *trek-schuit.*)

1632 *Sc. Acts Chas. I* (1870) V. 243/1 Also thair Trakboats, boats, crears, shippes more or lesse..Sall not be arrested. 1795 J. Phillips *Hist. Inland Navig.* 320 The public opening of the..navigation from sea to sea was made by the sailing of a track-barge...In the course of the voyage..the track-boat passed along..the great aqueduct over the river Kelvin. 1808–18 Jamieson, *Track-boat*, a boat used on a canal. 1824 in Sidney *Life R. Hill* (1834) 308 Mr. Hill went to Glasgow by the track boat, embarking at Grangemouth. 1908 *Westm. Gaz.* 27 Oct. 6/3 The journey was made by P. and O. steamer to Alexandria (sixteen days), thence in a track boat towed by tugs or horses to Atfeh (forty-eight miles along the Mahmoudieh Canal), thence by Nile steamer 120 miles to Cairo.

**Track-brake** to **-edge**: see Track *sb.* 13.

**Tracker**[1] (træ·kəɹ). [f. Track *v.*[1] + -er[1].] One who or that which tracks; one skilled in following a track or trail. In quot. *a* 1632, one who follows or walks in a path (*obs.*).

*Black tracker*, an Australian native employed by the government to track criminals.

1617 *Carte Papers* LXII. 438 If anie knowne Trackers bee vppon the track, the same tracker vppon reasonable hire of the seuerall tounes, shall followe the track vnto the end. *a* 1632 G. Herbert *Country Parson* xi. (1652) 51 The Countrey Parson, who is a diligent observer, and tracker of Gods wayes. 1640 Brome *Sparagus Gard.* III. iv, He..followes pretty feet and insteps like a hare tracker. 1810 Scott *Lady of L.* I. iv, The trackers of the deer. 1862 *Melbourne Leader* 5 July, The black trackers could only discover the tracks of six horsemen. 1904 *Blackw. Mag.* Nov. 674/2 The bloodhound is a wonderful tracker.

**Tra·cker**[2]. [f. Track *v.*[2]; cf. Du. *trekker.*]

**1.** One who tracks or tows a vessel; a tower; also, a towing-vessel, a tugboat.

1791–1823 Disraeli *Cur. Lit.* (1859) II. 143 The severe labour of the trackers, in China, is accompanied with a song. 1817 *Chron.* in *Ann. Reg.* 101/1 A Company in Leith have equipped a powerful steam-vessel, or tracker. 1864 Rawlinson *Anc. Mon.* II. vii. 174 As there was no room for rowers, trackers were engaged, who dragged the boat along by means of ropes. 1894 *Outing* (U. S.) XXIV. 363/2 We were awakened by the loud cries of the many trackers, making ready to draw the junks through the swift waters.

**2.** *Organ-building.* A strip or rod of wood forming part of the connexion between the key and the pallet, and exerting a pulling action: cf. Sticker.

1843 *Civil Eng. & Arch. Jrnl.* VI. 108/1 The machinery of the organ is so very extensive, that trackers, if placed in one line, would measure more than 5 miles. 1881 W. E. Dickson *Organ-Build.* viii. 95 Tracker. A flat riband of pine...Trackers..are now frequently slender round rods. 1887 W. S. Pratt in Gladden *Parish Problems* 435 The keys and stops operate an involved net-work of trackers, slides, rollers, levers, springs, and valves.

**b.** *attrib.*, as *tracker-action, -wire, -work.*

1904 *Athenæum* 12 Nov. 666/1 Our author adds that the *tracker action 'is dispensed with'. 1910 *Times* 16 Dec. 13/5 To have the organ taken down with the substitution of pneumatic action for the old 'tracker' action. 1852 Seidel *Organ* 64 Below the back end of the keys..the sling of a *tracker-wire is secured. 1878 E. J. Hopkins in Grove *Dict. Mus.* I. 485/1 If in *tracker-work..the total alteration amounts to no more than one eighth of an inch.

**Trackless** (træ·klės), *a.* [f. Track *sb.* + -less.] Without a track or path; pathless; not marked by a track; untrodden.

1656 Cowley *Pind. Odes, Muse* ii, Where Bird..did ne're Row through the trackless Ocean of the Air. 1708 *Brit. Apollo* No. 53. 3/2 A trackless Labyrinth of woe. 1801 Strutt *Sports & Past.* Introd. § 44 The recesses of a trackless wilderness. 1878 Lecky *Eng. in 18th C.* II. v. 66 The soldiers were easily..bewildered in the trackless mountains.

**b.** Leaving no track or trace.

1695 Blackmore *Pr. Arth.* v. 638 Then thro' the Heavn's their trackless Flight they take. 1864 [implied in Tracklessly]. 1890 'Boldrewood' *Col. Reformer* (1891) 426 His yacht..could sweep out unchallenged and trackless as the falcon. 1907 C. C. Brown *China in Leg. & Story* ii. 33 Its gray slabs worn by trackless feet, as the centuries went on.

**c.** Not running on a track or line of rails, while propelled by electric power from overhead conductors.

1909 *Westm. Gaz.* 22 Sept. 8/1 Leeds is now assured of a system of trackless trams. *Ibid.*, A splendid system of tramways, both trackless and otherwise.

Hence **Tra·cklessly** *adv.*, **Tra·cklessness.**

1847 Webster, Tracklessly, Tracklessness. 1864 Lowell *Fireside Trav.* 269 The cloud-shadows melted tracklessly toward the hills. 1868 Geo. Eliot *Sp. Gipsy* I. 83 Shall then pass away Like wind upon the waters, tracklessly.

**Track-leveller** to **-mile**: see Track *sb.* 13.

**Track-line**: see Track *sb.* 13, and Track-.

**Track-path, -road, -rope**: see Track-.

**Track-rail** to **-scraper**: see Track *sb.* 13.

**Track-schuyt, -scoot, -scout, -skuit,** anglicized forms of Trekschuit.

**Track-shoe** to **-walking**: see Track *sb.* 13.

**Trackway** (træ·kwēi). [f. Track *sb.* + Way.]

**1.** A path beaten by the feet of passers, a track; also, an ancient British roadway, a ridgeway.

1818 Kirby & Sp. *Entomol.* II. 98 Gould, speaking of his jet-ant (*F[ormica] fuliginosa*), says that they make several main track-ways, (streets he calls them,) with smaller paths striking off from them, extending sometimes to the distance of forty feet from their nest. 1826 W. A. Miles *Deverel Barrow* 8 The line of hill, south of Maiden-Castle, near Dorchester, where the British trackway runs for many miles. 1848 S. Rowe *Peramb. Dartmoor* 45 Trackways, under which designation those roads, or causeways, which cross the moor in various directions are generally known. 1891 T. Hardy *Tess* xi, They were no longer on hard road, but in a mere trackway.

**2. a.** A tramway. **b.** A railway (*Funk's Stand. Dict.* 1895).

1858 Simmonds *Dict. Trade*, *Track-way*, a tram-road.

**3.** [f. Track-.] A towing-path.

1873 *Act* 36 & 37 *Vict.* c. 34 *Preamble*, Any towing path and trackway on the bank of any navigable river.

**Track-work**: see Track *sb.* 13.

**Tract** (trækt), *sb.*[1] Also 5–6 **tracte.** [App. abbreviated from L. *tractātus* Tractate; not in any other lang.]

**I.** †**1.** Literary treatment or discussion. *Obs. rare.*

In some instances difficult to separate from sense 2.

[1432–50: see 2.] 1577 Hanmer *Anc. Eccl. Hist.* (1619) 245 It was our part to comprise in few words such things as required a severall tract. 1659 Bp. Walton *Consid. Considered* 14 They do assert and prove the plain contrary, and that not *obiter*, or by the by, but *ex professo*, in full tracts.

**2.** A book or written work treating of some particular topic; a treatise; a written or printed discourse or dissertation: = Tractate *sb.* 1. Now *rare* in general sense.

Formerly often applied to what would now be called 'books'.

1432–50 tr. *Higden* (Rolls) II. 257 For cause that a generalle tracte [L. *tractatus generalis*; Trevisa, tretysis ful and general] of the iiij. principalle realmes afore seide.., dothe require a large processe. *Ibid.* III. 219 The philosophres that were diuines..laborede and made tractes of God [L. *de Deo tractaverunt*; Trevisa, þei treted of God]. 1577 Hanmer *Anc. Eccl. Hist.* (1663) 84 This present Tract of mine is not made for any ostentation. 1614 Raleigh *Hist. World* II. (1634) 340 Palastina it selfe is but a Province, as I have noted in the beginning of this Tract. *a* 1677 Hale *Prim. Orig. Man.* I. ii. 69 The scope and end of my business in this Tract. 1825 McCulloch *Pol. Econ.* I. 38 In the course of the seventeenth century, a more than usual number of tracts were published on commercial and economical subjects. 1845 — *Taxation* II. iv. (1854) 183 Mr. Howlett.. has made some statements in his valuable tract on tithe.

**b.** Applied to a division of a book or literary work, treating of a separate subject or branch. *rare.*

1662 Stillingfl. *Orig. Sacr.* I. iii. § 3 Three books they tell us of, which Zertoost received by Revelation, or rather one book, consisting of three severall tracts, whereof the first [etc.]. 1891 J. E. H. Thomson *Bks. which influenced our Lord* I. x. 177 The Mishna is divided into six sections, each of these into ten tracts on an average, or sixty-one in all.

**3.** In later use: A short pamphlet on some religious, political, or other topic, suitable for distribution or for purposes of propaganda.

[1762 *Gentl. Mag.* Nov. 545/2 This little tract affords prescriptions for the soul.] 1806, 1816 [see c]. 1848 Thackeray *Van. Fair* ix, Whose sister, Lady Emily, wrote those sweet tracts, 'The Sailor's True Binnacle', and 'The Applewoman of Finchley Common'. 1851 Kingsley *Let.* in *Life* (1879) I. ix. 237 The barbarians..got into their addle pates that we were emissaries of Mazzini and Co. distributing political tracts. 1866 G. Macdonald *Ann. Q. Neighb.* xxx, Whether he only distributes tracts with condescending words. 1885 G. Meredith *Diana* xviii, Am I really as dull as a tract, my dear? 1911 A. R. Buckland in *Encycl. Brit.* XXVII. 177/2 A tract is understood to be brief and rather argumentative than educational. *Mod.* The British Museum library contains an immense collection of Civil War tracts.

**b.** *Tracts for the Times*: the title of a series of pamphlets on theological and ecclesiastical topics (known also as the *Oxford Tracts*, or simply *the Tracts*) started by J. H. Newman, and published at Oxford 1833–1841, on the doctrines of which the Tractarian movement was based.

The earlier of these were, in accordance with their title, brief pamphlets; but some of the later, e. g. that of Pusey on Baptism, were extended treatises, *tracts* in sense 2. The aim of the series was 'to arrest the advance of Liberalism in religious thought, and to revive' what the writers held to be 'the true conception of the relation of the Church of England to the Catholic Church at large' (*Churchman's Guide*). The last Tract, No. 90, by J. H. Newman, 'On Certain Passages in the XXXIX Articles', 'called forth a storm of reprobation; at the instance of Four Tutors, the Heads of the

Oxford Colleges pronounced censure upon the author', and at the request of the Bishop of Oxford the publication of the Tracts ceased. In the sequel, many who sympathized with the teaching of the Tracts (including at length Newman himself) seceded to the Church of Rome.

**1834** (*title*) Tracts for the Times. By Members of the University of Oxford. **1868** SIR J. T. COLERIDGE *Mem. Keble* xii. (1870) 276 It was Mr. Benson..who gave the authors and favourers of the Tracts the perfectly inoffensive name of Tractarian. **1881** FROUDE *Short Stud.* Ser. IV. (1883) 175 These were the views which we used to hear when the Tracts were first beginning. **1893** LIDDON, etc. *Life Pusey* I. xii. 277 The first Tracts are dated at the beginning of September (1833). They were generally short, several keeping within the suggested limit of four pages: they were chiefly concerned with the constitution, ordinances, and services of the Church.

**c.** *attrib.* and *Comb.*, as (in sense 3) *tract-distributing* adj., *distribution*, *-led* adj., *society*; (in sense 3 b, with capital *T*) *Tract divine, doctrine, man, movement, system, -writer.*

**1806** W. L. BOWLES *Banwell Hill* II. 360 The tract-led Miss, Who trots to every Bethel club. **1816** 'QUIZ' *Grand Master* VIII. Argt. 18 Let them, if they perceive impiety, Transmit it to the Tract Society. **1841** S. WILBERFORCE *Let.* 30 Mar., in Ashwell *Life* I. vi. 217 You know my dread of the 'Tract' doctrine of Reserve. **1843** *Chr. Lady's Mag.* XX. 211 The opinions of Oxford-tract men.. upon the divine efficacy of Sacraments. *Ibid.* 271 The pernicious errors broached.., by the Tract-writers of Oxford. **1846** D. WILSON *Exp. Lect. Col.* ii. 20 *note*, The Tract divines add to the three essentials required in the XIXth article a fourth. **1869** W. P. MACKAY *Grace & Truth* (1875) 43 Tract-distributors and pick-pockets. **1882** OGILVIE s.v., In this sense the word is frequently adjectivally used; as, *tract* society,..*tract* distribution, etc. **1893** LIDDON, etc. *Life Pusey* I. xii. 414 It was natural for the Tract-writers to honour the Fathers of the Church.

**II.** †**4. a.** Negotiation, treating; a treaty. (Cf. TRACTATE *sb.* 2.) **b.** Trade, traffic [cf. Pg. *trato* dealing, trade]. *Obs. rare.*

**1501** in *Lett. Rich. III & Hen. VII* (Rolls) I. 135 The kinges majestie had sent to him his seal for tract of pais bytwixt his grace and H. **1502** *Ibid.* 147 A tracte of accorde. **1582** N. LICHEFIELD tr. *Castanheda's Conq. E. Ind.* I. i. 3 They had beene in the Cayro, and understoode there much newes of Ormuse, and of theyr tract had with and into the Indies.

**Tract,** *sb.*[2] *R. C. Ch.* Also 4–5 **tracte,** 5 **tratt.** [ad. med.L. TRACTUS, q. v. (In Fr. *trait.*)] An anthem consisting of verses of Scripture, usually from the Psalms, sung instead of the Alleluia in the mass from Septuagesima till Easter Eve.

**1387** TREVISA *Higden* (Rolls) VII. 145 When forsoþe it was comen toward þe tracte [L. *Cum autem ad versum tractus ventum fuisset*] in whiche it is songen, *Scitote quoniam Dominus ipse est Deus.* c **1450** in Aungier *Syon* (1840) 327 From septuagesym in to ester thys tracte *Gaude Maria* schal be songe at lectren. **1483** CAXTON *Gold. Leg.* 412/1 Gelasyus and Gregory added therto collettis and sange to the lessons and gospellys graylles tracte and alleluya. **1483** *Cath. Angl.* 391/1 A Tracte (*A.* A Tratt), *sistema, tractus.* **1546** LANGLEY *Pol. Verg. De Invent.* v. viii. 108 b, The Tract Durandus saieth was deuysed by Teleophorus. **1624** DARCIE *Birth of Heresies* xviii. 74 In stead of which Alleluia is sung another song called a tract, with a loud voice, and a protracted note, in a graue kind of Musicke. **1867** C. WALKER *Ritual Reason Why* 155 These were called the *Tract*, from being drawn out (*tractus*) to a mournful cadence. **1877** J. D. CHAMBERS *Div. Worship* 331 The Tract was usually a mournful Psalm, or part of a Psalm.

**Tract** (trækt), *sb.*[3] Also 5–7 **tracte,** 6 **trackte,** 6–7 **trackt.** [ad. L. *tract-us* (*u*-stem), a drawing, dragging, pulling, trailing; a train, track, course, a tract of space or time, course, progress, duration, protraction, f. ppl. stem of *trahĕre* to draw, drag. In certain senses, this word fell together with TRACE *sb.*[1] and TRACK *sb.*, and was sometimes even used in the senses of these words; in others it corresponds with the cognate F. *trait*, OF. *traict*, also *tract*:—L. *tractus.*]

**I.** †**1.** The drawing out, duration, continuance, process, passing, or lapse *of time*; the course *of time*. Cf. L. *tractus temporum*, F. *trait de temps.*

**1494** FABYAN *Chron.* III. lvi. 36 This in tracte of tyme made hym welthy. **1575** FENTON *Gold. Ep.* (1577) 6 As tracte of time carryeth with it a lawe of forgetfulnesse of things past. **1651** N. BACON *Disc. Govt. Eng.* II. xxiv. 109 The Seasons now in tract were of short continuance. **1658** ROWLAND *Moufet's Theat. Ins.* 946 We conclude this art..to be very ancient, and derived to us by long tract of time. **1676** HALE *Contempl.* I. 294 In the tract of long life a man is sure to meet with more sicknesses. *a* **1734** NORTH *Exam.* I. ii. § 30 (1740) 45 Which being perpetually inculcated, in the Tract of a few Years, created in the People prodigious Resentments.

† **b.** Protraction (of time), deferring, putting off, dilatory proceeding, delay. (Cf. TRACT *v.*[2] 2.)

**1503–4** *Act* 19 *Hen. VII*, c. 28 *Preamble*, By whiche longe tracte of tyme the seid sueters..shulde be disconforted. **1523** WOLSEY in Fiddes *Life* II. (1726) 76 That no tract or deley bee used therein. **1600** HOLLAND *Livy* XXX. xvi. 751 They sought for nothing else but delaies and tract of time.

**c.** A space or extent of time, a period. (In later use regarded as *transf.* from 3.)

**1494** FABYAN *Chron.* v. cii. 76 Theodebertus..of his..vncles was greuously warred by longe tracte of tyme. **1524** WOLSEY in Strype *Eccl. Mem.* (1721) I. iv. 53 Considering the tract of time that is requisite. *a* **1548** HALL *Chron., Hen. V* 80 This short tyme and smal tract of my mortal life. **1615** G. SANDYS *Trav.* 143 A tract of three hundred sixty and foure yeares. **1799** J. ROBERTSON *Agric. Perth* 169 Waiting for a long tract of serene weather, which may not come. **1850** TENNYSON *In Mem.* xlvi. 9 A lifelong tract of time reveal'd. **1853** MAURICE *Proph. & Kings* iii. 43 Utterly unlike and separated by tracts of time and space. **1865** PALGRAVE *Hymn*, '*Thou say'st, Take up thy cross*' iii, Dim tracts of time divide Those golden days from me.

**2.** The continuance or continued duration *of* some action or state; the course or continuity *of* a narrative, etc.; a continued series. Now *rare* or *Obs.*

**1581** SIDNEY *Apol. Poetrie* (Arb.) 65 The whole tract of a Comedy, shoulde be full of delight. **1599** SANDYS *Europæ Spec.* (1632) 178 Yet tract of affliction, much misery, often over-reaching by subtilty of adversaryes, doth finally purge out those grosse-witted humours. **1632** LITHGOW *Trav.* IX. 407 They had wrot the whole tract of his abhominable vices to the Emperour. **1661** FELTHAM *Resolves* II. lviii. 307, I do not remember that we read the name of either Dice or Gaming in the tract of either Scripture. **1679** *Lauderdale Papers* (Camden) 261 A long continued tract of violence and oppressione upon ws. **1732** MACFARLANE *Geneal. Collect.* (1900) 310 He caused Apprehend and Execute at Crief for a train and tract of Depredations Macobertus Strowanus. **1773** ERSKINE *Inst. Law Scotl.* I. i. § 47 An uniform tract of decisions of the court of session..is.. accounted as part of our customary law. **1858** CARLYLE *Fredk. Gt.* IX. i. (1872) III. 73 Perhaps a sudden tract of good fortune..would have made me too proud.

**3.** A stretch or extent *of* territory, etc.; a space or expanse of land (more rarely, of water, air, etc.); a region, district. Cf. L. *tractus.*

**1553** EDEN *Treat. Newe Ind.* (Arb.) 8 The narrowe tracte of the Sea by the coastes of Grouelande. **1610** HOLLAND *Camden's Brit.* (1637) 126 All the Northerne tract of Britaine. **1654** EARL MONM. tr. *Bentivoglio's Warrs Flanders* 73 The Ocean first washing the said two Provinces for a long trackt of ground. **1725** DE FOE *Voy. round World* (1840) 280 This vast tract of land. **1776** TOPLADY *Hymn*, '*Rock of ages*' iv, When I soar through tracts unknown. **1814** CHALMERS *Evid. Chr. Revel.* x. 278 Those remote tracts beyond the limits of our astronomy. **1834–5** J. PHILLIPS *Geol.* in *Encycl. Metrop.* VI. 564/2 The great central plateau..is chiefly a granitic and porphyritic tract. **1886** STEVENSON *Kidnapped* 120, I spied a tract of water.. which..boiled white all over.

*fig.* **1817** CHALMERS *Astron. Disc.* iii. (1852) 88 We do think that this lays open a very interesting tract..of most legitimate and sober-minded speculation. **1902** F. W. H. MYERS *Wordsworth* viii. 90 Large tracts of it [the *Excursion*] have little claim to the name of poetry.

**b.** *Nat. Hist.*, etc. A region or area of some natural structure, as a mineral formation, or the body of an animal or plant; most commonly one extending longitudinally (cf. 8).

*spec.* (*a*) *Anat.* The whole extent of an organ or system of organs, as the *alimentary* or *digestive tract*, or a continuous longitudinal structure, such as one strand or division of a nerve-cord; *esp.* applied to particular regions of the brain or spinal cord, as the *olfactory, optic, pyramidal*, etc. *tracts.* (*b*) *Ornith.* A feathered area of the skin of a bird (= PTERYLA), as distinguished from a featherless *space.*

**1811** PINKERTON *Petralogy* II. 442 This pumice..commonly lies in long tracts, in the direction of which its vesicles are sometimes lengthened. **1841–71** T. R. JONES *Anim. Kingd.* (ed. 4) 437 The probable existence..of distinct tracts of nervous matter in the composition of the central chain of ganglia. **1867** Feather-tracts [see PTERYLA]. **1879** *St. George's Hosp. Rep.* IX. 127 General congestion of the alimentary tract. **1894** NEWTON *Dict. Birds* s. v. *Pterylosis*, The principal *pterylæ* or feathered tracts are as follows:— (1) Spinal tract...(2) Ventral tract...(3) Neck-tract [etc.].

*attrib.* **1899** *Allbutt's Syst. Med.* VI. 535 The tract fibres of each side must be connected with the anterior cornua on both sides. *Ibid.* VII. 79 An instance in which a tract degeneration was established.

**II.** † **4.** The action of drawing or pulling (in quots. *fig.*); attraction. *Obs. rare.*

**1616** B. JONSON *Devil an Ass* II. ii, He'll ne'r owne mee, But I am taken! the fine tract of it Pulls mee along! **1620** J. PYPER tr. *Hist. Astrea* I. VII. 226 She could feele the tracts of Loue.

†**5.** Drawing, or tracing (of lines). *Obs. rare.*

**1677** GILPIN *Demonol.* (1867) 22 Lines and figures are better known from mathematical instruction, than by their bare tract as written in dust. **1688** R. HOLME *Armoury* I. 19/1 The Ordinaries are made, and formed of Lines diversly composed; And according to the divers Tracts and Forms, of those said Lines, they do receive a divers Shape and variation of Names.

**III.** A material line drawn: = F. *trait* (see TRAIT).

†**6.** *Her.*: (*a*) = TRESSURE; (*b*) = TRACK *sb.* 7.

**1486** *Bk. St. Albans, Her.* e vj b, Off tractys in armys. Afore it is sayd of borduris in armys, now it folowith to se of tractis or lynys, and first of a symple tract; and they be calde tractis for as mych as the felde remaynyng of tharmys as wele with in as with owte, & an other lyne is drawyn of an other colowre..to the maner of a shelde. *Ibid.*, He berith asure a playn tract of golde. *Ibid.* e vij, Thys tract is other wyle dowbull as in tharmys of the kyng of Scottelonde. **1610** GUILLIM *Heraldry* I. v. 17 When the Field and the Circumference or Tract about the same,..be both of one metall, colour or furre, then shall you not terme it a bordure. *Ibid.* II. vii. 66, I purpose to present to your view a Threefold Orle or Tract, which doth include the twofold.

†**7.** A lineament, a feature; = TRAIT 4, 5. *Obs.*

**1606** SYLVESTER *Du Bartas* II. iv. I. *Trophies* 1101 Th' admired Tracts of a bewitching Face. **1632** LITHGOW *Trav.* I. 24 Like to the heauenly tract and resemblance of our blessed Sauiour. **1715** tr. *C'tess D'Aunoy's Wks.* 193 His Hair brown, his Tracts all regular, his Teeth fine. **1775** C. JOHNSTON *Pilgrim* 126 To account for some tracts in their national character.

**IV.** Senses approaching or coinciding with those of TRACK and TRACE.

**8.** Course, path, way, route; with *of* or possessive, the course or path traversed by a person, animal, or moving object: = TRACK *sb.* 3, 4. Now *rare* or *Obs.*: usually expressed by *track.*

(In quot. 1799, applied to a course or channel for water.)

**1555** EDEN *Decades* 255 Vnderstanding..that if I shulde sayle by the way of the northwest wynde, I shulde by a shorter tracte coomme to India [etc.]. **1616** W. FORDE *Serm.* 28 Like a bird in the aire, whose tract the aire closeth. **1665** SIR T. HERBERT *Trav.* (1677) 170 A loose and flying sand,..accumulated into such heaps as upon any great wind the tract is lost, and passengers (too oft) overwhelmed and stifled. **1726** SHELVOCKE *Voy. round World* 201 In the tract of the Manila ship. **1798** CHARLOTTE SMITH *Yng. Philos.* IV. 279 Perceiving that in the lane was certainly the most beaten tract, I hurried along it. **1799** J. ROBERTSON *Agric. Perth* 302 When the tract for conveying the water has been once made with judgment, it may remain for centuries. **1823** F. COOPER *Pioneers* v, The tract for the sleighs was much more limited. **1843** NICHOLSON *Hist. & Trad. Tales* 196, I..will pursue his tract no longer. **1865** ALEX. SMITH *Summ. Skye* (1880) 143 In Skye one is every now and again coming on the tract of the distinguished travellers.

**9.** *fig.* Course (of action, etc.); manner of proceeding, way, path: = TRACK *sb.* 5. *rare* or *Obs.*

**1566** PAINTER *Pal. Pleas.* I. Pref. 8 The other prescribeth a directe pathe to treade the tracte of this present life. **1581** LAMBARDE *Eiren.* II. ii. (1588) 125 In the Commission of the Peace, they are both conueied vnder this one tracte of speach. **1612** DRAYTON *Poly-olb.* Pref. A j, A Poeme.. whose vnusuall tract may perhaps seeme difficult, to the female Sex. **1632** J. FEATLY *Hon. Chast.* 19 Let it suffice that I walke in the vulgar tract, and divide sinne onely into originall and actuall. **1677** HALE *Contempl.* II. 25 In the same path and tract which leads us to Glorifie God, which is our Duty. **1752** HUME *Ess. & Treat.* (1777) II. 23 Any particular thought which breaks in upon the regular tract, or chain of ideas. **1834** H. MILLER *Scenes & Leg.* xxvii. (1857) 394 Men..who, seeing nothing very knowing in simple honesty, exert their ingenuity in the opposite tract.

**10.** A mark or impression marking the course of a person, animal, or thing; a footprint, trail: = TRACE *sb.*[1] 4, 5: cf. TRACK *sb.* 1. Now *rare* or *Obs.*; usually expressed by *track.*

*a* **1547** SURREY *Æneid* II. 920 A blasing sterre, dragging a brand of flame..By a long tract appointing us the way. **1565** JEWEL *Repl. Harding* (1611) 151 There appeared.. the very tracts and steps of Christs feet. **1585** HIGINS *Junius' Nomencl.* 390/1 *Orbita*, the trace, tract, or furrow of a cart wheele. **1595** *Blanchardyn* v. B j b, He had not ridden long, but he perceiued the tracktes & footsteps of a horse. **1607** SHAKS. *Timon* I. i. 50 But flies an Eagle flight ..Leauing no Tract behinde. **1632** GUILLIM *Heraldry* III. xiv. (ed. 2) 175 Termes of footing or treading...That of a Fallow Deere [or] Boare is termed Tract or Treading. **1709** DAMPIER *Voy.* III. II. 35, I saw the Tract of an Alligator here. **1807** in Halliwell *Life Shaks.* (1887) II. 143 There was only one waggon tract along the lane. **1857** H. MILLER *Test. Rocks* xi. 435, I was struck..to see how nearly the tract of a small shore crab along the wet sand, resembled them.

† **b.** = TRACK *sb.* 8. *Obs.*

**1542–3** *Act* 34 & 35 *Hen. VIII*, c. 26 § 47 If any goodes ..be stolen..thenne upon suite therof hadde and made, the tracte shalbe folowed from Towneshipp to Towneship.

†**11.** A mark remaining where something has been; an indication, vestige (*lit.* or *fig.*): = TRACE *sb.*[1] 6. *Obs.*

**1583** GOLDING *Calvin on Deut.* clxviii. 1040 Wee shall be handled with such rigour as shall make all them to tremble which see but the tracts thereof. **1610** HOLLAND *Camden's Brit.* (1637) 281 Walles, which, as men may see by their tract, tooke up a mile in circuit. **1615** G. SANDYS *Trav.* 225 But no tract therof [of the Labyrinth] remained in the days of Pliny. **1646** SIR T. BROWNE *Pseud. Ep.* I. x. 37 To obscure the diviner part, and efface all tract of its traduction. **1698** J. CRULL *Muscovy* 57 The Ruins appear now in some places six foot high,..the Tract being quite lost in others.

† **Tract,** *v.*[1] *Obs.* [ad. L. *tractāre* to handle, transact, manage, discuss, treat, freq. of *trahĕre* to draw. Cf. F. *traiter*, OF. *traicter*, rarely *tracter*, to manage, TREAT (Godef.).]

**1.** *trans.* To negotiate: = TREAT *v.* 1 b.

**1508** in *Lett. Rich. III & Hen. VII* (Rolls) I. 451 The l[ove and kindnes] that have been used in the tracting of our said mariage.

**2.** To deal with in speech or writing; to discuss or discourse (*trans.*, or *intr.* with *of*): = TREAT *v.* 2, 2 b.

**1529** *St. Papers Hen. VIII*, II. 149 Whiche thinge is not to be tracted, or retracted, till the Parliament. **1552** HULOET, Tract or treat of, *tracto.* **1588** A. KING tr. *Canisius' Catech.* 60 The sacraments..haue ane verray highe place in Christiane doctrine, and ar necessarie to be tractit of. **1607** TOPSELL *Four-f. Beasts* (1658) 396 Of all which kinde of traps shall be severally tracted: And first of all those which do catch Mice alive. *a* **1637** B. JONSON tr. *Horace's Art of Poetry* 202 The man, who..Saw many towns and men, and could their manners tract.

**3.** *trans.* To behave towards: = TREAT *v.* 7.

*a* **1548** HALL *Chron., Hen. IV* 15 b, The Erle..so gently and familiarly used and tracted the vulgare people. *Ibid., Rich. III* 46 b, Nothinge contented that the erle of Richmonde was in his dominion so vncurteously tracted and entreated.

† **Tract,** *v.*[2] *Obs.* [f. L. *tract-*, ppl. stem of *trahĕre* to draw; cf. *attract, contract, extract*, etc. f. ppl. stem. In some uses associated with TRACE *v.*[1] and TRACK *v.*[1] and [2].]

**I. 1.** *trans.* To draw, pull along, haul, tow. (Superseded by TRACK *v.*[2])

**1523** in *10th Rep. Hist. MSS. Comm.* App. v. 328 All..

goods and marchandis as shalbe labored, tracted, and adventured by ony of the inhabitants of this citie..oute of the haven and porte of the same, into ony where else. **1727** A. Hamilton *New Acc. E. Ind.* I. xi. 123 To carry a great Number of Men for tracting them up against the Stream, when the Winds are against them. **1769** Falconer *Dict. Marine* (1789) s. v. *Tract-scout* [= Du. *trekschuit*], It is usually tracted by a horse. **1769** [see *tracting* below].

**2.** To lengthen out, prolong, protract (time); to spend or waste in delay; to delay, put off.

**1527** Knight in Pocock *Rec. Ref.* I. xxviii. 57 The rivers not being always passable he hath of necessity tracted the time. **1529** in Froude *Hist. Eng.* (1856) I. iii. 192 The causes depending..may..be in such wise tracted and delayed, as your subjects suing in the same shall be put to importable charges. **1579–80** North *Plutarch* (1595) 606 He tracted time, & gaue them leisure to prepare to encounter his force. **1647** Lilly *Chr. Astrol.* xlix. 303 By dallying and tracting the time there shall be trouble.

**b.** *intr.* To be drawn out or prolonged, to continue: in *pres. pple.* protracted, continuous.

**1592** [see *tracting* below].

**3.** *fig.* To draw on, draw out; to induce.

**1615** [see *tracting* below].

**II. 4.** To go or travel along, tread, pursue (a path): = Trace *v.*$^1$ 3. Cf. Track *v.*$^1$ 3. (In quots. *fig.*)

**1579** Twyne *Phisicke agst. Fort.* II. xxxv. 212 This path is but litle tracted. **1613** Marston *Insatiate Countess* I. A ij b, [Death] From whose sterne Caue none tracts a backward path.

**5.** To pursue or follow up by the footprints or traces; also *fig.*: = Trace *v.*$^1$ 5, Track *v.*$^1$ 1.

**1577** Holinshed *Chron.* II. 1007/2 In the ende, they brought him to tract the steppes of lewde demeanor. **1590** Spenser *F. Q.* II. i. 12 By what meanes may I his footing tract? *Ibid.* vi. 39 As Shepheardes curre..Hath tracted forth some salvage beastes trade [=tread]. **1596** *Ibid.* VI. vii. 3 Well did he tract his steps as he did ryde. **1615** Sir E. Hoby *Curry-combe* To Rdr. 2 Hee that tracts a Fugitiue must take the By-path. **1654** Flecknoe *Ten Years Trav.* 43 Which false rumours I tracted from the very Fountain.

**6.** To draw, delineate: = Trace *v.*$^1$ 11.

**1611** Speed *Hist. Gt. Brit.* VI. xviii. (1623) 99 Having seen it [a wall] so tracted in an ancient Chorographicall Chart.

**7.** *intr.* ? To border *upon*. *rare*$^{-1}$.

**1611** Speed *Theat. Gt. Brit.* xiv. (1614) 27/1 [Of Barkshire] the South neere Kennet doth tract upon Hampshire.

Hence † Tra·cting *vbl. sb.* and *ppl. a.*

**1535** *Act 27 Hen. VIII*, c. 3 Without frustrate or wilfull delaye or tractyng of the tyme. **1592** Warner *Alb. Eng.* VII. xxxvii. (1612) 179, I heard a tracting sound. **1615** J. Stephens *Ess. & Char.*, *Huntsman* (1857) 202 The names of Foxe, Hare, and Bucke, be all tracting sillables; sufficient to furnish fifteen meales with long discourse in the adventures of each. Foxe drawes in his exploits done against Cubbes... Hare brings out his encounters [etc.]. **1769** Falconer *Dict. Marine* (1789), *Tracting*, the act of pulling any vessel..along the stream of a canal or river, by means of a rope.

**Tractability** (træktăbi·lĭti). [ad. L. *tractābilitās*, *-āt-*, f. *tractābilis* Tractable: see -bility, -ity.] The quality of being tractable; manageableness, docility.

**1531** Elyot *Gov.* I. xxi, Tractabilitie (which is to be shortly persuaded and meued). **1605** A. Warren *Poverties Patience* ii, Vaine Perswasion, that deludes Fond Tractability with fallacies. **1778** [W. Marshall] *Minutes Agric.*, *Digest* 41 A further proof of their tractability. **1849** Lytton *Caxtons* I. iii, He, wild man,..not yet civilized into the tractabilities of home.

**Tractable** (træ·ktăb'l), *a.* [ad. L. *tractābilis*, f. *tractāre*: see Tract *v.*$^1$, and cf. Treatable.]

**1.** That can be easily managed; docile, compliant, manageable, governable. (Of persons and animals, or their dispositions, etc.)

**1502** Atkynson tr. *De Imitatione* II. iii. 182 To be conuersaunt with meke, tractable or charitable company. **1548** Udall, etc. *Erasm. Par. Mark* Pref., The more noble courage and stomacke they be of, the more tractable they are. **1561** T. Norton *Calvin's Inst.* I. 37 Rather with tractable willingnesse to learn, than with sharpenesse of wit. **1611** Beaum. & Fl. *Knt. Burn. Pestle* II. i, I'm glad the girl Is found so tractable. **1738** Berkeley *Let.* 11 May, Wks. 1871 IV. 258 You have to do with people of no very easy or tractable spirit. **1832** Scott *Woodst.* ii, A large wolf-dog,..as tractable as he was strong and bold. **1855** Prescott *Philip II*, I. ii. (1857) 24 Philip..found the Aragonese legislature by no means so tractable as the Castilian.

**b.** Const. *to* with sb. or inf.; in quot. 1651, easily led or persuaded *to* or *to do* something.

**1509** Bp. Fisher *Funeral Serm. C'tess Richmond* Wks. (E.E.T.S.) I. 291 To god & to the chirche full obedyent & tractable. **1590** Greene *Never too late* (1600) 82, I..found him not onely guiltie of the crime, but tractable to be reclaimed. *c* **1645** in *Verney Mem.* (1907) I. 428 She is witty & very tractable to please. **1651** Baxter *Inf. Bapt.* 30 They are silly souls, and tractable to novelty.

† **c.** *transf.* of an action, etc. *Obs.*

*c* **1609** in *Capt. Smith's Virginia* III. xi. (1624) 89 He had oft brought the Salvages to a tractable trade. **1632** Lithgow *Trav.* v. 203 Their education to this tractable expedition is admirable.

**2.** Of things (usually concrete): Easy to manage, deal with, handle, or work; manageable.

**1555** Eden *Decades* 334 This metall [gold] is a body tractable and bryght. **1654** Earl Monm. tr. *Bentivoglio's Warrs Flanders* 57 On which side the ground was more tractable. **1726** Leoni *Alberti's Archit.* I. 27/1 The Nut Tree..is extremely tractable, and good for most uses. **1898** *Pall Mall Mag.* May 20 She had a small but exquisitely tractable voice. **1900** E. F. Scott *Fourth Gosp.* vii. 216 Elements .. not wholly tractable to his method of re-interpretation.

† **3.** That can be handled; palpable, tangible.

**1605** Willet *Hexapla Gen.* 203 These angels had palpable and tractable bodies. **1669** Gale *Crt. Gentiles* I. III. iii. 45 The visible and tractable Mater [matter]. **1694** Holder *On Time* i. 16 The other Measures..are of Continued Quantity, Permanent, and Visible, and for the most part Tractable; whereas Time is always Transient,..neither to be seen, nor felt, nor reserved.

† **4.** That one can 'do with' or put up with; tolerable, endurable. *Obs.*

**1605** *Tryall Chev.* v. i. in Bullen *O. Pl.* (1884) III. 339 As soone As the cool winds haue fand [= fanned] the burning Sunne And made it tractable for travaylers. **1692** Ray *Disc.* 237 Eternity is the very sting of Hell: take that out, and the Sinner will think it tractable enough.

**Tra·ctableness.** [f. prec. + -ness.] The quality of being tractable; tractability.

**1561** T. Norton *Calvin's Inst.* II. 100 Vnlesse he did frame vs to that tractablenesse by his spirit. **1600** Sir W. Cornwallis *Ess.* iii. D j b, The tractablenes of his people might keep them in peace. **1726** Leoni *Alberti's Archit.* I. 27/2 None of these [trees] for Tractableness can compare with the Linden. **1860** Holland *Miss Gilbert* v, A gentle sympathetic word would win her into tenderness and tractableness.

**Tra·ctably,** *adv.* *rare*$^{-0}$. [f. as prec. + -ly$^2$.] In a tractable manner; manageably; with docility.

**1611** Cotgr., *Tendrement*, tenderly,..gentlely, tractably. **1727** Bailey vol. II, *Tractably*, after a tractable Manner. Hence in Johnson and later Dicts.

† **Tractal,** *a.* *Obs.* *rare*$^{-1}$. [? irreg. (for **tractual*) f. L. *tractu-s* (see Tract *sb.*$^3$) + -al.] ? Intended to protract the time. (Cf. Tract *sb.*$^3$ 1 b.)

**1632** Lithgow *Trav.* III. 82 After tractall discourses, and deepe draughts of Leatick, reason failing, sleepe ouercame his sences.

**Tractarian** (træktē·riăn), *sb.* and *a.* [f. Tract *sb.*$^1$ + *-arian*; in 2, after *trinitarian*, etc.]

**A.** *sb.*

**1.** A writer, publisher, or distributor of tracts. *nonce-uses.*

(In quot. 1824, referring to the Religious Tract Society.)

**1824** *Man of Letters* 15 May 99 The superiority of the vulgar version will be acknowledged, we think, even by the tractarians themselves. **1851** *Illustr. Lond. News* 30 Aug. 270/2 The fanatical tract distributors of London..an itinerant distributor...The Tractarian was silent. **1900** *Speaker* 12 May 170/2 To revive his [James VI's] reputation as a poet or a tractarian.

**2.** A member of that school of High Churchmen which maintains the doctrines and practices set forth in 'Tracts for the Times' (see Tract *sb.*$^1$ 3 b).

**1839** C. Benson *Disc. Tradit. & Episc.* Pref. 3 The tractarians, that is, the authors, editors, and approvers of the *Tracts for the Times*, are Divines of acknowledged piety, and sincerity, and learning. *Ibid.* 5 The tractarians, if without offence we may so call them. **1841** Bp. D. Wilson *Let.* in Bateman *Life* (1860) II. xvi. 188 Her apostasy is like a standard-bearer fainting: and all aggravated by the opposite errors of the Tractarians. **1888** C. A. Lane *Notes Eng. Ch. Hist.* II. vi. xxix. 253 The Tractarians were the extreme wing of the modern 'High Church' party. **1892** F. Hall in *Nation* (N. Y.) 25 Aug. 145/1 Lawless in formation, certainly, is *Tractarian*; and yet it will live in history, to the exclusion of *Tractite*, *Tractuist*, and *Tractator*, all of which have been proposed in its stead.

**B.** *adj.* **1.** Of or belonging to the Tractarians (A. 2).

**1840** I. Taylor *Anc. Chr.* (1842) II. 144 *note*, One of the most recent .. publications of the Tractarian school. **1841** Bp. D. Wilson *Jrnl.* 18 Nov., in Bateman *Life* (1860) II. xvi. 193 Having given my booksellers..orders to send me the Tractarian Controversy publications. *a* **1873** S. Wilberforce *Ess.* (1874) II. 262 So strong a Romeward tendency amongst the members of the Tractarian party. **1896** R. Palmer *Fam. & Pers. Mem.* I. xxvii. 397 The 'Tractarian' forces were shattered by the loss of their leader.

**2.** Distributing tracts. *nonce-use.*

**1885** *Athenæum* 11 July 44 [Dr. Lansdell] was soon afterwards arrested for distributing tracts at railway stations... It is not very surprising that a policeman stopped the tractarian traveller.

Hence **Tracta·rianism,** the tenets or principles of the Tractarians, the Tractarian system; adherence to or maintenance of this; **Tracta·rianize** *v.*, *intr.* to teach, maintain, or practice Tractarianism (in **Tracta·rianizing** *vbl. sb.* and *ppl. a.*).

**1840** (*title*) Hints to Transcendentalists for working Infidel Designs through *Tractarianism. **1841** Bp. D. Wilson in Bateman *Life* (1860) II. xvi. 185 If he had not been imbued for seven years—steeped—in Tractarianism. **1899** Bp. Stubbs *Visitation Charges* (1904) 344 What is called the Oxford Movement, the movement represented by the *Tracts for the Times*, Tractarianism as it is still called. **1842** G. S. Faber *Prov. Lett.* (1844) II. 137 More than one young *Tractarianising Cleric. **1880** G. A. Simcox in *Macm. Mag.* No. 245. 399 The imputation of tractarianising clung to Wilberforce however he might try to separate himself from the Tractarians.

**Tractate** (træ·kteit), *sb.* Also 6 *Sc.* **tracteit**, 6–7 **tractat.** [ad. L. *tractātus* (*u*-stem) a handling, treatment, discussion, treatise, f. *tractāre*: see Tract *v.*$^1$ Cf. Prov. *tractat*, Sp. *tratado*, It. *trattato*, Fr. *traité*; also Ger. *tractat.*]

**1.** A book or literary work treating of a particular subject; a treatise.

**1474** Caxton *Chesse* 1 This first chappitre of the first tractate sheweth [etc.]. **1549** *Compl. Scot.* Epist. 6 To present to ȝour nobil grace ane tracteit of the fyrst laubir of my pen. **1641** Milton *Prel. Episc.* 3 Needlesse tractats stuff't with specious names. **1692** Ray *Disc.* III. ii. (1732) 411 A notable Passage taken out of Plutarch's Tractate. **1877** Morley *Crit. Misc.* Ser. II. 270 It was his own sense of the value of Liberty which led to the production of the little tractate. **1883** Edersheim *Life Jesus* (ed. 6) I. 401 In the Rabbinic tractate on the Samaritans.

† **b.** The subject treated of. *Obs.* *rare*$^{-1}$.

**1589** Nashe *Anat. Absurd.* 6 When as lust is the tractate of so many leaues, and loue passions the lauish dispence of so much paper.

† **c.** Literary treatment, discussion (*of* a subject).

**1586** Ferne *Blaz. Gentrie* Ep. Ded., A matter of it selfe so honorable, namely the tractate and handling of the nobilities and armes of generositie.

† **2.** Negotiation, dealing, transaction. *Obs.*

**1618** *Barnevelt's Apol.* F j, By reason of these fiue Regall Embassages, and tractates, it happened, that [etc.]. **1630** *R. Johnson's Kingd. & Commw.* 89 In Paris they dare talke of the Kings mistresses, intermeddle with all tractates of Parliaments and State.

† **Tra·ctate,** *v.* *Obs.* *rare.* [f. L. *tractāre*: see Tract *v.*$^1$, -ate$^3$.] *trans.* To handle, deal with.

**1657** Tomlinson *Renou's Disp.* 669 Things..onely Medicinal..should be tractated by Pharmacopolists alone.

† **Tracta·tion.** *Obs.* [ad. L. *tractātiōn-em*, n. of action f. *tractāre*: see Tract *v.*$^1$ and -ation.]

**1.** The handling or treating of a subject in discourse or writing; literary treatment, discussion.

**1570** Foxe *A. & M.* (ed. 2) 22/2 The tractation wherof .. I do refre..to them, that haue more leysure. **1628** Bp. Hall *Old Relig.* Ep. Ded. 6 A methode, and manner of Tractation, which might be of vse to plain vnderstandings. **1654** Z. Coke *Logick* 192 Tractation (or Handling) is the meditation of a Theme or matter to be done by Instruments of Art.

**b.** An instance of this; a passage or work treating of something; a discussion or treatise.

**1555** in Foxe *A. & M.* (1563) 974/2 He did ther intreate of the sacrament in that tractation *De cœna domini.* **1577** Harrison *England* II. v. (1877) I. 116, I might..make a long tractation of the round table. **1669** Gale *Crt. Gentiles* I. I. xi. 60 What I have..in this whole tractation laid down.

**2.** Conduct towards or dealing with a person or thing; treatment.

**1548** *Act 2 & 3 Edw. VI*, c. 23 § 2 Sentence for matrymonye, commanding solempnizacion, cohabitacion, consumacion and tractacion as becometh Man and Wyef to have. **1670** Maynwaring *Vita Sana* i. 22 Irregular and unfit tractation of Infants.

**3.** Handling, manipulation (in *lit.* sense). *rare.*

**1578** Banister *Hist. Man* I. 30 The prompt tractation, and handlyng, that now appertaineth to the hand. **1650** Bulwer *Anthropomet.* 217 They nourish it much by Art and often tractation.

**4.** Negotiation, dealing, treaty. *rare*$^{-1}$.

**1600** O. E. *Repl. Libel* II. v. 98 Any compact, packe, conspiracy, or tractation to any such purpose. [**1881** *Sat. Rev.* 17 Dec. 743/1 M. Gambetta thought that there might be even with Italy some sort of tractation. One of his hearers called out that this was quite a new word, and M. Gambetta ..replied that he had coined a word, because no existing word expressed the peculiarly delicate arrangement, or approach to an arrangement, which he had in his head.]

**5.** Use (of a word) in a particular sense. (= L. *tractatio*, Cicero *Part. Or.* v. 17.) *rare*$^{-1}$.

**1660** *Author Healing in Church* 26, I have thus done with the General and Theological Tractation of the words.

† **Tracta·tor.** *Obs.* [a. L. *tractātor*, agent-n. f. *tractāre*: see Tract *v.*$^1$ and -or 2 c.] One who treats of a subject; the writer of a tractate.

*a* **1638** Mede *Wks.* (1672) 386 Justin Martyr, Theophilus Antiochenus, Irenæus, or it may be another small Tractator or two. **1686** W. Hopkins tr. *Ratramnus* Dissert. ii. (1688) 25 Phil. Labbe numbers him among the Catholick Tractators, Radbert, Lanfranc, and Guitmund. **1725** tr. *Dupin's Eccl. Hist. 17th C.* I. v. 65 This Name of Treatise was given to it [sermon], because the Holy Scripture was explained in it; and it is upon that account that the Preachers were call'd *Tractators.*

**b.** *spec.* Any one of the writers of 'Tracts for the Times': see Tract *sb.*$^1$ 3 b.

**1842** Kingsley in *Life* (1877) I. 81 Talking of the Tractators—so you still like their tone! And so do I. **1844** R. M. Beverley *Ch. Eng. Examined* Pref. (ed. 2) 12 The Oxford tractators..write for this one object, to bring Christians from the Scriptures into tradition.

**Tractato·rian,** *a.* *Ch. Hist.* ? *Obs.* [f. late L. *tractātōri-us* (f. prec.) + -an.] In *tractatorian* or *tractatory letter*, late L. *epistola tractatoria*, a letter from a synod or council of bishops, so called from L. *tractātus* in the sense of a conference treating of sacred subjects. See Du Cange. Also **Tra·ctatory** *a.* in same sense; *sb.* a tractatory letter.

**1672–5** Comber *Comp. Temple* (1702) 510 St. Augustine, who excommunicated Primianus the Donatist, and sent his Tractatorian letter to all his fellow Bishops to avoid him. *Ibid.* 513 The Tractatorian Epistle, which the Bishops sent in the Name of the Church of Ptolemais to all her sister Churches. **1725** tr. *Dupin's Eccl. Hist. 17th C.* I. v. II. 69 They call'd those Tractatory Letters, by which the Metropolitans invited the Bishops of their Province to Synods. ..The Excuses of the Bishops who could not come to the Synod were wrote at the Bottom of the Letter which was sent to them, which they call'd Tractory, or Tractatory.

‖ **Tractatrix** (træktē·triks). Pl. **-trices** (-trisīz). [L. *tractātrix* (Martial, in sense 1), fem. of *tractātor* shampooer, also one who treats of a subject: see Tractator.]

**1.** A female shampooer. *rare*$^{-1}$.

**1874** M. Collins *Frances* II. 117 That stout Miss Susanetta, with her shrill voice, and her hands of the tractatrix, is a strange creature.

2. *Geom.* = TRACTRIX.
1828 in WEBSTER; hence in later Dicts.

**Tractatule** (træ·ktătiul). *rare.* [f. TRACTATE (or L. *tractātus*) + *-ule*, dim. suffix, as in *globule*, *granule*, etc.] A small tractate or treatise.
1892 *Sat. Rev.* 28 May 636/1 The first [volume] contains a much more mixed multitude of tractatules. 1901 N. SMITH in *Fortn. Rev.* Oct. 403 The carnal man cannot help sighing for a tractate—a tractatule even of the tiniest—on English verse, from the Venerable One.

**Tract-boat**, obs. form of TRACK-BOAT.

**Tracteit**, obs. Sc. form of TRACTATE.

‖ **Tractellum** (trække·lǒm). *Biol.* Pl. **tracte·lla.** [mod.L., f. L. *tract-*, ppl. stem of *trahĕre* to draw, after FLAGELLUM: cf. PULSELLUM.] The anterior flagellum of an infusorian, etc., which serves to draw the body after it in swimming. Hence **Tracte·llate** *a.* [-ATE[2]], furnished with a tractellum.
1880 KENT *Infusoria* I. 429 Among the free-swimming monoflagellate Infusoria.., where the locomotive appendage ..fulfils during natation the rôle of a tractellum. 1891 *Cent. Dict.*, *Tractellate*.

† **Tra·ctic.** *Obs. rare*[−1]. [irreg. f. L. *tract-āre* (see TRACT *v.*[1]), ? after *practic.*] = TRACTATE 1.
1651 N. BIGGS *New Disp.* § 287 In our Tractick of simple waters.

**Tractiferous** (trækti·fĕrəs), *a. nonce-wd.* [irreg. f. TRACT *sb.*[1] + -(I)FEROUS.] Carrying tracts.
1879 *Yachtsman's Holidays* 52 That curious freak of nature, a tractiferous yachtsman.

**Tractile** (træ·ktil, -əil), *a. rare.* [ad. late L. *tractil-is*, f. *tract-*, ppl. stem of *trahĕre* to draw: see -IL, -ILE.]
†1. Capable of being drawn out to a thread.
1626 BACON *Sylva* § 839 The Consistencies of Bodies.. Fragile, Tough, Flexible, Inflexible, Tractile or to be drawne forth in length, Intractile, Porous.
2. That may be drawn, as money from a bank.
1892 STEVENSON & L. OSBOURNE *Wrecker* vii, Eight thousand..was liquid and actually tractile in the bank.
¶ 3. Erron. used for TRACTIVE.
1839 *New Monthly Mag.* LVII. 539 The distinction they have drawn between the tractile capabilities of the horse and the dog.
Hence **Tractility** (trækti·lĭti), the quality of being tractile; in quot. 1838, *fig.* capacity of being drawn out or protracted.
1713 DERHAM *Phys.-Theol.* v. ix. 350 Silver, whose Ductility and Tractility are very much inferiour to those of Gold. 1838 B. CORNEY *Controversy* 9 His subject possesses tractility.

**Tracting**, *vbl. sb.*: see under TRACT *v.*[2]

**Traction** (træ·kʃən). [ad. med.L. *tractiōnem* (Albertus, *a* 1250), n. of action from *trahĕre*, *tract-um* to draw. So F. *traction*, Sp. *traccion*, Pg. *tracção*, It. *trazione*.]
1. The action of drawing or pulling; draught: opposed to *pulsion* or pushing, and (in *Dynamics*) to *pressure*.
*Force of traction*, the force exerted in or required for traction. *Line of traction*, the line along which this force acts. *Angle of traction*, the angle between the line of traction and the surface along which the body is drawn.
1656 tr. *Hobbes' Elem. Philos.* (1839) 343 Motion is distinguished into pulsion and traction. 1837 WHEWELL *Hist. Induct. Sc.* (1857) II. 32 Bodies, on which pressure and traction are exerted. 1843 *Penny Cycl.* XXV. 109/2 When the angle of traction..is 15 or 16 degrees, a horse pulls with good effect...An example of the force of traction exerted by steam. 1868 DUNCAN tr. *Figuier's Insect W.* Introd. 25 The cockchafer..possesses a power of traction equal to more than 14 times its own weight.
b. *Phys.* and *Path.* A drawing or pulling of a part or organ (in an animal or plant) by some vital process, as the contraction of a muscle, or the tension of some adherent part.
1615 CROOKE *Body of Man* 544 In the traction of the first the lid is depressed; in the traction of the latter it is lifted vp. 1669 HOLDER *Speech* 163 The Malleus, being fixed to an extensible Membrane, follows the Traction of the Muscle. 1802 PALEY *Nat. Theol.* xi. (ed. 2) 222 The claws do their office in keeping hold of the support..by the traction of the tendons, in consequence of the attitude which the legs and thighs take by the bird sitting down. 1875 BENNETT & DYER *Sachs' Bot.* 728 The layers which are less turgid and grow more slowly are exposed to a passive traction which promotes their growth. 1876 *Clin. Soc. Trans.* IX. 192 There was..a slight..traction of face to the right side when the patient laughed.
c. A drawing or pulling movement used in massage, etc.: in quot. 1841 applied to the use of metallic tractors (see TRACTOR 1).
1841 *Fraser's Mag.* XXV. 89 The effects produced by traction, or the rubbing of metallic tractors, tipped with little lumps of wax, on the parts affected by pain, are well known. 1887 D. MAGUIRE *Art Massage* iii. (ed. 4) 51 Tractions are movements used on the articulations by pulling one part while holding the other. 1901 *Westm. Gaz.* 28 Nov. 10/2 Traction of the tongue—that is, moving it about in a rhythmical manner—has produced wonderful results in restoring the apparently dead (especially children) to life. Dr. Laborde, of Paris, is the discoverer of the treatment.
d. *fig.* Drawing, attraction, attracting power.
1649 E. REYNOLDS *Hosea* v. 18 Our conversion and sanctification comes from..a supernaturall and omnipotent traction. *a* 1711 KEN *Christophil* Poet. Wks. 1721 I. 425 His Love in Suavities distills, Preventions, Tractions sweet, Devout Christ-hymning Heat. 1883 A. H. WELSH *Eng. Lit.* I. vi. 384 He [Macbeth] feels the resistless traction of fate.
2. *spec.* The drawing of vehicles or loads along a road or track; esp. in reference to the power by which this is done, as *horse*, *steam*, *electric traction*.
1822 IMISON *Sc. & Art* I. 27 Dividing the beam..that the point of traction may be as much nearer to the stronger horse. 1826 J. ADAMSON *Sk. Inform. Rail-Roads* 38 Every change..has..added to our powers of tracktion. 1902 *Daily Chron.* 1 July 4/6 The three stages are horse-traction, steam traction, and electric traction.
b. *transf.* (*a*) A vehicle driven by some special power, as a motor car. *nonce-use.* (*b*) *Stock Exch.* Stocks connected with traction, as tramways, etc.
1896 *Westm. Gaz.* 13 Nov. 5/2 They attended the Court, having ridden in ten miles on the offending traction. 1903 *Daily Chron.* 5 Nov. 8/7 The victory for Tammany early in the session reflected strength in tractions and other municipal utility stocks. 1905 *Ibid.* 4 May 5/7 Prices worked lower. Coalers and tractions showed some strength.
3. Short for *force of traction* (as a measurable quantity); the amount of rolling friction (also *traction of adhesion*) as measuring this (quot. 1877).
1825 J. NICHOLSON *Operat. Mechanic* 666 If the speed be increased from six miles an hour to eight, the horses have by no means 1-4th less work to do, supposing the friction a constant quantity, and the traction consequently the same. 1838 *Civil Eng. & Arch. Jrnl.* I. 350/1 A dynamometer, by which the traction might be measured with considerable accuracy. 1877 KNIGHT *Dict. Mech.*, *Traction*, the adhesive friction of a wheel on a rail, a rope on a pulley, etc.
4. *attrib.* and *Comb.*, as *traction company*, *installation*, *instrument*, *movement*, *power*; **traction aneurism, diverticulum** (see quots.); **traction-gearing**, an inexact name for *friction-gearing* (FRICTION *sb.* 5); **traction-load**, the weight of a locomotive engine or motor car which presses the driving-wheels upon the rail or ground so as to produce the requisite adhesive friction and prevent the wheel from slipping; **traction-splint** (*Surg.*), a splint with an attachment for pulling upon the limb; **traction-wheel**, a driving-wheel.
1891 *Cent. Dict.*, **Traction-aneurism*. 1899 *Syd. Soc. Lex.*, *T[raction] aneurism*, an aneurism most commonly seen in children, due to traction of the aorta from an incompletely atrophied ductus Botalli. 1897 *Allbutt's Syst. Med.* III. 364 *Traction diverticula generally occur on the anterior wall of the œsophagus. 1899 *Syd. Soc. Lex.*, *T[raction] diverticulum*, a circumscribed sacculation of the œsophagus from the traction of the circum-œsophageal adhesions. 1877 KNIGHT *Dict. Mech.*, **Traction-gearing*, an arrangement for turning a wheel and its shaft by means of friction or adhesion. 1879 *St. George's Hosp. Rep.* IX. 501 On three eyes a *traction instrument was used. 1887 D. MAGUIRE *Art Massage* iv. (ed. 4) 106 Executing..some *traction movements. 1908 *Westm. Gaz.* 13 Feb. 5/2 American machines..are geared so low as to give them a maximum of *traction power at the expense of speed. 1877 KNIGHT *Dict. Mech.*, **Traction-wheel*, a wheel employed in drawing or impelling a vehicle, as the driving-wheel of a locomotive or traction-engine.
Hence **Tra·ctional** *a.*, of or pertaining to traction.
1877 KNIGHT *Dict. Mech.* s.v. *Traction*, The tractional surface of a driving-wheel is the face of its perimeter.

**Tra·ction-e:ngine.** A steam-engine used for drawing heavy loads along an ordinary road; a road-engine (commonly as distinguished from a *locomotive* or railway-engine).
Also a similar engine used in agricultural work, e. g. for hauling the apparatus for thrashing to the required place, and then (as a stationary engine) driving the thrashing mechanism; or as a stationary engine for hauling a gang of ploughs across a field.
1859 *All Year Round* No. 30. 77, I met a huge lumbering Bonassus of a locomotive..staggering..about Agar-street, Strand. It was called, I believe, a Traction Engine, and will, no doubt, be useful in its generation. 1876 ROUTLEDGE *Discov.* 19 The idea has been successfully realized in the traction engines lately introduced. 1903 *Motor. Ann.* 202 The law regulating the employment of traction engines on public roads is the Locomotives' Act, 1898.

† **Tra·ctioner.** *Obs. rare.* [? f. TRACT *sb.*[1] 4, or TRACT *sb.*[3]] (?) One to whom a small parcel of land was leased: see quot.
1626 *Direct. to Ld. Deputy* in *S. P., Irel.* CCXLIII. 304 (P.R.O.) That such of the Natives as ought to have leases of certain small Parcells of land in the said Plantacions and are [known] by the name of *Tractioners*, may have the said Leases made unto them at reasonable and moderate rentes.

**Tractise**, obs. var. of TREATISE.

† **Tra·ctism.** *Obs.* [f. TRACT *sb.*[1] + -ISM.] = TRACTARIANISM. So † **Tra·ctite** = TRACTARIAN *sb.* (also *attrib.* = TRACTARIAN *a.*).
1834 WHATELY *Let.* in *Life* (1866) I. 241 Bishop..spoke for four hours, and the Tractites wrote about the removing of candlesticks. 1837 *Ibid.* 390 He perceived with me that the Hampden persecution was the first outbreak of Tractism. 1844 *Ibid.* II. 75 The Tractite path. 1844 in *Daily News* 4 Feb. (1869), I know that many of the opponents of the Tractites and not a few of the supporters expect that a church government would establish and extend Tractism.

† **Tractitian** (trækti·ʃăn). *Obs. nonce-wd.* [f. TRACT *sb.*[1], ? after *politician*, *practician*.] The writer of a tract or treatise. † **Tracti·tious** *a. Obs. rare*[−0] (see quot.).
1656 BLOUNT *Glossogr.*, *Tractitious*, that handleth, toucheth or intreats of. 1831 *Fraser's Mag.* III. 483 Such scrubby and execrable treatment as the reverend Tractitian has received from this reviewer of his Principles of Dissent.

† **Tra·ctive,** *sb. Sc. Obs.* [f. L. *tract-āre* to treat (cf. TRACT *v.*[1]) + -IVE.] = TRACTATE 1.
1558 Q. KENNEDY (*title*) Ane compendius Tractiue conforme to the Scripturis of almychtie God, ressoun, and authoritie. *a* 1575 *Diurn. Occur.* (Bann. Cl.) 62 The haill lordis past to the tolbuith, and thair proponit ane lang tractive, callit the confessioun of our faith.

**Tractive** (træ·ktiv), *a.* [f. L. *tract-*, ppl. stem of *trahĕre* to draw, drag + -IVE.] Having the property of drawing or pulling; used for traction.
1615 CROOKE *Body of Man* 179 The motion of the expulsiue faculty is one, and that of the tractiue another. 1691 T. H[ALE] *Acc. New Invent.* 118 Tractive and Pulsive forces upon swimming Bodies. 1839 *Civil Eng. & Arch. Jrnl.* II. 122/2 The tractive power of the driving wheels is very much reduced. 1859 SMILES *Stephenson* 199 The kind of tractive power to be employed in working the railway. 1894 *Athenæum* 25 Aug. 260/1 This has necessitated much heavier engines to increase the tractive force.
† b. *fig.* Attractive, enticing. *Obs. rare*[−1].
1658 T. MERITON *Love & War* IV. ii, If your own Queen by tractive Operation work effect.

**Tra·ctless,** *a. Obs.* or *arch. rare.* [f. TRACT *sb.*[3] 10 + -LESS.] = TRACKLESS.
1628 J. DOUGHTY *Serm. Church-schismes* 14 There want not infinite tractlesse mazes, wherein they can lurke vndiscerned. 1818 *Hervey's Medit.* 190 Ye Fish, that rove through tractless [*earlier edd.* trackless] paths of the sea. 1899 *Westm. Gaz.* 19 Dec. 2/1 In tractless wastes that stretch to Southern Pole, Her restless keel takes its unhindered way.

**Tractlet** (træ·ktˌlet). [f. TRACT *sb.*[1] + -LET.] A small tract.
1892 *Review of Rev.* 14 Apr. 413/2 This is a neatly-printed little tractlet. 1893 RICKETT *Quickening Caliban* xiii, Packets of picture-cards and tractlets. 1895 E. CHESTER in *Mission. Herald* (Boston, U.S.) Jan. 16 Tens of thousands of our Tamil handbills or tractlets..are scattered through the..Madura district.

† **Tra·ctly,** *adv. Obs. rare*[−0]. [f. L. *tract-us* drawn, drawn out, protracted + -LY[2].] See quot.
1552 HULOET, Tractlye or treatablye, or by space or leasure, *tractim*.

**Tractor** (træ·ktǫɹ, -əɹ). [Late or med.L. agent-n. from *trahĕre*, *tract-um* to draw: see -OR.]
1. *pl.* (in full (*Perkins's*) *metallic tractors*): Name of a device invented by Elisha Perkins, an American physician (died 1799), consisting of a pair of pointed rods of different metals, as brass and steel, which were believed to relieve rheumatic or other pain by being drawn or rubbed over the skin; see PERKINISM. *Obs.* exc. *Hist.*
1798 C. C. LANGWORTHY (*title*) A View of the Perkinean Electricity; or, an Inquiry into the Influence of Metallic Tractors. 1801 E. DARWIN *Zoon.* (ed. 3) II. 63 With the supposed existence of ghosts or apparitions, witchcraft, vampyrism..and American tractors, such theories..must vanish. 1825 SOUTHEY *Lett.* (1856) III. 499 His prayers may cure just as well as tractors or animal magnetism. 1885 WHITTIER *Pr. Wks.* (1889) II. 314 Jacob Perkins, in drawing out diseases with his metallic tractors, was quite as successful as modern 'faith and mind' doctors.
2. One who or that which draws or pulls something. a. In general sense.
1856 KANE *Arct. Expl.* I. 149 His limbs..splendid tractors for the sledge. 1880 *Daily Tel.* 23 Sept., The introduction of the iron road with its steam-horse for tractor.
b. *Surg.* 'An obstetric forceps' (Knight *Dict. Mech.* 1877). c. A traction-engine; a locomotive engine of any kind used for traction of loaded wagons, artillery, etc., on ordinary roads, or for drawing gang-ploughs; also, 'the frame and steel rope by which a gang of plows is drawn across a field by a traction-engine' (*Cent. Dict.* Suppl.).
1901 *Daily Chron.* 2 Aug. 6/4 These transformers supply the overhead trolley wires, which feed special 'electrical tractors' running along the towing-path, and in these tractors the drivers sit and control operations. 1902 *Ibid.* 29 Oct. 3/4 The County Council has not yet sanctioned the use of the tractor, but it will come before the members for consideration at an early date. 1903 *Motor. Ann.* 253 Rhodesia has appealed to motor manufacturers to supply motor-wagons or tractors for use specially in hilly country.
3. *Geom.* (See quot.)
1867 CAYLEY *Math. Papers* VII. 73, I use the term tractor' to denote a line which meets any given lines. *Ibid.*, Four given lines may be directrices (generating lines) of the same hyperboloid, viz. every tractor of any three of the four lines is then a tractor of all the four lines.
Hence **Tractora·tion**, the use of metallic tractors (see 1); also allusively; **Tra·ctoring** *ppl. a.*, using metallic tractors; **Tra·ctorism** = *tractoration*; **Tra·ctorist**, one who uses metallic tractors; **Tra·ctorize** *v.*, *intr.* to use metallic tractors; *trans.* to get by tractorizing (quot. 1803[2]); to treat with metallic tractors or similar appliances (quot. 1817); whence **Tra·ctorizing** *vbl. sb.* and *ppl. a.* (All more or less *nonce-wds.* and *Obs.*)
1803 (ed. 2) FESSENDEN (*title*) Terrible *Tractoration! A Poetical Petition against Galvanising Trumpery, and the Perkinistic Institution. 1861 O. W. HOLMES *Med. Ess.* Pref. (1891) 9 Homœopathy has not died out so rapidly as Tractoration. 1803 FESSENDEN *Terrible Tractoration* III. xxv, And you'll confound the *tractoring folks By Haygarth's tale. 1802–12 BENTHAM *Ration. Judic. Evid.* V. 189 The impostures that..have been seen acted on the spiritual and medical theatres: to exorcism, animal magnetism, and *tractorism. *Ibid.*, The operations..of the magnetist, and *tractorist no less so, in the expulsion of non-existent diseases. 1803 FESSENDEN (*title*) A Poetical Petition against *Tractorising Trumpery, and the Perkinistic Institution. *Ibid.* III. viii, To tractorise away our guineas. 1817 *Monthly*

*Mag.* XLIII. 293 Which cures were performed..by tractorizing them with rusty nails.

**Tractory** (træ·ktŏri), *a.* and *sb. rare.* [ad. L. *tractōri-us* of or for drawing, f. *tract-*, ppl. stem of *trahĕre* to draw: see -ORY.]

†**A.** *adj.* Serving for traction; tractive. *Obs.*

1684 tr. *Bonet's Merc. Compit.* x. 368 He shews the various uses of his..tractorie Machine which he invented.

**B.** *sb.* †**1.** Old name for some part of a plough: see quot. *Obs.*

1607 J. CARPENTER *Plaine Mans Plough* [xiii. 109 Now.. let vs first consider of the Soule, which is that Instrument wherewith being fastened to the Oxen, the Husbandman rippeth vp his land for the Seede] xviii. 127 (*heading*) The 5. part of the Soole, is the Tractorie. *Ibid.* xxvii. 160 The Tawe, or that yron Rope which embracing the Beame, assureth it to the Tractory.

†**2.** *Ch. Hist.* = TRACTATORY *sb. Obs.*

1709 J. JOHNSON *Clergym. Vade M.* II. 179 If they cannot come, to write their excuse in the Tractory. 1725 [see TRACTATORY].

**3.** *Geom.* = TRACTRIX.

1820 G. PEACOCK *Examples Diff. Calc.* I. xxiii. 174 The mechanical tractory of a straight line upon a perfectly smooth plane is an inverted semicycloid. 1853 GLYNN *Power Water* 140 Mr. C. Schiele of Oldham..is the proprietor of this mill, and the curve he has adopted is one discovered by Huygens, in his investigation of the cycloid. It is one of those singular and beautiful curves called 'tractories', and in this case it is produced by drawing the centre point of a radius bar along a straight line, which is the axis of the curve. 1864 WEBSTER, *Tractory, Tractrix*, the curve described on a plane by a heavy point attached to a string, and drawn along by moving the other end of the string.

‖**Tractrix** (træ·ktriks). *Geom.* Pl. tra·ctrices (-isīz). [mod.L. (Huygens) fem. of *tractor*: see TRACTOR, and cf. DIRECTRIX.] A curve such that the intercept on the tangent between its point of contact and a fixed straight line is constant; so called as being traced by the centre of gyration of a rigid rod of which one end is moved along the fixed straight line, or as being the form assumed by an inextensible string which is first laid straight upon a plane surface, and one end of it then drawn in a direction at right angles to that in which the string was laid. Also, one of a class of curves similarly traced, e.g. by movement along a fixed curve.

1727-41 CHAMBERS *Cycl.*, *Tractrix*, in geometry, a curve line, called also *catenaria*. [*Error*: the tractrix is the involute of the catenary, not the catenary itself.] 1843 *Penny Cycl.* XXV. 109/2 *Tractrix*, or *Tractory*, the name given to a curve described by a heavy point attached to a string, the other end of which is moved along a given straight line or curve. 1852 SALMON *Higher Plane Curves* vii. (1879) 289 The involute of the catenary is therefore a curve such that the intercept SN, on its tangent between the point of contact and a fixed right line, is constant. Such a curve is called the tractrix. 1877 B. WILLIAMSON *Int. Calc.* (ed. 2) vii. Ex. 9.

**Tract-scout**, obs. form of TREKSCHUIT.

†**Tra·cture.** *Obs. rare*⁻¹. [ad. med.L. *tractūra* (Du Cange), f. *tract-*, ppl. stem of *trahĕre* to draw: see -URE.] Drawing, attraction, enticement.

1658 MANTON *Exp. Jude* 6 Wks. 1871 V. 192 The angels being created pure, they had no lust within to incline them;.. there was no evil tracture, no tempter; how could they sin?

‖**Tractus** (træ·ktŏs). *R. C. Ch.* [med.L. *tractus*, a spec. use of L. *tractus* 'drawing, drawing out', fr. *trahĕre* to draw; 'quia trahendo, id est tractim, canitur': see Du Cange s.v.] = TRACT *sb.*[2]

*a* 1450 MYRC *Festial* 64 Scho layth downe Alleluia and oþyr songys of melody, and takeþe forþe tractus, þat ben songys of mowrnyng, and sykyng, and longyng. 1493 *Festivall* (W. de W. 1515) 5 b. 1854 HELMORE *Pract. Lect. Plain Song* 20 Graduals, Tractuses, Sequences, and Hymns.

**Tractyse**, obs. form of TREATISE.

**Tradable** (trē¹·dăb'l), *a.* Also tradeable. [f. TRADE *sb.* or *v.* + -ABLE.] That may be dealt with in the way of trade; marketable.

1599 ESSEX *Let. to Q. Eliz.* 25 June, in Moryson *Itin.* (1617) II. 35 Your good subiects may haue for their mony out of your Maiesties store, that which..may serue for their necessary defence, whereas if once they be tradable, the Rebels will giue such extreme and excessiue prices, that they will neuer bee kept from them. 1702 C. MATHER *Magn. Chr.* I. vi. (1852) 84 One ship..which they fraighted for England with the best part of their tradable estates.

**Tradal** (trē¹·dăl), *a.* [irreg. f. TRADE *sb.* + -AL.] Of or pertaining to trade; commercial.

1872 *Lond. & China Telegraph* 4 Mar. 171/1 The true English jealousy with which he has always guarded the port and its tradal interests from outside enemies. 1905 A. STEAD *Gt. Japan* (1906) 392 Bugbears placed in the way of Japan's tradal relations with foreign countries.

**Traddle**, dial. form of TREADLE.

**Trade** (trē¹d), *sb.* Forms: 4-6 *Sc.*, 7 trad, 4-7 *Sc.* traid, (5 tradde, 6 traude, trawde, thrade), 7 traide, 5 *Sc.*, 6- trade. [a. MLG. *trade* (*trâ*) fem., track (Schiller & Lubben), LG. *trade* (*traan* :—*traden*) track (Bremisch. Wbch.); also WFlem. *tra* (:—*trade*) walk, march, course (De Bo) :—OS. *trada* str. fem. footstep, track = OHG. *trata*, MHG. *trate*, *trat* str. fem. footstep, trace, track, way, passage, f. WGer. ablaut-series *tred-*, *trad-* to TREAD. App. introduced into Eng. in 14th c. from Hanseatic MLG., perh. orig. in nautical lang. for the 'course or track' of a ship; afterwards used in other senses of ME. *trede* TREAD. Cf. also Norw. and Sw. dial. *trad* (Rietz) in similar senses, and see TROD.

In Branch I, senses 1-4 run more or less parallel with the early senses of TREAD *sb.*; in sense 5 differentiation begins, and in branch II the sense-development of *trade*, from *c* 1550, turns sharply away from that of *tread*, which retains its close connexion with TREAD *v.* But in Sc., *tred* continued to represent both *trade* and *tread*: see under TREAD.]

**I.** †**1.** A course, way, path; with *possessive* or *of*, the course trodden by a person, or followed by a ship, etc.; = TREAD *sb.* 3. *Common trade*, a public thoroughfare. *Obs.*

*c* 1375 *Sc. Leg. Saints* xxxviii. (*Adrian*) 629 Sir adryane ..bad þame..To þe richt hand þe stere set, & dresse þame to hald þare trad In-to þe sey as þai first had. *c* 1400 *Sc. Trojan War* II. 1725 Dryvand thiddir..and hiddir, That þai mycht hald no certane traid. *c* 1425 WYNTOUN *Cron.* VII. x. 3266 The king..tuke þe se hamewartis his way, Hald- and þare traid fast by Orknay. *a* 1547 SURREY *Æneid* II. 587 A postern..there was, A common trade to passe through Priams house. 1552 HULOET, Trade, *via*. 1554 *Admiralty Crt., Exam.* 9. 28 Nov., The porte of Groyne standithe and is furthe of the right course and trade towards Cadix. 1561 *Ibid., Exam.* 13. 1 Apr., If the said pilott had followid the trade and course of thother Hamboroughe shippe. 1564 *Ibid., Libels* 35 No. 160 They feared their shippe woulde strike oon grownde yf he kepte that trade.

†**b.** *fig.* Cf. TREAD *sb.* 3 b. *Obs.*

1536 STARKEY *Let. to Cromwell* 24 July, in *England* (1878) p. xliii, You juge me more to be traynyd in phylosophye than in the trade of scripture. 1538 BALE *God's Promises* II, The covenaunt, whych I to Adam made, He regardeth not, but walketh a damnable trade. 1545 ASCHAM *Toxoph.* (Arb.) 98, I trust that you..haue so..noted the nature of it, that you can teache me as it were by a trade or waye how to come to it. 1547 *Homilies* I. *Serm. Gd. Works* III. (1859) 64 The right trade and pathway unto heaven. 1549 COVERDALE, etc. *Erasm. Par. Eph.* vi. 13 b, You shall not be lyke to the common trade of seruauntes. 1613 SHAKS. *Hen. VIII*, v. i. 36 Cromwell..Stands in the gap and Trade of moe Preferments.

†**2.** The track or trail of a man or beast; footprints; = TREAD *sb.* 1, 2. *Obs.*

13.. *Guy Warw.* (Caius) 4731 Than loked he aboute vnder the wode shawe: The trade of horse [*Auch.* hors traces] he there sighe. *c* 1470 HENRY *Wallace* V. 136 For thair sloith hund the graith gait till him ȝeid, Off othir trade [*ed.* 1570 tred] scho tuk as than no heid. 1537 *St. Papers Hen. VIII*, V. 97 Diverse of his tenauntes pursewed the trade with a slott hownd. 1590 SPENSER *F. Q.* II. vi. 39 As Shepheardes curre, that..Hath tracted forth some salvage beastes trade. 1591 — *Tears Muses* 275 The sacred springs..They trampled haue with their fowle footings trade. 1596 DALRYMPLE tr. *Leslie's Hist. Scot.* (S.T.S.) I. 21 The dog..seases not afor he find the trad of the fliaris.

†**b.** *transf.* The outer surface of the rim of a wheel, which makes the track or mark on the ground; the TREAD of a wheel. *Obs. rare*⁻⁰.

1556 WITHALS *Dict.* (1568) 18 b/1 *Orbita rotunditas*, a whele trade. *Ibid.*, The vtter parte of the whele, called the trade, *orbis*.

†**3.** Course, way, or manner of life; course of action; mode of procedure, method. *Obs.* or *dial.*

1456 SIR G. HAYE *Law Arms* (S.T.S.) 211 It war nocht lyke that thai folowit the trade of oure lord, quhilk in all his accioun was oure instructioun. *a* 1548 HALL *Chron.*, *Hen. IV* 2 Kyng Richarde..was nowe brought to that trade of liuyng that [etc.]. 1549-62 STERNHOLD & H. *Ps.* CXIX. v. i, Instruct me Lord, in the right trade Of thy statutes diuine. 1560 BIBLE (Genev.) *Prov.* xxii. 6 Teache a childe in the trade of his way, and when he is olde, he shal not departe from it. 1567 MAPLET *Gr. Forest* 77 The Cat.. is in hir trade and manner of liuing, very shamefast. 1571 *Calr. Carew MSS.* I. 410 Surety to leave their wicked thrade of life, and to fall to other occupation. 1633 BP. HALL *Hard Texts, N. T.* 176 In respect of the trade and course of their life. 1721 STRYPE *Eccl. Mem.* I. lii. 393 Commonly this was the trade: the better benefice, and the cure the more, the seldomer was the Parson or Vicar resident at home. *a* 1825 FORBY *Voc. E. Anglia* s. v., If this is to be the trade.

†**b.** A way or method of attaining an end; a contrivance, expedient. *Obs. rare.*

1572 J. JONES *Bathes of Bath* To Rdr. 1 The arte or trade of maintaining health. *Ibid.* Ep. Ded. 3 But also the Chyrurgians..may fynde a most apte trade of vnderstanding comprehended in few wordes. 1576 FLEMING *Caius' Dogs* (1880) 17 The water Spaniell,..hauing long, rough, and curled heare, not obtayned by extraordinary trades, but giuen by natures appointment.

**c.** A regular or habitual course of action; a practice or habit of doing something. *Obs.* exc. *dial.*

*c* 1586 C'TESS PEMBROKE *Ps.* LIX. i, Save me from those Who make a trade of cursed wrong. 1603 SHAKS. *Meas. for M.* III. i. 148 Thy sinn's not accidentall, but a Trade. 1608 — *Per.* IV. vi. 74 Now prittie one, how long haue you beene at this trade? 1616 R. C. *Times' Whistle* v. 1719 Now let me discourse of drunkennes, Which..is made Even a common ordinary trade. 1652 J. WRIGHT tr. *Camus' Nat. Paradox* VI. 134 Shee had long since forgot the Trade of running away. *a* 1716 BLACKALL *Wks.* (1723) I. 194, I do not make a Trade and Custom of it. 1755 *Man* No. 33. 4 But it now growing a trade in the family to send for *aquamirabilis*, the master..forbad his servants to fetch any. *Mod. dial.* He made a trade of going to their house.

†**d.** Used *advb.* in phr. *to blow trade*, of the wind, to blow in a regular or habitual course, or constantly in the same direction (cf. TRADE-WIND). So, of a ship, *to run trade* (rare). *Obs.*

1591-1600 J. JANE in Hakluyt *Voy.* (1600) III. 849 When we were shot in betweene the high lands [in Str. of Magellan], the wind blowing trade, without any inch of sayle, we spooned before the sea. 1670 NARBOROUGH *Jrnl.* in *Acc. Sev. Late Voy.* I. (1694) 84 Neither do I find the Winds to blow Trade; but they are veerable. 1719 DE FOE *Crusoe* 447 The Winds..seemed to be more steadily against us, blowing almost Trade, as we call it, from the East, and E.N.E. [in the China Sea]. 1720 — *Capt. Singleton* (1906) 198 The winds generally blow trade from the S. and S.S.E. from May to September. 1722 — *Col. Jack* (1840) 319 We ..kept our course W. by S.., running away, trade, as they call it, into the great gulf of Mexico.

†**4.** Practice; practical exercise, employment, or application. *Obs.*

1575 *Recorde's Gr. Artes* Pref. A v, Apt instrumentes,..if a man coulde applye them to vse, and by teaching of rules, frame them to better trade. *Ibid.* II. Ff j b, To acquainte your minde the better with yᵉ new trade of this rule. 1608 A. TODKILL in *Capt. Smith's Virginia* (1624) 66 The boates trimmed for trade, which..in their Iourney incountred the second Supply.

**5.** The practice of some occupation, business, or profession habitually carried on, esp. when practised as a means of livelihood or gain; a calling; formerly used very widely, including professions; now usually applied to a mercantile occupation and to a skilled handicraft, as distinct from a profession (PROFESSION 6 a), and *spec.* restricted to a skilled handicraft, as distinguished from a professional or mercantile occupation on the one hand, and from unskilled labour on the other.

In earliest use not clearly distinguishable from 3; the sense is developed by contextual additions, as *trade* (i. e. practice) *of husbandry*, *of merchandise*, *of fishing*, etc.

1546 *Reg. Mag. Sig. Scot.* 757/2 Except thai be in thair lefull marchandice, traudis and bissynes concerning the wynning of thair leving. 1583 STOCKER *Civ. Warres Lowe C.* I. 22 Againe to sette vppe, and place the accustomed trade of merchandise. 1601 SHAKS. *Jul. C.* I. i. 12 *Mur.* But what Trade art thou? Answer me directly...*Fla.* Thou art a Cobler, art thou? 1601 *Act* 43 *Eliz.* c. 2 § 1 For settinge to worke all such persons..[who] use no ordinarie or dailie trade of lief to get their livinge by. 1638 JUNIUS *Paint. Ancients* 100 His father consulting with his kinsfolkes about the trade he should put his sonne to, thought it best to make him a statuarie. 1656 in *Verney Mem.* (1907) II. 91 [If the boy were] to be fitted for a merchant or other trade. 1695 A. TELFAIR *New Confut. Sadd.* (1696) 1 Mackie..who is a Mason [*note* Stonecutter] by Trade, devoted his first Child to the Devil, at his taking of the Mason-Word. 1711 ADDISON *Spect.* No. 47 ¶ 7 A Neighbour of mine, who is a Haberdasher by Trade. 1737 *Gentl. Mag.* Mar. 189/1 Mr. Will. Potter, of Gainsborough,.. By Trade a Butcher. 1798 WORDSW. *Peter Bell* I. 201 A Potter, Sir, he was by trade. 1813 *Sk. Character* (ed. 2) I. 16 He was in trade; and...Miss Aucherly was well aware, his being in trade was an obstacle impossible to be surmounted. 1828 SCOTT *F. M. Perth* xix, Old Dorothy Glover, as she was called, (for she also took name from the trade she practised). 1856 FROUDE *Hist. Eng.* I. i. 43 No person was allowed to open a trade..unless he had first served his apprenticeship. 1860 LD. DENMAN in *All Year Round* 5 May 83 Every trade..is a business, but every business is not a trade. To answer that description, it must be conducted by buying and selling, which the business of keeping a lunatic asylum is not.

**b.** Anything practised for a livelihood.

1650 BAXTER *Saints' R.* III. xiv. § 9 Let men see that you use not the Ministrie only for a trade to live by. 1651 in *Verney Mem.* (1907) I. 482 The multitude of peasants in Savoye which practise the trade of bandittis. 1653 MILTON *Hirelings* Wks. 1851 V. 371 They would not then so many of them, for want of another Trade, make a Trade of thir preaching. 1659 B. HARRIS *Parival's Iron Age* 141 Souldiers desire not an end of War; because they have no other Trade to live. 1693 J. DRYDEN *Juvenal* XIV. 251 A Captain is a very gainful Trade. 1746 FRANCIS tr. *Horace, Epist.* II. i. 167 Unfit for War's tumultuous Trade. 1865 KINGSLEY *Herew.* i, Where learnedst thou so suddenly the trade of preaching? 1878 SIMPSON *Sch. Shaks.* I. 32 Her first venture in the trade which subsequently proved so profitable to her, that of buccaneering.

**6.** *The trade*: those engaged in the particular business or industry concerned or in question; *spec.* the publishers and booksellers; now more commonly, those engaged in the liquor trade.

1697 DRYDEN *Virg. Past.* IX. 44 A Member of the tuneful trade. 1791 BOSWELL *Johnson* 15 Apr. an. 1778 *note*, As Physicians are called the Faculty,..the Booksellers of London are denominated the Trade. 1837 SIR F. PALGRAVE *Merch. & Friar* Ded. 1 The reluctance with which the 'trade' engage in any work purporting to consist of ancient documents. 1868 JOYNSON *Metals* 63 Many thousands of tons of 'Bessemer metal'—for the 'trade' are not quite sure whether it is iron or steel. 1885 *Cyclist* 19 Aug. 1101/2 Interesting to Cyclists and the Trade. 1885 *Liverpool Echo* 14 Nov., The *Morning Advertiser*,..discussing the action of 'the Trade' in the coming contests, takes a very moderate view. 1886 C. E. PASCOE *Lond. of To-day* xxxix. (ed. 3) 329 Some of the publishing houses of London..are as ready to sell to the general public as to 'the trade'. 1903 *Westm. Gaz.* 7 Mar. 2/2 The House of Commons read a second time yesterday two Bills connected with 'the trade'. The first..was to bring home to the innkeeper his statutory liability to provide food as well as drink.

**b.** Any one of the corporations of craftsmen (usually seven in number) in a Scottish burgh, each of which formerly elected one or more members of the town-council.

1777 MAYNE *Siller Gun* I. i, Ae Simmer's morning, wi the sun The Seven Trades there Forgather'd. 1781 *Set of the Burgh* (of Hawick), Confirmed by Court of Session, that there presently are, and shall henceforth continue seven Incorporations within the said burgh, vizt.:—Weavers, Tailors, Hammermen, Skinners, Fleshers, Shoemakers, and Baxters, each of which shall..elect two quartermasters for each trade, to continue in office for one year. 1838 W. BELL *Dict. Law Scotl.* s.v. *Burgh, Royal*, In Edinburgh and Glasgow, the convener of trades and the dean of guild are *ex-officio* members of council. **1860** Cosmo Innes in Gordon *Hist. Moray* ii. (1882) 23 Do the Bailies and the 'Trades' fill the eye in their fine new Church..?

**II. 7. a.** *lit.* Passage to and fro; coming and going; resort. Now *dial.*

**1591** Sylvester *Du Bartas* i. v. 133 Some [fish] from the Sea..So both the Waters with free Trade frequenting. **1593** Shaks. *Rich. II*, iii. iii. 156 Ile be buryed in the Kings high-way, Some way of common Trade, where Subjects feet May howrely trample on their Soueraignes Head. **1624** Donne *Devot.* (ed. 2) 154 In Jacobs ladder, they which ascended and descended, and maintained the trade between heaven and earth. **1868** Atkinson *Cleveland Gloss.* s. v., A vast o' rabbits here, by the trade they make.

†**b.** *fig.* Mutual communication, intercourse, 'commerce', dealings. *Obs.*

**1602** Shaks. *Ham.* iii. ii. 346 Haue you any further Trade with vs? **1634** Massinger *Very Woman* iv. iii, Long was my travail, long my trade, to win her. *a* **1708** Beveridge *Thes. Theol.* (1710) I. 183 Free trade and commerce for grace and goodness for heaven and happiness.

**c.** To-do, 'work', fuss, commotion; trouble, difficulty. *dial.*

**1854** Miss Baker *Northampt. Gloss.* s.v., They make such a trade wi' me when I goo to see 'em. **1895** *Westm. Gaz.* 21 Sept. 2/1 What there was in him to make such a trade of, as his wife did, I could not see. **1899** *Leeds Merc., Supp.* 3 June (E.D.D.), They'll hae plenty o' trade on afore they mak' t' business pay.

**8.** Passage or resort for the purpose of commerce; hence, the buying and selling or exchange of commodities for profit; commerce, traffic, trading. † *To beat the trade*, to carry on business (*obs.*). See also Free trade.

**1555** Eden *Decades* 240 The trade of spices which was so commodious and profitable to hym. **1570** J. Campion in Hakluyt *Voy.* (1599) II. 114 A safe conduct from the great Turke, for a trade to Chio. **1604** *Ho. Comm. Jrnl.* I. 218/2 The Mass of the whole Trade of all the Realm is in the Hands of some Two Hundred Persons. **1611** *Reg. Mag. Sig. Scot.* 171/1 Cum privilegio aque de Clyde, mercature lie trafficque et trade ejusdem. **1670** R. Coke *Disc. Trade* 1 Trade is an Art of Getting, Preparing, and Exchanging things Commodious for Humane Necessities and Convenience. *a* **1687** Petty *Pol. Anat.* (1691) 34 Ann. 1664..was the best year of Trade that hath been these many years in Ireland. *a* **1692** Pollexfen *Disc. Trade* (1697) 91 The Trade to Swedeland and Denmark having of late Years carried from us great Sums of Money Annually. **1707** Hearne *Collect.* 12 Nov. (O.H.S.) II. 72 Dr. Davenant.. has writ..an Essay upon Ballance of Trade. **1818** Scott *Hrt. Midl.* ii, Contraband trade..is not usually looked upon, either by the vulgar or by their betters, in a very heinous point of view. **1835** *Penny Cycl.* III. 309/1 The balance of trade..is the difference between the aggregate amount of a nation's exports or imports, or the balance of the particular account of the nation's trade with another nation. **1889** *Nature* 19 Sept. 492/2 The struggle for the Eastern trade.

†**b.** A trading expedition. *Obs. rare*$^{-1}$.

**1725** De Foe *Voy. round World* (1840) 356 This new scheme of a trade round the World.

†**c.** A centre of trade, an emporium. *Obs. rare*$^{-1}$.

**1618** in Foster *Eng. Factories Ind.* (1906) I. 27 Surratt will never be a trade unles the Red Sea both supply yt and awe the Guzeratts.

**9.** With *a* and *pl.* An act of trading, a transaction, a bargain; *spec.* in politics, a private arrangement, a 'deal' or 'job'. Orig. *U.S. slang.*

**1829** *Massachusetts Spy* 18 Mar. (Thornton), When the business was completed, there was about an even trade between Mr. A. and Farmer G. **1835–40** Haliburton *Clockm.* (1862) 347 Havin' finished that are little trade, squire, there is another small matter I want to talk over with you. **1867** Lowell *Fitz Adam's Story* in *Heartsease & Rue* (1888) 158 Yet in a bargain he was all men's foe, Would yield no inch of vantage in a trade. **1888** Bryce *Amer. Commw.* II. iii. lxiii. 458 This is a Deal, or Trade, a treaty which terminates hostilities for the time.

†**10.** A fleet of trading ships under convoy. *Obs.*

**1747** *Gentl. Mag.* Nov. 519/1 The signal for the trade to make the best of their way. **1748** *Anson's Voy.* i. ii. 15 This squadron,..and the trade under their convoy,..tided it down the Channel. **1803** Nelson in Nicolas *Disp.* (1845) V. 194 On my arrival at Malta I ordered the Cyclops to proceed with the Trade from thence bound into the Adriatic.

**11.** Stuff, goods, materials, commodities; now *dial.*, usually in depreciatory use: rubbish, trash; in quot. 1697, implements, equipment.

**1645** T. Wilson (*title*) Childe's Trade; or the Beginning of the Doctrine of Christ, whereby Babes may have Milk, Children Bread Broken. **1670** Narborough *Jrnl.* in *Acc. Sev. Late Voy.* i. (1694) 27 These Herbs..for want of which fresh Trade several of my Men were falling into [the Scurvy]. *Ibid.* 58 Green Pease-leaves and such trade. **1697** Dryden *Virg. Georg.* iii. 535 His house, and household gods, his trade of war, His bow and quiver, and his trusty cur. **1707** Mortimer *Husb.* (1721) II. 177 They are sown at two Seasons of the Year; in the Spring with other like Kitchen Trade. **1777** *Horæ Subs.* 438 (E.D.D.), I took some trade, which I had of the doctor for my disorder. **1858** Simmonds *Dict. Trade, Trade*,..a Derbyshire mining term for refuse or rubbish from a mine. **1875** *Sussex Gloss.*, *Trade*, anything to carry; such as a bag, a dinner-basket, tools or shop-goods. **1889** Farmer *Americanisms* s. v., Medicine is also strangely named *trade* in Rhode Island.

**12.** Commodities for use in bartering with savages; also, native produce for barter.

**1847** J. Palmer *Jrnl.* 127 The value of fourteen dollars in trade would buy an ordinary horse. **1883** Chester in Lovett *J. Chalmers* vii. 239 About £50 worth of trade was distributed to the heads of families. **1884** *Pall Mall Budget* 22 Aug. 9/1 One of these boats has on board the 'trade', as we call the goods by which purchases are effected. **1897** Mary Kingsley *W. Africa* 517 Look what a lot of trade he threw away at that funeral of his wife.

**13.** Abbreviation of Trade-wind; chiefly in *pl.*

*c* **1796** T. Twining *Trav. Amer.* (1894) 14 The increasing unsteadiness of the wind denoted that we were upon the edge of the 'Trade'. **1806** Pinckard *Notes W. Ind.* I. xviii. 186 The delay..served but to augment the value of the ever-constant trades. **1853** Herschel *Pop. Lect. Sc.* iv. § 19 (1873) 157 The great and permanent system of winds known as the 'trades' and 'anti-trades'. **1857** C. Gribble in *Merc. Marine Mag.* (1858) V. 9 From this I carried a steady Trade, all sail set. **1880** Haughton *Phys. Geog.* iv. 188 The so-called north-east monsoons..are simply the usual Trades of the northern hemisphere. **1899** F. T. Bullen *Log Sea-waif* 213 The 'south-east trades' being notoriously steady and reliable in the Atlantic, while the north-east trades are often entirely wanting. **1899** 'Martello Tower' *At School & at Sea* 88 The trade slackened and became fitful.

**III. 14.** *attrib.* and *Comb.* **a.** attrib.: in sense 5, 'of or pertaining to a trade or calling', as *trade-body, -caste, -company* (Company *sb.* 6), *-guild, protection, skill, -work*; 'caused by or arising out of one's trade', as *trade disease, eczema, eruption*; in sense 8, as *trade advice, bill, competition, conflict, gamble, mart, partnership, product, profit, relation, reverse, rivalry, ship, site, supply, supremacy, town, use, value, wave, word*; in sense 12, 'pertaining to or used for barter', as *trade bag, blanket, boat, box, calico, chest, gin, glass, goods, gun, stuff*; **b.** instrumental, objective, etc., as *trade-bound, -destroying, -laden* adjs.; *trade-spoiler, -taxer.*

**1860** Reade *Cloister & H.* lxxxvi, Good *trade advice was to flow from the elders. **1907** *Chron. Lond. Mission. Soc.* Oct. 185/1 My mackintosh served as a blanket, and my *trade-bag as a pillow. **1892** Griffith tr. *Fouard's St. Peter* 268 *Trades-bodies, political assemblies, and societies for mutual aid. **1897** Mary Kingsley *W. Africa* 166 My back is against the *trade box, and behind that is the usual mound of pillows. **1891** E. Westermarck *Hist. Hum. Marr.* (1894) 372 [In India] there is an almost endless number of *trade-castes. **1876** B. Martin *Messiah's Kingd.* vi. i. 289 The embittered *trade-conflicts which distinguish our era. **1899** *Allbutt's Syst. Med.* VIII. 569 A patient suffering from a *trade eczema. *Ibid.* 914 Affections of the Skin produced by Occupations (*Trade Eruptions). **1853** Lynch *Self-Improv.* v. 122 There is much money-getting by *trade-gamble. **1897** Mary Kingsley *W. Africa* 664, I give an ..Analysis of Sample of *Trade-Gin. **1881** J. Hatton *New Ceylon* v. 136 The voyage up, with the *trade goods, is done in a canoe. **1874** Green *Short Hist.* iv. § i. 163 A wiser instinct of government led Edward to establish *trade-guilds in the towns. **1904** W. M. Ramsay in *Expositor* July 42 The workers in bronze were one of its numerous trade-guilds. **1873** R. F. Burton in Lady B. *Life* (1893) II. 20 Those who must often expose themselves..to Anglo-Ashanti *trade-guns. **1897** Mary Kingsley *W. Africa* 239 A picturesque series of canoes, fruit and *trade laden. **1904** *Speaker* 9 Apr. 31/2 A *trade-mart should be established. **1863** Fawcett *Pol. Econ.* iv. vii. (1876) 626 We have to ascertain whether rates are to be regarded as a deduction from *trade-profits, or whether they are a tax imposed upon the consumers of merchandise. **1883** *Chambers's Encycl.*, **Trade Protection Societies* are associations composed of merchants, tradesmen, and others,..for the promotion of trade, and for protecting the individual members from losses. **1897** *Boston* (Mass.) *Jrnl.* 3 Feb. 7/4 British subjects looking for friendly *trade-relations. **1874** Forster *Dickens* xi. i. (1907) 883 *Trade reverses at Glasgow had checked the success there. **1902** *Q. Rev.* July 243 The bitter *trade-rivalry with France. **1757** Dyer *Fleece* ii. Poems (1761) 103 The *trade-ship left his streams; the merchant shun'd His desart borders. **1872** Yeats *Growth Comm.* 301 A *trade site established twenty-one years earlier. **1693** W. Freke *Art of War* iii. 24 Is your war with a *Trade-state, pen them but in, and stop their Course. **1662** R. Mathew *Unl. Alch.* § 89. 156 That which is *Trade-stuff is fetcht more out of the Firr-tree, then out of the Scurff of Amber. **1888** Hasluck *Model Engin. Handybk.* (1900) 10 Purchased ..from the usual *trade-supplies. **1910** *Encycl. Brit.* VI. 789/2 Maintenance of *trade-supremacy in the eastern Mediterranean. **1903** *Speaker* 26 Sept. 597/1 The two sections—the 'food-taxers' and the '*trade-taxers'..can unite in office again. **1657** Owen *Commun. w. Father*, etc. iii. § 3 Wks. 1850 II. 244 According to the *trade use of the word, whence the metaphor is taken. **1891** *Daily News* 15 Apr. 2/5 No doubt the highest point in the *trade-wave has been reached and passed.

**15.** Special combs.: **trade allowance** (see quot.); **trade board**, a council regulating conditions of employment in certain trades; **trade cumulus**, the cumulus which collects in the trade-wind region in the day-time; the trade-wind cloud; **trade dinner**, a dinner at which representatives of a trade meet; **trade dollar**, a dollar issued by the U. S. A. for Asiatic trade: see Dollar 5; **trade-edition** (see quot.); **trade-English**, a broken English used by traders as a medium of communication with African natives, and also by natives speaking different languages; **trade-fixture**, a fixture put in for trade purposes (which remains the property of the tenant) (*Funk's Stand. Dict.* 1895); **trade-hall** (see quot.); †**trade-language**, a language used as a means of communication by people speaking different languages; **trade-master**, one who instructs a class in a trade or handicraft; **trade name**, (*a*) a descriptive or fancy name used to designate some proprietary article of trade; (*b*) the name by which an article or substance is known to the trade; (*c*) the name or style under which a business is carried on; **trade-officer**, in a penal institution: = *trade-master*; **trade price**, the price at which the wholesale dealer sells to the retailer; **trade-road**, a trade-route; **trade-room**, a room (in quot., on board ship) devoted to the storage and exchange of trade goods; **trade-route**, a route followed by traders or caravans, or by trading-ships; **trade-sale**, an auction held by and for a particular trade; **trade school**, a school in which handicrafts are taught; †**trade-way**, (*a*) ?beaten path; passage, thoroughfare; (*b*) the fairway of navigation. See also Tradecraft, -mark, -union, -wind.

**1858** Simmonds *Dict. Trade*, **Trade-allowance, Trade-price*, a wholesale discount, allowed to dealers or retailers on articles to be sold again. **1909** *Daily Chron.* 26 Mar. 6/4 To-day the President of the Board of Trade will introduce the new *Trade Boards Bill, dealing with what are known as 'sweated' trades. **1849** *N. & Q.* 1st Ser. I. 55/2 A custom.. which now passes under the designation of a '*Trade-Edition', the meaning..being, that the copyright, instead of being the exclusive property of one person, is divided into shares and held by several. **1897** Mary Kingsley *W. Africa* 432 That peculiar language, '*trade English'; it is not only used as a means of intercommunication between whites and blacks, but between natives using two distinct languages. *Ibid.* 434, I have a collection of trade English letters and documents, for it is a language that I regard as exceedingly charming. **1858** Simmonds *Dict. Trade*, **Trade-hall*, a meeting-hall, or sale-room in a town, for manufacturers or traders. **1662** Owen *Animadv. Fiat Lux* Wks. 1851 XIV. 142 [Latin] is the *trade-language of religion among learned men. **1888** *19th Cent.* Nov. 759 In our prisons the schoolmaster and the *trademaster take the place of the executioner. **1861** in Sebastian *Digest of Cases* 112 So far as the name was used..as a *trade name, the representatives of J. G. Loring were entitled under the Massachusetts Statute (Gen. St. c. 56) to restrain them [etc.]. **1878** Sebastian *Law of Trade Marks* 12 In imitation of trade names ..used as such and not as trade marks on goods. **1898** *Patent Office Reports* XV. 134 Goods marked with a trade name (i. e. Brazilian Silver). **1900** Hopkins *Law unfair Trade* 29 Proper names are not trade marks, and..there should not be such a thing as a technical trade name. **1904** A. Griffiths *50 Yrs. Public Service* xix. 269 Sometimes *trade officers, such as tailor, shoemaker, or serving mistress, helped themselves to materials from store. **1822** Scott *Nigel* Introd. Epist., You shall have it at *trade price. **1866** Livingstone *Last Jrnls.* (1873) I. i. 18 Our course is..in 'wadys', from which, following the *trade-road, we often ascend the heights. **1840** R. H. Dana *Bef. Mast* xiii. 28 The cargo having been entered in due form, we began trading. The *trade-room was fitted up in the steerage. **1876** R. E. Lytton *Lett.* (1906) II. xiv. 37 The *trade-routes have been re-opened. **1847** Webster, **Trade-sale*, an auction by and for the trade, especially that of the booksellers. **1861** *Chambers's Encycl.* II. 230/2 Trade sale. **1910** W. Parker in *Encycl. Brit.* XI. 352/2 The skins are sold in the trade sale as martens, but as there are many that are of a very dark colour and the majority are almost as silky as the Russian sable, the retail trade has for generations back applied the term of sable to this fur. **1898** *Engineering Mag.* XVI. 133/1 The Proficiency of the *Trade School Plumber. **1906** *Westm. Gaz.* 3 May 12/2 The day trade-schools provided by the Council for the training of boys and girls in certain trades after they leave the elementary schools. **1600** Surflet *Countrie Farme* v. iv. 665 Let them be ditched round about..to cut off the *trade waies of passengers. **1643** *Admir. Crt., Exam.* 58, 1 June, [A ship wrongly anchored in] the trade way.

**b.** Combinations with *trades* (pl. or for genitive *trade's*), as **trades-combination** = Trade-union; **trades committee**, a committee which regulates conditions of employment in a trade; †**trades-master**, one who has mastered a trade; a master workman (in quot. 1657, as distinct from a journeyman); **tradesperson**, nonce-singular of *tradespeople*. See also Tradesfolk, Tradesman, Tradespeople, Trades-union, Tradeswoman.

**1910** J. W. Harper *Soc. Ideal* xxxiii. 272 *Trades-combinations and masters' unions..are stages of progress. They are not final institutions. **1842** Cobden in Morley *Life* xii. (1902) 43/2, I would rather live under a Dey of Algiers than a *Trades Committee. **1612** R. Fenton *Usury* 96 If he be his *trades-master, he shall not stand in so great need of Gods blessing as other honest men do. **1657** J. Watts *Dipper Sprinkled* 174 Then to commence Merchant or Trades-master. **1886** E. Ward *Dress Reform Problem* iii. 50 A saving of trouble..both to the *tradesperson and the wearer.

**Trade** (trēɪd), *v.* Forms: see prec. [f. prec.]

†**1.** *trans.* To tread (a path); to traverse (the sea); *fig.* to go through, lead (one's life). *Obs.*

**1548** H. Harte (*title*) Godly Newe short treatyse instructyng euery parson howe they shulde trade theyr lyues in ye Imytacyon of Vertu and ye shewyng of vyce. **1551** Recorde *Pathw. Knowl.* To Rdr., I will not cease from trauaile the pathe so to trade, that finer wittes maie fashion them selues with such glimsinge dull light. **1556** in S. P. H. Statham *Dover Charters* (1902) 386 All others as tradethe and travaquythe the Narrowe Sease. **1598** Sylvester *Du Bartas* ii. ii. iii. *Colonies* 725 Timber-Trees (Whereof thou buildest Ships and Houses fair To trade the Seas). **1599** Nashe *Lenten Stuffe* (1871) 30 But I have traded them as frequently as the middle walk in St Paul's. *a* **1649** Drumm. of Hawth. *Conv. B. J. & W. D.* Wks. (1711) 226 They can hardly be compared together, trading diverse paths.

†**2.** *intr.* To tread, step, walk, go in a course.

**1591** Sylvester *Du Bartas* i. i. 473 This flowry Mansion where Mankind doth trade. **1618** in Foster *Eng. Factories India* (1906) I. 6 To trad by two at once. **1632** Lithgow *Trav.* x. 506 These once happy Iles, which long agoe my feet traded ouer. **1642** Rogers *Naaman* 503 Beware of..self-willednesse in Gods way, but humbly trade with him in it. **1651** Hobbes *Leviath.* II. xxiv. 127 By the labour of trading from one place to another.

† **3.** *trans.* To follow (a course) habitually; to practise; also, to use (something) regularly. *Obs.*

*a* **1562** G. Cavendish *Poems*, etc. (1825) II. 69 You, yong men all, That rageth in youthe and tradyth the courtly lyfe. **1563** Foxe *A. & M.* 851 That no man should speake of the sacramente, but with such wordes, as scripture doth trade, and beare. *c* **1570** in *Redforde's Play Wit & Sc.*, etc. (1848) 103 To those that lerne and trade vertue. **1579–80** North *Plutarch* (1676) 66 Being yet a young man, he devised to trade Merchandize. *a* **1631** Donne *Aristeas* (1633) 3 The Greeke Language which then was the most traded and vulgar through the whole Universe.

† **4.** To familiarize with the use, practice, or knowledge of something; to accustom or habituate *to* or *to do* something; to train (*up*) *in* or *with* some practice, etc.; to school, exercise. *Obs.*

**1553** Becon *Reliques of Rome* (1563) 23 b, Learned scholemaisters to trade vp the Christen youthe in good letters and liberall artes. **1563** B. Googe *Eglogs*, etc. (Arb.) 79 Trade thou thy selfe, in seruyng hym aboue. **1570** Levins *Manip.* 8/36 To Trade, *tradere, consuefacere.* **1575** *Recorde's Gr. Artes* Pref. A v, This man..dyd trade them to all suche thinges, as eyther were profitable or honest. **1577** Breton *Toyes Idle Head* (Grosart) 51/1 Desirous..to see Them both in learning traded up. **1603** H. Crosse *Vertues Commw.* (1878) 51 Being once taught to loath Vice, and traded in wel doing, from the cradle. **1652** Gaule *Magastrom.* 374 He had committed his sonne to a..sorcerer, to be brought up or traded in such arts as were interdicted by the laws.

† **5.** *intr.* **a.** To have dealings; to communicate, converse, have intercourse; to treat, negotiate (*with* a person). *Obs.*

**1553** Bale *Vocacyon* 19 b, From that daye..I traded wᵗ myselfe, by all possybylyte to set fourth that doctrine. **1582** N. Lichefield tr. *Castanheda's Conq. E. Ind.* 156 He would come and speake with him and trade for a peace. **1605** Shaks. *Macb.* III. v. 4 How did you dare To Trade and Trafficke with Macbeth, In Riddles, and Affaires of death. **1638** Brathwait *Barnabees Jrnl.* II. D ij, My Muse with Bacchus so long traded When I walkt, my legs denaid it. **1676** Glanvill *Seasonable Reflect.* 49 Should Satan send the most malignant spirits of Hell openly and professedly to trade for him.

**b.** To occupy oneself, be concerned *in* something; to deal, have dealings *in*. *Obs.* exc. as *fig.* from 6 b.

**1606** Shaks. *Ant. & Cl.* II. v. 2 Musicke, moody foode of vs that trade in Loue. **1618** Bolton *Florus* III. iii. (1636) 173 The Tigurins..trading in robberies, slipt away whither they could. *a* **1661** Fuller *Worthies, Westm.* (1662) II. 241 Hence it was that afterwards he traded so largely in experiments. **1818** Scott *Br. Lamm.* xxx[i], In private, however, she traded more deeply in the occult sciences.

**6.** *intr.* **a.** To resort *to* a place for purposes of trade. Hence, **b.** to engage in or carry on trade (*with* a person, *in* a commodity).

**a. 1570** J. Campion in Hakluyt *Voy.* (1599) II. 115 Englishmen did trade thither...If we should not trade thither, he should lose so much. **1575** in Tolstoy *1st 40 Yrs. Interc. Eng. & Russia* (1875) 161 Our subiectes trawding theither. **1650** Fuller *Pisgah* I. x. § 8 Little of the East-Indies being then known, and less traded to. **1735** Johnson *Lobo's Abyssinia, Voy.* iii. 18 Through this [channel] pass almost all the Vessels that Trade to, or from the Red-Sea. **1796** Morse *Amer. Geog.* I. 524 The people in West Jersey trade to Philadelphia. **1844** H. H. Wilson *Brit. India* I. 565 They traded with profit only to China.

**b. 1570** J. Campion in Hakluyt *Voy.* (1599) II. 115 In those dayes that we traded in those parts. **1608** R. Wiffin, etc. in *Capt. Smith's Virginia* (1624) 70 He found the Salvages more readie to fight then trade. **1660** F. Brooke tr. *Le Blanc's Trav.* 5 They [Dutch merchants] trade there [to Aman] in Cottons. **1718** *Free-thinker* No. 152 ℙ 2, I began to Trade for my self, in the Year Seventeen Hundred and Four. **1769** Cook *Voy. round World* II. ii. (1773) 311 Those who remained in the canoes traded with our people very fairly. **1776** *Trial of Nundocomar* 68/1, I used..to trade in salt. **1818** Scott *Rob Roy* xxxiv, I only trade now as wholesale dealer. **1892** *Photogr. Ann.* II. 671 Robert Cochrane, on behalf of self and partners, Henry Brooks and Edward Gaynor Robinson, trading as Henry Brooks and Co.

**c.** With sinister implication: To drive a trade *in* († *with*) something which should not be bought or sold; to traffic *in*.

**1663** Bp. Patrick *Parab. Pilgr.* xxi. (1687) 221 That cursed principle I named before, of trading with kindnesses, and putting them out to Use. **1737** *Gentl. Mag.* Mar. 155/2 The Clergy are continually trading in Benefices, wanting to change a worse for a better. **1843** Lytton *Last Bar.* I. ii, Tradest thou, too, for kisses? **1849** Macaulay *Hist. Eng.* v. I. 653 The chief justice was fast accumulating a fortune out of the plunder of a higher class of Whigs. He traded largely in pardons. **1853** Maurice *Proph. & Kings* viii. 133 Trading in religious arts and fears. **1878** Villari *Machiavelli* (1898) II. viii. 298 These men traded in war.

**d.** *To trade on* or *upon*: to make use of for one's own ends; to profit by; to take advantage of.

**1884** *Spectator* 4 Oct. 1289/2 All parties in the State repeat, demonstrate, and trade on that unanimity. **1885** Clodd *Myths & Dr.* I. v. 93 They..still trade on the fears and fancies of their fellows. **1907** *Verney Mem.* II. 233 Tom traded on his younger brother's fair fame.

† **7.** *trans.* To frequent for purposes of trade; to trade with (a country, etc.). *Obs.*

**1585** [see Traded 3]. *c* **1591** in *Lett. Lit. Men* (Camden) 77 The Companie of Merchauntes tradinge Muskovia havinge bene..preiudiced by the errors. **1598** Hakluyt *Voy.* I. 458 At the humble sute of the English merchants trading those countreys. **1638** Sir T. Herbert *Trav.* (ed. 2) 305 Since the Portugalls traded Indya they have shaven their heads. **1707** [see Traded 3].

† **8.** To carry in the way of trade; *to trade outward*, to export for trade purposes. *Obs. rare*⁻¹.

**1638** Sir R. Cotton *Abstr. Rec. Tower* 24 To permit all men bringing in Bullion to Trade outward the value thereof in domesticke Commodities at an abated Custome.

**9.** † To employ (money) in trade (*obs. rare*); to make (anything) the subject of trade, to trade in; to acquire or dispose of (also *to trade off*) by barter (*U.S.*); to buy and sell, to barter, to exchange.

*a* **1628** F. Grevil *Hum. Learn.* cxxvii, Changing, corrupting, trading hope and feare Instead of Vertues. **1660** T. Watson in Spurgeon *Treas. David* Ps. l. 22 The nonimprovement of talents...He had not spent it, only not trading it is sentenced. **1806** T. Ashe *Trav. Amer.* (1808) I. vi. 112 The words *buy* and *sell* are nearly unknown [in Erie, Pennsylvania]; in business nothing is heard but the word *trade.* **1830** Galt *Lawrie T.* II. i, I ain't a-going to trade her. **1834** Major J. Downing *Life & Lett.* (Boston, 1835) 39 To see what chance I could find to trade off my ax-handles. **1852** Mrs. Stowe *Uncle Tom's C.* xii, Trading negroes from Africa, dear reader, is so horrid!..But trading them from Kentucky—that's quite another thing! **1863** W. C. Baldwin *Afr. Hunting* vi. 167 Traded half a dozen large leather sacks from the Maccateese for beads, very cheap; they..are beautifully braided and sewn. **1904** M. Hewlett *Queen's Quair* I. vi, The peasant women, and girls also, do trade their legs by standing in the lagoon and gathering the leeches that fasten upon them to suck blood.

**Trade**, obs. pa. t. of Tread *v.*

**Trade bag, -board**, etc.: see Trade *sb.* 14–15.

**Tra·decraft.** [f. Trade *sb.* + Craft *sb.* in various senses.] † **a.** A trade-guild. **b.** Skill or art in connexion with a trade or calling. **c.** The craft or art of trading or dealing.

**1810** Combe *Picturesque* xxv. (1865) 370 And this same Hall their trade-craft found To be a sort of neutral ground. **1866** *Macm. Mag.* Oct. 432 There is tradecraft in literature as well as in painting. **1899** R. Whiteing *5 John St.* xxvi. 258 It is a lesson in tradecraft..to see how the girl holds her own with the dealers.

**Traded** (trēⁱ·dėd), *ppl. a.* and *a.* [f. Trade *v.* and *sb.* + -ed.]

**I.** † **1.** Of a road: Much used or trodden; often traversed; frequented; also *gen.* habitually used.

**1570–6** Lambarde *Peramb. Kent* (1826) 6 A populous citie, and a well traded highway. **1591** in Hakluyt *Voy.* (1600) III. 488 Heere be many Tygers..they vse the traded wayes. *a* **1631** [see Trade *v.* 3].

† **2.** Versed, skilled, practised; experienced; conversant, familiar. *Obs.*

**1548** Gest *Pr. Masse* in Dugdale *Life* (1840) App. 94 A great clerke and moch traded in auncient wryters. **1589** Nashe *Pref. Greene's Menaphon* (Arb.) 11 Sir Iohn Cheeke, a man of men, supernaturally traded in al tongues. **1606** Shaks. *Tr. & Cr.* II. ii. 64 Mine eyes and eares, Two traded Pylots 'twixt the dangerous shores Of Will, and Iudgement. **1654** H. L'Estrange *Chas. I* (1655) 17 A gentleman peculiarly qualifyed for and long traded in Sea exploits.

† **3.** Of a place: Frequented or resorted to for the purpose of trading. (Usu. with *well*, etc.) *Obs.*

**1585** T. Washington tr. *Nicholay's Voy.* IV. vii. 118 b, [The] cities of great Persia, wel traded with merchandize. **1610** Holland *Camden's Brit.* I. 450 A proper and fine burrough it is, well traded and pleasantly seated. **1652–62** Heylin *Cosmogr.* II. (1682) 94 Hannover,..well built, very strongly fortified, and not meanly traded. **1656** J. Chaloner in D. King *Vale Royall* IV. 30 It [the Isle of Man] is traded with 4. Market-Towns, Castle-Town, Douglas, Peel-Town, and Ramsey. **1707** Funnell *Voy.* (1729) 77 The biggest and best traded city in all America.

**II. 4.** Having a trade (of such a kind).

**1631** T. Powell *Tom All Trades* (1876) 170 The favour of great traded Merchants. *a* **1656** Hales *Gold. Rem.* I. (1673) 67 To see another man meanly clad, meanly housed, meanly traded.

**Trade dinner, dollar**, etc.: see Trade *sb.* 15.

† **Tra·de-fa·llen**, *a. Obs.* Fallen or broken in trade, bankrupt.

**1596** Shaks. *1 Hen. IV*, IV. ii. 32 Reuolted Tapsters and Ostlers Trade-falne. **1631** Heywood *1st Pt. Fair Maid of W.* I. i, Her father Sold hydes in Somersetshire, and being trade-fallne, Sent her to service. *a* **1632** T. Taylor *God's Judgem.* vii. (1642) 111 Many young Shop-keepers..through Drinking..have suddenly proved Trade-falne.

**Tradeful** (trēⁱ·dfŭl), *a.* [f. Trade *sb.* + -ful.] Full of trade; fully occupied or engaged in trading; † full of traffic; also *transf.* indicating busy trade.

**1594** Spenser *Amoretti* xv, Ye tradefull Merchants, that, with weary toyle, Do seeke most pretious things to make your gain. **1598** Sylvester *Du Bartas* II. i. IV. *Handie-Crafts* 23 Lo, how our Merchant-vessels to and fro Freely about our tradefull waters go. **1745** Warton *Pleas. Melanch.* 272 Through the naked street, Once haunt of tradeful merchants, springs the grass. **1845** Stocqueler *Handbk. Brit. India* (1854) 112 Shops and offices are shut up, or their tradeful hum and bustle all but stagnated.

**Trade-guild** to **-language**: see Trade 14, 15.

**Tradeless** (trēⁱ·dlės), *a.* [f. Trade *sb.* + -less.]

**1.** Without a trade; unskilled in any trade.

**1729** Young *Imperium Pelagi* v. xxi, O'er generous Glebe, o'er golden Mines Her beggar'd, famish'd, Tradeless Native roves. **1910** *Blackw. Mag.* Mar. 408/2 The semi-educated and tradeless worker.

**2.** Without or destitute of trade or commerce.

**1840** *Tait's Mag.* VII. 310 The Scotch nobility, in our tradeless days, were not sunk quite so low as the Italian nobility at present. **1897** Mary Kingsley *W. Africa* 371 The delta region is tremendously interesting..; but it is tradeless. **1900** H. G. Graham *Soc. Life Scotl. in 18th C.* VII. i. (1901) 233 Consigned to perpetual poverty in some tradeless village.

**Trade-mark** (trēⁱ·dmāɹk), *sb.* [f. Trade *sb.* + Mark *sb.*¹] A mark (now, one secured by legal registration) used by a manufacturer or trader to distinguish his goods from similar wares of other firms; usually a distinctive device or figure, a fancy name or trade name, or the name of an individual or firm, marked or impressed on the article or upon the package, etc., in or with which it is sold.

[**1571** *Letters Patent to R. Matthews* (in Edmunds *Patent Law* (1897) 885), To make the said haftes called Turky haftes for knyves, and for his marke to haue vpon the blade and hafte of the same knyfes..a halfe Moone.] **1838** Mylne & Craig *Reports of Cases* III. 338 The Court will grant a perpetual injunction against the use, by one tradesman, of the trade marks of another. **1862** *Act* 25 & 26 *Vict.* c. 88 § 1 The Expression 'Trade Mark' shall include any..Name, Signature, Word, Letter, Device [etc.]..lawfully used by any Person to denote any Chattel, or (in Scotland) any Article of Trade [etc.]..to be an Article or Thing of the Manufacture..of such Person, or to be an Article or Thing of any peculiar or particular Description made or sold by such Person. **1880** *Print. Trades Jrnl.* XXXI. 26 The owl is the trade-mark of the firm.

**b.** *fig.* A distinctive mark or token.

**1873** Browning *Red Cott. Nt.-Cap* 947 Trade-mark that stamps each word and deed. **1889** Doyle *Micah Clarke* 311 The trade mark upon your forehead is especially hard to overlook. **1898** Bodley *France* II. IV. vi. 406 Opportunists..utilised his name as the trade-mark of their parliamentary group.

**c.** *attrib.*, as *trade-mark name, registration.*

**1901** *Daily Chron.* 2 Dec. 7/1 A belated perambulator..with the trade-mark name of 'The Prince of Wales'. **1909** *Chem. & Druggist* 20 Feb. 315/2 Invented words should be protected by trade-mark registration; by themselves they cannot be copyrighted.

Hence **Tra·de-ma:rk** *v., trans.* to affix or imprint a trade-mark upon; **Tra·de-marking** *vbl. sb.*

**1904** D. Sladen *Lovers Japan* x, Bottled beer (made in Japan..and trade-marked with a big dragon). **1906** *Westm. Gaz.* 16 Mar. 5/2 The Bill..provided for the trade-marking of all imported beers.

**Trade mart, name**, etc.: see Trade *sb.* 14–15.

**Tradent** (trēⁱ·dĕnt). *Rom. Law. rare.* [ad. L. *trādens, trādent-*, pr. pple. of *trādĕre* to hand over, deliver.] The person who delivers or hands over any property to another.

**1880** Muirhead *Gaius* 580 The conditions upon which it carried the property were that the tradent was owner.

† **Trade·ntine**, *a. Obs. nonce-wd.* [f. *tra-* = Trans- + L. *dent-em* tooth + -ine.] Lying beyond or outside the teeth. **1653** [see Cidentine].

**Trader** (trēⁱ·dəɹ). [f. Trade *v.* + -er¹.]

**1.** One whose business is trade or commerce, or who is engaged in trading; a dealer or trafficker.

**1585** T. Washington tr. *Nicholay's Voy.* IV. xxv. 140 b, Great traders, with merchandise & ready monie. **1600** E. Blount tr. *Conestaggio* 55 The traders and handie-craftsmen who had not their kinsemen there. **1779–81** Johnson *L. P., Milton* Wks. II. 133 Neither traders, nor often gentlemen, thought themselves disgraced by ignorance. **1837** W. Irving *Capt. Bonneville* II. xx. 40 One of those general gatherings of traders, trappers, and Indians. **1848** J. Williams *Law Pers. Prop.* II. iv. 108 No farmer, grazier, common labourer, or workman for hire,..shall be deemed as such a trader liable to become bankrupt. **1886** L. O. Pike *Year Bks.* 13 & 14 *Edw. III* (Rolls) Introd. 83 Applicable to the servants of traders as well as to the servants of knights.

† **b.** A prostitute. *Obs. slang.*

**1682** Radcliffe *Poems* 45 Burdellos, T'encourage She-Traders and lusty young Fellows. **1693** *Humours Town* 39, I mean not Common Women, that live by Fornication, publick Traders. **1760** Foote *Minor* I. Wks. 1799 I. 247 Tip him an old trader, and give her to the knight.

**c.** A vessel engaged in trading; a trading ship.

**1712** *Lond. Gaz.* No. 5017/2 Ten sail of Irish Traders. **1862** *Catal. Internat. Exhib.* II. XII. 9 A trader for narrow rivers, with new arrangement of rudder. **1887** Mrs. Daly *Digging*, etc. *S. Australia* 296 The crews in the pearling schooners and small traders are very short-handed.

† **d.** A tradesman's token (Token *sb.* 10). *Obs.*

**1775** R. Twiss *Tour Irel.* (1776) 82 The want of small change [in 1727] was so great, that several persons were obliged to make copper and silver tokens, called *Traders*, which they passed as promissory notes among their workmen, customers, and neighbours.

† **2.** One who is occupied or concerned *in* something; a dealer. *Obs.*

**1668** Hale *Pref. Rolle's Abridgm.* a j b, The constant..course..of these great Traders in Learning, to bring in their several acquests therein..into a common Stock. **1673** [R. Leigh] *Transp. Reh.* 144 The nonconformists were great traders in Scripture. **1800** Coleridge *Piccolom.* I. x, That ancient trader In contraband negociations.

**Trade-road** to **-school**: see Trade *sb.* 14–15.

**Trades-** in *comb.*: see Trade *sb.* 15 b.

‖ **Tradescantia** (trædėskæ·ntiă). *Bot.* [mod. L. (Ruppius 1718), f. the name of John Tradescant (the elder), a 17th c. naturalist + -ia¹.] An American genus of perennial herbs (N.O. *Commelynaceæ*) characterized by three-petalled blue, white, pink, or purple ephemeral flowers having six stamens clothed with jointed hairs; spiderwort.

[**1629** Parkinson *Paradisus* 152 Phalangium Ephemerum virginianum Joannis Tradescant...Tradescant his spiderwort.] **1718** Ruppius *Flora Jenensis* 55 Tradescantia.] **1766** Lee *Introd. Bot.* App. (1788) 350/2 Spider-wort, Virginian, *Tradescantia.* **1866** *Treas. Bot.* 317 The filaments of the *Tradescantias* have jointed hairs, in which a granular movement is seen under the microscope.

**Tradesfolk** (trēⁱ·dzfouk). [f. as next + Folk.] People in trade; tradespeople: **a.** Artisans; **b.** Shopkeepers.

**1760–72** H. Brooke *Fool of Qual.* (1809) III. 21 This is holiday in the afternoon among us trades-folk. **1885** W. H. White *M. Rutherford's Deliv.* iii, The wine-merchant..by no means associating with the tradesfolk who displayed their goods in the windows. **1890** Pollard *Eng. Miracle Plays* Introd. 11 Philosophers, saints, mimes, jugglers, monks, nuns, bishops and tradesfolk have all to play their part.

**Tradesman** (trēⁱ·dzmæ̆n). Pl. **-men.** [f. *trade's*, gen. case of Trade + Man *sb.*[1]]

**1.** One who is skilled in and follows one of the industrial arts; an artificer, an artisan, a craftsman. Now *Sc.*, *local* (esp. *rural*) *English*, and *Colonial*.

**1597** Drayton *Heroical Epistles, Edward IV to Shores Wife* 117 The busie lawyer wrangling in his pleas,..The toyling trades-man, and the sweating Clowne. ? *a* **1600** *Robin Hood & Tanner* xxiii, 'What tradesman art thou?' said jolly Robin. **1625** Coke in *Commons Debates* (Camden) 131 The Master of the Ordinance was auntiently a tradesman vntill 37 Henry 8, and then it was conferd on a nobleman. **1657** in *Verney Mem.* (1907) II. 95 [His wish to be bound] apprintice unto some very good traydesman. **1657** R. Ligon *Barbadoes* (1673) 110 If they be Tradesmen, as, Carpenters, Joyners, Masons, Smiths. **1738** Swift *Pol. Conversat.* 27 If Things did not break or wear out, how would Tradesmen live? **1825** Jamieson, *Tradesman*, a name [in Scotland] restricted to a handicraftsman; all who keep shops being..called Merchants. *c* **1880** *Let. to Editor*, *Tradesman* in Australia does not mean a shopkeeper, but the man who works at a trade, i. e. the artisan. **1899** *Times* 25 Jan. 10 At the end of May a deputation of provincial tradesmen (in the Scotch sense) visited London...The carpenters and joiners came to terms with the employers.

**2.** One who is engaged in trade or the sale of commodities; *esp.* a shopkeeper.

**1601** Dent *Pathw. Heaven* 71 Couetousnesse..baneth our Gentlemen, it murthereth our Trades-men, it bewitcheth our Merchants. **1622** Malynes *Anc. Law. Merch.* 92 A Trades-mans shop, and a Merchants ware-house is taken to be publicke and open at the appointed times. **1655** E. Terry *Voy. E. Ind.* xxvi. 411 There are very many private men..who are Merchants, or Tradesmen that are very rich. **1695** Blackmore *Pr. Arth.* iv. 417 The Tradesman quits his Shop. **1717** Lady M. W. Montagu *Let. to Abbé Conti* 17 May, Most of the rich Tradesmen were Jews. **1766** Fordyce *Serm. Yng. Wom.* (1767) I. vii. 294 The daughters of plain tradesmen and honest mechanics. **1885** Miss Braddon *Wyllard's Weird* I. i. 30 This would give time for the tradesmen to get away from their shops. **1906** *Daily Chron.* 10 Feb. 4/7 'Tradesman', which in the north is used to denote a workman who has learned a trade, while in the south it is made to apply to a man who runs a business.

Hence **Tra·desmanship,** the quality or calling of a tradesman; *transf.* tradesmen collectively. Also *attrib.*

**1817** Bentham *Parl. Reform* (1818) 52 Say whether Tradesmanship honesty..is not worth all such other honesties put together. **1859** *Sat. Rev.* 10 Dec. 702/1 Tradesmanship in all its proprieties may stand aghast at the revelations of the inner life of a Strand shopkeeper's family.

**Tra·desmanlike,** *a.* [f. prec. + -like.] Like, or like that of, a tradesman; characteristic of a tradesman; in quot. 1862, workmanlike, skilful.

**1790** *Bystander* 344 A man of tradesmanlike appearance came and knocked at the door. **1862** Thornbury *Turner* I. 275 Crafty tradesmanlike alterations. **1870** Gladstone *Glean.* IV. v. 254 With a tradesmanlike devotion to her peaceful industry.

**Tra·despeople.** [f. *trade's*, gen. of Trade + People.] People engaged in trade; tradesmen, and their families and employees; shopkeepers.

**1728** Vanbrugh & Cib. *Prov. Husb.* v. ii, Those Tradespeople are the troublesomest Creatures! no Words will satisfy them! **1729** Fenton in *Waller's Wks.*, *Observ.* 60/2 No trades-people would trust her for any thing. *a* **1862** Buckle *Misc. Wks.* (1872) I. 579 The middle class of tradespeople were ignorant and poor.

**Tra·deswo:man.** Pl. **-women.** [f. as prec. + Woman.] A woman engaged in trade, or in a particular trade or calling; in quots. 1707, 1778, the wife of a tradesman.

**1707** *Reflex. upon Ridicule* ii. 212 New-vamped Tradeswomen, whose Dress and Train, and Furniture and Table, create Envy. **1778** Johnson 13 May, in *Boswell*, Tradeswomen (I mean the wives of tradesmen) in the city. **1889** *Sat. Rev.* 23 Feb. 218/1 The gentle lady must be put off, and the shrewd and thrifty tradeswoman must be put on.

**Trade-u·nion, trades-u·nion.** [f. Trade or pl. *trades* + Union.] An association of the workers in any trade or in allied trades for the protection and furtherance of their interests in regard to wages, hours, and conditions of labour, and for the provision, from their common funds, of pecuniary assistance to the members during strikes, sickness, unemployment, old age, etc.

**1835** Wordsw. *Postscript* iii. Poet. Wks. (1910) 966 It has no direct bearing upon clubs..nor upon political or trade-unions. **1842** Cobden in Morley *Life* xii. (1902) 43/2 Nothing can be got by fraternising with trade unions. They are founded upon principles of brutal tyranny and monopoly. **1887** Lowell *Democr.* 17 But the trade-unions are now debating instead of conspiring. **1896** L. Abbott *Chr. & Soc. Probl.* x. 272 The phrase 'trade union' came into existence about the year 1830 and the organization itself came into existence about the same time. **1906** *Westm. Gaz.* 6 Mar. 2/2 A trade union is a quasi-political association, rather than an association for carrying on business.

**1831** *Times* 18 Jan. 4/1 There is no doubt that these boys [spinners' apprentices at Haslingden] are kept in countenance by the 'Trades' Union'. **1834** Arnold *Let. to Chev. Bunsen* 29 Sept., You have heard..of the Trades' Unions, a fearful engine of mischief, ready to riot or to assassinate. **1868** Rogers *Pol. Econ.* ix. (1876) 88 The purpose of a trades-union is to keep up the price of labour, and if possible to enhance it. **1878** Jevons *Prim. Pol. Econ.* 61 A trades-union is a society of men belonging to any one kind of trade, who agree to act together as they are directed by their elected council, and who subscribe money to pay the expenses.

Hence **Trade-, trades-u·nionism,** the system, principles, or practice of trade-unions; **Trade-, trades-u·nionist,** a member of a trade-union; also *attrib.*

**1875** *N. Amer. Rev.* CXX. 215 The theory and possibilities of *trades-unionism. **1884** *Pall Mall G.* 10 Sept. 8/2 Although he was both a politician and a trade unionist, he could faithfully say trade unionism had always had his first care and attention. **1888** *Voice* (N.Y.) 14 Nov., China, it seems, is the cradle of tradesunionism, and boycotts are numerous. **1863** Fawcett *Pol. Econ.* ii. ix. (1876) 248 A social terrorism, very analogous to that by which *Trades-Unionists so frequently maintain their organizations. **1898** *Westm. Gaz.* 12 Jan. 3/2 Even another self-denying ordinance must be asked of the trade-unionist parent in this good cause.

**Trade-way,** etc.: see Trade *sb.* 14, 15.

**Tra·de-wind.** [f. Trade *sb.* + Wind *sb.* App. originating in the phrase *to blow trade*: see Trade *sb.* 3 d. Afterwards often shortened in nautical use to *trade*, in pl. 'the trades': see Trade *sb.* 13.

The name had in its origin nothing to do with *trade* in the sense 'commerce', or 'passage for the purpose of trading', though the importance of those winds to navigation led 18th c. etymologists (and perhaps even navigators) so to understand the term.]

†**1.** Any wind that 'blows trade', i.e. in a constant course or way; a wind that blows steadily in the same direction. *Obs.* exc. as in 3.

Originally applied to any wind having this character. But as it became gradually known that the only winds of which this is approximately true were the Indian monsoons, and the winds now so called, on each side of the equator in the Atlantic and Pacific Oceans, the name became restricted to these, and at length to the latter (senses 2 and 3). Also *fig.*

**1663** Cowley *To Drake's Ship* iv, The breath of Fame, like an auspicious Gale (The great Trade-wind which ne'er does fail), Shall drive thee round the World. **1666** Dryden *Ann. Mirab.* ccciv, But now, the Cape once doubled, fear no more; A constant trade-wind will securely blow And gently lay us on the spicy shore. *a* **1668** Davenant *Poems* Wks. (1673) 330 A Pilot, sure of faire Trade-Windes, The Helme in all the Voyage never hands. **1706** Phillips (ed. Kersey), *Trade-Wind*, a Wind that blows regularly at Sea, at certain Seasons of the Year, and serves to promote Trading Voyages. **1726** Shelvocke *Voy. round World* 385 Then came on the constant, or what may be call'd the trade wind on this [Pacific] coast [of America] blowing from the W.N.W, except in the night, that it comes about more Northerly. **1735** G. Hadley in *Phil. Trans.* XXXIX. 61 The same Principle..extends to the Production of the West Trade-Winds without the Tropicks. **1777** Colman in Sheridan *Sch. Scand.* Epil. 2, I, who was late so volatile and gay, Like a tradewind must now blow all one way. **1807** Crabbe *Parish Reg.* (1829) 17 But like a trade-wind is the ancient dame, Mild to your wish, and every day the same.

†**2.** Applied to the seasonal winds of the Indian Ocean; = Monsoon 1, 2. *Obs.*

The winter monsoon, from October to April, coincides in direction with the trade-wind of the North Atlantic; the summer monsoon blows in the opposite direction.

[**1634** Sir T. Herbert *Trav.* 8 Euery houre expecting these Anniuersarie winds, called by the Sea-men and Portugals, *Monzoons*; the property of which wind is to blow constantly one way, sixe moneths, and the other way, the other halfe yeare.] **1650** Fuller *Pisgah* i. vi. § 3 Rain,..like Trade-winds on some seas, came at set seasons. **1687** A. Lovell tr. *Thevenot's Trav.* iii. 1 That Season wherein there is a constant Trade-Wind upon that Sea, begins commonly at the end of October. **1720** De Foe *Capt. Singleton* (1906) 218 When we came in among the Spice Islands..we had a share of the monsoons, or trade-winds. **1794** Sullivan *View Nat.* I. 206 The constant or stated wind usually called the trade wind; and in some parts of the world, the monsoon. **1840** Thirlwall *Greece* VII. liv. 55 Some weeks were still to come before the trade-winds would set in from the north-east, when they would be perfectly favourable for the voyage.

**3.** Now *spec.* The wind that blows constantly towards the equator from about the thirtieth parallels, north and south; its main direction in the northern hemisphere being from the north-east, and in the southern hemisphere from the south-east. Cf. Anti-trade.

The N.E. trade is termed in Hawkins' *Voy. Florida* *c* 1565 (Hakl. Soc.) 25, 46, 'the ordinary breeze' (Breeze *sb.*[2] 1), the S.E. trade is termed by Linschoten 1583 *general windt*, 'the general wind', after Pg. *vento geral.*

[**1699** Dampier *Voy.* II. iii. 1 Trade-Winds are such as do blow constantly from one Point, or Quarter of the Compass, and the Region of the World most peculiar to them is from about 30 d. North to 30 d. South of the Equator.] **1712** E. Cooke *Voy. S. Sea* 446 Getting into the Trade-Winds, our Course was afterwards uniform. **1748** *Anson's Voy.* ii. ix. 224 We expected, upon the encreasing our offing from Quibo, to fall in with the regular trade-wind. **1821** R. Turner *Arts & Sc.* (ed. 18) 17 The trade-winds blow naturally from the N.E. on the north, and from the S.E. on the south of the line, throughout the whole year. **1835** Mrs. Somerville *Connex. Phys. Sc.* xv. (ed. 2) 147 There are many proofs of the existence of the counter currents above the trade winds. **1867** Denison *Astron. without Math.* 39 The heat of the torrid zone and its velocity of rotation produce the trade winds which blow constantly in the same directions in the same latitudes on the great oceans.

**b.** *attrib.*, as *trade-wind region*; **trade-wind cloud,** the trade cumulus (Trade *sb.* 15).

**1860** Maury *Phys. Geog. Sea* (Low) iv. § 255 The hottest place within the trade-wind regions is not at the equator. **1902** *Daily Chron.* 21 Aug. 7/1 As the darkness deepened a dull red reflection was seen in the trade-wind cloud which covered the mountain summit.

**Tradey,** variant of Trady.

†**Tra·diment.** *Obs. rare.* [ad. med.L. *trādimentum* (1190 in Du Cange), f. L. *trādĕre* to hand over, deliver; or a. OF. *trade-*, *tradiment* 'treason' (Godef.).] Treachery, perfidy, treason.

**1535** *St. Papers Hen. VIII*, II. 264 The Tholes entred by tradyment into Powers Courte. **1536** *Ibid.* 362 Beyng evicted, and recovered out of our possession by tradyment. **1561** T. Hoby tr. *Castiglione's Courtyer* ii. (1577) N j b, If it be true that it is such an abhominable profit and trespace to vse tradiment against a mans very enimy.

**Trading** (trēⁱ·diŋ), *vbl. sb.* [f. Trade *v.* + -ing[1].] The action of the verb Trade in various senses; *esp.* the carrying on of trade; buying and selling; commerce, trade, traffic.

**1590** [see b]. **1615** in *Buccleuch MSS.* (Hist. MSS. Comm.) I. 168 Either of us might assist each other in free Trading in those parts. **1645** Milton *Tetrach.* Wks. 1851 IV. 220 So to serve the commodity of insatiable trading, usury shall be permitted. **1654** *Nicholas Papers* (Camden) II. 82 Hee will stopp all tredding by sea that way. **1799** in Picton *L'pool Munic. Rec.* (1886) II. 219 To prohibit the trading for slaves. **1885** *Athenæum* 5 Sept. 302/1 Successful trading was not at that date quite so important.

**b.** *attrib.* and *Comb.*; in sense 'of, pertaining to, or connected with trade', as *trading course, line, origin*; 'intended for trade or barter', as *trading articles, cloth, goods*; 'frequented for, employed in, made or done for trading', as *trading centre, craft, journey, path, port, post* (Post *sb.*[3] 2 c), *ship, smack, station, tax, vessel, voyage*; †**trading-house,** a building in which barter was carried on in the savage parts of North America; **trading-place,** † (*a*) a place of resort or passage; (*b*) a place frequented for trade.

**1904** *Archæologia Æliana* XXV. ii. 255 *note*, The ports and *trading-centres of the Mediterranean. **1672** Sir W. Talbot *Discov. J. Lederer* 26 Your best Truck is a sort of course *Trading Cloth, of which a yard and a half makes a Matchcoat. **1676** in I. Mather *K. Philip's War* (1862) 99 That the Indian *Trading-houses..be suppressed. **1775** Adair *Amer. Ind.* 395 The ford of the old *trading path, where the enemy now and then passed the river. **1590** Greene *Never too Late* O iv, Flora did checker all her *trading place. **1719** De Foe *Crusoe* (1840) II. xii. 251 To put into the first *trading port. **1837** W. Irving *Capt. Bonneville* III. xxxiv. 205 Fort Wallah-Wallah is a *trading post of the Hudson's Bay Company. **1809** R. Langford *Introd. Trade* 111 The voyage may be..to several ports, which is called a **trading voyage.*

**Tra·ding,** *ppl. a.* [f. as prec. + -ing[2].] That trades, in various senses of the verb; *esp.* engaged in trade, commercial.

**1690** Child *Disc. Trade* (1698) 2 They have in their greatest councils of state and war, trading-merchants that have lived abroad in most parts of the world. **1697** Dryden *Virg. Georg.* iv. 20 These rob the trading citizens [bees]. **1711** Addison *Spect.* No. 69 ⁋ 1 Factors in the Trading World are what Ambassadors are in the Politick World. **1790** Burke *Fr. Rev.* 263 A great trading or manufacturing town. **1874** Green *Short Hist.* vi. § 3. 282 The trading and industrial classes.

*Comb.* **1727** [Dorrington] *Philip Quarll* Pref., Busy Worlds and Trading-Peopled Towns.

†**b.** That trades in or makes a trade of something (e.g. a public office or position). *Obs.*

**1787** Sir J. Hawkins *Johnson* 214 The duke of Newcastle ..gave him [Fielding] a nominal qualification of 100 l. a year, and set him up as a trading-justice, in which disreputable station he died. **1796** *Grose's Dict. Vulg. T.* (ed. 3), *Trading Justices*, Broken mechanics, discharged footmen, and other low fellows, smuggled into the commission of the peace, who subsist by fomenting disputes, granting warrants, and otherwise retailing justice. **1812** *Examiner* 30 Nov. 767/1 The Court treated the defendant as a systematic and trading libeller. **1839** Ld. Brougham *Statesm. Geo. III*, *Canning* 289 The common herd of trading politicians.

†**Tra·dit,** *v. Obs. rare*$^{-1}$. [f. L. *trādit-*, ppl. stem of *trādĕre* to hand over, deliver, f. *trans* across, over + *dare* to give. (Cf. *credit* f. L. *crēdit-*.)] *trans.* To deliver, to communicate.

**1657** Tomlinson *Renou's Disp.* 530 The most usual preparation, is after the manner we have tradited.

†**Tra·ditative,** *a. Obs. rare.* prob. an error for Traditive 1.

**1657–83** Evelyn *Hist. Relig.* (1850) I. 165 They fancy it very difficult to conceive how this deadly spot [of sin] should adhere so pertinaciously without some traditative emanation, seeing the body does not defile the Soul.

**Tradition** (trădi·ʃən), *sb.* Also 4–6 **-icion.** [a. OF. *tradicion*, *-iccion* (1292 in Godef.), in 15th c. *tradition*, = Pr. *tradition*, Sp. *tradicion*, It. *tradizione*, ad. L. *trāditio*, *-ōnem* 'delivery, surrender, handing down, a saying handed down, instruction or doctrine delivered', as in *traditio evangelica*, *catholica traditio* (Tertullian).]

**1.** The action of handing over (something material) to another; delivery, transfer. (Chiefly in *Law.*)

**1540** in R. G. Marsden *Sel. Pl. Crt. Adm.* (1894) I. 99 The byer..may entre and take possession of the said shipe goods..withowte any further tradicion or delyvery. **1601** W. Watson *Sparing Discov.* 13 In that a Priest is made by tradition of the Chalice, Patten, and Host into his hands. **1658** Bramhall *Consecr. Bps.* xi. 225 Then followeth.. lastly the tradition of the Bible into his hands. **1766** Blackstone *Comm.* II. xx. 307 A deed takes effect only from this tradition or delivery. **1773** Erskine *Inst. Law Scotl.* II. i. § 18 Tradition, which may be defined, the delivery of the possession of a subject by the proprietor, with an intention to transfer the property of it to the receiver. **1774** Bp. Hallifax *Anal. Rom. Law* (1795) 25 Justinian abolished the distinction, and gave to Tradition, or simple delivery, all the effects of the ancient Mancipation. **1884** *Cath. Dict.* (ed. 2) 626 Handing to the new priest the paten and chalice—an act commonly called the 'tradition of the instruments'.

†**2.** A giving up, surrender; betrayal. *Obs.*

**1482** *Monk of Evesham* (Arb.) 19 The office and seruice of owr lord ihesu cryste ys tradicion and passion was solenly songe. **1611** W. Sclater *Key* (1629) 103 By tradition or deliuering them vp to the power of Sathan. **1653** Manton *Exp. James* i. 13 Wks. 1871 IV. 92 A judicial tradition and delivering them up to the power of Satan and their own vile affections.

**b.** *spec.* in *Ch. Hist.* Surrender of sacred books in times of persecution: cf. Traditor 2.

**1840** Milman *Hist. Chr.* II. 369 The consecration of a bishop guilty of tradition, was the principal ground on which his election was annulled. *Ibid.* 371 Both denounced their adversaries as guilty of the crime of tradition. **1874** J. H. Blunt *Dict. Sects* (1886) 128/2 The crime of Tradition was a new one [Diocletian era]. [**1908** C. Bigg *Orig. Chr.* xxxvi. (1909) 484 In Gaul the Donatists themselves allowed that the sin of *traditio* had not occurred.]

**3.** Delivery, *esp.* oral delivery, of information or instruction. Now *rare.*

*a* **1500** Medwall *Nature* 60 Arystotell Whyche hath left in bokys of hys tradycyon How euery thyng by heuynly constellacyon Is brought to effecte. **1575** Gascoigne *Making of Verse* in *Steele Gl.*, etc. (Arb.) 33, I couet rather to satisfie you particularly, than to vndertake a generall tradition. **1605** Bacon *Adv. Learn.* II. xvi. § 1 The expressing or transferring our Knowledge to others .. I will tearme by the general name of Tradition or Deliuerie. **1667** Jer. Taylor *Dissuas. Popery* II. I. iii. 102 Tradition is any way of delivering a thing, or word to another; and so every doctrine of Christianity is by Tradition. I have deliver'd unto you, saith S. Paul, that Christ died for our sins. **1868** M. Pattison *Academ. Org.* vii. 327 A national institute for the preservation and tradition of useful knowledge.

†**b.** An ordinance or institution orally delivered.

**1382** Wyclif *Col.* ii. 8 Se ȝe that no man disseyue ȝou by philosofye and veyn fallace..vp the tradicioun of men, vp elementis of this world, and not vp Crist. **1563** Winȝet *Four Scoir Thre Quest.* § 63 Wks. (S.T.S.) I. 115 The Apostill St. Paull commandit in sindry places his traditionis to be keipet. **1565** Stapleton tr. *Staphylus' Apol.* 153 b, They putt out of S. Paule the worde *Traditions*, and put in his place sometime *Ordinaunces* sometime *Institutions*.

**c.** *Tradition of the Creed* (*Ch. Hist.*): oral instruction upon the Creed given to catechumens.

**1888** *Cassell's Encycl. Dict.* s.v., *Tradition of the Creed*,.. the instruction formerly given on certain days to the catechumens upon the Creed at mass. The time and place varied in different Churches. In the Mozarabic Missal it still retains its place before the Epistle on Palm Sunday. At Rome it took place on the Wednesday in Mid-Lent.

**4.** The action of transmitting or 'handing down', or fact of being handed down, from one to another, or from generation to generation; transmission of statements, beliefs, rules, customs, or the like, esp. by word of mouth or by practice without writing. Chiefly in phrase *by tradition.*

**1591** Savile *Tacitus' Hist.* (1604) 53 Old songs delivered to them, by tradition, from their fathers. **1625** N. Carpenter *Geog. Del.* II. xviii. (1635) 282 Some few customes preserued by tradition, not writing. **1626** Ailesbury *Passion Serm.* 3 Punishments which hung over their heads, and, by the tradition of just revenge, upon their children. **1658** Phillips, *Tradition*,..a bequeathing any Doctrine to posterity from age to age. **1725** De Foe *Voy. round World* (1840) 191 Rivetted in their minds by tradition from father to son. **1818** Hallam *Mid. Ages* ix. I. (1819) III. 335 The memory of Greece and Rome would have been feebly preserved by tradition. **1854** Milman *Lat. Chr.* IV. iv. (1864) II. 277 Fragments..tinged with Christian allusion in their later tradition from bard to bard.

**b.** quasi-personified, usually as a speaker. (Cf. Fame *sb.*[1] 1 b, Rumour *sb.* 2 b.)

**1658** Baxter *Saving Faith* 87 Tradition having published it, your labour is to be a great deal the more acceptable for the Authors sake. **1686** Aglionby *Painting Illustr.* i. 37 Paintings..which Tradition affirm'd to be Antienter than the Foundation of Rome. **1797** Ht. Lee *Canterb. T.*, *Old Woman's T.* (1799) I. 333 Tradition tells us of numberless miracles performed here! **1863** Mary Howitt *F. Bremer's Greece* II. xvi. 153 Wolves, so says tradition, first took gold to Delphi.

**5. a.** That which is thus handed down; a statement, belief, or practice transmitted (esp. orally) from generation to generation.

*c* **1380** Wyclif *Wks.* (1880) 392 I-bounden oonly by a posityue lawe or a tradycion þat þai han hem sijlfe made. **1432–50** tr. *Higden* (Rolls) II. 225 Matussale..lyvenge..to the grete floode of Noe, and 1100 longer, after the trewe tradicion. **1599** Shaks. *Hen. V*, v. i. 76 Go, go,..will you mocke at an ancient Tradition began vppon an honourable respect? **1704** Nelson *Fest. & Fasts* xiii. (1739) 159 The.. Traditions published under his Name are rejected..as spurious. **1851** D. Wilson *Preh. Ann.* (1863) II. IV. ii. 234 The traditions associated with these..monuments. **1872** Morley *Voltaire* i. (1886) 4 A collective religious tradition that had lost its virtue. **1878** Simpson *Sch. Shaks.* I. 4 Stucley's life has been surrounded with a complete cloud of traditions.

**b.** More vaguely: A long established and generally accepted custom or method of procedure, having almost the force of a law; an immemorial usage; the body (or any one) of the experiences and usages of any branch or school of art or literature, handed down by predecessors and generally followed. In quot. 1818, an embodiment of an old established custom or institution, a 'relic'.

**1593** Shaks. *Rich. II*, III. ii. 173 Throw away Respect, Tradition, Forme, and Ceremonious dutie. **1818** Lady Morgan *Autobiog.* (1859) 183 The duke is a tradition of the *grands seigneurs* of the courtly times of France, a tradition fast wearing out. **1865** R. W. Dale *Jew. Temp.* ix. (1877) 89 The glorious traditions of their race seemed against them. **1882** Freeman *Amer. Lect.* II. v. 381 The tradition is that a President [of U.S.] may be re-elected once and once only. **1891** *Leeds Mercury* 2 May 6/4 A scheme.. which was contrary to Conservative traditions.

**6.** *spec.* (*Theol.* and *Eccl.*) **a.** Among the Jews, Any one, or the whole, of an unwritten code of regulations, etc. held to have been received from Moses, and handed down orally from generation to generation and embodied in the Mishnah.

*c* **1380** Wyclif *Sel. Wks.* II. 78 But whi breken ȝe Goddis maundement, for ȝoure veyn tradicioun? **1382** — *Matt.* xv. 2 Whi thi disciplis ouerpassen, or breken, the tradiciouns [*gloss* or statutis] of elder men [**1534** Tindale, the tradicions of the elders]? **1585** Abp. Sandys *Serm.* i. 11 Vnder the name of doctrine receiued from Moses by word of mouth, without writing, that is to say tradition, the Scribes and Pharisees were able smoothlie to carie away any thing, til Christ recalled all things to the Lawe. **1613** Purchas *Pilgrimage* (1614) 170 When two Rabbins (saith their Talmud) maintaine contrary opinions, yet must not men contradict them, because both of them hath his Kabala or Tradition for the same. **1877** C. Geikie *Christ* II. xliv. 205 The commands or 'traditions' of the Fathers, handed down from the days of the Great Synagogue, but ascribed with pious exaggeration to the Almighty.

**b.** In the Christian Church, Any one, or the whole, of a body of teachings transmitted orally from generation to generation since early times; held by Roman Catholics to comprise teaching derived from Christ and the apostles, together with that subsequently communicated to the church by the Holy Spirit, and to be of equal authority with Scripture. Also (as in 4) the transmission of such teaching.

**1551** T. Wilson *Logike* (1580) 36 The Churche maie make Lawe, and appointe Tradicions, whatsoeuer thei be. **1562** *Articles of Religion* xxxiv, Whosoever..doth openly break the traditions and ceremonies of the Church which be not repugnant to the word of God. **1667** Milton *P. L.* XII. 512 The truth With superstitions and traditions taint. **1704** Nelson *Fest. & Fasts* v. II. (1739) 501 It being the Tradition of the Church. **1737** Challoner *Cath. Chr. Instr.* (1753) 213 The Sunday, or the Lord's-Day, which we observe by Apostolical Tradition instead of the Sabbath. **1867** Brande & Cox *Dict. Sc.*, etc., *Tradition*, in Theology ..is commonly employed to denote any doctrine or alleged fact, delivered or handed down, and received on the faith that the first to whom it was delivered received it from an authentic source.

**c.** Among Mohammedans, An account of sayings and doings of Mohammed, not contained in the Koran, but transmitted at first orally, and afterwards recorded; esp. those accepted as authoritative by the Sunnites or orthodox Mohammedans, but rejected by the Shiites: = Sunna.

**1718** Ockley *Hist. Saracens* II. 87 The Muslemans (who intitle themselves Sonnites, that is Observers of the Tradition, and Orthodox). **1727–41** Chambers *Cycl.* s. v. *Sonna*, There are also sectaries among the Mahometans, called Shiites, who reject the traditions of the Sonnites. **1860** Gardner *Faiths of World*, *Sonnah*, the Tradition of the Mohammedans, being the authentic record of the sayings and doings of the Prophet...There are six collections of the Sonnite traditions, and four of those of the Schiites.

**7.** *attrib.* and *Comb.*, as *tradition-bound*, *-following*, *-nourished*, *-ridden* adjs.; *tradition-monger*; **Tradition Sunday** (*Ch. Hist.*), a name for Palm Sunday, as the day of 'tradition of the creed' (see 3 c) in some churches.

**1719** J. T. Philipps tr. *Thirty-four Confer.* 5 Believing.. the Fables and Reveries of Tradition-mongers, your Poets and Doctors. **1888** *Cassell's Encycl. Dict.* s.v., *Tradition-Sunday.* **1895** *Westm. Gaz.* 17 May 7/2 To think that the tradition-bound Austria-Hungary, of all countries in Europe, should be the first to call a Pole to the post of Foreign Minister! **1901** *Academy* 26 Jan. 81/1 The prosy formula-ridden, tradition-following, go-by-rule eighteenth century. **1901** *Weekly Regr.* 19 Apr. 485/2 The tradition-nourished intellectual life so distinctive of the Catholic Church. **1910** *Westm. Gaz.* 25 June 2/3 Experiments..for the warning or encouragement of a more crowded and tradition-ridden island.

**Tradi·tion,** *v. rare.* [f. prec. sb.] *trans.* To transmit by tradition; to relate as a tradition.

**1640** Fuller *Joseph's Coat*, 1 *Cor. xi. 23* (1867) 43 Παρέδωκα ὑμῖν...English it as you please, 'I traditioned it unto you'. **1655** — *Ch. Hist.* VI. iii. 318 The following story is ..traditioned with very much credit amongst our English Catholicks. *a* **1661** — *Worthies, Somerset.* (1662) III. 20 This I may call a Charitable Curiosity, if true what is traditioned. **1872** *Daily News* 12 Aug., It is traditioned of Mr. Childers that he has been seen in a pea jacket.

So **Tradi·tioned** (-ʃənd) *a.* (*rare*⁻¹), having traditions of a kind specified by the prefixed word.

**1850** R. Simpson *Mem. Worth* iv. 47 The Crawick, a wild traditioned stream pours its waters into the Nith.

**Traditional** (trădi·ʃənăl), *a.* (*sb.*) [f. Tradition *sb.* + -al: cf. F. *traditionnel*, also med.L. *trāditiōnālis* (840) = *trāditōrius* Traditory.]

**1.** Belonging to, consisting in, or of the nature of tradition; handed down by or derived from tradition.

*a* **1600** Hooker *Eccl. Pol.* VI. v. § 7 In sundry traditional writings set down by their great interpreters and scribes. **1641** Milton *Prel. Episc.* Wks. 1851 III. 78 We esteem his traditionall ware, as lightly as Victor did. **1690** Locke *Hum. Und.* IV. xviii. § 10 There can be no Evidence that any traditional Revelation is of divine Original, in the Words we receive it, and in the Sense we understand it, so clear, and so certain, as those of the Principles of Reason. **1814** Scott *Wav.* lxxii, The traditional records of the respectable and ingenious Mrs. Grant of Laggan. **1911** H. M. R. Murray *Erthe upon Erthe* Introd. 23 The popular traditional version of the poem tended to become modified.

**b.** That is such according to tradition; asserted or related by tradition.

**1856** Stanley *Sinai & Pal.* v. 246 This traditional selection of Gerizim as the scene of the meeting with Melchizedek is further confirmed by all the circumstances of the narrative. **1874** Sayce *Compar. Philol.* viii. 302 The heirlooms of a traditional past. **1879** S. C. Bartlett *Egypt to Pal.* xxii. 455 Quarentania, the traditional region of the forty days temptation. **1908** [Miss Fowler] *Betw. Trent & Ancholme* 19 A traditional 'Rose of Sharon' survives from our great-grandmother's days.

†**2.** Observant of, bound by tradition. *Obs. rare.*

**1594** Shaks. *Rich. III*, III. i. 45 You are too sencelesse obstinate, my Lord, Too ceremonious, and traditionall... You breake not Sanctuarie, in seizing him. **1644** Milton *Judgm. Bucer* Wks. 1851 IV. 299 A pervers Age, eager in the reformation of Names and Ceremonies, but in realities as traditional and as ignorant as their forefathers.

† **B.** *sb.* A traditional belief or practice. *rare*⁻¹.

**1643** W. Greenhill *Axe at Root* 13 We stick too much to Mosaicalls, Prelaticalls, and Traditionalls.

Hence **Traditionality** (-æ·lĭti), traditional quality or character; a traditional belief or principle; **Tradi·tionalize** *v.*, *trans.* to render traditional.

**1834** *New Monthly Mag.* XLI. 455 We may trace a *traditionality, perhaps, in the style of representing Falstaff. **1840** Carlyle *Heroes* vi. (1858) 351 Many a man, doing loud work in the world, stands only on some thin traditionality, conventionality; to him indubitable, to you incredible. **1882** Davidson in *Encycl. Brit.* XIV. 860/2 [Longfellow's visit to Europe] *traditionalized his mind..and rendered him in some measure unfit to feel or express the spirit of American nature and life.

**Tradi·tionalism.** [ad. F. *traditionalisme*, or f. prec. + -ism.]

**1.** A system of philosophy which arose in the Roman Church *c* 1840, according to which all human knowledge (or, in a modified form of the system, all knowledge of religious and moral truth) is derived by traditional instruction from an original divine revelation.

[**1858** Lupus (*title*) La Traditionalisme et le Rationalisme examinés.] **1885** W. W. Roberts *Pontif. Decrees* Introd. 5 No sound Catholic could hold the opinions on Traditionalism taught at Louvain. **1885** *Cath. Dict.* (ed. 3), *Traditionalism*, a system of philosophy in which intellectual cognition, so far as the human mind is concerned, is reduced to belief in truth communicated by revelation from God, and received by traditional instruction through the medium of language, which was originally itself a supernatural gift. This system is also called *Fideism*, and is a reaction from the extreme of rationalism into an opposite extreme of anti-rationalism. De Bonald (d. 1840) is regarded as its author.

**2.** Adherence to traditional doctrine or theory; maintenance of, or submission to, the authority of tradition; excessive reverence for tradition: esp. in matters of religion.

**1860** Thirlwall *Rem.* (1877) I. 395 Without this, she would have fallen..under the blows, not of rationalism, but of traditionalism and superstition. **1869** *Spectator* 24 July 875 A conquest over the slavish legalism of the Pharisee and the timid traditionalism of the pious Jew. **1883** A. Roberts *O. T. Revision* ii. 29 Criticism and traditionalism are pitted against each other throughout the entire volume.

**Tradi·tionalist.** [f. Traditional + -ist.] An adherent of traditionalism; one who upholds the authority of tradition: = Traditionist 1. Also *attrib.*

**1875** E. White *Life in Christ* II. xvi. (1878) 188 If the Pharisaic doctrine of the oral law were the truth.., there was no reason why the Incarnate Wisdom of God should not confirm the doctrine of the traditionalists. **1881** *Nation* (N. Y.) XXXII. 425 The high-handed procedure of the traditionalist leaders. **1881** W. R. Smith *O. Test. in Jew. Ch.* xi. 326 The superciliousness with which traditionalists declare the labours of the critics to be visionary. **1906** *Edin. Rev.* July 208 To the traditionalist the reformer..is a profane person.

Hence **Tradi·tionali·stic** *a.*, of or belonging to traditionalists or traditionalism.

**1874** tr. *Ueberweg's Hist. Philos.* II. 339 De Bonald (1754–1840) was the chief of the so-called 'traditionalistic' school, the leading dogma of which was the divine creation of language.

**Traditionally** (trădi·ʃənăli), *adv.* [f. as prec. + -ly [2].] In a traditional manner; by, in the way of, or according to tradition.

**1646** Sir T. Browne *Pseud. Ep.* I. viii. 31 There are many things concerning the nature of simples, traditionally delivered, and to which I beleeve he gave no assent himselfe. *Ibid.* VII. xviii. 381 If that were true which is traditionally related by Strabo. **1764** Goldsm. *Hist. Eng. in Lett.* (1772) I. 211 The common law, which was traditionally delivered to them from their ancestors. 1859 C. Barker *Assoc. Princ.* i. 37 In an age..when private revenge was traditionally, if not legally, sanctioned. 1901 *Athenæum* 10 Aug. 198/1 The..effigy..of the maid of Normanton who was traditionally eaten by earwigs.

**Traditionary** (trădi·ʃənări), *a.* (*sb.*) [f. Tradition + -ary¹: cf. *additionary.* (In mod.L. *trāditiōnārius.*)]

1. = Traditional *a.* 1.

1661 Glanvill *Van. Dogm.* 249 Traditionary impositions. *a* 1677 Hale *True Relig.* i. (1684) 2 By Traditionary Transmission of many important Truths..from Ancestors to their Posterity. 1748 Hartley *Observ. Man* ii. iv. 396 The Corrupted Remains of some traditionary Revelation. 1802 Paley *Nat. Theol.* xviii. (ed. 2) 329 What can be the traditionary knowledge of a chicken hatched in an oven? 1857 Livingstone *Trav.* Introd. 1 Our grandfather was intimately acquainted with all the traditionary legends. 1868 Gladstone *Juv. Mundi* ii. (1869) 41 The traditionary, as opposed to the merely mythical, period.

b. = Traditional *a.* 1 b.

1835 Greswell *Parables* I. 442, I see the vestiges of a traditionary paradise in this dream of the poets. 1840 Hood *Up the Rhine* 314 Some two hundred yards distant stood the mill, in an Arabian waste, as remote from corn as the traditionary Mill of Buccleugh.

c. Characterized by tradition.

1844 Ld. Houghton *Palm Leaves, Burial Ground of Scutari*, 'Tis well to live and lord o'er those By whom his sires were most renown'd, But his fierce heart finds best repose In this traditionary ground.

†2. Observant of tradition; = Traditional *a.* 2.

1613 Purchas *Pilgrimage* iii. x. 247 They hate the Persians,..more then they doe the Christians: like as the Traditionary Iew doth the Textuarie, and the Papist the Protestant. 1666 Tillotson *Rule Faith* iii. x, Himself and his Traditionary Brethren.

B. *sb.* One who maintains or accepts the authority of tradition; a traditionalist. *rare.*

1727–41 Chambers *Cycl.* s. v., The traditionaries are what we more usually call rabbins and rabbinists, or talmudists. ..Hillel shone among the traditionaries, and Schammai among the textuaries. 1732 Neal *Hist. Puritans* I. 324 [quotes Strype (see Traditioner 1), with *traditionaries*].

Hence **Traditiona·rily** *adv.* = Traditionally.

1804 Mitford *Inquiry* xv. § 5 (ed. 2) 347 The antient Welsh airs, which have been transmitted traditionarily by ignorant harpers.

†**Tradi·tionate**, *a.* *Obs. rare*⁻⁰. [f. Tradition *sb.* + -ate².] Handed down by tradition, traditional. Hence †**Tradi·tionately** *adv.* (*obs. rare*⁻¹), by tradition, traditionally.

1593 Nashe *Christ's T.* 38 Not all thy seauenty Esdrean Cabalizers, who traditionately from Moyses receiued the Lawes interpretation, could euer rightly teach thee to diuine of the crucified Messias.

**Traditioner** (trădi·ʃənəɹ). *rare.* [f. as prec. + -er¹.] 1. = Traditionist 1.

1646 J. Gregory *Notes & Observ.* xxv. 122 The Easterne Traditioners meane by this the continuall sadnesse and contristation of heart. 1649 W. Sclater *Comm. Malachy* (1650) 48 The most superstitious Traditioners that ever lived. 1711 Strype *Life Abp. Parker* iv. xxviii. 435 In the Church of the Traditioners there is no other Disciplin than that which hath been maintained by the Antichristian Pope of Rome. 1868 Gladstone *Glean.* (1879) III. 58 We are all of us traditioners in a degree much greater than we think.

2. = Traditionist 2.

*c* 1882 J. Lucas *Studies Nidderdale* 41 Taken..from the dictation of a female traditioner.

**Traditionism** (trădi·ʃəniz'm). *rare.* [f. as prec. + -ism.] = Traditionalism 2.

1864 Webster, *Traditionism*, traditionalism. 1896 *Record* 13 Nov. 1127/1 The last reservation borders on traditionism.

**Traditionist** (trădi·ʃənist). [f. as prec. + -ist.]

1. One who accepts, adheres to, or maintains the authority of, tradition. a. *generally.*

1666 Tillotson *Rule Faith* iii. x, This fundamental difference about the rule of faith..is fully acknowledged by the traditionists themselves. 1706 Phillips (ed. Kersey), *Traditionist*, one that stands for Tradition. 1872 O. W. Holmes *Poet Breakf.-t.* viii. (1885) 207 The traditionists ..have insisted on eliminating cause and effect from the domain of morals.

b. In Moslem history: see quots. and Tradition 6 c.

1759 *Universal Hist., Mod.* II. 42 The great schism between the *Sonnites*, or *Traditionists*, that is, those of the Moslems who acknowledge the authority of the *Sonna*, or collection of moral traditions of the sayings and actions of Mohammed, and the *Shiites*, or partisans of Ali. 1847 *Ockley's Saracens* 82 *note*, Those who consider the caliphs preceding Ali as the rightful successors of Mohammed, are called Sonnites or Traditionists. 1864 *Reader* 30 Apr. 549/3 The language once used by the poets of the Desert, and employed by Mohammed and the traditionists.

c. In Judaism: cf. Tradition 6 a.

1840 Milman *Hist. Chr.* I. 69 The great schism in the Jewish popular creed, that of the traditionists and anti-traditionists.

2. One who gives vogue to, hands on, or records a tradition; a reporter or relater of traditions.

1759 Pilkington *Rem. Script.* v. 15 We are not able to ascertain who the Masorites or Traditionists were, that settled the present Standard of the Hebrew Scriptures. 1789 *Misc.* in *Ann. Reg.* 126/1 Traditionists of grievous tidings and narrators of heart-breaking events. 1841 D'Israeli *Amen. Lit.* (1867) 1 Priests and poets invented, and traditionists expatiated.

So **Tradi·tionize** *v., intr.* to deal in or give vogue to traditions; to support tradition.

1840 G. S. Faber *Christ's Disc. Capernaum* iv. 101 Ireneus..against the antiscripturally traditionising Gnostics.

**Tradi·tionless**, *a. rare.* [f. as prec. + -less.] Having no traditions.

1842 J. Wilson *Chr. North* I. 56 A Ruin nameless, traditionless—sole, undisputed property of Oblivion! 1907 *Daily Chron.* 18 June 3/1 A man whose traditions stop short at 1550 is likely to be wrong in so heartily condemning as traditionless..a nation that has gone on for another four centuries with magnificent..energy.

†**Tradi·tious**, *a.* *Obs. rare.* [f. Tradition: see -ous. Cf. *seditious.*] = Traditional 1.

1611 Speed *Theat. Gt. Brit.* (1614) 143/2 How palpably they are carried away by traditious obscurities. 1644 Quarles *Sheph. Oracles* iii, Be not deluded with traditious dreames.

**Traditive** (træ·ditiv), *a.* Now *rare.* [app. ad. obs. F. *traditif, -ive* (15th c.) traditional, f. L. *trādit-us*, pa. pple. of *trādĕre* to hand over, deliver: see -ive.]

1. Characterized by, belonging to, or being transmitted by, tradition; traditional, traditionary.

1611 Cotgr., *Traditif*, traditiue, or of tradition. 1638 Chillingw. *Relig. Prot.* i. ii. § 89. 85 If there be any Traditiue Interpretation of Scripture, produce it. 1642 Jer. Taylor *Episc.* (1647) 381 None of the Fathers ever expounded this place of Lay-Elders, so that we have a traditive interpretation of it in prejudice to the pretence of our new office. 1836 Keble *Serm.* viii. Postscr. (1848) 395 The question lay between traditive and private interpretation. 1879 M. Pattison *Milton* xiii. 206 That mysterious combination of traditive with original elements in diction, which Milton and Virgil, alone of poets known to us, have effected.

2. Orally delivered. *rare.*

1849 W. Fitzgerald tr. *Whitaker's Disput.* 553 Paul in this place mentions both traditive and written teaching, and that justly, considering the time.

**Traditor** (træ·ditǫɹ). Also 4 -ore, 5–8 -our. [a. L. *trāditor* deliverer, giver up, betrayer, agent-n. from *trādĕre*: see Tradit. With *traditour* cf. F. *traditeur* (Froissart). See also Traitor.]

†1. A betrayer, traitor. *Obs.* in general sense.

*c* 1375 *Sc. Leg. Saints* xxii. (*Laurentius*) 654 Þat man, þat wald tak, & haf Vtheris menis gud with Iniquite, With Iudas traditore suld he be. *c* 1450 *Maitland Cl. Misc.* III. 200 Item ane pharatrum for the sacrament. Item a traditour for the passioun. 1536 in Bolton *Stat. Irel.* (1621) 97 Thomas fitzGerald..who..like a most false disloyal traditour..rebelled against our soveraigne lord the king. ? 1681 in Somers *Tracts* I. 114 These Traditors of the Gospel have deserted the Plain Paths of Righteousness. 1696 Bp. Compton *Charge* 7 He becomes a Traditor in selling his Duty for a Morsel of Bread. *a* 1711 Ken *Lett.* Wks. (1838) 67 Yᵗ they might not have a Latitudinarian Traditour imposed on them, who would betray yᵉ baptismall faith. 1819 *Metropolis* I. 14 To our sex, he is a very traditore, and has.. planted thorns innumerable in the female breast.

2. *Ch. Hist.* One of those early Christians who in the great persecution under Diocletian, in order to save their own lives, delivered up their sacred books, vessels, etc., or betrayed their fellow-Christians: cf. Tradition 2 b.

1597 Hooker *Eccl. Pol.* v. lxii. § 7 There were in the Church it selfe Traditors, content to deliuer vp the Bookes of God by composition, to the end their owne liues might bee spared. 1634 'E. Knott' *Charity Maintained* i. vi. § 17 Whom they falsly affirmed to haue been ordained Bishop by those who were *Traditours*, or giuers vp of the Bible to the Persecutors to be burned. 1728 H. Herbert tr. *Fleury's Eccl. Hist.* II. 17 The Donatists pretended to prove, that Felix the Bishop of Aptonga was a traditor. 1849 W. Fitzgerald tr. *Whitaker's Disput.* 428 He says ..that there was no traditor in that succession from Peter to Anastasius. *attrib.* 1877 J. M. Fuller in *Dict. Chr. Biog.* I. 886/2 Exhorting him to cleave to those who had left the traditor-church.

†3. One who hands down a tradition. *Obs. rare*⁻¹.

1638 Chillingw. *Relig. Prot.* i. iii. § 44. 153 *note*, Saving the respect of the Tradition..From whatsoever Traditor it comes.

Hence †**Tradito·rian** *a.* (*obs. rare*⁻¹), †**Tradi·torous** *a.* (*obs. rare*⁻⁰, implied in †**Traditorously** *adv.*), traitorous, treacherous; **Tra·ditorship** (*Ch. Hist.*), the action of a traditor.

*a* 1734 North *Exam.* iii. viii. § 42 (1740) 615 The good Ignoramus Sherriff..stood up and maintained the City Rights against those *traditorian Court Slaves. 1536 in Bolton *Stat. Irel.* (1621) 97 Who..rebelled against our soveraigne lord the king, intending most falsly and *traditorously to take the said land of Ireland out of his possession. 1877 J. M. Fuller in *Dict. Chr. Biog.* I. 882/1 Not one present could claim to be free from *traditorship. One had thrown the gospels into the fire, another had offered incense to the gods, a third had delivered up small papers, but kept his codices. *Ibid.* 882/2 The emperor..subjected the alleged traditorship of Felix to a thorough examination (A. D. 313).

†**Tra·ditory**, *a. Obs. rare*⁻¹. [f. Traditor: see -ory². Cf. med.L. *trāditōrius*, in *trāditōria* (sc. *charta*, etc.), a deed of delivery or investiture: see Du Cange.] = Traditional 1, Traditive.

*a* 1653 G. Daniel *Idyll.* iv. 15 What the Ancients Speake From the first Symbole, Traditorie Truth Is soe indeed.

**Tradle**, obs. form of Treadle.

**Tradrille**, variant (or error for) Tredrille.

**Traduce** (trădiū·s), *v.* Also 6 traduse. [ad. L. *trādūcĕre* to lead across, transport, transfer, derive; also, to lead along as a spectacle, to bring into disgrace; f. *trans* across + *dūcĕre* to lead.]

†1. *trans.* To convey from one place to another; to transport. *Obs.*

1535 *St. Papers Hen. VIII*, VII. 610 The saide Duke of Angolesme shalbe traduced and brought hither into this Realme. 1650 Bulwer *Anthropomet.* 119 Matter is not traduced thorough the Body as it were by stone-gutters. *a* 1677 Hale *Prim. Orig. Man.* ii. vii. 183 We have no probable Evidence that any of their Descendents traduced the first Colonies of the American Plantations into America. 1678 Cudworth *Intell. Syst.* i. v. 706 Evil Demons..exagitating and disturbing the profitable humours,..partly by traducing the noxious into the principal parts.

†b. To put into another form or mode of expression, esp. into another language; to translate, render; to alter, modify, reduce. *Obs.* (exc. as an affectation after Fr. *traduire* or L. *trādūcĕre*, or with pun on sense 3; cf. 5).

*a* 1533 Ld. Berners *Gold. Bk. M. Aurel.* (1546) B v b, The auctoures and writers are dispraysed not of them that can traduce and compose werkes. 1552 Huloet s. v. *B*, That whyche they [Grecians] wryte with P. and Ph. is traduced in the Latine in B. 1574 J. Jones (*title*) A Briefe, Excellent and profitable Discourse of the naturall beginning of all growing and liuing things..Collected and tradused aswel forth of the best olde Wryters, as out of the new. 1674 Owen *Vind. Commun. w. God* Wks. 1855 II. 279 Being all of them traduced, and some of them transcribed, from the writings of the Socinians. 1814 Southey in *Q. Rev.* XII. 73 Milton has been traduced into French and overturned into Dutch. 1838 *Blackw. Mag.* XLIV. 615 Count Hypolite writes to us in flowery French, which we will traduce into our own plain English. 1850 Kingsley *Alt. Locke* iii, If ye canna traduce to me a page o' Virgil.

†c. To transfer from one use, sense, ownership, or employment to another. *Obs.*

1546 Langley *Pol. Verg. De Invent.* i. xiii. 25 This parte Socrates traduced and applyed from heauenly thinges, to the vse of lyfe. 1619 Sir A. Gorges tr. *Bacon's De Sap. Vet.* 83 In his description the Allegorie may bee applied and traduced to manners. 1632 Lithgow *Trav.* x. 441 An auncient and famous Kingdome,..not long ago traduced to the Castilian King by marriage. 1640 Bp. Hall *Episc.* iii. i. 218 It is traduced from that naturall sence, and used to signifie a man of some eminence in place and government.

†2. To pass on to offspring, or to posterity; to transmit, esp. by generation. *Obs.*

1568 H. B. tr. *P. Martyr's Comm. Romans* 85 b, To put vs in mynde, that originall sinne is by generation traduced from the parentes into vs. 1606 Bp. Hall *Medit.* i. xxix, Vertue is not traduced in [*Wks.* (1625) by] propagation, nor learning bequeathed by our will, to our heires. 1618 — *Contempl., N. T.* i. i, It is not in the power of parents to traduce holinesse to their children. 1646 Sir T. Browne *Pseud. Ep.* vi. x. 329 This complexion..is evidently maintained by generation, and by the tincture of the skin as a spermaticall part traduced from father unto son. 1733 Neal *Hist. Purit.* II. 399 The evangelical church..composing those religious models of Invocation and Thanksgiving, which they have traduced unto us as the Liturgies of St. James, Basil, and Chrysostom.

†b. *transf.* To produce as offspring, or in the way of generation; to propagate. (In passive often indistinguishable from 2.) *Obs.*

1599 Davies *Immort. Soul* v. viii, For tho' from Bodies, she [Nature] can Bodies bring, Yet could she never Souls from Souls traduce. *a* 1641 Bp. Mountagu *Acts & Mon.* vii. (1642) 409 There must be a supply of soules for men to be borne,..or soules must be traduced by propagation, as bodies are. *a* 1711 Ken *Hymns Evang.* Poet. Wks. 1721 I. 73 When God traduc'd by His propitious Might, Meal from Meal, Oyl from Oyl, as Light from Light.

†c. To derive, deduce, obtain *from* a source. (In passive often indistinguishable from 2.) *Obs.*

1615 J. Wright *Acc. Lady Jane Gray* in *Phenix* (1708) II. 35 Her Religion being traduc'd from the Instructions of her first Parents, and seconded by the learned Admonitions of them of the same Opinion. 1669 Gale *Crt. Gentiles* i. Introd. 3 Contemplations; which he..traduced, originally, ..from the sacred Oracles loged in the Jewish Church. 1709 O. Dykes *Eng. Prov. & Refl.* (ed. 2) 30 A great Part of us, is certainly traduc'd from our Parents.

3. To speak evil of, esp. (now always) falsely or maliciously; to defame, malign, vilify, slander, calumniate, misrepresent; †to blame, censure.

1586–7 *Reg. Privy Council Scot.* IV. 141 To detract, traduce and utter speichis full of dispyte. 1592 *Nobody & Someb.* in Simpson *Sch. Shaks.* (1878) I. 279 Do not traduce the King, hees vertuous. 1593 Abp. Bancroft *Daung. Posit.* ii. i. 41 They could not endure to heare her so traduced into all hatred and obloquy. 1602 Marston *Antonio's Rev.* ii. ii, My selfe then will traduce his guilt. 1680 Otway *Orphan* iii. i. 806 Has he supplanted me by some foul play, Traduc'd my Honour? 1697 Bentley *Phal.* Pref. (1699) 30 What pretense has he for traducing me here, as a proud and insolent man? 1781 Cowper *Expost.* 432 The man that dares traduce, because he can With safety to himself, is not a man. 1815 Kirby & Sp. *Entomol.* (1828) I. xi. 360 This curious insect so unjustly traduced by a vulgar prejudice.

†b. In various obsolete constructions: To state or affirm slanderously (something) *to be* so and so; to calumniously blame *for*, accuse *of*, charge *with.*

*c* 1618 Moryson *Itin.* iv. v. i. (1903) 437 They are confuted, who traduce the English tounge to be like a beggers patched Cloke, which they should rather compayre to a Posey of sweetest flowers. 1630 *R. Johnson's Kingd. & Commw.* 88 Yet are they traduced for many defects. 1632 Sir T. Hawkins tr. *Mathieu's Unhappy Prosperitie* 49 Those that traduce him of pride. 1643 Baker *Chron., Eliz.* 59 The Papists everywhere traduced the Queen for cruelty. 1649 Milton *Eikon.* xvi, The removing of liturgy he traduces to be done only as a thing plausible to the people. 1672 Marvell *Reh. Transp.* i. 39, I cannot warrant any man who hence took occasion to traduce him of Popery.

†c. To expose (to contempt); to bring dishonour upon, dishonour, disgrace. *Obs. rare.*

1605 Bacon *Adv. Learn.* i. iii. § 3 That which is most traduced to contempt. **1607** TOPSELL *Four-f. Beasts* (1658) 552 Likewise in..many other places of Scripture, whereby God himself must needs be traduced, if there be no Unicorn in the world. *a* **1661** HOLYDAY *Juvenal* 159 By their own ignoble actions they traduce, that is, disgrace their ancestors.

† **4.** To lead astray, mislead, seduce, betray. *Obs.*

*a* **1625** [see *traduced* below]. **1625** J. ROBINSON *Ess.* vii. Wks. 1851 I. 38 Many make their choice amiss, as..traduced by some vehement passion of anger, fear, envy, or the like. *a* **1660** *Contemp. Hist. Irel.* (Ir. Archæol. Soc.) I. 286 How those abortiue statists..swarve from theire said first holy principles, traduced to the possitiue opposition therof.

† **5.** To falsify, misrepresent, pervert, turn *into* (something bad). *Obs.*

**1643** MILTON *Divorce* II. xii. Wks. 1851 IV. 92 He there cites not the Law of Moses, but the licentious Glosse which traduc't the Law. *a* **1648** LD. HERBERT *Hen. VIII* (1683) 67 Who taking Texts..traduced the Sense thereof. *a* **1674** CLARENDON *Surv. Leviath.* (1676) 200 [It] hath in truth traduced the whole Scheme of Christianity into Burlesque.

Hence (in various senses: see above) **Traduced** (trădiū·st, *poet.* -diū·sėd) *ppl. a.*, **Tradu·cing** *vbl. sb.* and *ppl. a.* (whence **Tradu·cingly** *adv.*).

**1601** B. JONSON *Poetaster* v. iii, The malice of traducing tongues. *a* **1625** FLETCHER & MASS. *Laws of Candy* III. ii, I can forget the weakness Of the traduced Souldiers. **1645** MILTON *Tetrach.* Introd., Wks. 1851 IV. 137 The Canon Law..punishes the naming or traducing of any person in the Pulpit. *a* **1711** KEN *Urania* Poet. Wks. 1721 IV. 433 What they all clearly saw We only from traduc'd Sensation draw. **1721** BAILEY, *Traducingly*, slanderously. **1904** *Daily News* 4 May 4/2 His picture of the young Alexander..is less coloured by traducing rumour.

**Traducement** (trădiū·smĕnt). [f. prec. + -MENT.] The, or an, action of traducing; defamation, calumny, slander.

**1597** J. KING *On Jonas* (1618) 542 Innocent Christians, after their slanderous and false traducements, carried to their deathes. **1607** SHAKS. *Cor.* I. ix. 22 'Twere a Concealement worse then a Theft, No lesse then a Traducement, To hide your doings. **1839** *John Bull* 19 May, Lady..would have been unjustly immolated..by atrocious traducements there propagated. **1850** BLACKIE *Æschylus* II. 140 For 'gainst the stranger calumny Flows deftly from the tongue, and sweet traducement Costs not a thought.

**Traducent** (trădiū·sĕnt), *a. rare.* [ad. L. *trādūcent-em*, pr. pple. of *trādūcĕre* to TRADUCE.] Traducing, slanderous. **1730–6** in BAILEY (folio).

**Traducer** (trădiū·səɹ). [f. TRADUCE + -ER [1].] One who traduces.

**1.** A defamer, slanderer, calumniator.

**1614** RALEIGH *Hist. World* II. xxii. (1634) 474 Belike these traducers would commend no actions but of dead Princes. **1779** SHERIDAN *Critic* I. i, You are the greatest traducer of all other authors living. **1868** J. H. BLUNT *Ref. Ch. Eng.* I. 57 In spite of all that was afterwards alleged by Wolsey's enemies and traducers.

† **2.** One who deduces or derives. *Obs. rare.*

**1818** in TODD. **1864** WEBSTER cites FULLER.

**Traducian** (trădiū·siăn, -diū·ʃiăn), *sb.* and *a.* [ad. late L. *trādūciān-us*, deriv. of *trādux, -ducem* a layer or shoot for propagation, also in transferred sense: cf. TRADUCE *v.* 2, 2 b, and -IAN. The sense connects itself with that of the vb., 'to propagate, transmit to posterity'.] **a.** *sb.* (*a*) One who holds that the soul of a child, like the body, is propagated by or inherited from the parents. (*b*) (*less commonly*) One who holds the doctrine of the transmission of original sin from parent to child. **b.** *adj.* Applied to such doctrine or theory.

**1727–41** CHAMBERS *Cycl.*, *Traducians, Traduciani*, a name which the Pelagians anciently gave the catholics, because of their teaching that original sin was transmitted from father to children... At present some give the appellation *traduciani* to such as hold that the souls are transmitted to the children by the father. **1864** WEBSTER, *Traducian*, a believer in Traducianism. **1880** H. R. REYNOLDS in *Dict. Chr. Biog.* II. 240 The Ethiopians maintained a vigorous traducian doctrine of the origin of human souls. **1884** W. S. LILLY in *Fortn. Rev.* Jan. 127 The Traducian view—that the soul, like the body, is derived from the parent—has been held by theologians of much repute.

Hence **Tradu·cianism,** (*a*) the doctrine of the transmission of the soul from the parents (see a (*a*) above); (*b*) *rarely*, the doctrine of the hereditary transmission of original sin (see a (*b*) above); **Tradu·cianist,** a believer in traducianism in either sense; also *attrib.* or *adj.*; whence **Traduciani·stic** *a.*, pertaining to traducianists or traducianism.

**1848** R. I. WILBERFORCE *Doctr. Incarnation* iii. (1852) 32 This notion was called *Traducianism by the Schoolmen, the system opposed to it being termed Creationism. **1877** SHIELDS *Final Philos.* 199 Tertullian and Gregory of Nyssa had gone to the other extreme of traducianism or the notion of a physical propagation of the soul from parent to child. **1893** *Tablet* 18 Feb. 257 It is not allowable to any loyal Catholic to hold spiritual traducianism or generationism. **1858** J. C. ROBERTSON *Hist. Chr. Ch.* (1875) II. 152 Julian ..declared..that the God of the '*traducianists' (as he styled those who held that sin was derived by inheritance) was not the God of the gospel. **1872** LIDDON *Elem. Relig.* iii. 100 Augustine saw in the Traducianist doctrine an element of materialism. *Ibid.* 102 Of modern Traducianists, Delitzsch among Protestant, and Klee among Roman Catholic writers are perhaps the greatest. **1882–3** *Schaff's Encycl. Relig. Knowl.* III. 2318 He [Tertullian] adopts the *traducianistic view of hereditary sin.

† **Tradu·cible,** *a. Obs. rare*⁻¹. [f. TRADUCE *v.* + -IBLE: cf. *producible.*] Capable of being 'traduced' or transmitted; transmissible.

*a* **1677** HALE (J.), Oral tradition..were incompetent without written monuments to derive to us the original laws, because they are of a complex nature, and therefore not orally traducible to so great a distance of ages.

† **Tradu·ct,** *sb.*[1] *Obs. rare*⁻¹. [ad. L. *trāduct-us* sb. (*u*-stem), in same sense, f. *trādūcĕre* to lead across.] A passage, a channel.

**1535** STEWART *Cron. Scot.* (Rolls) III. 499 Syne on ane nycht that ilk traduct he brak, Quhair that thair enterit efter at his bak Richt mony sutheron with him that he led.

† **Tradu·ct,** *ppl. a.* and *sb.*[2] *Obs. rare.* [ad. L. *trāduct-us*, pa. pple. of *trādūcĕre*: see TRADUCE.] **a.** *ppl. a.* (const. as *pa. pple.*) Translated. **b.** *sb.* A translation.

**1534** (*title*) Erasmus's Funus, lately traducte into the vulgare Tonge, at the Request of a certayne Gentylman. **1541** R. COPLAND *Galyen's Terap.* 2 A ij, Whiche is the cause wherfore I haue traducte out of latyn in to frenche this fourth boke. *c* **1645** HOWELL *Lett.* II. xlviii, Things translated..lose of their primitive vigor..unless a paraphrasticall version be permitted, and then the traduct may exceed the Originall.

† **Tradu·ct,** *v. Obs.* [f. L. *trāduct-*, ppl. stem of *trādūcĕre*: see prec.] *trans.* To transmit, esp. by generation; to propagate: = TRADUCE 2, 2 b.

**1613** PURCHAS *Pilgrimage* I. v. 24 Although the Soule be not traducted (as they tearme it) and by generation conferred. *a* **1619** FOTHERBY *Atheom.* II. viii. § 2 (1622) 281 Our Nature, as it is now depraued in vs, and by the corrupt Conduicts of our sinfull Parents traducted vnto vs. **1657** W. MORICE *Coena quasi Κοινὴ* xxxiii. 306 This uncleannesse is alway diffused and traducted, as legal uncleannesse also was. **1659** H. MORE *Immort. Soul* II. xiii. § 6. 256 How this newly-created Soule is infused by God, no man knowes; nor how, if it be traducted from the Parents, both their Soules contribute to the making up a new one.

Hence † **Tradu·cter, -or,** one who 'traducts'; in quot. = TRADUCTIONIST.

**1682** H. MORE *Annot. Glanvill's Lux O.* 21 So weak an Illustration is this of what these Traducters would have.

**Traduction** (trădʊ·kʃən). [a. OF. *traduction* (13th c. in Hatz.-Darm.), or ad. L. *trāductiōn-em* 'leading across, transference, leading in triumph, public exposure'; in Christ.L. also in sense 3; also, in It. *traduzzione*, F. *traduction* 16th c., in sense of 'translation' into another lang.]

† **1.** Conveyance from one place to another; bringing over, transportation, transference. *Obs.*

? **1501** (*title*) A remembraunce for the traduction of the Princesse Kateryne, doughter to the right high and right myghty Prince the Kinge and Quene of Spayne. **1536** in Strype *Eccl. Mem.* (1721) I. App. lxxvi. 182 Concerning the traduction of the..Duke of Orleans into the realm of England there to bee educated. **1627** HAKEWILL *Apol.* (1630) 233 [That] the soule of the Baptist, or Elias, or of one of the Prophets, was by traduction passed into our Saviours bodie. *a* **1677** HALE *Prim. Orig. Man.* II. vii. 198 All the possibility there could be for traduction of the Brutes into America from the known World, could only be by Shipping.

† **b.** ? Course. *Obs. rare*⁻¹.

**1675** OGILBY *Brit.* Pref. 1 Some following the Natural Traduction of Rivers and Mountains.

† **2.** Translation into another language; *concr.* a translation. *Obs.* or *arch.*

*a* **1533** LD. BERNERS *Gold. Bk. M. Aurel.* (1546) B v, I confesse to deserue no merytes for my traduction. **1549** *Compl. Scot.* To Rdr. 10 He that hes the gyft of traductione, compiling or teching, his faculte is..honest. **1663** COWLEY *Pind. Odes* Pref., The verbal Traduction of him into Latin Prose. **1716** M. DAVIES *Athen. Brit.* III. 5 The Jesuit Rapin's Critical Parallels (whereof the English Traduction was so greedily bought up). **1822** SCOTT *Nigel* xxxii, Whilk we do not perceive even in the Latin version of the Septuagint, much less in the English traduction. **1823** BYRON *Juan* XI. xix. *note*, If there be any gem'man so ignorant as to require a traduction.

**3.** Transmission by generation to offspring or posterity; production, propagation; derivation from ancestry, descent. (Common in 17th c.; now *rare* or *Obs.*)

**1593** R. HARVEY *Philad.* 46 The vertues of men are euerlasting, yea and their bodies by traduction are immortall. **1600** O. E. *Repl. Libel* II. iii. 55 Pelagius going about to ouerthrow the traduction of originall sinne in the posteritie of Adam. **1617** HIERON *Wks.* (1620) II. 145 A great question, diuersly disputed to and fro, touching the traduction of the soule. **1640** BP. REYNOLDS *Passions* xxxii. 393 To have Being by Traduction, is, when the soule of the Child is derived from the soule of the Parent, by the meanes of Seed. **1652** N. CULVERWELL *Treat.* I. xi. (1661) 87 The Traduction of the Soul is inconsistent with the Immortality of it. **1875** E. WHITE *Life in Christ* III. xx. (1878) 282 From the first Adam they have received by traduction of being a nature which is animal and perishable.

† **b.** *gen.* Transmission; derivation; handing down, tradition. *Obs.*

**1646** SIR T. BROWNE *Pseud. Ep.* I. x. 37 Another Agent, who..proceedeth to obscure the diviner part, and efface all tract of its traduction. **1652** H. L'ESTRANGE *Amer. no Jewes* 50 The generall conflagration of all by fire might easily be conveyed by Sems off-spring, and traduction from Adam. *a* **1677** HALE *Prim. Orig. Man.* II. iii. 150 Arts have their successive invention and perfection and traduction from one People to another. **1727** DE FOE *Syst. Magic* I. i. (1840) 14 His wise dictates..which for so many ages were preserved by oral traduction, and were called the precepts of Noah. **1827** G. S. FABER *Orig. Expiat. Sacr.* 167 That altars and sacrifices were alike independently derived, both to Judaism and to Gentilism, from the common source of primeval Patriarchism: and this traduction he justly deems agreeable to both reason and to history.

† **c.** *transf.* Something transmitted or derived.

**1643** SIR T. BROWNE *Relig. Med.* II. § 14 God .. loves u[s] but for that part which is as it were himself, and the tra[duction] of his Holy Spirit. **1677** GALE *Crt. Gentiles* II. II[I.] 6 Corrupt traductions or broken traditions. **1794** G. WAKEFIELD *Exam. Paine's Age Reason* 49 If no written memo[rials] of the Jewish and Christian dispensations were..in existence, the present condition of the professors of these systems, as a traduction of believers in a certain system,.. cannot be accounted for.

† **4.** (rendering L. *traductio.*) A rhetorical figure consisting in the repetition of a word (or its derivatives) for some particular effect. *Obs. rare*⁻¹.

[**1589** PUTTENHAM *Eng. Poesie* III. xix. (Arb.) 213 Then haue ye a figure which the Latines call *Traductio*, and I the tranlacer: which is when ye turne and tranlace a word into many sundry shapes as the Tailor doth his garment, and after that sort do play with him in your dittie... Here ye see how..this word life is tranlaced into liue, liuing, liuely, liuelode.] **1626** BACON *Sylva* § 113 The Reports, and Fuges, have an Agreement with the Figure in Rhetorick,.. of Repetition, and Traduction. [**1875** E. J. PAYNE *Burke's Sel. Wks.* II. 297 The word is repeated, by the figure called *traductio*, in a contemptuous way.]

**5.** The action of traducing or defaming; calumny, slander, traducement. *rare.*

**1656** BLOUNT *Glossogr.*, *Traduction*, a conveying from one place to another, a translating; a slandering, defaming or traducing. **1793** J. WILLIAMS *Life Ld. Barrymore* 57 But who can restrain the dirty movements of Traduction and Illiberality? **1881** J. NICHOL *Death Themistocles* 17, I left traduction to its perjuries. **1889** *Daily News* 9 Apr. 2/6 The plaintiffs had a right to have their character preserved free of traduction.

**6.** *Logic.* (after *deduction, induction*): Transference or transition from one classification or order of reasoning to another.

**1847** JAS. BROUN *Let.* in De Morgan *Formal Logic* App. 332 When, abandoning one scheme of classification, we transfer our knowledge directly to another, we use traduction and traductive syllogism... In political science, what has been predicated by historians of men classed geographically is transferred to men classed according to constitutions of government by traduction. **1855** MISS COBBE *Intuit. Mor.* 76 By a process which modern logicians have happily named 'Traduction' we pass from one order of Reasoning [deductive] to the other [inductive]. **1870** JEVONS *Elem. Logic* xxv. 212 Each conclusion applies to just such an object as each of the premises applies to. To this kind of reasoning the apt name of traduction has been given.

Hence **Tradu·ctionist,** one who believes in the 'traduction' of the soul (see sense 3 above).

**1889** FARRAR *Lives Fathers* I. 232 He [Tertullian] maintains the views of the Traductionists, that the souls of all mankind are derived from Adam.

**Traductive** (trădʊ·ktiv), *a.* [f. L. *trāduct-* ppl. stem (see above) + -IVE.]

**1.** Having the property of being 'traduced' or transmitted; passing on to another; hereditary; traditional; derivative. Now *rare* or *Obs.*

**1657** W. MORICE *Coena quasi Κοινὴ* xxiv. 248 The punishments as wel as privileges are traductive, as in Attainders. **1670** MAYNWARING *Vita Sana* i. 4 Hereditary infirmities, and traductive debilities of Nature. **1741** WARBURTON *Div. Legat.* II. 355 Customs of Men..are all, whether civil or religious, traductive from one another. **1842** ORDERSON *Creol.* Pref., He has..ventured to draw from the sources of his memory traductive events.

**2.** *Logic.* Involving 'traduction'.

**1847** [see TRADUCTION 6].

**Trady** (trēɪ·di), *a. colloq.* [f. TRADE *sb.* + -Y: cf. *shady.*] Pertaining to or of the nature of trade.

**1899** *Cycling* 24 June 481/2 To my mind this worthy minister appears to be taking rather a tradey view of religion. **1901** *Academy* 26 Oct. 375/1 Book-Hunting... There are still possibilities in this least 'tradey' of trades.

**Tradyment,** variant of TRADIMENT *Obs.*

**Trafalgar** (trăfæ·lgăɪ, orig. and arch. træfălgā·ɪ). Name of a cape on the S. coast of Spain, famed for a great victory of the British fleet over the combined fleets of France and Spain on 21 Oct. 1805, in which Admiral Nelson was killed. Hence a common element in English names of streets and the like, as Trafalgar Square, London, formerly also of stage-coaches, fabrics, etc.; also, the former name of a large size of printing type: see quots.

**1826** *Haberdasher's Guide* 15 Trafalgar Cottons, for working muslins, &c. **1848** THACKERAY *Van. Fair* vii, Whither ..is the light four-inside Trafalgar coach carrying us? **1840** *Caslon's Printing Types*, Trafalgar. **1841** SAVAGE *Dict. Printing* 802 Trafalgar. 20 [lines contained in one foot]. *Ibid.* 803 Minion, Brevier, and Trafalgar, may be classed as irregular bodied letters, for they bear no specific regular proportion to any other size. **1888** JACOBI *Printers' Vocab.*, *Trafalgar*, a size of type one size larger than Twoline Double Pica and one size smaller than Canon.

† **Traffe.** *Obs. rare.* [Cf. OF. *treffe* used in a 14th c. document at Genoa to render It. *traffico* (Hatz.-Darm. s.v. *Trafic*).] Baggage: cf. TRAFFIC *sb.* 4 b.

**1566** ADLINGTON *Apuleius* 42 Sodenly the theeves returned home carefull and heavy, bringing no burthens with them, no not so much as traffe or baggage, save onely a maiden.

**Traffic** (træ·fik), *sb.* Forms: α. 6 traffigo, -ygo. β. 6 trafycke, (*Sc.* trafek, -eque, -eck); 6–7 trafick, -icke, 7–9 trafic. γ. 6 traffyque, -yk(ke, -icc, (*Sc.* traffeck, treffik, trefique), 6–7 traffícke, -ike; 6–8 trafficque, -ique, (*Sc.* traffect), traffick, 6– traffic. [In use soon after 1500, in various forms, cognate with the 15–16th c.

F. *trafique* (1441 in Godef.), *trafficque* (fem.), mod.F. *trafic* (m.) (Amyot 1559–74); Prov. *trafec, trafey*; Sp. *tráfico*, in 16th c. *tráfago*; Pg. *tráfego, tráfico*; It. *tráffico*, also, in 15–16th c. *trafico* (Florio), Venetian (*c* 1500) *traffigo*. The earliest Eng. forms are *traffykke* and *traffigo* (the latter as an alien word); the ordinary forms from 1549 to *c* 1680, *trafficque, -ique, -icke, -ike*, less usually *traf-*, were from the French of the same period; *traffick*, rare before 1600, became frequent in the 17th c. and in the form *traffic* the prevalent one in the 18th c. Some curious Sc. forms occur in the 16th c. The F. *traf(f)ic* was ad. It. *traffico*, which occurs in Pisan documents as early as 1323 (Bonaini, *Statuti inediti della citta di Pisa dal* XII *al* XIV *secolo* (1847) III. 457). OF. had also *trafit*, pl. *-itz* (1440 in Godef. *Compl.*). The sb. appears to have been the noun of action from the verb, It. *trafficare*, Sp. *trafagar*, Cat. *trafegar* to TRAFFIC, the ultimate source and etymology of which present difficulties: see Note below.]

**1.** The transportation of merchandise for the purpose of trade; hence, trade between distant or distinct communities; commerce.

1506 GUYLFORDE *Pilgr.* (Camden) 61 We founde also at Candy .ij. other galyes, Venysyans, ladynge maluesyes, called the galeys of Traffygo. *Ibid.*, We made sayle ayen, and so dyde the other .ij. galeys of Traffigo also in our company. 1549 THOMAS *Hist. Italie* A j b, How commodious the countrey is..to the trafficque of them that liue by merchaundise. 1568 GRAFTON *Chron.* I. 129 That passage and traffique of Marchaunts was forboden. 1596 SPENSER *F. Q.* VI. xi. 9 Merchants..wount To skim those coastes for bondmen there to buy, And by such trafficke after gaines to hunt. 1596 DALRYMPLE tr. *Leslie's Hist. Scot.* (S. T. S.) I. 38 A citie..to quhilke the frenche men and Spaniȝeards oft because of thair treffik sailed ouir. 1604 E. G[RIMSTONE] *D'Acosta's Hist. Indies* III. xix. 180 The greatest part of the habitation of the coast entertaines all the traffike of Spaine by sea. 1634 SIR T. HERBERT *Trav.* 43 Vessels of Traffique and Warre. 1651 HOWELL *Venice* 83 That the Venetians shold have free and safe trafic into the Pontick Seas. 1719 DE FOE *Crusoe* I. 296 It was not the Way to or from any Part of the World, where the English had any Traffick. 1860 MOTLEY *Netherl.* (1868) I. i. 7 Cadiz,..where the ancient and modern systems of traffic were blending like the mingling of the two oceans.

†**b.** (with *pl.*) A trading voyage or expedition.

*a* 1548 HALL *Chron., Edw. IV* 241 Thether was one of their common trafficques and ventes of all their Merchaundice. 1598 HAKLUYT (*title*) The Principal Navigations, Voiages, Traffiqves and Discoueries of the English Nation.

**2.** In wider sense: The buying and selling or exchange of goods for profit; bargaining; trade.

1568 GRAFTON *Chron.* I. 4 The honest and simple doings that before tyme had bene vsed..in their exchaunges and traffiques. 1604 R. CAWDREY *Table Alph.*, *Traffique*, bargayning. 1604 E. G[RIMSTONE] *D'Acosta's Hist. Indies* IV. iii. 210 The maner of the Indians trafficke..was to exchange, and give things for things. 1697 EVELYN *Numism.* i. 3 Antient Moneys..first used in Trafick. 1727 W. MATHER *Yng. Man's Comp.* 396 *Traffick* then is the Bartering, Bargaining, or Exchanging of one Man with another. 1785 BURKE *W. Hastings* Wks. 1813 XII. 202 Engaged in a low, clandestine traffic, prohibited by the laws of the Country. 1844 WILSON *Brit. India* III. 128 After a brief interval, Prome again became the seat of industry and traffic.

**b.** With *a* and *pl.*

1578 T. ELLIS in Hakluyt *Voy.* (1600) III. 40 We did coniecture, that they had either Artificers amongst them, or els a traffike with some other nation. 1604 E. G[RIMSTONE] *D'Acosta's Hist. Indies* V. xxx. 426 Those which made it a trafficke to buy and sell slaves. 1818 SCOTT *Hrt. Midl.* xxxii[i], She..had now, under pretence of a trifling traffic, resumed predatory habits.

**c.** *fig.*

1505 KILLINGWORTH in *Lett. Rich. III & Hen. VII* (Rolls) II. App. D. 381 As for K[ing] H[enry's] traffykkes they knewe theym wele ynough and better than ye did. 1570 BUCHANAN *Chamæleon* Wks. (1892) 46 The ouersey trafficque of mariage growing cauld. 1633 BP. HALL *Occas. Medit.* (1851) 139 Surely this very traffic of faculties is that, whereby we live;..one man lends a brain; another an arm; one, a tongue; another, a hand. 1697 DRYDEN *Virg. Georg.* IV. 227 The bees have common cities of their own,..beneath one law they live, And with one common stock their traffic drive. 1819 SCOTT *Ivanhoe* xli, I am stout enough to exchange buffets with any who will challenge me to such a traffic.

**d.** With sinister or evil connotation: Dealing or bargaining in something which should not be made the subject of trade.

1663 BP. PATRICK *Parab. Pilgr.* xxi. (1687) 220 Their courtesies are meer traffique, and they always expect to gain more than they give. 1702 *Eng. Theophrast.* 105 They make a Traffick of Honour, and pay for it with the wind of fair Words. 1790 BURKE *Fr. Rev.* 60 In this political traffick the leaders will be obliged to bow to the ignorance of their followers. 1818 COBBETT *Pol. Reg.* XXXIII. 686 It is notorious, that seats in the House of Commons are an article of traffic. 1880 MRS. FORRESTER *Roy & V.* I. 19 You make the most shameless traffic and barter of yourselves and each other. 1903 *Westm. Gaz.* 31 Dec. 2/3 Fruits of 'the traffic' occupy a prominent place in to-day's Metropolitan police-court reports. *Mod.* The white slave traffic; a traffic in souls and bodies.

**3.** *fig.* Intercourse, communication; dealings, business. Now *rare.*

*a* 1548 HALL *Chron., Edw. IV* 240 The quotidiane entercourse, trafficke and commutacion, which no smal season had ben practised, frequented, & excercised. 1560 DAUS tr. *Sleidane's Comm.* 339 b, That secreat trafficke, that thou haste with infidels. 1592 SHAKS. *Rom. & Jul.* Prol. 12 The fearful passage of their death-mark'd love..Is now the two hours' traffic of our stage. *a* 1628 F. GREVIL *Let. to Hon. Lady* v. Wks. 1870 IV. 285 Shee there vseth the traffique of wit. 1633 T. STAFFORD *Pac. Hib.* I. xv. (1821) 173 The President..returned him no Answer.., utterly refusing any further traffique with him. 1727 DE FOE *Syst. Magic* I. iii. (1840) 62 Perhaps they were not hardened enough at first for the carrying on such a traffick [intercourse with Satan]. 1825 JAMIESON, *Traffeck*, intercourse, familiarity. 1893 STEVENSON *Catriona* xxviii, Our traffic is settled.

†**4.** *transf.* Goods or merchandise in which trade is done; saleable commodities. Also *pl.* (quot. 1604) in same sense. *Obs.*

1555 EDEN *Decades* 157 They bowght them by exchaunge of golde and other of their trafycke. 1560 in Marsden *Sel. Pl. Crt. Admir.* (Selden) II. 119 In which shipps there be any merchaundizes or traffick apperteining to the ennemies. 1604 E. G[RIMSTONE] *D'Acosta's Hist. Indies* IV. xxii. 271 The Cacao..is so much esteemed amongest the Indians (yea and among the Spaniards) that it is one of the richest and the greatest traffickes of new Spaine. *c* 1710 CELIA FIENNES *Diary* (1888) 36 A Considerable ffaire is kept.., ye Traffique mostly hopps. 1716 GAY *Trivia* II. 10 You'll see a draggled damsel, here and there From Billingsgate her fishy traffic bear. 1778 BP. LOWTH *Transl. Isaiah* xxiii. 18 Her traffic and her gain, shall be holy to Jehovah: It shall not be treasured, nor shall it be kept in store.

†**b.** Baggage. *Obs. rare.*

1538 ELYOT, *Impedimenta*, is the caryage and trafyke, that goth with the hooste.

†**c.** A prostitute. Cf. TRADER 1 b. *Obs. rare.*

1591 GREENE *Disc. Coosnage* (1592) 15 These trafickes, these common truls I meane, walke abroad.

**d.** Worthless stuff, rubbish, trash; also, rascally people; rabble. *dial.*

1828 *Craven Gloss.*, *Traffick*, lumber, trash. 'There wor a deal of oud traffick to sell'..Rabble, low, rascally people, the canaille. 1869 *Lonsdale Gloss.*, *Traffic*, (1) lumber, rubbish. (2) Rabble, low, rascally people.

**5.** The passing to and fro of persons, or of vehicles or vessels, along a road, railway, canal, or other route of transport.

*a* 1825 FORBY *Voc. E. Anglia*, *Traffic*,..passing and repassing on a high road. Ex. 'There is a great deal of traffic on this road'. 1832 HT. MARTINEAU *Weal & Woe* ix, He sauntered along the pier, around which there was no busy traffic. 1886 C. E. PASCOE *London of To-day* xxvi. (ed. 3) 239 The traffic of omnibuses, cabs, carriages, and carts at this point is greater and more confusing than in any other part of London. 1894 SALA *London up to Date* 73 We have long since agreed to call street movement 'traffic'.

**b.** The amount of business done by a railway, etc., in the transport of passengers and goods; the account of or revenue from this.

1858 [implied in *traffic-return*: see 6]. 1883 *Pall Mall G.* 30 Nov. 5/2 It is obviously advisable that all the railways should adopt the same course, otherwise comparisons of traffic will become even more misleading than they are now. 1885 *Ibid.* 21 Nov. 5/2 Traffics are still decreasing, and this fact is all the more discouraging from the fact that the comparison is with decreased traffics. 1905 *Westm. Gaz.* 28 Sept. 9/1 Satisfaction is again expressed with this week's batch of Home Railway traffics.

**c.** A railway traffic-rate (RATE *sb.*[1] 6 b).

1899 *Daily News* 14 Mar. 9/1 The Grand Trunk Railway unconditionally withdrew the local traffics of January 6th, and agreed for the present to revert to former rates.

**6.** *attrib.* and *Comb.*, as, in sense 2, *traffic fellow, instinct*; in 5, *traffic block* (BLOCK *sb.* 19 a), *board* (BOARD *sb.* 8 b), *-entrance, -privilege, -rate, return* (RETURN *sb.* 9 c), *-road, staff, value*; instrumental, objective, and obj. genitive, as *traffic-manager*; *traffic-choked, -congested, -furrowed, -laden, -regulating, -thronged* adjs.; **traffic density**, the number of passengers and of tons of freight carried over any section of a railway in a given period (Webster 1911); **traffic mile**: see quot.; **traffic-taker**, a railway official whose business is to compile traffic returns.

1904 *Daily Chron.* 17 Feb. 7/2 *Traffic blocks are almost unknown. 1905 *Westm. Gaz.* 18 July 8/2 The authority which the Commission recommend to be established is a *Traffic Board. 1886 *Pall Mall G.* 19 Aug. 3/2 The *traffic-choked streets. 1886 T. HARDY *Mayor Casterbr.* ix, They..entered..by the back way or *traffic-entrance. 1590 GREENE *Royal Exchange* Ded., Wks. (Grosart) VII. 223 Merchaunts wyth theyr freendes, and *traffique fellowes. 1898 G. MEREDITH *Odes Fr. Hist.* 46 Their *traffic instincts hooded their live wits To issues. 1871 HOWELLS *Wedd. Journ.* (1892) 254 The stream athwart which the ferries sped their swift *traffic-laden shuttles. 1862 HELPS *Organiz. Daily Life* 30 A skilful *traffic-manager has been suffered to be too despotic in matters of traffic. 1911 WEBSTER (citing HADLEY), **Traffic mile* is a term designed to furnish an excuse for the erroneous practice of adding together two things (ton miles and passenger miles) which, being of different kinds, cannot properly be added. 1901 *Academy* 22 June 540/1 One sight amazes him..the effect produced when the *traffic-regulating policeman raises his hand. 1858 SIMMONDS *Dict. Trade*, **Traffic-return*, a periodical statement of the receipts for goods and passengers on a railway line. 1912 *Times* 19 Dec. 16/5 Canadian Pacific Railway shares opened above parity on the satisfactory traffic return.

Hence **Tra·fficful** *a.*, *nonce-wd.*, fully occupied with traffic; **Tra·ffickery**, *nonce-wd.* [-ERY], underhand dealing, intrigue; **Tra·fficless** *a.*, devoid of traffic.

*a* 1628 F. GREVIL *Sidney* ix. (1652) 107 Her *traffiquefull, and navigable river. *c* 1810 COLERIDGE in *Lit. Rem.* (1838) III. 387 This indiscreet *traffickery with Romish wares. 1892 *Black & White* Jan. 134/2 Stilled and trafficless streets.

[*Note.* It is clear that the verb and sb. arose in the commerce of the Mediterranean, and in the language of one of the nations by or with whom this was carried on. The earliest uses yet found are *trafficare* and *traffico* in the Pisan *Breve dell' ordine del mare*, cited above, which show both vb. and sb. in full established use in 1325. Etymologists are generally agreed in regarding the word as Romanic, and in seeing in the first element *tra* the regular It. repr. of L. *trans* across. Italian scholars also see in *-ficare* the derivative form of L. *facĕre* to do, make; *transficare* would thus be parallel to *transigĕre* to transact, or engage in transactions. But there are difficulties: see Diez, *traffico*, Körting, *transvicare*, etc. Some have suggested for the word an origin in Arabic, referring it to the verb *taraffaqa*, which sometimes means 'to seek profit'.]

**Traffic** (træ·fik), *v.* Inflected **trafficked** (-ikt), **trafficking.** Forms: see the sb. [ad. OF. *trafiquer* (1441 in Godef. *Compl.*), F. *traffiquer* (1529 in Hatz.-Darm.) = Cat. *trafegar*, Sp. *traficar* (in 16th c. *trafagar*), Pg. *traficar, trafeguear*, It. *trafficare* (known in 1325), *traficare* (Florio). As to etymology, see TRAFFIC *sb.* and Note there.]

**I.** Intransitive senses.

**1.** To carry on trade, to trade, to buy and sell; to have commercial dealings *with* any one; to bargain or deal *for* a commodity. Sometimes, To resort *to* a place for the purpose of trade: = TRADE *v.* 6 a.

1542 in *10th Rep. Hist. MSS. Comm.* App. v. 410 They that so would bargayn or trafique pertly or oppenly with any such merchauntes. 1555 EDEN *Decades* 317 They do not gladly permitte the Portugales to trafike in theyr kyngedome. 1585 T. WASHINGTON tr. *Nicholay's Voy.* IV. xi. 123 b, Vnto the ports..come to traffick, the merchants of Cambaia. 1613 H. SPELMAN *Relat. Virginia* in *Capt. Smith's Wks.* (Arb.) p. civ, Powhatan..carried our English to their storehouse where their corne was, to traffique with them. 1634 SIR T. HERBERT *Trav.* 53 Many Carrauans..trafiquing to the Portugall[s]. 1716 *Royal Proclam.* 18 Oct. in *Lond. Gaz.* No. 5480/1 Their Factors..should..Traffick, or Adventure into or from the..East-Indies. 1769 COOK *Voy. round World* I. ix. (1773) 93 They trafficked with us for cocoa-nuts and other fruit. 1800 WORDSW. *Brothers* 293 He was..A thriving man, and trafficked on the seas.

**b.** In a disparaging sense, or said of dealing considered improper: = TRADE *v.* 6 c: cf. prec. 2 d.

*c* 1657 in *Verney Mem.* (1907) II. 120 [He had made more money] than any man who trafficked in that desperate commodity—rebellion. 1696 PHILLIPS (ed. 5), *Trafic*,..us'd figuratively in an ill Sense, for trading in Simoniacal Contracts, and making an unlawful Gain of Spiritual things. Such a one has long Traffick'd in buying and selling his Countrey. 1853 J. H. NEWMAN *Hist. Sk.* (1873) II. I. ii. 82 He observed that it was somewhat more honourable to destroy idols than to traffic in them. 1854 J. S. C. ABBOTT *Napoleon* (1855) I. iv. 80 Beautiful and dissolute females..trafficking in their charms.

†**2.** *fig.* To have dealings or intercourse (*with* a person); to carry on negotiations; to be concerned, to busy or exercise oneself (*in* some matter). *Obs.*

1583 GOLDING *Calvin on Deut.* cxxi. 743 But there are meanes to trafique man with man. 1612 T. TAYLOR *Comm. Titus* ii. 13 (1619) 483 Who while they liue in earth, yet traffique and haue their conuersation in heauen. 1656 STANLEY *Hist. Philos.* v. (1701) 173/2 Hermodorus, of whom the Proverb, Hermodorus traffiques in Words. *c* 1721 MRQ. TULLIBARDINE *Let.* 24 Jan., in *10th Rep. Hist. MSS. Comm.* App. I. 126 On no pretence I trafick in any tainting politique. 1882 JAMIESON, *Trafeque*, to hold familiar intercourse. *Banffs.*

**b.** To have dealings of an illicit or secret character; to deal, intrigue, conspire (*with* some one, *in*, *for*, or *to do* something); to practise. (Cf. 1 b.)

1567 *Reg. Privy Council Scot.* I. 569 Trafficquand with the Papis Nunce. *a* 1649 DRUMM. OF HAWTH. *Hist. Scot.* (1655) 164 He also trafficked by the friends of..the Dowglasses and Humes to perswade them to a Return. 1681, 1735 [see *trafficking* below]. 1852 MISS YONGE *Cameos* II. ii. 17 Jeanne discovered that he was trafficking with her enemies and tampering with her friends.

**3.** *dial.* (See 4 b.)

**II.** Transitive senses.

†**4.** To traverse or frequent for the purpose of trading; to carry on trade in (a place). *Obs.*

1547 *Acts Privy Counc.* (1890) II. 130 The Kynges Majestes subjectes trafeking the seas. 1561 Q. ELIZ. in Hakluyt *Voy.* (1589) 362 Trade of marchandize with your Subiectes, and with other strangers trafiking your Realmes. 1611 W. SCLATER *Key* (1629) 36 Rome,..the seate of the Empire, trafficqued by all Nations.

**b.** To pass to and fro upon, to frequent (a road, etc.); to traverse. Also *intr.* To pass to and fro, walk or run about. *dial.*

*a* 1825 FORBY *Voc. E. Anglia*, *Traffic*, to frequent...'The new road will soon be trafficked'. 1850 MERRYWEATHER *Glimmerings* 52 Some would venture to traffic them in the day, but few would risk such perilous thoroughfares by night. 1877 *N. W. Linc. Gloss.*, *Traffic*, *v.* (1) To walk about without settled purpose. (2) To trespass upon other people's land. *A correspondent writes*, 'Our nurse used to scold us when children for trafficking up and down stairs.'

**5.** To carry on a trade in, to buy and sell; to dispose of (or † acquire) in the way of trade; to deal in; often with sinister implication; in quot. 1879, to barter *away*. Also *fig.* Now *rare.*

1597 DANIEL *Civ. Wars* VI. xviii, Whil'st wee..Ryot away ..whole Prouinces;..Traffique important Holdes, sell Fortresses. 1598 DALLINGTON *Meth. Trav.* N iv b, *Non patiar mercatores potestatum*, I will suffer none to traffique Offices. *a* 1628 F. GREVIL *Religion* Wks. 1870 I. 272 The world doth build without, our God within; He traffics goodness.

and she traffics sin. **1808** *Sporting Mag.* XXXII. 7 An assertion..that his Lordship had trafficked a seat for the Borough of Malton. **1879** *19th Cent.* No. 32. 673 The honour of the proud house of Este was being basely trafficked away. **1893** LANE-POOLE *Aurengzib* xii. 200 The young Prince was suspected of trafficking the Imperial honour with the Marathas.

†**6.** To negotiate (a matter). *Obs. rare.*

*a* **1649** DRUMM. OF HAWTH. *Hist. Scot.* (1655) 28 He trafficked the return of King James. *Ibid.* 207 Whilst they traffique this Marriage, many false accusations (as Plots laid against his person) are intended one after another at the Court.

Hence **Tra·fficking** *vbl. sb.* and *ppl. a.*

**1570** in Tolstoy *1st 40 Yrs. Interc. Eng. & Russ.* (1875) 103 Kept from traffiquing. **1580** *Nat. Covt. Ref. Princ. Reexhibited* (1787) 56 Trafficking Papists to be punished. *a* **1649** DRUMM. OF HAWTH. *Hist. Scot.* (1655) 11 The trafficking of a Marriage between Lewis the Daulphine..with Margaret Daughter to King James. **1681** in *Acts Parlt. Scotl.* (1875) XII. 44/1 They..shall never tolerate priests Jesuits nor traffecking Papists to abide in this Kingdome. **1735** in *Tablet* 19 Mar. (1910) 446/2 Trafficking Papists, I mean such as are continually employed in making Proselytes. **1835** MARRYAT *Pirate* ii, Grief is worth nothing in this trafficking world unless it is paid for. **1863** FROUDE *Hist. Eng.* VIII. viii. 132 Thus the antagonism went on, irritating Elizabeth..into dangerous traffickings with the Bishop of Aquila and his successor. **1903** W. N[EVILLE] *Penal Servitude* xiii. 170 Any officer found guilty of passing a letter out of prison would be liable to instant dismissal, as this comes under what is called 'trafficking'—an unpardonable offence.

**Trafficable** (træ·fikăb'l), *a.* [f. TRAFFIC *sb.* or *v.* + -ABLE.]

†**1.** Adapted or suitable for traffic or trading. *Obs. rare*⁻¹.

*a* **1603** T. CARTWRIGHT *Confut. Rhem. N. T.* (1618) 469 That being the most traffiqueable and Marchandable Citie of all Asia.

**2.** That may be bought or sold; marketable.

**1649** BP. HALL *Cases Consc.* i. (1654) 4 It is..in some cases a trafiqueable commodity. **1880** A. SOMERVILLE *Autobiog.* 90, I required what may be called trafficable material. **1889** *Sat. Rev.* 19 Oct. 422/1 [They] have been taught..to regard a vote as a commodity, traffickable.

**3.** Fit or suitable for passage to and fro.

**1890** *Goldfields of Victoria* 17 A good trafficable roadway. **1891** *Illustr. Lond. News* 17 Jan. 78/2 The streets are trafficable.

Hence **Trafficabi·lity**, **Tra·fficableness**, suitability for traffic or passage to and fro.

**1899** *Daily News* 16 Nov. 4/5 A paper dealing with.. London's treacherous 'trafficability' was read at the opening meeting of the 146th session of the Society of Arts.

**Trafficked** (træ·fikt), *ppl. a.* [f. TRAFFIC *v.* (or *sb.*) + -ED.] †**a.** That has trafficked or traded abroad; experienced in traffic (*obs. rare*); cf. *travelled*, *well-read*, *well-spoken*. †**b.** Traversed or explored for traffic or trade (*obs. rare*). **c.** Made the subject of traffic; dealt in as merchandise. **d.** Used for, or beaten or worn by traffic, as a road.

**1561** T. HOBY tr. *Castiglione's Courtyer* III. (1577) N v b, I vnderstood by merchaunt men a long time trafficked in that countrey. **1627** MAY *Lucan* VIII. (1631) 364 Let fortune then our sad, and ship wrack'd state Beyond the knowne, and trafficqu'd world translate. **1875** LANIER *Symphony* 234 O trafficked hearts that break in twain. **1909** *Westm. Gaz.* 30 Aug. 2/1 On lightly trafficked roads.

**Trafficker** (træ·fikəɹ). [f. TRAFFIC *v.* + -ER¹.]

**1.** One who is engaged in traffic or trade; a trader, merchant, dealer.

**1580** *Reg. Privy Council Scot.* III. 327 Divers..honest trafficquers of this cuntrie. **1615** tr. *De Monfart's Surv. E. Indies* 22 They are..great Traffickers. *a* **1727** NEWTON *Observ. Coin* (1730) 10 Traffickers in money will get above 6 per Cent by sending Gold to Spain. **1833** HT. MARTINEAU *Charmed Sea* v, The traffickers were exchanging their goods laboriously. **1863** GEO. ELIOT *Romola* iii, An itinerant trafficker in broken glass and rags.

**b.** With opprobrious force; cf. TRAFFIC *sb.* 2 d.

*a* **1785** GLOVER *Athenaid* XIII. Poems (1810) 124/2 Let these to some fell trafficker in slaves Be sold. **1839** JAMES *Louis XIV*, IV. 50 These traffickers in poison seem to have been seized with a sort of madness. **1869** *Echo* 28 Aug., Practices familiar to many generations of hardened traffickers in votes.

**2.** One who carries on an underhand or improper traffic (esp. between other parties); a go-between, a negotiator; an intriguer; a schemer.

**1570** in *Calr. Scott. Pap.* (1903) III. 384 Thome Bischop wes ye first trafficquar betuix ye bischop of Ros and ye said Johnne. **1687** *Royal Proclam.* in *Lond. Gaz.* No. 2221/4 For being Papists, Jesuits, or Traffickers, for hearing, or saying of Mass. **1879** FARRAR *St. Paul* I. 561 Lest any should say that he too, like the mass of traffickers around him, did but seek his own gain. **1893** STEVENSON *Catriona* ix. 96 The whole clan of old Jacobite spies and traffickers.

†**Traffle**, obs. variant of TAFFEREL, TAFFRAIL.

**1805** in Nicolas *Disp. Nelson* (1846) VII. 156 *note*, A Spanish two-decker..waved an English Jack from her traffle.

**Trafin, -e**, obs. forms of TREPHINE.

**Tragacanth** (træ·găkænþ). Also 6 **tragachant**, 7 **tragagant**, 8 **tragant**, **-anth**; see also ADRAGANT, DRAGANT, DRAGON². [a. F. *tragacante* (16th c.) = It., Sp. *tragacanta*, ad. L. *tragacantha* (Pliny), a. Gr. τραγάκανθα goat's-thorn, tragacanth-shrub, f. τράγος he-goat + ἄκανθα thorn.

The gum was called in L. *tragacanthum* (Celsus), whence Sp., Pg. *tragacanto*.]

**1.** A 'gum' or mucilaginous substance obtained from several species of *Astragalus* (see 2), by natural exudation or incision, in the form of whitish strings or flakes, only partially soluble in water: see quot. 1875. Used in medicine (chiefly as a vehicle for drugs) and in the industrial arts. Also a similar substance obtained from *Sterculia Tragacantha* of W. Africa. **a.** Commonly called *gum tragacanth*.

**1573** in Feuillerat *Revels Q. Eliz.* (1908) 199 Gum tragachant ii ounces. **1634** J. B[ATE] *Myst. Nat.* 33 With gum tragagant dissolued in faire water. **1643** STEER tr. *Exp. Chyrurg.* xiv. 57 Mixe it with the whites of Egges and Gum Tragacanth. **1714** *Fr. Bk. of Rates* 92 Gum Tragant per 100 Weight 02 10. **1811** A. T. THOMSON *Lond. Disp.* II. (1818) 65 Gum tragacanth is demulcent. **1830** LINDLEY *Nat. Syst. Bot.* 39 The Gum Tragacanth of Sierra Leone is produced by a species of Sterculia. **1875** BENNETT & DYER *Sachs' Bot.* 36 Gum-tragacanth consists of the cells of the pith and medullary rays of *Astragalus creticus*, *A. Tragacantha*, and other species, transformed into mucilage.

**b.** Called simply *tragacanth*.

**1601** HOLLAND *Pliny* XIII. xxi. I. 398 A pound of Tragacanth is worth thirteen deniers Romane. **1712** tr. *Pomet's Hist. Drugs* I. 181 Traganth or Tragacanth, is a white curl'd Gum made like little Worms. **1875** H. C. WOOD *Therap.* (1879) 577 Tragacanth is used in medicine only in the manufacture of troches and in suspending heavy powders.

†**2.** Any one of several low-growing spiny shrubs of the genus *Astragalus* (N.O. *Leguminosæ*), found in Persia and neighbouring regions, which yield gum tragacanth (see 1). *Obs. rare.*

**1601** HOLLAND *Pliny* XIII. xxi. I. 398 The same Iland hath the bush Tragacanth growing in it. **1741** *Compl. Fam.-Piece* II. iii. 373 Columbines, Spireas,..Spanish Broom,.. Tragacantha.

**3.** *attrib.*

**1813** MILBURN *Oriental Comm.* I. 110 Tragacanth gum, or as it is usually called gum dragon. **1836** J. M. GULLY *Magendie's Formul.* (ed. 2) 138 Tragacanth powder. **1876** HARLEY *Royle's Mat. Med.* 633 Tragacanth Bushes..are small, tangled, spiny bushes, resembling stunted varieties of ..furze. **1879** *Sat. Rev.* 8 Nov. 580/1 The tragacanth draught of the ancient Sophists is tolerated.

Hence **Tragaca·nthin** (also contr. **traga·nthin**), *Chem.*, the essential constituent of tragacanth and other gums: = BASSORIN. (See also quot. 1843.)

**1842** BRANDE *Dict. Sc.*, etc. s. v. *Tragacanth*, An analogous kind of gum is found in other plants, and the generic name of *tragacanthin* is sometimes applied to it. **1843** *Penny Cycl.* XXV. 114/1 An artificial substance prepared by boiling starch,..called tragacantin.

**Tragæ-comedy**, obs. form of TRAGI-COMEDY.

**Tragal** (trē·găl), *a. Anat.* [f. TRAG-US + -AL.] Pertaining to or situated upon the tragus.

**1891** in *Cent. Dict.* **1898** J. HUTCHINSON in *Arch. Surg.* IX. No. 36. 378 Those who have abundant vibrissæ very commonly, I believe, have these tragal tufts of hair also.

†**Tra·galism.** *Spanish Hist.* [ad. Sp. *tragalismo*, f. *trágala* in '*Trágala, perro!*' ('Swallow it, dog!', where 'it' refers to the Constitution), the refrain of a popular Constitutionalist song.] A designation for the principles of the Spanish Constitutional party of 1820 and succeeding years.

**1837** *Q. Rev.* July 68 The bloody tragedy of Spanish Tragalism. **1837** WALTON *Revol. of Spain* II. xii. 325 It was wished..merely to modify the existing plan so as to render it palatable abroad while *tragalism* was enforced at home.

[In Smart 1849 *Suppl.*, *Tragalism* (entered with a reference to *Q. Rev.* as above, but no quot.) is explained as 'Goatishness due to high feeding'. This absurd guess, based on a pseudo-etymological reference to Gr. τραγαλισμός ('the eating of dried fruits and sweetmeats', but imagined to be derived from τράγος goat) has been copied (with ingenious variations) in many recent dictionaries.]

†**Trage·diac**, *a. Obs. rare.* [f. L. *tragœdia* TRAGEDY + -AC; an anomalous formation for **tragedic*: cf. It. *tragedico* (Florio) and TRAGEDICAL.] Befitting tragedy; tragic in style.

**1782** ELIZ. BLOWER *Geo. Bateman* I. 205 Those ranting tragediac speeches. *Ibid.* III. 117.

†**Trage·dial**, *a. Obs. rare.* [f. as prec. + -AL.] Pertaining to tragedy; tragic.

*a* **1529** SKELTON *Agst. Scottes* 77 Melpomone, O Muse tragediall.

**Tragedian** (trădʒī·diăn). Also 4–5 **tragedyen**, **-ien**, (**tregedien**), 7–8 **tragœdian**. [ME., prob. a. OF. *tragediane* (1372 in Hatz.-Darm.), later and mod.F. *tragédien*, f. *tragédie* TRAGEDY: see -AN.]

**1.** A dramatist who composes a tragedy or tragedies; a tragic poet or author.

*c* **1374** CHAUCER *Boeth.* III. pr. vi. 60 (Camb. MS.) A tragedyen [*v. r.* tregedien] þat is to seyn a makere of dites þat hyhten tragedies. *a* **1631** DONNE *Poems* (1633) 165 Under this curled marble..Sleepe rare Tragedian Shakespeare, sleepe alone. **1671** MILTON *P. R.* IV. 261 What the lofty grave Tragœdians taught In Chorus or Iambic. **1875** SCRIVENER *Lect. Text N. Test.* 6 The dramas of the Greek tragedian Æschylus.

**2.** A stage-player who performs in tragedy; a tragic actor.

**1592** NASHE *P. Penilesse* (ed. 2) 26 b, The Tragedian that represents his person. **1602** SHAKS. *Ham.* II. ii. 342 What Players are they? *Rosin.*..The Tragedians of the City. **1602** MARSTON *Antonio's Rev.* II. iii, I will not swell, like a Tragedian, in forced passion of affected straines. **1693** DRYDEN *Persius' Sat.* v. 3 The well-lung'd Tragedians Rage. **1711** ADDISON *Spect.* No. 40 *ad fin.*, Mr. Powell..is excellently formed for a Tragœdian. **1870** L'ESTRANGE *Miss Mitford* I. vi. 200 No man can be a perfect tragedian who is not likewise a good actor in the higher branch of comedy.

†**3.** *fig.* A person concerned in a 'tragedy' or dreadful calamity; the victim, or inflicter, of a tragic fate. *Obs.*

**1592** WARNER *Alb. Eng.* IX. xlv. (1612) 214 The Tragedies and Tytles too of English Dukes did cease, Which Thomas, Duke of Norffolke, last Tragedian did increase. **1635** R. JOHNSON *Hist. Tom a Lincoln* (1825) 131 The Blacke Knight stayed from his desperate resolution, and from a bloody tragedian became the recoverer of his brothers life.

Hence **Trage·dianess** (*nonce-wd.*), a female tragedian.

**1822** *Blackw. Mag.* XII. 657 Was there to be a virtual *non-imprimatur* in force against our songstresses, romance-inditresses, tragedianesses, sonneteeresses?

**Trage·dical**, *a. rare.* [f. Gr. τραγῳδικ-ός befitting tragedy + -AL.] Of the nature, or having the character, of tragedy; tragical.

*a* **1548** HALL *Chron.*, *Hen. VI* 187 b, Thus you haue hearde the..tragedicall hystory of Kynge Henry the sixthe. **1891** W. S. GILBERT *Rosencrantz & Guild.* III, The poor author had hoped to have appalled you with his tragedical end!

‖ **Tragédienne** (traʒedie·n). [Fr., fem. of *tragédien* TRAGEDIAN.] A female tragedian or actor of tragedy; a tragic actress.

**1851** LONGF. in *Life* (1891) II. 221 We..called on Jenny Lind, and on Mrs. Warner, the tragédienne. **1866** *Standard* 7 Mar. 2/6 On Thursday night Miss Siddons, a young tragedienne..a great-granddaughter of *the* Siddons..made her first appearance..in the character of Juliet.

**Tragedietta** (trădʒīdiˌe·tă). [In form an It. dim. of *tragedia*: see -ETTA: cf. *comedietta*.] A slight or short tragedy; a dramatic sketch of tragic character.

**1891** *Pall Mall G.* 19 Oct. 2/3 My 'tragedy'—it is a very little one, a one-act tragedietta. **1902** *Daily Chron.* 2 July 3/1 One of them..might be called a 'tragedietta',..but, as a whole, they may be said to range from comedietta to farce.

†**Trage·dious**, *a. Obs.* [f. L. *tragœdi-a* TRAGEDY + -OUS.] Full of, or having the character of, tragedy; calamitous, tragic.

**1494** FABYAN *Chron.* VII. 670 Of whom [Richard III] tedyous it is to me to wryte the tragedyous hystory. **1565** J. HALLE *Hist. Expost.* 25 Most frivolous communications and tragedious doynges. **1616** J. LANE *Cont. Sqr.'s T.* x. 34 His late vncothe dreame was th' oracle of this tragedious schene. **1691** WOOD *Ath. Oxon.* I. 95 A true and most notable history,..in much part tragedious.

Hence †**Trage·diously** *adv.*, in tragic style.

**1602** WARNER *Alb. Eng.* XVI. cvi. 414 Our Histories tragediously doe varie hard Euents. **1658** COKAINE *Obstinate Lady* II. ii, The same blade Shall be the instrument, and I receive it Tragediously here on my knees.

**Tragedist** (træ·dʒĭdist). *rare*⁻¹. [f. TRAGEDY + -IST.] A writer of tragedy: = TRAGEDIAN 1.

**1823** G. DARLEY in *Lond. Mag.* Dec. 647/2 The *os magna sonans*..is the first great qualification for a tragedist, and this qualification the Author of the Bride's Tragedy most undeniably possesses.

**Tragedize** (træ·dʒĭdəiz), *v.* [f. TRAGEDY + -IZE: cf. *harmon-ize*, etc.]

**1.** *trans.* To act or perform as a tragedy; *fig.* to do or carry on tragically; in quot. 1593, to treat tragically, subject to a tragic fate.

**1593** NASHE *Christ's T.* (1613) 54 Like tragicke Seneca, I should tragedize my selfe, by bleeding to death in the depth of passion. **1599** — *Lenten Stuffe* 47 The nurse.. cowring on the backeside whiles these things were a tragedizing. **1623** [see TRAGEDIZED]. **1734** *Grub St. Jrnl.* 2 May 1/3 As woeful a tragedy as ever was tragedized on the British stage. **1827** *Blackw. Mag.* XXI. 736 This assuredly not less tragical tragedy than any that ever was tragedized by a company of tragedians.

**2.** *intr.* To perform as a tragedian; *fig.* to act or speak in tragic style.

**1756** TOLDERVY *Hist. 2 Orphans* IV. 105 If we do spend this money we can..tragedize for more. **1889** FARRAR *Lives Fathers* II. xiii. 14 Oh air and Oh virtue!—for I will tragedise a little! [tr. GREG. NAZ. *Ep.* v, More tragico exclamabo].

**3.** *trans.* To convert into a tragedy; to dramatize in tragic form.

**1811** *British Press* 19 Aug., *The Comedy of Errors*, tragedized. *a* **1849** H. COLERIDGE *Ess.* (1851) II. 177 Modern critics, aping the nicety of Athens, which forbade the tragedising of recent history, may think [etc.].

Hence **Tra·gedized** *ppl. a.*, **Tra·gedizing** *vbl. sb.*; also **Tra·gediza·tion**, the action of tragedizing.

**1623** COCKERAM, *Tragidized*, killed. **1796** *Sporting Mag.* VII. 329 The tragedization of Edward the Black Prince.

**Tragedy** (træ·dʒĭdi). Forms: 4–6 **tragedye**, (4–5 **tregeedie**, **tregedie**), 4–7 **tragedie**, 5 **-idie**, (**trajedi**), 5–6 **tragedi**, **-ide**, 6 **tragœdie**, (**trigide**, **-idy**), 5– **tragedy**. [ME. a. OF. *tregedie*, *tragedie* (14th c. in Godef.), ad. L. *tragœdia*, a. Gr. τραγῳδία, app. goat-song, f. τράγος goat + ᾠδή ode, song.

As to the reason of the name many theories have been offered, some even disputing the connexion with 'goat'. See L. H. Gray in *Classical Quarterly* VI. 60, and references there given.]

**1.** A play or other literary work of a serious or sorrowful character, with a fatal or disastrous conclusion: opp. to COMEDY¹ 1. †**a.** In mediæval use: A tale or narrative poem of this character.

*c* **1374** CHAUCER *Boeth.* II. pr. ii. 23 (Camb. MS.) The cryenges of tragedyes...Tragedye is to seyn, a dite of a prosperite for a tyme þat endith in wrecchydnesse. *c* 1374 — *Troylus* v. 1786 Go litel booke goo litell my tregeedie. *c* 1386 — *Monk's Prol.* 83 (Corpus) Or elles tregedys [*v.rr.* -ies, -ise] first wol I telle. *c* 1430 Lydg. *Misericordias* 65 At funeral feestys men synge tragedies With wooful ditees of lamentacioun. 1531 Elyot *Gov.* I. x, Than shall he, in redyng tragoedies, execrate and abhorre the intollerable life of tyrantes. 1593 Churchyard (*title*) The Earle of Murtons Tragedie.

**b.** Applied to ancient Greek and Latin works: the original (Dorian) being lyric songs, the later (Attic and Latin) dramatic pieces.

*c* 1430 Lydg. *Min. Poems* (Percy Soc.) 25 The tragidés divers and unkouth Of morall Senec. 1484 Caxton *Curiall* 11 As seyth Seneke in hys tragedyes, Age cometh to late to peple of smale howses. 1546 Langley *Pol. Verg. De Invent.* I. ix. 17 b, As the Alters were kindled with fyre, and the Goate layed on it, the Quire in honor of Bacchus, songe this Meter called a Tragedie. 1579 Lodge *Def. Poetry* (Shaks. Soc.) 24 Tragedies and Comedies..wer inuented..to no other purpose, but to yeelde prayse unto God for a happy haruest, or plentiful yeere. *a* 1637 B. Jonson *Horace's Art of Poetry* 312 Thespis is said to be the first found out The tragedy, and carried it about, Till then unknown, in carts, wherein did ride Those that did sing, and act. 1789 T. Twining *Aristotle's Treat. Poetry* II. § 12. 88 Now, the subjects of the best Tragedies are confined to a few families —to Alcmæon, Oedipus,..and others, the sufferers, or the authors, of some terrible calamity. 1873 Symonds *Grk. Poets* ix. 277 His Chorus were attired like Satyrs in goat-skins, to represent the woodland comrades of the god: hence came the name of *Tragedy* or Goat-song.

**c.** Applied to a modern stage-play.

1538 Bale *Thre Lawes* 1465 Companyons I want to begynne thys tragedye. 1597 Shaks. (*title*) An excellent conceited Tragedie of Romeo and Iuliet. 1611 — (*title*) The Tragedie of Cymbeline. 1641 Milton *Ch. Govt.* II. Pref., Wks. 1851 III. 146 The Apocalyps of Saint Iohn is the majestick image of a high and stately Tragedy,..intermingling her solemn Scenes and Acts with a sevenfold Chorus of halleluja's and harping symphonies. 1703 Farquhar *Inconstant* IV. iii, Cry then, handsomely; cry like a queen in a tragedy. 1775 Harris *Philos. Arrangem.* Wks. (1841) 316 This excellent tragedy [Macbeth]..is not only admirable as a poem, but is perhaps..one of the most moral pieces existing. 1838–9 Hallam *Hist. Lit.* III. III. vi. § 90. 339 Five of his sixteen plays are tragedies, that is, are concluded in death.

**2.** That branch of dramatic art which treats of sorrowful or terrible events, in a serious and dignified style: opp. to Comedy[1] 2. (Sometimes *personified.*)

1412–20 Lydg. *Chron. Troy* II. 852 Tragidie, who so list to knowe, It begynneth in prosperite, And endeth euer in aduersite; And it also doth þe conquest trete Of riche kynges and of lordys grete. 1508 Dunbar *Lament for Makaris* 59 [Death] That scorpioun fell hes done infek Maister Iohne Clerk, and James Afflek, Fra balat making & trigide. 1598 Meres *Palladis Tamia* 282 Plautus and Seneca are accounted the best for Comedy and Tragedy among the Latines. 1632 Milton *Penseroso* 97 Som time let Gorgeous Tragedy In Scepter'd Pall com sweeping by. 1757 W. Wilkie *Epigon.* Pref. 5 In Epic poetry, Tragedy, or any other of the higher kinds of poetical composition. 1861 Paley *Æschylus, Prometh.* (ed. 2) 799 *note*, This use is common in Homer, but rare in tragedy. 1900 W. L. Courtney *Idea of Tragedy* 12 Tragedy is always the clash of two powers—necessity without, freedom within.

**3.** *fig.* An unhappy or fatal event or series of events in real life; a dreadful calamity or disaster. (Cf. Comedy[1] 4.)

1509 Hawes *Past. Pleas.* xii. (Percy Soc.) 49 His chere is dolorus, As in bewaylyng a woful tragedy. 1535 Layton in *Lett. Suppress. Monasteries* (Camden) 76 To tell yowe all this commodie, but for thabbot a tragedie, hit were to long. 1617 Moryson *Itin.* I. 207 The warre of Hungarie made all those parts full of tragedies and miserie. 1657 Trapp *Comm. Job* i. 19 Lately at Witney..a scurrilous blasphemous Comedy was by the fall of the room wherein it was acted, turned into a Tragedy, as ending with the deaths of six. 1871 Freeman *Norm. Conq.* IV. xx. 572 The turning-point of William's reign, the tragedy of the fate of Waltheof.

†**b.** A doleful or dreadful tale; a passionate complaint. *Obs.*

1565 Jewel *Def. Apol.* II. xiii. (1611) 255 Iudge thou..how iust causes M. Harding had to mooue these Tragedies. 1594 Spenser *Amoretti* liv, I waile, and make my woes a Tragedy. 1611 Bible *Transl. Pref.* 2 Herevpon they raise vp a tragedie, and wish in their heart the Temple had neuer bene built. 1664 H. More *Myst. Iniq., Apol.* 538 Some would raise such Stirres and Tragedies about.

†**c.** With *of* or possessive: Sad story, unhappy fate, misery, misfortune; *esp.* sorrowful end, violent death. *Obs.*

1513 Douglas *Æneis* IV. Prol. 264 Sen I suld thi [Dido's] trigidy endite. *a* 1592 Greene *Alphonsus* I. Wks. (Rtldg.) 227/1 This sword..should the author be To make an end of this my tragedy. 1598–9 [E. Forde] *Parismus* I. (1661) 68, I fear he is destroyed by the treachery of that wicked homicide.., who is not contented with his tragedy, but also seeketh my destruction. 1617 Moryson *Itin.* I. 186 He ceased not to bewaile my misery, and to recount my Tragedy as if it had been the burning of Troy. 1678 Marvell *Growth Popery* Wks. (Grosart) IV. 412 Men sit by, like idle spectators, and still give money towards their own tragedy. 1738 Wesley *Psalms* XCI. iv, Thou..shalt look on and see The Wicked's dismal Tragedy.

¶**4.** Misused for Tragedian 1. *Obs. rare*⁻¹.

1460 Capgrave *Chron.* (Rolls) 49 Sophocles and Euripides ..were cleped Tragedies. Trajedi is as mech to sey as he that writith eld stories, with ditees hevy and sorowful.

**5.** *attrib.* and *Comb.*, as *tragedy-actor, -air, -drum* (Drum *sb.*[1] 3), *-god, -king, -player, -queen, speech, strut, -victim, -writer*; **tragedy-man** the chief tragic actor at a theatre.

1820 W. Tooke tr. *Lucian* I. 481 Lay aside your proper character and assume that of a *tragedy-actor. 1897 'A Hope' *Phroso* v, Her *tragedy-air was quite delightful. 1702 Steele *Funeral* IV. i. 59 He is a *Tragedy-Drum to one of the Play-Houses. 1820 W. Tooke tr. *Lucian* I. 505 Properties necessary for the equipment of a *tragedy-god. 1900 *Macm. Mag.* May 50/1 More like a *tragedy-king than a monarch of history. 1821 *Blackw. Mag.* X. 588 The vacant situation of *tragedyman. 1552 Huloet, *Tragedie player, *tragœdus.* 1848 Thackeray *Van. Fair* xlvi, She bowed me out of the room like a *tragedy queen. 1773 Goldsm. *Stoops to Conq.* v. i, A short *tragedy speech. 1791 Paine *Rights of Man* (ed. 4) 27 A *tragedy-victim expiring in show, and not the real prisoner of misery. 1552 Huloet, *Tragedie wryter, *tragicus, Sophocles.* *c* 1740 G. Walmsley in Hawkins *Johnson* (1787) 39 Johnson is a very good scholar and poet, and, I have great hopes, will turn out a fine tragedy-writer.

**Tragelaph** (træ·gĭlæf). Also in L. form **tragelaphus** (trăge·lăfŭs), pl. -i. [ad. L. *tragelaph-us*, a. Gr. τραγέλαφος, f. τράγος he-goat + ἔλαφος deer.]

**1.** (Rendering Gr. τραγέλαφος.) **a.** A name for some foreign species of capriform antelope or other horned beast, vaguely known to the ancients.

1398 Trevisa *Barth. De P. R.* XVIII. ci. (Bodl. MS.), Tragelaphus is icleped Ircocervus also and haþ þat name tragelaphus of trages þat is a gotte bucke and elephos þat is an herte. *Ibid.*, Tragelaphi..som beþ of þe kinde of þe herte. 1607 Topsell *Four-f. Beasts* (1658) 93 Of the first kinde of *Tragelaphus* which may be called a Deer-goat. *Ibid.* 94 There is another kinde..like a Deer..Pliny affirmeth, that they are found about the river Phasis, in Arabia and Arachotæ,..a City of India..which [beast] the Græcians call *Tragelaphos*, and the Germans, *Ein Brandhirse*...The figure of another *Tragelaphus*, or Deer-Goat, expressed by Bellonius..it wanteth a beard, and the hair thereof resembleth an Ibex-Goat..: the horns..like a Goats, but more crooked..which he never loseth. 1656 Blount *Glossogr.*, *Tragelaph* (*tragelaphus*), the great and blackish deere called a stone-buck, deer-goat, or goat-hart. 1774 Goldsm. *Nat. Hist.* (1862) I. II. v. 327 There is in the forests of Germany, a kind of stag, named by the ancients the *Tragelaphus*, and which the natives call the bran deer, or the brown deer.

**b.** *Myth.* A fabulous or fictitious beast compounded of a goat and a stag; hence *allusively.*

1644 Featly *Levites Scourge* 60 What Chimera's, Tragelaphusses, and Hippocentaurs dost thou talk of? *a* 1670 Hacket *Abp. Williams* II. (1693) 49 Tragelaphi, Satyrs and Griffins, Cocks and Bulls. 1818 R. P. Knight *Anc. Art & Mythol.* § 114. 88 Among the principal of these symbols [of Diana] is the deer,..which is sometimes blended into one figure with the goat, so as to form a composite fictitious animal called a Tragelephus. 1898 C. Thomas *Faust* I. p. lxiv, The 'tragelaph' had to be disposed of!

**2.** *Zool.* Any antelope of the modern genus *Tragelaphus*, as the S. African boschbok, *T. sylvaticus*, and the W. African harnessed antelope, *T. scriptus*, Speke's Tragelaph, *T. Spekii.*

1888 *Cassell's Encycl. Dict.*, Tragelaphus. 1908 Sir H. H. Johnston *Grenfell & Congo* II. xxxiii. 923 In Tragelaphs the Congo regions are well endowed. 1910 *Contemp. Rev.*, *Suppl.* Nov. 11 Two of these ruffians shot over fifty of the rare antelope called Speke's tragelaph.

So **Tragelaphine** (trăge·lăfəin) *a.*, belonging to the group *Tragelaphinæ* of antelopes, typified by the genus *Tragelaphus*; *sb.* an antelope of this group.

1891 Flower & Lydekker *Mammals* ix. 345 Tragelaphine Section...Includes large, so-called Bovine, Antelopes now mainly characteristic of the Ethiopian region. 1900 *Nature* 11 Oct. 585/1 If the markings of the Tragelaphines have the significance here attached to them, they should be better developed in the species that live in the bush than in those that frequent the open. 1905 P. C. Mitchell *Guide Gard. Zool. Soc.* (ed. 3) 43 The Tragelaphine Group (*Tragelaphinæ*) contains mostly large Antelopes with spirally-twisted horns.

†**Trage·mato·polist.** *Obs. rare*⁻⁰. [f. Gr. τραγηματοπώλης (Hesychius) + -ist, f. τραγήματ- dried fruit or sweetmeat.] A seller of sweets.

1656 Blount *Glossogr.*, *Tragematopolist* (*tragematopola*), he that sells comfits, carawaies and such other ware, made of sugar; a Confectioner. 1658 in Phillips.

**Traget, -our, -ry**: see Treget, etc.

**Tragi**, pl. of Tragus.

**Tragi-** (trædʒi), combining form repr. Tragic, in a few nonce-words on the model of Tragi-comedy, as *tragi-catastrophe, -farce, -farcical* adj. (See also under Tragi-comedy.)

1811 *Henry & Isabella* I. 169 The love of tragi-catastrophe, common to vulgar minds. 1893 *Sat. Rev.* 1 Apr. 342/1 The pitiable tragi-farce of French politics. 1896 *Daily News* 17 Jan. 6/3 The fantastic tragi-farcical experiment.

**Tragic** (træ·dʒik), *a.* and *sb.* Also 6 -icke, 7–8 -ick. [ad. L. *tragic-us*, a. Gr. τραγικ-ός of or pertaining to tragedy, f. τράγ-ος goat: see -ic; but in sense associated with τραγῳδία Tragedy. Cf. F. *tragique.*] **A.** *adj.*

**1.** Of, pertaining, or proper to tragedy as a branch of the drama; of the nature of tragedy; composing, or acting in, tragedy: opp. to Comic *a.* 1.

1563 *Mirr. Mag., Collingbourne* xv, Witnes theyr Satyr sharpe, and tragicke playes. 1590 Spenser *F. Q.* III. xii. 3 Yclad in costly garments fit for tragicke Stage. *a* 1637 B. Jonson *Horace's Art Poetry* 122 The comic matter will not be exprest In tragic verse. 1712 Addison *Spect.* No. 315 ⁋ 10 The ancient Tragick writers. 1788 Fitzpatrick *Prol. Sheridan's 'Critic'*, The tragic Queen to please a tasteless crowd, Has learnt to bellow, rant, and roar so loud. 1827 *Buckham's Theatre Grks.* (ed. 2) Pref. 6 The..Tragic and Comic metres. 1838 Thirlwall *Greece* III. xviii. 79 One of these exhibitions commonly followed each tragic performance, and it was always furnished by the tragic poet himself.

†**b.** *Tragic-comedy*: = Tragi-comedy. *Obs.*

1631 Mabbe (*title*) The Spanish Bawd, represented in Celestina: or, The Tragicke-Comedy of Calisto and Melibea. *c* 1650 Denham *Old Age* 664 On the world's stage, when our applause grows high For acting here life's tragic-comedy. 1653 H. More *Antid. Ath.* II. viii. § 3 All might prove but a Tragick-Comedy.

**c.** Befitting, or having the style of, tragedy: = Tragical 2.

1684 Winstanley *Eng. Worthies, Shaks.* 345 Never any exprest a more lofty and Tragick height. *a* 1718 Rowe (J.), Bid them dress their bloody altars With every circumstance of tragick pomp. 1837 Lockhart *Scott* xix *note*, Her [Mrs. Siddons'] tragic exclamation to a footboy during a dinner,..'You've brought me water, boy, I asked for beer'. 1888 A. K. Green *Behind Closed Doors* vi, He wasn't tragic, not a bit of it.

**2.** Resembling tragedy in respect of its matter; relating to or expressing fatal or dreadful events; connected with or excited by such events; sorrowful, sad, melancholy, gloomy; = Tragical *a.* 1.

1593 Shaks. 3 *Hen. VI*, v. vi. 28 My brest can better brooke thy Daggers point, Then can my eares that Tragicke History. 1667 Milton *P. L.* IX. 6, I now must change Those Notes to Tragic. 1718 Lady M. W. Montagu *Let. to Abbé Conti* 31 July, The tragic story that you are well acquainted with. 1751 Johnson *Rambler* No. 156 ⁋ 10 That the tragick and comick affections have been moved alternately with equal force. *a* 1780 Harris *Philol. Enquiries* Wks. (1841) 430 That pity and terror are the true tragic passions; that they truly bear that name, and are necessarily diffused through every fable truly tragic. 1819 Keats *Isabella* xxxi, Into her heart a throng Of higher occupants, a richer zest, Came tragic.

**3.** Resembling the action or conclusion of a tragedy; characterized by or involving 'tragedy' in real life; calamitous, disastrous, terrible, fatal. (In quot. 1876, Suffering calamity, extremely unhappy or unfortunate.)

1545 Joye *Exp. Dan.* viii. 129 b, Noble valeant princes.. haue there bene, which at last..haue had a miserable tragik ende. 1639 N. N. tr. *Du Bosq's Compl. Woman* II. 80 The Tragick effects of this levity. 1850 Carlyle *Latter-d. Pamph.* v. (1872) 181 In these tragic days. 1872 Yeats *Growth Comm.* 294 The tragic fate of many bold men. 1876 L. Stephen *Eng. Th. 18th Cent.* II. 372 Swift..is the most tragic figure in our literature. Beside the deep agony of his soul, all other suffering..is pale and colourless. 1907 *Verney Mem.* I. 98 Throughout his short life to its tragic close.

**4.** *Comb.*: (*a*) expressing combination of tragic with some other quality, as *tragic-comical, -humorous, -ironic*; (*b*) parasynthetic, as *tragic-fated.*

1839–40 W. Irving *Wolfert's R., Mountjoy* (1855) 47 Whenever my father looked me in the face, it was with such a tragic-comical leer. 1902 Monkshood & Gamble *R. Kipling* 155 Some side scene..of the great tragic-ironic. 1906 *Daily Chron.* 13 Mar. 3/4 The punishing, in a tragic-humorous manner, of a rascally set of owners. 1908 *Ibid.* 19 Nov. 3/2 At the time of the tragic-fated Struensee.

**B.** *sb.* **1. a.** A tragic actor: = Tragedian 2.

1587 *Mirr. Mag., Ferrex* i, Complayne I may with tragiques on yᵉ stage. 1837 Thackeray *Ravenswing* vi, 'That he is', said Canterfield, the first tragic.

**b.** A tragic poet or author: = Tragedian 1.

1594 R. Ashley tr. *Loys le Roy* 69 There hath bin a great companie of Tragicks, Comicks [etc.]. *a* 1619 Fotherby *Atheom.* II. ii. § 5 (1622) 203 Whereof two Tragicks haue giuen vs two notable instances. 1737 Savage *Public Spirit* 7 With lib'ral Light the Tragic charms the Age. 1827 *Buckham's Theatre Grks.* (ed. 2) Pref. 5 To give the student an idea of the manner in which he is expected to read the Tragics.

**2.** A tragic poem or drama, a tragedy. ? *Obs.*

*c* 1720 Prior *Written in Mezeray's Hist. France* 19 The man in graver tragick known. 17.. *The Link* in Dodsley *Coll. Poems* (1782) IV. 126 In epics and tragics.

**3.** *fig.* †Tragic fate (*obs.*); a tragic event, a disaster.

1689 Kirkton *Hist. Ch. Scot.* VIII. (1817) 310 This was her miserable tragick. 1857 Clough *Poems*, etc. (1869) I. 113 Whatever comes of it—pain and grief, suicide and murder, all the tragics you can think of.

**4.** quasi-*sb.* *The tragic*: that which is tragic; the tragic side of the drama, or of life; tragic style or manner.

1872 Morley *Voltaire* iii. (1886) 132 Sometimes they failed in reaching the tragic, through excessive fear of passing its limits.

**Tragical** (træ·dʒikăl), *a.* (*sb.*) [f. L. *tragic-us* (see prec.) + -al: see -ical. In earlier use than *tragic* or F. *tragique.*]

**1.** Of the nature of, or resembling tragedy in respect of its matter; relating to or expressing fatal or dreadful events; = Tragic *a.* 2.

Cf. F. *tragique*, 'tragicall, tragicke,..bloudie, deadlie, dolefull, dismall' (Cotgr.), It. *tragico*, 'tragicall, dismall, deadly' (Florio).

*c* 1489 Caxton *Blanchardyn* liv. 213 The vnfortunate report and tragicall tidings. 1596 *Edward III*, v. i. 105 So must my voice be tragicall againe, And I must sing of dolefull accidents. 1641 J. Jackson *True Evang. T.* I. 43 Eusebius was an eye-witnesse of these things, who tels a most tragicall story hereof. 1828 Duppa *Trav. Italy*, etc. 150 It represents the tragical fable of Hippolytus.

†**2.** Appropriate to or befitting tragedy; having the elevated or dignified style of tragedy; serious and stately; also, affectedly elevated, grandiose, pompous; (of language) grandiloquent, rhetorical, extravagant; (of aspect or manner) grave, formidable; = Tragic 1 c. *Obs.* (exc. as involved in 1 or 3).

1548 Udall, etc. *Erasm. Par. Mark* xii. 78 What with their

magnifik and hye titles, and what with their tragicall and masking apparell, as though they had bene almost god almighties peeres. **1565** Jewel *Def. Apol.* II. xiii. (1611) 255 He..would thinke these Tragical termes should beare some weight. For sober men seldome vse thus to cry without some cause. **1579** Lyly *Euphues* (Arb.) 137, I would haue tragical and stately stile shunned. **1591** Shaks. *1 Hen. VI*, III. i. 125 Why looke you still so sterne, and tragicall? **1673** *Lady's Call.* II. iii. § 2 Those tragical furies wherewith some women seem transported.

**b.** Excited with tragic feeling.

*c* **1592** Marlowe *Massacre Paris* II. vi, Though I seem mild and calm, Think not but I am tragical within. **1887** Miss Braddon *Like & Unlike* i, It will never do for Valentine to surprise us in this tragical mood.

**3.** = Tragic *a.* 3.

**1555** Eden *Decades* 144 The turmoyles and tragicall affayres of the Ocean. **1644** [H. Parker] *Jus Pop.* 22 The latter part of Neroes tragicall raign. **1716** Lady M. W. Montagu *Let. to Lady Rich* 1 Dec., The tragical end of an only son. **1784** P. Wright *New Bk. Martyrs* 797/1, I shall want assistance to help me upon this tragical stage [the scaffold]. **1871** Morley *Crit. Misc.* Ser. I. *Condorcet* (1878) 35 A destiny..as tragical as any in those bloody and most tragical days.

†**4.** = Tragic *a.* 1. *Obs.*

**1589** Puttenham *Eng. Poesie* I. xi. (Arb.) 41 They set forth the dolefull falles of infortunate and afflicted Princes, and were called Poets Tragicall. **1590** Shaks. *Mids. N.* v. i. 57 A tedious breefe Scene of yong Piramus, And his loue Thisby; very tragicall mirth. *Ibid.* 66, A play there is, my Lord,..And tragicall..it is: For Piramus therein doth kill himselfe. **1629** Wadsworth *Pilgr.* v. 47 They made a Tragicall-Comedy of our voyage, whereby they got much money and honour.

†**B.** *sb.* A tragical story or strain. *Obs. rare.*

**1606** G. W[oodcocke] *Hist. Ivstine* xix. 75 Hauing heard the Tragicall of what was become of them..they redoubled their griefes. **1621** Brathwait *Nat. Embassie* (1877) 119 Terpnus..did..sing on his Lute these wofull tragicalls.

**Tragicality** (trædʒikæ·lĭti). *rare.* [f. prec. + -ity.] Tragical quality or style; tragicalness.

**1843** Carlyle *Past & Pr.* III. iii, An air of supreme tragicality.

**Tragically** (træ·dʒikăli), *adv.* [f. as prec. + -ly[2]: see -ically.] In a tragical manner or style.

**1.** With tragic feeling or expression; † in early use, with loud or passionate complaint.

**1577** Vautrouillier *Luther on Ep. Gal.* 25 Paul might.. tragically have cried out against them: O ungracious world. *a* **1716** South *Serm.* (1727) VI. 427 Many complain and cry out very tragically of the Wretchedness of their Hearts. **1781** Gibbon *Decl. & F.* xviii. II. 116 He tragically lamented the cruel murder of Constans. *Mod.* A story very tragically told.

**2.** With calamitous, disastrous, or fatal issue.

**1583** in Hakluyt *Voy.* (1600) III. 154 Our voyage..ended tragically. **1602** Warner *Alb. Eng.* Epit. (1612) 384 This king that tragically raigned, being first deposed..tragically ended. **1693** Dryden *Juvenal's Sat.* Ded. (1697) 71 As his Provocations were great, he has reveng'd them tragically. **1885** *Manch. Exam.* 10 July 5/2 Their predictions have been only too tragically fulfilled.

†**3.** Grandiloquently, rhetorically. *Obs. rare*[−1].

**1678** Cudworth *Intell. Syst.* I. iv. § 36. 548 And accordingly is it said of Numenius by him [Proclus], that τρεῖς ἀνυμνήσας θεούς, he did τραγῳδῶν καλεῖν. πάππον, ἔγγονον, ἀπόγονον, having praised the Three Gods, Tragically or Affectedly called them, the Grandfather, the Son, and the Nephew.

**Tra·gicalness.** [f. as prec. + -ness.] Tragical quality.

**1667** *Decay Chr. Piety* xiv. ⁋ 2 As well in the tragicalness of the event, as the insolence of the undertaking. **1687** Boyle *Martyrd. Theodora* vi. (1703) 88 A spectacle, whose tragicalness his revenge would make acceptable to him. **1905** A. C. Benson *Upton Lett.* (1906) 208, I re-read *The Light that failed* for its abundant vitality and tragicalness.

**Tragicize** (træ·dʒisəiz), *v. rare.* [f. Tragic + -ize: cf. *criticize.*] *intr.* To speak or write in tragic style, to 'do the tragic'. (Cf. Tragedize 2.)

**1833–40** J. H. Newman *Ch. of Fathers* (1842) 129, I will tragicize a bit.

**Tra·gicly,** *adv. rare*[−1]. [f. Tragic *a.* + -ly[2].] = Tragically.

**1604** Stirling *Aurora, Elegy* iii. M j, But I shall sadly sing, too tragickly inclin'd, Some subiect sympathizing with my melancholious mind.

**Tra·gicness.** *rare*[−1]. [f. as prec. + -ness.] = Tragicalness.

**1667** Waterhouse *Fire Lond.* 124 By the Tragickness of all which, in Battails fought,..I lost Hundreds of Thousands of Men.

**Tragico-** (træ·dʒiko), combining form repr. Gr. τραγικός Tragic; as in **Tra·gico-hero·i-co·mic** *a.* (*nonce-wd.*) combining tragic, heroic, and comic elements. Also contracted Tragi-, q. v.

**1756** J. Warton *Ess. Pope* I. iv. 207 Bartolomeo Bocchini ..printed at Venice MDCXLI, a tragico-heroi-comic poem.

**Tragi-comedy** (trædʒiˌkǫ·mĕdi). Also 6 tragy-, 7 trage-, tragœ-; see also Comedy. [a. F. *tragi-comédie* (1545 in Hatz.-Darm.) = It. *tragicomedia* (Florio), ad. late L. *tragicōmœdia* (Lactantius *a* 325), syncopated from *tragico-cōmœdia* (Plautus); f. L. *tragicus* tragic + *cōmœdia* comedy.]

**1.** A play (or, *rarely*, a story) combining the qualities of a tragedy and a comedy, or containing both tragic and comic elements; sometimes *spec.* a play mainly of tragic character, but with a happy ending.

**1581** Sidney *Apol. Poetrie* (Arb.) 65 The right sportfulnes, is [not] by..mungrell Tragy-comedie obtained. [**1603** Harsnet *Pop. Impost.* xxiii. 150 Our Dæmonopoiia or Devil-fiction is Tragico-Comœdia, a mixture of both as Amphitryo in Plautus is.] **1640** Killigrew (*title*) The Prisoners. A Tragæ-Comedy. **1652** C. B. Stapylton *Herodian* Advt., He [Herodian] represents..the Emperors of that Age and their Courts, with Comedies, Tragedies and Tragicomedies. **1664** Flecknoe (*title*) Love's Kingdom. A Pastoral Trage-Comedy. **1770** Langhorne *Plutarch* (1879) I. 178/1 When tragedy took a graver turn, something of the former drollery was still retained, as in that which we call tragi-comedy. **1849** Macaulay *Hist. Eng.* v. I. 636 Shakspeare had borrowed from Whetstone the plot of the noble tragicomedy of Measure for Measure.

**2.** *fig.* An event or series of events of mixed tragic and comic character; a combination of pathetic and humorous elements in real life.

**1579–80** North *Plutarch* (1676) 619 His acts..may plainly shew, that all that was but a Tragi-comedy ceremoniously ended. *a* **1649** Drumm. of Hawth. *Cypress Grove* Wks. (1711) 126 Every one cometh there to act his part of this tragicomedy, called life. **1709** Steele *Tatler* No. 36 ⁋ 5 What heightened the Tragi-Comedy of this Market for Annuities. **1838** Lytton *Calderon* i, The Tragi-Comedy of Court Intrigue.

Hence **Tra·gi-come·dian,** an actor who performs in tragi-comedy; **Tra·gi-comedie·tta** (*nonce-wd.*), a slight or sketchy tragi-comedy.

*c* **1626** Middleton *Mayor of Queenborough* v. i, Comedians, tragedians, tragi-comedians. **1892** *Pall Mall G.* 12 May 3/1 Tragedy is a name not to be taken in vain, least of all by a poet of Mr. Swinburne's calibre. *Tragi-comedietta would have come nearer the mark.

**Tragi-comic** (trædʒiˌkǫ·mik), *a.* [f. Tragi- + Comic.] Having the character of a tragi-comedy; combining tragic with comic elements.

**1683** Cave *Ecclesiastici, Athanasius* 81 The Tragy-Comick Scene of Arsenius the Meletian Bishop. **1709** *Tatler* No. 68 ⁋ 3 You have a Tragi-comick Genius. **1790** Burke *Fr. Rev.* 11 In viewing this monstrous tragi-comick scene, the most opposite passions..succeed..each other..; alternate laughter and tears; alternate scorn and horrour. **1831** Southey in *Q. Rev.* XLIV. 276 A more tragi-comic history could not be imagined. **1840** *New Monthly Mag.* LVIII. 524 Screaming in ecstasy at the tragicomic termination of their attempt.

So **Tra·gi-co·mical** *a.*, of tragi-comic character (hence **Tra·gi-comica·lity,** tragi-comic quality, or an instance of this; **Tra·gi-co·mically** *adv.*, in a tragi-comical way). Also **Tra·gi-co·mi-opera·tical, -pa·storal** *adjs.* (*nonce-wds.*), combining the qualities of tragi-comedy and opera (or pastoral).

**1567** Fenton *Trag. Disc.* xiii. Argt. (1898) 238 A *tragicomiqual reaport. **1581** Sidney *Apol. Poetrie* (Arb.) 43 Some Poesies haue coupled together two or three kindes, as Tragicall and Comicall, wher-vpon is risen, the Tragicomicall. **1627** (*title*) A Tragi-Comicall History of ovr Times, vnder the borrowed names of Lisander and Calista. *a* **1661** Fuller *Worthies, Leicester.* (1662) II. 129 His tragicomical life, had a peaceable End. **1878** H. James *Europeans* i, It was extremely clever, and full of a sort of tragicomical power. **1897** *Q. Rev.* Jan. 182 His butterfly *tragicomicalities of romance. **1733** J. Bramston *Man of Taste* 22, I was *tragi-comically got. **1902** Swinburne in *Q. Rev.* July 25 The dissolution of a ruined household is.. tragicomically set before us. *c* **1778** Porson (*title* in *Daily Chron.* 29 Mar. (1902) 6/7), Out of the Frying-pan into the Fire..a *tragi-comi-operatical farce. **1714** Gay (*title*) The What d'ye call it: A *Tragi-Comi-Pastoral Farce. **1729** Hawker (*title*) The Wedding: A Tragi-Comi-Pastoral-Farcical Opera..The Overture, by Dr. Pepusch.

‖**Tra·gion, -ium.** *Herb. Obs.* [L. *tragion*, Gr. τράγιον, f. τράγος he-goat.] A name given by the Greeks to some strong-smelling plant or plants; identified by 16th c. herbalists with *Dictamnus albus* (*D. Fraxinella*, Lyte 343), and *Chenopodium vulvaria* (*Tragium Germanicum*, Lyte 548).

**1567** Maplet *Gr. Forest* 62 Tragion saith Diascorides, onely Crete & Cicilie bringeth forth. **1577** Grange *Gold. Aphrod.* F iij, The hearbe *Dictamus*, or Tragion. **1578** Lyte *Dodoens* III. xxi. 343 Of false Dictam...This herbe is called in Greeke τράγιον, in Latine *Tragium*: and is the first kind of *Tragium* described by Dioscorides. Some herboristes cal it *Fraxinella*. *Ibid.* v. iv. 549 We do call it in Greeke τράγιον: in Latine *Tragium*, that is to say, Goates herbe. And bycause you shall reade in Dioscorides of two other herbes called *Tragia*, to make some difference betwixt them, we do name this *Tragium Germanicum*: in Frenche, *Blanche putain*: in base Almaigne, Bocxcruyt: some call it *Vuluaria*, by whiche name it is knowen of the Herboristes of this Countrie:..I haue named it in Englishe, The ranke stinking Goate, or stinking Motherwort. **1587** Greene *Euphues* Wks. (Grosart) VI. 188 The herbe Tragion being once byt with an Aspis neuer groweth. **1706** Phillips (ed. Kersey), *Tragium*, a shrub..whose Leaves in Autumn stink like a Goat; also the Herb white Dittany.

**Tra·godra·ma.** *nonce-wd.* [f. Gr. τραγο-, combining form of τράγος (see Tragedy) + Drama.] A drama of tragic character.

**1793** [see Comodrama].

†**Trago·nce.** *Obs. rare*[−1]. [app. an altered form of *dragonce*, one of the 15–17th c. forms of the plant-name Dragons (*Arum Dracunculus*, now *Dracunculus vulgaris*); the variation of *d* and *t* being due to the confusion between *dragontia*, *-cia*, and *taragontia*, *-cia*, and the inclusion by 16th c. herbalists under Δρακοντία, *Dracontia*, or *Dracunculus*, of both Dragons (*Arum Dracunculus*) and Tarragon (*Artemisia Dracunculus*); an inclusion commemorated in the existing botanical names. See etymological note s. v. Tarragon.] = Dragons (or ? Tarragon).

**1575** Turberv. *Venerie* 43 She purgeth hir with the hearbe called Tragonce.

**Tragopan** (træ·gopæn). *Ornith.* [a. L. *tragopān*, Gr. τραγόπᾱν, name of a reputed bird in Ethiopia (perh. the bearded vulture); f. τράγος goat + Πάν Pan; in mod. Ornithology taken as the name of a genus (Cuvier, 1829).] A pheasant of the genus *Ceriornis* (formerly *Tragopan*), characterized by having a pair of erectile fleshy horns on the head; the species are found in India, China, etc.

[**1623** Cockeram III, *Tragoponadus*, a bird in Ethiope greater then an Eagle, hauing hornes like a Goate. **1706** Phillips (ed. Kersey), Tragopanas.] **1831** Gould *Birds fr. Himalaya* lxii, The genus Tragopan. **1847** Carpenter *Zool.* § 431 The Tragopans seem to connect the Pheasants with the Turkeys. **1882** *Athenæum* 27 May 671/1 Additions made to the [Zool. Soc.] menagerie during April..: a pair of black-headed tragopans (*Ceriornis melanocephala*);.. a male Cabot's tragopan (*Ceriornis Caboti*).

‖**Tragopogon** (trægoˌpōu·gǫn). *Bot.* [a. Gr. τραγοπώγων (Theophr.), f. τράγο-ς he-goat + πώγων beard.] A genus of Composite plants of which the common wild yellow-flowered English and European species, *T. minor* and *pratensis*, are known as Goat's-beard, and *T. porrifolius* with rose-coloured or purple flowers is cultivated for its esculent root under the name of Salsify.

**1706** in Phillips (ed Kersey). **1731** [see Salsify 1]. **1741** *Compl. Fam.-Piece* II. iii. 376 Products of the Kitchen Garden...Buglos, Borage, Tragopogon. **1830** [see Salsify 1].

**Tragule** (træ·giul). *Zool.* [ad. mod.L. *Tragulus*, dim. of *tragus*, Gr. τράγος goat.] A quadruped of the genus *Tragulus*, or of the family *Tragulidæ* of ruminants, found in India and Java, resembling small hornless deer; a chevrotain. So **Tra·gulid,** one of the *Tragulidæ*; **Tra·guline** *a.*, belonging to the *Tragulina*; also applied to a group of goat-like antelopes including the steenbok, *Nanotragus tragulus*; **Tra·guloid** *a.*, akin in form to the *Tragulidæ*; *sb.* a member of this group.

**1878** Bell tr. *Gegenbaur's Comp. Anat.* 559 This third portion [of the stomach] is wanting in the Tragulidæ and Tylopoda. **1883** *List Anim. Zool. Soc.* 176 Family *Tragulidæ*. Genus *Tragulus* [3 species]. **1891** *Cent. Dict.*, Tragule... Traguline... Traguloid, *a.* **1891** Flower & Lydekker *Mammals* 307 *Leptomeryx*, from the Miocene of the United States, is regarded as a Traguloid. **1896** tr. *Boas' Text Bk. Zool.* 509 The Tragulids (*Tragulidæ*) form a circumscribed group of small Ruminants without antlers; ..in most respects nearly allied to the Cervidæ.

‖**Tragus** (trē^i·gǒs). *Anat.* Pl. **tragi** (trē^i·dʒəi). [Late L., from *tragus*, a. Gr. τράγος he-goat, so named on account of the bunch of hairs which it bears: see quot. 1874.] A prominence on the inner side of the external ear, in front of and partly closing the orifice, opposite to the Antitragus, and in man usually bearing a tuft of hairs; specially developed in certain bats.

**1693** tr. *Blancard's Phys. Dict.* (ed. 2), *Tragus*, the extream Brim of the Ear. **1809** Abernethy *Dis. resemb. Syphilis* (1826) 127 Situated on the front of the ear, extending over the tragus. **1874** Roosa *Dis. Ear* (ed. 2) 19 Rufus of Ephesus, who was the first medical lexicographer, and who lived in the age of Pliny, used the names *helix*, *lobe*, *tragus*, and *anti-tragus*, still employed to describe the different parts of the auricle. **1904** *Speaker* 24 Dec. 315/2 The earlet, a curious development of the tragus in insectivorous bats.

**Traheen** (trahī·n). *Anglo-Irish.* [ad. Ir. *troighthín* (Dineen), *troighín* (O'Reilly), a little foot or sole, a soleless stocking worn without shoes; dim. of *troigh*, *troighth-* foot (pl. *troighthean*); cf. Gaelic *troidh* foot, pl. *troidhean.*] See quots.

**1817** Lady Morgan *France* (1818) I. 125 *note*, Partial covering of the leg is universal among the peasantry of Ireland, at this day, under the name of 'traheens'. **1836** W. H. Maxwell *Capt. Blake* II. iii. *note*, Traheeins are the legs of Connemara stockings, which case the limbs of the traveller, without cramping his toes.

†**Trahent,** *sb.* and *a. Obs. rare.* [ad. L. *trahent-em*, pr. pple. of *trahĕre* to draw.]

**A.** *sb.* App. short for Contrahent, contracting party, or applied to one of the claimants before they enter into a contract.

**1537** Cromwell in Merriman *Life & Lett.* (1902) II. 69 Euery point in the same [letter] bothe touching the title, the demeanors of the trahentes of both parties, And the seruice that may be don be eyther partie.

**B.** *adj.* Drawing, that draws.

**1661** Lovell *Hist. Anim. & Min.* 518 Potions,..used to evacuate humours, that doe not resist the trahent medicine.

‖**Tra·hison.** *rare.* [F. *trahison.*] Treason.

**1858** Kingsley *Red King* 73 Foul mishap and trahison. **1859** G. Meredith *R. Feverel* xxxix, She must see the trahison with her eyes.

†**Tra·htne,** *v. Obs.* [OE. *trahtnian*, f. *traht* text, passage, exposition.] *trans.* To expound.

*c* **1000** Ælfric *Hom.* I. 510 Hæȝmon trahtnað þis godspell. *Ibid.* II. 278 We woldon ȝefyrn trahtnian be ðam lambe. *a* **1050** *Liber Scintill.* lxv. (1889) 200 Mid were æwfæstum trahtna [*tracta*] be haliȝnysse. *c* **1200** Ormin 11680 Nimeþþ gom Off þiss þatt here iss trahhtnedd.

**Trahys,** obs. form of Trace *sb.*[2]

**Trahysh,** var. Traise *v. Obs.*, to betray.

**Traice, Traict,** obs. forms of Trait, Treat.

**Traictise,** obs. form of Treatise.

**Traid(e,** obs. f. Trade; pa. t. of Tray *v. Obs.*

**Traie:** see Tray. **Traifoyle,** obs. f. Trefoil.

**Traik** (trēk), *sb. Sc.* Also 6 traike, 8 trake. [Traik *sb.* and *v.* appear together in Sc. soon after 1500. Origin uncertain; with sense 1 cf. Sw. *tråk* 'troublesome task, painfulness, tiresomeness', *tråkig* adj., tiresome, troublesome, wearisome, and the vb. mentioned under Traik *v.* It is not clear that sense 2 is the same word, but cf. the vb.]

**1.** A plague, pestilence; mischief, disaster; also *fig.* of a person, one who is a 'pest' or 'plague'.

1513 Douglas *Æneis* III. ii. 141 Ane cruell pest and traik, ..Fell on our membris with sic infectioun, Was na remeid. *Ibid.* XI. xv. 59 This wench, this vengeabill pest or traike. 1739 A. Nicol *Poems* (1766) 20 The meikle trake come o'er their snouts. 1825 Jamieson s. v., He that has nae gear will hae nae traik.

**2.** 'The flesh of sheep that have died of disease or by accident' (Jamieson).

1802 Findlater *Agric. Peebles* xiv. 208 The sheep dying of disease are used as flesh meat, under the designation of *traik.* 1815 *Pennecuik's Descr. Tweeddale* Notes 95 The poor,..sluggish Tweeddale shepherd, fed with his dog upon traik (sheep that have died of some disease).

Hence **Trai·ky** *a.*, weak, worn out, fatigued.

1825 Jamieson, *Traik, traichie*, weak, in a declining state. 1846 in Brockett *N. C. Gloss.* (E. D. D.). 1884 J. Tait in *United Presb. Mag.* 157/2 Sometimes a treaky member of the flock can be utilized as food.

**Traik** (trēk), *v. Sc.* Also 6 trake, 6–9 traick. [Goes app. with Traik *sb.*, q. v.: origin uncertain, but cf. Sw. *tråka* to rub on, to tug, to drudge, Norw. *traaka* to struggle against, show disinclination to toil or work; to go with difficulty, go slowly, *traakes* to become tired or exhausted, *traakall* adj. unwilling, reluctant.]

**1.** *intr.* To decline in health, or be in declining health; to become worn out; to break down, collapse. Now *rare.*

1508 [see Traiked]. 1535 Stewart *Cron. Scot.* (Rolls) I. 423 Ane seiknes that is into the heid, Without the soner that it get remeid,..The memberis all will rycht sone tyne and traik. 1639 R. Baillie *Lett.* 28 Sept., Many of them died; and..the most part of all who remained traicked pitifullie. 1737 Ramsay *Sc. Prov.* xiv. 118 He's the gear that winna traik. 1834 Carlyle in Froude *1st Forty Years* (1882) II. xviii. 451 But for the kindness and helpfulness shown me on all hands I must have traiked.

**2.** To go idly about, to stroll; to wander, stray, go astray; *to traik after*, to come after, follow.

1818 Scott *Hrt. Midl.* xxiv, There isna a hussy..that you can bring within your doors, but there will be chields..coming traiking after them for their destruction. 1825 Jamieson, *Traik*..To wander so as to lose one's self; chiefly applied to the young of poultry, Dumfr. Hence the..phrase, 'He's nane o' the birds that traik', he can take good care of himself. 1842 J. Aiton *Domest. Econ.* (1857) 264 In half dozens they are tearing the thatch off the stacks, or they are 'traicking' through the corn-fields, each of them destroying with its feet quite as much as a sheep would eat.

Hence **Traiked, traikit** (trē·kėd, -it) *ppl. a. Sc.* **a.** wasted; worn out; **b.** of sheep or cattle: that has died a natural death; cf. Braxy; **Trai·king** *vbl. sb.*, strolling, wandering, 'walking out'.

1508 Dunbar *Flyting* 118 Bot now, in winter, for purteth thow art traikit. 1562 in Keith *Hist. Scot.* (1734) App. 96 Be the tempestuous Stormis of the Winteris past, the hale Gudis wer sa trakit, smorit and deid, that [etc.]. 1585–6 J. Melville *Let.* in *Wodrow Soc. Misc.* (1844) I. 439 Mr. Andrew has been a sore traicked man since he came home. *a* 1598 Rollock *Serm.* Wks. 1849 I. 437 The trakedest bodies that livis, even as gif they wer drawin throw an myre. *c* 1680 [F. Sempill] *Banishm. Poverty* 93, I call'd him Turk and traiked tyke. 1825 Jamieson, *Trakit*...1. Sore fatigued. 2. Wasted, brought into a declining state by being overdriven, starved, or exposed to the inclemency of the weather. 1828 J. Struthers *Hist. Scot.* II. 625 To butcher-meat, except..drowned calves and traiked sheep..they were total strangers. 1894 Crockett *Raiders* xxxv, His night-hawk traikings and trokings with a dozen hizzies.

**Trail** (trēl), *sb.*[1] Also 5 traille, trele, (6 treale), 5–7 trayle, 6–8 traile, 7 trayl. [Known in sense I from 14th c.; in other senses only from 15th c. or later. App. f. Trail *v.*[1]]

**I.** Something that trails or hangs trailing.

†**1.** The train of a robe or other garment. *Obs.*

13.. *Cursor M.* 28020 (Cott.) Yee leuedis..Thoru your trail bath wide and side, Es not at seke to find your pride. *c* 1440 *Promp. Parv.* 499/1 Trayle, or trayne of a clothe, *sirma.* 1688 R. Holme *Armoury* IV. xii. (Roxb.) 503/2 The traile or traine of this great mantle was layd on his left shoulder.

**b.** A trailing or hanging article of clothing.

1896 Barrie *Sent. Tommy* x, The shrewd blasts cutting through my thin trails of claithes.

**c.** A long trailing or loose-hanging slender mass of hair, fibres, or the like; 'any thing drawn to length' (J.).

1844 Mrs. Browning *Portrait* iii, Oval cheeks..Which a trail of golden hair Keeps from fading off to air. 1881 Blackmore *Christowell* iii, Running up to him, with her long grape-scissors in her hand, and a trail of bast around her neck.

**2.** A trailing ornament (carved, moulded, or embroidered) in the form of a wreath or spray of leaves or tendrils; a wreathed or foliated ornament.

[Some take this, and esp. 2 b, as belonging to Trail *sb.*[2]; prob. the two words tended to run together.]

*a* 1423 in *Archæologia* LXI. 171, ij Fiols of on sute of silver and gild, Graven aboute wt a traille of Ive levys. 1454 *Test. Ebor.* (Surtees) II. 175 A couered pece with a trele of roses opon ye couerynge. 1480–81 in Hope *Windsor Castle* (1913) 401 Ac lxii pedum de lez Traillez et Crestes. 1533 *Hampton Crt. Acc.* in E. Law *Hist. Hampton Crt.* (1885) 352 To Robert Skyngke..moulder of Antyke-worke, for a trayle of antyk sett in the great Joull-pece in the Kynges new Hall, conteynyng 71 yards in leyngthe, 8 inches brode, at 16 d. the yard. 1551 Sir J. Williams *Accompte* (Abbotsf. 1836) 52 A riche cope of crymsyn veluet..embrodred all ower with a traile and Fawcions of Venice golde. 1557–8 in Hope *Windsor Castle* (1913) 260 The armes of England and Spaine with the treales to the same. *a* 1618 Sylvester *Ode to Astræa* vii, That soft Sattin limme, With blew trayles enameld trimme. 1869 Boutell *Arms & Arm.* v. (1874) 78 A trail of foliage..filled the space between the angular bands.

**b.** A wreath or spray of (natural) leaves, etc.; a trailing tendril or branch. (Cf. 1 c.)

1598 Drayton *Heroic. Ep.* i. 117 A little Current..Which like a wanton Trayle creepes here and there. 1697 Dryden *Virg. Georg.* IV. 184 The late Narcissus, and the winding Trail Of Bears-foot, Myrtles green, and Ivy pale. 1725 *Bradley's Fam. Dict.* s. v. *Strawberry*, As soon as they shoot forth their Trails, you must take care to cut 'em. 1833 Ht. Martineau *Cinnamon & P.* iii, They had never entangled their feet in trails of the blue convolvulus. *a* 1861 T. Woolner *Beautiful Lady, Her Shadow* vii, Nigh clad in trails of tangled eglantine.

**c.** *attrib.* or as *adj.*

1533 *Hampton Crt. Acc.* in E. Law *Hist. Hampton Crt.* (1885) 352, 71 yardes in length and 8 inches brode, of trayle moldyd worke. 1644 Evelyn *Diary* 1 Apr., Next the streete side..are knotts in trayle or grasse worke. 1649 G. Daniel *Trinarch.* To Rdr. 104 Speed, Cutt in sippetts, Trussell, layd about For a trayle Garnish. 1684 *Lond. Gaz.* No. 1944/4 A Petticoat of Musk coloured Silk,..the Flowers Trail Silver.

**II.** Something trailed or made by trailing.

†**3.** A sledge [= L. *tragula*]. *Obs.*

1570 Levins *Manip.* 198/43 A Trayle, sledde, *traha.* 1576 in *Ripon Ch. Acts* (Surtees) 379 For a trayle to hym, 12 d. 1588 *Durham Wills* (Surtees) II. 330, ij long lethers, j traile, ij flekes, j nowt heck, 12s. 1600 D. Settle in Hakluyt *Voy.* III. 37 They frank or keepe certaine dogs..which they yoke togither, as we do oxen & horses, to a sled or traile: and so carry their necessaries ouer the yce and snow.

**4.** A drag-net [= L. *tragula*]. Also *trail-net*: see 16. (Also *fig.*)

1711 W. King tr. *Naude's Ref. Politics* v. 198 The first that made trails, and found out casting-nets to make men captives. 1807 P. Gass *Jrnl.* 29 The fish here are generally pike...What we caught were taken with trails or brush nets.

**5.** The hinder end of the stock of a gun-carriage, which rests or slides on the ground when the carriage is unlimbered. Cf. Train *sb.*[1] 20.

1768 J. Muller *Treat. Artillery* Vocab., *Trail*, is the end of the travelling carriage opposite to the wheels, and upon which the carriage slides, when unlimbered. 1803 Wellington in Gurw. *Desp.* (1837) II. 565 There is no remedy, ..excepting to lengthen considerably the trail of the carriage. 1868 *Rep. to Govt. U.S. Munitions War* 95 The gun is mounted on a field-carriage, with trail of the usual form.

**6.** Anything drawn behind as an appendage; a body or collection *of* things or persons, drawn along by, or following in the wake of, something or some one, or moving steadily along in a lengthened formation so as to suggest this; a train.

1621 Quarles *Argalus & P.* (1678) 85 A rising Sun.. From whence ten thousand trails of gold came down In waving points. 1697 Dryden *Virg. Georg.* I. 504 Seeming Stars..shooting through the Darkness..With..longTrails of Light. 1770 Langhorne *Plutarch* (1851) I. 282/1 Dreadful thunders..mingled with long trails of lightning. 1856 Mrs. Browning *Aur. Leigh* I. 86 From which long trail of chanting priests and girls. 1872 Black *Adv. Phaeton* xx, The wind was apparent in the hurrying trails of cloud.

**7.** A mark left where something has been trailed or has passed along; a trace, track. Also *fig.*

1610 Guillim *Heraldry* II. vii. (1660) 77 Upton tearmeth it in Latine, *Tractus* which signifieth a Trace, or Traile, because the field is seen both within and without it; and the Traile itselfe is drawn thereupon in a different colour. [See Tract *sb.*[3] 6 (*a*).] 1727 Gay *Fables* I. xxiv. 12 A snail, ..with slimy trail Crawls o'er the grass. 1817 Moore *Lalla R., Par. & Peri*, But the trail of the serpent is over them all. 1833 Marryat *P. Simple* xxix, I used to watch them [sharks] during the night watch, as their fins, above water, skimmed along, leaving a trail of light behind them. 1856 Mrs. Browning *Aur. Leigh* II. 21 Brushing a green trail across the lawn With my gown in the dew. 1864 Skeat *Uhland's Poems* 124 The heights were touched with May's fair golden trail. 1899 *Allbutt's Syst. Med.* VIII. 865 In the imperfectly washed, a trail of dirt marks the course of the burrow [of the itch insect].

**b.** *spec.* in astronomical photography, The line or trace produced by the motion of the image of a star across the plate during exposure.

1889 *Anthony's Photogr. Bull.* II. 185 On developing numerous stars will be found which are invisible to the naked eye. The stars will all leave trails, forming arcs of concentric circles whose center lies near the center of the plate. 1891 *Ibid.* IV. 83 When the plate is developed it will contain a series of lines or trails produced by the light of the star as it crossed the plate.

**8.** *spec.* The track or other indication, as scent, left by a person or animal, esp. as followed by a huntsman or hound, or by any pursuer. Also *fig.*

1590 Cokaine *Treat. Hunting* D ij b, Take your [otter] houndes to the place..and cast your traylors off vpon the trayle you thinke best. 1602 Shaks. *Ham.* IV. v. 109 How cheerefully on the false Traile they cry, Oh this is Counter you false Danish Dogges. 1607 Topsell *Four-f. Beasts* (1658) 120 The best manner to teach these hounds is to take a live hare, and trail her after you upon the earth;..afterward set forth your hound near the trail. 1741 *Compl. Fam.-Piece* II. i. 295 A sure Sign they are upon the Scent; that is, where the Fox hath passed that Night, it is called a Drag or Trail. 1805 Pike *Sources Mississ.* (1810) 38, I was determined..if we came on the trail of elk, to follow them..in order to kill one. 1806 *Ibid.* 57 My sentinel informed us, that some Indians were coming full speed upon our trail or track. 1827 J. F. Cooper *Prairie* iii, Did you ever run him upon the trail of carrion? 1837 W. Irving *Capt. Bonneville* (1849) 111 Vandenburgh put himself upon their trail, to trace them to their place of concealment. *a* 1859 Macaulay *Hist. Eng.* xxiv. (1861) V. 143 The Spanish Ambassador.. followed the trail with such skill and perseverance that he discovered, if not the whole truth, yet enough [etc.]. 1888 P. Lindley in *Times* 16 Oct. 10/5 The hound..took up the stale trail over some rather trying ground without a fault.

**b.** Something strong-smelling trailed or drawn along the ground to produce a scent for hounds to follow: = Drag *sb.* 6 b.

1763 *Brit. Mag.* IV. 553 They ran after a trail drawn by a man on horseback about 10 minutes before the hounds started. 1781 P. Beckford *Hunting* (1802) 85 A cat is as good a trail as any.

**9.** A path or track worn by the passage of persons travelling in a wild or uninhabited region; a beaten track, a rude path. (Chiefly in U.S. and Canada.)

1807 P. Gass *Jrnl.* 125 We proceeded down the river through dreadful narrows, where the rocks were in some places breast high, and no path or trail of any kind. 1875 Temple & Sheldon *Hist. Northfield, Mass.* 50 Indian Paths—which were narrow trails worn by the feet in marching single file—crossed the country in various directions. 1894 C. L. Johnstone *Canada* 81 A trail, as the Canadians call the tracks which do instead of roads.

**10.** *Geol.* A name for certain mixed glacial or other deposits resting upon older formations.

(So called as app. marking the track of floating ice.)

1866 O. Fisher in *Q. Jrnl. Geol. Soc.* 20 June 555, I have found that cylindrical pits and pipes are generally confined to soluble beds, and that the normal form of the cavities in clays, sands, and gravels is that of troughs or furrows. They are usually filled with materials derived from some neighbouring higher ground...For the sake of a name I shall call the materials which fill these furrows the 'trail'. 1882 Geikie *Text-bk. Geol.* VI. v. ii. § 2. 908 A remarkable bed of clay, loam, and gravel ('loess' or 'trail'). 1884 W. G. Smith in *Jrnl. Anthropol. Inst.* XIII. 358 The whole of the 'Palæolithic floor' is..covered with the 'warp and trail' belonging to the last geological period of great cold. 1897 *Archæol. Jrnl.* Dec. 375 Where the flints are buried, in the 'head' or 'rain wash' or 'run o' th' hills' or trail, or whatever we may call the surface accumulation.

**III.** Action of trailing.

**11.** The action of dragging oneself or something along, or of creeping or crawling; also *dial.*, a tiring walk. *rare.*

*a* 1547 Surrey *Æneid* II. 284 The serpents twine [=twain] with hasted traile they glide To Pallas temple. 1674 N. Fairfax *Bulk & Selv. World* 141 The souls business in the wagon or vehicle of the body is..rather to ride in state than to ride post, ennobling the body by its curious draughts and trails of enlivening sprightlinesses. 1876 *Whitby Gloss.* s. v., 'A lang trail', a tiresome journey.

**12.** The action of hunting by the trail; chase by the track or scent.

1669 Dryden *Wild Gallant* III. i, To come upon the spur after a trayl at four in the afternoon to destruction of cold meat and cheese. 1902 O. Wister *Virginian* ix, All winter he had ridden trail, worked at ditches during summer.

**13.** *Mil.* The act of trailing a rifle, or the position of it when trailed (see Trail *v.*[1] 2).

1833 *Regul. Instr. Cavalry* I. 29 The barrel..may be.. examined at the trail. 1847 *Infantry Man.* (1854) 30 *Trail Arms*...Bring it down to the trail on the right side. *Ibid.* 40 b, The short trail must never be used. 1892 Greener *Breech-Loader* 193 At the 'trail', that is, grasped in the right hand, the arm at full length, and the gun horizontal.

**14.** An act of drawing out, enticing, or befooling. *rare*$^{-1}$. 1847 [see Trail *v.*[1] 3 b].

**IV. 15.** A woman who trails her dress along the ground; an untidy woman, slattern, slut. *Sc.*

1825 Jamieson, *Trail*, a term of reproach for a dirty woman; as, 'Ye wile trail', you nasty hussy, *Aberd.* 1878 A. Paul *Rand. Writ.* 28 It is a very old saying..that no man should marry a trail, which meant a female who trailed her dress through the gutters. 1901 Trotter *E. Galloway Sk.* 102/2 Come, bring me quick, ye useless trail, The gully knife to sheer the kail.

**V. 16.** *attrib.* and *Comb.* (some of which may be from Trail *v.*[1]), as *trail-blazer, -hunting, -maker, -robbery, -trot*; *trail-weary* adj.; see also 2 c; **trail-bar**, a wooden bar for turning the trail of a gun-carriage in pointing the gun; **trail-board**, a carved piece in a ship: see quot.; **trail-car** (*U.S.*) = Trailer 6 a; **trail-cart** (*dial.*): see quots. 1770–1896; **trail-eye** = *trail-plate-eye*; **trail-handspike** = *trail-bar*; **trail lever**, 'a trailing lever hinged to the spindle-carriage of a spinning-mule' (*Cent. Dict. Supp.*); **trail-net**, a fishing-net that is trailed or drawn along, a drag-net; **trail-plank**, a plank for supporting the trail of a gun-carriage; **trail-plate**, an iron plate attached to the trail of a gun-carriage; hence

**trail-plate-eye**, an 'eye' or perforated piece fixed on the trail-plate, used in limbering up; **trail-rope**, a rope used for trailing or drawing something: (*a*) ? a tow-rope; (*b*) in a gun-carriage = PROLONGE; (*c*) a rope trailed on the ground to check the speed of a balloon; **trail-scent** = sense 8 b above (cf. TRAIN-SCENT); **trail-spade**, a projection at the lower end of the trail of a gun-carriage.

**1828** J. M. SPEARMAN *Brit. Gunner* (ed. 2) 116 *Trail Bearings. (Cast Iron.) **1908** *Daily Chron.* 19 May 3/2 Mrs. Hubbard's journey..with a small party of '*trail blazers' native to the ways of Labrador. **1704** J. HARRIS *Lex. Techn.* I, **Traile-board*, in a Ship, is a carved Board on each side of her Beak, reaching from her Main Stem to the Figure, or to the Brackets. **1770–4** A. HUNTER *Georg. Ess.* (1804) II. 370 To bruise out the grain by sledges or *trail carts. **1861** SMILES *Engineers* II. 109 Sledges or trail-carts were also used for the same purpose; but the most common instrument employed was the flail. **1896** CROCKETT *Grey Man* xii, A trail-cart,..a box with shafts like a carriage, but without wheels, mounted on a great brush of branches and twigs, which..scored the ground with a thousand ruts and scratches. **1887** *Pall Mall G.* 30 Mar. 6/1 Large numbers of *trail cattle, driven recklessly into Wyoming in 1881. **1890** NASMITH *Mod. Cotton Spinning Mach.* xi. 206 The traverse of the locking lever prior to locking is gradually lessened as the *trail lever slide L is lowered. **1892** — *Cotton Spinning* viii. 270 The shoulder R is pulled over the bowl carried at the end of the lever L, called the 'trail' lever, which is hinged to the carriage. **1901** *Wide World Mag.* VIII. 156/2 A couple of the *trail-makers visited the cabin and found the partners there. **1905** *Athenæum* 5 Aug. 183/2 A series of reprints or translations of the narratives of 'Trailmakers', from the earliest times to the close of the eighteenth century. **1820** JODRELL, **Trailnet*, or *Trawlnet*. **1877** KNIGHT *Dict. Mech.*, *Trail-net*, a net drawn or trailed behind a boat; or by two persons on opposite banks in sweeping a stream. **1859** F. A. GRIFFITHS *Artill. Man.* (1862) 115 One *trail plank...This plank is placed on the ground, so that the trail of a siege carriage may rest on it. **1828** J. M. SPEARMAN *Brit. Gunner* (ed. 2) 17 *Trail-plate Eyes. **1901** *Wide World Mag.* VIII. 154/2 The territory had been remarkably free from serious crime, and *trail-robberies were unknown. **1851** MAYNE REID *Scalp Hunters* xx, Mules and mustangs, picketed on long *trail-ropes. **1899** *Westm. Gaz.* 31 July 10/2 We opened the valve to hasten our descent before reaching it, and at 8.8 our trail-rope touched the ground. **1682** *Lond. Gaz.* No. 1711/8 A *Trail Scent for Hounds. **1781** P. BECKFORD *Hunting* (1802) 85 You say, you should like to see your young hounds run a trail-scent. **1904** *Sci. Amer.* 21 May 402/2 The carriage.. permits of checking the recoil without undue strain..through a *trail-spade provided with an elastic joint. **1897** *Outing* (U. S.) XXIX. 439/1 From the *trail-start to the death it had been no more than a 15-minutes' run. **1895** KIPLING *2nd Jungle Bk.* 134 They fell into the quick, choppy *trail-trot in and out through the checkers of the moonlight. **1894** *Outing* (U. S.) XXIV. 398/1 The once *trail-weary emigrant, the ranchman of to-day, does the freighting..from the railroad town.

† **Trail**, *sb.*[2] *Obs.* Forms: 5 **treylle**, 5–6 **trayle, traile**, 6 **trayll, treyle**, 8 **treil**, 7–8 **trail.** [Late ME. *treylle, trayle*, app. a. OF. *treille, traille* 'a bower or arbour of vine branches sustained by trellis-work' (Littré), also trellis, lattice work grating, grill (for window, door, etc.) = Pr. *treilla, trelha*:—L. *trichila*, later also *tricla*, bower, arbour, summerhouse: see also TRELLIS *sb.*[2]]

**1.** A latticed structure for training climbing plants upon; a trellis.

*c* **1460** SIR R. ROS *La Belle Dame* 184, I me withdrew.. And set me down aloon, behynd a trayle Ful of leves,..With grene withies y-bounden. **1565** COOPER *Thesaurus* s. v. *Brachium*, *Brachiata vinea*, a vine hauyng longe branches vpon trayles. **1693** EVELYN *De la Quint. Compl. Gard.* I. 132 Muscat-Grapes..ripen not so well when raised upon high Trails. **1727** *Bradley's Fam. Dict.* s. v. *Gardener*, To cut the Trees and Pallisades when there is need of it, as well as the Treils and Arbours.

**2.** A lattice; a grating; a grill.

**1485** CAXTON *Paris & V.* (1868) 64 Or they entred they opened a treylle whyche gaf lyght in to the pryson. *c* **1500** *Melusine* 328 He fonde a grete yron trayll, wherin were closed a hondred men..that the geaunt held for hys prysonners. **1552** ELYOT, *Clatro*..to shutte a wyndowe, specially a lattise window: To close with lattise grates, or treyles.

† **Trail**, *sb.*[3] *Obs.* [Aphetic shortening of ENTRAIL, orig. *entrai·le*.] Entrails, intestines, collectively; *esp.* those of certain birds, as woodcock and snipe, and fishes, as red mullet, which are cooked and eaten with the rest of the flesh.

**1764** SMOLLETT *Trav.* xviii. (1766) I. 291 The thrush is presented with the trail, because the bird feeds on olives. They may as well eat the trail of a sheep, because it feeds on the aromatic herbs of the mountain. **1772** WESLEY *Wks.* (1872) X. 387 Those that are fond of his bowels may put them in again, and swallow them as they would the trail of a woodcock. **1804** FARLEY *Lond. Art Cookery* 40 Baste them with a little butter, and let the trail drop on the toast. **1827** J. H. H. in Hone *Every-day Bk.* II. 94 Here [in France] they [larks] are always dressed with the trail, like snipes. **1846** SOYER *Cookery* 227 Take the flesh and trails of the woodcocks from the bones.

**Trail** (trēl), *v.*[1] Forms: 4–7 **traile, trayle,** 5 **traylle**, 5–6 **trailLe**, 6–7 **trale**, 6–8 **trayl**, 6– **trail.** [Occurs soon after 1300; agreeing in form with a late OE. *trægelian, træglian*, recorded only in the Prudentius Glosses (*Germania* n. s. XI. 398–9), glossing L. *carpĕre* 'to pluck, snatch, tear away or off', which does not so suit the ME. sense as to make its identity certain. ME. *trayle-n*, *traille*, was app. the same word as ONF. *traille-r* to haul or tow (a boat), 14th c. in Godef., and also as MLG. *treilen, tröilen* (1325 in Rügen, 14–15th c. in Brunswick, etc.), MFl. *treylen, treilen, treelen*, Fl., Du. *treilen*, LG. *treilen, treulen*, EFris. *treilen, trailen*, all 'to haul or tug (a boat)'. Cf. also LG., Du., Fl. *treil* tow-line; also ONF. *traille* (14th c.), *trele, tresle*, mod.Pr. *traillo*, Cat. and Sp. *tralla*, Pg. *tralha*, all meaning 'tow-line' or 'rope'. It is difficult to correlate the German and the Romanic words; but it is generally supposed that all go back to a late L. or Com. Romanic **tragulāre* 'to drag', f. L. *tragula*, meaning (inter alia) a 'drag-net', and a small *traha* or 'sledge', f. L. *trahĕre*, pop.L. **tragĕre* (F. *traire*) to 'draw, drag, haul'. This would also in form give OE. *trægelian*.

It is somewhat remarkable that while the earliest sense of both the OF. and MLG. words was 'to tow (a boat)', this specific use does not appear in ME., while the chief ME. uses do not appear on the continent. This detracts from the satisfactoriness of the derivation, which is still the best to which the known facts point: cf. also TRAIN *v.*[1], which similarly takes us back to L. *trahĕre*, **tragĕre* with a different suffix.]

**I.** Primary senses. Transitive.

**1.** To draw behind one; to drag along upon the ground or other surface (esp. something hanging loosely, as a long garment); also, to drag (a person) roughly, to hale; to haul.

*c* **1375** *Sc. Leg. Saints* xxvi. (*Nycholas*) 690 He hynt þe priour be þe hare,..& traylyt hyme ful angrely Our al þe floure here & þare. *a* **1380** *Minor Poems fr. Vernon MS.* liii. 356 Þei trompe bifore þis traiturs, and traylen hem on tres Þorow-out þe Cite. *c* **1489** CAXTON *Sonnes of Aymon* xx. 449 Ye shall see many knyghtes to traylle theyr bowelles thorughe the feeldes. **1530** PALSGR. 760/2 He was trayled upon a hardell thorowe al the towne, *il fust trayné sur vne herce par toute la ville.* *a* **1533** LD. BERNERS *Huon* cxxx. 475 Horses rynnynge abrode traylynge theyr brydels after them. **1623** in Foster *Eng. Factories Ind.* (1908) II. 231 A band of souldiers befor, marching with ther coulers trayled after. **1671** MILTON *Samson* 1402 They shall not trail me through thir streets Like a wild Beast. **1712–14** POPE *Rape Lock* III. 73 What boots..That long behind he trails his pompous robe? **1832** TENNYSON *Lady of Shalott* I. iii, Slide the heavy barges trail'd By slow horses. **1865** DICKENS *Mut. Fr.* I. x, The gentleman has trailed his stick after him.

**b.** To carry or convey by drawing or dragging, as in a vehicle or ship; sometimes said of something cumbrous figured as if dragged along, = 'drag' used dyslogistically. Also *dial.* to carry (dirt) on the feet into a house.

*c* **1435** *Torr. Portugal* 1316 They Reysed a gale with a saylle, The Geaunt to lond for to traylle. **1748** H. WALPOLE *Lett. to Mann* (1834) II. 232 The yacht is not big enough to convey all the tables and chairs and conveniences that he trails along with him. *a* **1763** SHENSTONE *Ballad* vi, A coach with a coronet trail'd her to Tweed. **1863** MRS. TOOGOOD *Yorks. Dial.* (MS.), The childer trail a lot o' moock in t' house. **1887** BOWEN *Æneid* III. 325, I, when our homes lay blazing, was trailed o'er sea.

**c.** To draw (the body or limbs) along wearily or with difficulty in walking, etc., esp. from disablement or exhaustion. So *refl.* to move along slowly and painfully, drag oneself along, crawl.

**1562** *Child-Marriages* 138 He..demaundid a tieth goose.. and she wold have gevin him none but one that haltid, and tralid the winge. **1566** BLUNDEVIL *Horsemanship* IV. cix. (1580) 50 b, The Horse will not lift that leg, but traile it nigh the ground. **1740** SOMERVILLE *Hobbinol* II. 404 Her wounded Parts Grov'ling she [a snake] trails along. **1863** W. C. BALDWIN *Afr. Hunting* ix. 413, I have no appetite, and trail my limbs after me as if they did not belong to me. **1908** SIR H. MAXWELL *Guide to Holyrood* 108 He trailed himself, a broken-hearted man, to Falkland Palace.

**2.** *Mil.* orig. To carry (a pike or similar weapon) in the right hand in an oblique position with the head forward and the butt nearly touching the ground; later *spec.* to carry (a lance or rifle) in a horizontal position in the right hand with the arm fully extended downward (as in the British army), or in an oblique position, grasping it just above the balance with the arm extended downward and slightly bent (as in the U.S. army). (Also, formerly, to carry (a pike) reversed, with the pointed head dragging along the ground, as at military funerals: see quot. 1688.) Phr. *To trail a pike*, to serve as a soldier (*arch.*).

**1549** *Compl. Scot.* vii. 70 The eldest of them vas in harnes, traland ane halbert behynd hym. **1565** CHURCHYARD *Chippes* (1575) 58 b, And still I hoept, the warres wold me aduaunce So trayld the piek, and world began a nue. **1622** FLETCHER & MASSINGER *Span. Curate* I. i, How proud..should I be To trail a pike under your brave command. **1688** R. HOLME *Armoury* III. xix. (Roxb.) 147/2 Trayle your pike, is to take it in the right hand vnder the head and hold it close to your side. In this posture they march. There is an other way of traileing the pike, which is by takeing the but end in the right hand holding it to the side, traileing or drawing the head after vpon the ground. In this posture they march at the funerall of a souldier. **1803** *Regulations for Exercise of Riflemen* 4 *Trail Arms.* The left hand seizes the rifle at the second pipe, the right close over the sight, and trails it on the right side at arm's length. **1825** SCOTT *Talism.* x, The soldiers wore the downcast..looks, with which they trail their arms at a funeral. **1833** *Regul. Instr. Cavalry* I. 161 The lance is 'trailed' by being carried in the right hand at the balance. **1870** LOWELL *Study Wind.* 92 Ben Jonson.. trailed a pike in the Low Countries. **1877** *Man. Field Artillery Exerc.* 62 Trail Arms. The Trail. Give the carbine a cant upwards with the right hand, seizing it close behind the back-sight, and bring it to a horizontal position at the full extent of the arm, fingers and thumb round the carbine. **1879** *Martini-Henry Rifle Exerc.* 13 Arms must never be trailed with fixed bayonets.

† **b.** Hence allusively *to trail a pen*, to write, to follow the occupation of a writer. *Obs. nonce-use.*

**1680** DRYDEN *Cæsar Borgia* Prol. 1 The unhappy man who once has trailed a pen Lives not to please himself, but other men.

**3.** *fig.* or in fig. context, with various implications: e. g. to drag forcibly *to* some course of action; to draw out, lengthen out in time, protract; to utter slowly, drawl; to 'drag *in*' irrelevantly; to subject to dishonour, 'drag in the dust'; etc.

**1604** T. WRIGHT *Passions* I. viii. 31 The sensitive appetite often..traleth and haleth the will to..follow her pleasures. **1648** CRASHAW *Music's Duel* 37 [She] Trayles her plaine Ditty in one long-spun note. **1649** BP. HALL *Cases Consc.* (1650) 396 As for Lyra, who is trayled in here, and cited. **1806** WORDSW. *Ode Intim. Immort.* v, Not in utter nakedness, But trailing clouds of glory do we come From God. **1806** G. AUSTIN *Chironomia* i. 38 The words..should not be trailed nor drawled, nor let to slip out carelessly. **1874** GREEN *Short Hist.* viii. § 3. 479 The policy which had so long trailed English honour at the chariot-wheels of Spain. **1891** E. & D. GERARD *Sens. Plant* III. III. xii. 81 There really is no reason for trailing out the matter longer.

**b.** To draw as by persuasion or art; to draw on; hence *colloq.* 'to quiz, befool' (Farmer *Slang*).

*a* **1717** PARNELL *Fairy Tale* 158 Then Will, who bears the wispy fire, To trail the swains among the mire. **1748** RICHARDSON *Clarissa* (1811) VII. lxvii. 276, I [was] so long trailed on between hope and doubt. **1847** C. BRONTE *J. Eyre* xvii, I..perceived she was (what is vernacularly termed) trailing Mrs. Dent; that is, playing on her ignorance: her trail might be clever, but it was decidedly not good-natured. **1900** KERNAHAN *Scoundrels & Co.* xxi, To see the Ishmaelites 'trail' a sufferer from 'swelled head' is to undergo inoculation against that fell malady.

**II.** Intransitive senses.

(But for the doubtful OE. *trægljan*, these form the earliest group in Eng. and perh. ought to be branch I.)

**4.** (*intr.* for *pass.* of 1.) To hang down so as to drag along the ground or other surface; to be drawn loosely behind (by a person, animal, or thing in motion).

**1303** R. BRUNNE *Handl. Synne* 3444 What sey ȝe men of ladyys pryde Þat gone traylyng ouer syde:..To soule helpe hyt myȝt do bote, Þat trayleþ lowe vndyr þe fote. *c* **1400** *Destr. Troy* 10358 Þat so worshipfull a wegh, as þe wight Troilus..Shuld traile as a traytor by the taile of his horse. *c* **1450** *Merlin* xiv. 211 Ther sholde ye se stedes and horse renne Maisterles, their reynes trailynge vndir fote. **1523** FITZHERB. *Husb.* § 141 That it [a gate] do not trayle and that the wyndes blowe it not open. **1633** P. FLETCHER *Purple Isl.* XII. xvi, His hanging dewlap trail'd along the golden sand. **1823** *Local Act 4 Geo. IV*, c. ii. § 98 If any Person..suffer any Timber..carried..upon wheel Carriages, to drag or trail upon the said Bridge or Roads. **1868–70** MORRIS *Earthly Par.* I. II. 620 The sound Of silken dresses trailing o'er the ground.

**b.** *Mil.* (*intr.* for *pass.* of 2).

**1677** *Lond. Gaz.* No. 1181/2 Amsterdam, March 19. Yesterday was performed the Funerals of the late Lieutenant Admiral de Ruyter, the proceeding was thus: 1. Marched two Companies of Soldiers, their Pikes trailing.

**5.** To hang down or float loosely from its attachment, as dress, hair, etc.; of a plant: to grow decumbently and stragglingly to a considerable length, so as to rest upon the ground or other support, as a stem or branch of a plant; to 'creep'.

*c* **1412** HOCCLEVE *De Reg. Princ.* 466 What help schal he, Wos sleeues encombrous so syde traille, Do to his lord? **1578** LYTE *Dodoens* I. vii. 13 It hath..small braunches ..creping or trayling alongst the ground. **1591** SPENSER *Ruines of Time* ii, Her yeolow locks,..About her shoulders careleslie downe trailing. **1687** A. LOVELL tr. *Thevenot's Trav.* II. 94 They cover this Table with a large pinked Carpet, which on all sides trails on the ground. **1776** WITHERING *Brit. Plants* (1796) III. 541 In open sunny situations it [*Prunella*] grows trailing,..but in woods it is upright. **1845** FORD *Handbk. Spain* I. 52 The Spanish horse's tail often trails to the very ground.

**6.** † To walk with long trailing garments (*obs.*); to drag one's limbs, walk slowly or wearily as if dragged along (often, following some person or thing: cf. 4); to move or go in extended order; to creep, crawl, as a serpent or other reptile.

**1303** R. BRUNNE *Handl. Synne* 3440 [see 4]. **13..** *Metr. Hom.* (Vernon MS.) in Herrig's *Archiv* LVII. 303 Ich [the devil] haue longe i-ben Þi lord and mad þe traile and [? in] gren In siclatoun and in scarlet. *a* **1400** *Sir Penny* 29 in *Map's Poems* (Camden) 360 He may ger tham trayl syde In gude skarlet and grene. **1513** DOUGLAS *Æneis* v. Prol. 11 Wantoun gallandis to traill in sumptuus wedis. **1608** TOPSELL *Serpents* (1658) 732 Like the Horned-serpent, so trails this elf on land. **1768** GOLDSM. *Good-n. Man* I. i, Nothing diverts me more than one of those fine old dressy things.. trailing through a minuet at Almack's. **1864** LOWELL *Fireside Trav.* 106 We trailed along, at the rate of four miles an hour. **1868** KINGLAKE *Crimea* (1877) III. i. 83 The cavalcade which had trailed in his wake. **1905** SIR F. TREVES *Other Side Lantern* II. vii. (1906) 73 The camels that trailed away from the city.

**b.** Of inanimate things: To move along slowly; to drift, glide, or flow slowly (*obs.*); sometimes, to move in the wake of something as if drawn along by it; to form a trail.

**1470–85** MALORY *Arthur* VII. xxxiv. 267 They..drewe their swerdes, and gafe grete strokes that the blood trayled to the ground. 1650 FULLER *Pisgah* IV. iii. 48 The water issuing thence trailed after them in all their removealls. 1754 J. LOVE *Cricket* I. 41 The dull Ball trails before the feeble Mace. 1822–34 *Good's Study Med.* (ed. 4) II. 68 Vesicular Erythema:..surface..covered with..minute vesicles..progressively trailing into the neighbouring sound parts. 1851 LONGF. *Gold. Leg.* IV. *Neighboring Nunnery* 59 Through the momentary gloom Of shadows o'er the landscape trailing.

**7.** To extend in a straggling line, to straggle.

1600 HAKLUYT *Voy.* III. 615 Cape Roxo is a low Cape and trayling to the sea-ward. 1905 J. B. FIRTH *Highways Derbyshire* vii. 98 The path..sometimes trails across the meadows.

**b.** *Trail off* (fig.): to 'go off' in a careless, casual, or indefinite way *into* something; to tail off.

1845 DICKENS *Cricket* iii, The soft-hearted Slowboy trailed off at this juncture into such a deplorable howl..that [etc.]. 1865 — *Mut. Fr.* II. xvi, Twemlow..trails off into '—actly so'.

**III.** Secondary senses, app. from TRAIL *sb.*1 2, 7–8.

**8.** *trans.* To decorate or cover with a trailing pattern or ornament; to adorn in the style of tracery. Const. *with*.

13.. *E. E. Allit. P.* B. 1473 Penitotes, & pynkardines, ay perles bitwene, So trayled & tryfled a traverce wer alle. 1399 LANGL. *Rich. Redeles* I. 47 Ypoudride wyth pete þer it be ouȝte, And traylid with trouþe, and treste al aboute. *c*1440 *Promp. Parv.* 499/1 Traylyn, a(s) cloþys, *segmento*,.. *sirino* [? *sirmo*]. 15.. *Househ. Bk. Earl Northumbld.* (1770) Notes 441, iiij Copes blew Sylk with red Orferes trayled with whitt Braunchis and Flowres. 1596 SPENSER *F. Q.* V. v. 2 A Camis light of purple silke.. Trayled with ribbands. 1870 ROCK *Text. Fabr.* Introd. i. 76 The golden ground is trailed all over with leaf-bearing boughs.

**9.** To follow the trail or track of, to track.

1590 COKAINE *Treat. Hunting* D ij b, An otter sometimes wilbe trayled a mile or two before he come to the holt where he lyeth. 1781 P. BECKFORD *Hunting* (1802) 150 Seeing the hare trailed to her form. 1788 *Gentl. Mag.* LVIII. I. 74/2 General Clarke..after trailing them upon several tracks, at last came up with them. 1880 HARTING *Brit. Anim. Extinct* I. 18 In later times the Bear was trailed with boar-hounds. 1910 *Contemp. Rev.* July 33 The ranch-man is away..trailing horse thieves.

**10.** To mark out (a trail or track); to trace out.

*c*1586 C'TESS PEMBROKE *Ps.* LIX. xiii, Abroad they range and hunt apace, Now that, now this, As famine trailes a hungry trace. 1600 HAKLUYT *Voy.* (1810) III. 546 By reason there met many wayes traled by the wild beastes, I lost my way. 1891 tr. *Didon's Christ* I. 410 The way of the Kingdom..is a way trailed with blood.

**b.** To make trails or tracks in; to make one's way through; see also quot. 1828 (*U.S.*).

1652 BENLOWES *Theoph.* XIII. xxvii, The Larks, wing'd travellers, that trail the skie. 1828 WEBSTER, *Trail*...In America, to tread down grass by walking through; to lay flat; as, to trail grass.

**11.** *intr.* To follow the trail or track of the game.

1741 *Compl. Fam.-Piece* II. i. 306 They will come Trailing along by the River Side. 1810 *Sporting Mag.* XXXV. 194 Mr. Yeatman's hare beagles trailed up to a hare in Pulham Furze. 1880 SHORTHOUSE *J. Inglesant* ii. 41 The hounds came trailing and chanting along by the river side.

**IV. 12.** *intr.* To fish by trailing a bait from a moving boat; *spec.* to fish from a trailer (see TRAILER 8).

1857 R. TOMES *Amer. in Japan* xiii. 308 Another cluster of fishing-boats..apparently trailing for fish. 1864 THOREAU *Maine W.* iii. 176 My companion trailed for trout as we paddled along.

**13.** *Billiards.* (See TRAILING *vbl. sb.* 1 c.)

**14.** *Cards.* At casino, To play a card that is useless for gaining a point. (Perh. *fig.* from 6.)

1909 in *Cent. Dict. Supp.*

† **Trail,** *v.*2 *Obs.* [a. OF. *treillier* to trellis, interweave, from *treille* TRAIL *sb.*2] *trans.* To provide with or train upon a trellis.

1398 TREVISA *Barth. De P. R.* XVII. clxxviii. (Bodl. MS.), Vines nedeþ to be trailed to be þe better susteyned.

**T rail**: see T 3 b.

† **Trai·lba:ston.** *Old Law.* Forms: (4 **traillebastoun**), 4–7 **traile-baston**, 4–5, 7– **trailbaston** (*pl.* 4 **-bastons**); also 4 **traile-, traylebastoun**, (4–5 **troille-**, **troyl(e-**, 6 **troyle-bastone**, 8 **trailbaton**); also 4 **trayne-bastoun**. [ME. a. AF. *traille-baston*, f. *traille* imper. of *trailler*, TRAIL *v.*1 + OF. *baston* stick, cudgel, club, lit. 'one who trails or carries a club or cudgel' (cf. *to trail a pike*).

Cf. for the formation, F. *coupe-bourse*, *coupe-gorge*, *porte-clefs*, *tue-chien*, and Eng. *cut-purse*, *cut-throat*, *pick-pocket*, *turnkey*, *kill-cow*, etc.]

One of a class of violent evil-doers in the reign of Edward I, who, as brigands or hired ruffians, bludgeoned, maltreated, and robbed the king's lieges, during his absence or absorption in foreign wars; also applied to their system of violence, for the suppression of which special justices were instituted in 1304–5; thence contextually applied also to the ordinances issued against them (*ordinatio de trailbastons*), and to the inquisitions, trials, courts, and justices (*justices sur les traylbastouns*, justices *for* or *of* trailbaston), appointed for their suppression. In living use from 1304 to *c* 1390; afterwards only a historical term, often misunderstood.

Evidence of the original application of *traille-baston* to the offenders is chiefly supplied by Anglo-Fr. and Latin writings, difficult to epitomize here. They may be seen in full in E. Foss *Judges of Eng.* vol. III. 28–36 (1851), and F. M. Nichols *Orig. Docmts. illustr. Criminal Law, time of Edw. I*, in *Archæologia* vol. XL (1866). The transference of the name of an offence to the legal process dealing with it, and even to its penalty, is a well-known phenomenon in the history of legal terms. In the 17th c. and later, many guesses were made at the origin of the name; thus the Justices of Trailbaston were fabled to be so called from their 'carrying the staff of justice', and by Coke, 'because they proceeded as speedily as one might draw a staff'.

1304–5 *Ordinance* in Camb. MS. Dd. vii. 6 lf. 61 (13..) Incipiunt Articuli Lincolnie qui dicuntur Traylebastoun. [in Brit. Mus. MS. Hargrave 336 *Les Articles de Trayne-bastoun.*]..Art. iij. De verberatoribus. De ceux qui sunt baturs e funt les grands bateries el pays, e qui sunt prestz e apparaylleez de estre loweez de tiele chose fayre solum ceo q' hom les vodra loweer ou purparleer, la baterie greyndre ou meyndre. 1305 (April) *Commission* (in Foss III. 31 (docketed)), De transgressionibus nominatis Trailbaston audiendis et terminandis. 1305 *Rolls of Parlt.* I. 178 (*Marginal note*) Ordinatio de trailbastons. *Ibid.* 201/1 Ad petitionem illorum qui steterunt in servicio Regis coram Justiciis de Trailebaston petentium remedium super eo, quod ubi plures homines fuerunt indictati de conspiraciis et aliis transgressionibus [etc.]. 1306 *Ibid.* 218/2 Les Justices qui sont ordenez pur entendre a les busoignes de Traillebaston. *c*1306 LANGTOFT *Chron.* in *Pol. Songs* (Camden) 319 Traylbastouns sunt nomez de cel retenaunce, En fayres et marchez se preferent fere covenaunce, Pur treys souz ou iiij, ou pur la valiaunce, Batre un prodomme ke unk fist nosaunce A cors Cristiene, par nuli temoygnaunce. *c*1306–7 *Outlaw's Song* ibid. 233 Je lur aprendroy le giw de Traylebastoun, E lur bruseroy l'eschyne e le cropoun, Les bras e les jaunbes, ce serreit resoun, La lange lur tondroy e la bouche ensoun. *c*1315 LANGTOFT *Chron.* in *Pol. Songs* (Camden) 320 Parmy Engletere gentz de graunz resouns Assignez sunt justizes sur les traylbastouns; Les uns par enquest sunt jugez à prisouns: Li altre alez à fourches à pendre environs. *a*1328 TRIVET *Chron.* (1845) 404 Hii justitiarii ab hominibus popularibus vocati sunt de Traylebastoun, quod sonat *Trahe baculum*. *c*1330 R. BRUNNE *Chron.* (1810) 328 Þe kyng herd alle þe fame, þe pleynt of ilka toun, & gaf þam a newe name, & cald þam Traile bastoun... The kyng þorgh þe lond did seke men o resons, & with þe justise þam bond, to site on Trailebastons. 1387 TREVISA *Higden* (Rolls) VIII. 295 Þat ȝere kyng Edward made hard inquisicioun aȝenst evel doers,..þat manere inquisicioun hiȝte trailbastoun. *c*1400 *Brut* clxxiii. 195 [He] lete enquere ..of alle þe mistakyngus and wrongus done þrouȝ misdoers in Engeland, of alle þe tyme þat he hade bene out of his realme, þat me callede 'Troylebaston'; and ordeynede þerto Iustices. 1494 FABYAN *Chron.* VII. 402. 1611 SPEED *Hist. Gt. Brit.* IX. x. § 46 Hee ordained Iustitiars for Trailbaston, who were to enquire of Man-slaughters, Ruffians, Disseisors, Boot-halers, Incendiaries, and other perturbers of the common quiet, and them to punish, by fine, death, and otherwise. *a*1618 RALEIGH *Prerog. Parl.* (1628) 18 The same yeere the King vsed the Inquisition, called *Traile Baston*. 1754 HUME *Hist. Eng.* (1761) I. xvi. 405 The renewal of the commission of trailbaton. 1851 Foss *Judges of Engl.* III. 36 Commissions of trailbaston continued to be issued at intervals till the middle of the reign of Richard II, when they finally ceased. 1853 PARKER *Turner's Dom. Archit.* II. i. 23 Strongholds for numerous bands of thieves, or 'trailbastons', as they were called. 1893 F. W. MAITLAND *Memoranda de Parl.* (Rolls) Introd. 53 *note*, This [Ordinatio de trailbastons in 1305] seems to be the first appearance in an official document of the curious word 'trailbaston'. There can be little doubt that it signified a 'club-man', a vagabond with a big stick.

**Trailed** (trēld), *ppl. a.* [f. TRAIL *v.*1 + -ED 1.]

**1.** Drawn behind, dragged along on a surface, etc. (see the verb); *Mil.* carried at the trail, as a pike or rifle; in quot. 1797, made by trailing something.

1653 H. COGAN tr. *Pinto's Trav.* xlii. 169 After them followed forty other Chariots,..full..of..Arms, and trayled colours. 1797 *Encycl. Brit.* (ed. 3) XVI. 11/2 In different parts of the course of this trailed track, small quantities of meal..should be laid. 1847 *Infantry Man.* (1854) 40 *b*, Trailed arms must never be used in field movements. 1865 *Pall Mall G.* 13 May 4 No amount of brushing could make their trailed dresses look quite clean again.

†**2.** Decorated with, or constituting, a trailing pattern or ornament. *Obs.*

1490 *Acta Dom. Concil.* (1839) 79 Ane goun of cramasy velvott, upon velvott droppit with gold, and lynit with trailyeit tweldore. 1552 HULOET, Traylled or purfled, *segmentatus*. 1878 NESBITT *Catal. Glass Vessels S. Kens. Mus.* 119 Pale green glass, with trailed ornament on the under surface.

**Trailer** (trēˑlər). Also 6 **trailor**, 6–7 **traylor**. [f. TRAIL *v.*1 + -ER 1.]

**1.** One who trails or drags something.

1808 *Sporting Mag.* XXXII. 134 The trailer indolently drags his stick after him. 1864 *Realm* 13 Apr. 2 Some trailer of coat-tails, looking out for a head to break.

†**2.** One who travels on foot (cf. TRAIL *v.*1 6); *esp.* a footpad. *Obs. slang.*

1591 GREENE *Art Conny Catch.* II. (1592) 4 Some base Priggar that..is a Trailer. The Trailer is one that goeth on foot.

**3.** A hound, or a huntsman, that hunts by the trail; one that follows a trail, a tracker.

1590 COKAINE *Treat. Hunting* B ij, You must chuse out.. two couple to be trailors of an olde Foxe and finders of him. *Ibid.* D ij b [see TRAIL *sb.*1 8]. 1859 MARCY *Prairie Trav.* v. 173, I have seen very few white men who were good trailers. 1899 *Scribner's Mag.* XXV. 16/1 The Texas Rangers..were splendid shots, horsemen, and trailers. 1903 *Forest & Stream* 24 Jan. 74/2 Bloodhounds..are not at all superior to the fox-hound as trailers.

**4.** Something that trails, drags along, or hangs draggling; *esp.* a trailing plant or branch (cf. *creeper*); in quot. 1613–39, a trailing decoration.

1613–39 I. JONES in Leoni *Palladio's Archit.* (1742) II. 45 This single Traylor does well, because of the Distance. 1832 TENNYSON *Eleänore* 38 Many a deep-hued bell-like flower Of fragrant trailers. 1870 LOWELL *Study Wind.* 15 A pair of orioles built on the lowest trailer of a weeping elm. 1880 MISS BIRD *Japan* I. 173 An ocean of trees entangled with a beautiful trailer. 1882 *Garden* 11 Feb. 106/3 Mikania pulverulenta..is a pretty trailer.

**5.** The rear wheel of a front-driven bicycle, or one of the rear wheels of a locomotive, as opposed to the *driver* or driving-wheel; a trailing-wheel.

1884 *Cycl. Tour. Cl. Gaz.* Nov. 341/2 The specimen..has a driving wheel of 36 inches, and a trailer measuring 24 inches. 1895 *Model Steam Engine* 58, 2nd, drivers or driving-wheels; 3rd, trailers or trailing wheels [of a locomotive]. 1906 *Westm. Gaz.* 25 Sept. 7/1 The Atlantic engine..had four driving wheels, two rear wheels which are called trailers, and four wheels in front of the drivers. Only the driving and trailing wheels had brakes.

**6. a.** A rail or road car designed to be drawn along by a motor vehicle. Also *attrib.*, as *trailer-car*, *-coach*, *-wagon*. **b.** A small carriage, usually a light chair on wheels, drawn along behind by a bicycle or tricycle.

1890 *Columbus* (Ohio) *Dispatch* 5 Aug., The line is to start with five motor cars for winter service, with some 'trailers' for excursion business. 1900 *Engineering Mag.* XIX. 737 By the adoption of a steam waggon and trailer, a full load of 5 tons being carried into Manchester twice a day. 1901 *Scotsman* 2 Mar. 12/5 The motor car, or motor car and trailer now so familiar in tramway practice. 1904 *Daily Chron.* 12 May 3/3 The Act of 1896..limited the weight of a motor-car to three tons unladen, and of a motor with trailer-wagon to four tons. 1909 *Times* 9 July 3/3 He was in a trailer attached to a motor-tricycle.

**7.** A kind of self-acting brake consisting of a prop attached to the rear of a vehicle, to catch on the ground and prevent the vehicle from running backwards down an incline; also called a *stopper*.

1877 in KNIGHT *Dict. Mech.*

**8.** A vessel used about 1800 in mackerel-fishing, having long poles or outriggers on each side, with baited lines about 20 fathoms long fastened to them.

1891 in *Cent. Dict.*

**Trailiness** (trēˑlinės). [f. TRAILY + -NESS.] The quality of being 'traily'.

1867 A. J. ELLIS *E. E. Pronunc.* I. iv. 324 [The] frequency [of final *e*'s in German] conveys no feeling of trailiness or weakness, as it does to the mere English reader.

**Trailing** (trēˑliŋ), *vbl. sb.* [f. TRAIL *v.*1 + -ING 1.]

**1.** The action of TRAIL *v.*1 in various senses. **a.** Dragging along, hanging down as a robe so as to drag, etc.: see the vb.

13.. *Min. Poems fr. Vernon MS.* xlviii. 194 Wher is þat gomen and þat song, Þat trayling & þat comelich ȝong, Þo haukes and þe houndes? 1377 LANGL. *P. Pl.* B. XII. 242 Þe pekok..may nouȝte fleighe heighe; Fro þe traillyng of his taille ouertaken is he sone. 1671 GREW *Anat. Plants* iii. App. § 9 In that [shade] all Strawberries delight; and by the trailing of the Plant is well obtain'd. 1865 TYLOR *Early Hist. Man.* iii. 37 The trailing is now done by horses only. 1886 WILLIS & CLARK *Cambridge* I. 579 The trailing of their chains [i. e. of the portcullises in heraldic devices] is as varied in design as that of the stalks and leaves of the roses. 1887 RUSKIN *Præterita* II. 265 The trailings and climbings of deep purple convolvulus.

**b.** The following of a trail, hunting by the trail.

1742 FIELDING *Jos. Andrews* III. vi, The best hound that ever pursued a hare;..good at trailing. 1902 *St. James' Gaz.* 31 May 20/1 One can understand the absorbing interest of trailing... Every animal leaves a trail. The expert even reads the story of a snake's trail.

**c.** *Billiards.* (See quot.)

1873 BENNETT & CAVENDISH *Billiards* 7 Trailing, that is following the ball with the mace to such a convenient distance from the other ball as to make it an easy hazard. *Ibid.* 8 In some games trailing was not allowed except by agreement.

**2.** *concr.* A trailing branch or shoot of a plant, a 'runner'; a trailing part or appendage.

1727 *Bradley's Fam. Dict.* s.v. *Garden*, Strawberries.. begin to shoot forth in January... You may cut off their Trailings in March. 1884 *Amer. Meteorol. Jrnl.* I. 8 A heavy, low flying..storm cloud with ragged trailings.

**Trai·ling,** *ppl. a.* [f. TRAIL *v.*1 + -ING 2.]

**1.** That trails (almost always in *intr.* sense); dragging or dragged behind, drifting along, hanging from something, etc.: see TRAIL *v.*1

13.. in *Rel. Ant.* II. 15 Ne be þi winpil nevere so jelu ne so stroutende, Ne þi faire tail so long ne so trailende. 1413 *Pilgr. Sowle* IV. xxxvi. (Caxton 1483) 84 A traylyng gowne of twelue yerdes wide solempnly dagged with huge bagge sleues. 1601 MARKHAM *Mary Magd. Lament.* Pref. 70 [She] made a towell of her trayling haires. 1784 COWPER *Task* v. 56 The trailing cloud [of tobacco-smoke] Streams far behind him, scenting all the air. 1858 G. MACDONALD *Phantastes* (1878) II. xix. 109 Walking with a..somewhat trailing and stumbling step.

**b.** Of a plant, or a branch, stem, or shoot of a plant: see TRAIL *v.*1 5.

1698 *Phil. Trans.* XX. 468 Stalks, round and most commonly upright, not square nor trayling. 1707 MORTIMER *Husb.* (1721) I. 161 The right sort hath long Stalks and trailing Branches. 1877–84 F. E. HULME *Wild Fl.* p. vi, Branches long, very trailing, slender; hooked prickles.

**2.** In specific technical applications. **a.** *Trailing wheel*, a wheel to which the motive force is not directly applied (opp. to *driving-wheel*), as one of the hinder wheels of a locomotive, or the rear wheel of a front-driving bicycle. Also applied to parts connected with this, as *trailing axle, spring*; so *trailing-weight*, that part of the weight of a locomotive which rests upon the trailing-wheels.

1849–50 WEALE *Dict. Terms, Trailing springs*, the springs fixed on the axle-boxes of the trailing wheels of a locomotive engine. *Ibid., Trailing wheels*. 1877 KNIGHT *Dict. Mech., Trailing-axle*, an axle behind the driving-axle in British locomotives. 1904 *Daily Chron.* 2 Feb. 6/6 Two pairs of coupled driving-wheels; then a single pair of trailing-wheels placed behind the fire-box.

**b.** *Trailing points*, on a railway, points directed away from a coming train (opp. to *facing points*). *Trailing horns* in a dynamo-electric machine: see quot. 1902.

1889 G. FINDLAY *Eng. Railway* 79 Trailing points..at a distance of 220 yards from the cabin. 1902 SLOANE *Stand. Electr. Dict., Following Horns*, in dynamo-electric machines, the projecting ends of the pole pieces towards which the outer uncovered perimeter of the armature turns. ..The leading horns are those away from which the armature rotates...Synonym—Trailing Horns. 1909 *Cent. Dict. Supp.* s.v. *Switch, Trailing-point switch*, in railroading, ..contrasted with facing-point switch.

Hence **Trai·lingly** *adv.*

1589 FLEMING *Virg. Georg.* IV. 65 Then is their sound heard heauier, and trailingly they hum. 1831 *Blackw. Mag.* XXX. 476 One of them..hangs trailingly along the mossy greensward. 1842 MRS. BROWNING *Grk. Chr. Poets*, etc. 59 Green vine-branches trailingly inclined.

**Trailless** (trēˑ·lˌlės), *a.* [f. TRAIL *sb.*[1] + -LESS.] Having no trails; trackless, pathless.

1884 BAILLIE-GROHMAN in *Century Mag.* XXIX. 195 Vast stretches of .. forest .. clothe their precipitous slopes .. in unbroken and perfectly trailless masses.

† **Trail-side**, *a. Sc. Obs.* [f. TRAIL *v.*[1] or *sb.*[1] + SIDE *a.*] That is so long as to trail.

1513 DOUGLAS *Æneis* XIII. vi. 18 In robbis lang also, or traill syde govn.

† **Trail wind**, app. erron. for *tail-wind*: see TAIL *sb.*[1] 12.

1679 *Admir. Crt. Exam.* 78. 23 Sept., They bore away for Jamaica with a trayl wind.

**Traily** (trēˑ·li), *a. dial.* and *colloq.* [f. TRAIL *sb.*[1] or *v.*[1] + -Y.] Characterized by trailing; slovenly; lazy; languid: see *Eng. Dial. Dict.*

1851 *Cumberld. Gloss., Traily*, slovenly. 1867 [implied in TRAILINESS]. 1902 *Westm. Gaz.* 23 Jan. 3/1 A muff..with a simple pretty bunch, not the traily extreme effect of the same flowers.

† **Trailye, trai·lʒe.** *Sc. Obs.* Also 5 trelʒe, 5–6 treilʒe, 6 treilie. [app. a. OF. *treillis*, var. of *treslis, trelis, treslie, tresli*, 'tissu à maille', network; cf. mod.F. *treillis* glazed calico, also sackcloth; but the Sc. word was evidently applied to some finer fabric.] A kind of cloth. (See also TRELLIS *sb.*[1]) Also *attrib.*

1490 *Acta Dom. Concil.* (1839) 158/1 Þat James Du..sall.. pay to Dauid Quhitehed..five stikkis of trelʒe of sindry hewis. 1495 *Acc. Ld. High Treas. Scot.* I. 226 Item, vj quarteris of quhit treilʒe..to be the King a harnes doublet. 1503 *Ibid.* II. 312 For ane maid doublat of trailʒe to him, vij s. vj d. 1507–8 *Ibid.* IV. 30 For ix½ elne blew trailʒe to be ane couch to the Quene. 1517 *Ibid.* V. 116 Blak trailʒe. 1542 *Inv. Roy. Wardr.* (1815) 92 Ane doublet of blak sating trailye. 1543 *Acc. Ld. High Treas. Scot.* VIII. 232 Fyve quarteris trailʒe to be his grace ane pair of sockis. 1566–7 *Mary's mourning-order at death of Darnley* in Chalmers *Mary* (1818) I. 207 Of treilie buccharem v elle.

**Train** (trēˑn), *sb.*[1] Forms: 4–6 trayn, 4–7 trayne, (5 treyne), 5–7 traine, 6–7 *Sc.* tryne, 6– train. [In origin representing two French sbs., *traîne* fem. (OF. also *traïne, trahine*) and *train* masc. (OF. *traïn*, also *trahin*), both held to be vbl. sbs. from *traîner* to drag, draw, etc. (see TRAIN *v.*[1]) and corresponding respectively to It. *traina*, and to Pr. *trahi*, Sp. *tragin* (Diez), It. *traino*. Even in OF., *traïn* and *traîne*, though generally distinct, were sometimes used in the same sense. In English, with the loss of final *e* in pronunciation and its consequent non-significance in spelling, *train* and *traîne* were used indifferently from the 14th c., and in the 17th *train* became the only spelling. On this account, and esp. because senses have arisen in Eng. which have no French prototypes, it is not possible satisfactorily to distinguish two words corresponding to F. *traîne* and *train*. The order here followed is therefore tentative and practical. The F. form, when it exists, is given, and it will be seen that branch II corresponds in the main to F. *traîne*, and branch III to F. *train*. Branches I and IV contain representatives of both F. words.]

**I.** Nouns of action from F. *traîner* or Eng. TRAIN *v.*[1] in various senses. All *Obs.*

† **1.** Tarrying, delay. [App. 'a dragging out' of time: cf. TRACT *sb.*[3] 1, 1 b. OF. *traîne, train* 'retard'.] In quots. 1553, *for a train* = for a while, for a little time. *Obs.*

*c* 1330 R. BRUNNE *Chron.* (1810) 263 For þe pes to haue, he mad so long a trayne. *Ibid.* 264 Þorgh Edward long trayne Gascoyn is born doun, Non defendes his chayne, but only Bayoun. 1489 CAXTON *Faytes of A.* I. xix. 60 Men holde and kepe the in talkyng as by a long trayne fyndyng alwayes somme controuersies that nede not... But onely for to passe tyme. 1553 *Respublica* V. vii. 1603 Thei wilbe heare soone, byde youe theim here for a traine. *Ibid.* ix. 1665, I leafte people heare for a traine to holde them talke.

† **2.** Course or manner of running (of a horse); a course of riding [F. *train* 'allure']. *Obs.*

1581 A. HALL *Iliad* VIII. 136 His horse he [Jupiter] beates, the ayre they clime, aloft they skimme amaine, Betweene the earth and welkin hie, they tread a iolly trayne. *a* 1625 FLETCHER *Woman's Prize* I. iii, A good tough train would break thee all to pieces. 1677 *Lovers Quarrel* 266 in Hazl. *E. P. P.* II. 264 Your choice horses are wild and tough, And little they can skill of their train.

† **b.** A particular gait of a horse: see quots.

1565 BLUNDEVIL *Horsemanship* I. iii. (1580) B j b, Their [Turky horses'] trauelling pace is neither amble, racke, nor trot; but a certaine kinde of easie traine. 1607 MARKHAM *Caval.* IV. i. (1617) 5 This shufling and broken incertaine pace, ..is neither amble nor trot, but a mixture of both, as taking his time keeping from trotting, and his motion of legges from ambling, and so compound this which is called a Traine or Racking.

† **3.** *Falconry.* (?) A short flight given to a hawk while being trained. [Not in F.] *Obs.*

1616 [see TRAIN *sb.*[2] 4].

† **4.** Training, education. [Not in F.] *Obs. rare*[−1].

1581 MULCASTER *Positions* Ep. Ded. (1887) 3 The generall traine and bringing vp of youth.

**II.** That which drags or trails, or is trailed.

**5.** An elongated part of a robe or skirt trailing behind on the ground; commonly worn by women of rank or fashion when in full dress, and by sovereigns and high officials on state occasions, and sometimes borne by a page or attendant as *train-bearer*. [OF. *train*, also *trainée*; mod.F. *traîne*.]

*c* 1440 *Promp. Parv.* 499/1 Trayle, or trayne of a clothe, *sirma*. *a* 1450 in Wr.-Wülcker 564/42 *Appendicium*, a lady trayne *et* a pendaunt of a gyrdyll. *Ibid.* 612/22 *Sirma, i. cauda vestis feminarum*, a trayne. 1457 *Coventry Leet Bk.* 299 Next folowed our seid souerayn lady, & the Duches of Buk[yngham] bere here Treyne. 1577 *F. de L'isle's Leg.* B vj, Would you..wishe that of her who by duetie ought euen to cary vp my trayne I should make my sister in Law? *a* 1600 *Bk. of Precedence* (E. E. T. S.) 26 A Baronesse may haue no trayne borne; but haueing a goune with a trayne, she ought to beare it her selfe. 1617 MORYSON *Itin.* III. 168 The ordinary Citizens Wiues haue their gownes made with long traines, which are pinned vp in the house. 1711 ADDISON *Spect.* No. 42 ¶ 1 The broad sweeping Train that follows her in all her Motions, and finds constant Employment for a Boy who stands behind her to open and spread it to Advantage. 1791–3 in *Spirit Pub. Jrnls.* (1799) I. 138 He trod on her crape train. 1798 JANE AUSTEN *Northang. Abb.* v, They..pinned up each other's trains for the dance. 1858 DORAN *Crt. Fools* 117 The period [time of Rich. II] when ladies in England first wore trains.

**b.** The tail or tail-feathers of a bird, esp. when long and trailing, as in the peacock; in *Falconry*, the technical name for the tail of a hawk. † Also formerly, the tail of a quadruped (*obs.*), or of an insect. [Not in F.]

1579 TWYNE *Phisicke agst. Fort.* I. xlii. 44 b, Declaryng howe well that byrde [hawk] flue,..how many feathers of the trayne, and how many of the winges are remaning or lost. 1579 SPENSER *Sheph. Cal.* May 281 His tayle he [the fox] clapt betwixt his legs twayne, Lest he should be descried by his trayne. 1591 SHAKS. 1 *Hen. VI*, III. iii. 7 Let frantike Talbot triumph for a while, And like a Peacock sweepe along his tayle, Wee'le pull his Plumes, and take away his Trayne. 1610 GUILLIM *Heraldry* III. xv. (1660) 178 The Lyon is one Colour, shaggie brested, with a certain tuft of haire in his traine. 1634 SIR T. HERBERT *Trav.* 211 [The dodo's] traine [is] three small plumes. 1639 T. DE GRAY *Compl. Horsem.* 24 The trayne [of a horse] long, not too thick, and falling to the ground. 1693 J. CLAYTON *Acc. Virginia* in *Misc. Cur.* (1708) III. 332 Their Turtle-Doves ..the whole Train is longer much than the Tails of our Pidgeons. 1852 R. F. BURTON *Falconry Valley Indus* viii. 76 A splendid goshawk,..with..a queenly train.

**c.** The tail of a comet; a luminous trail, such as that following a meteor. [Not in F.]

1602 MARSTON *Antonio's Rev.* I. iii, A blazing comet shot his threatning traine. 1602 SHAKS. *Ham.* I. i. 117 (Qo. 1604) As starres with traines of fier and dewes of blood, Disasters in the sunne. 1663 J. SPENCER *Prodigies* (1665) 32 The luminous tail or train of a Comet .. seems to the eye of ignorance the emblem of a flaming sword, or firy rod. 1860 TYNDALL *Glac.* I. ii. 17 In falling [it] leaves the light foaming mass..as a train in the air behind. 1909 CHAMBERS *Story of Comets* 137 The curvature of the train [of Donati's comet, 1858].

**6.** *poet.* Applied to the current of a river, etc., also to the elongated body of a serpent. [Not in F.]

[*c* 1586 C'TESS PEMBROKE *Ps.* LXXVIII. xx, All that rich land, where over Nilus trailes Of his wett robe the slymy seedy train.] 1667 MILTON *P. L.* VII. 306 Within those banks, where Rivers now Stream, and perpetual draw thir humid traine. 1695 BLACKMORE *Pr. Arth.* II. 153 Pure Crystal Rivers through the Meadows flow,..Their watry Train in Snaky Windings slides. 1727–46 THOMSON *Summer* 900 The green serpent..gathers up his train. *c* 1742 GRAY *Ignorance* 4. 1808 SCOTT *Marm.* III. Introd., Like streamlet..winding slow its silver train.

† **7.** Something dragged along the ground to make a scent or trail; a drag; also pieces of carrion or the like laid in a line or trail for luring certain wild beasts, as wolves, foxes, etc. into a trap [so F. *traînée*]. *Obs.*

1575 TURBERV. *Venerie* 187 Take a skynne of bacon..and when it is well broyled..dippe it and puddle it in this sawce ..and make a trayn therewith, and..if there be a foxe neare to any place where the trayne is drawne, he will followe it. 1607 TOPSELL *Four-f. Beasts* (1658) 527 The Hunters in some Countries..make a train with a Hogs liver sod, cut in pieces and anointed over with hony, and so anointing their shoes with Swines grease, draw after them a dead Cat, which will cause the beast to follow after very speedily. 1727 *Bradley's Fam. Dict.* s.v. *Animal*, For Beasts of Prey, as the Wolf, Fox, Badger, Pole-Cat,..you must make a Train; and when you come to any of the Places you have so prepared, throw four or five Bits of your Train-Carrion upon it, and of Chickens Guts for smaller Beasts.

**8.** The (visible) track of an animal. *rare*[−1]. [Cf. OF. *traîne* = trace.]

1908 *N. Hebrides Mag.* Jan. 19 The natives with me saw the train of a turtle on the sand. They thought to capture it, but did not succeed.

**III.** A suite or sequence of persons or things; a long series.

**9.** A number of persons following or attending on some one, usually a person of rank; a body of attendants, retainers, or followers; a retinue, suite; sometimes, the vehicles conveying the persons and baggage. [F. *train*, OF. *traînée*.]

*a* 1440 *Sir Degrev.* 1139 The Eorl and he with a trayn To the castel gan fare. 1513 DOUGLAS *Æneis* XIII. viii. 48 Al the chymmys riall rownd abowt Was fyllyt with thar tryne and mekill rowt. 1535 COVERDALE 1 *Kings* x. 2 She came to Ierusalem with a maruelous greate trayne. 1669 *Lond. Gaz.* No. 333/2 The Venetian Ambassador made his solemn Entry into this City, attended..by a large Train of Coaches. 1711 STEELE *Spect.* No. 113 ¶ 3 She has ever had a Train of Admirers. 1833 HT. MARTINEAU *Vanderput & S.* i, The long train of mourners. 1875 JOWETT *Plato* (ed. 2) I. 128 A train of listeners followed him.

**b.** *Mil.* The artillery and other apparatus for battle or siege, with the vehicles conveying them and the men in attendance, following or in readiness to follow an army. [F. *train*.]

1523 LD. BERNERS *Froiss.* I. lxxvi. 96 Syr Wyllyam Montagu..yssued out a horsbacke, and folowed couertly the hynder trayne of the scottes, who had horses so charged with baggage, yᵗ they might scant go any gret pace. 1643 CHAS. I *Treaty at Uxbridge* Wks. 1662 II. 527 The said Train of Artillery to be fitted in all points ready to march. 1712 STEELE *Spect.* No. 497 ¶ 2 A blunt honest fellow, who had a command in the train of artillery. 1810 WELLINGTON in Gurw. *Desp.* (1838) VI. 88 They have collected a train of artillery at Salamanca for the siege of Ciudad Rodrigo. 1900 *Daily News* 11 June 4/3 The military expression..'our trains', is apt to lead to misunderstanding..where the troops..have been actually travelling by railway trains.

† **c.** The rear of an army or body of soldiers. *Obs. rare.* [F. *train*.]

1598 BARRET *Theor. Warres* II. i. 28 How to turne their faces, making front of either flanke or traine. *Ibid.* III. ii. 55 The armed pikes..shall be..placed in the front and in traine of the battell.

**10.** *fig.* A set of attendant things, circumstances, or conditions; a series of consequences; in quot. 1638, something following, a sequel. Often in phr. *in the train of*, as a sequel to; so *in its train*.

1570 *Satir. Poems Reform.* xix. 101 That Kingdome sall come to greit ruyne Quhen that deuissioun hes his suit and tryne. 1638 R. BAKER tr. *Balzac's Lett.* (vol. II.) 23 For a traine to this first favour I require from you a second. 1721 BERKELEY *Prev. Ruin Gt. Brit.* Wks. III. 202 This vice draweth after it a train of evils. 1768 STERNE *Sent. Journ., Passport Paris*, The idea presented itself..with this in its train. 1833 HT. MARTINEAU *Brooke Farm* xii, Education came in the train of other good things. 1871 SMILES *Charac.* i. (1876) 9 There is no act, however trivial, but has its train of consequences.

**11.** A body of persons, animals, vehicles, etc., travelling together in order, esp. in a long line or procession; a succession of persons; *fig.* (chiefly *poet.*) a set or class of persons. [F. *train*.]

1489 CAXTON *Faytes of A.* I. xxiii. 70 A longe trayne of men of armes al clos togyder. 1591 SHAKS. 1 *Hen. VI*, II. ii. 34 Which of this Princely trayne Call ye the Warlike Talbot? 1698 FRYER *Acc. E. India & P.* 291 The best Hawks..fly in Trains like Wild Geese. 1746 FRANCIS tr. *Horace, Epist.* II. ii. 129 What milder Frenzy goads the rhiming Train? 1829 SCOTT *Anne of G.* vii, The caravans, or large trains of waggons, by which the internal commerce..was carried on. 1884 GILMOUR *Mongols* 287 Camels, trains of which..may be seen making their way along the crowded streets.

**12.** A number of things following one another in time or order; a series or course of actions, events, etc. **a.** A course of action in relation to its manner or purpose; method of procedure; manner of action; way of life; course, drift, or direction of a discourse, argument, etc. Now *rare* or *Obs.* (passing into b). [F. *train*.]

*c* 1530 (*title*) The ordre or Trayne of Warre, that a prynce or heed Captayne ought to take. 1534 MORE *Treat. Passion* Wks. 1330/2 They..corrupte some well mynded menne, before they perceyue the trayne of theyr craftye purpose. 1580 SIDNEY *Ps.* XV, He that leads of life an uncorrupted traine. *a* 1677 BARROW *Serm.* Wks. 1716 I. 39 God .. by secret methods and undiscernable trains, ordereth all events. 1756 HUME *Hist. Eng.* (1761) II. xxviii. 134 His splendid ostentatious train of life. 1836 *Random Recoll. Ho. Lords* xvi. 388 You never misapprehend the train of his reasoning.

**b.** In general: A series, succession, sequence (of actions, events, thoughts, or phenomena); a continuous course (of action, reasoning, etc.).

*c* 1645 HOWELL *Lett.* (1650) I. 445 A wife is the best or worst fortune that can betide a man throughout the whole train of his life. 1690 LOCKE *Hum. Und.* II. xiv. § 3 A train of Ideas, which constantly succeed one another in his Understanding. 1732 [see TRACT *sb.*[3] 2]. 1764 REID *Inquiry* v. § 5 Long and demonstrative trains of reasoning. 1769 ROBERTSON *Chas. V*, I. Wks. 1813 V. 165 A long train of fortunate events. **1858** BUCKLE *Civiliz.* (1871) II. viii. 582 The result of a long train of causes.

**c.** Proper sequence, order, or arrangement for some result; connected order; course, process: in phr. *in train* (formerly also *in a train*, and with defining adj., as *in (a) good train*).

**1528** GARDINER in Pocock *Rec. Ref.* I. xlii. 82 Everything in good train and order. **1591** SAVILE *Tacitus, Agricola* 260 Our men..were now in traine of winning the fielde. **1690** LOCKE *Hum. Und.* III. vii. § 2 It is not enough that a Man has Ideas clear and distinct..he must think in train. **1746** W. HORSLEY *Fool* (1748) II. 23 The Affairs of Europe hereby put in a happy Train. **1842** MACAULAY in *Life & Lett.* (1883) II. 114, I am..desirous to get on with my History, which is..in a fair train. **1885** 'MRS. ALEXANDER' *At Bay* x, Putting matters in train for the election.

**13.** A line of gunpowder or other combustible substance laid so as to convey fire to a mine or charge for the purpose of exploding it. Also *fig.* [It. *traina* (Florio); F. *traînée*.]

*a* **1548** HALL *Chron., Hen. VIII* 118 The Frenchmen..made traynes of gunpouder from strete to strete. **1677** W. HUGHES *Man of Sin* I. i. 4 A Mine was made, and Train was laid hereby for blowing up the Gospel it self. **1798** in Nicolas *Nelson's Disp.* (1846) VII. p. clviii, She [a ship] was set on fire by a train. **1839** *Civil Eng. & Arch. Jrnl.* II. 45/1 We were fortunate enough to witness two of these blasting operations...The order for firing the train given... In a few seconds after the ignition of the train, a rumbling sound, like that of..distant thunder was heard, and the..whole mass was lifted bodily from its base. **1850** GROTE *Greece* II. lxi. VII. 517 He..had already laid his train..for revolt. **1855** MACAULAY *Hist. Eng.* xxi. IV. 549 The spark had fallen: the train was ready: the explosion was immediate and terrible. After a tumultuous debate [etc.].

**b.** Pieces of carrion or the like laid in a line or trail for luring certain wild beasts: see sense 7.

**14.** An extended series of material objects or the like; a row, rank; *esp.* a series of things arranged in a definite order for some purpose; *rarely*, a continuous extent of something.

**1610** HOLLAND *Camden's Brit.* (1637) 343 Vpon this shore, lie out with a long traine certaine heapes in manner bankes or rampiers. **1664** POWER *Exp. Philos.* I. 43 Being layd of a row or train. **1763** W. ROBERTS *Nat. Hist. Florida* p. vi, Our more northern colonies..form one continued train along the whole eastern-side of North-America. **1774** M. MACKENZIE *Maritime Surv.* 76 When the Survey has been continued by a Train of stasimetric Triangles. **1863** LYELL *Antiq. Man* xviii. 356 Detached fragments of rock..in long parallel trains. **1878** ABNEY *Photogr.* (1881) 280 A train of prisms..set to the angle of minimum deviation.

**15.** A set of connected parts of mechanism which actuate one another in series; *spec.* (*a*) the set of wheels and pinions in a clock or watch which turns the hands (*going train*), or that which actuates the striking part (*striking train*); (*b*) a set or pair of rollers used in metal-working; a roll-train.

**1797** *Monthly Mag.* III. 464 Thus the progressive motion is communicated to the cotton spindles in the same manner as it is to the different parts of a common time-piece—by a train of wheels. **1831** BREWSTER *Nat. Magic* xi. (1833) 293 Motions are propagated..along a great variety of trains of mechanism. **1838** [see GOING *vbl. sb.* 6]. **1881** [see *roll-train*, ROLL *sb.*[1] 17]. **1884** F. J. BRITTEN *Watch & Clockm.* 266 The remarks on the train of a going barrel watch apply equally to the going train of a clock. **1885** C. G. W. LOCK *Workshop Receipts* Ser. IV. 307/2 The parts most likely to require repair in the striking trains of clocks.

**16.** A number of railway carriages, vans, or trucks coupled together (usually including the locomotive by which they are drawn). [So F. *train.*]

Orig. *train of carriages*, etc.; now one of the chief uses of the simple word: cf. 22 b.

*a* **1824** A. SCOTT *Ess. Rail-roads* in *Trans. Highland Soc.* (1824) VI. 29 By continually shifting the train of waggons at the head and foot of the inclined plane, from the one railway to the other. **1825** in W. Chambers *About Railways* (1865) 6 (Opening of Stockton and Darlington R.) The signal being given, the engine started off with this immense train of carriages. **1830** *Times* 17 Sept., The Northumbrian drawing the splendid train of carriages occupied by the Duke of Wellington...The Northumbrian locomotive engine, which had drawn the train of the Duke of Wellington. **1835** MARRYAT *Olla Podr.* vi, The trains went on well. **1837** *Cornish's Railway Companion* Title-p., The Company's charges from one station to another;..time of departure and arrival of each train, etc. **1839** W. CHAMBERS *Tour in Belgium* 73/1 We were speedily carried to the railway terminus, where a train of carriages was in waiting, with its locomotive engine hissing and chafing. **1855** LYNCH *Rivulet* LXII. ii, Thus through a distant valley's length Slow seems to glide the train. **1885** MABEL COLLINS *Prettiest Woman* x, A train left Warsaw early in the morning.

**b.** Hence, a line of vehicles coupled together.

**1883** GRESLEY *Gloss. Coal-mining, Journey*, a train or set of trams all coupled together.

†**17.** See quot. *Obs.* [Cf. F. *train*, 'nombre de vibrations qu'un mouvement d'horlogerie produit dans un temps déterminé' (Littré).] (Perhaps not Eng.)

**1704** J. HARRIS *Lex. Techn.* I, *Train*, is the Number of Beats which the Watch maketh in an Hour or any other certain time.

**IV.** Names of other things (chiefly material) derived from prec. branches.

†**18.** *Cookery.* A dish consisting of dates, figs, raisins, and almonds strung upon a long thread and covered with batter. *Obs.*

*c* **1450** *Two Cookery-bks.* 97 Trayne roste. Take Dates and figges..and þen take grete reysons and blanched almondes, and prik hem thorgh with a nedel into a threde of a mannys length,..rost the treyne abought the fire in þe spete;..cast the batur on the treyne as he turneth abought the fire. **14..** *Conuiuium domini de la Grey* ibid. 60 Le .ij. cours..Halybutte. Plays fryid. Trayne Roste. **14..** *MS. Douce 55* lf. 64.

†**19.** The carriage of a printing-press. [F. *train.*] (Perh. only French.) *Obs.*

**1594** R. ASHLEY tr. *Loys le Roy* 22 He maketh the train of the presse to roule [etc.].

**20.** Applied to various material objects that are dragged. **a.** The trail of a gun-carriage: see TRAIL *sb.*[1] 5.

**1769** FALCONER *Dict. Marine* (1776) II, *Crochets deretraite*, the eye-bolts, in the train of a gun-carriage, wherein are hooked the relieving tackles. **1815** [see *train-tackle* in 22 c].

**b.** A rough kind of sledge or sleigh used in Canada for transport. [Cf. F. *traîneau.*]

**1835** C. F. HOFFMAN *Winter in Far West* I. 210 At last a train [*note*, a rough kind of sled] and a couple of carioles drove up to the door. **1860** BARTLETT *Dict. Amer.*, *Train* (Fr. *traîneau*), a peculiar kind of sleigh used for the transportation of merchandise, wood, etc., in Canada.

†**c.** A drag-net, a seine. [F. *traîne.*] *Obs.*

**1576** FLEMING tr. *Caius' Dogs* (1880) 14 Such Dogges as serue for fowling...The first kinde of such serue the Hauke, The seconde, the net, or traine. **1609** BIBLE (Douay) *Hab.* i. 15 He drew it in his traine [L. *sagena*], and gathered it into his nette.

†**21.** A rope for dragging a plough or harrow. *local. Obs.*

**1798** *Statist. Acc. Scot.* XX. 260 The harrows are drawn side-ways by a train or side rope (like that used in a plough).

**V. 22.** *attrib.* and *Comb.* **a.** In sense 5, 'Having a train', as *train-dress, -gown, -petticoat, -skirt*; also **train-bearer**, an attendant who carries the train of a sovereign or other person; also *fig.*; so *train-bearing* adj.; **train-tea**, a tea-party on the occasion of a young lady's presentation at court.

**1722** *Lond. Gaz.* No. 6084/6 Sir Robert Rich his *Train-bearer sitting over-against him. **1838** Q. VICTORIA *Jrnl.* 28 June, I..went into a robing-room, where I found my eight train-bearers: Lady Caroline Lennox [etc.]. **1871** LOWELL *Pope* Prose Wks. 1890 IV. 56 No poet more often than he makes the second line of the couplet a mere train-bearer to the first. **1848** BUCKLEY *Iliad* 129 The *train-bearing Trojan women. **1792** *Trans. Soc. Arts* X. 199 The principal consumption in this cloth, is in *train-dresses for ladies' wearing. **1831** CARLYLE *Sart. Res.* I. vii, Wives of quality..have *train-gowns four or five ells in length; which trains there are boys to carry. **1678** *Lond. Gaz.* No. 1287/4 One long *Train petticoat of rich flowred Silk. **1876** T. HARDY *Ethelberta* II. 15 A light muslin *train-skirt. **1897** *Spectator* 16 Jan. 96/1 The '*train-tea' that celebrates the presentation at Court of an English girl in good society.

**b.** In sense 16, as *train hand* (HAND *sb.* 8), *train journey, -line, -load, -robber, -robbery, -service, -speed, -thief, -time, -wreck, -wrecker, -wrecking*; also **train-boy**, (*a*) *Coal-mining*: see quot. 1883; (*b*) (*U.S.* and *Canada*), a boy who sells newspapers, etc. on a railway train; **train-dispatcher** (*U.S.* and *Canada*), the officer who has charge of the running of trains on a railway; **train-ferry**, a ferry for conveying trains across a piece of water from one railway to another; so *train-ferriage*; **train-mile**, each mile of the aggregate distance run by all the trains on a railway in a given period, as a unit in estimating amount of traffic, working expenses, etc.; so *train-mileage*; **train-pipe**, a pipe connecting the source of power with the brakes on the cars in a continuous system of brakes on a railway train (also called *brake-pipe*); **train-road** = *train-way* (*a*); **train-shed** (*U.S.*), a roof supported by posts forming a shelter for one or more platforms at which trains stop; a roughly built or uninclosed railway station; **train-sheet**, a ruled sheet on which are recorded the movements of every train on a section of railway, according to information telegraphed from the various stations; **train-sickness**, a sickness or nausea to which some persons are subject when travelling by train; so *train-sick* adj.; **train-signal**, a method of signalling from the cars of a train to the engine by a continuous pipe (*Cent. Dict. Suppl.*); **train-staff**, (*a*) a staff delivered to an engine-driver as authority to travel over a single-line section of railway; (*b*) the staff of employees on a railway train; **train-stop**, an automatic apparatus, in connexion with a railway signal, for stopping a train; **train-way**, (*a*) a temporary line of rails for the conveyance of small loads, as in the course of construction of a railway; (*b*) a platform hinged to a wharf, with a line of rails upon which railway cars or trucks may run to and from a ferry-boat (*U.S.*).

**1883** GRESLEY *Gloss. Coal-mining*, **Train-boy*, a boy who rides upon the *train*, to attend to the rope attachments, etc. **1890** *Opelousas* (Louisiana) *Democrat* 19 Apr. 3/2 A boy who gets a position as train boy for our company must put up a certain amount of money as a guarantee. **1901** *Westm. Gaz.* 21 Feb. 10/2 Scarcely any observer has omitted to complain of the importunities of the train-boy [on American railways], with his merchandise of bananas and candies and chewing gum and dime novels. **1881** *Chicago Times* 14 May, John Converse is appointed assistant *train-dispatcher. **1897** *Month* Sept. 281 Behring Strait could be crossed by some powerful system of *train-ferriage. **1900** *Monthly Rev.* I. 41 The present route is across the lake by *train-ferry. **1894** *Westm. Gaz.* 3 Sept. 5/1 Many acts of heroism are reported, especially on the part of *train hands. **1908** *Daily Chron.* 11 Mar. 9/5 The *train-indicator, a huge framework confronting every passenger when he enters. There are eighteen clock faces, each of which tells the time at which the next train on the various lines departs. **1900** G. SWIFT *Somerley* 94 On our *train-journey home. **1882** *Macm. Mag.* XLV. 502 Arrival of the *train-loads of troops. **1894** T. M. COOLEY in *Forum* (N. Y.) Sept. 17 Train-loads of perishable goods were..ruined by delays which the strike had caused. **1898** *Engineering Mag.* XVI. 66 Of an American railway..the superintendent..is assisted by a *trainmaster, a roadmaster or division engineer,..and a chief dispatcher. **1864** WEBSTER, *Train-mile. **1868** *Q. Rev.* Oct. 300 The working expense per train-mile is 2*s.* 6*d.* **1892** *Daily News* 17 Feb. 2/6 The great industrial lines have run more train-miles, and therefore done more work, during the past half-year. **1868** *Q. Rev.* Oct. 301 A large proportion of the *train-mileage run..is useless, being far in excess of [public] requirements. **1909** *Great Central Railway Report* 6 Aug. 5 The strictest economy has been exercised in train mileage. **1889** FINDLAY *Eng. Railway* 120 While the train is running a continual vacuum is maintained in the *train-pipes. **1828** WEBSTER, **Train-road*..in mines, a slight rail-way for small wagons. **1877** KNIGHT *Dict. Mech.*, *Train-road*, a construction railway; a slight railway for small loads. **1892** GUNTER *Miss Dividends* (1893) 257 An institution..implacable in its pursuit of *train robbers, highwaymen, and others that raid the precious things the business community intrust to it. **1905** *Daily Chron.* 17 Apr. 4/5 There are two forms of criminal activity in which the United States enjoys an unenviable distinction. One of them is lynching and the other is *train-robbery. *Mod.* The *train-service to London has been improved. **1878** F. S. WILLIAMS *Midl. Railw.* 639 The *train setters and their foremen. **1892** *Pall Mall G.* 21 Nov. 7/3 The great iron and glass portal..will constitute the most extensive railway *train-shed in existence [at Philadelphia, U.S.]. **1909** *Daily Chron.* 22 July 7/1 Anyone to whom trains give the least sensation of vertigo should sit facing [the engine]...Children who are otherwise *train-sick will travel fairly well seated thus. **1906** *Westm. Gaz.* 27 Sept. 4/2 Many travellers suffer from *train-sickness. **1901** *Daily Chron.* 1 May 8/7 In these days when *train-speeds in Great Britain are mostly stationary. **1895** *Funk's Standard Dict.* s. v. *Staff*, *Train-staff. **1901** *Daily News* 16 Jan. 5/1 The Isle of Sheppey Light Railway is in single track..and it will be worked on the train-staff and ticket system. **1906** *Westm. Gaz.* 27 Apr. 7/1 The train staff having dealt so promptly with the trouble that the only sign of fire was a little smoke. *Ibid.* 27 Feb. 7/2 The *train-stop at the signal-post actuated the continuous brake, and thereby..brought the vehicle to a stand-still. **1892** *Pall Mall G.* 15 Mar. 2/1 It was *train-time, and I rose to leave him. **1881** *Chicago Times* 17 June, Running a car from a siding on the *train track. **1839** *Civil Eng. & Arch. Jrnl.* II. 46/1 The wagons when loaded..are easily pushed..down the *trainway to the face of the cliff. **1877** KNIGHT *Dict. Mech.*, *Train-way*, a hinged platform which forms a bridge leading from a wharf to the deck of a ferry-boat. **1891** *Boston* (Mass.) *Jrnl.* 26 Oct. 1/6 A *train-wrecker caught. **1885** *Manch. Exam.* 10 Jan. 5/1 An unsuccessful attempt at *train-wrecking.

**c.** In other senses: **train-bolt**, 'a bolt to which the training-tackle of a gun is hooked' (*Cent. Dict.*); †**train-horse**, a horse employed to draw artillery; **train-net** = sense 20 c; **train-rope**, **train-tackle**, a tackle hooked to the trail of a gun-carriage on board ship: see quot.; **train-service** (in sense 9 b); **train-shut** *a.*, shut by a train of wheels and pinions; **train-work**, a mechanism consisting of a series of parts (sense 15).

**1643** in *13th Rep. Hist. MSS. Comm.* App. I. 131 The county complains that we have not charged the *Train horse according to the letter of the Ordinance. **1710** *Lond. Gaz.* No. 4682/2 Train Horses..employed in drawing forty pieces of Artillery. **1864** *Glasgow Daily Herald* 24 Sept., There is as much damage done with *train nets as with trawl nets. **1887** *Spectator* 3 Sept. 1174 Their *train-services collected and equipped for a campaign. **1632** LITHGOW *Trav.* I. 5 Mine Epitaph shall sound, Of *traine-shut sluces, of the Thespian spring, Where chatring birds, Dodonean trees do sing. **1815** BURNEY *Falconer's Dict. Marine*, **Train-Tackle*,..a combination of pulleys, which is, during action, hooked to an eye-bolt, in the train of the carriage, and to a ring-bolt in the deck...Its use is, to prevent the gun from running out of the port whilst loading. **1867** SMYTH *Sailor's Word-bk.*, Train-tackle. **1876** PREECE & SIVEWRIGHT *Telegraphy* 92 The Morse involves a complicated and expensive *trainwork of mechanism.

† **Train**, *sb.*[2] *Obs.* Forms: 4–7 **trayne**, 4–5 **treyne**, **trayn**, 5 *north.* **trane**, 6–7 **traine**, 6–8 **train**. [a. OF. *traïne* guile, deceit, ruse (12th c. in Godef.), n. of action f. OF. *traïr*, (Fr. *trahir*) to betray; cf. *haine* (OF. *haïne*), *saisine*, f. *haïr*, *saisir*. Cf. the phrases 'withouten train', 'false train', etc. with OF. *sans traine*, *fausse traine*, etc.

In senses 2, 3, and 4 this word appears to be associated with senses 7 and 13 b of TRAIN *sb.*[1]]

**1.** Without *a* or *pl.*: Treachery, guile, deceit, trickery.

*c* **1400** *Destr. Troy* 3789 Ulexes..falsest in his fare, and full of disseit, Vndertaker of treyne, of talkyng but litill. *c* **1400** *Non-Cycle Myst. Plays* 7/67 We schal home tell, withouten trayn, Bothe word & werk, how hit was. *c* **1460** *Towneley Myst.* x. 330 Do wa, Ioseph,..Turne home to thi spouse agane, look thou deme in hir no trane, for she was neuer ffylde. **1590** SPENSER *F. Q.* I. vi. 41 Thou cursed Miscreaunt, That hast with knightlesse guile, and trecherous train, Faire knighthood fowly shamed. *a* 1600 *Flodden F.* VII. (1664) 70 Trusting his talk was void of trayne.

**b.** With *a* and *pl.* An act or scheme designed to deceive or entrap, a trick, stratagem, artifice, wile.

*c* 1330 R. Brunne *Chron.* (1810) 295 Þe kyng of Almayn[e] ..He mad a fals trayn[e]..He sent Edward to say, help him mot he nouht. *a* 1350 *St. Nicholas* 322 in Horstm. *Altengl. Leg.* (1881) 15 Now wote I wele, þou es vntrew..I trow ȝour law be bot a trayne. 1412–20 Lydg. *Chron. Troy* IV. 4904 Dredynge ay þat þese ilke tweyne Be som engyn or conspired treyne To þe Grekes wolden hym be-tray. 1529 Rastell *Pastyme, Brit.* (1811) 213 Mortymer was, by a trayne, taken in the castell of Notyngham. 1605 Shaks. *Macb.* IV. iii. 118 Diuellish Macbeth, By many of these traines, hath sought to win me Into his power. 1739 G. Ogle *Gualtherus* 23 An artless Mind, Unpractis'd in the Trains of Womankind. 1767 Mickle *Concub.* II. xlvi, The Nymph..With wylie Traines the Sonnes of Earth besett.

**2.** A trap or snare for catching wild animals; also *fig.* (In phrase *to lay a train*, associated with or merged in senses of Train *sb.*[1])

1390 Gower *Conf.* III. 241 Bot if a king his wille Fro lustes of his fleissh restreigne, Ayein himself he makth a treigne, Into the which if that he slyde, Him were betre go besyde. *c* 1420 ? Lydg. *Assembly of Gods* 773 That no maner trayne nor caltrop theryn wore. 1530 Palsgr. 282/2 Trayne a trappe, *atrappe*. 1624 Quarles *Sion's Elegies* iii. Poems (1717) 393, I seek my peace, but seek my peace in vain; For every way's a trap: each path's a train. *a* 1630 D. Hume *Hist. Ho. Douglas & Angus* (1644) 30 Fearing ..that there was some train laid for them, he turned about to have retired into the Castle. 1697 Dryden *Æneid* XI. 1056 Vain Fool and Coward,..Caught in the Train which thou thyself hast laid.

**3.** Something designed to lure an animal into a trap or snare; a lure, bait, decoy, enticement; also *fig.*

*c* 1407 Lydg. *Reson & Sens.* 6981 [The tiger] ys deceyved by meroures Which the hountys for socours Caste in the waye for a treyne. 14.. *Voc.* in Wr.-Wülcker 566/25 *Attractorium*, a trayne, *sed melius* a trays. 1548 Cranmer *Catech.* 97 b, Thou mayst make no traynes to bring him in to thy snare. 1602 *Hist. Eng.* in *Harl. Misc.* (Malh.) II. 464 The barbarous people..leaving their cattle abroad, as a train, to draw them [the Romans] within danger.

†**4.** A live bird attached to a line, or a lame and disabled bird, given as an enticement to a young hawk during its training. (Sometimes explained as the short flight which the hawk makes in trying to capture this: see Train *sb.*[1] 3.) *Obs.*

1496 *Acc. Ld. High Treas. Scot.* I. 287 Giffin to the man that brocht tua quyk herounis to the King, to make tranys to halkis,..ix s. *Ibid.* 291 Item, for a duke to be a trane to a halk..xij d. 1575 Turberv. *Falconrie* 117 When a sparow hawke is manned and reclaymed, then give her nine or ten traynes at the least, and when she killeth feede hir up alwayes. 1611 Cotgr., *Tome*, a traine with a lame and disarmed Heron, for the making of a young Faulcon. 1616 Surfl. & Markh. *Country Farme* 709 These flights are called traines, because they only traine or teach a young Hawke how to bestow her wing, and make her selfe victor ouer the prey.

† **Train,** *sb.*[3] *Obs.* (exc. in Train-oil). Forms: 5–6 trane, 6 treine, 6–7 trayne, traine, 6– train. [In 15–16th c. *trane*, a. MLG. and LG. *trân*, MDu. *traen*, Du. *traan*, whence mod.Ger. *tran*, and Da., Sw. *tran*; all meaning 'oil extracted or made to exude, spec. train-oil'; app. the same word as MLG. *trân, trâne*, MDu. *traen, trâne*, OHG. *trahan*, OS. **trahan*, pl. *trahni*, OLFrank. pl. *trâni* (Ger. *träne*) 'tear, drop', also gum or resin that exudes from trees, 'lacrymae arborum' (Kilian).] The earlier name of what is now called Train-oil.

1497 *Maldon, Essex, Burgh-Deeds* Bundle 72 No. 4 Possessiatus de uno barrello olei vocat. trane. 1515 *Sel. Cases Star Chamb.* (Selden) II. 92 The Crafte and misterie of Mercers hath vsed..othir grosse marchaundise as sopp, terre,..pik, Wax,..Trayne. 1545 *Rates of Customs* d j, Woll oyle called trane the tonne iiii li. 1602 Carew *Cornwall* I. 33 They pack them [pilchards] orderly in hogsheads..which afterwards they presse with great waights, to the end the traine may soke from them into a vessel placed in the ground to receyue it. 1712 A. van Leeuwenhoek in *Phil. Trans.* XXVII. 441 Upon several Parts of these little Membranes, there lay Fat, which..they call the Train. 1766 *Acc. Bks.* in *Ann. Reg.* 283/2 They don't drink train,..but use it in their lamps. 1802 *Trans. Soc. Arts* XX. 212 The cod-oil, or common train, brought from Newfoundland.

**b.** *attrib.* as *train-fat, -bottle.* (See Train-oil.)

1698 *Act* 10 *Will. III*, c. 14 § 7 Any Houses Stages Cook-Rooms Train-Fats or other Conveniencies for fishing there [Newfoundland]. 1707 *Lond. Gaz.* No. 4378/3, 23 Train-Fats burnt;..1568 Hogsheads of Train-Oil destroyed. 1797 Crantz in *Encycl. Brit.* (ed. 3) XIV. 610/1 Of the skins of the entrails [of the seal] they [Greenlanders] make their windows..; and they make train bottles of the maw.

**Train,** *v.*[1] Forms: 4–7 trayne, (5 treyne), 5–7 trayn, 6 (*Sc.*), 7 trane, 6–7 traine, 6– train. [ME. a. F. *traïn-er*, in OF. *traïner*, also *trahiner* (11th c. in Hatz.-Darm.); app. a deriv. of L. *trahĕre* (in pop.L. **tragĕre*, whence F. *traire*) to draw, drag; = Pr. *trahinar*; cf. Sp. *trajinar* to convey, '*traginar* to transport by pack-horses' (Minsheu), It. *trainare* 'to traine, to traile, to draggle or draw along the ground' (Florio).

Hatz.-Darm. suppose a sb. **tragina* from **tragere*, formed like *rapina, ruina*, fr. *rapĕre, ruĕre*, whence the vb. They do not identify this **tragina* with the existing *traine*, which is taken as a new formation from the vb. like *train*, masc.]

**I. 1.** *trans.* To draw or pull along after one; to drag, haul, trail. *Obs.* or *arch.*

*c* 1450 *Merlin* xviii. 299 He hente hir be the tresses and drough hir toward the horse trailinge..; and so he hath hir trayned and drawen. 1530 Palsgr. 383 To se the body of Hector so trayned by Achilles. 1607 Markham *Caval.* III. i. (1617) 9 This chase or sport we..call a Traine sent, because the sent which the Houndes hunt is trained alongst the fields. 1623 tr. *Favine's Theat. Hon.* VI. iv. 124 To traine the baggadge of the Christian Army there were three score thousand Chariots. 1667 Milton *P. L.* VI. 553 Behold.. the Foe Approaching..; in hollow Cube Training his devilish Enginrie [cannons]. 1831 Scott *Ct. Robt.* iii, He cannot be so false of word as to train me to prison under false pretexts.

**b.** *intr.* (for *pass.*) Of a garment: To hang down, esp. so as to drag or trail. Now *rare.*

1590 Spenser *F. Q.* II. iii. 27 Below her ham her weed did somewhat trayne. 1702 W. J. tr. *Bruyn's Voy. Levant* xxxi. 117 They let it [the tail] train down till they come to the lower End. 1789 Mrs. Piozzi *Journ. France* I. 184 A full black silk petticoat, sloped just to train a very little on the ground. 1827 [see Training *ppl. a.* 3].

†**2.** *fig.* (*trans.*) **a.** To draw out, lengthen out (in time), protract, spin out; also, to spend, pass (time, one's life); *esp.* to pass slowly or wearily, 'drag on'. Also *intr. Obs.*

*c* 1440 *Promp. Parv.* 499/1 Traynyn, or tranyyn, or longe taryyn (..*S.* or abydyn), *moror, differo.* 1539 [see Training *vbl. sb.* 1]. 1556 J. Heywood *Spider & F.* xcv. 8 To traine the time and tarie you..folli it weare. *a* 1560 Becon *Jewel of Joy* Wks. II. 5 Nether by letters nor yet by report..could we lerne wher you trained your life. 1652 J. Wright tr. *Camus' Nat. Paradox* x. 259 To seek a glorious Death.. rather than train so obscure and discontented a Life.

**b.** To draw *out* in length, to extend; to drawl, utter slowly (a word, phrase, name). *rare.*

1651 Cleveland *Smectymnuus* 10 A Name which if 'twere train'd would spread a mile. 1859 G. Meredith *R. Feverel* xlii, He trained out the [word] old.

†**c.** To draw after itself, draw *with* it; to involve as a consequence; to bring in its train. *Obs.*

1579 Fenton *Hist. Guicciard.* (1618) 12 If those small forces trained with them so great fortunes. 1619 Sir J. Finett in *Eng. & Germ.* (Camden) 63 A busynes that is lyke to trayn wyth it a consequence of continuall trouble.

†**d.** To strain the sense of. *Obs. rare*—[1].

1550 Bale *Eng. Votaries* II. 31 The scriptures he had so trayned with the rules of logycke, that by them he was able to maynteyne all falshede.

†**3.** To draw, lead, conduct, bring. *Obs.*

1549 Coverdale, etc. *Erasm. Par. Jude* 22 The Hebrues ..whom..Iesus trained out of the..bondage of the Egipcians. *c* 1586 C'tess Pembroke *Ps.* cv. xii, His chosen troopes with triumph on he traines. 1642 Chas. I *Declar.* 12 Aug. 16 Their resort was to the people, whom upon severall occasions they had trained down to Westminster.

**II. 4.** *fig.* To draw by art or inducement; to draw *on*; to allure, entice, decoy; to lead astray, deceive, take in. *arch.* (The most frequent early sense. ? Influenced by Train *sb.*[2])

1375 Barbour *Bruce* XIX. 354 The lord dowglas toward thaim raid;..Thame neir his battell for till trayne. ? *a* 1400 *Morte Arth.* 1683 Ȝe do bott trayne us..wyth trofelande wordez. 1412–20 Lydg. *Chron. Troy* III. 1015 His mortall foon þat..him to treyne leide out hoke & laas. 1588 T. Hughes *Misfort. Arth.* V. i. 88 So did his witte and feature feede that hope, Which falsely trainde me to this wofull hap. 1596 Shaks. 1 *Hen. IV*, V. ii. 21 We did traine him on. *a* 1694 Tillotson *Serm.* (1743) I. 237 Being insensibly trained on from one degree of wickedness to another. 1781 *Hist. Eur.* in *Ann. Reg.* 92/1 Being trained into a well-laid ambush. 1899 Goldw. Smith *United Kingd.* I. 200 He [Bruce] trained him [Comyn] to a church and stabbed him there.

†**b.** In good or neutral sense: To draw by persuasion; to persuade, induce, convert. *Obs.*

1526 in Strype *Eccl. Mem.* (1721) I. v. 67 The King had hopes to train the Emperor to reason by doulce methods. 1549 Coverdale, etc. *Erasm. Par. Thess.* 2 Howe easely you were trayned from the superstiscion of your forefathers,.. vnto the true wurshippe of God. 1612 Brerewood *Lang. & Relig.* 154 They have been by little and little brought and trayned to the Greek religion.

**III. 5.** To treat or manipulate so as to bring to the proper or desired form; *spec.* in *Gardening*, to manage (a plant or branch) so as to cause it to grow in some desired form or direction, esp. against a wall, or upon a trellis or the like.

*c* 1440 *Pallad. on Husb.* I. 1032 And bowis ore hit trayn So lough and rare, on hem that bees may dwelle. 1688 Evelyn *Diary* 24 Mar., His orangerie and gardens, where the wall fruit trees are most exquisitely nail'd and train'd. 1792 Mar. Riddell *Voy. Madeira* 9 The vines are trained and supported by poles. 1837 Lockhart *Scott* I. ix. 289 A garden..in which Scott delighted to train his flowers and creepers. 1852 O. W. Holmes *My Aunt* ii, Why will she train that winter curl In such a spring-like way? 1871 [see Trained *ppl. a.* 3]. 1888 *Nicholson's Dict. Gard.* s.v. *Training*, Sap flowing most forcibly into branches trained in an upright direction.

**6.** To subject to discipline and instruction for the purpose of forming the character and developing the powers of, or of making proficient in some occupation. (Also with *up.*) **a.** To instruct and discipline generally; to educate, rear, bring up.

1542 Udall *Erasm. Apoph.* Pref. *** ij b, For teachyng and trainyng young children. 1611 Bible *Prov.* xxii. 6 Traine vp a childe in the way he should goe. 1727 Gay *Fables* I. ix, Seek you to train your fav'rite boy? Each caution, ev'ry care employ. 1877 E. R. Conder *Bas. Faith* iii. 103 This protracted pupilage..is admirably calculated to train and perfect his moral character.

**b.** To instruct and discipline in or for some particular art, profession, occupation, or practice; to exercise, practise, drill; to make proficient by such instruction and practice (see also Trained *ppl. a.*). Const. *in, for, to.*

1555 W. Watreman *Fardle Facions* I. vi. 106 To be trayned, and exercysed in the feictes of warre. 1577–87 Holinshed *Chron.* I. 3/1 Bardus..was highlie renoumed..for inuention of dities and musicke, wherein..he trained his people. 1661 in *Verney Mem.* (1907) II. 170 To march, trayne and exercise his company, according to the moderne discipline of warr. *c* 1680 Beveridge *Serm.* (1729) I. 39 Such advocates as had been trained up in the civil law. 1823 Scott *Quentin D.* xxxi, To a false tale you will not desire me to train my tongue. 1859 *Musketry Instr.* 92 Bandsmen..fully trained to the use of the rifle. 1869 Huxley in *Sci. Opin.* 21 Apr. 464/1 He was thoroughly trained in the physical and chemical science of his day.

**c.** To discipline and instruct (an animal) so as to make it obedient to orders, or capable of performing tricks; to prepare a race-horse for its work.

1609 *Shuttleworths' Acc.* (Chetham Soc.) 181 Richard Eastwood, for his paynes and his coache, to trayne the horses theirin, xxx[s]. 1660 F. Brooke tr. *Le Blanc's Trav.* 166 These Lions..are..trained in parkes to hunt others. 1777 Priestley *Matt. & Spir.* (1782) I. xxii. 286 Dogs..may be trained to catch hares. 1872 J. F. Clarke *Self-Culture* i. (1880) 33 Animals can be trained by man, but they cannot train themselves. 1894 Astley *50 Years Life* I. 176 The present Robert Sherwood, who now trains at Newmarket.

**d.** To bring by a course of diet and exercise to the required state of physical efficiency for a race or other athletic feat.

1835–71 [see Training *vbl. sb.* 2 c]. 1887 Stevenson *Mem. & Portr.* vi. *Pastoral* 96 A threat of latent anger in the expression, like that of a man trained too fine and harassed with perpetual vigilance.

**e.** With *adv.* or *compl. adj.*: To bring into a specified condition by or as by athletic training. *Train off*, to throw off by training.

1879 *Spectator* 7 June 720 The beasts, always worn, for that terrible, incessant pulling trains them down almost visibly. 1891 Kipling *Light that Failed* viii. 165 You're disgracefully out of condition,..pure tallow born of over-feeding. Train it off, Dickie.

**7.** *intr.* for *pass.* To undergo or follow a course of instruction and discipline; in early quots., to go through a course of military drill, to drill.

1605 Stow *Ann.* 1310 The other 3000 citizens..shewed on the Miles end, where they trained all that day. 1685 Wood *Life* 28 June (O. H. S.) III. 146, 4 loades of muskets, pikes, etc...for the scholars to train with. 1811 Byron *Hints fr. Horace* 703 The youth who trains to ride, or run a race, Must bear privations. 1906 Beatrice Harraden *Scholar's Dau.* vii, My uncle thought I'd better train to be a doctor.

**b.** *intr.* With *adv.* To get into some condition by training; as *train on*, to improve in condition or form by training, to become more proficient; † *train off*, to get out of condition, lose one's vigour or skill, as by over-training; *train down*, to reduce one's weight with the object of getting fit for an event or feat. Also *fig.*

1776 E. Topham *Lett. fr. Edinburgh* 98 When they are young they dance extremely well; but afterwards (to speak in the language of the turf) they train off. 1810 *Sporting Mag.* XXXVI. 230 A hard round,..that convinced the judges of boxing that Blake had trained off. 1815 Byron *Let. to Moore* 10 Jan., It is impossible to read what you have lately done..without seeing that you have trained on tenfold. 1866 Maclaren *Training* 22 Under it a powerful man dwindles; and this, not from 'training down' as the phrase goes.

**IV.** † **8.** *trans.* To pursue by the 'train' or trail; to trace, track. *Obs.*

1583 [see Training *ppl. a.* 2]. 1592 Greene *Groat's W. Wit* C iij b, They followed and trayned the Foxe and Badger to the hole.

**b.** *Mining.* (See quots.)

1710 J. Harris *Lex. Techn.* II, *Training a Load*, in the Miner's Language, is searching for, and pursuing a Vein of Ore. 1895 *Funk's Standard Dict.*, *Train, v.*...5. In mining, to trace, as a lode to its head.

**9.** *intr.* †**a.** To walk in a person's train or retinue. *Obs. rare*—[1]. **b.** *Train off*: to draw off or away.

1633 P. Fletcher *Hymen* in *Poet. Misc.* 55 With her a troop of fairest wood-nymphs trains. 1825 T. Hook *Sayings* Ser. II. *Sutherl.* (Colburn) 27 James gradually trained off from the party. 1833 — *Widow & Marquess* ii, They [suitors] had trained off, upon finding..that Harriet's boasted fortune was visionary.

**10.** *trans.* To direct, point, or aim (a cannon or other fire-arm, or *transf.* a photographic camera); to bring by horizontal movement to bear (*on, upon*, the thing aimed at). Cf. Training *vbl. sb.* 4.

1841 Totten *Naval Text-Bk.* 417 *To train a gun*, to point it forward or abaft the beam. 1870 H. Meade *New Zealand* 236 A forty-pounder..trained on them during the conference. 1873 *Brit. Q. Rev.* 108 Their 'horizontal range', or the arc over which they could be trained, should be made small. 1889 G. Kennan in *Century Mag.* May 73/2 We set up the camera and trained it upon a part of the picturesque throng.

**b.** *intr.*

1891 *Cent. Dict.* s.v., *To train off*, to go off obliquely said of the flight of a shot.

**11.** *trans.* To convey by a railway train. *rare.*

1886 *Pall Mall G.* 14 July 14/1 Ship it [sewage] to Ireland..and let Paddy cart or train it away..to his potato patch or cornfield. **1892** *Field* 28 May 783/2 Ship the canoe on to the railway and train it right up the Wye valley.

**b.** *intr.* To go by train, travel by railway. Also *train it* (*colloq.*).

**1888** *Pall Mall G.* 2 Apr. 4/2 So exhausted were the men from the effect of the previous day's ride,..that all trained from Winchester to Farnham. **1888** *Harper's Mag.* Nov. 954/2 From Aberdeen to Edinburgh we trained it by easy stages.

**12.** *intr.* To act sportively, romp, 'carry on'. *U.S. colloq.*

**1889** Howells *Hazard New Fort.* II. viii, The girl broke into a fondly approving laugh at his drolling. 'Oh, I guess you love to train!' **1889** Farmer *Americanisms, To train.* New England girls use this term to denote acts of romping, or, to employ an English phrase, which seems its exact equivalent, *to train* is 'to carry on'.

†**Train,** *v.*² *Obs.* [f. Train *sb.*²; but prob. not always distinguished from Train *v.*¹]

**1.** *trans.* To lay (a train or snare); to set (a trap). Cf. Train *sb.*² 2.

**1412–20** Lydg. *Chron. Troy* IV. 4935 þat iustly þei may fallen in þe diche Whiche þei han made & for vs y-treyned.

**2.** *Falconry.* To entice (a hawk) by means of a live bird used as a lure. (Cf. Train *sb.*² 4.)

**1575** Turberv. *Falconrie* 117 Let the quayle wherewithall you trayne hir haue a feather pulled out of each wing and cast off the sparowhawke to hir a farre off.

**3.** *intr.* Of a hawk: To come to the train or lure.

**1579** Lyly *Euphues* (Arb.) 35 The fleetest fish swalloweth the delicatest bait:..the highest soaring Hauke traineth to yᵉ lure.

**Trainable** (trēⁱ·năb'l), *a.* [f. Train *v.*¹ + -able.] Capable of being trained; amenable to discipline and instruction; educable.

*c* **1550** (*title*) An Enterlude called Lusty Iuuentus, lyuely describing the frailtie of youth: of natur prone to vyce: by grace and good counsayll traynable to vertue. **1594** Carew *Huarte's Exam. Wits* iii. (1596) 30 Amongst horses..some there are more trainable than the rest. **1600** Holland *Livy* XXXIX. xl. 1049 This man was by nature so trainable and pliant to all alike, that [etc.]. **1869** *Daily News* 20 Aug., If there were skilled labour, or even trainable labour, to carry it on. **1872** Ruskin *Fors Clav.* (1896) I. xxii. 442 The horse, the noblest, because trainablest, of wild creatures.

**Trainage** (trēⁱ·nėdʒ). *rare.* [f. Train *v.*¹ + -age: cf. F. *trainage.*] The action of 'training' or drawing along; haulage; conveyance by train.

**1611** Cotgr., *Trainage*, trainage. **1817** *Mann. & Cust.* in *Ann. Reg.* 479/1 Fortunately (being the necessary conditions for good trainage) it [snow] had fallen on a ground already hardened by the frost. **1890** 'R. Boldrewood' *Col. Reformer* (1891) 42 Men in charge of droves..pursued the old and rugged road, not caring to use the swifter, costlier trainage.

**Trai·nba:nd, train-band.** Now *Hist.* [Abbrev. of *trained band*: see Trained *ppl. a.* 2.] A trained company of citizen soldiery, organized in London and other parts in the 16th, 17th, and 18th centuries. Also occas. applied to similar forces in other countries, e. g. the French *arrière-ban.*

**1630** *R. Johnson's Kingd. & Commw.* 28 In a hard battell there would appeare a great deale of difference betwixt an old beaten souldier..and a man of our traine bands of London. **1654** H. L'Estrange *Chas. I* 19 The Country Captains of the Train-bands were..very unskilfull and rude in the use of their Armes. **1670** Cotton *Espernon* I. II. 56 He commanded that in every Province, the Nobility, and Train-Bands should be ready to march. **1732** Pope *Ep. Bathurst* 214 To town he comes,..And heads the bold Train-bands. **1849** Macaulay *Hist. Eng.* v. I. 593 The trainbands of Wiltshire had mustered. **1851** Hawthorne *Grandfather's Chair* I. iii, Whenever a trainband of Salem was mustered.

**b.** *attrib.*

**1664** D. Fleming in *Extr. S. P. rel. Friends* II. (1911) 191 The Judges..were met..by all the Trainband horse of this county. **1674** Dean Grenville in *Surtees Misc.* (1858) 155 His Majestie hath a notorious Sott to his trainband captain. **1782** Cowper *Gilpin* i, A train-band captain eke was he Of famous London town. **1881** Besant & Rice *Chapl. of Fleet* I. iii, The train-band lieutenant..came swaggering to the inn.

Hence †**Trai·nba:nding** (*Obs. nonce-wd.*), raising of, or serving in, a trainband.

**1711** E. Ward *Vulgus Brit.* VIII. 95 Watching, Warding, and Trainbanding, Tho' Customs of an ancient Standing.

‖**Traineau** (trĕⁱnō·, ‖trɛno). [F. *traîneau*, in OF. *trahinel, traïnel*, deriv. of *traîner*: see Train *v.*¹] A sledge, sleigh; esp. one drawn by one or more horses over snow or ice.

[**1676** Lady Chaworth in *12th Rep. Hist. MSS. Comm.* App. v. 34 She hath also great pleasure in one of those sledges which they call *Trainias*, and is pulled up and down the ponds in them every day.] *a* **1715** Burnet *Own Time* (1753) III. iv. 10 He was driving the Princess upon the Snow in a Trainau. **1873** *Forest & Stream* 11 Dec. 273/2 Our traineau, heavily loaded, follows behind.

*attrib.* **1779** J. Moore *View Soc. Fr.* (1793) I. 398 Among the winter amusements of this place [Frankfurt], traineau parties may be reckoned.

**Trained** (trēⁱnd), *a.* [f. Train *sb.*¹ + -ed².]

**1.** Having a train, as a robe; having a luminous train, as a meteor (quot. 1686).

**1588** in *Aston's Manch. Guide* (1804) 25 A traynd gowne lyned wyth chamlett. **1686** Goad *Celest. Bodies* II. x. 291 Tayl'd and trayn'd Meteors. **1883** 'Sylvia' *Lady's Guide Dressmaking* 107, 2 trained petticoats. **1905** *Daily Chron.* 13 Nov. 8/1 The average middle-class English woman.. should never be tempted to wear a trained skirt out of doors.

†**2.** Attended by a train or retinue. *Obs. rare*⁻¹.

**1593** Nashe *Christ's T.* (1613) 4 He sent him not roially trained and accompanied like an Embassador.

**Trained** (trēⁱnd, *poet.* trēⁱ·nėd), *ppl. a.* [f. Train *v.*¹ + -ed¹.] In various senses corresponding to those of the verb.

†**1.** Drawn, trailed along, etc.; *fig.* attracted, allured, enticed. *Obs.*

**1579** Spenser *Sheph. Cal.* Oct. 24 Whereto thou list their trayned willes entice.

**2.** Disciplined; made proficient by discipline. **a.** *spec.* Subjected to military discipline and instruction, drilled; esp. in *trained band* = Train-band (now *Hist.*); so †*trained man, soldier*, a soldier belonging to a trainband (*obs.*).

**1570–6** Lambarde *Peramb. Kent* (1596) 70 The trained companies only shall resort to the places of their appointed Rendeuous. **1594** Sir H. Cocke in Ellis *Orig. Lett.* Ser. II. III. 175 Havinge..taken a perfect vyewe of all the Trayned Bandes. **1611** Bible *Gen.* xiv. 14 Abram..armed his trained seruants. **1617** Moryson *Itin.* II. 105 To haue six thousand of the trained bands in readines. **1644** Prynne & Walker *Fiennes' Trial* App. 25 Iames Powell of Bristoll, one of the Trained Souldiers of that City [called below Train Soldiers]. **1707** E. Chamberlayne *Pres. St. Eng.* II. xvi. (ed. 22) 217 Of the standing Militia, or Trained-Bands. **1827** Hallam *Const. Hist.* (1876) II. ix. 133 The citizens of London mustered their trained bands on holidays.

**b.** *gen.* Disciplined, instructed, educated; made proficient by discipline and instruction.

**1858** Hawthorne *Fr. & It. Note-Bks.* (1872) I. 21 The women ..have a trained expression that supplies the place of beauty. **1899** *Allbutt's Syst. Med.* VII. 855 To engage a trained hospital nurse. **1910** D. G. Hogarth in *Encycl. Brit.* I. 248/2 An Art, whose products cannot be confounded with those of any other..by a trained eye.

**3.** Of a plant: Artificially caused to grow in some desired way; of a woman's figure, made slender or shaped by wearing a corset.

**1766** *Compl. Farmer* s.v. *Peach-tree*, Such trees, which are of one year's growth from the budding,..will soon overtake in growth those which are called trained trees. **1786** Abercrombie *Gard. Assist.* 311 Those ready trained, denominated trained trees. **1871** *Figure Training* 90 Slender and elegantly trained figures.

**Trainee** (trēⁱnī·). [f. as prec. + -ee.] A person or animal undergoing training: correlative to *trainer.*

**1850** *Fraser's Mag.* XLI. 658 The trainers first double up one of his fore legs, which they bind fast with a cord; this they pull, and thus compel the trainee to come down upon his bent knee. **1861** *Temple Bar Mag.* IV. 58 The trainee is rubbed down dry. **1885** *Daily News* 16 Dec. 6/1 Let her ..ask whether she could be admitted as a lady pupil, as a trainee.

†**Trai·nel,** *sb. Obs.* Forms: 3–5 traynelle, 4 traynel(e, 6–7 trainel; 6–7 tranell, 7 trannell. [a. OF. *trainel* (13th c. in Godef.), a trammel or hobble for a horse, a fishing-net (14th c. in Littré).] (In some cases a graphical confusion between *trainel* and *tramel* seems possible.)

**1.** Some part of a horse's harness; perh. a hobble or trammel.

**1284** *Acc. Exch. K. R.* Bd. 97 No. 3 (P.R.O.) Pro cordis emptis..ad Traynell[is] et Loygnes factis pro eisdem [equis]. *Ibid.* m. 4 Pro loynes et traynellis. **c1341** *Durham Acc. Rolls* (Surtees) 541 In Traynels factis pro equis domini Prioris, viij d. In j traynel emp. pro equo Bursarii, iiij d. **1467** *Mann. & Househ. Exp.* (Roxb.) 389 Smythe the sadelere.. axsethe for..a new traynelle, viij.d.

**2.** A drag-net. Also *trainel-net.*

**1585** Higins *Junius' Nomencl.* 256/1 *Tragula..Traineau*, a trainel or drag net. **1601** Holland *Pliny* XVI. viii. I. 461 Much use there is of it [cork]..for flotes to trainels or dragnets. **1620** J. Wilkinson *Courts Leet* 122 No man ought to fish..but with such Nette or trannell as everie meash shall be two and a halfe inches wide. **1706** Phillips (ed. Kersey), *Trainel-Net, Tramel* or *Trammel*, a Drag-Net.

Hence †**Trai·nel** *v. Obs., intr.* to practise bird-catching with a drag-net (const. *for*).

**1530** Palsgr. 586/1, I hoble, I tranell for larkes, *je tremaille. Ibid.* 760/2, I tranell for larkes, *je trainelle.* **1676** Marvell *Mr. Smirke* 37 If a man went out by night on Tranelling, or Bat-fowling.

**Trainer** (trēⁱ·nəɪ). [f. Train *v.*¹ + -er¹.] One who or that which trains.

**1.** A person who (or thing that) educates or instructs; one who puts a person (or animal) through a course of training and exercise with a view to proficiency in something; an instructor; *spec.* † (*a*) one who trains or drills soldiers, a drill-sergeant (*obs.*); (*b*) one who trains persons or animals for some athletic performance, as a race; *spec.* one who trains race-horses. (Also with *up.*)

**1598** Barret *Theor. Warres* I. i. 6 The trayning of men.. done..by such sufficient Trayners. **1659** H. More *Immort. Soul* III. xvii. § 5. 508 As the basest men are the trainers up of the best sort of Dogs. **1812** *Sporting Mag.* XXXIX. 99 Mr. Price trainer at Newmarket. **1861** Paley *Æschylus, Agam.* 1599 *note*, Imprisonment and the pangs of hunger are first-rate trainers of the mind for teaching even old age. **1891** S. Mostyn *Curatica* 45, I took lessons in elocution... I cannot leave this part of my story without pausing to do honour to my trainer.

**b.** A member of a trainband, esp. when assembled for 'training' or drill; a militiaman. (In later use *U.S.*)

**1581–2** *Churchw. Acc. E. Budleigh* (ed. Brushfield) 19 Pd ..for makinge clean of the Caliuers for the trayners, xvjᵈ. **18..** *Mrs. Clavers' Western Clearings* 28 (Bartlett) The gentler sex partake..in the excitement, by running after the trainers. **1860** Bartlett *Dict. Amer., Trainers*, the militia when assembled for exercise.

**2.** †**a.** One who draws or drags. *Obs.* **b.** A string used in describing a circle. *rare*⁻¹.

**1648–60** Hexham, *Een Sleyper*, a Trainer, or a Dragger. *Een Sleyperesse*, a Traineresse or a Draggeresse. **1854** H. Miller *Sch. & Schm.* xxi. (1858) 459 There occurred on the.. sand, around decaying tufts of the bent-grass, deeply-marked circles, as if drawn by a pair of compasses or a trainer.

**3.** A frame upon which plants are trained. *rare*⁻⁰.

**1882** in Ogilvie (Annandale).

**4.** *Comb.*, as *trainer-like* adj.

**1836–48** B. D. Walsh *Aristoph., Knights* I. iii, That's a good trainer-like remark.

Hence † **Trai·neress** [-ess¹]. *Obs. rare*⁻⁰.

**1648–60** [see 2].

**Trainful** (trēⁱ·nful). [f. Train *sb.*¹ + -ful.] As much or as many (goods or passengers) as fill a railway train.

**1866** G. O. Trevelyan in *Macm. Mag.* Mar. 408 At Peschiera, the whole trainful—passengers, guards, and firemen —were forced to alight,.. our luggage was opened and emptied. **1885** *19th Cent.* Apr. 635 A trainful of troops.

**Trai·n-guard.** [f. Train *sb.*¹, in various senses + Guard *sb.*] †**a.** A train of attendants forming a guard. †**b.** A body of men in charge of the train of an army. **c.** The guard of a railway train.

**1650** Fuller *Pisgah* IV. v. § 32 Pharaohs daughter with her feminine train-guard. **1760** *MS. Audit Office* (Bodl.) 281/125. 7 d, Major Oughton and others for the Train Guard at the Battle of Culloden. **1897** *Pall Mall G.* 19 May 4/2 [In Denmark] The all-pervading militarism..of Germany has disappeared; the train-guard is no longer an exaggerated drill-sergeant.

**Training** (trēⁱ·niŋ), *vbl. sb.* [f. Train *v.*¹ + -ing¹.] The action of Train *v.*¹, in various senses.

†**1.** Drawing, trailing; drawing out, protracting, etc. *Obs.*

*c* **1440** *Promp. Parv.* 499/2 Tranyynge, or longe a-bydynge (*S.* trancyynge), *dilacio, mora.* **1539** Cromwell in Merriman *Life & Lett.* (1902) II. 182 The coldnes on that behalf & traynyng long of the matiers might helpe to conferme the said Counsaillours advises.

**2.** Discipline and instruction directed to the development of powers or formation of character; education, rearing, bringing up; systematic instruction and exercise in some art, profession, or occupation, with a view to proficiency in it; also, of an animal: see quots. 1697, 1874.

**1548** Udall *Erasm. Par. Luke* v. 61 b, In those thynges whiche concerne the bodye,..my trainyng of theim is somewhat with fauour and ientilnesse: but in such matiers as perteine to ye solle, it is a great waie streighter and sharper. **1600** J. Pory tr. *Leo's Africa* III. 148 Schooles.. freely bestowed for the training vp of youth. **1697** Dryden *Virg. Georg.* III. 321 When once he's broken, feed him full and high..Before his Training keep him poor and low. **1757** Foote *Author* I. Wks. 1799 I. 138 He's now in training as a waiter at the Cocoa-tree coffee-house. **1874** Carpenter *Ment. Phys.* I. i. § 24 (1879) 24 The process by which a Horse is taught any unusual performance—as when in 'training' for the Circus or the Stage. **1879** J. T. Rogers in *Cassell's Techn. Educ.* IV. 53/2 It would be absurd to assign the genius of Mozart to training.

**b.** *spec.* Military drill; *esp.* in former use, a public meeting or muster at a stated time for drill of militia and volunteer forces; now much used for the periodical camp work of the Territorials.

**1578** *Nottingham Rec.* IV. 179 Soldyours trayned with the Kallyver, thys Trayning beyng the 2 of October. **1581** Styward (*title*) The Pathwaie to Martiall Discipline, deuided into two Bookes...The Second Booke Entreateth of sundrie proportions and training of Caleeuers. **1598** Barret *Theor. Warres* I. i. 5 Our countrie Gentlemen and Citizens, who haue the trayning of their shires and townes. **1616** I. T. *A B C of Armes* A vj b, In time of Musters or Traynings. **1748** *Anson's Voy.* III. viii. 375 The training of land troops to the use of their arms. **1845** S. Judd *Margaret* I. xv, Hash,..at the Spring training, was punished..for disorderly behaviour.

**c.** The process of developing the bodily vigour and endurance by systematic diet and exercise, so as to fit for some athletic feat; the condition of undergoing this process, or of the resulting physical fitness.

**1835–6** *Todd's Cycl. Anat.* I. 510/1 By what in England is called training the bulk of the body may be..rapidly diminished. **1854** Dickens *Hard T.* I. ii, A professed pugilist; always in training. **1871** L. Stephen *Playgr. Eur.* x. (1894) 234, I was in good training.

**3.** Management (of a plant, etc.) esp. so as to produce the desired form or manner of a growth.

**1724** (*title*) A Treatise concerning the Manner of Fallowing of Ground, Raising of Grass-Seeds, and Training of Lint and Hemp. **1871** (*title*) Figure Training. **1888** *Nicholson's Dict. Gard., Training*.., as used in gardening, refers to the management of trees and plants..by regulating their branches to give all a fair amount of space and exposure to light...Also..so as to prevent the sap flowing to any one branch or part..at the expense of another.

**4.** The action of directing or aiming a fire-arm, etc., esp. by horizontal movement.

**1861** *Times* 23 July, The horizontal motion, or training, is effected by turning the shield itself, with the gun, crew, and platform on which they stand. **1870** *Daily News* 1 Feb., Where the fault lies is in bad training of the gun on to the object intended to be aimed at. **1885** *Pall Mall G.* 6 Jan. 2/2 Two [sights] being necessary for correct pointing at certain angles of training.

**5.** *attrib.* and *Comb.* (chiefly in sense 2), as *training-groom, -ground, -home, -place, -stable, -time*; **training-bank,** a bank constructed to deflect or direct a current (cf. *training-wall* below); **training-bit,** a special kind of bit used in training a vicious horse; **training-college,** a college for training persons for some particular profession; *spec.* a college for training teachers: cf. *training-school* below; **training-day,** a day devoted to training; *spec.* in former use, a stated or legally appointed day for the drilling of militia and volunteer forces; **training-halter,** a form of halter used in training horses: see quot.; **training-level,** a level (LEVEL *sb.* 1) used in training a gun; **training-pendulum,** a form of training-level with a pendulum; **training-post,** a post used in directing a current into a particular channel (cf. *training-bank, -wall*); **training-school,** a school in which pupils are trained for some special profession or occupation; *spec.* a school for training teachers, a normal school; **training-ship, -vessel,** a ship on which boys are trained for naval service; **training-wall,** a wall built to direct a current into the desired channel in a river, harbour, etc.

1911 *United Empire* July 489 Two moles and a *training bank are being constructed. 1877 KNIGHT *Dict. Mech.*, **Training-bit*, a wooden gag-bit used when training vicious horses. The cheeks are of iron, and are connected by a rod ..which passes through the wooden mouth-piece, having a head upon one end and a nut on the other. 1829 [**Training College* was in use in Ireland]. 1882 OGILVIE, *Normal school*..a school in which teachers are instructed in the principles of their profession and trained in the practice of it; a training-college. 1884 S. E. DAWSON *Handbk. Canada* 211 A theological training-college for priests. 1901 *Contemp. Rev.* Mar. 361 For years the supply of teachers exceeded the demand; now it is the other way, or soon will be, and that is one of the factors in the training college problem. 1676 WYCHERLEY *Pl. Dealer* II. i, As he passed by my window the last *training-day. 1880 MRS. ROLLINS *New Eng. Bygones* 56 This muster, or 'training-day',..when the militia was drilled in a vacant lot of some fortunate town. 1706 S. SEWALL *Diary* 27 May, Col. Noyes invites me to his *Training Dinner. 1816 *Sporting Mag.* XLVIII. 172 The defendant, a *training-groom to the Duke of Dorset. 1864 BOWEN *Logic* xiii. 450 To make them [the sciences] only the *training-ground, and not the field for the regular employment, of their mental powers. 1871 'M. LEGRAND' *Camb. Freshm.* xi, Newmarket Heath..is very little changed...The features of this matchless racecourse and training-ground remain pretty much the same. 1877 KNIGHT *Dict. Mech.*, **Training-halter*, a halter made in the same manner as a riding-bridle, with the exception of having short instead of long cheeks, which are provided with rings into which bit-straps may be buckled. 1905 *Westm. Gaz.* 3 Feb. 4/1 To avoid anything approaching institution or *training-home life. 1904 *Daily Chron.* 9 Feb. 3/3 In 1880 the Women's Training Home was established at Clapton and placed under the charge of Emma Booth...She was equal to the task, and well deserved the loving name of the 'Training Home mother'. 1867 SMYTH *Sailor's Word-bk.*, **Training-level*, a gravitating instrument for the same purpose as the training-pendulum. *Ibid.*, **Training-pendulum*, an improved pendulum to facilitate the accurate elevation and depression of guns on board ship. 1884 J. TAIT *Mind in Matter* (1892) 138 A world fitted to be the temporary abode and *training-place of spirits. 1884 *Pall Mall G.* 9 Dec. 12/1 Opening up a deep channel by the use of *training posts and the judicious use of dredging. [1814 *Brit. & For. School Soc., Bye Laws*, The school for children at the Borough Road, and the school for training of schoolmasters.] 1829 *Kildare Place Soc., Rep.*, To draw the attention of the public to these *Training Schools. 1897 GRENFELL & HUNT *New Classical Fragm.*, etc. lxvii. 101 Aurelius Asclepiades..agrees to hire from Aurelius Theon, the keeper of a training-school, probably at Arsinoe, the services of two dancing-girls. 1905 *Daily Chron.* 28 Apr. 7/5 In the 'danger' passage, between the two *training shafts of the fore barbette. c1860 H. STUART *Seaman's Catech.* 85 These men were never on board a ship before joining the *training ship. 1899 CROCKETT *Kit Kennedy* xxi. 145, I would have placed him [a boy] on a training ship and looked after him there. 1894 DOYLE *Mem. S. Holmes* 5 Where the Colonel's *training stable is situated. 1879 MᶜCARTHY *Own Times* II. xxviii. 349 The campaign had..only been a *training time for us. 1887 *Pall Mall G.* 25 Mar. 5/1 The French torpedo-boats fire bow torpedoes, whereas in our own boats the Whiteheads are shot from a *training-tube. 1908 *Month* Mar. 238 Large *training-vessels. 1883 *Specif. Alnwick & Cornhill Railw.* 43 The *training-walls are to be built of concrete, made of six parts of gravel to one of Portland cement.

**Training** (trēⁱ·niŋ), *ppl. a.* [f. as prec. (or from TRAIN *v.*²) + -ING².] That trains, in various senses.

†**1.** Drawing; *fig.* attracting, alluring, enticing.

1557 in *Tottell's Misc.* (Arb.) 202 Then finenesse thought by trainyng talke to win that beauty lost. 1567 TURBERV. *Poems* 52 Force not hir trayning truthlesse eies, but turne thy face away. 1590 C'TESS PEMBROKE *Antonie* 720 Th' enchaunting skilles Of her caelestiall Sp'rite, hir training speache.

†**2.** Tracking, pursuing. *Obs.*

1583 MELBANCKE *Philotimus* F f j, Diana in her trayninge chase delightes.

**3.** Having a train, trailing. Now *rare*.

1737 SAVAGE *Public Spirit* 7 The Tragic charms the Age; In solemn training Robes she fills the Stage. 1773 N. HOOKE *Rom. Hist.* (1830) I. 6 *note*, Ceres was represented..with a long training robe. 1827 MISS ROBERTS in *Lit. Souvenir* 147 The long training gowns, and flowing head-dresses.

**Trainless** (trēⁱ·nlės), *a.* [f. TRAIN *sb.*¹ + -LESS.]

**1.** Having no train; devoid of a train (as a robe, a meteor, a peacock).

1868 LOCKYER *Elem. Astron.* xxiv. § 305. 132 There was a region in which the meteors appeared trainless,..because they were directly approaching us. 1873 *Daily News* 7 Nov. 5/4 Priests whose trainless gowns showed they belonged to the order of Jesuits. 1904 *Ibid.* 21 Nov. 4 The peacock..that less than a month ago was a dowdy, trainless bird, has grown a 'tail' of bewildering beauty.

**2.** Devoid of (railway) trains; on which no trains are running.

1859 KINGSLEY *Misc., Agric. Crisis* II. 195 The money will be..surely in a better place than..in repudiated loans and trainless railroads. 1900 *Westm. Gaz.* 25 Aug. 4/3 Only two [railway] systems are now trainless.

**Trai·nman, train man.** Also with hyphen. [f. TRAIN *sb.*¹ (or *v.*¹) + MAN *sb.*¹]

†**1.** A man belonging to a trainband. *Obs.*

1654 H. L'ESTRANGE *Chas. I* (1655) 106 The Lord Mayor.. and the Sheriffs with a band of Train men, came down and made Proclamation.

**2.** A railway servant employed on a train. *U.S.*

1881 *Chicago Times* 30 Apr., All train men..now in employment on the road. 1897 KIPLING *Captains Courageous* 205 Old stories of the railroad that every trainman knows.

†**Trai·nment.** *Obs. rare.* [f. TRAIN *v.*¹ + -MENT.] An action or process of training.

1571 GOLDING *Calvin on Ps.* xxxii. 4. 119 So far unsufficient were the traynementes wherwith he had bin instructed. 1583 — *Calvin on Deut.* c. 615 The feast of Tabernacles was a traynment to the people of Israell. 1592 G. HARVEY *Four Lett.* iv. Wks. (Gr.) I. 229 That pretious Trainement is miserably abused, which should be the fountaine of skill.

**Trai·n oi·l, trai·n-oil.** [f. TRAIN *sb.*³ + OIL.] Oil obtained by boiling from the blubber of whales, esp. of the right whale; formerly also applied to that obtained from seals, and from various fishes.

c1553 CHANCELOUR in Hakluyt *Voy.* (1886) III. 40 They haue much oyle which wee call treine oyle. 1591 G. FLETCHER *Russe Commw.* (Hakl. Soc.) 11 An other..principall commoditie is their trane oyle, drawen out of the seal fish. 1661 LOVELL *Hist. Anim. & Min.* 229 Of the fat [of the tunny] is made Traine-oile for Clothiers. 1712 A. VAN LEEUWENHOEK in *Phil. Trans.* XXVII. 446 The Fat of a Whale,..out of which we boil the Train-Oyl. 1823 J. BADCOCK *Dom. Amusem.* 151 Soft Soap is made of train oil and a little tallow. 1865 PARKMAN *Champlain* ii. (1875) 210 Seeking..the more modest gains of codfish and train-oil.

*attrib.* 1842 BROWNING *Pied Piper* vii, A drawing the corks of train-oil-flasks. 1865 G. MACDONALD *A. Forbes* 18 Candles or train-oil lamps were burning in most..houses.

†**Trai·n-scent.** *Obs.* Also -sent, -cent: see SCENT *sb.* [f. TRAIN *sb.*¹ 7 or *v.*¹ 1 + SCENT *sb.*] Something 'trained' or dragged along the ground to make a scent for hounds to follow (= TRAIN *sb.*¹ 7); the sport of exercising hounds and horses by means of this (usu. in phr. *to hunt* or *run a train-scent*).

1603 T. M. *Progr. Jas. I*, E iij, There was prouided train-cents, and liue haires in baskets, being carried to the heath, that made excellent sport for his Maiestie. 1638 BROME *Antipodes* I. vi, They hunt trayne-sents with Oxen, and plow with Dogges. 1681 *Lond. Gaz.* No. 1608/4 There will be also a Plate given for Hounds running a Train-scent of four Miles. 1686 N. COX *Gentl. Recreat.* IV. (ed. 2) 93 Be careful to preserve his Speed till the last Train-scent.

†**Train soldier.** *Obs. rare.* A soldier belonging to a trainband or the militia, and not forming part of the standing army.

1630 *R. Johnson's Kingd. & Commw.* 329 The Garrison Souldier hath one and twenty shillings a moneth, the traine Souldier nothing. 1644 PRYNNE & WALKER *Fiennes' Trial* App. 25, I William Deane of the City of Bristoll, Baker, lately one of the Traine Souldiers there.

**Trai·nster.** = TRAINMAN 2.

1893 *Daily Graphic* 25 Nov. 18 He worked as trainster on a new railway track some way out of town.

†**Trai·ny,** *a. Obs. rare*⁻¹. [f. TRAIN *sb.*³ + -Y.] Having the quality of 'train' or train-oil.

1714 GAY *Trivia* II. 252 And where huge hogsheads sweat with trainy oil; Thy breathing nostril hold.

**Traipse**: see TRAPES.

**Trais,** obs. form of TRACE.

†**Traise, traish,** *v. Obs.* Forms: *α.* 4 trais, trayse; *pa. pple.* 4 **traised, traijst, traist, y-treyst,** (traysted), 6 *Sc.* **trasit.** *β.* 4 **traysch,** 5 **trays(s)hen, traisshe, tras(s)he, trahysh;** *pa. pple.* 4 **trayshed, traysoht,** etc. [f. F. *traiss-, trahiss-*, lengthened stem of *trahir* to betray: see TRAY *v.*, and cf. BETRAISE *v.*] *trans.* To betray.

*α.* a1300 *Cursor M.* 15497 Þou sal be traijst lauerd, to night. *Ibid.* 20042 Ur lauerd crist deied on rode and was traist. 13.. *Guy Warw.* (A.) 2517 He seyd, y-treyst we ben here. 1320-40 *Chron. Eng.* (Ritson) 830 Tho come the traitours..That heden traised Edmond. c1330 R. BRUNNE *Chron.* (1810) 61 Machog, þe Scottes kyng, þat wild þorgh traitourie Haf traised Edward þe kyng. c1350 *Will. Palerne* 2075 Has þat vntrewe treytour traysted me nouþe. a1352 MINOT *Poems* vii. 150 Þat daunce with treson was bygun, To trais þe bare with sum fals gyn. a1375 *Joseph Arim.* 624, I wol þe nout trayse. 1513 DOUGLAS *Æneis* IX. iv. 8 Drawbriggis befoir the ȝettis vprasit Junct to the wallis, at thai suld nocht be trasit.

*β.* c1330 R. BRUNNE *Chron. Wace* (Rolls) 5459 Wyst our folk we were þus trayscht [*v.r.* traist], Hit scholde make þem alle abayscht. c1400 *Rom. Rose* 3231 She hath [thee] trasshed, withoute ween. 1412-20 LYDG. *Chron. Troy* IV. 4562 To traisshe her toun þei hild it no repref. c1489 CAXTON *Blanchardyn* xlvi. 178 The good lady thenne hering the cursed and false traytours speke, saw wel that she was trahyshed of all poyntes.

**Traise,** obs. form of TRACE.

†**Traisement.** *Obs. rare*⁻¹. [a. OF. *traïssement*, f. *trahir*: see TRAISE and -MENT.] Betrayal, treachery.

c1380 *Sir Ferumb.* 4754 Godes for-bode..þat ich assentede to such a dede, To don hym such traysement.

**Traish,** var. TRAISE *Obs.*; obs. f. TRASH.

**Traisle, -il,** obs. Sc. forms of TRESTLE.

**Traison,** obs. f. TREASON. **Traiss,** obs. Sc. f. TRACE. **Traisse,** obs. f. TRASH.

†**Traist,** *sb. Sc.* and *north. Obs.* Forms: 4-6 **traiste,** 5 **trayste, treyst, trast,** 5-7 **traist.** [app. a. ON. **trøysti*, **treysti* (mod. Norw. dial. *trøyste* strengthening, strength, firmness), related to ON. *traust* sb., firmness, confidence, security, safety, trust, and to ON. *treysta, trøysta*, TRAIST *v.* Cf. Gothic *trausti* covenant. Cognate with TRUST, TREST, TRIST *sbs.*] Confidence, trust; assurance felt, received, or given.

c1340 HAMPOLE *Prose Tr.* 18 Puttande all his traiste and his desyre in hym [Ihesu]. a1400 *Relig. Pieces fr. Thornton MS.* (1867) 27 Þat we hafe trayste to com thedyre. c1400 *Apol. Loll.* 96 Sum tyme man is holpun bi treyst þat he haþ in o þing. 1456 SIR G. HAYE *Law Arms* (S. T. S.) 179 He wald geve lytill traist in that sauf condyt. c1500 *Lancelot* 1536 To wer on them In trast of victory. 1513 JAS. IV *Let.* in Hall *Chron., Hen. VIII* (1548) 30 Bastard Heron..slewe our warden vnder traist of dayes of metyng for iustice. 1596 DALRYMPLE tr. *Leslie's Hist. Scot.* I. (S.T.S.) I. 79 Thair hail traist, and al thair hope was in this opinione. 1678 SIR G. MACKENZIE *Crim. Laws Scot.* I. xi. § 16 (1699) 67 Where the Party Slain is under the Traist, Credit, Assurance, and power of the Slayer.

†**Traist,** *a.* (*adv.*) *Sc.* and *north. Obs.* Forms: 4 **treist, traste, trayste,** 4-5 **traiste, trayst, trast,** 5 **treyst,** 4-7 **traist.** [app. a. ON. *treystr*, pa. pple. of *treysta* (OTeut. **traustjan*) to make firm or strong, used in the sense of ON. *traustr* firm, strong, safe, secure, sure, trusty.]

**1.** Firm, strong; secure, safe.

a1300 *Cursor M.* 9883 Þis castel..a-pon þe marche it standes traist, O fede ne dredes it na fraist.

**2.** Assured, sure, confident, full of trust.

c1300 *Cursor M.* 17219 (Gött.) Þu mai be ful traist to spede. 1375 BARBOUR *Bruce* IX. 381 Þarfor sekir and trast þai war. c1375 *Sc. Leg. Saints* xxxii. (*Iustin*) 482 Þe feynd þane Wend he traste wes of þe man. c1475 *Rauf Coilȝear* 549 'Be thow traist', said the Coilȝear, 'man, as I am trew, I will not haist me ane fute faster on the way'.

**3.** Trusty, trustworthy; faithful, true.

c1330 R. BRUNNE *Chron.* (1810) 175 Ȝour wille is euer so gode, & ȝour treuth so treist. c1330 — *Chron. Wace* (Rolls) 8392 Lok þat ȝe be trewe & traist. 1412 in *15th Rep. Hist. MSS. Comm.* App. VIII. 10 Oure traiste and wele belofit cosyng, Schir William of Douglas. c1460 *Towneley Myst.* xxviii. 74, I saide if he nede be-stode to hym shuld none be trastir. c1461 in *Jarrow & Wearmouth* (Surtees) 246, I beseke ȝowe send furth a trayst mane. 1501 DOUGLAS *Pal. Hon.* I. xlix, Constant Lucrece, and traist Penelope. 1535 STEWART *Chron. Scot.* (Rolls) III. 166 Richt nobill men that war bayth traist & trew. 1620 *Reg. Mag. Sig. Scot.* 783/1 Our richt traist cowsing and counsellar Thomas Erle of Kellie.

**B.** *adv.* **a.** Firmly, securely. **b.** Confidently, assuredly.

c1470 *Golagros & Gaw.* 292 Trou ye full traist, My hecht sall haldin be for baill or for blis. *Ibid.* 415.

†**Traist,** *v. Sc.* and *north. Obs.* Forms: 3-4 **traiste,** 4 **treiste,** 4-5 **trayst(e,** 4-6 **traist, trast.** Pa. t. 4-5 **trast.** [ME. *traist, -en, trayst*, a. ON. (OW.Scand.) *treysta, trøysta* (OTeut. **traustjan*) to make firm, strong, or safe, to give firmness or security to, to confirm; refl. to make oneself secure, safe, or sure, with dat. or *til* to rely upon, trust to; f. *traustr* adj. strong, firm, safe, sure, trusty. Cognate with TRUST *v.*: see also TREST, TRIST.]

**1.** *trans.* To make secure or safe, to commit in trust; hence *refl.* to commit oneself with security or confidence, to trust, = sense 2.

c1375 *Cursor M.* 11868 (Fairf.) In quam þat we may traiste vs in. 1456 SIR G. HAYE *Law Arms* (S.T.S.) 179 He wald ..nocht traist his persone in it.

**2.** *intr.* To trust, have confidence, feel assured. (Const. *in, on, of, to,* or *inf.*)

a1300 *Cursor M.* 7491 He traistes al in his aun hand. a1300 *E. E. Psalter* cxxiv. 1 Þat traisten in Laverd ilk-on. 1340 HAMPOLE *Pr. Consc.* 1366 He may be called witty and wyse, Þat..on þis lyfe here traystes noght. 1375 BARBOUR *Bruce* V. 531 Þe king in hym trastit. c1375 *Sc. Leg. Saints* xxvi. (*Nycholas*) 538 Trastand thru hym to helpyn be. c1460 *Towneley Myst.* xxvii. 47 Thay wold for no tokynyng, ..Trast in that trew. 1530 LYNDESAY *Test. Papyngo* 331 Traistyng to chaip that faitale destanie. 1596 DALRYMPLE tr. *Leslie's Hist. Scot.* X. (S.T.S.) II. 385 Quhilk he mekle trasted in.

**b.** *trans.* with simple obj. (? *orig.* dative), or clause: To trust, have confidence in.

1375 BARBOUR *Bruce* VII. 179 May I trast the me to valk Till I a litill slepyng tak? c1470 HENRY *Wallace* I. 86 Ressawide he was and trastyt werray trew. 1473-4 *Acc. Ld. High Treas. Scot.* I. 49 It wes trastit the Duc of Glosister suld haue cummyn in. c1500 *Lancelot* 1129, I traist that neuer more was sen No man in feild more knyghtly hyme conten.

**c.** To expect with confidence.

1518 in *Peebles Burgh Rec.* (1872) 46 The said Johne, traisting trubill in the cuntre.

Hence †**Traisting** *vbl. sb.*, trusting, confidence.

*a* 1340 HAMPOLE *Psalter* lxx. 4 A stabile toure, til þe whilke we sail fle and be sykire in traystynge. 1456 SIR G. HAYE *Law Arms* (S.T.S.) 244 Thair lycht traisting in men that thai knew nocht.

**Traist**, pa. pple. of TRAISE *v. Obs.*; Sc. var. TREST, trestle.

†**Trai·stful**, *a. Obs.* [f. TRAIST *sb.* + -FUL. Cf. Sw. *tröstful* consolatory.] **a.** Sure, secure. **b.** Trustful, confident. **c.** Inspiring confidence, encouraging, comforting.

13.. *Cursor M.* 29009 (Cott.) Orisun agh for be Buxum, traistful, and priue. 1409 in *Exch. Rolls Scotl.* IV. ccxii, For the mare sikkirnes and traistful keping of..the forsaide thingis. 1533 GAU *Richt Vay* (S.T.S.) 32 He is callit our fader that is to ewerie chrissine man..ane traistful thing. *Ibid.* 45 Thir ar traistful wordis for al chrissine man.

Hence †**Trai·stfully** *adv.*, surely, confidently.

*c* 1470 *Golagros & Gaw.* 197, I may refresch yow with folk, to feght gif you nedis, With thretty thousand tald, and traistfully tight.

†**Trai·stfly**, *adv. Obs. rare.* [f. TRAISTY + -LY [2].] Trustfully, with confidence.

The usual variant of *traistly* in Cott. MS. of *Cursor M.*

13.. *Cursor M.* 10569 (Cott.) And siþen traistili [*Gött.* traystli] þe saand þai bade Quar-of þe angel þam bodword made. *Ibid.* 13422, 19950 [see TRAISTLY].

†**Trai·stly**, *adv. Obs.* [f. TRAIST *a.* + -LY [2].] **a.** With feeling of security, securely; with confidence or trust, confidently. **b.** Faithfully, trustily.

*a* 1300 *Cursor M.* 260 (Cott.) Traistli acountes sal we yeild. *Ibid.* 13422 (Gött.) þai gun trastli [*Cott.* traistili] trou fra þat dai in vr lauerd iesu. *Ibid.* 19950 (Edin.) Na hope of nan he wil forhu þat wil traistlic [*Cott.* traistili] in him tru. *a* 1340 HAMPOLE *Psalter* lxvii. 1 The prophet traistly couaitis that he wate is at cum. 1375 BARBOUR *Bruce* XVIII. 36 And war thai knyt witte ȝow, ȝe mycht The trastlyar abyde to ficht. *c* 1470 *Golagros & Gaw.* 744 The renkis of the Round Tabill, That has traistly thame tight to governe that gait. *c* 1520 M. NISBET *N. Test. in Scots* Acts ix. 27 In Damasc he did traistlie in the name of Jesu.

†**Trai·stness.** *Obs.* [f. TRAIST *a.* + -NESS.] **a.** Firmness, stability. **b.** Firm confidence, trust. **c.** Faithfulness, trustiness.

*a* 1300 *Cursor M.* 24054 (Cott.) Moder! traistnes of ur treuth, Do vs to reu al wit þi reuth. *Ibid.* 23645 (Gött.) þe gode..þir er for traistnes blith and glad. *a* 1340 HAMPOLE *Psalter* cv. 32 þe traystnes þat he had in oþer. 1456 SIR G. HAYE *Law Arms* (S.T.S.) 290 A gude Emperoure.. [suld] be full of traistnes and worthynes.

†**Traisty**, *a. Obs.* [f. TRAIST *sb.* or ? *a.* + -Y.] **a.** Secure, sure. **b.** Faithful, trusty.

13.. *Cursor M.* 59 (Gött.) For quen þu wenis traistiest to be, þu sal fra hir or scho fra þe. 1513 DOUGLAS *Æneis* v. x. 12 And in his traisty eir thus prevaly He rownis.

**Trait** (trē, trēt). Also 6 traite, 7 traict. [a. F. *trait*, in obs. F. *traict*, *tret*, draught, stroke, touch, line = Pr. *trait* feature:—L. *tractus* drawing, draught: see TRACT *sb.*[3]

The pronunciation trē, after mod. French, in the 19th c. considered in England the correct one, is becoming less general; in U.S. trēt is the established one.]

†**1.** 'Shot' of any kind, missiles; *orig.* arrows. *Obs. rare.*

*c* 1477 CAXTON *Jason* 112 Shoting on them arowes & other trait [*F. tirerent sur eulx saietes et aultre trait*].

†**2.** A drawing out; protraction; = TRACT *sb.*[3] I. *Obs. rare.*

1545 in Leadam *Crt. of Requests* (Selden) 169 Then.. tapper [= to appear] for heryng of the matter without any further traite of tyme.

†**3.** That which is drawn; a line, streak, stripe. *Sc. Obs. rare.*

1561 *Inv. Roy. Wardr.* (1815) 133 Item ane claith of estate of fresit claith of gold and traitis of violet silk partit equalie with violet velvot. [Cf. *below* Drauchtis of violett silk partit equalie with violett velvot.]

**4.** A stroke made with pen or pencil; a short line; a touch (in a picture).

1589 PUTTENHAM *Eng. Poesie* III. i. (Arb.) 150 The skilfull painters [chief praise] is in the good conueyance of his coulours and shadowing traits of his pensill. 1601 HOLLAND *Pliny* XXXV. xi. II. 550 In these [unfinished paintings] a man may (as it were) see what traicts and lineaments remaine to bee done. 1756 J. KENNEDY *Curios. Wilton Ho.* (1786) 45 The Traits are most beautiful, and the Sculpture of the very best Ages. 1823 J. BADCOCK *Dom. Amusem.* 141 The copy..is correct to a trait.

*fig.* 1860 WESTCOTT *Introd. Study Gosp.* vi. (1881) 340 The picture which he draws can be completed by traits taken from the other Evangelists. 1863 MARY HOWITT *F. Bremer's Greece* I. vi. 160 Let me now sketch some traits from that grand vision.

†**b.** Something penned; a line, passage, or piece of writing. *Obs.*

1572 ABP. PARKER *Corr.* (Parker Soc.) 414 In reading some words thereof..ye may think he hath mine information, but before God that trait was only of himself.

**5.** A line or lineament of the face; a feature.

1773 *Life N. Frowde* 52 The ten Thousand lovely Traits, that dwelt in every Feature of her radiant Face. 1809 *Med. Jrnl.* XXI. 329 The latter inherits the general exterior resemblance of his father, or even his shape, characteristic traits, looks, or voice. 1821 SHELLEY *Let.* 15 Aug., Her face is somewhat altered. The traits have become more delicate. 1860 EMERSON *Cond. Life, Behaviour* Wks. (Bohn) II. 385 A man finds room in the few square inches of the face for the traits of all his ancestors.

**6.** A particular feature of mind or character; a distinguishing quality; a characteristic.

1752 H. WALPOLE *Lett. to Mann* 28 Oct., A most sensible trait of the King. 1797 *Monthly Mag.* III. 494 That love of order, which is a remarkable trait in his character. 1803 NELSON in Nicolas *Disp.* (1846) VII. p. ccxxxi, A very excellent young man, and has all the traits for making an excellent seaman and naval officer. 1807 W. IRVING *Salmag.* iii. (1824) 38 Who have no national trait about them but their language. 1859 WRAXALL tr. *R. Houdin* xviii. 258 A pleasing trait of English manners and customs. 1897 GEN. H. PORTER in *Century Mag.* Sept. 744/1 Sheridan now began to exhibit those traits which always made him a tower of strength.

**b.** Of a thing.

1864 BOWEN *Logic* i. (1870) 7 The Concept refers to all the things whose common or similar attributes or traits it conceives. 1865 LIVINGSTONE *Zambesi* xxiv. 496 This trait was confined to the cool highlands. 1869 TOZER *Highl. Turkey* II. 269 The character of the tales has been altered.., yet..the original traits have..been preserved. 1871 JOWETT *Plato* I. 254 Some lesser traits of the dialogue may be noted.

**c.** A 'touch' *of* some quality. Now *rare.*

1815 W. H. IRELAND *Scribbleomania* 56 *note*, A poem.. wherein are to be found many traits of exuberant genius. 1830 MOORE *Byron* I. 328 A trait of pathos or high feeling, in comedy, has a peculiar charm. 1835 URE *Phil. Manuf.* 343 Many traits of almost parental kindness on the part of the masters.

**7.** A stroke: †**a.** of skill or cunning. *Double trait*, a stroke of double dealing. *Obs.*

*a* 1625 in Gutch *Coll. Cur.* I. 187 You deal with a Nation that hath playd more double Traits..than all the World beside.

**b.** of wit, sarcasm, pleasantry.

1704 SWIFT *T. Tub* Ded., Embellished with traits of wit so poignant and so apposite. 1781 H. WALPOLE *Let. to H. S. Conway* 16 Sept., In Voltaire's letters are some bitter traits on the King of Prussia. 1859 TENNYSON *Elaine* 320 When he fell From talk of war to traits of pleasantry.

**Trait, Traitee**, obs. ff. TREAT *v.*, TREATY.

**Traiter, -eres(se, -ere, -eri(e, -erous**: see TRAITOR, TRAITRESS, TRAITORY, TRAITOROUS.

‖**Traiteur** (tretör). [Fr. agent-n. from *traiter* to TREAT, to supply with food for money.] A keeper of an eating-house (in France, Italy, etc.) who supplies or sends out meals to order.

1751 SMOLLETT *Per. Pic.* xxxix, A party of those young sparks, at the house of a noted traiteur. 1763 — *Trav.* vi. (1766) I. 86 Your taylor, barber,..hatter, traiteur, and wine-merchant. 1828 [H. BEST] *Italy* 272 Our dinner was sent by the traiteur in a flat oblong basket. 1863 MISS BRADDON *Eleanor's Vict.* iv, I have a cup of coffee and a roll brought me every morning at nine from a *traiteur's* over the way.

**Traitie**, obs. form of TREATY.

**Traitor** (trē·tər), *sb.* Forms: α. 3 treitre, 5 trai-, traytre. β. 3–4 traitur, traytur, 3–7 traytour, (4–6 -oure), 3–8 traitour, 4–5 -oure, -ur(e, treitour, tretour, 4–6 *Sc.* trature, tratour, 5 tretowre. γ. 4 *Sc.* tratore, 4–5 traytore, 4–8 traytor, 5– traitor. δ. 6 traiter, 6–7 trayter. [a. OF. nom. *traitre* (= Prov. *traire*, F. *traître*) :—pop.L. *trādī·tor* for L. *trā·ditor* traitor, betrayer; also in acc. form OF. *traitor*, *-ur* (Roland, 11th c.), AF. *-our* (= It. *traditore*, Sp., Pg. *traidor*, Prov. *traidor*, Sard. *traitore*) :—L. *trāditō·rem*, agent-n. f. *trādĕre* to deliver, hand over, f. *trā-* (= *trans*) + *dare* to give, put.]

**1.** One who betrays any person that trusts him, or any duty entrusted to him; a betrayer. In early use often, and still traditionally, applied to Judas Iscariot.

α. *a* 1225 *Ancr. R.* 194 Heo biswikeð ou, & is ower treitre. *c* 1230 *Hali Meid.* 9 Ha habbeð itricchet te as treitres. 1485 CAXTON *Chas. Gt.* III. II. i. 231 To al crysten men thou hast ben traytre.

β, γ. *a* 1300 *Cursor M.* 11530 (Cott.) He was traitur fals in fai. *c* 1375 *Sc. Leg. Saints* vii. (*Jacobus Min.*) 29 þat wekit tratore Iudas. *Ibid.* xii. (*Mathias*) 242 þo he wyste he suld be traytore. 1377 LANGL. *P. Pl.* B. XIX. 435 Pieres þe plowman..trauailleth & tulyeth for a tretour also sore As for a trewe tydy man. 1382 WYCLIF *Mark* xiv. 44 The traitour hadde ȝouun to hem a tokene. 1548–9 (Mar.) *Bk. Com. Prayer, Collect St. Matthias*, In the place of the traytor Judas. 1657 TRAPP *Comm. Ezra* vii. 17 Said Christ, even to the very Traytour that did seek and suck his blood. 1867 M. ARNOLD *St. Brandan* iv, It is—Oh, where shall Brandan fly?—The traitor Judas, out of hell!

**2.** *spec.* One who is false to his allegiance to his sovereign or to the government of his country; one adjudged guilty of treason (including formerly *petit treason*) or of any crime so regarded. Also *fig.* or in extended sense.

*Traitor's Gate*, the river gate of the Tower of London by which traitors, and state prisoners generally, were committed to the Tower. In quot. 1678 *fig.*

α. 1474 CAXTON *Chesse* II. iv. (1883) 48 Slewe the traytre Goribalde. 1481 —*Godeffroy* cxvii. 176 Yf ony were vntrew & suche a traytre that wold destroye his countrey.

β, γ. *c* 1290 *S. Eng. Leg.* I. 38/146 'Ey, traytours', quath þe luþere Quen. 1297 R. GLOUC. (Rolls) 10693 In gibet hii were an honge, as to more vilte,..& so hii miȝte lerni traitour to be. *a* 1300 *Cursor M.* 11889 Aha! traiturs..i sale Hing yow bot ye mak me hale. 1375 BARBOUR *Bruce* IV. 19 Maknab, a fals tratour. *c* 1400 *Destr. Troy* 7899 But the triet men of Troy traitur hym cald. 1444 *Rolls of Parlt.* V. 111/2 He to be juged and demed as a Traitour, and suche execution to be don upon his body, as shuld be don uppon a Traitour atteint of hie Treson. 1591 SHAKS. *Two Gent.* IV. iv. 110 Vnlesse I proue false traitor to my selfe. 1606 — *Tr. & Cr.* v. vi. 5 Turne thy false face thou traytor. 1678 *Yng. Man's Call.* 31 Man enters into the world at traitors gate; born in sin, and conceived in iniquity. 1713 ADDISON *Ct. Tariff* ⁋ 23 He called [him] a lyar [and] a traytor. *a* 1771 GRAY *Dante* 7 If the telling may Beget the Traitour's Infamy. 1821 BYRON *Mar. Fal.* v. i, He is a traitor, and betray'd the state. 1881 BESANT & RICE *Chapl. of Fleet* I. 49 [Did] we not hack the limbs of our traitors, and stick them upon Temple Bar? *Mod.* A traitor in the camp; a traitor to the cause.

δ. 1583 LD. BURLEIGH *Exec. for Treason* (1675) 44 [They] ought to be adjudged Traiters. 1642 in *Verney Mem.* (1907) I. 242 Those thatt told you he was a trayter.

**3.** *attrib.* or as *adj.* That is a traitor, traitorous.

*a* 1300 *Cursor M.* 4397 (Cott.) Ne herd yee na wight how Yon traitur juu me wald sceind. *c* 1450 LOVELICH *Grail* lii. 275 A tretour boteler That kyng Marahans sone poysoned. *c* 1470 HENRYSON *Mor. Fab.* IV. ix, This wylie tratour tod On kneis fell. 1593 SHAKS. *Rich. II*, I. i. 102 False Mowbray..consequently like a Traitor Coward, Sluc'd out his innocent soule through streames of blood. 1700 DRYDEN *Pal. & Arc.* II. 568 Th' assassinating wife, the household fiend, And, far the blackest there, the traitor-friend. 1726 POPE *Odyss.* XXII. 93 He drew his traitor-sword, And like a lion rushed against his lord. 1837 A. TENNENT *Vis. Glencoe* 18 Some traitor spy, Meant to betray thee with a lie. 1887 J. M. FULLER in *Dict. Chr. Biog.* IV. 837/2 Judas the traitor-Apostle.

**4.** *Comb.*, as *traitor-led* adj., *-like* adj. and adv., *traitorwise* adv.

1594 *Warres Cyrus* 794 Or else Libanio..should die for his so traitorlike reuolt. 1598 in *Archpriest Controv.* (Camden) I. 210 Reputed by our Prince and countrye as trayterwise and disloyal. 1598 ROWLANDS *Betraying Christ*, etc. Gij b, Traitor-led troopes by night did apprehend him. 1721 STRYPE *Eccl. Mem.* III. l. 389 Heavy tidings came..that the French had won Calais..: for, traitor-like, it was said to be sold and delivered unto them.

†**Traitor**, *v. Obs.* [f. prec. sb.] **a.** *trans.* To make (any one) a traitor. **b.** *intr.* To act as a traitor.

16.. LITHGOW (Webster, 1864), But time, it traitors me. *a* 1649 DRUMM. OF HAWTH. *Thyrsis in Dispr. Beauty* Wks. (1711) 23/1 Most woful wretch! whom shining hair and eyes Lead to love's dungeon, traitor'd by a sight. 1656 S. H. *Gold. Law* 5 If it be said, that the King traytor'd such, or as it related to himself only.

**Traitoress**, variant of TRAITRESS.

†**Trai·torful**, *a. Obs. rare*[−1]. = TRAITOROUS.

*c* 1440 *York Myst.* xxxii. 300 Me lathes with my liff, so liffe I to lang. My traitourfull torne he turment my tene.

†**Traitorhead.** *Obs. rare*[−1]. In 4 treytorhede. [f. TRAITOR *sb.* + -HEAD.] = next.

1303 R. BRUNNE *Handl. Synne* 4204 þyr may no man so yware be..þat treytorhede ne wyl hym asayle.

**Traitorhood** (trē·tərhud). [f. as prec. + -HOOD.] The state or condition of a traitor; treachery.

*c* 1470 HARDING *Chron.* CXXIV. viii. (MS. Arch. Seld. B. 10, lf. 106 b), The Kynge with hoste one Roberte Mowbray Rode Who with the Kynge faughte of his traitourhode. 1871 RUSKIN *Fors Clav.* xi. 11 No more ashamed of Traitorhood, but invoking Traitorhood, as if it covered, instead of constituting, uttermost shame.

**Traitorism** (trē·təriz'm). [f. TRAITOR *sb.* + -ISM.] The practice or principles of a traitor.

1591 *Troub. Raigne K. John* II. (1611) I ij b, But wher fel traitorisme hath residence, There wants no words to set despight on worke. 1661 K. W. *Conf. Charac., Gd. old Cause* (1860) 62 The..most notorious cause of innovation and traitorisme. *a* 1734 NORTH *Exam.* II. v. (1740) 323 The Loyal Clergy of the Church of England at that time [*c* 1680].. are charged with Traitorism of their Principles. 1888 *Times* (weekly ed.) 29 June 8/1 There was no traitorism in the ranks. 1898 *Columbus* (Ohio) *Dispatch* 5 Jan. 7/1 Charges of conspiracy and traitorism were freely made.

†**Trai·torize**, *v. Obs. rare*[−1]. [f. as prec. + -IZE.] *intr.* (with *it*). To act as a traitor, play the traitor.

1656 S. H. *Gold. Law* 11 To Traytorize, Murther, and Thieve it, to bring your ends about.

**Trai·torling.** *nonce-wd.* [f. as prec. + -LING.] A petty or contemptible traitor.

*a* 1652 BROME *Queen & Concub.* III. x, There was not, But in the Queen, Petruccio, and my self, True Loyaltie in the Court. Away you Traytorling.

†**Trai·torly**, *a. Obs.* [f. as prec. + -LY [1].] Having the character of a traitor; traitorous.

*a* 1586 SIDNEY *Arcadia* III. xxvi. (1912) 506 That coward, and traytorly boy, who slewe my Uncle trayterouslie, and after ranne from me in the plaine field. 1611 SHAKS. *Wint. T.* IV. iv. 821 But what talke we of these Traitorly-Rascals? 1641 PRYNNE *Antip.* 5 An unhappie, if not perfidious Traytorly advice. 1668 ROLLE *Abridgm.*, *Tit. Action sur Case* (G.) pl. 8. 43 You are a Traytorly Rogue, you cheated your Father of all that ever he had.

†**Trai·torly**, *adv. Obs.* [f. as prec. + -LY [2].] Like, or in the manner of, a traitor; traitorously.

? *a* 1349 ? HAMPOLE *Wks.* (1895) I. 72 My trewest tresowre sa trayturly taken. 1387 TREVISA *Higden* (Rolls) III. 87 Whanne Ancus was dede, he sente traytourliche Ancus his sones an hontynge. *c* 1450 *Chron. London* (Kingsford 1905) 129 The viscount of Narbon that trayterly slew the duke of Borgoyn. 1535 STEWART *Cron. Scot.* (Rolls) II. 540 Sa tratourlie for to betrais ȝow all.

†**Traitoro·logy.** *Obs. nonce-wd.* [f. as prec. + -(O)LOGY, after *martyrology*.] A roll or register of traitors.

1647 VICARS *Just Correction*, etc. *of Scand. Bill* (title-p.) A succinct Traiterologie, in Answer to a lying Martyrologie.

**Traitorous** (trē·tərəs), *a.* Forms: 4 treterous, -tourous, 4–5 traytrous, 5–6 -torouse, 5–7 traitrous, 6 traytorous, -tourous(e, tra-

**terous, -turuse, traytorys, tretrous, 6–9 trayter-, traiterous, 6– traitorous.** [app. ad. OF. *traitreus, -eux* (*c* 1243 in Godef.), alteration of earlier *traitos, -eus, trahiteus*, conformed to *traitre*, TRAITOR. In Eng. having the appearance of being f. TRAITOR + -OUS.] Having the character of, or characteristic of, a traitor; treacherous; perfidious.

*c* 1380 *Sir Ferumb.* 5652 France had þo be delyured weel of a ful traytrous man. *c* 1477 CAXTON *Jason* 10 They that.. gyue them vnto these traytrous meuinges may in no manere haue rest daye ne nyght. 1535 COVERDALE *Isa.* lix. 12 Vsinge presumptuous & traytorous ymaginacions. 1568 GRAFTON *Chron.* II. 338 Aduoyde ye false trayterous and vngracious people. 1581 HAMILTON in *Cath. Tractates* (S.T.S.) 84 Maist traturuse tratures aganis thair soueran the Queinis maiestie. 1683 *Brit. Spec.* 170 A traitorous Crew of villanous Phanaticks. 1716 ADDISON *Freeholder* No. 31 ¶ 10 More of His Friends have lost their Lives in this Rebellion, than of His traiterous Subjects. 1812 G. CHALMERS *Dom. Econ. Gt. Brit.* 429 A spirit of disaffection.. followed.. by popular disturbances, and traiterous insurrection, affected her quiet, and interrupted her industry. 1871 R. ELLIS *Catullus* v. 12 So we shall not know, nor traitorous eye shall envy.

**Trai·torously,** *adv.* Forms: see prec.: also 4 **traytoures-, traytoursliche, traitoursly,** 5 **traytorsly,** 5–6 **-toursly.** [app. f. TRAITOROUS *a.* + -LY [2], but exemplified somewhat earlier; perhaps after OF. *traitreusement*, var. of *traiteusement* (13–14th c. in Hatz.-Darm.).] In a traitorous or treacherous manner; treacherously.

*c* 1330 R. BRUNNE *Chron. Wace* (Rolls) 14360 Conan his cosyn þere hym slew Treterously. 1387 TREVISA *Higden* (Rolls) I. 151 Þe firste Amazones were þe wyfes of Gothes, þat took wretche of hire housbondes deþ þat were traytouresliche i-slawe. 1388 WYCLIF *Ecclus.* xxxii. 19 He that doith tretourousli, schal be sclaundrid ther ynne. 1491 *Act 7 Hen. VII*, c. 15 Certeyn persones.. traiterously murdred.. John Mountague late Erle of Sarum. 1512 *Act 4 Hen. VIII*, c. 20 *Preamble*, John Tayler felonsly and traytoursly resetted one Archbold Armestrong. 1601 SHAKS. *All's Well* IV. iii. 339 You that haue so traitorously discouerd the secrets of your army. 1617 MORYSON *Itin.* III. 278 The Prince of Orange.. was in the yeere 1584 traiterously slaine. 1792 *Anecd. W. Pitt* I. vi. 152 Those who have traiterously conspired to rob him of his crown. 1867 FREEMAN *Norm. Conq.* I. v. 347 The very enemy with whom he had before traitorously leagued himself.

**Trai·torousness.** [f. as prec. + -NESS.] The quality of being traitorous; treachery.

1571 GOLDING *Calvin on Ps.* xxix. 2. 106 To abuse their highnesse too trayterousnesse. 1592 WYRLEY *Armorie* 136 Which citie yeelded was byth tretrousnes Of their Bishop. 1628 WITHER *Brit. Rememb.* VII. 2221 It is a kind of trait'rousnesse To give them more then due, as well as lesse. 1727 BAILEY vol. II, *Traitorousness*, Treasonableness, Perfidiousness. 1878 SIMPSON *Sch. Shaks.* I. 130 One of the arguments.. was the traitorousness of the attempt.

**Traitorship** (trē¹·təɹʃip). [f. TRAITOR *sb.* + -SHIP.] The function or action of a traitor. In quot. 1645, ? the personality of a traitor.

1645 WITHER *Vox Pacif.* 52 Nay, some among you are so void of reason, To buy their Traytorships. 1869 RUSKIN *Crown Wild Olive* iv. (1898) 184 Treasure.. which even our traitorship.. cannot sully. 1893 *Temple Bar Mag.* XCIX. 2 A sense of traitorship to his own nature.

† **Trai·tory.** *Obs.* Forms: 4 **traitre, -tere,** 4–5 **-terie,** 4–6 **-tourie,** 4–7 **-torie,** 5–6 **-tory;** 4 **traytrie,** 4–5 **-torye,** 4–6 **-tory, -tery(e,** 5 **-toury, -towrye, -tere,** 5–6 **-torie,** 6 **-tery, -terie;** 4 **traterie, -tourie,** 4–6 **-toury(e,** 5 **-towry, -tory,** 6 **-torie;** 5 **treitorie;** 5 **treytori,** 5–6 **-tory.** [f. TRAITOR + -Y: cf. *ancestry, mastery.*] The conduct or action of a traitor; treachery; treason.

1303 R. BRUNNE *Handl. Synne* 6248 Þou synnest þan wykkedly, And doust þe soule treytory. *c* 1330 — *Chron. Wace* (Rolls) 9698 Þey ȝede aboute þe court to spye Wher þey myght do þer trayterye. 13.. *K. Alis.* 3983 Thou schalt beo honged and to-drawe,.. For thou soche traytory wroughtest! *a* 1375 *Lay Folks Mass Bk.* App. IV. 44 ȝif he for traytrie weore take. 1375 BARBOUR *Bruce* IV. 22 It wes fer wer þan tratoury For to betreyss sic A persoune. *c* 1380 WYCLIF *Wks.* (1880) 26 In drede of treson of traitre aȝenst god and his lawe. 1390 GOWER *Conf.* III. 334 The king unto his Sone tolde Of Tharse thilke traiterie. 1402 *Pol. Poems* (Rolls) II. 28 Guiltie of traitorie to our realme. *a* 1450 MYRC *Festial* 13 Thre knyghtes also weren enpeched to þe Emperour of traytere. *c* 1450 *Mirour Saluacioun* 111 Of Judas & cosse & the traytourye. *c* 1485 *Digby Myst.* II. 400 He shall repent hys Rebellyous treytory. *c* 1500 KENNEDY *Passion of Christ* 299 Judas last, þat wrocht þe tratory. *c* 1537 *Thersites* (1820) 74 Imagin no tratourye againste your prince. *c* 1550 BALE *K. Johan* (Camden) 61 Never.. with owt moch traytery. 1570 LEVINS *Manip.* 106/17 Traytorie, *proditio.* 1571 in *Scot. Poems 16th C.* (1801) II. 280 To commit open tratorie. 1609 SKENE *Reg. Maj.* I. 112 Gif any man be convict of traitorie done to his overlord.

**Traitoursly,** obs. var. TRAITOROUSLY.

† **Trai·tously,** *adv. Obs.* Also 5 **traytous-,** 6 **trayteous-.** [after OF. *trai-, trayteusement, traitouse-, tra(h)iteusement*, f. *traitos, trayteus* (app. f. stem *trait-* of *trait-eur* + *-eus*, -OUS).] Traitorously.

*c* 1450 *Brut* cxxiii. 126 (Douce MS.) But þe Erl Godwyne.. falsly & traytously þouȝt to slee þo ij breþerne. 1489 CAXTON *Faytes of A.* IV. viii. 249 The prysoner had other traitously or by som otherwise assaylled whan they were but them two togyder. 1559 *Mirr. Mag., Rich. II* vii, Mine vncle Edmunde.. right trayteously arose.

**Traitress** (trē¹·três), **trai·toress.** Forms: 4 **traitores, -eresse,** (6 **-eres**), 4–7 **trayteresse,** (5 **-ures, tratouresse**), 5–6 **traytres(se,** (8 **-ess**), 5–7 **traitresse,** (6–7 **-oresse**), 7– **traitress.** [a. F. *traîtresse* (13th c. in Godef. *Compl.*), fem. of *traître* TRAITOR: see -ESS. In form *traitoress* f. TRAITOR + -ESS.] A female traitor; a traitorous or treacherous woman (or being personified as a woman). Sometimes in an attenuated or playful sense.

*c* 1369 CHAUCER *Dethe Blaunche* 620 (Fairf. MS.) Fortune.. The trayteresse [*v.r.* traitores] fals and ful of gyle That al behoteth and no thyng halte. *c* 1400 *Rom. Rose* 7391 That false tratouresse untrewe. *c* 1400 *Ywaine & Gaw.* 2587 That sho bitrayed hir lady, Als traytures sal sho haue hyr [= hire], Sho be brent her in this fir. *a* 1450 *Knt. de la Tour* (1906) 73 For a lytel thynge ye haue vndo yow, and haue be to me traitresse. *a* 1536 *Callisto & Melibæa* B iv b, Answere thou traytres how darst be so bold? 1601 SHAKS. *All's Well* I. i. 184 A Traitoresse, and a Deare. 1632 J. HAYWARD *Biondi's Eromena* 34 Mischievous and accursed Traitresse. 1651 tr. *De-las-Coveras' Don Fenise* 276 She saw the trayteresse Fregonde. 1702 ROWE *Tamerl.* IV. i, Death shall free me At once from Infamy and Thee, thou Traytress. *a* 1766 MRS. F. SHERIDAN *Nourjahad* (1767) 103 The traitoresses! they shall pay dearly for thus abusing my indulgence. 1769 BLACKSTONE *Comm.* IV. xiv. 203 If she [the wife] kills such divorced husband, she is a traitress. 1824 LADY GRANVILLE *Lett.* (1894) I. 255 The French Government released the little traitoresses. 1882 STEVENSON *Stud. Men & Bks.* (1905) 236 He [Knox] solemnly proclaims all reigning women to be traitoresses and rebels against God. 1884 TENNYSON *Becket* II. i. 50 *Henry.* Traitress! *Rosamund.* A faithful traitress to thy royal fame.

**b.** *attrib.* or as *adj. rare.*

1470–85 MALORY *Arthur* I. xxi. 67 Ye are the falsest lady of the world and the most traitresse vnto the kynges person. 1725 POPE *Odyss.* IV. 115 By the dire fury of a traitress wife.

**Traitrous, Traits, Traitt, Traitur,** obs. ff. TRAITOROUS, TRACE *sb.*[2], TREAT *v.*, TRAITOR.

**Traject** (træ·dʒekt), *sb.* [ad. L. *trājectus* a passing over, a place for crossing, f. *trājicĕre*, *trāicĕre* to throw across, f. *trans* across + *jacĕre* to throw. So F. *trajet, traject* (16th c.).]

**1.** A way or place of crossing over; *esp.* a place where boats cross a river, strait, or the like; a ferry. Less commonly, a route for crossing a tract of land.

*a* 1552 LELAND *Itin.* (1907) I. 51 The next *trajectus* from Kingston to the shore of Humbre in Lincolnshir is about a 3 mile to a place caullid Golflete. Yet the communer traject is from Kingeston to Berton apon Humber. 1657 THORNLEY tr. *Longus' Daphnis & Chloe* 39 The Bosphori; the Trajects, or the narrow Seas, swam over by Oxen. 1798 PYE *Naucratia* I. 57 Though his feet the traject often trace. 1810 SCOTT *Let. to Morrit* 9 Aug., in *Lockhart*, He would not again put foot in a boat till he had discovered the shortest possible traject. 1904 *Sci. Amer. Supp.* 5 Mar. 23553/3 As to the new Bagdad line, two different trajects were proposed.

**2.** The action or an act of crossing over water, land, a chasm, etc.; passage.

1774 PENNANT *Tour Scot. in 1772* 292 Land after a traject of four miles. 1828 A. CLARKE in *Life* xiii. (1840) 458 After a mile's traject [we] were in Lerwick. 1852 MUNDY *Our Antipodes* (1857) 30 We crossed the river by a punt running on a rope. The mode of traject is very inconvenient. 1875 *Wond. Phys. World* I. iv. 129 The only means of traject across these crevasses. 1882 E. O'DONOVAN *Merv Oasis* I. 124 During the whole traject I met with no living things save an enormous black eagle.

**b.** The action of carrying or conveying across; transport; transference. *rare.*

18.. *Athenæum* (Annandale), At the best, however, this traject was but that of the germ of life, which Sir W. Thomson, in a famous discourse, suggested had been carried to this earth from some other sphere by meteoric agency.

**3.** = TRAJECTORY *sb.* 1. *rare.*

18.. I. TAYLOR (Webster, 1864), The traject of comets.

**Traject** (trăˌdʒe·kt), *v.* [f. L. *trāject-*, ppl. stem of *trājicĕre*: see prec.]

† **1.** *trans.* To pass across, to cross (a river, sea, etc.). Also *intr. Obs. rare.*

1624 HEYWOOD *Gunaik.* I. 31 She.. trajecting many seas.. came at length into Egypt. *Ibid.* V. 231 The river Araxes, which he had late with a mightie host trajected. 1711 in *10th Rep. Hist. MSS. Comm.* App. V. 132 The Prince.. would have.. marched up by the river to Navan,.. and there have trajected. *Ibid.* 169 That induced General de Ginckle.. to traject the Shanon.

**2.** To carry or convey across or over; to transport. † **a.** (something material). *Obs.*

1635 HEYWOOD *Hierarch.* VIII. 510 He would traject them dry-foot through the seas. 1637 — *Dial.* xvi. Wks. 1874 VI. 236 The ferriman, who from the rivers brim Trajected thee. 1651 C. CARTWRIGHT *Cert. Relig.* I. 30 Him [Christ] we must mastigate, and chew by faith: traject, and convey him into our hearts as nutriment. 1684 T. BURNET *Th. Earth* I. 232 The notion.. that the rivers of paradise were trajected out of the other hemisphere into this by subterraneous passages.

**b.** To transmit (light, shadow, or colour).

1657 TOMLINSON *Renou's Disp.* Pref., Trajecting these lines through the sieve of our Crebrosity. 1661 GLANVILL *Van. Dogm.* 14 The shadow of a horse trajected against a wall. 1672 NEWTON in *Phil. Trans.* VII. 5101 To this way of Compounding Whiteness may be referr'd that other, by Mixing light after it hath been trajected through transparently colour'd substances. 1704 — *Optics* (1721) 57 A Prism, by which the trajected Light might be refracted either upwards or sideways.

**c.** To transmit (thought, words, etc.).

*a* 1711 KEN *Edmund* Poet. Wks. 1721 II. 169 By mutual Thoughts trajected either Soul Began each other sweetly to condole. 1863 COWDEN CLARKE *Shaks. Char.* xiii. 324 She compared him to that dervis who possessed the power of trajecting his soul into the body of any individual that suited his purpose. 1895 MACPHERSON *Ch. & Priory Monymusk* ii. 57 We can account for their name.. being even trajected into a longer and more distant period during which they had no existence at all.

**Trajectile** (trăˌdʒe·ktil, -əil), *a.* and *sb. rare.* [ad. mod.L. type **trājectil-is*: see TRAJECT and -IL. As a botanical term a. F. *trajectile* (Littré).]

**A.** *adj.* Capable of throwing or impelling across.

1838 I. TAYLOR *Home Educ.* 247 A trajectile force, leaping the voids of the universe. 1860 MAURY *Phys. Geog. Sea* (Low) ii. § 119 Arising from this difference in the rate of rotation and the trajectile force [of a cannon].

**b.** *Bot.* (See quot.)

1900 JACKSON *Gloss. Bot. Terms*, *Trajectile*.. when the connective completely separates the anther-cells.

**B.** *sb.* A body impelled through air or space. (Cf. *projectile*.)

1860 MAURY *Phys. Geog. Sea* (Low) ii. § 123 It [a current] should also move in a circle of trajection, or such as would be described by a trajectile moving through the air without resistance and for a great distance.

**Trajection** (trăˌdʒe·kʃən). [ad. L. *trājectiōn-em* a crossing over, transportation, n. of action f. *trājicĕre* to throw or convey across: see TRAJECT.]

**1.** The action of trajecting or fact of being trajected; a throwing or carrying across; passage through. † **a.** Passage across a river, etc. *Obs.*

1637 HEYWOOD *Dial.* xv. Wks. 1874 VI. 232 My due for thy trajection downe here lay. 1657–83 EVELYN *Hist. Relig.* (1850) I. 144 The spectre at the Rubicon, Caesar hesitating that trajection. 1690 T. BURNET *Th. Earth* II. 88 No long passage or trajection will be requir'd from shore to shore. 1711 in *10th Rep. Hist. MSS. Comm.* App. V. 133 The King observeing the Prince to attempt a trajection [of the Boyne] commanded his army to.. face to the enemy.

† **b.** The passing (of anything) through a sieve or the like. *Obs. rare.*

1657 *Physical Dict.*, *Trajection*,.. as cheese is strained from the whey. 1657 TOMLINSON *Renou's Disp.* 85 By common trajection.. or by a more peculiar colation.

**c.** Passage or transmission through any medium, or through space.

1652 GAULE *Magastrom.* 254 They might in all parts behold the trajections and motions of the starres. 1661 BOYLE *Cert. Physiol. Ess.* (1669) 166 Such Comets as have by a Trajection through the Ether, for a long time wander'd through the Celestial or Interstellar part of the Universe. 1686 GOAD *Celest. Bodies* II. i. 147 The Trajections and shooting of the Stars. 1713 DERHAM *Phys.-Theol.* VI. v. 365 The Trajection and Distribution of the Blood depends wholly on the Systole of the Heart. 1860 [see TRAJECTILE *sb.*].

**d.** Transmission (of light, heat, or other form of energy).

1633 T. ADAMS *Exp. 2 Peter* i. 19 Those upon earth that are said to have half a year night; yet are not without some trajection of light. 1661 BOYLE *Spring of Air* II. i. (1682) 21 Supposing light not to be made by a trajection of Atoms through Diaphanous bodies. 1704 NORRIS *Ideal World* II. iii. 189 Vision may be considered.. as it signifies the passing or trajection of the rays of light, with all their refractions thro' the several coats and humours of the eye.

**e.** *fig.*

1888 A. S. WILSON *Lyric Hopeless Love* cxxxvii, Not happiness but purpose drives The dim trajection of our lives. 1905 *Athenæum* 11 Feb. 174/1 His trajection of the ignorance of primitive man on this unknown immensity is very impressive.

† **2.** A perception transmitted to the mind; an impression, a mental image. *Obs.*

1594 *Zepheria* ii, When I empris'd.. The siluer lustre of thy brow t' unmask, Though hath my Muse hyperboliz'd trajections: Yet stands it aye deficient to such task. 1646 SIR T. BROWNE *Pseud. Ep.* VII. x. 357 The trajections of such an object [must] more sharpely pierce the martyr'd soul of John, then afterward did the nayls the crucifyed body of Peter.

**3.** Transposition; metathesis.

1612 BREREWOOD *Lang. & Relig.* 191 Ægypt is by them named.. not without some trajection of letters, כפתר for מצרים.

1649 ROBERTS *Clavis Bibl.* 289 Here is a more obscure Trajection or Transposition of the phrases in this verse. 1795 MACKNIGHT *Epist.* (1820) III. 95 The words are placed in the end of the verse by a trajection usual in Paul's writings. 1875 JOWETT *Plato* I. 152 You must suppose him to make a trajection of the word..' truly'. 1895 A. E. HOUSMAN in *Classical Rev.* Oct. 354/1 As a Corpus Poetarum is a work of reference.., there is some disadvantage in admitting even the most certain trajections.

**Trajectitious** (trædʒekti·ʃəs), *a. rare.* [f. late L. *trājectīcius* that is carried over (sea), f. L. *trāject-*: see TRAJECT *v.* and -ITIOUS [1].] Characterized by trajection or transport over the sea; over-sea, foreign.

1656 BLOUNT *Glossogr.*, *Trajectitious*, belonging to passage; As *trajectitious mony*, is that which is carried over the sea at the peril of the Creditor. 1855 LORENZ tr. *Van der Keessel's Sel. Theses* dlxxiv, In that kind of Exchange which is called local,.. mercantile or trajectitious.

**Trajectory** (trădʒe·ktəri), *a.* and *sb.* [ad. med. or mod.L. *trājectōri-us* pertaining to trajection (cf. late L. *trājectōrium* a funnel, *c* 400), whence F. *trajectoire* 'casting.. conveying through or over' (Cotgr. 1611); f. L. *trāject-*: see TRAJECT *v.*, and -ORY. The sb. corresponds to L. *trājectōria* (Newton) fem., in F. *trajectoire* sb. (in Cotgr.).]

**A.** *adj.* **1.** *Physics.* Of or pertaining to that which is thrown or hurled through the air or space.

1668 *Phil. Trans.* III. 807 To explaine that Trajectory rectilinear motion, he subjects the Comet of A. 1652 to a very rigid Calculus. 1851–9 MALLET in *Man. Sci. Enq.* 349 Reach the ground after describing a trajectory path.

**2.** *Physiol.* Said of a gland into which lymphatic vessels convey their fluids. ? *Obs.*

1747 tr. *Astruc's Fevers* 132 The common receptacles or trajectory glands of several lymphatic vessels.

**B.** *sb.* **1.** *Physics.* The path of any body moving under the action of given forces; by many modern writers restricted to that of a body not known to be moving, like a planet, in a closed curve or orbit; *esp.* the curve described by a projectile in its flight through the air.

Hence loosely used by gun-makers for the height to which a bullet rises above the line of sight, as 'the trajectory of this rifle is one inch in one hundred yards'.

1696 WHISTON *Th. Earth* I. (1722) 8 [This] must change its rectilinear into a curvilinear trajectory. 1704 J. HARRIS *Lex. Techn.* I, *Trajectory, of a Comet*, is the Line which by its Motion it describes. 1726 tr. *Gregory's Astron.* I. I. 73 Kepler, and several Philosophers after him, supposed the Trajectories of Comets to be right Lines. 1728 tr. *Newton's Treat. Syst. World* 142 If this problem was resolved, we should thence have a method of determining the trajectories of Comets to the greatest accuracy. 1795 HUTTON *Math. Dict.* II. 603 *Trajectory*, a term often used generally for the path of any body moving either in a void, or in a medium that resists its motion...Trajectory of a Comet is its path or orbit, or the line it describes in its motion. 1828 J. M. SPEARMAN *Brit. Gunner* (ed. 2) 395 To determine, by theory, the range of a shot, and the form of its trajectory in the air. 1843 MILL *Logic* VI. x. § 3 There might be others which, instead of an orbit, describe a trajectory, or a course not returning into itself. 1862 H. SPENCER *First Princ.* II. x. § 82 (1875) 252 It is common to assert that the trajectory of a cannon ball is a parabola.

**b.** *transf.* and *fig.*

1838 *Brit. Critic* XXIII. 1 An examination of..the somewhat eccentric trajectory of his [A. Knox's] thoughts. 1883 LOCKYER in *Times* 8 Dec. 10 We have..got a straight trajectory of the abnormal sunsets from the Seychelles to Brazil. 1883 *Cornh. Mag.* Feb. 217 That majestic spirit passes..through all the upward or downward trajectory between heaven and hell. 1889 BOYD CARPENTER *Perm. Elem. Relig.* Introd. 27 The trajectory of religion must rush away to the infinite beyond.

**2.** *Geom.* A curve or surface passing through a given set of points, or intersecting each of a given series of curves or surfaces according to a given law, e. g. at a constant angle.

1795 HUTTON *Math. Dict.* II. 603 Newton (Princip. lib. I. prob. 22) proposes to describe a Trajectory that shall pass through five given points. 1816 tr. *Lacroix's Diff. & Int. Calculus* 401 A problem celebrated from the earliest infancy of the Integral Calculus—the problem of Trajectories. Its object is to determine a curve which shall intersect all curves of a given species at a given angle. 1865 B. PRICE *Infin. Calc.* (ed. 2) 606 If the [constant] angle between the two curves is a right angle the trajectory is said to be orthogonal.

**3.** A projectile, as a bullet. *rare.*

1861 W. H. RUSSELL in *Times* 29 July, As far as I could judge, the men of the regiment were stout and strong material for arresting trajectories.

**Trajet** (‖ traʒe, træ·dʒėt). [a. F. *trajet*:—L. *traject-us*: see TRAJECT *sb.*]

**1.** A crossing, passage, 'run across'; = TRAJECT *sb.* 2.

1741 BERKELEY in Fraser *Life* viii. (1871) 268 You may.. come to Bath, and from thence..make a short trajet to our coast. 1825 T. HOOK *Sayings* Ser. II. *Sutherl.* I. 136 During the *trajet* from the Castle Inn at Marlborough. 1885 'MRS. ALEXANDER' *At Bay* iii, There is an earlier one ..by the Dieppe route, but you gain no time, for the *trajet* is longer. 1894 *Field* 1 Dec. 828/1 Made their trajet to Blessington town from Dublin.

**2.** The course or passage of a nerve or the like.

1849–52 *Todd's Cycl. Anat.* IV. 815/2 The trajet of the nerve is external to that of the internal jugular vein.

**Trak, Trake,** obs. forms of TRACK, TRAIK.

**Tra-la-la** (trā·lālā·), *int.* (*sb.*). A vocal utterance forming a musical phrase (usually ascending) expressive of gaiety or joy; also, a cadence or flourish on a horn or similar instrument.

1823 SCOTT *Quentin D.* ix, Lay on the dogs, in the name of the holy St. Hubert!—Ha! ha! tra-la-la-lira-la! 1835 T. MITCHELL *Aristoph., Acharn.* 1099 *note*, If the accent is thrown on the last syllable of this word [τήνελλα], it will approach very closely to modern imitative words of a similar kind: *Tirala! Tirala! Tralalla! Tralalla!* 1886 HISSEY *On Box Seat* 40 The cheery tra-la-la of the guard's horn.

**Tralatician** (trælăti·ʃăn), *a. rare.* [f. L. *trālātīci-us* (see TRALATITIOUS) + -AN.] = TRALATITIOUS 2, 3. So **Tralaticiary** (-i·ʃări) *a.*

1893 W. PETERSON in *Classical Rev.* Mar. 139/2 That portion of my commentary which represents what I may call the 'tralatician' element,—the ἀναγκαιότατα of textual interpretation. 1900 A. H. J. GREENIDGE in *Eng. Hist. Rev.* July 541 The annual and tralaticiary bill of outlawry which keeps people out of Italy.

† **Trala·tion.** *Obs. rare*⁻¹. [ad. L. *trālātiōn-em* = *translātiōn-em* a transferring, n. of action of *transferre* to TRANSFER.] The use of a word in a transferred or figurative sense; metaphor.

1620 BP. HALL *Hon. Mar. Clergy* I. § 14 According to the broad tralation of his rude Rhemists.

**Tralati·tion.** *rare*⁻⁰. [irreg. f. next.] = prec. 1864 in WEBSTER.

**Tralatitious** (trælăti·ʃəs), *a.* Also 9 -icious. [f. L. *trālātīci-us* usual, customary, common, metaphorical, tropical (f. *trālāt-*, ppl. stem of *transferre* and -ITIOUS [1]).]

**1.** Characterized by transference; *esp.* of words or phrases, metaphorical, figurative.

1645 TOMBES *Anthropol.* 5, I have planted, Apollo watered; but God gave the increase. Now these things cannot be conceived as tralatitious, for it is said, they were Ministers by whom they believed. 1650 FULLER *Pisgah* IV. vii. 138 Too often guilty of what may be termed tralatitious idolatry, when any thing..is loved, or honoured above, or even with God himself. 1688 R. HOLME *Armoury* III. 253/2 Tralatitious, or Artificiall sentences,..are Borrowed words, ..Termed also a Metaphor, Trope, Parable, or Simile. 1748 HARTLEY *Observ. Man* II. i. 63 A secondary and tralatitious Association. 1880 R. C. CHRISTIE *E. Dolet* 237, I give.. both its primary and its second or tralatitious meaning.

†**2.** Passed from hand to hand; common, ordinary, vulgar. *Obs.*

1653 WATERHOUSE *Apol. Learning* 4 By with-drawing those favours..which invigor'd Learning, and nourished men of deserts and worth,..and by appreciating things and persons more tralatitious and vulgar. 1656 BLOUNT *Glossogr.*, *Tralatitious*, transferred or transposed: of the common sort, ordinary, vulgar.

**3.** Handed down from generation to generation; traditional; also, repeated by one from another, as a statement.

1795 WYTHE *Decis. Virginia* 6 Where an estate of inheritance is acquired not by tralatitious act, as by estoppel, dissesin [etc.]. 1900 MARGOLIOUTH in *Expositor* Aug. 136 The subjects..and expressions are 'tralaticious', borrowed by one generation from another, in so long a series that it is now impossible to name or locate their originator. 1912 SIR W. RAMSAY in *Contemp. Rev.* Mar. 339 Self-satisfied contentment with tralaticious statements, borrowed from good books or teachers..and repeated in book after book.

Hence **Tralati·tiously** *adv.*, metaphorically.

1657 GAULE *Sap. Justif.* 91 Adams sin was not tropically and tralatitiously, but even litterally and properly, ours. 1669 HOLDER *Elem. Speech* 8 Language..properly..is that of the Tongue...Written Language is tralatitiously so called, because it is made to represent to the Eye the same Letters and Words, which are pronounced.

**Trale, Traleis,** obs. ff. TRAIL, TRELLIS.

† **Trali·neate,** *v. Obs. rare.* [f. It. *tralignare* 'to degenerate, to digresse, to growe from kinde' (Florio), repr. a L. type **tra(ns)līneāre*, f. TRA(NS)- + *līnea* LINE *sb.*[2]: see -ATE 3.] *intr.* To go out of the direct line; to deviate.

1700 DRYDEN *Wife of Bath's T.* 396 If you tralineate from your father's mind, What are you else but of a bastard-kind? 1745 ELIZA HEYWOOD *Female Spect.* No. 16 (1748) III. 193 If sons tralineate from their father's virtues, and each successive race degenerates from the former.

**Tra·lira·,** *int.* (*sb.*) Also redupl. **trallira, tral-lara.** A kindred vocal utterance to TRA-LA-LA, expressive of light-hearted gaiety.

1801 M. G. LEWIS *Grim White Woman* xix, Trallira! trallara! my old love, adieu! Trallira! trallara! I'll get me a new! 1819 SCOTT *Ivanhoe* xxxiii, Thou art one of those, who, with new French graces and Tra-li-ras, disturb the ancient English bugle notes.

Hence **Tra·-li-ra·** *v., intr.* to sing tra-li-ra.

1862 S. LANIER *Tournament* I. 10 Heart's palfrey caracoled gayly round, Heart tra-li-ra'd merrily; But Brain sat still, with never a sound, So cynical-calm was he.

† **Trall,** obs. var. of THRALL *v.*

*c* 1420 *Chron. Vilod.* 2300 He myȝt not passe ouȝt of þat stede He was ytrallyd in suche aray.

**Trall, Trallace, Trallop,** obs. ff. TRAWL, TRELLIS, TROLLOP.

† **Tralu·ce,** *v. Obs.* [ad. L. *trālūc-ēre* to shine across or through. Cf. It. *tralucere* (Florio).] *trans.* To shine through; = TRANSLUCE.

1591 SYLVESTER *Du Bartas* I. ii. 380 The turning Planets influence doth passe..through the glistring Tent Of the tralucing Fiery Element.

† **Tralu·cency.** *Obs.* [f. as next: see -ENCY.] = TRANSLUCENCY.

1599 R. LINCHE *Anc. Fict.* Fj, The perspicuous and coruscant tralucencie of the sun. 1646 SIR T. BROWNE *Pseud. Ep.* II. i. (1650) 42 The principle and most gemmary affection [of Crystall] is its Tralucency. 1649 G. DANIEL *Trinarch., Hen. V* cxci, Soe the Autumnall Gossamere, well-trimm'd In Deaw, retaines an odde Tralucencie.

† **Tralu·cent,** *a. Obs.* [ad. L. *trālūcent-em*, pr. pple. of *trālūcēre*: see TRALUCE. So It. *tralucente* (Florio).] = TRANSLUCENT. Hence † **Tralu·cently** *adv. Obs.*

1592 KYD *Sol. & Pers.* II. i, If loue of this my person,.. haue percst through thy tralucent brest. 1597 DRAYTON *Heroic. Ep., Edw. IV to Shore's Wife* Notes 57 Trees, whose gum is Amber, where Flies alighting are oftentimes tralucently imprisoned. 1608 B. JONSON *Masque Beauty* Wks. (Rtldg.) 548/2 In the centre of the throne was a tralucent pillar, shining with several coloured lights. 1664 POWER *Exp. Philos.* I. 42 They all seem like Fragments of Crystal, or Alum, perfectly Tralucent.

**Tram,** *sb.*[1] Also 4–5 **tramm(e, (traimm(e, traum(e),** 4–9 **trame.** [a. F. *trame*, OF. *traime*, *trème*, 12th c. in Godef. *Compl.*, (as in the late sense 1) woof of a web, also *fig.* cunning device or contrivance, machination, plot:—L. *trāma* woof. The literal sense of Fr. and L. appears in Eng. only in a technical use from mod.Fr. in 17th c.; but the fig. sense of 'machination' was adopted already in the 14th c., and app. gave rise to sense 3, which does not occur in French, but seems to belong here.]

**I. 1.** Woof or weft; *spec.* silk thread consisting of two or more single strands loosely twisted together; used for the weft or cross threads of the best silk goods. Also *tram silk.*

1679 *Lond. Gaz.* No. 1392/4, 6l. of fine black Worsted, some pounds of Raw trame. 1776–83 JUSTAMOND tr. *Raynal's Hist. Indies* III. 164 The silks of Naples, Sicily and Reggio, whether in organzin or in tram, are all ordinary silks. 1812 J. SMYTH *Pract. Customs* (1821) 214 Tram silk is considered in London as thrown silk, but not as organzine thrown silk. 1868 *Rep. U. S. Commissioner Agric.* (1869) 289 Two or three threads of raw silk twisted loosely two or four times to the inch is tram, shute, or woof. 1911 ALICE DRYDEN *Church Embroidery* 91 For working faces 'tram' silk should be used.

**II.** Chiefly *north. dial.* and *Sc.* †**2.** A cunning contrivance or device; a machination, plot, scheme.

13.. *Gaw. & Gr. Knt.* 3 þe tulk þat þe trammes of tresoun þer wroȝt. 1616 J. MAITLAND *Apol. W. Maitl. of Lethington* in *Misc.* (S. H. S., 1904) 187 That plot and trame to thamselfs and to manie others. 1866 J. E. BROGDEN *Provinc. Words Lincoln.*, *Trame*, 'gillery'.

†**3.** A mechanical contrivance; a machine, an engine; an implement, instrument, tool; in quot. 13.., tackle or gear of a ship. (Chiefly in *pl.*)

13.. *E. E. Allit. P.* C. 101 Then he tron on þo tres & þay her tramme ruchen. 1375 BARBOUR *Bruce* XVII. 245 He gert engynis and trammys ma [= make]. *a* 1400–50 *Alexander* 127 He toke traimmes him with to tute in þe sternes, Astralabus algate as his arte wald, Quadrentis coruen all of qu[h]yte siluyre full quaynte. *Ibid.* 286 þus as he tuke furth his toylis [= tools] & his trammys schewis. *Ibid.* 1296 Ser Balaan..Buskes him in breneis with big men of armes, With traumes [*v. r.* trawynns] & with tribochetis þe tild [*v. r.* towre] to asaile. *Ibid.* 1373 Quen he had tiȝt vp þis tram [*v. r.* trame (*i. e.* a siege-tower)] & þis tild rerid.

**Tram** (træm), *sb.*[2] [In sense 1, used in Sc. *c* 1500, and prob. earlier; app. the same word as LG. *traam* 'balk, beam, e. g. of a wheelbarrow or dung-sledge, tram, handle of a barrow or sledge, also a rung or step of a ladder, bar of a chair' (*Brem. Wbch.* 1771), EFris. *trame, trâm* beam of wood, rung or step of a ladder, bar of a chair, tram of a wheelbarrow; in MLG. *trame, treme*, MDu. *trame* balk or beam, rung of a ladder, etc.; WFlem. *traam, trame.*

The specific sense first found in Scotch is 'the tram of a barrow'. The further sense-development presents many difficulties, chiefly from the scarcity of early examples, and the fact that the various senses are from separate localities, so that they cannot be taken as showing any general development. But branch II, in which *tram* is a miners' term for the vehicle for carrying coal or ore (in its development from a hand-barrow, or at least a sledge, to a small 4-wheeled iron wagon) may, on the principle of *pars pro toto*, have arisen out of that of 'barrow-tram' in I. Branch III is more difficult, and is the *crux* of the word. But if it was short for something like 'tram-track', it might have arisen out of II; and if it was applied primarily to the wooden beams or 'rails' laid as wheel tracks, it might conceivably go back to the LG. sense of 'balk' or 'beam': evidence is wanting. From II or III used attributively came *tram-road* (in use in 1800), and the later *tram-way* (in use in 1825); also *tram-carriage* and the modern *tram-car*, known in 1868 and 1873 respectively, and before 1880 shortened in popular English use to *tram*, branch IV, which thus by a circuitous course 'harks back' to a sense akin to branch II.]

**I.** A shaft of a barrow or cart.

**1.** Each of the two shafts of a cart or wagon, a hand-barrow, or a wheelbarrow, the ends of which in a barrow form the handles. *Sc.*

These shafts are prolongations of the strong side-timbers of the frame or body of the structure: in a hand-barrow these are prolonged both ways, to form shafts or trams both before and behind, by which the two bearers carry the barrow; in a wheelbarrow they are prolonged in one direction to form the shafts, or trams, and in the other to form sockets for the axle of the wheel; in a cart they are prolonged in front to form the strong shafts or trams within which the horse walks, while their ends usually form short projections behind.

1500–20 DUNBAR *Poems* lii. 19, I wald scho war, bayth syd and bak, Weill batteret with ane barrow-tram. 1545 *Acc. Ld. High Treas. Scot.* VIII. 360 Ane pair of sled trammys to be lymmaris to ane of the saiddis falconis [guns]. *a* 1550 Barrow trammis, 1657 Barrow-trams [see BARROW *sb.*[3] 4]. 1766 *State of Proc., D. Macdonald* v. *A. Dk. of Gordon*, Pursuer's Proof 8, Light timber, such as stings and cart trams. 1786 BURNS *Inventory* 31 Ae auld wheelbarrow, mair for token, Ae leg an' baith the trams are broken. 1790 SHIRREFS *Poems* 360 Nor is the naig the worse to draw A wee while in the trams. 1830 GALT *Lawrie T.* IV. viii, I..sat down on the tram of the wagon. 1833 ALISON *Hist. Europe* (1849) II. vi. § 79. 75 Nearly an hour was..lost, by an accident to one of the trams of the royal carriage.

**b.** *transf.* In *pl.* The two upright posts of a gallows; also humorously, in *sing.*, a man's leg; particularly, a wooden leg.

*a* 1670 SPALDING *Troub. Chas. I* (1851) II. 4 Be order, the hangman brak his suord betuixt the crossis of Abirdein, and betuixt the gallowis-tramis standing thair. 1808–18 JAMIESON, *Tram*, in a ludicrous sense, the leg or limb; as *lang trams*, long limbs. 1882 *Ibid.*, Applied also to a person with long ungainly legs, *Clydes.* 1834 M. SCOTT *Cruise Midge* (1863) 48 He began to thunder at the low door with his pillar-like trams. *Ibid.* 206 It must have stumped along for fifty years on a leg of flesh and a tram of wood.

II. A framework, barrow, or the like, on which loads are dragged, carried, or supported.

**2.** *Coal-mining.* A quadrilateral frame or skeleton truck on which the corves were formerly carried; at first prob. carried like a hand-barrow, then dragged like a sledge, afterwards provided with low wheels on which to run; now in some colliery districts applied to the small iron truck which supplies the place of the earlier 'tram' and corve; in others to the part of the 'tub' (on wheels) to which the 'box' is bolted.

1516–17 *Durham Acc. Rolls* (Surtees) 293 Item, ad puteum [pit] de Hett,..j restis et j cruke de ferro..ij pykes, ij trammys, et ij shulys. 1585 *Wills & Inv. N. C.* (Surtees) II. 112, j long wayne without wheels, ij yron ax-nailes, and ij yokes, 6s. j cowpe, ij trams, and two ax-trees 2s. 8d. 1708 J. C. *Compl. Collier* (1845) 39 The Wages for the Barrow-Men is..about twenty pence a Day for each *Tram* (that is to say) for putting so many loaden Corves, as are carried on one Sledge or Tram in one Day to the Pit Shaft. 1789 BRAND *Hist. Newcastle* II. 681 Trams are a kind of sledges on which the coals are brought from the places where they are hewn to the shaft. A tram has four wheels, but a sledge properly so called is drawn by a horse without wheels. 1797 CURR *Coal Viewer* 9 Placing the corf upon a small frame or tram..and hooking or chaining one tram to another. 1817 FAREY *Derbyshire* III. 439 The Trams..have stout lower side pieces of wood which project at each end, and are hooped with iron which just meet together and receive the shock when the Trams overtake each other. 1839 URE *Dict. Arts* 982 An improvement..is to place the basket or corve on a small four-wheeled carriage, called a tram, or to attach wheels to the corve itself. 1841 J. HOLLAND *Hist. Fossil Fuel*, etc. 227 The coals..were conveyed..on trams, a narrow framework of wood mounted on four low wheels. 1851 GREENWELL *Coal-trade Terms Northumb. & Durh.* 54 Since the substitution of tubs, the trams have been attached to them. 1867 W. W. SMYTH *Coal & Coal-mining* 149 The northern method was to fill the coals..into a large basket (corve) of wicker..and to drag it on a small carriage, or tram,..to the crane-place on the main road. 1883 GRESLEY *Gloss. Coal Mining* 257 In South Wales *trams* constructed wholly of wrought iron or steel are much used...They have a carrying capacity of 25 cwt. 1888 NICHOLSON *Coal Trade Gloss.*, *Tram*, the term still applies to the part of a tub to which the box is bolted. 1894 *Northumbld. Gloss.* s. v., Trams and tubs are now made in one.

b. *transf.* The one or two lads in charge of a tram; also, the work performed by these.

1856 WHELLAN *Hist. Durham* 94 When a boy 'puts' or drags a load by himself he is designated a tram. 1894 *Northumbld. Gloss.* s.v., Sometimes tram was applied to the two lads in charge of it [the colliery tram]—called a 'tram of lads'. 'Half a tram', the work of one putter where two are engaged on a tram.

**3.** A quadrilateral frame or bench (like the body of a hand-barrow) supported on four legs or blocks, on which casks or the like stand, or at which an artisan works.

1818 W. MARSHALL *Review* II. 485 (E.D.D.) The cheese-tubs are placed on a small tram or bench. 1884 *S. Worc.* (Upton on Severn) *Gloss.*, *Tram* or *Tramming*, a framework, or a loose arrangement, of stout parallel rails on short legs, or blocks, for supporting casks. 1894 *S. E. Worc. Gloss.*, *Tram*, a strong square frame with four legs on which a wheelwright makes wheels; also a stand for casks.

III. A track of wood, stone, or iron; a tram-road or tramway.

**4.** A continuous line or track of timber beams or 'rails', or later of stone blocks or slabs, a parallel pair of which lines formed a tramway, originally in or from a mine. Hence, each of the wheel-tracks or 'rails' of a tram-road of an early type, or of a later tramway or railway.

[*a* 1734 NORTH *Life Ld. Keeper North* (1742) 136 The Manner of the Carriage [of coals in Northumberland in 1676] is by laying Rails of Timber, from the Colliery, down to the River, exactly streight and parallel; and bulky Carts are made with four Rowlets fitting these Rails; whereby the Carriage is so easy that one Horse will draw four or five Chaldron of Coals, and is an immense Benefit to the Coal Merchants.] 1826 J. ADAMSON *Sk. Inform. Rail-Roads* 6 The upper flat part [of a rail on a railway], along which the wheel rolls, we may, from its analogy to the old wooden rails, call the tram of the rail. 1834 N. W. CUNDY *Inland Transit* 1 The Manchester and Liverpool railroad, in my opinion, is constructed too narrow both in the trams and the space between them. 1838 SIMMS *Public Works Gt. Brit.* III. 3 He [Mr. Macneill] is laying stone blocks or trams for the wheels to roll upon. 1881 RAYMOND *Mining Gloss.*, *Tram*..One of the rails of a tramroad or railroad. [See also quot. 1825 in 5, and TRAM-LINE, -ROAD, -WAY.]

**5.** A road laid with such wooden planks or rails, or with parallel rows of stone slabs or of iron plates or 'rails', for the easier passage of loaded wagons, etc., in a coal-mine or above ground; a tram-road of an early type. (See also Note below.)

[1825 MACKENZIE *Hist. Northumbld.* I. 146 Square wooden rails laid in two right parallel lines, and firmly pegged down on wooden sleepers. The tops of the rail are plained smooth and round, and sometimes covered with plates of wrought iron. About the year 1786 cast-iron railways were introduced as an improvement upon the tram or wooden rail-way.] 1850 ANSTED *Geol.*, etc. § 1117 The loaded waggons, or corves, are conveyed along the tram by lads called putters. 1865 *Pall Mall G.* 27 June 10 Have they not trams in the suburbs of half our Lancashire towns, and is there not a tram on a grand scale for the use of those long ugly *Omnibus Americains* which ply between Paris and Versailles?

IV. Short for *tram-car* or the like.

**6.** A passenger car on a street tramway; a tram-car.

1879 WEBSTER Suppl., *Tram*, a car on a horse-railroad. *Eng.* 1880 MARY FITZ-GIBBON *Trip to Manitoba* vii. 71 To see if the trams were coming. 1883 G. H. BOUGHTON in *Harper's Mag.* Apr. 702/1 It was so easy to pop into the..tram. 1884 *Ibid.* Sept. 524/1 Taking the tram to Scheveningen. 1887 *Punch* 12 Mar. 130/2 She is left without a penny to pay for tram or bus. 1902 R. BAGOT *Donna Diana* xiii, The discordant clanging of the gongs of electric trams fall hideously on the ear.

**7.** An overhead or suspended carrier travelling on a cable.

1905 *Daily Chron.* 23 Sept. 8/1 (Supply of meat at Aldershot) Hoisting gear bears the carcases quickly away for dressing, and when that is done, an overhead carrying line, conveniently referred to as the 'tram', conveys them to the cooling room.

V. **8.** *attrib.* and *Comb.*, as *tram-bell*, *-boy*, *-carriage*, *-conductor*, *-driver*, *-load*, *-railway*, *-shed*, *-ticket*, *-wagon*, *-wheel*, *-whistle*, *-yard*; *-travelling* adj.; **tram-man**, a man employed on a tramway, *esp.* a tram-conductor or driver; **tram-rail**, (*a*) a plate-rail: see PLATE *sb.* 8; (*b*) each of the rails of a tramway. See also TRAM-CAR, -LINE, etc.

1905 *Daily Chron.* 14 Sept. 3/1 The incessant clanging of the *tram-bell [in Holland]. 1904 J. WELLS *J. H. Wilson* xi. 97 He..established societies for the *tram-boys [in collieries]. 1868 *Daily News* 22 July, Asking the moderate fee of twopence for its entire journey, the *tram carriage is like a rough omnibus without cushions turned inside out. 1892 ZANGWILL *Bow Mystery* 4 The *tram conductors' bells were ..ringing. 1904 *Daily News* 24 May 12 The crowded *tram-loads along this flowered highway of the West. 1892 ZANGWILL *Bow Mystery* 4 At an early meeting of discontented *tram-men. 1839 URE *Dict. Arts* 982 The rails are called *tram-rails, or plate-rails. 1900 *Westm. Gaz.* 5 Sept. 6/2 The tram rails had been watered in order to lessen friction, and accidents to cyclists are of constant occurrence in the same neighbourhood. 1894 *Daily News* 5 May 8/5 Of much advantage to the *tram-travelling public of South London. 1855 J. R. LEIFCHILD *Cornwall Mines* 150 That the ore may readily fall down to the level below them, whence it is carried in *tram-waggons to the shaft. 1825 J. NICHOLSON *Operat. Mechanic* 649 Fig. 644 represents a view of a rolley or *tram-wheel, calculated to move upon a plate railway. 1883 E. F. KNIGHT *Cruise Falcon* (1887) 40 Above the shrill scream of the *tram-whistle rises their shriller Babel. 1909 *London City Mission Mag.* Dec. 241/2 A stableman from an adjacent *tramyard.

(*Note.* The following quot. for *tram* is difficult to place. It has the appearance of belonging to sense 5; but its early date is at variance with this. No part of the road in or near the Bridgegate at Barnard Castle is now known as 'the tram', nor is there any tradition of the former existence of a tramway of any kind there. On the opposite or Yorkshire side of the Tees, the road running southward from the end of the bridge is protected from the river by a heavy stone wall locally known as 'the tram wall'; but this does not seem to answer to the words of the will.

1555 *Will of Ambrose Middleton* in *Wills & Inv. N.C.* (Surtees) II. 37 *note*, To the amendinge of the higheway or tram, from the weste ende of Bridgegait, in Barnard Castle, 20s.)

Hence **Tra·mful**, as much or as many as a tram or tram-car will hold; **Tramifica·tion** (*nonce-wd.*), the construction of a tramway; **Tra·mless** *a.*, (*a*) without shafts, as a cart (*dial.*); (*b*) having no trams or tramway facilities.

1905 *Daily News* 20 Sept. 6 The coal came up in little *tramfuls. 1834 *New Monthly Mag.* XL. 372 The whole object of that *tramification is the conveyance of goods—of heavy loads. 1850 A. MACLAGAN *Cronie O'Mine* Poems (1851) 174 A *tramless cart or a couterless plough. 1904 *Daily Chron.* 29 Mar. 3/6 Tramless Brixton..the Cars are to be Stopped for Two Months.

**Tram**, *sb.*$^3$ *Mech.* [Short for TRAMMEL *sb.*$^1$]

**1.** An instrument for describing ellipses; = TRAMMEL *sb.*$^1$ 4. 1884 in KNIGHT *Dict. Mech.* Suppl.

**2.** The condition of correct adjustment of one part to another (obtained by using the *tram-staff*); used in the phrases *in tram*, *out of tram*. Originally used in reference to the adjustment of millstones, thence extended to other mechanical adjustments.

1891 in *Cent. Dict.*; and in later Dicts.

**3.** *attrib.* and *Comb.*, as **tram-pot**, the step in which the toe of a millstone spindle revolves; **tram-staff**, a straight-edge used by millwrights in adjusting the millstone spindle (*Cent. Dict.* 1891).

1884 KNIGHT *Dict. Mech.* Suppl., *Trampot* (Milling), the seat in which the foot of the spindle is stepped.

**Tram** (træm), *v.*$^1$ [f. TRAM *sb.*$^2$]

**1.** *intr.* To travel by a tramway or on a tram-car (also *to tram it*). *colloq.* Also (*U.S.*), to drive or operate a tram-car (*Cent. Dict.* 1891).

1826 in *Northumbld. Gloss.* s.v., Liddell, why he from Durham came,..But home again he'd better tram. 1896 *Westm. Gaz.* 9 Apr. 7/2 The Walworthian has to tram to Greenwich. 1904 E. NESBIT *Phœnix & Carpet* x, They can tram it home.

**2.** *trans. Mining.* To convey (coal, ore, etc.) by a tram or trams.

1874 J. H. COLLINS *Metal Mining* (1875) 11 One sees..the ore and rubbish allowed to accumulate behind the men to a height of several feet before it is trammed back to the shaft. 1887 RAYMOND *Statist. Mines & Mining* 8 Tramming. 1889 *Eng. Illustr. Mag.* May 572/2 To 'tram' the coal from the working face..to the sidings where the horses take the waggons. 1893 *Pall Mall G.* 14 Jan. 1/3 In the level below ..only one man was saved, who had been tramming to the shaft the ore which he excavated on previous days.

b. To push (a tram or wagon) to and from the shaft in a mine.

1883 LE NEVE FOSTER in *Encycl. Brit.* XVI. 455/2 (*Mining*) This trolley (which is merely a small platform upon wheels) is pushed (*trammed*) to the shaft; the full kibble is hooked on to the winding-rope and drawn up, whilst an empty kibble is placed upon the trolley and trammed back along the level..where it is again loaded. *Ibid.*, The motive power for tramming wagons along the levels of metal mines is generally supplied by men or boys.

**Tram**, *v.*$^2$ [f. TRAM *sb.*$^3$] *trans.* and *intr.* To use a tram or tram-staff in adjusting spindles or axles, or in measuring, alining, or the like.

1891 in *Cent. Dict.* (implied in *tramming*); in later Dicts.

**Tram**, in *trim tram*: see TRIM-TRAM.

‖**Trama** (trē·mă, trā·mă). *Bot.* [L. *trāma* woof, weft, filling of a web.] The substance between the surfaces of the 'gills' of hymenomycetous fungi. Also called *intralamellar substance*, *dissepiment*. Hence **Tra·mal** *a.* (*Cent. Dict.* 1891).

1857 BERKELEY *Cryptog. Bot.* § 399 In Schizophyllum, the gills split in the direction of their trama. 1874 COOKE *Fungi* 23 In Lactarius and Russula the trama, or inner substance, is vesicular. 1875 BENNETT & DYER *Sachs' Bot.* 250 The substance of the lamella, called the *Trama*.

†**Tra·mble**, *v. Obs.* [Origin uncertain. Cf. Sw. dial. *tramla*, *trumla* to fall (Rietz).]

**1.** *intr.* To roll over and over; to tumble, fall headlong. *rare*$^{-1}$.

1609 BIBLE (Douay) *Job* xxx. 14 They haue broken violently vpon me, and are come trambling downe to my miseries [Vulg. *ad meas miserias devoluti sunt*].

**2.** *trans.* To wash (tin-ore) by agitating it in a trough of water (BUDDLE *sb.*$^2$) with a special shovel called a *trambling shovel*; to buddle; = TOZE *v.*$^2$

1671 *Phil. Trans.* VI. 2109 A man..with a Trambling shovel in his hand to cast up the Ore. *Ibid.* 2110 When this Buddle grows full, we take it up; here distinguishing again the Fore-head from the Middle and Tails; which are trambled over again. 1710 J. HARRIS *Lex. Techn.* II, *Trambling*, is the Term used in Dressing of Tin-ore, for washing it very clean in Water..with..a Trambling-shovel, and in a Frame of Boards, which they call a Buddle.

**Trambooze**: see TRAMPOOSE.

**Tram-car** (træ·m,kāɪ). [f. TRAM *sb.*$^2$ III. + CAR.] A public car or carriage running on a tramway for the conveyance of passengers; called earlier *tramway car*, and already in 1879 simply *tram* (TRAM *sb.*$^2$ 6). *Tram-carriage* (TRAM *sb.*$^2$ 8) is cited 1868.

1873 *Engineer* 28 Nov. 353 A trial of Grantham's steam tram car. 1876 *Ibid.* 26 May 400 A heavy vehicle such as an omnibus or a tram car. 1879 *Trans. Soc. Engineers* 195 The Italian tram cars enabled him to see nearly the whole of the city of Turin for..sixpence. 1883 F. M. CRAWFORD *Dr. Claudius* xiii, The ceaseless ring of the tram-cars stopping every few steps to pick up a passenger. 1905 R. BAGOT *Passport* iii, In a quiet and secluded position..undisturbed by the noise of the tram-cars.

*attrib.* 1880 *Proc. Inst. Mech. Engin.* 199 The flange of a tramcar wheel.

**Trame**, var. TRAM *sb.*$^1$

[**Tramiss.** Misreading of *traunss*, TRANCE.]

**Tra·m-line.** [f. TRAM *sb.*$^2$ 5 or 6 + LINE *sb.*$^2$: cf. *railway line.*] A tramway; also, a tram-rail.

1886 HARE *Story my Life* (1900) VI. xxiv. 9 We were taken back to the tram-line. 1895 ZANGWILL *Master* II. ix, The yellow sand scattered on slippery days along the tramlines. 1896 *Times* 30 Sept. 7/6 Tenders are to be sent in..to the tramline's offices. 1905 VISCT. RIDLEY in *Daily Chron.* 21 July 5/5 The Bill dealt with several new tramlines, three of which were uncontested and not very important.

**Trammel** (træ·mĕl), *sb.*$^1$ Forms: 5 **tramale**, **-ell**, **-elle**, (**tramaly**, 5–6 **-ely**), 5–6 **tramayle**, (6 *Sc.* **tramalt**), 6–7 **tramell**, 6–8 **-el**, 6–9 **trammell**, 7 **tramaile**, 6– **trammel**. [In sense 1, a. OF. *tramail* (*c* 1220 in Godef. *Compl.*), mod.F. *trémail* a fishing- or fowling-net, with three layers of meshes, = It. *tramaglio*, Sp. *trasmallo*, Pg. *trasmalho*:—late pop.L. *tramaculum* for *tri-*, *tremaculum* (in Salic Law, Hessels, Cod. I, xxvii. 20, *tremaclem*, v. rr. *tremalem*, *tremagilo*, *tramaculam*, *trimaclem*, *tremagolum*, *tremachlum*, etc.) a kind of fishing-net, generally explained as f. L. *tri-* three + *macula* mesh. In the Romanic langs. the prefix appears to have been taken as = *tra-*, L. *trans.* The history of the other senses here included is difficult: see Note below.]

I. **1.** A long narrow fishing-net, set vertically with floats and sinkers; consisting of two 'walls' of large-meshed netting, between which is a net of fine mesh, loosely hung. More fully TRAMMEL-NET.

The fish enters through the large mesh on one side, drives the fine netting through the large mesh on the other, and is thus trapped in a pocket or bag of the fine netting. Also sometimes applied to other kinds of fishing nets.

1363 [implied in TRAMMELLER 1].

*c* 1440 *Promp. Parv.* 499/1 Tramayle, grete nette for fyschynge (*K.* tramely, *H.*, *P.* tramaly), *tragum*. 14.. *Voc.* in Wr.-Wülcker 617/18 *Tramellum..quoddam genus retis*, ..a tramayle. 1467–8 *Durham Acc. Rolls* (Surtees) 92 Pro j rethe voc. Tramale, xxiiij$^d$. 1558 *Act 1 Eliz.* c. 17 § 3 No persone..shall fishe..with any maner of Nett, Tramell [etc.], but onely with a Nett or Tramell whereof every Meshe..shalbee [etc.]. 1633 P. FLETCHER *Pisc. Ecl.* v. xiv, Are thy lines broke? or are thy trammels tore? 1787 BEST *Angling* (ed. 2) 5 By fishing with trammels or flews in March or April. **1848** C. A. JOHNS *Week at Lizard* 242 The trammel is a long net, about five feet deep, with a double mesh, one large enough to allow the fish to pass through, the other much smaller. **1883** E. P. RAMSAY *Food Fishes N. S. Wales* 33 (Fish. Exhib. Publ.) They are usually taken for market with a Trammel, or Bag-net, set across the stream, or by hook and line.

**b.** A fowling-net; = TRAMMEL-NET b.

**1530** PALSGR. 282/2 Tramell to catche fysshe or byrdes, *trameau*. **1581** *Act* 23 *Eliz.* c. 10 § 6 To take any Partridges or Feasaunts by night, under any Tramell, Lowbell, Roadenette or other Engine. **1655** MOUFET & BENNET *Health's Impr.* (1746) 173 A Partridge taken in Flight, or a Lark dared with a Hawk, is worth ten taken with Nets, Springs and Trammels. **1895** QUILLER COUCH *Wand. Heath* 80 He and his mates went out and tilled the trammel.

**II. †2.** A hobble to prevent a horse from straying or kicking; also, a contrivance for teaching a horse to amble, consisting of lines and straps connecting the fore and hind feet on each side, with a strap over the back to which both lines were fastened for support. *Obs.*

*c* **1550** W. KETH *Tye the Mare, Tom Boy* 35 (Ritson) Yett wer thou much better In trammells to bynd her; A loock and a fetter Befor and behynd her. **1591** GREENE *Art Conny Catch.* II. (1592) 4 Whether they haue horse-locks or no,..in the night they take him or them away, and are skilfull in the blacke Art, for picking open the tramels or lockes. **1616** SURFL. & MARKH. *Country Farme* 133 It is called a Tramell when a Horses neere fore-legge and his neere hinder-legge..are so fastened together with leathers and cords, that he cannot put forward his fore-legge, but he must perforce hale his hinder-legge after it. **1675** *Lond. Gaz.* No. 1043/4 A..Nag..has all his paces, and swellings in his forelegs caused by the tramels. **1766** *Compl. Farmer*, *Tramel*,..made sometimes of leather, but more usually of ropes, fitted to a horse's legs to regulate his motion, and teach him to amble.

**3.** *transf.* and *fig.* Anything that hinders or impedes free action; anything that confines, restrains, fetters, or shackles. Chiefly *pl.*

*a* **1653** G. DANIEL *Idyll.* iii. 106 'Tis an easie Chord; ye Flax of Law Makes a soft Trammell. *a* **1680** BUTLER *Rem.* (1759) I. 266 To put his Wits into a kind of Tramels. **1709** STEELE & SWIFT *Tatler* No. 74 ¶ 4 The Gentleman is in the true Trammels of Love. **1787** MME. D'ARBLAY *Diary* 5 Jan., There seemed to be no opportunity..of liberating my evenings from official trammels. **1841** D'ISRAELI *Amen. Lit.* (1867) 462 The destiny of Spenser was..to wear the silken trammels of noble patrons. **1889** *John Bull* 2 Mar. 148/3 Throughout her career she [Geo. Eliot], for the most part, refused to bind herself by conventional trammels.

**4.** *Mech.* An instrument for describing ellipses (F. *compas à ellipse*), consisting of a cross with two grooves at right angles, in which slide pins carrying a beam or ruler with a pencil; also applied to the *beam-compass* (BEAM *sb.*[1] IV). Also *pl.*

So called because the motion of the beam carrying the pencil is trammelled or confined by the restriction of the pins to the grooves.

**1725** W. HALFPENNY *Sound Building* 7 Make the Tramel ..in the same Form as..in the Figure. **1780** LUDLAM in *Phil. Trans.* LXX. 378 The instrument for drawing ovals upon paper or board..is much in use among the joiners, and called by them the trammels. **1795** HUTTON *Math. Dict.* s. v., All the engines for turning ovals are constructed on the same principles with the Trammels: the only difference is, that in the Trammels the board is at rest, and the pencil moves upon it. **1875** *Carpentry & Join.* 118 We will now add one other method of striking elliptic curves, and describe..the instrument by which it is done. This is called a trammel. **1884** *Cheshire Gloss.* s. v., In working circular work, a staff of the radius of the circle is a trammel.

**III. 5.** A series of rings or links, or other device, to bear a crook at different heights over the fire; the whole being suspended from a transverse bar (the crook-tree), built in the chimney, or from a small crane or gallows, the vertical member of which turns in sockets in the jamb and lintel. Now *local Eng.* and *U.S.*

**1537** *Bury Wills* (Camden) 130 The tramely yn the chemney, and the racke on the soler. **1630** *Maldon, Essex, Documents* Bundle 217. No. 22 In the little butterye, i iron hooke to hange at the eand of a tramell, 2*d*. **1674** RAY *S. & E. C. Words* 77 A *Trammel*, an iron instrument hanging in the chimney, whereon to hang pots or kettles over the fire. **1866** WHITTIER *Snowbound* 136 The crane and pendent trammels showed. **1883** *Hampshire Gloss.*, *Trammel*, a hook to hang a boiler on. [An error.] **1889** LUCY LARCOM *New Eng. Girlhood* i. 22 We..sometimes smirched our clean aprons..against the swinging crane with its sooty pot-hooks and trammels.

**IV. †6.** *pl.* The plaits, braids, or tresses of a woman's hair; in quot. 1594 with play on sense 1.

(Sometimes erroneously explained as a net to confine the hair.)

**1589** GREENE *Menaphon* (Arb.) 25 She..wraps affection in the tramels of her haire. **1590** SPENSER *F. Q.* II. ii. 15 Her golden lockes she roundly did uptye In breaded tramels. *Ibid.* III. ix. 20 Her golden locks, that were in trammells gay Upbounden, did them selves adowne display And raught unto her heeles. **1594** GREENE & LODGE *Looking Glasse* G.'s Wks. (Rtldg.) 122/2 For women's locks are trammels of conceit, Which do entangle Love for all his wiles. **1669** A. BROWNE *Ars Pict.* 86 You may go over the hair, disposing into such forms, folds or tramels, as may become your Picture best. **1673** JORDAN *Lond. in Splend.* 12 A long fair Hair, the tramels tyed with small Ribon of all the light Colours.

**V. 7.** *attrib.* and *Comb.*, as †*trammel-boat* (? used in fishing with the trammel-net); *trammel-trick* [f. TRAMMEL *v.*]; **trammel-wheel**, a mechanical device for converting rotary into reciprocal motion, consisting of a wheel with grooves crossing each other, in which slide projections attached to a connecting-rod, so that the rod makes two up-and-down motions for each revolution of the wheel; also a modification of this.

**1614** T. GENTLEMAN *Way to Wealth* (1660) 9 The Pinks for barreld Fish, and Trammel boats. **1873** BROWNING *Red Cott. Nt.-cap* 176 Be theirs to drowse Trammeled, and ours to watch the trammel-trick! **1877** KNIGHT *Dict. Mech.*, Trammel-wheel.

[*Note.* French dictionaries have *trémail*, *tramail*, only in senses 1, 1 b. And indeed the sense-connexion of branches II, III, IV with I, and with each other, is obscure; some of them may perhaps be different words. But the identification of I and II is not confined to English. Du Cange quotes a med.L. statute of Piacenza, in which *tramaiolum* (?read *tramacolum*) is applied to a stick a cubit and a half long, ordered to be fixed to the necks of dogs to prevent them from running into vineyards or other places where they might do mischief; and he identifies this word with It. *tramaglio* and F. *tramail*, and refers to this word as known to be applied not only to a net, but to any kind of shackle or snare (*pedica*). Baretti's Ital. dictionary has *tramaglio* only as 'a trammel or drag-net', but Florio 1611 has it 'a tramell or ensnaring'.]

**†Trammel**, *sb.*[2] *Obs.* In 5 tramel, -ale, -aly. [Cf. OF. *tremuie*, *tremue*, *tremee* (all 14th c. in Godef.), *trameul*, *tremouille*, *tremuë* (Cotgr.), mod.F. *trémie* = Pr. *tremueia*, Cat. *tramuja*, It. *tramoggia*, Sicil. *trimoja*:—L. *trimodia*, a three-peck measure: see Diez, Scheler. Some med.L. and Romanic forms are affected by L. *trem-ĕre* to tremble. In Eng. apparently confounded with TRAMMEL *sb.*[1]] The hopper of a mill.

*c* **1440** *Promp. Parv.* 246/1 Hopur, of a mylle, or a tramale (*S.* tramel, *a* 1485), *taratantara*, *farricapsium*. *Ibid.* 499/1 Tramaly, of a mylle, *idem quod* hopur; *supra*; *et faricapsia*.

**Tra·mmel**, *v.* [f. TRAMMEL *sb.*[1]]

**†1.** *trans.* To bind up (a corpse). *Obs.*

**1536** in *Archæol.* XVI. 23 (Funeral Q. Kath.) The Corps must be sered, tramayled, leded, and chested. **1546–7** in Strype *Eccl. Mem.* (1721) II. App. A. 3 (Funeral K. Hen. VIII) Surely bound and trammel'd with cords of silk. *c* **1558** *Leland's Collect.* (1770) V. 308 Whoo [Q. Mary] after her Departuer was..cered, and tramelled in this Manner.

**2.** *intr.* To use a trammel-net; *trans.* to take (fish or birds) with a trammel-net.

**1588–1866** [see TRAMMELLING *vbl. sb.*]. **1846** *Bell's Life* 9 Aug. 7/5 Four men were caught trammelling pheasants.

**†3.** *trans.* To fasten together (the legs of a horse) with trammels (TRAMMEL *sb.*[1] 2); also, to put trammels on (a horse). *Obs.*

**1607** MARKHAM *Caval.* IV. ix. (1617) 45, I would haue you in any case..to tramell your horse aboue knee. **1610** — *Masterp.* II. clix. 468 After you haue tramelled all his foure legges. **1639** T. DE GRAY *Compl. Horsem.* 307 Tramell his fore-feet that he do not lye down.

**4.** *fig.* To entangle or fasten *up* as in a trammel.

**1605** SHAKS. *Macb.* I. vii. 3 If th'Assassination Could trammell vp the Consequence, and catch..Successe. **1819** KEATS *Lamia* II. 52 How to entangle, trammel up, and snare Your soul in mine. **1906** *Hibbert Jrnl.* Jan. 304 Mind is never either mere antecedent or mere consequent. It trammels up its before and hereafter.

**5.** *fig.* To hinder the free action of; to put restraint upon, fetter, hamper, impede, confine.

**1727** POPE *Let. to Gay* 6 Oct., Ill and vicious Habits, of which few or no men escape the infection, who are hackney'd and trammelled in the ways of a court. **1792** A. YOUNG *Trav. France* 236 We are little better than horses in a team, trammelled to follow one another. **1807** E. S. BARRETT *Rising Sun* II. 8 Till he had trammelled himself again with debts. **1865** SWINBURNE *Atalanta* 98 Ripe grasses trammel a travelling foot. **1883** LD. R. GOWER *My Remin.* I. i. 12 Like many great artists, when trammelled with a commission he seemed to lose power.

**6.** To fasten (a piece of work on the spindle of a lathe) with a clamp. *rare.*

**1833** J. HOLLAND *Manuf. Metal* II. vi. 134 The work must be trammelled to the nose of the spindle, by a contrivance called the dog and driver, the former being a sort of clutch, screwed upon the end of the work.

**†Tra·mmelet.** *Obs. rare.* [f. TRAMMEL *sb.*[1] 6 + -ET.] *pl.* Braids, tresses: cf. TRAMMEL *sb.*[1] 6.

**1654** HERRICK *Descr. Woman* 4 Like Aurora when with pearl she sets Her long discheveld rose-crownd trammelets.

**Tra·mmelled, -eled** (-ĕld), *ppl. a.* [f. TRAMMEL *sb.*[1] and *v.* + -ED.]

**1.** †**a.** Of hair: Braided or bound up in trammels.

**1609** HEYWOOD *Brit. Troy* v. lxxv, Is her haire browne? ..Browne trameld lockes best grace the brightest hew.

**b.** (See quot.)

**1753** CHAMBERS *Cycl. Supp.* s. v., A horse is said to be tramelled, that has blazes or white marks upon the fore and hind foot of one side;..so called from the resemblance the white foot bears to a half tramel. Cross-tramelled horse, is one that has white marks in two of his feet that stand crossways,..as in the far fore-foot, and the near hind-foot.

**2.** Confined by or as by trammels; fettered, shackled.

**1813** SCOTT *Rokeby* v. xxxiii, Harpool clasp'd His knees ..And round the trammelled ruffian clung. **1818** LADY CHARLEVILLE in *Lady Morgan's Autobiog.* (1859) 12 If your book be cut and garbled by those vile inspectors of a trammelled press. **1821** JOANNA BAILLIE *Metr. Leg.*, *Wallace* xvi, Who from their trammell'd country broke.

**Tra·mmeller, -eler.** *rare.* [f. as prec. + -ER[1]. Cf. obs.F. *trameilleur* a kind of boat (Godef.).]

**1.** ? A fisherman, or a boat, fishing with a trammel.

**1363** *Ministers Accts.* Bundle 1028, No. 15, P.R.O. (Rye), Et de xxx. s. receptis de quadam custuma vocata Cristschar' proveniente de piscaria batellorum..de Matheo Samon pro schar' de tramelers iiii. s. *Ibid.*, De consimili custuma ..de Roberto Bernhaud pro schars de tramelers xiii. s.

**2.** A fowler using a trammel-net.

**1581** *Act* 23 *Eliz.* c. 10 § 6 This Act shall not..extend to Lowebellers, Tramellers or others, whiche shall unwillinglye happen to take any Partridges. **1618** DALTON *Countrey Just.* 285 To bind trannellers [*sic*] for larkes, that they shall destroy no partridges.

**3.** One who or that which trammels or restrains.

**1864** in WEBSTER; and in later Dicts.

**Tra·mmelling, -eling,** *vbl. sb.* [f. TRAMMEL *v.* + -ING[1].] The action of the verb TRAMMEL in various senses. Also *attrib.* **trammelling-net** = TRAMMEL-NET.

**1588** LAMBARDE *Eiren.* IV. iv. 444 If any person..have taken..any Phesants or Partriches..by lowbelling or tramelling. **1616** SURFL. & MARKH. *Country Farme* 133 To be observed in the trammelling of Horses. **1688** R. HOLME *Armoury* III. xxii. (Roxb.) 277/1 A Long Nett, called a Tramelling Nett...The ends are fixed on long poles. **1826** HONE *Every-Day Bk.* I. 952 The larks..at Dunstable..are usually taken..with trammeling nets. **1866** *Daily Tel.* 5 Jan. 5/2 Trawling, shrimping, trammelling..methods deprecated by those who don't happen to practise them.

**Tra·mmellingly,** *adv.* [f. pres. pple. of TRAMMEL *v.* + -LY[2].] In a fettering manner.

**1884** J. W. HALES *Notes & Ess. Shaks.* 99 The exuberant growths of fancy cling around them trammellingly.

**Tra·mmel-net.** [f. TRAMMEL *sb.*[1] + NET *sb.*[1]] = TRAMMEL *sb.*[1] 1. Also *attrib.*

**1516** in Rogers *Agric. & Prices* III. 564. **1519** HORMAN *Vulg.* 277 b, Caste in the tramell nette ones more [*Inijce everriculum iterato*]. **1552** LYNDESAY *Monarche* 4771 In to thare Tramalt nett thay fangit ane fysche. **1580** HOLLYBAND *Treas. Fr. Tong*, *Vn Trameau*,..a tramell net. **1657** C. BECK *Univ. Charac.* L vij b, A tramel net or drag. **1787** BEST *Angling* (ed. 2) 63 They set trammel-nets baited, and leave them for whole days and nights, into which the fish enter of their own accord. **1884** *Daily News* 25 Dec. 3/6 A resolution prohibiting trammel-net fishing for salmon.

**b.** A fowler's net; = TRAMMEL *sb.*[1] 1 b.

**1648** HERRICK *Hesper.*, *Country Life* 65 Thy witty wiles to draw, and get The larke into the trammell net. **1669** WORLIDGE *Syst. Agric.* (1681) 252. **1768** PENNANT *Zool.* II. 235 The larker..makes use of a trammel net twenty-seven or twenty-eight feet long and five broad. **1882** BUCKLAND *Notes Anim. Life* 221 They [larks] are taken by thousands on dull nights with trammel nets.

**Trammer** (træ·məɹ). [f. TRAM *sb.*[2] or *v.*[1]]

**1.** *Coal-mining*, etc. A man or boy who removes the trams of coal, etc. from the workings; a putter.

**1839** URE *Dict. Arts* 982 Two persons called trammers are employed to transport the coals. **1878** DAVIES *Slate Quarrying* 117 The trammers..convey the slate blocks from the quarry to the dressers, and..also remove the waste. **1889** *Eng. Illustr. Mag.* May 572/2 Trammers are usually strong youths and prospective colliers. **1905** *Act* 5 *Edw. VII*, c. 9 § 2 Such persons if they are either in charge of working places or are holers, fillers, trammers, or brushers.

**2.** One who is employed on a tramway; also, a horse used to draw a tram-car.

**1889** *Even. News* 7 Oct., The trammers are equally worthy of public sympathy with the dock labourers. **1901** *Daily Chron.* 28 Dec. 9/7 The horses are good trammers, active, and fresh from work, and in good condition.

**Tramontane** (trămǫ·ntĕn, træmǫntē¹·n), *a.* and *sb.* Forms: 4 **tramountayne**, 7 **-mountain**, **-montan**, (6–8 **-ain**, 9 **-aine**), 6– **tramontane**; also in It. forms, 7–9 **tramontana**, 6–8 (*pl.*) **tramontani**; Lat. pl. 7 **tramontanæ**. See also TRANSMONTANE. [ad. It. *tramontana* north wind, pole-star, *tramontani* 'those folkes that dwell beyond the mountaines' Florio (= Sp., Pg. *tramontana* north wind, sunset), whence also Fr. *tramontane* north wind, pole-star, OF. *tramontan*(*e* sb. and adj. (13th c.) north wind, *tresmontaine* pole-star:—L. *transmontānus* beyond the mountains, f. *trans* across, beyond + *mons*, *mont-em* mountain: cf. *montān-us* of or belonging to mountains.]

**A.** *adj.* **1.** Dwelling or situated beyond, or pertaining to the far side of, the mountains (orig. and in reference to Italy, the Alps; in quots. 1806, 1840, referring to other mountains); hence, foreign; in quot. 1662 = occupied by a non-Italian.

**1596** NASHE *Saffron-Walden* Wks. (Grosart) III. 131 Were their stuffe by ten millions more Tramontani or Transalpine barbarous than balletry, he would haue prest it vpon Wolfe. *a* **1618** RALEIGH in Gutch *Coll. Cur.* I. 73 Tramontane, as well as Ultramontane Civilians will deem it otherwise. **1662** BARGRAVE *Pope Alex. VII* (1867) 50 The Italians have ever since taken care that St. Peter's chair shall never be a tramontan chair again. **1710** STEELE *Tatler* No. 222 ¶ 9 As for our Tramontain Lovers..A Man might as well serenade in Greenland as in our Region. **1781** GIBBON *Decl. & F.* xxxi. III. 245 The rustic, or even savage, aspect of those Tramontane warriors, often disguised a simple and merciful disposition. **1806** SCOTT *Let. to G. Ellis* 3 Mar., in *Lockhart*, To undertake your expedition to the tramontane region of Reged this season. **1820** *Edin. Rev.* XXXIV. 185 *note*, The clock in the clock-house built at Westminster in 1288..is usually considered as the earliest recorded instance of a Tramontane clock. **1840** *Blackw. Mag.* XLVII. 245 Our empire in India had waxed so powerful as to attract the envy of the Asiatic tramontane nations. **1884** J. S. BREWER *Reign Hen. VIII*, I. ix. 279 A tramontane ecclesiastic.

**b.** With the connotation 'uncouth, unpolished, barbarous'. Now *rare*.

**1739** CIBBER *Apol.* (1756) I. 233 This I have mention'd to shew not only our Tramontane Taste, but that [etc.]. **1784** COWPER *Task* IV. 533 Virtue is so scarce, That to suppose a scene where she presides Is tramontane, and stumbles all belief. **1796** CHARLOTTE SMITH *Marchmont* IV. 115, I..for a man of fashion had strange tramontane ideas. **1832** *Blackw. Mag.* XXXI. 101, I beg..if these can be your real sentiments, that you will keep them as private as possible. They are totally tramontane in this part of the world.

**2.** Of the wind: Coming across or from beyond the mountains; *spec.* in reference to Italy, Blowing from beyond the Alps: cf. B. 2.

**1705** ADDISON *Italy, Pavia* 27 That Side of the Church.. which faces the Tramontane Wind. **1794** SULLIVAN *View Nat.* IV. 236 Where no tramontane blasts could come from masses of snow. **1869** *Daily News* 10 Dec., I..was exposed to a tramontane wind as bitter as an oration of Mr. Roebuck, in his most sarcastic mood. **1877** A. J. ROSS *Mem. A. Ewing* vi. 63 A fierce tramontane wind usually blowing.

**B.** *sb.* †**1.** The north pole-star: originally so called in Italy and Provence, because visible beyond the Alps: cf. It. *tramontana* (Florio 1598), OF. *tresmontaine* (*c* 1295 in Godefroy). Also *fig.*

**13..** *E. E. Allit. P.* B. 211, I schal telde vp my trone in þe tramountayne. **1604** EDMONDS *Observ. Cæsar's Comm.* 40 Directions, both from the loadstone of reason, and tramontane of experience to shape an easie and successfull course. **1633** DRUMM. OF HAWTH. *Sp. to K. Charles, Jove* 9 The Tramontane which thy faire course directs, Thy Counsels shall approve by their effects.

**2.** In the Mediterranean and esp. in Italy, The north wind, as coming from beyond the Alps; hence generally, a cold wind from a mountain range. (Now usually in Italian form *tramontana.*)

**1615** G. SANDYS *Trav.* I. 38 The boysterous Tramontana.. here [Constantinople] most violently rages. **1664** EVELYN *Sylva* (1776) 316 [Florence and Rome] exposed to the nipping Tramontans (for so they call the Northern winds). **1721** BAILEY, *Tramontane..*, the North Wind. **1773** BRYDONE *Sicily* ii. (1809) 9 This morning..we have gotten a fine brisk tramontane (or North wind). **1794** SULLIVAN *View Nat.* I. 292 The deadening sirrocco wind, which is immediately succeeded by a *tramontana*, the *bise*. **1887** *Pall Mall G.* 21 Mar. 11/2 An excessively cold tramontana is blowing.

**3.** One who dwells beyond the mountains: orig. applied in Italy to foreigners beyond the Alps; also by these nations to the Italians; hence, a stranger, a foreigner; an outsider, barbarian.

**1593** NASHE *Christ's T.* Wks. (Grosart) IV. 184 Let not the Italians call you dulheaded Tramontain. **1622** BACON *Hen. VII* 97 Our Holy Father the Pope likes no Tramontanes [= French] in Italie. **1636** MASSINGER *Gt. Dk. Flor.* II. ii, A happiness Those tramontanes ne'er tasted. **1642** FULLER *Holy & Prof. St.* IV. iii. 251 Yet was it a great labour for a Tramountain to climb over the Alps to S. Peters Chair. **1703** STEELE *Tender Husb.* Epil., Till then forgive your Writers, that can't bear You shou'd such very Tramontanes appear. **1732** FIELDING *Miser* II. iii, Oh! child, you are quite a tramontane; I must bring you to like dear Spadille. **1811** MISS L. M. HAWKINS *C'tess & Gertr.* II. 52 See that horrible tramontane Major Brag who dined here to-day. **1855** MILMAN *Lat. Chr.* XIII. ix. VI. 181 The subtle Italians found themselves circumvented by the steady aggression of the Tramontanes.

†**Tramonta·tion.** *Obs. nonce-wd.* [n. of action f. It. *tramontare* 'to passe ouer the hils' (Florio), *tramontar del sole* sunset.] Setting (of the sun).

**1599** R. LINCHE *Anc. Fict.* K j, [The sun] vpon his tramontation and discent to the antipodes.

† **Tramort.** *Sc. Obs.* [app. f. L. *trā-*, *trans* beyond + *mors*, *mortem* death, *mortuus* dead. Cf. It. *tramortire* to fall into a swoon.] A putrefying carcass; a corpse.

**1508** DUNBAR *Flyting* 161 Thow Lazarus, thow laithly lene tramort. **15..** — *Poems* xxvi. 83 Mony stynkand fowll tramort. *Ibid.* xi. 20 Ane vgsum, vglye tramort. **1535** STEWART *Cron. Scot.* (Rolls) III. 117 Bayth pynd and puir like ony peild tramort.

**Tramosericeous** (træmosĭrĭ·ʃiəs), *a. Entom.* [f. mod.L. *tramosericeus*, f. L. *trāma* TRAM *sb.*[1]: see SERICEOUS.] Having a satiny lustre, as the elytra of certain beetles.

**1826** KIRBY & SP. *Entomol.* IV. xlvi. 284 Tramosericeous (*Tramosericeus*). The splendour of satin. Ex[ample] *Chlamys Bacca, monstrosa*, &c.

**Tramp** (træmp), *sb.*[1] [f. TRAMP *v.*[1]]

**1.** An act of tramping; a heavy or forcible tread, a stamp; hence, an injury to the foot of a horse caused by its setting one foot on another: cf. TREAD *sb.*

**1808–18** JAMIESON, *Tramp..*, the act of striking the foot suddenly downwards. **1844** STEPHENS *Bk. Farm* II. 397 [To horses] Tramps are dangerous, besides causing blemishes on the foot,..they may cause quittor. **1859** *Autobiog. Beggar Boy* 46 Having my right foot severely wounded on the instep, by the tramp of a horse. **1878** BROWNING *Poets Croisic* lxi, As the reed Is crushed beneath its tramp.

**2.** The measured and continuous tread of a body of persons or animals; hence, the sound of heavy footfalls.

**1817** MOORE *Lalla R., Fire-W.* iv, Heard'st thou not the tramp of men Sounding from yonder fearful glen? **1856** AYTOUN *Bothwell* II. iii, Does yet the court-yard ring with tramp Of horses and of men. **1889** QUILLER COUCH *Splendid Spur* (1895) 121 The monotonous tramp-tramp through the slush and mire of the roads. **1891** FARRAR *Darkn. & Dawn* xlvi, The tramp of the changing sentries..might be to her the echoing footfall of death.

*fig.* **1870** LOWELL *Among my Bks.* Ser. I. (1873) 186 To feel in her ears the dull tramp of the blood.

**3.** A bout of tramping or journeying on foot; a long, tiring, or toilsome walk or march; a trudge; a walking excursion (*colloq.*).

**1786** BURNS *Brigs of Ayr* 188 If haply Knowledge, on a random tramp, Had shor'd them wi' a glimmer of his lamp. **1822** T. BEWICK *Mem.* 138 This [journey] may be regarded as merely one of my 'tramps'. **1845** J. COULTER *Adv. Pacific* x. 120, I continued my tramp round the easternmost part of the island. **1859** JEPHSON *Brittany* xvii. 285, I doubted whether I should be in a condition for a tramp of thirty miles. **1873** TRISTRAM *Moab* ix. 170 Files of hundreds of camels slowly following each other in the weary tramp to Mecca. **1898** J. HUTCHINSON in *Arch. Surg.* IX. No. 34. 104 Much exhausted by a long tramp in hot weather.

**b.** *On* (*the*) *tramp*, on one's way from place to place on foot, esp. in search of employment, or wandering as a vagrant.

**1760** *Life & Adv. of Cat* 147 An English vagrant, on the common tramp (as they express it). **1813** T. MARTIN *Circle Mech. Arts* 608 When any of them are out of employ, they set out in search of a master, with a sort of Certificate from their last place. This is called going on the tramp. **1866** DORA GREENWELL *Ess.* (1867) 109 Some of the eight are in the army, some in the collieries, some on the tramp. **1888** 'J. S. WINTER' *Bootle's Childr.* iii, Just on tramp she seems to have been.

**4.** A person on the tramp; = TRAMPER 2; one who travels from place to place on foot, in search of employment, or as a vagrant; also, one who follows an itinerant business, as a hawker, etc.

**1664** in *Verney Mem.* (1904) II. 204 Thay goo so Lick trampis, so durty, tis a sham to see them. **1790** GROSE *Provinc. Gloss.* (ed. 2), *Tramp*, a tramp; a beggar. *Sussex.* **1808** *Agric. Mag.* III. 43 A certain class of wandering labourers known by the name of tramps. **1828** *Craven Gloss.*, *Tramp*, a pedlar; called also a tramper, an itinerant tinker, or one who travels with any kind of wares. **1842** *Rep. Sanitary Condition Labouring Classes* 357 The houses are stages for the various orders of tramps. **1860** RAMSAY *Remin.* Ser. I. (ed. 7) 157 A wretched woman, who used to traverse the country as a beggar or tramp. **1882–3** *Schaff's Encycl. Relig. Knowl.* II. 910/1 Monks, who..roamed about in the country, and really were neither more nor less than tramps of the most indolent and impertinent description.

**5.** In full, *ocean tramp*: A cargo vessel, esp. a steamship, which does not trade regularly between fixed ports, but takes cargoes wherever obtainable and for any port.

*c* **1880** [Remembered in colloquial use]. **1886** *Shipping Gaz.* 9 July, We think few will deny that the 'ocean tramp' is the product of competition. **1891** M. ROBERTS in *Murray's Mag.* June 795 The pure 'tramp' is not seen to its best advantage in seas whose ports are in connection with England by wire or submarine cable. **1891** [see OCEAN 3 c]. **1893** *Naut. Mag.* Mar. 212. **1900** F. T. BULLEN *Men of Merchant Service* iii. 21 The lowest type of tramp..is.. built so as to pass Lloyd's surveyor, but without one single item in her equipment that can be dispensed with.

**b.** *attrib.*, as *tramp steamer, vessel, trade.*

**1887** *Shipping Gaz.* 14 Jan., The day of building tramp steamers by means of money raised from single ship companies has passed away—for ever, we hope. **1891** *Pall Mall G.* 21 May 2/1 In many of our tramp boats there is need of great reform in the food supplied to our sailors. **1897** *Daily News* 26 Jan. 3/6 His complaint was against tramp vessels, which were often undermanned. **1902** *Westm. Gaz.* 5 June 4/2 Mr. R—,..who is largely interested in the 'tramp' trade,..also young Mr. R—,..who is also a large tramp owner. **1903** *Ibid.* 2 July 11/3 The volume of tramp shipping is six-sevenths of the whole..Tramp business cannot exist unless accompanied by cheap and good shipbuilding.

**6. a.** A plate of iron worn under the hollow of the boot to protect it in digging; also the part of the spade, etc., which is pressed upon by the foot. **b.** *Curling.* A piece of spiked iron fastened to the sole of the shoe to give a firm foot-hold on the ice.

**1825** JAMIESON, *Tramp*, a plate of iron worn by ditchers below the centre of the foot, for working on their spades. **1830** H. DUNCAN in *Poets Dumfries.* IX. (1910) 266 Gae get you besom, tramps, an' stane, An' join the friendly strife, man. **1844** [see *tramp-pick* in 7]. **1891** KERR *Maggie o' the Moss* 61 (E. D. D.) Wi' tramps on their feet, and besoms in han'. **1894** *Northumbld. Gloss.*, *Tramp*, the part of a spade on which the foot is placed to thrust;..an iron plate worn by drainers as a guard to the boot in digging.

**7.** *attrib.* (see also 5 b) and *Comb.*, as (in sense 4) *tramp-printer*, *-scarer*, *-ward*; *tramp-like* adj.; **tramp-cell**, a workhouse cell in which vagrants are lodged; **tramp-clog** = sense 6 a; **tramp-cock, tramp-coll** [COLL *sb.*[5]], a heap of hay compressed by treading; **tramp-house**, a lodging-house for tramps; **tramp-master**, a workhouse official charged with the control of the vagrants admitted; **tramp-pick** (*Sc.*), a narrow, pointed pick, with a tread, for breaking up stiff ground; **tramp-rick**, †**-ruck**, a rick or stack of hay compressed by treading.

**1905** *Daily Chron.* 22 Sept. 5/6 He was taken back to the workhouse, and placed in a *tramp cell. **1894** *Northumbld. Gloss.*, **Tramp-clog* or *tramp*,..a piece of iron plate..used as a guard where the spade is trodden in digging. **1775** *Ann. Reg.* II. 129/2 In these cocks, I allow the hay to remain until..I judge that it will keep in pretty large *tramp-cocks. **1825** JAMIESON, **Tramp-coll..*, a number of colls or cocks of hay put into one and tramped hard, in order that the hay may be farther dried. *Aberd.* **1850** [C. ROGERS] *Bairnsla Ann.* 42 (E.D.D.) A *tramp-hause. **1899** SIR G. DOUGLAS *Jas. Hogg* 146 In common tramp-houses, a death is..a godsend. **1904** *Daily Chron.* 29 Oct. 8/3 A *tramp-like personage stands sentinel complacently over a terrific bulldog. **1887** *Leamington Spa Courier* 30 Apr. 5/6 Persons willing to undertake the duties of *Tramp Master at the Workhouse. **1895** *Daily News* 5 Oct. 6/6 He maintained that..the trampmaster in Salford, had some knowledge of human nature. **1813** G. ROBERTSON *Agric. Surv. Kincardine* vi. 238 The *tramp-pick..is a kind of lever, of iron, about four feet long, and an inch square in thickness, tapering away at the lower end, and having a small degree of curvature there...It is fitted with a foot step..on which the workman presses with his foot. **1844** STEPHENS *Bk. Farm* I. 372 An iron tramp-pick to loosen the subsoil immediately under the mould, and raise the boulder stones...The tramp..is movable, and may be placed on either side to suit the foot of the workman, where it remains firm at about 16 inches from the point, which gradually tapers. **1895** *Westm. Gaz.* 17 Jan. 8/1 What the..foreman thought he at once 'spotted' as a *tramp-printer entered the office and asked to be allowed to try his hand at the case. **1799** J. ROBERTSON *Agric. Perth* 220 In making *tramp-ricks, they ought to be secured, by one rope over the top, in the direction of that point from which the most violent winds are expected to blow.., or by two transverse ropes, which is the surest way. **1812** SIR J. SINCLAIR *Syst. Husb. Scot.* I. 396 After it [hay] has been a short time in small cocks, it ought to be put up in what are called tramp ricks. **1588** *Exchequer Rolls Scot.* XXI. 412 For making of 36 dawarkis of hay..and for wynning and putting of the samyn in *tramp ruckis. **1905** *Blackw. Mag.* Dec. 817/2 The poor animal fulfils his function as a *tramp-scarer. **1906** *Westm. Gaz.* 14 May 12/2 [One] who, disguised as a tramp, has spent days and nights in *tramp-wards, lodging-houses, and shelters.

Hence **Tra·mpage**, the habit or condition of a tramp, vagrancy (*U.S.*); **Tra·mpdom**, the 'realm' or sphere of tramps; **Tra·mpess**, a female tramp; **Tra·mpish** *a.*, like or like that of a tramp; **Tra·mpishly** *adv.*, in a trampish manner; **Tra·mpism**, the practice of going on tramp.

**1894** *Chicago Advance* 3 May, A menace, a nuisance all along the line of their *trampage. **1897** *Plantation Missionary* (Oberlin, Ohio) Dec., The poor [may be] rescued from pauperism, trampage and crime. **1895** *Century Mag.* Oct. 945/1 The love of liquor brings more men and women into *trampdom. **1897** RAINE *Welsh Singer* 95 (E.D.D.) She was a *trampess who died in John Powys' barn. **1861** SALA in *Temple Bar Mag.* III. 299 A *trampish woman with a tambourine. **1890** *New York Sun* Feb., The depot policeman was shoving a trampish-looking man out of the place. **1889** *Harper's Mag.* Nov. 831/2 The battered folding-doors *trampishly lean against the walls. **1893** *Columbus* (Ohio) *Dispatch* 5 Sept., The plans will check idiotic processions and *trampism, and men who will not work will get out of the city. **1894** in *Review of Rev.* May 608/2, I make no defense of trampism nor vagabondage.

† **Tramp, trampe,** *sb.*[2] *Obs.* Also 7 trempe. [ad. Fr. *trempe* temper of steel (15th c.), f. *tremper* to TEMPER.] Temper of iron or steel. Also *fig.*

**1566** PAINTER *Pal. Pleas.* I. 98 b, If you doe euer make any proofe of trial to know of what trampe the arrowes of Loue be. *Ibid.* 166 b, The King of England..sent him an excellent harness with a sword of the self same tramp. **1581** RICH *Farew.* (Shaks. Soc.) 40 With what trampe bee wee tempered withall. **1581** A. HALL *Iliad* X. 179 His sword.. with point of perfect trampe. **1684** T. GODDARD *Plato's Demon* 40 Both Respect and Obedience too, will break, when bent with too much Rigor and beyond their Trempe.

**Tramp** (træmp), *v.*[1] [ME. *trampe-n* = Ger., LG. *trampen* (whence Da. *trampe*, Swed., Norw. *trampa*) to stamp:—OTeut. **tramp-*, 2nd grade of **tremp*, **tramp*, **trump* to stamp, tread (whence Goth. *ana-trimpan* to tread or press upon, also MHG. *trumpfen* to run, Norw. dial. *trumpa* to knock or push); a nasalized form of OTeut. **trep*, **trap*: see TRAP *sb.*[2]]

**1.** *intr.* To tread or walk with a firm, heavy, resonant step; to stamp.

**1388** WYCLIF *Prov.* vi. 13 He bekeneth with iȝen, he trampith [1382 tramplith, Vulg. *terit pede*] with the foot, he spekith with the fyngur. *a* **1485** *Promp. Parv.* 499/1 (MS. S.) Trampyn [*v. r.* trampelyn], *tero.* **1570** LEVINS *Manip.* 18/40 To Trampe, *strepitare.* **1865** KINGSLEY *Herew.* x, They had passed down the street, tramping and gingling and caracoling. **1877** TALMAGE *Serm.* 23 Hearest thou not the trembling of the ground, as the thunders of the judgment-day are tramping on?

**2.** *intr.* To tread heavily or with force (*on* or *upon* something); to stamp (*upon*): = TRAMPLE *v.* 3. *To tramp on any one's toes* (*fig.*), to infringe or encroach on his rights or privileges; to 'come down upon' with injurious effect; to take undue advantage of.

**1596** DALRYMPLE tr. *Leslie's Hist. Scot.* I. (S.T.S.) 123 Bewar that ȝe neuir trampe thairon [on a grave] with ȝour fute. **1641** *Ferguson's Sc. Prov.* (1785) 30 Tramp on a snail and she'll shoot out her horns. **1776** C. KEITH *Farmer's Ha'* xxxviii, The black cow has nae trampet yet Upo' your taes. **1839** URE *Dict. Arts* 768 [The hides] are then tramped upon by a workman walking repeatedly from one end of the vat to the other. **1862** SHIRLEY *Nugæ Crit.* xi. 477 It secures in practice my right, so long as I do not tramp on my neighbour's toes, to speak and think and act as I choose.

**3.** *trans.* To press or compress by treading; to tread or trample upon.

*Tramp down*, to crush down by heavy or vigorous treading; to suppress, to crush. *Tramp under one's foot* or *feet*, to tread or walk heavily upon; *fig.* to treat with contempt.

**1533** GAU *Richt Vay* (S. T. S.) 40/4 He suld tramp dwne the heid of the serpent. *Ibid.* 104/17 As the suine trampis the precious peirl onder thair feit. **1565** T. STAPLETON *Fortr. Faith* 86 b, The camamele, the more ye tread it and trampe it, the sweter it smelleth. **1581** N. BURNE *Disput.* in *Cath. Tractates* (S.T.S.) 167 Murther of spirituall magistratis..be tramping the memoriallis of al religione in guttaris. **1585** JAS. I *Ess. Poesie* (Arb.) 15 They see the painfull Vigneron pull the grapes: First tramping them, and after pressing now The grenest clusters gathered into heapes.

1844 STEPHENS *Bk. Farm* II. 266 A woman is appointed to tramp the straw, [and] spread it regularly over the mow that is forming. 1848 LYTTON *Harold* I. iii, No horse tramps the seeds we have sown for Harold the Earl to reap.

**b.** To tread (sheets, blankets, etc.) in a tub of soapy water, as part of the process of washing. *Sc.*

1798 *Monthly Mag.* Dec. 438/1 To tramp clothes. 1807 CARR *Caledonian Sk.* (1809) 226 In my way from Hopetounhouse to Linlithgow I saw the process of tramping, that is, of washing. 1842 AITON *Domest. Econ.* (1857) 112 Soak them [blankets, etc.], add to the water in which the linens were washed some soap, and also some of the preparation to produce a strong lather; rub or tramp them, then rinse and dry. 1871 C. GIBBON *Lack of Gold* viii, On washing days, it was tucked up above the knees to 'tramp the claes'.

**c.** *refl.* Of a horse: To injure itself by setting one foot on another: cf. TRAMP *sb.*[1] 1.

1844 STEPHENS *Bk. Farm* III. 847 The shoes usually worn by stallions are very clumsy, and..are apt to cause him tramp himself.

**d.** *To tramp flounders*, to catch flounders by stamping on the wet sand with the bare feet until they rise. *dial.*

1894 CROCKETT *Raiders* (ed. 3) 33, I must..proceed to the flats and tramp flounders for our breakfast.

**4.** *intr.* To walk; *esp.* to walk steadily or heavily; to trudge; to travel on foot; to go on a walking expedition (*colloq.*). Also *tramp it.*

1643 in *Verney Mem.* (1904) I. 302 Now the owld man must trampe on foote. 1720 *Humourist* 51 Your Hunters of News, who tramp it half a Score Streets, to know who has got a Wife or a Place. 1818 SCOTT *Br. Lamm.* xxi, My darling boy, whom I would tramp barefooted through the world for. 1820 CLARE *Rural Life* (ed. 3) 91 I've oft meant tramping o'er to see ye. 1840 DICKENS *Barn. Rudge* xlvii, These people, who go tramping about the country. 1862 W. J. STEWART in *Macm. Mag.* May 32 The miner must be prepared to tramp it to that part of the Quesnelle or Cariboo gold-fields.

**b.** To go about or travel as a tramp. *colloq.*

1891 in *Cent. Dict.* 1898 J. HUTCHINSON in *Arch. Surg.* IX. No. 34. 102 A man..who had tramped from Leeds in July weather, was seized by a fit on his arrival in London. 1909 *Bodleian* Mar. 7/1 I'd rather have tramped it than have gone in for any top-hatted occupation.

**5.** *trans.* To walk through or over with heavy or weary tread; to traverse on foot, *spec.* as a tramp.

*a* 1774 FERGUSSON *Ode to Bee* 45 Whether they tramp life's thorny way, Or thro' the sunny vineyard stray. *a* 1809 HOLCROFT *Mem.* (1816) I. 23, I and my mother were..tramping the villages to hawk our pedlary. *a* 1885 in J. Irving *West Scotl. in Hist.* 217 They..tramped the Trongate in pattens and caléche. 1894 HALL CAINE *Manxman* 10 He tramped the island in pursuit of his calling. 1895 P. HEMINGWAY *Out of Egypt* I. v. 55 He determined..to tramp the streets pretending to look for something to do.

**b.** To drive into or out of some condition by walking vigorously or steadily. *colloq.*

1853 KANE *Grinnell Exp.* xxvii. (1856) 220 Leaving the deck, where I have been tramping the cold out of my joints, I come below. 1892 *Field* 14 May 732/2 You will tramp your boots and feet into order.

**6.** *intr.* To make a voyage on a tramp steamer; also *trans.* to run (a tramp steamer). *colloq.*

1899 CUTCLIFFE HYNE *Further Adv. Capt. Kettle* viii, He heartily wished himself away back on the steamer, tramping for cargo. *Ibid.* x, You are making a good thing for us out of tramping the 'Parakeet'.

**7.** The verb-stem used *advb.*: cf. *bang*, etc.

1796 SCOTT *William & Helen* xlvii, Tramp! tramp! along the land they rode; Splash! splash! along the sea.

Hence **Tramped** (træmpt) *ppl. a.*; **tramped pike**, a large rick of hay compressed by tramping: cf. *tramp-cock, -rick*, TRAMP *sb.*[1] 7; **Tra·mping** *vbl. sb.* and *ppl. a.*; **tramping-card**, a certificate issued to a member of a trade organization, entitling him to maintenance while tramping in search of employment; **tramping-drum**, in *leather-dressing*, a revolving chamber in which hides are saturated with oil or dubbing to make them pliable (*Cent. Dict.* 1891); **tramping-machine**: see quot. 1904; **tramping-pestle**, one of the hammers in this machine.

1660 in *Archæologia* XI. 100 *Armorers Tooles.* Small Bickernes, Tramping Stakes, Round stakes, Welting stakes. 1791 MRS. RADCLIFFE *Rom. Forest* vi, They were alarmed ..by the tramping of horses near the abbey. 1828 SCOTT *F. M. Perth* xii, I am not so far to seek for a dwelling, that the same roof should cover me and a tramping princess like that. 1844 STEPHENS *Bk. Farm* III. 970 The large ricks thus formed are named tramped pikes. 1863 W. C. BALDWIN *Afr. Hunting* v. 112, I left..on a tramping tour into the Zulu country. 1878 E. SCHILLER *Eng. Germ. Fr. Technol. Dict.*, Tramping-pestle. 1893 J. MCCARTHY *Red Diamonds* I. 110 The tramping feet of the policemen. 1897 WEBB *Industr. Democracy* I. II. i. 153 And 'out-of-work pay', from the old-fashioned 'tramping card' to the modern 'donation' given when a member loses his employment by the temporary breakdown of machinery. 1904 *Sci. Amer., Supp.* 27 Feb. 23534/3 Tubbing is gradually giving way..to the 'tramping machine'...This machine is adapted from the French apparatus for fulling wool stock. It consists of two wooden hammers, which are moved alternately back and forth or up and down in a suitable receptacle, agitating the skins slowly and constantly,..and developing by friction the necessary heat, thus rendering the pelts soft and pliable.

† **Tramp**, *v.*[2] *Sc. Obs. rare.* Also 7 trampe. [ad. F. *tremper* to soak, steep (trans. and intr.), temper (iron or steel); also to be implicated (in); by metathesis from *tempρer, ad. L. *temperāre* to temper, qualify, modify: see TEMPER *v.*, TREMP. Cf. TRAMP *sb.*[2]] *trans.* To steep, soak; const. *in.* Also *intr.* for *pass.* Also *fig.*

1568 SKEYNE *The Pest* (1860) 35 Applicand the samin.. vpon the partis pectoralis, with ane lytill scarlote trampit in the decoctioun. 1570 BUCHANAN *Admonitioun* Wks. (1892) 24 Wt..hart..full of fellony toung trampit in dissait. 1597 LOWE *Chirurg.* (1634) 209 Let the end of the pellet or Uvula trampe in it.

**Tramper** (træ·mpəɹ). [f. TRAMP *v.*[1] + -ER[1].] One who or that which tramps.

**1. a.** One who treads heavily, a stamping person. **b.** One who tramples or treads on clothes, etc. in water, as part of the process of washing them; see TRAMP *v.*[1] 3 b. **c.** *pl.* Heavy boots for walking. *Sc.*

**a.** 1892 *Chamb. Jrnl.* 11 June 372 He is a quiet neighbour —no slammer or tramper. **b.** 1725 T. THOMAS in *Portland P.* VI. (Hist. MSS. Comm.) 111 [Here] we had the first sight of the Scotch 'trampers'...These trampers are the women that wash their linen cloth..by putting it into a large tub, into which one or two of them..get in, and instead of making use of hands, trample it with their bare feet. **c.** 1790 A. WILSON *Poems & Lit. Prose* (1876) II. 76 Rotten stockings, soleless trampers. 1824 J. WILSON *Noct. Ambr.* Wks. 1856 IV. 181 Hawick rig-and-fur stockins, and Thirlestane trampers a' studded wi' sparables.

**2.** A person who tramps or travels on foot, a pedestrian; *spec.* a tramp, a vagrant.

1760 in Earwaker *Manch. Constables' Acc.* (1892) III. 119 Pd three Trampers to Scotland. 1772 R. GRAVES *Spir. Quixote* (1783) I. 119 Because Squire Fielding..pretends that Tom Jones was harboured here, we shall be pestered with all the trampers that pass the road. 1818 SCOTT *Hrt. Midl.* xxv[i], D'ye think his honour has naething else to do than to speak wi' ilka idle tramper that comes about the town? 1825 BROCKETT *N. C. Words, Trampers*, beggars, who traverse extensive tracts of country, soliciting from door to door. 1829 E. ELLIOTT *Vill. Patriarch* III. v, Behold the tramper, with his naked toes! 1832 *Boston, Linc.*, etc. *Herald* 31 July 2/1 She never named the tramper woman to me again. 1848 DICKENS *Old C. Shop* xix, Passing numerous groups of gipsies and trampers on the road. 1908 *Sat. Rev.* 30 May 678/2 Tripper or tramper can get as much mountain air and walking as he wants without any Bill.

**Tra·m-plate.** [f. TRAM *sb.*[2] + PLATE *sb.*] One of the flat or flanged iron plates used in forming early tramways (in mines or above ground), instead of the wooden or stone 'trams' previously used.

1807 *Trans. Soc. Arts* XXV. 87 Improved tram-plates for carriages on rail roads. 1824 T. G. CUMMING *Rail & Tram Roads* 18 We find the flat rail, or tram plate, almost entirely superseded by the edge rail. 1829 *Mechanics' Mag.* XII. 132 The sort of rail employed is that called the edge-rail, in contradistinction to the flat rail or tram-plate. 1838 *Osborne's Guide to the Grand Junction Railway* 7 In the year 1776 Mr. Carr introduced the use of tram-plates in the Duke of Norfolk's colliery at Sheffield. These plates had an upright ledge or flange, from 2½ to 4 inches high, which served to keep the wheels of the trams or waggons on the line. 1851 GREENWELL *Coal-trade Terms Northumb. & Durh.* 16 The tram-plates, or other iron or metal way. 1894 [see PLATE *sb.* 8].

**Trample** (træ·mp'l), *sb.* [f. TRAMPLE *v.*] An act or the action of trampling.

1604 *Meeting of Gallants at Ordinarie* (Percy Soc.) 13 They ran..in the middle of the street, with such a violent Trample as if the Diuell had bene Coachman. 1641 MILTON *Reform.* II. ad fin., Under the despightfull controule, the trample and spurne of all the other Damned. 1821 CLARE *Vill. Minstr.* I. 93 Destruction's trample treads them down. 1856 R. A. VAUGHAN *Mystics* XIII. iii. (1860) II. 273 The earth shakes with the trample of a myriad hoofs. 1902 MRS. BARNES GRUNDY *Thames Camp* 143 The elephant is preparing for his final trample [on a man].

**Trample** (træ·mp'l), *v.* Also 5 trampel, 6 -pell. [ME. *trampel-en, trample-n*, in form a frequentative of TRAMP *v.*[1] (see -LE 3): cf. the analogous MHG., Ger., LG. *trampeln.*]

**1.** *intr.* To tread or walk heavily; to stamp. (In early use app. not differing in sense from TRAMP *v.*[1])

1382 WYCLIF *Prov.* vi. 13 He tramplith [1388 trampith, Vulg. *terit*] with the foot. 14.. *Beryn* 1350 He trampelid fast with his feet, & al to-tare his ere. *c* 1440 *Promp. Parv.* 499/1 Trampelyn (*S.* trampyn), *tero.* 1530 PALSGR. 760/2 The boyes trampell so over my heed, that I can nat slepe. 1590 SPENSER *F. Q.* I. vii. 37 His stubborne steed..Who under him did trample as the aire, And chauft that any on his backe should sitt. 1600 HAKLUYT *Voy.* III. 320 Certaine others..gathered their Ananas in the Indians gardens, trampling through them without any descretion. 1891 KIPLING *Light that Failed* x. (1900) 177 The Keneu and the Nilghai were trampling behind him, calling for Dick.

† **b.** *trans.* To tread, traverse; cf. TRAMP *v.*[1] 5; also *intr.* with *on. Obs. rare.*

1595 A. FLETCHER in Farr *S. P. Eliz.* (1845) II. 476 Walking rightly, Still trampling vertue's path. 1698 FRYER *Acc. E. India & P.* 128, I was the second Man [that] Trampled on the Top [of the mountain pass].

† **2.** *intr.* To go or travel on foot; = TRAMP *v.*[1] 4; also to go *between*, to act as an intermediary: cf. TRAMPLER b. *Obs. rare.*

1624 GEE *Foot out of Snare* xiii. 83 [He] hath rambled and trampled many miles abroad to bring nothing home. 1631 T. POWELL *Tom All Trades* (1876) 155 They [civil lawyers] admit of few or no Sollicitors, to trample betweene them and the Clyent. So that the Fee comes to them immediately and with the more advantage.

**3.** *intr.* with *on, upon, over.* **a.** *lit.* To tread repeatedly upon with heavy or crushing steps. Also in *indirect passive.*

1577 B. GOOGE *Heresbach's Husb.* II. (1586) 64 It delighteth to growe by high waies..and to be trode and trampled on. 1687 A. LOVELL tr. *Thevenot's Trav.* II. 86 For making of Terrasses, they lay..half a foot thick of Earth, but which sinks to far less being trampled and tread upon. 1798 *Monthly Mag.* Dec. 438/1 The Scotch lass..kilts (tucks) her petticoats above her knees and tramples or dances upon the linen, in a tub. 1879 H. PHILLIPS *Notes Coins* 10 A denarius of Julius Caesar bears an elephant trampling upon a snake.

**b.** *fig.* To treat with contempt; to violate the claims or rights of; to domineer or tyrannize over; † to encroach upon the rights of (*obs.*).

1646 J. HALL *Horæ Vac.* 93 Trample not on the imperfections of any. 1656 EARL MONM. tr. *Boccalini's Advts. fr. Parnass.* I. xxiii. (1674) 26 They should be trampled upon by the most barbarous Nations of the earth. 1692 tr. *Sallust* 152 [They] trample over your Faces magnificently, boasting their chief Pontificates. 1759 JOHNSON *Idler* No. 57 ⁋3 Wit tramples upon rules. 1799 NELSON in Nicolas *Disp.* (1845) IV. 82, I am jealous of being trampled upon. 1879 FROUDE *Cæsar* viii. 70 His friends..were being trampled upon by the populace whom he despised.

**4.** *trans.* To tread heavily and (esp.) injuriously upon; to crush, break down, or destroy by heavy treading; also *to trample down, under foot.*

1530 PALSGR. 760/2 Se howe this way is trampelled. 1596 MASCALL *Cattle* 71 To gather vp more cleane, and not for to trample so much vnder their feete. 1611 BIBLE *Matt.* vii. 6 Neither cast yee your pearles before swine: lest they trample them vnder their feet. 1650 TRAPP *Comm. Deut.* xvii. 2 He can as easily blast an oak, as trample a mushrome. 1725 [see TRAMPER 1 b]. 1813 SCOTT *Rokeby* v. xxxiii, Trampling down the dying man. 1833 HT. MARTINEAU *Manch. Strike* i. 11 He would trample us under foot if he could. 1853 WHEWELL *Grotius* III. 290 The lands of neutrals are not to be trampled. 1878 BROWNING *Poets Croisic* xxxvii, As an ox Tramples a flower-bed in a garden.

**b.** *fig.*

1583 BABINGTON *Commandm.* ii. 97 [If] our heartes were not altogether so hard trampled and beaten as they are. 1603 HOLLAND *Plutarch's Mor.* 982 To insult over Sparta..and at once to tread and trample under foot the high spirit and reputation of that city. 1675 E. WILSON *Spadacrene Dunelmensis* 14 Thus they trample all Learning under foot. 1793 COWPER *Bill Mortality* vii, Who trample order; and the day, Which God asserts His own, Dishonour. 1849 MACAULAY *Hist. Eng.* ii. I. 187 The party which had been vanquished, trampled down, and..annihilated.

**5.** *trans.* To put *in* or *out* by tramping or stamping; esp. *to trample out* (fire); in quot. 1848, to make or cause by trampling.

1573–80 BARET *Alv.* T 344 To tread or trample out: to wring out, *exculco.* 1842 BROWNING *Cristina* vii, The world's honours, in derision, Trampled out the light for ever. 1848 THACKERAY *Van. Fair* xii, I don't want Frederick to trample a hole in my muslin frock. 1858 FROUDE *Hist. Eng.* III. xiii. 113 The security against a spread of the conflagration was to trample it out upon the spot.

**Trampled** (træ·mp'ld), *ppl. a.* [f. TRAMPLE *v.* + -ED[1].] Beaten down or crushed by trampling; also *fig.* down-trodden, oppressed.

*c* 1440 *Promp. Parv.* 499/1 Tramplyd, *tritus.* 1592 *Arden of Feversham* IV. i. 3 The trampled pace Wherein he wount to guide his golden car. *a* 1764 LLOYD tr. *Henriade* Poet. Wks. 1774 II. 223 The trampled Law had lost its ancient force. 1842 TENNYSON *Locksley Hall* 156, I was left a trampled orphan, and a selfish uncle's ward.

**Trampler** (træ·mpləɹ). [f. TRAMPLE *v.* + -ER[1].] One who tramples, in various senses.

1580 HOLLYBAND *Treas. Fr. Tong, Trotteur, vn villotier*, a trotter, a trampler. 1611 COTGR., *Fouleur*, a treader (of grapes, &c.), a stamper, or trampler on. 1784 COWPER *Task* VI. 465 Th' injurious trampler upon Nature's law. 1816 BYRON *Ch. Har.* III. xx, The trampler of her vineyards.

† **b.** ? A go-between, intermediary; an attorney. *Obs. Cant.*

1608 MIDDLETON *Trick to Catch Old One* I. iv, [He] has been a trampler of the law, sir; and the devil has a care of his footmen. 1620 MIDDLETON & ROWLEY *World Tost at Tennis* 784 Pity your trampler, sir, your poor solicitor. 1630 J. TAYLOR (Water P.) *Water Cormorant* Wks. III. 13/2 The trampler is in hast, O cleere the way, Takes fees with both hands cause he cannot stay.

**Tra·mpling**, *vbl. sb.* [f. TRAMPLE *v.* + -ING[1].] The action of the verb TRAMPLE.

*c* 1440 *Promp. Parv.* 499/1 Trampelynge, *tritura.* 1530 PALSGR. 282/2 Tramplynge with fete, *marchage.* 1577 GOOGE tr. *Heresbach's Husb.* I. 45 Your Meddowes..Let them be kept from..trampling of Cattel. 1693 EVELYN *De la Quint. Compl. Gard.* II. 170 Bringing the Dung..(which cannot be done without much trampling on the Soil). 1828 SCOTT *F. M. Perth* iii, After some..trampling up and down stairs, Dorothy appeared. 1838 THIRLWALL *Greece* II. xv. 286 The universal silence was first broken by the trampling of the invaders, on the leaves with which the face of the woody mountain was thickly strewed.

**Tra·mpling**, *ppl. a.* [f. TRAMPLE *v.* + -ING[2].] That tramples, in various senses of the verb.

1581 SIDNEY *Astr. & Stella* lxxxiv, My Muse..Tempers her words to trampling horses feete More oft then to a chamber-melodie. 1608 MIDDLETON *Trick to Catch Old One* IV. v, A just judgment..upon usury, extortion, and trampling villany! 1697 DRYDEN *Æneid* III. 854 Trampling feet that shake the solid ground. 1839 LONGF. *Wreck of Hesperus* xvi, The sound of the trampling surf On the rocks.

**Trampolin, -ine** (træ·mpŏlin), *sb.* [f. It. *trampoli* stilts: cf. *trampolare* 'to go on stilts or high startops' (Florio, 1598).] A performance on stilts; also *attrib.* Hence **Tra·mpolin(e** *v.*, *intr.* to walk on or as on stilts. Also **Trampolino**: see quot. 1912.

1798 *Times* 28 June 7/1 Equestrian Performances with Oranges, Forks, Skipping Rope, Hat, Handkerchief, and a curious Equilibrium with a Hoop and Glass. Wonderful Trampolin Tricks, by Messrs. Smith [etc.]. 1833 M. SCOTT

*Tom Cringle* xi, [At the Negro Carnival] Then another tumblification of the whole party... Another trampoline. **1867** H. Kingsley *Silcote of Silcotes* xiii, She trampolining away to Hampstead with the children. **1912** Anne E. George *Montessori Method* ix. 141 One of the things invented by Séguin to develop the lower limbs..is the trampolino. This is a kind of swing, having a very wide seat.

**Trampoose** (træmpū·z), *v. U.S. slang. ? Obs.* Also **tramboozе, -pouse, -pouss(e.** [app. a capricious extension of Tramp *v.*[1]: cf. *vamoose, vampoose.*] *intr.* To tramp, trudge.

**1798** O'Keeffe *Wild Oats* ii. iii, I'd teach 'em to bring a gentleman's son tramboozing about the country. *a* **1818** D. Humphreys *Yankee in Eng.* (Bartlett), Some years ago I landed near to Dover, And seed strange sights, trampoosing England over. **1824** *Blackw. Mag.* XVI. 566 Mr. Moore was 'trampoosing' over America. **1825** J. Neal *Bro. Jonathan* I. 177 Trampoosing about all night. **1850** Porter *Tales of South & West* 44 (Bartlett) We trampoused along down the edge of the swamp.

So Trampoo·se *sb. rare*, a tramp, a trudge.

**1840** J. F. Cooper *Pathfinder* viii, I was with him in one of his trampooses.

**Trampsoun, -sown,** obs. ff. Transom.

**Tram-road** (træ·mˌrōud). [f. Tram *sb.*[2], sense 2 or 4 (more prob. the former) + Road.] Orig., in mining districts, a road having 'trams' or beams of wood, lengths of stone, or later, iron plates or 'rails' laid in two parallel lines, to form wheel-tracks for the easier transport of minerals in 'trams' or wagons; hence, generally, a track for vehicles thus made; = Railway *sb.* 1; now, in parliamentary language, a special track or narrow railroad for wagons or cars, as distinguished from a *tramway* laid down for tram-cars on an ordinary road or street. Also *attrib.*

(The name *tram-road* has been erroneously stated to be derived from the surname of Mr. Benjamin *Outram*, an engineer largely engaged in the construction of tram-roads for traffic, in some parts of the country (see quot. 1800). It is not improbable that, in some locality where tram-roads were a novelty, their name may have been associated in folk-etymology or by pre-scientific etymologers with that of the engineer. Unfortunately, the legend was recorded as a fact by S. Smiles in his *Life of George Stephenson* (1857), p. 59, whence it was quoted and repeated in popular publications, and is still widely current, although its absurdity, etymologically and otherwise, was clearly pointed out in 1882 by Professor Skeat in his *Dictionary of English Etymology*.)

[Cf. **1793** *Act* 33 *Geo. III*, c. 96 An Act..for making..Rail Ways and Stone Roads from such Canal to several Iron Works and Mines. **1799** *Commons Jrnl.* LIV. 613/1 A Bill for the making of Ways or Roads, usually called Railways or Dram Roads. *Ibid.* 664/1.] **1800** *Agreement* 18 Dec. in J. Lloyd *Old South Wales Iron Works* (1906) 143 The Monmouthshire Canal Company shall..make a good and sufficient tramroad, according to the plans of Benjamin Outram, ..Engineer, from the Tredegar Iron Works, to join their Canal near Risca Church. **1804** *Act* 44 *Geo. III*, c. 55 (*title*) An Act for making and maintaining a Railway or Tramroad from the Town of Swansea, into the Parish of Oystermouth in the County of Glamorgan. **1818** (*title*) Observations on the Proposed Railway or Tram-road from Stockton to the Collieries, by way of Darlington. **1824** T. G. Cumming *Rail & Tram Roads* 17 Such is the decided preference given to tram roads, that with the exception of about five miles..the whole are upon the tram plate principle. **1838** *Civil Eng. & Arch. Jrnl.* I. 328/1 Certain Improvements in the Construction of Railroads and Tramroads to facilitate the ascent and descent of Hills and inclined Planes. **1839** Ure *Dict. Arts* 982 The corves descend along the tramroads. *Ibid.* 994 In the dip-mine a double tram-road is laid. **1843** *Penny Cycl.* XXV. 118/1 Tram-road, a road prepared for the easy transit of trams or waggons, by the insertion, in its surface, of smooth beams of wood, blocks of stone, or plates of iron, as wheel-tracks. **1846** R. Ritchie *Railways* 12 Several tracks of continuous stone rails, usually termed tram roads, have been constructed. **1852** Wiggins *Embanking* 63 Good tram-road sleepers may be had at much less money. **1880** Disraeli *Endym.* lxii, Lancashire with..its tramroads and its railroads. **1881** Young *Ev. Man his own Mechanic* § 1091 The amateur will find his scaffold-boards very handy as a temporary tramroad for his barrow to run over. **1885** *Law Times Rep.* LI. 583/1 The tram-road upon which the steam motor was being driven. **1901** [see Tramway 1 b].

**b.** *fig.*

**1859** A. Sedgwick in *Darwin's Life & Lett.* (1887) II. 248 After a start in that tram-road of all solid physical truth. **1859** G. Meredith *R. Feverel* xxiii, The young man got on the tramroad of his passion, and went ahead.

**Tramson,** obs. form of Transom.

**Tramway** (træ·mwēi). [f. Tram *sb.*[2] + Way: cf. Tram-road, and *railroad, railway.*]

**1.** A track of parallel rails (originally flat planks of wood, afterwards lengths of stone or plates of iron), forming wheel-tracks for vehicles; a tram-road. **b.** Now *spec.* A track with rails flush with the road surface, laid in a street or road, on which tram-cars are run, for the conveyance of passengers. (For the distinction between *tramway* and *tram-road* in parliamentary language, see quot. 1901.)

**1825** E. Mackenzie *Hist. Northumbld.* I. 147 *note*, From recent experiments..it has been ascertained that upon an edge-railway one horse can work with a much greater load ..than upon a tram-way. **1830** *Mechanics' Mag.* XIII. 73 (*title*) Stone tramway in the Commercial Road...Tramway ..has been hitherto generally used to designate that description of iron railway in which flat rails or tram-plates level with the ground are employed. **1840** *Penny Cycl.* XX. 33/2 Stone tramways consist of wheel-tracks formed of large blocks of stone, usually granite, the surface of which is made so smooth as to offer very little resistance to the rolling of the wheels. **1846** R. Ritchie *Railways* 12 Tracks of continuous stone rails...In London..such tramways for short distances have long been in general use. **1854** W. H. D. Longstaffe *Darlington* 359 Wooden tramways still continued to be used..to almost our own day. **1861** Smiles *Engineers* II. 201 The adoption of tramways all round the quays. **1862** *Ibid.* III. 88 He [Trevithick] had the wooden tramway taken up in 1808, and a plate-way of cast iron laid down instead. **1882** *Rep. to Ho. Repr. Prec. Met. U. S.* 449 The ore is delivered by cars on a tramway, the descending car drawing up the empty one.

**b.** **1860** G. F. Train *Observ. Street Railw.* 3, I was surprized to find the progress made [in U. S.] in what the Americans term *Street Railways*, [and] the English *tramways*. **1863** P. Barry *Dockyard Econ.* 272 So early as 1801, Rennie reported upon the project of an iron rail or tramway between the east and west ends of London. **1864** Musgrave *Ten Days in Fr. Parsonage* I. i. 31 We still travel [more cheaply] on the French tramway. **1883** *Pall Mall G.* 14 Sept. 4/1 The first long electric tramway in the world will be opened to-day in county Antrim...The Portrush electric tramway. **1901** *Standing Orders Ho. Lords, Priv. Bills* 7 In these Orders..the term 'tramway' means a tramway laid along a street or road; the term 'tramroad' means a tramway laid elsewhere than along a street or road. **1911** *Edin. Rev.* July 52 Tramways pulse and jingle over the old Tournai Causeway.

**2.** *transf.* A cable or system of cables on which suspended cars travel. *U.S.*

**1872** Raymond *Statist. Mines & Mining* 318 The tram-way consists of two wire cables, each of which is six-tenths of an inch in diameter, extending from the lower adit on the Stevens lode to the base of the hill...All the ore will be sent to the base of the mountain by the tram-way.

**3.** *attrib.* and *Comb.*, as *tramway car, company, draught* (Draught *sb.* 1), *driver, man*; **tramway plate**, a plate-rail, = Tram-plate; **tramway terms**, the terms on which a municipality is legally able to acquire an existing tramway belonging to a private firm or company: see quot. 1902.

**1825** Tramway plate [see Plate *sb.* 8]. **1872** *Gentl. Mag.* Sept. 359 Asphalte pavements and tramway cars are modern blessings. **1874** *Ibid.* Apr. 454 In the great suburban boulevards the tramway-cars make locomotion alike swift, cheap, nasty, and dangerous. **1877** Gen. C. E. Gordon *Let.* 19 Nov. (in *Pearson's Catal.* (1888) 17), Camels will do well enough for tramway draughts. **1885** *Pall Mall G.* 22 Sept. 11/1 The concession allotted to the so-called tramway steamers [at Venice] is given for five years' time. **1894** *Westm. Gaz.* 6 July 6/2 He had always advocated fair play in dealing with the Tramway Companies. **1897** *Daily News* 7 Apr. 2/2 The tramway men themselves did not desire their hours and wages altered. **1901** D. B. Hall & Ld. A. Osborne *Sunshine & Surf* i, Down one of whose funnels, they say, two tramway cars can run abreast. **1902** A. Chamberlain in *Daily Chron.* 12 Dec. 8/7 Right to purchase..plant.. useful for Post Office purposes on what are commonly known as 'tramway terms'—that is, at its fair market value as plant in use.

Hence **Tra·mway** *v., trans.* to furnish with a tramway; *intr.* to travel by a tramway or tram.

**1871** Ruskin *Fors Clav.* iv. 24 The roads themselves beautifully public-tramwayed perhaps—and with gates set open enough for all men. **1900** *N. Brit. Daily Mail* 13 Feb. 4 Happy the man..who can exchange the dull prose of walking or of tramwaying for the poetry of motion..in..skating.

† **Trana·tion.** *Obs. rare.* [n. of action f. L. *trānāre* to swim across: see -tion.] A swimming or passing across, a crossing; also, a passing into another form, a transformation, metamorphosis.

**1654** Gayton *Pleas. Notes* ii. v. 52 The Metamorphosis, translation, or rather tranation of Arthur into a Crow. *Ibid.* iii. iii. 84 In his Tranation he lookt about, and saw under him (though a farre off) his Lord upon Rosinante, no bigger than a Toad upon a Ducking-stoole. **1664** Power *Exp. Philos.* iii. 159 The Magnetical Fluors..finding the grain..of the Stone to lye fit for their Tranation, do channel through to the opposite part of the Stone. **1719** *Glossogr. Angl. Nova*, *Tranation*, a swimming or flying over, a crossing athwart, a piercing.

**Trance** (trans), *sb.*[1] Also 4-6 **transe**, 4-7 **traunce**, 5-7 **traunse, trans,** 6 **trawnce,** 6-7 **traunss.** [a. F. *transe* fem., in OF. *transe* m. and f., passage, passage from life to death (*St. Alexis*, 12th c.), great apprehension or dread of coming evil (15th c. in Littré); verbal sb. f. F. *transir* to pass, depart (esp. from life), to die (12th c.), also (later) to benumb or be numbed by fear or cold, ad. L. *transīre* to pass over, cross, f. *trans* across + *īre* to go. (Cf. Sp. *trance* danger, last stage of life, Pg. *trance, transe* a dreadful circumstance; cf. It. *transito* 'a passage or going over; also a trance' Florio).

Palsgrave has 'Traunce a sickenesse, *trance*', and Cotgr. has 'also, a traunce or sowne; a great astonishment, amazement, or appallment', but these senses do not appear in Littré or Godef.; perh. they were Anglo-Fr.; otherwise the chief mod. sense of the Eng. word does not appear in F.]

†**1.** A state of extreme apprehension or dread; a state of doubt or suspense. *Obs.*

*c* **1374** Chaucer *Troylus* ii. 1257 (1306) Troylus..That lay, as doth þese loueres, yn a traunce By-twixen hope and derk desesperaunce. **1390** Gower *Conf.* III. 321 This cherles herte is in a traunce, As he which drad him of vengance. **1412-20** Lydg. *Chron. Troy* iv. 1536 Þe verray custom & þe pleyn vsaunce Of þis loveris, hangyng in a trance. *c* **1477** Caxton *Jason* 46 b, She was in a traunce what she shold saye to her. **1523** Ld. Berners tr. *Froiss.* I. cccxliii. 542 Thus these maters hanged in a traunce. **1577** Grange *Golden Aphrod.* etc. P ij b, In this traunce of troubles my trembling tongue was partly enioyned to silence.

**2.** An unconscious or insensible condition; a swoon, a faint; in mod. use, a state characterized by a more or less prolonged suspension of consciousness and inertness to stimulus; a cataleptic or hypnotic condition.

*c* **1386** Chaucer *Frankl. T.* 353 And longe tyme he lay forth in a traunce. *a* **1533** Ld. Berners *Huon* lxii. 215 She fell downe in a transe, more lyke to be deed than alyue. **1604** Shaks. *Oth.* iv. i. Stage direct., [Othello] Falls in a Traunce. **1617** Moryson *Itin.* i. 249 Most of the night he had lien in a trance. **1715-20** Pope *Iliad* xi. 462 Hector rose, recover'd from the trance. **1821** Byron *Two Foscari* i. i, Happy to escape to death By the compassionate trance, poor nature's last Resource against the tyranny of pain. **1852** H. Rogers *Eclipse of Faith* (1864) 296 Paulus thinks that Christ was only in a trance when he seemed to be dead. **1857** Dunglison *Dict. Med.* s.v. *Ecstasis*, In catalepsy, there is..complete suspension of the intellectual faculties. This last condition is in general described as trance. **1861** Geo. Eliot *Silas M.* vii, When Silas Marner was in that strange trance of his. **1899** *Syd. Soc. Lex.*, *Trance*, catalepsy; ecstasy. The hypnotic state: a prolonged abnormal sleep, in which the vital functions are reduced to a very low ebb, and from which the patients cannot ordinarily be aroused.

**3.** An intermediate state between sleeping and waking; half-conscious or half-awake condition; a stunned or dazed state.

*c* **1386** Chaucer *Sompn. T.* 508 The lord sat stille, as he were in a traunce, And in his herte he rolled vp and doun. *c* **1420** ? Lydg. *Assembly of Gods* 15 And as I so lay half in a traunse, Twene slepyng and wakyng he bad me aryse. *Ibid.* 2063 All thys I saw as I lay in a traunce. *c* **1530** Ld. Berners *Arth. Lyt. Bryt.* (1814) 245 The noble courte..is all in a traunce, in a maner halfe a slepe. **1549** *Compl. Scot.* xv. 123, I dee daly in ane transe. **1656** W. Montague *Accompl. Wom.* 17 [They] cannot imagine pensivenesse to be any thing but such a trans, as mad men or sick persons are in. **1757** Gray *Bard* 13 Glos'ter stood aghast in speechless trance.

**b.** A state of mental abstraction from external things; absorption, exaltation, rapture, ecstasy.

**1434** Misyn *Mending Life* xii. 128 With swetnes of godis lufe as [he] wer rauischyd in trans, meruelusly rauischid. **1594** Spenser *Amoretti* xxxix, Whylest rapt with joy resembling heavenly madnes, My soule was ravisht quite as in a traunce. **1598** Bacon *Sacr. Medit.*, *Impostors*, His ..conuersation towards God is full of passion, of zeale, and of traunssis [*mispr.* tramisses; orig. *plena excessus, et zeli, et extasis*]. **1632** Lithgow *Trav.* i. 32 This imaginary heauenly trance. **1696** Phillips (ed. 5), *Trance*, an Extasy, a Ravishment or Transportation of the Mind, which puts a Man beside himself. **1756-7** tr. *Keysler's Trav.* (1760) II. 238 The saint is represented lying in a trance. **1817** Moore *Lalla R.*, *Lt. of Haram* Wks. (1824) 313 As, in a kind of holy trance, She hung above those fragrant treasures.

**4.** *attrib.* and *Comb.*, as *trance-coma, -medium, -sleep, -state*; *trance-bound, -like* adjs.

**1825** J. Neal *Bro. Jonathan* I. 137 Waking out of a trance-like revery. **1849** H. Mayo *Truths Pop. Superstit.* v. 82 So are there three degrees of trance-sleep...The middle grade deserves to be called trance-coma. **1878** Emerson *Misc. Papers, Fort. Repub.* Wks. (Bohn) III. 389 The trance-mediums..exasperate the common sense. **1886** H. R. Haweis *Christ & Chr.*, *Light of Ages* v. 143 At Delphi..the priests ..uttered what a modern spiritualist would call *trance-speeches*; they became..what are known as *trance mediums*. **1903** F. W. H. Myers *Hum. Personality* I. 5 The exceptional trance-history of Emmanuel Swedenborg.

**Trance, transe** (trans), *sb.*[2] *Sc.* Also 6-7 **trans,** 6-9 **trans.** [Known from 16th c.: origin obscure. The sense is satisfied by L. *transitus*, which had the concrete sense 'passage, way through', as well as the abstract 'act of passing through or over'. But L. *transitus* could hardly have given Sc. *transs, trans* without passing through French, and the concrete sense is not recorded in OF.] A passage between buildings, or across between two streets; an entry, an alley, a close; also, a passage into, within, or through a house.

**1545** in Pennecuik *Blue Blanket* (1756) 34 Lands..lyand in the burgh of Edinburgh, upon the South-side of the high street thereof, betwixt the trans of the vennel called Hair's-closs, and the trans of the vennel called Borthwick's-closs. **1555** *Burgh Rec. Edinb.* (1871) II. 214 The Freir Wynd heid an ather syde of the trans of the Hie gait. *a* **1578** Lindesay (Pitscottie) *Chron. Scot.* (S.T.S.) I. 333 Quhilk was left waist of befoir, as transses and throw passagis. **1632** Lithgow *Trav.* x. 461 Carried..to the end of a Trance or stone-Gallery. **1659** Torriano, *Passaggio*..a trance from one room to another. *a* **1670** Spalding *Troub. Chas. I* (1851) II. 327 [He] causit draw his horss out of the stables into the transs. **1826** J. Wilson *Noct. Ambr.* Wks. 1855 I. 156 He had hardly put his hat on a peg in the transe. **1835** Hogg *Tales & Sk.* (1837) V. 222 So proud of 'squiring Lady Jane Gordon down the stairs and along the trance. **1883** *Chamb. Jrnl.* 210 From this single street [of Lerwick] steep lanes or trances lead up to the ridge.

*fig.* **1632** Rutherford *Lett.* (1862) I. 97 A little sight of that dark trance you must go through ere you come to glory. **1645** — *Tryal & Tri. Faith* Ded. (1845) 4 Time is but a short trance: we are carried quickly through it.

**b.** *attrib.* and *Comb.*, as *trance-door, -window.*

**1811** W. Aiton *Agric. Surv. Ayrs.* 114 The cattle.. entered by the same door with the family; the one turning to the one hand, by the trans-door to the kitchen, and the other turning the contrary way by the heck-door to the byre or stable. **1880** J. F. S. Gordon *Chron. Keith*, etc. 66 Several juveniles had..attempted to escape by 'the Trance window' on to the roof of the Weigh House. **1890** J. Service *Thir Notandums* v. 25 At the trance door Provost Painch's fit took the boss.

**Trance,** *sb.*[3] *dial.* Also **traunce.** [f. Trance *v.*[2]] ? A skip, a dance; applied ironically, as in 'a fine trance', to a long tedious walk or tramp, a long tiring round.

*c* **1746** J. COLLIER (Tim Bobbin) *View Lanc. Dial.* Wks. (1862) 40 I've had sitch o' traunce this Morning as eh neer had e'meh live. *a* **1800** PEGGE *Suppl. Grose, Trance*, a tedious journey. Lanc. **1885** *Cheshire Gloss., Traunce*, a tedious journey. 'He led me a fine traunce'.

† **Trance**, *sb.*[4] *Obs.* [a. Sp. *trance*, formerly *tranze* danger (see TRANCE *sb.*[1]), the original word in all three quots.] Danger, peril.

**1588** PARKE tr. *Mendoza's Hist. China* 356 They were themselues in the same trance and perill [*en el mismo tranze y peligro*], and as nigh their death. *Ibid.* 378 A very good warning vnto all..to flie from putting themselues into the like trance. **1612** SHELTON *Quix.* I. viii. (1619) 58 This thy Knight, who..finds himselfe in this dangerous trance [*en este riguroso trance*].

**Trance** (trɑns), *v.*[1] Forms: see TRANCE *sb.*[1] [In sense 1 a. OF. *transir* to pass away, to die: see TRANCE *sb.*[1]; in sense 2 f. TRANCE *sb.*[1]]

†**1.** *intr.* **a.** To 'pass away', to die. **b.** To swoon, faint. **c.** To be in extreme dread, doubt, or suspense. (In some early quotations these senses are difficult to distinguish.) *Obs.*

**1340** HAMPOLE *Pr. Consc.* 8158 Þai salle seme, whether þai lyg or stand, Als men in transyng, ay deghand. *a* **1350** *Assumpt. Mary* 325 in Horstm. *Altengl. Leg.* (1881) 116 Þan scho transed þare als fast, And þe saul fra þe body past. **14..** *Tundale's Vis.* 41 As he yn a transynge lay, Hys sowle was in a dredefull way. **1530** PALSGR. 761/2, I trawnce, I fall in a traunce or swounyng, *je me transis*...I feare me..he wyll dye, for he traunseth often, *je men doute,..quil mourra, car il se transit souuent.* *c* **1600** BUREL *Pilgr.* in Watson *Coll.* II. 48 Perplexit and vexit Betwixt houp and dispair, Quhyls transing, quhyls pansing, How till eschew the snair. **1632** LITHGOW *Trav.* I. 5, I trancing flye, I fall, I houering scale.

**2.** *trans.* To throw into a trance or a similar state; † to stupefy; to entrance, enrapture. Chiefly *poet.*

**1597–8** BP. HALL *Sat., Defiance to Envie* 33 And trance herself in that sweete extasey. *a* **1619** FLETCHER, etc. *Q. Corinth* II. iii, Why, where am I? How am I traunc'd and moap'd? i' th street—Heaven bless me. **1800** MOORE *Anacreon* xvii, Mingle in his jetty glances Power that awes, and love that trances. **1817** SHELLEY *Rev. Islam* v. xvii, I trod as one tranced in some rapturous vision. **1855** TENNYSON *Maud* II. IV. ii, When I was wont to meet her In the silent woody places..We stood tranced in long embraces. *fig.* **1830** TENNYSON *Mariana* ii, When thickest dark did trance the sky. **1865** J. THOMSON *Sunday up the River* IV. iii, What Sabbath peace doth trance the air! **1876** D. STEVENSON in *Gd. Words* 687 The world was tranced into a slumberous hush.

Hence **Tra·ncing** *vbl. sb.* and *ppl. a.*, entrancing.

**1340, 14..** [see sense 1]. **1856** MRS. BROWNING *Aur. Leigh* v. 512 That caressing colour and trancing tone Whereby you're swept away and melted in The sensual element. **1867** F. W. H. MYERS *St. Paul* 52 God with sweet strength, with terror and with trancing Spake in the purple mystery of dawn. **1873** E. BRENNAN *Witch of Nemi*, etc. 146 Let darkness make complete its trancing joy.

**Trance** (trɑns), *v.*[2] *Obs.* exc. *dial.* Forms: 4–9 **traunce**, 6– **trance** (also *dial.* 9 **trawnce**). [Origin and history obscure: see also TROUNCE. (The first quot. is also doubtful in form and sense.)] *intr.* To move about actively or briskly; to prance or skip; in later use applied ironically to moving over the ground with effort or speed; implying more rapidity than *tramp*.

*c* **1374** CHAUCER *Troilus* III. 641 (690) There was no more to speken [*v. rr.* skipen, schepe] nor to traunce [*MS. Harl.* 3943 taunce]. **1390** GOWER *Conf.* II. 72 He [Achelons] torneth him into a Bole..The ground he sporneth and he tranceth, Hise large hornes he avanceth. *a* **1560** ROLLAND *Crt. Venus* I. 192 The younkeir moir wantounlie did trance. *a* **1625** FLETCHER, etc. *Fair Maid Inn* v. i, Traunce the world over You shall never purse up so much gold as when you were in England. **1867** E. WAUGH *Factory Folk* xxii. 195 Thae'rt noan fit to trawnce up an' deawn o' this shap.

**Tranced** (trɑnst, *poet.* trɑ·nsėd), *ppl. a.* [f. TRANCE *v.*[1] + -ED[1].] In a trance; entranced. Also *fig.*

**1605** SHAKS. *Lear* v. iii. 218 There I left him traunst. *a* **1665** SIR K. DIGBY *Priv. Mem.* (1827) 44 A tranced angel. **1808** SCOTT *Marmion* VI. iv, Where oft Devotion's tranced glow Can such a glimpse of heaven bestow. **1820** KEATS *Hyperion* I. 72 A tranced summer-night. **1854** GRACE GREENWOOD *Haps & Mishaps Tour Europe* 62 One of his Madonnas so saintly beautiful in the tranced joy of her divine maternity.

Hence **Trancedly** (trɑ·nsėdli), *adv.*

**1830** TENNYSON *Arab. Nights* xiii, Then stole I up, and trancedly Gazed on the Persian girl alone. **1855** W. MORRIS in Mackail *Life* (1899) I. 59 The wren sings merrily, But the lark sings trancedly. **1893** *Nat. Observer* 22 July 246/2 To commune trancedly with the woodland spirit.

**Tranceful** (trɑ·nsfŭl), *a. rare.* [f. TRANCE *sb.*[1] + -FUL.] Full of trances; entrancing.

*a* **1883** A. MACLEAN in *Mem.* 120 That witchful, tranceful vision's fled. **1895** J. COOK in *Chicago Advance* 1290/1 Whip-poor-will, Let thy tranceful, tearful tune Charm the listening stars and moon.

† **Tranch**, *v. Obs.* Also 6 **traunche.** [a. F. *tranch-er* to cut: see TRENCH *v.*] *trans.* To carve (a sturgeon or other fish).

**1513** *Bk. Keruynge* (W. de Worde) A j b, Traunche that sturgyon. **1688** R. HOLME *Armoury* III. 78 Tranch that Sturgeon. **1840** H. AINSWORTH *Tower Lond.* II. xxxix, In the old terms of his art, he leached the brawn,..tranched the sturgeon, undertranched the tunny-fish, tamed the crab, and barbed the lobster.

‖ **Tra·nchant**, *a.* Also 6 **tranchaunt.** [= F. *tranchant* (trāñʃañ) cutting: see TRENCHANT.] Early form of TRENCHANT; also from 18th c. a loan-word from French; esp. in *fig.* sense: = TRENCHANT 2; also of colours, glaring, crude.

*a* **1529** SKELTON *Agst. Garnesche* III. 138 Your sworde ye swere, I wene, So tranchaunt and so kene. **1776** H. WALPOLE *Let. to W. Mason* 18 Feb., Modest as he is *tranchant* and sly as Montesquieu without being so *recherché*. **1812** *Edin. Rev.* Feb. 475 The Notes are written in a flippant, lively, *tranchant* and assuming style. **1832** L. HUNT *Poems* Pref. 22 Dryden had a tranchant sword, which demanded stoutness in the sheath. **1841** THACKERAY *2nd Funeral Napoleon* iii, The raw *tranchant* colours of the new banners.

‖ **Tranche.** [= F. *tranche* (trāñʃ), f. *trancher* to cut: see TRENCH. Now only as a loan-word from French.] A cutting, a cut; a piece cut off, a slice.

*c* **1500** *Melusine* xi. 43 The said fontayne, where as grett tranchis [*p.* 50 trenchis] or keruyng was made within the harde roche. **1893** P. FITZGERALD in *Month* July 337 Huge baskets..in which were huge *tranches* of bread.

‖ **Tranché** (trāñʃe), *a.* and *sb.* Also 7–8 **tranche.** [F. *tranché*, pa. pple. of *trancher* to cut, TRENCH *v.*]

**A.** *adj. Her.* Party per bend: see PARTY *a.* 3.

**1661** MORGAN *Sph. Gentry* II. i. 3 Josep[h]s Coat,..divided as Adams Shield and Chequered with Black and White, or Tranche with averse and different providences. **1704** J. HARRIS *Lex. Techn.* I, *Tranche*, a Word used by the French Armorists...Our English Heralds Blazon it..per Bend Counterchanged. **1725** COATS *Heraldry, Tranché*, in the French way of Blazon is us'd absolutely, without any addition to denote that honourable Partition which we call Party per Bend Dexter. *c* **1828** BERRY *Encycl. Her.* I. Gloss. **1882** CUSSANS *Handbk. Her.* xxiv. (ed. 3) 316.

**B.** *sb.* The edge of a coin milled or inscribed, to prevent clipping.

**1697** EVELYN *Numism.* vii. 225 The Circumscription about the *Tranché* or Edge.

‖ **Tranchefer** (trāñʃəfęr). *Obs.* or *arch. rare.* [F., f. *tranche* vb. imper. cut + *fer* iron.] A name given to a sword.

*c* **1530** LD. BERNERS *Arth. Lyt. Bryt.* (1814) 208 And Arthur drewe out Clarence, his good sworde;..also called traunchfer, that is for to say, cutter of yren. **1831** SCOTT *Ct. Robt.* xiii, We will go..and teach these Easterns how to judge of a knight's sword, by a single blow of my trusty Tranchefer.

**Trancum**, variant of TRANKUM *Obs.*

**Trane**, obs. form of TRAIN.

[† **Tranect.** *Obs.* Known only in the passage quoted, and prob. only a misreading or misprint of *traiect*, TRAJECT, in It. *traghetto* a ferry.

**1596** SHAKS. *Merch. V.* III. iv. 53 Bring them..Vnto the Tranect, to the common Ferrie Which trades to Venice.]

**Traneen** (trānī·n). *Irish.* Also **trau-, traw-, thra-, thrawneen.** [Anglicized spelling of Ir. *traithnín*, *trathnan*, a little stalk of grass (O'Reilly).] The crested dog's-tail grass, *Cynosurus cristatus*. (Often taken as the type of something of little or no value: cf. RUSH *sb.*[1] 2).

[**1808** J. WHITE *Ess. Grasses Irel.* 154 (Britt. and Holl. *Plant-n.*) Trathnin.] **1837** S. LOVER *Rory O'More* ii, You dare n't stand before any one with sich a thraneen as that in your fist. **1839** W. CARLETON *Fardorougha* iii, It's a bargin..I don't care a trawneen. **1842** S. C. HALL *Ireland* II. 74 She never cared a traneen for him, soul or body, and went off with a richer man. **1884** *Lays & Leg. N. Irel.* 20 Sorra a thrawneen you'll get from us more. **1899** *Blackw. Mag.* Mar. 572 But she'd not a traneen to her fortune.

† **Tra·ngam.** *Obs.* Also 7 **trangame**, 7–8 **-gham, -gum.** [Origin obscure: the first two quots. suggest that it was a fictitious law-term. Obs. after 1719, but recalled by Scott.

In quot. 1712 misquoted by Johnson as *trangram*, which erroneous spelling has been followed by later dictionaries, some of which further associate it with TANGRAM (known only from 1864). Cf. TRANKUM.]

An odd or intricate contrivance of some kind; a knick-knack, a puzzle; a toy, trinket; a gewgaw, trumpery ornament. Applied to anything which the speaker views with contempt.

*a* **1658** CLEVELAND *Engagement Stated* 21 When neither Arts nor Arms can serve to fight, And wrest a Title from its Law and Right, Must Malice piece the Trangum? and make clear The Scruple? **1672** EACHARD *Hobbs' State Nat.* 21 A Cause is a certain pack or aggregate of trangams, which being all packed up and chorded close together, they may then truly be said in Law to constitute a compleat and essential pack. **1676** WYCHERLEY *Pl. Dealer* III. i, But go, thou Trangame, and carry back those Trangames, Which thou hast stol'n or purloin'd. **1678** MRS. BEHN *Sir P. Fancy* IV. iii, Get you gone, and finefy your knacks and tranghams. **1679** OLDHAM *Sat. Jesuits* iv. (1682) 85 These [pretended sacred relics] are the Fathers Implements, and Tools, Their gawdy Trangums for inveigling Fools. [**1686** GOAD *Celest. Bodies* III. ii. 399 He, who looks upon Architecture and Fortification to be only Trangunims, is a Wise Man.] **1712** ARBUTHNOT *John Bull* III. vi, Hey day, what's here? What a Devil's the meaning of all these Trangams and Gimcracks, Gentlemen? **1719** J. ROBERTS *Spinster* 349 If they should rise from the dead now, and see you dressed up in your painted trangums, and East India rags, while all the poor Spinners hung about you crying for bread and for work. **1820** SCOTT *Abbot* xix, When yon usher..began to inquire what Popish trangam you were wearing...This comes of carrying Popish nick-nackets about you.

† **Trangdi·llio.** *Obs. rare.* [Origin unknown: some suggest a mistake for *twangdillio*, f. TWANG.] The twanging sound made by a musical instrument.

*a* **1704** T. BROWN *Pind. Petit. to Lds. in Counc.* Wks. 1730 I. 62 Even d'Urfey himself, and such merry fellows, That put their whole trust in tunes and trangdillioes, May hang up their harps and themselves on the willows.

**Trangle** (træ·ŋg'l). *Heraldry.* [a. obs. F. *trangle* (Cotgr. 1611), var. of *tringle*: see TRINGLE.] A diminutive of the fess; a bar or barrulet.

**1725** COATS *Heraldry, Trangle* is the Diminutive of a Fesse, by us commonly call'd a *Bar*. **1894** PARKER *Gloss. Her., Trangles*,..used by French heralds for bars and barrulets when their number is uneven, instead of *burelles*.

**Trank** (træŋk). *Glove-making.* [? ad. F. *tranche* a cutting.] An oblong piece of kid or other skin from which a glove is to be cut out; also, a glove-shape cut from this, before being sewn.

**1862** MRS. H. WOOD *Mrs. Hallib.* I. xxvi, The cutters cut the skins into tranks (the shape of the hand in outline) with the separate thumbs and forgits [= side-pieces of fingers]. **1894** *Times* 17 Aug. 9/4 Glove tranks, with or without the usual accompanying pieces. **1913** T. O. FARDON *Let. to Editor*, Two tranks, 2 thumbs, and 6 fourchettes are required to make a pair of gloves.

‖ **Trankeh, tranky** (tra·ŋke, -ki). Also 8–9 **trankey.** [a. Pers. ترانکه *trānkeh*, name in Persian Gulf for a pearl-diver's net, or perh. its adjectival deriv. *trānkī*, applied elliptically to a pearling-boat.] A small undecked vessel used in the pearl-fishery in the Persian Gulf.

**1727** A. HAMILTON *New Acc. E. Ind.* I. vii. 57 And then got Trankies (or Barks without Decks) and shipt what belonged to the English for Musskat. *Ibid.* 59 A sufficient Number of small Vessels, called Trankies, for their Transports. **1757** J. H. GROSE *Voy. E. Ind.* 28 Their trankys..are a kind of uncouth vessels, of seventy to a hundred tons. **1869** *Latest News* 17 Oct., The wind had fallen very light, and the trankies had taken in their sails, and were being impelled along slowly by means of the sweeps.

† **Tra·nkum.** *Obs.* Also **trancum.** [Altered form of TRINKUM, as in the reduplicated *trinkum-trankum*: perh. influenced by TRANGUM. Chiefly used by Scott.] A personal ornament; a trinket.

**1819** *Blackw. Mag.* V. 209 I'd be troubled to put on my trancums. **1822** SCOTT *Nigel* xxi, Come, my good boy,..never mind these trankums. **1824** — *St. Ronan's* xviii, That shawl must be had for Clara, with the other trankums of muslin and lace, and so forth. **1829** — *Doom Devorgoil* III. i, I had much ado To get these trankums on.

† **Tranla·ce**, *v. Obs. rare.* A word app. erroneously altered by Puttenham from *translate* or **tralate*, or the Latin equivalents. Used in one place in the sense 'to transpose'; in another in the sense 'to repeat a word in the shape of its various derivatives or cognates': cf. TRADUCTION 4.

In the latter sense, Day, three years earlier, had used *translate*, which in the sequel is used also by Puttenham himself. Collins app. took the word from Puttenham. So **Tranla·cer**: see quot.

[**1586** A. DAY *Eng. Secretary* II. (1625) 86 By translating of one word into diuers formes, as thus: What manhood call you this, so vnmanly to deale in those actions that especially appertaineth to a man? Here is this word *manhood* translated into *vnmanly* and to *man*.] **1589** PUTTENHAM *Eng. Poesie* II. (Arb.) 124 (End of cancelled pages) The same letters being by me tossed and tranlaced fiue hundreth times. *Ibid.* III. xix. 213 Then haue ye a figure which the Latines call *Traductio*, and I the tranlacer: which is when ye turne and tranlace a word into many sundry shapes as the Tailor doth his garment, and after that sort do play with him in your dittie..Ye see how..this word life is tranlaced into liue, liuing, liuely, liuelode: and in the latter rime this word wit is translated into weete, weene, wotte, witlesse, witty and wise: which come all from one originall. **1617** COLLINS *Def. Bp. Ely* II. vii. 273, I cast mine eyes vpon Theodorets owne texte, not as you trenlace and translate it at pleasure.

**Trannel**, obs. f. TREENAIL; var. TRAINEL *Obs.*

† **Trannet, tranet.** *Sc. Obs.* Some piece of horse harness: see quots.

**1504** *Acc. Ld. High Treas. Scot.* II. 433 Item to Johne Lethane, sadillar, for..ane trannet, ane molet bit tane for the Quenis stabile. **1506–7** *Ibid.* III. 209 Item, for ane tramtranet for hors to keip thaim fra struiking,..iij s.

† **Trano·nt, -oy·nt**, *v. Sc. Obs.* Also 5 **-ount, -ownt.** [Derivation unascertained.] *intr.* To shift one's position; *esp.* to do this rapidly and stealthily; to make a forced march, to steal a march *upon*. Hence † **Trano·nting** *vbl. sb.*

**1375** BARBOUR *Bruce* VII. 508 Schir Amery..vith sic tranonting..thoucht he suld suppriss þe kyng. *Ibid.* XVIII. 360 Kyng robert..Tranontit [*E.* -ountyt, *Hart* -oynted] swa on hym ane nycht, That, be the morne that it wes day, Cummyn in-till playn feld war thai. *c* **1425** WYNTOUN *Cron.* VIII. xxiv. 3717 Til Anande in tranowntynge þai coyme on þaim in þe dawynge. *c* **1450** HOLLAND *Howlate* 515 Sarazenis..tranoyntit with a trayne apon that trewe knycht. *c* **1470** HENRY *Wallace* VIII. 1564 Apon the morn the ost, but mar awys, Tranountyt north apon a gudlye wys. **1501** DOUGLAS *Pal. Hon.* II. lii, Thir ladyis..Uprais at last, commandand till tranoynt.

**Tranquil** (træ·ŋkwil), *a.* Also 7 **tranquill.** [ad. L. *tranquillus* quiet. Cf. F. *tranquille* (1470 in Godefroy *Compl.*).] Free from agitation or disturbance; calm, serene, placid, quiet, peaceful. **a.** Of the mind, or affairs.

**1604** SHAKS. *Oth.* III. iii. 348 Farewell the Tranquill minde; farewell Content. **1623** COCKERAM, *Tranquill*, quiet, peaceable. **1755** MRS. DELANY in *Life & Corr.* (1861) III. 328, I thank God all is tranquil again, after many fears and alarms. **1791** MRS. RADCLIFFE *Rom. Forest* i, Adeline appeared more tranquil than she had yet been. **1794** —

*Myst. Udolpho* xliii, She had sat..watching in tranquil melancholy the gradual effect of evening over the extensive prospect. **1872** HOWELLS *Wedd. Journ.* (1892) 66 They sat down for the tranquiller observance of the wharf.

**b.** Of the sea, the weather, a landscape, etc.

**1748** *Anson's Voy.* I. viii. 83 Relieved by approaching a warmer climate and more tranquil seas. **1807** CRABBE *Library* 52 The treasures of this tranquil scene. **1836** EMERSON *Misc., Nature* Wks. (Bohn) II. 143 In the tranquil landscape..man beholds somewhat as beautiful as his own nature. **1861–75** J. H. BENNET *Winter Medit.* I. v. 122 The ordinary notion of the Mediterranean is that of a blue and tranquil ocean lake.

**c.** Of things or actions: Steady, regular, even.

**1796** KIRWAN *Elem. Min.* (ed. 2) I. 434 Crystallized by tranquil fusion and slow refrigeration. **1827** FARADAY *Chem. Manip.* xiii. (1842) 293 The heating power of the tranquil flame is much economised..by using a jacket. **1836** RUSKIN *Præterita* I. vi. 298 How those winding roads steal with their tranquil slope from height to height.

† **Tranqui·lle.** *Obs. rare.* [sb. use of F. *tranquille*: see prec. Cf. L. *tranquillum* peace, quietness.] = TRANQUILLITY.

**1412–20** LYDG. *Chron. Troy* II. 1084 Þis addre..awakyd Priamus, And..Made him wery to lyuen in tranquille. *Ibid.* 1882 To trouble, allas, þe calm of his tranquille.

**Tranqui·llify,** *v. nonce-wd.* [f. L. *tranquill-us* + -(I)FY.] *trans.* = TRANQUILLIZE 1.

**1683** E. HOOKER *Pref. Pordage's Mystic Div.* 92 Whom..the allwise, allmighti and most mercifull God mai..sanctifi, tranquillifi and felicifi.

† **Tranqui·llitate,** *v. Obs. rare*$^{-1}$. [f. L. *tranquillitāt-em* (see next), or obs. F. *tranquilliter* (Cotgr.): see -ATE [3] 7.] *trans.* = TRANQUILLIZE.

**1657** TOMLINSON *Renou's Disp.* 629 Theriack complects all antidotes, which..tranquillitate diseases.

**Tranquillity** (træŋkwi·lĭti). Also 4–7 with *y* for *i*, *l* for *ll*, *-te*, *-tee*, *-tye*, *-tie* for *-ty*; 7–9 **tranquility.** [a. F. *tranquillité* (12th c. in Hatz.-Darm.), ad. L. *tranquillitāt-em*, f. *tranquill-us* TRANQUIL: see -ITY.] The quality or state of being tranquil; freedom from disturbance or agitation; serenity, calmness; quietness, peacefulness. **a.** Of the mind or affairs.

*c* **1374** CHAUCER *Boeth.* II. pr. iv. 29 (Camb. MS.) By tranquillite [*v. r.* -tee] of thi sowle. **1432–50** tr. *Higden* (Rolls) IV. 29 Lyvenge in peace and tranquillite after that tyme. **1535** COVERDALE *Prov.* xi. 23 The iust laboure for peace and tranquylite. **1610** DONNE *Pseudo-martyr* 17 That Court which is, *forum spirituale*, considers the publique tranquility. **1651** HOBBES *Leviath.* I. vi. 29 There is no such thing as perpetuall Tranquillity of mind, while we live here. **1838** THIRLWALL *Greece* II. xi. 27 A preliminary step toward the restoration of tranquillity. **1866** GEO. ELIOT *F. Holt* i, The tiny birds..hopped about in perfect tranquillity.

**b.** Of the weather, the elements, etc.

*c* **1450** tr. *De Imitatione* III. xxvii, Sey to..þe norþen wynde, 'blowe not'; & þere shal be gret tranquillite. **1545** JOYE *Exp. Dan.* Ep. Ded. A ij, Therfore is this tranquilite of the sea for that litle tyme, as a trwce taking in the winter, called the halcions dayes. **1748** *Anson's Voy.* I. viii. 82 We fully expected..to have experienced the celebrated tranquillity of the Pacifick Ocean. **1823** WORDSW. '*A volant Tribe of Bards*', The intense tranquillity Of silent hills, and more than silent sky. *a* **1854** H. REED *Lect. Eng. Lit.* x. (1855) 336 Bearing in..its own deep tranquillity, the reflection of the tranquillity of the heavens.

**Tranquillization** (træ:ŋkwiləizēⁱ·ʃən). [f. next + -ATION.] The action of tranquillizing.

**1797** W. TAYLOR in *Monthly Mag.* IV. 335 The conquest of Jerusalem, once accomplished, it would be natural for the Assyrian court to foster its tranquillization. **1850** HT. MARTINEAU *Hist. Peace* II. v. v. 256 How confidently did they..conclude that the tranquillization of Ireland was achieved! **1868** BRIGHT *Sp. Ireland* 14 Mar. (1878) 208, I was satisfied that was not the path of tranquillisation.

**Tranquillize** (træ·ŋkwiləiz), *v.* Also 8–9 **-ilise.** [f. TRANQUIL + -IZE, or ad. F. *tranquilliser* (15–16th c. in Hatz.-Darm.).]

**1.** *trans.* To render tranquil; to calm, soothe.

**1623** COCKERAM, *Tranquillize*, to quiet or pacifie. **1748** THOMSON *Cast. Indol.* II. xix, Joys without a name, That, while they rapture, tranquillize the mind. **1782** MISS BURNEY *Cecilia* VIII. ii, Tranquillize, I conjure you, your agitated spirits. **1835** WILLIS *Pencillings* I. iii. 22 It tranquillises the mind as well as the body. **1836** *Gentl. Mag.* Sept. 313/2 He [Lord Stanley] denied that the Bill..would 'tranquillize' Ireland, as it was called. **1860** TYNDALL *Glac.* I. xi. 78 A cigar which he lighted for the purpose tranquilized him.

**2.** *intr.* To become tranquil or quiet.

**1748** RICHARDSON *Clarissa* (1811) V. vii. 79 I'll try, as I ride in my chariot, to tranquillize. **1797** ANNA SEWARD *Lett.* (1811) IV. 396 How much better for England,..that hersons should tranquillize. **1814** BYRON *Corsair* II. iv. 46 'Twas but a moment's peevish hectic past Along his cheek, and tranquillised as fast.

Hence **Tra·nquillizing** *vbl. sb.* and *ppl. a.*

**1801** SOUTHEY *Thalaba* III. xxiii, The old Man tranquilly Up his curl'd pipe inhales The tranquillizing herb. **1850** LYNCH *Theo. Trinal* v. 80 Then [I] beheld the tranquillizing moon-rise. **1873** HAMERTON *Intell. Life* I. iii. (1876) 19 The tranquillizing of a sort of uneasiness.

**Tranquillizer** (træ·ŋkwiləizəɹ). [f. prec. + -ER [1].] One who or that which tranquillizes.

**1822–56** DE QUINCEY *Confess.* (1862) 241 A tranquilliser of nervous and anomalous sensations. **1891** T. HARDY *Tess* l, Nightfall..came as a tranquillizer on this March day.

‖ **Tranquillo** (traŋkwi·llo), *adv. Mus.* [It. *tranquillo* adj. TRANQUIL.] In a tranquil style or tempo; tranquilly.

**1854** *J. Schuberth's Mus. Hand-bk.* (ed. 4), *Tranquillamente, Tranquillo*, calmly, peacefully, tranquil. **1889** GROVE *Dict. Mus.*, *Tranquillo*, an Italian term, meaning 'calmly', 'quietly'. **1905** *Westm. Gaz.* 22 Apr. 12/1 Resting wilt thou Largo play, Presto or Tranquillo?

† **Tranqui·llous,** *a. Obs. rare.* Also 7 *erron.* **tranquilious.** [f. L. *tranquill-us* TRANQUIL + -OUS.] = TRANQUIL.

**1633** HEYWOOD *Rape Lucrece* Wks. 1874 V. 169 He..that may live in tranquillous pleasures. **1656** S. HOLLAND *Zara* (1719) 57 He was no foe to a tranquilious Subsistence.

Hence †**Tranqui·llousness** (Bailey, 1727, vol. II).

**Tranquilly** (træ·ŋkwili), *adv.* [f. TRANQUIL + -LY [2].] In a tranquil manner; calmly, quietly.

**1801** [see *tranquillizing*]. **1841** LANE *Arab. Nts.* I. 73 Tranquilly to sit by a mortal enemy. **1847** C. BRONTË *J. Eyre* xi, The reason they rest tranquilly in their graves now. **1851** HAWTHORNE *Snow Image*, etc., *Gt. Stone Face* (1879) 46 More years sped swiftly and tranquilly away.

**Tra·nquilness.** *rare.* [f. as prec. + -NESS.] Tranquil condition; = TRANQUILLITY. **1818** in TODD.

**Trans,** obs. form of TRANCE.

**Trans-,** *prefix.* The Latin preposition *trans*, 'across, to or on the farther side of, beyond, over', also used in comb., (1) with verbs, and their derived sbs. and adjs., e. g. *transīre* to go across, *transitio*, *transitor*, *transitus*, *transitīvus*, *transitōrius*; *transferre* to bear across, transfer, *translātus*, *translātio*, *translātor*, *translātīvus*, *translātīcius*; (2) with adjs. derived from sbs. (more strictly with sb. + adjectival suffix), as *transfluviālis* beyond the river, transfluvial, *transmarīnus* beyond sea, transmarine, *transmontānus* beyond the mountains, tramontane, *translīmitānus* beyond the boundary or frontier; esp. with adjs. in *-ānus*, *-īnus* from names of mountains, rivers, or districts, as *transalpīn-us*, *transaustrīn-us* (*Auster* south wind), *transdānubiān-us*, *transpadān-us* (*Padus* Po), *transrhēnān-us* (*Rhēnus* Rhine), *transtiberīn-us*, *transtigritān-us*. Before initial *s*, the *s* of *trans-* was generally but not always dropped, as in *transpicĕre* to look through, *tran-scendĕre* to transcend, *tran-scrībĕre* to transcribe, *tran-suĕre* to stitch through. In a number of verbs and their derivatives, *trans-* was reduced before a consonant to *trā-*, e. g. *trādĕre* to hand over, *tradūcĕre* to lead across, *trājicĕre* or *trāicĕre* to throw across, *trājectus* a crossing, *trānāre* to swim across.

In med.L. the number of these compounds was increased, and verbs formed also on sbs., as *transaccidentāre* to transpose the accidents, *transubstantiāre* to transmute the substance, *transnoctāre* to pass the night, *transviāre* to change the path or course of. They are also numerous in the modern Romanic languages. Many of the English words came through French; in OF. the inherited form was in *tres-*, as *trespasser* to trespass; the later adapted form is in *trans-*.

In English, *trans-* occurs in compounds representing those already used in Latin, and in others formed analogously from L. elements; also in compounds the second element of which is an English or other non-Latin word. The chief uses are as follows:

**1.** With the sense 'across, through, over, to or on the other side of, beyond, outside of, from one place, person, thing, or state to another': in verbs and their derivative sbs. and adjs. representing L. compounds, or formed etymologically on Latin elements; e. g. *transcolate*, *transcribe*, *transcript*, *transcription*, *transport*, *transportation*.

**2.** in verbs, etc. formed on Eng. vbs., adjs., or sbs., as *transboard*, *transearth*, *transfashion*, *tranship*, *trans-shape*, *transtime*.

**3.** in adjs. and their derivatives, representing L. adjs., or formed analogically on L. words, as *transmarine*, *transmural*; also on English sbs. or adjs., as *trans-border*, *-desert*, *-frontier*, *-polar*. These may have the sense 'across, crossing', or 'beyond, on the other side of', or both senses, as *trans-oceanic*. Special groups are:

**4.** in adjs. with the sense 'beyond, surpassing, transcending', as *transhuman*, *-material*, *-rational*.

**5.** in adjs., scientific terms (chiefly anatomical), with the sense 'through, across' (the thing denoted by the sb. implied), as *transapical*, *-frontal*, *-ocular*, *-uterine*.

**6.** in substantives with the sense 'transverse', as *trans-muscle*, *trans-stroke*. (*rare.*)

All words belonging to these six groups are treated in their alphabetical places as main words. In the two following groups *trans-* combinations are formed at pleasure, and examples only are here given with illustrative quotations in chronological order

**7.** in geographical adjs., formed on the names of rivers, seas, mountains, territories, etc., with the sense 'situated or lying beyond or on the other side of', as *trans-Adriatic*, *-Alleghanian*, *-Altaian*, *-Baikal*, *-ian*, *-Cantine* (the river Cam), *-Caspian*, *-Caucasian*, *-Danubian*, *-Egyptian*, *-Euphrat-es* (*-esian*, *-ic*), *-Gangetic* (Ganges), *-Grampian*, *-Indus*, *-Indine*, *-Jordan*, *-ic*, *-Juran* (Mt. Jura), *-Mersey*, *-Mississippi*, *-an*, *-Mosan* (R. Meuse), *-Severn*, *-Tiberine* (also *-Teverine*, It. *trasteverino*), *-Trentane* (R. Trent), *-Ural*, *-Volga*, *-Zambesian*, etc. (See also TRANSATLANTIC, TRANS-PACIFIC, TRANSKEI, TRANSLEITHAN.) Also from names of planets, *Trans-Martian*, *-Neptunian*, *-Uranian*, and in humorous nonce-use, as *trans-bedpost*.

**1612** DRAYTON *Poly-olb.* viii. 420 The Clees, like louing Twinnes,..that stand Trans-Seuerned, behold fair England tow'rds the rise. *a* **1641** BP. MOUNTAGU *Acts & Mon.* (1642) 144 Satrapaes of the Transeuphratesian Countreyes. **1655** FULLER *Hist. Camb.* (1840) 146 Monks' College..stood on the trans-Cantine side, an anchoret in itself, severed by the river from the rest of the University. **1756** C. LUCAS *Ess. Waters* II. 113 The transmosan territories of Liege. **1797** *Camb. Univ. Calendar* 18 That there cannot be a majority of transtrentane, or men born north of the Trent in the seniority. **1802** RANKEN *Hist. France* III. I. iii. 30 Burgundy Transjurane..now fell under the superiority of Germany. **1815** J. ADAMS *Wks.* (1856) X. 168 Our trans-Alleghanian States, in patriotism,..are at least equal to any in the Union. **1817** COLEBROOKE in *Trans. Linn. Soc.* XII. 352 Between the cis-gangetic and trans-gangetic regions. **1827** G. S. FABER *Sacr. Calend. Prophecy* (1844) II. 81 The transdanubian and transeuphratic conquests of Trajan. **1836** F. MAHONY *Rel. Father Prout, Barry* (1859) 503 Of an old transtiberine family, he claimed with the *trasteverini* unconditionated pedigree. **1840** MILMAN *Hist. Chr.* I. 177 On the remote border of his transjordanic territory. **1845** S. AUSTIN *Ranke's Hist. Ref.* II. 445 The generals now, under the eyes of the pope, demanded..as security for payment, the Transteverine city. **1854** MILMAN *Lat. Chr.* IV. ix. (1864) II. 424 Leo revenged himself by severing the Transadriatic provinces..from the Roman patriarchate. **1861** J. G. SHEPPARD *Fall Rome* i. 22 Pannonia was nearly equivalent to trans-Danubian Hungary. **1876** BLACKIE *Lang. & Lit. Scott. Highl.* 40 The quick sensibilities of trans-Grampian philologers. **1878** GLADSTONE *Prim. Homer* i. § 12. 15 Homer..gives an account of the trans-Egyptian Pygmæans. **1888** *Times* 9 Oct. 4/1 These outsiders..will also have to settle peacefully in the Russian Transcaspian. **1898** *Westm. Gaz.* 14 Feb. 2/1 Glimpses of the Jordan valley and the trans-Jordan hills. **1900** MARY C. WILSON *Irene Petrie* xiii. 305 A Campaign in trans-Himalayan lands. **1903** SIR H. H. JOHNSTON in *Times* 17 Feb., A Government Department..dealing with foreign (i.e., trans-Zambesian) labour.

**1852** R. GRANT *Hist. Physic. Astron.* xii. 166 M. Valz, of Marseilles, writing to M. Arago in 1835,..made the following..remarks relative to the probable existence of a Trans-Uranian planet. *Ibid.* 185 On the 2nd September, 1846, he [Mr. Adams] transmitted..an account of his further researches on the Trans-Uranian planet. **1879** *Nature* 27 Mar. 481/2 The Trans-Neptunian Planet..Observations made at Washington in 1850 of this supposed planet. **1885** CLERKE *Pop. Hist. Astron.* 98 He [Olbers] supposed that both Ceres and Pallas were fragments of a primitive trans-Martian planet.

**1864** MISS CORNWALLIS in *Sat. Rev.* XVIII. 463 Pray tell me about the trans-bedpost regions; my whole concern at present is the cis-bedpost—a very narrow domain.

**8.** in geographical adjs., formed as in 7, with the sense 'passing across, crossing', as in *trans-African*, *-Algerian*, *-American*, *-Andean* (*-ian*, *-ine*), *-Arabian*, *-Asiatic*, *-Australian*, *-Balkan*, *-Manchurian*, *-Mersey*, *-Mongolian*, *-Niger*, *-Pyrenean*, *-Saharan*, *-Siberian*, etc. Many of these occur also in sense 7.

**1880** *Nature* 4 Mar. 424/2 The future Transalgerian Railway Company. **1884** *Notes on Bks.* (Longman's) 31 May 247 The Transandine exploring and surveying expedition of 1871–2. **1886** *L'pool Courier* 16 Jan., Assisting in opening the trans-Mersey Railway. **1896** *Daily News* 30 Dec. 7/1 The trans-Siberian railway, one of the greatest engineering works of the century. **1898** *Chambers' Jrnl.* I. 543/2, 8000 feet above sea-level, the highest point to which the Trans-Andean railway had been carried. **1901** *Daily Chron.* 13 Nov. 3/3 The reported adoption..of the trans-American route for the conveyance of the Australian mails. **1903** *Ibid.* 17 Mar. 6/6 The project of a Trans-Pyrenean railway is thoroughly practicable. **1907** *Westm. Gaz.* 26 Oct. 16/3 This trans-African voyage of Mr. Savage Landor. **1908** *Edin. Rev.* July 146 The trans-Niger railway, destined to..open up to commerce a magnificent agricultural region.

*Pronunciation.* In the pronunciation of *trans-* in combination, great diversity prevails locally and individually in cultivated speech. This diversity affects both the vowel *a* and the consonant *s*.

Historically, the *a* is short (æ) as in *man*, *banns*, and it is so treated in nearly all pronouncing dictionaries. This pronunciation is retained in the north and west of England, in Scotland, in the United States, and by many speakers even in London and its surrounding area. But the general tendency in the London area to substitute for short (æ) before certain consonant groups (as in *chance*, *branch*, *demand*, *chant*, *pass*, *fast*, *ask*) the long vowel (ā) or something intermediate between (æ) and (ā), also affects *trans-*, so as to make its prevalent pronunciation (trāns) in this area, and hence to extend this pronunciation among individuals or groups in other districts. This diversity of pronunciation of original short *a* is compendiously indicated in this dictionary by the conventional symbol (ɑ), and this is accordingly used to indicate the varying pronunciation of the vowel in the *trans-* combinations. Under the stress, primary or subordinate, this (ɑ) means (æ) or (ā); when unstressed, it approaches or reaches (ǽ) or (ă), and sinks in some common words or in colloquial utterance to (ə), e. g. in *transfer* vb. (trɑnsfə̄·ɹ; trǣnsfə̄·ɹ, trănsfə̄·ɹ; trənsfə̄·ɹ).

The *s* of *trans-* is regularly (s) before a breath consonant, as in *tra·nscolate*, *transcha·nge*, *tra·nsfer*, *transfe·r*, *transpi·re*; also, of course, where *s* coalesces with initial *s* of the second element, as in *transcend*, *transcribe*, *transude*. In the South of England many use (trɑns-) in all *trans-* combinations, irrespective of what consonant or vowel follows. But many, even in the south, use (trɑnz-) before a liquid, or nasal, or any voiced consonant, and before a vowel, and this is more or less recognized by recent orthoepists. This is specially the case with the word *transact* and its derivatives, where (trɑnzæ·kt) appears to be the more prevalent pronunciation. It is to be observed also that the ordinary English school pronunciation of Latin *trans*, as a preposition and in combination, is (trænz) riming with *banns*, *plans*, and that many classical scholars retain this pronunciation in English in combinations in which the identity of the prefix with Latin *trans* is specially obvious, as in *trans-alpine*, *trans-danubian*, *trans-atlantic*, *trans-Pacific*, *trans-Jordan*, *trans-Caspian*, *trans-Siberian*. In this work (trɑns-) is given as the usual form (except in *transact*, etc.); but in words in which good authorities recognize (trɑnz-) as an alternative, this is indicated by adding (,-z-).

For the diverse treatment of *a* and *s* in these combinations, cf. Walker, Smart, Ogilvie (Annandale), Cassell's 'Encycl. Dict.', Webster, 'Century Dict.', Funk's 'Standard Dict.', and esp. Schröer *Neuenglisches Sprach-Aussprachwörterbuch*, Heidelberg, 1913, and Michaelis and Jones *A Phonetic Dictionary of the English Language*, Berlin, London, etc. 1913, in which the subject is treated by skilled observers.

**Transaccidentation** (trɑnsˌæ:ksidentē̆ⁱ·ʃən, -z-). [ad. Schol.L. *transaccidentātio* (Duns Scotus: the attribution to P. Lombardus in Marbeck is a mistake due to confounding commentary with text); after *transubstāntiātio*.] A transmutation of the accidents of the bread and wine in the Eucharist, as distinguished from *transubstantiation*, in which the substance alone is changed.

[*c* **1300** DUNS SCOTUS *Sent.* IV. xi. i. § 3 Transitio accidentis in accidens, magis diceretur transaccidentatio, quam transubstantiatio.] **1581** MARBECK *Bk. of Notes* 1101 Long after Boniface the third..did Petrus Lombardus [see above] bring vp these termes of Transmutation, and Transaccidentation. **1861** PEARSON *Early & Mid. Ages Eng.* 443 Such fables really involve a completely different doctrine, which might be called transaccidentation, but which no church has ever yet deliberately set forth. **1874** FISKE *Cosmic Philos.* I. 123 *note*, The schoolman..asserted that the individuality of the bread (its breadness) was exchanged for the individuality of Christ (his humano-divinity)... It was a noumenal, not a phenomenal change: the latter would have been [not transubstantiation, but] 'transaccidentation'.

**Transˌachero·ntic**, *a.* [TRANS- 7.] Lying beyond Acheron, a fabled river of the infernal regions; cf. TRANS-STYGIAN.

**1854** *Fraser's Mag.* XLIX. 88 His confused and monstrous transacherontic realm of life-after-death.

**Transact** (trɑnzæ·kt, trɑns-), *sb.* Now *dial.* Also 9 *Sc.* **-ack, -ac'**. [f. TRANSACT *v.*, or ad. L. *transactum* a thing completed, a transaction.] A transaction.

**1659** *New Lords Winding-Sheet* 4 The Transacts of Colonel John Barkstead hath been taken into consideration. **1871** W. ALEXANDER *Johnny Gibb* xli, We sit owre lang gin ance we begin an' clatter aboot our nain transacks. **1887** D. GRANT *Sc. Stories* (1888) 62 The followin' conversation wud tak' place in the coorse o' transac'.

**Transact** (trɑnzæ·kt, trɑns-), *v.* [f. L. *transact-*, ppl. stem of *transigĕre* to drive through, accomplish, f. TRANS- + *agĕre* to drive, do, act.]

**1.** *intr.* To carry through negotiations; to have dealings, do business; to treat; also, to manage or settle affairs. Now *rare.*

**1584-5** *Reg. Privy Council Scot.* III. 723 Quha..transactit and agreit with Mr. Patrik Gaittis..and be vertew thairof hes obtenit collatioun. **1623** BINGHAM *Xenophon* 79 The Trapezuntines..gaue the Grecians gifts of hospitalitie... They transacted likewise for the next neighbour Colchans. **1658-9** in *Burton's Diary* (1828) IV. 13 The last Parliament would never transact with them as Lords. We were turned out for it. **1683** CAVE *Ecclesiastici*, *Athanasius* 109 They transact Synodically in separate Assemblies. **1750** JOHNSON *Rambler* No. 74 ¶ 1 That..we may secure the love of those with whom we transact. **1872** SYMONDS *Introd. Stud. Dante* 266 Dante denounced the enemies of his country in his Comedy, and refused to transact with them.

**b.** *fig.* (Usually *dyslogistic.*) To have to do, to compromise.

**1888** *Athenæum* 24 Nov. 693/1 The plan..of 'transacting' with political convictions by acquiescence in, if not actually serving, governments the legitimacy of which the politician in his heart..denies. **1890** *Sat. Rev.* 4 Jan. 15/2 In his criticism..he seems to us a little to 'transact' with cant, or even not quite to have cleared his own mind of it. *Ibid.* 15 Nov. 571/1 He does not make the slightest attempt to 'transact' with naturalism or explain away the supernatural.

**2.** *trans.* To carry through, perform (an action, etc.); to manage (an affair); now *esp.* to carry on, conduct, do (business).

**1635** HEYLIN *Sabbath* II. (1636) 190 Provided..that the change be so transacted, that it produce no scandall or confusion in the Church of God. **1649** CROMWELL *Let.* Nov., Whilst these things have been thus transacting [= being transacted] here. **1709** STEELE *Tatler* No. 94 ¶ 1 In the Country wherein the Circumstances were transacted. **1751** JOHNSON *Rambler* No. 100 ¶ 1 Ignorance of what is transacting among the polite part of Mankind. **1776** ADAM SMITH *W. N.* I. ix. (1869) I. 99 A country fully stocked in proportion to all the business it had to transact. **1817** JAS. MILL *Brit. India* II. IV. v. 211 Affairs of no trivial importance were transacting in the Council.

**3.** To deal in or with; to traffic in, negotiate about; to handle, treat; to discuss. *arch.*

**1654** FULLER *Ephemeris Parl.* (title-p.), Containing the severall Speeches, Cases, and Arguments of Law transacted between his Majesty and both Houses. **1712** ARBUTHNOT *John Bull* II. iv, To have these usurers transact my debts at coffee-houses, and ale-houses; as if I were going to break up shop. **1767** S. PATERSON *Another Trav.* I. 406 Great sums are transacted. **1848** THACKERAY *Van. Fair* xxvi, While these delicacies were being transacted below.

†**4.** To carry, hand, or take over; to transfer.

[Cf. med.L. *transactāre* = *transferre* (1242 in Du Cange).]

**1621** ELSING *Debates Ho. Lords* (Camden) 71 The cause to be brought before us by *habeas corpus cum causa*, or the case to be transacted to the Kinge, and he to determyne yt. **1653** MANTON *Exp. James* i. 13 God's transacting our sin upon Christ is most satisfying to the Spirit. **1889** *Science* 29 Nov. 374 A paper..from which the following passages are transacted.

Hence **Transa·cted** *ppl. a.*, **Transa·cting** *vbl. sb.*

**1686** tr. *Chardin's Trav. Persia* 20 In all their Transacting together. **1752** J. LOUTHIAN *Form of Process* (ed. 2) App. 286 For transacted Processes and Decreets, the one Half of what they would have amounted to if extracted. **1854** J. GUTHRIE *Life J. Arminius* Pref. 2 There are other..transacted lives, which not to know..is a loss to the world. **1876** H. K. WOOD *Highw. Salvation* v. 69 There is the direct and personal transacting of a soul with the Saviour.

**Transa·ct**, *ppl. a. rare*⁻¹. [ad. L. *transact-us*, pa. pple. of *transigĕre*: see TRANSACT *v.*] Transacted. (Const. as pa. pple.)

**1854** SYD. DOBELL *Balder* xxviii, Night by night, when ..that mysterious sorrow is transact Unseen, and there is weeping in the air.

**Transaction** (trɑnzæ·kʃən, trɑns-). [ad. L. *transactiōn-em*, n. of action f. *transigĕre*: see prec. Cf. F. *transaction* (13th c. in Godef. *Compl.*).]

**1.** *Roman* and *Civil Law.* The adjustment of a dispute between parties by mutual concession; compromise; hence *gen.* an arrangement, an agreement, a covenant. Now *Hist.* exc. as in 3 c.

*c* **1460** *Oseney Reg.* 84 A stryfe..i-stered bytwene thabbot of Eynesham and N. clerke of Karsynton and thabbot of Oseney... In this maner in owr presence, be transaction, to be decidid. **1611** COTGR., *Transaction*, a transaction, accord, agreement, attonement. **1615** in *Buccleuch MSS.* (Hist. MSS. Comm. 1899) I. 167 [The Spice Trade] is appropriated to the Hollanders as well by right of Conquest as by Transaction. **1631** MASSINGER *Emperor East* III. iv, In this transaction, Drawn in express and formal terms, I have Given and consigned into your hands..my dear Eudocia! **1786** A. GIB *Sacr. Contempl.* i. 31 A covenant is a transaction between two parties.

**2.** The action of transacting or fact of being transacted; the carrying on or completion of an action or course of action; † the accomplishment of a result (*obs.*).

**1655** *Nicholas Papers* (Camden) II. 286 His carriadge in the transaction of the peace betweene the people of these countryes and Cromwell. **1658** PHILLIPS, *Transaction*, a finishing, or dispatching any businesse. **1782** MISS BURNEY *Cecilia* III. v, After the transaction of this affair. **1844** L. WOODS *Ch. Govt.* ii. 44 Any direction of Christ or..of his apostles respecting the transaction of business in the church.

**3.** That which is or has been transacted; an affair in course of settlement or already settled; a piece of business; in *pl.* doings, proceedings, dealings. Also *fig.*

**1647** CLARENDON *Hist. Reb.* I. § 18 Discoursing of the Court of France, and the transactions there. *a* **1656** BP. HALL *Serm.* 2 *Pet.* i. 10 Wks. 1837 V. 578 In our transactions with men, when we have an honest man's word for a bargain, we think it safe. **1726** SHELVOCKE *Voy. round World* Contents 1 Our most remarkable transactions there. **1755** DODDRIDGE *Hymn*, '*O happy day, that fixed my choice*' iii, 'Tis done; the great transaction's done; I am my Lord's, and He is mine. **1834** L. RITCHIE *Wand. by Seine* 192 Every marriage, every baptism, every fête, is a public transaction. **1863** MARY HOWITT *F. Bremer's Greece* I. i. 19 Every remarkable transaction obtained its stone-tablet on the Acropolis.

†**b.** A physical operation, action, or process.

**1662** SOUTH *Serm.* (1697) I. 49 There is not the least transaction of sense and motion in the whole man. **1794** J. HUTTON *Philos. Light* 261 Inertia is the law of action and passion by which motion is translated from one body to another..and, in this transaction, the rule observed is the actual weight of the bodies.

**c.** *Theol.* In reference to the Atonement, 'transaction' has been used in senses ranging from 1 to 3. (In sense 1 chiefly in deprecation.)

**1861** ABP. THOMSON *Aids to Faith* viii. 351 There is the danger lest the Atonement degenerate into a transaction between a righteous Father on the one side, and a loving Saviour on the other, because in the human transaction from which the analogy is drawn two distinct parties are concerned. **1876** MOZLEY *Serm.* viii. (1879) 169 Now I have nothing to do here with the mystery of this transaction; the question is the morality of it—how the act of one person can alter God's regards toward another. **1901** MOBERLY *Atonement & Personality* vii. 138 They seem to make atonement a transaction, historical, final, consummated long ago:—a transaction (I do not ask at this moment between whom; but..) far anterior to, and wholly outside of, the reality of ourselves. **1901** SANDAY *Life Christ in rec. Res.* v. ix. (1907) 249 So much at least seems to follow.., that the Scriptures do recognize a mysterious something which, in our imperfect human language, may be described as a 'transaction'.

†**4.** The action of passing or making over a thing from one person, thing, or state to another; transference. *Obs.*

*a* **1608** SIR F. VERE *Comm.* 69 Her Majesty being in hand with the States to make a transaction from the old treaty to the new. **1613-18** DANIEL *Hist. Eng.* (1621) 16 Putting on each others apparel and armes .. as if they made transaction of their persons each to other. *c* **1645** HOWELL *Lett.* (1650) II. II. 20 The transaction of these Provinces which the King of Spaine made as a dowry to the Archduke Albertus. **1691** SIR T. P. BLOUNT *Ess.* v. 127 Did not Commerce..by a continual Motion and Transaction render it [the world] wholesome, and profitable.

†**5.** The action of dealing with or handling a subject; treatment. Cf. TRANSACT *v.* 3. *Obs. rare.*

**1646** JER. TAYLOR *Apol. Liturgy* Pref. § 26 Those..Epistles and Gospels before the Communion..are Scriptures of the choicest, and most profitable transaction.

**6.** *pl.* The record of its proceedings published by a learned society. Rarely in *sing.* Cf. PROCEEDING *vbl. sb.* 2 c.

**1665** (*title*) Philosophical Transactions: Giving some Accompt of the present Undertakings, Studies, and Labours of the Ingenious in many considerable Parts of the World. *Ibid.* I. 75 In the first papers of these Transactions. *a* **1680** BUTLER *Rem.* (1759) I. 14 They all..Agreed to draw up th' Instrument, And..To print it in the next Transaction. **1805** *Phil. Trans.* XCV. p. iii, To reconsider the papers read before them, and select..such as they should judge most proper for publication in the future Transactions. **1877** A. B. EDWARDS *Up Nile* Pref. 8 The pages of scientific journals and the transactions of learned societies.

**Transactional** (trɑnzæ·kʃənăl, trɑns-), *a.* [f. prec. + -AL; cf. F. *transactionnel* (Littré).] Of, pertaining to, of the nature of, or involving a transaction; taking place in fact or reality.

**1858** BUSHNELL *Serm. New Life* 94 A relation wholly transactional. **1894** *Thinker* V. 155 The transactional revelation of principles and forces which are essential and eternal.

**b.** *Theol.*: see TRANSACTION 3 c.

**1901** MOBERLY *Atonement & Personality* ix. 218 What the thought of the present day would sum up as the 'transactional' theory of the atonement. **1901** SANDAY *Life Christ in rec. Res.* v ix. (1907) 244 The 'transactional' theory [of the Atonement]. **1905** *Speaker* 4 Feb. 440/2 The Atonement understood in an entirely forensic or 'transactional' sense.

Hence **Transa·ctionally** *adv.*, by means, or by way of a transaction; practically.

**1865** BUSHNELL *Vicar. Sacr.* IV. i. (1868) 452 The object is to give him a lesson transactionally. **1874** — *Forgiven. & Law* 59 Is it true that God must be gained or tempered transactionally, that is by acts in time, in order to the letting forth of grace upon his enemies?

**Transa:ctionee·r.** *nonce-wd.* [f. as prec. + -EER.] One who is concerned or has to do with transactions; in quots., with the published 'transactions' of a learned society.

**1700** (*title*) The Transactioneer, with some of his Philosophical Fancies; in two Dialogues. [A satire on Sir Hans Sloane and the Philosophical Transactions, by W. King, LL.D.] *Ibid.* Pref. 4, I have no personal Prejudice to the present Transactioneer or any of his Friends. **1700** J. RAY in *Lett. Lit. Men* (Camden) 205 The scurrilous Pamphlet entitled the *Transactioneer*.

**Transactor** (trɑnzæ·ktəɹ, trɑns-). [a. L. *transactor*, agent-n. f. *transigĕre*: see TRANSACT *v.*] One who transacts; a negotiator or intermediary; a manager, conductor, performer, doer.

**1611** COTGR., *Transacteur*, a transactor, dayes-man, accorder. **1653** J. HALL *Paradoxes* 159 He was a great Transactour for the Essex faction. **1660** MILTON *Pres. Means* Wks. 1851 V. 457 The transactors of our Affairs with forein Nations. **1863** KINGLAKE *Crimea* I. i. 7 Not a mere favourite of his sovereign, but the actual transactor of public business.

**Transalpine** (trɑnsˌæ·lpəin, -z-), *a.* (*sb.*) [ad. L. *transalpīnus* beyond or across the Alps, f. *trans*; TRANS- + *alpīnus* Alpine, f. *Alpēs* the Alps.]

**1.** That is situated beyond the Alps: **a.** Originally and usually as viewed from Rome or Italy, i. e. north of the Alps; also, dwelling in or belonging to a region beyond the Alps; also † *transf.* rude, uncultured (*obs.*). Cf. TRAMONTANE A. 1, 1 b.

**1590** GREENE *Orl. Fur.* (1599) 16 Found in the mountaines of Transalpine France. **1656** EARL MONM. tr *Boccalini's Advts. fr. Parnass.* I. xxiii. (1674) 23 Trans-Alpin writers, whose brains are thought to lie in their backs. **1659** LOVELACE *Poems* (1864) 225 Where then,..Lies our transalpine barbarous neglect? **1825** C. BUTLER *Bk. Rom. Cath. Ch.* 120 There certainly are some Transalpine territories in which the Cisalpine opinions on papal power prevail. **1837** WHEWELL *Hist. Induct. Sc.* (1857) III. 246 The first transalpine garden of this kind arose at Leyden in 1577. **1841** W. SPALDING *Italy & It. Isl.* I. 36 The Po is the only Italian river which can be compared with those of transalpine Europe. **1854** MILMAN *Lat. Chr.* VI. i. (1864) III. 373 Synods of Transalpine prelates, as at Rheims.

**b.** Beyond the Alps from England, or from Europe generally; Italian.

**1624** [SCOTT] *Votivæ Angliæ* Ded. 3 Those fiery Transalpine, and factious Transmarine English, who haue onely their bodies here, but their harts in Rome and Spaine. **1632** J. HOWELL in *Biondi's Eromena* b iij, So have I seen Transalpin grafts to grow, And beare rare fruit, remov'd to

Thames from Po. 1656 BLOUNT *Glossogr.*, *Transalpine*.., over or beyond the Alpes, forreign, Italian, on the further side of the mountains. 1718 ROWE *Prol. to Non-Juror* 34 To your Transalpine master's rule resort, And fill an empty abdicated court. 1765 WILKES *Let. fr. Naples* in *Corr. & Mem.* (1805) II. 200 This is my fourth letter to you since I have been transalpine.

c. Of or pertaining to the party in the Roman Church opposed to the Ultramontanes.

1794 in B. Ward *Dawn Cath. Revival* (1909) II. 63 The doctrine of the Deposing and Dispensing power of the Pope, ..doctrines which have for above a century been distinguished by the names of Ultramontane and Transalpine. 1826 [implied in TRANSALPINELY].

2. (Passing) across the Alps. *rare*.

1654 H. L'ESTRANGE *Chas. I* (1655) 104 In his Trans-Alpine expedition. 1744 in *10th Rep. Hist. MSS. Comm.* App. I. 282, I hope the K. of Sard$^a$ will harrass the Fr. and Sp$^{ds}$ in their transalpine march.

B. *sb.* A native or inhabitant of a country beyond or across the Alps: cf. 1 a and b above. *rare*.

1617 MORYSON *Itin.* III. 47 Old Writers..write, that the Diuine Law came from Italy to the Transalpines. 1622 BURTON *Descr. Leicester.* 92 Though those Transalpines account vs *Tramontani*, rude and barbarous,..yet may compare either with their olde Dante, Petrarch, or Boccace. 1634 W. TIRWHYT tr. *Balzac's Lett.* (vol. I.) 85 Those wise Transalpines themselves.., who thinke all such to be Scythians who are not Italians.

Hence **Trans,a·lpinely** *adv.* (cf. sense 1 c); † **Trans,a·lpiner** *Obs. rare* = TRANSALPINE B.

1826 G. S. FABER *Diffic. Romanism* (1853) 195 *note*, I recollect the practical cisalpine argument of Almain, from the flat judicial contradictoriness of the two *transalpinely infallible Popes, Nicolas III. and John XXII. 1599 NASHE *Lenten Stuffe* Wks. (Grosart) V. 238 As touching butter and cheese, the Hollanders cry By your leaue wee must goe before you, and the *Transalpiners with their lordly Parmasin..shoulder in for the vpper hand as hotly. 1657 EARL MONM. tr. *Paruta's Pol. Disc.* II. ix. 179 That all Transalpiners might be driven out of Italy, was a thing desired.. by all Italians.

**Transame**, obs. form of TRANSOM.

† **Trans,a·nimate**, *v. Obs. rare.* [Back-formation from next: see -ATE$^3$.] *trans.* To transfer the soul of (a person) from one body to another (also with the soul as obj.): = METEMPSYCHOSE *v.* Hence † **Transa·nimated** *ppl. a.*

1608 BP. J. KING *Serm.* 5 Nov. 31 The..strangest μετεμψύχωσις that euer was feigned by Poets, very incarnated, transanimated devils. 1613 PURCHAS *Pilgrimage* IV. xvii. 376 This Deuill doth transanimate his soule..into a dogge or other beast. 1625 — *Pilgrims* V. viii. § 3. 540 Being metamorphosed and transanimated from men to blockes. *a* 1641 BP. MOUNTAGU *Acts & Mon.* vii. (1642) 409 According to their beliefe, wicked mens soules be not transanimated at all.

**Tra·ns,anima·tion.** Now *rare.* [ad. med.L. *transanimātiōn-em* (410 in Jerome Epistle 124, 4), f. TRANS- + *anima* soul: see -TION.] Transmigration of the soul; = METEMPSYCHOSIS.

1574 EDEN tr. *Taisner's Bk. Navig.* Ded. (Arb.) p. xlvii, Yf it may be graunted..that the spirites of dead men may reuiue in other (after the opinion and transanimation of Pythagoras). 1612 SELDEN *Illustr. Drayton's Polyolb.* i. 14 This Pythagorean opinion of transanimation (I have like liberty to naturalize that word). 1727 A. HAMILTON *New Acc. E. Ind.* II. liii. 270 They have many Sects among them, but all agree in the Transanimation of Souls.

*fig.* 1871 EARLE *Philol. Eng. Tongue* vi. 241 As the pronoun passes into the still more subtle conjunction—so also do verbs graduate from particular to general use. Nor does the transanimation stop here.

**Transapical** (trans,æ·pikăl, -ē·pikăl), *a. Bot.* [f. TRANS- 5 + L. *apex, apic-em*, APEX: see APICAL.] Transverse to the apical axis (of a diatom).

1900 B. D. JACKSON *Gloss. Bot. Terms* 273 *Transapical*, ..at right angles to the apical axis, passing through the centre of the pervalvar (main longitudinal) axis of a Diatom; *transapical Plane*, the plane at right angles to both valvar and apical planes, passing through the pervalvar and transapical axis (O. Mueller).

**Trans,aqua·tic**, *a. rare.* [f. TRANS- 3: cf. AQUATIC.] Situated across the water or sea; transmarine.

1834 *Oxf. Univ. Mag.* I. 175 A durable connection between the mother country and her transaquatic daughters.

**Trans-atla·ntal**, *a. Anat.* [f. TRANS- 5 + L. *atlas, atlant-em* (see ATLAS) + -AL.] Transverse to, or crossing the atlas (vertebra).

1893 *Athenæum* 25 Mar. 382/2 Abnormal vertebræ of certain Ranidæ..in which the so-called 'atlas' possessed transverse processes and trans-atlantal nerves.

**Tra·nsatla·ntic** (trans,-, tranz,-), *a.*, *sb.* [f. TRANS- + ATLANTIC; cf. F. *transatlantique*.]

1. Passing or extending across the Atlantic Ocean.

1779 WILKES *Corr.* (1805) V. 212 After a long fruitless trans-atlantic voyage. 1892 *Chambers' Encycl.* IX. 403/2 In 1839 Mr. Samuel Cunard..came over to England from Halifax, determined to establish..a line of transatlantic steamships. 1895 *N. Amer. Rev.* Nov. 514 Of the utmost importance to all transatlantic travellers.

2. Situated or resident in, or pertaining to a region beyond the Atlantic; chiefly in European use: = American.

1782 JEFFERSON *Writ. & Corr.* (1894) III. 193 To suggest a doubt..whether nature has enlisted herself as a cis- or trans-Atlantic partisan. 1782 SIR W. JONES in *Mem.*, etc. (1804) 217 The sturdy transatlantic yeomanry, will neither be dragooned nor bamboozled out of their liberty. 1807 W. IRVING *Salmag.* xii. (1824) 199 His hat had the true trans-Atlantic declination towards his right ear. 1812 *Gen. Hist.* in *Ann. Reg.* 161/2 The civil war kindled in those regions between the native and transatlantic Spaniards. 1891 *Harper's Weekly* 19 Sept. 705/1 Salem had an aristocracy. The aristocrats were proud of their transatlantic ancestries.

B. *sb.* (absol. use of adj.): One who or that which is across the Atlantic; a native or inhabitant of a transatlantic country; *spec.* an American; also short for 'transatlantic steamer'.

1826 *Blackw. Mag.* Aug. 325/1 The Trans-Atlantics may hope to have some future share of European civilization. 1831 SCOTT *Jrnl.* (1890) II. 402 Count Robert, who is progressing, as the Transatlantics say, at a very slow pace indeed. 1883 *Contemp. Rev.* Aug. 227 A bed in a sleeping-carriage or a berth in a transatlantic. 1892 *Pall Mall G.* 17 Aug. 2/3 Cork, Killarney, and Dublin are this year crowded with transatlantics.

Hence **Trans,atla·ntically** *adv.*, in a transatlantic or American manner; in quot. 1846, across or while crossing the Atlantic; **Trans,atla·ntican, Trans,-atlantician** (-i·ʃăn) = TRANSATLANTIC B.; **Trans,-atla·nticism**, transatlantic character, nationality, or behaviour; a transatlantic or American idiom.

1846 *Blackw. Mag.* Apr. 501/1 [He] might, at that moment, be *transatlantically regaling himself at my particular expense. 1885 *Athenæum* 3 Jan. 10/2 She..had what is Transatlantically called 'a good time'. 1908 *Sat. Rev.* 25 July 120/1 It is transatlantically epigrammatic without being transatlantically smart. 1897 *Harper's Mag.* Apr. 724 English attentions to *transatlanticans savor either of patronage or servility. 1839 *Fraser's Mag.* XIX. 467 What has a *Transatlantician to do with European squabbles? 1907 *Daily Chron.* 16 Sept. 4/4 Trans-Atlanticians..are those who cross between New York and Liverpool or Southampton at least once a year. 1858 MOTLEY *Corr.* 6 June, The portentous aspect on the commonest occasions..which is apt to characterise *transatlanticism. 1895 *Pall Mall G.* 17 Oct. 4/1 The phrase..is only one more trans-Atlanticism.

**Trans,au·dient**, *a. nonce-wd.* [f. TRANS- + L. *audient-em* hearing, pr. pple. of *audīre* to hear; after *transparent*.] Permitting the passage of sound; capable of being heard through.

1854 LOWELL *Camb. 30 Yrs. Ago* Prose Wks. 1890 I. 80 Many a proprietor regretted the transaudient properties of canvas, which allowed the frugal public to share in the melody without entering the booth.

**Transboa·rd**, *v. rare.* [f. TRANS- 2 + BOARD *v.* 3.] *trans.* To transfer from one ship or vessel into another; to tranship.

1807 J. BARLOW *Columb.* VI. 38 Barks after barks the captured seamen bear, Transboard and lodge thy silent victims there. 1899 *Scribner's Mag.* July 69/1 The boat..for this [postal] service..is equipped with spacious mail-rooms, chutes for transboarding sacks [etc.].

**Trans-bo·rder**, *a.* [f. TRANS- 3 + BORDER *sb.*] Lying or living beyond a (or the) border; occupying territory outside the border.

1897 L. J. TROTTER *Life J. Nicholson* xv. (1908) 213 Younghusband was speaking about him to a trans-border chief. 1901 *19th Cent.* Apr. 711 Raised in fixed proportion from the transborder and cisborder clans. 1908 *Westm. Gaz.* 6 May 2/2 An Afghan..may be what, on the North-West Frontier, is called a 'Trans-border Pathan'—i.e., one of the independent tribes dwelling between British India and the Ameer of Kabul's territory.

**Transcalent** (tra·ns,kălĕnt, trans,kē·lĕnt), *a.* [f. TRANS- + L. *călēnt-em*, pr. pple. of *călēre* to be hot, to glow: see CALENT.

Etymologically the pronunciation is *tra·nscălent*; *transcā·lent* comes by false analogy with *translū·cent* and *transpā·rent* (in which the vowel is etymologically long).]

Having the property of freely transmitting radiant heat; pervious to heat-rays; diathermanous.

1834 E. TURNER *Elem. Chem.* (ed. 4) 107 Rock salt is remarkably diathermanous or transcalent. 1880 *Contemp. Rev.* Mar. 373 All bodies, so far at least as the heat of the sun is concerned, are more or less transcalent. 1896 *Allbutt's Syst. Med.* I. 269 The air rich in water vapour is less transcalent and translucent than in drier regions.

Hence **Tra·ns,calency**, the property of being transcalent; diathermaneity. 1864 in WEBSTER.

**Trans,calescent** (-kăle·sĕnt), *a. rare.* [f. TRANS- + L. *calēscent-em*, pr. pple. of *calēscĕre* to grow hot, to glow; cf. prec., and *fluorescent*.] Properly, Beginning to be transcalent; but in quot. = TRANSCALENT. So **Tra·ns,cale·scence**, the property of being transcalescent.

1850 GROVE *Corr. Phys. Forces* (ed. 2) 42 Bodies..shew a remarkable difference between their transcalescence, or power of transmitting heat, and their transparency... Rock-salt, the most transcalescent body known, may be covered with soot..and yet be found capable of transmitting..heat.

**Transcend** (transe·nd), *v.* Also 5-6 -send(e, (6 transsend). [ad. L. *tran(s)scend-ĕre* to climb over or beyond, surmount, f. TRANS- + *scand-ĕre* to climb. So OF. *transcender, -scendre* (14th c.).]

† 1. *trans.* To pass over or go beyond (a physical obstacle or limit); to climb or get over the top of (a wall, mountain, etc.). *Obs.*

1513 BRADSHAW *St. Werburge* II. 1461 That we may transcende this ryuer safe and sure. 1536 BELLENDEN *Cron. Scot.* (1821) I. 251 Gif ony Pichtis transcendit this dike to be punist na les than thay had offendit aganis the majeste of Romanis. 1602 FULBECKE *Pandectes* 4 In haruest he [the sun] transcendeth the other line of the Æquator and so being farre remoued from vs causeth winter. 1615 G. SANDYS *Trav.* IV. 254 Mountaines not to be transcended without much difficulty. 1695 LD. PRESTON *Boeth.* IV. 161, I have nimble Wings which can Transcend the Polar Height.

2. To pass or extend beyond or above (a non-physical limit); to go beyond the limits of (something immaterial); to exceed.

*a* 1340 HAMPOLE *Psalter* lx. 6 Þai ere a day þat contenys and transcendis þe warldis of all generaciouns. 1534 WHITINTON *Tullyes Offices* I. (1540) 45 They without doubt transende the due bonde of measure. 1559 W. CUNNINGHAM *Cosmogr. Glasse* 10 It transsendith the knowledge of man. 1643 BAKER *Chron.*, *Hen. VI* 75 He had transcended his Commission. 1662 STILLINGFL. *Orig. Sacr.* III. i. § 5 Infinity transcends our capacity of apprehension. 1713 YOUNG *Last Day* I. 48 'Twill raise thy wonder, but transcend thy praise. 1805 FOSTER *Ess.* IV. iii. 161 A genius almost transcending human nature. 1855 H. SPENCER *Princ. Psychol.* II. xvii. § 81 Unable as we are to transcend consciousness. 1875 JOWETT *Plato* (ed. 2) IV. 124 Ideas..derived from external objects as well as transcending them.

b. *Theol.* To be above and independent of: esp. said of the Deity in relation to the universe; see TRANSCENDENCE 1 b.

1898 ILLINGWORTH *Divine Immanence* iii. 71 It is through this power of self-consciousness..that spirit transcends matter. *Ibid.* 72 The divine presence..will be the presence of a spirit, which infinitely transcends the material order, yet sustains and indwells it the while. 1907 — *Doctr. Trinity* x. 196 On the other hand, we may..think of God as dwelling in the universe, without in any way transcending it. This means pantheism of one kind or another.

† c. *intr.* To go beyond, go farther. *Obs. rare*$^{-1}$.

1629 PARKINSON *Paradisi* (1904) 529 Hauing thus furnished you out a Kitchen Garden..let me a little transcend, and.. furnish them with some few other herbes.

3. *trans.* To go beyond in some respect, quality, or attribute; to rise above, surpass, excel, exceed.

*c* 1430 LYDG. *Min. Poems* (Percy Soc.) 8 In sighte transendyng alle erthely creatures. *a* 1529 SKELTON *Dethe Erle Northumbld.* 144 Transendyng far myne homly Muse. 1615 G. SANDYS *Trav.* I. 7 They imitate the Italians, but transcend them in their revenges. 1679 PENN *Addr. Prot.* II. i. (1692) 59 The Roman Church hath chiefly transcended other Societies in these Errors. 1766 FORDYCE *Serm. Yng. Wom.* (1767) I. vi. 222 Thy merits..far transcend them all. 1864 BURTON *Scot Abr.* II. ii. 191 The Poles also..strive to transcend one another in civility. 1866 R. M. FERGUSON *Electr.* (1870) 11 Electro-magnets far transcend permanent magnets in power.

† 4. *intr.* To ascend, go up, rise; to pass upward or onward. Also *fig.* *Obs.*

1513 BRADSHAW *St. Werburge* I. 190 Begyn we shall At the Cytee of Chester..And so transcendynge vp towarde Shrewysbury. *a* 1560 ROLLAND *Crt. Venus* II. 604 Bot quhen sic folk abone thair stait transcend. 1596 SIR J. DAVIES *Orchestra* cxii, Shee wheeles about, and ere the daunce doth end, Into her former place shee doth transcend. 1613 HEYWOOD *Silver Age* III. i. Wks. 1874 III. 135 Thy flowers thou canst not spare, thy bosome lend, On which to rest whil'st Phœbus doth transcend.

† b. *trans.* To ascend, to mount into. *Obs. rare.*

1601 B. JONSON *Poetaster* V. ii, It will be thought a thing ridiculous..that any poet..should, with decorum, transcend Cæsars chair.

5. *intr.* To be transcendent; to excel. *arch.*

1635 SWAN *Spec. M.* vii. § 3 (1643) 344 So one mans knowledge..transcends not seldome above the rest. *a* 1720 SHEFFIELD (Dk. Buckhm.) *Wks.* (1753) I. 260, I see no such distinction, nor wherein Man so transcends, except in arrogance. 1819 SCOTT *Ivanhoe* xxxiii, 'Thou art a mad knave', said the Captain, 'but thy plan transcends!'

† 6. *trans.* To cause to ascend or rise; to lift, elevate. *Obs. rare.*

1635 HEYWOOD *Hierarch.* VIII. 530 To that People thou a Law hast giv'n, Which from grosse earth transcendeth them to heav'n.

**Transcendence** (transe·ndĕns). [ad. med.L. *transcendentia*, f. L. *transcendent-em* TRANSCENDENT: see -ENCE. Cf. F. *transcendance* (18th c.).]

1. The action or fact of transcending, surmounting, or rising above; † ascent, elevation (*obs.*); excelling, surpassing; also, the condition or quality of being transcendent, surpassing eminence or excellence: = TRANSCENDENCY.

1601 SHAKS. *All's Well* II. iii. 40 In a most weake—..And debile minister, great power, great transcendence. 1644 DIGBY *Nat. Soul* x. § 7 There is a transcendence from science to science. 1678 *Lively Oracles* II. xix, God, in whom all those qualifications are united, and that in their utmost transcendences. 1744 HARRIS *Three Treat.* III. II. (1765) 215 That very Transcendence is an Argument on its behalf. 1802 ANNA SEWARD *Lett.* (1811) VI. 27 When we reflect that he had been excelled in every separate order of verse, justice may scruple the imputed transcendence. 1876 T. S. EGAN tr. *Heine's Atta Troll*, etc. 43 A temple, whose transcendence Indicates the Almighty's glory. 1907 ILLINGWORTH *Doctr. Trinity* xi. 226 We expect to see Divine action manifested through the operation of general laws, and not through their occasional transcendence.

b. *spec.* Of the Deity: The attribute of being above and independent of the universe; distinguished from *immanence* (see IMMANENT 1).

1848 R. I. WILBERFORCE *Doctr. Incarnation* III. (1852) 32 That Deistic theory of Transcendence, which supposes that the qualities of matter having been bestowed upon it by its Maker, everything has been left to go on by the impulse which was originally bestowed. 1856 R. A. VAUGHAN *Mystics* (1860) I. 214 Not always..able to embrace fully and together these two conceptions of transcendence and of immanence. 1896 *Chicago Advance* 16 Apr. 567/2 We have been accustomed to believe that nature reveals God in his immanence, but that Christ reveals God in his transcendence. 1907 ILLINGWORTH *Doctr. Trinity* x. 197 Divine immanence and divine transcendence are not mutually exclusive, but essentially correlative conceptions.

†**2.** Elevation or extension beyond ordinary limits; exaggeration, hyperbole. *Obs. rare.*

**1625** BACON *Ess., Adversitie* (Arb.) 504 This would have done better in Poesy; where Transcendences are more allowed. **1645** MILTON *Tetrach.* Wks. 1851 IV. 234 Why.. should they be such crabbed masorites of the Letter, as not to mollifie a transcendence of literal rigidity?

**3.** *Math.* The fact of being transcendental: see TRANSCENDENTAL 4.

**1902** *Encycl. Brit.* XXXI. 287/2 Lindemann by a similar process proved the transcendence of $\pi$.

**Transcendency** (trɑnseˑndĕnsi). [f. as prec.: see -ENCY.] The condition or quality of being transcendent; excess; surpassing excellency; with *pl.* a transcendent quality.

**1615** DAY *Festivals* xii. 341, I speake not against Lawfull Purchasing, it is that Transcendency I strike at, when Men depopulate whole Countries, to people the Land forsooth with Sheepe. **1662** EVELYN *Chalcogr.* Pref., Your modesty do's not permit me to run through all those Transcendencies. **1681** GLANVILL *Sadducismus* II. (1726) 462 The Essential Sanctity and singular Transcendency of the exalted nature of God. **1857** GLADSTONE *Oxf. Ess.* 8 The transcendency of his poetical distinctions has tended to overshadow his other claims and uses. **1886** *Westm. Rev.* Oct. 469 Christ..never reflected on transcendency and immanency.

**b.** The fact of transcending: = TRANSCENDENCE 1; an instance of this.

**1907** J. ORR in *Life of Faith* 9 Jan. 26/1 Such deviations from or transcendencies of the natural order we call miracles.

**Transcendent** (trɑnseˑndĕnt), *a.* and *sb.* Also -ant. [ad. L. *transcendent-em*, pr. pple. of *transcend-ĕre* to TRANSCEND. For the spelling with *-ant* cf. F. *transcendant* (14–15th c. in Hatz.-Darm.), also *ascendant, descendant.*]

**A.** *adj.*

**1.** Surpassing or excelling others of its kind; going beyond the ordinary limits; pre-eminent; superior or supreme; extraordinary. Also, loosely, Eminently great or good; cf. 'excellent'.

**1598** FLORIO, *Trascendente*, transcending, transcendent. **1611** COTGR., *Transcendant*, transcendant, surmounting, surpassing, exceeding. **1611** SPEED *Hist. Gt. Brit.* IX. ii. § 64 The Popes transcendent pleasure and power, being the strongest part of the Dukes title to the Crown. *a* **1637** B. JONSON *Goodwife's Ale* in *Athenæum* 1 Oct. (1904), When shall we meete agayne, and have a tast, Of that transcendant Ale we dranke of last? **1649** MILTON *Eikon.* 10 That transcendent Apostle Saint Paul. **1725** POPE *Odyss.* VI. 128 Nausicaa..shone transcendent o'er the beauteous train. **1754** RICHARDSON *Grandison* (1781) III. xxviii. 307 Such transcendant goodness of heart. **1807** CRABBE *Par. Reg.* I. 783 His own transcendant genius found the rest. **1865** SEELEY *Ecce Homo* v. (ed. 8) 48 A person of altogether transcendant greatness. **1878** GLADSTONE *Prim. Homer* vi. § 13. 73 Apollo is less transcendent in intellect [than Athenè].

†**b.** With *above, to*: greatly superior to. *Obs.*

**1634** RAINBOW *Labour* (1635) 35 Their clothings being by some degrees transcendant to needle worke even wrought with gold. **1634** HABINGTON *Castara* (Arb.) 16 If worth be not transcendant above the title. **1678** CUDWORTH *Intell. Syst.* I. iv. § 16. 286 Julian the Emperor..acknowledged besides the Sun, another Incorporeal Deity, transcendent to it. **1713** C'TESS WINCHELSEA *Misc. Poems* 202 If a fluent Vein be shown That's transcendent to our own.

†**2.** Of language: Elevated above ordinary language, lofty. *Obs.*

**1631** GOUGE *God's Arrows* III. § 15. 212 Those other high transcendent hyperbolicall phrases of the Prophet Isay. *a* **1653** — *Comm. Heb.* i. 5 (1655) 43 In this sense this high transcendent prophesie (Isa. ix. 6, 7) is to be taken.

†**3.** Of an idea or conception: Transcending comprehension; hence, obscure or abstruse. Cf. METAPHYSICAL 1 b. *Obs.*

**1624** GATAKER *Transubst.* 146 These are such transcendent subtilties, if not absurdities, as any metaphysics will afford. **1635** PERSON *Varieties* I. 3 Metaphysicks.. medleth with things transcendent and supernaturall. **1646** BP. MAXWELL *Burden Issachar* 31, I confesse, this Divinitie is so transcendent and Metaphysicall, that it exceeds my capacitie.

**4.** *Philos.* **a.** Applied by the Schoolmen to predicates which by their universal application were considered to transcend the Aristotelian categories or predicaments. See B. 1 a.

[*c* **1300** DUNS SCOTUS *Rep. Par. in Sent.* I. viii. v. § 13 Praedicata..quae dicuntur de Deo..sunt praedicata transcendentia..quidquid convenit enti antequam descendat in genera [i.e. the categories] est transcendens.] **1706** PHILLIPS (ed. Kersey), *Transcendent*,..in Logick, surpassing the Predicaments. **1872** LATHAM *Eng. Dict.* s.v. *Transcendental, Transcendent* is used by the scholastics and moderns, as opposed to immanent—meaning transcending the categories.

**b.** By Kant applied to that which transcends his own list of categories (explained as *a priori* conceptions of the understanding, which it necessarily employs in ordering its experience, but which have no validity outside of experience); hence, transcending or altogether outside experience; not an object of possible experience; unrealizable in human experience. (Distinguished by him from TRANSCENDENTAL 2 b.)

**1803** *Edin. Rev.* I. 258 Philosophy..is transcendent when ..it believes that the objects of our senses exist in a manner really known to us. **1815** COLERIDGE *Biog. Lit.* I. xii. (1870) 117 Those flights of lawless speculation, which, abandoned by all distinct consciousness, because transgressing the bounds and purposes of our intellectual faculties, are justly condemned, as transcendent. **1842** BRANDE *Dict. Sc.*, etc., s.v. *Transcendental*, Kant..draws a distinction between the *transcendental* and the *transcendent*...The *transcendent*..is that which regards those principles as objectively real to which Kant assigns only a subjective or formal reality, and consequently is by him regarded as beyond the limits of human reason altogether. **1877** E. CAIRD *Philos. Kant* II. x. 422 From the Kantian point of view both the question and the answer are transcendent. For they both involve the doctrine that the world is in space,..apart from its being known as such. *Ibid.* xiv. 523 And this synthesis is transcendent, i.e. it is a synthesis which cannot be represented as a phenomenon, or verified in sensuous experience. **1881** R. ADAMSON *Fichte* V. 112 *note*, For any question or theorem which might pass beyond possible experience, Kant reserved the term transcendent.

**5.** *Theol.* Of the Deity: In His being, exalted above and distinct from the universe; having transcendence. Distinguished from IMMANENT 1.

Originally often connoting the denial of Divine action or interference in mundane affairs.

**1877** D. PATRICK in *Encycl. Brit.* VII. 36/1 (*Deism*) Shaftesbury vigorously protests against the notion of a wholly transcendent God. Morgan more than once expresses a theory that would now be pronounced one of immanence. **1907** ILLINGWORTH *Doctr. Trinity* x. 194 To think of Him [God], in modern phrase, as transcendent, as above and beyond all relative and finite existence. *Ibid.* 195 It is theoretically possible..to conceive of God as simply transcendent, or simply immanent in the world. **1911** R. MACKINTOSH in *Encycl. Brit.* XXVI. 744/1 (*Theism*) God was apt to be thought of [in 18th c.] as purely transcendent, not immanent in the world.

**6.** *Math.* = TRANSCENDENTAL 4.

**1902** *Encycl. Brit.* XXXI. 287/2 Hermite first completely proved the transcendent character of *e* [see E (the letter) 5 a].

**B.** *sb.* [the adj. used *absol.*]

**1.** *Philos.* †**a.** A predicate that transcends, or cannot be classed under, any of the Aristotelian categories or predicaments. *Obs.*

Aristotle taught (*Metaph.* x. 2) that *being* and *unity* were neither categories, nor fell under any one category, but could be predicated in all the categories; in *Eth. Nic.* he says the like of *goodness*. Such predicates came to be called by the Schoolmen *transcendentia*, 'transcendents', as transcending the limits of the categories. Their enumeration as six, *Being, Thing, Something, One, True, Good* (found first in a treatise attributed to Thomas Aquinas, but thought by Prantl (*Gesch. der Logik* III. 245) to be subsequent to Duns Scotus), was in regular use down to the time of Kant.

[*c* **1300** DUNS SCOTUS *Op. Oxon. in Sent.* I. viii. iii. § 19 Transcendens quodcunque nullum habet genus sub quo contineatur, sed quod ipsum sit commune ad multa inferiora. **13..** in Thomas Aquinas *Opusc.* XLII. ii. (1490) K viij/2 Sunt autem sex transcendentia: videlicet *ens, res, aliquid, vnum, verum, bonum.*] **1581** W. FULKE in *Confer.* III. (1584) Y iij b, It is a transcendent, which is in all predicaments. **1640** G. WATTS tr. *Bacon's Adv. Learn.* III. iv. 143 All Relative and Adventive condicions and Characters of Essences, which we have named Transcendents; as Multitude, Paucity, Identity, Diversity, Possible, Impossible, and such like. **1652** GAULE *Magastrom.* 207 God is a transcendent, and is not under, nor yet within, the predicament of any part of the whole order of nature. **1697** tr. *Burgersdicius his Logic* I. iii. 6 Transcendents, as, Being, Thing, One, True, Good, which by their Community exceed all the degrees of Categories.

**b.** *transf.* A person or thing that transcends classification.

**1591** G. FLETCHER *Russe Commw.* (Hakl. Soc.) 37 In this number the lorde Borris..is not to be reckoned, that is like a transendent,..being the emperours brother in law. **1593** G. HARVEY *New Letter* Wks. (Grosart) I. 267 Hope is a Transcendent, and will not easily be imprisoned, or impounded in any Predicament of auncient or moderne Perfection. **1608** BP. J. KING *Serm. 5 Nov.* 23 Both were transcendents not to be placed in the classes or rankes of hitherto experienced or practised wickednesse. **1642** FULLER *Holy & Prof. St.* III. xxiii. 218 Fame falls most short in those Transcendents, which are above her Predicaments; as in Solomons wisdome. **1655** FULLER *Ch. Hist.* VII. i. § 37 Here I must set John Dudley Earl of Warwick (as a Transcendent) in a form by himself, being a competent Lawyer (Son to a Judge), known Soldier, and able States man, and acting against the Protector, to all these his capacities.

**c.** According to the Kantian philosophy: That which is altogether beyond the bounds of human cognition and thought. See A. 4 b.

*c* **1810** COLERIDGE in *Lit. Rem.* (1838) III. 221 Omnify the disputed point into a transcendant, and you may defy the opponent to lay hold of it. **1825** — *Aids Refl.* (1848) I. 260 Let X signify a transcendant, that is, a cause beyond our comprehension, and not within the sphere of sensible experience. **1837–8** SIR W. HAMILTON *Logic* xi. (1866) I. 199 The term transcendent,..he [Kant] applied to all pretended knowledge that transcended experience, and was not given in an original principle of the mind.

†**2.** One who or that which transcends or rises high above the ordinary rank of persons or things; a person or thing of great eminence. *Obs.*

**1593** G. HARVEY *Pierce's Super.* 18 Were..his lines such transcendentes, as his thoughtes..what an egregious Aretine should we shortly haue. **1612** W. SCLATER *Serm.* 8, I am loth to make them transcendents; yet such, sure, is their authoritie on earth *supra seriem.* **1613** PURCHAS *Pilgrimage* (1614) 175 The Cabalist as a super subtile transcendent, mounteth with all his industrie..from this sensible World unto that other intellectuall. **1679** V. ALSOP *Melius Inquir.* I. i. 73 'The command of a Superior will hallow an erroneous action', as a Transcendent in our Church speaks.

†**3.** That which transcends, surpasses, or excels something else, or things generally. *rare.*

**1613** PURCHAS *Pilgrimage* I. ii. 6 A Paradise, faire, shining, delightsome,..a meere transcendent, which eye hath not seene. **1658** COKAINE *Trappolin* III. ii, Your matchless eyes Transcendents of the brightest lightest stars.

†**b.** A transcendent or pre-eminent quality. *Obs.*

**1657–83** EVELYN *Hist. Relig.* (1850) I. 76 These are the transcendents and pre-eminences which this admirable heathen attributes to mankind.

†**4.** A 2- or 3-line capital letter such as those put at the beginning of books or chapters. *Obs. rare.*

**1602** WILLIS *Stenogr.* A iv b, A Transcendent, is a great Character, which extendeth it selfe further then the distance betweene the lines.

†**5.** *The transcendent*: the ascendancy, the superiority; = ASCENDANT B. 3. *Obs. rare.*

**1691** W. NICHOLLS *Answ. Naked Gospel* Pref. Cj, His Confidence has generally the transcendent of his Sincerity, which is the common fate of all Hereticks.

**6.** *Math.* A transcendental expression or function; a non-algebraical function; e.g. log $x$, sin $x$, $a^x$. See TRANSCENDENTAL *a.* 4.

**1809** IVORY in *Phil. Trans.* XCIX. 368 They belong to the class of elliptical transcendants. **1816** tr. *Lacroix's Diff. & Int. Calculus* 24 Those functions..not comprehended in the enumeration made in No. 14, are called transcendents. **1887** R. A. ROBERTS *Int. Calculus* I. 3 We might ..deduce their properties as we do in the case of the elliptic functions and the higher transcendents.

**Transcendental** (trɑnsendeˑntăl), *a.* (*sb.*) [ad. med.L. *transcendentāl-is* (*c* 1365, Wyclif *Materia & Forma* (1902) 242), f. as prec. + *-ālis*, -AL. Cf. F. *transcendental* (18th c.), obs. *-el* (16th c.).]

**1.** Of transcendent quality or nature; surpassing; excelling; exalted: = TRANSCENDENT *a.* 1.

(In quots. 1790–1868, more or less ironical or sarcastic.)

**1701** GREW *Cosm. Sacra* II. viii. 84 The Deity himself, tho' he perceiveth not Pleasure nor Pain..as we do; yet must needs have a Perfect and Transcendental Perception, both of Pleasure, and Pain, and of all other things. **1727** BAILEY vol. II, *Transcendental*, exceeding, going beyond, surpassing. **1790** BURKE *Fr. Rev.* 10 All these considerations ..were below the transcendental dignity of the Revolution Society. **1862** MERIVALE *Rom. Emp.* (1865) VI. xlviii. 59 His [the Emperor's] transcendental being was elevated above the restraints of all inferior existences. **1868** M. PATTISON *Academ. Org.* 6 It related to the transcendental parts of education.

**2.** *Philos.* **a.** *orig.* in Aristotelian philosophy: Transcending or extending beyond the bounds of any single category; = TRANSCENDENT *a.* 4 a. By 17th c. writers often made synonymous with *metaphysical.*

By Wilkins used with special reference to his own classification of things and notions.

**1668** WILKINS *Real Char.* II. i. 25 The most Universal conceptions of Things are usually stiled Transcendental, Metaphysic-all. *Ibid.* xii. 291 The words *sin, fault, trespass, transgression*,..being compounded with the Transcendental Particle, Diminutive or Augmentative,..denote a Peccadillo or small fault, or an Enormity or heinous crime. *Ibid.* 318 Those Particles are here stiled Transcendental, which do circumstantiate words in respect of some Metaphysical notion; either by enlarging the acception of them to some more general signification,..or denoting a relation to some other Predicament or Genus, under which they are not originally placed. **1676** GLANVILL *Ess.* i. 3 So different they [body and spirit] are in all things, that they seem to have nothing but Being, and the Transcendental Attributes of that, in common. **1682** H. MORE *Annot. Glanvil's Lux O.* 177 The Current Doctrine of Metaphysicians, who define Transcendental or Metaphysical Truth to be nothing else but the relation of the Conformity of things to the Theoretical..Intellect of God. **1710** BERKELEY *Princ. Hum. Knowl.* § 118 Those transcendental maxims which influence all the particular sciences. **1734** WATERLAND *Diss. Exist. First Cause* ii. 51 This is that pure, simple, absolute, transcendental Necessity, which the later School-men and Metaphysicians speak of. **1751** JOHNSON *Rambler* No. 131 ¶ 1 The wish for riches; a wish..so prevalent, that it may be considered as universal and transcendental. **1807** J. OPIE in *Lect. Paint.* ii. (1848) 270 Learn to see Nature and beauty in the abstract, and rise to general and transcendental truth, which will always be the same.

**b.** In the philosophy of Kant (1724–1804): Not derived from experience, but concerned with the presuppositions of experience; pertaining to the general theory of the nature of experience or knowledge, *a priori*; critical (see CRITICISM 2 c).

**1798** WILLICH *Crit. Philos.* 65 The division of transcendental logic into transcendental analysis and dialectic. *Ibid.* 182 The transcendental is opposed to the empirical. **1801** *Encycl. Brit.* Suppl. II. 355 Kant..calls all knowledge, of which the object is not furnished by the senses, and which concerns the kind and origin of our ideas, transcendental knowledge. **1803** *Edin. Rev.* Jan. 258 Philosophy..is transcendental, when..it investigates the subjective elements, which..modify the qualities or elements of the object as perceived. **1842** BRANDE *Dict. Sc.* etc., s.v., The transcendental he [Kant] defines to be that which, though it could never be derived from experience, yet is necessarily connected with experience, and which may be shortly expressed as the intellectual form, the matter of which is supplied by sense. **1872** MAHAFFY tr. *Kant's Prolegomena* 243 We must necessarily distinguish two sorts of idealism—transcendental and empirical. By the *transcendental idealism* of all phenomena, I mean the doctrine according to which we regard them all as mere representations, not as things *per se.* **1874** W. WALLACE *Hegel's Logic* § 42. 75 That unity of self-consciousness,..Kant calls transcendental..; and he meant thereby that this unity was only in our minds, and did not attach to the objects apart from our knowledge of them. **1877** E. CAIRD *Philos. Kant* II. v. 289 Transcendental is the word by which we have learnt to distinguish à priori ideas..so far as they enable us to know objects.

**c.** Used of any philosophy which resembles Kant's in being based upon the recognition of an *a priori* element in experience.

**1829** CARLYLE *Misc.* (1857) II. 74 The Idealist boasts that his Philosophy is Transcendental. **1842** EMERSON *Transcendentalist* Wks. (Bohn) II. 283 It is well known..that the Idealism of the present day acquired the name of Transcendental, from the use of that term by Immanuel Kant, of Konigsberg. **1872** MINTO *Eng. Prose Lit.* II. ix. 596 German transcendental philosophy. **1878** DOWDEN *Stud. Lit.* 47 The transcendental thinker [holds] that the mind contributes of its own stores ideas or forms of thought not derived from experience.

**d.** By Schelling 'transcendental philosophy' was used for the philosophy of mind as distinguished from that of nature.

**1903** ADAMSON *Developm. Mod. Philos.* I. 265 Philosophy of nature and philosophy of mind or transcendental philosophy are therefore at once parallel and complementary.

**3.** In uses derived from the philosophical sense: **a.** Beyond the limits of ordinary experience, extraordinary.

**1831** CARLYLE *Sart. Res.* II. v. (1858) 87 Sometimes it is even when your anxiety becomes transcendental, that the soul first feels herself able to transcend it. **1837** — *Fr. Rev.* III. I. i, Very frightful it is when a Nation..becomes transcendental. **1856** EMERSON *Eng. Traits* Wks. (Bohn) II. 104 This mental materialism makes the value of English transcendental genius. **1863** GEO. ELIOT *Romola* xxxix, That bust of Plato had been long used to look down on conviviality of a more transcendental sort. **1868** NETTLESHIP *Ess. Browning's Poetry* i. 34 Views..which, while less transcendental..are perhaps of more practical value.

**b.** Super-rational, superhuman, supernatural.

**1826** SCOTT *Woodst.* xiv, The dexterity with which he threw his transcendental and fanatical notions, like a sort of veil, over the darker visions excited by remorse. **1841** MYERS *Cath. Th.* IV. xvi. 265 A revelation which may justly be termed Transcendental—wholly incapable of being explained, but yet not incapable of being believed. **1850** WHIPPLE *Ess. & Rev.* (ed. 3) I. 228 It [poetry] thus transcends the sphere of the senses, and is, in a measure, transcendental. **1858** KINGSLEY *Lett.* (1878) II. 67 Below all natural phenomena, we come to a transcendental—in plain English, a miraculous ground. **1903** F. W. H. MYERS *Human Personality* I. p. xv, Transcendental vision, or the perception of beings regarded as on another plane of existence.

**c.** *Vaguely*, Abstract, metaphysical, *a priori*.

**1835** I. TAYLOR *Spir. Despot.* v. 212 Abstract and transcendental notions of an intolerant kind. **1840** THACKERAY *Paris Sk.-bk.* xv. (1872) 172 Having watched the Germans with their..mysterious transcendental talk. **1847** EMERSON *Repr. Men, Plato* Wks. (Bohn) I. 295 If he made transcendental distinctions, he fortified himself by drawing all his illustrations from sources disdained by orators and polite conversers. **1851** CARLYLE *Sterling* I. xv, To such length can transcendental moonshine, cast by some morbidly radiating Coleridge into the chaos of a fermenting life, act magically there. **1853** MAX MÜLLER *Chips* (1880) I. iii. 66 The exhausting atmosphere of transcendental ideas in which they [Hindus] lived. **1856** *N. Brit. Rev.* XXVI. 173 Proofs..that the most abstract and apparently transcendental truths in physical science will sooner or later add their tribute to supply human wants, and alleviate human sufferings. **1875** JOWETT *Plato* (ed. 2) I. 77 An unmeaning and transcendental conception. **1901** *Edin. Rev.* Apr. 427 He [Mill] rejected all transcendental conceptions.

**d.** Applied to the movement of thought in New England of which Emerson was the principal figure: see TRANSCENDENTALISM 1 b.

**1844** DICKENS *Mart. Chuz.* xxxiv, Two literary ladies present their compliments to the mother of the modern Gracchi...It may be another bond of union..to observe, that the two L.L.'s are Transcendental. **1887** CABOT *Memoirs of Emerson* I. vii. 249 [In the Boston or New England Transcendentalism] the transcendental was whatever lay beyond the stock notions and traditional beliefs to which adherence was expected because they were generally accepted by sensible persons.

**4.** *Math.* Not capable of being produced by (a finite number of) the ordinary algebraical operations of addition, multiplication, involution, or their inverse operations; expressible in terms of the variable only in the form of an infinite series.

The typical transcendental functions are sin $x$, $e^x$, log $x$.

**1706** PHILLIPS (ed. Kersey), *Transcendental Curves*,..are such Curves, as when their Nature or Property comes to be express'd by an Equation, one of the Variable or flowing Quantities there, denotes a Curve or crooked Line. **1811** HUTTON *Course of Mathematics* III. ix. 188 Transcendental or mechanical curves, are such as cannot be..expressed by a pure algebraical equation. Thus, $y = \log x$, $y = A$ . sin $x$, ..$y = A^x$, are equations to transcendental curves. **1843** *Penny Cycl.* XXV. 120 The roots of equations of the fifth and higher degrees are..transcendental: there is no mode of expression except by infinite series. **1879** CAYLEY in *Encycl. Brit.* IX. 818/2 The so-called circular functions..the exponential function..the logarithmic function..are all of them transcendental functions. **1882** GLAISHER *Ibid.* XIV. 773/1 The small group of transcendental functions, consisting only of the circular functions..sin $x$, cos $x$, &c.,..$e^x$, and log $x$. **1902** *Encycl. Brit.* XXXI. 287/2 There are numbers..which cannot be defined by any combination of a finite number of equations with rational integral coefficients. Such numbers are said to be *transcendental*.

**B.** *sb.* [the adj. used *absol.*] A transcendental conception, term, or quantity.

**1668** WILKINS *Real Char.* II. i. 24 The right ordering of these Transcendentals is a business of no small difficulty; because there is so little assistance or help to be had for it in the Common Systems. **1711** HICKES *Two Treat. Chr. Priesth.* (1847) II. 165 Generical terms come so near to the nature of transcendentals, that they are seldom capable of..exact definition. **1726** SWIFT *Gulliver* II. vii, As to ideas, entities, abstractions, and transcendentals, I could never drive the least conception into their heads. **1843** *Penny Cycl.* XXV. 120 The expression of the old transcendentals as recognised functions, and the writing of them accordingly, as log $x$, sin $x$, cos $x$, &c.

**Transcendentalism** (transende·ntăliz'm). [f. prec. + -ISM. Cf. F. *transcendantalisme* (Littré).]

**1.** Transcendental philosophy; a system of this; applied to that taught by Kant and other philosophers; also, to the idealism of Schelling.

**1803** *Edin. Rev.* Jan. 265 The theory of transcendentalism may therefore be a better dogmatism than others. **1817** T. L. PEACOCK *Melincourt* III. 40 He has thus discovered the difference between objective and subjective reality and this point of view is transcendentalism. **1851** CARLYLE *Sterling* I. viii. (1872) 46 He was thought to hold..alone in England, the key of German and other Transcendentalisms. **1866** DK. ARGYLL *Reign Law* ii. (ed. 4) 117 What is transcendentalism but the tendency to trace up all things to the relation in which they stand to abstract Ideas? **1878** DOWDEN *Studies in Lit.* 58 Transcendentalism, seeking the supernatural everywhere, loses sight of it as such.

**b.** The religio-philosophical teaching of the New England school of thought represented by Emerson and others: see quot. 1911.

**1842** EMERSON *Lect., Transcendentalist* Wks. (Bohn) II. 279 What is popularly called Transcendentalism among us, is Idealism. **1876** *N. Amer. Rev.* CXXIII. 468 Boston and its immediate neighborhood..really made up the kingdom ruled by Transcendentalism. **1887** CABOT *Emerson* I. vii. 248 The Boston or New England Transcendentalism had, as Dr. Hedge says, no very direct connection with the transcendental philosophy of Germany, the philosophy of Kant and his successors. **1911** *Encycl. Brit.* XXVII. 172/2 (*Transcendentalism*) The most famous example of the pseudo-philosophic use of the term is for a movement of thought which was prominent in the New England states from..1830 to 1850. Its use originated in the Transcendental Club (1836) founded by Emerson, Frederic Henry Hedge, and others. The movement had several aspects: philosophical, theological, social, economic.

**2.** Exalted character, thought, or language; also, that which is extravagant, vague, or visionary in philosophy or language; idealism.

**1831** CARLYLE *Sart. Res.* I. iii. (1858) 8 If through the high, silent, meditative Transcendentalism of our Friend we detected any practical tendency whatever, it was at most Political. **1837** THACKERAY *Carlyle's Fr. Rev.* Wks. 1900 XIII. 249 It teems with sound, hearty philosophy (besides certain transcendentalisms which we do not pretend to understand). **1859** SMILES *Self-Help* xi. (1860) 287 Nor did the lofty transcendentalism of his books by any means palliate the acted meannesses of his life. **1871** W. H. MILLER *Cult. Pleasure* Pref. (1872) 10 It is time, indeed, that the whole subject of happiness should be dragged down from the regions of transcendentalism.., and be made, if possible, to take its place in the highways and byeways of every-day life.

**3.** The quality or character of transcendent excellence; transcendency. *rare.*

**1840** CARLYLE *Heroes* iii. (1872) 80 Dante and Shakespeare.. dwell apart...In the general feeling of the world, a certain transcendentalism, a glory as of complete perfection, invests these two.

**Transcendentalist** (transende·ntălist). [f. as prec. + -IST. Cf. mod.F. *transcendantaliste* (Littré).] An adherent of some form of transcendentalism. Also *attrib.*

**1803** *Edin. Rev.* Jan. 267 We will admit to the transcendentalist his solitary noumenon, and its separate functions. **1829** CARLYLE *Misc.* (1857) II. 75 To a Transcendentalist, Matter has an existence, but only as a Phenomenon. **1840** *Boston Q. Rev.* 270 The men who are affected by it [the new movement] are called by their opponents, Transcendentalists. **1876** LOWELL *Among my Bks.* Ser. II. 32 Transcendentalist as he was by nature, so much so as to be in danger of lapsing into an oriental mysticism. **1879** R. H. HUTTON in *W. Bagehot's Lit. Stud.* Pref. Mem. 28 A thorough transcendentalist, by which I mean one who could never doubt that there was a real foundation of the universe distinct from the outward show of its superficial qualities, and that the substance is never exhaustively expressed in these qualities. **1882** *Athenæum* 17 June 767/1 Miss Peabody..was prominent in the old transcendentalist movement.

Hence **Transcendentali·stic** *a.*, of, pertaining to, or of the nature of transcendentalism; belonging to or held by transcendentalists.

**1892** *Monist* II. 265 If a philosophy denies the existence of transcendentalistic thought-entities or of any such things in themselves, which serve as cement to combine the *disjecta membra* of their world conception, it is generally declared to lead straight on to nihilism.

**Tra:nscendenta·lity.** *rare.* [f. as prec. + -ITY: cf. Ger. *transcendentalität* (D. Jenisch in *Kant Briefwechsel* 1902, III. 75).] Transcendental quality. (In quot. 1880 *humorous.*)

*a* **1846** SALISBURY cited in WORCESTER. **1880** W. S. GILBERT *Patience* I. 7 There is a transcendentality of delirium—an acute accentuation of supremest ecstacy.

**Transcendentalize** (transende·ntăləiz), *v.* [f. as prec. + -IZE.] *trans.* **a.** To render transcendent. **b.** To render transcendental; to idealize. Hence **Transcende·ntalized** *ppl. a.*

**1846** MOZLEY *Ess.* (1878) I. 233 The magnanimity, generosity, ardour, and refinement of ordinary virtue were transcendentalised in him. **1866** LIDDON *Bampt. Lect.* viii. (1875) 450 Nor is it to transcendentalize Him into an abstraction which mocks us when we attempt to grasp it as an unsubstantial phantom. **1875** *Contemp. Rev.* Nov. 996 How often even they are found seeking to transcendentalize their own religion, to escape from its old dogmas, and efface its ancient discipline! **1881** *Contemp. Rev.* Mar. 380 Some transcendentalized form of tolerance. **1883** *Century Mag.* XXIX. 200/2 The Venetian gondola, refined, transcendentalized.

**Transcende·ntally,** *adv.* [f. as prec. + -LY [2].] In a transcendental manner or degree; according to a transcendental system.

**1803** *Edin. Rev.* Jan. 277 Of moral duty it may be said, in like manner, that transcendentally it cannot exist. [**1842** MRS. BROWNING *Bk. Poets* Poems 1890 V. 241 Some have discovered that he [Shakspere] individualized, and some that he generalized, and some that he subtilized—almost transtranscendentally.] **1877** E. CAIRD *Philos. Kant* II. iii. 244 We hold that space and time are transcendentally ideal, i. e. that they have no objective validity..apart from the constitution of the sensibility through which they are apprehended.

¶ **b.** *erron.* = TRANSCENDENTLY.

**1870** *Eng. Mech.* 11 Mar. 636/2 The diamond, so transcendentally beautiful.

‖ **Transcendentia** (transende·nʃiă), *sb. pl. Obs. rare*[−1]. [L., neut. pl. of *transcendens* TRANSCENDENT.] Transcendent traits or qualities.

**1674** JOSSELYN *Voy. New Eng.* 89 There are certain transcendentia in every creature, which are the indelible characters of God, and which discover God.

**Transcendently** (transe·ndĕntli), *adv.* [f. TRANSCENDENT *a.* + -LY [2].] In a transcendent manner or degree; so as to transcend; surpassingly, supremely, pre-eminently.

**1623** GOUGE *Serm. Extent God's Provid.* § 1 He saith not simply, you are as good; but transcendently, more worth. **1638** SIR T. HERBERT *Trav.* (ed. 2) 85 His genius [is] so transcendently efflated with pride and ambition, that he beholds his equals with disdaine and anger. **1712** ADDISON *Spect.* No. 543 ¶ 1 It was the work of a Being transcendently wise and powerful. **1871** MORLEY *Crit. Misc., Carlyle* (1904) I. 164 The transcendently firm and clear-eyed intelligence of Goethe. **1907** *Verney Mem.* I. 71 Reserved for some transcendently important occasion.

**Transce·ndentness.** *rare.* [f. as prec. + -NESS.] The quality or character of being transcendent: = TRANSCENDENCY.

**1625** BP. MOUNTAGU *App. Cæsar* viii. 75 Why are you enraged against me, if I cannot attaine the measure of your transcendentnesse, but confesse my disability and imperfection? **1730** [see TRANSCENDINGNESS]. **1874** PUSEY *Lent. Serm.* 308 [S. Paul] piles up words upon words to utter as he may, that which is unutterable; the transcendentness of the might of the grace of God to usward.

† **Transce·ndiary.** *Obs. nonce-wd.* [? irreg. after *incendiary*, f. L. *transcend-ĕre* to TRANSCEND: see -ARY.] A transcendent person or thing; in quot., an eminent quality.

**1654** FULLER *Two Serm.* 60 Some grand Vices..infected the transcendiaries of their highest atchievements.

† **Transce·ndible,** *a. Obs. rare.* [f. as TRANSCEND + -IBLE.] Capable of being transcended or surmounted.

**1684–94** tr. *Plutarch's Mor.* (1874) II. 220 It appears that Romulus slew his brother, because he attempted to leap over a sacred and inaccessible place, and to render it transcendible and profane.

**Transcending** (transe·ndiŋ), *ppl. a.* [f. TRANSCEND *v.* + -ING [2].] That transcends; surpassing; supereminent; transcendent.

*a* **1529** [implied in TRANSCENDINGLY]. **1598** [see TRANSCENDENT A. 1]. **1641** *Vind. Smectymnuus* xiii. 113 A building of that transcending loftiness. **1713** DERHAM *Phys.-Theol.* IV. xii. 216 Man..being endowed with the transcending Faculty of Reason. **1852** MRS. JAMESON *Leg. Madonna* 196 An angel..might well prostrate himself as witness of the transcending miracle.

Hence **Transce·ndingly** *adv.*, transcendently; **Transce·ndingness**, transcendence.

*a* **1529** SKELTON *Replyc.* Wks. 1862 II. 232 Excellently enformed and transcendingly sped in moche high connyng. **1730** BAILEY (folio), *Transcendentness*, Transcendingness, Surpassingness. **1817** A. BONAR *Serm.* II. xx. 443 How transcendingly glorious does he appear! **1874** PUSEY *Lent. Serm.* 306 'That the transcendingness of the power', they say, 'may be of God, and not from us'.

**Transcension** (transe·nʃən). *rare.* [ad. med.L. *transcensiōn-em* (*c* 380 Jerome Ezech. Homil. XI. 1), n. of action from *transcend-ĕre* (ppl. stem *transcens-*) to TRANSCEND.] A passing beyond or above, transcendence.

*c* **1611** CHAPMAN *Hymne to Venus* 487 My muse, affecting first, thy fame to raise; Shall make transcension now, to others praise. **1886** *American* XII. 152 He laid great stress on miracles and all transcensions of law.

† **Transce·nt.** *Obs. rare.* [f. TRANSCEND, after *ascent*, *descent*.] The act of passing over or crossing.

**1621** G. SANDYS *Ovid's Met.* IX. ii. (1626) 177 Nor seekes the smoothest wayes: Nor by declining his transcent delayes.

† **Trans,cha·nge,** *v. Obs.* [f. TRANS- 2 + CHANGE *v.*: cf. obs. F. *transchangement* (Cotgr.).] *trans.* To transform; to transmute.

*a* **1598** ROLLOCK *Serm.* Wks. 1849 I. 398 Be schining it culd never sa transchange ane creature. *a* **1636** FITZ-GEFFRAY *Holy Transport.* (1881) 197 O Tygers into humane shape transchang'd. **1662** J. CHANDLER *Van Helmont's Oriat.* To Rdr., The which colour hath transchanged thee into black darkness; thou being a white and red Virgin.

† **Trans,cha·ngeative,** *a. Obs. rare.* [irreg. f. prec. + -ATIVE; cf. *talkative*.] Having the faculty of changing or tendency to change.

**1662** J. CHANDLER *Van Helmont's Oriat.* 157 The objects of taste sitting immediately in some body, cannot by reason of their corporeal thickness, form a transchangeative Image. *Ibid.* 244 The transchangeative virtue of the Archeus.

**Trans-cha·nnel,** *a.* [TRANS- 3, 8.] (Passing)

across a channel, esp. across the English or Irish Channel; crossing the Channel.

**1894** *Westm. Gaz.* 7 June 7/1 Trans-channel cycling. **1901** *Daily Chron.* 6 Sept. 6/2 The Admiralty Pier [at Dover] from which the trans-Channel passenger traffic is now conducted. **1909** *Westm. Gaz.* 12 July 7/1 The monoplane.. would not be ready to make the actual trans-Channel flight.

**Transchour**, obs. form of TRENCHER.

† **Trans,clou·t**, *v. Obs. nonce-wd.* [f. TRANS- 2 + CLOUT *sb.*[1] 4 b.] *trans.* To transform or disfigure with clouts or mis-shapen clothing.

**1647** WARD *Simp. Cobler* 25 Those women..disfigure themselves with such garbes, as not onely dismantles their native lovely lustre, but transclouts them into gant bar-geese.

† **Tra·ns,colate**, *v. Obs. rare.* [f. ppl. stem of mod.L. **transcōlāre* (after *percōlāre* to PERCOLATE), or obs. F. *transcouler* (Cotgr.) from same source + -ATE [3].] *trans.* To cause (liquid) to pass through a porous substance or medium; to strain, filter; = PERCOLATE *v.* 1. Hence † **Tra·nscolating** *ppl. a.*

**1615** CROOKE *Body of Man* 416 The vrine is transcolated through the flesh of the kidneis. **1661** LOVELL *Hist. Anim. & Min.* 315 The kidnies..are to draw, seperate, and transcolate whatever is serous and aqueous in the vessels, both veines and arteries. **1684** tr. *Bonet's Merc. Compit.* III. 93 Fortis transcolates the juices through Sand. **1817** PETTIGREW *Mem. Lettsom* III. 303 By transcolation, or by passing through the transcolating pores of all the solids.

† **Trans,cola·tion.** *Obs.* [f. as prec. + -ATION. Cf. obs. F. *transcoulation* (Cotgr.).] The process of transcolating; straining, filtration; = PERCOLATION a.

**1634** T. JOHNSON *Parey's Chirurg.* IX. i. (1678) 216 That solution of Continuity..which is generated by sweating out and transcolation, [termed] Diapedesis. **1662** STILLINGFL. *Orig. Sacr.* III. iv. § 6 Meer transcolation may by degrees take away that which the Chymists call the fixed salt. **1702** W. COWPER in *Phil. Trans.* XXIII. 1185 In Bruises when the Blood is extravassated, it goes off either by Transcolation or else causes an Abscess. **1817** [see TRANSCOLATING].

† **Trans,co·lorate**, *v. Obs. rare.* [f. TRANS- 2 + COLORATE *v.*] = TRANSCOLOUR. Hence † **Transco·lorated** *ppl. a.*, transcoloured.

**1823** J. BADCOCK *Dom. Amusem.* 43 The Transcolourated Writing.

**Trans,colora·tion, -coloura·tion.** Now *rare* or *Obs.* [f. TRANS- + COLORATION.] The action or process of transcolouring; change of colour.

**1664** POWER *Exp. Philos.* I. 74 Experiments in the Extraction, Commixtion, and Transcoloration of Tinctures. *c* **1790** IMISON *Sch. Art* II. 94 Among the most pleasing as well as surprizing phenomena of nature [are] the transcolourations produced by chemistry. **1827** *Blackw. Mag.* XXI. 781 True, through all transformations, and transfigurations, and transcolorations, to their original..forms, figures, and colours.

† **Trans,co·lour**, *v. Obs. rare.* [f. TRANS- 2 + COLOUR *v.*: cf. It. *transcolorare* 'to discolour or chaunge colour' (Florio).] *trans.* To change the colour of; to cause to change colour.

**1664** POWER *Exp. Philos.* I. 75 By its acidity is transcoloured into English Beer. **1669** COKAINE *Poems* 47 Do not believe I counterfeit, who think Verses in your praise would transcolour Inke. **1837** C. LOFFT *Self-formation* II. 262, I was never so transcoloured.

**Trans-co·ndyloid**, *a. Surg.* [f. TRANS- 5 + CONDYLE: cf. *condyloid*.] Traversing or cutting across the condyles.

**1885** *Buck's Handbk. Med. Sc.* I. 169/2 Hence this [Dr. W. Stokes'] amputation is generally known as the supracondyloid amputation, that of Carden being known as the trans-condyloid operation. **1899** *Syd. Soc. Lex.*, *Transcondyloid amputation of thigh.* Carden's operation.

**Trans-co·nscious**, *a. rare*[−1]. [TRANS- 4.] That is beyond or outside of consciousness or cognition.

**1865** MASSON *Rec. Brit. Philos.* ii. 96 He recognised the ideas of three supra-sensuous or trans-conscious objects—God, the Soul, and the World.

**Tra·ns-contine·ntal**, *a.* [f. TRANS- 3 + CONTINENTAL. Cf. mod.F. *transcontinental* (Littré).] That extends or passes across a continent; also, of or pertaining to the farther side of a continent.

**1869** J. A. POOR (*title*) Transcontinental Railway [from Atlantic to Pacific in U. S.]. **1876** J. A. ALLEN *Amer. Bison* (1877) 465 The great trans-continental emigrant route by way of the South Pass. **1883** W. J. SMITH in *19th Cent.* Nov. 841 The transcontinental railway which Queensland is about to construct. **1898** *Westm. Gaz.* 27 Sept. 6/1 Mr. R. L. J—, the well-known Trans-Continental cyclist, arrived safely in Khiva on the 5th inst.

† **Trans,co·rporate**, *v. Obs. rare.* [f. late L. *transcorporāre* (*a* 200 Irenæus): see -ATE [3], and cf. med.L. *transcorporātus* (Du Cange).]

**1.** *trans.* To change into a different body or substance; to transubstantiate.

**1570** FOXE *A. & M.* (ed. 2) 1314/1 Notwithstandyng that yͤ substance of bread and wyne was nowe banished out of the Sacrament, and vtterly transcorporated into the substance of Christes very body and bloud: yet was not this body eleuated..nor adored..till the dayes of Pope Honorius the 3.

**2.** *intr.* To migrate from one body to another; to transmigrate. Hence † **Transco·rporating** *ppl. a.*, holding the doctrine of transmigration.

Cf. TRANSINCORPORATION, and med.L. *transcorporatio.*

**1658** SIR T. BROWNE *Hydriot.* iv. 34 The Pythagorians and transcorporating Philosophers, who were to be often buried, held great care of their enterrment.

**Trans,co·rtical**, *a. Anat.* and *Path.* [TRANS- 5.] Crossing the cortex of the brain; in quot., caused by a lesion involving a cross-section of the cerebral cortex.

**1900** *Brit. Med. Jrnl.* 5 May 1104 This phenomenon the author considered analogous to the motor disturbances in the shape of aphasia which has been termed transcortical motor aphasia. **1901** *Lancet* 20 Apr. 1126.

**Trans,crea·te**, *v. nonce-wd.* [TRANS- 2.] *trans.* To create by or in the way of transmission.

**1834** COLERIDGE in *Lit. Rem.* (1839) IV. 166 Not the qualities merely, but the root of the qualities is transcreated. How else could it be a birth,—a creation?

**Tran,scri·bble**, *v. rare.* [f. TRANS- + SCRIBBLE *v.*, after *transcribe*.] *trans.* To transcribe carelessly or hastily. So **Transcri·bbler**, a careless or hasty transcriber.

**1746** GRAY *Let. to Wharton* in W. Mason *Mem.* (1807) II. 37 He [Aristotle] has suffered vastly from the transcribblers, as all authors of great brevity necessarily must. **1750** COVENTRY *Pompey Litt.* II. xii, He..once in a quarter of a year, took the pains to transcribble a sermon out of various authors. **1821** BYRON *Let. to Moore* 19 Sept., Such licentiousness of Verb and Noun as may tend to 'disparage my parts of speech' by the carelessness of the transcribblers.

**Transcribe** (trɑn,skrəi·b), *v.* Also 7 transscribe. [ad. L. *transcrībĕre*, f. *trans*, TRANS- + *scrībĕre* to write.]

**1.** *trans.* To make a copy of (something) in writing; to copy out from an original; to write (a copy). Also *absol.*

**1552** HULOET, Transcribe, *transcribo.* **1611** COTGR., *Transcrire*, to transcribe, to write or copie out. **1621** ELSING *Debates Ho. Lords* (Camden) 101 He coulde not tell whether all was transcrybed by his clerke. **1655** *Nicholas Papers* (Camden) II. 238 The enclosed leters..which I have desired your sonne for your beter satisfaction to transscribe. **1732** BERKELEY *Alciphr.* VI. § 3 The primitive Christians were careful to transcribe copies of the gospels. **1837** LOCKHART *Scott* I. v. 134 The Writer's Apprentice receives a certain allowance in money for every page he transcribes. **1850** MACAULAY in *Life & Lett.* (1913) II. xii. 266 Tomorrow I shall begin to transcribe again and to polish.

**b.** Less exactly: To copy or reproduce the matter or statements of (a writing or book) without regard to the wording; to quote, cite. Now *rare.*

*a* **1633** AUSTIN *Medit.* (1635) 221 A Tradition (which I find not in Abdias, Bishop of Babylon; nor in any of the common Legends that I thinke were almost all transcribed from him). **1646** SIR T. BROWNE *Pseud. Ep.* II. i. 50 Solinus who transcribed Plinie..hath in this point dissented from him. **1676** RAY *Corr.* (1848) 122 All which..makes me suspect he transcribed what he hath out of some writer, either Dutch, French, or Italian. **1726** POPE *Odyss.* V. Notes 285, I have sometimes used Madam Dacier as she has done others, in transcribing some of her Remarks without particularizing them. **1747** WESLEY *Prim. Physick* (1762) p. xviii, A few plain, easy rules. Chiefly transcribed from Dr. Cheyne. **1850** SCORESBY *Cheever's Whalem. Adv.* vi. (1858) 76 Which we have not room to transcribe here.

**2.** To write out in other characters, to transliterate; to write out (a shorthand account) in ordinary 'long-hand'; formerly also, to translate or render accurately in another language.

**1639** T. C[ARY] (*title*) The Mirrour which Flatters not.. Transcrib'd into English from the French [of La Serre],..And devoted to the well-disposed Readers. **1669** tr. *Beguinus' Tyroc. Chym.* To Rdr., It becomes every man, about to transcribe, or render the Works of another in his own native Tongue, neither to add any thing of his own, nor to omit of the Author's. **1724** A. COLLINS *Gr. Chr. Relig.* 138 All the books..were transcrib'd, as is usually suppos'd, out of the Hebrew into the Chaldee Character. **1875** RENOUF *Egypt. Gram.* 1 The omitted vowels are conventionally transcribed by the letter *e.* **1877** BROWNING (*title*) The Agamemnon of Æschylus transcribed by Robert Browning.

**b.** *Mus.* To adapt (a composition) for a voice or instrument other than that for which it was originally written. **1891** in *Cent. Dict.*

† **3.** *fig.* To copy or imitate (a person, his qualities, actions, etc.); to reproduce. *Obs.*

**1647** CRASHAW *Poems* 106 Thou and the lovely hopes that smile in thee Are ta'en out, and transcribed by thy great mother! **1664** EVELYN tr. *Freart's Archit.* Ep. Ded. 5 As many of those Illustrious Persons as by their large and magnificent Structures transcribe your Royal Example. **1709** WATTS *Hymn 'My dear Redeemer'* ii, Such love, and meekness so divine, I would transcribe, and make them mine. *a* **1729** ROGERS (J.), If we imitate their repentance as we transcribe their faults.

† **4.** To attribute or ascribe *to* another by transference. *Obs.*

**1561** T. NORTON *Calvin's Inst.* IV. xiv. (1634) 634 *margin*, Sacraments..be meanes whereby faith groweth, yet so that no power proper unto God be transcribed from him unto them. **1610** R. ABBOTT *Old Way* 15 The Papists..who haue transcribed the authority of Religion to mortall Men, to Doctors, and Fathers, and Councels. **1651** C. CARTWRIGHT *Cert. Relig.* II. 34 As he used to transcribe to the Father whatsoever divine power was in him, so the Apostle doth not improperly transferre to the Father that which was Christs most proper work.

**5.** *Roman Law.* To transfer, assign, make over *to* another; = L. *transcribere*: cf. TRANSCRIPTION 4.

**1880** [see *transcribed* below].

Hence **Transcribed** (-skrəi·bd) *ppl. a.*; **Transcri·bing** *vbl. sb.* and *ppl. a.*

**1700** P. LORRAIN in *Pepys' Diary*, etc. (1879) VI. 229 The transcribing of the Appendix. **1709** STEELE *Tatler* No. 19 ¶ 2 Small Quill-men and Transcribing Clerks. **1880** MUIRHEAD *Gaius* III. § 128 A literal obligation is created by transcribed entries; and these are made in two ways,—either from thing to person, or from person to person.

**Transcriber** (trɑn,skrəi·bəɹ). [f. TRANSCRIBE + -ER [1].] One who transcribes; a copyist or copier, as distinct from an original writer.

**1610** HOLLAND *Camden's Brit.* (1637), The carelesse negligence of transcribers. **1654** FULLER *Ephemeris* Pref. 3, I.. who have no commission to be an Authour, but a Transcriber. **1791** *Gentl. Mag.* Jan. 21/1 The dull transcribers of printed sermons. **1841** D'ISRAELI *Amen. Lit.* (1867) 218 Spurious writings..ascribed by ignorant transcribers to some ancient sage.

**Transcript** (trɑ·n,skript), *sb.* (*a.*) Forms: α. 3–4 transcrit, (3 traunscrit), 5 transcrite, (6 tancrete). β. 5–7 transcripte, (6 -scrypt), 5– transcript. [a. OF. *transcrit* (AF. also *transescrit*, *transecrit*) copy of a document, etc. (1221 in Godef.):—L. *transcript-um*, sb. use of pa. pples. of F. *transcrire*, and L. *transcrībĕre* to TRANSCRIBE. In 15th c. assimilated to the L. form *transcriptum* (evidenced from *c* 1200, in English use). A worn-down F. form *tancrist*, *tanscrit* (13th c. in Godef.), appears to be represented in 16th c. Eng. by *tancrete* (Skelton): see B.]

**1.** A written copy; also *transf.* a printed reproduction of this; *spec.* in *Law*, a copy of a legal record.

α. *c* **1290** *Beket* 551 in *S. Eng. Leg.* I. 122 Of ower olde lawes transcrit ȝe me take. *Ibid.* 553 Þe king him let a traunscrit take of his custumes echon. **1454** *Rolls of Parlt.* V. 248/1 That a transcrite of this same Act..be sent unto our seid Tresorer. **1522** [see B.].

β. **1467** *Mann. & Househ. Exp. Eng.* (Roxb.) 402 Item, for a transcripte of the offyce of Gorge, ij. s. **1481** *Coventry Leet Bk.* 493 A transcript of which lettre hereaftur ensueth. **1538** FITZHERB. *Just. Peas* 187 The clerke of the petit bagge to certify the transcrypt of every suche offyce. **1611** SPEED *Hist. Gt. Brit.* IX. viii. § 54 The Archbishop and other Barons, are so cunningly named in the Popes Transcript, as if [etc.]. **1642** CHAS. I *Answ. Declar. both Ho.* 1 July 36 That which now remains being but a Transcript of a Transcript. **1788** GIBBON *Decl. & F.* xliv. (1869) II. 637 Authentic transcripts were multiplied by the pens of notaries and scribes. **1803** in Gurw. *Wellington's Desp.* (1837) II. 117 *note*, The note that I addressed to him.., a transcript of which is contained in the enclosure. **1875** SCRIVENER *Lect. Text N. Test.* 15 The successive transcripts between the sacred autograph and the document before us.

**b.** A verbal or close translation or rendering. ? *nonce-use.* Cf. TRANSCRIBE *v.* 2.

**1871** BROWNING (*title*) Balaustion's Adventure: including a transcript from Euripides.

**2.** *transf.* and *fig.* A copy, imitation, reproduction; a representation, rendering, interpretation.

**1646** J. GREGORY *Notes & Obs.* Pref. (1650) 1 The Lesser worlds or men are but the Transcripts of the Greater, as Children and Bookes the Copies of themselves. **1647** CLARENDON *Hist. Reb.* I. § 53 Some Transcripts of such Expressions..he met with amongst the People. **1657** TRAPP *Comm. Job* iv. 3 Let our lives be a true transcript of our Sermons. **1711** ADDISON *Spect.* No. 166 ¶ 1 Words are the Transcript of those Ideas which are in the Mind of Man, and ..Writing or Printing are the Transcript of Words. **1781** COWPER *Expost.* 198 They only..Received the transcript of the eternal mind. **1860** WESTCOTT *Introd. Study Gosp.* vii. (ed. 5) 367 The Gospel of St. Mark is essentially a transcript from life. **1869** MᶜLAREN *Serm.* Ser. II. iii. (1875) 42 The artist that is satisfied with his transcript of his ideal will not grow any more.

**B.** *ppl. a.* Transcribed, copied.

*c* **1450** *Godstow Reg.* 102 A Transcripte charter of philippe Basset I-made to the mynchons of Godestowe. **1522** SKELTON *Why not to Court* 417 It shall be as he wyll Stop at law tancrete, An abstract or a concrete.

† **Tran,scri·pt**, *v. Obs. rare.* [f. L. *transcript-*, ppl. stem of *transcrībĕre* to TRANSCRIBE.] *trans.* = TRANSCRIBE. Hence † **Transcri·pting** *vbl. sb.*

**1592** G. HARVEY *Pierce's Super.* Wks. (Grosart) II. 123, I haue lost more labour then the transcripting of this Censure. **1609** *Sir T. Smith's Commw. Eng.* To Rdr. 2 Corruption of coppies, happening..by the often transscripting. **1633** T. STAFFORD *Pac. Hib.* III. xiii. (1821) 625 A Letter from Sir Robert Cecill unto the Lord Deputie, and the same transcripted..unto the President.

**Transcription** (trɑn,skri·pʃən). [ad. L. *transcriptiōn-em*, n. of action f. *transcrībĕre* to transcribe, or a. F. *transcription* (16th c. in Godef. *Compl.*).]

**1.** The action or process of transcribing or copying. Also *fig.*

**1598** FLORIO, *Trascrittione*, a transcription, a writing, or copying out. **1610** HEALEY *St. Aug. Citie of God* 548 The error was committed in the transcription of the copy from Ptolomies library. **1664** H. MORE *Myst. Iniq.* 93 By a diligent comparing of Copies upon every transcription. **1762** J. KENNEDY *Compl. Syst. Astronom. Chronol.* ad fin., Evidence which no transcription can corrupt. *a* **1848** R. W. HAMILTON *Rew. & Punishm.* i. (1853) 43 We might take the Decalogue and trace its transcription upon the soul of man. **1858** J. H. NEWMAN *Hist. Sk.* (1873) III. IV. xi. 416 Manual labour..applied to the transcription and multiplication of books..was a method of instruction.

**b.** Transliteration.

**1869** FARRAR *Fam. Speech* i. (1873) 10 He succeeded in demonstrating the law of transcription, and for the first time reading these names in their proper form. *Ibid.* 24 The transcription into Russian letters.

**2.** The product of this process; a transcript; a copy.

1650 *Vind. Hammond's Addr.* § 88 Besides this transcription, there is but one passage.., to which he thinkes fit to make reply. 1657 RUMSEY *Org. Salutis* Ep. Ded. (1659) 11 Most medicinal Books are usually but bare transcriptions from former Writers. 1696 PHILLIPS (ed. 5), *Transcription*, a Writing copied, or transcribed. 1882–3 *Schaff's Encycl. Relig. Knowl.* I. 116/2 A transcription of the work, made in the beginning of the third century.

**3.** *Mus.* The arrangement, or (less properly) modification, of a composition for some voice or instrument other than that for which it was originally written; an instance of this, a transcribed piece.

1864 in WEBSTER. 1878 E. J. HOPKINS in Grove *Dict. Mus.* I. 21/1 Variations or adaptations like the popular 'Transcriptions' of the present day. 1885 *Athenæum* 26 Dec. 851/1 To the musicianly ear the term 'transcription' has generally an unpleasant sound, because it frequently bears reference to some uncalled-for distortion of a composer's original idea.

**4.** *Roman Law.* A transfer, assignment (of a debt or obligation); = L. *transcriptio.*

1677 OWEN *Justif.* Wks. 1851 V. 170 This he [Paul] did by the transcription of both the debts of Onesimus to himself. 1880 MUIRHEAD *Gaius* III. § 129 There is transcription from thing to person when, for example, I enter to your debit a sum you already owe me by reason of a purchase, a conduction, or a partnership.

Hence **Transcri·ptional** *a.*, of, pertaining to, or of the nature of transcription; **Transcri·ptionally** *adv.*, on transcriptional grounds.

1881 WESTCOTT & HORT *Grk. N. T.* Introd. § 29 Transcriptional Probability is not directly..concerned with the relative excellence of rival readings, but merely with the relative fitness of each for explaining the existence of the others. 1905 J. R. HARRIS in *Expositor* Sept. 166 Traces of such transcriptional errors. 1907 H. S. CRONIN in *Eng. Hist. Rev.* Apr. 294 Both Latin versions must have had some transcriptional history. 1911 K. LAKE *Earlier Ep. St. Paul* 419 The omission is transcriptionally slightly the more probable reading.

**Transcriptitious** (tran͵skripti·ʃəs), *a. rare.* [f. L. *transcript-*, ppl. stem of *transcrībĕre* to TRANSCRIBE + -ITIOUS [1]. Cf. late L. *transcriptīcius*, *-ītius* belonging to a transfer or assignment.] Derived from or arising out of transcription; of the nature or character of a transcript.

1655–87 H. MORE *App. Antid.* (1712) 181 That there is no such Idea of God..as we have describ'd, neither Innate, nor Acquisititious, or Transcriptitious; because it involves in it the Notion of a Spirit. 1802–12 BENTHAM *Ration. Judic. Evid.* (1827) II. 436 Preappointed evidence may be distinguished into original and transcriptitious. *Ibid.* III. 396 Evidence..termed transcriptitious or transcriptural.

**Transcriptive** (tran͵skri·ptiv), *a.* [f. as prec. + -IVE; cf. *descriptive*, etc.]

**1.** Having the quality or habit of transcribing; given, devoted, or tending to transcription.

1646 SIR T. BROWNE *Pseud. Ep.* I. viii. 29 Although excellent and usefull Authors, yet being either transcriptive, or following the common relations of things, their accounts are not to be swallowed at large. *Ibid.* 33 He is to be embraced..as a transcriptive relator. 1823 BYRON *Let.* in *Eng. Stud.* (1897) XXIII. 453, I sent to Mrs. S—— a few Scenes more of the drama begun for her transcriptive leisure. 1888 CAVE *Inspir. O. Test.* viii. 455 Transcriptive Inspiration..moves the writers to write.

**2.** *Rom. Law.* Transferring obligation: cf. TRANSCRIPTION 4.

1875 POSTE *Gaius* III. § 131. 11 Transcriptive entries differ from mere entries of a person as debtor to cash.

Hence **Tran͵scri·ptively** *adv. rare*, in a transcriptive manner; by way of transcription.

1646 SIR T. BROWNE *Pseud. Ep.* I. vi. 21 Authors write often dubiously...Not a few transcriptively,..meerely transcribing almost all they have written.

† **Tran͵scri·ptor.** *Obs. rare.* [a. L. type **transcriptor*, agent-n. from *transcrībĕre* to TRANSCRIBE: cf. rare F. *transcripteur* (Littré).] = TRANSCRIBER.

1617 MORYSON *Itin.* II. 29 The Transcriptor fifty three shillings foure pence. 1811 in *2nd Rep. Rec. Irel.* 141 A Transcript of the Process..lodged with the Transcriptor and Foreign Apposer, previously to passing his Accounts for the year of his Sheriffalty.

**Tran͵scri·ptural,** *a.* [f. L. *transcript-us* transcribed, after *scriptural.*] = TRANSCRIPTIONAL.

1802–12 BENTHAM *Ration. Judic. Evid.* (1827) III. 223 Chains of written evidence in the form of transcriptural evidence. *Ibid.* V. IX. VI. ii. 516 Whether, provisionally at least, inferior evidence may not be employed..: transcriptural, for instance, instead of original. 1863 WESTCOTT in *Smith's Dict. Bible* II. 517/2 *note*, Two characteristic transcriptural errors occur in the passage.

† **Tran͵scrive,** *v. Obs. rare.* [f. TRANS- + SCRIVE *v.* (Cf. F. *transcrīv-*, stem of *transcrire* :—L. *transcrībĕre*.)] = TRANSCRIBE.

1665 in *Maitland Cl. Misc.* (1840) II. 524 For transcryveing a paper in a fine hand sent to London.

† **Trans͵cu·r,** *v. Obs. rare.* [ad. L. *transcurrĕre* to run across. Cf. OF. *transcourir* (12th–15th c. in Godef.).] *trans.* and *intr.* To run across or over; to run or rove to and fro.

1528 LYNDESAY *Dreme* 777 Tygris, Ganges, Ewphrates, and Nyle, Quhilk, in the est, Transcurris mony ane myle. 1626 BACON *Sylva* § 720 It is caused by the Fixing of the Minde upon one Object..whereby it doth not spatiate and transcurre, as it useth.

† **Trans͵cu·rrence.** *Obs. rare.* [f. as next: see -ENCE.] A running or passing over rapidly.

1656 BLOUNT *Glossogr.*, *Transcurrence*.., a running over, a passing over quickly. 1658 in PHILLIPS.

**Transcurrent** (trɑns͵kʊ·rĕnt), *a.* [ad. L. *transcurrent-em*, pr. pple. of *transcurr-ĕre.*]

† **1.** Running or passing across, over, or through.

1608 HIERON *Defence* III. 56 The honoring of a consecrated creature,..with an honor passant, or transcurrent, from and through it to the Creator. 1664 POWER *Exp. Philos.* III. 169 All the Circles of the Armillary Sphære are really.. inhærent in the Earth, by virtue of the transcurrent Atoms.

**2.** *Entom.* Extending or running transversely.

1826 KIRBY & SP. *Entomol.* IV. 349 Transcurrent...When a postfrænum is at first adnate to the sides of the postscutellum, and then diverges across the pannel to the base of the wings.

† **Trans͵cu·rsion.** *Obs.* [ad. late L. *transcursiōn-em*, n. of action f. *transcurrĕre* to run across.]

**1.** The action of running or passing across or through; a going or moving through, transition, penetration; also, a journey or passage through a country, across the sea, etc.

1624 WOTTON *Archit.* in *Reliq.* (1651) 307 Such notes as I have taken in my forraigne transcursions or abodes. 1626 BACON *Sylva* X. Pref., In a Living Creature..the Sense, and the Affects of any one Part of the Body, instantly make a Transcursion thorowout the whole Body. 1653 H. MORE *Antid. Ath.* II. xii. § 17 (1712) 84 To wonder at the transcursion of Comets. 1655 FULLER *Ch. Hist.* X. vi. § 6 The transcursion of Italians hither, added much to the discovery of the Papal abominations. 1665 HOOKE *Microgr.* xxxv. 166 To impede, for the greatest part, the transcursion of the Air.

**2.** *fig.* A running through a subject in discourse.

1641 H. L'ESTRANGE *God's Sabbath* 55 Not to expatiate too farre in collaterall transcursions. 1657 HOWELL *Londinop.* 41 Having made a short transcursion through the Government of the City of London.

**3.** Passage, lapse (of time).

1622 MABBE tr. *Aleman's Guzman d'Alf.* II. 44 Wisedome is the Daughter of Experience, which is gotten by the transcursion of Time. *Ibid.* 288 Nor was transcursion of time needfull in this case.

† **Trans͵cu·rsive,** *a. Obs. rare.* [f. L. *transcurs-*, ppl. stem of *transcurr-ĕre* + -IVE.] Characterized by running rapidly over a subject; cursory.

1599 NASHE *Lenten Stuffe* (1871) 8 In this transcursive reportory, without some observant glance, I may not overpass the gallant beauty of their haven. 1614 JACKSON *Creed* III. To Rdr. 5 b, To sift more of their arguments, then in these short transcursiue disputes I could.

† **Trans͵cu·rsory,** *a. Obs. rare.* [f. as prec. + -ORY [2]: cf. *cursory*, and late L. *transcursōri-us.*] = prec. Hence † **Transcu·rsorily** *adv. Obs. rare.*

1727 EARBERY tr. *Burnet's St. Dead* (1728) I. 238, I shall therefore just take a transcursory View of his Arguments. *Ibid.* II. 117, I have transcursorily taken a view of the Doctor's Notions.

**Transcurva·tion.** [TRANS- 6.] Transverse or lateral curvature (of the spine).

1822–34 *Good's Study Med.* (ed. 4) III. 263 This species offers us the four following varieties..γ Lateralis. Tetanic transcurvation.

**Transdialect** (trɑnsdəi·ălekt, -z-), *v. rare.* [f. TRANS- + DIALECT.] *trans.* To translate from one dialect into another.

1698 C. BOYLE *Bentley's Dissert.* (ed. 2) 52 If some Copyer ..thought that Ocellus's Physics would look better out of Doric, than in it, and therefore transdialected 'em. 1776 BURNEY *Hist. Mus.* I. 331 The poems under the name of Orpheus were written in the Doric dialect, but have since been trans-dialected, or modernised. 1830 J. DOUGLAS *Truths Relig.* (1832) 361 The book of Job appears to be the original Arabic of Job and his friends transdialected and amplified by Moses.

† **Transdi·gnify,** *v. Obs. rare.* [TRANS- 2.] *trans.* To transfer from one dignity or rank to another.

1655 J. SERGEANT *Schism Disarm'd* 212 The Popes Universal Power must be supposed to be transdignifi'd into a private Patriarchate.

**Transdiurnal** (trɑnsdəi͵ɔ̄·rnăl, -z-), *a. nonce-wd.* [TRANS- 3.] That is beyond the confines of day.

1848 LOWELL *Fable for Critics* 594 C[arlyle] shows you how every-day matters unite With the dim transdiurnal recesses of night,—While E[merson] in a plain, preternatural way, Makes mysteries matters of mere every day.

**Transduction** (trɑns͵dʊ·kʃən). *rare.* [ad. L. *transductiōn-em* (usually *trādūctiōnem*), n. of action f. *tra(ns)dūcĕre*: see TRADUCE.] The action of leading or bringing across.

1656 BLOUNT *Glossogr.*, *Transduction*, a leading over, a removing from one place to another. *a* 1816 BENTHAM *Offic. Apt. Maximized, Introd. View* (1830) 19 In lieu of *adduction*, as the purpose requires, will be subjoined *abduction*, *transduction*,..and so forth.

‖ **Transdu·ctor.** *Anat.* [L. agent-n. from *tra(ns)dūcĕre*: see prec.] That which draws across: applied to a muscle of the great toe.

[1890 BILLINGS *Med. Dict.*, Transductor hallucis.] 1899 *Syd. Soc. Lex.*, *Transductor*, syn. of *Transversus pedis.*

**Transe,** obs. form of TRANCE.

† **Transearth** (trɑns͵ɔ̄·ɹþ, -z-), *v. Obs. rare.* [f. TRANS- 2 + EARTH *sb.* or *v.*] *trans.* To move from one soil to another; to transplant.

1628 FELTHAM *Resolves* II. [I.] xix. 60 Fruites of hotter Countries, trans-earth'd in colder Climates.

† **Transeate** (trɑ·nsi͵eɪt), *v. Obs. rare*—[1]. [erron. f. L. *transe-o* I pass over (as if **transe-āre*) + -ATE [3].] *intr.* To pass over or across.

1657 TOMLINSON *Renou's Disp.* 221 The vinous parts of the wine transeating into vinegar.

**Transect** (trɑnse·kt), *v.* Also 9 transsect. [f. TRAN(S- + *sect-*, ppl. stem of L. *secāre* to cut: see SECT *v.*[2]] *trans.* To cut across; to divide by passing across; in *Anat.* to dissect transversely. Hence **Transe·cted** *ppl. a.*

1634 SIR T. HERBERT *Trav.* 161 Who with a Sword of a hundred Cubits length, cut off at one blow ten thousand Christians heads, and transected Taurus. 1846 DANA *Zooph.* (1848) 711 The concentric layers in these transsected knobs. 1861 E. T. HOLLAND *Iceland* in *Peaks, Passes*, etc. Ser. II. I. 8 The plain of Thing-vellir..is transected by numerous longitudinal crevasses in the lava. 1888 *Amer. Jrnl. Psychol.* May 448 The transsected sheaths of the tubules. 1890 O. CRAWFURD *Round Calendar in Port.* 178 The river Douro that transects the northern provinces of Portugal from east to west.

So **Transection** (trɑnse·kʃən) [cf. SECTION], the action of transecting; a transverse section.

1899 *Allbutt's Syst. Med.* VI. 518 Transection of the spinal cord above the lumbar enlargement depresses the knee-jerk for a time.

**Transelement** (trɑns͵e·lĭment), *v.* [ad. med. L. *transelementāre*, f. TRANS- + L. *element-um* ELEMENT.] *trans.* To change or transmute the elements of. Hence **Trans͵e·lementing** *vbl. sb.*

1567 JEWEL *Def. Apol. Ch. Eng.* II. 238 For, as he saith, wee are Transelemented, or transnatured, and changed into Christe, euen so,..wee saie, The Breade is Transelemented, or changed into Christes Body. 1583 FOXE *A. & M.* 1379/2 [Chrysostom] hath these same playne words, transelemented, and transformed. 1656 S. HOLLAND *Zara* (1719) 33 For that he remained for a time as one transelemented. 1812–29 COLERIDGE in *Lit. Rem.* (1838) III. 94 That the body of our Lord was not transelemented or transnatured by the *pleroma* indwelling, we are positively assured by Scripture. 1855 PUSEY *Doctr. Real Presence* Note Q. 186 The Divine gifts were amnesty of evils, removal of sin, transelementing of nature. 1878 GLADSTONE *Glean.* (1879) III. 264 The old monotheism was (so to speak) transelemented, and caricatured, into the gorgeous but gross and motley religion of the Greek and Italian peninsulas.

So † **Trans͵eleme·ntate** [med.L. *transelementātus*] *ppl. a.*, transelemented; **Trans͵eleme·ntate** *v.* = *transelement.*

1579 FULKE *Heskins' Parl.* 296 The bread & wine are transelementated into the vertue of his flesh & bloud. 1583 FOXE *A. & M.* 1382/1 The bread (sayth [Chrysostom]) is transelementate, and transmuted into an other substaunce then it was before. 1899 W. R. INGE *Chr. Mysticism* vii. 257 *note*, The last-named [Theophylact] goes on to say that 'we are in the same way transelementated into Christ'.

**Trans͵e:lementa·tion.** [n. of action from med.L. *transelementāre*: see above, and quot. 1896.] The action or process of changing the elements of something.

1550 HOOPER *Serm. Jonas* vi. S iij, The transelementacion and alteracion of the breade, no place of y[e] scripture commaundeth vs to beleue. 1624 F. WHITE *Repl. Fisher* 421 In Transubstantiation the matter is destroyed, and the quantitie and accidents remaine, and in Transelementation the matter remaineth, and the essentiall and accidentall formes are altered. 1654 JER. TAYLOR *Real Pres.* xii. ¶ 5 The name of Transelementation, which Theophylact did use, seems to approach nearer to signify the propriety of this mysterie, because it signifies a change even of the first elements. 1706 tr. *Dupin's Eccl. Hist. 16th C.* II. v. 53 If any one is offended with the new Term *Transubstantiation*, he will find that the Ancients used the terms *Conversion*, *Transmutation*, *Transformation*, *Transelementation*. 1855 PUSEY *Doctr. Real Presence* Note Q. 223 Through what the transelementation of our nature from mortal to immortal takes place. 1896 R. F. CLARKE in *Month* Feb. 207 A conversion (μεταβολή), a transmutation (μεταποίησις), a transelementation (μεταστοιχείωσις).

† **Trans͵e·minent,** *a. Obs. rare.* [f. TRANS- 4 + EMINENT.] Eminent beyond others; pre-eminent, supereminent. So † **Trans͵e·minency**, pre-eminence; † **Trans͵e·minently** *adv.*, pre-eminently.

1642 *Answ. Observ. agst. King* 19 What State businesses soever are fairely carried,..redound transeminently and really to the glory of the Crowne. 1660 BURNEY Κέρδ. Δῶρον (1661) 3 This is the transeminencie of the Persons, and they have the Illustrious Character of Kings. *Ibid.* 22 Our Soveraign Lord.., who hath Reigned in all ages, in the persons transeminent.

**Transempirical** (trɑns͵empi·rikăl), *a. rare.* [TRANS- 4.] Pertaining to things beyond the range of experiential knowledge; metempirical.

1906 W. JAMES in *Jrnl. Philos., Psychol.*, etc. 20 Dec. 712 A conclusion supposed to flow from the intrinsic absurdity of transempirical objects.

**Transept** (trɑ·nsept). Forms: 6 transsept, 7 -scept, 8– transept. [First found in 16th c., ad. med. or mod. (Anglo-)L. **transseptum*, f. TRANS- + SEPTUM, prop. *sæptum* hedge, fence, enclosure, f. *sæpīre* to hedge in, fence in, enclose. (Early history and actual origin unascertained.) Hence mod.F. *transept* (introd. 1828). The Anglo-L. *transeptum* is often used by Leland, and in one instance Englished as *transsept*; but the word was rare before 1700.] The transverse part of a cruciform church considered apart from the nave; also, each of the two subdivisions or arms of this (the *north* and *south transepts*).

1538-42 Leland *Itin.* (1907) I. ii. 131 It stode in the midle of the transeptum of the chirch. *Ibid.* iii. 239 One Sir John Scylley a knight and his wyfe sumtyme dwellyng in that paroche [Crideton] be buried in the north part of the transept [*ed.* 1711 transept] of this [church]. *Ibid.* 287 In Transepto Eccl. in Merid. parte. *Ibid.* 292 An exceding goodly Chapel in Transepto of Bishop Stillington and King. 1692 Wood *Ath. Oxon., Fasti* 821 His body was buried in the south Transcept or large south Isle joyning to the Choir of St. Peter's Church in Westminster. 1782 Warton *Hist. Kiddington* 8 The pediment of the southern Transept is pinnacled, not inelegantly, with a flourished Cross. 1815 J. Smith *Panorama Sc. & Art* I. 130 The part running north and south is called the cross or transept. 1870 F. R. Wilson *Ch. Lindisf.* 79 The chancel roof,..like those of the nave and transepts, is open-timbered.

**b.** *attrib.* and *Comb.*, as *transept aisle, chapel.*

1890 C. H. Moore *Gothic Archit.* iii. 160 Where there are no transept aisles..there are..no vertical divisions in the façade [end of transept]. 1900 *Yorkshire Archæological Jrnl.* XV. 281 The vaults of the presbytery and transept-chapels.

**Transeptal** (trǫnse·ptăl), *a.* [f. prec. + -al.] Of, pertaining to, or of the nature of a transept. Hence **Transe·ptally** *adv.*, in the manner of a transept.

1846 *Ecclesiologist* V. 152 A parclose..screening off the north transeptal chapel. 1856 *Ibid.* XVII. 88 A spacious narthex with the prescribed chapels..opening into it transeptally. 1884 *Ch. Times* XXII. 86 Exeter is noteworthy for its transeptal or 'paddle-box' towers. 1886 Willis & Clark *Cambridge* III. 261 The chapel is to the west of the hall, and has a transeptal antechapel.

**Trans-equato·rial**, *a.* [Trans- 3: cf. *equatorial.*] Situated on the other side of the equator; also crossing the equator.

1900 *Jrnl. R. Geog. Soc.* Apr. 381 The Southern, Australian, or trans-equatorial land of our hemisphere.

**Trans,esse·ntiate**, *v. rare.* [f. Trans- 1 + Essentiate *v.*] *trans.* To change from one essence or being into another. Hence **Trans,esse·ntiating** *vbl. sb.* So **Trans,esse·ntiate** *ppl. a.* [Essentiate *ppl. a.*], changed into another essence. (Const. as pa. pple.)

1675 Penn *Eng. Pres. Interests Consid.* Wks. 1782 III. 220 Here is no transessentiating or transubstantiating of being, from people to representative. 1839-52 Bailey *Festus* xxxv. 554 Curse transessentiate into blessing!

**Transetorious, -tory**, etc., obs. ff. Transitorious, Transitory, etc.

**†Tran,se·xion.** *Obs. rare.* [irreg. f. Trans- + L. *sex-us* Sex + -ion, after *connexion*, etc.] Change of sex.

1646 Sir T. Browne *Pseud. Ep.* iii. xvii. 147 Not only Mankinde, but many other Animals, may suffer this transexion, we will not deny, or hold it at all impossible. *Ibid.* 148 Surely it much impeacheth this iterated transexion of Hares, if that be true which Cardan and other Physitians affirm, that Transmutation of sex is only so in opinion.

**Transfashion** (trɑnsfæ·ʃən), *v.* [Trans- 2.] *trans.* To alter or change the fashion of, to transform.

1601 Deacon & Walker *Spirits & Divels* 134 He transmuted, transfashioned, transfigured, transformed, or metamorphozed himself into an angel. 1619 W. Sclater *Exp. 1 Thess.* (1630) 305 To see..our people so Cameleon-like transfashioned into [etc.]. 1855 Pusey *Doctr. Real Presence* Note Q. 233 God shall 'transfashion (μετασχηματίσει) our vile bodies, to be made like unto His glorious Body'.

**Transfeature** (trɑnsfī·tiŭɹ), *v.* [Trans- 2.] *trans.* To change the features of.

1875 Dora Greenwell *Liber Hum.* 33 Outward nature itself is transfigured and transfeatured to their view.

**Transfeminate** (trɑnsfe·mineⁱt), *v. rare.* [f. Trans- + L. *femina*: cf. Effeminate *v.*] *trans.* See quot. 1656. Hence **Transfe·minated** *ppl. a.*

1646 Sir T. Browne *Pseud. Ep.* iii. xvii. 148 These transfeminated persons were really men at first, although succeeding years produced the manifesto or evidence of their virilities. 1656 Blount *Glossogr., Transfeminate..*, to turn from woman to man, or from one sex to another. 1898 G. Meredith *Odes Fr. Hist.* 39 With a breath he blew them out, to beat their wings The way of such transfeminated things.

**Transfer** (trɑ·nsfəɹ), *sb.* [f. Transfer *v.*]

**1.** *Law.* Conveyance from one person to another of property, *spec.* of shares or stock.

1674 *Court Bks. Roy. Afr. Co.* (P.R.O.), [Form of acceptance] I do accept of —— his transfer of £— abovesaid the day and year abovewritten. 1693 *Act 5 Will. & Mary* c. 7. § 47 The Fee for examining..a Tickett or Tally in order to make a true Assignement or Transfer..shall..be One penny. 1694 *Bank of Eng. Charter* 27 July, There shall be constantly kept..a Register, or Book or Books, wherein all Assignments and Transfers shall be entered. 1727 Swift *What passed in Lond.* Wks. 1755 III. i. 189 All the Thursday morning was taken up in private transfers. 1766 Blackstone *Comm.* II. i. 9 The reciprocal transfer of property by sale, grant, or conveyance. 1788 Jefferson *Writ.* (1859) II. 367 Observations on the transfer of our domestic debt to foreigners. 1817 Jas. Mill *Brit. India* II. iv. i. 5 The office in which are effected the transfers of the Company's stock and annuities. 1836 J. Gilbert *Chr. Atonem.* vii. (1852) 204 The lowest case of legal transfer is that of a debt.

**2.** *gen.* The act of transferring or fact of being transferred; conveyance or removal from one place, person, etc. to another; transference; transmission.

1785 Burke *Corr.* (1844) III. 33 To remonstrate against the transfer of an immense sum of public money from the national service. 1811 J. Adams *Wks.* (1856) X. 3, I wait with patience for a transfer to another scene. 1843 Lytton *Last Bar.* i. iii, An amply sufficient cause for the transfer of his allegiance. 1870 Jevons *Elem. Logic* iv. 32 Equivocal words have become so by a transfer of meaning. 1877 Knight *Dict. Mech.* 1334/2 The third lithographic method is by transfer... The work is not drawn or engraved upon the stone direct, but is placed there in a completed condition from some source furnishing it. 1907 *Trans. Devon Assoc.* 50 The transfer of the county See to Exeter.

**b.** *Naut.* In tacking: The distance traversed at right angles to the line of advance.

1889 *Cent. Dict.* s.v. *Advance* 12, In naval tactics, the distance made by a ship under way, in the direction of her course, after the helm has been put to one side and kept there; opposed to *transfer*, the distance made at right angles to the original course.

**3.** A thing (*rarely*, a person) that is transferred; *spec.* writing, drawing, or a design, conveyed from one surface to another in lithography, photography, and the like.

1839 *Trans. Royal Soc.* IV. 133 Twenty-three specimens of photographs, made by Sir John Herschel, accompany this paper..copies of engravings and drawings, some reverse, or first transfers; and others second transfers or re-reversed pictures. 1864 Webster, *Transfer*..a soldier removed from one troop, or body of troops, and placed in another. 1877 Knight *Dict. Mech., Transfer*, an impression taken on paper, cloth, etc., and then laid upon an object and caused to adhere thereto by pressure. 1880 *Print. Trades Jrnl.* xxxi. 38 A transfer paper is prepared.., on which the transfer to be preserved is pulled. 1883 *Hardwich's Photogr. Chem.* 311 If a mat surface be desired, the transfer should be stripped from the glass before it is quite dry.

**4.** A means or place of transfer. Chiefly U.S. *spec.* **a.** *U.S. Post Office.* A telegraphic money-order. **b.** On a railway, etc.:

(*a*) A place at which trains or cars are transferred to a ferry for water transport; also, a ferry by which trains or cars are transported. (*b*) A siding connecting tracks at a crossing or on different levels (Webster 1911). (*c*) A transfer-ticket (*Cent. Dict.*). (*d*) The conveyance of passengers and luggage from one railway station to another, when these are not contiguous; hence *transfer-company*, a company which undertakes such conveyance between stations.

**c.** *Archery.* A sheet to which all scores are transferred from the target-papers.

1909 *Cent. Dict. Suppl.* s.v., The transfers are the official record from which the prize-list is made up.

**5.** *attrib.* and *Comb.*, as *transfer-boat, -clerk, -company* (4b), *-deed, -department, -form, office, -process, rate*; **transfer-book**, a register of transfers of property, esp. that of its shares or stock, kept by a joint-stock company; **transfer-day**, at the Bank of England, a day for the register of transfers of bank-stock; **transfer-elevator**, a crane for transferring cargo from one vessel to another; **transfer-fee**, that charged by a joint-stock company for registering a transfer; **transfer-gilding**, in ceramics, transfer of a pattern in gold, as from paper to unglazed ware; **transfer-ink**, ink used in lithography; **transfer-jar**, a jar used in the collection of gases over liquid; **transfer-lathe**: see quot.; **transfer-lithography**: see sense 3; **transfer-paper**, paper used in making transfers in lithography and other processes; **transfer-press**, in engraving, a transferring machine; **transfer-printing**, a process by which designs are printed on fictile and other ware (so **transfer-printed** adj.); also printing by means of lithography; **transfer-station** (*U.S.*), a point at which transfer-tickets are given, and passengers transferred from one car to another (*Cent. Dict. Supp.*); **transfer-table** (*U.S.*), a railway traverse-table; **transfer-ticket**, a ticket entitling a passenger to change from a conveyance to one on another line or route without re-booking or further payment; a through ticket; **transfer-work**, designs made by transferring or transfer-printing.

1888 *Daily News* 10 Dec. 6/8 The *transfer boat Maryland was conveying a section of a train from Washington to Boston across the Haarlem River, at midnight. 1694 J. Houghton *Collect. Improv. Husb. & Trade* V. No. 102 (13 July) The Seller goes to the Clerk of the Company..appointed to keep a Book of Alienations, called a *Transferr Book, and there he transferrs the Shares he has sold to the Buyer. 1701 *Lond. Gaz.* No. 3737/4 The Transfer Books of the Bank will be shut up from Monday the 15th Instant to Friday the 10th of October next, in order to a Dividend. 1746 Fielding *True Patriot* No. 10 The cash, transfer books, &c. removed to the tower, from the Bank. 1834 [S. Smith] *Lett. J. Downing* xxvi. (1835) 170 What the Treasury calls contingent drafts, and *transfer checks, and Treasury warrants. 1899 *Westm. Gaz.* 7 Sept. 7/1 It is nothing..for a *transfer clerk to wait for forty-five minutes at the Associated office. 1909 Eliz. L. Banks *Myst. Fras. Farrington* 159 These trunks had been delivered by a responsible *Transfer Company's waggon. 1771 *App. Chron.* in *Ann. Reg.* 209/2 He recollected it was not *transfer-day. 1884 Knight *Dict. Mech.* Suppl., **Transfer-elevator*, an elevator or crane for hoisting from one vessel into another. 1832 Babbage *Econ. Manuf.* xi. (ed. 3) 78 A single copy might be printed off with *transfer ink. 1827 Faraday *Chem. Manip.* xv. (1842) 322 Capped or *transfer jars are such as, being open above, have a cap cemented upon them, the latter being surmounted by a stop-cock. *Ibid.* xxiv. 627 Fill a transfer jar..with water..over the trough. 1877 Knight *Dict. Mech.*, **Transfer-lathe*, for..reducing large designs in relief to proportions suitable for coin. 1897 *Westm. Gaz.* 5 Apr. 7/3 To the average man the difference between 'lithography' and '*transfer-lithography' matters little. 1693 *Act 5 Will. & Mary* c. 7. § 54 The *Transfer Office above mentioned shall bee continued. 1858 Simmonds *Dict. Trade*, **Transfer-paper*, prepared paper used by lithographers; thin, unsized paper for taking copies of letters with a copying-press. 1878 Abney *Photogr.* (1881) 171 A piece of transfer paper (which is paper coated with gelatine subsequently rendered insoluble in water by alum or other such body) is placed in water of about 60° C., and softened. 1877 Knight *Dict. Mech.*, **Transfer-press*. 1865 *Athenæum* 25 Nov. 733/1 *Transfer-printing in pottery. 1905 *Daily Chron.* 24 Aug. 3/2 The single invention in porcelain decoration at our credit in the eighteenth century was transfer-printing. 1877 Knight *Dict. Mech.* 2368/2 Jacob Perkins, of Massachusetts, the inventor of the *transfer-process. 1861 *Massachusetts Stat.* 199 § 2 *Transfer ticket.

**Transfer** (trɑnsfɔ̄·ɹ), *v.* Also 5-7 -ferre, 7 -ferr. Inflected **transfe·rred**, etc. [a. F. *transfér-er* (3rd s. *transfère*) (14th c. in Littré), or its source, L. *transfer-re*, f. Trans- + *ferre* to bear, carry, bring.]

**1.** *trans.* To convey or take from one place, person, etc. to another; to transmit, transport; to give or hand over from one to another.

1382 Wyclif *Ezek.* xlviii. 14 Nether the first fruytis of the lond shuln be transferrid [*gloss* or born ouer, 1388 translatid], for thei ben halewid to the Lord. c1425 *St. Christina* xxxvii. in *Anglia* VIII. 133/35 Þe biggynge of the abbeye was transferred to a better place. c1430 *Art of Nombryng* 9 Put a cifre þer and transferre the article towarde the lift hande. 1516 in *Acts Parlt. Scotl.* (1875) XII. 36/2 It is thocht..that þe said governoure..suld transfer himselff to uthir cuntreis. 1624 Godwin *Moses & Aaron* (1641) 158 The moderne Jewes doe transferre the fault upon certaine proselyte Ægyptians who came forth with them. 1655 Stanley *Hist. Philos.* ii. (1701) 73/1 He first transferr'd Natural Philosophy out of Ionia to Athens. 1703 Moxon *Mech. Exerc.* 316 Divide one of these nine equal parts into two equal parts, and transfer that distance to the other eight equal parts. 1771 Goldsm. *Hist. Eng.* II. 357 Campegio..shortly after transferred the cause before the court of Rome. 1783 Burke *Rep. Affairs Ind.* Wks. XI. 42 If the court of directors should disapprove of his being transferred to Bengal. 1809 R. Langford *Introd. Trade* 86 For transferring £5690 Reduced Stock into the Four per Cents. 1818 in Willis & Clark *Cambridge* (1886) I. 573 Transferring three or four of the trees to another site. 1844 Ld. Brougham *Brit. Const.* vii. (1862) 94 The people's power being transferred to the representative body. 1860 Tyndall *Glac.* i. xxii. 151, I transferred my scrip to his shoulders, and led the way.

**b.** *fig.* esp. in Sematology: see quots.

1586 A. Day *Eng. Secretary* ii. (1625) 77 *Metaphora*, which is, when a word from the proper or right signification is transferred to another neere vnto the meaning. 1883 Murray *Eng. Dict.* Gen. Explan. p. xxi, As the primitive sense [of words] has been..transferred boldly to figurative and analogical uses.

**c.** *intr.* for *refl.* or *pass.*

1646 G. Daniel *Upon Virgil* 32 Wks. 1878 I. 22 But Wee..averre Soules are not lost, or Dye, but doe transfer. 1901 *Daily Chron.* 24 Oct. 3/4 He transferred later to the 19th Hussars, in which regiment he served in the Soudan campaign. 1911 Webster, *Transfer*, to change from one car, line, or the like, to another for continuing one's journey on a transfer.

**2.** *Law.* To convey or make over (title, right, or property) by deed or legal process.

1598 Florio, s. v. *Trascriuere*, To transfer or giue ouer his right to another. 1651 Hobbes *Leviath.* i. xiv. 67 My right is not transferred, but remaineth till I transferre it by some other Act. 1671 *Court Bks. Roy. African Co.* 19 Dec. (P.R.O.), I do transfer £500 of my subscription in the new joint stock of the Royal Company to the Rt. Hon. George Lord Berkeley. 1694 J. Houghton *Collect. Improv. Husb. & Trade* V. No. 102 [*Form*] 'I A. B. do hereby sell, assign, and transferr unto C. D. Ten Shares in the Joynt-Stock..with all the present and future Profits thereof'. 1771 *Junius Lett.* lxvii. (1797) II. 235 To this son-in-law..you meant to transfer the..property. 1818 Cruise *Digest* (ed. 2) IV. 65 A grant only transfers what the grantor may lawfully give. 1878 Jevons *Prim. Pol. Econ.* 14 Sometimes things can be literally handed over, like a watch or a book; sometimes they can be transferred by a written deed.

**3.** To convey (a drawing or design) from one surface to another, esp. (*a*) to a lithographic stone, to earthenware, glass, etc., by means of transfer-paper; (*b*) to a new back or ground, as an embroidered pattern, etc.

1839 Ure *Dict. Arts* 1017 This [roll of flannel] is used as a burnisher, one end of it being rested against the shoulder, and the other end being rubbed upon the paper; by which means it transfers all the engraved traces to the biscuit. 1860 *Ibid.* (ed. 5) III. 501 There are two distinct methods of printing in use for china and earthenware; one is transferred on the bisque..and the other is transferred on the glaze. The first is called 'press printing', and the latter 'bat printing'. 1877 Knight *Dict. Mech.* 2611/2 In engraving, a tracing may be made in pencil and transferred to the ground by running through the plate-press. An impression from a plate or stone may also be transferred to a stone.

Hence **Transferred** (-fɔ̄·ɹd) *ppl. a.*, conveyed from one person, place, sense, etc. to another.

1863 H. Allon *Mem. J. Sherman* 279, 102 members were added in 1839 and 63 in 1840, including transferred members. 1883 Murray *Dict.* Gen. Explan. p. xxi, The word was first taken into English..in a figurative, transferred, or specialized use. 1886 J. Ebsworth *Roxb. Ball.* VI. 165 As a transferred ballad, Dulcina was entered to John White and Thomas Langley, in the Registers of the Stationers' Company.

**Transferable** (trɑ·nsfĕrăb'l), *a.* [f. prec. + -able: cf. *preferable, referable.* See also Transferrable.] Capable of being transferred or legally made over to another; *spec.* of bills, drafts, cheques, etc.: assignable in the course of business from one person to another; negotiable.

1646 Sir T. Browne *Pseud. Ep.* vi. iii. 286 If we..fall upon consideration with what incongruity they are transferable unto others. 1711 Steele *Spect.* No. 149 ¶ 8 Take him in whom what you like is not transferable to another. 1874 *Act* 37 & 38 *Vict.* c. 3 § 5 The debentures..shall be transferable by the delivery of such debentures. 1909 *Westm. Gaz.* 8 Mar. 2/1 The adoption of the single transferable vote system of proportional representation.

Hence **Tra·nsferabi·lity,** the quality of being transferable.

1776 Adam Smith *W. N.* iv. iii. II. 66 Its easy and safe transferability, its use in paying foreign bills of exchange. 1875 Poste *Gaius* iii. Comm. (ed. 2) 431 The complete transferability of obligations was unknown to jurisprudence. 1893 *Nation* (N. Y.) 25 May 390/1 We shall [in political economy] regard transferability as meaning exchangeability.

**Transferal**: see Transferral.

**Transferee** (trɑnsfərī·). Also *erron.* -ferree. [f. Transfer *v.* + -ee.]

**1.** One to whom a transfer is made. (Chiefly in *Law*, as correlative to Transferor or Transferrer.)

1736 Bailey (folio) Pref., *Transférée*, the Person to whom any Thing is transferred. 1789–90 A. Hamilton in *Debates Congress* (1834) II. 2048 The transferable quality of stock..depends on the idea of complete security to the transferee. 1801 — *Wks.* (1886) VII. 187 A discrimination between original holders and transferees of the public debt. 1905 *Times* 3 Apr. 8/4 Mr. B. signed a blank transfer as transferee.

**2.** One who is transferred or removed; e. g. from one position or grade to another.

1892 *Daily News* 27 Oct. 5/5 The children removed under the law from gaols to reformatories in the past year have done fairly well; but, looking to the difficulty in inducing employers to take these transferees into their service, they urge [etc.]. 1899 *Educat. Rev.* XVIII. 27 No disgrace was entailed upon the transferees, who were advanced with the rest of that class at the regular promotion.

**Transference** (tra·nsfĕrĕns). Also 7–9 *erron.* -ferrence. [ad. L. type **transferentia* (used in med. or mod.L.; e.g. *a* 1541 by Paracelsus), f. *transferent-em*: see next and -ence.]

**1.** The action or process of transferring; conveyance from one place, person, or thing to another; transfer.

1760–72 H. Brooke *Fool of Qual.* (1809) I. 141 The transference was not difficult. 1776 Adam Smith *W. N.* v. ii. II. 467 The transference of stock or moveable property. 1791 Newte *Tour Eng. & Scot.* 127 In Argyleshire..it became common to convey land, and make other transferences of property in writing. 1827 Faraday *Chem. Manip.* xv. (1842) 323 Moderately-sized funnels..to assist in the transference of gas into vessels. 1839 *Morn. Herald* 13 June, A transference of power to the moneyed classes. 1875 Lubbock *Wild Flowers* i. 8 The transference of the pollen from one flower to another is..effected principally either by the wind or by insects. 1880 Swinburne *Stud. Shaks.* 258 A line too apt and exquisite to endure without injury the transference from its original setting. 1885 Watson & Burbury *Math. Th. Electr. & Magn.* I. 222 There is a transference, per unit time, of electricity *I* from the extremity *A* to the extremity of *B*.

**2.** *Sc. Law.* The procedure by which a depending action is transferred from a person deceased to his representative.

1681 Stair *Inst. Law Scot.* xv. § 10. 322 The Decreet will be effectual against all singular Successors, and subsequent Tennents without a new Decreet of Transferrence. 1765–8 Erskine *Inst. Law Scot.* iv. i. § 60 If the pursuer be dead, it is called a transference *active*..Where the defender dies, it gets the name of a transference *passive*. *Ibid.*, Yet a transference cannot proceed against a debtor's apparent heir, till the *annus deliberandi* be expired. 1838 W. Bell *Dict. Law Scot.* 999 Transferences are competent to inferior judges, only when the representatives reside within their jurisdiction, and the principal cause is in dependence before them.

† **Transferent** (tra·nsfĕrĕnt), *a. Obs. rare.* [ad. L. *transferent-em*, pr. pple. of *transfer-re* to transfer.] Effecting transference; in reference to sense: tropical, figurative.

1614 Raleigh *Hist. World* ii. vi. § 7 Tropicall or transferent, which applies the diuers formes and figures of naturall bodies, to signifie the dignities, fortunes [etc.]..of their Gods, and of men. 1651 C. Cartwright *Cert. Relig.* i. 46 In a Metaphoricall and transferent sense.

**Transferential** (trɑnsfĕre·nʃăl), *a.* [f. (mod.) L. *transferenti-a* Transference + -al.] Of or pertaining to transference.

1889 G. Allen in *Nature* 24 Jan. 290/2 So the Energy of Kinesis is seen to be a mere transferential mode from one kind of separation to another.

**Transferer** (tra·nsfĕrəɹ). [f. Transfer *v.* or *sb.* + -er [1].] One who or that which transfers: used sometimes for Transferrer, sometimes in the technical sense of Transferor.

1807 Joyce *Sci. Dial.* v. *Pneumatics*, This instrument is called the transferer. 1875 Ure *Dict. Arts* III. 620 (Pottery) This impression..is then laid by the transferer [*ed.* 1860 transferrer] upon the ware. 1884 W. H. Rideing in *Harper's Mag.* May 897/1 That the Bank may be sure that the transferer is the person he represents himself to be. 1906 *Daily News* 12 Jan. 12 Transfer of Labourers [in S. Africa]..It is provided in the sub-section that 'the transfer..shall be signed by the transferer, the transferee, and the labourer'. 1908 *Daily Chron.* 24 Apr. 11/7 Litho Transferer wanted.

**Transfero·graphy.** [f. Transfer *sb.* + -(o)graphy.] (See quot.)

1846 Worcester, *Transferography*, the art or act of copying inscriptions from ancient tombs, tablets, etc. *Williams.* 1864 in Webster. Hence in later Dicts.

**Transferor** (tra·nsfĕrǭɹ, -ǒɹ). Also *erron.* -ferror. [f. Transfer *v.* or *sb.* + -or.] One who transfers or makes a transfer or conveyance of property, etc. Esp. in legal use, correlative to *transferee*.

1875 Poste *Gaius* ii. (ed. 2) § 251 After the transfer of the inheritance the transferror continues heir, the transferee being sometimes quasi heir, sometimes quasi legatee. *Ibid.* Comm. 202 It confers property on the transferee, and discharges the transferor of an obligation. 1876 Digby *Real Prop.* iv. § 5. 200 The transferee stepping for all purposes into the place of the transferor. 1882 *Act* 45 & 46 *Vict.* c. 38 § 40 The receipt..for any money..discharges the payer or transferer therefrom.

**Transferotype**: see Transferrotype.

**Transfe·rrable,** *a.* Also 9 -ible. [f. Transfer *v.* + -able, on English analogies, as in *transferring, barrable. Transferrible* is a hybrid spelling between *transferrable* and analogical L. **transferibilis*. See also Transferable.] Capable of being or fit to be transferred.

*a.* 1660 R. Coke *Power & Subj.* 30 The offices..are alienable, communicable, and transferrable. 1714 *Act* 1 *Geo. I*, c. 21 § 19 That the said Capital or Joint Stock..shall be Assignable and Transferrable or Devisable. 1765 Blackstone *Comm.* I. viii. 328 A new species of money, always ready to be employed in any beneficial undertaking, by means of it's transferrable quality. 1872 O. W. Holmes *Poet Breakf.-t.* x, Sin was made a transferrable chattel. 1878 Abney *Photogr.* xxvi. (1881) 176 Transferrable prints.

*β.* 1832 Lyell *Princ. Geol.* II. 171 We believe the mean annual temperature of one zone to be transferrible to another. 1875 Poste *Gaius* ii. § 21 Similarly transferrible are estates in provincial lands.

Hence **Transfe·rrableness,** the quality of being transferrable.

1804 W. Taylor in *Ann. Rev.* II. 390 In reply to the objection of the transferrableness of machinery.

**Transferral** (trɑnsfǝ̄·răl). *erron.* transferal. [f. as prec. + -al: cf. *conferral.*] The action or fact of transferring; transfer, transference.

1863 *Cornh. Mag.* VII. 388 The transferal of Greenwich mean time into sidereal, and vice versâ. 1870 E. Mulford *Nation* x. 169 All acquisition of territory..is by the United States alone, and the immediate transferal is to the United States. 1875 Whitney *Life Lang.* v. 78 The old material of language is constantly suffering extension and transferral to new uses.

**Transferrer** (trɑnsfǝ̄·rəɹ). [f. as prec. + -er [1]. See also Transferer, -or.] One who or that which transfers.

1753 Hanway *Trav.* (1762) II. i. vii. 35 These transfers are made by the personal appearance of the transferrer. 1803 W. Taylor in *Ann. Rev.* I. 744 Compelling him to prove only against the immediate transferrer of the bill. 1825 J. Nicholson *Operat. Mechanic* 470 The impression when taken off the plate is given to a girl, called a cutter, who cuts it into shapes, and hands the parts to a woman (the transferrer), who puts them on the biscuit. 1860 H. Spencer *Soc. Organism* in *Westm. Rev.* Jan. 105 A system of vessels which continues ever after to be the transferrer of nutriment. 1862 *Catal. Internat. Exhib.* II. x. 17 This direct transferrer, invented by Mr. George Glover, is now generally used in the gradation of gas-holders for testing meters.

**Transferring** (trɑnsfǝ̄·riŋ), *vbl. sb.* [f. as prec. + -ing [1].] The action of the verb Transfer; transference.

1573 *Reg. Privy Council Scot.* II. 284 Thai obtenit ane decreit of transfering befoir the Lordis of Counsall and Sessioun. 1651 Hobbes *Govt. & Soc.* ii. § 7. 23 Words..effectuall towards the perfect transferring of his Right. 1688 *Act Sederunt* 26 July in Fountainhall *Hist. Not.* (Bann. Cl.) 882 After wakenings and transferrings are seen and returned, they need not byde the course of the roll, but may be summarly called and decerned, or debated. 1766 Blackstone *Comm.* II. xxx. 446 If it be a transferring of goods for money, it is called a sale. 1904 D. Cumming *Lithography* xx. 194 [Zinc and Aluminium] Plates with a fine grain or 'tooth'..suitable for all classes of transferring and printing.

*attrib.* 1827 Faraday *Chem. Manip.* xxiv. (1842) 634 Exhaust the retort.., attach it to a graduated transferring jar.

**Transfe·rro-, tra·nsferrotype.** *Photog.* [Irreg. f. Transfer + -type.] See quot. 1890.

1889 *Anthony's Photogr. Bull.* II. 322 This is not more trouble than the transferrotype process; it was, in fact, my familiarity with the double transfer carbon process which first suggested to me the transferrotype. 1891 *Ibid.* IV. 241 Eastman's transferotype paper answers well for decorating the tiles. 1890 Woodbury *Dict. Photogr.* 701 *Transferrotype*, a process of transferring bromide prints to any suitable support. [Description follows.] *Ibid.* 702 Warm tones.. may be obtained with transferotype paper.

† **Transfi·gurate,** *a. Obs. rare.* [ad. L. *transfigūrāt-us*, pa. pple. of *transfigūrāre*: see next.] Transfigured; having its figure or form altered: *spec.* in *Geom.* (see Transfigured).

1571 Digges *Pantom.* iv. Hh ij b, This transfigurate body [Dodecaedron] receiueth an internall Tetraedron, whose solide angles rest in the centers of his trigonall bases. *Ibid.*, Icosaedron within this transfigurate body may be described.

**Transfigurate** (trɑnsfi·giŭreɪt), *v.* Now *rare.* Pa. t. and pple. in Sc. 6 transfigurat. [f. ppl. stem of L. *transfigūrāre*, f. Trans- + *figūra* figure.] *trans.* = Transfigure. Hence **Transfi·gurating** *ppl. a.*

1432–50 tr. *Higden* (Rolls) II. 211 Thei may thro the permission of God transfigurate similitudes. *a* 1555 Ridley *Piteous Lament.* (1556) E iv, This our weake body shall be transfigurated and made lyke vnto christes glorious body. *a* 1560 Rolland *Crt. Venus* iii. 31 In ane tre scho was transfigurat. 1563 Winȝet *Four Scoir Thre Quest.* Wks. (S.T.S.) I. 87 Quhen he transfigurat His body afoir His passiour. 1600 F. Walker *Sp. Mandeville* 145 They can and do s[o] transfigurat themselues. 1819 Byron *Proph. Dante* iv. 3[...] High heaven is there Transfused, transfigurated. 1871 Morley *Crit. Misc.* Ser. i. *Carlyle* 219 [Carlyle's] epithet..shoot[s] like a sunbeam on to the matter, throwing a transfigurating light.

**Transfiguration** (trɑnsfigiŭrē·ʃən). [ad. L. *transfigūrātiōn-em* (Pliny), n. of action from *transfigūrāre* (see prec.). Cf. F. *transfiguration* (13th c. in Hatz.-Darm.). The specific sense [...] was from its ecclesiastical use the earlier in Eng.]

**1.** The action of transfiguring or state of being transfigured; metamorphosis.

*a* 1548 Hall *Chron., Hen. VI* 161 Ihon Cade..departed secretly in habite disguysed..but all his metamorphosis or transfiguracion, litle preuailed. 1567 Maplet *Gr. Forest* 7[...] He hath so often and so diuers transfiguration in colour. 1569 J. Sanford tr. *Agrippa's Van. Artes* 69 b, Ouide in his Transfigurations singeth in this sorte. 1607 Topsell *Four-f. Beasts* (1658) 361 Of the transfiguration of men into Lions, we shall say more afterward. 1650 Bulwer *Anthropomet.* (title-p.), Nations, fashioning and altering their Bodies from the mould intended by Nature; With Figures of those Transfigurations. 1836 Emerson *Nature, Idealism* Wks. (Bohn) II. 162 This transfiguration which all material objects undergo through the passion of the poet.

**2.** The change in the appearance of Jesus Christ on the mountain (Matt. xvii. 2; Mark ix. 2, 3).

*c* 1375 *Sc. Leg. Saints* i. (*Petrus*) 37 Criste..hym tuk to be hym by In his transfiguracion. 1497 Bp. Alcock *Mons Perfect.* D iij, This noble transfyguracoun thus shewed to his dyscyples. *a* 1691 Boyle *Greatn. Mind* i. ii. Wks. 1772 V. 557 How glorious it is in heaven, we may guess by what it was at his transfiguration here on earth. 1856 Dove *Logic Chr. Faith* v. i. § 2. 296 In that sublime spectacle called the transfiguration.

**b.** *Eccl.* The church festival commemorating this event, observed on the 6th of August.

*c* 1460 *Brut* cclv. 522 This Calixte instituted & ordeyned þe Feste of Transfiguracion of our Lorde to be halowed on Seynt Sixt day in August. 1510–11 *Rec. St. Mary at Hill* 274 Paid for brede, ale and wyne at þe fest of transfiguracion.

**c.** A picture or representation of this event.

1712 Blackmore *Creation* iii. 123 Did..Raphael's Pencil never chuse to fall? Say, are his Works Transfigurations all? 1753 Mrs. Delany in *Life & Corr.* (1861) III. 209, I have at last put the finishing stroke to the Transfiguration. 1838 Emerson *Addr., Lit. Ethics* Wks. (Bohn) II. 209 Say to the man of letters, that he cannot paint a Transfiguration.

**Transfigurative** (trɑnsfi·giŭrĕtiv), *a. rare.* [f. as Transfigurate *v.* + -ive.] Having the quality of transfiguring; that tends to transfigure.

1885 Fairbairn *Catholicism* (1899) II. iv. 76 A splendid example of the power of faith and of the creative and transfigurative force of the religious imagination.

**Transfigure** (trɑnsfi·giŭɹ, -fi·gəɹ), *v.* [ad. L. *transfigūrāre* to change the shape of (f. Trans- + *figūra* form, shape, figure); or a. F. *transfigurer* (12th c. in Hatz.-Darm.).]

**1.** *trans.* To alter the figure or appearance of; to change in outward appearance; to transform.

*a* 1300 *Cursor M.* 18497 (Cott.) Þai war transfigurd als tite, Was neuer i-wis snau sa quite. *a* 1340 Hampole *Psalter* xc. 6 When þe fende transfigurs him in aungel of light. *c* 1386 Chaucer *Knt.'s T.* 247 Venus, if it be thy wil Yow in this gardyn thus to transfigure. 1412–20 Lydg. *Chron. Troy* ii. 913 So craftily þei koude hem transfigure, Conformyng hem to þe chaunt[e]plure. *c* 1470 Henry *Wallace* vi. 91 Thow transfigowryt Wallace out off his weill. 1547 *Bk. Marchauntes* e viij b, Satan..by cautyle transfigurynge hym into an angell of lyght. 1589 Puttenham *Eng. Poesie* iii. xii. (Arb.) 174 Your single wordes may be many waies transfigured to make the meetre or verse more tunable and melodious. 1607 Topsell *Four-f. Beasts* (1658) 193 Wilde-goats are transfigured into many similitudes. 1855 Pusey *Doctr. Real Presence* Note Q. 230 The Sacraments, which, by the mystery of the sacred prayer, are transfigured into Body and Blood. 1880 McCarthy *Own Times* III. xxxii. 49 The mutiny was transfigured into a revolutionary war.

**b.** In reference to the Transfiguration of Christ.

*c* 1380 Wyclif *Sel. Wks.* II. 57 Þis gospel telliþ how þat Crist was transfigurid in siȝt of þree apostlis. *c* 1400 Maundev. (1839) x. 114 In þat hille Thabor, oure lord transfigured him before seynt Peter, seynt Iohn & seynt Iame. 1526 Tindale *Mark* ix. 2 And he was transfigured before them. 1911 J. A. Robinson in *Encycl. Brit.* XV. 381/2 They saw Jesus transfigured in a radiance of glory.

**c.** *intr.* for *refl. rare.*

1840 Browning *Sordello* ii. 214 He no genius rare Transfiguring in fire, or wave, or air, At will.

**2.** *trans. fig.* (in allusion to the Transfiguration of Christ): To elevate, glorify, idealize, spiritualize.

*c* 1380 Wyclif *Sel. Wks.* II. 58 Þus men sein þat transfigurie is turnyng into glorious forme. 1687 Boyle *Martyrd. Theodora* viii. (1703) 116, I think our notions will then be raised..and our love and other affections, will be transfigured, as well as our bodies. 1841 Myers *Cath. Th.* iv. ii. 185 His education becomes devotion, and his morality is transfigured into Religion. 1876 E. Mellor *Priesth.* i. 15 Temple, priest, and sacrifice were employed and transfigured into glorious spiritual significations. 1879 Farrar *St. Paul* (1883) 113 [Stephen's] whole being was transfigured by a consciousness which illuminated his very countenance.

† **3.** To transfer by a figure. (A literalism of translation.) *Obs.*

1382 Wyclif 1 *Cor.* iv. 6 This thing I haue transfigurid [Vulg. *transfiguravi*] in to me and in to Apollo; that in vs ȝe lerne.

Hence **Transfi·gured** *ppl. a.* († in *Geom.* (quots. 1571) applied to a solid in which plane faces are substituted for the original solid angles); **Transfi·guring** *vbl. sb.* and *ppl. a.*

*c* 1380 [see 2]. **1571** DIGGES *Pantom.* IV. Gg i b, This solides inscribed Octaedrons side is triple to the medietie of his contayning transfigured Tetraedrons side. *Ibid.* Gg iij b, A Transfigured Octaedron is a Geometricall Figure incompassed with 14 bases, whereof 8 are equall equiangle Hexagonall playnes, and the other 6 are equall squares. **1678** CUDWORTH *Intell. Syst.* I. v. 805 Bodies..luciform or lucid, like to our Saviour's then transfigured body. **1717** GARTH tr. *Ovid, Enchantm. Circe* 33 The dow'r desir'd is his transfigur'd friends. **1846** TRENCH *Mirac.* Introd. (1862) 93 Their transforming, transfiguring power. **1880** N. SMYTH *Old Faiths in New Light* iii. (1882) 98 It can shine, a steady and transfiguring light of life, for the world.

**Transfi·gurement.** *rare.* [f. prec. + -MENT: cf. OF. *transfigurement* (14th c. in Godef.).] = TRANSFIGURATION.

**1865** *Reader* No. 133. 57/1 By sudden transfigurement. **1878** GILDER *Poet & Master* 55 Then did the outer world.. Suffer a sudden strange transfigurement.

**Transfinite** (transfəi·nəit), *a.* (*sb.*) *Math.* [f. TRANS- 4 + FINITE.] Beyond or surpassing any finite number or magnitude: see quots. Also, as *sb.*, a transfinite number, etc.

**1903** *Nature* 3 Sept. 411/2 To readers unacquainted with [Cantor's] 'Mengenlehre', the introduction of transfinite numbers must appear rather startling. **1907** HOBSON *Funct. Real Variable* 177 Corresponding to a single transfinite cardinal number there is an infinity of transfinite ordinal numbers. **1907** *Athenæum* 14 Sept. 307/2 The simplest conception of a transfinite number may be gathered from the following illustration. A man walks along a road at a uniform pace, and the distance he goes is divided into intervals —½ mile, ¼ mile, ⅛ mile, and so on. The number of these intervals in the first mile is infinite, but the time taken is finite. We agree to regard the mile as ending with the ωth interval. If the next mile is divided in just the same way, then the intervals regarded as belonging to the same series will be the (ω+1)th, (ω+2)th, and so on. These numbers ω, ω+1, ω+2, are called by Cantor (who was the first to use them) transfinite ordinal numbers.

**Transfission** (transfi·ʃən). *Biol.* [f. TRANS- 1 or 6 + FISSION 2.] The transverse splitting of a cell or organism as a mode of reproduction; transverse fission.

**1891** in *Cent. Dict.*

† **Transfi·sticate,** *v. Obs.* (*humorous nonce-wd.*) [? f. TRANS- 1 + L. *fistūcare* to ram down or in (cf. FISTUCATE), with allusion to *fist.*] To strike or smash with the fist.

**1600** ROWLANDS *Lett. Humours Blood* iv. 64 For though your beard do stand so fine mustated, Perhaps your nose may be transfisticated.

**Transfix** (transfi·ks), *v.* [f. L. *transfīx-*, ppl. stem of *transfīgĕre*, f. TRANS- + *fīgĕre* to FIX. Cf. OF. *transfixer* (15th c. in Godef.).] *trans.* To pierce through with, or impale upon, a sharp-pointed instrument (also said of the instrument); to fix or fasten by piercing.

**1590** SPENSER *F. Q.* I. v. 50 The bold Semiramis, whose sides transfixt With sonnes own blade her fowle reproches spoke. **1626** MASSINGER *Rom. Actor* III. ii, Take A golden arrow to transfix her heart. **1797** MRS. RADCLIFFE *Italian* xxxiii, That monk seemed as if transfixed to the spot. **1802** PALEY *Nat. Theol.* xii. 109 The butcher-bird transfixes its prey upon the spike of a thorn, whilst it picks its bones. **1850** MRS. JAMESON *Leg. Monast. Ord.* (1863) 388 Being absorbed in rapturous devotion, she was transfixed, that is, received the Stigmata. **1875** JOWETT *Plato* (ed. 2) IV. 382 He delights..to transfix the Eristic Sophist with weapons borrowed from his own armoury.

**b.** *fig.* To pierce through (esp. with pain, grief, or other emotion); also, to render motionless (with astonishment, horror, etc.).

**1649** LOVELACE *Poems* 19 Transfixed Venus stood amas'd. *a* **1711** KEN *Hymnotheo* Poet. Wks. III. 76 Sent by a breaking Heart by Guilt transfix'd. **1791** COWPER *Odyss.* x. 303 His heart transfixt With anguish. **1840** DICKENS *Barn. Rudge* xix, Both of whom were so transfixed at sight of the ladies that..they..could do nothing but stare. **1863** GEO. ELIOT *Romola* iv, [He] stood transfixed, with his long dark eyes resting on the unknown man who had addressed him.

Hence **Transfixed** (-fi·kst, *poet.* -fi·ksėd) *ppl. a.*; *spec.* in *Her.*: see quots. *c* 1828 and 1894; **Transfi·xing** *ppl. a.*

**1661** BLOUNT *Glossogr.* (ed. 2), *Transfixed*.., sticked or thurst through. *c* **1828** BERRY *Encycl. Her.* I. Gloss., *Transfixed*, pierced through, as a boar's head, &c., transfixed with a spear, &c. **1854** KANE *Grinnell Exp.* xlvi. 429 Then the transfixed and transfixing vessels were both eaten up together by the greedy floes. **1859** SALA *Tw. Round Clock* (1861) 64 Their muskets—prudently divested of the transfixing bayonets. **1894** *Parker's Gloss. Her.* 456 Pierced with an arrow generally means the same as transfixed.

**Transfixa·tion.** *rare*⁻¹. [f. prec. + -ATION, after *fixation.*] Used for TRANSFIXION (sense b).

**1889** *Lancet* 9 Feb. 273/1 Had it [the nævus] been treated by the old method of transfixation and ligature, the infant would not improbably have sunk.

**Transfixion** (transfi·kʃən). [f. L. type **transfixiōn-em*, n. of action from *transfīgĕre*, *-fix-* to TRANSFIX: cf. L. *affixiōn-*, *crucifixiōn-*.] The action of transfixing or state of being transfixed.

**1609** BP. W. BARLOW *Answ. Nameless Cath.* 335 Hee.. shal finde both an explicit contradiction, and a double transfixion, like that stroake of Phinees..pearcing with one speech through two at once. **1628** BP. HALL *Serm. Gal.* ii. 20 Wks. 1837 V. 336 Six several times do we find that Christ shed blood; in his Circumcision, in his Agony, in his Crowning, in his Scourging, in his Affixion, in his Transfixion. **1844** *Phrenol. Jrnl.* Oct. 368 The head must have been embalmed, and must have been so before its transfixion.

**b.** *Surgery.* The process of piercing the limb transversely, and cutting from within outward, in amputation. (Cf. F. *transfixion*, Littré.)

**1872** T. BRYANT *Pract. Surg.* 1037 In cutting the posterior flap by transfixion..the Surgeon should always support it with his left hand. **1890** BILLINGS *Med. Dict.*, *Transfixion*, a piercing through, as in cutting a flap from within outward. *attrib.* **1883** *Daily News* 19 Feb. 4/8 Perhaps [the murderers] thought transfixion knives nothing worse than an improvement on the admittedly inefficient pikeheads of '48.

**Transfixture** (transfi·kstiŭɹ). *rare*⁻¹. [f. TRANSFIX, after FIXTURE.] The condition of being transfixed or fixed to the spot with some feeling.

**1886** T. HARDY *Mayor Casterbr.* II. xx. 278 Henchard waited—if that could be called a waiting which was a transfixture.

† **Transflee·t,** *v. Obs. rare*⁻¹. [f. TRANS- 2 + FLEET *v.*[1]] *intr.* To float or sail across.

*a* **1600** *Floddan F.* I. (1664) 2 Before King Henry past the Seas, And ere to France he did transfleet.

**Transfluent** (tra·nsfluˌĕnt), *a. rare.* [ad. L. *transfluent-em*, pr. pple. of *transfluĕre* to flow through.] Flowing across or through; in *Her.* said of a stream represented as flowing through a bridge.

*c* **1828** BERRY *Encycl. Her.* I. Gloss., *Transfluent*, an heraldic term, to express water appearing, in a coat, as if running through a bridge. **1847** PARKER *Gloss. Her.* 309.

**Transfluvial** (transflū·viăl), *a.* [ad. post-cl. L. *transfluviāl-is*, f. *trans*, TRANS- + *fluvi-us* a river: see -AL.] Situated or dwelling across or beyond a river: in quot. 1806 rendering Heb. עִבְרִי *ʕib'rī* 'one from the other side', i. e. from beyond the Jordan or ? the Euphrates.

**1806** W. TAYLOR in *Ann. Rev.* IV. 716 The term Hebrew, which signifies transfluvial,..was applied to the posterity of Abraham, because they came from beyond the Euphrates. **1862** S. LUCAS *Secularia* (1863) 92 As the lower curve..was intersected..by the river Avon, it included the transfluvial parishes of St. Mary Redcliffe, Thomas and Temple. **18..** LOWELL *Orient. Apol.* v, The sacred rites and laws of his Transfluvial rival.

So **Transflu·vian** *a.*, in same sense.

**1848** *Times* 18 Oct. 3/5 His successors were rather kings of Candahar, with some transfluvian provinces, than kings of India in our sense. **1865** *Daily Tel.* 12 Apr. 3 As long as this part of the Mississippi remained to the Confederates all the produce of the transfluvian region was theirs.

**Transflux** (tra·nsflʋks). *rare*⁻⁰. [f. TRANS- 1 + L. *flux-us* flowing, flux: cf. *efflux*, etc.] A flowing through, across, or beyond.

**1864** in WEBSTER. Hence in later Dicts.

**Transforate** (tra·nsfŏreɪt), *v. rare.* [f. ppl. stem of L. *transforāre* to bore or pierce through, f. TRANS- + *forāre* to bore, pierce.] *trans.* To pierce or bore through, perforate; *spec.* (*Surg.*) to perforate (the skull) in craniotomy.

**1727** BAILEY vol. II, *Transforate*, to make a hole through. **1775** ASH, *Transforated, Transforating*..(not much used).

**Transforation** (transforēɪ·ʃən). [ad. late L. *transforātiōn-em*, f. *transforāre*: see prec.]

† **1.** A seton; a thread or tape drawn through a fold of skin to maintain an issue. *Obs.*

**1597** A. M. tr. *Guillemeau's Fr. Chirurg.* cij b/1 The Needle for the Seton, or transforatione. *Ibid.* 39 b/2 All the which [cauteryes] haue but one onlye apertion, or two, and is then called a transforatione or Seton.

**2.** The action of transforating, as in craniotomy.

**1890** BILLINGS *Med. Dict.*, *Transforation*,..repeated perforation of the base of the fœtal skull in craniotomy.

**Transform** (transfǭ·ɹm), *v.* [ad. L. *transformāre*, f. TRANS- + *formāre* to form, f. *forma* form. Cf. F. *transformer* (14th c. in Godef. *Compl.*), also OF. *tresformer*.]

**1.** *trans.* To change the form of; to change into another shape or form; to metamorphose.

*c* **1340** HAMPOLE *Prose Tr.* 15 In transfourmynge of þe saule in þe Godhede. **1382** WYCLIF 2 *Cor.* iii. 18 Alle we.. ben transformyd into the same ymage. *c* **1400** MAUNDEV. (Roxb.) iv. 11 Of Ypocras daughter transformed from a womman to a dragoun. **1483** CAXTON *Cato* b vij b, This catte..is myn owne daughter the whiche by the plesure and wylle of god hath ben transfourmed in to a catte. **1548** UDALL, etc. *Erasm. Par. Mark* i. 5 b, That thynges of muche contrarietie maye easely be transformed, and tourned one into an other. **1590** SHAKS. *Com. Err.* III. ii. 151 And I thinke, if my brest had not beene made of faith, and my heart of steele, she had transform'd me to a Curtull dog, & made me turne i' th wheele. **1660** F. BROOKE tr. *Le Blanc's Trav.* 268 When Magicians shall have power to transform a humane body. **1813** SCOTT *Rokeby* I. xxxi, The victor sees his fairy gold, Transform'd, when won, to drossy mold. **1827** FARADAY *Chem. Manip.* xxiv. (1842) 618 Transform several small crystals of sulphate of nickel into a large one. **1853** J. H. NEWMAN *Hist. Sk.* (1873) II. I. ii. 65 To Samarcand.. we owe the art of transforming linen into paper.

**b.** *transf.* To change in character or condition; to alter in function or nature.

**1556** J. HEYWOOD *Spider & F.* ii. 5 My whole estate..Is here transformde from myrth to miserie. **1675** TRAHERNE *Chr. Ethics* 270 Love..transformes the most virulent affections into smooth, healing, perfective pleasures. **1796** MORSE *Amer. Geog.* I. 306 He transformed an undisciplined body of peasantry into a regular army of soldiers. **1852** H. ROGERS *Ecl. Faith* (1853) 16 A volume, which has transformed them from savages into men, and from idolaters into Christians.

**c.** *Math.* To alter (a figure, expression, etc.) to another differing in form, but equal in quantity or value.

**1743** EMERSON *Fluxions* 22 To transform the Fluxion.., assume [etc.]. **1884** tr. *Lotze's Logic* 332 These equations we transform in all sorts of ways by adding on new quantities, by subtracting others, by multiplication and division of the whole. **1885** WATSON & BURBURY *Math. Th. Electr. & Magn.* I. 155 We now proceed to transform this problem.

**d.** *Physics.* To change (one form of energy) into another, as mechanical energy into electricity, or electric energy into light or heat.

**1871** MAXWELL *Theory of Heat* (1875) 92 The total energy of any body or system of bodies is a quantity which can neither be increased nor diminished by any mutual action of those bodies, though it may be transformed into any of the forms of which energy is susceptible. **1878** W. GARNETT in *Encycl. Brit.* VIII. 208/2 All other forms of energy with which we are acquainted can be transformed into an equivalent amount of heat. **1902** J. LARMOR *ibid.* XXVIII. 164/2 There is a certain measurable quantity associated with each type of physical action..numerically identical with a corresponding quantity belonging to the new type into which it is transformed.

**e.** *Electr.* To change a current in potential, as from high voltage to low voltage, or in type, as from alternating to continuous. *Transform up*, to raise the voltage while decreasing the current. *Transform down*, to lower the voltage while increasing the current.

**1883** tr. HOSPITALIER *Mod. Applications of Electr.* (ed. 2) I. 142 All these apparatus have a common character; they receive electricity and give out electricity, which they transform according to their individual properties. **1888** S. P. THOMPSON *Dynamo-electr. Mach.* 486 At the generating station the alternating currents of low potential were to be transformed by means of an induction-coil to currents of high potential. **1897** SLOANE *Stand. Electr. Dict.* (1902) 547 Such dynamo could transform currents up or down. **1902** S. P. THOMPSON *Electr. & Magnet.* 502 To transform continuous currents from one voltage to another it is necessary to employ a rotating apparatus, which is virtually a combination of a motor and a generator.

**2.** *intr.* To undergo a change of form or nature; to change. Now *rare.*

**1597** BEARD *Theatre God's Judgem.* (1612) 68 Then did this iolly feast, to fast transforme. **1667** E. KING in *Phil. Trans.* II. 427 The Film does onely cover the Maggot, while she is transforming into an Ant. **1717** ADDISON tr. *Ovid, Transf. Cycnus* 11 His hair transforms to down, his fingers meet In skinny films, and shape his oary feet. **1747** GOULD *Eng. Ants* 52 The Female Aurelia's are generally the first which transform, and are those that make their Appearance in the Shape of large Flies. **1827** HOOD *Mids. Fairies* lxxxiii, Meanwhile I bade my pitying mates transform Like grasshoppers.

**Transform** (tra·nsfǫɹm), *sb. Math.* [f. prec. vb.] An expression derived from another by transformation.

**1853** SYLVESTER in *Phil. Trans.* CXLIII. I. 544 *Covariant*, a function which stands in the same relation to the primitive function from which it is derived as any of its linear transforms do to a similarly derived transform of its primitive.

**Transformable** (transfǭ·ɹmăb'l), *a.* [f. as prec. + -ABLE.] That may be transformed; capable of transformation.

**1674** GREW *Mixture* iii. § 1 All Principles are immutable; as we have above proved; and, therefore, not generable, formable, or transformable. **1870** H. SPENCER *Princ. Psychol.* I. vi. § 47 (ed. 2) 117 If the psychical force known as effort were transformable into a constant quantity of physical force. **1875** POSTE *Gaius* III. Comm. (ed. 2) 358 An obligation ..is always transformable, in the eye of the law, into the payment of a certain sum of money. **1902** J. LARMOR in *Encycl. Brit.* XXVIII. 166/2 Constituents..transformable into each other by chemical or physical action. **1904** *Daily Chron.* 28 Oct. 8/5 Justice..is such a transformable quality, that it is somewhat difficult to define it.

Hence **Transformabi·lity.**

**1875** POSTE *Gaius* III. Comm. (ed. 2) 358 This transformability of all Objects of obligation into money payments.

**Transfo·rmance.** *rare.* [f. as prec. + -ANCE: cf. *performance.*] = TRANSFORMATION.

**1611** CHAPMAN *May Day* II. iv, Take such a transformance, as you may be sure will keepe you from discouery. **1867** G. GILFILLAN *Night* vii. 220 Small need of such transformance upon thee.

† **Transfo·rmate,** *ppl. a. Obs. rare.* [ad. L. *transformāt-us*, pa. pple. of *transformāre* to TRANSFORM.] = TRANSFORMED.

**1571** DIGGES *Pantom.* IV. Hh iij b, Then is the superficial capacitie of the transformed Octaedrons Hexagonal playnes, equal to the whole superficies of Tetraedron transformate. *Ibid.* Ii j, The lesse semidiameter of the transformate Dodecaedrons trigonall bases.

**Transformation** (transfǫɹmēɪ·ʃən). [ad. late L. *transformātiōn-em* (Jerome, *a* 400), n. of action from *transformāre* to TRANSFORM. Cf. F. *transformation* (14th c. in Hatz.-Darm.).] The action of transforming or fact of being transformed.

**1.** The action of changing in form, shape, or appearance; metamorphosis.

**1432–50** tr. *Higden* (Rolls) II. 209 Monstruous transformaciones of men in to bestes be made..thro charmes of wicches. **1548** UDALL *Erasm. Par. Mark* i. 5 b, Transformacions and naturall chaungynges of thynges. **1555** EDEN *Decades* 43 *margin*, Fables much lyke Ouide his transformations. **1596** SHAKS. 1 *Hen. IV*, I. i. 44 Vpon whose dead corpes there was such misuse, Such beastly, shamelesse transformation. **1794** SULLIVAN *View Nat.* I. 112 Matter is capable of many seeming transformations, but no real transmutations have ever been discovered. **1864** BRYCE *Holy Rom. Emp.* xv. 260 No more than a man feels that perpetual transformation by which his body is renewed from year to year.

†**b.** A changed form; a person or thing transformed. *Obs. rare.*

**1598** SHAKS. *Merry W.* IV. v. 98 If it should come to the eare of the Court, how I haue beene transformed; and how my transformation hath beene washd, and cudgeld.

**c.** *Theatr.* More fully *transformation scene*: A mechanical disclosing scene in a pantomime; *spec.* the scene in which the principal performers were transformed in view of the audience into the players of the ensuing harlequinade.

**1859** *Punch* 5 Feb. 58/2, I have supped full of gorgeous transformations on which paint, coloured foils, Dutch metal ..have been lavished. **1881** *Playgoer* 1 Jan., A magnificent Transformation, a charming Watteau ballet scene. **1881** G. A. SALA in *Illustr. Lond. News* 1 Jan. 3/2 Two Grand Transformation Scenes. **1885** W. J. LAWRENCE in *The Theatre* Dec. 329 The account of the sixth scene is worthy of quotation, smacking as it does of the modern 'Transformation'. **1885** — in *Let.*, During the Grimaldi era the term 'transformation scene' referred to that particular juncture of the performance at which the good fairy changed the hero and heroine and their two persecutors in full view of the audience into Harlequin, Columbine, Clown and Pantaloon respectively.

**2.** *transf.* A complete change in character, condition, etc.

**1581** PETTIE *Guazzo's Civ. Conv.* II. (1586) 81 The simple soules not perceiuing that this their transformation or rather deformation, is no more seene than a pose in a mans face. **1602** SHAKS. *Ham.* II. ii. 5 Something haue you heard Of Hamlets transformation: so I call it, Since not th' exterior, nor the inward man Resembles that it was. **1746–7** HERVEY *Medit.* (1818) 59 To behold the prodigious transformation which has taken place on every individual. **1833** ALISON *Hist. Europe* I. i. § 60. 104 The transformation of France.. from a feudal Confederacy..to a compact and absolute monarchy. **1900** R. J. DRUMMOND *Apost. Teach. & Christ's Teach.* ix. 347 A regenerative transformation of humanity is practicable.

**3.** In scientific uses. **a.** *Zool.* Change of form in animal life, as in the successive transformations of insects, etc.; metamorphosis.

**1638** MAYNE *Lucian* (1664) 45 A Polypus I have seen, but would gladly learn its transformation from you. **1667** E. KING in *Phil. Trans.* II. 427 The black Speck..cast out of the Maggot in her transformation. **1774** GOLDSM. *Nat. Hist.* (1776) VIII. 7 Of the Transformations of the Caterpillar into its corresponding Butterfly or Moth. **1874** LUBBOCK *Orig. & Met. Ins.* i. 4 Linnæus classed them among the Coleoptera, from which however they differ in their transformations.

**b.** *Physiol.* and *Path.* Change of form or substance in an organ, tissue, vital fluid, etc.

**1834** J. FORBES *Laennec's Dis. Chest* (ed. 4) 587 Interstitial deposition, which..constitutes what is commonly termed transformation of the organ into a cancerous substance. **1843** J. A. SMITH *Product. Farming* (ed. 2) 75 The excrementitious matters of one organ come in contact with another during their passage through the plant or animal, and, in consequence, suffer new transformations. **1860** MAYNE *Expos. Lex.*, *Transformation*, term for a morbid change in a part, consisting in the conversion of its texture into one of a different kind, as of the soft parts into bone or cartilage.

**c.** *Math.* Change of form without alteration of quantity or value; substitution of one geometrical figure for another of equal magnitude but different form, as of a prism for a cylinder, or of one algebraical expression or equation for another of the same value; †formerly, also, alteration of the form of a solid figure by truncation of the solid angles: cf. TRANSFIGURED, TRANSFORMED.

*Transformation of co-ordinates*, an inaccurate but accepted expression for the substitution of a new set of co-ordinates, involving a transformation of the equation of the locus. Hence, in the case in which the new co-ordinates are measured in a different plane or space, *transformation* is extended to the relation of correspondence between the original and resulting loci, as in projection.

**1571** DIGGES *Pantom.* Epist. *ij b, A Discourse Geometricall of the fiue regulare or Platonicall bodyes [with] the manifolde proportions arising by mutuall conference of these solides Inscription, Circumscription or Transformation. **1706** PHILLIPS (ed. Kersey), *Transformation of an Equation*, (in Algebra) the changing of any Equation into one that is more easy. **1882** MINCHIN *Unipl. Kinemat.* 234 It will be convenient to speak of this quantity *K* as a modulus of transformation. **1885** WATSON & BURBURY *Math. Th. Electr. & Magn.* I. 157 The method of transformation used with conjugate functions.

**d.** *Physics.* Change of form of a substance from solid to liquid, from liquid or solid to gaseous, or the reverse; *Chem.* change of chemical composition, as by replacement of one constituent of a compound by another.

**1857** MILLER *Elem. Chem.* (1862) III. 67 In order to effect these transformations it is necessary to displace the hydrogen of the acid.

**e.** Change of energy from one form into another.

**1877** W. GARNETT in *Encycl. Brit.* VII. 583/2 The subject of which natural philosophy treats is the transformation of energy, which in all its phases takes place in accordance with two great principles known respectively as the principles of the conservation and the dissipation of energy. **1878** — *ibid.* VIII. 207/2 If subsequently we allow an equal amount of energy to undergo various intermediate transformations, but to be finally reduced to heat. **1902** *Ibid.* XXIX. 158 In succeeding years [from 1840] he [Joule] published a series of valuable researches on the agency of electricity in transformations of energy.

**f.** *Electr.* Change of a current into one of different potential, or different type, or both, as by a transformer (TRANSFORMER 2). Also *attrib.*

**1884** *Electrical Rev.* 26 July 64 Conditions for arranging a transformation coil, as regards its yield. **1911** *Encycl. Brit.* XXVII. 173/1 Transformers may be distinguished..in accordance with the type of transformation they effect.

**4.** An artificial head of hair worn by women.

**1901** *Daily News* 12 Jan. 6/7 Buying toupées, or even 'transformations', as those wigs are called which entirely cover the natural hair. **1903** *Westm. Gaz.* 6 Aug. 3/2 Hairdressers are known to make most of their returns by the producing of these transformations. **1906** *Referee* 9 Dec. 11/4 When he got to the exit door he discovered to his horror that he had dragged off the lady's 'transformation', and it was hanging to his sleeve-link.

**5.** *attrib.* and *Comb.*: **transformation-dancer** (*Theatr.*), one who dances successively in several costumes and characters; **transformation-jewel**, a jewel which may be worn in several ways; **transformation product**, *Chem.* a new compound formed by the decomposition or destructive distillation of a complex compound often existing in nature; **transformation scene**: see 1 c.

**1892** *Daily News* 29 Jan. 7/2 She was engaged generally upon the music hall stage... Her peculiar branch was transformation dancing...She was well known as a transformation dancer. **1892** *Pall Mall G.* 17 Mar. 1/3 French jewellers are devoting all their inventive genius to new designs for the setting of these transformation jewels.

Hence **Transforma·tional** *a.*, of or pertaining to transformation; **Transforma·tionist** = TRANSFORMIST 2.

**1888** MAX MÜLLER *Nat. Relig.* vi. (1889) 143 We ought to be transformationists and no longer evolutionists. **1894** *Athenæum* 10 Nov. 646/2 The distinction between 'combinational' and 'transformational' theories of experience.

**Transformative** (trɑnsfǭ·ɹmătiv), *a.* [ad. med.L. *transformātīvus* (Albertus Mag. *a* 1280), f. ppl. stem of L. *transformāre* to TRANSFORM: see -ATIVE. Cf. F. *transformatif* (neologism in Littré).] Having the faculty of transforming; fitted or tending to transform.

**1671** FLAVEL *Fount. Life* x. 30 The Light of Christ is powerfully Transformative of its Subjects. **1681** — *Meth. Grace* xxviii. 484 All communion with God is assimilating, and transformative of the soul into his image. **1806** A. KNOX *Rem.* (1844) I. 20 This high, heavenly, transformative Christianity. **1893** J. PULSFORD *Loyalty to Christ* II. 47 The One Divine formative and transformative Form.

†**Transforma·tor.** *Obs. rare*$^{-1}$. [agent-n., in L. form, from L. *transformāre* to TRANSFORM.] = TRANSFORMER.

**1617** COLLINS *Def. Bp. Ely* II. x. 420 No Transformators, no such sauage *Sarcophagi*, as S. Cyrill bends his penne against.

**Transformed** (trɑnsfǭ·ɹmd), *ppl. a.* [f. TRANSFORM *v.* + -ED$^1$.] Changed in form or character; in *Math.*, altered in form, but not in value. (In quot. 1413, 'misshapen'.)

In quot. 1571 applied to a solid figure modified by truncation of the solid angles (cf. TRANSFIGURED in same sense).

**1413** *Pilgr. Sowle* (Caxton 1483) IV. xxiv. 70 Beres ben brought forthe al fowle and transformyd. **1571** DIGGES *Pantom.* IV. Gg ij, A Transfourmed Cube is a figure geometrical enuironed with 6 equiangle Octogonall and 8 equilater triangular playnes or bases, whose sides are all equall. *Ibid.* Hh ij, A Transformed Dodecaedron. **1743** EMERSON *Fluxions* 29 Proceed thus till the transform'd Fluxion be as simple as possible. **1841** LANE *Arab. Nts.* I. 65 *note*, It was not imagined that this brute was the lost man in a transformed state. **1885** WATSON & BURBURY *Math. Th. Electr. & Magn.* I. 157 By substituting the coordinates..and placing on corresponding elements the same charges, the transformed system will be in equilibrium. **1904** J. OMAN *Vis. & Author.* III. iii. 190 The first Apostles, the humble, loyal, transformed ambassadors of Christ.

**Transfo·rmer.** [f. as prec. + -ER$^1$.]

**1.** One who or that which transforms.

**1601** DEACON & WALKER *Spirits & Divels* 208 He is no creatour of substances, no transformer of natures. **1765** J. BROWN *Chr. Jrnl.* (1814) 150 Sin, horrid transformer, how hast thou changed our God! **1883** J. D. FULTON *Sam Hobart* 18 The steam locomotive, the material transformer of the world.

**2.** *Electr.* An apparatus which transforms continuous currents from one voltage to another, or continuous into alternating currents or *vice versa.* (After F. *transformateur* (Hospitalier, 1882).)

**1883** tr. HOSPITALIER *Mod. Applications of Electr.* (ed. 2) I. 141 We designate by the term electric transformers apparatus in which electricity is no longer produced directly, but is transformed and changes its properties. **1884** *Electrical Rev.* 26 July 64 The present transformers, those of MM. Goulard and Gibbs, are..very similar to bobbins. **1886** G. FORBES in *Electrician* 26 Feb. 315 Induction coils used in this way have been called secondary generators or transformers. **1888** S. P. THOMPSON *Dynamo-electric Mach.* 484 For transforming from high pressures to low, several kinds of apparatus are known, namely:—..Induction-coils, also called for this purpose Secondary Generators, or Transformers, or Converters. **1891** *Times* 28 Sept. 13/6 From the transformer the currents are led to the four collecting rings of the motor, and a continuous current is taken off its commutator.

**b.** *attrib.*, as *transformer chamber, house, station.*

**1888** *Scribner's Mag.* Aug. 196/2 The development of a radically new and very interesting system, known as the secondary or transformer system. **1891** *Pall Mall G.* 12 Sept. 6/2 It furnishes the current for feeding 1,200 glow-lamps, partly fixed to a large frame in the transformer room, partly to a sort of signboard outside the hall. **1894** *Westm. Gaz.* 1 May 7/2 The current is conveyed to Rome on four copper cables. .. Outside the Porta Pia..it enters a transformer-house, where its pressure is reduced from 5,000 to 2,000 volts.

**Transfo·rming,** *vbl. sb.* [f. as prec. + -ING$^1$.] The action of the vb. TRANSFORM; transformation.

**1435** MISYN *Fire of Love* 40 Qwhat is lufe bott transfourmynge of desire In to þe þinge lufyd? **1580** HOLLYBAND *Treas. Fr. Tong*, *Transfiguration*, a transforming. **1633** P. FLETCHER *Purple Isl.* VI. lv, With quick and strange transforming. **1883** J. T. BURGESS in *Athenæum* 3 Nov. 569/1 The transforming of the south transept into the vestry.

**Transfo·rming,** *ppl. a.* [f. as prec. + -ING$^2$.] That transforms.

*a* **1653** BINNING *Serm.* (1845) 10 Love is an uniting and transforming thing. **1827** KEBLE *Chr. Y.*, 13*th Sunday Trin.* xviii, Our..Saviour's face..Bent on us with transforming power. **1842** I. WILLIAMS *Baptistery* I. ix. (1874) 107, I gaz'd Upon the footsteps of transforming time. **1907** W. M. RAMSAY in *Expositor* Jan. 72 The transforming hand of man was applied to it.

Hence **Transfo·rmingly** *adv.*

**1865** H. BUSHNELL *Vicar. Sacr.* ii. (1868) 68 He could not so powerfully and transformingly impress the fact. **1874** GEO. ELIOT *Coll. Breakf. P.* 771 That energy Which moves transformingly in root and branch.

**Transformism** (trɑnsfǭ·ɹmiz'm). [a. F. *transformisme* (Broca, *Congrès d'anthropol.* 1867, p. 401), f. *transformer* to TRANSFORM: see -ISM.]

**1.** *Biol.* The hypothesis that existing species are the product of the gradual transformation of other forms of living beings (*loosely*, such transformation itself); any form of the doctrine of evolution of species.

**1878** BARTLEY tr. *Topinard's Anthrop.* III. i. 527 Direct proofs as to transformism are not wanting. **1880** HUXLEY *Crayfish* vi. 318 We may suppose that crayfishes have resulted from the modification of some other form of living matter; this is what, to borrow a useful word from the French language, is known as..*transformism*. **1880** *Nature* 27 Jan. 307/1 Degraded plants, affording remarkable specimens of natural transformism. **1883** TYLOR in *Nature* 3 May 8/2 These processes of development, or evolution, or transformism were long ago recognised to no small extent by ethnologists.

**2.** The doctrine of gradual evolution of moral and social relations: *loosely*, such evolution itself.

**1885** *Athenæum* 17 Oct. 510/2 The transformist 'conference' at Paris last year was an eloquent lecture by M. Ch. Letourneau on the evolution of morals. The concluding remarks are as follows: 'In that which relates to education, I am sorry to differ entirely from the principal founder of transformism in morals, H. Spencer'. **1894** *Liberal* 24 Nov. 51/2 A laboratory in which the process of social transformism is carried on.

**Transformist** (trɑnsfǭ·ɹmist). [In sense 1, f. TRANSFORM *v.* + -IST; in sense 2, a. F. *transformiste* (Broca, 1867, as in prec.).]

**1.** One who is occupied in transforming. *humorous nonce-use.*

**1799** J. MACGOWAN *Dial. Devils* i. 11 As for the barbers, they are a set of transformists, established wholly by my dexterity.

**2.** An adherent of transformism. Also *attrib.* or as *adj.*

*a* **1879** PUSEY in *Athenæum* 19 July 83/1 We think the transformist theories a mere imagination. **1885** [see prec. 2.]. **1890** *Pop. Sc. Monthly* Dec. 257 Agardh..was a little too earnest a transformist, and believed that certain algæ could become animals.

Hence **Transformi·stic** *a.*, of or pertaining to transformism or transformists.

**1887** *Nature* 24 Feb. 389/2 In the chapter on the first appearance of man, the various transformistic theories are passed in review.

†**Transformity.** *Obs. nonce-wd.* [f. TRANSFORM, after *conformity.*] The state or condition of being transformed.

**1622** T. STOUGHTON *Chr. Sacr.* xiii. 175 The next words are, *But be ye transformed*...A plaine opposition betwixt that before, and this now spoken; betwixt that conformitie to this world, and this transformitie.

†**Transfou·nd,** *v. Obs. rare*$^{-1}$. [f. TRANS- 2 + FOUND *v.*$^3$; cf. L. *transfundĕre* to TRANSFUSE.] *trans.* To recast (metal) *into* (some other form).

*a* **1649** DRUMM. OF HAWTH. *Consid. to Parl.* Wks. (1711) 186 That all bells of steeples..be taken down and transfounded into pieces of ordnance.

†**Tra·nsfretate,** *v. Obs. rare*$^{-1}$. = TRANSFRETE.

**1653** URQUHART *Rabelais* II. vi, We transfretate the Sequan at the dilucul and crepuscul.

†**Transfreta·tion.** *Obs.* [ad. late L. *transfretātiōn-em*, n. of action f. *transfretāre*: see next.] The action of crossing or passing over a strait, channel, or narrow sea.

**1612** DAVIES *Why Ireland*, etc. (1747) 69 Since the last transfretation of King Richard the Second. *c* **1645** HOWELL *Lett.* IV. xxiii, She had a rough passage in her transfretation to Dover Castle. **1768** H. WALPOLE *Hist. Doubts* 90 Of this transfretation and Christening, Perkin, in his supposed confession, says not a word. **1782** S. PEGGE *Cur. Misc.* 60 Henry 2. levied numerous subsidies..for his transfretations (to use a Monkish word) into foreign parts.

†**Transfre·te,** *v. Obs.* Also 6 -fret, 7 -freat; *erron.* 6 -freit, 6–7 -freight. [ad. L. *transfretāre*, f. TRANS- + *fretum* a strait, channel; cf. OF. *transfreter* (*a* 1200 in Godef.).]

**1.** *intr.* To pass over a strait or narrow sea.

*c* 1540 tr. *Pol. Verg. Eng. Hist.* (Camden) I. 85 The Emperoure Severus..desierus to procure the destruction of Albinus, transfreted into Fraunce. *a* 1548 HALL *Chron., Hen. IV* 24 Declaryng also that..he wold transfret and passe the sea himselfe. 1567 DRANT *Horace, Ep.* vi. Dj, Treasure of greater gaine Then all the chaffer that transfretes from Portugal or Spaine. 1606 WARNER *Alb. Eng.* XIV. xci, Hence for Ireland at the least I must transfreat. 1653 WATERHOUSE *Apol. Learn.* 52 The Saxon Merchants ..Arm and Transfreight, and about the year six hundred eighty nine obtain the Rule over us.

**2.** *trans.* **a.** To convey across a strait or sea. **b.** To cross (a strait or sea).

1594 ? GREENE *Selimus* Wks. (Grosart) XIV. 266 T'await th' arriuall of some ship That might transfreit vs safely vnto Rhodes. 1595 *Locrine* I. i. 108 We..transfretting the Illirian sea, Arriued on the coasts of Aquitane. 1611 BRATHWAIT *Gold. Fleece, Sonn.* iv. G j b, With joyfull mirth..To haue transfreted such a Sea of woes. 1653 URQUHART *Rabelais* I. xxxiii. 151 Have we not..travelled and toyled enough, in having transfreted and past over the Hircanian sea?

**Transfro·ntal,** *a. Anat.* [TRANS- 5.] Crossing the forehead, or the frontal lobe of the brain.

1889 *Buck's Handbk. Med. Sc.* VIII. 152/1 The union of the subfrontal fissure, deeply with the precentral and the three transfrontal fissures.

**Trans-fro·ntier,** *a.* [TRANS- 3.] Lying, living, or done beyond the frontier of a country.

1877 LD. LYTTON *Lett.* (1906) II. xv. 481 The rudest and most unmanageable transfrontier chieftains. 1909 *Daily Chron.* 22 Jan. 3/4 A personal history of trans-frontier surveys and boundary demarcations.

† **Transfu·de,** *v. Obs. rare.* [irreg. f. L. *transfundĕre* (see TRANSFUSE), perf. tense *transfūd-ī.* Cf. *diffude, effude.*] *trans.* **a.** To transmit. **b.** To expend lavishly.

1432–50 tr. *Higden* (Rolls) I. 5 Withowte the sollicitude of writers scholde transfude [L. *transfunderet*] to vs the memory of thynges of antiquite. *Ibid.* VII. 153 So that y myȝhte transfude [L. *transfuderim*, v. r. *transfuderem*] my patrimony to youre utilite.

† **Tra·nsfuge.** *Obs. rare.* [a. F. *transfuge* (14th c. in Godef. *Compl.*), ad. L. *transfuga*, f. TRANS- + *fug-ĕre* to flee.] A deserter; a fugitive.

1548 *Privy Council Acts* (1890) II. 186 Certein Frenchemen ..demanded by the French King by treaty as transfuges. 1639 SEDGWICK *Milit. Disc.* 78 When a Souldier renounceth his colours, and becomes a transfuge, and runnes to the enemies side. [1855 LD. STANHOPE *Let. to Ticknor* 12 May in *Misc.* Ser. II. (1872) 18 The protection of deserters and *transfuges* is the invariable rule of every service in the world.]

So † **Tra·nsfuger,** in same sense; † **Transfu·gious** *a.*, that is a deserter.

1611 SPEED *Hist. Gt. Brit.* IX. xxiv. (1623) 1170 Scotland, the then Refuge of Traiterous transfugers. *Ibid.* 1181 That transfugious Champion.

† **Transfu·me,** *v. Obs. rare.* [ad. L. *transfūmā-re*, f. TRANS- + *fūmāre* to smoke, FUME.]

1623 COCKERAM, *Transfume*, to smoake thorow. 1656 in BLOUNT *Glossogr.*

† **Transfu·nd,** *v. Obs. rare.* [ad. L. *transfund-ĕre*: see next.] *trans.* = next.

1670 H. STUBBE *Plus Ultra* 121 Because this Transfunding of blood hath hitherto been looked on as the primary Invention. *a* 1677 BARROW *Serm.* (1687) I. viii. 97 Speech, that most natural, proper and easie means of..conveying, and, as it were, transfunding our thoughts and our passions into each other.

**Transfuse** (transfiū·z), *v.* [f. L. *transfūs-*, ppl. stem of *transfund-ĕre*, f. *trans*, TRANS- + *fundĕre* to pour. Cf. F. *transfuser* (17–18th c. in Hatz.-Darm.).]

**1.** *trans.* To pour (a liquid) from one vessel or receptacle into another.

1601 HOLLAND *Pliny* XXXIII. vi. II. 473 Ever and anon the troubled water ought to be transfused into a vessell of brasse, and clarified therein. 1664 POWER *Exp. Philos.* I. 4 The stings in all Bees are hollow and tubulous..so that when they prick the flesh, they do also, through that channel, transfuse the poyson into it. 1755 SMOLLETT *Quix.* II. IV. ii. (1803) IV. 141 Transfusing the contents of the bottles into their own bellies. 1829 *Chapters Phys. Sci.* 189 When water or any..fluid requires to be transfused from one vessel to another.

**2.** *transf.* and *fig.* To cause to 'flow' from one to another; to transmit; to diffuse into or through something; to cause to permeate; to instil.

*c* 1425 *St. Mary of Oignies* II. iv. in *Anglia* VIII. 165/15 As in a lighte [He] transfused hym-selfe þurgh alle þe body of þe seke. 1594 HOOKER *Eccl. Pol.* I. x. § 12 A naturall delight which man hath to transfuse from himselfe into others. 1605 B. JONSON *Volpone* III. v, Where we may so transfuse our wandering souls Out at our lips. 1618 HALES *Gold. Rem.* II. (1673) 9 The sole way of transfusing the principles of Christianity into men. 1709 SACHEVERELL *Serm.* 15 Aug. 4 It's..Influence is transfus'd thro' several.. Channels. 1877 MISS A. B. EDWARDS *Up Nile* ix. 240 The sun being..at its highest and the air transfused with light. 1880 E. WHITE *Cert. Relig.* (1881) 17 Their testimony, and teaching, and life, transfuse that certitude into those who receive their word.

**3.** *Med.*, etc. To transfer (the blood of a person or animal) into the veins of another; to inject (blood or other fluid) into the veins.

1666 *Phil. Trans.* 353 Take up the Carotidal Artery of the Dog or other Animal, whose Bloud is to be transfused into another of the same or a different Kind. 1743 tr. *Heister's Surg.* 305 The Blood of one Animal is transfused into the Veins of another. 1801 *Med. Jrnl.* V. 565 On transfusing red blood into the temporal artery, the animal remained lively and well.

**b.** To treat (a person) with transfusion of blood (or of some solution).

1897 *Allbutt's Syst. Med.* II. 948 We transfused the patient with saline solution containing sulphates. 1905 ROLLESTON *Dis. Liver* 268 He was transfused but died the same day.

Hence **Transfused** (-fiū·zd, *poet.* -fiū·zėd) *ppl. a.*; **Transfu·sing** *vbl. sb.* and *ppl. a.*

1652 BENLOWES *Theoph.* v. liv, The Primum Mobile do's seem immense And doth transfused Influence Through all inferiour Orbs..dispense. 1667 *Phil. Trans.* II. 490 The Conception of that Transfusing design. 1782 A. MONRO *Compar. Anat.* (ed. 3) Introd. 10 Changing their juices by transfusing of new liquors. 1842 LOUDON *Suburban Hort.* 91 They receive from the atmosphere the transfused light on every side. 1903 MORLEY *Gladstone* I. II. iv. 165 The transfusing alchemy of his rather smoky crucible.

**Transfuser** (transfiū·zəɹ). *rare.* [f. prec. + -ER [1].] One who or that which transfuses.

1889 *Nation* (N.Y.) 17 Oct. 319/2 The transfuser of Corean thought.

**Transfusible** (transfiū·zib'l), *a. rare.* [f. L. *transfūs-*, ppl. stem (see TRANSFUSE) + -IBLE: cf. *fusible.*] Capable of being transfused.

1661 BOYLE *Style Scriptures* (1675) 156 Expressions.. whose Penetrancy is as little transfusible into any other as the Sun's dazling Brightness..can be undetractingly Painted. 1826 MISS MITFORD *Village* Ser. II. 267 She could catch even the zest of a repartee, that most evanescent and least transfusible of all things.

**Transfusion** (transfiū·ʒən). [ad. L. *transfūsiōn-em*, n. of action from *transfundĕre* to TRANSFUSE. Cf. F. *transfusion* (1307 in Godef. *Compl.*).] The action of transfusing.

**1.** The action of pouring a liquid from one vessel into another; also *fig.* transference; transmission; translation.

1578 BANISTER *Hist. Man* I. 14 Nerves..pass through them [bones]..for the transfusion of sense into other partes. *c* 1645 HOWELL *Lett.* (1650) II. II. xlviii. 61 It is with languages as 'tis with liquors which by transfusion use to take wind from one vessell to another. 1700 DRYDEN *Fables* Pref. (1721) 24, I grant that something must be lost in all transfusion, that is, in all translations. *c* 1780 BURNEY in Boswell *Johnson* (1848) 71/2 *note*, He would find the transfusion into another language extremely difficult. 1835 *Fraser's Mag.* XII. 394 Of all poets, Theocritus is perhaps the least susceptible of transfusion. 1850 GROTE *Greece* II. lxviii. VIII. 595 Such persuasion had grown up gradually.., partly by insensible transfusion from others.

**2.** *Med.*, etc. The process of transferring the blood of a person or animal into the veins of another; the injection of blood or other fluid into the veins.

1643 *Plain English* 21 As if they..should, of a sudden, receive a Transfusion of Sheeps Blood from the others. 1678 PHILLIPS s. v., Transfusion of the blood is a late Anatomical invention experimented by the Royal Society. 1802 PALEY *Nat. Theol.* xxv. (ed. 2) 484 The experiment of transfusion proves, that the blood of one animal will serve for another. 1877 ROBERTS *Handbk. Med.* (ed. 3) I. 41 In some cases transfusion of blood is demanded, in order to save life and to replace the blood which has been lost.

**3.** *attrib.* and *Comb.*, as *transfusion apparatus, plan*; **transfusion cell** (*Bot.*), one of certain cells which remain thin-walled and thus permit the passage of water to the adjacent tissues; so *transfusion strand, tissue.*

1832 J. BROWN *Lett.* (1907) 25 Give me the latest information about the transfusion plan, specifying the quantities of salt [etc.]. 1875 BENNETT & DYER tr. *Sachs' Bot.* 466 Cells elongated in a direction transverse to the axis of the leaf.. leaving large intercellular spaces (Transfusion-Tissue of Mohl). 1877 KNIGHT *Dict. Mech.* 2613/2 Aveling's Transfusion-Apparatus. 1898 tr. *Strasburger's Text-bk. Bot.* I. i. 112 Special endodermal cells, directly external to the xylem strands, remain unthickened and serve as transfusion cells. *Ibid.* 111 Transfusion strands.

Hence **Transfu·sionist,** one who advocates or practises the process of transfusion of blood.

1889 *Pop. Sci. Monthly* Apr. 808 The early transfusionists reasoned, in the style of the Christian Scientists, that the blood is the life.

**Transfusive** (transfiū·siv), *a.* [f. L. *transfūs-*, ppl. stem (see TRANSFUSE) + -IVE. In med.L. *transfūsīvus* (Albertus Magnus, *a* 1280).] Having the quality of or a tendency to transfusion.

1677 W. HUGHES *Man of Sin* II. iv. 72 The Virgin Mary had a transfusive Virginity; which quenched all concupiscence in others towards her. 1850 J. HAMILTON in *Christian Sabbath* (1852) 132 The transfusive good humour which sent every one away with a purpose to come back. 1869 — *Mem. J. D. Burns* i. 11 The transfusive power of his large and exhaustless vitality.

Hence **Transfu·sively** *adv.*, with transfusion.

1635 HEYWOOD *Hierarch.* v. 278 When he his beames transfusiuely shall run Through Mars his Sphere.

† **Transgluti·tion.** *Obs. rare*$^{-1}$. [n. of action from late L. *transglutīre* to gulp down.] The action of swallowing; deglutition. So † **Transglu·tting** in same sense.

1541 R. COPLAND *Guydon's Quest. Chirurg.* F iij, The keye of Trachea arteria in the tyme of transgluttynge. 1650 BULWER *Anthropomet.* 118 There are many that drink without the moving of Transglutition.

**Transgredient** (transgrī·diĕnt, -z-), *a. rare.* [ad. L. *transgredient-em*, pr. pple. of *transgredī*: see TRANSGRESS *v.*] Transgressing. **a.** Violating a law or obligation. **b.** Passing beyond subjective limits; objective.

1837 SYD. SMITH *Wks.* (1850) 608 To paint the other branches of the Church as such slippery transgredient mortals. 1904 *Jrnl. Philos., Psychol. & Sci. Methods* 4 Aug. 426 Pragmatism..guarantees no objective or social certainty. Its standards are lacking in the essential character of a standard—transgredient reference and verifiability.

**Transgress** (tra·nsgres, -z-), *sb. rare.* ? *Obs.* [ad. L. *transgress-us* a passing over (*u*-stem), f. L. *transgredī*: see next. Cf. OF. *transgres*, 15th c. in Godef. (perh. the immediate source).] Transgression, trespass.

1578 in *Scot. Poems 16th C.* II. 196 There is na sanct may saif your saule Fra the transgres. 1624 HEYWOOD *Gunaik.* II. 73 There be many errors, excesses, and transgresses. *c* 1640 [SHIRLEY] *Capt. Underwit* v. ii, Well, sir, though your transgresse deserve no pardon, Yet I am charitable upon Condition. 1839 READE *Deluge* 112, I heard a Voice that spake within, And said such transgress was a sin.

**Transgress** (transgre·s, -z-), *v.* Also 6–7 **trans(e)gresse.** [app. a. F. *transgresser* (14th c. in Godef. *Compl.*), f. L. *transgress-*, ppl. stem of *transgredī* to step across, f. *trans* across + *gradī* to step.]

**1.** *trans.* To go beyond the bounds or limits prescribed by (a law, command, etc.); to break, violate, infringe, contravene, trespass against.

1526 *Pilgr. Perf.* (1531) 98 b, So they transgresse & breke the commaundement of god. 1550 CROWLEY *Epigr.* 757 Wyl ye transegresse my lawes? 1560 DAUS tr. *Sleidane's Comm.* 217 That he should suffer for transgressing themperours commaundement. 1660 *Trial Regic.* 126 That he that knew the Law so well should so much transgresse it. 1713 STEELE *Englishman* No. 50. 324 Too great an Inclination one way betrayed him to transgress the Rules of Charity. 1829 SCOTT *Anne of G.* xxii, Other points of etiquette were transgressed in their turn, after the repast was over. 1888 BRYCE *Amer. Commw.* II. xxxvii. 32 Where a statute passed by a State legislature is alleged to transgress the Constitution of the State.

**b.** *absol.*, or *intr.* (const. *against*): To break a law or command; to trespass, offend, sin.

1526 TINDALE 2 *John* 9 Whosoever transgresseth and bydeth not in the doctrine of Christ, hath not God. 1535 COVERDALE *Neh.* i. 8 Yf ye transgresse, then wil I scater you abrode amonge the nacions. 1599 SHAKS. *Much Ado* II. i. 260, I would not marry her, though she were indowed with all that Adam had left him before he transgrest. *a* 1699 LADY HALKETT *Autobiog.* (1875) 12, I did not transgresse against my Mother. 1875 JOWETT *Plato* (ed. 2) V. 50 That the two states should unite against a third which transgressed, was a great source of security.

† **c.** *trans.* To offend against (a person); to disobey. *Obs. rare.*

*a* 1619 FLETCHER *Bonduca* IV. ii, I never Blasphemed 'em, uncle, nor transgrest my parents. *a* 1625 — *Wom. Pleased* III. i, You are too Royal to me; To me that have so foolishly transgress'd you.

**2.** *trans.* To go or pass beyond (any limit or bounds).

*a* 1619 [see *transgressed* below]. 1641 WILKINS *Math. Magick* II. vi. (1648) 197 He advises that we should not.. transgresse the bounds of nature. 1686 PLOT *Staffordsh.* 322 Nor have these limits of human life been less transgresst by Men..than they have by women. *a* 1700 DRYDEN *Ovid's Metam.* xv. *Pythag. Philos.* 669 Hard mouthed coursers..Apt to run riot, and transgress the goal. 1829 LYTTON *Devereux* I. i, A man never known before to transgress the very slowest of all possible walks.

† **b.** *intr.* (*a*) To go beyond limits; to trespass (*on*). (*b*) To digress. *Obs.*

1662 GERBIER *Princ.* 22, I shall not spend time, and transgresse on the Readers patience, concerning the making of Clay, and burning of Bricks. 1689 tr. *Buchanan's De Jure Regni apud Scotos* 14 Let us return from whence we have transgressed.

Hence **Transgressed** (-gre·st) *ppl. a.* (in quot. *a* 1619, that has gone beyond ordinary limits, excessive); **Transgre·ssing** *vbl. sb.* and *ppl. a.*

1535 COVERDALE *Josh.* xxii. 22 Yf this be a transgressynge or trespacynge agaynst the Lorde. 1579 W. WILKINSON *Confut. Familye of Loue* b ij, She shall be guiltles of the transgressing. *a* 1619 FOTHERBY *Atheom.* II. ii. § 1 (1622) 198 So large.., and transgrest in her proportion. 1651 HOBBES *Govt. & Soc.* xiv. § 8. 217 Any one who hath suffered the punishment of the transgressed Law. *a* 1812 MᶜLEAN *Comm. Hebr.* (1847) I. 329 The punishment inflicted on his transgressing seed. 1907 *Blackw. Mag.* Feb. 177/1 He brought suits against transgressing shipmasters.

**Transgre·ssible,** *a. rare*$^{-0}$. [ad. late and med.-L. *transgressibilis*: see prec. and -BLE.] Capable of being transgressed.

1882 in OGILVIE; and in later Dicts.

**Transgression** (transgre·ʃən, -z-). [app. a. F. *transgression* (12th c. in Hatz.-Darm.), ad. L. *transgressiōn-em* a going over; later, a violation, transgression, sin, n. of action from *transgredi* to TRANSGRESS.]

**1.** The action of transgressing or passing beyond the bounds of legality or right; a violation of law, duty, or command; disobedience, trespass, sin.

1426 LYDG. *De Guil. Pilgr.* 1130 Transgressyoun ys for to say A goyyng fro the ryht[e] way, Or shortly, in sentement Brekyng off a comaundement. 1432–50 tr. *Higden* (Rolls) V. 213 Borne in as grete innocency and withowte synne as Adam was afore the transgression. 14.. *Cust. Malton* in *Surtees Misc.* (1888) 60 Alle odyr transgrescyons þ[t] towchys the lordes persons. 1494 FABYAN *Chron.* (1811) 342 Culpable in certayne artycles, towchynge transgressyon agayne the kynge. 1552 ABP. HAMILTON *Catech.* (1884) 27 Dedely synnis quhilke ar transgressionis of Gods commands. 1595 SHAKS. *John* I. i. 256 Heauen lay not my transgression to my charge. 1651 HOBBES *Leviath.* II. xxvi. 148 Punishments ordained beforehand for their transgression. 1722 DE FOE *Relig. Courtsh.* I. ii. (1840) 67 The children shall not be punished for the father's transgression. 1824 L. MURRAY *Eng. Gram.* I. 491 The transgression of this rule makes what are called harsh or forced metaphors.

**b.** The action of passing over or beyond. (Only as the etymological sense of the word.)

1623 COCKERAM, *Transgression*, a passing or going ouer. 1643 BURROUGHES *Exp. Hosea* (1652) 238 Sin is called by the name of Transgression..that is going beyond their bounds, going over the hedge. 1857 MAURICE *Ep. St. John* iii. 47, I call it transgression; that is, the passing over a boundary which was marked out for me. 1907 ILLINGWORTH *Doctr. Trinity* x. 190 Sin is always transgression, the overstepping of due bounds, the refusal to be limited.

**2.** *Geol.* The spread of the sea over the land along a subsiding shore-line, producing an overlap by deposition of new strata upon old.

1882 GEIKIE in *Nature* 13 July 242/2 In a section 'Upon Abrasion and Transgression', the author insists upon the paramount influence of the sea as an agent in planing down the surface of the land. 1903 CLAYPOLE in *Amer. Geol.* Aug. 91 The depression in southern Ohio, where the outcrop of the Corniferous limestone and the Corniferous-Hamilton is concealed by the transgression of the shale.

Hence **Transgre·ssional** *a.*, of or pertaining to transgression; of the nature of a transgression.

1690–1 LD. ROCHESTER *Let.* in Burnet *Own Times* (1823) VI. 284 Forgive this transgressional rapture, and receive my thanks..for your kind letter.

**Transgressive** (trɒnsgre·siv, -z-), *a.* [f. L. *transgress-*, ppl. stem (see TRANSGRESS) + -IVE. Cf. late L. *transgressīvus*.]

**1.** Having the character or quality of transgressing. **a.** Involving transgression; sinful.

1646 SIR T. BROWNE *Pseud. Ep.* I. x. 37 Adam..from the transgressive infirmities of himselfe might have erred alone, as well as the Angels before him. 1797 *Hist.* in *Ann. Reg.* 57/1 The powers assumed..were explicitly termed unconstitutional, and transgressive of the authority lodged in them by the laws.

**b.** Passing beyond some limit.

1735 H. BROOKE *Univ. Beauty* III. 30 Where the Solar Heat, and searching Air Transgressive, pierce our actuated Sphere.

†**2.** *Music.* ? Not coming in regular sequence; or ? Overlapping (cf. CONJUNCT B. 6). *Obs.*

1760 STILES *Anc. Gk. Mus.* in *Phil. Trans.* LI. 704 Systems were there considered as differing in respect, first, to magnitude; secondly, to genus; thirdly, to the being consonant or dissonant; fourthly, to the being rational or irrational; fifthly, to the being sequent or transgressive.

**3.** *Geol.* Overlapping: cf. TRANSGRESSION 2. (So Fr. *transgressif* (Littré).)

1854 [implied in TRANSGRESSIVELY]. 1860 MAYNE *Expos. Lex.*, *Transgressivus*,..applied to a couch or bed that becomes deposited on others of different natures and different levels by rising over them, so that it is necessarily more or less inclined: transgressive.

Hence **Transgre·ssively** *adv.*, in a transgressive manner; *spec.* in *Geol.* † (*a*) unconformably; (*b*) so as to overlap the formation next below it.

1847 WEBSTER, *Transgressively*,..by transgressing. 1854 MURCHISON *Siluria* viii. 169 The Silurian series overlap transgressively or unconformably the edges of the subjacent sandstone. 1879 GEIKIE in *Encycl. Brit.* X. 371/2 Upraised Lower Silurian rocks, upon the upturned and denuded edges of which the Carboniferous Limestone lies transgressively.

**Transgressor** (trɒnsgre·sɔɪ, -z-). Also 4–7 -our, 6 -er. [a. AF. *transgressour* = F. *transgresseur* (14th c. in Hatz.-Darm.), a. late L. *transgressōr-em*, agent-n. from *transgredī* to TRANSGRESS.] One who transgresses; a law-breaker; a sinner.

1377 LANGL. *P. Pl.* B. I. 96 And taken *trangressores* [*v.r.* transgressouris] and tyen hem faste. 1432–50 tr. *Higden* (Rolls) III. 263 He..did chide the transgressores of the lawes. 1463–4 *Rolls of Parlt.* V. 502/2 To committe the transgressours..to the next Gaole. 1526 TINDALE *Jas.* ii. 9 Ye commit synne, and are rebuked off the lawe as transgressours. — 11 Thou arte a transgresser off the lawe. 1638 *Penit. Conf.* viii. (1657) 235 His Conscience arraigneth him..as a Transgressor. 1667 MILTON *P. L.* XI. 164 Such title should belonge To me transgressour, who for thee ordaind A help, became thy snare. 1875 JOWETT *Plato* (ed. 2) V. 100 Whoever shall transgress the strains by law established is a transgressor of the laws.

**Transhape**, variant of TRANS-SHAPE.

†**Transhaw**, *a.* or *adv. Obs. rare.* Meaning and origin uncertain: perh. 'exposed' to the blast, opposed to 'borrow' sheltered from the blast.

1665 D. DUDLEY *Metallum Martis* (1854) 31 How to mend their Natures, by finning or setting the finery, lesse transhaw more borrow, which are terms of art, and by altering and pitching the works. *Ibid.*, If the work be set transhaw and transiring from the blast, the Iron is more coldshare, lesse Fined.

**Tranship** (trɒnˌʃi·p), *less commonly* **transship** (trɒnsˌʃi·p), *v.* *Jrnl.* [f. TRANS- + SHIP *v.*]

**1.** *trans.* To transfer from one ship to another; also *transf.*, from one railway train or other conveyance to another. Also *absol.*

1792 LD. MACARTNEY *Jrnl.* in Barrow *Life* (1807) II. 180 All the baggage and presents [were] put on board the large junks, to be transshipped into smaller ones. 1797 — *Emb. to China* II. i. 4 In order to tranship them. 1802 C. ROBINSON *Adm. Cas.* III. 247 He is not bound..either to tranship or to repair. 1813 WELLINGTON *Let.* 26 June in Gurw. *Desp.* (1839) X. 461, I am afraid it will be necessary to tranship the ordnance &c. into smaller vessels. 1846 ADDISON *On Contracts* II. ii. § 4 (1883) 494 If the vessel becomes disabled ..the master is bound to tranship and forward the cargo, if he has the means of transhipment at hand. 1876 CALLIS *Cutlery* 181 It was the practice of German manufacturers.. to..transship them without allowing them to land. 1900 *Blackw. Mag.* Oct. 559/1 He didn't give them time to transship enough provisions.

**2.** *intr.* Of a passenger: To change from one ship or other conveyance to another.

1879 ATCHERLEY *Boërland* 264 At East London..we transhipped into the steamship *African*. 1892 E. REEVES *Homeward Bound* 87 After going a mile or two we stopped, got out, and transhipped into another train. 1892 *Daily News* 18 Oct. 5/6 Passengers going by her had not to tranship either at Hong Kong or Shanghai. 1895 RAMSAY *Paul the Trav.* 283 He [Paul] had to transship in Troas.

**3.** *Comb.* in which *tra·nship* is app. = *transhipment*: as **tranship-shed**, a shed at a railway joint station for the transference of goods from one railway to another; **tranship-train**, a train running in connexion with a steamer into which the passengers tranship; **tranship-van**: see quot.

1903 *Westm. Gaz.* 14 Jan. 5/1 We have 'tranship', or road-vans, specially appointed to work on branches and at stations where there is not the heavy traffic. These take goods from a certain starting-point to be delivered at a number of roadside stations. 1903 *Ibid.* 21 Feb. 7/1 Inviting seven English and Scotch companies to co-operate in the matter of a tranship shed at Carlisle. 1904 *Daily News* 22 Oct. 9 When near the new station at Talacre the engine of a heavy tranship train jumped an obstruction... The guard of the disabled tranship hurried Chesterwards.

Hence **Transhi·pping** *vbl. sb.* (also *attrib.*).

1801 SIR WM. SCOTT in C. Robinson *Adm. Cas.* III. 259 If he [the master] had not the means of transhipping. 1816 TUCKEY *Narr. Exped. R. Zaire* iii. (1818) 88 The transhipping the stores..being finished. 1840 *Evid. Hull Docks Comm.* 121 The transhipping of them, either by rafts or small vessels. 1892 *Nation* (N.Y.) 1 Sept. 155/1 A better transshipping point.

**Transhi·pment, trans-shi·pment.** [f. TRANS- + SHIPMENT, or f. prec. + -MENT.] The action or process of transhipping or changing from one ship or other conveyance to another.

1796 VAUGHAN *Examination* 13 Landing a ship's cargo.. with as few intermediate trans-shipments as possible. 1813 WELLINGTON in Gurw. *Desp.* (1839) XI. 218, I am obliged to go through the details of all the orders for the transhipment. 1846 WARBURTON *Hochelaga* I. 259 The frequent locks and trans-shipment of the cargo must ever be a great embarrassment. 1856 *Farmer's Mag.* Nov. 424 The inconvenience of two transshipments, one at each end of the Erie Canal. 1885 LD. BLACKBURN in *Law Rep.* 10 App. Cas. 419 The cost of transhipment or reshipment, as the case may be. 1899 *Statesman* (Calcutta) 27 Sept., There exists communication by train from Siliguri to Gyabari with one transhipment. *attrib.* 1892 *Pall Mall G.* 24 Nov. 2/1, I refer especially to the transhipment trade. 1899 *Westm. Gaz.* 20 Dec. 9/1 Heavy dock charges [etc.] have lost the port the bulk of the transhipment business.

**Transhuman** (trɒnsˌhiū·măn, -z-), *a. rare.* [f. TRANS- 4 + HUMAN; after It. *trasumanar* in Dante.] Beyond the human; superhuman. So **Transhu·manate** [It. Dante *trasumanar*, Florio *tra(n)s-humanare*], **Transhu·manize** *vbs.*, *trans.* to make transhuman; **Transhumana·tion** [Florio *tra(n)s-(h)umanatione*], a making or becoming transhuman.

1812 CARY *Dante, Parad.* I. 68 Words may not tell of that transhuman change [*orig.* l. 70 trasumanar significar per verba Non si porio]. 1841 GALLENGA *Italy* i. (1848) I. 135 Dante's contact with God was trans-humanating. 1847 *Oxf. to Rome* (ed. 2) 215 A transhumanation takes place. 1872 LOWELL *Dante* Prose Wks. 1890 IV. 168 Souls..transhumanized to the divine abstraction of pure contemplation. 1885 A. J. BUTLER *Parad. of Dante* I. 70 To signify in words transhumanation were impossible. 1892 NORTON *Dante's Parad.* i. 4 Transhumanizing cannot be signified in words.

**Transience** (trɑ·nsiĕns, -z-; trɑ·nʃĕns, -ʒ-). [f. as TRANSIENT: see -ENCE.]

**1.** The action or fact of soon passing away; also, the condition or state of being transient, transiency.

1745 BROOKE *An Anthem* iv, Here, from time and transience won, Beauty has her charms resign'd. *a* 1822 SHELLEY *Ess. & Lett.* (1852) I. 184 A being..whose 'thoughts wander through eternity', disclaiming alliance with transience and decay. 1849 *Tait's Mag.* XVI. 8 Shadows..glide away, in transience fleet. 1875 JOWETT *Plato* (ed. 2) III. 126 Regarding the transience of pleasure as a proof of its unreality. 1905 *Westm. Gaz.* 22 Apr. 12/3 Any other explanation of the transience of French Protestantism.

**2.** The state or quality of being 'transient' in sense 2; = TRANSCENDENCE 1 b.

1882–3 *Schaff's Encycl. Relig. Knowl.* I. 370 [Calvinism] emphasizes at once the transience of God beyond, and the immanence of God within, the world.

**Transiency** (trɑ·nsiĕnsi, -z-; trɑ·nʃĕnsi, -ʒ-). [f. as prec.: see -ENCY.]

**1.** The quality or condition of being transient; brevity of existence; transitoriness.

1652 GAULE *Magastrom.* 96 How is it possible there should either be any..observation on the artists and art, in a transiency so imperceptible? 1805 W. TAYLOR in Robberds *Mem.* (1843) II. 98 A more eager popularity, like that of the 'Minstrel's Lay', would be symptomatic of transiency. 1812 COLERIDGE in *Lit. Rem.* (1836) I. 381 From their minuteness and transiency not calculated to stiffen or inflate the individual. 1831 *Blackw. Mag.* XXIX. 522 They try to perpetuate the transiency of emotions. 1905 F. YOUNG *Sands of Pleasure* I. v, Vaguely conscious of the transiency and instability of material life.

**2.** A transient thing or being. *rare.*

1866 CARLYLE *Edw. Irving* 318 Poor sickly transiencies that we are, coveting we know not what! 1881 PALGRAVE *Vis. Eng.* 200 On the trivialest transiencies fix'd, or plucking for fruit Dead-sea Apples and ashes of sin, more brute than the brute.

**Transient** (trɑ·nsiĕnt, -z-; trɑ·nʃĕnt, -ʒ-), *a.* (*sb.*) Also 7 *erron.* **transeant, -scient**; 7–9 (chiefly in sense 2) **transeunt.** [f. L. *transiens* (in oblique cases *transeunt-*, whence the form *transeunt*), pr. pple. of L. *transīre*, f. *trans* across + *īre* to go.]

**1.** Passing by or away with time; not durable or permanent; temporary, transitory; *esp.* passing away quickly or soon, brief, momentary, fleeting.

1607 *Schol. Disc. agst. Antichr.* I. i. 17 Whose parts are transeant and aereall, and presently vanishing. 1612 STURTEVANT *Metallica* v. 56 Instruments and means are said to be Transient, when in respect of their vse, they serue but once. 1659 PEARSON *Creed* (1839) 380 It containeth two distinct parts; one transient, the other permanent. 1662 J. DAVIES tr. *Mandelslo's Trav.* 261 They are transient showers soon over. 1713 BERKELEY *Guardian* No. 70 ¶ 8 The transient enjoyments of this life. 1813 SIR H. DAVY *Agric. Chem.* (1814) 282 This manure is transient in its effects, and does not last for more than a single crop. 1873 HAMERTON *Intell. Life* IV. v. (1875) 166 The few and transient hours that we can call our own.

**2.** Passing out or operating beyond itself; transitive; opposed to *immanent.* (Often spelt *transeunt* for distinction from sense 1.)

1613 PURCHAS *Pilgrimage* I. i. 4 The workes of God, which are either inward and immanent, or outward and transient. 1625 GILL *Sacr. Philos.* I. 98 You may observe a difference of actions, of which some are immanent, or indwelling in the doer..: some againe are transeunt, or passing from the doer upon that which is done. *a* 1677 HALE *Prim. Orig. Man.* 35 Those two great transeunt or emanant acts or works, the works of Creation and Providence. 1836–7 SIR W. HAMILTON *Metaph.* (1870) II. xxv. 118 An act of the mind going out of itself, in other words, a transeunt act. 1847 DE QUINCEY *Milton v. Southey & Landor* Wks. XII. 177 In metaphysical language, the moral of an epos or a drama should be immanent, not transient. 1890 *Athenæum* 8 Nov. 631/1 Volitionally reactive redintegration with its two stages, immanent and transeunt action.

**3.** Passing or flowing through; passing from one thing or person to another. Now *rare.*

1619 DENISON *Heav. Banq.* 341 If the worship at our receiuing did determine in the Sacrament, or were transient by it to God. 1644 [H. PARKER] *Jus Pop.* 57 They lurke between scripture and reason, and remain in a kind of transcient posture. 1671 GREW *Anat. Plants* i. (1682) 7 A Filtre to the transient Sap. *a* 1703 BURKITT *On N. T.* 1 Thess. ii. (1818) 16 Hereditary, and..transient from one generation to another. 1847 TENNYSON *Princess* v. 37 Away we stole, and transient in a trice From what was left of faded woman-slough To sheathing splendours..issued in the sun.

**4.** Passing through a place without staying in it, or staying only for a short time; in quot. 1731 of birds, migratory; *spec.* (*U.S. colloq.*) applied to a guest at a hotel, etc. (often *ellipt.* as *sb.*: see B. 2).

1685 BAXTER *Paraphr. N.T.*, *Mark* (1701) Introd., Whether this Mark was Bishop of Alexandria, or only a transient Evangelist there a while, is an Historical Controversie. 1713 SWIFT *Cadenus & Vanessa* 768 Love, hitherto a transient guest, Ne'er held possession of his breast. 1731 SIR J. CLERK in *Mem. W. Stukeley* (Surtees) I. 247 There are many transient fowls that come into Britain at certain seasons. 1740 W. DOUGLASS *Disc. Curr. Brit. Plant. Amer.* 3 The Author is not a transient Person, who from Humour or Caprice..may expose the Province. 1788 *Massachusetts Spy* 11 Dec. 3/2 A transient jockey came to the house of Mr. Jonathan Hubbey, and agreed to purchase a horse of him. 1822 MONTGOMERY *Hymn*, '*This stone to Thee in faith we lay*' v, But will, indeed, Jehovah deign Here to abide, no transient guest?

**5.** *Mus.* Introduced in passing, as a note, chord, etc. not belonging to the harmony, or to the key, of the passage; passing.

1801 in BUSBY *Dict. Mus.* 1838 G. F. GRAHAM *Mus. Comp.* 29/2 Passing notes, changing notes, transient notes, etc. 1878 F. TAYLOR in Grove *Dict. Mus.* I. 75/1 A so-called 'auxiliary note' (sometimes 'transient' or 'changing' note).

**B.** *sb.*

**1.** A transient thing or being; something passing or transitory, not permanent.

1652 SPARKE *Prim. Devot.* (1663) 279 If we (meanwhile) but rise from graves of sin And transients (which the most are buried in !). 1661 GLANVILL *Van. Dogm.* 81 A kind of stop or arrest, by the benefit of which the Soul might have a glance of the fugitive Transient. *a* 1674 TRAHERNE *Poet. Wks.* (1903) 18. 1860 BOYD *Recr. Country Parson* ii. 27 These gray transients have changed to shivering skeletons.

**2.** *U.S. colloq.* A person who passes through a place, or stays in it only for a short time; *spec.* a 'transient guest' at a hotel or boarding-house.

1880 MRS. ROLLINS *New Eng. Bygones* (1883) 84 My grandmother held these transients in low esteem. 1893 KATE SANBORN *S. California* 20 On an open, sunny site, and ..frequented by 'transients' and business men of moderate means. 1894 *Outing* (U.S.) XXIV. 260/1 Summer residents, transients, and all, had turned out early.

**Tra·nsiently** (see prec.), *adv.* [f. prec. + -LY [2].] In a transient manner; in passing through; briefly, momentarily; hastily.

1641 R. YOUNGE *Counterpoyson* 398, I have transiently found (in making up the Index) some literall mistakes, points misplaced, &c. 1649 J. H. *Motion to Parl. Adv. Learn.* 25 Some ends which I have transiently..glanced at. 1684 BAXTER *Parish Congreg.* 20 They might occasionally Communicate in our Parishes transiently. 1748 RICHARDSON *Clarissa* VI. xlvi. 69, I thought, transiently thought, that the tea..had an odd taste. 1826 SCOTT *Woodst.* iii. A smile passed transiently over his clouded brow. 1900 *Speaker* 29 Dec. 336/2 Not only transiently, but permanently declining.

**Tra·nsientness.** [f. as prec. + -NESS.] The quality or state of being transient; transience.

1667 *Decay Chr. Piety* x. ¶ 1 As they resemble the wind in fury.., so they might do also in transientness. 1698 NORRIS *Pract. Disc.* IV. 368 The Pleasure of this Life is.. in regard of its Transientness, like the Pleasure of a Dream. 1907 *Edin. Rev.* July 177 Suzanne..could not believe in the transientness of [Gibbon's affections].

**Transierd**: see TRANSIRE *v. Obs.*

**Trans,i·liac,** *a. Anat.* [f. TRANS- 5 + L. *ilium*: cf. ILIAC.] Lying across the ilium; extending transversely from one iliac bone to the other.

1891 in *Cent. Dict.*

**Transilience** (transi·liĕns). *rare.* [f. as next: see -ENCE.] A leaping from one thing to another, an abrupt transition: *spec.* in *Min.* abrupt transition of one mineral or rock into another.

1657 REEVE *God's Plea* 204 Man may haue..his diffluences, redundances,..and transiliences of speech. 1811 PINKERTON *Petralogy* II. 169 Rocks of black trap, surmounted by porphyry of the same base, the transilience being clear and palpable. 1830 HERSCHEL *Stud. Nat. Phil.* 330 Transferred by contact, or by sudden and violent transilience of the interval of separation..under the form of sparks and flashes.

So † **Transi·liency** [see -ENCY], the quality of being transilient; less correctly = prec. *Obs. rare*$^{-1}$.

1661 GLANVILL *Van. Dogm.* xii. 114 By an unadvised transiliency leaping from the effect to its remotest cause.

**Transilient** (transi·liĕnt), *a.* [ad. L. *tran(s)-silient-em*, pr. pple. of *tran(s)silīre* to leap across, skip over, omit, f. *trans* across + *salīre* to leap.] Leaping or passing from one thing or condition to another; in *Min.* said of one rock substance passing abruptly into another.

*Transilient fibres*, nerve-fibres passing from one convolution of the brain to another not immediately adjacent (*Syd. Soc. Lex.* 1899).

1811 PINKERTON *Petralogy* I. p. v, The Transilient Rocks, an interesting series, in which one substance.. passes into another, as granite into porphyry, trap into wacken. *Ibid.* 550 British rocks are often anomalous, or transilient, and can scarcely be reduced to precise denominations.

† **Transili·tion.** *Obs. rare*$^{-1}$. [ad. late L. *transilītiōn-em* (Augustine), n. of action f. *transilīre*: see prec.] The action of leaping over or 'skipping'; omission of intermediate numbers.

1582 T. WATSON *Centurie of Loue* lxxx, Founded by transilition or ouer skipping of number by rule and order, as from 1 to 3, 5, 7, and 9. *Ibid.* [see TRANSPOSITION 2].

**Transilluminate** (trans,il*ū*·mine*i*t), *v.* [f. TRANS- + ILLUMINATE *v.*] *trans.* To cause light to pass through; *spec.* in *Med.* to throw a strong light through (an organ or part) to discover the presence or cause of disease. So **Transillumina·tion**, the action or process of transilluminating.

1890 *Lancet* 1 Mar. 480/2 It [a tooth] was translucent by electric transillumination, showing that the pulp was living. 1900 *Ibid.* 25 Aug. 617/1 If in a darkened room the electric lamp used for transilluminating the frontal sinus was placed against the thyroid cartilage. 1901 *Ibid.* 11 May 1328/2 Transillumination is often used to find out if the antrum is diseased. 1912 KEITH *Human Body* i. 20 It may have occurred, however, to the onlooker that, since we can trans-illuminate the human body [*i.e.* with Röntgen-rays], it is no longer necessary to dissect it.

**Trans-impre·ssion.** *rare*$^{-1}$. [TRANS- 1.] An impression transferred or taken over (*from* something).

1812–29 COLERIDGE in *Lit. Rem.* (1838) III. 152 The very words, 'conception', 'comprehension', and all in all languages that answer to them, suppose this trans-impression from the mind.

**Trans,incorpora·tion.** [TRANS- 1.] Passage from one body to another; transmigration of the soul.

1810 W. TAYLOR in *Monthly Mag.* XXX. 47 The doctrine of the trans-incorporation of souls, or of their migration through successive human bodies, was taught..by a Jewish rabbi. 1843 ROBBERDS *Mem. W. Taylor* II. iv. 305 Its contents are full of curious information, more particularly those on the transincorporation of souls.

**Trans,i·nsular,** *a.* [f. TRANS- 3 + L. *insula* island: cf. *insular*.]

1. Crossing or going across an, or the, island.

1895 *Buffalo Current Hist.* (N.Y.) V. 404 When the colony [Newfoundland] would have to work its transinsular railway system. 1900 *Engineering Mag.* XIX. 684 Any trans-insular railroad project is chimerical.

2. *Anat.* Applied to a fissure of the brain that crosses the insula or island of Reil, and divides it into a cephalic and a caudal region.

1889 *Buck's Handbk. Med. Sc.* VIII. 160/1 Normal, human subfissures are..the transinsular and others crossing the surface of the insula.

‖ **Transire** (trans,əi·rĭ), *sb. Law.* [L. *transīre* to go across, pass over, f. *trans* across + *īre* to go.] A warrant issued by the custom-house, permitting the passage of merchandise.

1599 NASHE *Lenten Stuffe* (1871) 70 They would grant him his coquet, or *Transire.* 1656 in *Misc. Sc. Burgh Rec. Soc.* 30 Receiveing moneys for writeing bills, cocquetts, and transires. 1662 *Order Ho. Com. as to Customs* (1663) 9 A Transire or Let-passe from Port to Port in England. 1750 *Act 23 Geo. II*, c 29 § 2 No officer of his Majesty's customs shall sign or grant any cocquet, sufferance, transire, let-pass, warrant, or certificate..for exporting..such bar iron. 1888 *Act* 51 & 52 *Vict.* c. 24 § 5 (*a*) Any port..at which her transire is to be obtained.

† **Transire** (trans,əi·ɹ), *v. Obs. rare.* Also 6 transier. [irreg. f. L. *transīre* (see prec.), the inf. form being taken instead of the ppl. stem *transit-* (TRANSIT *v.*).] *intr.* To go or pass across; in quot. 1665, ? to lie transversely.

1592 WYRLEY *Armorie* 121 Pretended iorney if they onward hould, Transierd they were, as it was to me tould. 1665 D. DUDLEY *Mettallum Martis* (1854) 31 If the work be set transhaw and transiring from the blast.

**Trans,i·schiac** (-i·skiæk), *a. Anat.* [f. TRANS- 5 + L. *ischiac-us*, f. *ischi-um*: see ISCHIUM, and -AC.] Extending transversely from one ischial bone to the other.

1891 in *Cent. Dict.* 1899 in *Syd. Soc. Lex.*

**Trans-i·sthmian,** *a.* [f. TRANS- 3 + ISTHMUS: cf. *isthmian*.] Crossing or extending across an isthmus, esp. the Isthmus of Panama.

1885 GROVER CLEVELAND *Ann. Message to Congress U.S.A.* Dec., Our interests in any transisthmian route which may be opened. 1902 *Q. Rev.* Oct. 674 The Key to any possible trans-isthmian canal.

**Transit** (tra·nsit, -z-), *sb.* Also 5 **trancyte**, 5–7 **transite**. [ad. L. *transit-us* (-*ū* stem), verbal sb. from *transīre* to cross, f. *trans* across + *īre* to go. So It. *transito*, whence Fr. *transit* (17th c.).]

1. The action or fact of passing across or through; passage or journey from one place or point to another. Often in phrase *in transit*, L. *in transitu*.

*c* 1440 *Gesta Rom.* ii. 12 (Add. MS.) Above oure hede there is a transite of men [*Harl.* passage and goyng of peple]. 1716 M. DAVIES *Athen. Brit.* II. 171 Henry..of Huntington.., who writ ten Books *Historiæ Anglorum*, from the Transit and Introit of the Saxons hither, to the Year 1153. 1766 W. DIGBY in Jesse *Selwyn & Contemp.* (1843) II. 12, I lay at Gloucester in my transit. 1833 RITCHIE *Wand. Loire* 27 Sometimes..the transit from Nantes to Orleans takes two months! 1841 CATLIN *N. Amer. Ind.* xlvi. II. 87, I..made a transit across the prairies. 1853 KANE *Grinnell Exp.* vii. (1856) 50 Of the voyages to Lancaster Sound..the transit of the middle ice is the essential feature. 1877 BLACK *Green Past.* xxxii, In our rapid transit from place to place.

† b. *concr.* A way for passing, a passage.

*c* 1440 *Promp. Parv.* 499/2 Trancyte, where menn walke, *transitus.*

c. The passage or carriage of persons or goods from one place to another.

1800 COLQUHOUN *Comm. Thames* viii. 259 Property.. stationary on the Quays or in transit on the River. 1855 MACAULAY *Hist. Eng.* xiii. III. 254 While he governed, no prohibition..impeded the transit of commodities from any part of the island to any other. 1866 ROGERS *Agric. & Prices* I. xx. 504 The cost of carriage. Occasionally..this is charged in the value given, the transit being..undertaken frequently by common carriers. 1870 YEATS *Nat. Hist. Comm.* 62 The means of transit are so bad, that much good corn is left to rot upon the ground.

d. *transf.* A place at which a river may be crossed; a crossing. *rare.*

1852 GROTE *Greece* II. lxix. IX. 39 A..flourishing town, a centre of commerce enriched by the important ford or transit of the river Euphrates close to it.

2. *fig.* (in various senses.) A passing across; a transition or change; *esp.* the passage from this life to the next by death.

1657 W. MORICE *Coena quasi Κοινή*, Diat. v. 237 There can be no such transite from one kinde of action to another. 1765 H. WALPOLE *Otranto* iii. (1798) 50 To pray for her happy transit to a better life. 1810 KNOX & JEBB *Corr.* II. 19 The transit from autumn to winter. 1823 SCOTT *Quentin D.* vi, Speak a word of comfort to him ere he make his transit, Trois-Eschelles. 1859 HOLLAND *Gold F.* xv. 182 Old men..whose work of life is..done, and who may in peace.. sit down and wait their mysterious transit. 1871 EARLE *Philol. Eng. Tongue* § 276 This verb made an early transit to the weak form.

3. *Astrol.* The passage of a planet across some special point or region of the zodiac.

[1621 BURTON *Anat. Mel.* I. ii. I. iv, If ♄, by his revolution, or *transitus*, shall offend any of those radicall promissors in his geniture.] 1671 SALMON *Syn. Med.* I. xxix. 61 In Directions and Transits three things are to be considered; first the Significator, secondly the Promissor; thirdly the sign and house in which they happen. 1819 J. WILSON *Dict. Astrol.* s.v., The transits of the ☽ are said to cause all the daily passing events of a man's life, as she transits the △, ⚹, □, ☍, or ☌, of any particular house.

4. *Astron.* a. The passage of an inferior planet (Mercury or Venus) across the sun's disk, or of a satellite or its shadow across the disk of a planet; formerly also applied to an occultation of a star or planet by the moon, or of a star by a planet.

1669 FLAMSTEAD in *Phil. Trans.* IV. 1110 Let me desire those, who have fit..Instruments, to observe this Transit. 1704 J. HARRIS *Lex. Techn.* I, *Transit*, in *Astronomy*, signifies the passing of any Planet just by or under any Fixt Star; or of the Moon in particular, covering or moving close by any other Planet. 1769 M. CUTLER in *Life*, etc. (1888) I. 20 The 3d of this month happened the Transit of Venus over the sun's disk. 1769 COOK *Voy. r. World* I. xiii. (1773) 137 On Thursday the 1st of June, the Saturday following being the day of the Transit, I dispatched Mr. Gore in the long-boat to Imao. 1829 *Chapters Phys. Sc.* 398 The transits of Mercury and Venus are really eclipses of the sun. 1868 LOCKYER *Guillemin's Heavens* III. II. i. (ed. 3) 478 The value of the Sun's distance at present received has been deduced from the transits of Venus in 1761 and 1769. 1910 *Whitaker's Almanack* 88 Only Satellite IV [of Jupiter] will be visible at 2.30 a.m. February 24—Satellite II. being in transit, Satellite III. occulted, and Satellite I. eclipsed.

*transf.* 1859 in *Merc. Marine Mag.* (1860) VII. 65 The Shoal first seen was in transit with Embleton Island, bearing N.E. ¾ E.

b. The passage of a star or other celestial body across the meridian at its culmination.

1812 WOODHOUSE *Astron.* viii. 48 Two successive transits of a star over the meridian. 1834 MRS. SOMERVILLE *Connex. Phys. Sc.* vii. 61 While observing transits of the fixed stars across the meridian at Cayenne.

c. Short for *transit-circle, -compass, -instrument,* or *-theodolite*: see 5. *colloq.*

1843 *Penny Cycl.* XXV. 122/1 Transit, or Transit Instrument. *Ibid.* 122/2 Such an account of the transit as will enable any one to use it with tolerable success. 1879 NEWCOMB & HOLDEN *Astron.* 74 The meridian transit instrument, or briefly the 'transit'. 1897 *Edin. Rev.* July 66 The institution, furnished only with a transit when he took it in charge.

5. *attrib.* and *Comb.*, usually in relation to the conveyance of goods and passengers, as *transit-company, -depot, -road, -room, -time, -traffic, -way*; also **transit-circle**, an astronomical instrument consisting of a telescope carrying a large graduated circle, by which the right ascension and declination of a star may be determined by observation of it in transit (sense 4 b); a meridian-circle; **transit-clock**, a clock used in conjunction with a transit-instrument; **transit-compass**, an instrument, resembling a theodolite, used in surveying for the measurement of horizontal angles; **transit-duty**, a duty paid on goods passing through a country; **transit-instrument**, an astronomical telescope mounted on a fixed east-and-west axis, by which the time of the passage of a celestial body across the meridian may be determined; usually applied to one without a circle (cf. *transit-circle*); **transit-pass**, a warrant to pass through a country without payment of duty; **transit-theodolite** = *transit-compass*; **transit-trade**, trade arising out of the passage of foreign goods through a country.

1843 *Penny Cycl.* XXV. 133/1 A *transit circle may be made to answer both purposes. 1897 *Edin. Rev.* July 68 In 1851 a new transit circle, of great optical power and enormous mechanical stability, superseded Troughton's masterpiece of 1812. 1843 *Penny Cycl.* XXV. 130/1 To have a second clock called a journeyman, which strikes loudly and speaks as it were for the *transit clock. 1845 R. BROWN in *Mem.* ii. (1866) 28 We got into one of the *Transit Company's vans. 1887 MOLONEY *Forestry W. Afr.* 248 The Public Works Department of each Colony offers a ready *transit-depot for such contributions. 1776 ADAM SMITH *W. N.* v. ii. II. 515 In some small states duties..are imposed upon goods carried across the territory..from one foreign country to another. These are in some countries called *transit-duties. 1809 *State Papers* in *Ann. Reg.* 697/1 The transit duties on the goods thus imported or exported. 1812 WOODHOUSE *Astron.* vi. 32 It may be used as a *transit instrument: that is, the presence of a star on the meridian may be ascertained by it. 1889 *Pall Mall Gaz.* 2 Sept. 7/3 Less..than it cost foreigners to bring it to Pakhio under *transit-pass. 1861 J. NICHOL in *Mem.* (1896) 37 As regular as the *transit-room clock. 1862 *Catal. Internat. Exhib.* II. XIII. 3 A first-rate 6-inch *transit theodolite,..with vertical and horizontal circles. 1803 *Edin. Rev.* III. 243 Those..nations whose wealth has been promoted by the *transit trade. 1852 CONYBEARE & H. *St. Paul* (1862) II. xxiii. 329 The Valley of the Nile was the channel of an active transit trade in spices, dyes, jewels, and perfumes. 1903 *Expositor* May 335 Jerusalem had no natural command of the *transit-traffic. 1904 *Q. Rev.* Oct. 341 The trade-winds..contribute greatly to the salubrity and comfort of this *transit-way.

**Transit** (tra·nsit, -z-), *v.* [f. L. *transit-*, ppl. stem of *transīre*: see prec. Cf. L. *transitāre*, freq. of *transīre* (instanced in pr. pple. *transitāns* Cic.). In earlier use stressed *transi·te*.]

1. *intr.* To pass through or over; to pass away.

*c* 1440 *Gesta Rom.* xc. 415 The porter is the worlde; and right as by the porter so by the worlde we may transite. 1595 CHAPMAN *Ovid's Banq. Sence* (1639) 11 As Intellects themselves transite to each intelligible qualitie. 1775 'JOEL COLLIER' (Alex. Bicknell) *Mus. Trav.* (ed. 2) 68, I then transided to the gentleman himself. 1797–1803 FOSTER in *Life & Corr.* (1846) I. 173 The comets of the mind; they transit off. 1803 *Ibid.* 196, I have transited into another person. 1852 N. L. WALKER *Life in Spirit* xiii. (1853) 212 One or two transit off from our Divinity Halls annually.

2. *trans.* To pass across or through (something); to traverse, cross. Also *fig.*

1674 JEAKE *Arith.* (1696) 249, I have..transited Decimals and Astronomicals, and shall now apply myself to overlook Logarithmes. 1890 *Pall Mall Gaz.* 10 Mar. 3/1 Another line which would transit Germany, Russia,..Afghanistan, and India.

3. *Astrol.* To pass across (a sign, 'house', or special point, of the zodiac). Also *absol.* or *intr.*

1647 LILLY *Chr. Astrol.* lxvii. 409 When the unfortunate Anareta transits the degree ascending. 1686 GOAD *Celest. Bodies* III. ii. 403 Feavers..do annoy us, when the Heavenly Bodies Transit, or take up Station in such Parts of the Zodiack. 1819 J. WILSON *Dict. Astrol.* s.v. *Transits*, If the lord of the 8th..transit the cusp of the horoscope, it threatens death.

4. *Astron.* To pass across (the disk of a celestial body, the meridian of a place, or the field of view of a telescope). Also *absol.* or *intr.*

In quot. 1686 of the moon, to occult (a star or planet).

1686 GOAD *Celest. Bodies* I. xii. 49 The ☽ transiting ♀ that Night raised the Tides. 1755 B. MARTIN *Mag. Arts & Sc.* I. 45 In the Years 1753, 1786, 1799, in the Month of April, he [Mercury] will transit the Sun's Disk. 1833 HERSCHEL *Astron.* viii. 256 Rendering the planet invisible, unless..where it transits the sun's disc and appears on it as a black spot. 1870 PROCTOR *Other Worlds* viii. (ed. 2) 184 The markings seen on the third satellite, when transiting Jupiter's disc. 1878 LOCKYER *Stargazing* 354 The value of the divisions of the micrometer screw having been previously determined by allowing an equatorial star to transit.

**Transitable** (trɑ·nsităb'l), *a. rare.* [f. as prec. + -ABLE.] Capable of being passed across or over; affording means of transit.

1843 *Blackw. Mag.* LIV. 660 The river Chagre..is the nearest transitable point to Panama. 1866 RUSKIN in Spielmann *Life* (1900) 50 If you think it at all curable or transit-able, I'll advance her 20 pounds without interest. 1897 *Jrnl. R. Geog. Soc.* July 63 The efforts..made to open a transitable road to [the valley of the Rio Grande de Terraba] from the north..have proven futile.

‖ **Transita·rium.** *Obs. rare.* [mod.L., f. TRANSIT *sb.* 4 a; cf. *planetarium.*] An apparatus for illustrating the transit of a planet.

1761 *Brit. Mag.* II. 668 Earl Ferrers..presented to the [Royal] Society..a transitarium invented by his lordship for giving an ocular demonstration of the principles relating to the theory of that planet [Venus].

† **Transita·tion.** *Obs. rare.* [n. of action f. L. *transitāre*: see TRANSIT *v.* and -ATION.] The action of passing; passage. (In quots. *humorous.*)

1600–9 ROWLANDS *Knave of Clubs* 37 As on the way I Itinerated, A Rurall person I Obuiated, Interogating times Transitation. 1605 VERSTEGAN *Dec. Intell.* vii. 205.

**Tra·nsiter.** *rare.* [f. TRANSIT *sb.* or *v.* + -ER [1].] Name for a form of the apparatus usually called a 'recording micrometer', and attached to the eye-end of a transit telescope.

1902 *Science* (U.S.) 2 May 693/2 The actual arrangement in use at the Philadelphia Observatory, called for brevity a 'transiter'...The transiter seemed to furnish all the necessary facilities of motion and of recording, and..permitted elimination of all errors excepting that of bisection.

**Transition** (trɑnsi·ʒən, -si·ʃən, -zi·ʃən). [ad. L. *transitiōn-em*, n. of action f. *transīre, transit-* (see TRANSIT *v.*). Cf. F. *transition* (13–14th c. in Hatz.-Darm.).

(The first and prevailing pronunciation, contrary to the general analogy of words in *-tion*, is app. due (as suggested by Walker) to a desire to avoid the collocation of the two similar (voiceless) sibilants *s* and *ʃ*.)]

**1.** A passing or passage from one condition, action, or (rarely) place, to another; change.

1551 GARDINER *Explication, Of Transubstantiation* 123 In the mysterie of Christes person, there is no transition of the deitie into the humanite, or humanite into the deitie. 1621 G. SANDYS *Ovid's Met.* VI. (1626) 109 The vast sky painted with a mightie Bowe: Where, though a thousand seuerall colours shine, No eye their close transition can define. 1751 JOHNSON *Rambler* No. 172 ⁋ 7 A quick transition from poverty to abundance can seldom be made with safety. 1851 HAWTHORNE *Ho. Sev. Gables* xvii, Transition being so facile, what can be any man's inducement to tarry in one spot? 1862 SIR H. HOLLAND *Ess.* i. 1 We are living in an age of transition. 1899 STALKER *Christology of Jesus* v. 186 Death was..only a stage of transition to a higher form of life.

**2.** Passage in thought, speech, or writing from one subject to another.

1592 tr. *Junius on Rev.* vii. 1 This first verse is a transition. 1674 MILTON *P. L.* (ed. 2) XII. 5 Heer the Archangel paus'd..Then with transition sweet new Speech resumes. 1724 WATTS *Logic* IV. ii. vii. § 3 Acquaint yourself with all the proper..forms of transition from one part of a discourse to another. 1798 EDGEWORTH *Pract. Educ.* (1811) I. 115 The transition of attention from one subject to another. 1875 JOWETT *Plato* (ed. 2) V. 15 The Timaeus..one of his [Plato's] most finished works, is full of abrupt transitions.

**3.** *Mus.* † **a.** The passing from one note to another by means of a passing-note (*obs.*). **b.** The passing from one key to another, modulation; *spec.* a passing or brief modulation; also, modulation into a remote key.

1667 C. SIMPSON *Compend. Mus.* 88 A Note is somtimes broken to make a Transition by degrees to some other Concord. These Transitions or Breakings are commonly express'd in Quavers or Crochets. 1877 STAINER *Harmony* xii. § 150 A transition is the rapid passing through any key, without remaining sufficiently long in it to establish a modulation. 1889 PROUT *Harmony* x. (ed. 3) 101 Some writers use the term 'Transition', when the modulation is to a remote or unrelated key.

**4.** The passage from an earlier to a later stage of development or formation. **a.** *Geol.* Formerly *spec.* applied *attrib.* to certain early stratified rocks believed to contain the oldest remains of living organisms; now classified as Silurian: see quot. 1813.

1813 BAKEWELL *Introd. Geol.* (1815) 9 The lowest of the secondary rocks have..been called by the German geologists transition rocks, from the supposition that they were formed when the world was passing from an uninhabitable to a habitable state. 1815 W. PHILLIPS *Outl. Min. & Geol.* (1818) 116 To primitive rocks succeeds another class, which Werner denominates *Transition* rocks. 1823 BUCKLAND *Reliq. Diluv.* 117 It lies in a bed of transition limestone. 1834–5 J. PHILLIPS *Geol.* in *Encycl. Metrop.* VI. 593/2 On the East side of the transition ranges of the Wrekin and Wenlock Edge lies the Coalfield of Coalbrook Dale. 1839 MURCHISON *Silur. Syst.* I. xxxiv. 452 It also presents certain beds of transition between the limestone and the Old Red Sandstone. 1855 J. PHILLIPS *Man. Geol.* 104 The two parts connected by a transition band (upper caradoc). 1885 GEIKIE *Text-bk. Geol.* VI. II. ii. § 1. 658 Murchison was the first to discover that the so-called 'Transition Rocks' or 'Grauwacke' of early geological literature were capable of subdivision into distinct formations..he gave them the name of Silurian.

**b.** *Arch.* Change from an earlier style to a later; a style of intermediate or mixed character.

1835 R. WILLIS *Archit. Mid. Ages* i. 9 These may be called Imitation Specimens, to distinguish them from regular Transitions. 1842–76 GWILT *Archit.* Gloss., *Transition*, a term used to denote the passing from one period of a style to another, exhibiting features peculiar to both, some of which have not quite been given up, and some of which were beginning to be introduced. 1874 PARKER *Goth. Archit.* I. iii. 39 The remainder of the eleventh century may be considered as a period of transition.

**c.** *Philol.* The historical passage of language from one well-defined stage to another; e. g. from Old English or Anglo-Saxon to Middle English; or from Middle English to Modern English; hence applied to the interval occupied by this, and to the intermediate or transitional stage or form of the language during this interval.

1873–4 SWEET *Hist. Eng. Sounds* 160 We have..two periods of transition, one in which *nama* and *name* exist side by side, and another in which final *e* is beginning to drop...The former, commonly called Semi-Saxon.., is characterized by many far-reaching changes. I propose..to call the first the *Transition* period *par excellence*, distinguishing the two, when necessary, as first and second *Transition*, the more important one being generally called simply *Transition* or *Transition-English*. *Ibid.* 38 In the Transition period.. we are confronted by [a] curious and apparently inexplicable phenomenon. 1878 MURRAY *Eng. Lang.* in *Encycl. Brit.* VIII. 391/2 Transition Old English, or 'Semi-Saxon' 1120 to 1200...Transition Middle English 1400 to 1485...Many writers carry the Transition Old English down to 1250. *Ibid.* 397/2 The change of the language during the second period of Transition. *Ibid.* 402 Chronological Chart [has] Old English Transition 1123–1200. Middle English Transition, 1400–1485.

**5.** *attrib.*, as *transition form, species, stage, state*, etc.: see also 4 a and c. Often equivalent to TRANSITIONAL.

1805–17 R. JAMESON *Char. Min.* (ed. 3) 126 All the crystals that lie between two principal crystals, and form the transition of one into the other, constitute what is called a transition-suite. 1826 KIRBY & SP. *Entomol.* (1828) III. xxix. 161 Groups..connected by certain transition species. 1843 R. J. GRAVES *Syst. Clin. Med.* xxvii. 343 The most obstinate form [of the disease] generally selects such transition spots or intermediate tissues. 1853 J. SMITH *Treat. Mus.* 33 Transition or passing notes. 1856 FROUDE *Hist. Eng.* I. ii. 86 Wolsey..holding a middle place between an English statesman and a catholic of the old order, was essentially a transition minister. 1865 TYLOR *Early Hist. Man.* vii. 188 A very good example of this interesting transition work. 1884 J. TAIT *Mind in Matter* (1892) 50 The transition-stages set forth by revolutionists.

**Transitional** (trɑnsi·ʒənăl, -si·ʃ-, -zi·ʃ-), *a.* (*sb.*) [f. prec. + -AL.] Of or pertaining to transition; characterized by or involving transition; intermediate.

*c* 1810 COLERIDGE in *Lit. Rem.* (1838) III. 262 The Jewish Rabbis..represented the Millennium as the preparative and transitional state to perfect spiritualization. 1859 DARWIN *Orig. Spec.* vi. (1860) 172 By this theory innumerable transitional forms must have existed. 1867 A. J. ELLIS *E. E. Pronunc.* I. i. 30 Shakspere and Milton are transitional between Spenser and Dryden. 1867 FREEMAN *Norm. Conq.* I. i. 3 At a transitional period in the world's developement. 1874 PARKER *Goth. Archit.* I. iii. 58 The arches are transitional, two being round and two pointed.

**b.** *Transitional case* in grammar, a case in some languages expressing motion toward.

1890 A. S. GATSCHET *Gram. Klamath Lang.* 484 Transitional case in -na...This locative case-suffix..corresponds to our *to, toward, into, in.*

**B.** *ellipt.* as *sb.* (in quot. for *transitional cell*: cf. quot. 1904 s. v. MONONUCLEAR).

1904 *Brit. Med. Jrnl.* 10 Sept. 583 They [mononuclear white blood cells] become transformed in the blood (according to Ehrlich) into the transitionals.

Hence **Transi·tionally** *adv.*, **Transi·tionalness.**

1874 RUSKIN *Fors Clav.* xliv. 164 This plate of mine, melted down, after being transitionally serviceable to the burglar, will enter again into the same functions among the silver of the world. 1896 *Scot. Leader* 1 Jan. 7 A deep sense of the transitionalness of conclusions which were once thought to be for all time.

**Transitionary** (trɑnsi·ʒənări, -si·ʃ-, -zi·ʃ-), *a.* [f. as prec. + -ARY [1].] = TRANSITIONAL.

1685 H. MORE *Paralip. Prophet.* xxi. 181 This third Introductory Vision is a kind of Transitionary Introduction to the Opened Book-Prophecy. 1827 *Examiner* 630/2 The rapid, elastic, transitionary style of this actor. 1858 BUCKLE *Civiliz.* (1864) I. viii. 472 The transitionary state which France began to enter. 1900 *Literature* 14 July 28/1 The Induction..is essentially of a transitionary character.

**Transi·tionist.** *rare*⁻¹. [f. as prec. + -IST.] One who supports transition; in quot. *attrib.*

1856 E. G. K. BROWNE *Tractarian Movem.* (1861) 438 The advanced guard of the Transitionist party.

† **Transi·tious,** *a. Obs. rare*⁻⁰. [f. TRANSITION + -OUS.] Transitional. Hence † **Transi·tiously** *adv.* (*obs. rare*⁻¹), transitionally, by transitions.

1652 URQUHART *Jewel* Wks. (1834) 292 Speeches extending a matter..auxetically, digressively, transitiously.

**Transitival** (trɑnsitəi·văl, -z-), *a. Gram. rare.* [f. TRANSITIVE + -AL: cf. *adjectival, genitival*, etc.] = TRANSITIVE 2.

1871 EARLE *Philol. Eng. T.* § 270 This was a new and quite different verb, and should have had the transitival use.

**Transitive** (trɑ·nsitiv, -z-), *a.* (*sb.*) [ad. late L. *transitīvus* (Priscian), f. *transit-* (see TRANSIT) + *-īvus*, -IVE; in F. *transitif* (16th c.). With sense 1 cf. OF. *transitif* transient (13th c. in Godef.).]

†**1.** Passing or liable to pass into another condition, changeable, changeful; passing away, transient, transitory. *Obs. rare.*

1560 ROLLAND *Crt. Venus* I. 67 Thair waillit weid..Sa gay it was,..Sa wariant to sicht and transitiue. 1625 BRATHWAIT *Five Senses* 296 What availes it thee now to enjoy the transitive honours of this life? 1845 [implied in TRANSITIVENESS].

**2.** *Gram.* Of verbs and their construction: Expressing an action which passes over to an object; taking a direct object to complete the sense.

1571 [implied in TRANSITIVELY a]. 1590 STOCKWOOD *Rules Constr.* 64 A verbe transitiue..is such..as passeth ouer his signification into some other thing, as when I say, 'I loue God'. 1673 O. WALKER *Educ.* 153 Others are transient, when the Agent and Patient are divers, and are expressed by Verbs transitives, as striking, heating [etc.]. 1845 STODDART *Gram.* in *Encycl. Metrop.* (1847) I. 48/1 Verbs transitive and intransitive are, in other words, active and neuter; for the verb active is considered as passing over from the agent to the object, whilst the neuter is considered as not passing over.

**b.** as *sb.* A transitive verb.

1612 BRINSLEY *Lud. Lit.* 129 That other rule for the Acusatiue after the Verbe, is of Transitiues, whose action passeth into another thing.

**3.** *Philos.* Passing out of itself; passing over to or affecting something else; operating beyond itself; = TRANSIENT 2. (Opposed to *immanent.*)

1613 PURCHAS *Pilgrimage* I. i. 5 For all the proprieties of God are infinite, as they are immanent in himselfe, yet in their transitiue and forren effectes are stinted and limited to the modell and state of the creature. 1626 BACON *Sylva* § 70 Cold is Active and Transitive into Bodies Adjacent, as well as Heat. 1785 REID *Intell. Powers* II. xiv. (1803) I. 306 Logicians distinguish two kinds of operations of the mind; the first kind produces no effect without the mind, the last does. The first they call immanent acts; the second transitive. 1893 FAIRBAIRN *Christ in Mod. Theol.* II. II. iii. 441 It is of the essence of both to be transitive. Love regards an object whose good it desires; righteousness is the conduct which fulfils the desire of love.

**4.** Characterized by or involving transition, in various senses: that has something passing through it (*obs.*); that itself passes through stages; that forms a transition (real, or in thought) between two stages, positions, or conditions; that is in an intermediate stage or position; transitional; intermediate; transformational. Now *rare* or *Obs.*

1660 JER. TAYLOR *Duct. Dubit.* II. ii. rule vi. § 7 An image that is understood to be an image can never be made an idol; or if it can it must be by having the worship of God pass'd thorough it to God;..by being the analogical, the improper, the transitive, the relative (or what shall I call it) object of Divine worship. 1811 PINKERTON *Petralogy* I. 73 This transitive grunstein occurs in the Hartz. 1836 I. TAYLOR *Phys. The. Another Life* xii. (1847) 166 The preparations that are made by any of the transitive species of animals..for their approaching metamorphosis. 1854 F. BAKEWELL *Geol.* 5 The lower portion, resting on the crystalline rocks, being called the transitive series. 1860 MAYNE *Expos. Lex.*, *Transitivus*, applied by Werner to rocks or soils that present..the vestiges of organised bodies;..as forming the transition of soils from the first class to those of the third, with which they are nearly related: transitive. 1865 GROTE *Plato* I. xvii. 494 The transitive process, above described, represents the successive stages by which every adult mind has been gradually built up from infancy.

**5.** Of the application of words: Transferred. *rare.* ? *Obs.*

1810 D. STEWART *Philos. Ess.* II. I. i. 226 The greater part of the transitive or derivative applications of words depend on casual and unaccountable caprices of the feelings or of the fancy.

**6.** *Math.* In the theory of groups: see quots.

1890 *Cent. Dict.* s.v. *Group*, A group is called doubly, triply, or n times transitive if any set of 2, 3, n elements can be brought to any places. 1902 *Encycl. Brit.* XXIX. 121/1 If it is possible to find an operation S of the group such that O.S is any assigned one of the set of objects, the group is called *transitive* in respect of this set of objects. When this is not possible, the group is called *intransitive* in respect of the set.

**Transitively** (trɑ·nsitivli, -z-), *adv.* [f. prec. + -LY [2].] In a transitive manner; in the way of transition. **a.** *Gram.* In a transitive sense or construction; with a direct object.

1571 GOLDING *Calvin on Ps.* vii. 7. 20 The woord might also be taken transityvely for too settle or stablish David in his ryght. *a* 1638 MEDE *Wks.* (1672) 676 To construe the words transitively. 1737 WATERLAND *Doctr. Eucharist* v. 115 Ευλογειν is taken transitively in this very Case by the Apostle. *Mod.* Many verbs in English can be used both transitively and intransitively.

**b.** (See senses 3 and 4 of TRANSITIVE.)

1656 JEANES *Fulness Christ* 32 The divine properties are communicated to the humanity, not transitively, but intransitively. 1660 JER. TAYLOR *Duct. Dubit.* II. ii. rule vi. § 4 Vasquez..thinks it lawful to give Divine worship relatively or transitively to a man. 1822 T. TAYLOR *Apuleius* 310 It will always perceive intellectually, without transition, or transitively. 1855 PUSEY *Doctr. Real Presence* Note Q. 257 The bread still remains in its own substance; yet so that the whole proposition should be understood, not as actually, but transitively. 'This is my Body', i.e. passes into the body, or from this becomes the body.

**Tra·nsitiveness.** [f. as prec. + -NESS.] The quality or state of being transitive; in quot., transitoriness.

1845 J. H. NEWMAN *Ess. Developm.* 71 A belief in the transitiveness of worldly goods.

**Transiti·vity.** [f. late L. *transitīv-us* TRANSITIVE + -ITY.] = prec.: see TRANSITIVE 6.
1891 *Cent. Dict.*, *Transitivity*, the character of being transitive, as a group.

**Transitorily** (trɑ·nsitərili, -z-), *adv.* [f. TRANSITORY + -LY 2.] In a transitory manner; in passing through; temporarily, briefly, transiently.
1611 COTGR., *Casuellement*, ..vncertainly, transitorily. 1612 DONNE *Lett.* (1651) 92, I make account to be in London, transitorily, about the end of August. 1762 KAMES *Elem. Crit.* III. xix. 24 The mind is transitorily amused with the new object. 1847 *Illustr. Lond. News* 10 July 29/1 A flash of lightning now and then illuminated the entire panorama, but too transitorily to catch any of its features. 1899 CAGNEY tr. *Jaksch's Clin. Diagn.* vii. (ed. 4) 394 In acute lead-poisoning..large quantities of albumen are often transitorily present in the urine.

**Tra·nsitoriness.** [f. as prec. + -NESS.] The quality or condition of being transitory.
1590 NASHE *Pasquil's Apol.* I. D ij, In respect of the transitorinesse of worldly kingdoms. 1670 CLARENDON *Contempl. Ps.* Tracts (1727) 685 The vanity of this world, of the unsteadiness and transitoriness of all things in it. 1756 JOHNSON *Let.* 15 Apr. in Boswell, The uncertainty of fortune,.. the transitoriness of beauty. 1852 LEWIS *Observ. & Reason. in Pol.* I. 221 Written memorials are distinguished by permanence and solidity, as contrasted with the fugacity and transitoriness of oral tradition. 1899 INGE *Chr. Mysticism* i. 23 We may regard the spiritual world as endless duration opposed to transitoriness.

†**Transito·rious,** *a. Obs.* [f. late L. *transitōri-us* (see next) + -OUS.] = TRANSITORY.
1492 RYMAN *Poems* lxxxv. 1 in *Archiv Stud. neu. Spr.* LXXXIX. 255 This worlde is mutabilite That transitorious is. 1502 ATKYNSON tr. *De Imitatione* I. i. 154 Coruptible ryches, transetorious honours. 1550 BALE *Image Both Ch.* D vj b, Departynge from thys transitoryous lyfe. *a* 1598 ROLLOCK *Wks.* (Wodrow Soc.) II. 4 The creatures of God in themselues are but transitorious shadows.

**Transitory** (trɑ·nsitəri, -z-), *a.* (*sb.*) Also 4–5 **transitore**, 4–7 **-itorie**, 5 **-etorie**, **-itoire**, (**trancitorie**), 5–6 **transetory**, **-ytory(e**, **-itorye**, 6 *Sc.* **-itoir**. [ad. F. *transitoire* (12th c. in Godef. *Compl.*), ad. post-Aug.L. *transitōrius* having or allowing a passage through, in Chr.L. transient, passing, f. *transit-*: see TRANSIT *v.* and -ORY 2]

**1.** Having the quality of passing away; not lasting; fleeting, momentary, brief; transient.
*c* 1374 CHAUCER *Troylus* III. 778 (827) Now yf he wot þat Ioye is transitorie [*v.r.* trancitorie]. *c* 1375 *Sc. Leg. Saints* ii. (*Paulus*) 219 Þat eftire þis lyfe transitore Euire-lestand lyfe is me before. 1481 CAXTON *Myrr.* I. iv. 13 This world is not but a vayn thinge and transitoire. 1543–4 *Act* 35 *Hen. VIII*, c. 1 § 6 This Realme, after the Kinges transitorie lief,..shoulde be destitute of a laufull governour. *a* 1633 AUSTIN *Medit.* (1635) 279 So they are as transitorie as a Shepheards Tent. *Ibid.* 280 Like Things of that transitory nature, they begin to weare away. 1654 H. L'ESTRANGE *Chas. I* (1655) 3 That adventure..gave him also a transitory view of that excellent Lady. 1712 SWIFT *Wonderful Prophecy* (*heading*), This vain and transitory world will shortly be brought to its final dissolution. 1859 KINGSLEY *Misc.* (1860) II. 75 All the Continental Nations look upon our present peace as but transitory, momentary.

†**2.** Having a passage-way, allowing passage through. *Obs. rare.*
1613 GODWIN *Rom. Antiq.* (1625) 9 It had the name of *Forum Transitorium*, the transitorie Forum, because there was *Transitus, id est*, a way or passage through it into three seuerall market places.

**b.** Of the nature of a passage or transition; transitional. *rare.*
1592 tr. *Junius on Rev.* xix. 1 This chapter hath..two parts, one transitory or of passage unto the things that follow. 1906 *Rep. Vice-reg. Comm. Poor Law Ref. Ireland* I. 31 The transitory period between the old and new systems.

**3.** *Law. Transitory action*, an action in which the venue might be laid in any county.
1665 EVER *Tryals per Pais* x. 133 The Jurors of one County may finde any transitory thing done in another County. 1708 *Termes de la Ley* 419 An Action of Trespass for Battery, is transitory and not local. 1768 BLACKSTONE *Comm.* III. xxiii. 384 Actions transitory follow the person of the defendant, territorial suits must be discussed in the territorial tribunal. 1848 WHARTON *Law Lex.* 390/1 Personal actions are for the most part transitory, i.e., their cause of action may be supposed to take place anywhere.

†**4.** (app.) Trifling, of little moment. *Obs.*
1672 DRYDEN *Assignation* II. ii, You may scape with the loss of a Leg, or an Arm, or some such transitory Limb. 1673 — *Amboyna* II. i, Remember, no transitory sum, three hundred quadruples in your own country gold.

**B.** *sb.* †**1.** A transitory or fleeting thing. (Chiefly in *pl.*) *Obs.*
1649 ROBERTS *Clavis Bibl.* 367 A comfortable transitory enjoyment of transitories. 1654 WHITLOCK *Zootomia* 15 He that too closely imbraceth Transitories, is much the worse for them. 1665 GLANVILL *Scepsis Sci.* 50 This fleeting Transitory our Life.

†**2. a.** The transverse limb of the cross-staff (CROSS-STAFF 2). **b.** A transit-instrument. *Obs.*
(In sense a, Bourne has also *transvastory* and *transversary*.)
1574 BOURNE *Regiment for Sea* vi. (1577) 26 To take the heigth of the Sunne, to knowe the Altitude of the Pole aboue the Horizon, doo this...Put the Transitorie [ed. 1580, lf. 29 Transuastorie; ed. 1631, lf. 29 Transuersary] vpon the long staffe, then sette the end of the long staffe close at the corner of your eye [etc.]. [1578 — *Treas. Trav.* I. ix. 17 Concernyng the making of a Crosse staffe..you shal make an other short staff, called a Transuastorie, of two foote long, and in the very myddle of it you shall make a square hole.] *Ibid.* x. 18 b, If that the distaunce be further then the Transitorie wyl take, and the wal too shorte: then remoue the Plattes or wynges of the Transitorie to the markes, sixe ynches from both the endes of the Transitorie. 1751 *Phil. Trans.* XLVII. xxii. 159, I had several times seen Venus on the meridian with a three-foot transitory.

‖ **Transitu** (trɑ·nsitiū), in L. phr. *in transitu*: see ‖ IN 19; also as adj. in *transitu business*, etc.
1858 HOMANS *Cycl. Comm.* 452/1 The large increase of *transitu* business between the principal southern ports and the markets of Europe. *Ibid.* 453/1 Parties who operate in *transitu* cotton.

†**Tra·nsiture.** *Obs. rare.* [f. L. type **transitūra*: see TRANSIT and -URE.] Passing; passage.
1578 BANISTER *Hist. Man* I. 17 It yeeldeth ample scope.. to the transiture of meate and drinke. *Ibid.* 20 Two Processes..with larger holes for the transiture [*printed* -turie] of the Veyne, and Arterie vnto the Scull.

†**Tra·nsive,** *a. Obs. rare.* [f. *transe*, TRANCE *sb.*1 + -IVE.] Of the nature of a trance; of or pertaining to a trance.
1609 ARMIN *Maids of More-Cl.* (1880) 103 My mother's fast asleepe, and I awake, am in a transiue maze. 1609 — *Ital. Taylor* (1880) 149 These transiue apparitions dealt, As madmen in their fits.

†**Transje·ction.** *Obs. rare*—0. [n. of action f. L. *transjicĕre*, the uncontracted form of *trāicĕre*: see TRAJECT.] = TRAJECTION.
1656 BLOUNT *Glossogr.*, *Transjection*, a casting over, or thorow, an overthrowing.

**Transkei** (trɑns,kəi·), *sb.* (*a.*) [f. TRANS- 7 + *Kei*, a river of S. Africa.] A territory situated across the river Kei, which falls into the Indian Ocean, *c* 28° 20′ E., and was from 1847 to 1877 the boundary between Kafirland or Caffraria and Cape Colony, of which the Transkei territory now forms a part. Also *attrib.* or as *adj.* Hence **Trans,kei·an** *a.*
1879 *Whitaker's Almanack* 259/1 The area [of Cape Colony], including Basutoland and Transkei, 222,308 square miles. *Ibid.* 259/2 The Transkeian territories stretch from the Kei to Natal. 1898 *Ibid.* 515 (Cape Colony) The Transkei territories. *Ibid.*, (Principal events) Incorporation of all the Transkeian territories, except part of Pondoland, with the Colony, completed 1885; annexation of Pondoland 1894. 1899 *Daily News* 10 Oct. 7/1 The Pondos and the other Transkei tribes are not absolutely to be relied on. 1911 J. LENNOX *Missions S. Afr.* 81 A question of a much more difficult nature has exercised the Kafrarian and Transkeian Churches.

**Trans,la·de,** *v.* [TRANS- 2.] *trans.* To transfer the lading of one ship or carriage to another. Hence **Transla·ding** *vbl. sb.*
1881 *Daily News* 17 Mar. 5/3 A question of transit and the terminal charges for lading, unlading, and translading.

**Translatable** (trɑns,lē¹·tăb'l), *a.* [f. TRANSLATE *v.* + -ABLE.] Capable of being translated.
1745 H. WALPOLE *Corr.* (1846) II. 15, I..without having recourse to the Countess's translatable periods, am pleased with his company. 1830 MACKINTOSH *Eth. Philos.* Wks. 1846 I. 88 Modes of expression scarcely translatable into the only technical language in which that mind is wont to think. 1870 EMERSON *Soc. & Solit.* viii. 164 What is really best in any book is translatable.
Hence **Translatabi·lity, Transla·tableness.**
1867 LUDLOW *Fleeing to Tarshish* 115 To carry on his cogitations for him, with their accustomed wondrous translatability by the imagination. 1882 *Athenæum* 4 Mar. 278/1 We own to a certain scepticism as to La Fontaine's translatableness. 1911 MUNRO *Fundamentals* 31 The Translatability of Scripture.

†**Trans,late,** *a.* and *sb. Obs.* Also 7 **-at.** [ad. L. *translāt-us, -a, -um*, pa. pple.: see next.]
**A.** *adj.* Translated (see next); in quot. 1589, transferred in meaning, metaphorical.
1589 RIDER *Bibl. Schol.* Direct. for Rdr., First I place the proper Latine word vnder the figure of 1: then the figuratiue or translate vnder the figure of 2.
**B.** *sb.* Something translated; a translation. [Cf. L. *translātum* sb., OF. *translat* 13th c.]
1585–6 EARL LEYCESTER *Corr.* (Camden) 467, I sent to the register of the states for the act.., the translate whereof I send your honour hearein. 1619 CARLETON in *Eng. & Germ.* (Camden) 85 Divers lettres .. I have made transcripts of some, and translats of others. 1655 *Chym. Med. & Chyrurg. Addr.*, *Table*, A Translate of the Eleventh Chapter. 1668 *Lond. Gaz.* No. 254/4 The prohibitions made against the vending or reading any of the late Translates of the New Testament into French. 1803 COLLINS in Gurwood *Wellington's Desp.* (1837) III. 133 *note*, I..enclose a copy and translate of a note I..received from the Berai Rajah.

**Translate** (trɑns,lē¹·t), *v.* Also 4 (*Sc.*), 6 **translat**, 5–6 **traunslate**, 6 *Sc.* **translait**. Pa. t. and pple. **translated**; also 4–6 **translate**, (*pa. pple.*) **translat**. [Prob. first used in *translat(e* pa. pple., ad. L. *translāt-us*, pa. pple. of *transferre* to TRANSFER. The pa. pple. soon became *translat-ed*, and *translate* the verb stem (see -ATE suffix 3). But the verb may also immediately repr. F. *translater* (12th c. in Godef.). Cf. also med.L. *translātāre* (11th c. in Du Cange).]

**I. 1.** *trans.* To bear, convey, or remove from one person, place or condition to another; to transfer, transport; *spec.* to remove a bishop from one see to another, or a bishop's seat from one place to another, and, in Scotland, a minister from one pastoral charge to another; also, to remove the dead body or remains of a saint, or, by extension, a hero or great man, from one place to another.
*a* 1300 *Cursor M.* 9162 (Cott.) Helias was in þat squiare, Translated in a golden chiare. *Ibid.* 9220 Þe Iuues now er put o state And þair kingrik translate. *c* 1330 R. BRUNNE *Chron.* (1810) 208 Þis is þe same Hubert, þat we saw of nam, Þat translate S. Gilbert in þe hous of Sempyngham. *c* 1380 WYCLIF *Sel. Wks.* II. 318 We witen þat we ben translatid fro deþ to lyf. 1433 LYDG. *St. Fremund* 819 The Bysshop.. Translatyd hym to Dunstaple. 1432–50 tr. *Higden* (Rolls) II. 77 The seete of the metropolitan of alle Wales, whiche was translate afterwarde to Meneuia. 1517 TORKINGTON *Pilgr.* (1884) 49 Hys body was translat to Rome. 1529 S. FISH *Supplic. Beggars* (Arb.) 13 Then shall not youre.. power, crowne, dignitie..be translated from you. 1579 LYLY *Euphues* (Arb.) 41 Plante and translate the crabbe tree, where..it please you, and it wyll neuer beare sweete Apple. 1613 PURCHAS *Pilgrimage* (1614) 106 Hee translated the highest seat both of spirituall and Temporall Regiment to Jerusalem. 1625 in Willis & Clark *Cambridge* (1886) II. 445 He translated ye Vestrie. 1651 N. BACON *Disc. Govt. Eng.* II. xxviii. (1739) 131 This Headship was translated to the King. 1663 WOOD *Life* (O. H. S.) I. 472 After he had taken in another class of six there, he translated himself to the house of Arthur Tylliard an apothecary. *c* 1683 BURNET *Orig. Mem.* in *Own Time* (1902) I. Suppl. 67 Morley, made at first bishop of Worcester, and soon after..translated to Winchester. 1794 J. HUTTON *Philos. Light*, etc. 47 Heat is translated among bodies in a certain manner, and electricity in another. 1865 *Pall Mall G.* 11 Apr. 4 A discussion has arisen on the question whether the Charterhouse School ought or ought not to be translated into the country. 1869 FREEMAN *Norm. Conq.* III. xv. § 5. 518 The body of Harold, first buried under the cairn by Hastings, was afterwards translated to his own minster at Waltham. 1904 R. SMALL *Hist. U. P. Congregat.* I. 503 In 1829..the Synod at his own request, and without a vote, refused to translate.

**b.** To carry or convey to heaven without death; also, in later use, said of the death of the righteous.
1382 WYCLIF *Heb.* xi. 5 Bi feith Enok is translatid, that he schulde not se deeth; and he was not founden, for the Lord translatide him. 1387 TREVISA *Higden* (Rolls) II. 213 And so schulde þe body..be translated and chaunged in þe blisse of heuene wiþ oute deienge and deeþ. 1535 COVERDALE *Wisd.* iv. 10 He pleased God,..so that where as he lyued amonge synners, he translated him. 1702 *Lond. Gaz.* No. 3809/1 That after a long and happy Enjoyment of this your Earthly Crown, you may be translated to one Immortal. 1798 COLERIDGE *Fears in Solitude* 121 As if the wretch, Who fell in battle..Passed off to Heaven, translated and not killed. 1848 MRS. JAMESON *Sacr. & Leg. Art* (1850) 331 She was ninety years of age when the Lord translated her. 1904 JEBB in *Proc. Brit. Acad.* 3 Here, and here alone, the Hyperborean land is an Elysium to which mortals are translated without dying.

**c.** *Med.* To remove the seat of (a disease) from one person, or part of the body, to another. Now *rare* or *Obs.*
1732 ARBUTHNOT *Aliments* etc. 366 To translate the Morbifick Matter upon the Extremities of the Body. 1754 J. BARTLET *Farriery* (ed. 2) 105 The humours frequently settle, or are translated to the lungs, and other bowels. 1769 E. BANCROFT *Guiana* 394 The patient is either relieved, or the disease translated on the extremities. 1826 SOUTHEY in *Q. Rev.* XXXIV. 330 He could..cure a carbuncle..by making upon it the sign of a cross, and translate swellings from his pupil's arm to his own.

**d.** *Physics.* To move (a body) from one point or place to another without rotation: cf. TRANSLATION 1 f.

**II. 2.** To turn from one language into another; 'to change into another language retaining the sense' (J.); to render; also, to express in other words, to paraphrase. (The chief current sense.)
*a* 1300 *Cursor M.* 232 Þis ilk bok it es translate In to Inglis tong to rede. *c* 1350 *Will. Palerne* 167 For he of frensche þis fayre tale ferst dede translate. *c* 1385 CHAUCER *L. G. W.* 329 (*Balade*) Thow hast translatid the romauns of the rose. 1477 EARL RIVERS (Caxton) *Dictes* 2 It was translated out of latyn in to frenshe. 1589 PUTTENHAM *Eng. Poesie* I. xxxi. (Arb.) 75 Doctour Phaer one that.. excellently well translated into English verse Heroicall certaine bookes of Virgils Æneidos. 1689–90 TEMPLE *Ess. Poetry* Wks. 1731 I. 241 The first Change of Poetry was made by translating it into Prose. 1693 DRYDEN *Disc. Orig. & Progr. Satire* Ess. (ed. Ker) II. 92 'Tis only for a poet to translate a poem. 1776 JOHNSON 11 Apr., in *Boswell*, Poetry..cannot be translated; and, therefore, it is the poets that preserve languages. 1850 WHIPPLE *Ess. & Rev.* (ed. 3) I. 300 If the phrase, realizing the ideal, were translated into the phrase, actualizing the real, much ambiguity might be avoided. 1874 GREEN *Short Hist.* vii. § 1. 342 Retiring to Hamburg Tyndale translated the Gospels and Epistles.

**b.** *absol.* To practise translation; to make a version from one language or form of words into another; also *intr.* for *pass.*, of a language, speech, or writing: To bear or admit of translation.
*c* 1440 *Pallad. on Husb.* I. 735 Yet as myn auctor spak so wold I speke Sith I translate, and looth am from hym breke. 1576 FLEMING *Panopl. Epist.* 253 If you translate out of the Latine speach, into the Greeke. 1690 LOCKE *Hum. Und.* III. iv. § 9 This is to translate, and not to define, when we change two words of the same signification one for another. 1731 FIELDING *Author's Farce* II. v, The rogue had a trick of translating out of the shops as well as the languages. 1812 SOUTHEY *Omniana* II. 30 Claudian throughout would translate better than any of the ancients. 1827 — *Lett.* (1856) IV. 64 The Welsh, I suspect, is not a language which translates well. 1831 MACAULAY *Ess.*, *Johnson* (1887) 194 Sometimes Johnson translated aloud.

†**c.** To use in a metaphorical or transferred sense: see *translated*, quot. 1553, and cf. TRANSLATE *a.*, TRANSLATION 4. *Obs.*

**3.** *fig.* To interpret, explain; to expound the significance of (conduct, gestures, etc.); also, to express (one thing) in terms of another.

**1598** SHAKS. *Merry W.* I. iii. 54 He hath studied her will; and translated her will: out of honesty, into English. **1602** — *Ham.* IV. i. 3 There's matters in these sighes.. These profound heaues You must translate. **1850** MRS. JAMESON *Leg. Monast. Ord.* (1863) 55 The emblem has been translated into a fact, or rather into a miracle. **1892** WESTCOTT *Gospel of Life* 58 Right Doctrine is an inexhaustible spring of strength if it be translated into deed. **1903** *Westm. Gaz.* 26 Mar. 1/2 The delightful Norwegian master who..translates the nature of Norway..into music.

**III. 4.** To change in form, appearance, or substance; to transmute; to transform, alter; *spec.* in industrial use: of a tailor, to renovate, turn, or cut down (a garment); of a cobbler, to make new boots from the remains of (old ones).

*c* **1386** CHAUCER *Clerk's T.* 329 Vnnethe the peple hire knew for hire fairnesse Whan she translated [*v.rr.* transmewed, transformed] was in swich richesse. **1423** JAS. I *King's Q.* viii, How that eche estate As fortune lykith, thame will oft translate. **1487–8** *Rec. St. Mary at Hill* 138 For a man werkyng iij dayes & di. in the house..in translatyng of the steyer and in mendyng of wyndowes. **1536** BELLENDEN *Cron. Scot.* (1821) II. 72 Quhare he translatit the tempill of Apollo in ane abbay of his ordour. **1543–4** *Act 35 Hen. VIII*, c. 8 No man..shall cutt mynisshe or translate..any barrelles kilderkyns or firkyns. **1575–7** FENTON *Gold. Epist.* (1582) 160 To translate an auncient garment, and reduce him to the present fashion. **1590** SHAKS. *Mids. N.* III. i. 122 Blesse thee Bottome, blesse thee; thou art translated. **1621** BURTON *Anat. Mel.* I. ii. I. ii. (1628) 40 Nabuchadnezar was really translated into a beast. **1718** J. FOX *Wanderer* 14, I was waiting in Expectation of my own Change, and wondering..what Sort of Being I should be translated to. **1815** *Q. Rev.* Oct. 129 A place near Monmouth-street, where 'they translate old shoes into new ones'. **1905** PREECE & SIVEWRIGHT *Telegr.* viii. 194 Varley introduced repeaters at Amsterdam to translate the English double-current system of working into the Continental single-current system.

**5.** To re-transmit (a telegraphic message) by means of an automatic repeater.

**1855** [implied in TRANSLATING *station*].

**6.** To transport with the strength of some feeling; to enrapture, entrance. *arch.*

**1643** SIR T. BROWNE *Relig. Med.* I. § 49 That elegant Apostle, which seemed to have a glimpse of Heaven,..was translated out of himself to behold it. **1849** LONGF. *Ev.* I. iv. 104 Their souls, with devotion translated, Rose on the ardour of prayer. **1899** DIXON in Mackail *W. Morris* I. 115 There was no train...I was made aware of this by a fearful cry in my ears, and saw Morris 'translated'.

Hence **Transla·ted** (in quot. 1553, metaphorical: cf. TRANSLATE *a.*), **Transla·ting** *ppl. adjs.*

**1553** T. WILSON *Rhet.* (1580) 174 When thei maie haue most apt wordes at hand, yet wil thei of a purpose vse translated words. **1632** SHERWOOD *Eng. & Fr. Dict.* To Rdr., First the Proper [interpretation]; then, the Translated and Metaphoricall. **1687** T. BROWN *Saints in Uproar* Wks. 1730 I. 82 See these translating gentlemen translated to the quarter of lunaticks. **1727** POPE *Macer* 21 In a translated Suit, then tries the Town, With borrow'd Pins, and Patches not her own. **1729** SWIFT *Direct. Serv.* iv. Wks. (1869) 569 Your wages ..spent in translated red-heeled shoes. **1868** GLADSTONE *Juv. Mundi* ix. (1870) 364 Any deceased or translated hero. **1904** R. SMALL *Hist. U. P. Congreg.* I. 552 The court came to adjudicate upon a translating call to Mr. Jaffray from Dalry

**Translating** (trɑns,lēⁱ·tiŋ), *vbl. sb.* [f. TRANSLATE *v.* + -ING [1].] The action of the vb. TRANSLATE; translation, in various senses.

*c* **1460** FORTESCUE *Abs. & Lim. Mon.* xi. (1885) 137 With owt translatynge þeroff to any oþer vse. **1474** *Churchw. Acc. St. Mich., Cornhill* (Camden), Payde for translatyng of the meyres pue. **1535** in *Archæologia* IX. 246 For translating of a gowne of blacke veluette. **1601** R. JOHNSON *Kingd. & Commw.* (1603) 63 The translating of the Imperiall seate, from Rome to Constantinople. **1683** BURNET tr. *More's Utopia* Pref. 1 The refining and polishing a Language, ..the translating of Books into it. **1904** *Q. Rev.* July 7 Translating is a large industry, as any English reviewer of the last ten years can testify.

**b.** *attrib.*, as *translating-right*, *-trade*; **translating-relay** (*Telegr.*): see RELAY *sb.* 4; **translating-roller**, **-screw** (*Mech.*), a screw which moves a part of a mechanism in relation to the other parts; **translating-station** (*Telegr.*), a station at which an automatic repeater is introduced.

**1905** PREECE & SIVEWRIGHT *Telegr.* xi. 235 *Translating relays are required for the intercommunication between stations. **1911** WEBSTER, **Translating-roller* (*Ordnance*) a double-threaded screw for drawing a breech-block longitudinally from its place in the breech. **1891** *Cent. Dict.*, **Translating-screw*,..*spec.*, in breech-loading ordnance, a screw for moving in or out the wedge in the fermeture. **1855** *Patent Office Specif.* No. 314 The instruments are used in pairs at the *translating station. **1894** SALA *London up to Date* 263 The 'Cobbler's Last', that well-known organ of the boot and shoe '*translating' trade.

**Translation** (trɑns,lēⁱ·ʃən). [a. OF. *translation* (12th c. in Godef. *Compl.*), or ad. L. *translātiōn-em* a transporting, translation, n. of action f. *translāt-*, ppl. stem of *transferre* to TRANSFER.] The action of translating (or its result).

**I. 1.** Transference; removal or conveyance from one person, place, or condition to another.

*spec.* The removal of a bishop from one see to another; in the Church of Scotland, the removal of a minister from one charge to another; also, the removal of the body or relics of a saint to another place of interment.

*a* **1350** *St. Stephen* 211 in Horstm. *Altengl. Leg.* (1881) 30 Of þat ilk translacioun Es named saynt Steuyn inuencioun. *c* **1380** WYCLIF *Sel. Wks.* II. 318 Þis translacioun is better þan worldly translacioun of þe pope. **1447** BOKENHAM *Seyntys* (Roxb.) 30 Of summe relykys to make a translacyoun. **1473–4** *Acc. Ld. High Treas. Scot.* I. 52 The translacione of the parliament fra Sanctandros to Edinburgh. **1485** CAXTON *St. Wenefr.* 13 Her bones were broughte to thabbay of Shrewsbury, whiche translacion is halowed the 19 day of Septembre. **1597** HOOKER *Eccl. Pol.* v. lv. § 8 Ascension into heauen, is a plaine locall translation of Christ according to his manhood. **1612** BREREWOOD *Lang. & Relig.* 12 The translation of the imperial seat to Constantinople. **1635** SWAN *Spec. M.* (1670) 198 A fifth [effect of Earthquakes] is the translation of Mountains &c. unto some other places. **1647** N. BACON *Disc. Govt. Eng.* I. xi. (1739) 22 After the Translation of the Sea from Thetford to Norwich. **1647** CLARENDON *Hist. Reb.* I. § 188 The necessary forms for the Translation [of Laud from London to Canterbury]. **1777** J. ADAMS *Wks.* (1854) IX. 470 The rapid translation of property from hand to hand. **1869** FREEMAN *Norm. Conq.* III. xi. § 2. 34 That the Feast of the Translation of Saint Eadward should be kept..on the eve of the day of Saint Calixtus. **1910** in Halsbury *Laws of Eng.* XI. 400 *note*, The fees paid by the late Archbishop Magee on his translation to York amounted to £573 6*s*.

**b.** *fig.* of non-material things.

*Translation of a feast* (Eccl.), its transference from the usual date to another, to avoid its clashing with another (movable) feast of superior rank.

*c* **1530** T. COX *Rhet.* (1899) 82 Translacion of the faut is, whan he that confesseth his faut, sayeth that he dyd it, moued by the indignacion of the malycyouse dede of an other. **1552** ABP. HAMILTON *Catech.* (1884) 8 The translatioun of the sabboth day to the sonday. **1607** HIERON *Wks.* I. 151 Imputation: by which there is a kinde of translation or putting ouer of the beleeuers sinne vnto Christ, and of Christs righteousnesse to the beleeuer. **1681–6** J. SCOTT *Chr. Life* (1747) III. vii. 153 The very Translation of the Guilts of the People upon them. **1705** STANHOPE *Paraphr.* II. 549 A Translation of Punishment and Guilt, from the Person offering to the thing offered.

**c.** Removal from earth to heaven, *orig.* without death, as the translation of Enoch; but in later use also said *fig.* of the death of the righteous.

**1382** WYCLIF *Heb.* xi. 5 Enok .. bifore translacioun he hadde witnessing for to haue plesid God. **1682** SIR T. BROWNE *Chr. Mor.* II. § 6 Time, Experience, self-Reflexions, and God's mercies, make in some well-temper'd minds a kind of translation before Death. **1727** DE FOE *Syst. Magic* I. i. (1840) 12 A glorious example of such faith as was rewarded with an immediate translation of the person [Enoch] into heaven. **1760** G. WHITEFIELD *Let.* 29 Oct. (in *Pearson's Catal.* (1894) 64) Blessed be God for supporting me so well under the news of dear Mr. Polhill's sudden translation. **1878** GLADSTONE *Prim. Homer* v. 61 The Islands of the Blest, to which Menelaos has a promise of translation on his death.

**d.** *Med.* Transference of a disease from one person or part of the body to another. Now *rare* or *Obs.*

**1665** BOYLE *Occas. Refl.* II. xiii. (1848) 140 Madness..by the translation of the Humours into the Brain. **1732** ARBUTHNOT *Aliments* etc. 368 Translations of Morbific Matter in Acute Distempers. **1857** DUNGLISON *Dict. Med. Sc.*, *Metastasis*..translation. A change in the seat of a disease; attributed, by the Humorists, to the translation of the morbific matter to a part different from that which it had previously occupied.

**e.** *Astrol.* (See quots.)

**1658** in PHILLIPS. **1706** *Ibid.* (ed. Kersey), *Translation of Light and Nature*, a Phrase us'd by Astrologers, when a light Planet separates from a more weighty one, and presently joyns another more heavy. **1819** J. WILSON *Compl. Dict. Astrol.* 378 Translation of the light and nature of a planet is when a planet separates from one that is slower than itself and overtakes another by conjunction or aspect.

**f.** *Physics.* Transference of a body, or form of energy, from one point of space to another. *Motion* or *movement of translation*: onward movement without (or considered apart from) rotation; sometimes as distinguished from a reciprocating movement as in a wave or vibration.

**1715** tr. *Gregory's Astron.* I. (1726) I. 157 The Ratio of the Translations will be compounded of the Ratio of the Differences of the Angular Motions, and of the Ratio of the Distances from the Axis. **1794** J. HUTTON *Philos. Light & Heat* 47 We should conclude that the translation of heat, among bodies, is not performed according to the laws observed in that of light. **1854** MOSELEY *Astron.* viii. (1874) 34 This mass when left to itself will have two motions, one a motion of translation,..the other, a motion..of rotation. **1860** TYNDALL *Glac.* I. xxvii. 215 It was, for a time, a mere motion of vibration without any sensible translation. **1878** HUXLEY *Physiogr.* 171 The motion of the water is a movement of undulation and not of translation. **1884** J. S. RUSSELL (*title*) The Wave of Translation in its Application to the Three Oceans of Water, Air, and Ether.

**II. 2.** The action or process of turning from one language into another; also, the product of this; a version in a different language.

*a* **1340** HAMPOLE *Psalter* Prol., In þe translacioun i folow þe lettere als mykyll as i may. **1382** WYCLIF *N. T.* 595 Thei setten in her translaciouns oneli the names of thre thingis, that is of water, of blood, and of spirit. **1447** BOKENHAM *Seyntys* Introd. (Roxb.) 4 Thys translacyon..In to oure language. **1535** COVERDALE *Bible* Ded., I thought it my dutye..to dedicate this translacyon vnto youre hyghnesse. **1549** (*title*) The Byble in Englyshe, that is the olde and new Testament, after the translacion appoynted to bee read in the Churches. *a* **1568** ASCHAM *Scholem.* (Arb.) 92 Translation, is easie in the beginning for the scholer. **1581** PETTIE *Guazzo's Civ. Conv.* I. (1586) A iij, To present unto you the first sight of this my translation. *c* **1650** DENHAM *To Sir R. Fanshawe* 10 Nor ought a genius less than his that writ, Attempt translation. **1682** DRYDEN *Relig. Laici* 242 Various readings and translations. **1805** N. NICHOLLS *Corr. w. Gray* (1843) 37 Pope's translation of the Iliad stood very high in his estimation. **1837** LOCKHART *Scott* I. iii. 94 His translations in verse from Horace and Virgil were often approved by Dr. Adam. **1874** GREEN *Short Hist.* vi. § 3. 291 He [Caxton] stood between two schools of translation, that of French affectation and English pedantry.

**b.** *transf.* and *fig.* The expression or rendering of something in another medium or form, e. g. of a painting by an engraving or etching; also *concr.*

**1588** SHAKS. *L. L. L.* v. ii. 51 Some thousand Verses of a faithfull Louer. A huge translation of hypocrisie, Vildly compiled, profound simplicitie. **1812** R. H. in *Examiner* 30 Nov. 763/2 His translations on copper, to compare them with..verbal translations.., display much of the elegance of Pope. **1829** *Chapters Physical Sc.* xxiv. 308 That correctness of reasoning which..exhibits a faithful translation of the language of facts. **1829** *Examiner* 805/1 Engravers.. have here hung up their translations from the works of our landscape and other painters. **1864** *Athenæum* 27 Feb. 305/3 A system of copying which demands two translations,—that of the draughtsman and that of the chromo-lithographer.

**3.** Transformation, alteration, change; changing or adapting to another use; renovation.

**1382** WYCLIF *Heb.* vii. 12 Forsothe the presthod translatid, it is nede that and translacioun [1611 change] of lawe be maad. ?*c* **1470** ASHBY *Active Policy of Prince* 156 The ruine Of high estates, and translacion, That to vices and outrage dud incline, For the whiche thei suffred mutacion. **1534** MORE *Treat. Passion* Wks. 1344/1 The translacion or chaunging of it from thynges sensible to thynges intelligible. **1582** in Feuillerat *Revels Q. Eliz.* (1908) 349 Of wages, workemanship, Translations, Attendaunces. **1604** R. CAWDREY *Table Alph.*, *Translation*, altering, chaunging.

**b.** *spec.* (in workmen's use) The process of 'translating' boots (see TRANSLATE *v.* 4).

**1851** MAYHEW *Lond. Labour* (1861) II. 34 Translation..is this—to take a worn, old pair of shoes or boots, and by repairing them make them appear as if left off with hardly any wear. **1865** in Ruskin *Sesame* 90 Her son sat up the whole night to make the 'translations' [of old boots].

†**4.** *Rhet.* Transference of meaning; metaphor; = TRALATION. *Obs.*

**1538** ELYOT, *Metaphora*, a translation of wordes frome their propre sygnifycation. **1553** T. WILSON *Rhet.* (1580) 174 Men vse translation of wordes (called Tropes) for neede sake, when thei can not finde other. **1605** BACON *Adv. Learn.* I. vii. § 17 That excellent use of a metaphor or translation. **1652** URQUHART *Jewel* Wks. (1834) 292 With words diminishing the worth of a thing, tapinotically, periphrastically, by rejection, translation, and other meanes.

**III. 5.** *Law.* A transfer of property; *spec.* alteration of a bequest by transferring the legacy to another person.

**1590** SWINBURNE *Testaments* 280 Translation of a legacie is a bestowing of the same vpon an other. **1651** HOBBES *Leviath.* I. xiv. 67 All Contract is mutuall translation, or change of Right. **1754** ERSKINE *Princ. Sc. Law* (1809) 342 If the assignee conveys his right to a third person, it is called a translation. **1875** POSTE *Gaius* IV. Comm. (ed. 2) 490 No translation of property is operated by theft.

**6.** In long distance telegraphy, the automatic retransmission of a message by means of a relay.

**1866** F. M. FERGUSON *Electr.* (1870) 245 It would be advisable to..resend at the mid-station by translation. **1876** PREECE & SIVEWRIGHT *Telegr.* iv. § 113 The circuit can be divided, and the repeating station can work separately.. without translation.

**IV. 7.** *attrib.*, as *translation element*, *movement*, *right*, *work*; **translation wave**, an ocean wave with a propelling or forward impulse; a forced wave.

*a* **1704** T. BROWN *Amusem. Ser. & Com.*, *Voy.* ii. Wks. 1709 III. I. 14 He has so mortified himself..that the Translation-Bill may not pass. **1862** DANA *Man. Geol.* IV. 655 The ocean-waves, which the earthquake, if submarine, may produce, have an actual forward impulse, and are, therefore, forced or translation waves. *Ibid.* 729 The sound-wave may be felt before the translation wave, and may travel farther. **1862** H. SPENCER *First Princ.* II. v. § 56 (1875) 183 What we may call the translation element in Motion. **1898** P. MANSON *Trop. Diseases* i. 5 Slight translation movements of the pigment particles. **1906** *Westm. Gaz.* 15 Oct. 4/2 Their respective delegates have agreed to extend the period during which authors can protect their translation rights.

**Translational** (trɑns,lēⁱ·ʃənăl), *a.* [f. prec. + -AL.] Of or pertaining to translation. **a.** Belonging to, or consisting in, translation from one language into another.

**1813** E. HENDERSON *Let.* in *Life* (1859) 119 A translational exhibition of a certain notable portion of the Old Testament. **1869** *Contemp. Rev.* Feb. 134 Mr. Paley's editorial and translational labours. **1907** SALMON *Hum. Element in Gosp.* 244 Many of the variations in our Greek Gospels are simply translational.

**b.** *Physics.* Consisting in onward motion, as distinct from rotation, vibration, oscillation, etc.

**1867** THOMSON & TAIT *Nat. Phil.* I. I. § 107 Imagine this circle to be the inner edge of a fixed ring in space (directionally fixed, that is to say, but having the same translational motion as the earth's centre). **1898** SIR W. CROOKES *Addr. Brit. Assoc.* 25 The total energy of both the translational and internal motions of the molecules locked up in quiescent air at ordinary pressure and temperature is about 140,000 foot-pounds in each cubic yard of air.

†**Trans,lati·tious**, *a. Obs.* [f. L. *translātīcius*, *-ītius* traditional, customary, metaphorical, f. *translāt-*: see TRANSLATE *v.* and -ITIOUS [1]. Cf. obs. F. *translatice* (Cotgr.).]

**1.** Characterized by being transmitted, transferred, or carried from one person or place to another.

**1611** COTGR., *Translatice*, translaticious, translatiue; transposed, transferred. **1650** R. STAPYLTON *Strada's Low C. Warres* v. 138 Religion among Hereticks is not their own, but accidentall and translatitious. **1664** EVELYN *Sylva* I.

iv. § 8, I have frequently doubted whether it [the Elm-tree] be a pure Indigene or Translatitious. **1692** WASHINGTON tr. *Milton's Def. Pop.* vii, A delegated translatitious Majesty we allow, but that Majesty does chiefly and primarily reside in him, you can no more prove, than you can, that Power and Authority does.

**2.** Transferred in meaning; metaphorical; tralatitious.

**1637** J. WILLIAMS *Holy Table* 77 The translatitious and borrowed..appellation of that holy utensill. **1673** O. WALKER *Educ.* II. i. 228 It appears sometimes under a Metaphor, or some other translatitious expression.

Hence † **Translati·tiously** *adv.*, traditionally, by custom derived from others.

**1666** J. FRASER *Polichron.* (S.H.S.) 2 Translatitiously both in England and Low Countries of Scotland, we, by an inveterat custome derived from thence, doe say as yet Anderson, Jameson, Watson, Williamson, etc.

**Translative** (trɑnsˌlēⁱ·tiv, trɑ·nsˌlătiv), *a.* [ad. L. *translātīv-us* pertaining to transfer or translation (see TRANSLATE and -IVE); cf. F. *translatif* (14th c.) in legal use.] Involving or of the nature of translation (in various senses).

†**1.** Involving transference of meaning; metaphorical, tropical. *Obs.*

**1589** PUTTENHAM *Eng. Poesie* II. iii. (Arb.) 81 If our feete Poeticall want these qualities it can not be sayd a foote in sence translatiue as here. *Ibid.* III. xviii. 197 Properly.. Allegoria is when we do speake in sence translatiue and wrested from the owne signification.

**2.** Involving transference from one place to another; in *Physics*, of the nature of onward movement without rotation or reciprocation.

*a* **1682** SIR T. BROWNE *Wks.* (1835) IV. 370 We may improve their fruits without translative conjunction, that is, by insition of the scion upon his own mother. **1740** STACK in *Phil. Trans.* XLI. 418 It is allowed, that the translative Velocities of its Points cannot be in an inverted Ratio to the Roots of the Distances. **1875** HUXLEY & MARTIN *Elem. Biol.* (1877) 27 Watch the Brownian movements; note that they are simply oscillatory—not translative. **1883** *Nature* 15 Mar. 459/1 A screw's motion, which is partly translative along and partly rotative round a polar axis.

**3.** Tending or serving to translate or render; relating to translation, translational.

**1748** RICHARDSON *Clarissa* (1811) VIII. xi. 62 As the translative impulse (pardon a new word..) came upon me. **1819** G. S. FABER *Dispensations* (1823) II. 319 The sense of the Greek translative Diathekè is thus determined by the sense of the Hebrew original Berith. **1882** W. SHARP *Rossetti* iv. 311 Renderings specially admirable for translative excellence and inherent poetic merit.

**4.** *Law.* Expressing or constituting transference of property, etc.

**1875** POSTE *Gaius* II. Comm. (ed. 2) 172 Mancipation..might be used as a formality..of contract either translative or obligative.

**5.** *Gram.* (See quot. 1905.)

**1896** *Edin. Rev.* Jan. 84 The student [of Finnish] must remember the nominative, partitive,..prolative, translative, essive..and instructive [cases]. **1905** JESPERSEN *Hist. Eng. Lang.* 9 Translative, indicating the state into which anyone or anything passes.

**Translator** (trɑnsˌlēⁱ·təɹ). Also 4–6 -oure, 4–8 -our, 5 -ore, 6–7 -er. [a. OF. *translator*, *-our*, F. *-eur* (12th c. in Godef. *Compl.*), or L. *translātor*, agent-n. of *transferre*: see TRANSLATE and -OR.] One who (rarely, that which) translates.

**1.** One who translates or renders from one language into another; the author of a translation.

**13..** in Horstm. *Altengl. Leg.* (1878) 25/1101 Of al translatours in to latyn He was flour enditour fyn. *c* **1380** WYCLIF *Sel. Wks.* III. 96 Whiche word þe Ebru translatoure, Aquyla interpretid, 'and þe Lord confermede'. **1413** *Pilgr. Sowle* (Caxton) v. xiv. (1859) 82 The symple and vnsuffisaunt translatore of this litel book. **1509** BARCLAY *Shyp of Folys* (1570) 260 Go Booke,..By thy submission excuse thy Translatour [*rime* honour]. *a* **1680** BUTLER *Rem.* (1759) II. 405 A Translater dyes an Author, like an old Stuff, into a new Colour. **1778** WARTON *Hist. Eng. Poetry* II. Notes 19 Lapus de Castellione, a Florentine civilian, and a great translator from Greek into Latin, about the year 1350. **1837** LOCKHART *Scott* II. iv. 121 Mr. Cary, the translator of Dante.

**b.** One who renders a painting by engraving, or the like: cf. TRANSLATION 2 b.

**1855** *Gentl. Mag.* XLIII. 657/1 Mr. C. Blair Leighton.. lithographer..was one of the earliest translators of water and oil pictures by the chromatic process. **1888** W. P. FRITH *Autobiog.* III. vii. 159 The delightful art of Thomas [Landseer, the engraver], so thoroughly in sympathy with his brother [Edwin, the painter], places the producer in the front rank of the company of translators. **1897** *Daily News* 5 Feb. 8/6 Line engraving and mezzotint—both of them used largely in the service of the 'translators'.

**2.** One who transforms, changes, or alters; *spec.* a cobbler who renovates old shoes.

**1594** *Merry Knack* in Hazl. *Dodsley* VI. 566 As long as Jeffrey the translater is Mayor of the town. **1638** BRATHWAIT *Barnabees Jrnl.* A vj, That paltry Patcher is a bald Translater. *a* **1658** CLEVELAND *Gen. Poems* (1677) 23 I'm no Translator, have no vein To turn a Woman young again. **1693** *Humours Town* 77 The Jolly Translator, of Shoes, I mean, not Authors. **1700** T. BROWN *Amusem. Ser. & Com.* 130 The Cobler is Affronted, if you don't call him Mr. Translator. **1851** MAYHEW *Lond. Labour* I. 198/2 I'm a 'translator' by trade. **1886** *Daily News* 15 Oct. 3/6 'Translators', who cunningly metamorphose..old leather almost into new goods.

**b.** *transf. pl.* A 'translated' pair of shoes. *slang.*

**1851** MAYHEW *Lond. Labour* I. 51/2 To wear a pair of second-hand ones [boots], or 'translators' (as they are called), is felt as a bitter degradation.

**c.** (See quot.)

**1884** KNIGHT *Dict. Mech.* Supp., *Translator*,..an instrument whereby one form of energy is converted into another. For instance, the power of a prime motor, say a steam engine, is translated by means of a magneto-electric engine into electricity. **1891** in *Cent. Dict.*

†**3.** One who transfers or transports. *Obs.*

**1545** JOYE *Exp. Dan.* v. I v b, The changer and translator of kyngedoms and tymes. **1630** BRATHWAIT *Eng. Gentlem.* (1641) 53 That translator of the Median Empire to the Persians, victorious Cyrus. *a* **1633** AUSTIN *Medit.* (1635) 94 Constantine the Emperor (whom they make a great Translator of Bones) would not let them rest in their Graves.

**4.** An automatic repeater in long-distance telegraphy. Cf. TRANSLATION 6.

**1855** *Patent Office Specif.* No. 314 The use of translators in connection with submarine cables. **1876** PREECE & SIVEWRIGHT *Telegr.* iv. § 111 A distance is at last reached where direct working is impossible, and where it becomes necessary..to introduce mechanical repeaters or translators at some intermediate station to bring into play fresh currents.

**5.** *attrib.* and *Comb.*

**1885** *Pall Mall G.* 29 Jan. 4/2 The extraordinary merit of their translator-engravers. **1887** *Ibid.* 28 Sept. 2/2 [He] has fallen into the clutches of a 'translator-traitor' if ever there was one, who has not only corrected no blunder, but added an enormous mass of mistranslations and misprints. **1891** *Ibid.* 8 Dec. 3/1 A little spurt of undignified and vindictive petulance, a new form of translator-treachery.

Hence **Transla·torship**, the function of a translator (in quot. 1786 *humorously* with possessive as a title).

**1786** COWPER *Let. to Lady Hesketh* 11 Feb., You must return it [specimen of Homer]..to my translatorship. **1835** *Fraser's Mag.* XII. 53 An aspirant for the honours of translatorship.

**Translatory** (trɑnsˌlēⁱ·təri, trɑ·nsˌlătəri), *a.* [f. prec.: see -ORY [2].]

†**1.** Characterized by transferring from one to another. *Obs. rare.*

**1727** SWIFT *Art Polit. Lying* ¶ 6 Wks. 1755 III. I. 117 He divides Political Lyes into several species...The translatory is a lye, that transfers the merit of a man's good action to another who is [etc.].

**2.** Of or pertaining to physical translation; = TRANSLATIONAL b.

**1849** NOAD *Electricity* (ed. 3) 267 The negative tension of an insulated metal is sensibly augmented by giving a translatory motion to the gas which attacks its surface. **1860** TYNDALL *Glac.* II. xxix. 403 Owing to the quicker translatory movement. **1881** — *Floating Matter of Air* ii. 60 The Bacteria lost their translatory power, fell to the bottom, and left the liquid..clear.

**Translatress** (trɑnsˌlēⁱ·très). [f. TRANSLATOR + -ESS.] A female translator.

**1638** CHILLINGW. *Relig. Prot.* I. ii. § 91. 85 Which Card. Perron and his Translatresse so often translate false. **1759** DILWORTH *Pope* 76 By the French translatress Madam Dacier. **1865** *Even. Standard* 4 Feb., The celebrated French translatress of Darwin's work on the 'Origin of Species'.

**Transˌla·trix.** [fem., in L. form, of TRANSLATOR: see -TRIX.] = prec.

**1892** *Nation* (N. Y.) 18 Aug. 133/1 The translatrix knows her Greek well enough to do this. **1902** *Speaker* 4 Oct. 19/1 Is it the translatrix or Gregorovius himself who is guilty of [the mistake]?

† **Transˌlava·tion.** *Obs. rare*—[1]. [f. TRANS- 1 + L. *lavātiōnem*, n. of action fr. *lavāre* to wash, LAVE *v.*[1]] The action of 'laving' or ladling from one vessel to another.

**1601** HOLLAND *Pliny* xxxiv. xviii. II. 519 This translavation ought so long to be continued out of one vessell into another, untill such time as it have done casting any residence downward.

**Translay** (trɑnsˌlēⁱ·), *v. nonce-wd.* [TRANS- 2.] *trans.* To transfer and lay in a new position.

**1849** CLOUGH *Easter Day* 14 If not where Joseph laid Him first, why then Where other men Translaid Him after, in some humbler clay.

**Transleithan** (trɑnsˌləi·þăn), *a.* [f. TRANS- 7 + *Leitha*, name of a river.] Beyond the Leitha, a tributary of the Danube, which forms for a short distance the boundary between Hungary and the archduchy of Austria; hence, Magyar or Hungarian, as distinguished from the cis-Leithan provinces of the Austro-Hungarian empire. So **Transleitha·nian** *a.*

**1870** GLADSTONE *Glean.* IV. v. 201 [Hungary] has attracted to herself the Transleithan Slav population of the South. **1900** *Westm. Gaz.* 5 Jan. 1/3 A sort of tacit understanding that permeates almost all classes of Transleithanian society.

**Transˌle·ttering.** *nonce-wd.* [f. TRANS- 2 + LETTER *v.* + -ING [1].] = TRANSLITERATION.

**1802** W. TAYLOR in *Monthly Mag.* XIII. 12 It may seem strange to fix on a root, which his system of translettering would express by *shiv*.

**Transˌlimita·tion.** *rare.* [f. TRANS- 1 + L. *līmitātiōn-em* fixing of a limit, f. *līmit-em* boundary, limit. Cf. Sp. *translimitacion*.] The sending of troops across the frontier of a foreign state, for the preservation of order, etc.

**1845** W. H. KELLY tr. *L. Blanc's Hist. Ten Y.* v. iv. II. 445 All he [Mendizabal] had made up his mind to sanction was the system of *translimitation*, intended solely to deprive Don Carlos of the succours transmitted to him by the northern powers.

**Transliterate** (trɑnsˌli·tĕreⁱt), *v.* [f. TRANS- 1 + L. *littera* letter, written symbol + -ATE [3].] *trans.* To replace (letters or characters of one language) by those of another used to represent the same sounds; to write (a word, etc.) in the characters of another alphabet. Hence **Transli·terated** *ppl. a.*

**1861** MAX MÜLLER in *Sat. Rev.* 9 Mar. 247/1 Not only proper names, but the technical terms also of the Buddhist creed, had to be preserved in Chinese. They were not to be translated, but to be transliterated. But how was this to be effected with a language which, like Chinese, has no phonetic alphabet? **1861** G. MOORE *Lost Tribes* 158, I transliterate the words into modern Hebrew letters. **1871** EARLE *Philol. Eng. Tongue* § 190 To master this alphabet and transliterate passages of English into it. **1884** *American* VII. 378 The transliterated pages and the Devanagari can be kept in sight at the same time.

**Transliteration** (trɑnsˌlitĕrēⁱ·ʃən). [f. as prec. + -ATION.] The action or process of transliterating; the rendering of the letters or characters of one alphabet in those of another; *concr.* a word or writing thus rendered.

**1861** MAX MÜLLER in *Sat. Rev.* 9 Mar. 247/1 Even the Chinese were after a time unable to read—i. e., to pronounce—these random trans-literations. **1861** G. MOORE *Lost Tribes* 257 The transliteration into Hebrew presents a clear sense. **1862** RAWLINSON *Anc. Mon.* I. viii. 215 Too obscure or too illegible for transliteration. **1900** MARGOLIOUTH in *Expositor* Jan. 50 Till the most recent times no scientific method of transliteration had been invented.

**Transliterator** (trɑnsˌli·tĕreⁱtəɹ). [f. as prec. + -OR.] One who transliterates.

**1867** ELLIS *E. E. Pron.* I. iii. § 4. 191 Sanscrit transliterators. **1895** *Athenæum* 26 Oct. 575/3 Is it the last new idea of the Indian Government transliterator to put a dot under the *t* of Fathpûr, but not under the *h*?

**Translocalization** (trɑnsˌlōᵘ:kăləizēⁱ·ʃən). *rare*—[1]. [f. TRANS- 2 + LOCALIZATION.] Translocation, displacement; in quot., in reference to time.

**1888** *Amer. Jrnl. Psychol.* May 538 Patients..sometimes cannot repeat the same pseudo-experience twice alike, translocalizations in time being especially common.

**Translocate** (trɑ·nsˌlokeⁱt), *v. rare.* [f. TRANS- + LOCATE. Probably suggested by next, which was used much earlier.] *trans.* To remove from one place to another; to displace, dislocate.

*a* **1832** BENTHAM *Lang.* Wks. 1843 VIII. 325/1 Add, upon the model of *transfer*, and *transfuse*, translocate. **1887** *Amer. Nat.* Oct. 944 The ribs have been translocated from the original position..to the neurapophyses. **1899** *Syd. Soc. Lex.*, *Translocate*, the same as Dislocate.

**b.** *Veg. Physiol.* To subject to translocation.

**1911** in WEBSTER.

**Translocation** (trɑnsˌlokēⁱ·ʃən). [f. TRANS- + LOCATION.] Removal from one place to another; displacement; dislocation; † transmigration.

**1624** F. WHITE *Repl. Fisher* 424 Translocation of Christs bodie. **1625** N. CARPENTER *Geog. Del.* II. x. (1635) 174 A seperation was made by translocation of the parts of the Earth. **1665** SIR T. HERBERT *Trav.* (1677) 116 All defending the immortality of the Soul, and the translocation from one into another after death. **1677** CARY *Chronol.* II. I. I. xx. 152 There is..a casual translocation of the Numbers. *a* **1728** WOODWARD *Catal. Eng. Fossils* (1729) II. 4 *margin*, There happen'd certain Translocations at the Deluge. *c* **1814** COLERIDGE in *Lit. Rem.* (1838) III. 80 Translocation is not destruction. **1876** GLADSTONE *Homeric Synchr.* 79 A Revolution involving such extensive change, and such translocation of races. **1877** FOSTER *Phys.* I. ii. § 2 (1878) 79 The muscular contraction itself is essentially a translocation of molecules.

**b.** *Veg. Physiol.*: see quots.

**1900** B. D. JACKSON *Gloss. Bot. Terms*, *Translocation*.. the transference of reserve material from one part to another. **1911** WEBSTER, *Translocation*,..transfer of food materials or products of metabolism from one part to another by osmosis.

† **Transˌlu·ce,** *v. Obs. rare.* [ad. L. *translūc-ēre* to shine through, f. TRANS- + *lūcēre* to shine: cf. TRALUCE *v.*] *trans.* To shine through.

**1609** J. DAVIES *Holy Roode* (Grosart) 26/1 Let Ioy transluce thy Beauties blandishment.

**Translucence** (trɑnsˌliū·sĕns). [f. as next: see -ENCE.]

**1.** The action or fact of shining through.

**1826** COLERIDGE *Two Founts* 27 The soul's translucence thro' her crystal shrine! **1830** — *Lett., to Mrs. Gillman* (1895) 754 What appeared to you a translucence of the love of the good, the true, and the beautiful from within me. **1868** FARRAR *Silence & V.* i. (1875) 18 Nature, which is but the visible translucence of a divine agency working upon material things. **1875** MASSON *Wordsw.*, etc. 123 All the secrets of the earth's interior..are revealed in continuous translucence.

**2.** Transparency to light: = TRANSLUCENCY.

**1755** JOHNSON, *Transparency*, clearness; diaphaneity; translucence; power of transmitting light. **1847–9** *Todd's Cycl. Anat.* IV. 246/2 The epithelium beyond is of excessive delicacy and translucence. **1899** *Allbutt's Syst. Med.* VIII. 592 Having a wax-like translucence.

*fig.* **1859** I. TAYLOR *Logic in Theol.* 271, I admire the translucence of his character, and its strength.

**Translucency** (trɑnsˌliū·sĕnsi). [f. next: see -ENCY: cf. TRALUCENCY.] The quality or condition of being translucent; partial transparency: see quot. 1842. Also *fig.*

**1630** J. TAYLOR (Water P.) *Whore* Wks. II. 111/1 So one glance or glimpse of the translucencie of your eyes sundazeling corruscancy. **1646** SIR T. BROWNE *Pseud. Ep.* II. i. 52 Ice..its atoms are not concreted into continuity, which doth diminish its translucency. **1831** FARADAY *Exp. Res.* xlvi. 339 Different degrees of colour or translucency. **1842** BRANDE *Dict. Sc.*, etc., *Translucency*, semitransparency.

The term is chiefly used in descriptive mineralogy as applied to minerals which admit of a passage of the rays of light, but through which objects cannot be definitely distinguished. 1879 CALDERWOOD *Mind & Br.* 61 A chamber filled with a clear watery fluid, essential for the translucency of the external portion of the eye.

**Translucent** (trɑnsˌlʼū·sĕnt), *a.* [f. L. *translūcent-em*, pres. pple. of *translūcēre* to shine through: see TRANSLUCE, and cf. TRALUCENT.]

†1. That shines through; emitting penetrating rays. b. In quot. *a* 1652, thoroughly illuminated or luminous. *Obs. rare.*

1596 FITZ-GEFFRAY *Sir F. Drake* (1881) 97 The sunne, That latelie bright translucent splendour shed. *a* 1652 A. WILSON *Jas. I* (1653) 61 She had a translucent passage in the night, through the City of London, by multitudes of Torches. 1791 J. LEARMONT *Poems* 359 The Sun translucent from on high With locks of waving gold salutes the sky.

2. Through which light passes: = TRANSPARENT.

1607 TOPSELL *Four-f. Beasts* (1658) 153 The eye of man is translucent, and containeth in it a horny substance. 1634 MILTON *Comus* 861 Sabrina fair,..sitting Under the glassie, cool, translucent wave. 1725 POPE *Odyss.* I. 180 Replenish'd from the cool, translucent springs. 1847 LEWES *Hist. Philos.* (1867) I. 326 Water, air, and other bodies which are translucent. *fig.* 1891 SWINBURNE *Stud. Pr. & Poetry, Jrnl. Sir W. Scott* (1894) 23 The translucent treachery of such an impious imposture.

b. Now, more distinctively: Allowing the passage of light, yet diffusing it so as not to render bodies lying beyond clearly visible; semi-transparent.

1784 COWPER *Tiroc.* 120 A pane of thin translucent horn. 1846 GROVE *Corr. Phys. Forces* 29 The glass ceases to be transparent, though remaining translucent. 1851 WOODWARD *Mollusca* I. 66 The shell of the argonaut is thin and translucent. 1905 in *Westm. Gaz.* 17 Mar. 12/1 The windows of this classroom were once transparent, they are now translucent, and if not cleaned very soon will be opaque. *fig.* 1843 CARLYLE *Past & Pr.* II. ii, The old centuries melt from opaque to partially translucent, transparent here and there.

Hence **Transˌlu·cently** *adv.*, in a translucent manner or state; so as to be seen through.

1832 LYTTON *Eugene A.* I. i, So translucently pure and soft was her complexion. 1897 *Allbutt's Syst. Med.* III. 82 The skin..is translucently pale and shines like a mirror.

**Translucid** (trɑnsˌlʼū·sid), *a.* [ad. L. *translūcid-us* translucent: see prec. and -ID. Cf. F. *translucide* (16th c.).] = TRANSLUCENT 2, and now 2 b.

1626 BACON *Sylva* § 872 Which is most easily seen in the Eyes, because they are Translucide. 1651 *Life Father Sarpi* (1676) 18 How infusion by Art makes bark of Trees and Shells and Roots translucid. 1878 MISS J. YOUNG *Ceram. Art* (1879) 51 Porcelain is translucid, and therein differs from pottery, which is opaque.

†b. = TRANSLUCENT 1. *Obs. rare*$^{-0}$.

1727 [implied in TRANSLUCIDNESS].

Hence **Transˌlu·cidness** = next.

1727 BAILEY vol. II, *Translucidness*..the Quality of shining through, or permitting Light to shine through.

**Translucidity** (trɑnsˌlʼusi·dĭti). [ad. F. *translucidité* (16th c. in Hatz.-Darm.): see prec. and -ITY.] The quality or condition of being translucid; translucency.

1694 MOTTEUX *Rabelais* V. 254 The Flickermise flying through the translucidity of the corner'd Gate. 1798 MITCHELL tr. *Karsten's Min. Leskean Mus.* 367 The internal Lustre and the Translucidity are observable. 1855 tr. *Labarte's Arts Mid. Ages* xiv. 413 Owing to its translucidity.

**Translunary** (trɑ·nsˌlʼūnări), *a.* [f. TRANS- 3 + L. *lūna* moon, after *lunary*.] Lying beyond or above the moon: the opposite of *sublunary*; chiefly *fig.*, etherial, insubstantial, visionary. So **Translu·nar** *a.* (in some recent Dicts.).

1627 DRAYTON *Agincourt*, etc., *To H. Reynolds* 206 Neat Marlow bathed in the Thespian springs Had in him those braue translunary things. 1826 BEDDOES *Let.* Oct., Poems (1851) p. lviii, All my sublunary excursions this summer have been botanical; and my translunary ones..a thought or two for a didactic 'Boem'..on myology. 1892 *Century Mag.* June 183/2 A strayed visitor from some translunary sphere. 1902 AGNES M. CLERKE *Probl. Astrophysics* (1903) 2 The long-divorced sublunary and translunary worlds.

**Transˌma·ke**, *v.* [f. TRANS- 2 + MAKE *v.*, rendering Gr. μεταποιεῖν.] *trans.* To make into something different, to refashion. Hence **Transma·king** *vbl. sb.*

1844 *Dublin Rev.* Mar. 92 They [the sacramental symbols] are as it were *transmade*, made into a new thing, or, in the apt language of the Catholic dogma, transubstantiated. 1874 PUSEY *Lent. Serm.* 315 Those.. whom man could not have changed even by punishing, but the Word transmade, forming and fashioning them after its own will. 1909 D. STONE *Doctr. Eucharist* I. 72 [transl. St. Gregory of Nyssa] That body by the indwelling of God the Word was transmade (μετεποιήθη) to the dignity of Godhead.

†**Transˌmarinal**, *a. Obs. rare*$^{-1}$. [f. as next + -AL.] = TRANSMARINE.

1614 JACKSON *Creed* III. xiii. § 11. 137 Hart out of his transmarinall Catechisme, would gladly haue maintained it.

**Transmarine** (trɑnsˌmărī·n, -z-), *a.* (*sb.*) [ad. L. *transmarīnus*, f. *trans* across + *mare* sea, after MARINE. Cf. F. *transmarin* (12th c. in Godef.).]

1. That is beyond the sea; born, existing, situated, or found on the other side of the sea; over-sea.

1583 MELBANCKE *Philotimus* Aa j b, An aliaunt, or a transmarine straunger. 1610 T. HIGGONS *Serm. at Pauls Crosse* 3 Mar. (1611) 45 It was borne in transmarine and forraine parts. 1671 F. PHILLIPS *Reg. Necess.* 329 Purchasers of Transmarine Wares and Commodities. 1700 TYRRELL *Hist. Eng.* II. 723 Normandy, and the King's other Transmarine Dominions. 1807 G. CHALMERS *Caledonia* I. I. vi. 193 Contemporary authors..speak of the Scots, as a transmarine people. 1878 *N. Amer. Rev.* CXXVII. 189 If it [India] were the sole transmarine appendage to the crown.

2. Crossing or extending across the sea.

1860 GOSSE *Rom. Nat. Hist.* 84 Species [of birds] which are known to make long transmarine migrations. 1908 *Sci. Amer.* 15 Feb. 106/1 The remarkable transmarine railroad which is under construction from the mainland of Florida to Key West. 1908 F. HARRISON in *Trans. Roy. Hist. Soc.* Ser. III. III. 38 Pitt made all European questions subordinate to his transmarine, world-wide ambitions and schemes.

†B. *sb.* One born or dwelling beyond the sea; a native or inhabitant of a transmarine country.

1596 WARNER *Alb. Eng.* XI. lxv. (1602) 280 Perhaps, vnpossible..My loue should equall his, or I a trans-Marine be wrought. 1633 HEYWOOD *Eng. Trav.* II. ii, I am, quoth he, A Trans-marine by birth.

†**Transˌma·ritime**, *a. Obs. rare*$^{-1}$. [TRANS- 3.] = TRANSMARINE.

1610 BP. CARLETON *Jurisd.* 74 Transmaritim iudgments ought not to be admitted.

**Transˌmate·rial**, *a. rare*$^{-1}$. [TRANS- 4.] Beyond or transcending the material.

1903 *19th Cent.* Apr. 639 He ends by representing it [the subliminal self] as a hyperphysical spirit, whose origin is beyond matter, and whose functions are transmaterial.

**Transˌmateria·tion.** *rare*$^{-1}$. [f. TRANS- 1 + L. *māteriātiōn-em*: see MATERIATION.] Change of the matter of which a thing consists.

1866 HARPER *Peace thro. Truth* Ser. I. 159 If it be altered it must be either substantially, and that by Transubstantiation, or transformation, or transmateriation, or it must be accidentally.

†**Tra·nsmeˌate**, *v. Obs. rare*$^{-0}$. [f. ppl. stem of rare L. *transmeāre* to pass across (Pliny), f. *trans* + *meāre* to go, pass.] *trans.* To pass through or across. So †**Tra·nsmeˌable** *a.* [L. *transmeābilis*], that may be crossed, passable, †**Tra·nsmeˌant** *a.* [L. *transmeānt-em* pr. pple.], passing through.

1656 BLOUNT *Glossogr.*, *Transmeable*, to be, or that may be passed over. *Ibid.*, *Transmeate*, to passe or go beyond. 1657 *Physical Dict.*, *Transmea[n]t*, that passeth through the pores of the body, as through the bottom of a sieve. 1727 BAILEY vol. II, Transmeable..Transmeated.

†**Transmeation** (trɑnsˌmiˌēi·ʃən). *Obs. rare.* [n. of action from L. *transmeāre*: see prec. and -ATION.] A passing across or over.

1630 LORD *Banians* 52 They did hold, that there was a passage of soules of one creature into another, that this transmeation was of the soules of men into beasts, and of beasts into men. 1658 PHILLIPS, *Transmeation*, a passing through, or beyond.

**Transmedian** (trɑnsˌmī·diăn), *a.* (*sb.*) *Anat.* and *Zool.* [f. TRANS- + L. *medius* middle: cf. MEDIAN.] Passing or situated across the median line of the body; applied to certain muscles in brachiopods. Also as *sb.* a transmedian muscle. Also **Transˌme·dial** *a.*

1876 T. DAVIDSON in *Encycl. Brit.* IV. 193/1 Of the shell or valvular muscles..one pair are transmedians, each member passing across the middle of the reverse side of the shell. *Ibid.*, Transmedial or sliding muscles. 1881 *Cassell's Nat. Hist.* V. 261 The fifth pair of transmedians controls the movements from side to side of the beak or umbonal regions of the shell.

**Transmental** (trɑnsˌme·ntăl), *a.* (*sb.*) *rare.* [f. TRANS- 3 + L. *mens, ment-em* mind: cf. *mental*.] Existing beyond the mind; independent of or apart from human thought or perception; as *sb.*, a transmental existence or reality.

1907 *Jrnl. Philos., Psychol. & Sci. Methods* 17 Jan. 45 Should the reply be that some sort of transmental is implied, I would gladly recant, even though Professor James should still insist that the nature of that transmental is irrelevant to all human interests, even the most intellectual.

**Transmentation** (trɑnsˌmentēi·ʃən). *rare.* [f. TRANS- 1 + L. *mens, ment-* mind + -ATION; rendering Gr. μετάνοια afterthought, repentance. Cf. *mentation* and mod. 16th c. L. *transmentātio* (Goclenius in Du Cange).] Change of mind or thinking; mental conversion.

1647 TRAPP *Comm.* 2 *Cor.* vii. 9 *That ye sorrowed to repentance* Gr. To a transmentation, to a thorow change both of the minde and manners. 1657 REEVE *God's Plea* 63 Where there is μετάνοια, a new brayning, or a transmentation. 1835 J. HARRIS *Gt. Teacher* (1837) 181 Repentance, transmentation, a change of mind, was the indispensable condition of enrolment.

†**Transˌmeri·dian**, *a.* (*sb.*) *Obs. rare.* [f. TRANS- 7 + L. *meridiān-us* MERIDIAN.] Beyond the or a meridian. In quot. *absol.* as *sb.*, the region beyond the meridian in the Atlantic which separates the New from the Old World; the Western Hemisphere.

1500–20 DUNBAR *Poems* lxvi. 63 It micht have cuming in schortar quhyll Fra Calzecot and the new-fund Yle, The partis of Transmeridiane; Quhilk to considder is ane pane.

**Transmeridional** (trɑnsˌmĕri·diŏnăl, -z-), *a.* [f. TRANS- 3 + MERIDIONAL *a.* 4.] Crossing or traversing the meridian lines; running east and west.

1883 A. WINCHELL *World-Life* II. iii. (1889) 355 How the Mediterranean and Indian Ocean shores came to have general transmeridional trends. 1892 *Chambers' Encycl.* X. 505/2 The Caribbean Sea and the Mediterranean—those great transmeridional depressions.

**Transmew, transmue** (trɑnsˌmiū·), *v. Obs.* or *arch.* Also 4–5 -muwe, -mewe, 5 -mywe. [a. F. *transmue-r* (13th c. in Hatz.-Darm.), semi-learned form:—L. *transmūtāre* to change, TRANSMUTE, f. TRANS- + *mūtāre* to change: see MEW *v.*[1]] *trans.* = TRANSMUTE 1.

*c* 1374 CHAUCER *Troylus* IV. 439 (467) Thow most me first transmuwen [*v.r.* transmute] in a ston. *Ibid.* 802 (830) Ioies ..þat now transmuwed ben in cruel wo. *c* 1407 LYDG. *Reson & Sens.* 4323 She to A larke was transmewed. 1512 *Helyas* in Thoms *Prose Rom.* (1828) III. 81 His v. brethren and his sister, which were transmued in to swannes. 1590 SPENSER *F. Q.* I. vii. 35 Men into stones therewith he could transmew, And stones to dust, and dust to nought at all. *a* 1643 W. CARTWRIGHT *Ordinary* V. iv. in Hazl. *Dodsley* XII. 308, I, Robert Moth..do transmue my name to Geffery. 1748 THOMSON *Cast. Indol.* II. xlii, As if transmew'd to stone. 1820 SCOTT *Monast.* xxiii, To cast my riding slough, and to transmew myself into some civil form.

†b. *intr.* for *pass.* = TRANSMUTE 1 c. *Obs.*

*c* 1400 *Rom. Rose* 2526 In siker wise thou hir salewe, Wherwith thi colour wole transmewe. *c* 1407 LYDG. *Reson & Sens.* 303 Dame nature..Alle erthely thing repaireth newe ..Eche thinge..Which she seth faylle and transmywe. *a* 1461 — *Beware Doubleness* 44 Fortune's wheel..Whos cours standeth ever in doute For to transmew.

†**Transˌmigrable**, *a. Obs. rare*$^{-1}$. [f. L. *transmigrāre* to TRANSMIGR-ATE + -ABLE.] Capable of transmigration.

1689 G. HARVEY *Curing Dis. by Expect.* xvi. 120 Vegetables..whose fragrant scent is transmigrable with their humidity.

**Transmigrant** (trɑ·nsˌmigrănt, -z-), *a.* and *sb.* [f. L. *transmigrānt-*, ppl. stem of *transmigrāre*: see next.]

A. *adj.* That transmigrates. *rare.*

1654 GAYTON *Pleas. Notes* III. iii. 82 Such an Agonie and maw-Convulsions, that he thought his soule had been transmigrant and Errant from his Body. 1888 *Athenæum* 24 Nov. 695/2 They proceed to tell a secular story of transmigrant souls.

B. *sb.* †1. *orig.* One who transmigrates or leaves his own land and dwells in another: including the two notions of 'emigrant' and 'immigrant'.

1622 BACON *Holy War* Wks. 1879 I. 529/1 There are other bands of society, and implicit confederations. That of colonies, or transmigrants, towards their mother nation.

2. In recent use: A person passing through a country or place on his way from the country from which he is an emigrant to that in which he will be an immigrant. Used *spec.* in reference to the Aliens Act of 1905: see quot.

1894 WILLIS in *Rep. Bd. of Trade recent Immigr. fr. E. Europe* 10 The immigrants of [Russian and Polish] nationality formed..in 1892, 64 per cent. of all aliens (not being seamen and not known to be transmigrants) shown..to have come here from Hamburg. 1905 *Form of Return under Aliens Act*, A. Immigration Ports. Aliens Act, 1905. Transmigrants. That is, alien passengers (other than first-class passengers), who have in their possession prepaid through tickets, and in respect of whom security has been given that they will proceed to places outside the United Kingdom. 1910 *Daily News* 26 Feb. 4/2 Practically no aliens now arrive in this country for the purpose of settling here; they are nearly all transmigrants proceeding via England from the Continent to America.

b. Also said of migratory birds.

3. A soul which transmigrates.

1882 in OGILVIE (Annandale).

†**Tra·nsˌmigrate**, *ppl. a. Obs. rare*$^{-1}$. [ad. late L. *transmigrāt-us* (Isidore), pa. pple. of *transmigrāre*: see next.] Transferred, transported; cf. next, 1 b. (Const. as pa. pple.)

1430–40 LYDG. *Bochas* VIII. xx. (MS. Bodl. 263) 393/2 Iherusalem was whilom transmygrat, Ther trewe Prophetis for thei hadde in despiht.

**Transmigrate** (trɑ·nsˌmigrēⁱt, trɑnsˌməi·grēⁱt, -z-), *v.* [f. L. *transmigrāt-*, ppl. stem of (very rare) *transmigrāre*, f. *trans*, TRANS- + *migrāre* to MIGRATE. Cf. mod.F. *transmigrer* (16th c. in Godef.).]

1. *intr.* To remove or pass from one place to another; *esp.* of persons, or a tribe: to move from one place of abode to another, to migrate.

1611 CORYAT *Crudities* 91 The Longobardes..being exceedingly multiplied in their owne country, transmigrated into a bordering Island. 1646 SIR T. BROWNE *Pseud. Ep.* VI. x, This complexion..is evidently maintained by generation,..the Natives which transmigrate, omit it not without commixture. 1723 *Pres. St. Russia* II. 66 They are transmigrating from one Place to another. *a* 1797 H. WALPOLE *George II* (1847) I. ix. 269 The well affected clans might be induced to transmigrate to those settlements. 1898 *Westm. Gaz.* 1 Apr. 3/1 He found a wider space on the other side, so he transmigrated and slumbered in peace.

b. *trans.* in causal sense: To transfer, transport. (In quots. only in passive.)

1430–40 [see prec.]. 1635 HEYWOOD *Hierarch.* VII. Notes 463 Excellent Spirits..are rather transmigrated from the earth, to reigne with the Powers aboue. 1745 ELIZA HEYWOOD *Female Spect.* No. 11 (1748) II. 216 To try the experiment, Whether, by transferring the blood of one animal into another, the nature of the creature would be transmigrated also.

2. *intr. spec.* Of the soul: To pass after death into another body.

1606 SHAKS. *Ant. & Cl.* II. vii. 51 What manner o thing is

your Crocodile?..It liues by that which nourisheth it, and the Elements once out of it, it Transmigrates. **1616** B. JONSON *Epigr.* cxxxiii. 139 Their spirits transmigrated to a cat. *c* **1645** HOWELL *Lett.* (1650) II. 43, I think my soul would transmigrat into some tree, when she bids this body farewell. **1697** COLLIER *Ess. Mor. Subj.* II. (1709) 174 Methinks I should be loath to Transmigrate into a Child, or lie in a Cradle, with those few Things I have in my Head. **1883** GILMOUR *Mongols* xvii. 202 If souls do not transmigrate, where do they come from at birth, whither do they go at death?

**b.** *trans.* (causal). To cause to pass: cf. 1 b.

*c* **1559** R. HALL *Life Bp. Fisher* iii. (1655) 32 Luther's Soul was transmigrated into Henry the eighth. **1681** RYCAUT tr. *Gracian's Critick* 119 The Souls of evil livers, whom God.. had transmigrated into the Bodies of these irrational Creatures. **1876** A. B. GROSART in *Wordsworth's Pr. Wks.* I. Pref. 33 A monkey with a man's soul somehow transmigrated into it.

**c.** *transf.* and *fig.*

**1646** E. G. in M. L[uelyn] *Men-Miracles*, etc. A v, While the grosse Bodies of the Poets die, Their Souls doe onely shift. And Poesie Transmigrates, not by chance, or lucke. *a* **1711** KEN *Hymnotheo* Poet. Wks. 1721 III. 186 Desire.. To Love transmigrates when it dies. **1834** HT. MARTINEAU *Moral* IV. 144 The genius of society has before transmigrated through forms as horrid and disgusting as these. **1850** LYNCH *Theo. Trin.* v. 86 Philosophies die or transmigrate.

Hence **Tra·nsmigrated**, **Tra·nsmigrating** *ppl. adjs.*

**1682** T. FLATMAN *Heraclitus Ridens* No. 55 (1713) II. 98 Whether our Whigs..are not transmigrated Lice, who thrive and increase most in Hospitals and upon poor People? **1693** DRYDEN *Persius' Sat.* VI. 22 Who, in a drunken Dream beheld his Soul The Fifth within the Transmigrating roul. **1728** POPE *Dunc.* III. 49 Who knows how long, thy transmigrating soul Might from Bœotian to Bœotian roll! **1754** FOOTE *Knights* I. Wks. 1799 I. 62 The very abstract of penury! Sir John Cutler, with his transmigrated stockings, was but a type of him. **1898** *Westm. Gaz.* 28 July 2/3 To consider..more mundane matters, such as the number and characters of the transmigrating households.

**Transmigration** (trɑnsˌmigrēⁱ·ʃən, -məi-, -z-). [ad. late L. *transmigrātiōn-em* change of country (in Itala 1 Esdr. vi. 16 the Babylonian Captivity), n. of action from *transmigrāre*: see prec. Cf. F. *transmigration* (13th c. in Hatz.-Darm.).]

†**1.** The removal of the Jews into captivity at Babylon; sometimes used for the Captivity. *Obs.*

**1297** R. GLOUC. (Rolls) 196 Þe vifþe [age] was fram dauid to þe transmigracion Of babiloyne. **1382** WYCLIF *1 Chron.* v. 22 Thei dwelliden for hem unto the transmygracioun. **1430–40** LYDG. *Bochas* IV. iii. (MS. Bodl. 263) 216/2 How God wolde make a transmygracioun. In his kyngdam. **1579** J. STUBBES *Gaping Gulf* Bj, The whole people suffered a transmigration irretornable in Assiria. **1609** BIBLE (Douay) *2 Kings* xxv. 27 In the seven and thirteth yeare of the Transmigration.

†**b.** *transf.* The body of transmigrated people; the Jews of the Captivity. *Obs.*

**1609** BIBLE (Douay) *Jer.* xxviii. 4 Al the transmigration of Juda, that are entered into Babylon, I wil make to returne. — *Ezek.* xi. 24 And the spirite..brought me into Chaldee to the transmigration, in a vision in the spirite of God.

**2.** Passage or removal from one place to another, esp. from one country to another.

**1382** WYCLIF *Jer.* xiii. 19 Translatid is al Juda with parfit transmygracioun [1388 passyng ouere]. **1480** CAXTON *Chron. Eng.* III. (1520) 21 b/2 He put Nactanabo the kynge in Ethyopia and many Iewes in transmygracyon. **1534** MORE *Comf. agst. Trib.* III. Wks. 1237/2 Yf my transmigracion into a straunge countrey shoulde be any great griefe vnto me. **1630** T. WESTCOTE *Devon.* 51 Gentlemen's younger sons, who, by means of their travel and transmigration are very well qualified, apt, and fit to manage great and high offices in the republic. **1796** MORSE *Amer. Geog.* II. 419 The modern Italians are in a great measure free from..the transmigration of colonies. **1842** WESTCOTT in *Life* (1903) I. ii. 31 You have heard of my transmigration from Birmingham to Ludlow. **1858** H. W. BEECHER *Life Th.* (1859) 171 Birds in the hour of transmigration feel the impulse of southern lands. **1875** HADDAN in *Dict. Chr. Antiq.* I. 226/1 [According to] the author of the tract *De Translationibus*..the thing prohibited is 'transmigration' (which arises from the bishop himself, from selfish motives), not 'translation' (wherein the will of God and the good of the Church is the ruling cause). **1903** *Ardrossan & Saltcoats Herald* 1 May 2 The great Teutonic, Hungarian, Tartar, and Mongolian transmigrations.

**b.** *fig.* Of non-material things.

**1632** LITHGOW *Trav.* x. 500 Ignoble Gallants..swallow vp the honour of their..Predecessours, with..Gluttony, Lust, and vaine Apparell, making a Transmigration of perpetuity to their present Belly, and Backe. *a* **1711** KEN *Sion* Poet. Wks. 1721 IV. 397 Love instantly rejoin'd Love from the Lover's Mind, To God still am'rous Transmigrations makes. **1824** MISS FERRIER *Inher.* xxxiv, That enviable power of mental transmigration, which placed him..quite beyond the influence of her power.

†**3.** Transition from one state or condition to another; *esp.* passage from this life, by death; also *absol.* death. *Obs.*

**1576** FLEMING *Panopl. Epist.* 323 His ioyful estate of heauen, after his transmigration out of the labyrinth of this life. *a* **1631** DONNE *Serm.* lxi. (1640) 613 Enough for thy pilgrimage, enough for thy transmigration, enough for thy eternall habitation. **1675** T. PLUME *Life Bp. Hacket* (1865) 139 His placid departure, with as gentle a transmigration to happiness as..was ever heard of.

¶**b.** Loosely used for *transformation* or *transmutation* (cf. *transmogrification*). *Obs.*

**1618** N. FIELD *Amends for Ladies* II. i. in Hazl. *Dodsley* XI. 113 The teeth she had Have made a transmigration into hair: She hath a bigger beard than I. **1643** SIR T. BROWNE *Relig. Med.* I. § 39 Those strange and mysticall transmigrations that I have observed in Silkewormes.

**4.** *spec.* Passage of the soul at death into another body; metempsychosis. Also *fig.*

**1594** T. B. *La Primaud. Fr. Acad.* II. 527 This Transmigration of Soules they called Regeneration, because it was vnto them as it were a generation and newe birth. *a* **1625** FLETCHER *Woman's Prize* IV. v, I..know her To be a woman-wolf by transmigration. **1634** SIR T. HERBERT *Trav.* 38 The Bannyans..For they so much detest the slaughter of any creature, though a Louse..Imagining as did Pythagoras, the transmigration of mens soules into other creatures. **1709–10** STEELE *Tatler* No. 134 ¶ 1 A Discourse on the Transmigration of Men into other Animals. **1892** WESTCOTT *Gospel of Life* 153 The Myths of Plato will shew us how great an attraction this doctrine of transmigration exerts upon the imagination of men.

**5.** *Path.* The migration or passage of cells through a membrane or the wall of a vessel; the oozing of white blood corpuscles through the unruptured walls of the blood-vessels; diapedesis.

**1890** BILLINGS *Med. Dict.*, *Transmigration*, a moving across a limiting membrane or out of a vessel or cavity. **1899** *Syd. Soc. Lex.*, *Transmigration*, the passage of cells or particles through a membranous septum.

Hence **Transmigra·tionism**, the theory or doctrine of transmigration of souls; **Transmigra·tionist**, one who holds this doctrine; also *attrib.* or as *adj.*

**1888** F. W. H. MYERS in *Fortn. Rev.* Jan. 103 Is Traducianism conceivable?..Are we not driven back on some form of *Transmigrationism? **1884** *Chr. Commonwealth* 20 Mar. 545/1 Accessible to the influence of dead and buried Asiatic poetasters and *transmigrationists. **1903** F. W. MYERS *Hum. Personality* II. 267 Both the old traducianist and the old transmigrationist view would thus possess a share of truth.

**Transmigrative** (trɑ·nsˌmigrēⁱtiv, trɑnsˌməi·grătiv, -z-), *a.* [f. TRANSMIGRATE *v.* + -IVE.] Of, pertaining to, or characterized by transmigration; transmigratory.

**1727** D'URFEY *Eng. Stage Italianized* Argt., The Doctor brings the Queen to life by a transmigrative Secret. **1818** G. S. FABER *Horæ Mosaicæ* I. 147 That Adam, and Enoch, and Noah, were alike transmigrative incarnations of him. **1833** — *Recapit. Apostasy* i. 4 Those preëminent mundane patriarchs who were transmigrative reappearances of one and the same great universal father. **1844** — *Eight Dissert.* (1845) I. 284.

Hence **Transmigratively** *adv.*, by way of transmigration (of the soul).

**1818** G. S. FABER *Horæ Mosaicæ* II. 202 He himself was afterwards transmigratively born again in the body of his pontifical Successor Buddas-Addas. **1819** — *Dispensations* (1823) II. 74 Souls do not perish after death but flit transmigratively from one body to another.

**Transmigrator** (trɑ·nsˌmigrēⁱtəɹ, -z-). [f. as prec. + -OR.] One who or that which transmigrates: a transmigrant; a transmigrating spirit.

**1743** ELLIS *Knowl. Div. Things* ii. 122 Whenever we find a People begin to revive in Literature, it was owing..either to some Transmigrators from those Parts coming and settling among them, or else to their going thither for Instruction. **1837** LYTTON *Athens* II. 63 [Genius] the true spiritual transmigrator—it passes through all shapes, losing identity but not life and kindred to the Great Intelligence which is the Soul of matter.

**Transmigratory** (trɑnsˌməi·grătəri, -z-), *a.* [f. as prec. + -ORY[2]: cf. *migratory*.] Having the quality of transmigrating; of or pertaining to transmigration.

**1816** G. S. FABER *Orig. Pagan Idol.* I. 40 Reappearing.. agreeably to the transmigratory system. *Ibid.* II. 80 The latter [Noah] was deemed a transmigratory revival of the former [Adam]. **1871** ALABASTER *Wheel of Law* 90 They are reborn as angels..preparatory to reappearing in their last transmigratory existence as Buddha. **1893** HUXLEY *Evolution & Ethics* 19 That..each human being has his transmigratory representative.

†**Transˌmi·gure**, *v. Obs. rare*[—1]. Perversion of TRANSMIGRATE, after *transfigure*, or F. *transmigrer*.

**1687** WINSTANLEY *Lives Eng. Poets* 153 The soul of Aristotle was said to have transmigured into Thomas Aquinas.

†**Transˌmi·se**, *v. Obs.* Also 5–6 **-myse**. In earliest use in pa. pple. *transmised*, app. rendering F. pa. pple. *transmis*, *-mise*; cf. *demise*, *premise*, *promise*.] *trans.* To cause to pass or go; to send; = TRANSMIT.

**1480** CAXTON *Ovid's Met.* XIII. vii, Thyder had kynge Priamus transmysed and sent..his sone Polydorus. **1490** — *Eneydos* xiv. 52 The sonne..shal haue transmysed hys shynynge bemes. **1541** R. COPLAND *Guydon's Quest. Chirurg.* C ij, For the moste parte of the thynges that it [the liver] is composed is fleshely, blody, & therwith ben transmysed dyuers pypes or arteres. **1646** J. HALL *Horæ Vac.* 53 There being an innate desire in every man, to transmise himself unto posterity.

†**Transˌmi·ss**, *sb. Obs.* exc. *Hist.* [ad. L. *transmiss-us*, *-um*: see next.] A copy of an Irish Bill returned to the Irish Parliament with the king's approval.

**1764** *Jrnl. Irish Ho. Comm.* 11 May, Resolved That no Bill shall pass in this House until a Committee of this House shall compare the Transmiss with the original Heads of a Bill, and report, if any, and what alterations have been made therein, to the House. **1812** in *Rep. Comm. Pub. Rec. Irel.* (1815) 75 Transmisses of Public and Private Acts of Parliament.—The oldest Transmisses we could yet discover, are of the Reign of Henry VIII.

†**Transˌmi·ss**, *ppl. a. Obs. rare.* [ad. L. *transmiss-us*, pa. pple. of *transmittĕre* to TRANSMIT.] Transmitted. (Const. as pa. pple.)

**1647** H. MORE *Poems* 116 Souls..If they shoot out, be they equally transmisse Around this body? Or but upward start? *Ibid.* 181 Neither Speech nor Language is Where their voice is not transmisse.

†**Transˌmi·ss**, *v. Obs. rare.* [f. L. *transmiss-*, ppl. stem of *transmittĕre* to TRANSMIT. It occurs in the pa. pple. *transmiss'd*, app. representing L. *transmissum*. Cf. DISMISS.] = TRANSMIT.

*a* **1643** W. CARTWRIGHT *Ordinary* III. v, Any reversions yet? nothing transmiss'd?

**Transmissibility** (trɑnsˌmisĭbi·lĭti, -z-). [f. next + -ITY. Cf. F. *transmissibilité* (1812 in Hatz.-Darm.).] The quality of being transmissible.

**1828** in WEBSTER. **1847–9** *Todd's Cycl. Anat.* IV. 114/1 The associated pus has in reality nothing to do with the transmissibility of the diseases. **1875** BENNETT & DYER *Sachs' Bot.* 826 The hereditary transmissibility of acquired characters exhibits itself in a most marked way when it does not affect the whole of the parent-plant, but only a particular branch. **1894** *Pall Mall G.* 19 Nov. 1/2 He handles the transmissibility question with diffidence.

**Transmissible** (trɑnsˌmi·sĭb'l, -z-), *a.* [f. L. *transmiss-* (see TRANSMISS *v.*) + -IBLE. Cf. F. *transmissible* (16th c. in Hatz.-Darm.), and L. *remissibilis*, etc.] Capable of being transmitted.

**1644** BP. MAXWELL *Prerog. Chr. Kings* v. 59 It is transmissible to his Successor. **1660** BOND *Scut. Reg.* 138 God did declare it transmissible from Adam to the first born. **1798** MALTHUS *Popul.* III. i. (1806) II. 86 Transmissible and contagious disorders. **1869** DK. OF ARGYLL *Primeval Man* II. 39 Some varieties of form are effected..by domestication, and by constant care in the selection of peculiarities transmissible to the young. **1885** SIR E. FRY in *Law Rep.* 29 Ch. Div. 283 The right to a grant of administration is not transmissible.

**Transmission** (trɑnsˌmi·ʃən, -z-). [ad. L. *transmissiōn-em*, n. of action from *transmittĕre* to TRANSMIT. Cf. F. *transmission* (14th c. in Hatz.-Darm.).] The action of transmitting or fact of being transmitted; conveyance from one person or place to another; transference.

**1611** FLORIO, *Transmissione*, a transmission. **1626** BACON *Sylva* § 2 In the experiment of Transmission of the Sea-water into the Pits, the Water riseth; but in the experiment of transmission of the Water through the Vessels, it falleth. **1759** JOHNSON *Idler* No. 68 ¶ 2 Alphabetical writing made..the transmission of events more easy and certain. **1802–3** tr. *Pallas's Trav.* (1812) I. 82 On the transmission of the Black Sea through the Propontis, a great part of its shallow banks consequently became a saline steppe. *a* **1859** DE QUINCEY *Posth. Wks.* (1891) I. 308 One link in the transmission of the Homeric poems.

**b.** *Physics.* Conveyance or passage through a medium, as of light, heat, sound, etc.

**1704** NEWTON *Opticks* (1721) 238 Their Reflexion or Transmission depends on the constitution of the Air and Water behind the Glass. **1815** J. SMITH *Panorama Sci. & Art* I. 7 Which greatly retards the transmission of the heat. **1834** MRS. SOMERVILLE *Connex. Phys. Sc.* xvii. 147 The transmission of sound as well as light is impeded in passing through an atmosphere of variable density. **1881** SIR W. ARMSTRONG in *Nature* 8 Sept. 449/1 To force a transmission of heat from the fire to the water in the boiler.

**c.** *Biol.* The transmitting of the peculiar nature, or of some character, of an organism to its descendants; hereditary conveyance.

**1871** DARWIN *Desc. Man* II. xviii. II. 297 Equal transmission of ornamental characters to both sexes. **1880** E. R. LANKESTER *Degener.* 13 An organism..inherits, that is to say, is born with—the peculiarities of its parents; this is known as Transmission. **1890** *Sc. Gossip* XXVI. 66 Questions of protective resemblance and hereditary transmission.

**d.** *Mech.* Transference of motive force from one place to another; *concr.* a device for effecting this; *spec.* short for *transmission-gear* (see e).

**1906** *Daily Chron.* 28 June 2/7 There are four large and eleven smaller electric motors driving the transmissions. *Ibid.*, Improvements in devices for preventing accidents with transmissions. **1911** WEBSTER, *Transmission*,..*Horol.* the train of a watch, etc.

**e.** *attrib.* (chiefly in sense d): **transmission-gear**, mechanism for transmitting the power of an engine, etc.

**1833** BREWSTER *Nat. Magic* ix. 219 The sound will be partly reflected.., and the direction of the transmission wave changed. **1894** *Prospect. Tramway Motor Co.* 2 A transmission gear giving a wide range of continuously varying speed and inversely varying tractive effort. **1894** *Daily News* 3 Nov. 5/3 A large proportion of the sailors paid off there have gladly availed themselves of the transmission scheme. **1901** *Scaffolding* (ed. J. Black) 60 The endeavour to dispense with transmission gear between motor and machine constitutes to-day a recognised principle of construction [in cranes]. **1906** *Westm. Gaz.* 22 Jan. 8/1 The electricity will be conveyed at high pressure to a central spot on the transmission lines. **1908** *Ibid.* 14 Nov. 14/2 Double universal joints to maintain true alignment between the power- and transmission-shafts.

Hence **Transmi·ssionist**, one who holds the theory of the hereditary transmission of acquired characters; also *attrib.*

**1900** C. LL. MORGAN *Animal Behaviour* iii. § 5. 113 It forms a very pretty subject for transmissionists and their critics to quarrel over. *Ibid.* 114 Let us expand the transmissionist position a little further.

**Transmissive** (trɑnsˌmi·siv, -z-), *a.* [f. L. *transmiss-* (see TRANSMISS *v.*) + -IVE: cf. L. *remissivus* remissive.]

**1.** Having the quality or action of transmitting. **1649** G. DANIEL *Trinarch., Hen. V* ccclxxxvi, Harry (who gave more Of fate in his Transmissive veins, then both Could worke) yet wraps the Infant in that Cloth. **1834** MRS. SOMERVILLE *Connex. Phys. Sc.* xxv. 231 The transmissive power of certain substances having a dark colour exceeds by four or five times that of others perfectly diaphanous. **1903** *Union Mag.* Oct. 437/1 The function of the brain is not 'productive' but 'transmissive' of consciousness.

**2.** Having the quality of being transmitted. **1700** PRIOR *Carmen Seculare* 164 The Sire [may] inculcate to his Son Transmissive Lessons of the King's Renown. **1775** R. CHANDLER *Trav. Greece* (1825) II. 152 The native quickness of apprehension, which as if transmissive,.. is inherited even by the lower classes of the people. **1802-12** BENTHAM *Ration. Judic. Evid.* (1827) I. 68 Modifications of the genus of transmitted or transmissive evidence. **1887** L. P. MERCER *New Birth* (1890) 74 Transmissive dispositions and proclivities to evil, coming down a long line of tainted ancestry.

Hence **Transmi·ssively** *adv.*, by way of transmission; **Transmi·ssiveness.** **1881** SIR W. ARMSTRONG in *Nature* 8 Sept. 451/2 There will be a limit to the distance to which electricity may be profitably conveyed, but within that limit there will be wide scope for its employment transmissively. **1889** *Home Missionary* (N.Y.) Sept. 220 The aim is transmissiveness of the divine motive power.

**Transmissory** (trɑns,mi·sǝri, -z-), *a. rare.* [f. as prec. + -ORY[2]: cf. *promissory*.] = TRANSMISSIVE I. **1883** W. A. BUTLER in J. G. Butler *Bible Work* II. 235 Titles [of the Holy Spirit] which impress how truly his function is transmissory of perfections that dwell in Christ.

**Transmit** (trɑns,mi·t, -z-), *v.* [ad. L. *transmittĕre*, f. L. TRANS- + *mittĕre* to send.]

**1.** *trans.* To cause (a thing) to pass, go, or be conveyed to another person, place, or thing; to send across an intervening space; to convey, transfer. *a* **1400-50** *Alexander* 4335 Nouthire to toly ne to taunde transmitte we na webbis, To vermylion ne violett ne variant littis. **1544** COVERDALE *Let. to C. Hubert* Wks. (Parker Soc.) II. 509 Take care..that they be transmitted to me with the paper of Cephalæus. **1612** DAVIES *Why Irel.*, etc. (1747) 24 From this time forward untill the 17 year of King John..there was no army transmitted out of England to finish the Conquest. **1644** MILTON *Areop.* (Arb.) 46 That Eusebian book of Evangelick preparation transmitting our ears through a hoard of heathenish obscenities, to receive the Gospel. **1701** PENN in *Pa. Hist. Soc. Mem.* IX. 77 Hasten in my rents and debts, and transmit them with all possible speed. **1849** MACAULAY *Hist. Eng.* iii. I. 376 The expense of transmitting heavy goods in this way was enormous. **1880** C. R. MARKHAM *Peruv. Bark* iii. 273 They merely transmitted my letter to the Secretary of State, without any recommendation.

**b.** *intr.* (for *refl.*) To pass to the heirs. **1913** H. GOUDY in *Ess. Legal Hist. of Congr. Hist. Stud.* 208 Where..a delictal action was not strictly penal..it transmitted both actively and passively. *Ibid.* 218 In contracts the right of action almost invariably transmitted both to the heirs of the creditor and against the heirs of the debtor.

**2.** *fig.* To convey or communicate (usually something immaterial) *to* another or others; to pass on, esp. by inheritance or heredity; to hand down. **1629** BURTON *Truth's Triumph* 91 This word of faith.. wee shall transmit and conuay it, euen vnto posterity. **1651** HOBBES *Leviath.* III. xlii. 267 His Apostles..transmitted the same Spirit by Imposition of hands. **1710** PRIDEAUX *Orig. Tithes* v. 234 The House of Lords..had this power transmitted solely to them exclusive of the House of Commons. **1738** in *Nairne Peerage Evid.* (1874) 42 The said John Nairne..is likewise wholly disabled to take transmit or inherit any real or personal estate. **1828** DUPPA *Trav. Italy*, etc. 84 A glowing diffusion of light, of which Claude's finest pictures transmit but a faint resemblance. **1862** STANLEY *Jew. Ch.* (1877) I. xiii. 248 Samuel..had actually transmitted the office by hereditary succession to his sons. **1910** *Morning Post* 28 June 3/7 Capacity for milk-production, for early maturity [etc.]..are definitely fixed, and definitely transmitted from good sires.

**3.** *Physics* and *Mech.* To cause (light, heat, sound, etc.) to pass through a medium; also, of a medium, to allow (light, etc.) to pass through; to conduct. Also, to convey (force or movement) from one part of a body, or of mechanism, to another. Also *fig.* **1664** POWER *Exp. Philos.* I. 26 View her with a full light transmitted through a Burning-glass. **1751** JOHNSON *Rambler* No. 156 ₱ 2 Like light transmitted from room to room. **1795** LD. AUCKLAND *Corr.* (1862) III. 313 Imagination transmits some rays of your comfort at Beckenham to my pensive thoughts. **1831** LARDNER *Pneumatics* iv. 267 It is the nature of a fluid to transmit pressure equally in every direction. **1833** HT. MARTINEAU *Charmed Sea* iv. 54 How ..the atmosphere, in its now approaching state, becomes incapable of transmitting sound to any distance. **1842** PARNELL *Chem. Anal.* (1845) 29 Hydrosulphate of ammonia is prepared by transmitting sulphuretted hydrogen gas through solution of ammonia. **1862** *Catal. Internat. Exhib.* II. XII. 2 The motion of the handle on deck is transmitted..by means of a series of shaftings and tooth-wheels. **1866** ROSCOE *Elem. Chem.* (1871) 275 Gold..in thin films, transmits green light. **1878** HUXLEY *Physiogr.* 171 The motion is transmitted from particle to particle, to a great distance.

Hence **Transmi·tted** *ppl. a.*; **Transmi·tting** *vbl. sb.* and *ppl. a.* **1681** R. FLEMING *Fulfilling Script.* (1801) I. 430 Study the transmitting of truth and godliness. **1796** KIRWAN *Elem. Min.* (ed. 2) I. 271 By reflected light, blackish brown; but, by transmitted light, yellowish. **1800** HERSCHEL in *Phil. Trans.* XC. 458, I tried the transmitting capacity of the glass, by exposing it with the rough side towards the sun, over one of the transmitting holes of the apparatus. **1869** HADDAN *Apost. Succ.* iii. (1879) 56 The Church..has been held together compactly by the very fact of its transmitted orders. **1876** PREECE & SIVEWRIGHT *Telegraphy* 137 The battery which is connected to .. the transmitting portion of the apparatus.

**Transmit** (trɑ·ns,mit, -z-), *sb. rare.* [f. prec. vb.; cf. PERMIT *sb.*] An act of transmitting; an order of transmission. Also *attrib.*, as **transmit warrant**, a warrant authorizing transmission. **1672** BP. OF DERRY in *Essex Papers* (Camden) I. 26 That yo[r] Excell[cy] may not judge me heedles of that transmit to y[e] King before my leaving Dublin. **1741** W. WILSON *Contn. Def. Reform. Princ. Ch. Scot.* (1769) 407 Their petition could not get the common right of a transmit to the assembly. **1908** *Daily Chron.* 11 May 1/5 The Court signed a transmit warrant for the conveyance of Mrs. Cleary to Claremorris, and she left with the police escort yesterday.

**Transmittable** (trɑns,mi·tăb'l, -z-), *a. rare.* Also less correctly -ible. [f. as prec. + -ABLE; cf. ADMITTABLE.] That may be transmitted; transmissible. In quot. 1655, ? capable of being 'thrown' across. **1611** COTGRAVE, *Transmissible*, Transmittable. **1655** MRQ. WORCESTER *Cent. Inv.* § 73 A transmittible Gallery over any Ditch or Breach in a Town-wall. **1882** F. DARWIN in *Nature* 20 Apr. 581/2 A heliotropic stimulus is transmittable from one part of an organ to another. **1889** *Pall Mall G.* 1 Aug. 6 A virulent, contagious and transmittable disease.

**Transmittal** (trɑns,mi·tăl, -z-). *rare.* [f. as prec. + -AL.] The action of transmitting; transmission. *Letter of transmittal*, an official letter in which the recipient is informed that certain documents are transferred to his custody. *U.S.* **1724** SWIFT *Drapier's Lett.* vii, The prodigious profit which England receives by the transmittal thither of two thirds of the revenues of this whole Kingdom. **1813** *Brand's Pop. Antiq.* I. Pref. 7 In the transmittal of vulgar rites and popular opinions. **1904** *Athenæum* 18 June 788/1 The letter of transmittal..is dated July 1st, 1899.

**Trans,mi·ttance.** *rare.* [f. as prec. + -ANCE: cf. *admittance*.] The action of transmitting; transmission. **1855** in H. CLARKE *Eng. Dict.*; and in later Dicts.

**Trans,mi·ttant.** *rare*[−1]. [irreg. f. TRANSMIT *v.* or L. *transmittĕre* + -ANT. (L. analogy would give **transmittent*).] One who transmits; an official transmitter. **1855** MILMAN *Lat. Chr.* XIV. ii. VI. 406 The transmittants, the sole transmittants, of those graces and blessings which emanate from Christ.

**Transmitter** (trɑns,mi·tǝɹ, -z-). [f. TRANSMIT *v.* + -ER [1].] One who or that which transmits. **1727** SAVAGE *Bastard* 8 He lives to build, not boast a generous Race: No Tenth Transmitter of a foolish Face. **1775** JOHNSON *Tax. no Tyr.* 73 The transmitters of wrong. **1822** *New Monthly Mag.* V. 417 [Not] the inventor, but merely the 'transmitter' of a jest. **1874** L. STEPHEN *Hours in Library* (1892) II. i. 6 The great bulk of mankind are transmitters rather than originators of spiritual force. **1904** *Brit. Med. Jrnl.* 17 Sept. 672 The *stegomyia fasciata* (the transmitter of yellow fever).

**b.** *spec.* That part of a telegraphic or telephonic apparatus by means of which messages are transmitted or dispatched; a transmitting instrument: opposed to RECEIVER 7.

Also, the part of a stethoscope which transmits the sounds to the ear of the operator (quot. 1901).

**1876** PREECE & SIVEWRIGHT *Telegraphy* 251 The chief faults which are met with in the Transmitter are broken spiral springs and chains, or loose adjusting screws. **1878** G. B. PRESCOTT *Sp. Telephone* (1879) 9 The tone transmitter ..connected by a metallic conductor with the tone receiver.. at the distant station. **1888** *Pall Mall G.* 30 May 11/2 The operator sits watching at his transmitter on the Downs, while another attends in breathless expectation at the instrument in the Haymarket. **1889** PREECE & MAIER *Telephone* 5 The transmitter is the instrument into which the words are spoken. **1901** *Munsey's Mag.* XXIV. 522/2 Dr. Schmuetzer placed the stethoscope over his heart,.. with the rubber transmitters stuck in his ears. **1902** SLOANE *Electr. Dict.*, *Transmitter*, in general electric phraseology, any instrument which produces signals to be transmitted through a line or circuit...Thus the Morse key in telegraphy or the Blake transmitter in telephony are examples.

**c.** *attrib.* **1876** PREECE & SIVEWRIGHT *Telegraphy* 129 Fig. 90..contains a plan of the transmitter switch. **1892** *Pall Mall G.* 27 Apr. 7/2 A phonoporic receiver will not be actuated by impulses whose speed is regulated by a transmitter reed tuned to a different note from its own. **1904** *Electr. World & Engin.* 21 May 987 To overcome this difficulty [of being overheard by persons near] a transmitter hood has been patented. This is a metallic box adapted to be fastened upon the transmitter.

**Transmittible**, var. form of TRANSMITTABLE.

† **Trans,mo·dify**, *v. Obs. rare*[−1]. [f. TRANS- 2 + MODIFY.] *trans.* To modify in transmission. *a* **1774** TUCKER *Lt. Nat.* (1834) II. 673 Squibs of witticism, stolen and transmodified from the storehouse of philosophy.

**Transmogrify** (trɑns,mǫ·grifǝi), *v. vulgar* or *humorous.* Also 7-9 -mografy, -mography, -mogriphy, 8 -migrafy, -mugrify. [Origin uncertain: see Note below.] *trans.* To alter or change in form or appearance; to transform, metamorphose (utterly, grotesquely, or strangely). **1656** S. HOLLAND *Zara* vi. (1719) 33 So that he remained for a time as one trans-elemented. [*Note*] Meaning transmografide, or metamorphosed into a Mandrake. **1671** MRS. BEHN *Amorous Prince* III. iii, I wou'd Love would transmogriphy me to a maid now. **1688** SHADWELL *Sqr. Alsatia* III. i. 39, I know I am Transmography'd; but I am your very Brother, Ned. **1725** *New Cant. Dict.*, *Transmogrify*, or rather *Transmigrafy*. **1728** FIELDING *Love in Sev. Masques* v. iv. 68, I begin to think..that some wicked Enchanters have transmographied my Dulcinea. **1736** tr. *Ruggle's Ignoramus* III. 35 I'll go put on my other Dress, and be transmogrify'd to Dulman. **1751** WARBURTON *Lett.* (1809) 85 The first volume of the Divine Legation..is so transmogrified that you will hardly know it again. **1753** SMOLLETT *Ct. Fathom* xxiv, Thou art so transmographied, and bedaubed, and bedizened. **1786** BURNS *Addr. Unco Guid* v, Social life and Glee sit down,..Till, quite transmugrify'd, they 're grown Debauchery and Drinking. **1844** *Blackw. Mag.* LVI. 777 By proper clipping and pruning..an ingenious editor might transmogriphy these simple epistles into the philippics of Junius. *a* **1888** MARY HOWITT *Autobiog.* (1889) II. 278 It was transmogrified by the addition of two storeys and a flat roof.

**b.** To astonish utterly, confound. *dial.* **1887** P. M'NEILL *Blawearie* 84 We..made our way here and are quite transmogrified to find everything so outrageously transformed. **1888** *Berks. Gloss.* (E.D.S.), *Transmogrivied*,..surprised, greatly astonished.

[*Note.* If the original form was (as suggested in quot. 1725) *transmigrafy*, this may have been a vulgar or uneducated formation in *-fy* from TRANSMIGURE, or TRANSMIGRATE *vb.* (cf. TRANSMIGRATION 3 b). Apparently, it was originally *persons* that were 'transmografied', or metamorphosed.]

Hence **Transmo·grified**, **Transmo·grifying** *ppl. adjs.*; also **Transmo:grification** (-fikēi·ʃǝn), the action of transmogrifying, (strange or grotesque) transformation; **Transmo·grifier** (-fǝi,ǝɹ), one who transmogrifies. **1661** K. W. *Conf. Charac.*, *Hide-Parke Lady* (1860) 58 It must march at least thrice to the botchers for *transmogrification. **1694** MOTTEUX *Rabelais* v. ii. 6 The Transmogrification of the Macrobian Children into Swans. *a* **1878** SIR G. G. SCOTT *Recoll.* i. (1879) 47 The Tower..has undergone strange transmogrifications. *c* **1832** MRS. SHERWOOD in *Life* xxx. (1847) 529 We were led..over our *transmographied terrace. **1842** BARHAM *Ingol. Leg.* Ser. II. *St. Aloys*, The transmogrified Pagan perform'd his vow. **1676** *Poor Robin's Intell.* 13-20 June 2/1 A notable fewd between a Translator of Shooes and a *Transmogrifier of Garments, that is to say betwixt a Cobler and a Botcher. **1841** *Fraser's Mag.* XXIII. 338 Our modern transmogrifiers and parodists of ancient architecture. **1832** J. P. KENNEDY *Swallow B.* xliii, It [love] is the most *transmogrifying passion. **1904** *Longm. Mag.* Dec. 149 The transmogrifying process is being carried out only too rapidly.

**Transmontane** (trɑns,mǫ·ntēin, -mǫntēi·n), *a.* [In quot. *c* 1400 a. OF. *transmontane* adj. and sb., altered form of *tramontane*, pole-star, north pole, also *transmontanie* north wind (Godef.); in later use ad. L. *transmontānus*: see TRAMONTANE.]

**1.** Dwelling or situated beyond, or on the other side of, the mountains; = TRAMONTANE A. 1. **a.** From the Italian point of view: North of the Alps. **1727** BAILEY vol. II, *Transmontane*, dwelling or growing beyond the Mountains. **1826** K. DIGBY *Broadst. Hon.* II. *Tancredus* (1846) II. 20 The Britons, English, and other transmontane people. **1857** *Fraser's Mag.* LVI. 503 The proud citizens of Rome witnessed with indignation the influx of a crowd of transmontane artists. **1880** J. NICHOL *Byron* viii. 139 To abandon their transmontane plans, and agree to take up their head-quarters at Pisa.

**b.** In reference to other mountains, e. g. the Grampians in Scotland, the Rocky Mountains in N. America, the Blue Mountains in N. S. Wales. Also of traffic, across or over the mountains. **1884** *Science* 22 Feb. 220/1 Keeping back the migration..in order to monopolize this transmontane commerce. **1890** 'R. BOLDREWOOD' *Col. Reformer* (1891) 124 The transmontane towns. **1897** D. L. LEONARD in *Home Missionary* (N.Y.) Jan. 450 Just now [1842-6] it was that the entire transmontane region was added to the Union. **1900** W. WATT *Aberdeen & Banff* i. 4 The northern or transmontane Picts.

† **2.** *Transmontane star*, also absol. *transmontane*, the north pole-star; = TRAMONTANE B. 1. *Obs.* *c* **1400** MAUNDEV. (1839) xvii. 180 In þat lond, ne in many othere beȝonde þat, noman may see the sterre transmontane, ..þat wee clepen the lode-sterre. *Ibid.*, The sterre þat is clept the transmontayne. *Ibid.* 181 Aȝen þat transmontayne is the toþer sterre, þat is clept Antartyke.

Hence † **Transmonta·nian** *a. Obs. rare*[−1], of or pertaining to the non-Italian section of the Roman Church: cf. TRANSALPINE 1 c. **1624** T. SCOTT *Aphorisms of State* 8 Carion, Auentine, Cuspinianus, and other Transmontanian Writings.

**Transmorphism** (trɑns,mǭ·ɹfiz'm). *rare*[−1]. [f. TRANS- + Gr. μορφή form + -ISM: cf. METAMORPHISM.] Transformation of one thing into another, as in the process of evolution. **1888** SHOREY in *Amer. Jrnl. Philol.* IX. 417 The Democriteans evolve the higher from the lower by the operation of chance... We will..substitute for the guess of transmorphism the assertion of a metaschematism intentionally devised for ethical ends.

**Trans,mou·ld,** *v.* [f. TRANS- 2 + MOULD *v.*[2]] *trans.* To mould into another form or shape. **1855** PUSEY *Doctr. Real Presence* Note Q. 218 It seemed good to..the Maker of all things, to transmould (μεταπλαττειν) the living creature to incorruption. **1860** — *Min. Proph.* 259 God is all-powerful, and transmouldeth easily the nature of things which are, to what He willeth.

† **Trans,mou·nt,** *v. Obs. rare.* [f. TRANS- 2 + MOUNT *v.*] *trans.* To surmount; to pass over or across by mounting. **1600** HOLLAND *Livy* XLIII. xx. 1168 These embassadours having transmounted the top of the hill Scordus. **1601** — *Pliny* VIII. lviii. I. 233 The wild Asses [never] transmount that hill which devideth Cappadocia from Cilicia.

† **Trans,mo·ve,** *v. Obs. rare*[−1]. [In form, f. TRANS- 2 + MOVE *v.*, but in quot., app. mistakenly

used for *transmeue*, *-mewe*, *-mywe*, early forms of TRANSMEW, TRANSMUE, and rimed with *love*, *prove*.] *trans.* To transform, transmute, 'transmew'.

1590 SPENSER *F. Q.* III. xi. 43 Saturne..That to a Centaure did him selfe transmoue.

**Transmue**: see TRANSMEW.

**Transmundane** (trɑns₁mʊ·ndeɪn), *a.* [f. TRANS- 3 + L. *mund-us* world: cf. *mundane*.] That is or lies beyond the world.

1777 J. RICHARDSON *Dict. Persian, Arab.*, etc., Dissert. 29/1 Every ingenious critic may then, like Archimedes of old, require only some transmundane station on which to rear his engines; in order to shake to pieces the reason of man. 1859 G. MEREDITH *R. Feverel* iii, One of the most ancient theories of transmundane dominion and influence on mundane affairs. 1899 W. JAMES *Talks to Teachers on Psychol.* 24 Whatever of transmundane metaphysical insight..we may carry.

**Transmural** (trɑns₁miūə·răl), *a.* [f. TRANS- 3 + L. *mūr-us* wall: cf. *mural*.] That is beyond a wall or walls; *spec.* beyond the Roman Wall.

1851 D. WILSON *Preh. Ann.* (1863) II. III. ii. 67 Within the transmural province. 1911 *Edin. Rev.* Apr. 488 With the fourth century this transmural area was lost.

**Tra·ns-mu·scle.** [TRANS- 6.] A crossing or transverse muscle.

1836–9 *Todd's Cycl. Anat.* II. 956/2 We have seen similar trans-muscles lying above the membrane.

**Transmutability** (trɑns₁miūtăbi·lĭti, -z-). [f. next: see -ITY. Cf. med.L. *transmūtābilitās* (Aquinas, *a* 1274), It. *trasmutabilità* (Florio, 1611), F. *transmutabilité* (*Dict. Acad.*, 1762).] The quality of being transmutable; susceptibility of being changed into something else.

1611 FLORIO, *Trasmutabilita*, transmutability. 1669 W. SIMPSON *Hydrol. Chym.* 60 The transmutability of one salt into another. 1879 tr. *De Quatrefages' Hum. Spec.* 38 A variability which I fully accept, has nothing in common with the transmutability of Lamarck, Geoffroy, and Darwin. 1905 *Speaker* 26 Aug. 499/1 In chemistry..transmutability has survived merely as a wild and hopeless surmise.

**Transmutable** (trɑns₁miū·tăb'l, -z-), *a.* [ad. med.L. *transmūtābilis* (Albertus Magnus, *a* 1250), f. L. *transmūt-āre* to TRANSMUTE: cf. *mutable*.] Capable of being transmuted or changed into something else.

1460–70 *Bk. Quintessence* I. 14 Oure 5-essencie is þe instrument of alle vertues of þing transmutable if þei be putt in it, encreessynge an hundrid foold her worchingis. 1545 RAYNOLD *Byrth Mankynde* 20 By contynuall circulation of the matter transmutable, she maye brynge her pourpose to passe. 1652 FRENCH *Yorksh. Spa* ii. 6 All Elements are mutually transmutable into one the other. 1731 *Hist. Litteraria* II. 379 Animal Substances are..more easily transmutable into animal Juices than vegetable. 1879 tr. *De Quatrefages' Hum. Spec.* 39 Lamarck, Geoffroy, Darwin and his school, consider the species not only as variable but as transmutable. 1896 *Buffalo* (U. S.) *Current Hist.* VI. 3 *note*, Professor Dewar and others have shown the X rays to be transmutable into light rays affecting the eye.

†**b.** Liable to change, changeable, mutable.

*c* 1430 LYDG. *Min. Poems* (Percy Soc.) 197 The world unsuyr, fortune transmutable. 1509 HAWES *Conv. Swearers* v, Worldly rychesse is often transmutable. 1509 — *Past. Pleas.* xiii. (Percy Soc.) 51 They nothing thynke on fortune variable, Whyche al theyr ryches shal make transmutable.

Hence **Transmu·tably** *adv.*, in a transmutable manner; **Transmu·tableness**, transmutability.

1666 BOYLE *Orig. Formes & Qual.* I. ii, Some learned modern naturalists have conjectured at the easy transmutableness of water. 1680 — *Produc. Chem. Princ.* v. 265 The Aristotelian Hypothesis, of the transmutableness of what they call Elements. 1736 BAILEY (folio), *Transmutably*, in a manner capable of being chang'd.

**Transmutant** (trɑns₁miū·tănt, -z-). *Math.* [ad. L. *transmūtānt-em*, pr. pple. of *transmūtāre* to TRANSMUTE.] (See quot.)

1858 CAYLEY *Math. Papers* II. 515 We may say that the function obtained by replacing..the facients of a covariant or contravariant by the first derived functions of a contravariant or covariant is a Transmutant of the first-mentioned covariant or contravariant.

†**Tra·ns₁mutate,** *ppl. a. Obs.* [ad. L. *transmūtāt-us*, pa. pple. of *transmūtāre* to TRANSMUTE.] Transmuted. (Const. as pa. pple.)

1432–50 tr. *Higden* (Rolls) II. 343 Iupiter..putte her in a schippe in whom he had a bulle depicte, wherefore poetes feyne Iupiter to be transmutate in to the similitude of a bulle. 1668 BAXTER *Dying Th.* (1850) 156 As if the fiery part of the candle were annihilated or transmutate,..when the candle goeth out; and were not fire, and in action still.

†**Tra·ns₁mutate,** *v. Obs. rare.* [f. ppl. stem of L. *transmūtāre* to TRANSMUTE: see -ATE$^3$.] *trans.* = TRANSMUTE 1.

1632 VICARS *Æneid* v. 140 Here fortune her faire face first transmutated. 1659 STANLEY *Hist. Philos.* IX. (1687) 550/2 Solid Bodies, whose Elements are four, Fire, Water, Air, Earth; of all which, transmutated, and totally changed, the World consists. 1659 *Ibid.* XI. 763/1 By immixture of some small thing to be transmutated.

**Transmutation** (trɑns₁miutēi·ʃən, -z-). [a. F. *transmutation* (12th c. Hatz.-Darm.), or ad. late L. *transmūtātiōn-em*, n. of action from *transmūtāre* to change, shift, TRANSMUTE.] The action or process of transmuting or changing; the fact or condition of being transmuted or changed.

**1.** Change of condition; mutation; sometimes implying alternation or exchange. *Obs.* or *arch.*

*c* 1380 WYCLIF *Sel. Wks.* II. 297 þus seiþ James, þat at God is not transmutacioun. *c* 1384 CHAUCER *H. Fame* III. 879 Of dyvers transmutacions Of estates and eke of Regions. *c* 1398—*Fortune* I This wrecched worldes transmutacioun As wele and [*v. r.* or] woo, nowe poure and nowe honour. *c* 1449 PECOCK *Repr.* I. xviii. 107 In lengthe of tyme ful greet transmutacioun and chaunge is alwey maad in and aboute the circumstauncis of politik gouernauncis. *c* 1450 *Mankind* iii. 903 in *Macro Plays* 34 Thynke and remembyr, þe world ys but a wanite, as yt ys prowyd daly by d[i]uerse transmutacyon. 1570 FOXE *A. & M.* (ed. 2) 169/1 Busy you to purchase that palace that euer shal endure in ioy without transmutation. 1851 LONGF. *Gold. Leg.* III. 274 The constant change and transmutation Of action and of contemplation.

**2.** Change of one thing into another; conversion into something different; alteration, transformation. Also with *a* and *pl.* a case or instance of this.

1398 TREVISA *Barth. De P. R.* XIX. l. (xxxiii. in *Bodl. MS.* lf. 302 b/2), Þere may not be passinge transmutacion and chaunginge for þere is defaute of hete & of humoure. 1412–20 LYDG. *Chron. Troy* I. 58 That a sodeyn transmutacioun Was made of amptis to forme of men anon. 1545 RAYNOLD *Byrth Mankynde* 20 When that nature is dysposed to make a transmutation of any matter. 1594 PLAT *Jewell-ho.* III. 65 Alterations, transmutations, & sometimes euen real transubstantiations of white wine into Claret. 1692 BENTLEY *Boyle Lect.* iv. 139 The supposed change of Worms into Flies is no real transmutation. 1725 tr. *Dupin's Eccl. Hist. 17th C.* I. VI. iii. 237 He [Calvin] attacks Transubstantiation. He acknowledges that some of the Ancients made use of the Term Transmutation. 1782 PRIESTLEY *Corrupt. Chr.* II. VI. 7 It is too early..for..the transmutation of the bread and wine. 1879 tr. *De Quatrefages' Hum. Spec.* 9 Here..is no transmutation of force similar to that in a machine worked by electricity or heat. 1896 DK. ARGYLL *Philos. Belief* 69 The inconceivable power of transmutation exerted by that which we call life.

**3.** *spec.* **a.** *Alch.* The (supposed or alleged) conversion of one element or substance into another, esp. of a baser metal into gold or silver. Also *allusively*.

1478 *Coventry Leet Bk.* 422 To practise a true and a profitable conclusion in the Cunnying of transmutacion of metails. 1605 TIMME *Quersit.* III. 183 Alchymie..ordereth and finisheth the transmutations of things. 1750 JOHNSON *Rambler* No. 63 ¶ 7 Not one appears to have desisted from the task of transmutation, from the conviction of its impossibility. 1812 SIR H. DAVY *Chem. Philos.* 11 The processes supposed to relate to the transmutation of metals, and the elixir of life. 1872 YEATS *Techn. Hist. Comm.* 413 Alchemy, or the transmutation of metals, was virtually the parent of the modern science of chemistry.

**b.** *Law.* Transfer: usually *Transmutation of possession*, transfer or change of ownership.

1488–9 *Act 4 Hen. VII*, c. 4 An Acte for the passing and transmutacion of landes without Fyne. *Ibid.*, Such persones ..shall nowe lawfully make therof feoffmentes and transmutacion of possession by dede or dedis..without eny fyne for the said feoffement or transmutacion of possession. 1602 FULBECKE *1st Pt. Parallel* 33 He held that in euery exchaunge there must be a mutuall transmutation of the possession. 1818 CRUISE *Digest* (ed. 2) II. 358, IV. 149. 1876 DIGBY *Real Prop.* vi. 292 In these cases uses are said to be created by a conveyance operating by way of transmutation of possession; that is, they accompany one of the recognised modes of conveying the seisin at common law—feoffment, fine, or recovery.

†**c.** *Rhet.* Transferred use of a word; metonymy. *Obs. rare.*

1553 T. WILSON *Rhet.* 93 Transmutacion helpeth much for varietie, the whiche is when a woorde hath a proper signification of the owne, and beyng referred to an other thyng, hath an other meanyng.

†**d.** = TRANSMIGRATION 4. *Obs. rare*$^{-1}$.

1594 R. ASHLEY tr. *Loys le Roy* 68 b, The transmutation of soules from bodie to bodie.

†**e.** *Her.* = COUNTERCHANGING. Cf. TRANSMUTED b. *Obs.*

1610 GUILLIM *Heraldry* V. ii. 242 Counter-changing or Transmutation is an Entermixture of seuerall Metals or Colours, both in Field and Charge, occasioned by the apposition of some one or moe lines of partition.

**f.** *Biol.* Conversion or transformation of one species into another; *spec.* applied to the form of evolution or development propounded by Lamarck (1815–22). Also *attrib.*

1626 BACON *Sylva* § 525 The Transmutation of Plants, one into another, is *inter Magnalia Naturæ*: for the Transmutation of Species is, in the vulgar philosophy, pronounced Impossible:..but seeing there appear some manifest Instances of it, the Opinion of Impossibilitie is to bee rejected. 1691 RAY *Creation* II. (1692) 91 The most that can be inferred from hence is a transmutation of Species. 1722 WOLLASTON *Relig. Nat.* ix. 194 Transmutation of one species into another. 1859 PAGE *Handbk. Geol. Terms*, *Transmutation*,..a term adopted by Lamarck and his followers to express their hypothetical views of the derivation of existing species from preceding species, by slow and gradual Transmutations of one form of organisation into another form. 1863 LYELL *Antiq. Man* i. 3 Recent modifications of the Lamarckian theory of progressive development and transmutation. 1879 tr. *De Quatrefages' Hum. Spec.* 90 Their ideas may be arranged in two principal groups according as their authors favour a rapid or a gradual transmutation.

**g.** *Math.* †(*a*) = PERMUTATION 3 b (*obs.*). (*b*) = TRANSFORMATION 3 c (*rare* or *obs.*).

1674 JEAKE *Arith.* (1696) 576 Transmutation..serveth to show what Number of Changes may be made by any Number of..things in their Places or Positions. 1743 EMERSON *Fluxions* I. 53 The 21st and all the following Forms relate to the Transmutation of Fluxions.

**4.** *attrib.*, as *transmutation doctrine*, *theory*; **transmutation glaze**, trade name of a porcelain glaze having a changeable iridescent lustre.

1860 HUXLEY *Lay Serm.* xii. (1870) 306 The so-called 'transmutation' hypothesis considers that all existing species are the result of the modification of pre-existing species, and those of their predecessors, by agencies similar to those which at the present day produce varieties and races. 1876 tr. *Haeckel's Hist. Creat.* I. i. 4 The theory which, through Darwin, has been placed at the head of all our knowledge of nature, is usually called the Doctrine of Filiation, or the Theory of Descent. Others term it the Transmutation Theory.

Hence **Trans₁muta·tional** *a.*, of or pertaining to transmutation, esp. in sense 3 f.

1861 WILSON & GEIKIE *Mem. E. Forbes* ii. 41, I can find no room, however, for transmutational ingenuity in writing of Edward Forbes. 1907 *Edin. Rev.* Jan. 31 The crude transmutational theory.

**Trans₁muta·tionist.** [f. prec. + -IST.] One who believes in or advocates a theory of transmutation, esp. that of the transmutation of species in organic nature; a transformist. Also *attrib.*

It might also be, and prob. has been, applied to one believing in the transmutation of metals: an explanation given in Dictionaries from Worcester onward.

1844 *Monthly Rev.* Mar. 384 It is the doctrine of the Transmutationists. 1847 DARWIN in *Life & Lett.* (1887) I. 355 You have introduced several sentences against us Transmutationists. 1850 *Fraser's Mag.* XLII. 368 The author of the *Vestiges*, like the older transmutationists, assumes the mammals of the sea as the ancestors of the mammals of the land. 1866 *Reader* 20 Feb. 153/2 Owen.. pleads..strongly and manfully in favour of the transmutationist doctrine. 1909 *Q. Rev.* Oct. 421 When Darwin first propounded his doctrine of descent..there were few 'transmutationists'.

**Transmutative** (trɑns₁miū·tătiv, -z-), *a.* [ad. med.L. *transmūtātīv-us* (Albertus Magnus *Metaphys.*, *a* 1255), f. L. *transmūtāt-*, ppl. stem of *transmūtāre* to TRANSMUTE: see -IVE.] Having the quality of transmuting; tending to transmute; characterized by transmutation.

1611 SPEED *Hist. Gt. Brit.* IX. vi. (1623) 502 The great Elixar..hath so transmutatiue a faculty, as to make Copper seeme Gold. 1781 *Westm. Mag.* IX. 73 A kind of coagulation which may be called transmutative. 1841 HOR. SMITH *Moneyed Man* III. ii. 50 How little do we mark the effects of Time in ourselves; how suddenly and deeply are we struck by its transmutative touch in others. 1865 GROTE *Plato* I. i. 5 A generative, motive, or transmutative force.

**Trans₁mu·tatory,** *a. rare*$^{-1}$. [f. ppl. stem of L. *transmūtāre*: see next and -ORY.] = prec.

1616 DONNE *Serm.* (1661) III. 323 Love is..a transmutatory Affection, it changes him that loves, into the very nature of that that he loves.

**Transmute** (trɑns₁miū·t, -z-), *v.* Pa. pple. transmuted, also 5–6 transmute. [ad. L. *transmūtā-re*, f. TRANS- + *mūtāre* to change. (Occurs first as variant in MSS. of Chaucer's works.)]

**1.** *trans.* To alter or change in nature, properties, appearance, or form; to transform, convert, turn.

14.. *Chaucer's Troylus* IV. 439 (467) (MS. Gg. 4. 27) Þu muste me fyrst transmute [*v. r.* transmuwen] in to a ston. (14.. *Chaucer's Clerk's T.* 329 (Lansd. MS.) Vnneþ þe peple hire knewe for hire faireness Whan sche transmute was in suche rechesse.) 1494 FABYAN *Chron.* VI. clix. 149 The Emperour hauyng compassion of the forenamyd Barnarde, ..transmutyd the sentence of deth vnto perpetuyte of pryson, & losynge of his syght. 1545 RAYNOLD *Byrth Mankynde* 20 Y$^e$ lyuer: in whome the iuyce of meat, before of colour white, is transmutyd into red. 1583 MELBANCKE *Philotimus* D d iv, When Io was transmute of Ioue into an Hefars forme. 1660 SHARROCK *Vegetables* 29 The colour only or some other easily alterable accidents..are transmuted. 1871 TYNDALL *Fragm. Sc.* (1879) I. x. 310 To transmute its energy..into vibratory motion. 1890 *Century Mag.* May 48/2 The tendency of black plumage to become transmuted into white is a familiar..fact in breeding.

**b.** *Alch.* To change (one substance) into another, esp. a baser metal into gold or silver. Hence *allusively*. Also *absol.*

1610 DONNE *Pseudo-martyr* 94 By a new Alchimy, they doe not onely extract spirit out of euery thing, but transmute it all into spirit. *a* 1661 FULLER *Worthies, Worc.* III. (1662) 173 He is said to have transmuted a brass warming-pan (..onely warming it by the fire, and putting the Elixir thereon) into pure silver. 1750 JOHNSON *Rambler* No. 51 ¶ 11 Some alchymists have obstinately suppressed the art of transmuting metals. 1818 MRS. SHELLEY *Frankenst.* ii. (1865) 51 Metals cannot be transmuted. 1870 M. D. CONWAY *Earthw. Pilgr.* i. 29 You will find the pavements golden only when you can transmute them to gold.

†**c.** *intr.* for *pass.* To undergo transmutation; to change or turn *into* something else. *Obs. rare*$^{-1}$.

1675 G. R. tr. *Le Grand's Man without Passion* 139 His Strength transmutes into Temerity.

†**2.** *trans.* To remove from one place to another; to transport. [So late L. *transmūtāre*.] *Obs. rare.*

*a* 1700 *Life & Death Ld. Shaftsbury* in *Harl. Misc.* (1810) V. 372 His malady..that might transmute his soul into that endless happiness, which he had been so long labouring for. 1817 MAR. EDGEWORTH *Ormond* xxx, I was transmuted to Dublin, to be..lodged in Kilmainham.

Hence **Transmu·ting** *vbl. sb.* and *ppl. a.*

1579 FULKE *Heskins' Parl.* 155 Though we take the word of transmuting for changing, turning, transmuting, or transelementing,..yet meane they not chaunge of one substance into another. 1594 PLAT *Jewell-ho.* I. 45 The earth..by her inwarde heate and transmuting nature..will conuert [etc.]. 1846 TRENCH *Mirac.* i. (1862) 99 An ennobling of the common, and a transmuting of the mean. 1864 MUSGRAVE *Ten Days in Fr. Parsonage* II. v. 150 Efforts..made to employ public education of the poor as a transmuting power.

**Transmuted** (trɑns₁miū·tėd, -z-), *ppl. a.* [f.

prec. + -ED [1].] Changed in form or nature; altered; transformed.

1749 JOHNSON *Van. Hum. Wishes* ad fin., Patience, sov'reign o'er transmuted ill. 1805–6 CARY *Dante's Inf.* XXIX. 35 Who forged transmuted metals by the power Of alchemy. 1871 TYNDALL *Fragm. Sc.* (1879) II. ix. 183 Its matter is for the most part transmuted gas.

† b. *Her.* Of a charge on a field of two tinctures: Having the tinctures of the field reversed; = COUNTERCHANGED. *Obs.*

1486 *Bk. St. Albans, Her.* f ij, He berith quarterly Sable and Siluer with a Cheueron of the sayd colowris transmutit. 1572 BOSSEWELL *Armorie* II. 29, I terme these lyons transmuted because ye lyon first placed in ye fielde, is Sable, in Or, and the other is Or, in Sable. *c* 1828 in BERRY *Encycl. Her.* I. Gloss.

**Transmuter** (trɑnsˌmiū·tər, -z-). [f. as prec. + -ER [1].] One who or that which transmutes.

1826 SCOTT *Diary* 4 June, in *Lockhart*, The translator of Tasso and Ariosto, and in that capacity a noble transmuter of gold into lead. 1870 LOWELL *My Study Wind.* 254 Chaucer exposes the cheats of the transmuter of metals.

**Transˌmu·tive,** *a. rare*[−1]. = TRANSMUTATIVE.

1836 HOR. SMITH *Tin Trump.* (1876) 344 The Chymist, with transmutive art Extracts a poison and a bane.

† **Transˌmu·tress.** *Obs. rare*[−1]. [f. TRANSMUTER + -ESS.] A feminine transmuter.

1660 tr. *Paracelsus' Archidoxis* I. v. 76 This Tincture is a Transmutress of Bodies to a better State.

**Transˌmu·tual,** *a. rare*[−1]. [f. TRANS- 3 + MUTUAL.] Reciprocal, commutual.

1829 COLERIDGE in *Lit. Rem.* (1839) IV. 132 That very discipline, the capability of exercising which in its own specific nature without superinduction of a destructive and transmutual opposite, is the fairest and firmest support of their cause.

**Transmuwe, -mywe,** obs. ff. TRANSMEW.

† **Transˌna·te,** *v. Obs. rare*[−0]. [ad. L. *transnātāre* to swim over.] Hence **Transˌnata·tion, Transˌna·tion.**

1623 COCKERAM, *Transnate*, to swimme ouer. 1864 WEBSTER, *Transnatation*, the act of swimming across. 1911 *Ibid.*, *Transnation.*

**Transˌna·tural,** *a.* [f. TRANS- 4 + NATURAL.] † 1. That is beyond the order of nature; more than natural; supernatural. *Obs.*

1569 SANFORD tr. *Agrippa's Van. Artes* 70 Because they.. are supposed to be aboue nature, therefore they call them transnaturall or Metaphisicke. 1697 J. SERGEANT *Solid Philos.* 248 Great Scholars puzzle their Wits to find out Natural Causes for divers Effects, the true Reason for which is only owing to Trans-natural ones. 1700 —— (*title*) Transnatural Philosophy, or Metaphysicks.

2. Of which the nature is transmuted. *nonce-use.*

1907 E. H. COLERIDGE *C.'s Christabel* 29 The Geraldine of the First Part is a supernatural, of the Second Part a trans-natural being...The idea..of the second Part is.. physiological as well as mythological.

† **Transˌna·turalize,** *v. Obs. rare*[−1]. [f. as prec. + -IZE.] *trans.* = next.

1631 BRATHWAIT *Whimzies, Char. Pedlar* 140 He..turnes most impudent dogmaticall quacksalver. What transnaturalized elixers will this mercenarie mountebanke produce to delude the vulgar.

**Transˌna·ture,** *v.* Now *rare.* [f. TRANS- 2 + NATURE *sb.*] *trans.* To change the nature of.

1567 [see TRANSELEMENT]. 1583 STUBBES *Anat. Abus.* I. (1879) 54 Their curiosity, and nicenes in apparell..transnatureth them, makinge them weake, tender and infirme. 1627 J. CARTER *Plain Expos.* 72 The Soule, being set as a great Empresse in the bodie of man, hath a Favourite or Minion, to which it hearkeneth, and after which it is carried, yea, is euen so changed, and (as it were) transnatured by it, that if it be heauenly, the Soule is likewise heauenly; if earthly it maketh in like manner, an earthly Soule. 1657 REEVE *God's Plea* 156 Repentance..able to transnature and translate people. 1812–29 [see TRANSELEMENT].

Hence **Transˌnatura·tion,** change of nature. *rare.*

1873 F. HALL *Mod. Eng.* viii. 280 Save by effecting a total transnaturation or stagnation of the human mind, how could a language be prevented from undergoing changes?

**Trans-Neptunian**: see TRANS- 7.

† **Transˌnihila·tion.** *nonce-wd.* [f. TRANS- 1 + L. *nihil* nothing + -ATION.] Transformation (of nothing) into nothings.

1820 COLERIDGE *Lett., Convers.*, etc. I. 29 How and whence did this sterile Nothing split or multiply into plurality? Whence this portentous transnihilation of nothing into Nothings?

**Transnivean** (trɑnsˌni·viăn), *a.* [f. TRANS- 3 + L. *nive-us* snowy (f. *nix, niv-em* snow) + -AN.] Being or living beyond the snows (i.e. in quot. beyond the Himalayas).

1854 HOOKER *Himal. Jrnls.* I. v. 127 Earliest intercourse with the trans-nivean races.

† **Transˌno·minate,** *v. Obs. rare.* [f. ppl. stem of L. *transnōmināre* to change the name of, name over again: see TRANS- and NOMINATE.] *trans.* To change the name of. Hence † **Transno·minated** *ppl. a.*

1623 COCKERAM, *Transnominate*, to change one name for another. 1635 HEYWOOD *Hierarch.* VIII. Comm. 523 He also trans-nominated the two moneths of September and October, to Germanicus and Domitian; because in the one he was crowned, and in the other he was borne. 1657 GAULE *Sapient. Justif.* 22 Then seems it so much the more strange..that so many real effects should proceed from a poorly equivocal and transnominated cause.

† **Transˌnomina·tion.** *Obs.* [ad. late L. *transnōminātiōn-em*, rendering Gr. μετωνυμία metonymy: see TRANS- and NOMINATION. Cf. F. *transnomination* (Littré).] A change of name; *spec.* in *Rhet.* = METONYMY.

1561 T. NORTON *Calvin's Inst.* IV. xiv. 94 When the Apostle exhorteth the Ephesians to remembre that they were forein gestes of the testamentes,..he saith, that they were not partakers of Circumcision. Whereby he doth (by figure of transnomination) signifie that they were excluded from the promise it self, which had not receiued the signe of the promise. 1675 BROOKS *Gold. Key* Wks. 1867 V. 256 Oh, happy transnomination! Christ's bride being one with himself..is called, 'the Lord our righteousness'. 1715 KETTLEWELL *Chr. Obedience* 11 An ordinary figure..which the rhetoricians call a metonomie or transnomination, and that is a transferring of a word, which is the particular name of one thing to express another.

**Transˌno·rmal,** *a.* [f. TRANS- 4 + NORMAL.] Outside the bounds of the normal; beyond or above the normal.

1860 FARRAR *Orig. Lang.* (1865) 53 The 'transnormal' character of these tongues only proves that they are the work of minds incapable of all subtile analysis. 1875 A. W. WARD *Eng. Dram. Lit.* Introd. 23 The distinctive features which already his [Euripides'] quickwitted contemporaries found mirrored in his transnormal productions.

**Trans-oceanic** (trɑnsˌōuʃiˌæ·nik, -z-), *a.* [f. TRANS- + OCEANIC. Cf. F. *transocéanique* (Littré).] 1. Existing or situated beyond the ocean; also *transf.* pertaining to a region beyond the ocean.

1827 *Blackw. Mag.* XXII. 602 Their pristine transoceanic partiality for dram-drinking. 1872 *Daily News* 25 Mar., Then, England..employed her influence..in establishing the principle..of a threepenny rate for European letters, and a sixpenny rate for those intended for trans-oceanic countries. 1899 *Dublin Rev.* Jan. 67 Glimpses of a transoceanic world. 1902 J. LEIGHTON in *Publ. Circ.* 8 Feb. 156/2 This device was ..admired by our transoceanic relatives.

2. Passing or extending across the ocean.

1868 LYELL *Princ. Geol.* (ed. 10) II. III. xli. 420 We probably still remain ignorant of many means of transoceanic migration. 1884 *Q. Rev.* Apr. 453 The most vigilant supervision was exercised over the means of inland and transoceanic transport. 1892 *Times* 2 May 9/2 In 1871..the total transoceanic emigration from the United Kingdom was 252,435.

**Transˌo·cular,** *a.* [f. TRANS- 5 + L. *ocul-us* eye: cf. *ocular.*] Lying across the eye: applied to a longitudinal stripe or colour marking.

1872 COUES *Key N. Amer. Birds* 20 When these [lines] are continuous through the eye, they form a transocular line. 1876 *Proc. Zool. Soc.* 20 June 660 The crown being pure white, with only a transocular line on each side of the head.

**Transom** (træ·nsəm). Forms: 5 traunsum, -som, -sone, trampsoun, -sown, tramson, 6 trawnsom, (transumpt), transume, -same, 6–7 -sam, 6–9 -sum, -some, 7 -summe, 6– transom. [Late ME. *traunsum, -som*, of obscure history; but app. (as held by Prof. Skeat), a corruption of L. *transtrum*, of which it is the exact equivalent in sense. L. *transtrum* was a derivative of *trans*, or the root *tra-* across, with the instrumental *-trum* = Gr. -τρον, Indo-Eur. *-trom*.

No connecting forms between *transtrum* and *transum* have been found; but perh. the latter was a workmen's corruption, which had assumed this form before it came to be written down: cf. PEDIMENT. (Florio's spelling *transtroms* in 1598 and 1611 can only be taken as his own emendation of the Eng. word after It. *transtri*; he knew also the form *transoms*.)

The obscurity of the history is increased by the fact that senses 5 and 6 and the combination *transom-nail* are known of earlier date than the architectural and naval senses, which being those of L. *transtrum* would etymologically be earlier.]

1. In building, etc.: A cross-beam or cross-piece, esp. one spanning an opening to carry a superstructure; a lintel.

1487–8 *Rec. St. Mary at Hill* 137 Item, for v quarteres for traunsones, xd. 1519 HORMAN *Vulg.* 138, I hytte my heed ageynst the soyle or transumpt. 1538 ELYOT, *Transtra*, transoms which do go ouerwhart a house, also the seates etc.]. 1577 HARRISON *England* II. x, They are inforced for want of stuffe to vse no studdes at all, but only raysines, groundselles, transomes, and vpright principalles. 1598 FLORIO, *Transtri*, crosse or ouerthwart beames, transtroms [1611 Transtroms or crosse-beames]. *Ibid.*, *Trasti*...Also a transome or beame going crosse a house [1611 transoms or crosse beames]. 1667 PRIMATT *City & C. Build.* 63 Suppose a Shop-window to be twenty foot front,..the Brestsummer will take up twenty six foot of Timber,..the two Transums for the Stalls eight foot. 1682 WHELER *Journ. Greece* I. 18 [An arch] whose two Lintel-Posts, and Transome, are of three whole Stones. 1879 FARRAR *St. Paul* II. 12 [The Temple of Diana at Ephesus] Its doors..surmounted by transoms so vast and solid that the aid of miracles was invoked to account for their elevation.

b. The transverse top-beam of a gallows, a swing, or the like; the lintel stone of a trilith.

1615 G. SANDYS *Trav.* 56 Swinging vp and downe, as boyes do in bell-ropes: for which there be gallowses..of an exceeding height..by two ioyning ropes that are fastned aboue, they will swing themselues as high as the transome. 1796 MORSE *Amer. Geog.* II. 112 (Stonehenge) The transomes, or over-thwart stones, are quite plain. 1865 LUBBOCK *Preh. Times* v. (1878) 116 Circles of uprights and transoms at Stonehenge.

c. A beam resting across a saw-pit to support the log.

1885 *Cheshire Gloss.*, *Transom*, the cross piece of wood that holds up the log on a saw-pit. A *back-transom* is a spare one always kept under the log for safety. 1888 ELWORTHY *W. Somerset Gloss.*, *Transum*, a cross bearer used by sawyers to support the end of the piece. A spare support thrown across the pit would be also called a transum.

2. A horizontal bar of wood or stone across a mullioned window, dividing it in height; also, a cross-bar separating a door from the fan-light above it (Ogilvie, 1882).

1502 *Privy Purse Exp. Eliz. of York* (1830) 25 To John Conewey smyth for foure transoms and xij standardes [of iron for a window]. 1575 LANEHAM *Let.* (1871) 50 Foour great wyndoz a froont,..euery one a fyue foot wide, az many mo eeuen abooue them, diuided on all parts by a transum and Architraue. 1611 COTGR., *Meneau de fenestre*, the transome, or cross-barre of a window. 1663 GERBIER *Counsel* 19 The middle Transoms of them [windows] above six foot..since otherwise the middle Transome would be opposite to a mans eye. 1805 *T. West's Antiq. Furness* 365 The wooden mullions and transoms contained in the great [window] were placed there in 1796. 1871 *Athenæum* 29 July 151 The lancet windows of the principal story are long triplets, of ample width, and divided horizontally by broad transoms of sculptured work.

b. Short for *transom window*: A window divided by a transom; also a small window above the lintel of a door. *U.S. colloq.*

1844 KINGLAKE *Eöthen* v. 61 The transom that looks longwise through the street. 1882 *Harper's Mag.* Nov. 893 In trying to climb through the transom into the car he took hold of the guide rope. 1883 *Century Mag.* XXV. 588/2 The dim light that streamed into the room from the transom. 1908 W. CHURCHILL *Mr. Crewe's Career* x, The buzz of talk which he had heard through the closed transom.

3. In technical applications. † a. The vane of a cross-staff (CROSS-STAFF 2): see quot. 1696. *Obs.*

1594 BLUNDEVIL *Exerc.* VII. xii. (1597) 322 b, A new kind of crosse staffe, hauing 3 transames or crosses. 1696 PHILLIPS (ed. 5), *Transome*,..the Vane of a Cross Staff, or Wooden Member, to be set a-cross the cross Staff, having a Socket in it, upon which it slides stiff upon the Square of the Cross Staff, and may be set to any of the Graduations of it.

† b. The transverse member in a cross. *Obs.*

1615 G. SANDYS *Trav.* 184 For it [the Cross of Christ] was framed..of foure seuerall woods; the foot of Cedar, the bole of Cypresse, the transome of Palme, and the title of Oliue. 1658 SIR T. BROWNE *Gard. Cyrus* i. 96 Some [crosses] being right, and of one single peece without traversion or transome. 1864 R. S. HAWKER *Quest of Sangraal* 33 [The Southern Cross] a Pentacle of stars, whereof two shone for the Transome and three for the Stock.

c. A cross-piece connecting the cheeks of a gun-carriage.

1688 R. HOLME *Armoury* III. xviii. (Roxb.) 138/2 The transomes, are the peeces of wood which hold the cheekes or Limbres togather. 1828 J. M. SPEARMAN *Brit. Gunner* (ed. 2) 114 The 68-pounder carriage has, in addition to the breast transom.., a centre and horizontal one. 1853 STOCQUELER *Milit. Encycl.*, *Transoms*, in artillery, pieces of wood which join the cheeks of gun-carriages. There is but one in a truck-carriage, placed under the trunnion-holes; and four in a wheel-carriage—the trail, the centre, the bed, and the breast-transoms.

d. *Carriage-building.* In a perch-carriage, Each of two cross-timbers (*fore* and *hind transom*) framed across the perch, and upon which the springs are fixed.

1794 W. FELTON *Carriages* (1801) I. iii. 46 The fore transom, or fore spring-bar, is the most essential part of the cross framings. It is a strong timber fixed to the perch by means of a hooping-piece. 1877 G. G. THRUPP *Hist. Coaches* ii. 32 The carriage is composed of a transom in front with a perch..fastened to it.

e. Each of the transverse timbers joining the sides in the frame of a railway carriage bogie-truck.

1891 in *Cent. Dict.*

f. *pl.* On a railway: Cross-timbers laid between (or, formerly, beneath) longitudinal sleepers.

1838 *Civil Eng. & Arch. Jrnl.* I. 341/1 On the Great Western Railway..the longitudinal sleepers have been laid on transoms and piles. 1872 *Daily News* 15 July, For nearly a mile the transoms have been torn up and smashed, the ballast ploughed up, and the line otherwise injured. 1892 *Pall Mall G.* 23 May 1/3 The 'transoms' are the cross-timbers which hold the longitudinal sleepers at their proper distance apart.

g. The seat of a throne; also, a couch or seat built at the side of a cabin or state-room on board ship.

1883 F. M. CRAWFORD *Dr. Claudius* vii, The Duke was extended on a transom. *Ibid.* ix, He sat down on the transom. 1896 *Daily News* 19 May 5/2 Each throne has also been furnished with new transomes covered with crimson velvet.

4. *Shipbuilding.* † A cross-beam in the frame of a ship (*obs.*); *spec.* each of several transverse beams bolted to the stern-post, which support the ends of the decks and determine the breadth of the stern at the buttocks.

1545 ELYOT, *Canonia*, the transomes in a shyppe, whereon the hatches are made. 1584 B. R. tr. *Herodotus* II. xcvi. 94 They vnite and ioyne the plancks together..binding the same to many transomes that goe both crosse and longe wayes for the strength of the vessell. 1624 SIR W. MONSON *Tracts* (Navy Rec. Soc.) IV. 47 The transom is a timber that lies athwart the stern, and lays out the breadth of the ship at the buttock, which is her breadth from her tuck upwards. 1748 *Anson's Voy.* III. ii. 219 The long boat, which was at this time moored a-stern, was on a sudden canted so high, that it broke the transom of the Commodore's gallery. 1770 COOK *Voy. round World* II. vi. (1773) 398 The 27th and 28th were spent in refitting the ship.., fixing a transom for the tiller, getting stones on board. 1871 BLACKMORE *Maid of Sker* 65 Part of the taffrail was carried away, but the transom and transom-knees stood firm.

**b.** Short for *transom-frame* (see in 7); hence in *Boat-building*, a board similar in shape and position to a transom-frame: see quot.

**1857** P. COLQUHOUN *Comp. to Oarsman's Guide* 28 The stern-post is scarfed on, and upon it comes the transom, that heart-shaped piece of board, found in all cutter-built boats, and secured to the sax-board by transom grips or horizontal knees.

†**5.** Short for *transom-nail*. *Obs. rare.*

**1423** in Rogers *Agric. & Prices* III. 448/4 Hornchurch. Transom. 1 m. @ /10. **1427** *Rec. St. Mary at Hill* 65 Also payd for ij^m^l traunsum, þe m^l x d..xx d. Also pay for iij m^l sprigge, þe m^l ix d..xxvij d.

†**6.** ? A bolster; or part of a bedstead answering the same purpose. *Obs.*

The editor of the *Bury Wills* remarks 'the transome is usually considered to be that part of the bedstead which is between the two head-posts..but the general association of the word with feather beds would lead us to think the bolster was meant'.

[**1459**: ? implied in TRANSOMER.] **1463** *Bury Wills* (Camden) 23, ij peyre of good shetes, the trampsoun, the costerys of that chambyr. **1479** *Ibid.* 53 A traunson. **1482** MARG. PASTON in *P. Lett.* III. 288 To John Heyth a materas with a traunsom, a peire shetes, a peire blankettes, and a coverlight. **1522** *Bury Wills* (Camden) 115 A ffetherbed, ij trawnsoms, a matras, ij pelowes, iiij payer of schetes. [**1570** LEVINS *Manip.* 161/44 Ye Transome of a bed, *trabula*.]

**7.** *attrib.* and *Comb.*, as *transom-shaft*, *-stone*; *transom-shaped* adj. (2 b); **transom-bar**, the cross-bar over a door having a fan-light above it (*U.S.*); †**transom-eyed** *a.*, having a transom or beam (BEAM *sb.*[1] 3 c) in the eye; **transom-frame** (*Shipbuilding*), the aftermost 'square-frame' of a ship, giving shape to and supporting the stern, and bolted to the stern-post; **transom-grip** (*Boat-building*), an angular fastening analogous to a *transom-knee*; **transom-knee** (*Shipbuilding*), each of the curved timbers or angle-irons by which the transoms are fastened to the stern-timbers; **transom-lattice**, a transverse lattice; **transom-lifter**, an apparatus for controlling and fastening the fan-light over a door (*U.S.*); †**transom-nail**, a small size of nail, formerly in use; ? a lath nail; **transom-rib**, a transverse rib; **transom road** (*U.S.*), a railway track on longitudinal sleepers with transoms between them; **transom-stern** (*Shipbuilding*), a vessel's stern formed by or taking its shape from a transom; **transom-window** = 2 b: see quot. 1688.

**1909** *Cent. Dict. Supp.*, **Transom-bar*. **1601** BP. W. BARLOW *Defence* 67 Thus these *transam-eyed hypocrites can spie small motes in Vs. **1874** THEARLE *Naval Archit.* 85 A deep transverse frame, termed a '*transom frame', situated at the fore ends of the rudder-post, and connected thereto. **1857** *Transom-grip [see 4 b]. **1769** FALCONER *Dict. Marine* (1789), *Courbes d'arcasse*, the *transom-knees, or sleepers. *c* **1850** *Rudim. Navig.* (Weale) 156 *Transom-knees*, knees bolted to the transoms and the side of the ship. **1689** E. HOWARD *Caroloiades* 273 A *transom Lattise did divide that Room. **1359** *Letter-bk. G. London* lf. 83 Item in D. de lathes ij s. iij d. & ob. Item in Ml. & D. de *trasonna(i)l, xviij d. Item in Ml. & D. de Sprig' xv d. **1424** *Hornchurch Account* 2 & 3 Hen. VI. (New Coll. Oxf.), In .Ml. de traunsumnayl emptis pro domo capellani..x.d. **1835** R. WILLIS *Archit. Mid. Ages* vii. 85 The principal distinction between these [kinds of vaulting] and our own fan vaulting, is the substitution of lozenge-headed compartments in the fans for the English horizontal *transom rib. **1813** SCOTT *Rokeby* v. iv, The moon through *transom-shafts of stone, Which crossed the latticed oriels, shone. **1844** KINGLAKE *Eöthen* v. 60 The *transom-shaped windows suspended over your head. **1770** PENNANT *Zool.* IV. 53 In the interstices between the upright and *transome stones of Stone-henge. **1688** R. HOLME *Armoury* III. 473/2 A *Transome window, hath Cross barrs in it, at the third part of its height. **1837** MARY HOWITT *Rur. Life* III. v. (1862) 264 The state apartments are lofty and spacious, with numerous transom windows.

Hence **Tra·nsomed** (-səmd) *a.*, divided by or having a transom or transoms; †**Transomer**, (?) a case or slip for a bolster: cf. sense 6.

**1848** B. WEBB *Sk. Cont. Ecclesiol.* 276 The window is *transomed midway. **1876** T. HARDY *Ethelberta* (1890) 3 Lifting his eyes to the mullioned and transomed windows and moulded parapet above him. **1881** *Athenæum* 13 Aug. 216/1 The hall..is lighted by three transomed windows. **1459** *Paston Lett.* I. 480 Canvas in the Warderop and fyne Lynen Clothe of dyvers sortes..ix. berys for fetherbeddys. Item, iiij. *transomers.

†**Transon**, *v. Obs. rare.* Also 6 transsene. [ad. F. *tranςonner*, formerly also *transonner* (14–16th c. in Godef.) to cut into segments or pieces, cut up, carve, variant form of *tronçonner*, f. *tronçon*: see TRUNCHEON *sb.*] *trans.* To carve (an eel).

**1513** *Bk. Keruynge* in *Babees Bk.* (1868) 265 Transsene that ele. **1688** R. HOLME *Armoury* III. 78/2 Transon the Eel.

**Transonance** (trɑ·nsənăns). [f. TRANS- + L. *sonănt-em* sounding: see -ANCE.] The passage of the sound produced in one organ (e.g. the heart) through the substance of another (e.g. the lung).

**1909** in *Cent. Dict. Supp.*

**Trans,o·rbital**, *a.* [f. TRANS- 5 + ORBIT: cf. *orbital*.] Drawn or measured across between the orbits or eye-sockets.

**1852** DANA *Crust.* I. 92 Trans-orbital breadth small.

**Tra:ns-Paci·fic** (trɑns-, trɑnz-), *a.* [TRANS- 7, 8.] **a.** Across or crossing the Pacific Ocean. **b.** On the other side of the Pacific.

**1891** *Scribner's Mag.* Sept. 280/2 A newly organized trans-pacific service, running by way of Yokohama to Vancouver. **1897** *Daily News* 30 Jan. 6/1 The proposed 'All-British Trans-Pacific Cable'. **1906** *Athenæum* 17 Feb. 193/3 The Cardinal's Trans-Pacific experiences have accustomed him to such liberties.

**Transpadane** (trɑ·ns,pădēⁿn), *a.* (*sb.*) Also 7 -an. [ad. L. *transpadānus* adj. and sb., f. *trans* across + *Padus* the river Po, *padānus* of the Po. Cf. F. *transpadan, -ane* (Littré).] That is beyond the river Po (from Rome); opposed to *cis-padane*. **b.** *sb.* One living north of the Po.

*Transpadane Republic*, a republic formed by Bonaparte in 1796, consisting of Lombardy and part of Venetia.

**1617** MORYSON *Itin.* III. 106 Lombardy of old was part of Gallia Cisalpina, which the River Padus..divides into Cispadan (on this side the Po) and Transpadan (beyond the Po). *Ibid.*, Transpadane..containes the Dukedome of Milan. **1797** BURKE *Regic. Peace* iii. Wks. VIII. 311 Is it to the Cispadane or to the Transpadane republicks..that we address all these pledges? **1896** *Q. Rev.* Oct. 396 The enfranchisement of the Transpadane Gauls. *Ibid.*, So much for Caesar and his Transpadanes!

**Trans,pa·latine**, *a.* and *sb.* [TRANS- 5: cf. PALATINE *a.*[2]] **a.** *adj.* Extending transversely across either half of the palate. **b.** *sb.* The transpalatine bone in certain sauropsidan vertebrates.

**1891** in *Cent. Dict.* **1893** *British Museum Catalogue, Snakes* I. 71 Maxillary, palatine, and pterygoid movable; transpalatine present. **1899** in *Syd. Soc. Lex.*

**Trans,pa·lmar**, *a. Anat.* [ad. mod.L. *transpalmār-is*, f. TRANS- 5 + L. *palma* PALM *sb.*[2]: cf. *palmar*.] Extending across the palm of the hand, as the *transpalmar muscle*.

**1891** in *Cent. Dict.* **1899** in *Syd. Soc. Lex.*

†**Trans,pa·re**, *v. Obs. rare.* [f. after TRANSPARENT; cf. med.L. *transpārē-re*, f. *trans*, TRANS- 1 + *pārēre* to appear, show oneself; It. *transparere* (Florio, 1598).] *intr.* **a.** To be or become transparent. **b.** To appear or be visible through a transparent medium.

**1604** EARL STIRLING *Aurora* lxxiii, Oft haue I wish'd..That th' Alabaster bulwarke might transpare, And that the pillars rarer then they are, Might whiles permit some hapning rayes to passe. *Ibid.* xcix, But through the yce of that vniust disdane, Yet still transpares her picture and my paine. **1661** BLOUNT *Glossogr.* (ed. 2), *Transpare*.., to appear through, to be evident, or clear.

**Transparence** (trɑns,pēᵊ·rĕns). *rare.* [f. as next: see -ENCE, and cf. F. *transparence* (*c* 1400 in Godef. *Compl.*).] = TRANSPARENCY 1.

**1594** CAREW *Huarte's Exam. Wits* (1616) 84 That which cannot be read, with oyle is made legible, by yeelding thereto a brightnesse and transparence. **1598** FLORIO, *Trasparenza*, a transparence or through-light. **1619** DRAYTON *Man in Moon* 332 Cleere Amber..Through whose transparence you might easly see The beds of Pearle whereon the Gum did sleepe. **1845** R. W. HAMILTON *Pop. Educ.* x. (ed. 2) 270 Motive may be detected through the transparence of tendency. **1866** J. G. MURPHY *Comm. Exod.* xxiv. 10 Adamantine solidity, transparence, and brilliancy.

†**b.** *transf.* = TRANSPARENCY 2. *Obs.*

**1635** HEYWOOD *Hierarch.* IX. 575 The casements standing wide Clearely through that transparance is espy'de This Glutton. **1789** E. DARWIN *Bot. Gard.* IV. 343 O'er her light limbs the dim transparence plays, And the fair form it seems to hide, betrays.

**Transparency** (trɑns,pēᵊ·rĕnsi). [ad. med.L. *transpārēnti-a* (Du Cange), f. *transpārēnt-em*: see next and -ENCY.]

**1.** The quality or condition of being transparent; perviousness to light; diaphaneity, pellucidity.

*Thermal transparency*, perviousness to heat rays; diathermancy; cf. TRANSPARENT 1 b.

**1615** H. CROOKE *Body of Man* 556 It is like a thinne and pollished horne of a Lanthorn, not only in transparencie by which meanes it receiueth the light, but also in his substance. **1651–3** JER. TAYLOR *Serm. for Year* I. xviii. 238 His wife may, by seeing the beauties and transparency of that Crystall, dresse her minde and her body by the light of so pure reflexions. **1705** ADDISON *Italy* 26 The Clearness and Transparency of the Stream. **1750** tr. *Leonardus' Mirr. Stones* 36 A stone with a transparency, or a kind of brightness. **1830** HERSCHEL *Stud. Nat. Phil.* 141 Between transparency and opacity there would at first sight appear a direct opposition. **1860** MAURY *Phys. Geog. Sea* (Low) vi. § 313 The atmosphere is transparency itself. **1900** *Jrnl. Soc. Dyers* XVI. 7 The particles retain their form and transparency.

*fig.* **1843** CARLYLE *Past & Pr.* II. i, Written in its child-like transparency. **1866** GEO. ELIOT *F. Holt* v, The transparency of his talk..gave a charm even to his weaknesses.

**2.** That which is transparent; a transparent object or medium.

**1591** HARINGTON *Orl. Fur.* III. xvi, To make transparencies to meete in one And so convey the sunne-beames where you will. **1784** COWPER *Task* v. 151 A watery light Gleamed through the clear transparency.

**b.** *spec.* A picture, print, inscription, or device on some translucent substance, made visible by means of a light behind.

**1807** E. ORME (*title*) Essay on Transparent Prints, and on Transparencies in general. **1859** GULLICK & TIMBS *Paint.* 9 A mode of painting 'transparencies' as they would now be called, on linen.

*attrib.* **1855** W. WILLIAMS (*title*) Transparency painting on linen for decorative purposes.

**c.** A photograph or picture on glass or other transparent substance, intended to be seen by transmitted light. Also *attrib.*

**1874** CORBET *Venus at Isle of Desolation* 104 (Cassell), I took transparencies of the little photos. he took of my station. **1885** C. G. W. LOCK *Workshop Receipts* Ser. IV. 357/2 A negative or transparency is not fully developed much under 15 minutes. **1892** *Photogr. Ann.* II. 576 Various transparency printing frames. **1897** J. NICOL in *Outing* (U.S.) XXX. 496/2 The transparency plate and negative are placed in the printing frame exactly as in printing on paper.

†**3.** *Her.* An outline figure, or the shadow of a charge, without the charge itself, painted the same colour as the field, but of a darker tint: = ADUMBRATION 4. *Obs.*

**1610** GUILLIM *Heraldry* II. iii. 42 Adumbration or Transparency is a cleere exemption of the substance of the Charge..in such sort, as that there remaineth nothing thereof to be discerned, but the..bare proportion of the outward lineaments thereof. *Ibid.* vii. 65 The Orle..is an Ordinarie composed of a threefold line duplicated, admitting a Transparancie of the field, thorowout the..space therein enclosed. **1725** COATS *Dict. Her.* s. v. *Adumbration*, Some term such Adumbration, Transparency.

**4.** A burlesque translation of the German title of address *Durchlaucht*: cf. SERENITY 4.

**1844** THACKERAY *B. Lyndon* ix, Hobnobbing..with lovely excellencies, nay, with highnesses and transparencies themselves. *Ibid.*, Pippi..had kept back a note of hand 'her High Transparency' gave us. **1848** — *Van. Fair* lxii, His Transparency the Duke and his Transparent family..come and occupy the great box in the middle. **1895** *Westm. Gaz.* 7 Feb. 2/1 During the sojourn of grand transparencies beneath your Derbyshire roof.

**Transparent** (trɑns,pēᵊ·rĕnt), *a.* (*sb.*) Also 5 -paraunt, 6–7 -parant. [ad. med.L. *transpārēnt-em*, pr. pple. of *transpārēre* (= '*pellūcēre*' Du Cange), f. TRANS- + *pārēre* to appear, be visible. In 15th c. app. stressed *transparau·nt*, after F. *transparent* (14th c. in Hatz.-Darm.).]

**1.** Having the property of transmitting light, so as to render bodies lying beyond completely visible; that can be seen through; diaphanous.

**1413** *Pilgr. Sowle* (Caxton) I. iii. (1859) 4 The erthe seemyd me al clere and transparaunt, soo that I myght see clerely al that was withynne. **1432–50** tr. *Higden* (Rolls) VI. 425 A vesselle made of onichinus, transparente, and polischede by so subtile an arte þat [etc.]. **1588** SHAKS. *L. L. L.* IV. iii. 31 Nor shines the siluer Moone one halfe so bright, Through the transparent bosome of the deepe. **1667** MILTON *P. L.* VII. 265 The Firmament, expanse of liquid, pure, Transparent, Elemental Air. **1712–14** POPE *Rape of Lock* II. 61 Transparent forms, too fine for mortal sight. **1807** Transparent Prints [see TRANSPARENCY 2 b]. **1813** BAKEWELL *Introd. Geol.* (1815) 37 Uncrystallized quartz is seldom transparent, most frequently translucent, but sometimes opaque. **1868** LOCKYER *Elem. Astron.* iii. § 23 (1879) 125 Both head and tail [of a comet] are so transparent that all but the faintest stars are easily seen through them.

**b.** *transf.* Pervious to heat-rays.

**1871** B. STEWART *Heat* (ed. 2) § 178 It is probable that no substance is perfectly transparent with respect to heat. **1883** *Illustr. Lond. News* 24 Feb. 203/3 A table of various substances, some of which are opaque to light and transparent to heat, and the reverse.

†**c.** That shines through; penetrating, as light.

**1593** SHAKS. *2 Hen. VI*, III. i. 353 Like to the glorious Sunnes transparant Beames. **1593** T. WATSON *Tears of Fancie* xxxi, My loues transparent beames and rosy colour.

†**d.** Apparent or visible through something. Cf. TRANSPARE *v.* b. *Obs.*

**1609** DANIEL *Civ. Wars* IV. ii, Which, though..Thou ouerlay'st with fayrest colourings; Yet th' vnder-worke, transparent, shewes too plaine. **1712** STEELE *Spect.* No. 490 ¶ 7 To my fond Eyes she all transparent stood.

†**e.** Admitting the passage of light through interstices. *Obs. rare.*

**1617** MORYSON *Itin.* III. 141 Not farre thence is a transparant and pleasant, but little Wood. **1693** CONGREVE in *Dryden's Juvenal* XI. (1697) 280 He, whose thin transparent Rags, declare How much, his tatter'd Fortune wants repair.

**2.** *fig.* **a.** Frank, open, candid, ingenuous.

**1590** SHAKS. *Mids. N.* II. ii. 104 Transparent Helena, nature shewes art, That through thy bosome makes me see thy heart. **1635** R. CAREW in *Lismore Papers* (1888) Ser. II. III. 217 They are very well beloued for their ciuill and transparent carriage towards all sorts. **1878** T. HARDY *Ret. Native* I. iv, An ingenuous, transparent life was disclosed. **1891** E. PEACOCK *N. Brendon* II. 306 She was transparent as the daylight.

**b.** Easily seen through, recognized, understood, or detected; manifest, evident, obvious, clear. Cf. APPARENT 3.

**1592** SHAKS. *Rom. & Jul.* I. ii. 96 Then turne teares to fire: And these who often drown'd could neuer die, Transparent Heretiques be burnt for liers. **1638** CHILLINGW. *Relig. Prot.* I. ii. § 150. 111 Your Argument against us, is a transparent fallacy. **1710** STEELE *Tatler* No. 197 ¶ 5 In Courts, they make transparent Flatterers. **1867** FREEMAN *Norm. Conq.* I. v. 347 A transparent artifice..paralyses them. **1869** J. MARTINEAU *Ess.* II. 178 The fallacy of the remark is transparent. **1879** MᶜCARTHY *Own Times* II. xviii. 37 The transparent sincerity of his purpose.

**Trans,pa·rently**, *adv.* [f. prec. + -LY [2].] In a transparent manner or degree; so as to be seen through.

**1617** MORYSON *Itin.* III. 81 [Amber] after it is polished, becomes transparantly bright. **1628** tr. *Mathieu's Powerfull Favorite* 34 It is so minced and subtile, that falshood may be transparently seene through it. **1667** H. STUBBE in *Phil. Trans.* II. 497 The Sea was black and thick, not transparently blue, as before. **1851** HAWTHORNE *Snow Image, etc. Gt. Stone Face* (1879) 39 One enormous pane of glass, so transparently pure. **1861** *Sat. Rev.* 23 Nov. 526 The counter scheme..is much more transparently futile.

**Transˌpa·rentness.** *rare.* [f. as prec. + -NESS.] The quality of being transparent; = TRANSPARENCY 1.

**1727** in BAILEY vol. II. **1762** tr. *Busching's Syst. Geog.* VI. 619 The water..besides its perfect transparentness is of a most grateful taste. **1880** *Christy Carew* I. iii. 136 A dull night sky, starless, but with a clear transparentness.

**Transˌpa·rish,** *v. humorous nonce-wd.* [TRANS- 2.] *trans.* To transport beyond the parish.

**1819** SYD. SMITH in Lady Holland *Mem.* (1855) II. 187 If it blow before it rains, we shall all be up in the air in the shape of dust, and..transparished we know not where.

† **Transˌpa·ss,** *v. Obs. rare.* [= obs. F. *transpasser* 'to passe or goe through, to passe ouer' (Cotgr.), in med.L. *transpassāre* to go beyond (Du Cange), f. TRANS- + F. *passer*, med.L. *passāre* to pass. Cf. also It. *trapassare* 'to passe through, away, or over, to decease, to die' (Florio 1598), 'to passe from life to death' (ibid. 1611). Cf. TRESPASS *v.*]

**1.** *intr.* To pass away, depart, die.

**1592** DANIEL *Descr. Beauty* Wks. (1717) 422 Thy Form and flatter'd Hue, Which shall so soon transpass, Is far more fair than is thy Looking-glass.

**2.** *intr.* To pass or penetrate across or through; also *trans.* to pass beyond (a boundary or limit).

**1626** T. H[AWKINS] *Caussin's Holy Crt.* 176 It is impossible to deceyue God, whose eye..transpasseth through the abysses. **1629** MAXWELL tr. *Herodian* (1635) 320 Had transpassed the banks and bounds of the Roman Empire. **1646** J. GREGORY *Notes & Obs.* 74 The River Hyphasis..he transpassed, and set up Altars on the other side.

† **Transˌpa·ssable,** *a. Obs. rare.* [f. prec. + -ABLE.] Admitting of being passed through or over; capable of being crossed.

**1614** RALEIGH *Hist. World* I. (1634) 98 The navigable River of Tygris..which is everywhere transpassable by boates of great burthen. **1668** CULPEPPER & COLE *Barthol. Anat.* III. vi. 140 The foremore and deeper parts [of the lateral ventricles of the brain] are near to the Mammillary processes, and..they are in some manner transpassable.

† **Transˌpa·ssage.** *Obs. rare*⁻¹. [f. TRANS- 1 + PASSAGE: cf. prec.] Passage over or across.

**1603** DANIEL in *Florio's Montaigne* (1632) Pref. Verse, T'applaud his happy setling in our land: And safe transpassage by his studious care Who both of him and us doth merit much.

† **Transˌpa·tronize,** *v. Obs. rare*⁻¹. [TRANS- 2.] *trans.* To transfer from one to another the patronage of (something).

*a* **1609** WARNER *Alb. Eng.* IX. *To Sir G. Carey* ii, To transpatronize from him To you mine orphant Muse.

† **Transˌpea·r,** *v. Obs. rare.* Also -peer. [By-form of TRANSPARE, on analogy of *peer*, PEAR *v.*, *appear, compear.*] *intr.* To appear or become visible through something; also *fig.* to be apparent.

*c* **1645** HOWELL *Lett.* VI. lv, Those proofs..are not so clear, as those which break out, and transpeer through the dark clouds of adversity. **1654** Z. COKE *Logick* A ij, By this time then it transpears, That, as Nature needs Grace, so Grace desireth Nature.

**Transpeciate** (trɑnˌspī·ʃiˌeit), *v.* Now *rare.* [f. TRANS- + L. *speciēs* look, appearance, form, kind, SPECIES + -ATE 3.] *trans.* To change into a different form or species; to transform.

**1643** SIR T. BROWNE *Relig. Med.* I. § 30, I do not credit..that the Devil hath a power to transpeciate a man into a Horse. **1694** WESTMACOTT *Script. Herb.* (1695) 77 Revived and transpeciated into a quite different and highly useful form. **1721** BAILEY, *Transpeciated*,..changed from one species to another. **1894** G. S. HALL in *Forum* (N.Y.) May 309 There is no better test of educational institutions..than ..how far the lower has been transpeciated into the higher.

Hence **Tranˌspecia·tion,** transformation; change from one form or species into another.

**1867** MAUDSLEY *Physiol. Mind* 164 Transpeciation is a word used by Sir Thomas Brown which might be found useful at the present day. **1870** — *Body & Mind* 175 For the exaltation and transpeciation of force and material. **1883** — *Body & Will* II. iii. 132 First, that there has been what we may call a *nisus* of evolution in nature, and, secondly, that progressive transpeciations of matter have been events of it.

**Transˌpe·netrable,** *a. rare.* [f. TRANS- 1 + PENETRABLE.] Penetrable from side to side.

**1615** JACKSON *Creed* IV. II. vi. § 7 The body of the earth (which is not transpenetrable by any light) is directly interposed between the sun and moon.

**Transˌpe·ritone·al,** *a. Anat.* [f. TRANS- 5 + L. *peritonēum*: cf. *peritoneal.*] Traversing the peritoneal cavity. Hence **Transpe·ritone·ally** *adv.* So **Transpe·ritone** *a.*

**1891** *Cent. Dict.*, Transperitoneal. **1899** *Syd. Soc. Lex.*, Transperitone. **1900** *Lancet* 18 Aug. 487/1 A case of transperitoneal ligature of the left common iliac artery. **1903** *Ibid.* 6 June 1591/1 The external iliac artery was ligatured transperitoneally just below its origin.

**Transpicuous** (trɑnˌspi·kiuˌəs), *a.* [f. med. or mod.L. *transpicu-us*, f. L. *transpic-ĕre* to look or see through (f. TRANS- + *specĕre* to look), on analogy of *conspicuous, perspicuous.*] That can be seen through; pervious to vision.

**1638** WILKINS *New World* I. (1684) 75 Of this Opinion also was *Cæsar la Galla*, whose Words are these, 'The Moon doth there appear Clearest, where she is Transpicuous [*luna est transpicua*], not only through the Superficies, but the Substance also. **1667** MILTON *P. L.* VIII. 141 That light, Sent from her [the earth] through the wide transpicuous aire, To the terrestrial Moon. **1762–71** H. WALPOLE *Vertue's Anecd. Paint.* (1786) IV. 258 Light corridores, and transpicuous arbours through which the sun-beams play. **1910** *Athenæum* 9 Apr. 432/3 A region of mist..no instrument of science can render transpicuous to our eyes.

**b.** *fig.* Of language, etc.: Plain, clear in meaning; also *gen.* easily perceived or detected; manifest. Cf. TRANSPARENT 2.

**1877** PATMORE *Unknown Eros* I. 2 The lonely suns, the mystic hazes and throng'd sparkles bright That..In sweet transpicuous words, shall glow alway. **1896** T. HUTCHINSON in *Academy* 28 Mar. 256/1 Far-reaching and luminous thought..incarnated in language correspondingly grave and transpicuous, or ardent and sublime. **1908** *Month* Jan. 8 Why should we not have new words, so they be musical and their meaning transpicuous?

Hence **Tranˌspi·cuously** *adv.*, clearly (in meaning).

**1839–52** BAILEY *Festus* xx. 358 To speak transpicuously of things Divine Pertaineth not to nature.

**Transpierce** (trɑnsˌpīᵊ·ɹs), *v.* [a. F. *transpercer*, f. TRANS- + *percer* to pierce. Cf. TRESPERCE.]

**1.** *trans.* To pierce through from side to side (with the agent or the instrument as subject: cf. PIERCE *v.* 1).

**1594** DRAYTON *Idea* i, Then transpierce the Coarse. **1624** HEYWOOD *Gunaik.* III. 160 She snatcht up a sword with which she transpierst her selfe. **1697** DRYDEN *Æneid* II. 68 The sides transpierced return a rattling sound. **1725** POPE *Odyss.* x. 188, I launch'd my spear, and with a sudden wound Transpierc'd his back, and fix'd him to the ground. **1857** DUFFERIN *Lett. High Lat.* xii. (ed. 3) 364 He falls, transpierced by many wounds.

**b.** *transf.* and *fig.*: esp. said of the effect of emotion, and the action of wind, light, sight, etc.

**1598** DRAYTON *Heroic. Ep., C'tess Salisbury to Bl. Prince*, Is that great hart, that did aspire so hie, So soone transpersed with a womans eye? **1601** DANIEL *Civ. Wars* VI. cxiv, Whereof the proofe was such As sharpest pride could not transpearce the same. **1664** EVELYN *Kal. Hort., Mar.* (1729) 197 The sharp Easterly and Northerly Winds transpierce, and dry them up. **1788** GIBBON *Decl. & F.* xlvi. IV. 479 *note*, The eye of Tacitus seems to have transpierced the camp of the Parthians and the walls of the haram. **1841–4** EMERSON *Ess., Spir. Laws* Wks. (Bohn) I. 67 The divine question which searches men, and transpierces every false reputation.

**2.** To make one's way through; to pass through, penetrate; in quot. 1908, to extend through. *rare.*

**1604** W. HARBERT *Poems* (Grosart) 92 If England's loadestarre..Could the firme center's regiment transpearse. **1796** KIRWAN *Elem. Min.* (ed. 2) I. 93 Compound spar...In a porcelain heat, it vitrifies with the crucible, which it transpierces. **1908** *Athenæum* 6 June 701/3 A metal rod..transpierces the box.

Hence **Transpie·rced** *ppl. a.*; **Transpie·rcing** *vbl. sb.* and *ppl. a.*

**1592** DANIEL *Compl. Rosamond* Wks. (1717) 42 Transpiercing Rays of christal pointed Eyes. **1627–77** FELTHAM *Resolves* II. xlv. 247 Such transpiercings as rankle the flesh within. **1838** MRS. BROWNING *Isobel's Child* x, Dear Lord, who spreadest out above Thy loving, transpierced hands.

**Tranˌspi·nal,** *a. Anat.* [ad. mod.L. *transpīnālis*, f. TRANS- + L. *spīna* SPINE.] Of a muscle: Lying between two successive transverse vertebral processes; = INTERTRANSVERSE.

**Transpirable** (trɑnˌspəiᵊ·răb'l), *a.* [ad. med. or mod.L. *transpīrābilis*, or a. F. *transpirable* (*c* 1560 Paré): see TRANSPIRE and -ABLE.] Admitting of transpiration; capable of being breathed through.

**1578** BANISTER *Hist. Man* I. 7 Neither would substance of such, be anything so transpirable as were in that Case expedient. **1611** COTGR., *Transpirable*, transpirable, easie to breath out or through. **1674** R. GODFREY *Inj. & Ab. Physic* 69 So long as we live, our whole Body..is transpirable, and exspirable. **1687** A. LOVELL tr. *Thevenot's Trav.* I. 260 A Bardaque, or Pot, that is Transpirable. **1720** QUINCY tr. *Hodges' Loimologia* 212 The Body must be kept transpirable. **1870** ROLLESTON *Anim. Life* 121 To keep the gill-plates lubricated and transpirable by their secretion.

Hence **Transpirabi·lity,** the quality of being transpirable.

**1864–72** WATTS *Dict. Chem.* II. 821 Transpirability of Gases. **1870** ROLLESTON *Anim. Life* 35 The transpirability of the skin.

†**Tranˌspi·rately,** *adv. Obs. rare*⁻¹. [f. mod.L. **transpīrāt-us*, pa. pple. of *transpīrāre* to TRANSPIRE + -LY 2.] By or in the way of transpiration.

(But possibly a misprint for *transpiratively*.)

**1578** BANISTER *Hist. Man* I. 6 b, Those grosse..fumosities (which otherwise by the seamy Commissures, would transpirately euaporate).

**Transpiration** (trɑnˌspirēᵊ·ʃən). [ad. med. or mod.L. *transpīrātiōn-em*, n. of action from *transpīrāre* to TRANSPIRE; perh. through F. *transpiration* (1541 in Hatz.-Darm.).] The action or process of transpiring.

**1.** Exhalation through the skin or surface of the body; formerly, also, evaporation. Also *concr.* matter transpired.

**1562** BULLEYN *Bulwark, Dial. Soarnes & Chir.* 16 b, Expulsed, or auoided by inuisible transpiracion, whiche is one of the forces, or benefits of nature. **1605** TIMME *Quersit.* I. xv. 75 Mercury and sulphur doe vanish away by an insensible transpiration. **1707** *Curios. in Husb. & Gard.* 10[illegible] A viscous humour,..a plain Transpiration from the Plan[t] **1718** OZELL tr. *Tournefort's Voy. Levant* I. 131 It supple[s] and mollifies the Skin, thereby facilitating Transpiratio[n] **1826** KIRBY & SP. *Entomol.* IV. xli. 130 The substanc[e] secreted appears to be a transpiration through the pores o[f] the body. **1879** G. GLADSTONE in *Cassell's Techn. Educ.* IV. 204/1 The products of transpiration are always of a more or less oily nature. **1898** P. MANSON *Trop. Disease[s]* xxii. 338 The excessive loss of fluid by cutaneous transpiration creates a powerful thirst.

†**b.** Emanation, effluence. *Obs. rare.*

**1652** J. WRIGHT tr. *Camus' Nat. Paradox* x. 248 It i[s] probable that by some kinds of transpiration, or by the means of Spirits, things acted at a distance are conveyed to persons absent, and represented to them in their sleep. **167[5]** TRAHERNE *Chr. Ethics* 74 A mystery..perhaps founded in a grateful transpiration of spirits from one to the other.

**c.** *fig.* Outflow (of affection, etc.).

**1821–30** LD. COCKBURN *Mem.* 268 Always beloved for the constant transpiration of an affectionate and cheerful heart.

**2.** *Bot.* The exhalation of watery vapour from the surface of the leaves and other parts of plants, in connexion with the passage of water or sap through the tissues.

**1551** TURNER *Herbal* I. P ij, The floures and leues..whiche ..by ventyng out or transpiration maketh rype and digesteth. **1786** JEFFERSON *Writ.* (1859) II. 56 These leaves having a power of keeping themselves cool by their own transpiration, they impart no heat to the air by contact. **1878** MACNAB *Bot.* iv. (1883) 99 The water that plants give off as watery vapour by transpiration through the stomata.

*attrib.* **1895** OLIVER tr. *Kerner's Nat. Hist. Plants* I. 276 The bundles of woody cells and vessels..serve as conductors of the transpiration current. *Ibid.* 280 The stomata or transpiration-pores which pierce the epidermis of the leaf.

**3.** *Physics.* The passage of a gas or liquid under pressure through a capillary tube or porous substance.

**1867** HIRST in *Brande & Cox's Dict. Sc.*, etc. s. v., The transpiration of a gas is uninfluenced by the material of which a tube is constructed; it increases with pressure—the greater the density, the shorter the time of transpiration. **1870** ATKINSON tr. *Ganot's Physics* (ed. 4) § 132 For the same gas, the rate of transpiration increases, other things being equal, directly as the pressure.

**4.** The action or fact of something transpiring or becoming indirectly known; also, that which transpires (i. e. in quot. (*erron.*) happens). *rare.*

**1802–12** BENTHAM *Ration. Judic. Evid.* (1827) III. 110 Causes of transpiration..disclosure, with or without treachery, on the part of one or more of the co-delinquents. **1908** *Academy* 7 Mar. 529/2, 'I there prosecuted my enquiries and observed for myself what transpired'. The transpirations are disappointing.

†**Tranˌspi·rative,** *a. Obs. rare.* [f. ppl. stem of med. or mod.L. *transpīrāre* to TRANSPIRE + -IVE.] Having the quality of transpiring, or a tendency to transpire.

**1578** BANISTER *Hist. Man* I. 7 As if it should not haue passage out, after a certaine transpiratiue manner. **1662** J. CHANDLER *Van Helmont's Oriat.* 181 The whole arterial bloud..dispersed by the transpirative evaporation of the Body. **1753** N. TORRIANO *Gangr. Sore Throat* 55 The transpirative Matter,..carried back into the Mass of Humours, corrupts not only the Fluids,..but also the Solids.

**Transpiratory** (trɑnˌspəiᵊ·rătəri), *a. rare.* [f. as prec. + -ORY 2.] = prec.

**1855** in H. CLARKE *Eng. Dict.* Hence **1860** in WORCESTER; and in later Dicts.

**Transpire** (trɑnˌspəiᵊ·ɹ), *v.* [ad. med. or mod. L. **tran(s)spīrāre* (f. TRANS- + *spīrāre* to breathe), or a. F. *transpirer* (*c* 1560 in Paré).]

**1.** *trans.* To emit or cause to pass in the state of vapour through the walls or surface of a body; *esp.* to give off or discharge (waste matter, etc.) from the body through the skin; of plants: to give off (watery vapour); also, to exhale (an odour); to breathe forth (vapour or fire).

**1597** A. M. tr. *Guillemeau's Fr. Chirurg.* 40 b/1 When as we desire to transpire, and cause to evaporate, any venomouse vapours. **1647** CRASHAW *Hymn, 'Name of Jesus'*, With wider pores..More freely to transpire That impatient fire. **1664** EVELYN *Sylva* (1776) 29 It transpires the rest of the liquid at the Summites and tops of the branches into the atmosphere. **1774** GOLDSM. *Nat. Hist.* (1862) I. viii. 37 At the [quicksilver] mines near the village of Idra..some in a manner transpiring quicksilver at every pore. **1815** KIRBY & SP. *Entomol.* (1828) I. vi. 201 Aphides that transpire a cottony excretion. **1840** J. BUEL *Farmer's Comp.* 122 Some species transpiring their weight of moisture every twenty-four hours. **1878** MACNAB *Bot.* iv. (1883) 101 For the same reason cut flowers wither. The leaves transpire more fluid than the stem can take up. **1908** A. BENNETT *Old Wives' T.* III. ii, The air was heavy with the natural human odour which young children transpire.

**b.** To cause (a gas or liquid) to pass through the pores or walls of a vessel.

**1864–72** WATTS *Dict. Chem.* II. 820 The volume [of gas] transpired in equal times is inversely as the length of the tube. **1889** ANDERSON in *Nature* 19 Sept., Not only are gases occluded, but they are also transpired under favourable conditions of temperature and pressure.

**c.** *fig.* To cause to pass like breath. *rare.*

**1641** J. JACKSON *True Evang. T.* I. 37 As if Severus had transpired his soule into Maximinus,..he now became the Wolfe, and Leopard.

**2.** *intr.* Of a body: † To emit vapour or perfume; to give out an exhalation (*obs.*); of the animal body (or a person): to give off moisture through the skin; to perspire (*obs.* exc. as rendering Fr. *transpirer*); now only of plants: to give off watery vapour from the surface of leaves, etc.

1648 HERRICK *Hesper., Appar. of Mistr. Calling him to Elizium* 7 This, that, and ev'ry thicket doth transpire More sweet than storax from the hallowed fire. 1673 O. WALKER *Educ.* 68 Exercises and recreations..such..as may cause the body to transpire plentifully. 1844 KINGLAKE *Eöthen* xviii. (1864) 237, I saw that the Doctor was transpiring profusely. 1878 MACNAB *Bot.* iv. (1883) 102 When the plant is transpiring most rapidly and most water is moving through the stem, the wood cells and vessels are filled with air. 1885 *Jrnl. R. Microsc. Soc.* Oct. 826 If transpiration is suddenly stopped in branches which ordinarily transpire strongly, the leaves fall.

**3.** *intr.* Of a volatile substance: To pass out as vapour through pores (in the human body or any porous substance), to exhale; of a liquid: to escape by evaporation.

1643 DIGBY *Observ. Relig. Med.* (1644) 81 In bodies which have internall principles of Heat and Motion, much continually transpiring out to make roome for the supply of new aliment. 1687 A. LOVELL tr. *Thevenot's Trav.* II. 62 Through these Jars the water transpires and percolates into an earthen Vessel underneath. 1746–7 HERVEY *Medit.* (1818) 161 A fragrance .. peculiarly rich and reviving transpires from its opening tufts. 1794 G. ADAMS *Nat. & Exp. Philos.* II. xiii. 17 Moisture can transpire through our skin. 1815 KIRBY & SP. *Entomol.* (1818) I. ii. 29 One of those species [of Aphides] from the skin of which transpires a white cottony secretion. 1889 ANDERSON in *Nature* 19 Sept., Common coal-gas under high pressure transpires through the steel of the containing vessel.

**b.** *transf.* and *fig.* of non-material things.

1752 A. MURPHY *Gray's-Inn Jrnl.* No. 2 Anxiety and Solicitude, which soon transpire into the Face. 1753 *Ibid.* No. 51 An elegant Way of Thinking, which will be always sure to transpire into their Compositions. 1886 STEVENSON *Dr. Jekyll* ii, The mere radiance of a foul soul that thus transpires through, and transfigures, its clay continent.

†**c.** *trans.* To pass through the pores of. *Obs. rare*⁻¹.

1754 MILES in *Phil. Trans.* XLVIII. 526 Occasioned..by warm steams transpiring the earth.

**4.** *fig.* 'To escape from secrecy to notice' (J.); to become known, esp. by obscure channels, or in spite of secrecy being intended; to 'get wind', 'leak out'.

1741–2 HT. BUTLER *Mem.* (1841) II. 96 Yesterday's quarrel may transpire. 1748 LD. CHESTERFIELD *Let. Dayrolles* 26 Jan., This letter goes to you, in that confidence, which I.. place in you. And you will therefore not let one word of it transpire. 1754 RICHARDSON *Grandison* xxxvii. (1781) I. 265 Can he have so many Love-secrets, and yet will he not let them transpire to such a Sister? 1799 *Hull Advertiser* 1 June 2/4 The Hamburgh mail..has just arrived, but no particulars have transpired. 1821 JEFFERSON *Autobiog. & Writ.* (1892) I. 131 What passed between them did not transpire. 1856 FROUDE *Hist. Eng.* II. vii. 143 The conditions of the contract were not allowed to transpire. 1905 R. BAGOT *Passport* xxx, Not allowing the fact of there being any difficulty..to transpire to Donna Bianca.

¶**b.** Misused for: To occur, happen, take place. Evidently arising from misunderstanding such a sentence as 'What had transpired during his absence he did not know'. App. began in U.S. about 1800; registered in Webster's Dict. 1828 (not in Webster 1806).

[1802 M. CUTLER in *Life*, etc. (1888) II. 92 The most trying scene which has transpired through the course of this long and interesting discussion.] 1804 *Age of Inquiry* (Hartford, Conn.) 46 When..the reformation transpired in England.. almost the whole nation rejoiced. 1810 F. DUDLEY *Amoroso* I. 14 Could short-sighted mortality..foresee events that are about to transpire. 1828 WEBSTER, *Transpire*...3. To happen or come to pass. 1841 W. L. GARRISON in *Life* (1889) III. 16 An event .. which we believe transpired eighteen hundred years ago. 1848 DICKENS *Dombey* xxxii, Few changes—hardly any—have transpired among his ship's company. 1858 HAWTHORNE *Fr. & It. Note-bks.* I. 225 Accurate information on whatever subject transpired. 1883 L. OLIPHANT *Altiora Peto* I. 277 His account of what transpired was so utterly unlike what I expected.

¶**c.** Of time: To elapse. *Obs. rare. erron.*

1824 C. WORDSW. *Who wrote Eikon Basilike* 197 The interval of years which had transpired between the conversations and the account of them. 1827 — *Chas. I* 1 Whether in the interval which has transpired, the convictions at which I had arrived,..have been in any material degree confirmed, shaken, or modified.

Hence **Transpi·red** *ppl. a.*, **Transpi·ring** *vbl. sb.* and *ppl. a.*

1670 MAYNWARING *Physician's Repos.* 21 A strengthening or transpiring Medicine. 1693 A. VAN LEEUWENHOEK in *Phil. Trans.* XVII. 842 As to the Transpiring Parts of our Bodies. 1725 *Bradley's Fam. Dict.* s.v. *Antimony*, This Diaphoretick alone may be taken..in malignant Fevers, to facilitate the transpiring of the Venom thro' the Pores. 1827 FARADAY *Chem. Manip.* xv. (1842) 345 The transpired matter on the surface of the skin. 1895 OLIVER tr. *Kerner's Nat. Hist. Plants* I. 274 The sap in the transpiring cells becomes more concentrated.

**Transpirometer** (tranˌspəirǫ·mĭtəɹ). [f. TRANSPIRE (or its source) + -OMETER.] An apparatus for recording the amount of watery vapour transpired by a plant.

1904 *Science* 11 Mar. 424/2 An autographic transpirometer, ..records..on a drum the transpiration of a plant for a week.

**Transpiry** (tranˌspəi·ri). *rare.* [f. TRANSPIRE + -Y, after EXPIRY.] The fact of 'transpiring' or leaking out. In quot. misused for Occurrence.

1884 A. DANIELL *Princ. Physics* Introd. 3 All our arrangements..are subject to the transpiry of facts unknown or unforeseen at the time.

**Transplace** (tranˌsplēi·s), *v. rare.* [f. TRANS- + PLACE *v.*] *trans.* To change the place of, transpose; to oust from its position in favour of something else. (Also with the two things as obj.) Hence **Transpla·cing** *vbl. sb.*

1615 LAWSON *Country Housew. Gard.* (1626) 26 An artificiall transplacing or transposing of a twig, bud, or leafe, commonly called a graft. 1621 AINSWORTH *Annot. Ps.* xlii. 6 The Greeke readeth thus; the salvation of my face and my God; transplacing the Hebrew letters. 1641 WILKINS *Math. Magick* I. xi. (1648) 75 The transplacing of that Obelisk at Rome by Sixtus the first, was done in some few days by five or six hundred men. 1711 J. GREENWOOD *Eng. Gram.* 217 Of Transposition or the transplacing of words and sentences. *c* 1810 COLERIDGE in *Lit. Rem.* (1838) III. 205 'Not so killing but so secret'.., transplacing the sentences 'as secret though not so killing'. 1878 VILLARI *Machiavelli* (1898) I. 16 In the 'Decameron' Latin periods already transform and transplace Italian periods.

**Transplant** (tra·nsˌplant), *sb.* [f. next.]

**1.** That which is transplanted; *spec.* in forestry, a seedling transplanted once or several times.

1756 P. BROWNE *Jamaica* 163 Very few transplants of the kind thrive. 1885 P. MACOWAN *Rep. Cape Town Bot. Gard.* 1884. 9, A box of 25 transplants. 1898 F. WHITMORE in *Atlantic Monthly* Apr. 507/1 There was nothing for it but to sow seeds for transplants.

*fig.* 1891 M. DODS *Erasmus*, etc. 81 They do not appear as transplants in the writings of Plato.

**2.** The transferring of bacterial organisms from one medium to another for purposes of culture.

1900 *Jrnl. Exper. Med.* (U.S.) 25 Oct. 173 Both micro-organisms failed to survive the exposure, transplants failing to produce a growth on broth and on kidney.

**Transplant** (tranˌsplaˑnt), *v.* [ad. post-cl.L. *transplantāre* (Itala, Luc. xvii. 6), f. TRANS- + *plantāre* to PLANT. Cf. F. *transplanter* (16th c.).]

**1.** *trans.* To remove (a plant) from one place or soil and plant it in another. Also *fig.*

*c* 1440 *Pallad. on Husb.* III. 504 Transplaunte hem so, & some up wol they spring. 1555 EDEN *Decades* 135 Transplantyng the roote therof, [he] brought it from wyldenes to a better kynde. 1605 TIMME *Quersit.* I. xvi. 86 They are to be transplanted into home gardens. 1664 EVELYN *Kal. Hort., Aug.* (1729) 213 Transplant such Lettuce as you will have abide all Winter. 1768 STERNE *Sent. Journ.* I. *In the Desobligeant*, The man who first transplanted the grape of Burgundy to the Cape of Good Hope. 1842 TENNYSON *Amphion* x, Methods of transplanting trees.

**2.** To convey or remove from one place to another; to transport; *esp.* to bring (people, a colony, etc.) from one country to settle in another.

1555 W. WATREMAN *Fardle Facions* Pref. 9 Now gan thei tattempte..to transplante their progenie, and offspring into places unenhabited. 1606 in *Calr. S. P. Irel.* 553 The Grames and others to be transplanted into Ireland were charged with many children. *c* 1630 RISDON *Surv. Devon* § 308 (1810) 317 These lands were transplanted into the name of the Poultons. 1769 E. BANCROFT *Guiana* 120 The Bull and the Cow..have been successfully transplanted into Guiana. 1860 PUSEY *Min. Proph.* 43 The policy of transplanting nations..was adopted, as a regular part of Assyrian, Babylonian, and Persian policy. 1899 A. E. GARVIE *Ritschlian Theol.* v. vii. 211 We cannot even transplant ourselves into the religious life of a pious Israelite.

**3.** *Surg.* To transfer (an organ or portion of tissue) from one part of the body, or from one person or animal, to another.

1786 [see *transplanted* below]. 1906 *Daily Chron.* 22 Sept. 6/7 A..case in which a child..suffering from cretinism, had a portion of its mother's thyroid gland transplanted into its spleen. *Ibid.*, Successful experiments in transplanting the blood vessels of animals. 1909 *Westm. Gaz.* 5 July 6/3 A dachshund, to which the kidneys of a fox-terrier had been transplanted..was apparently in perfect health.

**4.** *intr.* †**a.** (for *refl.*) To leave one place of abode and settle in another; to emigrate. *Obs.*

1608 [see TRANSPLANTING]. 1655 *Clarke Papers* (Camden) III. 24 The Irish are unwilling to transplant or prove theire qualificacions, but they will bee forc'd to goe and make way for the English planters. 1662 *Jesuits' Reasons* (1675) 130, Why..not..take up your roots and transplant?

**b.** (for *pass.*) To bear transplanting.

1796 C. MARSHALL *Gardening* xv. (1813) 248 Peas will transplant, and therefore broken rows may be made up. 1817–18 COBBETT *Resid. U. S.* (1822) 302 Persons of advanced age, of settled habits,..do not..'transplant well'. Of all such persons, Farmers transplant worst. 1846 *J. Baxter's Libr. Pract. Agric.* (ed. 4) II. 361 *Transplanting.*—Swedish turnips transplant very well, like the common cabbage; but the true turnip, the white globe or yellow, do not transplant.

Hence **Transpla·nted** *ppl. a.*

1765 *Museum Rust.* IV. 232 A six-shilling book..on the subject of transplanted lucerne. 1786 J. HUNTER *Treat. Venereal Disease* VII. i. § 1 (1810) 586 The transplanted tooth fastened extremely well, and continued so for about a month. 1833 ALISON *Hist. Europe* (1849) I. i. § 37. 83 Any transplanted Irishman, found out of his district, might be put to death by the first person who met him.

**Transplantable** (tranˌsplaˑntăb'l), *a.* [f. prec. + -ABLE.] Capable of being transplanted.

1656 in P. H. Hore *Hist. Wexford* (1911) VI. 508 What popish proprietors of lands Transplantable, do yet remain untransplanted. 1824 MISS MITFORD *Village* Ser. I. (1863) 21 Cabbage-plants and celery, and all transplantable things. 1829 SOUTHEY *Sir T. More* (1831) II. 89 Old forms of government are not transplantable into new countries.

Hence **Transplantabi·lity**, capability of being transplanted.

1811 W. TAYLOR in *Monthly Mag.* XXXI. 448 The transplantability of the fossils. 1867 T. ARCHER in Macfarlane *Mem.* vii. 185 Some plants are famed for transplantibility.

**Transˌpla·ntar**, *a. Anat.* [f. TRANS- 5 + L. *planta* sole: cf. *plantar.*] Lying across the sole of the foot, as a *transplantar muscle.*

1891 *Cent. Dict.* cites COUES. 1899 in *Syd. Soc. Lex.*

**Transplantation** (tranˌsplantēi·ʃən). [n. of action from TRANSPLANT *v.*: cf. *plantation.* So F. *transplantation* (16th c.).]

**I.** The action of transplanting.

**1.** The removing of a plant from one place or soil and planting it in another.

1601 HOLLAND *Pliny* XVII. x. I. 510 Neither need they any remoouing or transplantation at all. 1764 *Museum Rust.* IV. 38 The culture of lucerne by transplantation. 1796 C. MARSHALL *Garden.* xviii. (1813) 296 In all transplantations, it is proper to shorten some of the roots. 1856 DELAMER *Fl. Gard.* (1861) 25 Take them up for division and transplantation every fourth summer at longest.

**2.** Transference or removal from one place to another; transportation; *esp.* the removal of people from one country and settling of them in another.

1606 in *Calr. S. P., Irel.* 551 The transportation and transplantation of the Grames and other[s]..into the realm of Ireland. 1614 PURCHAS *Pilgrimage* IV. viii. (ed. 2) 385 Those which haue beene here seated by the transplantations of Tamerlane and Ismael..out of other Countries. 1625 GILL *Sacr. Philos.* I. 96 Their foolish thoughts concerning the transplantation of soules. 1633 in Row *Hist. Kirk* (Wodrow Soc.) 360 That all such oaths and subscriptions at ministers entrie or transplantation be discharged. 1720 QUINCY tr. *Hodges' Loimologia* 80 The Transplantation of the Plague from Turkey to Holland. 1882–3 *Schaff's Encycl. Relig. Knowl.* II. 927/2 The Gnostics taught a transplantation of the highest order..into the pleroma.

**3.** The pretended magical cure of disease by causing it to pass to another person, or to an animal or plant. *Obs.* or *Hist.*

1655 S. BOULTON (*title*) Medicina Magica..containing the general Cures of all Infirmities, by way of Transplantation. 1663 BOYLE *Usef. Exp. Nat. Philos.* II. v. xi. 227 An Example of a most violent pain of the Arme, removed by Transplantation. 1730 BAILEY (folio), *Transplantation* by Approximation (in Nat. Mag.) which is more properly called Approximation, as when a Whitlow is upon a Finger, and is cured by rubbing a Cat's Ear, which is supposed to receive the Pain. 1854–67 C. A. HARRIS *Dict. Med. Terminol.*, *Transplantation*,..a pretended method of curing diseases by making them pass from one person to another.

**4.** *Surg.* The operation of transferring an organ or a portion of tissue from one part of the body, or from one person or animal, to another.

1813 J. THOMSON *Lect. Inflam.* 239 Besides those examples that are seen in the transplantation of the teeth, it must be confessed that instances of reunion among parts which had been entirely separated are very rare in the human body. 1881 in *Philad. Record* No. 3472. 2 The object aimed at was nothing less than the transplantation of bone. 1890 BILLINGS *Med. Dict.*, *Transplantation*, removal of a portion of living tissue from its normal position, and uniting it with living tissue in another place, in order to repair a defect or lessen deformity. 1909 *Westm. Gaz.* 5 July 6/3 The operation of kidney transplantation.

**II. 5.** That which has been transplanted; a transplanted company or body.

*a* 1641 BP. MOUNTAGU *Acts & Mon.* vii. (1642) 467 Salmanassar brought Colonies, and transplantations of mixed people from the countries beyond Euphrates. 1805 W. TAYLOR in *Ann. Rev.* III. 236 He would by propagating and sheltering the new transplantations, have given a vernal..luxuriance to the appearance of the whole surrounding growth.

**Transˌplantee·**. *rare*⁻¹. [f. as next + -EE¹ 2.] One who is transplanted.

*a* 1687 PETTY *Pol. Arith.* iv. (1691) 69 If the Nation who shall be admitted, shall be less able to prejudice and annoy the Transplantees into England than before.

**Transplanter** (tranˌsplaˑntəɹ). [f. TRANSPLANT *v.* + -ER¹.]

**1.** One who transplants. Also *attrib.*

1611 COTGR., *Transplanteur*, a transplanter. 1755 JOHNSON, *Transplanter*, one that transplants. 1827 STEUART *Planter's G.* (1828) 240 The failure and decay of the Top (the great opprobrium of Transplanters) is primarily to be ascribed to the entire want of skill in the preservation of these fibrous roots, on which the Tree mainly depends. 1852 *Meanderings of Mem.* I. 21 So thence uprooted with transplanter care, In other soil it scents another air.

**2.** An implement or contrivance for transplanting.

1828 WEBSTER, *Transplanter*,..2. a machine for transplanting trees. 1855 DELAMER *Kitch. Gard.* (1861) 16 The transplanter is a tool with handles at one end, and a couple of semicircular blades at the other, which, when closed, form a hollow cylinder. 1909 *Cent. Dict. Suppl.*, *Transplanter*, a horse-power machine used in setting out tobacco or other field plants.

**Transplanting** (tranˌsplaˑntiŋ), *vbl. sb.* [f. as prec. + -ING¹.] The action of the vb. TRANSPLANT in various senses.

1608 in *Buccleuch MSS.* (Hist. MSS. Comm.) 77 The natives ..will be at no charges in transplanting thither. 1655 FULLER *Ch. Hist.* x. Ded., Plants are much meliorated by transplanting. 1790 PALEY *Horæ Paul.* i. 2 The immediate transplanting of names and circumstances out of one writing into the other. 1883 G. B. GOODE *Fish. Indust. U. S.* 14 (Fish. Exhib. Publ.) The transplanting of fish was practised ..at the close of the last century. 1906 *Daily Chron.* 22 Sept 6/7 Professor Garré, of Breslau, delivered an interesting lecture on the transplanting of blood vessels and organs.

**b.** *concr.* That which is transplanted.

1889 *Lancet* 20 Apr. 801/1 Such colonies become so intimately fused with others that not seldom the transplantings from them turn out impure.

**c.** *attrib.* as *transplanting machine, wagon*, etc.

1786 ABERCROMBIE *Gard. Assist.* 172 The transplanting kinds, as cabbage, savoys, broccoli, celery, endive. 1827 STEUART *Planter's G.* (1828) 182 The best and simplest transplanting machine now known. *Ibid.* 223 A cursory idea of my own Transplanting Nurseries. 1877 KNIGHT *Dict. Mech.*, *Transplanting-apparatus*, a machine or truck for removing trees for replanting. 1884 *Ibid.* Suppl., Transplanting Wagon. 1904 R. SMALL *Hist. U. P. Congregat.* I. 19 He was now [in 1841] beyond the transplanting age.

**†Transˌpla·ntively,** *adv. Obs. nonce-wd.* [f. an assumed adj. **transplantive* (f. as prec. + -IVE) + -LY[2].] In the way of transplantation.

1606 WARNER *Alb. Eng.* xv. xciv. 376 Her heart to his, his heart to hers, transplantiuely did passe.

**Tranˌsple·ndency.** *rare.* [f. as next: see -ENCY.] The quality or condition of being transplendent; superéminent brilliancy or splendour.

1664 H. MORE *Antid. Idolatry* ii. 38 A supernatural and unimitable Transplendency of the Divine Presence.

**Tranˌsple·ndent,** *a. rare.* [f. TRANS- 1 + L. *splendent-em*, pr. pple. of *splendēre* to shine, be bright. Cf. *resplendent.*] Brilliantly translucent; resplendent in the highest degree.

*a* 1541 WYATT *Compl. Absence of Love* 49 The clere cristall, the bright transplendant glasse. 1622 R. PRESTON *Godly Man's Inquis.* i. 16 Our weakenesse is so great, and his Maiestie on the other side is glorious and transplendent. 1854 J. S. C. ABBOTT *Napoleon* (1855) I. xi. 198 Those energies now so transplendent on the banks of the Mississippi and the Ohio.

Hence **Tranˌsple·ndently** *adv.*, with surpassing splendour.

1664 H. MORE *Antid. Idolatry* ii. 36 The Divinity..is hypostatically, vitally and transplendently residing in this Humanity of Christ.

**Transˌpleu·ral,** *a. Surg.* [f. TRANS- 5 + L. *pleura*: cf. *pleural.*] Traversing the pleural cavity.

1891 in *Cent. Dict.* 1905 ROLLESTON *Dis. Liver* 149 A transpleural operation, letting out serous fluid from the pleura.

**Transˌpo·lar,** *a.* [f. TRANS- 3 + L. *polus* pole + -AR[1]: cf. *polar.*] Crossing the (north) pole or polar region.

1850 SCORESBY *Cheever's Whalem. Adv.* i. (1855) 3 Daring adventures after a north-east or transpolar route to India. 1900 *Scribner's Mag.* Sept. 296/1 That branch which passed by a transpolar migration..from Siberia into Greenland.

**†Transˌpo·nent,** *a. Obs. rare*[−1]. [ad. L. *transpōnent-em*, pr. pple. of *transpōnĕre* to TRANSPOSE.] Transposing, transferring: in quot. (*erron.*) = transferred; immanent by communication.

1612 R. SHELDON *Serm. St. Martins* 10 How the attributes, and diuine perfections, of God were transponent in Christ.

**Transˌpo·nible,** *a. rare*[−0]. [f. L. *transpōn-ere* to transpose + -IBLE.] Capable of being transposed; transposable. So **Transponibi·lity.**

1891 in *Cent. Dict.* 1902 in *Cassell's Encycl. Dict. Suppl.*

**Transpontine** (trɑnsˌpǫ·ntəin), *a.* [f. TRANS- 3 + L. *pons, pont-em* bridge + -INE[1]. Cf. F. *transpontin* (16th c. in Godef. *Compl.*).] That is across or over a bridge; *spec.* on the other side of the bridges in London, i. e. south of the Thames; *transf.* (from the style of drama in vogue in the 19th century at the 'Surrey-side' theatres), melodramatic, sensational.

1844 ALB. SMITH *Fort. Scatterg. Fam.* ix, It was Monday evening, sacred to the pits and galleries of transpontine theatres. 1860 MRS. P. BYRNE *Undercurrents Overlooked* I. 78 The..Metropolitan theatres, cispontine and transpontine. 1876 C. M. DAVIES *Unorth. Lond.* 130, I was wandering in transpontine London one Sunday morning. 1882 DE WINDT *Equator* 132 Triana, a transpontine suburb [of Seville], is worth a visit in the daytime. 1901 *Scotsman* 9 Apr. 5/4 A new drama strongly seasoned with transpontine flavour.

**Transport** (trɑ·nsˌpoɹt), *sb.* [f. next. Cf. F. *transport* transfer of rights (1312 in Godef. *Compl.*), med.L. *transportus* (Du Cange) transferment.]

**1.** The action of carrying or conveying a thing or person from one place to another; conveyance.

1611 FLORIO, *Trasporto*, a transportation, a transport. 1621 ELSING *Debates Ho. Lords* (Camden) 11 The Bill against transport of golde and sylver. 1674 JOSSELYN *Voy. New Eng.* 12 Undertaking the Transport of his Family. 1841 ELPHINSTONE *Hist. India* II. IX. i. 277 Availing himself of the Jamna and Ganges for the transport of his stores and part of his army. 1844 H. H. WILSON *Brit. India* III. III. vi. 251 Sale at prices sufficient to cover the whole cost of transport. 1875 BENNETT & DYER *Sachs' Bot.* 634 The Conducting Tissue for the transport of the formative materials. 1894 *Geol. Mag.* Oct. 470 In the same way the beds at Moel Tryfaen are regarded as examples of glacial transport.

†**b.** *fig.* Transference. *Obs.*

1653 URQUHART *Rabelais* I. ii, Many are now poor wandring beggars..whoare descended of..great Kings and Emperours, occasioned..by the transport and revolution of Kingdoms and Empires.

†**c.** Transfer or conveyance of property. *Obs.*

App. the earliest use in English. It is the regular term for 'transfer of shares' in the Minute Books of the East India Company 1624–28.

1456 SIR G. HAYE *Law Arms* (S.T.S.) 133 Men takis landis ..and syne makis transport of thame, and puttis tham in othir menis handis. 1523 LD. BERNERS *Froiss.* I. ccxii. 258 The sayde renounciacion, transportes, sessynge, and leauynge of all the sayde thynges. 1607 (Nov. 13) *E. India Co. Court Bk.* II. 59 (MS.) Notwithstanding the transport made at the last Court of Mr. Bramley's adventure by Agnes Smyth to Mr. Robert Sandie. 1682 SCARLETT *Exchanges* 55 By this Endorsement, he to whom the Bill is sent, is the true and right Possessor of it, and needs no further Assignation, Transport, or any other Title or Right.

†**2.** Transference of a word to a different meaning; metaphor. *Obs. rare.*

1589 PUTTENHAM *Eng. Poesie* III. xvii. (Arb.) 189 To call the top of a tree, or of a hill, the crowne of a tree or of a hill..because such terme is not applyed naturally to a tree, or to a hill, but is transported from a mans head to a hill or tree, therefore it is called by metaphore, or the figure of transport.

**3.** The state of being 'carried out of oneself', i. e. out of one's normal mental condition; vehement emotion (now usu. of a pleasurable kind); mental exaltation, rapture, ecstasy. Also with *a* and *pl.*, an instance of this, a fit of joy or rage; sometimes *transf.* an ecstatic utterance.

1658 PHILLIPS, A *Transport*,..also a sudden trance, or rapture of minde. 1663 BP. PATRICK *Parab. Pilgr.* xiii. (1687) 84 Can you imagine into what transports it will cast your soul to hear the praises of the Creator sung by all his Works? 1686 tr. *Chardin's Trav. Persia* 146 An unheard-of Transport of Fury. *a* 1715 BURNET *Own Times* an. 1660 (1766) I. II. 151 The letter was received with transports of joy. 1796 JANE AUSTEN *Pride & Prej.* l, When the first transports of rage..were over, he..returned to all his former indolence. 1854 J. S. C. ABBOTT *Napoleon* (1855) I. xxvi. 413 He was hailed with transport wherever he appeared.

**4.** A means of transportation or conveyance; orig. a vessel employed in transporting soldiers, military stores, or convicts; later, the horses, wagons, etc. employed in transporting the ammunition and supplies of an army; sometimes including the things so conveyed.

1694 [implied in *transport-ship*: see 6]. 1712 E. COOKE *Voy. S. Sea* 140 At Five in the Afternoon, the Transports row'd for the Town of Guayaquil. 1783 JUSTAMOND tr. *Raynal's Hist. Indies* VII. 72 [He] took three thousand men of regular troops or of militia, which he embarked upon twenty-five transports. 1834 NAPIER *Penins. War* XVI. iii. (Rtldg.) II. 341 From the scarcity of transports only 38 guns could be brought to the trenches. 1855 MACAULAY *Hist. Eng.* xiv. III. 411 The Dee was crowded with men of war and transports. 1879 A. FORBES in *Daily News* 13 June 5/5 That all-important element in campaigning, the transport, including in that term the animals, the waggons, and the supplies. 1897 S. L. HINDE *Congo Arabs* 86 One woman and a boy acted as transport. 1900 *Dundee Advertiser* 17 May 4 All our larger transport has arrived without mishap. The men and horses are standing the continuous strain admirably, notwithstanding the heavy roads.

**5.** A transported convict; a person under sentence of transportation. Now *rare.*

1767 *Chron.* in *Ann. Reg.* 58/2 Fourteen transports from Durham..were put on board..bound for Virginia. 1777 HOWARD *Prisons Eng.* (1780) 386 The county has for some years..clothed such transports as were quite indigent. 1817 *2nd Rep. Comm. Police Metrop., Min. Evid.* 392 Have you ever known any instances of returned transports obtaining licences to keep public houses? 1851 D. JERROLD *St. Giles* xix. 199 You don't mean to say..that you are an escaped transport?

**6.** *attrib.* and *Comb.*, as *transport-agent, -carriage,* †*felon, -hoy, -labour, -service, -wagon, worker,* etc.; †**transport-bill,** †**debenture,** a voucher given for a claim for transport services; †**transport brief, deed,** a transfer-deed; **transport-buoy,** a buoy used for the mooring and warping of vessels; **transport-rider** (*South Africa*), a goods carrier; so **transport-riding,** carriage of goods; **transport-ship, -vessel**: see 4.

1897 J. K. LAUGHTON in *Dict. Nat. Biog.* LII. 156/2 He was appointed *transport agent for the expedition to Egypt. 1710 *Lond. Gaz.* No. 4637/3 Lost.., four *Transport-Bills, ..being for two Months Freight each on the Ship *Success*, ..Signed by..her Majesty's Commissioners for Transportation. 1895 J. BROWN *Pilgr. Fathers* IV. 124 It was conveyed ..by a *transport brief or deed made on the 5th of May 1611. 1793 SMEATON *Edystone L.* § 102 The use that was made of *Transport Buoys, in the moving and mooring the king's ships in the Hamoaze. 1895 *Daily News* 18 Oct. 5/5 Dr. Hönig's new bicycle *transport-carriages for sick people. 1707 *Lond. Gaz.* No. 4311/3 A *Transport-Debenture for the Year 1697. No. 32. for 965 l. 3 s. 4 d. is lost. 1766 *Chron.* in *Ann. Reg.* 134/2 Three hundred *transport felons..have been shipped at Blackwall for the plantations. 1705 *Lond. Gaz.* No. 4167/3 This day came into Kingroad..two *Transport-Hoys. 1850 R. G. CUMMING *Hunter's Life S. Afr.* (1902) 10/2 The Dutchman along their road being very unfriendly and inhospitable to the English *transport-riders. 1909 R. CULLUM *Compact* xii. 143 Each waggon has two coloured transport-riders. 1900 HAGGARD *Black Heart* i, *Transport-riding—that is, in carrying goods on ox waggons from Durban or Maritzburg to various points in the interior. 1817 *Parl. Deb.* 584 A resolution then passed for 142,500*l.* for the *transport service. 1694 *Act 5 & 6 Will. & Mary* c. 23 § 3 The *Transport Shipps for the Warr of Ireland. 1701 *Lond. Gaz.* No. 3712/3 Several Transport Ships are arrived at Williamstad with Recruits. 1722 DE FOE *Col. Jack* ii, Coming to the common period of that kind of life, I mean to the transport-ship, or to the gallows. 1700 TYRRELL *Hist. Eng.* II. 795 Fourscore Cogs, a sort of small *Transport-Vessels. 1903 *Westm. Gaz.* 8 Apr. 5/2 The railwaymen, who are federated with the *transport workers, declining to handle any traffic which had been unloaded by 'free' labourers.

**Transport** (trɑnsˌpōə·ɹt), *v.* [ad. F. *transporter* (14th c. in Hatz.-Darm.), or its source L. *transportāre*, f. *trans* across + *portāre* to carry.]

**1.** *trans.* To carry, convey, or remove from one place or person to another; to convey across.

Formerly used in general sense: see quots.; now mostly restricted to the conveyance of persons, animals, and things as an organized operation, or with allusion to other senses.

1483 CAXTON *Gold. Leg.* 260 b/1 Where it shalle plese the to enhabyte it transporte me to the. 1490 — *Eneydos* x. 39 They were separed & transported in-to dyuerse places. 1494 FABYAN *Chron.* VII. ccxxii. 245 Dyuers bysshoppes sees were transported from one place to another; as Selwey to Chechester, Kyrton to Exetoʳ, Wellys to Bathe,..Dorchester to Lyncolne. *a* 1548 HALL *Chron., Edw. IV* 235 If the Duke of Britayne, would transporte hym into England. 1560 DAUS tr. *Sleidane's Comm.* 284 That he should neither make a brydge nor finde a foorde to transport his armie. 1579 *Galway Arch.* in *10th Rep. Hist. MSS. Comm.* App. v. 430 To tranchporte any manner tymber. 1599 SHAKS. *Hen. V*, II. Prol. 35 The Scene Is now transported (Gentles) to Southampton. 1606 in *Calr. S. P. Irel.* 551 To demise to the said Grames and such other persons as shall be transported ..120 quarters of land. 1632 LITHGOW *Trav.* x. 457 He made fast the doore, and transported the keyes. 1635 SWAN *Spec. M.* vii. § 3 (1643) 323 As a..Mirrour transporteth the light of the fire, or the sunne against a wall. 1709 STEELE *Tatler* No. 3 ⁋6 Mules to transport his Provisions and Ammunition. 1829 SCOTT *Anne of G.* ii, I have no wings to transport me from cliff to cliff. 1853 J. H. NEWMAN *Hist. Sk.* (1873) II. I. ii. 65 This region..receiving the merchandize of East and North, and transporting it by its rivers. 1856 KANE *Arctic Explor.* II. vi. 75 The dogs are indispensable in.. transporting us to Anoatoh. 1901 [see TRANSPORTABILITY].

**b.** *fig.* (app. the earliest use.)

*c* 1374 CHAUCER *Boeth.* III. pr. ix. 65 (Camb. MS.) The errour and folye of mankynde departeth and deuydeth it,.. and transporteth from verray and parfyt good to goodes þat ben false and vnparfyt. *c* 1475 *Partenay* 3739 And in to sorow transport our gladnesse. 1509 HAWES *Past. Pleas.* xxxi. (Percy Soc.) 150 Consyder well that your lusty courage Age of his cours must at the last transporte. 1652 G. COLLIER *Vind. Sabbath* (1656) 45 The Apostolick churches transported the exercises of that day to the Sunday. 1798 FERRIAR *Eng. Historians* 234 They transport our imagination to the scene. 1857 W. SMITH *Thorndale* 547 Man transports himself into nature, endues the great objects or powers of nature with human feelings, human will.

†**c.** To transfer or convey (property). *Obs.*

1523 LD. BERNERS *Froiss.* I. ccxii. 257 All the right that oure sayde brother hath.., he yeldeth and transporteth them to vs perpetually. *Ibid.* 258, 259 [see CESS *v.*[2] 2]. 1607 (July 31) *E. India Co. Court Bk.* II. 44 (MS.) Sir James Deane's letter to the Company that his stock of the 3rd voyage, being £200, be transported over to the accompt of Andrew Holdip his kinsman. *a* 1649 DRUMM. OF HAWTH. *Hist. Jas. II* Wks. (1711) 24 Transporting lands to themselves and their friends, distributing offices and places of the crown and state.

†**d.** *intr.* for *refl.* To transfer oneself to another place of abode; to emigrate. *Obs.*

*c* 1540 tr. *Pol. Verg. Eng. Hist.* (Camden No. 29) 143 Six months after that he had transported into Flanders. 1631 WEEVER *Anc. Fun. Mon.* 794 He required him (before he transported) to returne. 1633 T. STAFFORD *Pac. Hib.* II. x. (1821) 338 It shall be lawfull for any of the Inhabitants..to transport, without any molestation. 1675 tr. *Machiavelli's Prince* viii. (Rtldg.) 56 He transported into Africa.

†**e.** To remove from this world to the next: cf. TRANSLATE *v.* 1 b. *Obs.*

In quot. 1603, a euphemism for 'put to death, kill'. So taken by Schmidt in quot. 1590; but W. Aldis Wright takes it as, in Starveling's language, = 'transform, transfigure', comparing the use of 'translate' in III. i. 122.

1603 SHAKS. *Meas. for M.* IV. iii. 72 A creature vnprepar'd, vnmeet for death, And to transport him in the minde he is, Were damnable. (1590 — *Mids. N.* IV. ii. 4 He cannot be heard of. Out of doubt hee is transported.)

**2.** *spec.* **a.** *Sc. Ch.* To translate (a minister) from one charge to another.

1637–50 ROW *Hist. Kirk* (Wodrow Soc.) 164 There was an intention to have had four of the ministers of Edinburgh transported to other places. 1726 *Wodrow Corr.* (1843) III 257 Discharging them to be transported without the consent of the General Assembly, or declared transportable without consent of the people. *a* 1791 GROSE *Olio* (1796) 111 By transported we mean, in Scotland, removed to another parish. 1858 RAMSAY *Remin.* v. (1870) 118 A Seceding minister at Kircaldy. But I hear he expects to be transported soon. 1904 R. SMALL *Hist. U. P. Congregat.* I. 457 It was carried [in] 1830 by a great majority to transport.

**b.** *Sc. Eccl. Law.* To remove (the site of the church) to a different part of the parish.

1707 *Sc. Act Anne* c. 10 (1824) XI. 433/1 The transporting of Kirks,..or erecting and building of new kirks, being alwayes with the consent of the heritors of three parts..at least of the valuation of the parock whereof the kirk is craved to be transported or..new kirks to be erected and built. 1765–8 ERSKINE *Inst. Law Scot.* I. v. § 21 With more ample powers, of..transporting churches already built to more convenient places. 1838 [see TRANSPORTATION 2 b].

**c.** To carry away or convey into banishment, as a criminal or a slave; to deport.

1666 *Act 18 & 19 Chas. II*, c. 3 § 2 It shall be lawfull to and for the Justices..to transport or cause to be transported the said Offenders..into any of his Majestyes Dominions in America. 1667 PEPYS *Diary* 8 Sept., A prisoner being condemned at Salisbury for a small matter...They were considering to transport him to save his life. 1759 HUME *Hist. Eng.* III. lxi. 326 The rest were sold for slaves and transported to Barbadoes. 1849 MACAULAY *Hist. Eng.* ii. I. 177 It was provided that the offender should not be transported to New England.

**3.** *fig.* To 'carry away' with the strength of some emotion; to cause to be beside oneself, to put into an ecstasy, to enrapture.

1509 HAWES *Past. Pleas.* xxv. (Percy Soc.) 179 But loke hye his hart to transport. 1596 SPENSER *Hymne Heavenly Beautie* iii, Transported with celestiall desyre Of those faire formes. 1604 E. G[RIMSTONE] tr. *D'Acosta's Hist. Indies* I. xxi. 69 They stood transported with amazement. 1667

MILTON *P. L.* III. 81 Onely begotten Son, seest thou what rage Transports our adversarie? **1712** ADDISON *Hymn, 'When all thy mercies'* i, Transported with the view, I'm lost In wonder, love, and praise. **1840** DICKENS *Barn. Rudge* lxxi, Transported with the thought that rescue had at length arrived, Emma and Dolly shrieked aloud for help.

**Transportability** (trɑnsˌpōᵊɹtăbi·lĭti). [f. next + -ITY.] Capability of being transported; in early quots. referring to translation of ministers (see TRANSPORT *v.* 2 a, TRANSPORTATION 2 a).

**1651** *Reg. Comm. Gen. Assembly* 24 Feb. (S.H.S.) III. 538 The motion anent Mr. George his transportabilitie is waved. **1676** Row *Contn. Blair's Autobiog.* xi. (1848) 344 Mr. Blair supplicated the Presbytery of St Andrews for an act of transportability. **1846** in WORCESTER. **1883** *Century Mag.* July 430/2 The fever's..transportability was fearfully proven. **1901** *N. Amer. Rev.* Feb. 222 The Transvaal war has shown the transportability..of the heaviest artillery... The Boers transported their 'Long Tom' as they might have transported a piano.

**Transportable** (trɑnsˌpōᵊ·ɹtăb'l), *a.* [f. TRANSPORT *v.* + -ABLE. Cf. F. *transportable* (1812 in Hatz.-Darm.); mod.L. *transportābilis*.]

1. Capable of being transported.

**1582** *Reg. Privy Council Scot.* III. 530 In uptaking of the custum of all gudis transportabill furth of this realme. **1642** *Declar. Lords & Comm. to Gen. Assemb. Ch. Scot.* 13 [Soldiers] to be sent presently over to reside amongst them, or declared transportable. **1676** *Phil. Trans.* XI. 680 A Chest of Copper,..transportable by means of woodden barrs like a Sedan or Chair. **1726** [see TRANSPORT *v.* 2 a]. **1881** J. RUSSELL *Haigs* v. 105 Bringing off whatever was transportable on its own four feet. **1904** R. SMALL *Hist. U. P. Congregat.* II. 1 The Presbytery declared him transportable.

2. Involving or liable to transportation.

**1769** BLACKSTONE *Comm.* IV. xvii. 242 The statute.. makes it a felony transportable for seven years. **1815** MISS MITFORD in L'Estrange *Life* (1870) I. 323 It does not.. appear that he ever committed any hangable or transportable offence. **1840** GEN. P. THOMPSON *Exerc.* (1842) V. 371, I remember once discovering that I was living in the commission of transportable offences at the rate of two a-day.

Hence **Transˌpo·rtableness,** the quality of being transportable; liability to transportation.

**1727** in BAILEY vol. II. **1844** P. HARWOOD *Hist. Irish Reb.* 107 Transportableness for life.

† **Transˌpo·rtage.** *Obs.* [f. as prec. + -AGE. Cf. PORTAGE.] = TRANSPORTATION 1, TRANSPORT.

**1562** J. SHUTE *Cambini's Turk. Wars* 9 Almost..oute of hope of any transportage for them. **1600** HOLLAND *Livy* XLIII. xii. 1163 He should give order for their transportage thither. **1631** HEYWOOD *1st Pt. Fair Maid of West* I. i. Wks. 1874 II. 273 Such gold fit for transportage as I have, I'le beare along. **1637** — *Royall Ship* 12 Vessels..for the transportage of graine from one province to another.

So **Transpo·rtal, Transpo·rtance** [see -AL, -ANCE: cf. *importance*], transport, conveyance.

**1837** DARWIN in *Life & Lett.* (1887) II. 9 Let the powers of transportal be such. **1839** — *Voy. Nat.* ix. (1879) 187 To explain the transportal of these gigantic masses of rock. **1859** — *Orig. Spec.* iv. (1866) 104 So as to favour..the transportal of their pollen from flower to flower. **1893** SIR H. H. HOWORTH *Glacial Nightmare* II. 680 The transportal of drift in directions opposite to the movements of the ice. **1606** SHAKS. *Tr. & Cr.* III. ii. 12 Be thou my Charon, And giue me swift transportance to those fields. *c* **1611** CHAPMAN *Iliad* XVI. Comm. (1857) II. 105 Nor would Homer have any one believe the personal transportance of Sarpedon by Sleep and Death. **1615** BRATHWAIT *Strappado* (1878) 32 There's no fashion knowne, In forraine Courts,..But by transportance it doth come to thee. **1882** G. MACDONALD *Castle Warlock* xxxi, A doubtful denial of transportance.

† **Transpo·rtant,** *a.* *Obs.* *rare*$^{-1}$. [f. as TRANSPORT *v.* + -ANT.] Transporting, ravishing.

**1660** H. MORE *Myst. Godl.* VI. v. § 5. 227 So rapturous a Joy, and transportant Love.

**Transportation** (trɑnsˌpoɹtē·ʃən). [n. of action f. TRANSPORT *v.* + -ATION. Cf. L. (post-Aug.) *transportātiōn-em* transmigration, and F. *transportation* (1519 in Hatz.-Darm.).]

1. The action or process of transporting; conveyance (of things or persons) from one place to another.

Much used in 17th c. down to *c* 1660; afterwards gradually given up for *transport*, prob. to avoid association with penal transportation, sense 2 c.

**1540** *Act* 32 *Hen. VIII*, c. 14 § 2 For the fraight transportation conveyaunce or cariage of anny warres. *a* **1600** in Hakluyt *Voy.* III. 174 By reason of the transportation of raw wooll of late dayes more excessiuely then in times past. **1607** HIERON *Wks.* I. 371 Looke how the case stood with their transportation out of Ægypt into Canaan. **1615** G. SANDYS *Trav.* 26 Here is a Ferry for transportation into Asia. *a* **1656** USSHER *Ann.* VI. (1658) 331 Finding no ships there, for his transportation, he divided his army. **1679–88** *Secr. Serv. Moneys Chas. & Jas.* (Camden) 16 To the Bishop of London, for transportac'on of three Chaplains to the Leward Islands ..60 0 0. **1707** E. CHAMBERLAYNE *Pres. St. Eng.* I. vii. (ed. 22) 63 Upon the Three Articles of Exportation, Transportation or Re-exportation, and Importation, no Kingdom or State in the World can any ways match us. **1827** STEUART *Planter's G.* (1828) 264 It must make the Tree..more troublesome to be balanced during the transportation. **1855** PRESCOTT *Hist. Philip II*, I. 118 The transportation of the troops was going ..on. **1890** *Wisconsin Hist. Soc. Prospectus*, Upon any gift to the Society, transportation will be cheerfully paid.

b. *Geol.* The movement of land-waste by rivers, ocean-currents, glaciers, wind, etc.

**1830** LYELL *Princ. Geol.* I. 81 A geologist, who..sees the decomposition of rocks, and the transportation of matter by rivers to the sea. **1877** LE CONTE *Elem. Geol.* III. v. (1879) 516 The general direction of the scorings corresponds with that of transportation of the bowlders.

2. *spec.* a. *Sc. Ch.* The translation of a minister from one charge to another.

**1562** in Row *Hist. Kirk* (Wodrow Soc.) 24 Transportation declared lawfull where there is reason for it. **1663** BLAIR *Autobiog.* ii. (1848) 46 That assembly sets a note upon the act of my transportation. **1717** T. BOSTON in A. Thomson *Life* (1895) 129 In a time wherein there is so little need of transportations.

b. *Sc. Eccl. Law. Transportation of a church*, removal of the site of the church to a different part of the parish.

**1838** W. BELL *Dict. Law Scot.* s.v. *Transportation of Churches*, The form of applying for transportation is by a summons raised before the Teind Court, concluding for authority to transport, and to have the new church declared the regular parish church.

c. Removal or banishment, as of a criminal to a penal settlement; deportation.

**1669** in *10th Rep. Hist. MSS. Comm.* App. v. 95 If..the said Rice Havard [a condemned felon] doe give in security for his transportacion as before mentioned. **1678** BUTLER *Hud.* III. II. 197 Neither Chains, nor Transportation, Proscription, Sale, nor Confiscation. **1727** GAY *Begg. Op.* I. xiii, Were you sentenc'd to Transportation? **1879** McCARTHY *Own Times* II. xviii. 33 The sentence of death was changed into one of transportation for life.

3. *transf.* Means of transport or conveyance. *U.S.*

**1861** *Times* 29 July, We captured..all the enemy's camp equipage and transportation. **1869** T. W. HIGGINSON *Army Life* (1870) 236 There was no transportation to take us. At last, a boat was notified. **1890** *Century Mag.* Feb. 564/1 A lot of miscellaneous transportation, composed of riding horses, ambulances, and other vehicles. **1894** *Outing* (U. S.) XXIV. 234/2 Transportation is furnished for the horses of mounted officers.

b. A ticket or pass for travelling by a public conveyance. *U.S.*

**1909** in *Cent. Dict. Suppl.* **1911** in WEBSTER.

† 4. Transport (of feeling), rapture, ecstasy. *Obs.*

**1617** COLLINS *Def. Bp. Ely* II. vii. 286 Not onely in extasie and transportation..but in the daily forme of prayer. **1660** STANLEY *Hist. Philos.* IX. (1701) 373/1 A soul disturbed with anger or pleasure, or any other unbefitting transportation. **1690** LUTTRELL *Brief Rel.* (1857) II. 68 Which those poor people received with great transportations of joy.

5. *attrib.*, mostly in sense 1, as *transportation agent, company, money, rate, sentence, system*, etc.

**1573–4** *Privy Council Acts* (1894) VIII. 212 To aunswer the conduct, transportacion money and wages acording to her Majesties usuall entertainement. **1844** EMERSON *Lect., Yng. American* Wks. (Bohn) II. 303 The private transportation-shop. **1883** G. B. GOODE *Fish. Indust. U. S.* 67 (Fish. Exhib. Publ.) The construction of refrigerating transportation cars. **1888** BRYCE *Amer. Commw.* II. App. 670 All railroad, canal, and other transportation companies are declared to be common carriers. **1891** *Athenæum* 26 Dec. 862/3 There is not much in it about Siberia,..and the work is, in fact, one on the Russian transportation system. **1897** P. WARUNG *Tales Old Regime* 148 Her home record was bad, and most likely her transportation-sentence was life.

Hence **Transportaˑtional** *a.*, of, belonging or pertaining to transportation; **Transportaˑtionist,** one who favours the transportation of criminals.

**1888** J. T. GULICK in *Linn. Soc. Jrnl., Zool.* XX. 230 Transportational segregation, caused by activities in the environment that distribute the organism in different districts. **1840** GEN. P. THOMPSON *Exerc.* (1842) V. 26 On the whole, we seem to have flurried the transportationists.

**Transportative** (trɑnsˌpōᵊ·ɹtătiv), *a.* *rare*. [f. TRANSPORT *v.* + -ATIVE, after PORTATIVE.]

1. Adapted or liable to transportation; such as to be carried from place to place, portable.

**1643** TRAPP *Comm. Gen.* xxxii. 6 The Ark was transportative, till setled in Solomon's temple. **1657** *Ibid., Job* iv. 19 A tabernacle which hath no foundation, and is transportative. **1680** C. NESSE *Church-Hist.* 151 His ark should be no more transportative, but setled for a long season.

2. Having the quality of transporting.

**1886** A. WINCHELL *Walks Geol. Field* 46 The transportative power of the stream had become so abated.

**Transported** (trɑnsˌpōᵊ·ɹtĕd), *ppl. a.* [f. TRANSPORT *v.* + -ED [1].]

1. Conveyed from one place to another.

**1693** EVELYN *De la Quint. Compl. Gard.* I. II. x. 26 There is but little to be said..of Transported Earth,..it is a Novelty our Age has introduc'd in Gard'ning. **1830** LYELL *Princ. Geol.* I. 193 At the base of such hollow ravines was seen a wide and deep mass of ruins, consisting of transported earth, gravel, rocks, and trees.

b. Compulsorily carried to a distant country.

**1728** GAY *Polly* I. (1777) 18 Since he came over [to America] he married a transported slave. **1743** BULKELEY & CUMMINS *Voy. S. Seas* 20 Those Grandees..in a few Minutes look'd like a Parcel of transported felons. **1890** *Daily News* 18 Sept. 6/1 The transported of 1851 and of 1871 are looked upon as revolutionists who only got what they deserved.

2. 'Carried away' by excitement or vehement emotion; excited beyond self-control; enraptured.

**1600** E. BLOUNT tr. *Conestaggio* 247 Troublesome and transported subiects. **1685** BOYLE *Eng. Notion Nat.* v. 173 Like a passionate and transported thing, oppose it,..with such blind violence. **1746–7** HERVEY *Medit.* (1818) 29 The fondness of thy transported husband. **1874** MOTLEY *Barneveld* I. ii. 177 He had never seen a man so desperate, so transported.

Hence **Transpoˑrtedly** *adv.*, in a transported manner, in a transport; **Transpoˑrtedness.**

**1652** LOVEDAY tr. *Calprenede's Cassandra* I. 56 [She] *transportedly cryed out [etc.]. **1713** C'TESS WINCHELSEA *Misc. Poems* 27 Assemble here, you watry Race, Transportedly he cries. **1804** J. COLLINS *Scripscrap.* 28 The thief a new Region transportedly hails. *a* **1656** BP. HALL *Rem. Wks.* (1660) 420 Titular respects which those..can weild without any such taint or suspicion of *transportedness.

**Transportee** (trɑnsˌpoɹtī·). [f. as next + -EE.] A transported convict.

**1883** *Chambers' Encycl.* IX. 518/1 The criminal classes.. heard more about the success than the hardships of the transportees.

**Transporter** (trɑnsˌpōᵊ·ɹtəɹ). [f. TRANSPORT *v.* + -ER [1].]

1. One who transports.

**1535** *Act* 27 *Hen. VIII*, c. 14 § 1 The said..Tanners or other person transporter of the same Lether. **1562–3** *Act* 5 *Eliz.* c. 12 § 4 No..Carrier, Buyer or Transporter of Corne. **1615** G. SANDYS *Trav.* 209 A thing usuall it is betweene Tripoly and Aleppo..to make tame Doues the speedy transporters of their letters. **1744** J. PATERSON *Comm. Milton's P. L.* 305 The transporter of departed souls into hell. **1906** *Times* 21 Aug. 5/1 The result of the increased number of transporters is that the price of everything has fallen.

2. Any carrying apparatus; *esp.* a device for transporting coal from a quay or from one vessel to another.

*Transporter-bridge*, a bridge over a navigable waterway, high enough not to interfere with navigation, carrying a suspended platform or car which travels from bank to bank and conveys the traffic. So *transporter car*.

**1893** *Westm. Gaz.* 25 July 5/2 Mr. Temperley's ingenious contrivance for coaling rapidly... The 'transporter', as it is called, is made of steel, beam-shaped,..and fitted with an automatic travelling carriage suspended from the lower flange of the beam. **1894** *Ibid.* 31 July 7/1 The 'B' Fleet has now been coaled with exceptional rapidity and without recourse to the Temperly transporter. **1904** *Ibid.* 2 Sept. 10/2 The Runcorn Transporter Bridge, now being erected, has its towers made wholly of steel. They rise 190 ft. above high-water level. *Ibid.*, The transporter car..is suspended from the trolly by steel-wire ropes.

**Transporting** (trɑnsˌpōᵊ·ɹtiŋ), *vbl. sb.* [f. as prec. + -ING [1].] The action of the verb TRANSPORT; transportation.

**1500** in *10th Rep. Hist. MSS. Comm.* App. v. 391 After the transporting of the same to sell the said warres. **1574** in *Maitl. Cl. Misc.* I. 101 Transporting of certane quheit furth of this realme without lycence. **1612** J. MORE in *Buccleuch MSS.* (Hist. MSS. Comm.) I. 125 The transporting of Sir John Ogle's regiment to my Lord Chandos. **1712** J. JAMES tr. *Le Blond's Gardening* 209 Clay is not dear, unless in the Carriage and Transporting of it. **1849** MACAULAY *Hist. Eng.* ix. II. 531 He would be no party to the transporting of the prince into France.

b. *Naut.* (See quot.) Also *attrib.*

*c* **1850** *Rudim. Navig.* (Weale) 156 *Transporting*, moving a ship from one situation to another by hawsers only. *Ibid.*, *Transporting-blocks*, two snatch-blocks, fitted on each side above the taffrail to admit a hawser, when transporting the ship from one place to another.

c. *Sc.* See TRANSPORT *v.* 2 a, b.

**1707** [see TRANSPORT *v.* 2 b]. **1904** R. SMALL *Hist. U. P. Congregat.* I. 446 In September 1825 transporting calls came up to Mr. Ritchie from Dunfermline..and from the Potterrow. *Ibid.* 469 Mr. M'Gilchrist's mind was not up to the transporting point yet.

**Transˌpoˑrting,** *ppl. a.* [f. as prec. + -ING [2].] That transports.

1. That removes from one place to another; engaged in transportation.

*a* **1618** RALEIGH *Apology* 12 That we might have kept our Transporting ships with our men of War. **1830** LYELL *Princ. Geol.* I. 312 The direction and position of their destroying and transporting power. **1834–5** J. PHILLIPS in *Encycl. Metrop.* VI. 705/1 The transporting action of streams. **1886** *Academy* 7 Aug. 82/1 Michael is hurried into the transporting ship which founders with all on board.

2. *fig.* Causing transport, ecstasy, or rapture; ravishing, enchanting.

*c* **1655** A. SIDNEY *Love* (in *19th Cent.* Jan. (1884) 58), Epicureans allow soe much of it [Love] as conduceth to pleasure, but reject the transporting part. **1707** WATTS *Hymn*, '*My God, the spring of all my joys*' iv, My soul would leave this heavy clay At that transporting word. **1796** MRS. INCHBALD *Nature & Art* v, So did Henry survey, with transporting glory, his brother, drest for the first time in canonicals.

Hence **Transˌpoˑrtingly** *adv.*, in a transporting manner; ravishingly.

**1668** H. MORE *Div. Dial.* II. xi. (1713) 121 We see sundry Species of living Creatures this way the most pleasantly and transportingly provided for. *a* **1711** KEN *Hymnotheo* Poet. Wks. 1721 III. 54 [He] felt himself transportingly amaz'd.

**Transportive** (trɑnsˌpōᵊ·ɹtiv), *a.* *rare*. [f. TRANSPORT *v.* + -IVE.] Having the quality of transporting (*lit.* and *fig.*); tending to transport.

**1622** T. ADAMS *Eirenopolis* Wks. 1862 II. 315 It is the voice of transportive fury, 'I cannot moderate my anger'. **1633** — *Exp. 2 Peter* ii. 19 The running of our own ways, after our transportive fancies. **1899** T. C. CHAMBERLIN in *Jrnl. Geol.* Oct.-Nov. 669 As the declivity increased the cutting and transportive power of the drainage increased.

† **Transˌpoˑrtment.** *Obs.* [f. as prec. + -MENT. Cf. OF. *transportement* (13–16th c.).]

1. Transportation: = TRANSPORT *sb.* 1. *rare*$^{-1}$.

*a* **1619** FLETCHER, etc. *Q. Corinth* IV. i, Are not you he, when your fellow Passengers, Your last transportment being assayl'd by a Galley, Hid your self i' the Cabbin?

2. Vehement emotion, passion; rapture, ecstasy: = TRANSPORT *sb.* 3.

**1639** LD. DIGBY, etc. *Lett. conc. Relig.* (1651) 116 When they enveigh against Hereticks; their passions and transportments being at such times greatest. **1652** J. WRIGHT tr. *Camus' Nat. Paradox* XII. 325 To appease the frantick transportments of his Minde. **1686** tr. *Chardin's Coronat. Solyman* 81 Hairbrain'd, and violent actions, and full of a Transportment that truly savour'd of Extravagance.

**Transposable** (trɑnsˌpōu·zăb'l), *a.* [f. TRANSPOSE *v.* + -ABLE.] Capable of being transposed; interchangeable. Hence **Transposabi·lity.**

1879 WEBSTER *Suppl.*, Transposable. 1881 ARMSTRONG in *Nature* 8 Sept. 450/2 Heat, electricity and mechanical action, are all equivalent and transposable forms of energy. 1903 A. R. WALLACE *Man's Place in Universe* x. 195 The most important element in protoplasm..which confers upon it..its extreme mobility and transposibility, is nitrogen.

**Transposal** (trɑnsˌpōu·zăl). *rare.* [f. as prec. + -AL; cf. *proposal.*] Transposition.

1695 KENNETT *Par. Antiq.* ix. 106 A transposal from one fraternity to another. 1707 NORRIS *Treat. Humility* iv. 177 A strange turn and transposal of events. 1866 J. G. MURPHY *Comm. Exod.* xx. 17 The transposal of the first two clauses. 1868 MRS. WHITNEY *P. Strong* iii, Like the thing proof-readers put for a sign of a transposal.

†**Transˌpo·se,** *sb. Obs. rare.* [f. TRANSPOSE *v.*] = TRANSPOSITION.

1589 PUTTENHAM *Eng. Poesie* II. xii. (Arb.) 121 Of the Anagrame,..we may terme him, the poesie transposed or in one word a transpose. *Ibid.* 122 This man was very perfit and fortunat in these transposes. 1605 CAMDEN *Rem.* (1637) 175 This transpose of the letters in the name.

**Transpose** (trɑnsˌpōu·z), *v.* [a. F. *transposer* (14th c. in Hatz.-Darm.), f. TRANS- + *poser* to place: see POSE, COMPOSE.]

†**1.** *trans.* To change (one thing) *to* or *into* another; to transform, transmute, convert. *Obs.*

c1380 WYCLIF *Sel. Wks.* II. 387 Vertues ben transposid to vices. c1460 *Wisdom* 1005 in *Macro Plays* 68 Gyff a peny in thy lyve, with goode wyll To þe pore, & yt pleysythe Gode more þan mowntenyys [*MS.* mowyntenys] in to golde transposyde were; Ande aftir thy dethe, for the dysposyde. 1530 PALSGR. 761/1, I transpose, I chaunge or tourne a thyng... He hath transposed his house quyte newe, *il a transmué*, or *contourné sa mayson tout de nouveau*, or *toute neuue*. 1579–80 NORTH *Plutarch* (1676) 415 To transpose themselves from good Souldiers..to Labourers, Merchants, and Farmers. 1590 SHAKS. *Mids. N.* I. i. 233 Things base and vilde, holding no quantity, Loue can transpose to forme and dignity. 1605 — *Macb.* IV. iii. 21 That which you are, my thoughts cannot transpose; Angels are bright still, though the brightest fell.

†**2.** To change (a writing or book) *into* another language, style of composition, or mode of expression; to translate; to transfer; to adapt. *Obs.*

1390 GOWER *Conf.* II. 90 The Bible, in which the lawe is closed, Into Latin he [Jerome] hath transposed. 1552 HULOET, Transpose, *transcribo.* 1706 PHILLIPS (ed. Kersey), To *Transpose*,..to turn out of Verse into Prose, to change, or alter the Style. 1858 FABER tr. *Life of Xavier* 256 He spent them in transposing a copious exposition of the Apostle's Creed into Japanese.

†**3.** To change the purport, application, or use of; to apply or use otherwise; to give a different direction to; in bad sense, to corrupt, pervert; to misapply, abuse. *Obs.*

1509 BARCLAY *Shyp Folys* (1570) 106 They frowardly the sentence do transpose, And..By their corrupting and vnlawful glose,..bring to damnable heresie. 1548 GESTE *Pr. Masse* in Dugdale *Life* (1840) App. 101 Can the baptisme water be justly recompted a sacrament when it is transposed to other usage..namely..to christen belles, to washe our clothes withal? 1564 *Brief Exam.* B iv b, They toke..the salarie..consecrated to the Idolles.., and transposed it to finde the Ministers of the Church. 1644 MILTON *Educ.* Wks. (1847) 98/1 Nor should..any private friendship have prevailed with me to..transpose my former thoughts.

**4.** To remove from one place or time to another; to transfer, shift (*lit.* and *fig.*: now *rare* exc. as in 5); † to transplant (*obs.*); † to convey, conduct (*obs.*).

c1510 BARCLAY *Mirr. Gd. Manners* (1570) F iv, An olde tree transposed shall finde small auauntage. 1555 in Strype *Eccl. Mem.* (1721) III. App. xlvi. 139 Bisshope Barlo, after he was transposed and..discharged out of the bisshoprick of St. Davids. 1578 BANISTER *Hist. Man* v. 77 Many braunches are deriued from this veyne..transposing bloud to euery Membran. 1602 WARNER *Alb. Eng.* Epit. (1612) 389 Thus..was the Scepter transposed to the House of Lancaster. a1662 HEYLIN *Laud* (1668) 69 Transposing the Communion Table to the East end of the Quire. 1665 MANLEY *Grotius' Low-C. Warres* 671 To transpose his Horsemen, and afterwards his Carriages, into that part of the Sea-Coast. 1742 RICHARDSON *Pamela* III. 215 To..transpose his Affections to a worthier Object. 1887 RUSKIN *Præterita* II. vii. 243 As I transpose myself back through the forty years of desultory..reading.

**5.** To alter the order of (a set or series of things), or the position of (a thing) in a series; to put each of (two or more things) in the place of the other or others, to interchange; *esp.* to alter the order of letters in a word or of words in a sentence. (Now the ordinary sense.)

1538 ELYOT, *Metathesis*, where one letter is transposed from one place in a worde into an nother as *Tymber Tymbre.* 1571 GOLDING *Calvin on Ps.* lxxv. 5 Manye because they saw there could no handsom sence be picked out of the words, thoght the order to have bin transposed. 1605 CAMDEN *Rem.* 153 The letters of Elizabetha Regina transposed to signifie that happinesse..O Englands Soveraigne thou hast made vs happy: thus Elizabetha Regina, Angliæ Hera, Beasti. 1612 BRINSLEY *Lud. Lit.* xiv. (1627) 197 This one Verse is turned by transposing the words 104 wayes. 1691–8 NORRIS *Pract. Disc.* (1711) III. 171 Whose Notions ..are cross and transposed, that calls Evil Good, and Good Evil. 1706 [see TRANSPOSING]. 1833 J. HOLLAND *Manuf. Metal* II. 289 A common balance..should always be tested in this way:—Let a weight be put in one dish, and balanced by other weights in the other dish; let the weights be then transposed. 1861 PALEY *Æschylus* (ed. 2) *Supplices* 909 *note*, The following four verses Hermann transposes after 927. 1902 SLOANE *Electr. Dict.*, *Transposing*, a method of laying metallic circuits for telephoning. The wires at short intervals are crossed so that alternate sections lie on opposite sides of each other. It is done to avoid induction.

**b.** *Algebra.* To transfer (a quantity) from one side of an equation to the other, with change of sign.

1810 HUTTON *Course Math.* I. 222 Thus, if $x + 5 = 8$; then transposing 5 gives $x = 8 - 5 = 3$. c1865 in *Circ. Sc.* I. 456/2 The $3x$ is transposed: it is taken from the right and put on the left with changed sign.

†**6.** To discompose, disturb the mental composure of. *Obs. rare.*

1594 KYD *Cornelia* II. 214 Madam, you must not thus transpose your selfe; Wee see your sorrow, but who sorrowes not? 1621 BURTON *Anat. Mel.* II. III. v, Do something or other, let it [grief] not transpose thee.

**7.** *Mus.* To alter the key of; to put into a different key (in composition, arrangement, or performance).

1609 DOULAND *Ornith. Microl.* 26 To transpose is to remoue a song, or a Key from the proper place? 1715 (*title*) Melodies Proper to be Sung To..ye Psalms of David, Figur'd for the Organ, and..the Treble of each Melody Transpos'd for the Flute. 1845 E. HOLMES *Mozart* 30 He transposes *prima vista* the airs he accompanies. 1875 OUSELEY *Mus. Form* 71 At bar 23 the first subject is transposed into the key of E.

Hence **Transpo·sed** *ppl. a.*; **Transpo·sedly** (-ėdli) *adv.*

1609 DOULAND *Ornith. Microl.* 16 In transposed Songs. 1683 MOXON *Mech. Exerc., Printing* xxii. ¶ 8 He removes the other Transpos'd Page into the place of the first. 1771 LUCKOMBE *Hist. Print.* 447 If there be more than two Transpos'd Pages in the Sheet. 1889 F. TAYLOR in Grove *Dict. Mus.* IV. 161/2 Transposed editions of songs are frequently published, that the same compositions may be made available for voices of different compass. 1678 CUDWORTH *Intell. Syst.* I. v. 676 Writing down the..letters of the alphabet transposedly, any how.

**Transposer** (trɑnsˌpōu·zəɹ). [f. prec. + -ER[1].] One who transposes: esp. in sense 7.

1882 OGILVIE *Suppl.* s.v., The transposer has written the tune two tones higher. 1894 *Westm. Gaz.* 23 Apr. 1/3 Many great musicians are poor transposers.

**Transposing** (trɑnsˌpōu·ziŋ), *vbl. sb.* [f. as prec. + -ING[1].] The action of the vb. TRANSPOSE, in various senses.

1550 *Acc. St. Andrew's, Canterb.* (MS.), Item for the transposyng of a cope xviij d. 1559 MORWYNG *Evonym.* 141 By a certain *metempsychosin*, that is a transposinge of the soules or principal vertues. 1574 tr. *Marlorat's Apocalips* 210 b, The cup of his wrath...The transposing of the woorde Cup from his owne proper signification,..is very ryfe in the Scriptures. 1706 A. BEDFORD *Temple Mus.* vii. 156 We hardly meet with a Verse.., but with Transposing would admit of..Rhymes. 1908 *Contemp. Rev.* Apr. 414 There is not much more in it than a transposing of words.

**b.** *attrib.*: **transposing instrument** (*Mus.*), (*a*) an instrument having a mechanical device for transposing into a different key, as a *transposing harpsichord, organ, piano*; (*b*) a name for those orchestral instruments the parts for which are written in a different key from that in which they sound.

1840 *Penny Cycl.* XVIII. 142/2 This instrument was called by Mr. Trotter a transposing piano-forte. 1883 W. S. ROCKSTRO in Grove *Dict. Mus.* III. 433/1 In all these Scores, the Parts for the so-called 'Transposing-Instruments' correspond with the separate 'Parts' used in the Orchestra. 1889 A. J. HIPKINS *ibid.* IV. 160/1 Prætorius (A.D. 1619) speaks of transposing clavicymbals (harpsichords) which by shifting the keyboard could be set two notes higher or lower...Burney in his musical tour met with two transposing harpsichords; one..at Venice; the other..at Bologna.

**Transposition** (trɑnsˌpŏzi·ʃən). [prob. a. F. *transposition* (c1560 in Paré), or ad. med.L. *transposition-em* (Du Cange), n. of action from L. *transpōnĕre* (f. TRANS- + *pōnĕre* to place); but, like other nouns in *-position*, associated in F. and Eng. with *transposer*, TRANSPOSE *v.* etc.] The action of transposing, or condition of being transposed; the result of this.

**1.** *gen.* Removal from one position to another; transference.

1538 ELYOT, *Transcribere*, the transposition of a possession from one to an other. 1642 FULLER *Holy & Prof. St.* I. vii. 19 Well may masters consider how easie a transposition it had been for God, to have made him to mount into the saddle that holds the stirrop. 1678 CUDWORTH *Intell. Syst.* I. i. § 33. 42 This was the Doctrine of Pythagoras.., that no Real Entity perishes in Corruptions, nor is produced in Generations, but only new Modifications and Transpositions made. 1827 CARLYLE *Misc., Germ. Lit.* (1857) I. 30 A transposition of the critic into the author's point of vision.

†**b.** Translation into another language. *Obs.*

1653 LD. VAUX tr. *Godeau's St. Paul* A ij, To publish this elaborate transposition of your Lordships out of French into English.

**2.** Alteration of order, or interchange of position, esp. of letters in a word, or words in a sentence; metathesis; the result of such action; a word or sentence transposed.

1582 T. WATSON *Centurie of Loue* lxxx, By tables of transilition to decypher any thing that is written by secret transposition of letters. 1630 J. TAYLOR (Water P.) *Life & Death Virg. Mary* Wks. 22/1 For in an Anagram Iskariott is, By letters transposition, Traitor kis. 1675 BAXTER *Cath. Theol.* II. I. 248 Beza..thinks that a transposition of two Verses hath darkened these Texts. 1727 H. HERBERT tr. *Fleury's Eccl. Hist.* I. 62 There are so many..hyperbatons and transpositions, which render his stile difficult. 1818 SCOTT *Br. Lamm.* xxxiv, The mysterious transposition of the portraits. 1861 PALEY *Æschylus* (ed. 2) *Choeph.* 219 *note*, By the accidental transposition of the verses.

**3.** *Mus.* **a.** Alteration of key; the performance of a piece in a different key from that in which it is written, or the writing of a piece in a different key from the original; also *transf.* a transposed piece. †**b.** Inversion of parts in counterpoint (*obs.*).

1609 DOULAND *Ornith. Microl.* 26 Transposition is the remouing of a Song, or a Key from his proper place. 1740 (*title*) Calliope, or English Harmony: a Collection of.. English and Scots Songs,..with the Thorough Bass and Transpositions for the Flute. 1889 F. TAYLOR in Grove *Dict. Mus.* IV. 161/1 In transposition it often happens that a natural has to be represented by a sharp or flat, and *vice versa.*

**4.** *Algebra.* Transference of a quantity from one side of an equation (or one member of a proportion) to the other.

1664 POWER *Exp. Philos.* II. 130 Here is now four Proportionals, and by any three given, you may strike out [? = hit upon] the fourth, by Conversion, Transposition, and Division of them. 1674 JEAKE *Arith.* (1696) 622 In Transposition of the next Equation..the Signs are accordingly changed. c1865 *Circ. Sc.* I. 456/2 If known and unknown quantities are linked together, separate them by transposition.

**5.** *Anat.* Abnormal position of the organs of the body, e.g. the heart being on the right side; heterotaxy.

1857 DUNGLISON *Med. Lex.*, *Transposition of the Viscera* ..consists in the viscera being found out of the situations they ordinarily occupy. 1904 *Brit. Med. Jrnl.* 17 Dec. 1643 Heterotaxy, or transposition, the teratogenesis of which is still obscure.

Hence **Transposi·tional** *a.* (*rare*−1), of, pertaining to, or involving transposition.

a1800 S. PEGGE *Anecd. Eng. Lang.* (1814) 77 The most striking..error in pronunciation among the Londoners..lies in the transpositional use of the letters *W* and *V*...Thus they always say *Weal*, instead of *veal*..*Vicked*, for *wicked*.

**Transpositive** (trɑnsˌpǫ·zitiv), *a.* [f. TRANSPOSE *v.*, after *positive*, etc. Cf. F. *transpositif* (18th c.), and rare L. *transpositīva* (Quintil.).] Characterized by or given to transposition.

1783 BLAIR *Lect. Rhet.*, etc. I. vii. 122 The French Language..admits the least of inversion..; But the Italian retains the most of the antient transpositive character. 1869 A. W. POTTS *Lat. Pr. Comp.* (1870) II. ii. 40 The English language..is compelled to obey somewhat rigid rules in the arrangement of the words...The Latin language, on the contrary, is transpositive.

Hence **Transpo·sitively** *adv.* (in recent Dicts.).

**Transˌpo·sitor.** *rare*−1. [agent-n. in L. form from *transpōnĕre* (see TRANSPOSE); cf. F. *transpositeur* (1835 Dict. Acad.) and POSITOR.] One who transposes; a transposer.

1824 LANDOR *Imag. Conv., Southey & Porson* 43 We will lay aside the scrip of the transpositor and the pouch of the pursuer.

So **Transpo·sitory** *a.* (*rare*−1) = TRANSPOSITIVE.

1837 *Fraser's Mag.* XVI. 478 'Old England', in virtue of this transpository operation, evolves a *Golden Land.*

†**Transˌpou·r,** *v. Obs. rare.* [TRANS- 2.] *trans.* To pour from one to another, transfer by pouring.

1585 FETHERSTONE tr. *Calvin on Acts* xv. 9 Faith taketh that of Christ which it transpoureth into vs.

**Transˌpri·nt,** *v. rare.* [f. TRANS- 2 + PRINT *v.*] *trans.* To reprint from another book, etc. Hence **Tra·nsprint** *sb.*, that which is transprinted.

1825 COLERIDGE *Aids Refl.* (1848) I. 337 The celebrated conclusion of the fourth book of Paley's Moral and Political Philosophy, referred to in p. 268,..is here transprinted for the convenience of the Reader. 1827 BENTHAM *Mem. & Corr.* Wks. 1843 X. 577 A transprint of which, in a number of the *Examiner*, is likewise destined to accompany them.

**Transˌpro·cess.** *Anat.* [TRANS- 6.] A transverse process of a vertebra; a diapophysis.

1891 *Cent. Dict.* cites COUES.

**Transprose** (trɑnsˌprōu·z), *v.* [f. TRANS- 2 + PROSE *sb.* Orig. a nonce-word, to match TRANSVERSE *v.*[2], q. v.] *trans.* To turn into prose; to translate or render in prose. (Chiefly humorous.)

1671 VILLIERS (Dk. Buckhm.) *Rehearsal* I. i. (Arb.) 31 *Bayes*...I Transverse it; that is, if it be Prose, put it into Verse, (but that takes up some time); if it be Verse, put it into Prose. *Johns.* Methinks, Mr. Bayes, that putting Verse into Prose should be call'd Transprosing. *Bayes.* By my troth, a very good Notion, and hereafter it shall be so. 1672 MARVELL (*title*) The Rehearsal transpros'd: or, Animadversions upon a late Book, entituled, a Preface, shewing What Grounds there are of Fears and Jealousies of Popery. 1673 [R. LEIGH] *Transp. Reh.* 4 What Miracles men of Art can do by Transversing Prefaces and Transprosing Playes. 1681 DRYDEN *Abs. & Achit.* II. 443 Instinct he follows and no farther knows, For to write verse with him is to transprose. 1710 STEELE *Tatler* No. 194 ¶ 1, I shall transprose it, to use Mr. Bays's Term. 1732 [see TRANSVERSE *v.*[2]]. 1826 *Museum Criticum* I. 411 Babrius versified them [Æsop's apologues]: various persons, as Mr. Smith says in the Rehearsal, *transprosed* the choliambics of Babrius.

Hence **Transˌpro·sal**, the action of 'transprosing', or something 'transprosed'; **Transpro·ser**, one who 'transproses' (whence **Transpro·sership**); **Transpro·sing** *vbl. sb.*

1671 Transprosing [see above]. 1673 *S'too him Bayes* 4 Godsookers you'l spoil all my Transprosal. *Ibid.* 34, I.. bid your Transprosership heartily farewell. 1673 *Answ. to*

*A Seasonable Disc.*' 19 Has not the judicious Transproser a long Paragraph of the furious temper of these Clergy Men? **1718** J. TRAPP *Æneis* (1735) I. Pref. 81 Tho' the Translating of Poems into Prose is a strange, modern Invention; yet the French Transprosers are so far in the right; because their Language will not bear Verse.

**Trans,pu·lmonary,** *a.* [f. TRANS- 5 + L. *pulmo, pulmōn-em* lung: cf. *pulmonary.*] Acting or operated through the lungs: said of the respiration in birds, in which the lungs are connected with large air-sacs, into and out of which the air passes through the lungs.

**1902** G. B. HOWES in *Rep. Brit. Assoc.* 624 The respiratory process in the bird may be defined as *transpulmonary.*

† **Trans,qua·lify,** *v. Obs. rare*[−1]. [TRANS- 2.] *trans.* To change from one quality to another.

**1652** URQUHART *Jewel* Wks. (1834) 223 The fierceness of his foe was in a trice transqualified into the numbness of a pageant.

**Transrational** (transræ·ʃənăl), *a.* [TRANS- 4.] Going beyond or surpassing what is rational.

**1892** R. L. STEVENSON *Let.* in Myers *Human Personality* (1903) I. 302 The transrational felicity of the [dreamed] word..not one [syllable] was in itself significant, and yet the whole expressed to a nicety a voluminous distress of one in a high fever.

**Transre·al,** *a.* [TRANS- 4.] Beyond the real; outside the world of reality.

**1901** *Speaker* 3 Aug. 503/2 A foothold in the quicksands of time, 'a jumping-off ground' for his raids into the Transreal.

† **Transre·gionate,** *ppl. a. Obs. rare*[−1]. [f. TRANS- + L. *regiōn-em* region + -ATE [2].] Transferred to or inhabiting another region.

**1577** HARRISON *England* III. vi. (1878) II. 39 There are some cockescombs..in England, learning it abroad as men transregionate, which make account also of this pastime.

**Transrhenane** (transrī·nein), *a.* [ad. L. *transrhēnānus* adj. and sb., f. *trans* across + *Rhēnus* the Rhine. Cf. F. *transrhénan, -ane* (in Littré).] That is across or beyond the Rhine; hence, German as opposed to Roman or to French.

*a* **1727** NEWTON *Obs. Dan.* I. v. (1733) 54 Captains of the Transrhenane Franks in the reign of Theodosius. **1830** CROWE *Hist. France* I. 7 A fresh infusion of the ruder spirit of the Transrhenane race came to invigorate the already degenerated Franks of Gaul. **1835** *Fraser's Mag.* XI. 260 The crude chimæras of transcendental and transrhenane philosophy. **1913** *Eng. Hist. Rev.* July 561 The Germans obtained the very rudiments of civilization from the Kelts in their pristine transrhenane home.

**Transriverine** (transri·vərəin), *a.* [f. TRANS- 3 + RIVER: cf. *riverine.*] Situated across a (or the) river; transfluvial.

**1900** *Athenæum* 22 Dec. 824/2 The town [Birkenhead] was projected at first simply as a residential trans-riverine suburb of Liverpool.

† **Transs,** obs. spelling of TRANCE *sb.*

(In the following passage it has been variously taken as TRANCE *sb.*[1] 3 b, and as *sb.*[3]: see also Jamieson.)

*a* **1550** *Christis Kirke Gr.* v, He playt sae schill, and sang sae sweet, Quhyle Towsie tuke a Transs.

**Transsect**: see TRANSECT.

**Trans-segme·ntal,** *a. Anat.* [f. TRANS- 5 + SEGMENT: cf. *segmental.*] Passing across a segment; extending through one segment of a limb and terminating in another, as a nerve or vessel.

**1890** BILLINGS *Nat. Med. Dict.*, *Transsegmental arteries*, those which pass through a region to be distributed beyond.

**Transsene,** variant of TRANSON *v. Obs.*

**Trans-se·nsual,** *a.* [f. TRANS- 4 + L. *sensu-s* sense: cf. *sensual.*] Lying beyond or transcending the senses.

**1807** COLERIDGE in *Lit. Rem.* (1839) IV. 294 Confounding the..effects necessarily predetermined by the precedent causes..with the transsensual ground or actual power.

**Trans-sepu·lchral,** *a.* [f. TRANS- 3 + L. *sepulc(h)rum* sepulchre: cf. *sepulchral.*] That is beyond the sepulchre or tomb.

**1891** in *Cent. Dict.* **1911** in WEBSTER.

† **Trans-sha·pe, tran,sha·pe,** *sb. Obs.* [f. TRANS-SHAPE *v.*] Change of shape; transformation; metamorphosis.

**1611** HEYWOOD *Golden Age* IV. i, By our transhapes And guiles of loue. **1613** — *Silver Age* II. i, But her search He soone deluded in his slye trans-shapes. **1636** — *Love's Mistr.* I. i, Ile shew thee..What kind of people I commerst withall In my transhape.

**Trans-shape** (trans,ʃēⁱ·p), † **transhape** (tran,ʃēⁱ·p), *v.* Now *rare* (? *arch.*). [f. TRANS- + SHAPE *v.*] *trans.* To alter the shape or form of; to transform.

**1575** FENTON *Gold. Epist.* (1577) 332 The Oliue and Laurell, into the which were transhaped Lotus and Daphne. **1599** SHAKS. *Much Ado* v. i. 172 Thus did shee an howre together trans-shape thy particular vertues. **1638** HEYWOOD *Rape Lucrece* Wks. 1874 V. 179 Hee's from a toward hopefull Gentleman, Transeshapt to a meere Ballater. **1656** S. HOLLAND *Zara* (1719) 53 Till Soto by degrees was transhaped into a goodly Steed. **1659** *Lady Alimony* II. vi. E iv b, When th' Camel shall Transhape himself into a nimble Wesil,..I shall value you. **1855** SINGLETON *Virgil* I. 45 Or how he told of Tereus' limbs transshaped.

Hence **Trans-shaped** (-ʃēⁱ·pt) *ppl. a.*; **Trans-sha·ping** *vbl. sb.*

**1602** MARSTON *2nd Pt. Ant. & Mel.* IV. i, Rather put on some transhap't cavalier, Some habit of a spitting critick. **1909** tr. *Jusserand's Lit. Hist. Eng.* III. 140 Deeds of sorcery..: apparitions, evocations, transhapings.

† **Trans-shi·ft,** *v. Obs. rare*[−1]. [TRANS- 2.] *trans.* and *intr.* To shift across or away.

**1648** HERRICK *Hesper., Argt.* 9, I sing of times trans-shifting, and I write How roses first came red, and lillies white. *Ibid., On Himselfe*, When monarchies trans-shifted are, and gone, Here shall endure thy vast dominion.

**Trans-ship, -shipment**: see TRANSHIP, -MENT.

† **Trans-si·tuate,** *v. Obs. rare.* [TRANS- 2.] *trans.* To shift or alter the situation or position of.

**1630** DAVENANT *Cruel Brother* III, He chides Women, for wearing their Halfe-Ruffes, Which pinn'd behind transsciтuates the face.

**Trans-so·lid,** *a. rare.* [f. TRANS- 4 + SOLID *a.*] Beyond solid; of a density surpassing solidity.

**1898** J. W. POWELL *Truth & Error* v. 43 Geologic facts in a vast system lead to the induction that the centrosphere does not exist in the solid state; if it is metallic the weight reduces it to a trans-solid condition.

† **Trans-spi·rit,** *v. Obs. nonce-wd.* [TRANS- 1.] *trans.* To convey the spirit of (a thing) from one place or person to another.

**1652** W. AMES *Saints Security* 33 He is a Christian to purpose, who hath the Bible transpirited into his minde.

† **Trans-spi·ritualized,** *ppl. a. Obs. rare.* [TRANS- 4.] Spiritualized in a surpassing degree.

**1683** E. HOOKER *Pref. Pordage's Mystic Div.* 60 A littl incarnate Cherub..a very highly mystic and transspiritualized Person.

**Trans-ste·llar,** *a.* [f. TRANS- 3 + L. *stella* star: cf. *stellar.*] Existing or lying beyond the stars.

**1888** J. MARTINEAU *Stud. Relig.* II. III. ii. 270 Transstellar regions. **1893** FR. THOMPSON *Judgm. Heav.* iii. Poems 55 On the far crystalline pale of that transtellar Heaven.

**Trans-Stygian** (-sti·dʒiăn), *a.* [f. TRANS- 7 + L. *Styx, Styg-em*: cf. *stygian.*] That is on the other side of the Styx; infernal. (Cf. TRANS-ACHERONTIC.)

**1899** R. WALLACE *Geo. Buchanan* v. 91 Despising Pluto and the trans-Stygian penalties.

† **Trans-sty·le,** *v. Obs. rare.* [TRANS- 2.] *trans.* To transform or change the style or title of.

**1611** HEYWOOD *Gold. Age* III. i, Archas..by Ioues gift Pelasgia's seate hath wonne, Which after..He hath transstil'd Archadia by his name.

**Trans-subje·ctive,** *a.* Also **tran,subjective.** [TRANS- 4.] That transcends or is beyond subjective or individual experience as such.

**1887** R. ADAMSON in *Mind* Jan. 127 Pure, mere experience is simply such knowledge as the subject directly has of his own subjective processes. Anything else shows itself on the slightest analysis to contain trans-subjective reference or trans-subjective elements. **1899** JAS. WARD *Naturalism & Agn.* II. 170 The sun as transubjective object is not L's sun or M's sun or N's sun..but rather what is common to them all, neglecting what is peculiar to each. **1902** T. CASE in *Encycl. Brit.* XXX. 668/1 From this epistemology he derives the metaphysical conclusion that the things we know are indeed independent of my consciousness and of yours, taken individually, or, to use a new phrase, are 'trans-subjective'. **1911** JAS. WARD *Realm of Ends* vi. 124 By intersubjective intercourse [men] attain to the trans-subjective or truly objective, both in knowledge and in action.

† **Trans-su·bstancing,** *vbl. sb. Obs. rare*[−1]. [f. TRANS- 2 + SUBSTANCE + -ING [1], repr. med.L. *transubstāntiātio.*] = TRANSUBSTANTIATION.

*c* **1380** WYCLIF *Wks.* (1880) 345 Þus power þat prestis han standeþ not in trans-substansinge of þe oste.

**Transsude, Transsume,** etc.: see TRANSUDE, TRANSUME, etc.

**Trans,te·mporal,** *a. Anat.* [f. TRANS- 5 + L. *tempora* the temples: cf. TEMPORAL *a.*[2]] Crossing the temples; traversing the temporal lobe of the brain, as 'the transtemporal fissure'.

**1889** *Buck's Handbk. Med. Sc.* VIII. 157/1 The crossing of the temporal lobe ventrad of the supertemporal fissure by two transtemporal fissures.

† **Trans,tempora·tion.** *Obs. nonce-wd.* [f. TRANS- + L. *tempus, tempor-* time + -ATION.] Intermission of time, delay.

**1651** *Life Father Sarpi* (1676) 59, I would desire the Reader to tolerate a little transtemporation, and digression.

† **Trans,ti·me,** *v. Obs. nonce-wd.* [TRANS- 2.] *trans.* To change as to time.

**1647** WARD *Simp. Cobler* (1843) 16 To transplace or transtime a stated Institution of Christ,..is to destroy it.

**Transubstantial** (transʊbstæ·nʃăl), *a.* [f. TRANS- 1 + L. *substāntiăl-is*, f. *substantia* SUBSTANCE: cf. CONSUBSTANTIAL.] **a.** Changed or changeable from one substance into another; of or pertaining to transubstantiation. **b.** Made of something beyond substance; non-material, incorporeal.

**1567** *Gude & Godlie B.* (S.T.S.) 210 Gif God be transubstanciall In [= into] breid, with *hoc est Corpus Meum.* **1651** BIGGS *New Disp.* ⁋ 214 The transubstantial migration of the grapy juice of the papall Sacramentarians. **1892** E. C. STEDMAN in *Century Mag.* Apr. 821/1 The very stuff whereof the Muse fashions her transubstantial garments.

Hence **Transubsta·ntialism,** the theory or doctrine of transubstantiation; **Transubsta·ntialist,** one who holds this doctrine; **Transubsta·ntialize** *v.*, † (*a*) *trans.* to change from one substance to another, to transubstantiate; (*b*) *intr.* to hold or maintain the doctrine of transubstantiation (whence **Transubsta·ntializa·tion**); **Transubsta·ntially** *adv.*, by change of substance, in the way of transubstantiation.

**1842** G. S. FABER *Prov. Lett.* (1844) I. 183 The clause, through which Mr. Maitland would charge the Albigenses with acknowledged *Transubstantialism, could never have been uttered by themselves. **1838** — *Inquiry* 65 It is useful to let a Romanist himself exhibit the blasphemous heresy of the *Transubstantialists in all its naked deformity. **1850** BP. E. H. BROWNE *Exp. 39 Articles* XXVIII. i. (1874) 679 If there were no other alternative..we must perforce acknowledge, that they believed in a carnal presence, and were transubstantialists. For some presence they undoubtedly taught. **1647** TRAPP *Comm. Matt.* iii. 11 [The fire of the Spirit] spiritualizeth and *transubstantializeth us, as it were, into the same image from glory to glory. **1826** G. S. FABER *Diffic. Romanism* (1853) 246 Some..have rashly charged the Episcopal Church in Scotland with transubstantialising, because the ancient phrase occurs in her eucharistic liturgy. **1846** — *Lett. Tractar. Secess.* 180 The old phraseology, which Dr. Moehler confidently adduces as proof positive that the Primitive Church transubstantialised from the very beginning. **1826** — *Diffic. Romanism* (1853) 100 Specimens of such phraseology, by way of demonstrating the *transubstantialisation of the Primitive Church. **1577** tr. *Bullinger's Decades* (1592) 27 To expound the wordes of the Sacrament Sacramentally, and not *Transubstantially. **1579** FULKE *Heskins' Parl.* 428 Basil..beleeued the bread and wine to be made Christes body and bloud, he meaneth corporally and transubstantially.

**Tra·nsubsta·ntiate,** *ppl. a. Obs.* or *arch.* Also 5–7 **transs-**. [ad. med.L. *tran(s)substāntiāt-us*, pa. pple. of *tran(s)substāntiāre*: see next.] Transubstantiated. (Mostly const. as *pa. pple.*)

*c* **1450** *Mirour Saluacioun* 1886 Be the preest is brede to flesshe Transsubstanciate. *a* **1536** TINDALE *Declar. Sacram.* C vij, [They say] the breade and wyne are changed, turned, altered and transsubstancyat in to the very body and bloud of Chryste. **1550** CRANMER *Defence* 30 Yt holdeth, that breade is transubstantiate or tourned into the bodye, and wyne into the bloudde. **1571** FORTESCUE *Forest* 43 Sutche mercilesse and transubstantiate monsters. **1598** DALLINGTON *Meth. Trav.* B iij, He had transubstantiate this fat Fowle into fish. **1678** R. BARCLAY *Apol. Quakers* xiii. § 5. 459 The Bread, and..the Wine..which they say is Consecrate and Transubstantiate into the very Body of Christ. **1848** KINGSLEY *Saint's Trag.* I. ii. 194 To find the canvas warm with life, and matter A moment transubstantiate to heaven.

**Transubstantiate** (transʊbstæ·nʃi,eⁱt), *v.* Also **transs-**. [f. ppl. stem of med.L. *tran(s)substāntiāre* (Du Cange), f. TRANS- + *substāntia* SUBSTANCE. Cf. F. *transsubstantier* (14th c. in Godef. *Compl.*). App. first used in pa. pple.: cf. prec.] *trans.* To change from one substance into another; to transform, transmute.

**1584** R. SCOT *Discov. Witchcr.* III. ii. (1886) 45 She [a witch] confesseth that she transubstantiateth hir selfe. **1615** W. LAWSON *Country Housew. Gard.* (1626) 19 The sap..is consolidated and transubstantiated into the substance of the tree. **1670** PETTUS *Fodinæ Reg.* 44 The Philosophers stone ..which would..transubstantiate other Metals into..Gold and Silver. *a* **1711** KEN *Hymns Evang.* Poet. Wks. 1721 I. 98 He Water transubstantiated to Wine. **1870** HUXLEY *Lay Serm.* (1877) 133 A singular inward laboratory, which I possess, will..convert the dead protoplasm into living protoplasm, and transubstantiate sheep [*i.e.* mutton] into man.

**b.** *spec.* in *Theol.*: see TRANSUBSTANTIATION 2.

[*c* **1450**: see prec.] **1533** TINDALE *Supper of Lord* B iij, The wyne transsubstanciated into his bloud. **1651** C. CARTWRIGHT *Cert. Relig.* I. 122 After Consecration there is no longer the substance of Bread, but that the Bread is transubstantiated, and turned into the substance of Christs Body. *a* **1774** TUCKER *Lt. Nat.* (1834) II. 483 It is necessary the priest should call down His very body crucified upon the cross into the bread; which must be transubstantiated thereinto, or consubstantiated therewith. *a* **1819** GEO. HILL *Lect. Div.* (1821) III. 362 The practice of partaking in private of a small portion of what the priest has thus transubstantiated.

**c.** *transf.* and *fig.*

**1641** R. BROOKE *Eng. Episc.* 71 So large that no one man ..could sufficiently visit and over-see it except he get the Pope to Transubstantiate him also and so get a Vbiquitarian Body. **1675** OWEN *Author. Script.* Wks. 1851 VIII. 499 A private doctor of the Church of Rome may thus transubstantiate blasphemy into piety. **1759** STERNE *Tr. Shandy* II. ix, Never was a Dr. Slop so beluted, and so transubstantiated. **1884** J. TAIT *Mind in Matter* (1892) 125 Hints are transubstantiated into conceptions.

**d.** *absol.*

**1579** FULKE *Heskins' Parl.* 67 Ye Papistes call consecrating, to change ye substances, or to transubstantiat. **1641** R. BROOKE *Eng. Episc.* II. iii. 74 A Preist can Consecrate, and by Consecration Transubstantiate. **1667** MILTON *P. L.* v. 438 With keen dispatch Of real hunger, and concoctive heate To transubstantiate.

**e.** *intr.* for *pass.* To become transubstantiated.

**1851** W. ANDERSON *Exposure Popery* (1878) 84 If the cake be not genuine in respect of wheaten flour, and if the wine have been made of immature grapes, they will not transubstantiate.

Hence **Transubsta·ntiated** *ppl. a.*; **Transubsta·ntiating** *vbl. sb.* and *ppl. a.*

**1550** BALE *Apol.* 63 Those *transubstanciated Goddes, were knowne for no Goddes. **1654** JER. TAYLOR *Real Pres.* 47 The spiritual eating of him..may be done without their Transubstantiated flesh. **1718** J. CHAMBERLAYNE *Relig. Philos.* (1730) I. ii. § 5 A metamorphosed or transubstantiated Earth. **1849** SIR J. STEPHEN *Eccl. Biog.* (1850) I. 82 His faltering lips had closed on the transubstantiated elements. **1586** HOOKER *Serm. Justif.*, etc. § 11 As *transubstantiating of sacramental elements in the Eucharist. **1800** W. TAYLOR in *Monthly Mag.* X. 319 Scarcely marvellous enough for his *transubstantiating fancy.

**Transubstantiation** (trænsʊbstænʃi,ēⁱ·ʃən, -stænsi,ēⁱ·ʃən). Also **transs-**. [ad. med.L. *tran(s)substāntiātio* (in use in the 11th c.), n. of action fr.

*tran(s)substantiāre*: see prec. So F. *transsubstantiation* (14th c. in Godef. *Compl.*).

The L. form occurs as a current term, *c* 1070, in St. Peter Damian *Expos. Canonis Missæ* § 7 'Quando profertur ipsum pronomen ['Hoc'], nondum est transsubstantiatio'. (Migne *Patrologia* CXLV. 883.)]

**1.** The changing of one substance into another. (Often with allusion to sense 2.)

**1398** TREVISA *Barth. De P. R.* IX. xxxi. (MS. Add. 27944) lf. 129 Þanne þe cene day is day of reconciliacioun, of transubstanciacioun, of consacracioun, and of sacringe, of halewinge of oynement. **1477** NORTON *Ord. Alch.* v. in *Ashm.* (1652) 86 Whereby of Mettalls is made transmutation, Not only in Colour, but transubstantiation. **1574** NEWTON *Health Mag.* 23 Avicen sayeth that fleash is a meate comfortynge the body and of meere transubstantiation and conversion into bloud. **1594** PLAT *Jewell-ho.* III. 65 The Vintners practising..sometimes euen real transubstantiations, of white wine into Claret. **1651** HOBBES *Leviath.* IV. xlv. 361 The Gentiles..might excuse their Idolatry, by pretending..a transubstantiation of their Wood, and Stone into God Almighty. **1768** TUCKER *Lt. Nat.* (1834) I. 286 We look upon..the change of a substance from one species into another as a transubstantiation. **1872** O. W. HOLMES *Poet Breakf.-t.* xi. 362 It is no longer a wax doll for her, but has undergone a transubstantiation quite as real as that of the Eucharist.

**2.** The conversion in the Eucharist of the whole substance of the bread into the body and of the wine into the blood of Christ, only the appearances (and other 'accidents') of bread and wine remaining: according to the doctrine of the Roman Church.

Distinguished from *consubstantiation*, in which the elements of the bread and wine are held to coexist with the body and blood of Christ.

**1533** TINDALE *Supper of Lord* C iij b, S. Thomas theyr owne doctoure that made theyr transsubstanciacion confessethe that some there were that sayed that Christe dyd fyrste consecrate wyth other wordes, ere he nowe reachyng the bread to his disciple sayed, This is my bodie. *a* **1536** — *Declar. Sacram.* D iv, As concernyng the transsubstanciatyon I thinke that such a speche was among the olde doctours though they that came after vnderstode them amysse. **1558** BP. WATSON *Sev. Sacram.* viii. 45 The..church..did..well..when it inuented the worde of *Transsubstantiation*, to expresse the olde truthe,..that the former substaunces of breade and wine be conuerted and chaunged into the body and bloud of Chryste. **1579** FULKE *Heskins' Parl.* 73 Transubstantiation is not so olde as Damascene, neither was it receyued in the Greeke Church, neither is it at this daye. **1635** PAGITT *Christianogr.* 55 The word Transubstantiation is..first mentioned by Roger Hovenden, who flourished An. 1204. **1664** H. MORE *Myst. Iniq.* XV. 52 That Mysterious conceit of Transsubstantiation and the Idolatry thereon depending. **1678** *Act 30 Chas. II.* Stat. II. § 3 Such Peer or Member shall..audibly repeat this Declaration following. 'I *A. B.* do..testify and declare, That I do believe that in the Sacrament of the Lord's Supper there is not any Transubstantiation of the Elements of Bread and Wine into the Body and Blood of Christ at or after the Consecration thereof'. **1715** BENTLEY *Serm.* x. 362 By slow degrees Transubstantiation was enacted into an Article of Faith. **1839** KEIGHTLEY *Hist. Eng.* I. 83 As transubstantiation had not yet [11th c.] been established by the papal authority, it..formed no part of the public system of the Anglo Saxon church. **1901** BP. GORE *Body of Christ* ii. § 3. 118 The use..of the distinction of substance and accidents for the purpose of assisting the doctrine of transubstantiation was already familiar to Berengar,..he combats the proposed use of it, denying that the accidents can exist apart from their substance or 'subject', or apart from that of which they are attributes. **1901** B. J. KIDD *39 Art.* II. 230–1 It was a crude attempt to secure some real meaning to Our Lord's Words of Institution by the doctrine of a *physical* transubstantiation or change in the material elements. But the Schoolmen now came forward with a subtler defence...Hence the doctrine of a *metaphysical* transubstantiation was adopted [by the Realists].

Hence **Transubstantia·tionist**, one who holds the doctrine of transubstantiation. So **Transubstantia·tionite, -a·tionalist.**

*a* **1834** COLERIDGE in *Lit. Rem.* (1839) IV. 192 The Consubstantiationist, or the Transubstantiationist. **1839** J. ROGERS *Antipopopr.* VI. ii. 219 What Bedlam..contains madmen madder than the mad transubstantiationite? **1884** *N. & Q.* 23 Feb. 149/2 Dr. Samuel Pegge explained it ['please the pigs'] by 'An't please the pyx',..and so making it equivalent to *Deo volente* in the minds of transubstantiationalists.

**Transubstantiative** (trɒnsʊbstæ·nʃiătiv), *a.* [f. as TRANSUBSTANTIATE *v.* + -IVE; cf. CONSUBSTANTIATIVE.] Of the nature of transubstantiation. Hence **Transubsta·ntiatively** *adv.*, by way of transubstantiation.

**1826** G. S. FABER *Diffic. Romanism* (1853) 73 *note*, The fourth Council of Lateran..determined that the alleged material change in the elements, is not consubstantiative but transubstantiative. *Ibid.* 271 *note*, If, after his ascension, the humanity of Christ had been transubstantiatively changed into his Divinity.

†**Transubsta·ntiator.** *Obs.* [agent-n. in L. form, from med.L. *transubstantiāre* or TRANSUBSTANTIATE: see -OR. Cf. F. *transsubstantiateur* (16th c. in Godef. *Compl.*).] One who holds the doctrine of transubstantiation; a transubstantialist.

*a* **1555** RIDLEY *Declar. Lord's Supper* (1556) 53 b, Some amonge the transubstantiators..walke soe wilely and soe warely betwixte these ij..opinions. **1624** GATAKER *Transubst.* 82 As these Transubstantiators..say that the Bread in the Eucharist looseth its owne nature. *a* **1626** W. SCLATER *Exp. Rom. iv.* (1650) 143 Our Transubstantiatours..delude the simple, perswading the reall presence of Christs body. **1686** H. MORE *Real Pres.* ii. 12 These Transubstantiators have fallen..into that very absurdity, that they seemed so much to abhor from.

So **Transubsta·ntiatory** *a.* (*rare*⁻¹), implying or tending to transubstantiation.

**1878** E. JENKINS *Haverholme* 184 Transubstantiatory rather, is it not?

**Transudate** (trɒ·nˌsiudĕt), *sb.* [ad. mod.L. *transūdāt-us*, pa. pple. of L. *transūdāre* to TRANSUDE.] A substance transuded: = TRANSUDATION b.

**1876** tr. *Wagner's Gen. Pathol.* (ed. 6) 156 Most transudates taken from the cavities of dead bodies contain..generators of fibrin. **1899** *Allbutt's Syst. Med.* VIII. 500 In nasal catarrh or bronchitis we have..change of the normal transudate into a morbid exudate.

†**Tranˌsudate,** *v. Obs. rare.* [f. *transūdāt-*, ppl. stem of mod.L. *transūdāre* to TRANSUDE: see -ATE ³.] *intr.* = TRANSUDE.

**1684** BOYLE *Porousn. Anim. & Solid Bod.* viii. 128 That Mercury and Aqua fortis being digested together in a Bolthead, may, by rubbing the outside of the Glass, be made visibly and palpably to transudate.

**Transudation** (trɒnˌsiudēˈʃən). Also 7 transs-. [ad. mod.L. *tran(s)sūdātio*, f. L. *trans* across + *sūdātio* a sweating. Cf. F. *transsudation* (18th c.).] The action or process of transuding; the passing off or oozing out of a liquid through the pores of a substance.

**1612** WOODALL *Surg. Mate* Wks. (1653) 274 Transudation is, when in descensory distillation, the essence provoked, sweateth through, and is carried..into the receiver. **1661** BOYLE *Certain Physiol. Ess.* (1669) 192 The drops..proceeded not from the transudation of the Liquor within the Glass. **1794** SULLIVAN *View Nat.* I. xiv. 175 It causes transudations, evaporations, exhalations. **1848** CARPENTER *Anim. Phys.* 39 A simple transudation of the watery parts of the blood may take place..in the dead as in the living body.

*attrib.* **1899** CAGNEY *Jaksch's Clin. Diagn.* viii. (ed. 4) 418 Transudation fluids may be serous, sanious, or in rare instances, chylous.

**b.** *concr.* Something which is transuded.

**1650** H. BROOKE *Conserv. Health* 183 The more thick Transudation by the Ears. **1707** *Curios. in Husb. & Gard.* 101 The Manna of Calabria, and of Briançon, are only the Transudation of a Humour that breaths out of..Larch-Trees. **1897** *Allbutt's Syst. Med.* IV. 322 The amount [of proteids] present in the transudations of renal disease are far below those seen in the transudations of cardiac disease.

**Tranˌsu·datory,** *a.* [f. ppl. stem of mod.L. *tran(s)sūdāre*: see next and -ORY ².] Having the quality of transuding; characterized by transudation.

**1752** RANDOLPH *Virtues Bath-Water* 53 It does not..check the Exhalation of the transudatory Lymph. **1876** *Clin. Soc. Trans.* IX. 142 A cystoid or cicatrix, with their transudatory walls, favours the flow of intra-ocular fluids by exosmose.

**Transude** (trɒnˌsiū·d), *v.* Also 7 **transsude.** [ad. mod.L. *tran(s)sūdāre*, f. *trans* across + *sūdāre* to sweat. Cf. F. *transsuder* (18th c.).]

**a.** *intr.* To ooze through or out like sweat; to exude through pores (in the human body or anything permeable).

**1664** EVELYN *Sylva* 54 From the latter [*Picea*] transsudes a very bright and pellucid Gum. **1744** MITCHELL in *Phil. Trans.* XLIII. 108 In Winter, when they are..not covered with that greasy Sweat which transudes thro' them in Summer, their Skins feel more coarse. **1784** WEDGWOOD *ibid.* LXXIV. 383 Part of the water transudes through the vessel. **1877** ROBERTS *Handbk. Med.* (ed. 3) I. 31 The vessels become overloaded, and the fluid portion of the blood transudes.

**b.** *trans.* To ooze through (something) like sweat.

**1781** KERR in *Phil. Trans.* LXXI. 378 As the Lac liquifies twist the bag, and when a sufficient quantity has transuded the pores of the cloth, lay it [etc.]. **1814** W. C. WELLS *Ess. Dew* (1866) 110 The pans..are so porous that they readily permit water to transude them.

**c.** *trans.* in causal sense: To cause (something) to ooze through.

**1861** HULME tr. *Moquin-Tandon* II. IV. i. 214 A fluid which they disgorge or transude from some part of their body. **1877** ROBERTS *Handbk. Med.* (ed. 3) I. 26 The vessels may be so distended as to transude serum.

Hence **Transu·ded** *ppl. a.*, **Transu·ding** *vbl. sb.* and *ppl. a.*

**1756** NUGENT *Montesquieu's Spir. Laws* (1758) I. XIV. x. 326 After the transuding of the aqueous humour. **1772** *Phil. Trans.* LXII. 467 To let out extravasated or transuding fluids. *c* **1865** *Circ. Sc.* I. 333/1 A very great proportion of the transuded matters does not contribute to the nutrition. **1873** T. H. GREEN *Introd. Pathol.* (ed. 2) 319 The transuded serum usually differs from blood-serum in being of lower specific gravity.

†**Tranˌsu·lt,** *v. Obs. rare*⁻⁰. [ad. L. *tran(s)sultāre* to leap over, f. TRANS- + *saltāre* to leap.]

**1623** COCKERAM, *Transult*, to leape away. **1656** BLOUNT *Glossogr.*, *Transult*, to leap or jump over, to overleap.

**Transum**, obs. form of TRANSOM.

**Transume** (trɒnsiū·m), *v. Obs.* exc. *Hist.* Also 5–7 transsume. [ad. (post-Aug.) L. *tran(s)sūmĕre*, f. *trans* across, over + *sūmĕre* to take, seize; in med.L. *transsumĕre*, *transsumptāre*, to transcribe, make a copy of. Cf. OF. *transumer* (1482 in Godef.).]

**1.** *trans.* To make an official copy of a (legal) document; = EXEMPLIFY 7. *Obs.* exc. *Hist.*

**1482** in Rymer *Foedera* (1711) XII. 165/1 We have Decerned..the said Letters to be Exemplified and Transsumed. **1533** *St. Papers Hen. VIII*, I. 413 That the same Acte may be impressed, transumed, and set up on every churche dore. **1541** *Records of Elgin* (1903) I. 64 An transump and instrument transsumit out of Master Androis Cheves prothogall buik. **1545** *Reg. Privy Council Scot.* I. 10 The autentik copy of the said letter of merk autentikly transumyt in the toun of Arkis under the sele of the tabellioun and keparis of the sele of the vecunty of Arkis. **1598** D. WEDDERBURN *Compt Bk.* (S.H.S.) 157 David Ostlar..restis awin me a Crown for transuming Andro Ostlaris barnis Seasingis. **1693, 1765–8** [see TRANSUMPT *sb.*]. **1881** S. R. MACPHAIL *Relig. Ho. Pluscardyn* xi. 107 The original bull..having been produced in court to be transumed.

†**2.** To take from one to another, take over; to transfer, transport. *Obs.*

**1483** CAXTON *Pilgr. Sowle* IV. xxix. 76 This word statua, whiche that we transumen in to Englysshe, that is to mene an Image. **1627** W. SCLATER *Exp. 2 Thess.* (1629) 184 Termes properly belonging to time, are yet sometimes transsumed to denote what is pertinent to eternity. **1630** LORD *Relig. Persees* 17 The Angell..bade him close his eyes, and he would transume and rappe him up into that place of glory. **1656** [? J. SERGEANT] tr. *T. White's Peripat. Inst.* 382 Physicians affirm..the Seed of the Man disappears, being transum'd into the Flesh of the Woman.

†**3.** To transmute, change, convert (*into* something else).

**1579** FULKE *Heskins' Parl.* 155 The bread and wine are transsumed. *Ibid.*, Though we take the word of transuming for changing, turning, transmuting, or transelementing,..yet meane they not chaunge of one substance into another. **1652** CRASHAW *Carmen Deo Nostro* Wks. (1904) 249 With a well-bles't bread and wine Transsum'd, and taught to turn divine.

†**b.** *intr.* for *pass.* = TRANSMUTE *v.* 1 c. *Obs. rare.*

**1480** CAXTON *Ovid's Met.* xv. iv, They [the four elements] be wont to transume, that one into that other.

¶ Some instances of *transume* in early printed books or modern editions from MS. are mis-readings of *transmue*: see quots. below; and in some of the passages quoted above in senses 2 and 3, *transmue* was possibly the author's word. It is possible that sense 3 originated in this confusion of form between *transume* and *transmue*.

**1483** CAXTON *Gold. Leg.* 140/2 He..transumeth the payne perpetuell [*Fr. orig.* le muement de la paine de purgatoyre; *Lat. orig.* poenae purgatoriae..commutatio]..in to payne temporell. **1502** *Ord. Crysten Men* V. vi. (W. de W.) qq iv b, The soule shall be in suche wyse transumed [*Fr. orig.* transmuee] in god. **1543** *Harding's Chron.* CLXXVI. iv, Syr Hugh ..was transumed [*rimes* pursued, renewed] In high estate. **1909** ed. of Pecock's *Bk. of Faith c* 1456, p. 157 The siȝt is the principal outward wit, and therfore his name may be transumed [*MS.* (Trin. Coll. Camb.) transmued] in to the name of ech othere outward witt.

**Transumpt** (trɒnsʊ·mpt), *sb.* Also 5–6 *Sc.* transump, 5–7 transsumpt, 7 transumt. [ad. med.L. *tran(s)sumpt-um* transcript (Du Cange), f. ppl. stem of L. *tran(s)sūmĕre* (see prec.). Cf. OF. *transumpt* (15th c. in Godef.).] A copy, transcript; *spec.* a copy of a record, deed, or other legal document; an exemplification. (Chiefly in Sc. legal use from 16th c. to *c* 1870.) Hence, *action* or *decree of transumpt.*

**1480** *Acta Dom. Conc.* (1839) 50/1 Þe originale letter..or elles ane autentic transump þerof. **1541** [see TRANSUME 1]. *c* **1555** HARPSFIELD *Divorce Hen. VIII* (Camden) 195 The transumpt of the said brief was sent to the King's agents. **1677** GALE *Crt. Gentiles* II. IV. 54 What are the Ten Commandments..but a Transumt,..Abstract or rather extended Copie of the Law of Nature given to man in the beginning? **1693** STAIR *Inst. Law Scot.* (ed. 2) IV. xxxi. § 4 Although there be no express obligment to grant Transumpts, yet the Interest in common Evidents, is a sufficient Title to cause them be produced, to be Transumed. **1752** J. LOUTHIAN *Form of Process* (ed. 2) 283 For every Sheet of Decreets of Transumpt..0 14 6 Scots Money. **1755** CARTE *Hist. Eng.* IV. 118 A transumpt or copy was now taken of it. **1765–8** ERSKINE *Inst. Law Scot.* IV. i. § 53. 657 An action of transumpt,..is competent to any person who has a partial interest in a writing,..against him in whose custody the writing lies, to exhibit it. *Ibid.*, When a decree of transumpt is questioned upon a ground of falsehood alledged against the writing transumed. **1810** G. CHALMERS *Caledonia* II. III. vi. 274 The citizens of Edinburgh..paid the money on the production of such a transumpt. **1878** DIXON *Hist. Ch. Eng.* I. iii. 151 *note*, An instrument made on a transumpt of the Breve. *Ibid.*, A definition of transumpt, the word lately revived in the State Papers, for a copy made by authority, or an attested copy.

†**b.** A pictorial representation, sketch, or engraving (of a work of art). *Obs. rare*⁻¹.

**1629** MAXWELL *Herodian* b j *margin*, His [Commodus] naked Statue (as he plaid the Gladiator) is extant at Rome in the Fernesian Palace. See the Transumpt of it in M. G. Sandy's Iournall, p. 271.

†**Transu·mpt,** *ppl. a. Obs.* [ad. L. *transumpt-us*, pa. pple. of *transūmĕre* to TRANSUME.] 'Transumed', transferred, copied. (as *pa. pple.*)

**1495** *Trevisa's Barth. De P. R.* II. v. (W. de W.) b iij/2 They [angels] ben lyckened to other thynges that ben take and transumpte of materyall thynges.

**Transumpt,** obs. erron. form of TRANSOM.

†**Transu·mption.** ? *Obs.* Also 5 transs-. [ad. late L. *tran(s)sumptiōn-em* (Quintilian), n. of action f. *tran(s)sūmĕre* to TRANSUME. Cf. OF. *transumption* (15th c. in Godef.).]

**1.** Transcription, copying; a passage copied or taken from any author; a quotation.

**1412–20** LYDG. *Chron. Troy* Prol. 264 Veyn[e] fables, whiche of entencioun They han contreved by false trau sumpcioun, To hyde trouthe falsely vnder cloude. **1451** CAPGRAVE *Life St. Gilbert* 85 All þese transumpciones folowing rehersith our auctour to þis entent, þat men of religion schuld not haue fair condiciones owtward and euel inward,..and soo may men expounne all þe othir transumpciones. *a* **1716** SOUTH *Serm.* (1744) VII. ii. 28 It was not Paul's design, to use these words..by way of citation out of David; but having by a kind of transumption and accommodation borrowed those former words of his.

**2.** The action of taking over from one to another; transference or translation to another part or place.

**1615** CROOKE *Body of Man* 608 The aiery bodie..is nourished by blood brought by the Veines, and that *per Diadosin* that is by Transumption. **1656** E. REYNER *Rules Govt. Tongue* 213 Elijah informed Elisha of such things as should fall out in Israel after this transumption. **1684** tr. *Bonet's Merc. Compit.* VI. 242 A Sinus..out of which, sharp Ichores coming by transumption to the neck of the bladder.

**3.** *Rhet.* Transfer of terms; metaphor. See also quot. 1553.

*c* **1449** PECOCK *Repr.* II. xviii. 258 This colour of speche which in rethorick is clepid transsumpcioun. **1553** T. WILSON *Rhet.* (1580) 178 Transumption is, when by degrees wee goe to that, whiche is to bee shewed. As thus: Suche a one lieth in a darke doungeon, now in speakyng of darkenesse, we vnderstande closenesse, by closenesse, we gather blacknesse, and by blacknesse, we iudge deepenesse. **1624** BARGRAVE *Serm.* 7 Such parabolicall transumptions are to be expounded to the sense, not to the letter. **1677** GALE *Crt. Gentiles* II. IV. 280 The cause of this Transumtion is because we have not a word which properly signifies the stable mansion of Eternitie: wherefore we are forced to transfer, by way of similitude, our temporal words..to Eternitie. [**1880** LEWIS & SHORT *Lat. Dict.*, *Transumptio*, a taking or assuming of one thing for another, transumption, metalepsis, a transl. of μετάληψις, Quint. 8, 6, 37.]

**4.** *Logic.* In the Aristotelian logic (tr. Gr. μετάληψις), Conversion of a hypothetical proposition into a categorical one.

**1628** T. SPENCER *Logick* 293 Aristotle doth call all compound Syllogismes by the name of Hypotheticall, because they inferre the conclusion vpon the supposition of some part thereof: & doth divide them into such as conclude according vnto transumption: and qualitie (that is as Pacius vnderstands it), when the minor is taken out of the maior; as..If a man, then a living creature. But a man, therefore a living creature. [**1730–6** BAILEY (folio), *Transumptio* (with Schoolmen), a syllogism by concession or agreement, used where a question proposed is transferred to another with this condition, that the proof of this latter shall be admitted for a proof of the former.]

† **Transu·mptive,** *a. Obs.* or *arch.* [ad. L. *transumptīvus* (Quintilian), f. *transumpt-*, ppl. stem of *transūmĕre* to TRANSUME + *-īvus*, -IVE. Cf. OF. *transsumptivement* figuratively (Godef.).] Characterized by transumption; metaphorical.

**1597** DRAYTON *Heroic. Epist.*, *Rosamond to Henry II*, Annot., Meander is a riuer in Lycia...Heereupon are intricate turnings by a transumptiue and Metonimicall kind of speech, called Meanders. **1657** W. MORICE *Coena quasi Κοινὴ* xxvi. 265 Some..apply this text in an accommodate and transumptive sense. **1662** J. CHANDLER *Van Helmont's Oriat.* 153 It was yielded to by a liberty transumptive or of taking one thing for another, without taking heed. [**1876** LOWELL *Among my Bks.* Ser. II. 44 'The form or mode of treatment', he [Dante] says, 'is poetic, fictive, descriptive, digressive, transumptive'.]

**Transunite** (trans,yunəi·t), *v. rare.* [TRANS- 1.] *trans.* To unite across a space.

*c* **1652** GAULE *Magastrom.* 232 The fourth kind of phrenzie proceeds from Venus; and it doth, by a fervent love, convert and transunite the minde to God.

**Transuterine** (trans,yū·tərəin), *a. nonce-wd.* [f. TRANS- 3 + L. *uter-us* womb: cf. *uterine*.] Beyond or outside of the womb.

**1830** COLERIDGE *Ch. & St.* (ed. 2) 227 Do not the eyes, ears, lungs of the unborn babe, give notice and furnish proof of a transuterine, visible, audible atmospheric world?

**Transvaal** (trɑ·nsvāˑl, -z-). [f. TRANS- 7 + *Vaal*, a tributary of the Orange R. in S. Africa.] A former South African republic, now a state of the Union of South Africa, lying north of the Orange Free State, from which it is separated by the River Vaal.

*attrib.* **Transvaal daisy**, *Gerbera Jamesonii*, a composite plant, introduced from the Transvaal in 1888.

**1901** *Gardener* 12 Jan. 1049/1 The Transvaal Daisy..has been a bright patch for a long time...The large flame-coloured flowers..are a particularly fine sight.

Hence **Transvaa·ler**, a native or inhabitant of the Transvaal; **Transvaa·lian** *a.*, of or belonging to the Transvaal; **Transvaalite** (trɑnsvā·ləit, -z-) *Min.* [-ITE [1] 2.], a mineral consisting mainly of black oxide of cobalt, resulting from the alteration of cobalt arsenide, found at a cobalt-mine near Middleburg in the Transvaal.

**1887** RIDER HAGGARD *Jess* x, You [are] going to show us *Transvaalers how to do it, eh? **1899** *Daily News* 19 Dec. 3/5 That the position of the Britishers under the *Transvaalian oligarchy would, in the end, become absolutely unbearable. **1890** MACGHIE & CLARK in *Engin. & Mining Jrnl.* (N.Y.) L. 96 *Transvaalite. **1896** in CHESTER *Dict. Min.*

**Transvalua·tion.** [TRANS- 1.] An alteration of values; revaluation. So **Transva·lue** *v. trans.* to alter the value of, to re-value; **Transva·luer.**

**1898** *Contemp. Rev.* May 738 The transvaluation of all values—the reversal of all accepted ideals. **1906** *Q. Rev.* Jan. 64 A certain 'transvaluation' of the traditional judgments about the comparative merits of various tendencies in Greek philosophy. **1908** MOZLEY in *Contemp. Rev.* Apr. 425 Christianity..is the real transvaluer of all values. **1911** *Daily News* 20 Oct. 5 On such an island..all moral values would have to be transvalued.

† **Tra·nsvasate,** *v. Obs. rare*$^{-1}$. [f. ppl. stem of med.L. *transvāsāre*, f. TRANS- 1 + L. *vās* vessel. Cf. EXTRAVASATE.] *trans.* = TRANSVASE. So † **Transvasa·tion** [cf. F. *transvasation* (? 16th c. in Godef. *Compl.*)], the action or process of pouring out of one vessel into another.

**1601** HOLLAND *Pliny* XXXIV. xviii. II. 519 This transvasation ought so long to be continued out of one vessell into another, untill such time as it have done casting any residence downward. **1673** *Phil. Trans.* VIII. 6022 This Alcalisat odor is lost by transvasation, that salt being thereby steamed away. **1678** CUDWORTH *Intell. Syst.* I. iv. § 36. 619 For the Father and Son are not, as they suppose, tranvasated and poured out, one into another, as into an empty vessel; as if the Son filled up the concavity of the Father, and again, the Father that of the Son.

**Transvase** (trɑnsvēˑs), *v. rare.* [a. F. *transvaser* (12th c. in Hatz.-Darm.), f. TRANS- + L. *vās* vessel.] *trans.* To pour out of one vessel into another. Also *fig.* Hence **Transva·sing** *vbl. sb.*

**1839** URE *Dict. Arts* 587 The higher ouvreaux called the lading holes, because they serve for transvasing the liquid glass, are three in number. **1882** *Nature* 23 Feb. 388/1 Errors incident to the collection and the transvasing of the water. **1891** STEVENSON *Lett.* (1901) II. xi. 218 Something better to do than to transvase the work of others.

† **Transva·story.** *Obs.*, perh. corr. of *transversary*, used by Bourne interchangeably with TRANSITORY B. 2, TRANSVERSARY B. 2.

**Transve·ctant.** *Math.* [f. L. *transvect-*, ppl. stem of *transveh-ĕre* (see next) + -ANT.] An invariant or covariant derived from two binary forms by the operation of transvection.

**1876** [see next 2].

**Transvection** (trɑnsve·kʃən). [ad. L. *transvectiōn-em*, n. of action from *transveh-ĕre* (-*vect*-), f. *trans* across + *vehĕre* to carry.]

† **1.** The action of carrying or conveying from one place to another; transportation. *Obs.*

**1615** CROOKE *Body of Man* 325 The transvection or transportation of aer..to the same Lungs of the infant. **1680** H. MORE *Apocal. Apoc.* 330 The consummate salvation of the Saints, or their transvection into those eternal Mansions of glory. **1682** — *Annot. Glanvill's Lux O.* xiii. 105 That transposition..is..a transvection of them, rather than pulsion or traction.

**2.** *Math.* A method used by Clebsch and Gordan for deriving invariants and covariants from a product of two binary forms.

**1876** SALMON *Lessons Introd. Mod. Higher Algebra* (ed. 3) xix. 272 If $\phi$, $\psi$ be covariants..we can obtain from them the series of covariants $\phi_x{}^{p-k}\,\psi_x{}^{q-k}\,(\phi\psi)^k$...This operation, in German called *Ueberschiebung*, we shall call transvection, and the covariants generated we shall call transvectants of the two given covariants.

**Transve·ctor.** *Math.* [f. TRANS- + VECTOR.] In *Quaternions*, The sum of a vector and a provector.

**1853** SIR W. R. HAMILTON *Quaternions* (1866) 4 If a provector $BC$ be added to a vector $AB$, the sum is the transvector $AC$; or in symbols, I..$(B-A)+A=B$; and II..$(C-B)+(B-A)=C-A$.

**Transve·nom,** *v. rare.* [TRANS- 2.] *trans.* To transform into something poisonous.

*a* **1667** JER. TAYLOR, Envy..transvenoms the honey of another man's comfort into the poison of asps for its own bosom. **1816** COLERIDGE *Statesman's Man.* 26 That atheistic philosophy, which in France transvenomed the natural thirst of truth into the hydrophobia of a wild and homeless scepticism.

**Transverbate** (trɑnsvɔ̄·rbeˑit), *v. rare.* [f. TRANS- 1 + L. *verb-um* word + -ATE [3]; after *transliterate*.] *trans.* To translate verbally or word for word. So **Transverba·tion**, verbal translation.

**1885** *Athenæum* 14 Mar. 349/2 (*Philological Society*) Mr. B. Dawson read a paper on the Revised Version of the New Testament...He commended the accuracy of the revisers, but condemned their 'transverbation' of the Greek. **1896–7** H. HAIGH in *Bible Soc. Record* (N. Y.) Jan. 2 If we could take the Hebrew and the Greek and transverbate them it would be comparatively easy.

† **Transve·rberate,** *v. Obs. rare.* [ad. ppl. stem of L. *transverberāre*, f. TRANS- 1 + *verberāre* to beat.] *trans.* To strike through.

**1623** COCKERAM, *Transuerberate*, to strike thorow. **1640** G. WATTS tr. *Bacon's Adv. Learn.* III. iv. 147 The appetencies of Matter, and the most universall Passions, (which in either Globe are exceeding Potent, and transverberate [L. *transverberant*] the universall nature of things).

So **Transverbera·tion,** a striking through.

**1881** H. J. COLERIDGE *Life & Lett. St. Teresa* I. 24 The room in which Teresa received her mystical transverberation—the piercing of her heart by a fiery dart.

**Transversal** (trɑnsvɔ̄·ɹsăl, -z-), *a.* and *sb.* [ad. med.L. *transversāl-is* (*a* 1255 Albertus Magnus *Animal.* 13. 2. 1): see TRANSVERSE and -AL. Cf. F. *transversal* (16th c. in Hatz.-Darm.).]

**A.** *adj.* **1.** Lying or passing across; = TRANSVERSE *a.* 1.

*c* **1440** tr. *Pallad. on Husb.* VI. 179 A double cours of bourding..Oon transuersal, another cours directe. **1527** R. THORNE in Hakluyt *Voy.* (1589) 253 One of the transuersall lines. **1541** R. COPLAND *Guydon's Quest. Chirurg.* E iv, Openynge with two transuersall muscles. **1644** DIGBY *Nat. Bodies* xxvi. § 5. 236 The hart hath in the ventricles of it, three sortes of fibers:..the third, are transuersall or thwart ones. **1755** *Phil. Trans.* XLIX. 119 Flames, rays, and fiery corruscations, direct and transversal. **1831** FARADAY *Exp. Res.* xlvi. 358 The direct vibration of the luminous body may communicate transversal vibration..to the molecules of the ether. **1908** *Contemp. Rev.* Mar. 369 A scheme for the construction of a transversal line which would link Odessa and Varna.

† **2.** *Genealogy.* Collateral: = TRANSVERSE *a.* 2.

[*a* **1308** DUNS SCOTUS *Sent.* 4. 40. 6 Transversalis.] **1594** PARSONS *Confer. Success.* II. viii. 184 He was of the right discendant lyne of K. John, and the Cardinal was but of the collateral or transuersal lyne. **1907** [?implied in TRANSVERSALLY].

**3.** *Conch.* = TRANSVERSE *a.* 1 c. (So in F.)

**1835–6** *Todd's Cycl. Anat.* I. 710/2 All [shells] that are of greater breadth than length are named transversal.

**B.** *sb.* †**1.** Something transversal or lying athwart, a transverse line; *fig.* a deviation, digression. *Obs. rare.*

**1597** LOWE *Chirurg.* (1634) 256 Three kinds of fibres which are Rights, Obliques, and Transversals. **1620** SHELTON *Quix.* (1746) III. xxvi. 183 On with your Story in a direct Line, and fall not into your Crooks and your Transversals.

**2.** *Geom.* A line intersecting two or more lines, or a system of lines.

**1881** CASEY *Sequel to Euclid* 68 If two parallel lines be intersected by three concurrent transversals, the segments intercepted by the transversals on the parallels are proportional. **1885** EAGLES *Constr. Geom. Plane Curves* 15 Every transversal of a harmonic pencil is divided harmonically in the points in which it intersects the lines of the pencil. **1902** TOWNSEND tr. *Hilbert's Foundat. Geometry* 63 A segment [of a line] joining a vertex of a triangle with a point of the opposite side is called a *transversal*. A transversal divides the given triangle into two others having the same altitude and having bases which lie in the same straight line.

**b.** *Optics.* The line in which the plane of polarization of a beam of light intersects the wave-front; the transverse plane. **1909** in *Cent. Dict. Suppl.*

**3.** *Roulette.* A bet placed at the end of any three numbers taking them horizontally. Cf. TRANSVERSE B. 1 h. Also in Fr. form *transversale.*

*Transversale six*, a bet placed on the line, taking in the three numbers above and the three below.

**1895** G. MEREDITH *Amazing Marriage* ix, He stated that the number of 17 had won before. Abrane tried the transversal enclosing this favoured number.

‖ **Transversalis** (trɑnsvəɹsēˑ·lis). *Anat.* [med. and mod.L.: see prec.] A transverse muscle; one of the muscles, etc., that lie across various parts.

[**1704** J. HARRIS *Lex. Techn.* I, *Transversalis Colli*, is a Muscle of the Neck. **1827** ABERNETHY *Surg. Wks.* I. 292 The internal oblique and *transversalis* muscles.] **1872** HUMPHRY *Myology* 16 Between the external oblique and the transversalis.

**Transversa·lity.** [f. TRANSVERSAL + -ITY.] The condition or state of being transversal.

**1850** GREGORY *Reichenbach's Res. Magnet.*, etc. 421 We have placed beyond a doubt, the existence of transversality in the odylic phenomena. **1888** LD. RAYLEIGH in *Encycl. Brit.* XXIV. 450/1 The condition of transversality leads at once to the desired results.

**Transve·rsally,** *adv.* [f. as prec. + -LY [2].] In a transversal manner, transversely, athwart.

(In quot. 1641, app. = obliquely.)

**1641** WILKINS *Math. Magick* I. xviii. (1707) 77 The several Proportions of Swiftness and Distance in an Arrow shot Vertically, or Horizontally, or Transversally. **1762** tr. *Busching's Syst. Geog.* V. 39 A shield twice longitudinally divided and three times transversally with a scutcheon of pretence. **1907** *Daily Chron.* 19 Jan. 3/1 [In the opinion of some] 'Heredity goes transversally, sideways, not in straight lines'.

**Transve·rsan,** *a. Bot.* [f. as TRANSVERSE *a.* + -AN.] (See quot.)

**1900** B. D. JACKSON *Gloss. Bot. Terms* 274/1 *Transversan Plane*, that which passes through the centre of a Diatom frustule vertically to the pervalvar axis (O. Mueller).

† **Transve·rsant,** *a. Obs. rare*$^{-1}$. [f. as TRANSVERSE *v.*[1] + -ANT.] Crossing, transverse.

*c* **1440** *Pallad. on Husb.* I. 564 But maak this hous wherin they [thrushes] shal abide Light, clene, and playn, with perchis transuersaunt To sitte vppon.

**Transve·rsary,** *a.* and *sb.* [ad. L. *transversāri-us* lying across: see TRANSVERSE and -ARY. Cf. F. *transversaire* (Littré).]

† **A.** *adj.* Transverse. *Obs. rare*$^{-1}$.

*c* **1400** *Lanfranc's Cirurg.* 148 Þe wesant..haþ noon [brawnys] transuersarie, þat is to seie goynge ouerþwert, for wiþholdynge is not nedeful to him.

**B.** *sb.* †**1.** The transverse beam or member of a cross. *Obs. rare*$^{-1}$. [L. *transversarium* cross-beam.]

*a* **1608** DEE *Relat. Spir.* I. (1659) 185 Neither of the letters in the Transversary of the black Crosse.

**2.** A cross-piece or vane of a cross-staff. *Hist.*

**1594** J. DAVIS *Seaman's Secr.* (1607) 17 Your staffe so ordered, then moue the transversary upon your staffe to and fro as occasion requireth. **1638** OUGHTRED in Rigaud *Corr. Sci. Men* (1841) I. 31 For setting the degrees on the transversary. **1879** A. GEIKIE in *Encycl. Brit.* X. 187/1 The cross-staff was a very simple instrument, consisting of a graduated pole with cross pieces, called transversaries.., also graduated, which were fitted to work on it.

**Transverse** (trɑnsvɔ̄·ɹs, trɑ·nsvəɹs, -z-), *a.* (*sb.*, *adv.*, *prep.*) [ad. L. *transvers-us* turned or directed across, pa. pple. of *transvertĕre*: see TRANSVERT. Cf. F. *transverse* (16th c.).]

**1.** Lying across; situated or lying crosswise or athwart; *esp.* situated or extending across the length of something, *spec.* at right angles (opp. to *longitudinal*). Also const. *to*.

1621 BURTON *Anat. Mel.* I. i. II. iii, *Fibræ* are strings, white and solide, dispersed through the whole member, and are right, oblique, transuerse, all which haue their seuerall vses. *a* 1687 PETTY *Treat. Naval Philos.* I. i, Three perpendicular length-way sections..and..a transverse section of the Hull. 1784 COWPER *Task* I. 561 A kettle slung Between two poles upon a stick transverse. 1815 W. SHEPHERD, etc. *Syst. Educ.* (1822) II. 112 The influence is not exerted in a direction parallel to the wire through which the electricity passes but in a direction transverse to it. 1855 H. SPENCER *Princ. Psychol.* (1872) II. VI. ii. 7 In similar masses of matter which are subject..to the transverse strain, the power of resistance varies. 1870 F. R. WILSON *Ch. Lindisf.* 64 A transverse set of pews in the Chancel.

**b.** *Her.* Crossing the escutcheon from one side to the opposite one. (Cf. quot. 1610 in D.)

*c* 1828 BERRY *Encycl. Her.* I. Gloss., Transverse, and Transverse in point, to the dexter and sinister.

**c.** In a bivalve shell: Of greater breadth than length or height; having the longer diameter transverse to the hinge.

1822 J. PARKINSON *Outl. Oryctol.* 180 A transverse bivalve.

**d.** In special collocations: **Transverse artery,** *Anat.* one of the small branches given off at nearly right angles from the basilar; **transverse axis,** (*a*) an axis transverse to the main axis, as in a crystal; (*b*) *Geom.* the axis passing through the foci of a conic section (in an ellipse, the major axis): see AXIS[1] 7; **transverse bone,** *Zool.* in some reptiles, a bone connecting the pterygoid and maxilla; **transverse colon,** *Anat.* (see COLON[1]); **transverse fissure,** *Anat.* (*a*) the cleft below the hemispheres of the brain into which the pia mater extends to form the velum interpositum and choroid plexuses; (*b*) a short transverse cleft on the lower surface of the left lobe of the liver: **transverse ligament,** part of the cotyloid ligament; **transverse magnet,** a magnet formed by a combination of bar-magnets so that its poles are at the sides, not at the ends; **transverse magnetism, magnetization,** magnetization at right angles to the length of the bar; **transverse muscle,** *Anat.*, any one of various muscles extending across other parts; **transverse process,** a lateral process of a vertebra; **transverse sinus,** a simple network of veins connecting the two inferior petrosal sinuses; **transverse suture,** the suture between the frontal and facial bones; **transverse vein,** *Entom.* any one of the several short veins of the wings of an insect, connecting two longitudinal ones.

1857 DUNGLISON *Med. Lex.* 926/2 *Transverse artery of the face, arises from the temporal, passes transversely across the face..and gives its branches to the different muscles of the cheek. 1704 J. HARRIS *Lex. Techn.* I. s.v. *Latus Transversum*, The longest Diameter in the Ellipsis, which Apollonius calls the *Transverse Axis, or Diameter. 1878 BELL *Gegenbaur's Comp. Anat.* 59 The other connects the sides of the body, and is the transverse axis. 1840 E. WILSON *Anat. Vade M.* (1842) 101 The *transverse ligament is a strong ligamentous band. 1696 PHILLIPS (ed. 5), **Transverse Muscles*, the first pair shew themselves with a Membranous beginning, at the *Transverse Processes of the Vertebra of the Loyns. 1840 E. WILSON *Anat. Vade M.* (1842) 8 The transverse processes project one at each side from the laminæ of the vertebra. *Ibid.* 341 The *Transverse sinus passes transversely across the basilar process of the occipital bone. 1741 MONRO *Anat.* (ed. 3) 75 The *Transverse Suture runs quite cross the Face, from the external Canthus of one Orbit to the same Place of the other. 1860 MAYNE *Expos. Lex.*, *Transverse Suture*,..a suture which passes across the face, sinks down into the orbits, joining the bones of the skull to those of the face.

†**2.** Of kindred: Collateral, as between brothers, cousins-german, etc. *Obs. rare.*

1614 SELDEN *Titles Hon.* Pref. B iv, A Monster, that is not like him that got him, nor any other of the ascending or transuerse line. 1651 G. W. tr. *Cowel's Inst.* 154 This Discent ought to be to the next Heirs, Males or Females, in a direct or transverse line. 1660 JER. TAYLOR *Duct. Dubit.* II. iii. rule iii. § 9. 401 The Grand Parent of a Family; from whom the direct descendants are for ever to be reckon'd to the Kinred in the strait and proper line: but when once it goes to the transverse and collateral, they not onely have no title to the inheritance, but [etc.].

**3.** In combination with other adjs. (*Entom.*): **transverse-cubital, -medial** *adjs.* = TRANSVERSO-*cubital, -medial*; **transverse-quadrate** *a.*, quadrate with the transverse diameter the longer.

1840 tr. *Cuvier's Anim. Kingd.* 528 Having the thorax transverse-quadrate.

**B.** *sb.* [The adj. used *absol.*]

**1.** Something that is transverse: *spec.*

†**a.** A cross or transverse part or member. *Obs. rare.* †**b.** *Fortif.*? = TRAVERSE *sb.* 16. *Obs. rare.* **c.** The transverse axis of a conic section. **d.** See quot. 1867. **e.** A transverse muscle. **f.** *Arch.* (See quot. 1842–76.) **g.** The sprocket axle of a chain-driven motor-car. **h.** *Roulette* = TRANSVERSAL B. 3.

**a.** *a* 1633 AUSTIN *Medit.* (1635) 108 The Transverse of the Crosse..is held to have bin a peece, much about that length. 1634 BP. HALL *Contempl.*, *N. T.* IV. *Crucifixion*, Having fastened the transverse to the body of that fatal tree. **b.** 1704 J. HARRIS *Lex. Techn.* I, *Transverse*, in Fortification, is a little Trench bordered with two Parapets..which the Besiegers make quite thwart the Moat of the Place, to pass secure from Flank-shot, and to bring the Miners to the Bastions. **c.** 1743 EMERSON *Fluxions* 244 Let the Transverse of the Ellipsis = $2r$, Conjugate = $2c$. **d.** 1867 THOMSON & TAIT *Nat. Phil.* I. I. § 120 Mark a line..along its length, such that it shall be a straight line parallel to the axis...A line drawn from any point of the axis perpendicular to this side line of reference, is called the transverse of the rod at this point. **f.** 1842–76 GWILT *Archit.* Gloss. s. v. *Chambranle*, The top of a three-sided chambranle is called the transverse, and the sides ascendants. **g.** 1907 *Westm. Gaz.* 22 Nov. 10/1 Their manufactures include live axles of various types and sizes, transverses, change-speed and brake levers [etc.]. **h.** 1899 *Scribner's Mag.* XXV. 90/1 He placed eight louis on the number nineteen, and 1,200 francs on the line between nineteen and twenty-two, thus playing the 'transverse'.

†**2.** *By transverse* [L. *per transversum*], in a transverse position, crosswise; athwart. *Obs. rare.*

1596 SPENSER *F. Q.* VII. *Mutability* VII. lvi, Nothing doth firme and permanent appeare, But all things tost and turned by transverse.

**C.** *adv.* In a transverse direction or position; transversely, across, athwart. Now *rare* or *poet.*

1660 R. COKE *Justice Vind.* 41 When they are cut transverse, they are cut to right angles. 1671 MILTON *Samson* 209 These two proportiond ill drove me transverse. 1726 LEONI *Alberti's Archit.* I. 51/2 Beams across from one Wall to the other..are Columns laid transverse. 1798 BLOOMFIELD *Farmer's Boy*, *Spring* 93 And o'er the whole Giles once transverse again, In earth's moist bosom buries up the grain.

†**D.** *prep.* Across, athwart. *Obs. rare.*

1607 TOPSELL *Four-f. Beasts* (1658) 161 One of them descendeth, and goeth down into the Ditch, and standeth transverse or crosse the same. 1610 GUILLIM *Heraldry* III. xxii. 166 All Fishes being borne Transuerse the Escocheon must in blazon be termed Naiant.

**Transverse** (trɑnsvɜ̄·ɹs, -z-), *v.*[1] Now *rare.* [a. OF. *transverser* (13th c. in Godef.) = med.L. *transvers-āre* (Du Cange) to cross, f. L. *transvers-*, ppl. stem of *transvertĕre*: see TRANSVERT.]

**1.** *trans.* To pass or lie athwart or across; to cross, traverse. *rare.*

1430–40 LYDG. *Bochas* IX. x. (MS. Bodl. 263) 417/1 Ther shon wer..Richeli transuersed with gold weer. 1545 RAYNOLD *Byrth Mankynde* 7 In Latin: musculi transuersi: Bycause they transuerse or ouerthwart the belly. 1873 MIVART *Elem. Anat.* x. 413 The internal carotid transverses the petrous part of the temporal bone.

†**b.** *fig.* To act or speak in opposition to; to cross, thwart; in *Law* = TRAVERSE *v.* 12. *Obs.*

1387–8 T. USK *Test. Love* I. ii. (Skeat) l. 195, I trowe the strongest and the best that maie bee founde, woll not transuers thy wordes. 1628 SIR S. D'EWES *Jrnl.* (1783) 45 He was presentlie transversed and over-ruled by his flatterers. 1704 J. HARRIS *Lex. Techn.* I. s. v., To transverse an Indictment, is to take Issue upon the chief Matter, and to contradict or deny some Point of it. 1769 R. CUMBERLAND *Brothers* II. ii, That perverse hussey..threatens to transverse all my hopes.

†**c.** *intr. fig.* To go across or athwart; to run counter; to transgress *against*. *Obs. rare.*

1377 LANGL. *P. Pl.* B. XII. 284 Ac trewth þat trespassed neuere, ne transuersed aȝeines his lawe. 1393 *Ibid.* C. IV. 449 And ho so takeþ aȝen treuthe oþer transuerseþ aȝens reson Leaute shal do hym lawe.

**2.** *trans.* To turn upside down or backwards; to overturn, turn topsy-turvy. Now *rare* or *Obs.*

*c* 1520 BARCLAY *Jugurth* (1557) 18 As if thei wer belies of ships transversed or turned vp set downe. 1643 HOWELL *Parables on Times* Ep. Ded. 2 These sad confusions which have so unhing'd, distorted, transvers'd, tumbled and dislocated all things. 1738 WHITEFIELD in *Life & Jrnls.* (1756) 50, I could not but transverse the Prodigal's Complaint: How many are ready to perish with hunger, whilst I have enough and to spare. 1859 G. MEREDITH *R. Feverel* xiv, In love, it is said, all stratagems are fair, and many little ladies transverse the axiom by applying it to discover the secrets of their friends.

**b.** To convert into something different; to alter, transform. (Cf. TRANSVERSE *v.*[2])

1687 PRIOR & MONTAGU (*title*) The Hind and the Panther Transvers'd To the Story of The Country-Mouse and the City-Mouse. *c* 1700 SIR J. MONTAGUE in *N. & Q.* 7th Ser. (1889) VIII. 430/1 Making several essays to transverse.. other parts of the poem. 1702 *Modesty Mistaken* 5 Having transvers'd the two famous Lines of Sir J. Denham to the scandal of Bottled Ale.

Hence **Transve·rsed** *ppl. a.*, placed crosswise, crossing, transverse.

*a* 1711 KEN *Hymnotheo* Po. Wks. 1721 III. 85 His heav'nly Banner..Wrought with direct and with transversed Rays.

**Transve·rse,** *v.*[2] [f. TRANS- 2 + VERSE *sb.*; cf. TRANSPROSE. (Orig. as a kind of pun or play on prec.)] *trans.* To turn into verse; to translate or render in verse.

[1671 VILLIERS (Dk. Buckhm.) *Rehearsal* I. (Arb.) 31, I take a Book in my hand..if there be any Wit in't,..I Transverse it; that is, if it be Prose, put it into Verse.., if it be Verse, put it into Prose.] 1672 [H. STUBBE] *Rosemary & Bayes* 2 To pilfer from other men; and if they write in prose, he doth trans-verse them. 1732 FIELDING *Debauchees* Prol. 10 Old worn-out Jokes..Transvers'd from Prose, perhaps transpros'd from Rhimes. 1881 SAINTSBURY *Dryden* viii. 159 Having taken the fancy to transverse some Arthurian stories.

**Transversely** (trɑnsvɜ̄·ɹsli, -z-), *adv.* [f. TRANSVERSE *a.* + -LY[2].] In a transverse manner or direction; across, athwart; crosswise.

1650 BULWER *Anthropomet.* 225 Another membrane, which transversely..doth cover the chink of the Hymen. 1658 SIR T. BROWNE *Gard. Cyrus* i. 96 Not transversly or rectangularly intersected, but in a decussation, after the form of an Andrean or Burgundian cross. 1777 COOK *Voy. Pacific Ocean* II. i. (1784) I. 178 An open end, which represented an ellipse divided transversely. 1822 J. PARKINSON *Outl. Oryctol.* 180 A..transversely oblong bivalve. 1878 W. H. DALL *Later Preh. Man* 16 There are eighteen threads to the inch longitudinally and twenty-four transversely. 1884 BOWER & SCOTT *De Bary's Phaner.* 347 A layer of transversely elongated, partly thick-walled elements.

**Transve·rseness.** *rare.* [f. as prec. + -NESS.] The condition or state of being transverse.

1867 C. J. SMITH *Syn. & Antonyms* s. v. *Across*, Transverseness to a line of movement becomes opposition.

**Transversion**[1] (trɑnsvɜ̄·ɹʃən, -z-). *rare.* [n. of action fr. L. *transvert-ĕre* to turn across, TRANSVERT; cf. *conversion, inversion*, etc.] The action of turning across or athwart; intersection; a turning into something else, conversion, perversion, transformation; transposition.

1656 BLOUNT *Glossogr.*, *Transversion*, a turning away or crosse, a traversing, or going athwart. 1658 SIR T. BROWNE *Gard. Cyrus* i. 96 Nor shall we take in the mystical Tau, or the Crosse of our blessed Saviour, which having in some descriptions an Empedon or crossing foot-stay, made not one single transversion. 1671 [see next]. 1716–20 *Lett. fr. Mist's Jrnl.* (1722) I. 9 As if they intended a Transversion of Christendom to its first Paganism. 1870 LOWELL *Study Wind.* 331 A transversion common with him.

**Transve·rsion**[2]. [n. of action f. TRANSVERSE *v.*[2]] A turning into verse; *concr.* a metrical version of something.

(Quot. 1671 appears to combine this with prec.)

[1671 VILLIERS (Dk. Buckhm.) *Rehearsal* I. (Arb.) 31 My first Rule is the Rule of Transversion, or *Regula Duplex*, Changing Verse into Prose, or Prose into verse.] 1796 W. TAYLOR in *Monthly Mag.* I. 404 The following transversion of a passage from Ossian's Carthon, may give an idea of the practicability of such metres in the English tongue. 1898 *Q. Rev.* Jan. 100 Bayes's rules for the composition of plays..—the rule of transversion for instance.

**Transversive** (trɑnsvɜ̄·ɹsiv, -z-), *a.* *rare*[−1]. [f. L. *transvers-*: see TRANSVERSE *v.*[1] and -IVE.] Having the effect of crossing or thwarting.

1855 BAILEY *Mystic* 43 The will Of man, so oft transversive of the truth.

**Transverso-** (trɑnsvɜ̄·ɹso), used as combining form of L. *transvers-us* TRANSVERSE (see -O *suffix*), in a few rare scientific terms: **Transve:rso-cu·bital, Transve:rso-me·dial** *adjs.*, *Entom.* crossing the cubital, or the medial, cells of the wing, as certain nervures. **Transve:rso-spi·nal** *a.*, *Anat.* an epithet of several muscles attached to the transverse processes of the vertebræ. **Transve:rso-ve·rtical** *a.*, relating to, or expressing the ratio between, the transverse and vertical dimensions (greatest breadth and greatest height), as the *transverso-vertical index* in craniometry.

1857 DUNGLISON *Med. Dict.*, Transverso-spinal. 1891 *Cent. Dict.*, Transversocubital, Transversomedial, Transversovertical.

†**Transve·rt,** *v. Obs.* [ad. L. *transvertĕre* to turn across, f. *trans* across + *vertĕre* to turn.] *trans.* To turn across or athwart; to turn *into* something else, transform, convert; to turn about, reverse, overturn.

1432–50 tr. *Higden* (Rolls) II. 191 Somme men hauenge senowes as transuertede and ouercrossede thro alle the body, haue bene of grete myȝhte. *c* 1450 *Craft of Lovers* 419 Why mens langage wol procure and transuert The will of women and virgines innocent? 1552 HULOET s. v. *B*, In composicions B. is transuerted into these letters C. F. G. P. V. *Ibid.*, Preposterouse, out of order, overthwarth, transuerted. 1608 DOD & CLEAVER *Expos. Prov.* xi–xii. 143 They usually transuert their fauor and iustice, shewing mercy where they should exercise seuerity, and practising cruelty where they should shew mercy. 1651 HOWELL *Venice* 185 To transvert the Keys of Paradise into the Keys of a Prison. *a* 1660 *Contemp. Hist. Irel.* (Ir. Archæol. Soc.) III. 80, I maye lawfully saye, as our Saviour saide unto Saule,..transuertinge onely his name: Vllacke, Vllacke, cur me persequeris?

Hence †**Transve·rtible** *a. Obs.*, capable of being transverted.

?16.. [? SIR T.] BROWNE cited in Webster (1864).

†**Transve·st,** *v. Obs. rare.* [f. TRANS- 1 or 2 + L. *vestīre* to clothe, or Eng. VEST *v.*] *trans.* To clothe in other garments, e. g. those of the opposite sex; to disguise. Cf. TRAVESTY.

1652 J. WRIGHT tr. *Camus' Nat. Paradox* II. 42 How often did shee please her fancy with the imagination of transvesting herself, and by the help of a Man's disguise deceiving the eyes of those that watched her deportments? 1654 tr. *Martini's Conq. China* 199 No Man but some horrid wild Beast, or rather..some Devill transvested in our humane Nature.

†**Transview·,** *v. Obs. rare.* [TRANS- 2.] *trans.* To look through.

1602 J. DAVIES *Mirum in Modum* (Grosart) 9/2 Let vs with Eagles eyes without offence Transview the obscure things that do remaine.

†**Trans-vi·llage,** *v. Obs. nonce-wd.* [f. TRANS- 2 + VILLAGE *sb.*] *trans.* To transform or reduce (a town) to the size of a village.

1608 SYLVESTER *Du Bartas* II. iv. IV. *Decay* 242 Their Towns trans-villag'd, the Ten Tribes transported To a far Clime.

†**Transvola·tion.** *Obs.* [n. of action from L. *transvolāre* to fly across or over, pass across (in OF. *transvoler*, 14th c.), f. TRANS- + *volāre* to fly.] The action of flying or passing beyond the ordinary limits. (In quots. *fig.*)

1649 JER. TAYLOR *Gt. Exemp.* I. xii. 8 However Jesus had some extraordinary transvolations and acts of emigration beyond the lines of his ordinary conversation, it was but seldom. 1651 — *Serm. for Year* I. iv. 50 Extraordinary egressions and transvolations beyond the ordinary course of an even piety.

†**Transvo·lve,** *v. Obs. rare.* [f. TRANS- 1 + L. *volvĕre* to roll. Cf. L. *transvolvĕre* to roll past or by, to unroll.] *trans.* To roll over, overturn.

1644 Howell *Eng. Teares* 184 The great Deity of Heaven (who transvolves Kingdoms, and tumbleth down Kings in his Indignation). 1651 — *Venice* 179 Shall we admit in our free States an Authority, which..pretends to have power to controul, and transvolve the Dominions of others?

**†Transwa·ft**, *v. Obs. rare.* [f. Trans- 2 + Waft *v.*] **a.** *intr.* To float across through air or water. **b.** *trans.* To convey or carry across a river or sea. So **†Transwa·ftage** [cf. Waftage], a conveying or floating across.

1624 Heywood *Gunaik.* I. 31 From thence she came to Hæmus, and transwafted thence to a gulfe of Thracia, which by her was called Bosphorus. *Ibid.* IV. 209 In her transwaftage over the flood Evenus. 1635 — *Hierarch.* III. 128 Because Ioues Trull Europa, he from Sidon into Creet Transwafted, whilest the waue ne're toucht her feet.

**Transwri·tten**, *ppl. a. nonce-wd.* [Trans- 2.] Transcribed, or ? translated.

1874 Ruskin *Fors Clav.* xl, This is an ill written, and worse trans-written, human history, and not by any means 'Word of God'.

**†Trant**, *sb. north. dial. Obs.* [Origin obscure. Identical in form with Du. *trant* 'manner, way, method, kind', in MDu. also 'step, pace'. It is conceivable that from some of these senses there might arise the notion of 'shift, clever or cunning way or course, device, trick' (cf. F. *tour* and Eng. *turn*), but historical links are wanting.]

Cunning action, trickery; a stratagem, a trick (always in an evil sense).

13.. *Gaw. & Gr. Knt.* 1700 Summe fel in þe fute, þer þe fox bade, Traylez ofte a trayteres [? a travers], bi traunt of her wyles. c 1400 *Destr. Troy* 12210 For to take hit [Troy] by treason & trantis of hym. c 1440 *York Myst.* xxix. 234 Þis was a trante of a traytour. c 1460 *Towneley Myst.* xvi. 235 Hard I neuer sich a trant that a knafe so slight Shuld com lyke a sant and refe me my right. *Ibid.* xxv. 162, I know his trantes fro top to tayll.

**†Trant**, *v.*[1] *Obs. rare*$^{-1}$. [Goes with prec.] *intr.* To practise cunning devices; to employ cunning, craft, trickery, or deception.

13.. *Gaw. & Gr. Knt.* 1707 [The fox] trantes & tornayeez þurȝ mony tene greue.

**Trant**, *v.*[2] *rare.* Now *dial.* Also 6 **traunt.** [app. a back-formation from Tranter; cf. Peddle.] *intr.* To follow the occupation of a tranter. Hence **Tra·nting (trau·nting)** *ppl. a.*

1597–8 Bp. Hall *Sat.* IV. ii. 145 Who..had some traunting merchant to his sire, That traffick'd both by water and by fire. 1898 T. Hardy *Wessex Poems* 201 Naibour Sweatley ..Who tranted and moved people's things.

**Trant(e**, obs. form of Trente (at Cards).

**Tranter** (træ·ntəɹ). Now *dial.* Also 4–7 **traventer**, 6–7 **trauntor, trawnter**, 9 **traunter.** [*Tranter, traunter, trawnter* known from 1500, app. syncopated from *traventer* (see quot. 1601), in med. (Anglo-) L. *trāvetārius*, of uncertain origin.

A derivation formally possible for med.L. *trāvetārius*, would be that it was a corruption of L. **tra(ns)vectārius*, f. *transvehĕre* to transport, *transvectio* transportation.]

A word having various local uses: chiefly denoting a man who does jobs with his horse and cart; a carrier; a hawker or cadger with horse and cart; a huckster; also, one who buys up things to sell them elsewhere; †in 14–15th c. a tapster: see quots.

[1233 *Pat. Roll* 18 *Hen. III*, m. 17 Willelmus de Londonia trauetarius habet literas de conductu car[ucarum] suarum. [(in Calendar p. 32) Safe-conduct until Easter for William de London, the tranter, for his carts.] *Ibid.*, Willelmus de Norhamptona trauetarius Regis habet literas de saluo conductu. 1282 *Welsh Roll* No. 3. m. 2 d. (P. R. O.), Accepimus quod trauetarii et alii victualia et alia nobis et fidelibus nostris..in partibus Wallie necessaria ducentes. 1350 *Letter-Bk. F. Lond.* lf. 181 b, Item q' les garsouns des seriauntz.. cariage ne pregnont pluis des charettes ne de chivaux q' meister ne soit, et ceo de trauenters et chivaux q' sount allowers. [By Riley *Memorials London* (1868) 256 explained as 'Persons who let out carts on hire.] a 1400 *Litt. Red Bk. Bristol* (1900) II. 37 Diuerses trauenters de ceruoise. [*Ibid.* 38 Mettre a vendre ceruoys en trauentrie.]] 1500 *Gloucester Rec.* in 12*th Rep. Hist. MSS. Comm.* App. IV. 433 That alle maner of traunters and tapsters sel of the best ale a galon for 1 d qar. 1562 in Picton *L'pool Munic. Rec.* (1883) I. 79 No..trauntors shall buy any corn until the town be served. 1601 F. Tate *Househ. Ord. Edw. II*, § 51 (1876) 35 When he goeth..to make purveiance for poultry, he shal have with him the trauenters, which must be in the same office or some of them; these trauntors names shalbe entred in the warderobe. 1642 *Declar. Lords & Comm.* 31 Dec. 3 The robbing of the common Carriers and Trawnters. 1681 Blount *Glossogr.*, *Tranters*..are those that bring fish from the Sea-side in Wales to the Midland. Elsewhere call'd Ripiers. a 1700 B. E. *Dict. Cant. Crew*, *Tranter*, the same as *Crocker*. 1744–50 W. Ellis *Mod. Husbandm.* IV. II. 103 (E.D.S.) The word traunter I take to mean, strictly, any person that buys wheat in sacks to sell again in sacks. 1801 Mason *Suppl. Johnson*, *Tranters*..Country people, amongst whom alone this word is current, extend its meaning to all those who purchase any kind of provisions in order to sell them again. c 1880 *Bedford Dialect*, Mr. So-and-So the corn traunter bought 1500 quarters of wheat yesterday. 1891 T. Hardy *Tess* xvii, One of the family that used to do a good deal of business as tranters over there. 1899 C. K. Paul *Mem.* 60 He had become a 'tranter', doing odd jobs, haulage of manure, and the like. 1906 Sir F. Treves *Highways & Byways Dorset* Pref. 8 In this Sleepy Hollow they will find the untroubled life of the past,..will meet the tranter on the leisurely road.

Hence **†Tra·ntery** (in 4 trauentrie, 6 trawntrey), *Obs.* or ? *dial.*, the occupation of a tranter; retailing of ale, etc.; see also quot. 1670.

1330 *Kenfig Ord.* in Gross *Gild Merch.* (1890) II. 133 [from a 16–17th c. copy] Noe manner of person shall..cutt carne or trawntrey or ostrey hold, unless he be a burgess. a 1400 Trauentrie [see above]. 1670 Blount *Law Dict.*, *Trantery*, So in some Mannors they call the Money arising by Amercements of Alesellers and Victuallers, for breaking the Assise of Bread and Ale, as at Luston, and other Mannors in Herefordshire... But why so called *Quære*. 1706 in Phillips (ed. Kersey).

**Tra·ntles, †trantals**, *sb. pl. Sc.* [app. corruption of Trentals, taken as a type of trifling ceremonies.] Trifles, trifling or petty articles.

[1562 A. Scott *New Yeir Gift to Q. Mary* 89 Poems (S. T. S.) 4 Thai tyrit God with tryfillis, tvme trentalis, And daisit him with daylie darigeis.] 1697 Cleland *Poems* 88 Such are baptizing of bells, Hallowing Altars, Kirk and Cells.. For to impose gray Gowns, or Mantles, Or any such base Tritle Trantles. 1824 Mactaggart *Gallovid. Encycl.*, *Trantles*, bits of broken iron; odd things of hardware about a farm-house, same with *trantlums*; there are generally boles or holes about, where broken horse-shoon [etc.] be thrown; these are termed *trantle-boles*. a 1903 J. Lumsden *Toorle*, etc. 206 A' kind o' trantles they could find They braucht along!

**Tra·ntlum**, *sb.* (*a.*) *Sc.* Also 8 **trantlin, -lim.** [Extension of prec.] A trifle, knick-knack, toy; usually in *pl.*

1768 Ross *Helenore* I. 32, I came fiercelins in, An' wi' my trantlims made a rattlin dinn. 1776 C. Keith *Farmer's Ha'* xxix, They finger at the trantlims lang. 1841 W. Aitken *Poet. Wks.* 67 Your trantlums a' e'en break or burn. 1896 Crockett *Cleg Kelly* x, To the curbstane ye gang, wi' a' your traps and trantlums.

**b.** *attrib.* or as *adj.* Trifling.

1832 Rodger in *Whistlebinkie* (1890) I. 147 Their trantlum gear She couldna bear.

**Trap** (træp), *sb.*[1] Forms: 1 **treppe, træppe**, 3–5, 7 **trapp**, 4–6 **trappe**, 4– **trap.** [Late (and rare) OE. *treppe, træppe* (in *coltetræppe*), ME. *trappe, trapp*, agrees in form and sense with rare MDu. *trappe* trap, gin, snare, mod.WFlem. *traap, trape* (De Bo), in Kilian, 1599, '*trappe* (old word) mouse-trap, trap'; also with med.L. *trappa, trapa*, in Salic Law vii. 10 (MSS. of 8–9th c.), 'trap', OF. *trape* (12th c.), F. *trappe*, Prov. *trapa*, Pg. *trapa*, Sp. *trampa*; cf. also It. *trappola* (dim. of **trappa*); all in sense 'trap, pitfall, gin, snare'. The relations between the Romanic words and the Du. and Fl., and the relation of the latter to MDu. and MLG. *trappe, treppe* 'step, stair', are difficult to determine: see *Note* below.]

**1.** A contrivance set for catching game or noxious animals; a gin, snare, pitfall: cf. Man-trap, Mouse-trap, Rat-trap, Spring-trap.

In the common type, a spring or other device, released by the animal treading upon it, shuts the latter in, or catches hold of some part of it, in this case often killing it.

a 1000 Ælfric *Gloss.* in Wr.-Wülcker 95/13 Ic beswice fuȝelas hwilon mid neton . mid grinum, .. mid treppan (*decipula*). c 1386 Chaucer *Prol.* 145 She wolde wepe if that she saw a mous Kaught in a trappe. 1483 *Cath. Angl.* 391/2 A Trapp (*A.* Trape), *decipula, pedica.* 1484 Caxton *Fables of Æsop* I. xviii, The same lyon was take at a grete trappe. 1538 Elyot, *Decipula*, a grynne [*ed.* 1545 gyn] or trap to take byrdes. 1577 Googe tr. *Heresbach's Husb.* 156 b, I would rather counsell you to destroy your Rattes and Mise with Traps. 1597 G. Harvey *Trimming Nashe* Wks. (Grosart) III. 48 How happie the Rat caught in a trappe, and there dies a living death? 1599 Shaks. *Hen. V*, I. ii. 177 We haue.. pretty traps to catch the petty theeues. 1611 Bible *Jer.* v. 26 They lay waite as hee that setteth snares, they set a trap, they catch men. 1655 Mrq. Worcester *Cent. Inv.* § 72 It catcheth his hand as a Trap doth a Fox. 1719 De Foe *Crusoe* I. 171, I set three Traps..and going the next Morning I found them all standing, and yet the Bait eaten and gone. 1791 W. H. Marshall *W. England* (1796) II. 256 The Salmon Fishery of the Tavey...At one end of the dam, is a 'weir house' or Trap; on the principle of the vermin trap, whose entrance is outwardly large, but contracted inwardly, so as to..prevent the escape of the animal which has taken it. 1857 Tennyson *Geraint & Enid* 1571 A sudden sharp and bitter cry, As of a wild thing taken in the trap. 1883 *Fisheries Exhib. Catal.* 252 Fish Traps...Shrimp Trap. Eel Trap. Crab Traps. 19.. *Trade Catal.*, Patent automatic mouse trap. Balloon fly traps. Beetle trap. Patent trap for catching rats, stoats, weasel, rabbits, badger, otter, and other vermin and animals, also..all kinds of birds.

**b.** *transf.* and *fig.*, and in fig. expressions.

Often applied to anything by which a person is unsuspectingly caught, stopped, or caused to fall; also to anything which attracts by its apparent easiness and proves to be difficult, anything deceptive.

c 1200 Ormin 12301 He fandeþþ þa to lacchenn þe þurrh trapp off modiȝnesse. c 1386 Chaucer *Frankl. T.* 613 She wende neuere han come in swich a trappe. 1412–20 Lydg. *Chron. Troy* IV. 2659 Ȝif þei myȝt cacche hym in a trappe. 1509 Hawes *Past. Pleas.* xvi. (Percy Soc.) 64 Sodaynly my herte was in a trap By Venus caught. 1611 Bible *Rom.* xi. 9 Let their table be made a snare, and a trap, and a stumbling blocke. 1654 Bramhall *Just Vind.* iii. (1661) 40 The cruel statute of the Six Articles; which he made..as a trap to catch the lives of the Poor Protestants. 1765 Fordyce *Serm. Yng. Wom.* (1767) II. viii. 30 Let her lay traps for admiration. 1879 Dixon *Windsor* I. ii. 15 He resolved to take the Scottish invader in a trap. 1883 E. Pennell-Elmhirst *Cream Leicestersh.* 377 Two deep, hidden grips in midfield were nasty traps for blown horses.

**c.** Popularly applied to a police arrangement for the timing of motorists over a measured distance, in order to secure the conviction of such as exceed the legal speed-limit. Also *police-trap.*

1906 *Westm. Gaz.* 28 Aug. 4/2 The fear of the traps and the consequent fines is..an inducement to avoid tours in England...Car owners do not care to take the risks of the traps.

**2.** A movable covering of a pit, or of an opening in a floor, designed to fall when stepped upon; hence applied to any similar door flush with the surface in a floor, ceiling, roof, the top of a cab, or the like: cf. Trap-door.

13.. *Coer de L.* 4093 Doun ye scholde fallen there, In a pyt syxty fadme deep: Therfore beware,..At the passing of the trappe, Many on has had ful evyl happe. c 1374 Chaucer *Troylus* III. 692 (741) And with þat word he gan vn-do a trappe, And Troylus he brought In by þe lappe. 1470–85 Malory *Arthur* XIX. vii. 784 Sir launcelot that no peryl dredde..trade on a trap and the bord rollyd, and there sir Launcelot felle doune more than ten fadom in to a caue ful of strawe. 1682 Dryden *Mac Fl.* 212 Bruce and Longville had a trap prepared, And down they sent the yet declaiming bard. 1879 F. W. Robinson *Coward Consc.* II. vi, 'All right', said the cabman..as he closed the trap. 1838 Dickens *O. Twist* ix, He..drew forth..from some trap in the floor: a small box. 1904 Kipling in *Windsor Mag.* Jan. 228/2 Pyecroft..rising like a fairy from a pantomime trap. 1907 H. Wales *The Yoke* xviii, He pushed up the trap with his umbrella: 'Stop at the first jeweller's', he said to the [cab] driver.

**3.** The pivoted wooden instrument with which the ball is thrown up in the game of Trap-ball, q. v.; hence by extension, the game itself.

1591 [implied in Trapstick]. 1598 Florio, *Lippa*, a trap or cat, such as children play at. *Ibid.*, *Trappola*... Also a play that children vse called trap. 1637 Shirley *Hyde Park* II. iv. Div, I have heard you..in your younger [days] could play at trap well. 1652 J. Taylor (Water P.) *Journ. Wales* (1859) 26 The..laudable games of trapp, catt, stool-ball, racket, etc. 1719 D'Urfey *Pills* III. 162 We merrily Play At Trap. 1801 Strutt *Sports & Past.* II. iii. § 20 The trap..is generally made in the form of a shoe, the heel part being hollowed out for the reception of the ball; but boys and..rustics, who cannot readily procure a trap, content themselves with making a round hole in the ground.

**b.** *Trap* (*bat*) *and ball*: = Trap-ball.

1825 Hone *Every-day Bk.* I. 430 A game at trap-and-ball. 1868 Hughes *Tom Brown* (ed. 6) Pref. 11 Playing trap-bat-and-ball. 1877 *Cornh. Mag.* XXXVI. 368 To play trap-and-ball with Robin and Jack.

**4.** A device for suddenly releasing or throwing into the air an object to be shot at, as a pigeon.

1812 *Sporting Mag.* XL. 41 The trap was twenty-one yards from the gun. 1813 *Ibid.* XLI. 84 The parties fired with double-barrelled guns at two pigeons from a trap. 1892 Greener *Breech Loader* 234 It is wise to shoot pigeons at recognised clubs only..or experience at the trap may be very dearly bought.

**5.** *colloq.* or *slang.* Deceitful practice; trickery; fraud. *To understand trap*, to know one's own interest; *to be up to trap*, to be knowing or cunning.

1681 T. Flatman *Heraclitus Ridens* No. 5 (1713) I. 30 Well, Brother, I understand Trap. a 1734 North *Exam.* III. vii. § 63 (1740) 549 Some cunning Persons, that had found out his..Ignorance of Trap,..put him in great Fright, telling him he would certainly be hanged. 1785 Cowper *Let. to Lady Hesketh* 15 Dec., He understands booksellers' trap as well as any man. 1819 *Metropolis* II. 107 A papa too much up to trap to allow his offspring thus to be *had*. 1842 S. Lover *Handy Andy* ii, A clever, ready-witted fellow, up to all sorts of trap. 1902 *Westm. Gaz.* 14 Oct. 2/1 A 'policy' undistinguishable from trap in appearance.

**6.** *slang.* One whose business is to 'trap' or catch offenders; a thief-taker; a detective or policeman; a sheriff's officer.

1705 E. Ward *Hud. Rediv.* IV. v. 8 All girt with Chaps, Men, Boys, and Women, Traps Divers, Punks, and Serjeants Yeomen. 1800 *Sporting Mag.* XVI. 26 Send the traps to pull up Bounce and Blunderbuss. 1828 P. Cunningham *N. S. Wales* (ed. 3) II. 232 While the culprit stood quaking in the dock, surrounded by the traps of office. 1838 Dickens *O. Twist* xiii, 'Why, the traps have got him, and that's all about it', said the Dodger, sullenly. 1898 in M. Davitt *Life & Progr. Australia* xxxv. 192 A policeman is a 'Johnny', Or a 'copman' or a 'trap'. 1902 Snaith *Wayfarers* i, Expecting at every cast of the cards..to hear the boots of the 'traps' from Bow Street upon the stairs. 1905 *Daily News* 2 Jan. 9 Prisoner..said he was convicted upon the false evidence of a 'trap'—a Kaffir spy.

**7.** *colloq.* A small carriage on springs; usually, a two-wheeled spring carriage, a gig, a spring-cart. Cf. Rattletrap 2.

1806–7 J. Beresford *Miseries Hum. Life* VI. Introd., Bidding a long adieu to Bedlam in the shape of an inn..and a travelling trap for a sitting room. 1818 in *Illustr. Lond. News* (1884) 4 Oct. 315/3 His 'trap' was at the lodge, and ..he must be off. 1848 Thackeray *Van. Fair* lxvi, 'Hullo!' said he, 'there's Dob's trap'...The 'trap' in question was a carriage which the Major had bought for six pounds sterling. 1873 M. Collins *Squire Silchester* III. xiv. 143 Come with me to the stables. I'll have a trap out and drive to the Rectory. 1902 Buchan *Watcher by Threshold* 194 A trap shall be sent for you after dinner.

**8.** A device for preventing the upward escape of noxious gases from a pipe, as a double curve in or U-shaped section of the pipe, in which water stands.

1833 Loudon *Encycl. Archit.* § 464 No smell can penetrate upwards, it being intercepted by the trap and the water into which it dips. 1862 *Catal. Internat. Exhib.* II. x. 46 Traps to prevent effluvia from drains and gulleys. *Ibid.* XXXI. 24 Surface gutter with movable safety covers, sanitary traps. 1884 *Health Exhib. Catal.* 49/2 Water Closet of improved manufacture, ornamental bason and trap. 1892 D trap [see D I. 2].

**b.** Applied to various contrivances for preventing the passage of steam, water, silt, etc. Also, a ventilation door in a mine.

1877 Knight *Dict. Mech.*, *Steam-trap*, a self-acting device for the discharge of condensed water from steam-engines or steam-pipes. 1900 *Dundee Advertiser* 9 June 8 On the dead levels by the river the drainage water is run through tunnels piercing the embankments, each outlet having a trap or lock to prevent the tide from rushing up to drown the fields. 1900 *Daily News* 14 Feb. 3/2 Here and there [in a coal-mine]..are placed the ventilating doorways, or traps. At each of these sits the little trapper lad alone in the silent gloom. 1911 Webster, *Trap*,..a device to separate sand and silt from flowing water.

**9. a.** A recess in the butt of a musket or rifle, in which accessories are carried.

1844 [implied in *trap-plate*: see 11]. 1891 *Magazine Rifle Firing Exerc.*, *Aiming Drill*, The oil bottle is to be carried in the trap in the butt... Push the thong into the trap,..press down the end of the thong and close the trap. 1909 *Text-bk. Small Arms* 119 The short Springfield rifle is provided with a butt trap, containing a metal oil-bottle, holding oil at one end and a pull-through at the other.

**b.** The part of a stake- or trap-net in which the fish are confined.

1859 *Act* 22 & 23 *Vict.* c. 70 § 12 A clear Opening of at least Three Feet in Width in the Traps or Chambers of such Stake Net from the Bottom to the Top thereof.

**c.** *U.S.* = *trap-net* (see 11).

1888 Goode *Amer. Fishes* 216 Nets..similar in many respects to the so-called 'traps' of Seconnet River in Rhode Island. 1891 in *Cent. Dict.*

**10.** *Weaving.* A break in the threads of a warp; a faulty place resulting from this in woven cloth.

1871 Burnley *Phases Bradford Life* (1872) 197 Ere the loom ceases its motion, what is technically termed 'a trap' has occurred... A large number of 'ends' are broken, and must be tied neatly together again one by one before the work can proceed. 1883 *Gloss. Almondbury & Huddersfield* s. v., A bad place in the cloth is the consequence, and that is also called a trap. 1891 *Labour Commission Gloss.*, *Traps*, also called 'smashes' or 'mashes', are faults in weaving caused by the shuttle becoming *trapped*, which will break out the twist or warp threads for several inches in the width.

**11.** *attrib.* and *Comb.*, as *trap-bait*, *-cage*, *-catch*, *-chair*, *-lid*, *-load*, *-maker*, *-mouth*, *-setter*, *-setting*, *-tooth*, *-way*, *-window*; *trap-like* adj.; **trap-bat**, a bat used in playing trap or trap-ball; also, the game itself; **trap-board**, a perforated board in a Jacquard loom: see quot.; †**trap-bridge**, a drawbridge; **trap-cellar**, the space beneath the trap-doors in the stage of a theatre; **trap-creel**, a basket used for catching lobsters, etc.; **trap-crop**, a crop planted for the purpose of attracting insects or fungus from another crop; †**trap-ditch**, a ditch dug as a pitfall; **trap-drummer**, a street musician who plays a drum and other instruments at once; **trap-fisher**, one who fishes with a trap-net; **trap-hatch**, a hatch covered with a trap or trap-door; so **trap-hatchway**; **trap-hole**, a hole closed by a trap-door; also (*pl.*) pits dug in the ground to serve as obstacles to an enemy, *trous-de-loup*; **trap-hook**, a fish-hook fitted with a spring snap, a snap-hook; **trap-light**, a light having a device for trapping moths attracted by it; **trap-line**, the ensnaring filament in a spider's web; **trap-match**, a trap-shooting match; **trap-net**, a large net for catching fish: see quot. 1877; **trap-pit**, a deep pit in which beasts are trapped; also *fig.*; **trap-plate**, the hinged lid of the trap in a musket or rifle stock (see 9 a); **trap-poacher**, a poacher who traps game; **trap-point**, on railways, a safety-point (Point *sb.* B. 3 f) which prevents an unauthorized movement of a train or vehicle from a siding on to the main line by derailing it; **trap-seine** (*U.S.*), a kind of trap-net; **trap-shooter, -shot**, one who practises trap-shooting; **trap-shooting**, the sport of shooting pigeons, glass balls, etc., released from a spring trap; **trap-siding**, a siding on a gradient intended to intercept vehicles which break away from an ascending train and to derail them; **trap-tree**, the jack-tree, *Artocarpus integrifolia*, which provides gum for bird-lime; also (*U.S.*) a tree deadened or felled at a time when destructive beetles have entered the bark; **trap-twister, -winder**, in *Spinning*, a twisting or winding machine in which the roller or bobbin is stopped by a spring arrangement as soon as the yarn breaks (cf. 10); **trap-valve**: see quot.; **trap-weir** (*U.S.*), a trap-net (*Cent. Dict.* 1891).

1856 Kane *Arct. Expl.* I. xxvii. 356 The foxes seem tired of touching our *trap-baits. 1849 Lytton *Caxtons* ii. i, I wrote home to my father, modestly implying that I was short of cash, that a *trap-bat would be acceptable. 1865 *Athenæum* 11 Mar. 351/1 Kites could be flown, trap-bat indulged in. 1900 T. W. Fox *Mech. Weaving* vi. (ed. 2) 143 In or about..1830 William Jennings claimed the invention of a machine to work without hooks... In it a neck cord.. passes through a needle eye, through a perforated *trap board, that takes the place of a griffe, and is also threaded through a cross piece at the machine head where a loop is formed upon it, and a piece of twine passed through all the loops in one line, in order to prevent the cords from lifting. 1585 Higins *Junius' Nomencl.* 390/2 *Pons versatilis*, a draw-bridge: a falling bridg, or a *trap bridge. 1812 *Sporting Mag.* XXXIX. 26 A cage made upon the plan of the gold-finch *trap-cage. 1894 *Youth's Companion* 22 Nov. 562/4 For some weeks past our *trap-catch, both of eels and lobsters, had greatly diminished. *a* 1668 Lassels *Voy. Italy* (1698) II. 106 A chair of revenge, or a *trap-chair for an enemy. 1795 *Statist. Acc. Scot.* XVI. 516 A considerable quantity of lobsters and crabs..are taken, with *trap-creels. 1899 Massee *Plant Diseases* 26 The *trap-crop should consist of some plant readily susceptible to the disease it is intended to catch. 1657 Thornley tr. *Longus' Daphnis & Chloe* 16 Many such *Trap-ditches were digg'd in the fields. 1903 *Med. Record* 14 Feb. 268 *Trap-drummer's neurosis, a hitherto undescribed occupation-disease. 1820 Scoresby *Acc. Arctic Reg.* II. 204 The entrance is by a *trap-hatch at the bottom. 1903 J. Conrad & Hueffer *Romance* ii. iv, He slipped down the open trap-hatch near the window. 1799 *Hull Advertiser* 28 Dec. 3/2 A labouring man fell through a *trap hatchway at the house of..a baker. 1864 Webster, *Trap-hole. 1883 B. Phillips in *Century Mag.* Apr. 899/1, I discard all *trap-hooks, infernal machines working with springs, as only adapted for the capture of land animals. 1904 *Electr. World* 1 Oct. 563 Instruments..enclosed in a walnut casing with a *trap-lid. 1896 *U.S. Dept. Agric.*, *Cotton Plant*, *Bulletin* 331 Mally ..made extensive experiments with *trap lights for the moths. 1877 A. B. Edwards *Up Nile* xii. 332 Communicate by means of *trap-like openings with vaults below. 1895 *Westm. Gaz.* 29 Nov. 5/1 Pointing to the small trap-like exit under the judge's bench. 1889 H. C. McCook *Amer. Spiders* I. viii. 134 The *trapline of the Labyrinth spider differs..in being composed of several threads instead of a single line. 1894 A. Morrison *Mean Streets* 72 Helping with a heavy *trapload of luggage. 1907 *Daily News* 19 Feb. 6 If there were no rats, the *trap-makers of Birmingham would be out of work. 1895 *Outing* (U.S.) XXVII. 67/1 Expert shots assume many attitudes, as may be seen at any important *trap-match. 1894 G. Meredith *Ld. Ormont & Aminta* iv, Eyes bluish-grey..lively to shoot their meaning when the *trap-mouth was active. 1877 Knight *Dict. Mech.*, **Trap-net*, a fishing-net in which a funnel-shaped piece leads the fish into a pound from which extrication is not easy. 1904 Gallichan *Fishing Spain* 167 Lowering and raising the trap-nets are operations attended with peril. 1652 Benlowes *Theoph.* x. xiii, With dimpled chins, The *trap-pits where a fondling lies. 1849 A. Blackhall *Lays of North* 84 (E. D. D.) Reckless man, who..Revell'd in hell's trap-pit—drinking. 1844 *Regul. & Ord. Army* 106 New brass *trap plate and joint fitted to rifle. 1893 J. Watson *Conf. Poacher* 129 The *trap-poacher is only a casual. 1899 *Daily News* 5 July 3/5 A train, travelling from Blackpool to Birmingham, ran into the *trap points. Nine coaches were thrown on to an embankment. 1891 *Cent. Dict.*, **Trap-seine*, a trap-net specially adapted to take fish working down an eddy (Rhode Island). 1903 W. Blackwood *Local Veto & Bk.* xvi. 40 The *trap-setters and men-catchers were rapidly hastening the dynasty of Judah to its dissolution. *Ibid.*, What is our licensing system but a process of *trap-setting? 1899 Rider Haggard in *Longm. Mag.* July 247 The bruiser, the racing tout, the *trap-shooter and others equally ignoble are all 'sportsmen'. 1892 Greener *Breech Loader* 130 For ordinary *trap shooting a gun is required to shoot as closely as possible at the trap. *Ibid.* 94 Some *trap shots require their guns to carry as many as 6 in. high at forty yards. 1901 *Daily Chron.* 30 Sept. 5/1 He is reputed to be an excellent trap-shot. 1885 *Manch. Exam.* 19 Feb. 4/7 The engine left the line at a *trap siding and rolled down an embankment. 1868 Browning *Ring & Bk.* i. 1298 In its [the tiger-cat's] silkiness the *trap-teeth joined. 1884 W. S. B. McLaren *Spinning* (ed. 2) 237 Better than any winders for saving waste are *trap twisters where the yarn is not very soft. 1877 Knight *Dict. Mech.*, **Trap-valve*, a valve hinged on one side of its seat, and opening and closing like a shutter or trap-door, a *clack-valve*. 1904 Quiller Couch *Fort Amity* xxiii, Open the *trap-way and show us some light. 1884 W. S. B. McLaren *Spinning* (ed. 2) 237 There are many *trap winders for winding either single threads or two or more together. 1620 Middleton & Rowley *World Tost at Tennis* 456 His eyes look like false lights, cozening *trap-windows. 1836 Marryat *Midsh. Easy* xxxi, A small trap window in the roof.

[*Note.* The OE. *treppe*, *træppe*, and MFlem. *trappe*, WFlem. *traap*, *trape*, are generally held to be orig. either the same word as MDu. and MLG. *trappe*, 'stair, flight of steps, step', or a derivative of the same verbal stem **trapp-* (the non-nasalized original of **trampan* to tread, LG. *trappen*), for the supposed reason that a 'trap' was originally something laid for a beast to *tread* or step upon, and thus to be either caught by a gin or snare, or precipitated into a deep pit (cf. Pitfall). But it is difficult to conceive *trappe*, *treppe* used at once in the general sense 'stair or step', and in the very specific one of 'trap, snare, gin'. It has also to be noticed that it is only in MDu. or rather MFlem. that the word is known in both senses; for in OE. (and Eng. generally, down to 18th c.) *træppe*, *trap* had (like the Romanic *trappa*) only the sense of 'device for catching, gin, snare', while MLG. *trappe*, *treppe*, and thence mod.Ger., and the Scandinavian languages, have only the sense 'stair' or 'step of a stair'. (OHG. has a single instance of *trapa* wk. fem. as a gloss to L. *tenda*, but this rather looks like an adoption or re-adoption from med.L.) The actual relation of these words or senses is thus very obscure.]

†**Trap**, *sb.*[2] *Obs.* [Altered form of F. *drap* cloth, covering = Pr. *drap*, Sp. and Pg. *trapo*, It. *drappo*:—med.L. *drappus* cloth (Capit. Charles the Bald *a* 850), of uncertain origin: see Diez, and *Note* below.] A cloth or covering spread over the saddle or harness of a horse (cf. Trapper *sb.*[1]); a caparison; a trapping; *transf.* the hangings of a litter. (Usually in *pl.*)

13.. *K. Alis.* 1606 (Bodl. MS.) Þere men miȝtten quyk yseon Many hors wiþ trappe wryen. *Ibid.* 3416 Many trappe many croupere. 13.. *Coer de L.* 1515 A messanger ther com rydand, Upon a stede whyt so mylke, His trappys wer of tuely sylke. *a* 1400 *Octouian* 954 He bar thre rochys of seluer clere In scheld and trappys. 1513 Douglas *Æneis* xi. xv. 20 Hys rych mantill, of quham the forbreist lappis, Ratling of brycht gold wire, wyth gyltin trappys. 1721 Strype *Eccl. Mem.* III. iv. 36 The Queen [Mary, 1553] in her litter, richly garnished with cloth of gold, with two traps of white damask and cushions.

[*Note.* It is clear that 14th c. *trap* and *trappure* (later Trapper *sb.*[1]) correspond to OF. *drap* and *drapure*. The question is how these F. words in *dr-* have *tr-* in Eng. This may have been an Eng. change, due to influence of Trap in other senses. But the *trap* form may have existed in Anglo-Fr. or even in Fr. dialects. Du Cange has *trapus* (one example) for med.L. *drappus*; Pg. and Sp. have *trapo* 'clout, rag', formerly 'cloth', also *trapero* (draper), *trapería*, *trapajo*; med. (Anglo-) L. had *trappatura*, the ordinary equivalent of *trappure*, OF. *trappeüre*: see Trapper *sb.*[1]]

**Trap**, *sb.*[3] *Sc.* [app. = Du., MFlem. *trap* flight of steps, stair; MDu., early mod.Du. (Kilian) *trappe* step; OFris. *treppe* step of a ladder, etc., EFris. *trappe*, *trap* step (of a stair), also (= *trap-ledder*) ladder with broad flat steps instead of rungs, flight of steps; MLG. *trappe*, *treppe*, *troppe* flight of steps, stair, whence MG. *trappe*, *treppe*, Ger., LG. *treppe* stair; also (from MLG.), Da. *trappe*, Sw. *trappa*, Norw. dial. *trapp*, *tropp* flight of steps, stair. But the Sc. *trap* is by some referred directly to Trap *sb.*[1], as if short for *trap-ladder* or *trap-stair*, in sense of a ladder or stair leading up to a trap-door or trap-hole.] A ladder or movable flight of steps leading to a loft or the like.

[1756 Mrs. Calderwood in *Coltness Collect.* (Maitl. Cl.) 131 When we came to go up stairs to bed, there was a trap, which is the Dutch name for a stair.] 1808 Jamieson, *Trap*, a sort of ladder, a moveable flight of wooden steps. 1858 Simmonds *Dict. Trade*, *Trap*,..a sort of moveable ladder or steps. 1885 A. Munro *Siren Casket* (1889) 136 As you enter'd the door of the house from the street You confronted a trap or a ladder. 1899 J. Colville *Scott. Vernacular* 17 Against its wall stood the trap or ladder leading to the garret.

**b.** *attrib.* and *Comb.*, as *trap-like* adj.; **trap-ladder** [= WFlem. *trap-ladder*, *-leere*, EFlem. (Antwerp) *trapleer*, EFris. *trap-ledder* a ladder with flat steps, a 'pair of steps']; **trap-stair** = *trap*.

1855 Carlyle *Misc.*, *Prinzenraub* (1899) IV. 442 That other little Duke..who had built the biggest bassoon ever heard of; thirty feet high, or so; and was seen playing on it from a *trap-ladder. 1896 J. Lamb *Ann. W. Kilbride* ix. 244 A trap-ladder cost 2*s.* 6*d.* 1897 tr. *Balzac's Cousin Pons* 327 Reached by a short ladder, known among builders as a trap-ladder, there was a kind of garret. 1906 Dk. Argyll *Autobiog. & Mem.* I. ii. 18 Steep, *traplike wooden stairs. 1833 Loudon *Encycl. Archit.* § 164 The bottom [of the stair] might either project two double steps..; or a *trap stair, composed of the two lower steps, and made to fold up, might be resorted to. 1837 J. E. Murray *Summer in Pyrenees* II. 245 A little urchin came down a trap-stair at the further end. 1844 Stephens *Bk. Farm* I. 143 It enters from the straw-barn..by means of the stone or wooden trap-stair. 1847 H. Miller *First Impr.* xix. 368 Their terrace-like precipices, that rise over each other step by step—their trap-stairs of trappean rock,—for to this scenic peculiarity the volcanic rocks owe their generic name. 1850 R. Chambers *Burns' Life & Wks.* (1856) I. 145 Almost the only other apartment in the house is a kind of garret-closet, accessible by a narrow trap-stair ascending from the lobby.

†**Trap**, *sb.*[4] *Coal Mining*, etc. *Obs.* [History obscure; app. connected with the continental words *trap*, *trappe* step: see prec. (Perh. introduced by foreign miners in 16th c.)] A 'fault' in a seam of coal, also in a mineral vein or in any stratum; an up-throw or down-throw of the stratum (usually *trap-up* or *trap-down*). (Cf. *step-faults* applied to a series of faults in the same direction.)

1719 Strachey in *Phil. Trans.* XXX. 971 As..they are dug near the same Depth, it follows there must be a Trap, or several Traps down, which in all must amount to that Depth between the said Works. 1883 Gresley *Gloss. Coal-Mining*, *Trap-down* [in Bristol Coal-field], a fault which is a down-throw one... *Trap-up*, a fault which is an up-throw one.

Hence **Trap** *v.*[3] in *to trap up* or *down*, to be found at a higher or lower level after dislocation by a dike or fault: see quots.; whence **Trapping** *vbl. sb.*

1719 Strachey in *Phil. Trans.* XXX. 969 They observe, as they work to the South West, when they meet with a Ridg it Causeth the Coal to trap up, that is..they find it over their heads, when they are thro' the Ridg: but..when they work thro' a ridg to the North East, they say it traps down, that is, they find it under their feet. 1757 Da Costa in *Phil. Trans.* L. 233 The heavings, displacings, trappings, and breaks of the metallic veins. 1811 W. Taylor in *Monthly Mag.* XXXI. 448 Where there is a trapping down of the strata.

**Trap**, *sb.*[5] *Min.* Also 8 **trapp.** [a. Swed. *trapp* (Bergman 1766), so named from the stair-like appearance often presented by the rock, f. *trappa* stair: see Trap *sb.*[3]] A dark-coloured igneous rock more or less columnar in structure: now extended to include all igneous rocks which are neither granitic nor of recent volcanic formation.

[1794 Sullivan *View Nat.* II. 165 This is what the Swedes call *trapp*, or trapas, from stairs.] 1794 Schmeisser *Syst. Mineral.* I. 184 Trapp... Its name originates from the Swedish language. The term *trapp* describes a stone, which breaks in pieces of a rhomboidal figure, and consequently exhibits..steps like a stair case. 1796 Kirwan *Elem. Min.* (ed. 2) I. 227 Common Trap. Basalt of Werner. 1811 Pinkerton *Petralogy* I. 62 The volcanic eruptions, which are supposed to have produced the mountains of trap. 1863 A. C. Ramsay *Phys. Geog.* ix. (1878) 124 The rocks are pierced by..a white felspathic-looking trap, which has charred the coals at the points of junction. 1872 W. S. Symonds *Rec. Rocks* v. 146 A dyke of trap penetrates the rocks by means of a fissure.

**b.** *attrib.* and *Comb.*, as *trap-dike* (Dike *sb.* 9 b), *-granulite*, *-porphyry*, *-rock*, *-shale*, *-stone*, *-tuff*.

1796 Kirwan *Elem. Min.* (ed. 2) I. 355 Trap Porphyry..

sometimes..abounds..in quartz and felspar. **1811** SIR A. BOSWELL *Poet. Wks.* (1872) 102 Beneath his feet the trap-stone rung. **1813** BAKEWELL *Introd. Geol.* (1815) 118 Rocks in which hornblende forms a predominating ingredient, have been denominated trap rocks. **1821** R. JAMESON *Man. Mineral.* 401 Secondary Trap...The following are the different kinds of these rocks,.. Greenstone;.. Syenite;.. Amygdaloid;.. Wacke;.. Basalt; and.. Trap tuff. **1842** SEDGWICK in *Hudson's Guide Lakes* (1843) 241 Plumbago.. has..been found among coal strata near the sides of 'trap dykes'. **1853** in J. Phillips *Man. Geol.* (1855) 102 Roofing-slate,..alternating,..with porphyry, trappean conglomerate, trap-shale. **1855** J. PHILLIPS *Man. Geol.* 187 There are no trap dikes in this coal field. **1867** BURTON *Hist. Scot.* (1873) I. ii. 57 It is a small bar of trapstone. **1881** PREVOST in *Knowledge* No. 5. 85 The trap rocks, divisible into two great classes, called diorite and dolerite, contain soda, lime, magnesia, and potash.

† **Trap**, *sb.*[6] *Obs.* [a. OF. *trappe* a baking-tin for tarts (1395 in Godef.).] A kind of dish or pan, app. for baking.

?*c* **1390** *Forme of Cury* in Warner *Antiq. Culin.* 27 Make a crust in a trape. *c* **1420** *Liber Cocorum* (1862) 40 Fyrst make a fole trap.., Pynche hym, cowche hym þy flesshe þerby. *c* **1430** *Two Cookery-bks.* (E.E.T.S.) 54 Sew Trappe.

**Trap**, *sb.*[7]: see TRAPS, belongings, etc.

**Trap**, *v.*[1] [ME. *trappen* :—OE. **træppan* in *betræppan*, (*be*)*treppan* (BETRAP), f. *træp*, TRAP *sb.*[1] Cf. also ATTRAP, ENTRAP (from F.), which may have contributed to the Eng. vb.]

I. Transitive senses.

**1.** To catch in or as in a trap, entrap, ensnare.

[*a* **900** *Kentish Gloss.* 211 (Bosw.-T.) Hio [tr]e[p]te, *irretivit.*] *c* **1460** *Towneley Myst.* xiii. 371 Me thoght with a gyn A fatt shepe he trapt, bot he mayde no dyn. **1530** PALSGR. 761/1, I trappe, I take one by sleyght, or take any beest in a trappe or snare, *je attrappe* and *je trappe.* **1835** W. IRVING *Tour Prairies* xxiii. 211 Three persons are safer than a large number for trapping beaver. **1860** WARTER *Sea-board* II. 39 Wheat-ears, which all shepherds..trap on the Downs.

**b.** *fig.*

**1390** GOWER *Conf.* II. 218 Thus he, whom gold hath overset, Was trapped in his oghne net. *c* **1425** *Cast. Persev.* 2099 in *Macro Plays* 140, & þou, deuyl, with wyckyd wyl, In paradys trappyd us with tresun. **1509** HAWES *Past. Pleas.* xxix. (Percy Soc.) 143 Howe that my hart by Venus was trapt, With a snare of love. **1670** COTTON *Espernon* III. XI. 556 The Duke knowing, that..this was only a device to make him run into some error,..was not easie to be trap'd that way. *a* **1700** DRYDEN tr. *Ovid's Met.* XIII. *Sp. Ajax & Ulysses* 340 With ambush'd arms I trapp'd the foe, or tired with false alarms. **1885–94** R. BRIDGES *Eros & Psyche* July v, They alert with joy to see her trapt, Launch'd forth amain.

**c.** *fig.* with ref. to speech: To catch, pull up, or detect in a mis-statement. Also *Sc.* To detect and correct a classmate in an erroneous answer, or to answer a question which he cannot and 'take him down' (TAKE *v.* 80 b (*d*)).

**1630** PRYNNE *Anti-Armin.* 136 That contradicts their Doctrine, and traps them in a lye. **1681–6** J. SCOTT *Chr. Life* (1747) III. 601 The Jews having every Day Opportunity of conversing with them, they might have easily trapp'd them in their Relations. **1825** JAMIESON, *To trap*, to correct in saying a lesson at school, so as to have a right to take the place of him who is thus corrected. **1895** CROCKETT *Bog-Myrtle & Peat* 185 He had promptly 'trapped' his way to the head of the class...The operation of 'trapping' was simply performed. When a mistake was made in pronunciation, repetition, or spelling, any pupil further down the class held out his hand,..the 'trapper', providing always that his emendation was accepted, was instantly promoted to the place of the 'trapped'.

**2.** To furnish with traps; to set (a place) with a trap or traps (in quot. 1908 with arrangements for detecting law-breaking motorists, TRAP *sb.*[1] 1 c).

**1841** CATLIN *N. Amer. Ind.* II. lviii. 251 They assume the right of hunting and trapping the streams and lakes. **1908** *Westm. Gaz.* 8 Dec. 1/1 The owners of motors are not content to take them week by week down the same road, especially when that road is so well 'trapped' as is the highway to the London-by-the-sea.

**3.** To furnish (a drain, etc.) with a trap or traps, to prevent the ascent of foul air or gas.

**1862** *Catal. Internat. Exhib.* II. x. 46 The drains to be trapped and ventilated. **1881** B. W. RICHARDSON in *Gd. Words* XXII. 55 The chief drain has to be trapped outside the dwelling, a little way before it reaches the common sewer.

**4.** Chiefly *Mech.* To stop and hold or retain by a trap or contrivance for the purpose; to separate or remove by a trap:

e.g. to stop the shuttle of a loom in the warp; water, air, gas, heat in its passage; esp. anything suspended in water, or condensed from steam or gas, in a pipe.

II. Intransitive senses.

**5.** To practise catching wild animals in traps for their furs; also *gen.* to set traps for game.

**1807** P. GASS *Jrnl.* 78 Some Frenchmen who were out trapping caught 7 of them [beavers]. **1817** J. BRADBURY *Trav. Amer.* 18 *note*, Soon after he..trapped in company with a hunter named Potts. **1835** W. IRVING *Tour Prairies* xxiii. 210, I should like to come and trap on these waters all winter. **1894** *Times* 10 Dec. 10/2 The provisions of the Ground Game Act had not been observed; tenants were allowed to trap how and when they liked. **1905** D. WALLACE *Lure Labrador Wild* iii. 48 Tom Blake..had trapped at the..western end of Grand Lake.

**6.** To use, handle, or work a trap or traps.

**a.** (also with *it*) To use trap-doors on the stage in a theatrical performance. *nonce-use.*

**1886** *Sat. Rev.* 2 Jan. 20/1 Kazrac and the Demon go down and come up trap after trap...They should take a lesson of Mr. Conquest..(we know not whether or not that excellent artist still traps it).

**b.** To act as a 'trapper' in a coal-mine: see TRAPPER *sb.*[2] 2.

**1842** [see TRAPPING *vbl. sb.*[2]]. **1900** *Daily News* 14 Feb. 3/2 'How long have you been trapping?' 'Since I come down pit, six months ago.'

**c.** To handle or work a trap in trap-shooting: see TRAP *sb.*[1] 4, TRAPPER *sb.*[2] 3.

**Trap**, *v.*[2] [f. TRAP *sb.*[2]] *trans.* To adorn (a horse, mule, or the like) with trappings; to caparison. (Chiefly in *pa. pple.*) Rarely (in 19th c.) said in reference to a man.

**13..** [see TRAPPED *ppl. a.*[2]]. **1375** BARBOUR *Bruce* XIV. 289 The scottis all on fut war then, And thai on stedis trappit weill. *c* **1420** *Brut* 347 A mylke-white stede, sadelled and brydilled, & trapped with white cloth of golde. *Ibid.* 373 Al þe horsses drawyng þe chare were trappid yn blak. *a* **1548** HALL *Chron., Rich. III* 25 b, His horse trapped in blew veluet enbroudered with the naues of cartes burnyng of gold. **1621–3** MIDDLETON & ROWLEY *Changeling* I. i, Call your servants up, And help to trap your horses. **1631** HEYWOOD *Eng. Eliz.* (1641) 63 The Lady Elisabeth..rode in a chariot ..drawn with six horses trapt in cloth of silver. **1826** HOR. SMITH *Tor Hill* (1838) I. 29 Dudley hastily trapped himself for the field.

**b.** *transf.* and *fig.*

*c* **1412** HOCCLEVE *De Reg. Princ.* 489 Drapers and..skinners ..For suche folk han a special orisoune, That trapped is withe curses..til they be payed for her gere. **1577–87** HOLINSHED *Chron.* (1807) III. 345 One Agnes Daintie a butterwife..being first trapped with butter dishes, was then set on the pillorie. **1590** MARLOWE *2nd Part Tamburl.* I. i, Fair Europe..Trapt with the wealth and riches of the world. **1641** J. JACKSON *True Evang. T.* III. 178 A Prophecy so trapped with the ornaments of speech. **1903** *Daily Chron.* 10 Apr. 5/1 The old mess jacket was a gorgeous affair of innumerable gold buttons, with a gay scarlet waistcoat, also trapped with gold.

**Trap**, *v.*[3]: see under TRAP *sb.*[4]

**Trapan**: see TREPAN.

**Trap-ball** (træ·p,bǫl). [f. TRAP *sb.*[1] + BALL *sb.*[1]] A game in which a ball, placed upon one end (slightly hollowed) of a trap (TRAP *sb.*[1] 3), is thrown into the air by the batsman striking the other end with his bat, with which he then hits the ball away.

**1658** *Churchw. Acc. St. Marg. Westminster* (Nichols 1797) 64 One that played at trap-ball on the Lords day. **1740** CHESTERF. *Lett.* (1792) I. lxxi. 197 You will desire to excell all boys of your age at cricket, or trap-ball, as well as in learning. **1814** *Sporting Mag.* XLIII. 240 A game of trap-ball was played this month on the ice. **1909** *Daily Chron.* 27 Aug. 7/3 An inn..where..trap-ball is played on the lawn...The dictionary already calls it 'an old game'.

*attrib.* **1845** J. T. SMITH *Bk. Rainy Day* (1861) 18 On the eastern side of the house there was a trap-ball-ground.

**b.** A ball used in this game. *rare.*

**1713** S. SEWALL *Diary* 6 June, Boston..came down a Spit, and clear'd the Leaden throat, by thrusting out a Trap-Ball that stuck there.

**Tra·p-bri·lliant.** [app. f. Du. *trap* step (cf. next) + BRILLIANT *sb.*] In diamond-cutting, a form of brilliant in which each of the foundation squares is divided horizontally into two triangular facets at an obtuse angle (when viewed in elevation); also called *step-brilliant*, *split-brilliant.*

**1877** KNIGHT *Dict. Mech.* s.v. *Gem-cutting*, There are several varieties of brilliant cuts, known as—Half-brilliant.. Full brilliant..Split or trap-brilliant..Double brilliant or Lisbon cut. **1891** in *Cent. Dict.*

**Trap-cut.** [app. f. Du. *trap* step, stair + CUT *sb.*] A mode of cutting gems, chiefly used with emeralds, rubies, sapphires, etc.; also called *step-cut*, *degree-cut*: see quot. 1877.

**1853** O. BYRNE *Artisan's Handbk.* 225 The trap cut, or trapping, as it is called by lapidaries. **1865** EMANUEL *Diamonds* 98 The Trap or Step Cut. This is the most usual, besides being the most advantageous form of cutting emeralds and other coloured stones... There are generally only two or three steps from the table to the girdle. **1877** KNIGHT *Dict. Mech.*, *Trap-cut*, a mode of cutting gems in which the facets consist of parallel planes, nearly rectangular, arranged round the center of the stone.

**Trap-door** (træ·p,dōᵊɹ). [f. TRAP *sb.*[1] + DOOR.] A door, either sliding or moving on hinges, and flush with the surface, in a floor, roof, or ceiling, or in the stage of a theatre.

*c* **1374** CHAUCER *Troylus* III. 710 (759) 'Which weye be ye comen..?' Quod she...'Here at þis secre trappe dore', quod he. **1489–90** *Rec. St. Mary at Hill* 155 For viij ffoote di. tymber for o trapp dorr. **1579–80** NORTH *Plutarch* (1595) 1092 Aristippus..locked himself..in a litle high chamber with a trappe dore, and set his bed vpon it, and so slept. **1599** SANDYS *Europæ Spec.* (1632) 97 They have their trap doores or pit-falls in darke melancholy chambers. **1704** S. SEWALL *Diary* 12 Sept., Mrs. Tuthill falls through a Trap Door into the cellar. **1774** PENNANT *Tour Scot. in 1772* 93 The trap-door in the floor, contrived for the lowering in of the captives. **1840** DICKENS *Old Curiosity Shop* xxxv, Getting on the roof of the house through the trap-door.

**b.** *transf.* and *fig.*

**1648** GAGE *West Ind.* 82 Never to go to those parts, which were but snares and trap-dores to let down to hell. **1694** MOTTEUX *Rabelais* IV. xxxiv. 136 It no more open'd its Guttural Trap-door. **1860** P. P. CARPENTER in *Rep. Smithsonian Instit. 1859* 206 *note*, The operculum is a horny or shelly appendage to the end of the foot...It may be called ..the trap-door or toe-nail. **1869** J. MARTINEAU *Ess.* II. 94 The trap-door of some hidden paradox.

**c.** *Mining.* A door in a level for directing the ventilating current; a weather-door.

**1851** GREENWELL *Coal-trade Terms Northumb. & Durh.* 54 *Trapper*, a little boy whose employment consists in opening and shutting a trap-door when required. **1883** GRESLEY *Coal Mining Gloss.*, *Trap-door*, a small door, kept locked, fixed in a stopping or bolt, for giving access to firemen and certain others to the return air-ways, dams, or other disused places in a mine. **1886** J. BARROWMAN *Sc. Mining Terms* 68.

**d.** *Comb.* **Trap-door spider**, one of a group of large spiders, which make a nest in the shape of a tube with a hinged lid which opens and shuts like a trap-door; hence *trap-door nest*, etc.

**1826** KIRBY & SP. *Entomol.* III. xxxiv. 492 The trapdoor or mason spider (*Mygale cæmentaria*). **1864–5** WOOD *Homes without H.* vi. (1868) 116 Of all the burrowing spiders ..none is so admirable an excavator as the Trap-door Spider of Jamaica [*Cteniza*]. **1883** *Pall Mall G.* 29 Dec. 5/1 The trap-door spider is almost the typical natural curiosity of the Riviera. **1897** ANNE PAGE *Afternoon Ride* 58 The.. spider, decoyed out of his well-built trap-door nest.

† **Trape**, *v. Obs.* or *dial.* Also ? 5 trappe. [Origin obscure. If quot. *c* 1400 belongs here, it may possibly be = MDu. and MLG. *trappen* to tread, trample, in Kilian 'calcare, conculcare pedibus', in EFris. (Doornkaat-Koolman), to set down the foot with force and noise, to tramp.

But this is doubtful, as there is a long gap between 1400 and 1706, and *trape* is not phonetically identical with *trappe*. *Trape* of 1706–49 is moreover preceded 1593–1700 by TRAPES *v.*, of which it may have been a mutilated form.]

*intr.* = TRAPES *v.*

[*c* **1400** *Sowdone Bab.* 1802 Fal what so euer by falle, To the Soudon wole they trappe.] **1706** PHILLIPS (ed. Kersey), To *Trape*, to go idly up and down. **1721** in BAILEY. **1749** RICHARDSON *Let.* 4 Aug., in A. Dobson *Fielding* v. (1883) 139 The Lowest of all Fellows, yet in Love with a Young Creature who was traping after him.

**b.** = TRAPES *v.* 1 b.

**1875** *Sussex Gloss.* s.v., 'Her gown trapes along the floor'.

**Trape**, erroneous form of TRIPE [2].

**Trapes, traipse** (trēⁱps), *sb. colloq.* and *dial.* Also 9 **trapse.** [Goes with TRAPES *v.*, but of later appearance.]

**1.** An opprobrious name for a woman or girl slovenly in person or habits; 'a dangling slattern'.

**1676** *Poor Robin's Intell.* 11–18 Apr. 2/2 A lazy trapes that cares not how late she sits up, nor how long she lies in the morning. **1678** BUTLER *Hud.* III. II. 471 He found the sullen Trapes Possest with th' Devil, Worms, and Claps. *a* **1700** B. E. *Dict. Cant. Crew*, *Trapes*, a dangling Slattern. **1714** GAY *What d'ye call it* I. i, From Door to Door I'd sooner whine and beg,..Than marry such a Trapes. **1780** H. WALPOLE *Let. to Mason* 31 Aug., There was a trapes of a housekeeper. **1811** *Ora & Juliet* IV. 191 You and your dirty trapes. **1905** *Eng. Dial. Dict.* [cited from Lancash., Yorks. to Essex, Somerset].

**2.** An act or course of 'trapesing'; a tiresome or disagreeable tramp.

**1862** MRS. H. WOOD *Channings* (1866) 471 It's such a toil and a trapes up them two pair of stairs. **1866** MRS. LYNN LINTON *Liz. Lort.* I. xiii. 302 He..asked if the ladies would like to go down the mine?..his lass shouldn't go through such a trapse. **1887** T. HARDY *Woodlanders* xlviii, Leading folk a twelve-mile traipse. **1893** COUCH *Delectable Duchy* 196 A brave trapse all the way from Upper Woon.

**Trapes, traipse** (trēⁱps), *v. colloq.* Also 8–9 *dial.* **trapse**, 9 **traaps**; **traapess, trapas, trapass, trapess, trapez, trapus, traipass, traipess, traaypess**, etc. [Known *a* 1600. Evidently related to TRAPE *v.*, but the nature of their relation is not clear. In literary use, the spelling *traipse* and Pope's metrical use show the word as a monosyllable; but many modern dialects have it as two syllables.

If *trappe* *c* 1400 really belongs to TRAPE *v.*, that would appear to be the earliest word of the group, although *trapes* as vb. would be a deriv. of unusual form; but if not, *trapesing* of 1593 would be the earliest form recorded. The dialect forms *trapass*, *traipass* strongly recall OF. *trapasser*, *trepesser*, *trépasser* (still in Cotgr.), to pass over or beyond (see TRESPASS *v.*), though the senses do not exactly fit.]

**1.** *intr.* To walk in a trailing or untidy way; e.g. to walk or 'trail' through the mud; to walk with the dress trailing or bedraggled; to walk about aimlessly or needlessly. (Usually said of a woman or child.)

**1593** [see TRAPESING *vbl. sb.*]. **1647** in *Verney Mem.* (1907) I. 368 What soever wether comes I must goe trapesing a foote to yᵉ end of yᵉ lane. **1710** SWIFT *Jrnl. to Stella* 13 Dec., I am to go trapesing with Lady Kerry and Mrs. Pratt to see sights all this day. **1710–11** *Ibid.* 2 Mar., I was traipsing to-day with your Mr. Sterne. **1728** (ed. 1) POPE *Dunc.* III. 141 See next two slip-shod Muses traipse along. **1732** SIR C. WOGAN *Let. to Swift* 27 Feb., Ireland is left to trapes in her old draggle-tailed weeds by her own children. **1742** MRS. DELANY in *Life & Corr.* (1861) II. 189 We trapesed all over Babylon garden. **1824** MRS. CAMERON *Pink Tippet* II. 25, I would not go trapsing to school as she does. **1864** MRS. GASKELL *Wives & Dau.* ii, I've been out for these three hours trapesing about the grounds till I'm as tired as can be. **1869** *Punch* 16 Oct. 154/1 Draggletails trapseing along the street. **1884** L. F. ALLEN *New Amer. Farm-Bk.* 313 The frog, traipsing over the dewy fields. **1892** G. H. BILLINGTON in *Times* 1 Jan. 11/3, I only wish the children of the members of the Board..had to traipse a mile and a half to school.

**b.** To trail along the ground; to hang untidily.
1774 FOOTE *Cozeners* III. Wks. 1799 II. 184 These..skirts of the boy's are so light and genteel..: those we got made in the country trapes and dangle like a parcel of petticoats. 1887 *S. Cheshire Gloss.* s. v., Ah dait [= I doubt] it'll trapes, if yo han it made so long.

**2.** *trans.* To walk or tramp over; to tread, tramp (the fields, streets, etc.). *dial.*
1885 HALL CAINE *Shadow of Crime* xxiii, It's bad weather to trapes the fells. 1901 D. C. MURRAY *Ch. Humanity* v. 80 If you're to begin trapesing the streets again without a farthing in your pocket. 1902 *Monthly Rev.* Aug. 181 I'll gar you trapse the stone-floor bare-fit!

**b.** To tread (a dance) in a trailing way. *rare.*
1835 *Clouds of Aristophanes* ii. in *Blackw. Mag.* Oct. 526 She's not appearing Drest out Like the rest in filthy guise.. nor trapesing [*printed* trapering] forth a dirty minuet.

Hence **Trapesed** *ppl. a.*, trampled, bedraggled.
1884 G. H. BOUGHTON in *Harper's Mag.* Oct. 706/2 The town..looked messy and 'traipsed'. 1887 *S. Cheshire Gloss.* s.v., A woman with dirty garments was called 'a poor, trapes't thing'.

**Trapesing, traipsing** (trēⁱ·psiŋ), *vbl. sb.* [f. prec. + -ING [1].] The action of the verb TRAPES.
1593 BILSON *Govt. Christ's Ch.* xiv. 296 This t[r]apesing to and fro I impute rather to the rawnesse of your discipline.. This it is to wander in the desert of your owne deuises without the line of Gods worde, or leuell of his Church to direct you. 1800 MAR. EDGEWORTH *Out of Debt* i, Anything's better than trapesing through a shop. 1887 'H. SMART' *Cleverly Won* vii, If she thought trapesing about with the hounds was the way to get married, she was mistaken. 1895 T. HARDY *Jude* III. ii, The traipsing along to the station, the porter's 'B'your leave!' the screaming of the trains.

**Tra·pesing, trai·psing,** *ppl. a.* [f. as prec. + -ING [2].] That trapeses; going about in a slovenly manner.
1760 FOOTE *Minor* I. Wks. 1799 I. 244 One armful of good wholesome British beauty, is worth a ship-load of their trapsing, tawdry trollops. 1773 GOLDSM. *Stoops to Conq.* I. ii, The daughter, a tall trapesing trolloping, talkative maypole. 1886 HALL CAINE *Son of Hagar* I. vii, Beneath the traipseing feet of the people.

**Trapezate** (træpīzeⁱt), *a. rare.* [irreg. f. TRAPEZ-IUM + -ATE [2].] (See quot.)
1826 KIRBY & SP. *Entomol.* IV. xlvi. 264 Trapezate (*Trapezata*), quadrilateral with the four sides unequal, and none of them perfectly parallel.

**Trapeze** (trăpī·z). [a. F. *trapèze* in same senses, ad. L. TRAPEZIUM.]

**1.** An apparatus for gymnastic exercises and feats, consisting of a horizontal cross-bar suspended by two ropes in the manner of a swing.
Prob. orig. applied to a kind in which the ropes formed a *trapezium* (in sense 1 b) with the roof and cross-bar.
1861 *Sat. Rev.* 22 June 635 The ring is neither more nor less likely to cause death than the rope or the *trapèze*. 1865 *Public Opinion* 21 Jan. 81 His performances are of a very extraordinary character; among other things, he holds on to the trapeze by his teeth. 1877 BLACK *Green Past.* xxxvi, Will you..show the boys how to twist round a trapeze. 1880 *Encycl. Brit.* XI. 350/2 The trapeze consists of a horizontal bar suspended by ropes at a height of 4 or 5 feet from the floor. 1908 *Daily Chron.* 11 June 1/4 At this altitude of two miles above the ground her feet became entangled in the trapeze ropes.

**2.** = TRAPEZIUM. *rare*⁻⁰.
1864 in WEBSTER: hence in later Dicts.

Hence **Trape·zing**, performance on the trapeze.
1894 G. DU MAURIER *Trilby* I. 70 Fencing and boxing and trapezing seemed to be more in her line. 1905 *Daily Chron.* 6 June 3/1 People who are revivified by trapezings and comic songs have no individuality to be recreated.

†**Trape·zia.** *Obs.* [mod.L. *trapezia*, adj. fem. f. TRAPEZIUM, used absol. for *trapezia figura* trapezial figure or shape.] A quadrilateral figure other than a parallelogram; the 'trapezium' of Euclid, comprising the later trapezium and trapezoid.
1631 DE LA MAIN (*title*) The making, description, and use of a small portable Instrument for the Pocket..in form of a mixt Trapezia thus called a Horizontall Quadrant. 1693 J. WING *Heptarchia Math.* 64 A Table shewing the Area of Right-line Figures, as Squares, Triangles, and Trapezia's. 1752 A. FLETCHER *Univ. Measurer* I. 98 To reduce a Trapezia *ABCD* to a triangle. 1766 *Compl. Farmer* s.v. *Surveying*, Quadrangular figures..are either parallelograms or trapesias.

**Trapezial** (trăpī·ziăl), *a.* [f. mod.L. TRAPEZI-UM + -AL.]

**1.** Of or pertaining to a trapezium; having the form of a trapezium, trapeziform.
1681 tr. *Willis' Rem. Med. Wks.* Vocab., *Trapezial*, belonging to a geometrical figure, so called of four sides. 1703 T. N. *City & C. Purchaser* 249 At each corner of the Newel there is a trapezial Half-pace. 1852 DANA *Crust.* I. 312 Their trapezial or quadrate form.

**2.** *Anat.* Pertaining to the trapezium (in either sense), or to the trapezius muscle.
1891 *Cent. Dict.*, *Trapezial*, in *anat.*, pertaining to the trapezius: as, trapezial fibers or action. 1899 *Syd. Soc. Lex.*, *Trapezial*, pertaining to the *Trapezium* or *Trapezius*.

**Trape·zian,** *a. Cryst.* [f. as prec. + -AN. Cf. mod.F. *trapézien* (Littré).] Having trapeziform lateral faces in two rows between the two bases, as a crystal of barium sulphate.
1757 tr. *Henckel's Pyritol.* 23 Prismatical, trapezian, or irregular. 1805–17 R. JAMESON *Char. Min.* 203 A crystal is said to be..Trapezian, when its lateral surfaces consist of trapezia, which lie in two rows, between two bases, as in trapezian heavy-spar...It is a rectangular four-sided table, bevelled on the extremities, where the bevelling planes are trapeziums. 1828 in WEBSTER. Hence in later Dicts.

**Trapeziform** (trăpī·zifǭɹm), *a.* [f. TRAPEZ-IUM + -(I)FORM. Cf. F. *trapéziforme* (Littré).] Having the form of a trapezium; quadrilateral with only two sides parallel.
1776 J. LEE *Introd. Bot.* Explan. Terms, *Trapeziforme*, trapeziform. 1817 KIRBY & SP. *Entomol.* (1843) II. 145 The wax-pockets in the hive-bee..two trapeziform whitish pockets. 1834 MᶜMURTRIE *Cuvier's Anim. Kingd.* 375 In Mycterus,..the body is ovoid,..and the thorax trapeziform. 1868 *Rep. U. S. Commissioner Agric.* (1869) 100 The family Tenebrionidæ consists of insects..having the thorax square or trapeziform, and as broad behind as the base of the wing-cases (Westwood). 1890 *Cent. Dict.* s. v. *Projection*, *Trapeziform map-projection*, a map-projection in which the space between two meridians and two parallels is represented by a trapezoid [i. e. a trapezium].

**Trapezihedron**, erron. f. TRAPEZOHEDRON.

**Trapezio-** (trăpī·zio), used as combining form of TRAPEZIUM in the anatomical sense, as in **trapezio-metacarpal** *a.*, pertaining to the trapezium (bone) and the metacarpus.
1840 E. WILSON *Anat. Vade M.* (1851) 247 The..trapezio-metacarpal articulation.

**Trapezist** (trăpī·zist). [f. TRAPEZE + -IST.] A performer on the trapeze.
1888 *Star* 7 June 4/3 You may have heard of my sister Azella, the trapezist? 1893 *Westm. Gaz.* 10 Feb. 9/1 He has been a trapezist, a wire-walker, bar-performer, lifter of weights. 1905 *Ibid.* 11 Sept. 5/1 Aeronaut-trapezist killed.

†**Trapezite**, *a. Obs. rare*⁻¹. [app. f. TRAPE-ZIUM + -ITE.] Having the form of a trapezium (in Euclid's sense); trapezial.
1570 BILLINGSLEY *Euclid* x. Def. xi. 232 A figure..which may be any other rectiline figure, rectangled or not rectangled, triangle, pentagone, trapezite, or what so euer ells.

**Trapezium** (trăpī·ziŏm). Pl. **trapezia, -iums.** [a. mod.L. *trapezium*, ad. Gr. τραπέζιον, dim. of τράπεζα table, in geometry used by Euclid in the general sense (see 1 below), by Proclus (ed. Friedlein, p. 414) in sense 1 b. (The early Latin editions of Euclid 1482–1516 have not *trapezium*, but the Arabic *helmariphe*; *trapezium* is in the Basle ed. of 1546.)
With Euclid (*c* 300 B.C.) τραπέζιον included all quadrilateral figures except the square, rectangle, rhombus, and rhomboid; into the varieties of *trapezia* he did not enter. But Proclus, who wrote Commentaries on the First Book of Euclid's Elements A.D. 450, retained the name τραπέζιον only for quadrilaterals having two sides parallel, subdividing these into the τραπέζιον ἰσοσκελές, *isosceles trapezium*, having the two non-parallel sides (and the angles at their bases) equal, and σκαληνὸν τραπέζιον, *scalene trapezium*, in which these sides and angles are unequal. For quadrilaterals having no sides parallel, Proclus introduced the name τραπεζοειδὲς TRAPEZOID. This nomenclature is retained in all the continental languages, and was universal in England till late in the 18th century, when the application of the terms was transposed, so that the figure which Proclus and modern geometers of other nations call specifically a *trapezium* (F. *trapèze*, Ger. *trapez*, Du. *trapezium*, It. *trapezio*) became with most English writers a *trapezoid*, and the *trapezoid* of Proclus and other nations a *trapezium*. This changed sense of *trapezoid* is given in Hutton's Mathematical Dictionary, 1795, as 'sometimes' used—he does not say by whom; but he himself unfortunately adopted and used it, and his Dictionary was doubtless the chief agent in its diffusion. Some geometers however continued to use the terms in their original senses, and since *c* 1875 this is the prevalent use.]

**1.** *Geom.* **a.** Any four-sided plane rectilineal figure that is not a parallelogram; any irregular quadrilateral. (The Euclidean sense.)
[1551 RECORDE *Pathw. Knowl.* B iv, The fift sorte doth containe all other fashions of foure cornered figures, and ar called of the Grekes *trapezia*.] 1570 BILLINGSLEY *Euclid* I. Def. 34. 6 All other figures of foure sides besides these, are called trapezia, or tables. *Ibid.* 52 A trapesium hauing two sides parallels hath of necessitie the one of them longer then the other. 1660 BARROW *Euclid* I. Def. 33 All other quadrilateral figures besides these are called *Trapezia* or Tables. 1846 POTTS *Euclid* 5. 1862 TODHUNTER *Euclid* 5. 1906 HAMILTON & KETTLE *2nd Geometry Bk.* 39 Some terms for quadrilaterals are variously used by different writers. Here *trapezium* is used for all quadrilaterals that are not parallelograms.

**b.** *spec.* A quadrilateral having only one pair of its opposite sides parallel. (The specific sense to which the term was restricted by Proclus.)
The specific sense in Eng. in 17th and 18th c., and again the prevalent one in recent use.
[1570: see a.] 1698 FRYER *Acc. E. India & P.* 289 Geometrical Figures, like the Trapezium, or Square, in which the opposite sides are parallel. 1706 PHILLIPS (ed. Kersey), *Trapezium* (in *Geom.*) a Quadrilateral, or Square Figure, whose four Sides and Angles are not equal, but two of its Sides are parallel. 1721 BAILEY, *Trapezium*,..a Quadrilateral Figure in Geometry, whose opposite Sides are parallel to one another. 1788 [see TRAPEZOID *sb.* 1 a]. 1840 LARDNER *Geom.* 72 If the angles at the base of a trapezium be equal, its sides will be equal. 1862 TODHUNTER *Euclid* 5 Some writers propose to restrict the word *trapezium* to a quadrilateral which has two of its sides parallel, and it would be certainly convenient if this restriction were universally adopted. 1882 CASEY *Euclid* 45 A quadrilateral which has one pair of opposite sides parallel is called a *trapezium*. 1903 HALL & STEVENS *School Geom.* 56. 1903 BAKER & BOURNE *Elem. Geom.* 81. 1908 — *Elem. Mensuration* 48. 1909 GODFREY & SIDDONS *Geom. for Beginners* 77 A quadrilateral which has only one pair of sides parallel is called a trapezium. A trapezium in which the sides that are not parallel are equal is called an *isosceles* trapezium.

**c.** An irregular quadrilateral having neither pair of opposite sides parallel. (The usual sense in England from *c* 1800 to *c* 1875. Now *rare*.)
This is the *trapezoid* (τραπεζοειδές) of Proclus: see TRAPEZOID A. 1 a.
1795 HUTTON *Math. Dict.* II. 610/1 *Trapezium*,..a plane figure contained under four right lines, of which both the opposite pairs are not parallel. When this figure has two of its sides parallel to each other, it is sometimes called a *trapezoid*. 1807 — *Course Math.* II. 78 Lines are drawn in the fields on the plan, so as to divide them into trapeziums and triangles, the bases and perpendiculars of which are measured on the plan by means of the scale from which it was drawn. 1831 BREWSTER *Optics* xxv. 214 The solid called the icositetrahedron..is bounded by twenty-four equal and similar trapezia.

**2.** *Anat.* **a.** A bone of the wrist, articulating with the metacarpal bone of the thumb (so called from its shape); also, the corresponding bone in the lower animals; the first of the distal row of carpal bones. Also *trapezium bone*; Fr. *os trapèze*.
1840 E. WILSON *Anat. Vade M.* (1842) 70 The trapezium is too irregular in form to be compared to any known object. *Ibid.* (1851) 238 Groove in the scaphoid and trapezium bones. 1881 MIVART *Cat* 97 The trapezium is the smallest carpal and the most radial of the distal series.

**b.** (in full, *trapezium cerebri*.) A band of nerve-fibres in the *pons Varolii* of the brain.
1890 BILLINGS *Nat. Med. Dict.*, *Trapezium* (*cerebri*), in the pons Varolii a set of transverse fibres situated dorsally from the pyramids. In many animals..these fibres appear on the surface as an irregular quadrilateral area; hence the name.

**3.** *Astron.* A configuration of stars in the form of a trapezium; *esp.* that in the great nebula of Orion.
1851 NICHOL *Archit. Heav.* 143 All about the trapezium is a mass of stars. 1868 LOCKYER *Elem. Astron.* § 354 The constellation Hercules is easily recognised by..the trapezium formed by four of its stars. 1883 *Knowledge* 15 June 357/2 The famous trapezium [in the great nebula in Orion], consisting of four bright stars and two smaller ones.

**4.** = TRAPEZE 1. *rare.*
1856 *Encycl. Brit.* (ed. 8) XI. 169/2 The triangle and trapezium are two of the most amusing instruments in modern gymnasiums. 1862 A. MACLAREN *Milit. Syst. Gymnastic Exerc.* 92 The trapezium consists of a turned ash bar ..suspended by a rope at each end. *Ibid.* 93 The evolutions on the trapezium.

‖ **Trapezius** (trăpī·ziŏs). *Anat.* Pl. **trapezii** (-iˌəi). [mod.L. *trapezius* (*musculus*), adj. masc. f. *trapezium*: see prec.] Each of a pair of large flat triangular muscles (together forming the figure of a trapezium) extending over the back of the neck and adjacent parts. Also *trapezius muscle*.
[1693 tr. *Blancard's Phys. Dict.* (ed. 2), *Trapesius Musculus*, so called from its Geometric Figure.] 1704 J. HARRIS *Lex. Techn.* I, *T*[*r*]*apezius*, is a Muscle of the Shoulderblade, which serves to move it upwards, backwards, and downwards. 1831 R. KNOX *Cloquet's Anat.* 201 Its anterior surface is covered by the subclavius muscle, and the posterior by the trapezius. 1840 G. V. ELLIS *Anat.* 5 The great occipital nerve..perforates the trapezius muscle. 1860 O. W. HOLMES *Elsie V.* iii, The trapezius, lying diamond-shaped over the back and shoulders like a monk's cowl.

**Trapezohedron** (træːpīzohī·drŏn, -he·drŏn). *Geom.* and *Cryst.* Pl. **-hedra, -hedrons.** Also 9 **trapezoedron**, *erron.* **trapezihedron.** [f. *trapezo-*, used as combining form of TRAPEZIUM, after *tetrahedron*, etc. Cf. F. *trapezoèdre* (Littré).] A solid figure whose faces are trapeziums or trapezoids; as the icositetrahedron or deltohedron, with 24 faces, and the *trigonal trapezohedron*, with 6. Hence **Tra·pezohe·dral** *a.*, pertaining to or of the form of a trapezohedron.
1816–22 CLEAVELAND *Treat. Min. & Geol.* (ed. 2) I. 361 Another form [in Garnet] is a trapezoedron, or a solid presenting twenty four equal and similar, trapezoidal faces. 1828 WEBSTER, *Trapezihedron*, a solid bounded by twenty-four equal and similar trapeziums. 1847 — *Trapezohedron.* 1849 DANA *Geol.* xvii. (1850) 628 Garnet in trapezohedral crystals. 1868 — *Min.* 189 Quartz...Various trapezohedral forms...Many trapezohedrons in other positions. 1895 STORY-MASKELYNE *Crystallogr.* vii. § 257 The trigonal trapezohedron. *Ibid.* § 273 The trapezohedral tetartohedron. *Ibid.* § 274 The trapezohedra that occur on quartz belong to two correlative groups.

**Trapezoid** (træ·pĭzoid, trăpī·zoˌid), *sb.* and *a.* [ad. mod.L. *trapezoīdēs*, a. late Gr. τραπεζοειδής, neut. -ές table-like (Proclus 450), f. τράπεζα table: see -OID. Cf. F. *trapézoïde* (1652 in Hatz.-Darm.).]

**A.** *sb.* **1.** *Geom.* **a.** A quadrilateral figure no two of whose sides are parallel. (Often called by English writers (in 19th c.) TRAPEZIUM.)
This is the sense for which Proclus introduced the term τραπεζοειδές; it is retained in F. *trapezoïde*, Ger. *trapezoïd*, etc. See etymol. note to TRAPEZIUM.
1706 PHILLIPS (ed. Kersey), *Trapezoid*, a Geometrical Figure that has all its four Sides and Angles unequal, and no Sides parallel. 1753 CHAMBERS *Cycl. Supp.*, *Trapezoid*, in geometry, a plane irregular figure, having four sides, no two of which are parallel to each other. 1788 T. TAYLOR *Proclus' Comm.* I. 176 Of non-parallelograms, some have only two parallel sides,..others have none of their sides parallel. And those are called Trapeziums, but these Trapezoids. 1851 R. F. BURTON *Goa* 274 Its shape is a trapezoid, for though quadrilateral, none of its sides are equal or even.

**b.** With some: A quadrilateral figure having only two sides parallel: = TRAPEZIUM 1 b. ? *Obs.*
A misapplication of the term peculiar to English: now generally given up.

1795 HUTTON *Math. Dict.* II. 611/1 *Trapezoid* sometimes denotes a trapezium that has two of its sides parallel to each other. 1806 — *Course Math.* I. 291 A Trapezoid, or Trapezium having two Sides Parallel. 1846 POTTS *Euclid* 45 Sometimes an irregular four-sided figure which has two of its sides parallel, is called a trapezoid. 1879 in *Cassell's Techn. Educ.* II. 124 If any two of the sides are parallel to each other the figure is called a trapezoid. 1906 HAMILTON & KETTLE *2nd Geom. Bk.* 39 [Here] *trapezoid* [is used] for quadrilaterals that have one pair of parallel sides.

†**c.** Formerly applied to an irregularly quadrate solid with neither pair of sides parallel. *Obs.*

(Here *-oid* appears to have the same sense as in *ellipsoid, paraboloid.*)

1704 J. HARRIS *Lex. Techn.*, *Trapezoid* is a solid irregular Figure, having four Sides not parallel to one another. [The only sense given.] 1795 in HUTTON *Math. Dict.* II. 611/1 [as second sense].

**2.** *Anat.* A bone of the wrist, the second of the distal row of the carpus: so called from its shape. (Also in L.-Gr. form *trapezoides*; Fr. *trapézoïde.*)

1831 R. KNOX *Cloquet's Anat.* 135 The Trapezoides (*os multangulum minus*), is smaller than the trapezium. 1840 E. WILSON *Anat. Vade M.* (1842) 113 When seen from before, it has a quadrilateral form: it is named trapezoid. 1855 HOLDEN *Hum. Osteol.* (1878) 161 The trapezium and trapezoid form a shallow socket for part of the scaphoid.

**B.** *adj.* = TRAPEZOIDAL. (In all the quots. improperly used for TRAPEZIAL.)

1819 G. SAMOUELLE *Entomol. Compend.* 195 Thorax trapezoid, broad behind. 1826 KIRBY & SP. *Entomol.* IV. 264 Trapezoid... Quadrilateral, with two sides unequal and parallel. *Note.* We have departed from the more usual definition of *trapezoid*, 'An irregular figure whose four sides are not parallel', because the above is best suited to forms in insects. 1840 E. WILSON *Anat. Vade M.* (1842) 124 The internal lateral ligament is a broad and trapezoid layer of ligamentous fibres.

**b.** *Anat. Trapezoid body*: = TRAPEZIUM 2 b. *Trapezoid bone*: = A. 2. *Trapezoid ligament* (F. *ligament trapézoïde*), the CORACO-CLAVICULAR ligament. *Trapezoid line*: see quot. 1890.

1890 BILLINGS *Nat. Med. Dict.* s.v., *T[rapezoid] bone*, second bone of distal row of wrist... *T. line*, a rough ridge for attachment of trapezoid ligament on under surface of clavicle. 1899 *Allbutt's Syst. Med.* VI. 804 Degeneration of the trapezoid body.

**Trapezoidal** (træpĭzoi·dăl), *a.* [f. prec. + -AL: cf. F. *trapézoïdal* (Littré).] Having the form of a trapezoid; irregularly quadrilateral.

But sometimes misused for TRAPEZIFORM.

1796 KIRWAN *Elem. Min.* (ed. 2) I. 259 Oriental Garnet.. presenting either 12 rhomboidal planes, or 24 trapezoidal. 1831 R. KNOX *Cloquet's Anat.* 401 Each of these muscles occupies the side of the larynx; it is thin, flat, and of a trapezoidal figure. 1873 M. COLLINS *Squire Silchester* v, An irregular trapezoidal space, where..cattle and sheep are penned.

**b.** Having trapezoidal faces; trapezohedral.

1796 KIRWAN *Elem. Min.* (ed. 2) I. 36 When a fossil is broken into fragments, the shape of these is..sometimes cubical, rhomboidal, or pyramidal, or trapezoidal. 1805–17 R. JAMESON *Char. Min.* (ed. 3) 201 A Crystal is said to be ..Trapezoidal, when its surface consists of twenty-four equal and similar trapeziums [i.e. trapezoids]... Example, Trapezoidal garnet. 1822 J. PARKINSON *Outl. Oryctol.* 8 Its [coal's] fragments mostly cubical or trapezoidal.

So **Trapezoi·diform** *a.*

1826 KIRBY & SP. *Entomol.* IV. xlvi. 266 Trapezoidiform. ..Whose horizontal section is trapezoid.

**Trapfall** (træ·pfǫl). [f. TRAP *sb.*[1] + FALL *sb.*[2]: cf. PITFALL *sb.*] A trap consisting of a trap-door or covering over a pit or cellar arranged so as to give way beneath the feet. Also *fig.*

1596 SPENSER *F. Q.* v. ii. 7 In the same are many trap-fals pight, Through which the rider downe doth fall through oversight. 1610 HEALEY *St. Aug. Citie of God* 373 Avoide these damnable trap-falls of the devill. 1797 HOLCROFT tr. *Stolberg's Trav.* (ed. 2) III. lxxxvi. 132 She is accused of having contrived a trap-fall, in this palace. 1853 *Fraser's Mag.* XLVIII. 347 A manager, who entertains higher notions of his art..than that of a mere snare or trap-fall for audiences.

**Traphine**, obs. form of TREPHINE.

‖**Trapiche** (trapī·tʃe). [American Sp. *trapiche*, derivative of L. *trapētum* oil-press.]

**1.** A mill for crushing the sugar-cane; a sugar-mill; also, a sugar plantation.

1648 GAGE *West Ind.* 179 There was in my time a new Trapiche of Sugar. 1844 BRANTZ MAYER *Mexico* 197 On the east is another huge edifice where the boilers, engines, crushing machines, cooling vats, moulding apartments, etc., constitute the *trapiche* of the hacienda. 1896 *Nat. Geog. Mag.* July 242 The *trapiche* or sugar-cane press of the chief. Here two huge wooden rollers..pressed the cane stalks and large metal vessels received the juice.

**2.** A rude form of mill for grinding ores.

1881 RAYMOND *Mining Gloss.*, *Trapiche*, a rude grinding machine, composed of two stones, of which the upper is fastened to a long pole.

**Trapiferous** (træpi·fĕrəs), *a. Min. rare*—[1]. [f. TRAP *sb.*[5] + -(I)FEROUS.] Containing trap-rock.

1796 KIRWAN *Elem. Min.* (ed. 2) I. 382 Trapiferous Argillite.

**Tra·pish,** *a.* ? *Obs.* [f. TRAPES *sb.* + -ISH [1].] Like a trapes; slovenly; slatternly.

1705 ROWE *Biter* II. i, A Couple of the trapishest Creatures I ever saw in Masks. 1706 T. BAKER *Tunbr. Walks* v. i, Always trapish and dirty like an actress at a morning rehearsal. 1762 *Poetry* in *Ann. Reg.* 208 Now monstrous in hoop, now trapish, and walking With your petticoats clung to your knees, like a malkin.

**Trap-net**: see TRAP *sb.*[1] 11.

**Trappan,** obs. form of TREPAN.

**Trappean** (træ·pĭăn), *a. Min.* [f. TRAP *sb.*[5] + *-ean* (L. *-e-us* + -AN): cf. *marmorean.*] Pertaining to, of the nature of, or consisting of trap-rock.

1813 BAKEWELL *Introd. Geol.* (1815) 55 Domes of trappean porphyry. 1855 J. R. LEIFCHILD *Cornwall Mines* 271 A very fertile soil is formed from what is geologically called 'trappean ash', on the trap rocks. 1873 J. GEIKIE *Gt. Ice Age* xvi. 205 The trappean heights..between the valleys of the Clyde and the Irvine.

**Trapped, trapt** (træpt), *ppl. a.*[1] [f. TRAP *v.*[1] and *sb.*[1] + -ED.]

**1.** Caught in or as in a trap; also, caught in a mistake in class at school (*Sc.*).

*c* 1440 *Promp. Parv.* 499/2 Trappyd, or be-trappyd and gylyd.., *deceptus, illaqueatus.* 1552 HULOET, Trapped, *irretitus.* 1884 *Pall Mall G.* 8 Aug. 11/2, 3,000 trapped rabbits from this particular warren. 1894 H. NISBET *Bush Girl's Rom.* 93 'What do you want me to do?' asked the trapped gentleman. 1895 CROCKETT *Bog-myrtle & Peat* 185 The trapped boys sometimes rectified matters at the back of the school at the play-hour when fists became a high court of appeal and review.

**2.** Furnished with a trap or traps, as a drain, etc.

1892 T. B. F. EMINSON *Epidemic Pneumonia at Scotter* 10 Four..nominally trapped inlets.

**Trapped** (træpt, *poet.* træ·pĕd), *ppl. a.*[2] Also 7 **trapt.** [f. TRAP *sb.*[2] and *v.*[2] + -ED.] Protected or adorned with trappings.

13.. *Coer de L.* 3888 Kyng, eerls, barouns, knyghts, and squyers, Ryden ryally on trappyd destrers. 1375 BARBOUR *Bruce* XVI. 185 Trappit horss richt to the feit. *c* 1440 *Promp. Parv.* 499/2 Trappyd, wythe trapure, *faleratus.* 1602 *2nd Pt. Return fr. Parnass.* IV. ii, Mounted on a trapt Palfrey. 1885 B. HARTE *Maruja* iii, Cumbrous vehicles..drawn by gaily trapped mules.

**Trapped,** *ppl. a.*[3] [f. *trap* in TRAP-CUT + -ED.] Of a gem: Cut with the TRAP-CUT.

1875 KNIGHT *Dict. Mech.* 962/2 A thicker stone, trapped in two hights on the front and three on the back.

**Tra·pper,** *sb.*[1] *Obs.* exc. *Hist.* Forms: 4–6 **trappure,** 5 **trappor,** -**ere, trapure,** -**ur,** -**oure,** -**owre,** -**ere,** 5–6 **trappour(e,** -**ar,** 5–7 **traper,** 5–9 **trapper.** [ad. OF. **trapeüre*, **drapeüre*, *drapure* (*a* 1500 in Godef. 'chevaulx couvers de drapures diverses'), also AF. *drapeur* (Stat. 7 Edw. IV in Godef.); = med.(Anglo-)L. *trappātūra* (*a* 1450 in Du Cange): see TRAP *sb.*[2], *v.*[2] With later form cf. *bordure, border,* and -ER [2] 3.] A covering put over a horse or other beast of burden, made of metal or leather for purpose of defence, or of cloth for shelter and adornment; trapping; housing.

13.. *Coer de L.* 2262 Ten hundred stedes good and sure King Richard let array in trappure. *c* 1386 CHAUCER *Knt.'s T.* 1641 The scheeldes brighte testeres, and trappures; Gold hewen helmes, hauberkes, Cote Armures. *c* 1400 MAUNDEV. (Roxb.) xxvi. 123 Þai hafe..trappour to þaire hors. 1459 in *Paston Lett.* I. 477, j. pece of skarlot for trappars for horsys. 1463 *Mann. & Househ. Exp.* (Roxb.) 215 To John Wysnacke the same day,..ffor steynynge off my masterys traperys, iij. s. iiij. d. 1470–85 MALORY *Arthur* I. xvi. 58 The swerd.. cut thorow the trappere of stele. 1513 DOUGLAS *Æneis* VII. v. 194 Thair brusit trappouris and patrellis reddy boun. *a* 1548 HALL *Chron., Rich. III* 25 b, His horse trapped in blue veluet..which trapper was borne by fotemen from the grounde. 1621 QUARLES *Argalus & P.* (1678) 114 The Trappers seem to hover Like wings..As the horse pranc'd. 1891 *Athenæum* 23 May 670/3 His opinion that the long-shanked spur was for use when the horse was covered with a trapper. 1902 *Jrnl. Archæol. Inst.* Mar. 74 A chain-mail trapper beneath the textile.

*fig.* 1509 HAWES *Past. Pleas.* xxvii. (Percy Soc.) 132 The good knight Trouth..betrapped fayre and gaye Wyth shyning trappers of curiositie. 1600 SIR W. CORNWALLIS *Ess.* viii. F v, Al these blessings are the trapers of the furniture of Patience.

**Trapper** (træ·pəɹ), *sb.*[2] [f. TRAP *v.*[1] and *sb.*[1]]

**1.** One who sets traps or snares; *spec.* one engaged in trapping wild animals for their furs.

1768 PENNANT *Zool.* II. 338 The trappers..bait the trap with a meal worm..: Ten or a dozen nightingales have been caught in a day. 1827 J. F. COOPER *Prairie* II. i. 7 The hunters and trappers on La Platte. 1840 R. H. DANA *Bef. Mast* xiii. 31 Trappers and hunters..with their valuable skins and furs. 1857 TENNYSON *Enid* 1572 A sudden..cry, As of a wild thing taken in the trap, Which sees the trapper coming thro' the wood.

*attrib.* 1851 MAYNE REID *Scalp Hunt.* Pref. 6 My book is a trapper book. 1899 *Daily News* 27 Mar. 8/2 The authors tell us trapper stories and Red Indian tales.

**2.** A boy stationed to open and shut a trap-door for the passage of trams in a coal-mine. Also *trapper-boy, -lad.*

1815 *Ann. Philos.* VI. 114 The trappers have seats near their doors, and remain by them all the time the pit is at work. 1845 MRS. NORTON *Child of Isl.* 22 So lives the little Trapper underground; No glittering sunshine streaks the oosy wall. 1892 *Pall Mall G.* 19 Aug. 1/3 Mr. Keir Hardie ..began life as a trapper boy in a mine. 1900 [trapper lad: see TRAP *sb.*[1] 8 b].

**3.** One who manages a trap in trap-shooting: cf. TRAP *sb.*[1] 4.

*a* 1892 *Hurlingham Club Rules for Pigeon Shooting* § 6 If, in the opinion of the referee, the shooter is balked by any antagonist or looker-on, or by the trapper,..he may be allowed another bird. 1892 GREENER *Breech-Loader* 246 It is best to take no heed either of bystanders or trappers when going to the mark.

**4.** *colloq.* A horse which draws a 'trap'.

1883 *Pall Mall G.* 24 Apr. 4/1 The hard-worked 'trapper' ..munches his oats in solitude in many a stable. 1894 ASTLEY *50 Years Life* I. 57, I..made a journey to Tattersall's, and bought a very clever trapper, a bay mare.

†**Tra·pper,** *v. Obs. rare.* [f. TRAPPER *sb.*[1]] *trans.* To cover or adorn with trappings. Also *fig.*

1597 G. HARVEY *Trimming T. Nashe* Wks. (Grosart) III. 56 His fierie steedes trapperd in their caparisons. 1620 FELTHAM *Resolves* lxxxiii. 271 To see how Vice goes trapperd [*later edd.* trapped] with rich furniture. 1633 T. SCOT *Highw. God* 17 As for fear, it's too base an humour to trapper justice.

**Tra·ppiness.** *colloq.* [f. TRAPPY *a.*[1] + -NESS.] The quality of being 'trappy' or containing traps.

1885 *Field* 26 Dec. 884/1 There were broad pastures and large banks and ditches, innocent of trappiness for the most part, before the riders.

**Trapping** (træ·piŋ), *vbl. sb.*[1] Chiefly in pl. **trappings.** [f. TRAP *sb.*[2] and *v.*[2] + -ING [1].] A cloth or covering spread over the harness or saddle of a horse or other beast of burden, often gaily ornamented; a caparison.

1398 TREVISA *Barth. De P. R.* XVIII. xli. (Bodl. MS.), The colte is nouȝt..ihiȝt wiþ trappinge and gay harneys. 1553 EDEN *Treat. Newe Ind.* (Arb.) 15 *margin*, The riche trapping of the kinges horse. 1764 HARMER *Observ.* XXV. vi. 283 On a stately steed, with a rich saddle and fine trappings. 1817 MOORE *Lalla R.* (1824) 3 The embroidered trappings of the elephants.

**b.** *transf.* Chiefly *pl.* 'Ornaments; dress; embellishments; external, superficial, and trifling decoration' (J.). Also *fig.*

1596 NASHE *Saffron Walden* 114 Hee is neuer wont to keep anie man longer than the sute lasteth he brings with him, and then turne him to grasse and get one in newe trappings. 1601 SHAKS. *Twel. N.* V. i. 10 *Duke.* Belong you to the Lady Oliuia, friends? *Clo.* I sir, we are some of her trappings. 1602 — *Ham.* I. ii. 86 These, but the Trappings, and the Suites of woe. 1685 DRYDEN *Thren. August.* 330 He needs no Trappings of fictitious Fame. 1791 BOSWELL *Johnson* an. 1758 (1906) I. 201 A motto, the usual trapping of periodical papers. 1791 COWPER *Iliad* IV. 167 The stately trapping of some prince. 1859 HELPS *Friends in C.* Ser. II. II. vii. 136 To strip a man of all his trappings of birth, rank, and education.

Hence †**Tra·ppinged** (-iŋd) *a.*, adorned with trappings.

1654 GAYTON *Pleas. Notes* IV. xv. 252 What regard would be given to a Praetor without his trapping'd horse, the Gold Chain, and the Cap of maintenance?

**Trapping** (træ·piŋ), *vbl. sb.*[2] [f. TRAP *v.*[1] + -ING [1].] The action of TRAP *v.*[1] in various senses; catching by or as by a trap, etc.

1398 TREVISA *Barth. De P. R.* V. xi. (Tollem. MS.), Þan by trappynge of þe humoure, þat is conten[i]t, he makeþ þe teres falle oute of þe yen [*orig.* per alicationem contenti humoris oculos lacrymari faciunt]. *a* 1533 FRITH *Disput. Purgat.* (1829) 107 To that answereth he neither yea nor nay, for fear of trapping. ? 16.. *Country Gentleman's Vade M.* (Nares), For their art of trapping. 1842 *Rept. Comm. on Employment Children*, The employment.. assigned to the youngest children, generally that of 'trapping'. 1867 TROLLOPE *Chron. Barset* I. xxxiii. 286 [He] had his own very strong ideas about the trapping of foxes. 1890 *Lancet* 22 Nov. 1125/2 The defects in drainage arrangement, such as want of proper trappings..were very numerous.

**b.** *attrib.* and *Comb.*

1837 W. IRVING *Capt. Bonneville* i. (1849) 24 They detach bands..of trappers in various directions, assigning to each a portion of country as a..trapping ground. 1895 FRASER *Whaups of Durley* iii. 36 The trapping lesson, was..the most enjoyable part of the day's work. 1904 GALLICHAN *Fishing Spain* 164 One of these trapping-places [for trout]. 1904 *Westm. Gaz.* 3 Dec. 10/3 The Illicit Diamond Buying Act, said prisoner, was part of a trapping system.

**Trapping,** *vbl. sb.*[3]: see TRAP *sb.*[4]

**Trapping,** *vbl. sb.*[4]: see TRAP-CUT, quot. 1853.

**Tra·pping,** *ppl. a.* [f. TRAP *v.*[1] + -ING [2].] That traps or entraps: see TRAP *v.*[1]

*a* 1548 HALL *Chron., Hen. VII* 22 He allured and enticed with moost flatterynge woordes and trappynge termes, the lady Anne. 1551 T. WILSON *Logike* (1580) 85 b, They are called trappyng argumentes, because fewe that aunswered vnto them, can auoide daunger. 1821 CLARE *Vill. Minstr.* II. 63 Leave, oh leave the murky barn, Ere trapping spiders thee discern.

**Trappist** (træ·pist), *sb.*[1] (*a.*) [ad. F. *trappiste*, from *La Trappe*, name of the convent: see below.]

**1.** A monk of the branch of the Cistercian order observing the reformed rule established in 1664 by De Rancé, abbot of La Trappe, in Normandy.

1814 in Brackenridge *Views Louisiana* 288 To make the highest virtue to consist in silence, was reserved for the Trappists. 1836 LD. SHREWSBURY in E. Purcell *Life A. P. de Lisle* (1900) I. iv. 69, I..wish..to see a religious establishment on the premises; but I fancy we might have a much more useful one than a Trappist monastery. 1870 ROGERS *Hist. Gleanings* II. 24 The..most frivolous profligates have often become the most rigid..Trappists and Carthusians.

**b.** *attrib.* or as *adj.* Of or pertaining to this branch of the Cistercian order.

1847 BUNSEN *Ch. of Future* App. 307 The Count purchased the old Trappist Monastery. 1860 *All the Year Round* No. 74. 560 He intended to enter a Trappist convent. 1871 MORLEY *Crit. Misc.* Ser. I. 28 The Trappist theory of the conditions of virtue.

**2.** *transf.* A puff-bird of the genus *Monacha*, having inky-black plumage with white about the head; a NUN-BIRD. 1891 in *Cent. Dict.*

**Tra·ppist,** *sb.*[2] [f. TRAP *sb.*[1] or *v.*[1] + -IST.] A professional trapper (of wild animals).

1880 CARNEGIE *Pract. Trap.* 19 Hares do not offer so large

a field for work to the trappist as do rabbits. **1896** *Times* (weekly ed.) 380/4 Russian trappists almost denuded the coasts of animals.

**Trappistine** (træ·pistin, -īn). [f. Trappist[1] + -ine[3].]

**1.** A member of an order of nuns affiliated with the Trappists, founded in 1827. Also *attrib.*

**1884** *Cath. Dict.* 804/1 Mount St. Bernard in Leicestershire and the Trappistine convent of Stapehill in Dorset. **1896** C. K. Paul tr. *Huysman's En Route* vii. 100 She wandered..among the Trappistines in Switzerland.

**2.** A liqueur made by the Trappists. [So in Fr.]

**1891** in *Cent. Dict.*

**Trappoid** (træ·poid), *a. Min.* [f. Trap *sb.*[5] + -oid.] Resembling or allied to trap-rock.

**1842** in Phillips *Man. Geol.* (1855) 250 Upon this lies an often trappoid or magnesian conglomerate. **1854** Murchison *Siluria* xiii. 334 A reaggregated trappoid breccia. **1889** *Nature* 12 Dec. 140/2 In saucer-like hollows in the solid, tough, trappoid rocks.

**Trappose** (træ·pōus), *a. Min.* [f. as prec. + -ose.] Of, pertaining to, or of the nature of trap or trap-rock; trappean. Also **Tra·ppous** *a.* (*rare*—[0]).

**1796** Kirwan *Elem. Min.* (ed. 2) II. 175 Argillaceous Iron Stone...Of this sort also we may reckon the *Trappose Ore used..in Sweden. **1799** — *Geol. Ess.* 272 The black trappose matter that descends from the summit of the mountain to a torrent at its foot where it forms pillars. **1845** G. H. Smith in *Encycl. Metrop.* XXIII. 733/2 From Thunder Mountain, Westward, trappose-greenstone is the prevailing rock. **1828** Webster, *Trappous.

**Trappour, trappure**, obs. ff. Trapper *sb.*[1]

**Trappy** (træ·pi), *a.*[1] *colloq.* [f. Trap *sb.*[1] + -y.] Of the nature of a trap, 'catchy'; containing a trap or traps.

**1883** E. Pennell-Elmhirst *Cream Leicestersh.* 56 The jump into the lane is a trappy one. **1888** *Scott. Leader* 5 Apr. 4 Useless, trappy arithmetic, useless frivolities of grammar, the finesse of our exceptional spelling,..must all go if children are to be made more intelligent and observant. **1889** Baden-Powell *Pigsticking* 97 The trappy nature of the ground..due to the frequent occurrence of inexplicable holes. **1898** *Engineering Mag.* XVI. 108/1 The earlier engines, with their many cams, springs, gears, and trappy contrivances. **1904** *Daily Chron.* 16 Aug. 7/1 To permit 'trappy' off balls to pass by in such close proximity to his wicket as to make his admirers hold their breath.

**Tra·ppy**, *a.*[2] *rare.* [f. Trap *sb.*[5] + -y.] = Trappean, Trappose.

[**1828** Webster, *Trappous*...It ought to be *trappy*.] **1864** in Webster citing Wright. Hence in mod. Dicts.

**Traps** (træps), *sb. pl. colloq.* [A modern word of colloquial origin; app. shortened from *trappings*: see Trapping *vbl. sb.*[1] (Some take it as pl. of Trap *sb.*[1], as referring to the outfit of a trapper.)] Portable articles for dress, furniture, or use; personal effects; baggage; belongings.

**1813** Capt. R. M. Cairnes *Let.* 4 Apr. in *Dickson MSS.* (ed. J. H. Leslie, 1910) Ser. iii. 866 The rest [of the carriages] is for the Jolly Captain's Shirts and Stockings, &c., besides a mule for his other traps. **1828** *Craven Gloss.*, *Traps*, small tools or implements, always used in the plural number; equivalent to the classical *arma*. **1830** *Chron.* in *Ann. Reg.* 153/2 This was the general signal for getting our 'traps' on the ice. **1831** *John Bull* 7 Aug. 254 No one thought..that only three days afterwards he would be obliged to pack up his traps and be off. **1833** Marryat *P. Simple* xiii, I packed up my traps and went on shore. **1887** J. Ball *Nat. in S. Amer.* 194 To carry some of the traps with which a botanist is usually encumbered.

**Tra·pstick.** [f. Trap *sb.*[1] + Stick *sb.*] A stick used in the game of trap or trap-ball.

**1591** Percivall *Sp. Dict.*, *Paleta*, a trapsticke, *Bacillum lusorium*. *a* **1627** Middleton & Rowley *Span. Gipsy* ii. ii, If my woods, being cut down, can not fill this pocket, cut 'em into trap sticks. **1629** Shirley *Wedding* iii. ii, A boy of seven years old beat him with a trap-stick. **1764** T. Brydges *Homer Travest.* (1797) I. 272 On high In air he let his trapstick fly. **1862** Marsh *Lect. Eng. Lang.* 40 A mahogany box,..with..several trap sticks projecting through slots in the top of it.

**b.** *transf.* and *fig.*

**1680** *Honest Hodge & Ralph* 14 A meer trap-stick to bang the Phanaticks about. **1714** Addison *Spect.* No. 559 ⁋ 6 A foolish Swop between a Couple of thick bandy Legs, and two long Trapsticks that had no Calfs to them. **1796** *Grose's Dict. Vulg. T.*, *Trap Sticks*, thin legs, gambs.

**Tra-ra** (trā·rā, trārā·), *int.* and *sb.* An imitation of the sound of a horn, or some similar sound. (Cf. Tra-la-la.)

**1849** tr. *De la M. Fouqué's Sir Elidoc* 23 Hark, forward! hark, forward! Tra-ra, tra-ra! **1900** *Westm. Gaz.* 18 Jan. 4/2 It sounds as if a million kettle-drums were being played —a constant tra-ra-ra-ra, with the boom of the big guns.

**Tras, Trasche, Trase**, obs. ff. Trace, Trash.

†**Trase**, *v. Obs. rare.* [Derivation and meaning obscure. It has been suggested to be an early form of Trash *v.*[1], though the date is against this.]

*c* **1440** *York Myst.* xxxi. 3 Your tounges fro tretyng of trifillis be trased. *c* **1470** *Golagros & Gaw.* 675 Thair hors.. As trasit in vnquart quakand thai stand.

**Trash** (træʃ), *sb.*[1] Forms: (?4 **trasche**), 6 **trasshe, traish, trasse**, 6–7 **trashe**, 7 **traisse**, 6– **trash**. [With exception of the doubtful instance in 1 b, known only from 16th c.; origin obscure.

Cf. Norw. dial. *trask* lumber, trumpery, trash, baggage (which Falk & Torp refer to *tras* twig, sprig), Icel. *tros* rubbish, fallen leaves and twigs, and Norw. *trase*, Sw. *trasa* rags, tatters.]

**1.** That which is broken, snapped, or lopped off anything in preparing it for use; broken or torn pieces, as twigs, splinters, 'cuttings from a hedge, small wood from a copse' (*E. D. D.*), straw, rags; refuse.

**1555** *Bill in Chancery* in *Athenæum* 17 July (1886) 92/2 A carpenter's yarde, wherein he dothe laye his tymber and Trasshe. **1574** Hellowes *Gueuara's Fam. Ep.* (1584) 255 How wil he give wood to the Hospitall, that warmes himself by the trash of straw? **1670** Narborough *Jrnl.* in *Acc. Sev. Late Voy.* i. (1694) 108 The Woods..are so thick with Under-brush, old rotten Trees, and Leaves, and such Trash. **1675** Evelyn *Terra* (1729) 45 If you lay any Fern-brakes, or other Trash about them. *a* **1693** *Urquhart's Rabelais* iii. l. 401 They break..to very Trash the woody parcels. **1727** *Bradley's Fam. Dict.* s. v. *Cask*, The Trash, or gross Substance of pressed Grapes. **1763** *Brit. Mag.* IV. 464 The floor being thus prepared,..cover it with wet ground leaves or other tobacco trash. **1867** Baker *Nile Tribut.* ii. 53 Bamboos and reeds, with trash of all kinds, were hurried along the muddy waters.

**b.** An old worn-out shoe. *dial.*

The first quot. fits the sense; but its date, 150 years before any other example of the word, makes its place doubtful.

[*c* **1360** *E. E. Allit. P.* B. 40 Þen þe harlot with haste helded to þe table With rent cokrez at þe kne & his clutte [= clouted] trasches.] *c* **1746** J. Collier (Tim Bobbin) *View Lanc. Dial.* Gloss., *Trash*, unripe fruit; also an overworn shoe. **1828** *Craven Gloss.* s. v., In the plural *trashes*, a pair of worn-out shoes. **1885** Mrs. Banks *In his own Hand* iv, His week's tramp had..worn his shoes into trashes.

**c.** Broken ice mixed with water; trash-ice.

**1856** Kane *Arct. Expl.* I. xxvi. 342 Warped about one hundred yards into the trash.

†**d.** (?). *Obs.*

? *a* **1550** in *Brand's Pop. Antiq.* (1849) I. 120 For paulmeflowers, cakes, trashes, and for thred on Palme Sonday, viii[d].

**2.** *spec.* The refuse of sugar-canes after the juice has been expressed; cane-trash; also, the dried leaves and tops of the canes, stripped off while still growing, to allow them to ripen; field-trash.

**1707** Sloane *Jamaica* I. p. xlv, It was the custom to burn their Trash, which is the..remainder of the Sugar Canes after the juice is squeezed out. **1790** Castles in *Phil. Trans.* LXXX. 349 Burning the cane trash (or straw of the cane). *Ibid.* 356 The field trash (or the dried leaves and tops of the canes). **1793** J. B. Moreton *W. Ind. Cust.* 47 The [sugar-] canes being cut, and all the trash lopped off. **1842** [see Cane *sb.*[1] 10]. **1884** *Macm. Mag.* Nov. 19/2 Just before harvest, when the dead leaves or trash are thick around the canes.

**3.** Anything of little or no worth or value; worthless stuff; rubbish; dross. (Said of things material or immaterial.)

*c* **1518** Skelton *Magnyf.* 2164 As for his plate of syluer, and suche trasshe. **1604** Shaks. *Oth.* iii. iii. 156 Who steales my purse, steales trash. **1612** T. Taylor *Comm. Titus* ii. 14 (1619) 515 What can the Papist say now for his mony-masses, pardons, indulgences, and such trash? **1728** Young *Love Fame* iii. 192 Ambition feeds on trash. **1795** Mills in *Phil. Trans.* LXXXVI. 43 The great facility with which the gold might be separated from the trash. **1838** Thackeray *2nd Lect. Fine Arts* Wks. 1900 XIII. 284 Some..new pictures, in the midst of a great quantity of trash. **1852** Mrs. Stowe *Uncle Tom's C.* xix, What poor, mean trash this whole business of human virtue is!

**b.** *spec.*: see quot.

**1749** *Wealth Gt. Britain* 51 There are three kind of mark'd herring among the Dutch;..the last sort are called trash.

**c.** Worthless notions, talk, or writing; nonsense; 'rubbish', 'stuff'.

**1542** Udall *Erasm. Apoph.* E.'s Pref., Like trash & bagguage been those saiynges that are incidente in oracions. **1653** Milton *Hirelings* Wks. 1851 V. 383 Those Theological Disputations..rather perplex and leven pure Doctrin with scholastical Trash. **1737** Fielding *Hist. Register* i. Wks. 1784 III. 319 My Register is not to be fill'd..with trash for want of news. **1874** Burnand *My time* xxx. 293 Don't let me hear any more of such trash.

†**d.** Contemptuously applied to money or cash; 'dross'. *Obs. slang.*

(Cf. quot. 1604 in 3, which has prob. influenced later use.)

*a* **1592** Greene *Jas. IV*, iii. i, And therefore must I bid him provide trash, for my master is no friend without money. [**1601** Shaks. *Jul. C.* iv. iii. 26 Shall we now, Contaminate our fingers, with base Bribes? And sell..our.. Honors For so much trash, as may be grasped thus?] **1742** Young *Nt. Th.* vi. 218 Drudge, sweat,..for every gain, For vile contaminating trash. **1809** Malkin *Gil Blas* i. viii, Money! said he,..you have a poor opinion of Spanish charity, if you think that people of my stamp have any occasion for such trash upon their travels.

**4.** A worthless or disreputable person; now, usually, such persons collectively. *White trash*, the poor white population in the Southern States of America.

**1604** Shaks. *Oth.* v. i. 85, I do suspect this Trash To be a party in this Iniurie. **1750** Chesterf. *Lett.* 5 June, Prostitutes, actresses, dancing women, and that sort of trash. **1827** Scott *Chron. Canongate* v, Sheriffs, and bailiffs, and sic thieves and trash of the world. **1883** Fiske in *Harper's Mag.* Feb. 423/1 North Carolina was the paradise of the 'white trash'.

**5.** *attrib.* and *Comb.*, as *trash-eater, -monger, -reader, roof*; *trash-lined* adj.; **trash-bag**: see quot. 1688; also, old shoes; also, a disreputable or worthless person (*dial.*); **trash-house**, a building on a sugar-plantation where the stalks from which the juice has been expressed are stored for fuel; **trash-ice**, broken ice mixed with water (cf. 1 c); **trash-rack**, a rack set in a stream to prevent the passage of floating debris; **trash-reader**, a critical reader of novels and the like for a publisher; **trash-turner**, a metal plate in a sugar-mill, that guides the canes between pairs of rollers (Webster 1911).

**1688** R. Holme *Armoury* iii. xxii. (Roxb.) 278/1 A *Trash Bagg, of some called an Apron, wherein are seuerall pockettes ..to place the seuerall implyments..which the Angler hath occasion to use. **1886** *S. W. Linc. Gloss.* s. v., That son of hern's a regular trashbags. **1887** *S. Cheshire Gloss.*, *Trash-bag*, (1) a person whose boots or clothes are dirty, and generally who is slovenly in dress or habits, (2) in pl. old shoes. **1712** Steele *Spect.* No. 431 ⁋ 3 Find out some Name for these craving Damsels,..*Trash-eaters, Oatmeal-chewers, Pipe-champers [etc.]. **1793** J. B. Moreton *W. Ind. Cust.* 48 The canes..are..spread about the works till they dry, and then..carried to a long large shade, called a *trash-house, where they are piled, as being the only fuel for boiling the sugar. **1864** Webster, **Trash-ice*, crumbled ice mixed with water. **1891** *Cent. Dict.* cites Kane. **1894** J. E. Humphrey in *Pop. Sci. Monthly* XLIV. 496 Placed in *trash-lined bins. **1694** Motteux *Rabelais* V. 236 *Trashmongers and Spanglemakers. **1603** Florio *Montaigne* i. li. (1632) 167 Metonymia, Metaphore, Allegorie, Etimologie, and other such *trashnames of Grammar. **1913** J. B. Bishop *Panama Gateway* v. ii. 3 The entrances [of the penstocks] are closed by cast-iron head-gates and bar-iron *trash-racks. **1757** Smollett *Let.* 12 May in J. Irving *Bk. Dumbarton.* (1879) II. 197 Employed as a *trash reader for the *Critical Review*. **1902** in *Daily Rec. & Mail* 23 Aug. 5 Fine ash and sand rained down..with occasional showers of large stones. Some..were so hot as to set fire to the '*trash' roofs of huts..seven miles from the crater.

Hence **Tra·shify** *v.*, *trans.* to turn into trash, render trashy; **Tra·shless** *a.*, free from trash, purified from worthless elements.

**1663** Sir G. Mackenzie *Relig. Stoic* 36 Not suffering him to lay over his vitiousness upon Providence, a shift too ordinar amongst such as misunderstand the trashless Doctrine of the reformed Churches. **1831** *Examiner* 132/2 Thus is trash thrice trashified.

**Trash**, *sb.*[2] Now *dial.* [Goes with Trash *v.*[1], of which it may be the source, or the vbl. sb.] A cord used to check dogs in breaking or training them; a leash. Also *trash-cord*.

**1611** Markham *Country Content.* i. i. (1615) 15 Your Huntsmans lodging, wherein hee shall also keep his cooples, liams, collars, trashes, boxes. **1830** Scatcherd *Hist. Morley* 195 To 'Trash' signifies to clog, incumber, or impede, and accordingly..the rope tied by sportsmen round the necks of fleet pointers, to..check their speed, is hereabouts called a 'Dog Trash'. **1884** Speedy *Sport* iv. 43 It will be found in many cases necessary to use a trash-cord in breaking dogs. **1899** Dickinson *Cumberld. Gloss.*, *Trash cord*, a long slender rope fastened to the collar of a young pointer (or setter) if headstrong and inclined to run in.

**Trash** (træʃ), *v.*[1] *Obs.* exc. in sense 2. [Of obscure origin; perh. the 15th c. Trase is the same word.

As it is a hunting term, a French origin is naturally suspected, but the OF. *trasier, trachier* 'to draw a line through, strike out, efface', which agrees in form, does not explain sense 1, though it is app. the origin of sense 2.]

†**1.** *trans.* To check (a hound) by a cord or leash; hence *gen.* to hold back, restrain, retard, encumber, hinder. *Obs.*

**1610** Shaks. *Temp.* i. ii. 81 Who t' aduance, and who To trash for ouertopping. *a* **1619** Fletcher *Bonduca* i. i, I fled too, But not so fast;..he trasht me, Nennius. **1646** Hammond *Tracts* 31 Grieving the Spirit of God,..trashing of God in his course of grace. *a* **1660** — *Serm.* x. Wks. 1683 IV. 534 To incumber and trash us in our violent furious marches. **1837** De Quincey *Revolt of Tartars* Wks. 1862 IV. 145 There was not a chance for them, burdened and 'trashed' as they were, to anticipate so agile a light cavalry as the Cossacks.

**2.** To efface, obliterate. *western U.S.*

This was prob. a term of the French trappers.

**1859** Bartlett *Dict. Amer.*, *To trash a trail*, an expression used at the West, meaning to conceal the direction one has taken by walking in a stream.

**Trash**, *v.*[2] *Obs.* exc. *dial.* [app. f. Norse: cf. Sw. *traska*, Norw. *traske* :—*traðska* in the same sense.]

**1.** *intr.* To walk or run with exertion and fatigue, esp. through mud or mire.

**1607** W. S[mith] *Puritan* iv. i, A guarded Lackey to run befor't, and pyed liueries to come trashing after't. **1608** Middleton *Trick to Catch Old One* i. iv, I still trashed and trotted for other men's causes. **1654** H. L'Estrange *Chas. I* (1655) 59 To trash on foot in the mire on a rainy morning. *a* **1716** South *Serm.* (1744) X. 72 Those that trash through the mire and dirt. **1825** Brockett *N. C. Words*, *Trash*,.. to tramp about with fatigue. **1878** *Cumberld. Gloss.*, *Trash*, ..to walk quickly over wet ground. 'Trashan' through thick and thin for a heall day togidder'.

**2.** *trans.* To fatigue (with walking, running, or exertion); to wear out.

**1685** *Life Bp. Jewell* 36 Being naturally of a spare and thin Body, and thus restlesly trashing it out with reading, writing, preaching and travelling, he hastened his death. **1816** Scott *Bl. Dwarf* x, He hasna a four-footed creature but the vicious blood thing he rides on, and that's sair trashed wi' his night wark. **1821** Carlyle *Early Lett.* (1886) II. 5 The fineness of the weather did not prevent the journey from trashing me a good deal. **1911** *Blackw. Mag.* Nov. 605/2 The bullocks will be trashed.

**b.** *fig.* To labour (a point). [Cf. *thrash*.]

*a* **1670** Hacket *Abp. Williams* i. (1692) 87 Every Nation know their own way best, to what they are tied, as we know ours. He is a Busie-body that trasheth this in a Pulpit.

Hence **Tra·shing** *ppl. a.*, fatiguing, wearing out;

also **Tra·sh-mire** *dial.*, one who trashes in the mire.

1828 *Craven Gloss.*, *Trash-mire*, a slut. 1861 *Times* 25 Sept., They have had long marches, bivouacs in bad nights, and very trashing work.

**Trash**, *v.*³ [f. TRASH *sb.*¹]

1. *trans.* To free from trash or refuse; *spec.* to strip the outer leaves from (growing sugar-canes) so that they may ripen more quickly. Hence **Tra·shing** *vbl. sb.*; also **Tra·sher.**

1793 B. EDWARDS *Hist. Brit. Col. W. Ind.* II. v. i. 223 The ancient practice of trashing ratoons (i.e.) stripping them of their outward leaves, being of late..justly exploded. 1847 *Simmonds' Col. Mag.* Mar. 295 Plant-canes require at least four weedings and trashings before they are fit to shift for themselves. 1897 *Daily News* 23 June 15/3 In Northern Queensland..the white farmer and his family do most of the work themselves, except at 'trashing' time, when Kanakas are employed. 1902 *Q. Rev.* July 18 White men simply cannot work and 'trash' the cane in tropical Queensland. 1903 *Daily Chron.* 17 Sept. 6/7 The fierce rays of the torrid sun pouring down on the perspiring trashers of the cane.

2. To treat as trash; hence, to discard as worthless. 1909 in *Cent. Dict. Supp.*

**Trash-cord**: see TRASH *sb.*²

**Trashery** (træ·ʃəri). Also 6 trasshery. [f. TRASH *sb.*¹ + -ERY.] Trash collectively (in various senses); things of the nature of trash or rubbish.

1557 NORTH *Gueuara's Diall Pr.* 367 Water potts, platters, dishes, and other smal trasshery. 1813 SCOTT *Trierm.* II. Interl. iii, Who comes in foreign trashery Of tinkling chain and spur. 1832 in *Examiner* 537/1 It would seem to be time that these trasheries ceased! 1855 *Fraser's Mag.* LI. 201 The..little Jack-in-the-Green..is hardly to be discovered amongst the florid trashery in which he is involved.

**Trashify, Trashless**: see TRASH *sb.*¹

**Trashily, Trashiness**: see TRASHY.

†**Trash-nail.** *Obs.* Also 6 trashe, traishe nayle. [Derivation and specific sense uncertain. (Cf. *traverse nail* in TRAVERSE *sb.* 23.)] Some kind of nail (used app. in fixing up the stage or scenery for revels).

1556–7 in Swayne *Sarum Churchw. Acc.* (1896) 102 Trashe nayles, ij d. 1578 in Feuillerat *Revels Q. Eliz.* (1908) 308 Trashe nayle xiiiid. 1584 *Ibid.* 369 Threed, fire, candles, traishe nayle etc. 1620 THOMAS *Lat. Dict.*, *Clavi vmbellati*, ..Trash nailes.

**Trashtrie** (træ·ʃtri). *Sc.* [perh. a perversion of **trashry, trashery*: cf. *deviltry.*] = TRASHERY.

1786 BURNS *Twa Dogs* 63 Yet ev'n the ha' folk fill their pechan, Wi' sauce, ragouts, and such like trashtrie. 1896 J. SKELTON *Summers & Wint. at Balmawhapple* I. 161 Pope, and Swift,..feckless bodies wi' their fushionless English trashtrie.

**Trashy** (træ·ʃi), *a.* [f. TRASH *sb.*¹ + -Y.]

1. Of the nature of trash; rubbishy; worthless.

*a*1620 J. DYKE *Sel. Serm.* (1640) 286 Such slovenly meate, such trashy meat, such bitter meat. 1693 G. POOLEY in *Phil. Trans.* XVII. 675 The..sparry, stony, and trashy parts rise up to the top. 1868 *Athenæum* 14 Mar. 397/2 Trashy words set to trashy music. 1871 CARLYLE in *Mrs. C.'s Lett.* (1883) I. 14 Reading the trashiest heap of novels.

2. Encumbered with trash, that is, with the withered growth of the previous season. *U.S.*

1905–6 *Trade Catalogue* (Cent. Dict. Supp.), The high curve of the beam prevents fouling in trashy land.

Hence **Tra·shily** *adv.*; **Tra·shiness.**

1836 J. BROWN *Lett.* (1907) 34, I have been..feeling miscellaneously and therefore trashily. 1857 *Sat. Rev.* 10 Jan. 37/2 A work of uniform trashiness. 1880 VERN. LEE *Stud. Italy* II. ii. 26 A grand thought..mixed and amalgamated with trashiness.

**Traskite** (træ·skəit). *Ch. Hist.* Also 7 Thraskite, Threskite. [f. *Trask*, a surname + -ITE¹.] A follower of John Trask, who *c* 1617 began to advocate certain Jewish ceremonies, including the observance of the seventh-day Sabbath; now represented by the Seventh-day Baptists. Also †**Tra·skist** *Obs.*

1618 T. ADAMS *Bad Leaven* Wks. 1861 II. 343 There is a fourth leaven,..the mixing of law with gospel...This leaven might well..have moulded away, if there had not been a late generation of Thraskites to devour it as bread. 1631 WEEVER *Anc. Fun. Mon.* 54 Precisians, Disciplinarians, Iudaicall Thraskists. 1631 R. H. *Arraignm. Whole Creature* x. § 1. 78 Our Iudaizing Threskites. 1634 (Apr. 1) *Order Commiss. Eccles. Courts*, [To take measures for the suppression of] Brownists, Anabaptists, Arians, Traskists, Familists [etc.]. 1661 BLOUNT *Glossogr.* (ed. 2), *Thraskites*, are the followers of John Thraske. 1694 E. CHAMBERLAYNE *Pres. St. Eng.* III. (ed. 18) 377 Traskists, now called Seventh-day-men, who keep the Jewish Sabboth. 1874 BLUNT *Dict. Sects*, Traskites.

†**Trason**, *v. Venery. Obs.* Also 5 tresone. [Etymology obscure: the first part seems to be OF. *tras-*, *tres-*:—L. *trans* across, as in *trespass.*] *intr.* Of a roe: To cross or double before the hounds. Hence †**Tra·soning** *vbl. sb.*

1486 *Bk. St. Albans, Hunting* e ij b, When ye hunt at the Roo, then shall ye say thoore He crosses and tresones yowre howndys byfoore. 1575 TURBERV. *Venerie* xlv. 143 His [the roe's] crossings and doublings before the houndes are called Trasonings. 1688 R. HOLME *Armoury* II. 189/1. *a* 1700 B. E. *Dict. Cant. Crew*, *Trasoning* [printed *Trajoning*], when a Roe crosses and doubles. 1847–78 HALLIWELL, Trasenings.

**Trason, -oun**, etc., obs. ff. TREASON, etc.

**Trass** (træs). Also 8 traas, traass. [a. Du. *tras*, Ger. *trasz*, earlier *terra·s*, *tira·s*.] = TARRAS.

[1793 SMEATON *Edystone L.* § 201 Tarras. [*Note*] This substance, when prepared for use, is by the Dutch called *Tras*, from which our appellation of *Tarras* undoubtedly originates.] 1796 KIRWAN *Elem. Min.* (ed. 2) I. 354 Often mistaken for volcanic traass. 1811 PINKERTON *Petralogy* II. 427 The trass of the environs of Andernach, on the left bank of the Rhine, is a kind of puzzolana formed of small fragments of pumice, and several species of lavas...Trass is transported by water as far as Dort, to be reduced to powder in stamping mills worked by the wind...The Dutch also supply England with trass. 1838 *Civil Eng. & Arch. Jrnl.* I. 412/2 Tarras, or trass, is a bluish black cellular trap or lava, quarried at Andernach on the Rhine, into millstones. 1862 G. P. SCROPE *Volcanos* (ed. 2) 178 Both puzzolana and trass, when mixed up with lime, set readily under water.

**Trass, Trasse**, obs. ff. TRACE, TRASH *sb.*¹, TRUSS.

**Trassel**, obs. form of TRESTLE.

**Trassene**, error for *transsene*: see TRANSON *v.*

**Trasshe**, obs. f. TRASH, TRAISE *v. Obs.*, to betray.

**Trast**, var. TRAIST *Obs.*; obs. f. TREST.

**Trat** (træt). *local.* [Origin unascertained. Cf. TROT *sb.*¹ 6 and *v.* 5.] Also **trat-line**, a name on the east coast of England for a line having baited hooks hung along its length, laid near the water's edge, and fastened down at each end, to catch fish when the tide flows over it; a set line.

1894 *Daily News* 26 Apr. 6/5 At Deal..the catches of two boats consisted of nearly 700 fine whiting as well as codfish and dabs. These were taken on rods and 'trat' lines. 1905 in *Eng. Dial. Dict.* (from Yorkshire).

**Trat**, earlier northern form of TROT *sb.*²

**Trateric, -erous**: see TRAITORY, TRAITOROUS.

**Tratore, -orie, -ory, -our, -ouresse, -oury**: see TRAITOR, TRAITORY, TRAITRESS.

**Tra-trip**, variant of TREY-TRIP *Obs.*

†**Trattle**, *sb.*¹ Chiefly *Sc. Obs.* Also 6 (*pl.*) tratlis, trattillis, tratilis, trattils, tratelles. [n. of action from TRATTLE *v.*: cf. *tattle, prattle* as sbs.] Idle tales or talk; gossip; chatter.

1513 DOUGLAS *Æneis* VIII. Prol. 83 Off tratlis and tragedeis the text of all talk is. *a* 1592 GREENE *Jas. IV*, I. iii, But leave this trattle, and tell me what news. 1597 JAS. I *Demonol.* II. iv, Like old womens trattles about the fire.

**Trattle** (træ·t'l), **trottle** (trǫ·t'l), *sb.*² *local.* Also 6–7 tret(t)le, 6, 9 truttle. [Origin obscure: usually held to be related to TREDDLE.] *pl.* The rounded droppings of sheep, hares, rabbits, etc.

1547 BOORDE *Brev. Health* cxii. 42 b, If the egestion..doth loke like shepes tretles, there is abundance of coler adusted. 1598 FLORIO, *Tronzoli*, the dung or truttles of any cattle, as of sheepe. 1600 SURFLET *Countrie Farme* II. xii. 217 Break three or fower trottles of a goate or sheepe. 1639 T. DE GRAY *Compl. Horsem.* 62 His doung..hee putteth forth with round and hard trattles. *a* 1825 FORBY *Voc. E. Anglia*, *Trattles*,..the small pellets of the dung of sheep, hares, rabbits, &c. 1865 COCKAYNE in *Sax. Leechd.* II. Gloss. s.v. *Tyrdelu*, Called sheeps tredles in Somerset, trattles in Suffolk. 1877 *N. W. Linc. Gloss.*, *Trottles*, the dung of sheep, lambs, or rabbits. 1886 *S. W. Linc. Gloss.*, *Treddles*, *Truddles*, *Truttles.*

†**Tra·ttle**, *v.* Chiefly *Sc. Obs.* Forms: 5 tratyll, -el, -ill, tratle, 6 trattil, -ill, -yll, 6, 8 trattle; also *pres. pple.* 5 tratlyng, 5–6 *Sc.* tratland, *pres. pple.* and *gerund* 6–7 tratling; *pa. t.* 6 *Sc.* tratlit. [app. related in some way to TATTLE, but actually found earlier, and not in the sense 'stammer', in which *tattle* was first used. Probably echoic.] *intr.* and *trans.* To talk idly; to chatter, gossip.

*a* 1400 [see TRATTLING *vbl. sb.*]. *c* 1425 WYNTOUN *Cron.* VII. x. 3454 Ye rawe [=rave], & tratelys [*v.r.* tratlys] all foly. 1508 KENNEDIE *Flyting w. Dunbar* 313 Sen thow on me thus, lymmer, leis and trattillis. *a* 1555 BP. GARDINER in Foxe *A. & M.* (1563) 751 Ouer grosse opinions, to enter into your learned head, whatsoeuer the vnlearned woulde trattle. 1568 GRAFTON *Chron.* II. 107 He..vsed to trattle and talke more than ynough. *a* 1592 GREENE *Jas. IV* Induct., Many circumstances too long to trattle on now. *a* 1800 *Earl Richard* v. in Child *Ballads* (1885) III. 152/1 Better..Than thou canst keep thy clattering toung, That trattles in thy head.

†**Tra·ttler.** Chiefly *Sc. Obs.* In 5–6 tratlar, 6 -or, 7 -er. [f. TRATTLE *v.* + -ER¹.] One who 'trattles'; an idle talker, chatterer, gossip.

1456 SIR G. HAYE *Law Arms* (S.T.S.) 78 The tane is a grete tratlar, the tothir a still herkenare. 1500–20 DUNBAR *Poems* xli. 10 Be ȝe ane lear, that is werst of all, Be ȝe ane tratlar, that I hald als ewill. 1599 JAS. I Βασιλ. Δωρον (1603) 100 Where yee finde a tratler, away with him. 1670 RAY *Prov.* 260 A tratler is worse then a thief.

†**Tra·ttling**, *vbl. sb. Obs.* [f. TRATTLE *v.* + -ING¹.] The action of the verb TRATTLE; idle talking or chattering; gossiping.

*a* 1400 *Cursor M.* 27824 (Cott. Galba) Couatyse es ane euil syn...Of þis cumes tratilling of tresoune. *c* 1460 *How Gd. Wife taught Daughter* 17 (MS. St. John's, Camb.) Nocht oyss [=use] of tratlyng in the toune. 1570 *Satir. Poems Ref.* xxiii. 115 Thocht Lethingtoun with tratling he do trane thame. 1603 *Proph. of Waldhaue* (Bann. Cl.) 34 This taile that I tell you,..It is a tratling but trueth, the suth the to say.

†**Tra·ttling**, *ppl. a. Obs.* [f. as prec. + -ING².] That 'trattles'; chattering, tattling, gossiping.

1500–20 DUNBAR *Poems* xviii. 39 Thair tratling tungis that all furth temiss. 1559 AYLMER *Harborowe* P j b, The tratling Scot shal knocke out your chestes botoms. *a* 1585 POLWART *Flyting w. Montgomerie* 129 ȝet, tratling truiker, truth to tell [etc.].

**Trature, -uruse**, obs. ff. TRAITOR, TRAITOROUS.

**Trau**, var. THROW *sb.*¹ *Obs.*; obs. f. TROW *v.*

**Travail(e, -aill(e**, obs. ff. TRAVAIL, TRAVEL.

**Trauchle**, variant of TRACHLE *sb.* and *v.* *Sc.*

**Traue**, obs. form of TROW *v.*

**Traueil, -el, -eilous, -elous**, obs. ff. TRAVAIL, TRAVEL, TRAVAILOUS.

**Traught, Traul**, obs. ff. TROUGH, TRAWL.

**Traulism** (trǭ·liz'm). *rare.* Also in L. form traulismus. [ad. Gr. τραυλισμ-ός, f. τραυλίζειν to lisp, τραυλός adj. lisping, mispronouncing letters.] A stammering, stuttering.

[1589 R. HARVEY *Pl. Perc.* A ij, And so foorth following the Traulila-lilismus, as farre as Will Solnes stuttiing pronunciation may stumble ouer at a breath.] 1678 PHILLIPS (ed. 4), *Traulismus*,..a stammering repetition of the first syllable, or letter of a word, as *Tu-Tu-Tullius.* 1680 DALGARNO *Deaf & Dumb Man's Tutor* 128 Childish and ridiculous Traulisms. *a* 1800 S. PEGGE *Anecd. Eng. Lang.* (1803) 93 A stammering kind of syllable, rhetorically called a Traulismus. 1893 *Westm. Gaz.* 6 Oct. 2/1 A professor of elocution who has caught a trick of stammering from those whom he has cured of traulism.

‖**Trauma** (trǭ·mă). *Path.* [a. Gr. τραῦμα wound.] A wound, or external bodily injury in general; also the condition caused by this; traumatism.

1693 tr. *Blancard's Phys. Dict.* (ed. 2), *Trauma*,..a wound from an external cause. 1706 PHILLIPS (ed. Kersey), *Trauma*, a Wound. 1895 *Pop. Sci. Monthly* July 386 We have named this psychical trauma, a morbid nervous condition. 1899 *Allbutt's Syst. Med.* VI. 855 *Trauma* may lead to compression in one or other of the following ways.

**Traumatic** (trǫmæ·tik), *a.* and *sb.* [ad. late L. *traumatic-us*, ad. Gr. τραυματικός of or pertaining to a wound or wounds, f. τραῦμα, -ματ- wound. Cf. F. *traumatique* (16th c. in Godef. *Compl.*).]

A. *adj.* Of, pertaining to, or caused by a wound, abrasion, or external injury, as *traumatic erysipelas, insanity, idiocy*; † formerly, used for the cure of wounds, vulnerary, as a *traumatic balsam, herb.*

1656 BLOUNT *Glossogr.*, *Traumatick*, belonging to wounds or to the cure of wounds, vulnerary. 1676 WISEMAN *Chirurg. Treat.* I. iv. 29 Nature..was assisted the while by Traumatick Decoctions, &c. as in such cases is usual. 1835–6 *Todd's Cycl. Anat.* I. 163/1 Inflammation traumatic or idiopathic. 1869 G. LAWSON *Dis. Eye* (1874) 152 Traumatic Cataract, or cataract the result of an injury to the eye. 1913 *Times* 11 Aug. 13/3 Prof. V. Soubbotitch..presented his military experiences of traumatic aneurysms.

†**B.** *sb.* A vulnerary agent or remedy. *Obs.*

1683 SALMON *Doron Med.* I. 18 A very good Traumatick and Vulnerary. 1694 — *Bate's Dispens.* (1713) 496/2 An excellent traumatick and vulnerary.

Hence **Trauma·tically** *adv.*, in connexion with a wound or abrasion.

1866 A. FLINT *Princ. Med.* (1880) 143 Chronic pleuritis may be produced traumatically. 1897 *Allbutt's Syst. Med.* IV. 771 It [tonsillitis] may occur traumatically.

**Traumaticin** (trǫmæ·tisin). Also -ine. [f. as prec. + -IN¹.] (See quots.)

1857 DUNGLISON *Med. Lex.*, *Traumaticine*, a name given by Eulenberg to a solution of gutta-percha in chloroform, which is applied externally in various chronic cutaneous diseases. 1890 in BILLINGS *Nat. Med. Dict.* 1896 LYMAN in *Voice* (N. Y.) 9 Apr. 7/3 Another delicate, neutral, and durable dressing, termed traumaticin.

**Traumatism** (trǭ·mătiz'm). *Path.* [f. Gr. τραῦμα, τραυματ- wound + -ISM. Cf. F. *traumatisme.*] The action of a wound or external injury in producing a morbid condition; the condition so produced.

1857 DUNGLISON *Med. Lex.*, *Traumatism*,..the condition of the organism occasioned by a grave wound. 1876 DUHRING *Dis. Skin* 526 Anæsthesia may also result from traumatism. 1899 *Q. Rev.* July 274 Such [diseases] as are the consequence of inorganic poisons or traumatisms.

So **Traumatize** (trǭ·mătəiz) *v.*, *trans.* to inflict a wound upon, to wound (as in a surgical operation).

1903 *Therapeutic Gaz.* Feb. 100/1 In spite of the general insensibility the orifices retain their sensibility, the patient struggling when they are traumatized, though he will preserve no recollection of this.

**Traumato-** (trǭmătǫ), repr. Gr. τραυματο-, combining form of τραῦμα wound, in a few rare scientific terms, chiefly mod.Lat. ‖ **Trau:mato·cace** (-ǫ·kăsī) [Gr. κάκη badness], traumatic gangrene. ‖ **Trau:matoco·mium** [Gr. κομεῖν to tend], a hospital for the wounded. **Traumato·logy**, the scientific description of wounds. ‖ **Trau:mato-ne·sis** (-nī·sis) [Gr. νῆσις spinning], suture of wounds. ‖ **Trau:matopnœ·a** (-pnī·ă) [-πνοια breathing], the passage of air through a wound in the thorax during respiration. ‖ **Trau:matopy·ra** [πῦρ fire, fever-heat], traumatic fever. ‖ **Trau:mato-sapro·sis** [σαπρόειν to putrefy], traumatic gangrene.

1890 BILLINGS *Nat. Med. Dict.*, **Traumatocace*, traumatic gangrene. 1899 *Syd. Soc. Lex.*, *Traumatocace*, synonym of Hospital gangrene. 1857 DUNGLISON *Med. Lex.*, *Traumato-comium. 1899 *Syd. Soc. Lex.*, *Traumatology. 1890 BILLINGS *Nat. Med. Dict.*, *Traumatonesis. 1879 *St. George's Hosp. Rep.* IX. 245 No *traumatopnœa, no emphysema, no hæmoptysis. 1854–67 C. A. HARRIS *Dict. Med. Terminol.*, *Traumatopyra. 1860 MAYNE *Expos. Lex.*, **Traumatosaprosis*,..term for putrescence of a wound.

**Traumatol** (trǭ·mătǫl). [f. Gr. τραῦμα, τραυματ-

wound + -OL.] Trade-name of an iodo-orthocresol, a reddish powder used as a dressing for wounds.

1899 *Syd. Soc. Lex.*, *Traumatol*,..prepared by the action of iodine on oxytoluene.

**Traumatropism** (trǫmæ·tropiz'm). *Biol.* [Short for **traumatotropism*, f. Gr. τραῦμα wound, after *geotropism*, *heliotropism*, etc.] A peculiar growth or curvature of an organism (esp. a plant) resulting from a wound. So **Traumatro·pic** *a.*, of, pertaining to, or of the nature of traumatropism.

1898 R. BEER in *Nat. Science* June 390 The latent period ..can be greatly extended both in geotropism..and in traumatropism. *Ibid.*, It [a seedling of *Lupinus albus*] at once executed a traumatropic curvature.

**Traunce, -nse**, obs. ff. TRANCE. **Traunch, Trauncher, Traunchfer, Traunslate**, obs. ff. TRANCH, TRENCHER, TRANCHEFER, TRANSLATE.

**Traunt, Traunter, -or**: see TRANT, TRANTER.

**Traup(e, trauthe**, obs. ff. TROTH.

**Trauyl(l**, etc., obs. ff. TRAVAIL, TRAVEL, etc.

‖ **Travado** (trăvā·do). *Obs.* Also 8 travat. [Portuguese *travados* a kind of whirlwind, pl. of *travado*, pa. pple. of *travar* to twine, twist.] A sudden violent storm of wind and rain with thunder and lightning; a tornado.

[1625 PURCHAS *Pilgrims* II. VII. ii. § 6. 952 Very foule weather there with Thunder and Lightning, (which the Portugals call *Trauados*).] 1686 GOAD *Celest. Bodies* I. i. 2 Those Dire Tempests..known amongst us by the names of Spouts, Huracans, Tornados, Travados. 1770 J. R. FORSTER tr. *Kalm's Trav. N. Amer.* (1772) II. 63 A peculiar kind of storm called a Travat or Travado, happened to-day. 1867 SMYTH *Sailor's Word-bk.*, *Travado*, or *Travat*, a heavy squall, with sudden gusts of wind, lightning, and rain, on the coast of North America; like the African tornado.

**Travail** (træ·vĕl), *sb.*[1] Forms: (*v* before 1600 usually written *u*, in Sc. often *w*). *α.* 3–7 trauail, -ayl, 4–6 -ayll, -aille, -ale, 4–7 -aill, -aile, -ayle, 5–6 -aylle; 4 travail, 4–7 -aill, -aile, -ayle, 5 -all(e, 5–6 -ayll, -ale; *Sc.* 4–5 trawaill, -wailȝe, -aile, -ayle, (5 trewaill), 4–6 trawayll. *β.* traueylle, 4–7 -ell, -el, 5 -eyle, 6 -eill, -ille, -yll; 5 travelle, 5–7 travell, 5–8 travel, (7 travil); 5–6 *Sc.* trawel, -ell. [a. OF. *travail* suffering or painful effort, trouble (12th c. in Godef. *Compl.*) = Prov. *trebalh*, Sp. *trabajo*, Pg. *trabalho*, It. *travaglio*; vbl. sb. from *travailler*, etc.: see TRAVAIL *v.* OF. and Pr. had also fem. forms *travaille*, *trebalha*, labour, fatigue.]

(As to the diverse sense-development in Fr. and in Eng. see TRAVAIL *v.*)

**I. 1.** Bodily or mental labour or toil, especially of a painful or oppressive nature; exertion; trouble; hardship; suffering. *arch.*

*α.* *c* 1250 *O. Kent. Serm.* in *O. E. Misc.* 33 Clepe þo werkmen and yeld hem here trauail. *c* 1290 *S. Eng. Leg.* I. 61/247 [H]is trauail nis no þe lasse. *a* 1300 *Cursor M.* 9703 (Cott.) Qua wil for pes his trauaill [*v.rr.* trauayl] spend. *Ibid.* 20942 Was nan sua mikel trauael mad. 13.. *Ibid.* 12765 (Gött.) Ferli þaim toght hu he might last, Wid sua grete trauale [*other MSS.* trauaile] and fast. *c* 1375 *Sc. Leg. Saints* ii. (*Paulus*) 911 He tholit trawal ful gret. *c* 1386 CHAUCER *Frankl. T.* 889, I wol nat taken a peny of thee For al my craft ne noght for my trauaille [*v.rr.* -ayle, -aile]. 1390 GOWER *Conf.* III. 231 And lusti youthe his thonk deserveth Upon the travail which he doth. 1422 tr. *Secreta Secret.*, *Priv. Priv.* 152 His modyr that..with grete trauaill hym norishid. *Ibid.* 158 Ne be not al tymys in trauaille and in thoghtis. *c* 1470 HENRY *Wallace* VI. 672 We may thaim wyne, and mak bot lycht trawaill. 1549 CROWLEY *Last Trumpet* 268 Then holde thy selfe therwyth contente, As wyth the wage of thy travayle. 1570 *Satir. Poems Reform.* xvii. 13 Betuix gude and euill markand our trauaill [*rimes* saill, fraill]. 1596 DALRYMPLE tr. *Leslie's Hist. Scot.* I. (S.T.S.) I. 78 The diligens,..Industrie, and trauale of this Thanaus. 1597 HOOKER *Eccl. Pol.* V. lii. § 1 With care and trauaile to preserue this Article from..sinister construction. 1621 ELSING *Debates Ho. Lords* (Camden) App. 146 For which my paines and travaill they gave me two pesses a manne. 1660 JER. TAYLOR *Worthy Commun.* Introd. 1 Faint and sick with travaile and fear. 1826 E. IRVING *Babylon* I. II. 64 The common everyday travail of men in trade and handicrafts. 1867 F. FRANCIS *Angling* xiv. (1880) 489 Ah, what travail have I not endured in the pursuit of May fly hooks.

*β.* 13.. *Cursor M.* 89 (Cott.) Quat bote is to sette traueil [*v.rr.* -ail, -ayle, -aile] On thyng þat may not auail. [1375 (MS. 1487) BARBOUR *Bruce* VII. 45 We haf tynt þis trauell [*rime* avale].] 1382 WYCLIF *Gen.* xxxi. 42 Myn affliccioun and the traueil of myn hondis the Lord biheldе. *c* 1400 *Rule St. Benet* 1855 For vnto trauel wor we born, And al our elders vs be-forn. *c* 1450 *Merlin* ii. 26 He that ought doth for a gode man, lesith not his traueyle. 1530 PALSGR. 282/2 Traveyle, labour, *trauayl*. 1535 STEWART *Cron. Scot.* (Rolls) II. 191 This Conranus..Greit travell dalie did vpoun him tak. 1570 *Ane Tragedie* 32 in *Satir. Poems Reform.* x. 83 He to serue vs na traueil did spair. 1577 NORTHBROOKE *Dicing* (1843) 56 As Iob sayeth, a man is borne to trauel as the sparkes flee vpward. 1642 ROGERS *Naaman* To Rdr. § 1 A great peece of my travell in these Lectures. *a* 1770 JORTIN *Serm.* (1771) I. iv. 67 He wrought with labor and travel night and day. 1774 PENNANT *Tour Scot. in 1772* 225 After some travel [we] found the inside.

† **2.** With *a* and *pl.* A piece of bodily or mental labour; a work, a task; in *pl.* labours.

*c* 1350 *Will. Palerne* 4712 Þi tenful trauayles þow hast for me suffred. 1390 GOWER *Conf.* III. 133 Thei hadde a gret travail on honde. 1494 FABYAN *Chron.* VI. cxlix. 135 His manyfolde trauayllys, susteynyd for the weale of the realme. 1568 GRAFTON *Chron.* II. 10 One that much desyred to eschew the trauayles of Martiall affayres. *c* 1620 FLETCHER & MASSINGER *Trag. Barnavelt* V. i, Heaven direct And prosper theis your charitable traviles. 1690 PENN *Rise & Progr. Quakers* vi. (1834) 80 O it is a travail, a spiritual travail! 1724 A. COLLINS *Gr. Chr. Relig.* Pref. 21 He that seeketh her early shall have no great travels.

† **3.** The outcome, product, or result of toil or labour; a (finished) 'work'; *esp.* a literary work.

1563 SHUTE *Archit.* Fij b, I submyt my trauel, vnto allother..of like well wylling affection, wherwith I do offer this my poore atemptes and smal trauailes. 1597 MORLEY *Introd. Mus.* 183 The publication..of those neuer enough praised trauailes of master Waterhouse. 1624 WOTTON *Archit.* I. ad fin., I will conclude the first Part of my present Travel. The second remaineth concerning Ornaments.

**4.** The labour and pain of child-birth. Phr. *in travail* (Fr. *en travail*). Now chiefly *fig.*

1297 R. GLOUC. (Rolls) 237 Vor in travail of his beringe is moder was verst ded. *c* 1300 *St. Margarete* 283 Eni womman..in trauail of childe. 1512 *Helyas* in Thoms *Prose Rom.* (1828) III. 27 In great paine and travaille of bodye she childed .vi. sonnes and a faire doughter. 1535 COVERDALE *Ps.* xlvii[i]. 6 Feare came there vpon them, & sorowe as vpon a woman in hir trauayle. 1599 B. JONSON *Cynthia's Rev.* V. x, Doe you not see how his legs are in trauaile with a measure? 1611 BIBLE *John* xvi. 21 A woman, when shee is in trauaile, hath sorrow, because her houre is come. 1650 BULWER *Anthropomet.* 180 His wife dying after travel of a daughter. 1754–64 SMELLIE *Midwif.* II. 70 She felt all the Praeludia of an imminent travail. 1825 J. NEAL *Bro. Jonathan* III. 448 In the time of her travail. 1837 CARLYLE *Fr. Rev.* III. VI. vii, What a distracted City;..the Hour clearly in travail,—child not to be named till born! 1897 T. HARDY *Well-Beloved* II. xiii, Between the travail of the sea without, and the travail of the woman within.

† **5.** *transf.* The eclipse of a heavenly body. Cf. LABOUR *sb.* 7. *Obs. rare.*

1601 HOLLAND *Pliny* II. xii. I. 9 Seeing these things, and the paineful ordinarie travels (since that this tearme is now taken up) of the starres. [1627 HAKEWILL *Apol.* X. (1630) 82 Eclipses of the Sun and Moone, in which they are commonly thought to suffer, and to be as it were in travell during that time.] 1640 BP. REYNOLDS *Passions* i. 2 No eye gazeth on the Moone, but in her Travell.

† **6.** *transf.* The straining movement of a vessel in rough seas. (Cf. LABOUR *v.* 17.) *Obs. rare*⁻¹.

1687 A. LOVELL tr. *Thevenot's Trav.* II. 10 If the Vessel made but the least Travel, they thought themselves lost.

**II. 7.** Journeying, a journey.

For this and the senses derived from it, see TRAVEL *sb.*, the spelling under which these senses are now differentiated from the preceding.

**III. 8.** *attrib.* and *Comb.*, as **travail-pain, -pang**, pain or pang of child-birth (also *fig.*).

1814 SCOTT *Ld. of Isles* IV. xxvii, Thou heard'st a wretched female plain In agony of travail-pain. 1827 KEBLE *Chr. Y.*, *4th Sund. Trinity*, The travail pangs of earth must last Till her appointed hour. 1860 PUSEY *Min. Proph.* 86 The travail-pangs are violent, sudden, irresistible.

† **Travail, -aile**, *sb.*[2] *Obs.* [= F. *travail*, pl. *travails* (1467–8, *traval* in Godef. *Compl.*, in same sense). Cf. Cotgr., '*Travail*:..also the frame whereinto Farriers put vnrulie horses, when they shooe or dresse them.' Derivation disputed: by some referred to L. *trepālium* (see TRAVAIL *v.*), by others to L. **trabāculum*, or other deriv. of *trabs*, *trabem* beam, thing made of beams or timbers.] A kind of quadrangular frame in which restive horses are secured in order to be shod. Cf. TRAVE *sb.* 2.

1594 NASHE *Unfort. Trav.* Wks. (Grosart) V. 141 The trauaile wherein smithes put wilde horses when they shoo them. 1753 CHAMBERS *Cycl. Supp.*, *Travail*, in the manege. See the article Travice..This in some of the remoter parts of England goes by the name of a *break*; and is called in French *Travail*. 1771 *Misc.* in *Ann. Reg.* 177/2 *Trabale* is derived from *trabs*, from whence, as I conjecture, proceeds the word *travail* (*travise*), which..denotes that machine in which Farriers confine mettlesome and vicious horses in order to shoe them.

‖ **Travail, -aille** (travāi), *sb.*[3] [App. the same as F. *travail*, which in Canada (pronounced *travày*) is applied to the space between the two shafts of a vehicle in which the horse runs (cf. TRAVE *sb.* 1 b); this may well be originally the same word as prec., and ult. from L. *trabs*, *trabem* beam. *Travaux* is a false plural, found in books, for *travails*.] See quotations, and cf. TRAVOIS.

1865 MILTON & CHEADLE *N. W. Passage by Land* 171 A *travaille* is an Indian contrivance, consisting of two poles fastened together at an acute angle, with crossbars between. The point of the angle rests upon the back of the dog or horse, the diverging ends of the poles drag along the ground, and the baggage is put on to the crossbars. The Indians use these contrivances instead of carts. 1889 *Century Mag.* Jan. 339/2 In a month 'Richard's himself again', ready to fly over the grassy sward with his savage master or to drag the *travaux* and pack the buxom squaw. 1891 *Cent. Dict.*, *Travail*, A means of transportation, commonly used by North American Indians..Also called *travois*, *travee*.

**Travail** (træ·vĕl), *v.* Forms: *α.* 3–5 trauaille, 3–7 -aile, (4 -alle), 4–6 -aill, -ayle, -ayll(e, -ale, -all, 4–7 -ail, 6 -al. 4–5 travaylle, 4–6 -aille, 4–7 -ayle, -aile, 5 -ale, 5–6 -aill, 5– travail; 4–5 *Sc.* trawayll, -ale, 5 -aill. *β.* 4–5 traueil(e, -eyll(e, 4–6 -eyle, -ele, 5–7 -elle, -el, 6–7 -ell; 4–7 travele, 5 -eylle, 5–6 -eille, -eyl(e, 5–7 -ell, 5–9 travel. [ME. *travaill-en*, *-vaylle*, *-vaile*, *-veyle*, *-veile*, etc. (usually with *u*, or Sc. *w*, for *v*), a. OF. *travaillier*, *-vailler*, *-veillier*, *-veiller*, mod.F. *travailler* = Prov. *trebalhar* (also Pg. *trabalhar*, Sp. *trabajar*, It. *travagliare*); held by Romanic scholars generally to represent a late pop.L. or Com. Rom. **trepāliāre*, deriv. of *trepālium* (A.D. 582 in Du Cange), an instrument or engine of torture (prob. f. L. *trēs*, *tria* three + *pālus* stake, being so named from its structure). The etymological sense was thus 'to put to torture, torment', passing at an early stage into those of 'afflict, vex, trouble, harass, weary'. Through the refl. sense 'to trouble, afflict, or weary oneself', came the intrans. 'to toil, work hard, labour'. Thence also (as is generally thought) the verbal sbs. OF. *travail* m. and *travaille* f., ME. *travail*, *-aile*: see TRAVAIL *sb.*[1]

The sense-development has not followed the same course in French and in English. Thus English has not developed the simple sense 'work', for which the OE. word has lived on. On the other hand, French has not evolved the sense 'journey' = F. *voyager*, which appeared early in Anglo-Fr., and has become the main sense in English, and is differentiated by the spelling TRAVEL, while the more original senses, so far as they continue in use, retain the earlier spelling *travail*.]

**I. 1.** *trans.* To torment, distress, harass, afflict, vex, trouble; to weary, tire. *Obs.* or *arch.*

1303 R. BRUNNE *Handl. Synne* 6035 Þe fende yn-to hym was lope, And traueyled hym þre dayys with pyne. 1382 WYCLIF *Deut.* viii. 16 After that he trauelde thee and strengthide [1388 turmentid thee, and preuede], at the eende he hadde mercy of thee. 1387 TREVISA *Higden* (Rolls) IV. 473 Preostes schulde be worschipped to fore oþer men, and nouȝt i-travalled and i-greeved. 1483 CAXTON *Gold. Leg.* 192 b/1 They were wery and sore traueyled by the waye which was longe. *c* 1489 — *Sonnes of Aymon* iii. 70 For their strengthe, they trayueylle us moche. 1568 GRAFTON *Chron.* II. 252 He came thether in such haste, that hys horse and men were sore traueyled. 1627 *Lisander & Cal.* III. 39 Apt words to expresse the griefes, wherwith..we begin to be travelled. 1695 LD. PRESTON *Boeth.* Pref. 11 We are travelled with Uneasiness and Inquietude amidst our largest Enjoyments. 1816 SCOTT *Old Mort.* iv, I jalouse he wad hae liked to hae ridden by, but his horse..was ower sair travailed. 1832 [see TRAVAILED 1].

† **b.** *refl.* To put oneself to trouble, to weary or exert oneself, to labour or work hard: = Fr. *se travailler*, passing into the intr. sense 2. *Obs.*

*a* 1300 *Cursor M.* 22775 (Edin.) Þai..trauaild [*v.rr.* -ailled, -alid, -ailed] þaim on al wis To paien him in his seruis. *c* 1374 CHAUCER *Boeth.* III. pr. xi. 76 (Camb. MS.) Euery beest trauaylith hym to deffende and kepe the sauacion of hys lyf. 1556 *Aurelio & Isab.* (1608) I v, Whoo lovethe not, traveillethe not him selfe. 1581 PETTIE *Guazzo's Civ. Conv.* II. (1586) 99 To exercise and trauaile himselfe in gouerning his subiects with iustice.

† **c.** *trans.* To put to work, cause to work; to exert, employ, bring into action. *Obs.*

1390 GOWER *Conf.* II. 16 And if he wolde have holde him stille And nothing spoke, he scholde have failed: Bot for he hath his word travailed And dorste speke, his love he spedde. 1577 B. GOOGE *Heresbach's Husb.* III. (1586) 118 b, To trauell them [mares] moderately, will doe them rather good then harme. 1596 DANETT tr. *Comines* (1614) 328 The poore man that trauelleth and toileth his body to get foode. 1610 FLETCHER *Faithf. Sheph.* V. i, Let the floud..give remedy To greedy thirst, and travel not the tree That hangs with wanton clusters. 1630 EARL OF CORK in *Lismore Papers* (1888) Ser. II. III. 163, I haue with all affectionate zeale traveled my thoughts and stirred vp my best observacions [etc.].

† **d.** To shake, stir, 'work' (a thing) about.

*c* 1440 *Pallad. on Husb.* XI. 403 Seuen curnels of a pynappul do In oon sester of wyn that is impure And trauayle hit a tyme to and fro And aftir suffre hit to reste go. *c* 1440 *Anc. Cookery* in *Househ. Ord.* (1790) 455 Alway travaile hit wel over the fyre.

† **e.** *trans.* To labour at, to perform (some work, duty, or service). *Obs. rare*⁻¹.

1569 *Reg. Privy Council Scot.* I. 673 The Precheouris and utheris travelling the charge of ministerie within the kirk.

**2.** *intr.* (for *refl.*; cf. 1 b). To exert oneself, labour, toil, work hard. *arch.*

*c* 1250 *O. Kent. Serm.* in *O. E. Misc.* 34 Þos laste on ure habbeþ i-trauailed. 1303 R. BRUNNE *Handl. Synne* 10408 Y prey þe..To trauayle so moche for me. 13.. *E. E. Allit. P.* A. 549 Þenne þe fyrst bygonne to pleny & sayden þat þay hade travayled sore. 1423 JAS. I *Kingis Q.* lxx, As Tantalus I trauaile ay but-les. 1484 CAXTON *Fables of Æsop* VI. xvii, Who trauaylleth wel, he hath euer brede ynough for to ete. 1577 GOOGE *Heresbach's Husb.* 13 b, That he be not.. vnable to trauayle for age. 1615 W. LAWSON *Orch. & Gard.* (1623) 2 Such a Gardner as will conscionably, quietly and patiently, trauell in your Orchard. 1878 B. TAYLOR *Deukalion* I. ii. 22, I travail for my children.

*fig.* 1883 STEVENSON *Silverado Sq.* V. (1886) 76 Even in its gentlest moods the salt sea travails, moaning among the weeds or lisping on the sand.

**b.** Const. *about*, *for*, *in* (some matter), *to do* something. *arch.*

*c* 1290 *S. Eng. Leg.* I. 82/29 Ȝwat neode is it for to trauailli ferrore me to lede? *Ibid.* 350/161 Þou trauailest, he seide, a-boute nouȝt. *a* 1325 *Prose Psalter* xlviii[i]. 8 For þe pris of his raunsoun he shal trauail wyþ-outen ende. 1375 BARBOUR *Bruce* IX. 165 Thai had no-thing for to et, Bot gif thai trauailt it to get. *c* 1400 MAUNDEV. (Roxb.) ix. 33 Þis folk..trauailez nouȝt aboute tillyng of land. *c* 1489 CAXTON *Blanchardyn* vi. 26 In vayne he traueylled for to require her from him. 1559 BP. SCOT in Strype *Ann. Ref.* (1709) I. App. vii. 18, I shall nede to travell in provinge of the same. **1560** DAUS tr. *Sleidane's Comm.* 240 He wyll sende Ambassadours, whiche shall trauell for peace. **1612** T. TAYLOR *Comm. Titus* i. 7 (1619) 158 Truell not too much to be rich. **1678** WANLEY *Wond. Lit. World* v. i. § 93. 467/2 He travelled exceedingly for establishing the Peace of Christendom. **1704** SWIFT *T. Tub* Introd., I have been prevailed on..to travel in a compleat and laborious dissertation. **1897** W. BEATTY *Secretar* xxv. 213 Gif the meenisters uprightly travelled to punish vice.

† **c.** To work as a student, to study (*in* a subject or author). *Obs.*

**1551–1742** [see TRAVAILED 2]. **1570** T. WILSON *Demosthenes* Ded. 2 Maister Cheeke, hauing traueyled in Demosthenes as much as any one of them all.

**3.** Of a woman: To suffer the pains of child-birth; to be in labour. Also *fig.*

*a* **1300** [see TRAVAILING *vbl. sb.*]. **1388** WYCLIF *Rom.* viii. 22 And we witen, that ech creature sorewith, and trauelith with peyne [1382 childith] til 3it. **1470–85** MALORY *Arthur* VIII. i. 273 She byganne to trauaille fast of her child. **1565** *Reg. Privy Council Scot.* I. 396 The Countes of Buchane, quha than wes travelland with chyld. **1634** SIR T. HERBERT *Trav.* 14 Flowres which only Dame Nature trauels with. **1658** T. WALL *God's Revenge agst. Enemies Ch.* 56 Travelling with the pangs of a false zeal, they fall in labour of a monstrous Reformation. **1730** T. BOSTON *Mem.* App. 28, I have long travailed in pain about it. **1827** SCOTT *Surg. Dau.* viii, Her son, for whom she had travailed and sorrowed. **1860** PUSEY *Min. Proph.* 455 God's word..contains its own fulfilment in itself, and travaileth until it come to pass.

† **4.** Of a ship: To 'labour', to roll or pitch heavily and right itself with difficulty. *Obs. rare.*

*a* **1340** HAMPOLE *Psalter* ix. 34 Þi haly kirke..trauailand as a ship in gret stormes. **1390** GOWER *Conf.* III. 296 The yonge king makth mochel wo So forto se the Schip travaile.

**II.** † **5.** To journey, etc.: see TRAVEL *v.*, under which spelling these senses are now differentiated from the preceding.

**Travailed** (træ·vē̆ld), *ppl. a.* [f. prec. + -ED $^1$.]

**1.** Wearied in body or mind; troubled; harassed. *Obs.* or *arch.*

*c* **1420** *Prov.* in *Rel. Ant.* I. 233 Wele traveled wymen or wele traveled horsses were never good. *c* **1540** tr. *Pol. Verg. Eng. Hist.* (Camden) I. 79 Agricola issuinge owte of his tentes succored and refresshed his traveled soldiers. **1644** MILTON *Educ.* Wks. 1738 I. 140 Composing their travail'd spirits with the solemn and divine harmonies. **1832** L. HUNT *Poems* 255 Could my spirit..Slip from my travailled flesh.

† **2.** Experienced, versed, or learned (*in* a subject, etc.), as the result of working at it. (Cf. *well-read.*)

**1551** T. WILSON *Logike* (1580) A iij b, Your grace [Edw. VI] ..little needeth any helpe.., beeyng so well trauailed bothe in the Greke and in the Latine. **1647** TORSHELL *Design* 18 Daniel was a man..much travelled in Revelations. **1742** FIELDING *Jos. Andrews* II. ix, I am not much travelled in the history of modern times.

**3.** That is or has been in travail or child-bed.

**1842** R. S. HAWKER *Cornish Ballads*, etc. (1908) 130 A cottage bed, for there A travailed woman lay.

**Tra·vailer.** *Obs.* or *arch.* Also 4–5 **-our.** [ME. *travailour*, a. OF. *travailleor* one who harasses (*a* 1300 in Godef.), one who labours or travails (13th c.), agent-noun from *travaillier*: see TRAVAIL *v.* and -ER $^2$ 3.] One who travails or labours; † one who torments or harasses.

**1377** LANGL. *P. Pl.* B. XIII. 239 Alle trewe trauaillours and tilieres of þe erthe. *c* **1430** *Pilgr. Lyf Manhode* II. lxvii. (1869) 101 He ne is but a turmentour and a trauailour of folk. **1548** UDALL *Erasm. Par. Luke* xx. 155 Earnest trauaillers for yᵉ peoples behouf and profite. **1598** STOW *Surv.* 479 By profession busie Bees, and trauellers for their liuing in the Hiue of this common welth. **1611** SPEED *Hist. Gt. Brit.* IX. vi. § 107 Thomas Talbot an exact trauailer in genealogies.

**b.** A woman in labour.

**1388** WYCLIF 2 *Kings* xix. 3 Sones camen til to the child-beryng, and the traueler of childe hath not strengthis.

**Tra·vailing,** *vbl. sb. arch.* [f. TRAVAIL *v.* + -ING $^1$.] The action of the vb. TRAVAIL; labouring, toiling; labour of child-bearing; distress, fatigue, etc.

*a* **1300** *Cursor M.* 3487 (Cott.) In trauelling [*v. rr.* trauayling, -alyng]..Ful herd it was þair moder pain. **1362** LANGL. *P. Pl.* A. VII. 235 With techinge or with tilynge or trauaylynge of hondes. *c* **1440** *Alphabet of Tales* 402 He wiste not at sho was with childe to sho was evyn at travellyng. **1571** DIGGES *Pantom.* II. vi. M iij b, No small ease and discharge of laborsom trauayling. **1859** J. THOMSON *Cast. Indol.* i, Long years of restless travailing.

**Tra·vailing,** *ppl. a.* [f. as prec. + -ING $^2$.] That travails.

**1.** Labouring, toiling, hard-working. *Obs.* or *arch.*

*a* **1340** HAMPOLE *Psalter* viii. 7 Þa ere trauailand men gastly in haly kirke. **1456** SIR G. HAYE *Law Arms* (S.T.S.) 3 [To] put this travailland warld in pes and rest. **1579** FENTON *Guicciard.* (1618) 2 He was possessed with a mind trauelling, busie, & ambitious.

**2.** Of a woman: Suffering the pains of child-birth; in labour. Also *fig.*

*c* **1386** CHAUCER *Knt.'s T.* 1225 A womman trauaillynge was hire biforn. **1535** COVERDALE *Isa.* xlii. 14, I will crie like a trauelinge woman. **1641** MILTON *Reorfm.* II. Wks. 1851 III. 69 Let her cast her Abortive Spawne without the danger of this travailling and throbbing Kingdome. **1657** TRAPP *Comm. Esther* vii. 8 The pains of a travelling woman.

† **3.** Tormenting, harassing. *Obs.*

**1398** TREVISA *Barth. De P. R.* XVI. xlviii. (Bodl. MS.), Þe same stone [jet] boþe blacke and 3elow strengþeþ a3ens fantasies and a3ens..trauailinge fendes bi ny3t.

**Travailler**· see TREVALLY $^1$.

**Tra·vailous,** *a. Obs.* or *arch.* Forms: 4 trau-, traveilous, (trauyliouse), 4–5 trauelous, 4–6 trauailous, 5 trauaillous, traueyllous, (travelos), 6 trauaylous, 4–6, 9 travailous. [a. OF. *travaillos*, *traveilleus*, *-ous* toilsome (12th c. in Godef.), f. *travail* TRAVAIL *sb.*$^1$: see -OUS.] Full of or characterized by 'travail' or hard labour; toilsome; laborious; wearisome.

*c* **1340** HAMPOLE *Prose Tr.* 29 Lya [Leah] es als mekill at say as trauyliouse, and betakyns actyfe lyfe. *c* **1380** WYCLIF *Sel. Wks.* III. 273 Þe opyn meke and pore and traveilouse lif of Crist. **1382** — *Exod.* vi. 6, Y the Lord, that schal lede 3ow out of the traveilous prisoun of Egipciens. **1565** STAPLETON tr. *Bede's Hist. Ch. Eng.* 21 To take any more such trauaylous iourneis. **1888** DOUGHTY *Arabia Deserta* I. 59 Better his mother had been barren, than that her womb should have borne such a sorry travailous life.

Hence † **Tra·vailously** *adv. Obs. rare.*

*c* **1380** WYCLIF *Wks.* (1880) 439 Þei moten lyue, trewely, trauelously & perelously. **1382** — *Bible, Pref. Epist. St. Jerome* i, Plato to..thilk brynk of Itali,..ful traueilousli 3ede. **1382** — *Wisd.* xv. 7 The crockere, the nesshe erthe threstende, trauailously [Vulg. *laboriose*], maketh to oure vses eche vessel.

† **Tra·vailsome,** *a. Obs.* [f. TRAVAIL *sb.*$^1$ + -SOME.] Laborious; wearisome; toilsome.

**1549** CHALONER *Erasm. on Folly* O iv b, A travailsome and carefull life. **1577** tr. *Bullinger's Decades* (1592) 911 Ashamed ..of their trauelsome idlenesse. **1617** J. MOORE *Mappe Mans Mort.* II. vi. 137 Certaine sorrow, vncertaine pleasure, trauelsome labour, fearefull rest.

**Travaise,** obs. form of TRAVERSE.

† **Travale** (trăvā·l, travā·le). *Obs.* [Origin obscure.] In tambourine playing, a roll or drone-effect produced by drawing the wetted thumb over the parchment in a circular direction.

**1798** *Monthly Mag.* Feb. 136/1 Terms and characters necessary to be understood by the performer on the tambu-rino; such as the single travale, the double travale, the flamps. **1876** STAINER & BARRETT *Dict. Mus. Terms* s.v. *Tambourine*, To make the 'Travale'..draw your wetted thumb in a circular direction over the skin. The 'double-travale' is twice as quick.

**Travale, -alla, all(e)y:** see TREVALLY $^1$, $^2$.

**Travant,** variant of TRABANT.

**Travarse, -as, -ass,** obs. ff. TRAVERSE.

**Travat,** variant of TRAVADO, TREVAT.

**Tra·vated,** *a.* [Formed after It. *travata*, F. *travée* (Cotgr.), 'a bay of joists, the space between two beams' (Phillips 1706), f. L. type **trabāt-us*: cf. TRABEATED.] 'Noting a ceiling divided into a series of traves, or transverse bays' (Webster 1911).

† **Travature.** *Obs. rare*$^{-1}$. [ad. It. *travatura* (f. as prec. + *-ura*, -URE), 'a frame or ioyning together of beames of timber' (Florio).] A joist.

**1730** A. GORDON *Maffei's Amphith.* 327 The Modilions which are prominent inwardly..are hollowed cross-ways, and adapted for receiving the Travatures.

**Trave,** *sb. Obs.* exc. *dial.* [In sense 1, a. OF. *trave* beam: cf. It. *trave* beam:—L. *trabem*, acc. of *trabs* beam. Its application in sense 2 is difficult; but cf. F. *entrave* clog, fetter, shackle, hindrance, restraint.]

**1.** A (timber or wooden) beam.

**1395** in *Archæologia* XXIV. 313 Pro cariagio de ij traves pro justes de hospicio. **1574** *Richmond Wills* (Surtees) 251, ix hogesheads in the buttrie with the gantrees and traves there. *a* **1701** MAUNDRELL *Journ. Jerus.* 2 Mar. (1721) 7 For its Ceiling only some rude traves laid athwart it. *Ibid.* 28 Apr. (1732) 125 The Ceilings and Traves are..richly Painted.

**b.** *dial.* ? One of the shafts of a cart, or the shafts collectively. Also *attrib.*

**1823** E. MOOR *Suffolk Words* s.v., Horses harnessed ready for work, are said to be 'in the trave'—or, 'in the traves'. **1905** *Eng. Dial. Dict.* s.v., In phr. *to be in the trave*, of horses: to be harnessed ready for work.

**2.** A frame or enclosure of bars in which a restive horse is placed to be shod: cf. TRAVAIL *sb.*$^2$

*c* **1386** CHAUCER *Miller's T.* 96 She sproong as a colt doth in the traue. **1483** *Cath. Angl.* 391/2 Trave for to scho horse jn, *ferratorium, ergasterium.* **1613** R. CAWDREY *Table Alph.* (ed. 3), Traue, a place to shoe wilde horses in. **1656** BLOUNT *Glossogr.*, *Trave* (from the Fr. Travée, i. a bay of buildings), a trevise or little roome made purposely to shoo unbroken horses in. **1706** PHILLIPS (ed. Kersey), *Trave*, *Travel*, or *Travise*, a Place enclosed with Rails, to shoe an unruly Horse in. **1847–78** HALLIWELL, *Trave*, a frame into which farriers put unruly horses.

† **b.** *pl.* See quot. 1706. *Obs. rare*$^{-0}$.

**1706** PHILLIPS (ed. Kersey), *Traves*, a kind of Shackles for a Horse that is taught to amble, or pace. **1726** in *Dict. Rust.* (ed. 3).

**Trave,** dial. var. THRAVE, THREAVE, two shocks of corn. (Cf. med.L. *trava* in Du Cange.)

**1764** *Museum Rust.* II. xxxiii. 107 Some shock their sheaves setting them up in traves of six sheaves of a side, and two to cap them. *Ibid.*, If the sheaves were dry when the traves were set up. **1905** *Contemp. Rev.* July 95, I learned how to build a trave (which is by interpretation a shock or stook).

**Traveis,** obs. form of TRAVERSE, TRAVIS $^1$.

**Travel** (træ·vĕl, -v'l), *sb.* Forms: *a.* 4 travall, *Sc.* trawaile, -ale, 4–5 *Sc.* trawaill, trauaille, 4–7 -aile, 5 *Sc.* trawal, 5–7 trau-, travayle, 5–8 travail, 6 trauaylle, -eile, travaill, *Sc.* travale, 6–7 -aile. *β.* 5 *Sc.* trawel(l, 5–7 trauel(l, travell, (6 trauyll), 5– travel, (9 *Sc.* traivel). [orig. the same word as TRAVAIL *sb.*$^1$, in a specialized sense and form; the latter due to shifting of stress.]

† **1.** Labour, toil; suffering, trouble; labour of child-birth, etc.: see TRAVAIL *sb.*$^1$ 1–6.

**2.** The action of travelling or journeying.

*a.* *c* **1375** *Sc. Leg. Saints* xxv. (*Julian*) 9 Þe trawalouris.. for trawale ware wery. *c* **1400** MAUNDEV. (Roxb.) viii. 28 Þe way es comoun and wele ynogh knawen with all men þat vsez trauaile. *c* **1460** *Towneley Myst.* xiv. 94 That I may haue som beyldyng by, In my trauayll. **1500–20** DUNBAR *Poems* lxxxv. 36 Way stricht, cler dicht, to wilsome wicht, That irke bene in travale. **1561** T. HOBY tr. *Castiglione's Courtyer* I. (1577) E j b, After a yeares trauayle abrode. **1660** BLOUNT *Boscobel* I. (1680) 49 His feet..much galled with travail.

*β.* **1375** (MS. 1487) BARBOUR *Bruce* IV. 664 My twa sonnys with 3ow sall I Send to tak with 3ow 3our trawell [*rime* fale]. *a* **1533** LD. BERNERS *Huon* xxii. 65 Huon was wery of trauyll. *a* **1550** *Freiris of Berwik* 65 in *Dunbar's Poems* (S.T.S.) 287, I pray grit God him speid Him haill and sound in-to his travell. **1584** B. R. tr. *Herodotus* I. 33 The way is short, & the trauell easye. **1650** in *Verney Mem.* (1907) I. 464 The wayes are everywhere unsafe for travell. **1768** STERNE *Sent. Journ.* (1775) I. 72 (*The Rose*) The advantage of travel..was by seeing a great deal both of men and manners. **1897** *Westm. Gaz.* 11 Aug. 2/3 Continental travel is looking up. By travel we mean quick and comfortable travel.

**b.** With *a* and *pl.* An act of travelling; a journey. Now only in *pl.*, except *dial.*

**1559** W. CUNNINGHAM *Cosmogr. Glasse* Pref. A v b, His eloquence, prudence,..and other like vertues..insued of hys peregrinations, and travails. **1610** DAY *Festivals* iii. (1615) 56 He made (as it were) foure Travailes. *a* **1700** DRYDEN *Theodore & Hon.* 57 His travels ended at his country seat. **1753** C. GIST *Jrnls.* (1893) 84, I was unwilling he should undertake such a travel. **1821** CLARE *Vill. Minstr.* II. 182 In mortal wisdom, thou 'st already ran A circled travel of eternity. **1836** H. COLERIDGE *North. Worthies* (1852) I. 6 Soon after we find him on his travels in Italy. **1883** CLELAND *Inchbracken* iv. 28 Ye've had a sore traivel. *a* **1905** in *Eng. Dial. Dict.* s.v., (Westmoreland) Es ya wad see in a day's travel.

**c.** *pl.* (*ellipt.*) 'Account of occurrences and observations of a journey into foreign parts' (J.).

[**1591** (*title*) The Rare Trauailes of Iob Hortop.] **1706** PHILLIPS (ed. Kersey), *Travels*, Journeys, Voyages; or a Book giving a particular Account of such Voyages. **1710** *Tatler* No. 254 ⁋ 1 There are no Books which I more delight in than in Travels. **1798** MALTHUS *Popul.* (1878) 323 Some very intelligent Travels..written in 1810. **1841** ELPHINSTONE *Hist. India* I. 255 We possess the travels of a native of that country in India in the fourth century. *Mod.* He took Gulliver's Travels with him on his journey.

**d.** *transf.* Passage of anything in its course or path, or over a distance; movement.

**1742** YOUNG *Nt. Th.* IV. 713 [A comet] revisits earth, From the long travel of a thousand years. **1888** *Encycl. Brit.* XXIII. 701/2 The more the variety of characters is multiplied, the more 'travel' of the compositor's hand over the cases is necessary for picking them up. **1898** *Allbutt's Syst. Med.* V. 843 Cardiomotive force is equal to the output of the heart plus the resistance to the travel of the blood in the vascular system.

**e.** Passage over; traffic. *rare.*

**1830** HOOD *Haunted H.* I. xviii, Each walk as green as is the mantled pool For want of human travel.

**3.** A single movement of some part of mechanism, as a piston, slide-valve, etc.; also, the distance through which it moves; length of stroke.

**1841** *Civil Eng. & Arch. Jrnl.* IV. 251/2 To find..the travel of the valve corresponding to the travel..of the piston substitute. **1883** *Times* 8 Feb., A thin copper rod moved slowly backwards and forwards over them, with a travel of about 2 in. **1892** GREENER *Breech-Loader* 32 When the gun is fired the 'travel' of the mainspring is utilised as an automatically acting trigger. **1904** *Westm. Gaz.* 2 May 9/3 The incoming of 'three colour [printing] at one travel of paper'.

**4.** Capacity or force of movement.

**1816** SCOTT *Antiq.* xxx, The breaker was never able to bring her under command. She has more travel than any bitch I ever knew. **1844** STEPHENS *Bk. Farm* II. 625 A dog of high travel..will drive [sheep] hither and thither. **1892** *Daily News* 31 Dec. 3/4 A crew of men in the boat kept her rocking rapidly from side to side to give her more force and travel.

**5.** *attrib.* and *Comb.*, as *travel article*, *-book*, *-monger*; objective, as *travel-reader*, *-writer*; *travel-loving* adj.; instrumental, as *travel-broken*, *-disordered*, *-soiled*, *-spent*, *-stained*, *-tainted*, *-tattered*, *-tired*, *-toiled*, *-weary*, *-worn* adjs.

**1895** *Westm. Gaz.* 23 Apr. 7/1 A literary man who writes *travel articles in the Anglo-American magazines. **1878** BROWNING *La Saisiaz* 60 That rare nook..touched on by no *travel-book. **1856** KANE *Arct. Expl.* II. xx. 205 The condition of my own *travel-broken animals. **1840** DICKENS *Old C. Shop* xlvi, Dusty shoes, and *travel-disordered dress. **1768** BARETTI *Mann. & Cust. Italy* II. 324 Credit your *travel-mongers about the character of the Italians. **1810** SCOTT *Lady of L.* III. xxi, Panting and *travel-soiled he stood. **1847** MARY HOWITT *Ballads* 194 Neither to the other told How they were *travel-spent. **1840** DICKENS *Old C. Shop* xliv, Her *travel-stained dress. **1597** SHAKS. 2 *Hen. IV*, IV. iii. 40 *Trauell-tainted as I am. **1753** SMOLLETT *Ct. Fathom* (1784) 52/1 Our hero travel-tainted, lay sunk in the arms of profound repose. **1887** J. ASHBY STERRY *Lazy Minstrel* (1892) 218 Fast our *travel-time has sped. **1822** BYRON *Werner* I. i. 475 A poor sick man, *Travel-tired. **1821** SCOTT *Kenilw.* xxiv, Horses or light carriages to meet them, and bring them up without being *travel-toiled. **1856** E. FITZGERALD *Salaman* (1909) 47 Kurd..*Travel-weary, Fain would go to sleep. **1837** W. IRVING *Capt. Bonneville* I. v. 100 Both men and horses were..much *travel-worn. **1765** STERNE *Tr. Shandy* VII. iv, A *travel-writer would say, 'it would not be amiss to give some account of it'.

**Travel** (træ·vĕl, -v'l), *v.* Forms: see prec. [orig. the same word as TRAVAIL *v.*; cf. prec. Derivatives, as *travelled*, *-er*, *-ing*, etc. are usually spelt with *ll* in Gr. Britain, with single *l* in America.]

†**1.** To torment, distress; to suffer affliction; to labour, toil; to suffer the pains of parturition; etc.: see TRAVAIL *v.* 1–4.

**2.** *intr.* To make a journey; to go from one place to another; to journey. Also *fig.*

*α.* c 1290 *S. Eng. Leg.* I. 25/61 For ȝe þus i-trauailede beoth fram so ferre londe..Ich eov nelle greui nouȝt. c 1330 R. BRUNNE *Chron.* (1810) 3 He was of grete elde, & myght not trauaile. 1413 *Pilgr. Sowle* (Caxton) I. i. (1859) 1, I had longe tyme trauayled toward the holy Cyte of Ierusalem. 1548–9 (Mar.) *Bk. Com. Prayer*, *Litany*, To preserue all that trauayle by lande or by water. 1590 SPENSER *F. Q.* I. ii. 28 Long time they thus together traveiled. 1603 SHAKS. *Meas. for M.* I. iii. 14 He supposes me trauaild to Poland. 1691 NORRIS *Pract. Disc.* 94 Why should we..quit the Road.., if we may safely travail in it? 1714 GAY *Sheph. Week* Proeme, Other Poet travailing in this plain Highway of Pastoral.

*β.* c 1375 *Sc. Leg. Saints* xxxi. (*Eugenia*) 326 Sen scho mycht nocht trawel hym til. c 1410 *Sir Cleges* 16 To men, that traveld in londe of ware. 1483 *Cath. Angl.* 391/2 To Travelle, *itinerare*. a 1550 *Freiris of Berwik* 39 in *Dunbar's Poems* (S.T.S.) 286 For he wes awld, and micht nocht wele travell. 1594 NASHE *Unfort. Trav.* 68 He is no bodie that hath not traueld. 1600 SHAKS. *A. Y. L.* I. iii. 111 What danger will it be to vs,..to trauell forth so farre? 1697 DRYDEN *Virg. Georg.* IV. 147 A thirsty Train That long have travell'd thro' a Desart Plain. 1768 STERNE *Sent. Journ.* (1775) I. 15 (*Desobligeant*) An Englishman does not travel to see Englishmen. 1855 PALEY *Æschylus* Pref. (1861) 28 They have..pointed out the path in which succeeding editors should travel. 1901 W. R. H. TROWBRIDGE *Lett. Mother to Eliz.* iv. 13 [They] travelled down from London in a special Pullman attached to the Bristol express.

**b.** *To travel it*: to make a journey; *esp.* to go on foot.

1768 STERNE *Sent. Journ.* (1775) II. 135 (*Moulines*) To travel it through the Bourbonnois. 1903 *Speaker* 19 Dec. 293/1 Laird, I just travel't it.

**c.** *spec.* of a Methodist preacher: To go round a circuit. (Cf. quot. 1791 s. v. CIRCUIT 6.)

1789 [see TRAVELLING *ppl. a.* b]. 1791 HAMPSON *Mem. J. Wesley* III. 84 Every preacher was considered, when admitted to travel, as a member of conference. 1885 *Minutes Wesleyan Confer.* 8 The above have travelled two years. 1913 *Daily News* 17 July 4 On leaving Didsbury College he ..afterwards 'travelled', as the Methodists say, in the Brentford and Twickenham circuits.

**d.** To journey from place to place as a commercial traveller (TRAVELLER 3). Const. *in* the commodity for which the traveller solicits orders.

1830 LAMB *Let. to Wordsworth* 22 Jan., A rider in his youth, travelling for shops. 1898 *Westm. Gaz.* 2 May 5/2 One lady 'travels in balloons', it was said, meaning not that she soared aloft, but that she vended toy-balloons to drapers and others. 1906 B'NESS VON HUTTEN *What bec. Pam* 70 Mr. Bingle travelled in whisky. *Ibid.* 71 A gentleman who travelled in hygienic flannels. 1906 *Blackw. Mag.* Apr. 541/1 The Sophist who in ancient times 'travelled' in sophistry as our bagmen 'travel' in soap.

**e.** Of an animal: To walk or run; *spec.* of deer, to move on while browsing.

1877 C. HALLOCK *Sportsman's Gaz.* 88 If the deer is 'travelling', as it is called, one has to walk much faster. 1907 J. H. PATTERSON *Man-Eaters of Tsavo* xxii. 249 [The lion] was travelling leisurely, and I was delighted to find that I was gaining on him fast.

**3.** *transf.* To move, go; to pass from one point or place to another; to proceed, advance; to wander; *esp.* in mod. scientific use, to pass, to be transmitted.

1662 EVELYN *Chalcogr.* 29 Sculpture..travell'd and came to Rome. 1781 COWPER *Expost.* 582 Thy thunders travel over earth and seas. 1839 G. BIRD *Nat. Philos.* 129 Sound travels through different bodies with very different degrees of velocity. 1843 R. J. GRAVES *Syst. Clin. Med.* xxx. 400 Pains commencing in particular parts of the body, and travelling back towards the spine. 1878 HUXLEY *Physiogr.* 117 The earthquake-wave, as it travels along, causes the ground to rise and fall. 1911 E. RUTHERFORD in *Encycl. Brit.* XXII. 794/1 In an electric field, the positive ions travel to the negative electrode and vice versa.

**b.** *fig.* of some action figured as movement. *To travel out of the record*: see RECORD *sb.* 4 c.

1600 SHAKS. *A. Y. L.* III. ii. 326 Time trauels in diuers paces, with diuers persons. 1606 — *Tr. & Cr.* III. iii. 154 Honour trauels in a straight so narrow, Where one but goes a breast. 1664 MARVELL *Corr.* Wks. (Grosart) II. 181 His Royal Highness who hath travelled thorough all hearts. 1818 SCOTT *Hrt. Midl.* xxii, I must remind the learned gentleman that he is travelling out of the case before us. 1874 WHYTE MELVILLE *Uncle J.* viii, It seems that we are travelling out of the record.

**c.** Of a piece of mechanism: To move, or be capable of being moved, along a fixed course. (Cf. prec. sb. 3.)

1815 SCOTT *Guy M.* lvii, A large iron ring, which travelled upon the bar we have described. 1867 SMYTH *Sailor's Word-bk.*, *Travel*, [as] a thimble, block, &c., to run along on beams or ropes. 1892 *Photogr. Ann.* II, The top travels, so as to bring the case over another groove at the back.

**d.** *colloq.* To bear transportation.

1852 *Beck's Florist* Dec. 271 They do not..make good plants for exhibition, as they travel badly. 1887 J. B. SHEPPARD *Lit. Cantuarienses* (Rolls) I. Introd. 81 The monks knowing that so small a wine would not travel,.. always sold it on the spot.

**e.** To move on, esp. with speed. *colloq.* or *slang.*

1884 *Reports Provinc.* (E.D.D.), 'How he travels', said of a dog, running very fast. 1894 *Outing* (U.S.) XXIV. 473/1 The yachts were kept traveling from start to finish. *Mod.* That car is travelling, and no mistake! *Mod. U. S.* Keep travelling (= clear out, go on or away).

**4.** *trans.* (or with advb. accus.) To journey through (a country, district, space, etc.); to pass over, traverse (a road, etc.); to follow (a course or path).

†*To travel the road*, to practise highway robbery; cf. ROAD *sb.* 5 b.

1303 R. BRUNNE *Handl. Synne* 1952 Þarfore, y am come to þys cyte, And haue trauayled many a iurne. 1526 *Pilgr. Perf.* (W. de W. 1531) 8 Foure thynges be necessary to be..obserued of all them that entendeth to trauayle the same [journey]. 1578 LYTE *Dodoens* VI. iii. 659 Peter Belon..hath much haunted and trauayled the Ilande of Crete. 1644 EVELYN *Diary* 4 Nov., From hence we travell a plain and pleasant champain to Viterbo. 1682 HICKERINGILL *Black Non-Conf.* xvi, The Apostles that had the gift of Tongues travelled all Nations. 1706–7 FARQUHAR *Beaux Strat.* IV. ii, There's a great deal of address and good manners in robbing a lady; I am the most a gentleman..that ever travelled the road. 1823 F. CLISSOLD *Ascent Mt. Blanc* 21 Our path..now became far less dangerous than that we had just travelled. 1885 *Act* 48 & 49 *Vict.* c. 57 § 1 The senior judge..who actually travels that circuit. 1894 *Outing* (U.S.) XXIV. 366/2 The path was well traveled.

**b.** *fig.* or in *fig.* context.

1612 T. JAMES *Corrupt. Script.* To Rdr., Hauing now.. fully trauelled this vast wilderness of Sin. 1779 *Mirror* No. 16 ¶ 7 His brethren, travelling the same road, and subject to the like calamities with himself. 1784 COWPER *Task* III. 156 Some..travel nature up To the sharp peak of her sublimest height. 1822 SCOTT *Pirate* xviii, I have travelled books as well as seas in my day.

**c.** To traverse, cover (a specified distance).

1660 BLOUNT *Boscobel* III. (1680) 31 He passed through more dangers than he travailed miles. 1660 F. BROOKE tr. *Le Blanc's Trav.* 12 Having travelled five and forty dayes travail from Macharib. 1804 W. TENNANT *Indian Recreat.* II. 70 Their number is..greater than that of the miles you travel.

**5.** To cause to journey, to drive or lead from one place to another. Also *fig.*

1598 HAKLUYT *Voy.* I. 479 Their horses are but smal, but very swift and hard, they trauell them vnshod both winter and Sommer. 1607 TOPSELL *Four-f. Beasts* (1658) 242 In ancient time, if horses were to be travelled through snow, they made them boots of sackcloth to wear in their journey. 1784 R. BAGE *Barham Downs* I. 170 His masters..having travelled him through forty pages of Cornelius Nepos, advanced him to the dignity of Cæsar's commentaries. 1864 *Pall Mall G.* 4 Sept. 10/2 Graziers..stated that they prefer travelling their animals on foot distances of fifty, sixty, and seventy miles rather than exposing them to the cruelties exercised on them by the railway companies. 1891 *Melbourne Argus* 9 May 10/6 It would be advisable..not..to travel any stock at present.

**Travellable, travelable** (træ·vĕlăb'l), *a.* [f. TRAVEL *v.* + -ABLE.] Capable of being travelled over; adapted to travelling.

1602 CAREW *Cornwall* I. 53 b, The Westerne [roads] are better travaileable, as lesse subiect to these discommodities. c 1815 REES *Cycl.* s. v. *Road*, A line which is travellable at any season. 1858 BRIGHT *Sp. India* 24 June (1876) 22 More travelable roads than are to be found in the whole of India. 1886 HISSEY *On Box Seat* 125 The Government should keep the old main roads..in decent travellable order.

**Travelled, traveled** (træ·vĕld), *ppl. a.* [f. TRAVEL *v.* + -ED [1].]

**1.** That has travelled, esp. to distant countries; experienced in travel. Also with adv. as *far-travelled.* Also *transf.*

1413 *Pilgr. Sowle* (Caxton 1483) IV. xxxiii. 81 Auncyen trauayled men that ben experte in dedes of armes. 1525 LD. BERNERS *Froiss.* II. clxviii. 469 A well trauelled knight and well knowen. 1613 SHAKS. *Hen. VIII*, I. iii. 19 The reformation of our trauel'd Gallants. 1711 ADDISON *Spect.* No. 45 ¶ 3 One of these Travelled Ladies. 1780 *Mirror* No. 97 ¶ 18 Nothing can be more grotesque than her travelled language. 1821 BYRON *Juan* IV. lxxxviii, You Have got a travell'd air.

**2.** *Geol.* Of blocks, boulders, etc.: Transported to a distance from their original site, as by glacial action; erratic.

1830 LYELL *Princ. Geol.* I. 175 That the position..of a great portion of these travelled materials should now appear most irregular [etc.]. 1833 — *Elem. Geol.* xi. (1874) 146 The multitude of 'travelled' blocks and striated rocks. 1842 SEDGWICK in *Hudson's Guide Lakes* (1843) 196 The travelled bowlders of Shap granite. 1880 A. R. WALLACE *Isl. Life* vii. 106 The phenomenon of travelled or perched blocks is also a common one in all glacier countries.

**b.** Of earth or soil: That is not *in situ*; that has been brought to, or deposited in, the place where it is; made up, artificial. *Sc.*

1802 PLAYFAIR *Illustr. Hutton. Th.* 197, I am not sure whether this earth is travelled or not. 1805 FORSYTH *Beauties Scotl.* I. 16 The whole ground..is formed, not of natural, but of what builders term travelled earth. 1816 SCOTT *Antiq.* xxiii, It's travell'd earth that,..it howks sae eithly. 1839 D. D. BLACK *Hist. Brechin* xi. (1867) 253 Travelled or artificial earth has repeatedly been found.

**3.** Of a road, etc.: Frequented by travellers.

1882 B. HARTE *Flip* ii, It came..with voices in the travelled roads and trails.

**Traveller, traveler** (træ·vĕləɹ). Forms: 4 **travaillour**, 4–6 **travellour**, **-eiler**, etc. (see TRAVEL *v.*); 6– **traveller**, 9 *chiefly U.S.* **traveler**. [agent-noun f. TRAVEL *v.*: see -ER [2], and cf. TRAVAILER.] One who or that which travels.

**1.** A person who is travelling or going from place to place, or along a road or path; one who is on a journey; a wayfarer; a passenger.

c 1375 *Sc. Leg. Saints* xxv. (*Julian*) 20 Sic hope in-to sancte Iulyane þe traualouris þane had tane. c 1475 *Rauf Coilȝear* 82 Fyre, drink, nor meit, Nor nane vther eismentis for trauellouris behufe. 1552 ABP. HAMILTON *Catech.* (1884) 51 Certane travelars will nocht begin thair jornay on the satterday. a 1591 H. SMITH *Serm.* (1637) 327 A traveller passeth from towne unto towne, untill he come to his Inne. 1715–20 POPE *Iliad* XVI. 316 As wasps, provok'd by children in their play,..In swarms the guiltless traveller engage. 1828 WEBSTER, Traveler. 1843 MIALL in *Nonconf.* III. 429 The traveler, however, had a Scotch tongue in his head. 1886 C. E. PASCOE *London of To-day* xx. (ed. 3) 203 The 'Royal Forest Hotel' offers many attractions as a traveller's rest. 1889 'L. CARROLL' *Sylvie & Bruno Concl.* (ed. 2) Pref. 10 As to such words as 'traveler', I hold the correct principle to be, to double the consonant when the accent falls on that syllable: otherwise, to leave it single.

*fig.* 1387 TREVISA *Higden* (Rolls) I. 7 Among oþere noble trauaillours of þe þre pathes. 1631 T. POWELL *Tom All Trades* Title-p., An old Travailer in the sea of Experience. 1804 WORDSW. '*She was a phantom*' iii, A Traveller between life and death.

**b.** = TRAMP *sb.*[1] 4 (now *dial.*); *spec.* in Australia: see quot. 1896. Also, a travelling showman.

1763 *Gentl. Mag.* Sept. 461/2 Mrs. Jewel..was robbed..in the middle of the day by some Irish travellers. 1825 JAMIESON, *Traveller*, a beggar. 1851 MAYHEW *Lond. Labour* I. 243/2 There are many individuals in lodging-houses who are not regular patterers or professional vagrants, being rather, as they term themselves, 'travellers' (or tramps). 1896 *Australasian* 8 Aug. 249/2 (Morris) These travellers lead an aimless life, wandering from station to station, hardly ever asking for and never hoping to get any work. 1904 A. GRIFFITHS *50 Y. Public Service* xxiii. 347 These 'travellers' or 'foreigners' as they were styled locally, were responsible for a great part of the serious crime of the neighbourhood. 1906 *Gentl. Mag.* July 17 In some parts of the Midlands the tramp is generally known as the traveller.

**c.** *transf.* A sermon delivered by a preacher in various places on different occasions. *colloq.*

1892 *Pall Mall G.* 10 May 6/2 This sermon..was what is known amongst students as a 'traveller'. 1904 J. WELLS *Life J. H. Wilson* xxii. 205 His sermon on this subject was one of his 'travellers'.

**2.** *spec.* One who travels abroad; one who journeys or has journeyed through foreign countries or strange places.

1556 ROBINSON tr. *More's Utop.*, *P. Giles to Buslyde* (1895) p. xcvi, The very famous and renowmed trauailer Vlysses. 1600 SHAKS. *A. Y. L.* II. iv. 18 When I was at home I was in a better place, but Trauellers must be content. 1610 — *Temp.* III. iii. 26 Trauellers nere did lye, Though fooles at home condemne 'em. 1667 SPRAT *Hist. R. Soc.* 411 Cæsar ..had Conquer'd more Countries than most Travailers have seen. 1718 LADY M. W. MONTAGU *Let. to C'tess Mar* 10 Mar., We travellers are in very hard circumstances...If we tell anything new, we are laughed at as fabulous. 1834 L. RITCHIE *Wand. by Seine* 94 Some readers will think we are drawing our traveller's bow with a vengeance. 1885 *Encycl. Brit.* XIX. 404/1 Marco Polo (c 1254–1324) the Venetian, the most famous perhaps of all travellers. 1890 *Chambers' Encycl.* VI. 669/1 David Livingstone, missionary and traveller, was born at Blantyre..1813. 1913 MAURICE BARING *Lost Diaries* xvii. 177 The doctor..scoffed at the idea of the sea serpent, which, he said, was a travellers' tale.

**b.** *To play* (also, slang, *to tip*) *the traveller*: 'to tell wonderful stories, to romance' (Grose); hence, with *upon*, to deceive, befool, impose upon: in allusion to the mendacious or incredible character ascribed to 'traveller's tales'.

1739 BP. HERRING in *J. Duncombe's Lett.* (1773) II. 133, I am a little afraid, if I should be particular in my description, you would think I am playing the traveller upon you; but indeed I will stick religiously to truth. 1762 SMOLLETT *Sir L. Greaves* vi, Aha! do'st thou tip me the traveller, my boy? 1796 in *Grose's Dict. Vulg. T.* (ed. 3).

**3.** *spec.* (in full, *commercial traveller*: see COMMERCIAL 6): An agent employed by a commercial firm to travel from place to place showing samples of goods and soliciting custom.

1800 *Hull Advertiser* 19 July 2/4 That capital Inn..many years established as a Travellers' House. 1819 *Hermit in London* II. 186 Common bag-men styled travellers of the house of Messrs. So-and-So. 1830 N. S. WHEATON *Jrnl.* 497 At the Inn..I found a number of commercial travellers. 1851 MAYHEW *Lond. Labour* I. 381/2 Some tallymen who keep shops have 'travellers' in their employ, some of whom have salaries, while others receive a percentage upon all payments. 1894 *Times* 22 Jan. 13/4 Carpet travellers are now all out on their journeys, but are not sending in as many orders as could be wished.

**4. a.** A horse, or other beast of burden or draught, a vehicle, etc., that travels or goes along (fast, well, etc.). Cf. TRAVEL *v.* 3 e. **b.** Applied to birds making a long flight, or migrating.

1660 F. BROOKE tr. *Le Blanc's Trav.* 26 Dalascian Asses ..are good travellers,..they will go thirty miles a day without any wearinesse. 1874 J. W. LONG *Amer. Wild-fowl* i. 21 Frequently in spring continuous shooting may be had at 'travellers',.. i.e., ducks making long flights, often migrating. 1889 *Pall Mall G.* 21 Aug. 2/1 He stands 16 hands high, and looks every inch a traveller.

**5.** A piece of mechanism constructed to 'travel', run, or slide along a support; as a travelling crane, an overhead truck, a movable bridge bearing a crab for lifting and transporting heavy objects from one part to another of an engineering workshop or shed, a travelling or moving platform, etc.

1842 *Civil Eng. & Arch. Jrnl.* V. 359/1 The 'traveller' ..was moved forward from the other end of the dam. 1866 *Cycl. Usef. Arts* I. 2/2 Four pairs of balks.., where travellers are attached for holding the carcasses. **1896** *Allbutt's Syst. Med.* I. 369 The current is then increased by sliding the traveller of the rheostat from its maximum to a lower value. **1898** *Engineering Mag.* XVI. 80 A traveller, or portable platform,..is hoisted out, run across, and raised to the proper level, forming a level gangway..for the transit of passengers and goods from one platform to the other.

**b.** *Naut.* An iron ring or thimble running freely on a rope, rod, or spar; in quot. 1882, a rope on which such a ring slides; also, a rope or rod along which a yard may slide.

**1762–9** FALCONER *Shipwr.* II. 258 Some, travellers up the weather-back-stays send. **1790** *Naval Chron.* XXIV. 50 The hauling rope of the traveller got foul. **1840** R. H. DANA *Bef. Mast* Gloss., *Traveller*, an iron ring, fitted so as to slip up and down a rope. **1882** NARES *Seamanship* (ed. 6) 135 In sending the royal yard down..a weather top-gallant backstay can be used for a traveller. **1883** KELLY in *Harper's Mag.* Aug. 449/2 A jib,..hooked to a ring, called a traveller, ..is hauled out to the bowsprit by a tackle.

**c.** In ring-spinning, a metal ring or loop used to guide the yarn in winding it on the spindle.

**1853** URE *Dict. Arts* II. 832 Messrs. Sharp,..of Manchester, exhibited a throstle spinning frame on the 'ring and traveller' principle. **1877** KNIGHT *Dict. Mech.* 1944/1 As the spindles revolve, the thread passing through the traveler revolves it rapidly, and the horizontal bar ascending and descending alternately winds the yarn regularly upon the spools. **1884** W. S. B. MCLAREN *Spinning* (ed. 2) 167 The traveller..is to wind the yarn on to the bobbin and to affect the drag...By reducing the size of the traveller the drag can be made exceedingly slight.

**d.** *Theatr.* The mechanism for flying fairies, angels, ghosts, etc. above the stage.

**1859** SALA *Gaslight & D.* ii. 21 You may see the wires or 'travellers', used by 'flying fairies'.

**e.** *Angling.* A tackle which permits the bait to travel or move down the swim. Also *attrib.*

**1867** F. FRANCIS *Angling* i. (1880) 49 This kind of fishing, which is called 'traveller' fishing (the float being the traveller). *Ibid.* iv. (1883) 42 Barbel are taken with the traveller in the Nottingham fashion.

**6.** *attrib.* and *Comb.*, as *traveller fishing*, *float* (see 5 e), *monk*, *vocation*; *traveller-like* adj.

**1832** J. P. KENNEDY *Swallow B.* ix, I have not been idle in my traveller-vocation. **1847** W. CORY *Lett. & Jrnls.* (1897) 47, I felt more lively and traveller-like than I had before. **1907** T. C. MIDDLETON *Geog. Knowl. Time Discov. Amer.* 6 Cosmas Indicopleustes—the traveler-monk of Egypt [*c* 500–547].

**b.** Combinations with *traveller's*: **traveller's joy**, a name (given by Gerarde) for the wild shrub *Clematis Vitalba*, from its trailing over and adorning hedges by the wayside; **traveller's palm**, **traveller's tree**, names for certain trees which yield water or sap sought after by travellers to allay thirst, as *Ravenala madagascariensis* (*Urania speciosa*), N.O. *Musaceæ*, a palm-like tree of Madagascar whose hollow leaf-sheaths contain a store of water.

**1597** GERARDE *Herbal* II. cccxi. 739 Decking and adorning waies and hedges, where people trauell, and thereupon I haue named it the Traueilers Ioie. **1678** PHILLIPS (ed. 4), *Travailours-joy*, a sort of Herb called in Latin *Clematis*. **1776** WITHERING *Brit. Plants* (1796) II. 500 Traveller's-joy. Great Wild Climber. Virgin's Bower. Honesty. Hedges and shady places, in calcareous soil. **1885** LADY BRASSEY *The Trades* 177 We also saw [in Venezuela] many specimens of the *travellers' palm, each leaf of which..yields, when cut by the thirsty traveller, from half a pint to a pint of water. **1857** GOSSE *Omphalos* vii. 148 One of the stateliest of plants,—the *Traveller's Tree (*Urania speciosa*). **1883** *Encycl. Brit.* XV. 170/1 The traveller's-tree (*Urania speciosa*), with its graceful crown of plantain-like leaves.. supplying a quantity of pure cool water.

Hence **Tra·velleress** (*rare*), a female traveller.

**1820** KEBLE in Coleridge *Mem.* (1869) I. 99 A little sickliness now and then..on the part of some of my fellow-travelleresses. **1886** *Sat. Rev.* 21 Aug. 253/1 A much more common figure is the merely wrong-headed and cantankerous traveller—and particularly travelleress.

**Travelling, traveling** (træ·vĕliŋ), *vbl. sb.* [f. TRAVEL *v.* + -ING [1].] The action of the verb TRAVEL; journeying.

**1375** BARBOUR *Bruce* II. 283 Sen þai come owt off trawelling. **1382** WYCLIF *Jer.* xxix. 18 Wery trauailing to alle rewmes. *a* **1568** ASCHAM *Scholem.* (Arb.) 72 Disposed to prayse traueling, as a great commendacion. **1669** R. MONTAGU in *Buccleuch MSS.* (Hist. MSS. Comm.) I. 458 There has been so much snow that..there is no travelling for the post. **1738** CHESTERF. *Common Sense* No. 93 ⁋ 10 Travelling is, unquestionably, a very proper part of the education of our youth. **1847** HELPS *Friends in C.* I. vii. 112 Travelling is a great trial of people's ability to live together. **1875** URE *Dict. Arts* II. 538 The gas is said to bear travelling through this pipe very well.

**b.** *attrib.* = of travelling, as *travelling accomplishment*, *charge*, *companion*, *day*, *expenses*, *movement*, *pace*, *pay*, *power*, *propensity*; esp. in sense 'used, or adapted to be used, for or in travelling', or 'carried or taken with one when travelling', as *travelling album*, *arms*, *bag*, *baroscope*, *box*, *cap*, *carriage*, *chariot*, *chest*, *clock*, *commission*, *cup*, *dress*, *equipage*, *kitchen*, *pistol*, *suit*, *trunk*; **travelling-cabinet**, a small chest of drawers secured by outer doors so as to be safely portable on a journey: much used in 17th c. (*Cent. Dict.*); **travelling-carriage**, a strong carriage used for travelling before railways were introduced; **travelling-couvert** [F. *couvert* = COVER *sb.*[1] 7], 'a set of table utensils .. made to pack closely, for use in traveling' (*Cent. Dict.*); **travelling fellowship, scholarship**, a college fellowship or scholarship, given to enable the holder to travel for purposes of study or research; **travelling road**, *Mining* (see quot. 1883).

**1748** RICHARDSON *Clarissa* Wks. 1883 V. 495 A price that is often paid for *travelling accomplishments. **1709** HEARNE *Collect.* 7 Mar. (O.H.S.) II. 174 Whose hand and signet I have in my *traveling Album. **1689** in *Acts Parlt. Scotl.* (1875) XII. 52/1 To make use of horses and ordinary *travelling armes in the countrey. **1862** *Catal. Internat. Exhib., Brit.* II. No. 6932 Dressing cases, *travelling bags, and despatch boxes. **1669** BOYLE *Contn. New Exp.* xxii, The making of portable or *travelling baroscopes. **1835** WILLIS *Pencillings* I. vii. 43 The *travelling-books caution against sleeping in the carriage while passing these marshes. **1726** SWIFT *Gulliver* II. v, Glumdalclitch setting down my *travelling box, I went out of it to walk. **1859** JEPHSON *Brittany* i. 1, [I] pull my *travelling-cap over my eyes. **1798** S. LEE *Canterb. T., Yng. Lady's T.* II. 385 [He] purchased a *travelling-carriage. **1618** in J. Charnock *Hist. Mar. Arch.* (1801) II. 236 For *travelling charges to solicit for money. **1852** DICKENS *Bleak Ho.* xii, The *travelling chariot rolls on to the house. **1902** R. BAGOT *Donna Diana* ix, A *travelling clock on the writing-table. **1726** SWIFT *Gulliver* II. iv, It was always in my *travelling closet. **1813** COL. HAWKER *Diary* (1893) I. 67 The *travelling companion who was bundled into the mail. **1844** LOUISA S. COSTELLO *Béarn & Pyrenees* II. 88 In its snow-cold water I dipped my *travelling-cup. **1856** BONAR *Hymn, 'I heard the voice of Jesus say'* iii, In that light of life I'll walk Till *travelling days are done. **1844** J. T. HEWLETT *Parsons & W.* xxiv, While Madeline was changing her *travelling-dress. **1797** F. REYNOLDS *The Will* III. i, Suppose I try to get our *travelling-expences out of him? **1789** *J. Lewis' Mem. Dk. Glocester* 87 *note*, [Dr. Radcliffe] also founded two *travelling Fellowships for young Physicians. **1782** J. ADAMS *Diary* 26 July, I had on my *travelling gloves. **1825** J. NICHOLSON *Operat. Mechanic* 423 The rack..for regulating the *travelling-movement of the spinning or any other machine, on a rope-walk. **1815** *Chron.* in *Ann. Reg.* 57 Going over Uxbridge-common, at a regular *travelling pace. **1692** LUTTRELL *Brief Rel.* (1857) II. 401 On Friday next the persons belonging to the train for the descent enter into *travailing pay. **1782** MISS BURNEY *Cecilia* x. ii, My *travelling pistols were already charged. **1875** URE *Dict. Arts* II. 538 As to storage and *travelling power, Mr. Hastings..reports favourably. **1883** GRESLEY *Gloss. Coal-mining*, **Travelling road*, an underground passage..used expressly..for men to travel along to and from their working places. **1911** *Act 1 & 2 Geo. V*, c. 50 § 49 A person shall not ..travel or work in any travelling road or working place which is not so made secure. **1867** AUG. J. E. WILSON *Vashti* xxvii, Elsie was waiting to clothe me in my *travelling-suit. **1779** *Mirror* No. 17 ⁋ 13 A draw-bridge, which..exactly resembled the lid of a *travelling-trunk.

**Tra·velling, traveling,** *ppl. a.* [f. as prec. + -ING [2].] That travels, or goes from place to place; journeying, itinerant; moving; also *fig.*

**1375** BARBOUR *Bruce* VII. 241 'A travalland man, dame', said he, 'þat traualys heir throu þe cuntre'. *c* **1420** *Anturs of Arth.* li, These ij traueling men truly vppe thay take. **1495** *Act 11 Hen. VII*, c. 2 § 2 None other calling himself a Souldeour Shipman or travelyngman. **1605** SHAKS. *Macb.* II. iv. 7 By th' Clock 'tis Day, And yet darke Night strangles the trauailing Lampe. **1619–20** *Archdeaconry of Essex Minutes* lf. 241 (MS.) A travelinge or Wayfaringe woman. **1715** HEARNE *Collect.* (O. H. S.) V. 80 The two travelling Physitians, that are to be Dr. Radcliffe's Fellows of University College. **1827** MACKENZIE *Hist. Newcastle* II. 723 *note*, Fire-engines,..there is a travelling tank attached. **1837** H. EARLE in *Rep. Sel. Comm. Railw. Commun.* 60 For the purpose of having a travelling post-office, that they could sort the letters as they went on. **1867** F. FRANCIS *Angling* i. (1883) 12 Stream fishing..with a travelling or tripping bait, with or without a float. **1890** 'R. BOLDREWOOD' *Col. Reformer* (1891) 254 Great hordes of travelling sheep laid waste a portion of the run.

**b.** *spec.* of a Methodist preacher: see TRAVEL *v.* 2 c.

**1789** WESLEY *Wks.* (1872) IV. 464, I had much satisfaction in this Conference;..conversing with between forty and fifty travelling Preachers. **1825** *Mem. Isab. Wilson* 169 She came to reside..under the same roof as the Travelling Preachers near Wetherby.

**c.** Of plants: Creeping, or spreading by horizontal growth of the rootstock.

**1842** LOUDON *Suburban Hort.* 569 A new plantation may be made every six or seven years, or oftener,..if their travelling roots should grow out of bounds. **1885** *Pall Mall G.* 11 Feb. 5/1 To the number of curious plants,..a new specimen has lately been added which is described as the travelling plant. It is said to be of the lily of the valley species ..and has a root formed of knots, by which it annually advances about an inch..from the place where the plant was first rooted.

**d.** *Mech.* Constructed to 'travel' or move in a fixed course, either in a circuit or to and fro, as a crane, a platform or side-walk, etc.

**1834–47** J. S. MACAULAY *Field Fortif.* (1851) 70 To permit of a gun on a travelling carriage..being fired over the parapet. **1835** URE *Philos. Manuf.* 216 A novel mechanism adapted to the travelling-comb called the gill. **1862** *Catal. Internat. Exhib.* II. x. 21 Travelling Crane, the traversing motion being worked from the crab. **1873** *Iron* 5 July 23/3 Spier's Travelling Sidewalk. **1900** *Engineering Mag.* XIX. 701 At the Paris *Exposition*...The traveling sidewalk..is here carried out on a far larger scale than ever before attempted...It forms a continuous connection between the main portions of the exposition.

**Traventer**: see TRANTER.

**Traversable** (træ·vəɹsăb'l), *a.* [f. TRAVERSE *v.* + -ABLE.]

**1.** Capable of being traversed or crossed.

*a* **1656** USSHER *Ann.* vi. (1658) 218 Darius commanded it to be made all level, that it might be made the more traverseable for his horse. **1768** TUCKER *Lt. Nat.* (1834) I. 8 The land of philosophy..partly..traversable only by the speculative. **1812** *Examiner* 31 Aug. 557/2 Every quarter of the traversible globe. **1859** TENNENT *Ceylon* II. VII. ii. 121 Roads ..open and traversable at all seasons.

**2.** *Law.* Capable of being traversed or formally denied.

**1534** *Star Chamb. Cases* (Selden) II. 323 Eny other thyng, being materyall or trauersable, and not before aunswered confessed, avoyded, or trauersed, is true. **1588** W. LAMBARDE *Eiren.* IV. v. (1602) 473 It neither contained the place where, nor the person to whome the lether was sold, both which be materiall and trauersable. **1620** J. WILKINSON *Courts Leet* 110 A presentment made by fewer than by xii is traversable. **1726** AYLIFFE *Parergon* 70 The Bishops Certificate..is not Peremptory but Traversable. **1884** SIR H. COTTON in *Law Times Rep.* LI. 535/2 Returns such as this..have not generally been traversed..but it does not..follow that they are not traversable.

**3.** Capable of being traced continuously, as a geometrical figure.

**1905** J. C. WILSON *Traversing Geometr. Figures* I. § 29. 43 Resolution of a figure into a minimum of figures traversable in one traverse.

†**Traversant**, *a. Obs. rare.* [a. F. *traversant*, pr. pple. of *traverser* to cross: see -ANT.] Thwarting; unfavourable, inauspicious; = next.

14.. *MS. Cantab. Ff. I.* 6 lf. 137 (Halliw.) Thou hast a dominacioun traversaunt, Wythowte numbre doyst thou greeve.

**Traversary** (træ·vəɹsări), *a. Astrol.* [By-form of TRANSVERSARY, after L. *trāversus* = *transversus.*] Lying across, crossing; unfavourable, inauspicious.

**1851** K. H. DIGBY *Compitum* V. 2 Where men enter into the orbit which astrologers style a traversary planet. **1871** — *Ouranogaia* XII. 3 But all the earth feels not its dulcet ray. For traversary planets round us roll.

**Traverse** (træ·vəɹs), *sb.* Forms: 3–7 **trauers**, 4–8 **travers**, (4, 6 **trau-, traverce**, 5 **traverss**, 5–6 **trau-, travarse**), 5–7 **trauerse**, 5– **traverse.** Also *β.* 5 **travas, -vass**, 5–6 **trevass**, 5–7 **trauas**; 5 **trauest, trevesse**, 5–6 **traves**, 5–8 **treves**, 6 **traues**, 6–7 **travess, traveis, trau-, travesse**; 5–7 **travis**, 6 **trevis, trevys**, 6–7 **trauyce, traviss**, 6–8 **travice**, 7 **trauis, -ise.** See also TRAVIS, TREVIS. [Represents two OF. sbs., *travers* masc. (11th c.), and *traverse* fem. (12th c.), which, through the loss or misuse of final *e*, have fallen together in Eng. F. *travers* (dial. *travais*, *travars*, *travé*, in Prov. *travers*, Cat. *traves*, Pg. *traves* = It. *traverso*) is :—pop.L. *trāversum*, for L. *transversum*, neuter of *transversus*, TRANSVERSE *a.* F. *traverse* (Prov. *traversa*, Cat., Pg. *travessa*, It. *traversa*) is, according to Hatz.-Darm., chiefly from *traverser* TRAVERSE *v.*, but in some uses it appears to represent a late L. *trāversa* sb. fem. from pa. pple. of *transvertĕre* to TRANSVERT. From the falling together of these words under the current form *traverse*, and the rise in English of many new senses, it is not possible to distinguish the senses which belong etymologically to F. *travers* from those which belong to F. *traverse.*]

**I.** The action of TRAVERSE *v.* in a local sense.

**1.** The act of passing through a gate, or crossing a river, bridge, or other place forming a boundary (*obs.*): represented in quots. only by the sense, A toll paid on crossing the bounding-line of a town or lordship; = PASSAGE 5. *Obs.* exc. *Hist.*

Also called *toll traverse*: see TOLL *sb.*[1] 2 h.

[**1284** *Chanc. Inq. P. M. Edw. I* 40/6 (Norf.) (P. R. O.) De quadam consuetudine que vocatur travers et valet per annum 3*s.* **1292** BRITTON I. xx. § 1 Soit ausi enquis, quels del counté cleyment .. de aver lestage .. ou travers, ou toluen. [*Note, Traverse*, a toll paid for passing through the limits of a town or lordship.] **1347** *Inq. P. M. Edw. III*, File 86 (Norfolk Inq.) Est apud Brandone quedam custuma vocata 'travers' que est parcella manerii de Thefford.] **1598** KITCHIN *Courts Leet* (1675) 208 To have toll Travers is good. **1636, 1670** [see TOLL *sb.*[1] 2 h]. **1754** T. GARDNER *Hist. Dunwich*, etc. 134 *note*, Robert FitzRogers had customary Travers for Passage through Blythburgh and Walberswick. **1852** *Hull Shipping Dues Act* 2209 Certain tolls called..Toll Traverse. **1911** [see TOLL *sb.*[1] 2 h].

**2.** The action of traversing, passing across, or going through (a region, etc.); passage, crossing: orig. from side to side, but soon also from end to end, or in any course. Also *fig.* [= OF. *travers*, F. *traverse.*]

**1599** MARSTON *Sco. Villanie* II. vi. 199 Thinkst thou that I ..will once vouchsafe to trip A Pauins traverse? **1642** ROGERS *Naaman* 89 He led them a traverse of fourty yeares. **1658** PHILLIPS, Advt., Some Critticks perhaps will expect the names of Authours in the traverse of this Worke to be often set down. **1725** DE FOE *Voy. round World* (1840) 314 They were one-and-twenty days in this traverse. **1806** PIKE *Sources Mississ.* (1810) 67 In making a traverse of the lake, some of my men had their ears, some their noses, and their chins frozen. **1808** *Ibid.* II. 189, I determined to attempt the traverse of the mountain. **1902** *Speaker* 2 Aug. 485/1 He completed his traverse of Persia from north to south. **1904** P. FOUNTAIN *Gt. North-West* vii. 61 When a bay or inlet is come to, the crew [of the canoe]..like to strike straight across from headland to headland. In the technical language of the voyageurs this is termed making a traverse. **1907** G. D. ABRAHAM *Complete Mountaineer* 476 *Traverse*...Also used to define a climb up one side of a peak and down the other.

**3.** *Surveying.* A single line of survey carried across a region or through a narrow strip of country, by measuring the lengths and azimuths of a connected series of straight lines; used either where there is no general trigonometrical survey, or in filling up the details of one. Also, a tract of country so surveyed.

**1881** GEIKIE in *Nature* 6 Jan. 224/2 In about three months the traverses for the construction of the map were completed. *Ibid.* 225/1 The geological structure of different traverses of the country. **1887** *Encycl. Brit.* XXII. 706/1 In Indian Survey.. the traverses are executed in minor circuits following the periphery of each village and in major circuits comprising groups of several villages. **1900** H. M. WILSON *Topogr. Survey.* x. 195 Traverses made in connection with topographic mapping are of several degrees of accuracy.

**4.** The traversing or continuous tracing of a geometrical figure or part of one: see TRAVERSE *v.* 2 b.

**1905** J. C. WILSON *Traversing Geometr. Figures* I. § 2. 6 A traverse must exhaust the point at which it ends: for if any path from it were left untraversed, the traverse would leave the point by the path, and so it would not be the point at which the traverse ends. *Ibid.* § 9. 16 If the first traverse is a single path, that will be the characteristic of the whole traverse chosen.

†**5.** *Fencing.* The action or an act of traversing: see TRAVERSE *v.* 5, 15. Also *fig. Obs.*

**1547** HOOPER *Declar. Christ* xii. L vij, Marke the trauyce and pley betwene the law of God, and the conscience of Paule. **1599** G. SILVER *Paradoxes Defence* 61–2 This Cob was a great quareller...and..was sure by the cunning of his Trauerse, not to be hurt by anie man: for at anie time finding himselfe ouermatched would suddenly turne his backe and runne away...And this.. was called Cobs Trauerse. **1599** MARSTON *Sco. Villanie* III. ii. 225 Each gallant he doth meete He fronts him with a trauerse in the streete. **1706** FARQUHAR *Recruit. Officer* III. ii, [Direction] Plume and Brazen fight a traverse or two about the stage.

**6.** *Mountaineering.* An act of traversing or making one's way in a horizontal direction across the face of a mountain or rock (see TRAVERSE *v.* 21); also *concr.* a place where a traverse is made.

**1893** C. WILSON *Mountaineering* vi. 88 Short traverses are often difficult; you ascend a gully..as far as possible; and, when progress by that avenue is.. barred, a traverse is undertaken to the left or the right. *Ibid.* 90 We eventually accomplished the ascent by a long traverse which led round a corner and on to broken rocks. **1897** O. G. JONES *Rock-climbing* 113 Three o'clock found us still working westwards on the traverse. **1900** DENT *Mountaineering* 438 *Traverse*, sometimes used substantively to denote a surface of rock, snow, or ice that has to be crossed horizontally.

**II.** Senses denoting (or connected with) non-physical action (opposition, thwarting, or the like).

**7.** Something that crosses, thwarts, or obstructs; opposition; an obstacle, impediment; a trouble, vexation; a mishap; misfortune, adversity; *pl.* crosses. Now *rare.* [OF. *travers.*]

**1390** GOWER *Conf.* III. 384 His nature is so divers, That it hath evere som travers Or of to moche or of to lite. **1530** LYNDESAY *Test. Papyngo* 402 Quhate trauers, troubyll, and calamitie Haith bene in courte within thir houndreth ȝeris! **1654** H. L'ESTRANGE *Chas. I* (1655) 2 In the very nick of time (a strange traverse of Providence) dyes Pope Gregory, whose death put all to a stand. **1670** COTTON *Espernon* I. I. 34 He could not overcome those traverses, and difficulties, that his Majesties enemies still strew'd in his way. **1703** PENN in *Pa. Hist. Soc. Mem.* IX. 252 It is my lot to meet with traverses and disappointments. **1814** WORDSW. *Excursion* III. ad fin., Like traverses and toils Must he again encounter. **1900** MORLEY *Cromwell* iii. 48 In days of fierce duress, of endless traverses and toils.

**8.** *Law.* The traversing or formal denial in pleading of some matter of fact alleged by the other side; also, a plea consisting of this; also, ? a case in which a traverse is pleaded.

**1429** in *Calr. Doc. rel. Scotl.* (1888) 405 For declaracion of traverss made or to be made be assise. **1459** *Rolls of Parlt.* V. 371/1 Jugement [was] yeven for the Kyng, in the said traverse. **1542–3** *Act* 34 & 35 *Hen. VIII*, c. 5 § 15 Vntill the saide office be lawfully vndone by trauers or otherwyse. **1647** N. BACON *Disc. Govt. Eng.* I. xxiii. (1739) 41 That King put a Judge to death, for sentencing one to suffer death upon the Coroner's record, without allowing the Delinquent liberty of Traverse. **1780** BURKE *Sp. Econ. Reform* Wks. III. 247 His plea or traverse may be allowed as an answer to a charge, when a charge is made. **1824** H. J. STEPHEN *Pleading* 215 It is laid down as a rule that a traverse must not be taken upon matter of law. **1911** ODGERS *Comm. Law Eng.* v. xvii. II. 1214 The contradiction in terms of an allegation in the preceding pleading is technically known as a 'traverse'.

*transf.* **1575** LANEHAM *Let.* (1871) 17 If the dog in pleadyng woold pluk the bear by the throte, the bear with trauers woould claw him again by the skalp. *a* **1662** HEYLIN *Laud* II. 261 There was no Traverse to be made to this Dilemma. **1877** MORLEY *Crit. Misc.* Ser. II. 293 It is enough to meet them by a direct traverse, throwing the burden of proof upon them.

†**9.** A dispute, controversy. *At, in traverse*: in debate, in dispute. *Obs.*

*c* **1410** LYDG. *Life our Lady* in *MS. Soc. Antiq.* 134 lf. 18 (Halliw.) Whanne they were at travers of thise thre, Everiche holdynge his opinioun. *c* **1448** in *Rec. City Norwich* (1906) 345 The pryour of Norwich that tyme being in travers with the said meir and comonalte. *c* **1490** *Paston Lett.* III. 366 The matier depending in travers bitwixt the saide parties. **1524** in J. H. Glover *Kingsthorpiana* (1883) 64 The forseid land and grownds now in traves. **1553** GRIMALDE *Cicero's Offices* I. (1558) 27 If there bee a trauers in lawe: you shall rather defende your kinsman and frende than your neighbour. **1611** SPEED *Hist. Gt. Brit.* IX. xxiv. § 279 The LL. Generals.. would heare of no composition but for the Merchants ships onely, which whilest it was in trauise to and fro [etc.]. **1651** HOWELL *Venice* 2 These traverses twixt Saint Peter and Saint Mark could never shake Venice in the main of the Roman Religion.

†**10.** ? = PASSAGE *sb.* 13 c. *Obs.*

**1599** DALLAM in *Early Voy. Levant* (Hakl. Soc.) 25 The firste day of maye we saw there greatest traverses or sportes that they have in all the yeare. **1604** E. G[RIMSTONE] *D'Acosta's Hist. Indies* IV. xxxix. 315 The fooleries, tricks, traverses, and pleasant sportes they make when they are taught. **1643** J. M. *Soveraigne Salve* 11 The malignant traverses of our Calumniators.

†**b.** ? A passage from a discourse or writing. *Obs.*

**1608** PANKE *Fall of Babel* 56 He must needes meane by their own trauises out of him that Christ both spake and meant the bread when he said this is my body.

**III.** Senses denoting way across, crossing, way, path, track, course.

**11.** A passage by which one may traverse or cross; a way, pass; a crossing.

*a* **1678** MARVELL *Poems, Appleton Ho.* 17 The field In whose new traverse seemeth wrought A camp of battle newly fought. **1773** MRS. GRANT *Lett. fr. Mount.* (1807) I. viii. 66, I have got cold in these meadowy traverses. **1805** PIKE *Sources Mississ.* (1810) 22 The storm..burst upon us, in the Traverse, while making to Point de Sable. **1892** W. PIKE *North. Canada* 25 We put out..to paddle across the open traverse to the first of a group of islands.

**b.** *Arch.* (See quot.)

**1842–76** GWILT *Encycl. Archit.* Gloss., *Traverse*, a gallery or loft of communication in a church or other large building.

**12.** *Naut.* The zigzag track of a vessel sailing against the wind; with *a* and *pl.*, each of the runs made by a ship in tacking.

**1594** J. DAVIS *Seaman's Secr.* (1607) 46 A Travers is the varietie of the ships motion vpon euery alteration of Corses. **1644** MANWAYRING *Sea-Mans Dict.* 109 We call the way of the Ship (in respect of the points whereon we saile, and the Angles which the Ship makes in going to, and againe) the travers of the Ship. **1676** WOOD *Jrnl.* in *Acc. Sev. Late Voy.* I. (1694) 156 Courses *per* Traverse; true Course Protracted, with all impediments allowed, is North 43 d. **1762** *Gentl. Mag.* Mar. 99/1 This distance..may be increased tenfold by traverses which vessels must..make on such occasions. **1834** *Nat. Philos.* III. *Navig.* I. ii. § 17 (Usef. Knowl. Soc.) She will be found one mile to the west of that place at the end of the traverse, for the total amount of westings exceeds the eastings by one mile.

*β.* **1669** STURMY *Mariner's Mag.* II. 46 Agreeing so well with his Travisses at Sea. *Ibid.* II. v. 64 [see *traverse-scale*].

**b.** = *traverse-board*: see 23. ? *Obs.*

**1627** CAPT. SMITH *Seaman's Gram.* ii. 11 Vpon the Bittacle is also the Trauas, which is a little round boord full of holes ..vpon which..they keepe an account, how many glasses they steare vpon euery point.

**c.** *transf.* Each lap, length, or *pli* of a zigzag ascending road.

**1731** *Gentl. Mag.* Nov. 488/1 The Descent..is now firm, smooth and gradual, by 17 Traverses. **1775** JOHNSON *West. Islands* Wks. X. 353 We mounted by a military road cut in traverses.

**IV.** Concrete senses denoting something placed or extending across.

In these the popular forms *traves, -is*, etc., were very frequent: cf. TRAVIS, TREVIS.

**13.** A curtain or screen placed crosswise, or drawn across a room, hall, or theatre; also, a partition of wood, a screen of lattice-work, or the like. *Obs.* exc. *Hist.*

*c* **1374** CHAUCER *Troylus* III. 625 (674) Here after soone The voyde dronke, and trauers [*v. r.* traueres] drawe anoon. *c* **1386** — *Merch. T.* 573 Men drynken and the trauers [*v. r.* trauys] drawe anon. **1474** in *Househ. Ord.* (1790) 28 We will that our sayd sonne in his chamber and for all nighte lyverye to be sette, the traverse drawne anone upon eight of the clocke. **1589** PUTTENHAM *Eng. Poesie* I. xvii. (Arb.) 51 The floore..had in it sundrie little diuisions by curteins as trauerses to serue for seueral roomes where they might.. change their garments. **1605** B. JONSON *Volpone* v. iii. [Stage direct.] Volpone peeps from behinde a trauerse. **1700** FLOYER *Hot & Cold Bath.* I. iii. 55 Parted in the middle by a Travers of Wood. **1870** ROCK *Text. Fabr.* Introd. vii. 143 At top of and all along the travers ran the minstrel-gallery.

*β.* **1423** JAS. I *Kingis Q.* lxxxii, Ryght ouerthwert the chamber was there drawe A trevesse thin and quhite. *c* **1440** *Promp. Parv.* 499/2 Trauas, *transversum.* **1480** *Wardr. Acc. Edw. IV* (1830) 126 For making of ij travasses of grene sarsinett..iij s. **1488** *Acc. Ld. High Treas. Scot.* I. 100 For vij elne of tartar to a trevass. **1503** *Ibid.* II. 203 For xvj elne taffeti to be ane trevis to the Kingis bed. **1547** *Test. Ebor.* (Surtees) VI. 263 One traves for hir chamber of grene sarcenett and reide. **1613** BEAUMONT *Masque Inner T.* Argt., The fabricke was a mountaine with two descents, and severed with two travesses.

**b.** *fig.*

**1609** DANIEL *Civ. Wars* VIII. lxxxviii, He drawes a Trauerse 'twixt his greeuances. **1655** FULLER *Ornithol.* (1867) 261 It is the hanging of such Curtains and Traverses before our Deeds which keep up our Reputation.

**14.** A small compartment shut off or enclosed by a curtain or screen in a church, house, etc.; a closet. *arch.*

**1494** FABYAN *Chron.* VII. 473 Vpon a Saterdaye, the .xiiii. daye of the moneth of Octobre, both kynges beynge in .ii. trauersys, and in one chapell at Caleys, a masse was said before them. **1527** in Fiddes *Wolsey* (1726) II. 201 To the high alter wheare on the south side was ordeyned a goodlie travers for my Lord Cardinal. **1602** SEGAR *Hon. Mil. & Civ.* IV. xxii. 240 All Viscountesses may haue their gownes borne vp by a man...Also they may haue a Trauerse in their owne houses. **1633** DELL in *Ceremon. Coronat. Jas. I* (1685) 15 A little Traverse is to be made on the South side of the Altar .., for the King to..disrobe himself. **1902** *Westm. Gaz.* 11 Aug. 5/2 The King [Edward VII] went into his traverse and was there disrobed of his Imperial Mantle or Robe of State. *Ibid.*, In St. Edward's Chapel 'traverses', or dressing-rooms, had been curtained off for the use of the King and Queen.

*β.* **1526** *St. Papers Hen. VIII*, I. 172 Aftyr his first Masse was done, I wente unto hym, withyn his travesse. **1536** WRIOTHESLEY *Chron.* (Camden) I. 46 The King..then went into the traves that was made for him at the alters end. **1559** *Fabyan's Chron.* an. 1554. 562*/2 She [Q. Mary] went into a traueis [STRYPE traverse] made on the right side, and he into an other on the left side. **1593** in Hardman *Prayer-Bk.* (1890) 71 Her Majestie [Q. Elizabeth] entered her travess. **1605** *Ibid.* 157 Travase.

†**15.** A bar or barrier across anything; in quot. 1759 = BAR *sb.*[1] 15. *Obs.*

**1575** CHURCHYARD *Chippes* (1817) 152 With baskets big, and things to serue the turne A crosse the streete, a trauers made there was. **1654** H. L'ESTRANGE *Chas. I* (1655) 137 The Communion Table..to be placed at the East end,.. with..a woodden traverse of railes before it, to keep Profanation off. **1700** FLOYER *Hot & Cold Bath.* I. iii. (1706) 58 [Baptisteries] were parted in the middle by a Travers of Wood. **1759** ADM. HOLMES in *Naval Chron.* July (1810) XXIV. 117 The Dublin and Medway got over the traverse [in the River St. Lawrence].

**16.** *Fortif.* A barrier or barricade thrown across an approach, the line of fire, etc. as a defence; *spec.* (*pl.*) parapets of earth raised at intervals across the terreplein of a rampart or the covered way of a fortress, to prevent its being enfiladed. [= OF. *traverse.*]

**1599** HAKLUYT *Voy.* II. 81 The captaine caused to make the traverses upon the wall whereas the breach was. **1602** LD. MOUNTJOY *Let.* in Moryson *Itin.* (1617) II. 213 The enemy having raised from mountaine to mountaine, from wood to wood, and from bogge to bogge long Traverses, with huge and high Flanckers of great stones, mingled with Turffe. **1700** RYCAUT *Hist. Turks* III. 112 The Defendants ..sprang a Mine under the Ruins of the Ravelin; which threw so much Earth into the Traverses of the Enemy, as buried many of their Labourers. **1882** E. O'DONOVAN *Merv Oasis* II. xxxiii. 68 Opposite each gate was a large traverse, to protect it from artillery fire.

*β.* **1598** BARRET *Theor. Warres* v. i. 125 The parts of a Bulwarke are the Trauesses or flankers. **1622** F. MARKHAM *Bk. War* IV. iii. 132 Lading and carrying the earth in barrels, baskets, and wheele barrows, by which are framed the Trauesses or flankers of the Bulwarke.

**17.** A natural structure forming a transverse partition, as the diaphragm; anything lying transversely or across. [= F. *traverse.*]

**1604** T. WRIGHT *Passions* VI. 311 No man..can satisfie those demaunds..whether it [the Emmet] hath a Lyver, or no..whether a traverse or midriffe. **1657** THORNLEY tr. *Longus' Daphnis & Chloe* 136 His resolution was to imagine pleasure on this side the traverse.

**18.** Anything laid or fixed athwart or across; a cross-piece; a cross-beam in a timber roof; a transom; the transverse member in a cross; each of the rungs of a ladder (in quot. *fig.*), etc. [= F. *traverse.*]

**1708** J. CHAMBERLAYNE *St. Gt. Brit.* II. III. x. (1737) 429 The Traverse or Cross of the Sword being of Silver over Gilt, is in Length seventeen Inches and a Half. **1727–41** CHAMBERS *Cycl.*, *Traverse* is particularly used for a piece of wood or iron placed transversely, to strengthen and fortify another: such are those used in gates, windows, etc. **1730** A. GORDON *Maffei's Amphith.* 295 Two round Holes in the Stone of the Threshold,..and two others correspondent with them, in the Traverse above. **1766** ENTICK *London* IV. 197 Upon that ball was a cross, 15 feet high, whose travers measured six feet. **1793** BURKE *Conduct Minority* Wks. VII. 285 To make every man..cautious how he makes himself one of the traverses of a ladder, to help such a man ..to climb up to the highest authority. **1838** *Civil Eng. & Arch. Jrnl.* I. 198/1 The cast iron rail can be fixed to the blocks or bearers with the patent vertical ties, chairs, and traverses, or in any of the usual ways.

**19.** *Card-making.* A transverse section of a cardboard.

**1837** WHITTOCK, etc. *Bk. Trades* (1842) 100 The boards are first cut into slips, or, as they are termed, traverses, containing five cards each.

†**20.** The reverse side of a coin or medal. *Obs.*

**1622** PEACHAM *Compl. Gent.* xii. (1634) 119 *As.*.was worth a halfe-penny farthing. And it is discerned by this figure I. with the head or prowe of a Ship on the traverse; and Janus bifrons on the forepart.

¶**21.** *Her.* Stated to denote a bearing resembling a pile or a chevron turned sideways.

(But app. an error due to mistaking TRAVERSE *a.* 2, 2 b, for a sb.; Guillim, cited for this use, has the word only as adj.)

*c* **1828** BERRY *Encycl. Her.* I. Gloss., *Traverse*, sometimes termed a *doublet*, and, in French, *embrassé droit*, is a bearing, according to Guillim, resembling the cheveron, which issues from two angles of one side of the escocheon, and meets in a point about the middle of the other side.

**V.** Phrases and Combinations.

†**22.** Phrases. **a.** *At, in, on travers, traverse*, crossways, sideways, transversely; in flank; with a side glance, askance. *Obs.* (Cf. A-TRAVERS.) [OF. *à, en travers.*] See also 9.

*c* **1330** R. BRUNNE *Chron. Wace* (Rolls) 13394 Þe seriauntz & þe archers...were set..To kepe þe Romayns at trauers. *c* **1450** *Merlin* 262 He turned the heed in trauers, and made semblant as he hadde hym not herde. *Ibid.* 425 He loked proudly on trauerse. **1586** FERNE *Blaz. Gentrie* 29 Great peeces of tymber or logges of woode..set in trauerse ouer some passage, bridge or gate. **1659** Leak *Waterwks.* 14 They must be soldered a travers above the great Pipes. **1678** Moxon *Mech. Exerc.* iv. 66 Joyners work as well upon the Traverse..as with the Grain of the wood.

†**b.** *Through the travers*, lit. rendering of F. *par le travers*, through the transverse extent, through the breadth, across. *Obs.*

*c* **1489** Caxton *Sonnes of Aymon* xxviii. 576 [He] went ..thrugh the travers of the wodes wel the space of viii dayes.

**23.** *attrib.* and *Comb.* (sometimes of the verb-stem), as *traverse-rag* (see 13), *-sailing* (see 12); **traverse-board, travis-board**, *Naut.* a circular board marked with the points of the compass, and having holes and pegs by which to indicate the course of the ship (cf. 12); **traverse-book, travis-book**, a log-book; **traverse-circle**, a circular or segmental track on which a gun-carriage is turned to point the gun in any required direction; **traverse-drill**, a drill in which the boring tool has at the required depth a lateral motion; also, a drill in which the drill-stock is adjustable laterally on the bed; **traverse jury**, a jury empanelled to adjudicate on an appeal from another jury: see sense 8 and Traverse *v.* 12; **traverse line**, a line in a traverse-survey; **traverse-man**, one who makes the traverses (sense 3) in a topographical survey; **traverse-map**, a rough map, the main points on which have been determined by traversing: see Traverse *v.* 7; †**traverse-nail**, a kind or size of nail used in making partitions; **traverse-point**, the highest point of a mountain-pass; **traverse-saw**: see quot.; **traverse-scale, travis-**: see quot.; **traverse-survey**, a survey made for the purpose of locating the features of a country along a narrow strip, as for a canal, a railway, or a boundary line, as distinct from a general trigonometrical survey of the whole country; **traverse-warp machine**, a bobbin-net machine in which the warp traverses instead of the carriages.

*a* **1625** *Nomenclator Navalis* (MS. Harl. 2301), *Trauers bord is a board which they keepe in the Steeridg hauing the 32 pointes of the Compasse marked in it with little holes on every pointe like a Noddy-bord. **1626** Capt. Smith *Accid. Yng. Seamen* 11 The trauas boord. **1704** J. Harris *Lex. Techn.* I, *Traverse-Board*..upon it, by moving of a little Peg from Hole to Hole, the Steers-man keeps an account how many Glasses (that is, half Hours) the Ship Steers upon any Point. **1867** Smyth *Sailor's Word-bk.*, *Traverse-board*. *a* **1679** Sir J. Moore *Syst. Math.* (1681) I. 271 This account ruff taken off the Log-board, ought to be entred into a Book called a *Traverse Book or Log Book. **1727–41** Chambers *Cycl.* s.v. *Log*, They are entered into the log-book, or traverse-book, ruled and columned just as the log-board is. **1877** Knight *Dict. Mech.*, **Traverse-circle*, ..a circular track on which the chassis traverse-wheels of a barbette carriage, mounted with a center or rear pintle, run while the gun is being pointed. **1864** Webster, **Traverse-drill*, 1. a machine-tool for feeding a drill into the work. (*Local U.S.*) 2. A cotter-drill. (*Eng.*) **1877** Knight *Dict. Mech.*, *Traverse-drill*. **1823** *Rep. Sel. Comm. Sewers Metrop.* 15 We have never had any *traverse juries in the Tower Hamlets sewers within my recollection. **1900** H. M. Wilson *Topogr. Survey.* x. 195 *Traverse lines may be run in conjunction with a trigonometric survey to fill in the details. *Ibid.* 202 The *traverseman having set up and oriented his plane table. **1901** *Year-bk. U.S. Dept. Agric.* 121 When there are [no] accurate county maps it is almost impossible to carry on the soil survey except through the co-operation of State institutions which will undertake to make a *traverse map. *c* **1350** in Hope *Windsor Castle* (1913) 165 In xxx$^{\text{mi}}$ *Traversnail emptis pro parietibus camerarum canonicorum. **1358–60** *Ibid.* 216 In..lx mill. clavorum vocatorum travers. **1886** Ruskin *Præterita* I. ix. 304 This main pass of Jura..reaches its *traverse-point very nearly under the highest summit of that part of the chain. **1700** Congreve *Way of World* v. i, Dining behind a *traverse rag in a shop no bigger than a bird-cage. **1787** A. Clarke in *Life* (1840) App. 154 After much *traverse sailing, occasioned by the wind being almost directly opposite, we came to anchor. **1843** *Penny Cycl.* XXV. 169/2 Traverse sailing..is merely the sailing on different points of the compass, for short distances, in succession. **1877** Knight *Dict. Mech.*, **Traverse-saw*, a cross-cutting saw which moves on ways across the piece. **1669** Sturmy *Mariner's Mag.* ii. 46 A Portable most useful *Travis-Scale. *Ibid.* ii. v. 64 The Travis-Scale... An Instrument the most easie, ready, and necessary..for the working of Travises, and correcting your dead Reckoning. **1896** Markham in *Geog. Jrnl.* VII. 187 [He] set out to explore the river Madre de Dios...He was supplied with compass, sextant, and chronometer, and corrected his *traverse-survey by daily observations of the sun. **1839** Ure *Dict. Arts*, etc. 733 There are six different systems of bobbin-net machines. 1. Heathcoak's patent machine. 2. Brown's *traverse warp [etc.].

**Traverse** (træ·vəɹs), *a. rare.* Also 5, 7 **travers**, 7 **treverse**. [a. OF. *travers* (also in Cotgr. 1611):—late pop.L. and med.L. *trāversus* :—L. *transversus*: see Transverse *a.*]

**1.** Lying, passing, or extending across; cross, transverse.

**1426** Lydg. *De Guil. Pilgr.* 6999 Ouer my shuldere she yt [the scrip] caste And be-gan to bookele yt faste I travers wyse. **1598** Stow *Surv.* xl. (1603) 410 The ouersight and profites of a Crosse ferrie, or trauerse ferrie ouer the Thames ..before that any bridge was builded. **1625** Purchas *Pilgrims* II. vii. vi. 1122 The treverse wind..is so forcible..that it raiseth great heapes of sand. **1634** in *Archæologia* XXXV. 197 In the kitchen...A travers barre for the chimney. **1703** Maundrell *Journ. Jerus.* (1721) 112 The traverse part of the Cross. **1894** *Westm. Gaz.* 9 May 4/2 The explosions at the Waltham Cordite Factory..the strong traverse walls being blown to pieces.

†**2.** Slanting; oblique. *Obs.*

**1609** Holland *Amm. Marcell.* 412 With grim lookes and traverse cast of eye. **1610** Guillim *Heraldry* i. viii. 34 A Gusset..is formed of a Trauerse line drawne either from the Dexter or Sinister Chiefe point..tending to the Honour point, and descending from thence..to the extreme base parts of the Escocheon. *a* **1649** Drumm. of Hawth. *Fam. Ep.* Wks. (1711) 146 The deviser of this [chess] would represent unto us a game of state..the bishops..should be.. grave men, who by oblique, traverse and mystical ways.. should effectuate their master's designs and safety.

**b.** *Her. Parted per pile traverse*: said of the shield when divided by oblique transverse lines forming the figure of a pile (Pile *sb.*[1] 4) turned sideways.

**1638** Guillim *Heraldry* v. i. (ed. 3) 365 He beareth parted per pyle traverse, Argent, and Gules. **1704** J. Harris *Lex. Techn.* I. s.v., There is also a Partition of an Eschucheon used in Heraldry of this Figure, which they call Parted per Pile [*printed* Pale] Traverse, Argent and Gules.

**Traverse** (træ·vəɹs), *v.* Forms: 4–7 **trauerse**, (4 *Sc.* **trawers**), 5–7 **trauers, travers**, (6 **trauarse, trauerce**), 6– **traverse**. Pa. t. and pple. **traversed**: formerly often **traverst**. Also β. 5 **trauess**, 6 *Sc.* **trevess, treviss, treveiss**, 6–7 **traues, -ves**; 4–5 **trauys**, 5 **trauiss**, 6 **trauice**, 6–7 **trauise**, 7 **traviss**; 6–7 (9 *dial.*) **travish**; 6 **trauas, -ase, -aise**, 6–8 **travas**. [a. F. *traverser* (11th c.) to cross, thwart, f. *travers* Traverse *sb.* or *a.* Cf. Prov. *traversar*, Sp. *travesar*, Cat. *-essar*, It. *traversare*:—late pop.L. *trāversāre* for *transversāre*, in late L. to cross, throw across, f. *trāversus* = *transversus*, pa. pple. of *transvertĕre* to turn across: see Transvert *v.* The β-forms are popular corruptions, due to phonetic weakening of second syllable: cf. the Sp. and Cat. forms.]

**I.** To run across or through; to cross.

For intransitive uses related to these, see branch IV.

**1.** *trans.* †**a.** To run (something) through *with* a weapon; to pierce, stab (*obs.*); **b.** to pass through as a weapon, to penetrate, pierce. Now *rare.*

*c* **1400** *Laud Troy Bk.* 5841 With a spere he him trauersed. **1513** Douglas *Æneis* x. viii. 98 The schaft..throw the bordour of the scheyld swa persyt, Quhill fynaly in sum deyll it traversyt, And hurt a part of Turnus big body. **1613** R. Cawdrey *Table Alph.* (ed. 3), *Trauerse*, strike, or thrust through. **1846** Brittan tr. *Malgaigne's Man. Oper. Surg.* 410 The needles..traverse the intestine on the opposite side. **1878** Browning *La Saisiaz* 356 While I watch it [torture] traversing the human heart.

**c.** To cross (a thing) with a line, stripe, bar, barrier, or anything that intersects. In *passive*, To be crossed *with* lines, etc. Now *rare.*

*c* **1420** *Anturs of Arth.* 354 (Thornton MS.) In paulle purede with pane, fulle precyously dyghte, Trofelyte and trauerste wythe trewloues in trete. *a* **1548** Hall *Chron.*, *Hen. VIII*, 6 b, Two long gounes of yelowe satin, trauarsed with white satin. **1600** Dymmok *Ireland* (1843) 45 The rebells traversed the same [entrance] with a barricado with doble flancks. **1748** *Anson's Voy.* ii. vi. 196 They traversed the streets with barricadoes. *a* **1810** Tannahill *Poems* (1846) 37 His chequered robes excited their surprise, Richly travers'd with various glowing dyes.

†**d.** To get across (a horse); to mount, bestride.

**1438** *Bk. Alexander Gt.* (Bann. Cl.) 101 Bot he had nocht this counsale than, Trauersit his hors as michty man, He turnit nocht abasitly.

**e.** *Her.* To place across or crosswise (on the shield).

**1610** Bolton *Elem. Armories* 21 Three parallel Arrowes trauersed barre-ways.

**2.** To cross (a mountain, river, sea) in travelling; now *esp.* to pass or journey across, over, or through; to pass through (a region) from side to side, or from end to end; also, to pass through (a space or solid body), as rays of light, etc.

In quot. 1708, to pass the fingers across.

*c* **1489** Caxton *Sonnes of Aymon* iii. 105 Every man wente to hys countrey not the ryght waye but traversynge the mountaynes. **1590** Greene *Mourn. Garm.* (1616) 4 What Experience Vlisses got by trauersing strange Countries. **1667** Milton *P. L.* ix. 66 Thrice the Equinoctial Line He circl'd; four times cross'd the Carr of Night From Pole to Pole, traversing each Colure. **1708** J. Philips *Cyder* Poems (1778) 111 Blind British bards with volant touch Traverse loquacious strings. **1748** *Anson's Voy.* Introd. C iv b, The Manila ships are the only ones which have ever traversed this vast ocean. **1839** G. Bird *Nat. Phil.* 264 Currents of positive electricity will traverse the wire. **1868** Lyell *Princ. Geol.* (ed. 10) II. iii. xxxix. 355 The jaguar traverses with ease the largest streams. **1880** C. R. Markham *Peruv. Bark* 49 They traversed the valley of Chinchao. β. *a* **1533** Ld. Berners *Huon* xxxv. 111 Thou dydest swym in y$^{\text{e}}$ see, & trauesyd y$^{\text{e}}$ grete waues. **1585** T. Washington tr. *Nicholay's Voy.* ii. xi. 45 b, Trauishing this goulph, a Northerly wynde came full in the face of vs.

**b.** To trace (a geometrical figure, or part of one) continuously without lifting the pen or pencil. Also *intr.* or *absol.*

**1905** J. C. Wilson *Traversing Geometr. Figures* i. § 1. 5 To traverse in a figure, or in a part of it, is to trace a path along its lines, no line being traced twice over, ending at a point at which no path in the figure, or the given part of it, remains untraced. *Ibid.* § 9. 16 Rules for traversing figures which can be exhausted by a single traverse.

**3.** *fig.* (and in *fig.* context). To 'go through' (life, time, or anything figured as an extended space or region); to read through or consider thoroughly (a subject, treatise, etc.).

*c* **1477** Caxton *Jason* 4 Their lyf was trauersid in contynuelle bewailing. **1573** Tusser *Husb.* (1878) 137 Timelie to trauerse the thing that thou triue. *a* **1716** South *Serm.* (1744) X. 186 Traversing those several Scriptures, which these men alledge in the behalf of their opinion. **1823** Scott *Quentin D.* iv, Such were the thoughts which hastily traversed the mind of young Durward. **1874** Green *Short Hist.* vii. § 6. 398 It was in the years which we are traversing that England became firmly Protestant.

β. **1590** Nashe *Pasquil's Apol.* i. A iv, M. Bucer, Peter Martyr, and..the B. of Sarisburie, haue trauast our Church with as graue a gate as he. **1606** S. Gardiner *Bk. Angling* To Rdr., After thou hast but cursorily trauised this Treatise. **1616** W. Forde *Serm.* 4 We will, by Gods assistance.. travish the same ground we have began to tread.

**4.** Of a thing: To lie, be situated, extend, stretch, or 'run' across (something); to cross, intersect.

**1481** Caxton *Myrr.* ii. iii. 68 Thise two flodes [Tygris & Eufrates] trauerse many grete contrees. **1682** Sir H. Piers *Descr. Westmeath* in *Collect. de Rebus Hibern.* I. 65 The lintel that traverseth the head of the door is of one entire stone. **1683** *Brit. Spec.* 145 The Romans gave them their help to build another Wall of Stone,..traversing the Island in a direct line from East to West. **1748** *Anson's Voy.* ii. iii. 142 The country in the neighbourhood was so..traversed with mountains. **1829** I. Taylor *Enthus.* viii. 204 The dead solitudes of sand, traversed..by the Nile. **1835** W. Irving *Tour Prairies* xviii. 155 Deeply worn footpaths..traversing the country. **1851** Richardson *Geol.* viii. 270 Canals that everywhere traverse bone..called Haversian.

**5.** To go to and fro over or along; to cross and recross. *To traverse one's ground*, to move from side to side, in fencing or fighting.

**1590** Spenser *F. Q.* ii. viii. 35 So both attonce him charge ..With hideous strokes..That forced him his ground to traverse wyde. **1595** *Locrine* i. Prol. 5 A mightie Lion, ruler of the woods,..Traverst the groues. **1625** K. Long tr. *Barclay's Argenis* iv. xiii. 283 He..traversed his ground, came on, and gave backe, tyring his Enemy with change of play. **1829** Scott *Anne of G.* xxv, The Duke traversed the apartment with unequal steps, in much agitation. **1878** C. Stanford *Symb. Christ* v. 142 The spirit of evil traversing the earth to tempt the members of Christ's flock.

β. **1577** Harrison *England* ii. xiv. (1877) i. 265 To meet with his enimie in the plaine field..where he may trauaise his ground. **1592** Wyrley *Armorie, Capitall de Buz* 152 Trauasing Fraunce vp and downe at pleasure. **1613** Sir E. Hoby *Countersnarle* 27 Thus doth this Spider-Catcher travaise his ground, with a goodly flourish.

†**6.** *Carpentry.* To plane (wood) across the grain. *Obs.*

**1678** [see Traversing *vbl. sb.*]. **1703** T. N. *City & C. Purchaser* 268 *Traverse*, A Term in Joynery, signifying to plain a Board, (or the like) across the Grain.

**7.** *Surveying.* To determine the positions of points on the earth's surface by measuring the lengths and azimuths of a connected series of straight lines; to make or execute a traverse (Traverse *sb.* 3) of (a region); to delimit (an area) by thus determining the position of points on its boundaries; to trace the course of (a road, river, etc.) in this way.

**1874** C. C. King *Map & Plan Drawing* 69 The next operation is that of tracing, or, as it is technically called, 'traversing', any roads that may intersect the area, or if none be present, a line passing through that portion which contains the largest number of natural or artificial peculiarities. **1900** H. M. Wilson *Topogr. Survey.* x. 195 Their topography is most easily obtained by means of traversing. **1908** H. Lyons *Cadastral Surv. Egypt* 211 The province.. was divided up into sections..which approximated to districts, and these large blocks were traversed with care, the work being done by the more efficient of the staff who also traversed the villages lying on the boundary.

**II.** To turn, move, or bring (a thing) across.

**8.** *trans.* To alter the position of (a gun, etc.) laterally, so as to take aim. Also *absol.*

**1628** Digby *Voy. Medit.* (1868) 78 His men..were seene busie trauersing their gunnes vpon the Eagle. **1688** R. Holme *Armoury* iii. xviii. (Roxb.) 140/2 The laying or remoueing of a peece of Ordinance till it come to lie with the marke, is termed traversing of the peece. **1727–41** Chambers *Cycl.*, *Traverse*, in gunnery, signifies to turn or point a piece of ordnance..upon her platform. **1859** F. A. Griffiths *Artill. Man.* (1862) 196 No. 3..traverses with the handspike. **1899** *Westm. Gaz.* 30 Nov. 4/2 The gun can be traversed—that is, the direction of its aim laterally can be varied—by means of a wooden handspike.

β. **1622** R. Hawkins *Voy. S. Sea* (1847) 195 An English gunner..being travesing of a peece in the bowe, to make his shott, had his head carryed away with the first or second shott made out of our shippe. **1627** Capt. Smith *Seaman's Gram.* xiv. 65 To trauas a Peece is to turne her which way you will vpon her Platforme. **1644** Nye *Gunnery* ii. (1670) 2 There you may best observe, as the Peece is travissing, when you are in a direct line with the Mark. **1704** J. Harris *Lex. Techn.* I, *Travas*, a Term in Gunnery.

**b.** *intr.* To carry a gun so that it points at the head or body of another sportsman.

**1886** *Badminton Libr., Shooting* (1895) 177 Many men who shoot a great deal 'traverse' habitually, and the habit once acquired is most difficult to eradicate.

†**9.** To turn away, to divert; *fig.* to pervert. *Obs. rare.*

**1623** Sir E. Digby *Sp.* in Rushw. *Hist. Coll.* (1659) I. 132 For the Recovery of the Patrimony belonging to the King of Bohemia, now almost traversed from him, and in the possession of a powerful Enemy. **1689** Owen *True Nat. Gosp. Ch.* x. Wks. 1855 XVI. 183 It is the mystery of iniquity that hath traversed these things into..a posture unintelligible to spiritual wisdom.

**10.** To carry in a trailing manner; to trail. *dial.*

**1814** W. NICHOLSON *Peacock* III. 22 So ha'e I seen..mystic knighthood o' the apron; Wi' empty pride, in monkish gown, Travish a Bible thro' the town. **1824** MACTAGGART *Gallovid. Encycl.*, *Travish*, to carry after a trailing manner.

**III.** To direct oneself or act against.

**11.** *trans.* To act against, to go counter to; to cross, thwart, oppose.

*c* **1400** *Gosp. Nicodemus* 1301 (Galba MS.) He has me tenid and trauerst [**14**.. *v. r.* trauyst] ay in all þe werkes I haue wroght. **14**.. *Beryn* 3411 We submit vs all..nevir for to travers o word þat þow seyst. **1548** UDALL *Erasm. Par. Luke* xii. 119 The vnluckie ende of trauersing the lawe. **1652** NEEDHAM tr. *Selden's Mare Cl.* 2 Here..the difficultie ceased not, becaus som did travers the execution of the sentence. **1712** ARBUTHNOT *John Bull* IV. iii, He resolved to traverse this new project. **1771** LUCKOMBE *Hist. Print.* 274 To inclose a whole sentence between Parentheses..is traversing the intention of Parentheses. **1855** MACAULAY *Hist. Eng.* xvii. IV. 75 Berwick had sent Maxwell to watch their motions and to traverse their designs.

β. **14**.. [see α]. *c* **1460** *Towneley Myst.* xxv. 153 That trature trauesses vs all-way. *c* **1480** *Kyng & Hermit* 87 in Hazl. *E. P. P.* I. 17 When that they were travyst [? travayst] And of herborow were abayst.

†**b.** *intr.* To go (*against*), go counter. *Obs. rare.*

**1377** LANGL. *P. Pl.* B. XII. 284 Trewth þat trespassed neuere ne transuersed [*v. r.* trauersed] aȝeines his lawe. **1393** *Ibid.* C. IV. 449 Ho so takeþ aȝen treuthe oþer transuerseþ [*v. r.* trauerseth] aȝens reson.

**12.** *trans. Law.* To contradict formally (a matter of fact alleged in the previous pleading); to deny at law; *spec.* in phr. *to traverse an indictment*, to deny or take issue upon an indictment; *to traverse an office*, to deny or impeach the validity of an inquest of office. Also *absol.*

[**1292** BRITTON II. xxvi. § 2 Et autres plusours excepciouns ..porra le tenaunt traverser, et dire, qe il ne fust unques seisi.] *a* **1325** *MS. Rawl. B.* 520 lf. 96 b, Þer me ne mai noȝt vochen warant out of þe lignage bote onliche trauersen þe Entree. **1467** in *Eng. Gilds* (1870) 394 To travers the seid presentements or assessment for his acquitalle. **1553** T. WILSON *Rhet.* 47 In traversyng a cause before a judge. **1588** LAMBARDE *Eiren.* IV. xiii. 542 To Trauerse an Enditement..is to take issue vpon the chiefe matter therof, which is none other..then..to deny the point of the Enditement. **1647** N. BACON *Disc. Govt. Eng.* I. xxxvi. (1739) 54 In the answer of the Defendant, he either traversed the matter in fact, or confessed and justified, or confessed and submitted. **1791** HAMPSON *Mem. J. Wesley* II. 33 If they were disappointed at the quarter sessions,..they traversed and appealed to the upper courts. **1823** *Rep. Sel. Comm. Sewers Metrop.* 17 In all cases where the presentment of the jury is traversed,..that traverse must be tried by another jury, to be summoned by the sheriff, which is called a traverse jury. **1911** ODGERS *Comm. Law Eng.* V. xvii. II. 1214 Allegations of fact alone should be traversed, and these he must not traverse 'evasively, but answer the point of substance'.

†**b.** To affirm, by way of contradicting a charge or allegation. *Obs.*

**1491** *Act 7 Hen. VII*, c. 2 § 4 Yf..any man will travers that the seid Warrant is not the dede of hym that is named. **1654** FULLER *Two Serm.* 16 What will it benefit a Lamb to traverse his innocence in the pawes of a Lyon?

†**13.** To dispute; to discuss. *Obs.*

*c* **1440** *Partonope* 1772 Eche man did travers Others witte. **1503** HAWES *Examp. Virt.* xxviii, Longe haue they trauerst..Whiche of them sholde haue the preemynence. **1549** COVERDALE, etc. *Erasm. Par. 1 Cor.* 16 The matter.. muste bee trauersed before the commen officers. **1589** NASHE *Anat. Absurd.* Epist. ¶ iij, Amongst other talke which was generally traversed amongst us. **1599** — *Lenten Stuffe* (1871) 29, I could run ten quires of paper out of breath, in further traversing her rights and dignities.

**IV.** Intransitive senses allied to I and II.

These do not appear in Fr., in which *traverser* is always transitive. But in Eng. they sometimes appear earlier than the transitive senses to which they are specially allied.

**14.** *intr.* To move, pass, or go across; to cross, cross over; (of a ship) to tack. (Cf. 2 and 5.)

**1375** BARBOUR *Bruce* XVII. 532 So lang thai raid distroyande swa, As thai trauersit to and fra. **1517** TORKINGTON *Pilgr.* (1884) 6 We traversed owt of that Ryver into a nother lytell Ryver. **1677** W. HUBBARD *Narrative* Pref., Purchase wrote much, Hacluyt traversed farr. **1782** ELIZ. BLOWER *Geo. Bateman* II. 124 For some minutes he traversed backwards and forwards from the window to the door. **1897** *Scotsman* 14 May 6/1 The railway would so seriously injure the scenery of the valley and lake along which it would traverse.

β. **1438** *Bk. Alexander Gt.* (Bann. Cl.) 85 Daucline.. Trauissit challange for to maik. **1568** *Satir. Poems Reform.* xlvi. 53 Steir be the compas..Syne treveiss still, and lay abowt. *a* **1578** LINDESAY (Pitscottie) *Chron. Scot.* (S.T.S.) I. 213 Thair was tuo schipis..trevessing wpe and doune the firth. **1591** LYLY *Endym.* III. iii, We will trauice. Will you goe, sir? **1892** QUILLER COUCH *Three Ships*, etc. 179 Not a tint did he work, but kept travishing back and forth.

**b.** *fig.*

**1566** PAINTER *Pal. Pleas.* I. 90 This miserable louer, trauersing in seuerall mindes,..chaunged his mynde a thousand times in an hower. **1645** MILTON *Tetrach.* Wks. 1738 I. 250 That it does not traverse from the Closet of Conscience to the Courts of Civil or Canon Law. **1747** *Mem. Nutrebian Crt.* I. 203 We shall traverse back to some particulars of her education. **1824** GALT *Rothelan* II. xiii, His thoughts tossed and traversed like the inconstant clouds.

†**c.** In dancing: see quot. 1616. *Obs.*

**1584** B. R. tr. *Herodotus* II. 86 Many [women] trauise & daunce minionly. **1616** BULLOKAR *Eng. Expos.*, *Trauerse*, to march vp and downe or to moue the feete with proportion, as in dancing.

**15.** To move from side to side; to dodge (cf. 5); in quot. 1635 *trans.* to drive by 'traversing'. *Obs.* or *arch.*

**1470–85** MALORY *Arthur* X. xxx. 463 Thus they tracyd and trauercyd and hewe on helmes and hawberkes. *a* **1548** HALL *Chron., Hen. V*, 50 Thus this battaile continued iii long houres, some strake, some defended, some foyned, some trauersed, some kylled, some toke prisoners. **1598** SHAKS. *Merry W.* II. iii. 25 To see thee fight, to see thee foigne, to see thee trauerse. **1635** EARL STRAFFORD *Lett. & Disp.* (1739) I. 478 He shall be a very artificial Fencer..that traverseth me forth of my Ground. **1823** SCOTT *Quentin D.* xiv, To harass his antagonist, by traversing on all sides, with a suddenness of motion and rapidity of attack. **1858** MORRIS *Def. Guenevere* 13 The fight began,..Ever Sir Launcelot kept him on the right, And traversed warily.

†**16.** To digress. *Obs. rare.*

**1530** PALSGR. 761/2, I traverse, I go from one mater to an other...Nowe you leave the purpose and begyn to traverse.

**17.** To come or fall across each other; to cross. (Cf. 4.)

**1669** STURMY *Mariner's Mag.* I. ii. 17 It bloweth a storm —furle the Sail fast, and fasten the Yards, that they may not travers and gall.

**18.** To run freely in its proper socket, ring, channel, or course (as a rope); to turn or move freely from side to side on a traverse-circle (as a gun); to turn about on a pivot (as the needle of the compass). (Cf. 8.)

**1829** MARRYAT *F. Mildmay* xxiii, Sharp frosts..obliged us to pour boiling water into the sheaves of the blocks to thaw them, and allow the ropes to traverse. **1832** *Nat. Philos.* II. *Magnetism* iii. § 91. 22 (Usef. Knowl. Soc.) In moving ..towards the position which it thus tends to assume, the needle of the compass is said to traverse. **1849** CUPPLES *Green Hand* iv, The tiller-ropes cheeping as they traversed. **1851** *Ord. & Regul. R. Engineers* § 19. 94 Iron Traversing Platforms..so constructed, that..they may be made to traverse in any direction. **1856** KANE *Arct. Expl.* I. x. 113 It traversed freely by a ring on a loop or bridle. **1863** *Possibilities of Creation* 175 Let the head..have no power of traversing upon the atlas, and let that..spinal column.. become as stiff as an iron bar, and..poor humanity would be completely crippled.

**19. a.** *Falconry.* To move from side to side, to wriggle, as a hawk. **b.** *Manège.* To advance obliquely, as a horse: see quot. 1753.

**1486** *Bk. St. Albans, Hawking* a vij, Ye shall knawe it whan she puttith ouer she trauersith withe hir bodi. **1544** BETHAM *Precepts War* I. cxi. F v b, To take vp his horse with the spurres, that he may praunse, trauerse, and flyng wyth the heeles. **1610** GUILLIM *Heraldry* III. xx. (1660) 223 She [a Hawk] putteth over, when she removeth her meat from her Gorge, into her Bowels, by traversing with her body, but chiefly with her Neck, as a Crane..doth. **1753** CHAMBERS *Cycl. Supp.* s. v., A horse is said to traverse, when he cuts his tread cross-wise; throwing his croupe to one side, and his head to another. **1884** E. L. ANDERSON *Mod. Horsemanship* II. xii. 119 *Traversing* is the movement in which the horse passes to either side..upon two paths, the forehand following one, the hind-quarters, slightly retired, the other.

**20.** To advance or ascend in a zigzag line. (Cf. TRAVERSE *sb.* 12 c.)

**1773** JOHNSON *Let. to Mrs. Thrale* 6 Sept., Our way now lay over the mountains, which are not to be passed by climbing them directly, but by traversing.

**21.** *Mountaineering.* To make one's way in a horizontal or transverse direction across the face of a mountain or rock. (See TRAVERSE *sb.* 6.)

**1893** C. WILSON *Mountaineering* vi. 88 To traverse for some distance on steep snow or grass. *Ibid.* Gloss., *Traverse*,..(*a.*) to cross a mountain slope horizontally. **1897** O. G. JONES *Rock-climbing* 123 At the foot we joined up again and traversed round to the 'sheep walk'. *Ibid.* 269 The climber hangs by his hands,..and traverses across the face by sheer strength of his arms.

**V.** From TRAVERSE *sb.*

**22.** *trans.* To furnish or fortify with a traverse or traverses (see TRAVERSE *sb.* 16). *rare.*

**1828** J. M. SPEARMAN *Brit. Gunner* (ed. 2) 360 Of 170 shells, filled with powder, that were fired at the work when traversed, 58 took effect;..the effect on the traverses was considerable, and they were much ruined.

†**Traverse**, *adv.* (*prep.*) *Obs.* Also 5–7 travers. [Sometimes app. aphetic for A-TRAVERS *adv.* = F. *à travers*; sometimes advb. use of TRAVERSE *a.*] Across; crosswise; athwart; transversely.

*c* **1450** LOVELICH *Grail* liii. 211 Into A wast lawnde he happede there..and thus travers he Rod tyl Myd Nyht. **1525** LD. BERNERS *Froiss.* II. xli. 128 The erle..caused.. hyghe trees to be hewen downe, and layde trauers one ouer another. **1640** HOWELL *Dodona's Gr.* (1645) 2 A square of 550 miles travers. **1725** *Bradley's Fam. Dict.* s. v. *Willow*, Let them be copp'd Traverse, and not Obliquely, at one foot or somewhat more from the Ground.

**b.** *Traverse to, of*, right across; = B.

**1548** PATTEN *Exped. Scotl.* G vij, The furrowes laye trauers to their course. **1654** H. L'ESTRANGE *Chas. I* (1655) 68 Coming counter and travers of our Canon, they received the greater losse.

**B.** *prep.* Across. (Cf. A-TRAVERS *prep.*)

*a* **1548** HALL *Chron., Hen. VIII*, 3 After them came sir Thomas Brandon..clothed in tissue..and traverse his body, a greate Bauderike of Gold. **1610** HOLLAND *Camden's Brit., Scot.* II. 25 Hardly one by one can passe up, and that ..by Grees or steps cut out aslope travers the rock.

**Traversed** (træ·vəɹst), *ppl. a.* Also 6–7 trauerst. [f. TRAVERSE *v.* + -ED [1].]

**1.** Placed or laid across; crossed; transverse.

**1607** SHAKS. *Timon* V. iv. 7 [We] Haue wander'd with our trauerst Armes, and breathd Our sufferance vainly. **1621** LODGE *Summary Du Bartas* I. 286 The Stomake..closeth it selfe on euery side, by meanes of the trauersed fibers.

**2.** Passed or travelled over; traced continuously; penetrated, pierced.

**1599** T. M[OUFET] *Silkwormes* 61 Lifelesse in midway of their trauerst round. **1878** BROWNING *La Saisiaz* 357 Traversed heart must tell its story uncommented on. **1905** J. C. WILSON *Traversing Geometr. Figures* I. § 4. 10 If *B* was intermediate, the traversed lines at *B* are even in number.

**3.** Of a horse: see quots. Cf. TRAVERSE *v.* 19 b.

**1611** COTGR., *Travat*, a horse which is trauersed; viz. hath two white feet on the right, or left side. **1678** in PHILLIPS (ed. 4). **1720** W. GIBSON *Diet. Horses* i. 5 Those which are cross-traversed, having the Fore-foot on the Near Side, and Hinder Foot on the Far Side, or [vice versa] White.

**4.** *Her.* See quot., and cf. TRAVERSE *a.* 2, 2 b.

*c* **1828** BERRY *Encycl. Her.* I. Gloss., *Traversed*, (French, *contourné*) turned to the sinister side of the shield.

**Traversely** (træ·vəɹsli), *adv. rare.* [f. TRAVERSE *a.* + -LY [2].] Crosswise; transversely.

**1656** [? J. SERGEANT] tr. *T. White's Peripat. Inst.* 151 Being carry'd traversly by some motion of the Aire, 't is call'd a Gliding Star. **1738** WHELER in *Phil. Trans.* XLI. 100, I tied..at the End of the larger Arm, a Piece of Stick traversly. **1826** KIRBY & SP. *Entomol.* III. xxxv. 606 They [elytra] may..help them in flying traversely and before the wind.

**Traverser** (træ·vəɹsəɹ). Also 7 traueser. [f. TRAVERSE *v.* + -ER [1].] One who or that which traverses.

**1.** A person or thing that crosses or passes over.

**1613** M. RIDLEY *Magn. Bodies* 1 The two trauesers about the Sunne, called Venus and Mercury. **1830** HOWITT *Seasons* (1837) 3 A dismal time for the traversers of wide and open heaths.

†**2.** = TRAVERSE *sb.* 16. *Obs. rare.*

**1645** SLINGSBY *Diary* (1836) 159 Ye town..was made a kind of Garison wth some traversers and light works built about it.

**3.** *Law.* One who traverses a plea.

**1812** *Examiner* 21 Sept. 607/1 The traverser was prevented from hanging himself. **1886** DOWDEN *Shelley* (1887) I. vi. 240 The charge of Chief Justice Downes made clear the case against the traverser.

**4.** On a railway: A platform, moving laterally on wheels, by which trucks or carriages may be shifted from one set of rails to another parallel to it.

**1851** T. DUNN in *Pract. Mechanic's Jrnl.* III. 258, I was the first person who invented a traverser. **1878** F. S. WILLIAMS *Midl. Railw.* 643 The truck is now clear, and.. will be run on to the 'traverser', and..drawn sideways on to the next line of rails.

**Tra·verse-ta:ble.** [f. TRAVERSE *sb.* 12.]

**1.** *Naut.* A table from which the difference of latitude and departure corresponding to any given course and distance may be ascertained.

**1669** STURMY *Mariner's Mag.* IV. i. 141 By the Traverse-Table..you may find the Difference of Latitude and departure from the Meridian. **1706** PHILLIPS (ed. Kersey), *Traverse-Table*, a Paper on which are set down the Traverses, or Various Courses of the Ship, with the Points of the Compass. **1828** J. H. MOORE *Pract. Navig.* (ed. 20) 178 The variation is 11° 52′ E., and must be allowed..in all courses steered, or bearings taken by the compass, before they can be put in the Traverse Table. **1839** *Civil Eng. & Arch. Jrnl.* II. 352/1 He also shows how his traverse tables may be applied in setting out railway curves. **1843** *Penny Cycl.* XXV. 169/2 The traverse table is a table of double entry, into which, going with the angle of the course and the distance run, we find in two columns the corresponding departure, and length of the side called difference of latitude.

**2.** On a railway: = TRAVERSER 4. *U.S.*

**1864** WEBSTER, *Traverse-table*, (Railways), a platform with one or more tracks, and arranged to move laterally on wheels, for shifting cars, etc.; a traverser. **1877** in KNIGHT *Dict. Mech.*

†**Tra·verse-ways**, *adv. Obs.* [f. as next + -WAYS.] = next.

**1610** GUILLIM *Heraldry* II. vi. (1611) 61 A Canton parted trauerswaies whether it be from the dexter corner, or from the sinister, doth make two base squires.

**Tra·verse-wi:se**, *adv.* [f. TRAVERSE *a.* or *sb.* + -WISE.] Crosswise.

**1697** DAMPIER *Voy.* (1729) I. 336 The Beams or Bamboes ..are fasten'd traverse-wise to the Outlayers on each side.

**Traversible**, variant of TRAVERSABLE.

**Traversing** (træ·vəɹsiŋ), *vbl. sb.* [f. TRAVERSE *v.* + -ING [1].] The action of the verb TRAVERSE, in various senses.

**1589** NASHE *Martins Months M.* To Rdr., This our young masters Father..then was lept from the Bellfree, vp into the Chauncel of the Church..and vnder tooke the trauersing of greater matters. *a* **1642** SIR W. MONSON *Naval Tracts* III. (1704) 344/1 They [cannon] are..better in Traversing and Mounting. **1678** MOXON *Mech. Exerc.* iv. 65 This way of Cross-Grain'd working, is, by Workmen called Traversing. **1690** LEYBOURN *Curs. Math.* 641 Let these two Examples suffice for Traversing both by Protraction, Calculation, and by the Traverse Table. **1851** SIR F. PALGRAVE *Norm. & Eng.* I. 487 Amongst the marchings and traversings of the Northmen. **1883** *Contemp. Rev.* June 883 Forty years' laborious traversing of record offices and corporate archives. **1886** *Badminton Libr., Shooting* (1895) 177 The ..system of 'traversing'..cannot be too strongly deprecated. **1887** *Encycl. Brit.* XXII. 705/2 (*Surveying*) Traversing is a combination of linear and angular measures in equal proportion. **1895** *Westm. Gaz.* 25 Nov. 4/3 The 'traversing' or drawing sideways of the new bridge so that it would occupy..the place where the up line had formerly stood. **1905** J. C. WILSON *Traversing Geometr. Figures* 1 On the continuous description or traversing of Geometrical Figures.

b. *attrib.* and *Comb.*

**1825** J. NICHOLSON *Operat. Mechanic* 407 The alternate traversing motion is produced on the same principle as that applied to Baker's horizontal mangle. **1841** *Civil Eng. & Arch. Jrnl.* IV. 318/1 What is..termed the 'taking-up' or 'traversing motion' of the plank during..sawing. **1888** RUTLEY *Rock-Forming Min.* 18 Mechanical traversing arrangements..are rather an encumbrance than an advantage.

**Tra·versing,** *ppl. a.* [f. as prec. + -ING [2].] That traverses; crossing, transverse.

**1561** EDEN *Arte Nauig.* III. ix. 73 See also that the markes whiche you make in the yarde [= cross-staff], be trauersyng lines. **1771** LUCKOMBE *Hist. Print.* 476 In distributing of Musical Notes,..care ought to be taken to save the edges of the traversing lines from battering. **1865** GILLESPIE *Argt. Being & Attrib. God* III. ii. (1910) 93 Other lines, some of them..traversing lines, besides the main line of life.

b. In specific collocations: see quots.

*Traversing jury*, a traverse jury (see TRAVERSE *sb.* 23).

**1823** *Rep. Sel. Comm. Sewers Metrop.* 17 A traversing jury. **1828** SPEARMAN *Brit. Gunner* (ed. 2) 63 The guns are mounted on traversing platforms, and, in that case, fire over the epaulement. **1829** MARRYAT *F. Mildmay* xvii, The traversing beam of a steamboat. **1877** KNIGHT *Dict. Mech., Traversing-jack, a.* A jack used for engines or carriages upon the rails. *b.* A lifting-apparatus, the standard of which has a movement on its bed, enabling it to be applied to different parts of an object or used for shifting objects horizontally without moving the bed. *Ibid., Traversing-pulley*, a pulley so arranged as to traverse upon a rope or rod. **1878** F. S. WILLIAMS *Midl. Railw.* 664 Sidings and traversing tables will be laid between all these various shops, and also through them, so that there will always be more than one way by which trollies or trains can get in and out. **1884** C. G. W. LOCK *Workshop Receipts* Ser. III. 294/1 The traversing mandril should be made of the very finest steel. **1887** D. A. LOW *Machine Draw.* (1892) 96 The lever..for turning the horizontal screw of a traversing screw jack.

**Traversion** (trăvɔ̄·ɹʃən). *rare.* [f. TRAVERSE *v.* on the type of a L. *tra(ns)versiōnem: cf. TRANSVERSION.]

**1.** †**a.** The action of traversing or moving sideways in fencing: cf. TRAVERSE *v.* 5, 15 (*obs.*). **b.** The action of traversing a geometrical figure.

**1637** NABBES *Microcosm.* II. i. C ij b, I was..bred up in Mars his Fencing-schoole: where I..learn't..Time, motion and action; progression, reversion, and traversion; blowes, thrusts, falses [etc.]. **1905** *Westm. Gaz.* 30 Sept. 2/2 The general principles underlying this continuous traversion of figures, complete or incomplete.

† **2.** ? The transverse member of a cross. *Obs.*

**1658** SIR T. BROWNE *Gard. Cyrus* i. 96 Some [crosses] being..of one single peece without traversion or transome.

† **Tra·vers-ti·le.** *Obs.* [Origin of name obscure; in quot. 1703 referred to obs. F. '*travers* crosse, crosse-wise, thwart, ouerthwart, ill-placed, out of order' (Cotgr.).] See quots.

**1703** T. N. *City & C. Purchaser* 273 Travers. These Tyles are (by our common Bricklayers) call'd Travis, or Travas Tyles; but I suppose it should rather be Travers Tyles; for the word *Travers* is perfect French, signifying Irregularity; these .. Travers Tyles are .. irregular plain Tyles, viz. Such as have the Pin-holes broken out, or one of the lower Corners broken off. **1725** *Bradley's Fam. Dict.* s. v. *Tiles, Travers*, which they lay with the broken Ends upwards upon Rafters where pinn'd Tyles cannot hang. **1727-41** CHAMBERS *Cycl.* s. v. *Tyle*, Traverse Tyles.

**Travertine, -in** (træ·vəɹtin). Also **trevertine.** [ad. It. *travertino*, older *tivertino* 'a kind of stone to build withall' (Florio):—L. *tīburtīnus* TIBURTINE. Cf. F. *travertin*, in Cotgr. *trevertin.*] A white or light-coloured concretionary limestone, usually hard and semi-crystalline, deposited from water holding lime in solution; also called *travertine stone*; quarried in Italy for building. A less solid porous form is known as *calcareous tufa.*

[**1555** EDEN *Decades* 340 And [silver] is often tymes founde in an other stone lyke vnto Treuertino or in Treuertino it selfe.] **1797** HOLCROFT tr. *Stolberg's Trav.* III. lxxxviii. 455 They are..of the travertine stone. **1868** LYELL *Princ. Geol.* (ed. 10) II. III. xlvii. 544 Encrusted with a calcareous cement resembling travertin. **1875** MERIVALE *Gen. Hist. Rome* lxxix. (1877) 669 The travertine, or limestone of Tivoli, ..was used to a great extent to cover the plain brickwork. **1878** HUXLEY *Physiogr.* 122 At the falls of the Anio, the travertine has formed bed after bed to the thickness of four or five hundred feet.

b. *attrib.* Of, composed of, or of the nature of travertine.

**1797** [see above]. **1842** *Civil Eng. & Arch. Jrnl.* V. 171/2 The Italian fresco workers..sometimes used puzzolano mixed with Trevertine lime. **1909** *Eng. Rev.* Feb. 585 Sanger found these travertine mounds in every stage of development.

**Traves, -ess**(e, obs. forms of TRAVERSE.

† **Travested,** *pa. pple. Obs.* [An earlier formation than *travestied* pa. pple. of TRAVESTY *v.*; prob. intended as the repr. of It. *travestito*, F. *travesti*, on analogy of *vested, invested*, etc.] Disguised; travestied.

**1656** BLOUNT *Glossogr., Travested*, disguised or shifted in apparel; And metaphorically it may be applyed to any thing that is translated out of one language into another. **1687** MONTAGUE & PRIOR *Hind & P. Transv.* Pref. A iij, Homer has been Burlesque'd, and Virgil Travested without suffering any thing in their Reputation from that Buffoonry. **1725** BENTLEY *Rem. Collins' Disc. Freethink.* liv. III. 12, I see poor Lucan Travested, not apparel'd in his Roman Toga, but under the cruel Sheers of an English Tailor. **1752** WARBURTON *Serm. Ps. cxliv. 3* Wks. 1788 V. 30 To make God..the..inspector into human actions, is..returning him to the people, travested to the mortal size of local godship.

† **Travesteere,** *v. Obs. rare.* [= F. *travestir*, It. *travestire*: cf. Du. *travesteeren* (Keupers, 1901), Ger. *travestieren.*] *trans.* To travesty.

**1672** MARVELL *Reh. Transp.* I. 44 Who by a perverse Wit and Representation might travesteere the Scripture. **1673** [R. LEIGH] *Transp. Reh.* 144 He..makes conscience of using scripture..yet he makes none of travesteering it. **1675** V. ALSOP *Anti-Sozzo* III. ii. 132 They who first taught this.. Age to Travesteere serious matters.

**Travestier** (træ·vėstiˌəɹ). [f. TRAVESTY *v.* + -ER [1].] One who travesties.

**1883** EBSWORTH in *Roxb. Ballads* IV. 161 *note*, A solemn travestier of many old Songs (and Dramas). **1901** E. YARDLEY in *N. & Q.* 9th Ser. VII. 161/2 Anthony Hamilton ..travestier of the 'Arabian Nights'.

**Tra·vestiment.** *rare.* [f. TRAVESTY *v.* + -MENT.] An act of travestying; the wearing the dress of the opposite sex; a travesty.

**1832** *Examiner* 373/2 Miss E. Tree is to add to the amusements of Whit-Monday by playing *Romeo*. Though we do not advocate travestiements, we wish her success. **1892** *Graphic* 24 Dec. 778/3 The sight of these travestiments overcame the antique Spartan simplicity of the British toilettes.

**Tra·vestize,** *v. rare.* [f. TRAVESTY + -IZE: cf. *botany, botanize.*] *intr.* To practise travesty.

**1847** *Tait's Mag.* XIV. 811 You are travestising.

**Travesty** (træ·vėsti), *ppl. a.* and *sb.* Also 7–8 -ti, 7–9 -tie. [Originally a. F. *travesti*, fem. *travestie*, pa. pple. of (*se*) *travestir* (Montaigne *a* 1592), 'to disguise him, or take on another man's habit' (Cotgr.), ad. It. *travestire* to disguise (Florio), f. *tra-* = TRANS- + It., L. *vestire* to clothe. The adoption from It. in 16th c. accounts for the retention of *s* in Fr., as opposed to *vêtir, revêtir.* Made known in England in the title of Scarron's *Le Virgile Travesty en vers burlesques* (= Vergil travestied in burlesque verses), 1648, whence occasionally in other connexions, and at length as a sb., used first in Scarron's sense, and later in the etymological one.]

**A.** *ppl. a.* Dressed so as to be made ridiculous; burlesqued. (Const. as pa. pple.) *Obs.* or only as F.

*c* **1662** DAVENANT *Play House to Let* I. i, What think you Of Romances travesti..Burlesque and Travesti? These are hard words, And may be French, but not Law-French. **1664** COTTON (*title*) Scarronides: or, Virgile Travestie. A Mock-Poem. Being the First Book of Virgils Æneis in English, Burlésque. **1672** J. PHILLIPS (*title*) Maronides, or Virgil Travestie: Being a New Paraphrase upon the Fifth Book of Virgils Æneids in Burlesque Verse. **1673** O. WALKER *Educ.* II. iii. 245 Virgil we have seen publickly, and even the holy Writings we heard to have been, travesty. *a* **1774** TUCKER *Lt. Nat.* (1834) II. 130 One may laugh heartily at Virgil travestie, without either despising Cotton, or abating one's admiration of Virgil.

**B.** *sb.* **1.** A literary composition which aims at exciting laughter by burlesque or ludicrous treatment of a serious work; literary composition of this kind; hence, a grotesque or debased imitation or likeness; a caricature.

**1674** BUTLER *Hud.* I. III. Annot. 196 This Vickars..translated Virgils Æneides into as horrible Travesty in earnest, as the French Scaroon did in Burlesque. **1751** WARBURTON *Note Pope's Dunc.* II. 268 Accusing him..on a mere report from Edm. Curl, that he was Author of a Travestie on the first Psalm. **1789** BELSHAM *Ess.* II. xxxvi. 300 It..has sometimes the effect of a ludicrous travesti of the Odyssey. **1846** WRIGHT *Ess. Mid. Ages* I. v. 178 Those romances were but barbarous travesties of the original stories. **1871** FARRAR *Witn. Hist.* ii. 73 The vulgar travesty of a miracle alleged to have been wrought by a coarse soldier.

**2.** In etymological sense: An alteration of dress or appearance; a disguise. *rare.*

**1732** SIR C. WOGAN *Let. to Swift* 27 Feb., My design was to have travelled..*incognito*...But all my art and travestie was vain. **1823** BYRON *Juan* v. lxxiv, 'At least', said Juan, 'sure I may inquire The cause of this odd travesty?'

**Travesty** (træ·vėsti), *v.* [f. F. *travesti* pa. pple.: see prec. App. first used in the pa. pple. *travestied* = F. *travesti* or It. *travestito.* The simple vb. has not been found until after 1700. Cf. the history of TRAVESTED.]

**1.** *trans.* To alter in dress or appearance; to disguise by such alteration.

**1686** F. SPENCE tr. *Varillas' Ho. Medicis* 408 He slunk out of Rome thus ridiculously travesty'd. **1754** WARBURTON *Bolingbroke's Philos.* ii. 73 Old Naturalism thus travestied under the name of Religion, his Lordship bestows..on his own dear Country. **1827** SCOTT *Napoleon* Introd. ix. II. 305 Processions entered.., travestied in priestly garments. **1853** FELTON *Fam. Lett.* ix. (1865) 70 About ten courses of meat, so mixed, blended, and travestied with seasonings and vegetables, that it would puzzle a Philadelphia lawyer to tell what any of them is made of.

**2.** To turn into ridicule by grotesque parody or imitation; to caricature, burlesque.

**1673** BP. WARD *Apol. Myst. Gosp.* 42 Are the Mysteries of this Gospel..to be travestied or turned into Burlesque or Macaronique? **1756** J. WARTON *Ess. Pope* I. 57 One would imagine that John Dennis..had been here attempting to travesty this description of the restoration of Eurydice to life. **1874** MAHAFFY *Soc. Life Greece* vii. 197 The comic poets .. travestied known characters so as to make them hardly recognisable. **1888** BURGON *Lives 12 Gd. Men* II. vi. 87 The true version of a story which .. has been grossly travestied in the repetition.

Hence **Tra·vestied** (-tid) *ppl. a.*

**1864** *Ess. Social Subjects* 186 A reason which barely represents half your motives to yourself is sure to enter the other mind in such travestied guise as to convey nothing as you intend it. **1891** S. C. SCRIVENER *Our Fields & Cities* 68 Teaching the older histories from a travestied standpoint.

**Traveys, Travice,** obs. ff. TRAVERSE, TRAVIS.

**Travis** [1], **trevis** (træ·vis, tre·vis). Forms: α. 5 traveys, 6 traveis, 8 travice; β. 6 trevys, 9 trevis. [A variant of TRAVERSE *sb.* in sense of OF. *travers* (= 'travail, machine pour ferrer' in Godef., who cites 'Ung travers a ferrer chevaulx' from a document of 1472), ad. L. *traversum.*

In Eng. the word has undergone the same popular deformation as TRAVERSE *sb.* and *v.*, and is now identified in form with next, of which indeed in the Eng. Dial. Dict. it is treated as a sense.]

A framework or railed enclosure in which restive horses are put to be shod; a smith's shoeing shed; = TRAVE *sb.* 2.

α. **14..** *Voc.* in Wr.-Wülcker 617/19 *Tramerium*, traveys, *ergasterium idem est.* **1583** *Burgh Rec. Edinb.* (1882) IV. 287 To sett vp ane traveis of tymmer for shoing of horsis besyde his smiddy. **1727** BAILEY vol. II, *Travice*, a small Inclosure..consisting of four Pillars or Posts, kept together by cross Poles, for keeping in and holding unruly Horses in the time of Shoeing, or any other Operation. **1905** in *Eng. Dial. Dict.* s.v. *Traverse*, recorded from Cheshire, E. Anglia, Sussex.

β. **1530** PALSGR. 283/1 Trevys to shoe a wylde horse in, *trauayl a cheual.* **1831** YOUATT *Horse* xxii. (1847) 430 The trevis is a machine indispensable in every continental forge.

**Travis** [2], **trevis** (træ·vis, tre·vis). Also 8 **treves,** 8–9 **travisse,** 9 **trevesse, -vis, -ise, -iss, travis, -ise, -iss;** *Sc. dial.* **traivis, triviss, -ess, trivage;** *Eng. dial.* **travvis, travase, trivitch.** [dial. var. of TRAVERSE *sb.* q. v.

Similar forms occur as obs. or dial. variants in senses for which TRAVERSE is the current form; but in the following senses the altered forms are alone in use.]

**1.** A wooden partition $4\frac{1}{2}$ to 6 feet high, separating two stalls in a stable. (See TRAVERSE *sb.*, branch IV, of which this is a specific sense.)

**1818** SCOTT *Hrt. Midl.* xxv[i], Beyond the 'treviss', which formed one side of the stall, stood a cow. **1826** — *Woodst.* i, Stakes and trevisses of rough-hewn timber .. seemed to intimate that the hallowed precincts had been..made the quarters of a troop of horse. **1827** HOGG in *Blackw. Mag.* XXI. 69 As I was suppering the horses the night..behold I looks up, and there's my auld master standing leaning against the trivage. **1833** LOUDON *Encycl. Archit.* § 1070 The trevises to be 6 feet high at the front posts, and 4 feet and a half high at the hind posts. *Ibid.* § 1103 The back posts of the trivesses to be made of oak 6 inches square. **1844** STEPHENS *Bk. Farm* I. 125 The hind posts of travises should be of solid wood rounded in front.

**2.** A horse's stall in a stable.

(Bears the same relation to 1 as TRAVERSE *sb.* 14 to 13.)

**1756** MRS. CALDERWOOD in *Coltness Collect.* (Maitl. Cl.) 152 There were fifty-eight treveses in one end [of the stables]. **1859** J. BROWN *Rab & Fr.* (1862) 33 He [Rab] lay in the treviss wi' the mear, and wadna come oot. **1884** J. PURVES in *Gd. Words* Nov. 766/2 The horses crunching their food and rattling their halter-chains in the treviss. **1896** J. LUMSDEN *Battle of Dunbar*, etc. 13 Her neibor in the nearer triviss The maist redoubted naig alive is!

**3.** Comb. *Travis-* or *trevis-board, -boarding* (in a stable).

**1833** LOUDON *Encycl. Archit.* § 1070 $1\frac{1}{2}$-inch trevise-boards to be mortised into the hind post, which must be set 8 feet from the front wall. *Ibid.* § 1103 The trivess boarding to be 7 feet high in front, and 8 feet at the back end.

**Travis, -ish, -iss,** obs. forms of TRAVERSE.

**Travise, -ish, -iss,** obs. or dial. ff. TRAVIS.

‖**Travois, -voise** (travoi·, -voi·z), *sb. North Amer.* [Corruptions of TRAVAIL *sb.* [3], pronounced in Canada *travày* (travāi·), and by half-breeds of the Red River, Assiniboine, etc., *travòy* (travoi·), pl. *travòys.* This has been perverted by writers into an assumed F. *travois*, pl. *travois*, and this again englished as *travois, -voise*, pl. *-voises.* A form nearer to the original is preserved in the lumbermen's TRAVOY; see next word.

For the facts of the history we are indebted to Judge Prudhomme of St. Boniface, Winnipeg, through the good offices of Prof. Moyse of Montreal, and Prof. Rivard of Quebec.]

The primitive North American Indian means of transport, = TRAVAIL [3]. Also *attrib.*

**1885** *Boston* (Mass.) *Jrnl.* 31 Jan. 6/8 The pony..dragging that primitive Indian carriage, the travoise. **1892** J. RALPH in *Harper's Mag.* Mar. 508/2 On the plains they will have horses dragging travoises, dogs with travoises. **1896** G. B. GRINNELL *Story of Indian* ix. 156 Three vehicles were known to the primitive Indian—the travois in the south and the sledge in the north for land travel, and the canoe wherever there were water ways. **1899** *Daily News* 12 Jan. 6/1 Groups of silent men with bows and quivers at their backs, of women riding or leading patient pack ponies that dragged their travois. *attrib.* **1894** *Outing* (U.S.) XXIV. 448/2 An old travois pole which some squaw had discarded.

**Travoy** (trăvoi·), *sb.* [A broad vocalization of *travày*, Canadian pronunc. of French *travail*: see prec. So called from its analogy to the Indian *travày* or *travail.*] In *lumbering*, a sledge used in dragging logs; one end of the log rests on the sledge and the other trails on the ground.

**1878** *Lumberman's Gaz.* 2 Feb. 87 The haul at the former camp is too long to use travoys. *Ibid.* 9 Feb., The 'travoy' is kept busy on short hauls. *attrib.* **1901** *Munsey's Mag.*

XXV. 387/1 These 'travoy-roads'—the name comes from the French *travois*—have to be cleared by the 'swampers'. *Ibid.* 387/2 While the travoy road is in the process of construction.

Hence **Travoy·** *v. trans.* and *intr.*, to use a travoy, to haul (logs) by means of a travoy; whence **Travoy·ing** *vbl. sb.*

1878 *Lumberman's Gaz.* 2 Feb. 86 Travoying can be carried on to good advantage. *Ibid.* 87 Those who have short enough hauls to travoy are not much more than paying expenses. 1901 *Munsey's Mag.* XXV. 386/1 Second, it must be 'travoyed' from a hundred yards to a mile; third, it is hauled on sleighs as far as fifteen or sixteen miles; fourth, it is driven down a river, and I have known drives three hundred miles in length.

**Traw, trawe**: see THROW *sb.*[1], TRAVE *sb.* TROW *v.*, TRUE. **Trawaile, -al, -el, -ell,** etc., obs. Sc. spellings of TRAVAIL, TRAVEL. **Trawethe,** obs. f. TROTH.

**Trawl** (trǭl), *sb.* Also 7 trall, (troul, 8–9 trowl). [Origin and age obscure. If quot. 1481–90 belongs here, *trawelle* might be related to rare MDu. *traghel* drag-net (in *Teuthonista* 1475), referred by Verwijs and Verdam ult. to L. *tragula* drag-net. But the MS. reading is indistinct, and some would read *tramelle* (TRAMMEL *sb.*[1] 1).

Apart from quot. 1481–90, the vb. appears earlier than the sb., and may be its source, but is no less obscure in origin. The forms *troul, trowl* were perh. due to confusion with *trowl*, TROLL, another fishing term.]

**I. 1.** A strong net or bag dragged along the bottom of fishing-banks; a drag-net; = TRAWL-NET 1; esp. that now often distinguished as the *beam-trawl*, described in its modern form in quot. 1880. Also applied to a similar smaller drag-net used for the scientific investigation of the sea-bottom, dredging for deep-sea organisms, etc.

[1481–90 *Howard Househ. Bks.* (Roxb.) 192 My lorde Rekened with his netter and he had sent home to stoke a dragge of viij fadam yᵉ fadam xij d...Item a trawelle (?) of vij fadam, the Fadam vj d.] 1759 B. MARTIN *Nat. Hist. Eng.* I. *Isle of Wight* 120 Tho' the Method of using Trawls, which of late Years has prevailed, is no small Diminution of their Plenty, it being found by Experience to destroy the Spawn. 1763 ELLIS in *Phil. Trans.* LIII. 419 The Animal..was taken in a trawl in 72 fathoms water. 1834 [see TRAWL-NET 1]. 1877 W. THOMSON *Voy. Challenger* I. i. 17 A portion of a huge Pyrosoma..was brought up in the trawl. 1880 *Chambers's Encycl.* IX. 524 The *Trawl*, or *Beam-trawl*..is a triangular purse-shaped net, about 70 feet long, usually having a breadth of about 40 feet at the mouth, and gradually diminishing to 4 or 5 feet at the commencement of the *cod*, or smaller end.., which is about 10 feet long, and of nearly uniform breadth. The upper part of the mouth is secured to a wooden beam about 40 feet long, which keeps the net open; this beam is supported on two upright iron frames, known as the *trawl-heads* or *irons*. The under side of the net..is made with a deeply-curved margin attached to the ground-rope, the whole length of it in contact with the ground...Two stout ropes..are fastened, one to the front of each of the trawl-heads, the other ends united to form a bridle, to which is shackled a warp 150 fathoms long. By this warp the trawl is towed. *Ibid.* 525 A kind of trawl called the pole-trawl..is now used only in the south of Ireland. It is much less effective than the beam-trawl. 1884 *Science* IV. 225/2 American appliances for deep-sea investigation.—Trawls and Tangles. *Ibid.* 226/2 The method of attaching the bridle in the Challenger trawl was similar to that afterwards adopted for the Blake trawl. 1887 E. J. MATHER *Nor'ard of Dogger* ix. (1889) 114 The cry of the watch on deck, 'Haul here! haul the trawl! all haul! all haul!' roused me at 5 a.m.

†**2.** (?) The action of trawling, or (?) a trawling-ground. *Obs. rare.*

1630 in *Descr. of Thames* (1758) 76 No Trawler to work in Tilbury Hope after Michaelmas, with any Manner of Net under four Inches for Plaice all the Net over. And no Trawler to come upon any Trawl with any other Net at any Time of the Year.

**II. 3.** *U.S.* Applied to a buoyed line used in sea-fishing, having numerous short lines with baited hooks attached at intervals: see quot. 1864; a trawl-line. Cf. also *trawl-anchor, -buoy, -roller* in 4.

*To set, shoot,* or *throw a trawl*, to place a baited trawl-line in position for fishing; *to strip a trawl*, to examine a trawl-line in position and remove the fish caught

(The connexion of this with sense 1 is doubtful.)

1864 WEBSTER, *Trawl*,..a long line, sometimes extending a mile or more, having short lines with baited hooks attached to it, used for catching certain fish, as cod, mackerel, and the like. *Ibid.* s.v. *Trawl-line*, It is used in deep-sea fishing, and is over-hauled every hour or so by men in small boats, who remove the fish (*strip the trawl*) and rebait the hooks. 1897 KIPLING *Captains Courageous* 75, I helped bait up trawl ashore 'fore I could well walk.

**III. 4.** *attrib.* and *Comb.*, as *trawl-boat, -fish, -fisherman, -fishing, -hawse, -smack, -twine*; **trawl-anchor,** a small anchor for a trawl-line (*Cent. Dict.* 1891); **trawl-beam,** the beam which holds open the mouth of a trawl-net; **trawl-buoy,** a buoy for buoying up a trawl-line; **trawl-head** (see quots.); **trawl-keg,** a keg-buoy used in connexion with a trawl-line (*Cent. Dict.*); **trawl-line**: see sense 3; **trawl-man,** one trained to use a trawl or drag-net; one who fishes with a trawl-net (in either sense); **trawl-master,** the master of a trawler: see TRAWLER 2; **trawl-roller**: see quot.; **trawl-warp,** the warp or rope of a trawl-net; **trawl-wings** *sb. pl.*, towing-nets attached one to each side of a small beam-trawl for the collection of free-swimming animals. See also TRAWL-NET.

1904 KIPLING in *Windsor Mag.* Jan. 226/2 At no time could we see the trawler, though we heard the click of her windlass, the jar of her *trawl-beam. 1799 *Naval Chron.* I. 344 A mast for his *trawl boat. 1636 *Maldon, Essex, Borough Deeds* Bundle 110, lf. 4 Re[ceived] for the groundage of a boate that brought *trall fish, 2*d.* 1865 *Daily Tel.* 5 Jan. 5/1, 80,000 tons of 'trawl-fish' alone..are sent to the metropolis in [a year]. 1886 *York Herald* 10 Aug. 7/5 There was a good supply of trawl fish at to-day's market, brought in by cutters. 1907 *Q. Rev.* Jan. 163 Out of 600 bottles more than 54 per cent. were returned by *trawl-fishermen. 1895 *Daily News* 16 Apr. 5/2 The new law enacted by the Danish Government prohibiting the carrying of *trawl fishing-gear within the territorial waters of Iceland. 1904 *Daily Chron.* 24 Oct. 5/2 One shot..went straight through the mizzen-mast, and passed through the casing and the trawl-fishing board. 1904 *Blackw. Mag.* Dec. 730 The swirl of the water beneath the *trawl-hawse. 1858 LEWES *Sea-side Stud.* 277 Along the edge of the wide opening is a stout wooden beam, to the ends of which are fastened the *trawl heads, namely, thick flat semicircular bands of iron. 1880 [see sense 1]. 1883 *Fisheries Exhib. Catal.* 48 Improved Trawl-heads, capable of clearing with safety submarine cable and similar obstacles. 1883 *Standard* 13 Sept. 5/4 The 'bultow' is..a set line, called in some places a '*trawl line'. 1775 FALCK *Day's Diving Vessel* 25 An experienced *trawlman, accustomed to sweeping [dragging the sea-bottom]. 1864 [see TRAWL-NET 2]. 1902 *Scotsman* 3 Jan. 7/6 In Aberdeen, the headquarters of trawling, *trawlmasters ought to be more careful than anywhere else. 1877 KNIGHT *Dict. Mech.*, **Trawl-roller*, a roller having a number of grooves cut in its periphery, and attached to the side of the wherry or dory, and over which the trawls are drawn into the boat. 1895 *Daily News* 20 May 7/6 The *trawl smack Hilda also came in with a hand gone. 1864 WEBSTER, **Trawl-warp*, a rope passing through a block, used in managing or dragging a trawl-net. 1887 E. J. MATHER *Nor'ard of Dogger* (1888) 158 Our skipper..run out some eight-inch trawl-warp over each bow. 1884 *Science* IV. 227/2 Fig. 3. The *trawl-wings attached to the beam-trawl in use.

**Trawl** (trǭl), *v.* (Also 8 trowl, 9 troll.) [Goes with TRAWL *sb.* q. v.: cf. MDu. *traghelen* to drag, f. *traghel.*]

**1.** *intr.* To fish with a net the edge of which is dragged along the bottom of the sea to catch the fish living there, esp. flat-fish; to fish with a trawl-net or in a trawler.

1561 EDEN *Arte Nauig.* Pref. ¶ iv b, Certayne Fyshermen that go a trawlyng for fyshe in catches or mongers. 1630 in *Descr. Thames* (1758) 77 No Trawler that..doth use to Trawl to take Soal, Chates, Plaice or Thorn-back. 1778 *Eng. Gazetteer* (ed. 2) s. v. *Rye*, All the rest of the year they trowl for soles, plaise,..brills, &c. 1822 W. ROBINSON in J. A. Heraud *Voy. & Mem. Midshipm.* v. (1837) 91 We managed to trawl several times in going over these banks. 1866 *Daily Tel.* 16 Jan. 7/4 To think that..Columbus, in his most famous voyage of discovery, commanded a craft no bigger than the lugger in which the Brighton fisherman goes out trawling!

**b.** To drag or dredge: cf. DRAG *v.* 7 b.

1861 *Stockton Times* 15 Nov., The body was being trawled for on Saturday.

**c.** *trans.* To fish over (a ground) with a trawl-net; in quot. *fig.*

1906 *Academy* 10 Feb. 136/1 Mr. Macmichael has trawled every source of information.

**2.** *intr.* To drag a seine-net behind and about a shoal of herring, etc., in order to drive, enclose, and catch them. (Also *trans.* with the net as obj.: see quots.)

1864 *Glasgow Daily Herald* 24 Sept., Trawling went on in this loch without much objection till the trawlers went into the narrow waters above Otter Spit. If trawling was to be allowed inshore they would trawl out. 1880 *Chambers's Encycl.* IX. 525/1 The term trawling is commonly, although incorrectly, employed in Scotland to designate a particular mode of herring-fishing, which, however, is only seine-net fishing..on the principle of encircling shoals of fish, as has been practised in pilchard-fishing on the south coast of England from time immemorial. 1887 *Fisheries U.S.* Sect. v. II. 306 The net used for driving is 200 fathoms long, 8 fathoms deep, with meshes 6 inches square, made of 9-yarn rope...The net is trawled behind and about the herd [of seals] so as to drive them into the fiord and keep them there. Sometimes they rush under or over the net.

**3.** *trans.* To catch or take with a trawl or trawl-net. Hence **Trawled** (trǭld) *ppl. a.*

1864 *Glasgow Daily Herald* 24 Sept., I have seen the curers anxious to get the trawled herring. 1864 *Rep. Sea Fisheries Comm.* (1865) II. 1188/1, I believe I got the second shot of trawled fish that was ever fished in this country. 1883 *Fisheries Exhib. Catal.* (ed. 4) 175 Swatching and Trolling Old Hoods [seals]. 1890 *Philos. Mag.* Ser. v. Aug. 199 A specimen of Triassic conglomerate trawled seven miles south of the Deadman headland. 1906 *Daily Chron.* 15 Oct. 6/2 The steam trawler Herbert Ingram has landed at Boston a Royal sturgeon, which weighed 20 st...It was trawled up in the North Sea.

¶ **4.** Often confounded with *trowl*, TROLL *v.* (q.v.).

The following quot. appears to be the earliest instance of this confusion.

1701 *Cowel's Interpr.* s.v. *Trawlermen*, Hence to trowle or trawle with a Trowling-line for Pikes.

**Trawler** (trǭ·ləɹ). [f. TRAWL *v.* + -ER [1].]

**1.** One who trawls; one who fishes (*a*) *orig.* with a trawl or trawl-net; (*b*) in W. of Scotl., etc. as in TRAWL *v.* 2; (*c*) in *U.S.* with a trawl-line.

1599 [implied in *trawler boat*: see 3]. 1630 [see TRAWL *sb.* 2, *v.* 1]. 1652 *Order Council of State* May 31–June 10 in *First Du. War* (Navy Rec. Soc.) I. 258 The Council did not intend..that fishermen..trawlers and others..should be stayed. 1864 *Glasgow Daily Herald* 24 Sept., If trawling recommences all will become trawlers. *Ibid.*, The trawlers have damaged my nets, and stolen some of them, too.

**2.** A vessel employed in fishing with a trawl-net; now applied to a STEAM-TRAWLER.

1847 WEBSTER, *Trawler*, a fishing vessel which trails or drags a net behind it. (*Eng.*) 1848 *Life in Normandy* (1863) II. xiii. 254 When I was in a trawler we always studied the run of the tide..and ran as clear before it as we could. 1881 *Times* 21 Dec. 4/4 An action of salvage for services rendered by the owners, masters, and crews of the steam trawler Restless Wave, and the smacks Urgent and Harry Sinclair, to the iron ship Culzean. 1887 E. J. MATHER *Nor'ard of Dogger* ix. (1889) 114 The modern plan of fitting the trawlers with steam-power and coming home..into vogue.

**3.** *attrib.* and *Comb.*, as *trawler-boat, -fleet*; †**trawler-man**: see quots.

1599 *Admir. Crt. Exam.* 34, Jan. 31, There came..Thomas Segar with his *trawler boat. 1909 *Daily Chron.* 28 Dec. 1/4 The Picton Castle, a steam trawler belonging to the Castle *trawler fleet..has been capsized in the River Douro. 1633 *Stow's Surv. London* 19 Fishermen..stiled by the name of T[r]inckermen,..Hebbermen, Petermen, *Trawlermen, &c., that have lived (in precedent times) by very unlawfull fishing on this River. 1701 *Cowell's Interpr.*, Trawlermen. 1839–40 [see HEBBERMAN].

**Trawley,** variant of TROLLEY.

**Trawling** (trǭ·liŋ), *vbl. sb.* [f. TRAWL *v.* + -ING [1].] Fishing with a trawl-net or beam-trawl; also, the action of TRAWL *v.* in other applications. Also *attrib.* as *trawling apparatus, sloop, smack,* etc.

1561, 1689 [see TRAWL *v.* 1, TRINKING]. 1823 BYRON *Juan* XIII. cvi. *note*, Even net fishing, trawling, &c., are more humane and useful—but angling! 1858 LEWES *Sea-side Stud.* 276, I got initiated into the art and mystery of trawling, having made friends with a fisherman, master of a Trawler. 1864 *Glasgow Daily Herald* 24 Sept., When trawling was going on it took down the price of the herring... If the trawling commences again they may stop the drift-nets altogether, for they would get no fish. 1860 *Daily News* 20 Mar., A large number of trawling-sloops have been caught at sea, and much anxiety is felt for their safety. 1883 *Fisheries Exhib. Catal.* 7 Trawling Apparatus for Smacks and Yachts. 1887 E. J. MATHER *Nor'ard of Dogger* (1888) 114 Aboard a trawling-smack in one of the Yarmouth fleets. 1889 *Act* 52 & 53 *Vict.* c. 23 § 6 It shall not be lawful to use the method of fishing known as beam trawling or otter trawling within three miles of low water mark of any part of the coast of Scotland.

**Trawl-net.** [f. TRAWL *sb.* or *v.* + NET *sb.*[1]]

**1.** A fishing-net used in trawling; *esp.* = TRAWL *sb.* 1.

1696 *Phil. Trans.* XIX. 350 Here [Lincolnshire] are also good plenty of large Soals, taken in Troul-Nets, the Smacks being under Sail trailing them along. 1769 PENNANT *Zool.* III. 190 They [soles] are usually taken in the trawl-net; they keep much at the bottom. 1834 *Tait's Mag.* I. 125/2 The trawl-net scrapes along the ground; and as the flat fish breed in the channel, it appears that much injury and destruction has been done to the young fry when the trawl has been used near the shore. 1880 *Chambers's Encycl.* IX. 525/1 Smaller trawl-nets than those above described are used in bays and estuaries.

**2.** *Sc.* and *U.S.* Applied (erroneously) to a kind of seine-net used to surround and enclose shoals of herring and other fish.

1855 *Zoologist* XIII. 4670 The trawl-nets in Loch Fine. 1864 *Glasgow Daily Herald* 24 Sept., I think the trawl men might be content if they were allowed to use their trawl nets inshore without taking them into deep water.

¶ See also TROLLNET, with quot. 1558.

**Trawnter,** obs. form of TRANTER.

**Trawt,** obs. pa. pple. of TROW *v.*

**Trawth(e, trawþe,** obs. forms of TROTH.

†**Tray,** *sb.*[1] *Obs.* Forms: 1 treᵹa, 2 treȝe, 3 treiȝe, 3–4 treie, 4 trei, treye, trai, traie, 4–5 trey, tray, 5 trye, 5–6 traye, 6 *Sc.* tra. [OE. *treᵹa* (wk. masc.) trouble, pain = ON. *tregi* (wk. masc.), Goth. *trigō* (wk. fem.):—OTeut. **treg-on-, -ōn-*, f. **treg-*: see TRAY *v.*[1]] Pain, grief, affliction, trouble, vexation; esp. in alliterative phr. *tray and teen, teen and tray.*

*c* 700 *Cædmon's Gen.* 2274 (Gr.) Ic fleah wean,..treᵹan and teonan. *a* 1000 *Boeth. Metr.* v. 42 Forðæm þa tweᵹen treᵹan teoð tosomne. *c* 1020 *Rule St. Benet* iv. (Logeman) 20/10 Treᵹan debemus, ᵹedonne dæde ᵹeþyldelice ah forþyldian. *a* 1200 *Moral Ode* 371 Þer is blisse abuten treȝe [*v.r.* treiȝe]. *a* 1240 *Ureisun* 61 in *Cott. Hom.* 193 Muruhðe moniuold wið-ute teone and treie. 1357 *Lay Folks Catech.* 26 With-outen travaile or trey [*v.r.* tray] or passyng of tyme. *c* 1450 *Life St. Cuthbert* (Surtees) 112 Tene and tray of tormentoures. 1560 ROLLAND *Seven Sages* 17 Sum gettis plesure, vthers gettis tray and tene.

**Tray** (trēⁱ), *sb.*[2] Forms: 1 *trieᵹ, triᵹ, 4–7 trey, (*pl.* 4 treyes), 6 treie, traie, (7 trea), 4– tray (*pl.* 4 -es, 4– -s). [OE. **trieᵹ, triᵹ* = ON. **trøy*, OSw. (Dalecarl.) *trē* a corn-measure of definite capacity:—OTeut. **traujoᵐ*. For the form-history cf. HAY *sb.*[1], formerly (3–7) *hey*, OE. *hiᵹ*, ON. **høy, hey*, OSw. *hē*:—OTeut. **haujoᵐ*. The base *trau-* is in ablaut-relation with *treu-*, whence Goth. *triu*, OE. *treow* TREE, so that the primary sense may have been 'wooden (vessel)'.

It is remarkable that the word should appear so rarely in OE. and should be so common later. See on the etymol. Holthausen *Indog. Forsch.* XIX. 294, E. Lidén *ibid.* XVIII. 413.]

**1.** A utensil of the form of a flat board with a raised rim, or of a shallow box without a lid, made of wood, metal, or other material, of various sizes and shapes (round, oval, quadrilateral with rounded corners, etc.); now used for carrying plates, dishes, cups and other vessels, cards, etc., for containing and exhibiting small articles, as jewellery, natural history specimens, etc., and for various other purposes, as in mining, photography, chemistry, or other arts and sciences. (Often with defining word expressing its purpose, as *bread-tray, card-tray, tea-tray*, etc.: see these words.) Formerly more widely applied to shallow open vessels generally. In 13–14th c., app. also, as in OSwedish, name of a measure of capacity.

**10..** *Læceboc* in *Sax. Leechd.* II. 340 Nim þæt reade ryden, do on triȝ, hæt þonne stanas swiþe hate, leȝe on þæt triȝ innan. **1270** in *Sel. Cas. Law Merchant* (Selden Soc.) I. 7 Detinuerunt ei quinque marcas et quinque solidos..pro xj. treys [h]ordei sibi venditis. **1317** *Ibid.* 105 Cum simul emissent xx. treys carbonis maris. **13..** *Coer de L.* 1490 Bye us vessel gret plente, Dysschys, cuppys, and sawsers, Bolles, treyes, and platers. **1374** *Acc. John de Sleford* (Acc. Exch. K. R. 397/10, P.R.O.), Pro iiij trays de ligno precii pecie .iij. d. *c* **1475–1500** *Inv.* in Noakes *Worcester Mon.* (1866) 173 In duobus vasis de novo factis, vocatis trayes. **1494** FABYAN *Chron.* IV. lxix. 48, xii. Cophyns or Treys full of Erth he bare away vpon his shulders. **1553** EDEN *Treat. Newe Ind.* (Arb.) 18 They..haue theyr meate in great disshes or treys of copper. **1608** TOPSELL *Serpents* (1658) 659 Of a..healthy stock of Hornets..they have gathered three or four trays or baskets full of combes. **1639** HORN & ROB. *Gate Lang. Unl.* xl. § 434 Implements of a kitchin are..a trivet, a grater, treas, boles, water pitchers, platters. **1674** tr. *Scheffer's Lapland* 93 A kind of trey made of birch. **1848** THACKERAY *Van. Fair* vi, Sambo came into the room..with..a note on a tray. **1884** KNIGHT *Dict. Mech.* Supp. 893/1 *Thomson Battery* (Electricity), a modification of Menotti's battery, in which a copper tray replaces the copper plate, and contains the sulphate of copper crystals, and the superstratum of wet sawdust upon which rests the zinc element. **1885** R. BUCHANAN *Annan Water* vii, He soon returned carrying the tray, with teapot, cups, and saucers, [etc.].

**b.** In other uses: †(*a*) A mason's hod or vessel for mortar (*obs.*); (*b*) A butcher's tray: see quot. 1665; (*c*) A pig's trough.

**1350–1** *MS. Acc. Exchequer K. R.* Bundle 492. 27 (P.R.O.) Pro vj trayes emptis pro mortero imponendo iij s. **1573** TUSSER *Husb.* (1878) 37 A lath hammer, trowel, a hod, or a traie. **1573–80** BARET *Alv.* T 353 A Treie, or such hollowe vessell..that Laborers carrie morter in to serue Tilers, or Plasterers. **1611** COTGR., *Oiseau*..also, a Hodd; the Tray wherein Masons, &c., carrie their Mortar. **1665** HOOKE *Microgr.* xlvi. 197 Those hollow Trayes, in which Butchers carry meat. **1714** GAY *Sheph. Week, Friday* 65 No more her care shall fill the hollow tray, To fat the guzzling hogs with floods of whey.

**c.** *Ordnance.* See quot.

**1911** WEBSTER, *Tray*..a flat or curved piece of metal used to hold ammunition or any part of the mechanism of a gun; specif., in heavy cannon, a brass or steel part (called also *plugtray*) of the breech mechanism hinged on the rear.

**2.** *dial.* A hurdle.

**1829** [J. R. BEST] *Pers. & Lit. Mem.* 256 The hurdles or trays as we [in Lincolnshire] call them, in which the sheep are to be penned. **1832** *Stamford Mercury* 27 Jan. 2/5, 4 dozen of fence trays. **1851** *Jrnl. R. Agric. Soc.* XII. II. 402 The field..should be partitioned by 'trays' (or hurdles).

**3.** Part of the life-guard used on tram-cars and similar vehicles, a flat grid on which obstructions are picked up.

**1910** (April) *Board of Trade Mem., Tramways* [etc.] *on Public Roads.* (4) (*c*) The tray of the guard should be provided with a spring so as to hold the front edge down to the surface of the roadway when the tray is dropped. **1913** E. T. RUTHVEN-MURRAY *Let.*, If the car strikes anything on the track, the gate is pushed backwards and releases a 'trigger' (a catch sustaining the tray) which allows the tray to fall so that it slides along on the road and scoops up the obstruction.

**4.** *attrib.* and *Comb.*, as *tray-board, -load, -man, -monger*; *tray-like* adj.; **tray-battery** *Electr.* (see quot.); **tray-buggy** (*U.S.*), a buggy having a flat tray-like body; **tray-cloth**, a cloth or napkin placed upon a tray on which dishes, etc. are carried; **tray-galley**, in printing, a tray to which the type is transferred from the composing-stick; **tray-sheet**, a sheet of sheet-iron to be made into a tray.

**1884** KNIGHT *Dict. Mech.* Suppl., **Tray Battery* (*Electricity*), one in which the tray forms one of the elements of the combination. **1875** SIR T. SEATON *Fret Cutting* 42 The *tray-board should be five-eighths of an inch. **1890** 'R. BOLDREWOOD' *Miner's Right* xviii, A quiet horse and a light *tray buggy. **1897** *Westm. Gaz.* 25 Jan. 2/1 The poor fellow was borne to his rest on the shoulders of his friends, in a shallow, open *tray-coffin, the dead young face lying among flowers. **1896** T. L. DE VINNE *Moxon's Mech. Exerc., Printing* 407 The long *tray-galley of wood. **1906** R. WHITEING *Ring in New* 115 A small cabinet of *tray-like drawers. **1908** H. WALES *Old Allegiance* i. 13 When the servant had disappeared with the last *tray-load [of supper things]. **1764** *Poll Knts. of Shire Chelmsford 13th & 14th Dec. 1763*, Robert Dolphin *Traymonger. **1891** *Daily News* 9 Nov. 2/6 *Tray sheets for stamping purposes.

Hence **Tray·let** (*nonce-wd.*), a diminutive tray.

**1825** *Blackw. Mag.* XVII. 222 A small napkin-covered traylet, containing a cold sheep's head.

† **Tray**, *sb.*[3] *Obs. rare.* [app. f. TRAY *v.*[2]] Deceit, stratagem, ambush, trick.

*c* **1430** *Syr Gener.* (Roxb.) 7150 That we wer homward, I you pray, For euer I drede me of som fals tray. *c* **1440** *York Myst.* xxix. 60 Oure knyghtis þai are furth wente To take hym with a traye.

**Tray**, *sb.*[4] *Venery.* Also **trez.** [The same word as TREY three, in dice, cards, etc.; re-spelt after BAY *sb.*[6] Believed to go back in oral use to 18th c. at least.] The third branch of a stag's horn. Also *tray antler, tray tine.*

**1812** LD. GRAVES *Let.* (June 2) *to Ld. Ebrington in ref. to Stag-hunting Establmt. of Devon* (Exeter 1814) 14 His brow, bay, and tray antlers are termed his Rights. **1838** SCROPE *Art Deer-stalking* 2, 3 The stag's brow, bay and tray antlers are called his rights...A warrantable stag has brow, bay and tray, and two points on the tops of both horns. *Note.* I have taken my nomenclature from the Devonshire Hunt, as the best authority. It has been founded considerably above a century. **1863** KINGSLEY *Water-Bab.* ii. 62 You may know..what his rights mean, if he has them, brow, bay, tray, and points. **1884** JEFFERIES *Red Deer* iv, Close to the head a point springs from the beam and is curved upwards; this is called the brow point. Just over it a second starts,..this is called the bay. There is then an interval, till some way up the beam, or main stem, a third—the tray—appears. **1893** LYDEKKER *Horns & Hoofs* 269 The third the trez, tray, or royal tine. *Ibid.* 320 [The elk's] antlers..rise from the sides of the skull by a narrow beam ..without either brow, bez, or trez-tine.

† **Tray**, *v.*[1] *Obs.* Forms: 1 treȝian, 3 treȝe; *pa. t.* 3 traied, 4 traid; *pa. pple.* 3 treyde, 4 trayed. [OE. *tregian* (wk.), = OS. *tregan* (strong vb.) to rue, ON. *trega* (str.) to grieve:—OTeut. **treg-*: cf. TRAY *sb.*[1]] *trans.* To pain, grieve, trouble, vex, afflict.

*a* **1000** *Eadwine's Cant. Psalter* iii. 1 Drihten to hwi ȝemanifalde synt þa þe treȝiað oððe swencað me [*qui tribulant me*]. **1104** *O. E. Chron.* (Laud MS.), Eall þis wæs God mid to gremienne and þas arme leode mid to treȝienne. *c* **1250** *Gen. & Ex.* 3975 Quað balaam, 'for ðu treȝest me; Had ic an swerd, ic sluȝe ðe'. *a* **1300** *E. E. Psalter* v. 12 Out-put þam þar þai sal be, Lauerd for þai traied þe. **13..** *K. Alis.* 3046 (Bodl. MS.) Ich am so trayed þat neeȝ ich weþe!

† **Tray**, *v.*[2] *Obs.* Forms: 3–5 traye, (3 trayȝe), 3–6 traie, 4–6 tray (4 trai, 4–5 treie). [ad. OF. *traïr* (Roland 11th c.), F. *trahir* to betray:—late pop.L. **tradīre*, for L. *trādĕre* to deliver over, f. *tra-* (TRANS-) + *dare* to give.] *trans.* To betray.

*c* **1275** *Passion our Lord* 194 in *O. E. Misc.* 42 Mid þine valse cosse þu trayest monnes sune. *a* **1300** *Cursor M.* 15277 (Cott.) Þat i ha luued, he sal me trai [*Fairf.* tray]. **1377** LANGL. *P. Pl.* B. III. 123 Truste of hire tresore treieth ful manye. *c* **1400** *Laud Troy Bk.* 18053 Thei swore bothe to traye the toun. **1559** *Mirr. Mag.* (1563) Fiv, [To] punysh such as had my brother trayed. **1568** T. HOWELL *Newe Sonets* (1879) 117 A canckred poyson..Full closely coucht in pleasant bayte, with that poore soule to tray.

**Tray**, *v.*[3]: see TREY, TRAY *v.*

† **Tray**, *int. Obs.* [Exclamatory use of OF. *trai, tray*, pa. pple. of *traïr* to betray: see Godef. *Compl.*] Betrayed! Treachery! Treason!

*c* **1440** LOVELICH *Merlin* xiv. 14130 And evere he cride: 'Tray, tray, tray!' **1600–1** in *Hatfield Papers* (Hist. MSS. Comm.) XI. 46 But Orrell..did run and leap in the forefront with Sir Christopher Blount and Mr. Busshell, their weapons drawn, crying, 'Saw, Saw, Saw, Saw, tray, tray'.

**Tray**, obs. form of TREY, TROW *v.*

**Trayce**, obs. form of TRACE *sb.*[2]

† **Trayer.** *Obs. rare.* Also 5 **trayhour**, 6 **trayhor, trayor.** [ME. a. OF. *traieor, traior, trayeur*, nom. *traierre, trayeres* (*de vin*, etc.) (13th c. in Godef.), f. *trai-re* to draw (:—L. *trahĕre*): see -OR.] A drawer; a tapster.

**1473** *Rolls of Parlt.* VI. 96/2 Henry Fylongley, late Yoman trayer of our Celer. **1485** *Ibid.* 379/2 James Ederich, Yeoman Trayhour of oure Seller. **1526** in *Househ. Ord.* (1790) 234 That noe Hoggesheads be meddled with by the Trayhor untill that the said Groome-Grobber hath perused the same..whether it be drawne out as much as it ought to be, or not. **1596** SIR J. CÆSAR *Crt. Requests* (1597) 159 Tho. More, grome Trayor of the Kings Celler.

**Trayfle, -folde, -fole,** obs. ff. TREFLE, TREFOIL.

**Trayful** (trē¹·ful). [f. TRAY *sb.*[2] + -FUL.] As much as a tray will hold.

**1634–5** BRERETON *Trav.* (Chetham Soc.) 22 The kine give twenty seven great trease-full of milk. **1838** [MISS MAITLAND] *Lett. fr. Madras* (1843) 193 The Zemindar sent a very polite message with a tray-full of oranges. **1883** *Century Mag.* XXVI. 53 He has smashed a trayful of crockery. **1896** YOUNGHUSBAND *Hrt. Continent* vii. 170 Fruit is brought before you in huge trayfuls.

**Trayish,** variant of TRAISE *v. Obs.*, to betray.

**Trayl(e, trayll(e,** obs. forms of TRAIL.

**Traylles,** obs. form of TRELLIS.

† **Tray·ment.** *Obs. rare*—°. [f. TRAY *v.*[2] + -MENT; or a. OF. *traiement* (13th c. in Godef.).] Betrayal.

**1468** *Medulla Gram.* (in *Cath. Angl.* 30 *note*), *Prodicio*, a trayment.

**Trayn-, Trays-, Trayt-**: see TRAI-.

† **Trayne.** *Obs. rare*—¹. [Etymology obscure; perh. an error for *tayner.*] A fox's burrow or earth.

*c* **1400** MAUNDEV. (1839) xxvi. 267 In the time of Antecrist, a fox schall make there his trayne [*Roxb.* den; Fr. *vn vopil ferra sa taignere*], and mynen an hole, where kyng Alisandre leet make the ȝates.

**Trayor,** var. TRAYER *Obs.*

**Trays(e,** obs. ff. TRACE. **Trayse**: see TREY.

**Trayse, traysch,** etc., var. TRAISE, TRAISH.

**Trayson, -oun,** etc., obs. ff. TREASON.

**Trayte, -tee, -tye,** obs. ff. TREAT, TREATY.

† **Tray·thly,** *adv. Obs. rare.* Etymology and meaning obscure.

**13..** *E. E. Allit. P.* B. 907 For we schal tyne þis toun & trayþely disstrye. *Ibid.* 1137 & entyses hym to tene more trayþly þen euer In Iuda.

**Traytice, -yse,** var. TRETIS *a. Obs.* **Tray-trip,** var. TREY-TRIP *Obs.* **Traywe,** obs. f. TROW *v.*

**Traze,** obs. form of TRACE *sb.*[1]

**Trea,** obs. form of TRAY *sb.*[2], TREY.

† **Treacher** (tre·tʃəɹ). *Obs.* Forms: 3 **trichor**, 3–5 **-our**, 4 **trychor**, (**tryschor**), 5 **trychour**, **-eour, -eur**, 6 **trycher**; 4 **trechur, trecchour**, 4–6 (8) **trechour**, 5 **-ure**; 6 **trechor**, (**trachour**, **treitcheoure**), 6–7 **trecher**, 6–8 **treacher, -our**, 8 **-or.** [a. OF. *trecheor, -eur, tricheor, -eur* (12th c. in Godef.), F. *tricheur*, agent-n. (see -ER[2], -OR) fr. OF. *trechier, tricher* to cheat, trick: see TRECHE, TRICH *v.* Cf. Prov. *trichaire, trichador*, It. *trecchiero.*]

A deceiver, a cheat; one who deceives by trickery; *sometimes*, a traitor.

*c* **1290** *S. Eng. Leg.* I. 332/326 Þov art symon Magus, godes trichor. *Ibid.* 348/104 Askebert he was i-cleoped, a strong trichour, alas! ? *a* **1366** CHAUCER *Rom. Rose* 197 That is she that makith trechoures. **1481** CAXTON *Godeffroy* lxxx. 127 He was a trychour. **1513** DOUGLAS *Æneis* VIII. Prol. 97 Sum trachour [*v.r.* treitcheoure] crynis the cunȝe, and kepis corn stakis. **1591** SPENSER *M. Hubberd* 1255 Those same treachours vile. **1613** *Answ. Uncasing of Machivil's Instr.* G j b, If to Countrie thou hast a trechers heart. **1713** CROXALL *Orig. Canto Spenser* xxxv. (1714) 24 But smiling on the Treachour stood aloof. **1767** MICKLE *Concub.* I. xxxvii, The hungrie Trout the glitteraund Treachor eyes.

**b.** *attrib.* or as *adj.* Cheating, treacherous.

*c* **1400** *Rom. Rose* 6308 Forsothe I am a fals traitour God iugged me for a theef trichour. **1422** tr. *Secreta Secret., Priv. Priv.* 235 Whoso hath the neke ful shorte he is voucheous, deceyuant, and trechure. **1508** DUNBAR *Flyting* 55 The trechour tung hes tane ane heland strynd.

† **Trea·cherer.** *Obs.* Forms: 6 **trecherer, tretcherer**, 7 **treacherer.** [app. f. TREACHER-Y + -ER[1]: cf. *fripper-y, -er, adulter-y, -er.*] = prec. (In quot. 1592 with pun on *treasurer.*)

**1571** FORTESCUE *Forest* 104 b, The ribaulde and the graceless tretcherer. **1592** *Declar. Causes Gt. Troubles agst. Realm Eng.* 60 The Lord Trecherer I trust can giue her maiestie and the realme good accomptes of them. **1601** W. WATSON *Imp. Consid. Sec. Priests* (1675) 77 Stanley is a treacherer.

† **Trea·cherize,** *v. Obs. rare.* [f. TREACHER or TREACHERY + -IZE.] *intr.* To act in a treacherous manner; to play the deceiver or traitor. Hence † **Trea·cherizing** *vbl. sb.*

**1656** S. H. *Gold. Law* 4 Do they not by this render themselves Traytors, as contrary to trust, duty, and engagement, to trecherize it? *Ibid.* 10 Is not this to..go on in your Trecherizings, in hope of revenge and advancement?

† **Trea·cherly,** *adv. Obs. rare*—¹. [f. TREACHER + -LY[2].] = TREACHEROUSLY.

*c* **1394** *P. Pl. Crede* 475 Y pray þe, þou me telle More of þise tryflers, how trechurly þei libbeþ?

**Treacherous** (tre·tʃərəs), *a.* Forms: 4 **tricherous, -ows**; 4–7 **trecherous**, (4–5 **-us**, 5 **-owse, trecctherous**, 6 **trechrous**, 7 **tretcherous**), 6– **treacherous**, (6 **-ouse**). [a. OF. *trecher-, tricheros, -us, -eus* (12th c. in Godef.), f. *trecheur, tricheur* TREACHER: see -OUS.]

**1.** Of persons, their attributes or actions: Characterized by treachery; deceiving, perfidious, false; disloyal, traitorous.

*c* **1330** R. BRUNNE *Chron. Wace* (Rolls) 16519 Þe tricherous Saxons—þeyr tricherye vs euere mones. **1387** TREVISA *Higden* (Rolls) I. 357 Þe men beeþ variable and vnstedefast, trecherous and gileful. **1483** *Cath. Angl.* 392/1 Trecherus, *vbi* fals (*A.*). **1570** LEVINS *Manip.* 226/34 Treacherouse, *proditorius.* **1611** SHAKS. *Cymb.* IV. ii. 317 To write, and read, Be henceforth treacherous. **1644** EVELYN *Diary* 17 Nov., After a true tretcherous Italian guise. **1725** DE FOE *Voy. round World* (1840) 91 As fierce cruel treacherous and merciless a crew of human devils as any I have met with. **1897** MARY KINGSLEY *W. Africa* 329 A treacherous, thievish, murderous cannibal.

**2.** *fig.* Of things: Deceptive, untrustworthy, unreliable; of ground, ice, etc., unstable, insecure.

**1610** B. JONSON *Alch.* II. iii, O, yes, but I forgot. I haue ..One o' the treacherou'st memories, I doe thinke, Of all mankind. **1709** POPE *Ess. Crit.* 492 The treach'rous colours the fair art betray, And all the bright creation fades away. **1806–7** J. BERESFORD *Miseries Hum. Life* (1826) II. v, The ice proving treacherous. **1855** MACAULAY *Hist. Eng.* xiii. III. 335 Up steep crags, and over treacherous morasses, he moved as easily [etc.]. **1860** TYNDALL *Glac.* I. xv. 102 Over other [crevasses] a thin and treacherous roof was thrown. **1901** ALLDRIDGE *Sherbro* xxvi. 288 We scrambled over a treacherous-looking bamboo bridge.

**Trea·cherously,** *adv.* [f. prec. + -LY[2].] In a treacherous manner; by or with treachery.

*a* **1340** HAMPOLE *Psalter* xiii. 5 With þaire tongis tricherously þai wroght. **1596** SPENSER *F. Q.* V. vi. 26 A Spaniell wayting carefully Least any should betray his Lady treacherously. **1678** WANLEY *Wond. Lit. World* v. ii. § 6. 469/1 Gratian..was treacherously murdered. **1860** TYNDALL *Glac.* I. xi. 69, I stepped..upon a block of granite..; it treacherously turned under me.

**Treacherousness** (tre·tʃərəsnės). [f. as prec. + -NESS.] The quality of being treacherous.

**1610** BP. HALL *Apol. Brownists* xxiii, If you could..wash your hands of vnnaturall impietie, and trecherousnesse. **1647**

BOYLE *Let. to Hartlib* 8 Apr., Wks. 1772 I. p. xxxix, The treacherousness of my memory. **1865** *Ice-Caves of France* etc. 76 [He] had..experienced the treacherousness of this slope of ice.

**Treachery** (tre·tʃəri). Forms: 3–4 **tricherie, -eri, trycherye,** (3 **tricheriȝe**), 3–5 **tricherye,** (4 **trichcherye, tricchori,** 5 **trichery(e, trichory,** 6 **tritcherie**); 4–7 **trecherie, -ery,** (4 **-eri, -ori, trecchery, -eri, trecchry,** 4–5 **trecherie,** 5 **trechory, -ury, tretcherye,** 6 **-erie,** 5–6 **trecherye**), 6– **treachery,** (7 **treacherie**). [a. OF. *trecherie, tricherie* (12th c. in Godef.), F. *tricherie* treachery, f. *tricher* to cheat + *-erie*, -ERY. See TREACHER.] Deceit, cheating, perfidy; violation of faith or betrayal of trust; perfidious conduct.

*a* **1225** *Ancr. R.* 202 Þe Vox of ȝiscunge haueð þeos hweolpes: Tricherie & Gile, Þeofðe, Reflac [etc.]. *c* **1300** *Havelok* 2988 Hwou he woren with wronge ledde..with trecherie. **1422** tr. *Secreta Secret., Priv. Priv.* 231 Dysposyd to trechury and othyr ill tecchis. **1474** CAXTON *Chesse* III. iii. (1883) 94 To make amendes to them that by theyr tricherye they haue endomaged. **1596** SPENSER *F. Q.* V. iv. 46 But Talus usde, in times of jeopardy, To keepe a nightly watch for dread of treachery. **1599** DALLAM in *Early Voy. Levant* (Hakl. Soc.) 55 We doubted that some tritcherie would hapen unto us. **1611** COTGR., *Tricherie*, (whence, as it seemes, our trecherie) cousenage, deceit, a cheating, a beguiling. **1748** *Anson's Voy.* II. vi. 191 In case of any misconduct or treachery, he threatened..that the Pilots should be instantly shot. **1866** LIVINGSTONE *Last Jrnls.* (1873) I. x. 258 Treachery was suspected.

*fig.* **1896** *Allbutt's Syst. Med.* I. 268 Presenting some resemblance in climate to the Riviera, it [S. California] shares some of its drawbacks, treachery amongst them.

**b.** *esp.* The deception or perfidy of a traitor; treason against a sovereign, lord, or master.

*a* **1300** *Cursor M.* 18882 (Cott.) It most nu nede þe writte be fulfild..O iudas and his trecheri [*Gött.* trechori]. **13..** *Gaw. & Gr. Knt.* 4 Þe tulk þat þe trammes of tresoun þer wroȝt, Watz tried for his tricherie. *a* **1425** *Cursor M.* 15476 (Trin.) Bettur..to haue bene deed...Þen wiþ a kissyng on þis wise His lord done triccherye [*v. r.* tresun]. **1570** LEVINS *Manip.* 106/18 Traytorie, *proditio*. Treachery, *idem*. **1651** N. BACON *Dist. Govt. Eng.* II. xi. 98 They preferred the good of their Countrey above all; accounting trechery against it..to be a crime of great concernment. **1706** PHILLIPS (ed. Kersey), *Treachery*, Unfaithfulness, Disloyalty. **1911** G. MILLIGAN in *Encycl. Brit.* XV. 536/1 In ecclesiastical legend..Judas Iscariot is generally treated as the very incarnation of treachery.

**c.** With *a* and *pl.* An instance of this, an act of perfidy or treason.

*a* **1300** *Cursor M.* 3870 (Cott.) Laban said, 'frend, ful blethli.' Bot þar he did a trecheri. *c* **1300** *Havelok* 443 He þouthe a ful strong trechery, A trayson, and a felony,..forto make. **1586** J. HOOKER *Hist. Irel.* in *Holinshed* II. 142/1 They..revolve, as dogs to their vomits, so they to their treasons and treacheries. **1651** *Nicholas Papers* (Camden) I. 235 Hee that discovered to mee a trechery intended by one Tickell against mee in Ireland. **1726** LEONI *Alberti's Archit.* I. 66/1 Angles jutting out from..the Wall,..for treacheries, and for the safer throwing their Darts..are of some advantage to the Enemy. **1847** HELPS *Friends in C.* Ser. I. viii. 151 You hear a child reprimanded about a point of dress, or some trivial thing, as if it had committed a treachery.

**d.** *transf.* A substance that treacherously gives way under the feet.

**1870** LOWELL *Wks.* (1890) III. 277 Slumping clumsily about in the mealy treachery. **1886** G. ALLEN *Kalee's Shrine* xiii. 142 The intervening belt [of mud] was one huge waste expanse of liquid treachery.

†**Treachet.** *Obs.* A name for the lob-worm.

**1787** BEST *Angling* (ed. 2) 16 The Lob-worm, Dew-worm, Garden-worm, Twatchel, or Treachet.

† **Treachetour.** *Obs.* [? f. TRECHET *v.* + -OUR; or perh. a scribal or printer's error for **treacherour*, TREACHERER.] A deceiver, a traitor.

**1590** SPENSER *F. Q.* II. x. 51 The king was by a Treachetour Disguised slaine, ere any thereof thought. **1596** *Ibid.* VI. viii. 7 Ye caytiue treachetours vntrew.

**Treacle** (trī·k'l), *sb.* Forms: α. 4–6 **tryacle,** 4–7 **triacle,** 5 **tryacall, -cul, -kylle, -kell,** 6 **tri-, tryakle, tryackill,** 7 **triackle, -akcle**; β. 5 **tracle, treakill, -ylle,** 6 **treakil,** 6–7 **treakle,** 4– **treacle**; γ. *dial.* 9 **threeakle, traycle,** etc., *Sc.* **trykle.** [ME. *trya·cle, tria·cle*, a. OF. *triacle* (*a* 1200 in Godef. *Compl.*, s.v. *Theriaque*), beside *tiriacle* (1460), *teracle* (15th c.): = Prov. *triacla*, Sp., It. *triaca*, Pg. *triaga*, popular forms for Pr. *tiriaca*, Sp. *teriaca*, Pg. *theriaga*, It. *teriaca*, repr. a pop. late L. **triaca* for *thēriaca* :—Gr. θηριακή antidote against a venomous bite: see THERIAC, THERIACLE. The sense development in Eng. has proceeded further than in the Romanic langs.]

**I.** Original sense: chiefly *Obs.*

†**1.** *Old Pharm.* A medicinal compound, orig. a kind of salve, composed of many ingredients, formerly in repute as an alexipharmic against and antidote to venomous bites, poisons generally, and malignant diseases. Cf. THERIAC, THERIACLE. *Obs.*

As to its alleged composition, see THERIACLE.

**1340** *Ayenb.* 17 Vor-zoþe he is ine grat peril to huam alle triacle went in to uenym. *c* **1386** CHAUCER *Pard. Prol.* 28, I almoost haue caught a Cardynacle By corpus bones but I haue triacle [*v. r.* treacle]. **1390** *Earl Derby's Exp.* (Camden) 12 Pro factura unius pixidis de argento pro triacle imponendo. *a* **1400** HYLTON *Scala Perf.* (W. de W. 1494) III. xix, This oynement is precyous..for it is tryacle made of venym to destroy venym. *c* **1425** *St. Mary of Oignies* I. ix. in *Anglia* VIII. 143 Hee..ȝaf hym firste tryacul, þat hee myghte þe more priuely bringe in after venym. **1483** *Cath. Angl.* 392/1 Treakylle (*A.* Tryakylle), *tiriaca*. **1535** COVERDALE *Jer.* viii. 22, I am hevy and abashed, for there is no more Triacle at Galaad. **1545** J. HEYWOOD *Four P. P.* Plays (1905) 46 Richer is one box of this triacle Than all thy relics that do no miracle. **1628** WITHER *Brit. Rememb.* II. 315 A sixth of Cordials and Elixars prates; And some of Treacles, and of Mithridates. *a* **1658** CLEVELAND *Wks.* (1687) 18 Do study Salve and Triacle. **1693** SIR T. P. BLOUNT *Nat. Hist.* 348 The chief Use of Vipers is for the making of Treacle. **1804** *Med. Jrnl.* XII. 139 His anti-venereal treacle, well-known for curing the venereal disease, rheumatism, scurvy, old-standing sores.

†**b.** *transf.* Anything to which alexipharmic or antidotal virtue is ascribed; a sovereign remedy.

**1544** PHAER *Regim. Lyfe* (1560) L viij b, A nut is called the triacle of fish, shaled and sugred with a litle rose water. **1563** HYLL *Art Garden.* (1593) 75 Hearb grace..may well be kept for fiue yeares, and the leaues dryed, for all poysons, and a peculiar Triacle for the poor. **1727** *Bradley's Fam. Dict.* s.v. *Garlick*, To eat Garlick fasting is the Treacle of the Country People in the time of a Plague.

†**c.** In the names of particular kinds, with various qualifications, indicating place of origin, etc.; as *Treacle of Andromachus* = VENICE TREACLE; *Treacle of Genoa, Treacle of Flanders, London treacle, Roman treacle.*

**1479** J. PASTON in *P. Lett.* III. 259 Send me by the next man that comyth fro London ij pottys of tryacle of Jenne,—they shall cost xvj*d*. **1545** *Rates of Customs* c vj b, Tryacle of flaunders the barrell xx s. Tryacle of Jeane the pounde iiii d. **1586** *Ibid.* F j, Treacle of Flaunders the barrel xl.s. **1651** WITTIE tr. *Primrose's Pop. Err.* I. vii. 25 That ancient, and in all ages well approved Triacle of Andromachus, as also the Mithridate of Damocrates. *a* **1668** LASSELS *Voy. Italy* (1670) II. 213 The Apothecaries shop, where a Lay brother makes excellent Roman Treacle. *c* **1720** W. GIBSON *Farrier's Dispens.* v. III. (1734) 147 *London Treacle*...This seems to have been designed as a Succedaneum for the Mithridate, or Venice Treacle, and is that which the Country Apothecaries sell the Farriers under the general Name of Treacle, which many of the latter distinguish from the common Molossus-Treacle, by calling it, The Doctor's, or the Apothecaries Treacle. **1753** J. BARTLET *Gentl. Farrier* iii. 27 Genoa treacle twelve ounces, oil of anniseed one ounce.

**2.** *fig. Obs.* or *arch.*

*a* **1310** in Wright *Lyric P.* v. 26 Trewe triacle y-told with tonges in trone. **1340** *Ayenb.* 144 Þe oþer..hatte þe yefþ of pite. Þet is propreliche a dyau and a triacle a-ye alle kueadnesse, and nameliche aye þet uenim of zenne of enuie. *c* **1430** LYDG. *Min. Poems* (Percy Soc.) 236 The name of Jhesu! Geyn goostly venyms, holsomest tryacle. **1529** MORE *Dyaloge* IV. Wks. 273/2 Nowe tourne they the tryacle of holye scrypture quite into poyson. **1573** G. HARVEY *Letter-bk.* (Camden) 22 Let me understand a part how your London triacle hath wrouht against your Cambridg poisun. **1635** QUARLES *Embl.* v. xi. 42 Thou art the treacle that must make me sound. **1641** MILTON *Ch. Govt.* II. Concl., Wks. 1851 III. 178 With the sovran treacle of sound doctrine..to fortifie their hearts against her Hierarchy. [**1883** J. PARKER *Tyne Ch.* 267 Where is the triacle, the treacle, the balm, that drops its sacred healing on the soul's leprosy?]

†**3.** Entering into the names of plants formerly reputed to have medicinal virtues, as

*Churl's T.*, Garlic (*Allium sativum*); *Countryman's T.*, (*a*) Garlic; (*b*) Rue (*Ruta graveolens*); (*c*) Great Valerian (*V. officinalis*); *English T.*, Water Germander (*Teucrium Scordium*); *Poor Man's T.*, (*a*) Garlic; (*b*) Hedge Garlic (*Alliaria officinalis*). *Obs.*

**1398** TREVISA *Barth. De P. R.* XVII. x. (Tollem. MS.), Tame garlek..was not with oute cause clepid triacle of cherles [orig. *tiriacum rusticorum*]. **1538** TURNER *Libellus, Chamedrys*,..anglice Germander aut englysshe tryacle dicitur. **1548** — *Names of Herbes, Camedrys*,..in englishe Germander or englishe Triacle. **1551** [see ENGLISH *a.* 2 b]. **1578** LYTE *Dodoens* v. lxxi. 638 Garlyke..is good against all venome & poyson...Therefore Galen..called it poore mens Treacle. **1597** GERARDE *Herbal* App., Churles Treacle is *Allium*. **1611** COTGR., *Ail*, Garlicke, poore-mans Treacle. *Ibid.*, *Trissage*, Germaunder, English Treacle. **1661** J. CHILDREY *Brit. Baconica* 23 The Country men in Cornwall are great eaters of Garlick for healths sake, whence they call it there, the Country mans Treacle. **1745–7** T. SHORT *Med. Brit.* (ed. 2) 246 Rue..or the Country Man's Treacle. *Ibid.* 295 It [*Valeriana officinalis*] is called the Countryman's Treacle. **1866** *Treas. Bot.*, *Countryman's treacle*, an old name for *Ruta graveolens*.

**II. 4.** The uncrystallized syrup produced in the process of refining sugar; also sometimes extended to the uncrystallizable syrup that drains from raw sugar; = MOLASSES 1. (See Note there.)

**1694** WESTMACOT *Script. Herb.* (1695) 6 Good store of Molossus or common Treacle to sweeten it. **1727–41** CHAMBERS *Cycl.* s.v. *Sugar*, Sugar of syrop, or treacle... There are three kinds of syrops that run from sugar...The Dutch and German refiners first taught the islanders how to turn their treacle into sugar. **1731** [see MOLASSES 1]. **1789** MRS. PIOZZI *Journ. France* I. 84 Few of us could return..to..a roll and treacle. **1838** DICKENS *Nich. Nick.* viii, They have the brimstone and treacle..in the way of medicine. **1873** F. HALL *Mod. Eng.* 128 *note*, The very marked distinction between *molasses* and *treacle* is commonly ignored in America, where the latter is seldom heard. **1902** GREENOUGH & KITTREDGE *Words* 267 'Treacle' is applied indifferently to the 'spume of sugar', to 'maple syrup', and to 'molasses'.

**b.** An inspissated saccharine juice obtained from various trees and plants: see quots.

**1731–3** P. SHAW *Chem. Lect.* x. (1755) 193 A Kind of Treacle from Malt might be procured in cheap Years, for the Service of the Vinegar-maker, the Brewer, and the Distiller. **1753** CHAMBERS *Cycl. Supp.* s.v., Dr. Shaw, in his Essay on Distillery, has endeavoured to bring into use several sorts of Treacles, which..would serve..for the distillation of spirits, or the making of potable liquors. These are the inspissated juices or decoctions of vegetables: Such as the sweet juice of the birch, or sycamore. **1839** DARWIN *Voy. Nat.* xii. (1879) 256 Palm..Valuable on account of a sort of treacle made from the sap. **1902** [see 4].

**c.** *fig.* Something sweet or clogging; *esp.* complimentary laudation, blandishment; cf. BUTTER 1 f.

**1771** SMOLLETT *Humph. Cl.* 13 July, He began to sweeten the natural acidity of his discourse with the treacle of compliment and commendation. **1819** KEATS *Let.* 23 Aug., in Rossetti *Life* (1887) 146, I equally dislike the favour of the public, with the love of a woman; they are both a cloying treacle to the wings of independence. **1860** READE *Cloister & H.* lxxv, 'Oh, you nasty, cross old wretch!' screamed Catherine, passing in a moment from treacle to sharpest vinegar.

**III. 5.** *attrib.* and *Comb.*: in sense 1, as *treacle-box, -monger, -plaster, -pot, tap*; sense 4, as *treacle-pad* (see quot.), *phrase, -pot, -well*; *treacle-like* adj.; **treacle ale, beer,** a light ale or beer brewed from treacle and water; **Treacle Bible,** a collectors' name for any of the English versions or editions of the Bible having 'triacle' or 'treacle' where others have 'balm', as in Jer. viii. 22, etc.; **treacle-butter-cake,** see quot.; **treacle-carrier, treacle-conner,** contemptuous terms for an itinerant quack doctor or medical practitioner; **treacle-moon,** contemptuous for *honey-moon*; **treacle-parkin** = PARKIN; **treacle-posset,** a hot drink made of cider or milk and treacle; **treacle-vinegar, treacle-water,** a cordial distilled with a spirituous menstruum from Venice treacle, with other drugs and simples. See also TREACLE CLOVER, MUSTARD.

*a* **1833** A. PICKEN in *Casquet of Lit.* (1896) V. 195/2 Ye shall taste my wife's *treacle ale. **1806** *Naval Chron.* XV. 264 The liquor to which he was most partial was *treacle beer. **1899** *B. Quaritch's Rough List* No. 193. 40 Cranmer's Bible.. 1569...This is also a *Treacle Bible. **1457** *Will of Poole* (Somerset Ho.), A siluer *triacle boxe. **1828** *Craven Gloss.*, **Treacle-butter-cake*, oat cake spread over with treacle. **1621** MOLLE *Camerar. Liv. Libr.* III. xii. 187 These Mountebanks, *Triacle-carriers, and such other Dog-leaches. **1706** BAYNARD in Sir J. Floyer *Hot & Cold Bath.* II. 227 One of the Tribe of *Treacle-conners..whether Apothecary or Physician, I can't tell. **1871** GARROD *Mat. Med.* (ed. 3) 329 Tar is a reddish-black, *treacle-like liquid. **1411** *Close Roll 12 Hen IV*, m. 7 d, Henricus Kirtone..*Treacle-monger. **1815** BYRON *Let. to Moore* 2 Feb., The *treacle-moon is over, and I am awake and find myself married. **1906** *Daily Chron.* 5 Nov. 6/6 Once more the old '*treacle-pad trick' has been employed by burglars. Part of the window is smeared with treacle, which is then covered with a sheet of thick brown paper. **1626** *Art. agst. Dk. Buckhm.* in Rushw. *Hist. Coll.* (1659) I. 352 Strange effects to follow upon the applying of a *Treacle plaister. **1876** BRISTOWE *The. & Pract. Med.* (1878) 627 Frequent sipping of warm milk, barley-water, gruel, or '*treacle posset'. **1466** SIR J. PASTON in *P. Lett.* II. 293, I send yow..iij. *tracle pottes of Geane. **1769** J. BERRIDGE *Wks.* (1864) 444 Like children, always wanting the treacle-pot. **1841** CARLYLE in Froude *Life in Lond.* viii. (1884) I. 210, I fell first into sluggish torpor, then into *treacle-sleep, and so lay sound as a stone. *a* **1500** *Piers of Fullham* 228 in Hazl. *E. P. P.* II. 10 Yn tyme therfore tye up yowr *tryacle tappe; Let not to long thy fawset renne. **1727–41** CHAMBERS *Cycl.* s.v. *Theriaca*, Treacle water, and *treacle vinegar are found good preservatives against putrid air. **1727–41** CHAMBERS *Cycl.* s.v. *Water*, *Treacle-Water ..is directed..to be made of green walnuts, rue, carduus, marigold, baum, butter-bur-roots, burdock, angelica, masterwort, water-germander, Venice-treacle, mithridate, canary-vinegar, and lemon-juice, steeped and distilled...A more simple treacle-water, made from venice treacle, with an equal quantity of brandy and vinegar. **1909** *Blackw. Mag.* May 605/1 A University College varies its facial expression about as frequently as the Sphinx and about as violently as a *treacle-well.

**Trea·cle,** *v.* [f. prec. sb.]

†**1.** *trans.* To make into a 'treacle'; to give the qualities of a 'treacle' to. *Obs. rare*$^{-1}$.

*c* **1500** BOLLARD tr. *Godfredus on Palladius*, To make a vyne treaclede.

**2.** To smear or spread with treacle; to dose with (brimstone and) treacle; to sweeten or render palatable with treacle (also *fig.*).

**1838** DICKENS *Nich. Nick.* viii, A long row of boys waiting.. to be treacled. **1873** *Daily News* 11 Nov. 5/4 The pill may be treacled with apparent concessions. **1906** *Daily Chron.* 28 Mar. 1/7 'Treacle' thieves..treacled the window.., broke the glass with a brick, and stole eight trays of jewellery. *Mod.* We treacle the trunks of trees, in order to attract moths.

**b.** To catch (moths) by attracting them with treacle or the like spread on trees.

**1905** *Daily Chron.* 29 June 8/1 Country rambles with long-handled nets and cool summer night trips, 'treacling' moths.

**3.** *intr.* To flow as treacle, to trickle. *humorous nonce-use.*

**1899** 'A. HOPE' *King's Mirror* xxiii, I could almost see the words treacling from his thick lips.

Hence **Treacled** (trī·k'ld) *ppl. a.*, smeared with treacle; **Treacling** *vbl. sb.*

**1895** *Daily News* 11 Oct. 7/3 The thieves..smashed the window, having previously placed some treacled paper upon it to deaden the sound. **1903** *Daily Chron.* 10 June 7/2 There were barely enough flies to make a decent show on the treacled paper which constitutes his advertisement. **1913** *Daily Citizen* Oct. 4/2 The catching of insects by this method of treacling requires great experience before it is successful.

† **Trea·cle clo·ver.** *Herb. Obs.* A name given

by the herbalists to more than one leguminous plant; esp. to *Psoralea bituminosa*, a native of the Mediterranean and Levantine region.

1562 TURNER *Herbal* II. 158 b, The sede and the leaues of triacle clauer, dronken in water, help the pleuresye. 1578 LYTE *Dodoens* IV. xli. 500–1 Of the right Trefoyle, or Treacle Clauer...The flowers grow from the sides of the stalkes vpon long stemmes,..of a deepe blew or skye colour. 1579 LANGHAM *Gard. Health* (1633) 148 Treacle, or garden Clauer.. prouoketh vrine and termes, and cleanseth the matrix. 1884 MILLER *Plant-n.*, Treacle Clover, *Psoralea bituminosa*.

**Trea·cle mu·stard.** A name applied by 16th c. herbalists to the plant *Thlaspi arvense* on account of its supposed medicinal virtue; by later writers applied to *Clypeola Jonthlaspi*, and to *Erysimum cheiranthoides*.

1548 TURNER *Names of Herbs* 79 *Thlaspi*..may be named in englishe dysh-mustard, or triacle Mustard, or Boures Mustard. 1562 — *Herbal* II. 152. 1597 GERARDE *Herbal* II. xix. 205 Treacle Mustarde hath long broade leaues. 1712 tr. *Pomet's Hist. Drugs* I. 4. 1760 J. LEE *Introd. Bot.* App. 330 Treacle Mustard, *Thlaspi*. *Ibid.*, Treacle Mustard, *Clypeola*. 1856 GRAY *Man. Bot.* (1860) 35 *Erysimum*, Treacle Mustard. 1882 G. ALLEN *Colours Flowers* ii. 43 In treacle-mustard (Erysimum), the yellow is very pale, and the petals often become almost white.

† **Trea·cler.** *Obs. rare*$^{-1}$. [f. TREACLE *sb.* + -ER[1].] ? A vessel to contain 'treacle' of Genoa, or the like.

1415 *Will of Ld. Scrope* in *Promp. Parv.* 500 *note*, Tracleere argenteum et deauratum cum costis de birall.

**Treacle wormseed**: see WORMSEED.

**Treacly** (trī·kli), *a.* [f. TREACLE *sb.* + -Y.] Resembling treacle in quality or appearance; having the sweetness or sticky consistence of treacle; also *fig.* characterized by excessive sweetness: cloyingly sweet; sugared, honeyed.

1733 SHAW *Chem. Lect.* xi. (1755) 218 A proper, or rich, syrupy, or treacly Substance. 1800 W. TAYLOR in *Monthly Mag.* X. 317 It bestows..even on novelty of thought, a flat featureless mien, an insipid treacly sameness,..very unfavourable to impression. 1837 T. HOOD in *Mem.* (1860) I. 159 Whose book..although so treacley..does not please the natives. 1866 R. M. FERGUSON *Electr.* (1870) 243 India-rubber..some specimens of it having become treacly.

Hence **Trea·cliness**, treacly quality or condition.

1884 *Nature* 22 May 89/1 The property of viscosity or treaclyness possessed more or less by all fluids is the general influence conducive to steadiness.

**Treact, Treactise**, obs. ff. TREAT, TREATISE.

**Tread** (tred), *sb.* Forms: 3 (*pl.*) **treden, treoden**; 5 **trede, tredd**, (5–7 *Sc.*) **tred**; 6 *Sc.* **treade**, 9 *n. dial.* **treed**, *s. e. dial.* **trade**, 6– **tread**. [Early ME. *trede* (pl. *treden*), f. stem of OE. *tredan* to TREAD. Cognate with MDu. *trēde* m. and f., MLG. *trēde, tret* m., MHG. *trit*, Ger. *tritt* step, footstep, path, etc.; cf. also, from same root, TRADE, between which and *tread* in their earlier senses there is a close parallelism; see also TROD.]

**I. 1.** A footprint; the mark made in treading. *rare.*

*a* 1225 *Ancr. R.* 380 [He] scheaweð in ham his owene treden þet me trodde him in ham. *Ibid.*, Auh þe dunes underuoð þe treden [*v. r.* (MS. Titus 120) trodes] of him suluen. *c* 1230 *Hali Meid.* 15 He[e] seð þe folhen hire treoden. Meiden gan as heo dude. 1727 *Bradley's Fam. Dict.* s. v. *Animal*, An Otter's Tread is almost like that of a Badger, saving that his Toes..are longer one than another.

†**2.** A line of footsteps; the track or trail left by the steps or passage of a man or animal: = TRADE *sb.* 2. *Obs.*

*c* 1400 *Laud Troy Bk.* 1006 When he was comen to that stede, Ther he saw the schepes trede. 1513 DOUGLAS *Æneis* VIII. iv. 67 And, that thar tred suld na way be persaue, Onto his cave ay bakwartis by the talis To turn thair futsteppis he thaim harlis and tralis. 1570 *Satir. Poems Reform.* x. 340 Sum saw him weill, and followit his hors tred. 1570 *Henry's Wallace* v. 136 For thair sloith hund the graith gait till him ȝeid, Off othir tred [*c* 1470 trade] scho tuk as than no heid. 1727–41 CHAMBERS *Cycl.*, *Piste*, in the manage, the track or tread, which a horse makes upon the ground he goes over. 1815 SCOTT *Guy M.* xxiii, He passed a solitary house, towards which the horseman..had apparently turned up, for his horse's tread was evident in that direction. 1820 — *Monast.* xxxiv, I tracked the knight's horse-tread as far as near to the ford.

†**3.** A trodden or beaten way, a path, a track. *Obs.* exc. **b.** *fig.* path or way (of life or action).

14.. *Bone Flor.* 1882 Sche fonde a tredd and forthe ys gon ..To a noonre. 1628 FELTHAM *Resolves* II. [I.] xiii. 35 We wander in the tread of seuerall paths. *a* 1711 KEN *Psyche* Poet. Wks. 1721 IV. 229 When Jesus journy'd too and fro,.. The Female Vot'ries by you lead [= led] Still follow'd his instructive Tread. *a* 1862 BUCKLE *Civiliz.* (1869) III. iii. 132 Conditions which determine the tread and destiny of nations.

†**c.** Those who are on the ordinary way; the common 'run' of passers. Cf. TRADE *sb.* 1 b. *Obs.*

1615 CHAPMAN *Odyss.* XVII. 748 That the bread, Which now he begg'd amongst the common tread.

**4.** The action or an act of treading or trampling; a step.

*c* 1400 *Laud Troy Bk.* 13440 Thei drow him fro her hors tred. 1640 R. CHAMBERLAIN *Pref. Verses* in Brome *Antipodes*, On th' Antipodes..tis thus, Their feet do tread against the tread of us. 1671 FLAVEL *Fount. Life* v. 12 The least Tread awry may ingulph us in the Bogs of Error. 1733 W. ELLIS *Chiltern & Vale Farm.* 15 The tread of the Sheep makes this Ground turn before the Plow in a clotty Substance. 1812 J. WILSON *Isle of Palms* II. 379 Thy noiseless tread..Fell soft as snow on snow. 1823 J. F. COOPER *Pioneers* xxxviii, Louisa was startled by the low, cracking, but cautious treads, of some one approaching through the bushes. 1840 DICKENS *Old C. Shop* i, That incessant tread of feet wearing the rough stones smooth and glossy. 1843 J. SMITH *Forest Trees* 64 He gives a tread with his foot to render it firm. 1878 M. A. BROWN *Nadeschda* 18 She followed with her ears his tread.

**b.** Manner of treading; hence, style of walking.

1609 *Old Meg of Herefordsh.* (1816) 10 Howe doe you like this Morris-daunce of Hereford-shire?..Haue they not the right footing? the true tread? 1727 POPE *Lament. Glumdalclitch* 67 How wast thou wont to walk with cautious tread. 1812 BYRON *Ch. Har.* I. lxxiv, The ground, with cautious tread, is traversed o'er. 1840 R. S. HAWKER *Cornish Ball.*, etc. (1908) 89 Pause and move onward with obedient tread. 1850 MRS. BROWNING *Dead Pan* xi, Where O Juno, is the glory Of thy regal look and tread? 1881 LADY HERBERT *Edith* 7 She had the tread of an Empress.

**c.** *transf.* The quality or kind of the thing trodden upon; the sensation produced by treading on something (considered as an attribute of the thing). *rare.*

1819 KEATS *Lamia* 181 A sloping green of mossy tread.

**II. 5.** Course or manner of action; way of acting; *esp.* a habitual course; practice, custom; = TRADE *sb.* 3, 3 c. Chiefly *Sc.*

*Tred* is still the ordinary Sc. dial. word in all these senses = TRADE *sb.*, senses 3–9.

1562 *Reg. Privy Council Scot.* I. 212 Gif the tred wer nocht samekle usit be the inhabitantis of this realme. *a* 1572 KNOX *Hist. Ref.* Wks. 1846 I. 410 Quhat tred and ordour of doctrine thay have keipitt. 1572 *Satir. Poems Reform.* xxxiv. 10, I doe espy The Scottisch tred and nauchtie fassioun To be so bad. 1579 *Reg. Privy Council Scot.* III. 146 Following the bludie treade quhilk they and thair foirbearis of the same name had used of befoir. 1817 G. CHALMERS *Churchyard's Chips* Pref. 14 Three years..he saw the Emperor's wars: then homeward drew, as was his wonted tread. *Mod. Sc.* Ye mauna mak a tred o' gangin' there.

**6.** Regular occupation or business: = TRADE *sb.* 5. *Sc.*

1584 *Reg. Privy Council Scot.* III. 706 That na honest merchand..may peciablie travell nor use tred. 1588 *Ibid.* IV. 303 His Majesteis..subjectis ar havelie opprest and the tred of fisheing..gritlie impedit. 1596 *Sc. Acts Jas. VI* (1816) IV. 100/1 The following of ane lauchfull tred. 1603 *Reg. Mag. Sig. Scot.* 513/2 Cum libertate exercendi *the tred and traffique of merchandrice*. 1657 *Scott. Convention Rec.* III. 440 The whole tread only competent to merchandis of free burrows. *Mod. Sc.* What's the man's tred? This weather is bad for the tred. The tred o' the toon.

**7.** Coming and going; resort; intercourse; also, fuss, work; = TRADE *sb.* 7 a, 7 b, 7 c. *Sc. rare.*

1567 *Reg. Privy Council Scot.* I. 510 Having dalie and contenewall tred with the inhabitantis. 1591 *Ibid.* IV. 627 Not onlie sall thair tred in thai pairtis be cutt of, bot a cruell wear salbe denunceit aganis his majestie. *Mod. Sc.* What a tred aboot getting them off!

**III. 8. a.** *Farriery.* A bruise or wound of the coronet of a horse's foot, caused by setting one foot upon the other, or by over-reaching.

1661 LOVELL *Hist. Anim. & Min.* 62 The skinne wrapped about a horse's foot, that hath a tread, helpeth the same. 1754 BARTLET *Farriery* xxxix. (ed. 2) 313 A quittor..arises often from treads and bruises. 1846 J. BAXTER *Libr. Pract. Agric.* (ed. 5) I. 451 Quittor..a severe tread, which the horse accidentally inflicts upon itself in its endeavours to avoid falling upon its sides. 1894 *Northumbld. Gloss.* s. v. *Treed*, When a horse has injured himself by setting one foot on another he is said to have 'getten a treed'.

**b.** An act of treadling or pedalling a machine.

1680 MOXON *Mech. Exerc.* x. 188 Keeping exact time in Treads,..the Workman gives a quick Tread upon the Treddle. 1790 A. WILSON *Poems & Lit. Prose* (1876) II. 243 Whene'er the smooth tread I apply My shopmates deplore how I've sped.

**9. a.** The action of the male bird in coition. **b.** The cicatricula or chalaza of an egg; = TREADLE *sb.* 3.

**a.** 1674 N. FAIRFAX *Bulk & Selv. World* 124 An egg,..a thing that sprang from the impetus of the tread,..to be what 'tis, after laid by the Hen. 1725 *Bradley's Fam. Dict.* II. Pij b/2 A Hen..will lay Eggs without the Tread of the Cock, but these Eggs..are good for nothing to hatch. 1765 *Treat. Dom. Pigeons* 23 She will squat, and readily receive his tread, by which she is rendered prolific.

**b.** 1593 SOUTHWELL *St. Peter's Compl.* 51 Kill bad Chickins in the tread. 1647 *Husbandman's Plea agst. Tithes* 40 Whether the Cocks tread..be in every egge. 1796 MRS. GLASSE *Cookery* xx. 311 Strain off your eggs from the treads. 1871 HUXLEY *Anat. Vertebr. Anim.* (1882) 9 A patch of primary tissue;..the so-called *cicatricula*, or 'tread', which is observable in the new-laid egg, is of this nature.

**10.** Various technical senses.

**a.** The flat under side of the foot or of a shoe, which comes into contact with the ground in treading; the sole. **b.** A wheel track, a rut (*dial.*); the transverse distance between the two wheels of a cart or other vehicle; also, the width between the pedals of a bicycle or tricycle; the outer surface of a wheel, tire, or sledge runner; also, the rail surface on which the wheel bears. **c.** A shaped plate of iron worn under the hollow of the shoe to protect it in digging; a tramp. **d.** *Shipbuilding*: see quot. *c* 1850. **e.** The projecting foot-rest or step of a stilt (*Cassell's Encycl. Dict.* 1888). **f.** The upper side of the bed of a lathe between the headstock and back-centre (Knight *Dict. Mech.* 1877).

**a.** *c* 1720 W. GIBSON *Farrier's Guide* I. v. (1738) 76 The.. Plantaris, or Muscle of the Soal or Tread. 1898 J. HUTCHINSON in *Arch. Surg.* IX. No. 36. 337 The symptom..was pain under the tread of his left foot. **b.** 1735–6 PEGGE *Kenticisms*, *Tread*, a wheel-tread, rut, tract [i.e. track]. 1765 *Museum Rust.* IV. lix. 248 It would be less material what breadth the wheels themselves were of, so that their tread be flat. *Ibid.* 249 If carts were to have the distance of their [wheels] either equal to the greatest or least tread of the waggons, it would generally help to preserve and commode the roads. 1797 J. CURR *Coal Viewer* 25 Plain turn plates. Used for going round a turn. The trod or tread of these [tram-]plates are 4 inches broad. 1844 STEPHENS *Bk. Farm* III. 1163 This standard..has..been fixed at 4 feet 4 inches between the tread of the wheels. 1875 *Sussex Gloss.* s.v. *Trades*, 'You will never get your carriage down that laine, for it can't take the trades'. 1887 BURY & HILLIER *Cycling* 346 To keep 'the tread' of the machines, i.e. the width from pedal to pedal as narrow as possible. 1897 *Cycl. Tour. Cl. Gaz.* Sept. 399 A large hobnail..in the middle of the tread [of a pneumatic tire]. **c.** 1842 LOUDON *Suburban Hort.* 133 To save the shoes of the operator, a plate of iron about two inches broad, with leather straps, called a tread, is tied to his shoe. **d.** *c* 1850 *Rudim. Navig.* (Weale) 156 *Tread of the keel*, the whole length of the keel upon a straight line.

**11.** The horizontal upper surface of a step in a stair; also, the width of this from front to back; also, each of the rungs of a ladder.

1712 J. JAMES tr. *Le Blond's Gardening* 125 Each Step may have 15 or 16 Inches Tread, to five or six Inches Rise. 1791 SMEATON *Edystone L.* (1793) § 88 There was but one flat or tread of a step above the center of the house. 1833 LOUDON *Encycl. Archit.* § 239 One inch and a quarter oak treads with rounded nosings. 1838 *Civil Eng. & Arch. Jrnl.* I. 268/1 Ladders were of..rude construction..formed of two uprights with nailed treads or rounds on the face. 1884 *Health Exhib. Catal.* 49/1 Terra Cotta steps, with patent silicon treads. 1884 F. T. HODGSON *Stair-building* 12 Wall strings are the supporters of the ends of the treads and risers.

**b.** *Fortif.* A terrace at the back of a parapet, on which the defenders stand to fire over the parapet.

1834–47 J. S. MACAULAY *Field Fortif.* (1851) 3 The tread of the banquette..is made 3 feet wide, when the parapet is to be defended by a single rank. 1853 STOCQUELER *Milit. Encycl.*, *Tread*, of a banquette, the upper and flat surface on which the soldier stands whilst firing over the parapet.

**IV. 12.** *attrib.* and *Comb.*, as (sense 10 b) *tread cover, rubber, surface*; †**tread-behind**, a doubling; an evasion, artifice, shift; **tread-board**, the tread of a step = sense 11; also, each of the steps in a treadmill; † **tread-fowl**, the male bird; cf. 9 a; **tread-road** (*dial.*): see quot.; cf. *tread-way*; **treadsman** = TREADER; †**treadsole**, a door-sill; **tread-steps**, carriage-steps with flat treads; † **tread-way**, a roadway, thoroughfare. See also TREADMILL, TREAD-WHEEL.

1844 S. NAYLOR *Reynard the Fox* 20 His tricks and traps and *tread-behinds. 1908 *Westm. Gaz.* 16 Nov. 5/3 As regards the round and square *tread covers their imperviousness to cutting by flints [etc.]. *c* 1386 CHAUCER *Monk's Prol.* 57 Thou woldest han been a *tredefowel aright. 1894 *Northumbld. Gloss.*, *Treed-road, a beaten path. 1909 *Westm. Gaz.* 1 June 4/2 The rubber used in their non-skid is not ordinary '*tread' rubber. 1519 HORMAN *Vulg.* 237 The iewest..that the *tredisman..brouseth out of the grapis. *c* 1546 JOYE in Bp. Gardiner *Declar.* 14 The *tredsole or groundsole whereupon..the dore is turned and returned. 1837 W. B. ADAMS *Carriages* 87 *Tread Steps, for the coachman to mount by. 1896 *Godey's Mag.* Apr. 347/1 The *tread surface of the canvas tube was covered with two or three layers of the sheet rubber. 1630 T. WESTCOTE *Devon.* II. xxiii. (1845) 187 For whose more christian-like burial there is (in a spacious large *tread-way near the place of execution) a plot of ground enclosed with strong stone walls.

**Tread** (tred), *v.* Pa. t. **trod** (trǫd), *arch.* **trode** (trōud). Pa. pple. **trodden** (trǫ·d'n), **trod** (trǫd). Forms: see below. [OE. *tredan* (pa. t. *træd*, pl. *trǣdon*, pa. pple. *treden*); ME. *treden* (*trad, trēden, treden*), a Common Teut. strong vb., = OFris. *treda* (*trad, tred, trêd-, treden*), OS. *tredan* (*trad, trâd-un, treden*); MDu., MLG. *trēden*, Du., LG. *trēden*, OHG. *tretan* (*trat, trâtun*; *gi-tretan*), MHG., Ger. *treten*; Da. *træde*, Sw. *träda*, Norw. *treda*; OTeut. **tred-*; **trad-*, pl. **trǣd-*; *tred-*, of which a weak grade *trud-* gave Goth. *trudan* (**trap*, **trēdum*, *trudans*), and ON. *troða* (*trað*, *tráðum*; *troðinn*). Not certainly known outside Teutonic. In the 14th c. (in Hampole *a* 1340), either under Norse influence, or by assimilation to vbs. of Class IV (*brecan, bræc, brocen*), the pa. pple. *troden* (later *trodden, trode, trod*) began to be substituted for the original *treden*, although the latter in its shortened form *tred(e, tread* survived with some to the 17th c., and is still in dialect use. In the end of the 14th c. *troden* is found in the pl. of the pa. t., and from the 16th c. *trode, trod* also in the sing. Ormin has a weak pa. pple. *trededd* for *treden*, and a weak pa. t. *tredide, tredde* appears in the later Wyclifite version. Cf. OE. *treddian*, OHG. *trettôn*, ON. *treðja*, OTeut. type **tradjan*, perh. orig. intensive, but subseq. mixed up with the primary strong vb.]

**A.** Illustration of Forms.

**1.** *Inf.* and *Pres. stem.* 1 **tredan**, (**trædan**), 3–4 **treden**, 3–5 **trede**, (4 **tredde**), 4–7 **tred**, (5 **tredyn, tradde**), 6–8 **treade**, 6– **tread**. *Inflexions* 1 **trædað**, **trides**, **trideð**, 4 **tredeth**, 6 **treddis**.

*a* 700 *Beowulf* 1965 ȝewat him þa se hearda..sæ-wong tredan. *a* 800 *Riddles* viii. 1 Þonne ic hrusan trede. *Ibid.* lviii. 5 Trædað bearonæssas. *Ibid.* lxxxi. 24 Hio.. grundbedd trideð. *c* 825 *Vesp. Psalter* xc. 13 Ðu..trides leon & dracan. *a* 1000 *Ags. Ps.* (Th.) lv[i]. 1 Miltsa me, Drihten, forðon me man treteð. *c* 1200 Ormin 11946 Godess þeowwess gan onn himm & tredenn himm wiþþ fote. *a* 1340 Hampole *Psalter* vii. 5 þe enmy..tred [*conculcet*] in erth my lyf. *c* 1386 Chaucer *Knt.'s T.* 2160 The harde stoon.. on which we trede and goon. 1388 Wyclif *Rom.* xvi. 20 God of pees tredde Sathanas vndur ȝoure feet. *c* 1440 Tradde [see B. 11]. 1523 Fitzherb. *Husb.* § 21 Let hym beware, that he trede not to moche vppon the corne. 1535 Coverdale *Job* xl. 7 Treade all the vngodly vnder thy fete. 1567 *Gude & Godlie B.* (S.T.S.) 108 Thow sall..tred on the cruell Cocketrice. 1567 *Sc. Acts Jas. VI* (1814) III. 41 þame þat treddis hairis in þe snaw. 1570 Levins *Manip.* 206/1 To Treade, go, *gressus ponere*. 1583 Babington *Commandm.* viii. (1590) 354 Vntoothsome is that trueth euer, that treadeth downe my liking. 1596 Spenser *F. Q.* vi. ix. 27 Which.. under foot doth tread The mightie ones [*rime* dread].

**2.** *Pa. t.* α. 1 træd, 2–5 trad; 3–5 tradd, 4–5 trade, 5 tradde. β. 6 *Sc.* tred, (8 tread). γ. 6–9 trode, 6– trod (6 trodd). δ. *pl.* 1 trǽdon, 4 trêden, (treeden), 4–5 trōden, 5 trāden, trād, 6 trood, 4–9 trode, 6– trod. ε. (*weak conj.*) 4 treddede, *pl.* trediden, tredden, 5 treyde.

α. *a* 700 *Beowulf* 1882 Beowulf þanan..græs-moldan træd. *c* 1200 Ormin 2561 Forr ȝho tradd deofell unnderrfot. 1388 Wyclif *Ecclus.* xxiv. 11 Y trad bi vertu on the neckis of all excelent men. 1470–85 Malory *Arthur* xix. iv. 778 His hors..trade his [own] guttes..vnder his feet. 1481 Caxton *Reynard* xxxix. (Arb.) 105 The wulf trade forth to the foxe in grete wrath. 1484 — *Fables of Æsop* ii. xx, The oxe.. thradde and thrested her [the frog] with his fote. *c* 1489 — *Blanchardyn* xxiv. 89 The grasse wher vpon he trad.

β. 1560 Rolland *Seven Sages* 37 With feit [scho] it tred. 1737 Whiston *Josephus, Antiq.* ii. ix. § 7 Moses..tread upon it with his feet.

γ. 1535 Coverdale 2 *Kings* xiv. 9 A wylde beest..ran ouer yͤ hawthorne and trode it downe. [So 2 *Chron.* xxv. 18.] 1600 Heywood *2nd Pt. Edw. IV*, ii. iv. Wks. 1874 I. 139 Pity that ere awry she trod her shoe. 1738 Gray *Tasso* 15 Against the stream the waves secure he trod. 1823 Byron *Juan* vi. cxi, The way in which he trode. 1823 Scott *Quentin D.* xxvi, One of the bravest and most noble gentlemen that ever trode a court.

δ. ? *a* 1300 *Debate of Body & Soul* 423 Ther alle þe fendes fet it trode [*rime* brode]. 1377 Langl. *P. Pl.* B. xi. 347 Some [birds] troden hir makes and on trees bredden [C. xiv. 166 And some treden..and on trees bredden]. 1382 Wyclif 2 *Kings* ix. 33 The hors houes that treden [1388 to tredden] hyre. *c* 1420 *Chron. Vilod.* 2940, & nyst neuer where þey wenton ny trede. 1483 Caxton *Gold. Leg.* 173 b/2 They trad the corne in the feldes doun. 1526 Tindale *Luke* xii. 1 In so moche that they trood won another. 1535 Coverdale 2 *Kings* vii. 17 The people trode [Wycl. trade] vpon him, so that he dyed. *a* 1604 Hanmer *Chron. Irel.* (1633) 33 The Irish..trode not upon Scottish soile. 1715–20 Pope *Iliad* xv. 412 The wondering crowds the downward level trod. 1850 Hawthorne *Scarlet L.* Introd. (1879) 16 Trode the unworn street.

ε. (*weak conj.*) 1388 Wyclif 2 *Kings* xiv. 9 The beestis.. passiden, and tredden [*v.r.* treteden] doun the cardue. — *Luke* xii. 1 So that thei treden [*v.rr.* treeden, traden, trediden; 1382 troden] ech on othir. 1432–50 tr. *Higden* (Rolls) VII. 9 His feete..with whom he treyde [L. *pulsaverat*] the tumbe of blissede Odo.

**3.** *Pa. pple.* α. 1–3 treden, 3–4 i-trede, y-tredde, 6 tredden, tredd(e, 6–7 *Sc.* tred, 7 tread. β. 4–7 troden, (4 troddun), 6– trodden; 4 i-trode, 4–9 trode, (7 troad(e), 5– trod. γ. (*weak conj.*) 3 (*Orm.*) trēdedd.

α. *a* 900 tr. *Bæda's Hist.* iii. xvi. [xxii.] (1890) 224 Utworpen..&.fotum treden[e] & in eorðan ȝehwyrfde wæron. *c* 1315 Shoreham *Poems* i. 821 Namore ne greueþ hyt ihesus þane sonne [?stone] itrede in felþe. *c* 1410 *Master of Game* (MS. Digby 182) xxiv, If ye se it [the lair] gret and brode and wele ytrede. 1509 Barclay *Shyp of Folys* (1570) 208 They under foote are tred. *c* 1520 M. Nisbet *N. Test. in Scots, Rev.* xiv. 20 The lake was treddin [1388 Wyclif, troddun] without the citee. 1549 Coverdale, etc. *Erasm. Par. Rom.* 31 Lye they on the grounde and are tredde vnderfoote. 1580 Sidney *Ps.* xxxi. vi, Like a broken pott, in myer tredd. 1600 Hamilton *Facile Traictise* Ded., Brocht in contempt and tred vnderfut. 1608 Topsell *Serpents* (1658) 619 The Water-nep..which under-foot is tread [*rime* bed]. 1687 A. Lovell tr. *Thevenot's Trav.* ii. 86 Being trampled and tread upon.

β. *a* 1340 Hampole *Psalter* xvii. 42 þai sall be troden vndire my luf. *c* 1350 *Will. Palerne* 3402 Wit here horse troden. 1600 Holland *Camden's Brit.* (1637) 821 The Percies with it troden under foot. 1614 T. Adams in Spurgeon *Treas. Dav.* Ps. xiii. 5 Are trodden down by the poor. 1387 Trevisa *Higden* (Rolls) V. 379 Hym semede þat he [a cross] was nouȝt worþy to be trode [Caxton, trede] wiþ his feet. *Ibid.* VIII. 113 His baner was i-trode in þe fen. 1607 Topsell *Hist. Four-f. Beasts* (1658) 234 Hens do lay egges being not troad by a Cock. 1614 Earl Stirling *Domes-Day* iii. lxxx, Their empty channels may be troad on dry. 1621 Bp. Mountagu *Diatribæ* 359 To haue ..trod vnder foot the Law of God. 1725 Pope *Odyss.* v. 124 By mighty Jove's command..have I trod this pleasing land. 1774 Beattie *Minstr.* ii. vi, Which heretofore his foot had never trode.

γ. *c* 1200 Ormin 5728 Beo trededd dun.

**B.** Signification.

**1.** *trans.* To step upon; to pace or walk on (the ground, etc.); to walk in (a place); hence, to go about in (a place, etc.).

*a* 700 *Beowulf* [see A. 1]. 1362 Langl. *P. Pl.* A. x. 101 Selden Moseþ þe Marbelston þat men ofte treden. 1382 Wyclif *Deut.* xi. 24 Eche place that ȝoure foot tredith, shal be ȝour. 1591 *Troub. Raigne K. John* (1611) 26 Treading my Confines with thy armed troupes. 1594 ? Greene *Selimus* Wks. (Grosart) XIV. 212 Then let our winged coursers tread the winde. 1697 Dryden *Virg. Georg.* iii. 543 He who treads the bleak Meotian Strand. 1729 G. Adams tr. *Sophocles, Oedip. Colon.* i. v. II. 102 The Goddesses..whose Ground you have trod. 1802 Wordsw. *Sonn.* '*Here, on our native soil*', 'Tis joy enough and pride For one hour's perfect bliss, to tread the grass Of England once again. 1823 Chalmers *Serm.* I. 397 As hardy adventurers as ever trode the desert in quest of novelty. 1837 W. Irving *Capt. Bonneville* II. 53 The trapper stands..and gazes upon a promised land which his feet are never to tread.

**b.** Phrases. *To tread the stage* (*the boards*), to act upon the stage, to follow the profession of an actor (also *fig.* to write stage-plays). *To tread* † *clay, this earth, shoe-leather*, to be alive, to live; *to tread the deck*, to be on board ship, be a sailor; *to tread the ground*, to walk.

1691 G. Langbaine *Acc. Eng. Dram. Poets* 465 Shakespear by him reviv'd now treads the Stage. 1700 Dryden *Flower & Leaf* 182 Methought she trod the ground with greater grace. 1711 Steele *Spect.* No. 22 ¶ 2 One that never trod the Stage before. 1748 *Anson's Voy.* ii. xiii. 274 As skilful seamen as ever trod a deck. 1789 Burns *To Dr. Blacklock* x, She is a dainty chuckie, As e'er tread clay. 1825 Scott *Talism.* xxiv, The steeds..chafed on the bit, and trod the ground more proudly. 1828 J. T. Smith *Bk. Rainy Day* (1861) 255 A better man never trod shoe-leather. 1858 Lytton *What will he do* i. viii, She had never then trod the boards. 1868 Freeman *Norm. Conq.* II. viii. 164 No man that ever trod this earth was ever endowed with greater natural gifts.

**2.** To step or walk upon or along; to follow, pursue (a path, track, or road); also *fig.*

*a* 700 *Beowulf* 1353 On weres wæstmum wræc-lastas træd. 1551 Recorde *Pathw. Knowl.* To Rdr., I will not cease.. treading the paths of labour. 1697 Dryden *Virg. Georg.* iv. 517 The downward track he treads. 1754 Chatham *Lett. Nephew* vi. 40 Those who have trod the paths of the world before them. 1841 James *Brigand* xix, I never forget a path I have once trodden. 1884 W. H. White *Mark Rutherford's Deliverance* viii. (1892) 111 Yet he treads his path undisturbed.

**b.** † *To tread a person's steps* (*fig.*), to walk in the steps of, follow the example of (*obs.*); *to tread back one's steps* (*fig.*), to retrace one's steps (now *rare* or *obs.*).

1579 W. Wilkinson *Confut. Familye of Loue* 100 To.. tread the steppes of Gods sonne. 1641 J. Jackson *True Evang. T.* ii. 117 S. Philip..was fastened to the Crosse, and stoned to death, treading the steps both of his Master, and of Stephen. *a* 1704 T. Brown *Ess. on Women* Wks. 1711 IV. 152 They tread the Steps of their Parents, meerly by instinct. 1752 Foote *Taste* Ded. (ed. 4) 6 In the following Sheets her Steps have been trode with an undeviating Simplicity. 1777 Priestley *Matt. & Spir.* (1782) I. i. 7 The philosophical part of the world [may] tread back their steps. 1831 D. E. Williams *Life & Corr. Sir T. Lawrence* I. 243 We must tread back our steps.

† **c.** *To tread the feet of*, to trace the footprints of. *Sc. Obs. rare.*

1596 Dalrymple tr. *Leslie's Hist. Scot.* vi. (S. T. S.) I. 350 To schue thrie suofte horses backward, that..the persewer ..mycht not find how to tred the horses fute rycht.

**d.** *To tread a measure*, † *a dance*, etc., to go through a dance in a rhythmic or stately manner; to go through in dancing; so *to tread a march*. *arch.* and *poet.*

1577 Grange *Golden Aphrod.* M ij b, After these came Silenus..treadyng the hornpype. 1580 H. Gifford *Gilloflowers* (Grosart) 118 Thrice happy is their chaunce, That never knew to treade the lover's daunce. 1590 Greene *Orl. Fur.* Wks. (Rtldg.) 90/1 That did but Venus tread a dainty step. 1592 Shaks. *Ven. & Ad.* 1148 Teaching decrepit age to tread the measures. 1808 Scott *Marm.* v. xii, 'Now tread we a measure!' said young Lochinvar. 1810 — *Lady of L.* ii. vii, The proud march which victors tread. 1859 Jephson *Brittany* iii. 30 The favoured one who should tread a measure with her Imperial Majesty.

**3.** *intr.* To walk, go, pace; to set down the feet in walking; to step. Also said of the foot.

In quot. *c* 897 rendering L. *terere* of the Vulgate.

*c* 897 K. Ælfred *Gregory's Past. C.* xlvii. 357 Aworpen mon..bicneð mid ðæm eagum, & trit mid ðæm fet, & spricð mid ðæm fingre. *a* 1400–50 *Alexander* 1515 All þe brade stretis..þar he trede sulde. 1481 Caxton *Reynard* xxxix. (Arb.) 105 The wulf trade forth to the foxe in grete wrath. 1535 Coverdale *Deut.* xi. 24 All the places that the soles of youre fete treade vpon, shalbe yours. — *Ezek.* xliii. 19 Yͤ Leuites that..treade before me to do me seruyce. 1599 Shaks. *Hen. V*, iv. vii. 149 As arrant a villaine and a Iacke sawce, as euer his blacke shoo trodd vpon Gods ground. 1601 — *Jul. C.* i. i. 29 As proper men as euer trod vpon Neats Leather. 1632 Lithgow *Trav.* i. 22, I haue trod foure seuerall times from end to end of it. 1748 Thomson *Cast. Indol.* ii. xxxv, An honest sober beast, that..full softly trode. 1816 Byron *Prisoner of Chillon* xi, Avoiding only, as I trod, My brothers' graves without a sod. 1860 Tyndall *Glac.* i. xxi. 149, I crossed the glacier, treading with the utmost caution along the combs of ice.

**b.** *intr.* In phrases, esp. in fig. sense. *To tread on air*, to walk buoyantly or jubilantly; *to tread on eggs, on delicate ground, on thin ice*: see the sbs.

1481 Caxton *Reynard* xliii. (Arb.) 118 Eueriche of them tredeth in the foxes path and seketh his hole. 1580 Sidney *Ps.* xxv. vi, He doth..teach the humble how to tread. 1668 Denham *Prudence* Poems 147 Sense, her Vassal, in her footsteps treads. 1694 F. Bragge *Disc. Parables* xi. 381 Misery, and shame, and repentance, always tread close at the heels of wickedness. 1709 Pope *Ess. Crit.* 625 Fools rush in where Angels fear to tread [*rime* dead]. *a* 1734 North *Lives* (1826) I. 266 He had his jury to deal with, and if he did not tread upon eggs, they would conclude sinistrously. 1817 Jas. Mill *Brit. India* II. v. vi. 560 On the principal ground, however, the parliament..trode nearly blindfold. 1839 T. Mitchell *Aristoph., Frogs* 452 *note*, Was the author treading upon still more delicate ground than the Scholiast has imagined? 1874 W. Melville *Uncle J.* xxii, Leaving the gaol..Mr. Lexley seemed to tread on air.

**4.** *intr.* To step *on* (something in one's way); to put the foot down *upon* accidentally or intentionally, esp. so as to press upon.

*c* 1384 [see b]. *c* 1489 Caxton *Blanchardyn* xiv. 49 His courser..tradd vpon one of his armes. 1561 T. Norton *Calvin's Inst.* iii. 274 He will come..to think it vnlawfull.. to treade vpon a strawe lying a crosse. 1603 Shaks. *Meas. for M.* iii. i. 79 The poore Beetles that we treade upon. *c* 1643 Ld. Herbert *Autobiog.* (1824) 180 Finding my bare feet hurt by the stones I trod on. 1852 Mrs. Stowe *Uncle Tom's C.* xx, A body can't set their foot down without treading on 'em. 1887 Bowen *Æneid* ii. 380 When a traveller..Treads on a snake unseen.

**b.** Phrase. *To tread on any one's heels* or *toes* (also *fig.*); see the sbs.

*c* 1384 Chaucer *H. Fame* iii. 1063 Tho behynde begunne vp lepe And clamben vp on other fast..And troden [*v.r.* treden] fast on other heles. 1638 Junius *Paint. Ancients* 15 To come so neere as to tread upon their heeles. 1710 Addison *Tatler* No. 250 ¶ 11 If asking Pardon is an Attonement for treading upon ones Toes? 1711 Steele *Spect.* No. 153 ¶ 1 The Cocking young Fellow who treads upon the Toes of his Elders. 1868, 1879 [see Toe *sb.* 5 i]. 1896 Sir W. Walrond in *Libr. Mag.* Dec. 504 If they legislated too much they were bound to tread on somebody's toes.

**5.** *trans.* † **a.** To step or walk with pressure on (something) esp. so as to crush, beat down, injure, or destroy it; to trample. *Obs.* (exc. as in b.)

*c* 825 [see A. 1]. *a* 900 Fotum treden [see A. 3]. *a* 1000 *Ags. Ps.* (Th.) xc. 113 Þu..miht..bealde nu basiliscan tredan. *a* 1340 Hampole *Psalter* xxiv. 1 Wha sa ligges þare in, þe deuel tredis him. 1387 [see A. 3 β]. 1535 Coverdale *Luke* xii. 1 There were gathered together an innumerable multitude of people, in so much that they trode one another. 1573–80 Baret *Alv.* V 23 Treade a worme on the taile, and it turneth againe. 1656 B. Harris *Parival's Iron Age* (1659) 145 He was found amongst the dead, so trodden, and tumbled..that he was hard to be known. 1712 tr. *Pomet's Hist. Drugs* I. 160 To make 'em tight..they imploy Men to tread them [raisins] with their Feet.

**b.** With adverbial extension, as *to tread down, under foot, in the mire, to the ground, to pieces*, etc.; *to tread to death*, to kill by trampling.

*c* 1200 Ormin 2248 Alle þa þatt tredenn dun & cwenkenn All þatt tatt iss onnȝæness Godd. *c* 1290 *S. Eng. Leg.* I. 206/207 þe deoulene ornen opon hem and treden heom to þe grounde. 14.. *Sir Beues* 1195 (MS. M.) He..tredith hym vnder his fete In the dirte. 1523 Ld. Berners *Froiss.* I. ccccxxii. 739 In the thicke of the prease, they..were troden vnder fote to dethe. 1556 Olde *Antichrist* 99 b, The B. of Rome..is not ashamed to treade yͤ Lordes anointed neckes under his abominable feet. 1652 C. B. Stapylton *Herodian* xix. 159 Some he kils and some he treads to Jelly. 1678 Bunyan *Pilgr.* i. 79 He thought he should be..troden down like mire in the Streets. 1726 Swift *Gulliver* ii. viii, Being trod to death like a frog or a young puppy. 1823 Scott *Quentin D.* xvi, The wild boar of the forest, which treadeth down with his hoofs, and rendeth with his tusks.

**c.** *fig.* To crush, to oppress; to treat with contemptuous cruelty.

1526 *Pilgr. Perf.* (W. de W. 1531) 21 Tredynge vnder fote & vtterly despysynge all worldly pleasure & payne. 1652 in W. M. Williams *Ann. Founders' Co.* (1867) 32 For manie years extreamly trodden and kept under foote by the power and will of the Master. 1766 Goldsm. *Vic. W.* xxix, The luxuriant great ones of the world shall no more tread us to the earth. 1775 S. J. Pratt *Liberal Opin.* xlviii. (1783) II. 66 In the city, the spirit of humanity is too often trod under feet by the spirit of trade. 1857 Holland *Bay Path* xxix, Her memory..trodden under feet by malice, prejudice, and superstition. 1889 Gretton *Memory's Harkb.* 163 In his early days the masses were a good deal trodden down.

**d.** *intr.* for *pass.* To be trampled *down*.

1837 Carlyle *Fr. Rev.* III. ii. i, The Gironde..has trodden on it, and yet not trodden it down...It is a well-spring, as we said, this black-spot; and will not tread down.

**6.** *intr.* To trample *on* or *upon*. Also *fig.*

*c* 1000 *Ags. Gosp.* Luke x. 19 Ic sealde eow anweald to tredenne ofer næddran & snacan. *c* 1330 *Amis & Amil.* 2096 He..trad [*MS.* drad] on him in the slough. 1382 Wyclif *Luke* x. 19, I have ȝouun to ȝou power of defoulinge, [*gloss*] othir tredinge, on serpents, and scorpiouns. *c* 1450 tr. *De Imitatione* iii. xiv. 82 þat al men mowe goo over þee, and trede vppon the as vppon myre of the streete. 1590 Marlowe *2nd Pt. Tamburl.* iii. ii, Tread upon his neck, And treble all his father's slaveries. 1596 Dalrymple tr. *Leslie's Hist. Scot.* iv. (S.T.S.) I. 225 The sygne of the croce ..vpon the ground, quhairthrouche feit mycht haue occasione to tred or tramp thairvpon. 1683 *Col. Rec. Pennsylv.* I. 79 James Kilner Trode upon him on board the Ship. 1733 Fielding *Quix. in Eng.* ii. i, Each man rises to admiration by treading on mankind. 1818 Scott *Rob Roy* xxxix, A hatred as intense..as if my foot trode on your neck. 1884 Pae *Eustace* 79 Was he a worm to be trod on thus without turning?

**7.** *trans.* To press (something) downwards with the foot or feet in treadling or pedalling.

*To tread water*, in swimming, to move the feet as in walking upstairs, while the body is kept erect and the head above water.

1680 Moxon *Mech. Exerc.* xii. 209 The nearer the Fore-end of the Treddle you Tread, the easier you bring down the Pole. *Ibid.*, Tread the Treddle nimbly down. 1800 *Hull Advertiser* 15 Nov. 4/3, I always raised myself by treading water. 1853 Kane *Grinnell Exp.* xxxviii. (1856) 343 Seal breast-high, were treading water with their horizontal tails.

**8.** Of the male bird: To copulate with (the hen). Also *absol.*

*a* 1250 *Owl & Night.* 501 Sone so þu hauest itrede Ne myht þu leng a word iqueþe. 1377 [see A. 2 δ]. *c* 1386 Chaucer *Nun's Pr. T.* 358 (Ellesm.) He..fethered Pertelote twenty tyme And trad [14.. *Lansd. MS.* trade hire] as ofte. 1599 T. M[oufet] *Silkwormes* 24 Before the hardie Cocke

Beganne to tread, or brooding henne to clocke. **1614** MARKHAM *Cheap Husb.* (1623) 143 If your Henne be trodden with a carryon Crow, or Rooke,..it is mortall and incurable. *a* **1687** COTTON tr. *Martial* III. lviii. (1689) 59 I' th' Yards are seen, Cocks treading Rhodian Hens. **1721** BRADLEY *Philos. Acc. Wks. Nat.* 78 It is common for Cock Pheasants to tread the Hens of common Poultry. **1774** GOLDSM. *Nat. Hist.* (1776) V. 165 It matters not much whether she be trodden by the cock or no; she will continue to lay. **1910** A. PLATT tr. *Aristotle's De Generatione* III. viii. 751 When once the hens have been trodden, they all continue to have eggs almost without intermission.

**b.** *absol.* Of birds: To copulate.

**1486** *Bk. St. Albans, Hawking* a ij, We shall say that they [Hawks] trede. *a* **1659** OSBORN *Queries* Wks. (1673) 612, I my Self have seen both Swallowes and Hobbies build and tread upon their first Appearance. **1774** G. WHITE *Selborne* 28 Sept., The fact that I would advance is, that swifts tread, or copulate, on the wing.

†**c.** *trans.* with *out*: To engender, beget (off-spring). *Obs. rare*−1.

**1594** LYLY *Moth. Bomb.* I. i, As your Worship being wise begot a foole, so he being a foole may tread out a wise man.

**9.** *trans.* To thresh (corn) by trampling it on a threshing-floor: said of the oxen, etc. or of one using them; also with *out.* **b.** To press out the juice of (grapes) by trampling them in a vat. **c.** To tramp (clothes) in washing; see TRAMP *v.*1 3 c.

**1382** WYCLIF *Deut.* xxv. 4 Thow shalt not bynde the mouth of the oxe tredinge thi fruytis in the flore. — *Isa.* xvi. 10 Wyn in the presse he shal not trede, that to treden was wont; the vois of the trederes I toc awey. **1446** LYDG. *Two Nightingale Poems* ii. 155 It is [I], quod he, that trade it al alone. Withouten felawe I gan the wyne out-presse. **1577** B. GOOGE *Heresbach's Husb.* 42 b, Corne..in some place they..lyke to tread it out with Oxen. **1792** A. YOUNG *Trav. France* 31 This universal one of treading out the corn, with which all the towns and villages in Languedoc are now alive. **1801** *Farmer's Mag.* Aug. 313, I was long, and greatly prejudised against treading wheat. **1848** CLOUGH *Bothie* ii, The clothes that they trod in the wash-tub. **1871** B. TAYLOR *Faust* (1875) II. I. ii. 20 Who wine desires, let him the ripe grapes tread.

**10.** To make or form by the action of the feet in walking; *esp.* to beat (a path or track). Const. *out.*

*c* **1410** Wele ytredde [see A. 3 *a*]. **1552** HULOET, Tread out, *exculco, as.* **1563** *Homilies* II. *Rogation Week* IV. (1640) 235 The ancient terris of the fields, that old men beforetime with great paines did tread out. **1580** LYLY *Euphues* (Arb.) 450 Hee that diggeth the garden, is to be considered, though he cannot treade the knottes. **1856** FROUDE *Hist. Eng.* I. i. 51 Paths trodden by the foot-steps of ages. **1860** TENNYSON *Sea Dreams* 117 But she with her strong feet up the steep hill Trod out a path. **1865** VISCT. MILTON & CHEADLE *N.-W. Passage by Land* viii. (1867) 114 A track would require to be trodden out with snow-shoes to enable the dogs to travel.

**11.** *Horticulture.* To beat down and consolidate (soil) by treading; also with plants, etc. as object.

*c* **1440** *Pallad. on Husb.* II. 256 Sette hem depe..And tradde hem fast aboue. **1693** EVELYN *De la Quint. Compl. Gard.* II. 149 The first layer being thus compleated..the Gard'ner proceeds to lay the second, third, &c. beating them with the back of his Fork, or else treading them with his Feet. **1842** LOUDON *Suburban Hort.* 661 The ground should be previously trodden or rolled. **1845** *Florist's Jrnl.* 31 The whole should be gently trod with the feet.

**12.** *intr.* Of land (*tread loose*, hence ellipt. *tread*): To yield or give to the tread (? as after frost). *dial.*

**1847** *Jrnl. R. Agric. Soc.* VIII. I. 73 When the soil treads loose in the spring, it is very important to use the heavy roller, or some other means of consolidating the soil. **1891** MALDEN *Tillage* 49 When once the land 'treads' the horses are best in the furrow. *Ibid.* Gloss. s. v., Land is said to tread when it puddles or poaches under the feet of the horses employed upon it.

**13.** *trans.* With advbs.: To get or put into or out of some position or condition by treading; *esp.* to put *out* (fire) by treading. (See also 5 b, c.)

*To tread up* (partridges), to flush them by walking up to the covey (? in contrast to the practice of using dogs).

**1600** W. WATSON *Decacordon* (1602) 3 The fire..would breake out (if not troade out in time) of it selfe. *c* **1682** J. COLLINS *Salt & Fishery* 121 The Meat is..pack'd or trodden into Cask..with Salt betwixt every Lane or Lay. **1697** DRYDEN *Virg. Georg.* II. 314 Trample with thy Feet, and tread it in. *a* **1745** SWIFT *Direct. Servants* iii, Throw the [candle] snuff on the floor, and then tread it out, to prevent stinking. **1756** MRS. CALDERWOOD in *Coltness Collect.* (Maitl. Cl.) 118 One of them asked..would I have my toes trode off? 'Is your toes trode off?' said I. **1808** COL. HAWKER *Diary* (1893) I. 13, I trod up the whole covey. **1847** W. C. L. MARTIN *Ox* 168/1 Buried deep..with quick lime, and covered up with earth closely trodden down. **1849** MACAULAY *Hist. Eng.* i. I. 149 The flame of civil war.. was trodden out before it had time to spread. **1888** J. INGLIS *Tent Life in Tigerland* 8 The cattle had trod down all the dried leaves.

**b.** *To tread one's shoe awry* (*the shoe, one's foot, amiss*, etc.), to fall from chastity. See also AWRY A. 2 c. ? *Obs.* So *to tread one's shoes straight*, to conduct oneself circumspectly, to walk warily (*dial.*).

*c* **1422** HOCCLEVE *Min. Poems* xxiv. 66 No womman..But swich oon as hath trode hir shoo amis. **1520–1662** [see AWRY A. 2 c]. **1616** R. C. *Times' Whistle* VI. 2541 Due pennance thou deservst to doe For tredding thus awry thy slippery shoe. **1642** J. EATON *Honey-c. Free Justif.* 110 If she chance to tread her foot a little awry. **1870** E. PEACOCK *Ralf Skirl.* I. 112 They mun tread their shoes very straight or there'll be a row with our Squire.

Hence **Trea·ding** *ppl. a.*

**1562** J. HEYWOOD *Prov. & Epigr.* (1867) 214 There be mo treadyng cockes then one.

**Treader** (tre·dəɹ). [f. TREAD *v.* + -ER 1.]

**1.** One who or that which treads, in various senses.

**1382** WYCLIF *Amos* ix. 13 The erer shal cacche the reper, and treder of grape the man sendynge seed. **1538** ELYOT, *Lenobates*, a treader of grapes. **1599** T. M[OUFET] *Silkewormes* 33 Hence, sparrow treaders liue out scarce a year. **1601** R. JOHNSON *Kingd. & Commw.* (1603) 123 The Gothes and Vandales, the verie treaders downe of the Roman Empire. **1760** LAW *Spir. Prayer* II. 112 The seed of the woman, the treader on the serpent's head. **1826** SCOTT *Woodst.* xiv, A treader of mortar, or a bearer of a hod. **1869** *Pall Mall G.* 15 Nov. 3 More grapes were now thrown in, and again the treaders set to work. **1887** *Suppl. to Jamieson, Tredder*, a cock-bird, but generally applied to a [domestic] cock.

†**b.** See quot. *Obs.*

**1552** ELYOT, *Anteambulo*,..the vssher or treader that goeth before his maister.

**c.** One who is on the treadmill. *rare.*

**1824** SYD. SMITH *Wks.* (1859) II. 35/2 A treader, untried by a jury of his countrymen,.. striving against the law of gravity.

**2.** = TREADLE *sb.* 2. *rare.*

**1747** *Gentl. Mag.* Jan. 16/1 A wheel, to which motion was given by the foot by means of a treadle or treader.

**3.** = TREAD *sb.* 11.

**1881** YOUNG *Every Man his own Mechanic* § 1321 If a garden step or any other step with a treader of stone is required to be made.

**Treading** (tre·diŋ), *vbl. sb.* [-ING 1.]

**1.** The action of the verb TREAD in various senses.

*c* **1410** *Master of Game* (MS. Digby 182) xxiv, Ye may Jugge..an herte chaseable..by þe tredynge of þe grasse. **1523** FITZHERB. *Husb.* § 128 Well hardened with caryage and treading vpon. **1615** W. V[ALLANS] *Hon. Prentice* 33 A flat Marble stone..much defaced with treading, and neere worne out. **1709–10** STEELE *Tatler* No. 126 ¶ 4 He heard ..the Treading of one who approach'd. **1842** LOUDON *Suburban Hort.* 660 To press the soil on it firmly by treading.

**b.** *plural.*

*c* **1440** *Promp. Parv.* 501/1 Tredyngys, wythe the foote. **1535** COVERDALE *Song Sol.* vii. 1 O how pleasaunt are thy treadinges with thy shues. **1634** SIR T. HERBERT *Trav.* 20 The women..equall if not exceed the men in their more laborious treadings [in dancing]. **1760–72** H. BROOKE *Fool of Qual.* (1809) III. 89, I heard secret treadings and mutterings. **1865** *Englishm. Mag.* Feb. 147 With treadings slow and whisperings low Men sadly count the slain.

**2.** *concr.* Anything made by treading; *spec.* the footprint of a boar. See also COCK-TREADING.

**1573, 1655** [see COCK-TREADING]. **1575** TURBERV. *Venerie* 237 The footyng or print is called..of a Bore, the tracke or the Treading. **1731–3** TULL *Horse-Hoeing Husb.* xx. 295 Their [horses'] Treadings are cut so small by the Coulters, that the Earth is not kept from dissolving.

**3.** *attrib.* **Treading-mill** = TREADMILL; **treading-room**, a room in which the materials of porcelain are kneaded together by treading.

**1535** COVERDALE *Isa.* xli. 15, I wil make the a treadinge cart & a new flale, yt thou mayest throsshe & grynde the mountaynes. **1675** COTTON *Scoffer Scoft* 54 [Jove did] transform himself into a Swan, to try The treading way of Letchery. **1752** *Gentl. Mag.* Aug. 348 The next (on the ground floor) is the slip and treading rooms. **1830** SOUTHEY in *Q. Rev.* XLIII. 50 Road-making..which serves in those islands in place of the treading-mill.

**Treadle** (tre·d'l), *sb.* Forms: 1 **tredel**; 5 **tredel, -yl, -ylle, 6–9 treddle,** (8 **-el**), 7 **tredle,** (**treddle**), 8–9 **treadel, 6– treadle**; *β.* 7 **trydle, triddle** (also 9 *dial.*); *γ.* 7 **tradle,** 9 *dial.* **traddle.** [f. TREAD *v.* + -LE 1.]

†**1.** A step or stair. *Obs. rare*−0.

*a* **1000** *Ælfric's Voc.* in Wr.-Wülcker 117/6 *Bases*, tredelas, *uel* stæpas. *c* **1440** *Promp. Parv.* 501/1 Tredyl, or [*v.r.* of] grece, *gradus, pedalis.* *c* **1490** *Ibid.* 209/1 (MSS. K. & H.) Grece, or tredyl, *P.* or steyre, *gradus.* **1847–78** HALLIWELL, *Treddle*, the step of a stair, etc.

**2.** A lever worked by the foot in machines and mechanical contrivances, usually to produce reciprocating (as orig. in the loom) or rotary motion.

**14..** *Voc.* in Wr.-Wülcker 592/33 *Liciatorium*, a tredel. *Ibid.* 614/14 *Subpedium*, a tredel. **1483** *Cath. Angl.* 392/1 A Tredylle of ye lummys, *suppodium.* **1573–80** BARET *Alv.* T 347 The Treadle of a weauers loome, *insile.* **1608** TOPSELL *Serpents* (1658) 785 Consider the strange trydles of their Looms. **1667** in Pettus *Fodinæ Reg.* (1670) 35 Large Smelting Bellows with Beams, Frames, Swords, Triddles. **1680** MOXON *Mech. Exerc.* x. 183 Of the Treddle and Cross-Treddle. **1688** R. HOLME *Armoury* III. xxi. (Roxb.) 252/1 By the riseing and falling of the Tradles, these play vp and down. **1806** W. TAYLOR in *Ann. Rev.* IV. 772 Until the method of lifting it by treadels, or foot-staves. **1831** G. R. PORTER *Silk Manuf.* 215 Treadles on which the weaver presses his feet alternately. *Mod.* A sewing-machine worked by treadles.

**b.** A pedal of a bicycle or the like

**1887** MISS E. P. THOMPSON in *Monthly Packet* Jan. 88 My feet are unapt to move without the treadles under them. **1895** H. C. BEECHING *Poems, Going down hill on a bicycle* v, When the wheels scarce crawl, My feet to the treadles fall.

**c.** On a railway: see quot.

**1904** *Westm. Gaz.* 15 Nov. 10/1 There is an electric treadle just outside Shepherd's Bush Station which is operated by a brush fixed to the rear car of the train; and this operates on the block signal.

**3.** = TREAD *sb.* 9 b. Now *dial.*

**1658** SIR T. BROWNE *Pseud. Ep.* III. xxviii. (ed. 4) 225 The Grando or tredle are but the poles and establishing particles of the tender membrans. **1713** DERHAM *Phys.-Theol.* VII. iv. 391 At each end of the Egg is a Treddle, so called, because it was formerly thought to be the Sperm of the Cock. **1747** MRS. GLASSE *Cookery* vii. 70 The Treadels of the Eggs. **1794** G. ADAMS *Nat. & Exp. Philos.* I. v. 180 The chicken contained in embryo, in..the treadle of the egg.

†**b.** See quots. (Cf. TREAD *v.* 8, *sb.* 9.) *Obs.*

**1638** FORD *Fancies* III. iii, Whore, bitch-fox, treedle, fa la la la! [**1847–78** HALLIWELL, *Treddle*, a whore.]

**4.** *attrib.* and *Comb.*, as *treadle-board, -cord, -crank, -lever, -wire*; worked by a treadle or treadles, as *treadle-brake, -grindstone, -loom, -machine, -wheel*; also *treadle-shaking* adj.

**1881** YOUNG *Every Man his own Mechanic* § 550 Fastened to this shaft is the *treadle-board. **1903** *Westm. Gaz.* 20 Oct. 10/1 By slow degrees, we got the present serviceable *treadle brake that acts on the whole 'bus. **1766** *Compl. Farmer* s. v. *Flax*, The sword or upright timber-rod which turns the wheel by the *treadle-crank. **1902** MARSHALL *Metal Tools* 72 For larger tools..a *treadle grindstone.. will be found more convenient. **1839** URE *Dict. Arts* 269 A platform, which is raised up by a *treddle lever. **1882** FLOYER *Unexpl. Baluchistan* 45 The manufacturers sit in holes in their gardens before their rather clumsy *treadle-looms. **1893** A. S. ECCLES *Sciatica* 7 Working a *treadle sewing-machine for some hours. **1812** W. TENNANT *Anster F.* II. xxvi, Their *treadle-shaking feet now scour apace Through Gallow town. **1680** MOXON *Mech. Exerc.* x. 188 The *Treddle Wheel is used for small work only. **1880** CARNEGIE *Pract. Trap.* vi. 41 The *treadle wire itself may be flattened.

**Treadle** (tre·d'l), *v.* [f. TREADLE *sb.*]

**1.** *intr.* To work a treadle; to move the feet as if doing this; also, of a cyclist: to make one's way by treadling or pedalling one's cycle: also *trans.* with *way.* Hence **Trea·dling** *vbl. sb.*

**1891** T. HARDY *Tess* xxxv, In the strenuousness of his concentration he treadled fitfully on the floor. **1891** *Daily News* 7 Sept. 6/3 Two or three of these persecutor-cyclists were quietly treadling about the town as early as eight in the morning. **1896** *Ibid.* 25 July 8/1 We treadled our way swiftly through the..streets. **1912** *Ibid.* 21 Mar. 5 A little weakness which makes it difficult to do much treadling.

**2.** *trans.* To operate (a machine) by working a treadle.

**1906** H. BEGBIE *Priest* xvi, You'd be in Queer Street, treadling a sewing-machine for eighteen pence a day.

Hence **Trea·dler**, one who treadles.

*Treadler's cramp*, cramp of the legs affecting persons engaged in working treadle-machines.

**1891** *Lancet* 14 Feb. 410/1 Medical Society of London...A case of Treadler's Cramp. **1899** *Allbutt's Syst. Med.* VIII. 15 The lameness and the 'treadler's cramp' appeared simultaneously.

**Treadled** (tre·d'ld), *a.* [f. TREADLE *sb.* + -ED 2.] Having or furnished with a treadle or tread.

**1877** BLACKMORE *Erema* xxxv, With his treddled heel scraping the shoulder of his shining spade. **1894** — *Perlycross* 24 Nor linger for a moment at the treddled stile.

**Treadmill** (tre·dmil), *sb.* [f. TREAD *v.* + MILL *sb.*1] A horizontal cylinder made to revolve by the weight of persons treading on boards arranged as equidistant steps around its periphery. Formerly in use as an instrument of prison discipline.

**1822** (*title*) Description of the Tread Mill invented by Mr. William Cubitt of Ipswich, for the Employment of Prisoners. **1824** SYD. SMITH *Wks.* (1859) II. 36/1 The labour of the tread-mill is irksome, dull, monotonous, and disgusting to the last degree. **1836** GEN. P. THOMPSON *Exerc.* (1842) IV. 107 Religious observances of other people..forced upon us with a faggot or a treadmill. **1886** J. K. JEROME *Idle Thoughts* xii. 139 Too much getting up and down stairs.. puts one unpleasantly in mind of the tread-mill.

*transf.* and *fig.* **1827** SCOTT *Chron. Canongate* i, A kind of mental tread-mill, where you are perpetually climbing, but can never rise an inch. **1862** H. AÏDE *Carr of Carrlyon* I. 262 A return to the treadmill of London society. **1897** G. ALLEN *Typewriter Girl* xv, The squirrel who turns the unceasing treadmill of his cage. **1905** LYALL *Life Mrq. Dufferin* II. v. 173 He found himself again on the official treadmill.

*attrib.* **1849** E. B. EASTWICK *Dry Leaves* 5 There is no winding or sloping here...No! all is fair treadmill work. **1885** C. HARRISON in *Harper's Mag.* Mar. 548/1 Back again at the tread-mill round of business.

Hence **Trea·dmill** *v.*, *intr.* to labour on or as on the treadmill.

**1899** *Westm. Gaz.* 18 Nov. 3/2 My feet..slipped on the pedal till I was treadmilling clumsily with the middle instead of the ball of the foot. **1902** *Messenger* (N.S.W.) 5 Dec. 253 The..prison discipline of past days, in which treadmilling was the only work prisoners were permitted to do.

**Trea·d-so·ftly.** [f. imper. of TREAD *v.* + SOFTLY.] A name for a herbaceous perennial stinging plant (*Jatropha urens var. stimulosa*) of the southern United States; the spurge-nettle.

**1814** PURSH *Flora Amer. Septentr.* II. 602 *Jatropha stimulosa*..is a very injurious weed.., as it ruins the Negroes' feet when they tread upon it; from which it is known by the name of *Tread-softly.* **1884** in MILLER *Plant-n.*

**Trea·d-wheel,** *sb.* [f. TREAD *v.* + WHEEL *sb.*] A wheel rotated by the treading of persons or animals to give motion to machinery, to pump or raise water, etc.; *esp.* a wheel turned by the weight of a person or animal walking forward on the inside of its periphery; also, = TREADMILL.

*c* **1573** *Lansdowne MS. 101*, lf. 81 The Trade Whele where uppon men or horse stondyth. **1629** *Patent Specif.* (1856) No. 48. 1 An engine..which goeth downe to the bottome.. of the Worke where it is to be used either by a Treadwheele meanes, hands [etc.]. **1660** R. D'ACRES *Art Water-drawing* 12 Certain great hollow wheels, hanging perpendicularly, in which men tread (called by some tread-wheels) not unlike unto a dog in a spit-wheel. **1799** *Specif. Hardie's Patent* No. 2300 The steps..serve for the men to mount upon or dismount from the tread wheel. **1822** *Gentl. Mag.* July 9 A party of prisoners..working one of the Tread-wheels of the Discipline Mill, invented by Mr. Cubitt. **1839** I. TAYLOR

*Anc. Chr.* I. iii. 362 Ascetics.. wasting themselves to skeletons on the treadwheel of their devout taskwork.

Hence **Trea·d-wheel** *v., trans.* to inflict the discipline of the treadmill upon; whence **Trea·d-wheeling** *vbl. sb.*

**1831** *Lincoln Herald* 7 Oct. 4 Let these officials moderate their..fines, and treadwheeling.

† **Treaf,** *a. Obs. dial.* Also 7 **trefe.** [Etymology unknown.] Peevish, bad-tempered.

**1601** DENT *Pathw. Heaven* 389 Though her yoong suckling crie all night, and be exceeding treafe and waiward. **1627** J. CARTER *Plain Expos.* 16 They are pronounced blessed, not who are treafe, and teachie, irefull and snappish,..but the meeke who..submit themselues vnder the mightie hand of God. **1659** GAUDEN *Slight Healers* (1660) 34 To quiet the Trefe and Wayward people. **1691** RAY *S. & E. C. Words* (E.D.S.), *Treaf*, peevish, froward, pettish, very apt to be angry. Hence **1787** in GROSE *Provinc. Gloss.*

**Treager,** variant of TREGAR.

† **Treague** (trīg). *Obs.* [ad. med.L. *tregua, treuga, treugua* (*c* 1220 in Du Cange), = It. and Sp. *tregua*, Pr. *tregua, trega*, Pg. *tregoa*, ad. Goth. *triggwa* treaty, covenant, f. *triggws* true, sure. In OF. *trive, treve*, F. *trêve*: see also TREVE, TRUCE. (For form cf. LEAGUE.)] A truce.

**1590** SPENSER *F. Q.* II. ii. 33 Which to confirme, and fast to bind their league, After their weary sweat and bloody toile, She them besought, during their quiet treague, Into her lodging to repaire a while. *a* **1660** *Contemp. Hist. Irel.* (Ir. Archæol. Soc.) II. 174 A trumpeter..desiringe a treague or cessation of armes for a peremptorie time.

**Treaky,** var. *traiky* (see under TRAIK *sb.*).

**Treand, Treangell, -gle,** obs. ff. TREND, TRIANGLE. **Treas, Treasance**: see TRACE *sb.*[2], TRESANCE *Obs.*

**Treason** (trī·z'n), *sb.* Forms: 3-4 **treison,** 5-6 **treyson;** 3-5 (*Sc.* -6) **trayson, -one,** 4 (*Sc.* -6) **-oun,** 6 *Sc.* **-oune;** 4 (*Sc.* 6) **traison,** 4-6 **-oun;** 3-5 **tresun, -oun,** 3-7 **-on,** 4-5 **-une, -oune, -one,** 5 **-own;** 4 **tressun,** 5 **-on,** 5-6 **-one,** 6 *Sc.* **-oun;** 5- **treason,** (5 **-oune,** 5-7 **-oun,** *Sc.* 5-6 **trason,** 6 **-oun, -oune,** 7 **treassoune**). [a. AFr. *treysoun, tresun, treson, -oun*, = OF. *traïson* (11th c.), in mod.F. *trahison* = Pr. *traicio*, Cat. *traició*, Sp. *traición*, Pg. *traição* :—L. *trāditiōn-em*, n. of action from L. *trādĕre*, OF. *traïr*, F. *trahir* to deliver up, betray: see TRAY *v.*[2], TRAISE *v.*]

**1.** The action of betraying; betrayal of the trust undertaken by or reposed in any one; breach of faith, treacherous action, treachery.

*a* **1225** *Ancr. R.* 56 Dauid..dude..treison and monsleiht on his treowe kniht Vrie, hire louerd. *a* **1240** *Wohunge* in *Cott. Hom.* 279 Barabas a þeof þat wið tresun..hafde a mon cwelled. **1297** R. GLOUC. (Rolls) 2337 Vor hii..in trayson were cointe þat hii ssolde þen king sle. *a* **1300** *Cursor M.* 3882 (Cott.) Qui has þou don me sli tresum? *a* **1340** HAMPOLE *Psalter* ix. 29 Whas mouth is ful of weriynge & bitternes & treson. **13..** *K. Alis.* 1362 (Bodl. MS.) And he þat þe traisoun dede Was fore hakked in þat stede. *c* **1400** *Song Roland* 176 For men dred tresson wher they it finden, And thought on tresson þer trist was neuer. *c* **1400** MAUNDEV. (Roxb.) xi. 43 He had done treyson, when he slogh Vry. *a* **1450** *Knt. de la Tour* lxxiv. (1906) 96 It is treson whanne a man trustithe in her [his wife] and she discouered his counsaile. **1596** SHAKS. *Merch. V.* III. ii. 27 Vpon the racke Bassanio, then confesse What treason there is mingled with your loue. **1611** SIR W. MURE *Misc. Poems* i. 15 By subtil slight, or treassoune, To siege, and sack the Rampier of my ressoun. **1825** SCOTT *Talism.* i, From whom I should demand security, did I not know that treason seldom dwells with courage.

**2.** *Law.*

In old English law treason was either *High Treason*, an offence against the king's majesty or the safety of the commonwealth, or *Petit* or *Petty Treason*, an offence committed against a subject. Petit Treason is now punished only as murder, and High Treason is usually styled simply *treason*. Many acts of High Treason are now treated as *Treason felony*.

[**1292** BRITTON I. ix. § 1 Tresun est en chescun damage qe hom fet a escient ou procure de fere a cely a qi hom se fet ami. Et poet estre treysoun graunt et petit.]

**a.** *High Treason* or *Treason* proper: Violation by a subject of his allegiance to his sovereign or to the state.

Defined 1350-51 by Act 25 Edw. III, Stat. 5, c. 2, as compassing or imagining the king's death, or that of his wife or eldest son, violating the wife of the king or of the heir apparent, or the king's eldest daughter being unmarried, levying war in the king's dominions, adhering to the king's enemies in his dominions, or aiding them in or out of the realm, or killing the chancellor or the judges in the execution of their offices. In 1795 the offence was extended to actual or contemplated use of force to make the king change his counsels, or to intimidate either or both of the Houses of Parliament. But see *treason-felony* 4 b.

[**1292** BRITTON I. ix. § 2 Graunt tresoun est a compasser nostre mort, ou de nous desheriter de noster reaume, ou de fauser noster seal, ou de contrefere nostre monee ou de retoundre.] **1303** R. BRUNNE *Handl. Synne* 10258 Yn no þyng wote y more tresun, Þan brynge þy lorde to hys felun. **1473** WARKW. *Chron.* (Camden) 5 The Lorde Hungerforde was..behedede for hye treasoune. **1593** SHAKS. *Rich. II*, III. iii. 93 Tell Bullingbrooke..That euery stride he makes vpon my Land, Is dangerous Treason. *a* **1612** HARINGTON *Epigr.* IV. 5 Treason doth never prosper, what's the reason? For if it prosper, none dare call it Treason. **1660** *Trial Regic.* 31 To stand Mute in High-Treason, is all one, as to Confess the Fact. **1781** GIBBON *Decl. & F.* xvii. II. 60 A fatal maxim.. that in the case of treason, which included every offence that the subtlety of lawyers could derive from an hostile intention towards the prince or republic, all privileges were suspended. **1814** SCOTT *Wav.* xli, The charge brought against you of aiding and abetting high treason. **1902** *Westm. Gaz.* 12 June 10/1 At present there is only one species of treason—that known as high treason, by way of contradistinction to petty treason. **1907** *Verney Mem.* I. 34 Sir Robert Whittingham was attainted of treason. **1911** W. B. ODGERS & ODGERS *Comm. Law Eng.* I. 145 Writing treasonable words is, no doubt a more deliberate act than merely uttering them. But..if the writings be not published, they do not constitute an overt act of treason.

**b.** *Petit* or *petty treason*, treason against a subject; *spec.* the murder of one to whom the murderer owes allegiance, as of a master by his servant, a husband by his wife, etc. Now only *Hist.*

[**1351-2** *Rolls of Parlt.* II. 239/1 Il y ad autre manere de Treison, c'est assaver quant un Servant tue son Mestre.] **1496** *Ibid.* VI. 513/1 An Acte to make some Offences Petty Treason. **1580** G. HARVEY *Let. to Spenser* iv. Wks. (Grosart) I. 103 Reputing it Petty Treason to reuolt therefro. **1625** MASSINGER *New Way* III. ii, How! strike a Justice of Peace! 'Tis petty treason. **1763** *Brit. Mag.* IV. 273 Mary Head,..who was convicted at Chester assizes of petit treason, in killing her husband..was burnt. **1777** *Chron.* in *Ann. Reg.* 183/2 Joseph Armstrong was tried for petty treason, in poisoning his master's lady. **1828** *Act 9 Geo. IV*, c. 31 § 2 Every Offence, which before the Commencement of this Act would have amounted to Petit Treason, shall be deemed to be Murder only.

**c.** *Constructive treason*, action which though not actually or overtly coming under any of the acts specified in the Statute of Treason, was declared by law to be treason and punishable as such. *Misprision of treason*: see MISPRISION.

*a* **1714**, **1769** [see CONSTRUCTIVE *a.* 4 b]. **1882** LECKY *Eng. in 18th C.* xiii. III. 522 The charge [against Lord George Gordon] was what is termed by lawyers 'constructive treason'. It rested upon the assertion that the agitation which he had created and led was the originating cause of the outrages that had taken place.

**d.** In exclamatory use (in sense 1 or 2 a). Cf. TRAY *interj.*

**1388** WYCLIF 2 *Chron.* xxiii. 13 Sche to-rente hir clothis, and seide, Tresouns! tresouns! [**1539** BIBLE (Great), treason, treason]. **1470-85** MALORY *Arthur* IV. iii. 121 They herd a grete noyse and many cryed treson, treson. Alass, said kynge Arthur, we ben bitrayed. *a* **1491** J. ROSS *Hist. Reg. Angl.* (1716) 218 Sæpius se proditum clamans & dicens, Treson, Treson, Treson. **1593** SHAKS. *Rich. II*, V. iii. 72 Treason, foule Treason, Villaine, Traitor, Slaue. **1602** — *Ham.* V. ii. 334 *Ham.* Then venome to thy worke. (*Hurts the King.*) *All.* Treason, treason.

† **3.** With *a* and *pl.* An act of treason, in prec. senses; also, a species of treason. Also *fig.*

*c* **1330** R. BRUNNE *Chron. Wace* (Rolls) 7128 In casteles he sette garnysons ffor þe drede of oþer traysons. *c* **1330** — *Chron.* (1810) 172 His traitour ert þou now, þou did him a tresoun. **1474** CAXTON *Chesse* III. iii. (1883) 95 In assemblyng the peple thus to gyder they make moo traysons in the cytees than they make good alyances. **1593** SHAKS. *Rich. II*, III. ii. 51 His Treasons will sit blushing in his face. **1605** M. SUTCLIFFE *Brief Exam.* 2 Manifold rebellions and treasons against their princes. *a* **1709** ATKYNS *Parl. & Pol. Tracts* (1734) 23 By this means Men will be discouraged from discovering Treasons. **1708** *Termes de la Ley* 450 Petit Treason is a Treason of a lower degree; as if a Servant kill his Master, a Wife her Husband.

**4.** *attrib.* and *Comb.*, as *treason-charge, court, -law, -monger, -plot, -tavern, -worker*; *treason-canting, -hatching, -haunted* adjs.

**1682** *Dryden's Medall* To Author 26 All their *Treason-canting Priests. **1900** *Echo* 9 Jan. 2/7, I..was then discharged on the high *treason charge. **1900** *Daily News* 12 Nov. 5/2 At to-day's sitting of the *Treason Court, Mr. Schroeder..was released on bail. **1659** *Burton's Diary* (1828) III. 437 Her custom was..to come into the dining-room to him in her *treason-gown, (as I called it,) I telling him, that when she had that gown on, he should allow her to say anything. **1745** AYRE *Life Pope* II. 85 The sacred Character of a lurking, *treason-hatching Jesuit. **1871** J. HAY *Pike County Ball.* (1880) 110 Its stealthy echoes pour Through *treason-haunted regions. **1810** *Edin. Rev.* XVI. 105 The principles of *treason-law. **1746** M. HUGHES *Jrnl. Late Reb.* 5 Among all these *Treason-mongers, old Gordon, the Laird of Glenbucket is a notable Instance of Loyalty. **1839** LD. BROUGHAM *Statesm. Geo. III, Gibbs* 127 A rabble-leader or a treason-monger, a libeller or a blasphemer. **1640** YORKE *Union Hon.* 174 That bloody and damnable *treason-plot. **1681** DRYDEN *Abs. & Achit.* II. 459 Og from a *treason-tavern rolling home. **1553** in *Howell's St. Trials*, (1809) I. 788 Then shall there be men loving themselves, covetous, proud, disobedient to parents, *treason-workers.

**b. Trea·son-fe·lony,** an offence, formerly included among acts of treason, which by subsequent legislation has been removed from these, and is not punishable with death. So **trea·son-fe·lon,** one convicted of treason-felony.

Defined (though not so named) by the Crown and Government Security Act, 11 & 12 Vict. c. 12 (1848) by which treasons not directed at the person of the Sovereign were mitigated to felonies, punishable with penal servitude for life, or for a term of not less than five years.

**1865** *Annual Register* 252 The Attorney General said that the Act of Parliament respecting treason-felony created several offences and these were of three descriptions. **1865** *Times* 29 Nov. 10/2 Counsel for the prisoner was taken by surprise in finding bills for treason-felony instead of high-treason sent up to the grand jury. **1881** R. F. LITTLEDALE in *Academy* 29 Jan. 75 The experiences of a treason-felon. **1892** *Daily News* 26 Feb. 3/1 Out of the 23 treason-felony prisoners confined in British prisons during the last ten years, one had become insane.

**Trea·son,** *v. rare.* Forms: see prec.; also 4-5 **traysen, trassen.** [f. prec. Cf. OF. *traisonner* to betray.] *trans.* To betray; to act treasonably towards.

**13..** *K. Alis.* 723 Thy fadir hastow tresond here! *c* **1330** R. BRUNNE *Chron.* (1810) 105 Þei wer fulle wele knowen, þat wild haf tresond him. *c* **1374** CHAUCER *Troylus* IV. 410 (438) To traysen [*v.r.* trassen] a wight þat trewe is vn-to me. **1890** L. LEWIS *Proving of Gennad* XV. 104 Ere morning, thou shalt know who treasons thee.

**Treasonable** (trī·z'năb'l), *a.* [f. TREASON *sb.* + -ABLE.] Of the nature of treason; characteristic of or involving treason; perfidious, treacherous. (Orig. *Sc.*)

**1375** BARBOUR *Bruce* V. 550 Þis tratour ay Had in his thocht ..How he mycht best bring till ending Þis tresonabill vndirtaking. *c* **1470** HENRY *Wallace* XI. 829 Be this tresonabill concord Schyr Jhon suld be off all the Lennox lord. **1546** *Reg. Privy Council Scot.* I. 32 The tressonabill slauchter of umquhile David Cardinale Archbischop. **1596** DALRYMPLE tr. *Leslie's Hist. Scot.* x. (S.T.S.) II. 402 Thir trasonable trahitouris. **1634** *Documents agst. Prynne* (Camden) 27 In a most infamous, daungerous, and treasonable waye. **1675** tr. *Camden's Hist. Eliz.* an. 1601. 625 The Earl of Essex..had accused him as an Instigatour of him to this treasonable Attempt. **1741** RICHARDSON *Pamela* (1824) I. 110 So, Pamela, we have seized, it seems, your treasonable papers? **1818** HALLAM *Mid. Ages* viii. III. (1819) III. 233 Their participation in a treasonable conspiracy being manifest. **1855** MACAULAY *Hist. Eng.* xvii. IV. 18 The treasonable packet had been found in his bosom.

Hence **Trea·sonableness,** treasonable quality or character.

**1679** *Jenison's Popish Plot* Pref. 8 Treasonableness in point of Loyalty. **1727** in BAILEY vol. II.

**Treasonably** (trī·z'năbli), *adv.* [f. prec. + -LY[2].] In a treasonable manner. (Orig. *Sc.*)

*c* **1375** *Sc. Leg. Saints* xxvi. (*Nycholas*) 786 Þat cristine man tuk in hy Þe ymag þare tresonably. *c* **1470** HENRY *Wallace* VII. 914 Syne held it lang, quhill tratouris tresonably Causit his dede. **1549** *Compl. Scot.* viii. 72 Tha deserue as grite reproche as tha hed sellit traisonablye the realme to there enemeis. **1660** *Trial Regic.* 17 Did Maliciously, Treasonably, and Feloniously..condemn our late Soveraign Lord King Charls the First. **1839** JAMES *Louis XIV*, III. 18 The government of Mazarin..was treasonably assailed. **1884** *Manch. Exam.* 14 May 5/2 It was said that French military plans had been treasonably revealed.

**Treasone·tte.** *nonce-wd.* [f. TREASON *sb.* + -ETTE.] A small or petty act of treason.

**1824** LADY GRANVILLE *Lett.* (1894) I. 254 The absurdity of hunting out these treasonettes with such severity.

**Treason-felony**: see TREASON 4 b.

† **Trea·sonful,** *a. Obs. rare.* [f. as prec. + -FUL.] Full of treason; treasonous; treacherous.

**13..** *Cursor M.* 13960 (Cott.) Þe Iues..wit þair mani tressunful red, þai soght ihesu at do to ded. **1650** TRAPP *Comm. Num.* xvi. 14 They add rebellion to sin, and justifie their treasonful practices.

† **Trea·sonish,** *a. Obs. rare.* [f. as prec. + -ISH[1].] Of the nature of treason; somewhat treasonable.

**1672** EACHARD *Hobbes State Nat.* 98 Is not this very pragmatical and somewhat treasonish? **1681** T. FLATMAN *Heraclitus Ridens* No. 26 (1713) I. 169 Is not endeavouring to subvert it [monarchy] something like Treasonish?

**Trea·sonist.** *nonce-wd.* [f. as prec. + -IST.] One who practises or is concerned in treason.

**1796** COLERIDGE *Lett.* (1895) 179 Interesting to you, virtuous high-treasonist, and your friends the democrats.

† **Trea·sonless,** *a. Obs. rare*[−1]. [f. as prec. + -LESS.] Without or free from treason.

**1591** *Troub. Raigne K. John* xii. 84, I plead not guiltie, treasonles and free.

**Treasonous** (trī·z'nəs), *a.* [f. as prec. + -OUS.] Full of or abounding in treason; characterized by treason or treachery; treasonable.

*c* **1450** [implied in TREASONOUSLY]. **1593** NASHE *Christ's T.* Wks. (Grosart) IV. 196 Bannings, cursings, secrete murmurings, out-rage, murder, iniustice, all which are high treasonous trespasses against God. **1605** SHAKS. *Macb.* II. iii. 138 Against the vndivulg'd pretence, I fight Of Treasonous Mallice. **1784** *New Spectator* No. 18. 3 To prohibit such and such pieces, that were blasphemous, libellous, or treasonous. **1875** W. WARBURTON *Edw. III*, i. 21 That he had trepanned the Earl of Kent into a treasonous conspiracy.

Hence **Trea·sonously** *adv.*, in a treasonous manner.

*c* **1450** *Mirour Saluacioun* 2757 And Jhū crist with Judas kissis he tresovnously. **1821** MILMAN *Fortune* 181 Steep'd treasonously in great Pompey's gore.

† **Trea·sonry.** *Obs. rare*[−1]. [f. as prec. + -RY.] Treasonable practice or action.

*a* **1600** *Sang Outlaw Murray* 110 in Scott *Minstr. Scott. Bord.*, I am right rad of treasonrie.

† **Trea·sony.** *Obs. rare*[−1]. [f. as prec. + -Y.] = TREASON.

**16..** *Young Waters* xiv. in Child *Ballads* IV. (1886) 344 It is tauld me the day, sir knight, Ye've done me treasonie.

**Treasurable** (tre·ʒŭrăb'l), *a. rare.* [f. TREASURE *v.* + -ABLE.] Fit or worthy to be treasured; valuable; precious.

**1607** NORDEN *Surv. Dial.* v. 242 Many treasureable blessings lie hid from slouthfull men. **1811** *Henry & Isabella* II. 195 The treasurable object, for whom they were going to stake their existence. **1886** *Athenæum* 28 Aug. 265/3 His verses are a treasurable document to the literary student.

Hence **Trea·surableness,** treasurable quality.

**1898** *Weekly Reg.* 28 May 700 The..treasurableness of small and lovable things.

**Treasure** (tre·ʒiŭɹ, -ŭɹ, -əɹ), *sb.* Forms: 2–6 **tresor, 3–6 -ur, -our, 4–6 -ore, -oure, 5 -owre, -er, 5–6 -ure, 5 treysour, treasoure, 5–6 -our, 6 -or, 6– treasure.** (Also 4–5 **trissor,** 4–6 **tressour, 7 treassour; 4 thresur, 5–6 -our, -oure, 6 threasour, -ure.**) [In 12th c. *tresor,* a. OF. *tresor* (11th c. in Littré) :—pop.L. of Gaul **trēsaur-us* for cl.L. *thēsaur-us* (whence Pr. *thesaur,* OCat. *tesor,* Sp., It. *tesoro,* Pg. *thesouro*), a. Gr. θησαυρός treasure. Cf. the Sc. THESAUR.]

**1.** Wealth or riches stored or accumulated, esp. in the form of precious metals; gold or silver coin; hence in general, money, riches, wealth. Usually *collective,* without article or plural.

**1154** *O. E. Chron.* an. 1137 (Laud MS.), He hadde ȝet his tresor ac he to deld it & scatered sotlice. *a* **1225** *Ancr. R.* 150 Þe þet bereð tresor openliche in one weie þet is al ful of þeoues. *c* **1325** *Poem Times Edw. II* 321 in *Pol. Songs* (Camden) 338 Thurfte him noht seke tresor so fer. **13..** *Cursor M.* 16534 (Gött.) He kest þaim dune apon þe grund, threti penis þar fell. Bot þe Iuus..Þe thresur [*v. r.* tresour] forsok þai noght. *Ibid.* 24807 (Cott.) Wit trissor [*Edin.* tresori] son his scipp was tift. **1480** CAXTON *Chron. Eng.* IV. (1520) 31/2 Linus and..Cletus..were made to mynyster the treasoure of the chyrche to the people. **1597** J. PAYNE *Royal Exch.* 44 Where a mans threasure ys there is his hart. **1599** MASSINGER, etc. *Old Law* I. i, To fly my severe country; To turn all into treasure. **1686** tr. *Chardin's Trav. Persia* 71 A Man that..look'd upon five or six of those Pieces to be a great Treasure. **1695** LOCKE *Further Consid. Value Money* 23 Gold is Treasure as well as Silver, because it decays not in keeping, and never sinks much in its value. **1750** tr. *Leonardus' Mirr. Stones* 50 Some stones..preserve and increase treasure; others cure diseases. **1821** BYRON *Mar. Fal.* V. i, Goods, and jewels, and all kinds of treasure.

**b.** *pl.* in same sense.

*c* **1330** R. BRUNNE *Chron.* (1810) 98 Now is Henry..lord of mykelle þing, & riche man of tresours. ?*a* **1366** CHAUCER *Rom. Rose* 184 To take and yeve right nought ageyne, And gret tresouris up to leyne. **1474** CAXTON *Chesse* III. iv. (1883) 108 The resseyuours of the tresours royall. **1596** RALEIGH *Discov. Gviana* 9 Greate Cities, Townes, Temples, and threasures. **1838** *Murray's Hand Bk. N. Germ.* 45/1 The treasures of the once celebrated bank of Amsterdam ..were kept in the vaults below the building. **1857** RUSKIN *Pol. Econ. Art* 4 The last coin out of all their treasures.

**c.** *fig.*

**1382** WYCLIF *Luke* xviii. 22 Sille thou alle..and ȝyue to pore men, and thou schalt haue tresour in heuene. **1753** CHALLONER *Cath. Chr. Instr.* 128 The Treasure of the Church..are the Merits and Satisfactions of Christ and his Saints.

†**d.** A store or stock *of* anything valuable. *Obs.*

**1382** WYCLIF *Jer.* xli. 8 Wee han tresor in the feld, of whete, and of barly, and of oile, and of hony. **1604** E. G[RIMSTONE] *D'Acosta's Hist. Indies* IV. v. 217 The Creator hath furnished the Weast Indies with so great a treasure of silver. **1707** *Curios. in Husb. & Gard.* 55 A Treasure of central Fire, that manifests itself by the Vents of the Vulcanos.

†**e.** = TREASURE-TROVE. *Obs. rare.*

**1602** FULBECKE *1st Pt. Parall.* 16 A treasure properly is, when money or things of good value haue lyen from time out of minde hidden in the ground, so that no man now hath propertie in it.

**f.** *Treasure found*: see TREASURE-TROVE b.

**2.** *transf.* and *fig.* Anything valued and preserved as precious; also of a person, a 'jewel', 'gem' (*colloq.*).

*c* **1200** *Vices & Virt.* 135 Þat derworðe tresor, þat is, ðe hali gast. *a* **1340** HAMPOLE *Psalter* xxv. 11, I am rych in gostly tresoure. *c* **1530** H. RHODES *Bk. Nurture* in *Babees Bk.* (1868) 83 A seruaunt to suffer in anger, to his mayster is a treasure. **1611** SIR W. MURE *Misc. Poems* i. 79 To losse ane Infinit and endles treasour. **1663** BP. PATRICK *Parab. Pilgr.* xxxii. (1687) 393 A faithful friend is a strong defence: and he that hath found such an one, hath found a Treasure. **1791** BOSWELL *Johnson* 16 May an. 1778, Let me then comfort myself with the large treasure of Johnson's conversation which I have preserved. **1810** LADY GRANVILLE *Lett.* (1894) I. 18 My month nurse, a treasure, and the most respectable of dames. **1844** A. B. WELBY *Poems* (1867) 97 Our treasures are this little boy, contentment, peace, and health. **1907** *Verney Mem.* II. 60 The fine house and its treasures.

†**3.** A treasury; a treasure-house, a treasure-chest. *Obs. rare.*

[**1382** WYCLIF *1 Kings* xv. 18 Al the siluer and gold, that lafte in the tresours [*v. r.* tresories] of the hows of the Lord.] **1426** LYDG. *De Guil. Pilgr.* 8837 She tooke [hem] ful lowly ..And in hyr tresour vp hem layde. *c* **1475** *Pict. Voc.* in Wr.-Wülcker 782/5 *Hoc gazophilacium,* a tresure. **1550** CROWLEY *Epigr.* 185 Why can you neuer finde a time of leasure To se where the treasure will finde them workinge? **1596** DALRYMPLE tr. *Leslie's Hist. Scot.* x. (S.T.S.) II. 350 In the Quinȝehous or in the Kingis tresour.

**4.** *attrib.* and *Comb.,* as *treasure-box, -chamber, -chest, -coffer, -digger, -galleon, -giver, -hoard, -hunt, -hutch, -keeper, -room, -ship, -store, -vault,* etc.; *treasure-baited, -bearing, -laden* adjs.; **treasure-city**, a city in which supplies were stored; **treasure-flower**, local name of a South African composite flowering plant of the genus *Gazania,* esp. the species *G. Pavonia,* the peacock treasure-flower; **treasure-wheat**: see quot. See also TREASURE-HOUSE, -TROVE.

**1887** I. R. *Lady's Ranche Life Montana* 130 The robbers then rifled the *treasure-box, and rode off delighted with their booty. *a* **1547** in J. R. Boyle *Hedon* (1895) App. 80 Foure keys belonging the *tresasor [*sic*] chambere. **1823** SCOTT *Quentin D.* xxiii, Having carefully locked his treasure-chamber, the wealthy Fleming next conveyed his guest to the parlour. **1849** THACKERAY *Pendennis* xxiii[i], [She] had quite a little museum of locks of hair in her *treasure-chest. **1895** *Daily News* 23 Nov. 7/1 The treasure chests [for the Ashanti war] consist of heavy iron safes filled with specie..packed at the Bank of England. **1611** BIBLE *Exod.* i. 11 And they built for Pharaoh *treasure-cities, Pithom and Raamses. **1610** HOLLAND *Camden's Brit.* (1637) 106 Roman mony..in *treasure coffers. **1866** *Treas. Bot.,* *Treasure-flower, *Gazania.* **1898** G. MEREDITH *Odes Fr. Hist.* 51 Seen like some rare *treasure-galleon, Hull down, with masts against the Western hues. **1899** KIPLING *Stalky* vi, Three months ago he was commanding a *treasure-guard—a cart full of rupees to pay troops with—five thousand rupees in silver. **1898** *Folk-Lore* IX. 17 At Sidon, the so-called Alexander Sarcophagus was found by a *treasure-hunter. **1862** H. MARRYAT *Year in Sweden* II. 409 The great secret of *treasure-hunting is to hold your tongue. **1531** *Pilgr. Perf.* (W. de W.) 178 b, Graunt me lady..(o holy *tresour huche of God) one halfe farthinge to cast in to thy laude & prayse. **1567** *Trial Treas.* A ij b, One with *treasure lack his life framed. **1880** *Archæol. Cantiana* XIII. 455 It may have been a strong *treasure-room. **1900** H. BARBIE *In Mod. Spain* 25 Many of her *treasure-ships may have found their way to English ports. **1892** EARLE *Deeds Beowulf* 160 The grand *treasure-sword had been left behind. **1871** B. TAYLOR *Faust* (1875) II. III. 196, I hunted on the *treasure-trail. **1813** SCOTT *Rokeby* VI. iv, 'To Rokeby *treasure-vaults!' they quaffed, And shouted loud and wildly laughed. **1590** *Acts Privy Counc.* (1899) XIX. 117 Certaine wheats (called the *threasour wheats) belonging to everie church within that Island [Jersey]. [Cf. **1682** WARBURTON *Hist. Guernsey* (1822) 66 The trésors, which are certain rents anciently given for the repairs..to the churches..but have..been employed to uses merely secular.]

**Trea·sure,** *v.* [f. TREASURE *sb.* In Wyclif rendering *thēsaurizāre* of the Vulgate.]

**1.** *trans.* To put away or lay aside (anything of value) for preservation, security, or future use; to hoard or store up. Often *to treasure up.*

**1382** WYCLIF *Isa.* xxxix. 6 Alle thingus..that ben in thin hous, and that thi fadris han tresored. — *Baruch* iii. 16 Wher ben the princes..that siluer tresoren and gold? **1712–14** POPE *Rape Lock* v. 114 Some thought it mounted to the Lunar sphere, Since all things lost on earth are treasured there. **1769** COOK *Voy. round World* II. i. (1773) 281 Taking a Cheshire cheese from a locker, where it had been carefully treasured up for this occasion. **1821** SHELLEY *Ginevra* 131 As if the future and the past were all Treasured i' the instant.

†**b.** *absol.* To lay up treasure. (A literalism of translation.) *Obs. rare.*

**1382** WYCLIF *Ecclus.* iii. 5 As he that tresoreth, so and he that wrshepith his moder.

**2.** *fig.* To keep in store, lay up (e. g. in the mind, in memory).

**1382** WYCLIF *Jas.* v. 3 Ȝe han tressourid to ȝou wrath in the laste dayes. **1482** *Monk of Evesham* (Arb.) 61 The whyche..tresur to hem..the wrathe of owre sauyur ihesu cryste. **1631** GOUGE *God's Arrows* II. § 12. 148 God doth sometimes treasure up the sinnes of predecessours. **1741** WATTS *Improv. Mind* I. xvi. § 3 To acquire and treasure up a large store of ideas and notions. **1826** DISRAELI *Viv. Grey* v. xi, The ladies would treasure their energies for the impending ball. **1887** BOWEN *Æneid* III. 436 [I] Bid thee again and again in thy memory treasure the theme.

†**3.** To furnish or endow with treasures; to supply with treasure, to enrich. *Obs. rare.*

*c* **1600** SHAKS. *Sonn.* vi, Treasure thou some place, With beauties treasure. **1630** J. TAYLOR (Water P.) *Mem. Monarchs* II. Wks. II. 287/1 By a heauy taxe the King was treasur'd.

**4.** To hold or keep as precious; to cherish, prize.

**1907** *Verney Mem.* II. 403 Treasured as his most precious possessions. **1911** J. A. MACCULLOCH *Relig. Anc. Celts* xiv. 221 A feather was left at each house and carefully treasured.

Hence **Treasured** (tre·ʒiŭɹd) *ppl. a.,* stored, hoarded up, highly valued; **Trea·suring** *vbl. sb.*

**1602** *Archpriest Controv.* (Camden) I. 232 Every baker or brewer, for stewarding and treasuringe, must, by this newe device, be made equall with you. **1675** BROOKS *Gold. Key* Wks. 1867 V. 136 Wrath to come is treasured-up wrath. **1715–20** POPE *Iliad* VI. 359 The Phrygian queen to her rich wardrobe went, Where treasur'd odours breath'd a costly scent. **1856** KANE *Arct. Expl.* I. xxxi. 434 To give him a grating of our treasured potatoes.

**Trea·sure-hou:se.** A house, building, or chamber in which treasure is kept; a treasury.

*c* **1475** *Pict. Voc.* in Wr.-Wülcker 804/29 *Hoc gazafilacium,* a treserhouse. **1486** *Lichfield Gild Ord.* 24 We will and ordeyne that the one parte of the Indentures hereoff made,..remayne in the treasure-house of the seid cathedrall church. **1494** *Acc. Ld. High Treas. Scot.* I. 241 To put in the copburd in the Tressourhous. **1573–80** BARET *Alv.* T 351 The place where treasure is kept, a treasure house, *aerarium.* **1910** *Soc. Antiq. O. Sarum Excavation Fund* 5 In 1181–2 £9 1s were spent on the treasure-house within the tower.

**b.** *fig.*

**1552** LATIMER *Serm.* (1584) 302 b, The poore mans treasure house is his labour and trauayle. **1596** SHAKS. *Merch. V.* II. ix. 34 Why then to thee thou Siluer treasure house. **1890** 'R. BOLDREWOOD' *Col. Reformer* (1891) 135 Intellectual and artistic treasure houses. **1895** *Educat. Rev.* Oct. 223 The key which unlocks the treasure-house of literature.

**Treasureless** (tre·ʒiŭlės), *a.* [f. TREASURE *sb.* + -LESS.] Without treasure or treasures.

**1598** SYLVESTER *Du Bartas* II. i. III. *Furies* 809 Our fields are flock-lesse, treasure-lesse our Towns. **1868** G. MACDONALD *Seabd. Par.* xii, Man goeth treasureless to his grave.

**Treasurer** (tre·ʒŭrəɹ). Forms: 3–6 **tresourer, -urer, 4–7 -orer,** (4 **-orere, -oriere, -erour, -urrer,** 5 **-oreere, -owrere,** *Sc.* **-orair,** 6 **-ourar, trezerer**); 5–7 **thres-, 6–7 threasorer, -urer, -ourer; 6 treasorer, 6–7 -ourer, 6– treasurer.** [In 13–14th c. *tresorer, -ourer,* a. ONF. and AF. *tresorer* = OF. *tresorier,* f. *tresor* TREASURE, after late L. *thēsaurārius* (whence Pr. *thesaurier,* Sp. *tesorero,* Pg. *thesoureiro,* It. *tesoriere,* OSc. THESAURER): see TREASURE and -ER 2.]

**1.** One who has officially the charge of treasure; originally, a person entrusted with the receipt, care, and disbursement of the revenues of a king, noble, or other dignitary, of a state, city, or church; now, one who is responsible for the funds of a public body, or of any corporation, association, society, or club.

*Treasurer of a cathedral*: see quot. 1701.

*c* **1290** *Edmund Conf.* 394 in *S. Eng. Leg.* I. 442 At salesburi..prouendes of churches he hadde, and was tresurer [*v. r.* tresourer]. **1382** WYCLIF *Rom.* xvi. 23 Erastus tresorer, or kepere, of the cite, greetith ȝou wel. **1419** in *Surtees Misc.* (1888) 14 Maister Thomas Haxey, Tresorer of the Cathedrale Kirk of Seint Peter of York. **1607** COWELL *Interpr., Treasurer*...Most corporations through the kingdome, haue an officer of this name, that receiueth their rents, and disburseth their common expences. **1670** COVEL in *Early Voy. Levant* (Hakl. Soc.) 119 The two new Treasurers of the Turkey Company. **1701** *Cowell's Interpr., Treasurer in Cathedral Churches,* a Dignitary who was to take charge of the Vestments, Plate, Jewels, Reliques, and other Treasure belonging to the said Church. **1806** *Med. Jrnl.* XV. 357 The treasurer of each hospital must annually verify upon oath his accounts. **1913** *Kelly's Oxford Direct.* 148/2 Ashmolean Natural History Society,..G. C. Druce.., treasurer.

**b.** *Lord High Treasurer of England, of Great Britain,* also called *Treasurer, Lord Treasurer, High Treasurer, Treasurer of the Exchequer,* formerly, the third great officer of the Crown, controlling the revenues of the sovereign.

The office was put into commission several times in the 17th c., and definitely in the reign of George I, its duties being now discharged by five Lords of the Treasury: see TREASURY 3.

[**1292** BRITTON I. xix. § 10 Solom la discrecioun des Thresorers et des Barouns de nos Eschekers.] *c* **1330** R. BRUNNE *Chron.* (1810) 280 To Berwik cam þe kynge eschekere,.. Walter of Admundesham he was Tresorere. **1556** *Chron. Gr. Friars* (Camden) 71 Item the xj. day of October was made..the lord trezerer markes of Wynchester. **1562** in Feuillerat *Revels Q. Eliz.* (1908) 115 To the Threasourer and Chamberlaines of our Exchequier greeting. **1589** *Hay any Work* 27 Our L. high Chancellor, high Treasurer, and high Steward of Englande. **1607** COWELL *Interpr.* s. v., The Treasurer of England, who is a Lord by his office..vnder whose charge and gouernment is all the Princes wealth contained in the Exchequer. **1631** WEEVER *Anc. Fun. Mon.* 524–5 Lord Treasurers Remembrancer..maketh Proces against all Sheriffes..and Bayliffes, for their accounts. **1711** SWIFT *Jrnl. to Stella* 10 Apr., They talk of great promotions to be made: that Mr. Hardy is to be Lord-Treasurer. **1863** H. COX *Instit.* III. vii. 682 In earlier times, the Treasurer acted personally at the Exchequer.

**c.** *Lord High Treasurer of Scotland* (in Scotch, † *Lord* (*High*) *Thesaurer*), formerly, the officer having charge of the receipt and disbursement of the revenues of the kingdom, whose duty it was to examine and pass the accounts of the sheriffs and others concerned in levying the revenues, to receive resignations of lands, etc. In 1663 he was declared President of the Court of Exchequer.

**1473–89, 1685–1708** [see THESAURER]. **1877** *Accounts Ld. High Treasurer of Scotland* I. Pref. 13–14 In 1424 James I.. assigned two newly created offices, the Comptroller and the Treasurer. *Ibid.* 26 The earliest appointment of a Treasurer which remains on record is a letter under the Privy Seal 25 June 1526. *Ibid.* 34 None of these [accounts] are of earlier date than fifty years after the institution of the office; the earliest being of the year 1473–4.

**d.** *United States.* An officer of the Treasury Department, who receives and keeps the moneys, disbursing them only upon warrants drawn by the Secretary of the Treasury and duly recorded and countersigned; also an officer having the same function in each State.

**1790** HAMILTON *Wks.* (1886) VII. 52 The treasurer of the United States shall be the receiver of all payments for sales at the general land-office. **1821** J. Q. ADAMS in C. Davies *Metr. Syst.* III. (1871) 255 The weights were to be stamped ..in figures denominating their weight, and to be kept by the public treasurer. **1879** *Constit. California* Art. v. § 17 (in Bryce *Amer. Commw.* (1889) I. 695) A Secretary of State, a Controller, a Treasurer, an Attorney-General, and a Surveyor-General shall be elected at the same time and places.

**e.** In other official designations.

*a* **1505** in Kingsford *Chron. Lond.* (1905) 230 The Maister of his Requestes, and his Tresorer generall. **1533** WRIOTHESLEY *Chron.* (Camden) I. 18 Mr. Treasorer and Mr. Controwler of the Kinges howse. **1552** in *Vicary's Anat.* (1888) App. ii. 118 The Thresourer of ye Kinges maiesties Chambre. **1601** F. TATE *Househ. Ord. Edw. II* (1876) 6 The thresorer of the warderobe. **1607** COWELL *Interpr.* s. v., Then is there a Treasurer of the kings houshold..Treasurer of the Nauie, or Treasurer of the warres..Treasurer of the Kings chamber ..Treasurer of the Chauncerie..Treasurer of the Kings Wardrobe. **1613** *Voy. to Guiana* in *Harl. Misc.* (Malh.) III. 210 A treasurer-general for the plantations shall be resident in London. **1781** GIBBON *Decl. & F.* xvii. II. 54 The extraordinary title of *count of the sacred largesses,* was bestowed on the treasurer-general of the revenue.

**2.** *fig.* One who or that which is entrusted with the keeping of anything precious or valuable.

*a* **1300** *Cursor M.* 24672 (Edin.) To faintis was ti faiþe ne fere For þi þu was his tresorer [*Cott.* tresurrer]. **1340** *Ayenb.* 231 Þe drede of god is þe tresoriere þet þet tresor of madenhod lokeþ. *a* **1586** SIDNEY *Arcadia* I. (1622) 9 Knowing..that I shall finde your eares faithfull treasurers. **1671** BARROW *Serm. Ps. cxii. 9* Wks. 1687 I. 444 Rich men are indeed but the treasurers, the stewards, the caterers of God for the rest of men. **1831** SCOTT *Cast. Dang.* viii, The secrets of which thou seemest to be a too faithful treasurer. **1856** EMERSON *Eng. Traits, Aristocr.* Wks. (Bohn) II. 84 These lords are the treasurers and librarians of mankind.

**3.** [f. TREASURE *v.* + -ER [1].] One who treasures or hoards up; a hoarder, preserver, keeper *of* something precious.

**1597** J. PAYNE *Royal Exch.* 31 The wch noble vertu ought to be desirable to Lords, ladies, and the greatest Threasurers in the world. **1613** in *Crt. & Times of Jas. I* (1848) I. 247, I am a bad treasurer-up of names. **1631** B. JONSON *Underwoods, Epit. M. Drayton*, When thy ruins shall disclaim To be the treasurer of his name.

**Treasurership** (treˑʒŭrəɹʃip). [f. prec. + -SHIP.] The office of treasurer.

**1483** in *Lett. Rich. III & Hen. VII* (Rolls) I. 15 Thoffice of tresorership of Calais. **1529** *Act 21 Hen. VIII*, c. 13. § 31 Noo Deanery, Archdeaconry, Chauncellershippe, Tresourershippe, Chauntershippe, or Prebende in any Cathedrall or Collegyall Churche. *a* **1635** NAUNTON *Fragm. Reg.* (Arb.) 55 Then did the Queen..give him her assistance, and advanced him to the Treasurership. **1709** STRYPE *Ann. Ref.* I. xlv. 456 Being preferred..to a prebend of Winchester, and the treasurership of Sarum. **1886** DOBLE in *Hearne's Collect.* (O.H.S.) II. 456 He held the Treasurership of the Navy.

**Treasuress** (treˑʒŭrės). [In 15th c. *tresoresse* for *tresoreresse*, f. *tresorer*, TREASURER: see -ESS. Cf. OF. fem. *tresorière*.] A female treasurer.

*c* **1450** in Aungier *Syon* (1840) 287 The priores..schal depute a..suster experte in temporal rewle and gouernaunce for to assiste the tresouresses. *Ibid.* 292 The treseres and undertreseres. **1491** CAXTON *Vitas Patr.* (W. de W. 1495) I. cxxxviii. 151 The Tresoresse & moder of Orphanes. **1598** YONG *Diana* II. 57 One of my approoued friends, and treasouresse of my secrets. *a* **1688** DK. BUCKHM. *Instalm.* Wks. 1705 II. 84 A throng of Ladies, that did press To pay their Duty to the Treasuress. **1863** FABER *De Montfort's True Devotion Virg.* 12 He has made her the treasuress of all that His Father has given Him.

**Treasure-trove** (treˑʒŭɹ,trōuˑv). [Orig. two words, in AF. *tresor trové* = L. *thesaurus inventus*, in 15th c. rendered in Eng. **tresoure founden, founde, found**; in 16th c. with the Fr. form anglicized **treasure trovey, trove, trouve.**] *lit. Treasure found* (see b), i. e. anything of the nature of treasure which any one finds; *spec.* in *English Law*: Treasure (gold or silver, money, plate, or bullion) found hidden in the ground or other place, the owner of which is unknown.

In original use a merely descriptive phrase, of general application. But from an early period a distinction arose; treasure which had been lost (and not claimed), or voluntarily abandoned (of which the amount was naturally small and inconsiderable) was allowed to be kept by the first finder; while that which had been (certainly or presumably) hidden, was claimed by the Crown. This practically included all ancient treasure, and to this the name *treasure trove* was specifically restricted. To encourage the giving up of such treasure, when found, and to prevent the destruction of valuable antiquities, the finder now receives from the Crown four-fifths or nine-tenths of the value. (For full discussion, see Wm. Martin in *Law Quart. Rev.* (1904) XX. 27.)

[*a* **1190** GLANVILL *De Leg. et Consuet. Angl.* XIV. ii, Placitum de occultatione inventi thesauri fraudulosa. **1292** BRITTON I. ii. § 18 Et ausi apent a lour office de enquere de viel tresor trové en terre. **1348** *Year-bk. 22 Edw. III, Easter* (in Statham *Abridgement* (?1491) h ij), Thesaurum inuentum competit domino meo regi et non domino libertatis. *Ibid., Mich.* h ij b, Punysshement pur treasoure troue pris et emporte de werk de meere. **1443–4** *Year-bk. 22 Hen. VI, Mich.* (*ibid.* g viij), Cestuy a qui le proprete est auera tresoure troue. **1527** RASTELL *Expos. Terminorum*, *Tresour troue* est quant ascun money ou argent plate ou bolion est troue ascun leu et nul conust a quele properte est, doncques le properte de ceo apperteynt al roy et ceo est dit tresour troue [see 1567 below].]

**1550** *Acts Privy Counc.* N. S. (1891) III. 14 To go with certein persons that have offred to finde treasure trovey. **1567** *Expos. Terms Law* (1579) 180 b/2 Treasure founde is when any money, gold, or siluer, plate, or bolion, is found in any place, & no man knoweth to whom the property is, then the property thereof belongeth to the queene, and that is called treasure troue, that is to say treasure found. **1572** WOGAN in T. Wright *Q. Eliz. & Times* (1838) I. 442 One of the parties charged with the saide threasure trove. **1591** SYLVESTER *Du Bartas* I. v. 737 As wroth, that men upon his right should rove, Or theevish hands usurp his Treasar-trove. *c* **1634** COKE *Inst.* III. 132. **1765** BLACKSTONE *Comm.* I. viii. 295. **1776** ADAM SMITH *W. N.* II. i. (1869) I. 282 Treasure-trove was in those times considered as no contemptible part of the revenue of the greatest sovereigns in Europe. **1904** W. MARTIN in *Law Q. Rev.* XX. 32 From the present-day point of view..we may say that if the discovered treasure has not been hidden..it is not specifically treasure trove. *attrib.* **1868** G. STEPHENS *Runic Mon.* II. 515 They have been continually sent to the melting-pot, thanks to the old Treasure-trove law.

*fig.* *c* **1700** PRIOR *Dial. Dead* Poems (1907) 227 Substances, Identity, Diversity, and fifty other glorious Tresor-trouves, to which you [Locke], the Master of the Soil, have the only right and Property. **1864** TENNYSON *Aylmer's Field* 515 There the manorial lord too curiously Raking in that millennial touchwood-dust Found for himself a bitter treasure-trove.

† **b.** Rendered **treasure found.** *Obs.*

**1467–8** *Rolls of Parlt.* V. 583/1 Deodandes, Tresoure founden, and also all maner Goodes, Catelles and forfaitures. **1482** *Ibid.* VI. 205/1 Wrekke of the See, Tresour founde, and all such Issues, Fynes and amerciamentes. **1567** [see above]. **1651** G. W. tr. *Cowel's Inst.* 66 There is a propriety gained by finding, as in case of Treasure found,..by Treasure we mean an ancient hoarding of Money or other Mettall. **1670** BLOUNT *Law Dict.* s.v. *Treasure-trove*, The punishment for concealing Treasure found is imprisonment and fine. [**1887** *Act 50 & 51 Vict.* c. 71 § 36 A coroner shall continue as heretofore to have jurisdiction to inquire of treasure that is found, who were the finders, and who is suspected thereof.]

† **Trea·surous,** *a. Obs. rare.* [f. TREASURE *sb.* + -OUS: cf. *traitorous, treasonous.*] Full of or of the nature of treasure; precious.

*c* **1611** CHAPMAN *Iliad* To Rdr. 123 They fail'd to search his deep and treasurous heart. **1616** — *Homer's Hymns, To Earth* 29 Goddesse full of grace, And treasurous Angell t' all the humane Race.

**Treasury** (treˑʒŭri), *sb.* Forms: 3–5 **tresorye**, 3–6 **-orie**, 4–5 **-oury(e**, 4–6 **-ory**, 5 **-owrye**, **-owri**, 7 **-ury**; 5 **tresurry**, **-ie**, **tressurry**; 5–6 **thresory(e**; 5–7 **treasorie**, 6 **-ory**, **-urye**, 6–7 **-urie**, 6– **treasury.** [ME. a. OF. *tresorie* (11th c. in Godef.), f. OF. *tresor*, TREASURE (after med.L. *thesauria*: see THESAURY) + *-ie*, -Y.]

**1.** A room or building in which precious or valuable objects are preserved, *esp.* a place or receptacle for money or valuables (now *Hist.*); *transf.* the funds or revenue of a state or of a public or private corporation.

*c* **1290** *Beket* 2151 in *S. Eng. Leg.* I. 168 Þis luþere kniȝtes wenden a-non to is tresorie. *c* **1380** WYCLIF *Serm.* Sel. Wks. II. 211 Jesus biheld how þe puple caste moneye into þis tresorie. **1464** *Coventry Leet Bk.* 327 Þe remembrances of sich libertes as perteyned to Cheylesmore weren yn the Tresory of the Duch[y] of Lancastre. **1560** DAUS tr. *Sleidane's Comm.* 360 Mony..taken out of the common treasorie for the war. **1660** F. BROOKE tr. *Le Blanc's Trav.* 221 Gold..of her own proper treasury, and not her husbands. **1780** HARRIS *Philol. Enq.* Wks. (1841) 484 There was no more left in his treasury than forty-seven pieces of silver, and one of gold. **1840** THACKERAY *Barber Cox* July, Lady de Sudley thought a fête at Beulah Spa..might bring a little money into its treasury. **1849** ROCK *Ch. of Fathers* I. v. (1903) I. 287 In the treasury of the Cathedral at Aix-la-Chapelle there is a fine, whole, uncut chasuble.

**2.** *fig.* A repository of 'treasures'; a thesaurus; a 'treasure-house', 'storehouse'.

*c* **1384** CHAUCER *H. Fame* II. 16 In the tresorye hyt shette Of my brayn. **1535** COVERDALE *Job* xxxviii. 22 Wentest thou euer in to the treasuries off the snowe, or hast thou sene yͤ secrete places of the hale? **1673** *True Worship God* 61 The abundance of Divine Knowledg contained in the rich Treasury of Gods Word. **1772** PRIESTLEY *Inst. Relig.* (1782) I. Ded. 6 Value the scriptures, as a treasury of divine knowledge. **1861** PALGRAVE (*title*) The Golden Treasury of English Songs. **1879** P. BROOKS *Influence Jesus* iv. 209 Almost all men appropriate out of the great treasury of the language certain words which they make their own.

**3.** The department of state which controls the collection, management, and expenditure of the public revenue; *spec.* that of the United Kingdom; also that of the United States.

The office of Lord High Treasurer of Great Britain and Ireland is now discharged by a Treasury Board of Commissioners, the First Lord of the Treasury (who is usually, though not always, Prime Minister), the Chancellor of the Exchequer, and junior Lords not more that five in number, who act as party whips. The actual head of the department is the Chancellor of the Exchequer, who is assisted in his duties by the Financial Secretary in the House of Commons, and by the Permanent Secretary and his staff in the Treasury. The Patronage Secretary to the Treasury is the chief whip of the party in office.

All money raised by taxation or otherwise accruing to the Government is paid into the Consolidated Fund, the Exchequer account at the Bank of England. Money cannot be paid out of this account without requisitions and orders from the Treasury, authorized by votes of the House of Commons, and sanctioned by the Comptroller and Auditor General.

*c* **1383** in *Eng. Hist. Rev.* Oct. (1911) 742 Neiþir prelatis neiþir preestis..shulden han seculer officis, þat is chauncerie, tresorie, priuy seal, & oþere siche seculer officis in þe chekir. **1642, 1711, 1739, 1893** [see LORD *sb.* 11]. **1695** in *Calr. Treas. Pap.* I. Pref. 17 The King was graciously pleased to bestow on mee the place of Secretary to the Treasury. **1769** *Junius Lett.* xii. (1770) 58 With this precedent..every county in England, under the auspices of the treasury, may be represented as completely as the county of Middlesex. **1787** *Constit. U. S.* Art. i. § 9 No money shall be drawn from the Treasury, but in consequence of appropriations made by law. **1827** HALLAM *Const. Hist.* (1876) III. xv. 112 They saw Godolphin..still in the treasury. **1849** MACAULAY *Hist. Eng.* iii. I. 309 The lord treasurer..had eight thousand a year, and, when the treasury was in commission, the junior lords had sixteen hundred a year each. **1888** BRYCE *Amer. Commw.* I. xvii. (1889) I. 172 In the United States the Secretary of the Treasury sends annually to Congress a report containing a statement of the national income and expenditure. **1911** MAITLAND *Const. Hist.* 409 Nothing whatever can be done which involves the expenditure of public money without the consent of the Treasury.

**b.** The building where the Treasury Commissioners transact business; formerly also *Treasury Office.*

**1706** PHILLIPS (ed. Kersey), *Treasury*,..also the Treasury-Office. **1815** WRAXALL *Hist. Mem.* (1904) 483 The daily Newspapers..represented Lord Shelburne..advancing under cover of the night, to blow up the Treasury. **1879** *Whitaker's Almanac* 302/2 Government Offices .. Admiralty, Horse Guards, Treasury, War Office.

**4.** *Theatrical slang.* The weekly payment of a company of actors.

**1885** *Diary of Actress* 132 The engagement turned out as I feared, no money. They said Treasury would be at night, but there was nothing. **1885** J. K. JEROME *On the Stage* 159 On Saturday, we came to the theatre at twelve for treasury. The Captain was not there...He would be back by the evening..and treasury would take place after the performance. **1892** *Daily News* 8 Nov. 5/1 We must never lose sight of the fact that he had to provide 'treasury' at the week's end.

† **5.** = TREASURE *sb.* 1. *Obs.*

**1297** R. GLOUC. (Rolls) 7832 He het dele ek poueremen Muche of is tresorie. *Ibid.* 8431 Þis cristinemen so wel astored nere Of armes ne of tresorie. **13..** [see TREASURE *sb.* 1]. *c* **1440** *Alphabet of Tales* 196 Þe bisshop askid hym if he had fon any tresurrie. **1593** SHAKS. *2 Hen. VI*, I. iii. 134 Thy sumptuous Buildings, and thy Wiues Attyre Haue cost a masse of publique Treasurie. **1609** DANIEL *Civ. Wars* VIII. xlv, As he, who hauing found great Treasury. **1672** CAVE *Prim. Chr.* III. ii. (1673) 254 To impart the Treasuries of the Gospel.

**6.** *attrib.* and *Comb.*, as *treasury board*, *certificate*, *-chamber*, *-chest*, *-door*, *office*, *-vault*; **treasury-bench**, the front bench on the right hand of the Speaker in the House of Commons, occupied by the Leader of the House (usually the first Lord of the Treasury), and other members of the Government; **treasury-bill**, an instrument of credit, usually drawn for 3 or 6 months, issued by authority of Parliament to the highest bidder, when money is temporarily needed by the Commissioners of the Treasury; **treasury-bond**, an exchequer bond; **treasury chest fund**, a banking account not exceeding £1,000,000 from which advances are made for the public service at distant stations, accounted for and repaid by the departments concerned; **treasury department**, in the U.S. government, the finance department under the Secretary of the Treasury; **treasury lord**, one of the commissioners of the Treasury; **treasury letter** or **note**, a 'whip' issued by the government to its supporters in parliament; **treasury minute**, an administrative regulation for any department under the Treasury; **treasury note**, *U.S.* a demand note issued by the Treasury Department, receivable as legal tender for all debts (see also *treasury letter*); **treasury-warrant**, a warrant or voucher issued by the Treasury for any sum disbursed by the exchequer.

**1785** *Rolliad* (1790) 10 While on the *Treasury-Bench you, Pitt, recline. **1882** W. CORY *Mod. Eng. Hist.* II. 482 The House of Commons [in 1835] did not show any wish to make the Prime Minister sit on his own Treasury Bench. **1797** *Hist. Europe* in *Ann. Reg.* 198/1 If the advances on *treasury bills had been paid off when required. **1912** *Standard* 20 Sept. 7/4 The offering by rival quarters of lines of Treasury bills cannot be helpful to Chinese credit. **1855** *London as it is to-day* vii, The *Treasury Board holds its meetings here. **1858** SIMMONDS *Dict. Trade*, **Treasury bond*, a species of exchequer-bill. **1791** *Ann. Congress* (1849) III. 1071 *Treasury certificates issued in exchange for loan office settlement certificates. **1852** GROTE *Greece* II. lxxviii. X. 265 Thebes was commemorating her recent victory by the erection of a *treasury-chamber, and the dedication of pious offerings at Delphi. **1877** *Act 40 & 41 Vict.* c. 45 § 3 An account..showing the receipts and payments of the *Treasury Chest Fund, distinguishing those of the several Treasury chests. *Ibid.*, The Treasury may employ the Treasury Chest Fund to make temporary advances for any public service..to be repaid out of money appropriated by Parliament to such service. **1896** *Westm. Gaz.* 11 June 5/2 There was not a precedent for paying the expense of a military expedition out of the Treasury chest without such expedition having previously been sanctioned by Parliament. **1878** T. L. CUYLER *Pointed Papers* 54 A plain, coarsely-clad man..is seated in the *treasury-court of the Temple at Jerusalem. **1784** *Jrnls. Congress* 7 May, To revise the institution of the *treasury department. **1789** *Ann. Congress* 19 May (1834) I. 385 Mr. Madison moved..that there shall be a Treasury Department. **1892** A. B. HART *Form. of Union* 144 In establishing the Treasury Department a strong effort was made to create a Secretary of the Treasury as an agent of Congress. **1663** BP. HOPKINS *Serm. Vanity* (1685) 87 A seal set upon the *Treasury-door which none can break or violate. **1866** FELTON *Anc. & Mod. Gr.* II. II. iii. 298 He became a receiver of the public revenues, and acquired the name of *treasury-eater. **1778** H. WALPOLE *Last Jrnls.* II. 299 Not content with the usual *Treasury letters, Lord North issued a second batch, signed by himself, earnestly pressing attendance. **1812** *Act of Congress* 20 June, *Treasury notes shall be every where received in payment of all duties and taxes laid by the authority of the United States. **1815** *Deb. in Congress* 8 Dec. (1854) 1626 Having thus absorbed a portion of the Treasury note debt.. the Secretary of the Treasury proceeded to assign funds for the payment of the Treasury notes. **1899** *Westm. Gaz.* 24 Jan. 2/3 'Treasury Notes' are recognised by the student of our political history as the earliest form of Parliamentary 'Whips'. **1903** PORRITT *Unref. Ho. Comm.* I. xxv. 509 The circulars issued by the administration to its supporters became known as treasury notes in the reign of George III. **1812** *Sporting Mag.* XXXIX. 177 The danger I should be exposed to..if I disclosed their instructions, or the *Treasury-Orders. **1661** WOOD *Life* 1 Apr. (O.H.S.) I. 389 They conveyed themselves thro the cellar dore next to the *treasury-vault, locked it, and one of them put the key into his pocket. **1834** MACAULAY *Ess., Thackeray's Hist. Chatham* (1887) 319 Legge, the Chancellor of the Exchequer, refused to sign the *Treasury warrants which were necessary to give effect to the treaties. **1863** H. COX *Instit.* III. vii. 681 The Treasury warrant authorized the drawing an order upon the Tellers of the Exchequer.

Hence **Trea·sury** *v.* (*nonce-wd.*), in *pass.* to be honoured by the Treasury.

**1855** DICKENS *Dorrit* xxxiii, He was..Treasuried, Barred and Bishoped, as much as he would.

**Trea·suryship.** [f. prec. + -SHIP.] = TREASURERSHIP.

1700 TYRRELL *Hist. Eng.* II. 889 The King..required him to give an Account of his Treasuryship. 1876 BANCROFT *Hist. U. S.* III. xii. 179 George Grenville..took the treasuryship of the navy. 1903 *Daily Chron.* 30 July 3/6 The treasuryship of the connexional funds.

**Treat** (trīt), *sb.*[1] Forms: 4–6 **trete**, (5 **trett**, **treet**, **treyte**), 5–6 (9 *Sc.*) **tret**, 6 *Sc.* **treit**, 6–7 **treate**, (7 **trait**, **trayte**), 6– **treat**. [In branch I, f. TREAT *v.*; in II. from F. *trait*, or other derivative of the same stem.]

**I.** Senses arising out of TREAT *v.*

†**1.** The action or an act of treating, or discussing terms; parley, negotiation; agreement; treaty.

1375 BARBOUR *Bruce* x. 125 Schir alexander of Argill.. send tretis to þe king, And com his man but tarying. *Ibid.* XI. 35 [He] tald quhat tretis he had maid, And quhat day he thame [the English] gevyn had. *c* 1380 WYCLIF *Serm.* Sel. Wks. II. 248 In þis failen many men in tretes and acordis makynge. 1412–20 LYDG. *Chron. Troy* I. 2222 With-out assaut þe castel were y-ȝolde;..in swyche case longe trete were in veyne. 1448 *Paston Lett.* I. 75 That comynycasyon and trete schold be had betwyxt hys counsayle and myne. 1529 *Registr. Aberdon.* (Maitl. Cl.) I. 396 We þe saidis prowest bailȝeis consall and communite riplie auisit..be lang tret conuening togidder. 1590 SPENSER *F. Q.* III. viii. 16 [He] Bad that same boaster,..To leave to him that lady for excheat, Or bide him batteill without further treat.

†**2.** An entreaty, a beseeching. *Obs.*

1601 WEEVER *Mirr. Mart.* D iv, The king..Then vowes, prayes, treates; vowes, treates, and prayers vaine, From prayers, treates, and vowes he doth refraine. 1632 VICARS *Æneid* IV. 105 But none of all her treats or bitter teares Remove his thoughts. *a* 1660 *Contemp. Hist. Irel.* (Ir. Archæol. Soc.) II. 133 By word of mouth [he] made faire promises mingled with many treates.

†**3.** = TREATMENT 1; an instance of this. *Obs.*

1671 BUTLER *Ode to Du-Val* iii, France..That serves the ruder Northern Nations With Methods of Address and Treat. 1702 C. MATHER *Magn. Chr.* II. iv. (1852) 123 Those harsher and harder treats, which he sometimes had from the frowardness of not a few. *a* 1711 KEN *Hymnotheo* Wks. 1721 III. 286 All..Who had from him receiv'd injurious Treat.

†**b.** Treatment of guests or visitors; reception, entertainment. *Obs.*

1689 *Andros Tracts* I. 107 After a very unkind Treat, we humbly prayed his Excellency [etc.]. 1698 VANBRUGH *Æsop* II. i, I don't know how I shall return your friendly treat. *c* 1710 CELIA FIENNES *Diary* (1888) 148 Mr. Wm. Allen.. gave me a very civil treate, being an acquaintance of my Brother.

**4.** *concr.* An entertainment of food and drink, esp. one given without expense to the recipient; a feast, refection, collation. *Obs.* or merged in b.

1651 EVELYN *Char. Eng.* (1659) 32 They drink their crowned Cups roundly,..daunce after the Fiddle, kiss freely, and tearm it an honourable Treat. 1705 LUTTRELL *Brief Rel.* (1857) V. 536 According to the late acts, no money is to be spent or treats made upon account of elections. 1725 DE FOE *Voy. round World* (1840) 260 A very handsome table, covered with a cold treat of roasted mutton and beef. 1736 DRAKE *Eboracum* I. viii. 379 He performed all the exercises and gave the usual treat for the degree of doctor in divinity. 1819 WORDSW. *Waggoner* II. 46 Our treat shall be a friendly bowl.

**b.** Hence, An entertainment of any kind given gratuitously, esp. to children; a pleasure party or the like.

1683 KENNETT tr. *Erasm. on Folly* 156 For a concluding Treat you expect a formal epilogue. 1791 BURKE *App. Whigs* Wks. VI. 131 The Bastile could inspire no horrours into them. This was a treat for their betters. 1841 THACKERAY *Gt. Hoggarty Diamond* ii, I had promised a dozen of them a treat down the river. 1885 *L'pool Daily Post* 23 Apr. 5/2 Vanloads of happy urchins, bent on enjoying their Sunday school treat.

**c.** The action of treating or entertaining; one's part or turn to treat; an invitation to eat or drink.

1690 CROWNE *Eng. Friar* v. Wks. 1874 IV. 120 The bride is my kinswoman, so the treat to-night is mine, and I invite all this good company. 1888 LIGHTHALL *Yng. Seigneur* 135 'Shut up, Potdevin!' said the only man who understood English, fearful lest the second treat should go astray.

**d.** *To stand treat*: to bear the expense of a treat.

1837 MARRYAT *Dog-fiend* lv, Neither she nor the corporal would stand treat. 1841 THACKERAY *Gt. Hoggarty Diamond* ix, We had a very merry party at Vauxhall, Gus insisting on standing treat. 1885 'MRS. ALEXANDER' *Valerie's Fate* i, That stingy old thing..would not go into a cake-shop, though I offered to stand treat.

**5.** Something highly enjoyable; a great pleasure, delight, or gratification. Also rarely applied to a person as an emotional expression of commendation (quot. 1825). *colloq.*

[1802 PALEY *Nat. Theol.* xix. (ed. 2) 373 Carrion is a treat to dogs, ravens, vultures, fish.] 1805 E. DAYES *Wks.* 127 Here the admirer of nature will receive a high treat, from..woods, sinking into deep glens [etc.]. 1823 JEFFERSON *Writ.* (1830) IV. 385 Her 'Few Days in Athens'..has been a treat to me of the highest order. 1825 LADY GRANVILLE *Lett.* (1894) II. 13 Lord Dudley is a treat, and deserves his cutlets for the admirable despatch he wrote. 1880 MCCARTHY *Own Times* III. xxx. 4 His speeches were an intellectual treat. 1887–9 T. A. TROLLOPE *What I remember* II. 267 The excursion.. was another-guess sort of treat. 1901 ALLDRIDGE *Sherbro* xxiii. 237 An open shed-kitchen, so clean that it was quite a treat to look at it.

**b.** *A treat* (advb.): so as to gratify highly; extremely well; also (*gen.* or *ironically*) extremely, excessively. *vulgar colloq.*

1899 *Daily News* 8 May 4/2 This air makes yer liver work a fair treat. 1910 *Ibid.* 24 Dec. 4 I've begun with a white-washing job. It pays out my arms a treat.

**II.** Various obsolete or dialectal senses, not directly from the verb.

†**6.** In phr. *on* (*in*) *treat*, (*a*) ? at full length; in a series; (*b*) ? continuously, uninterruptedly, at length, at leisure. *Obs.* [Cf. OF. *à trait* 'lentement, posément, a loisir' (Godef.).]

? *a* 1400 *Morte Arth.* 3655 The maryneres..Towyne trvsselle one trete, trvssene vpe sailes. *c* 1450 MYRC *Par. Priest* 1174 Hath þy herte be wroth or gret When goddes serues was drawe on tret? *c* 1460 *Towneley Myst.* xxx. 130, For wysely he spekys on trete.

†**7.** *Med.* A plaster or ointment spread on a cloth. *Obs.* [? Aphetic for ENTRETE, OF. *entrait* adhesive plaster.]

*c* 1400 *Lanfranc's Cirurg.* 132 Take .iiij. partis of rosyn, & þe .v part of wex, & drawe abrood þat treet on a clooþ, & leie it on þe wounde. *a* 1450 *Stockh. Med. MS.* 87 For to make trete þat ys callyd playster of plombe. *Ibid.* 111 A tret for iche wound sanatyf. 1483 *Cath. Angl.* 393/1 Trett, *tractura, emplastrum.* 1562 TURNER *Herbal* II. 30 b, Wyth a cerote or treat made of waxe. 1639 T. DE GRAY *Compl. Horsem.* 304 This is a most soveraign treate or salve.

†**8.** = TREATISE *sb.* 1, b, c. *Obs.* [? A curtailed form of *tretis*, TREATISE, the *-is* being taken as pl. suffix. But cf. also F. *traité* treatise.]

*c* 1400 tr. *Secreta Secret., Gov. Lordsh.* 87 We shhall determyn after by a short trete, of propertez & vertuz of herbes. *c* 1440 *Promp. Parv.* 502/2 Trete (*H., P.* tretye or tretyce, *A.* tretyng), *tractatus.* *c* 1450 HOLLAND *Howlat* 307 At the forsaid trist quhar the trete tellis. *c* 1485 *Digby Myst.* IV. 3 Rede this trete. 1536 BELLENDEN *Cron. Scotland* (1821) I. p. liv, To schaw the auld maneris of Scottis.. under ane compendius treit. 1548 GEST *Pr. Masse* in H. G. Dugdale *Life* (1840) App. 72 Thys matteir..I have chosen ..too entreate upon, in respecte ye treate therof is..avaylable and nedeful. *a* 1555 PHILPOT *Exam. & Writ.* (Parker Soc.) 340 Let us proceed unto another treate of Florebell's.

†**9.** = TRACE *sb.*[2] 1, 2: chiefly in *pl.* traces. *Obs. rare.* [a. F. *traits*, earlier *traiz*, *trais*, whence Eng. *trays*, TRACE (taken as sing., with pl. *traces*).]

1611 COTGR., *Traict*,..a team-trace, or trait; the cord or chaine that runs betweene the horses, etc. 1613 MARKHAM *Eng. Husbandman* I. I. viii. (1635) 45 The Treates by which the Horses draw, being strong cords made of the best Hempe. 1620 — *Farew. Husb.* II. xiii. (1668) 61 To the big end of this harrow you shall fix a strong rope with a swingle-tree with Treats, Coller, and Harness. [*c* 1880 ELWORTHY *Let. to Editor*, Traces of rope, by which horses drag the plough. Still called *traites* in Dorsetsh. to distinguish from chain-traces.]

†**10.** A feature, lineament: = TRACT *sb.*[3] 7; cf. TRAIT 4. *Obs.*

1721 RAMSAY *Tea-t. Misc., O'er Bogie* iii, There a' the beauties do combine Of colour, treats and air.

**11.** *attrib.* †**Treat net**, some kind of fishing net; ? a drag-net (*obs.*).

1584 in *Descr. of Thames* (1758) 63 Treat Nets, Peter Nets, must be two Inches large in the Meish.

**Treat, treet,** *sb.*[2] Now *dial.* Also 7 **treate**, 9 **trait, -e**; (in sense 2) 3–4 **trait**, 3–5 **tret, treyt**, 5–7 **trayt**, 7 **treate, trete.** [Origin uncertain; perh. F. *trait*, *traite* pa. pple. drawn, withdrawn, extracted: but no sense 'bran' appears in F.]

**1.** The second of the three qualities of bran removed by bolting from wheaten meal.

(Halliwell has '*Trait*, the coarser meal, *Cornw.*'; but this is not given in any of the Cornwall Glossaries.)

1641 BEST *Farm. Bks.* (Surtees) 105 In every bushell of meale that commeth from the mill there is very neare a pecke of chizell drossed out; which, hereaboutes, is called *treate*, in the South-country, *branne.* 1829 BROCKETT *N. C. Words, Bye-bootings*, or *Sharps*, the finest kind of bran; the second in quality being called *Treet*, and the worst *Chizzel.* 1894 *Northumbld. Gloss., Treet*, the second quality of bran. The finest quality is called 'sharps' and the coarsest 'chizzel'. *a* 1905 SARAH HEWETT *MS. Collect.* (*Devon*) in *Eng. Dial. Dict.* s. v. *Trait*(*e*, Near Barnstaple I heard a farmer's wife say—'Yu ant atuked the traite out fine enough; there's a gude dayle o' the cuse bran long wi' this yer' [You haven't taken the treat out fine enough; there's a good deal of the coarse bran along with this here].

†**2.** Here app. belongs the denomination **Bread of trete** (AF. *pain de trayte*, med. (Anglo-)L. *panis de trete*, *treit*), also simply *trayt*, the second lowest and cheapest quality of bread specified in the Statute of Bread and Ale, 51 Hen. III, 1266; the name remained in use down to the 15th c.

Also discussed by the legal antiquaries of the 17th c. and later (in many cases with erroneous guesses: e.g. in Blount *Law Dict.* 1670, Phillips (ed. Kersey) 1706, Jamieson *Sc. Dict.* s. v. *Trayt*, etc.).

The Statute of 1266 specified three (or four) varieties of bread of fine flour, of which the standard form was the *wastel* (OF. *gastel*, F. *gâteau*), and three qualities of inferior bread, viz. bread of whole wheat, bread of trete, and bread of any kind of grain; the farthing loaf of trete was to weigh twice the weight of wastel, on account of the bran left in it.

1266 *Act* 51 *Henry III, Stat. Bread & Ale*, Quando quarterium frumenti venditur pro xij. d. tunc panis quadrantis de Wastello..ponderabit sex libras & sexdecim solidos ..Panis vero de trait [*v.r.* tret] ponderabit duos Wastellos. *c* 1290 FLETA II. ix. § 1 [*quoting prec.*] Panis de Treyt. *a* 1325 (Eng. tr.) *MS. Rawl. B.* 520 lf. 43 b, Of al hol bred þe furþingwort sal weie a Coket ant an half. Bred of trait sal weie tuuei wasteles. Bred of alle kunne corne sal weie tuuei cokettes. 14.. *Ipswich Domesday* in *Blk. Bk. Adm.* II. 175 Summe [bakers] maken wastel, ferst coket, and trayt all oonly; and summe symnel and trayt. 1420 *Marescalcia Prioris* in *Durham Acc. Rolls* (Surtees) 359 Non panem album nec tret, non pondera. 1425 *Ibid.* 371 Panis albus ob' minus per iij s. & panis de tret. 14.. *Iter Camerarii* c. 9 in *Acts Parl. Scot.* (1844) I. App. iv. 697 Tercio quod non panificant quodlibet genus panis ut lex burgi requirit, videlicet quachetum, wastellum, Symnellum, panem alsamyn, purum panem, et panem mixtum de treyt. 1609 SKENE *Chalmerlane Air* ix. in *Reg. Maj.* 150 b, Baksters sould be challenged that..4 They make not all kindes of bread, as law requyres; that is ane fage, symmell, wastell, pure cleane breade, mixed breade, and bread of trayt. 1607 COWELL *Interpr.* s.v., *Breade of treate*, anno 51 H. 3, Statute of breade, &c., what it signifieth, I cannot learne. *Ibid.* s.v. *Cocket*, In the statutes of bread and ale, made anno 51 H. 3 ..you have mention of bread coket, wastell bread, bread of trete, and bread of common wheate. 1674 JEAKE *Arith.* (1696) 74 Bread of Treet seems to be Houshold-Bread of the best Wheat unravelled, or ravelled through the coursest Boultel. 1863 *Chambers' Bk. Days* 15 Jan. I. 119/2 *Trete bread*, or *bread of trete*,..made of wheat meal once bolted, or from which the fine flour at one sifting had been removed. This was also known as 'bis' or brown bread, and probably owed its name to..bran being so largely its constituent.

**Treat** (trīt), *v.* Forms: 3–6 **trete**, 4–5 **treete**, 4–6 **tret**, (5 **treite, trette, treatte**), 5–6 **trayte**, **traict**(**e**, *Sc.* **trait**, 5–7 **treate**, 5–8 *Sc.* **treit**, (6 **treact, traite**, *Sc.* **traitt**), 6– **treat.** *Pa. t.* and *pple.* **treated** (4–6 **treted**(**e**, etc.); also *contr.* 5 **trete**, 6 *Sc.* **treit, trett**, 6–7 *Sc.* **treat**, 6– *Sc.* and *n. dial.* **tret.** [a. OF. *tretier*, *traitier* (12th c. in Godef.), F. *traiter*:—L. *tractāre* to drag, frequentative (intensive) of *trahĕre* to draw, pa. pple. *tractus*; cf. Pr. *tractar*, Sp. *tratar*, It. *trattare*.

The chronological order of senses in Eng. does not agree with that of L. *tractāre* or even of F. *traiter*. Senses 5 and 7 come nearest to the primary notion of *tractāre*.]

**1. a.** *intr.* To deal or carry on negotiations (*with* another) with a view to settling terms; to discuss terms of settlement; to bargain, negotiate.

1297 R. GLOUC. (Rolls) 10383 Þe verste day of octobre þis conseil bigan, Vor to trety of is lond þer was mani a man. *c* 1375 *Sc. Leg. Saints* xi. (*Symon & Judas*) 178 Or ellis ger þi fays be Rycht wondir fayne to tret with þe. 1390 GOWER *Conf.* I. 250 And aftir that of Mariage Thei trete and axen of hir wille. *c* 1430 LYDG. *Min. Poems* (Percy Soc.) 150 Begyn no trouble whan men trete of pees. 1568 GRAFTON *Chron.* II. 302 They treated for a peace betweene the two kinges, but nothing came to effect. 1617 MORYSON *Itin.* I. 195, I..was forced to treat with unknowne Merchants for taking money upon exchange. 1647 SPRIGGE *Anglia Rediv.* III. ii. (1854) 140 The governor beat a parley, desiring to treat. 1795 LD. AUCKLAND *Corr.* (1862) III. 353 My private opinion has ever been, that it is right in war to treat at all times. 1838–42 ARNOLD *Hist. Rome* III. xlv. 306 They began to treat with Marcellus for the surrender of Syracuse. 1895 *Times* 16 Jan. 14/2 The railway company..served upon Lord Gerard a notice to treat for certain land.

†**b.** *trans.* To handle or discuss (an affair) with a view to settlement; to negotiate, arrange, plan; rarely in bad sense, to plot (quot. 1622). In early use also with *obj. cl. Obs.*

1357 *Lay Folks Catech.* (T.) 46 Oure fadir the Ercebishop ..Has treted and ordayned for commune profet, Thurgh the consaile of his clergie, That ilkane that vndir him has kepynge of saules,..Teche and preche. 1375 BARBOUR *Bruce* IV. 177 Quhen þis cunnand þus tretit wes. 1406 *Rolls of Parlt.* V. 417/1 Come for to trete Pees or Trieues. 1465 CAXTON *Paris & V.* 52 He trayted that she shold haue of two barons that one. 1533 *Acc. Ld. High Treas. Scot.* VI. 154 Passing to the Newcastell to treit the peace. 1622 MABBE tr. *Aleman's Guzman d'Alf.* II. 154 Which of vs two treats falsehood, which intends diceit? 1658 BRAMHALL *Consecr. Bps.* v. 133 That these things should be treated, and concluded, and executed all at one meeting. *a* 1715 BURNET *Own Time* an. 1673 (1823) II. 30 He was treating a marriage with the archduchess.

**c.** With advb. extension: To bring or get (into or out of some position or condition) by negotiation.

1414 *26 Pol. Poems* xiii. 139 While ȝe trete, ay þey gete. Ȝe trete ȝoure self out of ȝoure riȝt. *c* 1440 LOVELICH *Merlin* 6554 A gret partye of the lond they hadden j-treted jnto here hond. 1681 *Moores Baffled* 3 They..advanced to besiege Tanger, but were violently repulsed, say some; others say, fairly treated off by the Portuguezes. 1882 SCHOULER *Hist. U. S.* II. 111 Eaton..indulged in some indiscreet reflections upon the administration for treating out himself and Hamet.

**2. a.** *intr.* To deal with some matter in speech or writing; to discourse. (In quot. 1509 *transf.* of pictorial representation.) Const. *of*, formerly also *on*, *upon*.

*c* 1374 CHAUCER *Troylus* I. 686 (742) Man maketh ofte a yerde With which þe makere is hym self beten In sondry maneres as þis wyse treten. 1382 WYCLIF 1 *Kings* iv. 33 [Solomon] tretyde of the beestis, and foulis. 1390 GOWER *Conf.* II. 215 To trete upon the cas of love,..I finde write a wonder thing. 1509 HAWES *Past. Pleas.* iv. (Percy Soc.) 17 The hall was hanged,..With cloth of arras..That treated well of a ful noble story. 1579 FULKE *Heskins' Parl.* 527 The Sixtieth Chapter treateth vpon this text. 1652 NEEDHAM tr. *Selden's Mare Cl.* 150 Objections..brought out of Writers treating of other matters. 1676 MOXON *Print Lett.* 3 The Roman Capitals have..been treated of. 1681 tr. *Belon's Myst. Physick* Introd. 46 The Author of this Discourse..having already..sufficiently..treated on that point. 1732 BERKELEY *Alciphr.* I. § 3 Certain writings of our divines that treat of grace. 1766 GOLDSM. *Vic. W.* xx, What subject did you treat upon? *a* 1873 DEUTSCH *Rem.* (1874) 173 This book.. treating of a most abstruse subject.

**b.** *trans.* To deal with (a subject) in speech or writing; to discuss. In mod. use often with mixture of sense 10: to deal with in the way of literary art.

*c* 1325 *Song of Yesterday* 155 in *E. E. P.* (1862) 137 Ensaumple here of i wol ȝou trete. *c* 1380 Wyclif *Last Age of Chirche* p. xxiii, Aftir þe opynioun of hem þat trete þis matir. 1382 — *Mark* ix. 32 What tretiden ȝe in the weie? *c* 1425 *Craft of Nombrynge* (E E.T.S.) 3 Þis boke tretys þe Craft of Nombryng. 1523 Ld. Berners *Froiss.* I. i. 1, I syr John Froissart, wyll treat and recorde an hystory of great louage and preyse. 1590 in Fuller *Ch. Hist.* (1655) ix. vii. § 27 That he [Thos. Cartwright] with others in some ..Conference..or..Assembly..did treat, and dispute..these six Articles. 1734 tr. *Rollin's Anc. Hist.* (1827) I. Pref. 2, I have already treated them at some length. 1860 Tyndall *Glac.* i. xii. 86 Questions which shall be treated under their proper heads. *Mod.* I wonder how he will treat the subject.

†**3. a.** To entreat, beseech, request (*trans.* and *absol.*); in quot. 1500–20, to get by entreaty. *Obs.*

*c* 1375 *Sc. Leg. Saints* xliv. (*Lucy*) 16 Hir modyr..Scho tretyt with hire for to ga. *c* 1400 *Sowdone Bab.* 1923 Thus thay treted him to and fro; At the laste he sayde, he wolde. *c* 1470 *Golagros & Gaw.* 1047, I trete for na favour. *Ibid.* 1066 Schir Gawyne tretit the knight to turn his entent. 1500–20 Dunbar *Poems* xvi. 14 Giftis fra sum ma na man treit. 1515 Barclay *Egloges* iv. (1570) Dj/2 To treate a tiran it is but thing in vayne. 1601 [see Treat *sb.*[1] 2]. 1630 J. Taylor (Water P.) *Laugh & be Fat* Wks. II. 74/2 He from thy labour treats thee to giue o're.

†**b.** *trans.* To speak to, address. *Obs. rare.*

*c* 1400 *Destr. Troy* 5309 Then Teutra þo triet men tretid o þis wise:—'Ye worshipfull weghes, well be you euer'. *Ibid.* 12844 Tretis hom truly all with tried wordes.

†**4.** To deal with, apply oneself to, work at, carry on, manage (something). *Obs.*

1375 Barbour *Bruce* i. 35 Off þaim I thynk þis buk to ma; Now god gyff grace þat I may swa Tret It, and bryng It till endyng. *c* 1450 tr. *De Imitatione* iii. iii. 67 Write my wordes in þin herte, and trete hem diligently. 1500–20 Dunbar *Poems* xx. 42 With all thy hart treit bissines and cure. 1562 Winȝet *Cert. Tractatis* ii. Wks. (S.T.S.) I. 21 He intendit to offer the signe onelie, and ȝe, to treit the veritie self of the sacrifice off the Kirk.

†**5.** To handle (in literal sense); in quot. 1607, ? to operate upon. *Obs. rare.*

1382 Wyclif *Col.* ii. 22 Nether ȝe schulen touche, nether taste, nether trete with hondis tho thingis. *c* 1440 *Pallad. on Husb.* i. 75 Loke yf hit be glewy, tough to trete. 1485 Caxton *Chas. Gt.* iii. 35 In especyall were ordeyned xij persones.. whych shold treate & see the relyques. 1607 Markham *Caval.* i. xix (1617) 83 Those barbarous..Horsemen, which with distempered hands, rough brackes, or t[w]ownd snaffles, doe treate and breake their horses mouthes.

†**6.** To manage, rule, govern (a person); to lead, induce (*to* some course of action); *refl.* to conduct oneself, behave. *Obs.*

1387 Trevisa *Higden* (Rolls) VII. 335 Þis Lanfrank tretede [*MS.* tredede] and bylad kyng William conquerour by an holy craft, nouȝt wiþ grym chidynge. 1425 *Paston Lett.* I. 21 The seyd priour and his brether, and I also, willen gladdely in these matieres be treted by yow. 1436 *Rolls of Parlt.* IV. 501/2 The more sufficient that men be of liflode ..þe more unlikly they are.. to be treted or moeved to perjurie. 1496 *Dives & Paup.* (W. de W.) i. xlii. 82/1 We may not treaten god ne put hym to no lawes. *a* 1550 in *Dunbar's Poems* (S.T.S.) 309/34 Treit weill thy self, and stand content.

**7.** To deal with, behave or act towards (a person, animal, etc.) in some specified way; to 'use' (well, ill, properly, reverently, etc.).

*c* 1374 Chaucer *Troylus* v. 134 And þat ye me wolde as youre broþer trete. 1375 Barbour *Bruce* i. 222 Alas! þat folk, þat euir wes fre,..War tretyt þan sa wykkytly, Þat þar fays þar Iugis war. *c* 1450 *St. Cuthbert* (Surtees) 552 Sho walde haue trete him all' a mys. 1572 *Satir. Poems Reform.* xxx. 79 Thy houshald trim and treit weill, thay confest. 1632 Lithgow *Trav.* vii. 332 There are many Turkish and Moorish slaues, very rudely treat. 1711 Steele *Spect.* No. 53 ¶ 2 That Mahometan Custom..of treating Women as if they had no Souls. 1746 Francis tr. *Horace, Epist.* i. ii. 15 Paris treats this Counsel with Disdain. 1816 J. Wilson *City of Plague* i. iv. 299 Treat his grey hairs with reverence. *c* 1850 *Arab. Nts.* 604 The caliph..spoke to the young man, whom he had seen treat his mare so ill.

†**b.** *intr.* To deal *with* in a specified way. *Obs.*

*c* 1400 *Rule St. Benet* 441 Þai þat wil hir lare despise.. With þam aw hir for to trete With preson & with penance grete. 1707 *Curios. in Husb. & Gard.* 242 He treats with Aristotle, as one might do with Moses.

**c.** *trans.* To consider or regard in a particular aspect and deal with accordingly. (Often with *as*.)

1456 Sir G. Haye *Law Arms* (S.T.S.) 122 Gif thare be ony thing..possible to be done, he sall nocht trait it to be impossible. 1844 Thirlwall *Greece* VIII. lxii. 147 The loss of so many captives was treated as a happy riddance. 1868 M. Pattison *Academ. Org.* ii. 35 The clergy are often treated as obstacles to the diffusion of knowledge. 1886 *Law Times* LXXXII. 94/1 Rules of judicial discretion.. are not to be treated as hard and fast rules that can never be broken.

†**8.** *spec.* To deal kindly with; to show kindness or respect to; to indulge, favour; to honour. *Obs.*

*c* 1440 *Alphabet of Tales* 128 Þe thrid confessur hard hym mekelie & spak frendlie vnto nym, & tretid hym. 1500–20 Dunbar *Poems* lxxvii. 60 Hir for to treit thai sett thair haill ingyne. 1549 *Compl. Scot.* xi. 92 He vil tret, cheris, and promes grit reches til ony of ȝou that vil adhere til hym. 1556 Lauder *Tractate* 27 To ponysche Vice, and treit virtew. 1581 *Satir. Poems Reform.* xliii. 134 Gif he did gud, God wald he sould be tret. 1596 Dalrymple tr. *Leslie's Hist. Scot.* ii. (S.T.S.) I. 136 He mekle delyted in hunting..he trett mekle the serkeis of wylde beistes.

**9.** To entertain, esp. with food and drink; to show hospitality to; to regale, feast, esp. at one's own expense, by way of kindness or compliment, or *spec.* of bribery, as at an election (see Treating *vbl. sb.* 5).

1500–20 Dunbar *Poems* lxxxii. 64 Thairfoir strangeris and leigis treit, Tak nocht ouer meikle for thair meit. *a* 1578 Lindesay (Pitscottie) *Chron. Scot.* xx. (S.T.S.) I. 91 Schir patrick gray satt downe to his denner and the erle treatit him and maid him guid cheir. 1644 Evelyn *Diary* 27 Feb., At an inn in this village is an host who treats all the greate persons in princely lodgings.. but they pay well for it. 1682 Luttrell *Brief Rel.* (1857) I. 162 The Morocco ambassadors attendants were treated yesterday by sir Thomas Boles, in Graies Inn. 1695 Prior *Prol. in Westminster Sch.* 16 Our generous scenes are for pure love repeated, And if you are not pleas'd, at least you're treated. 1709 Steele *Tatler* No. 95 ¶ 1 She had been searching her Closet for something very good to treat such an old Friend as I was. 1839 Thackeray *Fatal Boots* Feb., They gave me plenty of cakes and barley-sugar..I'd no need to spend my own money, for they would insist upon treating me. 1848 — *Van. Fair* xxxvi, Rebecca..ordered a bottle of sherry and a bread cake..to treat the enemy's lawyers.

**b.** *To treat* (a person, etc.) †*with* or *to*: To entertain with (food or drink, or any enjoyment or gratification); also *fig.* (sometimes *ironically*).

*a* 1550 in *Dunbar's Poems* (S.T.S.) 308/6 Sa mony ar thair ladeis treitis With triumphand amowres balleitis, And dois thair bewteis pryiss so he. 1662 J. Davies tr. *Olearius' Voy. Ambass.* 168 Some of the Caravan had been so treated with Aquavitæ, that being all dead asleep [etc.]. 1711 Budgell *Spect.* No. 161 ¶ 3 The Squire..treats the whole Company..with a Hogshead of Ale. 1712 Arbuthnot *John Bull* iii. viii, I treated the Lawyers, their wives, and daughters, with fiddles, hautboys, drums, and trumpets. 1735 Johnson *Lobo's Abyssinia, Descr.* xiv. 134 He treated us with the most opprobrious Language. 1852 Thackeray *Esmond* iii. iii, I treated her to the fiddles twice. 1897 'Tivoli' (H. W. Bleakley) *Short Innings* xiv, Dick had treated himself to two ices and a strawberry squash.

**c.** *absol.* or *intr.* To give, or bear the expense of, a treat or entertainment; to stand treat.

1710 Swift *Jrnl. to Stella* 11 Oct., I dined to-day with Dr. Garth and Mr. Addison, at the Devil Tavern, by Temple Bar, and Garth treated. 1720 Prior *Prol. to Orphan* 6 Our generous scenes for friendship we repeat; And if we don't delight, at least we treat. 1771 Smollett *Humph. Cl.* 23 June, The ladies treat with tea in their turns.

**10.** *trans.* To deal with in the way of art (literary, pictorial, musical, etc.); to handle or represent artistically, esp. in a specified manner or style.

1695 Dryden *Observ. Art Paint.* Wks. 1822 XVII. 493 Zeuxis and Polygnotus..treated..their subjects in their pictures as Homer did in his poetry. 1762–71 H. Walpole *Vertue's Anecd. Paint.* (1786) II. 134 Familiar subjects.. treated with great lustre and fullness of colouring. 1848 Mrs. Jameson *Sacr. & Leg. Art* (1850) 318 The life of St. Stephen..has been treated in mural frescoes. 1889 Parry in Grove *Dict. Mus.* IV. 27/1 The choral part [of Beethoven's 9th Symphony]..treats the theme in the form of variations apportioned to the several verses of the poem.

**11.** To deal with in order to some particular result. **a.** To deal with or operate upon (a disease or affection, a part of the body, or a person) in order to relieve or cure. Const. *with* a remedy or remedial process, *for* a disease, etc..

1781 *Med. Jrnl.* Mar. 150 The second class [of symptoms] are to be treated in the manner just now directed. *Ibid.* June 427 Seven patients in this disorder treated with mercury. 1797 *Encycl. Brit.* (ed. 3) XI. 347/1 A new-born infant, instead of being treated with syrups, oils, etc., ought to be allowed to suck the mother's milk. *Ibid.* 352/1 Cutaneous eruptions have been successfully treated with electrization. 1800 *Misc. Tracts* in *Asiat. Ann. Reg.* 327/2 The most adviseable method of treating the bite of a serpent. 1843 R. J. Graves *Syst. Clin. Med.* xxviii. 359 We were treating the woman for the pains I have..alluded to. 1875 Jowett *Plato* (ed. 2) I. 12 If his eyes are to be cured, his head must be treated. 1912 *Times* 19 Oct. 8/2 Making the necessary allocation of the insured persons to the doctors who will treat them.

**b.** To subject to chemical or other physical action; to act upon *with* some agent.

1816 Accum *Chem. Tests* (1818) 66 To treat the mineral water with the re-agents. 1845 McCulloch *Taxation* (1852) 334 Potato-starch when treated with sulphuric acid becomes sugar. 1903 *Times* 7 Mar. 7/5 These roads.. should..be treated with a steam roller.

Hence **Trea·ted** *ppl. a.* in various senses of the vb.

1710 Steele *Tatler* No. 195 ¶ 5 Three Times in Four the treated Persons have been Males. 1893 *Outing* (U.S.) XXII. 113/2 A glossy black substance,..which I concluded was highly treated asphaltum. 1897 *Daily News* 5 July 3/3 They were similar in all respects, except that one was made of 'treated' timber and the other of ordinary timber. 1905 *Daily Chron.* 10 Feb. 8/3 It is in shades that these treated metals are most effective.

**Treatable** (trī·tăb'l), *a.* Forms: 4–7 **tretable**, (5 **treteable**, **tretabill**, **-ylle**, 6 **-yl**), 5– **treatable**. [ME. *tretable*, a. F. *traitable* (13th c. in Godef.) :—L. *tractābilem*: see Tractable. In some senses f. Treat *v.* + -able.]

**1.** Easily handled or dealt with; tractable, manageable, docile; open to appeal or argument, 'easy to be entreated', affable. (Of persons, etc. or their attributes.) *Obs.* or *arch.*

1303 R. Brunne *Handl. Synne* 1992 Makayre ioyed þat þey were..so tretable; He þankeþ God þat he haþ founde So mylde wymmen yn wedlak bounde. *c* 1386 Chaucer *Pars. T.* ¶ 584 Man is a quik þing by nature and tretable to goodnesse. 1496 *Dives & Paup.* (W. de W.) x. v. 376/2 Yf he be meke & tretable, gyue hym [horse] a smothe brydel. 1578 *Chr. Prayers* in *Priv. Prayers* (Parker Soc.) 489 Thou ..art treatable and mild,..thou shewest mercy unto thousands. 1667 *Decay Chr. Piety* xvii. ¶ 10 Suffer themselves to cool into a treatable temper. 1711 Shaftesb. *Charac.* ii. ii. (1737) I. 238 Those arts, by which the people were render'd more treatable in a way of reason and understanding. 1888 Doughty *Arabia Deserta* I. 583 Nasr..had showed himself more treatable since the others' departure.

†**b.** Of things: Tractable; yielding to treatment, as a disease; flexible or ductile, as a metal.

1340 *Ayenb.* 94 God..huanne he nhesseþ þe herte, and makeþ zuete and tretable, ase wex ymered, and ase land guod and agrayþed. *Ibid.* 167 Gold..þe more hit is ine uere: þe more hit is clene and clyer and tretable. *c* 1425 tr. *Arderne's Treat. Fistula* 27 Considere þe lech bisily, þe wounde..if it be wele tretable and with-out hardnes. 1543 Traheron *Vigo's Chirurg.* ii. xi. 45 Yf the canker be tretable in the begynnynge,..and in suche parte of the bodye, that it maye seme possible to be rooted uppe.

†**c.** Of or in reference to actions, etc.: Gentle, easy, moderate, deliberate, not violent. *Obs.*

*c* 1430 *Stans Puer* 78 in *Babees Bk.* (1868) 31 Be soft in mesure, not hasti, but treteable. 1597 Hooker *Eccl. Pol.* v. xlvi. § 1 Somewhat there is why a vertuous minde should rather wish to depart this world with a kinde of treatable dissolution, then to bee suddainely cut off. 1612 T. Taylor *Comm. Titus* ii. 15 (1619) 536 Doctrine may be ponderous and waightie, where the speach is calme and treatable, stil waters often runne the deepest. 1690 Temple *Misc.* ii. *Gard. Epicurus* Wks. 1731 I. 182 In France, and the Low-Countries ..the Heats or the Colds, and Changes of Seasons, are less treatable than they are with us.

†**d.** Of utterance: Deliberate; distinct, clear, intelligible. *Obs.*

1450–1530 *Myrr. our Ladye* 55 To abyde vpon the tretable sayng of theyre seruyce, be yt neuer so werysom. 1561 Bp. Parkhurst *Injunct.* A iv, Whether the parsons..doth reade the common seruice with a lowde, distinct, and treatable voyce. 1632 G. Herbert *Country Parson* vi, [The parson's] voyce is humble, his words treatable and slow. 1641 Milton *Ch. Govt.* ii. Pref., Wks. 1851 III. 147 All these things with a solid and treatable smoothnesse to paint out and describe.

†**2.** Capable of being handled or touched, tangible; exposed to touch. *Obs. rare.*

1382 Wyclif *Heb.* xii. 18 Ȝe han not come to the tretable fyer [1388 the fier able to be touchid], and able to come to. 1541 R. Copland *Guydon's Quest. Chirurg.* H iij, What woundes of the bely are moste peryllous and moste dyfficyle to heale?..They in the myddes of the bely bycause the partyes there ben more treatable.

**3.** Capable of being or proper to be treated or dealt with.

1570 Levins *Manip.* 2/42 There be many other [adjs.] in *able*, deriued of Englishe verbes,..as..Treatable, worthy or able to be treated upon. 1657 J. Sergeant *Schism Dispach't* 614 More liable to the rigour of Martiall law and treatable as a greater enemy. 1741 Warburton *Div. Legat.* II. 44 Treatable by the common Rules of Art. 1833 Lamb *Elia* Ser. ii. *Barrenness Imag. Faculty*, From the moment that Sancho loses his reverence, Don Quixote is become a—treatable lunatic.

Hence **Trea·tableness**, the quality of being treatable; † in quots., tractability, docility; clearness of utterance; mildness of disposition.

1526 *Pilgr. Perf.* (W. de W. 1531) 144 b, In dede iustyce, in workes mercy, in maners discyplyne & tretablenes. 1546 Langley *Pol. Verg. De Invent.* i. x. 21 To..furnysh it with Elegance of termes & picked wordes:..to vtter it with comely gesture..for the conuenient treatablenesse thereof, doth teache and plainly declare the thing. 1700 Rycaut *Hist. Turks* III. 410 He commended the Wisdom of the present Vizier, his Humanity and Treatableness.

**Treatably** (trī·tăbli), *adv.* [f. Treatable + -ly 2.] In a treatable manner; † in quots., deliberately, distinctly, with clear utterance; without haste or violence, gently, easily, moderately.

1450–1530 *Myrr. our Ladye* 53 To vse theyr tongue to say yt tretably and dystynctely, wythout faylyng or ouerskyppnge of worde or sylable. 1527 Andrew *Brunswyke's Distyll. Waters* b iij b, Than make fyre vnder it that it may droppe treatably as yf you wolde tell the clock. 1612 Brinsley *Lud. Lit.* 151 You are to vtter each word leasurely and treatably; pronouncing euery part of it, so as euery one may write..as fast as you speake. 1693 Slare in *Phil. Trans.* XVII. 906 In the space of a Minute I have made Twelve Respirations, (when I was very sedate, and drew in my Breath very treatably).

†**Trea·tance.** *Obs. rare*—[1]. [f. Treat *v.* + -ance.] = Treatment 1.

1644 [H. Parker] *Jus Pop.* 54 Tis not sufficient to say, such a Nation was slavishly treated, they must prove, that there was cleer Law for that Treatance.

**Treatee** (trītī·). *rare.* [f. as prec. + -ee.] One who is treated or entertained: see Treat *v.* 9.

1841 J. T. Hewlett *Parish Clerk* III. 71 The interpretation of which was left to the treatees. 1884 Stockton in *Century Mag.* XXVIII. 588 Each took a cigar with that careless yet deferential manner which always distinguishes the treatee from the treator.

**Treater** (trī·təɹ). Forms: 5 *Sc.* **treyter**, 6 *Sc.* **tretar**, 7, 9 **treator**, 6– **treater**. [In sense 1, a. OF. *traiteor*, *traiteur* ambassador (1275 in Godef.); in other senses, f. Treat *v.* + -er [1].] One who treats, in any sense of the verb.

**1.** One who negotiates terms of settlement; a negotiator.

1489 *Barbour's Bruce* x. 125 Schir alexander of Argill.. send tretis [*Edinb. MS.* treyteris] to þe king, And com his man but tarying. 1550 *Reg. Privy Council Scot.* I. 91 Subscrivit be the commissaris, tretaris of the pece betuix France and Ingland. 1644 *Pr. Rupert's Jrnl.* 20 Nov. in *Eng. Hist. Rev.* (1898) XIII. 738 Treaters came with 27 propositions. *a* 1656 Ussher *Ann.* vi. (1658) 368 And he instead of a treater, played the traitor with them. 1859 W. Chadwick *Life De Foe* vi. 324 A misunderstanding among the treaters or negotiators. 1885 H. C. McCook *Tenants Old Farm*

ii. (1888) 13 A pedigree ante-dating William Penn,..his treaties and his aboriginal treators.

**2.** One who treats of or writes upon a subject.

**1594** BLUNDEVIL *Exerc.* (1636) A iij b, Modern Writers, and Treaters of that Art. **1892** A. C. DEANE *Frivolous Verses, Eng. Lit. Tripos* v, Here we possess highly-competent treaters, Ready to deal with all authors of note.

**3.** One who gives a treat, or stands treat; an entertainer, feaster.

**1692** E. WALKER tr. *Epictetus' Mor.* lvii, You may, 'tis true, your Appetite appease, But not your Company, nor Treater please. **1884** [see TREATEE]. **1906** *Daily Chron.* 19 June 6/3 Any hospitality which is likely to secure to the treater the goodwill of the treated, which has reference to some election,..is 'corrupt treating'.

**Treating** (trī·tiŋ), *vbl. sb.* [f. TREAT *v.* + -ING [1].] The action of the verb TREAT.

**1.** Negotiation of terms.

**1375** BARBOUR *Bruce* XIV. 8 He send and had treting With the erischry of Irland. *c* **1440** *Jacob's Well* 207 Be tretyng or counseylyng þei myȝte haue sped bettere. **1525** LD. BERNERS *Froiss.* II. cxix. [cxv.] 341 We be in treatynge togyther.., wherfore we wolde gladly make an exchaunge with certayne prisoners. **1638** R. BAKER tr. *Balzac's Lett.* (vol. II) 147 If in treating together, we should not sometimes violate the laws of our Art, [etc.].

**2.** Discoursing, discussion.

*c* **1450** tr. *De Imitatione* I. x. 10 Tretyng and talking of seculer dedes,.. lettiþ muche. **1720** WATERLAND *Eight Serm.* 114, I was once inclinable to defer the Treating of it some time longer.

**3.** Behaviour towards a person, etc.; usage.

**1549** *Compl. Scotl.* viii. 74 Al the gude treittyng that scottis men gettis in ingland changis in ane vile seruitude. **1588** A. KING tr. *Canisius' Catech.* 36 Irrewerent traicting of yᵉ name of god.

† **4.** Entreaty, beseeching. *Obs.*

**1595** DANIEL *Civ. Wars* II. lxxxix, With earnest 'treating she procur'd her Passe To come to him.

**5.** Regaling, feasting, entertaining; *spec.* the action of providing a person (wholly or partly at one's own expense) with food or drink at a parliamentary or other election in order to obtain (or in return for) his vote; bribery or corruption by feasting (illegal in Great Britain since 1854 by 17 & 18 Vict. c. 102, § 4).

**1709** STEELE *Tatler* No. 73 ¶ 14 An evil and pernicious Custom has of late..prevailed at the Election of Aldermen, by treating at Taverns and Alehouses, thereby engaging many unwarily to give their Votes. **1842** *Act* 5 & 6 *Vict.* c. 102 (*title*) An Act for the better Discovery and Prevention of Bribery and Treating at the Election of Members of Parliament. **1863** H. COX *Instit.* I. viii. 116 Treating..invalidates the vote of an elector treated.

**6.** *attrib.* † **Treating-house**, a house of entertainment or refreshment, an eating-house (*obs.*).

**1680** in *Verney Mem.* (1907) II. 369 Eate a Tart at the treating house by Knightsbridge. **1704** *Gentl. Instr.* III. (1713) 353 His first jaunt is to a Treating-house.

**Trea·ting,** *ppl. a.* [f. as prec. + -ING [2].] That treats, in any sense of the verb; in quot., negotiating, discussing terms.

**1820** A. RANKEN *Hist. France* VIII. I. iv. 95 The principal treating powers agreed to employ their endeavours in terminating the war.

**Treatise** (trī·tis, -iz), *sb.* Forms: 4–5 **tretis, -ys, -ice,** (4 **-es, -esse, -yss, -ies,** 5 **-ise, -yce),** 4–6 **tretyse,** (5 **treetise, -ys);** 5 **treatis,** 5–6 **-ys(e, -yce,** 6 **-es, -esse, -ice, -ize,** 6– **treatise.** *β.* 6 **tractise, -yse; traictise, treactise.** [a. AF. *tretiz* masc. (one instance *c* 1250 in Godef.) representing an OF. **traitëiz*, f. *traitier*, F. *traiter*, TREAT *v.* The forms *tract-*, *traict-*, *treact-* were 16th c. 'etymological' spellings after L.]

**1.** A book or writing which treats of some particular subject; commonly (in mod. use always), one containing a formal or methodical discussion or exposition of the principles of the subject; formerly more widely used for a literary work in general: see also b, c.

**13..** *Cast. Love* Introd., Her byginnet a tretys.. þat bisschop Grosteȝt made, ywis. *a* **1375** *Lay Folks Mass Bk.* App. IV. 1 Her techeþ þys tretys þenne Hou mon scholde here hys masse. *c* **1391** CHAUCER *Astrol.* Prol. 1 To lerne the tretis of the astrelabie. *c* **1400** *Cursor M.* 27548 (Cott. Galba) Here will I tell a schort tretice Made of þe seuyn dedly vice. **1422** tr. *Secreta Secret., Priv. Priv.* 236 Here endyth the tretyse of Physnomye, and begynnynge the tretyce of gouernaunce of helthe. **1493** *Dives & Paup.* (Colophon) Here endith a compendiouse treetise dyalogue of Diues & paup. **1526** TINDALE *Luke* i. 1 For as moche as many have taken in hond to compyle a treates off thoo thynges which are surely knowen amonge vs. — *Acts* i. 1 In my fyrst treatise (Deare frende Theophilus) I have written off all that Jesus began to do and teache. *c* **1530** *Crt. of Love* iv, That she, my lady, of her worthinesse, Accept in gree this little short treatesse. **1530** BAYNTON in *Palsgr.* Introd. 14 Whiche compendious tractyse..Whiche brefe traictise. **1542** UDALL *Erasm. Apoph.* E.'s Pref., This present treactise. **1588** *Marprel. Epist.* (Arb.) 27 In my next treatize, I shal proue the matter to be cleare. **1633** in *Verney Mem.* (1907) I. 76, I remember 'tis a letter, noe treatise, I have in hand. **1741–3** WESLEY *Extract of Jrnl.* (1749) 15 Turretin's history ..(a dry, heavy, barren treatise). **1869** FARRAR *Fam. Speech* iv. (1873) 107 You will see it stated in many modern treatises.

† **b.** A story, tale, narrative (spoken or written).

*c* **1374** CHAUCER *Troylus* IV. 642 (670) The whiche tale a-noon right as Criseyde Had herd, she..Ful bysily to Iuppiter by-soughte Yeue hym myschaunce þat þis tretis broughte. **1580** LYLY *Euphues* (Arb.) 226 To rehearse an olde treatise of an auncient Hermitte [etc.]. **1605** SHAKS. *Macb.* V. v. 12 The time ha's beene..my Fell of haire Would at a dismall Treatise rowze, and stirre.

† **c.** A descriptive treatment, description, account (*of* something). *Obs.*

**1570–6** LAMBARDE *Peramb. Kent* (1826) 151, I will here conclude the treatise of Dover. **1601** DOLMAN *La Primaud. Fr. Acad.* (1618) III. 686 The circles of the sphere,..the treatise whereof I refer to you.

† **2.** Negotiation, treating, discussion of terms; arrangement of terms. *Obs.*

*c* **1374** CHAUCER *Troylus* IV. 36 (64) Whan Calkas knew þis tretys sholde holde In Consistorie a-mong þe Grekes soone. **1375** BARBOUR *Bruce* XIX. 145 The scottis messingeres thar he fand Of pese and rest to haf tretise. The kyng wist schir yngerame ves vise. *c* **1440** *Partonope* 1336 Better..to dye Than in tretyse trust her curtesy. **1470–85** MALORY *Arthur* XX. xix. 831, I shalle sende a messager vnto my lord Arthur a treatyce for to take, for better is pees than allwayes warre. **1529** RASTELL *Pastyme, Hist. Brit.* (1811) 216 By the treatyse of the Countess of Henaude..a meane was made for a truse. *a* **1641** BP. MOUNTAGU *Acts & Mon.* iv. (1642) 253 Antony and Octavius were reconciled;..both ready and willing to yeeld to treatise, as standing in feare, the one of the other.

† **b.** A treaty; = TREATY *sb.* 3 a, b. *Obs.*

**1460** CAPGRAVE *Chron.* (Rolls) 216 Thanne [1354] was the town [Oxford] put under interdict..tyl a tretys was mad thus. *c* **1475** *Harl. Contin. Higden* (Rolls) VIII. 442 A tretys was made at Brugges. **1489** *Barbour's Bruce* XX. 47 (Edinb. MS.) And monymentis and lettrys ser, That thai off Ingland that tyme had,..In-till that tretyss wp thai gaff. **1530** PALSGR. 282/2 Treatyse bytwene two princes, *traicte, trete.* **1544** A. COPE *Scipio & Hannibal* 133 b, Also graunted in that treatise of peace.

† **3.** (?) An entreaty; = TREAT *sb.*[1] 2, TREATY 4. (But the quots. may possibly belong to sense 2.)

**1470–85** MALORY *Arthur* IV. xxv. 153 They asked herborow, but the man of the courtelage wold not lodge them for no treatyce that they coude treate. *Ibid.* VI. xv. 207 Syr launcelot leue that swerd behynde the, or thou wil dye for it. I leue it not sayd syr launcelot for no treatys.

Hence † **Trea·tise** *v., trans.* to make a treatise on, to treat or write of; † **Trea·tising,** writing of a treatise, treatment of a subject.

**1502** *Ord. Crysten Men* (W. de W. 1506) V. vii. 413 Yᵉ dampnacyon of the body that hath ben the meane of synne hath ben fyrst treatysed. **1605** HIERON *Short Dialogue* 15 Some..will..distast this your froothy and wordy treatising.

† **Trea·tiser.** *Obs.* Also 7 **-our, -or.** [f. prec. sb. or vb. + -ER [1].] The writer of a treatise.

**1604** HIERON *Wks.* I. 518, I remember a saying of S. Hieromes; 'I know..that I otherwise esteeme of the apostles then of other treatisers'. **1610** BP. HALL *Apol. Brownists* lv. 136 The poysoned workes of Origen, and other dangerous Treatisours. **1637** C. DOW *Answ. H. Burton* 169 Answering a Popish treatisor. **1646** R. BAILLIE *Anabaptism* (1647) 178 Unto those Arguments..the Treatiser adds nothing considerable.

† **Treatly, tretely,** *adv. Obs.* [f. TREAT *sb.*[1] + -LY [2].] = TREATABLY; deliberately.

*c* **1435** *Chron. London* (Kingsford 1905) 21 Holdyng the Scrowe in his hande..dystynctely and tretely he redde yt ouer.

**Treatment** (trī·tmĕnt). Also 6 **trait-,** *Sc.* **treit-.** [f. TREAT *v.* + -MENT. Cf. F. *traitement* (1255 in Hatz.-Darm.).]

**1.** Conduct, behaviour; action or behaviour towards a person, etc.; usage. (Const. *of* the person, etc. who is the object of the action.)

*c* **1560** A. SCOTT *Poems* (S.T.S.) iv. 46 Sic treitment is a trane To cleive thair quaver caice. **1585** Q. ELIZ. in *Four C. Eng. Lett.* (1880) 29 My ambassador writes so muche of your honorable traitment of him. **1647** CLARENDON *Hist. Reb.* I. § 49 This kind of Treatment was so ill suited to the Duke's great Spirit. **1719** DE FOE *Crusoe* I. 38 The generous Treatment the Captain gave me, I can never enough remember. **1809–10** COLERIDGE *Friend* (1865) 85 Had Luther been himself a prince, he could not have desired better treatment. **1907** *Verney Mem.* I. 280 Edmund complains of the treatment of the army by the treasurer.

**2.** Entertainment, feasting; an entertainment, banquet (= TREAT *sb.*[1] 4). *Obs.* exc. *dial.*

*a* **1656** USSHER *Ann.* VI. (1658) 437 As to the treatments of the guests, sometimes 1000, otherwhiles 1500 tables were most richly spread. **1715** tr. *C'tess D'Anois' Wks.* 452 He gave her Treatments, with enchanted Balls, and Comedies every Evening. **1725** POPE *Odyss.* XIV. 71 Accept such treatment as a swain affords.

**3.** Management in the application of remedies; medical or surgical application or service.

**1744** BERKELEY *Siris* § 95 Many are even rendered incurable by the treatment of inconsiderate physicians. **1781** *Med. Jrnl.* Feb. 98 The third part..relates to the pathology and treatment of disorders of the nerves. **1797** *Encycl. Brit.* (ed. 3) XI. 352/1 If this treatment prove very disagreeable to the patient. **1863** AITKEN *Pract. Med.* (1866) II. 65 Treatment is chiefly conducted by diet and by medicines. **1875** H. C. WOOD *Therap.* (1879) 380 Arsenic has long been used ..as a remedy in the treatment of cutaneous diseases.

**4.** Subjection to the action of a chemical agent. Also *attrib.*

**1828** WEBSTER s. v., The treatment of substances in chimical experiments. **1900** *Westm. Gaz.* 2 May 9/3 Four extra cyanide treatment tanks [for gold ore].

**5.** Action or manner of dealing with something in literature or art; literary or artistic handling, esp. in reference to style.

**1856** *Sat. Rev.* II. 322 The mode of treatment adopted by the Rouman balladists. **1879** H. PHILLIPS *Notes Coins* 8 The boldness of design and power displayed in the treatment of their subjects. **1889** PARRY in Grove *Dict. Mus.* IV. 20/2 The last movement [of Mozart's 'Jupiter' Symphony], with its elaborate fugal treatment, has a vigorous austerity.

**6.** Discussion of terms of settlement; negotiation. *rare.*

**1828** SIR W. NAPIER *Penins. War* III. i. (Rtldg.) I. 116 The stipulations of a treatment between the juntas.

**7.** (rendering F. *traitement*, sense 5 in Littré.) Salary, emolument. *nonce-use.*

**1852** *Fraser's Mag.* XLV. 170 The Professorship..is a very desirable appointment...Its 'annual treatments' (to borrow a delicate Gallicism) amount to four hundred a-year.

**Treator,** variant of TREATER.

**Treatrip(pe,** variant of TREY-TRIP *Obs.*

† **Trea·ture.** *Obs. rare*[−1]. [f. TREAT *v.* + -URE.] = TREATMENT I.

**1494** FABYAN *Chron.* VI. ccvi. 219 [Canute] sayde, 'All erthly kynges may knowe..that none is worthy to haue the name of a kynge but he that hath all thynges subiecte to his hestes, as here is shewed, by worchynge of his treature by this water'.

**Treaty** (trī·ti), *sb.* Forms: 4–5 **tretee,** 4–6 **trete, trety,** 5 **treetee, tretie, -ye, (tretty); traitee, -ie, -ye, traytee, -ye, (traytte, -ye,** 6 *Sc.* **treittie),** 5–7 **treatye,** 6 **-ee,** 6–7 **-ie,** 6– **treaty.** [ME. *trete, tretee*, a. AF. *treté*, OF. *traité, traitié*, ppl. sb. of *traiter* TREAT *v.*, and :—L. *tractātum* TRACTATE.]

† **1. a.** The treating of a subject in speech or writing; (literary) treatment; discussion. *Obs.*

**1382** WYCLIF *Ezra* Prol. 32 But that to short tretee I come [L. *sed ut ad compendium veniam*]. **1483** CAXTON *Cato* 3 The second partye pryncipal is the trayttye and alle the maner of this present book. **1552** HULOET, Treaty of any thyng, *dissertatio.* **1570–6** LAMBARDE *Peramb. Kent* (1826) 87 It followeth..that..I handle such particular places..as are mentioned in hystorie: in which treatie, I will observe this order. **1619** J. DYKE *Caveat Archippus* 10 That a full Treatie of the particulars..should come within..one houres discourse. *a* **1663** BP. SANDERSON in Spurgeon *Treas. Dav.* Ps. xix. 13 Such a presumptuous sin as we are now in treaty of.

† **b.** A work in which some subject is treated of; a treatise, dissertation; in early use, a story, narrative, written account (= TREATISE 1, b, c).

*c* **1400** tr. *Secreta Secret., Gov. Lordsh.* 90 The tretee folwand in þe whilk we sall determyn of singuleryte. *c* **1470** HENRY *Wallace* VII. 901 As witnes weill in to the schort tretty Eftir the Bruce, quha redis in that story. **1508** DUNBAR *Gold. Targe* heading, Here begynnys ane littil tretie intitulit the goldyn targe compilit be Maister Wilyam Dunbar. **1585** T. WASHINGTON tr. *Nicholay's Voy.* I. xv. 16 Villegaignon in his treaty which he hath made of the warres of Malta. **1646** SIR T. BROWNE *Pseud. Ep.* II. iv. 80 Sir Kenelme Digby in his excellent Treaty of bodies. *a* **1715** BURNET *Own Time* an. 1672 (1823) I. 567 In some sermons, and in some printed treaties, they charged the judges with corruption.

**2.** The treating of matters with a view to settlement; discussion of terms, conference, negotiation. Now *rare* or *Obs.* exc. in phr. *in treaty.*

*c* **1386** CHAUCER *Frankl. T.* 491 At after soper fille they in tretee [*v.r.* trete]. *c* **1450** *Brut* 491 þe Frensh men..labored to haue A traitie with þe King of Englond. *c* **1470** HENRY *Wallace* VII. 1267 Dunde thai gat sone be a schort trete. *c* **1500** *Melusine* XX. 113 In long treatee lyeth somtyme grete falshed. **1560** DAUS tr. *Sleidane's Comm.* 159 After a long treatie, albeit they coulde not throughlye agree, yet a trewce was made. **1615** G. SANDYS *Trav.* 234 A litle boate with a flag of treatie..to agree for the redemption of captiues. **1625** in Foster *Eng. Factories Ind.* (1909) III. 57 This was but yett in treatie. **1683** *Pennsylv. Archives* I. 70, I was in Treaty about your yea and nay going for an Oath. **1788** FRANKLIN *Autobiog.* Wks. 1840 I. 163 The treaty was conducted very orderly. **1881** MRS. L. B. WALFORD *D. Netherby* x, It appears he is in treaty for a place in the North.

**3.** † **a.** A settlement or arrangement arrived at by treating or negotiation; an agreement, covenant, compact, contract. *Obs.* exc. as in b.

**1427** *Rolls of Parlt.* IV. 318/2 My Lady of Gloucestre so be pourveyde fore be way of traitee or in other wise. **1469** *Plumpton Corr.* (Camden) 23 Sir John Malevera gave me a chalenge for him, & said he was outlawd under my trety: I told him I treted never; I bare your message to him. **1552** HULOET, Treaty or agreement, *pactio.* **1753** JOHNSON *Let. to J. Warton* 8 Mar., in *Boswell*, For descriptions of life, there is now a treaty almost made with an authour and an authouress.

**b.** *spec.* A contract between two or more states, relating to peace, truce, alliance, commerce, or other international relation; also, the document embodying such contract, in modern usage formally signed by plenipotentiaries appointed by the government of each state. (Now the prevailing sense.)

**1430–31** *Rolls of Parlt.* IV. 371/2 In ye Tretee of ye Pees, made nought longe agoo. **1545** ELYOT, *Fœdus*.., a treatie of peace, or league betwene princes. **1622** BACON *Hen. VII*, Wks. 1879 I. 760/1 A peace was concluded..being in effect rather a bargain than a treaty. **1671** EVELYN *Corr.* 31 Aug., The..height of the Warr..to the conclusion of it in the Treaty at Breda, 1667. **1776** ADAM SMITH *W. N.* IV. i. (1869) II. 24 By advantageous treaties of commerce, particular privileges were procured in some foreign state for the goods and merchants of the country. **1841** HAYDN *Dict. Dates* s. v., The first formal and written treaty made in England with any foreign nation was entered into at Kingston between Henry III and the dauphin of France..11 Sept. 1217. **1874** BANCROFT *Footpr. Time* viii. 195 A treaty of alliance with France. **1888** T. E. HOLLAND in *Encycl. Brit.* XXIII. 530/2 A treaty is a contract between two or more states. The term 'tractatus', and its derivatives..began to be commonly employed, in lieu of the older technical terms 'conventio publica', or 'foedus', from the end of the 17th century. In the language of modern diplomacy the term 'treaty' is restricted to the more important international agreements, especially to those which are the work of a congress, while agreements dealing with subordinate questions are described by the more general term 'convention'.

†**4.** Entreaty, persuasion, request. *Obs.*

c **1450** *Mirour Saluacioun* 3972 A wise womman..whilk turned the prince ire to pece thorgh hire tretee. c **1470** *Golagros & Gaw.* 1083 For ony trety may tyde..I wil noght turn myn entent. c **1470** HENRYSON *Mor. Fab.* II. (*Town & C. Mouse*) xxiv, With fair tretie yit scho gart hir ryse And to the burde thay went. **1606** SHAKS. *Ant. & Cl.* III. xi. 62 Now I must To the young man send humble Treaties, dodge And palter in the shifts of lownes. **1649** DAVENANT *Love & Hon.* II. i, The gentle Treaties, Sir, of love are fit For hours more happy.

†**5.** Treatment, usage; behaviour. *Obs. rare.*

**1630** B. JONSON *New Inn* I. i, *Host.* They call me Good-stock. *Lov.* Sir, and you confess it, Both in your language, treaty, and your bearing. **1654** tr. *Martini's Conq. China* 118 To partake of his sweet treaty, rather than of his cruelty. *Ibid.* 217 They were to expect no better Treaty from this Tyrants hands.

**6.** *attrib.* and *Comb.*, as *treaty-ally, -breaker, -money, -right, skill, -stipulation*; *treaty-breaking, -making* sbs. and adjs.; *treaty-bound, -sealed* adjs.; **treaty coast, shore**, a coast on or along which some foreign nation has certain rights guaranteed by treaty; **treaty-port**, a port opened to foreign commerce by a treaty (esp. applied to certain ports in China, Japan, and Korea, in relation to commerce with European nations).

**1904** *Daily Chron.* 1 Feb. 5/1 It would ill beseem King Edward, the *treaty-ally of the Mikado, to pay a visit to the Tsar. **1908** *Westm. Gaz.* 29 Feb. 3/1 The French are *treaty-bound to keep the open door. **1706** PRIOR *Ode to Queen* xx, Thus the Royal *Treaty-Breaker said. **1723** BLACKMORE *Alfred* x. 359 At his Tribunal let them be arraign'd Who *Treaty-breaking Principles maintain'd. **1909** *Daily Chron.* 7 July 3/1 Any delay in that grant would have led to an accusation of treaty-breaking. **1899** *Westm. Gaz.* 26 June 7/1 The whole *treaty coast is in a most excited state. c **1500** *Melusine* xxviii. 214 For to fulfyll..that he had promysed at *traytee makynge of the peas. **1856** KANE *Arct. Expl.* I. xvii. 210 They did not return: I had read enough of treaty-makings not to expect them too confidently. **1796** WASHINGTON *Let. to U. S. Ho. Repr.* 30 Mar., The *treaty-making power. **1763** SCRAFTON *Indostan* iii. (1770) 102 Demanded security for the payment of the remainder of the *treaty-money. **1881** J. HATTON *New Ceylon* iv. 114 With the *treaty ports of China and with Hong Kong we exchange annually upwards of twenty million pounds' worth of goods. **1901** *Westm. Gaz.* 4 Jan. 2/2 The extinction of the rights clearly possessed by France on the *Treaty Shore [of Newfoundland]. **1742** BLAIR *Grave* 500 Now vain their *Treaty-Skill! Death scorns to treat.

Hence (*nonce-wds.*) **Trea·ty** *v.*, *intr.* to make a treaty; *trans.* (with advb. extension), to bring or get (into some specified condition) by a treaty; **Trea·tyist**, one who frames or is bound by a treaty; **Trea·tyless** *a.*, having no treaty.

**1862** CARLYLE *Fredk. Gt.* XIV. ii. (1873) V. 152 In spite of treatyings innumerable. **1888** *Glasgow Even. Citizen* 3 Sept. 2/5 China must feel..irritated in having her people 'treatied' out of America and our Colonies. **1888** *Voice* (N. Y.) 26 Apr., A yearly addition of 150,000,000,000,000 of young codfish to vex future treatyists. **1892** *Nation* (N. Y.) 25 Aug. 137/3 There the negotiations hang, leaving these two high-protection countries in almost as helpless and ridiculous a plight as unhappy and treatyless England.

†**Treave**, obs. var. THRAVE, THREAVE *sb.* and *v.*

**1768** *Case of Jeffry Ruffle* 2 When cut down, the whole ought to be put into treaves of an equal size, and every tenth treave set out for the tythes. *Ibid.*, He tythed it at the times he gathered in his corn for treaving or loading, by separating and setting out every tenth sheaf.

†**Trebant**, obs. variant of TRABANT.

**1712** *Lond. Gaz.* No. 4967/1 His Majesty [at Vienna]..was on Horseback, preceded..by the Trebants, who are a sort of Yeomen of the Guards.

**Trebget, -got**, obs. forms of TREBUCHET.

**Treble** (tre·b'l), *sb.* Forms: see next. [a. OF. *treble*, sb. use of TREBLE *a.*]

**I. 1.** Anything threefold; a sum or quantity three times as great as another; the product of a sum or magnitude multiplied by three.

[**1324–5** *Rolls of Parlt.* I. 416/1 Que amounteront a treble & quatreble de lour coustages.] c **1430** *Art Nombryng* xi. (E.E.T.S.) 17 Thow most trebille the digit, and that triplat is to be put vnder the 3[rd] next figure towarde the right honde, And the vnder-treblle vnder the trebille. **1463** *Rolls of Parlt.* V. 502/2 Forfeiture..of the treble of his seid wages. **1475** *Ibid.* VI. 121/2 Uppon peyn of forfeiture of the treble of somoche as he so hath receyved or taken. **1799** WILSON in *Phil. Trans.* LXXXIX. 302 The equation of the halves, or quarters, or doubles, trebles, &c. of those functions.

**2.** In technical and elliptical uses. **a.** A triple barrier; an obstacle consisting of three successive fences.

**1569** STOCKER tr. *Diod. Sic.* III. xi. 120/2 Hys Campe which he with a treble of wood and earth fortified. **1895** *Daily News* 1 May 7/5 The fences..On one side of the ring..are arranged in a 'treble', just far enough apart to give room between for a horse to pull himself together for each effort.

**b.** *Paper-making* and *Printing*. A frame on which hand-made paper or printed sheets are hung to dry.

**1727–41** CHAMBERS *Cycl.* s.v. *Paper*, Carried up into the loft, and hung six or seven sheets together upon lines fastened to a thing called a Tribble, each tribble containing thirty lines ten or twelve foot long. **1766** C. LEADBETTER *Royal Gauger* II. xiv. (ed. 6) 371 The Sheets of Paper, taken from between the Felts, are laid one upon the other till the next Day and then are hung up, on Lines called Trebles, in the Drying-House. **1896** *Daily News* 23 Mar. 8/4 If time be no object, the sheets are hung on 'trebles' (the towel-horse is the domestic equivalent) in an ordinary room.

**c.** A kind of step-dance; the measure of or music for this. *dial.*

**1805** G. MCINDOE *Poems* 18 We'll sen' for fiddling Alic, and the piper he'll play treple. **1895** D. D. DIXON *Whittingham Vale* v. 67 A variety of step-dancing such as the 'treble', the single and double 'shuffle', the 'cut' [etc.].

**d.** *Whist.* A game (at short whist) in which one side scores five and the other none, counting three points to the winners.

**1870** HARDY & WARE *Mod. Hoyle* 30 If one side scores five while the adversaries have made not one point, the winning side makes a treble. **1876** A. C. WALKER *Correct Card* (1880) Gloss., *Treble*, scoring five before your adversary scores one.

**e.** *pl.* A quality or grade of small coal.

**1901** *Scotsman* 15 Oct. 4/8 There are four bush washers.. one for trebles.

**f.** A method of crocheting in which three loops of thread are carried on the hook; also a line or chain of crochet work done by this method.

**1882** CAULFEILD & SAWARD *Dict. Needlework* 127/2 s. v. *Crochet, Treble Stitch, Raised.*—Work three rows of Ribbed Stitch. Fourth row—work 2 Ribbed Stitches, and make a Treble for next, putting the hook into the stitch underneath it of the first row, work 2 Trebles in this way [etc.]. c **1900** THERÈSE DE DILLMONT *Encycl. Needlework, Crochet* 304 Trebles are little columns or bars made of loops or stitches... They are of different kinds; the half or short treble, the plain or ordinary treble [etc.].

**3.** One of three things or persons that are exact counterparts. *nonce-use* after DOUBLE *sb.* 2 b.

**1898** *Westm. Gaz.* 29 June 1/2 There are many 'doubles' in the House of Commons. There seem..to be in that assembly at least two groups of trebles.

**II. 4.** *Music.* The highest part in harmonized musical composition; the soprano part. Cf. TREBLE *a.* 2. [The musical use is supposed to have arisen from the fact that in early contrapuntal music the chief melody or *cantus firmus* was given to the tenor (TENOR *sb.* 4 a), the voice parts added above being the *discantus* or alto, and the *treble* (? third part) or soprano; but the history is somewhat obscure, esp. as *triplex, triplus* meant 'threefold' and not 'third', and in OF. *treble* was applied to a trio.]

c **1330** R. BRUNNE *Chron. Wace* (Rolls) 11263 Þo clerkes þat best couþe synge, Wyþ treble, mene, & burdoun. c **1430** LYDG. *Min. Poems* (Percy Soc.) 54 Thi [nasal] organys so hihe begynne to syng ther messe, With treble meene and tenor discordyng as I gesse. **1500–20** DUNBAR *Poems* xxxii. 19 All to small To sic ane tribbill to hald ane bace. **1567** *Trial Treas.* B iv, I will sing the trouble with all my harte. **1626** BACON *Sylva* § 109 In one of the lower Strings of a Lute, there soundeth not the Sound of the Treble,.. but only the Sound of the Base. **1782** BURNEY *Hist. Music* (1789) II. v. 456 The third and Triplum the highest or treble, of which term this was the origin. **1884** H. C. DEACON in Grove *Dict. Mus.* IV. 165 *Treble*..has been said to be a corruption of Triplum, a third part superadded to the Altus and Bassus. *fig.* **1532** MORE *Confut. Tindale* II. i. 95 His false translacyon wyth theyr farther false construccion, they thought sholde be the basse and the tenour wheruppon they wold synge the trouble wyth mych false descant. **1577** B. GOOGE *Heresbach's Husb.* III. (1586) 112 The grasiers trade the treble and the tillers occupation the base. **1638–56** COWLEY *Davideis* I. 458 Water and Air he for the Tenor chose, Earth made the Base, the Treble Flame arose. **1892** *Daily News* 16 Sept. 3/3 The dark tone of the ground..acts as bass to the treble of the silk.

**5.** A treble voice; also, a singer having a treble voice; one who sings the treble part.

? c **1475** *Sqr. lowe Degre* 782 Than shall ye go to your evensong, With tenours and trebles among. **1658** MARVELL *Poems, Music's Empire* 10 And Virgin Trebles wed the manly Base. **1719** D'URFEY *Pills* (1872) I. 7 The ravishing trebles delight every ear. **1801** STRUTT *Sports & Past.* IV. i. 254 Two celebrated trebles;..who occasionally made twenty shillings a day by ballad-singing.

**b.** *transf.* A high-pitched or shrill voice, sound, or note.

**1600** SHAKS. *A. Y. L.* II. vii. 162 His bigge manly voice, Turning againe toward childish trebble, pipes And whistles in his sound. **1647** H. MORE *Poems, Cupid's Conflict* vi, How well agreed the Brooks low muttering Base, With the birds trebbles. **1827** DISRAELI *Viv. Grey* VI. iii, 'So please your Serene Highness, I am here!' answered a very thin treble. **1855** TENNYSON *Brook* 40, I chatter over stony ways, In little sharps and trebles.

**6.** The string of treble pitch in a musical instrument; also, the chanter of a bagpipe.

**1562** J. HEYWOOD *Prov. & Epigr.* (1867) 186 Which string ..wouldst thou..harpe on? Not the base.., Nor the treble. **1623** LISLE *Ælfric on O. & N. Test.* Ded. xxxviii, What sports they now deuise With Treble and Drone, and Bonfiers, and Bels. **1682** DRYDEN *MacFl.* 46 At thy well-sharpened thumb,..The treble squeaks for fear, the basses roar.

†**7.** A musical instrument of treble pitch, as a violin. *Obs.*

**1634** *MS. Archd. Oxon, Berks.* c. 74 lf. 230 He plaied uppon a trebble in the house of Francis Iennings uppon a Sondaie. **1670** EACHARD *Cont. Clergy* 62 People..presently phansi'd the Moon, Mercury, and Venus to be a kind of violins or trebles to Jupiter and Saturn. **1710** in E. W. Dunbar *Soc. Life in Moray* (1865) 15, I can play on the Treble and Gambo, Viol, &c.

**b.** = *treble bell*: see TREBLE *a.* 2 b.

**1598–9** in Swayne *Sarum Churchw. Acc.* (1896) 147, ij newe gudgins for yᵉ Treble and nailes, 3*s.* 6*d.* **1652–3** *Ibid.* 227 The Sexton shall ring the Treable at 5 a Clocke in the Morning. a **1658** FORD, etc. *Witch Edmonton* II. i, Double Bells!..Trebles: buy me Trebles, all Trebles: for our purpose is to be in the Altitudes.

**8.** *attrib.* and *Comb.*, as **treble bob**: BOB *sb.*⁵; **treble-ringer**, the ringer of the treble bell in a peal.

**1872** Treble bob royal [see BOB *sb.*⁵]. **1899** *Westm. Gaz.* 31 Oct. 10/1 For sixty-seven years..Bunce was the treble ringer.

**Treble** (tre·b'l), *a.* and *adv.* Also 4–8 **trebble**, 6 **-il**; 5 **trebel, -yl(le, -ille, -ull**, 6 **treabell**, 6–7 **-ble**, 7 *Sc.* **treeble**; 5 **tribull**, 5–6 *Sc.* **trib(b)ill**, 5–7 **trible**, 7–8 (9 *dial.*) **tribble**; 5 **tryble, -ylle**; (6 **trouble**). [a. OF. *treble, trebble, treuble*, etc. (12th c. in Godef.):—pop.L. *triplus* for L. *triplex*. See also prec.]

**A.** *adj.* **1.** Consisting of three members, things, or sets combined; threefold; made of three thicknesses or layers of material; = TRIPLE *a.* 1.

c **1374** CHAUCER *Boeth.* IV. metr. vii. 115 (Camb. MS.) He drowh cerberus the hownd of helle by his treble cheyne. **1413** *Pilgr. Sowle* (Caxton) I. xxv. (1859) 30 Byndyng with double and treble boundes. a **1673** J. CARYL in Spurgeon *Treas. Dav.* Ps. cxl. 3 Serpents are..said to have a treble tongue, because, moving their tongue so fast, they seem to have three tongues. **1697** DRYDEN *Æneid* X. 1112 Thro' treble Plates it went Of solid Brass. **1781** GIBBON *Decl. & F.* xviii. II. 107 A treble inclosure of brick walls was defended by a deep ditch. **1832** R. & J. LANDER *Exped. Niger* II. xii. 183 They had formed themselves into a large treble circle. **1907** C. HILL-TOUT *Brit. N. Amer., Far West* vii. 130 A kind of shirt of double or treble elk-hide.

**b.** Of actions, conditions, etc.: Of threefold character or application; existing or occurring in three ways or relations; of three kinds.

**1390** GOWER *Conf.* III. 159 Thus thei worchen treble sinne, That ben flatours aboute a king. c **1450** *Mirour Saluacioun* 1529 The feend thoght crist to tempt be treble vice. **1571** GOLDING *Calvin on Ps.* lx. 6 The greate men were dubble and trebble traytours. **1694** F. BRAGGE *Disc. Parables* vii. 238 It would be a double and treble charity; 'twould provide for the happiness of both body and soul. **1818** SCOTT *Br. Lamm.* xii, It was attended with a treble difficulty. **1886** F. HARRISON *Choice Bks.* iii. 49 Every part and episode has its double and treble meaning.

**c.** Three times as much or as many; of three times the number or amount; triple.

**1423** *Rolls of Parlt.* IV. 257/2 Uppon peine de inprisonement..and trible dammages to the partie greved. **1489** *Barbour's Bruce* XVIII. 30 (Edin. MS.) Schir Eduard..said, that he suld fecht that day, Thouch tribill and quatribill war thai. **1563** W. COTHE in *15th Rep. Hist. MSS. Comm.* App. II. 32 It is not treble the company we have here, that is able to defend it. **1664** M. FELL in *Extr. S. P. rel. Friends* II. (1911) 187 People had theire goods distreaned trible the vallue of their fines. **1788** JEFFERSON *Writ.* (1859) II. 526 It sells..for treble the price of common whale oil. **1835** URE *Philos. Manuf.* 156 The roller A, moving with a treble surface velocity.

**2.** *Mus.* Of, pertaining to, or suited to the highest part in harmonized musical composition.

*Treble voice*: a voice ranging from about middle C to a twelfth or two octaves above it; a soprano voice. *Treble clef*: the G clef when placed (as usually) upon the second line of the stave.

c **1440** *Promp. Parv.* 501/1 Treblesonge (*K.* treble of orgene songe, *S.* trebyl songe), *precentus*. *Ibid.*, Trebyl syngare. **1530** PALSGR. 286/1 Wayte treble, *bussine*. **1674** PLAYFORD *Skill Mus.* 43 Increasing of the Voice in the Treble Part.. doth oftentimes become harsh. **1678** PHILLIPS (ed. 4), *Treble*, the highest part in Musick, called in Latin *Altus*. **1801** BUSBY *Dict. Mus.* Introd. 23 The Treble-cliff is used for the first or shrillest class, both of voice and instruments. **1876** STAINER & BARRETT *Dict. Mus. Terms* (1898) s.v., The treble or soprano voice is the most flexible of all vocal registers.

**b.** Hence in the names of musical instruments (or strings) of the highest pitch. Cf. *bass, tenor.*

*Treble bell*: the smallest bell of a peal.

**1530** PALSGR. 282/2 Treble stryng of an instrument, *chanterelle*. **1595–6** in Swayne *Sarum Churchw. Acc.* (1896) 145 A Rope for yᵉ Treabell bell, 2*s.* 5*d.* **1597** SHAKS. 2 *Hen. IV*, III. ii. 351 The Case of a Treble Hoeboy was a Mansion for him. **1674** PLAYFORD *Skill Mus.* 109 The Treble-Violin is a cheerful and spritely Instrument. **1872** ELLACOMBE *Ch. Bells Devon*, etc. 235 In 1718, two treble bells were added to the peal of S. Bride's.

**c.** High-pitched; high or sharp in tone; shrill.

**1562** J. HEYWOOD *Prov. & Epigr.* (1867) 110 In hir treble voyce, she fell so to cacklyng. **1602** MARSTON *Ant. & Mel.* III. Wks. 1856 I. 35 What trebble minikin squeaks here? **1727** GAY *Fables* xlvi. 15 A village cur,..Imagined that his treble throat Was blest with music's sweetest note. **1860** GEO. ELIOT *Mill on Fl.* III. vi, Bob spoke with a sharp and rather treble volubility.

†**d.** ? Upper. *Obs. rare.*

**1551** *Gray's N. Y. Gift* iii. in Furniv. *Ball. fr. MSS.* I. 418 Yet at this presence—ye shall vnderstand—The papest be Ranke, and on the treble hand: Som compford thé have; I cannott tell howe.

**3.** Special collocations. *Treble bar, treble gold stripe*, collectors' names for various moths: see quots. *Treble hook*, a fish-hook consisting of three single hooks fastened back to back. † *Treble letter*, a letter consisting of three sheets formerly charged triple postage (*obs.*). *Treble lock*, a lock operating by three turns of the key. *Treble star*, three stars so near (really or visually) as not to be separately visible without a telescope. † *Treble time* (*obs.*), triple time. See also in 2.

**1832** RENNIE *Conspect. Butterfl. & Moths* 201 The Tawny

*Treble Bar (*Argyromiges trifasciella*, Curtis)..Wings.. with three somewhat straight, equidistant, brown bands. *Ibid.*, The *Treble Gold Stripe (*Argyromiges tristigella*, Stephens). Wings..tawny-brown, with a straight silvery-golden band before, and a second in the middle. **1867** SMYTH *Sailor's Word-bk.*, **Treble-block*, one fitted with three sheaves or rollers. **1895** *Outing* (U. S.) XXVII. 222/2 Attached to each line were a sinker and a *treble hook, i. e., three hooks soldered together at such angles that when a fish has once gorged the thing, disgorgement is almost an impossibility. **1753** *Scots Mag.* July 328/2 The rates of double letters, are always double; of *treble letters, treble. **1805** *Act* 45 *Geo. III*, c. 11 § 1 For every single letter one penny; for every double letter twopence; for every treble letter or other letter under an ounce in weight three-pence. **1661** BAXTER *Mor. Prognost.* II. xxi. 50 There shall be a *Treble-Lock upon the Door of the Ministry. **1782** HERSCHEL in *Phil. Trans.* LXXII. 100 The beautiful *treble star in Monoceros's right fore-foot. **1686** PLOT *Staffordsh.* ix. 371 Seven bells rung together in peal...Their number excludes them, from ever being brought, either into common or *treble-time.

**B.** *adv.* **1.** In three ranks or rows, threefold; to three times the extent; three times over; trebly.

**13..** *K. Alis.* 6696 In hire mouth buth teth treble set. **1552** HULOET, Treble, *tripliciter*. **1563** A. NEVELL in B. Googe *Eglogs*, etc. (Arb.) 87 All these conclude him blest..And trible blest agayne. **1622** FLETCHER *Beggar's Bush* v. i, And I'll deserve it treble. **1675** WOOD *Life* 18 Sept. (O.H.S.) II. 322 Piers was double or treble paid by Dr. Fell. **1708** *Constit. Watermen's Co.* lvii, Every person offending therein, shall forfeit..treble as much as he or they respectively shall demand.

**2.** In a high-pitched tone; shrilly.

**1811** [implied in *treble-skirling*: see C. 2].

**C.** Combinations.

**1.** The adj. in combination. **a.** with sbs., as **treble-coursing**, the division of an air-current in a mine into three courses or channels; **treble-seam** (*Cricket slang*), a leathern cricket-ball stitched with three seams; **treble-tree**, an arrangement of swingle-trees for three horses abreast.

**1897** *Globe* 9 July 1/5 The old bowler..declared there was a lot of human nature in a *treble-seam. **1877** KNIGHT *Dict. Mech.*, **Treble-tree*, a whiffletree for three horses. An equalizer.

**b.** Parasynthetic combs. forming adjs., as *treble-barrelled, -breathed, -caped, -headed, -mailed, -piled, -rampired, -seated, -sinewed*; **treble-voiced**, having a treble or soprano voice.

**1784** *New Spectator* No. 1. 4 The ladies have assumed the *treble-caped great coat and belt. **1805** *Med. Jrnl.* XIV. 92 How our *treble-headed Pithon is to be augmented and increased. **1876** GEO. ELIOT *Dan. Der.* xxxvi, Gnawed by a double, a treble-headed grief. **1611** COTGR., *Tremaillé*, *treble-mailed. **1821** SCOTT *Kenilw.* xxiv, Velvet, single, double, *treble-piled. **1649** G. DANIEL *Trinarch., Hen. IV*, cxvii, As the wings of long-lost Day Breakes *treble-Rampierd Clouds. **1808** BENTHAM *Sc. Reform* 36 The permanent substitution of *treble-seated .. to single-seated judicature. **1606** SHAKS. *Ant. & Cl.* III. xiii. 178, I will be *trebble-sinewed, hearted, breath'd. **1552** HULOET, *Treble voyced, or shyll tuned, *acutus, a, um*.

**c.** With sbs., forming adjectives or attributive phrases, as *treble-cylinder, treble-shovel*; **treble-bite, treble-wedge-fast**, systems of breech-action in hand-guns.

**1892** GREENER *Breech-Loader* 22 With an efficient holding-down bolt, engaging with it as in the *treble-bite breech-action. **1877** KNIGHT *Dict. Mech.*, **Treble-cylinder Steam-engine*, an engine having a pair of large cylinders for the continuation of the expansion, one at each side of the small cylinder. *Ibid.*, **Treble-Shovel Plow*, one having three shares. A form of cultivator. **1881** GREENER *Gun* 174 Our patent *treble-wedge-fast action, with either hammerless or back-action locks and low hammers.

**2.** The adv. in comb. **a.** with pples., forming adjectives, as *treble-brandished, -damned, -refined, -ribbed, -riveted, -twisted*, etc.; **treble-dated**, living three times as long (as man); (in sense B. 2) *treble-skirling*. **b.** with vbs., as *treble-man, -shot*.

**1877** TENNYSON *Harold* I. i, Yon grimly-glaring, *treble-brandish'd scourge. **1824** COLERIDGE *Lett., to J. Gillman* (1895) 730 If he be not a *treble-damned liar. **1601** SHAKS. *Phœnix & T.* 17 Thou *treble-dated crow,..'Mongst our mourners shalt thou go. **1805** PIKE *Sources Mississ.* (1810) 51 We were obliged to take on but one sled at a time and *treble man it. **1694** SALMON *Bate's Dispens.* II. vi. (1713) 604/2 With its equal Weight of *trebble-refined Sugar. **1896** *Daily News* 14 Nov. 6/6 Besides deed-boxes, there were other receptacles..some *treble-ribbed with iron or copper. **1662** GERBIER *Princ.* 18 Casements *treble riveted, to keep out Wind and Rain. **1874** THEARLE *Naval Archit.* 131 For treble-riveted butt straps, nineteen diameters in breadth are required by Lloyd's. **1884** H. COLLINGWOOD *Under Meteor Flag* 74 Request Mr. Flinn to *treble-shot his larboard broadside. **1811** W. TENNANT *Anster Concert* xiii, High o'er the tenor sounded shrill The *treble-skirling women. **1867** BAKER *Nile Tribut.* ii. (1872) 32 A powerful hook, fitted upon *treble-twisted wire.

**Treble** (tre·b'l), *v.* [f. prec. Cf. OF. *trebler* (13th c. in Godef.).]

**1.** *trans.* To make three times as many or as great; to increase threefold; to multiply by three.

*a* **1325** *MS. Rawl. B. 520* lf. 32 ȝif þe contreie..ne ansuuerez noȝt..þe peine sal ben itrebbled. *c* **1430** *Art of Nombryng* xi. (E.E.T.S.) 17 Thow most trebille the digit. **1596** SHAKS. *Merch. V.* III. ii. 302 Double sixe thousand, and then treble that. **1666** SANCROFT *Lex Ignea* 28 His Insolence doubles and trebles the Vexation. **1720** *Lond. Gaz.* No. 5833/2 Which trebles the Duty..payable by the Exporter. **1885** DUNCKLEY in *Manch. Exam.* 20 July 6/1 During the present century the population has just about trebled itself.

**b.** To fold in three thicknesses; to make in three layers.

**1598** HAKLUYT *Voy.* I. 62 Caparisons for their horses made of leather artificially doubled or trebled vpon their bodies. **1638** SIR T. HERBERT *Trav.* (ed. 2) 316 A Cambolin of pure lawn..trebled on and about their naked shoulders.

**c.** To be three times as many or as much as.

**1615** G. SANDYS *Trav.* 115 Madein, A coyne of siluer that trebles the Asper for value. **1842** BORROW *Bible in Spain* xxxiv. (Pelh. Libr.) 250 A body of the Carlists,..whose numbers more than trebled his own.

**2.** *intr.* (for *refl.*) To grow to three times the number, amount, or size; to become threefold.

**1625** FLETCHER *Noble Gent.* II. i, Now I see your Fathers honours Trebling upon you. **1797–8** WELLINGTON in Owen *Desp.* (1877) 777 It has more than trebled since the peace of '83. **1815** SIMOND *Tour Gt. Brit.* I. 170 The rent of land has trebled in the last fifty years. **1882** PEBODY *Eng. Journalism* xix. 145 Mr. Levy reduced the price of the paper...The circulation doubled, trebled, quadrupled.

†**3.** *intr.* To emit a high-pitched or shrill sound; also, to sing the treble part to (const. *upon*) the lower parts or plain-song in a harmonized composition (in quots. *fig.*). *Obs.*

*c* **1425** *Cast. Persev.* 1900 in *Macro Plays* 134, I here trumpys trebelen al of tene. *a* **1591** H. SMITH *Wks.* (1866) I. 458 A nightingale..when she is in a pleasant vein, quavers and capers, and trebles upon it. **1606** S. GARDINER *Bk. Angling* 103 The singster of Israel hath .. giuen vs the Notes wee must alwayes treble vppon.

†**b.** *trans.* To utter in a high-pitched or shrill tone. *Obs. rare*$^{-1}$.

**1616** CHAPMAN *Homer's Hymn to Hermes* 645 He outrageously (when I accus'd him) trebled his reply.

Hence **Tre·bled** *ppl. a.*, made treble, threefold.

?*c* **1400** LYDG. *Æsop's Fab.* i. 23 With trebled [*v. r.* treble] laudis yeve to the trynité. **1653** R. SANDERS *Physiogn., Moles*, etc. 38 Divide the trebled number into two. *a* **1711** KEN *Preparatives* Wks. 1721 IV. 43 While I by trebled Zeal and Tears Strive to retrieve my careless Years.

†**Tre·blefold,** *a.* and *adv. Obs.* [f. TREBLE + -FOLD.] **a.** *adj.* Three times as great or numerous; threefold. **b.** *adv.* Three times as much, thrice over.

**1387–8** T. USK *Test. Love* I. iii. (Skeat) l. 152 Treble folde so mokell muste I suffer, ere tyme come of myne ease. **1561** T. HOBY tr. *Castiglione's Courtyer* I. (1577) C vij, They speake accompanying euery worde with certaine treblefolde sighes. **1587** Q. ELIZ. in H. Campbell *Love Lett. Mary Q. Scots* App. (1824) 62 God reward thee trebblefold in the double for the most troublesome charge so well discharged.

**Tre·bleness.** *rare.* [f. TREBLE *a.* + -NESS.]

†**1.** Treble quality (of sounds); high pitch.

**1626** BACON *Sylva* § 183 The Just and Measured Proportion of the Aire Percussed, towards the Basenesse or Treblenesse of Tones, is one of the greatest Secrets in the Contemplation of Sounds.

**2.** The quality of being threefold.

**1888** in *Cassell's Encycl. Dict.*

†**Trebler,** a treble-singer: see TRIBLER.

**Treblett,** erron. form of TRIBLET.

**Trebling** (tre·bliŋ), *vbl. sb.* [f. TREBLE *v.* + -ING$^1$.] The action of the verb TREBLE.

**1.** Increasing threefold; multiplication by three.

**1591** PERCIVALL *Sp. Dict.*, *Trasdobladura*, trebling, *triplicatio*. **1694** *Phil. Trans.* XVIII. 70 The doubling, trebling, quadrupling, &c. of Rations is performed by squaring, cubing, biquadrating, &c. of the terms.

**2.** *Naut.* See quots.

**1856** KANE *Arct. Expl.* I. xxxi. 423 The outside trebling or oak sheathing. **1867** SMYTH *Sailor's Word-bk.*, *Trebling*, planking thrice around a whaler's bows in order the more effectually to withstand the pressure of the ice.

**Trebly** (tre·bli), *adv.* [f. TREBLE *a.* + -LY$^2$.]

**1.** In a threefold degree or manner; triply.

**1590** SPENSER *F. Q.* I. xi. 22 Trebly augmented was his furious mood. **1629** WADSWORTH *Pilgr.* v. 47 She was left destitute, the..Iesuites being trebly paid. **1697** DRYDEN *Æneid* x. 1113 Linnen trebly rowl'd. **1814** SCOTT *Ld. of Isles* III. vii, Wicket and gate were trebly barr'd, By beam and bolt and chain. **1850** TENNYSON *In Mem.* cii. 16 This hath made them trebly dear.

†**2.** In a treble or high-pitched tone. *Obs. rare*$^{-1}$.

**1679** in *Verney Mem.* (1907) II. 330 A Mercy, $w^{ch}$ makes mee merrily & Trebly sing, Gaudiamus and Haleluia.

**Trebuchet** (tre·bŭʃet, ‖trebüʃe). Forms: α. 4 **trepejette, trepget,** 4–5 **-eget,** 5 **trepgett(e, trip-, trypgette,** 6 **trepegett, -gete, trepa-;** β. 4–5 **tri-, tre-, treybochet;** 5 **trebget** (*err.* **-got**); 6 **trabu-,** 7 **trebuschet,** (8–9 **trebucket**), 8– **trebuchet.** [In I, a. OF. *trebuchet*, also *trebuket, -busket, trabuchet* (12th c. in Godef.) siege-engine, bird-trap, mod.F. *trébuchet* trap, balance (= Prov. *trabuquet*, Sp. *trabuquete*, It. *trabocchetto*, med.L. *trā-, trēbuchētum*, Du Cange), f. OF. *tre-, tres-, trabucher* (11th c.) to overturn, overthrow, stumble, fall, in med.L. *trābuchāre*: see TRABUCH. The early α-forms (trepedʒe·t, etc.) are imitations of OF. *trebuchet* (trebŭtʃe·t). The word was obsolete in the 16th c.; from 18th c. historical and antiquarian. Sense 3 is from mod.Fr. In II, an application, in England, of med.L. *trēbuchētum* (see above), to the device known popularly from *c* 1200 as *cuck-stool, cucking-stool*. The Latin form remained app. as a legal term, rendered *trebuchet* in 17th c. by the legal antiquaries. Cf. **1611** COTGR., *Trebuchet*, a pitfall for birds; a pit, with a trap doore, for wild beasts; also, a paire of gold weights; also, an old-fashioned Engine of wood, from which great, and battering stones were most violently throwne.]

**I. 1.** A mediæval military engine for casting heavy missiles. *Hist.*

Described as consisting of a pivoted lever with a sling at one extremity, which was strained back against a heavy counterpoise, and then suddenly released. Cf. CATAPULT 1.

[**1224** *Close Roll* 8 *Hen. III*, m. 4 Facias usque Doura maeremium ad trubechetum nostrum faciendum. — 9 *Hen. III*, m. 24, viij. Roellas ereas quas fieri fecistis at trubechettum nostrum. **1377** *Rolls of Parlt.* III. 10/2 Un trebuchet outre ascun mesure qe l'en avoit unqes veeu.]

α. **13..** *Coer de L.* 5227 With trepeiettes they slungen alsoo. **1388** WYCLIF 1 *Macc.* vi. 20 Thei maden arblastis, [*gloss*] ether trepeiettis, that is, an instrument for to caste schaftis, and stoonys. *c* **1400** [see MANGONEL]. *c* **1420** *Brut* 428 The Kynge..leid therto his grete Gounnys, Trepgettis and Engenys, and bete adowne the wallis. **1520** *Caxton's Chron. Eng.* VII. 145/1 Gonnes, Engynnes, and trypgettes [**1482** trip-]. **1599** THYNNE *Animadv.* (1875) 41 'Trepegett' $yo^{u}$ expounde 'a Ramme to batter walles'. But the trepegete was the same that the mogonell. [**1896** *Eng. Hist. Rev.* Apr. 357 Eustace the monk was taken, and Stephen of Winchelsea..gave him his choice of having his head cut off on the trapget or the bulwarks [rather of being hurled from the trapget or having his head cut off on the bulwarks].]

β. *a* **1400–50** *Alexander* 1296 With traumes & with tribochetis þe tild to asaile. *c* **1400** *Siege of Troy* 838 in *Archiv neu. Spr.* LXXII. 33 An hundrid gynnys þer were vpset, Of Maungeneles and Treybochet. *c* **1440** *Promp. Parv.* 501/1 Trebget, for werre (*S.* trepgette), *trabucetum*. **1795** SOUTHEY *Joan of Arc* VIII. 198 Who kneeling by the trebuchet, Charged its long sling with death. **1825** SCOTT *Betrothed* viii, 'Well driven, trebuchet—well flown, quarrel!' cried the monk. **1885** C. W. C. OMAN *Art of War* 57 The feeble siege-artillery of the day, perrieres, catapults, trebuchets, and so forth.

†**2.** A trap or gin to catch small birds or beasts. *Obs. rare.* (So in Fr. from 14th c.)

**1362** LANGL. *P. Pl.* A. XII. 86 Þou tomblest wiþ a trepget ȝif þou my tras folwe. *c* **1440** *Promp. Parv.* 501/1 Trebget [*pr.* -got], sly instrument to take brydys or beestys (*S.* trepgette), *tendicule*.

**3.** A small delicately poised balance or pair of scales; an assay balance; a tilting scale. (So Fr.)

**1550** *Reg. Mag. Sig. Scot.* 105/1 Par de lie trabuschettis 15 sol. **1613** BP. FORBES *Comm. Rev.* xviii. § 6. 191 It is a hard thing to fall into the hands of the Lord: before whom all Nations are but as the droppe of a Bucket, or as the dust of a Trebuschet. **1871** M. C. LEA *Photogr.* 420 The French pattern of 'trebuchet', or tilting scale, now largely manufactured here. **1877** KNIGHT *Dict. Mech.*, *Trebucket*.

**II. 4.** An instrument of punishment, = CUCKING-STOOL, q. v.

[*c* **1200** *Chron. of Jocelin de Brakelond* (Camden) 38 Levaverunt homines de Illegga quoddam trebuchet, ad faciendam justiciam pro falsis mensuris panis vel bladi mensurandi. ?**1266–7** *Judicium Pillorie* in *Stat. Realm* (1870) I. 201/1 Paciatur judicium corporis, scilicet, Pistor Collistrigium, et Braciatrix trebuchetum vel castigatorium. *c* **1440** *Promp. Parv.* 107/1 Cukstole, for flyterys,..*turbuscetum, cadurca*. **1500** *Ortus Vocab.*, *Terbichetum*, a cokstole.] *c* **1640** J. SMYTH *Hundred of Berkeley* (1885) 143 Cucking stool and other Judicials, Collistrigia et trebuchets. **1667** E. CHAMBERLAYNE *Pres. St. Eng.* I. (1684) 48 Scolding women are to be set in a Trebuchet, commonly called a Cuckingstool..placed over some deep water into which they are let down and plunged under water thrice. **1769** BLACKSTONE *Comm.* IV. xiii. 169 A common scold,..if convicted, shall be sentenced to be placed in a certain engine of correction called the trebucket, castigatory, or cucking stool. **1867** *Cornh. Mag.* Jan. 38 A homely provision made for the punishment of mere bad language in the bridle and trebuchet or ducking-stool.

†**Trebuke,** variant of TRABUCH.

*c* **1482** J. KAY tr. *Caoursin's Siege of Rhodes* (1870) P 11 A man of Grece,..counseyled the Lord Mayster and the Rhodyans to make and ordeygne an engyne called Trebuke lyke a slynge, which was grete hye and myghty, and casted grete and many stones into the hoste of the Turkes.

†**Trebuler,** *a. Obs.* [f. *Trēbula*, name of a place: cf. *Trēbulāna vina* (Pliny).] ?Of Trebula.

**1606** S. GARDINER *Bk. Angling* ix. 158 The trebuler sort [of vines] that are thrust to the wall, that neuer growe high, or ouerdreepe others little.

**Trebuttar,** obs. form of TRIBUTARY.

**Trecche:** see TRECHE *v.*

**Trecc̆her, -erie, -erous, -our,** etc., obs. forms of TREACHER, -EROUS, -ERY, etc.

†**Trecentene,** *a. Obs. rare*$^{-0}$. [f. L. *trecentēnī* three hundred each.] (See quotation.)

**1656** BLOUNT *Glossogr.*, *Trecentene*, pertaining to three hundred.

‖**Trecento** (treˌtʃe·nto). [It., lit. 'three hundred', short for *mil trecento* 1300; cf. CINQUECENTO.] The fourteenth century (13..), as a period of Italian art, architecture, etc.; also *attrib.*

**1841** W. SPALDING *Italy & It. Isl.* II. 215 The vigour and expressiveness of the *trecento*. **1873** 'OUIDA' *Pascarèl* I. 9 The beautiful *trecento* windows were filled with eager faces. **1878** VILLARI *Machiavelli* (1898) I. III. viii. 149 The literature of the Trecento may be considered as exclusively Tuscan. **1899** *Westm. Gaz.* 17 Mar. 3/1 They treat..of the *trecento* painters, of Giovanni Bellini and the early Venetians.

Hence **Trece·ntist,** ‖**Trecenti·sta** (It., pl. -isti), an Italian artist, author, etc., of the 14th c.

**1821** BYRON *Juan* III. lxxxvi, In Italy he'd ape the 'Trecentisti'. **1883** C. C. PERKINS *Ital. Sculpt.* Introd. 23 The character of his work is so different from that of any other Italian trecentist.

†**Treche, trich,** *v. Obs.* Also 3 tricche, 5 trecche. [a. OF. *trichier, trechier* (3rd s. pres.

*triche, treche*), to deceive, cheat, in Picard *trikier*, (*trike*), mod.F. *tricher*, Prov. *trichar, triquar*, It. *treccare*. Ulterior origin uncertain: supposed by Diez to be from a German dialect (cf. also Mackel *Germ. elemente in franz.* 104); but others think from a late L. **triccāre* for L. *trīcārī* to trifle, shuffle, play tricks, f. *trīcæ* trifles, quirks, wiles, tricks (see Storm in *Romania* V. 172).

For the family of words belonging to this vb. see TREACHER to TREACHERY, also TRICHARD, and (more remotely) TRICK and its derivatives.]

*trans.* To deceive, cheat, betray, play false with.

*c* 1230 *Hali Meid.* 9 Nu þu sest þat ha habbeð itricchet te as treitres. *a* 1327 *Pol. Songs* (Camden) 69 Richard, thah thou be ever trichard, trichen shalt thou never more. *c* 1425 *Cast. Persev.* 253 in *Macro Plays* 84 Þese iij are nobyl, trewly I trowe, Mankynde to tenyn, & trecchyn a tyde.

**Treche**, var. TRESCHE *Obs.* **Trecher, -erous, -ery**, etc., obs. ff. TREACHER, -EROUS, -ERY.

† **Trechet**, *v. Obs. rare.* [deriv. of TRECHE *v.* (perh. error for *trecher*).] *trans.* To deceive, cheat, play false with. Hence † **Trechetting** *vbl. sb.* (See also TREACHETOUR.)

*c* 1330 R. BRUNNE *Chron.* (1810) 313 Þe[i] sent ageyn & said to kyng, 'it was no haunte Of certeyn sette & laid, to trechet þer conaunte. *Ibid.* 164 Whan he with trechettyng bi nyght away so ran, Wenes he our men Inglisse for to tretcher [*MS.* trecther] so?

**Trechmannite** (tre·kmănəit). *Min.* [? f. surname *Trechmann* + -ITE [1].] A rare mineral occurring in red rhombohedral crystals in the dolomite of the Binnenthal. It is prob. a sulpharsenite of silver. 1909 in *Cent. Dict. Suppl.*

**Trechometer** (trekǫ·mĭtəɹ). [a. F. *trechomètre*, f. Gr. τρέχ-ειν to run: see -METER.] An instrument which records the distance run by a vehicle.

1858 SIMMONDS *Dict. Trade*, *Trechometer*, a French machine for reckoning distances, specially adapted for vehicles.

**Trechor, -our, -ory, -ur, -ure, -ury**: see TREACHER, TREACHERY. **Trechoure**, obs. f. TRESSURE. **Treck-** in *treckschuit*, etc.: see TREK-. **Trecker**: see TRIGGER.

**Trecther**, scribal error for *tretcher* (cf. TREACHER): see TRECHET *v.* **Tred**, obs. f. TREAD.

**Tredding**: see TRADING *vbl. sb.* (quot. 1654).

**Treddle** (tre·d'l). Now *dial.* Forms: *α.* 1 tyrdel, 5 -dyl, 6 -dell, -dle, tirdil, turdyll, 6–7 terdle, 7 tir-, turdle; *β.* 5 tredel(e, triddil, tridel, trydelle, 7–9 truddle, 6– treddle; *γ.* 6 treatle. See also TRATTLE *sb.*[2] [ME. *tyrdyl*, etc. (whence by metathesis *tridil, treddle*), = OE. *tyrdel*, dim. of *tord*, TURD: see -EL *suffix* [1].] A pellet of sheep's or goat's dung: usually in *pl.*

*α.* *c* 1000 *Sax. Leechd.* II. 72 ȝenim gate tyrdlu. *Ibid.* 214 Haran tyrdlu. *c* 1440 *Promp. Parv.* 494/2 Tyrdyl, schepys donge. 1530 PALSGR. 281/2 Tyrdell. *Ibid.* 284/1 Turdyll shepes donge, *fient de brebis*. 1552 HULOET, Tyrdles of gootes or shepe, *rudus, eris*. 1563 HYLL *Art Garden.* (1593) 107 If you take the seeds of euery colour of Gilliflours and put them altogither into a thin small reed, or terdle of a sheep or goat. 1647 HEXHAM I, Sheeps dung or tirdles. 1671 SKINNER *Etymol. Ling. Angl.*, The Treddles *vel* Truddles, q. d. Turdles.

*β.* *c* 1410 *Master of Game* xi. (1904) 40 Men clepen þe steppes or þe marckes of þe Otere..and his fumes tredeles or spraintes. 14.. *MS. Lincoln Med.* lf. 291 (Halliw.) The triddils of an hare. 1483 *Cath. Angl.* 393/2 A Trydelle, *ruder*. 1577 B. GOOGE *Heresbach's Husb.* II. (1586) 55 b, Taking a Treddle of Sheepe, or Goates doung. 1601 HOLLAND *Pliny* XIX. xii. II. 33 The round treddles of a Goat. 1736 W. ELLIS *New Exper. Husb.* 25 Price for the neat Treddle, clear of all Hay, Straw, Flaff, or other Mixture. 1905 in *Eng. Dial. Dict.* from Lincoln, Herts, Kent, Surrey.

**Treddle**, variant of TREADLE.

**Treddling** (tre·dliŋ), *sb. dial.* In 5 tirdelyng; 9 also (*pl.*) trid(d)lings, treddlins. [f. TREDDLE + -ING [1].] Treddles of sheep, etc. in the mass.

*c* 1440 LYDG. *Hors, Shepe & G.* 381 Of the sheepe..To the lond gret profite doth his tirdelyng [*v. r.* tyrtelyng]. 1828 *Craven Gloss.*, *Tridlins*, excrement of sheeps. 1869 *Lonsdale Gloss.*, Treddlin's, Triddlin's. 1876 *Whitby Gloss.*, Triddlings.

† **Tre·decile**, *a.* or *sb. Astrol. Obs.* Also -il. [ad. mod.L. *tredecīl-is*, f. L. *trēs* three + *dec-em* ten; cf. *quartile, sextile*.] Denoting an aspect, introduced by Kepler, in which the planets are $\frac{3}{10}$ of a circle, i.e. 108°, apart. Cf. DECILE.

1647 LILLY *Chr. Astrol.* iii. 32 Of late one Kepler, a learned man, hath added some new ones as follow.. A Tredecile..consisting of 108 degrees. 1674 JEAKE *Arith.* (1696) 11 Aspects... Sesquiquintil or Tredecil. 1727–41 CHAMBERS *Cycl.*, *Aspect*, To the five ancient aspects, the modern writers have added several more; as decile, ..tridecile, ..[etc.]. 1819 J. WILSON *Compl. Dict. Astrol.* 101 The new aspects invented by Kepler are mostly produced by subdividing the others...The Tredecile, of 108°, is a quintile and half, or three deciles...Those arising from a division of the Δ or ✱ by 5 were [thought by Kepler to be] good; thus..the tredecile, being a quintile and a half, is good.

† **Trede·cuple**, *a. Obs. rare.* [f. L. *tredecim* thirteen, after *decuple*.] Thirteen times as great.

1570 BILLINGSLEY *Euclid* XVI. xxix. 453 To proue that an octohedron geuen, is tredecuple sesquialter to a trilater equilater pyramis inscribed in it.

**Tredel**, obs. form of TREADLE, TREDDLE.

**Tredge**, obs. form of TRUDGE.

**Tredrille, tredille** (tredri·l, -di·l). Also 8 tresdille, 9 tradrille. [f. QUADRILLE by substitution of *tre-* three for *qua(d-)*.] A card-game played by three persons, usually with thirty cards.

1764 H. WALPOLE *Let. to Earl Hertford* 8 June, Lady Albemarle was at tredille. 1767 LADY MARY COKE *Jrnl.* 2 May, The Duchess, Lady Blunt and I play'd at tresdille. 1769 *Ibid.* 15 June, I play'd at tredrille..with Madame de Viry and a French Officer for a shilling a fish. 1816 SINGER *Hist. Cards* 266 *Tredrille*, a modification of Quadrille which might be played by three persons...It was considered as very inferior to the game Quadrille played by four. 1821 LAMB *Elia* Ser. I. *Mrs. Battle's Opinions on Whist*, To explain to me how far it [ombre] agreed with, and in what points it would be found to differ from, tradrille. 1825 MRS. SHERWOOD *Bitter Sweet* II. 5 A hand at tredille or three-handed whist. 1860 T. L. PEACOCK *Gryll Gr.* xxiii, Quadrille is played with forty cards: tredrille usually with thirty: sometimes, as in Pope's Ombre, with twenty seven.

**Tree** (trī), *sb.* Forms: see below. [OE. *trēow, trīow*, OE., ME. *trēo*, etc. = OFris. *trē* (NFris. *trê, trǣ*), OS. *trio, treo, trew-* (MDu. in comb. *-tere, -tære*, Kilian); ON. *trē* (Da. *træ*, Sw. *trä* timber, *träd* tree); Goth. *triu*, gen. *triw-is* wood (wanting in OHG. and now also obsolete in LG. and Du.):—OTeut. **trewo-*, cognate with Skr. *dru* tree, wood, *dā·ru* wood, log, and with Gr. δρῦς oak, δόρυ spear; OSlav. *drievo* (from *dervo*) tree, wood, *drŭva* pl. wood, Russ. *de·revo, drevo·* tree, wood, Serv. *drvo* tree, *drva* wood, Czech *drva*, Pol. *drwa* wood; Lith. *dervà* pine-wood; also with OIr. *daur*, Welsh *derwen* oak. The modern Eng. *tree* is a regular repr. of OE. *trēo*, ME. *treo*; *trē* is the form in the Bestiary of *c* 1220; but the final prevalence of this over the other ME. forms *treow, trew, trow, trau*, was prob. assisted by its coincidence with Norse *trē*; *trē, tree* are the northern forms from *Cursor Mundi* onward. For form-history cf. KNEE.]

**A.** Illustration of Forms and Inflexions.

**1.** *Sing. nom.* 1 triow, (*late*) tryw, 1–2 treow, treu, (1) 3 trew, (1)–4 treo, 3–6 tre, 3– tree; 4 (*Kent.* trau, tra(u)w); trough; 5 *Sc.* trey, 6–7 trie. *dat.* 1 treowe, trēo, 2 treuwe, trewe, 4 trow(e, trauwe. [The development of OE. nom. acc. sing. was OTeut. **trewo*[m], *trewa, trew, trēu, trēo*, then with *w* from oblique cases (*trewes, treowes*, etc.), *trēow*, (*triow*).]

*c* 890 tr. *Bæda's Hist.* II. xi. [xiv.] (1890) 138 He..of treo [*v. r.* treowe] cirican ȝetimbrode. *c* 897 K. ÆLFRED *Gregory's Past. C.* xlv. 338 Ælc triow [*v. r.* treow] man sceal ceorfan. *c* 1000 *Ags. Gosp.* Matt. iii. 10 Ælc treow [*MS. B.* tryw, *Lind.* treu] þe godne wæstm ne bringð. *c* 1200 *Vices & Virt.* 27 Ðe treu of paradise. *c* 1200 *Trin. Coll. Hom.* 107 Of coren of eorðe, and of treuwe. *c* 1220 *Bestiary* 674 Ðus fel adam ðurȝ a tre, Vre firste fader, ðat fele we. *c* 1250 *Gen. & Ex.* 3301 A funden trew ðor-inne dede Moyses. *a* 1300 *Cursor M.* 657 (Cott.) Þis tree ys done in my friþe. 1340 *Ayenb.* 28 Ne in gerse, ne in busse, ne in trauwe. *Ibid.* 95 Þet trau of lyue. *Ibid.* 202 Þys traw wext and profiteþ. 13.. *K. Alis.* 6829 Alle tho That scholde with him to the trough go. 1393 LANGL. *P. Pl.* C. XXI. 200 Yf þei touchede þe treo and of þe frut eten. *c* 1530 R. HILLES *Common-Pl. Bk.* (1858) 140 Sone crokyth the tre that crokyed wyll be. 1535 STEWART *Cron. Scot.* (Rolls) II. 687 With the speir that wes of suir trie, He hit the king richt in at the e. 1573 TUSSER *Husb.* (1878) 109 Let Iuie be killed, Else trée will be spilled. *a* 1584 MONTGOMERIE *Ch. & Slae* 341 The trie sa hich of growth.

**2.** *Pl. nom.* *α.* 1 trēo, treow, triowu, treowu, -a, 1–2 treowe; 2 trowen, 2–4 treon, 3–6 trēn, 4 (troen), trene, 4–7 (–9 *dial.*) treen, 5 trenne, 5–6 treene. *β.* 2 treos, 2–3 (*Orm.*) trewwes, 2, 4 trewes, 2–5 tres, 3 troues, 3–4 trouwes, 3–5 treus, 4 trews, trowes, traues, trawes, 4–6 treis, 5 trese, 6 treys, *Sc.* treyis, 6–7 tries, 4– trees. [The development of OE. nom. acc. pl. was WGer. *trewu, trēu, trēo*; then again with *w* (from oblique cases), *trēow, treowu* (*-a*). The pl. *trēo* occurs in Vesp. Ps. and Lind. Gosp.]

*c* 825 *Vesp. Ps.* cxlviii. 9 Treo westemberu and alle cederbeamas. *c* 890 tr. *Bæda's Hist.* I. (1890) 26 Hit is weliȝ þis ealond on wæstmum & on treowum. *c* 897 K. ÆLFRED *Gregory's Past. C.* xl. 292 Sumu treowu he watrade. *a* 1000 *Epist. Alex. ad Aristot.* in Cockayne *Narrat.* 27 Eac þær wæron oþre treow. *Ibid.* 28 Ða halgan triow-swiðe wepen. *c* 1000 ÆLFRIC *Hom.* II. 588 Deorwurðe stanas, oþþe treowa. *c* 1175 *Lamb. Hom.* 5 Heo stiȝen uppe on þe godes cunnes treowe. *Ibid.* 41 He him sceawede heȝe treon. *c* 1200 ORMIN Introd. 13 Full gode treos inoȝhe. *Ibid.* 15468 Off gresess, & off tres. *c* 1200 *Trin. Coll. Hom.* 25 Gres and trowen. *Ibid.* 37 Hwile uppen trewes. *c* 1250 *Gen. & Ex.* 3305 Then [*i. e.* ten] and sexti palme tren. *c* 1275 LAY. 511 Alle hi solde hongie vppe heȝe troues. *a* 1300 *Cursor M.* 545 (Cott.) It groues tres [*Fairf.* trees] and gress. 13.. *Ibid.* 651 (Gött.) Of treis ..here es gode wone. ? *a* 1300 *XI Pains of Hell* 33 Þer beoþ bernynde treon. *a* 1325 *MS. Rawl. B.* 520 lf. 32 b, Þis statut ne portenez noȝt to grete hokes ne to oþere grete troen. *a* 1325 *Prose Psalter* xcv[i]. 12 Þan shul alle þe trews of þe wodes gladen. 13.. *K. Alis.* 6763 Þou shalt fynde trowes two. 1340 *Ayenb.* 25 Þe greatte traues. *Ibid.* 95 Uol of guode trawes. 1387 TREVISA *Higden* (Rolls) III. 445 Where þou knowe nouȝt þe treen [*v. r.* tren]. *a* 1400 *Pistill of Susan* 90 Turtils troned on trene. *c* 1400 Trees [see B. 1]. *c* 1400 *Yvaine & Gaw.* 2965 He loked in bitwix the trese. 1422 tr. *Secreta Secret., Priv. Priv.* 239 With lewys of trenne. *Ibid.* 243 The humours of tren and herbis. *c* 1430 LYDG. *Min. Poems* (Percy Soc.) 17 Twoo grene treene there grewe uprighte. *a* 1450 MYRC *Festial* i. 3 Treus and herbys. 1562–3 in Willis & Clark *Cambridge* (1886) II. 568, x greate tries at xxviij[s] the trie. 1563 *Mirr. Mag.* Induct. 2 With blustring blastes had al ybared the treen. 1565 *Satir. Poems Reform.* i. 45 Wynter windes..that doth l-bayre the tren. 1570 *Ibid.* xv. 50 All greinis and plesand treis [*rime* eyis]. 1596 DALRYMPLE tr. *Leslie's Hist. Scot.* VII. (S.T.S.) II. 17 Aple tries, and orchardis. 1600 FAIRFAX *Tasso* III. lxxv, The shadie tops of shaking treene. 1635, 1771, 1861 Trees [see B. 1]. 1843 E. JONES *Poems, Sens. & Event* 38 Vast interbranching treen.

**B.** Signification.

**1.** A perennial plant having a self-supporting woody main stem or *trunk* (which usually develops woody branches at some distance from the ground), and growing to a considerable height and size. (Usually distinguished from a *bush* or *shrub* by size and manner of growth; but cf. b.)

*c* 825, *c* 890, *c* 897 [see A. 2]. *c* 1000 ÆLFRIC *Gen.* iii. 6 Þæt treow wæs god to etanne. *c* 1175 *Lamb. Hom.* 109 Iliche þan treo þe bereð lef and blosman. *c* 1290 *St. Brendan* 41 in *S. Eng. Leg.* I. 221 Of treon and herbes, þikke i-novȝ. 1377 LANGL. *P. Pl.* B. XV. 327 A forest..ful of faire trees. 1398 TREVISA *Barth. De P. R.* XVII. i. (Tollem. MS.), A tre haþ..þe rynde, bowes, twigges, leues, blosmes, floures and frute. *c* 1400 *Destr. Troy* 12467 Trees thurgh tempestes tynde hade þere leues. 1481 CAXTON *Reynard* xii. (Arb.) 28 He brake a rodde of a tree. *c* 1530 R. HILLES *Common-Pl. Bk.* (1858) 140 Hyt ys a febyll tre thet fallyth at the fyrst strok. 1600 FAIRFAX *Tasso* VII. i, Through forrests thicke among the shadie treene. 1635 LAUD *Diary* 1 Dec., Many elm leaves yet upon the trees. 1771 *Junius Lett.* lvii. (1820) 298 He or his deputy were authorised to cut down..trees. 1861 BENTLEY *Man. Bot.* 540 Cunoniaceæ...Nearly allied to Saxifragaceæ, but differing from them in being trees or shrubs.

**b.** Extended to include bushes or shrubs of erect growth and having a single stem; and even some perennial herbaceous plants which grow to a great height, as the banana and plantain.

*c* 1340– [see ROSE-TREE]. *c* 1532 [see GOOSEBERRY 7]. 1640 [see PLANTAIN [3] 4]. 1649 [see CURRANT 4]. 1697 [see BANANA 1]. 1765 [see RASPBERRY 4]. 1855 BROWNING *Women & Roses* i, I dream of a red-rose tree. 1858 HOGG *Veg. Kingd.* 790 As a food, the Plantain is wholesome and agreeable. A tree generally contains three or four clusters.

**c.** Applied *fig.* or allusively to a person.

1594 SHAKS. *Rich. III*, III. vii. 167 The Royall Tree hath left vs Royall Fruit. 1807 WORDSW. *Force of Prayer* xiii, He was a tree that stood alone, And proudly did its branches wave.

**2.** The substance of the trunk and boughs of a tree; wood (esp. as a material of which things are made); timber. *Obs.* or *arch.*

*To go between the bark and the tree*: see BARK *sb.*[1] 6.

*c* 890 tr. *Bæda's Hist.* II. xi. [xiv.] (1890) 138 He þær hræde ȝeweorce of treo cirican ȝetimbrode. *c* 1122 *O. E. Chron.* an. 626 (Laud MS.) Þær he ær het ȝetimbrian cyrican of treowe. *c* 1290 *S. Eng. Leg.* I. 91/154 In one cheste of treo. ? *c* 1366 in Arnolde *Chron.* (1811) 138 Affixed w[t] nayles of irne or of tree. *c* 1440 *Partonope* 407 A brygge of stone and not of tree. *c* 1500 *Whole Prophecie of Scotland* 1603 (in Murray *Thomas of Erceldoune* Introd. p. xxxv), At Aberladie he shall light With hempen halters and hors of tree. 1531 ELYOT *Gov.* III. xvii, Eatyng his meate in a disshe of tree. 1638 JUNIUS *Paint. Ancients* 124 A horse made of maple tree. 1896 KIPLING *Seven Seas, Sea-Wife* iv, To ride the horse of tree [a ship].

**3.** A piece of wood; a stem or branch of a tree, or a portion of one, either in its natural state, or more usually (now always) shaped for some purpose. **a.** A pole, post, stake, beam, wooden bar, etc.; *esp.* (now only) one forming part of some structure, as a vehicle, plough, ship, etc.; usually as the second element in combinations, as AXLE-TREE, CHESS-TREE, CROSS-TREE, DOOR-TREE, DRAUGHT-TREE, ROOF-TREE, SWINGLE-TREE, etc.

971 *Blickl. Hom.* 187 Ond þa æfter þon het Neron ȝewyrcean mycelne tor of treowum & of mycclum beamum. *c* 1200 ORMIN 15835 Þatt temmple þatt wass wrohht Off trewwess & off staness. *a* 1300 *Cursor M.* 12399 (Cott.) Þe knaue þat þis timber fett..ouer scort he broght a tre. 1375 BARBOUR *Bruce* XIII. 238 Schetis..Thai festnyt in steid of baneris Apon lang treis and on speris. 1523 FITZHERB. *Husb.* § 3 The ploughe-beame is the longe tree aboue. *Ibid.* § 4 The sharbeame is the tre vnderneth, wherevpon the share is set. 1642 in J. Watson *Jedburgh Abbey* (1894) 85 Thrie scoir singill tries, threttie double tries, two hundred daills to be scaffolding and centtries. 1787 *MS. Deed*, Such trees and pipes as are now laid for conveying water from the said spring. 1848 KINGSLEY *Night Bird* 4 All night I heard a singing bird Upon the topmast tree. 1887 *Suppl. to Jamieson* s. v., A straight piece of rough timber used as a pole, lever, prop, or stay, is called a *tree*; as, a dyer's-*tree*, a raising-*tree* or lever for moving a mill-stone.

**b.** A stick, *esp.* a staff, cudgel: cf. PLANT *sb.*[1] 1 b. *Obs.* exc. *Sc.*

*c* 893 K. ÆLFRED *Oros.* IV. i. § 6 Hie namon treowu, & sloȝon on oþerne ende moniȝe scearpe isene næȝlas. *c* 1205 LAY. 25978 His fur he beten agon & muchele treowen læide on. *a* 1225 *Ancr. R.* 402 'Louerd', cweð heo to Elie, ..'lo! ich geder two treon'. 14.. *Emaré* 365 She was wax lene as a tre. *c* 1470 HENRY *Wallace* II. 97 A huntyn staff in till his hand he bar; Thar with he smat on Willȝham Wallace thair. Bot for his tre litill sonȝhe he maid. 1588 *Reg. Privy Council Scot.* Ser. I. IV. 270 The said Robert Lekky..maliciouslie straik and dang thame with rungis and treis. *c* 1680 *Songs of Scott.* (1893) 43, I am a puir silly auld man, And hirplin' ower a tree. 17.. *Gude Wallace* x. in Aytoun *Ballads Scot.* (1858) I. 56 He's gane to the West-muir wood, And there he pull'd a trusty tree.

**4. a.** The cross on which Christ was crucified, the holy rood. *arch.* and *poet.*

*a* **1000** *Rood* 25 (Gr.) Hwæðre ic..beheold hreowcearig hælendes treow. *c* **1275** *On Serving Christ* 30 in *O. E. Misc.* 91 As he for monkunnes neodes don wes on þe treo. **1382** WYCLIF *Acts* v. 30 The God of oure fadris reyside Jhesu, whom ȝe slowen, hangynge in a tree [TINDALE, and hanged on tree]. — 1 *Pet.* ii. 24 He..suffride, [*gloss*] or bar, oure synnes in his body on the tree. **1460** CAPGRAVE *Chron.* (Rolls) 106 A nayle, with whech oure Lord was nayled to the tre. **1596** R. COTTON *Armor of Proofe* xiv, Christ,.. who did our sinnes and foes to tree fast binde. **1635** PAGITT *Christianogr.* III. (1636) 52 Helena the Empresse found the Crosse, and adored the King, but not the Tree. **1707** WATTS *Hymn*, '*Alas! and did my Saviour bleed?*' iii, Was it for crimes that I had done He groan'd upon the tree? **1820** T. KELLY *Hymn*, '*We sing the praise of Him who died*' ii, He bears our sins upon the tree.

**b.** A gallows. Also † *dry tree*, *Tyburn tree.*

*c* **1425** *Cast. Persev.* 177 in *Macro Plays* 82 Pyncecras, Parys, & longe Pygmayne, And euery toun in Trage, euyn to þe dreye tre. **1500–20** DUNBAR *Poems* xvii. 28 Sum..nevir fra taking can hald thair hand, Quhill he be tit vp to ane tre. *a* **1533** LD. BERNERS *Huon* xviii. 49 Not lettynge for fere of any deth, though it be to go to the dry tre. **1535** COVERDALE *Esther* vi. 4 To hange Mardocheus on ye tre y[t] he had prepared for him. **1609** B. JONSON *Masque of Queens* ad init., From the dungeon, from the tree That they die on, here are we [witches]! *a* **1704** T. BROWN *Satire on Quack* Wks. 1730 I. 62 Though it was thy luck to cheat the fatal tree. **1818** SCOTT *Hrt. Midl.* iv, The area of the Grassmarket.. in the centre of which arose the fatal tree, tall, black, and ominous, from which dangled the deadly halter. **1847** KINGSLEY *Outlaw* x, And when I'm taen and hangit,.. ye'll steal me frae the tree.

**5.** The wooden shaft of a spear, handle of an implement, etc.; hence, a spear, lance (in phr. *to break a tree*). Now *dial.*

? *a* **1366** CHAUCER *Rom. Rose* 948 Ten brode arowis hilde he there,..But iren was ther noon ne stelle, For al was golde, ..Outake the fetheres & the tree. *c* **1400** *Laud Troy-Bk.* 12697 He was wounded with a spere..Hede & tre lefft bothe In him. *a* **1600** MONTGOMERIE *Misc. Poems* xlix. 24 We dout not bot they [thy knights] dar..be bold to brek a tre. **1611** COTGR., *Abrier d'Arbeleste*, the tree of a Crossebow. **1765** *Museum Rust.* III. 240 The person should have a spade.. about four inches broad, and eighteen inches long in the bit, ..with a tree in it of three feet six inches long. **1881** *Leicester Gloss.*, *Tree*, a wooden handle or stail.

† **b.** A wooden structure; applied *poet.* or *rhet.* to a ship; in quot. 1513 to the wooden horse at the siege of Troy. *Obs.*

**1382** WYCLIF *Wisd.* xiv. 1 Another thenkende to seilen,.. the tree berende hym. **1513** DOUGLAS *Æneis* II. i. 60 In this tree ar Grekis closit. **1535** COVERDALE *Wisd.* x. 4 Whan y[e] water destroyed y[e] whole worlde, wyszdome preserued the righteous thorow a poore tre. **1594** MARLOWE & NASHE *Dido* IV. iv, Here's Aeneas' tackling, oars, and sails...Oh, cursed tree, hadst thou but wit or sense, To measure how I prize Aeneas' love.

**c.** A wooden vessel; barrel, cask, 'the wood'. *Sc.*

**1513** *Acc. Ld. High Treas. Scot.* IV. 487 Item to hir in aile, full to seywart xxiiij last and a barrell,..ilk barrell contenand xij gallonis, price of the galloune xx d; summa of the last with the tree..xiij li. viij s. **1532** *Ibid.* VI. 156, xij ½ barrellis of aill, ilk barrell contenand v gallonis...Item, for xij treis to put the samyn intill, for ilk tree xviij d. **1656** TUCKER *Rep. Revenues Scot.* (Bann. Cl.) 10 The Scots use noe certaine vessells, but such as by a generall terme they call Trees,..some holding more or lesse gallons the tree. *a* **1814** RAMSAY *Scotl. & Scotsmen in 18th C.* viii. (1888) II. 78 The scourging a nine-gallon tree..consisted in drawing the spigot of a barrel of ale, and never quitting it..till it was drunk out.

**d.** The framework of a saddle: = SADDLE-TREE, q. v. for earlier quots.

**1535** STEWART *Cron. Scot.* (Rolls) III. 300 Ane hors he fand..Without saidill, curpall, tre, or brydill. **1591** GREENE *Art Conny Catch.* II. (1592) 5 His sadle is made without any tree. **1665** SIR T. HERBERT *Trav.* (1677) 314 Saddles of the better sort are usually of Velvet;..the trees are curiously painted. **1737** BRACKEN *Farriery Impr.* (1756) I. 328 If the Saddle be too narrow in the Tree. **1862** *Catal. Internat. Exhib., Brit.* II. No. 4721 Elliptical spring-seat saddle, and tree showing action of spring.

**e.** A block upon which a boot is shaped or stretched: = *boot-tree* (BOOT *sb.*[3] 8).

**1541** *Knaresborough Wills* (Surtees) I. 35, ij pair of boytte treys. **1596** NASHE *Saffron Walden* 17 Rayse thy conceipt on the trees, or..new corke it at the heeles, before it should thus walke bare-foote. **1766** [see *boot-tree*, BOOT *sb.*[3] 8]. **1839** THACKERAY *Fatal Boots* Nov., As I was polishing on the trees a pair of boots. **1891** KIPLING *Light that Failed* viii, As Dick..busied himself among the former's boots and trees.

**6.** Something resembling a tree with its branches.

**a.** A diagram or table of a family, indicating its original ancestor as the root, and the various branches of descendants; in full, *family* or *genealogical tree.* Also *fig.* a family, race, stock. (*b*) *Porphyrian tree* (*Logic*): see PORPHYRIAN.

**1297** R. GLOUC. (Rolls) 7255 Þo smot uerst þis tre aȝen to is kunde more [*i.e.* natural root]. *a* **1300** *Cursor M.* 1625 (Cott.) Bot first a tre,..I sal sette hire [*v.r.* here] of adam kin. **1693** STEPNEY in *Dryden's Juvenal* viii. 11 Vain are their Hopes, who fancy to inherit By Trees of Pedigrees, or Fame, or Merit. **1762–71** H. WALPOLE *Vertue's Anecd. Paint.* (1786) V. 305 Two genealogic trees. **1825** T. HOOK *Sayings* Ser. II. *Doubts & F.* v, A more honourable tree does not flourish in the archives of heraldry than ours. **1858** M. ARNOLD *Merope* 865 So dies the last shoot of our royal tree!

**b.** Any structure or figure, natural or artificial, of branched form.

*spec.* (*a*) (tr. *arbor* in med.L. phrases). An arborescent mass of crystals forming from a solution, as of silver (DIANA's *tree*), of lead (SATURN's *tree*), etc. (*b*) Applied to the spinal nervous system, consisting of the spinal cord and the nerves branching out from it. (*c*) A branched respiratory organ in Holothurians. (*d*) A worked design of tree-like form. (*e*) *Math.* A figure or diagram consisting of branching lines.

**1706**– [see DIANA 2]. **1843** R. J. GRAVES *Syst. Clin. Med.* xxx. 396 A certain portion of the extreme branches of the nervous tree. **1844** Lead-tree [see LEAD *sb.*[1] 12]. **1857** CAYLEY *Math. Papers* (1890) III. 242 On the Theory of the analytical Forms called Trees. **1865–8** WATTS *Dict. Chem.* III. 478 By the electro-chemical action of zinc in a solution of acetate of lead, it is deposited in an arborescent form, known under the name of *Saturn's Tree.* **1870** ROLLESTON *Anim. Life* Introd. 145 In the Holothurioidea these coeca take a great development, and are known as the 'lungs' or 'respiratory trees'. *Ibid.* 149 The left respiratory tree. **1879** *Unif. Reg.* in *Navy List* July (1882) 497/1 Tree of trimming braid at top of back.

**7.** Phrases. *At the top of the tree*, in the highest position: see TOP *sb.*[1] 14. *Up a tree* (*colloq.*, orig. *U.S.*), debarred from escape, like a hunted animal driven to take refuge in a tree; entrapped; in an awkward position, in a difficulty or 'fix'. *One cannot see the wood for the trees*: see WOOD *sb.*

**1774** FOOTE *Cozeners* I. (1778) 16 Master Moses is an absolute Proteus; in every elegance, at the top of the tree. **1782**– [see TOP *sb.*[1] 14]. **1825** J. NEAL *Bro. Jonathan* II. 103 If I didn't—I'm up a tree—that's a fact. **1839** THACKERAY *Major Gahagan* v, I had her in my power—up a tree, as the Americans say. **1857** HUGHES *Tom Brown* I. vii, 'What a pull', said he, 'that it's lie-in-bed, for I shall be as lame as a tree, I think'.

**b.** Phrases with *of.* *Tree of Buddha*, or *of wisdom* = BO-TREE. *Tree of chastity* = AGNUS CASTUS (*Treas. Bot.*); also called *chaste-tree* (CHASTE *a.* 9). *Tree of Diana*: see DIANA 2, and cf. 6 b (*a*) above. *Tree of heaven* = AILANTO. *Tree of Jesse*: see JESSE. *Tree of knowledge*, (*a*) loosely used as = next; (*b*) a figurative or symbolic expression for knowledge in general, comprising all its 'branches'. *Tree of the knowledge of good and evil*: see Gen. ii. 9, etc. *Tree of liberty*, a tree (or a pole) planted in celebration of a revolution or victory securing liberty (chiefly in reference to the French Revolution); also *fig.* *Tree of life*, (*a*) a tree symbolic of life or immortality, esp. that in the narrative of the garden of Eden (Gen. ii. 9, etc.); also *fig.*; (*b*) a shrub of the genus *Thuya*; = ARBOR VITÆ 1; (*c*) *Anat.* = ARBOR VITÆ 2. *Tree of mercy*, in mediæval legend, the allegorical tree which yielded the oil of mercy, and was at length to bear Christ for the healing of mankind. *Tree of Paradise*, the plantain (*Musa paradisiaca*). *Tree of Porphyry* (*Logic*): = PORPHYRIAN *tree.* *Tree of the universe*, the mythical ash-tree or *Yggdrasil* of Scandinavian mythology. *Tree of wisdom* = *tree of Buddha.*

*c* **1820** *Philos. Recreat.* 131 A curious Chemical Experiment, called the Tree of *Diana. *Note*, This is the modern silver tree. **1849** [see DIANA 2]. **1845** Tree of *heaven [see AILANTO]. **1898** *Daily News* 31 May 5/3 Some handsome specimens of tropical trees—the tree of heaven and the tulip tree. **1535** COVERDALE *Gen.* ii. 9 The tre of life in the myddest of the garden, and the tre of *knowlege of good and euell. **1848** LOWELL *Fable for Critics* 766 Their backs he salutes With the whole tree of knowledge torn up by the roots. **1765** *Universal Mag.* XXXVII. 376/2 (*Amer.*) Known by the name of the Tree of *Liberty ever since the memorable 14th of August. **1837** CARLYLE *Fr. Rev.* II. I. xii, A Tree of Liberty sixty feet high; and Phrygian Cap on it, of size enormous. **1890** LECKY *Hist. Eng.* xxvii. VII. 207 Trees of liberty had been planted in Antrim, and bonfires lit in consequence of French victories. **1382** WYCLIF *Gen.* ii. 9 The tree of *lijf in the mydle of paradys. **1599** DAVIES *Immort. Soul* XXXI. vii. (1714) 109 But Truth, which is eternal, feeds the Mind; The Tree of Life, which will not let her die. **1712** J. PETIVER in *Phil. Trans.* XXVII. 423 American Tree of Life. **1760** J. LEE *Introd. Bot.* App. 317 Tree of Life, *Thuya.* **1913** R. C. MACLAGAN *Our Ancestors* viii. 121 There was another locality for the Tree of Life. *c* **1375** *Canticum de Creatione* 620 in Horstmann *Altengl. Leg.* (1878) 132 And to þe tre of *mercy blyf Where out renneþ oyle of lyf His angel wil doun sende. *Ibid.* 695 To haue mercy on Adam,..And hem senden his angel fro hy To ȝeuen hem of þe tre of mercy Oyle, to helen him wyth. **1567** MAPLET *Gr. Forest* 63 The tree of *Paradise saith Cardane, is of short life, for the second yeare his bodie drieth vp and waxeth barraine: It beareth fruit like a cluster of Grapes, but in bignesse of an Apple. **1910** *Encycl. Brit.* IV. 739/1 The sacred Bo tree or tree of *wisdom.

**8.** *attrib.* or as *adj.* (in sense 2). Made or formed of 'tree', wooden: = TREEN *a.* 1. *Obs.* exc. *dial.*

*c* **1375** *Cursor M.* 12389 (Fairf.) Tree [*v.rr.* treen, trein] beddis coude he make. *Ibid.* 21048 Of tree wandis golde he wroȝt. **1402–3** *Durham Acc. Rolls* (Surtees) 217, j stane-trogh et j tre trogh. **1480** CAXTON *Chron. Eng.* IV. (1520) 37/1 In olde tyme the consecracyon..was made in tree vessell. **1587–8** *Burgh Rec. Edinb.* (1882) IV. 515 To caus mak ane pair of trey buits. **1599** *Lanc. Wills* (Chetham Soc.) III. 10 All other tree vessell whatsoever. **1640** R. BAILLIE *Canterb. Self-Convict.* 77 Their very tree-shoone. **1750** in *Cloud of Witnesses* (1778) App. 361 A cripple with a tree leg. **1881** *Leicester Gloss.* s. v., A 'tree leg' is a wooden leg.

**9.** *attrib.* and *Comb.* **a.** General attrib. (= 'of a tree or trees'), as *tree-avenue*, *-bark*, *-belt*, *-bole*, *-bough*, *-branch*, *-foliage*, *-foot*, *-fruit*, *-group*, *-life*, *-lore*, *-nursery*, *-root*, *-seed*, *-shadow*, *-soul*, *-stem*, *-stump*, *-trunk*, *-twig*, etc. **b.** Objective and obj. gen., as *tree-enchanter*, *-fancier*, *-feller*, *-lopper*, *-planter*; *tree-boring*, *-chopping*, *-climbing*, *-daubing*, *-felling*, *-growing*, *-haunting*, *-inhabiting*, *-lopping*, *-loving*, *-planting*, *-smearing* sbs. and adjs. **c.** Instrumental, as *tree-bordered*, *-clad*, *-covered*, *-crowned*, *-dotted*, *-fringed*, *-garnished*, *-girt*, *-lined*, *-planted*, *-set*, *-shaded*, *-skirted*, etc. adjs. **d.** Locative, as *tree-dweller*; *tree-dwelling*, *-feeding*, *-living*. **e.** Similative, etc., as *tree-great*, *-like* adjs.

**1910** HADDON *Races of Man* 74 Men still wear the *tree-bark loincloth and the women a tree-bark wrapper. **1836–48** B. D. WALSH *Aristoph.*, *Clouds* I. iv, Fly to the tops of the *tree-clad mountains! **1894** *Pop. Sci. Monthly* June 69 Such is the name of the *tree-dweller. **1908** SIR H. JOHNSTON *Grenfell & Congo* II. xxi. 507 These *tree-dwelling Pygmies. **1865** KINGSLEY *Herew.* xxx, Swaffham, Quy, and Waterbeach, and the rest of the *tree-embowered hamlets which fringed the fen. **1788** COWPER *Mrs. Throckmorton's Bullfinch* xi, The *tree-enchanter Orpheus. **1853** *Zoologist* II. 4035 Instances of *tree-feeding species. **1849** J. FORBES *Physic. Holiday* i, They..indulge in farming, gardening, *tree-felling. **1855** KINGSLEY *Heroes* III. (1868) 32 Round the *tree-foot was coiled the dragon. **1704** J. PITTS *Acc. Mohammetans* 66 They have but little *Tree-Fruit. **1601** WEEVER *Mirr. Mart.* E vij, *Tree-garnisht Cambriaes loftie mountaines. **1812** W. TENNANT *Anster F.* II. xxxiv, All the *tree-girt country-seats. **1904** SPENCER & GILLEN *North. Tribes Central Australia* xvii. 527 A visit to the *tree grave. **1600** FAIRFAX *Tasso* XI. xxxvii, With dreadfull hornes of iron tought *tree-great. **1871** DARWIN *Desc. Man* II. xvi. (1890) 489 *Tree-haunting birds. **1898** *Saga-Bk. Viking Club* Jan. 122 The *tree-life of Western Greenland. **1630** *R. Johnson's Kingd. & Commw.* 7 The hollow truncks of most *tree-like canes being full of water. **1776** WITHERING *Brit. Plants* (1796) II. 316 Stem tree-like. **1844** MRS. BROWNING *Lost Bower* iii, A little wood..As it climbeth .. Sideway from the *tree-locked valley. **1589** FLEMING *Virg. Bucol. & Georg.* 3 The *treelopper..Shall chaunt and sing. **1885–94** R. BRIDGES *Eros & Psyche*, *Aug.* xiv, The great hill-haunting and *tree-loving Pan. **1905** A. R. WALLACE *Life* II. 153 The gardens, the greenhouses, the *tree-nursery. **1864** H. WOODWARD in *Intell. Observer* V. 181 Piece of a Vase ornamented with a *tree pattern. **1825** COBBETT *Rur. Rides* (1885) II. 227 Experienced *tree-planters. *c* **1440** *Alphabet of Tales* 488 He sett hym down at a *tre-rute in þe son to comfurth hym. **1870** MORRIS *Earthly Par.* III. IV. 385 Like to a *tree-set garden. **1854** H. MILLER *Sch. & Schm.* xxiii. (1858) 499 A *tree-skirted glade. **1871** KINGSLEY *At Last* xi, We were aware, between the *tree-stems, of a green misty gulf. **1857** T. MOORE *Handbk. Brit. Ferns* (ed. 3) 56 A decaying mossy *tree-stump. **1894** H. NISBET *Bush Girl's Rom.* 200 There..sat the chief ..with his back against a *tree-trunk. **1914** MUNRO *Prehist. Britain* viii. 185 Only two or three..tree-trunk coffins have been found in Britain.

**10.** Special Combs. **a.** in names of plants, usually denoting species or varieties that grow to the stature or in the form of a tree, sometimes those that grow on trees; as *tree amaranthus*, *cabbage*, *carnation*, CELANDINE, *crane's-bill*, *fuchsia*, HOUSELEEK, MALLOW, *melon*, MIGNONETTE, ONION, *pea*, PEONY, POPPY, PRIMROSE, *rhododendron*, TOMATO, VIOLET, WILLOW, WORMWOOD; **tree aloe**, *Aloë dichotoma*; **tree azalea**, *Azalea* (*Rhododendron*) *arborescens*; **tree-beard**, (*a*) *Tillandsia usneoides*; (*b*) the lichen *Usnea barbata*; **tree cactus**, a tall-growing cactus, as the saguaro; **tree clover**, *Melilotus alba*; **tree cotton**, *Gossypium arboreum*; **tree cranberry** = CRANBERRY-*tree*; **tree germander**, *Teucrium fruticans* (Miller *Plant-n.*); **tree golden-rod** = GOLDEN-ROD *tree*; **tree-hair**: see quots.; **tree heath**, *Erica arborea*; **tree lily**, (*a*) a plant of the genus *Vellozia* (N.O. *Amaryllidaceæ*), comprising arborescent species found in Brazil and S. Africa, with lily-like flowers; (*b*) a name for the genus *Dracæna* (N.O. *Liliaceæ*); **tree lotus**, the nettle-tree, *Celtis australis*; = LOTE-TREE a; **tree lungwort**, (*a*) a lichen, *Sticta pulmonaria*, = LUNGWORT 5; (*b*) a boraginaceous plant, *Mertensia virginica* (cf. LUNGWORT 3 b); **tree lupine**, *Lupinus arboreus* of California; **tree medick**: see quot.; **tree nettle** = NETTLE-TREE 2; **tree onion**: see ONION 2; **tree orchid**, **orchis**, an orchid growing on trees, as those of the genus *Epidendrum*; **tree poke**, *Phytolacca dioica*; **tree purslane** = PURSLANE-*tree* (*b*); **tree sorrel**, *Rumex Lunaria*; **tree-tobacco**: see quot. (See also TREE-CREEPER 2, -FERN, -MOSS, -TREFOIL.)

**1786** ABERCROMBIE *Gard. Assist.* 115 India pink, mignonette,..*tree-amaranthus. **1884** MILLER *Plant-n.*, *Azalea arborescens*, Smooth Azalea, *Tree Azalea. **1861** BENTLEY *Man. Bot.* 675 *Tillandsia usneoides* is commonly called *Tree-beard or Old Man's Beard, from the..mass of dark coloured fibres, which hang from the trees in South America. **1829** *Glover's Hist. Derby* I. 199 The ten-thousand-headed cabbage, or *tree cabbage. **1884** *De Candolle's Orig. Cultiv. Plants* 406 Upper Egypt,..where we know the *tree-cotton to be wild. **1868** B. J. LOSSING *Hudson* 35 Here and there among the rocks..the *tree-cranberry appeared. **1712** J. PETIVER in *Phil. Trans.* XXVII. 420 Hermans round-leaved Cape *Tree Cranes-bill. **1597** GERARDE *Herbal* II. cciii. 532 Of *Tree Germander. **1866** *Treas. Bot.* 1161 **Tree-hair*, a name sometimes given to the dark wiry pendulous entangled masses of a lichen, *Cornicularia jubata*,..not uncommon on trees in sub-alpine woods. *Ibid.* 1197 The species [of *Usnea*]..are often called Tree Moss or Tree Hair. **1777** HUNTER in *Phil. Trans.* LXVIII. 40 The *erica ar-*

*borea* or *Tree-heath, a native of Spain and Portugal. **1907** *Gentl. Mag.* July 98/2 The big tree-heaths begin about 9500 ft. **1891** *Cent. Dict.* s. v. *Vellozia*, *Tree-lily. **1597** GERARDE *Herbal* III. clix. 1377 *Lichen arborum*, *Tree Lungwoort. **1882** *Garden* 3 June 381/1 The *Tree Lupine.. bears a profusion of yellow flowers. **1884** MILLER *Plant-n.*, *Medicago arborea*, Moon-Trefoil, *Tree-Medick. **1905** *Daily Graphic* 16 Jan. 4/4 The mummy-apple, a delicate *tree-melon. **1884** *Leisure Hour* Feb. 84/1 The *tree-pea, a shrub bearing pods very similar to those familiar to us all. **1842** J. AITON *Domest. Econ.* (1857) 287 The laburnums,.. the dwarf almond on the verge of the walks, and the *tree-peony. **1882** *Garden* 22 July 73/3 The *tree Purslane..is a loose, rambling plant. **1848** tr. *Hoffmeister's Trav. Ceylon*, etc., iv. 181 A forest of magnificent *Tree-Rhododendrons. **1753** CHAMBERS *Cycl. Supp.* s.v. *Sorrel*, The roundish-leaved *tree-sorrel. **1895** *Daily News* 28 Aug. 5/4 A very undesirable weed from the Argentine is spreading in the Canary Islands. This is the *Tree-tobacco... It is a troublesome pest in New South Wales and Victoria, where it is regarded as poisonous to cattle and horses.

**b.** in names of animals living in or on or frequenting trees, as *tree-ant*, *-bee*, *-beetle*, *-boa*, *-chafer*, -CUCKOO, *-falcon*, -KANGAROO, *-leech*, *-linnet* (Sc. *-lintie*), *-monkey*, -PARTRIDGE, -PIPIT, -SHRIKE, *-slug*, -SQUIRREL, -SWALLOW, -SWIFT, -WASP; **tree-asp**, a venomous serpent of the genus *Dendraspis*; **tree-bear** (*U.S. local*), a name for the racoon; **tree-bug**, any one of various hemipterous insects which feed upon the juices of trees and shrubs; **tree-butterfly**, a butterfly that lives among trees, as those of the S. African genus *Charaxes*; **tree-cat**, (*a*) a viverrine animal of the genus *Paradoxurus*, a palm-cat; (*b*) = *tree-fox*; **tree-crab**, a species of land-crab, *Birgus latro*, also called *palm-crab* (see PALM *sb.*[1] 7); **tree-cricket**, a cricket of the genus *Œcanthus*; **tree-crow**, (*a*) any one of various Oriental birds intermediate between crows and jays, as the genera *Crypsirhina*, *Dendrocitta*, etc.; (*b*) *wattled tree-crow*, a crow of the sub-family *Glaucopinæ*, a wattle-crow; **tree-dove**, any one of numerous arboreal species of pigeon of India, Australia, etc., belonging or allied to the genus *Macropygia*; **tree-duck**, a duck of the genus *Dendrocygna* or an allied genus; **tree-finch** = TREE SPARROW a; **tree-fish**: see quot.; **tree-fly**, a fly of the family *Xylophagidæ*; **tree-fox**: see quot.; **tree-hoopoe**, a bird of the genus *Irrisor*, a wood-hoopoe; **tree-hopper**, any one of various homopterous insects which live on trees; sometimes *spec.* the cicada; **tree-lark** = *tree-pipit*; **tree-lizard**, a lizard of the group *Dendrosaura*; **tree-lobster** = *tree-crab*; **tree-louse**, an aphis, a plant-louse; **tree-martin**, (*a*) an Australian bird, *Petrochelidon nigricans* (Morris *Austral Eng.*); (*b*) a S. American bird, *Progne tapera*; **tree-mouse**, (*a*) any species of mouse of arboreal habits; (*b*) see quot. 1897; **tree-oyster**, an oyster found upon the roots of the mangrove; **tree-pie**, a tree-crow of the genus *Dendrocitta*, found in India, China, and neighbouring countries; **tree-pigeon**, any one of various arboreal pigeons inhabiting Asia, Africa, and Australia; **tree-porcupine**, any porcupine of the subfamily *Sphingurinæ*, inhabiting America and the West Indies, living in trees, and having prehensile tails; **tree-rat**, an arboreal rodent, as those of the West Indian genera *Capromys* and *Plagiodon*; **tree-serpent**, **tree-snake**, any snake of arboreal habits, as those of the families *Dendrophidæ* and *Dipsadidæ* (both non-venomous); **tree-shrew**, an insectivorous animal of the genus *Tupaia*, a squirrel-shrew; **tree-tiger**, a name for the leopard (*Cent. Dict.*); **tree-warbler**, a bird of the genus *Hypolais* (sometimes reckoned as a subgenus of *Sylvia*). (See also TREE-CREEPER I, -FROG, -GOOSE, -SPARROW, -TOAD, -WORM.)

**1899** F. V. KIRBY *Sport E. C. Africa* xv. 163 A colony of those terrible insects, the red *tree-ants. **1891** *Cent. Dict.*, *Tree-bear. **1902** *Westm. Gaz.* 31 May 2/1 Joe produced from the recesses of his loose blouse a baby tree-bear and a handful of gum leaves. **1693** *Phil. Trans.* XVII. 612 He admires the..Contrivance of the Honeycomb, and particularly the *Tree-Bee. **1747** BAKER *ibid.* XLIV. 578 The *Tree-Beetle, or blind Beetle, vulgarly in Norfolk called the Dor. **1842** LOUDON *Suburban Hort.* 108 Besides the above-mentioned Ichneumonidæ, ants, field or *tree bugs, and many sorts of spiders, contribute..to the extirpation of various insects. **1869** R. TRIMEN in *The Cape & its People* (ed. R. Noble) 99 One of these *tree-butterflies, massive of thorax and broad and rigid of wing. **1885** HORNADAY 2 *Yrs. in Jungle* vii. 70 It proved to be a *tree-cat (*Paradoxurus musanga*). **1894** LYDEKKER *Royal Nat. Hist.* I. 457 The palm-civets, tree-cats, or toddy-cats, as they are indifferently called. **1704** PETIVER *Gazophyl.* II. xix, The great Brown-*Tree-Chaffer. **1816** KIRBY & SP. *Entomol.* xxiii. (1818) II. 321 The less savage but equally destructive tree-chafers (*Melolonthæ*). **1859** RIPLEY & DANA *Amer. Cycl.* VI. 63/1 They form the genus *œcanthus*, and are called *tree or climbing crickets. **1879** E. P. WRIGHT *Anim. Life* 246 Of the *Tree Crows we can only mention—The Benteot (*Crypsirhina varia*) of Java. **1872** COUES *N. Amer. Birds* 45 The crural feathers are..sometimes long and flowing, as in..our *tree-cuckoos. **1824** STEPHENS in Shaw *Gen. Zool.* XII. II. 98 *Tree Duck..inhabits the West India islands and the adjacent continent...It is said to make a whistling.. noise, and to build its nest in trees. **1668** CHARLETON *Onomast.* 66 *Falco Arborarius*,..the *tree-Falcon. **1783** LATHAM *Synopsis Birds* III. 252 *Tree Finch..is observed always to build on trees, and not in buildings like the House Sparrow. **1888** GOODE *Amer. Fishes* 263 *Sebastichthys serriceps*,..known as the '*Tree-fish', an appellation originating with the Portuguese..and without obvious application. **1904** P. FOUNTAIN *Gt. North-West* x. 104 The *tree-fox, or tree-cat, of the trappers..is *Mustela pennanti*, often called the fish-marten. **1873** *Cassell's Bk. Birds* III. 15 The *Tree Hoopoes (*Irrisor*) inhabit the forests of Africa... [They] pass their lives exclusively upon trees. **1836–9** *Todd's Cycl. Anat.* II. 868/2 The..*tree-hoppers..approach to the *Terebrantia*. **1850** GOSSE *Rivers of Bible* (1878) 286 Probably tree-hoppers, *cicadæ*, are meant. **1900** POLLOK & THOM *Sports Burma* II. 40 The *tree-leeches, so plentiful in forests..in Lower Burma, are a sad drawback to the pleasures of sport. **1844** *Zoologist* II. 508 Chaffinch, '*Tree-lintie'. **1797** *Monthly Mag.* III. 454/2 Bonnet..applied himself..to collecting..his experiments and observations concerning the *tree-louse and the worm. **1893** *Outing* (U. S.) XXII. 109/2 Swarms of *tree-monkeys congregate in chattering throngs. **1897** BLANCHAN *Bird Neighbors* 84 White-breasted Nuthatch (*Sitta carolinensis*)...Called also *Tree-mouse. **1904** *Q. Rev.* Oct. 472 The tree-mice and the veldt-rats. **1767** ELLIS in *Phil. Trans.* LVII. 432 The *Tree Oyster, and the Slipper Barnicle. **1901** *Daily Chron.* 28 Sept. 5/2 Proposal for increasing and improving the cultivation of tree-oysters. **1895** LYDEKKER *Royal Nat. Hist.* IV. 413 The common *tree-partridge (*A*[*rboricola*] *torqueolus*) ranging to an elevation of fourteen thousand feet. **1871** KINGSLEY *At Last* v, The *Tree Porcupine, or Coendou,.. climbs trees after leaves, and swings about like the monkeys. **1885** HORNADAY 2 *Yrs. in Jungle* xv. 171 Two *tree-rats (*Mus rufescens*) used to come into my hut from the jungle. **1731** MEDLEY *Kolben's Cape G. Hope* II. 163 The *Tree-Serpent is so call'd on account of her being seen mostly in trees. **1893** LYDEKKER *Royal Nat. Hist.* I. 312 With the *tree-shrews, or tupaias, we come to the first family of the true Insectivores. **1866–8** OWEN *Vertebr. Anim.* (L.), Some nocturnal *tree-snakes have a prolonged snout. **1881** SEEBOHM *Brit. Mus. Catal. Birds* V. 78 The Icterine *Tree-Warbler breeds in Central and Northern Europe, from the Atlantic to the Ural Mountains, extending northwards as far as the Arctic circle.

**c.** Other Special Combs.: **tree-agate**, a variety of agate with dendritic or tree-like markings (cf. MOSS-*agate*); **tree-bridge**, † (*a*) a wooden bridge (*obs.*); (*b*) a bridge formed by a fallen tree; **tree-burial**, the custom, among some tribes, of disposing of dead bodies by placing them in hollow trunks, or among the branches, of trees; **tree-calf** (*Bookbinding*): see quots.; **tree-claim** (*U.S.*), a 'claim' or piece of land allotted with the proviso that it shall become the property of the occupier after a fixed term on condition of his planting a certain proportion of it with trees; **tree-climber**, a person or animal that climbs a tree or trees; *spec.* (*a*) = TREE-CREEPER I; (*b*) a fish, the ANABAS or climbing perch; **tree-clipper** (*local*), the common tree-creeper (*Certhia familiaris*); **tree-coffin**, a prehistoric coffin made of a hollow tree-trunk; †**tree-cop** (*obs.*) = TREE-TOP; **tree-coupling**, in a vehicle, a piece connecting a 'single-tree' or swingletree and a double-tree; †**tree-crop** (*obs.*) = TREE-TOP; **tree-cult**, **-cultus** = *tree-worship*; **tree-deity** = *tree-god*; **tree-digger**: see quot.; **tree-drum**, a drum made from the trunk of a tree; **tree-god**, a divinity supposed to inhabit a tree, or a tree that is an object of worship; so **tree-goddess**; †**tree-honey** (*obs.*), a sweet juice or gum exuding from certain trees; **tree-house**, a house built in a tree (as by the natives of New Guinea) for security against enemies; **tree-iron**: see quot.; †**tree-jobber** (*obs.*) [JOBBER I], a woodpecker; **tree-legged** *a.* (*obs.* or *dial.*), wooden-legged; **tree-lifter**: see quot.; **tree-line**, the line or level on a mountain above which no trees grow (cf. *snow-line*); **tree-maker**, a maker of saddle-trees; **tree-man**, one of a race of men living in trees; **tree-marble**, **-marbling** (*Bookbinding*), marbling or staining in a tree-like branching pattern (cf. *tree-calf*); **tree-marking**, a tree-like or branched marking on the body of a person struck by lightning; **tree-milk**, a milky juice used for food, obtained from a tree or tree-like plant, as those called COW-TREE, or the COW-PLANT of Ceylon; **tree-nymph**, a nymph supposed to inhabit a tree; **tree-oil** = TUNG-*oil*; **tree-protector**, a contrivance for protecting the bark of a tree from injury by destructive insects, etc. (Knight *Dict. Mech.* 1877); **tree-pruner**, an implement for pruning trees; **tree-remover**, an apparatus for transplanting trees (Knight, 1877); **tree-rune**, one of a set of runes or alphabetic characters of branched or tree-like form; **tree-scraper**, an implement for scraping moss, dead bark, etc. from trees (Knight, 1877); **tree-spirit**, a spirit believed to inhabit a tree (cf. *tree-god*, *tree-nymph*); †**tree-stone**, a precious stone having tree-like markings (cf. *tree-agate*); †**tree-turned** *a.* (*obs.*), turned or changed into a tree; **tree-village**, a village consisting of *tree-houses*; **tree-wax**, any kind of wax produced from a tree, as Chinese wax, Japan wax; **tree-wool**, a woolly substance obtained from a tree, as pine-wool (PINE *sb.*[2] 7); †**tree-work** (*obs.*), work in wood, carpentry; so †**tree-worker**, a carpenter; **tree-worship**, worship rendered to trees or to the spirits supposed to inhabit them; so **tree-worshipper**, **tree-worshipping**.

**1596** DALRYMPLE tr. *Leslie's Hist. Scot.* v. (S.T.S.) I. 276 Thay..casting doune the *trie brig,..erected a fayre stane brig. **1839–52** BAILEY *Festus* xxvi. 446 To dare the broken tree-bridge across the stream. **1901** *Proc. Zool. Soc.* 2 Apr. 309 In the States of Patalung and Singgora..the Siamese practise a form of *tree-burial. **1879** *Cassell's Techn. Educ.* IV. 89 A third style of ornamentation is called *tree-calf. **1895** ZAEHNSDORF *Bookbinding* 28 Tree Calf.—Bright brown calf stained with acids in conventional imitation of the branches of a tree. **1890** L. C. D'OYLE *Notches* 44, I filed on the north-west quarter of 10 as a 'homestead', and the north-east quarter as a '*tree-claim'. **1879** JEFFERIES *Wild Life in S. Co.* 175 If you sit down on the elm butt..and watch quietly, before long the little *tree-climber will come. **1885** C. F. HOLDER *Marvels Anim. Life* 36 The tree-climber (*Anabas scandens*) one of which he had..captured. **1885** SWAINSON *Prov. Names Birds* 57 Tree Creeper.. *Tree clipper (Oxon). **1877** GREENWELL *Brit. Barrows* 32 *note*, Stowborough, Dorsetshire, where a body was discovered in 1767, in a *tree-coffin. *c* **1425** *St. Christina* x. in *Anglia* VIII. 123/21 She was constreyned to flee into *tree-coppys or touris, or in to þere summe hygh þinges. **1877** KNIGHT *Dict. Mech.*, **Tree-coupling*, a piece uniting a single to a double tree. **14..** *Childh. Jesus* 644 in Horstm. *Altengl. Leg.* (1878) 120 Alle þe chyldron..In to þe *tre-croppe hem toke. **1560** ROLLAND *Seven Sages* 66 The hird was sair feirit..That the tre crop he suld gar turne dounwart. **1905** CLODD *Animism* xiv. 74 In such customs and beliefs..are the materials of the manifold *tree-cults. **1871** TYLOR *Prim. Culture* xv. II. 202 The whole *tree-cultus of the world must by no means be thrown indiscriminately into the one category. **1911** *Encycl. Brit.* XXVII. 237/1 The powers of the *tree-deities. **1877** KNIGHT *Dict. Mech.*, **Tree-digger*, a kind of double plow employed in nurseries for cutting off the roots of trees which have been planted in rows. **1849** CUPPLES *Green Hand* xvii, I could make out the hollow booming of the African *tree-drum. **1905** W. E. GEIL *Yankee in Pigmy Land* v. 66 Their *tree-god, hideous and ridiculous. **1911** S. A. COOKE in *Encycl. Brit.* XXVII. 237/2 *note*, An African tree-god with priests and 'wives'. **1895** A. J. EVANS in *Folk-Lore* Mar. 21 A *Tree-Goddess akin to the Dryads of old. **1626** BACON *Sylva* § 848 It seemeth that there was, in old time, *Tree-Honey, as well as Bee-Honey. **1901** *Wide World Mag.* VI. 518/1 A New Guinea *tree-house. **1908** *Daily Chron.* 19 Mar. 6/6 A large store of ammunition in the shape of heavy stones is kept in the tree-houses, and is dropped with skill and discrimination upon the heads of..raiders. **1877** KNIGHT *Dict. Mech.*, **Tree-irons*, the irons connecting single to double trees, or the latter to the tongue of the vehicle. Also the hooks or clips by which the traces are attached. **1601** HOLLAND *Pliny* x. xxix, There be no wood-pecks or *tree-jobbers. **1832** BALLANTINE in *Whistlebinkie* (1890) I. 177 Ilk *tree-legged man, ilk club-taed laddie. **1844** G. GREENWOOD (*title*) The *Tree-lifter; or, a new method of transplanting Forest Trees. **1905** *Westm. Gaz.* 2 Sept. 2/3 Now we are high up, above the *tree-line. **1828** *Sporting Mag.* XXIII. 103 In making saddles..the trees of them are occasionally leaded by a *tree-maker. **1904** *Edin. Rev.* Apr. 348 The horrible little *tree-men discovered by Stanley. **1885** C. G. W. LOCK *Workshop Receipts* Ser. IV. 266/1 Marbling on leather is produced by small drops of colouring liquids, drawn..into veins, and spread into fantastic forms resembling foliage—hence often called '*tree-marble'. **1900** *Lancet* 27 Oct. 1199/2 There was numbness in both legs and *tree-marking on the left breast. **1831** KEIGHTLEY *Mythol. Gr. & It.* I. xvi. 206 The *Tree-nymphs (Hamadryades), who were born and died with the trees. **1901** *Trans. Yorksh. Dial. Soc.* May 82 An inscription in the cryptic characters, sometimes called '*tree-runes'. **1871** TYLOR *Prim. Cult.* I. xi. 430 The belief in *tree-spirits, and the practice of tree-worship. **1897** *Daily News* 1 May 8/1 Our Jack-in-the-Green was originally the human embodiment of the tree spirit. **1698** J. FRYER *Acc. E. India & P.* 215 *Tree-stones. Stones with the lively Representation or Form of a Tree thereon. **1605** SYLVESTER *Urania* lx, That sacred *Tree-turn'd Lady.. From whose pure locks your still-green Laurels grow. **1901** *Field* 27 Apr. 572/2 Another *tree village,..where I saw three houses erected on one tree. **1857** MILLER *Elem. Chem.* (1862) III. 267 The *tree wax of Japan consists of pure palmitin. **1870** ROCK *Text. Fabr.* i. (1876) 5 Embroidered with gold and *tree-wool. *c* **1205** LAY. 22899 Ich con of *treo-wrekes [= -werkes: *c* **1275** treo-workes] wunder feole craftes. **1382** WYCLIF *Isa.* xliv. 12 The crafti man *tree werkere. **1860** E. S. POOLE in *Smith's Dict. Bible* I. 95/2 (*Arabia*), The stone-worship, *tree-worship, &c., of various tribes. **1840** THORPE *Anc. Laws* II. 249 We forbid..*tree worshipings [*OE.* treowwurþunga].

**Tree**, *v.* [f. prec. sb.]

†**1.** *intr.* with *it*: To grow into a tree, attain the size of a tree. *Obs. rare*⁻¹.

**1650** FULLER *Pisgah* II. x. 210 Authors have affirmed that hyssope doth tree it in Judea.

**b.** *intr.* To take a tree-like or branching form, as a deposit from a solution under the influence of an electric current.

**1884** *Science* 17 Oct. 392/1 It will not prevent treeing.. which is one of the most serious defects of the Faure battery.

**2.** *trans.* To drive into or up a tree; to cause to take refuge in a tree, as a hunted animal, or a man pursued by a wild beast. (In quot. 1854 *refl.* = 3.) Also *fig.* to put into a difficulty or 'fix' (cf. *up a tree*, prec. 7).

*a* **1700** B. E. *Dict. Cant. Crew*, *Tree the Martern*, Dislodge him. **1834** [S. SMITH] *Lett. J. Downing* xxxii. (1835) 220 It wasn't long afore he tree'd a rakoon. **1854** THOREAU

*Walden* xii. (1863) 250 Some small squirrel which has treed itself for security. **1859** H. Kingsley *G. Hamlyn* v, It's no use,..you are treed, and you can't help yourself. If I give information you swing.

**b.** *Fox-hunting*: see quot.

**1781** P. Beckford *Hunting* (1803) 214 In some countries.. they have a method of treeing him. [*Note*] The intention of it is, to make the hounds more eager, and to let in the tail hounds. The fox is thrown across the branch of a tree, and the hounds are suffered to bay at him for some minutes before he is thrown amongst them.

**3.** *intr.* To climb up or perch upon a tree; *esp.* to take refuge in a tree from a hunter or pursuer.

*a* **1700** B. E. *Dict. Cant. Crew*, *A Martern Treeth*, Lodgeth. **1834** J. Hall *Kentucky* II. 191 The raccoon.. when the tree fell..was completely surrounded by his enemies, who took care to prevent him from again 'treeing'. **1866** *Reader* 3 Nov. 908 In America everything seems to 'tree' or perch—quail, grouse, snipes, and, lastly, foxes. **1902** P. Fountain *Mts. & Forests S. Amer.* v. 129 Then the hunter must tree for his life.

**4.** *trans.* To plant with trees. (Mostly in *pa. pple.*; cf. Treed 1.)

**1891** 'Annie Thomas' *That Affair* II. ix. 144 A secluded spot, well treed and shrubbed in.

**5.** Technical senses. **a.** To furnish with an (axle-)tree. **b.** To stretch or shape upon a tree, as a boot or saddle: see prec. 5 e, d. **c.** To fit (a spade, pick, etc.) with a wooden handle. **d.** To provide with supporting timbers or beams, as the roof of a coal-mine.

**1765** *Museum Rust.* IV. lix. 250 The edges of new wheels wear off much faster than the edges of old ones; and if treed a small matter wider, or narrower, the impediment is greatly encreased. **1856** *Chamb. Jrnl.* V. 26/2 A Wellington boot beautifully 'treed' and polished. **1864** Strauss *Eng. Workshops* 94 The holes for the nails and rivets are then punched out, and the tool [a shovel] is finally treed up. **1887** P. McNeill *Blawearie* 76 To warn the men to have their wall-faces all cleared up, and their roofs well treed.

Hence **Tree·ing** *vbl. sb.*

**1884** [see 1 b]. **1885** Newhall in *Harper's Mag.* Jan. 286/2 Wax finishes are so generally used for men's shoes that 'treeing' and 'dressing' with gum and blacking..are important. **1902** *Daily Chron.* 28 July 3/3 The American grouse differs essentially..from the British variety. All the different kinds frequently perch on trees; in fact..this habit of 'treeing' is characteristic of the breed.

**Treeangle**, obs. form of Triangle.

**Tree·-cree:per.**

**1.** A name for various birds which creep on the trunks and branches of trees; *esp.* the common European *Certhia familiaris*, or other species of the family *Certhiidæ*; also, a bird of the South American family *Dendrocolaptidæ*. Cf. Creeper 3.

**1814** *Sporting Mag.* XLIV. 184 A tree-creeper, one of our smallest birds. **1815** Kirby & Sp. *Entomol.* ix. (1818) I. 290 In America, the tree-creeper is furnished with a box at the end of a long pole to entice it to build in gardens, which it is..particularly useful in clearing from noxious insects. **1869** G. Rooper *Flood, Field & F.* (1874) 208 The pretty lady-like tree-creeper ran like a mouse up the tree. **1871** Darwin *Desc. Man* II. xvi. 206 An Australian tree-creeper (*Climacteris erythrops*).

**2.** A plant that creeps or climbs upon trees (cf. Creeper 4); *spec.* the African rubber-plant, *Landolphia florida*.

**1887** Moloney *Forestry W. Afr.* 94 The plant that produces it [india-rubber] is the giant tree-creeper (*Landolphia florida?*), covering the highest trees and growing principally on those near rivers or streams.

**Treed** (trīd), *ppl. a.* [f. Tree *sb.* or *v.* + -ed.]

**1.** Planted or covered with trees; wooded.

**1860** *All Year Round* No. 43. 403 Treed slopes high above the sea. **1909** *Blackw. Mag.* May 677/1 A little treed enclosure.

**2.** Driven to take refuge in a tree, as a hunted animal, or a man pursued by wild beasts.

**1891** *Tablet* 25 Apr. 660 Like a tree'd squirrel. **1894** *Times* 30 Mar. 14/1 He was alone and treed on a bitter cold night, with the lions..regularly patrolling the environs. **1902** *Outing* (U. S.) June 298/1 Old hunters throw the light of a torch upon a treed raccoon.

**3.** Decorated with a tree-like pattern: *treed calf* = *tree-calf* (Tree *sb.* 10 c).

**1892** J. H. Badley in *Pall Mall G.* 5 Oct. 2/1 A copy of ..'Self-made Men' in treed calf.

**Tree-fern.** A fern with an upright stem, growing to the size and form of a tree; as those of the genera *Cyathea* and *Alsophila*, found in tropical regions, and in Australia and New Zealand.

**1846** J. L. Stokes *Discov. Australia* I. viii. 251 The tree-fern..forms a canopy that perfectly excludes the piercing rays of even an Australian sun. **1871** Kingsley *At Last* xi, Calling a halt..to look at some fresh curiosity; now a tree-fern, now a climbing fern. **1886** A. Winchell *Walks Geol. Field* 150 Much of the coal-vegetation was of the nature of ferns,—some of them tree-ferns.

**Tree-frog.** Any frog of arboreal habits; often loosely used for *tree-toad*.

**1738** Mortimer in *Phil. Trans.* XL. 348, 71. *Rana viridis arborea*. The green Tree Frog. These Frogs are always found sticking to the under Sides of Leaves of Trees, and other Plants. **1802** Bingley *Anim. Biog.* (1813) II. 389 *Hylæ*, or *Tree-Frogs*,..are generally smaller than Frogs, and more elegant in all their proportions. **1849** Cupples *Green Hand* xv, At times the tree-frogs broke out in a loud clicking chirrup. **1860** Gosse *Rom. Nat. Hist.* 28 Then there come..sounds like the snoring of an oppressed sleeper,..or ..the groaning..of a ship's timbers in a heavy gale...These are produced by great tree-frogs.

**Treeful** (trī·ful), *sb. rare.* [f. Tree *sb.* + -ful 2.] A quantity or number that fills or crowds a tree (in quot. 1910, a Christmas tree).

**1837** *Blackw. Mag.* XLI. 418 All awoke..to the sound of a falling fountain, and a treeful of birds. **1910** *Daily News* 28 Dec. 6 A treeful of toys.

**Treeful** (trī·fŭl), *a. rare.* [f. Tree *sb.* + -ful 1.] Full of trees; abounding in trees.

**1855** Bailey *Mystic, Spir. Leg.* 83 Woods And treeful tracts. **1889** Hissey *Tour in Phaeton* 205 A level, green, and treeful country.

**Tree·-goose.** *Obs.* exc. *Hist.* A name for the barnacle-goose, formerly believed to be produced from a tree, in the form of the barnacle (cirriped): see Barnacle *sb.*[2] 1.

**1597** Gerarde *Herbal* III. clxvii. 1391 Foules whom we call Barnakles,..and in Lancashire tree Geese. **1622** Drayton *Poly-olb.* xxvii. 304 Those..trees..send from their stocky bough, A soft and sappy Gum, from which those Tree-geese grow, Call'd Barnacles by vs. **1655** H. More *Antid. Ath.* App. xiii. § 5 He also adds a story of another sort of Tree-geese which he gathered in their shells from an old rotten tree upon the shore of our English Coast. **1768** Pennant *Zool.* II. 452 These are the birds that..were believed to be generated out of wood, or rather a species of shell.. often found sticking to the bottoms of ships,..and were called Tree-geese. **1835** *Penny Cycl.* IV. 312/2.

**Treehood** (trī·hud). *rare.* [f. Tree *sb.*, after *manhood*, etc.] The state of a (full-grown) tree.

**1847** H. Miller *First Impr.* ix. 154 The saplings..have expanded into the dignity of full-grown treehood. *Ibid.* xvi. 292 Solid mid-aged treehood.

**Treeify** (trī·ifəi), *v. nonce-wd.* [f. as prec. + -(i)fy.] *trans.* To make or change into a tree.

**1848** Lowell *Fable for Critics* 31 Daphne—before she was happily treeified.

**Treeiness** (trī·inès). *rare.* [f. Treey + -ness.] The state or quality of being 'treey'.

**1904** *Academy* 27 Feb. 228/2 The suggestion of the leafage would give a sense of roundness and what one may call 'tree-iness'.

**Treeless** (trī·lès), *a.* [f. Tree *sb.* + -less.] Destitute of trees; containing no trees.

**1814** Wordsw. *Excurs.* II. 337 A quiet treeless nook. **1841** *Civil Eng. & Arch. Jrnl.* IV. 266/2 Another hundred years may see the United States a treeless country. **1873** J. Geikie *Gt. Ice Age* xxiv. 322 A bare and treeless state must have preceded the age of forests.

Hence **Tree·lessness.**

**1869** Lady Barker *Station Life N. Zealand* iv. (1874) 25 The utter treelessness of the vast Canterbury Plains. **1884** *Macm. Mag.* Nov. 18/2 A diminished rainfall warned the planters that treelessness means rainlessness.

**Treelet** (trī·lėt). *rare.* [f. as prec. + -let.] A little tree; a young tree, a sapling.

**1874** W. Cory *Lett. & Jrnls.* (1897) 372 A dozen dead treelets.

So **Tree·ling** [-ling [1]].

**1847** *Man in Moon* Feb. 103 These same treelings have an odd notion of coming out strong the first fine day in spring. **1883** O. W. Holmes in *53rd Cincinnati School Rep.* 99, I should delight in sending you a treeling.

**Tree·-moss** **a.** Any moss or moss-like plant that grows on trees; applied esp. to certain lichens. **b.** A moss-like plant of branched form like a miniature tree, as club-moss (*Lycopodium*).

**1611** Florio, *Musco*,..greene tree mosse. **1681** Grew *Musæum* II. II. 235 The Creeping Tree Mosse of America. **1766** J. Bartram *Jrnl.* 27 Jan., in Stork *Acc. E. Florida* 54 We encamped..on a bed of long tree-moss, to preserve us from the..damp ground. **1866** *Treas. Bot.* 1197 The species [of *Usnea*]..are often called Tree Moss or Tree Hair. **1884** Miller *Plant-n.*, Tree, or Beard, Moss, a name applied to various Lichens of the genera *Usnea*, *Ramalina*, *Cornicularia*, &c.; also to *Lycopodium Selago*. **1897–8** Britton & Brown *Amer. Flora* Index, *Tree Moss* [= The Fir Club-moss, *Lycopodium Selago*; The Cypress Spurge, *Euphorbia Cyparissias*].

**Treen** (trī·ĕn, trīn), *a. Obs.* exc. *dial.* Forms: 1 treowen, triwen, trywen, 4–6 trene, treyn, 4–7 trein, treene, 5 tren, trenne, 6 treine, treyne, (treing, tryen, 7 tryne), 4– treen. [OE. *trēowen*, etc., f. *trēow*, Tree + -en [4]: cf. Goth. *triweins* wooden.]

**1.** Made of 'tree' (Tree *sb.* 2); wooden.

*c* **1000** *Sax. Leechd.* II. 180 ȝetrifula on treowenum mortere. *c* **1000** Ælfric *Voc.* in Wr.-Wülcker 125 *Coturnus*, triwen sceo. *a* **1300** *Cursor M.* 12389 (Cott.) For plogh and haru.. Treen beddes for to make. **1375** Barbour *Bruce* x. 361 Of hempyn rapis ledderis ma, With treyn steppis bundin. **1422** tr. *Secreta Secret.*, *Priv. Priv.* 177 Ettynge of a tren dysshe. **1533** Bellenden *Livy* v. xviii. (S.T.S.) II. 210 Þe way þat ledis fra þe trene brig oure tiber. **1563–83** Foxe *A. & M.* 259/2 Some go on treen shoes or Pattins, some bare-footed. **1749** *Ann. of Banff* (New Spald. Cl.) I. 129 By 2 dales [= deals] for mending Treen-mare [Mare [1] 2 b] for the soldiers, £1. 14*s*. **1888** *Athenæum* 14 July 68 A treen paten of ancient date.

†**2.** Of or belonging to a tree or trees; in quot. 1670, obtained or made from trees. *Obs. rare.*

**1340–70** *Alex. & Dind.* 351 Wiþ trene bowus [L. *frondibus arborum*] we ben on þe body keuered. **1387** Trevisa *Higden* (Rolls) VIII. 237 A book also greet as a psawter, wiþ trene leves, i-wrete in Grew, Hebrew, and Latyn. **1545** *Records of Elgin* (New Spald. Cl.) I. 85 The trein corce [cross] anent the Gray freris vynd. **1590** Spenser *F. Q.* I. ii. 39 So left her, where she now is turnd to treen mould. **1670** Evelyn *Sylva* xvi. § 7. (ed. 2) 75 That a large Tract of the World almost altogether subsist on these Treen Liquors; Especially, that of the Date.

**Treen, treene**, obs. or dial. pl. of Tree.

**Treenail, trenail** (trī·nēl, tre·n'l), *sb.* Forms: 3–5 trenayl(e, 6 treenale, 7 trey naile, treenaile, tre-naile, tree-nell, 8 treenel, trenel, 7– treenail, trenail; *β.* 7–9 trennel, trunnel, (7–8 trunel, 8 trundle), 9 trennail. [f. Tree *sb.* + Nail *sb.*

Some confusion seems to have existed between this word and Trundle (small wheel or roller); cf. the *trun-* forms, and *trundles* in sense 'cylindrical pins or staves forming teeth of lantern-wheel'.]

A cylindrical pin of hard wood used in fastening timbers together, esp. in shipbuilding and other work where the materials are exposed to the action of water.

**1295** *Exch. Accts.* Bundle 5. No. 21 (P.R.O.) [Accts. of building a galley at Lyme.] In loco ij. operariorum per ij. septimanas qui perforaverunt Galeam et imposuerunt trenayl..iiij. sol. In iij. miliariis de trenayl emptis vj. sol. et. ix. den. **1495** *Naval Acc. Hen. VII* (1896) 164 C di Tre nayles xij[d]. [**1561–3** in Rogers *Agric. & Prices* (1882) III. 414/2–4 Tree nails, 6 *m.* 30 inch @ *c* 2/6..15 *m* 16 inch @ *c* 1/4..6 *c* 24 inch @ 2/-.] **1571** *Wills & Inv. N. C.* (Surtees) I. 361, iij houndrethe treenales viij[d]. **1627** Capt. Smith *Seaman's Gram.* ii. 4 The other parts of those plankes are made fast with good Tree-nailes and Trunnions of well seasoned timber. **1691** T. H[ale] *Acc. New Invent.* 118 Trenails. **1861** Smiles *Engineers* II. 39 *note*, Holes being bored through every piece of stone, one course was further bound to another by oak trenails. **1862** M. Hopkins *Hawaii* 98 The English seamen seizing some wooden treenails, struck the natives with them. **1864** *Daily Tel.* 30 July, The line was opened in 1854, and the chairs were then secured to the sleepers by Ransome's trenails.

*β.* *c* **1635** Capt. N. Boteler *Dial. Sea Services* (1685), Trennels. **1691** T. H[ale] *Acc. New Invent.* 22 The fastening of our Plank we perform with wooden Trunnels. **1711** W. Sutherland *Shipbuild. Assist.* 39 The Plank..fasten'd to the Timbers..with Trennels or Pins of Wood. **1769** *Nat. Hist.* in *Ann. Reg.* 100 *note*, Great square logs of pine, laid one upon another, and pinned together with oak trunels. **1776** G. Semple *Building in Water* 95 These Belts are to be ..pinned with Oak Trundles of about ½ Inch Diameter. **1828** Cunningham *N. S. Wales* 67 Cargoes consisting of wool, skins, ..trennails, and hides.

**b.** *attrib.*

**1497** *Naval Acc. Hen. VII* (1896) 313, ij lode of Trenayle wode. **1863** P. Barry *Dockyard Econ.* 110 Seventeenth in order stand the trenail-houses. For the year the expenditure in these houses was £4,411 11*s*. 10½*d*. **1867** Smyth *Sailor's Word-bk.*, *Tree-nail wedge*, a cross is cut in the tree-nail end, and wedges driven in, caulked.

Hence **Tree·nail** *v.*, *trans.* to fasten or secure (timbers) with treenails. (Chiefly in *pa. pple.*)

**1627** Capt. Smith *Seaman's Gram.* ii. 14 All the plankes to be treenailed to the beames. **1633** T. James *Voy.* 76 She was ready to be boulted and trenneld. **1793** Smeaton *Edystone L.* § 38 The balks, in all their intersections with each other, trenailed together. **1834** *Gentl. Mag.* CIV. I. 94/2 The timber head of a vessel,..built chiefly of oak timber, with some elm and fir, clinker built, and trunnelled.

**Treescape** (trī·skēɪp). *rare.* [f. Tree *sb.*, after *landscape*: see Scape *sb.*[3]] A landscape or scene consisting of or abounding in trees; a painting or drawing of such.

**1885** 'G. Stables' *Cruise 'Wanderer'* xi. (1886) 105 The treescapes, the wood and water peeps, are fine just before you reach Darlington. **1896** *J. Bamber & Co.'s Catal.* May 30/1 Treescape, Etching by F. E. Weirotter, with stream and figures.

**Treeship** (trī·ʃip). *rare.* [f. as prec. + -ship.] The condition of being a tree; existence as a tree.

**1791** Cowper *Yardley Oak* 61 Through all the stages..Of treeship—first a seedling,..Then twig; then sapling [etc.]. **1849** H. Miller *Footpr. Creat.* xiv. (1874) 246.

**Tree· spa:rrow.** Name for two distinct birds. **a.** *Passer montanus*, a species of sparrow, widely distributed in Europe and Asia, and found locally in Britain. **b.** *Spizella monticola*, a bird (not of the sparrow family) common in N. America.

**1770** Pennant *Zool.* IV. 17 Tree Sparrow. Mountain Sparrow. Common near Lincoln,..conversant among trees, but does not frequent houses. **1831** A. Wilson *Amer. Ornithol.* II. 252 *Fringilla Arborea*. Tree sparrow. The tree sparrow is six inches and a half long, and nine and a half in extent. **1889** *Science-Gossip* (U.S.) XXV. 145 As I neared a clump of cedars..a host of tree sparrows fluttered about me...These lively birds come to us from Canada in October and stay until April. **1897** *Times* 5 Jan. 5/4 The tree sparrow..is, in these islands, an exceedingly local..bird.

**Treet, treete, treetee, treetise**, obs. ff. Treat, Treaty, Treatise.

**Tree·-toad.** Any toad of arboreal habits, esp. those of the family *Hylidæ*, found chiefly in tropical America: often erroneously called *tree-frogs*.

**1778** J. Carver *Trav.* (1794) 253 Among the reptiles of North America there is a species of the toad, termed the tree toad, which is nearly of the same shape as the common sort, but smaller and with longer claws. **1855** Kingsley *Westw. Ho* xxi, When the sun went down, tree-toads came out.

**Tree·-top, tree top.** The top of a tree; the uppermost branches of a tree.

**1530** Palsgr. 233/1 Housetoppe or treetoppe. **1620** Middleton *Chaste Maid* III. iii, Perch at tree-top, And shake the golden fruit into hir lap. **1796** *Mother Goose's Melody* 15 Hush-a-by, baby On the tree top, When the wind blows the cradle will rock. **1821** Clare *Vill. Minstr.*, etc. (1823) I. 73 The sun each tree top mounted o'er. **1904** R. Bridges *Demeter* 318 As the light clouds fly O'er the tree-tops high.

**Tree:-tre·foil.** Forms: 6 tretrifoly, 6–7 -ie, 7 tree-trifolie, tre-trifoly, (trettifollie); 8–9

tree trefoil. The shrub *Medicago arborea*, also called *tree-medick* (TREE *sb.* 10 a); the κύτισος, *cytisus* of the ancients.
Not the genus *Cytisus* (L.) of botanists, nor the 'Cytisus' of florists (*Genista racemosa*).
1552 ELYOT, *Cytisus*, an herbe which is good to geue to cattell agaynst the rotte, some call it tretrifolie. 1601 HOLLAND *Pliny* XVI. xxiv. I. 471 The Elme, and the Tree-trifolie, are full of small and little braunches. 1657 S. PURCHAS *Pol. Flying-Ins.* I. xv. 94 Tre-trifoly with yellow knops. 1861 MISS PRATT *Flower. Pl.* II. 92 The Moon Trefoil, or Tree Trefoil (*Medicago arborea*).

**Treeward** (trī·wǫ̆ɹd), *a. nonce-wd.* [f. TREE *sb.* + -WARD.] Toward a tree or trees. So **Tree·wards** *adv.*
1854 *Tait's Mag.* XXI. 307 Birds are winging Treewards. 1869 *Routledge's Ev. Boy's Ann.* 584, I took care to be on the treeward side of the amputation.

**Treewe**, obs. form of TRUE.

† **Tree·-worm.** *Obs.* [f. TREE *sb.* + WORM *sb.*] The teredo or ship-worm.
1398 [see TEREDO 1]. 1398 TREVISA *Barth. De P. R.* XVIII. cxvi. (Bodl. MS.), A ful tender tre worme þat hatte teredo ..& is fulle nasche in kinde & ȝitte he þorleþ moste harde treen. 1483 *Cath. Angl.* 393/1 A Tre worme, *teredo*.

**Treey** (trī·i), *a. rare.* [f. as prec. + -Y.] Abounding in trees; well wooded.
1852 CLOUGH *Poems*, etc. (1869) I. 179 A sort of wide, tolerably rich, and treey upper valley. 1883 *Standard* 28 Dec. 5 There still linger treey tracks as wild as that 'savage wood'.

‖ **Trefa, trifa** (trē·fă, trəi·fă). *Jewish Ritual.* Also **trephah, tripha(h, (tryfer).** [repr. Heb. טְרֵפָה, Rabbin. טְרֵיפָה, *ṭ'rēphāh*, lit. 'that which is torn', flesh of an animal torn (or pounced upon fatally) by a wild beast (Lev. xvii. 15); f. טרף *ṭāraf* to tear, rend. In later use the word passed into the extended sense now used.] Flesh meat forbidden to be eaten by Jews because the animal has not been slaughtered in the manner prescribed by the Law. Also *trefa meat*. Opposed to KOSHER.
1851 MAYHEW *Lond. Labour* II. 120 Not being particular about eating 'tryfer,'—that is, meat which has been killed by a Christian. 1868 *Standard* 15 Dec. 6 The defendant ..pleaded..that meat killed and sold by a person not so licensed, was not 'kosher' meat, but 'trefa', and..unlawful to be eaten by Jews. 1892 ZANGWILL *Childr. Ghetto* I. 173 We decided that the fowl was tripha and could not be eaten. 1906 *Jewish Encycl.* XII. 109 s.v. *Terefah*, 'Terefah' in a broader sense includes also a regularly but unskilfully killed animal, in contradistinction to *Nebelah*. 1911 *Daily News* 11 Feb. 4 The Shechita Board notifies the Jewish public that the meat killed and sold under the supervision of the second rabbi is trifa—prohibited to be eaten by Jews.

**Trefallow, Trefe**, var. TRIFALLOW, TREAF.

**Trefele**, obs. f. TRIFLE. **Trefet, -ett**, obs. ff. TRIVET. **Treffle, Treffoyle**: see TREFLE, TREFOIL. **Trefine**, obs. form of TREPHINE.

**Trefle** (tre·f'l). Also 6 trayfle, 9 treffle. [a. F. *trèfle* (16th c. *treffle*, 1314 *tresfle*, in Hatz.-Darm.):—pop.L. *trifolum for cl.L. *trifolium*.]
†**1.** = TREFOIL 1. *Obs.*
1510 STANBRIDGE *Vocab.* (W. de W.) D ij b, *Trifolium*, trefle grasse. 1527 ANDREW *Brunswyke's Distyll. Waters* K j, Trayfles, Trifolium in latyn.
**2.** *Mil.* A mine having three chambers: see quots.
1756 MANNINGHAM *Compl. Treat. Mines* 104–5 [contains full description and figures]. 1853 STOCQUELER *Milit. Encycl.*, *Trefle* (*Trefoil*), a term used in mining, from the similarity of the figure to trefoil. The simple trefle has only two lodgments; the double trefle, four; and the triple one, six. 1877 KNIGHT *Dict. Mech.*, *Trefle* (*Fortification*), a mine with three chambers, like a trefoil.
**3.** A figure or arrangement like that of a triple leaf: = TREFOIL 3.
1877 COUES & ALLEN *N. Amer. Rod.* 151 Anterior lower molar of 5 to 8 prisms, of which the anterior forms an irregular treffle. 1889 *Pall Mall G.* 3 Jan. 4/1 The placing of the Maxim gun underneath the orchestra,..pointing across the ballroom... Around it was a trefle of harness and carbines.

‖ **Treflé, treflee** (trefle·, -ī·), *a. Her.* Also 9 trefflee. [F. *tréflé* having the form of a trefoil.] Adorned with trefoils: either along one edge, as a *bend treflé*, or at the end of each arm, as a *cross treflé* (in the latter case = BOTONÉ). So **Tre·fled**, tre·ffled *a.* (*Cent. Dict.* 1891).
1725 COATS *New Dict. Her.*, *Treflée*, a *Cross Treeflé*, is that whose Arms end in three Semicircles each representing the Trefoil or three-leav'd Grass. 1864 BOUTELL *Hist. & Pop. Her.* xix. § 5 (ed. 3) 314 A bend treflée vert. 1882 CUSSANS *Handbk. Her.* viii. 130 *Treflé*, ensigned with Trefoils. The Arms of Saxony, borne by the Prince of Wales, afford an example of a *Bend treflé*. 1892 *Jrnl. Cork Hist. Soc.* May 85 The special pattern of the cross is trefflee or trefoil.

**Trefoil** (trī·foil, tre·foil), *sb.* (*a.*) Forms: *α.* 5–7 trifolie, 5 tryfolye, 5–6 -foly, 6 -folly, 6–7 (9 *arch.*) trifoly. *β.* 5 treyfoyle, (iij.foili), 6 treifoile; traif-, treff-, (terf-, treef-), tryfoyle; 6–7 tri-, tre-, -foil(e, 7 trey-, (tree-) foile, 5– trefoil. *γ.* 5 trey-, trayfole, (6 -folde), 6–7 trifole, 7 trifol, tre-fole. See also TREFLE. [The *α*-forms appear to be directly ad. L. *trifolium*, f. *tri-* three + *folium* leaf, whence Sp. *trifolio*, It. *trifoglio*; the *β*-forms, from AF. *trifoil* (*c* 1265 in Wr.-Wülcker 556/33): cf. late OF. *trefeuil, -feul* (15th c. in Godef.), Pr. *trefueil*. The Fr. form *trèfle* represents a late L. *trifolum: cf. the *γ*-forms.]

**1.** A plant of the genus *Trifolium*, having triple or trifoliate leaves; a clover: commonly applied to species or varieties other (esp. smaller) than those cultivated under the name of 'clover'; often to the yellow-flowered *T. minus*, and also to the similar *Medicago lupulina*.
*α.* *a* 1450 *Stockh. Med. MS.* II. 666 in *Anglia* XVIII. 323 Of trifolie ȝif þou take þe jows. 1562 TURNER *Herbal* II. 5 Ye lefe [of Fenegreke] is lyke vnto trifoly. 1657 S. PURCHAS *Pol. Flying-Ins.* I. xv. 94 Another kinde of Trifoly with long red blossomes. 1840 BROWNING *Sordello* III. 2 Braid moonfern now with mystic trifoly.
*β.* *c* 1400 *Three Kings Cologne* 92 Þe leuys be liche treyfoyles. *c* 1440 *Pallad. on Husb.* I. 701 For wonte of gresse, on trefoil let hem byte. 1552 HULOET, Trifoyle herbe, *trifolium*. 1577 B. GOOGE *Heresbach's Husb.* I. 45 The best hearbe for Pasture or Meddowe, is the Trefoyle or Clauer. 1601 CHESTER *Love's Mart.* (1878) 82 Sweete trefoile, Weedwind, the wholesome Wormewood..Stone hearts tongue, Blessed thistle, and Sea Trifoly. 1610 GUILLIM *Heraldry* III. x. (1660) 146 The Treefoile is accounted the Husbandmans Almanack, because when it shutteth in the leaves it foretelleth raine. 1765 *Museum Rust.* IV. 120 Those useful grasses, the clovers and trefoils. 1815 ELPHINSTONE *Acc. Caubul* (1842) I. 387 They first soil them [horses] with trefoil, and then give them lucerne. 1830 *Withering's Brit. Plants* (ed. 7) III. 854 *note*, [St. Patrick] plucking a Trefoil, and thereby illustrating the mystery of the Trinity in Unity. *Ibid.*, Hence originated the custom of wearing the Shamrock, (a bunch of Trefoil) on the anniversary of that Saint [Patrick].
*γ.* [*c* 1420 Trayfole: see 3.] 1580 LYLY *Euphues* (Arb.) 376 As salfe..as sleeping in the grasse Trifole, where..no serpent ..dare venture. 1670 EVELYN *Sylva* (ed. 2) 3 The Tre-fole or Clover.
†**b.** *gen.* Any plant with trifoliate leaves, as wood-sorrel. *Obs. rare*$^{-1}$.
*c* 1425 tr. *Arderne's Treat. Fistula* 68 Panis cuculi alleluya, i. wodsour, is a treyfole growyng vnder buschez..a ful sour herbe.
**c.** With defining words, applied to particular species of *Trifolium*, or to plants of other genera having triple leaves, or otherwise resembling trefoil. **Bird's-foot trefoil**, a book-name for *Lotus corniculatus* and other species. **Bitumen** or **bituminous trefoil**, *Psoralea bituminosa*, a S. European evergreen shrub. **Bog trefoil**, *Menyanthes trifoliata*. **Hare's-foot trefoil**, *Trifolium arvense*. **Honeysuckle trefoil**, a former name for the white and red clovers (*Trifolium repens* and *T. pratense*). **Hop trefoil**: see HOP *sb.*[1] 4 b. **Meadow trefoil, Purple trefoil**, *T. pratense*, also the wild *T. medium*. †**Sea trefoil (trifoly)**, a name given by Turner to *Astragalus Glaux*. **Shrub trefoil**, the same as TREE-TREFOIL; formerly also identified with *Cytisus*, and by some applied to Yellow Jasmine; also to the Shrubby Trefoil of N. America. **Shrubby trefoil**, in Gerarde, app. the same as prec.; now the N. American hop-tree, *Ptelea trifoliata*; sometimes vaguely applied to other shrubby plants with trifoliate leaves. †**Sour trefoil**, an old name for wood-sorrel. **Strawberry-bearing** or **Strawberry-headed trefoil**, the strawberry clover, *Trifolium fragiferum*. **Sweet trefoil**: see quot. 1884. **Thorny trefoil**, a thorny shrub of the genus *Fagonia*, esp. *F. cretica*. **Water trefoil**, *Menyanthes trifoliata*. **White trefoil**, white or Dutch clover. **Yellow trefoil**, any yellow-flowered species of *Trifolium*, as *T. procumbens*; also *Medicago lupulina*. **Zigzag trefoil**, *Trifolium medium*. See also BEAN-TREFOIL, HEART *t.*, MARSH *t.*, MELILOT *t.*, MILK-*t.*, MOON-*t.*, SNAIL *t.*, TICK *t.*, TREE-TREFOIL.
1760 J. LEE *Introd. Bot.* App. 330 *Bird's foot Trefoil, *Lotus*. 1833 [see BIRD'S-FOOT 2]. 1658 ROWLAND *Moufet's Theat. Ins.* 1063 Take seed of *bituminous Trifoly. 1884 MILLER *Plant-n.*, *Psoralea bituminosa*, Bitumen Trefoil. *Ibid.*, *Menyanthes trifoliata*,..*Bog-Trefoil,..Marsh Trefoil, Water Trefoil. 1867 BABINGTON *Man. Brit. Bot.* (ed. 6) 85 *T*[*rifolium*] *arvense*..*Hare's-foot Trefoil. 1763 *Museum Rust.* I. 27 The sweet white-flowered, or *honeysuckle, trefoil. 1796 [see HONEYSUCKLE 8]. 1707 MORTIMER *Husb.* (1721) I. 41 The Yellow *Hop Trefoil. 1855– [see HOP *sb.*[1] 4 b]. 1578 LYTE *Dodoens* IV. xxxvi. 495 *Medow Trefoyle, or Common Trefoyle. 1785 MARTYN *Rousseau's Bot.* xxv. (1794) 367 *Purple Trefoil. Honeysuckle Trefoil, or Red Clover. 1548 TURNER *Names of Herbes* 40 *Glaux*.. may be called in englishe *sea Trifoly. 1597 GERARDE *Herbal* III. xiv. 1128 Of the *shrub Trefoile,..most do call it *Cytisus*, but we had rather name it *Trifolium fruticans*. 1640 PARKINSON *Theat. Bot.* 1466 Shrub Trefoile or the ordinary yellow Iasmine. 1771 J. R. FORSTER *Flora Amer. Septentr.* 6 Ptelea trifoliata. Shrub trefoil. Virginia. 1597 GERARDE *Herbal* III. xi. 1122 The first kinde of *Cytisus* or *Shrubbie Trefoile. *Ibid.* xiv. 1129. 1866 *Treas. Bot.* 936 *P*[*telea*] *trifoliata*, the Shrubby Trefoil of North America, is frequently grown in shrubberies. 1884 SARGENT *Rep. Forests N. Amer.* 31 Hop tree. Shrubby Trefoil. Wafer Ash. 1578 LYTE *Dodoens* IV. xliii. 503 This herbe is called.. in English Wood-sorel,..*Sower Trifoly. 1796 WITHERING *Brit. Plants* (ed. 3) II. 430 *Oxalis Acetosella*..Wood Sorrel ..Sour Trefoil. 1796 H. HUNTER tr. *St.-Pierre's Stud. Nat.* (1799) I. 10 One species..bears..it's seeds aggregated into the form of a strawberry, from which it derives the botanic name of *trifolium fragiferum*, the *strawberry-bearing trefoil. 1884 MILLER *Plant-n.*, *Melilotus cærulea*, *Sweet Trefoil. 1760 J. LEE *Introd. Bot.* App. 330 *Thorny Trefoil, of Candia, *Fagonia*. 1860 MAYNE *Expos. Lex.*, *Marsh Trefoil*, **Water Trefoil*, common names for the *Menyanthes trifoliata*, or buckbean. 1785 MARTYN *Rousseau's Bot.* xxv. (1794) 367 *White Trefoil, commonly called Dutch clover, has a creeping perennial stem... The *Yellow Trefoil, cultivated under this name, or that of Nonesuch. 1870 MORRIS *Earthly Par.* III. IV. 191 Some from amidst the daisies gleaned The yellow trefoil. 1796 WITHERING *Brit. Plants* (ed. 3) III. 651 *Zigzag Trefoil,..*Tr. medium*. 1843 *Penny Cycl.* XXV. 211/1 [*T. medium*] can be recognised by its zigzag stem, from which..it is sometimes called Zigzag Trefoil.

†**2.** A set or rosette of three leaves; the first three leaves of a young plant. *Obs. rare*$^{-1}$.
*c* 1440 *Pallad. on Husb.* III. 623 To make hem [mustard and colewort] hoor as frost..Let grounden glas go syfte on hem aboute, When theyr trefoyl or quaterfoyl is owte.
**3.** An ornamental figure representing or resembling a trifoliate leaf; *spec.* in *Arch.* an ornament with an opening divided by cusps so as to present or suggest the figure of a three-lobed leaf. (Cf. CINQUEFOIL, QUATREFOIL.)
1418 *E. E. Wills* (1882) 36 Wroght wit mapil leues and fret of .iij.foill. *c* 1420 *Anturs of Arth.* 510 (Thornton MS.) Trayfolede with trayfoles, and trewluffes by-twene. 1536 in *Antiq. Sarisb.* (1771) 198 Four Basons,..with Trifoils within pounced and chased in the midst with a Falcon of Gold. *a* 1548 HALL *Chron.*, *Hen. VIII* 207 A cote of greate riches, in braides of golde laied lose on Russet Veluet and set with Traifoyles, full of pearle and stone. 1551 SIR J. WILLIAMS *Accompte* (Abbotsf. Cl.) 76 Another paier of candelstickes chased withe trayfoldes. 1842–76 GWILT *Encycl. Archit.* Gloss., *Trefoil*, in Gothic architecture, an ornament consisting of three cusps in a circle. 1863 SIR G. G. SCOTT *Glean. Westm. Abb.* (ed. 2) 38 The tracery is not only in circles, but in quatrefoils and trefoils.
**b.** *Her.* A bearing conventionally representing a clover-leaf with its stalk; resembling a small cross with rounded leaves or lobes in place of the three upper arms.
1562 LEIGH *Armorie* 172 b, He bearethe Or, a Treffoyle, doble, slepped vert. 1622 PEACHAM *Compl. Gentl.* xvi. (1634) 206 Hee beareth Argent: a Cheveron Azure between 3 Treyfoiles Vert. The Treyfoile is the Herald of the Spring and the first grasse that appeareth; hereupon it was the Embleme of Hope. *c* 1828 BERRY *Encycl. Her.* I. Gloss., *Trefoil*, or Three-leaved Grass. This bearing often occurs in coat-armour.
**4.** *fig.* A set of three closely united.
1826 SCOTT *Mal. Malagr.* i. 48 One leaf of the holy Trefoil—one distinct and component part of the United Kingdoms. 1827 CARLYLE *Germ. Rom.* IV. 47 Among the children.. Wilhelm noticed Felix; the other two were the Angels of last night. The friendly trefoil came running towards him.
**5.** as *adj.* Three-leaved; consisting of three leaflets or lobes; having the figure of a trefoil or clover leaf; furnished with such figures.
1752 H. WALPOLE *Lett.* (1845) II. 440 A beautiful tomb, all in our trefoil taste. 1785 MARTYN *Rousseau's Bot.* xxv. (1794) 350 They are ternate, trefoil, or three-leaved. 1874 PARKER *Goth. Archit.* I. iv. 151 Small trefoil arches..between the corbels.
**6.** *attrib.* and *Comb.*, as *trefoil head, juice, leaf, seed*; *trefoil-headed, -like, -purpled* adjs.; *trefoil-wise* adv.; **trefoil burnet, trefoil green**, moths of which the larvæ feed on trefoil.
1825 OWEN & BLAKEWAY *Hist. Shrewsbury* II. 88 Six narrow pointed arches,..decorated with *trefoil heads. 1874 PARKER *Goth. Archit.* I. iv. 134 A window of two *trefoil-headed openings. 1619 SIR A. GORGES tr. *Bacon's De Sap. Vet.* 30 The Goate..doth greedily aspire To haue the *trifol iuyce passe downe her throate. 1758 MRS. DELANY in *Life & Corr.* (1861) III. 504 The receipt for tooth-ache is, 'Little *trefoil leaves, primrose leaves and yarrow pounded'. 1911 *Encycl. Brit.* XX. 399/2 The wood-sorrel, a small stemless plant with radical *trefoil-like leaves. 1782 J. SCOTT *Elegy* iii, The fragrant *trefoil-purpled field. 1765 *Museum Rust.* IV. 79 *Trefoil-seed, 2d. per pound. 1727–41 CHAMBERS *Cycl.* s.v. *Mistletoe*, Its flowers grow by three and three, *trefoil-wise. 1889 *Q. Jrnl. Geol. Soc.* Feb. 64 Groups of three globulites massed trefoilwise.

**Trefoiled** (trī·foild, tre·-), *a.* [f. prec. + -ED[2].] **1.** (Chiefly *Arch.*) Ornamented with a trefoil or trefoils; formed as a trefoil (sense 3).
*c* 1420 [see prec. 3]. 1815 J. SMITH *Panorama Sc. & Art* I. 154 The [window] heads being arched, are trefoiled or cinquefoiled. 1849 RUSKIN *Sev. Lamps* iv. § 27. 117 The wall in the trefoiled lights is curved. 1874 PARKER *Goth. Archit.* I. iv. 144 [Early English] Doorways are generally pointed or trefoiled.
**2.** Composed of, or having leaves composed of, three leaflets, trifoliate; *transf.* three-lobed.
1854 S. THOMSON *Wild Fl.* III. (ed. 4) 200 Trefoiled plants. 1892 M. STOKES *Six Months in Apennines* 19 Bursting from its trefoiled shell.

**Trefo·liated**, *pa. pple.* or *a.*, bad formation for TRIFOLIATED (after TREFOIL): = prec.
1835 R. WILLIS *Archit. Mid. Ages* v. 47 A quatrefoil, each of whose foils is trefoliated with an entire trefoil. 1900 *Daily News* 17 Mar. 4/6 On each section of the trefoliated leaves a blood-red spot was distinctly visible.

†**Tre·foot.** *Obs.* Also 6 treifoote, 7 trifoote, treefot. [f. L. *tres*, or OF. *treis* three + FOOT. Cf. OE. *trefet*, TRIVET.] A three-footed object; a tripod; a trivet.
1559 W. BAVAND tr. *Montanus' Comm. Weale* VII. i. 133 b, Thales..vnto whome..his..countreie men gaue the Golden treifoote whiche the Fisshermen had drawne vp. 1630 J. TAYLOR (Water P.) *Wks.* II. A a j, Euery man is not borne to make a Monument for the Cuckoo; to send a Trifoote home alone. 1634 T. JOHNSON tr. *Parey's Chirurg.* XXVII. ii. (1678) 664 A Kettle, set upon a Treefot. 1651 FRENCH *Distill.* i. 3 A Kettle, or a Pot set upon a Trefoot.

[**Trefte**, misreading of *treste*: see TRESS *v.*]

**Trefues**, obs. f. *treves*: see TREVE, TRUCE.

**Treg**, variant of TRIG *v.*[4], to fill full, cram.

†**Tre·gar.** *Obs.* In 7 treager, -s. [Corruption of *Treguier*, name of a place in Brittany. Cf. DOWLAS, LOCKRAM, POLDAVY.] A linen fabric made at Treguier; a kind of lockram.
1642 *Rates of Merchandizes* 72 (*Rates Inwards*) Lockerams..Treager, grest and narrow or common dowlasse, the

piece containing 106 ells £5.00.00. 1674 JEAKE *Arith.* (1696) 65 In 1 Piece of Lockram called Treagers, 106 Ells. 1721 C. KING *Brit. Merch.* I. 290 Thred Bruges, 22 Dozen. Tregar, 306 Pieces. Verdigrease, 327 lib.

**Tregedie**, obs. form of TRAGEDY.

† **Tre·get**, *sb. Obs.* Also *Sc.* 4 tryget, 6 traget, trigit, (? troget). [a. OF. *tresgiet, treget* (12th c. in Godef.) enchantment, magic, vbl. sb. of *tresgeter*: see TREGETOUR.] Jugglery; trickery, deceit.

*a* 1300 *Cursor M.* 8675 (Cott.) Sco..stal mi liuand child a-wai; Bot i kneu wel be light o dai O þis treget [*v. r.* tresun] sco had me don. *c* 1375 *Sc. Leg. Saints* x. (*Mathou*) 98 Þat gere fele men wene þat þai Throw tryget are goddis verray. *c* 1400 *Rom. Rose* 6267 Sith they cowde not perceyve His treget, and his cruelte. *Ibid.* 6825 By my treget I gadre & threste The gret tresour into my cheste. 1513 DOUGLAS *Æneis* IV. Prol. 247 Of thi trigittis [*ed.* 1553 tragetis] quhat toung can tell the trible?

**b.** *attrib.* or as *adj.* Juggling, deceitful.

1519 HORMAN *Vulg.* 280 b, A iugler with his treget [*pr.* troget] castis deceueth mens syght.

† **Treget**, *v. Obs. rare.* [a. OF. *tre(s)geter*: see next.] *intr.* To practise juggling tricks. Hence † **Tregetting** *vbl. sb.*

*c* 1440 *Promp. Parv.* 501/1 Tregettyn, *prestigior, pancracio. Ibid.* 501/2 Tregettynge, *mimatus, prestigium.*

**Tre·getour.** *arch.* Also 4 tregetowr, -ettur, trigettur, tri-, trygetoure, 4–5 tregetoure, -itour, -e, trigetour, 4–6 tregettour, 5 -etur, -ettowre, (trageotour), 6 try-, tragetour, treageter, trogeter, -ettar. [a. OF. *tre(s)geteo(u)r* (12th c. in Godef.) a juggler, mountebank, agent-n. of *tre(s)geter* to cast across or to and fro:—L. type **tra(ns)jectāre*, f. TRANS- + *jactāre* to throw, cast: see TRAJECT. Cf. It. *tragettatore* juggler; and, for sense, CAST *sb.* 24, CASTER 1.] One who works magic or plays tricks by sleight of hand; a conjurer; a juggler; hence, a trickster, a deceiver.

*a* 1300 *Cursor M.* 12247 (Cott.) A tregetur [*v. rr.* trigettur, tregit-, tregettour] i hope he be, Or elles godds self es he. 1340 HAMPOLE *Pr. Consc.* 4213 Als negremanciens and tregettours, Wiches and false enchauntours. *c* 1380 *Antecrist* in Todd *3 Treat. Wyclif* 128 Wiþ tregetours & tomblers, wiþ gestours & japeres. *c* 1520 *Treat. Galaunt* 106 in Furniv. *Ballads* I. 449 For trygetours & tryflours that tauernes haunte. 1533 tr. *Erasmus' Com. Crede* 65 b, These persons do make Christe a iuglere or a trogeter and a wonderfull deceiuer. 1609 HOLLAND *Amm. Marcell.* XXIII. v. 223 A dauncing Tregetour..was acting and counterfeiting certaine gestures that were commonly and usually taken up. 1819 SCOTT *Ivanhoe* xliii, The sewer thought I was dressed to bear a part in the tregetour's mummery. 1843 LYTTON *Last Bar.* I. ii, The more sombre *Tregetour*..promised to cut off and refix the head of a sad-faced little boy.

† **Tre·getry.** *Obs.* Also tregetrie, -re, tregettrie, -rye. [a. OF. *tre(s)geterie* (Godef.) enchantment, magic: see prec. and -ERY, -RY.] Juggling; deception, trickery.

*c* 1380 WYCLIF *Sel. Wks.* III. 410 Elles mot þei putt tregettrye and falsenes in Crist. *c* 1400 *Destr. Troy* 1624 Soche soteltie þai soght to solas hom with; The tables, the top, tregetre also. 14.. *Beryn* 2774 The wiche been so perfite of Nygramance, And of þe arte of apparence, and of tregetrie.

**Trehala** (trĭhā·lă). Also tricala. [ad. Turkish تيقالة *tīqālah*, native name.] The substance of the cocoons of a coleopterous insect, *Larinus maculatus*, found in Asia Minor; also called *trehala-manna, Turkish* or *Syrian manna.*

1862 WATTS *Gmelin's Handbk. Chem.* XV. 300 When pulverised trehala manna is treated with boiling alcohol, trehalose sometimes crystallises from the extract on cooling. 1868 — *Dict. Chem.* V. 878 *Trehala* or *tricala*, a substance imported from Persia, and consisting of the hollow cocoons of a coleopterous insect (*Larinus maculatus*). The larva of this insect eats the branches of *Echinops persica*, for the sake of the sugar, starch, and gum contained in them, and afterwards voids these substances to form its cocoon...Trehala has a sweetish taste, swells up in water, and is converted into a thick mucilaginous paste.

Hence **Trehalose** (trī·hălōᵘs, trĭhā·lōᵘs), *Chem.*, a white crystalline sugar, $C_{12}H_{22}O_{11}.2H_2O$, obtained by Berthelot in 1857 from trehala.

1862 MILLER *Elem. Chem.* (ed. 2) III. 73 The most important of these [varieties] is the common sugar, furnished by the sugar cane,..related to which are some others of small importance, viz. trehalose, melezitose, and melitose. 1865–8 WATTS *Dict. Chem.* III. 1068 *Mycose* or *trehalose.* $C_{12}H_{22}O_{11}$... Berthelot..obtained from trehala-manna..a sugar which he called trehalose, and at first regarded as different from mycose; but on further examination he was led to infer that the two are identical.

**Trei, treie**: see TRAY, TRY. **Treid**, obs. f. *tried*, pa. t. and pple. of TRY *v.* **Treifoile**, obs. f. TREFOIL. **Treigntalle**, obs. f. TRENTAL. **Treil**, var. TRAIL *sb.*[2] *Obs.*

**Treillage** (trē·lėdʒ, ‖ trę[l]yāʒ). Also 7 treilliage, 8 treilage. [a. F. *treillage* (16th c. in Hatz.-Darm.), f. *treille*, TRAIL *sb.*[2] + *-age*, -AGE.]

**1.** Lattice-work; a framework upon which vines or ornamental plants are trained; a trellis.

1698 W. KING tr. *Sorbière's Journ. Lond.* 28 At St. James's Park there were no Pavillions nor decoration of Treilliage and Flowers. 1712 ADDISON *Spect.* No. 477 ¶ 1 There are as many kinds of Gardening as of Poetry:..Contrivers of Bowers and Grotto's, Treillages and Cascades, are Romance Writers. 1830 GREVILLE *Mem. Geo. IV* 20 Apr. (1875) I. 335 A walk under a treillage of vines. 1907 *Edin. Rev.* Jan. 151 The garden is laid out with treillage and grass plot.

**b.** *attrib.*

1803 REPTON *Landscape Gard.* (1805) 104 Advantage may be taken of treillage ornaments to admit light. 1835 *Fraser's Mag.* XII. 524 Several vines trained over treillage-work.

**2.** A lattice or grill in a room.

1836 T. HOOK *G. Gurney* (new ed.) 35, I was placed in the manager's box, allotted the seat of honour behind the treillage.

Hence **Treillaged** *a.*, trellised.

1810 SHELLEY *Zastrozzi* iv, Their treillaged ornaments were silvered by the clear moonlight.

**Treille** (trēl). [a. F. *treille* (trę[l]y', trey') trellis, lattice:—L. *trichila* trellis for a vine: see TRAIL *sb.*[2]] **a.** *Her.* = TRELLIS *sb.*[2] 1 d.

1780 EDMONDSON *Heraldry* II. Gloss., *Trillise*, or *Treille*, a lattice. It differs from a fret in..that the pieces which compose it are not interlaced..but lie strait upon the undermost pieces, fixed with nails. 1889 ELVIN *Dict. Her.*, Treille, or Trillise.

**b.** *Lace-making.* See quot.

1882 CAULFEILD & SAWARD *Dict. Needlewk.* 500/2 *Treille*, one of the names by which the Réseau Grounds of Pillow and Needle Laces are distinguished from the Toile or pattern. The value of many laces is decided by the thickness or fineness of the thread used in the Treille, and the number of Twists given to the Bobbins when making it.

‖ **Treillis** (trę·[l]yi, treyi). Also (3 Anglo-L. treyliz), 8 trellis. [mod.F. *treillis*. Orig. the same word as TRELLIS, OF. *treliz*, L. **trilīcium*, f. *trilīx, -līcem*, the original sense of which it closely preserves. See TRELLIS.] A stout or coarse kind of cloth; in later use, buckram, sacking ('toile grossière pour sacs, vêtements de travail', Hatz.-Darm.; see also Littré s. v. senses 5, 6). See also TRAILYE.

[*c* 1250 *Faringdon Compotus* (MS. Barl. 49[2] lf. 6), Vna ulna canabi Valet. .ij. den. ob...Vna ulna buretell' Valet vnum den...Vna ulna treyliz Valet .iij. den.] 1706 PHILLIPS (ed. Kersey), *Trellis*,..also Cloth, otherwise call'd Buckram. 1714 *Fr. Bk. of Rates* 80 Treillis of Germany, per Piece of 10 Ells. 1858 SIMMONDS *Dict. Trade, Treillis*, a kind of coarse quilted linen, imported into France.

† **Trei·lȝe**, var. of TRAILYE *Sc.* a kind of cloth. Cf. also TREILLIS. This is perh. the meaning of *treilȝeis* in the following quot., which Ruddiman referred to F. *étrilles* currycombs, L. *strigulæ, strigiles* scrapers.

1513 DOUGLAS *Æneis* XII. ii. 92 Thar [stedis] lokrand manis and thar crestis hie Dressys wyth treilȝeis and camis honestlye.

**Trein, -e, treing**, obs. ff. TREEN *a.* **Treinke**, var. TRINK *sb.*[1] *Obs.* **Treip**, obs. Sc. f. TRIP. **Treische**, var. TRESCHE *Obs.* **Treison**, obs. f. TREASON. **Treist**, var. TRAIST *Obs.*; obs. Sc. f. TREST. **Treit**, obs. Sc. f. TREAT. **Treitcheoure**, var. TREACHER *Obs.* **Treitour, -tre**, obs. ff. TRAITOR. **Trei trippe**, var. TREY-TRIP *Obs.* **Treittie**, obs. Sc. f. TREATY.

**Trek** (trek), *sb. S. Africa.* [a. Cape Du. *trek* = Du. *trek* draw, pull, tug, march, f. *trekken*, TREK *v.*]

**1.** In travelling by ox-wagon, a stage of a journey between one stopping-place and the next; hence, a journey or expedition made in this way; also, journeying or travel by ox-wagon.

(Cf. *trek-tow* occurring in 1834.)

1849 E. E. NAPIER *Excurs. S. Africa* II. 1 First day's 'trek' in lower Albany. 1863 W. C. BALDWIN *Afr. Hunting* vii. 233, I joined Swartz..and went with him to Letloche, about fourteen days' trek. 1906 *Harper's Mag.* June 30/2 Distances in Africa are not reckoned by miles, but by treks or days.

**b.** An organized migration or expedition by ox-wagon.

1890 *Times* (weekly ed.) 28 Feb. 17/3 The proclamation of President Kruger forbidding the formation of a 'trek' to enter Mashonaland. 1901 *Scotsman* 8 Mar. 6/2 There had been a Boer trek into German South-west Africa, but it was only on a small scale. 1901 *Daily Chron.* 30 May 3/2 The men above-mentioned, or their sons,..led the great trek of 1836–9.

**c.** *transf.* and *fig.*

1895 J. G. MILLAIS *Breath fr. Veldt* v. 102 A big troop of guinea-fowls..following each other in their afternoon trek to the water. *Ibid.* vi. 123 From the sun-parched wilderness of Africa to art criticism is a big trek. 1902 CORNISH *Naturalist Thames* 67 The first [birds] to begin the 'trek' down the river are the early broods of water-wagtails.

**2.** *attrib.* and *Comb.*, as *trek-cattle, -ox*; trek-chain, trek-rope = TREK-TOW.

1900 *Daily News* 6 Apr. 3/1 The local supply of *trek cattle..from the farms of the Boers. 1850 CUMMING *Hunter's Life S. Afr.* (ed. 2) I. 220, I purchased..several excellent horses and *trek-oxen. 1906 *Harper's Mag.* June 29/1 The northernmost limit of the trek-ox in Africa. 1883 *Cornh. Mag.* Mar. 293 The oxen loosened from the *trek rope.

**Trek** (trek), *v. S. Africa.* [a. Du. *trekk-en* to draw, pull, tug, tow, march, travel; MDu., MLG., MHG. *trecken*, OWFris. *trekka*; orig. an intensive derivative of MDu., MLG. *trēken*, MHG. *trechen*, OHG. *trechan* to draw.]

**1.** *intr.* To make a journey by ox-wagon; hence, to travel, migrate; also, to go, proceed; to go away, depart (*slang*). Also *transf.* of wild animals.

1850 R. G. CUMMING *Hunter's Life S. Afr.* (1902) 12/2 [The elephants] turned their faces to the north-east, and trekked or migrated from their ancestral jungles to lands unknown. *Ibid.* 74/2 At dawn of day, we inspanned, and trekked about five hours in a north-easterly course. 1863 W. C. BALDWIN *Afr. Hunting* vi. 154 The wagons had been quietly treking along over an immense open country. 1891 *Spectator* 25 Apr. 583/2 A large body of them [Boers]—five thousand, it is said—therefore resolved to 'trek' into Mashonaland and establish a Republic upon the great plateau. 1895 J. G. MILLAIS *Breath fr. Veldt* ii. 25 The springbuck..were beginning to trek backwards and forwards uneasily. 1912 *Standard* 20 Sept. 7/1 He [the King] met the whole of the Third Division, who were trekking to their rest camps from their overnight bivouac.

**b.** *trans.* To cover (ground, a distance) by 'trekking'.

1890 SIR F. YOUNG *Winter Tour S. Africa* 118 The ground which I have myself treked.

**2.** *trans.* To draw or drag (a vehicle): said of oxen and other beasts of draught. Also *absol.*

1863 W. C. BALDWIN *Afr. Hunting* vi. 152 My oxen could not possibly trek my wagon through the heavy sands in their present condition. *Ibid.* viii. 309 We ultimately got the ox tied up to the wagon-wheel,..inspanned him next morning, and he treks well. 1893 H. M. DOUGHTY *Wherry in Wendish L.* 53 A farm horse..which trekked us for four or five miles.

Hence **Tre·kking** *vbl. sb.* and *ppl. a.*; also **Tre·kker**, one who 'treks'.

1850 R. G. CUMMING *Hunter's Life S. Afr.* (1902) 28/2 We..came upon an immense, compact herd of several thousand 'trekking' springboks. 1858 SIMMONDS *Dict. Trade, Trekking*, a colonial term in the Cape colony, for departing or leaving to settle in another country. 1891 *Times* 13 May 5/3 The committee of trekkers are having a copy taken..of the original documentary treaty. 1901 *Scotsman* 7 Mar., Heavy rains made trekking almost impossible. 1905 *Times* 4 Sept. 6/1 A score of trekkers [of the British Association] started in the morning in mule wagons for Kimberley.

‖ **Trekschuit, treck-** (tre·kskoit, ‖ -sχœüt). Forms: *α.* 7 draggescutte; 7–9 track-, 7–8 -scoute, 8 -skuit, 8 (9) -scoot, 8–9 -s(c)huyt, (8 trachtscoot, tract-scout); *β.* 8–9 treck-, 8 -schuyte, -scuit, -scoit, -scute, -scoot, 8–9 -schuit, 9 -schuyt, -shwytt, -shut, 8 trekschuyt, 9 trekschuit. (Cf. forms of SCHUIT, SCOUT *sb.*[3], SHOUT *sb.*[1]) [Du. *trekschuit*, formerly *-schuyt*, f. *trek* sb. or *trek-* vb.-stem of *trekken* to draw, pull, tug + *schuit*, MDu. *schûte* = MLG., LG. *schûte* boat, barge:—OTeut. **skûtô*, ME. *schûte*, ON. *skúta*: see SCHUIT and SHOUT *sb.*[1]] A canal- or river-boat drawn by horses, carrying passengers and goods, as in common use in Holland; a track-boat.

1696 *Caldwell Papers* (Maitl. Cl.) I. 174, 13 June. I went to Bruxelles in a Draggescutte. *Ibid.* 176 July 1st. I went in the Trackscoute fra yᵉ to Bruges. 1711 ADDISON *Spect.* No. 130 ¶ 4 As the Trekschuyt, or Hackney-boat, which carries Passengers from Leyden to Amsterdam, was putting off [etc.]. 1737 G. SMITH *Curious Relat.* I. i. 99 We took our Lodgings at the first Inn..where the Treckscutes landed. 1756 MRS. CALDERWOOD in *Coltness Collect.* (Maitl. Cl.) 131 There is no track-scoot goes from Helvest. 1769 *De Foe's Tour Gt. Brit.* III. 278 We should then travel with as much Safety, Certainty, and Dispatch, as in the Trachtscoots in Holland and Flanders. 1769 FALCONER *Dict. Marine* (1789), *Tract-scout*, a vessel employed to carry goods or passengers up and down the rivers or canals. 1772 *Tour Holland*, etc. 26 On Monday evening we went in the treckschuyte to Leyden. 1783 WESLEY *Jrnl.* 16 June, We set out in a trackskuit for the Hague. 1796 MORSE *Amer. Geog.* II. 335 Covered boats, called treckscuits, which are dragged along the canals by horses. 1816 SOUTHEY *Poet's Pilgr.* I. 26 Beside the busy wharf the Trekschuit rides. 1846 THACKERAY *Cornhill to Cairo* xv, Harmlessly as if we had been in a Dutch trackschuyt. 1893 STEVENSON *Catriona* xxii. 262, I.. arranged..to send on my chests by track-scoot to an address I had in Leyden. 1902 *Westm. Gaz.* 17 Nov. 3/2 It is a change from the tearing of motor-cars to note the slow progress of the *trekschuit.*

‖ **Trek-tow** (tre·ktōᵘ). *S. Africa.* [Cape Du., f. Du. *trek* sb. or vb.-stem (see TREK) + *touw* rope, cord, tow.] The central chain or cable of twisted hide attached to a wagon-pole, to which the yokes of the oxen are fastened.

1834 PRINGLE *Afr. Sk.* ii. 141 A strong central trace (trektow), formed of twisted thongs of bullock's or buffalo's hide. 1850 R. G. CUMMING *Hunter's Life S. Afr.* (ed. 2) I. 24 The waggon is steered by a pole, called the dissel-boom, to the end of which is fastened the trektow, a stout rope formed of raw buffalo-hide.

**Trelapse, -er**, variant of TRILAPSE, -ER.

**Trele**, obs. form of TRAIL *sb.*[2]

**Treles, -ez**, obs. forms of TRELLIS.

† **Trellis**, *sb.*[1] *Obs.*: see TREILLIS.

**Trellis** (tre·lis), *sb.*[2] Forms: 5–6 trelis, -ys, -es(e, 5 -ez, tril(l)es, 5–6 traylles, 6 treliss, -ies, trallace, treylles, trellesse, 7 trellize, treillis, 7–9 trellice, 8 trellies, 6– trellis. *Pl.* 5–6 trelis, -iz; 6 trelesez, treyl(le)sys, trellisses, 7 -izes; 9 -ises. *β. Sc.* 5 terlys, 6 trelies, traleis, tarlies, traylles, treylles, treilȝeis, (trailzeys), tirleise, -lis, tyrleis, 6–7 tirleis, -lies, 7 tirlace, 8 -lass, -less. [ME. a. OF. *treliz, -is*, fem. *trelice* (orig. adj.):—late pop.L. **trilīci-us*, f. L. *trilīx, -līcem* (in Isidore nom. *trilīcis*) = Gr. τρίμιτος, having three threads in the warp, f. L. *tri-* three

+ *licium* a thread of the warp; said of strong woven fabrics (cf. TREILLIS). OF. had also a rarer form *tresliz*, showing an early confusion of the prefix with OF. *tres-* :—L. *trans-*: so Pr. *treslitz*, It. *traliccio*, med.L. *trans-*, *trās-*, *trālicium*, a stout woven fabric. The application of the word to things woven of iron wire, gold, withes, etc. app. brought the sense into contact with OF. *treille*, Pr. *treilla*, *trelha*, med.L. *trelia*, *trillia*, etc. (see TRAIL *sb.*$^2$), and resulted in the later F. form *treillis* and the later signification 'lattice, grille'. Some of the 16th c. Scottish forms are difficult to distinguish from the pl. of *treilȝe*, TRAILYE.]

**1.** A structure of light bars of wood or metal crossing each other at intervals and fastened where they cross, with open square spaces between; used as a screen in window openings or the like; a window, gate, screen, etc. so constructed; a lattice; a grating. Now *rare*.

*a* **1400–50** Treles [implied in TRELLIS *v.* 1]. **1422** Trelys [see *trellis-window* in 3]. *c* **1440** *Promp. Parv.* 501/2 Trelys, of a wyndow, or oþer lyke (or grate..), *cancellus*. **1450–1** *Durham Acc. Rolls* (Surtees) 240 Et in ij Trelis emp. pro fenestra cove, vij d. **1498–9** *Ibid.* 101 Pro iij fenistris voc. trelez pro Scaccario Cellerarii et le Sethynghous. **1513–14** *Ibid.* 663 Pro ij trelesez ad ustrinum, vj d. **1531–2** *Durham Househ. Bk.* (Surtees) 74 Et Roberto Kyrver pro factura le treylsys 8 d. **1532–3** *Ibid.* 163 Pro factura le treyllesys. **1535** COVERDALE *Judg.* v. 28 His mother..cried piteously thorow the trallace. — *Prov.* vii. 6 Out of the wyndowe of my house I loked thorow the trelies. **1549** *Aberdeen Regr.* (1844) I. 271 Conuikit..for the strublance of Duncane Freser and ryving of his tirleise of his vyndok. **1553–4** *Burgh Rec. Edinb.* (1871) II. 285 Payit for ane tyrleis of irne to the portell of the counsal hous dure. **1582–8** *Hist. James VI* (1825) 46 Upoun the wyndo thairof, he..cuttit a small hole of the blak cloth that coverit the traleis. **1634** SIR T. HERBERT *Trav.* 49 The Windowes [at Gombroon]..in stead of Glasse vse wooden trellizes or casements. **1641** R. BAILLIE *Lett.* (Bann. Cl.) I. 316 (*Trial of Strafford*) At the back of the throne, there was two roomes on the two sydes; in the one did Duke de Vanden..and other French nobles sitt; in the other, the King, the Queen [etc.]; the tirlies, that made them to be secret, the King brake doun with his own hands; so they satt in the eye of all. **1768** STERNE *Sent. Journ.* (1775) II. 86 (*Passport, Hotel Paris*) The bird..attempting his deliverance, and thrusting his head through the trellis, pressed his breast against it, as if impatient. **1886** SHELDON *Flaubert's Salammbô* 21 Darting..glances through the golden trellisses into the silent apartments.

†**b.** An enclosure of lattice-work, a grating.

*c* **1500** *Melusine* lii. 329 Whan they that were in the traylles of yron herd it. **1555–6** *Burgh Rec. Edinb.* (1871) II. 364 Item, coft vij jestis to be ane tirleis to the deid banis at the south kirk dur. *Ibid.*, Item to Hennislie to cast the deid banis in the west tirleis iij s. **1593** *Rites of Durham* (Surtees 1903) 37 Y$^e$ highte of y$^e$ said trellesse was striken full of iron pikes..to thentent y$^t$ none should clyme ouer it.

**c.** Short for *trellis-door* or *-gate*: see 3. *Sc.*

?*c* **1800** *State, Fraser of Fraserfield* 194 (Jam.) At or near the westmost pole—there is a tirlass, at which a single person may enter.

**d.** *Her.* The figure of a trellis used as a charge. *In trellis*, with the pieces of which the charge is composed crossing and nailed at the joints, not interlacing.

**1823** SCOTT *Quentin D.* xxxiii, Sable, a musion passant Or, oppressed with a trellis gules, cloué of the second. **1882** CUSSANS *Her.* vii. (ed. 3) 120 Portcullis: An iron gate formed of bars armed at the base, and bolted in trellis. **1889** [see TRELLISED 2 b].

**2.** A similar framework used as a support upon which fruit-trees or climbing plants are trained.

**1513** DOUGLAS *Æneis* XII. Prol. 100 The wyne grapis ȝing Endlang the treilȝeis [ed. **1553** trailzeys] dyd on twystis hing. **1725** *Bradley's Fam. Dict.* s.v. *Pomegranate*, He must..take Care to plash all the Branches..against a Trellis made on purpose. **1766** *Compl. Farmer* s.v., Some persons ..erect trellises against their walls, extending from the inside of one pier to the nearest inside of the next. **1818** SHELLEY *Let. to Mrs. Shelley* 20 Aug., The vines are..trailed on low trellisses of reeds. **1850** *Beck's Florist* Feb. 59, I always fix the trellis on the pot at the time of potting. *fig.* **1861** S. WILBERFORCE *Let.* in *Life* (1881) II. xiii. 454 The earthly love becomes the trellice, up which the heavenly love creeps. **1894** H. DRUMMOND *Ascent Man* 193 Language formed the trellis on which Mind climbed upward.

**3.** *attrib.* and *Comb.*, as *trellis-border*, *-door*, *-frame*, *-gate*, *-grating*, *-hut*, *-lace*, *-pattern*; *trellis-covered*, *-shaded*, *-woven* adjs.; **trellis-window**, a window furnished with a trellis; see also quot. 1913. See also TRELLIS-WORK.

**1897** *Daily News* 12 Apr. 7/7 A pair of beakers, with baskets and sprays of flowers in *trellis borders. **1867** LADY HERBERT *Cradle L.* i. 14 The ladies..were conducted by black eunuchs through *trellis-covered walks. **1756** MRS. CALDERWOOD in *Coltness Collect.* (Maitl. Cl.) 219 They's chapells!..and a fine dressed-up Virgin in every one of them, and a *tirless door to let her be seen! **1897** R. N. BAIN tr. *Jókai's Pretty Michal* xxxii. 251 At the stroke of two, she was already in the shop below, the trellis-door of which, leading to the street, was closed. **1766** *Compl. Farmer* s.v. *Trellis*, For peach, nectarine, and apricot trees..the squares of the *trellis frame should not exceed three or four inches. **1697** in *Mem. Alloa* (1874) 66 To put on a *tirlace gate, with lock and key thereto. **1825** JAMIESON (1882), *Tirless-yett*, a turnstile. **1876** B. CHAMPNEYS in Willis & Clark *Cambridge* (1886) III. 238 *Trellis gratings fitted with adjustable valves. **1825** HONE *Every-day Bk.* I. 289 This saint lived in a *trellis hut. **1874** H. H. COLE *Catal. Ind. Art S. Kens. Mus.* 173 Bracelet. *Trellis pattern of plain and green glass beads. **1422** *Searchers Verdicts* in *Surtees Misc.* (1888) 16 The *trelys wyndowe at the somer hall. *a* **1651** CALDERWOOD *Hist. Kirk* (1843) II. 11 So Bothwellhauche shott at him with a hacquebutt, through a tirleis window. **1913** EDEN *Anc. Glass* 51 The branches of the tree or vine seemed to run in and out of a trellis, a circumstance which has given name to such windows—trellis windows. **1751** G. WEST *Education* xvii, Labyrinths involv'd and *trellice-woven bow'rs.

**Trellis** (tre·lis), *v.* Forms: see prec. [Almost always in pa. pple. *trellised* (tre·list), f. prec. + -ED. Cf. F. *treillisé* (14th c. in Godef. *Compl.*).]

**1.** *trans.* To furnish with a trellis or with lattice-work; to enclose in a trellis or grating.

*a* **1400–50** *Alexander* 3343 Þe thrid [step] of a Topas a-tyred & trelest & grauen. *c* **1470** HENRY *Wallace* XI. 197 A fell lyoun..With in a barrace,..Terlyst in yrn. **1593** *Rites of Durham* (Surtees 1903) 37 Aboue y$^e$ said dor, it was likewaies trellessed almoste to y$^e$ hight of y$^e$ valt aboue. **1634** SIR T. HERBERT *Trav.* 61 Windowes trellized very curiously. **1816** GALT *Life B. West* 92 Near a pile of ruins fringed and trellissed with ivy. **1883** 'VERNON LEE' in *Mag. Art* Nov. 3/1 Two villages, with..paved lanes trellised with grapes. *fig.* **1873** E. BRENNAN *Witch of Nemi* etc. 224 Some love that trelliseth the heart.

**2.** *intr.* To make a trellis. *rare.*

*c* **1520** *Mem. Ripon* (Surtees) III. 202 Will'mo Caruer trelyssyng et carvyng per j diem, 6*d.*

**3.** *trans.* To train (a plant) upon a trellis; to support on or as on a trellis. Also *fig.*

**1818** SHELLEY *Jrnl.* 26 Mar., The vines..are trellissed upon ..stakes. **1849** RUSKIN *Sev. Lamps* iv. § 34. 125 The living flowers..which..the French and Italian peasantry often trellis with exquisite taste about their casements. **1873** E. BRENNAN *Witch of Nemi* 5 A virgin round the summers of whose years Love trellissed joys to warp consuming fears.

**Trellised** (tre·list), *ppl. a.* [f. TRELLIS *sb.*$^2$ or *v.* + -ED.]

**1.** Furnished with a trellis or trellis-work; formed of trellis-work; trained upon a trellis.

**1472** *Durham Acc. Rolls* (Surtees) 94 Pro iiij Trillestwyndous empt. pro coquina. **1513** DOUGLAS *Æneis* III. iii. 10 The full mone..In throw the tirlist wyndo schane by nycht. **1656** BLOUNT *Glossogr.*, *Trellised*, crosse-barred, latticed, grated, with wood. **1814** SOUTHEY *Roderick* XVI. 28 Their trelliced vines. **1844** LEVER *T. Burke* xxvii, The trellised walls covered with honeysuckles and wild roses. **1889** S. LANGDON *Appeal to Serpent* ii. 42 Assisting the tendrils of a beautiful passion-flower to grasp the next highest bar of a trellised arch.

**2.** Shaped or arranged like a trellis; having a pattern or markings resembling a trellis.

**1664** POWER *Exp. Philos.* I. 5 The Common Fly..The like foraminulous perforations or trelliced eyes are in all Flyes. **1822** J. PARKINSON *Outl. Oryctol.* 40 Ramifications..disposed in a trellised form. **1828** TYTLER *Hist. Scot.* (1864) I. 320 [The armour of David earl of Huntingdon] is of the species called by the contemporary Norman writers the 'trellissed', and consists of a cloth coat, or vest,..intersected by broad straps of leather, laid on so as to cross each other, but to leave intervening squares of the cloth, in the middle of which is a round knob or stud of steel. **1835–6** *Todd's Cycl. Anat.* I. 712/1 These *striæ*, ridges and furrows, may cross one another, and the shell is then trellised. *a* **1873** LYTTON *Ken. Chillingly* II. ix, Its..trellised [wall-]paper.

**b.** *Her.* = LATTICED 2 c.

**1889** ELVIN *Dict. Her.*, *Treille* or *Trillise*, a Lattice, or Trellis, a pattern resembling fretty, but always nailed at each intersection; also termed Trellised cloué. **1894** in *Parker's Gloss. Her.* 586.

**Trellising** (tre·lisiŋ), *vbl. sb.* [f. TRELLIS *v.* + -ING$^1$.]

**1.** The action of TRELLIS *v.*; the making of, or furnishing with, a trellis.

**1474–5** *Durham Acc. Rolls* (Surtees) 95 Operantibus circa le trilessyng et facturam..fenestrarum.

**2.** *concr.* Trellis-work, a trellis.

**1860** *All Year Round* No. 41. 341 A gallery, latticed like a dairy window, behind which birdcage trellising women were admitted. **1913** MRS. WHARTON *Custom of Country* I. ix, Under the leafless trellising of a wistaria arbour.

**Tre·llis-work.** [f. TRELLIS *sb.*$^2$ + WORK *sb.*] Wood or metal work consisting of light cross-bars; = TRELLIS *sb.*$^2$ 1. Also, anything resembling this in structure or pattern. Also *attrib.*

**1712** J. JAMES tr. *Le Blond's Gardening* 74 Cabinets of Trellis-work altogether plain. **1739** GRAY *Let. to West* 21 Nov., Trellis-works covered with vines. **1814** WORDSW. *White Doe* IV. 49 Shades Of trellis-work in long arcades. **1822–34** *Good's Study Med.* (ed. 4) IV. 99 The corpus spongiosum as well as the corpora cavernosa [of the penis] are divided into cells or trellis-work by an infinite number of fine membranous plates. **1878** STUBBS *Const. Hist.* III. xviii. 214 The two kings met, with a grating of trellis-work between them, on the bridge of Pecquigny. **1898** *Westm. Gaz.* 10 Mar. 3/2 A very charming blouse..is that with a trellis-work. **1898** *Daily News* 5 Sept. 5/1 The tomb..was whitewashed all over and surrounded by a trelliswork fence. **1908** [MISS FOWLER] *Betw. Trent & Ancholme* 10 A Clematis Montana, surrounding the trellis-work frame.

**Trematode** (tre·mătōud), *a.* and *sb.* *Zool.* [ad. mod.L. *Trēmatōda* neut. pl., a. Gr. τρηματώδης having holes, perforated, f. τρῆμα hole, orifice.]

**A.** *adj.* Belonging to the class or order *Trematoda* or *Trematoidea* of parasitic worms, found in the bodies of various animals, having a flattish or cylindrical form, with skin often perforated by pores, and usually furnished with adhesive suckers; the flukes (FLUKE *sb.*$^1$ 2) are typical examples.

In Cuvier's classification the *Trematoda* constituted the second family of parenchymatous entozoa, containing besides the flukes some animals not now reckoned as trematodes.

**1836–9** *Todd's Cycl. Anat.* II. 121/1 The Trematode Order ..includes only two species infesting the human body. **1864** *Reader* 3 Dec. 712/1 He had discovered upon the angel-fish (*Squatina angelus*) a trematode worm of very singular organization, which will constitute a new genus. **1867** J. HOGG *Microsc.* II. iii. 567 One of the most remarkable of the Trematode helminths is Bilharzia haematobia of Cobbold. **1876** *Beneden's Anim. Parasites* Introd., Cestode and trematode worms.

**B.** *sb.* A trematode worm.

**1876** tr. *Wagner's Gen. Pathol.* 120 Trematodes are parasitic solitary flat-worms with inarticulate leaf-shaped bodies. **1904** *Brit. Med. Jrnl.* 17 Sept. 663 Sections of a minute adult trematode. **1905** *Q. Rev.* Apr. 488 The pearls in our fresh water mussel were formed by the larvae of a fluke (a trematode).

So **Tre·matoid** *a.* and *sb.*

**1882** OGILVIE (Annandale), Trematode, Trematoid, *a.* **1891** *Cent. Dict.*, Trematoid, *a.* and *n.*

† **Tre·mblable,** *a.* *Obs. rare.* [f. TREMBLE *v.* + -ABLE; cf. OF. *tremblable* (Godef.).] Fitted to cause trembling or fear; **a.** Demanding reverential fear; **b.** Causing dread or horror; dreadful.

**1560** DAUS tr. *Sleidane's Comm.* 318 That the Canon of the Masse..be spoken softlye, to the intente those tremblable misteries maye retaine theyr auncient dignities. **1609** G. BENSON *Serm.*, etc. 72 Which is tremblable and monstrous, there be some, who, when God smites them, they fly vnto a witch or an Inchauntresse, and call for succour. **1651** R. WITTIE tr. *Primrose's Pop. Err.* II. vi. 93 In this Country the Consumption is an evill so ordinary and tremblable.

**Tremble** (tre·mb'l), *sb.* Forms: see the verb. [f. TREMBLE *v.*]

**1.** An act or the action of trembling; a fit or state of trembling; a tremor; a vibration.

**1609** BIBLE (Douay) 2 *Esdras* xv. 37 They shal shake..and tremble shal take them. **1677** *Phil. Trans.* XII. 836 (According to him) Sound may be caused by the tremble of solid bodies without the presence of gross Air. **1719, 1760–72** [see b]. **1775** ASH, *Tremble* (s. *colloquial*, from the verb), a tremor. **1848** DICKENS *Dombey* xxvii, A terrible tremble crept over her whole frame. **1884** T. WOOLNER *Silenus* I. II. 21 Sitting beside the reeds He saw a tremble shivering thro' their leaves. **1894** 'IAN MACLAREN' *Bonnie Brier Bush, Cunning Sp. Drumtochty* (1895) 185 He micht gie a bit trimmil.

**b.** In colloq. phrases (*all*) *in*, *all of a tremble*, *on* or *upon the tremble*, trembling, esp. with agitation or excitement.

**1719** MISS HOWE in *Lett. C'tess Suffolk* (1824) I. 39 Mama has invited me to stay here,..which put me in such a tremble that I am hardly recovered. **1760–72** H. BROOKE *Fool of Qual.* (1809) II. 151, I am already all of a tremble. **1800** LAMB *Let. to Manning*, I am still on the tremble, for I do not know where we could go. **1818** COLERIDGE in *Lit. Rem.* (1836) I. 206 Why should I be in such a tremble all the while he talked? **1830** *Chron.* in *Ann. Reg.* 35/2 He seemed all of a totter and tremble.

**c.** Tremulousness or unsteadiness (of the voice) caused by emotion.

**1779** *Mirror* No. 54 ¶ 13 There is a melting tremble in her voice, which..is inimitably beautiful and affecting. **1848** DICKENS *Dombey* xxxiii, A deep impassioned earnestness.. that made the very tremble in her voice a part of her firmness.

**2.** *pl.* *The trembles*: Any disease or condition characterized by an involuntary shaking, as ague or palsy (esp. in sheep); the tremor due to mercurialism, delirium tremens, etc.; the 'shakes'; in N. Amer., milk-sickness (MILK *sb.* 10).

**1812** J. WALKER *Ess. Nat. Hist.* 525 Ovis in pascuis montosis morbo obnoxia est, hactenus insanabili,..the Trembles. **1848** A. S. TAYLOR *Poisons* xxxiii. 561 The disease produced by the use of the flesh or milk of animals fed in these districts, is known under the name of milk-sickness, or *trembles*. **1860** MAYNE *Expos. Lex.*, *Trembles*, a popular term for the disorder mercurial tremor. **1864** HAWTHORNE *S. Felton* (1883) 321 A hardness of hearing, and a dimness of sight, and the trembles. **1865** DICKENS *Mut. Fr.* IV. viii, What are popularly called 'the trembles' being in full force upon him. **1887** *Buck's Handbk. Med. Sc.* V. 9/1 The flesh of an animal suffering from trembles..would also produce the disease [milk-sickness].

**3.** The American aspen, *Populus tremuloides*.

**1749** in *Rep. Comm. Ho. Comm.* II. 246/2 (Hudson's Bay Co.) The Beavers chiefest Food is, the Poplar or Tremble. **1770** J. R. FORSTER tr. *Kalm's Trav. N. Amer.* (1772) II. 356 They likewise make use of those which grow on the asp-tree or tremble.

† **Tremble,** *a.* *Obs.* *rare*$^{-1}$. [ad. L. *tremulus*, after next.] Trembling.

**1568** TURNER *Herbal* III. 81 To be geuen..vnto them that haue the palsey, or any num or tremble member.

**Tremble** (tre·mb'l), *v.* Forms: *α.* 4–5 tremle, -el, -yl, (4 trenle, *Sc.* tremal), 5 -ylle, -ul, trymmel, 5–6 *Sc.* tri-, trymle, 6 *Sc.* trimm-, trymm-, -le, -yll, etc., trumle, 9 *Sc.* trimmil; *β.* 4–6 trem-, (trim-, trym-), -bel, -byl, etc., (6 trumbill), 4– tremble. [a. F. *trembler* (11th c. in Godef. *Compl.*):—pop. and med.L. *tremulāre* (Du Cange), by which the early *tremel*, *-le*, *-yl* form may have been influenced, f. L. *tremul-us* tremulous, f. *tremĕre* to tremble, quake, shake. Cf Prov. *tremblar*, Sp. *temblar*, It. *tremolare.*]

**1.** *intr.* Of persons (less commonly of animals), or of the body or a limb: To shake involuntarily as with fear or other emotion, cold, or weakness; to quake, quiver, shiver.

**1303** R. BRUNNE *Handl. Synne* 9390 Hys herte began to tremle and colde. **13..** *St. Cristofer* 629 in Horstm.

*Altengl. Leg.* (1881) 461 For ferde he tremlide ylka bone. *c* **1375** *Sc. Leg. Saints* xvi. (*Magdalena*) 877 He tremaland, as he mocht. *Ibid.* xxxiii. (*George*) 257 Fast tremeland. **1412–20** LYDG. *Chron. Troy* III. 5425, I..þat..Fele myn hond boþe tremble and quake. **1413** *Pilgr. Sowle* (Caxton 1483) I. xv. 11, I tremble as doth a leef vpon a tree. *c* **1475** *Rauf Coilȝear* 458 Trewlie that tenefull [a tiger] was trimland than. **1514** BARCLAY *Cyt. & Uplondyshm.* (Percy Soc.) 6 We tremble naked, and dye almost for colde. **1598** SYLVESTER *Du Bartas* II. i. III. *Furies* 204 At every word they trimbléd then for aw. *a* **1668** DAVENANT *Siege* II. i, I tremble like a tender Lamb, In a cold Winter night. **1681** FLAVEL *Meth. Grace* ix. 192 The bird that has been delivered out of the tallons of the hawk, trembles afterward at the noise of his bells. **1797** MRS. RADCLIFFE *Italian* i, He trembled with anxiety. **1820** W. IRVING *Sketch Bk.* I. 51, I felt Leslie's hand tremble on my arm. *a* **1850** ROSSETTI *Dante & Circ.* I. (1874) 94 Gives me full oft a fear that trembleth: So that I call on Death. *Ibid.* 167 Ah! Ballad, unto thy dear offices I do commend my soul, thus trembling.

**b.** *fig.* and *rhet.* To be affected with dread or apprehension, or with any feeling that is accompanied by trembling. Const. *at, for, to do* something.

*c* **1400** *Apol. Loll.* 55 W[h]o is þe formar and original cause.. of þis þus gret iuel, I drede ungly to sey, tremel and quake. **1552** LYNDESAY *Monarche* 6018, I trimyll tyll heir tell The terribyll Turmentyng of hell. **1562** WINȜET *Last Blast* Wks. (S. T. S.) I. 40 We exhorte ȝow..to feir and trimble at the feirfull exemplis of deid. **1717** LADY M. W. MONTAGU *Let. to C'tess Bristol* 1 Apr., The Grand Signior, with all his absolute power, trembles at a janissary's frown. **1766** GRAY *Kingsgate* 6 Earl Goodwin trembled for his neighbouring sand. **1778** COWPER *Hymn*, '*What various hindrances we meet*' iii, Satan trembles when he sees The weakest saint upon his knees. **1815** SHELLEY *Dæmon* 282 While human tongues Tremble to speak. **1911** MARETT *Anthropol.* ii. 43 Then man presumably killed game..on top of the Wealden dome, how many years ago one trembles to think.

**2.** Of things: To be agitated or affected with vibratory motion; to shake, quake, quiver.

*c* **1374** CHAUCER *Boeth.* I. met. i. 1 (Camb. MS.) The slake skyn tremblyth of myn emptyd body. *c* **1375** *Cursor M.* 24413 (Fairf.) Þe erþ be-gan to tremble & quake. **1484** CAXTON *Fables of Æsop* IV. xiv, Whan the toune is taken..the Country aboute..ouȝt to tremble and shake. **1555** EDEN *Decades* 322 The poynt of the needle styll respected the northe..sauynge that it sumwhat trembeled and declyned a lyttle. **1697** DRYDEN *Æneid* x. 418 They run their ships aground: the vessels knock,..and tremble with the shock. **1827** CARLYLE *Misc.*, *Richter* (1869) 20 Then began the Aeolian Harp of the Creation to tremble and to sound. **1908** [MISS FOWLER] *Betw. Trent & Ancholme* 39 A little Harebell trembling in the breeze.

**b.** Said of the tremulous or vibratory motion or effect of light, sound, speech, etc.

*c* **1400** [see TREMBLING *vbl. sb.*]. *c* **1440** *Partonope* 5790 Wyth voys tremelyng. *a* **1628**, **1634** [see TREMBLING *ppl. a.*]. **1708** POPE *Ode St. Cecilia* 17 In broken air, trembling, the wild music floats. *Ibid.* 114 Yet ev'n in death..Eurydice still trembled on his tongue. **1737** — *Imit. Hor.* II. vi. 189 Tell how the Moon-beam trembling falls. **1821** SHELLEY *Epipsych.* 548 Where the pebble-paven shore..Trembles and sparkles as with ecstasy. **1842** TENNYSON *Vision of Sin* 17 Low voluptuous music winding trembled.

**c.** *fig.*

**1819** SHELLEY *Fragm.*, *Questions* 8 A dream, Part of which comes true, and part Beats and trembles in the heart. *a* **1862** BUCKLE *Civiliz.* (1869) III. iii. 121 The liberties of Scotland..were trembling in the balance.

†**3.** *trans.* To regard with trembling or dread; to tremble at. (Cf. L. *tremĕre.*) *Obs. rare.*

**1382** WYCLIF *Isa.* lxvi. 2 To whom..shall I beholde, but to my porelet [Vulg. *pauperculum*] and contrit in spirit, and tremblende [*trementem*] my wrdis? **1450–1530** *Myrr. our Ladye* 185 Thy mother, whome the companyes of helles tremel and drede. **1565** T. STAPLETON *Fortr. Faith* 104 That whiche..the deuil, aboue al thinges, trembleth.

**4.** To cause to tremble or shake.

**1591** SPENSER *Virg. Gnat* 616 Either Scipion..To whom the ruin'd walls of Carthage vow'd, Trembling their forces, sound their praises lowd. **1649** G. DANIEL *Trinarch.*, *Hen. V*, xxv, The Palsey of the common Earth, Trembles my Quill. **1651** W. DURHAM *Maran-atha* (1652) 11 It was much that a prisoner should so soon tremble his Judge. **1746** TANSUR *New Mus. Gram.* 23 A Shake, or Trilloe,..is to shake, tremble, or warble your Voice, or Instrument. **1818** KEATS *Endym.* I. 468 Thou art as a dove Trembling its closed eyes. **1850** MRS. BROWNING *Woman's Shortcomings* ii, She trembles her fan.

**5.** *intr.* To pass tremulously. Chiefly *poet.*

**1730–46** THOMSON *Autumn* 151 Soon as the morning trembles o'er the sky And unperceived unfolds the spreading day. **1795** COLERIDGE *Eolian Harp* 46 Organic Harps..That tremble into thought. *a* **1817** T. DWIGHT *Trav. New Eng.* etc. (1821) II. 413 With a snail-like progress..we trembled through this part of our way. **1842** TENNYSON *Talking Oak* 161 A teardrop trembled from its source. **1864** LOWELL *Fireside Trav.* 295 On the dial of time the shadow has not yet trembled over the line that marks the beginning of the first century.

**6.** *trans.* *Tremble out*: To utter tremulously or falteringly.

**1868** ADAH I. MENKEN *Infelicia* 35 And trembling out prayers, and waiting to die.

Hence **Tre·mbled** *ppl. a.*, made to tremble.

**1819** KEATS *Ode to Psyche* 11 The whispering roof Of leaves and trembled blossoms.

**Tremblement** (tre·mb'lmĕnt). [a. F. *tremblement* (15th c. in Godef.), f. *trembler* to TREMBLE: see -MENT.]

**1.** The action or condition of trembling (*lit.* and *fig.*); vibration, agitation; also, an instance of this, a tremor.

**1677** GALE *Crt. Gentiles* II. IV. 147 It is..vapors within the bowels of the earth, raised up by subterraneous fires that cause Earthquakes and Tremblements. **1844** MRS. BROWNING *Lost Bower* iv, The wood..Thrills in leafy tremblement. **1867** JEAN INGELOW *Christ's Resurrect.* xvii, The waiting world doth quake with mortal tremblement.

**2.** A cause of trembling; a terror. *rare.*

**1677** GALE *Crt. Gentiles* II. IV. 131 Some read it thus, 'Ephraim was a tremblement to him that heard him', i. e. so long as he kept close to God he was formidable to al his enemies. **1895** *Daily News* 27 May 8/3 Italian villains, pirate marquises, 'and almost every possible tremblement'—fierce wars and faithful loves—do moralise his song.

**Trembler** (tre·mblər). [f. TREMBLE *v.* + -ER[1]: cf. F. *trembleur.*] One who or that which trembles.

**1.** One who trembles, esp. with fear; a timorous or terrified person.

**1552** HULOET, Trembler, *tremulus, i.* *a* **1660** HAMMOND *Serm. Matt. xi. 30* Wks. 1684 IV. 479 Those base submissions, that the covetous Mammonist or cowardly trembler drudges under. **1770** GOLDSM. *Des. Vill.* 199 Well had the boding tremblers learned to trace The day's disasters in his morning face. **1878** SEELEY *Stein* II. 531 A frightened trembler and maker of obeisances.

†**2.** A name given to those whose devotional exercises were accompanied by trembling, quaking, or shaking; *spec.* a Quaker. *Obs.* or *Hist.*

[**1678** R. BARCLAY *Apol. Quakers* xi. § 8 (1736) 359 Sometimes the Power of God will break forth;..every individual will be strongly exercised, as in a Day of Battle; and thereby Trembling and a Motion of Body will be upon most, if not upon all:..And from this, the name of Quakers, i. e. Tremblers, was first Reproachfully cast upon us.] **1689** R. WARE *Foxes & Firebrands* III. 198 These Sectaries..be as follows: 1 Independents..17 Quakers, or Tremblers. **1706** E. WARD *Hud. Rediv.* xv. 21 Of these quaint primitive Dissemblers, In old queen Bess's Days call'd Tremblers. *a* **1741** CHALKLEY *Wks.* (1766) 101, I was one called a Quaker, or Trembler. **1820** tr. *Trav. Cosmo III* (1821) 447 The sect of the Tremblers or Quakers was begun by James Naylor.

**3.** *transf.* Applied to **a.** a fish which gives an electric shock, as the electric eel of Africa; **b.** a bird or other animal which keeps up a shaking motion of the tail or body.

**1832** LYELL *Princ. Geol.* II. 106 The trembler, or *Silurus electricus* [belongs] to the rivers of Africa. **1867** SCLATER & SALVIN *Exotic Ornithol.* Pl. x, *Cinclocerthia ruficauda*, (Red-tailed Trembler). **1911** WEBSTER, *Trembler*, any of certain West Indian birds of the genera *Cinclocerthia* and *Rhamphocinclus*, of the family *Mimidæ*.

**4.** *Electr.* A vibrating spring blade which alternately makes and breaks the circuit in an induction coil.

**1877** *Telegr. Jrnl.* 15 Nov. 280/1 M. Trouvé, Paris, has made some improvements in the contact-breaker or trembler of induction coils. *Ibid.*, Vibrating stem of the trembler. **1903** *Motor. Ann.* 80 Troubles..caused through the petrol, float-jet, or tremblers not having been understood by the motorist. **1907** *Daily News* 10 Apr. 6 Next the trembler in the coil stuck, and the engine stopped.

**5.** *attrib.* (in sense 4), as *trembler-blade, -coil*; **trembler-bell**, an electric bell rung by a hammer attached to a trembler; also called *trembling bell.*

**1884** in *Jrnl. Franklin Inst.* (1886) CXXI. Supp. 69 Audible signals are given..on board the locomotive by a *trembler bell. **1905** PREECE & SIVEWRIGHT *Telegraphy* (new ed.) 254 There are many forms of these trembler bells, but the principle in all is alike. **1904** in *Westm. Gaz.* 28 May 5/3 The *trembler blade which governs the spark, and is in its turn controlled by the movement of the motor. **1908** *Ibid.* 6 Feb. 4/2 The ignition is effected by high-tension magneto and accumulator with *trembler-coil and self-starting switch.

‖ **Trembleuse** (trāṅblöz), *a.* or *sb. attrib.* [F., fem. of *trembleur* trembler; cf. Littré, '*Trembleuse*, tasse retenue dans sa soucoupe par une sorte de galerie'.] In *trembleuse cup*, a cup having a saucer with a '**well**', into which it fits so as to be kept from falling off.

**1883** *Daily News* 26 June 3/1 Sale of..china..a gros bleu trembleuse cup and saucer, exotic birds, 95*l*. **1893** *Auction Catal. Porcelain Cassiobury Park* 5 Old Sèvres Porcelain. 20. A Trembleuse Cup, Cover and Saucer. **1894** *Times* 16 June 7/6 A trembleuse cup and saucer, with landscape and trophies in medallions on white and gold ground.

**Trembling** (tre·mbliŋ), *vbl. sb.* [f. TREMBLE *v.* + -ING[1].] The action of the verb TREMBLE in various senses; in quot. 1902, *spec.* ague in sheep (see TREMBLE *sb.* 2).

**1303** R. BRUNNE *Handl. Synne* 4912 Ȝyf he lerne gylerye Fals wurde and feynt trenlyng [*v. r.* tremlynge]. **1382** WYCLIF *Eph.* vi. 5 Seruauntis, obeysche ȝe to fleishly lordis with drede and tremblyng, in symplenesse of ȝoure herte, as to Crist. *c* **1400** *Song Roland* 54 Trymlinge of tabers And tymbring soft. *c* **1440** *Promp. Parv.* 501/2 Tremelynge, or qwakynge, *tremor.* **1526** *Pilgr. Perf.* (W. de W. 1531) 112 b, Transformynge our gesture or countenaunce, as in tremblynge. **1647** H. MORE *Song of Soul* II. App. iv, All my spirits move with pleasant trembeling. **1693** LUTTRELL *Brief Rel.* (1857) III. 25 A ship from Jamaica brings that the earth there had some tremblings again. **1809–10** COLERIDGE *Friend* (1865) 2 At the sound of the word trembling came upon me. **1902** N. MUNRO in *Blackw. Mag.* Nov. 602/2 Sheep had been lost by the trembling.

**b.** *attrib.*, as *trembling fit*; †**trembling-stop**, a tremolo organ-stop.

**1659** LEAK *Waterwks.* 34 The Systemes and Measures of the Organ Pipes,..also of the manner of the Registers,..the Trembling stop, &c. **1856** KANE *Arct. Explor.* I. xvi. 191 Men..were seized with trembling-fits and short breath.

**Tre·mbling**, *ppl. a.* [f. as prec. + -ING[2].] That trembles, in various senses of the verb.

*a* **1400–50** *Alexander* 4914 (Ashm. MS.) Þe testre trased full of trones with trimballand wingis. **1526** *Pilgr. Perf.* (W. de W. 1531) 257 With tremblynge herte and holy fere, thynkyng hym selfe vnworthy to touche that moost holy body. *c* **1614** SIR W. MURE *Dido & Æneas* I. 269 A contrare blast Doth force his saile against the trembling mast. *a* **1628** SIR J. BEAUMONT *Bosworth F.* 66 Which like a twinkling Star, with trembling Light Sends radiant Lustre through the darksome Air. **1634** SIR T. HERBERT *Trav.* 207 The lookers on incessantly warble out soft trembling Musique. **1797** MRS. RADCLIFFE *Italian* xi, It was delivered in..low and trembling accents. **1877** FROUDE *Short Stud.* (1883) IV. I. x. 122 [He] let in the trembling wretches who had been shut out.

**b.** *transf.* Characterized or accompanied by trembling.

*c* **1430** LYDG. *Min. Poems, Pater Noster*, Atwyxe dred and tremblyng reuerence Astoned I am. **1613** SHAKS. *Hen. VIII*, I. ii. 95 Sixt part of each? A trembling contribution. **1794** BLAKE *Songs Exper.*, *Little Boy Lost* 10 In trembling zeal he seized his hair. **1818** SCOTT *Br. Lamm.* xxxv, To the butler's trembling entreaties..he at first returned no answer.

**c.** In specific applications: **trembling aixies** or **exies** (cf. ACCESS 10), the ague (*Sc.*); **trembling beef**, some dish of boiled beef (? *obs.*); cf. *trembling-piece*; **trembling bog**, bog-land formed over water or soft mud, which shakes at every tread, a quaking bog; so *trembling prairie*, in Louisiana, U.S.A.; **trembling-chair**: see quot.; **trembling eel**, the gymnotus; **trembling-grass**, quaking-grass (*Briza media*); **trembling-ill**, the ague in sheep (*Sc.*); **trembling palsy**, paralysis characterized by trembling of the extremities or the head (*Syd. Soc. Lex.*, 1899); **trembling-piece** [F. *pièce tremblante*], a joint of beef so interlarded with fat as to quiver; **trembling-poplar**, the Aspen, *Populus tremula*, also the N. American *P. tremuloides.*

**1808–18** JAMIESON, *Trembling Fevers*, the ague, Ang. *Trembling Aixes [*ed.* **1825** Exies]. **1818** SCOTT *Br. Lamm.* xi, The cookmaid in the trembling exies. **1806** A. HUNTER *Culina* (ed. 3) 238 *Trembling Beef. Take a brisket of beef, and boil it gently [etc.]. **1697** DRYDEN *Virg. Georg.* III. 653 He lives on standing Lakes, and *trembling Bogs. **1899** *Syd. Soc. Lex.*, **Trembling chair*, a vibrating chair used in the treatment of paralysis. **1807** JOYCE *Sci. Dialogues* xvi. (1846) 397 (*Electricity*) In Firmin's 'Natural History of Surinam' is some account of the *trembling eel. **1853** G. JOHNSTON *Bot. E. Bord.* 216 *Briza media*, *Trembling-grass: Quaking-grass. **1833** WILSON *Fr. & Eng. Dict.* s. v. *Tremblant*, *Trembling-piece. **1861** MISS PRATT *Flower. Pl.* V. 120 (Aspen, or **Trembling Poplar*)..is a middle-sized tree.

**Tremblingly** (tre·mbliŋli), *adv.* [f. prec. + -LY[2].] In a trembling manner; tremulously; with trembling; so as to tremble.

**1552** HULOET, Tremblyngly, *trepidanter.* **1581** A. HALL *Iliad* x. 183 He stoode so tremblingly, That one full wel might heare his teeth togither so to shake. **1617** COLLINS *Def. Bp. Ely* I. i. 95 Tremblingly we referre them to the heauenly censure. **1771** MME. D'ARBLAY *Early Diary* 3 July, That..agonizing sensibility which is tremblingly alive to each emotion of sorrow. **1863** W. PHILLIPS *Speeches* viii. 217 Tremblingly anxious to save Garrison's life.

**Tre·mblingness.** *rare*⁻⁰. [f. as prec. + -NESS.] The state of trembling; tremulousness.

**1727** BAILEY vol. II, *Tremulousness*, tremblingness.

**Trembly** (tre·mbli), *a. colloq.* [f. TREMBLE *v.* or *sb.* + -Y[1].] Full of trembling; tremulous.

**1848** LOWELL *Fable for Critics* (1865) 223 A single anemone trembly and rathe. **1848** DICKENS *Dombey* i, So trembly and shaky from head to foot. **1879** O. W. HOLMES *Archbishop & Gil Blas* 21 Is your voice a little trembly?

†**Tre·mebund**, *a. Sc. Obs.* [ad. L. *tremebundus* trembling, f. *tremĕre* to tremble.] Inclined to tremble; timorous, timid.

*c* **1560** A. SCOTT *Poems* (S.T.S.) xxvi. 56 Thay [women].. ar of nature tremebund.

†**Tremefa·ction.** *Obs. rare.* [ad. late L. *tremefaction-em*, n. of action f. *tremefacĕre* to cause to tremble.] Shaking, trembling. So † **Tremefacting** *ppl. a.*, that shakes or trembles.

**1597** A. M. tr. *Guillemeau's Fr. Chirurg.* 28/2 The Chyrurgiane must, without anye tremefactione, vse the same [lancet]. **1599** — tr. *Gabelhouer's Bk. Physicke* 197/2 The braynes of a Hare..will præevent the tremefactione both of handes and feete. *Ibid.* 207/2 Croockede, and tremefactinge Ioynctes.

**Tremefy** (tre·mĭfəi), *v. rare*⁻¹. [ad. L. *tremefacĕre* (see prec.), with -FY, prop. repr. L. *-ficāre*: cf. *satisfy.*] *trans.* To cause to tremble.

**1832** J. WILSON in *Blackw. Mag.* XXXI. 424 A nod that tremefies Olympus.

**Tremel**, obs. form of TREMBLE.

‖ **Tremella** (trĭme·lă). *Bot.* [mod.L. (Dillenius 1741), dim. from *tremulus*, *-ula* shaking, shivering.] A genus of amorphous hymenomycetous fungi consisting of tremulous gelatinous substance, typical of the N.O. *Tremellaceæ* or *Tremellineæ*, most species of which grow on decayed wood, but a few on the ground.

*Tremella Auricula* is known as Earth-jelly, *T. albida* as Fairy Bullet. *T. mesenterica* is conspicuous in dead hedges in winter from its orange tint.

**1760** J. LEE *Introd. Bot.* Table i, Tremella, Cryptogamia, Algæ. **1778** LIGHTFOOT *Flora Scot.* II. 901 *Tremella purpurea*... Little red-knobb'd Tremella. **1786** THOMPSON in *Phil. Trans.* LXXVII. 124 Any thing resembling tremella or that kind of green matter, or water moss, which forms upon the bottom and sides of the vessel.

Hence **Tremellaceous** (tremĕlē¹·ʃəs) *a. Bot.*, pertaining to the *Tremellaceæ* or *Tremellineæ*; **Treme·lliform** *a. Bot.*, of the form of the thallus in *Tremella* (Webster, 1911); **Treme·llin** *Chem.* [cf. F. *trémelline* (Littré)], (see quot. 1868); **Tre·melline** *a. Bot.*, pertaining to the genus *Tremella* or N.O. *Tremellineæ* (*Funk's Stand. Dict.*, 1895); **Tremelli·neous** *a. Bot.* = *tremellaceous*; **Tre·melloid** *a. Bot.*, resembling *Tremella* in form or substance; **Tre·mellose** *a. Bot.*, shaking, like *Tremella*, tremulous.

1860 MAYNE *Expos. Lex.*, *Tremellin. 1868 WATTS *Dict. Chem.* V. 878 *Tr[emella] mesenterica* was found by Brandes to contain, in the dry state,..5 pts. of a peculiar crystallisable resinous body, called tremellin. 1860 MAYNE *Expos. Lex.*, *Tremelloides*,..applied to a lichen, the membranous, delicate, and almost transparent expansions of which resemble those of the *Tremella*: *tremelloid. 1874 COOKE *Fungi* 72 Anomalous as it may at first sight appear to include these tremelloid forms with the dust-like fungi. 1887 W. PHILLIPS *Brit. Discomycetes* 333 *Calloria luteo-rubella*. ..Somewhat tremelloid. *Ibid.* 22 *Leotia lubrica*...Gregarious, somewhat cæspitose, *tremellose. *Ibid.* 420 *Tremellose*, shaking like jelly, of a jelly-like consistence.

† **Treme·nd**, *a. Obs. rare.* [ad. L. *tremend-us*: see next.] = TREMENDOUS.

1581 MARBECK *Bk. Notes* 346 Earthquakes, Thunderings and Lightenings, be tokens and tastes of Gods most treme[n]d and dreadfull power. 1650 TRAPP *Comm. Deut.* x. 8 That sacred and tremend function of the ministery.

**Tremendous** (trĭme·ndəs), *a.* Also 7–8 **tremenduous.** [f. L. *tremend-us* 'that is to be trembled at, fearful, dreadful, frightful, terrible', gerundive of *tremĕre* to tremble, tremble at: see -OUS. The by-form in *-uous* was shaped after adjs. from L. adjs. in *-uus*, as *conspicuous*.]

**1.** Such as to excite trembling, or awe; awful; 'dreadful; horrible; astonishingly terrible' (J.).

1632 LITHGOW *Trav.* x. 460 Hee, after many tremenduous threatnings, commanded the Scriuan to draw vp a Warrant. 1657–83 EVELYN *Hist. Relig.* viii. (1850) II. 17 Not blaspheming the tremendous name of God. 1661 BLOUNT *Glossogr.* (ed. 2), *Tremendous*.., greatly to be feared. 1689 T. PLUNKET *Char. Gd. Commander* 44 But the tremenduos Tetragramaton Will not, not always be a looker on. 1742 YOUNG *Nt. Th.* IV. 9 Black-boding man Receives, not suffers death's tremendous blow. 1796 J. MOSER *Hermit of Caucasus* I. 166 Rocks, torrents, and all the variety of tremenduous scenery. 1803 JANE PORTER *Thaddeus* ix, The air..was rendered livid and tremendous by long spires of fire. 1871 MACDUFF *Mem. Patmos* xi. 147 The Day, the Great day.. of His wrath...Now, to what does this tremendous description refer?

**b.** *absol.* That which is tremendous. *nonce-use.*

1742 YOUNG *Nt. Th.* v. 691 What heart of flesh Would trifle with tremendous? dare extremes? Yawn o'er the fate of infinite?

**2.** Hyperbolically, or as a mere intensive: Such as to excite wonder on account of its magnitude or violence; astounding; extraordinarily great; immense. (Cf. the similar use of *awful, frightful, terrible*, etc.) *colloq.*

1812 SOUTHEY *Ess.* (1832) I. 111 During the last forty years, a tremendous change has been going on. 1845 FORD *Handbk. Spain* I. 16 They..drive at a tremendous pace. 1866 G. MACDONALD *Ann. Q. Neighb.* vi, A tremendous splash reached my ears from the pond. 1882 FLOYER *Unexpl. Baluchistan* 91 He..evidently determined to smother his feelings in a tremendous dinner.

**b.** Extraordinary in respect of some quality indicated in context. *slang.*

1831 *Ch. Patronage Reporter* Jan. 26 Owing..latterly to the tremendous state of the weather. 1847 HELPS *Friends in C.* I. vii. 117 Over-managing people..are tremendous to live with. 1866 GEO. ELIOT *F. Holt* ii, This young Debarry is a tremendous fellow at the classics.

**Tremendously** (trĭme·ndəsli), *adv.* [f. prec. + -LY [2].] In a tremendous manner or degree; dreadfully; hence *colloq.* as a hyperbolical intensive: Exceedingly, extremely, excessively, very greatly.

1680 BAXTER *Cath. Commun.* (1684) 36 And Peter oft, and once tremendously..rebuk't by Christ. 1731 BAILEY, *Tremendously*, dreadingly. 1776 PENNANT *Zool.* (ed. 4) I. 177 White Owl: This species..will often scream most tremendously. 1817 SOUTHEY *Ess.* (1832) II. 43 The game was of the same kind, though the stake differed tremendously in magnitude. 1863 W. C. BALDWIN *Afr. Hunting* ix. 394 If he should have gone, I shall have some tremendously hard work for nothing. 1904 *Yorks. Post* 9 Sept. 4/3 How tremendously costly a thing naval 'supremacy' has become.

**Tremendousness** (trĭme·ndəsnės). [f. as prec. + -NESS.] The quality of being tremendous.

1727 BAILEY vol. II, *Tremendousness*,..tremendous Quality, Worthiness to be feared or dreaded. 1851 H. MELVILLE *Whale* xli, The pre-eminent tremendousness of the great Sperm Whale. 1894 *Chicago Advance* 3 May, It is good.. to recognize the tremendousness of death. 1906 *19th Cent.* June 974 Æschylus overpowers us with his tremendousness.

‖ **Tremie** (trē·mi). *Engin.* [F. *trémie*, OF. *tremuie*, *-uye* (mill-)hopper (*c* 1300 in Godef. *Compl.*) = It. *tramoggia* :—L. *trimodia* a three-peck measure, f. *tri-* three + *modius* peck.] A movable tube, widening at its upper end into a hopper, for depositing concrete under water.

1905 *Engineering Rec.* (N. Y.) 14 Jan. 53 Up to a height of 6 ft. below low water level, the concrete was deposited under water by means of a tremie. 1911 *Min. Proc. Inst. Civ. Engin.* CLXXXV. 9 The deposition of concrete..by means of tremies operated from scows.

‖ **Tremis** (trī·mis). *Rom. Antiq.* [L., f. *trēs* three, after *sēmis* half an as.] A Roman gold coin of the later emperors, the third part of an *as aureus*.

1706 PHILLIPS (ed. Kersey), *Tremissis*, or *Golden Triens*, a Roman Gold Coin worth five Shillings Sterling. 1756 NUGENT *Montesquieu's Spir. Laws* (1758) II. XXII. ii. 72 The sou of two tremises [F. *deux tremisses*] answered to an ox of twelve months.

**Tremle**, obs. form of TREMBLE.

‖**Tremocto·pus.** *Zool.* [mod.L., f. Gr. τρῆμα hole, pore + OCTOPUS.] A subgenus of Octopus having two large aquiferous pores on the back of the head.

1851 WOODWARD *Mollusca* I. 65 Between the branchiæ are two rows of brown or violet spots, like the pigment cells of the tremoctopus. 1878 BELL *Gegenbaur's Comp. Anat.* 327 Sometimes over a few of the arms only (4 in Tremoctopus), or over them all.

**Tremogram** (tre·mŏgræm). [f. Gr. τρέμειν to tremble, quiver + -GRAM.] **a.** A tracing recording involuntary muscular motion. **b.** An irregularity characterizing a person's handwriting: see quot. 1907. So **Tre·mograph** [-GRAPH], an instrument for recording involuntary muscular tremor.

1899 *Syd. Soc. Lex.*, *Tremogram*, the tracing of tremor made by means of the Tremograph. 1904 G. S. HALL *Adolescence* I. iii. 145 The tremograph, a thimble attached to a pivoted lever moving freely in all directions, showed that children could not hold the index-finger still for half a minute. 1907 P. FRAZER in *Jrnl. Franklin Inst.* Apr. 268 The curious marginal irregularities which accompany and seem to a certain degree to characterize the handwriting of each writer, which I have called 'tremograms'.

‖ **Tremolando** (tremola·ndo). *Mus.* Also **tremulando.** [It., pr. pple. of *tremolare* to shake, quaver, warble (Florio).] **a.** *adj.* (or *attrib.*) Tremulous, shaking. **b.** *adv.* In a tremulous or quivering manner; with a tremolo; used to indicate that a note or passage is to be thus rendered. **c.** *ellipt.* as *sb.* = TREMOLO 1, 2.

1852 SEIDEL *Organ* 24 Another absurd..contrivance is the tremulando, a register which..was to indicate the sobbing, sighing, and trembling of men. 1854 J. SCHUBERT *Mus. Hand-bk.* (ed. 4), *Tremolant*, a stop in german organs producing a tremolando effect. 1876–98 STAINER & BARRETT *Dict. Mus. Terms*, *Tremolando*,..(1) A chord or note played or bowed with great rapidity so as to produce a quivering effect. (2) Vibration of the voice in singing, arising from nervousness or a bad production; or used for the purpose of producing a special effect. *Ibid.*, *Tremolant*,..a fan-wheel by rotating in front of the wind chest causes a *tremolando*. 1887 *Athenæum* 26 Nov. 720/1 The violins accompany *tremolando* in descending thirds.

**Tremolant** (tre·mŏlănt). [a. G. *tremolant*, ad. It. *tremolante*, TREMULANT.] = TREMOLO 2.

1854 [see prec.]. 1876–98 STAINER & BARRETT *Dict. Mus. Terms*, *Tremolant*, or *Tremulant*, an organ and harmonium stop which causes the air as it proceeds to the pipes or reeds to pass through a valve having a moveable top...The up and down movement of the top of the valve gives a vibratory movement to the air which similarly affects the sound produced.

**Tremolite** (tre·mŏləit). *Min.* [Named 1796, f. *Tremola*, in Switzerland, where found + -ITE [1].] A white or grey (sometimes transparent) variety of AMPHIBOLE, composed of magnesia and lime, with little or no iron, occurring in fibrous masses or thin-bladed crystals. Also called *grammatite*.

1799 KIRWAN *Geol. Ess.* 219 Not far from St. Gothard, it is found mixed with tremolite, and stratified. 1807 T. THOMSON *Chem.* (ed. 3) II. 476 *Tremolite*..is a compound of silica and lime, or perhaps rather carbonate of lime. 1834–5 J. PHILLIPS *Geol.* in *Encycl. Metrop.* VI. 563/1 That [*sc.* marble] of Glen Tilt, characterized by its accompanying tremolites, lies in a quartzose mica slate. 1849 DANA *Geol.* xvii. (1850) 631 Acicular crystals of white hornblende or tremolite.

Hence **Tremoli·tic** *a.*, of the nature of, or containing tremolite, as *tremolitic marble*.

1879 DANA *Man. Geol.* (ed. 3) 70 Granular Limestone.. Varieties.—a. Statuary Marble;..Tremolitic; contains bladed crystallizations of..tremolite.

‖ **Tremolo** (tre·mŏlo). *Mus.* In 8 **tremola**; also 9 **tremulo.** [It. *tremolo* adj. trembling, shaking, quavering :—L. *tremul-us* TREMULOUS.]

**1.** A tremulous or vibrating effect produced on certain musical instruments or in the human voice in singing, esp. to express intensity of emotion: cf. VIBRATO.

[1724 *Short Explic. For. Wds. in Mus. Bks.*, *Tremola*, to Tremble, a particular Grace in Musick.] 1801 BUSBY *Dict. Mus.*, *Tremolo*, *Tremolante*, or *Tremente*, a word intimating that the notes are to be drawn out with a tremulous motion. 1865 MISS BRADDON *Sir Jasper* xvii, The trickling arpeggios and treble tremulos of a modern nocturne were all-sufficient. 1884 H. C. DEACON in Grove *Dict. Mus.* IV. 166/2 The instrumental tremolo is more nearly allied to the vocal vibrato. Indeed, what is called 'vibrato' on bowed instruments is what would be 'tremolo' in vocal music.

*attrib.* 1896 *Godey's Mag.* Feb. 195/1 Some cheap melodramatic stuff with *tremolo* shudders in the orchestra.

**b.** *transf.* and *fig.*

1877 LOCKHART *Mine is Thine* xviii, Her back still turned and a tremolo in her voice. 1897 *Daily News* 23 Nov. 6/2 He [a writer] executes so many tremolos and elaborate modulations on his theme.

**2.** A mechanical contrivance in an organ by which such an effect is produced; a tremulant. Also *tremolo stop*.

1867 AUG. J. E. WILSON *Vashti* xi, The..overwhelming pathos of the tones affected Dr. Grey much as the tremolo stop in some organ-overture in a dimly-lighted cathedral. 1869 M. J. MATTHEWS in *Eng. Mech.* 31 Dec. 385/3 A sixth is the 'tremolo', the least valuable of the lot.

**Tremor** (tre·mŏɹ, trī·mŏɹ). Also 4–9 **-our**, 5 **-oure.** [ME. *tremour*, a. OF. *tremor*, *-our* fear, terror (13th c. in Godef.), also a trembling or quivering (15th c.) :—L. *tremor*, *-ōrem*, f. *tremĕre* to tremble. In 17th c. reintroduced in L. form *tremor*.]

† **1.** Terror. *Obs.*

*c* 1374 CHAUCER *Troylus* v. 255 Swich a tremor [*v.r.* tremour] fele a-boute his herte That of þe feer his body sholde quake. 1490 CAXTON *Eneydos* xv. 60 To solace and dysporte thy self euermore wyth the thondre and weddrynges, for to gyue unto vs tremoure and feere. *Ibid.* xxii. 81 Horrible dremes & cruel, comen to-fore her in hir mynde that tormente her in tremoure merueyllous.

**2.** Involuntary agitation of the body or limbs, resulting from physical infirmity or from fear or other strong emotion; trembling: see quot. 1866.

[1611 SHAKS. *Wint. T.* I. ii. 110, I haue *Tremor Cordis* on me: my heart daunces.] 1615 CROOKE *Body of Man* 401 The disease called Tremor, or the shaking palsie. 1762–71 H. WALPOLE *Vertue's Anecd. Paint.* (1786) IV. 154 His lips are contracted by tremor. 1807 *Med. Jrnl.* XVII. 428 An approach to syncope, accompanied with more or less of universal tremor, and spasmodic twitchings, are said to have occurred. 1866 A. FLINT *Princ. Med.* (1880) 815 Tremor, that is, alternate contraction and relaxation of muscles in rapid succession, is a symptom of certain lesions of the nervous centres.

**b.** With *a* and *pl.* An instance of this; a fit of trembling.

1616 BULLOKAR *Eng. Expos.*, *Tremour*, a trembling. 1731 ARBUTHNOT *Aliments* v. (1735) 146 By its styptick and stimulating Quality it [tea] affects the Nerves..occasioning Tremors. 1813 J. THOMSON *Lect. Inflam.* 97 A tremor of the hands is often lessened or removed, for a while, by a dram, or some strong wine. 1871 R. ELLIS *Catullus* lxiv. 305 To a tremor of age their gray infirmity rocking.

**c.** *fig.* A nervous thrill caused by emotion or excitement; also, a state of tremulous agitation or excitement.

1754 RICHARDSON *Grandison* IV. vii. 51 He ceased speaking. I was in tremors. 1814 SCOTT *Ld. of Isles* VI. ii, The tremors that unbidden rise. 1838 DICKENS *Nich. Nick.* xxviii, He went about all day in a tremor of delight. 1866 G. MACDONALD *Ann. Q. Neighb.* xii, [She] drew herself up very haughtily..to hide her tremor.

**3.** A tremulous or vibratory movement caused by some external impulse; a vibration, shaking, quivering. *Earth-tremor*, an earthquake.

1635 HEYWOOD *Hierarch.* IX. 570 One of these Tremors lasted forty dayes, When six and twenty tow'rs and castles fell. 1656 BLOUNT *Glossogr.*, *Tremor*, quaking, trembling, shaking, great fear, also an earthquake. 1728 PEMBERTON *Newton's Philos.* 270 Motion consequent upon the tremors of the air, excited by the vibrations of sonorous bodies. 1830 LYELL *Princ. Geol.* I. 324 All countries are liable to slight tremors..when some great crisis of subterranean movement agitates an adjoining volcanic region. 1853 KANE *Grinnell Exp.* xxix. (1856) 250 The peculiar tremor of a cotton-factory. 1878 HUXLEY *Physiogr.* 187 Waves or tremors may be propagated in all directions through the solid ground.

**4.** A tremble or quaver in the voice; a tremulous sound or note.

1797 MRS. RADCLIFFE *Italian* ii, The tremor of his voice.. heightened its eloquence. 1838 LYTTON *Calderon* ii, There seemed a touch of true feeling in the tremour of his rich sweet voice. 1866 G. MACDONALD *Ann. Q. Neighb.* xxxi, There was a tremor in the old lady's voice more of disappointment and hurt than of anger.

**5.** *attrib.*, as **tremor disk**, the telescopic image of a star, as apparently enlarged by the vibration of the telescope and of the atmosphere; **tremor storm**, a prolonged series of earth-tremors.

1889 MILNE in *Nature* 31 Oct. 658/1 At certain seasons tremor storms are very marked. 1905 H. F. NEWALL in *Athenæum* 29 Apr. 534/1 On the general design of spectrographs for equatorials of large aperture, considered from the point of view of 'tremor discs'.

Hence **Tre·morful** *a. dial.*, **Tre·morous** *a. rare*, full of tremor; tremulous.

1901 'ZACK' *Tales Dunstable Weir* 39 'I'll not go nigh the maid', Martin cried, sort of tremorful. 1907 F. THOMPSON *New Poems, Orient Ode* 28 The tremorous nurse of joy.

**Tremorless** (tre·mŏɹlės), *a.* [f. TREMOR + -LESS.] Without tremor or excitement; untrembling, unshaken. Also *fig.*

1869 *Contemp. Rev.* XI. 43 A suicide, whose words, written just before he committed the act, prove his lucid and tremorless sanity. 1882 *Fraser's Mag.* XXV. 415 An albatross blown along by its outstretched tremorless wings. 1898 R. PRIMROSE in *Brit. Weekly* 6 Oct. 411/1 Brave men..with tremorless souls the worst can face.

Hence **Tre·morlessly** *adv.*, without tremor; without a ripple.

1890 CLARK RUSSELL *Ocean Trag.* III. xxxii. 187 The sea ..tremorlessly circling the island.

† **Tremp**, *v. Obs. rare.* [a. F. *tremp-er*: see TRAMP *v.*[2]] *trans.* To mix, temper.

1480 CAXTON *Ovid's Met.* x. vii, She gaf hym a dranke, tremped wt herbes & wyne.

**Trempe**, var. TRAMP *sb.*[2], temper. *Obs.*

**Tremulant** (tre·miŭlănt), *a.* and *sb.* Also erron. **-ent.** [ad. *tremulānt-em*, pr. pple. of late L. *tremulāre* to TREMBLE; in B. 2 repr. It. *tremolante* in same sense.]

A. *adj.* Tremulous; trembling.
1837 Carlyle *Fr. Rev.* I. v. ii, Hapless De Brézé; doomed to survive long ages, in men's memory, in this faint way, with tremulent white rod. 1884 *Pall Mall G.* 8 July 4/2 The Queen of the Opera can sing clean and firm, and with a touch of tremulant emotion, only just when and where it is wanted. 1899 *Allbutt's Syst. Med.* VI. 516 The muscular contractions which execute willed movements are themselves found..to be often slightly tremulant.

B. *sb. Mus.* 1. = Tremolo 2.
1862 *Catal. Internat. Exhib., Brit.* II. No. 3411, 9. Tremulant to swell. 1876 Hiles *Catech. Organ* iii. (1878) 20 A Tremulant is a contrivance that gives to the tone of any department of an Organ to which it may be applied, a waving, or undulating effect. 1903 *Westm. Gaz.* 26 Mar. 8/1 The largest organ in the world is being built..for the St. Louis Exhibition of 1904...There are to be ninety-nine mechanical appliances, thirty-six couplers, five tremulants, and forty-eight adjustable pistons.

2. = Tremolo 1.
1884 *Pall Mall G.* 30 Apr. 4/1 We strongly recommend Mesdames Durand and Laterner to subdue the tremulant in their voices.

**Tremulate** (tre·miŭleit), *v. rare.* [f. late L. *tremulāre* to tremble (Quicherat *Addenda*): see -ate 3 5, 6.]

1. *intr.* To tremble, vibrate; to palpitate, quiver.
1749 Abp. Rhys *Tour Spain & Port.* (1760) 92 Tender Limbs, that tremulate and wanton in the air. 1768 [W. Donaldson] *Life Sir B. Sapskull* I. xiv. 137 His heart flutter'd! and the whole man was tremulating with affection! 1813 T. Busby *Lucretius* II. iv. Comm. 34 The auditory nerve tremulates, and the brain is agitated.

2. *trans.* To cause to tremble or vibrate.
1764 Grainger *Sugar Cane* iii. 205 The faint breeze oft flags on listless wings, Nor tremulates the cocos airiest arch. 1813 T. Busby *Lucretius* I. iii. Comm. 8 No musician is provided..to tremulate the strings. *Ibid.* II. vi. Comm. 8 [The winds] tremulate whatever substances they encounter.

Hence **Tre·mulated, Tre·mulating** *ppl. adjs.*
1813 T. Busby *Lucretius* I. ii. 467 Those colours which.. Impress the tremulating nerves of sight. *Ibid.* II. iv. Comm. 27 Certain pulsations communicated to the air, by the tremulating organs of the voice. *Ibid.* 28 Substituting for his philosophy of vocal atoms, that of a tremulated medium.

**Tremulation** (tremiŭlēⁱ·ʃən). [n. of action f. Tremulate: see -ation.] The action or condition of trembling; an instance of this, a trembling.
1651 Wittie *Primrose's Pop. Err.* iii. xiii. 173 Hence do palsies, tremulations, and other evils arise. 1665 Hooke *Microgr.* lviii. 219, I have often taken notice of the tremulation of the Trees and Bushes. 1718 *Entertainer* No. 9. 67 Before most violent Eruptions of Mount Etna,..they feel Convulsions and Tremulations in the Earth thereabout. 1880 H. A. A. Nicholls in *Nature* 19 Feb. 373/2 The resistance to the volcanic force was too small to cause much tremulation.

**Tremulous** (tre·miŭləs), *a.* [f. L. *tremul-us* trembling, quivering, shaking (f. *trem-ĕre* to tremble, shake) + -ous.]

1. Of persons, their limbs, etc.: Characterized or affected by trembling or quivering from nervous agitation or weakness, of mental or physical origin; hence, fearful, timorous.
1611 Speed *Hist. Gt. Brit.* ix. viii. (1623) 569 The Monkes [being] very tremulous to enter matter of new intrications. 1667 *Decay Chr. Piety* xi. 310 The tender tremulous Christian, 'tis easie to discern how much he must be distracted and amaz'd by them. 1714 R. Fiddes *Pract. Disc.* I. 310, I shall appear to be of an abject and tremulous spirit. 1784 Cowper *Task* ii. 729 His voice unstrung Grew tremulous. 1897 R. Hichens *Londoners* (1902) 101 She gained the purple drawing-room on rather tremulous feet.

b. Said of writing, a line, or the like, done by a tremulous hand; hence, finely wavy.

2. Of things: Characterized by trembling or vibration; vibratory; easily caused to vibrate or tremble.
1616 Chapman *Homer's Hymns, To Mother of Gods* 4 That doth with Cymball sounds, delight her life; and tremulous diuisions of the Fife. 1664 Power *Exp. Philos.* i. 21 In my long Telescope I can some days see a tremulous Motion and Agitation of rowling fumes, and strong Atoms in the air. 1774 Goldsm. *Nat. Hist.* (1776) VI. 265 A tremulous motion which this animal [torpedo] is found to possess. 1815 J. Smith *Panorama Sc. & Art* II. 497 Gelatine, or jelly,..has a soft tremulous consistence. 1860 Farrar *Orig. Lang.* i. 6 The tremulous ripple on the surface of the sea.

b. Ready to vibrate in response *to* some influence; also *fig.* tremblingly sensitive or responsive.
1794 G. Adams *Nat. & Exp. Philos.* IV. xlix. 349 Columns of marble or porphyry are tremulous to thunder explosions, and to certain tones of an organ. 1867 H. Macmillan *Bible Teach.* i. (1870) 3 He is tremulous..to all the influences of the hour and scene.

†3. Affecting the organs of taste with a trembling or quivering sensation. *Obs. rare.*
1675 Grew *Disc. Tasts Plants* i. § 15 Tasts are either Still, as usually; or may be called Tremulous, as the Heat produced by *Pyrethrum*. 1707 *Curios. in Husb. & Gard.* 39 Grew..finds in Plants sixteen sorts of Tastes...16. Tremulous, as the Root of wild Pellitory.

4. Characterized by use of the tremolo in singing. (*nonce-use.*)
1884 *Pall Mall G.* 26 July 4/1 He quivered and shook himself all to pieces with the tremulous fever now so fashionable. 1887 *Daily News* 25 July 4/8 The tremulous vocalists one after the other failed to win popular favour.

**Tremulously** (tre·miŭləsli), *adv.* [f. prec. + -ly 2.] In a tremulous manner; tremblingly.
1730-6 Bailey (folio), *Tremulously*, with trembling, tremblingly. 1757 W. Wilkie *Epigon.* v. 127 Their lofty spires..O'er the pale ashes tremulously glow. 1811 Shelley *Let.* in Dowden *Life* (1886) I. iv. 167 Once I was tremulously alive to tones and scenes. 1886 *Manch. Exam.* 9 Jan. 5/1 The great Protestant and industrial interests stand tremulously on the watch.

**Tremulousness** (tre·miŭləsnės). [f. as prec. + -ness.] The state or quality of being tremulous.
1727 Bailey vol. II, *Tremulousness*, tremblingness. 1755 Johnson, *Trill*, quaver; tremulousness of musick. 1817 J. Evans *Excurs. Windsor*, etc. 74 His whole manner evidently marked by a nervous tremulousness. 1857 H. Spencer in *Fraser's Mag.* Oct. 401/2 This tremulousness of voice is very effectively used by some vocalists.

**Tremyl, -ylle,** obs. forms of Tremble.

**Tren, Trenail**: see Tree, Treen, Treenail.

**Trench** (trenᵗʃ), *sb.* Also 4-7 **trenche**, (6 **trenshe**, *Sc.* **treinch, trinch, -e, trynsch(e, trinsch(e**, 7 **trintch**). See also Tranche. [a. OF. *trenche* (1288 in Godef.), later OF. and mod.F. *tranche*, an act of cutting, a cut, a gash; a ditch or trench; a slice, etc., verbal sb. from OF. *trenchier*, F. *trancher* to cut, Trench *v.* See also Tranche. Many of the Eng. senses, wanting or obs. in mod.F., are supplied by *tranchée*.]

†1. A path or track cut through a wood or forest; an alley; a hollow walk. *Obs.*
c 1386 Chaucer *Sqr.'s T.* 384 And in a trench [*v.r.* trenche] forth in the park gooth she. c 1420 Lydg. *Thebes* i. in *Chaucer's Wks.* (1561) 358/2 As thei rengen the trenches by and by Thei heard a noise. 1575 Turberv. *Venerie* 98 By this word Trench is vnderstoode euery small way, not so commonly vsed...So is there also a difference betweene a Trench and a path. For trenches as I say, be wayes and walkes in a woode or Forest.

2. A long and narrow hollow cut out of the ground, a cutting; a ditch, fosse; a deep furrow. Also *fig.*
1489 Caxton *Faytes of A.* i. ix. 23 To lepen ouer trenchis or dyches. 1553 Eden *Treat. Newe Ind.* (Arb.) 13 They moued neare vnto the trenche or ditche of the castell. 1677 Yarranton *Eng. Improv.* 192 The River Dee must be carried in a large Cut or Trench through the lands..as far as Flint Castle, and then dropt by a large Cut, into the Deep Water below the Brewhouse. 1782 Miss Burney *Cecilia* vii. vi, How deep a trench of real misery do you sink, in order to raise this pile of fancied happiness! 1842 Tennyson *Audley Court* 41 Be shot for sixpence in a battle-field, And shovell'd up into some bloody trench. 1911 J. Ward *Roman Era in Brit.* viii. 140 A single trench disclosed broken pottery and charcoal.

3. *Mil.* An excavation of this kind, the earth from which is thrown up in front as a parapet, serving either to cover or to oppose the advance of a besieging force. Chiefly in *plural.* **a.** More particularly applied to the ditch or excavation.
c 1500 *Three Kings Sons* 42 That ther might be made grete trenches, that ther might be grete nombre of people hid theryn. 1513 Douglas *Æneis* xi. xvii. 104 Thai..delvys trynschis all the wallis abowt. a 1548 Hall *Chron., Hen. V*, 74 b, They without made mynes, cast trenches and shot gunnes dayly at the walles. 1623 Massinger *Bondman* ii. i, There are trenches too..In which to stand all night to the knees in water In gallants breeds the tooth-ache. 1879 *Cassell's Techn. Educ.* ii. 103/2 When this excavation is behind the mound it is called a trench.

b. *pl.* Including both the excavation and the mound or embankment: see quot. 1828. *To mount, relieve the trenches*: see quot. 1706. *To open trenches*: see Open *v.* 4 b, quot. 1853.
1585 T. Washington tr. *Nicholay's Voy.* i. xvii. 20 [They] did in the meane space diligently aduaunce their trenches and approaches for planting of their ordinance. 1607 Shaks. *Cor.* i. vi. 12, I saw our party to their Trenches driuen. a 1674 Clarendon *Hist. Reb.* xiii. § 22 Cromwell knew them too well to fear them..when there were no Trenches..to keep him from them. 1706 Phillips (ed. Kersey) s. v., Trenches are Works..either cut into the Ground..or else raised above it when rocky, with Bavins, Wooll-packs, Bags or Baskets filled with Earth. *Ibid., To Mount the Trenches*, is to go upon Duty in them. *To Relieve the Trenches*, is to relieve those that have been upon Duty there. 1777 Watson *Philip II* (1839) 95 By the advice of Dragut he resolved to extend his trenches and batteries, on the side next to the town. 1828 J. M. Spearman *Brit. Gunner* (ed. 2) 397 Trenches. A general term for all the approaches at a siege. 1848 Lytton *Harold* vii. iii, On the other side of the trenches were marching against them their own countrymen.

†c. Sometimes more particularly applied to the rampart, mound, or embankment. *Obs.*
1536 Bellenden *Cron. Scot.* (1821) I. 160 To bring treis to fill the fowseis,..otheris maid sindry instrumentis to breke down thair trinschis. 1560 Daus tr. *Sleidane's Comm.* 259 To bring yᵉ pionners to cast down their trenches. 1617 Moryson *Itin.* ii. 169 It was resolued that the ditches.. should bee deepned, and the trenches highthned. 1678 tr. *Gaya's Art of War* ii. 113 A Trench, a casting up of Earth by way of Parapet, with a Ditch or Foss on the side of the Enemy. 1693 in *Macfarlane's Geog. Collect.* (S.H.S.) II. 218 Ane ruinous tour surrounded with ane trintch of stone and earth. 1726 Leoni *Alberti's Archit.* II. 100/1 Severus threw up a trench a hundred and twenty two miles long.

d. *fig.* or *transf.*
1601 R. Johnson *Kingd. & Commw.* (1603) 23 The sea, which to the inhabitants is a deep trench against hostile inuasions. 1677 Gilpin *Demonol.* (1867) 299 A soul that is within the trenches of present peace. 1723 Mandeville *Fab. Bees* (1725) I. 66 Seducers..don't make their Attacks at Noon-day, but cut their Trenches at Night.

4. *transf.* Something resembling a trench. **a.** A cut, scar, furrow, or deep wrinkle in the face.
1588 Shaks. *Tit. A.* v. ii. 23 Witnesse these Trenches made by griefe and care. 1823 Scott *Quentin D.* vii, 'Thou name ladies' love, with such a trench in thy visage!' said Guthrie. 1830 Godwin *Cloudesley* II. xii. 185 Without trench or wrinkle, in his honest countenance.

b. *Anat.* and *Zool.* A cavity, pit, fossa.
1615 Crooke *Body of Man* 392 That cauity which is commonly called..the Trench or Spoone of the heart. 1631 Widdowes *Nat. Philos.* 62 From the trench of the veynes hang downeward white, narrow veynes. 1634 T. Johnson tr. *Parey's Chirurg.* iii. i. (1678) 54 The trench of the heart which..the Latines [called] *scrobiculus cordis*. 1846 Dana *Zooph.* (1848) 257 Bottom of trench convoluto-porous. *Ibid.* Gloss., *Trench* (Fossa), a meandering cell in the Meandrine Corals.

†5. A slice. Cf. Tranche. *Obs. rare.*
1558 Warde tr. *Alexis' Secr.* (1559) 70 Take..sixe Lemons cut in trenches.

†6. A trencher. *Obs. rare.*
(Perh. only in pl. *trenches* for *trenchers*.)
1602 in *Collect. Archæol.* (1863) II. 105 Pottes and cruses xxx..Trenches viij dossen.

†7. = Trenchefil, tranchefil (in both senses).
a. 1611 Cotgr., *Trenchefile*,..the trench, or trenching of a Crossebow string; that part thereof whereinto the neb of the arrow entreth.
b. 1607 Topsell *Four-f. Beasts* (1658) 251 The Indians were wont to use no bridles..but only..putting a long round trench through his [the horse's] mouth, to the edge whereof they fasten the rains, wherewithall they guide the beast. 1614 Markham *Cheap Husb.* i. ii. (1668) 16 Now and then drawing the trench to and fro in his Mouth. 1639 T. de Gray *Compl. Horsem.* 345 Tye it to his snaffle, trench, or bit. c 1720 W. Gibson *Farrier's Dispens.* ix. iii. (1734) 201.

†8. A griping or colic in the horse; also, a kind of worm infesting the horse. [= F. *tranchée*; cf. Cotgr., '*Trenchée*.., a fretting, wringing, or griping in the bellie..; the wormes, or bellie-ache.'] *Obs.*
1578 Lyte *Dodoens* ii. lxxiv. 246 It cureth the trenches or gryping payne in the small of the bellie or bowels. 1587 Mascall *Govt. Cattle, Horses* (1596) 133.

9. *attrib.* and *Comb.*, as *trench-cutting, -digger, -digging, -fighting, -guard, -lines, -work*; *trench-encircled, -like* adjs.; **trench-brace**, an extensible screw-brace or strut used to prevent the caving in of the side walls or to support the sheet-piling of a trench; **trench-cart** *Mil.*, a narrow hand-cart on which ammunition can be carried through the trenches; **trench-cavalier** *Mil.*, a high parapet constructed by the besiegers upon the glacis to command and enfilade the covered way of the fortress; **trench-drain, trench-elm**: see quots.; **trench-kitchen** *Mil.*, a field-kitchen where the fire is made in a small trench; **trenchman**, a labourer who opens trenches for pipe-laying; † **trench-master**, an officer in charge of the construction of trenches; **trench-planting**: see quot. 1905; † **trench-sergeant**, cf. *trench-master*. See also Trench-plough.
1877 Knight *Dict. Mech.*, *Trench-cart. 1834-47 J. S. Macaulay *Field Fortif.* (1851) 234 A return is then made to the trench, and the whole of the end of each is converted into a *trench cavalier. 1853 Stocqueler *Milit. Encycl.* 254/2 At the angle of the glacis, high breastworks, called trench cavaliers, are formed, to allow a plunging fire..to be directed into the covered-way. 1876 'Ouida' *Winter City* vi, Palestrina often saw its lord..plan *trench-cuttings to arrest the winter-swollen brooks. 1770 Langhorne *Plutarch* (1851) II. 1045/2 Making excursions to harass the *trench-diggers. 1846 *J. Baxter's Libr. Pract. Agric.* (ed. 4) I. 153, I have often had fine crops [of carrots] upon poor soils by *trench-digging the land to the depth of twenty inches. 1805 R. W. Dickson *Pract. Agric.* II. 923 *Trench Drain.—A deep ditch, or drain, which meets the trenches for the purpose of taking the water away speedily after the irrigation is performed. 1676 M. Cook *Forest-trees* xi. 50 The best sort [of Elm] is that which..shoots with a shoot not much less than a Sallow when it is lopped: it is called by some the *Trench-Elm, by others the Marsh-Elm. 1881 W. Cory *Lett. & Jrnls.* (1897) 468 A few bits of *trench-fighting. 1903 O. Causton in *Cornh. Mag.* Feb. 202 The long white *trench-graves on the summit move one more, perhaps, than any others in South Africa. 1849 Jas. Grant *Kirkaldy of Gr.* xxviii, He drove the *trench-guards down the Lawnmarket in disorder. 1900 *Westm. Gaz.* 19 Jan. 2/1 The *trench kitchen is more generally used in South Africa. 1908 *Blackw. Mag.* Apr. 502/1 A treble tier of *trench lines. 1577-87 Holinshed *Chron.* III. 1133/2 Edward Chamberleine esquier capteine of the pioners, sir Richard Leigh *trenchmaster. 1617 Moryson *Itin.* ii. 148 Captain Josias Bodley, Trench-Master. 1830 *Planting* 35 (Libr. Usef. Knowl.) Slit-planting..holing or pitting..*trench-planting..furrow-planting. 1905 *Terms Forestry* (U.S. Dep. Agric., Bulletin lxi.), *Trench planting*, a method of planting on dry ground, in which the seeds or young trees are set in trenches. *Syn.*: pit planting. 1755 *Mem. Capt. P. Drake* II. iii. 73 He would make me *Trench-Sergeant...In this Duty I was to attend in the Trenches twice a Day,..to have under my Command a Detachment of thirty unarmed Men ..to gather the Pick-axes, Shovels, Wheel-Barrows, etc. that should be left or scattered by the Workmen. 1884 *Mil. Engineering* (ed. 3) I. ii. 29 Fig. 1..represents this arrangement in a parallel executed by common *trench-work, and Fig. 2 in one constructed by flying trench-work.

**Trench** (trenᵗʃ), *v.* Forms: see the sb. [a. OF. *trenchier* (11th c. in Godef. *Compl.*), F. *trancher* to cut, hew, slice, etc. = Prov. *trencar*, *trinquar*, Catal. *trencar*, Sp., Pg. *trincar*; cf. It. *trinciare*. These Romanic forms are held to represent a popular L. **trincāre*, altered from L. *truncāre* to cut or lop off, f. *truncus* the trunk of a tree: cf. Truncheon. Our sense 1 is directly from OF. Senses 3–5 are either immediately from TRENCH *sb.* or largely influenced by it. Senses 6–8 are not in French; they prob. arose as figures from the action of extending military trenches so as to reach or touch the place besieged.]

**I.** To cut, make a cutting.

**1.** *trans.* To cut; to divide by cutting, slice, cut in pieces; to sever by cutting, cut off; to cut into, make a cut in; to cut *one's way*. Also *absol.*

**1483** CAXTON *Gold. Leg.* 104 b/2 Thomas is as moche to saye as..double or trenchyd and heuen. **1485** — *Chas. Gt.* II. x. 63 [He] gaf hym a stroke vpon his helme so sharply that he trenched moo than vc maylles. *c* **1510** BARCLAY *Mirr. Gd. Manners* (1570) Bj, Though the toth [of a serpent] trencheth, the tayle beareth poyson. **1513** DOUGLAS *Æneis* VI. iv. 32 Enee hym self..to the, Proserpyne, A ȝeld kow all to trynschit. *c* **1520** BARCLAY *Jugurth* (1557) 9 To bringe vnto him the heed of Hiempsal trenched from the body. **1725** POPE *Odyss.* x. 615 Draw thy falchion, and on every side Trench the black earth a cubit long and wide. **1856** BRYANT *Two Graves* 43 Trench the strong hard mould with the spade. **1867** FROUDE *Short Stud.* (ed. 2) 167 They are trenching their way thro' the weak place in the Pentateuch.

† **b.** To cut or carve *in* or *into* a surface. *Obs.*

**1591** SHAKS. *Two Gent.* III. ii. 7 This weake impresse of Loue, is as a figure Trenched in ice. **1665** J. WEBB *Stone-Heng* (1725) 148 Inscriptions cut or trencht in one of the Stones. —150 Those..had Epigraphs trencht into the Craggs.

† **c.** To make (a cut, gash, or wound) *in* or *into* something. *Obs. rare.*

**1592** SHAKS. *Ven. & Ad.* 1052 The wide wound, that the boare had trencht In his soft flanke. **1610** FLETCHER *Faithf. Sheph.* IV. ii, The wound by cruel knife Trencht into him.

**2.** To cut or make a cutting through a ridge or raised surface. The object of the vb. may be (*a*) the cutting made, (*b*) the ridge or surface cut through.

**1601** R. JOHNSON *Kingd. & Commw.* (1603) 50 For the ease of pilgrims..iournieng between Cair and Mecha, she began to trench a water course alongst the way. **1865** GEIKIE *Scen. & Geol. Scot.* ix. 238 The ridge is deeply trenched with gullies and narrow glens. *Ibid.* x. 285 If then the chain of the Sidlaws once ran unbroken to the south-west..how could the Tay trench it? **1881** GEIKIE in *Nature* 3 Nov. 1/1 In the general denudation of the country, deep valleys have been trenched through it.

**b.** *fig.* (with the surface cut or furrowed as *obj.*)

**1624** QUARLES *Job* xi. 50 Thy Hand hath trencht my cheekes with water-furrowes. **1787** BURNS *To Haggis* iii, His knife see rustic Labour dight,..Trenching your gushing entrails bright, Like ony ditch. **1840** R. H. HORNE *Gregory VII*, IV. i, Oft have I marked a deep awe trench his face. **1868** NETTLESHIP *Browning* iii. 95 A mouth..trenched on either side by early pronounced lines.

**c.** *Naut.* *To trench the ballast*: see quots.

**1627** CAPT. SMITH *Seaman's Gram.* vii. 33 To finde a leake, they trench the Ballast, that is, to diuide it. **1867** SMYTH *Sailor's Word-bk.*, *Trench the ballast*, to divide the ballast in a ship's hold to get at a leak, or to trim and stow it.

**d.** *To trench beaver*: to cut their dam, so as to catch the beavers.

(Cf. **1830** *Gardens & Menag. Zool. Soc.* I. 167 When the sheet of water they inhabit is merely kept up by a dam, they are..taken up by letting off the water, and leaving their huts completely dry.) **1822–34** *Good's Study Med.* (ed. 4) IV. 80 A young Chipewyan had separated from the rest of his band for the purpose of trenching beaver.

**II.** From TRENCH *sb.*; to do something to, with, or by a trench.

**3.** To cut a trench or trenches in (the ground).

**1530** PALSGR. 761/2, I trench the grounde, *je trenche*.. They have trenched a large myle and more. **1541** *Act* 33 *Hen. VIII* c. 35 The place..so broken dygged or trenched. **1870** N. F. HELE *Aldeburgh* iv. 25 We trenched the tumulus in a radiate manner, from the centre towards the circumference. **1872** G. DOWKER in *Archæol. Cantiana* VIII. 8 We subsequently trenched the surface of the platform.

**b.** *spec.* in *Agric.* and *Hort.* To make a series of trenches in digging or ploughing (a piece of ground), so as to bring the lower soil to the surface. *To trench up*, to lay (land) in trenches and ridges alternately (cf. RIDGE *v.* 2); *To trench down*, to bury (soil or weeds) in trenching. Also *absol.*

**1573** TUSSER *Husb.* (1878) 83 Thy garden plot latelie well trenched and muckt. **1649** in *Archæologia* X. 432 A muskmilion ground trenched, manured, and very well ordered. **1763** MILLS *Pract. Husb.* IV. 68 This may..be prevented by..trenching the ground up in ridges. **1793** *Trans. Soc. Arts* (ed. 2) V. 11, I trenched up the whole to the depth of eighteen inches. **1798** NICOL *Scotch Forcing Gard.* (ed. 2) 202 Trench three spits deep, by which the bottom and top are reversed, and the middle remains in the middle. **1799** J. ROBERTSON *Agric. Perth* App. 491 Many farmers were wont to trench down the low moss, and to cover it furrow deep, with clay taken out of the trench. *Mod.* The garden ought to be trenched.

**c.** *intr.* or *absol.* To dig a trench or trenches.

**1786** in J. Lloyd *Old S. Wales Iron Works* (1906) 34 Free power..to bore, dig, delve, and trench in, upon, or under the said..Parcel of land. **1833** HT. MARTINEAU *Tale of Tyne* i, Walter was..busy trenching in his garden. **1882** *Garden* 30 Dec. 577/1 Trench deeply..and as early in the winter as possible. *Ibid.*, When trenching..use half decayed manure.

† **d.** *intr.* Of a torrent: To cut its way. *Obs.*

**1613–16** W. BROWNE *Brit. Past.* II. i, As all the floods (Down trenching from small groves and greater woods) The vast insatiate Sea doth still devoure.

**4.** *trans.* To furnish with, set, or place in a trench. † **a.** To divert (a river) by means of a trench. *Obs. rare*$^{-1}$.

**1596** SHAKS. 1 *Hen. IV*, III. i. 112 A little Charge will trench him [the Trent] here, And on this North side winne this Cape of Land, And then he runnes straight and euen.

**b.** To set or plant in a trench.

**1678** R. L'ESTRANGE *Seneca's Mor.*, *Epist.* ix. (1696) 515 This would not have been..if you had Trenched them and Water'd them. *Mod.* Celery is usually trenched.

**c.** To bury in a trench.

**1870** *Standard* 14 Dec., They detail squads of their soldiers to trench their fallen comrades.

**d.** To drain (land) by means of open trenches or ditches; to ditch.

**1811** T. DAVIS *Agric. Wilts* App. 261 *Trenching or Guttering Land*, draining it with open drains. **1875** [implied in TRENCHER[2] 2].

**5.** *Mil.* To surround or fortify with a trench; to cast a trench *about*, *around* (a post, army, town, etc.); to entrench; also, to confine by means of a trench (*rare*, ? *obs.*).

*a* **1548** HALL *Chron.*, *Hen. V* 65 b, The Frenchmen diched, trenched and paled their lodgynges for feare of after clappes. *Ibid.*, *Hen. VI* 165 b, The place which they had trenched, dytched, and fortefied with ordenaunce. *Ibid.*, *Edw. IV* 220 b, The duke of Somerset..trenched his campe rounde about of suche an altitude, and so strongly. **1667** MILTON *P. L.* I. 677 Bands Of Pioners with Spade and Pickaxe arm'd Forerun the Royal Camp, to trench a Field, Or cast a Rampart. **1715–20** POPE *Iliad* XX. 175 A mound Of earth congested, wall'd, and trench'd around. **1827** KEBLE *Chr. Y.*, *10th Sund. Trin.* v, Now foes shall trench thee round, And lay thee even with earth. **1899** [see *trenched* below].

**b.** *fig.* To entrench.

**1601** ? MARSTON *Pasquil & Kath.* I. 113 Trench your selfe within the peoples loue. **1624** GEE *Foot out of Snare* 46 Trenching themselues in the Mines of their Labyrinths at home, or masking in their gold and siluer abroad. **1624** MASSINGER *Renegado* II. iv, A hermit in a desert, trenched with prayers. **1759** MASON *Caractacus* 52, I spy'd their helms 'Mid brakes and boughs trench'd in the heath below. **1838** CHALMERS *Wks.* XII. 81 One who..was..trenched among what he thought the speculations of orthodoxy.

† **c.** *intr.* To cast trenches, in siege works; in quot. 1623, to make one's way by trenching (*fig.*). *To trench at*: to lay siege to by means of trenches.

**1582–8** *Hist. Jas. VI* (1804) 231 The pyoneris hade trinchett in the castell hill of Edinburgh, and erectit a braid sconce to hyde thame. **1623** B. JONSON *Time Vind.* Wks. (Rtldg.) 636/1 The boy with buttons, and the basket-wench, To vent their wares into my works do trench! **1742** YOUNG *Nt. Th.* VI. 21 Like pow'rful armies trenching at a town, By slow, and silent, but resistless sap.

**III.** † **6.** *intr.* *To trench to* (*unto*): To extend in effect to; to extend so as to affect or touch. (Cf. TOUCH *v.* 20.) *Obs.*

**1612** BACON *Ess.*, *Judicature* (Arb.) 458 The thing deduced to Iudgement, may bee *meum et tuum*, when the reason and consequence thereof may trench to point of estate. *a* **1625** SIR H. FINCH *Law* (1636) 83 In law it is said the demise of the King, and a gift unto the King, without saying more, trencheth to his successors. **1628** COKE *On Litt.* 209 b, Because the money at the beginning trenched to the Feoffee in manner as a dutie. **1633** T. NASH *Quaternio* 234 If a man shall suborne two witnesses to depose a thing which trencheth to the life of a third person.

† **b.** *intr.* To extend or stretch (to a distance or in some direction); to trend. *Obs. rare.*

**1720** DE FOE *Capt. Singleton* viii. (1840) 133 The land trenched away to the west. **1775** ROMANS *Florida* App. 12 The shore is pretty bold too, except at the two ends, where the bars of said two rivers trench off a great way. *Ibid.* 19 From Hobé inlet we find the coast trenching about S 20 E or nearly S S E for about 3½ leagues.

**7.** † **a.** *To trench into* (*unto*): To 'cut' into, to enter into so as to affect or concern intimately. *Obs.*

**1621** ELSING *Debates Ho. Lords* (Camden) 59 This trencheth deeper unto us then we all conceave. A delinquent is brought before us, and, before yt was determined, resumed into the Kinges hands. **1622** MISSELDEN *Free Trade* (ed. 2) 131 It..is a matter that trencheth into the Supreme power and dignity of the King, and is peculiar to Him alone. **1641** W. HAKEWIL *Libertie of Subject* 91 A thing which trencheth as deepely into the privat interest of the Subject as the laying of Impositions.

**b.** *To trench on* or *upon*: To encroach or infringe (however slightly) *on* or *upon* a region which is the domain of another. † *To trench too near, too nigh*, = to come dangerously near infringing upon (*obs.*).

**1622** MABBE tr. *Aleman's Guzman d'Alf.* II. 15 The King ..being desirous to know, if any man of worth had presumed so farre to trench vpon what he had done. **1627** E. F. *Hist. Edw. II* (1680) 59 Nor may you trench too near your Soveraigns actions. **1629** N. CARPENTER *Achitophel* II. (1640) 78 [It] seemes to me to trench too farre on Gods Prerogative. **1647** N. BACON *Disc. Govt. Eng.* I. xl. 98 They would not allow their secular affairs to trench too nigh that days devotion. **1649** G. DANIEL *Trinarch.*, *Rich. II* ccc, But least my running Tent may Trench vpon Another's feild, I fixe my Pole downe here. **1799** J. ROBERTSON *Agric. Perth* 553 This scheme..may seem to trench on the liberty of individuals. **1865** MERIVALE *Rom. Emp.* VIII. lxiv. 116 He trenches a little on the night,..but no one finds the time long. **1866** MRS. H. WOOD *St. Martin's Eve* xiii, Though I squandered my own property, I have not trenched on yours.

**c.** in vaguer use, To come in thought, speech, or action close *upon* (something); to border closely *upon*, to verge *upon*; to approach *towards*; hence, to have a bearing *upon* or reference to (something).

**1635** HEYLIN *Sabbath* I. (1636) 190 Some..have trenched too neere upon the Rabbins, in binding men to nice and scrupulous observances. *a* **1639** W. WHATELEY *Prototypes* III. xxxix. (1640) 24 He did trench a little too neare upon an untruth. **1643** BAKER *Chron.*, *Hen. VI* 5 Knowing how far they trenched upon the Dukes destruction, and her own. **1691** *Case of Exeter Coll.* Pref. A ij b, Insignificant suggestions that trench nothing at all on the merits of the Cause. **1746** FIELDING *True Patriot* No. 23 They hold them [other persons and things] of no consequence,..unless they trench somewhat towards their own order or calling. **1841** D'ISRAELI *Amen. Lit.* (1867) 355 Some unlucky jest, trenching on treason, flew from the lips of the unguarded jester. **1876** C. M. DAVIES *Unorth. Lond.* 20 The opinions of this school—where they trench most closely on orthodoxy.

† **d.** *trans.* To trench or encroach upon. *Obs.*

**1626** B. JONSON *Staple of N.* v. vi, Who did? I? I trench the liberty o' the subiects?

Hence **Tre·nched**, **Tre·nching** *ppl. adjs.*

**1589** PUTTENHAM *Eng. Poesie* II. xi. (Arb.) 107 With sharpe Trenching blade of bright steele. **1596** SHAKS. 1 *Hen. IV*, I. i. 7 No more shall trenching Warre channell her fields. **1605** — *Macb.* III. iv. 27 Safe in a ditch he bides, With twenty trenched gashes on his head. **1763** MILLS *Pract. Husb.* IV. 322 Whatever..might afterward press down the trenched earth. **1899** *Daily News* 14 Dec. 5/5 The Highlanders formed up to renew the attack on the trenched kopje.

**Trenchancy** (tre·nᵗʃănsi). [f. next: see -ANCY.] The quality of being trenchant, 'sharp', or 'cutting'; incisiveness; causticity.

**1866** *London Rev.* 24 Nov. 568 Expected..to accept bitterness and passion for satire and trenchancy. **1877** MORLEY *Crit. Misc.* Ser. II. 390 Trenchancy whether in speaker or writer is a most effective tone for a large public. **1892** STEVENSON *Across the Plains* 203 With the same trenchancy of contrast.

**Trenchant** (tre·nᵗʃănt), *a.* (*sb.*) Also 4–5 **trenchaunt**, (5 **-aunte**), **-ande**, (5 *Sc.* **trensand**, 6 **trenchand**, 7 **trencheant**, **trinchante**); see also TRANCHANT. [a. OF. *trenchant* (mod.F. *tranchant*), pr. pple. of † *trenchier*, *trancher* to cut: see TRENCH *v.* and -ANT.]

**1.** Cutting, adapted for cutting; having a keen edge, sharp; † sharp-pointed (*obs.*). *arch.* and *poet.*

*c* **1330** R. BRUNNE *Chron. Wace* (Rolls) 4414 Nemny on þe heued he smot; Hit was trenchaunt, ouer fer hit bot. *c* **1380** *Sir Ferumb.* 537 Ich hem wolde wel conquere wiþ my swerd trenchaunt. *c* **1400** MAUNDEV. (1839) v. 47 This monstre ..hadde ij hornes trenchant on his forhede. *c* **1470** HENRY *Wallace* IV. 662 The trensand blaid to-persyt euirydeill. *c* **1477** CAXTON *Jason* 8 b, Jason smote another Centaure in the nekke with a trenchaunt arowe. **1590** SPENSER *F. Q.* I. i. 17 He..with his trenchand blade her boldly kept From turning backe. **1663** BUTLER *Hud.* I. i. 359 The trenchant Blade, Toledo trusty, For want of fighting was grown rusty. *a* **1774** GOLDSM. *Surv. Exp. Philos.* (1776) I. 236 The thin or trenchant end [of the wedge] is applied to the timber to be cleft, and the thick end struck upon by an hammer. **1830** TENNYSON '*Clear-headed friend*' ii, Nor martyr-flames, nor trenchant swords Can do away that ancient lie.

**b.** *Zool.* Of a tooth, bill, etc.: Having a cutting edge; sectorial.

**1831** MᶜMURTRIE *Cuvier's Anim. Kingd.* II. 136 In a fourth tribe [of fishes], the teeth are trenchant. It comprises two genera, *Boops* and *Oblada*. **1835–6** *Todd's Cycl. Anat.* I. 312/2 Trenchant bills which are..flattened horizontally. **1881** MIVART *Cat* 29 The lower molar..having a more completely trenchant form than any other tooth.

**c.** *transf.*, or in *fig.* or *allusive* use.

**1603** HOLLAND *Plutarch's Mor.* 30 Whose blood..now Trenchant Mars hath shed. **1809** W. IRVING *Knickerb.* VI. viii. (1849) 369 Pursuing its trenchant course, it severed off a deep coat pocket. **1851** GLADSTONE *Glean.* VI. lix. 39 Must it not be dangerous to place weapons so keen and trenchant in the hands of raw recruits? **1865** *Trav. by 'Umbra'* 10 Carve the impalpable and viewless air with thy trenchant paper knife. **1871** FREEMAN *Hist. Ess.* Ser. I. v. 117 The biographer of Edward [III], Mr. Longman, cannot wield the trenchant weapons of Lord Brougham.

**2.** *fig.* esp. of language: Incisive; vigorous and clear; effective, energetic.

*a* **1325** [implied in TRENCHANTLY]. **1663** BUTLER *Hud.* I. III. 882 Their Swords Were sharp and trencheant, not their Words. **1824** MISS MITFORD *Village* Ser. I. (1863) 208 Some trenchant repartee, that cuts off the poor answer's head like a razor. **1842** — in L'Estrange *Life* (1870) III. ix. 159 The most trenchant and violent writer of the 'Times'. **1877** OWEN *Wellesley's Desp.* p. xxxvi, For all these evils.. Wellesley devised prompt and trenchant remedies, most unpalatable to his employers.

**3.** *transf.* and *fig.* Sharply defined or outlined; clear-cut; distinct.

**1849** RUSKIN *Sev. Lamps* iii. § 14. 78 The use of the dark mass characterises, generally, a trenchant style of design. **1852** DANA *Crust.* II. 745 This subtribe has trenchant limits. **1873** H. ROGERS *Orig. Bible* ii. 78 The line of demarcation is seemingly most sharp and trenchant.

¶ **4.** *erron.* Capable of being cut.

**1824** LAMB *Elia* Ser. II. *Blakesmoor in H—shire*, What herald shall go about to strip me of an idea? Is it trenchant to their swords?

† **B.** *sb.* One who or that which cuts or severs; a cutter, a divider. *Obs. rare*$^{-1}$.

*a* **1660** *Contemp. Hist. Irel.* (Ir. Archæol. Soc.) I. 133 A turne-coate of lawfull confederacie, a trinchante of holy union, a scandall and reproofe of all Christian pietie.

† **b.** *Esquire trenchant*, an esquire carver; cf. ESQUIRE *sb.*[1] 1 c and 5, quot. 1797. *Obs.*

**1563** RANDOLPH in *Calr. Scott. Pap.* II. 3 A longe yonge man..one of her graces esquire trenchantes. [Cf. **1611** COTGR., *Trenchant, Escuyer,..valet trenchant*, a Caruer.]

**Trenchantly** (tre·nᵗʃăntli), *adv.* [f. prec. + -LY[2].] In a trenchant manner; 'cuttingly', incisively; sharply and effectively; definitely; so as to go to the root of a matter.

*a* **1325** *MS. Rawl. B.* 520 lf. 61 b, Him bi-houez to seggen trenchauntliche þat he is bastard. **1870** R. B. Brough *Marston Lynch* xiii. 116 He is trenchantly severe on better painters than himself. **1873** Hamerton *Intell. Life* vii. iii. (1875) 241 The educations of the two sexes were so trenchantly separated that neither had access to the knowledge of the other. **1877** Le Conte *Elem. Geol.* iii. (1879) 161 Groups of species confined within certain areas differing from other groups, sometimes overlapping them, sometimes trenchantly separated. **1896** W. C. Sidgwick in *Times* 11 Dec. 10/6, I hope the 'roughness of my methods' only means that I dealt trenchantly with his theories.

So **Tre·nchantness,** the quality of being trenchant.

**1892** *Temple Bar Mag.* Oct. 289 She..says so, with a trenchantness which brings up a little cloud of disappointed surprise.

† **Trenchefil, tranchefil.** *Obs. rare.* [a. F. *tranchefil* (Cotgr. *trenchefile*), f. *tranche*, imper. of *trancher* to cut + *fil* thread.]

**1.** In a double-stringed cross-bow, the part by which the two strings were united and into which the neb or tip of the bolt was set in shooting; the material of which this was made. Cf. Trench *sb.* 7 and quot. 1611 there.

**1369–1372** *Exch. Acc. K. R.* Bundle 178 No. 16 m. 4 (P. R. O.) Patricio Byker artillario Regis..lxiiij lb. fili pro cordis balistarum lij lb. trussyngthred lj. lb. di. trenchefyll.

**2.** Part of a bridle: according to Cotgrave, 'a snaffle, or the mouth of a snaffle, or watering Bit'.

**1730–6** Bailey (folio), *Bitt* (with Horsemen) in general signifies the whole Machine of a Bridle, as the Bit-mouth, the Branches, the Curb, the sevil Holes, the Tranchefil, and the Cross-chains. **1753** Chambers *Cycl. Supp.*, *Tranchefile*, in the manege, the cross chain of a bridle that runs along the bit-mouth, from one branch to the other.

† **Tre·nchepain.** *Obs. rare*$^{-1}$. [f. F. *tranche* vb. imperative, cut + *pain* bread.] A bread-cutter; an attendant who cut the bread at table.

*a* **1400** *Sir Perc.* 513 Bot thanne spak syr Gawayne, Was the kynges trenchepayne.

**Trencher**[1] (tre·nʼtʃəɹ). Forms: 4–5 **trencheour, -chour,** 4 **-chur,** 4–6 **-chor,** 5 **-chowre, trenschowre, -shoure,** ? 4, 5– **trencher.** (6 *Sc.* **trunsch(e)our, -owr, -zour),** 7 **trentcher.** [a. AF. *trenchour* = ONF. *trencheor* (1206 in Godef.), *tren-*, *trancheur*, = OF. *tranchouoir* (14th c. in Littré), *trencheoir* (Cotgr.), mod.F. *tranchoir*, f. †*trenchier*, *trancher* to cut, Trench *v.*, with suffix *-oir*, representing L. *-ātorium*. Godef. exemplifies the word in senses corresp. to both our branches I. and II.]

**I.** †**1.** A cutting or slicing instrument; a knife.

*c* **1330** R. Brunne *Chron.* (1810) 166 Fulle broþely & brim he kept vp a trencheour, & kast it at Statin,..His nese & his ine he carfe at misauentoure. *c* **1400** *Songs Costume* (Percy Soc.) 50 My baselard hath a trencher kene, Fayr as rasour scharp and schene. *c* **1410** *Master of Game* (MS. Digby 182) xxxiii, With a sharpe trenshoure kut as thyk as he canne þe flessh a doune to þe necke bone. *c* **1440** *Promp. Parv.* 501/2 Trenchowre, knyfe. **1553** *Acc. Ld. High Treas. Scotl.* X. 204 For ane cais to put sylver trunscheouris in of my lord governoures.

**II. 2.** A flat piece of wood, square or circular, on which meat was served and cut up; a plate or platter of wood, metal, or earthenware. *arch.* and *Hist.*

*c* **1308** *Song Times* in *Pol. Songs* (Camden) 204 A rowȝ bare trenchur, other a crust. **1360–70** *Durham Acc. Rolls* (Surtees) 175 In j pare de Trenchours pro priore, xij s. **1505** in *Exch. Rolls Scotl.* XII. 673, xxiiij poter dischis, xxiiij saw[s]aris, xij trunzouris. **1529** *Reg. Mag. Sig. Scot.* (1883) 177 A half galloun, a quart..a dische, a salsar and a trunscheour, extending to 1½ stanis of puder. **1547** *Bk. Marchauntes* b ij, Thei mak them kisse a trenchor or a small platter of gold, siluer, or lead: which thei name the platine. **1573–80** Baret *Alv.* T 357 A Trencher to eate meate on,..A broad trencher .. A round trencher. **1624** Capt. Smith *Virginia* iii. ii. 48 They imagined the world to be flat and round, like a trencher. **1696** Phillips (ed. 5), *Trencher*, a square, thin Plate of Wood, for People to cut their Meat upon. **1801** Mar. Edgeworth *Angelina* ii, The first dinner which she ate on wooden trenchers delighted her. **1895** Lyon *Chron. Finchampstead* 90 A very ancient oak table which had round places scooped out in it to receive a trencher or wooden basin for each person who dined at it.

† **3.** A slice of bread used instead of a plate or platter. *Obs.*

*c* **1380** Wyclif *Serm.* Sel. Wks. I. 115 Siche whelpis shulden ete trenchours of lordis. **1392** *Earl Derby's Exp.* (Camden) 218 In pane pro trenchors, v duc. di. *c* **1430** *Two Cookery-bks.* 41 Take whyte Brede, & kytte to trenchours. **1490** Caxton *Eneydos* xxxiv. 121 They sette hemselfe atte dyner, & made trenchers of brede for to putte theyr mete vpon. **1513** Douglas *Æneis* vii. iii. 26 Ne spair thai nocht at last.. Their fatale four nukit trunschowris for to eit.

**4.** A trencher and that which it bears; a supply of food; cf. Table 6 c. *arch.*

**1576** Fleming *Panopl. Epist.* 238 What benefites are obteined, by the sweate of other mennes labours, and also by the fatte crumbes of other mennes trenchers. **1612** Dekker *If it be not good* Wks. 1873 III. 280 Waite on the Priors Trencher soberly. **1659** W. Brough *Schism* 535 These new rabbis..are chaplains extraordinary to the trencher. **1667** L. Stucley *Gospel-Glass* xxii. (1670) 224 We have..brought our Children to live upon others trenchers. **1820** W. Irving *Sketch Bk., Spectre Bridegroom*, Even the poor relations paused for a moment from the indefatigable labours of the trencher.

**b.** In proverbial phrases, chiefly of obvious meaning. *To lick the trencher*, to toady; to play the parasite. *Trim as a trencher*: see quot. 1542.

**1542** Udall *Erasm. Apophth.* ii. 246 b, Fillyng vp as trymme as a trencher yͤ space that stood voide. **1589** Puttenham *Eng. Poesie* iii. xxv. (Arb.) 307 To speake faire to a mans face, and foule behinde his backe, to set him at his trencher and yet sit on his skirts. **1602** [see Lick *v.* 1 b]. **1649** Bp. Hall *Cases Consc.* iii. iii. (1654) 189 Carve you for your selfe and looke to your owne trencher. **1692** Washington tr. *Milton's Def. Pop.* viii. M.'s Wks. 1851 VIII. 185 You were there a few years ago, and began to lick a Cardinal's Trencher. **1852** Thackeray *Esmond* ii. xv, He will be at Roncq time enough to lick my Lord Duke's trenchers at supper.

**5.** *transf.* A flat board, circular or otherwise.

*c* **1511** *1st Eng. Bk. Amer.* (Arb.) Introd. 28/1 That Lande is so full of sande yat they muste goo vpon brode trenchers that they falle not & synke. **1669** Boyle *Contn. New Exp.* i. xli. (1682) 144 In the midst of the fixed Trencher (as we call a piece of solid wood shap'd like a Milstone). **1710** J. Clarke *Rohault's Nat. Phil.* (1729) I. 61 Water in a Pail is made to ascend up a Trunk, such as they shoot with, open at both Ends, and one End fixed in a Hole in a Trencher which exactly fits the whole Superficies; upon depressing the Trencher, the Water is forced up. **1825** Scott *Talism.* vi, At the barriers, when swords are blunted at point and edge, and spears are tipped with trenchers of wood, instead of steel pikes.

**b.** Applied to a butcher's 'tray'.

**1903** F. Markham *Recoll. Town Boy Westminster* 97 The butcher had his long trencher in which he carried his meat about.

**6.** *spec.* = Trencher-cap.

**1834** [implied in *trencherless*: see below]. **1848** Thackeray *Bk. Snobs* xiv, [The Master of a College's] crawler would have no objection to carry his trencher. **1862** Mrs. H. Wood *Channings* i, The boys began to file out, putting on their trenchers, as they clattered down the steps. **1906** *Daily Chron.* 26 Sept. 5/6 The girl students..in their red gowns and trenchers adorned with a red tassel.

**7.** *attrib.* and *Comb.* **a.** simple attrib., as *trencher-basket*, *-food*, *-house*, *-room*, *-side*; in sense 4, or in allusion to presence or entertainment at the table of a patron, as *trencher-analect*, *-art*, *-attendant*, *-buffoon*, *-companion*, *-critic*, *-fury*, *-hero*, *-knight*, *-labourer*, *-law*, *-mate*, *-philosopher*, *-poetry*, *-rascal*, *-saint*, *-schoolmaster*, *-service*, *-slave*, *-squire*, *-waiter*. **b.** objective, etc., as *trencher-carrier*, *-licker* (see 4 b), *-maker*, *-making*, *-scraper*, *-shifter*; also *trencher-like* adj. **c.** Special Combs.: **trencher-beard,** a beard resembling a trencher, i. e. large, flat, and square or round; † **trencher-bread,** bread made of unbolted flour for use as trenchers (sense 3); **trencher-coat,** in gilding: see quotation; **trencher-fed** *a.*, of fox-hounds: kept and fed by the several owners or members of the hunt, as distinguished from a pack that is kept in the hunt kennels; † **trencher-fee,** scraps of food given in alms; † **trencher-knife,** a pantry knife for cutting bread into 'trenchers'; † **trencher-loaf,** cf. *trencher-bread*; **trencher-plate,** a plate shaped like or used as a trencher; *spec.* in *Ceramics*, a flat earthenware plate with a narrow rim; also (*collective*) plate or precious metal of which trenchers were made; † **trencher-salt, -salt-cellar,** a small salt-cellar placed near a guest's trencher at table; **trencher-time,** dinner-time, meal-time. See also Trencher-cap, -chaplain, etc.

*a* **1643** W. Cartwright *Ordinary* iii. v, No gleanings, James? No *trencher-analects? *a* **1661** Holyday *Juvenal* (1673) 64 No man to rarer *trencher-art aspir'd. **1592** Nashe *Four Lett. Confut.* Wks. (Grosart) II. 224 Your *trenchor attendant..intends to tickle vp a Treatise of the barly kurnell, which you set in your garden. **1630** *Maldon, Essex, Documents* Bundle 217 No. 22, 1 *trentcher basket 6*d.* *a* **1668** Davenant *News fr. Plymouth* Wks. (1673) 3 Her Parent With a soure brow, and *Trencher Beard. *c* **1460** J. Russell *Bk. Nurture* 56 *Trencher bred iiij. dayes [old] is convenyent & agreable. **1596** Nashe *Saffron Walden* Wks. (Grosart) III. 143 He was to make a iourney to London ..to haue his blue coate (being destitute of euer another *trencher-carrier) credit him vp, though it were thrid bare. **1847–78** Halliwell, **Trencher-cloak*, a kind of cloak worn formerly by servants and apprentices. **1839** Ure *Dict. Arts* 613 Coat of assiette; *trencher coat. This is the composition on which the gold is to be laid. **1816** Scott *Old Mort.* iii[i], The *ci-devant* laird, once his patron, but now glad to be his *trencher-companion. **1598** Bp. Hall *Sat.* iv. iv. 23 Neuer haue I Salerne rimes profest To be some Ladies *trencher-criticke guest. **1887** A. E. Pease (*title*) The Cleveland Hounds as a *Trencher-Fed Pack. **1892** *Daily Tel.* 27 Aug., The oldest pack of regular, as distinguished from trencher-fed foxhounds. **1641** Brome *Jov. Crew* iii. Wks. 1873 III. 396 Dainty *Trencher-Fees, from a Gentleman's house; Such as the Serving-men themselves, sometimes, Would have been glad of. **1642** H. More *Song of Soul* i. ii. lxxx, Our mind cannot attend our *trencher-food. **1641** Milton *Ch. Govt.* ii. Wks. 1851 III. 149 A work..like that which flows at wast from..the *trencher fury of a riming parasite. **1607** G. Wilkins *Miseries Enforced Marr.* v. I iv, You knaue Slaue—*trencher-groome. Who is your maister? **1792** Wolcott (P. Pindar) *Churchwarden* iv. Wks. 1812 III. 111 The *Trencher Heroes hate All Obstacles that keep them from the plate. **1691** *Case of Exeter Coll.* 18 A little Room in the Colledge, called the *Trencher-house. **1392–3** *Earl Derby's Exp.* (Camden) 195 Clerico panetrie per manus eiusdem, pro j *trenchurknyff per ipsum empto. **1459** *Paston Lett.* I. 488 Item, j. trencher knyfe. **1588** Shaks. *L. L. L.* v. ii. 464 Some mumble-newes, some *trencher-knight. **1654** Whitlock *Zootomia* 506 This *Trencher-labourer will not drink with that Divine. **1597–8** Bp. Hall *Sat.* iv. iv. 21 When splenish morsels cram the gaping Maw, Withouten diets care, or *trencher-law. **1812** W. Tennant *Anster F.* iv. i, A *trencher-licker in Apollo's court. **1727** *Bradley's Fam. Dict.* s. v. *Blowing of Flower*, To shade it..with a *Trencher-like Board, or some other Device. *c* **1460** J. Russell *Bk. Nurture* 197, viij. louys bred with iij. or iiij. *trenchere lovis. **1588** in Lyon *Chron. Finchampstead* (1895) 212 James Redinge of Fynchamsted in the County of Barkes *Trenchermaker. **1733** W. Ellis *Chiltern & Vale Farm.* 98 The Trencher-maker is.. cautious of getting the Sap out of this Wood. **1815** Scott *Guy M.* vii, The art of *trencher-making, of manufacturing horn-spoons, and the whole mystery of the tinker. **1597** Hooker *Eccl. Pol.* v. ii. § 2 These *trencher-mates..frame to themselues a way more pleasant. **1605** Bacon *Adv. Learn.* i. iii. § 9 Those *Trencher Philosophers, which, in the later age of the Romane State, were vsually in the houses of great persons. **1580** Hollyband *Treas. Fr. Tong*, *Vne Assiette & trencheoir*, a *trencher plate. **1625** in Rymer *Fœdera* (1726) XVIII. 239/1 Sixe Trencher Plates of Goulde with Armes. **1641** in Rushw. *Hist. Coll.* iii. (1692) I. 281 For the relieving the present Necessity of Money, a Proportion of Plate should be melted for Coyn; and that the same shall be Trencher-Plate, and Dish-Plate. **1597–8** Bp. Hall *Sat.* i. i. 13 Such hunger-starven *trencher-poetrie. **1610** B. Jonson *Alch.* i. i, Away, you *trencher-raskall. **1691** *Case of Exeter Coll.* 8 And then she went to the *Trencher Room. **1649** G. Daniel *Trinarch., Hen. V*, lix, These *Trencher-Sts; full-paunch't Boetians. **1614** Tomkis *Albumazar* v. i. K j b, *Alb.* Shall I haue nothing? *Ron.* No, not a siluer spoone. *Fur.* Nor couer of a *Trencher-salt. **1625** in Rymer *Fœdera* (1726) XVIII. 238/2 A Trencher Salte of Golde in Forme of a Castle. **1681** *Lond. Gaz.* No. 1614/4 Two Silver *Trencher-Saltsellers, being marked within side S. W. E. **1609** Sir E. Hoby *Let. to T. H[iggons]* 23 The multiplicitie of Schools, needlesse Lecturers, and *trencher Schoolemasters. **1650** Weldon *Crt. Jas. I* (1651) 34 He had starved, had not a *Trencher-scraper, sometime his servant.. releived him with scraps. **1594** Nashe *Unfort. Trav.* Wks. (Grosart) V. 27 My state, you are not ignorant, depends on *trencher seruice. **1829** Scott *Ho. Aspen* ii. ii, Here's much to do about an old crazy *trencher-shifter. **1571** Golding *Calvin on Ps.* To Rdr. 9 There bee also certein *trencher-slaves, of whom David complaineth. **1617** Moryson *Itin.* iii. 113 The English were neuer more idle,..neuer more base ..trencher slaues, then in that age, wherein great men kept open houses for all commers. **1706** J. Dunton *Life & Err.* (1818) II. xiii. 485 Thou art a *Trencher-snake, a swallow-guest. **1628** Shirley *Witty Fair One* i. iii, How now, my officious *trencher-squire? **1692** R. L'Estrange *Fables* xxxiv, Trencher-Squires, that spend their time in Hopping from One Great man's Table to Anothers. **1846** Landor *Exam. Shaks.* Wks. II. 280/1 Did he discourse at all at *trencher-time? **1638** Ford *Lady's Trial* ii. ii, In your girl's days, you fell, forsooth, In love, and married..A *trencher-waiter.

Hence **Tre·ncherful,** as much as a trencher will hold; **Tre·ncherless** *a.*, without a trencher (in quot. a trencher-cap).

**1660** Pepys *Diary* 16 Feb., We went to the Sun Taverne in expectation of a dinner, where we had sent us only *trencherfulls of meat. **1883** Gilmour *Mongols* xxi. 266 A trencherful of hard sour masses of material. **1834** *Blackw. Mag.* XXXVI. 779 Pozzlethwayte was..cravat-less, hat-less, *trencher-less, and, alas! wig-less.

**Trencher**[2] (tre·nʼtʃəɹ). [f. Trench *v.* + -er[1].] One who trenches.

† **1.** One who carves; a carver. *Obs. rare.*

*a* **1625** Fletcher *Noble Gent.* iii. i, I was not born, I take it, for a trencher, Nor to espouse my mistress' dairy-maid.

**2.** One who cuts or digs trenches; one who trenches ground.

**1871** Blackie *Four Phases* i. 83 The trencher of the moral soil, not the planter of the seed. **1875** W. Alexander *Sk. Life among Ain Folk* 188 A 'tramp' to save the sole of his boot while operating as trencher or drainer. **1875** tr. *Comte de Paris' Civ. War Amer.* I. 397 All these works were executed by the soldiers, who showed themselves excellent trenchers.

**Tre·ncher-cap.** [f. Trencher[1] + Cap *sb.*[1]] A popular name for the academic or college cap, 'in shape thought to resemble an inverted trencher with a basin upon it' (Farmer and Henley); a 'mortar-board'. Also *transf.* one who wears a college cap, a collegian: cf. Catercap.

**1721** Amherst *Terræ Fil.* xxxv. (1754) 186 Neither do I find that these trencher-caps are more polite to their own dear countrymen, than they are to foreigners. **1796** *Grose's Dict. Vulg. Tongue* (ed. 3), *Trencher Cap*, the square cap worn by the collegians, at the universities of Oxford and Cambridge. **1811** *Chron.* in *Ann. Reg.* 74/1 His Royal Highness..was covered, during the whole time of his sitting ..,by a trencher cap, with a gold tassel. **1861** Hughes *Tom Brown at Oxf.* i, I walked about two inches taller in my trencher cap after it.

† **Tre·ncher-cha·plain.** *Obs.* A chaplain who eats at a patron's table; a domestic chaplain. *contemptuous.*

**1589** *Hay any Work* 37, I doe disdaine to deale with a contemptible trencher chaplaine. **1610** Boys *Expos. Domin. Ep.*, etc. Wks. (1630) 511 It is the fashion of parasites and trencher-Chaplaines to flatter, or at the least humour great men at their table. **1676** Marvell *Mr. Smirke* Wks. (Grosart) IV. 15 It savors of the liquorishness of a trencher-chaplain, little concerned in the 'curâ animarum'.

† **Tre·ncher-fly.** *Obs.* [f. Trencher[1] + Fly *sb.*[1], as a creature that infests the table.] A parasite.

**1590** Greene *Never too Late* Wks. (Grosart) VIII. 165 Fed vppon with Trencher flies, eaten aliue with flatterers. **1603** H. Crosse *Vertues Commw.* (1878) 29 He shall not want trencher-flies, clawbackes, and Sycophants. **1692** R. L'Estrange *Fables* No. 337. I. 294 To try, which of 'em were Friends, and which, only Trencher-Flies, and Spungers.

**Tre·ncher-friend.** ? *Obs.* A parasite; a toady.

**1590** Greene *Never too Late* Wks. (Grosart) VIII. 130 Flattering Gnatos, that only are time pleasers and trencher friends. 1607 SHAKS. *Timon* III. vi. 106 You Fooles of Fortune, Trencher-friends, Time Flyes, Cap and knee-Slaues. 1681 W. ROBERTSON *Phraseol. Gen.* (1693) 647 A Trencher friend; *amicus mensæ*. 1763 C. JOHNSTON *Reverie* II. 243 He gathered all his old pot-companions and trencher-friends about him, and fell to carousing as usual.

† **Tre·nchering.** *Obs. rare.* [f. TRENCHER[1] + -ING[1].]

**1.** *vbl. sb.* Devotion to the trencher; eating; feasting.

1594 HARINGTON *Nugæ Ant.* (1804) I. 170 Some men who love gameing,..some men who love wine, and some who love trencheringe.

**2.** Trenchers collectively.

1610 SHAKS. *Temp.* II. ii. 187 No more dams I'le make for fish,..Nor scrape trenchering, nor wash dish.

**Tre·ncher-man.** [f. as prec. + MAN *sb.*[1]]

†**1.** A cook or caterer. *Obs. rare.*

*a* 1586 SIDNEY *Arcadia* I. iv. (1912) 29 He had alreadie bene more fed to his liking, then hee could bee by the skilfullest trencher-men of Media.

**2.** A feeder; an eater; usually qualified, as *good, stout, valiant*, etc., one who plays a good knife and fork; one who has a hearty appetite.

1590 GREENE *Never too Late* Wks. (Grosart) VIII. 199 Mullidor tried himselfe so tall a trencher man, that his mother perceiued by his drift he would not die for loue. 1596 SHAKS. *Much Ado* I. i. 51 He's a very valiant Trencher-man, hee hath an excellent stomacke. 1663 DAVENANT *Siege* II. i, You Are a rare Trencher-man. 1694 MOTTEUX *Rabelais* v. Prol., Dry and hungry Souls, Pot and Trenchermen. 1805 *Sporting Mag.* XXVI. 52 One or two distinguished trencher-men. 1880 R. S. WATSON *Vis. Wazan* xii. 226 As much as would serve a valiant trencher-man in England for half a week.

**3.** One who frequents a patron's table; a parasite, dependent, hanger-on.

1599 NASHE *Lenten Stuffe* Ep. Ded., A dismall world for trenchermen, when theyr maisters bond shal not be so good as theirs. 1643 WITHER *Campo Musæ* 40 By these virtues, from a trencher-man A Princes Minion, riseth, now and than. 1849 THACKERAY *Pendennis* xx, Everybody knew old Pen, regular old trencher-man at Gaunt House, notorious old bore, regular old fogey.

So **Tre·ncher-wo:man.**

1891 T. HARDY *Tess* xxxiv, To be sure, 'a was always a good trencher-woman, as her face showed.

**Tre·nchful.** [f. TRENCH *sb.* + -FUL.] As many or as much as a trench holds or will hold.

1900 *Blackw. Mag.* July 125/2 The Commandant of the trenchful of Boers. 1901 'LINESMAN' *Words Eyewitness* vii. (1902) 151 Behind them again the advanced guard of a trenchful of curious private soldiers.

**Trenching** (tre·nʧiŋ), *vbl. sb.* [f. TRENCH *v.* + -ING[1].] The action of the verb TRENCH, in its various senses.

1543-4 *Act* 35 *Hen. VIII*, c. 10 Any digging trenching or breakinge of suche Grounde. 1632 SANDERSON *Serm.* (1657) I. 372 Sufficient to acquit..the Constitutions from that trenching upon Christian liberty, wherewith they are charged. 1799 J. ROBERTSON *Agric. Perth* 278 The trenching of land in the open fields..is not so expensive as is generally supposed. 1899 *Westm. Gaz.* 20 Nov. 7/3 Commandant Cronje had marked each step of his advance on the town by elaborate trenching.

**b.** *attrib.* and *Comb.*, as *trenching-fork, -knife, -plough, -spade, -system, -tool*; **trenching-plane**, a grooving-plane.

1875 *Encycl. Brit.* I. 335/2 To have those patches of ground..which are missed in ploughing, gone over with the *trenching-fork. *c* 1510 *Kalender of Sheph.* E v, A great bochery, where as Yreful men and women were thorowe persyd with *trenchyng knyues. 1859 F. S. COOPER *Ironmongers' Catal.* 134 *Trenching Plane. 1669 WORLIDGE *Syst. Agric.* (1681) 231 The *Trenching-Plough or Coulter is a certain Instrument used in Meadow or Pasture-ground, to cut out the sides of Trenches, Carriages or Drains. 1733 W. ELLIS *Chiltern & Vale Farm.* 326 The Trenching Plough, is either a Wheel or Foot-plough. 1904 *Daily News* 18 Aug. 8/1 Parties of soldiers..were going about the field with *trenching spades burying the dead. 1780 A. YOUNG *Tour Irel.* I. 17 Great quantities of potatoes planted in the *trenching way.

**Tre·nchlet.** *rare.* [f. TRENCH *sb.* + -LET.] A small or miniature trench.

1787 W. MARSHALL *Norfolk* II. 362 The trenchlets were shoveled, and the banks smoothed. 1793 — *W. England* (1796) II. 348 By running parallel trenchlets along the face of the slope.

[**Trenchman**, app. a misreading of *treuchman*, var. TRUCHMAN, an interpreter, DRAGOMAN.

1632 LITHGOW *Trav.* x. 460, I pleaded for a Trench-man, [it] being against their Law, to accuse or condemne a Stranger, without a sufficient Interpreter. 1666 *Despaut. Gram. Instit.* VII. (Jam.), *Interpres*, an interpreter or Trench-man. 1867 SMYTH *Sailor's Word-bk.*, *Trugman*..also called *trench-man*. 1879 BODDAM-WHETHAM *Roraima* 147 A strong active young fellow..acted as our trenchman.]

† **Tre·nchment.** *Obs. rare.* [f. TRENCH *v.* + -MENT, or aphetic for *entrenchment*.] A work formed by trenching; an entrenchment.

1604 E. GRIMSTONE *Hist. Siege Ostend* 214 The trenchments being finished, the besieged resolued to bandon the olde rampere. 1700 RYCAUT *Hist. Turks* III. 117 So many Trenchments, Retrenchments, and Palisadoes..that it was almost impossible for the Enemy to advance ten Paces.

**Trenchmore** (tre·nʧmōᵊɹ), *sb. Hist.* Also 6 -mour, -moore, 7 -moor. [Origin uncertain. Perhaps a place- or family-name.] An old English country dance, of a lively or boisterous nature; also, the air to which it was danced.

1551-2 in Feuillerat *Revels Edw. VI* (1914) 79 Thre garmentes of sarsenett..for them that daunsed trenchemore. 1579 GOSSON *Sch. Abuse* (Arb.) 33 Paris led the shaking of sheetes with Domitia, and Mnester [led] the Trenchmour, with Messalina. 1597 DELONEY *Gentle Craft* (1912) 154 Like one dancing the trench more he stampt up and downe the yard, holding his hips in his hands. 1611 BARREY *Ram Alley* III. i, Ile make him daunce a trenchmoor to my sword. *a* 1654 SELDEN *Table T.*, *King of Engl.* (1689) 28 In King Charles's time, there has been nothing but Trench-more [*mispr.* Fr—] and the Cushion Dance, *omnium gatherum*, tolly, polly, hoite come toite. 1776 SIR J. HAWKINS *Hist. Mus.* IV. IV. i. 392 In the..Rehearsal, the Earth, Sun, and Moon are made to dance the Hey to the tune of Trenchmore.

† **b.** quasi-*adv.* In a frisky, lively, or boisterous manner. *Obs.*

1577 STANYHURST *Descr. Irel.* in *Holinshed* II. 16/1 They beseet a diuine as well, as for..an ape to strike trenchmoore in a paire of buskins and a doublet. 1605 *Lond. Prodigal* I. ii, I' faith and thy tongue trips trenchmore. 1636 W. SAMPSON *Vow-Breaker* II. i. Dijb, We had a Wedding to day, and the young fry tickle trench-more.

Hence **Tre·nchmore** *v. nonce-wd.*, *intr.* to dance the trenchmore.

1598 MARSTON *Pygmal.* ii. 145 He doth curtsie, and.. Trenchmore with Apes, play musick to an Owle.

**Trench-plough, -plow** (tre·nʧ,plau), *v.* [f. TRENCH *sb.* or *v.* + PLOUGH *v.*] *trans.* and *intr.* To plough to the depth of two furrows, bringing the lower soil to the surface; to turn a second furrow-slice on the top of the first, by following in the same furrow with a plough set much deeper.

1731-3 TULL *Horse-hoeing Husb.* xix. 274 We Trench-plow where the Land will allow it. 1764 *Museum Rust.* III. xciv. 378 When I trench-plough a field, I go as deep with the second plough as four good horses and strong cattle can well draw. 1844 STEPHENS *Bk. Farm* I. 664, I trench-ploughed a field of 25 acres.

Hence **Tre·nch-plough** *sb.*, a plough designed or adjusted for trench-ploughing; **Tre·nch-ploughing** *vbl. sb.*, the action of the verb.

1763 *Museum Rust.* I. 343 If..the land had a trench-ploughing, it would be of great advantage. 1805 R. W. DICKSON *Pract. Agric.* I. 11 The Trench-Plough, which is so contrived as to turn up the ground to a great depth. 1844 STEPHENS *Bk. Farm* I. 499 A conduit..was built and covered with land stones obtained from the field by trench-ploughing.

**Trend** (trend), *sb.* [f. next.]

**1.** A rounded bend or circuit of a stream. *dial.*

*c* 1630 RISDON *Surv. Devon* § 253 (1810) 261 In the trend of Touridge,..stands Meeth. *a* 1874 MADOX-BROWN *Dwale Bluth* I. iv. (1876) I. 87 We'd dew best ter palch along ter th' trend i' th' holler hinder.

**2.** Wool (partly cleaned) wound in tops for spinning: cf. next, 2 b. *dial.*

1858 SIMMONDS *Dict. Trade*, *Trend*, clean wool.

**3.** *Naut.* **a.** That part of the shank of an anchor where it thickens towards the crown.

1794 *Rigging & Seamanship* I. 79 Several parts of the anchor are governed by the size of the trend, which is marked on the shank at the same distance from the inside of the throat as the arm measures..to the extremity of the bill. 1867 SMYTH *Sailor's Word-bk.*, *Trend of an Anchor*, the lower end of the shank, where it thickens towards the arms, usually at one-third from the crown.

**b.** The angle between the direction of the anchor-cable and that of the ship's keel.

1879 in WEBSTER Suppl.

**4.** The way something trends or bends away; the general direction which a stream or current, a coast, mountain-range, valley, stratum, etc. tends to take.

1777 *Horæ Subsecivæ* 438 (E.D.D.). 1803 W. TAYLOR in *Ann. Rev.* I. 438 Tracing the course of streams, or the trend of coasts. 1854 MURCHISON *Siluria* xii. 305 The trend and character of the marine currents. 1872 C. KING *Mountain. Sierra Nev.* i. 2 Numerous ridges..having a general north-east trend. 1876 A. H. GREEN *Phys. Geol.* (1877) 316 As we recede..along the trend of a belt of shale.

**b.** *fig.* The general course, tendency, or drift (of action, thought, etc.).

1884 *Chr. Commw.* 12 June 823/2 The trend of the thought and action of the churches is..towards the consecration of every department of life. 1912 LADY BURGHCLERE *Life Jas., 1st Dk. Ormonde* I. xii. 377 The general trend of affairs in Munster.

**Trend**, *v.* Also 7 treand, trent, 8-9 *dial.* trind. Pa. t. and pple. **trended**; also 4 *pa. t.* **trent, trend(e**, *pa. pple.* **trent, i-, y-trent**, 6 *pa. pple.* **trend**. [ME. *trenden*, OE. *trendan* (rare) :—OTeut. **trand-jan*, f. ablaut series **trend*: **trand*: **trund*, which appears also in OE. *trinde* round lump, ball, OFris. *trind, trund*, NFris. *trind*, MLG. *trint, trent, trunt* adjs. round, MLG. *trent* ring, circumference, boundary, Du. *trent* circumference, *omtrent* around, about; also Da., Sw. *trind* round. Ulterior relations obscure: cf. Falk and Torp. See also TRENDLE, TRINDLE, TRUNDLE.]

† **1.** *intr.* To turn round, revolve, rotate, roll; to turn or roll oneself about; also *fig.* *Obs.*

*a* 1000 *MS. Cott. Faust. A. x.* in *Anglia* I. 285 Se æppel næfre þæs feorr ne trenddeð, he cyð, hwanon he com. [*c* 1000 in Napier *O. E. Glosses* 5 *Teretes, i. rotundos*, sintrendende [*v. r.* sintredende], sinhwyrfende.] 13.. *Guy Warw.* (A.) 314 He went and trent [*Caius MS.* He wende, he trende] his bed opon, So man þat is wo bigon. 1398 [see TRENDING *vbl. sb.* 1]. 14.. *Beryn* 2038 The trowth woll be previd, how so men evir trend. 1654 VILVAINE *Epit. Ess.* I. 32 The whol frame doth round in her orb trend.

† **2.** *trans.* To cause (a thing) to turn round; to turn or roll (anything); to twist, plait, curl; *fig.* to revolve in one's mind. *Obs.* (exc. as in b).

*c* 1315 SHOREHAM vii. 78 A myȝt..Þat halt vp þerþe and sterren bryȝte Aboute itrent. *c* 1374 CHAUCER *Boeth.* III. met. xi. 79 (Camb. MS.) Lat hym rollen and trenden with-Inne hym self the Lyht of his inward syhte. *c* 1380 *Sir Ferumb.* 5881 Wyþ eȝene graye, and browes bent, And ȝealwe traces, & fayre y-trent. 1594 WILLOBIE *Avisa* (1880) 87 The Spindle that you see me driue, Hath fyld the spill so often trend. 1613-16 W. BROWNE *Brit. Past.* II. iii, Not farre beneath i'th valley as she trends Her siluer streame.

**b.** To wind (wool, partly cleaned) into tops for spinning. *dial.* (Cf. TRENDLE *sb.* 5.)

1777 [see *trended*]. 1794 *Young's Ann. Agric.* XXVI. 454 Herefordshire is the only county that I know which continues the practice of trinding (or winding the wool in tops, ready sorted in some degree for fine drapers). 1828 WEBSTER, *Trend, v. t.*, in rural economy, to free wool from its filth. (*Local.*)

† **3.** *intr.* To make a circuit, travel around or about the edge of a region or piece of land; to skirt, coast (*about, along*). *Obs.*

1580 in Hakluyt *Voy.* (1599) I. 437 You shall trend about the very Northerne and most Easterly point of all Asia. 1615 G. SANDYS *Trav.* 137 The maine Desarts: which all this while we had trented along, and now were to passe through. 1622 R. HAWKINS *Voy. S. Sea* (1847) 179 Trending about the cape, wee haled in east north-east, to fetch the bay of Atacames.

† **b.** More vaguely: To turn or direct one's course. *Obs.*

1618 in Foster *Eng. Factories India* (1906) 11 Their provisions trend from Mosambique to the Mulluccas. 1647 [see TRENDING *vbl. sb.* 2 b]. 1846 LANDOR *Imag. Conv.* Wks. I. 87/1 The religion of blood, like the beasts of prey, will continue to trend northward.

† **c.** *trans.* To coast along, skirt; to make the circuit of, to round (a point of land). *Obs.*

1600 HAKLUYT *Voy.* III. 206 We trended the said land about 9. or 10. leagues, hoping to finde some good harborough. 1602 CAREW *Cornwall* II. 98 b, From thence trending Penlee poynt, you discouer Kings Sand and Causam Bay.

**4.** *intr.* To turn off in a specified direction; to tend to take a direction or course expressed by the context; to run, stretch, incline, bend (in some direction), as a river, current, coast-line, mountain-range, territory, stratum, etc.

1598 HAKLUYT *Voy.* I. 104 The riuer of..Volga..issueth from the North part of Bulgaria..and so trending along Southward disimboqueth into a certain lake. 1610 HOLLAND *Camden's Brit.* I. 766 The shore treandeth out more and more. 1635 *Voy. Foxe & James to N. W.* (Hakl. Soc.) II. 354, I see the land trent to the Southward. 1779 FORREST *Voy. N. Guinea* 194 From the island of Ebus, the coast trends to the northward. 1860 MAURY *Phys. Geog. Sea* ii. § 116 In its course to the north, the Gulf Stream gradually trends more and more to the eastward. 1876 GREEN *Stray Stud.* 290 Their path lay along the coast trending round to the west. 1892 STEVENSON *Across the Plains* 232 The railroad trended to the right.

**b.** *fig.* To turn in some direction, to have a general tendency (as a discussion, events, etc.).

1863 G. A. LAWRENCE *Border & Bast.* xiii. 243 In which direction do the sympathies and interests of the Border States actually trend? 1886 DOWDEN *Shelley* I. iv. 164 The discussion..trended away from theology in the direction of politics. 1901 B. MEAKIN *Land of Moors* xx. 407 The Land of the Moors, which, as things trend to-day, must in time form part of her [France's] colony.

**c.** *trans.* in causal sense: To turn or bend the course of in a particular direction. *rare.*

1840 *Civil Eng. & Arch. Jrnl.* III. 109/1 Laying the several courses perpendicular to the face of the arch..and trending them to the abutments in an angle dependent on the given obliquity.

Hence **Tre·nded** (*dial.* **trinded**) *ppl. a.* (*spec.* of wool: see 2 b), **Tre·nding** *ppl. a.*; also **Tre·nder** (*dial.*), one employed in winding (cleaned) wool.

1777 *Horæ Subsecivæ* 438 (E.D.D.) Trinded wool, wool winded and fastned together with the 'rind of a tree'. 1794 [see TRENDING *vbl. sb.* 1 b]. 1805 LUCCOCK *Nat. Wool* 300 From the trended fleece of Herefordshire about one tenth of its weight is taken of coarse and inferior locks. 1828 WEBSTER, *Trender*, one whose business is to free wool from its filth. (*Local.*) 1856 J. MARTINEAU *Ess.*, etc. (1891) IV. 44 No treaty..can trace a boundary-line any more than a mountain-chain or trending coast can keep out the Almighty Maker of them both.

† **Trende**, *a.* *Obs. rare*[−1]. Perhaps 'rounded, circular'.

*c* 1400 *Sowdone Bab.* 940 O Thow, rede Marz Armypotente, That in the trende baye hase made þy trone.

**Trending** (tre·ndiŋ), *vbl. sb.* Also 8 **trinding**. [f. TREND *v.* + -ING[1].] The action of TREND *v.*

† **1.** Turning round, revolution, rotation. *Obs.*

1398 TREVISA *Barth. De P. R.* IX. i. (Tollem. MS.), Meuynge haþ cause firste and principally of trendynge [1535 trendlynge] aboute of heuen. *Ibid.* XI. x, Of his longe trendynge [1535 trendlynge] aboute comeþ his roundnesse.

**b.** The winding of wool in a top: see TREND *v.* 2 b. *dial.*

1794 *Young's Ann. Agric.* XXVI. 455 [I] send you, by Drew, a trinded top of wool..with the locks left out of it at trinding.

**2.** The fact or manner of turning, bending away, or taking a general (specified) direction, as a coast-line, etc.; general direction, trend.

1600 HAKLUYT *Voy.* III. A ij, For the space of fiue thousand leagues..considering the trending of the land. 1697 DRYDEN *Æneid* VII. 200 The Coasts and Trendings of the Crooked Shore. 1770 COOK *Voy. round World* III. i. (1773) 484 This point..may be known by the trending of the coast, which is north on the one side, and south-west on the other. 1823 SCORESBY *Jrnl. Whale Fish.* 472 Trending differs from bearing, inasmuch as it is..the direction of a coast or line of ice in regard to itself; whereas the bearing usually refers to the direction of an object, in regard to the place of an observer. 1863 KINGLAKE *Crimea* II. xvi. 222 The trending away of the hills leaves a hollow or recess.

†**b.** The action of continuing a course. *Obs.*

1647 G. TOOKE *Belides* 30 As a streame descending From his faire heads to sea, becomes in trending More puissant.

**Trendle** (tre·nd'l), *sb.* Forms: 1–5 **trendel**, 4–6 **-il**, 5 **-ill**, **-yl**, **-ull**, (**trenle**), 5–6 **trendell**(**e**, **-yll**, 7 **-al**, 4– **trendle**. [OE. *trendel* circle, ring, coronet, disk, orb, circus, = MLG. *trendel* round disk, MHG. *trendel*, *trindel* ball, circle, whence (acc. to Falk and Torp) OSw. *trindhel* circle, Sw. dial. *trinnel*; :—OTeut. **trendilo-*, f. root of TREND *v.* See also TRINDLE, TRUNDLE.]

†**1.** A circle, a ring, a coronet; a circular disk, orb; a ball, globe. *Obs.*

*a* 900 *O. E. Chron.* an. 806 An wunderlic trendel [*mirabilis corona*] wearð ateowed abutan ðare sunnan. *a* 1000 *Ags. Manual Astron.* in *Sax. Leechd.* III. 242 Ðaes monan trendel is symle ȝehal. *c* 1000 ÆLFRIC *Hom.* (Th.) II. 606 Seo lichamlice edwist, þæt is þære sunnan trendel. *c* 1050 *Byrhtferth's Handboc* in *Anglia* VIII. 333 Brevis [virgula] [i.e. ˘] ys anes trendles dæl þus licgende. 1388 WYCLIF *Isa.* xxix. 3, Y schal cumpasse as a round trendil [1382 a bal; *Vulg.* sphæram] in thi cumpasse,..and Y schal sette engynes in to thi bisegyng.

**2.** A wheel: = TRINDLE *sb.* 1, TRUNDLE *sb.* 1, 2. *Obs.* exc. *dial.*

1324 *Acc. Exch., K. R.* Bd. 165 No. 1. m. 4 (P.R.O.) Pro xxviij snekkes cum xxviij stapulis ad tenendum trendles ligni pro springaldis tendendis. *c* 1400 *Destr. Troy* 453 Hir Ene as a trendull turned full rounde, First on hir fader, for feare þat she hade. *c* 1440 *Promp. Parv.* 502/1 Trendyl, *troclea.* 1538 ELYOT, *Spiræ*, thynges whyche doo tourne and wynde in dyuers cerkles lyke a trendell...Also a cake made like a trendell. 1570 LEVINS *Manip.* 126/26 A Trendil, *rota.* 1887 *Suppl. to Jamieson, Trendle, trindle, trenle, trinle, trunle*, the wheel of a barrow, also the wooden portion of the wheel; a small wooden wheel such as is used for a trundle-bed.

†**3.** A suspended hoop or wheel on which tapers were fixed, forming a chandelier, used in churches on certain occasions before the Reformation. *Obs.*

1423 *Will Hodesole* (Somerset Ho.), Lego ad mantenendum le trendil ibidem. 1452 in *Berks., Bucks. & Oxon. Archæol. Jrnl.* Oct. (1903) 78 At yᵉ makyng of yᵉ Est[er] tapur & yᵉ trendull we spendyd iiij. d. 1476 *Croscombe Churchw. Acc.* (Som. Rec. Soc.) 57 Item for a rope for the Trendell..ixᵈ. 1502–3 in Kerry *Hist. St. Lawrence, Reading* (1883) 53 It. payed to John Turner for makyng of the Trendyll ij s...for corde to the same Trendyll, vj d...for tymber to make þe trendyll whele..for a bolte and a swevyll to the trendyll, ij d. 1524 *Churchw. Acc. St. Giles, Reading* 22 For makyng of the trendell xvijᵈ.

**4.** A vessel of flat rounded form; a round or oval tub used for various purposes; a circular trough or tray used by bakers. *dial.*

1493 *Yatton Churchw. Acc.* (Som. Rec. Soc.) 119 Thes be perselles that longyth to the Cherche howse..ix barellys..xxj trendyllys..ij trowys. 1516 *Ibid.* 135 Payd for hopyng a trendelle of yᵉ churche..iijᵈ. 1669 WORLIDGE *Syst. Agric.* (1681) 323 A *Trendle*, a flat Vessel, by some called a Kiver. 1847–78 HALLIWELL, *Trendle*,..a brewer's cooler. *West.* 1874 T. HARDY *Far fr. Madding Crowd* II. iii. 39 A clock with a face as big as a baking-trendle.

**5.** A bundle of (partly cleaned) wool 'trended' or wound up (see TREND *v.* 2 b). *dial.*

1805 LUCCOCK *Nat. Wool* 298 Sworn winders..are engaged to strip off the coarse part of the fleece and to wind up only the better kind of wool; to tie about half a dozen fleeces together, and to ticket the weight of each bundle, or as it is there called trendle.

**6.** Applied to various round or rounded objects (the identity of which cannot always be ascertained).

14.. *Voc.* in Wr.-Wülcker 571/19 *Catantrum*, a trendell. *Ibid.* 586/29 *Giraculum*, a trendel. *c* 1468 *Medulla Gram.* (*MS. Harl.* 1738, lf. 39/2), *Insubulus*, a websters trendyl. [*Insubuli* is rendered *web-beamas* in Wr.-Wülcker 188/4.] 1542 UDALL *Erasm. Apoph.* 29 A maiden..did..cast vp and receiue again one after another twelf trendles or roundles. 1766 *Compl. Farmer, Trendle*, any thing that turns round. 1887 *Suppl. to Jamieson, Trendle*,..a wooden roller on which a heavy block is moved along.

†**Trendle**, *v. Obs.* Forms: see prec.; also 3 **treondlin**. [f. prec. Cf. also TRINDLE, TRUNDLE.]

**1.** *trans.* To cause to roll or revolve; to roll: = TRUNDLE *v.* 1 a.

[*a* 1000 *Boeth. Metr.* v. 17 Atrendlod of ðæm torre.] 1382 WYCLIF *Judg.* vii. 13 Y sawȝ a sweuen, and it seemed to me, as a loof of barlich..to be trendlid and into the tentis of Madyan to goo doun. *c* 1420 *Liber Cocorum* (1862) 45 Take white pese,..Put hom in pot..Trendel hom in platere and pyke hom clene. *c* 1440 *Promp. Parv.* 502/1 Trendelyn a rownd thynge (*A.* trendlyn as with a rownde thynge), *trocleo, volvo.* 1552 HULOET, Trendle a ball, *proijcere pilam.* 1570 LEVINS *Manip.* 65/29 To Trendle, *rotare.*

**2.** *intr.* To roll, revolve: = TRUNDLE *v.* 1 b.

*a* 1225 *Leg. Kath.* 2361, & te riche lefdis Letten teares treondlin. *a* 1250 *Owl & Night.* 135 Þeyh appel trendli from þe treo. *c* 1400 *Laud Troy Bk.* 5954 Sche turnes & trendeles as doth a bal. *c* 1450 *Guy Warw.* (C.) 3712 He smote the sowdan with hys sworde, That the hedde trendyld on þe borde. 1495 *Trevisa's Barth. De P. R.* IX. i. (W. de W.) y ij/1 A thynge that trenlyth [*Bodl. MS.* trendeþ] rounde aboute chaungyth not place towchynge all the hole. 1598 YONG *Diana* 300 A certaine thing like a round ball..that ran trendling in the meadow before vs.

Hence †**Tre·ndling** *vbl. sb.* and *ppl. a.*

1495 *Trevisa's Barth. De P. R.* IX. i. (W. de W.) y ij/1 Some meuynge that is chaungynge of place is trenlynge [*Bodl. MS.* trendinge] and rounde wynded abowte. *a* 1577 GASCOIGNE *Flowers, Fruites of Warre* xliv, A tickell treasure, like a trendlynge ball.

†**Tre·ndled**, *a. Obs.* [f. prec. + -ED[1].] Rounded.

*c* 1220 *Bestiary* 737 Panter is an wilde der...He is blac.. Mið wite spottes sapen [shapen] al Wit [white] and trendled als a wel [wheel].

**Trendle tayle**: see TRUNDLE-. **Trendyl, -yll, Trendyll bed**, obs. ff. TRENDLE, TRUNDLE-BED.

**Trene**, obs. f. THRENE, TREEN; var. TRINE *v.*[2]

**Trenefald**, var. THRINFALD *Obs.*, threefold.

**Trenel, Trenite**, obs. ff. TREENAIL, TRINITY.

**Trenke**, var. TRINK *sb.*[1] *Obs.*, kind of net.

†**Trenket.** *Obs.* Also 5–6 **trynket.** [a. OF. (Picard) *trenquet*, OF. *trenchet*, f. *trenquer*, *trencher* to cut: see TRENCH *v.*] A knife; *spec.* a shoemaker's knife.

*c* 1440 *Promp. Parv.* 502/1 Trenket, sowtarys knyfe, *anxorium.* 1483 *Cath. Angl.* 392/1 A Trenket, *ansorium.* 1486 *Bk. St. Albans* f vij, A Trynket of Corueseris [= Shoemakers]. 1530 PALSGR. 283/1 Trynket a cordwayners toole. 1547 SALESBURY *Welsh Dict.*, *Tranket kyllell krydd*, Trenket. [Cf. 1611 COTGR., *Trenchet de cordoüannier*, a Shoomakers cutting-knife.]

**Trenlace, Trenle**: see TRANLACE, TRENDLE.

**Trenne, Trennel**: see TREE, TREEN, TREENAIL.

**Trensh-man**, error for *treush-man*, TRUCHMAN.

†**Trent.** *Obs.* [a. F. *trente* thirty, or ? abbreviation of *trental.*] = TRENTAL.

1389 in *Eng. Gilds* (1870) 8 On þe morwe to seie a trent of masses atte same ffreres.

**Trent**, obs. f., also pa. t. and pple., of TREND *v.*

**Trental** (tre·ntăl). Also 4–5 (9 *Hist.*) **trentale**, 4–6 **-alle**, 5 **-ayl**, **-el**, **-elle**, (**trintal**), 5–7 **trentall**, (6 **treigntalle**). [ad. med.(eccl.)L. *trentāle* (12th c. in Du Cange), f. pop.L. **trenta*, **trinta* (:—L. *trīgintā*, whence F. *trente* thirty) + *-āl-is*, *-āle*, -AL. So OF. *trentel* (12th c. in Godef.).]

**1.** A set of thirty requiem masses, said on the same day or on different days; also, the payment made for this. *arch.* and *Hist.*

13.. *Minor Poems fr. Vernon MS.* xxxiv. *heading*, Þe Pope trental. *Ibid.* lf. 303 Here bygunnet þe guldene trental þat ouȝte be loued swyþe wel. [Cf. xxxiv. 126 Let sei þeos Masses bi ȝoure hestes Wiþ-Inne þe vtaues of þe ffestes.] *c* 1386 CHAUCER *Sompn. T.* 16 Trentals seyde he, delieuren fro penaunce Hir freendes soules. *c* 1420 *Anturs of Arth.* 218 Were thritty trentales done, By-twene vnder and none. 1487 *Paston Lett.* III. 463 Every weke folowing unto my monthes mynde oon trentall, and iij. trentalles at my monthes mynde. 1530 LYNDESAY *Test. Papyngo* 695 With gret blys, bury we sall ȝour bonis, Syne trentalls twenty trattyll all at onis. 1531 *Wills & Inv. N. C.* (Surtees 1908) 127 Three treigntalles of masse. 1593 BELL *Motives Romish Faith* (1605) 24 For which Masses, Diriges, and Trentals, huge summes of money are giuen daily. 1694 MOTTEUX *Rabelais* (1737) V. 221 Obits, Trentals, and Services for the Dead. 1813 SCOTT *Rokeby* v. xxvii, Let mass be said, and trentals read. 1881 BRIDGETT *Hist. Holy Eucharist* II. xi. 150 St. Gregory's Trental..consisted of ten different masses three times repeated...According to..others they were said in thirty consecutive days, and even by thirty priests in one day.

†**b.** *transf.* A set or series of thirty. *Obs. rare.*

1508 KENNEDIE *Flyting w. Dunbar* 319 Thow says for thame few psaltris, psalmis, or creidis, Bot geris me tell thair trentalis of misdeidis. 1586 P. WYOT *Diary* Oct. in Chanter *Sk. Lit. Hist. Barnstaple* (1866) 92 On Sᵗ. Luke's day this yere there was a trental of sermons at Pylton.

†**c.** *loosely.* An elegy or dirge. *Obs.*

1648 HERRICK *Hesper.*, *Dirge upon Death of B. Stuart*, Soft silence let us have, While we this Trentall sing about thy grave. *Ibid.*, *To Julia*, Deare Julia, thou shalt have A trentall sung by virgins o're thy grave.

**2.** Used as = MONTH'S MIND, the commemoration service on the thirtieth day after burial. *arch.*

1659 H. L'ESTRANGE *Alliance Div. Off.* 302 The thirtieth [day] (called therefore..in old English the Months-mind, in after times the Trental). 1860 READE *Cloister & H.* ci, The convent will keep his trentals, but will feast, not fast.

**3.** *attrib.* and *Comb.*

1471 in *Somerset Medieval Wills* (1901) 222 Item, to Sir John Cerne to say a trentall mass for me, 2s. 6d. 1591 *Troub. Raigne K. John* (1611) 60 The arch prowd titled Priest of Italy,..Is busied now with trentall obsequies,..To ease their soules in painefull purgatorie.

‖**Trente.** Also 7–8 **trante.** [F. *trente* (trãnt) :—Com. Romanic **trinta*, **trenta*, for L. *trīgintā* thirty.]

†**1.** *Cards.* ? A combination of cards counting thirty, or the score gained by them. *Obs.*

1706 MRS. CENTLIVRE *Basset-Table* IV, I have lost a Trante and Leva, my ill fortune has not forsook me yet.

**2. Trente et quarante** (F. trãntekarãnt), in 7 erron. **trante a courante** [F. = thirty and forty], another name for the game of *rouge-et-noir* (in which thirty and forty are respectively winning and losing numbers).

1671 LADY MARY BERTIE in *12th Rep. Hist. MSS. Comm.* App. v. 22 Wee play sometimes at trante a courante. 1764 H. WALPOLE *Let. to Earl Hertford* 25 Nov., Hazard, *Quinze*, and *Trente-et-Quarante.* 1848 THACKERAY *Van. Fair* lxiii, A room for *trente-et-quarante* and roulette. 1892 F. WICKS *Veiled Hand* xviii, He would have one look at the *trente et quarante* table.

**Trentillment**, obs. var. TRINKLEMENT.

**Trentine** (tre·ntəin), *a.* [f. *Trent* (see def.) + -INE[1].] Belonging to Trent, a city of the Tyrol; *spec.* pertaining to the Council of Trent (1542–52, 1562–3): = TRIDENTINE. So †**Tre·ntish** *a.* in same sense; †**Tre·ntist**, an adherent of the doctrines of the Council of Trent.

1601 BP. W. BARLOW *Defence* 148 The Trentish Conuenticle confesseth, that it was no sacrament in the olde testament. *Ibid.* 149 Neither was it, say the Trentistes, a sacrament before Christes resurrection. 1675 J. SMITH *Chr. Relig. Appeal* I. 52 The Trentish Anathema would fall heavy upon me. 1826 C. BUTLER *Vind. Bk. Rom. Cath. Ch.* 108 The decree of the Trentine doctors which declared the attendances of Catholics at the Protestant services to be unlawful. 1851 GALLENGA *Italy* 149 Bands of armed peasants from the Trentine valleys had come to Milan.

**Trenton** (tre·ntən). *Geol.* A name given (*attrib.*, or *ellipt.* as *sb.*) to a limestone formation exemplified at Trenton Falls, New York, and hence to the group or series of Lower Silurian rocks to which it belongs.

1854 MURCHISON *Siluria* xvi. 413 From the 'Potsdam sandstone'..up to the slates and arenaceous schists over lying the Trenton limestone, the group so composed represents the Lower Silurian. 1873 DAWSON *Earth & Man* iv. 59 The Trenton. 1885 LYELL *Elem. Geol.* (ed. 4) 445 The Hudson River Group, and the Trenton Limestone, agree palæontologically with the Caradoc or Bala Group.

**Trenyte, -tie**, obs. forms of TRINITY.

**Treo**, obs. form of TREE.

†**Treouse**, *v. Obs.* [OE. *treowsian*, *trywsian*, early ME. *treosi-en*, *tr(e)ousi-en*, f. *treow* troth, faith.] **a.** *refl.* and *intr.* To pledge oneself, give assurance, engage. (Only OE.) **b.** *trans.* To prove to be true. **c.** *intr.* To rely *on.*

*a* 901 *Laws of K. Ælfred* c. 19 Gyf he hine trywsian wylle..ðæt he mot. *a* 1000 *O. E. Chron.* an. 972, Him comon onȝean .vi. cyningas and ealle wið [hine] trywsodon [*v. r.* ȝetreowsodon] ðat hi woldon [etc.]. *c* 1205 LAY. 8315 And þu hit nult ileuen..Ich hit wulle trousien. — 8489 Þas weord ich wulle þe treosien Þurh mine tirfulne god. — 9308 Þe king him treousede on, For he wes swa æht mon.

**Treouþe**, obs. form of TRUTH.

**Treowe, Treowthe**, obs. ff. TRUE, TRUTH.

**Trepan** (trĭpæ·n), *sb.*[1] Forms: 5–7 **trepane**, 5–6 **trapane**, 6 **trappan**(**e**, 7–8 **trapan**, 6– **trepan**. [a. F. *trépan* (also †*trapan*) a borer, surgical crown-saw (14th c.), ad. med.L. *trepanum* (Du Cange) a crown-saw, ad. Gr. τρύπανον a borer.]

**1.** A surgical instrument in the form of a crown-saw, for cutting out small pieces of bone, esp. from the skull.

*c* 1400 *Lanfranc's Cirurg.* 127 Þis schal be þe foorme of a trepane with þe whiche þe brayn scolle schal be trepaned wiþ. 1525 tr. *Jerome of Brunswick's Surg.* xxxiv. H j/2 If the bone be stronge, bore ther throughe many holes with the trappane. 1676 WISEMAN *Chirurg. Treat.* v. ix. 393, I began to work with the Trepan, which I much prefer before a Trephine, it being an Instrument which doth its work lightly, and cutteth the Bone equally. *a* 1715 BURNET *Own Time* an. 1660 (1766) I. 146 The operation of the trepan and the cure was counted one of the greatest performances of surgery at that time. 1846 BRITTAN tr. *Malgaigne's Man. Oper. Surg.* 166 The trepan is applied to the cranium, sternum, and to the tibia, in cases of sequestrum. The scapula has also been trepanned, the os coccyx, the inferior maxilla, &c.

†**2.** A military engine formerly used in sieges: ? for boring holes in walls. *Obs.*

1584 HUDSON *Du Bartas' Judith* III. 107 And there th' Inginers haue the Trepan drest, And reared vp the Ramme for battry best. 1608 SYLVESTER *Du Bartas* II. iv. IV. *Decay* 994 There-under (safe) the Ram with yron horn,..The boistrous Trepane, and steel Pick-ax play Their parts apace, not idle night nor day. 1610 W. FOLKINGHAM *Art of Survey* I. xiii. 45 Engines..Militarie; as Battering-Rams,.. Trepanes.

**3.** A boring instrument for sinking shafts. (Usually treated as F., *trépan.*)

1877 KNIGHT *Dict. Mech.*, *Trepan*..2. (French.) A workman's name for the steel at the foot of a boring rod. 1903 *Illustr. Lond. News* 10 Oct. 528 The great boring instrument or trêpan, rises and falls with a regular motion. 1903 *Daily Chron.* 22 Oct. 3/5 An 18 ft. shaft has reached a depth of nearly 1,100 ft., the small trépan having gone much further down.

**4.** *attrib.*, as **trepan hole**, a hole made in a bone by a trepan; **trepan saw**, a saw of the form of a trepan, a crown-saw.

1839 URE *Dict. Arts* 148 *A* is a pulley...It has the crown or trepan saw *a* fixed to it. 1899 *Allbutt's Syst. Med.* VII. 239 A piece of metal tubing..is screwed into the trepan hole.

**Trepan, trapan** (trĕ-, trăpæ·n), *sb.*[2] *Obs.* or *arch.* Also 7–8 **trapan**, (**trappan**). [A word of obscure and low origin, prob. originally a term of thieves' or rogues' slang. According to the known evidence, originally applied to a *person* in sense 1 below (quots. 1641, 1653). Thence arose the verb describing the action of such persons, TREPAN *v.*[2], found in various constructions 1656–62. Hence, finally, a second use of the sb. as a name of the action, 1665, sense 2 here. The earlier spelling of the sb. was *trapan*, probably formed in some way from TRAP *sb.*$^1$ or *v.*$^1$ The change to *trepan*, seen first in the vb., may have been due to association with TREPAN *v.*$^1$ (a much earlier and well known word), of which TREPAN *v.*$^2$ may have been supposed to be some sort of fig. application.

No F. *trapan* or *trapaner* in this sense is recognized by Littré, Hatz.-Darm., Cotgrave, Godefroy. Nor is there any reason to connect *trapan* with OProv. *trapon* 'sorte de piège', nor with It. *trapanare* = TREPAN *v.*$^1$]

**1.** A person who entraps or decoys others into actions or positions which may be to his advantage and to their ruin or loss. Also applied to an animal (quot. 1686).

**1641** T. JORDAN *Walks of Islington* II. ii. (1657) D ij b, If we had known you had been a Trapan, you should ne'r have been admitted into our company. **1653** (*title*) The Total Rout, or a Brief Discovery Of a Pack of Knaves and Drabs, intituled Pimps, Panders, Hectors, Trapans, Nappers, Mobs, and Spanners. **1686** J. DUNTON *Lett. fr. New-Eng.* (1867) 35 In colour he [alligator] is of a dark brown, which makes him the more imperceptable when he lies as a Trapan in the Waters. *a* **1734** NORTH *Exam.* I. ii. (1740) 119 He was a Rogue, and a manifest Trapan of the Earl's. **1855** MACAULAY *Hist. Eng.* xvii. IV. 32 Old associates who had once thought him a man of..spotless honour,..hinted their suspicions that he had been from the beginning a spy and a trepan.

**2.** [f. TREPAN *v.*$^2$] The action of entrapping; a stratagem, trick; a trap or snare.

**1665** *Surv. Aff. Netherl.* 131 So the Muscovite likely, upon a Trepan upon him, to be none of their mildest Foes, hath Engrossed the Comerce of the Caspian Sea. *c* **1668** *Roxb. Ball.* (1891) VII. 380 Beware of Trappans: Maids, look to your Hits. **1671** SOUTH *Serm., Worldly Wisdom* (1715) 341 There being a Snare, and a Trapan almost in every Word we hear. **1684** EARL ROSCOM. *Ess. Transl. Verse* 16 But what a thoughtless Animal is Man, (How very Active in his own Trepan!) **1823** SCOTT *Peveril* xlii, Aware, by experience, how many trepans, as they were then termed, were used betwixt two contending factions.

**Trepa·n**, *v.*$^1$ Forms: see TREPAN *sb.*$^1$ [f. TREPAN *sb.*$^1$, or F. *trépaner* (14th c. in transl. of Lanfranc).] *trans.* To operate upon with a trepan; to saw through with a trepan, as a bone of the skull. Also *absol.*

*c* **1400** *Lanfranc's Cirurg.* 127 [see TREPAN *sb.*$^1$ 1]. *Ibid.* 133 Þanne I stoppe þe sijk mannes eeris, þat he mowe not heere þe soun of þe yren þat trepaniþ. **1597** A. M. tr. *Guillemeau's Fr. Chirurg.* 10 b/1 We trepane or open the sculle. **1666–7** PEPYS *Diary* 28 Jan., Prince Rupert is.. so bad, that he do now yield to be trepanned. **1751** *Affect. Narr. of Wager* 145 The poor Surgeon..could..trapan a broken Scull. **1846** [see TREPAN *sb.*$^1$ 1]. **1899** *Allbutt's Syst. Med.* VII. 240 If the skull be trepanned during the condition of acute cerebral compression, the pulsation may be visibly increased.

**b.** In brush-making: see *trepanning*, quot. 1877, *trepanned*, quot. 1891.

Hence **Trepanned** (-æ·nd) *ppl. a.*, **Trepa·nning** *vbl. sb.* and *ppl. a.*: **trepanning-elevator**, see quot. 1877, and cf. ELEVATOR 2.

*c* **1400** *Lanfranc's Cirurg.* 127 Þis manere trepanynge suffiseþ to þee. **1597** A. M. tr. *Guillemeau's Fr. Chirurg.* 14 b/2 The edges of the trepannede perforatione beinge verye sharpe. **1759** ADAM SMITH *Mor. Sent.* I. II. iii. 72 A trophy.. of saws for cutting the bones, of trepanning instruments.. would be absurd. **1877** KNIGHT *Dict. Mech., Trepanning.* (*Brush-making.*) The tufts or bristles are drawn into the holes in the stock by means of wire inserted through holes in the edge, which are then plugged. *Ibid., Trepanning-elevator*, a lever for raising the portion of bone detached by the trephine. **1891** *Cent. Dict., Trepanned brush*, a drawn brush having the holes for the bristles drilled partially through the stock to meet lateral holes drilled from the edge or end. The tufts of bristles are drawn into these holes by strong silk or thread passing through the laterals.

**Trepan, trapan** (trĕ-, trăpæ·n), *v.*$^2$ *Obs.* or *arch.* Also 7 **trappan, trepane.** [f. TREPAN, TRAPAN *sb.*$^2$, q. v.] *trans.* To catch in a trap; to entrap, ensnare, beguile.

**1656** BLOUNT *Glossogr.*, To *Trepan*, or rather *trappan* (from the Ital. *Trappare* or *trappolare*, i. to entrap, ensnare, or catch in a gin) in the modern acception of the word, it signifies to cheat or entrap [etc.]. **1658** SLINGSBY *Diary* (1836) 431, I see that I am trepan'd by these two fellows. **1664** BUTLER *Hud.* II. III. 617 Some by the Nose with fumes trappan 'em, As Dunstan did the Devil's Grandamm [= Grannam]. **1745** *De Foe's Eng. Tradesman* (1841) II. xxxvi. 87 To lie upon the catch to trepan his neighbour. **1827** SCOTT *Surg. Dau.* vi, That he should have trepanned the friend who had reposed his whole confidence in him. **1894** CROCKETT *Raiders* 38 Fellows who would..trepan a lass from the Cumberland shore, or slit the throat of a Dumfries burgher.

**b.** To lure, inveigle (*into* or *to* a place, course of action, etc., *to do* something, etc.).

*a* **1661** FULLER *Worthies* (1662) II. 2 Some Setters trapanned him..to hear Masse. **1678** DRYDEN *Limberham* I. i, Hast thou trepan'd me into a Tabernacle of the Godly? **1700** S. L. tr. *Fryke's Voy. E. Ind.* 227 These Men trapan that sort of People to go a Voyage that commonly proves their Destruction. *a* **1715** BURNET *Own Time* (1766) II. 18 To make use of him to trepan a man to his ruin. **1829** SCOTT *Rob Roy* Introd., James Mohr Drummond was secretly applied to to trepan Stewart to the sea-coast, and bring him over to Britain. **1838–9** HALLAM *Hist. Lit.* III. III. vii. § 7. 353 Pallavicino having been trepanned into the power of the Pope, lost his head at Avignon.

**c.** To do (any one) *out of* (a thing) by craft or guile; to cheat or beguile *out of*; to swindle.

**1662** J. DAVIES tr. *Olearius' Voy. Ambass.* 163 Ten of those Rogues had trapann'd him out of 500. Crowns. **1725** DE FOE *Voy. round World* (1840) 12 The Spanish Captain..greatly enraged..at being..trepanned out of his ship. **1832** AUSTIN *Jurispr.* (1879) II. xxxvi. 629 Trepanned out of their interests by that ridiculous juggling.

Hence **Trepanned** (-æ·nd) *ppl. a.*; **Trepa·nning** *vbl. sb.* and *ppl. a.*; whence **Trepa·nningly** *adv.*, by cheating or strategy (Bailey, 1731).

**1670** WALTON *Lives, Hooker* 222 A slander which this Age calls Trepanning. **1682** in *Lond. Gaz.* No. 1714/5 That..Insinuating and Trapaning Association. **1701** GREW *Cosm. Sacra* 189 Some may think of Jael, that..she was no better than a Trapanning Hussy. **1702** C. MATHER *Magn. Chr.* III. II. v. (1852) 384 Pursevants employed for the trepanning and entrapping of them. **1824** GALT *Rothelan* I. II. xii. 259 The fate of the trapanned page. **1826** W. E. ANDREWS *Exam. Fox's Cal. Protestant Saints* 94 Trepanning questions about the power of the pope and the queen in spirituals were put to him.

**Trepanation** (trepănē·ʃən). [f. TREPAN *v.*$^1$ + -ATION; cf. F. *trépanation* (14th c. in tr. of Lanfranc).] The operation of trepanning; perforation of a bone, esp. of the skull, by a trepan.

*c* **1400** *Lanfranc's Cirurg.* 126 & þese, in as myche as touchinge trepanacioun, worchiþ best. **1597** A. M. tr. *Guillemeau's Fr. Chirurg.* 56 b/2 Opinione of Avicenna touchinge trepanatione. **1882** *Athenæum* 16 Dec. 817/2 Numerous cases of surgical and posthumous trepanation.

‖ **Trepang** (trĭpæ·ŋ). Also 8 **tripam**, 9 **tripang, trepong.** [Malay *trīpang* (Yule). The early form *tripam* was app. from Fr.] A marine animal, an echinoderm (*Holothuria edulis*), called also *sea-cucumber*, *sea-slug*, *sea-swallow*, or *bêche-de-mer*, eaten as a luxury by the Chinese.

**1783** JUSTAMOND tr. *Raynal's Hist. Indies* I. 277 [Celebes] furnishes..tripam, a species of mushroom, which increases in value in proportion to the roundness of it's form, and the blackness of it's colour. **1793** J. TRAPP *Rochon's Voy. Madagascar*, etc. 390 The tripam is a little spungy plant without root, and like a mushroom...It grows in great profusion in the island of Celebes. **1802** CAPT. ELMORE in *Naval Chron.* VIII. 380 Sea swallow (called beach de mar by the Portuguese, and trepong by the Malays). **1836** *Penny Cycl.* V. 188/2 The tripang swala, or sea-slug. **1879** WRIGHT *Anim. Life* 572 So far as we know, but one species is used for food. This, the Trepang of the Chinese (*Holothuria edulis*), is found in the Indian Ocean.

**b.** *attrib.* and *Comb.*, as *trepang-fisher*, *-fishery*.

**1846** J. L. STOKES *Discov. Australia* I. vii. 211 These lighter coloured people are Malays, captured from the Trepang fishers. **1878** P. L. SIMMONDS *Commerc. Prod. Sea* I. ix. 105 The trepang fishery of the Pacific and Eastern Seas. **1904** HOWITT *Native Tribes S. E. Australia* i. 26 The trepang fishers..are the Bugis, a Malayan people, who form the principal nation of the Island of Celebes.

† **Trepanize**, *v. Obs. rare.* [f. TREPAN *v.*$^1$ + -IZE.] = TREPAN *v.*$^1$

**1601** HOLLAND *Pliny* XVII. xxvii. I. 545 Even their bones also use to be trepanized and bored through as well as ours. **1684** *Contempl. St. Man* I. v. (1699) 47 Some have been cured by tripanizing the Scull, or drawing Bones from it.

**Trepa·nned**, *ppl. a.*$^1$ and $^2$: see TREPAN *v.*$^1$ and $^2$.

**Trepanner**$^1$ (trĭpæ·nəɹ). [f. TREPAN *v.*$^1$ + -ER$^1$.] One who operates with a trepan.

**1727** in BAILEY vol. II. **1775** in ASH; and in later Dicts.

**Trepa·nner**$^2$. *arch.* Also 7–8 **tra-**. [f. TREPAN *v.*$^2$ + -ER$^1$.] One who trepans; an entrapper, decoy, swindler.

**1658–9** in *Burton's Diary* (1828) IV. 157 There came several trepanners from Whitehall, it pleased God to keep us upright. *a* **1709** ATKYNS *Parl. & Pol. Tracts* (1734) 339 This Trapanning proves..that the Trapanner did bear a Spight and Malice against the Person trapanned. **1818** SCOTT *Rob Roy* xxxiv, The turmoils which the political trepanner..is ..putting into motion.

**Trepanning**, *vbl. sb.*$^1$ and $^2$, *ppl. a.*$^1$ and $^2$: see TREPAN *v.*$^1$ and $^2$.

**Trepas, -pase, -passe**, obs. ff. TRESPASS. See esp. TRESPASS *v.*

**Trepeget, -eiette, trepget**, obs. ff. TREBUCHET.

**Trepett**, var. TRIPPET *Obs.*

**Trephine** (trĭfəi·n, -fī·n), *sb.* Forms: 7 **trafine, trafin, trefine, traphine**, 8– **trephine.** [Orig. *trafine*, according to the inventor f. L. *trēs fīnēs* three ends (see quot. 1628), app. formed with reference to *trapan*, TREPAN *sb.*$^1$ (to which the later form *trephine* shows a nearer approach). F. *tréphine* is from Eng.] An improved form of trepan, with a transverse handle, and a removable or adjustable sharp steel centre-pin which is fixed upon the bone to steady the movement in operating.

**1628** WOODALL *Viaticum* Wks. (1639) 313 The Trafine..an Instrument of myne owne composing,..although it may be said to be a derivative or Epitomy of or from the Trapan.. I thought fit to put the name of a Trafine upon it (*a tribus finibus*) from the three ends thereof. **1656** RIDGLEY *Pract. Physic* 172 Raise it with a Trepan, or a Trefine. **1767** GOOCH *Treat. Wounds* I. 304 That kind of trepan, called the *trephine*, is now in general use,..it is more commodious than the other. **1855** H. SPENCER *Princ. Psychol.* (1873) I. I. iv. 70 When by means of a trephine, the depressed portion of bone is cut out, the brain..at once resumes its duties.

*transf.* **1854** BADHAM *Halieut.* 441 The patient may plunge and writhe, but the operation of trephine goes on, and soon ..does the lamprey push his tongue through the bony plates of the skull, and draw it back, with a sample of brains adhering.

**b.** *attrib.*, as *trephine hole*, *opening*, *saw* (cf. TREPAN *sb.*$^1$ 4).

**1877** KNIGHT *Dict. Mech., Trephine-saw*, a crown-saw; a cylindrical saw with a serrated end, to make a circular kerf by the rotation of the saw. **1878** T. BRYANT *Pract. Surg.* I. 220 The trephine opening was filled in by a tough membrane. **1891** W. H. WHITE in *Jrnl. Physiol.* XII. 247 The same sized trephine hole was made in the skull.

**Trephi·ne** (see prec.), *v.* [f. prec.] *trans.* To operate upon with a trephine. Also *absol.*

**1804** ABERNETHY *Surg. Obs.* 174 Which opinions would induce us to trephine in cases of slight depression [of bone in fractured skull]. **1860** O. W. HOLMES *Elsie V.* xxvi, He was trephined at Greenwich Hospital. **1892** 'G. TRAVERS' *Mona Maclean* (1893) III. 102 A fractured skull came in.. and I waited to see them trephine. **1899** *Allbutt's Syst. Med.* VI. 293 The sinus is then exposed by trephining the mastoid.

Hence **Trephined** (-əi·nd, -ī·nd) *ppl. a.*, **Trephi·ning** *vbl. sb.* (also *attrib.*); also **Trephina·tion**, the operation of trephining.

**1862** *Catal. Internat. Exhib., Brit.* II. No. 3552 Trephining Instruments. **1874** ROOSA *Dis. Ear* 425 Many cases of trephination of the mastoid. **1886** *Athenæum* 24 Apr. 557/2 A skull..which exhibits a remarkable instance of post-mortem trephining. **1891** *Ibid.* 19 Sept. 390/3 Amulets from portions of the trephined skulls.

**Trepid** (tre·pid), *a. rare.* [ad. L. *trepid-us* scared, alarmed.] Trembling; agitated; fearful.

**1650** W. BROUGH *Sacr. Princ.* (1659) 421 Trembling, and chilness and confusion in the powers of action..a stupid, trepid, troubled motion. **1675** tr. *Machiavelli's Prince* vi. (Rtldg.) 39 The defence is so trepid and faint. **1760–72** H. BROOKE *Fool of Qual.* (1809) IV. 25 [He] presented his trepid hand to conduct the fair .. to her carriage. **1859** THACKERAY *Virgin.* lxx, The poor little trepid creature, panting and helpless under the great eyes.

Hence **Tre·pidly** *adv.*, **Tre·pidness.**

**1727** BAILEY vol. II, *Trepidness*, Trepidity, Fearfulness. **1911** *Daily News* 13 Nov. 4 With a show of boldness, but really trepidly and distrustfully.

**Tre·pidant**, *a. rare.* [ad. L. *trepidānt-em*, pr. pple. of *trepidāre* to TREPIDATE.] Trepidating, trembling with fear or agitation.

**1892** *Black & White* 2 July 2/2 In either party are many trepidant hopes and fears. **1907** F. THOMPSON *Sel. Poems* 50 Its keys are at the cincture hung of God, Its gates are trepidant to His nod.

Hence **Tre·pidancy**, the quality of trepidating.

**1845** POE *Tales, Fall of Ho. Usher*, Futile struggles to overcome an habitual trepidancy.

† **Tre·pidat, -ate**, *a. Obs. rare.* [ad. L. *trepidāt-us*, pa. pple. of *trepidāre*: see next.] Agitated, disturbed. (Cf. TREPIDATION 3.)

**1605** S. DOVE *Confut. Atheism* 19 The celestiall spheres in continuall volubilitye..their diurnall or daylye course from the East to the West, their retrograde and vyolent motion from the West to the East, their trepidat motion from the South to the North.

**Trepidate** (tre·pide'ɪt), *v. rare.* [f. ppl. stem of L. *trepidāre* to hurry, bustle, be agitated or alarmed. Cf. OF. *trepider* (14th c. in Godef.).] *intr.* To tremble with fear or agitation; also simply, † To shake, be agitated (*obs.*).

**1623** COCKERAM, *Trepidate*, to tremble for feare. **1653** R. G. tr. *Bacon's Hist. Winds* 364 Let the eighteenth Motion be the Motion of Trepidation, to which (as is understood by Astronomers) we give no great credit...In which bodies being not altogether well placed..doe trepidate or agitate continually. *a* **1774** TUCKER *Lt. Nat.* (1834) II. 126 Vanity.. insinuates among our pores,..trepidates through the nerves, ..and runs throughout the whole constitution. **1854** *Fraser's Mag.* L. 355 A thing which causes our mind to trepidate with quaking fear.

Hence **Tre·pidating** *ppl. a.*

*a* **1774** TUCKER *Lt. Nat.* (1834) II. 620 A calm and steady alertness..never anxious nor trepidating. **1866** J. B. ROSE tr. *Ovid's Met.* 202 The flush of pain And panting breath, and trepidating vein.

**Trepidation** (trepidē·ʃən). [ad. L. *trepidātiōn-em*, n. of action fr. *trepidāre*: see prec. Cf. F. *trépidation* (15th c.).]

**1.** Tremulous agitation; confused hurry or alarm; confusion; flurry; perturbation.

**1607–12** BACON *Ess., Of Seditions & Troub.* (Arb.) 414 There vseth to be more trepidacion in Courtes vponn the breaking out of troubles then were fitt. *a* **1639** WOTTON *Election Dk. Venice* in *Reliq.* (1651) 176 The success of that great day, in such trepidation of the State made every man meritorious. **1780** JOHNSON *Let. to Mrs. Thrale* 9 June, They did their work at leisure..without trepidation, as men lawfully employed. **1796** MME. D'ARBLAY *Camilla* I. 323 Miss Margland..in equal trepidation from anger and from fear. **1879** M. ARNOLD *Mixed Ess., Geo. Sand* 318, I found a large party assembled. I entered with some trepidation.

**2.** Tremulous, vibratory, or reciprocating movement; vibration; oscillation, rocking; an instance of this; also, involuntary trembling of the limbs, as in paralytic affections; tremor.

**1605** BACON *Adv. Learn.* II. ii. § 8 Massiue bodies..haue certaine trepidations and wauerings, before they fixe and settle. **1696** J. EDWARDS *Demonstr. Exist. & Provid. God* I. p. xii, Earth-quakes and trepidations of the earth. **1750** JOHNSON *Rambler* No. 1 ¶ 13 My impatience..will not suffer me to attend any longer the trepidations of the balance. **1822–34** *Good's Study Med.* (ed. 4) III. 227 A considerable degree of trepidation reached occasionally to her finger's end. **1837** WHEWELL *Hist. Induct. Sc.* (1857) II. 240 The trepidation of the body struck perpetually generates a new sound. **1899** *Syd. Soc. Lex., Trepidation*, a rhythmic movement of the foot in certain forms of paraplegia and in epilepsy.

**3.** *Astron.* A libration of the eighth (or ninth)

sphere, added to the system of Ptolemy by the Arab astronomer Thabet ben Korrah, *c* 950, in order to account for certain phenomena, esp. precession, really due to motion of the earth's axis.

*a* 1631 DONNE *Valedict.* Poems (1633) 193 Moving of th' earth brings harmes and feares, Men reckon what it did and meant, But trepidation of the spheares, Though greater farre, is innocent. 1653 [see TREPIDATE *v.*]. 1667 MILTON *P. L.* III. 483 They pass the Planets seven, and pass the fixt, And that Crystalline Sphear whose ballance weighs The Trepidation talkt, and that first mov'd. 1670 EACHARD *Cont. Clergy* 52 Up presently to the primum-mobile, and the trepidation of the firmament. 1834 *Penny Cycl.* II. 532/2 Thabet ben Korrah..about A.D. 950..revived an old notion ..(not mentioned by Ptolemy, but by Theon [A.D. 385]) of a variation in the position of the ecliptic, which has been called a *trepidation.*

**Trepidatory** (trėpi·dătəri), *a.* [f. as prec. + -ORY [2].] Of, pertaining to, or characterized by trepidation or tremor.

1881 G. F. RODWELL in *Knowledge* 16 Dec. 130/2 The most severe shock lasted for 70 seconds, and combined oscillatory, trepidatory, and rotatory movement. 1890 W. O'BRIEN *When we were Boys* 191 'You are joking', he said, in the trepidatory tone of one who had just heard the last Trumpet was about to sound.

**Trepidity** (trėpi·dĭti). [f. L. *trepid-us* TREPID + -ITY.] Agitation, alarm, fearfulness.

1721 BAILEY, *Trepidity*, trembling, fearfulness. 1807 W. TAYLOR in *Ann. Rev.* V. 193 Pecuniary cowardice is far viler than animal trepidity. 1898 *Westm. Gaz.* 7 Sept. 7/1 It was with some trepidity that..one looked out of the window.

**Tres,** obs. f. *trees*, pl. of TREE; obs. f. TRESS.

†**Tres-,** a. F. *très* (trę) adv. 'very':—L. *trans* beyond; formerly in occasional Eng. use prefixed to adjs., properly French (or identical in form with French), as *treschristien* [= mod.F. *chrétien* Christian], *tresgrand* (very great), *tresnoble*, *trespuissant*, *tres-royal*; sometimes to English adjs., as *tres-sacred*, *tres-splendent.* Hence rarely in derived sb., as *trespuissance.*

1572 *Satir. Poems Reform.* xxxviii. 19 Thy style was *Treschristien, maist Cristen King. 1605 BROUGHTON *Corrupt. Handl. Relig.* 104 The trespas is doubtles *tresgrand. 1587 FLEMING *Contn. Holinshed* III. 1977/1 Of this *tresnoble and *trespuissant monarch, I find these few verses. 1577–87 HOLINSHED *Chron.* I. 181/1 The *trespuissance of Cnute, the amplenesse of his dominions. 1647 WARD *Simp. Cobler* 57 *Tres-Royall Sir, I once againe beseech you. 1600 W. WATSON *Decacordon* (1602) 49 The same *tres-sacred bodie..was both dead and buried. 1648 *Petit. East. Assoc.* 12 To behold..our *Tres-splendent Crown carried into a desolate Wardrope.

**Tresai·el, tresay·le.** *Obs.* exc. *Hist.* Forms: 5–6 **tresaill**, 6 **tresaioul**, 7–8 **tresaile**, 8 **tresail**, 6–9 **tresayle**. [AF., formed after BESAIEL; cf. F. *trisaïeul* (16th c. in Godef. *Compl.*), f. *tri-*, TRI- + *aïeul* grandfather, AIEL.] A grandfather's grandfather; a great-great-grandfather.

1491 *Ordin. Yarmouth* in H. Swinden *Gt. Yarm.* (1772) 135 King Henry tresaill of our sovereigne lord the kyng that now is. 1550 J. COKE *Eng. & Fr. Heralds* § 35. (1877) 66 His [Charlmayne's] tresaioul, named Pepyn. 1607 COWELL *Interpr.*, *Cosenage*.., is a writ, that lyeth where the tresaile (that is, *tritavus*, the father of the besaile, or of the great grandfather) is seysed in his demesn as of fee, at the day of his death, of certaine lands or tenements, and dyeth: and then a straunger entreth and abateth. 1768 BLACKSTONE *Comm.* III. x. 186 If it mounts one degree higher, to the tresayle or grandfather's grandfather,..the writ is called a writ of cosinage, or *de consanguineo.*

b. *Writ of tresayle*: see quot.

1772 *Jacob's Law Dict.* (ed. 9), *Tresayle*, the name of a writ, to be sued, on ouster, by abatement, on the death of the grandfather's grandfather; now obsolete. 1848 in WHARTON *Law Lex.*

†**Tresance.** *Obs.* Also 5 **-auns, -aunce**, 5–6 **-awnce, -ens(e**, 6 **treasance**. [ad. med.L. *tresantia*, *trisantia*, of uncertain meaning, but app. the covered passage round a cloister: see Du Cange, ed. 1887. Etymology obscure: perh. *tres-* = L. *trans-*.]

1. A passage in or through a house; a corridor.

1428 in Heath *Grocers' Comp.* (1869) 6 The seide parlore and the tresance lattizid, glazid, and selyd. [1429–30 in Hope *Windsor Castle* (1913) 395 Pro factura ostii de la tresaunt in capella.] *c* 1440 *Promp. Parv.* 502/1 Tresawnce, in a howse.., *transitus.* *c* 1475 *Crabhouse Reg.* (1889) 58 The tresense fro the chawmbur dore to the halle dore. 1519 HORMAN *Vulg.* 291 b, I mette hym in a tresawnce: where one of the bothe muste go backe. 1579 TWYNE *Phisicke agst. Fort.* I. cxviii. 148 His other Gallerie and large Treasance. [1851 TURNER *Dom. Archit.* I. v. 233 (Roll of 35 Hen. III) Wainscote also the tresance [*tresancia*] between the hall and the aforesaid bed-chamber.]

2. ? A window; ? a lattice or screen.

1510 STANBRIDGE *Vocab.* (W. de W.) B j b, *Transcenna*, a tresens. [1525 est fenestra in summitate domus.] 1530 PALSGR. 282/2 Tresens drawen over an estates chambre, *ciel.*

†**Tresche.** *Obs.* Also **treische, treche.** [a. OF. *tresce*, *tresche* a dance, merry gathering (12th c. in Godef.); cf. It. *tresca* 'a kind of Antike or merrie dance' (Florio); 'a country-dance' (Baretti).] A dance, revel, merry-making.

*Tresche of giants*, a popular name of prehistoric stone-circles. Cf. CAROL *sb.* 4.

*c* 1290 *S. Eng. Leg.* I. 88/65 Huy sounguen ofte..and treches [*v.r.* tresches] huy gonne lede. 1297 R. GLOUC. (Rolls) 1221 Þe kinges neueu & þe erles neueu of kent..In þat noble tresche [*v.rr.* treische; companye; reuel] strif bigonne arere. *Ibid.* 3062 Þat was þe treche of geans, vor a quointe worc it is Of stones al wiþ art ymad, In þe world such non is..Þus was stonheng uerst ymad, þat men al day yseþ. *Ibid.* 7067 Roberd þis noble duc as he wende ouerlond A wel vair maide as him þoȝte in a tresche [*v. rr.* one treche: a strete] he vond.

**Trese,** obs. f. *trees*, pl. of TREE.

†**Tresemay·ns.** *Obs.* [= OF. *treis* (*trois*) *semaines* three weeks.] The space of three weeks.

1545 in Leadam *Crt. of Requests* (Selden) 168 The tenauntes ..shall brynge afor theym at Westminster the tresemayns of Ester next commyng all suche auncient Courte Rolles and Recordes.

‖**Tresette** (‖ trese·tte, trese·t). Also **trisette, trissett, tresset.** [Ital. *tresette*, f. *tre* three, *sette* seven, F. *tré-sept.*] An Italian card-game for four persons, played with a pack of 40 cards (the 8, 9, and 10 of each suit being excluded), in which the 3 and 7 are the winning cards.

1785 C'TESS ROSENBERG *Ess.* II. 109 A priest who used to come every day to make up my father's party at trisette. 1858 MISS BRIGHTWELL *Life Linnæus* 172 Mostly played at the Swedish game of trissett. 1902 tr. *Ct. Kielmansegge's Diary* 57 We were home by dinner-time, and spent that evening..at Richmond, playing a game of tresset amongst ourselves. 1903 *Review of Rev.* Aug. 250/2 He liked..to sit down..to a four-cornered card game of tresette.

†**Tresge·t.** *Obs. rare*[−1]. [a. OF. *tresgiet*, *tresget* act of throwing across, darting (12th c. in Godefroy), n. of action fr. *tre(s)geter*: cf. TREGET.] Casting of darts.

13.. *K. Alis.* 7383 (Bodl. MS.) Wel hij fiȝtten on þe pleyn Wiþ tresget [*v. r.* target] wiþ rerẹmeyn.

†**Tresgressor.** *Obs. rare*[−1]. Altered form of TRANSGRESSOR, with F. *tres-* = L. *trans-*, as in *trespass.*

1549 *Compl. Scot.* xiv. 118 Ane tresgressor that hed committit cryme.

‖**Tresillo** (tresī·lʸo). [Sp., factitious dim. of *tres* three.] A Spanish card-game; = OMBRE.

1829 W. IRVING in *Life & Lett.* (1864) II. 403 The countess comes up to the Alhambra with a little party to play at Tresillo. 1878 H. H. GIBBS *Ombre* 4 The game [Ombre] is now played in Spain under the name of *Tresillo*, meaning a threesome game.

**Tresle,** obs. form of TRESTLE.

†**Tresmountai·n,** *a. Obs. rare*[−1]. [a. OF. *tresmontaine* polestar (13th c. in Godef.), with *tres-* = *tras-*, *trans-*: see TRA-, TRANSMONTANE.] = TRANSMONTANE 2; cf. TRAMONTANE B. 1.

*c* 1430 *Pilgr. Lyf Manhode* IV. xxiii. (1869) 189 Summe j drawe to þe pitee of þe ryal magestee of god,..summe ooþere to þe sterre tresmountayne.

**Tresnoble**: see TRES-. **Treson, Tresor, -our,** obs. ff. TREASON, TREASURE.

**Trespass** (tre·spăs), *sb.* Forms: 3–7 **trespas**, (4–5 **trispas, trispase**), 4–6 **trespace**, 4–7 **trespasse**, (5 **truspas, trespaas**, 6 **tresspas, treaspas**), 7– **trespass.** β. 4 **trepas, -pase**, *pl.* **-pasis.** [ME. *trespas*, a. OF. *trespas* passing across, passage, transgression of an order or law, offence, vbl. sb. fr. *trespasser*, mod.F. *trépasser* to pass away, die: see TRESPASS *v.* The legal application of the words seems specially English.]

1. A transgression; a breach of law or duty; an offence, sin, wrong; a fault.

*c* 1290 *S. Eng. Leg.* I. 23/152 He [St. Dunstan]..for-ȝaf hem [his servants] heore trespas..And a-soylede hem of heore sunnes. *c* 1330 R. BRUNNE *Chron.* (1810) 171 Þei did a foule trespas, it was vnsemly þing. 1382 WYCLIF *Matt.* vi. 14 ȝif ȝee shulen forȝeue to men her synnys, and ȝoure heuenly fadir shal forȝeue to ȝou ȝoure trespassis. *a* 1425 *Cursor M.* 822 (Trin.) Furst shulde he bie dere þat trespace [*rime* grace]. *c* 1440 *Alphabet of Tales* 502 In þat mene while.. it [a soul] mot hafe done suche penance for þe truspas at it had done, at it mot hafe bene delyverd fro payn. 1526 TINDALE *Matt.* vi. 12 [see TRESPASS *v.* 3 b]. *Ibid.* 14 And [= if] ye wyll not forgeve men there trespases, no more shall youre father forgeve your treaspases. 1611 SHAKS. *Wint. T.* I. ii. 265 Be plainer with me, let me know my Trespas. 1687 A. LOVELL tr. *Thevenot's Trav.* II. 179, I lookt upon it as a Trespass against human prudence, to run the hazard a second time of being hindered to go into the Indies. 1768 BLACKSTONE *Comm.* III. xii. 208 Trespass, in it's largest and most extensive sense, signifies any transgression or offence against the law of nature, of society, or of the country in which we live. 1831 SCOTT *Ct. Robt.* v, My head..is at your imperial command, prompt to pay for the unbecoming trespass of my tongue.

2. *Law.* In a wide sense, Any violation or transgression of the law; *spec.* one not amounting to treason, felony, or misprision of either.

*c* 1290 *Beket* 462 in *S. Eng. Leg.* I. 119 It nas neuere lawe ne riȝt, double dom to take For o trespas. *c* 1330 R. BRUNNE *Chron.* (1810) 50 Edrik was hanged on þe toure, for his trispas. 1421 *Coventry Leet Bk.* 24 Noo Osteler bake no maner of bred in hur houses, nodur mannys bred ne horsebred, to sell, up the payne of vj s. viij d. at every trespas. 1428 *Surtees Misc.* (1888) 5 His trespas of forgeyng and utteryng of fals osmunds and castyng of fals tyn. 1472–5 *Rolls of Parlt.* VI. 157/1 Trespasses doon with force and armes ayenst your peas. 1553 T. WILSON *Rhet.* 49 Sometimes a man is accused of felonye, and yet he proueth his offence to be but a trespace. 1651 G. W. tr. *Cowel's Inst.* 211 The word Trespasse..comprehends every violation of the Law. But our discreet Lawyers call only private crimes Trespasses, and make distinctions even amongst these. 1895 POLLOCK & MAITLAND *Hist. Eng. Law* II. viii. § 3. II. 510 Trespass (*transgressio*) is the most general term that there is; it will cover all or almost all wrongful acts and defaults. Every felony, says Bracton, is a trespass, though every trespass is not a felony. In a narrower sense therefore *trespass* is used [in 13th c.] as a contrast to *felony.*

β. *c* 1308 in *Pol. Songs* (Camden) 197 Of feloni hi ne taketh hede, Al thilk trepas is a-go.

3. *Law. spec.* Any actionable wrong committed against the person or property of another; also short for *action of trespass.* **a.** *Trespass to person.*

13.. *Cursor M.* 29391 (Cott. Galba) Of him þat dose a light trispase To prest or clerk vnwitandly. 1444 *Coventry Leet Bk.* 203 In satisfaccion of the trespas doon to hym the tyme þat he was beeton. 1767 COMYNS *Digest* V. 534 Trespass to the Person may be by Menace, Assault, Battery or *Mayhem.* 1822 HAMMOND *Comyns' Digest* VII. 495 A throws a squib among the people at a market, it lights near B who throws it from him, C does the same, and it strikes D and puts out his eye: D has trespass *vi et armis* against A. 1876 POLLOCK *Leading Cases done into Eng.* 17 And now 'gainst Shepherd, for loss of eye, Question is, whether trespass will lie.

b. *Trespass to goods.*

1590 SWINBURNE *Testaments* 183 If the testator make diuerse executors, and do bequeath to the one of them the residue of his goodes;..if the other executor enter thereunto, hee is subiect to an action of trespasse. 1768 BLACKSTONE *Comm.* III. 257 He may bring an action of trespass for taking away his goods. 1863 H. COX *Instit.* II. ix. 523 Another remedy for the unlawful taking of goods is by action of trespass, to recover damages for the loss of goods. 1909 HOLDSWORTH *Hist. Eng. Law* III. 271 The place of appeal was taken by the semi-criminal action of trespass *de bonis asportatis.* 1913 *Laws Eng.* (ed. Halsbury) XXVII. 865 The gist of an action of trespass is an unlawful taking or removing or damaging of a personal chattel.

c. *Trespass to land.* A wrongful entry upon the lands of another, with damage (however inconsiderable) to his real property.

*c* 1455 *Forest Lawis* c. 21 in *Acts Parl. Scot.* (1844) I. 692 Of trespas in forest of Baron. [1472–3 *Rolls of Parlt.* VI. 43/2 Noo persone nor persones, which have taken any..profittes of any of the premisses, or have entred and doon trespas.] 1768 BLACKSTONE *Comm.* III. xii. 209 In the limited and confined sense..it signifies no more than an entry on another man's ground without a lawful authority, and doing some damage, however inconsiderable, to his real property... Every unwarrantable entry on another's soil the law entitles a trespass by breaking his close. 1818 CRUISE *Digest* (ed. 2) IV. 319 If a person grants a piece of ground in the middle of his estate; he at the same time impliedly grants a way to it, and the grantee may pass over the land of the grantor..without being guilty of a trespass.

d. *Trespass on the case*, a form of action now obsolete in which the damage complained of is a result not immediate, but consequential of an unlawful act. So called from the L. name of the writs (*brevia de transgressione super casum*) under which it was brought; also the name of the writ itself.

1429 *Rolls of Parlt.* IV. 346/1 Speciall actions of dette or trespasse uppon her cas. 1641 *Termes de la Ley* 257 If not that it bee a trespasse upon the case, and then the words *Vi et armis* are left out, and in lieu thereof the writ shal say in the end thereof, *Contra pacem.* 1768 [see CASE *sb.*[1] 6 e]. 1875 POSTE *Gaius* III. Comm. (ed. 2) 473 What was done by the introduction of the action of Trespass on the Case, was exactly analogous to what the praetors did. 1888 F. POLLOCK in *Encycl. Brit.* XXIII. 454 In the 16th century, a special form of 'trespass on the case' became, under the name of *assumpsit*, the common and normal method of enforcing contracts not made by deed, and remained so till the middle of the present century.

4. A passing beyond some limit. Now generally associated with TRESPASS *v.* 4. *rare.*

16.. *Jolly Pinder of Wakefield* ii. in Child *Ballads* (1888) III. 131 There is neither knight or squire..Dare make a trespasse to the town of Wakefield. 1681 tr. *Belon's Myst. Physick* 46 Some small Trespasses beyond the Rules of Physick. 1798 CHARLOTTE SMITH *Yng. Philos.* I. 49 He was frequently involved in scrapes for harmless frolics and trespasses out of bounds.

5. An encroachment, intrusion *on* or *upon*: cf. TRESPASS *v.* 5.

1769 GOLDSM. *Hist. Rome* (1786) II. 23 Mankind are ever most offended at any trespass on ceremony. 1799 JEFFERSON *Writ.* (1859) IV. 287, I know the extent of this trespass on your tranquillity. 1805 *Med. Jrnl.* XIV. 575 Would not a publication of this kind be a species of trespass on the board of health, lately instituted in Ireland? 1830 GLADSTONE in Morley *Life* (1903) I. App. 639 One trespass more I must make on your patience.

6. *attrib.* and *Comb.*, as *trespass act*, *-board* (BOARD *sb.* 2 b), *-fine*, *money*, *-offering* (cf. SIN-OFFERING); *trespass-chiding* adj.

1906 F. S. OLIVER *A. Hamilton* II. iii. 121 By this victory he smashed the *Trespass Act. 1908 *Nation* 21 Nov. 299/1 These writers have a disregard of all *trespass-boards. 1847 TENNYSON *Princ.* v. 36 Boys that slink From ferule and the *trespass-chiding eye. 1611 BIBLE 2 *Kings* xii. 16 The *trespasse money, and sinne money was not brought into the house of the Lord. 1535 COVERDALE *Lev.* v. 15 Yf a soule trespace..he shal brynge his *trespaceofferinge vnto the Lorde. 1845 KITTO *Cycl. Bibl. Lit.* s. v. *Adultery*, Bringing a trespass offering (a ram) to the door of the tabernacle, to be offered in his behalf by the priest.

**Tre·spass,** *v.* Forms: 4–6 **trespas, -pace, -passe**, (4–5 **trispas**, 6 **treaspas**), 6– **trespass.** β. 4–6 **trepasse**, 6 **-pase.** [f. TRESPASS *sb.*; or a. OF. *trespasser* to pass beyond or across, mod.F. *trépasser* to pass away, die, Pr. *tras-*, *tres-*, *trapassar*, Sp. *traspasar*, It. *trapassare*, med.L. *transpassare* to pass beyond, f. L. *trans* beyond (F. *très*) + *passare*, etc. to PASS. (The chief sense in Eng. attaches itself rather to the Eng. sb. than to the Fr. verb.)]

**1.** *intr.* To commit a transgression or offence; to transgress, offend; to sin. Also *fig.*

1303 R. BRUNNE *Handl. Synne* 4250 He..þat may, and wyl nat, here hys messe, ..he trespasyþ more yn þe lay. 13.. *Seuyn Sag.* (W.) 3921, I trispast namare than did he. 1382 WYCLIF *Sel. Wks.* III. 514 Summe prelatis þat trespaceden. 1387 TREVISA *Higden* (Rolls) V. 153 He had i-trespassed. *c* 1430 *Syr Tryam.* 1062 Yf he had trespaste oght. 1591 SPENSER *Virg. Gnat* 365 Not vnto him that neuer hath trespast, But punishment is due to the offender. 1797 MRS. RADCLIFFE *Italian* ix, Father Schedoni would be the last among us so to trespass. 1805 WORDSW. *Waggoner* I. 112, I trespassed lately worse than ever.

*β.* *c* 1400 *Lanfranc's Cirurg.* 98 (Add. MS.) ȝif þat þe blode trepasse [*Ashm. MS.* trespace] onlye in qualyte, amende hym.

**b.** Const. *against* († *to, unto, for*).

1303 R. BRUNNE *Handl. Synne* 1217 Þou hast trespast apertly Aȝens þys comaundment so hy. ? *a* 1366 CHAUCER *Rom. Rose* 1036 Who so durste to hir trespace, Or til hir folk, in werk or dede. *c* 1380 *Antecrist* in Todd *3 Treat. Wyclif* (1851) 135 He preied forȝyveness of his Fadre for hem þat trespassedd for hym. *c* 1386 CHAUCER *Melib.* ¶ 911 Ye haue mysborn yow and trespassed vn-to me. 1426 *Paston Lett.* I. 26, I have nought trespassed ageyn noon of these iij. 1523 FITZHERB. *Husb.* § 168 To forgyue them that haue trespaced to the. 1770 BURKE *Pres. Discont.* Wks. II. 341 He trespasses against his duty who sleeps upon his watch. 1845 M. PATTISON *Ess.* (1889) I. 22 He would not..trespass against the law and the canons.

†**2.** *trans.* with the matter of the trespass as object: To do (something wrong); to commit. *Obs.*

1375 BARBOUR *Bruce* XI. 553 For he thoucht that he suld amend That he trespassit had. 14.. *Eng. Fragm. Med. Service-Bks.* 8 To forȝeue alle maner of men and women þat þey haue trespased to the. *Ibid.* 9 Alle þe sennes that i haue trespased aȝens the wilful passioun of oure lord. 1542 UDALL *Erasm. Apoph.* 229 b, The offense euen of it self was hainous & besides that, trespaced in the emperours owne doughter. 1591 SPENSER *Virg. Gnat* 448 The faults which life hath trespassed. 1631 MAY tr. *Barclay's Mirr. Mindes* I. 25 It begins to censure with much rigour, the trespassed errours of the same.

†**3. a.** To transgress, violate (a law, etc.) *Obs.* [So in OFr.]

1483 CAXTON *G. de la Tour* d vij b, She had trespaced his commaundement. *a* 1536 TINDALE *Pathway* Wks. (1573) 385/2 To punish vs if we trespasse the law and good order. 1613 DANIEL *Hist. Eng.* I. (1650) 223, I must not so much trespasse Vertue, as to overpasse one memorable particular.

*β.* 1523 LD. BERNERS *Froiss.* I. ccxxxiii. 323 These lordes and knightes..durst nat trepase the popes commaundement.

†**b.** To offend against, wrong, violate (a person). *Obs.*

1427 in *10th Rep. Hist. MSS. Comm.* App. v. 294 If ony man shal trespasse or ly by ony nurishe or apprentise. 1523 LD. BERNERS *Froiss.* I. cclxxx. 420 They had greatly trespassed the prince, wherof than they repented them, but than they coulde not remedy it. 1526 TINDALE *Matt.* vi. 12 And forgeve vs oure treaspases, even as we forgeve them which treaspas vs. 1556 J. HEYWOOD *Spider & F.* xix. 7 At the least thou hast trespassed me.

**4.** *Law. intr.* To commit a trespass (see TRESPASS *sb.* 2); *spec.* to enter unlawfully on the land of another, or on that which is the property or right of another. Const. *on, upon.*

*c* 1455 *Forest Lawis* c. 21 in *Acts Parl. Scot.* (1844) I. 692 Item gif a fre man happyn to trespas [orig. *delinquat*] in þe forest of ony baroun to quham þe king be fre charter has granted a forest.. All þat is fundin with him trespassand in þe forest. 1590, 1651 [implied in TRESPASSER 2; cf. also sense 5]. *a* 1718 PRIOR *Epitaph* 20 Each Virtue kept it's proper Bound, Nor Trespass'd on the other's Ground. 1755 JOHNSON, *Trespass*, 2. to enter unlawfully on another's ground. 1843 PRESCOTT *Mexico* (1850) I. vi. 160 The lad answered, 'It was the king's wood, and he would punish him with death if he trespassed there.' 1844 in Ashbee *Last Rec. Cotswold Commun.* (1904) 37 Pd. Wm. Hands for..preventing Cattle from Trespassing on the Corn 4 weeks. 4 s. 1858 LYTTON *What will he do* III. viii, I trust we are not trespassing. 1880 *Chambers' Encycl.* IX. 535/1 If he is..trespassing with intent to catch or kill game, he may in some cases be apprehended and given into custody...If..A.'s cattle trespass on B's land, B can impound them.

*fig.* 1818 KEATS *Endymion* IV. 870 No pearl Will trespass down these cheeks.

**5.** *intr. fig.* with *on* or *upon*: To make an improper or uninvited inroad on (a person's time, attention, patience, etc.); to intrude on or upon the rights or domain of; to encroach on, infringe.

1652 URQUHART *Jewel* 274, I am afraid that I have trespassed a little upon the patience of the Reader. 1663 *Flagellum or O. Cromwell* (ed. 2) 5 Herein he trespassed upon that respect and lenity due and usual to Children of his Birth and quality. 1724 DE FOE *Mem. Cavalier* (1840) 231 We made bold..to trespass upon the country for a few horses. 1803 *Med. Jrnl.* IX. 53 Fearing that I have already trespassed on the limits of your Journal. *a* 1881 A. BARRATT *Phys. Metempiric* (1883) 206 Science is on those occasions trespassing on Metempiric, and is talking about things of which it cannot possibly know anything.

†**6.** *intr.* (in form **trepass.**) To pass beyond this life; to die. Also *trans.* in *to trepass this life. Trepassed*, deceased. (The only sense in which this vb. is preserved in mod.F.) *Obs. rare.*

14.. [implied in TRESPASSEMENT]. 1523 LD. BERNERS *Froiss.* I. xx. 29 As soone as I am trepassed out of this worlde. *Ibid.*, Soone after thys, noble Robert de Bruse, Kyng of Scotland, trepassed out of this vncertayne worlde. *Ibid.* ccxxix. 305 To gyue ayde and helpe, and to recomforte his cosyn, the wyfe of therle Charles trepassed. *a* 1533 — *Huon* vii. 17 It is .vii. yere syns he trepasyd thys lyfe.

Hence **Tre·spassed, Tre·spassing** *ppl. adjs.*

1631 Trespassed [see sense 2]. 1731–3 TULL *Horse-Hoeing Husb.* xix. 277 A very good Crop (except part of it, which being eaten by the trespassing Sheep..was somewhat blighted). 1788 D. GILSON *Serm. Pract. Subj.* xiv. (1807) 265 One trespassing Egyptian might thrust him away. 1824 G. C. RENOUARD *Ceylon* in *Encycl. Metrop.* (1845) XVI. 445/2 As all trespassing beasts are forfeited, the poor natives who live in the neighbourhood of plantations, are often deterred from rearing cattle.

† **Tre·spassable,** *a. Obs. rare.* Also 5 trepassable. [f. as TRESPASS *v.* + -ABLE; in sense 1 a. OF. *trespassable* that may be crossed (12th c.).]

**1.** That may be passed through or crossed.

*c* 1400 MAUNDEV. (1839) xvii. 182 All the parties of see & of lond han here appositees habitables or trepassables.

**2.** Subject or liable to an action of trespass.

1681 DEGGE *Parson's Counsellor* (ed. 3) 169 The Parson may have an Action of Trespas against any body that shall do any Trespassable act in the Church, or Church-yard.

**Tre·spassage.** *rare.* [f. TRESPASS *v.* + -AGE.] A trespassing, a trespass.

1874 W. BRUCE *Hebrew Odes* 74 Is there any God like the Lord above Who passeth over trespassage?

† **Tre·spassant,** *a. Obs. rare.* [a. AF. *trespassant*, pr. pple. of *trespasser*: see TRESPASS *v.* and -ANT.] That trespasses.

1587 HARRISON *England* II. xi. (1877) I. 226, I would wish the partie trespassant, to be made bond or slaues vnto those that receiued the iniurie.

† **Trespa·ssement.** *Obs. rare.* [a. OF. *trespassement* (12th c. in Godef.), F. *trépassement*: see TRESPASS *v.* and -MENT.] A passing away (from life); departure, decease.

14.. in *Wars Eng. in France* (1864) II. 523 Incontynent aftir his [Henry V's] trespasement..Johne, duc of Bedforde ..was made regente. 1475 *Bk. Noblesse* (Roxb.) 41 Frome the second yere of his reigne..into the day of his trespassement the space of .vij. yere.

**Trespasser** (tre·spăsəɹ). Forms: 4–5 trespasour, 4–6 -passour, -oure, 5 -pasor, -owre, -passor, 5–6 -pacer, 6 -passar, 6– trespasser. [ME. a. AF. *trespassour* = OF. *trespasseor*, agent-n. of *trespasser* to TRESPASS.] One who trespasses.

**1.** A transgressor, a law-breaker; a wrong-doer, sinner, offender.

[1292 BRITTON I. xxi. § 11 Touz trespassours encountre la forme de nos estatuz.] 1362 LANGL. *P. Pl.* A. I. 94 And take trespassours and teiȝen hem faste. 1387 TREVISA *Higden* (Rolls) VII. 117 Of þe whiche statut þe firste trespasour was þe erle. 1450–1530 *Myrr. our Ladye* 75 And forgyue vs oure trespasses, as we forgyue oure trespassoures. 1535 COVERDALE *Josh.* vii. *heading*, The trespacer is stoned vnto death. 1648 *Petit. East. Assoc.* 26 We see no reason, why ..our Trespassers be our Judges. 1742 J. GLAS *Lord's Supper* v. vi. 234 The Trespasser humbles himself to confess his Fault.

**2.** *Law.* One who commits a trespass; *esp.* one who trespasses on the lands of another.

*c* 1455 *Forest Lawis* c. 22 in *Acts Parl. Scot.* (1844) I. 692 Item gif ony wylde best be fundyn dede or wondyt and þe trespassour be nocht fundyn, at þe next mut þar aw to be inquisicioun made. 1590 SWINBURNE *Testaments* 237 Whosoeuer as a meere trespasser, entereth into the goods of the testator. 1651 G. W. tr. *Cowel's Inst.* 231 The party following them [stray beasts], and endeavouring to keep them from committing Damages, is no Trespasser. 1700 TYRRELL *Hist. Eng.* II. 1108 Concerning Trespassers in Parks. 1837 DICKENS *Pickw.* xix, Remind me to have a board done about trespassers, and spring guns, and all that sort of thing, to keep the common people out. 1895 POLLOCK & MAITLAND *Hist. Eng. Law* II. 166 The man who has bought or hired goods from a trespasser, how has he broken the king's peace and why should he be sent to gaol?

*fig.* 1702 NORTH *Let.* 6 Dec., in *Lives* (1890) III. App. 247 If I am too much a trespasser on your better time.

†**3.** *Rhet. lit.* 'That which oversteps or passes beyond'; hyperbaton. *Obs. rare*$^{-1}$.

1589 PUTTENHAM *Eng. Poesie* III. xii. (Arb.) 180 To all their speaches which wrought by disorder the Greekes gaue a general name (*Hiperbaton*) as much to say as the (*trespasser*).

**Trespassing** (tre·spăsiŋ), *vbl. sb.* [f. TRESPASS *v.* + -ING [1].] The action of the verb TRESPASS.

*a* 1340 HAMPOLE *Psalter* c. 4 Doand trispasyngis i hatid [*Vulg.* facientes preuaricaciones odiui]. 1388 WYCLIF *Rom.* iv. 15 Where is no lawe, there is no trespas, nethir is trespassyng. 1561 T. NORTON *Calvin's Inst.* III. 266 They winking at their own trespassings. 1852 CHR. ROSSETTI *Poems* (1904) 148/2, I..weep for my trespassing. 1886 *Pall Mall G.* 7 Oct. 4/2 Trespassing, in English law..is distinctly not a criminal offence; the trespasser cannot be 'given into custody', as the notice-boards have it.

**Tre·spassory,** *a.* [f. TRESPASS *sb.* + -ORY [2].] Pertaining to or of the nature of a trespass.

1888 POLLOCK & WRIGHT *Possession in Comm. Law* 131 Possession originally obtained by consent cannot become trespassory.

† **Trespe·rce,** *v. Obs. rare*$^{-1}$. [a. OF. *trespercier* (12th c. in Godef.), f. *tres*:—L. *trans*, TRANS- + *percier* to PIERCE.] *trans.* To pierce through, transpierce.

1483 CAXTON *G. de la Tour* K iij, A suerde shold trespeice her sowle and her herte.

**Trespuissance, -ant**: see TRES-.

**Tress** (tres), *sb.* Forms: *pl.* 3 tressene, 4– tresses, (5 -is, trissis); *sing.* 4–6 tresse, (6 *Sc.* tres), 6– tress. See also TRACE *sb.*[3] [a. F. *tresse*, in OF. *tresce* a plait or braid of hair (12th c. in Littré, etc.) = Pr. *tressa, treza*, It. *treccia*, beside the vb. F. *tresser*, OF. *trecier*, It. *trecciare* 'to plaite, to tie..vp in tresses, as womens haires are' (Florio). In Sc. and some Eng. dialects this appears also in the forms *trais(s* and *trace*: see TRACE *sb.*[3], *v.*[3] The OF., Pr., and It. sbs. point to a late L. or Romanic *tricia, trecia*, which appears in med.L.: see Du Cange.

For the derivation, Diez favours a form **trichea* (or **trichia*) f. Gr. τρίχα threefold, taking the primary sense to be 'a triple plait'. Hatz.-Darm. take *tresse* as vbl. sb. from the vb. *tresser*.]

**1.** A plait or braid of the hair of the head, usually of a woman: cf. TRACE *sb.*[3] 1.

13.. *Seuyn Sag.* (W.) 478 With both honden here yaulew here Out of the tresses sche hit tere. *c* 1384 CHAUCER *Knt.'s T.* 191 Hir yelow heer was broyded in a tresse Bihynde hir bak, a yerde longe I gesse. *a* 1400–50 *Alexander* 3450 Hire hede vn-helid was on hiȝe & hild all in trissis. *c* 1440 *Promp. Parv.* 502/1 Tresse, of heere, *trica.* 1530 PALSGR. 282/2 Tresse of heer, *tresse.* 1581 PETTIE *Guazzo's Civ. Conv.* III. (1586) 136 b, Certain women, whereof one had her tresses crossed in such sort vpon her head, that they made the likenesse of two hearts bound together. 1590 SPENSER *F. Q.* II. ix. 19 Her yellow golden heare Was trimly woven and in tresses wrought. 1613 R. CAWDREY *Table Alph.* (ed. 3), *Tresses*, lockes of hayre broyded vp. 1717 LADY M. W. MONTAGU *Let. to Lady Rich* 1 Apr., Their beautiful hair [was] divided into many tresses, hanging on their shoulders. 1777 ROBERTSON *Hist. Amer.* I. II. 92 Their black hair..was bound in tresses around their heads. 1793 EARL MACARTNEY *Jrnl. Emb. China* 4 Aug., [Their hair] is platted in a tress, and falls down the back.

**b.** (By extension) A long lock of hair (esp. that of a woman), without any sense of its being plaited or braided; mostly in pl. *tresses.* (The usual current sense.)

*c* 1290 *S. Eng. Leg.* I. 325/82 Heo drovȝ of hire tressene and caste a-wei. *c* 1384 CHAUCER *H. Fame* I. 230 A queynt array As she had ben an hunteresse With wynde blowynge vpon hir tresse. *c* 1450 *Merlin* xviii. 298 She was all discheuelee in her heer, and Taurus hir heilde be the tresses and drough hir after his horse. 1595 WEEVER *Epigr.* IV. xxii. (1599) E vj, Rose-checkt Adonis with his amber tresses. 1696 PHILLIPS (ed. 5), *Tresses*, said of the Hair, when it hangs down in dishevell'd Locks. 1717 POPE *Sappho to Phaon* 85 Nor braids of gold the varied tresses bind, That fly disorder'd with the wanton wind. 1824 W. IRVING *T. Trav.* I. I. vi. 75 Her long dishevelled tresses hanging to the ground. 1871 R. ELLIS *Catullus* lxvi. 47 What shall a weak tress do, when powers so mighty resist not?

**c.** *transf.* and *fig.* (and in fig. context). Applied to long leafy shoots or tendrils, rays of the sun, etc.

1423 JAS. I *Kingis Q.* i, In Aquary, Cinthia the clere Rynsid hir tressis. 1598 SYLVESTER *Du Bartas* II. i. IV. *Handicrafts* 139 Somtimes the Plane, somtimes the Vine they shear, Choosing their fairest tresses. *c* 1620 Z. BOYD *Zion's Flowers* (1855) 145 My sonnes..will by the tresses snatch The fittest time. 1641 J. TRAPPE *Theol. Theol.* v. 205 The radiant tresses of the sun. 1810 T. L. PEACOCK *Genius of Thames* 65 The weeping willow droops to lave Its leafy tresses in the wave. 1875 TRISTRAM *Moab* ii. 29 Luxuriant tresses of maiden-hair fern.

**d.** (*Our*) *Lady's tresses*: see LADY'S TRACES.

†**2.** A flat plait or braid (of interwoven threads, fibres, hairs, rushes, straw, etc.) Cf. TRACE *sb.*[3] 2, 3. *Obs.*

1491 CAXTON *Vitas Patr.* (W. de W. 1495) I. xxxvi. 38 b/2 Saynt Anthonye made a tresse for to make a lytyll basket. 1542 *Inv. Roy. Wardrobe* (1815) 82 Ane cott of variand taffatie with ane small walting tres of gold [cf. 1539, p. 32 trais of gold]. 1550 *Acc. Ld. High Treas. Scot.* IX. 455 Item, xvj elnis tressis put on the saittis of the saidis chiris.

†**3.** *Her.* = TRESSURE 2. Cf. TRACE *sb.*[1] 10. *Obs. rare.*

1577 HOLINSHED *Chron.* I. *Hist. Scot.* 358/2 They beare in their armes the Lion and Lillyes, wyth the tresse in fourme and fashion as the King of Scotlande beareth hys.

**4.** *attrib.* and *Comb.*, as *tress-lifting, -like, -shorn, -topped* adjs.

1819 KEATS *Lamia* I. 207 Down through *tress-lifting waves the Nereids fair Wind into Thetis' bower. 1647 R. STAPYLTON *Juvenal* xv. 277 Th'orphane..Whose *tresse-like haire, and eyes still dropping pearle. 1845 KITTO *Cycl. Bibl. Lit.* s. v. *Babylon*, It bears spreading and ever-green branches,..adorned with long tress-like tendrils. 1866 J. B. ROSE tr. *Ovid's Met.* VIII. 234 And matrons Eveninan, *tresses-shorn. 1871 BROWNING *Balaust.* 1323 Past the pines *Tress-topped.

Hence **Tre·ssful** *a.*, full of or fully furnished with tresses; **Tre·ssless** *a.*, having no tresses; **Tre·sslet**, a little tress.

1606 SYLVESTER *Du Bartas* II. iv. III. *Magnif.* 734 Pharo's faire daughter..Was queintly dressing of her *Tress-full head Which round about her to the ground did spread. 1865 CARLYLE *Fredk. Gt.* xx. iii. (1873) IX. 51 The Bernburg Officers, tragically *tressless in their hats. 1882 J. WALKER *Scotch Poems* 136 A glossy *tresslet of her lint-white hair.

**Tress,** *v.* Now *rare* exc. in *pa. pple.* Also 4 tresce. [ME. a. F. *tresser*, OF. *trecier* (12th c. in Littré) = Pr. *tressar, trezar*, It. *trecciare* to arrange in a tress, braid, plait; goes with TRESS *sb.*

The OF. form *trecier* indicates a late L. type **triciāre*, f. *tricia, trecia* (or **trichia*): see TRESS *sb.*]

**1.** *trans.* To arrange (hair) in tresses.

? *a* 1366 CHAUCER *Rom. Rose* 569 And with a riche golde treasour Her hede was tressed queintly. 1390 GOWER *Conf.* III. 255 And hou hir yelwe her was tresced And hire atire so wel adresced. *c* 1440 *Promp. Parv.* 502/1 Tressyn heere, *trico.* 1623 tr. *Favine's Theat. Hon.* II. iv. 78 The Sicambrians were observed by their yellow haire, tressed and knit in cordons. 1827 ROBERTS *Voy. Centr. Amer.* 29 The hair was worn long and tressed behind with a cord. 1867 *Morn. Star* 19 Sept., Neither sex wears any covering on the head, preferring to tress..that with which nature has provided them.

b. To arrange or dispose (threads, etc.) in braids. 1862 [see *tressing* below]. 1904 *Westm. Gaz.* 24 May 1/3 The tiny fingers threw the bobbins swiftly from side to side, moved the pins on the pricked paper pattern, tressed the lace that had to be finished before eventide.

2. *intr.* Of the hair: To fall in tresses; to admit of being arranged in tresses.

1867 *Morn. Star* 19 Sept., The hair of the Abyssinians is ..sufficiently long to tress well.

Hence **Tre·ssing** *vbl. sb.*

*c* 1425 *St. Mary of Oignies* I. i. in *Anglia* VIII. 135/34 Tressynge & tiftynge of here. 1862 *Catal. Internat. Exhib., Brit.* II. No. 4542, Skilful tressing, and most careful workmanship and finish, in which the exhibitor endeavoured not to be surpassed by any of his fellow competitors.

**Tress,** obs. form of TRACE *sb.*[2], TREST *sb.*[2]

**-tress,** ending of feminines of agent-nouns in *-ter*, *-tor*, etc., usually short for *-ter-ess*, *-tor-ess*: as in *actress*, *auditress*, *huntress*, *mistress*, *seamstress*, *songstress*, *traitress*, *vintress*: see -ESS[1].

**Tres-sa·cred,** most sacred: see TRES-.

‖ **Tresseau** (treso). [Fr. :—OF. *tressel*, deriv. of *tresse* TRESS.] Applied to a vine, of which the grapes grow in a much elongated cluster. Also *attrib.*

1763 MILLS *Pract. Husb.* IV. 381 If some plants of the tresseau, whose fruit never ripens easily, are mixed with the pineaus, it is..because our forefathers..judged it necessary to add these tresseaus. *Ibid.* 382 A reasonable proportion of the tresseau grape should always be planted with the others in sandy soils.

**Tressed** (trest, *poet.* tre·sėd), *ppl. a.* and *a.* [f. TRESS *sb.* and *v.* + -ED.]

1. Of the hair: Arranged in tresses; braided.

*c* 1386 CHAUCER *Wife's Prol.* 344 Ye wommen shul apparaille yow..noght in tressed [*v. rr.* trussede, tressede] heer and gay perree. 1500–20 DUNBAR *Poems* xlvi. 77 Hir goldin tressit hairis redomyt. 1579 SPENSER *Sheph. Cal.* Apr. 12 He plongd in payne his tressed locks dooth teare. 1612 tr. *Benvenuto's Passenger* II. 573 In two faire eyes, or in the tressed lockes.

2. Having or furnished with tresses; often as the second element in a parasynthetic compound, as *gold-tressed*.

13.. *K. Alis.* 5393 (Bodl. MS.), Hij weren..tressed in þe nekkes as a woman. 1412–20 LYDG. *Chron. Troy* IV. 2645 Firy Titan, gold-tressed in his spere. 1601 WEEVER *Mirr. Mart.* Cviij, A Comet..Bearded, or trest, or stretching forth his taile. 1623–4 MILTON *Paraphr. Ps. cxxxvi.* 30 He.. caus'd the Golden-tressed Sun All the day long his cours to run. 1758 *Poetry* in *Ann. Reg.* 413 The silver tressed Summer's gone. 1830 TENNYSON *Recoll. Arab. Nts.* xiii, A brow of pearl Tressed with redolent ebony.

**Tressel, -il,** etc.: see TRESTLE.

**Tressilate** (tre·sileⁱt), *v. rare.* [ad. F. *tressaillir* to thrill, tremble, f. *tres-* :—L. TRANS- + *saillir* to jump.] *intr.* To start with sudden agitation, as with a thrill of surprise, joy, etc.

1889 D. C. MURRAY *Danger. Catspaw* xiv, The ladies tressilated deliciously. The crime began to take an air of romance.

**Tresson, -oun, -un,** obs. forms of TREASON.

**Tres-splendent,** *a.*, 'most' or 'very illustrious': see TRES-.

**Tressure** (tre·ʃiŭı, tre·ʃŭı). Forms: *α.* 4–6 **tressour**, (5 **-owre, tresour, -ewyr, treasour, trissoure,** 7 **tresseur**); *β.* 5 **tressur, trussure,** 6 **treasure,** 5– **tressure**; *γ.* 5 **trechoure**. [ME. *tressour* represents OF. *tresseor*, *-eour*, also *tressoir*, *tressoer* (13th c.) :—L. **triciātōrium*: see -OUR; ME. *tressure* = OF. *tressure*, *-eure* (12–13th c.): see -URE; f. F. *tresse* TRESS.]

†1. A ribbon or band worn round the head; a net with which a woman's tresses are confined; a head-dress; also, app., the arrangement of her hair in tresses, her *chevelure*. *Obs.*

*a* 1310 in Wright *Lyric P.* xxxvii. 105 The ryche ledies in huere bour, That wereden gold on huere tressour. 13.. *Gaw. & Gr. Knt.* 1739 Þe hazer stones Trased aboute hir tressour, be twenty in clusteres. ?*a* 1366 [see TRESS *v.* 1]. *c* 1420 *Metr. Life St. Kath.* (Halliw.) 11 Maxent..bad anon hys turmentours Do hange hur be hur tresourys. *c* 1425 *Voc.* in Wr.-Wülcker 656/17 *Hoc tricatorium*, tressure. *c* 1475 *Pict. Voc.* ibid. 792/18 *Hec tricatura*, a tresewyr. 1483 *Cath. Angl.* 392/2 A Tressowre, *trica*, *tricatura*. *Ibid.* 394/1 A Trissoure of A woman hedde, *cincinnus*,.. *trica*, *tricatura*, *cincinnaculus*.

2. *Her.* A diminutive of the orle (ORLE 1 a), consisting of a narrow band of one-quarter the width of the bordure; usually borne counterfleury, or double and fleury counterfleury, as in the arms of Scotland. Formerly also called *trace* (TRACE *sb.*[1] 10), *tract* (TRACT *sb.*[3] 6 (*a*)).

*a* 1440 *Sir Degrev.* 635 Hure botenus was toore, Anamelede with azoure; With topyes and trechoure Overtrasyd. *Ibid.* 1031 He beres in cheef of azour, Engrelyd with a satur, With doubule tressour. 1572 BOSSEWELL *Armorie* II. 41 b, Without mention made of anye tracte, or Tressour Counterflorie. 1592 WYRLEY *Armorie, Ld. Chandos* 77 Two Ermin Lions passant crowned gold, With Scottish treasure. 1611 COTGR., *Trescheur*, a Tracke, or Tresseur (in Blason). 1704 J. HARRIS *Lex. Techn.* I, *Tressure*, a term in Heraldry for an Orle when it is flowered; and if there be two of them, it is called a double Tressure. 1707 E. CHAMBERLAYNE *St. Gt. Brit.* II. ii. (ed. 22) 90 In the second place, Or, within a Double Tressure, Counter-flower'd Lys, Gules, a Lyon Rampant of the Second, for the Royal Arms of Scotland. 1808 SCOTT *Marm.* IV. vii, The double tressure might you see, First by Achaius borne. 1857 J. PATERSON *Hist. Regality Musselburgh* 180 Three crescents within a double tressure.

3. *Numism.* An ornamental enclosure, circular or of several arches, containing the type or distinctive device, found on many gold and silver coins of former centuries.

1745 M. FOLKES *Eng. Silver Coins* 16 He..omitted the double tressure surrounding the head upon the former groats. 1817 RUDING *Annals Coinage* III. 400 In a double tressure of ten arches with trefoils in the outer angles, the English Lion [etc.]. 1841 HAWKINS *Silver Coins* (1876) 206 Edward III. 1327 to 1377...The Groats were struck at London or York: the type has the bust of the king, front face, within a double tressure of nine arches. 1898 G. B. RAWLINGS *Brit. Coinage* 39 Gold florin of Edw. III...*Rev.* A short ornate beaded cross, enclosed by a tressure of four arches, with a lion in each angle.

Hence **Tre·ssured** *a.*, provided with (in quot. *loosely*, borne upon) a tressure.

1805 SCOTT *Last Minstr.* IV. viii, The tressured fleur-de-luce he [Thirlestane] claims To wreathe his shield.

**Tressy** (tre·si), *a.* [f. TRESS *sb.* + -Y.] Resembling, characterized by, or adorned with tresses.

1614 SYLVESTER *Bethulia's Rescue* III. 230 Like two Popplars which..their tressie Tops doe hide Amid the Clouds. 1795 COLERIDGE *Lewti* 10 Pendent boughs of tressy yew. *a* 1845 HOOD *Ruth* iv, Her hat, with shady brim, Made her tressy forehead dim.

†**Trest,** *sb.*[1] *Obs.* Forms: 4–5 **treste,** 4–6 **trest.** [A parallel form to TRAIST *sb.*, TRIST *sb.*, TRUST *sb.* It may in some instances be a variant of *traist* (which is probable at least for the 16th c. Scotch use); but is viewed by Morsbach as a variant of *trist*.] Confidence, assurance, trust.

*a* 1300 *Floriz & Bl.* 408 Al mi trest is þe upon. 1422 tr. *Secreta Secret., Priv. Priv.* xl. 198 Iosue..by the grete treste that he had in god, comanded the Sone and the mone. 1570 *Satir. Poems Reform.* xxiv. 48 To hing, As tratouris sould, for schuitting vnder trest. *a* 1600 MONTGOMERIE *Misc. Poems* xxx. 23 Sen he took me vnder trest.

**Trest** (trest), *sb.*[2] Now only *Sc.* and *dial.* Forms: *α.* 4–6 **treste,** 6 *Sc.* **treist,** 5– **trest.** *β.* 5 *Sc.* **trast,** 6 *Sc.* **traist.** *γ.* 5 **tryste,** 5–6 **tryst,** 6 **trist.** *δ.* 6 **triss,** 6–9 **tress.** [a. OF. *treste*, var. of *traste*, orig. *trastre*, *trestre* (12–13th c. in Godef.) :—L. *transtrum*, **trāstrum* cross-beam, transom; cf. obs. It. *trasto*, pl. *trasti* the benches of a galley, transoms (Florio), which has also lost the second *r*.]

1. = TRESTLE 1.

13.. *Seuyn Sag.* (W.) 3874 The kinges dener wele was grayd; Thai set trestes and bordes on layd. 13.. *E. E. Allit. P.* B. 832 Þe trestes tylt to þe woȝe & þe table boþe. 1432 *Test. Ebor.* (Surtees) II. 22, j met bord wᵗ j pare trystes. *c* 1470 HENRY *Wallace* x. 40 Thai..Past our the bryg; Wallace gert wrychtis call, Hewyt trastis: wndyd the passage all. 1501 DOUGLAS *Pal. Hon.* III. lxx, Traists, formis, and benkis, war poleist plane. 1565 in Hay Fleming *Reform. Scotl.* (1910) 610 Ane aikin burd standand on treistis. 1627 MAY *Lucan* x. 133 High tresses golden tables bore. 1665 J. FRASER *Polichron.* (S.H.S.) 197 The trests and supporters of the oaken table. 1825 SCOTT *Betrothed* xiv, When the boards and tresses on which the viands had been served were withdrawn. 1886 J. BARROWMAN *Sc. Mining Terms*, *Tress*, a trestle; the fulcrum for the lever used in boring.

†b. A rest used with a harquebus or other fire-arm: = TRESTLE 4 a. *Obs.*

1513 *Acc. Ld. High Treas. Scot.* IV. 527, ij cartis with gwnstainis,..the cran with the traistis for the gwn. 1515 *Ibid.* V. 15 Four gret eschin treis to mak trestis for hacbuschis. 1543–4 *Ibid.* VIII. 248 For fraucht of thre boittis witht the said artalȝe, having tressis,..and other necessaris convenient thairfore.

2. A tripod; a three-legged stool: = TRESTLE 2. Now *dial.*, and variously used.

1483 *Cath. Angl.* 393/2 A Tryste (*A.* A Tristylle), *tripos*, *tristula*. 1513 DOUGLAS *Æneis* III. vi. 11 God Apollois divinationis, Vnder his trestis and burdis at Delphos schene. 1547–64 BAULDWIN *Mor. Philos.* (Palfr.) 10 Certaine fishers found a golden treste or triuet, on which was written 'sapienti', that is, Giue this to a wise man. *a* 1800 PEGGE *Suppl. Grose*, *Trest*, a strong large stool. Lanc. 1882 *Lanc. Gloss.*, *Trest*, a strong bench; a butcher's block [cf. sense 1].

†**Trest,** *a.* *Obs.* [A parallel form to TRAIST *a.*, TRIST *a.*[1]: cf. TREST *sb.*[1] and next.]

1. Firm, strong: = TRAIST *a.* 1.

*c* 1470 *Golagros & Gaw.* 526 He..Turnit to ane hie toure, that tight wes full trest.

2. Confident, sure: = TRAIST *a.* 2.

*a* 1300 *Cursor M.* 17219 Þou mai be ful trest to spede.

3. Trusty, faithful: = TRAIST *a.* 3.

*c* 1560 A. SCOTT *Poems* (S.T.S.) ix. 28 Ane constant hairt bayth trest & trew. 1566 *Inv. Roy. Wardrobe* (1815) 177 Service done..be our trest cousing Johnne now erle of Mar. 1584 HUDSON *Du Bartas' Judith* v. 134 So shall you finde me,..as faithfull, secret, trest, and trew.

Hence † **Tre·stly** *adv. Obs.*, confidently.

*a* 1568 in *Bannatyne Poems* (Hunter. Cl.) 213 Thair is nocht faithfulnes fundin in to this erd; Now is nocht thre may trestly trow in the ferd.

†**Trest,** *v.* *Obs.* Forms: 3 **treste(n,** 5–6 **trest**; also 4 *pa. t.* **treste.** [A parallel form to TRAIST *v.*, TRIST *v.*, TRUST *v.* Morsbach considers it a phonetic variant of *trist*. But in the northern and Sc. examples it may be merely a variant spelling of *traist*, perh. under English influence.]

1. *refl.* To commit oneself securely, to trust (*in*, *of*, *on*): cf. TRAIST *v.* 1.

*a* 1250 *Prov. Ælfred* 505 in *O. E. Misc.* 132 On him þu maist þe tresten. 1422 tr. *Secreta Secret., Priv. Priv.* xl. 198 That neuer he shold hym treste of the helpe of his god.. This kynge Ezechie hym trested in god.

2. *intr.* To trust (*of*, *to*, or with *inf.*): = TRAIST *v.* 2.

*c* 1275 LAY. 17941 For sealde he aswint þat to him seolue tresteþ. 13.. *Sir Beues* (A.) 3520 Meche a [= he] treste to Arondel. *c* 1400 *Apol. Loll.* 66 Wan þe man trestiþ of þis absolucoun, wening him siker..& mendiþ not. 1405 in *Roy. & Hist. Lett. Hen. IV* (Rolls) 159 Treste ȝe nought to no Leutenaunt. *c* 1425 *XI Pains of Hell* 347 in *O. E. Misc.* 221 Y pray ȝou seris trest wele hereto. *c* 1560 A. SCOTT *Poems* (S.T.S.) xxii. 17 Ay tresting for to speid.

b. *trans.* with simple obj. (? *orig.* dative), or clause: = TRAIST *v.* 2 b.

*c* 1275 LAY. 2351 Ac he nam one hired man þat wel he treste con. 1500–20 DUNBAR *Poems* xiii. 11 Is na man thair that trestis ane vther. *c* 1560 A. SCOTT *Poems* (S.T.S.) xxx. 8 Trest weill this taill is trew. 1570 *Satir. Poems Reform.* xvii. 183 He may, I trest, set vs at rest.

**Trest,** obs. form of TRYST.

**Trestle** (tre·s'l), *sb.* Forms: *α.* 4–5 **trestele,** 4–6 **-el, -ell(e, -ill(e,** 5 **-iel, -ul,** 5–6 **-yll(e,** 6 **-il, -yl,** 4– **trestle**; 4–6 **tresselle,** 6–8 **-ell,** 7 **-il, -al,** (**tresle**), 5–9 **tressel,** 7–9 **tressle**; (6 *Sc.* **traisle,** 7 **threstle,** 8 **trassel**). *β.* 5–6 **trystell(e,** 6 **-el, tristell, -il, -ill(e, tristle, trys(s)elle, trisselle.** *γ.* 5 **trostyle,** 6 **-ell, trustyll,** 7–8 **trussell,** 7–9 **-el,** (8 **trusle**), 8–9 **trussle,** 9 **trustle.** [ME. *trestel*, a. OF. *trestel* (12th c. in Hatz.-Darm., mod.F. *tréteau*) a transom, beam :—pop.L. **transtellum*, dim. of *transtrum* beam: see -LE 2 and cf. TREST *sb.*[2] Pop.L. **transtellum* would normally have given OF. *trastel*, but cf. *treste*, TREST *sb.*[2] from *transtrum*.]

1. A support for something, consisting of a short horizontal beam or bar with diverging legs, usually two at each end; *esp.* one of a pair or set used to support a board so as to form a table.

13.. *Coer de L.* 102 They sette tresteles, & layde a borde. *c* 1400 *Brut* clxxxvii. 206 Þis Piers of Gauaston..went into þe Kyngus tresorie..and toke þe table of golde, wiþ þe tresteles of þe same, and meny oþere riche gewelles. 1495 *Naval Acc. Hen. VII* (1896) 196 Mete tables in the Captayns Caban and..Trystelles for the same. 1522 in *Archæologia* XXV. 457 A tabill & the trostells. 1525 LD. BERNERS *Froiss.* II. clvii. [cliii.] 434 These burgesses sette downe the lytter on two trestels. 1543 *Ludlow Churchw. Acc.* (Camden) 15 Payde for makynge of the tryselle..ij d. 1572 in Feuillerat *Revels Q. Eliz.* (1908) 165 Tables and tressells. 1688 R. HOLME *Armoury* IV. xii. (Roxb.) 502/1 Then was the Body ..set on a Tressell between two crosses, and couered with a large purple veluett pall. 1703 T. N. *City & C. Purchaser* 3 Horses, or Trussels,..to lay the Poles..on whilst they are boring. 1743 in H. S. Wyndham *Ann. Cov. Gard. Theatre* (1906) II. 312 A Mountebank's stage and tressells. 1792 A. YOUNG *Trav. France* 217 In Italian inns..the bedstead is usually four forms, like trussels, set together. *a* 1800 PEGGE *Suppl. Grose*, *Trussell*, a stand for a barrel. Kent. 1806–7 J. BERESFORD *Miseries Hum. Life* XVIII. 195 The proverbial obstinacy of the pig rather increases than diminishes when he is laid on the tressel for execution. 1838 DICKENS *O. Twist* v, An unfinished coffin on black tressels. 1861 WRIGHT *Ess. Archæol.* II. xiv. 41 The Anglo-Saxon table was formed merely by placing a board upon trestles at the time of eating.

†2. A three-legged stool or seat; a tripod. *Obs.*

*c* 1440 *Promp. Parv.* 503/1 Trostyle, *tristellus*, Kylw. *et* Dicc. *tripos*, Comm. 1552 HULOET, Trestle, *tripus*,..whych hath thre fete. 1561 T. NORTON *Calvin's Inst.* IV. 151 These be the answers, of the Holy see, these be yᵉ Oracles of the Apostolike trestle. *Margin*, Apollo among yᵉ Heathen gaue..Prophecies at a threefooted boord or trestle. 1570 LEVINS *Manip.* 126/28 A Tristil, *tripes*. 1656 BLOUNT *Glossogr.*, *Trestle* (*tripus*), a three footed-stool, or any thing with three feet, a trevet. 1658 in PHILLIPS.

b. A three-legged frame or stand for a support; a tripod. Now *dial.*

1790 ROY in *Phil. Trans.* LXXX. 165 We made shift, by the help of a long beam, and a moveable trestle by way of fulcrum for it to rest upon, to get the instrument up to the top of its own proper scaffold. 1795 *Ibid.* LXXXV. 435 The plank and bar were supported on five of the tressels, or tripods, belonging to the Royal Society. 1828 *Craven Gloss.*, *Tressel*, a frame to support a scaffold, made of three feet.

3. *Her.* A low stool or bench used as a bearing: usually represented with three legs.

1610 GUILLIM *Heraldry* IV. ix. (1611) 213 He beareth gules, a fesse Humet, or, betweene three trestles argent...This charge..is of some..taken..for a Table. 1894 *Parker's Gloss. Her.*, *Tressel*, a three-legged frame to support a table, borne chiefly by branches of one family.

4. In various specific uses. †a. A support or rest for a harquebus or other early fire-arm (see REST *sb.*[1] 11 a): = TREST *sb.*[2] 1 b. *Obs.* b. A framework consisting of upright (or more or less inclined) pieces with diagonal braces, used to support a bridge or other elevated structure. c, d. See quots. e. One of the timber props or shores used to support a ship while being built. †f. A stand or frame for candles or tapers burning in religious worship. *Obs.* g. = TRESTLE-TREE (*Century Dict.*).

a. 1497 *Naval Acc. Hen. VII* (1896) 95 Trestelles for

hakbusses. **b.** 1796 MORSE *Amer. Geog.* I. 438 [A bridge] 160 feet long and 22 feet wide, supported by two wooden trussels, and two stone pillars. 1811 WELLINGTON in Gurw. *Desp.* (1838) VIII. 351 A certain quantity of timber for the construction of a pile engine and of a Trustle. 1861 SMILES *Engineers* II. 183 The centres spanning the whole width of the arch were composed of eight ribs each, formed in one piece, resting upon the same number of solid wedges, supported by inclined tressels placed upon longitudinal bearers, firmly fixed to the offsets of the piers and abutments. 1900 *Jrnl. Sch. Geog.* (U. S.) Apr. 135 There is not a difficult grade or an embankment or trestle of any importance between New York and Buffalo. **c.** 1823 NICHOLSON *Pract. Build.* iv. 231 Trussels, four-legged stools for ripping and cross-cutting timber upon. 1882 YOUNG *Ev. Man Own Mech.* § 517 A trestle, or sawing-stool. **d.** 1839 URE *Dict. Arts*, etc. 378 The horse or trestle consists of a strong wooden frame... Upon the middle of this..two uprights and a strong cross beam, for supporting the thick plank upon which the skins are worked. 1875 *Ure's Dict. Arts* III. 93 A high *trussel* is frequently used, across which the leather is thrown, after undergoing any of the processes. **e.** 1860 LONGF. *Wayside Inn* I. *Build. Long Serpent* xvi, Then they launched her from the tressels, In the ship-yard by the sea. **f.** 1523 *Will R. Broster* (Somerset Ho.), ij s to make a Trisell to brenne at Masse. 1546 *Ludlow Churchw. Acc.* (Camden) 26 Payde for a trisselle and holy candelles.

**5.** *transf.* and *fig.*: esp. (*pl.*) applied to the legs.

1610 B. JONSON *Alch.* IV. iii, He lookes in that deepe ruffe, like a head in a platter Seru'd in by a short cloake vpon two tressils. *c* 1620 T. ROBINSON *Mary Magd.* 232 Or rather cast a due-deuoted glaunce Vpon the marble tressels vnder plac't: But then her douelike feete themselues aduance. *Ibid.* 1471 Happy wert thou to touch y^e tressells bare Of thy beloued, heau'nly paramour. 1649 G. DANIEL *Trinarch., Hen. IV*, ccxciii, The Bishop w^th his Colleague Arundel, Were the first Tressells vnto Henrie's Throne. 1650 B. *Discolliminium* 16, I must not cut off her..legs.., and set her upon Tressels.

**6.** *attrib.* and *Comb.*: **trestle-bed**, a portable or movable bed supported upon trestles, as used in a hospital tent, etc.; **trestle-board**, a board laid upon trestles to form a table; **trestle-bridge**, a bridge supported upon trestles or trestlework (see 4 b); †**trestle-candle**: cf. 4 f; **trestle-post**: cf. 4 b; **trestle-table**, a table made of a movable board or boards laid upon trestles; **trestlework**, a framework composed of a series of trestles (of wood or iron) fastened together, for supporting a bridge or viaduct, esp. on a railway.

1870 DISRAELI *Lothair* lx, Princesses..might be seen by the *tressel beds. 1856 C. W. MOORE (*title*) New Masonic *Trestle-Board, adapted to the work and lectures as practised in the Lodges..of Knights Templars in the United States of America. 1867 BRANDE & COX *Dict. Sc.*, etc., s. v., Two or more [trestles] are used for carrying a bridge, called a *trestle bridge. 1889 G. FINDLAY *Eng. Railway* 62 A temporary trestle bridge was erected. 1559 *Ludlow Churchw. Acc.* (Camden) 90 For ij li...of *tryssille candelle. 1799 A. YOUNG *Agric. Lincoln.* 74 He has..conducted the water to a very large wheel, in troughs, upon *trussle-posts 20 feet high. 1891 *Cent. Dict.*, *Trestle-table. 1905 *Macm. Mag.* Nov. 4 A small white bell-tent,..at its door a long trestle-table was set out with a bench on either side. 1861 W. H. RUSSELL in *Times* 10 July, The road led to a cypress swamp, over which the engines bustled..at a perilous rate along a high *trestlework.

Hence **Tre·stle** *v. trans.*, to place upon trestles; **Trestled** (tre·s'ld) *a.*, provided with or supported upon trestles; **Tre·stlewise** *adv.*, in the manner of a trestle (in quot., ? upon trestles); **Tre·stling**, a structure of trestles, trestlework.

1879 *Daily News* 7 Apr. 3/3 Having disembarked and 'tressled' their boats, the two crews returned to Putney. 1885 B. HARTE *Maruja* v, The black *tresselled bed. 1434 *E. E. Wills* (1882) 102 A litil tabel peynted *trestelwise. 1887 *N. York Tribune* 20 May (Cent.), *Trestling.

**Trestle-tree.** *Naut.* Forms: see TRESTLE. [f. TRESTLE *sb.* + TREE *sb.* 3 a.] *pl.* Two strong pieces of timber fixed horizontally fore-and-aft on opposite sides of a mast-head, to support the cross-trees, the top, and the fid of the mast above.

*a* 1625 *Nomenclator Navalis* (Harl. MS. 2301) *Tressel-trees*, are ioyned to the Cross-trees and doe lie crosse each other, and serue to the same vse, theie differ onlie that the Tressel trees ar those w^ch goe Long-ships, the other thwart ships. 1626 CAPT. SMITH *Accid. Yng. Seamen* 12 The trussell trees or crosse trees. 1804 A. DUNCAN *Mariner's Chron.* Pref. 16 Certain timbers fixed upon the hounds and cheeks of the masts, and called the trestle trees, and cross-trees. *c* 1860 H. STUART *Seaman's Catech.* 76 The trussle-trees..are usually made of oak. 1911 E. GOSSE *Poems, Ships on Sea* iii, Less steadfast, o'er the trackless wave I strayed, And follow still their vanishing trestle-trees.

**Tresun**, obs. form of TREASON.

**Tret** (tret), *sb. Comm. Obs.* exc. *Hist.* [Known *c* 1500; origin and history obscure.

Generally conjectured either to be identical with OF. and AF. *tret*, variant of *trait* act of drawing, draught, etc. (see TRAIT), or to represent OF. *traite* 'a draught..a transportation, vent outward, shipping ouer; and an Imposition vpon commodities exported, or so transported' (Cotgr.): cf. It. *tratta* 'permission or priuilege to transport from out any country any merchandice..also that custome that is paid for things carried out' (Florio); see also med.L. *tracta* in Du Cange. These senses of the Fr., It., and med.L. words do not satisfactorily explain the commercial use of *tret* in Eng.; but it is possible that the term may have originated in connexion with a single class of commodities or of transactions, and have been extended by 1670 to others. See Du Cange s. v. *tracta*; also Skeat *s.v.*, and E. Weekley in *Trans. Philol. Soc.* June 1909. Cf. also CLOFF, DRAFT 1, DRAUGHT 13.]

An allowance of 4 lb. in 104 lb. (= $\frac{1}{26}$) on goods sold by weight after the deduction for tare.

The reason or ground of the allowance was apparently forgotten already in the 17th c., and has been variously given since: see quots.

*a* 1500 in *Arnolde's Chron.* 47/2 Your said suppliant shulde be rebated for the tare of euery of the said xij bales iiij ll. and for the cloff of euery off the said xij bales ij ll. Som. lxxij ll. and for the tret of y^e same peper cxxxvij ll. 1670 BLOUNT *Law Dict.* s. v. *Tare and Tret*, The other [Tret] is a consideration allowed in the weight for wast, in emptying and reselling the Goods. 1674 *Lond. Gaz.* No. 892/4, 59 Bails at fifteen pence, and 17 Sacks at sixteen pence a pound, with Tret and Tare as Custom. 1674 JEAKE *Arith.* (1696) 82 There is an Overweight allowed by Merchants called Tret, which is 4 lb. upon every Hundred of 112 lb. 1678 PHILLIPS (ed. 4), *Tret*, a certain allowance that is made by Merchants, before a Commodity is garbled from its refuse [1706 ed. Kersey adds] as Dust, Moats, &c., which is always 4 in every 104 Pounds. 1711 STEELE *Spect.* No. 136 ▸ 7 There is my little Merchant,..there's my Man for Loss and Gain, there's Tare and Tret. *a* 1850 J. GRAY *Introd. Arith.* (ed. 100) 58 What is the value of 12 bales of pepper..tare 3 lb. per bale, allowing also tret and cloff? 1882 BITHELL *Counting-ho. Dict.*, *Tret*, an allowance made for wear, damage, or deterioration in goods during transit from one place to another.

†**Tret**, *a. Obs. rare*^−1. [App. a shortened form of TRETIS.] = TRETIS. (Cf. TRETY *a.*)

*c* 1470 HENRY *Wallace* IX. 1928 Braid breyst and heych, with sturdy crag and gret; His lyppys round, his noys was squar and tret [*ed.* 1570 treit].

**Tret, Tretabill, -ble, Tretar**, obs. ff. TREAT, TREATABLE, TREATER. **Tretcherer, -ous, -ye**: see TREACHER, -OUS, -Y. **Trete**, obs. f. TREAT, TREATY. **Treteable**, obs. f. TREATABLE. **Tretee, Tretes, -esse**, obs. ff. TREATY, TREATISE. **Treterous**, obs. f. TRAITOROUS. **Tretice, -is(e, Tretie**, obs. ff. TREATISE, TREATY.

†**Tretis**, *a. Obs.* Forms: 4 tretys, 5 tretis, -ise, -ez, traytice, -yse. [a. OF. *traitis*, *tretis* slender, graceful, well-built (12th c. in Godef.) :–pop.L. type **tracticius* drawn-out, slender, f. *tract-us*, pa. pple. of *trahĕre* to draw: see -ITIOUS[1].] Well-proportioned, neat, graceful, handsome.

?*a* 1366 CHAUCER *Rom. Rose* 932 That other bowe was.. Tretys and long, of good fasoun. *c* 1380 *Sir Ferumb.* 5883 Hure vysage was fair & tretys. *c* 1386 CHAUCER *Prol.* 152 Hire nose tretys [*Hengwrt* tretez, *Camb.* tretis], hir eyen greye as glas. 1490 CAXTON *Eneydos* xxix. 112 Her forehed brod and highe ynoughe, the browes traytice and broun. *Ibid.*, The necke [of Dydo]..longe ynoughe..and traytyse on the backe syde.

**Tretour, (-owre), -ourous**, obs. ff. TRAITOR, TRAITOROUS. **Tretrifolie, -y, trettifollie**, obs. ff. TREE-TREFOIL. **Tre-trip**, var. TREY-TRIP *Obs.* **Trett(e, Tretty**, obs. ff. TREAT, TREATY. **Trettle**, obs. f. TRATTLE *sb.*[2]

†**Tre·ty**, *a. Obs. rare*^−1. = TRETIS *a.*

*c* 1450 *St. Cuthbert* (Surtees) 7362 He had a lange trety face.

**Trety, -ye**, obs. ff. TREATY. **Tretys**, obs. f. TREATISE; var. TRETIS *Obs.*

**Treu**, obs. f. TREE, TROW, TRUE. **Treuage, Treuandise, Treuant, Treuce, Treuchman**: see TREWAGE, TRUANDISE, TRUANT, TRUCE, TRUCHMAN. **Treuges, treuis, Treugth**, obs. ff. TRUCE, TRUTH. **Treukour**, obs. Sc. f. TRUCKER. **Treuliche, -ly**, obs. ff. TRULY. **Treumph**, obs. Sc. f. TRIUMPH.

†**Treunt**, *v. Obs. rare.* [Etymol. obscure: has some likeness to TRANONT.] *intr.* ? To depart.

?*a* 1400 *Morte Arth.* 1976 Trussene fulle traystely, and treunt there-aftyre. *Ibid.* 2017 This traytour has treunt this tresone to wyrche! He has the cete forsett appone sere halfez. *Ibid.* 3900 Than the traytoure treuntede the Tyseday thar-aftyre, Trynnys in with a trayne tresone to wirke.

**Treus**, obs. pl. of TREE; obs. f. TRUCE. **Treush-man**, obs. f. TRUCHMAN. **Treut, treuth(e, treuþ(e**, obs. ff. TRUTH. **Treuwes, treux, treuys**, obs. ff. TRUCE.

†**Trevally**[1]. *Obs.* or *dial.* Forms: 7 trevall, (travailler), travalley, 7–8 travally, 7, 9 *dial.* trevally. [perh. a corruption of REVEILLE.]

**1.** A signal made by beating the drum; also attrib., *trevally-beat*. Also *transf.*

1645 R. SYMONDS *Diary Civ. War* (Camden) 224 When the trevall was beate, and they lett downe their bridge for their scouts. 1675 CROWNE *Country Wit* II. i, Beat a Travalley on the drums of their ears. 1685 B. RINGROSE *Bucaniers Amer.* II. IV. 10 We heard..a small arm discharged, and after that a drum beating a Travailler. 1688 R. HOLME *Armoury* III. xix. (Roxb.) 154/2 The seuerall Beates or points of warre are these..14 A Revally, or Trevally, and ruvalley. 1698 FRYER *Acc. E. India & P.* 144 The next Morning I..Landed presently after Travally-Beat. 1798 O'KEEFFE *Highland Reel* I. ii, Your rattan would be the drumstick of the corps, to beat the travally on my back—row-dy-dow!

**2.** A disturbance, a noisy 'to-do'.

1819 *St. Patrick* I. 162 (Jam.) Gin ye could airt me tae ane o' them [runnigates], we wad let you see a fine trevallie. 1866 KENNEDY *Irish Celts* 19 (E.D.D.) There was such a thravally ruz..about it. 1881 *Cumberland Gloss.*, *Trevally*, disturbance, quarrelling.

‖**Treva·lly**[2]. Also -valley, -valli, -valla, travalley, -vale. [Supposed to be an alteration of CAVALLY.] A name applied in Australasia to several sea-fishes, mostly of the family *Carangidæ* or Horse-Mackerels.

Six species of *Caranx*, *Neptonemus*, and *Teuthis*, to which the name is applied, are enumerated by Morris *Austral English*.

1883 E. P. RAMSAY *Food-Fishes N. S. Wales* 20 The white trevally, *Caranx georgianus*,..on the New South Wales coast..seldom..weighing over 1½ to 2 lbs., is found on the shores of Queensland of a much greater size. 1883 *Fisheries Exhib. Catal.* (ed. 4) 184 The Collection also contains..the.. 'Trevalley'. 1886 SHERRIN *Fishes of New Zeal.* 99 Dr. Hector says: 'The trevalli is the arara of the Maoris, or the trevalli or cavalli of the fishermen...The fish known as trevalli in the Dunedin district is a different fish. 1890 *Victorian Statutes, Fisheries Act*, Schedule 2, Travale.

**Trevass**, obs. form of TRAVERSE, TRAVIS *sb.*

†**Trevat** (tre·vāt). *Obs.* Also **travat, trivet, trevette** (*Cent. Dict.* 1891). [Derivation unascertained.] An instrument with a sharp blade formerly used for cutting the loops which form the pile of velvet, Wilton carpets, etc., when handwoven.

1831 G. R. PORTER *Silk Manuf.* 279 Running a sharp instrument called a trevat along the groove of the wire. 1844 G. DODD *Textile Manuf.* vi. 203 A cutting instrument called a trevat..severing the pile-threads. 1864 *Q. Rev.* July 31 These rows of loops are afterwards cut through by an instrument now called a 'trevat', and thus the peculiar surface of velvet is given. 1877 KNIGHT *Dict. Mech.*, Trivet. 1888 *Encycl. Brit.* XXIV. 467/1 Along this groove a cutting knife called a trivet is run to cut the loops. 1914 (Apr. 21) *Let. fr. Tomkinson & Adam, Kidderminster*, The word, as we understand it here, is spelt 'Travat', and [the specimen] is so labelled in the Museum; but the knife has been out of use so many years that only men who are 80 years of age or thereabouts remember anything of it.

†**Treve.** *Obs. rare.* Also 5 trieue (for trieve), 6 trefue (for trefve). [a. F. *trêve*, OF. also *trive* (12th c. in Godef. *Compl.*), *trieve* (*c* 1275), also *truive*, *trueve*, *true*; = Pr. *treva*, *treg(u)a*, Sp., It. *tregua*, med.L. *tregua*, *treuga*, *treugua*, Com. Romanic type **treuwa* (Darmesteter), from Germanic. In OF. often, in Eng. always, in pl. *treves* (cf. *unes triuwes*, Froissart). Ultimately the same word as TRUCE (ME. *trewes* pl. of *trewe*), q. v. for its further etymology.] = TRUCE.

1406 *Rolls Parlt.* V. 417 Come for to trete Pees or Trieues. 1410 in *Proc. Privy Council* (1834) I. 325 That ferme pees other longe and goode trieues..may be accordede and stablisshede. 1523 (Dec. 18) SAMPSON & JERNINGHAM *Let. to Wolsey* (MS. Cott. Vesp. C. II. 228: See *St. Papers Henry VIII*, VI. 211), The French men requiryd treves for v or vi monethis...The Lord Chauncelier enteryd in to the communication off a peace or treves...Iff the King our mastre might know thEmperour determinid to a peace or treves...He nevyr wold enclyne or gyue hering to owthir peace or treves. 1550 NICOLLS *Thucyd.* 132 b, The Beotians made trefues for tenne dayes onely. *Ibid.* 134 b, Wyllynge to compryse the..Corinthyans in the trefues of tenne dayes.

†**Trevee·r**, *v. Obs. rare.* [? ad. F. *trevirer* for *chavirer* to capsize, upset, f. *tre-* = TRANS- + *virer* to whirl, roll.] *trans.* ? To upset.

1636–7 *Admir. Crt. Exam.* 115. 24 Jan., Six butts of the articulate shipp's ladinge..were by reason the said shipps giveing waie in foule weather treveered, and one of them was quite out and the other aboute one third out.

**Treveiss**, obs. form of TRAVERSE *v.*, TRAVIS. **Treverse**, obs. f. TRAVERSE *a.* **Trevertine**, var. TRAVERTINE. **Treves, -ess(e**, obs. ff. TRAVERSE, TRAVIS. **Trevet**, obs. f. TRIVET. **Trevice**: see TRAVIS[1]. **Trevis, -iss**, obs. ff. TRAVERSE, TRAVIS. **Trevit**, obs. f. TRIVET.

†**Trew**, *v. Sc. Obs.* [f. *trew*, obs. sing. of *trewes*, TRUCE.] *trans.* To protect by a truce.

*c* 1425 WYNTOUN *Cron.* VII. viii. 1654 Þe lordis of Northumbyrlande Askyt trewis at þe Kynge..Tyl þe fest of þe Trynyte He grantyde thaim trewit for to be.

**Trew**, obs. f. TREE, TROW *v.*, TRUCE, TRUE.

†**Trew·age, tru·age.** *Obs.* Forms: 3–6 truage, treuage, 4 truwage, 4–5 trowage, 4–6 trewage, 4–7 trouage, 5 triwage, trywage. [a. OF. *treuage* (12th c. in Godef.) tribute, f. OF. *trëud*, *trëu* (Roland, 11th c.) :–L. *tribūt-um* TRIBUTE + -AGE.] Tribute.

*c* 1275 LAY. 7189 Romleode Com to þissere þeode, And setten truage in þisse lond [*c* 1205 and sette ȝeld a þisse londe]. *Ibid.* 25044 Nou axeþ þorh cunde truage of þis londe. *c* 1330 R. BRUNNE *Chron.* (1810) 7 Grete treuage þei toke of þis lond here. *c* 1400 tr. *Secreta Secret.*, *Gov. Lordsh.* 57 Þerfore trowages and þe kynges rentys encresys. *c* 1440 *Generydes* 1792 Defende your lande that it pay noo trewage. 1525 LD. BERNERS *Froiss.* II. xl. 125 When he hath wonne a countrey..he desyreth nothynge but truage. 1530 PALSGR. 283/1 Truage, trybute, *treuaige*. 1593 NASHE *Christ's T.* (1613) 104 Our God..asketh no other treuage at our handes for giuing, but asking and thanksgiuing. 1661 MORGAN *Sph. Gentry* II. viii. 102 At Rome hastily will I be: not to give you Truage but to have Truage of you.

**b.** Toll, custom; payment for some privilege.

*c* 1380 *Sir Ferumb.* 1731 'Ȝe mote furst', quaþ þe Sarazyn, 'syþþe ȝe þyder fondeþ, For þe truwage make fyn þat to þis brigge longeþ'. 14.. *Cov. Corp. Christi Pl.* I. 524 Nor also aleond stranger throȝ my realme pas, But the[y] for there truage do pay markis fyve. 1596 WARNER *Alb. Eng.* x. lx, For their Charters did they offer..to undergo all Truage, Taxe and Charge. 1657 HOWELL *Londinop.* 49 Wooll Key, where was used to be the Trouage of Woolls.

¶ Misused for 'homage'.

**1592** NASHE *P. Penilesse* (ed. 2) 31 As he should stoop to doo him truage, he might seaze vpon his throat and stifle him.

Hence †**Trew·ager** *Obs.*, one subject to tribute, a tributary. (Cf. *homager.*)

*c* **1330** R. BRUNNE *Chron.* (1810) 45 Þe folk wild not suffre to be treuwageres.

**Trewaill, Trewbut(e, Trewcht,** obs. Sc. ff. TRAVAIL, TRIBUTE, TRUTH. **Trewand, -ant, -andise,** etc., obs. ff. TRUANT, TRUANDISE *Obs.*

**Trewce,** obs. form of TRUCE.

†**Trewe.** *Obs. rare.* [a. OF. *trëu*, older *trëud* (Roland, 11th c.): see TREWAGE.] Tribute. *Bring to trewe*, to subject to tribute, make tributary.

*c* **1330** R. BRUNNE *Chron. Wace* (Rolls) 4600 Al my conqueste preise y nought, Bot þe Bretons to trewe be brought. *Ibid.* 11921 To aske hym trewe, hit is for nought.

**Trewe, Trewell,** obs. ff. TRUCE, TRUE, TROWEL.

†**Trewe·rne.** *Obs.* [prob. from a place or personal name.] A wagon or truck of some kind.

**1667** in Pettus *Fodinæ Reg.* xxv. (1670) 38 One great Trewerne with Iron wheels to carry out deads belonging to the Addits.

**Trewes, trewice, -is,** obs. ff. TRUCE.

**Treweth(e, trewht,** obs. ff. TRUTH. **Trewit,** obs. f. TRIVET. **Trewker,** obs. Sc. f. TRUCKER. **Trewliche, -lie,** obs. ff. TRULY. **Trewmph,** obs. Sc. f. TRIUMPH.

**Trews** (trūz), *sb. pl.* Also 6 trewis, (8–9 truis). [ad. Irish *trius*, Gael. *triubhas*, sb. sing., ad. Eng. TROUSE (singular, with pl. *trouses*), but from the final (sound of) *s* treated as a plural, with no singular in use: cf. *drawers, breeches.*] Close-fitting trousers, or breeches combined with stockings, formerly worn by Irishmen and Scottish Highlanders, and still by certain Scottish regiments.

*a* **1568** MONTGOMERIE *Misc. Poems* liv. 3 Smoir cunary takin trewis breikles McBradȝan. [**1581** A. TROLLOPE *Let.* 12 Sept. in *Cal. St. Papers, Irel.* 1574–85, 318 They had ech of them a hatt, a lether jerken, a payre of hosen, which they called trowes, and a payre of broges.] *a* **1653** Z. BOYD *Zion's Flowers* (1855) Introd. 19 Content to weare the Irish trews. **1728** RAMSAY *Tea-t. Misc., Highland Laddie* ii, I'd take young Donald without trews, With bonnet blew, and belted plaidy. [**1746** *Act* 19–20 *Geo. II*, c. 39 § 17 The Plaid, Philibeg, or little Kilt, Trowse, Shoulder Belts, or whatsoever of what peculiarly belongs to the Highland Garb.] **1771** PENNANT *Tour Scot. in 1769* (1794) 210 The truis were worn by the gentry, and were breeches and stockings made of one piece. **1790** BURNS *On Battle of Sheriffmuir* iii, Had you seen the philibegs, And skyrin tartan trews, man. **1808** SCOTT *Marm.* v. v, The chequer'd trews, and belted plaid. **1834** PLANCHÉ *Brit. Costume* 338. **1860** KNIGHT *Pop. Hist. Eng.* VI. viii. 134 *note*, Prince Charles Edward is painted as wearing the truis, the breeches and stockings in one piece, or hose pantaloon. **1911** C. F. ATKINSON in *Encycl. Brit.* XXVII. 585/1 Highland regiments wear tartan kilt..; Lowland regiments (also Scottish Rifles, Highland Light Infantry, and all mounted officers) tartan trews.

Hence **Trew·sman,** one who wears trews; a Highlander.

**1819** SCOTT *Leg. Montrose* iv, We have a wheen canny trewsmen here.

**Trews, trewse, trewyce, -ys,** obs. ff. TRUCE.

**Trewþ(e, trewthe,** obs. forms of TRUTH.

**Trey** (trē¹), *sb.* Forms: 4–7 treye, 6–9 tray, 7 trye, 5– trey. [a. OF. and AF. *treis, trei*, F. *trois*, dial. *tray* = Prov. *treis*, nom. *trei*, Sp. *tres*, It. *tre*:—L. *trēs* three.]

**1.** The three at dice or cards. **a.** *Dice.* That side of the die that is marked with three pips or spots; a throw which turns up this side.

*c* **1386** CHAUCER *Pard. T.* 325 Seuene is my chaunce, and thyn is cynk and treye [*Corpus, Lansd.* fyue and þre]. *c* **1450** *Bk. of Brome* 17 Ȝowr cast wosse sysse and dobyll trey. **1588** SHAKS. *L. L. L.* v. ii. 232 *Qu.* Hony, and Milke, and Suger: there is three. *Ber.* Nay then two treyes,.. Methegline, Wort, and Malmsey; well runne dice: There's halfe a dozen sweets. **1668** DRYDEN *Evening's Love* III. i, Two sixes and a trey wins it. **1772** FOOTE *Nabob* II. Wks. 1799 II. 301 Tray, ace, or two deuces. **1910** *Nation* 1 Jan. 566/1 There's luck under the deuce but none under the tray.

**b.** *Cards.* That card of any suit which is marked with three spots. *rare.*

**1680** COTTON *Compl. Gamester* xv. (ed. 2) 93 The best Putt-Cards are first the Trey, next the Deuce. **1816** SINGER *Hist. Cards* 195 The trey presents us with the separation of a lover and his mistress. **1896** J. K. BANGS *House-boat on Styx* v, I do not know a trey of diamonds from a silver salver.

†**c.** In proverbial phrase *ere you can say trey-ace* (see 3), of which *treis, trayse* appears to be a contracted form. *Obs.*

**1390** GOWER *Conf.* I. 142 Al sodeinliche, as who seith treis, Wher that he stod in his Paleis, He tok him fro the mennes sihte. *c* **1400** *Laud Troy Bk.* 8917 A man schuld not so sone say 'trayse', As he fel ded & held his payse. *a* **1553** UDALL *Royster D.* III. iii. (Arb.) 48 Bydde them high apace. *M. Mery.* I wyll be here with them ere ye can say trey ace.

**2.** *slang.* The number three, in various connexions; a set of three; a threepenny piece.

**1896** VIZETELLY tr. *Zola's Rome* 372 Stake their luck on a cardinal, just as they nurse a 'trey' in the lottery. **1897** MARSHALL *Pomes* 71 (Farmer) And the magistrate..left but very little doubt That the moons she'd have to do would be a tray. **1907** *Daily Chron.* 26 July 4/7 One easily sees why it [threepence] is a 'tray'.

**3.** *Comb.* **trey-ace,** a throw that turns up trey with one die and ace with the other; so **trey-deuce**; **trey-point** = sense 1; †**trey-table,** a dicing-table; †**trey-trace,** (?).

*a* **1553** *Trey ace [see 1 c]. **1725** LD. STANHOPE in *C'tess Suffolk's Lett.* (1824) I. 186 Wishing you all imaginable success at Trey-ace, Commerce, or whatever else may be the prevailing diversion. **1680** COTTON *Compl. Gamester* xxxiii. *Hazzard* (ed. 2) 122 Five [has] but two chances, Trey Ace and two Deuces, or *Trey Deuce and Quater Ace. **1657** C. BECK *Univ. Char.* L vij b, A *tray point on a die. **1646** EVELYN *Mem.* (1857) I. 249 There is also a bowling-place, a tavern, and a *trey-table. **1575** R. B. *Appius & Virg.* Bj, With hey tricke, how trowle, trey trip, and *trey trace.

**Trey, tray,** *v.* [app. f. TREY *sb.*] app. To divide or deal (a pack of cards) into three heaps in order to separate the suits (in the order of which new cards are or were packed), before shuffling in the usual way.

(This is the explanation given by the majority of those who answered a query as to this word in the *Pall Mall Gazette* of 5 Jan. 1914. Two of these, Mr. R. H. Macaulay, M.A., and Mr. C. B Lacey, both resident in India in 1888, remember the word as there used in this sense. Several other explanations were suggested, e.g. that *tray* was for F. *trier* to pick out.)

**1888** *Times* 15 Feb. 8/2 Two new packs were opened, and were 'trayed' and shuffled in the usual way. Dr. Sanders had one of the packs cut to him, and proceeded to deal. He turned up the Knave of Clubs, and on sorting his hand found that he had the other 12 trumps.

**Trey,** obs. Sc. f. TREE. **Trey, treye:** see TRAY.

**Treybochet,** obs. f. TREBUCHET. **Treyfoile, -fole, -foyle,** obs. ff. TREFOIL.

†**Treygobe·t.** *Obs.* [Evidently, *trey go bet* = three go better: cf. *hey-go-bet* (HEY 3); but origin unknown.] Name of an old game at dice.

**1426** LYDG. *De Guil. Pilgr.* 11623 Pleye at the ches, pley at the tablys, At treygobet & tregetrye, In karyyng & in Iogolory. *c* **1554** *Interlude of Youth* C iij, Syr I can teache you to play at the dice..The Treygobet and the hasarde also. **1587** M. GROVE *Pelops & Hipp.* (1878) 117 On bench with clownes whole peny vp, at trey gobet to play.

**Treylle,** var. TRAIL *sb.*[2] *Obs.* **Treylles, treylsys:** see TRELLIS. **Treyn, treyne:** see TRAIN, TREEN *a.*, TRINE *v.*[2], 3. **Trey-sail,** obs. f. TRYSAIL. **Treyse,** obs. f. TRACE *sb.*[2] **Treyson, -oun,** obs. ff. TREASON. **Treyst (y-treyst),** pa. pple. of TRAISE *v. Obs.* to betray; var. TRAIST *Obs.* **Treyte, Treyter,** obs. f. TREAT *sb.*, TREATER. **Treytori, -ory,** var. TRAITORY.

†**Trey-trip.** *Obs.* Also 6–7 trea-, 7 tray-, trei-, tre-, tra-. [app. f. TREY *sb.* + TRIP *v.* (?).] A game at dice, or with dice, in which success probably depended on the casting of a trey or three.

**1564–78** BULLEYN *Dial. agst. Pest.* (1888) 94 He is plaiyng at the trea trippe with our hoste sonne. **1575** [see *trey-trace*, TREY *sb.* 3]. **1588** *Marprel. Epist.* (Arb.) 38 Because the gamesters..wan all his monie at trey trip. **1602** in *Sir R. Cecil's Corr.* x. (1766) 127 There is great danger of being taken sleepers at tray-trip, if the King sweep suddenly. **1617** *Machiavell's Dogge* B j b, But leauing Cardes, lett's goe to dice awhile, To Passage, Treitrippe, Hazarde or Mumchaunce...And trippe without a Treye makes had I wist To sitte and mourne among the sleepers ranke. **1636** DAVENANT *Wits* Wks. (1673) 195 My Watch are playing above at Trea-trip For some Suffolk Cheese. **1639** MAYNE *City Match* II. iv, Find himself business at tre-trip i'th'hall. **1660** TATHAM *Rump* IV. i, It seems he plays better at tratrip with thee then thy husband Ireton did.

**Treyumphe,** obs. f. TRIUMPH. **Treyvette,** obs. f. TRIVET. **Trezerer,** obs. f. TREASURER.

**Tri-** (trai, *occas.* tri), *prefix*, a. L. *tri-* and Gr. τρι-, combining form of *trēs*, τρεῖς three, τρίς thrice.

The *i*, etymologically short in Greek and Latin, was in Latin sometimes lengthened, esp. in numerals (*trīcēnī, trīgintā*, etc.). In Eng. it is now usually long and diphthongal (əi), except in derivatives before two consonants, as *triple, triptych*, also in *trilogy, trimeter*. In scientific books *tri-* is often represented by the numeral, as *3-bracteate*, 3-carbon.

**I.** Forming adjs. (and derived sbs. and advbs.) with the senses:

**1.** Having, characterized by, or consisting of (*rarely*, belonging or relating to) three (of the things denoted by the second element).

**a.** In comb. with adjs. derived from sbs. (usually L. or Gr.), or less commonly with the sb. without adjectival termination. **Triacno·dal** *Geom.*, having three acnodes or conjugate points (see CONJUGATE *a.* 6 a). **Tri·act, Tria·ctinal, Tria·ctine** *Zool.* [Gr. ἀκτίς, ἀκτῖν- ray], having three rays: said of a sponge-spicule. **Trialate** (trəiˌēˑlĕt), *Nat. Hist.* [L. *āla* wing], three-winged (*Cent. Dict.* 1891). **Tria·nnulate** *Zool.* [L. *annulus* ring], having or consisting of three rings. **Tria·nthous** *Bot.* [Gr. ἄνθος flower], having three flowers. **Tria·rctic** (see quot.). **Tria·rcuated** [L. *arcu-s* bow, ARCH], three-arched. **Tria·real,** comprising or divided into three areas. **Tria·xon, -o·nian, -onid** [Gr. ἄξων axis], of sponge-spicules: having three axes; = TRIAXIAL. **Triba·silar** *Anat.*, designating a bone formed by union of three bones at the base of the skull. **Tribla·stic** *Zool.* [Gr. βλαστός germ], having three layers (epiblast, mesoblast, hypoblast) in the blastoderm of the embryo. **Tribra·cteate** *Bot.*, having three bracts; so **Tribra·cteolate,** having three bracteoles or minute bracts. **Trica·rinate, -ated** *Nat. Hist.* [L. *carīna* keel], having three keels or ridges. **Tricarpe·llary, Trica·rpellate** *Bot.*, consisting of or having three carpels. **Trica·rpellite** [ad. mod.L. *Tricarpellītēs*], a fossil tricarpellary nut-like fruit, found in the London Clay. **Trica·rpous** *Bot.* [Gr. καρπός fruit], 'bearing three fruits or three carpels' (*Syd. Soc. Lex.* 1899). **Tricau·dal, Tricau·date** [L. *cauda* tail], having three tails or tail-like processes, as the *retrahens auris* or *tricaudālis* muscle, or the hind margin of the posterior wings in some *Lepidoptera*. **Trice·llular,** having or consisting of three cells. **Trice·ntral,** having three centres; so †**Tricentre·ity,** the fact or attribute of having three centres. **Tricepha·lic, Trice·phalous** [Gr. τρικέφαλος, f. κεφαλή head], having three heads, three-headed. **Tricolu·mnar,** having three columns; arranged in or occupying three columns of print. **Tricornigerous** (trəi-kǫɹni·dʒĕrəs) [late L. *tricorniger*, f. *cornu* horn: see -GEROUS], **Trico·rnute, Trico·rnuted,** three-horned; having three horn-like processes. **Tricoryphean** (-kǫrifī·ăn) [Gr. κορυφή peak], having three peaks. **Trico·state** [COSTATE], three-ribbed. **Tricotyle·donous** *Bot.*, having three cotyledons. **Tricruno·dal** *Geom.*, having three crunodes. **Tricru·ral** [L. *crūs, crūr-* leg], three-legged; consisting of three branches radiating from a common centre. **Tridia·metral,** having three diameters. **Tridi·gitate,** (*a*) *Zool.* having three digits (fingers or toes); (*b*) *Bot.* digitate with three leaflets, ternate; so **Tridi·gital, Tridi·gitated.**

(*Continued on next page.*)

**1873** SALMON *Higher Plane Curves* 245 The quartic is a *triacnodal curve composed of a trigonoid figure within the triangle and of the three vertices as acnodes. **1886** LENDENFELD in *Proc. Zool. Soc.* 560 The calcareous triaxon spicules have only three rays—*triact. [**1886** *Proc. Zool. Soc.* 21 Dec. 563 *Triactina*, with three rays.] **1891** *Cent. Dict.*, *Triactinal. **1887** SOLLAS in *Encycl. Brit.* XXII. 416 (Fig. 12) *c*, triod (triaxon *triactine). **1901** *Proc. Zool. Soc.* 5 Mar. 197 The sixth [segment] is *triannulate. **1891** *Cent. Dict.*, *Trianthous. **1883** A. R. WALLACE in *Nature* 22 Mar. 482/2 Heilprin..seeks to show that the Neoarctic and Palæarctic should form one region, for which he proposes..'*Triarctic Region', or the region of the three northern continents. **1822** J. PARKINSON *Outl. Oryctol.* 264 A series of *triarcuated, imbricating, transverse slips. **1897** *Allbutt's Syst. Med.* II. 142 Gresswell, under the names '*triareal' and 'pentareal', has described certain peculiarities of the tongue. **1886** *Triaxon [see *triact*]. **1887** *Amer. Nat.* Oct. 938 A *triaxonian star with five or six rays. **1911** *Encycl. Brit.* XXV. 729/1 Sponges with a skeleton composed of siliceous spicules,..either *triaxonid and hexactinellid in form, or derivable from the triaxonid..type. **1878** BARTLEY tr. *Topinard's Anthrop.* v. 173 Cretinism, according to [Virchow] is due to the synostosis of the *tri-basilar bone—that is to say, of the spheno-basilar suture, and the suture of the body of the anterior sphenoid and the posterior sphenoid. **1890** H. M. STANLEY *Darkest Africa* II. xxi. 22 *Tri-bladed and four-bladed knives were shown to me. **1901** *Science* 6 Dec. 891/2 A possible basis for a division of the '*triblastic' animals into two parallel but independent series. **1870** HOOKER *Stud. Flora* 305 Flowers..in 1- or more-flowered *3-bracteate spikelets. *Ibid.* 321 Flowers..minutely *3-bracteolate. **1834** MEDWIN *Angler in Wales* I. 258 Along the *tri-breakered sea-shore. **1897** *Proc. Zool. Soc.* 2 Feb. 198 Dorsal scales very strongly *tricarinate. **1802** SHAW *Gen. Zool.* III. 54 *Tricarinated Tortoise. **1872** OLIVER *Elem. Bot.* II. 253 A *tricarpellary pistil. **1900** B. D. JACKSON *Gloss. Bot. Terms*, *Tricarpellate. [**1859** PAGE *Handbk. Geol. Terms*, **Tricarpellites*.., fossil nut-like fruits from the London clay, so called from their consisting of three carpels or seed-cells.] **1882** OGILVIE, Tricarpellite. **1891** *Cent. Dict.*, *Tricarpous. **1860** MAYNE *Expos. Lex.*, *Tricaudalis*, having three tails; three-tailed: *tricaudal. **1891** *Cent. Dict.*, *Tricaudate. *Ibid.*, *Tricellular. **1900** in B. D. JACKSON *Gloss. Bot. Terms.* **1642** H. MORE *Song of Soul* II. iii. II. vi, The second way that makes the soul *tricentrall. *Ibid.* I. viii, The *Tricentreity Of humane souls. **1913** *19th Cent.* Aug. 284 The dual monarchy is not only bicephalic.. but..*tricephalic. **1891** *Cent. Dict.*, *Tricephalous. **1907** *Daily News* 13 Mar. 2 The *Tri-Church Conference of the Congregational, United Brethren, and Methodist Protestant Churches of the United States. **1865** *Pall Mall G.* 15 June 9 The *tricolumnar 'Historicus' favours the *Times* at his usual length with a letter. **1892** *Athenæum* 4 June 725/1 Fifty-six pages of index, mostly tricolumnar. **1819** KEATS *Let. to G. & Georgiana Keats* 13 Mar., The black badger with *tri-cornered hat. **1903** *Bradford Antiq.* July 348 Tricornered bits of wood. **1727** BAILEY vol. II, **Tricornigerous*.., bearing or having three Horns. **1891** *Cent. Dict.* cites WESTWOOD for *Tricornute. **1816** G. S. FABER *Orig. Pagan Idol.* II. 502 The Mount of Olives; which he adopted as the local *tricoryphean Meru or Ida of his apostasy. **1861** BENTLEY *Man. Bot.* (1870) 146 If a ribbed leaf has 3 ribs.. it is said to be 3-ribbed or *tricostate. **1828** BRANDE in *Lancet* 14 June 323/1 Containing three [cotyledons], *tricotyled[on]ous. **1873** SALMON *Higher Plane Curves* 245 If the ellipse cuts each side in two real points, then the quartic is *tricrunodal. **1873** HOOKER tr. *Le Maout's Bot.* 915 The macrospores are marked on one hemisphere with a *tricrural line. **1891** *Cent. Dict.*, *Tridiametral,..*Tridigitate. **1881** *Tridigital [see BIDIGITATE]. **1900** B. D. JACKSON *Gloss. Bot. Terms, Tridigitate*,..thrice digitate, ternate. **1811** SHAW *Gen. Zool.* VIII. 105 *Tridigitated Kingfisher..is a native of New Holland;..the legs and feet red, with three toes only.

**Tri-** *prefix.* **I. 1.** (*Continued from preceding page.*)

**Tridynamous** (trəidi·nămǝs) *Bot.* [after DIDYNAMOUS, TETRADYNAMOUS], having six stamens of which three are longer than the others. **Tri-eleme·ntary,** composed of three elements. **Trifa·sciated** *Zool.* [L. *fascia* band], having or marked with three bands. **Trifau·cian** [L. *trifaux* (Vergil *Æn.* vi. 417), f. *faucēs* throat], having three throats. **Trifilar** (trəifəi·lăɹ) [L. *filum* thread], consisting of three threads. † **Trifi·stulary** [L. *fistula* pipe], having three pipes or tubes. **Triflagellate** (trəiflæ·dʒělět) *Biol.*, having three flagella, as an infusorian. **Triflo·ral, Triflo·rous** *Bot.* [L. *flōs, flōr-* flower], bearing three flowers (on one stem); three-flowered. **Trifo·veolate, -ated** *Entom.*, having three foveolæ or shallow pits. **Triga·stric** *Anat.* [after DIGASTRIC], having three bellies, as a muscle. **Trigene·ric** *Gram.* [GENERIC], of three genders. **Trigla·ndular** *Bot.* [mod.L. *glandula* (GLANDULE), dim. of *glans* acorn], 'having three nuts or nutlets in one involucre' (*Cent. Dict.* 1891). **Trigu·ttulate** *Nat. Hist.* [GUTTULATE], having three spots like small drops. **Trihemeral** (trəihe·mĕrăl) [Gr. τριήμερος, f. ἡμέρα day], lasting three days. **Trihilate** (trəihəi·lét) *Bot.* [HILUM]: see quot. **Trihyposta·tic,** existing in three 'hypostases' or 'persons': see HYPOSTASIS 5 (*b*). **Tri·jugate, Tri·jugous** *Bot.* [L. *jugum* yoke; cf. *trijugus* triple], having three pairs of leaflets: said of a pinnate leaf. **Trila·biate** *Nat. Hist.* [L. *labi-um* lip], three-lipped. **Trilame·llar, Trila·mellated, Trila·minar, Trila·minate** *Nat. Hist.* [LAMELLA, LAMINA], having or consisting of three layers. **Trilo·phodont** *a. Zool.* [Gr. λόφος ridge + ὀδούς, ὀδοντ-tooth], having molar teeth with three transverse ridges, as the genus *Trilophodon* of mastodons. **Trilophous** (tri·lǝfǝs) [Gr. λόφος crest], having three rays forked, as a sponge-spicule. **Trilu·minar, Trilu·minous** [L. *lūmen* light], 'having three lights' (Bailey, 1727). **Trima·stigate** *Biol.* [Gr. μάστιξ, -ῑγ- whip] = *triflagellate.* **Trime·mbral,** 'having, or consisting of, three members' (Webster, 1864). **Trimu·scular,** furnished with three muscles. **Trinoctial** (trəinǫ·kʃăl) [L. *nox, noct-* night], belonging to or lasting three nights. **Trinu·cleate** *Biol.*, having three nuclei. **Trio·cular** [L. *oculus* eye], having three eyes. **Triope·rculate** *Nat. Hist.*, having three opercula (see OPERCULUM). **Triortho·gonal** *Geom.* [ORTHOGONAL], pertaining to or consisting of three systems of lines or surfaces, each intersecting the other two at right angles. **Trio·vulate** *Bot.*, having three ovules. **Tripa·leolate** *Bot.*: see quot. **Tripa·pillated** *Zool.*, having three papillæ. **Tripa·schal** [PASCHAL], including three passovers. **Triphasic** (trəifēi·zik), having or exhibiting three phases. **Triphyle·tic** [Gr. φυλετικ-ός, f. φυλέτης tribesman, φυλή tribe]: see quot. **Tripo·lar,** having or characterized by three poles. **Triprostho·merous** *Comp. Anat.* [f. *prosthomere,* f. Gr. πρόσθεν forwards + μέρος part], consisting of three prosthomeres, i. e. somites which, with their parapodia, have passed forwards from the thorax. **Triprostyle** (trəiprǫ·stəil) [PROSTYLE], of an ancient temple: having a portico with three pillars in front (also said of the portico). **Tripu·nctal** [med.L. *tripunctālis* (Wyclif), L. *punct-um* point: cf. PUNCTAL], occupying three points in space. **Tripu·nctate** [L. *punct-um* point], marked with three points or dots. **Tripu·pillate** *Entom.* [cf. PUPILLATE], having three 'pupils' or included spots, as an ocellated spot on an insect's wing. **Tripyra·midal** *Cryst.*, characterized by three types of pyramid: applied to a class of the hexagonal system. **Triquadra·ntal** *Geom.*, formed by three quadrants, as a spherical triangle. **Trirecta·ngular,** having three right angles, as a spherical triangle (Worcester, 1860). **Trirhombohe·dral** *Cryst.*, characterized by three types of rhombohedron: applied to a class of the hexagonal system. **Trisceptral** (trəise·ptrăl), having, or pertaining to, three sceptres. **Trise·nsory,** pertaining to or affecting three of the senses. **Trise·palous** *Bot.*, having or consisting of three sepals. **Trise·ptate,** having three septa or partitions. **Trise·rial** (whence **Trise·rially** *adv.*), **Trise·riate,** arranged in three series or rows. **Trise·tose** *Entom.*, bearing three setæ or bristles (*Cent. Dict.* 1891). **Trisi·nuate, Trisi·nuated,** having three sinuses or inward curves, as the margin of an insect's wing. **Trispe·rmous** *Bot.* [Gr. σπέρμα seed], containing three seeds. **Trispi·nose, Trispi·nous** *Nat. Hist.*, having three spines. **Trisplanchnic** (trəisplæ·ŋknik) *Anat.* [Gr. σπλάγχνα viscera], applied to the sympathetic nerve, as having connexions with the viscera of the three great cavities (cranial, thoracic, abdominal) of the body. **Trisporic** (trəispǫ·rik), **Trisporous** (trəispōᵊ·rǝs) *Bot.*, having or consisting of three spores. **Tristachyous** (trəistæ·kiǝs) *Bot.* [Gr. στάχυς ear of corn, spike], having three spikes. **Tristigma·tic, Tristi·gmatose** *Bot.*, having three stigmas. **Tristy·lous** *Bot.*, having three styles. **Trive·rbal** [L. *verb-um* word], consisting of three words. **Trive·rbial** [f. L. *tria verba* three words]: see quot. **Trive·rtebral** *Anat.*, consisting of three vertebræ united. **Trivi·rgate** *Zool.* [L. *virga* twig, rod, stripe], marked with three streaks or stripes. **Trivolu·minous,** consisting of three volumes; composing a work in three volumes. **Trizo·mal** *Geom.* [Gr. ζῶμα girdle], applied to a curve having an equation of the form $\sqrt{U}+\sqrt{V}+\sqrt{W}=0$: cf. POLYZOME, and *tetrazomal* s. v. TETRA-.

**b.** With Eng. sbs. (without adj. ending); chiefly nonce-wds. instead of the usual formations in *three-*: as *tri-church, -letter, -party, -phase.*

**c.** Occas. with sb. + -ED [2] (instead of the usual *three-. . ed*): as *tri-bladed, -breakered, -cornered, -faced, -legged, -membered, -pointed, -sceptred, -shaped, -zoned.*

1866 ODLING *Anim. Chem.* 25 Comparing *tri-elementary bodies of this kind with tri-elementary mineral substances. 1835 BURNES *Trav. Bokhara* (ed. 2) II. 162 The great *trifaced idol of Elephanta. 1777 PENNANT *Zool.* (ed. 4) IV. 75 Tellina..*Trifasciated, with a very brittle shell. 1802 SHAW *Gen. Zool.* III. 542 Trifasciated Snake. 1716 M. DAVIES *Athen. Brit.* II. To Rdr. 41 Those reviving Hydra's and Triceptick or *Trifaucian Cerberus's have been often and are are still daily baffl'd and defeated. 1903 *Nature* 5 Feb. 334/1 An inertia table..in which an aluminium ring was supported by a *trifilar suspension. 1646 SIR T. BROWNE *Pseud. Ep.* III. xii. 132 Nor will the solitude of the Phænix allow this denomination, for many there are of that species, and whose *trifistulary bill and crany we have beheld our selves. 1891 *Cent. Dict.*, *Triflagellate..*Trifoveolate. 1860 WORCESTER, *Trifloral. 1771 J. R. FORSTER *Flora Amer. Septentr.* 25 Ranunculus abortivus..*triflorous. 1861 HAGEN *Synopsis Neuroptera N. Amer.* 193 Each side with a fuscous, *trifoveolated stripe. 1676 *Phil. Trans.* XI. 770 He makes an ingenious supposition of a *trigastrick muscle. 1880 EARLE *Philol. Eng. Tongue* § 420 The old adjective had.. even a double set of *trigeneric inflections. 1887 W. PHILLIPS *Brit. Discomycetes* 27 Sporidia 8, narrowly fusiform, bi- or *tri-guttulate. 1840 G. S. FABER *Prim. Doctr. Regen.* II. vi. 140 You were thrice plunged into the Water,..symbolically exhibiting the *trihemeral continuance of Christ in the sepulchre. 1866 *Treas. Bot.*, *Trihilate, having three apertures, as some sorts of pollen grains. 1862 NEALE *Hymns East. Ch.* 32 Three co-eternal, co-enthroned,..*Trihypostatic Essence. 1880 GRAY *Struct. Bot.* (ed. 6) 417/2 Pinnate leaves are unijugate, with a single pair of leaflets, bijugate, with two pairs, *trijugate, with three pairs [etc.]. 1819 *Pantologia*, *Trijugous leaf,..a pinnate leaf with three pairs of leaflets. 1856-8 W. CLARK *Van der Hoeven's Zool.* I. 192 Body anteriorly obtuse,..Mouth *trilabiate. 1900 B. D. JACKSON *Gloss. Bot. Terms*, *Trilamellar. 1822 J. PARKINSON *Outl. Oryctol.* 186 One [tooth of the shell].. slightly *trilamellated. 1882 SLADEN in *Jrnl. Linn. Soc.* XVI. 243 The spinelets are..regularly *trilaminate. 1844 TUPPER *Crock of G.* ii, A ricketty triangular and *trilegged table. 1902 *Westm. Gaz.* 6 Aug. 6/1 A new telegraphic code has been invented..known as Baldrey's *Tri-Letter Code...Every word in any language is represented by three letters only. 1909 *Cent. Dict.* Supp., *Trilophous. 1891 *Cent. Dict.*, *Trimastigate. 1626 PRYNNE *Perpet. Regen. Man's Est.* 331 A threefold and *trimembred objection. 1875 C. C. BLAKE *Zool.* 108 The larynx is *trimuscular. 1623 COCKERAM, *Trinoctial, belonging to three nights. 1880 MUIRHEAD *Gaius* Digest 623 *Manus*,..avoidance of it by trinoctial interruption. 1887 W. PHILLIPS *Brit. Discomycetes* 254 Sporidia..*3-nucleate or pseudo-septate. 1844 TUPPER *Heart* iv, Men.. being neither naturally monocular nor *triocular. 1900 B. D. JACKSON *Gloss. Bot. Terms*, *Trioperculate. 1891 *Cent. Dict.*, *Triovulate. 1866 *Treas. Bot.* 1172 *Tripaleolate, consisting of three pales or paleæ, as the flower of a bamboo. 1891 *Cent. Dict.* cites H. ALLEN for *Tripapillated. 1907 *Daily Chron.* 11 Mar. 4/4 The great danger ahead of Australia is..her *tri-party system of government, which places parties in office that do not command the confidence of the country. 1883 SCHAFF *Hist. Chr. Church* (ed. 2) I. § 16. 130 Three theories [of the length of Christ's public ministry],..designated as the bipaschal, *tripaschal, and quadripaschal schemes, according to the number of Passovers. 1900 *Engineering Mag.* XIX. 778/2 The Central Station of the '*Tri-Phase' Company at Asnières, Seine..which will furnish tri-phase currents to Paris. 1901 *Buck's Handbk. Med. Sc.* III. 105 In the frog's heart the variation shown by the capillary electrometer is diphasic. For the human heart the later work seems to show a *triphasic current. 1900 B. D. JACKSON *Gloss. Bot. Terms*, *Triphyletic,..used of hybrids containing the blended strains of three species. 1605 SYLVESTER *Du Bartas* II. i. III. *Lawe* 487 'Gainst the *tri-pointed wrathfull violence Of the drad dart. 1865 MANSFIELD *Salts* 33 The general idea of a *tripolar compound, the simplest form of which is supposed to be water. 1894 BATESON *Variation* xvi. 430 Tripolar division of nucleus in embryonic tissue of Trout. 1902 E. R. LANKESTER in *Encycl. Brit.* XXV. 700 Arthropoda—Hexapoda. Head shown by its early development to be *triprosthomerous. 1841 *Civil Eng. & Arch. Jrnl.* IV. 118/2 Only the portico part of the temple (a Corinthian hexastyle, *triprostyle) advanced into the enclosed area in front. 1897 DZIEWICKI *Wyclif's De Logica* III. Introd. 23 If the Equator consist of *tripunctal atoms, it cannot be a circle. 1841 *Penny Cycl.* XX. 74/2. 1872 NICHOLSON *Palæont.* 491 Oval or elliptical *tripunctate areoles. 1826 KIRBY & SP. *Entomol.* IV. xlvi. 287 An ocellus is called bipupillate, *tripupillate, etc., when there are two, three, etc. of these spots. 1896 C. W. CROCKETT *Elem. Plane & Sph. Trigon.* 126 A *triquadrantal triangle has three sides each equal to a quadrant. *Ibid.*, A *trirectangular triangle is also triquadrantal. *a* 1886 FERGUSON *Ogham Inscript.* (1887) 153 This symbol in a bi-sceptral form traverses the crescent; in a *tri-sceptral form, the other emblem. 1792 J. BARLOW *Conspir. Kings* 78 The *trisceptred prince, of Austrian mould..Theresa's son. 1895 *Edin. Rev.* Jan. 108 A '*trisensory hallucination', 'visual', 'auditory', and 'tactile'. 1903 F. W. H. MYERS *Human Personality* I. 254. 1830 LINDLEY *Nat. Syst. Bot.* 286 *Trisepalous calyx. 1874 COOKE *Fungi* 27 The spores..at first unilocular, but afterwards *triseptate. 1860 WORCESTER, *Triserial, *Triseriate (Bot.), in three rows, one below another. *Gray.* 1866 *Treas. Bot.* 1174 *Triserial*, in three rows. 1891 *Cent. Dict.*, *Triserially, in three series; so as to be triserial. 1613 HEYWOOD *Silver Age* III. Wks. 1874 III. 156 The triple-headed dogge..Hels *tri-shap't porter. 1891 *Cent. Dict.*, *Trisinuate. 1849 JOHNSTON in *Proc. Berw. Nat. Club* II. No. 7. 366 The frontal margin *trisinuated. 1760 J. LEE *Introd. Bot.* II. (1765) 159 *Rhamnus*, with a *trispermous Fruit. 1819 G. SAMOUELLE *Entomol. Compend.* 93 Interior antennæ with the first joint of the peduncle *trispinose. 1828 STARK *Elem. Nat. Hist.* II. 162 Thorax granulated, carinated, *trispinous. 1826 KIRBY & SP. *Entomol.* IV. xxxvii. 4 Called the great sympathetic, the intercostal, or *trisplanchnic nerves. 1857 DUNGLISON *Med. Lex.*, *Trisplanchnic Nerve*.. Great sympathetic, Intercostal, Ganglionic or vertebral nerve. 1866 *Treas. Bot.* 1174 *Trisporic. 1891 *Cent. Dict.*, *Trisporous. *Ibid.*, *Tristachyous. *Ibid.*, *Tristigmatic..*Tristigmatose. 1900 B. D. JACKSON *Gloss. Bot. Terms*, Tristigmatic. 1891 *Cent. Dict.*, *Tristylous. 1900 in B. D. JACKSON *Gloss. Bot. Terms.* 1817 JAS. MILL *Brit. India* I. II. vi. 279 The *triverbal phrase, and the triliteral syllable. 1768 BLACKSTONE *Comm.* III. xxvi. 424 In the Roman calendar there were in the whole year but twenty eight judicial or *triverbial days allowed to the praetor for hearing causes [*note*, Otherwise called *dies fasti, in quibus licebat praetori fari tria verba, do, dico, addico*]. 1871 HUXLEY *Anat. Vertebr. Anim.* viii. 341 The last cervical and the anterior dorsal vertebræ [in *Glyptodon*] are ankylosed together into a single '*tri-vertebral' bone. 1863 *Ibis* Jan. 15 *Acc[ipiter] nisoides*..closely resembles the preceding one, *A. nisus*, but is smaller, with *trivirgate throat. 1857 READE *Course of True Love* 191 Paper is not absolutely valueless, whatever the *trivoluminous may think. 1892 *Athenæum* 31 Dec. 914/2 In tri-voluminous fiction. 1867 CAYLEY *Math. Papers* VI. 485 On the *Trizomal Curve and the Tetrazomal Curve. 1840 R. HORNE *Gregory VII*, v. iv. (ed. 2) 100 *Tri-zoned Jove's star-set eternity.

**2.** Triply; three times; in three ways, directions, etc. **Tricu·rvate,** 'curved in three directions, as a sponge-spicule' (*Funk's Stand. Dict.*). **Trie·qual,** constituting three that are equal. **Trigoneu·tic** *a.* [Gr. γονεύειν to generate], producing three broods in a year, as certain insects (cf. *trivoltine* in 4 b); so **Trigoneu·tism. Trila·rcenous,** three times convicted of larceny. **Triqua·drifid** *Bot.* [QUADRIFID], having three lobes each deeply divided into four segments. **Triqui·nate** *Bot.* [QUINATE], having three lobes each divided into five. **Tri·sonant** [L. *sonānt-em* sounding], sounding in three ways; in quot. *loosely*, comprising three classes of vocal sounds. **Trisquare** (trəi·skwēəɹ), 'three-square; having three equally wide plane faces' (*Cent. Dict. Suppl.* 1909). **Trita·ctic** *Geom.* [L. *tact-*, ppl. stem of *tangĕre* to touch: cf. TACTIC *a.*[2]], having or involving three coincident points of contact. Also TRITERNATE. **b.** *spec.* in *Cryst.* denoting forms having three ranges of facets, the number in each range being expressed by the second element: as **tri-dodecahe·dral** (12), **tri-hexahe·dral** (6), **tri-octahe·dral** (8); also **tri-rhomboi·dal,** having eighteen faces occupying the positions of those of three different rhomboids.

1805-17 R. JAMESON *Char. Min.* (ed. 3) 205 *Tri-dodecahedral red silver-ore..a six-sided prism, acuminated on the extremities with three planes, and truncated on all the edges. 1839 BAILEY *Festus* v. (1848) 44 Injustice, hate, uncharitableness, *Triequal reign round earth, a Trinity of Hell. 1805-17 R. JAMESON *Char. Min.* 204 *Trihexahedral, ..when [the crystal's] surface consists of three..ranges of planes, disposed six and six above each other...Tri-hexahedral nitrate of potash..; a six-sided prism, acuminated on both extremities with six planes. 1823 SYD. SMITH *Botany Bay* Wks. (1850) 369 The man of three juries, who has three times appeared at the Bailey, *trilarcenous. 1805-17 R. JAMESON *Char. Min.* 205 *Tri-octahedral sulphat of lead,..a four-sided pyramid,..the edges of the common base truncated, the angles on it very deeply bevelled, the bevelling planes set on the lateral edges, and the bevelling edges again deeply truncated, so that the crystal..consists of three rows of planes, of which each row contains eight planes. 1833 HOOKER *J. E. Smith's Eng. Flora* V. I. 113 The upper leaves..are *tri-quadrifid. 1891 *Cent. Dict.*, *Triquinate. 1805-17 R. JAMESON *Char. Min.* 202 *Trirhomboidal; this, in the Wernerian Crystallography, is a double six-sided pyramid, with alternately broad and narrow lateral planes,..and..acuminated on the extremities with three planes, which are set on the smaller lateral planes. Example, Tri-rhomboidal calcareous-spar. 1876 DOUSE *Grimm's L.* xlvii. 97 The priority of any one of the known *tri-sonant systems over the others is untenable.

**3.** In combination with an adj. (usu. in *-ly*) derived from a sb. denoting a period of time: Comprising three —, lasting three —, occurring or appearing every three (days, etc.); also (*loosely*) occurring three times (a day, etc.); those in *-ly* are also used as advbs. = every three (days, etc.) or three times a (day, etc.): as *tridaily*; *triho·ral* [L. *hora* hour]. See also TRIMONTHLY, -WEEKLY; TRIANNUAL, -DIURNAL, etc.

1887 *Science* IX. 79 The system of *tridaily [meteorological] observations. 1860 WORCESTER cites LD. ELLESMERE for *Trihoral.

**II. 4.** Forming sbs., with the senses: **a.** Something consisting of or equivalent to three (of the things denoted by the second element); a triple —. ‖ **Triachæ·nium** (irreg. -akenium) *Bot.* [mod.L.: see ACHENE], a fruit composed of three achenes. **Tri·aster** *Biol.* [Gr. ἀστήρ star: cf. DIASTER], a figure bearing some resemblance to three conjoined stars, resulting from a tripolar division of a nucleus. † **Tricube** *Math. Obs.*, the third power of a cube, a ninth power. † **Tridiapa·son** *Mus. Obs.* [DIAPASON 1], an interval of three octaves, a twenty-second. † **Trifluctua·tion** *Obs.* [L. *fluctus* wave]: see quot. **Trihemio·bol** [Gr. τριημιωβόλιον], an ancient Greek coin of the value of $1\frac{1}{2}$ obols. **Triju·nction**, a junction or union of three. † **Trimi·llion**, the third power of a million; also (quot. 1707) a thousand thousand millions, i. e. a billion (= TRILLION in both senses: cf. etymology of BILLION). **Tri:millionai·re** [after *millionaire*], a person possessed of three millions of money (pounds, dollars, francs, etc.). **Tri·pair** *Math.*, a set of three pairs. † **Tripa·palty** [PAPALTY], a period during which there were three rival popes. † **Triqua·drate** *Math. Obs.* [QUADRATE *sb.*[1] 1 b], the third power of a square, a sixth power. **Tristigm** (trəi·stim) *Geom.* [Gr. στίγμα prick, point], a system of three points with the straight lines connecting them (*Cent. Dict. Suppl.* 1909).

**b.** Something having, or related in some way to, three (of the things denoted or indicated by the second element). **Tricephal** (trəise·fǎl) [Gr. τρικέφαλος adj., f. κεφαλή head: see *tricephalic* in I. 1 a], a three-headed figure or image of a deity. ‖ **Trio·rchis** [mod.L., f. Gr. ὄρχις testicle; cf. τριόρχης]: see quot. 1857. **Tri·plane**, an aeroplane with three supporting planes; also *attrib.* **Triquate·rnion** *Math.*, an expression of the form $q_1 + \omega q_2 + \mu q_3$, where $q_1$, $q_2$, $q_3$, are quaternions, and $\omega$ and $\mu$ are commutative with quaternions. **Tri:sacramenta·rian**, one who recognizes three and only three sacraments. **Trivo·ltine** [Ital. *volta* turn, time], a silkworm of a breed which yields three cocoons in a year.

**c.** Something (denoted by the second element) having three of some characteristic part, or related to three things. **Tri-car** (-machine, -mobile, -motor-car), a motor-car with three wheels; a motor tricycle with a seat for a person or a carrier for luggage in front. **Trice·ptor** *Phys. Chem.* [L. *-ceptor* = *captor* taker], an intermediary body having three haptophorous groups. **Trico·aster**, a combination of a three-speed gear with a 'coaster' brake on a cycle. † **Tri-plura·lity**, a plurality in which three benefices are held at once. **Tripy·ramid** *Cryst.*, a triangular pyramid, as a form in certain calcareous spars. **Tri-schism** (*nonce-wd.*), schism of three parties. **Tri-spear** (*nonce-wd.*), a trident.

1882 OGILVIE, *Triachenium, triakenium. 1900 B. D. JACKSON *Gloss. Bot. Terms*, Triachænium. 1894 BATESON *Variation* I. xvi. 431 *note*, A case of the presence of *triasters in two bilaterally symmetrical tracts of the blastoderm of Loligo. 1909 J. W. JENKINSON *Experim. Embryology* 30 Triaster, a tripolar figure with three spindles. 1904 *Sat. Rev.* 20 Feb. 228/1 The development of the *tri-car is especially important. *Ibid.*, There is a great future for the useful tri-car. 1906 *Westm. Gaz.* 21 Aug. 4/2 Experience is going to show that the final form of the tri-car for delivery purposes will be of a very different pattern. 1888 RHYS *Hibbert Lect.* i. 81 *note*, The wide distribution of the *tricephal has induced M. Mowat to declare for the improbable hypothesis, that it was..but the Roman Janus..naturalized in Gaul. 1902 VAUGHAN & NOVY *Cellular Toxins* (ed. 4) 132 The intermediary body [usually an] 'amboceptor'.. may be a *triceptor, quadriceptor, etc. 1908 *Daily Chron.* 21 Nov. 9/4 He made use of the Sturmey-Archer *Tricoaster, which is the three-speed gear in association with a foot-acted brake. 1674 JEAKE *Arith.* (1696) 273 Some to shorten..the long Names of..Higher Powers..call.. φφ a Bicube, φφφ a *Tricube &c. 1811 BUSBY *Dict. Mus.* (ed. 3), *Tri-Diapason. 1646 SIR T. BROWNE *Pseud. Ep.* VII. xvii. 377 Τρικυμία..is a concurrence of three waves in one, whence arose the proverb, τρικυμία κακῶν, or a *trifluctuation of evils. 1887 B. V. HEAD *Hist. Numorum* 336 There are also *trihemiobols..of later style, for the Pegasus on the obverse has pointed wings. 1887 *Athenæum* 29 Jan. 164/2 To have the *trijunction of Tibet, India, and Burma focussed within the four corners of a map. 1707 *Curios. in Husb. & Gard.* 155 These ten Thousand Willows ..will produce each of them likewise a hundred more. Thus we have a Million; then a hundred Millions: next come the Tens of Bimillions; then the *Trimillions. 1806 [see TRILLION]. 1848 *Tait's Mag.* XV. 646 A *tri-millionaire buys it for a deer-forest. 1905 *Westm. Gaz.* 28 Dec. 7/3 Returning home in a *tri-motor-car. 1650 H. MORE *Observ.* in *Enthus. Tri.*, etc. (1656) 92 If you have not a sleight of Art to Metamorphize your selves into *Triorchises. 1857 DUNGLISON *Med. Lex.*, *Triorchis*, one who has three testicles. 1878 CAYLEY *Math. Papers* X. 450 We have thus..a system of..63 hexpairs; and selecting at pleasure any three pairs out of the same hexpair, we have a system of (63×20=)1260 *tripairs. 1651 N. BACON *Disc. Govt. Eng.* II. xvii. (1739) 89 During the *Tripapalty much money had been levied..to serve for the recovery of the Popedom to one of an English interest. 1908 *Times* 3 Oct. 6/3 Experiments with a *triplane machine. 1909 *Westm. Gaz.* 4 Mar. 4/2 In machines of the biplane and triplane types. 1425 *Rolls of Parlt.* IV. 290/2 That mony a Parsone..have pluralite, and somme *tripluralite. [1753 CHAMBERS *Cycl. Supp.*, **Tripyramides*,..the name of a genus of spars...The bodies of this genus are spars, composed of single pyramids, each of three sides,..affixed by their bases to some solid body.] 1828 WEBSTER, Tripyramid. 1674 JEAKE *Arith.* (1696) 273 Some..call ʒʒ a Biquadrate, ʒʒʒ a *Triquadrate. 1902 G. COMBEBIAC cited in *Cent. Dict. Supp.* for *Triquaternion. 1727–41 CHAMBERS *Cycl.*, **Trisacramentarians*,..a sect..who admit of three sacraments, and no more...There have been several trisacramentarians among the protestants, who allowed of baptism, the eucharist, and absolution, as sacraments. 1896 J. H. WYLIE *Hist. Eng. Hen. IV*, III. 388 Instead of schism, *tri-schism, which threatened to become centi-schism. 1887 MORRIS *Odyss.* v. 292 His hand the *tri-spear grasping.

**III. 5.** In Chemical nomenclature, in the names of compounds and derivatives, with general sense 'three', 'three times'.

**a.** Prefixed to names of compounds of elements, radicals, or groups, names of salts, etc., to signify three atoms, groups, or equivalents of these elements or radicals in combination with another element or radical; e.g. **tribromide**, a compound of 3 atoms of bromine with another element or radical, as *tribromide of boron*; **trisulphate**, a compound of three $SO_4$ groups with a metal or radical (or in earlier nomenclature of three $SO_3$ groups with a basic oxide). So **trichloride, -cyanide, -fluoride, -hydride, -iodide, -oxide, -sulphide** (*-sulphuret*); **triacetate, -carbonate, -chlorate, -cyanate, -hydrate, -phosphate, -thionate**, etc. Also in names of some organic compounds, referring to their composition, as TRIAMIDE, TRIAMINE, and the compound ethers or esters of glycerin with acids, as TRIACETIN, **tributyrin, -palmitin, -stearin**, etc. See also TRISILICATE.

In early nomenclature, *tri-* or *tris-* prefixed to the name of a salt meant 3 molecules not of the acid, but of the base; thus 3 PbO.$C_4H_6O_3$ was called *tris-* or *tri-acetate of lead*; similarly $B_3O$ was called *trioxide of* any element B.

1826 HENRY *Elem. Chem.* I. 591 Tri-phosphate of lime. 1850 DAUBENY *Atomic Theory* (ed. 2) 112 When the number of proportionals of base is 2, the prefix *di* or *dis* is adopted; when 3, *tris*; when four, *tetrakis*...*tris*ilicate of iron, 3 of base to 1 of silicic acid. 1860 SCOFFERN *Orr's Circle of Sciences, Chem.* (new ed.) 467 The most important is the tris or triacetate [of lead]. 1856 FOWNES *Chem.* (ed. 6) 607 Three compounds of stearic acid with glycerin..which M. Berthelot distinguishes as monostearin, bistearin, and tristearin. 1863–72 WATTS *Dict. Chem.* I. 895 The metals which form trichlorides are antimony, arsenic, bismuth, gold, molybdenum, thallium, vanadium, and probably indium. 1866 ROSCOE *Elem. Chem.* xvi. 142 Arsenic unites with chlorine, bromine, and iodine, to form arsenic trichloride, tribromide, and triiodide. *Ibid.* xxiv. 207 Metallic antimony occurs native, but its chief ore is the trisulphide.

**b.** Prefixed to adjs., or to sbs. used attrib., in the names or descriptions of acids, alcohols, compound ethers or esters, oxides, salts, etc.; e.g. *trisodic* or *trisodium*, (a salt) containing 3 atoms of sodium; *triethylic* or *triethyl* (a compound) containing 3 ethyl groups. So *trihydric* or *trihydrogen*, *tricalcic* or *tricalcium*, *triargentic* or *tri-silver*, *tricarbon*, *trichloric*, *trimethylic* or *trimethyl*, *triplumbic*, *trithionic*, *triacetic*, etc.

1866 ODLING *Anim. Chem.* 108 We meet with still less oxidised tricarbon molecules. 1869 ROSCOE *Elem. Chem.* xv. 154 The three atoms of hydrogen in trihydrogen phosphate may be replaced by three different metals. 1873 WATTS *Fownes' Chem.* 340 A trisodic orthophosphate, sometimes called subphosphate. *Ibid.* 451 Triplumbic tetroxide, or Red lead. 1888 MUIR & MORLEY *Watts' Dict. Chem.* I. 99 Alcohols are classed as monohydric, dihydric, trihydric..according to the number of hydroxyl-groups which they contain.

**c.** Prefixed to the names of elements or radicals, or their combining forms (as *azo-*, *bromo-*, *chloro-*, *hydro-*, *hydroxy-*, *iodo-*, *nitro-*, *oxy-*, *sulpho-*, *thio-*: see these) entering into the name of a compound, to signify that three atoms or groups of the element or radical are present, or are substituted for hydrogen, in the substance designated by the rest of the name: as *tribro:mobe·nzene*, $C_6H_3Br_3$, in which three of the hydrogen atoms of benzene, $C_6H_6$, are replaced by three bromine atoms; so *trimethylbenzene*, $C_6H_3(CH_3)_3$; *trie:thylca·rbinol*, $C(C_2H_5)_3OH$; *trime·thylamine*, $N(CH_3)_3$; *trichlorhydrin*, $C_3H_5Cl_3$; so *tribromhydrin*, etc. Combinations of this kind are formed when wanted, and are unlimited in number: only a few are mentioned in this work: see TRIBROM-, TRICHLOR-, etc.

**d.** In verbs and their pples. derived from sbs. as in a, as **tribrominated, trichlorinated**, in which three hydrogen atoms have been replaced by atoms of bromine or chlorine; **trihydrated**, containing three molecules of water.

1857 MILLER *Elem. Chem.* III. 47 Trichlorinated Dutch Liquid. 1868 Trihydrated: see TRIHYDRATE.

**IV. 6.** Forming verbs (and derivatives), as TRI-FALLOW, TRISECT, TRISECTION, q. v.

**Triable** (trəi·ǎb'l), *a.*[1] [a. AF. *triable*, f. as TRY *v.* + -ABLE.] That may be tried.

**1.** *Law.* Capable of being judicially tried in a court of law; liable to judicial trial. Also *transf.* **a.** Of a cause or offence.

1429 *Rolls of Parlt.* IV. 346/1 What issue triable be enquest..happethe to be taken..that hit be tried be enquest of the corps of the saide Shire. 1495 *Act 11 Hen. VII*, c. 21 Plees..triable by any Jury or Inquest. 1600 TATE in Gutch *Coll. Cur.* I. 8, I hold all appeals triable in the King's Bench lawfull. 1770 BURKE *Pres. Discont.* Wks. II. 339 A direct simple issue..triable by plain men. 1865 NICHOLS *Britton* II. 161 *note*, A writ of right, triable by battle or great assise.

**b.** Of a person.

1554 *St. Trials, Sir N. Throckmorton* (1730) I. 76/1 The Partie triable..shall finde himselfe in much worse case, than before when those cruell Lawes stoode in force. 1577–87 HOLINSHED *Chron.* III. 1113/2 The principall and accessaries in felonie and murther be triable and punishable by the common law. 1697 tr. *C'tess D'Aunoy's Trav.* (1706) 243 All that belong to the Inquisition being not subject to or tryable by any other Jurisdiction. 1757 J. LIND *Lett. Navy* ii. 99 All persons are triable by court martials. 1883 *Sat. Rev.* 10 Feb. 170/2 Englishmen are now triable for all kinds of misdemeanours and crimes..in the High Court at Allahabad.

**2.** That may be ascertained, tested, or proved.

1612 STURTEVANT *Metallica* (1854) 27 A triable Inuention is an inuention whose worth and goodnesse cannot certainly appeare before trialls and experiments. 1626 DONNE *Serm.* xxi. (1640) 202 The matter is matter of faith..considerable, and triable by reason. 1660 BOYLE *New Exp. Phys. Mech.* i. 28 In our above-mentioned first Experiment, and..others tryable in our Engine. 1706 BAYNARD in Sir J. Floyer *Hot & Cold Bath.* II. 210 She had tried all things triable.

Hence **Tri·ableness**. 1847 in WEBSTER.

† **Tri·able**, *a.*[2] *Obs. nonce-wd.* [f. TRI- + -ABLE.] Divisible into three.

1647 WARD *Simp. Cobler* 55 Whatsoever is duable or triable, is fryable.

**Triacad** (*Anc. Greek History*): see TRIAKAD.

**Triacanthoid** (trəi,ǎkæ·nþoid), *a.* and *sb.* *Ichth.* [f. mod.L. *Triacanthus*, generic name (f. Gr. τρι-, TRI- + ἄκανθα spine) + -OID.] **a.** *adj.* Belonging to or having the characters of the family *Triacanthidæ* of plectognath fishes, typified by the genus *Triacanthus*. **b.** *sb.* A fish of this family.

1891 in *Cent. Dict.*

**Triacetic**: see TRI- 5 b and ACETIC.

**Triacetin** (trəi,æ·sǐtin). *Chem.* [f. TRI- 5 a + ACET(IC + -IN[1] (the termination of the compound ethers of glycerin: see ACETIN).] Glyceryl triacetate, $C_3H_5(OC_2H_3O)_3$, the compound ether or ester of glycerin or glycerol, $C_3H_5(OH)_3$, and acetic acid, $C_2H_4O_2$, the three H atoms of the OH groups in glycerol being replaced by three acetyl groups, $C_2H_3O$; also called *acetic triglyceride*; a colourless liquid boiling at 258–259° C.; it is found in the oil of the seeds of the spindle-tree.

1858 FOWNES *Elem. Chem.* (ed. 7) 504 Berthelot has pointed out three classes of compounds which glycerin is capable of forming...With acetic acid, for instance, it forms three combinations..monacetin, diacetin, and triacetin.

**Triachænium, Triacnodal**: see TRI- 4 a, 1.

**Triacle**, obs. form of TREACLE.

**Triacontad** (trəi,ǎkǫ·ntæd). [ad. Gr. τριακοντάς, -αδ-, f. τριάκοντα thirty.] The number thirty, or a set of thirty. So **Triaconta,ëterid** (-etiə·rid) [ad. Gr. τριακονταετηρίς, -ιδ-, f. τριακονταετής adj. of or for thirty years], a period of thirty years, or a festival recurring every thirty years; **Triacontahedral** (-hī·drǎl, -he·drǎl) *a.* [Gr. ἕδρα base, side], contained by thirty faces, esp. by thirty rhombs, as a crystal; **Triaco·ntarchy** (triak-) *Anc. Gr. Hist.* [ad. Gr. τριακονταρχία, f. ἀρχή rule], the rule of the Thirty at Athens (see THIRTY A. 1 c); **Triaconter** (trəi,ǎkǫ·ntəɹ) [ad. Gr. τριακοντήρης], an ancient Greek galley with thirty oars.

1621 BP. MOUNTAGU *Diatribæ* 258 Their Ogdoades, Duodecads, *Triacontads,..and all the Æones, blasphemous speculations. 1839 *Fraser's Mag.* XX. 202 The *Triacontaëterid of the pillar of Rosetta—the grand period of the Panegyres, or festivals of the gods, which returned each thirty years. *Ibid.* 328 The great triacontaëterid or panegyry of the resurrection. 1805–17 R. JAMESON *Char. Min.* (ed. 3) 201 A Crystal is said to be..*Triacontahedral when its surface consists of thirty rhombs. 1852 GROTE *Greece* II. lxxii. IX. 259 Isokrates, who speaks with indignant horror of these Dekarchies,..denounces those features which they had in common with the *Triakontarchy at Athens. 1859 RAWLINSON *Herodotus* IV. cxlviii. III. 124 Theras..took ship, and sailed, with three *triaconters, to join the descendants of Membliarus. *Note*, Triaconters were vessels of 30 oars, 15 on each side.

**Triact, -actinal, -actine**: see TRI- 1.

**Triad** (trəi·æd). Also 6–7 -ade. [f. L. *triad-*,

stem of *trias*, a. Gr. τριάς, τριαδ-, a group of three. Cf. F. *triade* (1564 in Hatz.-Darm.).]

**1.** A group or set of three (persons, things, words, attributes, etc.); three collectively or in connexion.

**1546** *St. Papers Hen. VIII*, XI. 341 Two thynges I noted in thEmperour, diligent herynge of me, and good wordys; yf deadis shal nowe folowe accordingely, the triade shall be perfecte. **1614** T. ADAMS *Divell's Banket* 28 Sometimes they daunce in Triades, by threes. *a* **1774** TUCKER *Lt. Nat.* (1834) II. 228 Descend, celestial Graces, sacred Triad. **1862** MERIVALE *Rom. Emp.* VI. liii. 128 The triad of matricides, Nero, Orestes, Alcmæon. **1898** J. T. FOWLER *Durham Cath.* 49 Three triads of Lancet windows.

**b.** The number three (in Pythagorean philosophy).

**1660** STANLEY *Hist. Philos.* IX. (1701) 381/1 The Triad is the first number, actually odd, and the first perfect number, and middle, and proportion. **1875** JOWETT *Plato* (ed. 2) I. 485 The triad or number three is uneven.

**2.** Specific uses. **a.** Applied to the Trinity. [repr. Gr. τριάς trinity, used by Theophilus of Antioch and Clement of Alexandria, *a* 200.]

**1661** BP. G. RUST *Origen & Opin.* 19 There is nothing in that blessed Triad he describes which can be called Creature. **1721** BAILEY, *Triad*..the Trinity. **1806** T. MAURICE *Fall of Mogul* I. ii, Divine, ineffable, eternal triad! **1909** H. B. SWETE *Holy Spirit in N. T.* II. i. 124 [What] He [Jesus] had taught concerning these Three Persons by presenting Them as at once a Triad and a Unity.

**b.** A group of three associated or correlated deities, beings, or powers.

*a* **1746** HOLDSWORTH *Rem. Virgil* (1768) 83 Virgil..means the great Triad of deities first received all over the East. **1813** PRICHARD *Phys. Hist. Man* vii. § 6. 394 We see the attributes of the three persons of the Triad, united in one figure, which represents the supreme Deity, holding conjoined the characters of Creator, Preserver, and Destroyer. **1907** ILLINGWORTH *Doctr. Trinity* vii. 130 The many artificially arranged triads,..like that of Brahma, Siva, and Vishnu in India.

**c.** In Welsh literature: A form of composition characterized by an arrangement of subjects or statements in groups of three.

[**1611** SPEED *Hist. Gt. Brit.* VI. liv. § 12. 189 The Booke *Triades* mentioned by the Author of the Reformed History of Great Britaine.] **1852** MISS YONGE *Cameos* (1877) I. xxxii. 274 Instructions were still oral, and for convenience of memory were drawn up in triads, or verses of three. **1868** SKENE *Four Anc. Bks. Wales* I. 28 As early as the date of the Black Book of Caermarthen some of the Welsh traditions appear under the form of short triads, and that MS. contains a fragment of what were probably the earliest—the Triads of the Horses.

**d.** *Mus.* A chord of three notes, consisting of a given note with the third and fifth above it; e. g. a common chord (without the octave).

The third may be *major* or *minor*, the fifth *perfect*, *augmented*, or *diminished*; hence the triad is described by these adjs. accordingly.

**1801** in BUSBY *Dict. Mus.* **1881** BROADHOUSE *Mus. Acoustics* xv. 320 There are within the octave only three triads or chords of three notes which are consonant. **1889** PROUT *Harmony* viii. § 181 A chord..containing a major third and an augmented fifth..is called an augmented triad.

**e.** *Chem.* A trivalent element or radical, i. e. one which combines with three atoms of hydrogen or other monovalent element or radical.

**1865** *Reader* 1 Apr. 372/2 The family of triatomic atoms or triads, consisting of nitrogen and its analogues, gold and boron. **1865–8** WATTS *Dict. Chem.* III. 964 There are four triad metals properly so called, namely, aluminium, thallium, indium, and gold. **1868** FOWNES *Elem. Chem.* (ed. 10) 252 Each element is connected with others by a number of lines, or connecting bonds, corresponding to its degree of equivalence; a monad being connected..by only one such bond, a triad by three.

**f.** *Biol.* (*a*) A group of three cells, e. g. spores. (*b*) A tertiary unit of organization consisting of an aggregate of dyads: cf. DYAD 2 b. Also *attrib.*, as *triad-deme*: see DEME *sb.*[2] 2.

**1876** tr. *Schützenberger's Ferment.* 52 The two spores connected together have only one plane surface, the triads have two. **1883** [see DEME *sb.*[2] 2].

**g.** *Pros.* A group of three lines having different rhythms. **1885** [see DYAD 2 c].

**h.** *Math.* (*a*) A set of three things, esp. in *Geom.* of three points. (*b*) In Quaternions, An indeterminate product of three vectors.

**1850** CAYLEY *Math. Papers* I. 481 Forming with seven letters..a system of seven triads containing every possible duad. **1885** LEUDESDORF *Cremona's Proj. Geom.* 37 If the triad *ABC* be projected from *S* upon $s_1$ (giving $A_1B_1C_1$), and the triad *A'B'C'* be projected from *S* upon $s_2$ (giving $A_2B_2C_2$); then the triads $A_1B_1C_1$ and $A_2B_2C_2$ will be in perspective.

**i.** *Cryst. Triad axis*, an axis of trigonal symmetry. **1909** in *Cent. Dict. Supp.*

**3.** *Triad Society* [tr. Chinese *San Ho Hui*, lit. 'three unite society', i. e. 'triple union society', according to Giles meaning 'the union of Heaven, Earth, and Man']. A secret Chinese society, formed in the reign of Yung Chêng, 1723–36, with the alleged purpose of ousting the Manchu dynasty; now having a large membership in Southern China and various foreign countries. Hence *Triads* = members of the Triad Society.

**1821** W. MILNE *Acc. Triad Society* in *Trans. Royal Asiatic Soc.* (1827) I. 240 The name .. seems .. to be the *San hŏ hwuy*, i. e. 'The Society of the Three united, or the Triad Society'. **1836** SIR J. DAVIS *Chinese* xi. II. 15 The *San-hŏ-hoey*, or Triad Society...The name seems to imply that when Heaven, Earth, and Man combine to favour them, they shall succeed in subverting the present Tartar dynasty. **1848** S. W. WILLIAMS *Middle Kingd.* I. viii. 395 The English government of Hongkong, enacted in 1845, that any Chinese living in that colony who was ascertained to belong to the Triad Society, should be declared guilty of felony, be imprisoned for three years, and after branding expelled the colony. **1900** *Daily News* 13 Nov. 9/3 The programme of the Triads. **1907** *Daily Chron.* 28 May 1/7 A rebellion has broken out in Kwantung. About 30,000 persons, headed by the Triad Secret Society, have risen.

**Triadelphous** (trəiˌăde·lfəs), *a. Bot.* [f. TRI- + Gr. ἀδελφός brother + -OUS, after DIADELPHOUS.] Of stamens: United by the filaments into three bundles. Of a plant: Having the stamens so united.

**1830** LINDLEY *Nat. Syst. Bot.* 87 Stamens [of the Pea tribe]..either distinct or monadelphous, or diadelphous; very seldom triadelphous. **1896** HENSLOW *Wild Flowers* 18 In the St. John's worts, they [the filaments] are grouped into clusters..of three or five. These are therefore triadelphous and pentadelphous.

**Triadic** (trəiˌæ·dik), *a.* (*sb.*) [f. TRIAD + -IC.] Of, pertaining to, or constituting a triad; consisting of triads.

**1788** T. TAYLOR *Proclus* I. 123 We shall find a line [to be] monadic; but a superficies dyadic, and a solid body triadic. **1839** BAILEY *Festus* viii. (1848) 95 Nature's great Triadic principle, in all things seen. **1850** CAYLEY *Math. Papers* I. 481 On the triadic arrangements of seven and fifteen things.

**b.** *Triadic canon* (*Gr. Ch.*): a hymn (CANON[1] 7 b) in honour of the Trinity.

**1862** NEALE *Hymns East. Ch.* 160 It would be impossible without wearying the reader, to translate the whole of the Triadic Canons.

**c.** *Chem.* That is a triad; trivalent.

**1882** in OGILVIE (Annandale).

**d.** *Anc. Pros.* (*a*) Containing three different metres or rhythms. (*b*) Composed of groups of systems, each of which contains three unlike systems. **1891** in *Cent. Dict.*

**e.** Of or belonging to the Welsh Triads.

**1849** T. STEPHENS *Lit. Kymry* 447 The Triadic form is frequently seen in the poems of Aneurin, and Llywarch Hen. **1906** C. SQUIRE *Mythol. Anc. Brit.* v. 52 We learn..that the battle of Camlan was one of the 'Three Frivolous Battles of Britain',..and that the usual 'Three' alone escaped from it, though Arthur himself is, in spite of the triadic convention, added as a fourth.

**B.** *sb. Math.* In Quaternions, A sum of products of three vectors.

So **Tria·dical** *a.*, = *triadic*; **Tria·dically** *adv.*, according to triads, in the manner of a triad (in quot. 1860, in sense 2 c: cf. e above).

**1837** WHEWELL *Hist. Induct. Sc.* (1857) I. 223 The intellectual gods produce all things triadically. **1860** J. J. THOMAS *Brit. Antiq.* 214 The gallant Cymro triadically repeated..several englynion. **1890** *Dublin Rev.* Jan. 60 *note*, A transcript of an old Triadical commentary.

**Triadism** (trəi·ădiz'm). [f. as prec. + -ISM.] Method, system, or principle of triads; arrangement in groups of three; threefold constitution.

**1846** T. W. JENKYN *Baxter's Wks.* Pref. Ess. 50 The method which Baxter adopted for systematizing the doctrines of Theology may be called Triadism. [Cf. TRICHOTOMIZE.] **1909** A. R. COLQUHOUN in *Q. Rev.* Apr. 672 The suggestion that triadism should supersede dualism as the basis of the [Habsburg] monarchy supposes the erection of a third (i. e. a Slav) State.

**Triadist** (trəi·ădist). *Welsh Lit.* [f. as prec. + -IST.] A composer of triads (see TRIAD 2 c).

**1868** T. NICHOLAS *Pedigree Eng. People* 197 *note*, Caer-Llion, as the seat of King Arthur, obtains from the Triadist pre-eminence even superior to the two Municipia, London and York.

**Triæne** (trəiˌī·n, trəi·īn). *Zool.* [ad. Gr. τρίαινα trident.] A kind of sponge-spicule.

Variously described as 'a rhabdus having at one end three prongs or "cladi" diverging at equal angles', and 'a tetraxon spicule with 1 long and 3 equal shorter tangential rays'.

**1887** SOLLAS in *Encycl. Brit.* XXII. 417/1 (*Sponges*) A particular case of the cladose rhabdus,..of the most frequent occurrence, is the triæne.

Hence **Triænostrongyle** (trəiˌīnoˌstrǫ·ndʒil) [Gr. στρογγύλος rounded], a triæne in which the main arm is blunt at the end; **Triæ·nostyle** (-stəil) [Gr. στῦλος pillar, STYLE], one in which it is sharp; **Triæ·notyle** (-təil) [Gr. τύλη cushion], one in which it is blunt and rounded.

**1909** in *Cent. Dict. Supp.*

**Triage** (trəi·edʒ). [a. F. *triage* (14th c. in Hatz.-Darm.), n. of action f. *trier* to pick, cull: see TRY *v.* and -AGE.] The action of assorting according to quality. Also *attrib.*; hence *concr.* (see quots.)

**1727–41** CHAMBERS *Cycl.* s. v. *Wool*, Each fleece consists of wool of divers qualities, and degrees of fineness, which the dealers therein take care to separate...If the triage, or separation be well made, in 15 bales there will be [etc.]. **1825** *Gentl. Mag.* XCV. I. 216/1 These [pickers] sort the [Coffee] berries into three classes; 'best quality', 'middling', and the third of all the bad broken berries .. is called 'triage coffee'. **1880** *Spons' Encycl. Manuf.* I. 705 The broken beans [of coffee], or 'triage', must also be separated by hand from the dust. **1880** *Daily News* 28 Oct. 3/8 Coffee.—..Costa Rica;..Triage 59*s.* 6*d.*

**Triagonal** (trəiˌæ·gŏnăl), *a.* [Erroneous formation for TRIGONAL, after *tetragonal*, *pentagonal*, etc.; cf. TRIALOGUE.] Triangular.

**1822** SCOTT *Pirate* xv. *note*, They change ranks, and place themselves in a triagonal figure. **1879** *Proc. U. S. Nat. Museum* II. 270 Ostracionts with triagonal, tetragonal, or pentagonal carapaces.

**Triakad, triacad** (trəi·ăkæd). *Anc. Gr. Hist.* [ad. Gr. τριακάς, -αδ-, the number thirty (also as below): cf. TRIACONTAD.] 'At Athens, a political division of the φυλή containing thirty families; at Sparta, either 30 families ($\frac{1}{10}$ of an oba), or 10 families ($\frac{1}{30}$ of an oba)' (Liddell and Scott). Cf. OBE.

**1846** GROTE *Greece* II. viii. II. 602 Herodotus tells us that Lycurgus established the military subdivisions peculiar to Sparta—the Enômoties, the Triakads, and the Syssitia. **1868** SMITH *Smaller Dict. Grk. & Rom. Antiq.* (ed. 7) 389/1.

**Triakis-** (trəi·ăkis), repr. Gr. τριάκις thrice; used in combination in *Geom.* and *Cryst.* in **Tri·akisˌi·cosahe·dron, Tri·akisˌo·ctahe·dron, Tri·akisˌte·trahe·dron** (pl. in all cases **-hedra**), names of solids derived respectively from the icosahedron, octahedron, and tetrahedron by erecting a triangular pyramid on each face, thus multiplying the original number of faces by three. (In *Geom.* specially applied to those forms in which the pyramids are of such altitude as to make all the solid angles regular.) Hence in derived adjs., as **Tri·akisˌo·ctahe·drid.**

**1878** GURNEY *Crystallogr.* 89 The form..called the triakisoctahedron. **1895** STORY-MASKELYNE *Crystallogr.* vii. § 174. 199 The triakisoctahedron or octahedrid pyramidion ..the more acute the pyramidion the more nearly it approximates in aspect to a rhomb-dodecahedron. *Ibid.* § 187. 220 Triakisoctahedrid forms met with in combination. *Ibid.* § 189. 224 The triakistetrahedra..(tetrahedrid pyramidia).

**Triakontarchy**: see TRIACONTARCHY.

**Trial** (trəi·ăl), *sb.*[1] Also 6 *Sc.* triel, 6–7 *Sc.* tryel(l, 6–7 tri-, tryall, 7–8 (9 *dial.*) tryal. [= AF. *trial*, *triel*, f. *trier* to TRY, instanced in 16th c., but prob. earlier: see -AL. Cf. Du Cange s. v. *triallum.*] The action or fact of trying or being tried, in various senses of TRY *v.*

(The senses are here arranged not according to the chronological order of the quotations cited, but in accordance with the sense-development seen in TRY *v.* and TRIABLE.)

**1.** *Law.* The examination and determination of a cause by a judicial tribunal; determination of the guilt or innocence of an accused person by a court.

Hence to *bring* (a person or cause) *to trial*; to *put* (a person) *on his trial*, to *stand* (*one's*) *trial*, etc.; also *trial by the country*, *by jury*, *by proviso*, etc.: see these words.

*a* **1577** SIR T. SMITH *Commw. Eng.* (1633) 189 The clarke asketh him how he will be tried and telleth him he must say, by God and the countrie, for these be the words formall of his triall after inditement. **1651** HOBBES *Leviath.* II. xxvi. 146 In the ordinary trialls of Right, Twelve men of the common People, are the Judges. **1712** ARBUTHNOT *John Bull* App. iii, So Jack resolved; but he had done more wisely to have put himself upon the trial of his country. **1838** THIRLWALL *Greece* IV. 73 He was brought to trial..Theramenes, lately his intimate friend, became his accuser. **1885** *Manch. Exam.* 10 July 5/1 In this case the parties were first put upon their trial. **1911** *Act* 1 *& 2 Geo. V*, c. 6 § 9 (1) Any sheriff or his lawful deputy before whom a writ of inquiry or a writ of trial is executed.

**b.** The determination of a person's guilt or innocence, or the righteousness of his cause, by a combat between the accuser and accused (*trial by battle*, *by* (*single*) *combat*, *by wager of battle*, *by the sword*); 'a combat decisive of the merits of a cause' (Schmidt); see also *trial by* ORDEAL. These methods of trial are now abolished; but expressions originally referring to them are still in fig. use. Thus, war is often spoken of as a 'trial by battle' with God for judge.

**1593** SHAKS. *Rich. II*, I. i. 81 Ile answer thee in any faire degree, Or Chiualrous designe of knightly triall. **1595** — *John* II. i. 286 Those soules That to their euerlasting residence, Before the dew of euening fall, shall fleete In dreadfull triall of our kingdomes King. *Ibid.* 342 England thou hast not sau'd one drop of blood In this hot triall more then we of France. **1600** — *A. Y. L.* I. ii. 199 Let your faire eies, and gentle wishes go with mee to my triall. **1617** [see COMBAT *sb.* 1]. **1641** [see BATTLE *sb.* 2]. **1738** GLOVER *Leonidas* III. 564 By single combat were the tryal vain. **1819** *Act* 59 *Geo. III*, c. 46 Whereas..the Trial by Battel in any Suit, is a Mode of Trial unfit to be used; and it is expedient that the same should be wholly abolished..be it..enacted, That ..in any Writ of Right now depending, or which may hereafter be..commenced, the Tenant shall not be received to wage Battel, nor shall Issue be joined nor Trial be had by Battel. **1868** G. PRYME *Autobiog. Recoll.* vii. (1870) an. 1818. 133.

**2.** The action of testing or putting to the proof the fitness, truth, strength, or other quality of anything; test, probation.

**1526** *Pilgr. Perf.* (W. de W. 1531) 108 The tryall of our fayth, & examinacyon or proue of our hope. **1548** UDALL, etc., *Erasm. Par. Mark* viii. 53 b, Nowe maketh he a triall howe much his disciples haue profited ghostly. **1600** J. PORY tr. *Leo's Africa* IX. 339 The most certaine triall of these horses is when they can ouertake the beast called Lant or the Ostrich in a race. **1604** E. G[RIMSTONE] *D'Acosta's Hist. Indies* IV. vi. 221 The triall of mettall by fire. **1695** WOODWARD *Nat. Hist. Earth* I. (1723) 23 They answer all Chymical Tryals in like Manner as the Sea-Shells do. **1903** *Motor. Ann.* 145 The Automobile Club..held a series of practical and official brake trials in Welbeck Park.

**b.** The fact or condition of being tried by suffering or temptation; probation. † In quot. *c* 1550, temptation (*obs.*). (Cf. 9.)

*c* 1550 CHEKE *Matt.* xxvi. 41 Can ie not watch oon hour with me, watch and prai yt ie enter not into trial. 1644 MILTON *Areop.* (Arb.) 45 That which purifies us is triall. 1755 YOUNG *Centaur* i. Wks. 1757 IV. 108 Is not this stretching out our boldness even beyond the day of tryal? 1871 MACDUFF *Mem. Patmos* vi. 71 The hour of trial—the testing hour of suffering arrived.

† **3.** Inquiry or investigation in order to ascertain something; examination, elucidation. *To take* (*get*) *trial*, to make inquiry. *Sc. Obs.*

1557–72 *Diurnal Occur.* (Bann. Cl.) 72 Ane conventioun ordanit to convene in Sanctandrois for taking tryell of the matter aboue writtin. 1575 in *Maitl. Cl. Misc.* I. 126 To be diligent for gaitting of tryall of the deid barne that wes cassin furth in Foresteris wynd. *a* 1657 SIR W. MURE *Ps.* cxxxix. 3 My pathes, my lying doun thou eyest, And narrow tryall takes.

**4.** Action, method, or treatment adopted in order to ascertain the result; investigation by means of experience; experiment. *Rule of trial and error*: see POSITION 3.

1570 LEVINS *Manip.* 13/14 A Tryall, *experimentum.* 1608 BACON *Comment. Sol.* Wks. 1868 IV. 63 A collection of phainomena, of surgery, destillations, minerall tryalls. 1726 LEONI *Alberti's Archit.* II. 106/1 In what season it is best to make these tryals has not been..declared. 1806 HUTTON *Course Math.* I. 256 They may be all readily solved by the following easy rule of Double Position, sometimes called Trial-and-Error. 1812 WOODHOUSE *Astron.* xxxix. 387 Astronomers have sought, by the indirect methods of trial and conjecture, to avoid them. 1907 *Verney Mem.* I. 536 He will have some alders set in the wet places..for a trial.

† **b.** The result ascertained by testing; effect; efficacy. (Cf. PROOF *sb.* 7.) *Obs. rare.*

1559 MORWYNG *Evonym.* 30 They giue it to drinke against the fittes of the falling sycknes with maruellous tryall.

† **5.** *transf.* Evidence, proof. *Obs.*

1532 FRITH *Let.* Wks. (1573) 81/1 What can be more triall of a faythfull hart, then to aduenture not onely to ayde and succour by the meanes of other,..but also personally to visite the poore oppressed? 1577 HARRISON *England* II. vi. (1877) I. 153, I will not saie..if I should, I could easilie bring my triall. *a* 1586 *Satir. Poems Reform.* xxxvi. 86 Thow..gave gud tryell of thy lytill treuth. *a* 1670 SPALDING *Troub. Chas. I* (1851) II. 33 Thir newis turned to nothing, for there wes no tryel found that sic materis were trew.

**6.** A testing of qualifications, attainments, or progress; examination.

*spec.* the examination prescribed by Presbyteries for the licensing of preachers or the ordination of ministers; also, in Scotland, the public probation of a Lord of Session; (*pl.*) at Eton College, Harrow, and other schools, the terminal examination; at Oxford and Cambridge, short for *trial eights* (see 13).

1672 *Mem. J. Fraser* in *Sel. Biog.* (Wodrow Soc.) II. 309 After trial of my gifts and conversation by several exercises and pieces of trial..they agreed to trust me in the name of Christ with the dispensation of the Gospel. 1706 *Act 6 Anne* c. II. Art. xix, No writer to the signet [shall] be capable to be admitted a lord of the session unless he undergo a private and publick tryal on the civil law. 1708 J. CHAMBERLAYNE *St. Gt. Brit.* (1710) 425 The Manner of Admission into this Society [*sc.* the Faculty of Advocates] is..sometimes, tho' rarely, by a Trial in the Scots Law. 1710 T. HALYBURTON *Mem.* ii. (1824) 238, I underwent the other parts of my private trials and on May 1, 1700 was ordained at Ceres. 1815 SCOTT *Guy M.* xix, He went to stand trial for his license as a preacher. 1847 in Hare *Story my Life* (1896) I. 223 We are busy at our Trial, which we do with our masters in form. 1849 HARPER *E. Erskine* i. 11 Mr. Erskine was after the usual trials licensed by the Presbytery of Kirkcaldy. 1905 VACHELL *The Hill* ix, If we put our backs—and heads —into Trials, we can easily get a remove. 1908 G. D. LAW in Boston *Acc. Life* 84 *note*, The trials of a probationer about to be ordained were similar to those of a divinity student applying for licence. 1908 *Westm. Gaz.* 7 Oct. 12/1 The ceremony..which every Scottish judge has to 'pass', is called his 'trials'.

† **7.** The fact of undergoing or experiencing; experience. *To have* (or *make*) *trial of*, to experience. *Obs.*

1600 J. PORY tr. *Leo's Africa* v. 257 Whereof I my selfe haue had often triall. 1631 WEEVER *Anc. Fun. Mon.* 512 Henries command was a Law; of which Cromwell had a triall. 1656 EARL MONM. tr. *Boccalini's Advts. fr. Parnass.* I. xxiii. (1674) 26 Tyrants, by whom they made trial of the most deplorable miseries. 1657 — tr. *Paruta's Pol. Disc.* 72 Even Augustus himself made trial of many Insurrections in Spain, Germany, and in the Eastern parts. 1687 A. LOVELL tr. *Thevenot's Trav.* I. 178 We had a tryal then of these Panniers, and for my part I was much at my ease.

**8.** An attempt to do something; an endeavour, effort. (In quot. 1614, an attempt to gain.)

1614 RALEIGH *Hist. World* v. iii. § 11 [He] went to a greater enterprise; euen to fight in tryall of the Empire. 1638 SIR T. HERBERT *Trav.* (ed. 2) 72 Ecbar is poysoned;..after foureteene dayes violent torment and trialls to expell the poyson, yeelds up his ghost. 1720 SWIFT *Fates Clergymen* Wks. 1755 II. II. 24 But this I confess is a trial too dangerous often to engage in. 1793 SMEATON *Edystone L.* § 98, I proposed to make a trial for landing if the weather should suit. 1853 LYNCH *Self-Improv.* i. 6 If you take away trial, you get rid of failure, but of success too. 1860 TYNDALL *Glac.* I. xviii. 128 He said he would make the trial.

**9.** That which puts one to the test; *esp.* a painful test of one's endurance, patience, or faith; hence, affliction, trouble, misfortune. (Cf. 2 b.)

1754 RICHARDSON *Grandison* (1781) III. i. 9 How would such a creature..have behaved under such tryals? 1831 SCOTT *Cast. Dang.* xiv, Trials by which the most generous affections may be soured. 1838 DICKENS *Nich. Nick.* iv, All people have their trials. 1865 — *Mut. Fr.* I. iv, Lavinia has not known the trial that Bella has known. 1885 'MRS. ALEXANDER' *At Bay* ix, Her life has been a very trying one. ..I trust its trials will soon be over.

**10.** Something that serves as a sample or proof of a manufacture or material, or of the skill of a maker or operator, the progress of an operation, etc.; *spec.* in *Pottery manuf.* a piece of clay or the like by which the progress of the firing process may be judged; a trial-piece.

1608 R. WIFFIN etc., in *Capt. Smith's Wks.* (Arb.) 128 Capt. N. being dispatched with the tryals of pitch, tarre, glasse, frankincense, and sope ashes, with that [=what] clapbord and wainscot could bee provided. 1609 ? N. POWELL *ibid.* 154 Wee..produced a triall of glasse; made a well.. re-couered our Church [etc.]. 1825 J. NICHOLSON *Operat. Mechanic* 469 In different parts of the oven..rings of Egyptian black clay are placed, as trials, by which an experienced fireman can tell how much longer the process must be carried on. 1870 J. ROSKELL in *Eng. Mech.* 18 Feb. 548/2 If the Copper is intended for rolling purposes, then a large sample termed a trial is taken.

† **b.** See quot. *Obs. rare.*

1611 COTGR., *Languette*,..the tryall, or cocke of a ballance.

**c.** Short for *trial-ball, trial-gallop.*

1884 *Illustr. Lond. News* 1 Nov. 410/3 Three guineas for a 'lose' (besides four guineas for every private 'trial'). 1897 'TIVOLI' (Bleakley) *Short Innings* vi, 'That was a trial!' he explained. 'It was the second ball!' cried Tuckett.

**11.** A sieve or sifting screen. Now *dial.*

1825 J. NICHOLSON *Operat. Mechanic* 446 The spout.. receives the bark from the stones, and conveys it into the tryal..which tryal is wired, to shift or dress the bark as it descends from the stones. 1885 *Cheshire Gloss.*, *Trial*, a coarse sieve in a winnowing machine.

**12.** Phrases. *On trial* (sense 2), on the basis or condition of being tried, as *to take* a person or thing *on trial*, to take subject to the condition of being satisfactory when tried. *To be on* (*his, her,* or *its*) *trial* (2, 6), to be in a state of probation until it is seen how he or it will succeed or work. See also *to put* a person *on his trial*; *to bring to trial*; *to stand* (*one's*) *trial* in sense 1.

1741 WESLEY *Wks.* (1872) I. 301 The others were put upon trial again. 1889 JESSOPP *Coming of Friars* iii. 133 During the thirteenth century they [the monks] were, so to speak, upon their trial. 1904 H. PAUL *Hist. Eng.* I. 409 Speaking at the Trinity House on the 9th of June [1855], Prince Albert declared that Constitutional government was on its trial, and urged the duty of placing more confidence in the Ministers of the Crown. [But Pr. Albert's words, as given in *Illustr. Lond. News* 16 June, 1855, and other newspapers, were 'Gentlemen, our Constitutional Government is undergoing a heavy trial' [etc.]. See also Th. Martin *Life of Pr. Consort* (1874–9).] *Mod.* I will take the maid for a month on trial. You may have the dust-extractor three days on trial.

**13.** *attrib.* and *Comb.* Of or pertaining to trial; made, done, used, or taken for or as a trial: as *trial animal, -chord, -correction, day, -examination, -feat, -fire, -ground, heat* (HEAT *sb.* 10), *-hole, -hour, -impression, lot, marriage, match* (Cricket), *number, -ordeal, -pan, parlour, plot, race, stone, time, -working, -yard*; also *pl.*, as *trials cap, man, secretary*; also **trial balance**, in book-keeping by double entry, an addition of the whole of the entries on each side of the ledger, when the sum of the debits ought to balance the sum of the credits; **trial bar**, 'a cuboid used by turners for testing the inclination of planes' (*Cent. Dict. Suppl.* 1909); **trial bit**, an adjustable bit for measuring a horse's mouth (Knight *Dict. Mech.* 1877); **trial-book**, a book in which a cashier enters sums paid and received so as at any time to take out a trial balance of cash in hand; **trial case** = *trial sight*; **trial cock** (see quot.); **trial court**, a court before which trials take place in the first instance; distinguished from an appeal court; **trial eight**, *Boat-racing*, an eight-oared boat's provisional crew, from among whom some members of the final eight may be chosen; **trial glasses** (*pl.*), a set of graduated glasses for ascertaining the requirements of defective vision; **trial-jar** (see quot.); **trial judge, t. justice**: cf. *trial court*; **trial jury**, a petty jury, distinguished from a grand jury (Webster, 1911); **trial lawyer**, a lawyer practising in a trial court; **trial-list**, the register of causes or prisoners to be tried; the calendar (*Cassell's Encycl. Dict.* 1888); **trial-piece**, something made or taken as a specimen; *spec.* a coin or the like struck as a test of the die, or as a specimen of the design; **trial plate**, in assaying coin (see quot.); **trial proof**, a proof taken from a plate during the process of engraving to show its state; **trial sight** (see quot.); **trial (spectacle) frame**, an adjustable frame with revolving graduated fittings to hold *trial glasses* (q.v.); **trial square**, a try-square (Knight *Dict. Mech.* 1877); **trial-trip**, a trip taken to test the speed and other qualities of a vessel, etc.

1905 *Brit. Med. Jrnl.* 27 May 1141 The dose which the *trial animals stood will set up serious symptoms in the infected ones. 1890 *Times* 11 July 13/5 Witness drew his attention to the figures in the cashier's *trial-book, and asked how he accounted for them. 1901 *Daily Chron.* 23 Nov. 9/5 A '*Trials' cap is eagerly sought after, and the inclusion of 'Old Blues' robs other men of their chance. 1889 BRINSMEAD *Hist. Pianoforte* 187 The *trial-chord, when struck, should produce a rapid beat or series of undulations of sound. 1825 J. NICHOLSON *Operat. Mechanic* 167 *Trial or gauge cocks.. to ascertain the height of the water in the boiler. 1867–77 G. F. CHAMBERS *Astron.* I. xi. 129 Applying this..to the eclipses in the form of a *trial-correction. 1907 *Westm. Gaz.* 4 Apr. 2/1 The new law permits the Government to appeal from certain judgments of the *trial Court. 1593 SHAKS. *2 Hen. VI*, III. i. 114 That Doyt that ere I wrested from the King..Be brought against me at my *Tryall day. 1878 STUBBS *Lect. Med. & Mod. Hist.* (1886) 157 [The Crusades] were the *trial-feat of the young world. 1598 SHAKS. *Merry W.* v. v. 88 With *Triall-fire touch me his finger end. 1891 *Cent. Dict.*, *Trial glasses. 1895 *Arnold & Sons' Catal. Surg. Instrum.* 125 Spectacle Frame, plain, for Trial Glasses. 1878 URE *Dict. Arts* IV. 323 The Mont Cenis tunnel formed the greatest *trial-ground ever brought to the attention of inventors and makers of either rock-drills or air-compressors. 1909 *Westm. Gaz.* 29 May 9/4 Arrangements have been made for aeroplane flights..at Wembley, where an excellent stretch of suitable trial-ground exists. 1894 A. ROBERTSON *Nuggets*, etc. 212 He turned from side to side, apparently looking for a digger's *trial-hole that would suit his purpose. 1907 SIR W. M. RAMSAY in *Expositor* Sept. 203 The terms of our firman permitted.. the making of trial-holes. 1847 MARY HOWITT *Ballads*, etc. 317 In this, the fiercest *trial-hour, My doubting soul sustain! 1879 H. PHILLIPS *Addit. Notes Coins* 1 There are also leaden *trial-impressions of the dies. 1877 KNIGHT *Dict. Mech.*, **Trial-jar*, a tall glass vessel used for containing liquids to be tested by the hydrometer. 1908 *Westm. Gaz.* 11 June 2/1 They..gave orders for *trial lots [of soft wire-rods]. 1897 *Outing* (U.S.) XXIX. 485/1 The result is a lot of fast *trial-machines, all of one general family. 1905 *Daily Chron.* 1 July 6/4 Both crews are awarded their distinctive medals, and every member may wear the 'Trials' cap—the white flannel cap with the crossed oars. The '*Trials' man is out of the ruck. 1833 NYREN *Yng. Cricketer's Tutor* 58 The whole country round would flock to see one of their *trial matches. 1884 F. J. BRITTEN *Watch & Clockm.* 273 The Greenwich method of arriving at the *trial number. 1874 RAYMOND *Statist. Mines & Mining* 500 Inasmuch as the samples of ore were not large in quantity, they commenced making small *trial-pans. 1555 BRADFORD *Let.* in Foxe *A. & M.* (1570) 1834/2 You are in the schole-house and *triall parlour of the Lord. 1663 *Inscr. Simon's Petit. Crown*, Thomas Simon most humbly prays your Majesty to compare this his *tryall piece with the Dutch [etc.]. 1830 [E. HAWKINS] *Anglo-French Coinage* 64, I cannot consider this as current money, neither does it exactly come under the description of a trial piece. 1859 *Edin. Rev.* CIX. 377 Cicero attempted to make words, and his trial-pieces were very neat..struck of good metal. 1904 *Westm. Gaz.* 11 July 10/2 Some interesting trial-pieces..executed in true fresco on a suitable ground before beginning to paint on the wall. 1883 *Encycl. Brit.* XVI. 484/1 Pieces cut from *trial plates of standard fineness,..being assayed against the coins under examination. 1906 *Westm. Gaz.* 20 Aug. 3/1 The county [Gloucestersh.] happens to be one which affords a great variety of experiment owing to the variety of its soils...Hence the advent of the *trial plots. 1891 *Cent. Dict.*, *Trial proof. 1900 *Westm. Gaz.* 8 Nov. 1/3 These rare mezzotints are all in trial proof state. 1903 *Daily Chron.* 3 Aug. 3/3 The prints exist in a far less 'restricted' number than he imagines, and are not by any means chiefly trial-proofs. 1847 *Illustr. Lond. News* 10 July 23/2 The first day is to be occupied with the *trial races. 1884 KNIGHT *Dict. Mech.* Supp., **Trial Sight* (Optical), an oculist's case of trial lenses, etc., for testing sight. *Ibid.* 903/2 A *trial spectacle frame, with double grooves to each eye, graduated to 180°...Used for finding the axis of imperfect vision in astigmatism or cylindrical cornea. 1877 W. R. COOPER *Egypt. Obelisks* xxii. (1878) 126 A *trial stone for every idle Greek or ignorant tourist to cut his initials upon. *c* 1841 ARNOLD in Stanley *Life* (1845) II. x. 300 The first seventy years of the eighteenth century,..the abused *trial time of modern Europe. 1860 PUSEY *Min. Proph.* 79 It was a long trial-time, in which they were taught entire dependance upon God. 1858 SIMMONDS *Dict. Trade*, **Trial-trip*, an experimental trip. 1902 ELIZ. L. BANKS *Newspaper Girl* 211, I wouldn't let any reporter take the trial trip, anyway. 1905 A. R. WALLACE *Life* II. 182 The house being used for prospecting purposes and *trial-workings.

† **Trial**, *sb.*² *Obs. rare.* In 5 **tryall.** [App. an ignorant combination of TRI- + -AL.] A group or set of three, a triad. (In the second quot. confusedly used for each one of the three.)

? *a* 1500 *Chester Pl.* i. 7, I am the tryall of the trynitie that neuer shall be twynninge. *Ibid.* 17 These three tryalls in a Trone and true Trynitie Be grounded in my godhead, exalted by my excellence.

**Tri·al**, *a. Gram.* [f. L. *tri-*, stem of *trēs, tria* three + -AL, after *dual.*] Applied to a 'number' or inflected form denoting three, in some languages of New Guinea and Polynesia; = TRINAL *a.* 3.

1886 J. INGLIS *In New Hebrides* ix. 99 There are four numbers in the personal pronouns [used by the Aneityumese], the singular, the dual, the trial, and the plural; as *I, we two, we three,* and *we all.* 1911 *Bible in World* July 206/2 The Kiwai language is one of the most difficult in New Guinea.. The verb..distinguishes singular, dual, trial (3) and plural number both in the subject and object.

**Trialate**: see TRI- 1.

**Trialism** (trəi·ăliz'm). [f. as prec. + -ISM, after *dualism.*]

**1.** The doctrine of the threefold constitution of man, as body, soul, and spirit, or other three separate essences. 1891 in *Cent. Dict.*

**2.** A union of three states or countries.

1908 *Westm. Gaz.* 16 Jan. 2/1 The substitution of a Trialism, consisting of Austria, Hungary, and Bohemia,..

for the present Dualism. **1911** *Q. Rev.* July 260 There has been revived in Austria the idea of 'trialism', that is to say, the amalgamation of all the Servo-Croatian countries of the Monarchy into a unit, which, with the German States and Hungary, would form a kind of federal empire.

**Triality** (trəiˌæ·lĭti). *rare.* [f. as prec., after *duality, plurality.*]

†**1.** The holding of three benefices at once. *Obs.*

*a* **1529** SKELTON *Col. Cloute* 564 Of tryalytes, And of tot quottes, They commune lyke sottes. **1536** *Act* 28 *Hen. VIII*, c. 16 § 4 Pluralities, unions, trialities, appropriacions..And other bulles, breves, and faculties. **1587** HARRISON *England* II. ii. (1877) I. 63 So plentifullie gat he by his perquisits, as elections, procurations, appeales, preuentions, pluralities, tot quots, trialities [etc.]. **1637** BASTWICK *Litany* II. 9 The Pope selleth nonresidences, pluralityes, trialityes, totquots, the Prelats doe the same.

**2.** The condition or quality of being threefold.

**1872** DORAN *Mem. Gt. Towns* xiii. (1878) 294 Dr. Wigan ..not only wrote on the Duality of the Mind, but on the Triality (if we may coin a word), the threefold excellence, of the Brighton atmosphere.

**Trialogue** (trəi·ălǫg). [Erroneous formation on supposed analogy of *dialogue*, the first syllable of this being mistaken for the prefix DI-[2] = two. Cf. med.L. *trialogus* (Wyclif).] A dialogue or colloquy between three persons.

**1532** MORE *Confut. Tindale* Wks. 431/2 As though it wer a dyalogue, or rather a tryalogue betwene himself, the messenger and me. **1691** WOOD *Ath. Oxon.* I. 21 Trialogue between Tho. Bilney, Hugh Latimer, and W. Repps. **1721** D'URFEY *Two Queens Brentford* v. i, This Epilogue..is a Trialogue, and to be perform'd between Sol, Rain, and Boreas. **1900** G. W. E. RUSSELL *Conf. Bks. & Men* 150 A trialogue, called 'A contention between a wife, a widow, and a maid'.

**Triamide** (trəi·ămǝid). *Chem.* [f. TRI- 5 a + AMIDE.] A compound in which the three acid hydroxyls (OH) of a tribasic acid are replaced by three amidogen groups ($NH_2$): the hydrogen of the amidogen groups may be replaced by metals or by one or more monovalent radicals; e.g. citramide, $C_3H_4(OH)(CO.NH_2)_3$, the triamide of citric acid, $C_3H_4(OH)(CO.OH)_3$; cyanuramide or melamine, $C_3N_3(NH_2)_3$, the triamide of cyanuric acid, $C_3N_3(OH)_3$. For the earlier view of the structure of triamides, see quot. 1863–72.

**1862** MILLER *Elem. Chem.* (ed. 2) III. 427 As an instance of a *secondary triamide*, phenylcitramide may be given. **1863–72** WATTS *Dict. Chem.* I. 173 *Primary Triamides.*—They represent 3 molecules of ammonia, in which 3 atoms of hydrogen are replaced by a triatomic acid-radicle:—Phosphamide..$N^3.(PO)'''.H_6$. **1866** ODLING *Anim. Chem.* 19 $C_3N_3(H_2N)_3$ Cyanuric triamide.

**Triamine** (trəi·ămǝin). *Chem.* [f. TRI- 5 a + AMINE.] A carbon compound containing three amidogen or amino-groups ($NH_2$), but excluding the amides, in which the amidogen may be viewed as replacing acid hydroxyl groups; the hydrogen of the amidogen groups may be replaced by one or more monovalent radicals: see also quot. 1868.

**1868** FOWNES *Elem. Chem.* (ed. 10) 882 Triamines. These are bases derived from..three molecules of ammonia.. $N_3H_9$, by substitution of..trivalent alcohol-radicals for a part or the whole of the hydrogen. A portion of the hydrogen may at the same time be replaced by univalent alcohol-radicals. **1887** TIDY *Mod. Chem.* (ed. 2) 758 Aniline red is a salt of base *rosaniline*, $C_{20}H_{19}N_3$. This..is a triamine.

**Trian** (trəi·ăn), *a. Her.* [app. f. L. *trēs, tria* three + -AN.] In *trian aspect*: see quot.: cf. THREE-QUARTERED b.

*c* **1828** BERRY *Encycl. Her.* I. Gloss., *Trian-aspect*, showing three-fourth parts of the body, as an eagle, &c. in a trian-aspect: it is what painters term three-quartered.

‖**Triandria** (trəiˌæ·ndriă). *Bot.* [mod.L. (Linnæus 1735), f. mod.L. *triandr-us*, f. Gr. τρεῖς three + ἀνήρ, ἀνδρ- man, male, taken as = stamen: see -ANDROUS.] The third class in the Linnæan Sexual System, comprising plants having hermaphrodite flowers with three stamens not cohering; also an order in some classes, comprising plants with three stamens. So **Tria·nder** (*rare*), a triandrous plant; **Tria·ndrian, Tria·ndrious,** and (usually) **Tria·ndrous** *adjs.*, having three stamens; belonging to the class (or order) *Triandria.*

**1828** WEBSTER, **Triander.* **1748** LINNÆUS *Hortus Upsaliensis* Classis iii. 13 *Triandria. **1760** J. LEE *Introd. Bot.* II. xxiii. (1788) 139 Of the twentieth Class, *Gynandria*.. Order II, *Triandria*, comprehending such Plants as have three Stamina. **1828** WEBSTER, **Triandrian.* **1786** ABERCROMBIE *Gard. Assist., Arrangem.* 35 Willow tree..Common white leaved...*Triandrious, white barked. **1830** LINDLEY *Nat. Syst. Bot.* 261 [Irideæ] differ from Amaryllideæ..in being *triandrous. **1870** HOOKER *Stud. Flora* 430 Hierochloe...Holy Grass..upper flower 2-sexual 2-androus; 2 lower male, 3-androus.

**Triangle** (trəi·æŋg'l, trəiˌæ·ŋg'l), *sb.* Also 5 **tri-, tryangyl,** 5–7 **tryangle,** 6 **triangil, tryanghel,** 6–7 **triangill;** 5–6 **treangle,** 6 **treeangle, treangell.** [a. F. *triangle* (13th c. in Godef. *Compl.*), or ad. its source, L. *triangulum*, sb. neut. from *triangulus* adj. three-cornered, f. *tri-*, TRI- + *angulus* ANGLE.]

**1.** *Geom.*, etc. A figure (usually, a plane rectilineal figure) having three angles and three sides.

In *mod. Geom.* a triangle is regarded as a system of three points not collinear, together with the three straight lines joining them; or as a system of three straight lines each intersecting the two others at different points.

*Circular triangle*, a plane triangle formed by three intersecting circular arcs. *Spherical triangle*, a triangle formed by three arcs upon the surface of a sphere: see SPHERICAL. *Triangle of forces*, the theorem in statics that if three forces in one plane, acting at one point, be in equilibrium, three straight lines in that plane parallel to their directions will form a triangle whose sides are proportional to their magnitudes.

**1398** TREVISA *Barth. De P. R.* XVII. cviii. (Tollem. MS.), Some [nuts] ben distinguid in þe cop as it were with þe schap of a triangle [orig. *per formam trianguli*]. *c* **1400** *Lanfranc's Cirurg.* 258 Þe nose is maad of .ij. boones in þe maner of a triangle in þis maner. ΔΔ. **1551** RECORDE *Pathw. Knowl.* I. Defin., A triangle is nothinge els to say, but a figure of three corners. **1560** DAUS tr. *Sleidane's Comm.* 451 Betwyxt Caleis, Arde and Grauelyn, Townes..set as it were a treangle. **1646** SIR T. BROWNE *Pseud. Ep.* 25 In every triangle, two sides which soever be taken are greater then the side remaining. **1781** GIBBON *Decl. & F.* xvii. II. 3 The figure of the imperial city [Constantinople] may be represented under that of an unequal triangle. **1885** LEUDESDORF *Cremona's Proj. Geom.* 145 A series of theorems..relating to the inscribed pentagon, quadrangle, and triangle..a series of correlative theorems relating to the circumscribed pentagon, quadrilateral, and triangle.

**b.** A figure of this form used symbolically (e.g. an equilateral triangle as a symbol of the Trinity), or in magic or necromancy. In *Her.* a figure of this form as a bearing; *in triangle*, said of three or more bearings arranged in the form of a triangle.

**1584** R. SCOT *Discov. Witchcr.* XV. ii. (1886) 322 He is a lier, except he be brought into a triangle, and there he speaketh divinelie. **1766** PORNY *Heraldry* (1787) 175 Azure, three Trouts fretty in Triangle Argent. **1810** SOUTHEY *Kehama* XIX. viii, The sacred Triangle.. Holding the Emblem which no tongue may tell. *c* **1828** BERRY *Encycl. Her.* I. Gloss., *Triangle*, this sometimes occurs as a bearing in coat-armour. See Cross of Triangles, or twelve triangles in cross. **1864** BOUTELL *Her. Hist. & Pop.* xix. § 5. (ed. 3) 311 A nail in every point thereof, in triangle. **1894** *Parker's Gloss. Her.* s. v., Charges may be described as *fretted in triangle*, e.g. in the arms of Troutbeck (under *Salmon*)... The insignia of the Isle of Man are sometimes blazoned as *flexed in triangle.*

**c.** *fig.* A group or set of three, a triad.

**1621** T. WILLIAMSON tr. *Goulart's Wise Vieillard* 129 In this sacred triangle is included the renouncing of our selues. **1659** WHITING (*title*) Old Jacob's Altar, newly repaired; or, the Saints Triangle of Dangers, Deliverances, and Duties. **1907** *Daily Chron.* 5 Dec. 3/4 Mrs. Dudeney's novel..deals with the eternal triangle, which, in this case, consists of two men and one woman.

**2.** Something having the form of a triangle; any three-cornered body, object, or space.

*a* **1618** SYLVESTER *Mem. Mortalitie* II. lx, Th' Earth cannot fill thy heart's unequall Angles, Thy heart's a Triangle, the earth's a Round. **1788** GIBBON *Decl. & F.* l. (1846) V. 2 The Arabian peninsula may be conceived as a triangle of spacious but irregular dimensions. **1791** NEWTE *Tour Eng. & Scot.* 120 The present fort, which is a triangle, has two bastions. **1843** CARLYLE *Past & Pr.* II. i, In what wig and black triangle dost thou walk abroad? **1847** MRS. A. KERR tr. *Ranke's Hist. Servia* i. 13 The Servians..in the first half of the 14th century..formed the strongest power of the Illyrian triangle. **1895** R. W. CHAMBERS *King in Yellow, Demoiselle D'Ys* i, A long wavering triangle of water-fowl drifted southward over our heads.

*spec.* **natural objects.*

**b.** *Palmistry.* A triangular figure made by three of the lines of the hand: see quot. 1653.

*c* **1460** METHAM *Wks.* (E.E.T.S.) 86 A tryangyl that ys off one length, evyn on alle partys..betokynnyth bodyly strengh and bold off herte. *Ibid.*, The fyrste lyne ys the fyrst parte off the tryangyl, and yt gothe aboute the hylle of the thombe. **1653** R. SANDERS *Physiogn.* 58 This Triangle is made in the hand by three Lines, that of Life, the middle natural Line, and that of the Head.

**c.** *Astron.* The constellation *Triangulum*, north of *Aries*, characterized by three stars in the positions of the angular points of an isosceles triangle.

Also, *Triangulum minus*, the Lesser Triangle, a constellation immediately south of this, introduced by Hevelius in 1690, but now disused; *Triangulum australe*, the Southern Triangle, a modern constellation near the South Pole.

**1551** RECORDE *Cast. Knowl.* (1556) 265 By hir [Andromeda's] lefte foot is ther a small constellation..commonly called the Triangle. **1868** LOCKYER *Guillemin's Heavens* (ed. 3) 334 The Altar and the Southern Triangle, which lie along the Milky Way in looking towards the pole.

**d.** *Anat.* Applied, with defining words, to the triangular areas bounded by certain muscles: as

*Triangles of the neck, anterior* (subdivided into the *submaxillary triangle* and the *superior* and *inferior carotid triangles*) and *posterior* (subdivided into the *occipital* and *subclavian triangles*); *Triangle of Petit*, above the crest of the ilium; *Scarpa's tr.*, in the upper part of the thigh.

**1846** BRITTAN tr. *Malgaigne's Man. Oper. Surg.* 147 The inferior triangle of the popliteal space is bounded on each side by the heads of the gastrocnemius. **1876** *Clin. Soc. Trans.* IX. 41, I removed all the enlarged glands in front of the sterno-mastoid, and thus cleared the anterior triangle of the neck. **1897** *Allbutt's Syst. Med.* IV. 418 [An abscess] may open superficially in the loin through the triangle of Petit.

**e.** *Entom.* A triangular marking or space on an insect's wing.

**1832** [see 4]. **1891** *Cent. Dict., Triangle*...In *entom.* a large three-sided cell found in the wings of many dragon-flies..often called the *discoidal* triangle, to distinguish it from the *internal* triangle, which adjoins it on the inner side, and the *anal* triangle, which lies close to the anal border of the wing.

**f.** A species of box-fish of triangular form, as *Ostracion trigonum.*

***artificial objects.*

**g.** A small ornament or piece of jewellery of a triangular form.

**1528** *Will of W. Mores* (Somerset Ho.), A triangill of siluer and gilte. **1529** *Will of Leigh* (ibid.), My corsse gurdell wt the Treeangle of flowres of silver and golde. **1531** *Rec. St. Mary at Hill* 48 A demysent [girdle] with..a pendantte a treangell of selver and gelt. **1632** J. HAYWARD tr. *Biondi's Eromena* 120 This Iewell..a triangle of three rich diamonds, each angle..enriched with a great pearle.

†**h.** *Eccl.* A stand or frame on which copes were hung up. *Obs.*

**1532** in *Archæol. Cant.* (1872) VIII. 124 Item a treangle for copys, a presse [*Editor's Note*, a crane or stand for hanging copes]. **1538** in *Archæologia* XLIII. 226, ij chestes and the tryangle for the same ornaments to be hengyd. **1849** ROCK *Ch. of Fathers* II. vi. 43 [A doubtful statement].

†**i.** (More fully *triangle virginal*), an early kind of keyboard stringed instrument. *Obs.*

[**1661** PEPYS *Diary* 14 June, I sent to my house by my Lord's order his shipp and triangle virginall.] **1662–3** *Ibid.* 18 Mar., This day my tryangle which was put in tune yesterday, did please me very well.

**j.** A musical instrument of percussion, consisting of a steel rod bent into a triangular form, but open at one corner; it is struck with a small straight steel rod. Also *transf.* = TRIANGLER.

**1801** in BUSBY *Dict. Mus.* **1811** LADY GRANVILLE *Lett.* (1894) I. 21 We play upon the..guitar, triangle, and castagnettes. **1878** F. HUEFFER in Grove *Dict. Mus.* I. 28/1 He is said to have accepted the appointment of supernumerary triangle at the Gymnase. **1913** *Times* 14 May 8/5 The only percussion (even the usual drums are excluded) consists of triangle and cymbals.

**k.** Name for a kind of large tripod composed of three poles or spars joined at the top, bearing a pulley for hoisting heavy weights, or for weighing: see also quot. 1867.

**1699** EVELYN *Kal. Hort.* (ed. 9) 63 If the Tree be too ponderous to be lifted perpendicular by the Hand alone, by applying a Triangle and Pully..draw out the Tree. **1707** MORTIMER *Husb.* (1721) I. 187 Set up three Poles (like unto a Triangle wherewith they usually weigh heavy Ware) spreading at the Bottom. **1867** SMYTH *Sailor's Word-bk.*, *Triangle*,..a machine formed by spars for lifting weights, water-casks, &c. Also, a stage hung round a mast, to scrape, paint, or grease it. **1873** in *5th Rep. Dep. Kpr. Irel* 26 The Records were lowered through the aperture in the centre of the floor by means of a rope, supported by a triangle raised over the opening.

**l.** *Mil.* (Usually *pl.*) A tripod, orig. formed of three halberds stuck in the ground and joined at the top, to which soldiers were formerly bound to be flogged; a structure resembling this.

[**1796** GROSE *Dict. Vulg. T.* s. v. *Halbert*, Soldiers of the infantry, when flogged, being commonly tied to three halberts, set up in a triangle, with a fourth fastened across them.] **1847** in WEBSTER. **1853** STOCQUELER *Milit. Encycl.*, *Triangles*, a wooden instrument consisting of three poles so fastened at top that they may spread at bottom in a triangular form...An iron bar, breast high, goes across one side of the triangle. The triangles were used in some regiments for..inflicting military punishments. **1871** G. LAWRENCE *Anteros* i. (1872) 11 He was unsparing both of his tongue and of the lash—the triangles were an honoured institution in those days. **1897** P. WARUNG *Tales Old Regime* 29 Already, at Molong [Australia], there is one military-post and a triangles, and at Wellington Valley there is another military-post and another triangles.

**m.** *Pottery.* A triangular piece of baked ware, with points projecting from the angles, placed between pieces of biscuit ware to prevent their adhering to each other when baking.

**1877** in KNIGHT *Dict. Mech.*

**n.** *Angling.* A set of three hooks fastened together so that their barbs are at the angular points of a triangle.

**1867** F. FRANCIS *Angling* iv. (1880) 116, I had used a single flight of small brazed triangles. **1904** GALLICHAN *Fishing Spain* 145 The flying triangles are to blame. It is not often that one loses a fish hooked on the tail triangle.

**o.** A drawing-instrument in the form of a right-angled triangle of wood, vulcanite, etc.; a set square.

**1877** KNIGHT *Dict. Mech.*, *Triangle*... A three-cornered straight-edge,..for drawing parallel, perpendicular, or diagonal lines. It has one right angle, the two others being each of 45°, or one of 30° and the other of 60°.

**3.** Collectors' name for certain moths. See also 4.

**1832** RENNIE *Conspect. Butterfl. & Moths* 55 The Triangle (*Gr[aphiphora] Triangulum*, Ochsenheimer) appears the end of July. *Ibid.* 164 The Triangle (*P[seudotamia] trigonana*, Stephens). Near London.

**4.** *Comb.*, as *triangle-marked* adj.; **triangle moth**, *Limacodes asellus*; **triangle-ways** *adv.* (*rare*) = TRIANGLEWISE.

**1689** *Lond. Gaz.* No. 2485/4, 16 silver Trencher-Plates;.. marked with a Cypher triangle-ways. **1832** RENNIE *Conspect. Butterfl. & Moths* 228 The Triangle-marked Purple (*G[racillaria] purpurea*, Haworth). Wings..purple, with a three-cornered central halfband...The Triangle-marked Red (*G. stigmatella*, Stephens)...The Triangle Marked Buff (*G. ochracea*, Haworth).

†**Triangle,** *a. Obs.* [ad. L. *triangulus*, f. TRI- + *angulus* corner.] Having three angles; three-cornered, triangular. Also quasi-*adv.* In the form of a triangle, triangularly.

**1474** CAXTON *Chesse* 136 In one of the corners was made a tour treangle as a shelde. **1525** tr. *Jerome of Brunswick's Surg.* B ij/1 The bony part [of the nose] hath .ij. tryangle bonis. *a* **1548** HALL *Chron., Edw. IV*, 201 b, Three hilles, not in equal distaunce,..but liyng in maner although not fully triangle. **1660** BLOOME *Archit.* A j, *Gutta*, are drops sometime round, sometime in Triangle fashion. **1661** [see TRIANGLE *sb.* 2 i]. **1803** SHAW *Gen. Zool.* IV. II. 444 Triangle Sparus [a fish]. Mentioned by Cepede from Commerson: native of the Indian seas.

*Comb.* **1655** MRQ. WORCESTER *Cent. Inv.* § 69 A little triangle scrued Key. *Ibid.* § 71 A Key perfectly square,..no heavier then the triangle-scrued Key.

**Triangle,** *v. rare.* [f. TRIANGLE *sb.*]

† **1.** *intr.* ? To lie or extend in the form of a triangle. *Obs.*

**1595** *Aberdeen Regr.* (1848) II. 129 The said wmquhill Mr Androis yard dyk ascendis south eist..triangling throw an[d] athort the hedis of the yardis of the said vmquhill Badie.

**2.** *trans.* To flog at the triangles (*sb.* 2 l).

**1879** L. WINGFIELD *Lords of Strogue* III. iv. 110 His henchman had been well triangled..to extort evidence against his master.

**Triangled** (trəi·æŋg'ld, trəi,æ·ŋg'ld), *a.* Forms: see TRIANGLE *sb.*; also 5 **triangulit,** 6–7 **-uled.** [f. as prec. + -ED; cf. L. *triangulāt-us.*]

† **1.** Three-cornered, triangular. *Obs.*

**1486** *Bk. St. Albans, Her.* e v, Euery body triangulit is moore of lengthe then of brede and naamly conyt. *a* **1505** in Kingsford *Chron. Lond.* (1905) 250 A Cupbourde of 6 stages height, beyng Tryangled. **1570** BILLINGSLEY *Euclid* XI. def. x. 314 If the base of a Pyramis be a triangle, then is it called a triangled Pyramis. **1613** ZOUCH *Dove* 24 Triangl'd Sicily. **1688** R. HOLME *Armoury* III. 293/2 There are Round, Square, Triangled,..many cornered,..Pies.

† **b.** *Arith.* = TRIANGULAR 2 b. *Obs. rare*⁻¹.

**1603** HOLLAND *Plutarch's Mor.* 796 It [the number of nine] standeth of two triangled numbers, to wit, a senarie and a ternarie.

**2.** Arranged in a triangle; situated at the angular points of a triangle. ? *Obs.*

**1610** GUILLIM *Heraldry* III. xxiii. (1611) 167 Fishes are borne..Imbowed, extended, endorsed..fretted and triangled. **1632** LITHGOW *Trav.* IV. 135 In one of these triangled points..standeth the Pallace of the Great Turke.

**3.** *Her.* Divided into triangles by crossing lines.

*c* **1828** BERRY *Encycl. Her.* I. Gloss., *Triangled* and *Triangléе*, formed into triangles, as indentings point in point.

**Triangler** (trəi·æŋglər). [f. as prec. + -ER¹.] A performer on the triangle in a musical band.

**1840** *New Monthly Mag.* LX. 79 Mr. Gamut not knowing where to find another professional triangler. *a* **1868** M. J. HIGGINS *Ess.* (1875) 251 His grandson, who had lately been elevated to the post of triangler in the band of the Duke of York's school.

† **Tri·anglewi·se,** *adv. Obs.* [f. TRIANGLE *sb.* or *a.* + -WISE.] In the manner or form of a triangle; triangularly.

**1523** FITZHERB. *Husb.* § 4 Somme plowes haue a bende of yron tryanglewise, sette there as the plough eare shulde be. **1597** A. M. tr. *Guillemeau's Fr. Chirurg.* 18 b/1 When as we cutte the skinne, we must doe it triangle wyse. **1670** NARBOROUGH *Jrnl.* in *Acc. Sev. Late Voy.* I. (1694) 62 They lie Triangle-wise one of another.

† **Tria·nglify,** *v. Obs. nonce-wd.* [f. as prec. + -[I]FY.] *trans.* To make into or arrange in a triangle or triangles.

**1589** FLEMING *Virg. Georg.* III. 49 Vnder Septentrio (or Charles waine, seuen stars trianglifide).

App. an erroneous rendering of *septem subjecta trioni* (Verg. *Georg.* iii. 381), *trioni* being dat. of *trio* plough-ox: see SEPTENTRION.

**Triangular** (trəi,æ·ŋgiŭlăı), *a.* (*sb.*) Also 6–7 **-er, -are,** (7 **triangler**). [ad. late L. *triangulār-is*: see TRIANGLE and -AR¹. Cf. OF. *triang(u)lier* (13th c. in Godef.).]

**1.** Having, or arranged in, the form of a triangle; contained by three sides and angles; three-cornered, three-sided.

**1541** R. COPLAND *Guydon's Quest. Chirurg.* E iv, The bony substaunce [of the nose] hath two trianguler bones wherwith the brydge is reysed vp. **1590** SPENSER *F. Q.* II. ix. 22 The frame thereof seemd partly circulare, And part triangulare. **1644** EVELYN *Diary* 3 Feb., A triangular brick building. **1776** WITHERING *Brit. Plants* (1796) II. 375 *Populus*... Leaves nearly triangular, toothed and angular. **1825** SCOTT *Talism.* i, His triangular shield suspended round his neck.

**b.** Situated at the angular points of a triangle. (In quots. quasi-*adv.*) ? *Obs.*

**1622** DRAYTON *Poly-olb.* xxii. 1152 Three..hils that stand Trianguler. **1707** MORTIMER *Husb.* (1721) II. 74, 3 or 4 quarter Stakes set triangular or quadrangular.

**c.** Having three edges, as a prism or pyramid; three-edged, trihedral, triquetrous.

**1644** DIGBY *Nat. Bodies* xxix. § 1. 257 Those..cunning in Optikes..by refractions..make all sortes of colours out of pure light: as we see..in..triangular glasses, or prismes. **1665** SIR T. HERBERT *Trav.* (1677) 384 Other strange Fish we had..some were globous, others triangular. **1727–41** CHAMBERS *Cycl.* s. v. *Pyramid*, The pyramid is said to be triangular, quadrangular, &c. as the base is triangular, quadrangular, &c. **1807** HUTTON *Course Math.* II. 262 To find the Number of Balls in a Triangular Pile. **1852** MRS. STOWE *Uncle Tom's C.* vi, The small, sharp, triangular beech-nuts lay scattered thickly on the ground. **1873** E. SPON *Workshop Receipts* Ser. I. 330/2 Triangular glovers' needles for sewing up skins.

**d.** Contained by triangles, as a solid figure; of which the faces are triangles. *rare.*

**1805–17** R. JAMESON *Char. Min.* (ed. 3) 144 Triangular Dodecahedron..consists of two six-sided pyramids, joined base to base.

**2.** Pertaining or relating to a triangle: as *triangular compasses*, a kind of compasses with three legs, used for taking off triangles; *triangular co-ordinates* (*Geom.*), a kind of trilinear co-ordinates. *Triangular quadrant*: see quot. 1706.

**1701** MOXON *Math. Instr.* 21 Triangular Compasses, containing 3 Legs or Feet, to take off at once any Triangle used on Maps, Globes, etc. **1706** PHILLIPS (ed. Kersey), *Triangular Quadrant*, is a Sector with a loose Piece to make it an Equilateral Triangle; having the Calendar graduated on it, with the Sun's Place, Declination, &c. It is an Instrument of great Use in the Arts of Dialling, Navigation, and Surveying. **1807** T. YOUNG *Lect. Nat. Philos.*, etc. I. x. 102 Triangular compasses are sometimes used for laying down a triangle equal to a given triangle.

**b.** Arith. *Triangular numbers* (also *ellipt.* as sb. pl. *triangulars*), the first series of POLYGONAL numbers (1, 3, 6, 10, 15, 21, etc.), obtained by continued summation of the natural numbers 1, 2, 3, 4, 5, 6, etc.: see quot. 1837.

**1706** W. JONES *Syn. Palmar. Matheseos* 165 In a Rank of Triangulars their Sums are called Triangulars or Figurates of the 3d Order. **1796** HUTTON *Math. Dict.* I. 468/2 The triangular numbers 1, 3, 6, 10, 15, &c. **1806** — *Course Math.* (1810) I. 214 The sides or faces in either the triangular or square piles, are called arithmetical triangles; and the numbers..in these, are called triangular numbers. **1837** BABBAGE *Bridgew. Treat.* 37 They are called triangular numbers because a number of points corresponding to any term can always be placed in the form of a triangle.

**3.** *fig.* Relating to or taking place between three persons or parties, three-sided; also, constituting a triad or set of three, threefold, triple.

**1812** JEFFERSON *Writ.* (1830) IV. 175 The triangular war must be an idea of the Anglomen and malcontents. **1816** T. L. PEACOCK *Headlong Hall* xv, Avarice, luxury, and disease constitute the triangular harmony of the life of man. **1871** W. WHITE *Jrnls.* (1898) 244 We had an interesting triangular talk. *Mod.* In these elections there will be several triangular contests.

**4.** *Comb.*: **a.** parasynthetic, as *triangular-bodied, -headed, -leaved, -pointed, -spotted*; also *triangular-wise* adv. **b.** *Bot.* in combination with other adjs. of form, as *triangular-cordate, -crenate, -dentate, -hastate, -ovate, -rhomboid, -subulate.*

**1707** MORTIMER *Husb.* (1721) I. 189 Placing another Row at the Ends where the forked Sticks meet Triangular-wise. **1731** MILLER *Gard. Dict.* s. v. *Aloe*, The upright triangular-leav'd viscous Aloe. **1768** PARSONS in *Phil. Trans.* LVIII. 194 The triangular-headed Cameleons. **1804** SHAW *Gen. Zool.* V. 420 Triangular-bodied, unarmed Trunk-Fish. **1823–5** SIR J. E. SMITH *Eng. Flora* (1828) II. 9 Mercury Goose-foot. Leaves triangular-arrow-shaped, entire. **1870** HOOKER *Stud. Flora* 264 Scrophularia nodosa..leaves ovate or tri-angular-cordate. **1887** W. PHILLIPS *Brit. Discomycetes* 99 Margin triangular-dentate.

**Triangularity** (trəi,æŋgiŭlæ·rĭti). [f. as prec. + -ITY; cf. med.L. *triangulāritās* (Duns Scotus, *a* 1308: prob. older).] The quality of being triangular; triangular form.

*a* **1688** CUDWORTH *Immut. Mor.* (1731) 14 Things are White by Whiteness, and Black by Blackness, Triangular by Triangularity, and Round by Rotundity. *a* **1751** BOLINGBROKE *Ess., Hum. Knowl.* v. Wks. 1754 III. 436 We say, for instance, not only that certain figures are triangular, but we discourse of triangularity. **1788** T. TAYLOR *Proclus' Comm.* I. 48 Its triangularity would be essential, supposing every species of triangles but the isosceles extinct. **1805** R. P. KNIGHT *On Taste* I. iii. (ed. 2) 38 It partook..of the qualities of the immutable idea of triangularity.

**Tria·ngularly,** *adv.* [f. as prec. + -LY².] In a triangular way; in the form or manner of a triangle.

**1604** T. WRIGHT *Passions* v. 221 The heart..of man triangularly respecteth the blessed Trinitie, every corner a Person, and the solide substance your common Essence. **1610** NORDEN *Spec. Brit., Cornw.* (1728) 70, 3 whyte stones sett trianguleriy as pillers supportinge another stone. **1681** GREW *Museum* III. I. v. 307 A Spar with Crystals Triangularly pointed. **1702** W. J. *Bruyn's Voy. Levant* xxxiv. 134 This Town is Triangularly built.

**b.** *fig.* As three parties to a transaction (cf. TRIANGULAR 3).

**1892** *Sat. Rev.* 31 Dec. 758/2 The Russian refusal to negotiate 'triangularly' with England and China.

† **Tria·ngulary,** *a. Obs.* [f. as TRIANGULAR: see -ARY².] = TRIANGULAR 1.

**1622** MABBE tr. *Aleman's Guzman d'Alf.* II. 191 A kinde of triangulary sayle. **1653** URQUHART tr. *Rabelais* I. xliv. 197 Lifting up in the upper part of the scul the two triangularie bones called sincipital.

**Triangulate** (trəi,æ·ŋgiŭlĕt), *a.* (*sb.*) [ad. med.L. *triangulāt-us* triangular (Albertus Magnus, *a* 1255), f. L. *triangul-um* TRIANGLE: see -ATE²; but possibly pa. pple. of med.L. **triangulāre* vb.]

**1.** Having three angles, triangular; in later use only in *Nat. Hist.*, applied to parts or structures of triangular form.

**1611** HOPTON *Speculum Topogr.* II. ii. 187 Be it round, square, triangulate, or multiangulate. **1819** G. SAMOUELLE *Entomol. Compend.* 166 Antennæ with the three last joints forming an oblong triangulate mass. **1852** DANA *Crust.* I. 307 A few species have a somewhat triangulate and subrostrate form.

**2.** Made up or composed of triangles. (In later use in *Nat. Hist.*) † Also as *sb.* a figure made up of triangles (*obs.*).

**1610** HOPTON *Baculum Geodæt.* VI. xiv. 135 The sides of a tryangulate are more by 2, then the tryangles whereof he is made. **1611** — *Speculum Topogr.* I. ii. 7 Of Triangulates. A Triangulate is a mixt figure composed of Triangles, and may be resolued into the same againe. **1766** *Compl. Farmer* s. v. *Surveying*, Right-lined figures..are either triangles or triangulate, that is, such as are compounded of, and resolvable into triangles.

**3.** *Nat. Hist.* Marked with triangles; having triangular markings.

**1891** *Cent. Dict.* s. v., A triangulate bar is generally formed of triangles with their bases together..; it is a form of ornamentation common on the wings of *Lepidoptera*.

Hence **Tria·ngulately** *adv.*, in a triangulate manner; triangularly; so as to form triangles.

**1852** DANA *Crust.* I. 428 Carpus triangulately dilated at inner margin. **1891** *Cent. Dict.* s.v., A margin or surface marked triangulately with black.

**Triangulate** (trəi,æ·ŋgiŭleⁱt), *v.* [f. L. *triangul-um* + -ATE³, or f. ppl. stem of med.L. **triangulāre*: cf. also F. *trianguler.*]

**1.** *trans.* *Surveying* (also *transf.*, as in *Astron.*). To measure and map out (a region or territory) by tracing a series or network of triangles from a base-line and measuring their sides and angles; to determine (e. g. a distance or altitude) in this way. Also *absol.*

**1833** HERSCHEL *Astron.* iv. 157 We may, as upon the earth, triangulate, by measuring..their [the stars'] angular distances from each other. **1855** F. GALTON in *Cambr. Ess.* 93 A running survey of a new country is best made by triangulating as much as is practicable. **1891** *Cent. Dict.* s. v., To triangulate the height of a mountain.

*fig.* **1860** O. W. HOLMES *Elsie V.* xix, A sagacious person, ..who has triangulated a race, that is taken three or more observations from the several standing-places of three different generations.

**b.** *gen.* or *allusively*. To mark out into triangles.

**1853** KANE *Grinnell Exp.* xxvi. (1856) 212 The entire plain is triangulated with ice-barricades. **1879** J. TIMBS in *Cassell's Techn. Educ.* IV. 343/2 The system of wires.. stretching across the sky-line of great thoroughfares, and visibly triangulating the metropolis in every direction.

**2.** To divide or convert into triangles.

**1864** WEBSTER, *Triangulate*..2. To make triangular. **1901** C. W. BROWN in *Cycl. Tour. Cl. Gaz.* July 298/2 A plan which completely triangulates the four-sided figure of the frame and converts it into two distinct triangles.

Hence **Tria·ngulating** *vbl. sb.* and *ppl. a.*

**1861** WILSON & GEIKIE *Mem. E. Forbes* x. 280 He was ready and eager to avail himself of a triangulating cruise with Lieutenant Spratt. *Ibid.* 290 Messrs. Spratt and Forbes proceeded to make the triangulating observations.

**Triangulated** (trəi,æ·ŋgiŭleⁱtėd), *ppl. a.* and *a.* [f. as prec. adj. or vb. + -ED.]

**1. a.** = TRIANGULATE *a.* 1. **b.** Formed into a triangle. **c.** Converted or divided into triangles; composed of triangles.

**1610** HOPTON *Baculum Geodæt.* II. i. 18 If right lined, whether a Tryangle or Tryangulated? **1752** J. HILL *Hist. Anim.* 286 The triangulated Ostracion. **1897** *Westm. Gaz.* 6 Dec. 9/1 A [bicycle] frame..worthy of attention is that known as the 'triangulated', designed by Mr. C. W. Brown for ladies' machines.

**2.** Measured or mapped out by means of triangles, as in surveying. (In quot. *fig.*)

**1894** *Thinker* VI. 344 There may be a vast terra incognita lying back of the triangulated regions of consciousness.

**Triangulation** (trəi,æŋgiŭlēⁱ·ʃən). [ad. med.L. *triangulātiōn-em* (Abelard, *a* 1142), n. of action from **triangulāre* to TRIANGULATE. So F. *triangulation* (1835 in *Dict. Acad.*).] The action or process of triangulating.

**1.** The tracing and measurement of a series or network of triangles in order to survey and map out a territory or region.

**1818** *Blackw. Mag.* III. 463 The English triangulation, begun by General Roy. **1826** T. DRUMMOND in *Phil. Trans.* CXVI. II. 334 Slieve Snaght, the highest hill of Innishowen, ..forms an important point in the triangulation, which connects the North of Ireland with the western islands of Scotland. **1863** A. C. RAMSAY *Phys. Geog.* xxxi. (1878) 550 The triangulation of Scotland for the Ordnance Survey. **1864** J. HUNT tr. *Vogt's Lect. Man* Index, Triangulation of the skull.

**2.** Division of a rectilinear figure into triangles.

**1891** *Cent. Dict.*, *Triangulation*, 1. A making triangular; formation into triangles.

**Triangulato-** (trəi,æŋgiŭlēⁱ·to), used as combining form of med. or mod.L. *triangulātus*, TRIANGULATE *a.*, in terms of *Nat. Hist.* denoting a combination of this with another form, as *triangulato-e·xcavate, -o·vate, -subo·vate* adjs.

**1849** DANA *Geol.* App. I. (1850) 714 Very broad triangulato-ovate. **1852** — *Crust.* I. 630 This segment is deeply triangulato-excavate posteriorly.

**Tria·ngulator.** [a. mod.L. *triangulātor* (Pontanus, *a* 1500), agent-n. from **triangulāre* to TRIANGULATE.] One who triangulates. **1891** in *Cent. Dict.*

**Triangulo-** (trəi,æ·ŋgiŭlo), used as combining form of L. *triangulum* TRIANGLE, in **triangulo-pyramidal, triangulo-triangular** *adjs.*, applied to certain series of figurate numbers: see quots., and cf. PYRAMIDAL 4, TRIANGULAR 2 b.

[**1646** F. VIETA *Opera* 294 In prima adfectione per unitatis crementum, in secunda per numeros triangulos, in tertia per numeros pyramidales, in quarta per numeros triangulo-triangulos, in quinta per numeros triangulo-pyramidales.] **1715**

*Phil. Trans.* XXIX. 183 A series of Fractions..whose Numerator is a given Number and Denominators are triangular or pyramidal or triangulo-triangular Numbers, &c. **1785** HUTTON *Math. Tables* 7 The several orders of figurate numbers, which he [Vieta] calls triangular, pyramidal, triangulo-triangular, triangulo-pyramidal.

**Tria·nguloid,** *a. rare.* [f. L. *triangul-um* TRIANGLE + -OID.] Resembling a triangle; of somewhat triangular form.

**18..** H. SPENCER (O.), A trianguloid space.

† **Triannual** (trəi,æ·niuăl), *a. Obs. rare.* [f. TRI- 3 + ANNUAL.] Occurring every three years; lasting for three years; = TRIENNIAL.

**1640** *Par. Acc. St. Barth. by Exchange* in *Archæologia* XLV. 78 Pd. the ringers for joy of the tryannual Parliament, o. 2. 6. **1656** EARL MONM. tr. *Boccalini's Advts. fr. Parnass.* I. lxix. 133 He was deputed a Triannual President of the Isle of Negrapont.

¶ **b.** Occurring thrice a year.

**1901** *Daily Chron.* 8 June 5/2 The ladies..we learn..will hold 'tri-annual invitation meetings'...That, we suppose, means an invitation once in four months.

**Triannulate**: see TRI- 1.

**Triantelope** (trəi,æ·ntĭlǒup). *Australia.* Also **triantulope.** Popular corruption of TARANTULA, applied to a large spider of the genus *Voconia.*

**1846** C. P. HODGSON *Remin. Australia* 173 The tarantulas, or 'triantelopes' as the men call them, are large, ugly spiders. **1909** *Daily Chron.* 13 Apr. 4/7 What is a 'triantelope'?..Originally it was the children's..way of saying tarantula, but people generally came to adopt it.

**Trianthous**: see TRI- 1.

**Tria·psal,** *a.* [f. TRI- + L. *aps-is, apsid-em* APSE + -AL.] Having three apses. Also **Tria·psidal.**

**1849** FREEMAN *Archit.* I. viii. 191 A vestige of the triapsal termination of the basilicas. **1875** — *Venice* (1881) 131 The arrangement of the triapsidal basilica. **1883** *Mag. of Art* June 338/2 It is triapsal, the transepts as well as the choir ending in a semi-circle. **1898** J. T. FOWLER *Durham Cathedr.* 22 The original triapsidal east end.

**Triarch** (trəi·ɑɹk), *sb.* [f. TRI- + *-arch* in *tetrarch*: cf. Gr. τρίαρχος chief ruler, and next.]

**1.** The ruler of one of three divisions of a country or territory.

**1886** J. BURY in *Jrnl. Hellenic Stud.* VII. 314 These three lords were called the *terzieri* (*tierciers*) of Negroponte. Hopf calls them *Dreiherrn*, and we may call them *triarchs*. *Ibid.* 321 William laid claim..to the north of Euboia, calling himself a triarch.

**2.** In Fourier's social organization: A ruler of the third (ascending) rank.

**1848** *Tait's Mag.* XV. 706 There will be duarchs for four phalanx, triarchs for 12, tetrarchs for 48, and so on until the douzarch reigns over a million.

Hence **Tri·archate,** *rare*⁻¹ [cf. *patriarchate*], an association of three rulers.

**1881** HARTSHORNE *Glance 20th C.* 15 Then, the triarchate; is it not surprising? Pope, Patriarch, and Primate of Canterbury! Roman, Greek, and Anglican, united at last!

**Triarch** (trəi·ɑɹk), *a. Bot.* [f. TRI- + Gr. ἀρχή beginning, origin.] Arising from three points of origin, as the woody tissue of a root: cf. DIARCH.

**1884** BOWER & SCOTT *De Bary's Phaner.* 354 As a rule the xylem-plates are diarch in Lupinus varius,..triarch in Pisum sativum,..tetrarch in Phaseolus. *Ibid.* 363 Triarch and tetrarch bundles sometimes occur in thick roots of species which are usually diarch. **1895** [see TETRARCH *a.*].

† **Tri·archist.** *Obs. rare*⁻¹. [f. TRI- + Gr. ἀρχή beginning + -IST.] One who maintains the existence of three original principles of being.

**1678** CUDWORTH *Intell. Syst.* I. iv. § 13. 216 Plutarch was both a Triarchist and a Ditheist,—an assertor of Three Principles, but of Two Gods.

**Triarchy** (trəi·ɑ̈ki). [f. TRI- + Gr. -αρχία government, or ad. Gr. τριαρχία triumvirate.]

**1.** The government or jurisdiction of a triarch; one of three divisions of a country ruled by triarchs.

**1601** HOLLAND *Pliny* V. xviii. I. 101 There lye betweene and about these citties, certaine Royalties called Triarchies, containing every one of them as much as an whole countrey.

**2.** Government by three rulers or powers jointly; three persons associated in government, a triumvirate. Cf. TETRARCHY 2.

**1656** BLOUNT *Glossogr.*, *Triarchie* (*triarchia*), a government, where three are in like authority. **1658** in PHILLIPS. **1859** *Morn. Star* 28 Apr. 4/3 The Emperor of the French..proposed to the Queen that the pentarchy of the five Powers should be put an end to, and a triarchy of France, England, and Russia, be established in its stead. **1892** *Nation* (N. Y.) 20 Oct. 305/3 He proposed to establish a sort of triarchy, which was to consist of the Emperor of Austria and the King of Prussia..and a sovereign to be chosen periodically by and from the heads of the smaller principalities.

**3.** A group of three districts or divisions of a country each under its own ruler.

**1660** HOWELL *Parly Beasts* 143 [The rational soul] dividing her Empire into a Triarchy,..governs by three Viceroys, the three Faculties. **1799** S. TURNER *Anglo-Sax.* I. II. x. 355 The island, though nominally under an hexarchy, was fast verging into a triarchy. **1888** *Voice* (N. Y.) 27 Dec., Three ambitious little kingdoms..Greece, Servia and Bulgaria. This triarchy cannot long endure; one must take the lead, with the prospect of absorbing the others.

**Triarctic** to **Triareal**: see TRI- 1.

† **Tria·rian,** *a.* (*sb.*) *Obs.* [f. L. *triāri-ī* (see TRIARY) + -AN.] Consisting of *triarii* (see TRIARY); also *allusively.* **b.** *sb.* (*pl.*) The *triarii.*

**1642** *View of Print. Book int. Observat.* 39 The Triarian legion, in which they put their last and chiefest strength. **1658** PHILLIPS, Triarians. **1663** COWLEY *Ode Restor. Chas. II* xi, Let our weak Days lead up the Van; Let the brave Second and Triarian-Band, Firm against all impression stand. **1715** M. DAVIES *Athen. Brit.* I. 65 His best Veteran and Triarian, Regular Troops.

**Tri:arti·culate,** *a.* [f. TRI- 1 + L. *articulus* joint + -ATE [2].] Three-jointed.

**1826** KIRBY & SP. *Entomol.* III. 518 Flies..with triarticulate antennæ. **1875** C. C. BLAKE *Zool.* 296 The Colopoda..—The feet are very short,..indistinctly triarticulate.

† **Tri·ary.** *Obs.* Pl. **triaries.** [ad. L. *triāri-ī*, sb. pl. (see below), f. *trēs, tri-* three.] *pl.* (also *collect. sing.*) The *triarii*, or soldiers of the third line in the ancient Roman army. Also *fig.* or *allusively.*

**1533** BELLENDEN *Livy* IV. ix. (S.T.S.) II. 79 Seand þe Inemyis sett ernistlie to wyn þe tentis, he Ischit on þare richt hand with ane feirss cumpany of triaris. **1589** IVE *Du Bellay's Instr. Warres* 76 Naming..the Souldiers of the fyrst battaile *Hastaries*; those of the second *Princes*, and those of the third *Triaries.* **1663** COWLEY *Ess. in Verse & Prose, Danger Procrast.*, If I should draw upon you all my forces out of Seneca and Plutarch upon this subject, I should overwhelm you, but I leave those as Triary for your next charge. **1679** V. ALSOP *Mel. Inquir.* II. viii. 368 This is the last retreat of these Gentlemen; hither they retire as to their Triary and strong reserves.

**Trias** (trəi·æ̆s). [a. late L. *trias*, a. Gr. τριάς the number three: see TRIAD. In 2, a. Ger. *Trias.*]

**1.** The number three; a set of three, a triad.

**1610** BOLTON *Elem. Armories* 182 One is onely best: next to that the Trias, Ternio, or number three, and so the rest of the Odde to Fifteen. **1635** HEYWOOD *Hierarch.* II. 68 Sometimes, what's proper vnto Man alone, Is giuen to this Trias, three in One: As, when we attribute vnto him Wings. **1728** H. HERBERT tr. *Fleury's Eccl. Hist.* I. 250 This is the first time that we meet in the ancients with the word *Trias*, or Trinity in this sense. **1864** *Daily Tel.* 9 Sept., A people with whom drinking, smoking, and spitting are the Trias of social bliss.

**2.** *Geol.* Name for the series of strata lying immediately beneath the Jurassic and above the Permian; so called because divisible, when typically developed (as in Germany), into three groups (*Keuper, Muschelkalk,* and *Bunter Sandstein*); represented in Britain by the Upper New Red Sandstone and associated formations.

**1841** MURCHISON, etc. in *Proc. Geol. Soc. Lond.* (1842) III. 403 The Trias of German geologists. **1842** SEDGWICK in *Hudson's Guide Lakes* (1843) 204 In France and Germany the series of rocks..admits of a triple division (called 'Trias', or the 'Triassic system'). **1876** PAGE *Adv. Text-Bk. Geol.* xvi. 289 The reason for regarding the Trias as mesozoic. **1912** *Return Brit. Museum* 169 A slab of Rhynchocephalian and other footprints from the Trias of Storeton, Cheshire.

*attrib.* and *Comb.* **1855** J. PHILLIPS *Man. Geol.* 248 Bands of red and blue trias-like sandstones and clays. **1867** W.W. SMYTH *Coal & Coal-mining* 240 Reaching coal beneath the Permian and Trias formations.

**Triassic** (trəi,æ·sik), *a. Geol.* [f. TRIAS + -IC.] Of or belonging to the Trias; *Triassic system* = TRIAS 2.

**1841** SIR P. G. EGERTON in *Proc. Geol. Soc. Lond* (1842) III. (*title of paper*) A Notice on the Occurrence of Triassic Fishes in British Strata. **1868** LYELL *Princ. Geol.* (ed. 10) II. III. xlix. 592 A long narrow island..composed partly of granite and partly of triassic sandstone. **1889** *Science-Gossip* XXV. 122/2 The Triassic and Permian formations show a time of 'great physical disturbance,..volcanic eruptions discharging vast beds..of lava and layers of volcanic ash'.

**Triaster**: see TRI- 4 a.

**Triatic** (trəi,æ·tik), *a. Naut.* [Origin obscure; app. f. TRI- three.] In *triatic stay*: see quots.

**1841** DANA *Seaman's Man.*, *Triatic Stay*, a rope secured at each end to the heads of the fore and main masts, with thimbles spliced into its bight, to hook the stay tackles to. **1867** SMYTH *Sailor's Word-bk.* [as in Dana, with this addition] This term applies also to the jumper-stay, extending in schooners from the mainmast-head to the foremast-head, clearing the end of the fore gaff. **1895** *Funk's Stand. Dict.* s.v., *Triatic stay* (*Naut.*), a device consisting of two pendants attached respectively to the foremast-head and mainmast-head, and having thimbles spliced to the other ends, to which the third part, or span, is attached, as are also the stay-tackles; used principally for hoisting boats in and out of a vessel.

**Triatomic** (trəi,ătǫ·mik), *a. Chem.* [f. TRI- + ATOM + -IC.] **a.** Having three atoms in the molecule. † **b.** = TRIVALENT. *Obs.* **c.** Containing three hydroxyl groups (OH); = TRIHYDRIC *a.*[1]

**1862** MILLER *Elem. Chem.* (ed. 2) III. 53 To the triatomic group [of elements] belong nitrogen, phosphorus, arsenic, antimony, bismuth, and gold. **1863–72** WATTS *Dict. Chem.* I. 464 To classify them [primary hydrides and chlorides] in four principal groups, thus: Monatomic, Diatomic, Triatomic, Tetratomic. **1872** *Ibid.* VI. 237 Nitrogen, which combines with 3 atoms of hydrogen, is triatomic, triadic, or trivalent. **1882** ROSCOE *Elem. Chem.* xxxv. 320 The possible number of derivatives of the triatomic alcohols is much larger than that of either of the preceding classes. **1894** *Times* 18 Aug. 10/3 No doubt the passage of..the diatomic form of the substance to the triatomic form..takes place with evolution of heat. **1903** *Edin. Rev.* Oct. 393 It [radium] can ozonise oxygen—that is, condense it by rendering its molecules tri-atomic.

**Tria·xal,** *a.* [f. TRI- 1 + L. *axis* AXIS + -AL.] Having three axes: said in *Geom.* of co-ordinates; in *Zool.* of sponge-spicules. Also (more regularly) **Tria·xial** *a.*

**1886** *Proc. Zool. Soc.* 21 Dec. 581 A regular triaxial network is formed. **1891** *Cent. Dict.* s.v., Triaxal coördinates. **1896** DK. ARGYLL *Philos. Belief* 110 The intercalation of triaxial spiculae, at the proper intervals or interspaces.

**Triaxon, Triaxonian**: see TRI- 1.

**Triazine** (trəi,æ·zəin). *Chem.* [f. TRI- 5 a + AZ(OTE + -INE [5].] A general term, invented by Widman (1888), for compounds the molecules of which contain a cyclic group consisting of three carbon and three nitrogen atoms.

These may be arranged in three ways: (1) the consecutive or vicinal form, also called *osotriazine*; (2) the unsymmetrical; (3) the symmetrical, also called *cyanidine*: thus (1) $N\left\langle{}^{N.C}_{N.C}\right\rangle C$, (2) $N\left\langle{}^{N.C}_{C.C}\right\rangle N$, (3) $N\left\langle{}^{C.N}_{C.N}\right\rangle C$.

**1894** *Jrnl. Chem. Soc.* LXVI. I. 57 New Triazole and Triazine Derivatives. **1900** SMITH *Richter's Org. Chem.* II. 604 Alkyl- and phenyl-derivatives of symmetrical triazine or cyanidine are obtained.

**Triazo-** (trəi,æ·zo). *Chem.* [f. TRI- 5 c + AZO-.] A formative of the names of compounds containing three atoms of nitrogen arranged in a ring, thus $-N\left\langle{}^{N}_{\dot{N}}\right.$, as *triazobenzene*, $C_6H_5N\left\langle{}^{N}_{\dot{N}}\right.$. It has also been used somewhat differently, as in *triazoacetic acid*, $N_2\left\langle{}^{CH(CO_2H).N_2}_{CH(CO_2H).N_2}\right\rangle CH(CO_2H)$. Also *attrib.* as in *triazo compounds, derivatives*, etc.

**1896** *Jrnl. Chem. Soc.* LXX. I. 338 Ethylic diazoacetate ..with concentrated alkali, triazoacetic acid. **1901** *Ibid.* LXXX. I. 104 Preparation of Azoimides (Triazo-compounds) ..p-*Triazobromobenzene* forms crystals melting at 20°. **1910** DESCH & LAPWORTH in *Chem. Soc. Ann. Reps.* VII. 124 Substances containing the triazo-group, $N_3$.

**Triazole** (trəi,æ·zōul). *Chem.* Also **-ol.** [f. TRI- 5 a + AZ(OTE + *-ole* (= *oleum* oil).]

**a.** A general term for compounds the molecules of which contain a cyclic group consisting of three nitrogen and two carbon atoms. The ring may be arranged in two ways, $N\left\langle{}^{C.N}_{C.\dot{N}}\right.$ and $N\left\langle{}^{C.C}_{N.\dot{N}}\right.$.

**b.** A compound having the formula $C_2H_3N_3$ and containing a triazole ring with two double bindings. Five isomers are possible, and are variously named; e. g. *triazole, osotriazole, isotriazole.*

**1888** MUIR & MORLEY *Watts' Dict. Chem.* I. 423 Triazol. A name given to the hypothetical $C_2H_3N_3$. **1894** [see TRIAZINE]. **1900** SMITH *Richter's Org. Chem.* (ed. 3) II. 512 Triazole, $C_2H_3N_3$, melting at 121° and boiling at 260°, is obtained from formamide and formhydrazide.

**Tribade** (tri·băd, ‖ triba·d). [a. F. *tribade* (16th c.), or ad. its source L. *tribas, -ad-*, Gr. τριβάς, τριβαδ-, f. τρίβειν to rub.] A woman who practises unnatural vice with other women. Also *attrib.*

**1601** B. JONSON *Forest* x. *Præludium*, Light Venus..with thy tribade trine, invent new sports. **1890** H. H. ELLIS *Criminal* iii. § 7. 106 Such emblems are common among pæderasts and tribades.

Hence **Tri·badism, Tri·bady.**

**1811–19** *Woods and Pirie v. Gordon* (*Index Catal. Libr. Surgeon-General's Office U. S. A.* XIV. 752), Lady C. G... who had charged them with the practice of tribadism. **1864** tr. *Caspar's Forensic Med.* (N. Syd. Soc.) III. 335 Tribadism. Even in the Old Testament there is distinct allusion to this form of sexual aberration. **1882** PAYNE *1001 Nights* II. 156. **1909** *Cent. Dict. Suppl.*, Tribady.

**Tribal** (trəi·băl), *a.* [f. L. *trib-us* TRIBE + -AL: hence mod.F. *tribal* (Littré).] Of or pertaining to a tribe or tribes; characteristic of a tribe.

**1632** LITHGOW *Trav.* VI. 296 They are..of colour Tauny, boasting much of their triball Antiquity. **1740** WARBURTON *Div. Legat.* V. iii. 240 Even the tribal Sceptre was established long after the death of Jacob. **1849** STEPHENS *Bk. Farm* (1891) III. 409 The white face has been well described as the 'tribal badge' of the Hereford [ox]. **1906** PETRIE *Relig. Anc. Egypt.* viii. 58 Of these some are probably tribal gods.

Hence **Tribally** (trəi·băli) *adv.*, as a tribe; in the manner of, or in relation to a tribe.

**1890** *Science* 27 June 383/2 It is probable that Professor Putnam is not justified in concluding that the people of the two sections were tribally identical. **1908** F. SPENCE *Chr. Reunion* vii. 109 *note*, The election (federally or tribally) of the elders of the Ecclesia by its members.

**Tribalism** (trəi·băliz'm). [f. TRIBAL + -ISM.] The condition of existing as a separate tribe or tribes; tribal system, organization, or relations.

**1886** *Edin. Rev.* Apr. 443 No national life, much less civilisation, was possible under the system of Celtic tribalism. **1893** GOLDW. SMITH *Ess.* 176 National churches have lapsed into something very like tribalism in this respect [about war]. **1898** *Weekly Reg.* 29 Oct. 561 Those who have set the maxims of Christ above those of narrow tribalism.

So **Tri·balist** *rare*, a tribesman.

**1888** in *Cassell's Encycl. Dict.*

**Tribasic** (trəibē̆i·sik), *a. Chem.* [f. Gr. τρι-, TRI- + βάσ-ις base + -IC.] Having three bases.

**1.** Of an acid: Having the property of exchanging three atoms of hydrogen for three of potassium or sodium, and thus forming a salt; e. g. phosphoric acid, $H_3PO_4$, which reacts with sodium hydroxide, NaOH, forming trisodium phosphate, $Na_3PO_4$. Of a salt: Containing three molecules of the basic oxide; e. g. tribasic lead acetate.

In the first half of the 19th c., the acid oxide was considered to be the acid itself (not as now when *acid* means the compound of this oxide with water), and *tribasic acid* was applied to an oxide which united with three equivalents of base to form a salt: hence the name.

**1837** GRAHAM in *Phil. Trans.* 62 A new nomenclature of these salts..I offer for consideration..Tribasic phosphate of water..(3 HO, $PO_5$). Tribasic phosphate of water and soda..(NaO, 2 HO, $PO_5$). Tribasic phosphate of soda and water..(2 NaO, HO, $PO_5$). Tribasic phosphate of soda..(3 NaO, $PO_5$). **1849** D. CAMPBELL *Inorg. Chem.* 317 Salts which are isomorphous with the salts of tribasic phosphoric acid. **1862** MILLER *Elem. Chem.* (ed. 2) III. 255 The..synthetic experiments of Berthelot..have shown that the ordinary varieties of natural fats and oils, are the tribasic ethers of the triatomic alcohol glycerin. **1875** *Ure's Dict. Arts* (ed. 7) III. 863 *Phosphates of Soda*...The principal are the normal tribasic phosphate, the well-known rhombic phosphate [etc.]. **1899** CAGNEY *Jaksch's Clin. Diagn.* vii. (ed. 4) 378 Being a tribasic acid, it forms three classes of salts—acid, neutral, and basic.

†**2.** Of an element: = TRIATOMIC b. *Obs.*

**1862** MILLER *Elem. Chem.* (ed. 2) III. 52 Triatomic or Tribasic elements, each atom of which is in combination equivalent to $H_3$ or three atoms of hydrogen. **1880** CLEMINSHAW *Wurtz' Atom. The.* 204 Nitrogen has been represented as a tribasic element derived from the type of three condensed molecules of hydrogen.

**Tribasilar**: see TRI- 1.

**Tribbill, tribble**, obs. var. TREBLE.

**Tribbler**: see TRIBLER.

**Tribe** (trəib), *sb.* Forms: *α.* 3 (*pl.*) **tribuz**, 4–6 **tribu**, (*pl.* **-us**), 5 **trybu-s**. *β.* 4–6 **trybe**, (7 *Sc.* **tryb**), 4– **tribe**. [In earliest form, ME. *tribu*, a. OF. *tribu*, Sp., Pg. *tribu*, It. *tribù*, *tribo*, a. L. *tribus* (*u*-stem); but as the OF. has not been found in the sing. before 14th c. the ME. *tribuz* of 1250 may directly represent L. *tribūs* pl. The later *tribe* may have been f. L. *tribus* on the usual pattern of derivatives from L. sbs. in *-us*.

L. *tribus* is usually explained from *tri-* three and the verbal root *bhu*, *bu*, *fu* to be. It is thought by some to be cognate with Welsh *tref* town or inhabited place.

The earliest known application of *tribus* was to the three divisions of the early people of Rome (attributed by some to the separate Latin, Sabine, and Etruscan elements); thence it was transferred to render the Greek φυλή, and so to the Greek application of the latter to the tribes of Israel. This, from its biblical use, was the earliest use in English, the original Roman use not appearing till the 16th c.]

**1.** A group of persons forming a community and claiming descent from a common ancestor; *spec.* each of the twelve divisions of the people of Israel, claiming descent from the twelve sons of Jacob.

*Ten Tribes*, the tribes of Israel which revolted from the House of David, leaving only Judah and Benjamin to the kingdom of Judah. Their history after their deportation by Shalmaneser is lost, and they are often referred to as the *Lost Tribes*, whose identification in remote regions has been a matter of frequent speculation.

*α. c* **1250** *Gen. & Ex.* 3813 Ðoȝ he wenen ðat god sal taken Of ðo .xii. tribuz summe mo. *c* **1449** PECOCK *Repr.* II. vi. (Rolls) 173 In her tribu or kinred..as in the hous of Miche...The Tribu of Dan. **1481** CAXTON *Godeffroy* clxxi. 253 Whan the .x lygnages or trybus departed fro the heyer of Salamon And helde them to Ieroboam. **1526** *Pilgr. Perf.* (W. de W. 1531) 24 b, Shall syt in trones..& iudge the xii tribus of Israel. **1531** ELYOT *Gov.* I. ii, Wherfore ix partes of them which they called Tribus forsoke hym, and elected Hieroboaz..to be theyr kynge.

*β. c* **1380** WYCLIF *Wks.* (1880) 365 Þe trybe or kynrede of leuy. **1390** GOWER *Conf.* III. 279 Of whom..The tribes [*v.r.* tribus] tuelve of Irahel Engendred were. **1480** CAXTON *Chron. Eng.* III. (1520) 20 b/2 The dukes were euer of the trybe of Iuda. **1535** COVERDALE *Ps.* lxxvii. 67 He refused the tabernacle of Ioseph, and chose not the trybe of Ephraim. **1671** MILTON *Samson* 1540 An Ebrew, as I guess, and of our Tribe. **1715–20** POPE *Iliad* II. 431 In tribes and nations to divide thy train. **1819** SCOTT *Ivanhoe* xxxvi, Where dwelt a Jewish Rabbi of his tribe. **1866** *Smith's Smaller Dict. Bible* (1907) 487/1 Samaria retained its dignity as the capital of the ten tribes...In B.C. 721, Samaria was taken,..and the kingdom of the ten tribes was put an end to. *Ibid.* 487/2 Since the deportation of the ten tribes by Shalmaneser. **1910** *Encycl. Brit.* I. 315/1 A circumstance which led Bernier to speculate on the Kashmiris representing the lost tribes of Israel.

**b.** A particular race of recognized ancestry; a family.

*c* **1400** MAUNDEV. (1839) viii. 67 With his wyf Eue..he gatt Seth; of whiche tribe, þat is to seye, kynrede, Ihesu Crist was born. **1617** SIR R. WINWOOD *Let.* 29 July, in *10th Rep. Hist. MSS. Comm.* App. I. 102 The howse of Austria for many yeares together interchangeably hath maried in their owne trybe. **1623** COCKERAM, *Tribe*, a kindred. **1667** MILTON *P. L.* XII. 23 And dwell Long time in peace by Families and Tribes Under paternal rule. **1719** WATTS *Hymn*, '*Jesus shall reign*' vii, In Him the tribes of Adam boast More blessings than their father lost. **1838** LYTTON *Alice* I. vi, To what tribe of Camerons do you belong?

**2.** *Roman Hist.* One of the traditional three political divisions or patrician orders of ancient Rome in early times (see quot. 1842); later, one of the 30 political divisions of the Roman people instituted by Servius Tullius, and in B.C. 241 increased to 35.

**1533** BELLENDEN *Livy* I. xvii. (S.T.S.) I. 96 Þe toun of rome was dividit..in sindri partis, and euery ane of þir partis war callit tribis, be thirllage of tribute þat þai aucht to pay to þe king..þir tribus pertenit na thing to þe distribucioun and nowmer of centuries. **1560** DAUS tr. *Sleidane's Comm.* 412 Themperor..abrogateth all the tribes, and restoreth the same state of the common weale. **1600** HOLLAND *Livy* I. xliii. 31 b, Having divided the citie into foure Wards, according to the quarters and hils; those parts which were inhabited, he [Servius Tullius] called Tribes, of the word Tribute (as I suppose). **1611** B. JONSON *Catiline* II. i, I ha' been writing all this night..unto all the tribes And centuries for their voices, to help Catiline In his election. **1842** *Smith's Dict. Grk. & Rom. Antiq.* 994/1 The three ancient Romulian tribes, the Ramnes, Tities, and Luceres,..to which the patricians alone belonged, must be distinguished from the thirty plebeian tribes of Servius Tullius. **1902** W. M. RAMSAY in *Expositor* Jan. 25 Citizenship necessarily implied membership of one of the tribes of which the city was composed.

**b.** *Grecian Hist.* Rendering the Greek φυλή.

**1697** POTTER *Antiq. Greece* I. ix. (1837) 57 Cecrops..divided them [the Athenians] into four φυλαί, or tribes; each tribe he subdivided into three parts. **1842** *Smith's Dict. Grk. & Rom. Antiq.* 990/2 In the earliest times of Greek history mention is made of people being divided into tribes and clans. *Ibid.* 991/2 Of the Dorian race there were originally three tribes. *Ibid.* 993/1 [At Athens] the Tribes or Phylae were divided..each into three φρατρίαι (a term equivalent to fraternities). *Ibid.* 993/2 Solon..abolished the old tribes, and created ten new ones, according to a geographical division of Attica.

**c.** *Irish Hist. Tribes of Galway*: the families or communities of persons having the same surname.

**1834** *Encycl. Brit.* (ed. 7) X. 306/1 After..1270, it [Galway] became the residence of a number of enterprising settlers...Of these settlers, the principal families, fourteen in number, are still known by the name of the Tribes of Galway...These families became so closely connected by intermarriages, that dispensations are frequently requisite for the canonical legality of marriages among them at present. **1898** *Westm. Gaz.* 10 Oct. 2/1 A day at least must be given to Galway—the 'City of the Tribes'.

**d.** A division of some other nation or people.

**1693** TATE *Juvenal* xv. 194 [Teach] stragling Mountainers, for publick Good, To Rank in Tribes, and quit the savage Wood. **1784** COWPER *Task* v. 222 When man was multiplied and spread abroad In tribes and clans. **1788** GIBBON *Decl. & F.* xlii. (1869) II. 554 The nation was divided into two powerful and hostile tribes.

†**e.** A division of territory allotted to a family or company. *Obs. rare.*

**1643** BAKER *Chron.*, *Jas. I* 158 Now they began to divide the Country [Bermudas] into Tribes and the Tribes into Shares.

**3.** A race of people; now applied esp. to a primary aggregate of people in a primitive or barbarous condition, under a headman or chief.

**1596** SHAKS. *Merch. V.* I. iii. 111 For suffrance is the badge of all our Tribe. **1604** — *Oth.* III. iii. 175 Good Heauen, the Soules of all my Tribe defend From Iealousie. *Ibid.* v. ii. 349 Of one, whose hand (Like the base Indean) threw a Pearle away Richer then all his Tribe. **1745** ? RANDALL *Hymn*, '*Behold, the mountain of the Lord*' iv, Him shall the tribes of earth obey, Him all the hosts of heaven. **1823** J. MARSHALL *Const. Opin.* (1839) 273 Territory..occupied by numerous and warlike tribes of Indians. **1835** THIRLWALL *Greece* I. iv. 113 The Ionians were a Hellenic tribe, who took forcible possession of Attica and a part of Peloponnesus. **1836** W. IRVING *Astoria* I. xiii. 214 Engaged in trading expeditions..among the tribes of the Missouri. **1875** MAINE *Hist. Inst.* iii. 65 The tribes themselves, and all subdivisions of them, are conceived by the men who compose them as descended from a single male ancestor. *Ibid.* 69 In some cases the Tribe can hardly be otherwise described than as the group of men subject to some one chieftain.

**4.** A class of persons; a fraternity, set, lot. Now often *contemptuous*.

*c* **1600** SHAKS. *Sonn.* cvii, Ile liue in this poore rime, While he insults ore dull and speachlesse tribes. *a* **1684** EARL ROSCOM. *Prol. to Dk. York at Edin.* 2 Folly and vice are easy to describe, The common subjects of our scribbling tribe. **1712** ADDISON *Spect.* No. 529 ¶ 6 There is another Tribe of Persons who are Retainers to the Learned World...I mean the Players or Actors of both Sexes. **1719** SWIFT *To Yng. Clergym.* Wks. 1755 II. II. 4 Professors..in most arts and sciences are generally the worst qualified to explain their meanings to those, who are not of their tribe. **1796** BURKE *Reg. Peace* ii. Wks. VIII. 218 The tribe of vulgar politicians are the lowest of our species. **1843** RUSKIN *Arrows of Chace* (1880) I. 18 Dr. Waagen is a most favourable specimen of the tribe of critics. **1850** J. H. NEWMAN *Diffic. Anglic.* I. xii. (1891) I. 388 Perish sooner a whole tribe of Cranmers, Ridleys, Latimers, and Jewels!

**b.** *Tribe of Ben*, a name applied to themselves by literary associates and disciples of Ben Jonson in his later life. ('*Sealed*' appears to refer to Rev. vii. 3–8.)

*a* **1637** B. JONSON *Underwoods* lxv. (*title*) An epistle, answering to one that asked to be sealed of the Tribe of Ben. *Ibid.* 78 Now stand, and then, Sir, you are Sealed of the Tribe of Ben. **1911** SIR A. W. WARD in *Encycl. Brit.* XV. 505/1 At the festive meetings where he ruled the roast among the younger authors whose pride it was to be 'sealed of the tribe of Ben'.

**5. a.** *Nat. Hist.* A group in the classification of plants, animals, etc., usually forming a subdivision of an order, and containing a number of genera; sometimes used as superior and sometimes as inferior to a family; also, loosely, any group or series of animals.

**1640** PARKINSON (*title*) Theatrum Botanicum: the Theater of Plants..Distributed into sundry Classes or Tribes, for the more easie knowledge of the many Herbes [etc.]. **1667** MILTON *P. L.* XI. 279 O flours..Who now shall reare ye to the Sun, or ranke Your Tribes? **1672** GREW *Idea Philos. Hist. Plants* § 2 We commonly say, *Centaurium Majus and Minus*, *Chelidonium Majus and Minus*,..which yet are distinct Species, and of very different Tribes. **1766** *Compl. Farmer* s. v. *Vegetable*, Vegetables, according to the analyses made of them by chemistry, are distinguishable into two grand tribes, the acid and the alkaline. **1774** GOLDSM. *Nat. Hist.* (1776) III. 256 This tribe of the cat kind with spotted skins and a long tail. **1832** HT. MARTINEAU *Life in Wilds* v, A tribe of birds whose habit is to unite in flocks. **1880** GRAY *Struct. Bot.* ix. § 1. (ed. 6) 326 *Tribe* has been for a generation or two..established in both kingdoms, as a grade inferior to order and superior to genus.

**b.** A class, group, kind, or sort of things.

**1731** in *10th Rep. Hist. MSS. Comm.* App. I. 269 The slimy tribe of Snails and Worms. **1744** BERKELEY *Siris* § 87 The whole tribe of chronical diseases. **1776** G. CAMPBELL *Philos. Rhet.* I. v. (1801) I. 114 Under it I include these three tribes: experience, analogy and testimony. **1822–34** *Good's Study Med.* (ed. 4) I. 446 The same tribe of medicines will generally be found useful in the third variety. **1844** STEPHENS *Bk. Farm* II. 678 It is..a member of the harrow tribe of implements.

**6.** A number or company of persons or animals; a 'troop'; in *pl.*, large numbers, 'flocks'.

**1711** POPE *Temp. Fame* 356 Then came the smallest tribe I yet had seen, Plain was their dress, and modest was their mien. **1820** SCORESBY *Acc. Arctic Reg.* II. 209 The same tribe of whales were seen in the latitude of 78°. **1833** HT. MARTINEAU *Brooke Farm* i, There were tribes of children in most of the cottages. **1909** *Blackw. Mag.* Feb. 160/2, I could fancy her..writing lengthy epistles to a tribe of nieces.

**7.** *attrib.* and *Comb.*, as *tribe-book*, *-chief*, *-chieftainship*, *-guest*, *-land*, *-league*, *-man*, *-mark*, *-name*, *-territory*; *tribe-invited*, *-like* adjs.

**1893** P. WHITE *Hist. Clare* 12 He must have used..the *tribe-books then in existence. **1864** BRYCE *Holy Rom. Emp.* xii. (1889) 189 The first barbarian kings had been *tribe chiefs. *Ibid.* Supp. Ch. 424 The German kingdom..was then passing from primitive *tribe-chieftainship into a feudal monarchy. **1746** P. FRANCIS tr. *Horace*, *Ep.* I. xiii. 17 A *Tribe-invited Guest Carries his Cap and Slippers to a Feast. **1872** E. W. ROBERTSON *Hist. Ess.*, *Rome* 248 The *tribe-land, in early times, was probably divided into local districts corresponding with the Centuries of the tribe. **1899** BARING-GOULD *Bk. West* II. 102 The old tribeland or principality of Gallewick was reduced in the Middle Ages to a Manor. **1864** BRYCE *Holy Rom. Emp.* viii. (1889) 116 The five or six great tribes or *tribe-leagues which composed the German nation. **1859** R. F. BURTON *Centr. Afr.* in *Jrnl. Geog. Soc.* XXIX. 90 If he suspect that it belongs to a fellow *tribeman. **1884** W. WRIGHT *Empire Hittites* 129 The scratchy *tribe-marks of the Bedawin. **1886** CONDER *Syrian Stone-Lore* ix. (1896) 323 *note*, The *tribe-names of Arabia may be best explained by the early linguistic condition in which the abstract and the comparative were unknown. **1876** tr. *Keil & Delitzsch's Ezekiel* II. 384 Every *tribe-territory shall stretch from the Jordan to the Mediterranean.

**b.** Combinations with *tribe's*, as TRIBESMAN, q. v.; *tribesfolk*, *tribespeople*, *tribeswoman*.

**1888** DOUGHTY *Arabia Deserta* I. viii. 222 There is no Beduwy so impious that will chide and bite at such, his own *tribesfolk. **1888** in *Jrnl. Anthrop. Inst.* Aug. (1889) 90 He sent me a list of a number of the *tribespeople. **1853** HICKIE tr. *Aristoph.* (1872) II. 404, I come with water to rescue my fellow *tribes-women being on fire. **1899** W. CANTON in *Expositor* Feb. 130 There were tribeswomen who were hospitable enough to welcome the young mother.

**Tribe**, *v. rare.* [f. prec. sb. Cf. *to class*, *to group*.] *trans.* To classify in tribes; also, to group or place in the same tribe *with*.

**1696** BP. NICOLSON *Eng. Hist. Libr.* i. 19 Our Fowl, Fish, and Quadrupeds are well Trib'd by Mr. Willughby and Mr. Ray. **1838** [see *tribed* below]. **1852** *Meanderings of Memory* I. 104 Her nature may with thine be tribed.

Hence **Tribed** (trəibd) *ppl. a.*, divided into tribes.

**1838** S. BELLAMY *Betrayal* 65 Trib'd Decapolis Ye need not seek.

**Tri·beless**, *a.* [f. TRIBE *sb.* + -LESS.] Belonging to no tribe.

**1819** SHELLEY *Prometh. Unb.* III. iv, Man Equal, unclassed, tribeless, and nationless. **1875** POSTE *Gaius* I. Comm. (ed. 2) 126 The tribeless man (*aerarius*) forfeited his vote and became incapable of military service.

**Tribelet** (trəi·blėt). [f. as prec. + -LET.] A small tribe.

**1855** BAILEY *Spir. Leg.* in *Mystic*, etc. 69 The hill Altäic named the almighty god, By Tchudic tribelets of the age of mounds. **1873** DIXON *Two Queens* II. VII. iv. 25 An Irish tribelet, who had swept across the land. **1899** OLIVE SCHREINER in *Fortn. Rev.* July 1 They were split up into endless tribelets.

**Tribeship** (trəi·bʃip). [f. as prec. + -SHIP.] The condition or position of being a tribe; the members of a tribe collectively, or their territory. *Free tribeship*, *sceptre t.*, the position of being a free tribe or the 'sceptre-tribe'.

**1782** J. BROWN *Comp. View Nat. & Rev. Relig.* IV. i. 291 The Sceptre Tribeship, or power of Supreme Government ..is now long ago departed. **1840** J. WILSON *Our Israelitish Origin* vi. (1865) 69 The greater part of the tribeship of Judah lay South of Jerusalem. **1862** W. BARNES in *Macm. Mag.* Mar. 412/1 Trial by Jury seems..to have been practised by the Celtic people..in their times of free tribeship.

**Tribesman** (trəi·bzmæ̆n). [f. *tribe's*, genitive of TRIBE *sb.* + MAN *sb.*[1] (Cf. *clansman*.)] **a.** A man belonging to a tribe; a member of a tribe. Chiefly *pl.* **b.** With possessive, a man of one's own tribe, a fellow-tribesman.

**1798** SOUTHEY *Rose* 28 For her Her tribes-men sigh'd in vain. **1837** WHEELWRIGHT tr. *Aristoph.* II. 117 Why spare our stones, my fellow tribesmen? **1883** *Standard* No. 18465. 5/2 To make a meal off the grasshopper with the tribesmen of the Sierra Nevada. **1893** ELIZA R. SUTHERLAND in Barrows *Parl. Relig.* I. 635 An animal dying of itself may not be eaten by a tribesman, but might be sold to a stranger. **1905** *Times* 13 Sept. 3/3 A patrol..has been fired on by Tebetekentzy tribesmen.

**Tribill, trible**, var. TRIBUL, TRIBULE.

**Tribit**, obs. form of TRIBUTE.

**Tri-bladed, -blastic**: see TRI- 1 c, a.

†**Tribler, tribbler,** app. obs. for **trebler*, a treble-singer.

1539 *Wills & Inv. N. C.* (Surtees 1908) 162 To Robte Belryngar xij d. To everye on of the Tribulars xx d. 1546 *Yorks. Chantry Surv.* (Surtees) II. 361, vj choresta-riez, vj tribblers, one orgayne player. *Ibid.*, The vj triblers for ther yerlie stipend lijs vjd.

**Triblet** (tri·blėt). Also 8 triboulet, 9 treblett, tribolet. [= F. *triboulet* in the sense 'wooden cylinder used by goldsmiths for rounding articles' (Littré); of uncertain origin: see Littré.] A cylindrical rod or mandrel used for forging nuts, rings, tubes, etc., or for drawing lead-pipe. Also *attrib.*: *triblet tubes*, thin tubes which slide one upon the other, as in a telescope.

1611 COTGR., *Triboulet*, a Triblet; the toole whereon Goldsmiths and Clockmakers put Rings, and little wheeles, when they file, or otherwise worke, them. 1736 AINSWORTH *Lat. Dict.* I, A triblet, or triboulet (goldsmith's tool for making rings). 1778 NAIRNE in *Phil. Trans.* LXVIII. 854 In the uppermost room stood a large iron triblet, of about three feet in height. 1853 URE *Dict. Arts* I. 724 A mandril, ..which consists of a long rod of iron, having a short steel treblett on its end. 1877 KNIGHT *Dict. Mech.* s. v., The nut having been cut from the bar, the hole is punched and enlarged by the triblet. 1895 *Model Steam Engine* 95 Triblet drawn tube (i.e., tube made by drawing a steel mandrel through the inside as well as drawing the outside through a hole).

**Tribochet**, obs. form of TREBUCHET.

**Triboluminescence** (tri:bo,liūmine·sĕns). [f. Gr. τρίβος rubbing + LUMINESCENCE.] The quality of emitting light under friction or violent pressure.

1889 *Philos. Mag.* Sept. 151 According to the mode of excitation I distinguish Photo-, Electro-, Chemi-, and Tribo-luminescence. 1899 *Nature* 27 Apr. 618/1 The name triboluminescence has been applied by E. Wiedemann to an emission of light not due to rise of temperature which occurs on crushing certain substances. *Ibid.* 619/1 Crystals of saccharin which, when freshly prepared, flash brilliantly on crushing,..after a few weeks' preservation show no appreciable triboluminescence.

Hence **Tribolumine·scent** *a.*, exhibiting triboluminescence.

1904 W. G. LEVISON in *Science* 27 May 827/2 A zinc-blende from Utah..was the most intense tribo-luminescent substance..yet investigated.

**Tribometer** (trəibǫ·mĭtəɹ). [ad. F. *tribomètre*, f. as prec. + *-mètre*, -METER.] An instrument for estimating sliding friction.

*a* 1774 GOLDSM. *Surv. Exp. Philos.* (1776) I. 293 He [Muschenbrook] calls it a Tribometre, a name compounded ungrammatically enough, but it means a measurer of friction. 1870 C. DRAPER in *Eng. Mech.* 28 Jan. 478/3 This apparatus [a loaded beam of wood] is called a *tribometer*. 1877 KNIGHT *Dict. Mech.*, *Tribometer*, an apparatus resembling a sled, used in estimating the friction of rubbing surfaces.

**Tribophosphorescent** (tri:bo,fǫsfŏre·sĕnt), *a.* [f. as prec. + PHOSPHORESCENT.] = TRIBOLUMINESCENT. So **Tribopho·sphoro,scope**, an instrument for examining triboluminescence.

1904 W. G. LEVISON in *Science* 27 May 826/1 Note on a Tribophosphoroscope, and the Duration and Spectrum of Tribophosphorescent Light.

**Tribowne**, obs. Sc. form of TRIBUNE *sb.*[1]

**Tribrach**[1] (trəi·bræk, tri·b-). *Prosody.* In 6 tribracchus, 8 tribrachus, 8–9 -ys; 7 tribrack. [ad. L. *tribrachys*, a. Gr. τρίβραχυς, f. TRI- + βραχύς short. Cf. F. *tribraque* (Littré).] A metrical foot consisting of three short syllables.

1589 PUTTENHAM *Eng. Poesie* II. xiii. (Arb.) 133 For your foote tribracchus of all three short, ye haue very few trissillables. 1602 T. CAMPION *Art Eng. Poesie* iv. 11 We may vse a Spondee or Iambick and sometime a Tribrack or Dactile. 1706 PHILLIPS (ed. Kersey), *Tribrachus*, or *Tribrachys*, (Gr.) a Foot in Greek and Latin Verse, consisting of three short Syllables; as Populus. 1827 TATE *Grk. Metres* in *Theat. Grks.* (ed. 2) 436 Of all the resolved feet, the Tribrach in Trochaic verse with its ictus on the first syllable ..is most readily recognised by the ear as equivalent to the Trochee. 1885 GOODELL in *Trans. Amer. Philol. Assoc.* XVI. 88 The plain tribrach is frequent in every one's reading.

Hence **Tribrachic** (trəibræ·kik) *a.*, consisting of three short syllables; also, composed of tribrachs.

1866 BLACKIE *Homer & Iliad* I. 401 If the range of pure tribrachic measure, or of tribrachs intermingled with trochees, appears much wider in our song-books than in volumes of poetry written to be read.

**Tribrach**[2] (trəi·bræk). [f. TRI- + Gr. βραχίων arm.] A figure or object having three arms or branches; *spec.* a prehistoric flint implement of this form. So **Tribrachial** (trəibrē·kiăl) *a.*, having three arms or branches.

1873 A. WAY in *Archæol. Jrnl.* XXX. 28 The implement ..is of a form that may be designated tribrachial, having three branches radiating from the centre. *Ibid.* 31 The unique tribrachial implement. *Ibid.*, The flint tribrach was presented..by the late Dr. Martin in 1853, with other objects from Ventnor. 1897 SIR J. EVANS *Anc. Stone Implem. Gt. Brit.* iv. 78 A singular instrument chipped out of flint, like three celts conjoined..,so as to form a sort of tribrach.

**Tribracteate**, etc.: see TRI- I.

**Tribrom-, tribromo-** (trəi,brōu·m(o)). *Chem.* [f. TRI- 5 c + BROM(O-.] A formative signifying that three atoms of bromine are substituted for hydrogen in the substance designated by the rest of the name; e. g. *tribromobenzene*: see TRI- 5 c.

1852 ANDERSON in *Q. Jrnl. Chem. Soc.* IV. 117 The yellow precipitate thus obtained is the hydrobromate of tribromocodeine. 1900 SMITH *Richter's Org. Chem.* II. 92 Aniline, acted upon by..bromine, yields..Tribromaniline.

**Tribromhydrin** (trəi,brōum,həi·drin). *Chem.* [f. TRI- 5 a + *bromhydr(ic* + -IN[1] (termination of the compound ethers of glycerin: see ACETIN).] Glyceryl tribromide, $C_3H_5Br_3$, a haloid ester or compound ether of glycerin or glycerol, $C_3H_5(OH)_3$, in which the three OH groups are replaced by bromine atoms.

1862 MILLER *Elem. Chem.* (1869) III. 326 Glycerin forms with hydrobromic acid compounds analogous to those which it yields with hydrochloric acid, such as *monobromhydrin* ($C_3H_7BrO_2$), *dibromhydrin* ($C_3H_6Br_2O$), and *tribromhydrin* ($C_3H_5Br_3$). 1899 SMITH *Richter's Org. Chem.* I. 474 Tribromhydrin fuses at 16°, and boils at 220°.

**Tribromide**: see TRI- 5 a and BROMIDE.

**Tribual** (tri·biuăl), *a.* [f. L. *tribu-s* TRIBE + -AL: cf. *gradu-al*, *manu-al*. (L. had in this sense *tribuārius*.)] Of, belonging or pertaining to a tribe; tribal.

1650 FULLER *Pisgah* II. x. 207 The first tribuall defection to idolatry Dan was guilty of. *a* 1661 — *Worthies, Leicester.* (1662) II. 126 The Tribual Lisping of the Ephramites. 1817 G. S. FABER *Eight Dissert.* (1845) I. 229 We are apt to fancy, that this extraordinary people have no tribual distinctions among themselves. 1822–34 *Good's Study Med.* (ed. 4) IV. 268 It would..have been a much greater improvement..to have employed hydrops as a generic, instead of hydropes as a tribual or family name. 1881 BENTHAM in *Jrnl. Linn. Soc.* XVIII. 287 Observations on the most important tribual and subtribual characters.

Hence **Tri·bually** *adv.*, by tribes, tribally.

1817 G. S. FABER *Eight Dissert.* (1845) II. 181 Here, apparently, they were first tribually planted, when Nimrod and his baffled Cuthim migrated from Babel to Ashur.

†**Tri·bul**, *v.* Chiefly *Sc. Obs.* Forms: 4–6 trible, tribul(e, 6 tribull, -bill, -bil. [a. OF. *triboler, -bouler, -buler*, etc. (12th c. in Godef.), ad. L. *trībulāre* to press, oppress, afflict: see TRIBULATION.] *trans.* To bring tribulation upon; to distress, harass, afflict.

*a* 1325 *Prose Psalter* xxxviii[i]. 9 Man for-soþe in likenes passeþ; ac in vayn he hys tribled [*v. r.* sturblyd]. 1375 BARBOUR *Bruce* IV. 58 It wes gret pite for to heir Folk till be tribulit on þis maneir. 1456–70 in *Acts Parlt. Scotl.* (1875) XII. 20/2 Part of ewyl myndit personis..wrangis and tribulis ws and our pwr tenentis. 1563 WINȜET *Wks.* (S.T.S.) II. 28 Men of corruptit mynd,..tribuland thair wit about quæstions and stryfe of wordis. 1572 EARL ARGYLE *Let.* in *Munim. Irvine* (1890) I. 60 Quhatsomevir persone or personis..sall attempt to tribull, molest, harme or injure the foirsaidis provest, baillzies [etc.].

Hence †**Tri·bular** *Sc. Obs.*, one who distresses or afflicts; †**Tri·bulness** *Sc. Obs.* = TRIBULE; †**Tri·bulous** *a. Sc. Obs.*, full of tribulation.

1574 *Reg. Privy Council Scot.* II. 395 The saidis declarit tratouris,..and *tribularis of the commoun weill. *c* 1375 *Sc. Leg. Saints* xxiv. (*Alexis*) 327, & neuir for ony *tribulnes Spak he II..mare ore les. 1563 WINȜET *Four Scoir Thre Quest.* To Rdr., Wks. (S.T.S.) I. 51 That quhilk the Prophete spak..apperis in thir our *tribulus dayis almaist fullelie complete.

**Tribulage** (tri·biŭlėdʒ). *local.* Now *Hist.* [ad. med.L. *trĭbulāgium* (*trubl-*), f. *trĭbulum* threshing-sledge (in med.L. app. some other crushing-machine): see -AGE.] A species of poll-tax formerly levied on each tin-miner in some of the stannaries: see quots. Cf. TRIBULARY.

[1296–7 *Ministers' Accts.* 24–5 *Edw. I* (*Bailiff's Accts. Edmund of Cornw.*) (P.R.O.), *Perquisita stagnariorum.* Idem reddit compotum de cxj solidis vij denariis de minutis amerciamentis Nigre More hoc anno et de vj solidis de Trublagio hoc anno. 1338 — 12 *Edw. III* 816/11 De x solidis iij denariis de quadam consuetudine vocata Tribulagium videlicet de quolibet homine operante cum tribula, obolum.] 1537 *Let. Hen. VIII* in Rymer *Foedera* (1712) XIV. 581/1 Concedimus eidem Johanni Greynfeld Tribulagium nostrum, sive consuetudinem vocatam le Tribulage, infra Hundreda nostra de Penwyth et Kerr. 1906 G. R. LEWIS in *Victoria County Hist., Cornwall* I. 537/1 Tribulage, a poll tax levied in Blackmore at the rate of ½*d.*, and in Penwith and Kerrier at ⅓*d.*..for each labouring tinner. *Ibid.* 538 *note*, The Civil War brought with it the final extinction of tribulage, dublet, and the fine of tin. 1908 — *Stannaries* v. 140 The tax known as 'tribuiage', or 'shovel money', which represents the only attempt at a capitation tax in the Cornish stannaries, was paid in two stannaries only, Penwith and Kerrier, and, after 1342, Blackmore. *Ibid.* 141 The record of tribulage payments is necessarily incomplete from the fact that the duty was collected and paid to the receiver by the head bailiff, and often included in their accounts with the perquisites of the stannary courts.

†**Tri·bulance.** *Obs. rare.* [a. OF. *tribulance* (*a* 1300 in Godef.), f. *tribuler*, ad. L. *trībulāre*: see TRIBULATION and -ANCE.] Tribulation.

1560 ROLLAND *Crt. Venus* II. 531 Greit tribulance, or famine accidentaill.

**Tribular** (tri·biŭlăɹ), *a. rare*⁻⁰. [f. L. *tribūl-is* one of the same tribe with another + -AR.] Tribal.

1864 in WEBSTER; whence in later Dicts.

**Tribular**: see TRIBLER.

†**Tri·bulary.** *Obs. rare*⁻¹. [f. as TRIBULAGE + -ARY.] = TRIBULAGE.

1467–8 *Rolls of Parlt.* V. 610/2 Thoffice of Baillyf of oure Stannarie of Penwith and Kerye..togeder with alle þe tribularye within oure said Stannarie commyng.

†**Tri·bulate**, *ppl. a. Obs. rare.* In 6 *Sc.* tribulat. [ad. L. *trībulāt-us*, pa. pple. of *trībulāre*: see next.] Tribulated. (Const. as *pa. pple.*)

1560 ROLLAND *Crt. Venus* III. 32 [Q]uhen he on sey be storme was tribulat.

**Tribulate** (tri·biŭleˡt), *v.* [f. L. *trībulāt-*, ppl. stem of *trībulāre*; or perh. from TRIBULATION, q. v.] *trans.* To afflict; to oppress; to trouble greatly.

*a* 1637 N. FERRAR *110 Consid.* (1638) 122 If such a one be needy, tribulated, and afflicted, it is because it so pleaseth God. 1829 LANDOR *Imag. Conv., Cdl. Albani & Picture-Dealers* Wks. 1846 II. 7/2 The Pontifical Chancery and the Ruota Criminale would never tribulate gallant men in this guise. 1845 CARLYLE *Cromwell* IX. (1871) IV. 136 Otherwise tribulated by subaltern authorities. 1885 S. COX *Expositions* I. xxiii. 306 'He will tribulate them that tribulate you', says St. Paul to the Thessalonians.

**Tri·bulated**, *ppl. a.* [f. L. *trībulāt-us* pa. pple. of *trībulāre* (see next) + -ED[1].] Subjected to tribulation, afflicted.

1682 DEWSBURY *Gen. Epist.* 6, I dearly beseech you.. that you Watch over the Tender and Tribulated ones. *a* 1715 NELSON *T. à Kempis' Chr. Exerc.* III. xvi. 140 The Comforter of the afflicted and Tribulated. 1858 CARLYLE *Fredk. Gt.* v. ii. (1872) II. 67 Friedrich's Sister, Father, Mother, were tribulated, almost heartbroken.

**Tribulation** (tribiŭlēˡ·ʃən). *arch.* Also 4–6 try-, -cion, etc. [a. OF. *tribulacion* (12th c. in Godef. *Compl.*), ad. Chr.L. *trībulātiōn-em* (Itala *a* 200, etc.), n. of action from L. *trībulāre* to press, oppress, afflict, f. *trībul-um* a threshing-sledge, app. f. *trī-*, var. stem of *ter-ĕre*, *trīvi*, *trītum* to rub, grind + *-bulum*, forming names of instruments.]

**1.** A condition of great affliction, oppression, or misery; 'persecution; distress; vexation; disturbance of life' (J.).

*c* 1330 R. BRUNNE *Chron.* (1810) 206 He lyued in wo & strife, & in tribulacioun. *c* 1374 CHAUCER *Troylus* v. 988 Myn herte is now in tribulacion. 1382 WYCLIF *Matt.* xxiv. 21 Thanne schal be greet tribulacioun. *c* 1440 *Gesta Rom.* viii. 22 (Harl. MS.) To þis Cite is a þorny wey and a sharp, *scil.* penaunce and tribulacion in erþe. 1534 MORE *Comf. agst. Trib.* I. Wks. 1158/1 Tribulacion is euery such thing as troubleth and greueth a man either in bodye or mynde. 1667 MILTON *P. L.* XI. 63 Tri'd in sharp tribulation, and refin'd By Faith and faithful works. 1696 PHILLIPS (ed. 5), *Tribulation*, Affliction, Misery; generally spoken of that which a Christian takes in good part, as being inflicted by the hand of God. 1862 *Sat. Rev.* 8 Feb. 141 The sufferers..are sustained in their tribulation by the proud consciousness that they are assisting to uphold a great national principle.

**b.** With *a* and *pl.* An affliction.

*a* 1225 *Ancr. R.* 402 None wateres, þet beoð worldliche temptaciuns ne tribulaciuns..ne muwen þeos luue acwenchen. *a* 1450 *Knt. de la Tour* (1906) 75 Many tribulacions and euylls. 1526 *Pilgr. Perf.* (W. de W. 1531) 11 b, Ye paynes, aduersitees, tribulacyons..& all other labours & besynesses of this worlde. 1667 MILTON *P. L.* III. 336 The just shall ..after all thir tribulations long See golden days.

†**c.** One who or that which causes trouble. (In quot., app. a cant name for a gang of disturbers.)

1613 SHAKS. *Hen. VIII*, v. iv. 65 These are the youths that thunder at a Playhouse..that no Audience but the tribulation of Tower Hill, or the Limbes of Limehouse, their deare Brothers, are able to endure.

†**2.** The condition of being held in pawn or pledge. *Obs. slang.*

1663 DRYDEN *Wild Gallant* I. ii, Sirrah, Boy, fetch my Suit with the Gold Lace at Sleeves from Tribulation. 1764 *Low Life* (ed. 3) 15 Pawnbrokers..busy in altering the Dates of Cloaths under Tribulation.

†**Tribule.** *Sc. Obs.* Also trible, -ill, -il. [f. as TRIBUL *v.*] Tribulation, distress, affliction.

1513 DOUGLAS *Æneis* IV. Prol. 247 Of thi trigittis quhat toung can tell the trible [*v. r.* tribill]? 1549 *Compl. Scot.* ix. 75 Afflictione ande tribil. 1563 WINȜET *Four Scoir Thre Quest.* To Rdr., Wks. (S.T.S.) I. 49 Thai suffer in this lyfe ..that be diuers tribulis thai mot enter..in the lyfe eternall. *Ibid.* 63 For na trible of tyme nor tyrannie of man.

**Tribuloid** (tri·biŭloid), *a. Bot.* [f. mod.L. *Tribulus* + -OID.] (See quot.)

1900 B. D. JACKSON *Gloss. Bot. Terms*, *Tribuloid* (εἶδος, resemblance), like the fruit of *Tribulus*, beset with sharp bristles, echinate (Heinig).

‖**Tribuna** (tribū·na). *Obs.* [It. and med.L. *tribūna*, f. L. *tribūnus* TRIBUNE *sb.*[1]] An octagonal saloon in the Galleria degli Uffizi at Florence containing many famous paintings and statues.

1644 EVELYN *Diary* 20 Nov., The quire, roofe and paintings in the Tribuna are excellent. 1756–7 tr. *Keysler's Trav.* (1760) II. 19 That admirable chamber called *la Tribuna*, or *l'Octogone*, which name it derives from its octangular figure...On entering the tribuna, the eye is immediately struck with six marble statues standing in the center, among which is that famous statue, called the Venus de Medicis.

**Tribunal** (trəi-, tribiū·năl), *sb.* (*a.*) Also 6 try-, 6–7 -all. [ad. L. *tribūnāl*, *-āle* sb. neut., a tribunal, judgement seat, f. *tribūn-us* TRIBUNE *sb.*[1]: see -AL. Cf. F. *tribunal* (13th c. in Hatz.-Darm.), perh. the immediate source; also Sp., Pg. *tribunal*, It. *tribunale*. By Spenser stressed *tribuna·l* as in French.]

**1.** Originally, A raised semicircular or square platform in a Roman basilica, on which the seats of the magistrates were placed; a dais; a raised throne or chair of state; a judgement seat (also *fig.*).

1526 *Pilgr. Perf.* (W. de W. 1531) 212 We all shall stande before the tribunall of god. 1590 SPENSER *F. Q.* III. v. 53

And crowne your heades with heavenly coronall, Such as the Angels weare before Gods tribunall. **1642** in *10th Rep. Hist. MSS. Comm.* App. IV. 429 Making 2 Tribunalles or seates for the judges at the last assizes. **1702** ECHARD *Eccl. Hist.* (1710) 612 They will be both read in the day of Judgment, before the Tribunal of Jesus Christ. **1833** CRUSE *Eusebius* V. i. 170 Those around the tribunal cried out against him.

**2.** A court of justice; a judicial assembly.

**1590** SPENSER *F. Q.* II. ix. 53 Painted faire..with picturals Of Magistrates, of courts, of tribunals. **1610** HOLLAND *Camden's Brit.* (1637) 177 The Tribunals, or Courts of Justice in England. **1667** MILTON *P. L.* III. 326 When thou..shalt.. from thee send The..Arch-Angels to proclaime Thy dread Tribunal. **1687** T. BROWN *Saints in Uproar* Wks. 1730 I. 82, I am forced to appeal to your impartial tribunal. **1835** ALISON *Hist. Europe* (1847) IV. xiv. 137 On the 14th October [1793] the Queen was brought before the Revolutionary Tribunal. **1867** FREEMAN *Norm. Conq.* I. vi. 574 The judgement of a competent tribunal is always worth something.

**b.** *fig.* Place of judgement or decision; judicial authority.

**1635** QUARLES *Embl.* II. xiii. 49 Go up, my soul, into the tribunal of thy conscience. **1734** tr. *Rollin's Anc. Hist.* (1827) I. 153 The field of battle is a tribunal without partiality and cabal. **1817** BENTHAM *Parl. Reform* Introd. 222 By the tribunal of public opinion it ought to be taken as and for confessional evidence. **1875** WHITNEY *Life Lang.* viii. 150 Our recognition of the community as final tribunal which decides whether anything shall be language or not.

†**3.** = TRIBUNE *sb.*[2] 1, 2. *Obs.*

**1644** EVELYN *Diary* 7 Nov., [In Rome] the..Churches of St. Cosmo and Damiano,..a pretty odd fabriq, with a Tribunal, or Tholus within, wrought all of Mosaic. *Ibid.* 12 Nov., The tribunal of the high altar is of exquisite worke. **1694** *Ibid.* 5 Oct., Placing columns on pilasters at the East tribunal [of St. Paul's]. **1722** J. RICHARDSON *Statues, etc. Italy* 319 The Tribunal, or *Mezzo Cupola* of Dominichino. **1797** *Encycl. Brit.* (ed. 3) VII. 300/2 The..Venus of Medici..stands in a room called the Tribunal [*Tribuna*].

**B.** *attrib.* or as *adj.*

**1.** Pertaining to, of the nature of, or authorized by a tribunal.

**1554-5** BRADFORD *Let.* 16 Feb. in Coverdale *Lett. Martyrs* (1564) 471 A thing wherof I doute not to answer..before the tribunal seat of Iesus Christ. **1560** ROLLAND *Crt. Venus* II. 1020 Or Rhamnusia in hir sait Tribunall. **1610** *Histrio-m.* VI. 91 Affliction is the perfect way That leads to Joves tribunall dignity. **1645** MILTON *Tetrach.* Wks. 1851 IV. 216 A law to suffer a kind of tribunall adultery. **1708** PRIOR *Mice* 37 When we meet at God's tribunal throne.

†**2.** Of or pertaining to a tribune. *Obs. rare.*

**1577** HANMER *Anc. Eccl. Hist.* (1663) 21 A sign being given from the tribunal seat. **1577-87** HOLINSHED *Chron.* I. 34/1 Narcissus went vp vnto the tribunall throne of Plautius, to declare the cause of his comming. **1670** *Narr. Long Parl.* in Somers *Tracts* (1748) I. 32 Persons..of a tribunal Spirit and Temper.

Hence **Tribu·nalled** *a.*, having or seated on a tribunal; †**Tribu·nalship** = TRIBUNESHIP.

**1654** R. CODRINGTON tr. *Iustine* XIII. 213 The chief Tribunalship of the Camp was given to Seleuchus. **1852** *Meanderings of Memory* I. 32 Tribunalled judge, he weds the weaker cause, Holds sternly up as he lays down the laws.

†**Tribunary,** *a. Obs. rare.* [f. TRIBUNE *sb.*[1] + -ARY. Cf. OF. *tribunaire* (14th c. in Godef.).] Of or pertaining to tribunes; tribunitian, tribunitial.

**1612** W. SHUTE *Fougasse's Venice* i. 8 Now the Tribunarie Gouernment..shall be rightly termed Infancie.

**Tribunate** (tri·biunĕt). [ad. L. *tribūnāt-us*, f. *tribūnus* TRIBUNE *sb.*[1]: see -ATE[1]. Cf. F. *tribunat.*]

**1.** The office of tribune; tribuneship; government by tribunes.

**1546** LANGLEY *Pol. Verg. De Invent.* II. iii. 38 b, During that office [dictatorship] all other magistrates were abrogated except the Tribunate or Prouostship of the commons. **1603** HOLLAND *Plutarch's Mor.* 877 The Tribunate was an empeachment, inhibition, and restraint of a magistracie, rather than a magistracie it selfe. **1746** MELMOTH tr. *Pliny's Lett.* VII. xxii. (1748) II. 410, I so strongly pressed you to confer the Tribunate upon my friend. **1869** SEELEY *Lect. & Ess.* ii. 35 The great Roman Revolution which began with the tribunate of Gracchus and ended with the battle of Actium.

**2.** *French Hist.* A representative body of legislators established under the constitution of the year 8 of the Revolutionary calendar (1800–1).

[**1804** *Ann. Rev.* II. 85/2 Our author was present at a sitting of the tribunat, in the Palais Royal.] **1827** SCOTT *Napoleon* xv, A Tribunate of one hundred deputies. **1861** M. ARNOLD *Pop. Educ. France* 136 Both in the Tribunate and in the Legislative Body his measure encountered strenuous resistance. **1905** *Edin. Rev.* July 90 Benjamin Constant and nineteen others were turned out of the Tribunate. *attrib.* **1802** in *Spirit Pub. Jrnls.* VI. 394 [Bonaparte] planted the hedges with *legislative* and *tribunate* shrubs, and apparently gave them a good root in the earth.

**Tribune** (tri·biun, trəi·-), *sb.*[1] Also 4 *Sc.* tribone, -owne, trybone, 5 -bun(e, 7–8 tribun. [ad. L. *tribūnus*, lit. 'head of a tribe', f. *tribu-s* TRIBE; cf. F. *tribun* (13th c. in Hatz.-Darm.).]

**1.** A title designating one of several officers in the Roman administration; *spec.* **a.** *Tribune of the people* (L. *tribūnus plebis*), one of two (later five, then ten) officers appointed to protect the interests and rights of the plebeians from the patricians. **b.** *Military tribune* (L. *tribūnus mīlitāris*), one of six officers of a legion, each being in command for two months of the year.

*c* **1375** *Sc. Leg. Saints* xxii. (*Laurentius*) 171 Þane was þare a mychtty tribowne. *Ibid.* xxxiii. (*George*) 22 Quhare he wes mad..a trybone. & þu sal wit, a tribone is he þat [of] þe thred-part of a cyte or of a cunctre kepare is; & a tribone is als I-wise þat trybut gadris to þe king..& he his tribune als, þu kene, to quham ansueris a thousand men. **1387** TREVISA *Higden* (Rolls) II. 273 After consuls, tribunes plebis and dictatores rulede the comounte anon to Iulius Cesar his tyme. **1456** SIR G. HAYE *Law Arms* (S.T.S.) 45 Ane othir maner of officiaris..callit trybunys. **1533** BELLENDEN *Livy* IV. iii. (S.T.S.) II. 61 The ȝere iij^c^x. fra þe first fundatioun of rome was þe first tyme þan ony tribunis militare war create with power consulare. **1678** R. L'ESTRANGE *Seneca's Mor.* I. xv. (1696) 77 He that is a Tribune, would be a Prætor. **1741** MIDDLETON *Cicero* I. Pref. 36 A new order of Magistrates, of their own body, called Tribuns. **1838-42** ARNOLD *Hist. Rome* I. viii. 139 The tribune's power of protection enabled him to interpose in defence of the unfortunate. **1879** FROUDE *Cæsar* iv. 37 He forced his way steadily upwards..to the rank of military tribune.

**2.** *transf.* and *fig.* An officer holding some position analogous to that of a Roman tribune; a judge; a protector of the rights of the people; a popular leader, a demagogue.

**1587** HARRISON *England* II. v. (1877) I. 109 The cheefe or high tribune of the excheker is of custome called lord cheefe baron. *a* **1660** *Contemp. Hist. Irel.* (Ir. Archæol. Soc.) II. 147 Himself alone with his fewe Conatian tribunes..will disannull all this. **1756** NUGENT *Gr. Tour, Italy* III. 78 Venice was originally a democratical state, under consuls and tribunes...The Tribunes were succeeded by the Doges. **1853** MACAULAY *Biogr., Atterbury* (1860) 13 By the body of the clergy he was regarded as the ablest and most intrepid Tribune that had ever defended their rights. **1882** W. CORY *Mod. Eng. Hist.* II. 283 Mr. Cobbett..took his seat on the Treasury Bench. To have a tribune of the people sitting between Ministers..would be a hindrance to business.

Hence †**Tribu·nian** *a. Obs. rare*, of or pertaining to a tribune.

*a* **1693** *Urquhart's Rabelais* III. xxxix. 328, I give out Sentence in his favour, unto whom hath befallen the best Chance by Dice; Judiciary, Tribunian, Pretorial, what comes first.

**Tribune** (tri·biun, trəi·-), *sb.*[2] Also 7 tribun. [a. F. *tribune* (1409 in Godef. *Compl.*), ad. It. and med.L. *tribūna* (914 in Du Cange), taking the place of L. *tribūnāle* TRIBUNAL.]

**1.** = TRIBUNA.

**1645** EVELYN *Diary* 27 Feb., The edifice without is Gotiq, but very glorious within, especialy the roofe, and one tribune well painted. *a* **1668** LASSELS *Voy. Italy* (1670) II. 103 There are divers other pictures in that vaulted Tribun in Mosaick worke. **1843** *Penny Cycl.* XXVI. 249/2 The apartment of the Imperial Gallery at Florence, which is called the Tribune (Tribuna).

**2.** The semicircular or polygonal apse of a basilica or basilican church, usually domed or vaulted.

*a* **1771** GRAY *Archit. Gothica* Wks. 1843 V. 332 The difference between the body and ailes of the choir at Peterborough, with the east side of the transept, and the semicircular tribune which finishes the same choir. **1794** W. HUTCHINSON *Hist. Cumberld.* I. 155 *note*, Warwick church, remarkable for its tribune or rounded east end. **1841** W. SPALDING *Italy & It. Isl.* III. 157 The length of the church, from the principal entrance to the end of the tribune, is 601 feet. **1874** PARKER *Goth. Archit.* Gloss. 329 *Tribune*, the semicircular space at one end of the Basilica, for the judges. In Churches copied from the Basilicas it was retained as the apse.

**3.** A raised platform or dais; a rostrum; a pulpit; the throne or stall of a bishop.

**1762-71** H. WALPOLE *Vertue's Anecd. Paint.* (1786) III. 61 A large inscription over the tribune at the end of the hall. **1790** BURKE *Fr. Rev.* 46 Any of the discoursers in our pulpits, or on your tribune;..Dr. Price, or..the Abbé S[i]eyes. **1842-76** GWILT *Archit.* Gloss. s.v. *Apsis*, The bishop's throne being raised by steps above the ordinary stalls..was sometimes called *exhedra*, and in later times *tribune*. **1850** W. IRVING *Mahomet* xiv. (1853) 87 A pulpit or tribune..to which he ascended by three steps. **1866** GEO. ELIOT *F. Holt* xxiv, Mr. Lyon was seated on the school tribune or dais at his particular round table. **1885** WOODROW WILSON *Congress. Govt.* ii. 127 Members [of the French Chamber of Deputies] do not speak from their seats..but from the 'tribune'..a box-like stand,..resembling those narrow, quaintly-fashioned pulpits ..still to be seen in some of the oldest of our American churches.

**4.** A raised and seated area or gallery, esp. in a church; also applied to stands at continental race meetings (F. *tribune*).

**1865** *Pall Mall G.* 13 June 5 Last year..it was easy to move about from the saddling-ring to the tribunes, to get places in the latter to sit down, and to promenade in front of the tribunes, with plenty of elbow-room. **1865** *Times* 1 Aug. 7/4 There were not more than 45 or 50 ladies in the 'tribunes'—the low galleries on the side of the hall are so called. **1870** DISRAELI *Lothair* lxvi, The church was crowded; not a chair or tribune vacant. **1883** *Mag. Art* June 338/2 The unfamiliar storey is known as a tribune, and runs immediately above the nave at the point usually occupied by the triforium. It is a lofty gallery. **1891** *Winchester Word-Bk., Tribunes*, large pews in ante-chapel reserved for ladies. (Obs.) **1904** PRINCESS RADZIWILL *Recoll.* ix. 160, I never left the tribune from which ladies were allowed to hear the debates.

**Tri·bune,** *v.* [f. TRIBUNE *sb.*[1]] †**a.** *trans.* To regulate or control by tribunal authority. *Obs. rare*[—1]. **b.** *intr.* To play the tribune (*Funk's Standard Dict.* 1895).

**1647** WARD *Simp. Cobler* (1843) 52 These Essentialls, must not be Ephorized or Tribuned by..a few mens discretion.

**Tribuneship** (tri·biunʃip, trəi·-). [f. TRIBUNE *sb.*[1] + -SHIP.] The office of a Roman or other tribune; the term of this office. Also *transf.*

**1541** PAYNEL *Catiline* li. 74 b, The senate decreed, that Metellus shuld leaue vp his trybuneshyp and Cesar his pretorshyp. **1603** HOLLAND *Plutarch's Mor.* 877 This Tribuneship having taken originally the first beginning from the common people, is great and mighty in regard that it is popular. **1636** E. DACRES tr. *Machiavel's Disc. Livy* I. xiii. 72 The accustomed Religion help'd well..for the restitution of the Tribunship to the Nobility. **1756** WARD in *Phil. Trans.* XLIX. 699 The year 50, which answers to the ninth tribuneship of Claudius. **1842** W. C. TAYLOR *Anc. Hist.* xv. § 6 (ed. 3) 440 Becoming a candidate for the tribuneship,..[he] was elected without much opposition. **1849** MACAULAY *Hist. Eng.* vi. II. 41 The crimes which had disgraced the stormy tribuneship of Shaftesbury.

**Tribunitial, -icial** (tribiuni·ʃăl), *a.* [f. L. *tribūnīci-us* + -AL. Cf. OF. *tribunicial* (14th c. in Godef.).] Of or pertaining to a Roman tribune; tribunitian. Also *transf.*

**1598** GRENEWEY *Tacitus' Ann.* III. xii. (1622) 81 Tiberius ..sent letters to the Senate, requesting the Tribuniciall authority for Drusus. **1621** JAS. I *Answ. to Petit. Comm.* in Rushw. *Hist. Coll.* (1659) I. 46 If you would give as good ear to them, as you do to some Tribunitial Orators among you. **1783** BLAIR *Lect. Rhet.* (1813) I. xiii. 295 Those terrible tribunitial harangues, by which he inflamed..the citizens of Rome. **1858** BUSHNELL *Nat. & Supernat.* xii. (1864) 380 Reason may be allowed to have a tribunitial veto against it. **1885** G. SALMON in *Academy* 5 Dec. 368/1 The tribunicial power was conferred on Trajan in the month of October.

**Tribunitian, -ician** (tribiuni·ʃăn), *a.* [f. as prec. + -AN. Cf. F. *tribunicien* (14th c. in Hatz.-Darm.).] Of, belonging or pertaining to a Roman tribune, or the office of tribune.

**1533** BELLENDEN *Livy* III. iv. (S.T.S.) I. 255 Þis auctorite tribuniciane was devisit to þe vniuersall proffitt and supporte of þe ciete. **1598** GRENEWEY *Tacitus' Ann.* VI. iv. (1622) 126 By a Tribunitian law it was brought vnto halfe one in the hundred; and in the end Vsury was wholly forbidden. **1730** A. GORDON *Maffei's Amphith.* 342 The Tribunitian *Viatores* had places. **1842** DE QUINCEY *Pagan Oracles* Wks. 1858 VIII. 180 The very same reason which had obliged Augustus not to usurp..the tribunitian office. **1891** FARRAR *Darkn. & Dawn* lx, He would exercise his ancient tribunician privilege, and veto a decree of condemnation.

**b.** *transf.* and *fig.* Having the power of veto like the Roman tribunes; popularly appointed; demagogic; factious.

**1637** HEYLIN *Answ. to Burton* 80 Mass. Prinne is of a factious Tribunitian spirit. **1783** *Town & Country Mag.* 19 He must..exercise a tribunitian power of..preventing the exhibition of what the nominal physician prescribes. **1846** LANDOR *To J. Forster* Wks. II. 675 Steadfast Cromwell's tribunitian throne. **1854** MILMAN *Lat. Chr.* VII. i. (1864) IV. 21 The tribunitian fury of ecclesiastical demagogues. **1888** *Pall Mall G.* 20 Jan. 2/2 The association would be..a great associated tribune of the people, with more than tribunitian powers.

†**Tribuni·tious,** *a. Obs. rare.* [f. as prec. + -OUS.] Factious or violent, after the manner attributed to the Roman tribunes; = TRIBUNITIAN b.

**1600** HOLLAND *Livy* XXXIV. ii. 853 Yours will the blame bee, if yee have brought women now to raise and stirre up tribunitious seditions. **1625** BACON *Ess., Counsell* (Arb.) 87 Let them not come in Multitudes, or in a Tribunitious Manner.

**Tribu·nitive,** *a. rare.* [irreg. f. L. *tribūnus* TRIBUNE *sb.*[1], by false analogy with such words as *unitive*, *punitive*, etc.] Of or pertaining to a tribune or popular champion.

**1856** GOLDW. SMITH in *Oxford Ess.* 310 Whatever democratic or tribunitive spirit it might have.., would not be corrupted by evil communications with hereditary despotisms.

**Tributable** (tri·biutăb'l), *a.* [f. TRIBUTE *sb.* + -ABLE.] Liable to pay tribute; subject to tribute.

**1830** W. TAYLOR *Hist. Surv. Germ. Poetry* II. 126 He ought not be waited on for nothing, To whom so many heads are tributable.

**Tributary** (tri·biutări), *a.* and *sb.* [ad. L. *tribūtāri-us*: see next and -ARY[1]. Cf. F. *tributaire* (12th c. in Godef. *Compl.*).]

**A.** *adj.* **1.** Paying tribute; subject to imposts.

**1382** WYCLIF 1 *Macc.* xiii. 39 ȝif eny other thing was tributarye [*gloss*] or bounden to tribut, in Jerusalem, nowe be it not tributarie. **1422** tr. *Secreta Secret., Priv. Priv.* xxxiii. 185 Al..by-came lyeges and Subiectes tributarijs by grete othis for ham and hare kyngedomes and lordshuppes. **1494** FABYAN *Chron.* II. xlviii. 31 At those dayes a great parte of yᵉ worlde was trybutary to Rome. **1570-6** LAMBARDE *Peramb. Kent* (1826) p. xii, These therefore were by Iulius Cæsar subdued to the Romane Empire, and their countrie made a tributarie Province. **1665** DRYDEN *Ind. Emp.* I. ii, This Charles is some poor Tributary Lord. **1786** BURKE *W. Hastings* III. III. xxviii. Wks. XI. 460 As far independent as a tributary prince could be. **1845** STOCQUELER *Handbk. Brit. India* (1854) 9 Many states, hitherto independent, were compelled to become tributary to the Company.

**b.** *fig.*

*c* **1412** HOCCLEVE *De Reg. Princ.* 89 Þat fretynge aduersarie Myn hert[e] made to hym tributarie. **1577** HELLOWES *Gueuara's Chron.* 232 Traiane did vse to say, that Rome was more tributarie then any place of the world: for that they could not eate, but if it were giuen them from other kingdomes. **1796** BURNEY *Mem. Metastasio* II. 218 Productions..for which they used to be tributary to the industry of other nations.

**2.** *transf.* and *fig.* Furnishing subsidiary supplies or aid; subsidiary, auxiliary, contributory; also said of a stream or river which flows into another.

**1611** SHAKS. *Cymb.* IV. ii. 37 Th'emperious Seas breeds Monsters; for the Dish, Poore Tributary Riuers, as sweet Fish. **1764** GOLDSM. *Trav.* 49 For me your tributary stores combine. **1860** TYNDALL *Glac.* I. vii. 57, I climbed up among the tributary glaciers. **1878** HUXLEY *Physiogr.* 5 With reference therefore to the rivers tributary to the Thames. **1899** *Allbutt's Syst. Med.* VI. 651 The neuralgia may affect the whole of the tributary nerves of the plexus.

**3.** Paid or offered as tribute; of the nature of tribute; contributory.

**1588** SHAKS. *Tit. A.* I. i. 159 Loe at this Tombe my tributarie teares, I render. **1632** LITHGOW *Trav.* II. 55 They pay a yearly tributary pension vnto the great Turke. **1771** *Poetry* in *Ann. Reg.* 206 Immortal fame Shall grace with tributary praise thy name. **1780** COWPER *Table Talk* 112 Many a dunce, whose fingers itch to write, Adds, as he can, his tributary mite. **1814** SCOTT *Ld. of Isles* I. i, Each minstrel's tributary lay Paid homage to the festal day.

**4.** Of which one bears the cost; expensive.

**1632** LITHGOW *Trav.* I. 9 The chargeable expences of a tributary iourney. *Ibid.* III. 114 This tributary, tedious, and sumptuous peregrination.

**B.** *sb.* (Absolute use of the adj. So in Fr.)

**1.** One who pays tribute. Also *fig.*

[*c* **1375** *Sc. Leg. Saints* xii. (*Mathias*) 123 With trybvtaris he fled þane to þe towne of Ierusaleme.] **1432–50** tr. *Higden* (Rolls) I. 275 For Sicambri were tributaryes to thempyre of Rome vn to the tyme of Valentinian. **1535** COVERDALE *1 Macc.* i. 4 He..subdued yͤ londes and people with their prynces, so that they became tributaries vnto him. **1612** DAVIES *Why Ireland*, etc. (1787) 10 The Irish Lords did only promise to become tributaries to King Henry the Second. And such as pay only tribute..are not properly subjects but sovereigns. *a* **1704** T. BROWN *Alsop's St. Conform.* Wks. 1711 IV. 119 Living a constant Tributary to those Vermin the Bailiffs. **1866** ROGERS *Agric. & Prices* I. xx. 509 A tributary and vassal to the English monarch.

**2.** *transf.* and *fig.* One who or that which furnishes subsidiary supplies or aid. **a.** *spec.* A stream contributing its flow to a larger stream or lake; an affluent, feeder.

(Not in TODD 1818, WEBSTER 1828, or CRAIG 1849.)

**1836** W. IRVING *Astoria* III. 261 A fortified post and port ..commanding the trade of that river and its tributaries. **1846** MᶜCULLOCH *Acc. Brit. Empire* (1854) I. 35 The Medway can hardly be called a tributary of the Thames; but..it falls into the æstuary of the latter. **1866** M. ARNOLD *Thyrsis* xi, What sedged brooks are Thames's tributaries. **1897** MARY KINGSLEY *W. Africa* 354 Two new rivers..both of which he surmised were tributaries of the Congo.

**b.** Of other things.

**1859** CORNWALLIS *Panorama New World* I. 137 At the foot of this terraced hill was the necropolis, and near it its tributary, the Bendigo Hospital. **1859** GEO. ELIOT *A. Bede* ii, The lower sphere might be said, at a rough guess, to be thirteen times larger than the upper, which naturally performed the function of a mere satellite and tributary. **1870** EMERSON *Soc. & Solit., Bks.* Wks. (Bohn) III. 84 The great metropolitan English speech, the sea which receives tributaries from every region under heaven.

Hence **Tri·butarily** *adv.*, **Tri·butariness.**

**1727** BAILEY Vol. II, *Tributariness*, the Condition or State of those that pay Tribute. **1847** WEBSTER, *Tributarily*, adv. in a tributary manner.

**Tribute** (tri·biut), *sb.* Also 4 **trebute, tribuyt, -uit, -it,** 4–6 **tribut, trybut, -e,** 5 *Sc.* **trewbut, -e.** [ad. L. *tribūtum*, neut. of *tribūtus*, pa. pple. of *tribu-ĕre* to assign, give, pay. Cf. F. *tribut* (15th c. in Hatz.-Darm.), and the semi-popular and inherited OF. forms *trebus* (14th c. in Godef. *Compl.*) and *treu*: see TREW.]

**1.** A tax or impost paid by one prince or state to another in acknowledgement of submission or as the price of peace, security, and protection; rent or homage paid in money or an equivalent by a subject to his sovereign or a vassal to his lord.

**1340–70** *Alex. & Dind.* 710 Þei..taken of ȝou tribit þat traie is to paie, Of ȝoure offringus alle ofte in þe ȝere. ? *a* **1400** *Morte Arth.* 114 With-owttyne more trouflyng the trebute we aske, That Julius Cesar wane wyth his jentille knyghttes! **1490** CAXTON *Eneydos* xxxi. 117 They of Athenes muste sende eueri yere for a trybute to the kynge Mynos of Crete..seuen men and seuen wymen. **1560** DAUS tr. *Sleidane's Comm.* 41 b, Germany is muche impouerished with warres..and with tributes. **1610** SHAKS. *Temp.* I. ii. 113 He..Confederates..with King of Naples To giue him Annuall tribute, doe him homage. **1781** GIBBON *Decl. & F.* xvii. (1869) I. 470 A large portion of the tribute was paid in money. **1843** *Penny Cycl.* XXVII. 503/2 Edgar..liberat[ed] the Welsh from the payment of the tax of gold and silver on condition of an annual tribute of three hundred wolves. **1872** FREEMAN *Gen. Sketch* xii. § 14 (1874) 225 The successes of the Turks were largely owing to their taking a tribute of children from their Christian subjects.

**b.** Hence contextually, The obligation or necessity of paying this; the condition of being tributary, as *to lay a tribute on*. *Under*, † *on tribute*: under obligation to pay tribute (also *fig.*: cf. 2).

**1377** LANGL. *P. Pl.* B. XIX. 37 Wonyeth þere none But vnder tribut & taillage as tykes & cherles. *c* **1470** HENRY *Wallace* V. 589 Still scho duelt on trewbute in the toune, And purchest had king Eduuardis protectioune. **1535** COVERDALE *Prov.* xii. 24 A diligent hande shal beare rule, but the ydle shal be vnder tribute. **1609** BIBLE (Douay) *ibid.*, The hand ..which is slothful, shal serve under tributes. **1662** BP. HOPKINS *Serm.* 1 *Pet.* ii. 13 (1685) 4 If a fast did only lay a tribute upon our eyes. **1793** R. HALL *Apol. Freed. Press* iv. 50 His imperial fancy has laid all nature under tribute.

**2.** *transf.* and *fig.* Something paid or contributed as by a subordinate to a superior; an offering or gift rendered as a duty, or as an acknowledgement of affection or esteem.

**1585** T. WASHINGTON tr. *Nicholay's Voy.* IV. xxvii. 145 b, The euils..wherof by the tribute of death, they were deliuered. **1665** SIR T. HERBERT *Trav.* (1677) 39 His Father ..having paid Nature her last Tribute..the year before. **1671** MILTON *P. R.* III. 258 From his side two rivers flow'd, ..Then meeting joyn'd thir tribute to the Sea. **1750** GRAY *Elegy* 80 Some frail memorial..Implores the passing tribute of a sigh. **1806** *Med. Jrnl.* XV. 318 The committee..also declare, that they cannot conclude their report, without returning a just tribute of acknowledgement to the illustrious author of this discovery, Dr. Jenner. **1850** *Syd. Smith's Wks.* I. 8/1 *note*, I cannot read the name of Malthus without adding my tribute of affection for the memory of one of the best men that ever lived. **1860** HOOK *Lives Abps.* I. vi. 323 To the merits of Grimbald no higher tribute could have been paid.

**3.** In *Mining* (originally in the tin-mining of Cornwall; now in general use). **a.** The proportion of the value of the ore raised, paid by the miners to the owners or lessors of the land or their representatives. **b.** The proportion of ore raised or its value, paid to the miners by the owners of the mine or land, in payment of their labour. **c.** Hence, *to work on tribute*, or *on the tribute system*, to work on the plan of paying or receiving certain proportions of the produce. **d.** Work performed in excavating and dressing the ore, as distinguished from *tut-work*, which consists in sinking shafts, driving of adits, and similar preparatory operations.

**a. 1778** PRYCE *Min. Cornub.* 330/1 *Tribute*, [called] a *Cope* [in] North of England, a consideration or share of the produce of a Mine either in money or kind..paid by the Takers or Tributors to the original Adventurers or owners, for the liberty granted to the Takers of enjoying the Mine, or a part thereof, called a Pitch, for a limited time. **1886** *N. Zealand Herald* 1 June 6/7 Tributes were let to several parties, whose contributions to the company during the year amounted to £153 19s. 6d. The receipts showed calls to be £1573 4s., tributers £153 19s. 6d., sundries (such as crushing, interest, and overdraft) £47 9s. 6d.: total, £1774 13s. **1911** C. BOYD in *United Empire* July 393 The Tributor is a small gold-miner..paying tribute on his holding.

**b. 1832** BABBAGE *Econ. Manuf.* xxvi. (ed. 3) 252 *Tribute*, which is payment for raising and dressing the ore, by means of a certain part of its value when rendered merchantable. **1855** J. R. LEIFCHILD *Cornwall Mines* 143 The ores so raised are sold every week, and the miner immediately receives his tribute or per centage for which he agreed to work. **1865** R. HUNT *Pop. Rom. W. Eng.* Ser. I. (1871) 90 The inducements of very high 'tribute' were held out to the miners.

**c. 1869** R. M. BALLANTYNE *Deep Down* xxviii. 359 When a man works on 'tribute' he receives so many shillings for every twenty shillings' worth of ore that he raises during the month. **1875** *Melbourne Spectator* 12 June 63/2 The company pleaded that the mine was let on tribute. **1877** RAYMOND *Statist. Mines & Mining* 85 The Wyoming and Pittsburgh are worked on tribute. **1885** *Money Market Rev.* 29 Aug. (Cassell), Some twelve men are now working old dump, concentrating on tribute.

**d. 1839** *Penny Cycl.* XV. 246/1 The dead work is denominated 'tutwork', and the raising of ores 'tribute'. *Ibid.*, The mode of payment adopted in tutwork and tribute is entirely different: in the former case..the miner..is paid at so much per fathom..; in the latter case..the miner receives a certain percentage on the actual value [of the ore], being paid at the rate of so many shillings in the pound upon that value.

**4.** *attrib.* and *Comb.*, as *tribute-bribe*, *-coin*, *-gatherer*, *-offer*, *-payer*, *-payment*, *-piece*, *-quittance*, *-river*, *-roll*; in sense 3, as *tribute-man*, *-pitch* (PITCH *sb.*[2] 12), *system*, *-taker*, *work*; *tribute-bearing*, *-paying* adjs.; **tribute-children,** children surrendered as tribute. See also TRIBUTE-MONEY.

*a* **1661** HOLYDAY *Juvenal* (1673) 21 Yet in his life Paid *tribute-bribes to his own conscious wife. **1603** KNOLLES *Hist. Turks* (1638) 332 Far the greatest part of these *tribute children, taken from their Christian parents,..hee caused to be dispersed into euery city and country of his dominion in Asia. **1630** *R. Johnson's Kingd. & Commw.* 510 *margin*, The *Iemoglans*, or tribute-children. **1582** N. T. (Rhem.) *Matt.* xxii. 19 Shew me the *tribute coine. And they offred him a penie. **1552** HULOET, *Trybute gatherer, *telo*. **1649** MILTON *Eikon.* iv, They had stoned his tribute-gatherer. **1839** DE LA BECHE *Rep. Geol. Cornw.*, etc. xv. 503 It seems they worked in different parties..like the *tribute-men of the mines. *a* **1586** SIDNEY *Arcadia* II. xvii, Fair streames ..let the *tribute-offer of my teares unto you, procure your stay a while with me. **1552** HULOET, *Trybute payer, *stipendarius*,..*tributarius*. **1598** HAKLUYT *Voy.* I. 60 From what countrey soeuer tribute payers, or ambassadours come vnto him. **1860** J. CAIRNS *Mem. J. Brown* vi. 186 The true Christian doctrine of civil obedience and *tribute paying. **1592** KYD *Sp. Trag.* I. iii, Is our embassadour dispatcht for Spaine?..And *tribute paiment gone along with him? **1610** HOLLAND *Camden's Brit.* (1637) 101 Whether these *tribute-pieces were coined by the Romans..I may not easily affirme. **1778** PRYCE *Min. Cornub.* 189 A *Tribute-Pitch consists of a few fathoms in length on the course of the Lode [in a Copper Mine]. **1865** R. HUNT *Pop. Rom. W. Eng.* Ser. I. (1871) 105 She was promised no end of good luck..and Jan the best luck in tribute-pitches. **1819** SHELLEY *Prometh. Unb.* III. iii, Indus and its *tribute rivers. **1605** SYLVESTER *Du Bartas* II. iii. IV. *Captaines* 119 A thousand Streamlings that ne'er saw the Sun, With *tribute silver to his service run. **1872** R. B. SMYTH *Mining Statist.* 83 There does not appear any very good reason why prospecting ventures should not, as a rule, be established on the *tribute system. **1883** *Encycl. Brit.* XVI. 449/2 The third method is that which is known as the tribute system. The miner working on tribute..gives the mining company all the ore he extracts at a certain proportion of its value, after he has paid all the cost of breaking it, hoisting it to the surface, and dressing it. **1778** PRYCE *Min. Cornub.* 189 A *Tribute-Taker, as well as every other Miner in a Bal, obliges himself and partners to lend a hand gratis at the capstan whenever required. **1874** J. H. COLLINS *Metal Mining* 127 What are the advantages and disadvantages of the different forms of 'tut work' as compared with '*tribute work'?

**Tribute** (tri·biut), *v.* [f. prec. sb.]

†**1.** *intr.* To yield tribute; *trans.* to pay as tribute. *Obs. rare.*

*c* **1440** *Pallad. on Husb.* IV. 555 But hem I sette in wel pastyned londe, And they tributed with felicite. **1570** LEVINS *Manip.* 196/26 To Tribute, *tribuere*. **1654** WHITLOCK *Zootomia* 302 Amorous Trifler, that spendeth..his Afternoones in discourse with Paint, or Lust, tributing most precious Minutes, to the Scepter of a Fanne.

**2.** *Mining. trans.* and *intr.* To work on tribute. Hence **Tri·buted** *ppl. a.*; **Tri·buting** *vbl. sb.* and *ppl. a.*

**1855** J. R. LEIFCHILD *Cornwall Mines* 143 Tributing..is a business requiring keen judgment and close application. *Ibid.* 152 Dolcoath miners,..tut-working and tributing, to send up copper for coinage, for tea-urns, for tea-kettles, and for trinkets. **1909** *Westm. Gaz.* 29 Dec. 10/4 All the tributing parties, owing to their being unable to earn a living, threw up their contracts. **1912** *Times* 19 Dec. 19/1 From all of the tributed properties they were receiving revenue.

**Tri·bute-mo:ney.** Money paid in tribute.

**1526** TINDALE *Matt.* xxii. 19 Let me se the tribute money. And they toke hym a peny. **1706** ARBUTHNOT *Serm.* Misc. Wks. 1751 II. 185 Let down your Nets; and you may fetch your Tribute-Money out of your Fishes. **1814** SCOTT *Wav.* xv, Paying the arrears of tribute money. **1881** W. W. NEWTON *Childr. Serm.* xii. 67 The tribute money was about one shilling and threepence.

**Tributer:** see TRIBUTOR.

**Tributor, tributer** (tri·biutəɹ). Also (5 -ir), 5–6 -our, 6 tribitour. [f. TRIBUTE *v.* (or ? *sb.*) + -OR, -OUR (after agent-nouns from L. or F.), and -ER[1] (on English analogies). Cf. rare late L. *tribūtor* one who gives.]

†**1.** One who pays tribute. Also *fig. Obs.*

**1483** *Cath. Angl.* 393/2 A Tributir, *tributarius*. **1534** WHITINTON *Tullyes Offices* III. (1540) 152 That the cytes that Lucius Scylla made fre..shulde be tributers agayne. **1547** BOORDE *Introd. Knowl.* xxiv. (1870) 181, I am a Venesien..For part of my possession, I am come tributor to the Turke. **1588** PARKE tr. *Mendoza's Hist. China* 60 The prouince of Santon 3. millions and 700. thousand tributers. **1596** FITZ-GEFFRAY *Sir F. Drake* (1881) 70 The mighty Silver-river..His tributorie sandes to him reveal'd; Nor sdained it to be a tribitour, Vnto the Oceans mightie Emperour. *a* **1648** LD. HERBERT *Hen. VIII* (1683) 435.

†**2.** A giver, bestower. *Obs. rare*⁻¹.

*a* **1548** HALL *Chron., Hen. V* 50 b, Almightie God geuer & tributor of this glorious victory.

**3.** *Mining.* A miner who works 'on tribute': see TRIBUTE *sb.* 3 c.

**1778** PRYCE *Min. Cornub.* 188 The Tributor..has several persons concerned with him. *Ibid.* 330/1 [see TRIBUTE *sb.* 3 a]. **1855** J. R. LEIFCHILD *Cornwall Mines* 147 The ore sold for £182:2:2, and, as the tribute was 7*s.* 6*d.* in the pound, the share for the tributers was £68:5:9. **1875** *Melbourne Spectator* 29 May 46/1 A fight between the few Europeans employed on the works and the Chinese tributers. **1877** *Encycl. Brit.* VI. 218/1 Capitalists, landowners, inventors, Cornish tributers..are all brought under the stimulating influence of self-interest. **1886, 1911** [see TRIBUTE *sb.* 3 a]. **1902** *Daily Record* 1 Oct. 4 The concessions by the late Boer Government..have got into hands so grasping that their excessive terms to tributors for water-rights and power have kept a large area of these fields fallow.

**Tributorian** (tribiutōᵊriăn), *a. rare.* [f. late L. *tribūtōri-us* TRIBUTORY + -AN.] Of or pertaining to tribute or payment.

**1880** MUIRHEAD *Gaius* IV. § 72 There is the tributorian action against a father or owner, whose son or slave has with his father's or owner's knowledge invested his *peculium* in merchandise.

†**Tributo·rious,** *a. rare.* [f. as prec. + -OUS.]

**1727** BAILEY vol. II, *Tributorious*, pertaining to Distribution.

†**Tri·butory,** *a.* and *sb. Obs.* [ad. (jurid.) L. *tribūtōrius* of or concerning payment, f. *tribūtor*, agent-n. from *tribu-ĕre* to bestow, give, pay: cf. *contributory*. Superseded by the nominal derivative TRIBUTARY.]

**A.** *adj.* Paying tribute; = TRIBUTARY *a.* 1.

*c* **1460** FORTESCUE *Abs. & Lim. Mon.* iii. (1885) 115 The peple..sought helpe of the Romayns, to whom thai hade be tributori. **1530** PALSGR. 283/1 Trybutorie, *tributayre*. **1585** T. WASHINGTON tr. *Nicholay's Voy.* III. xiii. 95 [They] are not tributorie in any gabels or money taxes. **1596** [see TRIBUTOR 1]. **1615** G. SANDYS *Trav.* 219 My father..that rich country tributory made.

**B.** *sb.* = TRIBUTARY *sb.* 1.

**1585** T. WASHINGTON tr. *Nicholay's Voy.* II. vii. 37 They became tributories vntoo the prince of the Turkes. [But cf. I. ix. 12 A newe Kyng, vnto whom they..rendred them selues as his tributaries.]

**Tributyrin** (trəi͵biū·tirin). *Chem.* [f. TRI- 5 a + BUTYRIN.] Glycerol tributyrate, $C_{15}H_{26}O_6$, the compound ether or ester of glycerin and butyric acid: cf. TRIACETIN: a colourless oily liquid, boiling at 285° C., the characteristic constituent of butter-fat.

**1855** *Q. Jrnl. Chem. Soc.* VII. 282. **1863–72** WATTS *Dict. Chem.* I. 697 Tributyrin..is a neutral, oily liquid, with an odour analogous to that of [monobutyrin and dibutyrin], and a pungent taste, with irritating aftertaste.

**Tricalcic** (trəi͵kæ·lsik), also **Trica·lcium,** *a. Chem.* [f. TRI- 5 b + CALCIC, CALCIUM.] Applied to a salt containing three atoms of calcium; e.g. *tricalcic* or *tricalcium phosphate*, $Ca_3(PO_4)_2$, a salt of calcium and orthophosphoric acid, $H_3PO_4$.

**1871** VALENTIN *Pract. Chem.* 147 Hydric disodic phosphate gives a bulky white precipitate of tricalcic phosphate. **1876** HARLEY *Royle's Mat. Med.* 61 The ashes of bones..

consist chiefly of tricalcic phosphate. 1911 *Jrnl. Chem. Soc.* C. II. 396 Action of a solution of Sodium hydroxide on Tricalcium phosphate.

**Tricapsular** (trəikæ·psiŭlăɪ), *a. Nat. Hist.* [f. TRI- + L. *capsula* CAPSULE + -AR.] Having three capsules.

1694 *Phil. Trans.* XVIII. 278 Tricapsular Seed-vessels. 1760 J. LEE *Introd. Bot.* II. xxix. (1765) 145 In *Aconitum* some are tricapsular, and others quinquecapsular.

**Tri-car** to **Tricaudate**: see TRI- 4 c, 1 a.

**Tricarbon** (trəi·kā·ɹbǫn), *a. Chem.* [f. TRI- 5 b + CARBON.] Containing or derived from three atoms of carbon, as the *tricarbon* series of hydrocarbons.

1866 [see TRI- 5 b]. 1866 ROSCOE *Elem. Chem.* xxvii. 239 Whilst $CH_4$ is the type of the mono-carbon series, $C_2H_6$ is that of the di-carbon series, and similarly, $C_3H_8$ that of the tri-carbon series. *Ibid.* xxx. 273 Tricarbon Series: Propyl alcohol $C_3H_8O$.

**Tricchery, -ori**, obs. forms of TREACHERY.

† **Trice**, *sb.*[1] *Obs. rare.* Also 5 **tryys, -st, -ste.** [a. MDu. *trîse*, *trijs*, Du. *trijs* windlass, pulley, hoisting-block = MLG. *trîsse*, *trîtse* tackle, hoisting-rope (whence also Da. *tridse*, *trisse*, Sw. *trissa* sheave, pulley, Ger. *trieze* crane, pulley). Cf. TRICE *v.*] A pulley or windlass.

1357-8 *Ely Sacr. Rolls* (1907) II. 178 In j trice empt. de Domino Priore 6s 8d. *c* 1440 *Promp. Parv.* 503/1 Tryyste, wyndas [*v. rr.* tryys, tryyst], *machina, carchesia.* 1462-3 *Norwich Sacr. Roll* (MS.), Pro le trice ad trahendum plumbum, xx d. In fune et hawuseris pro le trice, iij s. ix d.

**Trice** (trəis), *sb.*[2] Forms: 5-6 **tryse, 6 tryce, 6-7 trise, 6- trice.** [Found first in phrase *at a trice*, app. originally 'at one pull or tug, at one effort', *trice* being app. verbal sb. from TRICE *v.*; soon passing into the sense 'at once, immediately, in a moment, instantly', whence in later use the simple sb. comes to be equal to 'instant, moment'. Cf. the sense-development of Fr. † *à un coup*, *à coup*, † *tout à un coup*, *tout d'un coup*, orig. 'at a stroke', hence 'at once, immediately, instantly'.

The later phrase *in a trice* recalls the Sp. *en un tris* instantly, orig. 'in a crack' (CRACK *sb.* 2), from *tris* the noise made by cracking or breaking of glass; but the Eng. phrase 'at a trice' appears too early for Spanish influence. Rather are the English, French, and Spanish phrases parallels expressing suddenness of action.]

**1.** † **a.** *At a trice, lit.* at a single pluck or pull; hence, in an instant; instantly, forthwith; without delay. *Obs.*

*c* 1440 *Ipomydon* 392 The howndis..Pluckid downe dere all at a tryse. *a* 1530 HEYWOOD *Love* (1534) B iv, At dore were this trull was, I was at a tryce. 1540 PALSGR. *Acolastus* N j b, Open the dores at ones, or at a tryce. 1603 HARSNET *Pop. Impost.* 59 They made sure to have a Devil readie at a trice. *a* 1635 NAUNTON *Fragm. Reg.* (Arb.) 49 True it is, He had gotten the Queens eare at a trice.

† **b.** *With a trice* in same sense. *Obs.*

1515 BARCLAY *Egloges* iii. (1570) B vj/2 Sometime thy bedfelowe is colder then is yse, To him then he draweth thy cloathes with a trice. *a* 1566 R. EDWARDES *Damon & Pithias* (1571) H j, Now Pithias kneele downe,..And with a trise thy head from thy shoulders I wyll conuay. 1577 NORTHBROOKE *Dicing* (1843) 129 The gaine gotten by this playe at dyce, when all is gotten with a trice ouer the thumbe, without anye trafficke or loane. 1625 *Gonsalvio's Sp. Inquis.* 140 Immediatly after this confession thus by them made, they broke their necks with a trice.

**c.** *In a trice* († *on a trice*) in same sense.

1508 SKELTON *P. Sparowe* 1131 To tell you what conceyte I had than in a tryce, The matter were to nyse. 1553 BECON *Reliques of Rome* (1563) 266 The Aungells..maye as a man would say in a trise go downe vnto them. 1577-87 HOLINSHED *Chron.* II. 31/1 Suddenlie..in a trice it skippeth to the top of the rocke. 1610 SHAKS. *Temp.* v. i. 238 On a trice,.. Euen in a dreame, were we diuided from them. 1699 LD. TARBUT in *Pepys' Diary*, etc. (1879) VI. 195 In a trice, from words they came to blows. 1782 COWPER *Gilpin* xxx, In a trice the turnpike-men Their gates wide open threw. 1847 C. BRONTË *J. Eyre* xx, I'll make you decent in a trice. 1872 BLACK *Adv. Phaeton* ix, A fire is lit in a trice.

† **2.** One single attempt or act; the time taken for this; an instant or moment; a very brief period. *Obs.*

1579 TOMSON *Calvin's Serm. Tim.* 899/2 Wee shall marueile howe the deuill coulde so deceiue vs at the first trice. 1589 R. HARVEY *Pl. Perc.* (1590) 5 Stand by a trice, but looke you depart not the court. 1597-8 BP. HALL *Sat.* IV. vii. 57 The whiles the likerous priest spits euery trice. 1605 SHAKS. *Lear* I. i. 219 That she..should in this trice of time Commit a thing so monstrous. *a* 1618 RALEIGH *Advice of Son* (1651) 8 Nothing would be so much esteemed as a short trice of time, which now by days, and moneths, and years, is most lavishly misspent. 1668 WILKINS *Real Char.* 186 By Time..Instant, Moment, Trice, Nick.

† **Trice**, *sb.*[3] *Obs.* Origin and meaning obscure. (Variously conjectured to be a variant or erroneous form of TRACE *sb.*[1] in sense 'way, course (of action)', or of TRIST, TRYST.)

*c* 1460 G. ASHBY *Dicta Philos.* 598 A kynge sholde not sett hym selfe in myche price, Ner his counseil haue of hym gouernance, Ne ofte use huntyng, keping wele his trice, Ner take any newe way by ignorance. [*L.* Decet regem non multum appreciare seipsum, nec gubernari suo consilio, nec vti frequenter venacione, nec incedere semita quam ignorat.]

**Trice** (trəis), *v.* Also 4-7 **tryce, trise, 5-6 tryse**; 8-9 *erron.* **trace.** [a. MDu. *trîsen*, Du. *trijsen* to hoist = MLG. *trîssen*, *trîtsen*, whence also Da. *trisse*, Ger. *triezen* to hoist. Ulterior history obscure.]

† **1.** *trans.* To pull; to pluck, snatch, draw with a sudden action; rarely, to carry off (as plunder). *To trice* one *out of* a thing, to do one out of it by sudden force. *Obs.*

*c* 1386 CHAUCER *Monk's T.* 535 By god out of his sete I wol hym trice [*v. rr.* tryce, trise]. 1421-2 HOCCLEVE *Dial.* 208 in *Min. Poems* 117 Whan that deathe shall men from hence trice. 1446 LYDG. *Nightingale Poems* i. 336 Deth wyll you trise, ye wot not how ne whenne. *c* 1450 LOVELICH *Grail* xiii. 20 In the tyme Of the chas, Alle Tholomes harneis Itrised was. 1500-25 in *Thoms' Anecd.* (Camden) 31 Sir William..makes no more adoe but trices him up, and throwes him into the Thames. 1540 PALSGR. *Acolastus* Argt. C j, After he was left naked and triced away from al his goodes, or bereued of al that euer he had. 1600 W. WATSON *Decacordon* (1602) 103 Vntill they might get him triced out of their way. 1611 SPEED *Hist. Gt. Brit.* IX. viii. § 38 Thus to be triced out of that which so vehemently..he tooke care to see effected. 1618 BOLTON *Florus* (1636) 106 Wee neverthelesse had tryced him out of most of her Townes and Countries.

**2.** To pull or haul with a rope; *spec.* (*Naut.*) usually with *up*, to haul or hoist up and secure with a rope or lashing, to lash up.

? *a* 1400 *Morte Arth.* 832 They trisene vpe þaire saillez, And rowes ouer the ryche see. 1579-80 NORTH *Plutarch* (1676) 401 They threw him down a Rope from the wall, which he tyed about his middle, and so was triced up by it. 1622 R. HAWKINS *Voy. S. Sea* (1847) 105 We cast a snare about his neck and so tryced him into the ship. 1627 CAPT. SMITH *Seaman's Gram.* iv. 18 Ropes fast triced together with handspikes. *Ibid.* v. 22 Bunt lines is..a small rope.. to trice or draw vp the Bunt of the saile. 1688 R. HOLME *Armoury* III. xv. (Roxb.) 34/2 They trise vp the anchor from the Hawse to the top of the fore-castle. 1836 MARRYAT *Midsh. Easy* x. 28 All the wet sails were also spread on the booms or triced up in the rigging. 1907 *Macm. Mag.* Feb. 316 Aft there, two of you,..and trice the ladder up.

Hence **Tri·cing** *vbl. sb.*; also *attrib.* as *tricing-batten, -line, -rope*: see quots.

1404 *Durham Acc. Rolls* (Surtees) 397, iiij trasys ij trysyng rapis. 1627 CAPT. SMITH *Seaman's Gram.* I. viii. 36 For slinging the yards, bousing or trising. 1769 FALCONER *Dict. Marine* (1776), *Tracing-Line* [ed. 1815 *Tricing-Line*],..a small cord..used to hoist up any object to a higher station... Such are the tracing-lines of the awnings, and those of the yard tackles. 1804 A. B. in *Naval Chron.* XII. 381 [He] cut one of the tricing lines of the netting. 1836 E. HOWARD *R. Reefer* xlv, My tricing-up to the truck. *c* 1850 *Rudim. Navig.* (Weale) 156 *Tricing battens*,..to which the sailors trice-up the middle of their hammocks out of the headway. 1909 *Athenæum* 30 Mar. 339/2 The tricing-up of a refractory midshipman to the mast-head.

**-trice**, *suffix*, a. F. *-trice*, ad. L. *-trīx*, *-trīce-m*, or It. *-trice*; in Latin forming feminines to agent-nouns in *-tor*. In Eng. formerly used in many words, as in *corruptrice*, *directrice*, *genetrice*, *imperatrice*, *mediatrice*, *oratrice*, *salvatrice*, *victrice*, also (from *deserter*) *desertrice*. Modern Eng. prefers the form -TRIX from the L. nominative, esp. in legal and learned words; but, in others, generally substitutes the compound suffix -TRESS.

**Tricellular**: see TRI- 1 a.

**Tricenary** (trəisī·nări), *a.* and *sb.* Also 5 *erron.* **tricenn-.** [ad. L. *trīcēnāri-us* of, pertaining to, or consisting of thirty, f. *trīcēnī* thirty each.]

**A.** *adj.* Of or pertaining to thirty; containing, or lasting, thirty days. ? *Obs.*

1655 STANLEY *Hist. Philos.* III. (1701) 75/2 After Solon's time, the Civil year..consisted of Months,..alternately of twenty nine, and thirty days, at Athens, though divers places of Greece..did not for a long time after part with their tricenary Months. 1671 H. M. tr. *Erasm. Colloq.* 389 Tricenary and yearly Masses.

**B.** *sb. R. C. Ch.* [med.L. *tricēnārium*, Du Cange.] A series of masses said on thirty consecutive days: cf. TRENTAL.

1482 *Monk of Evesham* (Arb.) 94 That sche schulde orden to be seyde for me. v. tricennarijs of messys. 1911 A. M. BUCHANAN tr. *Contempl. Life* xxi. 101 Numerous anniversary Masses are said, and the suffrages for the dead are increased by tricenaries, during which Masses are offered on thirty consecutive days.

So **Tricena·rious** *a.* (*rare*—⁰) = *tricenary* adj. (In some mod. Dicts. misspelt **tricennarious**, and confused in form and sense with TRICENNIAL.)

1656 BLOUNT *Glossogr.*, *Tricenarious*, of or belonging to thirty. [1836 SMART, *Tricennial*, belonging to the number thirty; *Tricennarious* is less used. 1882 OGILVIE (Annandale), *Tricennarious*, tricennial; belonging to the term of thirty years.]

† **Trice·nnal.** *Obs.* [ad. med.(Anglo-)L. *trīcennāle*, in form neuter of L. *trīcennālis* of or belonging to thirty years, f. *triciēs* thirty times + *annus* year, but app. erroneously used for a tricenary or trental.] = TRICENARY B.

1537 tr. *Latimer's 2nd Serm. bef. Convoc.* E ij, Your forefathers sawe somwhat whiche made this constitution, against the venalitie and sale of Masses, that vnder peine of suspending, no priest shuld sell his sayinge of tricennals, or annals. [1707 FLEETWOOD *Chron. Prec.* (1745) 109 Tricennalia were called Trentals from Trigintalia, and in English, a months-mind, because the service lasted a month or 30 days, in which they said so many masses.]

**Tricennial**, *a. rare*—⁰. [f. L. *trīcenni-um* period of thirty years (f. *triciēs* thirty times + *annus* year) + -AL.] Of or belonging to thirty years.

1656 BLOUNT *Glossogr.*, *Tricennial*, of thirty or thrice ten years. 1731 BAILEY, *Tricennial*, belonging to the Term of 30 Years. 1864 WEBSTER, *Tricennial*, of, pertaining to, or consisting of, thirty years; occurring once in every thirty years.

**Tricentenary** (trəise·ntĭnări, -sentī·nări), *a.* and *sb.* [f. TRI- + CENTENARY: cf. L. *trecentēnī* three hundred each.] = TERCENTENARY.

1846 WORCESTER, *Tricentenary*, a period or space of three hundred years. *Ec[lectic] Rev[iew]*. 1882 OGILVIE (Annandale), *Tricentenary*, *n.* 1. That which consists of or comprehends three hundred; the space of three hundred years. 2. The commemoration of any event which occurred three hundred years before, as the birth of a great man; as, Shakspere's *tricentenary*. Called also *Tercentenary*. *Tricentenary*, *a.*, relating to or consisting of three hundred; relating to three hundred years; as, a *tricentenary* celebration. Called also *Tercentenary*.

So **Tricentena·rian**, a person 300 years old.

1889 *Academy* 20 July 34/3 Perhaps the interior of the Antarctic continent may yield a crop of tricentenarians, since, according to Herodotus, the most wonderful things are generally found at the extremities of the earth.

**Tricentennial** (trəisente·niăl), *a.* and *sb. rare.* [f. TRI- + L. *centenni-um* a space of a hundred years + -AL: cf. prec.] = TERCENTENNIAL.

1882-3 *Schaff's Encycl. Relig. Knowl.* II. 1051/2 The great national Luther tri-centennial of 1817. 1893 *Cycl. Rev. Current Hist.* (U. S.) III. 311 The tricentennial exercises were held in the exposition building.

**Tricentral** to **Tricephalous**: see TRI- 1 a, 4 b.

**Triceps** (trəi·seps), *a.* and *sb.* [a. L. *triceps*, *tricipit-em* three-headed, f. TRI- + *-cep-s*, *-cipit-*, deriv. form of *cap-ut* head. Cf. F. *triceps* (16th c.).]

**A.** *adj.* Three-headed (in quot. 1577 *loosely*, consisting of three heads); *spec.* of a muscle: Having three heads or points of origin (see B).

1577 GRANGE *Golden Aphrod.*, etc. R ij b, The Triceps head of Cerberus. 1804 ABERNETHY *Surg. Obs.* 99 An agitation of fluid was felt beneath the triceps muscle in the inside of the arm. 1881 MIVART *Cat* 96 A rough process or 'tuberosity', into which the triceps muscle is inserted.

**B.** *sb.* A triceps muscle; *spec.* that of the thigh (*triceps extensor cruris*, *t. femoralis*) and that of the upper arm (*t. extensor cubiti*, *t. humeralis*).

1704 J. HARRIS *Lex. Techn.* I, *Triceps*, is a Muscle of the Thigh, so called from its three Heads or Beginnings. 1846 BRITTAN tr. *Malgaigne's Man. Oper. Surg.* 211 The brachial [artery]..between the biceps and the internal portion of the triceps. 1860 O. W. HOLMES *Elsie V.* iii. (1887) 33 The triceps..furnishes the *calf* of the upper arm.

Hence † **Trice·ptic** *a.* (*nonce-wd.*) [irreg. for TRICIPITAL], three-headed.

1716 M. DAVIES *Athen. Brit.* II. To Rdr. 41 Those.. Triceptick or Trifaucian Cerberus's.

**Triceptor**: see TRI- 4 c.

‖ **Triceratops** (trəise·rătǫps). *Palæont.* [mod.L., f. Gr. τρικέρατ-ος three-horned + ὤψ face.] A genus of gigantic predentate dinosaurs of the family *Ceratopsidæ*, having a strong nasal horn, besides two large pointed horns above the eyes; found in the Laramie beds of the United States.

1892 *Pall Mall G.* 22 Mar. 7/1 In the same neighbourhood also has been discovered recently another reptilian monster called the triceratops, which had an enormous bony frill around the back of its neck..measuring six feet across... The animal, though tremendously massive, was only thirty feet long. 1910 *Spectator* 21 May 838/2 The oddest is the gigantic triceratops, the three-horned herbivorous dinosaur.

**Tricesail**, variant of TRYSAIL.

**Trich**, variant of TRECHE *v. Obs.*, to cheat.

**Trichæsthesia** to **Trichauxis**: see TRICHO-[1].

† **Tri·chard.** *Obs.* [a. OF. *trichart*, mod. Norm. dial. *trichard*, f. *trichier*, *trechier*, TRECHE *v.*] A deceiver, a cheat.

*a* 1327 *Pol. Songs* (Camden) 69 Richard, thah thou be ever trichard, trichen shalt thou never more.

**Trichechine** (tri·kěkəin), *a.* and *sb. Zool.* [f. mod.L. *Trichech-us* (Artedi 1705-35; f. Gr. θρίξ, stem τριχ- hair + ἔχ-ειν to have; applied to the manatee 'quia solus inter pisces fere hirsutus est'); name (now disused) of a genus including the manatee and walrus: see -INE[1].] **a.** *adj.* Belonging to or having the characters of the family *Trichechidæ* or walruses. **b.** *sb.* An animal of this family, a walrus. So **Trichechodont** (trike·kodǫnt) [Gr. ὀδούς, ὀδοντ- tooth] *a.*, characterized by molar teeth like those of the manatee, with cusps confluent into two or more transverse crests; *sb.* an animal having such molar teeth; **Tri·chechoid** *a.* and *sb.* = *trichechine*.

[1842 BRANDE *Dict. Sci.*, etc., Trichechus.] 1887 COPE *Orig. Fittest* vii. 249 Many of the Tapirodonts have the Trichecodont type of mandibular teeth. *Ibid.* 255 Trichecodonts. —The Mastodons and Elephants form a most complete series between this form and the Bunodonts. 1888 *Cassell's Encycl. Dict.*, Trichechine. 1891 *Cent. Dict.*, Trichechoid.

**Tricherie, -erous**, obs. ff. TREACHERY, -EROUS.

**Trichi** (tri·tʃi). *colloq.* or *slang.* Also **trichy.** Short for TRICHINOPOLI (cigar).

1877 R. F. BURTON *Sind Revisited* I. i. 7 We smoked, generally Manilla cheroots, now supplanted by foul Dindigals and fetid 'Trichies'. 1886 YULE & BURNELL *Hobson-Jobson*, *Trichies* or *Tritchies*, the familiar name of the cheroots made at Trichinopoly; long, and rudely made, with a straw inserted at the end for the mouth. 1889 *Blackw.*

*Mag.* Aug. 238, I had smoked a trichy whilst lazily watching the fleecy clouds.

‖ **Trichiasis** (triki,ǟ·sis, trikəi·ăsis). *Path.* [Late L., a. Gr. τριχίασις (Galen), f. τριχιᾶν to be hairy.] **a.** Introversion of the eye-lashes; also, growth of an extra row of eye-lashes beneath the normal ones. **b.** A disease in which small filamentous bodies are passed in the urine: = PILIMICTION. **c.** A disease of the breasts in suckling women, in which the nipples crack into fine fissures.

**1661** LOVELL *Hist. Anim. & Min.* 340 The trichiasis, when haires grow under the natural, and prick the eye. **1693** tr. *Blancard's Phys. Dict.* (ed. 2), *Trichiasis*,..hairy Urine, such as by reason of pituitous Humours Hairs seem to swim in. **1706** PHILLIPS (ed. Kersey), *Trichiasis*, or *Trichosis*, a growing of much Hair: Also a fault in the Eyelids when there is a double row of Hairs. **1839–47** *Todd's Cycl. Anat.* III. 82/2 One of the operations for trichiasis is to extirpate the roots of the eye-lashes. **1857** DUNGLISON *Med. Lex.*, *Trichiasis*...This name has been given..1. To a disease of the kidneys or bladder, in which filamentous substances, resembling hairs, are passed in the urine...2. To a painful swelling of the breasts, in child-bed women, when the milk is excreted with difficulty. **1878** T. BRYANT *Pract. Surg.* I. 312 The hair bulbs may become displaced, causing the eyelashes to be misdirected—'trichiasis'.

‖ **Trichidium** (triki·diŏm). *Bot.* Pl. **-ia.** [mod.L., f. Gr. θρίξ, τριχ- hair: cf. ANTHERIDIUM.] A simple or branched hair-like body which supports the spores in certain fungi, as *Geaster*.

**1842** BRANDE *Dict. Sci.*, etc., *Trichidium*, a netted filamentous organ..in which the spores of some kinds of fungi are included. **1866** *Treas. Bot.*, *Trichidium*, a hair which bears the spores of such fungals as *Geastrum*.

‖ **Trichina** (tri·kină, trikəi·nă). *Zool.* Pl. **-æ.** Also in anglicized form (or from Fr.) **trichine.** [mod.L. *Trichina* (whence F. *trichine*), f. Gr. τρίχινος adj. 'of hair', f. θρίξ, τριχ- hair.] A genus of minute parasitic nematoid worms; *esp.* the species *T. spiralis*, which infests man and various animals, the adult inhabiting the intestinal tract, and the larvæ migrating to and becoming encysted in the muscular tissue, causing TRICHINOSIS.

**1835** *Trans. Zool. Soc.* I. 323, I have seen in..the diseased muscle, groups of minute oblong vesicles..these may..be germs of the *Trichina*. **1858** COPLAND *Dict. Pract. Med.* III. 1399 The *Trichina* having found a resting place, a cyst closely adhering to the tissues is formed round it. **1875** tr. *von Ziemssen's Cycl. Med.* III. 651 To exterminate the rat is to exterminate trichinæ.

*attrib.* **1857** tr. *Küchenmeister's Anim. & Veg. Parasites* (Syd. Soc.) I. 351 The spot to which it reached during the trichina-life. (**1865** *Even. Standard* 12 Dec. 5/2 The trichine disease continues its ravages at Hadersleben.) **1897** *Allbutt's Syst. Med.* II. 1051 Examination of the rats of different countries proves the extreme liability of this rodent to trichina infection. **1901** *Mem. & Lett. Sir J. Paget* iii. 58 Epidemics of this trichina-fever.

Hence **Tri·chinal** *a.*, of or pertaining to the trichina (in quot. 1857 *spec.* the larva); **Trichi·natous** *a.* erroneous formation for TRICHINOUS; ‖ **Trichiniasis** (trikinəi·ăsis) [mod.L.: cf. *elephantiasis*] = TRICHINOSIS; **Tri·chinid**, a worm of the family *Trichinidæ*; **Trichiniferous** (trikini·fĕrəs) *a.* [-FEROUS], containing or conveying trichinæ; **Trichinize** (tri·kinəiz) *v.*, *trans.* to infect with trichinæ (hence **Tri:chiniza·tion**, **Tri·chinized** *ppl. a.*); **Trichinoid** (tri·kinoid) *a.*, resembling or allied to *Trichina*.

**1857** tr. *Küchenmeister's Anim. & Veg. Parasites* (Syd. Soc.) I. 346 It is almost impossible to determine during the *Trichinal existence, to which of the two sexes the mature animal would belong. **1885** A. W. BLYTH in *Leisure Hour* Jan. 25/2 This ham..was discovered to be swarming with..trichinal cysts. **1870** NICHOLSON *Man. Zool.* xxvi. I. 152 If ..a portion of *trichinatous muscle be eaten by a warm-blooded vertebrate, and so introduced into the alimentary canal, an immediate development of young Trichinae is the result. **1854–67** C. A. HARRIS *Dict. Med. Terminol.* s.v. *Trichina*, The disease..called *Trichiniasis or Trichina disease. **1871** SIR T. WATSON *Lect. Princ. & Pract. Physic* (ed. 5) II. 636 Within a month after the dinner 20 of these persons had died of, and more than 80 were then suffering from, 'trichiniasis'. **1869** E. A. PARKES *Pract. Hygiene* (ed. 3) 195 The eating of raw *trichiniferous pork is the chief cause of the propagation of the entozoon to man. **1864** *N. Syd. Soc. Year-bk. Med.* 175 Experiments with picro-nitrate of potash on *trichinised rabbits. **1866** *Standard* 19 Feb., The cat and the dog were both trichinised experimentally.

**Trichinopoli** (tritʃinǫ·pŏli). Also **-poly.** Name of a district and city in the Madras presidency; used *attrib.*, as *Trichinopoli cigar*, *work*; also *absol.* = T. cigar (*colloq.* abbreviated to TRICHI).

**1863** *Reliquary* Oct. 68 It [an Irish brooch] has also an attached silver chain, of that peculiar construction known as Trichinopoly-work. **1887** DOYLE *Stud. Scarlet* I. iii, He ..smoked a Trichinopoly cigar. *Ibid.* I. iv, Such an ash as is only made by a Trichinopoly.

**Trichinoscope** (tri·kino-, trikəi·noskoup). [f. TRICHINA + -SCOPE.] An instrument for examining meat in order to detect the presence of trichinæ (*Cent. Dict.* 1891).

**Trichinosis** (trikinōᵘ·sis). *Path.* [mod.L., f. TRICHIN-A + -OSIS.] A disease caused by the introduction of trichinæ into the alimentary canal, and the migration of their embryos or larvæ into the muscular tissue; characterized by digestive disturbance, slight fever, swelling, pain, and lameness in the muscles, etc. Also *attrib.*

**1866** *Daily Tel.* 18 Jan. 5/2 Learned professors have declared that a large proportion of the flesh of swine sold in the markets of Berlin..is poisoned by a dreadful distemper called trichinosis—by myriads of trichinæ. *Ibid.*, A congress of *savants* and medical men to confer on the great trichinosis question. **1890** B. A. WHITELEGGE *Hygiene & Public Health* ix. 211 Trichinosis in man is generally due to the consumption of the imperfectly cooked flesh of a pig suffering from the disease.

Hence **Trichinosed** (tri·kinōᵘzd) *ppl. a.*, infected with trichinosis, or with trichinæ; **Trichinotic** (-ǫ·tik) *a.*, pertaining or relating to trichinosis.

**1881** *Daily News* 3 Feb., The rejection by Italy and Germany of whole cargoes of American trichinosed bacon has glutted with it the French market. **1889** *Lancet* 4 May 901/2 The very long duration of the disease is a slight argument also against the trichinotic view.

**Trichinous** (tri·kinəs), *a.* [f. TRICHINA + -OUS.] Infested with trichinæ; affected with, or of the nature of, trichinosis.

**1857** tr. *Küchenmeister's Anim. & Veg. Parasites* (Syd. Soc.) I. 353 In pigeons fed with trichinous mole's flesh, Herbst found many free Trichinæ. **1866** *Reader* 10 Feb. 154/3 The town of Hadersleben in the Hartz was the scene of a terrible outbreak of a trichinous disease, resulting in the death of some eighty people.

**Trichite** (tri·kəit, trəi·-), *sb.* [f. Gr. θρίξ, τριχ- hair + -ITE[1]; in *Min.*, a. Ger. *trichit* (Zirkel, 1867).]

**1.** *Min.* A name for very minute dark-coloured hair-like bodies occurring in the substance of some vitreous rocks.

**1868** DANA *Min.* (ed. 5) 805 The name *Trichite*..is applied by Zirkel..to microscopic capillary forms, often curved, bent, or zigzag,..opaque and black or reddish-brown, of undetermined nature, which he detected in some..glassy..volcanic rocks. **1879** RUTLEY *Study Rocks* x. 162 Trichites ..are minute elongated bodies resembling small hairs or fibres.

**2.** *Zool.* A name for extremely fine siliceous fibres found in certain sponge-spicules, or for such spicules themselves: see quot. 1887. Also *attrib.*

**1887** SOLLAS in *Encycl. Brit.* XXII. 418/1 (*Sponges*) A curious group of flesh spicules are the *trichites*. In this group silica..forms within the scleroblast a sheaf of immeasurably fine fibrillæ or trichites...The trichite sheaf may be regarded as a fibrillated spicule. **1890** *Cassell's Nat. Hist.* VI. 322 In other forms, the trichites grow radiately outward .., and becoming thickened with age, produce a trichite-stellate, or, if they are very numerous, a trichite-globate or globate spicule.

**3.** *Bot.* (See quot.)

**1900** B. D. JACKSON *Gloss. Bot. Terms* 275 *Trichite*, a needle-shaped crystal of amylose in starch grains, stated to form the latter by aggregation (A. Meyer).

Hence **Trichitic** (-i·tik) *a.*, pertaining to or of the nature of a trichite, or containing trichites.

**1879** RUTLEY *Stud. Rocks* x. 170 Minute granules and trichitic bodies.

† **Tri·chite**, *a. Obs. rare.* [f. as prec.] Characterized by very fine fracture, so as to resemble or suggest hairs or fine filaments.

**1764** PLATT in *Phil. Trans.* LIV. 41 The shells of the trichite kind. *Ibid.*, *note*, The more debased sort breaks in a hairy trichite manner.

**Trichiurid** (triki,yūᵊ·rid). *Ichthyol.* [f. mod.L. *Trichiuridæ* pl. (see -ID[3]), f. *Trichiūrus*, properly *Trichūrus*, generic name, f. Gr. θρίξ, τριχ- hair + οὐρά tail.] A fish of the family *Trichiuridæ* (the hair-tails), typified by the genus *Trichiurus*, characterized by a ribbon-like body and a long filament at the end of the tail. Also **Trichiure.** So **Trichi,u·riform**, **Trichi,u·roid** *adjs.*, having the form of the fishes of this genus or family.

[**1774** GOLDSM. *Nat. Hist.* (1862) II. III. i. 294 Trichurus.] **1819** *Pantologia*, *Trichiurus*, Trichiure...1. *T. lepturus*, Silver-trichiure. **1854** BADHAM *Halieut.* 407. **1865** *Athenæum* 20 May 688/1 A new form of Trichiuroid Fishes. **1891** *Cent. Dict.*, Trichiuriform. **1895** *Funk's Standard Dict.*, Trichiurid.

**Trichlor-, trichloro-** (trəi,klōᵊ·ro). *Chem.* [f. TRI- 5 c + CHLOR(O-.] A formative analogous to TRIBROM(O-, expressing the substitution of three atoms of chlorine for hydrogen, as in *trichlorobenzene*, $C_6H_3Cl_3$; so *trichloracetic* acid, $CCl_3 . CO_2H$, etc.

**1845** HOFMANN in *Mem. & Proc. Chem. Soc.* II. 286 Trichloraniline..$C_{12}H_4Cl_3N$..procured..by the direct action of chlorine on aniline or the chlorinated base. **1876** HARLEY *Royle's Mat. Med.* 339 The aldehyde thus formed is immediately attacked by the chlorine and converted into hydrochloric acid and trichloraldehyde or chloral. **1912** THORPE *Dict. Appl. Chem.* II. 44 Chloroform, *Trichloromethane* $CHCl_3$..was discovered by Liebig in 1831.

**Trichlo·rate, Trichlo·ride**: see TRI- 5 a.

**Trichlorhydrin** (trəi,klōᵊɹ,həi·drin). *Chem.* [f. TRI- 5 a + *chlorhydr*(*ic* + -IN[1] (termination of the compound ethers of glycerin: see TRIACETIN).] Glyceryl trichloride, $C_3H_5Cl_3$, a haloid ester or compound ether of glycerin or glycerol, $C_3H_5(OH)_3$, in which the three OH groups are replaced by chlorine atoms.

**1862** MILLER *Elem. Chem.* III. 281 Trichlorhydrin .. is a neutral liquid, insoluble in water.

**Tricho-**[1] (triko, trəiko), before a vowel **trich-** (trik, trəik), ad. Gr. τριχο-, τριχ-, combining stem of θρίξ hair, in many terms of botany, zoology, etc. ‖ **Trichæsthe·sia** *Path.* [mod.L., f. Gr. αἴσθησις feeling], a form of paræsthesia consisting in a sensation as of a hair on the skin. ‖ **Trichangia** (-æ·ndʒiă) *sb. pl.* [f. Gr. ἀγγεῖον vessel], the capillary blood-vessels; hence ‖ **Tricha·ngiecta·sia, -e·ctasis** *Path.* [f. Gr. ἔκτασις extension], dilatation of the capillaries. ‖ **Trichatro·phia** *Path.* [see ATROPHY], atrophy of the hair-bulbs, causing brittleness of the hair. ‖ **Trichau·xis** [f. Gr. αὔξη, αὔξησις increase], excessive growth of hair. ‖ **Trichobacte·ria**, (*a*) the filamentous or thread-like bacteria; (*b*) bacteria which possess flagella (Dorland *Med. Dict.* 1900–13). **Tri·choblast** *Bot.* [Gr. βλαστός germ, taken as = cell], name for certain special cells or idioblasts resembling hairs. ‖ **Trichobranchia** (-bræ·ŋkiă) *Zool.* [BRANCHIA], (in pl. -æ), name for the gills, set with filaments, of certain decapod crustaceans; hence **Tricho·bra·nchial** *a.*, pertaining to or of the nature of such gills; **Trichobra·nchiate** *a.*, having or characterized by such gills. **Trichoca·rpous** *a.* *Bot.* [Gr. καρπός fruit], having hairy fruit (*Cent. Dict.* 1891). ‖ **Trichocephalus** (-se·fălŏs) *Zool.* [mod.L. (Goeze, 1782), f. Gr. κεφαλή head], a genus of parasitic nematoid worms, having the head filamentous; hence **Trichoce·phalid**, a worm of the family *Trichocephalidæ*, typified by this genus; **Trichoce·phaloid** *a.*, resembling or akin to the genus *Trichocephalus*. ‖ **Trichocla·sia, -o·clasis** [Gr. κλάσις fracture], brittleness of the hair. ‖ **Trichocrypto·sis** [Gr. κρυπτός concealed], disease of the hair-follicles. **Tri·chocyst** (-sist) *Zool.* [CYST: named by Allman 1855], one of a number of minute rod-like bodies, each containing a coiled protrusible filament, found in the cuticle of many *Infusoria*, resembling the thread-cells of cœlenterates; hence **Trichocy·stic** *a.* (*Cent. Dict.* 1891). ‖ **Trichodectes** (-de·ktīz) [Gr. δέκτης receiver, beggar], a genus of insects parasitic on quadrupeds; *T. lotus* is the dog-louse; *T. sphærocephalus*, the red-headed sheep-louse. **Tricho·do·ntid** *Ichthyol.*, a fish of the family *Trichodontidæ* [mod.L., f. *Trichodon* (Tilesius, 1811), f. Gr. ὀδούς, ὀδοντ- tooth], a sand-fish; so **Tricho·do·ntoid** *a.*, akin to the sand-fishes. **Tri·chogen** (-dʒen) [-GEN], a hypodermal cell, in insects and other arthropods, from which a hair arises. **Tricho·genous** *a.*, producing, or promoting the growth of, hair. **Trichoglo·ssine** *a.*, *Ornith.* [Gr. γλῶσσα tongue], belonging to the subfamily *Trichoglossinæ* or brush-tongued parakeets, of which *Trichoglossus Swainsonii* (Swainson's lory) is a well-known Australian example. **Tri·chogyne** (-dʒəin) *Bot.* [Gr. γυνή woman], a hair-like process forming the receptive part of the female reproductive organ or procarp in certain algæ and fungi; hence **Trichogynial** (-dʒi·niăl), **Trichogynic** (-dʒi·nik) *adjs.* **Trichomonad** (-mǫ·næd) *Zool.* [MONAD 4], an infusorian of the genus *Trichomonas*, characterized by several flagella and hair-like processes; some species are parasitic in man and other animals. **Trichomy·cterine, -my·cteroid** *adjs.*, *Ichthyol.* [Gr. μυκτήρ nostril], belonging respectively to the subfamily *Trichomycterinæ* and the family *Trichomycteridæ* (or *Pygidiidæ*) of fishes (cat-fishes), found in S. American rivers (*Cent. Dict.*); also as *sbs.* **Trichono·tid** *Ichthyol.* [Gr. νῶτος back; from the long hair-like dorsal ray of the species *Trichonotus setigerus*], a fish of the family *Trichonotidæ*; so **Trichono·toid** *a.* and *sb.* **Trichopa·thic** *a.* [Gr. πάθος suffering], relating to diseases of the hair; so **Tricho·pathy** [-PATHY], treatment of diseases of the hair. **Trichophocine** (-fōᵘ·səin) *a.*, *Zool.* [Gr. φώκη seal], belonging to the subfamily *Trichophocinæ* or hair-seals (*Cent. Dict.*). **Tri·chophore** (-fōᵊɹ) [Gr. -φόρος bearing], (*a*) *Bot.* (see quot. 1860: ? *obs.*); (*b*) *Bot.* the structure which bears the trichogyne in florideous algæ; (*c*) *Zool.* one of several projections of the integument in certain annelids, from which spring bundles of setæ or bristles; **Trichopho·ric** (-fǫ·rik) *a.*, pertaining to or of the nature of a trichophore; **Tricho·phorous** *a.*, bearing hairs or hair-like bodies; of the nature of a trichophore. **Tricho·pter** *Entom.* [Gr. πτερόν wing], a member of the group *Trichoptera* of neuropterous insects, characterized by specially hairy wings; a caddis-fly; so **Tricho·pteran** *a.* = *trichopterous*; *sb.* = *trichopter*; **Tricho·pterist**, one who studies the *Trichoptera*; **Tricho·pterous** *a.*, belonging to or having the characters of the *Trichoptera*, hairy-winged. **Trichopterygid** (-pte·ridʒid) *Entom.* [Gr. πτέρυξ wing], *sb.* a member of the family *Trichopteryˈgidæ* of clavicorn beetles, having the wings fringed with hairs, and comprising the smallest beetles known; *a.* belonging to or having the characters of this family; so **Trichopteˑrygoid** *a.* **Trichoptile** (trikǫˑptil) *Ornith.* [Gr. πτίλον down], a hair-like prolongation of the sheath of a growing feather, forming part of the downy covering of the young of certain birds; hence **Trichoˑptilar** *a.*, pertaining to or of the nature of a trichoptile. ‖ **Trichorrhœˑa** [Gr. -ῥοια flowing], falling off of the hair. ‖ **Trichoschisis** (-ǫˑskisis) [Gr. σχίσις splitting], splitting of the hair. **Trichosoˑmatous** *a., Zool.* [Gr. σῶμα body], belonging to the division *Trichosomata* of flagellate *Infusoria*. ‖ **Triˑchosporaˑngium**, pl. **-ia** (also anglicized **trichoˑsporange**) *Bot.*, Thuret's term for the multilocular sporangium of certain fucoid algæ, which appears to consist of jointed hairs (distinguished from Oosporangium); hence **Trichosporaˑngial** *a.* **Triˑchospore** *Bot.*, a spore or conidium borne upon a filamentous stalk, in certain fungi. **Trichostoˑmatous** *a., Zool.* [Gr. στόμα mouth], belonging to the order *Trichostomata* of *Protozoa*, having the mouth and pharynx provided with vibratile membranes and cilia, by the movements of which particles of food are drawn in. **Trichothaˑllic** *a., Bot.* (see quots.).

**1902** *Nature* 7 Aug. 360/1 On a new form of tactile sensibility, *trichesthesia, by MM. N. Vaschide and P. Rousseau. **1857** Dunglison *Med. Lex.*, *Trichangia..*Trichangiectasia. **1890** Billings *Nat. Med. Dict.*, *Trichangiectasis..*Trichatrophia..*Trichauxis. **1882** Vines *Sachs' Bot.* 85 These cells..present the appearance, when the petiole is broken across..of tough, slender hairs projecting out of the tissue. For idioblasts of this kind I [Sachs] propose the term *Trichoblast, in order to express their resemblance to many epidermal trichomes. **1878** *Proc. Zool. Soc.* 4 June 776 They.. may be called '*trichobranchiæ', in contradistinction to the lamellar gills or 'phyllobranchiæ', which are met with in a large number of other Crustacea. **1891** *Cent. Dict.*, *Trichobranchial. **1878** *Proc. Zool. Soc.* 4 June 777 Among the *trichobranchiate Podophthalmia, the Euphausidæ possess no other than podobranchiæ. **1880** E. R. Lankester in *Nature* 12 Feb. 355/2 Crayfishes..differ from prawns..in being 'trichobranchiate' in place of 'phyllobranchiate'. **1819** *Pantologia*, *Trichocephalus, a genus of the class vermes. **1846** *Proc. Amer. Phil. Soc.* IV. 232 He had found the tricocephalus in the human cœcum after death. **1897** *Allbutt's Syst. Med.* II. 1048 Found in association with a high degree of trichocephalus infection. **1895** *Funk's Standard Dict.*, *Trichoclasia..*Trichoclasis. **1890** Billings *Nat. Med. Dict.*, *Tricho-cryptoses. **1900–13** Dorland *Med. Dict.*, Trichocryptosis. **1859** J. R. Greene *Man. Anim. Kingd.*, *Protozoa* 66 In the cortical layer of Bursaria, certain peculiar fusiform bodies or '*trichocysts' have been detected, and from these Prof. Allman states that he has observed the emission of minute filaments [resembling] the urticating organs of the fresh-water polype. **1880** Kent *Infusoria* I. 249 A sheaf-shaped fascicle of rod-like trichocysts. **1876** tr. *Beneden's Anim. Parasites* 71 The *trichodectes of the dog has lately attracted the especial notice of naturalists. **1898** Packard *Text-bk. Entomol.* 188 Each of these pores communicates with a hair-forming hypodermal cell, called by Graber a **trichogen*. **1853** E. Wilson *Healthy Skin* (ed. 4) Index, *Trichogenous remedies. **1879** A. R. Wallace *Australas.* iii. 59 The *Trichoglossidæ, or brush-tongued Lories. **1875** Bennett & Dyer *Sachs' Bot.* 212 The term *Trichogyne is given to a long thin hair-like hyaline sac, which serves as a receptive organ, and springs from a structure..called the Trichophore. The latter is a body usually consisting of several cells. **1877** Huxley *Anat. Inv. Anim.* Introd. 29 The protoplasmic body of the trichogyne, which unites with the spermatozooids, does not undergo division itself. **1882** Vines *Sachs' Bot.* 238. **1900** B. D. Jackson *Gloss. Bot. Terms*, **Trichogynial*, relating to a trichogyne. **1891** *Cent. Dict.*, *Trichogynic. **1861** Hulme tr. *Moquin-Tandon* II. vii. 407 The *Trichomonads..form irregular masses with the particles of thickened mucus. **1889** J. M. Duncan *Clin. Lect. Dis. Wom.* xxii. (ed. 4) 179 At one time it was supposed that the discovery of trichomonads, or a leptothrix, or a vibrio, would decide whether it was venereal or not. **1891** *Cent. Dict.*, *Trichopathic. **1900–13** Dorland *Med. Dict.* **1860** Mayne *Expos. Lex.*, **Trichopathy*, a term proposed..for the system of treating diseased affections of the hair. *Ibid.*, *Trichophorus*...Name by Nees von Esenbeck for the filamentous base of mushrooms, when the filaments, by their agglutination, form a kind of membrane: a *trichophore. **1875** [see *trichogyne*]. **1877** Huxley *Anat. Inv. Anim.* v. 229 Stiff hair-like appendages..developed within diverticula of the integument, or trichophores, in which their bases always remain enclosed. **1882** Vines *Sachs' Bot.* 238 In the true Florideæ..a lateral row of cells bears at its apex a closed hair-like prolongation, the trichogyne, and is hence termed the *Trichophore*. **1891** *Cent. Dict.*, *Trichophoric. **1892** *Jrnl. Linn. Soc., Bot.* XXIX. 74 Not unfrequently this trichophoric apparatus consists of three cells—two basal trichophoric cells and the trichogyne. **1864** Webster, *Trichopter. **1826** Kirby & Sp. *Entomol.* IV. xlvii. 379 The existence..of the collar in the *Trichoptera. **1835** Kirby *Hab. & Inst. Anim.* II. xx. 318 The *Trichoptera* (Caseworm-flies) have four hairy membranous wings. **1842** Brande *Dict. Sci., Art*, etc., *Trichopterans. **1897** *Naturalist* 115 Neuropterists and *trichopterists have commenced..as lepidopterists. **1816** Kirby & Sp. *Entomol.* (1818) II. xxi. 243 *Phryganea grandis* ..is a *trichopterous insect. **1826** *Ibid.* IV. xlvii. 375 There is no tendency in the saw-flies towards a Trichopterous type. **1891** *Cent. Dict.*, *Trichopterygid. **1895** *Funk's Standard Dict.*, *Trichopterygoid. **1900** *Ibis* Oct. 665 The actual feather-sheath makes its appearance, pushing before it its *trichoptilar appendage, which has now become abraded. *Ibid.* 654, I shall term these thread-like structures *trichoptiles. **1860** Mayne *Expos. Lex.*, *Trichorrhœa. **1857** Dunglison *Med. Lex.*, *Trichoschisis. **1891** *Cent. Dict.*, *Trichosporange. **1900** in B. D. Jackson *Gloss. Bot. Terms*. **1887** *Trans. Roy. Soc. Edin.* XXXII. 591 The *trichosporangial form [of fruit of *Ectocarpus*] is well known. **1857** Berkeley *Cryptog. Bot.* § 67. 88 The two organs called Oosporangia and *Trichosporangia by Thuret. **1909** *Cent. Dict. Suppl.*, *Trichostomatous. **1890** *Athenæum* 29 Nov. 743/1 The formation of the plantlets by *trichothallic gemmation from the tufts of..hairs..on the old thallus of *P[unctaria] plantaginea* and *P. latifolia*. **1900** B. D. Jackson *Gloss. Bot. Terms*, *Trichothallic*..when the shoot ends in one or more multicellular hairs or tufts of such.

**Tricho-** [2] (triko, trəikǫ), combining form repr. Gr. τρίχα, τριχῇ in three, triply: used in a few more or less technical words. These are modern, formed on the analogy of Gr. compounds in διχο-, Dicho-. (Gr. compounds in τριχο- are only from θρίξ, τριχ- hair: see prec.) **Trichocladose** (trikǫˑklădōus) *a. Zool.* [Gr. κλάδος shoot], having triple or trifurcate *cladi* or secondary rays, as a sponge-spicule. **Trichotriæne** (-trəi,īˑn) *Zool.*, in sponge-spicules, a triæne of which each of the three *cladi* is trifurcate. See also Trichotomic, etc.

**1887** Sollas in *Encycl. Brit.* XXII. 416 (Fig. 13) (*Sponges*) *p*, amphitriæne (this is trichoclادose). *Ibid.* 423/2 Canal system diplodal. Spicules trichotriænes.

**Trichodal** (trikōuˑdăl), *a. Zool.* [f. Gr. τριχώδης hair-like (f. θρίξ, τριχ- hair: see -ode) + -al.] Extremely thin: applied to a sponge-spicule.

**1888** Sollas in *Challenger Rep.* XXV. p. lviii, Both the rhabdus and the style may..be..immeasurably thin (trichodal, τριχώδης, hair-like).

**Trichoid** (triˑkoid), *a. rare.* [ad. Gr. τριχοειδής (applied by Galen to the capillary blood-vessels), f. θρίξ, τριχ- hair + εἶδος form: see -oid.] Resembling hair or a hair; hairlike; capillary.

**1854–67** C. A. Harris *Dict. Med. Terminol.*, *Trichoid*, resembling a hair.

**Trichoˑlogy.** [f. Gr. θρίξ, τριχ- hair: see -ology.] The study of the structure, functions, and diseases of the hair. Hence **Tricholoˑgical** *a.*, pertaining to or engaged in trichology; **Trichoˑlogist**, one who is versed in trichology.

**1860** Mayne *Expos. Lex.*, *Trichology*, term for the doctrine of the hair. **1887** *Standard* 28 Oct. 5/3 The Elements of Trichological Science. *Ibid.*, The Trichologists study the physiology and the diseases of the hair. **1895** J. J. Raven *Hist. Suffolk* 253 Something may be discoverable by craniology, trichology, odontology. **1913** *Daily News* 4 Oct. 9 The study of the hair is becoming a science with a national institute of its own—the National Institute of Trichologists.

‖ **Trichoma** (trikōuˑmă). Pl. **trichoˑmata.** [mod.L., a. Gr. τρίχωμα a growth of hair, f. τριχοῦν to cover with hair.]

**1.** *Path.* A disease of the hair: = Plica 1.

**1799** Hooper *Med. Dict.*, *Trichōma*, a disease of the hair. See *Plica polonica*. **1857** Dunglison *Med. Lex.*, *Trichoma*, Capillamentum, Plica.

**2.** *Bot.* Each of the filaments composing the thallus in algæ of the order *Nostochineæ*.

**1866** *Treas. Bot.*, *Trichoma*, the filamentous thallus of algals, as *Conferva*. **1879** W. G. Farlow *Marine Algæ* (1881) 11 In..the Nostochineæ, the cells are..attached to one another in the form of filaments, to which the name of *trichomata* is given.

Hence (from sense 1) **Trichoˑmaphyte** (-fəit) [Gr. φυτόν plant], a cryptogamic growth formerly supposed to cause trichoma; **Trichoˑmatose** *a.*, affected with trichoma.

**1857** in Dunglison *Med. Lex.*

‖ **Trichomanes** (trikǫˑmănīz). *Bot.* [L. (Pliny), a. Gr. τριχομανές a kind of fern (cf. τριχομανία a mania or passion for long hair).] A genus of ferns, having filamentous outgrowths from the margins of the fronds; the bristle-ferns.

**1562** Turner *Herbal* II. 157 b, Trichomanes (that is our English Maydens heare). **1706** Phillips (ed. Kersey), *Trichomanes*, the Herb Maiden-hair or Goldilocks. **1757** Parsons in *Phil. Trans.* L. 401 We see the leaves of ferns of several kinds, polypodium, tricomanes, and other capillary plants. **1885** Lady Brassey *The Trades* 234 Such ferns as trichomanes, hymenophyllums, and many others growing in the greatest luxuriance.

Hence **Trichoˑmanoid** *a.*, resembling or akin to the ferns of this genus.

**1900** in B. D. Jackson *Gloss. Bot. Terms*.

**Trichome** (tri-, trəiˑkōum). *Bot.* [ad. Gr. τρίχωμα (see Trichoma); cf. Caulome.] The general name for any outgrowth of the epidermis or superficial tissue of a plant, as hairs, scales, prickles, etc.

**1875** Bennett & Dyer tr. *Sachs' Bot.* 129 We may term all appendages of other parts which originate as outgrowths of epidermis-cells, whatever their form and function, Hairs (Trichomes). Thus the so-called paleæ and sporangia of Ferns are trichomes. **1876** *Encycl. Brit.* IV. 90/1 Hairs, scales, prickles, &c.,..all have been embraced under the general name *trichome*.

**Trichophyte** (triˑkǫfəit). Chiefly in mod.L. form **Trichoˑphyton.** [f. Gr. θρίξ, τριχ- hair + φυτόν plant.] A genus of minute fungi, parasitic on the skin; esp. the species *Trichophyton tonsurans*, which produces ringworm.

**1862** H. Macmillan in *Macm. Mag.* Oct. 463/1 Another variety of tric[h]ophyton or hair-plant which luxuriates on the beard. **1876** Duhring *Dis. Skin* 70 The trichophyton, giving rise to three affections, tinea circinata, tinea tonsurans, and tinea sycosis. **1898** P. Manson *Trop. Diseases* xxxvii. 579 Itching rings, or segments of rings, of trichophyton infection. **1899** *Allbutt's Syst. Med.* VIII. 779 Conglomerative pustular perifolliculitis..due to one of the trichophyton fungi. *Ibid.* 855 Sabouraud thinks it probable that the trichophytes, or some of them, may exist independently as saprophytes.

Hence **Trichophytic** (-fiˑtik) *a.*, of or pertaining to a trichophyte; **Trichophytoˑsis**: see quot. 1890.

**1890** Billings *Med. Dict.*, *Trichophytosis*, disease of the skin produced by the tric[h]ophyton fungus. **1899** *Allbutt's Syst. Med.* VIII. 854 It is rare to find the same species of large-spored fungus in any two cases of trichophytic ringworm. *Ibid.* 863 Lesions of trichophytic appearance. *Ibid.*, Lesions having the circinate form..characteristic of trichophytosis.

**Trichor, -our, -ory**: see Treacher, Treachery.

**Trichord** (trəiˑkǭɹd), *sb.* and *a.* [ad. Gr. τρίχορδος three-stringed, f. τρι-, Tri- three + χορδή string, Chord.] **a.** *sb.* A musical instrument of three strings; a three-stringed lyre or lute. **b.** *adj.* Having three strings to each note: applied to a pianoforte in which most of the keys have three strings each.

**1776** Burney *Hist. Mus.* I. 211 Though so ancient and honourable an origin has been assigned to the Dichord and Trichord. **1866** Mrs. Riddell *Race for Wealth* xxiii, One of Collard's Repetition Trichord grand pianos.

‖ **Trichosis** (trikōuˑsis). *Path.* [med. or mod.L., a. Gr. τρίχωσις growth of hair (f. τριχοῦν 'to cover with hair', in pass. 'to be hairy').] **a.** = Trichiasis a. **b.** = Trichoma 1.

**1693** tr. *Blancard's Phys. Dict.* (ed. 2), *Trichosis*, the same with *Trichiasis*. **1706** Phillips (ed. Kersey), *Trichiasis*, or *Trichosis*, a growing of much Hair. **1890** Billings *Med. Dict.*, *Trichosis*, disease of the hair, plica.

**Trichotomic** (trikǫ-, trəikǫtǫˑmik), *a.* [f. Gr. τρίχα triply + -τομ-ος cut + -ic, after Dichotomic.] = Trichotomous.

**1873** Wagner tr. *Teuffel's Hist. Rom. Lit.* I. 442 A certain fondness of trichotomic composition. **1880** *Athenæum* 25 Dec. 851/3 To construct..the whole sum of human knowledge on the plan of a trichotomic system of self-division. **1882–3** *Schaff's Encycl. Relig. Knowl.* III. 2394/1 The trichotomic view [of human nature] is found in the New Testament.

**Trichotomism** (tri-, trəikǫˑtŏmiz'm). [f. as prec. + -ism: cf. Dichotomism.] A trichotomous system; trichotomy.

**1912** W. Gemmel *Diamond Sutra* 17 *note*, In later ages.. trichotomism was taught as to the nature of all Buddhas.

**Trichotomist** [1] (tri-, trəikǫˑtŏmist). *nonce-wd.* [f. Gr. *τριχοτόμος adj. hair-cutting (implied in τριχοτομεῖν to cut the hair) + -ist.] A hair-cutter.

**1875** R. F. Burton *Gorilla L.* (1876) I. 205 Whatever absurdity in hair may be demanded by the trichotomists and philopogons of Europe, I can at once supply it to any extent from Africa.

**Trichotomize** (tri-, trəikǫˑtŏməiz), *v.* [f. as next + -ize: cf. Dichotomize.] *trans.* To divide into three parts; to arrange or classify in three divisions, or in groups of three. Also *absol.* Hence **Trichoˑtomist** [2], one who trichotomizes or practises trichotomy.

**1651** *Fuller's Abel Rediv.*, *Colet* (1867) I. 121 The latter [sayings, etc.] he intended to trichotomize, or reduce unto ternaries. **1681** Baxter *Councels Yng. Men* Catal. *j, Shewing that Trinity in Unity is imprinted on the whole Creation, and that Trichotomising is the just distribution in Naturals and Morals. **1846** T. W. Jenkyn *Baxter's Wks.* Pref. Ess. 50.

**Trichotomous** (tri-, trəikǫˑtŏməs), *a.* [f. Gr. τρίχα triply + -τομ-ος cut + -ous; cf. Dichotomous.]

**1.** *Bot.* Dividing into three branches; so branched that each successive axis divides into three.

**1800** *Misc. Tr.* in *Asiatic Ann. Reg.* 273/2 Peduncles axillary,..trichotomous. **1806** Galpine *Brit. Bot.* § 29 Aira. ..Culm almost naked: pan[icle] spreading trichotomous. **1880** S. Yosino in Sir E. J. Reed *Japan* II. 44 *note*, Its stem and branches are trichotomous.

**2.** Making three divisions, classes, or categories; involving or of the nature of trichotomy.

**1855** N. Lindley *Introd. Jurisprudence* App. 85 The passages cited..are all against the trichotomous and in favour of the dichotomous division of *culpa*. **1899** Robertson in *Expositor* May 351 A trichotomous psychology.

Hence **Trichoˑtomously** *adv.*

**1830** Lindley *Nat. Syst. Bot.* 204 Flowers in regular cymes, branched bi- or trichotomously. **1853** Royle *Mat. Med.* (ed. 2) 444 Panicles short, trichotomously divided.

**Trichotomy** (tri-, trəikǫˑtŏmi). [f. Gr. τρίχα triply + -τομία cutting: after Dichotomy.] Division into three; arrangement or classification in three divisions, classes, or categories.

**1610** Healey *St. Aug. Citie of God* 303 This Trichotomy or triple division doth not contradict the other Dichotomy. **1734** J. Kirkby tr. *Barrow's Math. Lect.* viii. 119 His [Aristotle's] trichotomy..into Hypotheses, Definitions, and Axioms. **1836–7** Sir W. Hamilton *Metaph.* xli. (1870) II. 416 It remained..for Kant to establish..the decisive trichotomy of the mental powers. **1868** *Contemp. Rev.* VII. 598 Popular theology is rather founded on the dichotomy of man into body and soul, than on the Christian trichotomy of body, soul, and spirit.

**Trichroic** (trəikrōu·ik), *a.* [f. Gr. τρίχρο-ος, τρίχρους three-coloured + -IC: cf. DICHROIC.] Having or showing three colours; *spec.* of crystals, exhibiting three different colours when viewed in three different directions.

1881 S. P. THOMPSON in *Nature* 15 Sept. 465/2 Di- or trichroic absorption is a general property of all coloured crystals other than those of the cubical system. 1888 RUTLEY *Rock-Forming Min.* 100 Such crystals are said to be trichroic.

**Trichroism** (trəi·kro,iz'm). [f. as prec. + -ISM. Cf. F. *trichroïsme.*] The property of being trichroic: *spec.* **a.** *Cryst.*: see prec.

1847 WEBSTER cites Dana. 1860 in MAYNE *Expos. Lex.* 1865–8 WATTS *Dict. Chem.* III. 670 Some biaxial crystals exhibit trichroïsm; thus certain Brazilian topazes of a yellowish rose tint in the direction of the median line, are violet when viewed along the complementary line, and yellowish white perpendicular to the plane of the axes. 1881 S. P. THOMPSON in *Nature* 15 Sept. 465/2 Crystals in which the electric conductivity differs in three different directions will exhibit trichroism.

**b.** *Nat. Hist.* The occurrence of three different colorations in three varieties of a species, as in certain birds and insects.

1899 SHARP in *Cambr. Nat. Hist.* VI. vi. 351 *H[eliconius] erato* exhibits the very rare condition of trichroism, the hind wings being either red, blue, or green.

**Trichromatic** (trəi,kromæ·tik), *a.* [f. Gr. τρι-, TRI- + χρωματικός CHROMATIC; Gr. has τριχρώματος.] Having, showing, or pertaining to three colours; trichroic: *spec.* **a.** *Optics.* Having or relating to the three fundamental colour-sensations (red, green, violet) of normal vision. **b.** Applied to lithographic printing in three colours; also to a photographic process by which the natural colours are reproduced by super-position or combination of photographs taken in three different-coloured lights.

1891 in *Cent. Dict.* [in sense a]. 1896 C. G. ZANDER *Photo-trichromatic Printing* Pref., Trichromatic printing does not make the headway it deserves. *Ibid.* 36 The Young-Helmholtz theory of trichromatic vision. 1900 *Westm. Gaz.* 14 Nov. 2/1 'A Handbook of Photography in Colours'.. by Messrs. Thomas Bolas, Alexander Tallent, and Edgar Senior. The curious will find every phase of trichromatic photography expounded. 1904 *Daily News* 17 Aug. 5 Trichromatic Toy-Books...I noticed the other day that a large toy-book..was done entirely by the three-colour process—literally three printings in all.

So **Trichro·matism**, the quality of being trichromatic; *spec.* (*a*) = TRICHROISM b; (*b*) combination of three different colours, as in painting or colour-photography; **Trichro·matist**, one who uses (only) three different colours or pigments.

1854 *Blackw. Mag.* LXXVI. 330 With the unsparing use of these three unmitigated colours only..decorators..should style themselves Trichromatists [not Polychromatists]. 1895 *Funk's Stand. Dict.*, Trichromatism.

**Trichromic** (trəikrōu·mik), *a.* [f. Gr. τρι-, TRI- + χρῶμα colour + -IC: cf. DICHROMIC.] Three-coloured, three-colour; = TRICHROMATIC.

In quot. 1900 applied to abnormal vision in which only three different colours are perceived.

1881 LE CONTE *Sight* 63 Herschel regarded normal vision as trichromic. 1897 *Daily News* 6 Jan. 3/3 By the method of trichromic photography..the colours of natural objects were shown. 1900 EDRIDGE-GREEN in *Lancet* 4 Aug. 323/1 A person whose colour vision is trichromic may see a spectrum of the same length as the normal-sighted, but he sees only three colours—red, green, and violet.

**Trichronous** (trəi·kronəs), *a. Anc. Pros.* [f. Gr. τρίχρον-ος, of three times or measures (f. τρι-, TRI- + χρόνος time) + -OUS.] Containing or consisting of three times or *moræ*; having the duration of three short syllables: = TRISEMIC.

1889 *Cent. Dict.* s.v. *Dichronous*, A dichronous long (that is, an ordinary long, equal to two shorts, distinguished from a trichronous or other protracted long).

**Trichur**, variant of TREACHER *Obs.*

**Tricipital** (trəisi·pităl), *a. rare*⁻⁰. [f. L. *triceps, -cipit-em* + -AL.] = TRICEPS A.

1891 in *Cent. Dict.*

**Tricircular** (trəisə·ɹkiŭlăɹ), *a. Geom.* [f. TRI-1, 2 + CIRCULAR.] **a.** Referred to three fixed circles: said of a system of co-ordinates. **b.** Passing three times through each of the circular points at infinity: said of a curve.

1876 CAYLEY *Math. Papers* IX. 562 The sextic is a tricircular sextic having the three points *A, B, C* for foci.

**Trick** (trik), *sb.* Forms: 5–6 **trik,** *pl.* **trikkes,** 6–7 **tricke,** 6– **trick,** (7 **trike**). [In sense 1, a. OF. *trique*, Picard and Norman form of *triche* deceit, treachery, cheating, Norm. dial. *trique* trick (Moisy), going with, and prob. verbal sb. from, *trikier*, Norm.-Picard form of *trichier, trechier, trecier* to deceive, cheat, mod.F. *tricher* = Prov. *trichar, triquar*, It. *triccare* to cheat; cf. also TRECHE *v.*, TREACHER, etc. Both sb. and vb. have in Eng. had developments of signification unknown to F. *triche* and *tricher*.

The origin of the Romanic word is disputed. It was held by Diez to be of German origin; he compared Du. *trek* 'drawing, pull, which has also the sense 'trick, cunning'. But most Romanic scholars refer it to a late L. or Com. Rom. *triccāre, alteration of *trīcāre, trīcarī*, 'to trifle, play tricks', f. *tricæ* 'trifles, toys', also 'subterfuges, quirks, wiles, tricks': see Storm in *Romania* V. 172, Ulrich in *Zeitschr. f. Rom. Phil.* IX. 566.]

**I. 1.** A crafty or fraudulent device of a mean or base kind; an artifice to deceive or cheat; a stratagem, ruse, wile; esp. in phrase *to play* (*show*) *one a trick, to put a trick* or *tricks upon*: see PLAY *v.* 9, PUT *v.*[1] 23 d, and cf. sense 2.

*c* 1412 HOCCLEVE *De Reg. Princ.* 2286 Of suche vnknyghtly trikkes he nat roghte. 1560 ROLLAND *Seven Sag.* 82 Quha can excuse.. Sic ane fals trik sa trymlie playit to him? 1570 LEVINS *Manip.* 120/23 A Trick, *facinus*. 1588 GREENE *Pandosto* (1607) 4 Vnder the shape of a friend to shew him the tricke of a foe. 1622 in Foster *Eng. Factories Ind.* (1908) II. 138 [Watching their opportunity] to put a tricke uppon us. 1649 JER. TAYLOR *Gt. Exemp.* II. Ad Sect. xii. 54 Let every man.. deale with justice, noblenesse, and sincerity..without trickes and stratagems. 1707 J. STEVENS tr. *Quevedo's Com. Wks.* (1709) 350 Such..Sayings..As for Instance,..do not put Tricks upon Travellers. *c* 1740 CAREY *God save the King* ii, Frustrate their knavish tricks! 1790 BURKE *Fr. Rev.* 150 Ashamed, as of a silly deceitful trick. 1842 TENNYSON *Lady Clare* 73 Play me no tricks. 1867 FREEMAN *Norm. Conq.* I. v. 347 He was again at his old tricks [*O. E. Chron.* an. 1003 his ealdan wrenceas]. 1888 BRYCE *Amer. Commw.* II. lviii. 404 Public opinion, deterring even bad men from the tricks to which they are prone.

**b.** Without article: Trickery, fraud. *rare.*

1833 NYREN *Yng. Cricketer's Tutor* 78 His word was not always to be depended on..he would now and then shuffle, and resort to trick.

**c.** An illusory or deceptive appearance; a semblance, sham. ? *arch.* or *Obs.*

1592 KYD *Sp. Trag.* III. xii, Art thou not sometimes mad? Is there no trickes that comes before thine eies? 1781 COWPER *Conversation* 782 And all her love of God..A trick upon the canvass, painted flame. 1856 WHITTIER *Panorama* 207 In this poor trick of paint You see the semblance, incomplete and faint, Of the two-fronted Future.

**2.** A freakish or mischievous act; a roguish prank; a frolic; a piece of roguery or foolery; a hoax, practical joke.

1590 SHAKS. *Com. Err.* I. ii. 80 Or I shall breake that merrie sconce of yours That stands on tricks, when I am vndispos'd. 1605 *Tryall Chev.* v. ii. in Bullen *O. Pl.* III. 346 That's a tricke..to mocke an Ape. 1687 A. LOVELL tr. *Thevenot's Trav.* I. 61 These Buffoons are always playing some foolish Tricks amongst themselves to make him laugh. 1796 MME. D'ARBLAY *Camilla* III. 252 If any one plays their tricks upon me, they shall pay for their fun. 1846 MRS. CARLYLE *Lett.* (1883) I. 367 Fortune has played me such a cruel trick this day. 1888 *Pall Mall G.* 10 Oct. 4/1 If they were more numerous they could afford to play tricks.

**b.** A capricious, foolish, or stupid act; a thing done without full thought or consideration. Usually *contemptuous* or *depreciative.*

1591 SHAKS. *Two Gent.* IV. iv. 43 Did'st thou euer see me doe such a tricke? 1598 — *Merry W.* II. ii. 117 That were a tricke indeed! 1603 — *Meas. for M.* II. ii. 121 Proud man, Drest in a little briefe authoritie..Plaies such phantastique tricks before high heauen As makes the Angels weepe. 1693 CONGREVE *Old Bach.* IV. v, I hope you don't mean to forsake it; that will be but a kind of a mongrel cur's trick. 1829 CARLYLE *Misc.* (1857) II. 115 It were but a fool's trick to die for conscience.

**3.** A clever or adroit expedient, device, or contrivance; a 'dexterous artifice' (J.); a 'dodge'.

1573 TUSSER *Husb.* (1878) 123 Gather the lowest, and leauing the top, Shall teach thee a trick, for to double thy crop. 1588 SHAKS. *L. L. L.* v. ii. 466 Som Dick That.. knowes the trick To make my Lady laugh. 1618 BOLTON *Florus* (1636) 76 There also, the Carthaginians vented another new trick of their trade. 1638 JUNIUS *Paint. Ancients* 307 This was a meere tricke of the Painter. 1752 HUME *Ess. & Treat.* (1777) I. 107 (*Eloquence*) The moderns.. reject with disdain all those rhetorical tricks. 1815 JANE AUSTEN *Emma* xvi, Making..a trick of what ought to be simple. 1896 *Boston* (Mass.) *Jrnl.* 21 Nov. 7/3 The novelist ..knows the tricks of his trade.

**4.** The art, knack, or faculty of doing something skilfully or successfully. ? *arch.*

1611 SHAKS. *Cymb.* III. iii. 86 Nature prompts them In simple and lowe things, to Prince it, much Beyond the tricke of others. 1667 PEPYS *Diary* 5 Apr., Several that had got ground..for charity, to build sheds on, had got the trick presently to sell that for 60*l.* which did not cost them 20*l.* 1825 SCOTT *Talism.* xxvii, Thou art even matchless at the trick of the sword. 1897 KIPLING *Captains Courageous* ii, Thet was right smart fer a passenger. There's more trick to it in a sea-way.

**5.** A feat of dexterity or skill, intended to surprise or amuse; a piece of jugglery or legerdemain.

1606 SHAKS. *Tr. & Cr.* v. ii. 24 A iugling tricke, to be secretly open. 1697 DRYDEN *Æneid* Ded., Ess. (ed. Ker) II. 201 Like Merry-Andrew on the low rope, copying lubberly the same tricks which his master is so dexterously performing on the high. 1738 SWIFT *Pol. Conversat.* 56 You have more Tricks than a Dancing Bear. 1848 THACKERAY *Lett.* 28 July, The wizard..asked them..if they didn't like a trick he had just performed.

**6.** *concr.* †**a.** Something devised or contrived; a clever contrivance or invention. *Obs. rare.*

*a* 1548 HALL *Chron., Hen. V* 48 b, Sence that tyme, they haue imagined caltrappes, harowes and other newe trickes. 1601 B. JONSON *Ev. Man in his Hum.* (Qo.) II. iii, This brasse varnish being washt off, and three or foure other tricks [*Fol.* patches] sublated.

**b.** A trifling ornament or toy; a trinket, bauble, knick-knack; hence *pl.*, small and trifling articles; 'traps', personal belongings or effects (*U.S.*).

*a* 1553 C. BANSLEY *Treatise* xviii. (Percy Soc.) 6 Take hede .. Least youre wives raymente, and galante trickes doo make youre thryfte full bare. 1596 SHAKS. *Tam. Shr.* IV. iii. 67 A knacke, a toy, a tricke, a babies cap. 1599 HAKLUYT *Voy.* II. I. 64 The women of this countrey weare aboue an hundreth tricks and trifles about them. 1821 SCOTT *Kenilw.* xvii, These court tricks, and gambols..are the tricks and trinkets that bring fair fortunes to farthings. 1877 C. HALLOCK *Sportsman's Gaz.* 640 Camp 'tricks' should be kept in their places, not thrown helterskelter, or left lying where last used. 1894 MARY J. JAQUES *Texan Ranch Life* xxvi. 258 There was no need to pack our 'tricks' for England, we were assured, since we should never return to Texas; to say nothing about sailing. *a* 1904 A. ADAMS *Log Cowboy* xiii, After I get a shave..and buy what few tricks I need.

**II. 7.** A particular habit, way, or mode of acting; a characteristic quality, trait, practice, or custom. (Usually, a bad or unpleasant habit.)

1576 FLEMING *Panopl. Epist.* 244 It is not my propertie to be enuious against other (which is a tricke incident to a great number). 1581 PETTIE *Guazzo's Civ. Conv.* III. (1586) 129 A maide of ripe yeeres, who is hardlie brought to..leaue her olde ill tricks, if she haue taken anie. 1596 SHAKS. *1 Hen. IV*, v. ii. 11 The Foxe, Who ne're so tame, so cherisht, and lock'd vp, Will haue a wilde tricke of his Ancestors. 1650 FULLER *Pisgah* II. xii. 251 The lazy trick of the wild Irish..who to save pains, burn the straw, so to part the grain from it. 1688 PENTON *Guard. Instr.* (1897) 23 The danger in great Schools of..learning ill Tricks. 1709 STEELE *Tatler* No. 8 ¶ 5 My Valet de Chambre knows my University-Trick of reading there [in Bed]. 1754 EARL CHATHAM *Lett. Nephew* v. (1804) 35 The trick of laughing frivolously is by all means to be avoided. 1791 SIR J. REYNOLDS in Boswell *Johnson* an. 1739 (1848) 42/1 Those motions or tricks of Dr. Johnson are improperly called convulsions. 1884 *Cassell's Fam. Mag.* Mar. 220/2 The Wey..has a trick of overflowing its banks.

**8. a.** A habit or fashion of dress. Also *fig. arch.*

1543 BECON *Nosegay* E iij, Some tyme we followe the fasshyon of the Frenche men. Another time we wil haue a tricke of the Spanyyardes. 1564–78 BULLEYN *Dial. agst. Pest.* (1888) 17 Fine knottes vppon his girdle after Frances trickes. 1760 C. JOHNSTON *Chrysal* (1822) III. 147 He threw himself at her feet in all the trick of woe. 1874 R. W. BUCHANAN *Poet. Wks.* III. 150 In the very trick of woe he clad His features.

**b.** A characteristic expression (of the face or voice); a peculiar feature; a distinguishing trait.

1595 SHAKS. *John* I. i. 85 He hath a tricke of Cordelions face. 1605 — *Lear* IV. vi. 108 The tricke of that voyce, I do well remember: Is't not the king? 1847 LYTTON *Lucretia* II. iv, He detected..even the trick of his walk. 1881 BESANT & RICE *Chapl. of Fleet* II. i, An old-fashioned bearing and trick of speech.

**c.** The mode of working a piece of mechanism, etc.; the system upon which a thing is constructed.

1663 BP. PATRICK *Parab. Pilgr.* xx. (1687) 203 If you will have so much patience, I will discover to you the trick of it, and shew you by what mechanical powers this liveless Engine.. is stirred. 1819 SHELLEY *Cenci* v. iv. 6 He frowned, as if to frown had been the trick Of his machinery. 1888 J. PAYN *Myst. Mirbridge* xxi, No one who did not know the trick of it could have opened yonder safe.

**9.** *Naut.* The time allotted to a man on duty at the helm; a spell; a turn; esp. in *to take* or *stand one's trick* (*at the wheel*, etc.). Also *transf.*

1669 STURMY *Mariner's Mag.* IV. i. 138 Seamen when their trike or turn have been out, and the Log hove. 1769 FALCONER *Dict. Marine* (1789) s. v. *Spell*, The spells..to steer the ship; which..is generally called the *trick*. 1835 MARRYAT *Jac. Faithf.* xviii, His duty is to take his trick at the wheel. 1892 M. GIBBS in *Science* 19 Aug. 99 The male [robin], who shares the duties of sitting, when going to take his trick, almost invariably flies..in the same path. 1912 [see *trick-duty* in 13].

**III. 10.** *Her.* A sketch in pen and ink of a coat of arms; *in trick*, sketched in pen and ink. (Perhaps a different word: see TRICK *v.*)

1572 BOSSEWELL *Armorie* II. 30 b, The tricke of this cote I toke, as I found it paynted on a Table, in a parishe churche of Nottingham. 1610 BOLTON *Elem. Armories* 87 Drawing the blacke lines, which giue the shape,..lastly they sometime call it a Tricke. 1792 *Gentl. Mag.* Jan. 21/1 A large manuscript collection of arms in trick, done in the reign of Elizabeth. 1890 DILLON in *Archæologia* LII. 130 The flags are only shown in trick with the heraldic tinctures noted. 1908 *Let. of Richmond Herald of Arms* (MS.), Not a painting of the Coat of Arms, but a trick, i.e. a pen and ink sketch with all the heraldic colours marked on it.

**IV. 11.** *Card-playing.* The cards (usually four) played, and won or 'taken' in one round, collectively; hence *to take a* or *the trick. Odd trick*: see ODD *a.* I.

In quots. 1599, 1602, a hand of cards (*obs.*): in other early quots. with a play upon other senses.

1599 MASSINGER, etc. *Old Law* III. i, Here's a trick of discarded cards, of us! 1602 HEYWOOD *Woman Kill'd* Wks. 1874 II. 123 Many a deale I haue lost, the more's your shame. You haue seru'd me a bad tricke. 1607 TOURNEUR *Rev. Trag.* III. iv, Wee'll get thee out by a trick...You know a trick is commonly foure Cardes. 1611 COTGR., *Mornifle*, ..a tricke at Cards. 1622 MABBE tr. *Aleman's Guzman d'Alf.* I. 1 Leauing..to others..to play out that tricke of Cards for mee. *a* 1658 CLEVELAND *Smectymnuus* 21 A Murnival of Knaves Pack'd in a Trick. 1688 R. HOLME *Armoury* III. xvi. (Roxb.) 73/2 A Trick, is as many cards as is won at one laying downe either at the game of Whisk or Picket. 1778 C. JONES *Hoyle's Games Impr.* 51 (*Whist*) The Odds then is 2 to 1 in Favour of B's winning of a Trick. 1837 DICKENS *Pickw.* vi, Impossible to have made another trick. *a* 1839 PRAED *Poems* (1864) II. 63 Well—four by honours, and the trick!

**V.** Phrases and Combinations.

**12.** Phrases. **a.** *A trick worth two of that,* a

much better plan or expedient (cf. 3). **b.** *To do the trick*, to accomplish one's purpose, do what is wanted.

**a.** **1596** SHAKS. 1 *Hen. IV*, II. i. 41 Nay soft I pray ye, I know a trick worth two of that. **1654** H. L'ESTRANGE *Chas. I* (1655) 65 Old Sir John Savil found a trick worth two of that, he had a project would bring in double that mony. **1773** GRAVES *Spir. Quixote* III. xv, I was thunder-struck..; but she said, 'she knew a trick worth two of that'. **1855** THACKERAY *Newcomes* i, Best be off to bed, my boy—ho, ho! No, no. We know a trick worth two of that. 'We won't go home till morning, till daylight does appear.'

**b.** **1812** J. H. VAUX *Flash Dict.*, Do the Trick. **1823** EGAN *Grose's Dict. Vulg. T.*, *Do the trick*, to accomplish any robbery, or other business successfully;..a man who has imprudently involved himself in some great misfortune, from which there is little hope of extrication, is declared by his friends..to have done the trick for himself. **1872** *Punch* 9 Nov. 196/1 Pail of whitewash and box o' paints will do the trick. **1895** G. MEREDITH *Amazing Marriage* xv, I've brought him safe;..He'll do the trick today.

**13.** *attrib.* and *Comb.* (chiefly in sense 5): Of, pertaining to, or of the nature of a trick or tricks, as *trick change*, *-cycling*, *-dealer*, *fall*, *-riding* (so *trick-ride* vb.), *-shower* (SHOWER *sb.*²), *-work*, *-writing*; in senses 9 and 11, *trick-duty* (see quot.), *-making*, *-taking*; skilled in or trained to perform tricks (sense 5), as *trick-animal*, *-cyclist*, *-dog*, *-donkey*, *-horse*, *-pony*; made or used for performing tricks, as *trick-bag*, *-chair*, *-cycle*, *-dagger*, *-property*, *-staircase*, *-sword*, *-wig*; also **trick-doctor**, ? a negro sorcerer; **trick-line** *Theatr.*, a strong fine line used in pantomime transformations; so **trick-scene**, a transformation scene.

**1884** *World* 3 Dec. 16/2 The original stud from which the renowned breed of *trick-animals, pink-eyed and piebald, has sprung. **1910** *Nation* 22 Jan. 665/1 A hocus-pocus loaf out of a conjuror's *trick-bag. **1904** *Daily Chron.* 23 Aug. 3/2 It is of a piece with..the murder of Ithocles in an 'engine', otherwise *trick-chair. **1896** *Westm. Gaz.* 8 Jan. 2/3 Quick changes—'*trick changes' is perhaps more technical a term—were accomplished with remarkable ingenuity. **1901** *Wide World Mag.* VIII. 140/1 An open space here afforded room for a little figure-skating, or rather *trick-cycling. **1903** *Daily Chron.* 20 May 8/3 A young *trick-cyclist..met with a fatal accident to-day while practising looping the loop. **1889** P. A. BRUCE *Plant. Negro* 116 The *trick doctor..employs the arts of the Obeah practitioners ..with the arts of the Myal. **1886** C. SCOTT *Sheep-Farming* 204 A well-trained and experienced collie excels in sagacity all others of the dog family. His was not the intelligence of the *trick dog. **1881** *Chequered Career* 120 If you don't pay us our accounts, we will collar your *trick-donkey. **1912** *Boston Transcript* 24 July 7/3 Company reduces the time for those who do *trick duty [refers to telephone exchange; a night trick is 7 hours' duty between 10 p.m. and 7 a.m.]. **1861** *Windsor Express* 5 Oct., The well-known American Circus..45 *trick and ring horses. **1908** *Westm. Gaz.* 4 Jan. 14/1 All aces are valuable as honours in a 'trump' game, as well as in their *trick-making capacity. **1908** *Daily Chron.* 31 Dec. 4/4 Special masks for the grotesques and '*trick' properties will often break into a couple of hundred pounds. **1887** *Bicycl. News* 10 Sept. 371/2 Probably Maltby will be matched against Temple..to *trick-ride. **1885** *Cyclist* 19 Aug. 1088/2 He entertained the spectators with a *trick-riding performance. **1677** *Descr. Diamond Mines* in *Misc. Cur.* (1708) III. 255 Light Women-Dancers, and *Trick-Shewers. **1899** *Daily News* 9 Jan. 6/6 The King..rolls head over heels down a '*trick' staircase. **1901** A. DUNN *Bridge* 52 A sequence of cards equal for *trick-taking purposes, such as king, queen, knave. **1888** *Pall Mall G.* 1 Sept. 3/1 A *trick wig, with the hanging hair..on a spring piece that allows this fringe to turn over back or down over the forehead. **1876** 'OUIDA' *Winter City* vi, The little Meissonier pictures were clever, if they were mere *trick-work and told no story. **1894** *Westm. Gaz.* 5 July 8/1 Article-writing is to a great extent *trick-writing. To 'catch on' they must dogmatise in pointed commonplace.

**Trick** (trik), *v.* [In branch I not found till late in the 16th c.; app. f. TRICK *sb.* (The date of appearance is too late to refer it directly to Norman-Picard F. *trikier*, *triquer*.) Branches II and III are a little earlier, and may perh. be of different origin; the last is especially difficult to connect with the primary sense of the verb. Cf. sense 10 of the sb.]

**I. 1.** *trans.* To deceive by a trick; to cheat.

(In quot. 1630 with word-play on *trick* and *trump* at cards.)

**1595, 1606** [see TRICKING *vbl. sb.* 1, TRICKER 1]. **1630** B. JONSON *New Inn* I. i, When she [Fortune] is pleas'd to trick or tromp mankind, Some may be coats, as in the cards; but, then, Some must be knaves. **1706** E. WARD *Wooden World Diss.* (1708) 94 However he tricks his Captain in other Things, his Plate and Dishes are every Day forth coming. **1802** MAR. EDGEWORTH *Moral T.* (1816) I. xiii. 104 To trick a gauger was thought an excellent joke. **1852** THACKERAY *Esmond* I. vii, He was often tricked about horses, which he pretended to know better than any jockey. **1884** W. C. SMITH *Kildrostan* I. ii. 235 'Tis plain I have been tricked and overreached.

**b.** To cheat *out of*; to deprive *of* by trickery.

**1698** FRYER *Acc. E. India & P.* Contents p. vii, Syddy Jore trick'd out of his Life by Bullul Caun. **1727** GAY *Begg. Op.* I. ii, She tricks us of our money. **1888** BRYCE *Amer. Commw.* III. lxxxi. 66 His belief that he who makes the wealth of the country is tricked out of his proper share in its prosperity.

**c.** To beguile *into*; to induce *into* by trickery.

**1706** E. WARD *Wooden World Diss.* (1708) 68 The Tide-waiter, voluntarily trick'd into a Game at All fours. **1801** CHARLOTTE SMITH *Lett. Solit. Wand.* II. 240 Her contempt of one who could so basely contrive to trick her into his power. **1874** GREEN *Short Hist.* ix. § 3. 625 To trick them into approval of a war with Holland.

**d.** *absol.* or *intr.* To practise trickery, to cheat.

*a* **1700** DRYDEN *To Mr. Granville* 23 Thus they jog on, still tricking, never thriving. **1701** PENN in *Pennsylv. Hist. Soc. Mem.* IX. 73 If in the least he tricks, use him accordingly. **1909** *Nation* 2 Oct. 11/2 To the ignorant and superstitious everything tricks and deludes.

**2.** To get or effect by trickery or cheating. *rare.*

**1662** in *Verney Mem.* (1907) II. 178 London is a Theife will trick your purse as well as mine. **1895** G. S. STREET *Introd. to Congreve's Comedies* 25 The trick..of a tricked marriage is common in Congreve.

**3.** *intr.* To play tricks *with*; to trifle *with*.

**1881** STEVENSON *Virg. Puerisque*, etc. (1895) 162 We may trick with the word life..until we are weary of tricking. **1913** *Daily News* 23 Sept. 5 The fireman was 'tricking' with girls on the platform.

†**4.** *trans.* To sophisticate or adulterate (wine, etc.). *Obs. rare.*

**1594** PLAT *Jewell-ho.* III. 66 This makes the Vintners to tricke or compasse all their naturall wines, if they bee a little hard, with Bastarde to make them sweeter. **1662** [see TRICKING *vbl. sb.* 1].

**II. 5.** *trans.* To dress, array, attire; to deck, prank; to adorn (usually with the notion of artifice). Const. *with*, *in*. Also *intr.* with *it*. Also *fig.*

? *a* **1500** *Mylner of Abyngton* 457 in Hazl. *E. P. P.* III. 117 The wenche she was full proper and nyce,.. For she coulde tricke it point device. *a* **1553** C. BANSLEY *Treat.* xii. (Percy Soc.) 5 Sponge up youre vysage, olde bounsynge trotte, and tricke it wyth the beste, Tyll you tricke and trotte youre selfe, to the devyls trounsynge neste. *a* **1592** GREENE *George-a-Greene* Wks. (Rtldg.) 266/2 Some peasants trick'd in yeoman's weeds. **1632** MILTON *Penseroso* 123 Till civil-suited Morn appeer, Not trickt and frounc't..But Cherchef't in a comly Cloud. **1759** MASON *Caractacus* Poems 1830 II. 138 His clemency,..trick'd and varnish'd by your glossing penmen. **1873** BROWNING *Red Cott. Nt.-cap* III. 408 The late death chamber, tricked with trappings still. **1890** R. BRIDGES *Shorter Poems* II. 1 What musical array Tricks her sweet syllables.

**b.** Often strengthened with *up*, *off*, *out*.

*c* **1533** LATIMER *Let.* in Foxe *A. & M.* (1563) 1316/1 A poore purgatory. So poore y[t] it should not be able to fede so fatte, and tricke vp so many idell and slouthful lubbers. *c* **1590** GREENE *Fr. Bacon* x. 38, I cannot trick it up with poesies. **1622** BACON *Hen. VII* 27 That the King..to blinde the eyes of simple men had tricked up a Boy in the likenesse of Edward Plantagenet. **1727** GAY *Begg. Op.* III. v, To trick out young Ladies, upon their going into Keeping. **1821** *Examiner* 19/2 She was well tutored and tricked off for the occasion. **1822** SCOTT *Fam. Lett.* 18 Feb., I must trick out my dwellings with something fantastical. **1878** E. JENKINS *Haverholme* 153 Tricking out tables to look like altars.

**c.** *transf.* To dress *up*, to prepare (food). *rare.*

**1824** W. IRVING *T. Trav.* I. 10 A slight repast had therefore been tricked up from the residue of dinner.

†**6.** To arrange, adjust, trim. Often in phrase *to trick and trim*. Cf. TRIG *v.*⁴ *Obs.*

**1552** ELYOT s.v. *Caesaries*, *Repexa caesaries*, a busshe twise or thrise kemed and tricked. **1570** LEVINS *Manip.* 120/33 To trick, or trim, *concinnare*. **1579–80** NORTH *Plutarch* (1676) 624 Being not of authority..to take the stern in hand, and govern the ship, he took himself to tricking the sails. **1639** S. DU VERGER tr. *Camus' Admir. Events* 206 He consumed so much time..in tricking and trimming his head. **1770** M. BRUCE *Elegy* viii, On the green furze..The linnet sits, and tricks his glossy plumes. **1810** SOUTHEY *Kehama* VIII. ii, No human hand hath trick'd that mane From which he [the steed] shakes the morning dew.

**III. 7.** To sketch or draw in outline; to delineate or trace the outline of (*obs.*); *spec.* in *Her.*, to draw (a coat of arms) in outline, the tinctures being denoted by initial letters (*o*, *a*, *s*, etc.) or by signs. Also with *out*.

(In many passages incorrectly used or confused with sense 5.)

**1545** ELYOT, *Adumbro*..some do suppose that it signifieth, to trycke a thynge, or drawe it grossely, as paynters doo at the begynnyng. **1562** LEIGH *Armorie* (1597) 106 This cote I had in the Monasterie of Saint Katherins besides the Towne of Rone, which for the rarenes therof I tricked. **1594** CAREW *Huarte's Exam. Wits* viii. (1596) 111 The boy ..with his pen can tricke a horse to the life. **1657** WOOD *Life* 14 Aug. (O. H. S.) I. 223 He..tricked out with his pen the ichnography of the church and cloyster and buildings adjoyning. **1859** *Symonds' Diary* (Camden) Introd. 14 The ..shields of arms recorded in the MS. are..'tricked',..thus necessitating a description of the bearings. **1908** H. HALL *Formula Bk.* I. 123 The feature of these instruments [Chancery Warrants]..being the technical description of the arms which are usually tricked on the original.

†**Trick,** *a.* and *adv.* *Obs.* [In use from *c* 1530 to 1630, very common from *c* 1550 to 1600. Origin obscure: it does not seem to be connected in sense with TRICK *sb.* or *v.* On the other hand its two senses correspond closely to senses 2 and 3 of TRIG *a.* The latter was at that time only northern; midland and southern speakers may have associated it with the known sb. and vb. *trick*, and adopted it in this form. Often alliteratively coupled with *trim*.]

**A.** *adj.* **1.** Smart, adroit, clever, nimble, 'neat'. *rare.* Cf. TRIG *a.* 2.

(Quot. 1545 may belong to sense 2.)

**1542** [implied in TRICKLY *adv.*] **1545** ASCHAM *Toxoph.* (Arb.) 28 Two bowes..whereof the one is quicke of cast, tricke and trimme both for pleasure and profyte: the other is a lugge slowe of cast, folowing the string. ? *a* **1550** *Schole Ho. Women* 100 in Hazl. *E. P. P.* IV. 109 So trick a way they haue to kisse With open mouth and rowling eyes. **15..** *Six Ballads w. Burdens* (Percy Soc.) 8 Say-well in wordes is proper and trycke. **1589** WARNER *Alb. Eng.* VI. xxx. (1612) 147 Trimmest fidling on the trickest kit. **1593** LODGE *Phillis*, etc. (Hunter. Cl.) 71 Sweet chaines of honny speech, Deliuered by a trick Herculean tongue Able to tice all eares.

**2.** Trim, neat, handsome, in form or feature; smart, 'fine', ornate in dress. Cf. TRIG *a.* 3, 3 b.

*c* **1530** REDFORDE *Play Wit & Sc.* (1848) 1 See That all thynges be cleane and trycke abowte ye. **1533** J. HEYWOOD *Play of Weather* Plays (1905) 123 As dearly my youth I might have sold As the trickest and fairest of you all. *a* **1548** HALL *Chron.*, *Hen. VIII* 70 A tricke waggon, on the which sat a ladie richely appareled. *a* **1553** C. BANSLEY *Treat.* xxiv. (Percy Soc.) 7 Lustye wylfull wyll wyll.. cause the tryckeste of you all, to synge a carefull songe. **1570** LEVINS *Manip.* 120/40 Trick, *nitidus*, *concinnus*. **1581** A. HALL *Iliad* II. 39 Bryseis his tricke and gallant trull. *a* **1586** SIDNEY *Arcadia* III. (1629) 390 A neighbour mine.. That maried had a tricke and bonny lasse. **1630** W. FREAKE *Doctrines Jesuits* 43 Gay Gownes..wherewith hee can make her both tricke and trimme.

**B.** *adv.* **1.** Cleverly, 'neatly', 'finely'.

**1564–78** BULLEYN *Dial. agst. Pest.* (1888) 94 He plaieth tricke vpon the Gitterne. **1584** PEELE *Arraignm. Paris* I. i, But tell me, wench [Flora], hast done't so trick indeed? [i.e. deck'd the earth with parti-colour'd flowers].

**2.** Neatly, smartly, elegantly, 'trigly'.

**1594** GREENE & LODGE *Looking-Glasse* G.'s Wks. (Rtldg.) 122/2 Unless you coy it trick and trim. **1615** BRATHWAIT *Strappado* (1878) 190 A sumptuous graue, Which garnisht is without full tricke and trim. *a* **1658** CLEVELAND *Myrtle-Grove* 50 Her gamesome Hair..in wild Rings ran trick about the air.

**Tricked** (trikt), *ppl. a.* Also 7 **trickt.** [f. TRICK *v.* + -ED¹.] **a.** Done or made by trickery. **b.** Artfully decked or adorned; dressed up.

**1549** COVERDALE, etc. *Erasm. Par. Jas.* 35 Not in subtill reasonynges..or tricked fyne termes of eloquence. *a* **1619** FLETCHER, etc. *Knt. Malta* I. i, Thou trickt up toy. **1837** LYTTON *E. Maltrav.* III. iii, Affected, tricked-out, well-dressed children. **1868** SWINBURNE *Blake* 69 A special colour or savour which redeems the offences of a tricked and tinselled style. **1869** BLACKMORE *Lorna D.* xxi, This pretty youth, so tricked and slender, seemed nothing but a doll to me. **1895** [see TRICK *v.* 2].

**Tricker¹** (tri·kəɹ). [f. TRICK *v.* + -ER¹.]

**1.** One who plays tricks or practises trickery; a cheat, deceiver, trickster; also, one who plays a trick or prank.

**1562** J. HEYWOOD *Prov. & Epigr.* (1867) 107 This tricke.. Brought to this tricker nother muse nor mase. **1606** *Choice, Chance*, etc. (1881) 7 Leaue tricks to trickers. *a* **1734** NORTH *Lives* (1826) II. 418 All the various species of politicians and trickers. *a* **1849** H. COLERIDGE *Ess.* (1851) II. 135 These trickers unwittingly speak truth.

†**2.** One who tricks out, decks, or artfully adorns.

*a* **1553** C. BANSLEY *Treat.* xxx. (Percy Soc.) 8 A wanton tricker..Wyth a double fardyngale and a caped cassoc, moche lyke a players gowne. **1567** *Triall Treas.* (1850) 24 She hath an amiable face; A tricker, a trimmer, in faith that she is, The goddess of wealth, prosperitie and bliss. **1600** KEMP *Nine Daies Wond.* i. A iij, Caualiero Kemp.. onely tricker of your Trill-lilles, and best bel-shangles betweene Sion and mount Surrey.

**3.** One who tricks a coat of arms.

**1586** FERNE *Blaz. Gentrie* To Gentl. Inner Temple, I did alwaies abhor the nude title and bare skill of a Blazoner, things common to each painter and tricker of armes. **1688** R. HOLME *Armoury* I. 2/2 Every Painter, Tricker, or a meer Blazoner of Arms, will not serve to make..an absolute Herauld.

†**4.** Some tool used by burglars. *Obs. rare.*

**1592** GREENE *Art Conny catch.* II. D iij, He [the curber] hath his trickers, which are engines of Iron so cunningly wrought, that he wil cut a barre of Iron in two with them.

**Tri·cker²**, early and dial. form of TRIGGER¹. Hence **Tricker-firelock,** a hand fire-arm of the middle of the 17th c., discharged by pulling a trigger; **Tricker-lock,** name in the 17th c. for a gun-lock furnished with a trigger, whether a *match tricker-lock*, or a *wheel tricker-lock*.

**1629** *Schedule* in Meyrick *Antient Armour* (1824) III. 100 For a match tricker-lock compleat..1*s.* For a handle or guard of a tricker..vi*d.* For furnishing and setting of a tricker lock in place of a feare lock, with a handle, tricker, and tricker pynnes. ii*s.* vi*d.* **1824** MEYRICK *ibid.* 88 The tricker-lock, I conceive, to be that furnished with a hair-trigger, as it is now called. **1855** *Jrnl. Brit. Archæol. Assoc.* XI. 255 Mr. G. Wright exhibited..a fine example of the lock of a Tricker firelock,..exhumed..from the battle-field of Worcester [1651]. The rising piece above the pan is furrowed, to facilitate the production of the sparks from the pyrites or flint.

**Trickery** (tri·kəri). [f. TRICK *sb.* + -ERY.] The practice of tricks; deceitful conduct or practice; deception, artifice; imposture.

**1800** PARR *Spital Serm.* Wks. 1828 II. 394 Good sense without the trickeries of art, good language without the trappings of rhetoric. **1824** MISS MITFORD in L'Estrange *Life* (1870) II. ix. 174 He has a great deal of real sensibility, mixed with some trickery. **1825** T. HOOK *Sayings* Ser. II. *Man of Many Fr.* (Colburn) 91 Versed in all the experimental trickeries of science. **1881** JOWETT *Thucyd.* I. 118 We rely not upon management or trickery, but upon our own hearts and hands.

**Tri·ckful,** *a. rare.* [f. TRICK *sb.* + -FUL.] Full of tricks; tricky. Hence **Tri·ckfully** *adv.*

**1775** S. J. PRATT *Liberal Opin.* xlviii. (1783) II. 17, I was ..as thoughtless, and as trickful as the best, or rather—the worst of them. *c* **1790** MRS. LARPENT in *19th Cent.* Aug. (1913) 312 Mrs. Siddons..acted well, Kemble stiffly, trickfully, yet in one sense sensibly!

†**Tri·ckify,** *v.* *Obs. rare.* [f. TRICK *v.* or TRICKY *a.*: see -FY (cf. *beautify*, *prettify*).] *trans.* To trick, deck, adorn: = TRICK *v.* 5.

1678 E. COOKE *Naked Breasts & Shoulders* 56 They could better imploy their time, than in so adorning and trickifying their Bodies.

**Trickily** (tri·kili), *adv.* [f. TRICKY *a.* + -LY [2].] In a tricky manner.

1895 *Treas. Relig. Thoughts* (N. Y.) Oct. 459/1 Actually enforcing laws trickily made to be evaded. 1899 H. M. GREY *Moorish Captivity* iii. 34 The current twirled very trickily through the narrow channel between the reefs.

**Trickiness** (tri·kinės). [f. as prec. + -NESS.] The quality of being tricky; deceitfulness; also intricacy, complexity.

1723 *Caldwell Papers* (Maitl. Cl.) I. 250 Allowing a child's prevaricating, and laughing at its little trickiness and cunning. 1868 *Morn. Star* 19 June, A good deal of trickiness in the matter of petitions has lately been discovered. 1885 *Spectator* 8 Aug. 1041/1 Even the brilliance of his literary expression is beginning to be suspected of trickiness. 1894 BARING-GOULD *Kitty Alone* III. 56 Her simple mind..with no trickiness or dissimulation in it.

**Tricking** (tri·kiŋ), *vbl. sb.* [f. TRICK *v.* + -ING [1].] The action of TRICK *v.*

**1.** The action of cheating, deceiving, or beguiling; trickery, deceit; in quot. 1662, † the sophistication of wine (*obs.*).

1595 *Enquiry Tripe-wife* (1881) 145 Your valorous assaults against The Tricking of the Tripe-wife. 1662 CHARLETON *Myst. Vintners* (1675) 203 The Transmutation or Sophistication of Wines, which they call Trickings or Compassings. 1799 W. GILPIN *Serm.* I. ix, [The world] will shew you, that tricking, and deceit of various kinds, are very consistent with christianity. 1810 W. WILSON *Hist. Dissent. Ch.* III. 46 The disingenuous arts of craft and tricking.

**2.** Dressing up, decking out, ornamentation (in quot. 1598 *concr.*).

1549 COVERDALE, etc. *Erasm. Par. Eph.* Prol. C ij, Men fynely broughte vp in trickynge of termes and tounges. 1598 SHAKS. *Merry W.* IV. iv. 79 Go get vs properties And tricking for our Fayries. 1695 BP. J. SAGE *Article* Wks. 1844 I. 371 So much needless ostentation, so much odd external tricking about it.

**3.** Sketching or drawing in outline; *spec. Her.* the delineation of armorial bearings in black and white: see TRICK *v.* 7.

1562 LEIGH *Armorie* ad fin., The olde order in trickyng of all maner of Armes, is to vse one letter for one word. O. Or. Yelowe [etc.]. 1864 *Lond. & Middlesex Archæol. Soc. Trans.* II. 58 The authority for this engraving is a tricking in a volume at the College of Arms.

**Tri·cking,** *ppl. a.* [f. as prec. + -ING [2].] That tricks; cheating, deceiving; using trickery.

1697 DRYDEN *Virgil, Life* (1721) I. 71 The Craft and Tricking part of Life, with which Homer abounds. 1790 BURKE *Fr. Rev.* Wks. V. 302 The degenerate fondness for tricking short-cuts, and little fallacious facilities. 1815 SCOTT *Guy M.* xlvii, All the world knows him to be sordid, mean, tricking, and I suspect him to be worse.

Hence **Tri·ckingly** *adv.*, so as to cheat, artfully.

1833 *Fraser's Mag.* VII. 244 The small portion of notice which you condescend to bestow on Mr. Lytton Bulwer in the Magazine of this month, so trickingly put to the well-known ritornella of 'Whiston and Ditton'.

**Trickish** (tri·kiʃ), *a.* [f. TRICK *sb.* + -ISH [1].]

**1.** Characterized by or given to tricks or trickery; rather tricky, crafty, or cunning.

1705 STANHOPE *Paraphr.* II. 391 The little trickish Arts of Dissimulation. 1760 J. ADAMS *Diary* 18 Dec., His habitual trickish, lying, cheating disposition. 1879 MCCARTHY *Own Times* II. xviii. 19 The somewhat cunning and trickish agitation which O'Connell had set going.

**2.** = TRICKY 2; TICKLISH *a.* 5.

1900 C. LEE *Cynthia* v. 72 Terr'ble trickish work. 1907 *Black Cat* June 24 It was trickish work handling a canoe among those pounding logs and frequent dead-heads.

Hence **Tri·ckishly** *adv.*, **Tri·ckishness.**

1788 V. KNOX *Winter Even.* xxxiv. (1790) I. 291 That odium, which..has branded the whole tribe with charges of duplicity ..and trickishness. 1824 *Examiner* 57/1 Religion, trickishly wedded to Priestcraft. 1897 SARAH GRAND *Beth Bk.* xxii, It was another instance of the trickishness of her memory.

**Trickle** (tri·k'l), *sb.*[1] [f. TRICKLE *v.*] A falling or flowing drop; a tear; a small quantity of liquid; a small fitful stream.

1580 HOLLYBAND *Treas. Fr. Tong, Pleur*, a teare, a trickle. So 1611 in COTGRAVE. 1730–6 BAILEY (folio), *Trickle*, a drop. 1855 BROWNING *Another Way of Love* iii, Delicious as trickles Of wine poured at mass-time. 1857 MRS. GATTY *Parab. fr. Nat.* Ser. II. (1868) 12 The waterfall..was reduced to a miserable trickle. 1897 'A. HOPE' *Phroso* ix, Vlacho's blood began to curl in a meandering trickle from beneath the curtain.

*fig.* 1853 C. BRONTË *Villette* viii, No flow, only a hesitating trickle of language. 1895 BARING-GOULD *Noémi* v, But it [money] comes in in trickles and goes out in floods. 1897 MARY KINGSLEY *W. Africa* 637 It will only serve to bring down the little trickle of native trade.

**Tri·ckle,** *sb.*[2] Variant of *triddle*, TREDDLE. Cf. also dial. *tricklings* in *Eng. Dial. Dict.*

1598 FLORIO, *Cacarelle*, the trickles or dung of sheepe, goates, rats or conies. 1639 O. WOOD *Alph. Bk. Secrets* 23 Sheepes trickles.

**† Tri·ckle,** *a. Obs. rare.* [f. TRICK *sb.* or *v.* + -LE I (as in *brittle*), but apparently influenced by TICKLE *a.*] Tricky, treacherous; ticklish; requiring caution; = TRICKY *a.* 2.

1579 SPENSER *Sheph. Cal.* July 14 In humble dales is footing fast, The trode is not so trickle [*v. r.* tickle]. 1594 WILLOBIE *Avisa* (1880) 136 Such trickle trades procure a suddaine fall.

Hence **† Tri·ckleness.** *Obs. rare*[—1].

*a* 1618 J. DAVIES *Wittes Pilgr.* (Grosart) 45/2 O Time.. That neuer mou'st, but dost my Sences moue To mind thy flight, and this lifes tricklenesse.

**Trickle** (tri·k'l), *v.* Forms: 4–6 **trekel,** (4 *Sc.* **trygle,** 4–5 **trikle, trekil,** 6 *Sc.* **trigle, -il),** 5 **trikel, -il, trekyl, -ll,** 5–6 **trickil, -el, -ell,** 6 **tryckel,** (**triccle, trycle,** 7 **truckle),** 6– **trickle:** see also TRINKLE *v.*[1] [History doubtful. In the first Chaucer passage (sense 1) one MS. out of seven, the Lansdowne, has *strikle*, which is taken by Prof. Skeat as the original form (the initial *s* being lost after a prec. word in *-s*, e. g. *teres*), and this as a freq. or dim. of ME. *striken* to strike (the reading of two of the Chaucer MSS.) occurring twice elsewhere in sense 'flow' ('ase strem that striketh stille', 'strikeð a stream ut of þæt stanene þruh'), OE. *strican* to strike, also to go, move, run. As to form and sense, this is possible; but no other ME. examples of *strikle* are known, so that the evidence is scanty.

(Cf. however MHG. *strîchen* to strike, also to move, travel, wander, and Ger. *streichen*, said of a ship as 'das Schiff streicht durch die Wellen'.)]

**1.** *intr.* **a.** Originally said of tears: To flow or fall in successive drops.

*c* 1375 *Sc. Leg. Saints* xxii. (*Laurentius*) 278 Þane laurence handis one hym lad With t[r]ygland terys. *c* 1386 CHAUCER *Prioress' T.* 222 Hise salte teeris trikled [*v. rr.* trekelede, stryked, striked, strikled] doun as reyn. — *Sompn. T.* 156 With many a teare triklyng [*v. rr.* trynkelynge, trillyng] on my cheke. *a* 1400–50 *Alexander* 4974 Þar trekild doun of þa teres of iemmes [gems], Boyland out of þe barke bawme & mirre. 1513 DOUGLAS *Æneis* IV. vi. 66 (ed. 1553) Be al thir teris trigilland [*ed. Small* tringling] ouer my face. *Ibid.* VI. xi. 14 The teris trigling [*ed. Small* thringling] ouer his chekis ran. 1548 UDALL *Erasm. Par. Luke* vii. 74 The fete of Iesus beeyng well washed with teres tryclyng down from hir yies. 1565 GOLDING *Ovid's Met.* I. (1593) 12 The bitter teares did trickle downe their cheeke. 1702 POPE *Sappho* 200 And silent tears fall trickling from my eyes. 1843 LEVER *J. Hinton* xi, Tears of..joy trickled slowly down her cheeks.

**b.** Of other liquids; rarely of powders or granulated substances. Also, to flow in a very scanty and halting stream.

1526 *Pilgr. Perf.* (W. de W. 1531) 249 b, Yssued out blode & water..lyke droppes tricclyng downe to the grounde. 1610 HOLLAND *Camden's Brit.* (1637) 583 From his spring heads Trent trickleth downe. 1683 WARE *Hunting of Romish Fox* v. 87 The Blood..ran thrô the crevises of the Crown of Thorns, and truckled down the Face of this Image. 1725 DE FOE *Voy. round World* (1840) 261 The hill or gullet where the water trickled down from the rocks. 1866 G. MACDONALD *Ann. Q. Neighb.* iii, The flour was trickling down out of two wooden spouts. 1871 L. STEPHEN *Playgr. Eur.* (1894) x. 241 A small glacier trickles into the desolate valley.

**c.** *transf.* and *fig.*

1628 [see TRICKLING *vbl. sb.*] 1728 POPE *Dunc.* III. 201 Fluent nonsense trickles from his tongue. 1758 JOHNSON *Idler* No. 7 ℙ 4 The rivulets of intelligence which are continually trickling. 1899 *Allbutt's Syst. Med.* VIII. 5 What can be more wonderful than to see a man's thoughts trickling from the end of his pen at the rate of nearly a word a second! 1901 *Scotsman* 11 Mar. 9/1 Then another thousand rupees came trickling in.

**2.** *intr.* To emit falling or flowing drops; to drip or run (*with* tears, blood, etc.); to shed tears.

*c* 1400 *Destr. Troy* 8058 Yf the ton ee with teres trickell on hir chekes. 1582 STANYHURST *Æneis* I. (Arb.) 32 Fast he stood: and tricklyng dyd speake. 1611 BIBLE *Lam.* iii. 49 Mine eye trickleth downe and ceaseth not. 1865 DICKENS *Mut. Fr.* III. ix, His hand was trickling down with blood.

**3.** *trans.* To emit or give forth in successive drops or a thin fitful stream; also, to cause to trickle; to pour drop by drop, or in a fitful stream.

1602 MARSTON *Antonio's Rev.* V. v, The vaines..Trickling fresh goare about my fist. 1671 WOODHEAD *St. Teresa* I. xxii. 147 We behold him..trickling blood. 1746–7 HERVEY *Medit.* (1818) 186 Ye gushing Fountains, that trickle potable silver through the matted grass. 1854 DICKENS *Hard T.* II. i, The mills..oozed and trickled it [oil]. 1863 READE *Hard Cash* xxi, With adroit and tender hands they.. trickled stimulants down her throat. 1878 T. L. CUYLER *Pointed Papers* 144 He knows every wound that trickles its silent drops from the bleeding spirit.

**b.** *fig.* with *off* or *out*: To let go one by one.

1657 REEVE *God's Plea* 26 Thus doth the voluptuous man measure out his time, trickle out his hours. 1907 *Blackw. Mag.* July 36/2 The company commanders begin to trickle off their men.

**Tri·cklet.** [f. TRICKLE *sb.* + -LET (or -ET).] A small or minute trickle; a minute streamlet.

1880 *Daily Tel.* 28 Oct., Merely the result of tricklets of perspiration. 1886 RUSKIN *Præterita* I. ix. 292 A tricklet here at the bottom of a crag. 1888 R. L. STEVENSON in *Scribner's Mag.* Oct. 511/1 A tricklet of a stream divides them.

**Trickling** (tri·kliŋ), *vbl. sb.* [f. TRICKLE *v.* + -ING [1].] The action of the verb TRICKLE; also *concr.* that which trickles.

1628 GAULE *Pract. The.* (1629) 34 The slow tricklings of his Mercie;..the full streame of outward blessings. 1814 BYRON *Lara* II. xvii, The tides [of blood]..In feebler, not less fatal tricklings flow. 1863 BARING-GOULD *Iceland* 134 Shale..wet with tricklings from the rock overhead.

**Tri·ckling,** *ppl. a.* [f. as prec. + -ING [2]] That trickles: see the verb.

*c* 1375 [see TRICKLE *v.* 1 a]. 1513 DOUGLAS *Æneis* XIII. iv. 23 With habundans of mony trigland teir Wetand thar brestis. 1557 in *Tottell's Misc.* (Arb.) 215 Not euery tricklyng teare doth argue inward paine. *c* 1586 C'TESS PEMBROKE *Ps.* LXXVIII. vii, The trickling springs to such huge rivers grew. 1665 SIR T. HERBERT *Trav.* (1677) 181 Rivers..which after a long trickling race..disembogue themselves into the Caspian. 1791 COWPER *Iliad* IV. 170 Stained with thy trickling blood. 1848 EDMESTON *Sacr. Poetry* (1868) 202 Dry the trickling tear.

**† Tri·ckly,** *a.*[1] *Obs. rare.* [f. TRICK *a.* + -LY [1]: cf. *goodly, sickly, weakly.*] Smart-looking, showy.

1573 TUSSER *Husb.* (1878) 164 Though trickly to see to, be gallant to wiue, Yet comely and wise is the huswife to thriue.

**Trickly** (tri·kli), *a.*[2] *rare.* [f. TRICKLE *sb.* or *v.* + -Y.] Characterized by trickling.

1876 MISS BROUGHTON *Joan* II. x, Her boots no longer rattle, nor do cold and trickly rills race down the nape of her neck. 1910 *Westm. Gaz.* 12 Mar. 15/2 The heron is ever on the look-out to use his long neck for a quick blow and trickly gulp.

**† Tri·ckly,** *adv. Obs.* [f. TRICK *a.* + -LY [2].] **a.** Cleverly. **b.** Neatly, smartly, trigly, finely.

1542 UDALL *Erasm. Apoph.* 108 Feactely & trickely representing..a certain lasciuious playe. 1581 A. HALL *Iliad* III. 58 The place was trickly decked vp. 1592 GREENE *Groat's W. Wit* (1617) 21 The olde womans daughter was trickly attyred. 1599 MINSHEU, *Limadamente*, exquisitly, trickly. 1608 H. CLAPHAM *Errour Left Hand* 103 In shadowie plots, the Vipers, Monkscowle groes, Which with his yellowe flower full trickly shoes.

**† Tri·ck-madam.** *Obs.* [a. F. *trique-madame* (1545 in Hatz.-Darm.), of uncertain origin.] An old name of one or more species of Stonecrop, formerly used in salads; called also PRICK-MADAM and TRIP-MADAM.

According to Lyte, Prick-madam was the plant now called *Sedum reflexum*, and Wild Prick-madam, *S. album*; according to Littré, *trique madame* in France is 'l'orpin blanc', or 'trique blanche', ? *Sedum album*; according to Eugène Rolland *Flore populaire* VI. 108–110, *trique-madame* is in France applied indiscriminately to *Sedum acre* and *S. album*, but it is doubtful if the name was ever applied in England to the former (Biting Stonecrop or Wall Pepper).

1600 SURFLET *Countrie Farme* II. xvi. 223 Tricke-madam doth nothing feare the cold. *Ibid.* II. lx. 397 Steepe the seedes for a certaine time in the iuice of trick-madame. 1699 EVELYN *Acetaria* 70 Trick-madame..is cooling and moist. 1725 *Bradley's Fam. Dict.* s. v. *Sallet*, The Cimes and Tops of Trick-Madam, when young and tender, drest as Purslain, is a frequent Ingredient in our cold Sallet.

**Trickment** (tri·kmėnt). *rare.* [f. TRICK *v.* + -MENT.] Decoration, adornment.

In earliest use app. heraldic ornament; cf. HATCHMENT.

*a* 1619 FLETCHER, etc. *Knt. of Malta* IV. ii, A new tomb, new trickments too. *a* 1619 — *Mad Lover* V. iv, No tombe shall hold thee But these two armes, no Trickments but my teares. *a* 1843 SOUTHEY in *Fraser's Mag.* (1868) LXXVIII. 106 Other poets,..forced their verses with far-fetched conceits and tawdry trickments of art.

**† Tri·ckness.** *Obs. rare.* [f. TRICK *a.* + -NESS.] The condition or quality of being 'trick'; neatness, smartness, or trigness of attire.

1600 ABP. ABBOT *Exp. Jonah* 593 He saw some as proud, and glad of their tricknesse, as Ionas was of his shadow.

**Trickology** (trikǫ·lŏdʒi). *nonce-wd.* [f. TRICK *sb.* + -OLOGY.] The science of trickery. Hence **Tricko·logist**, a trickster.

1723 (*title*) Trickology, or a Letter of Advice to a Student of Medicine. *Ibid.* 4 Trickology, which a Greek would name *Technology*, a Part by far more witty and lucrative than all the other five. *Ibid.* 20 A serious Sense of Religion..shall never make a good Trickologist.

**Tricksical, Tricksily**: see under TRICKSY *a.*

**Tricksiness** (tri·ksinės). [f. TRICKSY *a.* + -NESS.] The quality or condition of being tricksy.

**1.** Artful smartness of apparel. *rare.*

*a* 1553 C. BANSLEY *Treat.* xix. (Percy S.) 6 Loke well, ye men, to your wives trycksynes, whyche is to shamefull wyde.

**2.** Playfulness, sprightliness; mischievousness.

1846 D. JERROLD *Chron. Clovernook* Wks. 1864 IV. 439 The tricksiness of an extravagant spirit. 1871 G. MEREDITH *H. Richmond* II. 21 Pride in their physical prowess, their dexterity, ingenuity, and tricksiness, and their purity of blood. 1876 GEO. ELIOT *Dan. Der.* I. vii, There was none of the latent fun and tricksiness which had always pierced in her greeting of Rex.

**3.** Deceptiveness, trickiness.

1888 J. T. WALKER *Reason. Chr.* 2 The Judge points out ..its tricksiness and capacity for self deception.

**† Tri·cksing,** *ppl. a. Obs. rare.* [as if f. a vb. **tricks* + -ING [2]; cf. TRICKSY *v.* and TRICKING.] Tricking, cheating, treacherous.

1681 COTTON *Wond. Peak* (ed. 4) 45 Some of which hanging tablets [stones], as he still Made further progress up the tricksing hill, He found so loose, they threatned as he went To sweep him off and be his Monument.

**Tricksome** (tri·ksŏm), *a.* [f. TRICK *sb.* or *v.* + -SOME.]

**1.** Given to playing tricks; = TRICKY *a.* 1.

1648 *Church-lands not to be sold* 48 The Pope had made.. the necessity,..that he might fleece the Clergy; which that just Councel well weighing,..made him finde some other tricksom way, to salve his necessity. 1761 *Antiq.* in *Ann. Reg.* 169/2 The Dracs, supposed to be malicious, or at least tricksome demons. 1821 *New Monthly Mag.* III. 555/2 Mr. Kemble was often artificial; but all his art was employed on those passages where Mr. Kean is merely tricksome. 1858 LYTTON *What will he do?* x. v, I have been a trick-some shifty vagrant.

**2.** Playful, sportive, frolicsome.

1815 J. SCOTT *Vis. Paris* (ed. 2) I. ii. 17 Some ladies..their flowing shawls..and tricksome gait, bade our young gentlemen prepare their compliments in a new language. **1824** *Examiner* 107/2 A tricksome youth full of mischievous merriment. **1832** L. HUNT *Poems, To J. H.* 27 My tricksome Puck. **1870** F. JACOX *Rec. Recluse* I. xii. 249 [He] has pictured Handel with..his delicacies and tricksome graces.

**b.** Of music.

**1820** L. HUNT *Indicator* No. 60 (1822) II. 60 The most tricksome harmonies and accompaniments of Mozart and Beethoven. **1822** *Examiner* 266/1 The situations are often too serious, and the devotion too solemn, to allow of tricksome passages.

**Trickster** (tri·kstəɹ). [f. TRICK *sb.* or *v.* + -STER.] One who practises trickery; a rogue, cheat, knave.

**1711** *Medley* No. 39 The other..was such a Lubbard Trickster, so awkward at Mischief, that he deserv'd only to be laugh'd at. **1741** RICHARDSON *Pamela* II. 260 Tho' I have won the Game, I hope, Sirs, I am no Trickster. **1844** DISRAELI *Coningsby* IX. vi, The Whigs were known to be feeble; they were looked upon as tricksters. **1879** MCCARTHY *Own Times* II. xviii. 2 Diplomatists..commissioned to act as tricksters. **1879** DIXON *Windsor* II. xvi. 171 The woman whom he knew to be a trickster.

*attrib.* **1889** *Voice* (N. Y.) 7 Mar., The bad faith so frequently shown by trickster party leadership.

Hence **Tri·ckstering**, the action of a trickster (also *attrib.*); **Tri·ckstress**, a female trickster.

**1821** SCOTT *Kenilw.* xxxvi, I like not this lady's tampering and *trickstering with this same Edmund Tressilian. **1883** *Times* 12 July 10 Due to political trickstering directed against Mr. Bradlaugh. **1889** J. J. THOMAS *Froudacity* 77 Since the trickstering days of Governor Irving. **1870** E. H. PEMBER *Trag. Lesbos* viii. 119 Nay, young *trickstress, nay!

**Tricksy** (tri·ksi), *a.* Also 6–7 **tricksie, -sey, trickesie, trixsie, trixy.** [app. f. *tricks*, pl. of TRICK *sb.* + -Y, with the natural meaning 'given to, distinguished by, or abounding in tricks'.]

**1.** Artfully trimmed or decked; spruce, smart, fine.

**1552** LATIMER *Serm., John xv. 12* (1572) 153 Let them go as tricksie as they wil in this world, yet for all that they be foule and filthy inough before God. **1577** KENDALL *Flowers Epigr.* 19 b, Thou wandrest trixsie trimsie fine, with crispt and curled heare. **1589** FLEMING *Virg. Georg.* III. 51 When he is new become againe, Hauing cast off his skin, and tricksie trim with youth afresh. **1598** FLORIO, *Immarzapanato*, become or made fine,..sweete, or daintie,..trickesie, and trim as a marchpane. **1631** *Celestina* VII. 88 To see every thing so trimme and tricksie about you. *a* **1820** J. R. DRAKE *Culprit Fay* iv. (1835) 12 Their little minim forms arrayed In the tricksy pomp of fairy pride! **1852** D. G. MITCHELL *Dream Life* 150 The tricksy panoply that he has wrought out of the mettle of his classics.

**2.** Full of or given to tricks or pranks; playful, sportive; mischievous, capricious, whimsical.

**1596** SHAKS. *Merch. V.* III. v. 74, I doe know A many fooles..Garnisht like him, that for a tricksie word Defie the matter. **1598** MARSTON *Sco. Villanie* II. Prol., Tricksey tales of speaking Cornish dawes. **1604** DEKKER *Honest Wh.* I. xi. Wks. 1873 II. 63 [Stage-direction] Enter Candido like a Prentise. *Wife.* Why how now mad-man, what in your tricksi-coats? **1610** SHAKS. *Temp.* v. i. 226 *Ariel.* Sir, all this seruice Haue I done...*Prospero.* My tricksey Spirit. **1831** CARLYLE *Sart. Res.* I. iv, A rich, idiomatic diction, picturesque allusions, fiery poetic emphasis, or quaint tricksy turns. **1871** R. ELLIS *Catullus* ii. 5 My lady..Bends her splendour awhile to tricksy frolic. **1895** CROCKETT *Love Idylls* (1901) 125 The tricksy maid clapped her hands and laughed merrily.

**3.** Full of tricks or deception; tricky, crafty, cunning, cheating.

**1766** GOLDSM. *Vic. W.* xxvi, I still continued tricksy and cunning, and was poor, without the consolation of being honest. **1809–10** COLERIDGE *Friend* (ed. 3) I. 25 The tricksy humilities of the ambitious candidates for the favorable suffrages of the judicious public. **1856** R. A. VAUGHAN *Mystics* (1860) I. 241 Willoughby had to tell of the escapades of tricksy trout.

**4.** That is apt to play tricks upon one; that needs cautious handling: = TRICKY *a.* 2, TICKLISH.

**1835** WILLIS *Pencillings* I. xxi. 146 The second and third stories are ornamented with tricksy-looking iron balconies. **1862** *Morn. Star* 21 May, Kidderminster is a tricksy borough. Its people have a knack of taking their own way. **1900** H. SUTCLIFF *Shameless Wayne* i, A lass is tricksy handling ut sich times.

Hence **Tri·cksical** *a.*, inclined to be tricksy or to play tricks; **Tri·cksily** *adv.*, in a tricksy or sportive manner.

**1866** ALGER *Solit. Nat. & Man* III. 163 The heathen deities,..that once tricksily danced over the classic landscapes. **1889** *Pall Mall G.* 28 May 3 Imagination is, indeed, a tricksical jade.

† **Tri·cksy,** *v. Obs. rare.* In 6 **trixie.** [f. prec.] *trans.* To make 'tricksy' or spruce.

**1598** FLORIO, *Nimfarsi*, to trim, to smug, to trixie, to decke or spruce himselfe vp as a nimphe.

**Trick-track**: see TRIC-TRAC.

**Tricky** (tri·ki), *a.* [f. TRICK *sb.* + -Y.] Characterized by or full of tricks.

**1.** Given to the practice of crafty or deceitful tricks; characterized by trickery.

**1786** BURNS *To Auld Mare* v, Tho' ye was trickie, slee, an' funnie, Ye ne'er was donsie. **1812** WALKER in P. Graham *Agric. Surv. Stirling* 401 A minister..paid in kind from the small tricky heritors, who are imposing upon him grain of the worst quality. **1831–54** LD. COCKBURN *Jrnl.* ii. (1874) 113 As Lord President he was tricky. **1868** E. EDWARDS *Ralegh* I. ii. 27 Very characteristic..of the tricky and tortuous policy of Elizabeth's government.

**b.** Skilled in performing clever tricks or dodges.

**1887** *Daily News* 19 May 3/3 It had gained many prizes, and was what he might call a tricky dog. **1890** L. C. D'OYLE *Notches* 63, I used to be what they call a 'tricky' hunter. **1901** *Essex Weekly News* 29 Mar. 8/3 His partner..was the trickiest forward on the field.

**2.** Having the deceptive character of a trick; containing unexpected difficulties; needing cautious action or handling; risky, catchy, ticklish. *colloq.*

**1887** SAINTSBURY *Hist. Elizab. Lit.* iv. (1890) 111 One of the tricky things called echo sonnets. **1887** *L'pool Daily Post* 14 Feb. 5/7 Accompanying certain recitations with music, which at first appeared a rather tricky experiment. **1891** KIPLING *Light that Failed* i, Revolvers are tricky things for young hands to deal with.

**Triclad** (trəi·klæd, tri·kläd), *a.* and *sb. Zool.* [ad. mod.L. *Triclada*, neut. pl., f. TRI- + Gr. κλάδος branch.] **a.** *adj.* Belonging to the division *Triclada* or *Tricladida* of turbellarian worms, having a main intestine with three branches. **b.** *sb.* A worm of this division. (Cf. POLYCLAD.)

**1888** ROLLESTON & JACKSON *Anim. Life* 579 Bundles of dorso-ventral muscle-fibres, &c. in *Nemertea* and Triclad *Turbellaria*. *Ibid.* 672 Transverse fission has been observed in the Triclads *Planaria subtentaculata*..and *Polycœlis cornuta*. **1909** J. W. JENKINSON *Experim. Embryol.* 273 The reunion of separated blastomeres in Triclads.

† **Tri·clasite.** *Min. Obs.* [ad. Ger. *triclasit* (Hausmann 1808), f. Gr. τρι-, TRI- + κλάσ-ις breaking, fracture + -ITE [1].] Obsolete synonym of FAHLUNITE.

**1835** *Encycl. Brit.* (ed. 7) XII. 37/1 Triclasite. Specific Gravity 2·61 to 2·66. **1850** ANSTED *Elem. Geol., Min.* etc. § 401 Fahlunite, Triklasite, Hydrous silicate of alumina with magnesia, oxide of iron, and oxide of manganese. **1868** DANA *Min.* (ed. 5) 485 The name triclasite alludes to three cleavages, and is therefore bad, as they are not cleavages of the species, but in part of the original iolite.

**Tricla·vian.** [f. TRI- + L. *clāvus* nail + -IAN.] One who holds that only three nails were used at the crucifixion of Christ. Hence **Tricla·vianism.**

**1838** G. S. FABER *Inquiry* 398 The author of the Noble Lesson, whom I suppose to have been a Triclavian, mentions the five wounds. *Ibid.* 397 Pope Innocent III finally and infallibly determined, that four nails were used, and that the Roman soldier pierced the right side of Christ; a decision, which of course stamped the brand of heresy upon Triclavianism.

**Triclinate** (trəi·-, tri·klineɪt), *a. Cryst.* [f. TRI- + L. *clīnāt-us* inclined.] = TRICLINIC.

**1837** DANA *Min.* 40 On examining the figure of anorthite..we..have no room for a doubt, that this crystal is triclinate. **1849** — *Geol.* App. II. (1850) 732 Cleavage oblique, probably indicating triclinate crystallization.

† **Tricline.** *Obs.* Also 5 **-yne.** [ad. L. *triclīnium*: see below: cf. OF. *triclin*, 14th c., *tricline*, 15th c.] = TRICLINIUM.

*c* **1440** *Pallad. on Husb.* I. 391 And half as high thyn chamber & tricline [*v.r.* -clyne] Thou make, as hit is mesure long by lyne. **1492** RYMAN *Poems* xii. 9 in *Archiv Stud. neu. Spr.* LXXXIX. 181 O floure of all virginitie..O triclyne of the trinitie.

**Triclinial** (trəikli·niăl), *a.* [f. TRICLINI-UM + -AL.] Pertaining to a triclinium. So **Tricli·niarch** [ad. L. *triclīniarchēs*, Gr. *τρικλινιάρχης: cf. ARCHITRICLINE], the president of a feast; † **Tricli·niary** *a.* [ad. L. *triclīniāris*] = *triclinial.*

**1874** I. TAYLOR *Etruscan Researches* iii. 47 The couches on which the corpses repose have a *triclinial arrangement. **1656** BLOUNT *Glossogr.*, *Tricliniarck (*tricliniarches*), the master of the dining chamber or room, the huicher. **1892** *Harper's Mag.* Dec. 131/1 There is no need thus to punish your tricliniarch. **1646** SIR T. BROWNE *Pseud. Ep.* v. vi. 243 From this *Tricliniary disposure, we may illustrate that obscure expression of Seneca. **1695** J. EDWARDS *Perfect. Script.* 133 This was their posture..on their tricliniary beds.

**Triclinic** (trəikli·nik), *a. Cryst.* [f. Gr. τρι-, TRI- + κλίν-ειν to incline, lean, slope + -IC.] Applied to that system of crystalline forms in which the three axes are unequal and obliquely inclined (also called *anorthic*, *tetartoprismatic*, or *doubly oblique*); belonging to this system.

**1854** DANA *Min.* Introd. (ed. 4) 29 In the Triclinic System, the three axes are unequal, and all the intersections are oblique. **1869** ROSCOE *Elem. Chem.* (1871) 267 Copper sulphate..crystallizes in large blue crystals belonging to the triclinic system. **1897** GEIKIE *Anc. Volcanoes Gt. Brit.* I. 27 The bottom of the flow was thickly crowded with triclinic felspars and augites.

‖ **Triclinium** (trəikli·niŏm, triˌkləi·niŏm). *Roman Antiq.* Pl. **-ia.** [L. *triclīnium*, a. Gr. τρικλίνιον, dim. of τρίκλῑνος, as sb. a dining-room with three couches, f. κλίνη couch, bed.] A couch, running round three sides of a table, on which to recline at meals; a table-couch; also, a room for eating in; a dining-room.

**1646** SIR T. BROWNE *Pseud. Ep.* VII. xviii. 381 Fishponds, Gardens, Tricliniums. **1797** S. LYSONS *Rom. Antiq. Woodchester* 17 These [apartments] occupy the situation assigned by Vitruvius for the *triclinia* of the spring and autumn. **1848** MRS. JAMESON *Sacr. & Leg. Art* (1850) 106 In the Triclinium of the old palace of the Lateran.

**Triclinoˌhe·dric,** *a. Cryst.* [f. as TRICLINIC + Gr. ἕδρα base.] = TRICLINIC. So **Triclinohe·dral** *a.*

**1837** DANA *Min.* 15 Oblique Rhomboidal Prism...It..forms the class *Triclinata*...*Note.* Triclinohedral of Naumann. **1882** OGILVIE (Annandale), Triclinohedric.

**Tricoaster**: see TRI- 4 c.

**Tricoccous** (trəikǫ·kəs), *a. Bot.* [f. TRI- + COCC-US + -OUS.] Of a fruit: Composed of three *cocci* or carpels; also of a plant, having a fruit of this kind. Also **Trico·ccose** *a.*

**1697** *Phil. Trans.* XIX. 396 Tricoccos Shrubs called Widdow-Wayles. **1703** J. PETIVER *ibid.* XXIII. 1458 The Berry is perfectly tricoccose. **1707** SLOANE *Jamaica* I. 124 A tricoccous, rough seed-vessel. **1845** LINDLEY *Sch. Bot.* vii. (1858) 114 The fruit of this order is tricoccous; that is, it consists of 3 carpels.

**Tricolic** (trəikǭu·lik), *a. Gr. Pros.* [f. Gr. τρίκωλος (f. τρι-, TRI- + κῶλον limb, clause) + -IC.] Consisting of three cola: see COLON [2] 1. So **Trico·lon,** a period consisting of three cola.

**1706** PHILLIPS (ed. Kersey), *Tricolon*,..a Stanza, or Staff of three Verses. **1891** *Cent. Dict.*, Tricolic.

**Tricolorous** (trəikv·lərəs), *a.* [f. late L. *tricolor, -ōr-em* (see next) + -OUS.] = next, A.

**1891** in *Cent. Dict.*

**Tricolour, tricolor** (trəi·kvləɹ), *a.* and *sb.* [ad. late L. *tricolor, -ōrem* adj. (Priscian *c* 500), and F. *tricolore* adj. (often in phr. *drapeau tricolore*: see A. 2, B. 2).]

**A.** *adj.* Having three colours; three-coloured.

**1.** *Nat. Hist.* (in form **tricolor**).

**1866** *Treas. Bot.*, *Tricolor*, consisting of three colours. **1900** in B. D. JACKSON *Gloss. Bot. Terms.*

**2.** Of a flag, cockade, etc.; esp. of the national flags of France, Italy, and Mexico: see B. 2.

**1815** SOUTHEY in *Q. Rev.* July 482 (tr. *Napoleon*) Tear down those colours which the nation has proscribed; mount the tricolour cockade. **1832** tr. *Sismondi's Ital. Rep.* xvi. 362 The French general Baraguai d'Hilliers entered the city..and planted..the tricolour banner on St. Mark. **1860** W. G. CLARK in *Vac. Tour.* 56 [They] made haste to take all the tricolor flags from their windows. **1886** *Pall Mall G.* 3 July 8/2 Many..supporters had also donned tricolour rosettes.

**B.** *sb.* (Not so used in French.)

**1.** *Gardening* (in form **tricolor**). Short for *Amarantus tricolor*, a species of amaranth from China, cultivated for its brightly coloured leaves, compounded of green, yellow, and red.

**1786** ABERCROMBIE *Gard. Assist.* 239 Fine balsams, cockscombs, tricolors, etc.

**2.** A tricolour flag, cockade, etc.; *esp.* the national flag of France adopted at the Revolution, consisting of equal vertical stripes of blue, white, and red.

**1798** SCOTT *War-song* viii, If ever breath of British gale Shall fan the tri-color [*rime* shore]. **1815** BYRON *On the Star of 'the Legion of Honour'* iv, A rainbow..Of three bright colours. *Note*, The tri-colour. **1832** MARRYAT *N. Forster* xli, The French tricolour hardly had time to blow clear. **1837** CARLYLE *Fr. Rev.* I. v. v, Red and Blue, our old Paris colours: these, once based on a ground of constitutional White, are the famed Tricolor,—which (if Prophecy err not) 'will go round the world'. **1847** DISRAELI *Tancred* IV. ii, The flag of England has beaten even the tricolour. **1855** W. MORRIS in Mackail *Life* (1899) I. 82 The Russian tricolour, horizontal stripes of blue, red, and white. **1870** *Daily News* 1 Dec., An unpretending house..has a sentry at the gate, and a North German tricolour displayed above the garden wall.

**Tricoloured, -colored** (trəi·kv:ləɹd), *a.* (Often with hyphen.) [f. TRI- + COLOURED, after prec., simulating a parasynthetic compound, as *three-coloured.*] = prec. A.

**1795** *St. Papers* in *Ann. Reg.* 234/2 That tri-coloured standard [of 1789, when the red and blue of Paris were added to the white of the French King]. **1797** S. & HT. LEE *Canterb. T., Frenchm. T.* (1799) I. 234 Each wore a tri-coloured ribbond in his hat. **1806** A. DUNCAN *Nelson* 98 The tri-colored cockade..caught his eye. **1840** MACAULAY *Ess., Ranke* (1887) 592 The tricoloured flag floated on the top of the Castle of St. Angelo.

**Tricolumnar**: see TRI- 1.

‖ **Tricon** (tri·kǫn). *Cards.* [F. *tricon*: origin unknown; perh. jocularly f. L. *tri-* three + *con-*, CON-, together.] In certain card games, as Commerce: see quots.

**1798** *Sporting Mag.* XII. 142 The tricon is three tens, three nines, three fours, or any three cards of the same rank. **1850** *Bohn's Hand-Bk. Games* 329 At this game [Commerce] are three parts: 1st, That which takes place of all others, called the tricon, or three cards of the same denomination, similar to pair-royal at Cribbage.

**Triconodont** (trəiˌkǭu·nǫdǫnt), *a. Zool.* [f. TRI- + Gr. κῶνος cone + ὀδοντ- tooth: cf. CONODONT.] Having molar teeth with three conical cusps, as the extinct genus *Triconodon* or family *Triconodontidæ* of mammals (supposed to be marsupials); also said of such teeth. So **Triconodo·ntid,** an animal of this family; **Triconodo·ntoid** *a.*, belonging to or having the characters of this family; *sb.* = *triconodontid*; **Trico·nodonty,** the condition of being triconodont.

**1881** *Q. Jrnl. Geog. Soc.* XXXVII. 378 The fourth premolar of *Triacanthodon* approaches the triconodont or true molar type. **1895** *Funk's Standard Dict.*, Triconodontid, Triconodontoid. **1897** *Amer. Nat.* Dec. 998 The triconodont crown..was predominant in the Lower Jurassic period. *Ibid.* 999 Both the 'haplodont' and 'triconodont' crowns are seen to-day among the Cetacea. **1899** *Proc. Zool. Soc.* 2 May 571 The famous theory of the gradual complication, of triconodonty and trituberculy, is an untenable hypothesis.

**Tri:consona·ntal,** *a.* [f. TRI- + CONSONANTAL.] Consisting of or containing three consonants: said chiefly of the radical words of the

Semitic languages. Hence **Triconsona·ntalism,** triconsonantal formation. So **Triconsona·ntic** *a.*

**1863** *Smith's Bible Dict.* III. 1539/1 It is more than probable that the triconsonantal has been evolved out of a biconsonantal root. *Ibid.*, The bisyllabism [of the Hebrew verb] is in reality triconsonantalism, the vowels not forming any part of the essence of the root. **1869** FARRAR *Fam. Speech* iii. (1873) 88 The root of the Semitic verb is always triliteral, or rather triconsonantic.

**Tricorn** (trəi·kǫɹn), *a.* and *sb.* Also (as or after Fr.) **tricorne.** [ad. F. *tricorne* or L. *tricornis* three-horned, f. *tri-*, TRI- + L. *cornū* horn.]

**A.** *adj.* Three-horned; having three horns or horn-like projections; *spec.* applied to a cocked hat with the brim turned up on three sides.

**1844** HOBLYN *Dict. Med. Terms, Tricorne*,..a term applied to each lateral ventricle of the brain, from its three-horned shape. **1864** M. J. HIGGINS *Ess.* (1875) 201 With their tricorn hats they looked very much like Knaves of Spades. **1883** A. WALLIS in *N. & Q.* 6th Ser. VIII. 363/1 A white bob-wig surmounted by a tricorne hat completes the ordinary costume of a gentleman living in the second Georgian period. **1909** *Daily Graphic* LXXX. 13/1 An ermine tricorne hat.

**B.** *sb.*

**1.** An (imaginary) creature with three horns.

**1760** *Impostors Detected* III. viii. II. 78 These creatures were distinguished..by a lump on their heads,..supported by three small protuberances; from whence they were called Tri-corns. **1823** [see BICORN]. **1895** F. E. HULME *Nat. Hist. Lore & Leg.* 147 What can have..suggested the idea of such a very unpleasant tricorn, it is impossible to say.

**2.** A tricorn hat: see A.

**1876** G. MEREDITH *Beauch. Career* ii, A shocking bad, bald, brown-rubbed old *tricorne*. **1903** J. CONRAD & HUEFFER *Romance* v. i, He wore a large and shadowy tricorn.

So † **Trico·rnous** *a.* (*obs. rare*$^{-0}$), three-horned.

**1656** in BLOUNT *Glossogr.*

**Tri-cornered, -cornigerous, -cornute,** etc.: see TRI- 1 c, 1.

**Tricorporal** (trəikǭ·ɹpŏrăl), *a.* [f. TRI- + L. *corpus, corpor-* body + -AL: cf. *corporal.*] Having three bodies; three-bodied. So **Trico·rporate, Trico·rporated** *adjs.* in same sense, *spec.* in *Her.*: see quots.; also **Trico·rporous** *a.* (*rare*$^{-0}$).

**1730–6** BAILEY (folio), **Tricorporal*, that hath three bodies. **1822** T. TAYLOR *Apuleius* III. 59 Coequal to the destruction of the tricorporal Geryon, or the three-headed Cerberus. **1731** BAILEY vol. II, **Tricorporate, Tricorporous*, that hath three bodies. *c* **1828** BERRY *Encycl. Her.* I. Gloss., *Tricorporate* is said when the bodies of three beasts are represented issuing from the dexter, sinister, and base points of the escocheon, and meeting conjoined to one head in the centre point. **1572** BOSSEWELL *Armorie* II. 42 *Tricorporated. **1610** GUILLIM *Heraldry* III. xv. (1611) 141 A Tricorporated Lion issuing out of the three corners of the Escocheon all meeting vnder one head. **1727** BAILEY vol. II, **Tricorporous.*

**Tricoryphean, -costate**: see TRI- 1.

**Tri·cosane, tri-i·cosane.** *Chem.* [f. Gr. τρία three + εἴκοσι twenty + -ANE.] A hydrocarbon belonging to the paraffin series, containing 23 atoms of carbon.

**1894** MUIR & MORLEY *Watts' Dict. Chem.* IV. 793 *n*-Tricosane $C_{23}H_{48}$ (melting point 48°C.)...Obtained also by fractional distillation of paraffin oil from brown coal...Glittering plates. **1902** *Jrnl. Chem. Soc.* LXXXII. I. 734 Pennsylvania Petroleum..furnished a small proportion of a solid tricosane, $C_{23}H_{48}$, which melts at 45°.

† **Tricot**[1]. *Obs. rare*$^{-1}$. [Allied to OF. *tricotage* chicanery, trickery (Godef. *Compl.*), *tricotement* chicane (*c* 1400 in Godef.), *tricoterie* 'cousenage, cheating, trecherie, deceit, in the following of a suit, etc.' (Cotgr.), which imply a vb. **tricoter* to cozen, cheat, and perh. a sb. **tricot*; but these do not appear in this sense, unless they are fig. uses of *tricoter* to knit, *tricot* knitting.] Trickery, fraud.

*c* **1430** *Pilgr. Lyf Manhode* III. xxvi. (1869) 150 The oother hand..is cleped..tricot..and disceyuaunce.

‖ **Tricot**[2] (trīko). [F. *tricot* knitting, knitted work, f. *tricoter* to knit; of uncertain origin.] Knitting; knitted work or fabric; a woollen fabric, knitted by hand, or by machinery in imitation of hand-knitting; also, name of a woollen fabric (see quot. 1904). Also short for *tricot-stitch.*

**1872** BROWNING *Fifine* iii, The human beauty..Tricot fines down if fat, padding plumps up if lean. **1882** CAULFEILD & SAWARD *Dict. Needlework* 128/2 Make a Foundation chain ..and work a row of Tricot. **1893** A. ZIMMERN tr. *Blümner's Home Life Anc. Grks.* xii. 440 The costume and the tricots, as well as the grotesque masks, are worthy of notice. **1898** *Daily News* 5 Mar. 6/4 A mourning walking dress in woollen tricot. **1904** *Woollen Draper's Terms* in *Tailor & Cutter* 4 Aug. 480/1 *Tricots*, a woollen fabric, with diagonals running straight across the piece, and something like cassimere handle.

**b.** *attrib.*, as *tricot-stitch, tricot-work.*

**1880** *B'ham Weekly Post* 2 Oct. 1/5, I have an interminable piece of trico work in hand, which has been my resource for several years. **1882** CAULFEILD & SAWARD *Dict. Needlework* 128/1 *Tricot stitch*... The easiest of crochet stitches, but only suitable for straight work; it is usually worked with Berlin or fleecy wool, and a wooden hook, and is suitable for couvrepieds, counterpanes, muffatees, mufflers, and other warm articles.

† **Tricotee,** *sb. Obs.* Also 7 **trick-a-tee,** 8 **tricotez.** [a. F. *tricotets*, also *tricotée* (Lamonnoye in Littré), f. *tricoter* to dance in a lively manner: origin uncertain.] A lively kind of old dance. Hence † **Tricotee** *v.* (with *it*), to dance this. *Obs.*

**1659** *Lady Alimony* I. ii. A iij b, A Monkey dancing his Trick-a-tee on a Rope. **1664** COTTON *Scarron.* IV. (1741) 120 Poor Dido..tho' oppressed with Woe and Care, cut Capers, and Tricotee'd it barefoot. **1667** FLECKNOE *Damoiselles à la Mode* IV. ii. 80 The dancing Bears shall dance the Tricotees with him for a wager. *a* **1701** SEDLEY *Grumbler* II. i, Will you have a minuet, Sir?..What then? (here he names half a dozen dances) The trocanny, tricotez, rigadon?

**Tricotyledonous**: see TRI- 1.

**Tricquet,** variant of TRIQUET *Obs.*

**Tricrotic** (trəikrǫ·tik), *a. Physiol.* [f. TRI-, after DICROTIC; cf. Gr. τρίκροτος rowed with triple stroke, as a trireme.] Of the pulse or a sphygmographic tracing: Having or showing three undulations for each beat of the heart. *Tricrotic wave*, the third of such undulations. So **Tri·crotism,** tricrotic condition; **Tri·crotous** *a.* = *tricrotic.*

**1876** tr. *Wagner's Gen. Pathol.* (ed. 6) 630 The pulse of aged persons is tricrotic. **1877** ROBERTS *Handbk. Med.* (ed. 3) II. 21 This form of pulsation is sometimes called tricrotous. **1890** BILLINGS, *Tricrotic wave*, the third curve of the sphygmogram. **1891** *Cent. Dict.*, Tricrotism. **1913** DORLAND *Med. Dict.* s.v. *Pulse, Tricrotic pulse*, one that is marked by three abnormally distinct sphygmographic waves to the pulse-beat.

**Tricrunodal, -crural**: see TRI- 1.

**Tric-trac** (tri·k,træ·k). Also 7– **trick-track.** [a. F. *tric-trac*, † *trique-trac* (16th c. in Littré; cf. also *jeux de triquetactz*, Godef. *Compl.*); so called from the clicking sound made by the pieces in playing the game: F. *tric-trac*, an echoic word (15th c.), applied to various clicking noises.] An old variety of backgammon: = TICK-TACK 2.

[**1653** URQUHART *Rabelais* II. vii. 41 The trictrac of the knocking Friars.] **1687** SEDLEY *Bellamira* IV. i, I lost three sets at back-gammon, and a tout at trick-track. **1690** R. DAVIES *Jrnl.* (Camden) 78, I taught them to play grand tric-trac. **1788** *Gentl. Mag.* Dec. 1071/1 One of the kinds of trictrac used in Europe. **1852** THACKERAY *Esmond* I. iv, He loved to play at cards and tric-trac with him. **1897** DOWDEN *Fr. Lit.* V. i. 336 The destiny of nations is satirically viewed as a vulgar game of trick-track.

*attrib.* **1800** MAR. EDGEWORTH *Belinda* xxx, There's Mrs. Delacour leading Miss Portman off into the trictrac cabinet. **1819** LAMB *Let. to Miss Wordsworth* 25 Nov., In the trick-track board, where the hits are figured.

**Tricube, Tricurvate**: see TRI- 4 a, 2.

**Tricuspid** (trəikʊ·spid), *a.* (*sb.*) [ad. L. *tricuspis, -cuspid-em* three-pointed, f. *tri-*, TRI- + *cuspis* point: cf. F. *tricuspide* (Littré).] Having three cusps or points. **a. Tricuspid valve** or **valves** (*Anat.*): the valve consisting of three triangular segments (or, as otherwise regarded, the set of three triangular valves) which guards the opening from the right auricle into the right ventricle of the heart. Also *absol.* or as *sb.*; hence *attrib.*, as *tricuspid murmur, obstruction, opening, regurgitation*, etc.

**1670** *Phil. Trans.* V. 2097 We did also observe two Ventricles with the tricuspid [and] sigmoid-valves. **1834** J. FORBES *Laennec's Dis. Chest* (ed. 4) 547 In hypertrophy of the right ventricle..the thickening..is always a little greater in the vicinity of the tricuspid valves. **1872** HUXLEY *Physiol.* ii. 36 On the right side there are..three of these broad pointed membranes, whence the whole apparatus is called the tricuspid valve. **1877** ROBERTS *Handbk. Med.* (ed. 3) II. 10 Said to accompany tricuspid obstruction. *Ibid.* 43 Tricuspid Regurgitation. **1898** *Allbutt's Syst. Med.* V. 786 Valvular incompetence..at the tricuspid opening. *Ibid.* 869 We may notice occasionally..a tricuspid systolic murmur.

**b.** Of various structures, as a tooth, leaf, etc.: also *absol.* or as *sb.* a tricuspid tooth.

**1849** *Florist* 212 There is something very striking..about their tricuspid petals, and quaint, lively markings. **1856** WOODWARD *Mollusca* III. 449 The central teeth are..tricuspid in Loligo. **1881** J. ANDERSON *Scot. in Early Chr. T.* iii. 130 In the West Highland crosses they are..terminated by a peculiar conventional, tricuspid leaf.

So **Tricu·spidal, Tricu·spidate, Tricu·spidated** *adjs.* in same sense.

**1822–34** *Good's Study Med.* (ed. 4) I. 520 The *tricuspidal valve, with the..sigmoid valve of the pulmonary artery.. never exhibit bony deposits. **1852** SALMON *Higher Plane Curves* vi. (1879) 253 The quartic is tricuspidal. **1752** J. HILL *Hist. Anim.* 11 The Brachionus, with..a *tricuspidate tail. **1881** BAKER in *Jrnl. Linn. Soc.* XVIII. 280 Stigma capitate, obscurely tricuspidate. **1822** J. PARKINSON *Outl. Oryctol.* 197 An inequivalved..shell; *tricuspidated at the base. *Ibid.* 275 Teeth of cartilaginous fishes..triangular, conical, single pointed, tricuspidated, tridentated.

**Tricu·ssate,** *a. Bot.* [irreg. f. DECUSSATE, with substitution of TRI- for *de-*.] (See quot.)

**1900** B. D. JACKSON *Gloss. Bot. Terms, Tricussate*, used for whorls of three leaves each, the leaves of each whorl alternating with those above and below.

**Tricyanate, Tricyanide**: see TRI- 5 a.

**Tricycle** (trəi·sik'l), *sb.* [a. F. *tricycle*, used in sense 1 in 1827; in sense 2 in Dict. Acad. 1878; f. TRI- + Gr. κύκλος circle, wheel: cf. BICYCLE.]

†**1.** A three-wheeled coach or omnibus drawn by two horses, formerly used in Paris. *Obs.*

**1828** *Chron.* in *Ann. Reg.* 185/1 Tricycles.—Christmas-day was rendered memorable to the Parisians by the starting of this new species of carriage... The tricycle is a kind of coach, mounted on three wheels; it is drawn by two horses only.

**2.** A velocipede with three wheels (now usually one in front and one on each side behind), driven by treadles actuated by the feet, or (*motor tricycle*) by a small motor attached.

**1868** *London Society* Nov. 411 The tricycle, or three-wheeled Velocipede, is easier to guide and safer to use than the bicycle. **1881** *Philad. Record* No. 3459. 2 M. Trouve riding at ease through the streets of Paris upon a tricycle driven by stored-up electricity. **1896** Motor tricycle [see MOTOR A. 5]. **1902** *Encycl. Brit.* XXVII. 325 As far back as 1883 or 1884 the whole of Europe had been covered by women on tricycles.

*attrib.* and *Comb.* **1885** *Graphic* 21 Feb. 186/1 An Englishman..tricycle-riding the country. **1896** *Daily News* 28 May 3/2 Infantry bring up a tricycle Maxim gun.

Hence **Tri·cycle** *v.*, *intr.* to ride a tricycle (whence **Tri·cycling** *vbl. sb.* and *ppl. a.*); **Tri·cycler, Tri·cyclist,** one who rides a tricycle; **Tricy·cular** *a.* [irreg. after *vehicular*; cf. BICYCULAR], pertaining to tricycles.

**1883** *Sat. Rev.* 28 July 107/2 The modern heroine..rides, boats, *tricycles, and plays lawn-tennis. **1902** *19th Cent.* Nov. 764, I was tricycling homeward one evening. **1881** *Daily News* 18 July 5/5 Some member of Parliament should take the matter up, so as to relieve the steam *tricyclers from the restriction. **1888** J. & E. R. PENNELL *Sent. Journ.* 180 A meeting of tricyclers was not an every-day occurrence in their town. **1882** *Standard* 15 May 2/8 *Tricycling divisions of bicycle clubs. **1882** RICHARDSON in *Gd. Words* 177 Mr. Browning called my attention to *tricycling as a healthful recreation. **1878** *Prospectus Bicycle Touring Club*, Any amateur Bicyclist or *Tricyclist—lady or gentleman—is eligible for election to the Bicycle Touring Club. **1887** *Times* 9 Apr. 5/5 The tricyclists were formed into the main column. **1870** *Belgravia* Feb. 444 The latest contrivance in that way comes more under the *tricycular head.

**Tricyclic** (trəisəi·klik, -səi·klik), *a.* [f. Gr. τρι-, TRI- + κύκλος circle + -IC.]

**1.** *Bot.* Arranged in three whorls.

**1900** in B. D. JACKSON *Gloss. Bot. Terms.*

**2.** *Chem.* Of a carbon compound: Having three rings or closed chains of atoms in its structural formula; e. g. phenanthrene. (Ger. *tricyklisch.*)

**1891** *Jrnl. Chem. Soc.* LX. 1258 The two best known tricyclic compounds, anthracene and phenanthrene.

‖ **Tridacna** (trəi-, tridæ·knă). *Zool.* [mod.L. (Da Costa 1776), f. Gr. τρίδακν-ος eaten at three bites, f. τρι-, TRI- + δάκν-ειν to bite.] A genus of bivalve molluscs, including the *Tridacna gigas* or Giant Clam, the largest bivalve shell known. Also *attrib.*

**1776** DA COSTA *Conchol.* 294 A Tridacna, the Bason Conch or Clamp. **1860** WRAXALL *Life in Sea* xiv. 299 The giant Tridacna, which is five feet broad, forms entire submarine banks. **1904** *Athenæum* 24 Sept. 419/1 In graves at Rubiana were found rings of tridacna shell and other objects of the same material carved in a fretwork design.

So † **Tridacnan** *a. Obs. rare*$^{-0}$.

**1623** COCKERAM, *Tridacnan*, any thing that is so big that must be cut in three pieces, or morsels, ere it can be eat.

**Tridactyl** (trəidæ·ktil), *a.* Also **-yle.** [ad. Gr. τριδάκτυλ-ος, f. τρι-, TRI- + δάκτυλος finger, digit.] Having three fingers or toes.

**1812** SHAW *Gen. Zool.* VIII. 104 Tridactyle Kingfisher. **1822** J. PARKINSON *Outl. Oryctol.* 321 The feet of this animal were tridactyle. **1877** LE CONTE *Elem. Geol.* I. (1879) 431 Only three functional toes on the hind foot, which therefore formed a tridactyl track. **1912** *Return Brit. Museum* 179 A tridactyl Reptilian foot-print.

**Trida·ctylous,** *a.* [f. as prec. + -OUS.]

**1.** = prec.

**1828** in WEBSTER. **1851** MANTELL *Petrifact.* i. § 3. 65 The foot-tracks are, for the most part, tridactylous (three-toed). **1856–8** W. CLARK *Van der Hoeven's Zool.* II. 379 Feet tridactylous, palmate, with hallux none.

† **2.** *Chem.* Applied to a compound of an atom of one element with 3 atoms of another, as $SO_3$. *Obs.*

**1865** MANSFIELD *Salts* 483 The simple molecule Sn...does not imitate the molecule Sb. in forming tridactylous compounds either with O. or with H.

**Tridaily**: see TRI- 3.

**Triddil, Triddle**: see TREADLE, TREDDLE.

‖ **Tride** (‖ trīd, trəid), *a.* ? *Obs.* [F. *tride* 'terme de manège, vif, serré' (Littré), a. Eng. *tread* in sense 'gait, pace'.] (See quots.)

**1727** BAILEY vol. II, *Tride* (with Horsemen), short and swift. *Tride-pace*, is a going of short and thick Motions, tho' united and uneasy. *Tride-career*, a fast Gallop that has its Times and Motions short and nimble. To work Tride..upon Volts, is to mark his Time with his Haunches short and ready. [Also in later Dicts. and Cyclopædias.]

**Tride,** obs. f. *tried*, pa. t. and pple. of TRY *v.*

**Tridecane** (trəi·dĭkēn). *Chem.* [f. Gr. τρία three + δέκα ten + -ANE.] A colourless liquid hydrocarbon of the paraffin series, containing 13 atoms of carbon; its melting point is –6° C. and boiling point 234° C.

**1894** MUIR & MORLEY *Watts' Dict. Chem.* IV. 793 Tridecane, $C_{13}H_{28}$. **1902** *Jrnl. Chem. Soc.* LXXXII. I. 733 Hydrocarbons in Pennsylvania Petroleum...Tridecane [etc.].

So **Tridecyl** (trəi·dĭsil) [-YL], the radical ($C_{13}H_{27}$) contained in tridecane. Hence **Tridecy·lic** *a.* in *tridecylic acid*, $C_{13}H_{26}O_2$; also called **Trideco·ic** or **Tridecato·ic** *acid.*

**1868** WATTS *Dict. Chem.* V. 880 Tridecyl. **1880** *Jrnl. Chem. Soc.* XXXVIII. 34 Tridecylic, Pentadecoic, [etc.] Acids.. The discovery of tridecoic and pentadecoic acids makes the list of fatty acids complete as far as stearic acid. **1913** THORPE *Dict. App. Chem.* (ed. 2) V. 529 Tridecatoic or Tridecylic Acid..crystallises in thin plates; m. p. 40·5°.

† **Tri͵dece·nnary,** *a. Obs. rare*⁻¹. [An irregular formation from L. *tredecim* thirteen.] Intended to mean: Of or pertaining to the number thirteen.
(By the form, it ought to mean 'Of thirteen years'.)
**1783** Robertson *Hist. Amer.* (ed. 4) III. 385 Computed.. first by what he calls a tridecennary progression of days from one to thirteen,..and then by a septenary progression of days from one to seven, making in all twenty.

**Tri·decila·teral,** *a. rare.* [irreg. f. L. *tredecim* thirteen + Lateral.] Thirteen-sided.
**1882** Vines *Sachs' Bot.* 205 The shoot itself may be said to be tri-, quadri-, quinqui-, octo-, trideci-lateral, &c.

**Tridecile, Tridel:** see Tredecile, Treddle.

**Trident** (trəi·dĕnt), *sb.* (*a.*) [ad. L. *tridens, trident-em*, f. *tri-* three + *dens, dent-em* tooth. Cf. F. *trident* (13–14th c. in Godef. *Compl.*).]
**1.** An instrument or weapon with three prongs.
**a.** *esp.* A three-pronged fish-spear or sceptre as the attribute of the sea-god Poseidon or Neptune, also figured as borne by Britannia.
**1599** Nashe *Lenten Stuffe* (1871) 18 In the swing of his trident he constituted two lord admirals ouer the whole navy of England. **1607** Shaks. *Cor.* iii. i. 256 He would not flatter Neptune for his Trident, Or Ioue, for 's power to Thunder. **1612** Dekker *Lond. Triumph.* Wks. 1873 III. 241 In his hand he holds a siluer Trident, or Three-forked Mace. **1697** Dryden *Æneid* i. 208 The God himself with ready trident stands, And opes the deep, and spreads the moving sands. **1849** James *Woodman* vii, Some serrated at the edges like Neptune's trident. **1898** Rawlings *Brit. Coinage* 113 In 1797 we have the first English regal copper penny... Britannia seated to right, the union shield at her side, a palm branch in her right hand and a trident in her left.
**b.** A three-pronged spear used by the *retiarius* in ancient Roman gladiatorial combats.
**1693** Stepney in Dryden *Juvenal* viii. (1697) 209 As Retiarius he Attacks his Foe; First waves his Trident ready for the throw, Next casts his Net. **1891** Farrar *Darkn. & Dawn* xxxix, He flung down net and dagger and trident, and, retreating to the barrier, stood there with folded arms.
**c.** *fig.* or in *fig.* context.
**1638** R. Baker tr. *Balzac's Lett.* (vol. II.) 202 The Syllogisme, which by the saying of a Grecian is the Trident and Mace of Philosophie, is in your Writings all painted and perfumed. **1698** Congreve *Birth of Muse* 109 To Worlds remote, she [Britannia] wide extends her Reign, And wields the Trident of the stormy Main. **1804** A. Duncan (*title*) The British Trident; or, Register of Naval Actions. **1812** Wellesley *Parl. Deb.* 30 Nov., To concede the points.. would be to throw into her hands the trident of the main.
**2.** *transf.* Applied to something resembling a trident in shape or configuration, as a three-pronged fork, a piece of land with three promontories.
**1730** Swift *Let. to Gay* 10 Nov., Tell her Grace, that the ill management of forks is not to be help'd when they are only bidential..her Grace hath cost me thirty pounds to provide Tridents for fear of offending her. **1869** Tozer *Highl. Turkey* I. 101 The two other peninsulas, which form the trident of Chalcidice.
**3.** *Geom.* Name of a plane cubic curve of a form suggesting a three-pronged weapon; also *trident curve*. Also called *Cartesian parabola* (Parabola b).
**1710** J. Harris *Lex. Techn.* II, *Trident* is a Name given by Sir Is. Newton to that kind of Parabola, by which D'Cartes constructed Equations of six Dimensions. **1795** Hutton *Math. Dict.* II. 191 Cartesian Parabola.. $xy = ax^3 + bx^2 + cx + d$.. being Newton's 66th species of lines of the 3d order, and called by him a *Trident*. **1864** Cayley *Math. Papers* V. 364 The Trident Curve.
**4.** *attrib.* and *Comb.*, as *trident-bearer, -swayer, tooth*; *trident-armed, -bearing, -shaped* adjs.
**1866** J. Conington *Æneid* i. 226 He, *trident-armed, each dull weight heaves. **1749** G. West *Odes Pindar* i. Anti-str. v, Invocating oft the name Of the *Trident-bearing God. Strait the *Trident-bearer came. **1871** Kingsley *At Last* xiv, A curious *trident-shaped stand..on the horns of which garlands of flowers are hung as offerings. **1904** C. Lanier *Sonn.* in *Daily Chron.* 21 Apr. 3/2 *Trident-swayer of emotion's trembling sea! **1901** G. Meredith tr. *Iliad, Reading of Life* 128 The God drives deep his *trident teeth.
**B.** as *adj.* Having three prongs or forks; tridental. Also *fig.*
**1589** Greene *Menaphon* (Arb.) 24 Neptune..with his trident mace. **1648** Earl Westmoreland *Otia Sacra* (1879) 97 A Trident mischief that doth wound, Requires a Treble Patience to afford Relief. **1864** [see 3 above]. **1910** *Expositor* Aug. 139 He is represented..hurling the trident lightning and with a huge club.

**Tridental** (trəide·ntăl), *a.*¹ [f. as prec. + -al.]
†**1.** Bearing a trident. *Obs. rare.*
**1635** Quarles *Embl.* i. ii. iv, The white-mouth'd Water now usurpes the Shore, And scornes the pow'r of her trydentall Guide.
**2.** Of, pertaining to, or of the nature of a trident; three-pronged, trifurcate.
**1648** Gage *West Ind.* vii. 20 Catching one with a tridentall iron Fork. **1791** Cowper *Iliad* v. 458 The bold Son of Amphytrion with tridental shaft Her bosom pierced. **1843** R. H. Horne *Orion* iii. iii. 166 Now had Poseidon with tridental spear Torn up the smitten sea. **1892** *Graphic* 28 May 637/2 These picturesque tridental bays have contributed backgrounds to many of the artist's pictures.

**Tride·ntal,** *a.*² *rare*⁻⁰. = Tridentine. Hence **Tride·ntally** *adv.*, in accordance with the Tridentine decrees.
**1842** G. S. Faber *Prov. Lett.* (1844) II. 49 A very possible advance, from the fourth century, to the yet more fully instructed, because tridentally instructed, sixteenth.

**Tridentate** (trəide·ntĕt), *a. Bot.* and *Zool.* [f. Tri- + L. *dentāt-us* toothed: see -ate² 2.] Having three teeth or tooth-like processes; three-pronged, three-pointed.
**1760** J. Lee *Introd. Bot.* ii. xxii. (1765) 124 Corolla..either ..tridentate; or quinquedentate. **1852** Dana *Crust.* i. 662 The only species..have the front of the carapax deeply tridentate. **1856–8** W. Clark *Van der Hoeven's Zool.* I. 313 Tarsi with tridentate claws.
So † **Tride·ntated** *a. Obs.* in same sense.
**1752** J. Hill *Hist. Anim.* 35 The grey Fly..with tridentated marks on the abdomen. **1822** J. Parkinson *Outl. Oryctol.* 275 Numerous teeth of cartilaginous fishes..triangular,..tricuspidated, tridentated.

**Tridented,** *a.* [f. as Trident + -ed.]
**1.** (trəide·ntėd). Three-toothed, three-pronged; = Tridentate.
**1620** Quarles *Jonah* Sect. vi. F ij, Neptune..Held his tridented Mace vpon the South. **1816** *Encycl. Perthensis* V. 639/2 The pappus [is] monophyllous and tridented.
**2.** (trəi·dėntėd). Having or furnished with a trident.
**1624** Quarles *Sion's Elegies* iii. 12 Tridented Neptune. **1866** J. B. Rose tr. *Ovid's Met.* viii. 236 Unto Neptune tridented I prayed.

†**Tride·ntifer.** *Obs. rare.* [a. L. *tridentifer*, f. as Trident + *-fer* bearing.] He who bears a trident; the wielder of the trident; Neptune.
**1600** Tourneur *Transf. Metamorph.* xl, Is that great gift Tridentifer presents, To make faire passage for his foule intents?
So **Tridenti·ferous** *a.*, trident-bearing.
**1656** in Blount *Glossogr.* **1727** in Bailey vol. II.

**Tridentine** (tri·dĕntəin, trəide·ntəin), *a.* and *sb.* [ad. med.L. *Tridentīn-us*, f. *Tridentum* the city of Trent.] **A.** *adj.* Of or pertaining to the city of Trent in Tyrol, or to the Council of the Roman Catholic Church held there (1545–63).
**1561** Barlow in H. N. Birt *Eliz. Relig. Settlement* x. (1908) 424 Thomas Stapleton and Edward Goddeshalfe..as it is bruited were the last summer at Tridentine Council. *a* **1711** Ken *Hymnarium* Poet. Wks. 1721 II. 134 The Faith Nicene he spake exact, But when to that the Tridentine he tack'd, This a new Gospel is. **1849** Sir J. Stephen *Eccl. Biogr.* (1850) I. 475 The most promising quarrel which had arisen in the Church since the close of the Tridentine Council. **1901** Bp. Gore *Body of Christ* iv. § 4 (1907) 257 When they [Protestants] rejected the Tridentine doctrine of the Melchizedekian priesthood.
**B.** *sb.* One who accepts and conforms to the decrees of the Council of Trent; an orthodox Roman Catholic.
*a* **1836** R. H. Froude *Rem.* (1838) I. 434 [In answer to the statement that] the Romanists were Schismatics in England, but Catholics abroad, [Froude replied] No, they are wretched Tridentines every where. *a* **1882** *Dublin Rev.* (Ogilvie), Anglicans have styled Catholics of the present day Tridentines.
So **Tri·dentize** *v. rare, intr.* to conform to the Tridentine decrees.
**1826** G. S. Faber *Diffic. Romanism* (1853) 110 [It] is evident to common sense, and will readily be admitted by the tridentising Romanist.

**Tri͵deri·vative.** *Chem. rare.* [Tri- 5 c.] A derivative containing three substituted atoms of radicals of the same kind; a tri-substitution product.
**1875** *Jrnl. Chem. Soc.* XXVIII. 567 Contributions to our knowledge of the Connection between the Bi- and Tri-derivatives of Benzene. **1891** *Cent. Dict.* s. v., Trichloracetic acid is a triderivative of acetic acid.

**Tridge,** dial. and obs. form of Trudge *v.*

**Tridiametral, -diapason, -digital,** etc.: see Tri- 1, 4 a.

**Tri-dimensional** (trəi͵dime·nʃənăl), *a.* [f. Tri- 1 a + Dimensional.] Having or exhibiting three dimensions, as a solid body. Hence **Tri-dimensiona·lity,** the condition or quality of being of three dimensions (in quot. 1894 loosely used).
**1875** Cayley in *Phil. Trans.* CLXV. 678 Theorem C, in the particular case of *tridimensional space. **1894** *Nation* (N. Y.) 23 Aug. 145/1 The tridimensional graphs of Wislicenus. **1906** *Athenæum* 19 May 612/3 An ingenious series of star charts..which when looked at through red and green spectacles exhibit the stars as appearing in tri-dimensional space. **1894** *Nation* (N. Y.) 13 Sept. 192/2 There are three fundamental color-sensations..; but there is nothing corresponding to this *tri-dimensionality in the vibrations themselves. **1901** Titchener *Exper. Psychol.* I. ix. 138 The two figures will approach each other, and at last will overlap...At the moment of complete overlapping, the cone stands out with an almost startling tridimensionality.

**Triding:** see Trithing.

**Tridiurnal** (trəi͵dəi͵ɜ·ɹnăl), *a.* [f. Tri- 3 + Diurnal.] **a.** Comprising three days. **b.** Occurring three times a day.
**a. 1828** J. Sterling *Ess.*, etc. (1848) II. 45 Various minor periods,..monthly, weekly, tridiurnal, and daily. **b. 1884** *Athenæum* 10 May 602/1 He..commenced to make tridiurnal meteorological observations and to issue a daily weather report.

**Tri-dodecahedral:** see Tri- 2 b.

‖**Tri-domi·nium.** [In form mod.L., f. Tri- + L. *dominium* lordship, rule, Dominion.] The joint rule of three powers or states: applied to that of Gt. Britain, Germany, and United States in Samoa.
**1899** *Westm. Gaz.* 1 Mar. 2/3 Herr von Bülow..is reported to have said with regard to Samoa that the Tri-dominium had failed. **1900** *Edin. Rev.* Apr. 499 The break up of the unworkable tridominium..has been satisfactory to all parties.

**Tridrachm** (trəi·dræm). *Gr. Antiq.* [ad. Gr. τρίδραχμον, f. τρι-, Tri- + δραχμή Drachm.] A silver coin of ancient Greece, of the value of three drachms: see Drachm 1.
**1771** Raper in *Phil. Trans.* LXI. 469 Their larger Coins above the Drachm were, the Didrachm, the Tridrachm, and the Tetradrachm. **1827** Robinson *Archæol. Græca* v. xxvi. (ed. 2) 550, 3 dr[achmæ] or tridrachm, 1/11¼. **1842** *Smith's Dict. Grk. & Rom. Antiq.* s.v. *Drachma*, Among those [silver coins] now preserved, the tetradrachm is commonly found; but we possess no specimens of the tridrachm, and only a few of the didrachm.

**Triduan** (trəi·diu͵ăn), *a.* Also 7 -ane. [ad. L. *trīduān-us*, f. *trīduum*: see below and -an.] Lasting for three days (in quot. 1600 *transf.*); also, occurring every third day.
**1597** J. King *On Jonas* (1618) 299 The triduan rest of Christ in the graue, must bee vnderstood by the figure *synecdoche*, a part put for the whole. **1600** W. Watson *Decacordon* (1602) 48 To raise a triduane Lazarus from death to life againe. **1658** Phillips, *Triduan*, (Lat.) continuing three dayes. **1755** Johnson, *Triduan*, 1. Lasting three days. 2. Happening every third day.

‖**Triduo** (trī·duo). *R.C.Ch.* [It. and Sp. *triduo*:—L. *trīduum*: see below.] A three days' prayer or festal celebration.
**1848** Manning *Jrnl.* in *Life* (1895) I. xix. 402 Then was sung the *Veni Creator* (a triduo for the Roman State at this time). **1869** *Life of Marg. M. Hallahan* (1870) 473 We are meditating a great Triduo to our Holy Mother. **1871** *Echo* 28 Feb., The Cardinal Vicar is at present occupied in getting up triduos for the tercentenary of the Battle of Lepanto.

‖**Triduum** (trəi·diu͵ɒm). [L. *trīduum*, prop. neut. of **trīduus* adj. (sc. *spatium*), f. *tri-*, Tri- + *diēs* day.] **a.** A period of three days; *esp.* in *R.C.Ch.* the last three days of Lent. **b.** = Triduo.
**1883** Schaff *Hist. Church* II. xi. lxxi. 525 The mysterious triduum between the crucifixion and the resurrection. **1885** *Pall Mall G.* 7 Nov. 7/2 Yesterday there commenced at the Church of the Servite Fathers..a Triduum to celebrate an event of interest in the early history of our Royal family. **1910** *Universe* 3 June 9/1 A solemn Triduum in honour of the feast of Corpus Christi was preached in St. Mary's Cathedral, Edinburgh.

**Tridymite** (tri·dimait). *Min.* [ad. Ger. *tridymit* (vom Rath 1866), f. Gr. τρίδυμος threefold, f. τρι-, Tri- + -δυμ-ος, as in δίδυμος twin; named in allusion to its compound forms consisting of three individual crystals.] A crystallized form of silica, occurring in small hexagonal tables, found in trachyte and other igneous rocks.
**1868** Dana *Min.* (ed. 5) 805 Tridymite occurs in small hexagonal tables, colorless and transparent, which are usually compound, and mostly of three individuals. **1888** Rutley *Rock-Forming Min.* 130 Tridymite is essentially a volcanic mineral.

**Tridynamous:** see Tri- 1.

**Trie, Trielie,** early forms of Try *a.*, Tryly.

**Trie,** obs. form of Tree, Try *v.*

**Tried** (trəid), *ppl. a.* [f. Try *v.* + -ed¹.]
**1.** Separated from the dross or refuse; of metals: purified, refined; of fat: rendered, clarified; of an egg-yolk: separated from the white; of flour, etc.: sifted, bolted, fine. Mostly *Obs.*
*Tried out*, said of a whale the blubber of which has been cut off, melted down, and run into casks.
**13..** *K. Alis.* 828 (Bodl. MS.) Riche rede I tried golde. **13..** *Coer de L.* 6342 Tryyd sylvyr and tresore fyn. **1382** Wyclif *Ex.* xvi. 31 The taast of it as of tryed floure with hony. *c* **1430** *Two Cookery-bks.* 51 Take fayre y-tryid ȝolkys Raw, & Sugre, an pouder Gyngere. **1611** Cotgr., *Argerite*, the (Siluer-coloured) foame of tried lead. **1627** Capt. Smith *Seaman's Gram.* xv. 75 Legs of Mutton..with tried sewet or butter. **1639** T. de Gray *Compl. Horsem.* 304 Take..of old tryed hogs grease one pound.
†**2.** Chosen, select, choice; excellent. *Obs.*
**13..** *E. E. Allit. P.* B. 1317 He trussed hem in his tresorye in a tryed place. **1362** Langl. *P. Pl.* A. i. 126 Treuþe is tresour triedest on eorþe. *c* **1400** *Destr. Troy* 1840 Fro Priam, full prist,..That in Troy truly is a triet kyng. *Ibid.* 10842 A tryet ost Of grekes..were gedrit. **1581** A. Hall *Iliad* v. 97 Dame Iuno of the tryed horsse in hand doth take the raynes.
†**b.** As *sb.* Distinguished one. *Obs.*
*c* **1400** *Destr. Troy* 13791 To the toumbe of þat tried truly ho yode.
**3.** Proved or tested by experience or examination.
*c* **1412** Hoccleve *De Reg. Princ.* 2097 Deth hath but smal consideracioun Vnto þe vertuous,..No more..Than to a vicious maistir losel tried. *c* **1440** *Promp. Parv.* 502/2 Tryyd,..*probatus, examinatus.* **1508** Kennedie *Flyting w. Dunbar* 513 Cankrit Caym, tryit trowane, Tutiuillus. **1583** Stubbes *Anat. Abus.* ii. (1882) 100 Choose foorth certeine persons of a tried conuersation. **1604** G[rimstone] *D'Acosta's Hist. Indies* ii. vii. 95 It is approoved by many tryed experiences. **1724** De Foe *Mem. Cavalier* (1840) 277 He [was] an old tried soldier. **1760** R. Brown *Compl. Farmer* ii. 17 My design is..to promote tried experiments. **1841** W. Spalding *Italy* III. 82 Public men of tried abilities.
Hence † **Tri·edly** *adv. Obs.*, in a tried manner; choicely; experiencedly.
*c* **1400** *Destr. Troy* 3054 Hir tethe þat tryetly were set, Alse qwyte & qwem as any qwalle bon. *Ibid.* 10583 Þai tild vp a toure, triedly wroght. **14..** *Langland's P. Pl.* B. Prol. 14, I seigh a toure on a toft trielich [*MS. O.* triedliche] ymaked. **1549** Coverdale, etc. *Erasm. Par.* 1 *Peter* iv. 12 That thing..whyche wente long ago before in the triedly proued prophetes. **1557** *Tottell's Misc.* (Arb.) 141 So triedly did he treade..That fortune found no place to geue him once a check.

**Triedral**, obs. variant of TRIHEDRAL.

**Tri-elementary**: see TRI- 1.

† **Triˌe·nnal**, *a.* and *sb. Obs. rare.* Also 4 tri-, tryenal(e, -ennal(e, -el, trinel. [ad. med.L. *triennāl-e* (sc. *officium*), neuter of *triennālis* of three years: cf. F. *triennal* (16th c.).]

**A.** *adj.* = TRIENNIAL. *rare*—°.

1611 COTGR., *Triennal*, triennall, of three yeares.

**B.** *sb.* A dispensation or indulgence for three years. (In 14th c. a disyllable = *trī·nal*.)

1362 LANGL. *P. Pl.* A. VIII. 157 [I] diuinede þat Dowel Indulgence passede, Bienals and Trienals and Busschopes lettres. *Ibid.* 166 Bote trustene to Trienals [B. VII. 170 triennales; C. X. 330 triennels] treuly me þinkeþ Is not so syker for þe soule sertes, as do-wel. *c* 1380 WYCLIF *Sel. Wks.* III. 400 Biggynge of beneficis, of indulgensis and trinels, pardouns, and veyne privilegies.

**Triennial** (trəiˌe·niăl), *a.* and *sb.* Also 7 tryenniall, triennuall, 8 trienial. [f. L. *trienni-s* of three years, *trienni-um* a space of three years (f. *tri-*, TRI- + *annus* year) + -AL. Cf. prec.]

**A.** *adj.* **1.** Existing or lasting for three years, three-years'; changed every three years.

*Triennial Act* (*Eng. Hist.*), an act of 1640, limiting the duration of parliament to three years; also the name given to an act of 1694, following an earlier one of Charles II, providing against any longer intermissions of parliament than three years. Cf. sense 2.

1640 *Jrnls. Ho. Comm.* II. 83 Amendments..to the Bill of Triennial Parliaments. 1643 PRYNNE *Sov. Power of Parl.* II. 25 The Admiralls Patents (which anciently were..but annuall or Triennuall at most). *c* 1645 HOWELL *Lett.* (1650) I. 70 My friends, whom I so much long to see after this triennial separation. 1701 *Lond. Gaz.* No. 3756/9 Whenever the Dissolution of this Present..Parliament shall happen, either by Virtue of the Trienial Act, or Prerogative Royal. 1807 HORSLEY *Serm.* (1812) II. 316 We, in the writings of the evangelists have a complete summary of his [Christ's] triennial preaching. 1863 H. COX *Instit.* I. vi. 35 The Triennial Act of William III limited the duration of Parliament to three years at the furthest.

**2.** Recurring every three years.

1642 HOWELL *For. Trav.* (Arb.) 77 If these Lights grow dim, there is a Trienniall Snuffer for them. 1663 BLAIR *Autobiog.* v. (1848) 77 Primate Usher's triennial visitation. 1782 T. WARTON *Hist. Kiddington* 8 To the bishop for Procurations, on account of his triennial visitation. 1821 MISS MITFORD in L'Estrange *Life* (1870) II. vi. 140 We have been very gay..with our triennial theatricals. 1872 YEATS *Growth Comm.* 182 There was a triennial change of officers.

**B.** *sb.* **1.** A period of three years; a triennium.

1661 *Sir H. Vane's Politics* 13 During our Principality, which breathed out many Triennials. 1892 *Min. Nat. Counc. Congr. Ch.* (U.S.) 143 No other triennial in the history of the society has a tithe of the work in the way of..printed appeals.

**2.** An event recurring every three years; *spec.* the visitation of his diocese by a bishop every three years.

1640 *Archdeaconry of Essex Minutes* 29 July (MS.) We were this day inhibited for the Bp's. of London's tryenniall, by Gilson. 1724 BP. DOWNES in *Nicolson's Epist. Corr.* 576 The expence of the Triennial may leave your pocket empty.

Hence **Triennia·lity** [cf. F. *triennalité*], the condition of being triennial.

1806 W. TAYLOR in *Ann. Rev.* IV. 240 The parliament..produced fewer great men during its trienniality, than since the prolongation. 1817 BENTHAM *Parl. Reform* Introd. (1818) 283 Moderate reform insists at stopping at the stage indicated by the word trienniality.

**Triennially** (trəiˌe·niăli), *adv.* [f. TRIENNIAL *a.* + -LY [2].] Every three years; once in three years.

1689 in *6th Coll. Papers rel. Pres. Juncture* 25 The Parliament to be chosen Triennially, and to meet Annually. 1727 BAILEY vol. II, Triennially. 1806 W. TAYLOR in *Ann. Rev.* IV. 714 It appears that the tithe ought to be levied triennially. 1881 *Chamb. Jrnl.* No. 914. 419/1 The gorgeous festival given..triennially at the Crystal Palace.

† **Trie·nniated**, *a. Obs. rare.* [f. L. *trienni-um* (see below) + -ATE + -ED.] Made triennial. (In quot., as the second element of a compound.)

1661 *Sir H. Vane's Politics* 8 By obliging sundry eminent Chieftans of our long-trienniated Assembly.

‖ **Triennium** (trəiˌe·niŏm). [L., prop. neuter of **triennius* adj. (sc. *spatium*), f. *tri-*, TRI- + *ann-us* year.] A space or period of three years.

1847 BUNSEN *Church of Future* v. 119 The first theological examination follows upon the academical triennium. 1876 BOURNE *Life Locke* I. ii. 52 He adopted the less usual course of shortening his triennium by two terms. 1894 *Nation* (N.Y.) 14 June 444/1 Just home from his triennium in Germany.

‖ **Triens** (trəi·enz). Pl. **trientes** (trəiˌe·ntīz). [L., = third part.] The third part of anything; *spec.* in *Rom. Antiq.* a copper coin worth one-third of the as; also in later times, a gold coin, one-third of the aureus: cf. next.

1601 HOLLAND *Pliny* xxxiv. xiii. II. 513 The Servilij..have among them a certaine peece of brasse coine called a Triens (*i.* the third part of a Romane Asse) which they doe keepe and feed with silver and gold...I will set downe..the verie words of old Messala: The house (quoth he) of the Servilij hath a certaine sacred Trient. 1693 tr. *Blancard's Phys. Dict.* (ed. 2), *Triens*, the third part of a physical Pound. 1706 PHILLIPS (ed. Kersey), *Triens* (Lat.), the third part of the Roman Pound, or Coin call'd *As*, weighing four Ounces: Or the third of any entire Thing divisible into twelve Parts.

† **Trient.** *Obs.* [ad. L. *triens, trient-em* third part.] **a.** The ancient Roman copper coin called *triens*: see prec. **b.** An angle of 120°, comprising one-third of the circumference of a circle; in *Astrol.* = TRINE B. 2 (also *adj.* = TRINE A. 2).

1563 HYLL *Art Garden.* (1593) 24 When they are asunder 120 degrees, which is called a triangle, Trygon, or Trient aspect. 1601 [see TRIENS]. 1657 TOMLINSON *Renou's Disp.* 160* Three ounces..or at most a trient, that is four ounces. 1657 *Physical Dict.*, *Trient*, a third part. 1673 WALLIS in Rigaud *Corr. Sci. Men* (1841) II. 570 If the angle be more than a trient, and less than two trients, whose subtendant ..I suppose to be the chord of a trient increased by one of the arches.

† **Trie·ntal**, *a.* and *sb. Obs. rare.* [ad. L. *trientālis*, f. *triens, trient-em*: see TRIENT and -AL.]

**A.** *adj.* Pertaining to or constituting a third part (e.g. $\frac{1}{3}$ of a foot in length, of a pound in weight, etc.).

1656 BLOUNT *Glossogr.*, *Triental* (*trientalis*), of or being four inches broad or ounces in weight. 1891 *Cent. Dict.*, *Triental*, *a.* of the value of a triens; of or pertaining to the triens, or third part.

**B.** *sb.* An ancient Roman drinking-vessel containing one-third of a *sextarius*.

1656 BLOUNT *Glossogr.*, *Triental* (Lat.), a vessel containing the third part of *Sextarius*, half our Pint. 1789 MADAN tr. *Persius* iii. (1795) 91 But a trembling comes on whilst at his wine, and the warm triental He shakes out of his hands.

**Triequal**: see TRI- 2.

**Trier** (trəi·əɹ). Forms: 4–5 **triour**, 5 **tryoure**, 6 **trior**, **tryar**, 7 **triar**, 6– **trier**, **tryer**; in senses 2 and 4, also 6–8 **triour**, 7 **tryor**, 8–9 **trior**. [f. TRY *v.* + -ER [1]; in the early form *triour*, a. AF. **triour* (-OUR) in legal use. Cf. F. *trieur*.]

**1.** One who examines and determines a cause or question; one who examines judicially; a judge.

*c* 1330 R. BRUNNE *Chron.* (1810) 250 Þe triours alle þat caste, & put þer saw tille on. 1472 *Coventry Leet Bk.* 382 These persons folowyng be ordeyned & chosen to be triours within þis Cite to determyn variances betwixt parties within þis Cite as touchyng metes & bondes & Gutters & such oþer. *a* 1586 SIDNEY *Arcadia* III. Wks. 1724 II. 693 The almighty powers, whom I invoke as triers of mine innocency, and witnesses of my well-meaning. 1645 *Ordinance* in Neal *Hist. Purit.* (1736) III. 293 That certain persons be appointed Triers..to determine the validity of Elections. 1659–60 *Free Parl.-Letany* iii, From Vow-breakers & Kingtryers—Libera nos, Domine! 1809 JEFFERSON *Writings* (1830) IV. 128 The testimony..is the more grateful, as proceeding from eye-witnesses and observers, from triers of the vicinage. 1821 SCOTT *Kenilw.* xi, To get old Gaffer Pinniewinks, the trier of witches,..to comprehend Wayland Smith. 1821–30 LD. COCKBURN *Mem.* ii. (1874) 101 A dexterous and practical trier of ordinary cases. 1885 DIXON *Hist. Ch. Eng.* III. 377 The bishop himself was to be the chief trier.

**2.** *pl.* Two persons appointed by a court of law to determine whether a challenge made to the panel of jurors, or to any of them, is well founded.

[*a* 1377 *Rolls of Parlt.* II. 400/1 Sur quele chose furent esleuz Triours par la Court, qe disoient qe le Viscounte fust eidaunt et bien voillant a la partie du dit Evesqe.] 1511 in W. H. Turner *Sel. Rec. Oxford* (1880) 4 He commawnded the ij tryarse in the King's name to tell Hullys parte owt of the dore [of the gildhall]. *c* 1570 *Pride & Lowl.* (1841) 18 Ye shall have triers two or three, That shall judge of their [jurymen's] indifferencie. 1665 EVER *Tryals per Pais* ix. 128 When any challenge is made to the Polls, two tryors shall be appointed by the Court, and if they try one indifferent, and he be sworn, then he and the two tryors shall try another. 1768 BLACKSTONE *Comm.* III. xxiii. 363. 1863 H. COX *Instit.* II. iii. 354 Two triers appointed by the Court.

**3.** *Hist. pl.* A committee appointed by the King to determine to which court petitions should be referred, and if necessary, to report them to the parliament. The practice was disused in 1886.

[1332 *Rolls of Parlt.* II. 68/1. 1485 *Ibid.* VI. 268/1 Et sount assignez Triours des Petitiones de Gascoigne, et d'autres Terres et Paiis de par dela, et des Isles [names follow].] 1844 T. E. MAY *Treat. Parl.* xix. 301 Receivers and triers of petitions were appointed...The triers were committees of prelates, peers, and judges [etc.]...By them the petitions were examined...The functions of receivers and triers of petitions have long since given way to the immediate authority of Parliament at large. 1878 STUBBS *Const. Hist.* § 757 III. xx. 452 As soon as the opening speech of the chancellor was ended, the names of the receivers and triers of petitions were read by the clerk of the crown. The receivers were clerks or masters in chancery; the triers were selected by the king from the list of the lords spiritual, the lords temporal, and the justices. [1886 *Jrnls. Ho. Lords* CXVIII. 19/2 Les Triours des Petitions, etc. as in 1485.]

**4.** *pl.* Members of the House of Lords sitting as a jury at the trial of a peer for treason or felony. In full, *lords triers*.

1539 *Act* 31 *Hen. VIII*, c. 10. § 9 Peres that shalbe called hereafter to be triours of suche treasons. 1596 WARNER *Alb. Eng.* x. lvi. (1612) 246 These Noble Tryers, iustly then examining the Cause. 1676 C. HATTON in *Hatton Corr.* (Camden) 134 Ther were 31 Lords tryers present. 1794 BURKE *Rep. Lords' Jrnls.* Wks. 1842 II. 607 A course of precedents, in a legal court, composed of a peer for judge, and peers for triers. 1831 MACKINTOSH *Hist. Eng.* II. vii. 198 Queen Anne and her brother Rochford were tried..before the duke of Norfolk,..assisted by twenty-six 'lords triers', who in some degree performed the functions of jurors in this tribunal. 1849 MACAULAY *Hist. Eng.* vi. II. 39 The high steward was sole judge of the law; and the lords triers formed merely a jury to pronounce on the question of fact. Jeffreys was appointed high steward. 1855 *Ibid.* xviii. IV. 158 The Lords insisted that every peer should be entitled to be a Trier. The Commons were with difficulty induced to consent that the number of Triers should never be less than thirty six.

**5.** *Church Hist.* One of a body of commissioners appointed in 1654 'for the approbation of all public preachers and lecturers before their admission to benefices'. Also *transf.*

1655 *Clarke Pap.* (Camden) III. 53 His Highnesse..left Mr. Cordwell, the minister, to bee concluded by the Tryers of London. 1657 [see EJECTOR 1]. 1664 BUTLER *Hud.* II. II. 813 And do they not as Triers sit To judge what Officers are fit? *a* 1691 BAXTER in *Reliq.* (1696) 72. 1691 WOOD *Ath. Oxon.* I. 861 Afterwards he enjoyed two livings successively without examination by the Tryers. 1808 W. WILSON *Hist. Dissent. Ch.* I. 471 The Commissioners were in all thirty-eight..and were commonly known by the name of Tryers. 1862 VAUGHAN *Nonconformity* 186 The number of ministers ejected by the Triers was considerable.

**6.** An umpire in sports or games. Now *dial.*

1607 MARKHAM *Caval.* III. (1617) 79 These Tryers are certaine indifferent Gentlemen, chosen by both the parties that make the match, who are to see that there be faire play, and that the Articles be fully performed on both parties. 1747 J. RELPH *Poems* 16 At spworts, if I was trier. 1826 *Sporting Mag.* XVIII. 321 A trier, or stickler as he is commonly called, is an umpire. 1888 ELWORTHY *W. Somerset Word-bk.*, *Trier*, the umpire at a wrestling, cudgel-playing, or any other match.

**7.** One who or that which tests or proves something; a prover; a tester or test.

*a* 1483 *Liber Niger Edw. IV* in *Househ. Ord.* (1790) 75 This seyde sergeaunt, or the yoman tryoure, or the groome tryoure,..dayly to be redye in the hall. 1538 ELYOT, *Spectatores*, beholders, triers of money. *a* 1541 WYATT *Poet. Wks.* (1861) 169 Of good and bad the tryers are these twain. 1552 HULOET, Tryers, *comprobatores*. 1607 SHAKS. *Cor.* IV. i. 4 You were vs'd To say, Extreamities was the trier of spirits. 1610 BP. CARLETON *Jurisd.* Pref., When it was examined by vnskilfull and deceitfull triars,..taking vpon them to be triars of truth. 1712 BUDGELL *Spect.* No. 307 ¶ 7 There should be certain Triers or Examiners..to inspect the Genius of every particular Boy. 1760 *Cautions to Officers of Army* 162 There was formerly in the Army, particularly in Queen Ann's Time, a Sett of Officers in most Corps, who were called Provers, or Tryers; these upon a young Officer's joining the Regiment,..without any Cause picked a Quarrel with him: when, if the young Man acquitted himself with Honour, and escaped with Life, he passed the Rest of his Time quietly enough. 1796 CAPT. BOWEN in *Naval Chron.* XXIII. 368, I ordered one gun to be fired, as a trier of her intention. 1817–18 COBBETT *Resid. U. S.* (1822) 98 They are the best of triers. Whatever they prefer is sure to be the richest thing within their reach. 1869 SPURGEON *Treas. Dav.* Ps. lxxiii. 21 God is frequently called..the Trier of the hearts and reins.

**8.** One who (or that which) tries out or separates (metal, honey, grain, oil, etc.) from impurities.

1523 LD. BERNERS *Froiss.* I. ccccii. 699 They set but lytell by the manassyng of a sonne of a tryer of hony. *a* 1637 B. JONSON *Eupheme's Mind* vii, Disdaining any tryer, 'Tis got where it can try the fire. 1725 *Phil. Trans.* XXXIII. 262 The Triers, that open them [whales] when dead,..never observed any Grass, Fish, or any other Sort of Food in the right or Whalebone Whale. 1869 *Lonsdale Gloss.*, *Trier*, a corn-screen.

† **9.** One who finds *out* or tries to find out by search or examination. *Obs.*

1547–64 BAULDWIN *Mor. Philos.* (Palfr.) 65 Law is the finder & trier out of truth. 1563 FOXE *A. & M.* 1297/1 Mayster Thomas Bilney..a trier out of Sathans subtleties.

**b.** *spec.* (See quot.)

1778 *Eng. Gazetteer* (ed. 2) s. v. *Youle*, Youle, York, E. Rid. ..Here are a sort of people, called triers, who with a long piece of iron search into the soft boggy ground hereabouts for subterraneous trees.

**10.** One who tries or attempts to do something; in *Cricket slang*, a player who perseveres in trying to win.

1891 in *Cent. Dict.* 1897 *Daily News* 28 July 11/5 He trusted they would remember that even when the eleven did badly they were always tryers. 1903 *Daily Chron.* 24 Feb. 3/2 Mr. Bernard Capes may be described, in the language of the cricket-field, as 'a great try-er'.

**11. a.** Something devised to try or test quality. **b.** Something that is trying or difficult, or that tries one's patience or mettle.

1797 *Encycl. Brit.* (ed. 3) VIII. 238/1 Though the common powder-triers may show powder to be better than it really is, they can never make it appear to be worse than it is. 1893 *Field* 11 Feb. 187/2 The district being a trier, many and various were the mishaps. 1901 *U. S. Dept. Agric., Year-bk.* 237 These samples are drawn by means of a 'trier', or clover-seed sampler, which is thrust through the bag, allowing the seed to run out at the open end of the trier.

**12.** *Trier on*, one who 'tries on' garments in order to test the fit; *spec.* an assistant to a clothier or dressmaker who helps customers to try on garments, or who displays their style by wearing them (= MODEL *sb.* 11 b).

1895 *Blackw. Mag.* Apr. 557 The girl bethought herself of the 'tryer-on' [*cf. above* 'a young woman, discharging in perfection her function of wearing clothes so skilfully as to tempt buyers with them']. 1900 *Westm. Gaz.* 12 Jan. 5/3 The 'tryers-on'..had spent nearly four hours in hard work.

**Trierarch** (trəi·ĕrāɹk). *Gr. Hist.* Also 7 -arck, 9 -arc. [ad. L. *triērarch-us*, or its Gr. source τριήραρχος, -άρχης, f. τριήρης trireme + -αρχος ruling, ruler. Cf. F. *triérarque* (Oresme, 14th c.).] **a.** The commander of a trireme. **b.** A citizen who, singly or in conjunction with others, was charged with the duty of fitting out a trireme or galley for the public service.

1656 BLOUNT *Glossogr.*, *Trierarck*.., the mr. of a Ship or Galley. 1697 POTTER *Antiq. Greece* I. xxvi. (1715) 158 The

Trierarchs, and Overseers of the Navy. **1734** tr. *Rollin's Anc. Hist.* XIII. vii. (1827) V. 290 The..Trierarchs..were appointed to fit out the galleys in time of war.

**Trierarchal** (traiˈĕrāɹkăl), *a.* [f. as prec. + -AL.] Of or pertaining to a trierarch or trierarchs. So **Triera·rchic, -ical** *adjs.* [Gr. τριηραρχικός].

**1837** WHEELWRIGHT tr. *Aristophanes* II. 127 The city had been full of martial tumult and trierarchal clamour. **1853** GROTE *Greece* II. lxxxvii. XI. 381 Demosthenes belonged to a trierarchic family. **1866** FELTON *Anc. & Mod. Gr.* I. II. xii. 502 The fitting out of war-ships, called the trierarchic liturgy. **1891** *Athenæum* 25 July 128/1 The law of Periander in 357 B.C...placing 1,200 citizens in the trierarchical symmories.

**Trierarchy** (traiˈĕrāɹki). [ad. Gr. τριηραρχία, f. τριήραρχος TRIERARCH.] The position or office of a trierarch; the equipment and maintenance of a trireme or other vessel, as a public service or 'liturgy'; the system by which a fleet was thus maintained. **b.** 'The trierarchs collectively' (Ogilvie, 1882).

**1837** BULWER *Athens* II. 462 Extraordinary liturgies—such as the Trierarchy or equipment of ships which entailed also the obligation of personal service on those by whom the triremes were fitted out. **1839** THIRLWALL *Greece* VI. xlv. 51 The citizens who were liable to the charges of the trierarchy. **1850** GROTE *Greece* II. lv. VII. 47 As a rich young man, also, choregy and trierarchy became incumbent upon him. **1869** A. W. WARD tr. *Curtius' Hist. Greece* II. III. iii. 477 The trierarchy, i.e. the obligation incumbent upon the citizens to make the ships belonging to the state ready for sea, to hire crews, etc.

**Triet**, obs. form of TRIED.

**Trieteric** (traiˌĭteˑrik), *a.* and *sb.* *Antiq.* [ad. Gr. τριετηρικός, L. trietēricus, f. τριετηρίς a festival celebrated every third, i.e. alternate, year, f. τρι- three + ἔτος year.]

**A.** *adj.* Taking place every alternate year, as the festivals of Bacchus and other divinities.

**1656** BLOUNT *Glossogr.*, *Trieterick*.., that is every third year. **1847** LEITCH tr. *C. O. Müller's Anc. Art* § 390 The Mænads at the trieteric festival on Mount Parnassus thought they descried the satyrs and heard their music. **1852** GROTE *Greece* II. lxxv. IX. 477 *note*, The Isthmian games were trietêric, that is celebrated in every alternate year. **1911** *Athenæum* 15 Apr. 493/3 Dr. Farnell has..a theory of 'trieteric' agricultural rites.

**B.** *sb.* (also *pl.*) A festival, esp. of Bacchus, celebrated every alternate year.

**1592** R. D. *Hypnerotomachia* 90b, As in the daunce called Thiasus, in the trieteric [*pr.* -ie; *orig.* Trieterici] of Bacchus. **1627** MAY *Lucan* v. 86 To whome in mixed sacrifice The Theban wiues at Delphos solemnize Their trieterickes.

So † **Triˌeteˑrical, Triˌeteˑrican** *adjs. Obs.* = A.

**1646** J. GREGORY *Notes & Obs.* xxi. 106 The trietericall sports,..that is the mysteries of Bacchus. **1775** ASH *Suppl.*, *Trieterican*, belonging to the trieterica.

**Triethyl** (traiˌeˑþil). *Chem.* [f. TRI- 5 + ETHYL.] **a.** A formative denoting the presence of three ethyl groups, $C_2H_5$, in a compound, as **trieˑthylbiˑsmuthine**, $Bi(C_2H_5)_3$, **triethyl phosphine**, $P(C_2H_5)_3$; see also *Triethylamine* below. **b.** *spec.* denoting the substitution of three ethyl groups for three hydrogen atoms in the substance designated by the rest of the name; e.g. **trieˑthylbeˑnzene**, $C_6H_3(C_2H_5)_3$, in which three ethyl groups take the place of three H atoms in benzene, $C_6H_6$; so **trieˑthylmeˑthane**, $CH(C_2H_5)_3$ from methane, $CH_4$; **trieˑthylcaˑrbinol**, $C(C_2H_5)_3OH$; **trieˑthyluˑrea**, $CONH(C_2H_5)N(C_2H_5)_2$. Also used attrib., as *triethyl phosphate*, $(C_2H_5)_3PO_4$. Hence **Triethyˑlic** *a.* = triethyl *attrib.*

**1858** FOWNES *Elem. Chem.* (ed. 7) 615 Triethylstibine $SbAe_3$. **1873** — *Chem.* 587 Triethylic borate is formed by the action of boron trichloride on alcohol. **1868** WATTS *Dict. Chem.* V. 880 Triethylglycerin or Triethylin..is a liquid having a pleasant ethereal odour. **1889** MUIR & MORLEY *Watts' Dict. Chem.* II. 506 Tri-ethyl-phosphine. ..Colourless mobile liquid. Its odour is very penetrating but not disagreeable.

Hence **Triethylamine** (traiˌeˑþilămain), the tertiary amine of ethyl, $N(C_2H_5)_3$, in which the three hydrogen atoms of ammonia, $NH_3$, are replaced by three ethyl groups; formerly also called *Triethyl ammonia* and *Triethylia*.

**1850** DAUBENY *Atom. The.* viii. (ed. 2) 242 Triethylamine, consisting of 3 atoms of ethyle replacing 3 of hydrogen. **1857** MILLER *Elem. Chem.* III. 211 Triethylia..is also a soluble, volatile, and powerful base. **1858** FOWNES *Elem. Chem.* (ed. 7) 595 Triethylamine, Triethyl-ammonia...is a colourless, powerfully-alkaline liquid, boiling at 91° C.

**Trieues, -eux, -ewis**, obs. ff. TREVE, TRUCE.

**Triexoctoedron**, var. TRI-HEXOCTAHEDRON.

**Tri-faced**: see TRI- I c.

**Trifacial** (traifēˑʃăl), *a.* *Anat.* [f. TRI- + FACIAL.] A name for the fifth pair of cranial nerves (also called TRIGEMINAL), which divide into three branches supplying the face and some adjacent parts. Also *transf.* pertaining to or affecting the trifacial nerves.

**1840** G. ELLIS *Anat.* 82 Branches of..the first, second, or third divisions of the fifth or trifacial nerve. **1842** E. WILSON *Anat. Vade M.* (ed. 2) 407 The Trifacial Nerve is analogous to the spinal nerves in its origin by two roots. **1863** J. DEAN *Gray Subst. Medulla Obl.* etc. II. i, I have not been able to discover any connection between these columns and the trifacial or auditory roots. **1899** *Allbutt's Syst. Med.* VI. 662 A carious tooth may set up a trifacial neuralgia.

† **Triˑfaˑllow**, *v.* *Obs.* Also 8 try-, tre-; see also THRY-FALLOW. [app. altered from the earlier *three-*, *thry-fallow*, after TWIFALLOW, or under the influence of TRI- prefix as in *tri-weekly*, *triennial*, etc.] *trans.* To plough (land) a third time in the course of its lying fallow. Also *absol.*

[**1573**, **1641**: see THRY-FALLOW]. **1610** W. FOLKINGHAM *Art of Survey* I. ii. 43 Orders and seasons for fallowing, twifallowing, trifallowing and seed-furre. **1681** WORLIDGE *Dict. Rust.* s.v. *Fallow*, Thus may you fallow, twifallow, and trifallow; that is once, twice, or thrice plough it before the seed-time. **1707** MORTIMER *Husb.* (1721) I. 53 About the latter end of July or beginning of August, is the time of Try-fallowing, or last plowing before they sow their Rye or Wheat. **1766** *Complete Farmer*, *To Trefallow*, to plough land the third time before sowing.

**Trifarious** (traifēˑriəs), *a.* *rare.* [f. L. *trifāri-us* (compared by some with Gr. τριφάσιος in same sense) + -OUS.]

**1.** Of three sorts; facing three ways.

**1656** BLOUNT *Glossogr.*, *Trifareous* (*trifarius*), of three manner of wayes. *c* **1800** BP. MILNER in Husenbeth *Life* (1862) 39 No longer prate on huge Briareus, On monstrous triple bodied Geryon; For I have seen a real trifarious Protesting—Catholic—Presbyterian!

**2.** *Bot.* Arranged in three rows.

**1846** WORCESTER, *Trifarious*,..in three rows. **1857** BERKELEY *Cryptog. Bot.* § 565 Leaves trifarious, the third row smaller than the others.

**Trifasciated, -faucian**: see TRI- I.

† **Triˑferous**, *a.* *Obs. rare.* [f. L. *trifer* (f. TRI- + *-fer* bearing) + -OUS.] Thrice-bearing; bearing fruit or flowers thrice a year.

**1656** BLOUNT *Glossogr.*, *Triferous* (*trifer*), that brings forth fruit thrice a year. *a* **1682** SIR T. BROWNE *Tracts* 70 Some are biferous and triferous which bear twice or thrice in the year.

**Trifet**, obs. form of TRIVET.

† **Triff-traff.** *Obs.* In 6 **tryfetrafe.** [app. a reduplicated form of TRAFFE baggage: cf. *trish-trash*, redupl. from *trash*. But it may also be associated with *riff-raff*.] Trumpery, trash, rubbish; = RIFF-RAFF[1] 2.

**1547** *Bk. Marchauntes* bj b, Of brotherhodes, inuentions, tradicions, deceptions, lawes and wythout nombre of such tryfetrafe, wherby they can meruelously well drawe money to them.

**Trifid** (traiˑfid), *a.* [ad. L. *trifid-us*, f. *tri-*, TRI- + *fid-*, stem of *findĕre* to split.]

Split or divided into three by deep clefts or notches; three-cleft; *esp.* in *Bot.* and *Zool.*

**1753** CHAMBERS *Cycl. Supp.* s.v. *Leaf*. **1760** J. LEE *Introd. Bot.* II. ix. (1765) 93 Such as have Trifid Corollæ. **1769** PENNANT *Brit. Zool.* III. 320 The tail is naturally bifid, but in many is trifid. **1872** MIVART *Elem. Anat.* ii. 50 In the Howling Monkeys we find a trifid spine. **1895** *Pop. Sci. Monthly* Sept. 692 As far back as 1800 Pliny Moody had observed trifid markings upon sandstones.

**b.** *gen.* Divided into three parts, or of the nature of such division; tripartite. *rare.*

**1871** EARLE *Philol. Eng. Tongue* viii. 417 In that chapter the third section assumed a trifid form. **1902** *Sat. Rev.* 6 Dec. 711/1 The old trifid division of mammals.

**Trifilar** to **Triflagellate**: see TRI- I.

**Trifle** (traiˑf'l), *sb.* Forms: α. 3–5 **trufle**, (3–4 **truyfle**), 4 **trufel, truffle**, (**trewful**), 4–5 **truful**, 5 **-fulle, truffulle, truffille.** β. 4 **trofle, trofil**, 4–5 **trofel**, (5 **trowful**). γ. 4 **tryffel**, 4–5 **trifil**(**e**, **-ful**, (4 **tryuol, trefle**, 4–5 **-fele**), 4–6 **tryfel, -fyl, -fle**, 4–7 (8 *Sc.*) **triffle**, 5 **tryfil, trifelle, triffol**, 5–6 **tryfell**(**e**, 6 **-fille, -full**(**e**, **-fyll**(**e**, (**tryefull**), **trifill, -fulle, triffelle, triffill**(**e**, 7 **triffel, tryffel, -le**, 4– **trifle.** [ME. *trufle*, etc., a. OF. *trufle* (13th c. in Godef.), *treufle*, *truffle* (1370), parallel forms of *trufe*, *truffe*, 'moquerie, tromperie' (1265 in Godef.), = It. *truffa*, 'a cozening, cheating, conicatching' (Florio), Pr., obs. Sp. and Pg. *trufa*, 'a gibe, a iesting or ieering' (Minsheu); of uncertain origin. The phonology of the word in English presents difficulties; but *trufle*, with *ü*, would give later *tryfle*, *triffle*; and *u* sometimes varied dialectally with *o*, as in the ME. *trofel*. The short *ĭ* indicated by *ff* in *tryffel*, *triffol*, *triffle*, appears from the 14th to the 18th c.; but *trifle* with single *f* is ambiguous, and does not show when *trĭfle* became *trīfle*.

For the ulterior etymology, Diez was inclined to identify F. *truffe*, *trufle* with *truffe*, Pr. *trufa* (Littré), a TRUFFLE, a subterranean edible fungus. But it is app. only in F. (and Prov.) that the two words have the same form, and no connexion of sense has been ascertained: see TRUFFLE.]

† **1.** A false or idle tale, told (*a*) to deceive, cheat, or befool, (*b*) to divert or amuse; a lying story, a fable, a fiction; a jest or joke; a foolish, trivial, or nonsensical saying. *Obs.*

The shades of sense cannot always be distinguished.

α. *a* **1225** *Ancr. R.* 106 Þeos ant oðre trufles þet he bitrufleð monie men mide. **1297** R. GLOUC. (Rolls) 8613 Wanne me sede him of suche wondres..to trufle [*v.rr.* trifle, tryffel] he it wende. **1340** *Ayenb.* 58 Þe bourdes and þe trufles uol of uelþe and of leazinges. **1390** GOWER *Conf.* III. 344 Mi Sone, unto the trouthe wende..And lete all othre truffes [*v.rr.* trifles, triffles] be. **1393** LANGL. *P. Pl.* C. XXI. 151 Hit is trufle [*v. rr.* tryfle, triful, trewful] þat þou tellest. *c* **1440** *York Myst.* v. 125 Allas! þat I..trowed þe trufuls þat þou me saide. *Ibid.* xxxi. 300 But telle vs nowe some truffillis betwene vs twoo. **1483** *Cath. Angl.* 395/2 Truffillis, *nuge*, *gerra*.

β. **13..** *Cursor M.* 253 (Cott.) To wast þair liif, in trofel and truandis. *Ibid.* 27623 (Cott. Galba) Of pride cumes.. sang of trofils [*Cott.* truful] or lesing. **1340** HAMPOLE *Pr. Consc.* 183 Many has lykyng trofels to here. *c* **1400** *Rule St. Benet* 1735 Tales of trofils þai sal non tel.

γ. **1303** R. BRUNNE *Handl. Synne* 5031 Þys yche tale ys no tryfyl, For hyt ys wryte yn þe bybyl. **13..** *Gaw. & Gr. Knt.* 108 Talkkande bifore þe hyȝe table of trifles ful hende. **1377** LANGL. *P. Pl.* B. XVIII. 147 It is but a trufle [*v. rr.* tryfule, truyfle] þat þow tellest. *c* **1380** WYCLIF *Wks.* (1880) 442 Iapis & gabbingis or oþere tryuolis. *c* **1440** *Generydes* 4664 These are butt triffolys and delayes. **14..** *Voc.* in Wr.-Wülcker 617/42 *Trufa*, a trefele. *c* **1440** *Promp. Parv.* 502/2 Tryfle, *trufa*. *c* **1518** SKELTON *Magnyf.* 1142, I am yet as full of game As euer I was, and as full of tryfyls [*rime* nyfyls]. **1548** UDALL, etc. *Erasm. Par. Matt.* xv. 67 The Phariseis teache and obserue supersticiously these folysh tryfles. **1681** W. ROBERTSON *Phraseol. Gen.* (1693) 1258 Nifles and trifles; vain tales of Robin Hood; *aniles fabulæ*.

**2.** Hence, A matter of little value or importance; 'a thing of no moment' (J.); a trivial, paltry, or insignificant affair.

*c* **1290** *S. Eng. Leg.* I. 412/345 Þare-fore mot ech holi man ..tuyrne is herte to some truyfle. **1340** *Ayenb.* 142 Þer treteþ he of his greate quereles hueruore alle oþre niedes him þingþ trufles. *c* **1380** WYCLIF *Sel. Wks.* II. 185 Worldli goodis, fame of þe world, and oþer trifilis. **1513** MORE *Rich. III* (1883) 48 Leneth mi lord thi master so muche to such trifles? **1585** *Reg. Privy Council Scot.* IV. 32 The materis..wer bot triffillis in respect of uthiris of greitar importance. **1604** SHAKS. *Oth.* III. iii. 322 Trifles light as ayre, Are to the iealious, confirmations strong As proofes of holy Writ. **1706** E. WARD *Wooden World Diss.* (1708) 33 He's a mighty exact Man about Trifles. **1758** JOHNSON *Idler* No. 23 ⁋ 7 There is scarcely any man without some favourite trifle which he values above greater attainments. **1833** HT. MARTINEAU *Brooke Farm* ix. 110 Some trifles went wrong in the cottage. **1882** PEBODY *Eng. Journalism* xxii. 176 A Society journal, dealing..with the trifles of the day.

**b.** Without article. *rare.*

**1768** TUCKER *Lt. Nat.* (1834) I. 219 The advantage of virtue over vice and trifle does not lie in the very act, but in the consequences. *Ibid.* 620 As well in matters of trifle as of moment.

† **c.** *transf.* A worthless person; a trifler. *Obs.*

*c* **1475** *Pict. Voc.* in Wr.-Wülcker 806/21 *Hic nugigerulus*, a trifelle. *a* **1623** FLETCHER *Love's Cure* III. iv, *Syav.* Pray wear these trifles. *Clara*...You are a trifle, wear your self, sir, out. **1675** TRAHERNE *Chr. Ethics* 392 You will look as like a trifle, a knave, or a fool, as one of them; and be as very a mad man. *a* **1716** SOUTH *Serm.* (1744) XI. 18 It shews him to be a fop, a trifle and a mere picture.

**3.** *concr.* A small article of little intrinsic value; a toy, trinket, bauble, knick-knack.

**1375** *Will of Eliz. Lister* (Somerset Ho.), A goun et vnum triffle sȝelf egged. *a* **1400-50** *Alexander* 1894 Þe trufils þat ȝe to me sent, þe herne-pan, þe hand-ball, þe hatt made of twiggis. **1530** PALSGR. 283/1 Tryfell, a knacke, *friuolle*. **1630** *R. Johnson's Kingd. & Commw.* 196 Divers sorts of Linnen-cloth, with innumerable other small trifles. **1719** DE FOE *Crusoe* I. 44 To purchase..for Trifles, such as Beads, Toys, Knives, Scissars, Hatchets, Bits of Glass, and the like; not only Gold Dust,..Elephants Teeth, &c. but Negroes. **1756** MRS. CALDERWOOD in *Coltness Collect.* (Maitl. Cl.) 148 If you buy a triffle..then they are very civill. **1912** *Daily Graphic* 31 Dec. 13/2 These elegant trifles [hat-pins] are made in a variety of graceful designs.

**4.** A literary work, piece of music, etc., light or trivial in style; a slight or facetious composition; a bagatelle. Often used in meiosis.

**1579** LYLY *Euphues* (Arb.) 106 If Lucilla reade this trifle, shee will straight proclaime Euphues for a traytour. **1665** BOYLE *Occas. Refl.*, *Disc. Occas. Medit.* (1848) 1 The Trifles of this kind, your Commands make me trouble you with. *a* **1704** T. BROWN *1st Sat. Persius* 66 Read his trifles, and scarce in one line You'll find him guilty of the least design. **1751** EARL OF ORRERY *Remarks Swift* vi. (1752) 47 Poems to Stella, and trifles to Dr. Sheridan, fill up a great part of that period. **1837** KEITH *Bot. Lex.* 2 Anacreon, in one of his little trifles in honour of drinking, makes the very trees of the forest drink. **1884** W. C. SMITH *Kildrostan* 47 A little song—A trifle..Which I had writ for Mairi once to sing.

**5.** A small sum of money, or a sum treated as of no moment; a slight 'consideration'.

*c* **1595** CAPT. WYATT *R. Dudley's Voy. W. Ind.* (Hakl. Soc.) 39 The Captaine præsentinge him with a trifle from our Generall, hee [etc.]. **1615** G. SANDYS *Trav.* 116 Giving a trifle for oile, about midnight we departed. **1746** FRANCIS tr. *Hor. Sat.* II. iii. 214 'What will it cost? Nay, hold!'— 'A very trifle.'—'Sir, I will be told.'—'Three pence.' **1762–71** H. WALPOLE *Vertue's Anecd. Paint.* (1786) II. 157 Some not suiting the places, were brought back, and sold for a trifle after the death of my father. **1818** SCOTT *Let.* 30 Apr. in Lockhart *Life* (1837) IV. iv. 138, I could bet a trifle the doors, &c. will arrive the very day I set out.

**b.** An insignificant quantity or amount.

**1722** DE FOE *Plague* (1884) 132 Here is fifty thousand.., within a Trifle. **1911** BEVERIDGE *North Uist* v. 63 Nor can it ever have afforded more than a mere trifle of arable soil.

**c.** *A trifle* (advb.): To a trifling or slight extent; in a small degree, a little; somewhat, rather.

**1859** READE *Love me Little* xi, The bank itself was small and grave and a trifle dingy. **1860** G. MEREDITH *E. Harrington* xi, The chairman welcomed them a trifle snubbingly. **1887** JESSOPP *Arcady* vii. 214 Jehu is a trifle below middle height. **1892** *Speaker* 3 Sept. 291/2 We may inquire, perhaps, if it be not a trifle arrogant.

**6.** † **a.** A dish composed of cream boiled with various ingredients. *Obs.* **b.** A light confection of sponge-cake or the like, flavoured with wine or spirit, and served with custard and whipped cream.

**1598** FLORIO, *Mantiglia*, a kinde of clouted creame called a foole or a trifle in English. **1688** R. HOLME *Armoury* III. 85/1 *Triffel*, is Cream boiled with Sugar, Mace and Cinnamon. **1736** BAILEY *Househ. Dict.* 571 To make a Trifle. Boil a quart of cream,..sweeten it,..put to it two spoonfuls of rennet; let it stand till it comes like cheese. **1781** COWPER *Let.* 18 Feb., There is some froth, and here and there a bit of sweetmeat, which seems to entitle it justly to the name of a certain dish the ladies call a trifle. **1836–9** DICKENS *Sk. Boz, Bloomsbury Christening*, There were fowls, and tongue, and trifle, and sweets, and lobster salad. **1860** O. W. HOLMES *Elsie V.* vii. (1891) 110 That most wonderful object of domestic art called trifle,..with its charming confusion of cream and cake and almonds and jam and jelly and wine and cinnamon and froth.

**7.** Name for a kind of pewter of medium hardness; in *pl.* also, articles made of this.

**1610–11** [implied in TRIFLER 3]. **1612–13** in Welch *Hist. Pewterers' Co.* (1902) II. 61 Att wch tyme was Syzed by them theis seuerall parcells of Tryffles as followe vizt: Great duble bells wth peper boxes & baules...The greate beakr..Middle beaker..Smale beaker..The great beere bowle...The large wrought Cupps..[etc.]. **1668–9** *Ibid.* 140 It is..agreed..that..every person that taketh Hollow-ware of any workman & returneth not him for the same ½ plate mettle and ½ London Trifles, shall pay unto such workman for want of plate mettle after the rate of 3s 6d per Cent and deliver him good London Trifles. **1839** URE *Dict. Arts* 952 The English tradesmen distinguish three sorts, which they call plate, trifle, and ley pewter; the first and hardest being used for plates and dishes; the second for beer-pots; and the third for larger wine measures. **1875** KNIGHT *Dict. Mech.* 1677/1 To regulate the quality..a button of pure tin weighing 182 grains was employed; a similar button of plate-pewter would weigh 183½ grains; of trifle, 185½ grains; and of ley, 198½ grains.

**8. a.** *attrib.* or as *adj.* Trifling.

**1607** TOPSELL *Four-f. Beasts* 170 This is no trumpery tale, nor trifle toy.

**b.** *Comb.*, as *trifle-bearer*, *-dish*, *-monger*, *-worship*; **trifle-pewter** = sense 7; **trifle-ring**, 'a ring having some hidden mechanism or play of parts, as a gimmel-ring, puzzle-ring, or one composed of three or more hoops working on pivots' (*Cent. Dict.*).

**1561** WITHERS tr. *Calvin's Treat. Relics* A ij, Certaine *trifle bearers, who..did exercise a most vilainous and filthy kynd of cariyng hyther, and thether reliques of martyrs. **1859** LANG *Wand. India* 107 The soup..was served up in a *trifle-dish which had formed part of a dessert service belonging to the 9th Lancers. **1819** *Hermit in London* III. 81 These selfish *trifle-mongers. **1875** KNIGHT *Dict. Mech.* 1677/1 The *trifle-pewter has, tin 83; antimony 17; with a good deal of lead occasionally. *a* **1860** J. A. ALEXANDER *Gosp. Jesus Christ* xv. (1861) 203 The exchange of spiritual life for..factitious morals and a senseless *trifle-worship.

Hence (*nonce-wds.*) **Tri·fledom**, the realm of trifles; **Triflet** (trəi·flėt), a small trifle (in sense 4).

**1895** *Daily News* 8 Nov. 3/2 A skit upon the Haymarket piece..described..as 'A Trilby Triflet'. **1903** *Westm. Gaz.* 22 Sept. 2/3 Twin synonyms of frolic mild,..Are ye from Trifledom exiled?

**Trifle** (trəi·f'l), *v.*1 Forms: (3 **bitrufle(n)**, 4 **treoflen, trufly, trofel, -le, trofulle**, 5 **trufylle, tryfulle, trefele, troufle, tryffle, trifel, -ful**, 5–6 **tryfle**, 6 **tryffel, tryfell, -fyll, -ful, trifyll**, (7 **triffle**), 6– **trifle**. [ME. a. OF. *truffle-r*, *truiffle-r*, parallel form of *truffer*, *trufer*, *trupher* (13th c. in Godef.) to make sport of, deceive, jeer or laugh at, = It. *truffare* 'to cozen, to cheate, to coniecatch' (Florio): cf. *truffe*, *trufle*, *truffle* mockery, cheating: see TRIFLE *sb.*]

†**1.** *trans.* To cheat, delude, befool; to mock. *Trifle out*, to dismiss with mockery. *Obs. rare.*

[Cf. *a* **1225** Bitrufle: see TRIFLE *sb.* 1 a. *c* **1290** *S. Eng. Leg.* I. 412/323 Wel bi-trufleth he þat folk.] *a* **1450** MYRC *Festial* 194 Symon Magvs..trifuld þe pepull to holde hym an holy man. **1523** LD. BERNERS *Froiss.* I. cc. 237 Than the comons of the cite beganne to saye, howe dothe our bysshop tryfle and mocke vs. **1533** TINDALE *Supper Lord* E ij b, To tryful out ye trouth wyth tauntes and mockes, as More doth.

†**2.** *intr.* To say what is untrue, to jest in order to cheat, mock, amuse, or make sport. *Obs.*

*c* **1305** *St. Dunstan* 74 in *E. E. P.* (1862) 36 Treoflinge heo smot her and þer. **1340** *Ayenb.* 214 Naȝt uor to iangli, uor to lheȝȝe, ne uorto trufly. *c* **1430** *Chev. Assigne* 48 He was trewe of his feyth & loth for to tryfulle. *c* **1440** *Promp. Parv.* 502/2 Tryflon, or iapyn (*K.* trifelyn,..*P.* tryfflyn), *trufo, ludifico.* **1483** *Cath. Angl.* 395/1 To Trufylle, *nugari,..neniari, trufare.* **1538** ELYOT, *Ineptio*.., to tryfle. **1551** ROBINSON tr. *More's Utop.* I. (1895) 98 The vyle bondemen skoffynge and tryfelynge amonge them selfes. **1573–80** BARET *Alv.* T 366 To trifle, to do, or speake a thing vnmeete for the purpose, *inepto.* **1602** SHAKS. *Ham.* II. i. 112, I feare he did but trifle, And meant to wracke thee.

**b.** *Trifle with*: To treat with a lack of seriousness or respect; to 'play' or dally with.

**1523** LD. BERNERS *Froiss.* I. ccccix. 712 Sirs, methynke the frenchmen do but tryfell with me, and with the countre of Flaunders. **1530** PALSGR. 562/1, I gest, I bourde or tryfyll with one, *je bourde.* **1605** SHAKS. *Lear* IV. vi. 34 Why I do trifle thus with his dispaire, Is done to cure it. **1670** COTTON *Espernon* I. III. 133 At last the Duke nettled to see himself so pursu'd, and trifled withal by his Enemy, commanded [etc.]. **1769** *Junius Lett.* xxxv. (1820) 168 This is not a time to trifle with your fortune. **1794** MRS. RADCLIFFE *Myst. Udolpho* xii, I let him see that I was not to be trifled with. **1852** MRS. SMYTHIES *Bride Elect* xliii, He shall not trifle with your affections. **1869** FREEMAN *Norm. Conq.* III. xii. 253 Trifling with what ought to be solemn engagements.

†**c.** So *trifle it*. *Obs.*

**1563** FOXE *A. & M.* 1190/1 Bradford desired my lord Chauncelor not to trifle it, saying that he wondred his honoure woulde make solemne oths (made to God) trifles in that sorte. **1657** J. SERGEANT *Schism Dispach't* 577 You have broke the Unity of the former church (and not of the court onely, as you trifle it) which you were in.

**3.** *intr.* To toy, play (*with* a material object); to handle or finger a thing idly; to fiddle, fidget *with*.

*c* **1460** J. RUSSELL *Bk. Nurture* 287 Put not youre hands in youre hosen..nor pikynge, nor trifelynge ne shrukkynge. **1530** PALSGR. 549/1, I fydell, I tryfle with my handes, *je fretille mes mayns.* **1618** M. BARET *Horsemanship* I. 75 If when he standeth..he coueteth to goe backe, or trifle with his body or feete, then [etc.]. **1715** POPE *2nd Ep. Miss Blount* 17 O'er cold coffee trifle with the spoon. **1842** TENNYSON *Will Waterpr.* xxix, Silent gentlemen, That trifle with the cruet. **1865** DICKENS *Mut. Fr.* I. ii, He trifles quite ferociously with his dessert-knife.

**b.** *trans.* To play with. *rare.*

**1817** KEATS *Endym.* IV. 210 Young Bacchus stood, Trifling his ivy-dart.

**4.** *intr.* To dally, loiter; to spend time idly or frivolously; to waste time.

? *a* **1400** *Morte Arth.* 2932, I red thowe trette of a trewe, and trofle no lengere. **1560** DAUS tr. *Sleidane's Comm.* 114 b, He trifleth and dalieth thus with doubtfull wordes. **1638** SIR T. HERBERT *Trav.* (ed. 2) 133 Let us now triffle no longer, but view the City. **16..** EVELYN *Diary* 21 Oct. an. 1632 Whiles I was now trifling at home I saw London. **1751** JOHNSON *Rambler* No. 153 ¶ 5 While I was thus trifling in uncertainty. **1856** OLMSTED *Slave States* 91 They must have 'trifled' a great deal, or they would have accomplished more than they had.

†**5.** *trans.* To pass or spend (time) frivolously or idly; to waste (time). *Obs.* exc. as in b.

**1586** J. HOOKER *Hist. Irel.* in Holinshed II. 157/2 He still lingered and trifled the time and came not. **1596** SHAKS. *Merch. V.* IV. i. 298 We trifle time, I pray thee pursue sentence. **1611** HEYWOOD *Gold. Age* IV. i. Wks. 1874 III. 66 Wee haue trifled the night till bed-time. **1697** CONGREVE *Mourn. Bride* II. vii, I haue not leisure to reflect, or know, Or trifle time in thinking. **1742** R. BLAIR *Grave* 572 Fain would he trifle time with idle talk.

**b.** esp. with *away*, † *off*, to fritter away idly. † With *forth*, *out*, to defer or put off idly.

**1532** HERVET *Xenophon's Househ.* 59 b, His worke men and laborers..trifyll away the day. *Ibid.*, His folke..trifle forth the time. **1609** HOLLAND *Amm. Marcell.* 305 He a long while trifled out the time. **1613** SHAKS. *Hen. VIII*, v. iii. 179 Come Lords, we trifle time away. **1657** J. WATTS *Dipper Sprinkled* 86 Trifle away paper with needless repetitions. **1774** *Trinket* 172 *Une affaire de cœur*, is at best a silly business, yet mighty necessary to trifle off that trifle, life. **1818** SCOTT *Hrt. Midl.* vi[i], Why do you trifle away time in making a gallows?—that dyester's pole is good enough for the homicide.

†**6.** To make a trifle of; to render trivial or insignificant. *Obs. rare*−1.

**1605** SHAKS. *Macb.* II. iv. 4 This sore Night Hath trifled former knowings.

**7.** *intr.* To act (or speak) in an idle or frivolous way, esp. in serious circumstances.

**1736** BUTLER *Anal.* II. v. Wks. 1874 I. 207 A person rashly trifling upon a precipice. **1779** *Mirror* No. 60 One of the most important lessons to be learned in life, is that of being able to trifle upon occasion. **1815** SCOTT *Guy M.* xviii, I cannot help trifling, Matilda, though my heart is sad enough. **1867** AUG. J. E. WILSON *Vashti* xxviii, 'Oh, Salome! you have trifled.' 'No, sir. Take that back. I never stoop to trifling; and the curse of my life has been my almost fatal earnestness of purpose'.

**8.** *trans.* To utter or pass in a trifling manner.

**1822** LAMB *Elia* Ser. I. *Old Actors*, She used him for her sport..to trifle a leisure sentence or two with. **1825** C. M. WESTMACOTT *Eng. Spy* I. 226 Trifles a little badinage.

**Tri·fle,** *v.*2 *dial.* [Eng. Dial. Dict. suggests deriv. from OE. *trifulian*, *tribulian*, *getrifulian*, ad. L. *trībulāre* to thresh, bruise, pound, grind, f. *trībulum* threshing-sledge; this seems probable, though no examples are known between the 11th and 17th c., and the sense is not exactly identical.] *trans.* To beat or trample down (standing corn or grass).

[*c* **1000** ÆLFRIC *Voc.* in Wr.-Wülcker 114/26 *Pilurus, uel pistor*, se þe pilaþ, *uel* tribulaþ.] *c* **1000** *Sax. Leechd.* II. 150/3 Eft withier rinde ȝebærn to ahsan do eced to trifula swiðe. *Ibid.* 186/10 Menge eall togædere & trifolige. *c* **1050** *Gloss.* in Wr.-Wülcker 423/25 *In tritura*, in trifelunge. **1641** BEST *Farm. Bks.* (Surtees) 54 A mower..may mowe (with as much ease) amongst ranke barley as other, if it stande streight, and bee not trifled, neyther with the winde, nor with cattle-feete. **1846** BROCKETT *N. C. Words* (ed. 3), *Trifled-corn*, corn that has fallen down, in single ears, mixed with standing corn. **1893–4** *Northumbld. Gloss.*, *Trifled*, beaten down with wind or rain; applied to grass or grain.

**Trifler** (trəi·flər). Forms: (4 **troifiard**), **triffler(e, -our, triflere**, 4–6 **trifeler**, 4–7 **tryfler**, 5 **trufeler, truffilere, tryfflare, tryfelare, -fulere, -fuller, (-pheler), trifulere**, 6 **tryfelar, -fullar**, 6–7 **triffel(l)er, tryf(f)eler**, 6– **trifler**. [a. OF. *trufleor*, *-eour*, *-eur*, nom. *trufflere* (beside *trufeor*, *truffeur*, etc., all 13th c.) liar, cheat, trifler, agent-n. from *truffer*, *truffler*: see TRIFLE *v.*1 and -ER 2. Also with other suffixes: see -ER1.] One who trifles.

**1.** A teller of feigned or idle stories, one not to be believed or taken seriously; a jester, a joker; a nonsensical speaker; a worthless fellow.

**1382** WYCLIF *Wisd.* ii. 16 As trifleres [1388 triffleris, *marg.* trifeleris; that is, men of no vertu; L. *nugaces*] wee ben eymed of hym. *c* **1394** *P. Pl. Crede* 475 Telle More of þise tryflers hou trechurly þei libbeþ? *Ibid.* 742 Y miȝt tymen þo troifiardes to toilen wiþ þe erþe, Tylyen & trewliche lyven & her flech tempren! **1399** LANGL. *Rich. Redeles* III. 118 Þe tale of a trifflour. *c* **1420** ? LYDG. *Assembly of Gods* 685 Tregetours, trypheleis, feyners of tales. *c* **1425** *Voc.* in Wr.-Wülcker 651/11 *Hic nugator*, trifulere. *c* **1440** *Promp. Parv.* 502/2 Tryfelare.., *trufator, nugax.* **1483** *Cath. Angl.* 395/1 A Trufeler (*A.* Truffilere), *gerro,..nugifer, nugigerulus.* **1519** HORMAN *Vulg.* 77 Thys felowe is a tryfullar, leude, of no truste, or reputacion. *a* **1533** LD. BERNERS *Gold. Bk. M. Aurel.* (1546) I i v, Gamners and trifelers, and such other iuglers. **1576** FLEMING *Panopl. Epist.* 399 Then Poggius the babbler, the trifler, the railer.

**2.** One who is not serious or earnest in what he does; one who wastes his time on trivialities; a frivolous person.

**1607–12** BACON *Ess.*, *Beauty* (Arb.) 210 A man cannot tell whether Appelles or Albert Durere were the more trifler. **1710** PALMER *Proverbs* 244 Many a one will prove but a trifler in Latin or Greek, who in his mother-tongue might have appear'd to advantage. **1756** JOHNSON in W. Payne *Game of Draughts* Ded., Triflers may find or make any thing a trifle. **1781** COWPER *Charity* 355 The solemn trifler with his boasted skill. **1818** SCOTT *Br. Lamm.* xxxiii, At present, I have no leisure for the disputes of triflers. **1833** MACAULAY *Ess.*, *War Succession Spain* (1887) 280 Harley, we believe, was a solemn trifler,—St. John a brilliant knave. **1872** MORLEY *Voltaire* i. (1886) 4 Erudition figures him as shallow and a trifler.

**3.** One who works in the kind of pewter called 'trifle' (see TRIFLE *sb.* 7).

**1610–11** in Welch *Hist. Pewterers' Co.* (1902) II. 56 It was ordered..that..the tryflers shall have for ther ware as they do delyver to the company..mettall and money and vppon the complaynt of any of those tryflers wch ar not so payed it is ordered that they shall have x *d.* a pound for ther mettall and also to be fynd. **1612–13** *Ibid.* 61 A meeteinge..of certen tryffeleres for the Syzeinge of wares. **1614–15** *Ibid.* 68 Triffelers.

† **Triflery.** *Obs. rare*−1. In 4 **triphilrie**. [a. AF. **truflerie* = OF. *truferie* (13th c.), f. *truffer*, *trufler*: see TRIFLE *v.*1 and -RY.] False, feigned, vain, or idle speech or action.

**13..** *Cursor M.* 10131 (Gött.) Þis bok es of na triphilrie [*Cott.* ribodi; *Fairf.* iapery; *Trin.* iaperie], Bot of godd and vr leudy.

**Trifling** (trəi·fliŋ), *vbl. sb.* [f. TRIFLE *v.*1 + -ING 1.] The action of the verb TRIFLE; jesting or frivolous talk; fooling; idle, foolish, or frivolous conduct or practice; frivolous delay or waste of time; † also *concr.* (*pl.*) trumpery (quot. *c* 1540).

**1382** WYCLIF *Wisd.* iv. 12 Forsothe the priue desceyuyng of trifling [L. *fascinatio nugacitatis*] derkneth goode thingus. ? *a* **1400** *Morte Arth.* 114 With-owttyne more trouflynge the trebute we aske. *c* **1460** [see TRIFLE *v.*1 3]. **1530** PALSGR. 283/1 Tryflynges, scoffynges, *fredaines.* *c* **1540** HEYWOOD *Four P. P.* A iv b, Euery pedler In euery trifull must be a medler Specially in womens triflynges, Those vse we chieflye aboue all thynges. **1586** J. HOOKER *Hist. Irel.* in Holinshed II. 163/1 He returned his answer by a letter ..vsing therein nothing but triflings and delaies. *a* **1694** TILLOTSON *Serm.* (1742) III. 345 What a frivolous contention, what a trifling in serious matters. **1768** CHESTERF. *Let. to Godson* 15 Sept., Wit if you have any, and..agreable trifling or *badinage.* **1840** KINGSLEY *Lett.* (1878) I. 50 You are not bigoted by the solemn trifling of the schools. **1873** M. ARNOLD *Lit. & Dogma* (1876) p. xi, All other religious discussion is idle trifling. **1885** *Manch. Exam.* 4 May 5/2 Speeches..marked by a good deal of brilliant trifling.

**Tri·fling,** *ppl. a.* [f. as prec. + -ING 2.]

†**1.** Cheating, befooling, false, feigning. *Obs.*

? *a* **1400** *Morte Arth.* 1683 Ȝe do bott trayne vs to daye wyth trofelande wordez! **1547** *Bk. Marchantes* e vj, Was there no suche folysh fayned triflyng deceite in England. *a* **1548** HALL *Chron.*, *Hen. IV* 17 The kyng gaue many friuolus and trifelyng aunswers. **1560** DAUS tr. *Sleidane's Comm.* 37 b, So trifelynge & wicked a doctrine should haue bene dispised of all men.

**2.** Behaving idly or frivolously; not serious; frivolous; foolish.

**1535** COVERDALE 1 *Tim.* v. 13 Not onely are they ydell but also tryflinge & busybodies speakynge thinges which are not comly. **1659** *Gentl. Calling* (1696) 92 Shall more and baser be sought out, every the triflingest and vilest Entertainment? **1703** ROWE *Ulyss.* IV. i, Oh trifling, idle Talker. **1709** STEELE *Tatler* No. 109 ¶ 4 The trifling Way the Women have in spending their Time, and gratifying only their Eyes and Ears. **1885** *Athenæum* 23 May 661/1 The perverse intrusion of trifling thoughts at agonizing moments.

**3.** Of little moment or value; paltry, trumpery; insignificant, petty.

**1538** STARKEY *England* I. iii. 94 Delycate wynys, fyne clothys,..and a thousand such tryfelyng thyngys. **1645** EVELYN *Diary* 25 Jan., The worke of 10 years study for a trifling reward. **1659** *Gentl. Calling* (1660) 139 [One] that for every the triflingest injury expects..to be avenged seventy and seven fold. **1722** DE FOE *Plague* (1754) 8 Those were trifling Things to what followed immediately after. **1814** *Rep. Comm. Publ. Rec. Irel.* (1815) 75 To receive some trifling sum by way of Fee. **1869** FREEMAN *Norm. Conq.* III. xi. 66 The danger..was comparatively trifling.

**Tri·flingly,** *adv.* [f. prec. + -LY 2.] In a trifling manner or degree.

**1547–64** BAULDWIN *Mor. Philos.* (Palfr.) 126 See that thou swearest not..falsely & vntruely, or vainely & triflingly. **1601** DEACON & WALKER *Answ. to Darel* 123 You deale too triflinglie with your ignorant Reader. **1759** GOLDSM. *Pol. Learn.* ii, When philosophy became abstruse, or triflingly minute. **1763** WILKES *Corr.* (1805) I. 173 However triflingly this affair may have been talked of, it is, in reality, of very serious and general consequence. **1865** G. MEREDITH *Rhoda Fleming* vi, He had winced triflingly at one or two expressions.

**Tri·flingness.** [f. as prec. + -NESS.] The quality of being trifling; triviality, pettiness.

1581 SIDNEY *Apol. Poetrie* (Arb.) 71 The triflingnes of this discourse, is much too much enlarged. 1752 CARTE *Hist. Eng.* III. 507 Ross and his colleagues shewed the triflingness of this excuse. 1821 *J. Smith's Sel. Disc.* Pref. 10 A profitable companion; nothing of vanity and triflingness in him. 1912 *19th Cent.* Nov. 1023 The triflingness of free negro agricultural labour.

**Trifloral, Triflorous**: see TRI- 1.

† **Triflous**, *a. Obs. rare.* Also 6 **tryfelous, triflelous.** [app. f. TRIFLE *sb.* + -OUS: cf. OF. *trufous* (13th c.).] Trifling; insignificant, trivial; frivolous.

1509 BP. FISHER *Fun. Serm. C'tess Richmond* Wks. (E. E. T. S.) I. 291 Tryfelous thynges that were lytell to be regarded. 1535 — *Ways Perfect Relig.* ibid. 384 How light, & howe triflelous a thing it is. 1662 J. CHANDLER *Van Helmont's Oriat.* 43 It is a Childish and triflous thing. *Ibid.* 340 These races of vapours out of the Stomack, are triflous.

**Trifluctuation**: see TRI- 4.

**Triflu·or-, Trifluo·ro-.** *Chem.* [f. TRI- 5 + FLUOR(O-.] A formative analogous to TRICHLOR(O-, expressing the substitution of 3 atoms of fluorine for hydrogen, as in *trifluoromethane* or *fluoroform*, $CHF_3$, from methane, $CH_4$; so *trifluorethylene*, $CF_2:CHF$, from ethylene, $CH_2:CH_2$.

1899 *Jrnl. Chem. Soc.* LXXVI. I. 197 Trifluorotoluene ($C_6H_5.CF_3$) is not decomposed at high temperatures, and not attacked by water, alkalis.

**Triflu·oride**, *Chem.*: see TRI- 5 a and FLUORIDE.

1850 DAUBENY *Atom. The.* x. (ed. 2) 338 The gaseous trifluoride of boron, which contains no hydrogen. 1880 ROSCOE & SCHORLEMMER *Chem.* II. ii. 319 Antimony Trifluoride, $SbF_3$, is obtained as a dense snow-white mass, by distilling antimony with mercury fluoride.

**Trifoil, -fol(e**: see TREFOIL.

**Trifold** (trəi·fōuld), *a. rare.* [f. TRI- + -FOLD: cf. BIFOLD.] Threefold, triple.

1579 LYLY *Euphues* (Arb.) 142 Ther is amongst men a trifold kinde of life, Actiue..Speculatiue...The third is..a lewde lyfe, and idle and vaine life. 1867 J. B. ROSE tr. *Virgil's Æneid* 228 The trifold janitor Of Stygian Orcus. 1900 G. H. KINGSLEY *Sport & Trav.* 416 The trifold affection existing between the three.

**Trifoliate** (trəifōu·liĕt), *a.* [f. TRI- + L. *foliāt-us* leaved: cf. *trifolium* TREFOIL.] Three-leaved; *esp.* in *Bot.* consisting of three leaflets, as a compound leaf; also of a plant, having such leaves; *transf.* having the form of such a leaf.

1753 CHAMBERS *Cycl. Supp.* s.v. *Leaf.* 1756 ELLIS in *Phil. Trans.* XLIX. 867 The pinnated one called by the gardeners the poison ash, did not strike so deep a black as the other two trifoliate ones. 1845 LINDLEY *Sch. Bot.* v. (1858) 56 Leaves stalked, trifoliate; leaflets toothed. 1897 *Allbutt's Syst. Med.* III. 148 The pelvic brim [in some cases of osteomalacia] assumes a trifoliate form.

Also **Trifo·liated** *a.*, **a.** *Bot.* = prec.; **b.** *Arch.* Having or consisting of trefoils: see TREFOIL *sb.* 3.

1698 J. PETIVER in *Phil. Trans.* XX. 315 The Leaves of this are many times only trifoliated. 1733 MILLER *Gard. Dict.* (ed. 2) s.v. *Leaves*, A Trifoliated Leaf, is a digitated Leaf, consisting of three Fingers, as the Trefoil. 1850 INKERSLEY *Styles Archit. France* 309 The Clerestory window-archway..is divided into three pointed trifoliated lights. 1863 WALBRAN *Mem. Fountains Abbey* (Surtees) 147 A trifoliated canopy.

**Trifolie**, variant of *trifoly*: see TREFOIL.

**Trifoliolate** (trəifōu·liŏlĕt), *a. Bot.* [f. TRI- + med.L. *foliolum* leaflet, dim. of L. *folium* leaf: see -ATE [2].] Consisting of three leaflets, or having leaves of this form; trifoliate. (Abbrev. *3-foliolate.*)

1828 in WEBSTER. 1868 LOSSING *Hudson* 35 The bright trifoliolate oxalis, or wood-sorrel. 1870 HOOKER *Stud. Flora* 242 Leaves alternate 3-foliolate.

‖ **Trifolium** (trifōu·liŏm, trəi-). *Bot.* [L. *trifolium* (Pliny), f. *tri-*, TRI- + *folium* leaf. Cf. TREFOIL.] A large genus of leguminous plants, with trifoliate leaves, and flowers mostly in close heads; including many valuable fodder-plants, known as *clovers* or *trefoils*: *spec.* in recent agricultural use, applied to the species *T. incarnatum.*

[*c* 1000 ÆLFRIC *Voc.* in Wr.-Wülcker 133/22 *Trifolium* geaces sure, *uel* þrilefe. *c* 1625 *Names of Plants* ibid. 556/33 *Trifolium*, [F.] trifoil, [Eng.] wite clouere.] 1541 R. COPLAND *Galyen's Terap.* 2 F iij, Verbascum soden, and leaues of trifolium. 1596 LODGE *Marg. Amer.* 23 The fortunate husband, well trained to yoake and plough, learned of trifolium who lifteth up her leaves against tempest. 1885 *Manch. Exam.* 16 June 5/1 A large quantity of trifolium..has grown with immense rapidity.

*attrib.* 1900 *Westm. Gaz.* 15 Mar. 10/1 Several varieties of the great *trifolium* family lay claim to the honour of being the true 'St. Patrick's Cross'.

**Trifoly, Trifoote**: see TREFOIL, TREFOOT.

**Triforial** (trəifōᵊ·riăl), *a.* [f. next + -AL.] Of, pertaining to, or constituting a triforium.

1848 B. WEBB *Cont. Ecclesiol.* 45 Each of these arches is situated below a blank triforial arcade of two arches. 1854 J. L. PETIT *Archit. Stud. France* 37 The triforial arches of Amiens and Evreux. 1861 BERESF. HOPE *Eng. Cathedr. 19th C.* vi. 217 Previously to its reappearance in Germany, the triforial gallery had made good its position elsewhere.

‖ **Triforium** (trəifōᵊ·riŏm). *Arch.* Pl. **-ia.** [med.(Anglo-)L., found first in Gervase of Canterbury, *c* 1185; then, from him, in Battely's ed. of Somner *Antiquities of Canterbury*, 1703. In these, referring only to Canterbury Cathedral; in current English use, and in reference to cathedrals generally, only since 1800. Mentioned by Viollet-le-Duc, *Dict. d'Architecture* 1868, as introduced into architectural nomenclature by the English archæologists. Etymology unknown: see Note below.] A gallery or arcade in the wall over the arches at the sides of the nave and choir, and sometimes of the transepts, in some large churches. Originally applied to that in Canterbury Cathedral; in the nineteenth century extended as a general term.

[*c* 1185 GERVASE (of Canterbury) *Tract. de Combust. et Repar. Cant. Eccl.* Wks. (Rolls) I. 13 Hic murus chorum circuiens in circinatione illa pilariorum in capite ecclesiæ in unum conveniebat. Supra quem murum via erat quæ triforium appellatur, et fenestræ superiores.] 1703 N. BATTELY *Somner's Antiq. Canterb.* II. I. iv. 16 The former Quire had but one Triforium, now there are two round the Quire, and one in each side Isle of the Quire. *Ibid.*, A multitude of Marble Pillars..placed about the double Triforium, one above the other. 1726 J. DART *Hist. Canterb. Cath.* 8. 1774 GOSTLING *Walk Canterbury* 150 Above these large windows is a walk which Mr. Battely calls a triforium. 1815 J. SMITH *Panorama Sc. & Art* I. 155 Another..distinction of these arches, in large buildings, is the absence of the triforium or gallery. 1833 DALLAWAY *Disc. Archit. Eng.*, etc. 95 Above them [pointed arches] are the triforia, continued through every part. 1848 *Builder* 8 July 328/2 A discourse was..delivered by Prof. Willis, on the triforium of ancient churches...The only ancient work in which such a term could be found..was a history of Canterbury (by Gervase), in which it occurred in three places..He [Willis] verily believed that the modern term was a clumsy latinization of 'thoroughfarium'. 1868 A. K. H. BOYD *Less. Mid. Age* 368 The nave [at Norwich], of fourteen bays, vaulted in stone, and with the heavy round arches of the triforium as large as those below, makes the choir, of four bays, ending in a pentagon, seem small in comparison. 1874 PARKER *Goth. Archit.* Gloss. 329 *Triforium*, or *Blind-story*, the middle story of a large church, over the pier-arches and under the clere-story windows.

*attrib.* 1835 R. WILLIS *Archit. Mid. Ages* vii. 87, *ff* is the clerestory string, and *gg* the triforium string. *Ibid.* ix. 137 *note*, The clerestory wall is recessed back over the triforium gallery. 1835 WHEWELL *German Churches* (1842) 103 These intermediate vaulting shafts spring from the triforium tablet. [*Note.*] The running tablet or cornice below the triforium. 1905 BOND *Goth. Archit.* 519 The term *triforium*..is often used, not of the arcade, but of the space at the back of the arcade. So that it means sometimes the triforium arcade, sometimes the triforium chamber.

[*Note.* On the face of it, *triforium* looks like a normal L. formation (cf. *tricennium, triennium, trifinium, trifurcium*) from *tri-* three or thrice + *fores* 'a door of two leaves' = 'something consisting of or containing three doors'. Hence it has been explained as referring to a gallery or arcade with triple openings, as found at Amiens and in some other cathedrals; but this is not the case in Canterbury cathedral, to which alone the term was applied down to 1800, so that the explanation is not consistent with the facts. Others have suggested formation from L. *forāre* to bore, pierce, with *tri-* for F. *tres*, L. *trans*. Various other conjectures have been offered (see e.g. *N. & Q.* series 2, vol. IV. 269, 320, 371, 481, 522; V. 57, etc.); but none of them are satisfactory. The word itself may have been erroneously formed or misapplied by Gervase: see also med.L. *triforium* in the sense 'border, ornamental bordering' in Du Cange.]

**Triform** (trəi·fǫɹm), *a.* [ad. L. *triformis*, f. *tri-* + *forma* FORM: cf. F. *triforme* (15th c. in Godef.), perh. the source in quot. *c* 1450.]

**1.** Having a triple form; combining three different forms; formed or composed in three parts.

*c* 1450 *Mirour Saluacioun* 683 This temple of Salomon had on it pynacles thre Be whilk the triforme Auriole of marye takened may be. 1660 STANLEY *Hist. Philos.* IX. (1701) 379/2 Something which hath beginning, middle and end. To such a form and nature they attributed the number Three, saying, That whatsoever hath a middle is triform. 1678 CUDWORTH *Intell. Syst.* I. v. 673 Centaurs, and Scyllas, and Chimæras,..mixtly boviform and hominiform, biform and triform animals. 1805–17 R. JAMESON *Char. Min.* (ed. 3) 202 A crystal is said to be..Bi-form, tri-form, when it contains a combination of two or three remarkable forms.

**2.** Existing or appearing in three different forms.

1623 COCKERAM, *Triforme*, hauing three formes or fashions. 1667 MILTON *P. L.* III. 730 The neighbouring Moon..With borrowd light her countenance triform Hence fills and empties. 1678 CUDWORTH *Intell. Syst.* I. iv. § 17. 304 Damascius..tells us..that Orpheus introduced τριμορφον θεὸν, a Triform Deity. 1684 T. BURNET *Th. Earth* I. 164 This epistle..taught that the heavens and the earth had chang'd their form, and would do so again..; so as the same world would be triform in success of time. 1742 tr. *Algarotti on 'Newton's Theory'* II. 161 Her triform Goddess we before admired. 1847 LEITCH tr. *C. O. Müller's Anc. Art* § 206 In the representation of the tri-form Hecate. 1867–77 G. F. CHAMBERS *Astron.* I. xii. 136, I [Galileo] have observed the most distant planet [Saturn] to be tri-form. 1879 H. W. WARREN *Recr. Astron.* viii. 169 Huyghens..solved the problem of the triform appearance of Saturn.

**3.** *erron.* Triangular.

1621 J. TAYLOR (Water P.) *Superbiæ Flagellum* Wks. 34/2 That heights, depths, bredths, triforme, square, oval, round, And rules Geometricall in beards are found.

So **Tri·formed** (-fǫɹmd), **Trifo·rmous** *adjs.* in same senses; **Trifo·rmity** (*rare*⁻⁰) [late L. *triformitās* (Claudian)], the quality of being triform.

1644 DIGBY *Nat. Bodies* xxiii. § 8. 212 That which is most watry, is fittest to fabricate the body..of the *triformed plant. *a* 1662 HEYLIN *Laud* (1668) 368 Governed by a Tryformed Presbytery of Pastors, Elders, and Deacons. *a* 1739 JARVIS *Quix.* I. IV. xliii. (1885) 242 O thou triformed luminary, bring me sweet tidings of her! 1816 G. S. FABER *Orig. Pagan Idol.* I. 413 She [Sphinx] was likewise triformed, blending together in one figure a lion, a virgin, and a bird. 1727 BAILEY vol. II, **Triformity*, the having three Forms or Shapes. 1841 WILKINSON *Mann. Egypt.* Ser. II. I. xii. 232 The idea entertained by the Pagan Egyptians of a '*triformous Deity',..who assumed different names according to the triad under which he was represented.

**Trifo·rmol.** [f. TRI- 5 + *form(aldehyde)* (see FORM-) + -OL.] A commercial name of paraformaldehyde (see PARA- 2), used as an antiseptic.

1907 WOOD *U. S. A. Dispens.* 1604 *Paraformaldehyde, Triformol*..may be considered as a polymerized formaldehyde.

**Triforoid** (trəi·fŏroid), *a.* (*sb.*) *Zool.* [f. mod.L. *Triforis* (f. TRI- + *foris* door, opening) + -OID.] Belonging to or having the characters of the family *Triforidæ* of gastropods, typified by the genus *Triforis*. **b.** *sb.* A gastropod of this family.

1891 in *Cent. Dict.*

**Trifoveolate, -foveolated**: see TRI- 1.

**Trifurcate** (trəifɒ̄·ɹkĕt), *a.* [f. L. *trifurc-us* three-forked, f. *tri-*, TRI- + *furca* FORK + -ATE [2]. Cf. mod.F. *trifurqué* (Littré), *trifourche* (Cotgr.), also F. *trifurcation* (Bonnet).] Divided into three branches like the prongs of a fork; three-forked, three-pronged, trichotomous. Also *fig.* So **Trifu·rcal** *a.* (*rare*⁻¹); **Tri·furcate** *v.*, *intr.* to divide or branch into three; **Tri·furcated** *a.* = *trifurcate* adj.; also, having some part, as a fin, trifurcated, as the *trifurcated blenny* or *hake*; **Trifurca·tion**, division into three branches, or the point at which this takes place; † **Trifu·rcous** *a. Obs. rare*⁻⁰ = *trifurcate* adj.

1716 M. DAVIES *Athen. Brit.* III. *Suppl. Diss. Drama* 8 Whether he took himself to be affronted..and consequently that he deserv'd such *Trifurcal Repartees. 1811–31 BENTHAM *Logic* App., Wks. 1843 VIII. 291/2 Instead of bifurcate, two-pronged, suppose the plan of division, for example, *trifurcate, three-pronged. 1866 R. M. FERGUSON *Electr.* (1870) 97 Occasionally when darting between the clouds and the earth, it breaks up near the latter into two or three forks, and [lightning] is then called bifurcate or trifurcate. 1887 SOLLAS in *Encycl. Brit.* XXII. 417/1 (*Sponges*) The arms of a triæne may bifurcate..or they may *trifurcate. 1894 *Geol. Mag.* Oct. 438 The primary ribs of the Australian fossil..trifurcate more regularly. 1727 BAILEY vol. II, **Trifurcated*,..three-forked. 1769 PENNANT *Zool.* III. 131 A very singular trifurcated spine. 1836–9 *Todd's Cycl. Anat.* II. 933/2 The antenna on one side..was trifurcated. 1884 M. MACKENZIE *Dis. Throat & Nose* II. 224 In two cases there was *trifurcation of the trachea. 1656 BLOUNT *Glossogr.*, **Trifurcous*,..three-forked.

**Trig** (trig), *sb.*[1] [Goes with TRIG *v.*[1]; the vb. being app. the source of the sb.]

**1.** A wedge or block placed under a wheel or cask to prevent it from rolling; hence in a mine, a bar used as a brake for the wheel of a tram; also *U.S.*, a brake-shoe, a skid; in extended use applied to any material, as hay or gravel, laid on a slide to check the motion of a sledge going over it. In quot. 1647 *fig.* Cf. TRIGGER [2].

Its fig. use in quot. 1647 points to an earlier literal use: see also TRIG *v.*[1]

1647 R. STAPYLTON *Juvenal* xvi. 62 Nor is his suite in danger to be stopt, Or with the trigges of long demurrers propt. 1830 SEBA SMITH *Major J. Downing* (1860) 72 I've seen the wheels chocked with a little trig not bigger than a cat's head. 1858 SIMMONDS *Dict. Trade, Trig*, a wedge or block to prop up a cask, or to stop a wheel. 1883 GRESLEY *Gloss. Coal Mining, Trig*, a sprag used for stopping or putting the brake on trams, wagons, &c. 1886 J. BARROWMAN *Sc. Mining Terms* 68 *Trig*, a piece of wood laid in front of a waggon wheel to stop its motion.

†**2.** *Thieves' slang.* See quot. *Obs.* (perh. a different word, or ? belonging to TRIG *sb.*[2])

1812 J. H. VAUX *Flash Dict.*, *Trig*, a bit of stick, paper, &c., placed by thieves in the keyhole of..the door of a house, which they suspect to be uninhabited; if the trig remains unmoved the following day, it is a proof that no person sleeps in the house. This..is called trigging the jigger.

**Trig**, *sb.*[2] Also 7 **trigg.** Now *dial.* and in workmen's speech. [Goes with TRIG *v.*[2], of obscure origin.] A line traced, cut, or marked out on the ground, as a boundary or centre line, a guide for a cutting, etc.; the line or score at which a player at bowls, quoits, curling, etc. stands, or from which runners start in a race; hence *to foot* or *toe the trig*; also *dial.* a shallow trench, gutter, or small ditch, a narrow path or track (*Eng. Dial. Dict.*).

1648 DAVENANT *Long Vac. in Lond.* 98 Now Alderman in field does stand, With foot on Trig, a Quoit in hand. 1688 R. HOLME *Armoury* III. xvi. (Roxb.) 70/1 The Trigg is the place or mark on which the players are to set one foot, or foot the Trigg, when they deliuer their Bowles. 1796 *Grose's Dict. Vulg. T.* (ed. 3), *Trig*, the point at which schoolboys stand to shoot their marbles at taw; also the spot whence bowlers deliver the bowl. 1843 *Civil Eng. & Arch. Jrnl.* VI. 22/1 He is also..to preserve the centre or trig line, especially in curves. 1893–4 *Northumbld. Gloss.*, *Trig*, the starting line in a race, which may be either a stretched cord, a stick, a post, or an imaginary boundary. 1895 *E. Anglia Gloss.*, *Trig*, (2) The mark from which a ball is delivered.

**Trig**, *sb.*[3] *dial.* or *colloq.* [f. TRIG *v.*[3]] A trot, a hurried walk; a tramp on foot, a trip.

1884 HOLLAND *Cheshire Gloss.* (E.D.S.) s.v., He's allus uppo th' trig (always in a hurry). 1888 *Blackw. Mag.* Sept. 392 The goings on of himself and his comrade on the 'great trig' in the wilds of the Scotch Highlands. *attrib. Ibid.*

396 Nothing remained but to declare the 'trig' field season at an end.

**Trig** (trig), *a.* (*sb.*[4]) Forms: 2–7 **trigg**, 6 (*Sc.*) **tryg**, 7 **trigge**, 5– **trig**. [a. ON. *tryggr* faithful, trusty, trustworthy, secure (Norw., Sw. *trygg*, Da. *tryg* secure, safe, sure); = Gothic *triggws* true, faithful: see TRUE. Orig. northern Eng. and Sc.; in general literary use in 19th c.]

(The sense development between 1200 and 1500 is not very clear, and the order of senses given is mainly chronological; perhaps sense 4 ought to stand before 3. Cf. the note to TRIM *a.*, which is to a great extent applicable also to TRIG.)

**I. 1.** True, faithful; trustworthy, trusty. Now only *north. dial.*

*c* 1200 ORMIN 6177 Þin laferrd birrþ þe buhsumm beon & hold & trigg & trowwe. 1818 T. THOMPSON *Canny Newcassel* in Midford, etc. *Coll. Songs* (1819) 8 For Geordy aw'd dee,—for my loyalty's trig. 1829 BROCKETT *N. C. Words, Trig*, true, faithful. 1893–4 *Northumb. Gloss., Trig*, neat, spruce, true, reliable.

**II. †2.** Active, nimble, brisk, sprightly, alert. *Sc.*

*c* 1470 HENRYSON *Mor. Fab.* VII. (*Lion & Mouse*) i, Ane trip of myis..Richt tait and trig, all dansand in ane gyis. 1513 DOUGLAS *Æneis* XII. Prol. 184 Litill lammis Full tait and trig socht bletand to thar dammis. 1724 RAMSAY *Eagle & Robin* 23 A tunefull Robin trig and ȝung.

**3.** Trim or tight in person, shape, or appearance; of a place, Neat, tidy, in good order. Chiefly *Sc.* and *dial.*

1513 DOUGLAS *Æneis* IX. x. 89 The beste sal be full tydy, tryg, and wycht. 1697 R. PEIRCE *Bath Mem.* I. iv. 71 Her..Foot and Leg [were] as shapely, strong, and trigge. *Ibid.* vi. 107, I, by chance, met her trigg and lusty, in the Market-Street. 1816 SCOTT *Antiq.* xxiv, And it's like some o' them will be sent back to fling the earth into the hole, and mak a' things trig again. 1821 GALT *Ayrsh. Legatees* x, The wonted ornaments of every trig change-house kitchen. 1824 SCOTT *St. Ronan's* xxviii, A damsel so trig and neat that some said she was too handsome for the service of a bachelor divine. 1837 R. NICOLL *Poems* (1843) 126 My Sandie was the triggest lad That ever made a lassie glad. 1889 *Scribner's Mag.* Aug. 168/1 Bait is a dirty substitute for the trig fly.

**b.** Trim or neat in dress; smartly-dressed; spruce, smart, well-dressed.

1725 RAMSAY *Gentle Sheph.* I. ii, Few gang trigger to the kirk or fair. 1821 CLARE *Vill. Minstr.*, etc. II. 96 Trig as new pins, and tight's the day was long. 1825 BROCKETT *N. C. Words, Trig*, neat, trim; or rather tricked out, or what is called fine. 1873 HOWELLS *Chance Acquaint.* iv, The trig corporal, with the little visorless cap worn so jauntily. 1884 *Century Mag.* XXVIII. 541 The stylish gait and air of the trig little body who wore them. 1893 'J. S. WINTER' *Aunt Johnnie* II. 181 She really looked very smart and trig and jaunty.

**4.** In good physical condition; strong, sound, well; also, firm, steady; in quot. *a* 1722, *advb.*

1704 LOCKE *Let. to Churchill* 27 June, in Fox Bourne *Life* (1876) II. 546, I hope..that I may congratulate your safe return, strong and trig as you were before. *a* 1722 LISLE *Husb.* (1757) 270 A man will keep so much the greater awe over [oxen when ploughing], and will make them go trig. 1847–78 HALLIWELL, *Trig*, (5) well in health. *West.* (6) sound and firm. *Dorset.* 1858 *Brit. Q. Rev.* LVI. 548 Those noble [Greek and Roman] youths..sitting on the bare backs of their chargers, and guiding them with their hands;..they do not sit badly considering they have not the advantages ..of pig's skin and stirrups to keep them square and trig. 1890 AMELIA E. BARR *Olivia* xvii. 351, I wish I was in mid-ocean all trig and tight. Then I would enjoy such a passion of wind.

**5.** Prim, precise, exact; in depreciative use: Cut and dried, smug. *rare.*

1793 J. PEARSON *Political Dict.* 38 Trig and demure, the [girl] comes back. 1832 J. P. KENNEDY *Swallow B.* viii, A certain trig and quaint appearance given by his tight dark-colored small-clothes. 1868 TUCKERMAN *Collector* 74 A trig nurse, with Saxon ringlets, dragging a petulant urchin. 1872 H. W. BEECHER in *Chr. World Pulpit* II. 341 Our system of trig and prig theology. 1876 BLACKIE *Songs Relig. & Life* 137 A little man, smooth, and close-shaven, very trig, and smug.

**6.** Full, distended, stuffed to the utmost, 'tight'. *north. dial.*

1811 WILLAN *W. Riding Gloss.* (E.D.S.), *Trig*,..full, distended. 1825 BROCKETT *N. C. Words, Trig* a., full. 1905 in *Eng. Dial. Dict.* from Cumbld., Yorksh., Lincolnsh. *Ibid.* (N. Lincoln), 'Thoo mon't shuv no moore i'to that bag, it's oher trig noo'.

**†B.** *sb.*[4] A trim, spruce fellow; a dandy, a coxcomb. *Obs.*

1610 B. JONSON *Alch.* IV. vii, You are a Pimpe, and a Trig, And an Amadis de Gaule, or a Don Quixote.

Hence **Tri·gly** *adv.*, **Tri·gness.**

1728 RAMSAY *Lure* 40 What fowl is that,..that stands sae trigly on your hand? 1821 GALT *Ann. Parish* ii. 29 The lassies, who had been at Nanse Banks's school, were always well spoken of..for..the trigness of their houses, when they were..married. 1853 KANE *Grinnell Exp.* ii. (1856) 18 Their spars had no man-of-war trigness. 1896 J. TWEEDDALE *Moff* i. 14 Fields were subdivided by trigly cut hedges.

**Trig**, *v.*[1] Inflected **trigged, -ing.** [Etymology uncertain: perhaps ad. ON. *tryggja*, ODa. *trygge* to make firm or secure, from *tryggr* firm, sure, true.

This derivation fairly suits the sense; the difficulty being that *to trig* (in this sense) is not a northern or Sc. word, but is at home in dialects south of the Thames, which makes a Norse origin unlikely.]

**1.** *trans.* To make firm or fast; to prevent from moving; *esp.* to apply a wedge, block, or the like, to (a wheel) in order to stop or retard its motion.

1591 PERCIVALL *Sp. Dict., Calzar*, to shoo. *Calceare*, to trig a wheele [*mod. Sp. Dict., calzar*, to shoe..to stop a wheel]. 1651 CARTWRIGHT *Poems* (Nares), Times wheels are trig'd, and brib'd to make a stand. *a* 1661 HOLYDAY *Juvenal* (1673) 155 With free Chariot, fat Damasippus hurries; he, (He! even the consul) triggs the wheel. 1726 *Dict. Rust.* (ed. 3) s. v. *Trigger*, An Iron to Trig or Stay a Wheel. 1802 in *Spirit Pub. Jrnls.* VI. 235 Our friend Haterius should be trigged like a cart-wheel on an inclined plane. 1830 SEBA SMITH *Major J. Downing* (1860) 72 They make pesky bad work, trigging the wheels of Government. 1845 S. JUDD *Margaret* III. (1871) 397, I stand ready to trig the wheels in all the steep places.

**2.** To support or shore up with a wedge; to wedge up; to prop. Often with *up.*

1711 W. SUTHERLAND *Shipbuild. Assist.* 26 Shores, which ought to be placed on Timber Foundations, called Sholes, and well nog'd or trig'd. 1883 BARING-GOULD *J. Herring* xiv, She made him raise the hearthstone, and trig it up with a piece of granite. 1899 — *Bk. West* xvii, To prevent the springs being broken..the axle-trees had been 'trigged up' below with blocks of wood.

**†3.** *Thieves' slang.* See TRIG *sb.*[1] 2. *Obs.*

Hence **Tri·gging** *vbl. sb.*

1667 FLAVEL *Saint Indeed* (1754) 148 The wheels being oiled with delight, run nimbly, and have often need of trigging. 1682 — *Fear* vi. 78 Our thoughts run nimbly.. like oyled wheels, and have need of trigging.

**Trig**, *v.*[2] *dial.* Inflected **trigged, -ing.** [Goes with TRIG *sb.*[2]: origin of both obscure.

(As Du. *trekker* has become in Eng. *trigger*, it is conceivable that Du. *trekken* 'to draw a line' might become *trig*; but nothing corroborative of such an origin has been found.)]

*trans.* To make a score on (the ground) for a player at bowls, quoits, etc., to stand at; also, to mark out (ground) with a line or shallow trench. *Trig out*, to mark out or trace, as a boundary line. Also *absol.*

1706 PHILLIPS (ed. Kersey), *Trig*,..to set a mark to stand at, in playing at Nine-pins. 1727 BAILEY vol. II, *Trigged*, having a Mark set to stand in playing at Nine Pins. 1843 [implied in TRIGGER[3]]. 1881 MISS JACKSON *Shropsh. Word-bk., Trig*,..to make shallow furrows, or trigs, as between seed-beds for onions, carrots, etc.—'I trigged the ground afore I put the seed in'. 1893 H. PEASE *Borderland Stud.* 36 Gravely he consulted with his 'marrow' (mate) who 'trigged' for him.., carefully noted the indicated line. *a* 1905 *MS. Gloss.* (Warwick) in *Eng. Dial. Dict.* s. v. *Trig* v.[1], Plots of ground let for building are trigged out, i. e. the boundaries are marked by cutting a small trench in them. 1914 H. F. RUTTER (M. Inst. C. E.) in *Let.*, I have been asked scores of times by a ganger [over navvies] 'Could you come and trig out the centre line for us, Sir?'

**Trig**, *v.*[3] Now *dial.* Also 6 **trigge**, 7 **trigg**; infl. **trigg-.** [Origin unknown.] *intr.* To trot; to walk quickly or briskly; to trip; also *to trig it*; *spec.* (*slang*) see quot. 1796; also *trans.* or with advb. acc., as in *to trig the country*, to tramp; *to trig* (a distance).

1599 NASHE *Lenten Stuff* 49 Away to the landes ende they trigge. 1647 TRAPP *Comm.* 2 *Thess.* i. 3 How oft are we sitting down on earth,..till affliction call to us, as the angel to Elijah, 'Up, thou hast a great way to go', and then we trigg. *a* 1652 A. WILSON *Inconstant Lady* II. i, Hee triggs it to Romilia's. *a* 1680 T. GOODWIN *Blessed State* xii. Wks. 1703 V. III. 83 His Servant..(who must presently, without more ado, trig and Foot it after his Master). 1700 T. BROWN *Amusem. Ser. & Com.* 66 She ..Trig'd away Hand in Hand with the Gentleman. 1796 *Grose's Dict. Vulg. T.* (ed. 3), *To trig it*, to play truant. *a* 1825 FORBY *Voc. E. Anglia, Trig*, to trot gently; or trip as a child does after its nurse. 'They trigged off together'. 1872 HARTLEY *Yorksh. Ditties* Ser. II. 72 Mony a mile he had to trig One sweltin' summer day. 1891 B. GREGORY in *Wesl. Meth. Mag.* 56 A travelling tailor, having 'trigged the country' in search of work as far as 'Newrak'.

**Trig**, *v.*[4] Now *dial.* Infl. **trigg-.** [f. TRIG *a.* 3, 6; with both senses cf. TIGHT *v.*[3]]

**I. 1.** *trans.* To make trig or trim, to trim, to make tidy or neat; now often, to dress smartly or finely. *Trig out*, to dress or deck out. Chiefly *Sc.* and *north. dial.* Hence **Tri·gging** *vbl. sb.*, the action of the verb; *concr.* finery.

1696 *Song*, '*This is no my ain House*' i, Sin' ho claimed my daddy's place I downa bide the triggin o't. 1724 RAMSAY '*This is no my ain house*' i, Mine ain house I'll like to guide, And please me with the trigging o't. 1793 RITSON *N. Garland* (1809) 71 He rigg'd and trigg'd, and rid away. 1877 R. W. THOM *Jock o' Knowe* 54 Beauty..shines divine when seen Trigged oot in love and charity. 1896 KIPLING *Seven Seas, Rhyme Three Sealers* 62 He has rigged and trigged her with paint and spar. 1897 W. BEATTY *Secretar* xxx. 243 (Fifeshire) She had gotten me into her room to see that I was trigged out as I should be.

**II. 2.** *trans.* To fill full, to stuff, cram. (Cf. to fill 'tight'.)

1660 H. MORE *Myst. Godl.* IV. iii. 105 By how much more a mans skin is full freg'd with flesh, blood and natural Spirits. 1771 SMOLLETT *Humph. Cl.* 15 May, O Molly! the sarvants at Bath..lite the candle at both ends. Here's nothing but ginketting, and wasting, and thieving, and tricking, and trigging. 1790 GROSE *Provinc. Gloss.* (ed. 2) Supp., *Trig thy kite*, fill thy belly. 1825 BROCKETT *N. C. Words, Trig*, to fill, to stuff. 1828 *Craven Gloss.* s. v., 'He's trigg'd his hamper;' that is, he has filled his belly. 1905 in *E. Dial. Dict.* from Cumbld., Westmld., Durham, Yorksh.

**Trigamist** (tri·gămist). [f. as TRIGAMY + -IST.] †One who has been married three times (*obs.*); now, one who has three wives or husbands at the same time. Cf. BIGAMIST. Also *attrib.*

1656 BLOUNT *Glossogr., Trigamist*,..he that hath had three wives. 1854 *Tait's Mag.* XXI. 316 We could have spared..the memorials of the trigamist Doctor. 1895 *Daily Tel.* 28 Nov. 7/2 Collis being already a bigamist or trigamist. 1899 RODWAY *Guiana Wilds* 266 The Church would not permit me to baptize a trigamist, and the chief would not part with either of his wives.

**Trigamous** (tri·gắməs), *a.* [f. Gr. τρίγαμ-ος thrice married (f. τρι- + γάμος wedding) + -OUS.]

**1.** Characterized by, involving, or living in trigamy.

1886 *Pall Mall G.* 25 Jan. 4 'The Man with Three Wives' never lives in the trigamous state. 1900 P. F. WILLERT in *Eng. Hist. Rev.* July 590 Bigamous and trigamous marriages. 1908 *Daily Chron.* 22 Jan. 5/5 All three combine to avenge the treachery of the trigamous husband.

**2.** *Bot.* Having male, female, and hermaphrodite flowers in the same head. (Cf. POLYGAMOUS 3.)

1842 BRANDE *Dict. Sc.*, etc., *Trigamous*,..containing three sorts of flowers in the same flower-head; that is to say, males, females, and hermaphrodites. 1900 in B. D. JACKSON *Gloss. Bot. Terms.*

**Trigamy** (tri·gămi). [ad. late L. *trigamia*, a. Gr. (eccl.) τριγαμία, f. τρίγαμος: see prec. So F. *trigamie* (Littré).]

**1.** *Eccl. Law.* Marriage for the third time after the death of former wives or husbands. ? *Obs.*

1615 G. SANDYS *Trav.* 82 For them [priests] it is lawfull to marry: but bigamy is forbidden them, and trigamy detested in the Laity. 1727–41 CHAMBERS *Cycl., Trigamy*, a third marriage; or the state of a person who has been married three times...In the ancient church, trigamy was only allowed to such as had no children by their former marriages.

**2.** The state of having three wives or husbands at the same time; the crime of contracting a third marriage while two previous spouses are alive.

*a* 1634 COKE *On Litt.* III. xxvii. (1648) 88 The difference between Bygamy, or Trigamy, &c. and Polygamy. 1706 PHILLIPS (ed. Kersey), *Trigamy*, (Gr.) the having three Husbands or three Wives at once. 1884 *Chr. World* 16 Oct. 795/5 A woman 30 years of age was charged with trigamy, all three husbands being still alive.

**Trigastric**: see TRI- I.

**Trigeminal** (trəiˌdʒe·minăl), *a.* (*sb.*) *Anat.* [f. L. *trigemin-us* born three at a birth (see below) + -AL.] A name for the fifth pair of cranial nerves, from their dividing into three branches: also called TRIFACIAL. Also *absol.* as *sb.*

1830 R. KNOX *Béclard's Anat.* 349 The nerves of the arteries belong either to the sympathetic nerves, or to the spinal and trigeminal nerves. 1872 HUXLEY *Physiol.* xi. 264 Each nerve of the fifth pair is very large..and, having three chief divisions, is often called trigeminal. 1899 *Allbutt's Syst. Med.* VI. 744 Such pain follows the distribution of peripheral branches of the trigeminal.

**b.** Pertaining to, occurring in, or affecting the trigeminal nerve.

1874 GARROD & BAXTER *Mat. Med.* (1880) 22 In cases of intercostal and trigeminal neuralgia. 1899 *Allbutt's Syst. Med.* VII. 354 The trigeminal anæsthesia affects either the whole of the region..or only that supplied by special divisions.

**Trige·minous**, *a.* [f. as prec. + -OUS.]

**1.** (See quots.) *rare.*

1656 BLOUNT *Glossogr., Trigeminous* (*trigeminus*), threefold, three at a birth. 1658 PHILLIPS, *Trigeminous*, (Lat.) three brought forth at a birth; also treble, or threefold.

**2.** *Anat.* = TRIGEMINAL. 1891 in *Cent. Dict.*

**3.** *Bot.* = *trijugate* (see TRI- 1).

1900 in B. D. JACKSON *Gloss. Bot. Terms.*

‖ **Trigeminus** (trəiˌdʒe·minŏs). *Anat.* [L. *trigeminus* born three at a birth, f. TRI- + L. *gemin-us* born at the same birth.]

**†1.** A former name for the complexus muscle (COMPLEXUS[2]). *Obs.*

[1704 J. HARRIS *Lex. Techn.* I, *Complexus*, a Muscle of the Head, serving to move it backwards. It is also called *Trigeminum*, because it hath plainly a three-fold beginning, and seems to be compounded of 3 Muscles.] 1706 PHILLIPS (ed. Kersey), Trigeminus or Trigeminum.

**2.** The trigeminal nerve. Also *attrib.*

1875 tr. *von Ziemssen's Cycl. Med.* II. 574 Neuralgia in the branches of the trigeminus nerve. 1899 *Allbutt's Syst. Med.* VII. 354 Tactile sensibility may be impaired in the region of the trigeminus on the side of the lesion.

[**† Trigen**, app. an error of some kind for *triger*, TRIGGER[2], appearing first in 1659; whence in Phillips *New World of Words* 1678, and in many subsequent Dictionaries.

1659 HOOLE tr. *Comenius' Visible World* lxxxv. 175 He.. stoppeth the wheel with a trigen [*sufflamine*] in a steep descent. 1678 PHILLIPS (ed. 4), *Trigen*, a kind of Pole whereby a Coach or Waggon is stopped from going too fast down a Hill. 1688 R. HOLME *Armoury* III. 339/2. 1847–78 HALLIWELL, *Trigen*, a skidpan for a wheel.]

**Trigeneric**: see TRI- I.

**Trigenic** (trəiˌdʒe·nik), *a.* *Chem.* [app. f. TRI- 5 b + Gr. γένος kind + -IC: the acid was so named by Liebig and Wöhler, 1846, regarding it as the product of *three kinds* of substances, cyanic acid, aldehyde, and ammonia.] In *trigenic acid*, $NH:2(CO.NH):CH.CH_3$, also called ethylidene (or ethidene) biuret, as being biuret, $NH:2(CO.NH_2)$, in which two atoms of H are replaced by ethylidene, $CH.CH_3$; it crystallizes in small prisms, slightly soluble in water.

1868 WATTS *Dict. Chem.* V. 883. 1882 *Jrnl. Chem. Soc.* XLII. 168.

**Trigentale, -all**, obs. forms of TRIGINTAL.

†**Triger**, corruption of *chigger*, CHIGOE.

**1782** P. H. BRUCE *Mem.* 426 Trigers..get through the soles of peoples feet and lodge between the skin and the flesh.

**Trigesimal** (trəiˌdʒe·simăl), *a. rare.* [f. L. *trīgēsim-us* thirtieth + -AL.] †**a.** Thirtieth. *Obs.* **b.** *loosely.* Consisting of thirty (i. e. in quot., days).

**1637** SALTONSTALL *Eusebius' Constantine* 141 The trigesimall yeare of his raigne. **1839** *Fraser's Mag.* Aug. 203/1 The upper part may originally have been a crescent, implying monthly...The figure thus connects itself with the monthly trigesimal period.

**Trigetour, -ettur**, var. TREGETOUR *Obs.*

**Trigger**[1] (tri·gəɹ). Forms: *α.* 7–8 (9 *dial.*) **tricker**, (7 **trycker**); *β.* 8 **triger**, 7– **trigger.** [In form *tricker*, ad. Du. *trekker* a trigger, f. *trekken* to pull: see TREK. The form *trigger* occurs in 1660, but *tricker* remained the usual form down to *c* 1750, and is still in dialect use from Scotland to the English Midlands.]

**1.** A movable catch or lever the pulling or pressing of which releases a detent or spring, and sets some force or mechanism in action, *e.g.* springs a trap.

**1621** MARKHAM *Prev. Hunger* 39 Hard by this loope [of the net] shall there be fastened..a little broad thin trycker, made sharpe and equall at both ends. *Ibid.* 40 The loope and the tricker. **1735** *Phil. Trans.* XXXIX. 84 That Tricker has a Pin. **1764** *Museum Rust.* III. lxv. 298 The triggers to throw the rake behind the roots. **1853** SIR H. DOUGLAS *Milit. Bridges* vi. (ed. 3) 301 The ram was worked by hand-ropes (fig. 8) attached to the fall, which is a much quicker way than by the trigger and drop. **1885** C. G. W. LOCK *Workshop Receipts* Ser. IV. 428/2 (Photography) A trigger is provided for releasing the shutter. **1913** E. T. RUTHVEN-MURRAY *Let.* 30 Dec., If the tram-car strikes anything on the track, the gate is pushed backwards and releases a 'trigger' (in this case a catch sustaining the tray) which allows the tray to fall so that it glides along on the road and scoops up the obstruction.

**2.** *spec.* A small steel catch which, on being 'drawn', 'pulled', or pressed by the finger, releases the hammer of a gun-lock. Hence *to pull trigger*, to fire a gun (*at, on*).

*α.* **1622** F. MARKHAM *Bk. War* I. ix. 35 Let the Cocks and Trickers be nimble to goe and come. **1660** BOYLE *New Exp. Phys. Mech.* xiv. 89 We took a Pistol.., and..ty'd to the Tricker one end of a string. *Ibid.* 100 The Trigger was pull'd. **1759** ADAM SMITH *Mor. Sent.* II. iii. (1781) 161 Each of them draws the tricker of a gun. **1828** MOIR *Mansie Wauch* xii, It was an act of desperation to draw the tricker.

*β.* **1660** [see *α*]. **1688** CAPT. J. S. *Art of War* 17 Your musquet being levelled breast high with your fingers upon the trigger. **1753** HANWAY *Trav.* (1762) II. I. xi. 58 We could not pull the trigers of their muskets. **1868** *Rep. to Govt. U. S. Munitions War* 24 The trigger is pulled, *h* is drawn down and the spring, released, darts the needle through the guide into the cartridge, the blunt end of the needle sharply striking the fulminate and thus igniting the charge. **1888** 'R. BOLDREWOOD' *Robbery under Arms* xlix, Not once or twice..you've pulled trigger on me.

**b.** A lever or snib in a cross-bow the pulling or pressing of which releases the string.

**1681** GREW *Musæum* I. v. iii. 113 Just as when a Cross-Bow is let off by pulling down the Tricker. **1688** R. HOLME *Armoury* III. xvi. (Roxb.) 77/1 The string is..lett fly by a Tricker or button. **1846** GREENER *Sc. Gunnery* 12 It remained thus until the trigger of the cross-bow suggested a contrivance to convey, with equal certainty and greater rapidity, the burning match to the pan.

**3.** In *fig.* and *allusive* uses. *In the drawing of a trigger*, in a moment, instantaneously. *Quick on the trigger*, quick to act in response to a suggestion, to take advantage of a situation, or the like.

**1706** FARQUHAR *Recruit. Officer* I. i, This is the cap of honour, it dubs a man a gentleman in the drawing of a tricker. **1871** TYNDALL *Fragm. Sc.* (1879) II. ii. 12 Prayer is the trigger which liberates the Divine power. **1905** *Daily Chron.* 16 Feb. 4/5 A born musical leader, fertile in ideas, quick on the trigger.

**4.** *attrib.* and *Comb.*, as *trigger-catch, -detent, -guard* (GUARD *sb.* 16 d), *-jig* (JIG *sb.* 6), *-line, -plate, -pull, -pulling, -string, -touch*; **trigger area**, *Phys.* and *Path.*, a sensitive area of the body, irritation of which causes some special effect in another part (so *trigger point*); **trigger-block**, a piece of mechanism in a steam-engine, which automatically allows the steam-valve to close when a certain speed is attained; **trigger finger**, (*a*) the forefinger of the right hand, with which the trigger of a fire-arm is pulled; (*b*) *Path.* an affection of a finger (see quot. 1890); **trigger-fish**, a fish of the genus *Balistes*; so called because the large first ray of the dorsal fin is depressed by depression of the second, like the hammer of a gun-lock by the trigger; **trigger-hair**, *Zool.* a fine hair or filament at the mouth of a thread-cell in some cœlenterates, which operates like a trigger in emission of the stinging-hair; **trigger-plant**, a plant of the genus *Candollea* (formerly *Stylidium*), characterized by the two stamens being united with the style into a highly irritable column; **trigger point**, *Phys.* and *Path.* (cf. *trigger area* above). See also *tricker-firelock, tricker-lock* (TRICKER[2]).

**1891** *Cent. Dict.*, *Trigger area. **1900** DORLAND *Med. Dict.* (1913), *Trigger area*, an area stimulation or irritation of which may cause physiologic or pathologic changes in another area. **1893** D. K. CLARK *Steam Engine* III. 58 A square *trigger-block..slides vertically through..the catch-block. **1861** FAIRBAIRN *Iron* 123 The movement of the roller *o* causes the shoulder of the rod P to get under the point of the *trigger-catch *u*; the valve is by these means kept closed till the whole force of the blow is struck. **1868** *Rep. to Govt. U. S. Munitions War* 24 The small lock-tube is drawn back, pulling with it..the needle-bolt, till the shoulder *a* is caught behind the trigger-catch. **1881** GREENER *Gun* 470 The *trigger-comb arrangement is very ingenious, and is such that the barrels may be fired simultaneously or in quick succession, by adjusting a small screw. **1868** *Rep. to Govt. U. S. Munitions War* 24 The needle-bolt, and with it the needle, is held back by the shoulder *a*, catching against the *trigger-detent *h*. **1829** W. H. MAXWELL *Stories of Waterloo* I. 223 Removing Mr. Clinch's *trigger-finger. **1890** BILLINGS *Med. Dict.*, *Trigger finger*, sudden arrest of the movement of extension (or, less frequently, of flexion) of one of the fingers, until a special effort is made, when the movement is completed with a snap or jerk. **1882** OGILVIE, *Trigger-fish. **1884** *Longm. Mag.* Mar. 529 Trigger-fish and trunk-fish. **1908** *Westm. Gaz.* 3 Oct. 6/1 It penetrates into the body of the oyster in the expectation of its host being broken up and eaten by the trigger-fish. **1859** *Musketry Instr.* 38 To see that every man holds his rifle firmly with the left hand;..that the fingers of the right hand are behind the *trigger guard. **1868** *Rep. to Govt. U. S. Munitions of War* 51 The breech-block..works vertically in the shoe, being depressed or elevated by a hinged lever, fitting with a catch, over the trigger-guard. **1795** R. DODD *Rep. Hartlepool* 16 The seaman, standing with the *trigger-line in his hand, at a sufficient distance from the gun's recoil. **1884** MILLER *Plant-n.*, *Trigger-plant, *Stylidium graminifolium* and other species. **1860** *All Year Round* No. 71. 500 The stock is divided into..lock-side, head, small, trigger-guard, *trigger-plate, trigger [etc.]. **1891** *Cent. Dict.*, *Trigger point. **1900** in DORLAND *Med. Dict.* (1913). **1892** GREENER *Breech-Loader* 187 Gentlemen ..should state exactly what weight the *trigger pulls are desired. **1906** *Sub Target Rifle* 13 For practice in *trigger-pulling it is of great advantage. **1892** *Photogr. Ann.* II. 885 The exposure is made by pneumatic or *trigger release.

Hence **Tri·ggerless** *a.*, without a trigger.

**18..** ? BROWNING *Miniature* iv. (in *The Sibyl* (Rugby Sch.) 1 Apr. 1893), Arquebuses and pistols triggerless.

**Trigger**[2] (tri·gəɹ). [f. TRIG *v.*[1] + -ER[1].]

**1.** A device or appliance to retard or stop the motion of a vehicle descending a slope. Now *dial.*

**1591** PERCIVALL *Sp. Dict.*, *Estornija de carro*, the trigger of a cart, *sufflamen.* **1611** COTGR., *Enrayer vne rouë*, to stay, or hold a wheele backe with a Trigger. *Enrayoir*..a Trigger, the staffe thats put before a cart-wheele, to keepe it from ouer-throwing, or ouer-hastie going. **1631** ANCHORAN *Comenius' Gate Tongues* 88 To the wheeles are put triggers [L. *sufflamina*, F. *les enrayoirs*]. **1648** HEXHAM *Dutch Dict.*, *Radt-sperre*.., that which is put into the Wheele, lest the Cart be overthrowne, or a Trigger [*ed.* 1678 triger]... *Rede, ofte Wagen-span*, the Trigger of a Wheele to stay it. *a* **1661** HOLYDAY *Juvenal* (1673) 282 The souldier..has not his estate worn-out with such delay, like a waggon-wheell with the trigger that stops it. **1681** W. ROBERTSON *Phraseol. Gen.* 1246/2 A Trigger to stay a Cart wheel up hill, *sufflamen.* **1888** ELWORTHY *W. Som. Word-bk.*, *Trigger*, anything used to trig or block. 'Here! thick gurt stone 'll do vor a trigger.'

*fig. a* **1661** HOLYDAY *Juvenal* xvi. (1673) 279 Their means ne're, without fruit, Are gaul'd with the long trigger of a suit.

**b.** See quot.

**1893** *Wilts. Gloss.*, *Trigger*, the rod let down to 'trig up' the shafts of a cart.

**2.** *Ship-building.* A support holding the dog-shore in position; also *transf.* the dog-shore itself.

**1867** in SMYTH *Sailor's Word-bk.* **1877** KNIGHT *Dict. Mech.*, *Trigger*...A piece of wood placed under a dog-shore to hold it up until the time for launching. **1896** *Strand Mag.* XII. 324/2 This obstacle, known variously as the 'trigger', 'dagger', or 'dog-shore', is usually a short length of hard-wood interposed—in a sloping direction, and in such a way as to promptly yield to a smart downward blow—between fixed projections on the side of the standing ways and of the sliding ways. **1899** *Daily News* 16 Jan. 7/3 The last blocks had been knocked away and the Oceanic was held in place only by a 'trigger' on each side. These huge triggers of cast steel..work in hydraulic pistons, and fit into slots of the sliding ways. **1900** *Engineering Mag.* XIX. 681 From these triggers, dog shores, bearing only about one-quarter of an inch outside of the fulcrum, extend up against the keel.

**Tri·gger**[3]. [f. TRIG *v.*[2] or *sb.*[2] + -ER[1].] **a.** See quot. 1843. **b.** = TRIG *sb.*[2]

**1843** HARDY in *Proc. Berw. Nat. Club* II. No. 11. 56 Two men, named triggers, must see that when the race for the succeeding cast of the bowl has concluded, the straw is exactly between the feet of the party whose turn it is to dismiss the bowl. **1891** H. JOHNSTON *Kilmallie* xix. II. 110 (*Curling*) The second, third, and fourth players, on each side, footed the trigger, and sent their stones hurtling along the as yet unpolished ice towards the goal.

**Trigide, Trigil**, obs. ff. TRAGEDY, TRICKLE.

**Trigintal** (trəiˌdʒi·ntăl). Now only *Hist.* Also 5–6 **-gen-**. [ad. med.L. *trīgintāle*, f. L. *trīgintā* thirty: see -AL.] = TRENTAL. Also *attrib.*

**1491** *Cartular. S. Nicholai Aberdon.* (New Spald. Cl.) I. 257 Ye Songe mess with note on ye morne yerefitre at Sanct nicholess alter, and trigental of saidis messis in ye oulk followinge. **1530** in *N. & Q.* 9th Ser. VI. 414/1 An hole trigintall of masses to be saide in the churche where I shalbe buryed. **1726** AYLIFFE *Parergon* 190 Trentals or Trigintals were also a number of Masses, to the Tale of Thirty,..instituted (as pretended by St. Gregory). **1898** A. F. LEACH *Beverley Act Bk.* I. p. lxxx, The annuals, trigintals..with legacies and Lenten tithes are worth 20 marks.

**Triginte·nnial**, *a. rare*[-1]. [f. L. *trīgintā* thirty + *-enni-um* (f. *ann-us* year) + -AL.] Taking place once in thirty years.

**1894** *Yale News* (New Haven, Conn.) 29 June, About twenty-five members of the class were present at their trigintennial reunion.

**Trigintise·xtuple.** *rare*[-1]. [f. L. *trīgintā* thirty + **sextuplex*, f. *sextus* sixth, as in *duplex, triplex*, etc.] The product obtained by multiplying a given quantity by 36.

**1690** LEYBOURN *Curs. Math.* 349 If any Root be Multiplied by 6 the Product shall be the Root of the Trigintisextuple.

**Trigit**, variant of TREGET, *Obs.*

‖ **Trigla** (tri·glă). *Ichth.* [mod.L. *trigla* (Linn. 1758), a. Gr. τρίγλη, -λα, the red mullet, whence also It. *triglia* (tri·lʸa).] A genus of fishes, family *Triglidæ*, the gurnards; any species of this genus.

**1752** J. HILL *Hist. Anim.* 265 The red Smoothheaded Trigla, without any beards. The King of the Mullets. *Ibid.* 267 The red Trigla..The Red Gurnard. The French call it Marrude. **1854** BUSHNAN in *Circ. Sc.* (1865) I. 294/2 The trigla utters a grunting sound when it is taken out of the water.

**Triglandular**: see TRI- I.

**Trigle**, obs. Sc. form of TRICKLE.

**Triglochid** (trəiglōᵘ·kid), *a. rare.* [f. Gr. τριγλώχῑς, -ῑν- (f. τρι-, TRI- + γλωχίς, γλωχῖν point of an arrow) + -ID[2].] Having three points; tricuspid. Also **Triglo·chin** *a.*

**1760** J. LEE *Introd. Bot.* III. xviii. (1765) 213 *Triglochid*, three pointed. **1836–9** *Todd's Cycl. Anat.* I. 581/1 This valve..receives the name of the..triglochin valve.

**Trigloid** (tri·gloid), *a.* and *sb. Ichth.* [f. Gr. τρίγλη TRIGLA + -OID.] **a.** *adj.* Belonging or akin to the group *Trigloidea* or family *Triglidæ* of fishes, typified by the genus TRIGLA. **b.** *sb.* A fish of this group or family. Also **Tri·glid.**

**1888** *Proc. U. S. Nat. Museum* XI. 577 He especially instanced the Triglids and Dactylopterids as two groups which exhibit great diversities. *Ibid.* 588 The Trigloid, Cottoid, Gobioid, and Lophioid families... To even still greater a degree are the Agonoids, the Trigloids, and Dactylopteroids divergent.

**Triglot** (trəi·glǫt), *a.* and *sb.* [f. Gr. τρι-, TRI- + γλῶττα tongue, after *polyglot.*] **a.** *adj.* Of a book or writing: In three languages. **b.** *sb.* A book, esp. a Bible, in three languages.

**1882–3** *Schaff's Encycl. Relig. Knowl.* III. 1864 A Samaritan Pentateuch Triglot, .. Hebrew .. Samaritan .. Arabic. **1890** (*title*) The Triglot Bible. Comprising the Holy Scriptures of the Old and New Testament in the Original Tongues, the Septuagint, the Syriac (of the New Testament) and the Vulgate Versions, in parallel columns. **1901** H. BROWNE (*title*) Triglot Dictionary of Scriptural Representative Words in Hebrew, Greek, and English.

**Trigly**: see under TRIG *a.*

**Triglyceride** (trəiˌgli·sĕrəid). *Chem.* [f. TRI- 5 (irregularly used) + GLYCERIDE.] A compound in which three acid radicals are united by oxygen to glyceryl; i. e. they replace the three H atoms of the OH groups in glycerin or glycerol, $C_3H_5(OH)_3$; e. g. stearin is called the triglyceride of stearic acid.

**1860** DEBUS in *Q. Jrnl. Chem. Soc.* XII. 243. **1895** LEWKOWITSCH *Benedikt's Oils, Fats, Waxes* 46 Glycerol ..deporting itself like a trihydric base, is able to combine with three radicles of fatty acids...The resulting compounds are called 'triglycerides'. **1912** THORPE *Dict. App. Chem.* (ed. 2) I. 577 The glycerides of butter fat contain butyric, caproic, caprylic, capric, lauric, myristic, palmitic, stearic, and oleic acids, as triglycerides.

**Triglyph** (trəi·glif). *Arch.* Also *erron.* 7–9 **tryglyph**, 7 **triglife, -iphe**, 8–9 **trigliph.** Formerly in L. form **triglyphus**, pl. **-i.** [ad. L. *triglyphus* (Vitr.), a. Gr. τρίγλυφ-ος thrice-grooved, f. τρι-, TRI- + γλυφή carving. So F. *triglyphe* (1545 in Hatz.-Darm.).] A member or ornament in the Doric order, consisting of a block or tablet with three vertical grooves or glyphs (strictly, two whole grooves, and a half-groove on each side), repeated at regular intervals along the frieze, usually one over each column, and one or two (see DITRIGLYPH 2) between every two columns.

**1563** SHUTE *Archit.* C ij b, The Canalicoli, standing vpright within the Triglyphi... Bitwixte the .2. Triglyphos, you shall set Methopa. **1624** WOTTON *Archit.* in *Reliq.* (1651) 230 A sober garnishment..of Triglyphs and Metopes alwayes in the Frize. **1704** J. HARRIS *Lex. Techn.* I, *Triglyph*..is a Member of the Frize of the Dorick Order. **1797** HOLCROFT tr. *Stolberg's Trav.* (ed. 2) III. xc. 528 A triglyph ..was nine feet and a half high. **1823** P. NICHOLSON *Pract. Build.* 467 The architrave and trigliph, representing the beams and joists [of a primitive building]. **1871** B. TAYLOR *Faust* (1875) II. I. vii. 76 The pillared shaft, the triglyph even rings, I think, indeed, the whole bright temple sings.

Hence **Tri·glyphal** *a.* = *triglyphic* (*a*); **Tri·glyphed** (-glift) *a.*, furnished or adorned with triglyphs; in quot. 1880 as *pa. pple.*, ? carved in the manner of a triglyph; **Trigly·phic, Trigly·phical** (*rare*[-0]) *adjs.*, (*a*) pertaining to or of the nature of a triglyph; (*b*) 'containing three sets of characters or sculptures' (Webster, citing Gliddon).

**1890** MARQUAND in *Amer. Jrnl. Archæol.* VI. 54 The Egyptian scotia..is replaced in the Greek entablature by the *triglyphal frieze. **1837** *Penny Cycl.* VII. 217/2 The plain capital composed of merely an echinus and abacus, and a *triglyphed frieze, enable us to pronounce at once that the order is the Doric. **1849** FREEMAN *Archit.* II. ii. 110

Some Sicilian examples exhibit the triglyphed frieze. **1880** F. W. PERCIVAL in *Academy* 4 Sept. 173 The hair..represented in long parallel tresses distinctly triglyphed in the rock. **1847** WEBSTER, **Triglyphic*, **Triglyphical*. **1866** RUSKIN *Crown Wild Olive* App. (1898) 219 They attack Brandenburg, under its Triglyphic protector.

**Trigness**: see under TRIG *a.*

**Trigon** (trəi·gǫn). Also 7 trygon, 7–8 trigone. [ad. L. *trigōn-um*, ad. Gr. τρίγων-ον triangle, neuter of τρίγωνος, f. τρι-, TRI- + -γων-ος -angled, -cornered.]

**1.** A figure having three angles and three sides; a triangle.

**1600** FAIRFAX *Tasso* II. li, Let Ismen with his squares and trigons war. *a* **1628** SIR J. BEAUMONT *Bosworth F.* 346 When the Cranes direct their Flight on high,..they in a Trigon fly. **1694** MOTTEUX *Rabelais* IV. Prol. (1737) 78 An equilateral Trigone. **1806** HUTTON *Course Math.* I. 272 An Equilateral Triangle is also a Regular Figure of three sides ..being also called a Trigon. **1859** F. A. GRIFFITHS *Artil. Man.* (1862) 333 Trigon..Heptagon..Octagon.

**2.** *Astrol.* **a.** A set of three signs of the zodiac, distant 120° from each other, as if at the angles of an equilateral triangle; = TRIPLICITY 3. (Also *fig.* or *allusively.*) **b.** The aspect of two planets distant 120° from each other; = TRINE *sb.* 2.

**1563** [see TRIENT]. **1589** WARNER *Alb. Eng.* VI. xxxi. (1612) 158 She Euen at the firie Trigon shall your chiefe Ascendant be. **1593** G. HARVEY *Pierce's Super.* 100 His zeale to God, and the Church, was an aery Triplicity: and his deuotion to his Prince, and the State, a fiery Trigon. **1597** SHAKS. 2 *Hen. IV*, II. iv. 288. *a* **1633** AUSTIN *Medit.* (1635) 7 If the Astronomers hold there was a great Trigon of Constellations at his [Christ's] Birth: I am sure here is a great Trigon of Trigons, at his Conception. **1644** LILLY *Eng. Proph. Merlin* (title-p.) The beginning, and end of the Watry Trygon: An entrance of the fiery Triplicity. **1664** BUTLER *Hud.* II. III. 905 Some..Affirm the Trigons chopp'd and chang'd, The wat'ry with the fiery rang'd. **1704** HEARNE *Duct. Hist.* (1714) I. 23 Saturn and Jupiter.. having run through all the four Trigons, meet again, according to Kepler, at the end of 800 Years. **1819** JAS. WILSON *Compl. Dict. Astrol.* s. v. *Triplicity*, The first trigon is composed of ♈, ♌, and ♐, and is therefore called the fiery triplicity.

**3.** †**a.** A triangular instrument used in surveying; also, one used in dialling. *Obs.*

**1590** J. BLAGRAVE *Baculum Familliare* (title-p.) A Booke of the making and vse of a Staffe, newly inuented by the Author, called the Familiar Staffe,..which..staffe..readily performeth all the seuerall vses of the Crosse staffe, the Quadrate, the Circle, the Quadrante, the Gunners Quadrante, the Trigon, [etc.]. **1704** J. HARRIS *Lex. Techn.* I. s. v., In Dyaling there is sometimes used an Instrument of a Triangular Form, which is called, a Trigon.

†**b.** A triangular fort. *Obs.*

**1688** R. HOLME *Armoury* III. xvi. (Roxb.) 98/1 A Trigon, a figure of a fort with three corners.

**c.** An ancient lyre or harp of triangular form.

**1727–41** CHAMBERS *Cycl.* s. v., The trigon was a kind of triangular lyre, invented by Ibycus. **1776** HAWKINS *Hist. Mus.* I. II. ix. 247 The Trigon..was..struck either with a quill, or beaten with little rods. **1879** STAINER *Music of Bible* 11 Attempts to shew that the *kinnor* was a trigon, or three-cornered harp.

**4.** *Zool.* A bivalve of the genus *Trigonia*.

**1835** KIRBY *Hab. & Inst. Anim.* I. viii. 263 The Trigons, nearly related to the cockle, are mostly fossils.

**5.** Name of an ancient game at ball (Gr. τρίγων, L. *trigōn* ('lusum trigonem', Hor. *Sat.* I. vi. 126)).

**1842** W. SMITH *Dict. Gr. & Rom. Antiq.* 761/2 The most favourite game at ball seems to have been the trigon or *pila trigonalis*,..played at by three persons, who stood in the form of a triangle.

**6.** *Comp. Anat.* The triangle formed by the three cusps of the upper molars in primitive mammals.

**1897** H. F. OSBORN in *Amer. Nat.* Dec. 1002 Our studies among the Mesozoic mammals have left no doubt that the upper and lower triangles, or 'trigon' and 'trigonid', were derived from the reptilian protocone by the addition of lateral cusps...The 'trigon' was essentially a cutting apparatus, so perfect that many mammals retained it without further evolution.

**Trigonal** (tri·gŏnăl), *a.* (*sb.*) [ad. L. *trigōnāl-is*, f. *trigōn-um*: see prec. and -AL.]

**1.** Of, pertaining or relating to, a trigon or triangle; of the form of a triangle, having three angles, triangular. (In q. 1570 = TRIANGULAR 2 b.)

*Trigonal co-ordinates* (*Geom.*), a system of co-ordinates related in a particular way to trilinear co-ordinates, invented by S. Levi in 1876.

**1570** BILLINGSLEY *Euclid* VII. def. x. 186, 6 in diuers respectes is a lineall number..and also a trigonall or trianguler number. **1571** DIGGES *Pantom.* IV. def. viii. T j b, When any equiangle triangle..is..described within a circle..[its] sides are called the trigonal..Cordes of that circle. **1849** FREEMAN *Archit.* II. v. 170 A fine lofty pile, with..three trigonal apses. **1891** *Cent. Dict.* s. v., A linear equation in trigonal coördinates of the first class represents a cubic [curve].

**b.** *Geom.* and *Cryst.* Applied to a solid figure with triangular faces, or having some other relation to a triangle. Also, Having a relation to three angles: as *trigonal quoin*, a solid angle contained by three plane angles; *trigonal symmetry*, the symmetry of a figure or body which coincides with its original position after rotation about an axis through an angle of 120° or 240°.

**1878** GURNEY *Crystallogr.* 38 If three symmetral planes and no more intersect in the same straight line, it is called an axis of trigonal symmetry. **1891** *Cent. Dict.* s. v. *Trisoctahedron*, The trigonal trisoctahedron has each face an isosceles triangle. **1895** STORY-MASKELYNE *Crystallogr.* iv. § 79. 98 A plane figure may..be symmetrical with regard to a point within it as a pole of symmetry...Where $n = 2$, or $= 3$, 4, or 6, the symmetry may be defined as being *diagonal*, *trigonal*, *tetragonal*, or *hexagonal*. *Ibid.* vii. § 180. 211 The trigonal dodecahedron,..a tetrahedron with a three-faced pyramid on each of its faces. *Ibid.* § 257. 302 The trigonal trapezohedron..has trapezoids for its faces, which meet in two trigonal quoins.

**2.** Triangular in section, triquetrous: now *esp.* in *Zool.* and *Bot.*

**1571** DIGGES *Pantom.* IV. xi. Y iij b, The solide of Tetraedron may..be parted into 4 equal Trigonal Pyramides. *a* **1728** WOODWARD *Nat. Hist. Fossils* (1729) I. 158 Spar of a yellow Hue, shot into numerous trigonal pointed Shoots. **1753** CHAMBERS *Cycl. Supp.* s. v. *Leaf*, *Trigonal Leaf*, one much like the triquetrous, only that..the several faces are each hollowed in form of channels. *Ibid.*, *Lilium*, the lilly.. The pistil..finally becomes an oblong and trigonal fruit. **1854** WOODWARD *Mollusca* II. 225 Shell impunctate, oblong, or trigonal. **1895** W. M. MACPHERSON *Monymusk* v. 76 A plain roundheaded door with a trigonal hood.

**3.** *Astrol.* Relating to, or of the nature of, a trigon (in either sense): see prec. 2.

**1603** SIR C. HEYDON *Jud. Astrol.* xxi. 470 All trigonall aspects doe accord. **1635** SWAN *Spec. M.* v. § 2 (1643) 105 The Trigonall revolution..of the Planets [cf. TRIGON 2 quot. 1704].

†**4.** Of or pertaining to a trigon (TRIGON 3 a). Also as *sb.* short for *trigonal instrument*. *Obs. rare.*

**1593** FALE *Dialling* 39 Your Diall being made, and the Stile placed therein: take your Trigonall Instrument, and set it upon the Stile, so that the whole Diameter thereof may stand plaine upon the edge or upper part, the centre A, of your Instrument...Then fasten a thread at the uppermost end of your Trigonall in every line of the signes so yᵗ you may direct downeward by the centre A, to the plat of your Diall: and..then moving the Trigonall on the right hand, so that the thread may be stretched on the left hand, make there likewise a prick upon the plat.

**B.** *sb.* **1.** See A. 4.

**2.** *Anat.* = TRIGONE, TRIGONUM 2 (*Cent. Dict.*).

Hence **Tri·gonally** *adv.* (*rare*—⁰), triangularly (*Cent. Dict.* 1891).

**Trigonate** (tri·gŏnět), *a. Zool.* [f. as prec. + -ATE [2].] = prec. adj. 1 and 2.

**1815** STEPHENS in Shaw *Gen. Zool.* IX. I. 226 Female without the white trigonate spot beneath the chin. **1828** STARK *Elem. Nat. Hist.* II. 203 *A*[*mmothea*] *Caroliniensis*,..back with three trigonate tubercles.

**Trigone** (trigōᵘ·n, trəi·gōᵘn). *Anat.* [a. F. *trigone* (trigo·n), ad. L. *trigōn-um* TRIGON.] The triangular area at the base of the urinary bladder, between the openings of the ureters and urethra.

**1835–6** *Todd's Cycl. Anat.* I. 385/1 The posterior part of the trigone is thinner than the anterior. **1876** GROSS *Dis. Bladder* 137 The usual seat of villous tumor is the trigone. **1898** P. MANSON *Trop. Diseases* xxxii. 503 In the trigone of the bladder, there are..patches of inflammatory thickening.

**Trigone**, obs. form of TRIGON.

**Trigonel** (tri·gŏnel). *rare*—¹. [ad. F. *trigonelle*, or mod.L. *Trigōnella* (Linnæus, 1737), dim. of L. *trigōna*, fem. of *trigōn-us* adj., a. Gr. τρίγωνος (see TRIGON); so called from the triangular appearance of the flowers.] A plant of the genus *Trigonella*, N.O. *Leguminosæ*.

**1884** *De Candolle's Orig. Cultivated Pl.* 112 Trigonel, or Fenugreek—*Trigonella fænum-græcum*.

Hence **Trigone·lline** *Chem.* [f. mod.L. *Trigōnell-a* + -INE [5]], an alkaloid occurring in the seeds of fenugreek, in hempseed, and in peas, and prepared artificially from nicotinic acid.

**1886** *Jrnl. Chem. Soc.* L. 85, Jahn's *Trigonelline*, $C_7H_7NO_2 + H_2O$, crystallises in colourless, flat prisms, of feeble saline taste; it is readily soluble in water.

**Trigonellite** (trigŏne·ləit). *Palæont.* [ad. mod.L. *Trigōnellītēs* (given as a generic name), f. mod.L. *Trigōnella*: see prec. and -ITE [1] 2 a.] A fossil of triangular form and shelly consistence, found in the Kimmeridge clay; 'probably the operculum of a cephalopod' (Lyell).

[**1748** J. HILL *Hist. Fossils* 646 That kind [of Cockle] call'd by authors Trigonella...This kind..approaches to a triangular figure.] **1831** MURCHISON in Phillips *Man. Geol.* (1855) 301 Hard, compact, not oolitic, containing brachyphyllum, ferns, and trigonellites. **1851** WOODWARD *Mollusca* I. 80 They were described in 1811, by Parkinson, who called them trigonellites. **1885** LYELL *Elem. Geol.* xx. (1885) 295.

**Trigoneutic, -goneutism**: see TRI- 2.

‖**Trigonia** (trəigōᵘ·niă). *Conch.* [mod.L. generic name, f. as TRIGON + -IA [1].] A genus of bivalve molluscs having a shell of triangular form.

**1837** *Encycl. Brit.* (ed. 7) XV. 343/1 The trigonia now forms along with castalia, the small family of Trigonées. **1851** WOODWARD *Mollusca* I. 11 The cockle and trigonia have the foot bent, enabling them to make short leaps. **1883** *Fisheries Exhib. Catal.* (ed. 4) 176 Collection of Trigonias ..exhibited by Dr. J. C. Cox, F.L.S. of Sydney.

Hence **Trigoniacean** (trəigoᵘni͵ēi·ʃiăn), **a.** *adj.* belonging to the group *Trigoniacea* of bivalve molluscs, typified by the genus *Trigonia*; **b.** *sb.* a mollusc of this group. In recent Dicts.

**Trigonic** (trəigǫ·nik), *a. rare.* [ad. Gr. τριγωνικός triangular, f. τρίγωνος: see TRIGON and -IC.] Of or pertaining to a trigon or triangle.

*Trigonic co-ordinates* (*Geom.*), a system of co-ordinates invented by W. Walton in 1868, determining a point in a plane by the angles subtended at the point by the sides of a fixed triangle.

**1788** T. TAYLOR *Proclus* I. 54 The soul from material triangles or circles, forms in herself the trigonic, or circular species.

So † **Trigo·nical** *a. rare*, = TRIGONAL 3.

**1644** LILLY *Merlinus Angl.* To Rdr. A j b, The Government of the World by the seven Planetary Angels under the severall Trygonicall Revolutions of Saturne and Iupiter.

**Trigonid** (tri·gŏnid). *Comp. Anat.* [f. TRIGON + -ID (arbitrarily used).] The triangle of cusps of the lower molar teeth in primitive mammals.

**1897** [see TRIGON 6].

**Trigono-** (tri·gŏno, trigōᵘ·no), combining form repr. Gr. τρίγωνο-ς adj. three-cornered, triangular, neut. τρίγωνον as sb. a triangle; used in several scientific terms. **Trigonoce·phale, -ce·phalous** *adjs.*, *Zool.* [Gr. κεφαλή head], having a triangular head, as a serpent of the genus *Trigonocephalus*; so **Trigonocepha·lic** *a. Anthrop.*, having a malformation of the skull, caused by premature closing of the medio-frontal suture, in which the sides are flat and converge to an apex in front; **Trigonoce·phaly**, the condition of being trigonocephalic. **Trigonocerous** (-ǫ·sĕrəs) *a.*, *Zool.* [Gr. κέρας horn], having horns of triangular section. **Trigonocu·neate** *a.* [L. *cune-us* wedge], triangularly wedge-shaped. **Trigo·nodont** *a.*, *Comp. Anat.* [Gr. ὀδούς, ὀδοντ- tooth], having the primitive cusps of the molar teeth arranged in a triangle. **Trigo·notype**, *Geom.* [Gr. τύπος figure, image, TYPE], name for a trigonal trapezohedron (*Cent. Dict.* 1891).

**1865** *Morn. Star* 13 Mar., A *trigonocephale black serpent, brought over in 1842, is alive. **1878** BARTLEY tr. *Topinard's Anthrop.* v. 176 **Trigonocephalic*, skull triangular at the top anteriorly, supposed to be owing to the medio-frontal synostosis. *Ibid.* Index, *Trigonocephaly. **1904** DUCKWORTH *Morphol. & Anthropol.* x. 253 A skull which viewed from above presents a peaked or rostrated appearance and has been described as triangular or trigonocephalic. **1848** SMART, **Trigonocerous*, having three-angled horns,—applied to a species of fossil stag. **1864** in WEBSTER. **1822** J. PARKINSON *Outl. Oryctol.* 224 *Trigono-cuneate, rather smooth on the upper part, longitudinally sulcated. **1897** H. F. OSBORN in *Amer. Nat.* Dec. 1002 '*Trigonodont' is most appropriate because the first step in molar morphology is to identify the primitive triangle.

**Trigonoid** (tri·gŏnoid), *a.* and *sb. Geom.* [ad. Gr. τριγωνοειδής of triangular form: see TRIGON and -OID.] **a.** *adj.* Resembling a triangle; approximately triangular. **b.** *sb.* A plane figure contained by three circular arcs of equal radius meeting at angles; a species of curvilinear triangle. So **Trigonoi·dal** *a.*, (*a*) *Nat. Hist.* = *trigonoid* adj.; (*b*) *Geom.* 'like a trigonoid' (*Cent. Dict.* 1891).

**1822** J. PARKINSON *Outl. Oryctol.* 217 Subcordated, trigonoidal. **1873** SALMON *Higher Plane Curves* 245 The quartic is a triacnodal curve composed of a trigonoid figure within the triangle and of the three vertices as acnodes.

**Trigonometer** [1] (trigŏnǫ·mĭtəɹ). [f. TRIGONOMETRY, on analogy of *chronometer*, *thermometer*: see -METER.] A name given to various trigonometrical instruments.

**1767** J. FERGUSON *Tables & Tracts* (1771) 80 Mr. Mungo Murray..contrived a very useful instrument..which he calls The Armillary Trigonometer. **1796** HUTTON *Math. Dict.*, *Armillary Trigonometer*, an instrument..consisting of five semicircles..so divided and graduated, as to serve for expeditiously resolving many problems in astronomy, dialling, and spherical trigonometry. **1828** *Amer. Jrnl. Sc.* XIV. 270 A trigonometer..which may be conveniently carried in the pocket. **1860** in *Abridgm. Specif. Patents Optical*, etc. *Instr.* (1875) 345 An improved mathematical or plotting instrument [denominated by the inventor] a protracting trigonometer.

**Trigono·meter** [2]. [f. TRIGONOMETRY, on analogy of *geometer*, and the like.] A person versed in trigonometry; *spec.* one engaged in a trigonometrical survey.

*a* **1852** MACGILLIVRAY *Nat. Hist. Dee Side & Braemar* (1855) 92 We arrived at the centre of the broad top..seating ourselves on the base of the pyramidal cairn of the Trigonometers. **1902** *Westm. Gaz.* 10 Nov. 12/2 Kabru is..higher than Aconcagua—its height is,..according to the trigonometers, above 24,000 ft.

**Trigonometric** (tri:gŏno͵me·trik), *a.* [f. TRIGONOMETRY + -IC: perh. through F. *trigonométrique* (1762 in *Dict. Acad.*).] = next.

**1811** PINKERTON *Petral.* I. 184 The mountains, on which their trigonometric operations had conducted them. **1862** C. P. SMYTH *Three Cities in Russia* II. 186 The trigonometric operations require the observer..to be for long periods under canvass.

**Trigonometrical** (tri:gŏno͵me·trikăl), *a.* [f. TRIGONOMETRY or mod.L. *trigonometria* + -IC + -AL; after *geometrical*, etc.] Of, pertaining to, or performed by trigonometry.

*Trigonometrical functions*, those functions of an angle, or of an abstract quantity, used in trigonometry, viz. the sine, tangent, secant, etc.: see TRIGONOMETRY. *Trigonometrical survey*, a survey of a country or region performed by triangulation and trigonometrical calculation.

**1666** [implied in TRIGONOMETRICALLY]. **1690** LEYBOURN *Curs. Math.* 552 To find the Altitude..by Trigonometrical Calculation. **1706** W. JONES *Syn. Palmar. Matheseos* 278 Any three..being given, the other three may be found by Trigonometrical Calculation. **1758** MURDOCH in *Phil. Trans.*

L. 543 A table of the trigonometrical analogies. **1801** CAPT. W. MADGE (*title*) Account of the Operations carried on for accomplishing a Trigonometrical Survey of England and Wales, 1797. **1807** HUTTON *Course Math.* (1811) II. 3 A Trigonometrical Canon is a table showing the length of the sine, tangent, and secant, to every degree and minute of the quadrant, with respect to the radius, which is expressed by unity or 1. **1860** TYNDALL *Glac.* I. xi. 69 A pyramid of stones used as a trigonometrical station by Professor Forbes.

**Tri:gonome·trically,** *adv.* [f. prec. + -LY [2].] In a trigonometrical manner; by means, or by the method, of trigonometry.

**1666** COLLINS in Rigaud *Corr. Sci. Men* (1841) I. 115 Problems that seem easy trigonometrically, but not so analytically. **1751** J. STUART in *Lett. Lit. Men* (Camden) 382 An exact Map of all the Province of Attica trigonometrically surveyed. **1859** R. F. BURTON *Centr. Afr.* in *Jrnl. Geog. Soc.* XXIX. 8 Such as cannot be ascended should be measured trigonometrically.

**Trigonometrician** (trigǫnǫmĕtri·ʃăn). [f. TRIGONOMETRIC: see -ICIAN.] = TRIGONOMETER [2]. So **Trigono·metrist.**

**1884** *Manch. Exam.* 4 Oct. 5/4 The base-line of the trigonometrist admits of fresh refinements in precision. **1900** *Athenæum* 18 Aug. 223/3 The autobiographer became a trigonometrician, and astronomer at large.

**Trigonometry** (trigǫnǫ·mĕtri). [ad. mod.L. *trigōnometria* (B. Pitiscus 1595), f. Gr. τρίγωνο-ν triangle + -μετρία measurement. So Fr. *trigonométrie* (1629 in Hatz.-Darm.).] That branch of mathematics which deals with the measurement of the sides and angles of triangles, particularly with certain functions of their angles or of angles in general (the SINE, COSINE, TANGENT, COTANGENT, SECANT, and COSECANT), and hence with these functions as applied to abstract quantities; thus including the theory of triangles, of angles, and of (elementary) singly periodic functions.

Trigonometry comprises *plane trigonometry*, which treats of plane triangles and angles, and *spherical trigonometry*, which treats of spherical ones, i.e. those described on the surface of a sphere.

[**1595** B. PITISCUS (*title*) Trigonometria: sive De Solvtione Triangvlorvm Tractatus breuis & perspicuus.] **1614** (*title*) Trigonometry: or The Doctrine of Triangles. First written in Latine, by B. Pitiscus.., and now Translated into English, by Ra. Handson. **1631** R. NORWOOD (*title*) Trigonometrie. Or, The Doctrine of Triangles: Divided into Two Bookes: The first shewing the mensuration of Right lined Triangles: The second of Sphericall. **1738** *Gentl. Mag.* Jan. 13/1 A few Calculations by Trigonometry. **1816** PLAYFAIR *Nat. Phil.* II. 13 It often happens..that the stars must be observed when they are not on the meridian, and their positions..must then be derived from spherical trigonometry. **1854** KINGSLEY *Alexandria* i. 31 For the purpose of working out this theory he [Hipparchus] required a science of trigonometry plane and spherical: and this he accordingly seems to have invented.

‖ **Trigonon** (trigōu·nǫn). *Antiq.* [a. Gr. τρίγωνον triangle, a musical instrument of this form.] = TRIGON 3 c.

**1727–41** CHAMBERS *Cycl.*, *Trigon, trigonon*, .. a musical instrument, used among the ancients. **1847** LEITCH tr. *C. O. Müller's Anc. Art* § 425. 505 A concert of female players on the flute, the cithern and the trigonon. **1864** ENGEL *Mus. Anc. Nat.* 195 The trigonon ought..more properly to be classed with the lyre than with the harp.

**Trigonous** (tri·gǫnəs), *a. Nat. Hist.* [f. Gr. τρίγων-ος (see TRIGON) + -OUS.] = TRIGONAL 2.

[**1760–88** J. LEE *Introd. Bot.* Gloss., *Trigonus caulis*, a three-sided stalk.] **1821** W. P. C. BARTON *Flora N. Amer.* I. 114 Capsule truncate, trigonous. **1828** STARK *Elem. Nat. Hist.* I. 259 *Dendrocolaptes*,.. Bill depressed and trigonous at the base. **1870** HOOKER *Stud. Flora* 245 Convolvulus arvensis..seeds 4, obtusely 3-gonous.

‖ **Trigonum** (trigōu·nǫ̆m). [L., ad. Gr. τρίγωνον triangle: see TRIGON.]

**1.** *Antiq.* A musical instrument: = TRIGON 3 c.

**1727–41** CHAMBERS *Cycl.* s.v. *Music*, Of stringed instruments we hear of the lyra or cithara, the psalterium, trigonum, sambuca [etc.]. **1801** BUSBY *Dict. Mus.*, *Trigonum*, or *Triangular Harp*, an instrument supposed to have been of Phrygian invention. *Ibid.*, From Sophocles we learn, that a certain musician..was so admirable a performer on the Trigonum,..that [etc.].

**2.** *Anat.* = TRIGONE.

**1879** *St. George's Hosp. Rep.* IX. 322 The walls of the bladder were slightly hypertrophied, and there was a small ulcer on the left half of the trigonum.

† **Trigony** (tri·gŏni). *Obs. rare*[−1]. [ad. Gr. τριγονία third generation, f. τρι-, TRI- + γόν-ος, γονή offspring, family, generation.] Threefold generation or production.

**1660** HOWELL *Parly Beasts* 140 Man is that great Amphybium in whom lye Three distinct Souls by way of trigony.

**Trigram** (trəi·græm). [f. Gr. τρι-, TRI- + γράμμα, -ατ-, line, letter, or γραμμή stroke, line.] **a.** An inscription of three letters; also, = TRIGRAPH (Webster 1864). **b.** A figure or character formed of three strokes. **c.** *Geom.*, etc. A set of three lines; *spec.* the figure formed by three straight lines in one plane not intersecting in the same point; also more generally, any figure composed of three elements.

**1606** BIRNIE *Kirk-Buriall* (1833) 17 Inscryving their tombes with a trigram of D. M. S. **1801** J. HAGER *Babylon. Inscr.* 54 What connexion is there between the first trigram, or three united strokes, to represent heaven, and..the second trigram,..three broken ones, to represent the earth? **1882** *Athenæum* 2 Sept. 297/1 The hexagrams..are composed each of a double trigram... The trigrams consist of three lines one above the other. **1897–8** *Ann. Rep. Bur. Amer. Ethnol.* 842 The swastika itself merely represents two superposed trigrams.

So **Trigramma·tic, Trigra·mmic** *adjs.*, consisting of three letters (= TRILITERAL) or sets of letters; **Trigra·mmatism** = TRILITERALISM.

**1834** *Encycl. Brit.* (ed. 7) VIII. 560/1 The trilingual, or rather trigrammatic stone of Rosetta. **1839** DONALDSON *New Cratylus* § 70 (1850) 107 Their apparent [Semitic] trigrammatism, their etymological disintegration, and the tertiary condition in which their oldest remains are found, must be referred to the constant intermixtures, re-unions [etc.]. **1846** WORCESTER, *Trigrammic*, containing three letters. *Thomson.* **1847** WEBSTER, *Trigrammatic*, containing three sets of characters or letters. *Gliddon.*

**Trigraph** (trəi·graf). [f. Gr. τρι-, TRI- + γραφή writing, drawing.] A combination of three letters denoting a simple sound, as *eau* in F. *beau*, *sch* in Ger. *schaf.* **1836** in SMART; hence in later Dicts.

**Trigraphy** (tri·grăfi). *Geom.* [f. after HOMOGRAPHY: see TRI-.] A group of three sets of points or lines having a relation analogous to that of *homography* between two (see HOMOGRAPHY 1); that branch of geometry which deals with such relations. Hence **Trigraphic** (trəigræ·fik) *a.*, pertaining to trigraphy.

**1895** J. W. RUSSELL in *Proc. Lond. Math. Soc.* XXVI. 446 (*title*) Applications of Trigraphy... Trigraphic ranges... A trigraphy projects into a homographic trigraphy. *Ibid.* 448 Given the trigraphic relation, to construct the vague points. *Ibid.* 450 Trigraphic Pencils. *Ibid.* 452 Trigraphic Properties of a Quadric Surface.

**Triguttulate**: see TRI- 1.

‖ **Trigynia** (trəi͵dʒi·niă). *Bot.* [mod.L. (Linnæus), f. TRI- + Gr. γυνή woman, taken as = female organ, pistil.] An order in many classes of the Linnæan System, comprising plants having three pistils. Hence **Tri·gyn,** a plant of the order *Trigynia*; **Trigy·nian, Trigy·nious** *adjs.*, of or belonging to the order *Trigynia*; **Trigynous** (tri·dʒinəs) *a.*, having three pistils.

[**1748** LINNÆUS *Hortus Upsaliensis* 23 Trigynia.] **1760** J. LEE *Introd. Bot.* II. viii. (1765) 92 *Trigynia*, comprehending such Plants as have three Styles. **1775** ASH, *Trigynous*, having three pistils. **1806** GALPINE *Brit. Bot.* 64 Hypericum. ..Fl[owers] trigynous. **1828** WEBSTER, Trigyn..Trigynian. **1846** WORCESTER cites LINDLEY for *Trigyn.* **1860** MAYNE *Expos. Lex.*, *Trigynius, a, um*...*Bot*...trigynious.

**Trihedral** (trəihī·drăl, -he·drăl), *a.* (*sb.*) *Geom.*, *Cryst.*, *Nat. Hist.*, etc. Also **triedral.** [f. Gr. τρι-, TRI- + ἕδρα base + -AL.] Of a solid figure or body: Having three sides or faces (in addition to the base or ends); bounded laterally by three surfaces; triangular in section. *Trihedral angle* or *quoin*, a solid angle formed by three surfaces meeting at a point.

**1789** A. CRAWFORD in *Med. Commun.* II. 355 Obtuse trihedral pyramids. **1812** SIR H. DAVY *Chem. Philos.* 125 Thus 6 particles may compose an octoedron or triedral prism. **1839–47** *Todd's Cycl. Anat.* III. 267/2 The inferior molars are..divided into two triedral portions. **1878** GURNEY *Crystallogr.* 85 The trihedral quoins of the rhombic dodecahedron. **1880** HUXLEY *Crayfish* iii. 116 Each of these joints is trihedral, the outer face being convex; the inner, flat; and the upper concave.

**B.** *sb. Geom.* A trihedral figure; the figure determined by three planes meeting at a point (*Cent. Dict. Suppl.* 1909). Also **Trihe·dron.**

**1828** WEBSTER, *Trihedron*, a figure having three equal sides. **1860** WORCESTER cites DAVIES.

**Trihemeral, -hemiobol**: see TRI- 1, 4 a.

**Trihemimer** (trəi·hĕmi·məɹ). *Anc. Pros.* Usually in Lat. form **trihemi·meris** (also tri͵e-). [ad. mod.L. *trihēmimeris*, ad. Gr. type *τριημιμερής consisting of three halves, f. τρι- + ἡμι- half + μέρ-ος part: cf. HEPHTHEMIMER, PENTHEMIMER.] A group or catalectic colon of three half-feet; esp. as constituting the first part of a hexameter, preceding the cæsura. Hence **Trihemi·meral** *a.*, applied to a cæsura occurring in the middle of the second foot.

**1704** J. HARRIS *Lex. Techn.* I, *Triemimeris*, is a Branch of the Cæsura of a Latine Verse, when after the first Foot of the Verse there remains an odd Syllable, which helps to make the next Foot. **1871** *Public Sch. Lat. Gram.* (1876) 529 The next best form is obtained by uniting with the hephthemimeral cæsura the trihemimeral, in the middle of the second foot. *Ibid.* 550 In both verses the rhythm is helped by the trihemimeris.

**Trihemitone** (trəihe·mitoun). *Mus.* ? *Obs.* [ad. Gr. τριημιτόνιον, f. τρι-, TRI- + ἡμιτόνιον HEMITONE.] An interval of three semitones, or a tone and a semitone; a minor third; esp. that used in the ancient Greek (Pythagorean) scale.

**1694** W. HOLDER *Harmony* (1731) 61, I would..call the greater Third (as the Greeks do) *Ditone*,..and the Third Minor, *Trihemitone*.., as consisting of three half-Tones, (or rather of a Tone and half a Tone). **1746** *Phil. Trans.* XLIV. 268 The Trihemitone of the Ancients falls short of the third Minor by a Comma. **1753** CHAMBERS *Cycl. Supp.* s.v. *Interval*, Trihemitone of the Greek Scale, or deficient third Minor, 32/27,..Third Minor, 6/5,..Trihemitone Major, 4096/3375.

**Tri-hexahedral**: see TRI- 2 b.

† **Tri-hexoctahe·dron.** *Geom. Obs.* In 8 triexocto-. [f. TRI- 2 + HEXOCTAHEDRON.] A solid figure having 18 (= 3 times 6) square and 8 triangular faces.

**1765** KIRBY *Perspective made Easy* (ed. 3) 45.

**Trihilate**: see TRI- 1.

**Trihydrate** (trəi͵həi·drĕ̇t). *Chem.* [f. TRI- 5 a + HYDRATE.] A compound containing three molecules of water combined with an element or radical or with another compound; also, a compound containing three hydroxyl groups, OH, united to an element or radical; e.g. *bismuth trihydrate*, which may be regarded as $Bi_2O_3, 3H_2O$ or as $Bi(OH)_3$. So **Trihydrated** *a.*, combined with three molecules of water.

**1854** SCOFFERN in *Orr's Circ. Sc.*, *Chem.* 374 A crystallized trihydrate of phosphoric acid results. **1868** WATTS *Dict. Chem.* IV. 83 Nitrates..Copper also forms a trihydrated salt, $Cu''N^2O^6.3H^2O$. **1873** — *Fownes' Chem.* (ed 11) 391 The trihydrate is the ordinary gelatinous precipitate obtained by treating solutions of aluminium salts. **1888** MUIR & MORLEY *Watts' Dict. Chem.* I. 145 Aluminium..Trihydrate. ..Occurs native, in hexagonal fibrous crystals, as *gibbsite*, and *hydrargyllite*.

**Trihydric** (trəi͵həi·drik), *a.*[1] *Chem.* [f. TRI- 5 + Gr. ὕδωρ water + -IC.] Containing three hydroxyl groups, OH; thus glycerin or glycerol, $C_3H_5(OH)_3$, is a trihydric alcohol; pyrogallic acid or pyrogallol, $C_6H_3(OH)_3$, is a trihydric phenol.

**1866** FRANKLAND *Lect. Notes* 269 Relations of Glycerin to the Trihydric Acids, Glyceric Acid,..and Tartronic Acid. **1881** FRANKLAND & JAPP *Lect. Notes* (ed. 3) II. 105 Trihydric Alcohols. Glycerin..series. These alcohols contain three semimolecules of hydroxyl. **1900** SMITH *Richter's Org. Chem.* (ed. 3) II. 140 The phenols, like the alcohols, are distinguished as mono-, di-, and trihydric, according to the number of hydroxyl groups which have entered.

**Trihydric,** *a.*[2] *Chem.* = TRIHYDROGEN (which is now preferred).

**1866** ROSCOE *Elem. Chem.* xv. 136 The three atoms of hydrogen in trihydric [*ed.* 1869 trihydrogen] phosphate may be replaced by three different metals. **1887** TIDY *Modern Chem.* (ed. 2) 163.

**Trihydro-** (trəi͵həi·dro). *Chem.* [f. TRI- 5 + Gr. ὑδρο-, combining form of ὕδωρ water: see HYDRO-.] A formative denoting that the compound contains the elements of three molecules of water, $H_2O$, united to the substance designated by the rest of the name; e.g. *trihydrostrychnine*, $C_{21}H_{28}N_2O_5$, which differs from strychnine, $C_{21}H_{22}N_2O_2$, by $3H_2O$.

**1879** *Jrnl. Chem. Soc.* XXXVI. 387 Another basic substance was obtained, *trihydrostrychnine*.

**Trihy·drogen,** *a. Chem.* [TRI- 5 b.] Containing 3 atoms of hydrogen in combination, as *trihydrogen phosphate*, $H_3PO_4$. **1869** [see TRIHYDRIC *a.*[2]].

**Trihypostatic** to **Trijunction**: see TRI- 1, 4.

**Tri-icosane**: see TRICOSANE.

**Tri-iod-, tri-iodo-.** [TRI- 5 c.] A formative analogous to TRIBROM(O-, TRICHLOR(O-, expressing the substitution of three atoms of iodine for hydrogen, as in *tri-iodobenzene*, $C_6H_3I_3$, *tri-iodomethane*, etc.

**Tri-i·odide**: see TRI- 5 a and IODIDE.

† **Trike,** *v. Obs. rare*[−1]. [Derivation obscure. Some conjecture that it is the primitive of *trikel*, TRICKLE *v.*, and meant 'to flow down': cf. TRILL *v.*[2] 3; others that it may be for *strike.*] *intr.* To hang down, descend, fall in a flowing manner.

*a* **1310** in Wright *Lyric P.* (Percy Soc.) 35 Hire gurdel of bete gold is al, Umben hire middel smal, that triketh to the to.

**Tril,** obs. form of TRILL.

† **Trilabe.** *Obs. rare*[−0]. [According to Mayne, 'f. Gr. τρεῖς three + λαβ-εῖν to lay hold on'. Cf. ASTROLABE.] A surgical instrument with three expansible prongs: see quot.

**1860** MAYNE *Expos. Lex.*, *Trilabe*, name of an instrument for extracting foreign bodies of sufficiently moderate size from the bladder through the urethra, having three branches capable of being expanded in the bladder, and then closed on the object to be withdrawn.

**Trilabiate** to **Trilaminate**: see TRI- 1.

† **Trilapse, trelapse,** *a.* and *sb. Sc. Obs.* [f. L. *tri-*, TRI- + *laps-us* pa. pple. fallen, sb. a fall.] **A.** *adj.* That has fallen for the third time into a sin or offence; also said of the offence.

**1593** in *Maitl. Cl. Misc.* I. 56 James Pirrhie trilaps in adultery. **1597** *Ibid.* 128 Hellen Allan..confessis..that the samin fault is trelaps in hir persone. **1600** *Presbyt. Rec. Stirling* in Ferguson *Alex. Hume* (1899) 282 The penalties paid by adulterers and trelaps fornicaturs to be devoted to the reparatione of ye brig of Tullibody. **1651** *Humbie Kirk-sess. Rec.* in *Maitl. Cl. Misc.* I. 440 Declaring her to the session to be trilapse in fornication.

**B.** *sb.* A third lapse or fall (into a sin or offence).

**1651** in *Maitl. Cl. Misc.* I. 441 Isobell Spence entred in sackcloth..to give satisfaction for her trilapse in [= into] fornication. **1725** *Presbyt. Rec.* in Cramond *Ann. Banff* (1893) II. 82 George Barclay had openly confessed his trelapse. **1776** in J. Mill *Diary* (1889) 133 This being a relapse to the woman and a trelapse to the man.

Hence † **Trila·pser** (tre-) *Sc. Obs. rare*⁻¹, one who lapses or falls a third time.

1649 *Rec. Dingwall Presb.* (S. H. S.) 148 Trelapsers in fornication be brought before the Presbyterie.

**Trilarcenous**: see TRI- 2.

† **Trilater**, *a. Obs. rare.* [ad. L. *trilater-us*: see next.] = next.

1570 BILLINGSLEY *Euclid* xvi. xxix. 453 To proue that an octohedron geuen, is tredecuple sesquialter to a trilater equilater pyramis inscribed in it.

**Trilateral** (trəilæ·tĕrăl), *a.* and *sb.* [f. L. *trilater-us* three-sided + -AL. Cf. F. *trilatéral.*]

**A.** *adj.* Contained by three sides; three-sided.

1660 BARROW *Euclid* I. Def. xx, Three sided or Trilateral figures are such as are contained under three right lines. 1788 T. TAYLOR *Proclus* I. 173 Euclid appears to me to have made a separate division into angles and sides, from considering this alone, that every triangle is not also trilateral. 1828 *Hutton's Course Math.* II. 136 The quadrilateral space *EAA'E'* is double the trilateral space *AA'F*. 1875 MERIVALE *Gen. Hist. Rome* xviii. (1877) 102 Two powers now remained to struggle for the dominion of the trilateral island [Sicily].

**B.** *sb.* A three-sided figure; a triangle.

1766 *Compl. Farmer* s. v. *Surveying*, Triangles are figures comprehended under three right lines, and..might be better called trilaterals. 1870 *Observer* 9 Oct., From the canal, round the trilateral of St. Denis, to the Seine about Argenteuil, the Prussian Guards..have their stations. 1885 LEUDESDORF *Cremona's Proj. Geom.* 31 It follows that the triangles (trilaterals) *bcd*, *b'c'd'* are also in perspective.

Hence **Trilatera·lity, Trila·teralness,** the quality of being trilateral; **Trila·terally** *adv.*, in a trilateral form, triangularly.

1837–8 SIR W. HAMILTON *Logic* xi. (1866) I. 208 [A] triangle [is distinguished] from every other class of mathematical figures, by the single character of *trilaterality. 1847 WEBSTER, **Trilaterally*. 1727 BAILEY vol. II, **Trilateralness*, the having three Sides.

**Trilemma** (trəile·mă). [formed after DILEMMA: see TRI-.] A situation, or (in *Logic*) a syllogism, of the nature of a DILEMMA, but involving three alternatives instead of two.

1672 P. HENRY *Diaries & Lett.* 16 Feb. (1882) 250 Wee are put hereby to a Trilemma either to turn flat Independents, or to strike in with yᵉ conformists, or to sit down in former silence. 1690 C. NESSE *O. & N. Test.* I. 375 Joseph..prudently answers the..trilemma, the..three-horned argument. 1725 WATTS *Logic* III. ii. §6 This sort of argument may be..composed of three..members, and may be called a Trilemma. *a* 1860 SEARS (Worcester), We stand in a trilemma, and we must adopt one of three sets of conclusions. 1887 FOWLER *Deductive Logic* v. (ed. 9) 120 We may form a Trilemma, Tetralemma, &c., by increasing the number of antecedents or consequents or both.

**Triles,** obs. f. TRELLIS. **Tri-letter**: see TRI- 1 b.

**Trilineal** (trəili·nĭăl), *a.* (*sb.*) *Geom.* [f. TRI- + post-cl.L. *līneālis* LINEAL.] = next. Also as *sb.* a trilineal figure.

1715 tr. *Gregory's Astron.* I. (1726) I. 45 The infinitely small trilineal Figures. 1807 HUTTON *Course Math.* II. 115 To each add the trilineal *IAE*. 1891 *Pall Mall G.* 20 Oct. 6/1 Dr. Barrett..addressed the students,..he said, 'Never mind about trilineal co-ordinates, go in for music.'

**Trilinear** (trəili·nĭăɹ), *a. Geom.* [f. TRI- + L. *līneāris* LINEAR, f. *līnea* line.] Of, contained by, or having some relation to, three lines (including curved as well as straight lines).

*Trilinear co-ordinates*, a system of co-ordinates determining a point in a plane by its distances, measured in three fixed directions, from three fixed straight lines forming a triangle.

1715 tr. *Gregory's Astron.* III. (1726) I. 379 The trilinear Figure *ALS* is to the whole Ellipse, as the trilinear Figure *AGS* to the whole Circle. 1807 HUTTON *Course Math.* II. 115 The Sector or Trilinear Space contained by an Arc of the Curve and two Radii. 1896 *Yale Univ. Grad. Course Instr.* 70 A course in analytical geometry...It includes the use of determinants and trilinear coördinates.

**Trilineate** (trəili·nĭĕt), *a. Zool.* [f. TRI- + L. *līneāt-us* streaked, striped, f. *līnea* LINE: see -ATE² 2.] Marked with three lines or streaks. So **Trili·neated** *a.*

1802 SHAW *Gen. Zool.* III. 543 Trilineated Snake..marked throughout the whole length by three black lines or narrow stripes..Native of Africa. 1803 *Ibid.* IV. 472 Trilineated Sparus..with the body marked on each side by three longitudinal spotted brown lines. 1891 *Cent. Dict.*, Trilineate.

**Trilingual** (trəili·ŋgwăl), *a.* [f. TRI- + L. *lingua* tongue, after *lingual*; cf. L. *trilinguis* in same sense.] Speaking or using, written or expressed in, or relating to three languages.

1834 *Encycl. Brit.* (ed. 7) VIII. 560/1 The trilingual, or rather trigrammatic stone of Rosetta. 1851 LAYARD *Pop. Acc. Discov. Nineveh* Introd. 13 What are called the Trilingual inscriptions of Persia. 1904 MORLEY in *19th Cent.* Oct. 578 Whatever we may think of..the trilingual heresy [that worship could be offered only in three languages]. 1907 *Athenæum* 7 Dec. 719/1 The literature of England up to the end of the fourteenth century is trilingual, English, Latin, or Anglo-Norman.

**Trili·nguar,** *a. rare.* [f. as prec. + -AR.] **a.** Having, or uttered with, three tongues; three-tongued. **b.** = prec.

1824 *New Monthly Mag.* XI. 424 We have no three-headed dog chained at the gate of Tartarus to startle the visitants by his tri-linguar latrations. 1830 MAUNDER *Dict.*, *Trilinguar*, consisting of three languages.

**Triliteral** (trəili·tĕrăl), *a.* (*sb.*) [f. TRI- + L. *littera* letter + -AL.] Consisting of three letters.

1751 WESLEY *Wks.* (1872) XIV. 150 A [Hebrew] Root is usually triliteral, like פָּעַל [*pāʿal*]. 1869 FARRAR *Fam. Speech* iii. (1873) 88 The root of the Semitic verb is always triliteral, or rather triconsonantic. 1884 H. D. TRAILL in *Macm. Mag.* Oct. 444/1 Ignoramus..may annoy him even more than the triliteral Saxon..'ass'.

**B.** *sb.* A triliteral word or root.

1828 WEBSTER, *Triliteral, sb.*, a word consisting of three letters. 1839 PAULI *Analecta Hebraica* v. 41 Consonants were added to the original bi-literal words, and thus triliterals arose. 1896 W. H. WARD in Hilprecht *Rec. Res. in Bible Lands* 180 The proper names of persons and cities resist the attempt to reduce them to Semitic triliterals or to Aryan roots.

Hence **Trili·teralism,** the use of triliteral roots, as in Semitic languages; **Trilitera·lity** (cf. F. *trilittéralité*), **Trili·teralness,** triliteral character; **Trili·terally** *adv.*

1841 *Fraser's Mag.* XXIII. 484 May not this habit.. account for the Hebrew triliteralism? 1874 SAYCE *Compar. Philol.* ii. 77 The Semitic languages..entirely..built upon the principle of triliteralism. 1875 WHITNEY *Life Lang.* xii. 248 The triliterality of the roots and their inflection by internal change. 1902 GRIFFITH in *Encycl. Brit.* XXVII. 728/1 The triliterality of Old Egyptian.

**Trilith** (trəi·liþ). Orig. (and still often) in Gr. form **trilithon** (trəi·liþǫn). [ad. Gr. τρίλιθον, neut. of τρίλιθος adj., of three stones, f. τρι-, TRI- + λίθος stone; so mod.F. *trilithe*.] A prehistoric structure or monument consisting of three large stones, two upright and one resting upon them as a lintel.

α. 1740 W. STUKELEY *Stonehenge* iv. 22 This *adytum*..is in truth compos'd of certain *compages* of stones, which I shall call *trilithons*, because made, each of two upright stones, with an impost at top. 1881 T. HARDY *What Shepherd Saw* in *Changed Man*, etc. (1913) 190 A Druidical trilithon, consisting of three oblong stones in the form of a doorway. 1904 WINDLE *Rem. Prehist. Age Brit.* 185 An ellipse of hewn sarsen trilithons, with mortise and tenon connections.

β. 1851 D. WILSON *Preh. Ann.* (1863) I. iii. 93 A trilith or complete cromlech, consisting only of three stones. 1852 WRIGHT *Celt, Rom. & Saxon* ii. 59 Stones..arranged in what the French archæologists term triliths. 1867 PEARSON *Hist. Eng.* I. 78 Circles of monoliths or triliths, sometimes surrounding what seems an altar.

**b.** (in form **trilithon**) repr. Gr. τρίλιθον applied to the Jupiter temple at Bálbec, in the wall of which there are three gigantic stones lying end to end.

1847 LEITCH tr. *C. O. Müller's Anc. Art* § 269. 262 Of the trilithon at Balbec there are to be seen stones as much as 60 feet in length. 1881 *Athenæum* 6 Aug. 174/2 She [Mrs. G. Sumner] attributes the trilithon temple of Baalbek.. to those mysterious Phœnician builders.

Hence **Trilithic** (trəili·þik) *a.* (erron. **trilitho·nic**), pertaining to or of the nature of a trilith.

1834 *Gentl. Mag.* Feb. 175 Having what may almost be called the unique trilithonic construction. 1872 LATHAM *Eng. Dict.*, Trilithic.

† **Trill,** *sb.*¹ *Obs. rare.* Also 6 **tryle.** Origin and meaning uncertain.

1558 *Cal. Anc. Rec. Dublin* (1889) 470 Wheare the bouchers of this cittie and ther servaunts dothe contynuallie cut trills out of every hyde,..every person may laufully seise and take..all and every suche tryle as shalbe founde. 1654 in W. M. Myddelton *Chirk Castle Acc.* (1908) 47 For makeinge trills and pullies for the weaver's loome.

**Trill** (tril), *sb.*² Also 8 **tril.** [Goes with TRILL *v.*³; ad. It. *trillo*, beside *triglio*, 'a quaver or warble in singing' (Florio); so F. † *tril, trille.*]

**1.** *Mus.* **a.** A tremulous utterance of a note or notes, as a 'grace' or ornament: = TREMOLO or VIBRATO. **b.** A rapid alternation of two notes a degree apart; a shake.

1649 LOVELACE *Poems* 120 Far lesse be't Æmulation To passe me, or in trill or Tone Like the thin throat of Philomel. 1662 PLAYFORD *Skill Mus.* I. xi. (1674) 47 The Trill..is upon one Note only. 1710 STEELE *Tatler* No. 222 ⁋ 10, I..have attributed many of his [a vocal musician's] Trills and Quavers to the Coldness of the Weather. 1785 BURNS *Cotter's Sat. Night* xiii, The sweetest far of Scotia's holy lays: Compar'd with these, Italian trills are tame. 1801 RANKEN *Hist. France* I. 488 The beats, the trills, the shakes, and accents of the Italians. 1886 *Appleton's Ann. Cycl.* XI. 87 This even and continuous roll [of the canary-notes] is as perfect as the trill of any instrument.

**2.** *transf.* A tremulous high-pitched sound or succession of notes, esp. in the singing of birds.

*a* 1704 T. BROWN *Praise Drunkenness* Wks. 1730 I. 37 The Drunkard's voice is hoarse and manly, not like the squeaking trils of an Eunuch. 1745 WARTON *Inscript. Hermitage* ii, Within my limits lone and still The blackbird pipes in artless trill. 1865 DICKENS *Mut. Fr.* III. xii, There was quite a fresh trill in his voice. 1884 MRS. C. PRAED *Zéro* iv, There was the trill and full chirrup of the chaffinch.

**3.** *Phonetics.* The pronunciation of a consonant, esp. *r*, with vibration of the tongue or other part of the vocal organs; a consonant so pronounced.

1848 A. J. ELLIS *Essentials Phonetics* 50 There may be three trills belonging to this group. *Ibid.* 51 Persons who are unable to execute the trill. 1867 A. M. BELL *Visible Speech* 55 The sign of 'trill'..denotes a vibration of the *uvula*;..of the point of the *tongue*;..of the *lips*. 1877 SWEET *Handbk. Phonetics* § 102 Trills are a special variety of unstopped consonants. 1889 A. J. ELLIS *Early Eng. Pronunc.* 643 Uvular trill.

**Trill,** *sb.*³ *dial.* [Variant of THRILL *sb.*⁴, THILL¹.] The shaft of a cart or wagon. Also *attrib.*

1688 R. HOLME *Armoury* III. 339/2 The Trills, or Sides of the Cart, which the horse is to stand between. *Ibid.* 340/1 The Trill Horse, that next the Cart, and beareth the sides up with a Back band lying on the Trill Sadle. 1726 *Dict. Rust.* (ed. 3) s.v. *Cart*, The Trill-Hooks and Back-band, which holds the Sides of the Cart up to the Horse. 1766 *Compl. Farmer* s.v. *Spiky-roller*, Let the trills be placed just on the middle of each frame. [1905 *Eng. Dial. Dict.*, *Thrill*, recorded from South Cheshire, but now 'less commonly used than formerly'. Also *Thrill-bars, Thrill-gears; Thrill-horse*, or *Thriller*, the shaft-horse.] [Randle Holme, with whom the Dictionary entries begin, was a native of Chester.]

† **Trill,** *sb.*⁴ *Obs.* [Cf. DRILL *sb.*⁴, a furrow.] A hot-air channel in a green-house, etc.; a flue.

1707 MORTIMER *Husb.* (1721) II. 191 One part of it may have Trils made under the Floor to convey warmth from the Stoves made on the back side of the House, the better to preserve it from Cold or Dampness.

**Trill** (tril), *v.*¹ Now *dial.* or *arch.* Forms: 4–6 **tril(le, tryl(le,** 6 **tryll,** 6– **trill.** [ME. *trille*: cf. Sw. and Norw. *trilla*, Da. *trilde, trille*, to roll, trundle, wheel; also EFris. *trullen, trüllen* to roll, turn round. See also TIRL *v.*³]

**1.** *trans.* To turn (a thing) round, to cause to revolve or rotate; = TIRL *v.*³ 1. **a.** To twirl, twiddle, whirl, spin.

*To trill the bones* (slang): to throw the dice with a spinning motion; cf. 'whirl the bones', BONE *sb.* 5 a.

*c* 1386 CHAUCER *Sqr.'s T.* 308 But whan yow list to ryden any where Ye mooten trille [*v. r.* trylle] a pyn stant in his [the brazen horse's] ere. *Ibid.* 313 And whan ye come ther as yow list abyde, Bidde hym descende, and trille [*v. rr.* tryl, -le, tril] another pyn. 1530 PALSGR. 762/1, I tryll a whirlygyg rounde aboute, *je pirouette*...I tryll, *je jecte*. 1547 SALESBURY *Welsh Dict.*, *Troi whirligwgan*, tryll a whyrlygyg. *c* 1550 R. WEVER *Lusty Juventus* D iij, I wyll trill the bones while I haue one grote. 1570 LEVINS *Manip.* 123/43 To Tril, *circumuertere*. 1616 J. LANE *Cont. Sqr.'s T.* IV. 417 So taught her how to trill the pinn in th'eare, Which th'horse, at willes quicke call, heard anie wheare. 1873 WILLIAMS & JONES *Somerset. Gloss.*, *Trill*, to twirl. 1885 BURTON *Arab. Nts.* (1887) III. 141. Thereupon the Prince trilled the pin.

**b.** To roll, bowl, trundle (a ball, a hoop, etc.); to move (a thing) on wheels or castors. Also *fig.*

1408 CLIFTON tr. *Vegetius' De Re Milit.* IV. xvii. (MS. Digby 233, lf. 220 b/2) Þese toures mot haue crafty whelus Imaad to trille hem liȝtliche to þe walles. *c* 1440 *Promp. Parv.* 502/2 Tryllyn, or trollyn, *volvo*, Cath. 1542 UDALL *Erasm. Apoph.* 42 b, Eris..had trilled along the table a golden apple. *c* 1572 GASCOIGNE *Fruites Warre* lxvii, As fortune trilles the ball. 1642 HOWELL *For. Trav.* (Arb.) 29 As wise as he, who carried the coach-wheele upon his back, when he might have trilled it before him all along. 1650 — *Giraffi's Rev. Naples* I. 91 The huge concourse of people..which were so thick, that one might have trill'd a bal upon their heads. 1673–4 ALLESTREE *Let.* 7 Jan. in Fox Bourne *Locke* (1876) I. vi. 321, I had acknowledged the receipt of yours..long since, had I not been trilled on in a constant expectation of being [etc.]. 1905 in *Eng. Dial. Dict.* s.v., (E. Kent) There now, let me see how nicely you can trill your hoop.

† **2.** *intr.* Of a wheel, ball, etc.: To revolve, spin, roll, trundle. *Obs.*

1531 ELYOT *Gov.* I. xxvii, If it [tennis-ball] trille fast on the grounde. 1681 RYCAUT tr. *Gracian's Critick* 142 Sometimes it [the ball] was tossed so high, that it was out of sight, anon so low..it bounded and trilled on the ground.

Hence **Tri·lling** *vbl. sb.*

*c* 1410 LOVE *Bonavent. Mirr.* xviii. (1908) 112 As we mowe see alday many men and wommen berynge bedes with trillynge on the fyngres and waggynge the lippes, bot the siȝt caste to vanytees.

**Trill,** *v.*² *arch.* Forms: 4–6 **trylle,** 4–7 **trille,** (? 5 **tryle**), 6–7 **tril,** 6– **trill.** [Perh. a distinct sense-development of prec. But cf. the synonymous DRILL *v.*²; also Ger. *trillen* 'to flow whirling or rolling', cited by Grimm from a 17th c. writer, and taken by him as a form of *drillen* to turn.]

**1.** *intr.* Of tears, water, a stream: To roll, to flow in a slender stream, the particles of water being in constant revolution, with a more continuous motion than is expressed by *trickle*; to purl. (Sometimes (as in quot. 1613) including the notion of musical sound, as in TRILL *v.*³)

13.. *St. Erkenwolde* 322 in Horstm. *Altengl. Leg.* (1881) 273 Teres trilled adoun & one þe toumbe lightene. *c* 1386 CHAUCER *Sompn. T.* 156 (Harl. MS.) With many a teere trilling [*v. rr.* triklyng, trynkelynge] on my cheeke. *a* 1541 WYATT *Poems, Compar. Love to Stream*, From these hie hilles as when a spring doth fall, It trilleth downe with still and suttle course. 1613 W. BROWNE *Brit. Past.* I. v, Two springs arise and delicately trill In gentle chidings through an humble dale. 1667 DRYDEN & DAVENANT *Tempest* II. iv, A cold sweat trills down o'er all my limbs. 1769 *De Foe's Tour Gt. Brit.* I. 230 Water, which trills through Marble Troughs, one below another. 1815 SCOTT *Guy M.* xxii, A little dell, through which trilled a small rivulet.

**b.** *intr.* To flow or run with thrilling effect. (Perh. meant for THRILL *v.*¹ 4 b.)

1740 SOMERVILLE *Hobbinol* I. 71 What Extasies of Joy Trill'd through thy Veins, when..they strok'd thy grizly Beard.

**2.** *trans.* To cause to flow in this way. † *Trill off*, to drain off, drink up (*obs.*).

*c* 1485 *E. E. Misc.* (Warton Cl.) 65 One truth let ever thi tong tryle. 1589 NASHE *Almond for Parrat* 12 b, A boule of Beere..you tooke..from before him, and trilled it off without anie more bones. 1591 SYLVESTER *Du Bartas* I. v. 825 The other [Pelican]..Tears her own bowells, trilleth-out her blood To heal her young. 1649 G. DANIEL *Trinarch.* To Rdr. 55 The Pumpe of Witt..trills a Coppie, that the Spunges may Lick vp what he hath Squeez'd. 1867

Aug. J. E. Wilson *Vashti* xxv, When I have trilled a fortune into that abhorred vacuum, my pocket, I shall go down to the Tigris, and catch the mate to Tobias' fish.

† 3. *intr.* To fall or hang down in a flowing manner; to stream, trail. *Obs.*

*a* 1400 *Sir Beues* (E.) 1665 Hys heere tryllyd doun too hys ffoote. *c* 1440 *Brut* 462 A bawdrik of gold aboute his neck, trillyng doun behynde hym. 1609 Bp. W. Barlow *Answ. Nameless Cath.* 11 His Picture drawn with two ropes about his neck, and his bowels (like an other Iudas) trilling downe his body.

Hence **Tri·lling** *vbl. sb.* and *ppl. a.*

1567 Turberv. *Pyndara's Answ. to Tymetes* Epit., etc. 27 Not shed my trilling teares vpon thy moisted face? 1582 Stanyhurst *Æneis* ii. (Arb.) 43 Tears with trilling shal bayne my phisnomye deepelye. 1637 B. Jonson *Sad Sheph.* ii. ii, Twa trilland Brooks, each (from his Spring) doth meet. 1665 Hooke *Microgr.* xx. 129 The droppings or trillings of Lapidescent waters in Vaults under ground. 1713 Steele *Guard.* No. 50 ⁋ 2 The trilling of rivulets.

**Trill**, *v.*$^3$ [Appears *c* 1667, ad. It. *trillare*, in Florio 1611 also *trigliare* (not in 1598), 'to quaver or warble in singing', cognate with *triglio*, *trillo*: see Trill *sb.*$^2$ (It. *trillare* is usually referred to a German source: cf. Trill *v.*$^4$)]

1. *intr.* To sing with vibratory effect; to sing a trill or shake, to 'shake'; of a voice, etc.: To sound with tremulous vibration.

1666–7 Pepys *Diary* 7 Feb., My wife..proud that she shall come to trill, and..I think she will. 1667 *Ibid.* 7 Sept., I did tell him of my intention to learn to trill. 1841 D'Israeli *Amen. Lit.* (1867) 402 This consonance trills in the simple carol of the African women. 1856 Capern *Poems* (ed. 2) 54 And music trilled o'er moor and mead. 1884 *St. James' Gaz.* 29 May 6/2 At least four nightingales.. trilling in whole-hearted chorus.

2. *trans.* To utter or sing (a note, tune, etc.) with tremulous vibration of sound.

*a* 1701 Sedley *Poet. Pieces* Wks. 1722 II. 15 The Nightingale her mournful Story trills In yonder Hawthorn Shade. 1727–46 Thomson *Summer* 746 The sober suited songstress trills her lay. 1810 Scott *Lady of L.* iv. xxiv, So blithely he trilled the lowland lay. 1840 Dickens *Old C. Shop* xv, The lark trilled out her happy song. 1860 Gosse *Rom. Nat. Hist.* 28 Like that charming bird-voice, it was beautifully trilled or shaken. 1862 Miss Braddon *Lady Audley* ix, Sitting down to the piano to trill out a ballad.

b. To cause (an instrument or the voice) to vibrate with a tremulous sound.

1848 Dickens *Dombey* iii, The man who trilled the little bell of the Dutch clock as he went along. 1848 A. J. Ellis *Essentials Phonetics* 49 The tongue assumes precisely the same position as for *s*, but the tip is now trilled.

3. To pronounce (a consonant, esp. *r*) with a vibration of the tongue (or other vocal organ) and the corresponding auditory effect; = Roll *v.*$^2$ 4 c.

1848 A. J. Ellis *Essentials Phonetics* 95 To show that the *r* is..trilled. 1873 J. A. H. Murray *Dial. S. Co. Scotl.* 120 R is in Scotch..in all positions trilled sharply with the point of the tongue. 1887 *Pronunc. Latin* (Camb. Philol. Soc.) 5 Trilled 'r' as in French (or Scotch): more strongly trilled than in English 'Opera', 'herring'.

Hence **Trilled** (trild) *ppl. a.*, **Tri·lling** *vbl. sb.* and *ppl. a.*; whence **Tri·llingly** *adv.*, in a trilling manner, with trilling; also **Tri·ller**, one who trills.

*a* 1700 Dryden (Todd), Am I call'd upon the grave debate, To judge of trilling notes and tripping feet? 1749 Fielding *Tom Jones* v. x, The sweet trilling of a murmuring stream. 1753 *Scots Mag.* XV. 40/2 Ye angels, catch the trilling sound. 1848 A. J. Ellis *Essentials Phonetics* 68 *Veer-ing, car-ing* [etc.] lose their trilled..*r*. 1854 Bushnan in *Circ. Sc.* (*c* 1865) I. 292/2 Its song is composed of several strains, each consisting of trilling and warbling notes variously modulated. 1873 T. L. K. Oliphant *Sources Stand. Eng.* 323 A triller of Italian trills must be known as a vocalist. 1887 Trilled [see sense 3]. 1887 *Eng. Illustr. Mag.* Sept. 779 As many finches, singing trillingly. 1888 Sweet *Eng. Sounds* 25 We have, lastly, the trilling of open consonants [especially English and German r]. 1894 *Outing* (U. S.) XXIV. 230/2, I had failed to subsist on the manna of the Covenanters or a high-trilled Te Deum.

† **Trill**, *v.*$^4$ *Obs. rare.* [Etymology obscure. Cf. MDu. *trillen*, *drillen* to move to and fro, vibrate, vacillate, Du. *trillen* to shiver, shake, EFris. *trillen* to shake or rock from side to side.] *trans.* To rock (a cradle).

*c* 1425 *Fest. of Ch.* viii. in *Holy Rood* (E.E.T.S.) App. 213 ȝit myȝt þe mylde may amon Her cradel trille to and fro, And syng, Osye, thi song!

**Trill**: see Tirl *v.*$^3$ (senses 1 b, 3).

† **Trilla·do.** *Obs. rare.* [f. Trill *sb.*$^2$ + -ado.] A trilling or trill in music.

1721 D'Urfey *Operas*, etc., Pref., Equal with the buzzing and squeaking Trilladoes of the Italian.

**Trilles**, obs. form of Trellis.

**Trillet** (tri·lėt). [f. Trill *sb.*$^2$ + -let (? -et).] A little or tiny trill; in quot. *fig.*

1878 Lanier *To mocking-bird* 1 Trillets of humor,—shrewdest whistle-wit.

**Trillibub** (tri·libɒb). *Obs.* exc. *dial.* Forms: 6 trylly-, trylybubbe, 7 trilla-, 6–9 trillibub; 6 trully-, trullibub(be, 7– trullibub. Cf. Trollibobs, -bags. [Origin obscure.] Chiefly (now always) *pl.*: Entrails, the inwards of an animal.

Often in the alliterative collocation *tripes and trillibubs*.

1519 Horman *Vulg.* 155 b, Let vs haue trypis, chetterlyngis, and tryllybubbys ynough [*aulicoctia ad satietatem*]. 1542 Boorde *Dyetary* xvii. (1870) 276 All the inwardes of beestes and of fowles, as the..trypes, and trylybubbes. 1599 Massinger, etc. *Old Law* iii. ii, I hope my guts will hold, and that's e'en all A gentleman can look for of such trillibubs. 1785 Grose *Dict. Vulg. T.*, *Tripes and trullibubs*, the entrails, also a jeering appellation for a fat man. 1823 Moor *Suffolk Words*, *Trullibubs*, a low coarse term among butchers for the entrails generally of animals. 1883 *Hampsh. Gloss.*, *Trullibubs*, the intestines.

b. Applied to a person or animal. (See also *Eng. Dial. Dict.* s. v. *trolly-bags*.)

1600 Dekker *Gentle Craft* iv, Run wife, bid your maids, your trullibubs, make ready my fine mens breakfasts. 1614 B. Jonson *Bart. Fair* i. iii, There cannot be an ancient Tripe or Trillibub i' the Towne, but thou art straight nosing it. 1785 [see above].

† c. In alliterative collocation *tricks and trillibubs*. In quot. 1632, *trilly bubkins* is a nonce diminutive. *Obs.*

1632 Brome *Novella* i. ii, Such Curles, such Purles, such Tricks and Trilly bubkins As Mayds would turne no Mayds almost to see 'hem! 1637 Shirley *Hyde Park* iii. ii, I forgive thee, and forget thy tricks And trillabubs...Wenches must have their ways.

† **Trilli·l**, *adv. Obs.* Also tri-, trylill, trill-lill. [A kind of onomatopœic prolongation of Trill *v.*$^2$] With the sound of flowing liquid. Hence † **Trillil** *v.*, to drink with a trilling sound.

*a* 1592 Greene *Jas. IV*, Wks. (Rtldg.) 202 O Sir the wine runs trillill down his throat. 1599 Nashe *Lenten Stuffe* 40 Whereas in wodden Mazers, and Agathocles earthen stuffe, they trillild it off before. 1600 *Look About You* ix. C ij b, We'll drinke trylill, Ifaith. 1609 Dekker *Ravens Alm.* B ij b, Amongst gentlemen that haue full pursses and those that crie trilill, let the world slide. 1635 Heywood *Philocoth.* 55 He that cryes trill-lill boyes, is a Rhetoritian.

**Trilling** (tri·liŋ), *sb.* [= Da., Sw. *trilling*, Norw. *trinnling*, Du. *drieling*, Ger. *drilling* triplet, f. Tri- + -ling.] One of a set of three. a. One of three children born at the same birth; a triplet. b. *Min.* A crystal composed of three individuals.

1846 Worcester, *Trilling*, one of three children born at the same birth. *For. Q. Rev.* 1864 in Webster (citing Wright). 1896 Chester *Dict. Min.*, *Tridymite*,..f. τρίδυμος, 'triplet', because often found in trillings.

**Trilling**, *vbl. sb.* and *ppl. a.*: see Trill *v.*$^{1-3}$.

**Trillion** (tri·lyən). [= F. *trillion* (N. Chuquet, *c* 1484), It. *trillione*, from the stem of *million* with substitution of *tri-*: cf. *billion*.] The third power of a million; a million billions, i. e. millions of millions. (In France and local U.S., a thousand 'billions', i. e. an English billion: see Billion.)

The terms *billion, trillion, quadrillion*, etc., up to *nonillion*, are explained by N. Chuquet, in his *Triparty de la Science des Nombres* (lf. 2 r) printed in *Bullettino di Bibliografia e di Storia delle Scienze Matematiche* XIII. 593 (Roma 1880); also in the *Arismetique* of Ét. de la Roche, 1520. Both of these early writers explain *billion, trillion*, etc. as successive powers of a million, the trillion being the third power of a million, 'a million of millions of millions', as always used in England. According to Littré, it was only in the middle of the 17th c. that the erroneous custom was established of dividing series of figures above a million into groups of three, and calling a thousand millions a billion, and a million millions a trillion, an entire perversion of the nomenclature of Chuquet and De la Roche, an error unfortunately followed by some in the United States.

1690 Locke *Hum. Und.* ii. xvi. § 6 [see Billion]. 1696 Jeake *Arith.* 14 Others..call..the nineteenth place Trillion. 1706 W. Jones *Syn. Palmar. Matheseos* 8 Then the 3d. Point from Units stands under Trillions. 1802 in *Spirit Pub. Jrnls.* VI. 337 He wished also to purchase the words billions, trillions, and quadrillions, in order to make his constituents comprehend the immensity of their burdens, and the profundity of his arithmetic. 1806 Hutton *Course Math.* (1810) I. 5 Millions of millions, or bi-millions, contracted to billions, millions of millions of millions, or tri-millions, contracted to trillions. 1867 Denison *Astron. without Math.* 226 You will find the tons in..the earth [to be] 5842 with 18 cyphers after it or 5842 trillions of tons.

Hence **Trillionaire** (trilyənēə·ɹ) [after *millionaire*], one possessing property worth a trillion of pounds, dollars, or other standard coin.

1873 M. Collins *Miranda* I. 194 The trillionaire might turn patriot and pay the National Debt without feeling it. 1886 *Tinsley's Mag.* Oct. 323 A few trillionaires and struggling persons of that description.

**Trillionth** (tri·lyənþ), *a.* and *sb.* [f. prec. + -th.] a. *adj.* The ordinal adjective corresponding to 'trillion'. b. *sb.* One part out of a trillion.

1848 *Fraser's Mag.* XXXVII. 647 The millionth of a grain is a common dose; and a trillionth, octillionth, even a decillionth, very usual ones. 1851 Ruskin *Sheepfolds* 16 The seven-millionth or trillionth of its collective evidence.

‖ **Trillium** (tri·liǒm). *Bot.* [mod.L. (Linnæus, 1753), in allusion to the triple leaves.] A genus (chiefly North American) of perennial endogenous herbs (N.O. *Trilliaceæ*, formerly referred to *Smilaceæ*) bearing a whorl of three thin short-stalked or stalkless leaves at the summit of a simple stem, with a solitary flower in the middle. In America also called *wake-robin*. Also, a plant of this genus.

1760 J. Lee *Introd. Bot.* (1788) 300 *Trillium*, Herb True-love of Canada. 1846 *Penny Cycl., Supp.*, Trillium. 1873 'Susan Coolidge' *What Katy Did at Sch.* vii, Each walk ..ended in some delightful discovery, trilliums, dog-tooth violets, apple-trees in blossom, or wild strawberries turning red. 1885 Gatty *Juliana H. Ewing* iii. 48 Trilliums are amongst the North American plants which have lately become fashionable. 1904 Farrer *Gard. Asia* 162 Tangles of bamboo, illuminated by the snowy stars of trillium.

‖ **Trillo** (tri·lo). [It. (Florio, 1611), f. *trillare*, Trill *v.*$^3$] A shake or quaver· = Trill *sb.*$^2$

1651 Stanley *Poems* 201 Nightingales their trillo practise here. 1656 Blount *Glossogr.*, *Trillo*,..an excellent grace in singing; being an uniform trembling or shaking of the same Note. 1661 Pepys *Diary* 30 June, Myself humming to myself the trillo, and found by use that it do come upon me. 1721 D'Urfey *Two Queens Brentford* iv. i, The Relish and Story in't shall vie with all the Opera Trillo's in Europe. 1815 *Hist. J. Decastro* I. 232 A trillo from Old Comical threw her into convulsions.

b. *transf.* and *fig.*

1672 W. de Britaine *Interest Eng. in Dutch War* 25 My Genius never prompted me to the least Trillo of Grandeur. 1713 Addison *Guard.* No. 124 ⁋ 8 To dream On mossy pillows, by the trilloes Of a gentle purling stream.

**Trill-trill**, *sb.* and *v.* Reduplication of Trill *sb.*$^2$ and *v.*$^3$, representing a repeated or continued trill or trilling. So also **Trill-rill** *int.*

1849 Cupples *Green Hand* xv, You heard a low, half-smothered, small sound, deeper down, as it were, fill up the break with its throbbing and trill-trilling, as if just *one* land-cricket or a grasshopper did it. 1859 Cornwallis *New World* I. 160 The trill trill of many a gaudy plumaged tenant of the woods. 1903 *Academy* 21 Feb. 186/2, I heard the thrush to-day..'Trill-rill!' he kept on trilling.

**Tri·lobal**, *a. rare*$^{-1}$. [f. mod.L. *trilob-us* three-lobed + -al.] = next.

1884 *Athenæum* 5 July 21/1 Trilobal are the windows, each lobe..counterchanged of three, like the Tresham shield.

**Trilobate** (trəi·lobeˈt, trəilōᵘ·bėˈt), *a. Nat. Hist.* [f. Tri- + mod.L. *lobātus*: see Lobate.] Having or consisting of three lobes, three-lobed.

1785 Martyn *Rousseau's Bot.* xviii. 260 A trilobate capsule, of three valves and three cells. 1803 Shaw *Gen. Zool.* IV. 487 Trilobate Labrus [a fish] size of a Carp..native of the African seas. 1806 Galpine *Brit. Bot.* 61 Alchemilla... L[eaves] flat, trilobate, incised. 1877 Coues *Fur Anim.* ix. 274 The exterior pair [of incisors] are..obscurely trilobate.

So **Tri·loba·ted** *a.* = *trilobate*; **Triloba·tion**, trilobate condition; **Trilo·be** *v.*, *trans.* to divide into three lobes; **Trilobed** (-lōᵘbd) *a.* = *trilobate*.

1775 Ash, *Trilobated, having three lobes. 1890 *Amer. Jrnl. Archæol.* VI. 594 Pointed windows..trilobated or with elaborate tracery. 1872 Nicholson *Palæont.* 161 In some cases..this *trilobation is only obscurely marked. 1826 Kirby & Sp. *Entomol.* xxx. III. 114 [The head] is *trilobed, each lateral lobe being divided into three smaller ones. 1872 Nicholson *Palæont.* 160 Order Trilobita.—Crustaceans in which the body is usually more or less distinctly trilobed.

**Trilobite** (trəi·lobəit, tri·-). *Palæont.* [ad. mod.L. *Trilobītes* (Walch, 1771), f. Gr. τρι-, Tri- + λόβ-ος lobe (of the ear, etc.) + -ite$^1$.] A member of a large group of extinct arthropodous animals, characterized by a three-lobed body; allied to the extinct Eurypterids and the existing King-crabs (*Limulus*), and like them of doubtful affinity, having been usually classed as crustaceans, sometimes as arachnids; their remains are found abundantly in Palæozoic rocks, esp. the Silurian.

1832 J. Green *Monogr. Trilobites N. Amer.* 14 The fossil remains of the trilobite family. 1833 Lyell *Princ. Geol.* III. 195 A limestone, containing trilobites and other fossils of our mountain and transition limestones. 1842 H. Miller *O. R. Sandst.* ix. (ed. 2) 209 The Trilobite has a wide geological range, extending from the upper Cambrian rocks to the upper Coal Measures. 1860 *All Year Round* No. 50. 563 A creature called a Trilobite, very much like an immense woodlouse. 1873 Dawson *Earth & Man* iii. 44 The body was composed of numerous segments, each divided transversely into three lobes, whence they have received the name of Trilobites. *attrib.* 1854 Murchison *Siluria* ix. 194 The trilobite-flags of Builth.

Hence **Trilobitic** (-i·tik) *a.*, pertaining to, of the nature of, or containing trilobites.

1839 *Civil Eng. & Arch. Jrnl.* II. 148/2 Until we come to trilobitic schist. 1872 W. S. Symonds *Rec. Rocks* iii. 51 The absence of the trilobitic genus, Olenus, from the Menevian group. 1875 Croll *Climate & T.* xviii. 294 Those strange trilobitic-looking fishes of that era.

† **Tri·lobous**, *a. Obs. rare.* [f. mod.L. *trilob-us* three-lobed + -ous.] = Trilobate.

1753 Chambers *Cycl. Supp.* s. v. *Leaf*, *Trilobous Leaf*, one divided into three lobes.

**Trilocular** (trəilǫ·kiŭlăɹ), *a. Nat. Hist.* [f. Tri- + L. *locul-us* small receptacle, dim. of *locus* place + -ar$^1$.] Having three cells or compartments, as the capsule of a plant, or the heart of a reptile. Also **Trilo·culate** *a.* (*Cent. Dict.* 1891).

1753 Chambers *Cycl. Supp.*, *Capsule*,..sometimes contains only one cell or cavity, sometimes more;..called *unilocular*; ..*bilocular*, *trilocular*. 1785 Martyn *Rousseau's Bot.* xvi. (1794) 185 Ipomæa has..a trilocular capsule. 1845 Lindley *Sch. Bot.* i. (1858) 16 [The pistil] is either *bilocular*, *trilocular*, *multilocular*, or otherwise. 1861 Hulme tr. *Moquin-Tandon* ii. ii. 54 Amphibia... Their heart, trilocular or bilocular.

**Trilogical** (trəi-, trilǫ·dʒikăl), *a.*$^1$ [f. Trilogy + -ical.] Of or pertaining to a trilogy. So **Trilo·gic** *a.*; **Trilogist** (tri·lŏdʒist), the author of a trilogy.

1866 Felton *Anc. & Mod. Gr.* I. i. xi. 201 The trilogical form appears to have been an enlargement of the original tragic outline. 1889 Haigh *Attic Theatre* 22 In it the trilogic form of composition is brought to the highest perfection. 1913 *Daily News* 8 Aug. 7/1 Mr. Onions is the first of the English trilogists to consummate his undertaking.

**Tri-logical** (trəi,lǫ·dʒikăl), *a.*$^2$ *rare.* [f. Tri- 1 + Logical.] Relating to or dealing with three subjects of discourse.

1836–7 Sir W. Hamilton *Metaph.* xli. (1870) II. 416 Kant ..was the philosopher to whom we owe this tri-logical classification [of mental phenomena into knowledge, feelings, will].

**Trilogue** (trəi·lǫg). [f. TRI- + Gr. λόγος word, discourse.] A group of three words or sayings (cf. next, 3), as the Welsh triads.

1834 MEDWIN *Angler in Wales* I. 283 These trilogues or triads..are easily retained in the memory.

**Trilogy** (tri·lŏdʒi). [ad. Gr. τριλογία (see def. 1), f. τρι-, TRI- + λόγος discourse: see -LOGY. Cf. F. *trilogie*.]

**1.** *Gr. Antiq.* A series of three tragedies (originally connected in subject), performed at Athens at the festival of Dionysus.

1836 THIRLWALL *Greece* III. xviii. 73 A trilogy, which comprised three distinct tragedies. 1842 BRANDE *Dict. Sc.* etc., s. v., All the plays of Æschylus, and the Henry VI of Shakspeare, are examples of a trilogy. 1850 GROTE *Greece* II. lxvii. (1862) VI. 25 To three serious dramas or a trilogy.. the tragic poet added a fourth or satyrical drama.

**2.** Any series or group of three related dramatic or other literary works.

1661 BLOUNT *Glossogr.* (ed. 2), *Trilogie*,..a speaking or writing in three parts. 1820 T. MITCHELL *Aristoph.* I. p. cxxvi, That immortal Trilogy of Plato, which has been embalmed by the tears of all ages. 1841 TRENCH *Parables* xxii. (1877) 376 These parables are thus a trilogy. 1875 JOWETT *Plato* (ed. 2) III. 679 The other great Platonic trilogy of the Sophist, Statesman, Philosopher. 1877 DOWDEN *Shaks. Prim.* vi. 90 The trilogy consisting of I and II Henry IV and Henry V.

**3.** *transf.* and *fig.* A group of three related utterances, sayings, subjects, etc.

1835 T. MITCHELL *Aristoph., Acharn.* 249 *note*, What Theophrastus evidently intended for a trilogy of characters, ..each rising above the other in want of shame and an absence of decency. 1837 CARLYLE *Fr. Rev.* III. I. v, Thus they three, in wondrous trilogy, or triple soliloquy. 1879 FARRAR *St. Paul* I. 581 *note*, His fundamental trilogy of Christian virtues—faith, hope, love.

**Trilophodont** to **Triluminous**: see TRI- 1.

**Trim** (trim), *sb.* Also 6–7 **trym, trimme**, 7–8 **trimm.** [f. TRIM *v.*]

I. Nautical senses.

**1.** The state of being trimmed or prepared for sailing; esp. the condition of being 'fully rigged and ready to sail' (Onions *Shaks. Gloss.*).

1590 SHAKS. *Com. Err.* IV. i. 90 The ship is in her trim, the merrie winde Blowes faire from land. *c* 1595 CAPT. WYATT *R. Dudley's Voy. W. Ind.* (Hakl. Soc.) 59 Our good shipp beinge putt in her best trym..Captaine Jobson caused the collers..to be advanced in the topps, poope and shrowdes of our shipp. 1628 DIGBY *Voy. Medit.* (Camden) 36, I found my shippe to be in perfect good trimme. 1874 BURNAND *My Time* xxix. 279 Their yacht..was kept in trim all the year round. 1878 BESANT & RICE *Celia's Arb.* xii, Don't let the boy think the vessel has got out of trim after all these years.

**2. a.** The most advantageous set of a ship in the water on her fore and aft line; also with qualification, as *good, better, best, bad trim.* **b.** Adjustment of the sails with reference to the direction of the wind and the ship's course. **c.** The condition of being properly balanced. **d.** The difference between the draught forward and the draught aft (cf. TRIM *v.* 13).

1614 GORGES *Lucan* III. 111 Of any ship to find the trimme, In wrought seas how she best might swimme. 1674 PETTY *Disc. Dupl. Proportion* 28 Different Velocities, arising from the different Trim of the same Ship,..the best Trim being that which makes least resistance. 1704 J. HARRIS *Lex. Techn.* I, *Trimm of a Ship*, is her best Posture, Proportion of Ballast, and hanging of her Masts, &c. for Sailing;..to find the best way of making any Ship to Sail swiftly, is called finding her Trim. 1748 *Anson's Voy.* Introd. 10 The discovery of her most eligible position in the water (usually stiled her Trim). 1764 REID *Inquiry* vi. § 22 A ship requires a different trim for every variation of the direction and strength of the wind. 1769 FALCONER *Dict. Marine* (1789), *Out of Trim*, the state of a ship when she is not properly balanced for the purposes of navigation. 1793 SMEATON *Edystone L.* § 170 They must..always be in sailing trim. 1839 *Civil Eng. & Arch. Jrnl.* II. 323/1 To preserve the trim of the ship, by keeping the centre of gravity in its proper position. *a* 1845 HOOD *Pain in Pleas.-Boat* 5 Bill, shift them bags of ballast aft—she's rather out of trim! 1867 SMYTH *Sailor's Word-bk.*, *Trim*, the set of a ship on the water, whether by the head or the stern, or on an even keel. It is by the disposition of the ballast, cargo, masts, and other weight which she carries, that a vessel is best adapted for navigation... *Trim of the hold*, the arrangement of the cargo, &c., by which a vessel carries sail well [etc.].

**e.** In vague non-technical use, The general appearance or look of a ship: cf. 3.

1757 GRAY *Bard* 73 In gallant trim the gilded Vessel goes. 1837 DISRAELI *Venetia* VI. ii, I cannot exactly make out its trim; it scarcely seems a merchant vessel.

II. General senses.

**3.** Adornment, array; equipment, outfit; dress: usually in reference to style or appearance; hence sometimes nearly = guise, aspect.

1596 SHAKS. 1 *Hen. IV*, IV. i. 113 They come like Sacrifices in their trimme. 1623 MASSINGER *Bondman* I. i, I'd court Bellona in her horrid trim As if she were a mistress. *a* 1646 VISCT. FALKLAND *Marr. Night* I. (1664) B ij b, A brave and Courtly Girle: has trim and dazle enough of white and red, to attract the eye. 1798 WORDSW. *Idiot Boy* xviii, She sees him in his travelling trim. 1818 SCOTT *Br. Lamm.* xxxii, Bucklaw, in bridegroom trim. 1838–9 FR. A. KEMBLE *Resid. in Georgia* (1868) 58 The Sunday trim of the poor people. *fig.* 1637 HEYLIN *Antid. Lincoln.* Pref. A j b, One that conjectured of the house by the trimme or dresse, would thinke it very richly furnished. 1646 G. DANIEL *Poems* Wks. (Grosart) I. 38 The Earth doth now begin To flourish, in her Sweet and glorious Trimme. 1650 T. VAUGHAN *Anthroposophia* 65, I would not have Thee look here for the Paint, and Trim of Retorick. 1784 COWPER *Task* III. 357 Nature in her cultivated trim Dressed to his taste, inviting him abroad.

†**b.** *The trim*: the prevailing mode; the fashion. *Obs. rare.*

1603 DANIEL *Def. Ryme* F v, Being now the trym, and fashion of the times, to sute a man otherwise cannot but giue a touch of singularity. 1628 FORD *Lover's Mel.* I. iii, Not like a lady of the trim. 1638 — *Fancies* IV. i, Is't possible? why, you are turned a mistress, A mistress of the trim.

†**c.** with *a* and *pl.* A piece of personal adornment, an ornament; a style of dress or array; also *fig. Obs.*

1579–80 NORTH *Plutarch* (1676) 228 For her Purple Gowns, or for other such pretty fine trims of Gold, as women use to wear. 1647 WARD *Simp. Cobler* (1843) 25 If I see a trimme, far trimmer than she that weares it. 1675 PENN *Eng. Pres. Interest* i, Civil Affairs..may be peaceably transacted under the different Liveries, or Trims of Religion.

**d.** The act of trimming or condition of being trimmed (cf. TRIM *v.* 9).

1608 ROWLANDS *Humors Looking Glasse* 4 Many antique faces passe, From Barbers chaire vnto his glasse, There to beholde their kinde of trim. *Mod. colloq.* The barber will give you a trim.

†**e.** = TRIMMING *vbl. sb.* 2 a. *Obs.*

1665 SIR T. HERBERT *Trav.* (1677) 143 The gold..that was laid..upon the trim of Vests, was..in as perfect lustre as if it had been but newly done.

**f.** The dressings of a house; 'the visible woodwork, as the base-boards, door and window-casings, etc.' (*Cent. Dict.*). *U.S.*

1884 *N. York Even. Post* 14 Apr. (Cent. D.), No wood having been used in construction except for floors, doors, and trim. 1885 HOWELLS *Silas Lapham* (1891) II. 54 The trim of the doors and windows was in light green and the panels in salmon.

**4.** Condition, state, or order, esp. for work or action of any kind: usually qualified by an adj. (Now the chief general sense.)

1628 FELTHAM *Resolves* II. [I.] xlv. 132 If we looke vpon him, in another trimme of the minde: how smooth hee is. 1666 G. ALSOP *Maryland* Ded., I am so my self, and the world, as far as I can perceive, is not much out of the same trim. 1749 SMOLLETT *Gil Blas* XI. xiv, They had almost dined, and consequently were in a trim for disputing. 1782 COWPER *Gilpin* 162 The Calender, amazed to see His neighbour in such trim. 1803 WELLINGTON in Gurw. *Desp.* (1837) I. 476, I am in good marching trim. 1856 KANE *Arct. Expl.* II. i. 9, I can hardly keep my charts..in any thing like decent trim. 1882 ROXBURGH in Jean L. Watson *R. S. Candlish* ii. 25 Matters were at length in trim for my settlement. 1891 *Field* 7 Mar. 344/2 With the excellent present trim of the water, and fish feeding, anglers should take advantage of the few days left.

**b.** Hence *in* (†*the*) *trim, into* (*to*) *trim*, in or into proper condition or order.

1827 SCOTT *Napoleon* lxv, Soldiers whose hearts were in the trim. 1828 — *F. M. Perth* iii, One of your hermits that..brings himself to trim by fasting and penance. 1879 RUSKIN *Hortus Inclusus* lvi. (1887) 68 [My] eyes, head, feet, and fingers, all fairly in trim. 1886 HUXLEY in *Life & Lett.* (1900) II. viii. 129, I will give him a dose of that remedy when once I get into trim. 1890 'R. BOLDREWOOD' *Col. Reformer* (1891) 179 The barque was empty and the whaling gear in trim.

**5.** (orig. *fig.* from 2.) The nature, character, or manner of a person or thing; his or its 'way'.

1706 E. WARD *Wooden World Diss.* (1708) 31 Those that knew his Trim, us'd to load him well with Ale and Salmon. 1771 T. HULL *Sir W. Harrington* (1797) III. 53 Our brother ..never is ten minutes in the company of a woman without finding what he calls the trim of her. 1787 BECKFORD *Italy* (1834) II. 22 That I allow; but such, you know, is my trim and I cannot help it. 1818 SCOTT *Hrt. Midl.* xxxvii[i], His wife knows his trim, and I have not the least doubt that the matter is quite certain. 1824 R. STUART *Hist. Steam Engine* 206 The water which is heated under a great pressure..is forced into [that] in the common boiler, and heats it to any degree suited to the nature or trim of the engine.

**Trim,** *a.* (*adv.*) Forms: 6– **trim**; also 6 *Sc.* **trume, trvme; trym, trymme, tryme;** 6–7 **trimme,** 7 **trimm, trimn.** [History obscure. OE. had an adj. *trum*, 'firm, stable, strong, sound, robust' (not known in the cognate langs.); whence also in prehistoric time the vb. *trum-jan, OE. *trymman*, TRIM *v.* No example of *trum* is known after OE. times, but the negatives *untrum* infirm and *untrumnesse* infirmity survived to *c* 1200–1225. Afterwards, like TRIM *v.*, the adj. disappears till after 1500. The modern adj. *trim* does not answer in form, nor directly in sense, to *trum*; but in both it goes with the verb. It would appear therefore to be a deriv. of the verb (or, if both came down in ME., to have been conformed to the verb).]

In many early quotations it is difficult or impossible to infer the exact shade of meaning intended. Cf. TRIG *a.*

**1.** In good condition or order; well prepared, furnished, or equipped; fit, competent, proper, suitable; hence, sound, good, excellent, fine, beautiful. (Often a vague term of approval.)

1503–13 [implied in TRIMLY *adv.* 1]. *c* 1530 H. RHODES *Bk. Nurture* 504 Better is it to beate a prowde man then for to rebuke him, For he thinkes in his owne conceyte he is wyse and very trim. 1567 DRANT *Horace, Art Poetry* A iv, For the sage ryghte seriouse wordes be trim. 1577 HOLINSHED *Chron.* II. 992/2, xl great carreuelles, and thirtene trymme Barques throughly furnished and appoynted with good mariners and men of warre. 1583 *Leg. Bp. St. Androis* 879 Ane burges man..Having a trvme schop in the toun. *a* 1585 POLWART *Flyting w. Montgomerie* 551 (Harl. MS.) The blaired bucke and bystour..Hes right trume [*v.r.* trim] teathe, somwhat sett in a thrawe. 1588 SHAKS. *Tit. A.* V. i. 96 'Twas trim sport for them that had the doing of it. 1590 SPENSER *F. Q.* III. i. 36 Fragrant violets, and Paunces trim. *Ibid.* 40 Sweet birdes..Ay caroling of love and jollity, That wonder was to heare their trim consort. 1636 JAMES *Iter Lanc.* (Chetham Soc.) 6 Gilbert Stone, being for y^e^ time a trimme man of his penne. 1725 POPE *Odyss.* IV. 1032 The vessel rides,..In all her tackle trim to quit the shore. 1817 BYRON *Beppo* xcvi, The ship was trim.

†**b.** (?) Firm. (But perh. sense 1.) *Obs.*

1549 COVERDALE, etc. *Erasm. Par. Jas.* i. 28 It taketh no rote in a briery place, ne in marice, nether in the sande..but it requireth a pure, a trymme, and a substauncial grounde. 1565 W. ALLEN in Fulke *Confut. Purg.* (1577) 449 Doe you not see here a trimme faith and a substantiall?

**2.** Neatly or smartly made, prepared, or arranged; elegantly or finely arrayed, dressed, or 'got up'; having a neat, spruce, or tidy appearance or effect. **a.** Of things: chiefly in sense 'neat, properly made and properly kept'; † formerly sometimes of dress, smart, pretty, beautiful.

*c* 1521 J. CLERK *to Wolsey* in Ellis *Orig. Lett.* Ser. III. I. 258, ij bokys..coverd with clothe off gold..the porteur, fascio[un] and tryme deckyng of the said bokis. 1542 UDALL *Erasm. Apoph.* 246 b, Fillyng vp as trymme as a trencher y^e^ space that stood voide. 1567 *Gude & Godlie B.* (S.T.S.) 37 Ze [= ȝe] set on schone vpone his feit, The quhilk are trim and wounder meit. 1574 tr. *Marlorat's Apocalips* 37 This place of Paradise was better furnished and trimmer than other places. 1675 HOBBES *Odyssey* 232, I him gave a purple double vest, A sword, and coat edged with fringes trim. 1717 BERKELEY *Tour Italy* Wks. 1871 IV. 537 Laurel hedges, but not so trim as ours. 1740 SOMERVILLE *Hobbinol* I. 150 See with what Pomp The gaudy Bands advance in trim Array. 1771 PENNANT *Tour Scotl. in 1769*, 31 The gardens are..trim to the highest degree. 1789 MME. D'ARBLAY *Diary* 21 Aug., Captain Molloy's large boat..was very trim and neat, and had all its rowers new dressed. 1840 DICKENS *Barn. Rudge* xxiii, Mr. Chester..completely attired..in the trimmest fashion of the day. 1849 MACAULAY *Hist. Eng.* ii. I. 201 The large and stately mansions, the trim villas. 1886 RUSKIN *Præterita* I. v. 168 The houses on each side with trim stone pathways up to them.

**b.** Of persons (rarely animals): Neat, 'trig', comely; neatly, smartly, or † finely dressed or adorned.

1548 UDALL, etc. *Erasm. Par. Matt.* vii. 50 The swyne is not the trymmer for the precious stones. 1552 HULOET, Trymme, *bellulus, a, um*; loke in trycke...Trymme wenche gorgiously decked, *phalerata fœmina.* 1650 BULWER *Anthropomet.* 155 These paintings..whereby the said women think themselves more trim and beautiful. 1681 W. ROBERTSON *Phraseol. Gen.* 1247/1 A very trim woman, *cultissima fœmina.* 1877 MAR. M. GRANT *Sun-maid* ii, He was rested from his long journey, trim, brushed, and polished. 1888 ANNA K. GREEN *Behind Closed Doors* iv, A trim and quiet girl came tripping to the door.

†**c.** 'Tight' (?), elegantly-shaped, well-made, handsome, good-looking. *Obs.*

1568 T. HOWELL *Newe Sonets* (1879) 146 So streight, so square, so trym was he, So fayre of forme, so wyse, so sage. 1578 LYTE *Dodoens* II. i. 148 Iupiter..turned her into a trim heaffer. 1600 J. PORY tr. *Leo's Africa* VIII. 304 In the day-time he shall see none but trim and beautifull women. 1635 BROME *Sparagus Gard.* II. ii, I warrant you, he is a trim youth? 1649 G. DANIEL *Trinarch., Rich. II* lxxviii, The Trimmest fellowes of this Regiment Envie'd the Gentry.

†**3.** In ironical use: cf. 'fine', 'nice', 'pretty', in similar use. *Obs.*

1569 J. SANFORD tr. *Agrippa's Van. Artes* 14 b, They.. haue spoken of nothinge but trimme trifles. 1573 G. HARVEY *Letter-Bk.* (Camden) 9 Here was stuf gud plenti to furnish up a trim tragedi. 1581 J. BELL *Haddon's Answ. Osor.* 66 Hath hee not made a trimme speake agaynst us? *a* 1586 SIDNEY *Arcadia* (1622) 370 A trim purchase you haue made of your owne shame. 1611 BEAUM. & FL. *Maid's Trag.* II. ii, And there's Another of 'em, a trim cheating souldier, I'le maul that Rascal. 1634 HEYWOOD & BROME *Witches Lanc.* III. Wks. 1874 IV. 217 O you are a trim mother are you not? 1680 OTWAY *Ca. Marius* IV. i, News quotha? Trim News truly.

**4.** In parasynthetic combinations.

1873 B. HARTE *Fiddletown*, etc., *D. Varden* 87 Trim-bodiced, bright-eyed, roguish-lipped. 1840 DICKENS *Old C. Shop* xv, Then came the trim-hedged fields on either hand.

**B.** *adv.* †**1.** = TRIMLY 1. *Obs.*

*c* 1540 J. REDFORD *Mor. Play Wit and Sc.* (Shaks. Soc.) 37 His toong servth him now trym. 1549–62 STERNHOLD & H. *Ps.* xxxv. 26 Let not their hartes reioyce and cry, There, there, this geare goeth trim. 1573 TUSSER *Husb.* (1878) 11 He plainly taught how good from naught may trim be tride. *c* 1613 MIDDLETON *No Wit like Woman's* V. i, Now the bells they go trim, they go trim.

**2.** = TRIMLY 2.

1529 *Supplic. to King* (E.E.T.S.) 49 Tryme decked horses, to ryde..lyke a lorde. 1590 SPENSER *F. Q.* II. vi. 2 A litle Gondelay, bedecked trim With boughes and arbours woven cunningly. 1594, 1615 Trick and trim [see TRICK *adv.* 2]. 1742 COLLINS *Ode Manners* 17 Like a bride, so trim array'd.

**3.** *Comb.*, as *trim-cut, -dressed, -kept*, etc., adjs.

1813 SCOTT *Trierm.* II. v, Sick of flower and trim-dress'd tree, Long for rough glades, and forest free. 1861 THACKERAY *Four Georges* i. (1862) 23 The trim-cut forest vistas. 1873 MISS BROUGHTON *Nancy* III. 9 The little trim-swept drive. 1889 J. K. JEROME *Three Men in Boat* 77 The trim-kept villas on the other side.

**Trim** (trim), *v.* Infl. **trimmed, -ing.** Forms: (1 **trymman, trymian, treman**), 6 **trymme, tryme,** (**treme**), **trym,** 6–7 **trimme,** 6– **trim,** (7 **trime**). [The existing senses of this verb begin early in the 16th c. Before 1550 the word had become exceedingly common in nearly all its chief senses. OE. had a verb *trymman* or *trymian* :—**trumjan* to make firm or strong, strengthen, confirm, set (a force) in array, settle, arrange, etc., f. OE. *trum* adj. firm, strong, sound, steadfast, stable, etc. So far as the *form* is concerned, *trymman, trymian* would naturally become *trym, trim* by 1500; the *sense* 'make fit, make ready, prepare, fit out' might also arise out of the OE. The difficulty is that not one certain example of the verb in any sense is known during the Middle English period, and that it comes upon the scene in the 16th c., like a new word, quickly laid hold of to supply many needs. But as no other source is known, it is generally held that *trim* is identical with the OE. *trymman*, and that the verb (perh. along with TRIM *a.*), must have been preserved in spoken use, or in some dialect, for four centuries, without appearing in the extant literature.

OE. had also the compounds *ȝetrymman* to confirm, strengthen, encourage, also intr. (for refl.) to grow strong, gain or recover strength, and *betrymian* to beset with a force, besiege, environ, with 3 examples as late as *c* 1225 (see BITRUM); *Genesis & Exodus*, *c* 1250, has also two instances of a vb. *trim-en* to 'be pregnant, conceive', or perhaps to 'give birth'; but none of these show any approach to the modern senses. The OE. senses and that in *Gen. & Ex.* are here prefixed as possibly bearing upon the later history.]

**I.** (Only OE.) †**1.** *trans.* To make firm or strong; to strengthen, confirm; to give as security; to arm or array (a force); to settle, arrange; to encourage, comfort, exhort.

*a* 800 *Cædmon's Gen.* 276 (Gr.) Þæt he west and norð wyrcean ongunne, trymede ȝetimbro. *a* 800 *O. E. Chron.* an. 430 Þæt he hiera ȝeleafan trymede. *c* 840 in Kemble *Cod. Dipl.* II. 5 Ic Berhtwulf..ðas mine ȝesaldnisse trymme and fæstna in Cristes rode tacne. *c* 893 K. ÆLFRED *Oros.* IV. x. § 2 Þæs on merȝen Hannibal ȝefor to þære byriȝ, & beforan ðæm ȝeate his folc ȝetrymede, þe mon haett Collina...Ac hie hie butan þæm ȝeate anȝean Hannibal trymedon. *c* 897 — *Gregory's Past. C.* xv. 88 Ne ȝe ðone weall ne trymedon ymb hiera hus on ðæm dæȝe þe him niððearf wæs. *c* 950 *Lindisf. Gosp.* John v. 31 ȝif ic cyðnisse ic trymmo [*perhibeo*] of mec. 971 *Blickl. Hom.* 91 Men ȝehyraþ myccle stefne on heofenum swylce þær man fyrde trymme & samniȝe. *a* 1000 *Ags. Ps.* (Th.) ciii. 15 Hlaf trymeð heortan mannes. 10.. *O. E. Chron.* an. 1052 Hi..ȝeræddon þæt man tremede gislas on æȝðer healfe.

[†**b.** (Early ME.) *intr.* To become pregnant, conceive; ? to bring forth. *Obs.* (Perhaps does not belong to this word.)

*c* 1250 *Gen. & Ex.* 1024 Bi ðan sal sarra selðe timen, Ðat ȝ[h]e sal of a sune trimen. *Ibid.* 1198 Ȝhe wurd wið child, on elde wac, And trimede and clepede it ysaac.]

**II.** (Mod.Eng.) †**2.** To put into proper condition for some purpose or use; to prepare, make ready; to dress; to get (land) into condition for cropping, to till; to cultivate (a tree). *Obs.*

1517 TORKINGTON *Pilgr.* (1884) 55 The bestys that we rode vpon, [were] ryght weke and ryght simple, and evyll trymed to Jorney with. 1523 LD. BERNERS *Froiss.* I. lix. 80 He raysed an engyn in yᵉ Castell, the which was not very great, but he trymmed it to a poynt [*orig.* lattrempa bien et apoint]. 1578 LYTE *Dodoens* VI. xxvii. 692 In Brabant..the Corriers and Leather dressers .. do trimme and dresse Leather like Spanishe skinnes. 1593 SHAKS. *Rich. II*, III. iv. 56 He had not so trim'd And drest his Land, as we this Garden. 1645 in W. M. Williams *Ann. Founders' Co.* (1867) 98 Thomas Embry .. did trim and make up Brass Works for persons not free of the Company. 1725 DE FOE *Voy. round World* (1840) 71 Casks..which their coopers assisted us to trim, season and fit up.

**3.** To fit out (a ship, etc.) for sea. *arch.* *spec.* † To caulk, clean, and dress a ship's bottom: see quot. 1711 (*obs.*).

*c* 1513 E. HOWARD in Ellis *Orig. Lett.* Ser. III. I. 147 Ther be redy..at c. shippes of warre..they be very well trymmed and will not faill to comme owte and fight with us. 1525–6 in Ellis *Orig. Lett.* Ser. II. I. 221 Our..Sovereyn Lorde shall within fewe yerys loose his seyd Shypps..except they be new kalkyd and trymmyd. 1542 *Lam. & Piteous Treat.* in *Harl. Misc.* (Malh.) I. 235 Seuen galleyes stronge and well trymmed. 1585 T. WASHINGTON tr. *Nicholay's Voy.* I. viii, The Arsenal,..into which are hayled vppe and trymmed the gallies and other vessels. 1613 SHAKS. *Hen. VIII*, I. ii. 80 As rau'nous Fishes doe a Vessell follow That is new trim'd. 1711 W. SUTHERLAND *Shipbuild. Assist.* 165 To *trim* a Ship; to load and equip her, and put her into a condition for Sailing; also to calk, clean, and dress a Ship, and do any small matter in repairing her. 1850 BLACKIE *Æschylus* II. 258 Xerxes..Trimmed vain fleets for thy undoing.

†**4.** To put (something broken, worn, or decayed) into good condition or working order; to repair, restore, put right. *Obs.*

*c* 1520 *Mem. Ripon* (Surtees) III. 204 Will'mo Caruer tremyng dorythes & lokes & alias. 1548 UDALL, etc. *Erasm. Par. Mark* i. 14 Who were also trymmyng and mendyng theyr nettes. 1569 SPARKE *Sir J. Hawkins' 2nd Voy.* (Hakl. Soc.) 11 He trimmed the maine mast of the *Iesus*, which in the storme aforesaid was sprung. *a* 1628 PRESTON *Breastpl. Love* (1631) 114 Your soules need to be trimmed every morning as well as the body. 1633 MUNDAY *Stow's Surv.* 905 The repairing and trimming of this Church..was in the yeere of our Lord God 1600. *a* 1687 PETTY *Treat. Naval Philos.* I. ii, All the forementioned Incurvations are to be trimmed and repaired by reconciled lines.

**5.** *spec.* To put (a lamp, fire, etc.) into proper order for burning, by removing any deposit or ash, and adding fresh fuel; also, to cleanse or cut level (a wick); by extension, to renew the burned-out carbons or electrodes of (an arc lamp). Also *fig.*

1557 N. T. (Genev.) *Matt.* xxv. 7 Then all those virgins arose, & trymmed their lampes [So *Rhem.* (1582) & 1611; WYCLIF (1382) anourneden, (1388) araieden; TINDALE (1526), COVERDALE (1535), *Great* (1539), *Bishops'* (1568) prepared]. *a* 1701 MAUNDRELL *Journ. Jerus.* (1732) 71 The dayly employment of these Recluses is to trim the lamps. 1764 GOLDSM. *Trav.* 14 Where cheerful guests retire To pause from toil, and trim their evening fire. 1794 MRS. RADCLIFFE *Myst. Udolpho* xxvi, He stopped for a moment to trim the torch. 1819 WIFFEN *Aonian Hours* (1820) 134 Vesper has trimmed up his lamp for the night. 1902 SLOANE *Stand. Electr. Dict.* App., *Trimming*, the renewal of the carbons in an arc lamp.

†**6.** To provide or furnish *with* what is necessary for the purpose in view; to equip, supply. *Obs.*

1523 WOLSEY in *St. Papers Hen. VIII*, VI. 188, 50,000 souldeours largely and plenteously furnished eskipped and trymmed. 1552 HULOET, Trymme a gardeyn wyth beddes. 1552–3 in Feuillerat *Revels Edw. VI* (1914) 93 Cupid shalbe a letell boy howe mvst be tremmed with a bow and arrows blinfelde. 1557 N. T. (Genev.) *Luke* xxii. 12 Then he shal shewe you a great hie chamber trimmed [1611 furnished]. 1630 J. LEVETT *Ord. Bees* (1634) 20 Do you not usually dresse and trim your hives with some hony, or other sweet liquor, before you put any swarm into them? 1667 PEPYS *Diary* 20 July, And..is married to him that is new come, and hath new trimmed the house.

**7.** To array, dress (const. *in* or *with* something); to make comely, adorn, dress *up* (also with *out*).

*c* 1516–21 DK. BUCKHM. *to Wolsey* in Ellis *Orig. Lett.* Ser. III. I. 216 He dowtid that I was not soo well trymmed as I wolde desir to be. 1525 LD. BERNERS *Froiss.* II. ccxlvii. [ccxliii.] 759 All the armorers in London were sette a worke to trymme men in their harnesse for the iustes. 1557 N. T. (Genev.) *Rev.* xxi. 2 That holy citie..prepared as a bryde trymmed for her housbande. 1604 T. WRIGHT *Passions* v. § I. 151 Salomon..exhorteth vs..not to looke vpon a woman trimmed and decked vp. 1697 DRYDEN *Virg. Georg.* III. 734 The Victim Ox..Trim'd with white Ribbons, and with Garlands drest. 1756 W. DODD *Fasting* (ed. 2) 10 To be deck'd and trimm'd out..in the pride of dress. 1903 N. MUNRO in *Blackw. Mag.* Jan. 81/1 She hastened to trim herself before the moon revealed her.

**8.** *spec.* To decorate (a hat, garment, etc.) with ribbons, laces, feathers, flowers, braids, embroideries, or the like, so as to give it a finished appearance; also, of a thing, to form the trimming of. Also *fig.*

1547 in Feuillerat *Revels Edward VI* (1914) 11, vj Black vellett Cappes..trymyd with damaske golde & Syluer. 1581 SIDNEY *Apol. Poetrie* (Arb.) 59 And who readeth Plutarchs eyther historie or philosophy, shall finde, hee trymmeth both theyr garments, with gards of Poesie. 1793 MME. D'ARBLAY *Let.* May, Miss Kitty trimmed up her best cap, and tried [it] on. 1796 JANE AUSTEN *Pride & Prej.* xxix, When I have bought some prettier-coloured satin to trim it with fresh. 1859 *Habits Gd. Soc.* iv. (new ed.) 184 Her dress was white, trimmed down on either side with single roses. 1859 W. COLLINS *Q. of Hearts* iii, Trimmed with white braid.

**9.** To dress (the hair or beard); to clip (the hair), or to clip the hair of (a person); sometimes, to shave (a person); also, to dub (a cock).

1530 PALSGR. 762/2, I trymme, as a man dothe his heare or his busshe...Trymme my busshe, barber, for I intende to go amongest Ladyes to day. 1592 LYLY *Midas* III. ii, How sir will you be trimmed? wil you haue your beard like a spade, or a bodkin? 1607 *Nottingham Rec.* IV. 283 We present the barbr..for triming men in serves tyme vppon the Sabott Daye. 1611 BIBLE 2 *Sam.* xix. 24 And Mephibosheth..had neither dressed his feete, nor trimmed his beard [COVERDALE (1535) combde, *Great* (1539) shauen, *Geneva* (1560), *Bishops'* (1568) dressed], nor washed his clothes. *a* 1625 in Strutt *Sports & Past.* (1801) III. vii. § 20 A dunghill cock, neatly cut and trimmed for the battle. 1652 in *Verney Mem.* (1907) I. 485 The Razors and Sizars hee Trimmed withall. 1748 SMOLLETT *Rod. Rand.* lxiv, I sent for another barber and suffered myself to be trimmed. 1856 R. W. PROCTER *Barber's Shop* xxi. (1883) 203 The era of the flying barbers, when shops were few, and gentlefolk were trimmed at home. *fig.* 1600 *Dr. Dodypoll* v. ii. in Bullen *O. Pl.* III. 158 The Marchant I perceive hath trimde you, Doctor, And comb'd you smoothlie.

**10.** *fig.* To beat, thrash, trounce; also, to reprimand, reprove, upbraid, scold (cf. 'to give one a dressing').

App. at first an ironical use of sense 2, but afterwards often with allusion to 8, 9 or other sense: cf. the colloq. phr. *to trim one's jacket*, and the ironical use of DRESS *v.* 9, ARRAY *v.* 10. With quots. *a* 1518, 1638, cf. TRIM-TRAM *sb.*

*a* 1518 SKELTON *Magnyf.* 2234 Tushe! these maters..are but soppys in ale; Your trymynge and tramynge by me must be tangyd. *c* 1550 R. WEVER *Lusty Juventus* D j, Tell me .. who it was, And I wyl trim the knaue, by the blessed masse. 1638 FORD *Fancies* III. iii, *Sec.* My razor shall be my weapon, my razor. *Spa.* Why, has not come to the honour of a beard yet; he needs no shaving. *Sec.* I will trim him and tram him. 1748 SMOLLETT *Rod. Random* iii, None of your jaw, you swab,..else I shall trim your lac'd jacket for you. 1822 SCOTT *Nigel* xxxiii, Some that remember..how I trimmed them about the story of hearkening behind the arras. 1882 *Mrs. Raven's Tempt.* I. 232 Mrs. Raven stood trimming Worsfold and his wife about harbouring the woman.

**11.** To cut off the excrescences or irregularities of; to reduce to a regular shape by doing this. Also with the part removed as object. In quot. 1879 *absol.* Also with *up*. Also *fig.*

1594 CAREW *Huarte's Exam. Wits* ix. (1596) 120 A wodden chest knobby and nothing trimmed on the outside. 1664 EVELYN *Kal. Hort.*, *Feb.* 60 Trim up your Palisade Hedges, and Espaliers. 1761 CHURCHILL *Apol.* Poems 1763 I. 72 See tortur'd Reason how they pare and trim And like Procrustes, stretch or lop the limb. 1879 BROWNING *Ivan Ivan.* 36 His axe now trimmed and toyed With branch and twig. 1885 *Law Times* LXXIX. 187/2 The farmer has.. no inclination..to trim the roadside hedges. 1891 *Labour Commission Gloss.*, *Trimming castings*, the operation of trimming off with chisel and file the 'runners', i.e. rough edges of metal castings. 1893 J. A. HODGES *Elem. Photogr.* (1907) 105 The manner in which it [a print] has been trimmed and mounted.

**b.** *transf.* See quots.

1895 *Funk's Standard Dict.*, *To trim the shore*, to follow the shore-outline: said of fish. 1901 *Blackw. Mag.* Nov. 692/2 They [migrating birds] always 'trim' the shore—that is pass close over the headlands.

**12.** *Carpentry.* To bring (a piece of timber, etc.) to the required shape; *spec. to trim in*, to fit or frame (one piece) to or into another; cf. TRIMMER 4, *trimming-joist* (TRIMMING *vbl. sb.* 7).

1679 MOXON *Mech. Exerc.* ix. 153 This Newel serves also for a Post to Trim the Stair-Case too. 1703 T. N. *City & C. Purchaser* 268 When Workmen fit a piece into other Work, they say they trim in a piece. 1833 LOUDON *Encycl. Archit.* § 83 The whole properly trimmed (framed round, leaving a clear opening,) to the chimney shafts. 1842–76 GWILT *Encycl. Archit.* Gloss. s. v., A piece of workmanship fitted between others previously executed, which is then said to be *trimmed in* between them.

**13.** *Naut.* To distribute the load of (a ship or boat) so that she floats on an even keel; in quot. 1580, to steady, as with cargo or ballast.

*To be trimmed* (so much) *by the head* (or *stern*), to be built or laden so as to draw (so much) more water at the bows than at the stern (or the reverse).

1580 H. SMITH in Hakluyt *Voy.* (1598) I. 448 With all hands she did lighten her sterne, and trimme her head. 1627 CAPT. SMITH *Seaman's Gram.* vi. 27 Trim the Boat is to keepe her straight. 1668 CULPEPPER & COLE *Barthol. Anat.* I. ix. 18 That so the Body may be equally as it were poised, and ballanced, or trimmed, as the Watermen speak of their boats. *c* 1720 PRIOR *Bibo & Charon* 5 Trim the boat, and sit quiet, stern Charon replied. 1800 *Local Act* 39 & 40 *Geo. III*, c. x § 42 The Lighter trimmed so as to make the same swim at equal Marks at the Stem and Stern thereof. 1820 SCORESBY *Acc. Arctic Reg.* II. 475 For the purpose of trimming the ship more by the stern.

**b.** *intr.* (for *refl.* or *pass.*) of a ship or boat.

1861 HUGHES *Tom Brown at Oxf.* ii, While he had been sitting quiet and merely paddling,..the boat had trimmed well enough. 1889 WELCH *Naval Archit.* i. 7 When the excess draft is aft,..the vessel is said to trim by the stern.

**c.** *transf.* To adjust (the balance) so as to equalize it.

1817 JAS. MILL *Brit. India* II. v. i. 338 How easily the balance among those powers might have been trimmed. 1840 THIRLWALL *Greece* VII. liii. 23 The only way to secure the Macedonian ascendancy.., was to trim the balance of power. 1864 COBDEN *Speeches* (1878) 492, I wanted to trim the scales to prevent there being an undue preponderance in favour of the other side.

**14.** *Naut.* To adjust (the sails or yards) with reference to the direction of the wind and the course of the ship, so as to obtain the greatest advantage. Const. *to*.

*To trim by* or *on a wind*, to set the sails so as to sail as nearly as possible against the direction of the wind: see BY A. 9, B. 1 d. *To trim full* or *sharp*: see FULL A. 11, SHARP *adv.* 2.

1624 CAPT. SMITH *Virginia* II. 24 Nor had we a Mariner nor any had skill to trim the sayles. 1627 — *Seaman's Gram.* ix. 42 All your Sheats, Brases, and Tackes are trimmed by a winde. 1667 DRYDEN & DAVENANT *Tempest* I. i, Trim her right before the wind. 1669 STURMY *Mariner's Mag.* I. ii. 17 Thus have you all the Sails trimm'd sharp, full, and by a Wind. 1697 *Lond. Gaz.* No. 3315/1, I crouded Sail to Leeward to him, trimming my Sails on a Wind tho' I went before it. 1748 *Anson's Voy.* III. v. 342 That which was the stern of the proa, now becomes the head, and she is trimmed on the other tack. 1836 H. ROGERS *J. Howe* i. (1863) 8 The..dexterous pilot..will trim his sails to every variation of wind. 1899 F. T. BULLEN *Log Sea-waif* 336 A little south-easterly breeze sprang up, to which we trimmed the yards.

**b.** *absol.* or *intr.* Also *fig.*

1697 DAMPIER *Voy.* (1729) I. 145 Next Morning we again trimm'd sharp, and made the best of our way to the *Lobos de la Mar*. 1706 E. WARD *Wooden World Diss.* (1708) 21 If the Wind and Tide of Affairs prove too violent, he then certainly trims about. 1833 R. MUDIE *Brit. Birds* (1841) I. 110 The kite feels the first action of the revolving air as if it were a breeze, trims to it, and is borne upward in a spiral. 1857 C. GRIBBLE in *Merc. Marine Mag.* (1858) V. 9 Trimmed on the starboard tack, and made all possible sail.

**c.** *transf.* and *fig.* To turn, adjust, adapt.

1779 COWPER *Pineapple & Bee* 12 Having wasted half the day, He trimmed his flight another way. 1821 SCOTT *Kenilw.* xxxiv, He could scarce have missed shipwreck, knowing..so little how to trim his sails to a court gale. 1847 EMERSON *Poems* (1857) 187 As the bird trims her to the gale, I trim myself to the storm of time. 1898 *Allbutt's Syst. Med.* V. 958 We must trim our treatment according to the phases and peculiarities of the individual.

**15.** To stow or arrange (coal or cargo) in the hold of a ship, or carry it to the hatches when discharging; also to shift (coal) in a ship's hold, etc.; also, to arrange (coal) as it is loaded on a truck. Cf. *coal-trimmer* (COAL *sb.* 16).

1797 BAILEY & CULLEY *Agric. Northumberld.* 7 Trimming 2s. 6d. keelman's beer 1s. 4d. per chaldron. 1828 JOPLIN *Views Currency* 14 Corn can be warehoused at Hull, and trimmed and turned for about 2s. per quarter per annum. 1838 *Civil Eng. & Arch. Jrnl.* I. 397/1 The coals cannot be trimmed in the ships so fast. 1884 *Manch. Guard.* 24 Jan. 5/1 The cargo was properly stowed and trimmed. 1886 J. BARROWMAN *Sc. Mining Terms* 68 To *Trim*, to arrange by hand the coals on a truck while being loaded.

16. *intr.* (also with *it*). To modify one's attitude in order to stand well with opposite parties; to move cautiously, or 'balance' between two alternative interests, positions, opinions, etc.; also, to accommodate oneself to the mood of the times.

1685 SOUTH *Serm.* (1697) I. 456 Gross, fulsome juggling with their Duty, and a kind of Trimming it between God and the Devil. 1687 DRYDEN *Hind & P.* III. 666 [Non-resistance] A passive term which..trims betwixt a rebell and a king. *a* 1700 B. E. *Dict. Cant. Crew*, *To Trim*, to hold fair with both sides. 1766 EARL MARCH in Jesse *Selwyn & Contemp.* (1843) II. 67 Lord Mansfield trimmed in his usual manner, and avoided declaring his opinion. 1888 BURGON *Lives 12 Gd. Men* II. ix. 217 Nothing knew he..of a disposition to trim with the times.

†**b.** *trans. Trim away*: To waste (time) in indecision. *Obs. rare.*

1687 DRYDEN *Hind & P.* III. 501 He who heard what every fool could say Would never fix his thoughts, but trim his time away.

**c.** *trans.* To modify according to expediency.

1885 *Daily Tel.* 6 Nov. (Cassell), Lord Hartington is not the sort of statesman to trim his opinions according to the expediency of conciliating or not conciliating.

Hence **Trimmed** (trimd) *ppl. a.*; in sense 8 often as the second element in an instrumental combination, as *blue-*, *ermine-*, *flower-*, *gold-*, *lace-trimmed*, etc.: see also these words.

*c* 1532 DU WES *Introd. Fr.* in *Palsgr.* 922 A goodly lady meke, trymmed, *dame gaillarde, benigne, cointe.* 1649 in *Verney Mem.* (1907) I. 448 A paire of French trimed gloves. 1892 *Photogr. Ann.* II. 57 To mark the mount at each corner of the trimmed print.

**Trimachy** (tri·măki, trəi·-). *rare.* [f. Gr. τρι-, TRI- + -μαχία, μάχη fight, battle, combat.] **a.** A series of three battles. **b.** 'A contest among three' (*Cent. Dict. Suppl.* 1909).

1887 F. M. CRAWFORD *Saracinesca* i, Count Bismarck had only just brought to a successful termination the first part of his trimachy; Sadowa and Sedan were yet unfought.

**Trimacular** (trəimæ·kiŭlăɹ), *a. Nat. Hist.* [f. TRI- + L. *macula* spot + -AR [1].] Having or marked with three spots. So **Trima·culate** [mod.L. *trimaculāt-us*], **Trima·culated** *adjs.*

1769 PENNANT *Zool.* III. 206 The Trimaculated Wrasse... On each side of the lower part of the back fin were two large spots, and between the fin and the tail another. 1888 *Cassell's Encycl. Dict.*, *Trimacular.*

**Trimastigate, -membral,** etc.: see TRI- 1 a, c.

**Trimble,** obs. form of TREMBLE.

†**Tri·mboat.** *Obs.* In 6 **tryme-**. [First element uncertain.] Some kind of fishing-boat used in the 16th c. on the Thames. So **Trimnet** (trimmenet), and app. **Trymle boat**: see quot.

1558 *Act 1 Eliz.* c. 17 § 1 No person..withe any maner of ..Trollnett Trimmenet Trymebote Stalbote Weblyster..or ..any Heling Nett or Trymle Bote..shall take and kyll any yong Broode Spawne or Frye of Eeles Salmon Pyke or Pyckerell.

**Trimelic** (trəime·lik), *a. Gr. Antiq.* [f. Gr. τριμελής (f. τρι-, TRI- + μέλος song, melody) + -IC.] Consisting of three melodies in different modes.

1850 MURE *Lit. Greece* III. 44 The celebrated trimelic or tripartite nome,..consisting of three parts or strophes, each in one of the three chief..modes..Dorian, Phrygian, and Lydian.

**Trimelli·tic,** *a. Chem.* [f. TRI- 5 + MELLITIC.] In *trimellitic acid*, a colourless compound, $C_6H_3(COOH)_3$, unsymmetrical benzene-tricarboxylic acid, obtained by the oxidation of colophony by means of nitric acid. So named in 1870, by Baeyer, who prepared it from mellitic acid.

1872 WATTS *Dict. Chem.* VI. 813 Trimellitic Acid..is moderately soluble in water.., and crystallises..by slow evaporation in nodular groups of indistinct crystals.

†**Trimenstre,** *a. Obs. rare.* [f. L. *trimenstris*, erron. form of *trimestris*: see TRIMESTER.] Ripening in three months.

*c* 1440 *Pallad. on Husb.* I. 260 Trymenstre seed in heruest forto sowe In londis cold is best.

So **Trime·nstruous, Trime·nsual** *adjs.* (*rare*—⁰) [f. TRI- + MENSTRUOUS, etc.]: see quots.

1656 BLOUNT *Glossogr.*, *Trimenstruous*, of three moneths age. 1658 in PHILLIPS. 1891 *Cent. Dict.*, *Trimensual*, happening every three months.

**Trimerous** (tri·mĕrəs, trəi·-), *a.* [f. mod.L. *trimer-us* (ad. Gr. τριμερής, f. τρι-, TRI- + μέρος part) + -OUS.] Having, consisting of, or characterized by three parts: *spec.* **a.** *Bot.* Having the parts of the flower, or the leaves, in series or whorls of three. **b.** *Entom.* Consisting of three segments or joints, as the tarsi in certain insects (see *trimeran* below); of an insect, having such tarsi (= *trimeran*).

1826 KIRBY & SP. *Entomol.* III. xxxv. 685 Trimerous insects are those whose tarsi consist of only three joints. *Ibid.* IV. xlvii. 378 Tarsi mostly trimerous, rarely dimerous. 1845 LINDLEY *Sch. Bot.* viii. (1858) 129 *note*, *Trimerous* means that they [parts of a flower] are a power of 3. 1857 HENFREY *Bot.* 226 *Schizandraceæ*..calyx and corolla 3-merous. 1869 *Student* II. 12 Polymerous leaves may be dimerous, trimerous, etc. according to their number of meriphylls. 1875 BENNETT & DYER *Sachs' Bot.* 570 Among the dimerous and trimerous flowers of the orders Polycarpæ and Cruciflorae.

So **Trimeran** (tri·mĕrăn) *Entom.*, *adj.* belonging to the division *Trimera* of beetles, or of hymenopterous insects, characterized by trimerous tarsi; *sb.* an insect of either of these divisions; **Trimere** (trəi·miəɹ) *Zool.*, a division of the third order in the supporting reticular skeleton of extinct siliceous sponges; **Trimerite** (tri·mĕrəit) *Min.*, a rare silicate of glucinum, manganese, and calcium, occurring in pinkish pseudo-hexagonal crystals, shown by their optical properties to be combinations of three triclinic individuals (*Cent. Dict.* 1891).

1842 BRANDE *Dict. Sci.*, etc., **Trimerans, Trimera*,..the name of a section of Coleopterous insects, including those which have each tarsus composed of three articulations. 1909 *Cent. Dict. Suppl.*, *Trimere. 1896 CHESTER *Dict. Names Min.* 274 **Trimerite*, Silicate of glucinum, manganese, and calcium, found in brilliant pinkish crystals.

**Trimesic** (trəime·sik), *a. Chem.* [f. TRI- 5 + MES(ITYLENE + -IC.] In *trimesic acid*, $C_6H_3(CO_2H)_3$, symmetrical benzene–tricarboxylic acid. (So named by Fittig, 1867, when he obtained it from mesitylenic acid, and found it to be tribasic.)

1889 ROSCOE & SCHORLEMMER *Chem.* V. 138 Trimesic acid ..crystallizes in hard, transparent, thick prisms, which melt above 300°.

**Trimester** (trəime·stəɹ). [ad. F. *trimestre* sb. (Cotgr., 1611), ad. L. *trimestris* adj., f. TRI- + *mensis* month.] A period or term of three months.

1821 S. WESTON (*title*) A Trimester in France and Swisserland; or, a three months' journey..from Calais to Basle. 1895 *Current Hist.* (U. S.) V. 573 The cause of the insurgents seems to have made good progress in the third trimester of the revolt. 1907 *Westm. Gaz.* 6 Feb. 12/1 His two trimesters at Bonn University barely sufficed for him to attend a score of lectures.

So †**Trimestre** *a. Obs. rare*—⁰ = next.

1623 COCKERAM, *Trimestre*, of three moneths.

**Trimestrial** (trəime·striăl), *a.* (*sb.*) [f. L. *trimestris* (see prec.) + -AL.] Consisting of or containing three months; occurring or appearing every three months. **b.** as *sb.* A quarterly publication.

1693 J. BEAUMONT *On Burnet's Th. Earth* II. 96 By others it's made Trimestrial, and by others to consist of Six Months. 1824 MEDWIN *Convers. Byron* I. 171 People who read nothing but these trimestrials. 1855 *Tait's Mag.* XXII. 630 The complaint of a trimestrial contemporary. 1865 MAFFEI *Brigand Life* I. 81 He levied a regular trimestrial tax upon all cattle-dealers.

Also (less correctly) **Trime·stral** *a.*

1824 BP. BLOMFIELD in *Mem.* (1863) I. iv. 101, I have been busier for the last three months than ever I was before for any trimestral portion of my life. 1829 GEN. P. THOMPSON *Exerc.* (1842) I. 52 The fiend is up again and doing, till Vishnu array himself in trimestral or monthly incarnation, to return him to his deep. [Referring to the *Quarterly Review*.] 1881 MRS. LYNN LINTON *My Love* xii, Their trimestral visit..had to be paid.

**Trimetallic** (trəimĭtæ·lik), *a.* [after BIMETALLIC: see TRI-.] Pertaining to or using three metals as currency. So **Trime·tallism,** the use of a triple standard of currency.

1887 *Contemp. Rev.* Dec. 812 The metal coinage system of the world is not..'mono-metallic', nor 'bi-metallic', but 'trimetallic'. 1897 *Westm. Gaz.* 8 Oct. 2/3 Here is a correspondent in the *Times*..who asks, 'Why not Trimetallism?'

**Trime:tapho·sphate.** *Chem.* [TRI- 5 a.] A triple polymer of a metaphosphate, sodium mono-metaphosphate being $NaPO_3$.

1894 MUIR & MORLEY *Watts' Dict. Chem.* IV. 107.

**Trimeter** (tri·mĭtəɹ, trəi·-), *sb.* and *a. Pros.* Also 6 **trymeter,** 8 **trimetre.** [ad. L. *trimetrus* adj. and sb., a. Gr. τρίμετρος adj., f. τρι-, TRI- + μέτρον measure (see METRE *sb.*[1] 4).]

**A.** *sb.* A verse of three measures; i. e. in trochaics, iambics, or anapæstics, of three dipodies (= six feet); in other rhythms, of three feet; *esp.* the *iambic trimeter*, the usual verse of the dialogue in ancient Greek plays.

1567 DRANT *Horace, Art Poetry* A viij, The foote of Syllabs shorte and long Iambus hath to name..and trymeter the verse (which of the same Consists) is cawld. *a* 1637 B. JONSON *Horace, Art Poetrie* 381 This foot yet, in the famous trimeters Of Accius and Ennius, rare appeares. 1789 T. TWINING *Aristotle's Treat. Poetry* (1812) II. 445 The hexameter is but one third longer than the Iambic trimeter; their respective times being 24, and 18. 1850 BROWNING *Christmas Eve* xviii, Or Turklike brandishing a scimetar O'er anapæsts in comic-trimeter. 1859 *Sat. Rev.* 20 Aug. 225/2 Mr. Whyte and..Mr. Thomas..have translated the *Inferno* into English trimeters.

**B.** *adj.* Of a verse: Consisting of three measures.

1706 PHILLIPS (ed. Kersey), *Trimetrum*,..a Trimeter Verse of three Measures, an Iambick of six Feet. 1886 C. A. BRIGGS *Messianic Proph.* v. 143 Psalm xviii..is of eight strophes, of fourteen trimeter lines each.

**Trimethyl** (trəime·þil). *Chem.* [f. TRI- 5 + METHYL.] **a.** A formative denoting the presence of three methyl groups, $CH_3$, in a compound, as **trimethyl-arsine,** $As(CH_3)_3$, **trimethyl-phosphine,** $P(CH_3)_3$: see also *Trimethylamine* below. **b.** *spec.* denoting the substitution of 3 methyl groups for 3 hydrogen atoms, in the substance designated by the rest of the name; e.g. **trimethylbenzene,** $C_6H_3(CH_3)_3$, in which 3 methyl groups have taken the place of 3 H atoms in benzene, $C_6H_6$; so **trimethyl-methane,** $CH(CH_3)_3$, from methane, $CH_4$, **trimethyl-carbinol,** $C(CH_3)_3.OH$, etc. Also used *attrib.* as **trimethyl phosphate,** $(CH_3)_3.PO_4$. Hence **Trimethy·lic** *a.* = **trimethyl** *attrib.*

1866 ROSCOE *Elem. Chem.* xxxi. 281 Trimethylarsine is a colourless liquid. 1868 WATTS *Dict. Chem.* IV. 608 Trimethylphosphine is a transparent, colourless, mobile liquid, heavier than water, having a strong refracting power, and an indescribably nauseous odour. 1873 WATTS *Fownes' Chem.* (ed. 11) 767 Trimethyl-benzene is susceptible of three isomeric modifications.

Also **Trime·thylamine,** the tertiary amine of methyl, $N(CH_3)_3$, in which all the 3 hydrogen atoms of ammonia, $NH_3$, are replaced by 3 methyl groups; a volatile liquid with a penetrating fishy odour; formerly also called *Trimethyl ammonia* and *Trimethylia.* **Trime·thylene,** $CH_2\langle{}^{CH_2}_{CH_2}$, a colourless gas; *trimethylene-diamine*, a poisonous ptomaine.

1857 MILLER *Elem. Chem.* III. 210 *Trimethylia*...This alkali..is found in considerable quantity in the roe of herrings. 1866 ODLING *Anim. Chem.* 87 Trimethylamine $(CH_3)_3N$, a frequent constituent of stale brine in which herrings and other fish have been pickled. 1872 GARROD & BAXTER *Mat. Med.* (1880) 408 The Hydrochlorate of Trimethylamine is a stable compound, in long needle-shaped crystals, very deliquescent, soluble in water and in alcohol.

**Trimetric** (trəime·trik), *a.* [f. TRI- + Gr. μέτρον measure (or, in sense 2, f. as TRIMETER) + -IC.]

**1.** *Cryst.* Applied to that system of forms having three unequal axes mutually at right angles: = ORTHORHOMBIC.

1837 DANA *Min.* 15 *Classis Trimetrica*, or the Trimetric System. 1873 WATTS *Fownes' Chem.* (ed. 11) 281 The bases of these monoclinic forms are identical in form with those of the trimetric system.

**2.** *Pros.* Consisting of three measures.

1889 *Amer. Jrnl. Philol.* July 224 The theory that the hexameter is a combination of two trimeters..is old and familiar;..a tetrameter (tetrapody) is assumed as the original verse, which became a trimeter (trimetric colon) as a result of..the combination.

**Trime·trical,** *a.* [f. as prec. + -AL.] **a.** *Pros.* = prec. 2. *rare*—⁰. **b.** *Trimetrical Classic*, a loose expression for the 'three-character classic', a Chinese elementary school-book written in lines of verse, each line consisting of three characters.

1828 WEBSTER, *Trimeter*, *Trimetrical*, consisting of three poetical measures. 1900 A. H. SMITH in *Westm. Gaz.* 28 June 3/3 He was set the usual task in the Trimetrical Classic. 1908 *China's Millions* Mar. 40/1 For a nation to pass within the life-time of a generation from the Trimetrical Classic to the study of John Stuart Mill.

**Trimillion, -millionaire:** see TRI- 4 a.

**Trimle,** obs. or dial. form of TREMBLE.

**Tri·mly,** *a. rare.* [f. TRIM *a.* + -LY [1].] Having a trim character.

1858 MRS. GORE *Heckington* I. xiii. 274 Estates and mansions [so] left..are now..of rare occurrence in our trimly island.

**Trimly** (tri·mli), *adv.* [f. TRIM *a.* + -LY [2].] In a trim manner.

†**1.** Effectively, thoroughly, soundly, properly; cleverly, featly, neatly, nicely; finely, well. *Obs.*

1503–13 DUNBAR *Poems* liii. 200 Quhen I saw hir sa trimlye dance, Hir guid conwoy and countenance. 1556 OLDE *Antichrist* 171 Being trymlye furnished in false wyles and lies. 1579–80 NORTH *Plutarch* (1676) 489 Little showers.. which..make the Earth bring forth all things very trimly. 1600 FAIRFAX *Tasso* VI. xcvii, This formost hazard had she trimly past. 1623 LISLE *Ælfric on O. & N. Test.* Pref. 11 Harke ye..how trimly this sounds in English. 1679 C. NESSE *Antid. agst. Popery* 133 Scaliger truly and trimly told the Jesuits.

**2.** So as to be neat, elegant, or smart in appearance or effect; neatly; finely, smartly.

1523 [COVERDALE] *Old God & New* (1534) P j, They shall haue trymly garnyshed & decked the aulters with many ymages. 1545 ELYOT, *Candide uestitus*, trymmely apparayled. ..*Concinne*, properly, honestly, trymly. 1588 PARKE tr. *Mendoza's Hist. China* 331 The women [with] their haire trimly kembed and dressed. 1645 MILTON *Colast.* Wks. 1851 IV. 348 The stuff, though very cours and thredbare, garnisht and trimly fac't with the commendation of a Licencer. *c* 1728 SOMERVILLE *To A. Ramsay* 65 In all her richest head-geer trimly clad. 1879 BUTCHER & LANG *Odyssey* VII. 107 All manner of garden beds, planted trimly.

†**Tri·mmage.** *Obs. rare*—¹. [f. TRIM *v.* + -AGE.] = TRIMMING *vbl. sb.* 2.

1693 *Lond. Gaz.* No. 2892/4 A Copper colour'd Coat with black Trimmage.

**Trimmenet:** see under TRIMBOAT.

**Trimmer** (tri·məɹ). [f. TRIM *v.* + -ER [1].]

†**1.** app. A canopy. *Obs. rare.*

1518–19 *Rec. St. Mary at Hill* 303 As towchyng the tabernacles, trymmers, is that a workman shall se them & he to shew his best advice in it. *a* 1548 HALL *Chron.*, *Hen. VIII* 73 Vnder yᵉ trimmer, anticke images of gold. 1559 *Dunmow Churchw. Acc.* lf. 42 b (MS.), For making ii yrons and iiii staples for the trymmer over the rood, iiᵈ.

**2.** One who trims; one who repairs, adjusts, makes neat or smart, etc.; *spec.* **a.** a tailor's, dressmaker's, or milliner's assistant; **b.** a finisher in coach-making; **c.** see quots. 1881, 1891. Often as second element, as in *hat-trimmer*, etc.

1555 W. WATREMAN *Fardle Facions* II. viii. 167 The yndians are..greate deckers and trimmers of them selues.

1580 HOLLYBAND *Treas. Fr. Tong*, *Racoustreur*, a minder or trimmer of things. 1591 PERCIVALL *Sp. Dict.*, *Afeytador*, a barber, a trimmer, a decker, *tonsor*, *fucator*, *ornator*. 1621 T. WILLIAMSON tr. *Goulart's Wise Vieillard* 115 That man a trimmer of a garden of pleasure. 1652 N. CULVERWELL *Treat.* I. xi. (1661) 88 He calls God.. the Painter, and Trimmer of the Soul. 1850 KINGSLEY *Cheap Clothes* 17 If to the trimmer we return an answer that is considered 'saucy', we are fined 6*d.* or 1*s.* 1879 *Melbourne Argus* 24 Dec. 2/1 Trimmers [coachmaking] get from £2 10s. to £3 10s. per week. 1881 *Guide Worcester Porcelain Wks.* 8 The trimmer..removes any superfluous glaze. 1891 *Labour Commission Gloss.*, *Trimmers*, skilled workmen engaged in shaping and pressing hosiery goods. 1902 SLOANE *Stand. Electr. Dict.* App. s. v. *Trimming*, The work of a lamp trimmer frequently includes cleaning the feed rod of the upper carbon with a cloth so as to ensure smooth action of the clutch.

**3.** One who or that which cuts, clips, prunes, etc.; *spec.* †a barber (*obs.*); also, an implement or machine for trimming edges in industrial processes.

1583 STUBBES *Anat. Abus.* II. (1882) 50 What say you of the barbers and trimmers of men? 1653 URQUHART *Rabelais* I. lv, At the going out of the halls..were the perfumers and trimmers, through whose hands the gallants past. 1751 SMOLLETT *Per. Pic.* (1779) II. xl. 37 Peregrine mentioned this assassination to his own trimmer. 1810 *Sporting Mag.* XXXV. 263 The defendant's witnesses..described as croppers, dockers, nickers and trimmers [of horses]. 1876 SPURGEON *Commenting* 4 Calvin..was no trimmer and pruner of texts. 1883 R. HALDANE *Workshop Receipts* Ser. II. 99/2 Trimmers' paste requires to be smooth,..and possessed of great adhesive qualities. 1889 *Anthony's Photogr. Bull.* II. 364 With..the straight-edge to guide the knife or trimmer, cut first one side and then..the three others.

**4.** *Arch.* A short beam framed across an opening (as a stair-well or hearth) to carry the ends of those joists which cannot be extended across the opening; also, a brick-trimmer (BRICK *sb.*[1] 10). Also *attrib.*

1654 in E. B. Jupp *Carpenters' Co.* (1887) 316, 2 foote 9 inches from the backe of the Chimney to the Trimmer peece or binding Joyst. 1737 *Salmon's Country Build. Estimator* (ed. 2) 62 Remember to measure the Trimmers that support the Hearths taking the Length by the Girt of the Arching of them. 1833 LOUDON *Encycl. Archit.* § 234 Four-inch brick trimmer arches to be turned where required.

**5.** One who trims between opposing parties in politics, etc.; hence, one who inclines to each of two opposite sides as interest dictates.

Applied orig. in this sense to Lord Halifax and those associated with him (1680–90), but by him accepted in the sense 'one who keeps even the ship of state'; hence 'one who changes sides to balance parties' (J.).

1682 DRYDEN *Dk. Guise* Epil. 33, 38 We Trimmers are for holding all things even.—Yes—just like him that hung 'twixt Hell and Heaven...You Trimmers shou'd, to poize it, hang on t'other. 1682 *Character of a Trimmer* 2 A Trimmer, one neither Whigg nor Tory, is a Hater of Anti-christ, an Abominator of Enthusiasm. 1685 EVELYN *Mem.* 7 May, Those whom (by way of hateful distinction) they call'd Whiggs and Trimmers. 1704 *Faction Displ.* xiv, The Patriot's Soul disdains the Trimmer's Art. 1739 WESLEY *Wks.* (1872) I. 183 Nor is it possible for all the trimmers between God and the world to elude the consequence. 1809 W. IRVING *Knickerb.* v. i. (1849) 262 He who wavers in seeking to do what is right gets stigmatized as a trimmer. 1888 T. HARDY *Wessex T.* (1889) 201 One of the trimmers who went to church and chapel both.

**6.** One who or that which trims or trounces (see TRIM *v.* 10); a stiff competitor, fighter, etc.; a slasher; a stiff letter, article, bout, run, blow, throw of the ball, etc. *colloq.*

1776 FOOTE *Bankrupt* III. Wks. 1799 II. 126 *Pep.* Don't you think the public would bear one skirmish more..? I have a trimmer here in my hand. *Plast.* To which I have as tart a retort. 1804 NELSON in Nicolas *Disp.* (1846) VI. 163, I shall write the Dey of Algiers a trimmer. 1816 SCOTT *Antiq.* xi, I will shew you his last epistle, and the scroll of my answer—egad, it is a trimmer! 1827 *Sporting Mag.* XXI. 141 Amongst the young hounds I noticed some trimmers. 1828 *Ibid.* XXII. 117 We found in Man Wood, and killed him [the fox] after a trimmer of fifty minutes. 1882 *Daily Tel.* 17 May, Mr. H. was clean bowled by a trimmer from Barnes.

**7.** One whose business is to stow the cargo or coal in loading a ship, or to shift it from one place to another in the hold; also, a mechanical contrivance for doing this; also, one who arranges the coal in loading trucks.

1836 SIR G. HEAD *Home Tour* 331 These men called trimmers, whose business it is to level the cargo as it comes tumbling below. 1890 *Sci. Amer.* 7 June 360/1 The coal handling plant..may be resolved into three parts: The elevators..; the trimmers, which take the coal from the elevators and deposit it upon the heaps; and finally the reloaders. 1891 *Labour Commission Gloss.*, *Trimmers*, men on board ship whose duty is to go into the coal bunkers of a vessel and to place the coals within reach of the fireman...When a ship is loading grain in bulk, the trimmers move the grain from the point under the hatchway to the ends of the ship.

†**8.** *pl.* Ropes and yards for trimming the sails of a ship: see TRIM *v.* 14. *Obs. rare*—[1].

1630 tr. *Camden's Hist. Eliz.* IV. 32 Their Masts and Trimmers ouerthrowne, their Cables cut.

**9.** *Angling.* (*a*) A float of cork, wood, etc., to which a line, with baited hook, is attached; used on lakes and ponds for taking pike; (*b*) a peg surmounted by a reel on which the line is wound, driven into the bank of a stream for the same purpose; a bank-runner.

1799–1815 [implied in *trimmer-angling*, *-fishing*: see b.]. 1840 BLAINE *Encycl. Rur. Sport* § 3638 The bank trimmer is much in use on the lakes of England, the lochs of Scotland, [etc.]. 1845 LUBBOCK *Fauna Norfolk* ii. 90 He launched his fleet of trimmers, pike finding a ready sale at his own door. 1854 L. LLOYD *Scandinav. Adv.* I. 189 Trimmers, or night-lines, were also much used in my vicinity. 1873 G. C. DAVIES *Mount. & Mere* iii. 18 The trimmers are baited with dead roach, and, luckily for the pike and the fair sportsman the eels get the largest share of the bait.

**b.** *attrib.* and *Comb.*, as *trimmer-angling*, *-bait*, *-cork*, *-fishing*, *-hook*, *-line*.

1799 G. SMITH *Laboratory* II. 264 An approved Method of Trolling, and Trimmer-fishing. 1815 T. F. SALTER *Angler's Guide* (title-p.), Trolling, Bottom and Float-Fishing, Fly-Fishing, and Trimmer-Angling. 1840 BLAINE *Encycl. Rur. Sport* § 3638 A large hooked arrow armed with strong twine might be shot over the trimmer line...The cord [should be wound] on round the groove in the flat trimmer cork. *Ibid.* § 3639 Let the trimmer-hook be sufficiently large. 1863 ATKINSON *Stanton Grange* (1864) 194 The trimmer-bait had been taken by a nice half-pound trout. 1867 F. FRANCIS *Angling* iv. (1880) 133 *note*, It is trimmer-fishing in disguise.

Hence **Tri·mmering** *vbl. sb.*, trimmer-fishing.

1870 *Observer* 9 Oct., Trimmering, trolling, live bait fishing, spinning, fly fishing. *attrib.* 1888 FENN *Dick o' Fens* x. *heading*, A trimmering expedition.

**Trimmill**, obs. or dial. form of TREMBLE.

**Trimming** (tri·miŋ), *vbl. sb.* [f. TRIM *v.* + -ING[1].] The action of the verb TRIM.

**1.** Making trim, putting in order, equipment, preparation; repairing, putting right; *spec. Naut.* the fitting out, repairing, or cleaning the bottom of a ship: see TRIM *v.* 2–6.

1519–20 *Rec. St. Mary at Hill* 304 Paid for Trymmyng of the courten of our ladys tabernacle...Paid to a carpenter for Trymmyng of the peyse of the pyx. 1585 T. WASHINGTON tr. *Nicholay's Voy.* II. vi. 36 The trimming and gathering of the mastick. *c* 1595 CAPT. WYATT *R. Dudley's Voy. W. Ind.* (Hakl. Soc.) 30 Such things which wee weare to have from the carvells for the speedie dispatchinge of our admeralls trimminge. *a* 1642 SIR W. MONSON *Naval Tracts* II. (1704) 254/2 Upon the return of the clean Squadron to Sea, whilst the other Squadron is in Trimming.

**b.** Adornment, decoration, dressing up; making neat or smart; also cutting, clipping, shearing (*lit.* and *fig.*); †*spec.* cutting of the hair (*obs.*).

*a* 1536 *Calisto & Mel.* A iij b, What trimyng what payntyng, to make faynes. 1554–5 in Feuillerat *Revels Q. Mary* (1914) 176 Counterfet pearle for the trymynge & garnishing of the womens hedpeces and fruntes of their visars. 1583 STUBBES *Anat. Abus.* II. (1882) 50 They [the barbers] haue inuented such strange fashions and monstrous maners of cuttings, trimmings, shauings. 1638 *Archdeaconry Essex Min.* lf. 3 b (MS.) Edwardus Geary presentatus for trymeing of men on the Saboath day in tyme of divine service. 1693 *Vestry Bks.* (Surtees) 258 For the Beadle's blew cote trimming and making, 19 s. 6 d. *a* 1700 B. E. *Dict. Cant. Crew*, *Trimming*, Cheating People of their Money. 1723 MANDEVILLE *Fab. Bees* (1733) I. 320 To have them all whole and tight in the same Cloaths and Trimming must add to the comliness of the sight. 1886 C. SCOTT *Sheep-Farming* 171 Trimming is the modelling or clipping from time to time of the already rough shorn sheep.

**c.** *pl.* Pieces cut off in trimming something; parings, cuttings, scraps.

1805 R. W. DICKSON *Pract. Agric.* I. 116 Where there are coppices of young wood,..fences..may be formed at very small expence by the trimmings from them. 1846 SOYER *Cookery* 27 The trimmings of any description of game..may be used for making the above sauce. 1857 MILLER *Elem. Chem.* III. 667 The strongest glue..from the ears and refuse trimmings of thick hides in general. 1881 *Daily Tel.* 23 Feb., The scraps and trimmings of joints,..good meat, true meat, often cut from the primest parts of the animal. 1912 *Daily News* 21 Mar. 4 The bodger's fire of beech trimmings.

**2.** *concr.* Adornment, array; *esp.* **a.** Any ornamental addition to the bare fabric of a dress, etc. Also *fig.* Chiefly *pl.*

In quot. 1625 = the trappings of the sacrificial victim. Cf. quot. 1697 in TRIM *v.* 7.

1625 K. LONG tr. *Barclay's Argenis* IV. v. 255 Must this pompe, this attire, this beauty, be the trimmings to offer mee a Sacrifice to Sicilies infernall gods? *a* 1654 SELDEN *Table-T.*, *Relig.* (Arb.) 102 Every Man has a Doublet: So every Man has his Religion: We differ about Trimming. 1684 *Contempl. St. Man* II. v. (1699) 178 What Fool is so sottish as to bestow precious Trimming upon a Penitential Garment? *a* 1713 ELLWOOD *Autobiog.* (1765) 24 Those unnecessary Trimmings of Lace, Ribbands, and useless Buttons. 1850 H. ROGERS *Ess.* II. iv. 205 Discourses..garnished with a trimming of French terms and phrases. 1906 *Temple Bar Mag.* Jan. 33 Tunics..of darker grey with 'trimmings'.

**b.** *pl.* Accessories, usual accompaniments; e. g. to the bare fabric of a house, to a joint of meat, etc.

1612 T. BODLEY *Will* in Macray *Ann. Bodleian* (1880) 407 There shelues, deskes, seates, and other needeful trimings. 1828 MISS MITFORD *Village* Ser. III. 47 The leg of mutton and trimmings had been paid for over and over. 1837 DICKENS *Pickw.* xxxvii, A boiled leg of mutton with the usual trimmings. 1858 GEN. P. THOMPSON *Audi Alt.* II. lxx. 11 Style, which is only the trimmings of the dish. 1884 *St. James' Gaz.* 29 Apr. 4/2 Agricultural and mechanical implements, house trimmings, locks, latches, and hinges.

**3.** A beating, a drubbing; a sharp censure.

*a* 1518 [see TRIM *v.* 10]. 1675 V. ALSOP *Anti-Sozzo* Pref., They..would doubtless interpose, and bestow a deserved Trimming upon the Book, and make it doe Penance in its own sheets. 1763 LD. HALIFAX *Let.* 24 Sept., in 10*th Rep. Hist. MSS. Comm.* App. I. 360 That superficial pert Gentleman has got a thorough trimming from the Duke. 1787 MRS. TRIMMER *Two Farmers* (1788) 21 It was a cruel trick and he deserves a good trimming for it. 1823 PYNE *Wine & Walnuts* (1824) I. xviii. 215 He expected another trimming on the usual topic, his vanity.

**4.** *Naut.* The adjustment of a ship's balance, load, sails, etc. as in TRIM *v.* 13, 14.

1627 CAPT. SMITH *Seaman's Gram.* viii. 34 The Master is to see the cunning of the ship, and trimming of the sailes. *Ibid.* xi. 54 The trimming of a ship doth much amend or impaire her sailing...To finde her trim, that is, how she will sail best.

**5.** The action of balancing or poising; the stowing or arrangement of cargo or coal in the hold of a ship in such a way as to keep her trim.

*c* 1796 T. TWINING *Trav. Amer.* (1894) 96 The wagon..was so often depressed in the soft ground and old ruts on one side, that the passengers were obliged to press towards the other. Without this perpetual trimming we should certainly have been overturned. 1893 *Times* 10 July 13/6 The apparatus..has a working capacity of 100 tons per hour, and by it all trimming of the cargo is obviated. 1911 *Act* 1 *& 2 Geo. V*, c. 41 § 1 Work done..in connection with the stowing or discharging of cargoes..or the trimming of coal on board that ship.

**6.** *fig.* Balancing between opinions or parties so as to remain in favour with both sides: see TRIM *v.* 16.

1696 C. LESLIE *Snake in Grass* (1697) 223 Having themselves serv'd all turns, that ever happen'd in their time,.. they had the Face to upbraid others for their Changing and Trimming. 1760 LAW *Spir. Prayer* II. 91 Management, prudence, or an artful trimming betwixt God and mammon, are here all in vain. 1827 SCOTT *Jrnl.* 22 Dec., An attempt to govern *par bascule*—by trimming betwixt the opposite parties. 1882 A. BAIN *Jas. Mill* iv. 194 The opposition was founded on Brougham's trimming to the Church.

**7.** *attrib.* and *Comb.*, as *trimming-blade*, *-hook*, *-tool*; in sense 2 a, *trimming-maker*, *-manufacturer*, *-merchant*, *-shop*. **b.** Special combs. (in some of which *trimming* may be the *ppl. a.*), as **trimming-basin**, a barber's basin; **trimming-board**, a board on which paper is trimmed; **trimming-can**: see quot.; **trimming-joist**, a joist into which the end of a trimmer (sense 4) is fitted; **trimming-machine**: see quot.; **trimming-piece** = *trimming-joist*; **trimming-room**, **-shear**: see quots.; **trimming spout**, a jointed spout delivering grain, sand, or the like from an elevator into a ship or truck, so as to distribute it over the available space (*Cent. Dict.*, *Suppl.* 1909); **trimming-tank**, a water-tank in the bow or stern of a ship which is filled or emptied as the trim of the ship demands.

1683 *Lond. Gaz.* No. 1820/4 A Silver *Trimming-Bason and a Pot, two Silver Candle-sticks. 1868 *Rep. U. S. Commissioner Agric.* (1869) 255 Figure 8 represents the *trimming hook, and Figure 9 the *trimming blade. 1858 SIMMONDS *Dict. Trade*, **Trimming-can*, a small tin vessel with a spout, for pouring oil into a table-lamp. 1667 PRIMATT *City & C. Build.* 81 Binding-Joysts with their *Trimming-Joysts. 1679 MOXON *Mech. Exerc.* viii. 137 These Joysts, Trimmers and Trimming Joysts, are all to be pinned into their respective Mortesses. 1877 KNIGHT *Dict. Mech.*, **Trimming-machine*, 1. a species of lathe for trimming the edges of stamped hollow-ware, such as sheet-metal pans...2. (*Boot-making*), a machine for trimming the edge of uppers. 1819 *Lond. Post Off. Direct.* 84 Crooks' & Co. *Trimming-makers, 98 Wood-street. 1896 C. K. PAUL tr. *Huysman's En Route* II. vi. 262 The religious trimming-makers could trim these watered and plain silks with silver and gold. 1833 LOUDON *Encycl. Archit.* § 234 The trimmer arch, *w*, is shown abutting against the *trimming piece. 1881 *Guide Worcester Porcelain Wks.* 27 The ware..is then taken.. into the *trimming room, where any superfluous glaze is taken off. 1877 KNIGHT *Dict. Mech.*, **Trimming-shear*, a machine for trimming wool borders on..mats. 1854 M. T. MORRALL *Hist. Needle Making* (ed. 2) 22 Which soon brought them [needles] into demand in the *trimming shops of London. 1903 *Q. Rev.* July 119 The *trimming-tanks..assist in keeping the boat on an even keel.

**Tri·mming**, *ppl. a.* [f. as prec. + -ING[2].] That trims, in various senses of the verb; making trim, adorning, decorating; clipping, paring; *colloq.* or *slang*, 'stunning', 'rattling', excellent.

1559 MORWYNG *Evonym.* 187 We will referre amongste the trimmyng waters also, those waters wherwith whelkes and litle Pushes or Biles in the face, are made hoale. 1778 EARL CARLISLE in Jesse *Selwyn & Contemp.* (1844) III. 341 Such trimming gales as would make such a landsman as you stare. 1825 *Sporting Mag.* XV. 340, I did not minute this run, but..it must have been a trimming one. 1828 *Ibid.* XXI. 297 Lord Cleveland's hounds have..had a trimming day in their Bedale country. 1896 *Daily News* 31 Jan. 5/5 Expert dressmakers, forewomen, embroiderers, and trimming-women have been recruited for her wardrobe workroom.

**b.** Following a neutral or middle course between opposed principles or parties, esp. when this is done to stand in favour with both.

1683 *Trimmer Catechised* 1 You follow..the Old Trimming Jews..who sometimes worship God, and sometimes Baal. 1685 WOOD *Life* 23 Apr. (O.H.S.) III. 141 It was [a] luke-warm, trimming sermon. 1686 W. HOPKINS tr. *Ratramnus* Dissert. ii. (1688) 32 He now passeth at best but for a Trimming Catholick, with F. Cellot and his Friends. *c* 1780 SIR J. HARRIS in Bancroft *Hist. U. S.* (1876) VI. xlix. 359 An ambiguous and trimming answer was given. 1793 G. ROSE in *Ld. Auckland's Corr.* (1862) III. 165 The politics of his paper were very trimming.

Hence **Tri·mmingly** *adv.*

1718 *Free-thinker* No. 118 ¶ 3 He will neither philosophize Trimmingly, nor reason Intemperately. 1789 A. C. BOWER *Diaries & Corr.* (1903) 97 The next day I had the gout trimmingly [cf. quots. 1778–1828 above].

**Trimmle**, obs. or dial. form of TREMBLE.

**Trimness** (tri·mnės). [f. TRIM *a.* + -NESS.]

The quality or condition of being trim; neatness, smartness, spruceness, fineness.

1552 HULOET, Trymnes, *polities, ei.* 1565 COOPER *Thesaurus, Commendatur..verborum splendore et copia..* commended..for trimnes & plentie of woordes. 1576 FLEMING *Panopl. Epist.* 240 In turning them [his verses] in a foreigne tonge, much of their worthinesse and trimnesse is diminished. 1580 HOLLYBAND *Treas. Fr. Tong, Mignonneté,* trimmenesse, neatenesse, finenesse. 1727 BAILEY vol. II, *Trimness,* Neatness, Gayness, Spruceness in Dress. 1820 L. HUNT *Indicator* No. 61 (1822) II. 63 To shew the trimness of her anckles. 1886 J. R. REES *Diversions Bk.-worm* i. 8 The very wilderness..makes the trimness of other gardens appear paltry and forbidding.

**Trimnet**: see under TRIMBOAT.

‖**Tri·moda nece·ssitas.** *Old Eng. Hist.* Usually erron. **trinoda n.** [Late L., = *trimoda,* fem. of *trimodus* adj. 'of three kinds', (Isidore *Orig.* II. xvii, *De trimodo dicendi genere*), f. TRI- + *modus* mode, manner, *necessitas* necessity, exigency, need, obligation.

The phrase occurs only once, viz. in an OE. Charter attributed to K. Cædwalla of Wessex, 685–88, but actually in a MS. of about 975. Thence erroneously cited in 1614 by Selden as *trinoda necessitas,* whence in other 17th c. legal antiquaries and dictionaries, and thence in 19th c. historians and legal writers, and usually taken to mean *three-knotted* from L. *nōdus* knot. See article by W. H. Stevenson in *Eng. Hist. Rev.* Oct. 1914; also G. J. Turner in *Encycl. Brit.* (ed. 11) XXVII. 287/1.]

A collective appellation for the three great obligations upon land-holders in Anglo-Saxon times, of maintaining bridges and fortresses, and rendering military service, in OE. *brycgbōt, burhbōt,* and *fyrd.* (There was no collective OE. term for the three.)

*c* 975 *Charter of Cædualla* an. 680 in Kemble *Cod. Dipl.* I. 24 Ego cædualla rex..hanc donationis meæ cartulam scribere iussi, et absque trimoda necessitate totius christiani populi, id est arcis munitione, pontis emendatione, exercitii congestione, liberam perstrinxi. 1614 SELDEN *Titles of Honor* II. viii. 301 Those three; repairing of Bridges, Tax for Warre, and Castle gard, or repairing them: as of what no land should or could be discharged. They are called by a speciall name *Trinoda Necessitas* in a Patent by K. Cedwalla to Wilfrid first Bishop of Selesey. 1691 BLOUNT *Law Dict.* (ed. 2), *Trinoda necessitas,* i. Expeditio, Pontis, & Arcis reparatio. 1701 *Cowell's Interpr., Trinoda Necessitas,* a threefold necessary Tax or Imposition, to which all Lands were subjected in Saxon Times. 1874 STUBBS *Const. Hist.* I. v. 95 The duty of 'burh-bot', which formed part of the *trinoda necessitas,* and was incumbent on every owner of land, threw the burden of repairing the fortifications on the land-owning townsmen of the particular *burh.* 1876 DIGBY *Real Prop.* i. 13 The *trinoda necessitas,* to which all lands were subject.

†**Trimo·dial,** *a. Obs. rare*—⁰. [f. L. *trimodia* or *trimodium,* a measure of three modii or pecks, f. TRI- + *modius* peck + -AL.]

1656 BLOUNT *Glossogr., Trimodial,* pertaining to a measure of three bushels.

**Trimontane** (trəimǫ·ntěⁱn), *a. nonce-wd.* [f. TRI- + L. *montānus*: see MONTANE, and cf. L. *Trimontium,* place-name.] Having, or having some relation to, three mountains or hills; in quots., belonging to Boston in Massachusetts. So **Trimou·ntain** *a.* in same sense; *sb.* (in *pl.*) a set or group of three hills.

1837 HAWTHORNE *Twice-told T.* (1851) II. i. 8 From this station,..Gage may have beheld his disastrous victory on Bunker Hill, (unless one of the tri-mountains intervened). 1840 — *Biog. Sk., Mrs. Hutchinson* (1879) 169 The dusk has settled..upon..the Trimountain peninsula. 1885 E. C. STEDMAN in *Century Mag.* XXIX. 511 It has required some independence..for a trimontane [i. e. Bostonian] poet to be a progressive and speculative thinker.

**Trimo·nthly,** *a.* [TRI- 3.] **a.** Occurring every three months. **b.** Lasting or extending over three months.

1869 J. D. BURNS *Mem. & Rem.* vi. 104 Our trimonthly Communion. 1870 *Cornh. Mag.* July 66 The trimonthly homes of country squires. 1879 *Daily News* 1 Dec. 6/5 Annual as opposed to bi-monthly or tri-monthly budgets.

**Trimoric** (trəimǫ·rik), *a. Pros.* [f. TRI- + MORA¹ 3 + -IC.] Containing three *moræ*; having the length of three short syllables.

1901 P. GILES *Man. Compar. Philol.* § 271 (ed. 2) 230 In the difference of accentuation between οἶκοι and οἴκοι we have probably traces of the difference between original dimoric and trimoric diphthongs. Final diphthongs when dimoric allow of the circumflex on a foregoing long syllable; when trimoric they do not.

**Trimorphic** (trəimǭ·ɹfik), *a.* [mod. f. Gr. τρίμορφ-ος (f. τρι-, TRI- + μορφή form) + -IC.] Having, or existing in, three forms: *spec.* **a.** *Bot.* Having flowers with pistils and stamens of three different relative lengths. **b.** *Zool.* Exhibiting three different forms (colorations, etc.) in different individuals of a species, or of a colony of polyps. **c.** *Cryst.* Of a substance: Occurring in crystals of three fundamentally different forms with the same chemical composition.

1866 DARWIN *Orig. Spec.* iv. (ed. 4) 111 The reciprocally dimorphic and trimorphic plants. 1870 NICHOLSON *Man. Zool.* 19 When two such distinct forms exist the species is said to be 'dimorphic', and when three are present it is called trimorphic. 1870 HOOKER *Stud. Flora* 147 Lythrum Salicaria..Flowers trimorphic in respect of length of style and filaments in 3 sets of individuals. 1888 ROLLESTON & JACKSON *Anim. Life* 238 The worker bee is a dimorphic female; the soldiers and workers among the Termites are trimorphic with the fully-formed male and female.

So **Tri·morph,** *Cryst.* a trimorphic substance, or each of its three different forms; **Trimo·rphism,** trimorphic condition, occurrence in three different forms (of a plant, animal, or crystalline substance); **Trimo·rphous** *a.* = *trimorphic.*

1860 WORCESTER, **Trimorphism,* the property of crystallizing in three different forms. *Dana.* 1862 DARWIN in *Life & Lett.* (1887) III. 301 If I can only prove..it [Lythrum] is a grand case of trimorphism, with three different pollens and three stigmas. 1866 — *Orig. Spec.* ii. (ed. 4) 50 There are, however, other cases, namely of dimorphism and trimorphism,..which certain animals of either sex, and certain hermaphrodite plants, habitually present. Thus..the females of certain species of butterflies..appear under two or even three conspicuously distinct forms. 1875 LUBBOCK *Wild Flowers* iii. 77 Of the foreign species of Oxalis some are dimorphous, some *trimorphous. 1878 GURNEY *Crystallogr.* 83 Titanium dioxide is trimorphous, for it not only crystallises as Anatase and Rutile, but also as Brookite. 1909 *Cent. Dict. Suppl.,* Trimorph.

**Trimountain**: see TRIMONTANE.

**Trimsie**: see TRICKSY *a.* 1 (quot. 1577).

**Trim-tram** (tri·m,træ·m), *sb.* (*a.*) *Obs.* exc. *dial.* Also 9 *dial.* **trin tran.** [In I. app. f. TRIM *a.,* with varied reduplication; in II. and III., app. whimsical applications of I.; but perh. distinct words.]

**I.** (Cf. *flim-flam, jim-jam, whim-wham.*)

†**1.** app. A personal ornament of little value; a pretty toy or trifle; a gew-gaw. *Obs.*

1523 SKELTON *Garl. Laurel* 130 A trym tram for an horse myll it were a nyse thyng. *a* 1529 — *El. Rummyng* 76 After the Sarasyns gyse, With a whym wham, Knyt with a trym tram, Vpon her brayne pan. 1548 PATTEN *Exped. Scotl.* Pref. c iv, From yᵉ fondnes of his trimtrams and gugaws. 1560 BECON *Jewel of Joy* Wks. II. 19 b, A frenche hode wyth an edge of golde, besydes pearles and precious stons and suche other trime trames. 1667 F. VERNON *Oxonium* 24 [Undergraduates] making Trimtrams with Rushes and flowers.

†**2.** An absurd or silly device or practice; an absurdity; a piece of nonsense. *Obs.*

1533 MORE *Answ. Poysoned Bk.* Wks. 1114/2, I haue as you se so wel auoyded his ginnes and his grinnes & all his trimtrams. *c* 1550 R. WEVER *Lusty Juventus* in Hazl. *Dodsley* II. 66 Holy kneeling, holy censings, And a hundred trim-trams mo. 1568 W. FULWOOD *Enimie Idlenesse* I. B vij, Whether that sorcerers do vse to ryde vpon a Byzom, and practise such other like trim trams. 1582 STANYHURST *Æneis* II. (Arb.) 46 But loa, to what purpose do I chat such iangleryе trim trams? 1708 *Brit. Apollo* No. 16. 2/2, I have some Thoughts with an old Trim Tram To venture on the Marriage Whim Wham.

**3.** In riming jingles; sometimes referring to similarity or equal treatment of two of different position. Now *dial.* (Cf. *giff-gaff.*)

1583 MELBANCKE *Philotimus* D iij b, Trim tram, neither good for God nor man. *a* 1627 MIDDLETON & ROWLEY *Span. Gipsy* IV. iii, Trim, tram, hang master, hang man! 1681 T. FLATMAN *Heraclitus Ridens* No. 19 (1713) I. 131 Well, Trim tram, like Master like Man. 1760–62 SMOLLETT *Sir L. Greaves* xiii, They thought you as great a nincompoop as your squire—trim tram, like master, like man. 1877 T. GIBSON *Leg.,* etc. *Westmoreld.* 50 Trin tran, sike like master sike like man, A lazy life brings scant or scan.

†**4.** *attrib.* or as *adj.*

1615 SIR E. HOBY *Curry-combe* v. 223 Wee dare not say the Master and man might bee trim-tram and confederate. 1632 BROME *North. Lasse* I. v, What a Trim-tram trick is this? the Master and the man both brain-cras'd. 1762 BRIDGES *Burlesque Homer* (1772) 411 (Farmer) He's telling some long trim-tram story.

**II.** †**5.** A shrimp-net having a triangular wooden frame resting on the ground in front of the beam (*Funk's Stand. Dict.*). *attrib.* **Trim-tram man,** one who uses this net in shrimping. *Obs.*

1590 *Cal. St. Papers, Dom.* 692 Regulations for hooks..whitebait, shrimp leaps and trim trams. 1746 R. GRIFFITHS *Ess. Conserv. Thames* Index 277 Draggermen (or Trimtrammen).

**III. 6.** A lich-gate; also a gate which opens in a V-shaped enclosure, a kissing-gate. *dial.*

1842 *Church Builder* Apr. 45 *note,* In..parts of Devonshire and Cornwall Lichgates are called Trim-trams. 1893 *Wilts. Gloss., Trim-tram,* a gate which swings in a V-shaped enclosure of post and rail, so as to prevent cattle from passing through.

**Trimuscular**: see TRI- 1.

**Trin** (trin). [perh. f. TRINE *sb.,* conformed to TWIN.] *pl.* Three children or young born at one birth: = TRINE *sb.* 3. Also *sing.* one of such; also *attrib.* or as *adj.* Cf. THRIN *sb.*

1831 *Blackw. Mag.* XXIX. 998 The teeming matron is near her time, and from her bulk you may back her for trins. 1844 STEPHENS *Bk. Farm* (1849) I. 597/2 In a small flock of 50 Leicester ewes, 48 of them had twins, and 2 trins. 1875 FURNIVALL in *Lovelich's Grail* I. 291 *note,* Trins are always born: two males and one female. 1887 — in *J. Lane's Cont. Sqr.'s T.* p. viii. *note,* Spenser..made the fay-born trin brethren, Priamond, Dyamond, and Triamond, fight Camballo..to see which of them could win Canace.

**b.** *transf.* (*Min.*) A compound crystal of three individuals, a trilling.

1868 DANA *Min.* (ed. 5) 805 *Tridymite,*..in allusion to its compound forms of three individuals, or trins, from τρίδυμος.

**Trinacrian** (trəinēⁱ·kriăn), *a.* [f. L. *Trīnacria* Sicily, a. Gr. Τρινακρία, taken as f. τρι-, TRI- + ἄκρα point, cape; but orig. Θρῑνακίη, f. θρῖναξ trident.] Of Sicily, Sicilian; hence, three-pointed.

1640 HOWELL *Dodona's Gr.* (1645) 49 The Trinacrian Vespers, and Bartholomean Massacre, were nothing to this. 1667 MILTON *P. L.* II. 661 Vex'd Scylla bathing in the Sea that parts Calabria from the hoarce Trinacrian shore. 1871 RUSKIN *Fors Clav.* x. (1896) I. 201 Only the Trinacrian legs of [the Isle of] Man.

So **Trinacrite** (tri·năkrəit) *Min.,* a brown variety of PALAGONITE. (Now considered as a rock.)

1854 DANA *Min.* (ed. 4) II. 166 Trinacrite..is dull brown and cleavable or micaceous, and is mixed with..Siderosilicite. 1868 WATTS *Dict. Chem.* V. 240 *Siderosilicite,* a mineral forming, together with trinacrite, a brown mass on the tufa..at Cape Passaro, the southernmost point of Sicily.

**Trinal** (trəi·năl), *a.* Also 6–7 **trinall,** 7 **trienall.** [ad. late L. *trīnāl-is* (Adamnan), f. L. *trīn-us,* pl. *trīnī* three each, threefold: see -AL.]

**1.** Composed or consisting of three parts; threefold; triple; trine.

1590 SPENSER *F. Q.* I. xii. 39 Singing before th' eternall Majesty, In their trinall triplicities on hye. 1622 P. HANNAY *Sonn.* xx, O Trinall-one, one God and Persons three. 1629 MILTON *Ode Nativity* 11 Wherwith he wont at Heav'ns high Councel-Table, To sit the midst of Trinal Unity. *a* 1843 SOUTHEY in *Fraser's Mag.* (1868) LXXVIII. 118 Tercets, or the trinal verse of Dante. 1871 FRASER *Life Berkeley* x. 396 The relations which contribute to form distance, and trinal extension. 1907 F. HARRISON *Philos. Common Sense* p. xxviii, The synthesis is necessarily dual, or often trinal, in idea.

†**2.** *Astrol.* = TRINE *a.* 2. *Obs. rare*—¹.

1561 EDEN *Arte Nauig.* II. vii. 33 Trinall aspecte, is when betwene the planettes shal be foure signes, which are .120. degrees.

**3.** *Gram.* Applied to a 'number' or inflected form expressing three. Also *absol.* as *sb.*

1853 *Proc. Philol. Soc.* (1854) IV. 60 A trinal as well as a singular, a dual, and a plural number. 1881 *Trans. Victoria Inst.* 26 The form of the plural in some languages shows that it was originally a trinal.

Hence **Trina·lity,** the quality of being trinal.

1864 SHEDD *Hist. Chr. Doctr.* III. i. (1869) 243 Some of the theologies of pagan antiquity contain intimations of trinality in the Divine Being.

**Trinary** (trəi·nări), *a.* and *sb. rare.* [ad. late L. *trīnāri-us* of three kinds (Isidore *Orig.* III. vi): cf. L. *ternārius* TERNARY.]

**A.** *adj.* Consisting or composed of a set of three; threefold; triple; ternary.

1474 CAXTON *Chesse* IV. ii. (1883) 166 For the trynary nombre conteyneth iii parties whiche make a perfect nombre. 1882 G. ALLEN in *Nature* 17 Aug. 374 The inner palea exhibits rudiments of two sepals,..making up, with the outer palea, a single trinary whorl. 1884 MARY BOOLE in *Athenæum* 23 Aug. 238/1 Ascribing to the Eternal a dividedness projected from the trinary nature of the human faculties.

†**B.** *sb.* A set or group of three; a triad; a trio.

1596 FITZ-GEFFRAY *Sir F. Drake* (1881) 22 The gracefull Graces faire triplicitie, Of moderne Poets rarest trinarie. 1654 VILVAIN *Epit. Ess.* IV. lxxx. 83 In England a Trinary of Peers Renound for riches was in divers yeers.

**Trinch, Trinchet**: see TRENCH, TRINKET *sb.*³

**Trinck, Trinckam, Trinckle,** etc.: see TRINK, TRINKUM, TRINKLE, etc.

**Trinco·malee·.** Name of a harbour on the north-east coast of Ceylon: *attrib.* in **Trincomalee wood**: see quots.

1842 *Penny Cycl.* XXIV. 448/1 The Trincomalee-wood used at Madras for making the Massoola boats is the produce of Berrya Ammonilla. 1866 *Treas. Bot.* 138 The tree [*Berrya Ammonilla*] is a native of the Philippine Islands and Ceylon,..and is considered the best wood in the island for making oil casks...It is exported in large quantities under the name of Trincomalee wood.

**Trincum, Trind**: see TRINKUM, TREND *v.*

**Trindle** (tri·nd'l), *sb.* Forms: 4–6 **trindel,** (5 **-ylle,** 6 **-al, -ell, -ill(e**; 4 **tryndall,** 5 **-yl, -el,** 5–6 **-elle, -yll, -ylle,** 6 **-ell, -ull, tryndle, trynle, tryneyll,** 7–9 *Sc.* **trinle,** 9 *Sc.* **trinnel, trinnle),** 6– **trindle;** also 8–9 *Sc.* **trintle.** [Early ME. *trindel,* a parallel form to TRENDLE, corresp. to MHG. *trindel,* from **trendilo-*: see also the various *trind-* forms under TREND *v.,* and cf. TRUNDLE *v.*]

**1.** A wheel; *esp.* a 'trundle' or lantern-wheel in a mill; also, the wheel of a wheelbarrow: = TRENDLE *sb.* 2, TRUNDLE *sb.* 1, 2. *Obs.* exc. *dial.*

*c* 1343 *Durham Acc. Rolls* (Surtees) 543 In j pari de Trindelis. [1391 *Mem. Ripon* (Surtees) III. 106 In tryndallo pro j porta infra cymiterium, 3*d.*] 14.. *Nom.* in Wr.-Wülcker 696/13 *Hec troclia,* a trindylle. 1455–6 *Durham Acc. Rolls* (Surtees) 241 Pro j pare de le tryndylles empto pro molendino de Milburn. 1531 *Lett. & Papers Hen. VIII,* V. 180 For working of the tryndyll of the myll at Hampnes Castell. 1587 *Shuttleworths' Acc.* (Chetham Soc.) 41 For a pere of myllne trynles, ijˢ xᵈ. 1594 *Ibid.* 89 For makinge of a whelebarrowe trindle iiijᵈ. 1786 BURNS *The Inventory* 33 Ae auld wheelbarrow..I made a poker o' the spin'le, An' my auld mother brunt the trin'le. 1855 E. WAUGH *Sk. Lanc. Life* (1857) 65 He..order't th' wheelbarrow wi' spon-new trindle t' be fotcht.

†**b.** A spindle: cf. TRENDLE *sb.* 5. *Obs.*

1483 *Cath. Angl.* 393/2 A Tryndelle of A webster, *insubulus* (A. *infusillus*), *troclea.* *Ibid.* 412/2 A Weffer tryndylle, *insubulus, troclea.*

†**2.** A roll or coil (?) of wax taper, used for light in mediæval churches. (Its nature is disputed: see quots. 1796 and 1852.) *Obs.* exc. *Hist.*

(App. something different from TRENDLE *sb.* 3.)

1537 in *Reliquary* Jan. (1893) 40 Itm' ij new tryneylls of waxe lytylle wasted. 1547 EDW. VI. *Injunct.* § 28 Also, that they shall take awaie, vtterly extincte, and destroye, all shrines,.. candelsticks, tryndilles or rolles of waxe, pictures, paintynges [etc.]. **1559** Q. ELIZ. *Injunct.* § 23 Trindals, and Rolles of wax. [**1796** PEGGE *Anonym.* (1809) 42 *Trindilles* or *trindals* ..may mean cakes of wax, which being round are therefore called *trindles*, or *trundles*. **1852** ROCK *Ch. of Fathers* III. ix. 237 In some..instances it is likely that these long strings of wax taper were..coiled up..into folds, so as to form what we are to understand by *trindles* or rolls of wax.]

† **3.** Something of rounded form, as a pellet of sheep's or goat's dung. *Obs.*

**1607** TOPSELL *Four-f. Beasts* (1658) 203 The same Physitian prescribeth Goats trindles to be drunk in Wine against the Jaundise. **1660** HOWELL *Parly Beasts* 123 The very trindles drunck in wine are good against the Jaundise.

**b.** See quot. 1825. *dial.*

**16..** in *Daily News* 27 Dec. (1911) 3/2 To make a Haggisse Puddinge. Take a Calfe Trindle, a quart of Creame, halfe a dozin Egges, a Manshett, a pound of Currans, with Cinamon, Ginger, Nuttmegge, Mace, and Cloves, and Suger, and a little Rose water. **1825** JAMIESON, *Trinnel*, calf's guts.

**4.** *Bookbinding.* Each of several flat pieces of thin wood or metal, shaped something like toy horse-shoe magnets, by which (in pairs) the stitched, glued, and rounded back of a book is held flat while the front edge is ploughed.

On the withdrawal of the trindles, the back resumes its convex form and the front edge becomes concave.

**1818** *Art Bk.-binding* 16 Put the trindles between the back of the book and the paste-boards. **1885** C. G. W. LOCK *Workshop Receipts* Ser. IV. 239/2 A piece of thin millboard or 'trindle' is put between the hind board and the book.

**Tri·ndle,** *v. Obs.* or *dial.* Forms: see prec. [A parallel form to TRENDLE. Form history not clear. The OE. *tryndyl-* seems to imply derivation from the grade *trund-*: see TREND *v.*]

† **1.** *trans.* To make round, to round. (Only OE.)

*c* **1000** ÆLFRIC *Voc.* in Wr.-Wülcker 152/5 *Circumtectum*, tryndyled reaf.

**2.** *trans.* To cause (a wheel, etc.) to revolve; to cause (a ball, hoop, cask, etc.) to roll along a surface; to trundle.

**1595** BARNFIELD *Cynthia* x, A golden Ball was trindled from aboue. **1637** RUTHERFORD *Lett.* (1862) I. 272 He hath other things to do than to play with me and to trindle an apple with me. **1808–18** in JAMIESON, *Trintle, trinle*, *v. a.*

**3.** *intr.* To revolve or turn round (as a wheel, spindle, etc.); to roll (as a ball, hoop, cylinder, etc.) along a surface.

*c* **1400** *Ywaine & Gaw.* 3259 Sir Ywain..strake his nek-bane right in sonder,..His hevid trindeld on the sand. **1530** PALSGR. 762/2, I tryndell, as a boule or a stone dothe, *je roulle.* **1815** SCOTT *Guy M.* xlviii, If we were ance out o' this trindling kist o' a thing. **1894** BLACK *Highl. Cousins* I. 35 Your ball strikes the face of the hill and..comes quietly trintle, trintle, trintling down the slope.

**Trindle-bed, -tail**: see TRUNDLE-BED, -TAIL.

**Trine** (trəin), *a.* and *sb.* Also 4–7 **tryne**. [a. F. *trin, trine* (13th c. in Littré):—L. *trīn-us* threefold, f. *trēs, tria* three.]

**A.** *adj.* **1.** Threefold; triple.

*Trine compass*, threefold space, i. e. heaven, earth, and sea.

*c* **1386** CHAUCER *Sec. Nun's T.* 45 The eterneel loue and pees That of the tryne compas lord and gyde is. *c* **1450** *Cov. Myst.* ix. (1841) 88 Recomendyng me to that Godhyd that is tryne in trone. *a* **1550** BELLENDEN in *Bannatyne Poems* (Hunter. Cl.) 8/153 Thow Godheid trine, rignand in vnitie. **1656** BLOUNT *Glossogr.*, *Trine, trinus*, of three years old, or pertaining to the number three. **1675** BAXTER *Cath. Theol.* I. I. 40 By his Trine influx of Power, Wisdom, and Goodness. *a* **1711** KEN *Hymns Festiv.* Poet. Wks. 1721 I. 248 To teach the Faith of Godhead Trine. **1735** BERKELEY *Reasons* § 17 The trine dimensions of a cube generated by motion. **1868** GLADSTONE *Juv. Mundi* viii. (1870) 227 He [Zeus] is the governor of the air..; the eldest of the trine brotherhood.

**b.** *Trine immersion* (also *trin-immersion*), the immersion of a person three times in baptism, in the name of the three Persons of the Trinity. So *trine affusion, aspersion.*

**1637** GILLESPIE *Eng. Pop. Cerem.* II. ix. 37 When the Arrians abused Trin-immersion in Baptisme. *Ibid.*, The Ceremony of Trin-immersion. **1657** J. WATTS *Dipper Sprinkled* 54 She hath given over her old way of the Trine-immersion, and is upon the new path of Trine-aspersion. **1884** G. T. STOKES in *Contemp. Rev.* Apr. 600 If immersion cannot be used, trine affusion may suffice, accompanied by fasting.

**2.** *Astrol.* Denoting the 'aspect' of two heavenly bodies which are a third part of the zodiac, i.e. 120°, distant from each other. Also, Connected with or relating to a trine aspect. Also *fig.* Favourable, benign: cf. quots. 1581, 1614 in B. 2.

**1477** NORTON *Ord. Alch.* vi. in Ashm. *Theat. Chem. Brit.* (1652) 100 Cause them to looke with a Trine aspect. **1594** BLUNDEVIL *Exerc.* IV. xliv. (1636) 502 You shall find the Moone to be in a trine aspect with the Sunne. **1605** DRAYTON *Man in Moon* 459 How the Signes in their Triplicities, Be simpathizing in their Trine consents. **1609** C. BUTLER *Fem. Mon.* v. (1623) Lj, If hir Princely Grace Vouchsafe with Trine Aspect reply to make. **1790** SIBLY *Occult Sc.* (1792) I. 143 A trine aspect, △.

**B.** *sb.* **1.** A group of three; a triad.

**1552** LYNDESAY *Monarche* 5681 Gregor, Ambrose, and Augustyne, With Confessoris, are tryumphand tryne. **1591** SYLVESTER *Du Bartas* I. ii. 383 Rightly may we call those Trines (Fire, Aire and Water) but Heav'n's Concubines. *c* **1614** SIR W. MURE *Dido & Æneas* III. 291 O furyes! O Vindictive tryne. *a* **1711** KEN *Hymns Evang.* Poet. Wks. 1721 I. 40 Believe, repent, and love, this easy Trine. **1874** A. J. ELLIS in *Phil. Trans.* XXIII. 16 A *duodene*..consists of 12 tones, forming four *trines* of major Thirds arranged in three *quaternions* of Fifths.

**b.** *spec.* The Trinity; in first quot. = TRINITY 1 b.

*a* **1568** *Bannatyne Poems* (Hunter. Cl.) 79/7 Off a will, substance, and equalite,..To be laud in tryne and vnite. **1613** W. BROWNE *Brit. Past.* I. v, Thou by whose hand the sacred Trine did bring Us out of bonds. *a* **1711** KEN *Hymnarium* Poet. Wks. 1721 II. 68 O holy, holy, holy Trine, Me for thyself refine. **1827** KEBLE *Chr. Y., Trin. Sunday*, Eternal One, Almighty Trine!

**2.** *Astrol.* A trine aspect. Phr. *in trine.*

**1581** N. WOODES *Conflict Consc.* II. i. B iij, Now murthering Mars..With amiable tryne, apply to my beame. **1614** TOMKIS *Albumazar* II iii, Coniunctions, And fortunate aspects of Trine and Sextile. **1761** *Brit. Mag.* II. 465 The planets, with their conjunctions, oppositions, signs, circles, cycles, trines, and trigons. **1837** WHEWELL *Hist. Induct. Sc.* (1857) I. 176 When she was nearly in trine, and in sextile with the sun.

**3.** *pl.* Three children (or young) at a birth; triplets.

**1628–9** *Faversham Par. Reg.* (MS.), Samuell..Elizabeth.. Marie..Trines of John Juyce [and] Susan. **1706** *All Saints, Canterb. Par. Reg.* (MS.), Jane and Mary 2 of ye trines of Wm Plummer [buried]. **1844** STEPHENS *Bk. Farm* II. 610 The two lambs which constituted the trines were..taken away to relieve the ewes. **1867** J. CAMPBELL *Balmerino* IV. v. 325 He..baptized in the parish three times trines.

† **Trine,** *v.*[1] *Obs.* Also 4–5 **tryne**, 5 **trien.** [Aphetic f. ME. *atrine-n, etrine-n*, ATRINE:—OE. *æthrinan* to touch, f. *æt-* AT- + *hrinan* to touch.]

*trans.* To touch.

*c* **1200** *Trin. Coll. Hom.* 21 Whu shal þat wurðe, siððen wapman me ne trineð? **1340–70** *Alex. & Dind.* 132 Sent was a vois sone fro heuene, þat non trinde þe tres. **1393** LANGL. *P. Pl.* C. XXI. 87 For alle hij were vnhardy þat houede þer oþer stode, To touche hym oþer to tryne [*v. rr.* trien, trine, trinen, turne] hym oþer to take hym doun and graue hym. *c* **1400** *St. Alexius* (Trinity) 429 Ac hy ne dorste hem tryne [*Laud* ouer him trine].

† **Trine,** *v.*[2] *Obs.* Also 4–6 **tryne**, 5 **treyne, trene**; *pa. t.* 4 **tron(e**, 5 **treyned, trynyd.** [Of Scand. origin: cf. OSwed. *trina* (pret. *trān*) to go, step, march, Da. *trine*, older *trene* (pret. *trēn*).]

*intr.* To go, march, step. (Chiefly in allit. verse.)

**13..** *E. E. Allit. P.* C. 101 Then he tron on þo tres & þay her tramme ruchen. ?*a* **1400** *Morte Arth.* 1757 With trompes thay trine, and trappede stedes. *Ibid.* 4189 Than the traytoure..Trynnys in with a trayne tresone to wirke. *a* **1400–50** *Alexander* 4888 He..Gas him vp be degreces to þe grete lawe, Trenes to þe topward þat touched to þe cloudis. **1560** ROLLAND *Crt. Venus* I. 189 [The twa] did tryne with diueris countenance.

**b.** *trans.* with cognate obj.

**13..** *E. E. Allit. P.* A. 1112 To-warde þe þrone þay trone a tras. *Ibid.* B. 976 Trynande ay a hyȝe trot þat torne neuer dorsten. *a* **1400** *Pistill Susan* 225 But ȝit we trinet [*v. r.* trynyd] a trot, þat traytor to take. ?*a* **1400** *Morte Arth.* 4055 The trays of the traytoure he trynys fulle euenne.

**c.** apparently preserved in Rogues' Cant.

**1622** FLETCHER *Beggar's Bush* III. iii, *Hig.*..Let the Quire Cuffin: And Herman Beck strine, and trine to the Ruffin. *Clause.* Now interpret this unto him. *Hig.*..Let the Constable, Iustice, and Divell go hang. **1815** SCOTT *Guy M.* xxviii, No wonder that you scour the cramp-ring, and trine to the cheat sae often. **1826** — *Woodst.* xxxvi, We trine to the nubbing cheat to-morrow.

**d.** (Perh. arising from a shortening of the phrase *trine to the cheats* = go to the gallows, be hanged). To hang (*intr.* and *trans.*).

**1567** HARMAN *Caveat* 37 Their end is..hanginge, whiche they call trininge in their language. *Ibid.* 85, I towre [see] the strummel [straw] trine [hang] vpon thy nabchet [cap]. *Ibid.* 86 Tryning on the chates..hange on the gallowes. **1608** DEKKER *Lanthorne & Candle-light* B ij b, [From thence] to be Tryn'de on the Chates. **1610** ROWLANDS *Martin Mark-all* E ij, If you will make a word for the Gallous, you must put thereto this word *Treyning*, which signifies hanging; and so Treyning Cheate is as much to say, hanging things, or the Gallous. *a* **1700** B. E. *Dict. Cant. Crew, Trine*, to Hang; also Tyburn. *Ibid.* s. v. *Wap*, Let her trine for a Make,..let her hang for a Half-penny.

**Trine,** *v.*[3] *rare.* [f. TRINE *a.* or *sb.*]

**1.** *trans.* To put or join in a trine aspect.

*a* **1700** DRYDEN *Pal. & Arcite* III. 389 By fortune he [Saturn] was now to Venus trined, And with stern Mars in Capricorn was join'd. **1840** BROWNING *Sordello* IV. 603 'Tis done! and now deter Who may the Tuscan—once Jove trined for her—From Friedrich's path!

**2.** To make a trine or triad of.

**1834** *Tait's Mag.* I. 658/1 The Isthmian *now* of each Eternity, Trining the has-been, being, and to-be.

† **Tri·nehood.** *Obs. rare*⁻¹. In 5 **tryne-hode.** [f. TRINE *a.* + -HOOD.] Threefold state; Trinity.

**1471** RIPLEY *Comp. Alch.* Pref. i. in Ashm. *Theat. Chem. Brit.* (1652) 121 O Tryne hode in Deite.

† **Tri·nely,** *adv. Obs. rare*⁻¹. [f. TRINE *a.* + -LY[2].] Triply, in a threefold manner.

**1606** SYLVESTER *Du Bartas* II. iv. II. *Magnif.* 1341 The greater World hath but one Sun to shine, The lesser but one Soule, both but one God, In Essence One, in Person Trinely-odde.

**Trinervate** (trəinə̄·ɹvĕt), *a. Nat. Hist.* [f. TRI- + L. *nervus* NERVE + -ATE[2]; cf. mod.L. *trinervis.*] Having three nerves or veins. Also **Tri-ne·rve, Trine·rved** *adjs.*, three-nerved.

**1811** A. T. THOMSON *Lond. Disp.* II. (1818) 45 Thin, cordate..trinerved leaves. **1819** *Pantologia, Trinerve leaf*,.. having three nerves or unbranched vessels meeting in the base of the leaf. *Ibid.*, Trinervate. **1866** *Treas. Bot.*, *Trinerved, trinervis*, having three ribs, all proceeding from the base. **1891** *Cent. Dict.*, Trinervate..Trinerve.

**Trinfauld**, var. THRINFALD *Obs.*, threefold.

**Tring** (triŋ). *Ornith. rare.* [ad. mod.L. *tringa* (Linn.), generic name, formed app. after Gr. τρύγγας, name of some bird.] Any species of bird of the genus *Tringa* (which name is more frequent in use), commonly called Sandpipers. So **Tri·ngine** *a.*, of or pertaining to the genus *Tringa*; **Tri·ngoid** *a.*, resembling the genus *Tringa.*

[**1674** RAY *Words, Water Fowl* 90 Tringa major.] **1752** J. HILL *Hist. Anim.* 476 The red-legged Tringa. **1757** [see *coot-footed* s. v. COOT *sb.*[1] 5]. **1757** *Phil. Trans.* L. 255 This bird is like in shape to most others of the tringa or snipe kind. **1796** MORSE *Amer. Geog.* I. 212 Red coot footed Tring, *Tringa Rufa.* Spotted Tring, *Tringa maculata.* Little Trings of the sea shore. Sand Birds. **1816** J. BIGELOW in *N. Eng. Jrnl. Med. & Surg.* V. 338 A species of plover or of tringa.

**Tringham**: see TRINKUM.

**Tringle** (tri·ŋg'l). [a. F. *tringle* (16th c.), in Cotgr. *tringle, trangle*, 'a Curtaine-rod; and more generally, a peece of round yron, or wire,.. vsed for [various purposes]; also, a flat sticke, or lath-like peece of wood'. In OF. *tingle* beam (1328 in Godef.): cf. mod.Du. *tengel* flat lath.

Hatz.-Darm. derive the OF. from the Du. word; but as the latter is app. only mod.Du., and not mentioned even by Kilian (see Franck, Van Wijk), it may be from the Fr. word.]

**a.** *Arch.* (See quot. 1696.) **b.** A curtain-rod, or any long slender rod. Cf. TRANGLE.

**1696** PHILLIPS (ed. 5), *Tringle*, a little square Member, which is directly upon every Triglyph, under the Platband of the Architrave; from whence hang down the Pendant Drops of the Dorick Order [**1706** (ed. Kersey), *adds*] A Curtain-Rod, a Lath that reaches from one Bed-post to another. **1704** in J. HARRIS *Lex. Techn.* I. **1881** W. E. DICKSON *Organ-Build.* xii. 151 A long rod or tringle of wood, connecting all these arms by pins passing through them and itself.

**Tringle,** variant of TRINKLE *v.*[1], to trickle.

‖**Tringlette** (trẽŋgle·t). [F. (1690 in Furetière), dim. of *tringle*: see above.] A pointed stick used to open the cames or grooved leaden bars which hold the panes in fretwork or diamond-paned windows (Knight *Dict. Mech.* 1877). (In Fr. also, the piece of glass in such a pane, Littré.)

**Tringum-Trangum**: see TRINKUM.

‖**Trinidado** (trinidā·do). *Obs.* or *arch.* [Sp. adj. from *Trinidad* (= Trinity) an island of the West Indies.] A kind of tobacco from Trinidad.

**1599** BUTTES *Dyets drie Dinner* Ep. Ded. Aa j b, Here is a Pipe of right Trinidado for him. **1600** ROWLANDS *Lett. Humours Blood* ii. 8 To drinke a pipe of Trinedado. **1889** DOYLE *Micah Clarke* 180 A pipe of Trinidado is all I require.

† **Trin-imme·rsion**: see TRINE *a.* 1 b.

**Trinitarian** (trinitē^ə·riăn), *a.* and *sb.* [f. 16th c. L. *trīnitāri-us* (f. *trīnitās* TRINITY) + -AN.

*Trinitarius* sb. occurs in Servetus, *2nd let. to Calvin* *a* 1553, also in Prince N. Radzivil *Let. to Calvin* 1564 (Calvin Wks. 1879 XX. 332). Cf. F. *trinitaire*, TRINITARY.]

**A.** *adj.* (In senses 1, 2, 4 with capital T.)

**1.** *Ch. Hist.* Belonging to the order of the Holy Trinity: see B. 1.

**1628** L. OWEN *Unmask. Monks* 24 Of the Trinitarian Friars. In the time of..Pope Innocentius the third, the Friers who are called Trinitarians, began to shew themselues to the world. **1725** *Lond. Gaz.* No. 6355/1 Father Navajas, a Trinitarian Fryar. **1885** *Cath. Dict.* (ed. 3) s. v., At the dissolution there were eleven Trinitarian houses in England, five in Scotland, and one..in Ireland.

**2.** *Theol.* Relating to the Trinity; holding the doctrine of the Trinity (opp. to *Unitarian*).

In early use, *Trinitarian heretic*, one holding heretical views as to the Trinity: cf. B. 2 b.

**1656** BLOUNT *Glossogr.*, *Trinitarian* hereticks, otherwise *New Arians* are those that deny the blessed Trinity, and all distinction of the Divine persons. **1775** ASH, *Trinitarian*, belonging to the Trinity, acknowledging the Trinity. **1838–9** HALLAM *Hist. Lit.* IV. IV. ii. § 28. 37 We do not find much of importance written on the Trinitarian controversy. **1899** A. E. BURN *Introd. Creeds* ii. § 6. 22 An unbroken traditional use of the Trinitarian [baptismal] formula.

**3.** Forming a trinity; consisting of or involving three in one; triple, threefold.

**1812** *Reflector* II. 159 Our polygraphs, our trinitarian writing-desks. **1889** B. JONES in *Co-operative News* 22 June 644 The fund would not be there, if it were not for this trinitarian combination of effort [of labourer, capitalist, consumer]. **1910** *Daily News* 30 Dec. 4 France, Russia, and England do not constitute a trinitarian group or threefold entity in foreign affairs.

**4.** Belonging to Trinity College (in Cambridge, Oxford, or Dublin). *nonce-use.*

*a* **1876** M. COLLINS *Pen Sketches* (1879) I. 50 Concerning Cam wrote our pleasant Trinitarian poet [Jas. Payn].

**B.** *sb.* (With capital T.)

**1.** A member of the religious order of the Holy Trinity, founded in 1198 to redeem Christian captives from Mohammedans: = MATHURIN.

All the churches and houses of the order were dedicated to the Holy Trinity.

**1628** [see A. 1]. **1656** BLOUNT *Glossogr.*, *Trinitarians*, a religious order. See *Mathurins*. *Ibid.*, *Mathurins*, Friers so called, being of the order of the Holy Trinity, whose principal institute is to redeem poor Christian Captives from the slavery of the Turk. **1688** R. HOLME *Armoury* III. 179/2 The Trinitarians, or Monks of the Order of the Trinity, begun Anno 1211. **1905** *Westm. Gaz.* 11 Sept. 3/1 Down Mark-lane and through Crutched Friars, where the famous Trinitarians of old had their monastery.

**2.** *Theol.* One who holds the doctrine of the Trinity of the Godhead; a believer in the Trinity.

1706 Phillips (ed. Kersey) s. v., The Orthodox that believe the Trinity are also call'd Trinitarians by the Socinians. 1708 Swift *Abol. Chr.* Misc. 1731 I. 109 They make a Difference betwixt nominal and real Trinitarians. 1850 Robertson *Serm.* Ser. iii. iv. (1872) 45 There are..Trinitarians who are practically Tri-theists, worshipping three Gods.

†**b.** In earlier use, 'applied particularly to certain sectaries whose opinion as to the Trinity was not orthodox' (Littré) = *Trinitarian heretic* in A. 2; including Antitrinitarians or Unitarians.

1565 Harding *Confut. Apol.* 133 There are many other sectes..to witte, Osiandrines, Adiaphoristes, Antinomians, Newe Maniches,..Trinitarians. 1658 Phillips, *Trinitarians*, a sort of Hereticks that deny the Mystery of the Trinity [1706 (ed. Kersey) *adds*] and all distinction of the Divine Persons.

**3.** A member of Trinity College (Cambridge, Oxford, or Dublin). *nonce-use.*

1852 C. A. Bristed *5 Yrs. Eng. Univ.* (ed. 2) 48 The outcries of the Trinitarians waxed more and more boisterous. 1899 *Literature* 28 Jan. 89 Trinity College, Oxford...The story of each period is supplemented by a list of the most notable amongst contemporary Trinitarians.

Hence **Trinitaˈrianism**, the doctrine of Trinitarians; Trinitarian belief; **Trinitaˈrianize** *v. trans.* to make Trinitarian.

1775 Ash, *Trinitarianism*,..the doctrine of a Trinity of persons in the Godhead. *a* 1817 *Merivale's Reports* III. 357 A sect of Protestant Dissenters called Unitarians, professing themselves to be opposed to Trinitarianism. 1833 Arnold *Let.* 9 Mar., in Stanley *Life & Corr.* (1845) I. vi. 358 If we could get rid of the Athanasian Creed, and of some other instances of..the technical language of Trinitarianism, many Unitarians would have a stumbling-block removed. 1852 De Morgan in Graves *Life Sir W. R. Hamilton* (1889) III. 404 In your versification of the Te Deum you Trinitarianize it.

†**Triˈnitary.** *Obs.* [ad. 16th c. L. *trīnitāri-us*: see Trinitarian. Cf. F. *trinitaire* (Calvin, 1560).] = Trinitarian B. 1, 2, 2 b.

1561 Norton tr. *Calvin's Inst.* i. xiii. 39 The name of the Trinitie was so hatefull, yea so detestable to Seruetto, that he sayde, that all the Trinitaries, as he called them, were vtterly godlesse. 1581 Allen *Apol.* 20 These present Protestants, Anabaptists, Puritans, Trinitaries, and other wolues of what heare so euer,..daily decay and discouer their owne malice and folly. 1693 tr. *Emilianne's Hist. Monast. Ord.* 135 Of the Order of the Mathurines, or Trinitaries.

**Trinitrate** (trəiˌnəiˈtreᵗt). *Chem.* [f. Tri- 5 + Nitrate.] A compound formed from three molecules of nitric acid, $HNO_3$, by the replacement of the three hydrogen atoms by a trivalent element or radical; e. g. *bismuth trinitrate*, $Bi'''(NO_3)_3$; *glyceryl trinitrate*, $C_3H_5'''(NO_3)_3$, (= Trinitrin).

1868 Watts *Dict. Chem.* IV. 83 The [hydrated] trinitrates of aluminium and bismuth .. evolve unaltered nitric acid. 1880 Roscoe & Schorlemmer *Treat. Chem.* II. ii. 338 Bismuth Trinitrate..is obtained in large transparent triclinic prisms. 1912 Thorpe *Dict. Appl. Chem.* (ed. 2) II. 773 The most important is glyceryl trinitrate, or nitroglycerin.

**Triniˈtride.** *Chem.* [f. Tri- 5 + Nitr(ogen + -ide.] A compound formed from hydrazoic acid or azoimide, $HN_3$, by replacement of the hydrogen by a metal; as *sodium trinitride*, $NaN_3$.

1911 *Jrnl. Chem. Soc.* C. ii. 693 Corrosion of some metals in Sodium Trinitride Solution.

**Triniˈtrin.** *Chem.* [f. Tri- 5 + Nitr(ic + -in[1] (see Acetin).] The compound ether or ester of glycerol or glycerin with nitric acid, $C_3H_5(O.NO_2)_3$, also called *glyceryl trinitrate* or more commonly and less correctly *nitroglycerin*; an oily liquid discovered in 1847, which when struck explodes violently; largely used in making dynamite and other explosives.

1866 Roscoe *Elem. Chem.* xxxvi. 316 If the nitric acid employed..be concentrated, a new compound called Trinitrine or Trinitro-glycerine, is formed. 1898 *Allbutt's Syst. Med.* V. 996 Trinitrine should be prescribed if any sign of intolerance of the iodides be noticed.

**Trinitro-** (trəinəiˈtro), before a vowel **trinitr-**. *Chem.* [f. Tri- 5 + Nitro-.] **a.** A formative denoting that three nitro-groups, $NO_2$, have replaced three hydrogen atoms in the substance designated by the rest of the name, the nitrogen atoms being directly joined to carbon atoms; e. g. **trinitrophenol** or picric acid, $C_6H_2(NO_2)_3(OH)$, in which three H atoms of phenol have been replaced by three $NO_2$ groups, the N atoms directly joined to three C atoms. So **trinitrocresol**, $C_6H(CH_3)(OH)(NO_2)_3$, from cresol; **trinitronaphthalene**, $C_{10}H_5(NO_2)_3$ from naphthalene, $C_{10}H_8$, etc. Also *attrib.*, as *tri-nitro carbolic acid.*

1851 *Q. Jrnl. Chem. Soc.* III. 75 A third compound is formed, in which 3 eq. of hydrogen are replaced by hyponitric acid: this is Trinitranisol. 1869 Roscoe *Elem. Chem.* xxxix. 381 Tri-nitro-phenol [1866, xxxix. 336 tri-nitro carbolic acid] or picric acid, is a bright yellow crystalline body.

**b.** In earlier nomenclature, *trinitro-* included cases in which the nitrogen atoms of the $NO_2$ groups were attached by oxygen atoms to the carbon atoms of the substance designated by the rest of the name; such compounds are now called Trinitrates; e. g. **triniˈtroglyˈcerin**, $C_3H_5(O.NO_2)_3$ (also Trinitrin), now called *glyceryl trinitrate.* So **triniˈtro-ceˈllulose** or gun-cotton, a powerful explosive, considered to be $\{C_6H_7O_2(O.NO_2)_3\}x$, derived from cellulose, $\{C_6H_{10}O_5\}x$, by replacement of OH groups by $O.NO_2$ groups of nitric acid, $HO.NO_2$, the molecule being some unknown multiple of the formula. (See also quot. 1910.)

1864 Mills in *Jrnl. Chem. Soc.* XVII. 158, I prepared trinitro-glycerin for this purpose. 1866 [see Trinitrin]. 1875 H. C. Wood *Therap.* (1879) 589 The true explosive gun-cotton, that which is alone adapted for gunnery, is trinitrocellulose. 1897 *Daily News* 9 Feb. 7/4 Mr. Maxim..took the two most powerful smokeless explosives, nitroglycerine and tri-nitro-cellulose. He mixed them by dissolving them in something which would dissolve both. 1910 Walker & Mott *Holleman's Org. Chem.* (ed. 3) 293 In the nitration of cellulose the final product is trinitro-oxycellulose..the formation of the trinitro-compound is accompanied by oxidation of the cellulose...$(C_{24}H_{40}O_{21})x$.

**Trinity** (triˈnĭti). Forms: 3–6 **trinite, -yte,** (4 **trinte,** 4–6 **trynite, -yte,** 5 **trynete**), 4 **trini-, tryni-,** 5 **trynytee**; 4–5 **trenite,** (4 **-ete,** 4–6 **-yte,** 6 **-eti, -etee, -ytie**); 4–6 **trynitie,** 6 **triniti,** 6–7 **trinitie,** 6- **trinity.** Also β. 5 **ternyte,** 6 **ternitie.** [a. OF. *trinite* (in 11th c. *trinitiet, -itet*), also *trinetei, trenite, ternite* (= Pr., Sp. *trinidad*, Pg. *trindade*, It. *trinità*) :—L. *trīnitāt-em* (nom. *trīnitās*) 'a triad, a trio', in Christian use from Tertullian (195–220), f. *trīnus*: see Trine. Also in other langs. from L., e. g. Ir. *trionnoid*, Gael. *trionaid*, Welsh *trindod*; Ger. *trinität*.

L. *trīnitās* in Christian use rendered Gr. τριάς, used in this sense by Theophilus of Antioch, fl. 180, and by Clement of Alexandria, *c* 150–212. After Tertullian (*Adv. Prax.* xxv.) L. *trīnitās* is used by Cyprian, Hilary, Marius Victorinus, Priscillian, Jerome, Augustine, and others.]

**1.** The state of being threefold, threefoldness, threeness. **a.** in non-theological sense.

?*c* 1425 *Lucidarie* vi. (1909) 6 Nyne ordres of aungels..Whi nyne of angels? For þe trynyte þat is in hem in þe nombre of nyne, þat is þries þre. 1850 Robertson *Serm.* Ser. iii. iv. (1872) 52 It is a trinity—a division in the mind of God.

**b.** *spec.* in theological use: applied to the existence of one God in three persons. (In early use esp. in phr. 'God in trinity', i. e. in threeness.)

*a* 1300 *Cursor M.* 2708 Toward him com childir thre, Liknes o god in trinité. *c* 1320 R. Brunne *Medit.* 1 Alle myȝty god yn trynyte, Now & euer wyþ vs be. *c* 1400 *Ywaine & Gaw.* 2205 Thorgh grace of god in trenyte, I sal the wreke of tham al thre. *c* 1450 *Merlin* i. 8 Belevest thow not in the fadir, sone, and holy goste, and that these thre persones be oon god in trynite? 1548–9 (Mar.) *Bk. Com. Prayer, Athanasian Creed*, So that..the vnitie in trinitie, and the trinitie in vnitie, is to be wurshipped. 1673 Milton *True Relig.* Wks. 1851 V. 410 For terms of Trinity, Triunity, Co-essentiality, Tripersonality, and the like, they reject them as Scholastic Notions, not to be found in Scripture. 1719 Waterland *Vind. Christ's Div.* xxii. 336 As to Those who take Trinity and Tritheism for Synonymous Terms, They may go on to value Themselves upon it. 1907 Sanday *Life Christ in Rec. Research* v. ix. 232 The doctrine of the Trinity is essentially a doctrine of Trinity *in* Unity. The basal truth is that God is one.

**2.** The three 'persons' or modes of being of the Godhead as conceived in orthodox Christian belief; the Father, Son, and Holy Spirit as constituting one God; the triune God. (Now always with capital T; often *the Holy Trinity, the Blessed Trinity.*)

(There is possibly an instance of an early form *trineteð* = ONF. *trinitet*, in Layamon 29533; but both MSS. are defective, one reading merely *ðes nome*, and the other ... *nete his name* (the rest being burnt).)

*a* 1225 *Ancr. R.* 26 Ȝette me ham, holi þrumnesse Trinite, iþe wurðschipe of þe. *a* 1300 *Cursor M.* 129 (Gött.) Þat es, þe haly trinite, Þat all has wroght wit his beute. 1390 Gower *Conf.* III. 87 The hihe almyhti Trinite, Which is o god in unite. *c* 1450 Lydg. *Merita Missæ* 46 in *Lay Folks Mass Bk.* App. v. 149 Werships Ewyr the Ternyte. 1516 in *Acts Parlt. Scotl.* (1875) XII. 37/1 Ȝoure hienes..quhais grace..the trinite have in his blissit keping. 1587 Golding *De Mornay* xxxiv. (1592) 552 The Kingdome whose king is the Trinitie, whose Lawe is Charitie, and whose measure is eternitie. 1677 Gale *Crt. Gentiles* II. iii. 48, I shal not denie but that these blind heathens..might have some..imperfect traditions concerning a Trinitie. 1827 Heber *Hymn*, '*Holy, holy, holy*' i, God in three Persons, blessed Trinity! 1849 R. I. Wilberforce *Doctr. Holy Bapt.* (1850) 18 It was the Second, not the Third Person of the Ever-blessed Trinity who became the Incarnate Mediator.

**b.** A symbolical figure representing the three persons of the Godhead.

1496–7 *Rec. St. Mary at Hill* 33 Item, a gylt Table of the Trynete, for to sett on the high Aulter. 1503–4 *Ibid.* 252 Payd to the glassyng of þe gret vynddow vythe þe Trenyte in the southe yell [= aisle]. [*c* 1828 Berry *Encycl. Her.* I. Gloss., *Trinity*, the heraldic device for the representation thereof is composed of roundles and lines.]

**c.** *ellipt.* The festival of the Holy Trinity; Trinity Sunday (see 6).

[1215–30 *S. Osmundi Consuet.* xxi. 4 in *Reg. S. Osmund* (Rolls) I. 38 Festum Sanctæ Trinitatis.] *c* 1290 *St. Brendan* 229 in *S. Eng. Leg.* I. 225 Þo com atte trinite þis gode man. 13.. *Guy Warw.* (A.) 705 It was at þe holy trinite, Þerl dubbed sir Gij þe fre. 1624 Laud *Diary* 6 June, Second Sunday after Trinity, I preached at Westminster.

**3.** Any combination or set of three (persons, beings, things, principles, etc.) forming a unity, or closely connected; a triad, trio.

1542 *St. Papers Hen. VIII*, IX. 251 We might ones be joyned to gidre in a ternitie, as the Pope thEmpereur and the King of Portugal be. 1633 G. Herbert *Temple, Starre* v, Then with our trinitie of light, Motion, and heat, let's take our flight. 1694 F. Bragge *Disc. Parables* iii. 84 The lust of the flesh, the lust of the eyes, and the pride of life;..that Trinity which the generality of men adore. *a* 1711 Ken *Hymns Festiv.* Poet. Wks. 1721 I. 268 Thus coalesce in sacred Lays, A Trinity, Love, Joy, and Praise. 1883 W. Binns in *Chr. Globe* 13 Sept. 823/2 Siva, the destroying deity of the Indian trinity. 1906 Petrie *Relig. Anc. Egypt* xii. 79 The formal theology of the schools which grouped gods together in trinities or enneads.

**4.** In full, *Herb Trinity* (med.L. *herba Trinitatis*): an old name for **a.** the heart's-ease or pansy, *Viola tricolor*, from the three colours of the flower; **b.** *Anemone Hepatica*, from the three-lobed leaf.

1597 Gerarde *Herbal* ii. ccxcix. 703 Harts ease is named ..of others *Herba Trinitatis* or Herbe Trinitie, by reason of the triple colour of the flowers. *Ibid.* ii. ccclxxxvii. 1032 Noble Liuerwoort is called *Hepatica trifolia*,..and Herbe Trinitie. *a* 1700 B. E. *Dict. Cant. Crew, Hearts-ease*,..an Herb called by some the Trinity,..or Pansies. 1864 *N. & Q.* 3rd Ser. V. 60/2 The well known name of Herb Trinity given to the *Anemone hepatica.*

**5.** Colloquial abbreviation for *Trinity College.*

1757 Gray *Let.* 17 Apr., The Duke of Bedford is now here [Cambridge] to settle his son at Trinity. *c* 1765 — *Satire* 11 The Master of Trinity To him bears affinity.

**6.** *attrib.* Dedicated to or connected with the worship of the Holy Trinity, as *Trinity aisle, altar, guild, light*; bearing a figure or symbol of the Trinity, as *Trinity ring, window*; occurring (blossoming, etc.) about the season of Trinity Sunday (see below), as *Trinity fair, honeysuckle, tide*; belonging to or connected with the Trinity House (see below), as *Trinity Brethren* (sb. pl.), *Corporation, due, high-water mark, man, pilot, standard, waterman, yacht*; also † **Trinity grass**, an old name for some species of trefoil; **Trinity-herb** = herb trinity (see 4 a); **Trinity House**, shortened title of a guild or fraternity originally established at Deptford, incorporated in the reign of Henry VIII, having the official regulation of British shipping; **Trinity Monday** (*rare*), the day after Trinity Sunday; **Trinity Sunday**, the Sunday next after Whit-Sunday, observed as a festival in honour of the Trinity; **Trinity term**, the fourth of the terms or sessions of the High Court of Justice in England: see Term *sb.* 5; since 1873 called officially *Trinity Sittings*, and now beginning on the Tuesday following Trinity Sunday; also one of the university terms, which at Oxford is continuous with Easter term, the two being reckoned for most purposes as one.

1579 in Cranage *Churches Shropsh.* (1912) II. 945 Towards the reparations of the wyndoo in the *triniti ylle [= aisle]. 1536 in *Luton Trinity Guild* (1906) 214 Item payd to the paynter for makynge of a border for the *trenyte awter..6*s.* 1850 Coote *Admiralty Practice* 59 The Court will direct the attendance of the *Trinity Brethren to be written for. *Ibid.*, The Court is assisted by two elder Brethren of the *Trinity Corporation at the hearing of every suit for collisions. 1783 in *Late Meas. Ship-Owners in Coal-Trade* (1786) 63 *Trinity dues per Cocket. 1507 in *Charters &c. Edinb.* (1871) 191 Thair said *Trinite faires yeirlie to begin on the Monninday next eftir Trinitie Sonday. 1545 Elyot, *Lagopus*, an herbe of the kynd of trefoyles called *trinitie grasse. 1657 C. Beck *Univ. Char.* L viij, Trinity grass or hare-foot. 1423 *Coventry Leet Bk.* 47 The brethren and systren of the *Trinyte guylde of Couentre. 1566 *Act* 8 *Eliz.* c. 13 § 1 The..Mayster Wardens and Assistauntes of the *Trinytie Howse ..shall..set up suche..Beakons, Markes and Signes for the Sea..as to them shall seeme moost meete. *a* 1642 Sir W. Monson *Naval Tracts* iii. (1704) 339/1 A Master is to be chosen by the Trinity-House. 1534 in *Luton Trinity Guild* (1906) 208 Item payd for xij li. wex for ye *trenytie lyght..6*s.* 1698–9 *Act* 11 *Will. III*, c. 21 § 2 Every Person..who..shall be employed in..navigating any Lighter..on the River Thames (*Trinity Man Fisherman Ballast Man..excepted). 1771 *Order Bk. B. Junior Bursar Trinity Coll. Oxford* 39 (MS.) May 27..*Trinity Monday. Ordered that a general Court be held at Wroxton, Oct. 29. 1819 J. H. Newman *Lett.* (1891) I. 37. 1867 Freeman in Stephens *Life* (1895) I. vi. 386 So we shall anyhow meet on Trinity Monday. *a* 1903 'Merriman' *Last Hope* i, The tottering headstones of certain master mariners and *Trinity-pilots. 1877 W. Jones *Finger-ring* 487 A rare and curious '*Trinity' ring, turned out of one piece of ivory. 1837 *Civil Eng. & Arch. Jrnl.* I. 33/1, 16 feet under the high-water of *Trinity standard. 1426–7 *Rec. St. Mary at Hill* 65 Þe monday after *Trenite sonday. 1911 *Encycl. Brit.* (ed. 11) XXVII. 286 From Trinity Sunday onwards all Sundays until the close of the ecclesiastical year are reckoned as 'after Trinity'. 1540 *Act* 32 *Hen. VIII*, c. 21 § 2 The full terme of the said *Trinitie Terme shall..begynne..the Fryeday next after Corpus Christi day. 1669 [see Hilary]. 1899 *Oxford Univ. Cal.*, May 20, Oxford Trinity or Act Term begins. May 30, Trinity Law Term begins. 1511 *Pilton Churchw. Acc.* (Som. Rec. Soc.) 61 Item for ij tapers agenst *trynyte tide..xx*d*. 1841 L. J. Bernays tr. *Couard's Serm. Ch. Hist.* xii. 154 During the coming Trinity tide. 1724 *Lond. Gaz.* No. 6249/9 Thomas Measant,..*Trinity-Waterman. 1525–6 *Rec. St. Mary at Hill* 332 For mendyng of the *trynite wyndowe of the Sowthe side of the church. 1825 Hone *Every-day Bk.* I. 726 The *Trinity-yacht..lay off St. George's.

Hence **Triˈnityhood** (*nonce-wd.*), the condition or character of being a trinity.

1886 *Trinitas Trinitatum* xxvii. 267 We have seen the Majesty of the Divine Trinityhood vindicated, in the triumph of the Second Adam over Satan.

**Triniunity**, variant of TRINUNITY.

† **Trink**, *sb.*[1] *Obs.* Also (4 *pl.* treinekys), 4–6 trynk, treinke, 5 trenke, (trimke, trymke), 5–6 trynke, (6 trungke), 7 trinck(e, trinke. [Origin obscure. Known in AF. (or English in AF. context) from 14th c., and in use till 17th c.; but almost confined to legal enactments. It has been compared as to form with It. *trinca* a cable, Sp. *trinca* rope, cord, *trincas* lashings (Diez), but evidence of connexion with these is wanting.]

A kind of fixed fishing-net formerly used in the Thames and other rivers, concerning which ordinances were made from 14th c. onward.

1311 *Liber Horn City of London* lf. 221 b (MS.) Item ylia un autre manere de Reys qe um apele Treinekys la largesce de 1 pouz et di. 1344 *Letter Bk. F. London Recds.* lf. 80 b, Compertum est..quod predicta retia vocata Treinkes non sunt largitatis in Mallio..nisi dimidii pollicis ad plus. Ideo consideratum est quod comburantur. 1376 *Rolls of Parlt.* II. 331/2 Qe touz les Trynks par entre Loundres & la miere soient oustez. 1423 *Act 2 Hen. VI*, c. 12 § 1 Salvez a chescun son droit & title en les Weres Kydelx & Trymkes avantditz. *Ibid.* c. 19 § 1 Item ordeignez est & establiz qe la stacion des Reis & engines appellez Trynkes et de toutz autres maneres reis qe sont..fichez & attachez.. soit toutoutrement defenduz...Purveux toutfoitz qe bien lise as possessours des ditz Trynkes..peschier ovec eux..les entraihantz et conveiantz par main come autres peschours [cf. TRINKER, quot. *c* 1485]. 1485 *Letter-Bk. L. Lond.* lf. 208 b, That the Nettes called Trenkes be of the largenes of ii Inches in the Masshe in the fore part and an Inche & half large..in..the later part. 1556 *Chron. Gr. Friars* (Camden) 10 This yere [1405] alle the kydelles and trungkes thorowghout the Temse from the towne of Stanes..unto the watter of Medevey..by the mayer & commonalte of London were dystrowyd and brent. 1630 *Lex Londinensis* (1680) 211 That no Trinckerman or other Fisherman shall buy any Trincke..until he be allowed and thought fit by the Lord Major of London..and seventeen Trinks allowed, and no more. [1688 R. HOLME *Armoury* III. xxii. (Roxb.) 278/1 A Trink, was of old a Kind of Nett to fish withall.]

b. Short for *trink-boat*: see d.

1557 *Admir. Crt. Lib.* 27 (2) No. 131 Proprietarii duarum naviculanum vocatarum ij Trynkes.

c. A fisherman who uses a trink; a trinkerman.

1630 *Lex Londinensis* (1680) 210 That no Trincke shall stand in any Byrth more than is allowed him to stand. *Ibid.* 212 That each Trincke shall every dark and foggy night hang forth out of his said Trinck-boat one Lanthorn. *Ibid.*, That every Trincke shall at all times and seasons take up.. his Anchor at the time of his leaving off from fishing.

d. *attrib.* and *Comb.*: **trink-boat**, a fishing-boat with a trink; **trink-cable**, a cable used with a trink; **trink-man** = TRINKERMAN; **trink-net** = *trink.*

1630 *Trinck-boat [see c above]. 1630 *Lex Londinensis* (1680) 212 That every *Trincke Cable be no more then twenty fathom long at the most. 1689 in Strype *Stow's Surv.* (1754) II. v. xxvii. 480/2 All *Trinke-Men shall yearly, at the Guildhall-Chappel, present themselves before the Lord-Mayor or Water-Bailiff. 1584 *Order Conserv. Thames* in Strype *Stow's Surv.* (1754) I. I. ix. 42/2 No Fishermen, Garthmen..or Tynkermen, shall..make any.. Stalker Nets, *Trynck Nets, Purse Nets, Casting Nets [etc] except they be 2 Inches in the Mash.

† **Trink**, *sb.*[2] *Obs. rare*$^{-1}$. [? Nasalized form of TRICK *sb.* 8 a.] Style of adornment; fashion.

1575 LANEHAM *Let.* (1871) 36 Hiz beard smugly shauen; and yet hiz shyrt after the nu trink, with ruffs fayr starched, sleeked, and glistering like a payr of nu shooz.

**Trink**, *sb.*[3] *Sc.* and *dial.* Also 7 **trinck.** [perh. a. Norm. (Picard) *trenque, trencque*, northern form of OF. *trenche, tranche* TRENCH.] A trench, channel, watercourse (natural or artificial).

1592 *Aberdeen Regr.* (1848) II. 77 That na channell, stanes, sand, nor any uther thing be cassin in the trink of the watter, or within the fluid merk, out of schippis, craris, or bottis. 1603 *Ibid.* 239 That the haill trinck of the water salbe drawn doun the South syd of the Lochfeild croft..and eist syd of the said loch in the auld trinck to be cassin deper and wyder, and that the water trinck on the south-vest syd of the said locht.. salbe stoppit and condamnit. 1812 J. HENDERSON *Agric. Surv. Caithn.* 200 The lower end in an oblong trink in the earth or floor. 1825 JAMIESON, *Trink, trenk*, app. synon. with Eng. *trench.* 1859–99 in *Eng. Dial. Dict.*

† **Tri·nker.** *Obs.* [f. TRINK *sb.*[1] + -ER[1].] **a.** = TRINK *sb.*[1] **b.** = TRINKERMAN. Also in comb. † **trinker-boat** = *trink-boat* (see TRINK *sb.*[1] d).

*c* 1485 tr. *Act 2 Hen. VI*, c. 19 (MS. Harl. 4999, lf. 185 b), That the stacioun of nettis and engynes cald Trynkers and al other maner nettis whiche bien..ficched and attached..be al vtterly defended...Purveied alwey that it be lieful to the possessours of the saide Trynkers..to fisshe with hem..in drawyng and conveiyng bi hande as other fisshers don [cf. TRINK *sb.*[1] quot. 1423]. 1615 E. S. *Britain's Buss* in Arber *Garner* III. 650 Those pernicious Trinkermen, who with trinker-boats destroy the river of Thames, by killing the fry and small fish there.

So **Tri·nking**, the action of fishing with a trink.

1689 in Strype *Stow's Surv.* (1754) II. v. xxvii. 480/1 That no Person..use or practice Trincking, Stow-boating, Trawling, or Catching of Fish, or Bait, on the Lord's-Day..upon Forfeiture of 20 *s.*

**Trinkerman** (tri·ŋkəɹmæn). Pl. **-men.** Also *erron.* 6–7 tynker-, 7–8 tin(c)kerman. See also TINKLERMAN. [f. TRINKER: cf. FISHERMAN.] A man who fishes with a trink (see TRINK *sb.*[1]); the title of a class of fishermen on the Thames.

1538 *City of London Recds.* Jrnl. 14 lf. 111 (MS.) Fyrst yt ys agreed that the Trynkermen shal begynne to occupye theyre occupacion at Saynt James day. 1542 *Lett. & Pap. Hen. VIII*, XVII. 15 Considerations why the trynker men cannot save small brood and fry of fish. 1584 Tynkermen [see *trink-net*, TRINK *sb.*[1] d]. 1615 [see TRINKER-*boat*]. 1720 STRYPE *Stow's Surv.* (1754) I. I. vii. 34/1 Whereas there are a certain Company of Fishermen, called Trinkermen (or Tynkermen) frequenting the River of Thames, eastward. 1868 in *Windsor Express* 22 Aug., The old fishermen—'trinkermen' as they are termed—in the tidal way are praying devoutly for a continuance of rain.

† **Tri·nkery**, *sb.* or *a. Obs. rare*$^{-1}$. [? f. TRINKET *sb.*[1] Perh. error or misprint for *trinketry* or *trinkety.*] ? Adornment; in quot. *attrib.* or *adj.* Serving for adornment, ornamental.

1582 STANYHURST *Æneis* IV. (Arb.) 99 As yet in her pincking not pranckt with trinckerye trinckets.

**Trinket** (tri·ŋkėt), *sb.*[1] Also 6 tryn-, trinkett(e, 7 trinckett. [Origin uncertain; has the form of a diminutive in -ET.

From the similarity of form, it has been suggested that this is the same word as TRENKET or *trynket*, a small knife, spec. a shoemaker's knife. But to such a transition of sense the general sense-history of the word from 1533 offers no confirmation. Another suggestion, supported by other words with *trink-* for *trick-*, is that this may be in some way related to TRICK *sb.* or *v.*; cf. esp. TRICK *sb.* 6 b; but here also evidence is wanting. Godefroy has a single instance of OF. *tryncle*, 1474, evidently denoting a piece of jewellery: cf. sense 2.]

† **1.** Any small article forming part of an outfit; usually *pl.* the tools, implements, or tackle of an occupation; paraphernalia, accoutrements, 'traps'.

*a* 1536 *Calisto & Mel.* A vj, I haue..sene her trynkettes For payntyng thynges inumerable Squalmys & balmys. 1560 DAUS tr. *Sleidane's Comm.* 114 b, A conjuror.. had all his trynkettes and furniture concerning suche matters in a redinesse. 1573 TUSSER *Husb.* (1878) 36 Husbandlie furniture [in the stable]..A line to fetch litter, and halters for hed, With crotchis and pinnes, to hang trinkets theron, And stable fast chained, that nothing be gon. 1583 STUBBES *Anat. Abus.* II. (1882) 49 Cheese, fagots, pots, pannes, candles, and a thousand other trinkets besides. 1598 HAKLUYT *Voy.* I. 62 The poorer sort of common souldiers haue euery man his leather bag or sachell well sowen together, wherin he packs vp all his trinkets. 1606 S. GARDINER *Bk. Angling* 48 Sundrie and many are the trinkets that belong to fishing. 1693 DRYDEN *Juvenal's Sat.* VI. 212 Pack up with all your Trinkets, and away. 1787 W. TAYLOR *Poems* 67, I' se gie her..A rock an' reel, pot, pan, an' wheel, An' mony mae usefu' trinkets.

† **b.** Applied to articles of food: A sweet, a dainty trifle. *Obs.*

1587 *Wills & Inv. N. C.* (Surtees) II. 158, xij lbs of synnamount comffettes 20/-. For banketinges disshes, as socatte and sewgar trinkettes, 10/-. 1822 SCOTT *Nigel* xxiii, Let Tim send the ale..with a bit of diet-loaf, or some such trinket.

**2.** A small ornament or fancy article, usually an article of jewellery for personal adornment.

*a* 1533 LD. BERNERS *Gold. Bk. M. Aurel.* Let. v. (1535) Ff ij, But I wold wyt..what goodly trinkettes ye hope to were in the straytnes of the Sepulchre. 1577 HARRISON *England* II. vii. (1877) I. 168 To receiue some other trinket newlie deuised by the fickle headed tailors. 1585 T. WASHINGTON tr. *Nicholay's Voy.* II. vii. 37 b, They were many chaines, tablets, and other trynkets of gold. 1674 tr. *Scheffer's Lapland* 89 The weight of the trinkets they [Lapp women] carry about them doth commonly weigh twenty pound. 1713 GAY *Fan* I. 115 Each trinket that adorns the modern dame, First to these little artists ow'd its frame. 1726 SWIFT *Gulliver* II. iv, Trinkets, of which the girl was very fond, as children at her age usually are. 1774 GOLDSM. *Nat. Hist.* (1776) VI. 396 The tortoise-shell of which such a variety of beautiful trinkets are made. 1849 MACAULAY *Hist. Eng.* iv. I. 473 Half as much as he proposed to expend in covering his wife with trinkets. 1863 KINGLAKE *Crimea* (1876) I. i. 14 Down to the giving of trinkets and ribbons, he was not forgetful.

† **3.** *fig.* Applied esp. to the decorations of worship, and to religious rites, ceremonies, beliefs, etc. which the speaker thinks vain or trivial. *Obs.*

1538 LONDON in *Lett. Suppress. Monasteries* (Camden) 224, I have pullyd down the image of your lady..with all trynkettes abowt the same, as schrowdes, candels, images of wexe, crowches, and brochys. 1549 COVERDALE, etc. *Erasm. Par. Col.* i. 1 Iewishnes and superstitious Philosophie.. superstitiously also honouryng the Sunne, the Moone, and starres, with suche other smal trinkettes of this worlde. *a* 1591 H. SMITH *Serm.* (1625) 50 Then they invented purgatory, masses, prayers for the dead, and then all their Trinkets. 1655 FULLER *Ch. Hist* II. ii. § 20 The Administration of that Sacrament was not loaded with those Superstitious Ceremonies..of Crossing, Spittle, Oyl, Cream, Salt, and such like Trinkets.

**4.** *attrib.* and *Comb.*, as *trinket-box, -case, -maker.*

1809 MALKIN *Gil Blas* IX. i. (Rtldg.) 309 A goldsmith's daughter! exclaimed I..Can you think of tying me up to a trinket-maker? 1825 T. HOOK *Sayings* Ser. II. *Sutherl.* I. 142 Repeating the question about Grace's trinket-box. 1841 MRS. MOZLEY *Lost Brooch* II. xv. 109 The trinket case was on the toilette table, and open. 1906 W. CHURCHILL *Ld. R. Churchill* II. xvi. 250 The place-hunters and trinket-seekers who surrounded them.

† **Tri·nket**, *sb.*[2] *Obs.* Also 6 trankett. [Origin and history obscure.

App. a local word of Cheshire and Lancashire; possibly a particular use of prec.; but according to Ray 1691 from Welsh *trànked.* Owen Pugh (1832) has this word as '*tranced* an earthen vessel or cup, such a cup with a handle, as is in common use'; but no etymology of the word is known in Welsh, and it may have been borrowed from a neighbouring Eng. dialect.]

A small drinking vessel; a cup, mug; a porringer.

1541–2 *Will W. Davenport* (Bramhall, nr. Stockport) in *Lanc. & Chesh. Wills* (Chetham Soc. 1857) I. 80 In y[e] kechen ..xij pottengers, xij salsers, xv trankettis, iij potthookis. 1621 GILL *Logon. Angl.* (ed. 2) 37 *Trinkets*, instrumenta doliariorum quibus vinum ab uno vase exhaurifur in aliud. 1691 RAY *N. C. Words* (E.D.S.), *Counterfeits and Trinkets*, porringers and saucers. *Chesh. Ibid.*, *Trinket*, a porringer. *Chesh.* from Welsh *trànked.* *a* 1700 B. E. *Dict. Cant. Crew*, *Trinkets*, Porringers. *c* 1705 DE FOE *True Relat. Appar. Mrs. Veal* Wks. 1840 V. 348 I'll warrant you, this mad fellow ..has broke all your trinkets. But, says Mrs. Bargrave, I'll get something to drink [tea] in, for all that.

† **Tri·nket**, *sb.*[3] *Obs.* Also 6–7 -ette, trinquet, 7 trinchet. [Identical with (and prob. a.) F. *trinquet* (15–16th c. in Hatz.-Darm.) a foremast, also its sail; in Cotgr. 1611, 'properly the top or top-gallant on any mast'; in mod.F. dictionaries 'the foremast in a lateen-rigged vessel'. According to Hatz.-Darm., ad. It. *trinchetto* 'a small saile called a trinket' (Florio), 'the fore-sail' (Baretti); = Sp. *trinquete* 'the foremast, the fore saile' (Percival); Cat. *triquete*, Pg. *traquete* (Jal). Cf. also F. *trinquette* (15–16th c.), 'a triangular sail, a kind of lateen sail' (Littré), a fore-stay sail, a storm-jib; so Sp. *trinquetilla.* If the original application was to a sail, the meaning may have been a three-cornered sail, from L. *triquetrus*; but Jal takes the name as primarily designating a mast. See Diez, Littré, Jal.] A kind of sail; *esp.* the triangular sail before the mast, in a lateen-rigged vessel.

In Holland's Livy it represents L. *dolon*, which Isidore (XIX. iii. 3) defines as 'minimum velum et ad proram defixum'.

1555 EDEN *Decades* 195 They..sayle with twoo sayles as with the master sayle and the trinkette. 1596 THOMAS *Lat. Dict.* (1606), *Dolo*, a small saile in a ship called a Trinket. 1600 HOLLAND *Livy* XXXVI. xliv. 943 b, Hee set up the trinkets [L. *dolones*] or small sailes, meaning to make way into the deepe. 1648 HEXHAM *Dutch Dict.*, *Focke, ofte Focke-zeyl*, a small saile at the prow of a ship, called a Trinket. 1658 EARL MONM. tr. *Paruta's Wars Cyprus* 63 That they might keep company, they used only the Trinchet. *Ibid.* 134 The Turkish gallies sayled..with their Trinchetsayl onely, very close together. 1697 POTTER *Antiq. Greece* III. xvi. (1715) 134 Δόλων, the Trinket, or small Sail in the Fore-deck.

**b.** See quots., and cf. Cotgr. cited in etymology above. (Perh. an error.)

1656 BLOUNT *Glossogr.*, *Trinquet*.. is properly the top or top-gallant on any mast, the highest saile of a ship. So 1707 in *Glossographia Anglicana Nova.*

**Tri·nket**, *sb.*[4] *local.* [dim. of TRINK *sb.*[3]: see -ET.] A small or narrow channel or watercourse.

1880 *Antrim & Down Gloss.*, *Trinket*, a small artificial water-course. 1888 H. C. HART in *N. & Q.* 7th Ser. VI. 372/2 *Trinket*..is used about Dublin and also in the northern counties, with the sense of 'a little stream or watercourse by the roadside'. 1901 *Blackw. Mag.* Sept. 362/1 A smack drew through the fine mist in the Firth [of Forth], and sailing up the trinket, landed Provost Trail on the east pier-head.

† **Tri·nket**, *v.*[1] Chiefly *Sc. Obs.* Also 9 trinquet. [Origin unknown (unless connected with TRINKET *sb.*[1] 3, or TRICK *sb.* or *v.*). Cf. also TRINKLE *v.*[3]] *intr.* To have clandestine communications or underhand dealings *with*; to intrigue *with*; to act in an underhand way, prevaricate.

1647 [see *trinketing* vbl. sb. below]. 1651 *Mr. Love's Case* 37 Was there any such Article..by which he stood in Conscience bound to trinket with the declared and professed Enemies of the State? 1676 FOUNTAINHALL in M. P. Brown *Suppl. Dict. Decis.* (1826) III. 67 If the witness be found lying and trinketing in thir, it vilifies and derogates much from the weight and faith of his testimony. *a* 1734 NORTH *Exam.* I. ii. § 63 (1740) 63 Had the Popish Lords.. not trinketed with the Enemies of that [the Crown] and themselves. 1819 SCOTT *Ivanhoe* xxxviii, Tampering and trinketing with hellish cures. 1821 — *Kenilw.* xxxvi, A woman, who trinkets and traffics with my worst foes!

Hence † **Tri·nketer**[1], one who has underhand dealings; a secret trafficker; an intriguer; † **Tri·nketing** *vbl. sb.*, underhand dealing or trafficking.

1651 *Mr. Love's Case* 40 Mr. [Chr.] Love with the rest of his fellow *Trinketers, divided their thoughts and endeavors between doing of mischief..and the keeping themselves out of danger. 1821 SCOTT *Kenilw.* ix, If he becomes thus a trinketer with Satan. 1646 R. BAILLIE *Lett.* 1 Dec. (1841) II. 412 The King, all his lyfe, hes loved *trinketting naturally and is thought to be much in that action now with all parties. 1647 *Hamilton Papers* (Camden) 149 Some talk confidently of fresh trinketting with the King. *a* 1716 SOUTH *Serm.* (1717) VI. 126 By their Tricks and Trinketting, between Party and Party. 1827 SCOTT *Surg. Dau.* i, To abhor all trafficking or trinketing with Papists.

**Tri·nket**, *v.*[2] *rare.* [f. TRINKET *sb.*[1]] *trans.* To deck *out* with trinkets.

1863 SALA *Capt. Dangerous* III. viii. 265 The Girls for sale are apparelled in a sumptuous manner, bathed, perfumed, and trinketed out.

† **Tri·nketer**[2]. *Obs.* [f. TRINKET *sb.*[1] + -ER[1] 1.] One who attaches importance to trinkets: in quots. used contemptuously in reference to Romish religious observances, etc.: see TRINKET *sb.*[1] 3.

1583 MELBANCKE *Philotimus* C iij, These two deludinge trinketters. 1659 HEYLIN *Certamen Epist.* 321 Neither of which (..necessity nor essentiallity) hath hitherto been ascribed to the Cross in Baptism, by any of the greatest Trinketers in the Church of Rome.

So † **Tri·nketing** *a. nonce-wd.*, having to do with trinkets, toys, or trivial rites and ceremonies.

1679 BP. CROFT *Let. Popish Idol.* 23 Silly Women..pleased with Toys, which makes the weaker Sex much incline to the trinketting Ceremonies of the Papists.

**Trinketry** (tri·ŋkėtri). [f. TRINKET *sb.*[1] + -RY, after *jewelry*.] Trinkets collectively; articles of personal decoration or of ornament viewed as trinkets or toys. Also *fig.*

1810 SOUTHEY *Kehama* XIII. xiii, Ear-drop, nor chain, nor arm, nor ankle-ring, Nor trinketry on front, or neck, or breast. 1839–40 W. IRVING *Wolfert's R.* (1855) 205 In those days there were no country stores in those parts, with their artificial finery and trinketry. 1892 *Critic* 23 Jan. 47/2 Plain, entirely accurate, not unmusical prose, unencumbered with the trickery and trinketry required by verse. 1911 F. N. STREATFEILD *Remin.* xiii. 147 A General, with much trinketry on his manly bosom.

**Tri·nkety**, *a. colloq. rare.* [f. TRINKET *sb.*[1] + -Y.] Of the nature of a trinket or thing of little importance; trivial, paltry.

1817 SCOTT *Let. to Miss J. Baillie* 26 Sept., in Lockhart *Life*, A series of little trinketry sort of business, and occupation, and idleness, have succeeded to each other.

†**Trinkilo.** *Obs. rare.* App. perversion of TRINKET *sb.*[1], simulating a Sp. or It. form.

1631 BRATHWAIT *Whimzies, Char. Pedler* 138 It is a pretty thing to observe how hee carries his trinkilo's about him.

**Trinking**: see under TRINKER.

**Trinkle** (tri·ŋk'l), *v.*[1] *Sc.* and *dial.* Also 5–6 **trynkel**, 6 **-kle**; *β.* 6 **tringle, thringle.** [app. a nasalized modification of TRICKLE *v.*[1]]

**1.** *intr.* To trickle, to flow or fall drop by drop. Also *fig.* Hence **Tri·nkling** *ppl. a.*

14.. *Chaucer's Sompn. T.* 156 (Camb. MS. Gg. 4. 27) With manye a tere trynkelynge [*v.rr.* trilling, triklyng] on myn cheke. 1513 DOUGLAS *Æneis* IX. v. 58 With teris trynkeland our his chekis and face. *a* 1600 MONTGOMERIE *Sonn.* lv. 10 My trinkling teirs, the presents I propyne. 1687 MACFARLANE *Geog. Collect.* (S.H.S.) III. 145 Burns..are seen trinkling down the green Hills. 1794 BURNS '*O Mally's meek*' 14 Her yellow hair..Comes trinkling down her swan-white neck. 1828 *Craven Gloss.*, *Trinkle*, to trickle. 1832 MOTHERWELL *Jeanie Morrison* ix, Tears trinkled doun your cheek. *β.* 1513 DOUGLAS *Æneis* VI. xi. 14 The teris thringling [*ed.* 1553 trigling] furth our his chekis ran. 1535 STEWART *Cron. Scot.* (Rolls) II. 558 So mony teir come tringland fra his ene.

**2.** *trans.* To cause to trickle; to shed (tears).

*a* 1605 MONTGOMERIE *Cherrie & Slae* (revision) iv, Quhairon Apollos paramouris Had trinklit mony a teir.

Hence **Tri·nkle** *sb. Sc.* = TRICKLE *sb.* 1.

1887 *Jamieson's Dict., Suppl.*, *Trinkle*, a drop, series of drops, falling or fallen, as from a leaking vessel or a spout; a continuous dropping, or a slender thread of falling liquid; ..a trinkle of blood. 1905 in *Eng. Dial. Dict.*

**Tri·nkle,** *v.*[2] *dial.* [Altered f. TINGLE, TINKLE.]

**1.** *intr.* To tingle, thrill.

1644 R. BAILLIE *Lett.* 2 Apr. (Bann. Cl.) II. 154 The maine chance is in the North, for which our hearts are trinckling.

**2.** To tinkle, make a tinkling sound.

1827 COLERIDGE in *Hone's Every-day Bk.* II. 115 The noises give an impulse to the icy trees, and the woods all round the lake *trinkle*. 1892 *Field* 28 May 805/2 The pilot..watched her [a yacht] trinkling through the water.

† **Tri·nkle,** *v.*[3] *Obs.* Also 7 **-ckle,** 8 **-cle.** [app. orig. an alteration (erroneous or intentional) of TRINKET *v.*[1]] *intr.* To treat secretly or in an underhand way, intrigue (*with*); = TRINKET *v.*[1]

1672 MARVELL *Reh. Transp.* I. 310 Others..have made it their business to trinkle with the Members of Parliament, for obstructing it. 1677 *Sec. Packet Advices to Men of Shaftesb.* 28 No Temporal Lordships must look to thrive by trinkling with them, unless they will truckle to 'em too. 1683 TEMPLE *Mem.* Wks. 1731 I. 394 They were suspected to have trinkled at least with Holland about raising Seditions, and perhaps Insurrections in England. 1688 *Vox Cleri pro Rege* To Rdr., Let her [the Church] then take heed how she trinckles with the Crown, and be afraid of bringing down the Royal Thunder upon her own Head.

**b.** *trans.* ? To provoke, incite.

1685 COTTON tr. *Montaigne* III. 180 We have need to be trinckled and tickled by some such niping incitation as this. 1705 HICKERINGILL *Priest-cr.* II. Wks. 1716 III. 91 Can you blame them therefore, by all Arts, to trinkle a Popishly-affected Prince..or some silly well-meaning Bigot, to draw his Weapon? *Ibid.* III. 180 That such Wretches..would trincle the Tackers, and Priest-ridden Bigots, to endeavour to exclude all other English-Men from their Liberties.

**Tri·nklement.** Now *dial.* Also 6 **trentill-, trintlment.** [Irregularly f. TRINKET *sb.*[1] or OF. *tryncle* trinket, jewel (1474 in Godef.).] Adornment; in *pl.* 'trinkets, knick-knacks' (E.D.D., Lancash.).

1582–3 *Wills & Inv. N. C.* (Surtees) II. 61 Trentillment of houshold 10/- One siluer cupp 40/-. 1586 *Ibid.* 129 Wooden vessell, tubbes, and other trintlmentes of howsholde, 10/-. In the Seller. Tubbes, with other trintlmentes 10/-. *a* 1675 LIGHTFOOT *Rem.* (1700) 245 You see all the Trinklements of Popery, and the Pope and Friars hanging on. ? 1857 J. T. STATON *B. Shuttle* 8 (E.D.D.) Owd-fashunt, un valuable trinklaments.

**Trinklet** (tri·ŋklėt). *rare.* Also 6 **trincklet.** [app. an alteration of TRINKET *sb.*[1], after diminutives in -LET; cf. *giglet.*]

† **1.** ? A woman decked out with 'trinkets' or finery. *Obs. rare*[−1].

*c* 1550 *Pryde & Abuse Wom.* 52 in Hazl. *E. P. P.* IV. 234 Oure trotte, our trotte, our lustye trotte,..Is nowe become a trickynge one, And a wanton trincklet agayne.

**2.** = TRINKET *sb.*[1] 2, 3.

1897 J. KENSIT in *Westm. Gaz.* 15 Jan. 7/3 His lordship is now reintroducing the trinklets of Rome, by the wearing of a mitre upon his head. 1898 *Westm. Gaz.* 29 Nov. 5/2 A jewel robbery..the greater part of the jewels and trinklets.. being taken. 1909 *Nation* 6 Mar. 862 Ornaments of show, Trinklets and mirrors—these can go Outside.

**Trinkum** (tri·ŋkǒm). Now *dial.* or *colloq.* Also 7 **trinckam, trinkom,** 8–9 **-cum,** 9 **-krum.** [app. a humorous alteration of *trinket*, with latinized ending.] A trinket.

1667 COTTON *Scarron.* IV. 125 Scarce had she thus dispos'd her trinckums, When up the Stairs, behold the Queen comes. 1699 J. DUNTON *Life & Err.* (1818) II. xvii. 537 Good store of holy water..and of several other consecrated trinckams. 1774 *Poetry* in *Ann. Reg.* 224 Very fine ladies with very fine incomes, Which they finely lay out on fine toys and fine trincums. 1819 SCOTT *Let. to J. Richardson* 22 Aug., in *Lockhart*, He had a world of trinkums to get, for you know there goes as much to the man-millinery of a young officer of hussars as to that of an heiress on her bridal day. 1892 SARAH HEWETT *Peas. Sp. Devon.* 136, I put a vew trinkrums about a 'undered yers old in a smal box.

Also reduplicated, **Tri·nkum-tra·nkum** (also **tringum-trangum, tringham trangham**) *slang* and *dial.*; also *attrib.*

*a* 1700 B. E. *Dict. Cant. Crew*, *Tringum-Trangum*, a Whim, or Maggot. 1702 STEELE *Funeral* II. ii, Come, come, this is not one of your Tringham Trangham witty things, that your poor poets write. 1718 MOTTEUX *Quix.* I. III. vi. (1749) 154 Toralva..comes after him bare-foot..with a pilgrim's staff in her hand, and a wallet at her back wherein.. she carry'd a piece of a looking-glass,..a broken pot with paint, and I don't know what other trinkums trankums to prink herself up. 1821 GALT *Ann. Parish* xii, Trinkum-trankum flowers and feathers. 1842 *Blackw. Mag.* LI. 23 Cheap gun shops, trinkum-trankum shops.

**Trinoctial**: see TRI- 1.

**Trinodal** (trəiˌnōu·dăl), *a.* [f. TRI- + L. *nōd-us* knot, NODE + -AL; cf. L. *trinōdis*.] **a.** Having three knots. *rare*[−0]. **b.** *Bot.* Having three nodes (NODE *sb.* 2 b), as a stem. **c.** *Geom.* Having three nodes (NODE *sb.* 7), as a curve.

1656 BLOUNT *Glossogr.*, *Trinodal*.., that hath three knots, three-knotted. 1866 *Treas. Bot.* 1172 *Trinodal*, having three nodes only. 1873 SALMON *Higher Plane Curves* vi. (1879) 255 The other will be a trinodal quartic.

So **Trinode** (trəi·nōud), *Geom.* a combination of three nodes at one point of a curve; **Trino·dine** *a.* = *trinodal* a.

1866 J. B. ROSE tr. *Ovid's Fasti* I. 612 Alcides grappled him; and broke With club trinodine,..The caitiff's head. 1891 *Cent. Dict.*, Trinode.

**Trinoda necessitas**: see TRIMODA N.

**Trinomial** (trəinōu·miăl), *a.* and *sb.* [Formed with TRI- after BINOMIAL, q. v.]

**A.** *adj.* **1.** *Math.* Consisting of three terms, as an algebraical expression.

1704 J. HARRIS *Lex. Techn.* I, *Trinomial-Root*, in Mathematicks, is a Root consisting of three parts connected together by the Sign +; as *a*+*b*+*c*. See *Binomial*. 1743 EMERSON *Fluxions* I. 83 The Fluents of the Trinomial or compound Binomial Fluxions. *c* 1865 *Circ. Sc.* I. 483/2 The..multiplier will be trinomial.

**2.** *Nat. Hist.* Consisting of three terms, the first being that of the genus, the second that of the species, the third that of the subspecies or variety, instead of the two former only; involving or characterized by three terms, as a system of nomenclature. (Cf. BINOMIAL A. 2.)

1865 DARWIN *Lett.* (1903) I. 474, I have sometimes..speculated on what nomenclature would come to, and concluded that it would be trinomial. 1884 *Nature* 10 July 257/1 More than ten years ago..Dr. Coues, in his 'Key to the North American Birds', first began to adopt the trinomial nomenclature which is now so generally accepted by American ornithologists.

**B.** *sb.* **1.** *Math.* An expression consisting of three terms connected by + or −.

1674 JEAKE *Arith.* (1696) 294 If three Quantities be conjoyned, and but three, they are sometime called Trinomials. 1706 W. JONES *Syn. Palmar. Matheseos* 171 To raise any Trinomial..to any given Power. *c* 1865 *Circ. Sc.* I. 473/1 The square of a binomial consists of three terms; that is, it is a trinomial.

**2.** *Nat. Hist.* The name of a subspecies or variety when composed of three terms (the names of the genus, species, and subspecies or variety).

1884 *Proc. Boston Soc. Nat. Hist.* 19 Mar. 166 According to recent lists all names are to be trinomials, either through duplication or addition.

Hence **Trino·mialism,** the trinomial system of nomenclature, or the use of trinomial names (see A. 2); **Trino·mialist,** one who uses or advocates this system; **Trinomia·lity,** the quality or character of being trinomial; **Trino·mially** *adv.*, in a trinomial manner; by the use of trinomial names.

1884 *Academy* 5 July 13/3 Dr. Coues..showed how useful '*trinomialism' was in describing species which over the vast extent of North America varied to an extent hardly realised in the Old World. 1898 *Nature* 30 June 196/2 Mr. Blanford has not yet brought himself to accept the principle of trinomialism for birds. 1884 *Proc. Boston Soc. Nat. Hist.* 19 Mar. 168 Some *trinomialists disclaim responsibility for the repetition or duplication. 1891 *Cent. Dict.*, *Trinomiality. 1884 *Nature* 10 July 257/2 There has been..a consensus of opinion..that they [the Yellow Wagtails] ought to be treated *trinomially.

**Trinominal** (trəinǫ·minăl), *a. rare.* [f. TRI- + L. *nōminālis* NOMINAL.] Having three names; in *Nat. Hist.* = TRINOMIAL A. 2.

1674 BLOUNT *Glossogr.*, *Trinominal* (*trinominalis*), that hath three names. 1691 W. NICHOLLS *Answ. Naked Gospel* 90 No farther distant from Socinianism, than a Trinominal Deity is different from him that is personally one, without such nominal Distinction. 1882 OGILVIE (Annandale), *Trinominal, a.*, same as *Trinomial*.

† **Tri·nomy**[1]. *Math. Obs. rare.* [formed with TRI- after BINOMY.] = TRINOMIAL B. 1.

1571 DIGGES *Pantom.* IV. xxi. Cc iij b, By reduction of the former Trinomye to a Binomye.

**Trinomy**[2] (tri·nǒmi). *rare.* [f. TRI- + Gr. -*νομία*, -NOMY.] A threefold law, rule, or arrangement.

1838 *Fraser's Mag.* XVIII. 556 Its greatest pivot consists in the fundamental trinomy of understanding, discerning, and contempering.

**Trinquet**, var. TRINKET *sb.*[3] and *v.*[1] *Obs.*

**Trinsch**, obs. Sc. form of TRENCH.

**Trintch, Trinte**, obs. ff. TRENCH, TRINITY.

**Trintle**, Sc. and dial. variant of TRINDLE.

**Trintlment**, obs. form of TRINKLEMENT.

**Trinucleate**: see TRI- 1.

**Trinu·ndine.** *Rom. Antiq. rare*[−1]. [ad. L. *trinundin-us*, f. TRI- + *nundina*: see NUNDINE.] A period including three successive nundines, i. e. seventeen days.

1891 FARRAR *Darkn. & Dawn* xix, Onesimus was doomed to the scourge, as well as to a trinundine of solitude on bread and water.

† **Trinu·ne, trin-une,** *a. Obs.* Also 7 **trine une, triniune.** [f. L. *trīn-us* (or its pl. *trīni*) three each, TRINE + *ūnus* one.] Three in one: = TRIUNE. So † **Trinu·ned** *ppl. a.*, combined as three in one; † **Trinu·nion,** † **Trinu·nionhood,** † **Trinu·nity** (also **triniunity**), state of being triune, trinity in unity.

1620 T. GRANGER *Div. Logike* 73 That we are bound to worship the *trin-vne God with faith. 1681 J. SCOTT *Chr. Life* I. (1684) 10 The Mysterious Trin-un-Divinity. 1610 W. FOLKINGHAM *Art of Survey* I. iii. 5 Opall Paderas, with their *Trineuned luster. 1603 J. DAVIES *Microcosmos* 207 But that same onely-wise *Trin-vnion Workes Miracles, wherein all wonder lies. 1612 — *Muse's Sacr.* (Grosart) 32/2 Who (were it possible) art more compleate in Goodnesse, then thine owne *Trin-vnionhood! 1650 F. CHEYNELL (*title*) The Divine *Trinunity of the Father, Son, and Holy Spirit. 1673 MILTON *True Relig.* 7 As for terms of Trinity, Triniunity, Coessentiality, Tripersonality, and the like, they reject them as Scholastic Notions, not to be found in Scripture. 1694 R. BURTHOGGE *Reason & Nat. Spirits* 279 He makes the same application of it to the Divine Trin-unity that Laurentius Valla doth.

**Trio** (trī·o, trəi·o). [a. F. *trio* (*a* 1600 in Hatz.-Darm., according to whom) a. It. *trio*, f. *tre* three, 'formed in imitation of *duo*'.]

**1.** *Mus.* A composition for three voices or instruments; also, a company of three performers singing or playing such a composition.

1724 *Short Explic. For. Wds. in Mus. Bks.*, *Tria*, or *Trio*, Musick in Three Parts is so called, either for Voices or Instruments, or both together. 1727–41 CHAMBERS *Cycl.*, *Trio*, in music; a part of a concert wherein three persons sing; or more properly a musical composition consisting of three parts. 1775 MME. D'ARBLAY *Early Diary* (1889) II. 134 It seemed to be a sort of *trio* between an old woman, a young woman, and a young man. 1824 BYRON *Juan* XVI. xlv, Oh! the long evenings of duets and trios! 1885 'MRS. ALEXANDER' *At Bay* iii, Mademoiselle Antoinette and Elsie, assisted by the singing-master, were performing a trio.

**b.** Name for a second or subordinate division of a minuet or other dance movement, or of a scherzo or march; commonly in a different key and style from the main division, which is repeated after it.

Supposed to be so called because originally written for three instruments or in three parts.

1840 *Encycl. Brit.* (ed. 7) XXI. 387/1 The term *trio* is also applied to a movement in ¾th time, which often follows the minuet in a piece of instrumental music. 1889 F. CORDER in Grove *Dict. Mus.* IV. 172/2 How the second minuet acquired the name of Trio is not quite clear. Bach only calls it so in the few instances in which it is written in three parts—as opposed to the minuet in two. *Ibid.* 173/1 By the time of Haydn the term Trio is firmly established, and even in his earliest works..there are two minuets, each with a trio.

**2.** A group or set of three: **a.** of persons.

[1763 MRS. BROOKE *Lady J. Mandeville* (1820) 55 Foreseeing we should be a very awkward party to-day *à trio*, I sent..to ask three or four very agreeable girls..to come and ramble all day with us in the woods.] 1789 H. WALPOLE *Let. to Mrs. H. More* 22 Apr., The lady flowers and their lovers enter in pairs or trios. 1836 W. IRVING *Astoria* xliv. III. 38 The trio of Kentucky hunters, Robinson, Rezner, and Hoback. 1904 *Verney Mem.* II. 59 Chatting with this trio of charming cousins.

**b.** of things or animals; in quot. 1777 a stanza of three lines; in *Cricket*, three runs.

1777 tr. *Chesterfield's Lett.* I. xxxv. Misc. Wks. II. 110, I will tell you very frankly, I could as soon get off fifty thousand of his *trios* as fifty. 1856 KANE *Arct. Expl.* II. xiii. 132 [Walrus] surging in loving trios from crack to crack. 1873 EARLE *Philol. Eng. Tongue* (ed. 2) § 109 The general adoption of this trio of vowel-sounds as the basis of phonology. 1882 *Daily Tel.* 24 June, At 237 Studd resumed in place of Ramsay, but was almost at once driven by Giffen for a trio.

**c.** *Cards.* At piquet, a combination of three aces, kings, queens, or knaves in one hand.

1891 in *Cent. Dict.*

**Triobol** (trəi·ǫbǫl, trəiˌǭu·bǫl). Also in L. form **triobolus.** [ad. Gr. *τριώβολον*, f. *τρι-*, TRI- +

ὀβολός OBOL.] An ancient Greek coin of the value of three obols, or half a drachma.

[1693 tr. *Blancard's Phys. Dict.* (ed. 2), *Triobolon*, half a Dram.] **1837** WHEELWRIGHT tr. *Aristoph.* II. 190 She bates her tongue for my triobolus. **1842** *Smith's Dict. Grk. & Rom. Antiq.* s. v. *Drachma*, Specimens of the tetrobolus, triobolus, diobolus..are still found. **1887** B. V. HEAD *Hist. Numorum* 316 Tetradrachms, Drachms, and Triobols.

†**Trio·bolar**, *a. Obs.* Also 6–7 triobular. [ad. med.L. *triōbulār-is* (Du Cange), f. L. *triōbol-us*: see prec. and -AR.] *lit.* Worth three obols; in use always *fig.*, of little or no worth, vile, paltry, mean, contemptible. (Cf. *twopenny-halfpenny*.)

**1585** T. WASHINGTON tr. *Nicholay's Voy.* Ep. Ded., Common men, (I meane not triobular mates) men I say, of base descent and linage. **1593** ABP. BANCROFT *Daung. Posit.* II. iii. 48 Railing pamphlets; many of them but triobolar chartals. **1647** MAYNE *Serm. agst. False Proph.* 11 It may pass currant amongst the Balladmongers for a triobolar Ballad.

Also †**Trio·bolary** (also -ulary) *a.* in same sense.

**1644** FEATLEY *Levites Scourge* 7 Libelled in all the triobulary pasquils printed the first and second weeke of October. **1653** GAUDEN *Hierasp.* 504 There are many such whining people, penurious protestants, triobolary Christians. **1700** T. BROWN *Amusem. Ser. & Com.* 48 Seeing their Qualities ridicul'd by every Triobolary Poet.

**Tri-octahedral, -ocular**: see TRI- 2 b, 1.

**Trioctile** (trəi|ǫ·ktil, -təil). *Astrol.* [f. TRI- + L. *octo* eight, after *quartile, sextile*.] An aspect of two planets distant from each other three-eighths of the whole circle, i. e. 135 degrees; the sesquiquadrate.

**1727–41** CHAMBERS *Cycl.* s. v. *Aspect*, To the five ancient aspects, the modern writers have added several more; as decile, containing the tenth part of a circle; tridecile,.. biquintile,..semisextile,..quincunx.., to the astrological phvsicians we owe octile, containing one eighth; and trioctile, containing three eighths. **1795** HUTTON *Math. Dict.*, *Trioctile*,..which some call the *sesquiquadrans*.

**Triod** (trəi·ǫd). *Zool.* [ad. Gr. τρίοδος a place where three ways meet, f. τρι-, TRI- + ὁδός way.] Name for a simple triradiate sponge-spicule, consisting of three rays inclined at angles of 120°.

**1887** SOLLAS in *Encycl. Brit.* XXII. 416/2 Fig. 12..*c*, triod (triaxon triactine).

**Triodontoid** (trəi|odǫ·ntoid), *a.* (*sb.*) *Ichth.* [f. mod.L. *Triodon, -ont-* (f. Gr. τρι-, TRI- + ὀδούς tooth; so called from the divided upper jaw and undivided lower jaw, suggesting three teeth) + -OID.] Resembling or allied to the genus *Triodon* of plectognath fishes. **b.** *sb.* A fish of this genus or family. **1891** in *Cent. Dict.*

‖ **Triœcia** (trəi|ī·ʃiă). *Bot.* [mod.L. (Linnæus), f. Gr. τρι-, TRI- + οἶκος house: cf. DIŒCIA, MONŒCIA.] The third order in the Linnæan class *Polygamia*, comprising plants having male, female, and hermaphrodite flowers on different individuals. Hence **Triœcious** (-ī·ʃəs) *a.*, **Tri|oi·cous** *a.*, belonging to this order, or having the flowers thus distributed (whence **Triœ·ciously** *adv.*); **Triœcism** (-ī·siz'm), triœcious character or condition.

**1760** J. LEE *Introd. Bot.* II. xxvi. (1765) 138 **Trioecia*, comprehending such Plants as have the Polygamy on three distinct Plants. **1860** MAYNE *Expos. Lex.*, *Triœcius*, *Bot.* ..*triœcious. **1866** *Treas. Bot.*, *Triœcious*, *Trioicus*, having male flowers on one individual, female on another, and hermaphrodite on a third. **1891** *Cent. Dict.*, *Triœciously ..*Trioicous.

**Triole** (trəi·ōul, trī·ōul). *Mus. rare.* [dim. of TRIO: cf. F. *triolet* TRIOLET.] = TRIPLET 2 c.

**1880** S. LANIER *Sc. Eng. Verse* iii. (1909) 116 In the first bar a process exactly reversing that..described for the triole is used with singular effect. A triole [music] .. indicates that the three notes [music] are to be played in the time of two [music]'s; but we may reverse this and indicate that two [music]'s are to occupy the time of three [music]'s.

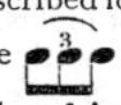

**Triolein** (trəi|ōu·lī|in). *Chem.* [f. TRI- 5 + OLEIN.] One of the glycerides of oleic acid, or oleates of glyceryl: see quots.

**1855** *Q. Jrnl. Chem. Soc.* VII. 282 Berthelot..prepared ..Triolein...It is identical with natural olein. **1868** WATTS *Dict. Chem.* IV. 195 Triolein is liquid at 100°. In contact with the air it gradually turns acid. **1873** — *Fownes' Chem.* (ed. 11) 626 Oleic acid forms three glycerides, viz. monolein..; diolein..; and triolein $(C_3H_5)(C_{18}H_{33}O_2)_3$, which are produced by heating oleic acid and glycerin together.

**Triolet** (trəi·ǒlėt, trī·-). [a. F. *triolet* (1538 in Godef., used in senses 1 and 3), dim. of *trio*; but see Hatz.-Darm for a different origin.]

**1.** *Verse.* A stanza of eight lines, constructed on two rimes, in which the first line is repeated as the fourth and seventh, and the second as the eighth.

**1651** P. CAREY (*title*) Trivial Poems, and Triolets. Written in obedience to Mrs. Tomkin's commands. **1836** F. MAHONY *Father Prout* (1860) 208 To his fostering care the poetry of France is indebted for..the triolet. **1878** DOWDEN *Stud. Lit.* 394 This writer excels in sonnets, and that in triolets. **1880** F. HUEFFER in *Macm. Mag.* Nov. 51 Such a poem as the following triolet, by Mr. Robert Bridges, is perfect of its kind. 'When first we met we did not guess' [etc.].

†**2.** *Cards.* Term for one-third of the stakes at the game of Beast. *Obs.*

**1680** COTTON *Compl. Gamester* xxiv. (ed. 2) 108 He that hath three of any sort, that is, three fours, three fives, three sixes, and so forth, takes up the Triolet.

‖ **3.** *Mus.* = TRIPLET 2 c. *rare*⁻⁰. (Properly Fr.) **1888** in *Cassell's Encycl. Dict.*

**Triology** (trəi|ǫ·lŏdʒi). [f. TRI- + -OLOGY. (Not on Greek analogies.)]

**1.** = TRILOGY.

**1837** *For. Q. Rev.* XIX. 447 Three tragedies thus formed together a Triology. **1898** *Westm. Gaz.* 14 Apr. 3/1 Mr. Meredith's 'Napoleon', the second instalment of his triology on France,..appears in the current number of *Cosmopolis*. **1900** *Dundee Advertiser* 29 Nov. 2 Mr. Fenton treats the Epistles to the Romans, Corinthians, and Hebrews as a 'Triology' designed to show 'the Christian Faith in its Intellectual, Social, and Spiritual aspects'.

**2.** A doctrine or system of three or a triad.

**1894** *Thinker* V. 346 The monotheistic idea of All-Father soon gave place to that of a triology.

**Trional** (trəi·onæl). *Pharm.* [f. TRI- 5 + ending of SULPH)ONAL, because it contains three ethyl groups.] Trade-name of the synthetic narcotic drug diethylsulphonemethylethylmethane, $CH_3(C_2H_5)C(SO_2C_2H_5)_2$, resembling sulphonal.

**1889** *Jrnl. Chem. Soc.* LVI. 1233 Trional..crystallises in lustrous tables, melts at 76°, and dissolves in 320 parts of cold water. **1896** *Allbutt's Syst. Med.* I. 225 By the substitution in Sulphonal of a molecule of ethyl $(C_2H_5)$ for a molecule of methyl, trional is formed. **1913** THORPE *Dict. App. Chem.* (ed. 2) V. 530 Trional..is employed in medicine for the same purpose as sulphonal and tetronal.

‖ **Triones** (trəi|ōu·nīz), *sb. pl.* Also 7 in anglicized form **trions.** [L. *triōnēs* ploughing-oxen, also as here.] A name for the seven principal stars in *Ursa Major*, also called *Charles's Wain*.

**1594** GREENE & LODGE *Looking Glass* G.'s Wks. (Rtldg.) 134/1 The fair Triones with their glimmering light Smil'd at the foot of clear Bootes' wain. **1615** CROOKE *Body of Man* 340 There are seauen wonders of the world,..seauen greater and lesser Triones in heauen. **1654** VILVAIN *Epit. Ess.* VI. 51 The Heav'ns sevn Trions show. **1795** HUTTON *Math. Dict.*, *Triones*,..Charles's Wain.

**Trionychoid** (trəi|ǫ·nikoid), *a.* (*sb.*) *Zool.* [ad. mod.L. *Trionychoidea*, neut. pl., f. TRIONYX, generic name: see -OID.] Belonging to the suborder *Trionychoidea* of *Chelonia*, typified by the genus *Trionyx* of soft-shelled turtles. **b.** *sb.* A turtle of this suborder.

**1886** GÜNTHER in *Encycl. Brit.* XX. 469/1 A distinct Trionycoid genus. **1889** NICHOLSON & LYDEKKER *Palæont.* II. liii. 1117 The marked resemblance of the palate and the general aspect of the Trionychoid skull to that of existing Pleurodira.

**Trionym** (trəi·onim). [f. Gr. τριώνυμ-ος having three names, f. τρι-, TRI- + ὄνομα name.] A name consisting of three terms; a trinomial name in botany or zoology; = TRINOMIAL B. 2. So **Trionymal** (trəi|ǫ·nimăl) *a.* = TRINOMIAL A. 2, TRINOMINAL.

**1656** BLOUNT *Glossogr.*, *Trionimal*.., that hath three names. [**1691** TOMLINSON in Ray *N. C. Words* s. v. *Brock*, The animal is trionymus, *badger, brock*, or *gray*.] **1884** COUES in *Auk* Oct. 321 *Trionym*, an onym consisting of three terms. **1884** J. A. ALLEN *ibid.* 352 Even a trinomial (or trionymal) system..fails to meet the requirements of the case.

**Trionyx** (trəi·|ǒniks, trəi|ōu·niks). *Zool.* [mod. L. *triōnyx*, f. Gr. τρι-, TRI- + ὄνυξ nail; cf. Gr. τριώνυχ-ος having three nails.] Name of a genus of chelonian reptiles, so called because only three of the five toes have nails. There are several species, including *T. triunguis, sinensis, ferox*, the Nilotic, Chinese, and American Trionyx.

**1835** KIRBY *Hab. & Inst. Anim.* II. xxii. 433 The Trionyx, also, a kind of tortoise, devours them [the young crocodiles] as soon as hatched. **1878** BELL *Gegenbaur's Comp. Anat.* 427 These are wanting in Trionyx. **1896** *List Anim. Zool. Soc.* 570 *Trionyx muticus*, Unarmed Trionyx; Hab. North America.

**Trioperculate** to **Triovulate**: see TRI- 1, 4 b.

**Trior, triour**: see TRIER.

**Triose** (trəi·ōus). *Chem.* [f. TRI- 5 + -OSE ².] **a.** Group name of the sugars containing three atoms of carbon, $C_3H_6O_3$; the two possible cases are *aldotriose*, $CH_2OH.CHOH.CHO$, and *ketotriose*, $CH_2OH.CO.CH_2OH$. **b.** It has also been used as a group name and as a termination for the trisaccharides, i. e. those sugars which break up on hydrolysis into three simple sugars.

**1894** MUIR & MORLEY *Watts' Dict. Chem.* IV. 531 [Sugars] are designated according to the number of carbon atoms they contain: thus, pentose containing $C_5$,..Triose $C_3H_6O_3$, glycerose. **1894** M'GOWAN *Bernthsen's Org. Chem.* (ed. 2) 317 Sugars of the above [cane sugar] group are termed '*-bioses*', e. g. milk sugar is lacto-biose. Similarly raffinose is a '-triose', Mele-triose. **1895** *Athenæum* 26 Jan. 123/1 [A paper] 'Presence of a Triose in Starch Transformation Products' [was read].

**Trioxide** (trəi|ǫ·ksəid). *Chem.* [f. TRI- 5 + OXIDE.] A compound of three atoms of oxygen with an element or radical; e. g. *sulphur trioxide*, $SO_3$; *nitrogen trioxide*, $N_2O_3$.

**1868** FOWNES *Elem. Chem.* (ed. 10) 134 A series of oxides containing quantities of oxygen in the proportion of the numbers 1, 2, 3, united with a constant quantity of another element, are distinguished as *monoxide, dioxide*, and *trioxide* respectively. **1911** ROSCOE & SCHORLEMMER *Treat. Chem.* (ed. 4) I. 723 Boron Trioxide, $B_2O_3$,..is obtained when boron burns in the air, or in oxygen.

**Trioxy-** (trəi|ǫ·ksi). *Chem.* [f. TRI- 5 + OXY- ².] A formative denoting the presence of three atoms of oxygen in a compound; most commonly used as a substitute for *trihydroxy-*, denoting that three hydroxyl groups, OH, have replaced three hydrogen atoms in the compound designated by the rest of the name.

Thus pyrogallol, $C_6H_3(OH)_3$, is one of the three *trioxybenzenes*, being derived from benzene, $C_6H_6$, by the replacement of three hydrogen atoms by three OH groups.

**1863** *Fownes' Chem.* (ed. 9) 494 Trioxethylenamine. **1880** MILLER *Elem. Chem.* III. 552 *Trioxynaphthalene*: $C_{10}H_5(OH)_3$, is formed in a similar manner. **1900** SMITH *Richter's Org. Chem.* (ed. 3) II. 230 Trioxybenzoic acids, $(HO)_3C_6H_2CO_2H$. Three of the six possible isomerides are known.

**Trip** (trip), *sb.*¹ Also 5 **tryp**, 5–7 **trippe**, 6 **tryppe**, 7–8 **tripp**. [f. TRIP *v.*]

(The order of the senses here is not chronological, but follows that of the verb.)

**I. 1.** The action or an act of tripping or moving lightly and quickly; a light lively movement of the feet; tripping gait or tread; the sound of this.

**1600** in Bodenham *Eng. Helicon* O iij, More fine in trip, then foote of running Roe. **1694** DRYDEN *Love Triumph.* IV. i, Yonder comes Dalinda; I know her by her trip. **1747** R. FORBES *Lyon in Mourning* (1895) I. 117 Some..used to take a dance in the cabin..they could not prevail with her to take a trip. **1814** SCOTT *Wav.* xxxvii, He sometimes could distinctly hear the trip of a light female step. **1871** B. TAYLOR *Faust* (1875) I. xxii. 200 How each his legs in nimble trip, Lifts up and makes a clearance.

†**b.** *spec.* A kind of step in dancing. *Obs.*

**1599** B. JONSON *Cynthia's Rev.* II. iv, Both the swimme and the trip are properly mine, euery body will affirme it, that has any iudgement in dancing.

†**c.** *fig.* app. A step *towards* accomplishing something. *Obs. rare.*

**1682** BUNYAN *Holy War* 6 The King..takes them in the very nick and first tripp that they made towards their design, convicts them of the treason [etc.].

**2.** *fig.* *In the trip of a minute*, in the movement or passage of a minute, in a minute's space.

**1728** VANBR. & CIB. *Prov. Husb.* IV. i. 59 They'll whip it up, in the Trip of a Minute. **1899** *Literature* 25 Nov. 515/1 Mr. Zangwill's [prologue] has caught the 'trip' of the old fashioned prologue.

**3.** A short voyage or journey; a 'run'. Apparently originally a sailor's term, but very soon extended to a journey on land. **a.** A short voyage or run of a ship, between two points, or to a point and back again; each of a series of short runs made by a ship or boat; hence also, a short voyage in a ship.

**1691** T. H[ALE] *Acc. New Invent.* 12 [A vessel pronounced] not to be fit for her being adventured to Sea..for more than a small tripp. *Ibid.* 15 Making a Tripp for England. **1743** BULKELEY & CUMMINS *Voy. S. Seas* 106 After three or four Trips return'd, and anchor'd where we came from. **1754** RICHARDSON *Grandison* IV. lvi, It will be what mariners call a *trip* to England. **1769** COOK *Voy. round World* II. i. (1773) 293 The little boat was obliged to make three trips before we could all get over to the rest of the party. **1773** *Life N. Frowde* 81 We were one Voyage to Dantzic and Hamburgh, another to Copenhagen and Stockholm,..During all these Trips, my Polly and I wrote to each other. **1852** MRS. STOWE *Uncle Tom's C.* xxxi, The good steamer *Pirate*, which lay at the levee, ready for a trip up the Red River. **1867** SMYTH *Sailor's Word-bk.*, *Trip*, an outward bound passage or short voyage, particularly in the coasting trade. **1879** FROUDE *Caesar* xvi. 270 Two trips were required to transport the increased numbers.

**b.** A short journey or run on land; *esp.* each of a series of journeys or runs over a particular route.

(The meaning in quot. *c* 1440 is doubtful.)

[*c* **1440** *York Myst.* xviii. 133 An aungell..bad me flee With hym and þe On-to Egipte. And sertis I dred me sore To make my smale trippe.] **1699** DAMPIER *Voy.* II. III. viii. 94, I pass'd the Isthmus twice, and was 23 days in the last Trip that I made over it. **1706** E. WARD *Wooden World Diss.* (1708) 53 If ever he make a Trip by Land, it's a Wonder. **1856** KANE *Arct. Expl.* II. xvi. 169 The food I could bring from the vessel by occasional trips with my dog-team. **1901** *Daily News* 3 Jan. 6/4 These two men work on eight-trip shifts, each trip consisting of an eastward and westward journey. **1906** *Ibid.* 22 Dec. 6 The 'bus-driver ..is paid by 'trip', and anxious to get his trips done.

**c.** A short journey (by sea or land) for pleasure or health, an excursion (more fully *pleasure trip*); in later use often applied to such a journey whatever its length. Also applied to a passage by rail provided at a fare lower than the usual; a *cheap trip*, an excursion; occas. short for 'party of trippers' or 'trip-train'.

This arose imperceptibly out of **a** or **b**, and it is not easy to fix its first use.

*c* **1749** LADY LUXBOROUGH *Lett. to Shenstone* (1775) 159 If you would take a trip to this little Retreat at this melancholy season. **1774** GOLDSM. *Nat. Hist.* (1776) I. 152 A passage over the Alps, or a journey across the Pyrenees, appear pretty trips or excursions, in the comparison. **1812** *Religionism* 25 Lectureship Will meet th'expences of a country trip. **1861** THORNBURY *Turner* (1862) I. 18 Later trips to Margate made him love Kent and the sea. **1880** *Sat. Rev.* 2 Oct. 423/2 On inquiring..what it all means, he is told that 'a trip is in' from some large manufacturing town, and his peace is gone, for that day at least. **1884** *Times* (weekly ed.) 29 Aug. 14/1 [They] hurry off on flying trips to Kerry or Connemara.

† **d.** An account or description of a journey. *Obs.*
**1712** SWIFT *Lett. Eng. Tongue* Wks. 1755 II. I. 189 Those monstrous productions, which under the name of trips, spies, amusements, and other conceited appellations, have over-run us for some years past.

**e.** Each run or voyage of a fishing vessel; also (*U.S.*) the catch or take of fish during a single run; the proceeds of a trip in fish. **1891** in *Cent. Dict.*

**f.** *Mining.* A train of cars run in and out of a mine as a single unit. **1909** in *Cent. Dict. Suppl.*

**4.** *Naut.* A single board or reach in tacking; a tack. Also *transf.* a run on land.
**1700** T. BROWN *Amusem. Ser. & Com.* 34, I Tack'd about, and made a Trip over Moor-fields. **1708** *Constit. Watermen's Co.* lxi, If any Tilt-Boat-Master .. shall .. turn to Windward in any of the said Boats except one Trip in each particular Reach. **1722** CAPT. OGLE in *Lond. Gaz.* No. 6091/3 The wind took me a-head and I made two Trips. **1867** SMYTH *Sailor's Word-bk.*, *Trip*..also denotes a single board in plying to windward.

**II. 5.** 'A stroke or catch by which the wrestler supplants his antagonist' (J.); a sudden catching of a person's foot with one's own so as to cause him to lose his balance and stumble or fall.
**1412–20** LYDG. *Chron. Troy* II. 1867 Sodeynly to make hym doun to falle, And with a trip, þrowe hym on þe bake. **1530** PALSGR. 283/1 Tryppe in wrastlyng, *crochet, jambet.* *Ibid.* 762/2, I gyve one a tryppe, or caste my foote byfore hym to gyve hym a fall. **1697** DRYDEN *Virg. Georg.* II. 776 The Groom..stript for Wrestling, smears his Limbs with Oyl, And watches with a Trip his Foe to foil. **1760–72** H. BROOKE *Fool of Qual.* (1809) III. 20 [He] gave a slight trip to his..assailant, who instantly fell. **1825** SCOTT *Betrothed* xxxii, I knew the old De Lacy's back-trip as well as thou.

**b.** *fig.*
*c* **1430** *Hymns Virg.* (1867) 75 Til deeþ þee caste with a trippe of dissaite. **1601** SHAKS. *Twel. N.* v. i. 170 Or will not else thy craft so quickely grow, That thine owne trip shall be thine ouerthrow? **1660** WINSTANLEY *Eng. Worth.* Pref. 3 The trips that Writers cunningly give one another. **1884** SHARMAN *Hist. Swearing* iii. 39 Socrates..held at a just appreciation the trips and sallies of Athenian manhood.

**c.** In coursing: see quots.
**1856** 'STONEHENGE' *Brit. Sports* (ed. 2) I. III. viii. § 2 A Trip or Jerk occurs when a dog in attempting to kill his hare, lays hold of her but loses her again; these score half-a-point. **1890** A. R. STARR in *Upland Shooting* 466 The trip is an unsuccessful effort to hold a rabbit, although the greyhound may touch him, or even tumble him.

**6.** A stumble or mis-step caused by striking one's foot against an object so as to lose one's equilibrium. † *To hang on the trip*, to hang on the point of falling or toppling over (*obs.*).
**1681** COTTON *Wond. Peak* (ed. 4) 42 Jutting Stones that, by the Earth left bare, Hang on the trip, suspended in the air. **1687** A. LOVELL tr. *Thevenot's Trav.* III. 45 Elephants ..are the surest footed of all Beasts of Carriage,..it is very rare to see them make a trip. **1710** STEELE *Tatler* No. 231 ¶ 2 The poor Animal being now almost tired, made a second Trip. **1846** *J. Baxter's Libr. Pract. Agric.* (ed. 4) I. 419 If the [horse's] toe dig into the ground before the foot is firmly placed, a trifle will cause a trip and a fall. **1884** MARTINEAU in *Mem. Anna Swanwick* iii. (1903) 147 A bruise which I got through a trip-up and fall upon some rough rocks.

**b.** *fig.* Cf. TRIP *v.* 8 b, c.
**1584** LYLY *Campaspe* I. ii, It is a signe by the trip of your tongue..that you haue done that to day, which I haue not done these three dayes. (*Psyllus*) What is that? (*Manes*) Dined. **1649** G. DANIEL *Trinarch., Hen. IV* i, The Pulse of Nature neuer giues one trip.

**c.** *Mil.* A contrivance for tripping an enemy.
**1862** *Catal. Internat. Exhib.* II. XI. 14/2 Trip for Checking Infantry and Cavalry..formed by laying the bands singly on the ground three or four feet apart, edge-wise and buttoned.

**7.** A mistake, blunder; a fault; a slip, lapse; a false step; a slip of the tongue. † *To take* or *have in a trip* (also † *to take trip*), to catch tripping, to detect in an error (*obs.*).
(In some cases *take in a trip* seems to have been misunderstood to mean 'take in a trap'.)
**1548** UDALL, etc. *Erasm. Par. Mark* x. 63 Yᵉ other desired more to take him in a trip, then to be healed: to proue him, rather then to learne. **1551** ROBINSON tr. *More's Utop.* I. (1895) 91 [To] fynde some hole open to set a snare in, wherewith to take the contrarie parte in a trippe. **1579** FULKE *Refut. Rastel* 725 He is taken tardie in his owne trip. **1594** J. DICKENSON *Arisbas* (1878) 69 Thus fell Loue into a trip: Thus she galde him with a quip. **1604** N. D. *3rd Pt. Three Convers. Eng.* 214 Sutcliffe, being taken trip by E. O... beateth himselfe vp and downe pittifully. **1628** MILTON *Vacation Exerc.* 3 And mad'st imperfect words with childish tripps, Half unpronounc't, slide through my infant-lipps. **1773** J. BERRIDGE *Wks.* (1864) 130 A trip in one point would have spoiled all. **1841** BP. WILBERFORCE in *Croker Papers* (1884) 23 July, An occasional trip in the performance was what threw you out.

**III. 8.** *Mech.* A contrivance that trips (see TRIP *v.* 14); a projecting part of some mechanism which comes into momentary contact with another part so as to cause or check some movement. (Cf. TRIP-HAMMER.)
**1906** *Westm. Gaz.* 6 Mar. 10/1 To protect trains in foggy weather, when the arms and lights of signals are obscured, the automatic train-stop has been installed...A little arm is raised to a vertical position and strikes a trip on the front motor-car of the passing train. By this operation current is cut off. **1907** *Daily Chron.* 8 Aug. 2/3 In dismounting the pedal is again held against the trip, and by it the rider swings himself comfortably out of the saddle to drop on his foot as the cycle is still moving along.

**IV. 9.** *attrib.* and *Comb.* (in some cases perh. from the vb.-stem); in sense 3, as *trip-card, -committee, -fund, -mileage, -taking*; in sense 8, describing an appliance for catching, releasing, or actuating some part, or a machine operated by such a device, as *trip-coil, -cord, -cut-off, -die, -lever, -motion, -piece, -pin, -wagon, -wheel*; also **trip-catch**, a catch which holds the trip or releasing device until it is tripped; † **trip-coat**, ?a turn-coat; **trip-dial**, in a cyclometer, a dial on which the mileage of each trip is registered; **trip-engine**, a steam-engine having a *trip valve-gear* (*Cent. Dict. Suppl.* 1909); **trip-gear**, short for *trip valve-gear* (*Cent. Dict.* 1891); **trip-hook**, some instrument of torture (perh. an error; cf. GADGE *sb.*); **trip-line**, in *Lumbering*, a light line attached to the dog-hook, or to a cable, by which these are recovered or returned; **trip money**: see quot.; **trip-rate**, the rate of payment by the trip: see *trip-system*; **trip-shaft**: see quot.; **trip-sill**: see quot.; **trip-slip**, a strip of paper in which a car conductor registers the number of fares taken on each trip (*U.S.*); **trip system**, a system of payment of men in charge of a train, omnibus, or the like by the trip or journey; † **trip-taker**, one who 'takes another in a trip', a fault-finder; **trip-train**, a mineral train which is intended to make a certain number of trips, out and home, in the day; also, an excursion train; **trip valve-gear**, a valve-gear in which the steam is cut off by the tripping of a lever which holds open the steam-valve. See also TRIP-HAMMER.
**1897** *Outing* (U. S.) XXX. 492/2 Road-rides are scheduled on cards distributed among the members. These *trip-cards are a commendable feature. **1880** TOLHAUSEN tr. *Uhland's Corliss-Engines* 193 The edge of a *trip-catch fastened on the eccentric strap, will approximately move on an elliptical path, and trip up against a steel catch-plate fastened on the extremity of the inlet valve-spindle. *a* **1619** FLETCHER *Mad Lover* I. i, Twenty of your *trip-coats turn their tippets. **1903** *Trans. Amer. Inst. Elect. Engin.* 657 (Cent. Supp.) *Trip-coil. **1884** KNIGHT *Dict. Mech.* Supp., **Trip Cut Off*, an arrangement to disconnect one portion of the valve motion from the other, so as to allow the cut-off valve to close with great rapidity. **1907** *Daily Chron.* 27 Mar. 9/5 For all-round purposes a double cyclometer with '*trip' dial is preferable. **1884** *Pall Mall G.* 11 Sept. 4/1 At the mills and workshops..weekly payments are received towards the *trip fund...The tickets are supplied .. a fortnight beforehand, the trip committee being responsible for the issue and the payment of those actually used. **1846** BROWNING *Soul's Trag.* I. 333 The glowing *triphook, thumbscrew and the gadge. **1904** *Sci. Amer. Suppl.* 23 July 23880 On this stem is fixed a *trip lever, C, which holds B against A by the spring, D. **1905** *U. S. Dept. Agric., Logging terms*, **Trip-line*, a light rope attached to a dog hook, used to free the latter when employed in breaking a jam...*Syn.* throw line. *Ibid.*, *Haul back*, a light wire rope..used to return the cable. *Syn.*...trip line. **1909** *Westm. Gaz.* 17 June 4/2 The Jones Speedometer ..registers up to sixty miles an hour, and is fitted with season and *trip mileage. **1891** *Labour Commission Gloss.* s. v. *Money*, **Trip money*, a term used on canals to mean a payment in addition to tonnage; a bonus given in addition to wages. **1907** *Daily Chron.* 27 Mar. 9/6 The 'Little *Trip Motion'. **1908** *Ibid.* 6 June 8/3 The trip motion.. consists of a catch which holds the cranks and pedals at a certain position. **1901** *Westm. Gaz.* 25 Nov. 8/3 Their grievance is that *trip rates paid them are inadequate, and do not admit of a fair wage. **1864** WEBSTER, **Trip-shaft*, (Steam eng.), a supplementary rock-shaft, worked by hand, for starting an engine. **1905** *U. S. Dept. Agric., Logging terms*, **Tripsill*, a timber placed across the bottom of the sluiceway in a splash dam, against which rest the planks by which the dam is closed. **1894** *Labour Commission Gloss.* s. v., The *trip system on railways is the equivalent of the piece-work system in productive industries. **1556** ROBINSON tr. *More's Utopia* (Arb.) 35 *margin*, *Triptakers. **1897** *Daily News* 31 May 2/7 The second and fourth weeks in June being very largely given up to *trip-taking and rejoicing. **1894** *Labour Commission Gloss.* s. v. *Trip System*, The men working a *trip train are paid a full week's wages. **1907** *Daily News* 28 June 6 He had come by a trip train to Skegness. **1903** *Electr. Rev.* 8 Aug. 197 Engines with Corliss *trip-valve gear driven by separate eccentrics. **1874** RAYMOND *Statist. Mines & Mining* 405 From these the chargers can take the ore in quantities to suit. A *trip-wagon, holding one charge, is generally used. **1877** *Ibid.* 429 A fan B, to give the puffs of air; a *trip-wheel, lever, and spring to operate the fan.

**Trip**, *sb.*[2] Also 4 **tryppe**, 5 **tripe**, 5–6 **trippe**, 6 *Sc.* **trype**, 7 **tripp.** [Etymology obscure: perh. related to *troop*.]

† **1.** A troop or company of men. *Obs. rare.*
(App. in contemptuous use.)
*c* **1330** R. BRUNNE *Chron.* (1810) 203 Me þouht kyng Philip inouh was disconfite, Whan he & alle his trip [orig. *tut sun hoste*] for nouht fled so tite. *a* **1578** LINDESAY (Pitscottie) *Chron. Scot.* (S.T.S.) II. 157 Think not it wilbe ane trype [*v.r.* troup] of men of weir of France that will.. conqueis this realme.

**2. a.** A small flock (of goats, sheep, hares, etc.). *Obs.* exc. *local.*
**1305** [implied in *tripherd*]. *a* **1400** *Sir Perc.* 186 Scho.. with hir tuke a tryppe of gayte, With mylke of thame for to bayte To hir lyves fode. *c* **1410** *Master of Game* (MS. Digby 182) v, Þat men calle a trippe of tame swyne, and of wylde swyne it is called a soundre. *c* **1470** in *Hors, Shepe. & G.* etc. (Caxton 1479, Roxb. repr.) 31 A Trippe of gete. A Trippe of hares. *c* **1470** HENRYSON *Mor. Fab.* IV. xix. *Ibid.* v. (*Parl. Beasts*) xxxvi, Ane trip of lambis dansing on ane dyke. *Ibid.* VII. (*Lion & Mouse*) i, Ane trip of myis.. Richt tait and trig, all dansand in ane gyis. **1513** DOUGLAS *Æneis* III. iv. 24 Trippis eik of gait, but ony keipar, In the rank gersis pasturing on raw. **1556** WITHALS *Dict.* (1568) 14 b/2 A flocke or trippe of goates. **1575** TURBERV. *Venerie* 235 Huntesmen vse to saye an Heard of harts and hindes, buckes and does: and a Trippe of Gotes and Geates. **1584** in *Five Crt. Rolls Gt. Cressingham, Norfolk* (ed. Chandler 1885) 80 A certeyn trippe of sheep. **1674** RAY *S. & E. C. Words* 77 A Trip of sheep i. e. a few sheep, Norf. **1807** VANCOUVER *Agric. Devon* (1813) 101 They are generally owners of trips or small flocks of sheep, depastured upon Exmoor. *a* **1905** in *Eng. Dial. Dict.* (Norfolk), I ha' got a trip of sheep.

**b.** A small flock of wild-fowl.
**1805** MACKINTOSH *Driffield Angler* 294 Trip of dotterel. **1826** COL. HAWKER *Diary* (1893) I. 291 A fine trip of wigeon. **1859** FOLKARD *Wild-Fowler* III. 276 Trip after trip [of wild-fowl] passes over his head in rapid succession. **1893** *Daily News* 28 Feb. 5/4 Wild ducks..are seen hurrying across the lawn with large 'trips' of young ones.

**3.** *Comb.* † **tripherd**, a goatherd, or shepherd.
**1305** *Compotus of Bolton Abbey* in Whitaker *Hist. Craven* (1805) 330 In pane pro triphyrdes sarculant' metent'. **1317** *Ibid.* 338 Pro Tripherds.

† **Trip**, *sb.*[3] *Obs.* In 4–5 also **trippe, trype, trep.** [Derivation uncertain.]

**a.** ? A piece of rind of cheese. **b.** *E. Anglian dial.*: see quots. *a* 1825, 1849.
*c* **1386** CHAUCER *Sompn. T.* 39 Yif hym a busshel whete Malt or Reye A goddes kechyl or a trype [*v.rr.* trip, -pe, trep] of chese. **1823** MOOR *Suffolk Words* s.v., 'Is that a cream cheese?' 'No, it is only a trip.' *a* **1825** FORBY *Voc. E. Anglia*, *Trip*, *s.*, a small cheese, made in summer, to be eaten in its soft and curdy state, or it soon becomes dry, tough, and uneatable. **1849** RAYNBIRD *Agric. Suffolk* 301 *Trip*..differs from cream-cheeses as having no cream in, and being thicker.

† **Trip**, *sb.*[4] *Obs. rare.* [Cf. THRIP (*a* 1700).] Threepence.
**1600** T. HILL *Art Vulgar Arith.* III. x. 261 b, The same Vingtin is woorth our trip or English 3d.

**Trip** (trip), *v.* Also 4 **trep**, 4–6 **tryp(pe**, 4–7 **trippe**, 5 *Sc.* **treip**, 6 **trype**, 6–8 **tripe**, 8 **tripp**, 9 *dial.* **thrip.** [a. OF. *treper, triper, tripper* (12th c. in Godef.) to strike (the ground) with the foot in sign of joy or of impatience, to leap, dance, also to trample or strike with the feet; in Cotgr. 'to hop, skip, trip, or foot it up and downe; also to stampe, trample on, tread under foot'; = Pr. *trepar* to hop, spring (Diez); of Lower Frankish origin: cf. MDu. *trippen* (Kilian, Du. *trippelen*) to skip, trip, hop, LG. *trippen, trippeln*, Fris. *tripje*; in ablaut relation with Du. *trappen*, G. *trappen, trappeln*, in OE. *treppan* to tread, trample: cf. G. *treppe* step.]

**I.** To tread or step lightly or nimbly.

**1.** *intr.* To move lightly and nimbly on the feet; to skip, caper; to dance; † of a horse: to caper, prance (*obs. rare*—1). *arch.*
*c* **1386** CHAUCER *Miller's T.* 142 In twenty manere koude he trippe [*v. r.* trip] and daunce After the scole of Oxenford[e] tho. — *Sqr.'s T.* 304 This hors anoon bigan to trippe [*v. r.* tryppe] and daunce. *c* **1430** *Pilgr. Lyf Manhode* IV. ix. (1869) 180, j carolle, j trippe, j daunce. *c* **1560** A. SCOTT *Poems* (S. T. S.) v. 9 Now in May to madynis fawis With tymmer wechtis to trip in ringis. **1598** SHAKS. *Merry W.* v. v. 97 About him (Fairies) sing a scornfull rime, And as you trip, still pinch him to your time. **1610** — *Temp.* IV. i. 46 Each one tripping on his Toe, Will be here with mop, and mowe. *c* **1633** MILTON *Arcades* 99 Nymphs and Shepherds dance no more..Trip no more in twilight ranks. **1796** R. P. KNIGHT in *New Ann. Reg., Poetry* 152 No fairies now, or dapper elves are seen, By Fancy's eye, light-tripping o'er the green. **1849** JAMES *Woodman* ii, He found the young sisters..tripping in the green wood with the fairies of nights.

**b.** *intr.* with *it.*
**1579** LYLY *Euphues* (Arb.) 115 If [she have] no cunning to daunce, request her to trippe it, if no skill in musicke, profer hir the Lute. **1632** MILTON *L'Allegro* 33 Com, and trip it as ye go On the light fantastick toe. **1712** ARBUTHNOT *John Bull* IV. viii, The Family tripped it about, and capered like hail-stones bounding from a marble floor. **1833** HT. MARTINEAU *Brooke Farm* ix. 112 The young folks tripped it away on the grass.

† **c.** *transf.* Of the heart: To beat excitedly. *Obs.*
*c* **1430** *Pilgr. Lyf Manhode* II. cvi. (1869) 115 Myn herte hoppeth for ioye, and lepeth and trippeth.

† **d.** *trans.* To step or tread on. *Obs. rare.*
*c* **1380** *Sir Ferumb.* 241 Garyn his gode stede hym fette, Þat was in spaygne iboȝt; Þe erld lep vp wyþ oute lette, His styrop trepede he noȝt.

**2.** *trans.* **a.** To perform (a dance) with a light lively step. *rare.*
**1627** DRAYTON *Nymphidia* xli, Eu'ry Mayde..The Hornepype neatly tripping. **1660** F. BROOKE tr. *Le Blanc's Trav.* 406 They dance and trip Moresco Sarabrands to them again. **1812** LADY NAIRNE *Caller Herrin* in R. Ford *Harp Perthshire* (1893) 112 He can trip the spring fu' tightly.

**b.** To tread lightly and nimbly, dance upon.
**1749** SHENSTONE *Irregular Ode* 72 The sportive graces trip the green. **1808** A. SHARPE in R. Ford *Harp Perthshire* (1893) 93 Ghosts of the slain trip Corunna's lone shore. **1887** P. M'NEILL *Blawearie* 43 Nannie had been a short time at the dance, and had tripped the floor with both the joiner and the blacksmith.

**3.** *intr.* To go, walk, skip, or run with a light and lively motion; to move with a quick light tread; also with *it*, and in phr. † *to trip and go.*
? *a* **1400** *Morte Arth.* 3713 Alle trompede they trippe one

trappede stedys. *c* **1470** HENRYSON *Mor. Fab.* v. (*Parl. Beasts*) xi, The lark, the maueis..treipand fra tre to tre. **1576** FLEMING *Panopl. Epist.* 405 That you should in stormy weather, and durtie wayes,..come tripping to mee in your silken sleppers. **1579** GOSSON *Sch. Abuse* (Arb.) 25 Trype and goe, for I dare not tarry. **1588** SHAKS. *L. L. L.* IV. ii. 144 Trip and goe, my sweete, deliuer this Paper into the hand of the King. **1712** TICKELL *Spect.* No 410 ¶ 1, I dismissed my Coach at the Gate, and tripped it down to my Counsel's Chambers. **1870** ROCK *Text. Fabr.* I. 240 Hares tripping within a park. **1883** S. C. HALL *Retrospect* II. 173 She..tripped before us up the stairs to the drawing-room.

**b.** *transf.* and *fig.*

**1662** STILLINGFL. *Orig. Sacræ* III. i. § 18 Wee see..with what facility the mind..trips over mountains, crosseth the ocean. *a* **1774** TUCKER *Lt. Nat.* (1834) II. 126 Vanity.. mingles among our vital juices, trips along the tongue, dances upon the eyes. **1854** ALFORD in *Life* (1873) 237 So many notes tripped backwards and forwards between us. **1884** W. C. SMITH *Kildrostan* 86 There's a nice breeze tripping on the Loch.

**c.** *Angling.* See quots.

**1867** F. FRANCIS *Angling* i (1883) 8 The line [is] plumbed, so that the float shall carry the hook just off the bottom, now and then perhaps touching it, or 'tripping'. *Ibid.* ii. (1880) 66 The right depth..for the worm to trip or drag slowly over the bottom.

**d.** quasi-*trans.* = RUN *v.* 37 a.

**1850** BLACKIE *Æschylus* II. 64 Far liefer would I lackey this bare rock Than trip the messages of Father Jove.

**4.** *trans.* To cause to trip or go nimbly; to send *forth* trippingly.

**1598** E. GILPIN *Skial.* (1878) 20 Come trip the dice, haue at your box (Madame) Ile cast at all. **1616-61** HOLYDAY *Persius* (1673) 294 His dainty palate tripping forth his words. **1901** 'ZACK' *Dunstable Weir* 191 When her zot under the big fig tree, thripping her lace-bobbins in and out.

**5.** *intr.* To make a trip or short excursion. Also *to trip it.*

**1664** ETHEREDGE *Comical Revenge* Prol., If you shou'd, we and our Comedies Must trip to Norwich, or for Ireland go. **1699** J. DUNTON *Life & Err.* (1818) II. 613 The gentleman who tripped lately to Ireland. **1767** H. WALPOLE *Let. to G. Montagu* 31 July, I shall trip to Paris in about a fortnight. **1878** M. C. JACKSON *Chaperon's Cares* I. xiii. 177 Persuaded Mr. Kirke to trip it to Brighton for the good of his health. **1892** BESANT in *Illustr. Lond. News* Summer No. 1 The trippers have not yet begun to trip.

**II.** To strike with the foot so as to cause stumbling (and derived senses).

(App. an English development of sense.)

**6.** *trans.* To cause to stumble or fall by suddenly arresting or catching the foot; 'to throw by striking the feet from the ground by a sudden motion; to strike the feet from under the body' (J.). Also with *up*, †*down*. Often with the heels, foot, etc., as object, esp. in the phrase ***to trip up one's heels***.

*c* **1425** *Cast. Persev.* 3426 in *Macro Plays* 179 He wende þat he schulde a levyd ay, tyl dethe trypte hym on his daunce. **1530** PALSGR. 762/2 Why dyd you tryppe him as he was ronnyng? **1592** GREENE *Art Conny Catch.* III. 32 The other following tript vp his heeles. **1592** SHAKS. *Ven. & Ad.* 722 The earth, in love with thee, thy footing trips. **1605** SHAKS. *Lear* I. iv 95 *Ste.* Ile not be strucken, my Lord. *Kent.* Nor tript neither, you base Foot-ball plaier. *Ibid.* II. ii. 32, 126. **1627** DRAYTON *Nymphidia* lvii, A Stump doth trip him in his pace, Downe comes poore Hob vpon his face. *a* **1653** GOUGE *Comm. Hebr.* xi. 20 (1655) III. 84 The verb..signifieth to supplant, or to trip down, which is oft done with the heel. **1711** ADDISON *Spect.* No. 42 ¶ 1 The right adjusting of her Train, lest it should chance to trip up her Heels. **1786** MME. D'ARBLAY *Diary* 13 Aug., I have come on prodigiously..in the power and skill of walking backwards, without tripping up my own heels. **1828** SCOTT *F. M. Perth* iv, Henry Smith, parrying the blow.., tripping him at the same time, gave him a severe fall. **1884** BROWNING *Ferishtah, Shah Abbas* 144 What lay on floor to trip your foot?

**b.** *fig.* or in *fig.* context.

*a* **1548** HALL *Chron., Hen. VI* 122 b, The Frenchmen .. determined to trippe and deceiue them by their accustomed seruaunt, called master Treason. **1551** BP. GARDINER *Explic., Transubstantiation* 109 b, There was neuer man tryppyd himselfe more hansomely to take a fall, then this auctour doth. **1597** SHAKS. 2 *Hen. IV*, v. ii. 87 To trip the course of Law, and blunt the Sword That guards the peace. **1653** HOLCROFT *Procopius* II. 29 The former fight, wherein not our cowardise, but some cross fortune tript us. *a* **1774** TUCKER *Lt. Nat.* (1834) II. 118 The free-thinker..loves to pick holes..to trip up an adversary at unawares. **1872** BLACKIE *Lays Highl.* 62 Hasty winter..Came, and tripped the summer's heels.

†**c.** *intr.* *To trip at*: to attempt to trip or overthrow. *Obs. rare.*

**1633** HEYWOOD *Eng. Trav.* v. Wks. 1874 IV. 87 Though their riots tript at my estate, They haue not quite orethrowne it.

†**d.** *trans.* *To trip off*: to throw off. *Obs. rare.*

**1674** N. FAIRFAX *Bulk & Selv.* 173 At the very time of my writing this, Half..should be fairly tript off.

**e.** In coursing: see quot., and cf. TRIP *sb.*[1] 5 c.

**1859** STONEHENGE *Brit. Sports* (ed. 4) I. III. viii. § 2 A tripping or jerking the hare to be reckoned one point...It has been said, when a hare is tripped or jerked that the dog ought to have held her.

**7.** To overthrow by catching in a fault or blunder; to detect in an inconsistency or inaccuracy.

**1557** N. T. (Genev.) *John* xv. 20 *note*, To be diligent to espie fautes to trippe one in. **1586** J. HOOKER *Hist. Irel.* in *Holinshed* II. 105/1 Being tript by the councell in his tale, was committed to the Fleet. **1611** SHAKS. *Cymb.* v. v. 35 These her Women Can trip me, if I erre. *a* **1625** FLETCHER *Noble Gent.* III. i, He must..Be a better Statesman than yourself that can Trip me in anything.

**8.** *intr.* To strike the foot against something, so as to hop, stagger, or fall; to stumble *over* an obstacle; to make a false step.

*c* **1440** *Promp. Parv.* 503/1 Tryppyn, or stoomelyn, *cespito.* **1530** PALSGR. 762/2 My horse stombled nat, he dyd but tryppe a lytell. **1579** G. HARVEY *Let. to Spenser* Wks. (Grosart) I. 23 A good horse that trippeth not once in a iourney. **1637** HEYWOOD *Dial.* Wks. 1874 VI. 291 Run not so fast, lest thou shouldst trip perhaps. *a* **1760** I. H. BROWNE *Design & Beauty* Poems (1768) 100 Tumblers trip but to conceal their art. **1833** MARRYAT *P. Simple* xvii, I tripped over my sword, and nearly fell on my nose. **1867** TROLLOPE *Chron. Barset* II. xlix. 61 He would have tripped at the upward step at the cathedral door had she not been with him. *fig.* **1581** MULCASTER *Positions* xxxvii. (1887) 150 Neither will I touch the other two, vnles I fortune to trip vpon them by chaunce. *a* **1716** SOUTH *Serm.* (1744) XI. 167 They may sometimes out of infirmity trip into a perjury, a murder or an adultery.

**b.** Said of the tongue: To stumble in articulation; to falter in speaking.

**1526** *Pilgr. Perf.* (W. de W. 1531) 163 b, To saye his seruyce with stoppynge & tryppynge of tonge. **1598** DRAYTON *Heroic. Ep.* ii. 9 With the earnest Haste, my Tongue oft trips. **1690** LOCKE *Hum. Und.* III. x. § 33 Drinking..till his Tongue trips, and his Eyes look red, and his Feet fail him. **1706** PHILLIPS (ed. Kersey), To *Trip*, to stumble with the Feet, or falter with the Tongue.

**c.** *Horology.* Of an escape-wheel: To fail to release itself from the pallet; see also quot. 1850 s.v. TRIPPING *vbl. sb.* 2.

**1850-79** [see TRIPPING *vbl. sb.* 2]. **1884** F. J. BRITTEN *Watch & Clockm.* 89 Gravity escapements were rather regarded with suspicion as having a tendency to trip.

**9.** *intr.* To fall into an error; to make a mistake or false step; to commit a fault, inconsistency, or inaccuracy.

**1509** BARCLAY *Shyp of Folys* (1570) 39 Thy finger lay before thy lips, For a wise mans tonge without aduisement trips. **1584** B. R. tr. *Herodotus* I. 37 b, Least he were taken vp for triping and conuicted of a lye. **1726** SWIFT *Gulliver* IV. xi, After many endeavours to catch me tripping in some part of my story [etc.]. **1864** TENNYSON *Grandmother* vii, Jenny had tript in her time. **1871** TYNDALL *Fragm. Sc.* (1879) II. vii. 93 How I rejoiced when I found an author tripping.

**III.** †**10.** *Naut. intr.* To tack. *Obs. rare.*

**1687** A. LOVELL tr. *Thevenot's Trav.* II. 118 Thus did we trip to and again in that Streight, the wind continually shifting and turning.

**11.** *Naut. trans.* To loose (an anchor) from its bed and raise it clear of the bottom by the cable or a buoy rope. Also *intr.* for *pass.*

**1748** *Anson's Voy.* II. i. 112 We .. set the sails, which fortunately tripped the anchor. **1797** S. JAMES *Narr. Voy. Arabia*, etc. 16 We tripped our small bower. **1825** H. B. GASCOIGNE *Nav. Fame* 50 A greater force each steady shoulder plys, The Anchor Trips, and from the mud does rise. **1840** R. H. DANA *Bef. Mast* xxv, Everything was sheeted home and hoisted up, the anchor tripped and cat-headed, and the ship under headway. **1882** NARES *Seamanship* (ed. 6) 199 Sail must be made before tripping the anchor. **1903** *Union Mag.* Oct. 447/1 The usual plan is to take in the chain till it is straight up and down and then to trip the anchor by paying the boat off.

**12.** *trans.* To tilt; *spec. Naut.* to give (a yard) the necessary cant in sending it down; also, to lift (an upper mast) in order that it may be lowered.

**1840** R. H. DANA *Bef. Mast* xxiii, [The royal yards] were all tripped and lowered together. **1841** — *Seaman's Man.*, *Tripping Line*, a line used for tripping a topgallant or royal yard in sending it down. **1885** *Encycl. Brit.* XXI. 821/1 (*Ship-building*) The chain then draws the bolt, and in falling trips the cradle from under the bottom.

**13.** *intr.* To tilt or tip up; of the floors of a ship, to be strained or twisted out of their horizontal position.

**1869** SIR E. J. REED *Shipbuild.* ii. 23 The floors are comparatively free to trip, by the keelson riding along the keel. **1874** THEARLE *Naval Archit.* 72 The hogging strains peculiar to long, narrow ships tend to produce a tripping of the floors; or an alteration in the form of the space.. enclosed by keel, keelson, and floors. **1888** ELWORTHY *W. Somerset Word-bk.*, *Trip*, v. i. to move on a pivot or fulcrum. A paving stone not evenly bedded when stepped upon is apt to log—this is to trip.

**14.** *trans.* To release (a catch, lever, or the like) by contact with a projection; to operate (a mechanism) in this way. Cf. TRIP *sb.*[1] 8.

**1897** *Daily News* 4 Nov. 6/4 An automatic parachute was to spread itself to make the descent and 'trip' the camera as it gracefully came to earth.

**Tripair, -paleolate**: see TRI- 4 a, 1.

**Tripal, trypal** (trəi·păl), *a.* and *sb.* [f. TRIPE *sb.*[1] + -AL.]

†**A.** *adj.* Of or pertaining to the tripes or entrails. *Obs. rare.*

**1709** [W. KING] *Usef. Transact. Philos.* Mar.-Apr. 47 Microscopical Observations on the Membranes of the Intestines, and other Trypal Vessels.

**B.** *sb.* A tall, lanky, or slovenly person. *Sc.*

**1809** SKINNER *Poems, Christmas Ba'ing* 4 But a lang trypall there was Snap, Cam' on him wi' a bend. **1871** W. ALEXANDER *Johnny Gibb* x. (*dial.*), Mair smeddum..nor the like o' that gawkie trypal.

**Tripalmitin** (trəi,pæ·lmitin). *Chem.* [f. TRI- 5 + PALMITIN: cf. TRIACETIN.] A crystalline substance, also called *palmitin* or *glyceryl tripalmitate*, $C_3H_5(C_{16}H_{31}O_2)_3$, occurring in palm-oil and in many animal and vegetable fats and oils, and prepared synthetically by Berthelot.

**1855** *Q. Jrnl. Chem. Soc.* VII. 283 Natural margarin and palmitin.. as well as the artificial compounds identical with them, appear indeed to be trimargarin and tripalmitin. **1913** THORPE *Dict. App. Chem.* (ed. 2) IV. 78 By heating palmitic acid with glycerol, the mono-, di-, and tri- palmitins are prepared.

**Tripam, -pang**, obs. forms of TREPANG.

†**Trip-and-go, trip-go**, *sb. phr. Obs.* [See TRIP *v.* 3.] The action of tripping and going; one who trips and goes, or who uses this expression.

**1532** MORE *Confut. Tindale* Wks. 685/2 [Water] receiueth shortly the steppes of euery man, yea and of euery woman to, but she gete her on a pace, with trip and go quikly and walke wonderous light. **1601** CHETTLE & MUNDAY *Death Earl Huntington* v. i. K j, Should any of these no forsooths, These pray awayes, these trip and goes, these tits, Deny mee. **1611** in *Coryat's Crudities* Panegyr. Verses h ij, So nimble Tom, the traueller Trip-goe.

**Tripapalty, -papillated**: see TRI- 4 a, 1.

**Tripart** (trəi·paɹt), *a. rare.* [f. TRI- + PART *sb.*] = TRIPARTITE *a.*; threefold; in quot. 1592, taking place between three parties, three-sided.

**1592** WYRLEY *Armorie* 137 Which tripart combate was so noblie fought As sick prince tooke pleasure it t'behould. **1630** GOODALL *Tryall Trav.* Ded., To the Thrice Noble And Illustrious Lady :..Elizabeth..These tripart tryalls of trauell are consecrated by Baptist Goodall. **1791** COWPER *Iliad* XV. 230 By distribution tripart we received Each his peculiar honours.

†**Tri·part**, *v. Obs.* Also 6 try-. [f. TRI- + PART *v.*] *trans.* To divide into three parts.

Chiefly in pa. t. and pple. *triparted*, Sc. *-it*: cf. next.

**1528** LYNDESAY *Dreme* 202 The Patrimonie and rent.. Quhilkis suld haue bene tryppartit in to thre. **1567** *Gude & Godlie B.* (S.T.S.) 210 Quhy war ȝe sa vnnaturall, As..Tripartit and deuydit him? **1621** QUARLES *Esther* Div. Poems (1717) 134 He That's born, may challenge but one part of three Triparted thus.

So **Tripa·rtible** *a.* [f. TRI- + L. *partibilis* divisible], separable into three parts or pieces.

**1860** WORCESTER cites GRAY.

**Tripa·rted**, *ppl. a.* [f. OF. *triparti* or L. *tripartitus*: see -ED.] = TRIPARTITE *a.*

**1424** in *Calr. Pat. Rolls* VI. 29 The mair and the aldermen..be thise presents triparted..make and ordeyne thise constitutiouns and restreynts. *c* **1456** PECOCK *Bk. of Faith* (1909) 298 In the stories clepid Ecclesiastik Storie and Tripartid Stori. **1514** in *Eng. Gilds* (1870) 146 Vnto twoo parties of thes Indentourz triparted,..the seid Maister & brethern hath putt ye common seal. **1586** FERNE *Blaz. Gentrie* 175 As they [crosses] are to be seen biparted, or diuided into 2 parts, so also may they be borne in Armes, triparted ouer the whole feeld. **1688** R. HOLME *Armoury* III. 270/2 Some blazon this..triparted, if it end in three points. **1866** *Treas. Bot.* 1172 *Triparted*, *Tripartite*, parted to the base in three divisions.

Hence **Tripa·rtedly** *adv.*

**1569** *Reg. Privy Council Scot.* II. 5 That the articles of this treaty may be accorded tripartedlie.

**Tripartient** (trəi,pā·ɹʃiĕnt), *a.* and *sb. rare.* [f. TRI- + L. *partient-em* dividing.] See quot.

**1706** PHILLIPS (ed. Kersey), *Tripartient*, any Number that divides another into three equal Parts, without any Remainder. Hence **1721** in BAILEY; and in later Dicts.

**Tripartite** (trəi,pā·ɹtəit, tri·paɹtəit), *a.* (*sb.*) Also 5 **trypartite, -tyte**, 5-6 **tripertite, -tyte.** [ad. L. *tripartīt-us*, f. *tri-* three + *partītus*, pa. pple. of *partīrī* to divide.]

**1.** Divided into or composed of three parts or kinds; threefold, triple.

*c* **1420** LYDG. *Assembly of Gods* 1031 Freewyll, Vertew & Vyce, as trypartyte [*rimes* lyght, wyght]. **1432-50** tr. *Higden* (Rolls) II. 161 Of the tripartite langage of Saxones, ..the weste men of Englonde sownde and acorde more with the men of the este..then the men of the northe with men of the sowthe. *Ibid.* III. 275 Oon Socrates Cassiodorus commendethe in his story tripartite. **1592** WARNER *Alb. Eng.* VIII. xliii. (1612) 206 Of Brittish race and many, and of Saxon Princes some, Whose blood by Normaine mixture now is tripartite become. **1609** HOLLAND *Amm. Marcell.* 56 Hee divided the nights according to a tripartite or threefold function, For sleepe, for affaires of State, and for his booke. **1647** CLEVELAND *Poems, Smectymnuus* 44 Like to an *Ignis fatuus*, whose flame Though sometimes tripartite, joynes in the same. **1745** J. MASON *Self Knowl.* I. ii. (1853) 14 Man is..a tripartite Person; or a compound Creature made up of three distinct Parts, viz. the Body, which is the earthy or mortal Part of him, the Soul, which is the animal or sensitive Part; and the Spirit or Mind, which is the rational and immortal Part. **1848** GALLENGA *Italy* I. IV. iii. 468 Though still nominally tripartite, Italy, for all commercial and intellectual purposes, was one. **1861** O'CURRY *Lect. MS. Materials* 347 The Tripartite Life of St. Patrick. **1900** *Westm. Gaz.* 15 Feb. 10/1 The folding bicycle...This detachable machine is known as the 'Tripartite', because it is made to disconnect into three separate parts.

**b.** Involving, or of the nature of, division into three parts.

**1576** FLEMING tr. *Caius' Dogs* (1880) 2, I wyll expresse and declare in due order, the grand and generall kinde of English Dogges, .. making a tripartite diuision. **1596** HARINGTON (*title*) An Anatomie of the Metamorphosed Aiax. Wherein by a tripertite method is plainly, openly and demonstratiuely declared [etc.]. **1785** BURKE *Nabob of Arcot* Wks. 1842 I. 331 They prevailed on him to propose a tripartite division of that vast country. **1856** MERIVALE *Rom. Emp.* (1865) IV. xxxix. 370 The tripartite division of the earth's surface is a tradition of unknown antiquity. **1882-3** *Schaff's Encycl. Relig. Knowl.* I. 724 A tripartite division into philosophical, historical and practical theology.

**2.** Made in three corresponding parts or copies, as an INDENTURE (q. v.) drawn up between three persons or parties, each of whom preserves one of the copies.

**1442** in *Proc. King's Counc. Irel.* (Rolls) 275 He was bounde by endenture tripartite to kepe the peas. *a* **1483** *Liber Niger* in *Househ. Ord.* (1790) 74 One indenture trypartite; the one to remayne with these Butlers purveyours ..the other parte, with the clerke of buttillary..the thirde parte to remayne in the countyng-house. **1592** WEST *1st Pt. Symbol.* § 47 D, These deedes indented are not only bypartite..but also may be made tripartite, that is of three parts. **1643** BAKER *Chron., Hen. IV* 36 They [Earls of Northumberland and Worcester, and Henry Hotspur] agreed upon a Tripartite Indenture under their hands and seales, to divide the Kingdome into three parts. *a* **1743** SOMERVILLE *Sweet-Scented Miser* 62 By precedents a bond can write, Or an indenture tripartite.

**3.** Engaged in or concluded between three parties.

**1497** in Ellis *Orig. Lett.* Ser. I. I. 50 The tripartite Warre ..determyned ayenst the said Turk, and how the Hungaries, Boyams, and the Polans..shall make werre by land [etc.]. **1577–87** HOLINSHED *Chron.* III. 862/1 The articles of the league tripartite, agreed betwixt the emperour, the king of England, and the French king. **1665** MANLEY *Grotius' Low C. Warres* 666 George Count Solmes, Ernestus of Nassau, ..and Vere General of the English,..Govern'd the Army by a Tripartite Command. **1775** L. SHAW *Hist. Moray* iii. (1882) 402 A parsonage..the patronage whereof was once tripartite between the King, Marshal, and Duffus. **1857** GEN. P. THOMPSON *Audi Alt.* I. xxiv. 88 The tripartite treaty which virtually exists among three of the leading powers of the world.

**4.** *Her.* **a.** Applied to the field when divided into three parts of different tinctures: = TIERCÉ. **b.** Applied to a cross or saltire when each of its members consists of three narrow bands with spaces between. Also TRIPARTED, † TRIPARTITED.

**1796** STEDMAN *Surinam* II. xix. 79 The arms [of Surinam] are tripartite, which I apprehend to be some of those of the house of Somelsdyke, the West India company, and the town of Amsterdam.

**5.** Consisting of three parts or divisions, as a member or organ of an animal or plant.

**a.** *Zool.* and *Anat.*

**1658** ROWLAND *Moufet's Theat. Ins.* 936 A black bill or beak, hardish, tripartite. **1668** CULPEPPER & COLE *Barthol. Anat.* IV. iv. 163 It is inserted into the three Intervals of the four upper Ribs, being tripartite. **1911** J. W. JENKINSON *Sea Urchin* 270 These larvae had a mouth and a typically tri-partite gut.

**b.** *Bot.*: *spec.* of a leaf, etc., Divided into three segments nearly to the base. (Abbrev. *3-partite.*)

**1753** CHAMBERS *Cycl. Supp.* s.v. *Leaf*, Tripartite Leaf. **1862** DARWIN *Fertil. Orchids* ii. 90 The stigmatic surface is differently shaped, being more plainly tripartite. **1870** HOOKER *Stud. Flora* 256 Solanum Dulcamara..leaves ovate or cordate, sometimes 3-partite.

**6.** *Math.* Involving three sets of variables.

**1869** CAYLEY *Math. Papers* VI. 464 The quantic is unipartite, bipartite, tripartite, &c., according as the number of sets is one, two, three, &c.

**B.** *sb.* † **a.** A tripartite indenture (see 2). *Obs.*

**b.** A book, document, or treatise in three parts.

**1480** *Coventry Leet Bk.* 445 The people..in Hasil-wode, ..throwen don thornes, ffirs, fern, brome; diggen turves, & such other; where be the tripartite they owe nothyng to haue there but comien of pasture to their bestes cominable. **1657** R. MOSSOM (*title*) The Preacher's Tripartite, in Three Books. **1788** GIBBON *Decl. & F.* xliv. (1836) 757 The tripartite [*tripertita*] of Aelius Paetus..was preserved as the oldest work of jurisprudence. **1861** O'CURRY *Lect. MS. Materials* 350 Father Colgan's deductions from the text of the Tripartite [cf. quot. 1861 in sense 1 above].

† **Tripartite,** *v. Obs. rare.* [f. as prec.] *trans.* To divide into three parts, or among three persons.

*c* **1470** HARDING *Chron.* XV. i. (*MS. Ashm. 34*, lf. 13 b), Whanne he [Brutus] had the Ile alle Trypartytede [*v.r.* (*MS.*) tripertited; *ed.* 1543 tripertyted] He callede the Chyef logres aftir locryne. **1633** GERARD *Descr. Somerset* (1900) 103 Reginald Prouse whose son's daughters, married to the Earls of March Mortimer, to the Lord Zouche, and to the Earl of Pembrooke Hastings, tripartited these lands. **1641** J. JACKSON *True Evang. T.* III. 165 The Text at the first was tripartited, and two of those parts are already handled.

¶ **b.** *erron.* To divide (in general).

**1653** T. BROOKS *Precious Remedies* (1658) 275 *margin*, The Counsellor saith, A States-man should be thus tripartited, his will to God, his love to his Master, his heart to his Countrey, his secret to his friend, his time to businesse.

† **Tripartited,** *ppl. a. Obs.* [f. as prec. + -ED [1].] Divided into or composed of three parts; made between three parties: = TRIPARTITE *a.*

**1426** *Anc. Deed* A. 10383 (P.R.O.) in *Catalogue* IV. 547 This endenture tripartitit beres wittenes that [etc.]. **1486** *Bk. St. Albans, Heraldry* C vij b, Off a cros tripartitid florishid. *a* **1548** HALL *Chron., Hen. V* 68 b, A truce tripertited betwene the .ii. kynges and the duke and their countreys was determined. **1612** DRAYTON *Poly-olb.* xv. 257 In Britaine here we find, our Severne, and our Tweed, The tripartited ile doe generally divide. **1650** T. BAYLY *Herba Parietis* 3 So many tripartited walls, with benches for to sit upon.

**Tripartitely** (see TRIPARTITE *a.*), *adv.* [f. TRIPARTITE *a.* + -LY [2].] In a tripartite manner; in or into three parts.

**1656** W. D. tr. *Comenius' Gate Lat. Unl.* § 584 The Body [is divided] tripartitely into head, trunk, joynts or Limbs. **1752** J. HILL *Hist. Anim.* 561 The Dasypus, with the covering tripartitely divided. The African Armadilla.

**Tripartition** (traipaɹti·ʃən). [f. L. *tripartītus*: see TRIPARTITE *a.* and -TION.] Division into three parts; partition among three; † *Arith.* division by three (*obs.*).

**1652** SPARKE *Prim. Devot.* (1663) 293 St. Augustine giveth another and very proper tripartition. **1691** tr. *Emiliane's Frauds Rom. Monks* (ed. 3) 103 He divided the vast Revenues of his Abby into three parts...Almost all the Abbots of France, Germany and Italy..made a Tripartition of the Revenues of their Abbies. **1853** TH. ROSS *Humboldt's Trav.* III. xxxii. 309 The tripartition of the Cordilleras, and.. the spreading of their branches. **1908** J. MASSIE in *Daily Chron.* 14 May 4/4 It is the principle of this Bill—its tripartition of Irish University education—that I do not like.

† **Tripa·rtitory,** *a. Obs. rare*—[1]. [f. as prec. + -ORY [2].] Composed of three ingredients: = TRIPARTITE *a.* I.

**1651** BIGGS *New Disp.* ¶ 246 The other three, in this tripartitory [*erron. printed* -atory] secretion shall even then be worse naughty packs then the solitary bloud.

† **Tripa·rty,** *v. Obs. rare.* = TRIPARTITE *v.*

**1543** [see quot. *c* 1470 s. v. TRIPARTITE *v.*].

**Triparty** *a.*, **Tripaschal**: see TRI- 1 b, a.

**Tripe** [1] (traip). Also 5 *Sc.* trip, 5–6 **trippe**, 6 **tryppe**, 5–8 **trype.** [a. OF. *tripe*, *trippe* entrails of an animal (13th c. in Hatz.-Darm.), mod.F. *tripe* (whence Sp., Pg. *tripa*): ulterior source uncertain.]

**1.** The first or second stomach of a ruminant, esp. of the ox, prepared as food; formerly including also the entrails of swine and fish.

*Plain tripe* is the first stomach, paunch, or rumen, *honeycomb tripe* the second, or reticulum.

**a.** With *a* and *pl.* as an individual thing. Now *rare.* (Usually plural.)

*a* **1300** *Sat. People Kildare* xviii. in *E. E. P.* (1862) 155 Hail be ȝe hokesters dun bi þe lake wiþ..tripis and kine fete and schepen heuedes. **14..** *Nom.* in Wr.-Wülcker 741/30, 31 *Hoc strutum*, *Hec tripa*, a tripe. *c* **1483** CAXTON *Dialogues* 26/27 We shall breke our fast with trippes, Of the lyver, of the longhe. **1533** ELYOT *Cast. Helthe* (1541) 22 The inwarde of beastes, as trypes and chytterlynges. **1556** WITHALS *Dict.* (1568) 48 b/2 *Omasum*, is one of the foure partes of a beastes mawe very fatte, calde a tripe. **1655** MOUFET & BENNET *Health's Impr.* (1746) 201 The Taste of Tripes did seem so delicate to the Romans, that they often killed Oxen for the Tripes sake. **1767** STERNE *Tr. Shandy* IX. xxi, 'I'm loaded with tripes', says the second. **1880** R. OWEN in *Sanctorale Catholicum* Mar. 133 Then the priest, bearing tripes hot from the spit, approached as if to give to Pionius.

**b.** *collect. sing.* as the name of this substance.

**13..** *K. Alis.* 1574 (Bodl. MS.), Ribaudes festeþ also wiþ tripe. *c* **1430** *Two Cookery-bks.* I. 18 Trype of Turbut or of Codelynge. Take þe Mawes of Turbut, Haddok, or Codelyng, & pyke hem clene [etc.]. **1682** DRYDEN *Abs. & Achit.* II. 473 To what would he on quail and pheasant swell That ev'n on tripe and carrion could rebel? **1771** GOLDSM. *Haunch of Venison* 82 At the bottom [of the table] was tripe, in a swinging tureen. **1840** DICKENS *Barn. Rudge* xxxi, A steaming supper of boiled tripe and onions.

**2.** The intestines, bowels, guts, as members of the body; hence, the paunch or belly including them. *arch.* or *low.* Commonly in *pl.*

*c* **1470** HENRYSON *Orpheus & Eurydice* 298 Ane grysly grype,..with his bill his baly thro[w] can bore, Baith maw, mydred, hart, lever, & tripe [*v. rr.* trype, trip], He ruggit owt. *a* **1529** SKELTON *Ph. Sparowe* 307 Of Inde the gredy grypes Myght tere out all thy trypes! *c* **1645** HOWELL *Lett.* (1650) II. lv. 71 The Turke when he hath his tripe full of pelaw, or of Muton and Rice, will go to natures cellar. **1774** J. COLLIER *Mus. Trav.* (1785) 82 Dead cats, rotten puppies, the tripe of a dead horse. **1806–7** J. BERESFORD *Miseries Hum. Life* (1826) XX. 250 Poor Margery's tripes Are the martyrs of gripes.

**b.** Applied opprobriously or contemptuously to a person; also *bag of tripe.*

**1595** *Eng. Tripe-wife* (1881) 150 Saist thou me so, thou Tripe, thou hated scorne? **1614** B. JONSON *Bart. Fair* IV. v, *Alice.* Thou Sow of Smithfield, thou. *Ursula.* Thou tripe of Turnebull. **1614, 1785** Tripe or Trillibub [see TRILLIBUB]. **1822** COBBETT *Weekly Reg.* 349 Any great, bloated, squeaking, bag of tripe. **1825** JAMIESON s. v. *Trypal*, A tall, meagre person is denominated 'a long tripe o' a fallow'.

**3.** *transf.* and *fig.* (in various applications).

**1676** D'URFEY *Mad. Fickle* II. i. (1677) 11 You Dog,.. Udsbores, I'le beat thee into a Tripe. *a* **1704** T. BROWN *Contin. Quaker's Serm.* Wks. 1709 III. II. 4 Sowse us therefore, in the Powdering-Tub of thy Mercy, that we may be Tripes fit for the Heavenly Table. **1892** *Spectator* 24 Dec. 930/2 This book..very vulgar..it is a dish of literary and artistic 'tripe-and-onions'. **1895** CROCKETT in *Cornh. Mag.* Oct. 341 He swore that he could make a song..that would be worth a shopful of such 'tripe'.

**4.** *attrib.* and *Comb.*, as *tripe-broth*, *fritter*, *soup*; *tripe-gut*; *tripe-cart*, *-house*, *-shop*; *tripe-dealer*, *-dresser*, *-monger*, *-seller*, *-selling*; *tripe-like*, *-visaged* adjs.; **tripe-cheeks**, a person with coarse blowzy cheeks; **tripe-club**, a society which meets to eat tripe; **tripe-man**, one who prepares and sells tripe as a business; **tripe-stone** *Min.*, see quot. 1816; † **tripe-wife** *sb.*, a female tripe-dresser; hence † **tripe-wife** *v.*, *trans.* to make into, or like, a tripe-wife; **tripe-woman** = *tripe-wife.*

**1747** tr. *Astruc's Fevers* 308 Physicians prescribe on this occasion anodyne lenient clysters of *tripe-broth. **1912** *Dollar Mag.* Dec. 182 Neither of us had seen a *tripe-cart before. **1599** PORTER *Angry Wom. Abingd.* H iij b, What needst thou to care, whipper-Ienny, *Tripe-cheekes. **1710** (*title*) The Swan *Tripe-Club: A Satyr on the High-Flyers. **1868** *Daily News* 19 June, The tripes of bullocks are purchased wholesale by the *tripe-dressers. **1906** *Break-fast Menu S. Y. 'Argonaut'* 9 July, *Tripe Fritters. **1659** TORRIANO, *Bottaccio*, the greatest *tripe-gut in an ox. **1897** *Allbutt's Syst. Med.* II. 941 Inflammation of the stomach and bowels accompanied by peculiar *tripe-like wrinklings of the mucous membrane. **1621** BP. MOUNTAGU *Diatribæ* 114 Cleon the Currier, and Agoracritus the *Tripe-man. **1851** MAYHEW *Lond. Labour* II. 7/2 These portions [of the bullock] form what is styled the tripe-man's portion. **1621** BP. MOUNTAGU *Diatribæ* 540 He.. vseth κοιλίας belly, or, Inwards of a Beast, as speaking vnto him, whom hee maketh a *Tripe-monger. **1597** A. M. tr. *Guillemeau's Fr. Chirurg.* 54 b/2 A *Tripe-seller..had his membrane *Dura mater* cleft asunder. **1621** BP. MOUNTAGU *Diatribæ* 540 Hee..saith, *For not Tithing thy Tripes*, intending..that *Tripe-selling was his raising trade. **1829** MARRYAT *F. Mildmay* xx, My mother keeps a *tripe-shop. *a* **1735** ARBUTHNOT *Harmony in Uproar* Misc. Wks. 1751 II. 34 To invite you to eat a *Tripe-soup and Fricassey of Sheep's Trotters. **1816** CLEAVELAND *Min.* 122 Concreted sulphate of barytes...These stalactites..from some resemblance to the intestines, have received the name of *tripe stone. **1597** SHAKS. 2 *Hen. IV*, v. iv. 9 Thou damn'd *Tripe-visag'd Rascall. **1580** HOLLYBAND *Treas. Fr. Tong*, *Tripière*, a *trype wife. **1595** *Eng. Tripe-wife* (1881) 146, I haue heard him that trickt the Tripe-wife sweare, till her husband abused him. *a* **1652** BROME *City Wit* IV. ii, Was not thy mother a notorious Tripe-wife? **1647** WARD *Simp. Cobler* 26 When I consider how women ..haue *tripe-wifed themselves with their cladments. **1598** FLORIO, *Trippara*, a *tripe-woman.

Hence † **Triped** (traipt) *a. Obs. rare*, made into or dressed as tripe.

**1597** *Bk. Cookerie* B ij b, Triped mutton. Take a paunche of a Sheepe faire scowred [etc.].

† **Tripe** [2]. *Obs.* Forms: 5–6 **trype**, 6 **tryp**, **trip**, (7 **trape**), 7–8 **tripe.** [a. OF. *tripe* (1374 in Godef. *Compl.*; cf. also *triperie* 1275), 'étoffe de laine ou de fil travaillée comme le velours'; according to Littré, so called from its resemblance to the interior of the paunch of ruminants.] An imitation velvet of wool or thread; 'mock-velvet', velveteen, fustian. Also *tripe of velvet* (F. *tripe de velours*), and *tripe velvet*; hence also † **Triped** (**trypit**, **tript**) *a.* applied to velvet.

*c* **1430** *Brut* 459 Clothed in scarlet, with furred hodes, and round standynge cappes of Trype. **1542–3** *Acc. Ld. High Treas. Scot.* VIII. 176 Ane elne trype velvet, price xiiij *s.* **1565** in Hay Fleming *Reform. Scotl.* (1910) 609 Twa stuillis coverit with trypit wellwott. **1598** FLORIO, *Trippa*, a kinde of tripe veluet that they make womens saddles with, called fustian of Naples. **1612** *Inv.* in A. McKay *Hist. Kilmarnock* (1880) 308 Four cuschownis of tripe veluet. **1656** *Acts & Ordin. Parl.* c. 20 *Rates* (Scobell) 467 Fustians called.. Naples Fustians, Trape, or Velure plain. [cf. **1660** *Act 12 Chas. II*, c. 4 (*Schedule of Rates*) Naples fustians tript.] **1714** *Fr. Bk. of Rates* 80 Tripes of Velvet, per Piece of 10 Ells 03 10.

**Tripedal** (tri·pĭdăl, trəi·pēdăl, trəipī·dăl), *a. rare.* [ad. L. *tripedāl-is*, f. *tri-*, TRI- + *pēs*, *ped-* foot: see -AL.] † **a.** Having a length or extent of three feet. *Obs. rare*—[0]. **b.** Having three feet, three-footed. So † **Tripeda·neous** *a.* [f. L. *tripedāne-us* + -OUS] = sense a. *Obs. rare*—[0].

**1623** COCKERAM, *Tripedall*, three foot long. **1656** BLOUNT *Glossogr.*, *Tripedanious*, *Tripedal*..that is three foot long. **1658** in PHILLIPS. **1856** *Chamb. Jrnl.* 29 Mar. 202/2 The "baked 'tato" man, with his brightly-polished..tripedal or quadrupedal apparatus. **1878** MISS J. J. YOUNG *Ceram. Art* (1879) 113 The Japanese dragon is a tripedal representative of the species.

‖ **Tripe de roche** (trīp də rɔʃ). [F., 'rock tripe', from the appearance of the thallus.] A name originally given in Canada to various edible lichens of the genera *Gyrophora* and *Umbilicaria*, which afford a slightly nutritious but bitter and purgative food. Also called *rock tripe.*

**1809** A. HENRY *Trav.* 221, I found a very high rock, and this covered with a lichen, which the Chipeways call *waac*, and the Canadians, *tripe de roche.* **1861** H. MACMILLAN *Footn. fr. Page Nat.* 99 A bitter and nauseous lichen, to which the name of *Tripe de Roche* (Gyrophora) has been given, as if in mockery.

**Tripela**: see TRIPOLI (polishing powder).

**Tripe·nnate,** *a. Bot. rare*—[0]. [f. TRI- + PENNATE.] = TRIPINNATE.

**1828** in WEBSTER. **1900** in B. D. JACKSON *Gloss. Bot. Terms.*

**Tripeptide** (trəipe·ptəid). *Chem.* [Named by Fischer, 1902, f. TRI- 5 + PEPT(ONE + -IDE.] A compound containing the residues of three amino-acids united by the joining of NH in one residue to CO in another; e. g. alanyl-glycyl-glycine, $NH_2.CH(CH_3).CO-NH.CH_2.CO-NH.CH_2.CO.OH$, is a tripeptide formed from alanine, $NH_2.CH(CH_3).COOH$, and two glycine molecules, $NH_2.CH_2.CO.OH$.

**1903** *Jrnl. Chem. Soc.* LXXXIV. I. 799 The ethyl ester is very easily formed when the tripeptide is acted on by alcoholic hydrochloric acid. **1908** PLIMMER *Chem. Const. Proteins* II. 23 Carbethoxyl-glycyl-glycyl-leucine ester.. was the first known representative of a tripeptide.

**Tri-personal** (trəipɔ̄·ɹsənăl), *a. Theol.* [f. TRI- + L. *persōna* PERSON + -AL.] Consisting of or existing in three persons: said of the Godhead (see PERSON *sb.* 7 a); also, relating to the three persons of the Godhead.

**1641** MILTON *Reform.* II. Wks. 1851 III. 68 Thou..one Tri-personall Godhead, looke upon this thy poore and almost spent, and expiring Church. **1859** G. BUSH *Swedenborg's Doctr.* (1875) 25 Those who oppose the tripersonal scheme [of the Trinity] will be accused of rejecting a Trinity in any sense whatever. **1871** H. MACMILLAN *True Vine* iii. (1872) 88 In our creation as body, soul, and spirit, God exhibited the tri-personal aspect of His nature.

Hence **Tripe·rsonalism**, the doctrine or theory of three persons in the Godhead; **Tripe·rsonalist**, one who holds this doctrine; **Tripersona·lity**, the condition of being tripersonal, existence in three persons; **Tripe·rsonally** *adv.*, in a tripersonal manner, in three persons.

**1886** N. F. RAVLIN *Progress. Th. Gt. Subj.* i. 14 Jesus..did not speak the truth, if the popular doctrine of *tripersonalism be true. **1846** WORCESTER cites CLISSOLD for *Tripersonalist. **1855** SMEDLEY, etc. *Occult Sciences* 109 The modern Jews, in opposition to the tripersonalists, consider the whole as attributes. **1673** MILTON *True Relig.* 7 *Tripersonality [see TRINUNITY]. **1836** CARLYON *Early Years* 290 The Tripersonality of the Deity is the very corner-stone of our religion. **1901** MOBERLY *Atonement & Personality* 154 The Three Persons are neither Three Gods, nor Three parts of God. Rather they are God Threefoldly, God *Tri-personally.

**Tripertite**, obs. form of TRIPARTITE.

**Tripery** (trəi·pəri). [a. OF. *triperie* (13.. in Godef. *Compl.*), f. *tripe* TRIPE [1]: see -ERY.] **a.** A place where tripe is prepared or sold. †**b.** In contempt, Action pertaining to the tripes or entrails (*obs. rare*).

**1611** COTGR., *Triperie*, a Triperie; a market, street, or shop wherein tripes are vsually sold. **1651** BIGGS *New Disp.* ⁋ 150 To speake of that piece of Tripery, of washing the Guts with a Clyster. **1656** in BLOUNT *Glossogr.* [from Cotgr.]. **1854** *Q. Rev.* Sept. 282 Slaughter-houses, triperies, bone-boiling houses, gut-scraperies.

**Tripet**, obs. form of TRIPPET.

**Tripetalous** (trəipe·tăləs), *a. Bot.* [f. TRI- + L. *petalum* PETAL + -OUS.] Having, or consisting of, three petals. Also † **Tripe·talose** *a. Obs.* So **Tripe·taloid, Tripetaloi·deous** *adjs.* (of a six-parted perianth) having three of the segments petaloid.

[**1688** R. HOLME *Armoury* II. 118/1 *Tripetala*, or *Tetrapetala*, Flowers which consist of 3 or 4 leaves.] **1830** LINDLEY *Nat. Syst. Bot.* 283 The *tripetaloid flower and polyspermous fruit of Xyris. **1866** *Treas. Bot.* 1173 *Tripetaloid*, consisting of six parts, of which three resemble petals, and three are green and small. **1830** LINDLEY *Nat. Syst. Bot.* 254 These water-plants are readily distinguished from all other monocotyledons by their *tripetaloideous flowers. **1698** PETIVER in *Phil. Trans.* XX. 332 The Flowers [are] *tripetalose. **1704** J. HARRIS *Lex. Techn.* s.v. *Petala*, Plants are distinguished into Monopetalous,..*Tripetalous, and Pentapetalous. *c* **1711** PETIVER *Gazophyl.* VIII. lxxi, A blew flowred tripetalous Plant, with Lilly Leaves. **1800** HURDIS *Fav. Village* 136 Fair tripetalous depending flowers.

**Tripgette, -go**: see TREBUCHET, TRIP-AND-GO.

**Tri·p-ha:mmer.** [f. TRIP *sb.*[1] or *v.* + HAMMER.] A massive machine-hammer operated by a tripping device, as a wheel with projecting teeth, a cam, or the like, by which it is raised and then allowed to drop; a tilt-hammer. Also *fig.*

[**1809** (Oct. 14), A trip hammer was patented by the United States to John Smith, Otsego County, New York.] **1824** *Debates in Congress* 18 Feb. (1856) 1572 Our committee on manufactures, while it keeps in motion its wheels and trip-hammers, has kindly condescended to superintend our ploughs and sheep-folds. **1831** J. HOLLAND *Manuf. Metal* I. 128 A blast furnace, forge, trip-hammer, shop, and mills. **1848** LOWELL *Fable for Critics* 893 When the heart in his breast like a trip-hammer beats. **1854** EMERSON *Lett. & Soc. Aims, Eloquence* Wks. (Bohn) III. 190 What character, what infinite variety, belong to the voice! sometimes it is a flute, sometimes a trip-hammer.

*attrib.* *a* **1864** GESNER *Coal, Petrol.* etc. (1865) 321 To bore the well with an auger, instead of a trip-hammer motion. **1883** H. TUTTLE in *Harper's Mag.* Nov. 825/2 Chisels acting on the trip-hammer principle. **1896** KIPLING *Seven Seas, M'Andrew's Hymn* 45 Oh for a man to weld it then, in one trip-hammer strain.

**Triphane** (trəi·fēⁱn). *Min.* [a. F. *triphane* (Haüy, 1801), f. Gr. τριφανής appearing threefold; so called from exhibiting three lustrous cleavages (Littré *Suppl.*).] A synonym of SPODUMENE.

**1816** CLEAVELAND *Min.* 251 *note*, Spodumene. Jameson. Triphane, Hauy. **1819** *Gentl. Mag.* May 448/2 Triphane has been recently found by Dr. MacCulloch in the granite of Glen Elg. **1850** ANSTED *Elem. Geol., Min.*, etc. § 415 Spodumene or Triphane, another felspathic mineral, with a yet larger proportion of silicate of lithia in the place of silicate of potash.

**Triphase, -phasic**: see TRI- 1 b, a.

**Triphen-, tripheno-.** *Chem.* [f. TRI- 5 + PHEN-, PHENO-.] A formative of names of compounds containing three radical groups formed from the benzene or phene group, $C_6H_6$, by loss of hydrogen atoms; e.g. *triphe·nazine*,

$$C_6H_4{<}^{N}_{N}{>}C_6H_2{<}^{N}_{N}{>}C_6H_4.$$

**1890** *Jrnl. Chem. Soc.* LVIII. 491 The dye..regarded by the author as triphenodioxazine. **1892** MUIR & MORLEY *Watts' Dict. Chem.* III. 830 Triphenazine Dihydride $C_{18}H_{12}N_4$.

**Triphe·nin.** *Pharm.* [app. f. TRI- 5 (referring to the three carbon atoms in propionyl) + PHEN(ETIDIN + -IN [1].] Propionylphenetidin, $CH_3CH_2CO.NH.C_6H_4.OC_2H_5$, i.e. phenetidin, $NH_2.C_6H_4.OC_2H_5$, in which one of the hydrogen atoms of the amino-group, $NH_2$, is replaced by propionyl, $CH_3CH_2CO$; a synthetic drug with antipyretic and antineuralgic properties.

**1896** *Merck's Ann. Rep.* 155 Triphenin..White crystalline flakes, freely dissolving in alcohol..melting point of 120–121° C. **1911** MAY *Chem. Synth. Drugs* 74 Para-propionyl-phenetidine (*Triphenin*) is similar to *phenacetin*.

**Triphe·nyl-.** *Chem.* [f. TRI- 5 + PHENYL.] A prefix denoting that three phenyl groups, $C_6H_5$, are substituted for three hydrogen atoms in the substance designated by the rest of the name; e.g. *triphenylacetic acid*, $C(C_6H_5)_3.CO_2H$, from acetic acid, $CH_3.CO_2H$. So **Triphenylmethane**, $CH(C_6H_5)_3$, from methane, $CH_4$; **Triphenylmethyl-**, $C(C_6H_5)$ —, from methyl, $CH_3$. But this term may also indicate the presence of three phenyl groups and one methyl group, $(C_6H_5)_3(CH_3)$; **Triphenylcarbinol**, $C(OH)(C_6H_5)_3$, from carbinol, $CH_3OH$; **Triphenylamine**, formerly triphenylia, $N(C_6H_5)_3$, from ammonia, $NH_3$; **Triphenylrosaniline**, $C(OH)\{C_6H_4.NH(C_6H_5)\}_2\{C_6H_3(CH_3).NH(C_6H_5)\}$, from rosaniline, $C(OH)\{C_6H_4.NH_2\}_2\{C_6H_3(CH_3).NH_2\}$; the hydrochloric acid derivative of this is a blue dye-stuff. So also **Triphe·nylated** *a.*, containing three phenyl groups.

**1858** FOWNES *Elem. Chem.* (ed. 7) 601 Triphenylamine. **1862** MILLER *Elem. Chem.* (ed. 2) III. 444 Triphenylia. **1871** *Jrnl. Chem. Soc.* XXIV. 143 An alcoholic solution of triphenylguanidine absorbs large quantities of cyanogen. **1880** FRISWELL in *Jrnl. Soc. Arts* 445 The hydrochloride of triphenylrosaniline. **1893** THORPE *Dict. App. Chem.* III. 874 Triphenylrosanilines. The triphenylated derivatives of ordinary rosaniline may be subdivided into two classes: crystalline and uncrystallisable blues. **1894** MUIR & MORLEY *Watts' Dict. Chem.* IV. 2 Tri-phenyl-benzene $C_{24}H_{18}$ i.e. $C_6H_3Ph_3$.

**Triphilrie**: see TRIFLERY.

**Triphony** (tri·fŏni). *Mus.* [ad. med.L. *triphōnia* (see below), f. Gr. τρι- three + φωνή voice.] In early mediæval music, Diaphony for three voices. (In quot. 1827 *gen.* A sound of three together.)

**1827** CARLYLE *Germ. Rom.* II. 278 Then resounded a louder triphony of clear crystal bells. [**1889** ROCKSTRO in Grove *Dict. Mus.* App. s.v. *Diaphonia*, When a third Part was added, by doubling the Organum in the Octave above, the form of composition was called Triphonia.] **1899** *Spectator* 20 May 723 A service with the chants sung in unison, the organ accompanying with triaphony [*sic*].

**Triphthong** (tri·fþǫŋ). Also 7 triphthonge, tripthong, 8 triphthongue. [f. TRI-, after DIPHTHONG; cf. F. *triphtongue* (1550 in Godef. *Compl.*).] A combination of three vowel sounds in one syllable; also loosely applied to a combination of three vowel characters, more correctly called TRIGRAPH. (Cf. DIPHTHONG.)

**1599** MINSHEU *Span. Gram.* (1623) 9 A triphthong is a sounding of three vowels into one syllable with one breath together, and that after five sorts. *a* **1637** B. JONSON *Eng. Gram.* I. v, The Tripthong is of a complexion, rather to be fear'd than lov'd. **1668** WILKINS *Real Char.* 371 A common Assertion..That no one syllable can consist of three Vowels, and consequently that there can be no Tripthongs. **1706** PHILLIPS (ed. Kersey), Triphthongue. **1711** J. GREENWOOD *Eng. Gram.* 244 A Triphthong is, when three Vowels meet together in one Syllable; as *eau* in Beauty: but this we pronounce *Buty*. **1889** PITMAN *Man. Phonogr.* (new ed.) § 41 The double vowels heard in the words *ice, owl, ay, boy*, and the triphthong *wī*, are represented by small angular marks.

Hence **Triphthongal** (trifþǫ·ŋgăl) *a.*, pertaining to or of the nature of a triphthong.

**1748** *Phil. Trans.* XLV. 403, 7 vocal Notes or Vowels,.. struck, as one may say, in diphthongal or triphthongal Chords with each other.

**Triphyletic**: see TRI- 1 a.

**Triphylite** (tri·filəit). *Min.* [f. Gr. τρι- three + φυλή tribe + -ITE [1], because it contains three bases.] A compound phosphate of iron, manganese, and lithium, occurring in greenish-grey or bluish crystals. Orig. called **Triphyline** (tri·filin) [ad. Ger. *triphylin* (Fuchs, 1834)].

**1836** *R. D. & T. Thomson's Rec. Gen. Sci.* III. 476 Triphylline.., from its consisting of three phosphates. It is described by Fuchs as being crystalline, cleaving in four directions; one of the cleavages is vertical to the others. **1850** Triphylline [see TRIPLITE]. **1868** DANA *Min.* (ed. 5) 542 Triphylite and triplite, like other minerals containing protoxyd of manganese, undergo easy alteration by oxydation and hydration.

**Triphyllous** (trəifi·ləs), *a. Bot.* [f. Gr. τρίφυλλ-ος (f. τρι-, TRI- + φύλλον leaf) + -OUS.] Having or consisting of three leaves; *spec.* of a calyx or corolla, trisepalous or tripetalous.

**1760** J. LEE *Introd. Bot.* II. xxxii. (1765) 156 *Ranunculus*, with a triphyllous Calyx and polypetalous. **1762** EHRET in *Phil. Trans.* LIII. 82 At the base of this broad petal is situated an irregular unequal-divided triphyllous periantheum. **1866** *Treas. Bot.* 1173 *Triphyllous*, having the leaves in a whorl of three; also, having only three leaves.

**Tri·physite.** [f. TRI- + Gr. φύσις nature + -ITE [1] 1 a: see MONOPHYSITE.] See quot.

**1874** J. H. BLUNT *Dict. Sects* (1886) 599/2 *Triphysites*, those divines who..A.D. 684, 688..declared a belief not only in Christ's distinct Divine and Human natures, but also in a third nature resulting from the union of the two.

† **Tripilous,** *a. Obs. rare*[−1]. [f. L. *tri-* three + *pil-us* hair + -OUS.] Having three (anal) hairs.

**1671** *Phil. Trans.* VI. 2255 Some of them [insects] had stings and were tripilous, and others not.

**Tripinnate** (trəipi·neⁱt), *a. Bot.* [f. TRI- + PINNATE.] Of a leaf: Triply pinnate; having leaflets pinnately arranged on tertiary petioles similarly arranged: see PINNATE *a.* 1 a, and cf. BIPINNATE. (Abbrev. *3-pinnate.*)

**1760** J. LEE *Introd. Bot.* III. vi. (1765) 188 *Tripinnate*, or *Triplicato-Pinnate*, when a Petiole bears many Folioles, each of which are Bipinnate. **1870** HOOKER *Stud. Flora* 170 Daucus Carota; leaves 3-pinnate. **1880** GRAY *Struct. Bot.* iii. § 4 (ed. 6) 104 Tripinnate or Thrice Pinnate leaves of a regular sort are rare.

So **Tripi·nnated** *a.* in same sense; **Tripi·nnately** *adv.*, in a tripinnate manner; **Tripinnatifid** (-æ·tifid), **Tripinna·tisect** *adjs.*, triply pinnatifid, or pinnatisect; tripinnately divided half-way, or quite, to the base.

**1845** LINDLEY *Sch. Bot.* iv. (1858) 26 *b*, *A[nemone] Pulsatilla* (Pasque Flower). Leaves tripinnatifid with linear acute segments. **1847** W. E. STEELE *Field Bot.* 95 *A[donis] autumnalis*..; leaves 3-pinnatifid. **1857** HENFREY *Elem. Bot.* § 94 Where tripinnatisect leaves have filiform segments, the term dissected is usually employed. **1876** HARLEY *Royle's Mat. Med.* 583 Leaves tripinnated, with fine capillary segments like those of fennel. **1891** *Cent. Dict.*, Tripinnately.

† **Tri·pla.** *Mus. Obs.* [a. L. *tripla*, fem. of *triplus*: see TRIPLE *a.*] Triple proportion between one note and another; triple time or rhythm. Also *attrib.*

**1549** *Compl. Scot.* vi. 37 There vas mony smal birdis.. singand..in accordis of mesure of diapason prolations, tripla ande dyatesseron. **1597** MORLEY *Introd. Mus.* 29 Tripla.. is that which diminisheth the value of the notes to one third part: for three briefes are set for one. **1659** C. SIMPSON *Division-Violist* I. 8 Of Tripla's. Sometimes the Grounds themselves are Tripla-Time; consisting (usually) either of three Semibreves, or three Minims, or three Crochets to a Measure. **1728** R. NORTH *Mem. Music* (1846) 104 For songs he approved onely the soft vein, such as might be called a step tripla.

† **Tri·plage,** *a. Obs. rare.* [app. f. TRIPLE + -AGE (irregularly used).] Triple, threefold.

**1526** in Dillon *Customs of Pale* (1892) 85 Upon paine of m[l] markes to the kinge, and amendes to the partie grevid by triplage damage. *Ibid.*, By triplage freholdurs dammage.

† **Triplar,** *a. Obs.* Also -are, -er. [ad. late L. *triplāris*, f. *triplus* TRIPLE.] = TRIPLE *a.*; cf. TRIPLA.

*c* **1470** HENRYSON *Orpheus & Eurydice* 227 (Bann. MS.) Thair leirit he tonis proportionat, As duplare, triplare [*v.r.* triplar, -er] and emetricus.

**Triplasian** (trəiplēⁱ·siăn, -ʃăn), *a. rare.* [f. Gr. τριπλάσι-ος three times as much or as many, threefold + -AN.] Threefold, triple. So **Triplasic** (trəiplæ·zik) *a.* in same sense; **Tri·plasy** (see quot. 1900).

**1678** CUDWORTH *Intell. Syst.* I. iv. 288 The Persian Magi to this very day, celebrate a Festival Solemnity in honour of the Triplasian (that is, the Three-fold or Triplicated) Mithras. *Ibid.* 290 The Persian Trinity (or Triplasian Deity). **1816** G. S. FABER *Orig. Pagan Idol.* II. 415 The triplasian Mithras. **1864** J. HADLEY *Ess.* v. (1873) 98 Beside these three ratios of arsis and thesis,..Aristoxenus mentions two others: the triplasic, in which the two parts of the foot are as 3 to 1 [etc.]. **1900** B. D. JACKSON *Gloss. Bot. Terms*, *Triplasy*.., the division of an organ into three analogous structures (Fermond).

† **Tri·plate,** *ppl. a.* and *sb. Obs.* [ad. med.L. *triplāt-us*, pa. pple. of *triplāre* to triple (Johannes de Janua, *a* 1286).] **a.** *ppl. a.* Multiplied by three; triplicated, triple. **b.** *sb.* The product of a number multiplied by three. So † **Tri·plated** *ppl. a.*, triple, threefold; † **Tripla·tion**, multiplication by three, tripling.

*c* **1430** *Art of Nombryng* 17 Thow most trebille the digit, and that triplat is to be put vnder the .3.[rd.] next figure towarde the right honde. *Ibid.* 18 After-warde..settyng away alle that is ouer the hede of the triplat nombre. *Ibid.*, Nother me shalle not cesse of the fyndynge of that digit, neither of his triplacioun,..tille it come to the first figure. **1486** *Bk. St. Albans, Her.* E vij, Off tractis triplatit and quatriplatit othyrwyle..He berith golde a trace triplatit of Siluer. **1501** DOUGLAS *Pal. Hon.* I. xli, Fresche ladyis sang in voice virgineall..Proportionis fine with sound celestiall, Duplat, triplat, diatesserial [etc.]. **1542** RECORDE *Gr. Artes* (1575) 167 Triplation is multiplying by 3. **1574** H. BAKER *Well-spring Sci.* (1617) 76 Example of Triplation. If you will triple $^3/_5$, you must diuide $^3/_5$ by $^1/_3$ [etc.].

**Triple** (tri·p'l), *sb.* Forms: see next. [sb. use of TRIPLE *a.*; cf. OF. *triple* in sense 5 below (*c* 1450 in Godef. *Compl.*).]

**1.** A triple quantity, sum, or number; thrice as much or many; the product of a number multiplied by three.

*c* **1425** tr. *Arderne's Treat. Fistula* 30 Of alle þise herbes, ..take euen porcion, outtake of wodebynde, of whiche..be taken þe triple or quadriple. **1557** RECORDE *Whetst.* N iij b, Multiplie that triple, by the same quotiente. And set it doune vnder the first triple. **1674** JEAKE *Arith.* (1696) 195 Triple the Root, and multiply this triple by the Root. **1789** T. TAYLOR *Proclus* II. 16 Not only the doubles, but also the triples, and all multiples of the same quantity. **1830** H. ANGELO *Remin.* I. 327 To add more than triple to his income.

† **b.** A set or series of three; a triad. *Obs. rare.*

1653 R. G. tr. *Bacon's Hist. Winds* 203 This triple of Principles hath been introduced by the Chymists. 1654 WHITLOCK *Zootomia* 464 The Sins, or Judgments of others may make this Triple of Petitions out of that unparallel'd Paterne.

**2.** In technical and elliptical uses. †**a.** *Mus.* Triple measure or rhythm. *Obs.* **b.** A triple star. **c.** A magic lantern having three optical tubes combined in one.

1597 MORLEY *Introd. Mus.* 9 Where it comprehendeth three semibriefes, as in a triple. 1890 C. A. YOUNG *Uranography* § 32, 11 Monocerotis, a fine triple. 1892 *Photogr. Ann.* II. 531 Optical lanterns. Single lanterns. Biunials and triples.

**3.** *Bell-ringing.* A peal rung on seven bells with the tenor, i. e. the eighth, behind; the bells interchanging each time in three sets of two.

1798 in *Gentl. Mag.* Apr. (1825) 298/2 A full and compleat peal of grandsire tripples, consisting of 5040 changes. 1872 ELLACOMBE *Ch. Bells Devon*, etc. iii. 238 A peal of 'London Union Triples'. 1902 *Westm. Gaz.* 23 Oct. 12/2 A boy of fourteen..took part in ringing 1,260 changes, which constitutes a quarter-peal of Grandsire Triples.

†**4.** = TREBLE *sb.* 7 b. *Obs. rare*$^{-1}$.

*a* 1553 UDALL *Royster D.* (Arb.) 88 The Peale of belles rong by the parish Clerk, and Roister Doisters foure men. The first Bell a Triple.

†**5.** = TREBLE *sb.* 4. *Obs. rare*$^{-1}$.

1600 FAIRFAX *Tasso* XVIII. xxiv, The humaine voices sung a triple hie.

**Triple** (tri·p'l), *a.* (*adv.*) Forms: 6 **tryple**, (**treeple**), 7 **tripill**, 7–8 (9 *U.S.*) **tripple**, 6– **triple**. [a. F. *triple* (16th c. in Godef. *Compl.*), or ad. L. *triplus*, a. Gr. τριπλοῦς, = L. *triplex* threefold.]

**1.** Consisting of three members, things, or sets combined; threefold; = TREBLE *a.* 1.

1551–2 in Feuillerat *Revels Edw. VI* (1914) 78 One sute of tryple aparrell of whighte satten. 1587 HARRISON *England* III. viii. in *Holinshed* I. 233/1 The triple tillage of an acre dooth cost 13 shillings foure pence before the saffron be set. 1589 PUTTENHAM *Eng. Poesie* II. i. (Arb.) 78 The Philosopher gathers a triple proportion,..the Arithmeticall, the Geometricall, and the Musicall. *c* 1620 T. ROBINSON *M. Magd.* 1132 There stood ye Monarche of this tripple Isle. 1697 DRYDEN *Æneid* VI. 563 The triple porter of the Stygian sound, Grim Cerberus. 1776 WITHERING *Brit. Plants* (1796) II. 266 A triple thorn beneath the buds. 1847 GROTE *Greece* II. xxiii. III. 536 The trireme or war-ship with a triple bank of oars. 1874 H. H. COLE *Catal. Ind. Art S. Kens. Mus.* 127 Triple rows of chains.

**2.** Having three applications or relations; existing or occurring in three ways or characters; of three kinds; = TREBLE *a.* 1 b.

1567 GOLDING *Ovid's Met.* VII. (1603) 79 b, By triple Hecats holy Rites. 1587 *T. Norton's Calvin's Inst.* IV. xii. § 15. 414 *margin*, [There is] a triple vse of fasting. 1651 HOBBES *Leviath.* II. xxxi. 187 From hence there ariseth a triple Word of God,..to which Correspondeth a triple Hearing. 1675 BAXTER *Cath. Theol.* II. VIII. 173 The Sun ..whose triple Influx Motion, Light, and Heat, affecteth all things. 1860 MOTLEY *Netherl.* (1868) I. i. 10 Their choice was triple.

**3.** Three times as much or many; of three times the measure or amount; multiplied by three.

1550 CROWLEY *Last Trump.* 955 If any man do the desyre Him to defend in doinge wronge, Though he woulde geue the triple hire, Yet geue none eare unto his songe. 1557 RECORDE *Whetst.* E iij, For .9. is triple to .3: and .12. is triple to .4. 1614 RALEIGH *Hist. World* II. (1634) 478 Great conquests are won to repay the charges of Warre with triple interest. 1756 C. LUCAS *Ess. Waters* I. 169 The quantity should not be less than triple the weight of the solids consumed. 1793 SMEATON *Edystone L.* 195 The detached figure ..shews a part of the top of the wall..to a triple scale. 1806 HUTTON *Course Math.* I. 344 Each pyramid is the third part of the prism, or the prism is triple of the pyramid.

†**4.** That is one of three; third. *Obs. rare.*

1601 SHAKS. *All's Well* II. i. 111 One [receipt] which..He bad me store vp, as a triple eye, Safer then mine owne two. 1606 — *Ant. & Cl.* I. i. 12 You shall see in him (The triple Pillar of the world) transform'd Into a Strumpets Foole.

**5.** Special collocations.

*Triple alliance*, an alliance of three states or powers, esp. that of England, Sweden, and the Netherlands in 1668, of France, Great Britain, and the Netherlands in 1717, and of Germany, Austria-Hungary, and Italy in 1883; also *transf.* *Triple bob major*, app. an error for *treble bob major*: see BOB *sb.*[5] *Triple change* (*Bell-ringing*), one in which three pairs of bells change places. *Triple counterpoint*, three-part counterpoint in which the parts may be interchanged without breaking the rules. *Triple crown*, a threefold crown; *spec.* (*a*) the papal tiara; also, a heraldic bearing representing this = TIARA 2 b; (*b*) in horse-racing, the winning of the three races known as the 'Two Thousand Guineas', the 'Derby', and the 'St. Leger' (also *attrib.*). *Triple entente* (Fr.), an understanding as to political action between three powers. *Triple first*, at Cambridge University, a first class in three triposes; also, one who obtains this. *Triple fugue* (*Mus.*), a fugue having three subjects. *Triple gown*: see quot. †*Triple grass*, the genus *Trifolium*. *Triple hat*, the papal tiara. †*Triple Lady's traces*, a species of orchid with three tubers. *Triple line*, *plane*, *point* (*Geom.*), a line, plane, or point formed by the coincidence of three lines, planes, or points. *Triple phosphate* (*Chem.*), phosphate of ammonium and magnesium. *Triple pit* (*Mining*), a shaft divided into three compartments lengthwise: see quot. *Triple plane*: see *triple line*. *Triple play*, in baseball, play in which three men are put out. *Triple point* (*Geom.*), a point common to three branches of a curve, or at which the curve has three tangents: see *triple line*. †*Triple progression* (*Mus.*): see quot. †*Triple proportion*: = *triple ratio*. *Triple quartan* (*ague*), a quartan ague in which the paroxysms occur in sets of three. *Triple ratio*, the ratio of three to one. *Triple rime* (*rhyme*): see RHYME *sb.* 3 c (but in quot. 1872 = TERZA RIMA). *Triple rhythm* (*Mus.*), a threefold rhythm consisting of one heavy and two light accents or beats. *Triple salt* (*Chem.*), a salt containing three different bases. *Triple screw*, a screw having three consecutive threads of the same pitch (*Cent. Dict.* 1891). *Triple star*, a treble star (see TREBLE *a.* 3). *Triple suspension* (*Mus.*): see quot. *Triple tail*, a fish, *Lobotes surinamensis*, in which the dorsal and anal fins are extended so as to resemble tails. *Triple tertian* (*ague*): cf. *triple quartan*. *Triple time* (*Mus.*), a rhythm of three beats in the bar; also *compound triple time* (see COMPOUND *a.* 2 f). *Triple unite*: see UNITE. Also TRIPLE TREE.

1668 TEMPLE *Lett.* xv. (1699) 56 Monsieur de Witt: Who, he said, hindred them from being received into the *Triple-Alliance. 1715 ADDISON *Drummer* v. i. (1722) 39 But here comes the Triple-Alliance [three Rogues]. 1799 *Monthly Rev.* XXX. 528 This design..gave rise to the Triple alliance ..to support the treaty of Utrecht. 1858 G. DUFF *Pol. Surv.* 18 A triple commercial and political alliance between France, Belgium, and Holland. 1906 *Westm. Gaz.* 26 Oct. 2/3 The alleged renewal of the Triple Alliance between Germany, Austria-Hungary, and Italy. 1809 W. IRVING *Knickerb.* (1861) 42 The bells..rang a *triple bobmajor on the joyful occasion. *a* 1845 BARHAM *Ingol. Leg.*, *Wedding-day* 94 The blithe 'College Youths'.. Accustomed, for years, to pull bell-ropes for wagers, Rang faster than ever; their 'triple-bob-majors'. 1872 ELLACOMBE *Ch. Bells Devon* iii. 232 After 1677..Stedman..appears to have introduced the method of double and *triple changes. 1869 OUSELEY *Counterp.* xvii. 134 *Triple and quadruple counterpoints.. consist of three or four melodies so interwoven that any of them may become a correct bass to the others. 1876 STAINER & BARRETT *Dict. Mus. Terms*, *Triple counterpoint*, a counterpoint in three parts, so contrived that each part will serve for bass, middle, or upper part as required. 1555 EDEN *Decades* 226 A *triple crowne much lyke the popes. 1593 SHAKS. 2 *Hen. VI*, I. iii. 66. 1624 BEDELL *Lett.* iv. 78 In one scutchion with the crosse Keyes and triple crown in the crest. 1780, 1894 [see TIARA *sb.* 2 b]. *a* 1854 H. REED *Lect. Eng. Hist.* viii. (1855) 272 The triple crown of the papacy. 1897 *Daily News* 7 Sept. 5/1 What the sporting prophets love to call the 'triple crown',..the Two Thousand, the Derby, and the St. Leger. 1901 *Daily Chron.* 20 July 9/1 The triple-crown winner stood a sound 6 to 4 on chance. 1914 *Times* 5 Aug. 7/4 First came the Franco-Russian Alliance, and later on the Anglo-French, and the Anglo-Russian agreements, which paved the way for the diplomatic group known as the *Triple Entente. 1876 STAINER & BARRETT *Dict. Mus. Terms* s.v. *Fugue*, Fugues have been divided..By number of subjects; as a double fugue, having two subjects; a *triple fugue, three subjects, &c. 1834 *Tait's Mag.* I. 720/2 The double or *triple gowns (the Judges with the double and triple salaries). 1562 BULLEYN *Bulwark, Bk. Simples* (1579) 32 *Trifolium*, called the three leaued grasse. [*margin*] *Triple grasse. 1840 CARLYLE *Heroes* iv. (1858) 285 You with your tiaras, *triple-hats,..stand on Devil's Lie, and are not so strong! 1611, 1785 *Triple Ladies traces [see LADY'S TRACES]. 1857 *G. Bird's Urin. Deposits* (ed. 5) 276 The *triple phosphate which is precipitated artificially from urine..is a neutral salt. 1899 CAGNEY tr. *Jaksch's Clin. Diagn.* vii. (ed. 4) 388 It [urine] deposits on standing a more or less abundant deposit of fat-laden and swollen leucocytes and triple-phosphate crystals. 1839 URE *Dict. Arts* 970 A shaft is to be divided into three compartments, one for the engine pumps, and two for raising coals,..which is denominated a *triple pit. 1896 KNOWLES & MORTON *Baseball* 103 **Triple play*, a play in which the ball is handled quickly enough to retire three men. 1873 B. WILLIAMSON *Diff. Calc.* (ed. 2) xiv. § 209 If the lowest terms in the equation of a curve be of the third degree, the origin is a *triple point. 1801 BUSBY *Dict. Mus.*, **Triple Progression*, an expression in old music, implying a series of perfect fifths. 1557 RECORDE *Whetst.* C j, Proportion .. Doble, *Triple, Quadriple. *a* 1696 SCARBURGH *Euclid* (1705) 180, 12 compared to 4 is Multiple Proportion, and named triple. 1625 HART *Anat. Ur.* II. v. 79, I went to a Canon who lay sicke of a *triple Quartane ague. 1727–38, 1866 *Triple rhyme [see RHYME *sb.* 3 c]. 1872 LOWELL *Dante* Prose Wks. 1890 IV. 158 In the form of the verse (triple rhyme) we may find an emblem of the Trinity. 1800 tr. *Lagrange's Chem.* I. 248 When the quantity of ammonia corresponds with that of the nitrate of magnesia necessary to form a *triple salt, the precipitation is then checked. 1868 WATTS *Dict. Chem.* V. 886 *Triple salts*, a name sometimes applied to salts containing three different bases, such as microcosmic salt. 1831 *Encycl. Brit.* (ed. 7) IV. 47/1 M. Struve has also taken notice of 52 *triple stars. 1876 STAINER & BARRETT *Dict. Mus. Terms* s.v. *Suspension*, Two suspended notes form a double suspension; three a *triple suspension, and so on. 1803 SHAW *Gen. Zool.* IV. 80 The tail..appears as if composed of three distinct parts,..hence the name of Triurus, or *Triple-Tail, applied to this fish by Commerson. 1888 GOODE *Amer. Fishes* 148 The 'Flasher' or 'Triple-tail'..is spoken of by various authors as the 'Black Triple-tail'. 1822–34 *Good's Study Med.* (ed. 4) I. 607 The fifth species [of ague] consisting of double tertians, *triple tertians, unequal tertians, duplicate tertians. 1662 PLAYFORD *Skill Mus.* I. viii. (1674) 28 Pricks of Perfection are used for perfecting Notes, and are only used in the *Triple-Time. 1749 J. MASON *Numbers in Poet. Comp.* 74 If..we banish our slow Tunes, and sing only Triple-Time Tunes to pure Iambic Measure. 1889 F. TAYLOR in Grove *Dict. Mus.* IV. 174/1 When a bar of triple time consists of two notes only the accent is always on the longer note.

**B.** *adv.* To three times the amount or extent; in a threefold manner; triply; thrice. See also C. 2.

1606–1897 [see C. 2]. 1641 in Cochran-Patrick *Rec. Coinage Scotl.* (1876) I. Introd. 31 Coining of the Stirling coper monie .. could not have been done the ordinare way for triple more charges. 1643 R. BAILLIE *Lett. & Jrnls.* (1841) II. 71 Triple more already than ever was taught in Scotland. 1692 BENTLEY *Boyle Lect.* iii. 85 If we had double or triple as many.

**C.** Combinations.

**1.** The adjective in combination. **a.** Parasynthetic combs., as *triple-arched*, *-barbed*, *-bodied*, *-coloured*, *-crested*, *-crowned*, *-edged*, *-formed*, *-gemmed*, *-hatted*, *-lived*, *-nerved*, *-piled*, *-rayed*, *-ribbed*, *-stranded*, *-throated*, *-towered*, *-turreted*; **triple-awned**, in *triple-awned grass*, = *three-awned* (THREE B. III. 2). Also TRIPLE-HEADED.

1906 *Daily News* 4 Sept. 6 The construction of the *triple-aisled nave [of Strassburg Cathedral]. 1819 KEATS *Eve St. Agnes* xxiv, A casement high and *triple-arch'd there was. 1848 BUCKLEY *Iliad* 204 Wounding him on the shoulder with a *triple-barbed arrow. 1905 *Daily Chron.* 22 Sept. 1/7 He is now in a cell *triple-barred and double-locked. 1840 BROWNING *Sordello* I. 201 The *triple-bearded Teuton come to life! 1583 MELBANCKE *Philotimus* D d j, The *triple-bodied Pluto. 1728 POPE *Dunc.* II. 248 At some sick miser's *triple-bolted gate. 1855 MILMAN *Lat. Chr.* XIV. x. (1864) IX. 358 The *triple-chorded harmony of faith, holiness, and charity. 1660 F. BROOKE tr. *Le Blanc's Trav.* 140 *Triple-coloured tortoises. 1667 MILTON *P. L.* XI. 897. 1717 FENTON *Odyss.* XI. Poems 126 To drag to light the *triple-crested Dog That guards Hell's massy Portal. 1679 BEDLOE *Popish Plot* Ep. A j b, Their *Tripple Crown'd Idol at Rome. 1776 DA COSTA *Conchology* 21 A *triple-edged spear or sword. 1606 SYLVESTER *Du Bartas* II. iv. II. *Magnificence* 921 A great Cornaline, Where some rare Artist..Hath deeply cut Time's *triple-formed Front. 1840 CARLYLE *Heroes* iv. (1858) 286 A black spectral Nightmare and *triple-hatted Chimera. 1709–10 STEELE *Tatler* No. 118 ¶ 1 To deal with them as Evander did with his *triple-lived Adversary. 1811 WILLDENOW *Bot.* (new ed.) § 42 A leaf is said to be..*Triple-nerved.., when out of the side of the middle rib above the base there arises a nerve running towards the point. 1851 MRS. BROWNING *Casa Guidi Wind.* I. 830 On *triple-piled Throne-velvets sit at ease to bless the poor. 1847 LD. LINDSAY *Chr. Art* I. 124 Our Saviour is represented..distinguished by the *triple-rayed nimbus. 1847 W. E. STEELE *Field Bot.* 47 Root-leaves crowded..petals rounded, *triple-ribbed. 1629 FORD *Lover's Mel.* IV. ii, The dog, whose *triple-throated noise Hath rous'd a lion from his uncouth den. 1611 COTGR., *Fourchier à trois dents*, a *triple-toothed forke. *c* 1828 BERRY *Encycl. Her.* I. Gloss. s. v. *Triple*, *Triple-towered gate, double-leaved. *a* 1550 in Baring-Gould & Twigge *West. Armory* (1898) 3 Barnestaple Towne: Arg: a *triple turreted tower gul: betweene 3 ogresses.

**b.** in combination with sbs., forming adjectives or attributive phrases, as *triple-compartment*, *-cylinder*, *-expansion* (see EXPANSION 7), *-hearth*, *-line*, *-lock*, *-rack*, *-shift*, *-wick*; **triple-screw**, having three screw-propellers.

1882 *Rep. to Ho. Repr. Prec. Met. U. S.* 293 The main working shaft, which is *tripple compartment. 1877 KNIGHT *Dict. Mech.*, **Triple-cylinder engine*, a steam-engine employing three cylinders. 1886 *Pall Mall G.* 21 Sept. 13/2 These steamers..are provided with *triple expansion engines. 1893 J. A. HODGES *Elem. Photogr.* (1907) 17 The '*triple-extension' type [of camera]. 1877 RAYMOND *Statist. Mines & Mining* 339 The Bennett Mill carries ten stamps, six *triple-hearth reverberatory roasting-furnaces [etc.]. 1889 RIDER HAGGARD *K. Solomon's Mines* 220 The Greys filed off in a *triple-line formation. 1895 *Daily News* 14 Mar. 5/5 The ticket will be dropped in a *triple-lock box. 1892 *Photogr. Ann.* II. 545 Large size (patent) *triple-rack telescopic front tubes. 1901 *Daily Mail* 30 Oct. 5/3 A series of six *triple-screw 14,865 ton battleships. 1892 *Photogr. Ann.* II. Advt., *Triple Wick Lamps,..Four Wick Lamps.

**2.** The adverb in combination. **a.** with pa. pples. or adjs., as *triple-compound*, *-compounded*, *-dyed*, *-endowed*, *-refined*, *-roomed*, *-turned*, *-twined*.

1897 *Daily News* 14 June 6/6 Two sets of *triple-compound engines, each self-contained. 1775 ADAIR *Amer. Ind.* 69 A double, or *triple-compounded [word]. 1606 SYLVESTER *Du Bartas* II. iv. II. *Magnificence* 729 Their long strong sarcels, richly *triple-di'd Gold-Azure-Crimsin. 1824 MISS MITFORD *Village* Ser. I. (1863) 130 A *triple-refined taste. 1610 HEALEY *St. Aug. Citie of God* XV. xxvi. 566 The arke..had roomes aboue those vpper roomes, and so was called *triple-roomed, being three stories high. 1606 SHAKS. *Ant. & Cl.* IV. xii. 13 *Triple-turn'd Whore, 'tis thou Hast sold me to this Nouice. 1804 J. COLLINS *Scrip-scrap.* xi, Bath deems a *triple-twin'd Laurel thy Due.

**b.** with pres. pples., as *triple-barking*, *-flashing*.

1733 SWIFT *On Poetry* 214 To Cerberus they give a sop, His *triple-barking mouth to stop. 1903 *Daily Chron.* 27 Feb. 7/7 A light vessel, say one showing a ten-mile range *triple-flashing red light.

Hence (*nonce-wds.*) †**Tri·plefold** *adv.*, triply, threefold; †**Tri·plewise** *adv.*, in a triple manner.

1570 FOXE *A. & M.* (ed. 2) 36/1 To these is gyuen pardon from the Pope, double and triplefold more, then to any other good worke of charitie. 1594 MARLOWE & NASHE *Dido* v. i, Ganges..Whose wealthy streams may wait upon her [Troy's] towers, And triple-wise entrench her round about.

**Triple** (tri·p'l), *v.* Forms: see TRIPLE *a.*; also 5 **threpil**, **-el**, **tryple**. [ad. med.L. *triplāre* (see TRIPLATE); cf. F. *tribler* (1484 in Godef. *Compl.*), Prov. *triplar.*]

**1.** *trans.* To make three times as great or as many as before; to multiply by three; to make threefold; to treble.

1375 (MS. 1487) BARBOUR *Bruce* XVIII. 30 And said, that he suld fecht that day, Thouch Tryplit or quadruplit [*Edin. MS.* (1489) tribill and quatribill] war thai. *a* 1400–50 *Alexander* 1476 Þe bischop..Comandis to ilka creatour to crie þurȝe þe stretis, To thre dais on a thrawe be threpild [*v.r.* threpelytt] to-gedire. 1542 RECORDE *Gr. Artes* (1575) 115 To double the remayner of poundes, and triple the remayner of shillings. 1564 *Reg. Privy Council Scot.* I. 297 Thair abone impresonment to be tripled. 1620 in Foster *Eng. Factories Ind.* (1906) 208 Private traders..who confesse they triple their principall between that place and Bantam. 1655 *Clarke Papers* (Camden) III. 23 His Highnesse..tripled the guards, and scoured the citty and 4 miles round with horse. *a* 1774 GOLDSM. *Surv. Exp. Philos.* (1776) I. 128 The body goes on with the double impression, and receives also a new one which triples it. 1795 *Hist.* in

*Ann. Reg.* 17/1 She was determined to double and even triple her army. **1820** LAMB *Elia* Ser. I. *Two Races of Men*, He will return them [books]..with usury; enriched with annotations, tripling their value. **1858** BUCKLE *Civiliz.* (1864) II. i. 119 The export of foreign commodities was tripled.

**b.** To fold in three thicknesses. *rare*—0.

**1573–80** BARET *Alv.* T 376 *Triple*, to..fold a thing three times.

**c.** *spec.* in *Mech.* To alter (a steam-engine) from single or double expansion to the triple-expansion type; also, to fit (a vessel, etc.) with triple-expansion engines.

**1891** [see TRIPLING *vbl. sb.* 1 b].

**2.** To amount to three times as many as. *rare*—1.

**1589** in Hakluyt *Voy.* (1599) II. II. 145 Their losse I can assure you did triple ours, as well in quality as in quantity.

**3.** *intr.* To grow to three times the former number or amount.

**1799** W. TAYLOR in *Monthly Rev.* XXVIII. 526 Our author hesitates whether wages have not tripled. **1805** SYD. SMITH in Lady Holland *Mem.* (1855) II. 15, I..was pleasing myself with the notion..that your income was tripling and quadrupling in value. **1839** *Times* 11 June, Within the last twenty years it [crime] has tripled.

**Tripled** (tri·p'ld), *ppl. a.* [f. prec. + -ED 1.] Made triple or threefold; multiplied by three.

**1583** STUBBES *Anat. Abus.* II. (1882) 98 This tripled commandement,..Feede my sheepe, feede my sheepe, feede my sheepe. **1621** MIDDLETON *Sun in Aries* Wks. (Bullen) VII. 349 Behold yon Fountain with the tripled crown. **1698** DRYDEN *Ep. to Motteux* 35 Time, action, place, are so preserved by thee That even Corneille might with envy see The alliance of his tripled Unity. **1790** R. MERRY *Laurel of Liberty* (ed. 2) 30 They force its tripled walls.

‖ **Triplegia** (trəiplī·dʒiă). *Path.* [mod.L., f. Gr. τρι- three + πληγή stroke; cf. HEMIPLEGIA.]

**1899** *Allbutt's Syst. Med.* VI. 894 Hemiplegia..when added to the paraplegia of spinal origin, makes up a clinical picture of a triplegia. **1900–13** DORLAND *Med. Dict.*, *Triplegia*,.., hemiplegia with paralysis of one limb on the opposite side.

**Triple-headed,** *a.* Having three heads; three-headed.

**1581** A. HALL *Iliad* v. 87 Iuno..stricken so did stand By triple headed sheering shafte, ysent by Herculs hand. **1605** DRAYTON *Pastorals* iv. 30 Such monster-tamers..As haue tyde vp the triple-headed hound. *a* **1658** CLEVELAND *Wks.* (1677) 94 The Tripleheaded Turn-key of Heaven with the Tripleheaded Porter of Hell. **1775** ADAIR *Amer. Ind.* 29 Proserpine and Cerberus were triple-headed. **1847** LD. LINDSAY *Chr. Art* I. 84 The triple-headed, bat-winged, horned and hoofed monster of the later middle ages.

**Tripleness** (tri·p'lnės). *rare.* [f. TRIPLE *a.* + -NESS.] The quality or condition of being triple; triplicity.

*c* **1881** HORT in *Expositor* June (1907) 489 When there is tripleness and at the same time not mere co-ordination but progression.

**Triplet** (tri·plėt). Also 8 **triplit.** [f. TRIPLE, after DOUBLET; cf. F. *triplet* (Littré).]

**1.** A set of three; three persons or things combined or united.

**1733** SWIFT *Legion Club* 183 Such a triplet could you tell Where to find on this side hell? **1824** L. MURRAY *Eng. Gram.* (ed. 5) I. 444 A very frequent succession of words and phrases, in couplets, or triplets, is also a great blemish in composition. **1851** AIRY *Presid. Addr. Brit. Assoc.* 43 Observing stations should be selected..in triplets: the three stations of each triplet having relation to the north boundary, the centre, and the south boundary of the shadow. The Russian Government has..actually equipped six triplets.

**2.** In various specific uses. **a.** Three successive lines of verse, esp. when riming together and of the same length.

**1656** EARL MONM. tr. *Boccalini's Advts. fr. Parnass.* II. xiv. (1674) 153 Berni, the Head of those Italian Poets, who have..written facetious things in Triplets. **1697** [see 3]. **1751** EARL ORRERY *Remarks Swift* (1752) 188 One of his strictest rules in poetry was to avoid triplets. **1800** MALONE *Life Dryden* 525 He sent a second messenger to the bookseller, with a very satirical triplet. **1862** BORROW *Wild Wales* lix. (1911) 311 He was a poet by nature, having a muse wonderfully glib at making triplets and quartets.

**b.** *pl.* Three children at a birth; *sing.* one of three at a birth.

**1787** GARTHSHORE in *Phil. Trans.* LXXVII. 351 [Of] triplets, or three born at once, we find comparatively..few instances in..any..country. **1860** TANNER *Signs Pregnancy* (1862) 110 The presence of three distinct [uterine] double sounds, not isochronous, warrants the diagnosis of triplets. **1905** *Daily News* 25 Jan. 9 His mother said she..had two other boys the same age..The troublesome triplet was remanded.

**c.** *Mus.* A group of three notes to be played in the time of two of the same time-value.

**1801** in BUSBY *Dict. Mus.* **1848** RIMBAULT *Piano* 23 When three notes of one sort are joined together, and have the figure 3 placed over or under them, they are called a Triplet,..and are to be performed in the time of two only of the same kind. **1862** ERNST PAUER *Programme* 8 Mar., With triplets continually increasing in rapidity.

*transf.* **1860** RUSKIN *Unto this Last* iv. § 82 Triplets of birds and murmur and chirp of insects.

**d.** *Arch.* A window of three lights.

**1849** FREEMAN *Archit.* II. I. vii. 180 The genuine triplet with the higher central light seems hardly to be found in Italy. **1868** *Daily News* 22 July, A window in the Abbey Church, consisting of a triplet of lancets at the west end of the nave.

**e.** A combination of three plano-convex lenses in a microscope, etc.; also, a microscope having three lenses.

**1837** *Encycl. Brit.* (ed. 7) XV. 36 Sir David Brewster has made triplets in which two of the lenses are fluids and the third a solid. **1867** [see 3].

**f.** A counterfeit jewel: see quot., and cf. DOUBLET *sb.* 5.

**1877** *Five Yrs.' Penal Servitude* iv. 274 A triplet is made as follows:—Two colourless topazes are prepared for the back and the front. Between these is neatly placed a piece of blue glass, and the three are stuck together with Venice turpentine.

**g.** A tandem bicycle for three riders.

**1894** *Daily News* 3 Sept. 3/3 On a triplet, [they] started to create a record for their type of machine, and succeeded ..in riding the fastest mile ever ridden at Herne-hill.

**h.** *Geom.* A system of three families of surfaces such that one of each family passes through each point of space. **1891** in *Cent. Dict.*

**i.** *Naut.* Three links between the cable and the anchor-ring. **1891** in *Cent. Dict.*

**3.** *attrib.* **Triplet lily,** the American genus *Triteleia*, N.O. *Liliaceæ*, having the parts of the flower regularly arranged in threes.

**1697** DRYDEN *Æneid* Ded. fj, I frequently make use of Triplet Rhymes. **1867** J. HOGG *Microsc.* I. i. 13 The first triplet achromatic object-glass. **1874** H. H. COLE *Catal. Ind. Art S. Kens. Mus.* App. 287 This bas-relief represents a god with several triplet heads and a great number of hands. **1884** MILLER *Plant-n.*, *Triteleia*, Triplet-Lily. **1892** *Photogr. Ann.* II. 548 Microscope and micro-polariscope, fitted with Mr. Hughes's patent 5in. triplet condensers. **1900** *Daily News* 21 Apr. 6/3 New amateur triplet records were established..from two miles up to 28 miles.

**Triple tree.** *Cant.* Now *Hist.* or *arch.* [TREE *sb.* 4 b.] A gallows (in reference to its three parts).

*a* **1634** RANDOLPH *Hey for Honesty* IV. i, This is a Rascal deserves to ride up Holborn, And take a pilgrimage to the triple-tree, To dance in Hemp Derricks Caranto. **1707** J. STEVENS tr. *Quevedo's Com. Wks.* (1709) 181 Being come to the tripple Tree, he..set his Foot on the Ladder. **1862** SALA *Ship Chandler* i. 5 Busy as was the triple tree.., they could not hang all the rogues they convicted.

**Triplex** (trəi·-, tri·pleks), *a.* (*sb.*) [a. L. *triplex, -plic-* threefold, f. *tri-* three + *plic-* to fold.] Triple, threefold. Also *absol.* as *sb.*

**1601** SHAKS. *Twel. N.* v. i. 41 The triplex..is a good tripping measure, or the belles of S. Bennet,..may put you in minde, one, two, three. [**1654** D. CAWDREY (*title*) Diatribe Triplex: or A threefold Exercitation Concerning 1. Superstition. 2. Will-worship. 3. Christmas Festivall.] **1655** HAMMOND (*title*) An account of Mr. Cawdry's Triplex Diatribe. **1656** S. HOLLAND *Zara* (1719) 71 So that now there is like to be a trouble in Triplex. **1911** W. TEMPLE *Nat. Personality* viii. 112 We are not so compelled to speak of three centres of consciousness in the Deity; rather we should speak of a triplex consciousness.

Hence **Triple·xity** = TRIPLICITY.

**1895** in *Funk's Stand. Dict.*

**Tripley,** obs. form of TRIPLY *v.*

**Tripli-** (tripli), short for *triplici-*, combining form of L. *triplex* TRIPLE, occurring in a few rare adjs. (chiefly *Bot.*), as **triplico·state** = *tricostate* (TRI- 1 a); **tri·pliform** = TRIFORM 1; **tripli-nerved** = TRINERVATE.

**1866** *Treas. Bot.* 1173 *Triple-nerved, Triplinerved, Triplinervis*, the same as Triple-ribbed. **1869** INMAN *Symbolism* Introd. 12 One symbol was tripliform, the other single. **1879** WEBSTER Suppl., Triplicostate.

**Triplica·nd.** *Sc. Law.* [ad. L. *triplicānd-*, gerund. stem of *triplicāre* to TRIPLICATE.] The tripling of the feu-duty for one year; a triple feu-duty so paid. Cf. DUPLICAND.

**1898** *Mem. Jas. E. Fyfe* 39 The superior rubbed his hands over an annual duty of £30 an acre, with a triplicand every twenty-first year.

**Triplicate** (tri·plikĕt), *a.* and *sb.* [ad. L. *triplicāt-us*, pa. pple. of *triplicāre* (*rare*) to triple.]

**A.** *adj.* Threefold, triple; forming three exactly corresponding copies; consisting of or related to three corresponding parts.

**1432–50** tr. *Higden* (Rolls) I. 239 A triplicate honor was ȝiffen to a kynge..hauenge victory, in his commenge to the cite of Rome. **1512** *Act 4 Hen. VIII*, c. 19 § 10 One parte of the seid Writyng triplicate to be indented shall remayne with the seid Commissioners. **1528** in Burnet *Hist. Ref.* (1679) I. Records II. iv. 25 Certain Expeditions Triplicat; the one unto the Prothonotar Gambora, the other unto Gregory de Cassali, and the third unto me. **1756** *Gentl. Mag.* Oct. 461/1 It was always customary to make double and triplicate bills of loading. **1862** BEVERIDGE *Hist. India* III. VIII. iii. 333 The conclusion of a triplicate treaty by the British government, the Maharajah, and Shah Shujah-ul-Moolk. **1902** W. M. ALEXANDER *Demonic Possession N.T.* iii. 61 There are..duplicate or triplicate narratives of these three cases.

**b.** *Triplicate proportion, ratio*: the proportion or ratio of cubes (third powers) in relation to that of the radical quantities.

**1660** BARROW *Euclid* v. Def. x, When 4 magnitudes A, B, C, D are proportional, the first A shall have a triplicate ratio to the fourth D of what it had to the second B. **1674** PETTY *Disc. Dupl. Proportion* 44 Like pieces of Timber, that are in cubical or triplicate proportion of their Sides, are strong but according to duplicate proportion, or the Squares of their respective Sides. **1718** QUINCY *Compl. Disp.* 45 The Gravity of Bodies decreases in a Triplicate, but their Surface in a Duplicate Proportion of their Diameters. **1806** HUTTON *Course Math.* (1810) I. 314 The Ratio of the First [quantity] to the Third, will be duplicate or the Square of the Ratio of the First and Second; and the Ratio of the First and Fourth will be triplicate or the cube of that of the First and Second, and so on.

**c.** *Triplicate quartan* (*ague*) = *triple quartan* (TRIPLE *a.* 5).

**1822–34** *Good's Study Med.* (ed. 4) I. 613 Quartanus triplicatus. Triplicate quartan.

**d.** In combination, as *triplicate-ternate* (*Bot.*) = TRITERNATE.

**1847** in WEBSTER. **1900** B. D. JACKSON *Gloss. Bot. Terms*, *Triplicate-ternate*, triternate (Crozier).

**B.** *sb.* **1.** One of three things exactly alike, *esp.* one of three copies of a document; *pl.* three things exactly alike.

**1762–71** H. WALPOLE *Vertue's Anecd. Paint.* (1786) II. 23 *note*, There are three portraits of himself,..and three triplicates of his mistress. **1801** WELLINGTON in Gurw. *Desp.* (1837) I. 284, I have the honor to enclose the triplicate of a letter to the Governor of Bombay. **1835** BATMAN in Cornwallis *New World* (1859) I. 410, I busied myself in drawing up triplicates of the deeds of the land I had purchased. **1859** TENNENT *Ceylon* II. VII. v. 200 Not only a duplicate, but a triplicate of the desecrated relic were regarded with undiminished adoration both in Pegu and Ceylon.

**b.** *In triplicate*: in three exactly corresponding copies or transcripts. Also *transf.*

**1810** WELLINGTON in Gurw. *Desp.* (1838) VI. 170 Desire Captain Eliott to send his account of the expenditure in Triplicate. **1860** HOOK *Lives Abps.* II. vii. 412 The constitutions were written in triplicate. **1894** *Times* 7 Aug. 6/2 Many of the trains..were run in duplicate and triplicate.

†**2.** Triplicate ratio; third power, cube. *Obs. rare.*

**1767** MURDOCH in *Phil. Trans.* LVIII. 28 The accelerative force of A..will be increased in the triplicate of that ratio.

**Triplicate** (tri·plikeit), *v.* [f. L. *triplicāt-*, ppl. stem of *triplicāre* (see prec.), f. *triplex*, triple.]

**1.** *trans.* To multiply by three; to increase threefold; to triple.

**1623** COCKERAM, *Triplicate*, to triple, or doe a thing three times. **1652** BENLOWES *Theoph.* x. lxi, Could'st thou engross Cathaiahs Gems And more than triplicate Romes triple diadems. **1717** B. TAYLOR in *Phil. Trans.* XXX. 614 This Formula will also triplicate the number of true Figures in *Z.* **1871** *Daily News* 19 Jan., They have thus triplicated the defences of a tract they had judged to be exposed.

**2.** To make or provide in triplicate; to make the triplicate of; to repeat a second time.

**1639** GENTILIS *Servita's Inquis.* (1676) 851 They might.. reply, and triplicate the same request with greater instance. **1653** R. SANDERS *Physiogn.* 249 Such a person usually reiterates and triplicates his words, to little purpose. **1879** G. MEREDITH *Egoist* xxxvi, We are in danger of duplicating [wedding-presents] and triplicating and quadruplicating.

Hence **Tri·plicating** *ppl. a.*

**1906** *Hibbert Jrnl.* Apr. 598 Hegel's argument was a kind of trinity: i.e. it moved in a triplicating way,—thesis, antithesis and synthesis.

**Tri·plicated,** *ppl. a.* [f. prec. + -ED 1.] Made threefold; triple. *Triplicated proportion*, triplicate proportion.

**1635** WINGATE Λογαριθμοτεχνία 69 Having three numbers given, to finde a fourth in a triplicated Proportion. **1678** [see TRIPLASIAN]. **1753** CHAMBERS *Cycl. Supp.* s. v. *Bridge*, The piers being only thirteen feet thick, yet serving to support an immense weight of a triplicated arcade. **1851** C. L. SMITH tr. *Tasso* XI. vii, The flaming quire Of Heaven in triplicated order dighted.

**Triplication** (triplikēi·ʃən). [a. F. *triplication* (Godef.), or ad. L. *triplicātiōn-em*, n. of action from *triplicāre* to TRIPLICATE.]

**1.** The action or process of making threefold, or multiplying by three; also, the result of this.

**1610** HEALEY *St. Aug. Citie of God* XIX. ii. (1620) 708 These twelue sects are produced by the triplication of these foure. **1674** JEAKE *Arith.* (1696) 24 Triplication..is to add the given number to the double of the same. **1798** W. PALGRAVE *Let.* in *Parr's Wks.* (1828) VIII. 103 The triplication of the assessed taxes. **1893** *Nation* (N.Y.) 23 Mar. 213/3 A duplication or triplication of teachers of theology entered into my ideal of the school.

**2. a.** *Civil* and *Canon Law.* The plaintiff's reply to the defendant's duplication, corresponding to the surrejoinder at common law. **b.** In *Common Law* sometimes applied (after Britton) to the rejoinder.

[**1292** BRITTON III. xiv. § 6 Et si le pleyntif die, qe il fust seisi par acun feffement, a ceo soit respoundu par triplicacioun, cum desus est dit.] *a* **1577** SIR T. SMITH *Commw. Eng.* (1609) 67 Where the law is not doubtful, according to the matter conteyned in the declaration, answer, replication, rejoynder, or triplication, the Judge out of hand decideth it. **1651** G. W. tr. *Cowel's Inst.* 243 Our Lawyers call a Duplication, as well in the Chancery, as in other Courts a Rejoinder, and a Triplication a Sur-rejoinder. **1726** AYLIFFE *Parergon* 251 There are also Triplications, which the Plaintiff objects to the Defendant's Duplication. **1865** NICHOLS *Britton* II. 116 Nevertheless in some cases the plaintiff may have a valid replication..But the tenant may answer by way of triplication, that [etc.]. **1880** MUIRHEAD *Gaius* IV. § 128 If this..for any reason be really inequitable to the pursuer, still another clause is necessary on the other side for his relief, which is called a triplication. **1895** POLLOCK & MAITLAND *Hist. Eng. Law* II. ix. § 4. 613 The exception may be met by a replication, the replication by a triplication and so on *ad infinitum.*

*transf.* **1593** G. HARVEY *Pierces Super.* Wks. (Grosart) II. 112 For any my briefe Triplication, he will prouide a Quadruplication at large. **1621** [see DUPLICATION 3 b]. **1649** ROBERTS *Clavis Bibl.* 344 Eliphas his Triplication, or third Opposition against Job.

**Triplicative** (tri·plike¹tiv), *a.* [f. L. *triplicāt-*, ppl. stem of *triplicāre* to TRIPLICATE + -IVE.] Having the quality of tripling.

1839–52 BAILEY *Festus* (ed. 5) 509 The esoteric truths which nature veiled, Of the one triplicative essence.

**Triplicato-** (triplikē¹·to), combining form repr. L. *triplicātus* TRIPLICATE, rarely used in a few botanical terms instead of the simple *tri-*, as **triplicato-pinnate** *a.* = TRIPINNATE, **triplicato-ternate** *a.* = TRITERNATE.

[1753 CHAMBERS *Cycl. Supp.* s. v. *Leaf, Triplicato-ternatum.*] 1760 J. LEE *Introd. Bot.* III. vi. (1765) 188 *Triternate*, or *Triplicato-Ternate*; when a Petiole bears three Folioles that are each of them Biternate. 1866 *Treas. Bot.* 1173 *Triplicato-pinnate*, the same as Tripinnate.

**Triplicature** (tri·plike¹tiūɹ). [f. L. *triplicāt-*, ppl. stem of *triplicāre* to TRIPLICATE, after DUPLICATURE: see -URE.] Triplication.

1891 in *Cent. Dict.*

† **Tripli·citate**, *v. Obs.* [f. late L. *triplicitāt-*, TRIPLICITY + -ATE ³.] *trans.* To triple.

1657 TOMLINSON *Renou's Disp.* 720 Efficacious in curing the Dropsie, if the quantity of Cypress be triplicitated.

**Triplicity** (tripli·sĭti). [ad. late L. *triplicitāt-em*, f. L. *triplex, -icem*: see TRIPLEX and -ITY. Cf. F. *triplicité* (14–15th c. in Hatz.-Darm.).]

**1.** The quality or condition of being triple; threefold character or existence; tripleness, threefoldness.

1555 EDEN *Decades* 1 One god whom we honour in triplicitie of person. 1624 HEYWOOD *Gunaik.* VI. 268 To this three-fold age, I compare the triplicitie of the Muses. 1690 BURNET *Th. Earth* III. 10 This triplicity of the heavens and the earth is the first, obvious, plain sence of the apostle's discourse. 1705 HEARNE *Collect.* 12 Dec. (O.H.S.) I. 126 The Triplicity of the Crownes. 1850 L. HUNT *Autobiog.* I. ii. 45 He was clergyman, physician, and lawyer, at once. How this singular triplicity came to take place, I cannot say.

**2.** A combination or group of three things, beings, or attributes; three things collectively; a triad, trio, triplet.

1585 S. R. (*title*) The Choise of Change: Containing the Triplicitie of Diuinitie, Philosophie, and Poetrie. 1590 SPENSER *F. Q.* I. xii. 39 Many an Angels voice Singing before th'eternall majesty, In their trinall triplicities on hye. 1607 TOPSELL *Four-f. Beasts* (1658) 451 The Panther..is joyned with the Lion and the Wolf, to make up the triplicity of ravening Beasts. 1660 WATERHOUSE *Arms & Arm.* 143 Solomon, Marcus Antoninus, and our late King James, a triplicity of unparalleld Majesties. 1899 F. M. CRAWFORD *Via Crucis* vi. 71 A most perfect triplicity of beauty, grace and elastic strength.

† **b.** A multiple by three; three times the amount. *Obs. rare*—¹.

1646 SIR T. BROWNE *Pseud. Ep.* IV. xii. 218 Affirming.. what receiveth motion in the seventh, to be perfected in the Triplicities; that is, the time of conformation..from motion unto the birth [is] treble.

**3.** *spec.* in *Astrol.* A combination of three of the twelve signs of the zodiac, each sign being distant 120° or the third part of a circle from the other two: = TRIGON 2 a.

Each of the four triplicities is named after one of the 'elements', of whose qualities it is supposed to partake; thus *airy t.* = Gemini, Libra, Aquarius; *earthy t.* = Taurus, Virgo, Capricornus; *fiery t.* = Aries, Leo, Sagittarius; *watery t.* = Cancer, Scorpio, Pisces.

1398 TREVISA *Barth. De P. R.* VIII. ix. (Bodl. MS.) lf. 80/1 Þese howses beþ icleped þe howses of triplicite and somme of exaltacioun, for þilke signes þat accordeþ in one kinde makeþ triplicite and have .o. name. *c* 1532 DU WES *Introd. Fr.* in *Palsgr.* 1054 The sayd xii signes..ben devided by foure triplicites. 1584 R. SCOT *Discov. Witchcr.* XIII. vii. (1886) 243 In Aries, Leo, and Sagittarie is a certain triplicitie. 1650 R. GELL *Serm.* 8 Aug. 45 Talk not to them of fiery, aiery, watry, earthly triplicities. 1815 SCOTT *Guy M.* iii, I will calculate his nativity according to the rule of the 'Triplicities', as recommended by Pythagoras, Hippocrates, Diocles, and Avicenna. 1855 SMEDLEY, etc. *Occult Sciences* 307 The Four Triplicities is another distribution of the twelve signs into groups of three.

† **b.** *fig.* or *allusively. Obs.*

1573 G. HARVEY *Letter-bk.* (Camden) 140 So many influences and triplicityes of loove. 1647 *Husbandman's Plea agst. Tithes* 70 The fiery triplicitie..of Bishops, Priests, and Deacons. 1680 *Hon. Cavalier* 15 The Pope, the Fanatick, and the Turk, that Fiery Triplicity of the World.

**Triplicostate, -form, -nerved**: see TRIPLI-.

**Tripling** (tri·pliŋ), *vbl. sb.* [f. TRIPLE *v.* + -ING ¹.]

**1.** The action of the verb TRIPLE.

1603 FLORIO *Montaigne* (1634) 94 It is a great..wonder for a man to double himselfe; and those that talke of tripling, know not, nor cannot reach unto the height of it. 1630 DELAMAIN *Grammelogia* **j, The doubling, tripling [etc.] of Circles. 1853 SIR W. R. HAMILTON *Lect. Quaternions* ii. 53 Two successive acts, of negatively doubling and negatively tripling, compound themselves into the single act of positively sextupling.

**b.** *spec.* See TRIPLE *v.* 1 c.

1891 *Times* 26 Oct. 4/3 There is a fair amount of tripling of engines in old vessels ordered.

**2.** *concr.* **a.** *pl.* Three children at a birth; triplets.

1858 LEWES *Sea-side Stud.* 246 This multiplication of individuals from one egg, this production of twins, or triplings, is a constant fact.

**b.** *Min.* A compound crystal made up of three independent individuals; a trilling, trin.

1895 STORY-MASKELYNE *Crystallogr.* § 157 Such crystals are triple, quadruple, &c. hemitropes (or triplings, fourlings, &c.).

**Triplite** (tri·plait). *Min.* [ad. Ger. *triplit* (Hausmann, 1813), f. Gr. τριπλοῦς threefold, in reference to its three cleavages: see -ITE ¹.] A phosphate of iron and manganese (often containing fluorine), of a brown or blackish colour, with cleavage in three directions mutually at right angles.

1850 ANSTED *Elem. Geol., Min.* etc. § 447 Hureaulite, Heterozite, and Triphylline, or Triplite, are phosphates of manganese and iron. 1868 DANA *Min.* (ed. 5) 543.

**Triplo-** (triplo), before a vowel **tripl-**, combining form repr. Gr. τριπλόος, τριπλοῦς threefold, triple; occurring in a few rare scientific terms. (Cf. TRIPLI-.) **Triploblastic** (-blæ·stik) *a., Biol.* [Gr. βλαστός germ], having three germinal layers (epiblast, mesoblast, and hypoblast: cf. BLASTODERM) in the embryo; belonging to the division *Triploblastica*, a synonym of CŒLOMATA, including the majority of animals; cf. *diploblastic* s. v. DIPLO-. **Triplo-caulescent** (-kǭle·sĕnt), **-caulous** (-kǭ·ləs) *adjs., Bot.* [L. *caulis* stem], having a tertiary system of axes or stem-branches. ‖ **Triplo·pia**, anglicized **tri·plopy**, *Path.* [Gr. ὤψ eye: cf. DIPLOPIA], an affection of the eyes in which objects are seen triple.

1888 *Cassell's Encycl. Dict.*, *Triploblastic. 1890 BILLINGS *Med. Dict.*, *Triploblastic*, having three germ-layers. 1900 B. D. JACKSON *Gloss. Bot. Terms*, **Triplo-caulescent*.. when a plant has a third (tertiary) system of axes. **Triplocaulous*..possessing ternary axes (Pax). 1860 MAYNE *Expos. Lex.*, **Triplopia*, a term for..disordered vision in which objects are tripled. 1903 F. W. H. MYERS *Hum. Personality* I. 479 Cases, where ciliary spasm..led to.. triplopia. 1863 ATKINSON tr. *Ganot's Physics* VII. vi. 463 A single eye may also be affected with *triplopy, but in this case the third image is exceedingly weak.

**Triploid** (tri·ploid). *Surg. rare.* ? *Obs.* [ad. mod.L. *triploides*, f. Gr. τριπλό-ος: see prec. and -OID.] (See quot.)

[1706 PHILLIPS (ed. Kersey), *Triploides.*] 1750 *Mem. R. Acad. Surg. Paris* I. 162–3 The instruments hitherto used to raise the bones of the cranium depressed on the dura mater are..the triploid...This instrument has three feet or branches like a tripod.

**Triploidite** (tri·ploidəit). *Min.* [f. TRIPL(ITE + -OID + -ITE ¹.] A hydrous phosphate of iron and manganese, allied to TRIPLITE.

1878 *Amer. Jrnl. Sc. & Arts* Ser. III. May 398 Triploidite.. occurs in crystalline aggregates whose structure is parallel-fibrous to columnar.

**Triplu·mbic**, *a. Chem.* [f. TRI- 5 + L. *plumb-um* lead + -IC.] Containing three atoms of lead; e. g. *triplumbic tetroxide*, $Pb_3O_4$.

1866–8 WATTS *Dict. Chem.* IV. 566 *Triplumbic phosphate*, $Pb^3P^2O^8$, is obtained as a white, earthy, amorphous precipitate. 1905 NEWTH *Inorg. Chem.* (ed. 11) 648 Triplumbic Tetroxide..is obtained when lead carbonate, or monoxide, is subjected to prolonged heating in contact with air.

**Triply** (triplai·), *sb. Sc. Law. Obs.* exc. *Hist.* [ad. OF. *triplique* (*treplicque*, 1392–3 in Godef. *Compl.*); cf. also REPLY, DUPLY, QUADRUPLY.] A third reply; a pursuer's reply to a defender's rejoinder; a surrejoinder. Also *allusively*.

1531 in *10th Rep. Hist. MSS. Comm.* App. I. 71 Notwithstanding the rights, replies and triplies produced on the part of John Kynross, not proved. 1643 BAILLIE *Lett., to W. Spang* 7 Dec. (1841) II. 109 When, upon every proposition by itself, and on everie text of Scripture..the replyes, and duplies, and triplies, are heard. 1678 SIR G. MACKENZIE *Crim. Laws Scot.* II. xxiii. § 9 (1699) 253 After they have ended, His Majesties Advocat speaks, but there are no Duplys, or Triplys used. *a* 1693, 1760, 1820, 1881 [see DUPLY]. 1695, 1762 [see QUADRUPLY].

So **Triply·** *v.* [cf. OF. *tripliquer* (1310 in Godef.)], to make a triply or reply to a defender's rejoinder (*trans.* and *intr.*).

1504 in *Charters &c. of Stirling* (1884) 68 Till obiect, except, and aganesay, to repley, dupley, tripley, and quadrupley. 1662 *Justiciary Records* (S. H. S. 1905) 44 Triplied by Birnie. He oppones the answers. 1678 SIR G. MACKENZIE *Crim. Laws Scot.* I. xxiv. § 4 (1699) 123 To which it was triplyed, that the Act of Parliament, discharging Usurary Wadsets doth not discharge Tacks. 1766 *State of Proc., Dk. Roxburgh* v. *Pringle* 7 Duplied for the Defender..Triplied for the Pursuer, That as..this Question must go to Proof [etc.].

**Triply** (tri·pli), *adv.* [f. TRIPLE *a.* + -LY ².] In a triple degree or manner; three times.

1660 R. COKE *Power & Subj.* 191 If he will purge himself he may do it triply. 1826 DISRAELI *Viv. Grey* II. ii, His large library table, once triply covered with official communications. 1885 MISS BRADDON *Wyllard's Weird* III. xxxi. 210 She had heard her husband proclaim himself triply an assassin.

*Comb.* 1785 MARTYN *Rousseau's Bot.* xxxii. (1794) 490 The common Fern..has superdecompound, or triplypinnate fronds. 1819 *Pantologia*, *Triply-ternate*, triternate. 1865 MRS. L. L. CLARKE *Common Seaweeds* iii. 67 Fan-like, rose-coloured varieties, or triply-branched. 1899 RODWAY *Guiana Wilds* 27 A triply-armed clump of palms.

**Tri·p-madam.** *Herb.* Also 7–8 tripe-madam(e. [a. F. *tripe-madame*, according to Hatz.-Darm. an alteration of the earlier *trique-madame*, TRICK-MADAM. Taken from De La Quintinye by Evelyn, and thence in later herbalists and horticulturists. The earliest Eng. form was PRICK-MADAM.] = TRICK-MADAM.

1693 EVELYN *De La Quint. Compl. Gard.* II. VI. 202 Tripe-Madam is one of our Sallet-Furnitures; it is used chiefly in the Spring when it is tender. 1707 MORTIMER *Husb.* (1721) II. 177 Trip Madam is propagated of Seeds, Cuttings, or Slips; 'tis used in Salads in Spring. 1879 PRIOR *Brit. Plants, Trip Madam*..a plant used as a treacle or vermifuge, *Sedum reflexum*.

**Tripod** (trəi·pǫd), *sb.* and *a.* Also 7 **trypod**, 7–8 **tripode**. [ad. L. *tripūs, tripod-*, a. Gr. τρίπους, -ποδ- adj., three-footed, also as sb., f. τρι- three + πούς, ποδ- foot.]

**A.** *sb.* **1.** *Gr.* and *Rom. Antiq.* A three-legged vessel; a pot or cauldron resting on three legs; a similar ornamental vessel, often presented as a prize, or as a votive offering (see also 2).

[1370 *Mem. Ripon* (Surtees) II. 130 Item unum tripod ferri.] *c* 1611 CHAPMAN *Iliad* XVIII. 308 He gaue command to his neare souldiers, To put a Tripod to the fire, to cleanse the festred gore From off the person. 1697 DRYDEN *Æneid* V. 146 Within the circle, arms and tripods lie, Ingots of gold and silver heap'd on high. 1791 COWPER *Iliad* VIII. 333 A tripod, or a chariot with its steeds. 1834 LYTTON *Pompeii* II. ix, In the centre..was a small altar on which stood a tripod of bronze. 1853 HUMPHREYS *Coin-Coll. Man.* iv. (1876) 35 The principal type of the coinage of Crotona is the tripod.

**2.** *spec.* A vessel of this kind at the shrine of Apollo at Delphi, on which the priestess seated herself to deliver oracles. Hence *allusively*, the Delphic oracle; any oracle or oracular seat.

1603 HOLLAND *Plutarch's Mor.* 1356, I will not be affraid to affirme that this reason properly is the Tripode or three footed table as one would say, and Oracle of trueth. *c* 1645 HOWELL *Lett.* (1892) II. 637 Pythagoras, whom the Tripod [= oracle of Apollo] pronounc'd the wisest Man. 1790 BURKE *Fr. Rev.* 99 Dr. Price, in whom the fumes of his oracular tripod were not entirely evaporated. 1839 THIRLWALL *Greece* xliii. V. 271 He compelled the prophetess by threats to mount the tripod, and pronounce a declaration. 1874 SAYCE *Compar. Philol.* i. 4 He [the comparative philologist] is ready to take his seat on the tripod.

**3.** A seat, table, or other similar structure with three legs; *esp.* a three-legged stool.

1656 BLOUNT *Glossogr.*, *Tripode* (*tripodium*), a three footed stool, any thing that hath three feet. 1710 ADDISON *Whig Exam.* No. 1 ⁋ 3 Three legs is a joint-stool, called in the Sphinx's country a tripode. 1798 BLOOMFIELD *Farmer's Boy, Spring* 193 A friendly tripod forms their humble Seat. 1870 EMERSON *Soc. & Solit.* Wks. (Bohn) III. 2 Each must stand on his glass tripod, if he would keep his electricity. 1887 J. NICHOLSON *Beacons E. Yorksh.* 13 *note*, The brandrith is literally an iron tripod.

**4.** A three-legged support of any kind; *esp.* a frame or stand with three (diverging) legs, usually hinged at the top, for supporting a camera, compass, or other apparatus.

1825 J. NICHOLSON *Operat. Mechanic* 185 A sort of tripod, having a flat ring of brass for its upper, and another for its lower part. 1893 J. A. HODGES *Elem. Photogr.* (1907) 15 Cameras..intended to be used whilst supported on a tripod, and designated 'stand-cameras'.

**5.** *Tripod of life, vital tripod* (fig.): see quot.

1834 J. FORBES *Laennec's Dis. Chest* (ed. 4) 1 The heart, lungs, and brain constitute, according to the happy expression of Bordeu, the tripod of life. 1857 DUNGLISON *Med. Lex.*, *Tripod, Vital.* 1872 HUXLEY *Physiol.* i. 19.

**6.** *Anat.* and *Zool.* **a.** A bone or other structure with three processes; a tripodal bone, etc. **b.** A sponge-spicule with three equal rays (*Cent. Dict. Suppl.* 1909).

1888 ROLLESTON & JACKSON *Anim. Life* 883 *Plectellaria*, without shell,..or with an incomplete one, either a basal tripod without ring,..or a sagittal ring usually without tripod. 1891 *Cent. Dict.* s. v., The premaxillary bone of birds is a tripod.

**7.** *attrib.* and *Comb.*, as *tripod-head, -leg, -top*; *tripod-covering, -mounted* adjs.

1614 GORGES *Lucan* V. 173 Pythons Trypod-couering hide. 1872 C. KING *Mountain. Sierra Nev.* xii. 257 Playfully drumming the frail crest with our tripod legs. 1889 *Anthony's Photogr. Bull.* II. 160 A few duplicate screws for camera and tripod head..will be of much use. 1893 *Photogr. Ann.* 40 There is no tripod-top screw to lose. 1900 *Westm. Gaz.* 25 May 4/2 A tripod-mounted gun.

**B.** *adj.*

**1.** Having or resting upon three feet or legs; three-footed, three-legged; of the form of a tripod.

*Tripod race* (quot. 1870), a THREE-LEGGED race.

1715–20 POPE *Iliad* XXIII. 50 Th' attending heralds,..With kindled flames the tripod-vase surround. 1779 FORREST *Voy. N. Guinea* 373, I found many Badjoo boats,..all of them having the tripod mast. 1794 MRS. RADCLIFFE *Myst. Udolpho* xxvi, A tripod lamp that stood on the stairs. 1833 T. HOOK *Parson's Dau.* I. iv, A cedar bagatelle board..on silver tripod stand. 1870 *Routledge's Ev. Boy's Ann.* July Suppl. 9/2 Tripod race. 1877 KNIGHT *Dict. Mech.*, *Tripod jack*, a screw-jack supported on three legs, connected to a common base-plate.

**2.** ? Uttered as from the tripod, oracular; or ? Three feet long (*fig.*: cf. SESQUIPEDALIAN A. 1).

1798 EDGEWORTH *Pract. Educ.* (1811) II. 29 He may be taught with much care and cost to speak tripod sentences. 1834 MAR. EDGEWORTH *Helen* vii, Some pages of 'The Rambler'..I liked not at all; its tripod sentences tired my ear.

**Tripodal** (tri·pǒdăl), *a.* [f. L. *tripod-*, TRIPOD + -AL.] Of the form of, or pertaining to, a tripod; three-footed, three-legged (in quot. 1843, performed on three legs, i. e. with a staff to support one's steps: cf. Gr. τρίποδας ὁδούς, Æsch. *Agam.*

80); *Anat.* having three rays or processes, as a bone. So, in same sense, **Tripodial** (tripōu·diăl), **Tripo·dian**; **Tripodic** (trəipǫ·dik) (applied to a method of walking in some insects in which two legs on one side and one on the other move together), **Tripo·dical** (in quot. 1643 *fig.* oracular, authoritative: cf. prec. A. 2).

1774 T. West *Antiq. Furness* (1805) 10 The *tripodal copper vessel. 1843 G. Wilson *Let.* in *Life* vii. (1860) 306 Yesterday I made a tripodal journey round the garden. 1872 Coues *N. Amer. Birds* 23 This is a three-pronged or tripodal bone. 1845 Birch in *Classical Museum* III. 418 Immediately before him is a *tripodial vessel or caldron. 1797 *Encycl. Brit.* (ed. 3) X. 252/2 The *tripodian lyre of Pythagoras. 1801 Busby *Dict. Mus.* (1811), *Tripodian*, a stringed instrument, said to have been invented by Pythagoras the Zacynthian, which, on account of the difficulty of its performance, continued in use but for a short time. It resembled in form the Delphic Tripod, whence it had its name. 1891 H. H. Dixon in *Nature* 8 Jan. 223/2, I have observed this '*tripodic' walk in earwigs, water scorpions, aphides, and some beetles. 1643 Howell *Twelve Treat.* (1661) 249 Judges..whose judgement in points of Law shold be onely *tripodicall and sterling. 1656 Blount *Glossogr.*, *Tripodical*, that hath three feet, three footed. 1850 *Ecclesiologist* X. 179 A sort of tripodical shallow vessel.

**Tripody** (tri·pŏdi). *Pros.* [f. Tri-, after Dipody.] A group or verse of three feet.

1883 Jebb *Oedipus Tyrannus* p. lxx, This verse forms a.. sentence of three dactyls, a dactylic tripody. 1891 *Harper's Mag.* Mar. 570/2 There are hundreds of [folk-songs] in Hungarian music consisting of dipodies, tetrapodies, tripodies, pentapodies, and hexapodies.

**Tri-pointed, -polar**: see Tri- 1 c, a.

**Tripoli** (tri·pŏli). Also 7 -ie, 7–8 -y, (8 tripela). [= F. *tripoli* (16th c. in Godef. *Compl.*), f. *Tripoli*, a region in North Africa, or town of the same name in Syria, where found.] A fine earth used as a polishing-powder, consisting mainly of decomposed siliceous matter, esp. that formed of the shells of diatoms; called also *infusorial earth* or *rotten-stone*.

1601 Holland *Pliny* xxxv. vi. II. 530 Tripolie or goldsmiths earth. 1665 Hooke *Microgr.* Pref., With a little Tripoly, rub them till they come to be very smooth. 1777 G. Forster *Voy. round World* II. 355 A sort of tripoly, which is called rotten-stone by some miners. 1797 *Encycl. Brit.* (ed. 3) VII. 608/2 The common tripela, or Tripoli, used to polish glass and stones. 1830 Lyell *Princ. Geol.* I. 214 That admixture of clay and silica, called tripoli. 1869 tr. *Pouchet's Universe* (1871) 21 Some tripolis of a red colour are employed in house-painting.

**b.** *attrib.*

1677 Plot *Oxfordsh.* 78 That very lasting brightness.. receiv'd from the Gold-smiths Tripoli-stone. 1825 J. Nicholson *Operat. Mechanic* 755 To polish Varnish.—This is effected with pumice-stone and Tripoli earth. 1839 G. Roberts *Dict. Geol.*, *Tripoli powder*.., used for polishing fossils, &c. It is itself the remains of fossil insects. 1868 Dana *Min.* (ed. 5) 199 Tripolite..(*c*) *Tripoli slate* (Polishing slate..), a slaty or thin laminated variety, fragile.

Hence **Tri·poline** *a.*, of or pertaining to tripoli; **Tri·polite** *Min.*, an infusorial variety of opal-silica, constituting one of the kinds of tripoli; **Tri·polith** [Gr. λίθος stone], trade name for a kind of cement: see quot.

1759 Da Costa in *Phil. Trans.* LI. 193 The layers of fossil wood in this mountain, having been saturated with the Tripoline particles,..thereby composed a stone. 1868 Dana *Min.* (ed. 5) 199 Infusorial Earth, or Earthy Tripolite, a very fine-grained earth looking often like an earthy chalk, or a clay. 1882 *Athenæum* 30 Sept. 438/1 The new binding material 'tripolith',..is composed of sulphate of lime (gypsum), coke powder, and precipitated oxide of iron.

**Tripos** (trəi·pǫs). See also Tripus. [app. irreg. alteration of L. *tripūs* Tripod, after Greek words in *-os*.]

†**1.** A three-legged vessel, seat, or frame: = Tripod A. 1, 3, 4. *Obs.*

1621 Burton *Anat. Mel.* To Rdr. (1628) 41 Thales sent the golden Tripos..to Bias, Bias to Solon, &c. 1697 W. Derham in *Phil. Trans.* XX. 4 For which purpose a Tripos may be best, whose Legs open and shut by Joynts at the Top. 1745 D. E. Baker *ibid.* XLIII. 540 A most curious antique Tripos of Metal. 1827 G. Higgins *Celtic Druids* 27 They were made of thin laminæ of gold—something like the triposes of the ancient Peruvians.

†**b.** *spec.* = Tripod 2. *Obs.*

1589 Greene *Menaphon* (Arb.) 22 Posting from Arcadia to the Tripos where Pithia sate. 1606 Marston *Parasit.* I. ii. B j, What, in the name of prophesie?..Speake, thou three legd Tripos, is thy shippe of Fooles a flote yet? [perh. sense 2.] 1679 Dryden *Troil. & Cress.* Pref., The inspiration was still upon him, he was ever tearing it upon the tripos. 1756 J. Kennedy *Curios. Wilton Ho.* (1786) 30 The two Griffins and the Tripos are the Symbols of Apollo. 1780 J. Duché *Disc.* (1790) I. xv. 285 Whatsoever the thrice-great Hermes delivered as oracles from his sacred tripos.

**2.** *Cambridge University.* Formerly: **a.** A bachelor of arts appointed to dispute, in a humorous or satirical style, with the candidates for degrees at 'Commencement' (corresponding to the Terræ filius at Oxford): so called from the three-legged stool on which he sat. **b.** A set of humorous verses, originally composed by the 'Tripos', and (till 1894) published at Commencement after his office was abolished (in full, *tripos verses*: see e). **c.** The list of candidates qualified for the honour degree in mathematics, originally printed on the back of the paper containing these verses (in full, *tripos list*: see e).

1659–60 Pepys *Diary* 26 Feb., Mr. Nicholas, of Queen's College [Cambr.], who I knew in my time to be Tripos with great applause. 1665 J. Buck in Peacock *Stat. Cambr.* (1841) App. B. p. lxx, The Senior Proctor calleth up the Tripos, and exhorteth him to be witty, but modest withall. *Ibid.* p. lxxi, The Bedels also are to deliver the Tripos's Verses to the V.C., Noblemen, Drs etc. 1696 Phillips (ed. 5), *Tripos*,..the Name which is given at Cambridge, to him that is called the *Terræ Filius* at Oxford. 1797 *Cambr. Univ. Cal.* 157 A List of those who have received Honors, on commencing Bachelors of Arts; copied from the Triposes. 1841 Peacock *Stat. Cambr.* App. A. p. x. *note*, He was called the *bachelor of the stool*, or *tripos*, which gave the name to the day: he was generally selected for his skill and readiness in disputation, and was allowed..considerable license of language. 1851 *Coll. Life t. Jas. I*, 89 Thos annual verses which still bear the name of tripos.

**d.** Hence, in current use: *orig.* The final honours examination for the B.A. degree in mathematics, consisting of two parts (formerly *first* and *second tripos*, now the *Mathematical Tripos*, Parts I. and II.); *later*, extended to the subsequently founded final honours examinations in other subjects (*Classical Tripos*, *Theological Tripos*, etc.).

1842 *Cambr. Univ. Cal.* 27 First Tripos Day. On the Day after Ash-Wednesday, at one o'clock, the bell rings for the first Tripos...The second Tripos is on the Thursday after Midlent Sunday. 1865 *Reader* 4 Mar. 245/2 The Mathematical and Classical Triposes. 1875 in Willis & Clark *Cambridge* (1886) III. 234 The Oriental Triposes attract a fair number of Candidates. 1905 *Edin. Rev.* Oct. 440 Not only had three new Triposes been established.

**e.** *attrib.*, as *tripos candidate*; **tripos day**, (*a*) either of the two days on which the 'Tripos' disputed; (*b*) a day on which a tripos (examination) is held; **tripos list**, the list of successful candidates in a tripos; **tripos paper**, †(*a*) a paper containing the tripos list (*obs.*); (*b*) any one of the papers of questions set in a tripos (examination); **tripos speech**, the humorous or satirical speech delivered by the 'Tripos'; **tripos verses** (see b above).

1904 *Expositor* Mar. 219 He develops into a *Tripos candidate. 1842 *Tripos day [see 2 d]. 1847 Webster s.v. *Tripos-paper*, Tripos day, *tripos examination. 1901 *Q. Rev.* Apr. 598 His ordinary '*tripos' lectures kept strictly to business. 1841 Peacock *Stat. Cambr.* 71 *note*, The earliest *Tripos list which appears in the *Cambridge Calendar* is for the year 1753. 1818 Macaulay in *Life & Lett. Z. Macaulay* xi. (1900) 343 Desirous to return loaded with medals or distinguished on the *tripos-paper. 1876 L. Stephen *Eng. Th. 18th C.* II. xii. vi. 360 He seems to have been suspended from his degree for a *tripos speech. 1828 Gunning *Ceremonies Cambr.* 84 *note*, First Tripos. The Writers of the *Tripos Verses.

**Tripot**, erron. spelling of Try-pot.

**Trippant** (tri·pănt), *a. Her.* [a. OF. *trippant*, pres. pple. of *tripper* to Trip.] = Tripping *ppl. a.* 3.

1658 in Prestwich *Respublica* (1785) 192 A bucke trippant Gules, attired Or. *c* 1828 Berry *Encycl. Her.* I. Gloss., *Trippant*, or *Tripping*, a term used to express a buck, antelope, hart, hind, &c. when represented with the right foot lifted up, and the other three feet, as it were, upon the ground, as if trotting. 1898 *Tit-Bits* 25 June 512/2 Crest, a stag trippant; arms, a chevron between three roundles.

**Trippe**, obs. form of Tripe[1].

**Tripper** (tri·pəɹ). [f. Trip *v.* + -er[1].] One who or that which trips.

**1.** One who dances; one who moves with light, sprightly steps; in quot. *a* 1847 *transf.* applied to a shoe or slipper.

*c* 1380 Wyclif *Wks.* (1880) 246 A daunsere, a trippere on tapitis. 1576 Gascoigne *Grief of Joye* iv. Wks. (Roxb.) II. 299 Dancyng delights are like a whyrlyng wheele..Thes tryppers strive to throwe theire braynes awaye As wheeles voyde water. 1594 Nashe *Unfort. Trav.* Wks. (Grosart) V. 106 [The ostrich] outstrippeth the nimblest trippers of his feathered condition in footmanshippe. 1691 Dryden *King Arthur* iv. i, Ye Sylvan trippers of the green. *a* 1847 Eliza Cook *When I wore red shoes* i, What were Cinderella's slippers To my pair of fairy trippers?

**2.** One who or that which causes to stumble. Also *tripper-up*; *spec.* in *slang*: see quots. 1887, 1904.

1605 Camden *Rem.* (1657) 76 A tripper, or supplanter. 1860 C. A. Collins *Eye-witness* vi. 81 He has either been tripped up, or has stumbled..The tripper up..will..come in for certain remarks which are the reverse of complimentary. 1887 *Daily Chron.* 18 Nov. (Farmer), A witness at the East End inquest yesterday alluded to 'trippers up'..'A man who trips you up and robs you'. 1904 Sweeney *Scotland Yard* xii. 313 Women known as trippers up, who preyed on drunken seamen. 1905 W. E. Geil *Yankee in Pigmy Land* iv. 44 Roots were encountered. They were regular trippers.

**3.** One who or that which stumbles (*lit.* and *fig.*).

1806 W. Taylor in *Ann. Rev.* IV. 560 A sipper is a tripper. 1856 *Titan Mag.* Nov. 415/1 Our [church] service is spoil'd by..The trippers—the clippers—the impudent skippers. 1903 *Union Mag.* Nov. 513/1 Dr. Young's camel was a 'tripper' and it stumbled and threw the Doctor over its head.

**4.** One who goes on a trip, or short journey or voyage for pleasure; an excursionist. *colloq.*

*Cheap tripper*, one who travels by a cheap trip.

1813 *Drakard's Paper* 3 Oct. in Ashton *Mod. Street Ballads* (1888) 80 Trippers to the seaside for a week. 1851 *Eliza Cook's Jrnl.* 19 July 177 The Tripper is the growth of railways and monster trains. 1872 Hartley *Yorkshire Ditties* Ser. ii. 140 A lot of cheap trippers 'at's just com'd for a day. 1899 Kitchin in *Ruskin in Oxford* etc. (1904) 154 The modern tripper leaves only desolation and dirty paper behind him.

**b.** *attrib.* and *Comb.*

1904 *Daily Chron.* 17 Sept. 3/1 These pictures were painted in tripper haunts. 1907 H. Wyndham *Flare of Footlights* xii, Pull us down to the island. The tripper element won't be so conspicuous there. 1909 *Westm. Gaz.* 7 Aug. 4/3 The tripper-thronged part of the island.

**5.** A street railroad conductor or other employee who is paid by the trip or journey. *U.S.*

1891 in *Cent. Dict.*

**6.** *Mech.* A contrivance for tripping; a trip.

1870 *Eng. Mech.* 14 Jan. 430/1 To each rod a tripper or pallet is affixed. 1893 *Jrnl. R. Agric. Soc.* Dec. 717 As soon as the sheaf has attained the required size it automatically raises a tripper. 1908 *Blackw. Mag.* Jan. 59/2 The tripper works the air-delay valve.

**Trippet**[1] (tri·pĕt). Forms: 4–5 **tripet**, **trypet**, 5 **trepett**, 6 **tryppyt**, 7 **trippett**, 9 **-it**, 8– **trippet**. [In sense 1 a. OF. *tripot*, *-pout* (*a* 1350 in Godef.). But in 2–4 associated with or formed from Trip *v.*, *sb.*[1]]

†**1.** An evil scheme; a malicious trick or plot. *Obs.*

*c* 1330 R. Brunne *Chron. Wace* (Rolls) 2911 Ne schal nought Brenne bede me trypet [*Petyt MS.* treget]. *a* 1400 *Leg. Rood* viii. 41 Fouled is my fayre fruit, þat neuer dude tripet ne truit. *Ibid.* 480 Truyt and tripet to helle shal sterue.

†**2.** An act of tripping up, a trip. *Obs.*

1430–40 Lydg. *Bochas* vi. ii. (MS. Bodl. 263) 306 To his pride I [Fortune] gaff a gret tripet. *c* 1450 *Mankind* 113 in *Macro Plays* 5 Take yow here a trepett! *a* 1550 *Image Hypocr.* i. 456 in *Skelton's Wks.* (1843) II. 420/1 In your holy armes,..Devoutly to clipe it, To caste her with a tryppyt. 1714 Parkyns *Inn-play* (ed. 2) 42 The Hanging Trippet is when you put your Toe behind your Adversary's Heel, on the same side, with a design to hook his Leg up forwards, and throw him on his Back.

**3.** The piece of wood pointed at the ends used in tip-cat; the 'cat'; also the game itself. Also *attrib.*, as *trippet-stick*. *north. dial.*

*c* 1440 *Promp. Parv.* 503/1 Trypet, *tripula*, *trita*. 1624 *N. Riding Rec.* (1885) III. ii. 199 Fr. Milnes ordered to be whipped for that he..did on Easter day last in the time of afternoon service play in the Churchyard at Aislaby at a game called Trippett. 1825 Brockett *N. C. Words*, *Trippit and Coit*, a game similar to spell and ore...Called *Trippit* and *Rack* in parts of *North*. The trippit is a small piece of wood obtusely pointed. 1828 *Craven Gloss.*, *Trippet*, the 'cat' or piece of wood in the game of tip-cat... The player with his bat, called a trippet stick, strikes it smartly at the end, which causes it to rise in a rotatory motion, high enough to strike it before it falls. 1873 Harland & Wilkinson *Lanc. Leg.* 152 Trippet. This game is played in the fields..It is still practised by the colliers... The trippet is about two inches long, and is made of holly.

**b.** The trap used in trap-ball; the game of trap-ball.

1825 Brockett *N. C. Words.*

**4.** *Mech.* See quot. and cf. Trip *sb.*[1] 8.

1877 Knight *Dict. Mech.*, *Trippet* (Machinery), a projection intended to strike some object at regularly recurrent intervals.

**Trippet**[2] (tri·pĕt). Now *north. dial.* Also 6 **-ett**, **tripett**, 7–9 **tripet**. [Cf. OF. *trepied*, *tripié*, *tripier* (12th c. in Godef. *Compl.*), and Trivet.] A trivet.

1563 *Richmond Wills* (Surtees) 169 A gyrdle, a brandrett, a speitt, and a trippett. 1570 Levins *Manip.* 87/42 A Trippet, *tripus*, *odis*, *hic.* 1581 *Inv.* in *Trans. Cumb. & West. Arch. Soc.* X. 40 *Item.* Spitt and tripett. 1677 Gale *Crt. Gentiles* II. iii. 60 Which Machine was called from its three Pillars, Tripos, as it were of three feet, much of the same forme with the usual Tripet. 1820 Shelley *Hymn to Mercury* x. 7 Her household stuff and state, Perennial pot, trippet, and brazen pan. 1894 *Northumbld. Gloss.*, *Tripet*, an iron grating placed on the top of (and across) the kitchen fire for pans to rest on; a trivet.

**Tripping** (tri·piŋ), *vbl. sb.* [f. Trip *v.* + -ing[1].]

**1.** The action of the verb Trip in transitive senses.

1591 Percivall *Sp. Dict.*, *Traspie*, tripping, *supplantatio.* 1601 Breton (*title*) No Whippinge, nor Trippinge: but a kinde friendly Snippinge. 1760–72 H. Brooke *Fool of Qual.* (1809) I. 163 The mysteries of bruising, of wrestling, and of tripping. 1862 *Catal. Internat. Exhib.* II. xii. 26 Martin's patent anchor..easy tripping and fishing, great lightness. 1880 *Times* 12 Nov. 4/4 It was only lately that Rugby school abandoned the 'hacking' and 'tripping' which made football dreaded by anxious mothers.

**2.** The action of the verb Trip in intransitive senses. Also *tripping up*; in quot. 1857 *spec.* the curvature of a boat's keel.

1594 Nashe *Terrors Night* Wks. (Grosart) III. 273 Their daintie feete in their tender birdlike trippings, enameld (as it were) the dustie ground. 1603 Holland *Plutarch's Mor.* 1072 Answeres and oracles as touching..the tripping and stumbling of the foot. 1693 *Apol. Clergy Scot.* 14 [They] are very glad when they can discover the trippings of their Adversaries. 1733 S. Knight in *Bibl. Topogr. Brit.* (1790) III. 167 It is very easy to discover his trippings. 1828 Carlyle *Misc.*, *Goethe's Helena* (1857) I. 145 Fine warblings and trippings on the light fantastic toe. 1840 Hood *Up Rhine* 36 Tripping up the Rhine, instead of taking my place at Woodlands. 1850 Denison *Clock & Watch-m.* 77 The hook at the end of the slope will not catch the tooth as it ought to do, and two or three teeth will slip past at once: this is called tripping. 1857 Colquhoun *Comp. Oarsman's Guide* 31 *Shear* is the rising of the gunwale of a boat towards head and stern; *gamber* is the same on the keel; otherwise called tripping up. 1879 *Cassell's Techn. Educ.* IV. 371/1 This error called 'tripping', is also produced if there is much space between the detent and the wheel. **1894** *Forum* (N. Y.) Oct. 158 Slips, hesitations, and tripping in speech, which, once made, could never be recalled.

**3.** *attrib.* and *Comb.*, as *tripping-block*; **tripping-line** (*Naut.*), a light line for tilting the yards (see TRIP *v.* 12); also, a line for manipulating a drogue; **tripping string**, a line set by burglars to trip possible pursuers.

**1620** SHELTON *Quix.* II. iv. 26 What doe I know, whether ..the Deuill hath set any tripping-blocke before me, where I may stumble and fall? **1841** R. H. DANA *Seaman's Man.*, *Tripping line*, a line used for tripping a topgallant or royal yard in sending it down. **1882** NARES *Seamanship* (ed. 6) 260 Drogues..are towed..mouth foremost by a stout rope, a small line termed a tripping-line, being fastened to the apex. **1891** *Daily News* 31 Dec. 4/7 The doors..having first been securely fastened..and tripping strings having been stretched across the pathways and lawn.

**Tri·pping,** *ppl. a.* [f. as prec. + -ING 2.] That trips, in various senses.

**1.** Moving quickly and lightly; light-footed; nimble. Also *fig.*

**1567** DRANT *Horace, Epist.* xiv. E v, Thou hast no trippinge trull to mince it with the now That thou mighst foote it vnto her. **1568** *Satir. Poems Reform.* xlvi. 56 Thir tripand tyddis may tyne ws aw. **1684** BUNYAN *Pilgr.* II. Introd. Verses 185 When little Tripping Maidens follow God, And leave old doting Sinners to his Rod. **1708** PRIOR *Turtle & Sparrow* 37 The tripping Fauns and Fairies came. **1807** SCOTT *Let. to Southey* 1 Oct. in Lockhart *Life*, A tripping Alexandrine stanza. **1851** D. JERROLD *St. Giles* i. 2 A quick, tripping footstep sounds in the deserted street. **1880** LD. ACTON *Lett. to Gladstone* (1904) 6 You will find his conversation, easy and tripping as it is, very inferior to his writings.

**2.** Stumbling, erring, sinning.

**1577** tr. *Bullinger's Decades* (1592) 296 The Lord beginneth..with the bridle to checke the mouth of his tripping Church. **1580** HOLLYBAND *Treas. Fr. Tong*, *Chevaux qui brunchent*, stumbling or tripping Iades. **1646** GATAKER *Mistake Removed* 31 The tripping toung sometimes tels truth. **1703** ROWE *Fair Penit.* Epil., The tripping Dame cou'd find no Favour. **1903** G. MATHESON *Repr. Men Bible* Ser. II. 287 Where the tripping are trodden down, where the weak are weeded out by the strong.

**3.** *Her.* Of a buck, stag, etc.: Walking, and looking toward the dexter side, with three paws on the ground and one fore-paw raised; the same as *passant* of other animals. *Tripping-counter* = COUNTER-TRIPPANT.

**1562** LEIGH *Armorie* 90 b, An Vnicorne trippyng, Sable. **1610** GUILLIM *Heraldry* III. xiv. (1611) 131 He beareth Azure, three Buckes tripping. *c* **1828** BERRY *Encycl. Her.* I. Gloss., *Tripping-counter*, or *counter-trippant*, is when two bucks, &c. are borne trippant contraryways, as if passing each other out of the field. **1864** BOUTELL *Her. Hist. & Pop.* x. 62 Stags,..when in easy motion, they are tripping. **1870** ROCK *Text. Fabr.* I. 40 Two giraffes, with one leg raised—may be better described as tripping.

**4.** In names of mechanical appliances that trip or are tripped (cf. TRIP *v.* 14); as *tripping-coil*, *-lever*, *-relay* (*Cent. Dict., Suppl.* 1909); **tripping-valve**: see quot.

**1877** KNIGHT *Dict. Mech.*, *Tripping-valve*, one moved recurrently by the contact of some other part of the machinery.

Hence **Tri·ppingness.**

**1827** *Examiner* 738/1 Too much of trippingness in the walk. **1890** FANNY MURFREE *Felicia* xi, The basso could not forgive the soprano for the trippingness of her execution.

**Trippingly** (tri·piŋli), *adv.* [f. prec. + -LY 2.] In a tripping manner.

**1590** SHAKS. *Mids. N.* v. i. 402 This Ditty after me, sing and dance it trippinglie. **1602** — *Ham.* III. ii. 2 Speake the Speech I pray you..trippingly on the Tongue. **1819** *Blackw. Mag.* IV. 719 Her songs came trippingly off the tongue. **1858** CAPERN *Ball. & Songs* 89 Down the hill, towards the mill, Turned the maiden trippingly.

**Trippist** (tri·pist). *colloq. rare.* [f. TRIP *sb.* + -IST.] = TRIPPER 4.

**1792** *Gentl. Mag.* Dec. 1129/1 Allowing that this Tourist, or Trippist, has told the truth. **1886** *Modern Society* 16 Jan. 117 (Farmer) With returning appetite came the desire to the convivial ocean trippists to set sail again for the Mediterranean. **1895** *B'ham Inst. Mag.* Oct. 202 A testimonial illuminated on parchment by one of the lady trippists.

**Tripple** (tri·p'l), *sb. S. Africa.* [f. TRIPPLE *v.*2] A horse's gait, resembling the amble.

**1880** GILLMORE *On Duty* 296 A slow tripple—a pace similar to what is designated 'racking' in North America. **1887** RIDER HAGGARD *Jess* (1899) 4 He put the tired nag into a sort of 'tripple' or ambling canter much affected by S. African horses. **1901** *Field* 9 Mar. 322/1 This 'tripple' is between a fast walk and slow trot.

**Tri·pple,** *v.*1 *Obs.* exc. *dial.* [freq. of TRIP *v.* + -LE 3.] *intr.* To trip, move lightly; to dance, skip.

*c* **1630** RISDON *Surv. Devon* § 308 (1810) 315 Where, fearless of the hunt, the deer securely stood, And trippling freely, walk'd a burgess of the wood. **1851** W. ANDERSON *Rhymes* (1867) 42 (E.D.D.) He trippled, he danced, an' he sung.

**Tri·pple,** *v.*2 *S. Africa.* [a. Du. *trippelen*, f. *trippen* to trip, skip.] *intr.* To go at a tripple.

**1899** G. H. RUSSELL *Under the Sjambok* iv. 49 They [Boers]..getting into their saddles, slowly trippled away (a kind of run, neither gallop, canter, or trot). **1903** *Longm. Mag.* Dec. 151 That easy hand canter usual in such Free State horses as do not tripple.

Hence **Tri·ppling** *vbl. sb.* and *ppl. a.*; also **Tri·ppler,** a horse that tripples.

**1901** *Field* 9 Mar. 322/1 The Boer never rides his horse at the trot, but at a quick walk or canter, and a step peculiar to the country and called 'trippling', or, as we should style it, ambling. **1905** *Blackw. Mag.* Oct. 526/1 He could still hear the trippling patter of the other rider. **1909** R. CULLUM *Compact* xi. 132 Can't I even persuade you to ride my 'tripler'?

**Triprosthomerous, -prostyle**: see TRI- 1 a.

†**Trip-skin.** *dial. Obs.* [Cf. TRIP *sb.*3] See quots.

*a* **1825** FORBY *Voc. E. Anglia* s. v. *Rock*, Wool..is spun ..by being drawn out and formed into yarn by the finger and thumb, and pressed by the hand on the trip-skin. *Ibid.*, *Trip-skin*..1. A piece of leather, worn on the right hand side of the petticoat, by spinners with the rock, on which the spindle plays, and the yarn is pressed by the hand of the spinner. 2. The skinny part of roasted meat which before the whole can be dressed, becomes tough and dry, like a trip [cheese] overkept.

**Tripsome** (tri·psŏm), *a.* [f. TRIP *sb.*1 or *v.* + -SOME.] Characterized by tripping; nimble. Hence **Tri·psomely** *adv.*

**1819** *Blackw. Mag.* V. 401 The shortened notes more tripsomely tipped over than in the modern airs. **1846** MRS. GORE *Eng. Char.* (1852) 52 He beholds the tripsome feet of Lady Clementina flit by him. **1847** — *Castles in Air* xvi, An elf-like pigmy..walking tripsomely by my side. **1890** *Sat. Rev.* 13 Dec. 688/2 Sprightly style and tripsome metre.

**Tript**, variant of *triped* (see TRIPE 2).

**Tripterous** (tri·ptĕrəs), *a. Bot. rare*—°. [f. TRI- three + Gr. πτερόν wing, after DIPTEROUS.] Having three wings, or wing-like expansions.

**1866** *Treas. Bot.*, *Tripterous*, three-winged. **1900** in B. D. JACKSON *Gloss. Bot. Terms.*

**Triptote** (tri·ptǒut), *sb.* and *a. Gram.* Also 7–8 **triptot.** [ad. L. *triptōta* (pl.) nouns that have only three case-endings, a. Gr. τρίπτωτα, pl. neuter of τρίπτωτο-ς with three case-endings, f. τρι-, TRI- + πτωτός falling (πτῶσις case). Cf. F. *triptote*.] **a.** *sb.* A noun (or other word) used in three cases only. **b.** *adj.* Having only three cases.

**1612** BRINSLEY *Pos. Parts* (1669) 102 *Q.* What words do you call Triptots? *A.* Such as have but three cases in the singular number. **1656** BLOUNT *Glossogr.*, *Triptote* (*triptoton*), a Noun having but three cases. **1658** in PHILLIPS. **1751** WESLEY *Wks.* (1872) XIV. 40 Triptots, which have three Cases; as, *opis*, *opem*, *ope*. **1886** *Encycl. Brit.* XXI. 651/1 The nominative of the so-called 'triptote' nouns has, as in classical Arabic, the termination *u*.

**Triptych** (tri·ptik). Also **triptic.** [f. TRI- after DIPTYCH; cf. Gr. τρίπτυχος consisting of three layers, and It. *triptica*, F. *triptyque* (Littré).]

**1. a.** *Antiq.* A set of three writing-tablets hinged or tied together. **b.** A card made to fold in three divisions. Also *attrib.*

**1731** GALE in *Phil. Trans.* XXXVII. 161 The Diptychs and Triptychs that were covered with Wax, served only for common Occurrences. **1885** E. M. THOMPSON in *Encycl. Brit.* XVIII. 154/1 These triptychs then were *libelli* of three tablets of wood, cleft from one piece and fastened together, like the leaves of a book, by strings passed through two holes pierced near the edge. *Mod. Advt.*, Confirmation Triptych. A small-folding Triptych Certificate Card.

**2.** A picture or carving (or set of three such) in three compartments side by side, the lateral ones being usually subordinate, and hinged so as to fold over the central one; chiefly used as an altar-piece.

[**1848** MRS. JAMESON *Sacr. & Leg. Art* (1850) 227 In a tabernacle or triptica by Niccolo Frumenti, the central compartment represents the raising of Lazarus.] **1849** CURZON *Visits Monast.* 366 The most valuable reliquary of St. Laura is a kind of triptic. **1852** MRS. JAMESON *Leg. Madonna* Introd. (1857) 53 A Triptych is an altar-piece in three parts. **1896** *Church Times* 14 Aug. 154 There is no east window, but above the altar is an exquisite triptych.

So in Fr. form ‖ **Triptyque** (triptīk), applied to a threefold card used as an international passport by associations of motorists.

**1908** *Westm. Gaz.* 21 Jan. 4/2 The triptyque, or special card which opens the doors to half-a-dozen countries, and relieves its holder of much bewildering formula when touring abroad. **1909** *Daily Chron.* 9 July 8/3 The adoption of the triptyque, or international passport, for balloons and aeroplanes such as is now in use for motor-cars.

**Tripudiary** (trəipiū·diări), *a. rare.* [f. L. *tripudi-um*: see TRIPUDIATE *v.* and -ARY 1.]

**1.** *Rom. Antiq.* Denoting a species of divination (called *tripudium*) from the behaviour of birds, esp. of the sacred chickens, when fed.

**1646** SIR T. BROWNE *Pseud. Ep.* I. iv. 16 The conclusions of Southsayers in their Augurial, and Tripudiary divinations, collecting presages from voice or food of birds. **1656** BLOUNT *Glossogr.*, *Tripudiary divination* was by bread rebounding on the ground, when it was cast unto birds, or chickens.

**2.** Of or pertaining to dancing. (*affected.*)

**1819** H. BUSK *Vestriad* III. 396 Which from my data, dicta, and decrees, At once the art tripudiary frees.

So **Tripu·dial** *a.* [cf. med.L. *tripudiālis* (1237 in Du Cange), OF. *tripudial* (13th c. in Godef.)] in sense 2 above.

**1716** M. DAVIES *Athen. Brit.* II. 138 Theatrical Decorations of Musical, Comical, and Tripudial Interludes.

**Tripudiate** (trəipiū·di,eit), *v.* Now *rare* and *affected.* [f. L. *tripudiāt-*, ppl. stem of *tripudiāre* (collat. form *tripodāre*), f. *tripudium* a beating the ground with the feet, a leaping or dancing, a religious dance (prob. f. *tri-* three + *pod-* (cf. Gr. ποδ-, foot). Cf. OF. *tripudier* (14th c. in Godef.).]

**1.** *intr.* To dance, skip, or leap for joy, or with excitement; to exult.

**1623** COCKERAM, *Tripudiate*, to daunce. *a* **1641** BP. MONTAGU *Acts & Mon.* iii. (1642) 205 Such..could not but jubilate, tripudiate, feele extraordinary motions and affections of joy. *a* **1670** HACKET *Cent. Serm.* (1675) 589 The Earth did rejoice and tripudiate when the Saviour came forth alive out of the belly of the Grave. **1891** *Sat. Rev.* 8 Aug. 158/1 He..will..tripudiate upon the platform because his party have made a long legislative score.

**2.** To trample, stamp, or jump (*on* or *upon*) in contempt or triumph.

**1888** *Sat. Rev.* 5 May 524/1 On poor Colonel Slade..he tripudiates with all the chivalry of the 'varray perfit gentil knight' of controversy that he is. **1891** *Ibid.* 7 Nov. 520/1 He tripudiates a little..on the unfortunate Mediæval and Modern Languages Tripos. **1895** FARRAR *Gathering Clouds* I. 131 The people tore down the image, tripudiated on its shattered fragments.

So **Tripu·diant** *a.* [ad. L. *tripudiānt-em*, pres. pple. of *tripudiāre*: see above], dancing; *fig.* exultant, triumphant; **Tripudia·tion** [ad. late L. *tripudiātiōn-em*, n. of action f. *tripudiāre*], the action of dancing or leaping, esp. in token of joy or excitement; exultation; **Tripudist** (tri·piŭdist), one given to 'tripudiating'.

*a* **1626** W. SCLATER *Exp. 4th ch. Rom.* (1650) Ep. Ded., A kind of *tripudiant joy, and exultation of spirit. **1668** H. MORE *Div. Dial.* III. xxxvi. (1713) 283 How transported are my Spirits, how triumphant and tripudiant! **1870** *Sat. Rev.* 26 Feb. 275/1 Fast young peeresses and..tripudiant matrons. **1623** COCKERAM II, Dancing, **Tripudiation*. **1629** H. BURTON *Truth's Triumph* 295 After a goodly flourish and triumphall tripudiation, as if the field were already won. **1709** J. JOHNSON *Clergym. Vade M.* II. 110 The word implies tripudiation, or immodest dancing. **1885** *Sat. Rev.* 12 Dec. 769/2 The rest of his speech was mere tripudiation. **1833** DOUCE *Dance of Death* i. 6 These riotous and irreverent *tripudists and caperers appear to have possessed themselves of the churchyards to exhibit their dancing fooleries.

**Tripunctal** to **Tripupillate**: see TRI- 1.

‖ **Tripus.** *Obs. rare.* [L. *tripūs*, a. Gr. τρίπους TRIPOD.] **a.** = TRIPOS 2 a. **b.** = TRIPOD A. 1.

**1670** EACHARD *Cont. Clergy* 37 Wits..who never..were at all inspir'd from a Tripus's, Terræ-filius's, or Prævaricator's speech. **1697** BENTLEY *Phal.* (1699) 458 Gelon..made a Golden Tripus of xvi Talents, and sent it to Delphi a Donary to Apollo.

**Tripylæan, -ean** (tripilī·ăn), *a.* and *sb. Zool.* [f. mod.L. *Tripylæa*, neut. pl. (f. Gr. τρι-, TRI- + πύλη gate) + -AN.] **a.** *adj.* Belonging to the division *Tripylæa* of radiolarians, characterized by having three openings into the central capsule. **b.** *sb.* A radiolarian of this division.

**1888** ROLLESTON & JACKSON *Anim. Life* 879 (*Radiolaria*) Some tripylean *Phaeodaria*, i. e. those with three apertures to the central capsule. **1902** *Cassell's Encycl. Dict., Supp.*, Tripylæan *a.* and *s.*

**Tripyramid** to **Triquaternion**: see TRI- 4 a–c, 2, 1 a.

†**Triquet,** *sb.* and *a. Obs. rare.* Also 6 tricquet. [f. L. *triquetrus*: see TRIQUETROUS.] **a.** *sb.* A triangle; in quot., a set of verses arranged in the form of a triangle. **b.** *adj.* Triangular.

**1589** PUTTENHAM *Eng. Poesie* II. xi. (Arb.) 105–6. *Ibid.* 107–8 Of the Triangle or Triquet...A certaine great Sultan of Persia called Ribuska, entertaynes in loue the Lady Selamour, sent her this triquet reue[r]st pitiously bemoning his estate...To which Selamour to make the match egall,.. answered in a standing Triquet. **1656** BLOUNT *Glossogr.*, *Triquet* (*triquetrus*), having three corners, triangular.

‖ **Triquetra** (trəikwe·tră, -kwī·tră). [L., fem. of *triquetrus*: see Walde.] †**a.** A triangle. *Obs.* **b.** An ornament of triangular shape, formed of three interlaced arcs or lobes. Also *attrib.*

**1586** FERNE *Blaz. Gentrie* 48 A coate-armor, wherin something would be borne resemblant somewhat to the signes of that art [heraldry], as Circles, Spheres, Triquetras, Pyramides, &c. **1706** PHILLIPS (ed. Kersey), *Triquetra*, a Triangle, or three-cornered Figure. **1845** PETRIE *Round Towers Irel.* II. iii. 323 That curious triangular figure, known among medallists by the name of triquetra..formed by the ingenious interlacing of a single cord or line. **1887** J. R. ALLEN *Early Chr. Symbolism* 111 The foot [of the Irish Cross] is finished off..with a triangular point and a triquetra knot.

**Triquetral** (trəikwe·trăl, -kwī·trăl), *a.* [f. L. *triquetr-us* (see below) + -AL.] = TRIQUETROUS.

*Triquetral bones*, small bones of irregular triangular form, sometimes found in the sutures of the skull; also called *Wormian bones.*

**1646** PRYNNE *Laud* 124 Plate for the Chappell...A triquetrall Censor. **1804** SHAW *Gen. Zool.* V. 420 Triquetral Trunk-fish. **1861** HAGEN *Synopsis Neuroptera N. Amer.* 159 Abdomen triquetral.

**Trique·tric,** *a. rare*—°. [f. TRIQUETR-A + -IC.] 'Pertaining to the triquetra' (*Cent. Dict.* 1891).

**Triquetrous** (trəikwe·trəs), *a.* [f. L. *triquetrus* three-cornered, triangular + -OUS.] Three-sided, triangular; in *Nat. Hist.* of triangular cross-section, three-edged, trihedral, triangularly prismatic or pyramidal.

**1658** SIR T. BROWNE *Gard. Cyrus* ii. 40 The *lithostrota* or figured pavements of the ancients, which consisted not all of square stones, but were divided into triquetrous segments.

1752 J. Hill *Hist. Anim.* 27 The grey wood Spider, with a triquetrous body. 1826 Kirby & Sp. *Entomol.* III. xxxiii. 432 Almost universally they [the mandibles of insects] incline to a triquetrous or three-sided figure. 1870 Hooker *Stud. Flora* 291 Lamium, Dead-nettle..nutlets 3-quetrous. 1872 Oliver *Elem. Bot.* App. 309 Fruits ovoid, acutely triquetrous.

Hence **Trique·trously** *adv.*
1884 in Stormonth *Dict.*

**Triquinate**: see Tri- 2.

**Triradial** (trəirēi·diăl), *a.* [f. Tri- + L. *radius* ray: see Radial and -al.] = next. Hence **Trira·dially** *adv.*
a 1886 Ferguson *Ogham Inscript.* (1887) 123 They are tri-radial groups corresponding to the..symbol of the Trinity. 1891 *Cent. Dict.*, Triradially.

**Triradiate** (trəirēi·diˌĕt), *a.* (*sb.*) [f. as prec.: see Radiate *a.* and -ate² 2.] Having or consisting of three rays; radiating in three directions from a central point; three-rayed, trifurcate.
1846 Patterson *Zool.* 60 Three beautiful little semicircular horny saws, arranged in a triradiate manner, so that their edges meet in the centre. 1874 Cooke *Fungi* 36 The triradiate spores of Asterosporium. 1875 Huxley in *Encycl. Brit.* I. 754/2 Each pterygoid..is a triradiate bone, with an anterior, an inner, and a posterior, or outer, ray.

B. *sb.* A triradiate sponge-spicule.
1887 Sollas in *Encycl. Brit.* XXII. 417/1 (*Sponges*) The shorter paired rays being termed basal, and the whole spicule a sagittal triradiate. 1911 A. Dendy in *Encycl. Brit.* XXV. 722/1 The triradiates and quadriradiates..are not simple spicules, but spicule-systems formed of three or four rays each originating independently from its own scleroblast.

So **Trira·diated** (-eitĕd), *a.* = *triradiate*; **Trira·diately** *adv.*, in a triradiate manner (*Cent. Dict.* 1891); **Triradia·tion**, radiation in three directions; also, a triradiate figure or structure.
1786 *Phil. Trans.* LXXVI. 160 The cavity..is divided into..chambers or compartments by solid transverse septa, which communicate with each other by a triradiated aperture. c 1900 *Buck's Handbk. Med. Sc.* II. 177 The callosal eminence.., the hippocamp, and the occipital eminence form an irregular triradiation.

**Trirectangular**: see Tri- 1.

**Trireme** (trəi·rīm), *sb.* and *a.* Also 7 tryreme. [ad. L. *trirēmis*, f. *tri-* three + *rēmus* oar; cf. F. *trirème* (c 1352 in Godef. *Compl.*).]

A. *sb.* An ancient galley (originally Greek, afterwards also Roman) with three ranks of oars one above another, used chiefly as a ship of war.
1601 Holland *Pliny* vii. lvi. I. 190 Aminocles the Corinthian built the first Trireme with three rowes of ores to a side. 1656 Blount *Glossogr.*, *Trireme* (*trirēmis*), a Galley wherein every oare had three men to it, or a Galley that hath three oares on every side. 1662 J. Bargrave *Pope Alex. VII* (1867) 118 They having then no such ships as we have now, their byremes and tryremes being but pittiful boats. 1776 Burney *Hist. Mus.* I. 185 In the triremes, or vessels of three banks of oars, there was always a *tibicen*, or flute-player. 1868 *Smith's Dict. Gr. & Rom. Antiq.* (ed. 7) 262/1 Triremes..were..divided into two classes: the one consisting of real men-of-war, ..and the other of transports.

B. *adj.* Having three ranks of oars.
1697 Potter *Antiq. Greece* iii. xiv. (1715) 124 Trireme, quadrireme, and quinquereme Gallies, which exceeded one another by a Bank of Oars. 1839 Thirlwall *Greece* VII. lvi. 165 A fleet was to be equipped of forty trireme galleys.

**Trirhombohedral, -rhomboidal**: see Tri- 1 a, 2 b.

**Tris-** (tris), *prefix*, repr. Gr. τρίς thrice (which occurs as prefix, τρισ-, in numerous Gr. compounds, chiefly adjs.): used in Eng. in a few technical words of various kinds, and in Chemistry.

1. See Trisagion, Trisdiapason, Trismegist, Trisoctahedron, Tristetrahedron.

2. *Chem.* † a. Used in the early part of the 19th century, after T. Thomson (*First Princ. Chem.* (1825) I. p. xx), prefixed to the modified name of the chlorous element or of the acid, denoting that three atoms or molecules, not of this element or acid, but of the other component, are present in the compound named; e.g. *trisphosphuret of copper*, a compound of one atom of phosphorus and three atoms of copper; *trisacetate of lead*, a compound of one molecule of acetic acid and three molecules of lead oxide. (Cf. Tri- 5 a, note.) *Obs.*
1836 [see Trisnitrate]. 1848 R. D. Thomson *School Chem.* 39 Greek numerals denote an increase in the base, as $B_2O$ is a *Disoxide*, or *Dinoxide*, while BO is a *trisoxide*. The same nomenclature is applied to the acids.

b. Now used prefixed to the names of complex radicals or compounds, signifying that the whole complex is present thrice over, and not merely the single element or radical immediately following the prefix; e.g. *trisbenzene-azophenol*, $C_6H_2(N:NC_6H_5)_3OH$, a compound containing three $N:NC_6H_5$ groups substituted in phenol, $C_6H_5OH$; *tristhio-dimethyl-benzaldehyde*, $\{C_6H_3(CH_3)_2.CHS\}_3$, in which the whole group is present thrice.
1907 *Jrnl. Chem. Soc.* XCII. i. 800 Trisbenzeneazoresorcinol, $C_6H(OH)_2(N_2Ph)_3$.

**Trisaccharide** (trəiˌsæ·kărəid). *Chem.* [f. Tri- 5 + L. *saccharum* sugar + -ide. (Not f. Tri- + Saccharide.)] A carbohydrate which on hydrolysis reacts with $2H_2O$, yielding three molecules of monosaccharides (sugars having the general formula $C_nH_{2n}O_n$); e.g. *raffinose*, $C_{18}H_{32}O_{16}$, which yields dextrose, fructose, and galactose; *gentianose*, $C_{18}H_{32}O_{16}$, which yields fructose and two molecules of dextrose.
1910 Armstrong *Simple Carbohydrates & Glucosides* 49 The best-known trisaccharide is raffinose, which is often found..in the sugar beet.

**Trisacramentarian**: see Tri- 4 b.

‖ **Trisagion** (trisæ·giǫn, -ē·giǫn). Also 4–9 in Lat. form **trisagium**; also 9 **trishagion**; also in masc. form **trisagios**. [a. Gr. (τὸ) τρισάγιον, the eucharistic hymn, neut. of τρισάγιος thrice holy, f. τρίς thrice + ἅγιος holy.] An ancient hymn, used especially in the Oriental Churches, beginning with a threefold invocation of God as holy. Also loosely applied to the 'angelic hymn' called Ter-sanctus or Sanctus, q. v.
1387 Trevisa *Higden* (Rolls) V. 11 He ordeyned þat trisagium, þat is, 'Sanctus, sanctus, sanctus,' schulde be songe at masse. 1635 Pagitt *Christianogr.* 99 The Trisagion being solemnly sung, the Copt Priest beginneth the Consecration. 1654–6 Trapp *Comm. Isa.* vi. 1 The prophet Isaiah..heareth the *trisagion* of the blessed angels. 1710 Wheatley *Bk. Com. Prayer* vi. § 19 Of the Trisagium. a 1711 Ken *Christophil* Poet. Wks. 1721 I. 483 O may I with Seraphick Heat Trisagions while I live repeat. 1885 *Notes on Angels* 56 In the Tris-Hagion or Ter Sanctus of the Communion Office. 1894 F. Watson *Bk. Genesis true Hist.* v. 89 He [Isaiah] hears the Seraphim chanting the Trisagion.

**Trisceptral, -sceptred, -schism**: see Tri- 1 a, c, 4 c.

† **Trisdiapa·son.** *Mus. Obs.* [f. Tris- + Diapason, after Disdiapason.] An interval of three octaves, a twenty-second; a note three octaves above or below a given note. (Cf. *tri-diapason*, Tri- 4 a.)
1677 Plot *Oxfordsh.* 293 And so will strike an under trisdiapason, or a 22d. 1706 Phillips (ed. Kersey), *Tris-Diapason*, or *Triple-Diapason*..a Chord, otherwise call'd a Triple Eighth.

**Trise**, obs. form of Trice *sb.*² and *v.*

**Trisect** (trəi·sekt), *a. Bot. rare.* [f. Tri- + L. *sect-us* cut, as in *palmatisect*, *pinnatisect*.] Of a leaf: Divided into three lobes quite to the base, but not articulated so as to form separate leaflets.
1899 Heinig *Gloss. Bot. Terms*, *Sect*, completely divided from margin to midrib into distinct parts, in comp. as *trisect*.

**Trisect** (trəise·kt), *v.* [f. Tri- + L. *sect-*, ppl. stem of *secāre* to cut, after Bisect.] *trans.* To divide into three equal parts (esp. in *Geom.*); sometimes *gen.* to divide into three parts.
1695 Alingham *Geom. Epit.* 44 Trisect any side..in the points *d* and *e*. a 1696 Scarburgh *Euclid* (1705) 88 From hence 'tis manifest, how to trisect a Right angle. 1786 *Phil. Trans.* LXXVI. 16 Mr. Graham..perceived..how very much more easy a given line was to bisect than to trisect or quinquesect. 1822 De Quincey *Confess.* 146 Could not I have reduced it a drop a day, or by adding water, have bisected or trisected a drop? 1876 A. J. Evans *Through Bosnia* ii. 48 We found the dwelling-houses trisected into a sleeping-room, a kitchen, and a store-room.

Hence **Trise·cted** *ppl. a.* (in *Bot.* = Trisect *a.*); **Trise·cting** *vbl. sb.*
1694 *Phil. Trans.* XVIII. 70 So the halving, trisecting, quartering, &c. is performed by extracting the Square Root, the Cubick, Biquadratick Roots, &c. of the Terms. 1809 Cavendish *ibid.* XCIX. 227 In trisecting, the greatest error we are liable to does not exceed that of bisection in a greater proportion than that of 4 to 3. 1828 Webster, *Trisected*, divided into three equal parts. 1866 *Treas. Bot.* 1174 *Trisected*, cut deeply into three parts.

**Trisection** (trəise·kʃən). [n. of action f. Trisect *v.*, after L. *sectiōnem* Section: see -tion, and cf. F. *trisection* (1690 in Hatz.-Darm.).] The action of trisecting; division into three equal parts; rarely *gen.* division into three.
1664 Power *Exp. Philos.* iii. 187 The Trisection of an Angle. 1786 *Phil. Trans.* LXXVI. 16 The division of the arc of 90..required trisections and quinquesections. 1842 De Quincey *Pagan Oracles* Wks. 1858 VIII. 193 Into this trisection I shall decompose the coarse unity of the question presented by Van Dale. 1885 Leudesdorf *Cremona's Proj. Geom.* 295 The point *Q* is one of the points of trisection of the arc.

**Trisector** (trəise·ktəɹ). [f. Trisect *v.* + -or.] One who or that which trisects; *spec.* in quot. 1872, one who attempts the trisection of an angle.
1864 *Athenæum* 27 Aug. 276/3 The trisector of an angle. 1872 De Morgan *Budget of Paradoxes* 71 He is sometimes ranked with the trisectors.

So **Trise·ctory** *a.*, having the property of trisecting: applied to certain curves used in the trisection of an angle (*Cent. Dict.* 1891); **Trise·ctrix** [see -trix], a line that trisects; *spec.* a curve used in the trisection of an angle (*ibid.*, *Suppl.* 1909).

**Triseme** (trəi·sīm), *a.* and *sb. Anc. Pros.* [ad. Gr. τρίσημος, f. τρι-, Tri- + σῆμα sign.] a. *adj.* = *trisemic* (see below). b. *sb.* A trisemic foot. So **Trisemic** (trəisī·mik) *a.*, containing, consisting of, or equivalent to three moræ or short syllables.
1885 Goodell in *Trans. Amer. Philol. Assoc.* XVI. 88 This metre is logaœdic, trisemes and cyclic dactyls, as well as tribrachs and inverted trochees, being substituted freely for pure trochees. 1894 Gildersleeve *Lat. Gram.* (ed. 3) 459 Syncopè and Protraction (triseme long).

**Trisensory** to **Tri-shaped**: see Tri- 1 a, c.

**Trisette**, variant of Tresette.

† **Trish-trash.** *Obs.* [A reduplicated form of Trash *sb.*¹; cf. Mish-mash.] Trash, rubbish, worthless stuff.
1542–5 Brinklow *Lament.* 14 b, All the trishtrashe that Antichrist hath solde vs. 1583 Golding *Calvin on Deut.* cix. 669 That a man shall seeme a wolfe vnto vs, or that such trishtrash shall get the vpper hand of vs. 1602 *How to Choose Good Wife* ii. i. C iv b, He that minds trish trash.

**Trisilicate** (trəiˌsi·likĕt). *Chem.* and *Min.* [f. Tri- + Silicate.] A compound of one or more basic oxides with silicon dioxide or silica, $SiO_2$: a. in early nomenclature denoting a compound of silicon dioxide with three equivalents of the base (see note s. v. Tri- 5 a); thus *trisilicate of iron* denoted a compound of three equivalents of iron oxide and one of silicon dioxide, then called silicic acid; b. now used for compounds derived from hypothetical *trisilicic* acids, formed of three molecules of silicon dioxide ($SiO_2$) with varying numbers of water molecules; e.g. $3\,SiO_2 . 2\,H_2O$; $3\,SiO_2 . 5\,H_2O$. c. In Mineralogy, denoting a silicate in which the oxygen in the silicon dioxide bears to the oxygen in the basic oxides the ratio 3 : 1. So **Trisilicic** (trəiˌsili·sik) *a.*: see b.
1850 Daubeny *Atom. The.* (ed. 2) 112 Trisilicate of iron [denotes] 3 of base to 1 of silicic acid. 1868 Watts *Dict. Chem.* V. 243 Silicates are sometimes distinguished by names which express directly the oxygen-ratio in the base and acid..1 : 3 Trisilicates. *Ibid.* 251 Bohemian glass-tubing consists of potassio-calcic trisilicate, $2(K^2O . 3\,SiO^2)\,3\,(Ca''O . 3\,SiO^2)$. 1902 Miers *Mineralogy* 208 Albite, $Na_2O . Al_2O_3 . 6\,SiO_2$ or $NaAlSi_3O_8$...According to [its] oxygen ratio, therefore ..Albite is a trisilicate. 1905 Newth *Inorg. Chem.* (ed. 11) 637 By the partial withdrawal of water from three molecules of silicic acid a number of hypothetical trisilicic acids may be derived...Felspar, or orthoclase, is a trisilicate, $Al_2K_2(Si_3O_8)_2$. 1911 Roscoe & Schorlemmer *Treat. Chem.* (ed. 4) I. 920 Derivatives of trisilicic acid, $H_4Si_3O_8\,[3\,Si(OH)_4 - 4\,H_2O]$.

**Trisinuate, -ed**: see Tri- 1 a.

**Triskele** (tri·skīl). Also in quasi-Gr. form **triskelion** (triske·liǫn), erron. **tri·skelos.** [f. Gr. τρι-, Tri- + σκέλος leg; cf. τρισκελής three-legged.] A symbolic figure consisting of three legs or lines radiating from a common centre.
1857 Birch *Anc. Pottery* (1858) I. 164 On some other Sicilian tiles the potter had placed the triskelos, or three legs, as an emblem of the country. 1880 B. Head *Guide Coins & Medals Brit. Mus.* 23 The Triskelion is supposed by some to be a symbol of the sun. 1885 *Athenæum* 27 June 826/2 Panels, on which were sculptured designs such as the 'sunsnake', the swastika, and the triskele. [1914 *Brit. Mus. Return* 110 The rare staters..bear respectively a triskeles of human legs..a wheel..and a crescent.]

**Trismegist** (tri·smĭgist), anglicized form of L. *trismegistus*, Gr. τρισμέγιστος 'thrice-greatest' (cf. F. *trismégiste*), title of the Egyptian Hermes (see Hermes 3): in quots. used allusively. So **Trismegi·stian**, **Trismegi·stic, -ical** *adjs.*, belonging or ascribed to, following, or having the character of Hermes Trismegistus.
1657 H. Pinnell *Philos. Ref.* A viij, He that listed himselfe a true Chymist, had faire hopes to become a great Trismegist. 1678 Cudworth *Intell. Syst.* i. iv. 307, Δεύτερον θεόν, as the Hermaick or Trismegistick Writers call it, *The Second God.* *Ibid.* 323 Books, called Hermetical and Trismegistical. 1694 Motteux *Rabelais* v. xlvi, Is this all that the Trismegistian Bottle's Word means? 1913 *19th Cent.* Jan. 178 The extant tractates and fragments of this Trismegistic literature.

‖ **Trismus** (tri·zmɒs). *Path.* [mod.L., ad. Gr. τρισμός = τριγμός a scream, also a grinding, rasping.] Tetanus or tonic spasm of the muscles of the neck and lower jaw, causing the jaw to close rigidly; lock-jaw. (Rarely extended to tetanus in general.)
1693 tr. *Blancard's Phys. Dict.* (ed. 2), *Trismus*, the grinding of the Teeth, or a Convulsion of a Muscle of the Temples, whereby the Teeth gnash whether one will or no. 1704 in J. Harris *Lex. Techn.* I. 1806 *Med. Jrnl.* XV. 44 This man had a slight cut in the palm of one of his hands.. which was healed several days prior to his seizure with trismus. 1897 *Trans. Amer. Pediatric Soc.* IX. 77 There is trismus of the hands and feet.

† **Trisni·trate.** *Chem. Obs.* [f. Tris- + Nitrate.] Old name for a nitrate supposed to contain three equivalents of basic oxide and one equivalent of nitric anhydride (then called nitric acid). Cf. Tris- 2 a.
1836 *Pharm. R. Coll. Physic.* 217 Trisnitrate of Bismuth was formerly employed as a cosmetic under the name of magistery of Bismuth..represented to possess anti-spasmodic powers. 1850 Daubeny *Atom. The.* iii. (ed. 2) 112 Trisnitrate of alumina [denotes] 1 of acid to 3 of the earth. 1876 Harley *Royle's Mat. Med.* 252 Trisnitrate of bismuth.

**Trisoctahedron** (tri:sǫktăhī·drǫn, -he·drǫn). *Geom.* and *Cryst.* [f. Tris- + Octahedron.] A solid figure having 24 faces, every three of which correspond to one face of an octahedron: either with triangular faces (= *triakisoctahedron*), or with

trapezoidal faces (= *deltohedron, icositetrahedron*, or *trapezohedron*). Hence **Tri·soctahe·dral** *a.*, pertaining to or having the form of a trisoctahedron.
1847 WEBSTER (citing DANA), Trisoctahedron. 1891 *Cent. Dict.*, Trisoctahedral.

**Trisonant**: see TRI- 2.

**Trispast** (tri·spæst). *rare.* [ad. L. *trispastos* (Vitruvius), a. Gr. τρίσπαστος adj., f. τρι-, TRI- + σπά-ειν to draw, pull.] An (ancient) apparatus with three pulleys for hoisting heavy weights.
1706 PHILLIPS (ed. Kersey), *Trispast* (Gr.), an Engine that consists of three Pulleys. 1819 in *Pantologia*; and in later Dicts.

**Tri-spear** to **Trisquare**: see TRI- 4 c, 1 a, 2.

**Trispective** (trəi͵spe·ktiv). *Geom.* [f. after PERSPECTIVE: see TRI-.] A relation, analogous to *perspective* (PERSPECTIVE *sb.* 3 c) between three trigraphic ranges of points: see TRIGRAPHY.
1895 J. W. RUSSELL in *Proc. Lond. Math. Soc.* XXVI. 450 Three ranges situated as above may be said to be in trispective, *O* being the centre of trispective.

**Triss, Trisselle, Trissett**: see TREST, TRESTLE, TRESETTE.

† **Trist,** *sb.*$^1$ *Obs.* Also 3–5 **triste**, 4–5 **tryst**(e, (5 **thrist**). [App. etymologically related to TRAIST, TRUST; but the nature of the relation is not clear; see further under TRUST *sb.*] Confidence, faith; confident expectation, hope: = TRUST *sb.* 1, 2.
c1200 *Trin. Coll. Hom.* 75 Trist to longe lif letteð þe mannes shrifte. 1303 R. BRUNNE *Handl. Synne* 7228 Of swych, here wombes are here Cryst; Þat ys here loue, þat ys here tryst. c1330 — *Chron.* (1810) 103 My triste is laid on þe duke Roberd. c1374 CHAUCER *Troylus* I. 98 (154) Thei hadde a relyk hight Palladion That was hire tryst [*v.rr.* trist, trost] a bouen euerichon. c1380 WYCLIF *Sel. Wks.* III. 431 Siche signes drawen fro love of Crist þo þat setten so meche trist in hem. 1388 — *Matt.* ix. 22 Jhesus turnede, and say hir, and seide, Douȝtir, haue thou trist [1382 trust]. c1400 *Apol. Loll.* 30 He haþ no tryst of preching..he haþ only þe name of prest. 1413 *Pilgr. Sowle* (Caxton) II. xliii. (1859) 49 Thylke also, that vppon the tryste of mercy haue leyn in theyr lustes to theyr lyues ende. c1440 *York Myst.* xviii. 13 All my triste, lord, is in þe. 1483 *Cath. Angl.* 393/2 Triste, *fiducia ex bona consciencia est, confidencia temeritatis est, & cetera.*

† **Trist,** *sb.*$^2$ *Obs.* Forms: 4 **tryste**, 4–5 **tryst**, **triste**, 5 **trest**, **treste**, **tryyst**. [a. OF. *triste* (12th c. in Godef.); cf. TRISTRE: in med.L. *trista, tristra*. Derivation obscure; perh. the same word as prec.] An appointed station in hunting.
c1330 R. BRUNNE *Chron. Wace* (Rolls) 858 To venerye he gaf his tent; An herde of hertes sone þey met, At a triste [*v.r.* at triste] to schete, Brutus was set. 14.. *Voc.* in Wr.-Wülcker 613/22 *Statuncula*, a tryst. c1440 *Promp. Parv.* 503/1 Tryyst, merke, *limes*, C. F. *meta.* 1470–85 MALORY *Arthur* XVIII. xxi. 764 They..coude wel kylle a dere bothe at the stalke & at the trest. [1607 COWELL *Interpr.*, *Tritis*, alias *Tristis*, is an immunitie from that attendance, in the forest, whereby euery man dwelling in the forest, is tyed to be readie, houlding of a Greyhound, when the Lord of the Forest is disposed to chace. 1799 *Sporting Mag.* XIII. 321 The diversion named the *Traist* or *Trista*. 1882 J. F. S. GORDON *Hist. Moray* III. v. 102 He..sounded with his horn the death-note of many a deer in the trystas which he held with his nobles in the royal forests.]

b. *gen.* A station assigned; appointed place, rendezvous. Cf. TRYST *sb.* 4.
c1330 R. BRUNNE *Chron.* (1810) 157 Acres þan is his [K. Richard's] triste, opon þe Sarazin feendes, To venge Jhesu Criste þiderward he wendes. *Ibid.* 179 Þe Inglis at þer triste bifor þam bare alle doun, & R. als him liste þe way had redy roun.

**Trist,** *sb.*$^3$: see TRIST *a.*$^2$

† **Trist,** *a.*$^1$ *Obs.* Also 4 **tryst**, **tryste**, 5 **triste**. [Goes with TRIST *sb.*$^1$]
1. Confident, sure: = TRUST *a.* 1.
1340–70 [implied in TRISTLY]. c1400 *Ywaine & Gaw.* 3888 Of him ye myght be trist inogh.
2. Trusty, trustworthy, faithful: = TRUST *a.* 2.
c1330 R. BRUNNE *Chron. Wace* (Rolls) 1108 Anacletus graunted wel, ȝyf Brutus wold be tryst as stel Þat his lyf he wolde hym saue. *Ibid.* 3564 Þe walles he reisede trist & trewe. c1400 *Destr. Troy* 12634 To trye out the truthe with his trist hond, On what buerne so was bold þe batell to take. 1540 *Registr. Aberdon.* (Maitl. Cl.) I. 416 Letter from þe King praying his trist consalour þe bischop and weilbelouit clarkis of Abirdene to consent.

**Trist,** *a.*$^2$ (*sb.*$^3$) (*obs.* or *arch.*); in ordinary use now only as Fr. ‖ **triste** (trīst). Also 5 **tryst, tryste.** [a. F. *triste* (10th c. in Godef. *Compl.*) = Prov. *trist, triste*, Sp., Pg. *triste*, It. *tristo*, ad. L. *tristis* sad, sorrowful, gloomy.]
1. Feeling or expressing sorrow; sad, sorrowful, melancholy.
c1420 LYDG. *Thebes* 1956 Whan Tydeus hadde told his tale, Ethiocles, trist and wonder pale, his conceyt first in maner hath refreyned. 1474 CAXTON *Chesse* II. v. (1883) 71 Hyt apperteyneth not to a prynce that ony man shold departe sorowfull or tryste fro hym. 1513 DOUGLAS *Æneis* XI. vi. 2 Thyr messingeris, all trist and wobegon, Returnit haymwartis into thar maist neid. 1600 FAIRFAX *Tasso* XIII. xxix, A bitter sorrow by the hart him bit,..sad, silent, trist, Alone he would all day in darknes sit. 1702 VANBRUGH *False Friend* I. i, I staid in Flanders, very trist for your loss. 1775 MISS BURNEY *Early Diary* (1889) II. 112 The Russian nobleman..had a most *triste*, foreign countenance. 1820 W. IRVING *Life & Lett.* (1864) II. 18 The populace have a more triste and grave appearance. 1851 SIR F. PALGRAVE *Norm. & Eng.* II. 410 His hitherto cheerful countenance [was] *triste* and worn.

b. Characterized by or causing sorrow; sad, doleful, lamentable.
c1450 *St. Cuthbert* (Surtees) 6741 Eftirward fell tyme triste. 1513 DOUGLAS *Æneis* X. v. 142 The comete stern sanguynolent, Wyth hys red cullour trist and violent. 1667 WATERHOUSE *Fire Lond.* 83 Not more trist to other parts of the World and to this nation in general, then to Me in particular. 1768 EARL CARLISLE in Jesse *Selwyn & Contemp.* (1843) II. 285 It is a *triste* reflection. 1888 'P. CUSHING' *Blacksmith of Voe* II. xi. 267 What a trist fate, elenge, sombre, and pitiful!

2. Devoid of interest or liveliness; dull, depressing, dismal, dreary. (Only in form *triste*, as Fr.)
?1756 H. WALPOLE *Lett.* Aug. (1846) III. 239 The great apartment is vast and triste, the whole leanly furnished. 1805 EMILY CLARK *Banks of Douro* II. 135 To live constantly at my house will be a situation too triste for you. 1835 *Court Mag.* VI. 188/2 A family going to Bath..without introductions to the *élite* of the town, will pass a most *triste* and deplorable winter. 1894 MRS. H. WARD *Marcella* III. 158 Life was often triste and dull in the great house.

† B. *sb.*$^3$ Sadness, sorrow, affliction. *Obs. rare.*
a1510 DOUGLAS *K. Hart* II. 380 That is ane sing [= sign] befoir ane hevie trist!

Hence **Tri·steness**, dullness, dreariness. *rare.*
1866 MARK LEMON *Wait for the End* xxxiv. 442 The mirthfulness of the guests..was in pleasing contrast to the tristeness of the morning gathering.

† **Trist,** *v. Obs.* Forms: 3–5 **triste**, 4–6 **trist**, **tryst**(e, (6–7 *Sc.* **thrist**). *Pa. t.* 4 **tristide**, 5 **tristed**; usually contr. 3–5 **triste**, 5 **trist, tryst.** [Goes with TRIST *sb.*$^1$: cf. TRAIST *v.*, TRUST *v.*]
1. *intr.* To have confidence; to confide, rely (*in, on, upon, to*): = TRUST *v.* 1.
a1250 *Owl & Night.* 760 Ich kan wit & song manteine Ne triste ich to non oþer maine. c1330 R. BRUNNE *Chron. Wace* (Rolls) 1697 He triste to mykel on his myght. c1374 CHAUCER *Troylus* V. 1709 O Pandarus that in dremes for to triste Me blamed hast. c1380 WYCLIF *Wks.* (1880) 347 Whoso fayliþ in feiþ he is fals to god, & tristiþ not to hijs treuthe. 1382 — *Mark* vi. 50 He spak with hem, and seide to hem, Triste ȝe, I am; nyle ȝe drede. ?a1400 *Arthur* 428 Arthour..tryst on god, & was wel payd. c1430 *Pilgr. Lyf Manhode* I. v. (1869) 3 Seint Peeter, in whom he wel triste, and certeyn wel mihte triste in him. c1475 *Songs & Carols* (Percy Soc.) 11 Few be trew to tryst upon.
2. *trans.* To have confidence in, rely on: = TRUST *v.* 2.
a1272 *Luue Ron* 56 in *O. E. Misc.* 94 Nis he neuer treowe ifunde. Þat him tristeþ he is amed. 1390 GOWER *Conf.* II. 257 He tok to him suche as he triste In secre. 1430–40 LYDG. *Bochas* I. x. (MS. Bodl. 263) 48/2 As a brother sholde his brother triste. a1500 *Childe of Bristow* 154 in Hazl. *E. P. P.* I. 116 Frendship, sone, is ylle to triste.
3. To expect confidently, hope: = TRUST *v.* 3. (Const. with clause, or *intr.* with *of.*)
c1200 *Trin. Coll. Hom.* 217 Ich triste þat he nele neng bi mine wrihte. a1400–50 *Alexander* 1344 Of þe takyng of tire tristed þai no lenger. 1433 *Rolls of Parlt.* IV. 425/1 He takith hym nowe so nygh, tristyng yat it shall lyke the Kyng.
4. To believe: = TRUST *v.* 4. (With simple obj. or clause.)
1340–70 *Alisaunder* 489 Sir, I tolde you trouth, trist yee no nooþer. c1380 WYCLIF *Wks.* (1880) 33 Þey..dysceyuen ..lordis & ladies..& maken hem to triste þat it is almes to distroye trewe men. ?a1400 *Arthur* 545 Þer ys no man wel nye, y tryste, Þat can be waar of hadde wyste.
5. To give credit to (a person for goods); to supply (goods *to* a person) on credit: = TRUST *v.* 7. *Sc.*
1583 *Leg. Bp. St Androis* 1046 Ye wald doe weill gif ye wald thrist me...Ye salbe payit...Your tristene sall not be for nought. 1609 SKENE *Reg. Maj.*, *Burrow Lawes* cxxx. 136 Browsters, Fleshers, and Baikers sall lenne (and thrist) to their neighbours aill, flesh, and bread, sa long as they buy fra them.

**Trist,** obs. f. TREST, TRYST. **Tristachyous**: see TRI- 1 a. **Triste**: see TRIST *a.*$^2$ **Tristearin**: see TRI- 5 a. **Tristell,** obs. f. TRESTLE.

† **Tristen,** *v. Obs. rare.* [irreg. f. TRIST *v.* + -EN$^5$.] = TRIST *v.* Hence † **Tristening** *vbl. sb.* (Cf. TRUSTEN.)
1382 WYCLIF 2 *Cor.* i. 15 And in this tristnynge [1388 tristyng, *Vulg.* confidentia] I wolde firste come to ȝou. 1388 — *Eph.* iii. 12 [see TRUSTEN].

**Tristene,** Sc. f. *tristing* vbl. sb.: see TRIST *v.* 5.

**Tristesse.** Also 4 **tristesce**, 5 **trystesse**, (**tristresse**), 6 **tristes.** Now only as F. (tristeˑs). [ME. a. OF. *tristesce, -tece, -trece* (12th c. in Godef. *Compl.*), F. *tristesse*, = Prov. *tristicia, tristessa*, Sp., Pg. *tristeza*, It. *tristezza* :—L. *tristitia* sadness, f. *tristis* sad.] Sadness, grief, melancholy.
1390 GOWER *Conf.* II. 115 He withinne his thought conceiveth Tristesce, and so himself deceiveth. c1425 LYDG. *Dance Macabre* x, Mine old ioyes been turned into tristesse. 1485 CAXTON *Paris & V.* 11 He ledde hys lyf in grete trystesse and sorowe. c1489 — *Blanchardyn* iv. 20 Þe palays and the cyte were tourned from Ioye vnto tristresse. 1547 HOOPER *Declar. Christ* v. Eiij b, *Ezeb.*.signifithe ether affliction, rebellion, sorow, tristes, trauel, or peyne. 1797 SCOTT *Fam. Lett.* (1894) I. 6 If it will help to banish *Tristesse*, let me again assure you that every thought of my heart shall be directed to insure your happiness. 1856 EMERSON *Eng. Traits* xvi. 162 Nature..too much by half for man in the picture, and so giving a certain *tristesse*.

**Tristetrahedron** (tri͵s͵tetrăhīˑdrǫn, -heˑdrǫn). *Geom.* and *Cryst.* [f. TRIS- + TETRAHEDRON.] A solid figure having 12 faces, every three of which correspond to one face of a tetrahedron: either with triangular faces (= *triakistetrahedron*), or with trapezoidal faces. (Cf. TRISOCTAHEDRON.)
In recent Dicts.

† **Tri·stful,** *a.*$^1$ *Obs. rare*$^{-1}$. In 5 **trystefull**. [f. TRIST *sb.*$^1$ + -FUL 1.] Trustworthy: = TRUSTFUL *a.* 1.
c1440 *York Myst.* xxv. 514 Hayll! talker trystefull of trew tales!

**Tristful** (tri·stfŭl), *a.*$^2$ *arch.* Also 5 **trystefull.** [f. TRIST *a.*$^2$ + -FUL 1.] Full of sadness; sad, sorrowful; dreary, dismal: cf. TRIST *a.*$^2$
1491 CAXTON *Vitas Patr.* II. (W. de W. 1495) 180 b/1 Entryng in his hermytage he founde hym trystefull and sore to the deth. c1500 *Melusine* 305 That message was the cause of the trystefull dolour of the departyng of his wyf. 1602 SHAKS. *Ham.* III. iv. 50 This solidity and compound masse, With tristfull visage as against the doome, Is thought-sicke at the act. 1748 RICHARDSON *Clarissa* (1811) VIII. lv. 251 How will thy tristful visage be illuminated by it! 1880 BROWNING *Dram. Idylls* Ser. II. *Pietro of Abano* xxi, Then did Peter's tristful visage lighten somewhat.
Hence **Tri·stfully** *adv.*
1847 in WEBSTER. 1880 W. WATSON *Prince's Quest* (1892) 31 The day, begun Tristfully, trailed an ever wearier wing.

**Tristich** (tri·stik). *Pros.* [f. TRI-, after DISTICH; cf. Gr. τριστιχία a union of three verses, f. τρίστιχος three-rowed, f. τρι- three + στίχος row.] A group of three lines of verse; a stanza of three lines.
1813 T. BUSBY tr. *Lucretius* II. VI. *Comm.* p. ix, Much of the thought contained in the subjoined tristich of Ovid, is evidently derived from the original of this. 1864 PUSEY *Lect. Daniel* vi. 316, Ps. x..has 3 tristichs (verses divided into 3). 1886 C. A. BRIGGS *Messianic Proph.* III. ii. 82 *note*, In the third part, a tristich, the three sons appear.
Hence **Tristichic** (tristi·kik) *a.*, characterized by tristichs.
1882–3 *Schaff's Encycl. Relig. Knowl.* III. 1955 A closed train of thought which is unrolled after the distichic and tristichic ground-form of the rhythmical period.

**Tristichous** (tri·stikəs), *a. Bot.* [f. Gr. τρίστιχ-ος (see prec.) + -OUS.] Arranged in, or characterized by, three rows or ranks.
1857 HENFREY *Elem. Bot.* § 62 The tristichous or three-ranked arrangement, which is common among the Monocotyledons. 1887 *Jrnl. Educ.* Dec. 520 The quincuncial or tristichous arrangement could be..indicated by fractions.

† **Tristi·fical,** *a. Obs. rare*$^{-0}$. [f. L. *tristific-us* adj., saddening (f. *tristis* sad + *-ficus*, -FIC) + -AL.]
1656 BLOUNT *Glossogr.*, *Tristifical*.., that makes sad or heavy.

**Tristigm** to **Tristigmatose**: see TRI- 4 a, 1 a.

**Tristil, -ill**(e, obs. forms of TRESTLE.

† **Tri·stily,** *adv.*$^1$ *Obs.* Forms: see TRISTY *a.*$^1$ [f. TRISTY *a.*$^1$ + -LY$^2$.]
1. Trustfully; confidently, boldly; securely: = TRUSTILY 1.
c1380 WYCLIF *Wks.* (1880) 42 Goo þei [friars] tristiliche for almes, and hem nediþ not to be a-schamyd. 1382 — *Acts* ix. 27 Barnabas..telde..how in Damask he [Paul] dide tristily in the name of Jhesu. 1388 — *Prov.* iii. 23 Thanne thou schalt go tristili in thi weie, and thi foot schal not snapere. c1410 LOVE *Bonavent. Mirr.* (1907) 149 The euerelastynge lyf in heuene, that thei tristily hopen to haue by his gracious byheste.
2. Faithfully, truly: = TRUSTILY 2.
c1330 R. BRUNNE *Chron. Wace* (Rolls) 4864 Þer to han hated, & fomen ben, Þat syþen han loued to-gedre wel, Tristiloker þan ony stel. 1380 *Lay Folks Catech.* 1181 Þis is nedful to alle þat tristyly lyuys. a1400 *Pistill of Susan* 340 (Cotton MS.) Telle me tristili [*other MSS.* treuwely, trewly, trwly], er þow þy lyfe tyne. c1400 *Destr. Troy* 8739 A tabernacle triet & tristyly wroght.
3. Certainly, surely: = TRUSTILY 3.
?a1366 CHAUCER *Rom. Rose* 1166 (Glasgow MS.) If she hadde an enemy, I trowe that she coude tristely [*v. r.* craftily] Make hym fulle soone hir frend to be. 1393 LANGL. *P. Pl.* C. IV. 498 He þat seceþ sapience fynde he shal þat foleuþ Tristilich a teneful tixt.

† **Tri·stily,** *adv.*$^2$ *Obs. rare.* In 5 **trystily.** [f. TRISTY *a.*$^2$ + -LY$^2$.] Sadly, sorrowfully.
c1450 *St. Cuthbert* (Surtees) 4408 Elfride lay wakand all'ane, He thoght trystily and made his mane.

† **Tri·stiness.** *Obs.* [f. TRISTY *a.*$^1$ + -NESS.] Trustiness, faithfulness.
1408 CLIFTON tr. *Vegetius De re milit.* (MS. Digby 233) lf. 185 b/1 Wheþer he haue good tristinesse in knyghthod.

† **Tristi·tiate,** *v. Obs. rare*$^{-1}$. [f. L. *tristitia* sadness + -ATE$^3$.] *trans.* To affect with sadness, to sadden. So † **Tristi·tious** *a. Obs. rare*$^{-1}$, full of sadness, sorrowful.
1628 FELTHAM *Resolves* II. [I.] xli. 122 Nor is there any whom Calamity doth so much tristitiate, as that hee neuer sees the flashes of some warming ioy. 1694 MOTTEUX *Rabelais* V. 248 Their plaisant Notes tristitious Thoughts confound.

† **Tri·stive,** *a. Obs. rare*$^{-1}$. [f. TRIST *a.*$^2$ + -IVE.] Sad, doleful, mournful.
1578 T. PROCTOR *Gorg. Gallery* P iv, Though death hath shapte his most untimely end Yet for his prayse my tristive tunes I send.

**Tristle,** obs. form of TRESTLE.

† **Tri·stly,** *adv. Obs.* [f. TRIST *a.*$^1$ + -LY$^2$.] Confidently; securely; boldly: = TRUSTLY *adv.* 1.
1340–70 *Alex. & Dind.* 513 Þat þou mihte trystli trye þe

treweste lawe. *a* 1400–50 *Alexander* 1632 He me thrett to be tra [=thra, thro], & for no thyng turne, Bot tyre me titely þarto & tristly to wend. 1408 CLIFTON tr. *Vegetius De re militari* (MS. Digby 233) lf. 183 b/2 No man dredeþ to fulfille in dede þat he tristly troweþ he hath wel lerned.

**Tristnynge**: see TRISTEN.

† **Tristour.** *Obs. rare*$^{-1}$. [a. OF. *tristur*, *-teur*, *-tor* (12th c. in Godef.), f. *triste* sad; = L. type **tristōr-em*: cf. F. *hauteur*.] Sadness, grief.

*c* 1380 *Sir Ferumb.* 2373 Þe Amiral hem tolde with tristour by him how it is y-went.

† **Tristre.** *Obs.* Also 4 trystor, -ere, -er, 5 -yre, tristur. [a. OF. *tristre* (12th c. in Godef.), phonetic variant of *triste*, TRIST *sb.*[2] (In OF. *tristre* appears later than *triste*; but in ME. *tristre* is the earlier.)] = TRIST *sb.*[2]

*a* 1225 *Ancr. R.* 332 Tristre is þer me sit mid þe greahundes forte kepen þe hearde, oðer tillen þe nettes ajean ham. 13.. *Gaw. & Gr. Knt.* 1146 A hundreth of hunteres, as I haf herde telle, of þe best; To trystors vewters 3od. *c* 1410 *Master of Game* (MS. Digby 182) xv, Þe baytyng of þe bull and huntyng of þe wilde boore,..with grehoundes at þe tristre. *c* 1460 *Towneley Myst.* xxx. 208, I stande at my tristur, when othere men shones. 1483 *Cath. Angl.* 393/2 Trystyre, *staciuncula* (A.).

† **Tristsum,** *a. Sc. Obs. rare*$^{-1}$. [f. TRIST *a.*[2] + -SOME.] Sad, woeful, lamentable.

1567 *Satir. Poems Reform.* iv. 75 I wat it wald mak ony haill hairt sair For to reuolue my tristsum tragidie.

† **Tri·sty,** *a.*[1] *Obs.* Also 4 tristi, trysti, 4–5 trysty. [f. TRIST *a.*[1] + -Y [1].]

**1.** Trustful, confident: = TRUSTY *a.* 1.

*c* 1325 *Spec. Gy Warw.* 477 Put al þin hope in god almiht, And tristi hope to him þou haue. 1382 WYCLIF *Prol. Bible* iii. 4 This..shulde make men trysty in Goddis help.

**2.** Trustworthy, faithful: = TRUSTY *a.* 2.

13.. *E. E. Allit. P.* B. 763 If ten trysty in toune be tan in þi werkkez, Wylt þou mese þy mode & menddyng abyde? *c* 1375 *Cursor M.* 13365 (Fairf.) Þe bridegome dide þidder calle His maste tristi [*Cott.* specialiest] frendis alle. *c* 1450 *St. Cuthbert* (Surtees) 7806 Þai were tristy, and a bote bryng To lede þein his body. 1483 *Cath. Angl.* 393/2 Tristy, *vbi* trewe (*A.*).

**b.** Of things: Reliable; secure: = TRUSTY *a.* 2 b.

13.. *Cast. Love* (Halliw.) 690 On trysti [*v. r.* trusti] roche heo stondeth fast. 1340–70 *Alisaunder* 952 Till hee had take þe toune þat tristy was holde. *c* 1350 *Will. Palerne* 1147 Boþe partiȝes prestly a-paraylde hem..Of alle tristy a-tir þat to batayle longed.

† **Tri·sty,** *a.*[2] *Obs.* Also 5 trysty. [f. TRIST *a.*[2] + -Y [1].] Sad, sorrowful; in quot. 14.., dark or dull-coloured (= SAD *a.* 8).

? *c* 1400 LYDG. *Æsop's Fab.* III. 88 The sheepe condempned, tristy and pale of hewe. 14.. *Epiph.* in *Tundale's Vis.* (1843) 114 Ne forred with armyn nor with trysty gray. ? *a* 1600 in Ashm. *Theat. Chem.* (1652) 264 The King was tristy and heavy of cheere.

**Tristylous**: see TRI- 1 a.

**Trisu·bstituted,** *a. Chem.* [TRI- 5 c.] Containing three substituted atoms or radicals. So **Trisubstitu·tion.**

1904 *Jrnl. Phys. Chem.* Apr. 298 Trisubstituted acids are less associated than disubstituted acids, and these latter less than monosubstituted acids. *Mod.* Trichloracetic acid is a trisubstitution product.

‖ **Trisul** (trisū·l), **trisula** (trisū·lă). [Skr. *triçūla*, f. *tri-* three + **çūla* spit, spear-head.] A three-pointed figure or ornament, used as an emblem of the Hindu god Siva, and also as a Buddhist symbol.

1871 ALABASTER *Wheel of Law* 249 On the great toe is the Trisul. 1876 J. FERGUSSON *Hist. Indian Arch.* I. iv. 97 The trisul or trident emblem which crowns the gateways may..represent Buddha himself. 1905 *Protestant Observer* Aug. 117/3 The trisul appears on a large medal of the Great Exhibition, 1851, with two fishes (Pisces) under Victoria and Albert.

† **Tri·sulc, tri·sulk,** *a.* (*sb.*) *Obs.* [ad. L. *trisulc-us* three-cleft, f. *tri-*, TRI- + *sulcus* furrow. Cf. F. *trisulce* (*trisulque*, 16th c. in Godef. *Compl.*).] Three-cleft, three-forked, trifurcate: esp. as an epithet of the lightning or thunderbolt, after L. *trisulcum fulmen* (Varro), *Jovis telum trisulcum* (Ovid), etc.

1609 HEYWOOD *Rape Lucrece* I. ii, That hand That flings the trisulke thunder. 1611 — *Gold. Age* v. i, Jupiter..Who thunder and the trisulke lightning beares. 1650 BULWER *Anthropomet.* xiv. 142 The Tongue of man is not double, or trisulke, or bisulke, as in some creatures. 1653 URQUHART *Rabelais* II. xxxii, Jupiter confound me with his trisulk lightning if I lie! 1656 BLOUNT *Glossogr.*, *Trisulk* (*trisulcus*), having three edges, or three furrows. 1658 in PHILLIPS.

**B.** *ellipt.* as *sb.* A thunderbolt.

1637 HEYWOOD *Dial.* iv. Wks. 1874 VI. 160 Hand once againe thy Trisulk, and retire To Oeta, and there kindle't with new fire. 1638 SIR T. HERBERT *Trav.* (ed. 2) 239 They ..never..looke upon him, least the fulgor of his aspect might peradventure prove no lesse formidable than the Trisulk of Iupiter. 1646 SIR T. BROWNE *Pseud. Ep.* II. vi. 100 If we consider the threefold effect of Jupiters Trisulk, to burn, discusse and terebrate.

**Trisulcate** (traisʊ·lkĕt), *a.* [f. as prec. + -ATE [2].] **1.** = prec. adj.

1719 D'URFEY *Pills* III. 322 Him, that hurls the Bolt trisulcate. 1866 J. B. ROSE tr. *Ovid's Met.* 61 By whose right hand are hurled The flames trisulcate.

**2. a.** *Bot.* Marked with three furrows or grooves, three-furrowed.

1891 in *Cent. Dict.* 1900 in B. D. JACKSON *Gloss. Bot. Terms.*

**b.** *Zool.* Divided into three digits, as a foot; tridactylous. (Cf. BISULCATE.) 1891 in *Cent. Dict.*

So **Trisu·lcated** *a. rare* = 2 a above.

1703 PETIVER in *Phil. Trans.* XXIII. 1428 The Fruit whole is about the bigness of a midling Nut, smooth, blackish and trisulcated.

**Trisulph-, trisulpho-** (traisʊlf, traisʊlfo). *Chem.* [f. TRI- 5 + SULPH(URIC.] A formative of the names of carbon compounds containing three $SO_2$ groups, or three $SO_2 . OH$ groups, and derivatives of the latter. (TRISULPHONE, and TRISULPHONIC, with TRISULPHONATE, now also express these meanings.)

1867 GRIESS in *Jrnl. Chem. Soc.* XX. 101 Trisulphodiphenylenic Acid..its composition may also be expressed in two different ways, viz. $C_{12}H_6 . S_3H_4O_{11}$, or $C_{12}H_6 . S_3H_6O_{13}$. 1875 WATTS *Dict. Chem.* VII. 1111 $N^vH^2(SO^3K)^3$ Trisulphammonate of potassium...$ON^v(SO^3K)^3$ Trisulphoxyazate of potassium.

**Trisulphate** (traisʊ·lfĕt). *Chem.* [f. TRI- 5 + SULPHATE.] A compound formed from three molecules of sulphuric acid, $H_2SO_4$, by replacement of the hydrogen by a metal or radical, and thus containing three $SO_4$ groups; e. g. *aluminium trisulphate*, $Al_2(SO_4)_3$; *glyceryl and hydrogen trisulphate*, $(C_3H_5)'''H_3(SO_4)_3$.

1880 ROSCOE & SCHORLEMMER *Treat. Chem.* II. ii. 312 Antimony Trisulphate, $Sb_2(SO_4)_3$, .. crystallizes .. in long glistening silky needles.

**Trisulphide** (traisʊ·lfəid). *Chem.* [f. TRI- 5 + SULPHIDE.] A compound of an element or radical with three atoms of sulphur; e. g. *boron trisulphide*, $B_2S_3$; *arsenic trisulphide*, $As_2S_3$; *potassium trisulphide*, $K_2S_3$.

1866 ROSCOE *Elem. Chem.* xxiv. 207 Metallic antimony occurs native, but its chief ore is the trisulphide. 1888 MUIR & MORLEY *Watts' Dict. Chem.* I. 516 Bismuth Trisulphide, $Bi_2S_3$, occurs native as bismuth glance. 1905 *Jrnl. Chem. Soc.* LXXXVIII. II. 245 Golden-yellow leaflets of arsenic trisulphide are formed.

**Trisulphone** (traisʊ·lfōun). *Chem.* [f. TRI- 5 + SULPHONE.] A compound in which carbon radicals are linked to other carbon radicals by the intervention of three $SO_2$ groups, the sulphur atoms being directly joined to the carbon atoms; e. g. *triethylsulphonemethylmethane*, $C(CH_3)(SO_2 . C_2H_5)_3$; *trisulphone acetone*,

$$(CH_3)_2C : \{SO_2 - C(CH_3)_2\}_2 : SO_2.$$

So **Trisulphonic** (traisʊlfǫ·nik) *a.*, in *trisulphonic acid, amide, chloride*, etc., compounds of three $SO_2 . OH$, $SO_2 . NH_2$, $SO_2 . Cl$, etc., groups with a trivalent element or radical, the sulphur being directly joined to the element or carbon of the radical; e.g. *amine-trisulphonic acid*, $N(SO_2 . OH)_3$; *benzene-trisulphonic acid*, $C_6H_3(SO_2 . OH)_3$; *benzene-trisulphonic chloride*, $C_6H_3(SO_2Cl)_3$; **Trisu·lphonate**, a salt of a trisulphonic acid.

1874 SCHORLEMMER *Carbon Comp.* 199 A series of sulphonic acids..substitution products of marsh gas,..the third is methenyltrisulphonic acid, $CH(SO_3H)_3$. 1879 WATTS *Dict. Chem.* VIII. I. 259 Benzenetrisulphonic acid, $C^6H^3(SO^3H)^3 + 3H^2O$, crystallises in long flat deliquescent needles. 1886 *Jrnl. Chem. Soc.* L. 623 Benzenetrisulphonic chloride melts at 184°; the amide melts at 306°. 1892 *Ibid.* LXII. 614 Attempts to prepare a tetrasulphone by the action of sodium on haloid trisulphones and of phenylthiochloride on trisulphonates [gave] negative results.

**Trisyllabic** (trəi-, trisilæ·bik), *a. erron.* triss-. [a. F. *trissyllabique* (16th c. in Godef. *Compl.*), f. L. *trisyllab-us*, a. Gr. τρισύλλαβος of three syllables, f. τρι- three + συλλαβή syllable: see -IC. For spelling cf. note s. v. DISYLLABIC.] Consisting of or involving three syllables. So **Trisylla·bical** *a.* in same sense; **Trisylla·bically** *adv.*, as or in three syllables; **Trisy·llabism,** trisyllabic character; **Trisy·llabize** *v.*, *trans.* to make trisyllabic.

*a* 1637 B. JONSON *Eng. Gram.* I. vii, All nouns *trisyllabic [are accented] in the first [syllable]. 1861 PALEY *Æschylus* (ed. 2) *Persians* 467 *note*, Trisyllabic form of the more Attic ᾄσσω. 1882 F. T. PALGRAVE in *Spenser's Wks.* (Grosart) IV. p. xxx, In some the..trissyllabic rhyme is used. 1656 BLOUNT *Glossogr.*, **Trisyllabical* (*trisyllabicus*), that hath three syllables. 1658 in PHILLIPS. 1801 CHENEVIX in *Phil. Trans.* XCI. 195 *note*, In trisyllabical nouns, the first or second syllable is usually accented. 1858 DE QUINCEY *Mrq. Wellesley* Wks. 1858 VIII. 20 *note*, The *Annesley* family ..do not pronounce their name *trisyllabically .. viz., Ann-es-ley, but as if *Anns* (in the possessive case) *-ley*. 1884 E. EINENKEL *St. Kath.* p. xxxii, The older forms..are not very remote from genuine *trisyllabism. 1866 *Pall Mall G.* 12 Apr. 9 The Marquis finds it convenient to *trisyllabize that plebeian appellation.

**Trisyllable** (trəi-, trisi·lăb'l), *sb.* (*a.*) *erron.* 7 tress-, 6– triss-. [f. TRI- + SYLLABLE: cf. Gr. τρισύλλαβος of three syllables, F. *trissyllabe* (16th c. in Godef. *Compl.*), Sp. *trisilabo*.] A word, or a metrical foot, of three syllables. In quot. 1718, trisyllabic or 'triple' rime (*nonce-use*).

1589 PUTTENHAM *Eng. Poesie* II. iii. (Arb.) 82 To euery bissillable they allowed two times, and to a trissillable three times, and to euery polisillable more, according to his quantitie. 1630 J. TAYLOR (Water P.) *Cast over Water* Wks. II. 158 When a tressillable a verse doth end, 'Tis harsh, 'tis paltry, and it doth offend. 1718 SWIFT *To Sheridan* 31 But now I find my Muse but ill able, To hold out longer in Trissyllable. *a* 1771 GRAY *Corr.* etc. (1843) 303 As to trissyllables, as their accent is very rarely on the last, they cannot properly be any rhymes at all. 1875 POSTE *Gaius* Pref. (ed. 2) 6 The word 'Gaius' is a trisyllable in the classical period. 1887 COOK *Sievers' O. E. Gram.* 133 [They] sometimes take *u* after the manner of the trisyllables.

**B.** as *adj.* = TRISYLLABIC. (In quot. 1817 [1], having trisyllabic or 'triple' rimes.)

1766 BP. LOWTH *Larger Confut. Bp. Hare* 36 [Bentley] gives examples of trissyllable feet, namely, Bacchiac and Cretic feet, in English Verse. 1817 COLERIDGE *Biog. Lit.* 31 An innocent amusement from the riddles, conundrums, trisyllable lines, &c., &c., of Swift. *Ibid.* 178 Double and trisyllable rhymes, indeed, form a lower species of wit.

**Trit-**: see TRITO-. **Tritactic**: see TRI- 2.

**Tritagonist** (traitæ·gŏnist). [ad. Gr. τριταγωνιστής an actor who plays the third part, f. τρίτος third + ἀγωνιστής combatant, actor.] The third actor in a Greek tragedy.

1890 *Athenæum* 28 June 841/3 Creon, although said to be the tritagonist, entered by the central door. 1907 A. E. HAIGH *Attic Theatre* 283 The tritagonist took what in modern times would be called the 'heavy' parts.

**Tritaph** (trəi·taf). *Archæol.* [f. Gr. τρι-, TRI- + τάφος tomb: cf. *cenotaph*.] A group of three cists or chambers in a prehistoric tomb.

1904 WINDLE *Rem. Preh. Age Eng.* viii. 181 This circle.. consists of six symmetrically arranged sets of cysts, each a tritaph, i. e. two tangential and one radial.

† **Tri·tarchy.** *Obs. rare.* [f. Gr. τρίτ-ος third + -αρχία government.] Rule or government by three persons: irregularly used for TRIARCHY 2.

1647 M. HUDSON *Div. Right Govt.* II. iv. 96 Intestine and bloody dissentions..created by the Tritarchie of Simon, Iohn, and Eleazer.

**Tritcherie**, obs. form of TREACHERY.

‖ **Trite** (tri·tī), *sb. Anc. Gr. Mus.* [a. Gr. τρίτη, fem. of τρίτος third (sc. χορδή string).] Name of the third string or note (counting from the highest) in each of the higher tetrachords.

1603 HOLLAND *Plutarch* Explan. Words, *Trite Diezeugmenon*, The third of disjuncts, a string or note in the scale of musicke C *sol fa ut*. *Trite Hyperbolæon*, A treble string; the third of Exceeding or treble; F *fa ut*. *Trite Synemmenon*, or *Syzeugmenon*, The third of the Conjuncts, a string or note in musicke, B *fa*, B *mi* in rule. 1776 BURNEY *Hist. Mus.* (1789) I. i. 16 *Trite*, the third string from the top of the two last tetrachords. 1801 in BUSBY *Dict. Mus.*

**Trite** (trəit), *a.* [ad. L. *trītus*, pa. pple. of *terĕre* to rub.]

**1.** Worn out by constant use or repetition; devoid of freshness or novelty; hackneyed, commonplace, stale.

*a* 1548 HALL *Chron.*, *Hen. V* 40 b, Accordyng to the trite adage: He must liberally spende that will plentefully gayne. 1607 *Puritan* III. v. 162, I would not haue my Arte vulgar, trite, and common. 1654 WHITLOCK *Zootomia* 384 A Saying not triter than truer. 1762–71 H. WALPOLE *Vertue's Anecd. Paint.* (1786) V. 133 It is a trite observation, that gunpowder was discovered by a monk. 1818 SCOTT *Br. Lamm.* xviii, An art of building up a character for wisdom upon a very trite style of commonplace eloquence. 1837–9 HALLAM *Hist. Lit.* (1855) I. I. vii. § 32. 407 The story told by Erasmus of Colet is also a little too trite for repetition. 1885 *Athenæum* 28 Mar. 401 The theme of Death can no more wear trite than the theme of Love.

**2.** Well worn; worn out by rubbing; frayed; of a road or path, well-trod, beaten, frequented.

1599 B. JONSON *Cynthia's Rev.* I. iii, If my behaviours had beene of a cheape or customary garbe; my accent, or phrases, vulgar; my garments trite. 1656 BLOUNT *Glossogr.*, *Trite*, worne, over-worne, old, threedbare, much used, common. 1682 SIR T. BROWNE *Chr. Mor.* I. § 25 Unexpected Emergences, whereby we pass not our days in the trite road of affairs affording no Novity. 1855 *Fraser's Mag.* LI. 272 Specimens of the bronze coinage of the later empire; ..mostly trite and faceless. 1861 G. F. BERKELEY *Sportsm. W. Prairies* vii. 98 The woods were..unbroken save by the straight trite line of hasty locomotion.

**Tritely** (trəi·tli), *adv.* [f. prec. + -LY [2].] In a trite or commonplace manner.

1691 WOOD *Ath. Oxon.* (L.), Other things are mentioned by Baleus and Pitseus very tritely, and with little satisfaction to the reader. 1870 *Pall Mall G.* 5 Dec. 10 Keeping order among the band—'order', as he tritely observed, 'being necessary everywhere'.

**Tritencephalon**: see TRITO-.

**Triteness** (trəi·tnės). [f. TRITE *a.* + -NESS.] The quality of being trite; commonplaceness.

1727 BAILEY vol. II, *Triteness*, wornness, the being much worn. 1755 JOHNSON, *Triteness*, staleness; commonness. 1780 *Mirror* No. 80 There is one class of writers to whom the charge of triteness does..very little apply. 1791–1823 D'ISRAELI *Cur. Lit.* (1858) III. 63 *note*, Triteness and triviality are fatal to a proverb. 1910 *Scott. Hist. Rev.* Oct. 17 Telling his story with the triteness and circumspection of a lawyer.

**Triternate** (traitə̄·ɹnĕt), *a. Bot.* [f. TRI- 2 + TERNATE *a.*] Thrice ternate: see quots. (Abbrev. *3-ternate*.) Hence **Trite·rnately** *adv.*

1760 J. LEE *Introd. Bot.* III. vi. (1788) 202 Triternate, or Triplicato-Ternate; when a Petiole bears three Folioles that are each of them ternate. 1835 LINDLEY *Introd. Bot.* (1848) II. 360 *Triternate*, when the common petiole divides into three secondary petioles, which are each subdivided into three tertiary petioles, each of which bears three leaflets. 1856 A. GRAY *Man. Bot.* (1860) 20 A large triternately compound leaf. 1870 HOOKER *Stud. Flora* 168 Peucedanum officinale; leaves 3-ternately pinnate.

**Tritheism** (trəi·þiˌiz'm). [f. TRI- + THEISM; cf. Gr. τριθεΐα (f. τρι-, TRI- + θεός God), F. *trithéisme* (1727 in Littré).] Belief in three Gods; *esp.* an interpretation of the doctrine of the Trinity according to which the three Persons are three distinct Gods. (Cf. next.)

1678 CUDWORTH *Intell. Syst.* I. iv. 604 This Trinity is no other than a kind of Tritheism, and that of gods independent and co-ordinate too. 1719 WATERLAND *Vind. Christ's Div.* Contents, This Assertion,..that there is no Medium between Tritheism and Sabellianism. 1855 MACAULAY *Hist. Eng.* xvii. IV. 51 In his zeal against Socinians and Sabellians, he [Sherlock] used expressions which might be construed into Tritheism. 1910 SANDAY *Christologies* i. 12 The doctrine of the Trinity is not Tritheism.

**Tritheist** (trəi·þiˌist). [f. TRI- + THEIST; cf. F. *trithéiste* (Littré).] A believer in three Gods; *esp.* one who holds that the three Persons of the Trinity are three distinct Gods.

Chiefly in controversial use; applied *spec.* to a sect of Monophysites in the sixth century who denied the consubstantiality of the three Persons of the Trinity.

1608 WILLET *Hexapla Exod.* 323 They which hold not the distinction of three persons onely, but the diuision also of the substance, as the Tritheists. 1715 *Wodrow Corr.* (1843) II. 17 Roell is not thought Arian or Socinian in the great point of the Deity of Christ, but rather a Tritheist. 1850 ROBERTSON *Serm.* Ser. III. iv. (1872) 45 There are in almost every congregation..Trinitarians who are practically Tri-theists, worshipping three gods. 1903 H. L. GOUDGE 1 *Cor.* Introd. 30 S. Paul certainly is no Tritheist; the Son and the Spirit never obscure the Father for a moment.

Hence **Tritheˌi·stic, Tritheˌi·stical** *adjs.*, of, pertaining to, or believing tritheism.

1698 SOUTH *Serm.* III. Ded. A iv b, Reprinting exploded Tritheistick Notions. 1708 H. DODWELL *Nat. Mort. Hum. Souls* 44 Our Adversaries will appear to be the Tritheistical Gobarus's, as to this Particular of the Heresies then condemned in the Tritheists. 1822 JEFFERSON *Writ.* (1830) IV. 354 Missionaries..from the tritheistical school of Andover. 1827 ARNOLD in *Life & Corr.* (1844) I. ii. 50 The tritheistic notions of the Trinity.

**Tritheite** (trəi·þiˌəit). Also 6–8 -it. [ad. Gr. τριθεΐτης, late L. *tritheïta* (Isidore), f. τρι- three + θεός god; cf. F. *trithéite*.] = TRITHEIST.

1585–7 T. ROGERS *39 Art.* v. (1633) 24 The Tritheites; which affirme the holy Ghost to be inferiour vnto the Father. 1597 HOOKER *Eccl. Pol.* v. xlii. § 13 The blasphemies of Arrians, Samosatenians, Tritheits, Eutychians, and Macedonians. 1691 W. NICHOLLS *Answ. Naked Gospel* 98 Gregorius Paulus,..was first a Tritheite, and afterwards an Unitarian. 1725 tr. *Dupin's Eccl. Hist. 17th C.* I. VI. v. 252 He [Servetus] crudely affirms, that they who distinguish three Persons in the Godhead, are Tritheites who admit of three Gods. *attrib.* 1708 H. DODWELL *Nat. Mort. Hum. Souls* 42 The Author of the Tritheit Heresy, Johannes Philoponus. 1887 C. J. BALL in *Dict. Chr. Biog.* IV. 319/1 An approach to the Tritheite standpoint.

**Tritheocracy** (trəiþiˌǫ·krăsi). *nonce-wd.* [f. TRI- + THEOCRACY.] Rule or government by three Gods; a group of three Divine beings exercising joint rule.

1850 BUSHNELL *God in Christ* 115 Father, Son and Holy Ghost are, in their view, socially united only and preside.. as a kind of celestial tritheocracy over the world.

**Trithing** (trəi·ðiŋ), **thrithing** (þrəi·ðiŋ). Forms: 3 triting, 3–4, 8–9 trithing, 7 -e, 8 triding; 4 thrythyng, 7–8 thrithing: see also RIDING *sb.* [Late OE. *þriðing, *þriding, ad. ON. *þriðjung-r* 'thirding', third part. The form *thrithing* was still known to the 17th c. legal writers; but *trithing* is also found in early times, and in modern legal and historical works. The form *þriding or *thriding lost its initial after *east, west,* and *north*, as in 13th c. *Northredyng*, now *North Riding*.]

**1.** = RIDING *sb.* Now only *Hist.* Also in *comb.* **Trithing-reeve** = *trithinger*: see below.

[*a* 1150 *Law Edw. Conf.* c. 31 Erant etiam alie potestates super wapentagiis, quas trehingas uocabant, scilicet super terciam partem prouincie. Et qui super ipsam dominabantur, uocabantur þrehingrefes [*v. r.* trehingreues], ad quos deferebantur cause que non poterant diffiniri in wapentagiis.] *c* 1290 FLETA II. lxi. § 23 Sciendum [est] quod aliæ potestates erant super wapentakia, quæ tritinga dicebantur, eo quod erat tertia pars provinciæ; qui vero super eos dominabantur, trithingreves vocabantur, quibus differebantur causæ quæ non wapentakiis poterint diffiniri in Schiram. 1295–6 Trithing [see RIDING *sb.* 1]. 1313–14 *Eyre of Kent* (1910) I. 32 De wapentagiis & Trithingis positis ad firmam. 1333 *York Memo. Bk.* (Surtees) I. 144 Artificiariorum in tribus trithingis infra comitatum Ebor. 1593 NORDEN *Spec. Brit., M'sex* I. 7 Yorkeshire..is diuided into Rydings, which may be also called ðriþingas, all which parts conteine in them certain hundreds in euerie of which was conteined ten teoþunges, of us called Tithings, conteining ten men, whereof it was also called tienmentale, a colledge or corporation of ten men. 1701 *Cowell's Interpr.*, *Thrithing-Reve*, the third part of a County, or three or more Hundreds or Wapentachs, were called a *Triding* or *Trithing*; such sort of Portions are the Laths in Kent, the Rapes in Sussex, and the Ridings in Yorkshire. And those who govern'd these Trithings, were thereupon called *Trithing-Reves*, before whom were brought all Causes that could not be determined in the Wapentakes, or Hundreds. 1747 CARTE *Hist. Eng.* I. 309 Some mention another subdivision of counties into three portions called thence *trithings* (corruptly ridings). 1765 BLACKSTONE *Comm.* I. Introd. iv. 116 Where a county is divided into three of these intermediate jurisdictions, they are called trithings, which were antiently governed by a trithing-reeve. 1874 STUBBS *Const. Hist.* I. v. 100 *note*, In the trithing he sees the threefold division of the land allotted to the Norse odallers.

**2.** Division into three parts, tripartition. *rare*[−1].

1879 HAIGH in *Yorks. Arch. Jrnl.* V. 205 The distinct trithing of two of the divisions [in a dial] is evidence of knowledge of the complete Hindu system.

Hence †**Tri·thinger, thri·thinger**, the governor of a trithing.

1314–15 *Rolls of Parlt.* I. 291/2 Viscountes, Thrythyngers, & autres Baillifs [de Counte de Nicole].

**Trithio-** (trəiþəiˌo). *Chem.* [f. TRI- 5 + THIO-.] Prefix denoting that three atoms of sulphur have been substituted for three atoms of oxygen in the substance designated by the rest of the name; e. g. *trithiocarbonic acid*, $H_2CS_3$, derived from carbonic acid, $H_2CO_3$; *trithiocarbonate*, a salt of this acid. In many cases, however, *tri-* refers to the whole substance and not to the sulphur alone; e. g. *trithio-acetaldehyde*, $(CH_3CHS)_3$, a compound of three molecules of thio-acetaldehyde, $CH_3CHS$.

1894 MUIR & MORLEY *Watts' Dict. Chem.* IV. 692 Tri-Thio-Citric Ether $C_3H_5O(CO.SEt)_3$.. Oil, smelling like mercaptan. 1899 SMITH *Richter's Org. Chem.* (ed. 3) I. 203 Trithio-formaldehyde $(CH_2S)_3$, melts at 216°. 1910 WALKER & MOTT *Holleman's Org. Chem.* (ed. 3) 348 Carbon disulphide..With alkali-metal or alkaline-earth-metal sulphides it yields trithiocarbonates.

**Trithionic** (trəiþəiˌǫ·nik), *a. Chem.* [f. TRI- 5 + Gr. θεῖον sulphur + -IC.] In *trithionic acid*, $H_2S_3O_6$, an acid containing three atoms of sulphur in the molecule, discovered by Langlois in 1842 (*Ann. Chim. Phys.* IV. 77), known only in aqueous solution, which is inodorous, sour, and bitter, and in its salts, the **Trithi·onates.**

1844 *Chem. Gaz.* II. 66 Berzelius..separates the acids of sulphur into monothionic acids (sulphuric and sulphurous acids), dithionic acids..trithionic acid (Langlois' sulphated hyposulphuric acid). 1848 *Ibid.* VI. 369 Trithionic Acid is obtained dissolved in water when the solution of the trithionate of potash is decomposed with the fluosilicate of potash. 1913 THORPE *Dict. Appl. Chem.* (ed. 2) V. 308 Trithionic acid..on attempting to concentrate [the solution], even *in vacuo*, it decomposes into sulphur, sulphur dioxide, and sulphuric acid.

**Tritical** (tri·tikăl), *a.* [f. TRITE *a.*, with play on *critical*.] Of a trite or commonplace character.

1709 SWIFT (*title*) A Tritical Essay upon the faculties of the mind. 1762 [see TRITICALLY]. 1841 D'ISRAELI *Amen. Lit.* (1867) 285 To sermonise with a tedious homily or a tritical declamation. 1869 *Contemp. Rev.* X. 125 To have every book of the Bible dealt with..with the same tendency to 'tritical' reflections.

Hence **Tritica·lity, Tri·tically** *adv.*, **Tri·ticalness**; so **Tri·ticism** (after *criticism*; cf. also *witticism*).

1835 CARLYLE in *Corr. Carlyle & Emerson* 13 May (1883) I. 71 Our Ex-Chancellor has been promulgating *triticalities ..against the Aristocracy. 1762 STERNE *Tr. Shandy* VI. xi, 'Tis all tritical, and most *tritically put together. *c* 1714 POPE, etc. *Mem. M. Scriblerus* vii, A *Triticalness or Mediocrity in the Thought. 1824 SCOTT *Redgauntlet* Let. xii, Weary, flat, and stale *triticism.

†**Triti·cean**, *a. Obs. rare*[−0]. [f. L. *trītice-us* wheaten (f. *trīticum* wheat) + -AN.] (See quot.)

1656 BLOUNT *Glossogr.*, *Triticean* (*triticeus*), wheaten, of wheat. 1658 in PHILLIPS.

**Triticeous** (triti·ʃəs, -iəs), *a.* [f. as prec. + -OUS.] Resembling a grain of wheat. *Triticeous cartilage* or *nodule* (mod.L. *cartilago triticea*), *Anat.*, each of two small cartilaginous nodules one on each side of the larynx.

[1890 BILLINGS *Med. Dict.* s.v. *Cartilago*, *C[artilago] triticea*, a small cartilaginous nodule found in lateral thyrohyoid ligament on each side.] 1891 *Cent. Dict.* s.v., Triticeous nodule. *Ibid.*, *Triticeus*, the triticeous cartilage of the larynx.

**Triticin** (tri·tisin). *Chem.* [f. L. *trītic-um* wheat (in mod.Bot.L. a generic name, including couch-grass) + -IN [1].]

†**1.** Name given to the gluten of wheat by Hermbstaedt (*Erdmann's Jrnl. Techn. Chem.* (1831) XII. 11); also applied to a substance obtained from potato starch (see quot. 1838). *Obs.*

1838 T. THOMSON *Chem. Org. Bodies* 652 [In preparing amidin, or the soluble part of starch from potato starch] The triticin is retained by the cloth. 1860 MAYNE *Expos. L.*, *Triticin*, term by Hermbstædt for the gluten of wheat.

**2.** A carbohydrate, $C_{12}H_{22}O_{11}$ or $(C_6H_{10}O_5)_n$, obtained from the roots of couch-grass, *Triticum repens*, and so named by Müller (*Arch. Pharm.* (1873) II. 508); it is a tasteless hygroscopic powder, very soluble in water, and lævorotatory; when boiled with dilute acids it changes into lævulose.

1874 *Jrnl. Chem. Soc.* XXVII. 171 The quantity of triticin present in the dried roots of couch-grass varies from 3·5 to 7·8 per cent. 1888 *Ibid.* LIV. 246 From *Dracaena australis* the author has obtained a carbohydrate, 6 $C_6H_{10}O_5 + H_2O$, which very closely resembles triticin. 1890 *Ibid.* LVIII. 227 Triticin..from the root of *Dracaena rubra*, melts at 140°..Triticin, from *Triticum repens*, melts at 160°.

**Triticoid** (tri·tikoid), *a. Bot.* [f. as prec. + -OID.] Resembling the wheat-plant.

1858 *Jrnl. R. Agric. Soc.* XIX. I. 103 Henslow has also found a triticoid form of *Ægilops squarrosa*.

**Tritish** (trəi·tiʃ), *a. rare*[−1]. [f. TRITE *a.* + -ISH [1].] Somewhat trite. So **Tritism** (trəi·tiz'm), trite or commonplace character.

1779 T. TWINING in *Recreat. & Stud.* (1882) 60 The notes.. seem now and then to be tritish. 1785 *Rolliad* (1812) 137 A solid truth in the observation of Horace which its tritism does not destroy.

**Trito-** (tritǫ, trəitǫ), before a vowel **trit-**, combining form repr. Gr. τρίτος third, occurring in several technical, mostly scientific, terms (usually corresponding to terms in PROTO-, and DEUTERO- or DEUTO-). **1.** Generally.

‖ **Tritencephalon** (-ense·fălǫn) [mod.L., f. Gr. ἐγκέφαλος brain], the third of the three primary cerebral vesicles of the embryo; also, the hindmost segment of the brain of an insect. **Tri·tocere** (-sĭᵊɹ) [Gr. κέρας horn], that tine of a deer's antler which is third in order of development (*Cent. Dict.* 1891). ‖ **Tritocerebrum** (-se·rĭbrǫm), *erron.* -on [mod.L., f. L. *cerebrum* brain], = *tritencephalon*; hence **Tritoce·rebral** *a.*, pertaining to or constituting a tritocerebrum. **Tri·tocone**, the posterior external cusp of a premolar tooth. **Tri·to-Isai·ah** [after DEUTERO-*Isaiah*], a later author to whom a third section of the book of Isaiah is attributed by some critics. **Tritome·sal** *a.* [Gr. μέσος middle], applied to a series of cells in the wings of hymenopterous insects, now usually called the submedian second discoidal and first apical cells. **Trito·to·xin**: see quot. 1904 s.v. *prototoxin* (PROTO- 2 b). **Tritove·rtebra**, in Carus's nomenclature (1828), applied to the bones of the limbs reckoned as the third set of vertebræ; hence **Tritove·rtebral** *a.*, pertaining to or of the nature of a tritovertebra. **Trito·vum**, a third stage of an ovum, succeeding the deutovum. **Tritozooid** (-zōᵘ·oid), a tertiary zooid, produced from a deuterozooid.

1910 *Encycl. Brit.* XIII. 425/2 This anterior or 'brain' mass consists of three lobes (the prot-, deut-, and *tritencephalon of Viallanes). *Ibid.* 418/2 An 'intercalary' or *tritocerebral segment has been demonstrated..in various insect embryos. 1898 PACKARD *Text-bk. Entom.* 231 Viallanes first..divided the brain of adult insects into three regions or segments; i. e. the 'protocerebron', 'deutocerebron', and '*tritocerebron'. *Ibid.* 237 The œsophageal lobes (Tritocerebrum). 1896 *Proc. Zool. Soc.* 5 May 563 (*Premolars*) The antero-external cusp (protocone of Scott) ..develops first, the antero-internal or deuterocone second, and the tetartocone third, the *tritocone being wanting. 1908 *Athenæum* 7 Nov. 565/2 A *Trito-Isaiah besides a Deutero-Isaiah. 1826 KIRBY & SP. *Entomol.* III. xxxv. 632 The medial areolets..form three distinct series; these may be called the protomesal, deuteromesal, and *tritomesal. *c* 1860 S. KNEELAND, JR. in *Amer. Cycl.* XIII. 424 (Cent. Dict.) [Carus] makes what he calls proto-, deuto-, and *trito-vertebræ. 1902 *Cassell's Encycl. Dict., Supp.*, *Tritovertebral. 1877 HUXLEY *Anat. Inv. Anim.* vii. 385 In the Acarus of the Mouse, Claparède observed that the deutovum stage is followed by a *tritovum. 1861 J. R. GREENE *Man. Anim. Kingd., Cœlent.* 74 The medusoids budded by *Sarsia* are, probably, *tritozoöids.

†**2.** In *Chemistry*, formerly used, after T. Thomson (*Syst. Chem.* (1804) I. 103), in naming the third oxide, sulphuret, iodide, etc. in a series in ascending order (cf. PROTO- 3 a, DEUTO- 1). *Obs.*

1806–1850 [see TRITOXIDE]. 1825 T. THOMSON *First Princ. Chem.* II. 481 Tritosulphuret of potassium.

‖ **Tritoma** (tri·tǫmă, *incorrectly* trəitōᵘ·mă). *Bot.* [mod.L., f. Gr. τρίτομος thrice-cut, f. τρι- three + -τομος cut; from the capsule splitting into three valves.] A genus of liliaceous plants (also called *Kniphofia*), natives of South Africa, with spikes of scarlet or yellow flowers; several species in cultivation are popularly called *flame-flower* or *red-hot poker*.

1882 *Garden* 13 May 325/2 Tritomas..produce a grand effect in autumn. 1900 *Blackw. Mag.* Apr. 574/2 The tritomas, blazing up red-hot.

**Triton** (trəi·tǫn). Also 6–7 **tryton.** [a. L. *Trītōn*, Gr. Τρίτων, in sense 1.]

**1.** *Gr.* and *Rom. Myth.* Proper name of a sea-deity, son of Poseidon and Amphitrite, or of Neptune and Salacia, or otherwise of Nereus; also, one of a race of inferior sea-deities, or imaginary sea-monsters, of semi-human form.

1584 R. SCOT *Discov. Witchcr.* VII. xv. (1886) 122 They have so fraied us with bull beggers, spirits, witches,..tritons, centaurs, dwarfes, giants, imps [etc.]. 1593 PEELE *Order of Garter* Wks. (Rtldg.) 585/2 A trump more shrill than Triton's is at sea. 1656 BLOUNT *Glossogr.*, *Triton*, a god of the sea, also a weathercock. 1661 J. CHILDREY *Brit. Baconica* 102 A Triton or Man-fish was taken on the shore of Portugal. *a* 1764 LLOYD *Chit-Chat* Poet. Wks. 1774 I. 193 Tritons which in the ocean dwell, And only rise to blow their shell. 1806 WORDSW. *Sonnet 'The world is too much with us'*, So might I..hear old Triton blow his wreathèd horn. 1887 BOWEN *Virg. Æneid* v. 824 Tritons swift on the deep with the hosts of Phorcus parade.

*attrib.* 1801 ELIZ. SCOT *Alonzo & Cora* 146 He prays the Triton-train To still the blustring winds, and smooth the main.

**b.** A figure of a Triton in painting, sculpture, etc.; in *Her.* represented as a bearded man with the hind quarters of a fish, and usually holding a trident and a shell-trumpet (cf. MERMAN).

1601 HOLLAND *Pliny* IX. V. I. 236 A certain sea goblin, called Triton, sounding a shell like a Trumpet or Cornet:..in forme and shape like those that are commonly painted for Tritons. 1722 RICHARDSON *Statues, &c. Italy* 116 Upon the Decks of the Ships there are Tritons. 1849 CLOUGH *Amours de Voy.* III. ii, It looked at me there from the face of a Triton in marble.

**c.** *fig.* and *allusively*: esp. applied to a seaman, waterman, or person connected in some way with the sea; in quot. 1900 to a large ship. *Triton of* or *among the minnows* (and similar phrases): see MINNOW 1 b.

1589 NASHE *Anat. Absurd.* Epistle, My tongue is too to base a Tryton to eternise her praise. 1607 [see MINNOW 1 b]. 1638 SIR T. HERBERT *Trav.* (ed. 2) 12 Neptune sweld with rage in such impatience, that the Tritons (Marriners) grew agast. *a* 1704 T. BROWN *Walk round Lond., Thames* Wks. 1709 III. III. 57 From their Lowzy Benches up started such a noizy multitude of old grizly Tritons. 1817 COLERIDGE *Lay Serm.* 387 The wretched ambition of figuring as the triton of the minnows. 1900 *Q. Rev.* Jan. 80 These vessels [Atlantic liners] are the Tritons of the Sea. 1908 *Nation* 26 Dec. 497/2 On his own side he is a Triton among the minnows.

**2.** *Zool.* **a.** A genus of marine gastropods with trumpet-shaped shells; an animal, or shell, of this genus or of the family *Tritonidæ*. Also called *Triton's shell.*

1777 PENNANT *Zool.* IV. 61 Lepas. Acorn. Its animal the Triton. The shell multivalve. 1835 KIRBY *Hab. & Inst. Anim.* I. ix. 297 Others which live by prey, as the strombs, the helmet-shells, and the tritons. 1842 *Penny Cycl.* XXII. 53/2 *Triton variegatus*, the marine trumpet or Triton's shell. 1861 P. P. CARPENTER in *Rep. Smithsonian Instit.* 1860, 185 The *Personæ*, or Mask-shells, are Tritons with a broad thin inner lip and curiously twisted mouth.

**b.** An extensive genus (now divided) of newts; an animal of this genus or group.

1839 *Encycl. Brit.* (ed. 7) XIX. 160/2 Genus Triton, *Laur.* Aquatic salamanders...Commonly called newts...The crested triton...The spotted triton. 1861 HULME tr. *Moquin-Tandon* II. v. ii. 288 Triton, or Aquatic Salamander. 1909 *Contemp. Rev.* Apr. 446 The lost leg of a lizard, or the amputated leg of a triton, can be readily regenerated.

Hence (*nonce-wds.*) **Tri·toness**, a female Triton; **Trito·nic** *a.*, of or pertaining to a Triton or Tritons; **Tri·tonize** *v., intr.* to play the Triton (see 1 c above); **Tri·tonly** *adv.*, like or in the manner of a Triton.

1614 GORGES *Lucan* IX. 377 To her selfe the name she chose Of *Trytonesse. 1836 *Foreign Q. Rev.* XVII. 161 To conjure up fairy scenes and *tritonic festivals. 1841 *Blackw. Mag.* XLIX. 486 There alone is that petty vanity of *tritonizing among the minnows properly rebuked. 1599 NASHE *Lenten Stuffe* Wks. (Grosart) V. 229 Mercuriall..hath..noysed the name of our Ilande and of Yarmouth so *Tritonly. 1888 G. MEREDITH *Hard Weather* 16 Is the land ship? we are rolled, we drive Tritonly.

**Tritone** (trəi·tōun). *Mus.* [ad. med.L. *tritonus*, ad. Gr. τρίτονος, f. τρι-, TRI- + τόνος TONE.] An interval consisting of three whole tones; an augmented fourth. (Also formerly in Latin form.)

1609 DOULAND *Ornith. Microl.* 20 A Tritone doth exceed the Consonance of a Diatessaron. 1730 *Treat. Harmony* 7 The Leaps of the False Relations, viz. of a Tritonus, and of a Semidiapente are..forbidden. 1775 STEELE in *Phil. Trans.* LXV. 76 Tritones, or sharp fourths, above the upper minims. 1789 BURNEY *Hist. Mus.* (ed. 2) III. vii. 344 The Tritonus..consisting of three tones, without the intervention of a semitone, is extremely difficult to sing. 1854 *Cherubini's Counterpoint* 11 It now remains to be demonstrated how and why the Tritone is a false relation in harmony.

**Tritonioid** (trəitōu·niˌoid), *a. Zool.* [f. mod.L. *Tritonia*, generic name + -OID.] Resembling or allied to the genus *Tritonia*, belonging to the family *Tritoniidæ* of opisthobranchiate gastropods.

1891 in *Cent. Dict.*

**Tritonoid** (trəi·tŏnoid), *a. Zool.* [f. mod.L. *Triton*, generic name + -OID.] Resembling or allied to the genus *Triton* (TRITON 2 a); belonging to the family *Tritonidæ* of tænioglossate gastropods. 1891 in *Cent. Dict.*

**Tritonous** (trəi·tŏnəs), *a. rare*—1. [f. TRI- + Gr. τόν-ος TONE + -OUS; cf. *monotonous*.] Consisting of three tones or notes.

1847 GOSSE *Birds Jamaica* 194 The Flycatcher..is pertinacious in its tritonous call.

**Tritor** (trəi·tǭɹ). *Zool.* [a. L. *trītor* a rubber, grinder, f. *terĕre, trīt-* to rub, grind.] A specially hard and white ridge or prominence on the teeth of some fishes, as those of the genus *Chimæra*.

1889 NICHOLSON & LYDEKKER *Palæont.* xlviii. 950 One or more triturating ridges, or prominences, differing in appearance from the rest of the tooth, which may be conveniently termed tritors. 1897 PARKER & HASWELL *Zool.* II. 178 Each..tooth has its surface slightly raised into a rounded elevation.., known as a tritor.

† **Tri·tory.** *Obs. rare.* [ad. med.L. *trītōri-um*, f. L. *trīt-*, ppl. stem of *terĕre* to rub, thresh: see -ORY 1. Cf. *Ælfric's Vocab.* (Wr.-Wülcker 107/2), '*Trītōrium*, þerscel', THRESHEL, a threshing-instrument, a flail, which separates the grain from the straw and chaff.] A vessel for separating liquids of different densities.

1660 tr. *Paracelsus' Archidoxis* I. x. 143 The Pure [Spirit] will Swim at top, Separate it by a Tritory, or Separating Glass. [1693 tr. *Blancard's Phys. Dict.* (ed. 2), *Tritorium*, the same with *Infundibulum*. 1758 *Elaboratory laid Open* Introd. 30 *Tritoriums*, or separating funnels. 1860 MAYNE *Expos. Lex.*, *Tritorium*, term for a mortar; also a glass for separating oil from water in distillation; formerly used the same as *Infundibulum*, according to Ruland and Johnson, and Paracelsus.]

† **Tritoxide** (trəit-, tritǫ·ksəid). *Chem. Obs.* [f. TRIT(O- + OXIDE.] The third of the series of oxides of a metal or radical, containing the next higher proportion of oxygen to the *deutoxide*. (Now expressed by *trioxide* or other term indicating the actual proportion: cf. PROTOXIDE, DEUTOXIDE.) Sometimes improperly used to denote a compound containing three proportions of oxygen (= TRIOXIDE).

1806 *G. Adams' Nat. & Exp. Philos.* I. App. 538 Minium, the tritoxide of lead. 1812 SIR H. DAVY *Chem. Philos.* 369 The dark brown oxide [of manganese]..must be a tritoxide or an oxide containing three proportions of oxygene. 1850 DAUBENY *Atom. The.* xi. (ed. 2) 371 In certain states of disease, a peculiar compound, called by Mulder the tritoxide of proteine, makes its appearance.

† **Tri·trace.** *Obs. Cant.* [app. f. TRY *v.* + TRACE *v.*, with allusion to *trey-trace* (TREY *sb.* 3).] In *troll hazard of tritrace*, name of an 'order of knaves': see TROLL *v.* 15 b.

† **Tri·ttle.** *Obs.* Also 6 **tryttle.** [Phonetic variant of TRATTLE *sb.*2] A pellet of sheep's or goat's dung: = TRATTLE *sb.*2, TREDDLE.

1526 *Grete Herball* ccxxx. (1529) N iv b, Gottes tryttles or tordes. 1624 GEE *Foot out of Snare* 35 To gild-ouer and make acceptable any Pils, though being nothing else but sheeps trittles.

**Trittle-trattle,** *int.* and *sb. Sc. rare.* In 6 **trittyll trattyll, -ill, -il.** [Reduplication of TRATTLE *sb.*1, idle talk. Cf. TITTLE-TATTLE.]

**A.** *int.* An exclamation expressing contempt.

1529 LYNDESAY *Complaynt* 245 Now trittyll, trattyll, trolylow,..thow dois bot mow. 1535 — *Satyre* 4366 *Dil.* Better bring hir to the Leitches heir. *Fol.* Trittill trattill! Scho may nocht steir.

**B.** *sb.* (in *pl.*) **a.** Foolish or idle talk; nonsense. **b.** Trifles, gewgaws, knick-knacks.

1563 WINȜET *Wks.* (S.T.S.) II. 82/15 That thow be nocht temerouslie sclanderit..be euery wane manis trittil trattilis. 1896 CROCKETT *Grey Man* ii. 13 At the fair..buying of trittle-trattles at the lucky-booths.

**Trit-trot.** [Reduplication of TROT.] A word imitating the sound of trotting.

*c* 1840 *Maypole Song*, All round the maypole, trit-trit trot, Our fine maypole shall never be forgot. 1912 COUCH *Poison Island* xii. 75 There come wafted to our ears..the trit-trot of hoofs approaching.

**Trituberculate** (trəitiubə̄·ɹkiŭlět), *a. Comp. Anat.* [f. TRI- + L. *tūbercul-um* tubercle + -ATE 2.] Having three tubercles, as a tooth; relating to or characterized by such teeth. Also **Tritube·rcular** *a.* So **Tritube·rculism, Tritube·rculy,** the condition of being tritubercular, or the presence of tritubercular teeth; **Tritube·rculist,** one who holds that the molar teeth of mammals are modifications of tritubercular teeth.

1883 COPE in *Proc. Amer. Philos. Soc.* (1884) 324 The type of superior molar tooth..was triangular or *tritubercular. 1890 *Nature* 20 Mar. 466/2 The tritubercular molar consists of three cusps, cones, or tubercles, arranged in a triangle, and so disposed that those of the upper jaw alternate with those of the lower. 1835-6 *Todd's Cycl. Anat.* I. 563/1 Molars..with *tri-tuberculate transverse ridges. 1902 *Sat. Rev.* 6 Dec. 711/2 The..fossil Theromorpha with multituberculate teeth,..those with trituberculate teeth. 1890 *Nature* 20 Mar. 466/2 It appears probable..that '*trituberculism', as this type of tooth-structure may be conveniently termed, was developed from a simple cone-like tooth during the Mesozoic period. 1891 FLOWER & LYDEKKER *Mammals* ii. 32 We also find trituberculism differentiating into a secodont and a bunodont series. 1896 *Proc. Zool. Soc.* 5 May 590 There is no evidence to show that this type of upper molar arose in the way suggested by *trituberculists. 1888 H. F. OSBORN in *Amer. Nat.* 1068 The almost universal predominance of *trituberculy in the early geological periods. 1902 *Sat. Rev.* 6 Dec. 711/2 Mr. Beddard..gives..the rival theories of trituberculy and multituberculy.

**Triturable** (tri·tiŭrăb'l), *a. rare*—1. [= F. *triturable* (16th c. in Godef. *Compl.*), f. *triturer* or late L. *trītūrāre* to TRITURATE: see -ABLE.] Capable of being triturated.

1646 SIR T. BROWNE *Pseud. Ep.* II. i. 53 Crystall..is..triturable, and reduceable into powder, by contrition.

**Tritural** (tri·tiŭrăl), *a. rare*—1. [f. L. *trītūra* TRITURE + -AL.] Adapted for trituration.

1901 *Proc. Zool. Soc.* 5 Mar 172 The armoured Chelonian..The roof of the mouth between this tritural border is raised into a dome with the concavity downwards.

**Triturate** (tri·tiŭreˈt), *v.* [f. late L. *trītūrāt-*, ppl. stem of *trītūrāre* to thresh, f. L. *trītūra* TRITURE. Cf. F. *triturer* (16th c.).] *trans.* To reduce to fine particles or powder by rubbing, bruising, pounding, crushing, or grinding; to comminute, pulverize; also, to mix (solids, or a solid and a liquid) in this way. **a.** *Pharm., Geol.*, etc.

[1623 COCKERAM II, *To thresh corne*, triturate.] 1755 JOHNSON, *Triturable*..(from triturate). 1771 T. PERCIVAL *Ess.* (1777) I. 60 The mixture was well triturated in a marble mortar. 1796 KIRWAN *Elem. Min.* (ed. 2) II. 224 Sometimes brittle, sometimes tough according to the proportion of Mercury principally when triturated. 1826 HENRY *Elem. Chem.* II. 99 Triturate in a mortar, and put the mixture..into a phial. 1862 DANA *Man. Geol.* § 51. 49 Rock made from shells..triturated into a calcareous earth by the sea.

**b.** *Phys.* said of the action of the molar teeth, the gizzard, etc. upon the food.

1822 [see *triturating* below]. 1835-6 *Todd's Cycl. Anat.* I. 311/1 It [the food] is triturated..by the mandibles certainly [in Parrots]. 1851 CARPENTER *Man. Phys.* (ed. 2) 269 By the act of mastication..the food is triturated and mingled with the salivary secretion. 1881 DARWIN *Veg. Mould* 18 Worms swallow many little stones,..it is probable that they serve, like mill-stones, to triturate their food.

**c.** *fig.*

1848 LANDOR *Imag. Conv.* Ser. v. *Thiers & Lamartine*, At first we were tickled, at last we were triturated. 1881 *Scribner's Mag.* Aug. 542 The raw ingredients of our national admixture are supplied quite as rapidly as the whirl and stir of the popular system can triturate and commingle them.

Hence **Tri·turated, Tri·turating** *ppl. adjs.*

1777 COOK *Voy. Pacific* II. viii. (1784) I. 331 Where the shore is low, the soil is commonly sandy, or rather composed of *triturated coral. 1791 COWPER *Iliad* II. 508 The triturated barley grain First duly sprinkling. 1839 DARWIN *Voy. Nat.* xix. (1852) 439 Gorges..through which the whole vast amount of triturated matter must have been carried away. 1898 P. MANSON *Trop. Diseases* xxxv. 547 Three or four ten- to thirty-grain doses of well triturated thymol in cachets. 1822 J. PARKINSON *Outl. Oryctol.* 312 In this [fossil elephant's] tooth..there are only thirteen plates, nine ..of which are seen on the *triturating surface. 1835-6 *Todd's Cycl. Anat.* I. 318/2 The triturating action of the gizzard. 1860 MAURY *Phys. Geog. Sea* (Low) § 41 The abrading, triturating power of water.

**Trituration** (tritiŭrēˈ·ʃən). [ad. late L. *trītūrātiōn-em*, n. of action from *trītūrāre* to TRITURATE; cf. F. *trituration* (14th c. in Godef. *Compl.*).] The action or process of triturating; reduction to fine particles or powder by friction; comminution, pulverization. **a.** *Pharm., Geol.*, etc.

1646 SIR T. BROWNE *Pseud. Ep.* IV. vii. 197 A pumice-stone powdered is lighter then one entire,..for..abatement can hardly be avoyded in the Trituration. 1756 C. LUCAS *Ess. Waters* I. 46 Earths..are..reduced to the utmost tenuity by trituration or grinding. 1833 LYELL *Princ. Geol.* III. 2 Disputing..whether sand and pebbles were the result of aqueous trituration. 1872 YEATS *Techn. Hist. Comm.* 318 By the continual trituration of the runner, the ore is reduced and amalgamation effected.

**b.** *Phys.*: see TRITURATE *v.* b.

1731 BAILEY vol. II, *Trituration*, (in Physick) the action of the Stomach on the food. 1740 CHEYNE *Regimen* 73 Blood Globules, by their Rotundity, Volubility, and Elasticity, resist Trituration, that is, Digestion. 1802 PALEY *Nat. Theol.* xvi. (1817) 140 Without the trituration of the gizzard; a chicken would have starved upon a heap of corn.

**c.** *transf.* A mass produced, or medicine prepared, by trituration.

1890 BILLINGS *Med. Dict., Trituration*...2. A preparation directed by the U. S. P[harmacopœia]...*T. of elaterin*, elaterin 10, saccharum lactis 90; triturate (U. S. P.). 1898 P. MANSON *Trop. Diseases* viii. 153 He injected bouillon containing a trituration of one of these flies into a guinea-pig.

**d.** *fig.*

1832 I. TAYLOR *Saturday Even.* 344 The royal Image and Superscription by the trituration and corrosion it undergoes in the common world becomes continually less and less distinct. 1856 MERIVALE *Rom. Emp.* (1865) IV. xl. 528 Wealthy nobles..whose means were in process of trituration under the pressure of the imperial imposts. 1909 *Edin. Rev.* July 214 This trituration of the people has produced a multitude of dialects.

**Triturator** (tri·tiŭreˈtəɹ). [a. late L. *trītūrātor*, agent-n. from *trītūrāre* to TRITURATE.] One who or that which triturates; an instrument or apparatus for triturating, esp. for grinding drugs.

1864 *Reader* 17 Dec. 770/2 Hammers or triturators. 1893 E. A. BUTLER *Household Insects* 137 The gizzard..appears to act more as a strainer than as a triturator.

**Tri·turature.** *rare.* [f. late L. *trītūrāt-* (see TRITURATE) + -URE.] = TRITURATION.

1846 WORCESTER, *Triturature*, a wearing by rubbing or friction. *Smith.*

† **Triture** (tri·tiŭɹ), *sb. Obs.* [ad. L. *trītūra* a rubbing, a threshing, f. *trīt-*, ppl. stem of *terĕre* to rub; cf. F. *triture* (1610 in Hatz.-Darm.).]

**1.** Friction or galling (of a yoke). *rare*—1.

1607 J. CARPENTER *Plaine Mans Plough* 221 The oxe accustomed to the yoke or triture..dooth often..returne to the yoke againe.

**2.** Pounding or grinding; comminution; trituration.

1657 TOMLINSON *Renou's Disp.* 57 Humectation, Infection or Triture are wont to be reduced to Infusion. 1718 QUINCY *Compl. Disp.* 12 The continual Triture has the same Effects upon it, as repeated Sublimation. 1767 PERCIVAL in *Phil. Trans.* LVII. 226 The powder and the water were well incorporated by triture. 1790 WEDGWOOD *ibid.* LXXX. 308 To try whether this tedious process of solution could be expedited by triture or calcination, some of the mineral was rubbed in a mortar.

Hence † **Tri·ture** *v., Obs., trans.* to triturate.

1773 CLEGG in *Phil. Trans.* LXIV. 49 Four penny-weights of each of the astringents..were tritured in plain water.

† **Trityl** (trəi·til). *Chem. Obs.* [ad. F. *trityle* (Chancel, 1853), so called as being the third of the series of alcohol radicals of the form $C_nH_{2n+1}$: see TRITO- and -YL, and cf. TETRYL, PENTYL, HEXYL, etc.] The radical $C_3H_7$, now called PROPYL. Hence † **Tri·tylene** = PROPYLENE, † **Trity·lic** *a.* = PROPYLIC, etc.

1854 *Q. Jrnl. Chem. Soc.* VI. 287 Propionic Alcohol..to

which the author [Chancel] gives the name *Hydrate of Trityl*. **1856** FOWNES *Elem. Chem.* (ed. 6) 474 Trityl-alcohol, or hydrated oxide of trityl. We prefer the name propylic alcohol. **1857** MILLER *Elem. Chem.* III. 27 Tritylic or Propylic Alcohol $C_6H_8O_2$. *Ibid.* 28 Propylic (Tritylic) Ether.. $C_6H_7O$. *Ibid.* 190 *Tritylene, Propylene.* ..Reynolds obtained this gas mixed with marsh gas. **1868** WATTS *Dict. Chem.* V. 887 Trityl (better known as Propyl). *Ibid.* 888 One of the earliest .. recognitions of the trityl-group is to be found in Chancel's note..(1853), which describes a trityl-alcohol. *Ibid.* 891 Tritylamine, or Propylamine... Bright, colourless, highly refracting, very mobile liquid. *Ibid.* 892 Tritylene, or Propylene, $C_3H_6$.

**Tritylodontoid** (trəi:tilǫdǫ·ntoid), *a.* and *sb.* *Palæont.* [f. mod.L. *Tritylodon, -ont-* (f. Gr. τρι-, TRI- + τύλος knob + ὀδούς, ὀδοντ- tooth) + -OID.] **a.** *adj.* Resembling the genus *Tritylodon*, or belonging to the family *Tritylodontidæ*, of extinct monotreme mammals, found in the Triassic and Jurassic formations, and characterized by trituber-cular molar teeth. **b.** *sb.* A member of this family. In recent Dicts.

**Trium-fe·minate.** *nonce-wd.* [f. L. *trium*, gen. pl. of *trēs* three + *fēmina* female, woman + -ATE[1], after TRIUMVIRATE.] A group of three women associated in government.

**1873** M. COLLINS *Miranda* I. 75 These three formed a trium-feminate, and governed despotically that corner of the quarterdeck.

**Triumph** (trəi·ʊ̆mf), *sb.* Forms: 4–7 **triumphe, tryumphe,** (5 **treyumphe, trihumphe, triumphee,** 6 **triump, tryhumphe, tryoumffe,** *Sc.* **trywmph, trieumph, treumph(e, trewmph),** 6–7 **tryumph,** 6– **triumph.** [ME. a. OF. *triumphe* (12th c.), F. *triomphe*, = Prov. *triomfe*, Sp. *triunfo*, Pg. *triumpho*, It. *trionfo*, ad. L. *triumph-us* (older form *triumpus*); cf. Gr. θρίαμβος hymn to Bacchus.]

**1.** *Rom. Hist.* The entrance of a victorious commander with his army and spoils in solemn procession into Rome, permission for which was granted by the senate in honour of an important achievement in war. Also *transf.*

[*c* **893** K. ÆLFRED *Oros.* II. iv. § 2 Heora an consul..forsoc þone triumphan [L. *triumphum*], þe him mon ongean brohte.] *c* **1374** CHAUCER *Anel. & Arc.* 43 With his tryumphe and laurer corovned thus..Let I this noble prince Theseus Toward Athenes in his wey ryding. **1398** TREVISA *Barth. De P. R.* XVII. xlviii. (Tollem. MS.), The lauri tre is propirly halowed to triumphes, worschipe of victoures. *c* **1430** LYDG. *Min. Poems* (Percy Soc.) 25 Where is Julius, proudest in his empire, With his triumphes moost imperiall? **1593** SHAKS. *Rich. II*, III. iv. 99 What was I borne to this: that my sad looke, Should grace the Triumph of great Bullingbrooke? **1600** HOLLAND *Livy* III. lxiii. 131 This was the first time that ever any triumph was granted by the voices of the people, without the authoritie and assent of the Senatours. **1703** ROWE *Ulyss.* I. i, Where is the Triumph shall go forth to meet him? **1838–42** ARNOLD *Hist. Rome* III. xlvi. 321 Marcellus was anxious to obtain a triumph for his conquest of Syracuse.

†**b.** *transf.* in the 'philosopher's game'. *Obs.*

*c* **1600** *MS. Sloane 451* lf. 1 In it men fight and striue together by the art of comptynge.. whether may (the enimies kinge beinge taken) erect a triumphe in his aduersaries campe. *Ibid.* 1 b, You may make your triumphe, as well of your enimies men taken as of your owne vntaken. **1801** STRUTT *Sports & Past.* IV. ii. (1876) 415 It is..certain that the great object of each player is to take the king from his opponent, because he who succeeds may make his triumph and erect his trophy.

**2.** *transf.* The action or fact of triumphing; victory, conquest, or the glory of this; also, a signal success or achievement. Also *fig.*

*c* **1400** *Sowdone Bab.* 913 Of the treyumphe he bare the flour In dispite of Mahounde. *c* **1412** HOCCLEVE *De Reg. Princ.* 3213 He..hadde of folkes dethes suche pitee, That.. Al his tryumphe was to hym but peyne. **1548–9** (Mar.) *Bk. Com. Prayer, Visitation of Sick*, That thou mayest haue perfit victory and triumph against the deuil, sinne, and death. **1567** *Gude & Godlie B.* (S.T.S.) 59 For vs he sched his precious blude, With greit tryumph vpon the rude. **1632** LITHGOW *Trav.* III. 119 Like a naked table wherein nothing is painted: euen so is Thebes and her past tryumphs defac'd. **1735** POPE *Ep. Lady* 225 Wisdom's triumph is well-tim'd Retreat. *a* **1835** SIR D. SANDFORD *Rise & Progr. Lit.* (1847) 40 Of that airy and extravagant spirit,..the Attic comedy, in its first estate, was at once the triumph and the type. **1853** J. H. NEWMAN *Hist. Sk.* (1873) II. I. iv. 191 It was the triumph of civilization over brute force.

†**b.** *transf.* The subject of triumph. *Obs. rare.*

**1671** MILTON *Samson* 426 Our Foes Found soon occasion thereby to make thee Thir Captive, and thir triumph.

†**3.** Pomp, as of the procession described in 1; splendour; glory; magnificence.

**1494** FABYAN *Chron.* lxix. 47 After whiche victory .. the sayd Constantyne ..was receyued of the Senate with moost triumphe. **1560** ROLLAND *Seven Sages* 6 With all triumph hir funerall seruice Was dewlie done. **1671** MILTON *Samson* 1312 This day to Dagon is a solemn Feast, With Sacrifices, Triumph, Pomp, and Games. **1718** *Free-thinker* No. 68 ¶9 This Ceremony is not performed..with the usual Pomp and Triumph.

†**4.** A public festivity or joyful celebration; a spectacle or pageant; *esp.* a tournament. *Obs.*

**1502** ARNOLDE *Chron.* (1811) p. xli, At the same triumphe the Kinge made lvii Knightis. **1568** GRAFTON *Chron.* II. 682 When publique playes or open triumphes should be shewed, or set forth abrode in the stretes. **1593** SHAKS. *Rich. II*, v. ii. 52 What newes from Oxford? Hold those Iusts & Triumphs? **1630** *R. Johnson's Kingd. & Commw.* 200 Many Chambers full of Masking garments, and other abiliments for triumphs and pastimes both for Land and Water. **1660** F. BROOKE tr. *Le Blanc's Trav.* 276 The River Nile..advances moderately, not doing any dammage: and when it comes they make a generall triumph. *a* **1721** PRIOR *Ode on Coronation* iv, His Peoples blessings greater than his own, And he that gives the Triumph triumphs least. **1825** HONE *Every-day Bk.* I. 1446 The printed descriptions of these processions [Lord Mayor's show] are usually entitled 'Triumphs'. [**1903** *Edin. Rev.* Apr. 459 Every event in life was made a pretext for fêtes, processions, and 'triumphs'.]

**5.** The exultation of victory or success; elation; joy; rapturous delight.

**1582** N. LICHEFIELD tr. *Castanheda's Conq. E. Ind.* I. xxviii. 71 That the rest of the Fleete shoulde weye their Ankors, the which..they did begin with great diligence and triumph that the Marriners made. **1604** R. CAWDREY *Table Alph., Triumph*, great ioy outwardly shewed. **1667** MILTON *P. L.* VII. 180 Great triumph and rejoycing was in Heav'n When such was heard declar'd the Almightie's will. **1761** GRAY *Fatal Sisters* 54 Songs of joy and triumph sing! **1891** E. PEACOCK *N. Brendon* II. 57 There was triumph on his countenance.

**b.** *In triumph*, triumphant, rejoicing in victory or success; triumphantly. (Orig. *fig.* from 1.)

**1593** SHAKS. *3 Hen. VI*, III. iii. 18 Let thy dauntlesse minde still ride in triumph, Ouer all mischance. **1667** MILTON *P. L.* x. 537 To see In Triumph issuing forth thir glorious Chief. **1697** DRYDEN *Virg. Georg.* III. 15, I, first of Romans shall in Triumph come From conquer'd Greece, and bring her Trophies home. **1810** SCOTT *Lady of L.* II. xix, Hail to the chief who in triumph advances!

**c.** *To ride triumph*, to ride at full tilt. ? *Obs.*

**1761** STERNE *Tr. Shandy* IV. xvi, To have so many jarring elements breaking loose, and riding triumph in every corner of a gentleman's house.

†**6. a.** A trumpet blast of victory. **b.** *pl.* Shouts of triumph or exultation. *Obs.*

**1566** STAPLETON *Ret. Untr. Jewel* Epistle, It is to blowe the Triumphe before the Victory. **1602** MARSTON *Ant. & Mel.* I. Wks. 1856 I. 10 Hark how Piero's triumphs beat the ayre. **1704** J. TRAPP *Abra-Mule* v. i, The loud Triumphs of the shouting Soldiers.

†**7.** A triumphal arch. Also *transf. Obs. rare.*

**1644** EVELYN *Diary* 7 Nov., The people were now generally busye in erecting temporary triumphs and arches with statues and flattering inscriptions. **1656** EARL MONM. tr. *Boccalini's Advts. fr. Parnass.* I. lxxix. (1674) 107 Triumphs, Trophies, Statues, and such like things, which are so familiarly seen built in your Streets. **1658** *Hist. Christina Q. Swedland* 319 The triumphs or statues of Sugar with which they had adorned the table.

†**8.** *Cards.* **a.** = TRUMP *sb.*[2] 1. *Obs.*

*Terrestrial triumph* = TAROC, TAROT.

**1529** LATIMER *1st Serm. Card* in Foxe *A. & M.* (1563) 1300/2 The game that wee wyll playe at, shall bee called the triumphe... Lette therefore euery Christian manne and woman playe at these cardes, that they maye haue and obteyne the triumph; you must marke also that the triumphe muste apply to fetche home vnto hym all the other cardes, whatsoeuer sute they bee of. **1598** FLORIO, *Gérmini*,..a kinde of playing-cards which we call terrestriall triumphs. [**1606** SHAKS. *Ant. & Cl.* IV. xiv. 20 Shee..has Packt Cards with Cæsars, and false plaid my Glory Vnto an Enemies triumph.]

†**b.** An obsolete card-game; = TRUMP *sb.*[2] 1 b.

**1529** [see 8 a]. **1554** *Interlude Youth* C iv, At the cardes I can theche you to play, At the triump [*ed.* **1561** triumph], and one and thyrtye. **1594** CAREW *Huarte's Exam. Wits* viii. (1596) 112 Playing at Cent, and at Triumph. **1626** tr. *Boccalini's New-found Politicke* III. xiii. (*heading*), A Poetaster for playing at Cards, and deuising the Game called Triumph or Trump, is brought before Apollo.

**9.** *attrib.* and *Comb.*, as *triumph-bough, -day, -hour, -path, -robe, -salute, -song, -tear, -tune, -wise*; *triumph-decking* adj.; also †**triumph-church**, the Church triumphant; **triumph-gate**, the gate through which a triumphing general entered Rome; in quot. *transf.*

*a* **1637** B. JONSON *Sad Sheph.* I. ii, [Why should not] each of us cut down a *triumph-bough? *c* **1620** in Farr *S. P. Jas. I* (1847) 318 Shyne bright in the *Triumph Church, faire soule, That in the Militant has shyn'd so longe. **1593** SHAKS. *Rich. II*, v. ii. 66 For gay apparell against the *triumph day. **1827** POLLOK *Course T.* x. 109 Great triumph-day of God's Incarnate Son. **1646** SIR R. FANSHAW tr. *Guarino's Faithf. Sheph.* IV. iv. 165 Ye *triumph-decking Lawrell boughs, Empale my glorious and victorious brows. **1880** G. MEREDITH *Tragic Com.* (1881) 143 This handsome, undaunted, *triumph-flashing man. **1848** ELIZA COOK *Old Palace* i, Its *triumph-gates were flinging wide. **1892** R. F. TOWNDROW *Garden*, etc. 65 The elms are clad in *triumph-robes of gold. **1844** *Regul. & Ord. Army* 37 The forts and batteries from which *Triumph Salutes are usually fired. **1561** DAUS tr. *Bullinger on Apoc.* (1573) 154 b, The voyces of the glade and ioyfull sort, singing true and eternall *triumph-songes in heauen. *c* **1586** SIDNEY *Ps.* LXVI. i, All lands.. With *triumph tunes Gods honor sound. **1565** GOLDING *Ovid's Met.* IV. (1593) 95 In *triumph-wise accomplishing her hest.

**Triumph** (trəi·ʊ̆mf), *v.* Forms: see prec. sb. [a. OF. *triumpher* (13th c.), F. *triompher*, = Prov. *triomfar*, Sp. *triunfar*, Pg. *triumphar*, It. *trionfare*, ad. L. *triumphāre*, f. *triumphus* TRIUMPH.]

**1.** *intr.* To celebrate a Roman triumph.

**1530** PALSGR. 762/2, I tryumphe for a conquest or a victorye gotten... It was a marvaylouse syght to se the Romaynes tryumphe, whan they had the vyctorie of their ennemyes. **1607** SHAKS. *Cor.* II. i. 194 Would'st thou haue laugh'd, had I come Coffin'd home, That weep'st to see me triumph? *a* **1656** USSHER *Ann.* vi. (1658) 675 Upon the Ides of December, Q. Pedius Triumphed for Spain. **1764** GIBBON *Misc. Wks.* (1814) IV. 375 He triumphed for his victories over the great Mithridates. **1846** KEIGHTLEY *Notes Virg., Bucol.* x. 26 The custom of the Roman generals, when triumphing and attired as Jupiter, to have their faces tinged with *minium*.

**2.** To be victorious; to prevail; to gain the mastery. Const. *over*, † *against*, † *on*, † *of*, † *in*.

**1508** DUNBAR *Poems* vii. 2 Renownit, ryall, right reuerend and serene Lord, hie trywmphing in wirschip and valoure. *a* **1520** — *Poems* xxxvii. 39 He deit triumphand, he raiss and wan the feild. **1548–9** (Mar.) *Bk. Com. Prayer, Private Baptism*, To triumph againste hym [the devil], the worlde, and the fleshe. **1590** SPENSER *F. Q.* II. x. 56 [Bunduca]..Triumphed oft against her enemis; And yet, though overcome.., Shee triumphed on death. **1593** SHAKS. *Lucr.* 77 Those two armies that would let him go Rather then triumph in so false a foe. **1610** HOLLAND *Camden's Brit.* (1637) 39 Nations twice triumphed of. **1667** MILTON *P. L.* XII. 452 He shall ascend With victory, triumphing through the aire Over his foes and thine. *c* **1708** LADY M. W. MONTAGU *Lett., to Miss A. Wortley* 27 Aug. (1887) I. 37 Destiny triumphs over all your efforts. **1838** THIRLWALL *Greece* II. xvi. 342 After praying them to remember his good will, if the cause of Greece triumphed, he rode away.

†**b.** *trans.* To cause to triumph. *Obs. rare.*

*a* **1571** JEWEL *On Thess.* (1611) 143 God..hath triumphed the name of his Christ. **1582** N. T. (Rhem.) *2 Cor.* ii. 14 Thankes be to God, who alwaies triumpheth vs in Christ Iesus.

†**c.** To triumph over; to conquer. *Obs.*

**1603** B. JONSON *Sejanus* I. i, We, that,..were born Free, equal lords of the triumphed world, And knew no masters, but affections. **1626** MASSINGER *Rom. Actor* II. i, Two and thirty legions, that awe All nations of the triumphed world. **1667** MILTON *P. L.* x. 572 So oft they fell Into the same illusion, not as Man Whom they triumph'd once lapst.

†**3.** *intr.* To be in a state of pomp or magnificence. Cf. prec. 3. *Obs.*

**1483** CAXTON *Gold. Leg.* 388 b/2 Thou shalt tryumphe as a quene in my royame. **1538** STARKEY *England* I. iv. 131 Yongur bretherne go a beggyng, where as the eldur hath tryumphyd and lyuyd in plesure. **1553** *Respublica* v. v. 1472 Making these newe Ladies of hir werie, We shoulde thrihumphe & reigne. **1568** [see TRIUMPHING *vbl. sb.*].

**4.** 'To rejoice for victory'; to be elated at another's defeat, discomfiture, or the like; 'to insult upon an advantage gained' (J.); hence, to rejoice, exult, be elated or glad; to glory.

**1535** COVERDALE *Ps.* xii[i]. 2 How longe shal myne enemie triumphe ouer me? *Ibid.* xciii[i]. 3 How longe shal the vngodly tryumphe? **1565** JEWEL *Repl. Harding* (1611) 371 S. Paul triumphed of that thing that in the world was so deepely despised. **1572** tr. *Buchanan's Detection* Oj, Quhen rage..shall ragingly triumph vpon the goods and blude of poore subiectis. **1591** SHAKS. *1 Hen. VI*, I. vi. 8 France, triumph in thy glorious Prophetesse. **1594** — *Rich. III*, III. iv. 91 Triumphing at mine enemies. **1617** MORYSON *Itin.* I. 74 They..triumph of diuers Citizens borne heere. **1746** FRANCIS tr. *Hor., Sat.* II. iii. 48 Good sir, don't triumph in your own disease. **1825** SCOTT *Betrothed* viii, The laugh and the song..which triumphed by anticipation over their surrender.

*fig.* **1593** SHAKS. *Lucr.* 12 To praise the cleare vnmatched red and white, Which triumpht in that skie of his delight. *Ibid.* 1388 In great commaunders, Grace, and Maiestie You might behold triumphing in their faces. **1593** — *Rich. II*, III. ii. 77 The blood of twentie thousand men Did triumph in my face.

†**5.** *intr. Cards.* To trump. *Obs. rare.*

**1563** [see TRIUMPHING *ppl. a.*]. **1626** B. JONSON *Fortunate Isles* Wks. 650/1 The four knaves entertain'd for the guards Of the kings and the queens that triumph in the cards.

Hence **Tri·umphed** *ppl. a.*

**1603, 1626** [see sense 2 c].

**Triumphable** (trəi·ʊ̆mfăb'l), *a. rare.* [f. prec. + -ABLE.] That may be triumphed in or over.

**1768** *Woman of Honor* I. 157 No .. very triumphable success.

**Triumphal** (trəi,ʊ·mfăl), *a.* (*sb.*) [ad. L. *triumphālis*, f. *triumphus* TRIUMPH, or a. OF. *triumphal* (*trionfal*, 12th c. in Godef. *Compl.*), F. *triomphal*: see -AL.]

**1.** Of, pertaining to, or of the nature of a triumph; celebrating or commemorating a triumph or victory.

*Triumphal arch* (†*arc*), an arch (sometimes threefold) erected, first by the Roman emperors and also in modern times, in commemoration of a victory; also a temporary structure of this kind. *Triumphal chaplet, garland, wreath*, the laurel wreath worn by the victor at a Roman triumph. *Triumphal images*, the laurel-wreathed statues which a triumphing general might bequeath to his descendants. *Triumphal ornaments*, the insignia of triumphing generals, consuls, etc.; also, the privileges or distinctions bestowed on them.

**1430–40** LYDG. *Bochas* IV. i. (MS. Bodl. 263) 211/2 The tryumphal [crowns] maked wer of gold Offred in tryumphes to worthi Emperours. **1463** ASHBY *Prisoner's Refl.* 209 Thou may be in heuyn memyall Seruaunt thorough thy tryumphall victory By mekenes and werkes merytory. **1495** *Trevisa's Barth. De P. R.* XVII. xlviii. (W. de W.) P ij/2 The lauri tree..is properly halowed to triumphal worship of Conquerours. **1539** TONSTALL *Serm. Palm Sund.* (1823) 15 The crosse is now euery where amongest Christen men erected..as an arche triumphal ageinst the deuyll. **1542** UDALL *Erasm. Apoph.* 254 b, The garlande triumphal [was made] of golde. **1550** SIR T. HOBY *Trav.* (1902) 36 A verie bewtifull triumphall arke of the Emperor Nerva. **1591** SAVILE *Tacitus, Agricola* (1622) 200 That all the honours of triumphall ornaments, image triumphall,..should be awarded vnto him in Senat. **1601** HOLLAND *Pliny* XXII. iii. II. 115 The Chaplet Triumphall, which they ware who entred with triumph into Rome. **1681** *Lond. Gaz.* No. 1631/1 A Triumphal Arch was Erected near the first Gate. **1706** PHILLIPS (ed. Kersey), *Triumphal Crown*,.. a Crown at first made of Laurel, and afterwards of Gold, which the Cities usually sent to the Victorious General, to wear on the Day of his Triumphal Entry. **1776** GIBBON *Decl. & F.* xi. (1846) I. 323 The triumphal car of Aurelian ..was drawn.. either by four stags or by four elephants. **1835** T. MITCHELL *Acharn. Aristoph.* 1099 *note*, A triumphal ode in honour of Hercules. **1884** *Pall Mall G.* 28 Aug. 1/1 The Prime Minister has arrived at Midlothian after a triumphal progress.

†**2.** Victorious, triumphant. *Obs.*

**1513** DOUGLAS *Æneis* VIII. iv. 47 Wyth proud spulȝe arryving triumphall. **1618** BOLTON *Florus* (1636) 31 He returned home to his Oxen, a tryumphall husbandman.

**B.** *sb.* †**1.** An ode of triumph or victory; a pæan. *Obs. rare.*

**1589** PEELE *Eclogue* Wks. (Rtldg.) 561/2 Man, if triumphals here be in request, Then let them chant them that can chant them best. **1589** PUTTENHAM *Eng. Poesie* I. xxiii. (Arb.) 61 Our Triumphals written in honour of her Maiesties long peace.

†**2.** A token of triumph. *Obs. rare*⁻¹.

**1671** MILTON *P. R.* IV. 578 The Fiend..to his crew..brought Joyless triumphals of his hop't success, Ruin, and desperation, and dismay.

†**3.** A triumphal car or chariot. *Obs. rare*⁻¹.

**1633** SHIRLEY *Triumph Peace* Introd., The four triumphals, or magnificent chariots, in which were mounted the Grand Masquers.

†**4.** A triumphal celebration; a triumph. *Obs.*

**1592** SYLVESTER *Tri. Faith* i, A sacred Virgin's stately Triumphals. **1675** G. R. tr. *Le Grand's Man without Passion* 37 As he makes her to assist at her Triumphals, he will have her the constant companion of her Labours.

**Triumphancy** (trəi‚ʊ·mfănsi). [f. TRIUMPHANT: see -ANCY.] The state or quality of being triumphant.

**1592** WYRLEY *Armorie* 153 Which Hector like with great triumphancie Had conquerd kings through magnanimitie. **1652** SPARKE *Prim. Devot.* (1663) 287 His triumphancy,.. his translation from earth to heaven. **1701** BEVERLEY *Apoc. Quest.* 17 Constantines Victorious Triumphancy over Paganism. **1892** PATER *Wks.* (1901) VIII. 51 In all the triumphancy of his later days at Rome.

**Triumphand**, Sc. form of TRIUMPHING *ppl. a.*

**Triumphant** (trəi‚ʊ·mfănt), *a.* (*sb.*) [ad. L. *triumphānt-em*, pres. pple. of *triumphāre* to TRIUMPH, or a. F. †*triumphant*, *triomphant* (15th c.): see -ANT.]

**1.** Celebrating a triumph or victory; of, pertaining to, of the nature of, or befitting a triumph; triumphal. Now *rare.*

**1531** ELYOT *Gov.* III. xxi, They wold haue set his image in triumphant apparaile within the capitole. *a* **1548** HALL *Chron., Hen. VIII* 48 b, An arche triumphante, whiche shalbe made at the place where the iustes shalbe. **1591** SHAKS. 1 *Hen. VI*, I. i. 22 Like Captiues bound to a Triumphant Carre. **1651** H. L'ESTRANGE *Smectymnuomastix* 6 Let us..chant that triumphant Ode which..the Children of Israel sung upon the overthrow of the Egyptians in the red sea. **1719** DE FOE *Crusoe* (1840) I. xiv. 246 The triumphant feast..after a victory. **1876** FREEMAN *Hist. Sk.* 50 That long procession of triumphant virgins..bearing their gifts to their Lord on the knees of His Mother.

**2.** That has achieved victory or success; conquering; 'victorious; graced with conquest' (J.)

*Church Triumphant*: see CHURCH 4 b.

**1494** FABYAN *Chron.* 442 Kyng Edwarde.. gaue to the sayde Scottys batayll, and of them had tryumphaunte victorye. **1526** *Pilgr. Perf.* III. liv. (W. de W. 1531) 251 b, Let vs gyue praysynges to god for the chirche triumphant. **1575–85** ABP. SANDYS *Serm.* xiv. (Parker Soc.) 283 He is that triumphant prince, which hath most victoriously vanquished and thrown under foot our enemies. **1683** *Brit. Spec.* 134 Whilst in all other Provinces..Cruelty and Slaughter were Triumphant, the Christians here began to repair their demolished Churches. **1704** HEARNE *Duct. Hist.* (1714) I. 401 The Spartan State which became afterwards so Triumphant in Greece. **1819** BYRON *Mazeppa* I. i, The power and glory of the war..Had pass'd to the triumphant Czar. **1878** BROWNING *La Saisiaz* 267 There is no reconciling.. Goodness with triumphant evil.

†**b.** *transf.* Of or gained by conquest. *Obs. rare*⁻¹.

*c* **1600** SHAKS. *Sonn.* cli, My soule doth tell my body that he may Triumph in loue, flesh..doth point out thee As his triumphant prize.

†**3.** Splendid; glorious; magnificent; noble; notable. *Obs.*

**1494** in *Lett. Rich. III & Hen. VII* (Rolls) I. 394 A tryhumphant sight. **1568** GRAFTON *Chron.* II. 419 King Henrie maried Iane Duches of Briteyne..and with all triumphant pompe conueyed her through the Citie of London to Westminster. **1592** SHAKS. *Rom. & Jul.* V. iii. 83 Ile burie thee in a triumphant graue. **1606** — *Ant. & Cl.* II. ii. 190 She's a most triumphant Lady, if report be square to her. **1696** PHILLIPS (ed. 5), *Triumphant*, Victorious, Magnificent, Pompous, Superb.

**4.** Rejoicing or exulting for or as for victory; triumphing; exultant.

**1594** SHAKS. *Rich. III*, III. ii. 84 Thinke you, but that I know our state secure, I would be so triumphant as I am? **1604** R. CAWDREY *Table Alph.*, *Triumphant*, reioycing for the conquest. **1794** MRS. RADCLIFFE *Myst. Udolpho* xxxi, The cavaliero thought..he was to be called to no account, but was to go off triumphant. **1827** LYTTON *Pelham* lx, The papers..were filled with the most triumphant abuse and ridicule of the Whigs. **1907** *Verney Mem.* I. 206 The triumphant cries of an immense multitude.

†**B.** *sb.* [cf. obs. F. *triumphant* (Godef. *Compl.*).] One who triumphs; a victor, conqueror. *Obs.*

**1562** J. SHUTE *Cambini's Turk. Wars* 18 b, The number of the triumphantes was in maner infinite, thei had no desyre but to robbe. **1629** J. M. tr. *Fonseca's Devout Contempl.* 242 Saint Chrysostome reports of the Roman Triumphantes, That some entred Rome in Chariots drawne with pyde Horses. **1696** AUBREY *Misc.* (1721) 185 It hath been observed, That after Triumphs, the Triumphants have been sick in Spirit. **1812** SOUTHEY *Omniana* I. 227 Triumphant generals in Rome wore Rouge...Our fair ever-blushing triumphants have secured to themselves the charm of picturesque cheeks.

**Triumphantly** (trəi‚ʊ·mfăntli), *adv.* [f. prec. + -LY ².] In a triumphant manner; victoriously; exultantly; 'with insolent exultation' (J.); †magnificently.

*a* **1548** HALL *Chron., Hen. VIII* 194 He would be so triumphantly installed without makyng the kyng priuye. **1595** SHAKS. *John* II. i. 309 The dancing banners of the French, Who are at hand triumphantly displayed To enter Conquerors. **1675** TRAHERNE *Chr. Ethics* 438 A man, that sees and knows the glory of his high and heavenly estate, does all things triumphantly. **1791** BOSWELL *Johnson* 21 Mar. an. 1783, While he went on talking triumphantly, I was fixed in admiration. **1855** MACAULAY *Hist. Eng.* xv. III. 504 Walker's accusers..brought calumnious accusations which were triumphantly refuted.

†**Triumphate**, *a. Obs. rare*⁻¹. [ad. L. *triumphātus*, pa. pple. of *triumphāre* to TRIUMPH.] Triumphed over, conquered.

**1471** RIPLEY *Comp. Alch.* V. li. in Ashm. *Theatr. Chem. Brit.* (1652) 160 My doctryne therefore remember wyttyly, And passe forth toward the Syxth Gate, For thys the Fyfthe ys tryumphate.

**Triumphator** (trəi·ŏmfēⁱtǫɹ). [a. L. *triumphātor* one who triumphs, a conqueror, agent-n. f. *triumphāre* to TRIUMPH. Cf. OF. *triomphateur* (14th c.).] A conqueror; *spec.* a Roman general who was granted a triumph; hence *transf.*

**1611** SPEED *Hist. Gt. Brit.* IX. vi. § 61 The most noble King of England, and Triumphator of Ireland. **1876** T. S. EGAN tr. *Heine's Atta Troll* etc. 80 Vict'ry is at last decided, And the day, the triumphator Treads..On the necks of all the mountains.

So †**Triu·mphatrice**, *Obs. rare* [cf. F. *triomphatrice* (1769 in Littré)], a female who triumphs.

**1430–40** LYDG. *Bochas* IV. Prol. vi. (MS. Bodl. 263) 207/2 Dilligence, cheef triumphatrice Of slogardie, necligence & slouthe.

**Triumpher** (trəi·ŏmfəɹ). [f. TRIUMPH *v.* + -ER ¹.] One who triumphs.

**1.** One who celebrated a Roman triumph.

**1542** UDALL *Erasm. Apoph.* 305 Of whom [Cicero] Plinius ..saieth..[Thou] diddest as worthyly deserue to haue the garlande of a triumpher for thy toung, as euer had any other before for the swearde. **1661** MORGAN *Sph. Gentry* III. iv. 34 The Triumpher made his entrance in his Royall Chariot and was met by the Senators in their robes. **1737** L. CLARKE *Hist. Bible* (1740) I. IX. 609 On entering the capitol he did not, as other Triumphers used to do, put any of his captives to death.

**2.** A victor, conqueror.

**1540** COVERDALE *Fruitf. Less.* V. (1593) Oo j, The glorious triumpher ascending vp to heauen with great victorie. **1603** H. CROSSE *Vertues Commw.* (1878) 17 An Antidote against pride, and a valiant tryumpher ouer flaming desires. **1760** C. JOHNSTON *Chrysal* (1822) III. 313 A vain ambition of triumphing over the triumpher. **1848** W. H. KELLY tr. *L. Blanc's Hist. Ten Y.* I. Introd. 17 In that uninterrupted succession of calamities..what are all these famous triumphers,..all these haughty distributers of empires?

**Triumpherate, -ery**, obs. erron. ff. TRIUMVIRATE, TRIUMVIRY (by confusion with *triumph*).

**Triumphing** (trəi·ŏmfiŋ), *vbl. sb.* [f. TRIUMPH *v.* + -ING ¹.] The action of the verb TRIUMPH.

**1568** GRAFTON *Chron.* II. 255 There was great triumphyng and iustyng the space of .xv. dayes. **1623** in Foster *Eng. Factories Ind.* (1908) II. 240 In Goa ther hath bine great triumfinge and much rejoysinge att this newes. **1777** BRAND *Pop. Antiq.* App. 402 The antient Hoc-tide, an old Saxon Word, importing the Time of Scorning or Triumphing. *c* **1850** NEALE *Hymns East. Ch.* (1866) 144 Thou..Hast made them [heaven and earth] one by..Thy triumphing.

**Tri·umphing,** *ppl. a.* [f. as prec. + -ING ².] That triumphs, in various senses; triumphant.

**1500–20** DUNBAR *Poems* lxxxvi. 19 Tryumphand tempill of the Trinite. *Ibid.* lxxxvii. 9 O hye trivmphing peradiss of joy. **1563** FOXE *A. & M.* 1297/2 For yᵉ chief (as their triumphing card) he [Latimer] limited the hart. **1618** G. STRODE *Anat. Mortalitie* 214 The blessed and triumphing Church in heauen. **1660** *Charac. Italy* 6 Her streets..did shine with triumphing Cæsars and Consuls in their trophæal Chariots. **1721** DE FOE *Mem. Cavalier* II. 293 With a triumphing Enemy at our Heels. **1868** LYNCH *Rivulet* CXL. i, With adoring homage..And spirit triumphing.

Hence **Tri·umphingly** *adv.*, triumphantly (now *rare* or *Obs.*).

**1552** LYNDESAY *Monarche* 3937 He rose..On the thrid day, tryumphandlye. **1645** BP. HALL *Remedy Discontent* xvii. 97 The good soul..can triumphingly say, O Death, where is thy sting? **1680** C. NESSE *Church Hist.* 72 Free-grace..rides triumphingly over all the incapacities.

†**Triu·mphous,** *a. Obs. rare.* [f. L. *triumph-us* TRIUMPH + -OUS.] = TRIUMPHANT. Hence †**Triu·mphously** *adv.*

*c* **1468** in *Archæologia* (1846) XXXI. 337 The Duke adressid hym, horssid and armid, tryhumphoslye accompanyd wᵗ lordis unto the felde. **1501** DOUGLAS *Pal. of Hon.* Verses to Jas. IV, i, Triumphous laud with palme of victorie. **1546** *Primer Hen. VIII* 145 Jesus, a King most merveilous, Noble, excellent, & triumphous.

†**Tri·umphress.** *Obs. rare.* [f. TRIUMPHER + -ESS.] A female triumpher.

*c* **1780** MONSEY in Jeaffreson *Bk. Doctors* (1860) II. iv. 84 Kill the Triumphress, and avenge my wrong.

**Triumvir** (trəi‚ʊ·mvəɹ). Also 7 -ver. Pl. **-virs,** or in L. form **-viri** (-virəi). [a. L. *triumvir*, usually in pl. *triumvirī* (also *trēsvirī*), back-formation from *trium virōrum*, gen. pl. of *trēs virī* three men.] *Rom. Hist.* One of three magistrates or public officers forming a committee charged with one of the departments of the administration; also, a member of the coalition of Pompey, Cæsar, and Crassus, B.C. 60 (first triumvirate), or of the administration of Cæsar, Antony, and Lepidus, B.C. 43 (second triumvirate).

**1579–80** NORTH *Plutarch* (1595) 940 M. Anthony the Triumuir. **1600** HOLLAND *Livy* VI. xxi. 232 They created certaine *Quinqueviri* for the division of the Pomptine lands: and *Triumviri* for the planting of a colonie at Nepet. **1697** DRYDEN *Æneid* Notes 626 Virgil had..describ'd the Miseries which Rome had undergone betwixt the Triumvirs and the Common-wealth-Party. **1704** HEARNE *Duct. Hist.* (1714) I. 378 Three Men called *Triumviri* were yearly appointed to be Judges what Lands were Public and what Private. **1814** BYRON *Corsair* II. xv, Yet be the soft triumvir's fault forgiven. **1847** TENNYSON *Princ.* VII. 116 By axe and eagle sat, With all their foreheads drawn in Roman scowls..The fierce triumvirs.

**b.** *transf.* and *fig. pl.* Three persons (or things) associated in power or authority; cf. TRIUMVIRATE 2, 3; *spec.* in the French Revolution: see quot. 1895.

**1619** PURCHAS *Microcosmus* v. 34 Those *Triumviri*, the Liver, Heart, and Braine. **1788** *Gentl. Mag.* Jan. 16/2 Those triumviri in the republick of letters, Lipsius, Casaubon, Scaliger. **1837** CARLYLE *Fr. Rev.* III. VI. vii, Saint-Just is standing motionless,..Couthon ejaculating, 'Triumvir?'.. Robespierre is struggling to speak. **1894** *Q. Rev.* July 98 Keble, Newman and Pusey have been called its Triumvirs. **1895** *Edin. Rev.* Oct. 388 The Triumvirs, as they were called, —that is, Robespierre, Couthon, and St. Just.

Hence **Triu·mvirship,** triumvirate.

**1597** BEARD *Theatre God's Judgem.* (1612) 411 In the beginning of his triumuirship. **1870** *Echo* 7 Nov., The narrow escape we have had from another Reign of Terror, under the triumvirship of..MM. Flourens, Pyat, and Blanqui.

†**Triu·mviracy.** *Obs. rare.* [f. as TRIUMVIRATE: see -ACY.] = TRIUMVIRATE.

**1678** R. L'ESTRANGE *Seneca's Mor.* (1776) 260 In the triumviracy he made use of his sword.

**Triumviral** (trəi‚ʊ·mvirăl), *a.* [ad. L. *triumvirāl-is*, f. *triumvir*, TRIUMVIR.] Of or pertaining to a triumvir or a triumvirate.

**1579** TWYNE *Phisicke agst. Fort.* I. xlii. 60 b, He was thought to haue condemned certayne in the Triumuiral proscription. *a* **1671** LD. FAIRFAX *Mem.* (1699) 82 The army had three Generals, Lesly, Manchester and Fairfax...This Triumviral Government. **1862** MERIVALE *Rom. Emp.* III. xxxi. 448 The triumviral commission which gave him the government of one third part of the empire.

**Triumvirate** (trəi‚ʊ·mvirĕt). Also 6–7 -virat, 7 -verat, *erron.* **triumpherate.** [ad. L. *triumvirāt-us*, f. *triumvir*, TRIUMVIR: see -ATE ¹.]

**1.** *Rom. Hist.* The position, office, or function of the triumviri, or of a triumvir; an association of three magistrates for joint administration: see TRIUMVIR.

**1601** HOLLAND *Pliny* XXXV. xi. II. 546 A pretie jest..reported..as touching Lepidus: It happened during the time of his Triumvirat. **1606** SHAKS. *Ant. & Cl.* III. vi. 28 He frets That Lepidus of the Triumpherate, should be depos'd. **1718** ROWE tr. *Lucan* I. 182 The fierce Triumvirate combin'd in peace. **1841** W. SPALDING *Italy & It. Isl.* I. 89 Cæsar's ..weaker rivals.., Antony and Lepidus, who had formed with him the Second Triumvirate.

**2.** By extension: Any association of three joint rulers or powers.

**1584** *Leycesters Commw.* (1641) 86* What doe you thinke ..of this new Triumvirat so lately concluded about Arbella? *c* **1650** DENHAM *On Fletcher's Wks.* 30 When Jonson, Shakespear, and thyself,..swayed in the triumvirate of wit. **1741–2** H. WALPOLE *Lett. to Mann* (1834) I. 64 A triumvirate who hate one another more than any body they could proscribe. **1861** *Sat. Rev.* 23 Nov. 526 He wishes Germany to be ruled by a triumvirate of Ministers.

*fig.* **1643** SIR T. BROWNE *Relig. Med.* I. § 19 There is in our Soul a kind of Triumvirate, or triple Government of three Competitors. **1649** MILTON *Eikon.* xxii. Wks. (1847) 323/2 That violent and lawless triumvirate within him, under the falsified names of his reason, honour, and conscience. **1898** C. MARTYN in *Voice* (N.Y.) 9 June 6/4 The third member in his triumvirate of powers was a robust conscience.

**3.** Less exactly, A group or set of three persons (*rarely* things) thought of together, but not necessarily associated in fact; a trio; *esp.* three persons of authority or distinction in any sphere.

**1654** H. L'ESTRANGE *Chas. I* (1655) 145 June the 14. a Triumvirate of Libellers, Mr. Prin,..Dr. Bastwick,..and Mr. Burton..received a severe censure in the Star-chamber. **1748** RICHARDSON *Clarissa* Wks. 1883 VIII. 197 How I cursed the censoriousness of this plaguy triumvirate! A parson, a milliner, and a mantua-maker! **1873** LOWELL *Among my Bks.* Ser. II. 2 The great triumvirate of Italian poetry, good sense, and culture. **1898** W. GRAHAM *Lost Links* 117 The triumvirate of the young century [Byron, Shelley, Keats].

**4.** *attrib.* or as *adj.*

**1586** T. B. *La Primaud. Fr. Acad.* I. 659 Brutus and Cassius..slew Cæsar: wherupon..the triumvirate war was opened against them. **1624** CAPT. SMITH *Virginia* v. 181 A petition..vnto the triumuerat Gouernors. **1849** *Morning Chron.* 3 Feb., A triumvirate leadership..Mr. Herries, Lord Granby, and Mr. Disraeli.

†**Triu·mviry.** *Obs.* Also *erron.* **triumphery.** [? for L. *triumvirī*, pl. of TRIUMVIR.] = TRIUMVIRATE.

**1588** SHAKS. *L. L. L.* IV. iii. 53 *Lon.* Am I the first $y^t$ haue been periur'd so? *Ber.* I could put thee in comfort, not by two that I know, Thou makest the triumphery. **1656** EARL MONM. tr. *Boccalini's Advts. fr. Parnass.* 222 The City pretor..accusing the Triumviry of having exceeded the bounds of their authority.

**Triunal** (trəi,yū·năl), *a. poet. rare.* [f. as next + -AL.] = next.

*a* **1711** KEN *Hymnarium* Poet. Wks. 1721 II. 64 In the same Hymn the mystic four Triunal God adore. **1855** BAILEY *Mystic* 13 The true, triunal God.

**Triune** (trəi·yūn, *occas.* trəiyū·n), *a.* (*sb.*) [f. TRI- + L. *ūnus* one.] Three in one; constituting a trinity in unity. **a.** of the Godhead; also of heathen deities.

**1635** QUARLES *Embl.* V. viii. 31 The Son and heir to heav'n's Tri-une Jehove. *a* **1711** KEN *Hymns Festiv.* Poet. Wks. 1721 I. 270 We firmly God Triune believe. **1832** I. TAYLOR *Saturday Even.* (1834) 471 The economy of human Salvation has..signalised the distinction of the Triune Nature. **1904** BUDGE *3rd & 4th Egypt. Rooms Brit. Mus.* 82 A figure of..a singing woman of Amen-Rā, adoring the triune form of the sun-god.

**b.** *gen.* (often with allusion to a.).

**1705** PENN in *Pa. Hist. Soc. Mem.* X. 73 Humility, fear, and love are the triune qualities of a true Christian. **1867** GOLDW. SMITH *Three Eng. Statesmen* (1882) 8 The triune despotism of the Privy Council, the Star-Chamber, the Court of High Commission. **1874** L. MORRIS *Ode Fair Spring Morning* 55 Youth, dawn, springtide, triune miracle!

**c.** Being three at a birth; 'trin'. *rare* $^{-1}$.

**1771** *Stanhope* (*Durham*) *Par. Register Baptisms* 21 Dec. (MS.), Thomas, William, and George, triune sons of Thomas Thistlewaite.

**B.** *sb.* A being that is three in one; a group of three things united; a trinity in unity.

**1605** TIMME *Quersit.* II. ii. 108 It hath pleased the omnipotent Creator to..showe himself a Unitrine or Triune. *a* **1711** KEN *Sion* Poet. Wks. 1721 IV. 363 The great Triune in Counsel far above. **1866** R. S. CANDLISH *1st Ep. John* xlvi. 516 The 'three in one' unitedly, 'the Triune'. **1879** G. MEREDITH *Egoist* I. v. 67 She had money and health and beauty, the triune of perfect starriness.

**Triungulin** (trəi,ɒ·ŋgiŭlin), *a.* and *sb. Entom.* [f. TRI- + L. *ungula* claw + -IN $^2$.] **a.** *adj.* Having three claws on each leg, as the larvæ of the *Meloidæ* or blister-beetles in their first stage. **b.** *sb.* A triungulin larva.

**1891** *Cent. Dict.*, Triungulin, *n.* **1899** *Cambr. Nat. Hist.* VI. 270 The eggs of the blister-beetle..giving rise to little larvæ of the kind called triungulin, because each leg is terminated by three tarsal spines or claws. *Ibid.* 301 The young triungulins.

**Tri-u·nial,** *a.* (*sb.*) [f. TRI-, after BI-UNIAL.] Applied to a magic lantern having three optical tubes combined in one: also ellipt. as *sb.*

**1891** *Daily News* 3 Dec. 5/5 A lecturer..who was provided ..with what was described as 'a magnificent triunial'.

**Triunity** (trəi,yū·nĭti). [f. TRIUNE + -ITY, or f. TRI- + UNITY.]

**1.** The state or attribute of being three in one. **a.** of the Godhead: cf. TRINITY 1 b.

**1653** H. MORE *Conject. Cabbal.* (1713) 157 The Præexistence of the Soul, and the Triunity in the Godhead, which Pythagoras taught. **1673** [see TRINITY 1 b]. *a* **1711** KEN *Hymns Evang.* Poet. Wks. 1721 I. 271 We guess from Man's co-eval Three, At God's ador'd Triunity. **1825** COLERIDGE *Aids Refl.* (1848) I. 134 The Scriptural..idea of God will, in its development, be found to involve the idea of the Triunity.

**b.** *gen.*: cf. TRINITY 1 a.

**1816** COLERIDGE *Lay Serm.* 340 There exists in the human being..no mean symbol of Tri-unity, in reason, religion, and the will. **1894** ILLINGWORTH *Personality* iii. (1895) 71 The family..its abstract triunity being..personally realised in father, mother, and child.

**2.** Three in one; a set or group of three constituting a unity. **a.** The Godhead conceived as three 'persons': = TRINITY 2.

**1621** T. BEDFORD *Sin unto Death* 15 Nor is it possible to offend any one person of this Tri-vnitie, but the iniurie doth redound to them all. *a* **1834** COLERIDGE in *Lit. Rem.* (1839) IV. 210 Instead of one Tri-unity we might have a milleunity...Sherlock..had not the clear idea of the Trinity.

**b.** *gen.* = TRINITY 3.

**1646** *Unhappy Game Scotch & Eng.* 8 Then were it a Triunity, and not a Bi-unity.

So **Tri,u·nifica·tion,** the action of making to be three in one; **Triu·nion** = *triunity*; **Triunita·rian,** a believer in the triunity of the Godhead: = TRINITARIAN B. 2.

**1892** *Nation* (N.Y.) 20 Oct. 305/3 To secure..the *triunification of Germany. **1650** T. VAUGHAN *Anima Magica* To the Author, And fix the roving thoughts in one Inseperate *Triunion. **1819** G. S. FABER *Dispensations* (1823) I. 188 Jewish commentators..cannot be said to have any of (what the Socinians would call) the prejudices of the *Triunitarians. **1859** LD. ACTON *Lett.* (1909) 103 The triunion representing Germany in that triumvirate would also..be president of the new Germanic confederation.

**Trivage,** dial. corruption of TRAVIS $^2$.

**Trival,** obs. erron. form of TRIVIAL.

**Trivalent** (trəi·vălĕnt, tri·v-), *a. Chem.* [f. TRI- + L. *valēnt-em,* pr. pple. of *valēre* to be worth.] Having the combining power of three atoms of hydrogen or other univalent element; combining with three atoms of a univalent element or radical.

**1868** FOWNES *Elem. Chem.* (ed. 10) 251 Trivalent elements or Triads. **1876** TILDEN *Chem. Philos.* 143 The group $PO_1$ is trivalent, and so it holds together the two atoms of sodium and one atom of hydrogen in one molecule. **1880** CLEMINSHAW *Wurtz' Atom. The.* 260 The ammonia type [represented] the combination of a trivalent atom with three univalent atoms. **1888** MUIR & MORLEY *Watts' Dict. Chem.* I. 524 The atom of B [Boron] is trivalent in gaseous molecules.

Hence **Trivalence** (trəi·vălĕns, tri·v-), the quality of being trivalent.

**1888** *Athenæum* 21 July 102/2 The trivalence of the metals of the aluminium group.

**Trivalve** (trəi·vælv), *sb.* and *a. Nat. Hist.* [f. TRI- + VALVE, after *bivalve.*] **a.** *sb.* A shell having three valves. **b.** *adj.* Having three valves. Also **Tri·valved, † Triva·lvous, Triva·lvular** *adjs.*

**1776** DA COSTA *Conchology* 278 These Shells are *trivalves, and have two large valves, with a small valve placed between them, near to the hinge. **1891** *Cent. Dict.*, Trivalve, *a.* and *n.* **1856** W. CLARK *Van der Hoeven's Zool.* I. 190 Head *trivalved. **1681** GREW *Musæum* II. I. iv. 198 *Trivalvous, i.e. composed of three Sides or Plates joyned together by the length of the Shell. **1693** SIR T. P. BLOUNT *Nat. Hist.* 60 Bauhinus Pictures it [the Ginger plant]..with a trivalvous Cod. **1785** MARTYN *Rousseau's Bot.* xx. (1794) 278 Purslain has..a capsule of one cell..; in some species it opens horizontally, in others it is *trivalvular.

**Trivant,** dial. var. TRUANT. Hence (*nonce-wds.*) **Trivanting** *a.*, playing the truant; **† Trivantly** *a.* or *adv.* ? idle or idly.

**1621** BURTON *Anat. Mel.* I. ii. III. xv. 181 These men.. cannot distinguish betwixt a true Schollar, and..him that by reason of a voluble tongue, and some triuantly [*ed.* 1624 *adds* Polyanthean] helps, steales and gleanes a few notes from other mens harvests. **1624** *Ibid.* Democr. to Rdr. (ed. 2) 8 A trifler, a triuant, thou art an idle fellow. **1851–85** Trivant, trivent in *Eng. Dial. Dict.* from Chesh., Leic., Northants., and Oxf. [**1863** SALA *Capt. Dangerous* I. iv. 90 Those trifling and trivanting gentlewomen that pull diseases on to their pates with drums and routs, and late hours.]

**Trivariant** (trəivēə·riănt), *a. Physical Chem.* [f. TRI- 5 + VARIANT *a.*] Applied to a system having three degrees of freedom or variable factors; e.g. one in which the temperature, pressure, and concentration of the components can be varied independently without destroying the nature of the system.

**1902** TREVOR in *Jrnl. Phys. Chem.* VI. 136, I would therefore suggest..that when the variance is successively zero, one, two, three..the system be said to be in an Invariant, Univariant, Bivariant, Trivariant..state. [Cf. **1904** A. FINDLAY *Phase Rule and its Applications.*]

**†Trive,** *v. Obs.*, nonce-abbreviation of CONTRIVE.

**1573** TUSSER *Husb.* (1878) 137 Teach timelie to trauerse the thing that thou triue. *marg.* True for contriue.

**Trivector** (trəive·ktəɹ). *Geom.* [f. TRI- + VECTOR.] A set of three vectors, i.e. *radii vectores* (see RADIUS 3 e) from the same point.

**1869** CAYLEY *Math. Papers* VII. 400 We should have the focus and three points on the orbit; or (what is the same thing) three radius vectors from the focus, say a 'trivector'.

**Triverbal** to **Trivertebral**: see TRI- 1.

**Trivess,** Sc. dial. form of TRAVIS $^2$.

**Trivet** (tri·vĕt). Forms: ?1 trefet, 5 trevid, treued, trefet, -ett, 5–6 trevette, 5–9 trevet, 6 trevyt, treyvette, trivette, tryvette, 6–7 trevett, tryvet, trivett, 7 trifet, 7–9 trevit, (9 *dial.* trewit), 6– trivet. [*Trefet* occurs in a 12th c. copy of a 10th c. document (see below), otherwise it is not known till the 15th c.; it appears to be this word, and to represent L. *triped-em,* nom. *tripes* three-footed, f. *tri-* three + *pēs, ped-* foot; cf. OF. *trepied, tripié, trespieds,* TRIPPET $^2$.

11.. *Rec. Gifts of Adeluuold* (963–84) in Birch *Cart. Sax.* III. 367, vi bidenfate & ii cuflas & þry trogas & lead & trefet & ix winterstellas & i fedelsswin.]

**1.** A three-footed stand or support: = TRIPOD A. 3, 4. Now *rare* exc. as in b.

**1526** *Pilgr. Perf.* (W. de W. 1531) 37 b, And by sayenge of theyr pater noster make a treuet go rounde about the hous. **1594** PLAT *Jewell-ho.* II. 23 A large Balneo, wherein you may place sixe or eight glasse bodies..each of them fastened to a leaden trivet, $y^t$ they may stand steady in the water. **1653** H. MORE *Antid. Ath.* II. ii. § 14 (1712) 47 Who perceiving that his Iron Trevet..had three Feet and could stand expected also that it should walk. **1782** BECKFORD *Italy, &c.* (1834) I. v. 347 [They] shifted their trivets from cow to cow. **1888** DOUGHTY *Arabia Deserta* II. 146 Abdullah made a trivet of reeds, and balancing thereupon his long matchlock..he fired.

**b.** *spec.* A stand for a pot, kettle, or other vessel placed over a fire for cooking or heating something: orig. and properly standing on three feet; now often with one or two vertical projections by which it may be secured on the top bar of a grate.

**1416** *Maldon, Essex, Court Rolls* Bundle 10 No. 3 Districtus est per 1 trevet, 1 patell. de eneo. *c* **1483** CAXTON *Dialogues* 8/5 The ladle of the pot about the fyre; Treuet for to sette it on. **1561** HOLLYBUSH *Hom. Apoth.* 36 Put the same into a newe pot, set it by the fyre vpon a treuet. **1683** MOXON *Mech. Exerc., Printing* xi. ¶ 23 This Caldron is set upon a good strong Iron Trevet. **1755** HALES in *Phil. Trans.* XLIX. 342 In Devonshire, they set the pans of milk on trivets, making fires under them, to give the milk..a scalding. **1838** DICKENS *O. Twist* xii, He sat over the fire with a saveloy and a small loaf in his left hand..and a pewter pot on the trivet. **1875** M. COLLINS *Sweet & Twenty* I. xviii, A defiant kettle sang upon a trivet.

**c.** *Her.* A bearing representing the three-footed stand used in cooking, usually as viewed from above, the three feet being shown around the edge.

*a* **1550** in *Baring-Gould & Twigge's West. Armory* (1898) 3 Arg: a trivet sab. **1688** R. HOLME *Armoury* III. xiv. (Roxb.) 7/2 He beareth Argent, a three square Trevett, sable.

**† d.** *pl. dialectal* (**trewets, truets**): see quot.

**1674** RAY *S. & E. C. Words* 77 *Trewets* or *Truets,* Pattens for Women, *Suff.*

**e.** Applied allusively to prehistoric stone structures. (See also quot. 1892 in 4.)

**1596** SPENSER *State Irel.* Wks. (Globe) 643/1 These..greate stones..which some vaynlye terme the old Gyaunts Trivetts.

**† 2.** A three-footed vessel, as a pot, cauldron, etc.; chiefly *Antiq.* = TRIPOD A. 1. *Obs.*

**1547–64** BAULDWIN *Mor. Philos.* (Palfr.) 10 Certaine fishers found a golden tresle or triuet. **1612** *North's Plutarch* 1231 Pausanias..offered a triuet of gold vnto the temple of Delphes. **1676** HOBBES *Iliad* IX. 118 Seven fire new Trevets.

**† b.** = TRIPOD A. 2. *Obs.*

**1577–87** HOLINSHED *Chron.* III. 1238/1 Who suppose euerie blast of their mouth to come foorth of Trophonius den, and that they spake from the triuet. *a* **1641** BP. MOUNTAGU *Acts & Mon.* iii. (1642) 205 Shee [Cumana Sibylla] composed her selfe upon a golden Trifet, and..uttered what by Inspiration was suggested to her.

**3.** Phr. *As right as a trivet,* thoroughly or perfectly right (in reference to a trivet's always standing firm on its three feet).

**1835** HOOD *Dead Robbery* x, 'I'm right', thought Bunce, 'as any trivet'. **1837** DICKENS *Pickw.* l, 'I hope you are well, sir'. 'Right as a trivet, sir', replied Bob Sawyer. **1868** HELPS *Realmah* ii. (1876) 24 All goes as right as a trivet.

**4.** *attrib.* Three-footed; having three feet, legs, or supports: = TRIPOD B. 1.

**1481–90** *Howard Househ. Bks* (Roxb.) 45 To Tomas pewterer for..a trefet vesel iiij.d. **1700** DRYDEN *Ovid's Met.* VIII. *Baucis* 84 The Trivet-Table of a Foot was lame. **1892** H. OWEN in *Owen's Descr. Pembrokeshire* 254 *note,* [They call the stone *Gromlegh*..There are other stones..in the Countrey adioyneinge as *Legh y tribedd* neere Ricordstone..] 'The trivet (or tripod) stone',..so called because of its three supporters.

Hence **Tri·vetwise** *adv.*, in the manner of a trivet.

**1859** R. F. BURTON *Centr. Afr.* in *Jrnl. Geog. Soc.* XXIX. 418 The fireplaces are three stones or clods, placed trivetwise upon the ground.

**Trivet,** variant of TREVAT.

**Trivial** (tri·viăl), *a.* (*sb.*). [ad. L. *triviālis,* in sense 5 below, f. *trivium* (see TRIVIUM); cf. F. *trivial* (16th c. in Godef. *Compl.*).]

**I. 1.** Belonging to the TRIVIUM of mediæval university studies.

**1432–50** tr. *Higden* (Rolls) VI. 333 Sche..hade noble auditors and disciples, to whom sche redde the arte triviale [L. *trivium legeret*]. **1515** BARCLAY *Egloges* iv. (1570) Cvj/1 If they haue smelled the artes triuiall, They count them Poetes hye and heroicall. **1597–8** BP. HALL *Sat.* IV. i. 173 Hath.. thrise rehearsed them in his triviall floare. **1807–8** SYD. SMITH *Plymley's Lett.* x. Wks. 1859 II. 178/2 The Protestants may likewise retain their trivial and grammar schools. **1904** KER *Dark Ages* 27 Plato does not allow the mediæval classification of Dialectic as a Trivial Art along with Grammar and Rhetoric.

**† 2.** Threefold, triple. *Obs. rare* $^{-1}$.

Cf. late L. use of *triviālis* (Arnobius).

**1432–50** tr. *Higden* (Rolls) I. 25 Giraldus of Wales, which describede Topographie of Irlonde, Itinerary of Wales, and the Lyfe of Kinge Henry the Secunde, under a triuialle distinccion [L. *sub triplici distinctione*].

**† 3.** Placed where three roads meet. *Obs. rare* $^{-1}$.

**1614** SELDEN *Titles Hon.* 129 Their other sacred Triuiall Statues.

**4.** *Zool.* Belonging to the TRIVIUM of an echinoderm. **1891** in *Cent. Dict.*

**II. 5.** Such as may be met with anywhere; common, commonplace, ordinary, everyday, familiar, trite. Now *rare* (passing into 6).

**1589** NASHE *Pref. Greene's Menaphon* (Arb.) 9 A few of our triviall translators. **1610** HEALEY *St. Aug. Citie of God* VIII. v. 291 It is triuiall in the Schooles: 'Nothing is in the vnderstanding that was not first in the sense'. **1665** GLANVILL *Scepsis Sci.* i. 8 The most ordinary and trivial Phænomena in nature. **1704** F. FULLER *Med. Gymn.* (1711) 37 Explain the manner of this by a trivial Observation. **1827** KEBLE *Chr. Y., Morning* xiv, The trivial round, the common task. **1895** MACEWEN *Life Dr. Cairns* 161 This..is now the trivial definition and ground principle.

**6.** Of small account, little esteemed, paltry, poor; trifling, inconsiderable, unimportant, slight.

**1593** SHAKS. *2 Hen VI,* III. i. 241 We haue but triuiall argument, More then mistrust, that shewes him worthy death. **1655** FULLER *Ch. Hist.* II. i. § 5 To demurre to the Truth of his so frequent Miracles, being so Redundant in working them on Triviall Occasions. **1790** BURKE *Fr. Rev.* 94 They..are ready..to abandon for a very trivial interest what they find of very trivial value. **1869** FREEMAN *Norm. Conq.* III. xii. 251 The offence..could..be passed by as altogether trivial.

**7.** *Nat. Hist.* Applied to names of animals and plants: **a.** to a Latin name added to the generic name to distinguish the species: = SPECIFIC A. 5; **b.** to a name in common as distinct from scientific use: Popular, vernacular, vulgar.

**a. 1759** B. STILLINGFL. *Misc. Tracts* (1762) Pref. 16 In the last edition of his *Systema naturæ* he [Linnæus] has mentioned above 1500 species of insects, has..given them classical, generical, and trivial or specifical names. **1815** KIRBY & SP. *Entomol.* (1843) I. 181 *Scolytus destructor*, whose trivial name well characterises the..severity of its ravages. **1902** C. D. SHERBORN *Index Animalium* p. vii, All trivial names are entered as if they were masculine, *e.g. nigra* will be found under *niger*.

**b. 1815** BURROW *Elem. Conchol.* 193 The following List of English Trivial Names will be found useful to purchasers of shells, as dealers most frequently adopt them. *Ibid.* 194 Trivial Names. Linnæan Name. Lepas. English Name. Acorn Shell. **1901** *Spectator* 17 Aug. 216/1 The trivial name for the whole family of terns..is 'sea-swallow'.

**III. 8.** *Comb.*, as *trivial-minded* adj. (whence *trivial-mindedness*).

**1872** GEO. ELIOT in Cross *Life* (1885) III. 161 We should.. have patience with their trivial-mindedness. **1905** A. R. WALLACE *My Life* II. 383 Even in the most trivial-minded [I] was able to find some common ground of interest.

**B.** *sb.*

†**1.** = TRIVIUM 1 (in quot. *transf.*). *Obs. rare*$^{-1}$.

**1432–50** tr. *Higden* (Rolls) I. 5 The triuialle [L. *trivium*] of the vertues theologicalle and quadriualle of the cardinalle vertues.

**2.** *pl.* The three subjects of study constituting the TRIVIUM. Now only *Hist.*

**1481, 1522** [see QUADRIVIAL A. 2, B. 2]. **1630** HALES *Gold. Rem.* (1673) 282 In the Trivials and Quadrivials, as old Clerks were wont to name them. **1691** WOOD *Ath. Oxon.* II. 181 Peter Heylyn..profiting in Trivials to a miracle, especially in Poetry. **1716, 1886** [see QUADRIVIAL B. 2].

**3.** A trivial matter; a triviality, trifle. Usually *pl.*

**1715** M. DAVIES *Athen. Brit.* I. 288 'Tis scarce worth disputing..about such trivials. **1886** TUPPER *My Life as Author* 334 Take these twelve as samples of many more such trivials.

**4.** *Math.* 'A coefficient or other quantity not containing the quantities of the set considered' (*Cent. Dict.* 1891).

**Trivialism** (tri·viăliz'm). *rare.* [f. prec. + -ISM.] Trivial character, triviality; something of trivial character, a triviality.

**1830** H. N. COLERIDGE *Grk. Poets* (1834) 6 It will be a matter of wonder..that such trivialisms..could ever pass for genuine poetry. **1882** OGILVIE cites CARLYLE.

**Trivialist** (tri·viălist). *rare.* [See -IST.]

**1.** A student of 'trivials': see TRIVIAL B. 2.

**1716** M. DAVIES *Athen. Brit.* III. 3 Fitter for Veterans and Criticks in Closets and Libraries, than for Tyronists and Trivialists in Schools.

**2.** One who pursues or deals in trivialities.

**1829** CARLYLE *Misc.* (1840) II. 173 Voltaire..was, therefore, ..no Philosopher, but a highly accomplished Trivialist.

**Triviality** (triviæ·lĭti). [f. L. type **triviālitāt-em*, f. *triviālis* TRIVIAL; cf. F. *trivialité* (Cotgr. 1611), It. *triuialità* (Florio 1598), Sp. *trivialidad*, Pg. *trivialidade*: see -ITY.]

**1.** The quality of being trivial; commonplace or trifling character.

**1598** FLORIO, *Triuialità*, homelines, triuiality. **1817** COLERIDGE *Biog. Lit.* 106 My severest critics have not pretended to have found in my compositions triviality. **1862** BORROW *Wild Wales* lxxxix. III. 228 The loss of the house was a matter of triviality compared with that of the library. **1874** L. STEPHEN *Hours in Library* (1892) II. ii. 39 The genuine excellence which underlay the superficial triviality of Crabbe's verses.

**2.** With *a*, or (commonly) in *pl.*: Something trivial; a trivial matter, affair, characteristic, remark, etc.; a trifle.

**1611** COTGR., *Trivialitez*, Triuialities; triuiall, sleight, common, homelie, ordinarie matters. *c* **1664** BARROW in Rigaud *Corr. Sci. Men* (1841) II. 37, I..find little but repetitions and trivialities. **1831** CARLYLE *Sart. Res.* I. xi. (1858) 45 A..Letter, full of compliments,..dining repartees, and other ephemeral trivialities. **1843** — *Past & Pr.* III. vi, The Practical labour of England is not a chimerical Triviality. **1877** BLACK *Green Past.* v, Archery meetings and croquet parties and such trivialities.

**Trivialize** (tri·viăləiz), *v.* [f. TRIVIAL + -IZE; cf. mod.F. *trivialiser* (Littré).] *trans.* To make trivial; to render commonplace or trifling.

**1846** LANDOR *Imag. Conv., Southey & Landor* Wks. II. 168/1 Milton has ennobled it [the sonnet] in our tongue, and has trivialised it in that [Italian]. **1895** W. PLATT *Women* 147 Trivialising marriage into the enjoyment of a mere instinct.

**Trivially** (tri·viăli), *adv.* [f. as prec. + -LY [2].] In a trivial manner.

**1.** Commonly, ordinarily, familiarly; in a commonplace or trite way. Now *rare* or *Obs.*

**1625** BACON *Ess., Greatn. Kingd.* (Arb.) 473 Neither is Money the Sinewes of Warre (as it is triuially said). **1647** TRAPP *Comm. Matt.* xi. 17 He is the best preacher, saith Luther, that delivereth himself vulgarly, plainly, trivially. *a* **1661** HOLYDAY *Juvenal* (1673) 211 He thinks it more unhappiness ..to die with a divided carcase, then with a whole one:.. the whole body being not usually so trivially exposed to scorn, as the head, when divided from the body. **1818** SOUTHEY in *Q. Rev.* XVIII. 9 Leah and Rachel were..used almost as trivially for examples by poets as by theologians.

**2.** In a trifling, slight, or paltry way; in the way of trifling, frivolously.

**1649** J. H. *Motion to Parl. Adv. Learn.* 26 Their youth so trivially spent. **1710** STEELE *Tatler* No. 207 ¶ 2 Minds which are not trivially disposed. **1858** O. W. HOLMES *Aut. Breakf.-t.* viii. (1883) 161 You speak trivially, but not unwisely.

**Tri·vialness.** Now *rare.* [f. as prec. + -NESS.] = TRIVIALITY 1.

*a* **1687** H. MORE *App. Def. Philos. Cabbala* xi. § 1 As for the pretended Trivialness of the Fifth and Sixth Days work. **1732** STACKHOUSE *Hist. Bible* (1767) IV. VI. v. 212 The vast distance of the place and trivialness of the errand. **1855** MILMAN *Lat. Chr.* XIV. ii. (1864) IX. 77 In the puerility and trivialness of their wonders they even surpass the Western Hagiologies.

**Tri-vi·ded,** *ppl. a. nonce-wd.* [f. TRI-, after *divided*.] Divided into three. So **Tri-vi·sion** [after *division*], division into three.

**1896** J. H. WYLIE *Hist. Eng. Hen. IV*, III. 388 Instead of di-vision they had tri-vision. **1900** — in *Athenæum* 4 Aug. 146/2 Instead of three Popes and a tri-vided faith.

†**Tri·vious,** *a. Obs. rare.* [f. L. *trivium* (see TRIVIUM) + -OUS.] = TRIVIAL *a.* 5, 6.

**1583** MELBANCKE *Philotimus* M j b, Intricate endles triuious toylings. **1677** GALE *Crt. Gentiles* II. IV. 219 Upon as sleight and trivious reasons.

**Trivirgate**: see TRI- 1.

**Triviss,** Sc. dial. variant of TRAVIS [2].

‖**Trivium** (tri·viŏm). [L. (f. *tri-*, TRI- + *via* way), a place where three ways meet; in med.L. in sense 1 below.]

**1.** In the Middle Ages, the lower division of the seven liberal arts, comprising grammar, rhetoric, and logic. (Cf. QUADRIVIUM.)

**1804** RANKEN *Hist. France* III. iv. 308 They included all learning in the seven liberal arts; of which grammar, rhetoric, and dialectics, formed what they called Trivium. **1837** HALLAM *Hist. Lit.* I. I. i. § 3. 3 The trivium and quadrivium, a course of seven sciences, introduced in the sixth century. **1886** S. S. LAURIE *Rise Universities* 64 The ..instruction given by Gerbert at Rheims about 1000 A.D. seems to have been simply a full and extended trivium.

**2.** *Zool.* The three anterior ambulacra of an echinoderm. (Cf. BIVIUM.)

**1870** ROLLESTON *Anim. Life* 142 To divide the five rays [in *Asterias*] into a 'bivium', between which the madreporic tubercle lies, and a 'trivium', the two lateral arms of which lie on either side of the arm which is opposite to that tubercle. **1877** HUXLEY *Anat. Inv. Anim.* ix. 570 In the fossil genus, Dysaster, this separation of the ambulacra into trivium and bivium exists naturally.

**Trivoltine, Trivoluminous**: see TRI- 4 b, 1 a.

**Triwe,** obs. form of TRUE.

**Tri-weekly** (trəi₁wī·kli), *a.* and *adv.* [TRI- 3.]

**A.** *adj.* **a.** Occurring every three weeks, or lasting for three weeks. **b.** Usually, Occurring, appearing, or operating three times every week.

**1832** (May 17) W. T. BARRY in *Amer. State Papers* (1834) XV. 348 The line of stages connecting Philadelphia and Delaware with the Eastern shore of Maryland and Virginia, has been increased from a bi-weekly, to a tri-weekly line. **1843** *Penny Cycl.* XXVI. 14/2 Semi- or tri-weekly newspapers. **1895** R. H. SHERARD in *Bookman* Oct. 16/2 The tri-weekly supplement of *La Lanterne*. **1903** *Daily Chron.* 15 Jan., The tri-weekly expresses running across Siberia.

**B.** *adv.* **a.** Every three weeks. **b.** Three times a week.

**1884** G. P. KEESE in *Harper's Mag.* July 300/1 A line of ..coaches has been established, leaving tri-weekly. **1901** *Daily News* 12 Jan. 5/3 In consequence of military restrictions..the advertisement sheet which has been appearing every week will be issued tri-weekly.

**Triwes, triws,** obs. forms of TRUCE.

**-trix,** *suffix*, ending of Latin feminine agent-nouns (with stems in *-trīc-*, acc. *-trīcem*, whence Fr. *-trice*: see -TRICE), corresponding to masculines in *-tor*, as *adjūtrix* female helper, *bellātrix* female warrior, *imperātrix* female commander, empress, *inventrix* female discoverer, *vēnātrix* huntress, etc.; sometimes used adjectively, as *victrix* victorious, *ultrix* avenging. Several of these nouns were adopted in Eng., from ancient or mediæval Latin, in the 15th c. and later, as ADMINISTRATRIX, CONSOLATRIX, CREATRIX, EXECUTRIX, MEDIATRIX, PERSECUTRIX, TESTATRIX, etc.; and others formed on the analogy of them, as INHERITRIX, NARRATRIX, PERPETRATRIX, etc. In Geometry, words in *-trix* denote straight lines (*linea* being understood), as BISECTRIX, DIRECTRIX; more rarely curves or surfaces, as INDICATRIX, TRACTRIX. The suffix has occasionally been loosely used to form nonce-feminines to agent-nouns in *-ter*, as PAINTRIX instead of the regular *paintress*. The commoner suffix in Eng. is -TRESS: see also -TRICE.

**Trixie, trixsie, trixy,** obs. ff. TRICKSY.

**Trizomal**: see TRI- 1.

**Tro, troa,** obs. ff. TROW *v.* **Troad,** obs. pa. pple. of TREAD *v.*; obs. f. TROD *sb.* **Troak,** obs. f. TRUCK. **Troan,** var. TRON; dial. f. TRUANT.

**Troat** (trōut), *v. Venery.* Also 7 **troyte, trout, throat**; 9 *erron.* **froat.** [Cf. OF. *trout* (Godef.), also *trut*, an interjection for urging on hunting dogs, asses, sheep. Cf. also ROUT *v.*[3] to bellow.] *intr.* To cry or bellow: said of a buck at rutting time; cf. BELL *v.*[4] 2, BELLOW *v.* 2, GROAN *v.* 2. Hence **Troa·ting** *vbl. sb.* and *ppl. a.*

**1611** COTGR. s. v. *Réer*, In tearmes of hunting we say, that ..the fallow troytes or croynes. *Ibid.*, *Rere*, to bellow as a Stag, to troute as a Buck. **1650** FULLER *Pisgah* III. ix. 338 Here..the throating Bucks [are said] to lodge. *a* **1700** B. E. *Dict. Cant. Crew* s.v. *Buck*, A Buck Groaneth or Troateth, makes a Noise at Rutting time. **1727** *Bradley's Fam. Dict.* s. v. *Buck-hunting*, He groans and troats, as a Hart belleth. **1847–78** HALLIWELL, *Troat*, to bellow, said of the buck. **1900** *Sporting Phraseology* in *Shooting Times* 15 Dec. 15/1 *Froating* or *troating*, call of buck.

**b.** Said of a swan.

**1839** G. DARLEY *Nepenthe* I. (1897) 20 And [the swan] troats for joy, too proud for song.

**Troath,** obs. f. TROTH. **Trobel, -bil, -ble, -bul(l, -byll,** obs. ff. TROUBLE.

†**Trobellion,** obs. var. TOURBILLION, whirlwind.

*c* **1450** *Merlin* xx. 324 Merlin by crafte made soche a trobellion a-rise that ther lefte nother tente ne pavilon stondinge.

**Trobelows, -lys,** obs. forms of TROUBLOUS.

**Trocar** (trōu·kaɪ). Also 8 **trochart,** (**trois-quarts, -quart**), 8–9 **trocart, trochar.** [ad. F. *troquart*, *trois-quarts* (1694), *trocart* (1762), f. *trois* three + *carre* side, face of an instrument; so called from its triangular form.] A surgical instrument consisting of a perforator or stylet enclosed in a metal tube or cannula, used for withdrawing fluid from a cavity, as in dropsy, etc.

**1706** PHILLIPS (ed. Kersey), *Trochar*, a Cane, or Pipe made of Silver, or Steel, with a sharp-pointed End, us'd in tapping those that are troubled with the Dropsy. **1739** HUXHAM in *Phil. Trans.* XLI. 644 A very small hollow Needle with Perforations, as in that used by some instead of the Trocar. **1744** WARRICK *ibid.* XLIII. 16 My Apparatus was a large Trois-quarts, made on purpose, and dipped in Oil; an Injector[etc.]. **1751** *Ibid.* XLVII. xl. 268 The common trocarts did not seem proper. **1758** J. S. *Le Dran's Observ. Surg.* (1771) 216 He perforated it with the *Troisquart*. **1861** HULME tr. *Moquin-Tandon* II. VI. iv. 304 The Ticks plunge their beaks into the skin in the same way as one may thrust in a trochar. **1876** GROSS *Dis. Bladder* 32 If abscesses point, they must be opened with the knife, or trocar.

*attrib.* **1863–76** CURLING *Dis. Rectum* 101 A sharp trocar-needle can be passed through the canula. **1905** ROLLESTON *Dis. Liver* 54 There was..fibrinous peritonitis around the site of the trocar punctures.

†**Troch,** obs. Sc. form of THROUGH *prep.*

**1573** TYRIE *Refut.* in *Cath. Tractates* (S. T. S.) 29 To expose thame self troch sic wane subterfugis.

**Troch,** Sc. form of TROUGH; var. of TROCHE.

‖**Trocha** (trō·tʃa). *Mil.* [Sp.] A strategic line of defences, as trenches, blockhouses, etc.; a military cordon.

**1896** *Daily News* 9 Dec. 7/5 The Spanish force,..near Punta Brava [Cuba], on the western side of the trocha. **1898** *Ibid.* 13 Apr. 3/1 These trochas have at every corner and at frequent intervals along the sides what are called forts, but which are really small blockhouses. **1902** R. T. HILL in *Encycl. Brit.* XXVII. 306/1 A corps of 20,000 men was stationed on this *trocha* or military cordon.

**Trochaic** (trokē·ik), *a.* and *sb. Pros.* [a. F. *trochaïque* (*c* 1550 in Godef. *Compl.*), or ad. L. *trochaic-us*, ad. Gr. τροχαικός, f. τροχαῖος: see TROCHEE.]

**A.** *adj.* **1.** Of a verse, rhythm, etc.: Consisting of, characterized by, or based on trochees.

**1589** PUTTENHAM *Eng. Poesie* II. xiii. (Arb.) 136 Verses where the sharpe accent falles vpon the first and third, and so make the verse wholly Trochaicke. **1776** BURNEY *Hist. Mus.* (1789) I. vi. 73 The dialogue admitted, occasionally, Trochaic verses. **1835** T. MITCHELL *Acharn. Aristoph.* 190 *note*, In the structure of the comic trochaic tetrameter catalectic, the nice points of tragic verse are freely neglected.

**2.** Of a foot, etc.: Of the nature of a trochee; consisting of a long (or an accented) followed by a short (or an unaccented) syllable.

*Trochaic spondee*, a spondee having the accent or *ictus* upon the first syllable.

**1756–82** J. WARTON *Ess. Pope* II. 213 An intermixture of those different feet (iambic and trochaic particularly) into which our language naturally falls. **1827** TATE *Grk. Metres* in *Theatre of Greeks* (ed. 2) 426 In the two following lines will be found specimens of..the Trochaic Spondee in all its places. **1888** H. W. CHANDLER *Elem. Grk. Accentuation* I. i. (ed. 2) 2 A word with a trochaic ending and accented penultimate must be properispome.

**B.** *sb.* A trochaic verse or foot.

**1693** DRYDEN *Juvenal* Ded. (1697) 44 One Poem consisted only of Hexameters; and another was entirely of Iambiques; a third of Trochaiques. **1756–82** J. WARTON *Ess. Pope* (ed. 4) I. ii. 55 He conjures the powers below in beautiful trochaics. **1827** TATE *Grk. Metres* in *Theatre of Greeks* (ed. 2) 427 This nicety of structure in the long Trochaic of Tragedy.

Also **Trocha·ical** *a.* (*rare*); hence **Trochaica·lity**, trochaic character.

**1755** JOHNSON, *Trochaical*, consisting of trochees. **1910** *Sat. Rev.* 18 June 791/1 A trochee of quite excessive trochaicality.

**Trochal** (trǫ·kăl, trōu·kăl), *a.* [f. Gr. τροχός wheel + -AL.]

**1.** *Zool.* Resembling a wheel; rotiform: as the *trochal apparatus*, *disk*, or *organ* of the Rotifera, an organ of locomotion consisting of two rings of cilia surrounding the mouth. **b.** Having a trochal apparatus, as a rotifer: = TROCHATE (*Cent. Dict.*).

**1841–71** T. R. JONES *Anim. Kingd.* (ed. 4) 482 The space between the two layers of the trochal disk. **1888** ROLLESTON & JACKSON *Anim. Life* 632 Class Rotifera. Unisegmental Vermes with a retractile trochal apparatus at the anterior end of the body. **1899** *Syd. Soc. Lex.*, *Trochal organ*, the characteristic oral organ of the Rotifera.

**2.** Revolving like a wheel or top. *rare*$^{-0}$.

**1891** in *Cent. Dict.*

**Trochalopod** (trǫ·kălopǫd, trokæ·lŏpǫd), *sb.* (*a.*) *Entom.* [f. mod.L. *Trochalopod-a*, neut. pl., f. Gr.

τροχαλός adj. running, rolling + πούς, ποδ- foot.] A member of the *Trochalopoda*, a group of heteropterous insects in which the posterior coxæ have a rotary motion. **b.** *adj.* Belonging to the *Trochalopoda*. Also **Trochalopodous** (trǫkälǫ·pǒdəs) *a.*

1870 *Ann. & Mag. Nat. Hist.* Sept. 233 The coxæ of trochalopodous Heteroptera are round. 1909 *Cent. Dict. Suppl.*, Trochalopod.

**Trochanter** (trokæ·ntəɹ). *Anat.* and *Zool.* [a. F. *trochanter* (Paré, 16th c.), a. Gr. τροχαντήρ (in sense 1), f. τρέχειν to run.]

**1.** A protuberance or process in the upper part of the thigh-bone, serving for the attachment of certain muscles; usually, as in man, two in number, the *great trochanter* (*t. major*) for the external rotator muscles, and the *lesser trochanter* (*t. minor*) for the ilio-psoas muscle.

1615 CROOKE *Body of Man* 997 The great Trochanter..the lesser Trochanter. These two processes are ioyned together by a line which buncheth out behind. 1741 MONRO *Anat. Bones* (ed. 3) 279 The Muscles inserted into these two Processes being the principal Instruments of the rotatory Motion of the Thigh, have occasioned the Name of Trochanters to the Processes. 1881 MIVART *Cat* 282 Between the great trochanter and the tuberosity of the ischium.

**2.** *Entom.* The second joint of an insect's leg, next to the coxa (COXA 2); sometimes consisting of two joints (cf. TROCHANTIN b).

1816 KIRBY & SP. *Entomol.* xxii. (1818) II. 286 These legs ..vary in larvæ of the different orders; but they seem in most to have joints answering to the hip (*coxa*); trochanter; thigh (*femur*); shank (*tibia*); foot (*tarsus*), of perfect insects. 1861 HULME tr. *Moquin-Tandon* II. VI. i. 310 Each limb [of the Sarcoptus Scabiei] consists of a hip, trochanter, small trochanter, thigh, leg, and tarsus.

Hence **Trochanterian** (-tīə·riăn) (*rare*—⁰) [F. *trochantérien*], **Trochanteric** (-te·rik) *adjs.*, pertaining to a trochanter; *trochanteric fossa* = digital fossa (see DIGITAL A. 2).

1842 E. WILSON *Anat. Vade M.* (1851) 254 The trochanteric fossa of the femur. 1857 DUNGLISON *Med. Lex.*, *Trochanterian.* 1890 HUMPHRY *Old Age* 16 Liability to fracture..especially remarkable in the trochanteric part and neck of the thigh-bone.

**Trochantin** (trokæ·ntin). *Anat.* and *Zool.* [a. F. *trochantin*, f. *trochanter* (see above).] **a.** The lesser trochanter: see TROCHANTER 1. *rare*—⁰. **b.** *Entom.* The proximal joint of the trochanter (TROCHANTER 2) when two-jointed. Hence **Trochanti·nian** *a.* [F. *trochantinien*], pertaining to the trochantin.

[1857 DUNGLISON *Med. Lex.* s. v. *Trochanter*, Chaussier, by the word *trochanter*, means the larger process; the smaller he calls *trochantin.*] *Ibid.*, *Trochantinian.* 1898 PACKARD *Text-bk. Entomol.* 95 The coxa usually has a posterior subdivision or projection, the trochantine; sometimes, as in Mantispa, the trochantine is obsolete.

**Trochar, -art,** variants of TROCAR.

**Trochate** (trōᵘ·keᶦt), *a. Zool. rare.* [f. as TROCHAL + -ATE ².] **a.** Furnished with a trochal apparatus, as a rotifer. **b.** = TROCHAL 1.

1891 in *Cent. Dict.*

† **Troche,** *sb.*¹ *Venery. Obs.* Also 7 **troch**, in Dicts. *erron.* **torch.** [a. OF. *troche* (13th c. in Godef.) cluster, mass, also in sense 2 below; in Twety *Art de Venerie* (*a* 1327) in sense 1, with which cf. OF. *trocheure* (14th c. in Godef. *Compl.*), F. *trochure.* Cf. also TROCHED, TROCHING.]

**1.** A cluster of three or more tines at the summit of a deer's horn; distinguished from a *fourche* (*i. e.* fork) of two tines.

*c* 1410 *Master of Game* (MS. Digby 182) xxxiii, And þenne þe lorde shulde take vppe þe hertes heede by þe reght syde bitwene þe sureale and þe fourche or troche. 1586 FERNE *Blaz. Gentrie* 194 As a perfect wood-man..to name the Sommeites, troches, or tynes, of the hornes. 1623 COCKERAM I. s. v. *Pollard*, Torch. 1651 DAVENANT *Gondibert* II. xxxiv, His [a stag's] spacious Beame..From Antlar to his Troch had all allow'd.

**2.** An ornamental button consisting of or set with three or more jewels in a bunch.

1434 in Rymer *Fœdera* (1710) X. 593/2 Withynne which Tablet ar xl Troches, iche Troche conteynyng iv Peerles. 1576 in Nichols *Progr. Q. Eliz.* (1823) II. 2 A border containing vii buttons or troches of gold, in every of them iii smale rubyes, and viii buttons or troches of golde, in every of them iv mene perle. 1625 in Rymer *Fœdera* (1726) XVIII. 238/1 A Cupp of Goulde with a Cover..garnished with.. one and twentie Troches of Pearles, three Pearles in every Troche.

Hence † **Troche** *v. Obs.*, *intr.* to develop a troche or troches.

1413–22 *Venery de Twety* in *Rel. Ant.* I. 151 Now wyl we speke of the hert,..Whan an hert hath..forched on the one syde, and troched on that other syde, than is he an hert of .x. and of the more. And whan..that he hath troched on boothe parties of the hed, he is of xij. and of that lasse. *c* 1450 in *Twici's Art of Hunting* etc. (1908) 108 When he trochithe on that one side of v & on the other side of vj he is of xvj de greynders.

**Troche** (trōᵘʃ, trōᵘtʃ, trōᵘk), *sb.*² *Pharm.* Forms: *pl.* 6 **troschies,** (**trocis**), 7 **trosches, trotches,** 7–8 **trochies,** 7– **troches**; *sing.* 7 **trosche,** 7– **troch, troche.** [An altered form of TROCHISK, originating in the plural *troschies*, *trochies*, taken as *trosches*, *troches*, implying a sing. *troschie*, *trochie*, in vulgar and commercial use often pronounced and sometimes written *trochee* (trōᵘ·ki), like TROCHEE. The spellings *trosch*, *troche* simulate French, and the pronunciation (trōᵘ·ki) is conformed to that of L. *trochiscus.*] A flat round tablet or lozenge, made of some medicinal substance powdered, worked into a paste with mucilage or the like, and dried; = TROCHISK.

*a.* 1597 GERARDE *Herbal* II. ccxcvi. 696 Troschies, or little flat cakes. 1714 *Phil. Trans.* XXIX. 68 The Trochies made of the Gall..a Cordial Sudorifick.

*β.* 1601 HOLLAND *Pliny* xx. xviii. II. 68 There bee certaine ordinarie trosches made of Poppie seed beaten into pouder, which with milke are..vsed by way of a liniment to bring sicke patients to sleepe. 1639 T. DE GRAY *Compl. Horsem.* 234 Make of it little cakes or trotches, as broad as a groat. 1656 RIDGLEY *Pract. Physick* 260 Troches of Capers, of Harts-tongue. 1681 GREW *Musæum* III. I. v. 297 A little round, flat, and blackish Stone, resembling a Medicinal Troch. 1769 PENNANT *Zool.* III. 22 The medicine was.. given in form of a powder or troche. 1811 A. T. THOMSON *Lond. Disp.* (1818) 709 *Trochisci.* Troches..are little cakes or tablets composed of powders combined with sugar and mucilage. [1857 DUNGLISON *Med. Lex.*, *Trochiscus*.., a troch or round table..; a solid medicine, prepared of powders, incorporated by means of mucilage, crumb of bread, juices of plants, &c.] 1875 H. C. WOOD *Therap.* (1879) 19 Troches, or lozenges, are gummy pellets or disks, so made as to dissolve slowly in the mouth.

**Trocheameter** (trǫkiˌæ·mītəɹ). [app. erron. f. Gr. τροχός wheel (cf. τροχιά wheel-track) + -METER.] = TRECHOMETER.

1857 LIVINGSTONE *Trav.* iii. 59 Our trocheame[te]r showed that we had made but twenty-five miles. *Note.* This is an instrument which, when fastened on the waggon-wheel, records the number of revolutions made. 1903 J. G. C. ANDERSON *Journ. Pontus* vii. 47 An accident happened to my trocheameter, so that I am unable to give the exact length of this section of the road.

† **Tro·ched,** *a. Venery. Obs.* [ad. OF. *troche* (14th c. in Godef.), as if f. TROCHE *sb.*¹ + -ED ².] Having a 'troche', as a deer's horn; also said of the deer.

*c* 1410 *Master of Game* (MS. Digby 182) xxiv, If he be troched of iii. he is an herte of xii. 1413–22 *Venery de Twety* in *Rel. Ant.* I. 151 Whan he is troched on boothe sydes of .vi. than is he of .xxiij. atte fulle. 1611 COTGR. s. v. *Troché*, *Teste de cerf trochée*, Troched, or whose top is diuided into three or foure small branches.

**b.** Also (by analogy) said of a tower furnished with pinnacles or battlements. *rare.*

13.. *E. E. Allit. P.* B. 1383 With koynt carneles aboue, coruen ful clene, Troched toures bitwene twenty spere lenþe. 13.. *Gaw. & Gr. Knt.* 795 A better barbican þat burne blusched vpon neuer; And innermore he be-helde þat halle ful hyȝe, Towre telded bytwene trochet ful þik.

**Trochee** (trōᵘ·kī). *Pros.* Also in Gr.-Lat. form 6 **trocheus,** 6–7 (9) **trochæus.** [ad. L. *trochæus*, ad. Gr. τροχαῖος, prop. adj. (*sc.* πούς foot) running, tripping, f. τρόχος a running, course, f. τρέχειν to run; cf. F. *trochée* (1572 in Hatz.-Darm.).] A metrical foot consisting of a long followed by a short syllable; in accentual verse, of an accented followed by an unaccented syllable. Also called CHOREE.

1589 PUTTENHAM *Eng. Poesie* II. xiii. (Arb.) 133 For your Trocheus of a long and short ye haue these words *mānĕr*, *brōkĕn*, *tākĕn*, *bōdiĕ*, *mēmbĕr*, and a great many moe. 1603 HOLLAND *Plutarch's Mor.* 1259 A Trochæus was put in stead of a Pæon. 1603 DANIEL *Def. Rhyme* G j b, If we shold say the state of China, which neuer hard of Anapestiques, Trochies, & tribracques, were grosse, barbarous, and vnciuile. *a* 1771 GRAY *Corr.* etc. (1843) 240 The measure.. is Dimeter-Iambic, but admits of a Trochee, Spondee, Amphibrachys, Anapæst, &c. in almost every place. 1803 COLERIDGE *Met. Feet* i, Trochee trips from long to short.

† **b.** = TRIBRACH. *Obs. rare*—¹.

1586 W. WEBBE *Eng. Poetrie* (Arb.) 69 A foote of 3 sillables..is either simple or myxt. The simple is eyther *Molossus*, that is of three long,..or *Trochæus*, that is of 3 short.

**Trochee, trochies**: see TROCHE *sb.*²

**Tro·che(e)ize,** *v.* [f. TROCHEE + -IZE.] *trans.* To turn into a trochee, to make trochaic.

*a* 1834 COLERIDGE *Notes & Lect.* (1849) I. 319 A dibrach.. trocheized..by the *arsis* or first accent damping, though not extinguishing, the second. 1907 OMOND *Eng. Metrists* ii. 83 An Italian priest said to him, 'You dactylize and trocheeize every thing'.

**Trochid** (trǫ·kid). *Zool.* [f. mod.L. *Trochidæ*, f. *Trochus*, generic name: see TROCHUS and -ID ³.] A mollusc of the family *Trochidæ*; a top-shell.

1861 P. P. CARPENTER in *Rep. Smithsonian Instit.* 1860, 215 The shells are not pearly as in the Trochids. *Ibid.* 216 A conical Trochid.

**Trochiferous** (troki·fĕrəs), *a. Zool. rare*—⁰. [f. Gr. τροχός wheel (see TROCHUS) + -[I]FEROUS.] Bearing a wheel-like or trochal organ, as a rotifer; rotiferous.

1899 in *Syd. Soc. Lex.* 1909 in *Cent. Dict. Suppl.*

**Trochiform** (trǫ·kifǫɹm), *a. Zool.* [f. TROCHUS + -[I]FORM.] Having the form of a trochus or top-shell; top-shaped; = TROCHOID *a.* 2.

1822 J. PARKINSON *Outl. Oryctol.* 250 The single trochiform shell, *Trochus Anglicanus* of Lister. 1875 C. C. BLAKE *Zool.* 257 The shell is ear-shaped, spiral, or trochiform.

† **Tro·chil.** *Obs.* Also 7 **-yle.** [ad. L. *trochilus.*] = TROCHILUS ¹ 1.

1604 DRAYTON *Owle* 411 For the base Trochyle thinketh it no payne, To scowre vile Carion for a savoury gayne. 1638 SIR T. HERBERT *Trav.* (ed. 2) 323 He [the crocodile] opens his chaps to let the little Trochil pick his teeth, which give it feeding.

**Trochile,** anglicized form of TROCHILUS ².

**Trochilic** (troki·lik), *a.* and *sb. rare.* ? *Obs.* [f. Gr. τροχίλος, taken in sense of τροχός wheel + -IC.] **a.** *adj.* Of or pertaining to rotary motion; relating to wheels. **b.** *sb.* The science or art of rotary motion. Also **trochilics.**

1570 DEE *Math. Pref.* c iv b, Bycause the frute hereof..is in Wheles, it hath the name of *Trochilike*: as a man would say, Whele Art. 1605 CAMDEN *Rem.* 138 By Arte Trochilick. 1641 WILKINS *Math. Magick* II. xiv. (1648) 265 Some principles in Trochilicks, or the art of wheel-instruments. 1646 SIR T. BROWNE *Pseud. Ep.* v. xviii. 260 Horologies composed by Trochilick or the artifice of wheeles. 1648 PETTY *Advice to Hartlib* 6 Making Watches and other Trochilick motions. 1696 in PHILLIPS (ed. 5).

**Trochilidine** (troki·lidəin), *a. Ornith.* [f. mod.L. *Trochilidæ* (f. *Trochilus*: see next) + -INE ¹.] Belonging to or characteristic of the family *Trochilidæ* or humming-birds. So **Trochi·lidist**, one who studies the *Trochilidæ*.

1861 GOULD *Trochilidæ* III. Pl. 142 The name of Floresi will also always be held in high regard among Trochilidists for the fine collections of Humming-Birds obtained by him. 1881 NEWTON in *Encycl. Brit.* XII. 358/1 *note*, 'Trochilidists' in giving their measurements do not take these extraordinary developments into account. 1885 *Proc. Zool. Soc.* 1 Dec. 887 The characters presented in the Trochilidine skeleton.

‖ **Trochilus** ¹ (trǫ·kilǒs). *Ornith.* Also *erron.* 7–9 **troculus,** 8 **trochulus.** [L. *trochilus*, a. Gr. τροχίλος, f. τρέχειν to run.]

**1.** A small Egyptian bird (not certainly identified) said by the ancients to pick the teeth of the crocodile. Also *allusively* (in quot. 1856 *attrib.*).

1579 LYLY *Euphues* (Arb.) 44 The birde Trochilus lyueth by the mouth of the Crocodile and is not spoyled. 1596 LODGE *Marg. Amer.* (Hunter. Cl.) 48 Why the swanne hateth the sparrow, the eagle the *Trochilus*, the asse the bee [etc.]. 1615 G. SANDYS *Trav.* II. 100 A little bird called *Troculus*, doth feede her selfe by the picking of his teeth. *a* 1658 CLEVELAND *Char. Country-Comm.-Man* Wks. (1687) 74 So the poor Souldiers live like Trochilus, by picking the Teeth of this sacred Crocodile. 1856 R. A. VAUGHAN *Mystics* (1860) II. IX. iii. 134 This troculus service—the picking the teeth of the gorged ecclesiastical crocodile. 1910 THOMPSON tr. *Aristotle's Hist. Anim.* 612 When the crocodile yawns, the trochilus flies into his mouth and cleans his teeth.

**2.** An alleged name for some species of wren, or other small European bird.

[1678 RAY *Willughby's Ornithol.* II. xi. 227 The golden-crown'd Wren: Regulus cristatus...The Trochilus of Pliny and Aristotle.] 1706 PHILLIPS (ed. Kersey), *Trochilus*, the fin-footed Runner; a Bird so call'd because it always runs; a Wren.

**3.** A Linnæan genus of American birds, originally including all the then known humming-birds; now greatly restricted.

In first quot. app. used for some other small bird.

1672 JOSSELYN *New Eng. Rarities* 7 The Troculus, a small bird, black and white, no bigger than a Swallow. 1752 J. HILL *Hist. Anim.* 502 The gold and purple Trochilus. The yellow Humming-bird. 1796 STEDMAN *Surinam* II. xxv. 219 The trochulus, or humming-birds, were so thick among the tamarind-trees, that they resembled a swarm of bees.

‖ **Tro·chilus** ². *Arch.* Also 7–8 anglicized as **trochile** (trǫ·kəil). [L., app. the same word as prec.: cf. Gr. τροχιλία the sheaf of a pulley.] A concave moulding; = SCOTIA, CASEMENT 1: esp. in classical architecture.

1563 SHUTE *Archit.* D iij, The nethermost Trochilus or Scotia. 1664 EVELYN tr. *Freart's Archit.* 125 Trochile is that cavity appearing next to the Torus. 1789 P. SMYTH tr. *Aldrich's Archit.* (1818) 117 At Tivoli, the ends of the channels and the cavity of the trochile or casement are not round but square. 1842–76 GWILT *Archit.* Gloss., *Trochilus*, ..an annular moulding whose section is concave like the edge of a pulley..more commonly called a *scotia.* 1845 PARKER *Gloss. Archit.* 330 *Scotia*, or *Trochilus*, a hollow moulding constantly used in the bases of columns, &c., in classical architecture.

**Trochin** (trōᵘ·kin). *Anat. rare*—⁰. [a. F. *trochin* (Chaussier), app. arbitrarily f. TROCHANTER; cf. TROCHANTIN.] (See quot.) Hence **Trochi·nian** *a.* [F. *trochinien*].

1857 DUNGLISON *Med. Lex.*, *Trochin*...Chaussier has given this name to the smaller of the tuberosities at the upper extremity of the os humeri; because it gives attachment to one of the rotator muscles of the arm,—the subscapularis. *Trochinian*, that which belongs or relates to the trochin.

† **Tro·ching.** *Venery. Obs.* [f. TROCHE ¹ + -ING ¹.] A 'troche', or troches collectively; a branching into a troche.

*c* 1410 *Master of Game* (MS. Digby 182) ii, If þer be thre or .iiii. or mo, it is ycleped trochynge. *Ibid.* xxiv, þe trochynge..hye and gret. 1660 HOWELL *Parly of Beasts* iv. 62 Such branch'd horns, such spilters [*sic*] and trochings on their heads, as that goodly Stagg bears. 1678 PHILLIPS (ed. 4), *Trochings*,..the small little branches on the top of the Deers-head, divided into three or four.

† **Trochi·scate,** *v. Obs.* [f. L. *trochisc-us* (see next) + -ATE ³.] *trans.* To make into 'trochisks'.

1657 TOMLINSON *Renou's Disp.* 580 [Pills] of..choyce Rhabarb, Agarick trochiscated. 1662 H. STUBBE *Ind. Nectar* vi. 112 Half a dram of Rhubarb trochiscated.

‖ **Trochi·scus.** *Pl.* **-isci.** [L.] = next.

† **Trochisk** (trōᵘ·kisk). *Obs.* Forms: 5 **trocis,** 6 **-cysce, -cyske, -cisque,** 6–7 **-ciske, -chiske, -chisce, -chisque, -chis,** 7 **-cisk, -chisc(k, -chisch, -chisq,** 7–8 **trochisk,** (*erron.* 5 **-ciste,** 6 **-chist,** 7–8 **-chiste**); also, in L. form **trochiscus.** [a. F. *trochisque* (*trocisque, trocisse,* 1425 in Godef. *Compl.*) = It. *trochisco,* Ger. *trochisk*; ad. L. *trochiscus,* a. Gr. τροχίσκος small wheel, small globe, pill, lozenge, dim. of τροχός wheel.] A medicated tablet or disk; a (round or ovate) pastille or lozenge; = TROCHE *sb.*[2]

c **1400** *Lanfranc's Cirurg.* 211 Þou schalt purge him with trocis de turbit, or wiþ anoþer medicyn þat purgiþ fleume. c **1425** tr. *Arderne's Treat. Fistula* (E.E.T.S.) 91 When.. it is cold..enforme þerof trocistes. **1525** tr. *Jerome of Brunswick's Surg.* F j b/2 Therof make a trocysce. **1541** R. COPLAND *Guydon's Formul.* U ij b, Trociskes..be put to powdre, and with swete wyne incorporate, and be made to trociskes. **1545** RAYNOLD *Byrth Mankynde* R ij, Temper the hole masse into litell roundels or trociskes. **1576** BAKER *Jewell of Health* 109 Let Trochistes or lytle flat balles be made therof. **1612** WOODALL *Surg. Mate* Wks. (1653) 64 Trochisks of Minium..mundifie sordid ulcers. **1625** GILL *Sacr. Philos.* i. 17 Poysons..rightly used..may be helpefull..: as it appeares in the trocisks of the vipers flesh. **1658** ROWLAND *Moufet's Theat. Ins.* 1056 The Dose is one Trochis, with one ounce of wine. **1665** G. HARVEY *Advice agst. Plague* 21 Perfume your sheets..by burning the said Trochisces in a warming pan. **1748** tr. *Vegetius' Distemp. Horses* 136 Give him..one Trochisk a Day dissolved in Water.

**Trochite** (trǭ·kəit, trōᵘ·kəit). *Palæont.* Now *rare* or *Obs.* [ad. mod.L. *trochītēs,* f. Gr. τροχός wheel: see -ITE[1].] A name for the detached wheel-like joints of encrinites: = ENTROCHITE, ENTROCHUS.

**1676** BEAUMONT in *Phil. Trans.* XI. 726 One Trochite.. has round inlets or sockets. **1815** W. PHILLIPS *Outl. Min. & Geol.* (1818) 141 Transition Limestone..contains petrifactions of marine animals, as corallites, encrinites, pentacrinites, entrochites, and trochites. **1853** TH. ROSS *Humboldt's Trav.* III. xxxii. 391 A heap of turbinites and trochites.

Hence **Trochitic** (troki·tik) *a.* (*rare*⁻⁰), of the nature of or pertaining to a trochite or trochites.

**1891** in *Cent. Dict.*

**Trochiter** (trǭ·kitəɹ). *Anat. rare*⁻⁰. [a. F. *trochiter* (Chaussier), altered from TROCHANTER.] (See quot.) Hence **Trochite·rian** *a.* [F. *trochitérien*].

**1857** DUNGLISON *Med. Lex., Trochiter*.., the larger of the two tuberosities at the upper extremity of the os humeri; so called because it affords insertion to rotator muscles.—Chaussier. *Trochiterian,* in the language of Chaussier, means any thing belonging or relating to the trochiter.

‖ **Trochlea** (trǭ·kliă). *Anat.* [L. *trochlea*: cf. Gr. τροχιλία, -χιλέα, -χαλία sheaf of a pulley.] A pulley-like structure or arrangement of parts, with a smooth surface upon which some other part, as a bone or tendon, slides;

*spec.* (*a*) the surface of the inner condyle of the humerus at the elbow-joint, with which the ulna articulates; (*b*) the cartilaginous loop through which the superior oblique muscle of the eye passes; (*c*) the orifice of the metathorax in hymenopterous insects, through which the tendon of the abdomen passes.

**1693** tr. *Blancard's Phys. Dict.* (ed. 2), *Trochlea,* the same that *Bathmis.* **1826** KIRBY & SPENCE *Entomol.* xxxvi. III. 701 Here the upper orifice in the trunk is the pulley (*trochlea*), the tendon is the rope (*funiculus*), and the abdomen is the weight to be lifted. **1854** OWEN *Skel. & Teeth* (1855) 64 The distal end of the tibia forms a transverse pulley or trochlea. **1857** DUNGLISON *Med. Lex., Trochlea,* a pulley;..for example, the articular surface at the lower extremity of the os humeri; so called from its forming a kind of pulley on which the ulna moves...Also, the cartilaginous pulley over which the tendon of the trochlearis muscle passes, at the upper and inner part of the orbit.

**Trochlear** (trǭ·kliăɹ), *a.* [ad. mod.L. *trochleār-is,* f. *trochlea*: see prec. and -AR.]

**1.** *Anat.* Belonging to or connected with a trochlea, as a muscle, nerve, etc.; forming a trochlea, pulley-like, as a surface of a bone, etc.

*Trochlear fossa, t. spine,* parts of the frontal bone connected with the trochlea of the eye. *T. muscle,* the superior oblique muscle of the eye. *T. nerve,* each of the fourth pair of cranial nerves, the motor nerves for the trochlear muscles. *T. nucleus,* a nucleus in the brain from which the trochlear nerve arises.

**1681** tr. *Willis' Rem. Med. Wks.* Vocab., *Trochlear muscle,* a muscle made almost like a windlas or pully. **1808** BARCLAY *Muscular Motions* 304 In many cases..the particular direction in which several muscles act..is regulated by trochlear ligaments or pulleys. **1870** N. F. HELE *Aldeburgh* iv. 29 A trochlear end of a humerus. **1875** SIR W. TURNER in *Encycl. Brit.* I. 840/2 The patella moves up and down the trochlear surface of the femur.

**2.** *Bot.* Pulley-shaped; circular and contracted in the middle like the wheel of a pulley, as the embryo of *Commelynaceæ.*

**1830** LINDLEY *Nat. Syst. Bot.* 255 It [Spiderwort] has scarcely any affinity with Palms, except in its trochlear embryo.

So **Trochle·ariform** (-æ·rifǭɹm) *a., Bot.* [f. mod.L. *trochleāri-s* + -FORM; irreg. for **trochleiform,* f. TROCHLEA + -FORM] = sense 2 above; ‖ **Trochle·aris** (-ēᵊ·ris), *Anat.* [mod.L. (see above), sc. *musculus* or *nervus*], the trochlear muscle, also the trochlear nerve; **Tro·chle·ary** *a., Anat.* (*rare*) = sense 1 above; **Tro·chle·ate** *a., Bot.* = sense 2 above (*Cassell's Encycl. Dict.* 1888).

**1895** *Funk's Stand. Dict.,* *Trochleariform. **1693** tr. *Blancard's Phys. Dict.* (ed. 2), **Trochlearis,* the upper, or greater oblique Muscle of the Eye. **1842** *Penny Cycl.* XXII. 78/2 The pulley of the trochlearis muscle of the eye. **1890** BILLINGS *Med. Dict., Trochlearis*...2. Trochlear nerve. **1828** WEBSTER, **Trochleary,* pertaining to the trochlea; as, the trochleary muscle,..the trochleary nerve...*Parr.*

**Trocho-** (trǭko), before a vowel **troch-** (trǭk), combining form repr. Gr. τροχός wheel, disk; occurring in several scientific words. **Trocheidoscope** (-əi·dǒskoᵘp) [after KALEIDOSCOPE], a rotating disk with coloured sectors, for showing combinations of colours (*Cassell's Encycl. Dict.* 1888). **Trochelminth** (trǭ·kelminþ) [Gr. ἕλμινς, ἑλμινθ- worm], a rotifer. **Tro·choblast** [Gr. βλαστός germ], one of the embryonic cells giving rise to the prototroch in the trochophore larva of marine annelids. **Tro:chocepha·lic** (-sĭfæ·lik) *a.* [Gr. κεφαλή head], having a round form of skull due to premature union of the parietal and frontal bones; so **Trochocephaly** (-se·făli), the condition of being trochocephalic. **Trochoceracone** (-se·răkōᵘn) [Gr. κέρας horn, κῶνος cone], a nautiloid shell with loose flattened coils, as those of the fossil genus *Trochoceras*; so **Trochoceran** (trǫkǫ·sĕrăn) *a.,* having the form or character of such a shell (*Cent. Dict. Suppl.*). **Tro:chocœlomate** (-sī·lōᵘmĕt) *a.,* belonging to the *Trochocœlomata,* a proposed division of *Metazoa,* containing animals having radiated cœlomes (= *Radiata*). **Trocho·meter** [-METER] = TRECHOMETER (Worcester 1846). **Tro·chophore** (-fōᵊɹ) [Gr. -φόρος bearing], **Tro·chosphere** (-sfiᵊɹ), a larval form constituting a stage in the development of most molluscs and of certain worms, esp. marine annelids, characterized by a spheroidal body with a ring of cilia; also *attrib.*; hence **Trochospheric** (-sfe·rik), **-sphe·rical** *adjs.,* pertaining to or having the form of a trochosphere. **Trochozoon** (-zōᵘ·ǫn) [Gr. ζῷον animal], one of the *Trochozoa,* a collective name for those molluscs, annelids, etc. which pass through a trochosphere larval stage, or for such larvæ; also for a hypothetical ancestral group of animals from which these are assumed to be derived.

**1904** *Amer. Nat.* July–Aug. 500 Cells..identical in origin with the 'primary *trochoblasts' of the annelids. **1878** BARTLEY tr. *Topinard's Anthrop.* v. 176 *Trochocephalic, very round skull. *Ibid.* Index 547/1 *Trochocephaly. **1884** HYATT in *Proc. Boston Soc. Nat. Hist.* 5 Mar. 113 We can readily transform a protocoelomate into a *trochocoelomate by destroying the horizontal parts of the partitions between the ampullae. **1892** J. A. THOMSON *Outlines Zool.* xi. 182 By far the most important larval form among Annelids is that known as the Trochosphere or *Trochophore. **1909** J. W. JENKINSON *Experim. Embryol.* 213 Eight instead of the usual four macromeres were found in the Trochophore larva. **1883** E. R. LANKESTER in *Encycl. Brit.* XVI. 648/1 [In the Limpet the] Diblastula..acquires a ciliated band, and becomes a nearly spherical *Trochosphere. **1888** ROLLESTON & JACKSON *Anim. Life* 454 The Mollusca with the exception of *Cephalopoda* pass through a typical larval development, in two stages—a Trochosphere and a Veliger stage. **1899** *Syd. Soc. Lex.,* *Trochospheric. **1891** *Cent. Dict.,* *Trochospherical. **1890** *Nature* 22 May 94/1 The author's conclusions are, that the *Balanoglossus*..has originated from a *trochozoon which acquired some features in common with worms.

**Trochoid** (trǫ·koid, trōᵘ·koid), *sb.* and *a.* [ad. Gr. τροχοειδής round like a wheel, f. τροχός wheel + εἶδος form: see -OID; cf. F. *trochoïde* (1658 in Hatz.-Darm.).] **A.** *sb.*

**1.** *Geom.* A curve traced by a point on or connected with a rolling circle; *orig.* = CYCLOID 1: now usually restricted to the *curtate* and *prolate cycloids,* traced respectively by points within and without the circle; also extended to curves similarly generated by a circle rolling upon another circle, either inside it (HYPOTROCHOID) or outside it (EPITROCHOID).

**1704** J. HARRIS *Lex. Techn.* I. s. v., A Curve Line..called a Cycloid or Trochoid. **1711** W. SUTHERLAND *Shipbuild. Assist.* 59 The Cycloids or Trochoids. **1867** DENISON *Astron. without Math.* 86 *note,* That curve is called a trochoid, but when the tracing point is on the circumference it becomes a cycloid. **1881** C. W. BOURNE in *Eng. Mech.* No. 874. 377/1 The bar AB is jointed to a bar BC, so that while AB revolves round A as centre, BC can also revolve round B as centre, then a curve will be described by the point C...Every such curve is comprised under the name 'trochoid'.

**2.** *Zool.* A gastropod of the family *Trochidæ*; a top-shell.

**1839** *Penny Cycl.* XIV. 317/2 Mollusca...Class III. Gastropoda...Order 6. Pectinibranchiata. Family of Trochöids.

**3.** *Anat.* A trochoid articulation, a pivot-joint.

**1860** in WORCESTER; hence in later Dicts. [Cf. quot. 1857 in B. 3.]

**B.** *adj.*

**1.** *Geom.* = TROCHOIDAL 1. *rare*⁻⁰.

**1882** OGILVIE (Annandale), *Trochoid, a.* 1. Trochoidal.

**2.** *Conch.* Top-shaped, conical with flat base, as the shells of the genus *Trochus* or family *Trochidæ*; *Zool.* belonging to the family *Trochidæ.*

**1859** J. R. GREENE *Man. Anim. Kingd., Protozoa* 16 If ..the spiral passes obliquely round an axis, the shell assumes a more or less pyramidal form, and is termed 'trochoid'. **1861** P. P. CARPENTER in *Rep. Smithsonian Instit.* 1860, 213 The..African group *Collonia* have small Trochoid shells.

**3.** *Anat.* Applied to a pivot-joint, in which one bone turns upon another with a rotary motion.

**1857** DUNGLISON *Med. Lex., Trochoid*.., an articulation, in which one bone turns upon another, like a wheel upon its axle. **1860** MAYNE *Expos. Lex., Trochoides,*..resembling a wheel: trochoid. *Anat.* Applied to a movable connexion of bones in which one bone rotates upon another, as the first cervical vertebra upon the odontoid process of the second.

**Trochoidal** (trǫkoi·dăl), *a.* [f. prec. + -AL.]

**1.** *Geom.* Having the form or nature of a trochoid; pertaining or relating to trochoids: see prec. A. 1.

**1799** YOUNG in *Phil. Trans.* XC. 137 A similar chord bent into a trochoidal curve. **1861** W. FROUDE *Rolling of Ships* (1862) 23 The wave would be more accurately represented by some member of the cycloidal or trochoidal family than by the curve of sines.

**2.** *Conch.* = TROCHOID B. 2. *rare*⁻⁰.

**1891** in *Cent. Dict.*

**3.** *Anat.* = TROCHOID B. 3. *rare.*

**1882** OGILVIE (Annandale) s. v. *Trochoid,* A trochoidal articulation.

Hence **Trochoi·dally** *adv.,* in a trochoidal manner or course.

**1855** DE MORGAN in Graves *Life Sir W. R. Hamilton* (1889) III. 519 A book..showing that the earth moves trochoidally if the sun has motion.

‖ **Trochus** (trōᵘ·kǒs, trǫ·kǒs). Pl. **trochi** (-kei), also **trochuses.** [L., a. Gr. τροχός, f. τρέχειν to run.]

**1.** *Gr.* and *Rom. Antiq.* A wheel or hoop, used in athletic exercises or as a plaything.

**1706** PHILLIPS (ed. Kersey), *Trochus,* a Wheel, a Top for Children to play with. **1734** tr. *Rollin's Anc. Hist.* (1768) I. Pref. 88 The exercises of leaping, throwing the dart, and that of the trochus or wheel. **1847** LEITCH tr. *C. O. Müller's Anc. Art* § 351. (1850) 427 Ganymede with trochus.

† **2.** = TROCHE[2]. *Obs. rare*⁻¹.

**1748** tr. *Vegetius' Distemp. Horses* 85 Three Trochus's or Cakes of Sinoper.

**3.** *Zool.* **a.** A genus of gastropod molluscs, having a top-shaped or conical shell; the type of the family *Trochidæ* or top-shells.

**1753** CHAMBERS *Cycl. Supp., Trochus,*..a genus of shells. **1774** GOLDSM. *Nat. Hist.* (1776) VII. 33 The trunk of the Trochus is fleshy, muscular, supple, and hollow. **1851** WOODWARD *Mollusca* (1856) 12 The trochi and purpuræ are found at low-water, amongst the sea-weed. **1859** H. KINGSLEY *G. Hamlyn* xxxiv. (1894) 325 They fell to gathering shells...Trochuses, as big as one's fist.

*attrib.* and *Comb.* **1774** GOLDSM. *Nat. Hist.* IV. 22 Snails of the trochus kind. **1889** *Science-Gossip* XXV. 168 Trochus-shaped rotulites.

**b.** The internal ring of cilia in the trochal organ of a rotifer.

**1888** ROLLESTON & JACKSON *Anim. Life* 632 The trochal apparatus..appears to consist typically of an internal præoral ring of long cilia, the trochus, and an external ring of finer cilia, the cingulum.

**Trock, Trocker,** Sc. ff. TRUCK, TRUCKER.

**Trocle,** obs. form of TRUCKLE.

**Troco** (trōᵘ·ko). [app. altered from It. *trucco* 'a billiard-boord, also the play at billiards' (Florio, 1611); or Sp. *truco* the game of TRUCKS, q. v.] See quot.

[**1598** FLORIO, *Trucco,* a kinde of play with balles vpon a table called billiards; but properly a kinde of game vsed in England with casting little bowles at a boord with thirteene holes in it.] **1882** OGILVIE (Annandale), *Troco,* an old English game revived, formerly known as 'lawn-billiards' ..played on a lawn with wooden balls and a cue ending in a spoon-shaped iron projection. [But app. never so called in English. See TRUCKS.]

**Troctolite** (trǫ·ktələit). *Min.* Also **trok-.** [ad. Ger. *troktolit* (Von Lasaulx, 1875), f. Gr. τρώκτης a kind of sea-fish (taken as = trout) + λίθος stone: see -LITE.] (See quot. 1892.)

**1883** *Science* I. 342/2 The term 'troktolite' is the equivalent of the more common 'forellenstein'. **1892** *Chambers' Encycl.* X. 301 *Troctolite* (trout-stone), a variety of Gabbro, composed almost entirely of white felspar..and dark olivine.

**Troculus,** erron. form of TROCHILUS[1].

**Trod** (trǫd), *sb.* Now *dial.* Forms: 1– **trod**; 6 **troad, trood, trodd, -e,** 6–7 **trode.** [OE. *trod* neut. (also *trodu* fem., acc. *trode*) = ON. *troð* treading, trampling, OHG. *trota* winepress (cf. mod. Norw. dial. *trod* fem. foot-board, step), f. ON. *troða,* Goth. *trudan* to tread, ablaut variants of WGer. *tredan* to tread.]

† **1.** Tread, footprint, track, trace. *Obs.*

*Beowulf* (Z.) 843 Secga ænegum þara þe tir-leases trode sceawode, hu he..on weᵹ þanon..feorh-lastas bær. **946–961** *Laws of Edgar* I. c. 5 Gyf him hundred bedrife trod on oðer hundred. a **1225** *Ancr. R.* 380 (MS. Titus) Þe dunes underuoð þe trodes [*v. r.* treden] of him suluen. c **1420** *Chron. Vilod.* 513 Þey nyste neuer where he was a-go, Ne of his trodus no sygne þer nasse. **1551** SIR R. BOWES in *Eng. Border Hen. VIII* (1847) II. 18 They may lawfullye followe there [stolen] goodes either wᵗʰ a sleuthe hounde the trodd thereof, or ellse by suche other meanes as they best can devise. **1563** in Bp. W. Nicholson *Leg. Marchiarum* (1705) 127 Providing the Parties grieved to follow their lawful Trode with Hound and Horn, with Hue and Cry and all other accustomed manner of fresh Pursuit.

**b.** *Hot-trod*: see HOT *a.* 12.

**2.** A trodden way; a footpath, path, way. *dial.*

**1570** LEVINS *Manip.* 155/32 A Trod, path, *callis, is, hæc.* *a* **1575** PILKINGTON *Expos. Neh.* iv. 13 (1585) 60 God and the world cannot be friends: and that maketh so few Courtiers to tread this trodde. **1578** *Paradise Dainty Devises* A iij, And takes us from the trod, which guides to en[d]lesse gayne And sets us in the way that leades to lasting payne. **1596** SPENSER *F. Q.* VI. x. 5 He chaunst to come, far from all peoples troad. **1642** H. MORE *Song of Soul* IV. xxvii, Thus in the middle trod I safely went, and fairly well have row'd. **1678** PHILLIPS (ed. 4), *Trode*, (old word) signifying a path. **1825** BROCKETT *N. C. Words*, *Trod*, a foot path through a field. **1897** *Speaker* 4 Sept. 260/2 The lane and 'trod' must have saved me the mile or more.

**3.** The tread of a wheel (TREAD *sb.* 10 b). *dial.*

**1797** CURR *Coal Viewer* 20 The rim [of the corf wheel] is 1½ inches broad on the trod or face. **1825** J. NICHOLSON *Operat. Mechanic* 645 Making the wheels and spokes of cast iron, with hoops, tyres, or trods, of malleable iron.

**4.** *Comb.*, as †**trod-gate**, †**trod-way**, trodden way or track.

*a* **1400–50** *Alexander* 2988 Alexander..Ay trottis him to þe trod-gate [*Dublin MS.* troyde-gate] as him þe torche wyssis. **1661** J. CHILDREY *Brit. Baconica* 164 The Coals grow so near the surface..that the Cart wheels turn them up in the trod-ways.

**Trod** (trǫd), *ppl. a.* [Shortened from TRODDEN.] = TRODDEN: chiefly as second element; also with adv., as *trod-down*.

**1632** MILTON *L'Allegro* 131 Then to the well-trod stage anon. **1638** W. LISLE *Heliodorus* x. 177 To see their trod-downe fellowes hurt. **1897** H. N. HOWARD *Footsteps Proserpine* 48 Mingled with elf-trod moss.

**Trod**, *v. Obs.* or *dial.* [f. TROD *sb.*] **a.** *trans.* To follow the footprints or track of; to track, trace. **b.** *intr.* (*U.S.*) To pursue a path.

*a* **1225** *Ancr. R.* 232 Betere is þe þet troddeð wel & ofsecheð wel ut his owune feblesce þen he þet meteð hu heih is þe heouene. **1619** SIR J. SEMPIL *Sacrilege Handled* App. 49 To trode Tithes then vp as neare as may be, euen to Adam, from the Law. **1825** JAMIESON s.v., To 'trod a thief'. **1909** *N. York Observer* 2 Sept. 316/1 Trodding to Self-Support. The Home Mission Committee of Buffalo Presbytery has set itself earnestly to the task of bringing its dependent churches to self-support.

**Trod** (trǫd), pa. t. and pple. of TREAD *v.*; obs. pa. pple. of TROW *v.*

**Trodden** (trǫ·d'n), *ppl. a.* [Late ME. *troden*, taking the place of OE. and ME. *treden*, pa. pple. of TREAD; imitating such pa. pples. as *holpen*, *stolen*, from *help*, *steal*.] That has been walked, stepped, or trampled upon (also *fig.*): see senses of TREAD *v.* Also in comb., as DOWN-TRODDEN.

**1545** ELYOT, *Pressatus*, oppressed, charged, troden downe. **1590** SPENSER *F. Q.* I. iii. 10 The troden gras, In which the tract of peoples footing was. **1700** DRYDEN *Ovid's Met.*, *Acis, Polyphemus*, etc. 94 More revengeful than a trodden snake. **1760–72** H. BROOKE *Fool of Qual.* (1809) I. p. x, I was as a trodden worm, and turned. *a* **1849** J. C. MANGAN *Poems* (1859) 421 There's hope, too, for his trodden thralls.

**b.** Of a path, etc.: Formed or marked by treading; beaten.

**1576** FLEMING *Panopl. Epist.* 226 *margin*, Pouertie the troden path to vertuous conuersation. **1615** W. LAWSON *Country Housew. Gard.* (1626) 19 To walke in the plaine trodden path. **1870** MORRIS *Earthly Par.* III. IV. 34 Now by trodden way and wild Goes Heimir long.

**Trode**, arch. pa. t. and pple. of TREAD *v.*

†**Trod-net.** *Obs.* Also 6 **trodenette.** [Origin uncertain.] Some kind of fishing-net.

**1523** FITZHERB. *Surv.* 10 b, In some rinnyng waters, the lordes tenauntes haue lybertie by custome to fysshe with shouenettes, trodenettes, small pytches, and suche other. **1562–77** LEIGH *Surv.* (1596) F iv, Fishing, with..casting nets..trod-nets, and such like.

**Troe**, obs. form of TROW.

**Trofe, Troffe**, obs. forms of TROUGH, TURF.

**Trofel, -fil, -fle**, obs. forms of TRIFLE.

**Trögerite** (trö·gərəit). *Min.* [Named (1871) after R. Tröger of Neustädtel, Saxony: see -ITE [1].] A hydrous arseniate of uranium, occurring in thin lemon-yellow tabular crystals.

**1872** DANA *Min.* App. i. 16.

**Troget, -eter, -ettar**, var. TREGET, TREGETOUR.

**Trogh(e, Troght**, obs. ff. TROUGH, TROTH.

**Troglodyte** (trǫ·g-, trōu·glodəit), *sb.* (*a.*) Also 6–8 -ite. [ad. L. *trōglodyta*, ad. Gr. τρωγλοδύτης, f. τρώγλη hole + δύειν to get or go into.]

**1.** One of various races or tribes of men (chiefly ancient or prehistoric) inhabiting caves or dens (natural or artificial); a cave-dweller, cave-man.

**1555** W. WATREMAN *Fardle of Facions* I. vi. 93 The Troglodites myne them selues caues in the grounde, wherin to dwell. **1614** RALEIGH *Hist. World* I. (1634) 52 Which Regions..(I mean that of Niger, and that of Prester John and the Troglodytes). **1642** HOWELL *For. Trav.* (Arb.) 51 They were Troglodites, and had no dwelling but in the hollowes of the rocks. **1842** W. C. TAYLOR *Anc. Hist.* xii. § 4 (ed. 3) 336 Some..Cappadocians were and continue to be Troglodytes, or dwellers in caves. **1851** D. WILSON *Preh. Ann.* (1863) I. ix. 251 The Troglodytes of post-pliocene ages.

**2.** Applied to various species of animals. †**a.** Some kind of deer or other horned quadruped. *Obs.*

**b.** A bird of the genus *Troglodytes*; a wren. *rare*—°.

**c.** An anthropoid ape of the genus *Troglodytes*, as a gorilla or chimpanzee.

**1661** LOVELL *Hist. Anim. & Min.* Introd., The hornes, in the stagge are ramous, .. the Phrygian have moveable hornes, the Troglodyte direct to the earth. [**1706** PHILLIPS, *Troglodytes* or *Passer Troglodytes*, a little Bird call'd a Wren.] **1774** GOLDSM. *Nat. Hist.* (1862) I. VII. i. 491 The Troglodyte of Bontius, the Drill of Purchas, and the Pigmy of Tyson, have all received this general name—oran-outang.

**d.** Applied allusively to an animal or plant.

**1817** KIRBY & SP. *Entomol.* (1818) II. xxi. 265 The caterpillar of another moth (*Noctua subterranea*, F.)..remains, a true Troglodyte,..in its cell under ground. **1845** LONGF. *To a Child* 99 The cavernous..homes Of wandering..tribes of ants..These hapless Troglodytes. **1856** GRINDON *Life* iii. (1875) 29 That sullen troglodyte, the *Lathræa*, of the woods.

**3.** *fig.* A person who lives in seclusion; one unacquainted with the affairs of the world; a 'hermit'. Also, a dweller in a hovel or slum; a person of a degraded type like the prehistoric or savage cave-dwellers.

**1854** H. ROGERS *Ess.* II. i. 11 Some would make him..such a very Troglodyte in metaphysics that he was not properly acquainted even with such writers as Descartes or Hobbes. **1879** G. MACDONALD in *Graphic* Christmas No. 5 The girl who had been from her very birth a troglodyte, stood in the glory of a southern night. **1905** *Sat. Westm. Rev.* 25 Feb. 3 A belief worthy only of troglodytes inaccessible to Imperial ..thought.

**4.** *attrib.* or *adj.* That is a troglodyte, cave-dwelling; of or belonging to a troglodyte or troglodytes.

**1704** SWIFT *T. Tub* x. (1709) 119 Hear the words of the famous Troglodyte Philosopher. **1785** LATHAM *Gen. Synopsis* V. 229 Troglodyte Rail...These inhabit New Zealand. **1827** BUCKINGHAM *Trav. Mesopot.* I. 58 Large caves, and smaller grottoes;..any other Troglodyte habitations. **1873** H. SPENCER *Stud. Sociol.* vi. 119 Aboriginal man, of troglodyte or kindred habits.

Hence (or from the L. or Gr.) **Tro·glody·tal** *a.*, pertaining to or characteristic of a troglodyte; †**Tro·glodytan** = *troglodyte* (sense 1); **Tro·glodytish** *a.*, resembling or characteristic of a troglodyte; **Tro·glodyti:sm**, the condition of a troglodyte, the habit of dwelling in caves.

**1845** S. JUDD *Margaret* II. i. (1871) 160 Coming up from their dark *troglodytal abodes. **1607** TOPSELL *Four-f. Beasts* (1658) 225 People of Arabia called *Erembi*, which some call *Ichthyophagans*, and **Troglodytans*. **1866** *Sat. Rev.* 3 Mar. 256/2 The most perfect type of *troglodytish women does not care even for theology or religion. **1867** *Chambers' Encycl.* IX. 557/1 Perhaps we shall not be far wrong if we regard *Troglodytism as the primitive state of all..mankind.

**Troglodytic** (trǫg-, trōuglǫdi·tik), *a.* Also 6 -it-. [ad. L. *trōglodytic-us*, a. Gr. τρωγλοδυτικός, f. τρωγλοδύτης: see prec. and -IC.]

**1.** Inhabited or frequented by troglodytes; pertaining to or characteristic of a troglodyte.

**1585** T. WASHINGTON tr. *Nicholay's Voy.* IV. xi. 122 b, The part of this Arabia bordering vpon Ethyopia by the auncients called Trogloditick. **1665** SIR T. HERBERT *Trav.* (1677) 36 Upon the Æthiopick or Trogloditick shoar. **1841** W. SPALDING *Italy & It. Isl.* I. 313 In the deep rocky valley of Ispica, are cliffs cut out into numerous habitations...This curious Troglodytic city, still occupied by a few peasants. **1874** WITHROW *Catacombs of Rome* (1877) 152 So habituated did he become to this troglodytic existence.

**2.** Having the habits of a troglodyte; cave-dwelling.

**1676** EVELYN in *Aubrey's Nat. Hist. Surrey* (1719) I. Pref. 8 In the sandy Banks about Albury, do breed the Troglodytic Martines, who make their Boroughs in the Earth. **1833–4** J. PHILLIPS *Geol.* in *Encycl. Metrop.* (1845) VI. 698/2 Many parts of the Mediterranean shores were anciently possessed by Troglodytic nations. **1894** WINDLE *Tyson's Philol. Ess. Pygmies* Introd. I. 21 These tribes..are said to be pigmy in stature, troglodytic, and still in the Stone Age.

**3.** Resembling a troglodyte; of a degraded type like the cave-dwellers; also *fig.* not interested in or conversant with affairs.

**1871** J. A. SYMONDS in *Life* (1895) II. 77 Uttering..these little bat squeaks of a Troglodytic creature. **1886** STEVENSON *Dr. Jekyll* ii. (ed. 2) 25 God bless me, the man seems hardly human! Something troglodytic..? **1910** *Blackw. Mag.* Feb. 169/2 A respectable troglodytic peer.

So **Troglody·tical** *a.*

**1841** T. A. TROLLOPE *Western France* I. ix. 164 The whole [calcareous bank]..is hollowed out into a vast number of.. troglodytical habitations.

**Troglodytid** (troglǫ·ditid). *Ornith.* [f. mod.L. *Troglodytidæ*, f. *Troglodytes*, generic name: see TROGLODYTE and -ID [3].] A bird of the family *Troglodytidæ*, including wrens, mocking-birds, etc. So **Troglodytine** (troglǫ·ditəin) *a.*, belonging to the subfamily *Troglodytīnæ*; **Troglodytoid** (troglǫ·ditoid) *a.*, akin to the *Troglodytidæ*.

**1890** *Field* 12 Apr. 517/3 Other families may be ultimately added to this Troglodytine group. **1895** *Funk's Stand. Dict.*, Troglodytid..Troglodytoid.

**Trogon** (trōu·gǫn). *Ornith.* [mod.L., Gr. τρώγων, pr. pple. of τρώγειν to gnaw.] A bird of the genus *Trogon* or family *Trogonidæ*, widely distributed in tropical and subtropical regions, esp. in the New World, and characterized by soft plumage of varied and usually brilliant colouring.

**1792** SHAW *Mus. Lever.* 177 The Leverian Trogon...Violaceous Trogon with a gloss of green-gold; wings black; abdomen white. **1838** J. GOULD (*title*) A Monograph of the Trogonidæ, or Family of Trogons. **1879** E. P. WRIGHT *Anim. Life* 277 The Golden Trogon (*Trogon resplendens*) has the greater portion of its plumage apparently composed of burnished gold. **1907** *Spectator* 23 Mar. 452/1 In the Miocene period..among the birds of French forests were trogons and parrots. **1910** *Q. Rev.* July 137 The beautiful Central American Quezal, or King of the Trogons, ranges ..from greenish bronze, through golden green, green, indigo, to purple and then into grey-black.

Hence **Trogonid** (trogǭu·nid), a bird of the family *Trogonidæ*; **Trogonine** (trōu·gǒnəin), **Trogonoid** (trōu·gǒnoid) *adjs.*, belonging to or having the characters of the *Trogonidæ*.

**1890** H. SEEBOHM in *Ibis* Jan. 31 In the Picine arrangement, whether typical or Trogonine, the front plantar does not lead to the second toe. **1891** *Cent. Dict.*, Trogonoid. **1895** *Funk's Stand. Dict.*, Trogonid.

**Trogositid** (trōugǫ|səi·tid), *sb.* and *a.* *Entom.* [ad. mod.L. *Trōgosītidæ*, f. *Trōgosīta*, name of the typical genus, f. Gr. τρώγειν to gnaw + σῖτος grain.] **a.** *sb.* A clavicorn beetle of the family *Trogositidæ*. **b.** *adj.* Belonging to the *Trogositidæ*. So **Trogositoid** (trōugosəi·toid) *a.*, allied to the *Trogositidæ*.

**1895** in *Funk's Stand. Dict.*

**Troian(e, -en**: see TROJAN.

**Troic** (trōu·ik), *a.* [ad. Gr. Τρωικός, f. Τρώς, name of the mythical founder of Troy.] Pertaining or relating to ancient Troy; Trojan.

**1831** KEIGHTLEY *Mythol. Anc. Greece* (1854) 440 Contains much Troic matter. **1878** GLADSTONE *Homer* ii. 32 The Troic expedition.

**Troich**, obs. Sc. f. TROUGH. **Troie**, obs. f. TROY.

‖**Troika** (troi·kă). [Russ. тройка.] A Russian vehicle drawn by three horses abreast.

**1842** tr. *Kohl's Russia* xxv. 202 One of his [Orlowsky's] best, and best-known pictures is his 'Courier'. A Russian troika is carried on at full speed by three wild horses. **1904** *Daily Record & Mail* 22 Apr. 4, I crossed the Baikal in a troika, a basket sleigh on wooden runners, drawn by three horses abreast.

†**Troil**, *v. Obs. rare.* [a. OF. *troillier, truillier, treuiller* (*c* 1250 in Godef.), ad. MHG. *trüllen.*] *trans.* To dupe, beguile, deceive.

**1393** LANGL. *P. Pl.* C. XXI. 321 Thus with treison and with trecherie þow troiledest hem boþe.

**Troilite** (trōu·iləit). *Min.* [f. the name of Dominico Troili, who described a meteorite containing this mineral which fell in 1766 (Dana): see -ITE [1].] A sulphide of iron found in meteorites.

**1868** DANA *Min.* (ed. 5) 57. **1903** *Daily Chron.* 12 Sept. 3/1 Troilite..is one of the dozen or so minerals found in meteorites that are not found on our earth.

**Troillebastone**, variant of TRAILBASTON.

**Trois, troiss**: see TROY (weight), TRUSS.

**Trois point** (trwa point). [F. *trois* three + POINT *sb.*[1] B. 3 g.] The third point from the outer end in either table of a backgammon-board.

**1745** HOYLE *Backgammon* viii. § 7. 50, 5 Men upon his Adversary's Ace Point, and 3 Men upon his Adversary's Trois Point. **1870** HARDY & WARE *Mod. Hoyle, Backgammon* 143 You must then endeavour to secure your adversary's cinque, quatre, or trois point.

**Trois-quart(s**: see TROCAR.

‖**Trois-temps** (trwatañ). [Short for F. *valse à trois temps* waltz in triple time.] The ordinary form of waltz, as distinguished from the more rapid DEUX-TEMPS. Also *trois-temps waltz*.

**1859** *Habits of Gd. Society* v. (new ed.) 209, I was at a public ball at Caen..and was amused to find the *trois-temps* danced with a peculiar shuffle, by way of compromise between conscience and pleasure. *Ibid.*, They..danced a polka, a gallop and a *trois-temps* waltz.

**Troite**, obs. form of TROUT.

**Trojan** (trōu·dzăn), *a.* and *sb.* Also 4 **Troien**, 4–5 **Troiane**, 4–6 **Troyan**, 4–7 **Troian**, 5 **Troienne**, 6 **Troyane**, -en(e. [Formerly *Troyan*, *Troian* (troi·ăn); ad. L. *Trōiānus*, f. *Trōja* Troy.

The spelling *Troian* app. stood originally for *Troyan*; later it prob. represents *Trojan*.]

**A.** *adj.* Of or pertaining to ancient Troy or its inhabitants.

*c* **1374** CHAUCER *Troylus* II. 825 Antigone..Gan on a troyan lay to syngin clere. **1412–20** LYDG. *Chron. Troy* II. 8591 For Achilles þouȝt it dide hym good With his swerde Troyan blood to schede. **1490** CAXTON *Eneydos* xxv. 91 The troienne folke is alle..descended of the forsworne laomedon. **1574** R. BRISTOW *Motives* (1599) 7 b, The Troian horse. **1581** A. HALL *Iliad* v. 92 Through all the camp Troyene So honord..as he King Priams sonne had bene. **1649** OGILBY tr. *Virgil's Georgicks* I. (1684) 72 Long since enough we with our Blood did pay What might the Trojan Perjury defray. *a* **1721** PRIOR *Pallas & Venus* I The Trojan Swain had judg'd the great Dispute. **1835** THIRLWALL *Greece* I. 149 We..pass ..out of the mythical circle..into that of the Trojan war.

**B.** *sb.* **1.** An inhabitant or native of Troy. (In quot. 1910 used allusively.)

[*c* **893** K. ÆLFRED *Oros.* I. viii. § 4 Ymb ealra þara Troiana ȝewin to asecȝenne.] *c* **1330** R. BRUNNE *Chron. Wace* (Rolls) 158 Of manyon he reknes & sayes, both of Troiens & of Gregeis. *c* **1385** CHAUCER *L. G. W.* 933 *Dido*, The hors.. Thour which that many troyan [*v. r.* many a troian] muste sterue. **1503** HAWES *Examp. Virt.* vii, To the Troyans story lette hym resort. **1579** E. K. *Gloss. Spenser's Sheph. Cal.* July 147 Paris, who thereupon with a sorte of lustye Troyanes, stole her [Helena]. *c* **1620** T. ROBINSON *Mary Magd.* 122 Thousand

Hellens faire,..And as many Troians braue. **1835** THIRLWALL *Greece* I. 33 The Pelasgians..in the Trojan war..side with the Trojans against the Greeks. **1910** M. G. KYLE *Fundamentals* 31 The Hittites have in one respect been the Trojans of Bible History.

**2.** *colloq.* **a.** A merry or roystering fellow; a boon companion; a person of dissolute life; also (in later use only) as a vague term of commendation or familiarity: a good fellow (often with the alliterative epithet *true* or *trusty*). Cf. GREEK *sb.* 5.

[**1588** SHAKS. *L. L. L.* v. ii. 681 Fellow Hector..Vnlesse you play the honest Troyan, the poore Wench is cast away.] **1600** KEMP *Nine Daies Wond.* C ij, He was a kinde good fellow, a true Troyan. **1663** BUTLER *Hud.* I. i. 620 There they say right, and like true Trojans. **1762** BP. FORBES *Jrnl.* (1886) 208, I was most hospitably entertained by that honest old Trojan Mr. Sutherland. **1827** SCOTT *Surg. Dau.* v, None are so scrupulous as I am about making promises. I am as trusty as a Trojan for that. **1888** F. COWPER *Captain of Wight* (1889) 84 Eustace, my Trojan, don't you call me a goose again.

**b.** A brave or plucky fellow; a person of great energy or endurance: usu. in phr. *like a Trojan.*

[**1387** TREVISA *Higden* (Rolls) II. 255 ȝif we wil mene þat þey [the people of Ilium] beeþ stronge we clepeþ hem Troians.] **1846** NEWMAN in Ward *Life* (1912) I. iii. 114 Working like a Trojan. **1882** JAMIESON, *Trojan*, a name applied to a person of uncommon size, strength, daring, or endurance. **1897** G. ALLEN *Type-writer Girl* xvii. 179, I worked hard at that gown...Dear little Elsie helped me with it like a Trojan.

**3.** *Entom.* A name given by Linnæus to certain species of butterflies, chiefly tropical, distinguished by crimson spots on the wings from allied species called *Greeks*.

**1832** T. BROWN *Bk. Butterflies & M.* (1834) I. 142 The Imperial Trojan. *Papilio Priamus.* **1863** BATES *Nat. Amazon* iii. (1864) 62 Those species of Papilio..so conspicuous in their velvety black, green, and rose-coloured hues, which Linnæus..called 'Trojans'.

Hence **Tro·janry** (*nonce-wd.*), body or company of Trojans. See also TROYANISH, TROYISH.

**1667** COTTON *Scarron.* IV. 135 Dido..Ran..to spie, What was become o' th' Trojanry.

† **Troke, truke,** *v. Obs.* (exc. *dial.*) Forms: 1 **trucian,** 2–3 **truke,** 3 **trukie,** 3–4 **troke,** 5 **truche,** (8 *dial.* **truck**). [OE. *trucian*, ulterior origin unascertained.]

**1.** *intr.* To fail; to be wanting or lacking.

*c* **1000** ÆLFRIC *Hom.* (Th.) II. 42 Ne trucað heora nan ana ðurh unmihte. *c* **1205** LAY. 16416 Þa iseh Hængest þæt his help trukede [*c* **1275** trokede]. *a* **1225** *Ancr. R.* 68 Bute ȝif þe ilke þridde, oðer stu[n]de trukie. *c* **1250** *Gen. & Ex.* 105 Til domes-dai ne sal it troken. *a* **1800** PEGGE *Suppl. Grose* s. v., A cow is said to truck when her milk fails. North.

**b.** with dative of person.

*c* **1122** *O. E. Chron.* an. 1090, He undergeat þæt his ȝesworene men him trucedon. *a* **1225** *Ancr. R.* 230 ȝif bileaue him trukede. *a* **1240** *Lofsong* in *Cott. Hom.* 213 Bihold, heie louerd, hu monnes help trukeð me.

**c.** To fail or be unable *to do* something. *rare*$^{-1}$.

*a* **1400–50** *Alexander* 1988 Loo here a gloue full of graynes .. And þou truches [*Dubl. MS.* And yf þou thynkes] þaim to tell [L. *quod si facere non valebis*], þen [etc.].

**2.** *trans.* To deceive, beguile.

*c* **1175** *Lamb. Hom.* 35 Heo us truket þenne we lest weneð. *a* **1225** *Juliana* 7 Ah ha truste upon him þat ne truked na mon. **13..** *Sir Beues* (A.) 3268 Ful wel him þouȝte..Þat him trokede a gret gile, For he was in þe castel be-loke.

Hence † **Troking** (**truking**) *vbl. sb.*, failure, lack; deceit; also † **Troke** (**truke**) *sb.* (*rare*$^{-1}$), failure, want, lack.

*c* **1175** *Lamb. Hom.* 79 Ierusalem bitacneð griþes sihþe, and ierico trukinge of lihte. *a* **1225** *Ancr. R.* 12 Þis nis bute a trukunge & a fals gile. *c* **1250** *Gen. & Ex.* 3508 Help ðe nedful ðat he ne be dead, for truke of ðin helpe.

**Troke, Troker,** Sc. ff. TRUCK, TRUCKER [1].

**Trokel, -ell, -ill,** obs. forms of TRUCKLE.

† **Tro·ker, tru·ker.** *Sc. Obs.* Forms: 5–6 **truker,** 6 **trukour, treukour, truikour, -er, trouker, trucour,** 7 **trewker.** [f. TROKE *v.* + -ER [1].] A deceiver, cheat; a rascal, rogue.

*c* **1470** HENRYSON *Mor. Fab.* IX. (*Wolf & Fox*) xxii, Staf or sting yone truker for to strike. **1530** LYNDESAY *Test. Papyngo* 1001 Agane our wyll, those treukouris bene intrusit. **1535** STEWART *Cron. Scot.* (Rolls) II. 511 With diligence and bissie cuir tha woik, And mony trucour in the tyme tha tuik. **1560** ROLLAND *Seven Sages* 78 The treuth now ȝe haue spyit Of that Truikour. *a* **1578** LINDESAY (Pitscottie) *Chron. Scot.* (S.T.S.) I. 221 Thir fallis trukeris quhilk cause ȝour grace to beleif ewill on my handis. *a* **1585** POLWART *Flyting w. Montgomerie* 225 Thy doytit dytings soone denie, Trouker, or I thy trumperie trie.

**b.** *attrib.* or as *adj.*

**1596** DALRYMPLE tr. *Leslie's Hist. Scot.* VIII. (S.T.S.) II. 58 Mony at this tyme mony trukour tragidies in the cuntrie stiret vp. **1650** *Dalgety Sess. Rec.* in W. Ross *Past. Wk. in Covenant. Times* ix. (1877) 172 William Skinstone .. did sclandour him in calling him a trewker lowne.

**Troktolite,** variant of TROCTOLITE.

**Troll** (trǭl), *sb.* [1] Also 6 **trowell,** 7 **trole, troul, trowle,** 7–9 **trowl.** [app. f. TROLL *v.*; but in some uses the derivation is uncertain.]

**1.** The act of trolling; a going or moving round; routine or repetition.

**1705** ROWE *Biter* I. i, Make up the Troll of the Sentence, as merrily conceited Persons are us'd to do. **1790** BURKE *Fr. Rev.* 274 The troll of their categorical table might have informed them that there was something else..besides substance and quantity.

**2.** A song the parts of which are sung in succession; a round, a catch.

**1820** W. IRVING *Sketch Bk., Little Britain* (1865) 306 The famous old drinking trowl from Gammer Gurton's Needle. **1856** KANE *Arct. Expl.* I. xix. 233 It is sad..to miss..the joyous troll of his ballads.

† **3.** A little wheel; *spec.* an angler's reel or winch on a fishing-rod. *Obs.*

[Cf. OF. *trueil* (Godef. *Compl.*), F. *treuil* windlass, winch.]

**1570** LEVINS *Manip.* 57/15 A Trowell, *rotula.* **1662** VENABLES *Experienced Angler* iv. 47 With your troul wind up your line till you think you have it almost streight. **1670–1** *Act* 22 & 23 *Chas. II*, c. 25 § 6 If any person..shall ..use any..Nett..Angle, Haire Noose, Troll or Speare.

**4.** *Angling.* **a.** The method of trolling in fishing for pike, etc.: see TROLL *v.* 13.

**1681** CHETHAM *Angler's Vade-m.* xli. § 7 (1689) 312 It's not so good for the Trowl as snap. **1688** R. HOLME *Armoury* II. 324/2 *Trowl*, a fishing for a Pike: and this is by walking, and the line to run on a winch, that it may be winded up, or let out at pleasure. **1794** *Sporting Mag.* III. 247 Both at trowl and snap, cut away one of the fins. **1847** T. BROWN *Mod. Farriery* 902 At both troll and snap some persons have two or more swivels to their line.

**b.** A lure used in trolling, as a *trolling-spoon* (see TROLLING *vbl. sb.* 4).

**1869** *Cornh. Mag.* Apr. 419 The many artificial trolls which have been..invented for salmon and trout-angling.

**5.** A kind of low cart: = TROLLEY *sb.* 1. *local.*

**1663** [implied in *trollful*: see below]. **1810** *Hull Improv. Act* 56 Any cart waggon sledge troll dray. **1870** *Murray's Handbk. E. Counties* 224/2 They [the 'rows' of Yarmouth] are traversed by..a sort of horse-wheelbarrow, called 'trolls' or 'trolly-carts'. **1882** BUCKLAND *Notes & Jottings* 192 When the trawlers [at Yarmouth] come in laden with fish they transfer them to very large boats..and thence into trolls, which are backed into the water.

**6.** *attrib.* and *Comb.*: **troll-line** = *trawl-line* (see TRAWL *sb.* 4); **troll-plate** (see quot.).

**1888** EARLL in Goode *Amer. Fishes* 195 The smack fishermen of Charleston catch a few on *troll-lines during..spring and early summer. **1877** KNIGHT *Dict. Mech.*, **Troll-plate* (*Machinery*), a rotating disk employed to effect the simultaneous convergence or divergence of a number of objects; such as screw-dies in a stock, or the jaws of a universal chuck.

Hence **Tro·llful,** as much as fills a troll (sense 5).

**1663** P. HENRY *Diaries & Lett.* (1882) 143 August 1. Hay carry'd in out of ye great meadow, three trolefuls.

**Troll** (trǭl), *sb.* [2] Also **trold, trolle.** See also TROW *sb.* [4] [a. ONorse and Swed. *troll*, Da. *trold* (whence Da. *trylla, trylde*, Sw. *trolla* to charm, bewitch, ON. *trolldómr* witchcraft).

(Adopted in English from Scandinavian in the middle of the 19th c.; but in Shetland and Orkney, where the form is now TROW (in 1616 *troll*), it has survived from the Norse dialect formerly spoken there.)]

In Scandinavian mythology, One of a race of supernatural beings formerly conceived as giants, now, in Denmark and Sweden, as dwarfs or imps, supposed to inhabit caves or subterranean dwellings: see quotations, and cf. TROW *sb.* [4]

**1616** *Dittay Sheriff Court Shetland* 2 Oct. (Jam. s. v. *Trow*), The said Catherine for airt and pairt of witchcraft and sorcerie, in hanting and seeing the Trollis ryse out of the kyrk yeard of Hildiswick. **1851** BORROW *Lavengro* xxx. (1911) 188 A laidly Trold has dragged it there. **1856** EMERSON *Eng. Traits, Ability* Wks. (Bohn) II. 34 The Scandinavian fancied himself surrounded by Trolls—a kind of goblin men, with vast power of work and skilful production. **1865** BARING-GOULD *Werewolves* iv. 40 In the Hrolfs Saga Kraka, we meet with a troll in a boar's shape, to whom divine honours are paid. **1865** WHITTIER *Tent on Beach, Kallundborg Church* 14 But the sly Dwarf said, 'No work is wrought By Trolls of the Hills, O man, for naught.' **1867** BRANDE & COX *Dict. Sc.*, etc. s. v., These Trolls are superior to man in strength and stature, but far beneath him in mind. **1869** TOZER *Highl. Turkey* II. 273 A boy's escape from a Troll or an enchanted horse.

**b.** *attrib.* That is a troll, as *troll-maiden, -wife, -woman*; belonging to or inhabited by trolls, as *troll-garden, -land, -marsh*; also **troll-bull,** a supernatural being in the form of a bull; **troll-drum,** a drum used in Lappish magical rites; **trollman,** a magician or wizard.

**1902** *Folk-Lore* June 185 On 'Old Holy Kings' Night' black *troll-bulls come up from the sea and visit the byres. **1894** *Jrnl. Hellenic Stud.* XIV. 270 In Lapland..designs of this character ornamented the *troll-drums of the magicians till within a recent period. **1864** KINGSLEY *Rom. & Teut.* i. (1875) 1 Fancy to yourself a great *Troll-garden. **1886** J. CORBETT *Fall of Asgard* I. 65 This is no *Troll-land, but a fair place that Thor has kept for you. *Ibid.* 36 They had wanted to drive her away for a *troll-maiden. **1865** BARING-GOULD *Werewolves* viii. 108 Property..imparted to them by the *Trollmen. **1886** J. CORBETT *Fall of Asgard* I. 59 Over the lake..and over the *Troll marsh to the valley. **1851** THORPE *Northern Mythol.* I. 113 Hedin met in the forest a *Troll-wife riding on a wolf, with a rein formed of serpents. **1862** H. MARRYAT *Year in Sweden* II. 390 Herve Ulf, on his way to matin-song, was accosted by a *Trolle woman.

**Troll** (trǭl), *v. arch.* and *dial.* Forms: 4–5 **trolle,** 6 **trol,** 6–7 **trole,** 6– **troll;** 5–9 **trowl,** 6–7 **trowle, troule,** 6–8 **troul;** 5–9 **trull,** (5 **trulle**); 8–9 *Sc.* **trow.** [A word or series of words of uncertain origin, and of which all the senses do not go closely together. It is generally derived from OF. *troller*, a hunting term, 'to quest, to go in quest of game, without purpose', of which Godefroy has one instance. This survives in mod. French (see Littré). Godefroy has also one example of *traller*, in Littré *trôler* 'to lead or walk in all directions indiscriminately, to run here and there, to run about, ramble'. These may well be the same word, and *trôler* is by many referred to Ger. *trollen* 'to roll', though the senses are not the same. Both senses are found in English, but the word has also other senses not found in German or French.]

**I.** † **1.** *intr.* To move or walk about or to and fro; to ramble, saunter, stroll, 'roll'. *Obs.*

**1377** LANGL. *P. Pl.* B. XVIII. 296 And þus hath he trolled [*v.r.* tollid] forth þis two & thretty wynter. [**1561**: see 15 b.] **1691** tr. *Emilianne's Frauds Rom. Monks* (ed. 3) 107 Another sort of Pilgrims..who spend their time in trouling from one place of Devotion to another.

**2.** *trans.* To move (a ball, bowl, round body) by or as by rolling; to roll, bowl, trundle; to turn over and over, or round and round; to roll (the eyes); to throw (dice); *spec.* to trundle (a bowl) at the game of bowls (also *absol.*); also, to knock *down* by bowling.

*c* **1425** *St. Eliz. of Spalbeck* in *Anglia* VIII. 117/12 Sche myghte not holde hir heed vpon a pillow..but..trollid it hyderwarde and þyderwarde. *c* **1450** *Two Cookery-bks.* 95 Put all in a treen boll, and trull [*v. r.* twille] hit to-gidre with thi honde. **1572** [see TROLL-MADAM]. **1599** PORTER *Angry Wom. Abingd.* (Percy Soc.) 8 Let them trowle the bowles vppon the greene; Ile trowle the bowles in the buttery. **1628** LE GRYS *Barclay's Argenis* 77 Shee trowled her angry eyes on euery side. **1647** FANSHAW *Civ. Wars Rome* Poems 301 The forbidden Dice to trowle. **1665** T. A. *Excell. Roy. Hand* 9 Taking a few Pease out of his Pocket,..he troll'd them along the Floor. **1699** J. DUNTON *Life & Err.* (1818) II. 594 The Duke was then flinging the first bowl. Next trowled the Bishop. **1821** GALT *Ann. Parish* xlv, The sinner..who loves to troll his iniquity like a sweet morsel under his tongue. **1822** SCOTT *Nigel* xxi, As I was wont to trowl down the ninepins in the skittle-ground. **1841** THACKERAY *Drum* I. iii, My Grandsire was trolling the [drum-]sticks.

**3.** *intr.* To roll; also, to turn round and round; to spin, whirl.

**1581** MULCASTER *Positions* xix. (1887) 80 Children when they had their whirling gigges vnder the deuotion of their scourges, caused them to troule about the broad streates. **1626** BRETON *Fantasticks, Easter Day* (1857) 330 The Lovers eyes doe troule like Tennis balls. **1664** POWER *Exp. Philos.* I. 18 Mites..trolling to and fro with this mealy dust..sticking to them. **1730** SWIFT *Death & Daphne* 88 How pleasant on the Banks of Styx, To troll it in a Coach and Six! **1818** SCOTT *Hrt. Midl.* l, This is Lady—Lady—these tamn'd Southern names rin out o' my head like a stane trowling down hill. **1855** SINGLETON *Virgil* I. 80 Waggons..That lazy troll.

**II. 4.** *intr.* To move nimbly, as the tongue in speaking; to wag. Also said of a person. *Obs.* or *arch.*

*a* **1616** BEAUMONT *Ex-ale-tation of Ale* xxxiv, Fill him but a boule, it will make his tongue troule. **1638** FORD *Fancies* III. iii, His tongue trouls like a mill-clack. **1828** *Blackw. Mag.* XXIV. 166 See how she trolls with the tongue.

**b.** *trans.* To move (the tongue) volubly. ? *Obs.*

**1667** MILTON *P. L.* XI. 620 To sing, to dance, To dress, and troule the Tongue, and roule the Eye. **1747** [? UPTON] *New Canto Spencer's F. Q.* xviii. 12 How they troul the Tongue and roll the Eye.

† **5.** *fig. trans.* To turn over in one's mind; to revolve, ponder, contemplate. *Obs. rare*$^{-1}$.

**1685** F. SPENCE tr. *Varillas' Ho. Medicis* 107 His Holiness ..had trolled in his understanding so black a crime.

**III.** † **6.** *trans.* To cause to pass from one to another, hand round among the company present; esp. in phrase *to troll the bowl.* Hence *troll-the-bowl* as sb., a tippler, carouser. *Obs.*

**1575** *Song* in *Gammer Gurton* II. B j b, Then dooth she trowle, to mee the bowle. **1599** PORTER *Angry Wom. Abingd.* B ij b, Where be..these trowle the bowles, these greene men? **1600** DEKKER *Gentle Craft* (1862) 4 Trowl the bowl, the jolly nut-brown bowl.

† **7.** *intr.* Of the vessel or its contents: To move or pass round the company; to circulate, be passed round. *Obs.*

**1620** MIDDLETON *Chaste Maid* III. ii. 77 Now the cups troll about To wet the gossips' whistles. **1651** *Miller of Mansf.* 9 Nappie Ale..in a browne Bole Which did about the Board merrily trowle. **1808** SCOTT *Marm.* VI. Introd. 65 The wassel round, in good brown bowls, Garnish'd with ribbons, blithely trowls.

† **8.** *intr.* To come *in* abundantly like a flowing stream; to 'roll' in. *Obs.*

**1576** GASCOIGNE *Steele Gl.* (Arb.) 68 He that can winke at any foule abuse As long as gaines come trouling in therwith. *a* **1627** MIDDLETON & ROWLEY *Spanish Gypsy* I. (1653) C ij, This little Ape gets money by the sack full, It troules upon her. **1630** J. TAYLOR (Water P.) *Jacke-a-Lent* Wks. I. 117/1 The pide-coat Mackrell, Pilchard, Sprat, and Soale, To serve great Jacke-a-Lent amaine doe trole. **1689** HICKERINGILL *Ceremony-Monger* Concl. iii. Wks. 1716 II. 482 The Council of Sardica..saw this Develish Mischief coming trowling into the Church.

† **9.** *trans.* To cause to roll or flow (*in*). *Obs.*

**1573** TUSSER *Husb.* lix. (1878) 137 That trustily thriftines trowleth to thee. **1599** NASHE *Lenten Stuffe* (1871) 40 To trowl in cash throughout all nations.

**IV. 10.** *trans.* To sing (something) in the manner of a round or catch; to sing in a full, rolling voice; to chant merrily or jovially. Cf. Roll *v.*[2] 4 b. Const. *forth, out.*

Perh. originally *fig.* from 6 = to sing in succession, as a round or catch (each line being as it were passed on to the next singer).

1575, 1586 [see Trolling *vbl. sb.* 2]. 1610 Shaks. *Temp.* iii. ii. 126 Will you troule the Catch You taught me but whileare? 1672 Shadwell *Miser* i, If thou wert just now trolling out Hopkins and Sternhold. 1813 Scott *Rokeby* iii. xxviii, But, hark! our merry-men so gay Troll forth another roundelay. 1863 Geo. Eliot *Romola* ix, He could touch the lute and troll a gay song.

**b.** *intr.* To sing in this way; to carol, warble.

1879 Stevenson *Trav. Cevennes* 132 He trolled with ample lungs. 1881 — *Virg. Puerisque* 281 Pan, the god of Nature, ..trolling on his pipe until he charmed the hearts of upland ploughmen.

**11.** *intr.* Of bells: To give forth a recurring cadence of full, mellow tones; of a song: to sound or be uttered in a full, rolling, or jovial voice; *transf.* of a tune: to be present in or recur constantly to the mind, to 'run in one's head'.

1607 [see Trolling *ppl. a.*]. 1678 Dryden *Kind Keeper* iii. i, I have had..a Tune trouling in my Head. 1682 H. Aldrich *Upon Christ Church Bells Oxf.*, O the bonny Christ Church Bells.. they.. trowle so merrily, merrily. 1813 [see Trolling *ppl. a.*]. 1890 Barrie *My Lady Nicotine* xxx. 239 He strolled away, an air from 'The Grand Duchess' lightly trolling from his lips.

**12.** *trans.* To utter nimbly or rapidly; to recite in a full rolling voice. Also *intr.* of speech.

1625 B. Jonson *Staple of N.* iv. iv, If he runne To his Iudiciall Astrologie, And trowle the Trine, the Quartile and the Sextile. 1709 Mrs. Manley *Secret Mem.* I. 185 The old Ones Discourse trouls all upon Virtue. 1850 L. Hunt *Autobiog.* III. xix. 50 They speak well out, trolling the words clearly over the tongue. 1874 Blackie *Horæ Hellen.* 292 Greek trimeters may be trolled off from the British tongue, as glibly as any hexameters.

**V. 13.** *Angling. intr.* To angle with a running line (? *orig.* with the line running on a 'troll' or winch); also (*trans.*) to fish (water) in this way; *spec.* **a.** to fish for pike by working a dead bait (usually on a gorge hook) by a sink-and-draw motion; **b.** (*trans.* and *intr.*), to angle with a spinning bait: = Spin *v.* 12 a, b; **c.** in *U.S.* and *Sc.* use (perh. through association with *trail* or *trawl*), to trail a baited line behind a boat. Also *fig.*

In quot. 1606 perh. confused with Trawl.

1606 S. Gardiner *Bk. Angling* 28 Consider how God by his Preachers trowleth for thee. 1651–7 [see Trolling *vbl. sb.* 3]. 1675 Crowne *Country Wit* v, Here have I been angling and trowling for my Father-in-law, and have had him at my hook all day. 1682 Nobbes *Compl. Troller* (1822) 226 In some places, they troll without a rod, or playing the bait, as I have seen them throw a line out of a boat, and so let it draw after them as they row. 1711 Gay *Rural Sports* i. 264 Nor drain I ponds the golden carp to take, Nor trowle for pikes, dispeoplers of the lake. 1764 Goldsm. *Trav.* 187 The peasant..With patient angle trolls the finny deep. 1814–24 Col. Hawker *Instr. Yng. Sportsm.* 173 Trolling, or spinning a minnow, is the other most general mode of trout fishing. 1831 *Encycl. Brit.* (ed. 7) III. 144/2 *Trolling*, in the more limited sense of the word, signifies catching fish with the gorge-hook, which is composed of two, or what is called a double eel-hook. 1864 Webster, *Troll*, ..to angle..with a hook drawn along the surface of the water. 1881 *Harper's Mag.* Nov. 831, I troll a cast of flies. 1891 Lang *Angling Sk.* 5 Trolling a minnow from a boat in Loch Leven—probably the lowest possible form of angling.

†**14.** *fig. trans.* To draw on as with a moving bait; to entice, allure. *Obs.*

1565 Golding *Ovid's Met.* ii. (1593) 33 They troll me downe to lower waies. 1638 Ford *Lady's Trial* v. i, I foster a decoy here, And she trowls on her ragged customer. 1684 J. Goodman *Winter-even. Confer.* i. (1705) 21 The hopes he is fed withal trowls him on.

**VI.** †**15.** *Phrases.* **a.** *Hawking.* (?)

*a* 1529 Skelton *Ware the Hauke* 116 With troll, cytrace [? trytrace], and trouy, They ranged, hankin bouy. 1575 R. B. *Appius & Virginia* B j, With hey tricke, how trowle, trey trip, and trey trace Trowle hazard in a vengeance.

†**b.** *Troll and troll by, Troll hazard, Troll with*, as sbs., names for various 'orders of knaves': see quot, and cf. sense 1. *Obs. Cant.*

1561 Awdelay *Frat. Vacab.* (E.E.T.S.) 12 Troll and Trol by, is he that setteth naught by no man nor no man by him. Troll with is he that no man shall know the seruaunt from ye Maister...Troll hazard of trace is he that goeth behynde his Maister as far as he may see hym...Troll hazard of tritrace, is he that goeth gaping after his Master.

**Troll**, obs. form of Trowel.

**Trolldom** (trǭ·ldəm). [= Sw. *trolldom*:—ONorse *trolldómr*: see Troll *sb.*[2] and -dom.] The practice of trolls, witchcraft.

1891 Atkinson *Moorland Par.* 76 *note*, The entire category of 'trolldom' or witchcraft.

**Trolleite** (trǫ·lī̆əit). *Min.* [ad. Sw. *trolleit* (Blomstrand, 1867), named after the Swedish chemist Trolle-Wachtmeister: see -ite[1].] A hydrous aluminium phosphate, occurring in pale green compact masses. 1868 Dana *Min.* (ed. 5) 577.

**Troller** (trǭ·ləɹ). Forms: see Troll *v.* [f. Troll *v.* + -er[1].]

**1.** One who trolls catches, songs, etc.: see Troll *v.* 10.

*a* 1734 North *Lives* (1826) II. 205 He was a great troller of songs. 1824 Miss Mitford *Village* Ser. i. (1863) 113 A troller of profane catches.

**2.** *Angling.* One who trolls for pike, etc.: see Troll *v.* 13.

1651–7 T. Barker *Art of Angling* (1659) 30 The best Trouler for a Pike within this Realm of England. 1682 Nobbes (*title*) The Compleat Troller, or the Art of Trolling. 1820 T. F. Salter (*title*) The troller's guide; a practical treatise on the art of trolling or fishing for jack and pike. 1894 *Field* 1 Dec. 838/2 The trollers killed ten.

**b.** A trolling-rod.

1688 [see *trolling-rod* s.v. Trolling *vbl. sb.* 4].

**Trolley, trolly** (trǫ·li), *sb.* Also trawley. [? f. Troll *v.*; cf. *lorry, rolley, rulley.*]

**1.** Locally applied to a low cart of various kinds, e.g. a costermonger's cart; at Yarmouth, a narrow cart or sledge adapted for the 'rows' or narrow alleys (Row *sb.*[1] 4 c). Cf. Troll *sb.*[1] 5 and *trolley-cart* in 4 below.

1823 Moor *Suffolk Words* s.v., Sich roads! We got rarely jounced i' the trolly. 1870 *Pall Mall G.* 25 Aug. 4 The prisoner was leading his horse in a trolly along Fairfield-road, Bow.

**2.** A low truck without sides or ends, esp. one with flanged wheels for running on a railway, or a track of rails in a factory, etc. Cf. Bogie 1.

1858 Simmonds *Dict. Trade, Trolley*, a kind of railway vehicle. 1861 Smiles *Engineers* II. 201 The goods in the London Docks are hauled in trollies, waggons or hand-barrows from ship to ship. 1862 Mrs. H. Wood *Mrs. Hallib.* xix, I'll send in a trolley of coal. 1881 Raymond *Mining Gloss.* s.v., The two-wheeled trolly is used in a rolling-mill to wheel the puddle-balls to the squeezer. 1881 H. W. Nicholson *From Sword to Share* xxv. 182 The train..was made up of some dozen sideless trucks, or trawleys. 1885 *Law Times* 16 May 47/1 A porter..put all the luggage on a trolley..and wheeled the trolley on to the platform.

**3.** A grooved metallic pulley which travels along, and receives current from, an overhead electric wire, the current being then conveyed by a *trolley-pole* or other conductor to a motor, usually that of a car on a street railroad; also called *trolley-wheel* (see 4). Also applied to any pulley running along an overhead track, as in a *trolley-scale* (see 4).

1891 in *Cent. Dict.* 1902 Sloane *Stand. Electr. Dict.* s.v., Trolleys are principally used on electric railroads. 1909 *Cent. Dict. Suppl.* s.v. *Abattoir scales*, The meat, suspended from hooks attached to a trolley traveling on a telpherage system or overhead track, is run upon a short section of track which forms the weighing-platform of the scales... Another form of scale employs a trolley for weighing materials in transit, with a scale-beam attached directly to the trolley and traveling with it. Called a *trolley-scale.*

**b.** Short for *trolley-car*: see 4. *U.S.*

1891 *Month* LXXIII. 24, I jumped off the trolley. 1908 *Daily Chron.* 20 Jan. 4/4 To go anywhere in Boston you must take a tram..(they call it a trolley).

**4.** *attrib.* and *Comb.*, as *trolley-journey, -load, system*; **trolley-bar** = *trolley-pole*; **trolley-car** (*U.S.*), an electric car driven by means of a trolley (see 3); **trolley-cart** (*local*), a Yarmouth trolley (see 1); **trolley coal**, coal conveyed on trolleys or street trucks for sale; **trolley-ear, trolley-hanger**, a contrivance for supporting and insulating a trolley-wire; **trolley-frog** (see quot.); **trolley-harp, trolley-head**, the holder at the end of a trolley-pole which supports the trolley-wheel; **trolley-hook**, a hook used for replacing a trolley-wheel when it slips off the wire (*Funk's Stand. Dict.* 1895); **trolley-line**, a line of electric cars run by means of trolleys (*ibid.*); **trolleyman**, a man employed to drive a trolley or a trolley-car; **trolley-pole**, a hinged pole on an electric car, supporting the trolley (see 3), and conveying the current from the overhead wire; **trolley-rail**, a rail conveying current to the motors on an electric railway; **trolley-road**, an electric tram-line worked on the trolley system (*U.S.*); **trolley-scale**, a scale for weighing meat or other commodities, in which the scale-beam is attached to a trolley travelling on an overhead track, as in a market or warehouse; **trolley-wheel** = sense 3; **trolley-wire**, an overhead electric wire supplying current to the trolleys of electric cars.

1891 *Pall Mall G.* 30 Oct. 6/2 On the top of the car is a '*trolley bar'. 1895 *Pop. Sci. Monthly* Apr. 758 The lazy barges will perhaps rival in bustle the *trolley car on land. 1865 *Daily Tel.* 25 Aug., Yarmouth ingenuity..hit upon the notion of the '*trolly cart'..a sledge, about 12 ft. long, but not much more than a yard in breadth, mounted upon wheels less than 3 ft. high. 1890 *Daily News* 18 Mar. 4/6 They further increased the price of house coal by 2s. a ton, and *trolly coal by 1s. 6d. per ton. 1898 Houston *Dict. Electr.*, **Trolley Ear*, a metal piece supported by an insulator to which the trolley wire is fastened. **Trolley Frog*, the device to which the trolley wire is attached, employed for causing a car to deviate from one line to another. *Ibid.* s.v. *Hanger*, A *trolley hanger on a straight trolley line. 1904 *Electr. World & Engin.* 18 June 1167 *Trolley-harp. 1896 A. Morrison *Child of the Jago* 190 To start..on a *trolley-journey. 1898 *Daily News* 22 Oct. 3/5 A *trolley-load of foreign silks, velvets, and fancy woollen goods. 1897 *Ibid.* 23 Feb. 7/4 The number on strike at Sunderland is 111, including 51 *trolleymen. 1900 *Ibid.* 11 June 3/2 The strike of street trolley (electric tramcar) men [at St. Louis]. 1895 *Funk's Stand. Dict.*, *Trolley-pole. 1897 *Daily News* 19 July 8/4 The electricity is transmitted to the motors on the car by means of trolley poles, or 'fishing rods', which ..glide along the wire as the car runs. 1897 *Trans. Amer. Inst. Electr. Engin.* 355 *Trolley-rail. 1895 *Information* 6 July 3/2 This electric railroad is practically a very heavy and substantially built *trolley road. The trolley wire..is hung from very heavy poles. 1909 *Trolley-scale [see 3]. 1892 *Daily News* 4 Oct. 5/1 An intra-mural elevated railway is being constructed...Its cars will be moved by electric traction on the '*trolley' system. 1891 *Pall Mall G.* 30 Oct. 6/2 A small grooved '*trolley wheel ..runs against the under side of the overhead wire. 1895 *Trolley wire [see *trolley road*].

Hence **Tro·lley** *v., trans.* to convey by trolley; *intr.* to travel by trolley; **Tro·lleyful**, as much or many as a trolley will hold; **Tro·lleyize** *v. trans.* to adapt to the trolley system, as a tramline (*U.S.*).

1882 W. E. Baxter *Winter in India* viii. 84 Mr. Prestage ..had arranged that we should be '*trollied' down the mountains instead of going in the train. 1900 *Daily News* 21 Mar. 5/4 These two officers trollied along the line..till they got close to Springfontein Station. 1900 *Ibid.* 21 May 4/1 A procession of three hundred young men dragging a *trolleyful of ladies. 1895 *Pop. Sci. Monthly* Apr. 751 Every species of tramway..becomes *trolleyized.

**Troll flower.** Also 6 trol flower. [tr. Ger. *trollblume* (whence app. mod.L. generic name *Trollius*, C. Gesner *c* 1555, and F. *trolle*); app. f. stem of *troll-en* to roll, in reference to the globular shape of the flower. (Dr. Prior's statement in quot. 1879 appears to be erroneous.)] A book-name for the Globe-flower (*Trollius europæus*).

1578 Lyte *Dodoens* iii. lxxii. 418 Byside these kindes of Ranunculus is yet another strange kinde.., the whiche is called Troll flowers. *Ibid.* 419 The Trol flowers grow upon the mountaynes of Switserlande. 1879 Prior *Pop. Names Brit. Plants* (ed. 3), *Troll-flower*, the globe-flower, from Sw. *troll*..a malignant supernatural being, a name..given to this plant on account of its acrid poisonous qualities.

**Tro·llibags, -bobs.** *dial.* Also trolle-, trolly-, -bags, -bods. [Variant of Trillibub.] Entrails, intestines: generally with *tripes.*

1824 Mactaggart *Gallovid. Encycl.* s.v. *Raens*, And when he fins a sheep fa'en aval, Her trolly-bags he can unravel. *a* 1825 Forby *Voc. E. Anglia*, *Trollibags s.*, the intestines. 1828 *Craven Gloss.*, *Trollibobs* ..is generally preceded by tripes; as 'tripes and trollibobs', intestines. 1876 *Whitby Gloss.*, *Trollebods*, a roll or complication of entrails. 1876 *Mid-Yorks. Gloss.*, *Trollybods*..entrails.

**Trolling** (trǭ·liŋ), *vbl. sb.* Also 5–9 trowling, 6–8 trouling. [f. Troll *v.* + -ing[1].] The action of the verb Troll in its various senses.

**I. 1.** Rolling, revolution.

*c* 1440 *Promp. Parv.* 503/1 Trollynge, or rollynge, *volucio.* 1613 Day *Dyall* v. (1614) 98 Concerning the Heavens they perceived such aequabilitie of motion, such turning and trolling of them.

†**b.** 'Rolling' or 'streaming' in; abundant influx. *Obs.*

1614 T. Adams in Spurgeon *Treas. Dav.* Ps. xiv. 1 Extortion batters in the usurer's affections by the trolling in of his moneys.

**II. 2.** Singing in the manner of a round, or in a jovial style; in quots. applied contemptuously to antiphonal singing.

1575 *Brieff Disc. Troubles Franckford* (1846) 206 The trollinge and descantinge of the Psalmes. 1586 in Neal *Hist. Purit.* (1732) I. 480 The service of God is grievously abused by..ringing and trowling of psalms from one side of the Choir to another.

**III. 3.** *Angling.* The action or practice of fishing by the methods described s.v. Troll *v.* 13.

But in *trolling-line* (quot. 1888 in 4), app. confused with *trawling*; cf. Trawling, Trawl-net, Trollnet.

1651–7 T. Barker *Art of Angling* (1820) 22 The manner of his trouling was with a hasell rod. 1682 [see Troller 2]. 1725 T. Taylor in *Portland Papers* VI. (Hist. MSS. Comm.) 88 The late Duke..took great delight in that kind of fishing for them [pike] which is termed 'trowling'. 1787 Best *Angling* (ed. 2) 43 The walking bait is that which the fisher attends to himself, and is called trowling. 1860 G. H. K. *Vac. Tour.* 167 If you..will go and spin a butter-fish for lythe,..you will there first discover what sport trolling can be. 1888 Goode *Amer. Fishes* 62 In trolling from a boat at least 300 feet of line should be used. 1910 H. T. Sheringham in *Encycl. Brit.* II. 28/2 The use of the drop-minnow, which is trolling on a lesser scale.

**4.** *attrib.* (in sense 3), as *trolling-bait, -fly, -hook, -line, -rod, -spoon, -tackle.*

1891 *Cent. Dict.*, *Trolling-bait. 1898 *Blackw. Mag.* Nov. 630/1 Many reaches of the Tay are fished by *trolling-fly. 1891 *Cent. Dict.*, *Trolling-hook. 1701 *Cowell's Interpr.* s.v. *Trawlerman*, To trowle or trawle with a *Trowling-line for Pikes. 1888 Goode *Amer. Fishes* 187 They live at sea and are caught by the use of trolling-lines. 1688 R. Holme *Armoury* iii. 103/1 A *Trowling Rod, or a Trowler, hath a ring at the end of the Rod for the Line to run through, when it runs off a Reele. 1844 J. T. Hewlett *Parsons & W.* xi, I..bought a short, strong trolling-rod. 1883 *Century Mag.* XXVI. 382 The Florida bass are taken with the hand-line and *trolling-spoon. 1910 H. T. Sheringham in *Encycl. Brit.* II. 28/2 (*Angling*), The traditional form of *trolling-tackle was such that the bait had to be swallowed by the pike before the hook would take hold.

**Tro·lling,** *ppl. a.* [f. Troll *v.* + -ing[2].] That trolls, in various senses of the vb.; rolling.

1581 A. Hall *Iliad* iv. 73 A wood ful fit to forge the trolling wheeles Of chariots. 1607 *Lingua* v. ix. L j b, The pleasing changes that a well tun'd Corde Of trowling bells will make. 1659 Wood *Life* (O. H. S.) I. 287 His voice was a bass,..very strong and exceeding trouling, but he wanted skill. 1813 T. Busby *Lucretius* II. v. 1792 Relieved by many a trolling song.

† **Tro·ll-madam.** *Obs.* Forms: 6 troule in madame, trol in madam, trowe maddam, trolemadame, 7 trol-madame, troll-my-dame, troll-medam, trou-madame, 8 troll-madame, 8–9 trou-madame. [app. an alteration of F. *trou-madame* (f. *trou* hole) by association with TROLL *v.*] A game played by ladies, resembling bagatelle: see quot. 1572. = HOLE *sb.* 10 a.

**1572** J. JONES *Bathes Buckstone* 12 The Ladyes, Gentle Women, Wyues and Maydes maye..haue in the ende of a Benche eleuen holes made, intoo the which to trowle pummetes or Bowles of leade..or also of Copper, Tynne, Woode ..the pastyme Troule in Madame is termed. *margin*, Trol in Madam. **1573** in Gage *Hengrave* (1822) 199 A frame of wood upon w^ca they play w^th pellets, called trowe maddam. **1606** HOLLAND *Sueton.* Annot. 18 The game of young Gentlewomen called of some Trol-Madame. **1611** SHAKS. *Wint. T.* IV. iii. 92 A fellow (sir) that I haue knowne to goe about with Troll-my-dames. **1666** *Third Advice to a Painter* 19 He plays with Danger, and his Bullets trouls, As 'twere at Trou-Madam through all the holes. **1689** *Lond. Gaz.* No. 2503/4 If any Persons have occasion for Tables, and Table-men,..and Troll-Madams, they may be furnished. **1774** H. WALPOLE *Let. to C'tess Upper Ossory* 30 July, I would not for the world have a table of trou-madame without a king and a queen. **1819** *Blackw. Mag.* IV. 564 A harmless quiet kind of sport, like shuttlecock, or trou-madame. or nine-pins.

† **Tro·llnet.** *Obs. rare*^−1. A kind of net declared illegal in the Act cited.

It is doubtful whether it is connected with TRAWL, TRAWLER, TRAWL-NET, or TRAIL *v.*, since it seems to relate to fishing for river fish which are not caught with drag-nets or by trawling; but cf. *trawler-man* (TRAWLER 3).

**1558** *Act* 1 *Eliz.* c. 17 § 1 No Person..withe any..Crele, Rawe, Fagnett, Trollnett..shall take..Spawne or Frye of Eeles, Salmon, Pyke or Pyckerell.

† **Trollo·ll,** *v. Obs. rare*^−1. [Reduplicated form of TROLL *v.*] *intr.* (with *it*). To sing in a rollicking style, to troll.

*a* **1734** NORTH *Examen* I. ii. § 130 (1740) 101 They got drunk and trolloll'd it bravely.

**Trollop** (trǫ·ləp), *sb.* Also 7 **trolops**, *dial.* 7–9 **trallop**, 9 **trollops, trallops.** [? Connected with TROLL *v.*; for the termination cf. *gallop*, *wallop*.]

**1.** An untidy or slovenly woman; a slattern, slut; also, sometimes, a morally loose woman, a trull.

In quot. 1615 *transf.* of hounds.

**1615** WITHER *Sheph. Hunt.* Ecl. ii, Such wide-mouth'd Trollops that 'twould doe you good To heare their loud-loud Echoes teare the Wood. **1621** BRATHWAIT *Nat. Embassie*, etc. (1877) 196 The Parsons wife, a lusty Trolops. *a* **1626** MIDDLETON *Mayor of Queenborough* IV. i. 4 To greet thy grace, thy queen, and her fair trollops. **1682** in *East Anglian* Sept. (1904) 327 Many rayleing opprobrious Speeches and Invectives against the said Elizabeth, calling her Tripe and Trallop. **1742** FIELDING *Jos. Andrews* I. viii, That impudent trollop, who is with child by you. **1846** D. JERROLD *Mrs. Caudle's Curtain Lect.* xxxii, But for that trollop..her quarter's up on Tuesday, and go she shall. **1887** JESSOPP *Arcady* vii. 210 The husband of a dirty trollop who can neither cook nor sew.

**2.** Anything draggling, or hanging loosely and untidily. *Sc.*

**1872** WEDGWOOD *Dict. Eng. Etym.* (ed. 2), *Trollop*, a large piece of rag, especially wet rag. **1882** JAMIESON, *Trollop*, a large, unseemly, straggling mass of anything.

Hence **Tro·llop** *v.* (*Sc.*), *intr.* (*a*) to hang loosely and untidily, to draggle; (*b*) to act or dress like a trollop, to be slovenly; † **Trollopee·**, name for a loose dress worn by women in the 18th century; **Tro·lloping, Tro·llopish, Tro·llopy** *adjs.*, like or characteristic of a trollop, ungainly, slovenly.

**1872** WEDGWOOD *Dict. Eng. Etym.* (ed. 2) s. v., Banff, **trollop*, to hang in a wet state; 'The bairn cam in wee 'ts frockie a' trollopin' aboot its leggies'. **1882** JAMIESON, To *Troll*, *Trollop*,..to walk, work, or dress in a slovenly manner. **1756** *Connoisseur* No. 134 ⁋ 7 A burgess's daughter ..who appeared in a *Trollopee or Slammerkin, with treble ruffles to the cuffs. **1762** *Songs Costume* (Percy Soc.) 240 With your flounces and furbelows, sacks, trollopees. **1733** DUCHESS OF QUEENSBERRY *Let. to Swift* 10 Nov., I did not cut and curl my hair like a sheep's head, or wear one of their *trolloping sacks. **1773** GOLDSM. *Stoops to Conq.* I. ii, The daughter, a tall trapesing, trolloping, talkative May-pole. **1876** MISS BROUGHTON *Joan* iv, With such a trolloping length of uncurled curls down their backs. **1864** WEBSTER, *Trollopish. **1748** RICHARDSON *Clarissa* (1811) VIII. xli. 157 Their gowns, made to cover straddling hoops, hanging *trollopy, and tangling about their heels. **1864** MISS YONGE *Trial* II. 133 In the front..stood a trollopy-looking girl.

**Trolly** (trǫ·li). Also 7–8 **trolly-lolly.** [Cf. Flemish *tralje*, *traalje*, trellis, lattice, mesh, network (De Bo). *Kant* (q. 1882) is Flem. for 'edge, border, lace, point'.] Name of a kind of lace: see quots. Also *attrib.*

*a* **1700** B. E. *Dict. Cant. Crew*, *Trolly-lolly*, coarse Lace once much in fashion, now worn only by the meaner sort. **1756** MRS. DEWES in *Mrs. Delany's Life & Corr.* (1861) III. 434 She is..dressed much better than I ever saw her. I fancy her friend Mrs. Egerton has vamped her up with a trolly hood. **1882** CAULFEILD & SAWARD *Dict. Needlework* 501 *Trolly Laces*..are Pillow Laces, made in Normandy, in Flanders, and in Buckinghamshire, and Devonshire,..their ground..is an imitation of the Antwerp Trolly Net or Point de Paris Ground, and is made with twists, while the pattern is outlined with a thick thread like that used in the old Flemish Laces, and known as Trolle Kant. **1891** *Cent. Dict.* s. v. *Trolley*, Honiton lace made with a trolley ground. **1895** *Funk's Stand. Dict.* s. v. *Trolley*, *T*[*rolley*]-*thread*, one of the threads outlining the pattern of trolley-lace.

**Trolly,** variant of TROLLEY.

**Trolly-lolly** (trǫ·li,lǫ·li), *int.* [Cf. TROLLOLL.] A refrain of a song, expressing careless gaiety or jollity. Also in nonce (threatening) use as *vb. trans.* (quot. 1723). So † **Trolylow** (also as an expression of contempt), **Trololay·** *Sc.* (in conjunction with HOGMANAY). Also † **Trolly trolly** (? *int.* or *a.*), expressing contempt.

**1362** LANGL. *P. Pl.* A. VII. 109 Þenne seten summe and songen atte ale, And holpen him to herien wiþ 'Hey! trolly-lolly!' [1377 B. VI. 118 'how! trolli-lolli!' **1393** C. IX. 123 'hoy! troly! lolly!']. **1529** LYNDESAY *Complaynt* 245 Now trittyll, trattyll, trolylow,..thow dois bot mow. *c* **1530** *Hickscorner* 690, I was not gladde, perde! but now: Hey, trolly, lolly! Let us se who can descaunt on this same. **1567** *Triall Treas.* (1850) 5 Hey howe, troly lowe; hey dery, dery. *a* **1693** *Urquhart's Rabelais* III. xxxvi. 298 Wishy, washy; Trolly, trolly. **1723** *Case of Edward Collins* 11 She said to her I'll trolly-lolly you. **1792** *Caledonian Mercury* 2 Jan. (Jam. s. v. *Hogmanay*), The cry of *Hogmanay Trololay*, is of usage immemorial in this country.

**Trolops**: see TROLLOP.

‖ **Trombash** (trǫ·mbæʃ). Also **trum-.** [Native name in the Soudan.] A kind of boomerang used by the Soudanese. Also *fig.*

**1867** BAKER *Nile Tribut.* xx. (1872) 346 A curious weapon, the *trombash*, used by these people. **1876** C. C. LONG *Central Africa* xvii. 237 Central Africa is a deadly pestiferous country, in spite of the 'trumbash' to the contrary by travellers. **1884** A. GREGORY in *Fortn. Rev.* Mar. 382 They use many weapons, lances and sickle-bladed knives and trumbashes, a kind of boomerang with mischievous-looking iron prongs and points.

† **Tro·mbe.** *Obs. rare.* Also **trompe, trumbe.** [ad. It. *tromba* a hand-grenade, *tromba di fuoco* 'a kind of casting wild-fier' (Florio, 1598); cf. obs. F. *trombe* a hollow humming-top.

With *trompe* cf. TRUMP *sb.*[1] hollow tube, trumpet, etc.]

**a.** A hollow tube filled with explosives; a hand-grenade. **b.** A mortar for firing rockets.

**1560** WHITEHORNE *Ord. Souldiours* xxix. 39 b, Trombes or trunkes of fyre. *Ibid.*, Putte in the trumbe a handfull of serpentine poulder vnmixte. **1588** LUCAR tr. *Tartaglia's Colloq. Arte Shooting* App. 85 How you may make a Trunke or Trombe which will shoote fireworkes. **1591** *Garrard's Art Warre* 317 For preparations against the assault you must not be destitute of all sorts of arteficial fire, as Trompes, Granades, Bullets.

**Trombe,** variant of TROMPE [2], blast apparatus.

**Trombidiid** (trǫmbi·di,id), *a.* and *sb. Zool.* [ad. mod.L. *Trombidiidæ*, f. *Trombidium*, the typical genus: see -ID [3].] **a.** *adj.* Of or pertaining to the *Trombidiidæ*, a family of mites. **b.** *sb.* A mite of this family. **1891** in *Cent. Dict.*

**Trombolite,** variant of THROMBOLITE.

**1850** ANSTED *Elem. Geol.*, *Min.* etc. § 506 Trombolite and Pelocronite are varieties [of Phosphori-calcite].

**Trombone** (trǫ·mbōun, trǫmbōu·n), *sb.* [ad. It. *trombone* 'a bace or great sackbut, a great trump' (Florio, 1598), also, a blunderbuss, augmentative of *tromba* trumpet. Cf. F. *trombon* (16th c. in Godef.).]

**1.** *Mus.* A large loud-toned brass instrument of the trumpet kind, consisting of a long tube bent twice upon itself, and ending in a bell mouth; the U-shaped bend nearer the mouth-piece is of double telescoping tubes, sliding upon one another, so that the length of the sounding tube may be adjusted to produce the desired note.

It is also made with valves and pistons instead of the slide (*valve-trombone*).

**1724** *Short Explic. For. Wds. Mus. Bks.*, *Trombone*, a very Large or Bass Trumpet, though more properly a Sackbut. **1813** *Examiner* 10 May 303/2 Every violin, bassoon, and trombone. **1856** MRS. C. CLARKE tr. *Berlioz' Instrument.* 151 There are four kinds of trombones, each of which bears the name of the human voice to which it bears the nearest resemblance in quality of tone and compass. **1881** BROADHOUSE *Mus. Acoustics* 234 The Trumpet..and the Trombone its natural bass. **1889** W. H. STONE in Grove *Dict. Mus.* IV. 176 In A.D. 1520 there was a well-known Posaunenmacher named Hans Menschel, who made slide Trombones as good as, or perhaps better, than those of the present time. **1892** SYMONDS *Life Michel Angelo* (1899) II. xi. 65 A sense-deafening solo on a trombone.

*attrib.* **1886** *Academy* 16 Oct. 267/1 Why..are Handel's trombone parts persistently ignored? **1893** B. ABBOTSFORD *But* vii. 40 The 'it' [man] with the trombone voice. **1906** KROPOTKIN *Mem. Revolutionist* (1908) I. viii. 47 Behind each one of us a violinist or a trombone player stands. **1908** *Westm. Gaz.* 23 July 4/2 It does not concern them whether the [motor-engine] cylinders are as big as beer-barrels, or the stroke as elongated as a trombone-slide.

**b.** One who plays this instrument.

**1848** DICKENS *Dombey* xxxi, An artful trombone lurks and dodges round the corner.

**c.** A reed-stop in the organ of similar tone.

**1837** *Stranger's Guide York* (ed. 6) 78 Trombone..Wood open diapason.

‖ **2.** (trombō·ne), pl. **tromboni** (-nī). = BLUNDERBUSS I.

**1754** RICHARDSON *Grandison* (ed. 7) III. 258, I beat down his Trombone, a kind of Blunderbuss, just as he presented it at me. **1794** MRS. RADCLIFFE *Myst. Udolpho* xxxi, When we came up, we fired our tromboni, but missed. **1797** — *Italian* xxi, He fired his trombone in the air, when every rock reverberated the sound. **1843** BORROW *Bible in Spain* xxxiii, He then discharged his trombone just over my head.

Hence **Trombonist,** = 1 b; **Trombony** *a. colloq.*, pertaining to or characterized by the trombone.

**1891** *Cent. Dict.*, *Trombonist. **1897** *Weekly Sun* 19 Sept. 3/4 A trombonist in our tontine band. **1908** *Times* 8 July 7/2 Herr Steidl..showed us how a trombonist and a clarinetist ought to be educated. **1899** A. LAYARD *Musical Bogeys* 44 The *Trombony Bogey is terribly thin. **1913** *Daily News* 6 Sept. 6 The Prelude to Act III of 'Lohengrin'..is a trombony piece of music.

**Trombone,** *v. rare.* [f. prec. sb.]

**1.** *trans.* To move to and fro as in playing the trombone (*humorous*).

**1879** HARLAN *Eyesight* vi. 70 The age..when we commence to 'trombone our newspaper' in search of the receding near point of distinct vision. **1893** W. H. HUDSON *Idle Days Patagonia* xi, The redskin..is never observed to trombone his newspaper.

**2.** *intr.* To play the trombone; also *transf.* to make a sound like a trombone.

**1888** H. DRUMMOND *Tropical Africa* i. 18 The hippopotami ..tromboning at us within pistol-shot kept us awake.

**Trome,** variant of TRUME.

**Trommel** (trǫ·mĕl, -'l). *Mining. U.S.* [a. G. *trommel* DRUM.] A rotating cylindrical sieve or buddle used for washing and sizing ores.

**1877** in KNIGHT *Dict. Mech.* **1886** tr. *Callon's Lect. Mining* xxiii. III. 27 A trommel is a barrel in the form of a cylinder or of a truncated cone, horizontal or slightly inclined.

**Tromometer** (tromǫ·mĭtəɹ). [f. Gr. τρόμος trembling + -METER.] An instrument for measuring or detecting faint earth-tremors. Hence **Tromometric** (trǫmome·trik), **Tromome·trical** *adjs.*, of or pertaining to the tromometer or its use; **Tromometry** (tromǫ·mĕtri), the measuring of earth-tremors, the scientific use of the tromometer.

**1878** *Nature* 12 Sept. 533/1 The instruments, particularly the tromometer, were continually agitated. **1883** J. MILNE in *Trans. Seismol. Soc. Japan* VII. I. 13 As to the cause of tromometric movements we have a field for speculation. **1887** G. H. DARWIN in *Fortn. Rev.* Feb. 271 The 'normal tromometer' of Bertelli..is a simple pendulum,..with an arrangement for observing the dance of the pendulum-bob with a microscope. **1895** *Funk's Stand. Dict.*, Tromometry. **1898** *Nature* 1 Dec. 104/2 The subject to which he [Rossi] devoted the greatest attention was perhaps tromometry, in connection with which he devised many instruments. **1901** *Daily Record & Mail* 22 July 7 'Trommetric' observations (states 'Science Siftings') have been made at the observatory near the summit of Mount Etna.

**Tromp,** obs. form of TRUMP; var. TROMPE.

† **Tro·mpant,** *a. Obs. rare*^−1. [a. F. *trompant*, pres. pple. of *tromper*: see TRUMP *v.*[2]] Cheating, deceiving, dishonest.

**1605** *Lond. Prodigal* IV. ii, Him..Who makes a trompant life his daily sport.

**Trompat, -er(e,** obs. forms of TRUMPET, -ER.

† **Trompe** [1]. *Obs. rare*^−1. [a. OF. *trompe* (Godef.), f. *tromper* to deceive: cf. TRUMP *v.*[2]] Deceit, deception.

**1547** *Bk. Marchauntes* a vij, Beholde here the trompe the paynted glosse of theyr malycyousnes.

‖ **Trompe** [2] (trōnp). Also **trombe, tromp.** [F. *trompe, trombe.*] An apparatus for producing a blast, in which water falling in a pipe carries air into a receiver, where it is compressed, and thence led to the blast-pipe; a water blowing-engine. Also *attrib.*

**1828** WEBSTER, *Tromp*, a blowing machine formed of a hollow tree, used in furnaces. **1839** URE *Dict. Arts* 824 The trompe, or water-blowing engine. *Ibid.* 825 The ordinary height of the trompe apparatus is about 26 or 27 feet to the upper level of the water cistern. **1881** RAYMOND *Mining Gloss.*, *Trombe* or *Trompe*, (Fr.), an apparatus for producing an air-blast by means of a falling stream of water, which mechanically carries air down with it, to be subsequently separated and compressed in a reservoir or drum below. **1894** BOWKER in *Harper's Mag.* Jan. 418 About the middle of the seventeenth century the tromp was introduced.

**Trompe,** obs. f. TRUMP; var. TROMBE *Obs.*

**Tromper, Tromperie, -ery, Trompet, -ette,** obs. ff. TRUMPER, TRUMPERY, TRUMPET.

‖ **Trompille** (‖ tronpī·y, trǫmpi·l). *rare*^−0. [F., f. *trompe*, TROMPE [2]; cf. F. *trompillon.*] Each of the holes or tubes by which air is admitted to the water-pipe of a trompe.

**1828** WEBSTER, *Trompil*, an aperture in a tromp. **1891** *Cent. Dict.*, Trompille.

**Trompour, -e,** obs. ff. or var. TRUMPER.

**Tron** (trǫn), **trone** (trōn), *sb. Sc.* and *north. dial.* Also 6 **tronne, throne, troyne,** 7, 9 **troan.** [ME. a. OF. *trone* (Godef.):—L. *trutina*, a. Gr. τρυτάνη balance, pair of scales.]

**1.** (Chiefly *Sc.*) A weighing machine; a pair of scales or other machine for weighing merchandise; a public weighing apparatus in a city or (burgh) town; also called 'the king's trone'. Now *Hist.*

[*c* **1290** *Fleta* II. xii. § 15 Quod fideliter colligant..ulnas, tronas, stateras, et pondera cujuslibet generis, tam pro pane quam pro aliis rebus venalibus provisa et habita. **1365** *Stat. David II*, c. 39 in *Acts Parlt. Scot.* (1844) I. 139/1 Extitit ordinatum, quod sit trona ad lanas ponderandas in burgis Regiis, per singulos portus Regni.] **1477** in *Charters &c. Edinb.* (1871) 141 Sic like gudis that suld be weyit to be vsit at the Ouer Bow, and a trone set thare. *a* **1500** in *Arnolde's Chron.* (1811) 101 The marchaunt may make his wolle to be weyen at the kyngis trone yf he will. 1609 SKENE *Reg. Maj., Stat. David II* 44 (see 1365 above) The Chalmerlane sall cause..mak ane Trone for weying of woll in all the Kings burghis. 1742 in J. Paterson *Hist. Regality Musselburgh* (1857) 82 Repair the cross and the trone in the town of Musselburgh. 1824 G. CHALMERS *Caledonia* III. VI. viii. 654 The trone for weighing goods being established at the bottom of the tower, the Church obtained the name of the Trone Church. *a* 1850 J. GRAY *Arithm.* (ed. 100) 12 The Tron Pound kept at Edinburgh is equal to 9622·67 Troy Grains; it varies, however, in different places and for different purposes. 1886 MASSON *Edinb. Sk.* 29 Markets..each having its own 'tron' or weighing apparatus.

**b.** The post of this was used as a pillory, or place of public exposure and punishment of offenders.

1449 *Sc. Acts Jas. II*, c. 9 (1814) II. 36/1 And fra þai [beggars] haf no*t* to lefe aponne þat þar eris be nalyt to þe trone or to ane vthir tre and cuttit of and bannyst þe cuntre. 1515 *Burgh Rec. Edinb.* (1869) I. 156 He was adiugeit to be had to the trone and thair strikkin throw the hand and banist this towne. 1650 *Acts Sederunt* 6 Feb. (1790) 69 They ordain the said John Rob to be sett upon the Trone with a paper upon his head, bearing thir words; (This John Rob is sett heir for being an false informer of witnesses), and ordaines his lugg to be nailed to the Trone be the spaice of ane hour. 1731 *Gentl. Mag.* Mar. 123/2 He shall have his Lugs tacked to the muckle Trone with a Nail of twal a Penny.

**c.** Contextually, The place where the tron was set up; a market-place, market; in quot. 1821 *fig.*

1500–20 DUNBAR *Poems* lxxxii. 24 At your hie Croce, quhair gold and silk Sould be, thair is bot crudis and milk; And at ȝour Trone bot cokill and wilk. *a* 1572 KNOX *Hist. Ref.* Wks. 1846 I. 121 The Englismen seing no resistance, hurlled..cannounes up the calsay to the Butter-throne. 1725 RAMSAY *Gentle Sheph.* I. ii, I'll..win the vogue at market, tron, or fair, For halesome, clean, cheap, and sufficient ware. 1821 GALT *Ann. Parish* xxxvii, Irville..is an abundant trone for widows and other single women. 1891 H. HALIBURTON *Ochil Idylls* 65 At the very trons in touns It [snow]'s knee-deep lyin.

**d.** Short for *tron weight*: see 3.

1801 RANKEN *Hist. France* I. I. v. 429, 1200 bundles of hay, of 4 pounds weight each..is..327 stone Trone on the Scotch acre.

**2.** (*pl.*) *north. dial.* A weighing-machine; a pair of scales, a steelyard or spring balance.

1825 BROCKETT *N. C. Words, Trones*, a steel yard. 1863 MRS. TOOGOOD *Yorksh. Dial.* (MS.), Go and borrow the trones to weigh the hay.

**3.** *attrib.* **Tronman (trone-man)**: see quot. 1808–25; **tron(e-pound**, the pound of *tron weight*, varying locally from 21 to 28 ounces avoirdupois; so **tron(e-stone** (see quots.); **tron(e weight**, the standard of weight used at the tron.

1808–25 JAMIESON, *Trone-men, the name given to those who carry off the soot swept from chimneys, because they had their station at the *Trone*, Edinburgh. 1896 SMEATON *Ramsay* vii. 182 Tronmen with their bags of soot. 1683 *Repr. Advantages Manuf. Woollen-cloath* 4 Wooll (not worth 8sh. Scots the *Trone-pound). 1565 *Reg. Privy Council Scot.* I. 375 Fourtie thowsand *troyne stane wecht. 1795 HUTTON *Math. Dict., Trone-Stone*, in Scotland, according to Sir John Skene, contains 19½ pounds. 1882 OGILVIE (Annandale) s.v. *Trone*, The later tron stone..contained 16 tron pounds, the tron pound being equivalent to 1·3747 lbs. avoirdupois. 1593 *Reg. Mag. Sig. Scot.* 815/1 Cum potestate crucem foralem cum lie trone et *trone-wechtis habendi. 1618 *Sc. Acts Jas. VI* (1816) IV. 587/2 That Weght called of old the Trone weght to be allvtterlie abolisched. 1799 J. ROBERTSON *Agric. Perth* 346 Cheese..sold by tron weight, having twenty-one ounces to the lb. 1812 SIR J. SINCLAIR *Syst. Husb. Scot.* I. 58, 150 to 200 stone of hay, trone weight, is carried by each two-horse cart, to..Perth and Dundee.

Hence **Tron (trone)** *v.*, *trans.* to weigh at the tron.

1609 SKENE *Reg. Maj.* I. 152 Tronars sould be challenged, that they keip not their office in troning..of wooll, bot they trone the samine to some men, and not to others. 1861 RILEY *Liber Albus* 124 That no foreign merchant or other shall sell or buy any wares that ought to be weighed or troned, except by our own beam or tron.

**Tron**, obs. f. THRONE; pa. t. of TRINE *v.*[2] *Obs.*

**Trona** (trōu·nă). *Min.* [a. Swed. *trona* (1773), app. from Arabic طرون *trōn*, apocopate form of نطرون *natrūn*, NATRON, ad. Gr. *νίτρον* soda (Dozy).] Native hydrous sodium carbonate, found in various places in N. Africa and America.

1799 KIRWAN *Geol. Ess.* 497 The trona was not deprived of its water of crystallization. 1850 ANSTED *Elem. Geol., Min.* etc. § 371 Trona, Urao, Hydrous sesqui-carbonate of soda. 1866 LAWRENCE tr. *Cotta's Rocks Class.* (1878) 51 Trona.. forms a crust on the ground on mountain slopes..in Peru.

**Tronage** (trōu·nėdʒ). [a. AF. *tronage*, f. OF. *trone* TRON: see -AGE.] The weighing of merchandise at the tron; a charge or toll upon goods so weighed; the right of levying such charge.

[1200 *Rot. Chart.* (1837) 35/2 Teneant predictam feriam.. cum stallagio et theloneo, pesagio et tronagio, et cum omnibus aliis libertatibus. 1290 *Rolls of Parlt.* I. 47/2 Mercatores..conqueruntur quod per deceptionem tronagii, & suptilitatem manuum ponderantium, decipiuntur de Catallis suis. 1347–8 *Ibid.* II. 213/1 Les ditz Citeinz ount este quitz de tronage, pesage des leins, & de merces.]

*a* 1325 *MS. Rawl. B.520* lf. 20 b, Þe lord king grauntez þat ..of..tollage, tronage, passage, pontage..lith fram nou forth ward assise of nouele disseisine. *a* 1500 in *Arnolde's Chron.* (1811) 100 To tronage perteinen thoos thingis that shalbe weyen by the trone of yᵉ kyngis. 1603 STOW *Surv.* 564 It [London] auayleth the prince in Tronage [*ed.* 1598 Tonnage], Poundage and other her customes, much more then all the rest of the realme. 1607 COWELL *Interpr., Tronage*..is a kind of tolle..taken (as it seemeth) for weying. 1766 ENTICK *London* (1776) I. 334 The tronage, that is to say, the weighing of lead. 1860 *All Year Round* No. 76. 614 Here, was formerly kept the royal steelyard, or beam, for the tronage of imports.

Hence **Tro·nager** = TRONER.

1885 H. HALL *Hist. Custom-Revenue Eng.* II. vi. 123 The sacks..and the bales..were successively weighed at the 'beam' by a special officer, the 'tronager' or 'tronour'.

**Troncheon, -ion, -on, -oun, Troncke, Trondle**, obs. ff. TRUNCHEON, TRUNK, TRUNDLE.

**Trone**: see TRON.

**Trone**, obs. f. THRONE; pa. t. of TRINE *v.*[2] *Obs.*

**Tro·ner.** *Sc.* and *north. dial. Obs.* exc. *Hist.* Forms: 5 tronner, 5–7 tronar, 7 -our, 8 -or. [ad. med.L. *tronārius*, f. *trona* TRON.] An official who had charge of the weighing of merchandise at the tron.

[1365 *Stat. David II*, c. 39 in *Acts Parlt. Scot.* (1844) I. 139/1 Et sit in quolibet loco tronarius.] *c* 1450 *Iter Camerar.* c. 15 in *Acts Parlt. Scot.* (1844) I. App. iv. 698/2 Of Tronaris. At þai keip nocht þar office in assayande woll bot sum þai assay ande oþer sum þai spar for mede in scath to þe king. 1507 *Reg. Privy Seal Scotl.* I. 219 Tronaris and uther officiaris. 1609 [see COCKET *sb.*[1] 1 b, TRON *v.*]. 1789 BRAND *Hist. Newcastle* II. 150 *note*, The office of tronor and poisor of Newcastle upon Tyne. 1885 [see TRONAGER].

† **Tro·ngle**, *v. Obs. rare*⁻¹. [Echoic.] In vbl. sb. **Tro·ngling**, a ringing or tingling in the ears.

1398 TREVISA *Barth. De P. R.* XI. ii. (Tollem. MS.) In eeren wynde makeþ also whistelynge and tronglynge [*Bodl. MS.* trongelinge] and ryngynge [*orig.* sibilum et tinnitum].

**Tronion**, obs. form of TRUNNION.

‖ **Tronk** (trǫŋk). [Cape Dutch, ad. Pg. *tronco* trunk, stock (of a tree), the stocks, by extension 'prison'. (Unknown in Du. of Holland.)] A prison.

1693 *Gov. Rec. Fort St. George, Madras*, The justices.. committed him to the Custody of the Talliars in the Trunke, but on the 21 September last, he made his escape by breaking through the Prison wall. 1863 LADY DUFF GORDON *Lett. fr. Egypt*, etc. (1875) 259 He..informed me he had just been in the Tronk. 1897 *Daily News* 31 Mar. 6/4 Discomfort inflicted by the Boers on their prisoners in the tronk at Pretoria. 1905 *Blackw. Mag.* Sept. 389/1 You shall be caught. You shall go to tronk.

**Tronk, tronke**, obs. forms of TRUNK.

**Tronsoun**, obs. form of TRUNCHEON.

**Troo**, obs. or Sc. form of TROW *v.*

**Troocheman**, obs. f. TRUCHMAN, interpreter.

**Trood**, obs. f. TROD (*sb.*, and pa. t. of TREAD *v.*).

**Trookyll**, obs. form of TRUCKLE.

**Troolie** (trū·li). Also 8 troelie, 9 troely, (in Dicts.) trooly. [Corruption of Tupi *tururi*.] A name for the immense entire leaf of the bussu-palm (*Manicaria saccifera*), often thirty feet in length and four or five in breadth, used in the lower Amazon region for thatching. Also, the tree itself. Also *attrib.*, as *troolie leaf, palm, tree*; **troolie hut**, a hut thatched with troolies.

1769 E. BANCROFT *Guiana* 13 Troelies are a leaf near thirty feet in length, serving for the thatch of houses. *Ibid.* 103 Troolies are, perhaps, the largest leaves..hitherto discovered. 1825 WATERTON *Wand. S. Amer.* I. (1903) 12 The troely, one leaf of which will defend thee from both sun and rain [*Note* (1903) The Troolie palm]. *Ibid.* (1882) 30 The low and swampy parts near creeks where the troely tree grows. 1847 M. J. HIGGINS *Ess.* (1875) 227 An Indian.. barn, open at the sides, and thatched thickly with troolie leaves at the top. 1899 RODWAY *Guiana Wilds* 20 Lying on the bed in the troolie hut.

**Trooly, Troone**, obs. ff. TRULY, THRONE.

**Troop** (trūp), *sb.* Forms: 6 trowp, (troppe), 6–7 troup, trowpe, troope, 6–8 troupe, (7 trope), 6– troop. [a. OF. *trope* (13th c.), F. *troupe* (16th c.), = Prov. *trop*, Sp., Pg. *tropa*, It. *truppa*, prob. :—late L. *troppus* 'flock', of which the ulterior origin is uncertain.]

**1. a.** A body of soldiers.

1545 LISLE in *St. Papers Hen. VIII*, I. 829 Your enymyes ..assemblyd more and more in gret troupes. 1598 BARRET *Theor. Warres* III. i. 42 Your Musketiers being deuided into sundrie troupes, of 30, 40 or 50 in a troupe. 1610 HOLLAND *Camden's Brit.* (1637) 527 Amid the thickest troupes of his enemies in the battaile of Agincourt. 1794 MRS. RADCLIFFE *Myst. Udolpho* xv, The travellers frequently distinguished troops of soldiers moving at a distance. 1838 LYTTON *Leila* II. ii, In this troop..rode many of the best blood of Spain. 1852 THACKERAY *Esmond* III. vii, Esmond perfectly well remembered seeing the old lady sitting up in the bed.. that morning when the troop of guard came to fetch her.

**b.** A number of persons (or things) collected together; a party, company, band.

1584 R. SCOT *Discov. Witchcr.* X. ix. (1886) 150, I marvell againe, that no bodie else heareth nor seeth this troope of minstrels. 1601 ? MARSTON *Pasquil & Kath.* II. 95 The glooming morne..hath..forc'd the sacred troupes of sparkling stars into their priuate Tents. 1615 G. SANDYS *Trav.* 42 Liuing in wandring troupes according to the Scythian Nomades. 1711 ADDISON *Spect.* No. 130 ⁋ 1 We saw at a little Distance..a Troop of Gipsies. 1833 HT. MARTINEAU *Manch. Strike* i. 1 The children dispersed in troops.

**c.** Of animals: A herd, flock, swarm.

1587 MASCALL *Govt. Cattle* (1596) 237 Fold for sheepe... Make your pennes..in some drie ground, and make also partitions thereinto to receiue small troups of forty or moe. 1604 E. G[RIMSTONE] *D'Acosta's Hist. Indies* IV. xxxiii. 299 In Peru there is such store of pastures and feedings, as..every man feedes his troupes where he pleaseth. 1719 DE FOE *Crusoe* (1840) I. xx. 358 We perceived two or three troops of wolves. 1812 CARY *Dante, Parad.* XXXI. 6 A troop of bees. 1847 TENNYSON *Princ.* IV. 150 As flies A troop of snowy doves athwart the dusk.

**d.** Used to indicate a great number; a 'lot'; esp. in *pl.* 'flocks', 'swarms'.

1590 SHAKS. *Com. Err.* V. i. 81 A huge infectious troope Of pale distemperatures, and foes to life. 1596 DALRYMPLE tr. *Leslie's Hist. Scot.* IX. (S.T.S.) II. 193 Our folkis, in hope to obteine the hous, in troupis rinis to, bot agane ar dung doune. 1605 SHAKS. *Macb.* V. iii. 25 That which should accompany Old-Age, As Honor, Loue, Obedience, Troopes of Friends. 1658 *Whole Duty Man* xvii. § 18 We find this sin of self-love set by the Apostle in the head of a whole troop of sins. 1794 LD. AUCKLAND *Corr.* (1862) III. 198 Lady Auckland and the troop are all in perfect health. 1881 BESANT & RICE *Chapl. of Fleet* II. i. (1883) 120 There is no time, for a woman, like the time when she..is courted by a troop of lovers.

† **e.** A company of performers: = TROUPE.

1779 SHERIDAN *Critic* I. i, Your first inquiry would be, whether they had brought a theatrical troop with them. 1835 T. MITCHELL *Acharn. Aristoph.* 1043 *note*, This prize-feast is..a frequent source of encouragement to his orchestral troop.

**2.** *pl.* Armed forces collectively. Also *fig.*

1598 BARRET *Theor. Warres* 136 Fraunce and Flanders, too full of his pencionary troupes. 1605 SHAKS. *Lear* IV. v. 16 Our troopes set forth to morrow. 1671 LADY M. BERTIE in *12th Rep. Hist. MSS. Comm.* App. V. 22 My brother Peregrine and all the troopes are to show in Hide Parke beefore the Prince of Orange. 1732 LEDIARD *Sethos* II. VIII. 143 Certain sums of money to raise troops. 1835 T. MITCHELL *Acharn. Aristoph.* Introd. p. xvii, It was a war of native and self-paid troops against troops foreign and purchased. 1854 COBDEN *Speeches* (1878) 319 The courage displayed by our troops.

**3.** *Mil. spec.* A subdivision of a cavalry regiment commanded by a captain, corresponding to a *company* of foot and a *battery* of artillery.

1590 SIR J. SMYTH *Disc. Weapons* Ded. 5 b, Souldiors.. disordering themselues vpon euery light occasion both in battallion, squadron and troupe. 1641 EVELYN *Diary* 12 Sept., Here were now 16 companies and 9 troopes of horse. 1703 MARLBOROUGH *Lett. & Disp.* (1845) I. 117 Lord Raby's regiment of dragoons..is of eight troops. 1832 *Regul. Instr. Cavalry* III. 45 *Troop*—The half of a Squadron. Troops are called Right and Left in each Squadron.

**b.** The command of a troop.

1813 WELLINGTON in Gurw. *Desp.* (1838) XI. 187 Just at this moment there is a troop vacant for purchase in the regiment of Life Guards. 1842 THACKERAY *Fitz-B. Pap.* Pref. (1887) 14 His papa would have purchased him a troop—nay, a lieutenant-colonelcy—some day, but for his fatal excesses.

**4.** *Mil.* A signal on the drum for troops to assemble in readiness for marching; the assembly. (Cf. quot. 1667 in TROOP *v.* 1.)

1688 R. HOLME *Armoury* III. xix. (Roxb.) 153/2 The drumer is to beat all maner of beats, as a Call, a Troope, a March, a Preparative. 1706 PHILLIPS (ed. Kersey) s. v., The Troop, which is the second beat of the Drum,..for the Men to repair to their Colours. 1803 *Instruct. Infantry* (ed. 3) 13 The Music plays the Troop. 1845 S. JUDD *Margaret* I. xiii, Tony's beat of the troop was the signal for the soldiers to assemble.

**5.** *attrib.* and *Comb.*: in sense 2, as *troop-boat, column, -ship, -steamer, -traffic, -train, -transport*; in sense 3, as *troop-gelding, -leader* (cf. LEADER[1] 6), *-leading, -orderly, sergeant* (*-major*), *-stable*; also *troop-lined, -thronged* adjs.; **troop-bird** (*U.S.*), a troopial (Worcester 1860, citing Gray); **troop-boot** (*U.S.*), a cavalry boot; **troop-fowl** (*local U.S.*), a scaup-duck; **troop-horse**, (*a*) a cavalry horse; † (*b*) *collectively*, horsemen for a troop.

1816 in *Century Mag.* LIX. 623/1 He had taken ten gunboats from the Neapolitans, and several *troop-boats. 1885 E. CUSTER *Boots & Saddles* x. 107 The general..wore *troop-boots reaching to his knees. 1702 *Lond. Gaz.* No. 3790/8 A bright-bay *Troop-Gelding 15 hands and half high. 1640 *Bk. War Comm. Covenanters* 1 The Committie ordaines, that, the *troupe horss to be leviat furth of the Stewartrie for the service of the publict. 1856 LEVER *Martins of Cro' M.* xxxvi, The sound of troop-horses passaging to and fro.. now interrupted the colloquy. 1832 *Regul. Instr. Cavalry* II. 29 The *Troop Leaders are to be on the pivot flank. 1889 *Pall Mall G.* 3 July 4/3 The procession followed the *troop-lined route. 1896 *Westm. Gaz.* 10 Mar. 5/3 He was *troop-orderly that day. 1688 R. HOLME *Armoury* III. xviii. (Roxb.) 134/1 The *Troup, or Holster pistall, this is longer then the fore said [girdle pistol] by as much againe. 1838 JAS. GRANT *Sk. Lond.* 92 The Troopers..being allowed..to call for as much tobacco, technically termed '*Troop-sand', as they could consume at the sitting. 1853 STOCQUELER *Milit. Encycl.* s.v. *Serjeant-Major*, A *Troop Serjeant-major receives 3s. [per day]. 1889 W. S. GILBERT *Foggerty's Fairy* etc. (1892) 108 He was now troop-sergeant, and one of the smartest men in the squadron. 1862 THACKERAY *Philip* xvi, I certainly did suffer most cruelly on board that horrible *troop-ship. 1855 WHYTE MELVILLE *Gen. Bounce* xx, Their task consisted of lounging about a *troop-stable, attired in undress uniform, to watch the men cleaning and 'doing up' their respective horses. 1862 *Catal. Internat. Exhib.* II. XII. 13 Model of Government *troop steamer for the Lower Indus. 1893 GOSSE *Questions at Issue* 270 The breaking-out of cholera in a *troop-train.

**Troop** (trūp), *v.* [f. prec. sb.]

**1.** *intr.* To gather in a company; to come together; to flock, assemble.

1565 COOPER *Thesaurus, Agglomero*,..to prease or gather thicke to gether, as souldiours doe: to trowpe. 1588 SHAKS. *Tit. A.* II. i. 113 There will the louely Roman Ladies troope. 1604 E. G[RIMSTONE] *D'Acosta's Hist. Indies* IV. xxxiii. 300 These wilde kine have so multiplied..that they troupe together in the fields and woods by thousands. 1667 MILTON

*P. L.* vii. 297 As Armies at the call Of Trumpet..Troop to thir Standard. **1795** Burke *Let. to W. Elliot* Wks. 1842 II. 244 Multitudes, hardly thought to be in existence, would appear, and troop about him. **1799–1805** Wordsw. *Prelude* v. 260 She left us destitute, and, as we might, Trooping together.

†**2.** **a.** *trans.* To gather or assemble (individuals) into a troop or company. Also *refl.* To associate or consort *with* a number of others, to go in company. *Obs.*

*c* **1590** Greene *Fr. Bacon* vii. 3 The king..trooped with all the western kings That lie alongst the Dantzic seas by east. *Ibid.* xii. 16, I came not, troop'd with all this warlike train. **1590** — *Orl. Fur.* Wks. (Rtldg.) 91/2, I vow..To troop myself with such a crew of men As [etc.]. **1620** [G. Brydges] *Horæ Subs.* 410 Amongst some of them hee should troope himselfe.

**b.** *intr.* To associate *with*.

**1592** Shaks. *Rom. & Jul.* i. v. 50 So shewes a Snowy Doue trooping with Crowes, As yonder Lady ore her fellowes showes. **1605** — *Lear* i. i. 134 All the large effects That troope with Maiesty. **1864** Lowell *Fireside Trav.* 195 The descendants of Sabine pigeons..trooping with noisy rooks and daws. **1880** Kinglake *Crimea* VI. ix. 299 He would troop with the accusing throng.

**3.** *intr.* To walk, go, pass; *colloq.* (with *off*, *away*, etc.) to go away, 'be off', 'pack'. Cf. March *v.*[2] 2.

**1590** Shaks. *Mids. N.* iii. ii. 382 And yonder shines Auroras harbinger; At whose approach Ghosts wandring here and there, Troope home to Church-yards. **1700** T. Brown *Amusem. Ser. & Com.* 32, I thought 'twas Time to troop off to an Eating-House. **1708** Mrs. Centlivre *Busie Body* iv. ii, Get out of my house,—go troop. **1782** Eliz. Blower *Geo. Bateman* I. 147 Pack up your cloaths, Miss Pert, for ..you shall troop from hence to-morrow. **1860** G. Meredith *Evan Harrington* xlv, The place is ours till we troop.

**4.** *intr.* To march in rank; to walk or pass in order. Also *fig.* Now somewhat *colloq.*

**1592** Wyrley *Armorie* 148 Now close to troupe, then goodly to deraine. **1598** Barret *Theor. Warres* iii. ii. 70 Sundry small troupes, trouping round about the battell. **1635** Barriffe *Mil. Discip.* lxxiii. (1643) 199 Those files which formerly gave fire in the meane time trooping backe. **1682** H. Aldrich *Upon Christ Church Bells Oxf.*, Yᵉ verger troops before yᵉ Deane. **1698** Fryer *Acc. E. India & P.* 130 My Indians..trouped by three or four wretched Towns. **1820** W. Irving *Sketch Bk.* I. 63 (*R. van Winkle*) He was generally seen trooping like a colt, at his mother's heels. **1883** S. C. Hall *Retrospect* II. 40 The days..trooped forward as peacefully as..the soft white clouds. **1893** *Nation* (N. Y.) 22 June 453/2 As the spring months troop by, they bring a succession of fruits.

**b.** *trans.* To cause to march in a troop.

**1872** T. Cooper *Life* 238 At six we were trooped off.

**5.** *intr.* To come or go in great numbers; to pass in flocks or troops; to flock (*in*, *out*, etc.).

**1610** Bolton *Elem. Armories* 51 The rest of proofes which troup-vp close to their quarter,..who can but embrace? **1629** Milton *Christ's Nativity*, *Hymn* xxvi, The flocking shadows pale Troop to th' infernall jail. **1784** Cowper *Task* v. 61 Now from the roost..Come trooping at the house-wife's well-known call The feather'd tribes domestic. **1862** Mrs. H. Wood *Mrs. Hallib.* i. xiv, All the children trooped in at once. **1910** A. M. Fairbairn *Stud. Relig. & Theol.* II. viii. iii. 519 The address delivered, the Jews trooped out of the synagogue.

**6.** *trans.* (*Mil.*) *To troop the colour* (or *colours*): to perform that portion of the ceremonial known as Mounting of the Guard in which the colour is received. Also *absol.*

The first Standing Order on the subject (but not containing the word) is dated May 1755; but the appellation may date back to Marlborough's time, as it is known that there were Campaign orders on the subject of Mounting of the Guard which do not appear to have been preserved. See 'General Regulations, Orders, and Warrants, 1717–1766', MS. in the War Office Library, in which the ceremonial is fully described.

**1803** *Instruct. Infantry* (ed. 3) 11 To Troop or send for the Colours. **1816** *Chron.* in *Ann. Reg.* 8/1 After the trooping of the colours had taken place the detachment..received the Eagles. **1861** G. F. Berkeley *Sportsm. W. Prairies* xiv. 233 In mounting guard they 'troop' as much as we do. **1893** *Times* 5 June 6/1 The ceremony called trooping the colour which dates back to the times of Marlborough. **1894** *Ibid.* 1 June 10/1 First the colour was trooped, and then followed a march past in column.

**7.** To transport (troops).

**1882**, **1894** [see Trooping *vbl. sb.* b.]

**Trooper** (trū·pəɹ). [f. Troop *sb.* + -er [1].]

**1.** A soldier in a troop of cavalry; a horse soldier.

The term was used in connexion with the Covenanting Army which invaded England in 1640. It was used in the English Army in 1660. In the first establishment of Horse Regiments after the Restoration, the strength of a troop of horse was 1 Captain, 1 Lieutenant, and 60 Troopers.

**1640** *Bk. War Comm. Covenanters* 1 That ilk trouper have for the twa pair of the 40 dayes lone appoyntit be the Committie of Estaites xviij libs. **1694** Luttrell *Brief Rel.* (1857) III. 296 [They] were all mounted on gray and white horses, and new clothed, and are more like troopers than dragoons. **1703** Marlborough *Lett. & Disp.* (1845) I. 164 The troopers might embark with the two regiments of foot. **1844** H. H. Wilson *Brit. India* I. 199 The escort..consisted of but two companies of native infantry and sixteen troopers. **1877** *Field Exerc. Infantry* 331 Two or more troopers should be with each support, to carry intelligence.

**b.** In various colloq. and slang phrases, esp. *to swear like a trooper*.

**1785** Grose *Dict. Vulg. T.* s.v., You will die the death of a trooper's horse, that is with your shoes on, a jocular method of telling any one he will be hanged. **1810** *Sporting Mag.* XXXVI. 122 The fellow..swore like a trooper. **1812** Lady Granville *Lett.* 12 Sept. (1894) I. 41 William Lamb laughs and eats like a trooper. **1842** S. Lover *Handy Andy* xli, Jack was heard below, swearing like a trooper. **1854** Badham *Halieut.* 443 A friend of his, 'eques fortissimus', i.e. one who lied like a trooper. **1884** Symonds *Shaks. Predecess.* iv. 160 Juventus..swears like a trooper.

**2.** A horse ridden by a trooper; a troop-horse; a cavalry horse.

**1640** Sir J. Lessley in *Antiq. Rep.* (1809) IV. 436 The tag'd tail'd trooper that stands in the staw. **1791** 'G. Gambado' *Ann. Horsem.* iv. (1809) 84 Instead of his capering like a Trooper, he hangs down his head and tail. **1855** Whyte Melville *Gen. Bounce* xx, How he gave it you..about riding that old trooper instead of your own charger! **1901** *Field* 9 Feb. 163/3 These expenses take too much off the price paid for a trooper.

**3.** In Australia: A mounted policeman.

**1858** McCombie *Hist. Victoria* viii. 100 A violent effort [was] made by the troopers on duty to disperse an assemblage which occupied the space of ground in front of the hustings. **1864** J. Rogers *New Rush* ii. 51 A trooper spies him snoring in the street.

**4.** A troop-ship.

**1872** 'Aliph Cheem' (Yeldham) *Lays of Ind* (1876) 204 The gallant trooper 'Crocodile' is getting under weigh. **1880** *World* 13 Oct., Of those in the Euphrates, one of the Imperial troopers, four were down simultaneously with sunstroke. **1896** Newnham-Davis *Three Men & a God* 79 The last hired trooper of the season was going home in the early spring, taking in her a draft of the regiment.

†**5.** *Cant.* A half-crown. *Obs.*

*a* **1700** B. E. *Dict. Cant. Crew*, *Trooper*, a half Crown.

**Troopial, troupial** (trū·piăl). *Ornith.* [ad. F. *troupiale* (Brisson 1760), f. *troupe* troop, from its living in flocks.] A name given to various species of birds of the American family *Icteridæ*; *esp.* the icteric oriole. Also *attrib.*

[**1825** Waterton *Wand. S. Amer.* (1882) 26 You hear the pretty songster called Troupiale pour forth a variety of sweet and plaintive notes.] **1825** Bonaparte *Amer. Ornith.* I. 27 Yellow-headed Troopial. *Ibid.* 28 Red-winged Troopial. *Ibid.* 31 All the species of Troopial are peculiar to America. **1863** Bates *Nat. Amazon* vii. (1864) 168 Flocks of a handsome bird belonging to the Icteridæ or troupial family. **1892** W. H. Hudson *Nat. La Plata* 283 A scarlet-breasted troupial of La Plata. **1895** Newton *Dict. Birds*, Troopial.

**Trooping** (trū·piŋ), *vbl. sb.* [f. Troop *v.* + -ing [1].] The action of the verb Troop.

**1809** *Howell's St. Trials* I. 142/2 Not for any assemblings or troopings by them formerly made within the kingdom of England, but [etc.]. **1816** [see Troop *v.* 6]. **1885** *Manch. Exam.* 8 June 4/7 The chief event..was the trooping of the colours on the Horse Guards Parade. **1888** Stevenson *Black Arrow* 167 The great trooping of black clouds, and the cold squalls that followed one another. **1893** L. Killeen *Soldiers at Sea* 32 When the trooping is over for the year, the troopships lie idle in Portsmouth Harbour. **1907** *Westm. Gaz.* 2 Dec. 12/1 The completion of a dream of 'trooping', by means of which the South-Western moves our sailors and soldiers to and from the coast in any part of England without detraining for other lines.

**b.** *attrib.*

**1647** *Caldwell Pap.* (Maitl. Cl.) I. 110 Quhat they depursed..for trouping horses furnishit be them, quartering of troupers, and monethlie mantinance. **1696** *Lond. Gaz.* No. 3147/4 A Trooping Saddle trimmed with blue. **1882** *Pall Mall G.* 24 June 8/1 The preparation of the *Serapis* and *Crocodile* for the Indian trooping season can be suspended if found necessary, and they can be employed as supplementary transports. **1894** *Scott. Leader* 17 May 5 The Admiralty has chartered two P. & O. steamers..to begin the trooping service in September.

**Troo·ping**, *ppl. a.* [-ing [2].] That troops.

**1582** Stanyhurst *Æneis* iii. (Arb.) 83 Heere..fields of Salent with trouping clustered armye Lyctius Idomeneus dooth keepe. **1728–46** Thomson *Spring* 135 The little trooping birds. **1823** Chalmers *Serm.* I. i. 24 His people ..come in trooping multitudes around him. **1843** J. Martineau *Chr. Life* (1867) 464 Whose trooping images the dawning light does not disperse.

†**Troo·pmeal**, *adv. Obs. rare.* [f. Troop *sb.* + -meal.] By troops, in a troop or troops.

**1600** Holland *Livy* v. xxx. 200 The Nobles old and young, came troup-meale..into the hall. *c* **1611** Chapman *Iliad* xvii. 634 So troope-meale Troy pursu'd a while.

**Troo·pwise**, *adv. rare.* [f. Troop *sb.* + -wise.] By or in troops.

**1820** W. Tooke tr. *Lucian* I. 560 *note*, Wolves are frequently seen going troopwise.

**Troose**, var. Trouse, trews, trousers.

**Troostite** (trū·stəit). [Named after Prof. G. Troost of Nashville, Tennessee: see -ite [1].]

**1.** *Min.* A variety of Willemite, with admixture of iron and manganese, occurring in reddish hexagonal crystals.

**1835** C. U. Shepard *Treat. Min.* II. 247 Troostite..is found at Sterling (N. J.) associated with Franklinite. **1850** Ansted *Elem. Geol., Min.* etc. § 448 Troostite, or Troolite, is a variety [of Bi-silicate of Manganese] containing iron. **1868** Dana *Min.* (ed. 5) 262 Willemite..Silicate of Zinc...The crystals of..New Jersey are often quite large, and pass under the name of *troostite*.

**2.** *Metallurgy.* A transitional constituent of steel: cf. Martensite, Pearlite 2, Sorbite [2].

**1902** *Encycl. Brit.* XXIX. 572/2 Austenite, troostite, sorbite, and other constituents [of iron] have also been described.

Hence **Troostitic** (-i·tik) *a.*, pertaining to or consisting of troostite (*Cent. Dict. Suppl.* 1909).

**Trooze**, variant of Trouse, trews, trousers.

†**Tropæ·an**, *a. Obs. rare*[−1]. [f. L. *tropæ-us* adj. (Pliny) + -an: cf. Gr. τροπαία (sc. πνοή) an alternating wind, one which blows back from sea to land' (L. & Sc.), f. τρόπος turning.] Blowing from sea to land; *tropæan winds*, sea-breezes.

**1686** Plot *Staffordsh.* 44 The frequent rains brought by the Tropæan winds from the Irish Seas.

**Tropæolaceous** (tropī͵olēi·ʃəs), *a. Bot.* [f. mod.L. *Tropæolāce-æ* (f. Tropæolum) + -ous: see -aceous.] Belonging to the Natural Order *Tropæolaceæ*, typified by the genus *Tropæolum*; regarded by some as a division of *Geraniaceæ*.

**1909** in *Cent. Dict. Suppl.*

**Tropæolin** (tropī·ŏlin). Also -ine. [f. next + -in [1], -ine [5]; from the resemblance of the colour to that of the flowers of some species of *Tropæolum*.] Any one of several orange dyes, of complex composition, belonging to the class of sulphonic acids.

**1880** Friswell in *Jrnl. Soc. Arts* 446 This body has been used as a dye, under the name of Tropæoline O. **1881** Watts *Dict. Chem.* VIII. 1857 Diazinsulphonic Acids..Sulphoxybenzenephenols...Some of them are dye-stuffs, known in commerce as tropæoline, chrysoïdine, roccelline, &c. **1897** *Allbutt's Syst. Med.* II. 522 Watery solution of tropæolin.

‖**Tropæolum** (tropī·ŏlŏm). *Bot.* Pl. -a (and in Eng. form -ums). [mod.L. (Linnæus, 1737), f. Gr. τρόπαιον trophy; so called from the resemblance of the leaf to a shield and the flower to a helmet.] A South American genus of herbs (N.O. *Tropæolaceæ* or *Geraniaceæ*), mostly of trailing or climbing habit, with irregular spurred flowers, usually deep orange or yellow; several species are cultivated as ornamental plants, and are commonly called Indian Cress, and (erroneously) Nasturtium.

**1785** Martyn *Rousseau's Bot.* xxxi. (1794) 481 The nectary is found on the calyx in *Tropæolum*. **1815** J. Scott *Vis. Paris* (ed. 2) App. 287 The hedges are interlaced with twining *Tropæola*, *Passion flowers*, and *Convolvuli*. **1866** *Treas. Bot.* 1178/1 The Tropæolums are remarkable for possessing an acrid taste, similar to that which exists among the *Cruciferæ*. **1901** *J. Black's Carp. & Build., Home Handicr.* 45 Passion flowers, convolvuluses, and tropæolums running up and around the window.

‖**Tropæum** (tropī·ŏm). Also 6 tropheum, 7–9 trophæum, 9 tropæon. [L. *tropæum*, *trophæum*, ad. Gr. τρόπαιον trophy.] = Trophy. (Now only *Antiq.*, in *lit.* sense.)

**1549** *Compl. Scot.* xvii. 149 This last tryumphe of laure tre vas callit *tropheum*, quhilk signifeis ane ioyful victoree. **1570–6** Lambarde *Peramb. Kent* (1826) 307 They..enacted in their Chapter house, that..Saint Cuthbertes feast (as a Tropheum of their victorie) shoulde be holden double, both in their Church and Kitchen. **1847** Leitch tr. *C. O. Müller's Anc. Art* § 200 (1850) 189 Below, a tropæon is erected by Roman legionaries and auxiliaries. **1901** *Athenæum* 5 Jan. 24/2 [The] massive foundations..are too deep and strong for anything but a very large tower or trophæum.

**Tropal** (trōu·păl), *a. Geom.* [f. L. *trop-us* Trope + -al.] Pertaining to or constituting a trope: see Trope 8.

**1875** Cayley *Math. Papers* IX. 519 The quartic surface has also four tropes (planes which touch the surface along a conic)...The conic of contact or tropal conic in each plan being the intersection of the plane with the before-mentioned quadric surface. *Ibid.* 520 Ordinary tropal planes each touching the surface in a proper conic.

‖**Troparion** (tropæ·riǫn, -ēᵊ·riǫn). Pl. -ia. [a. Gr. τροπάριον, dim. of τρόπος Trope (sense 5).] In the Greek Church: A short hymn, or a stanza of a hymn; also, = Troper.

**1850** Neale *Hist. Eastern Ch.* I. 832 *note* b, A Canon, in the usual services, consists of nine odes; each ode is divided into an uncertain number of troparia, generally three, four, or five. *Troparion* is the generic term for all the short hymns of which the services of the Greek Church almost entirely consist. **1876** Stainer & Barrett *Dict. Mus. Terms* (1898), *Troparion*, an office-book of the Greek Church containing the sequences or chants sung after the lessons.

**Tropary, tropery** (trōu·pəri). *Eccl.* [ad. med.L. *troparium*, *troperium*, f. L. *tropus* Trope (sense 5).] = Troper.

**14..** *Nom.* in Wr.-Wülcker 719/34 *Hic troporius*, a tropery. **1725** J. Lewis *Life Pecocke* (1744) 158 It was usual to swear on the tropery or t[r]oper, a book of sequences. **1882** *Church Q. Rev.* 276 A very considerable number of the Service Books in use..in Anglo-Saxon times survive...They consist of Sacramentaries or Missals, Troparies, Passionals [etc.].

**Trope** (trōup). Also 6 troope, 7 trop. [ad. L. *tropus* a figure of speech, ad. Gr. τρόπος a turn, f. τρέπειν to turn; cf. F. *trope* (1554 in Godef. *Compl.*). Sometimes app. repr. Gr. τροπή (cf. 3).]

**1.** *Rhet.* A figure of speech which consists in the use of a word or phrase in a sense other than that which is proper to it; also, in casual use, a figure of speech; figurative language.

**1533** Tindale *Supper of Lord* Cv, If ye be so sworne to the litteral sense in this matter, that ye will not in these wordes of Christe, Thys is my bodye, &c., admitte in so playne a speache anye troope. **1573** Tusser *Husb.* xxviii. (1878) 68 Christmas is onely a figure or trope. *a* **1638** Mede *Wks.* (1672) 349 That usual Trope of Scripture, by a part, or that which is more notable or obvious in any kind or rank of things, to imply the rest. **1693** Dryden *Juvenal* (1697) p. liii, Where the Trope is far fetch'd, and hard, 'tis fit for nothing but to puzzle the Understanding. **1779** Sheridan *Critic* i. i, Your occasional tropes and flowers suit the general coarseness of your stile, as tambour sprigs would a ground of linsey-wolsey. **1783** Blair *Lect. Rhetoric* xiv. I. 275 Tropes..consist in a word's being employed to signify something that is different from its original and primitive meaning; so that if you alter the word, you destroy the Figure. **1837** Macaulay *Ess., Bacon* (1887) 428 Irony is one of the four primary tropes. **1876** Gladstone *Homeric Synchr.* 262 To treat as a poetical trope this idea of kings as god-born or god-reared. **1888** Bryce *Amer. C.* III. cxi. 597 [American] rhetoric is Rhodian rather than Attic, overloaded with tropes and figures.

*attrib.* **1799** Han. More *Fem. Educ.* (ed. 4) I. x. 221 By this negligence in the just application of words, we shall be.. much misled by these trope and figure ladies.

†**2.** In Gregorian Music, A short distinctive cadence at the close of a melody. *Obs.*

**1603** Holland *Plutarch's Mor.* 1358 To let passe therefore the five positures of the Tetrachords, as also the first five tones, tropes, changes, notes or harmonies. **1605** Bacon *Adv. Learn.* ii. v. § 3 Is not the trope of music, to avoid or slide from the close or cadence, common with the trope of rhetoric of deceiving expectation? **1626** — *Sylva* § 113.

†**3.** [= Gr. τροπή.] The 'turning' of the sun at the tropic; also = Tropic A. 2. *Obs. rare.*

**1677** Gale *Crt. Gentiles* II. iv. 258 The Sun has..its annual Tropes and Vicissitudes, what they call Solstices, whereby it is nearer to or remoter from us. **1735** H. Brooke *Univ. Beauty* iv. 169 Now 'thwart the trope, or zone antartic steer.

†**4.** *Logic.* = Mood *sb.*2 1. *Obs. rare.*

**1656** Stanley *Hist. Philos.* viii. (1701) 315/1 Of Moods or Tropes there are two kinds, one of Indemonstrables,..the other of Demonstrables.

**5.** In the Western Church, A phrase, sentence, or verse introduced as an embellishment into some part of the text of the mass or of the breviary office that is sung by the choir.

(Tropes were discontinued at the revision of the missal under Pope Pius V in the 16th cent.)

**1846** Maskell *Mon. Rit.* I. p. xxxvii, The Tropes..were ..sung either before or after the Introit and Hymns in the service of the Mass. **1853** Rock *Ch. of Fathers* IV. xi. 21 A.. practice..had..grown up..in the north and western quarters of Christendom..of weaving certain pious sentences, called by the Romans 'festive praises', by the Franks 'tropes', between the words of the psalm in the introit at mass. **1894** W. H. Frere *Winchester Troper* p. ix, 'Trope'..is the regular word to describe additions to the Introit, Offertory and Communion, and is also more rarely found in connection with the Ite missa est or Benedicamus at the close of Mass.

**6.** In the Moravian Church, One of the three divisions forming the 'Unity of the Brethren'.

[**1780** B. La Trobe tr. *Cranz's Hist. Brethren* 355 In.. 1749..the administration of the Reformed tropus in the Unity of the Brethren was tendered to, and accepted by, the Bishop of Sodor and Man, Thomas Wilson.] **1809** Bogue & Bennet *Hist. Dissenters* (1833) II. i. 64 The three different classes of persons who compose the Unity, bear among the brethren the name of tropes or tropuses.

**7.** In Greek Philosophy: see quots.

**1866** Ferrier *Grk. Philos.* I. xv. 467 Of these tropes or Sceptical arguments Sextus enumerates ten. **1910** R. D. Hicks *Stoic & Epicurean* 376 Ænesidemus undertook to arrange the whole material at the disposal of the Sceptic in his contention against the dogmatic position under ten heads or tropes. The word trope properly denotes procedure; the ten tropes were intended to contain the means of refuting dogmatism in all possible forms, and to provide directions for stating every line of available argument which could lead to negative conclusions and paralyse assent.

**8.** *Geom.* The reciprocal of a node on a curve or surface; in different cases, a multiple tangent or tangent plane, or a plane or developable surface touching the given surface in a particular way.

**1869** Cayley *Math. Papers* VI. 330 Using 'trope' as the reciprocal term to node. **1875** [see Tropal].

**Tropee**, obs. form of Trophy.

**Tropeic** (tropī·ik), *a. Ichth.* [f. Gr. τρόπις keel + -ic.] Applied to the ventral fold in certain sharks. **1895** in *Funk's Stand. Dict.*

**Tropeine** (trōu·pi,əin). *Chem.* [Arbitrarily altered from Tropine.] Generic name for the esters or compound ethers of tropine.

**1883** *Science* I. 401/2 A series of derivatives, called by the author tropeines, results from the action of various organic acids with hydrochloric acid upon tropine. **1895** in *Funk's Stand. Dict.*

†**Tropel.** *Obs. rare.* Also (*pl.*) 5 troplys, 7 trowples. [a. OF. *tropele* (*a* 1200 in Godef.), dim. f. OF. *trope* Troop: see -el 2.] A small troop or company.

**1375** Barbour *Bruce* xiii. 275 Thai scalit in tropellis [*v.rr.* troplys, trowples] ser. *c* **1400** *Laud Troy Bk.* 5577 Paris come thenne with his tropel, With alle his knyghtes hardi and fel.

**Troper** (trōu·pəɹ). *Eccl.* (now only *Hist.*) Also 5 **tropere, tropoure, tropure,** 8 **tropar.** [OE. *tropere*, ad. med.L. *troperium* (see Tropary); cf. OF. *tropier, troper* (12th c. in Godef.).] A book containing tropes (Trope 5); also, a book containing sequences; a sequencer.

*a* **1073** *Charter Bp. Leofric* in Thorpe *Charters* 430, ii. fulle sangbec.. & i. tropere & ii. salteras. *a* **1400–50** *Alexander* 1568 With tablis & t[r]opoures. *c* **1400** *Laud Troy Bk.* 9369 The Bible ne no Missale,..The Grael ne the Tropere. *c* **1475** *Pict. Voc.* in Wr.-Wülcker 755/3 *Hoc troparium*, tropere. *a* **1746** Lewis in Gutch *Coll. Cur.* II. 169 A Tropery, or book of Sequences. It was called in English a T[r]oper. **1894** W. H. Frere *Winchester Troper* p. vi, The Tropers practically represent the sum total of musical advance between the ninth and the twelfth century.

**Tropery**: see Tropary.

†**Trophæ·al,** *a. Obs.* [f. L. *trophæ-um* Trophy + -al.] Pertaining to or adorned with trophies.

**1646** J. Gregory *Notes & Obs.* (1650) 163 He stiled himself thus Augustus Cæsar Octavianus Trophaeall. **1660** *Charac. Italy* 6 Her streets of old did shine with triumphing Cæsars and Consuls in their trophæal Chariots.

**Trophæum**: see Tropæum.

**Trophal** (trōu·făl), *a. Zool.* [f. Troph-i + -al.] Pertaining to or forming the trophi.

**1902** D. Sharp in *Encycl. Brit.* XXIX. 500/1 The appendages of the posterior three, or trophal, segments become the parts of the mouth.

**Trophe, -ee,** obs. forms of Trophy.

**Trophesy** (trǫ·fīsi). *Path.* [irreg. f. Gr. τροφή nourishment, with ending app. after *dropsy, palsy.*] 'Defective nutrition due to disorder of the trophic nerves' (Dorland *Med. Dict.* 1900–13). Hence **Trophesial** (trofī·ʃiăl, -ziăl) *a.*, pertaining to trophesy; in quot. 1899, pertaining to nutrition: = Trophic.

**1883** E. C. Mann *Psychol. Med.* 349 (Cent. Dict.) Excessive thought, with mental anxiety,..is much more exhausting, and therefore more commonly followed by trophesies. **1891** *Cent. Dict.*, Trophesial. **1899** *Allbutt's Syst. Med.* VIII. 408 A morbid cerebral condition impairing psychical and trophesial function. *Ibid.* 409 The trophesial function of the cortex.

‖**Trophi** (trōu·fəi), *sb. pl. Zool.* [mod.L., pl. of *trophus*, a. Gr. τροφός feeder, f. τρέφειν to nourish.] A collective name for the mouth-parts in insects, as organs for seizing and preparing the food. Also applied to the parts of the pharynx in rotifers, having a similar function.

**1826** Kirby & Sp. *Entomol.* xxxiii. III. 355 *Trophi*, the different instruments or organs contained in the mouth, or closing it, and employed in manducation or deglutition. They include the *Labrum, Labium, Mandibulæ, Maxillæ, Lingua*, and *Pharynx.* **1833** Lyell *Princ. Geol.* III. 277 The antennæ, tarsi and trophi are generally very obscure or distorted. **1888** Rolleston & Jackson *Anim. Life* 633 Class Rotifera...The mouth leads into an oesophagus, followed..usually directly by a muscular pharynx or mastax containing the chitinous jaw-apparatus or 'trophi'...The shape of the 'trophi' is variable.

**Trophic** (trǫ·fik), *a.* (*sb.*) *Biol.* [ad. Gr. τροφικός, f. τροφή nourishment: see -ic. Cf. F. *trophique.*] Of or pertaining to nutrition; *spec.* of certain nerves and nerve-centres, Concerned with or regulating the nutrition of the tissues.

**1873** A. Flint *Physiol. Man, Nervous Syst.* ii. 80 Centres attached to the sensory system of nerves, which have, as far as we know, a purely trophic influence over the nerves. **1875** H. C. Wood *Therap.* (1879) 559 Nerves which preside over nutrition,—the so-called trophic nerves. **1894** *Lancet* 3 Nov. 1030 The large amount of wasting of the muscles.. might suggest the possibility of a trophic lesion. **1899** *Allbutt's Syst. Med.* VII. 124 Another affection of the lower limbs, possibly trophic,..is rupture of the tendo Achillis.

**B.** *sb.* Something that promotes nutrition.

**1893** E. S. D'Odiardi *Med. Electricity* 54 The second class is composed of trophics, or nutrients, *i. e.*, promoters of nutrition.

So **Tro·phical** *a.* (*rare*) = *trophic* adj.; hence **Tro·phically** *adv.*, in relation to nutrition.

**1857** Dunglison *Med. Lex., Trophical Nerves*, the organic nerves, or nerves of the sympathetic system. **1900** *Lancet* 23 June 1779/2 This..implies continuity of the protoplasm of one neurone with another, but trophically and genetically the two are independent.

**Trophied** (trōu·fid), *a.* Also 8 **trophy'd.** [f. Trophy *sb.* or *v.* + -ed.]

**1.** Adorned with a trophy or trophies. Also *fig.*

**1622** Drayton *Poly-olb.* xxx. 159 From whose stone-trophied head, it [the echo] on to Wendrosse went. **1718** Rowe tr. *Lucan* viii. 1122 The Name that wont the trophy'd Arch to grace. **1798** S. Rogers *Epist. Friend* 200 Thro' trophied tombs of heroes and of kings. **1844** H. G. Robinson *Odes Horace* i. xii, The peaceful reign Of Numa, or the proudly trophied state Of Tarquin. **1905** Capt. Glasfurd *Rifle Ind. Jungle* 387 That mighty head shall be accorded the post of honour on already well-trophied walls.

**2.** Formed into or constituting a trophy.

*a* **1843** Southey *Comm.-pl. Bk.* IV. 55/1 The trophied armour damp gleaming to the central fire. **1887** *Daily News* 16 May 5/7 The Exchange was..tastefully decorated, each window..having its trophied flags and shield.

**Trophilegic** (trǫfile·dʒik), *a. Biol.* [irreg. f. Gr. τροφή nourishment + L. *legĕre* to gather, to collect + -ic. (Perhaps suggested by L. *frūgĭlĕgus* fruit-gathering.)] Collecting nutriment.

**1898** *Nature* 3 Nov. 15/1 The trophilegic action of the fronds [of ferns], in connection with which certain arrangements have been observed, destined to facilitate the passage of water to the roots.

**Trophism** (trǫ·fiz'm). *Phys.* [f. Gr. τροφή nourishment + -ism.] The process of nutrition of the tissues; 'direct trophic influence' (Dorland *Med. Dict.* 1900–13).

**1878** A. Hamilton *Nerv. Dis.* 444 Various depraved conditions of sensibility, motility, and trophism may follow.

**Tropho-** (trǫ·fo), combining form repr. Gr. τροφή nourishment, f. τρέφειν to nourish: entering into various technical terms, chiefly of biology and allied sciences. **Tro·phoblast** [-blast], a layer of cells external to the embryo, having the function of supplying it with nourishment; also applied by some to the morbid growth in cancer, as held to be an abnormal development of the same tissue; hence **Trophobla·stic** *a.*, relating to or consisting of trophoblast. **Trophoca·lyx** [Calyx], a cup-shaped body from which the placenta is developed in certain mammals, as bats and moles. **Tro·phocyte** (-səit) [-cyte], each of a set of cells forming one of the constituents of the fatty tissue in adult insects. **Tro·phodisc, -disk,** a disk-shaped body from which the placenta is developed in certain mammals, as rabbits. ‖ **Tropholecithus** (-le·sipŏs) [mod.L., f. Gr. λέκιθος yolk], the nutritive yolk of an ovum; hence **Trophole·cithal** *a.* **Tropho·logy** [-logy], that department of physiology which deals with nutrition. ‖ **Trophone·ma** (pl. -ne·mata) [mod.L., f. Gr. νῆμα thread], each of the glandular villi of the uterus in certain viviparous fishes, which supply nutriment to the embryos. ‖ **Tro:phoneurosis** (-ōu·sis), pl. **-oses** (-ōu·sīz) [Neurosis], any one of a class of functional disorders due to derangement of the trophic action of the nerves; hence **Trophoneurotic** (-ǫ·tik) *a.*, pertaining to or of the nature of trophoneurosis. **Tropho·pathy** [Gr. -παθεια suffering], any derangement of nutrition, esp. of a tissue. **Tro·phophore** (-fōəɹ) [ad. Gr. τροφοφόρος bringing nourishment], any one of the wandering amœboid nutritive cells in a sponge which give rise to gemmules or embryos. **Trophophoric** (-fǫ·rik) *a.* [f. as prec. + -ic], having the function of supplying provisions. **Trophophorous** (-ǫ·fŏrəs) *a.* [f. as prec. + -ous], pertaining to or of the nature of a trophophore. **Tro·phoplasm** (-plæz'm), Nägeli's term for that portion of the protoplasm of a germ or cell which is supposed to furnish nutriment to the *idioplasm*; hence **Trophopla·smic** *a.*, pertaining to or of the nature of trophoplasm. **Tro·phoplast,** Meyer's term for a specialized granule of protoplasm in a vegetable cell: = Plastid 2. **Tro:phopo·llen** [cf. *trophosperm* below], a proposed name for the partition of the loculus of an anther. **Tro·phosome** (-sōum) [Gr. σῶμα body], the aggregate of nutritive zooids of a hydrozoan (distinguished from *gonosome*); hence **Trophoso·mal** *a.* **Tro·phosperm** [ad. F. *trophosperme* (Richard, *a* 1819), f. Gr. σπέρμα seed], a proposed name for the placenta of a seed-vessel. **Tro·phosphere,** a spherical body (consisting of the *trophoblast* and the *trophospongia*) from which the placenta is developed in certain mammals, as hedgehogs. ‖ **Trophospongia** (-spǫ·ndʒiă) [mod.L. (Hubrecht), f. Gr. σπογγιά sponge], a compact layer of cells between the trophoblast and the decidual tissue; hence **Trophospo·ngial, -ian** *adjs.* ‖ **Tropho·ta·xis** [mod.L.: cf. Taxis 6], = *trophotropism.* **Trophotro·pic** *a.*, pertaining to or exhibiting trophotropism. **Tropho·tropism** [Gr. -τροπος turning: after *heliotropism*, etc.], reaction of an organism or cell to the stimulus of a source or supply of food by movement towards or away from it (*positive* or *negative t.*). **Trophozoite** (-zōu·əit) [Gr. ζῷον animal: cf. -ite 1 3], a sporozoon (endoparasitic protozoon) in its growing stage, when it is absorbing nutriment from its host. **Tropho·zooid** (-zōu·oid), a nutritive zooid of any colonial organism, as a hydrozoan.

**1889** Hubrecht in *Q. Jrnl. Microsc. Sci.* Dec. 299 This striking difference between somatic mesoblast and *trophoblast becomes still more accentuated in the next developmental phases. *Ibid.* 385 If we agree..to designate the outer layer alone as trophoblast, the outer layer plus a thin layer of somatic mesoblast without blood-vessels as diplotrophoblast [etc.]. **1907** *Contemp. Rev.* Sept. 411 A cancer is 'irresponsible trophoblast'. **1889** Hubrecht (as above) 301 Mesoblastic warts, ridges, and outgrowths being soon surrounded on three sides by the *trophoblastic proliferation. **1907** *Contemp. Rev.* Sept. 410 The trophoblastic theory of cancer. **1889** Hubrecht (as above) 359 The *trophocalyx (as this specialized region may conveniently be called, both in the bat and the mole, per analogiam with the trophosphere of the hedgehog and the trophodisc of the rabbit). **1904** *Jrnl. Roy. Microsc. Soc.* Oct. 527 Imaginal Adipose Tissue in Muscidæ.—Ch. Pérez has made a study of this tissue, which consists of two kinds of elements—*trophocytes and œnocytes. **1889** Hubrecht (as above) 323 Corresponding regions of the rabbit might be indicated by the name of *trophodisc, that of the bat and mole of trophocalyx. **1891** *Cent. Dict.*, *Tropholecithal. **1879** tr. *Haeckel's Evol. Man* I. viii. 216 The nutritive yolk (*vitellus nutritivus*, or *tropholecithus)..is a mere appendage of the true egg-cell, and contains hoarded food-substance,..so that it forms a sort of storehouse for the embryo in the course of its evolution. **1890** Billings *Med. Dict.*, *Trophology, science of nutrition. **1891** *Proc. Roy. Soc.* 19 Mar. 363 We propose to term the villiform structures of the uterine mucous membrane in Selachians, which essentially secrete nutriment, *trophonemata. *Ibid.* 365 Transverse sections of a trophonema shew [etc.]. **1857** Dunglison *Med. Lex.*, *Trophoneuroses, morbid conditions of the process of nutrition, owing to modified nervous influence. **1876** tr. *Wagner's Gen. Pathol.* 292 Many forms of disease rarely occurring, but..highly characteristic and very evident to the senses, tropho-neuroses. **1896** *Allbutt's Syst. Med.* I. 179 Facial hemi-atrophy and scleroderma from their distribution would suggest a trophoneurosis. **1891** *Cent. Dict.*, *Trophoneurotic. **1897** *Allbutt's Syst. Med.* II. 47 The so-called 'varieties' or 'forms' of leprosy..(2) the *smooth* (also called 'anæsthetic', 'non-tuberculated', 'tropho-neurotic', etc.). 1890 *Lancet* 8 Mar. 535 The belief of the writers that *trophopathy..has more to do with the cause of the so-called incurable diseases than the profession gives credit to. 1890 BILLINGS *Med. Dict.*, *Trophopathies*, disorders of nutrition. 1891 *Cent. Dict.*, *Trophophore, *Trophophorous. 1892 LD. LYTTON *King Poppy* I. 67 *note*, Official ranks, civil, military, and *trophophoric. 1893 tr. *Weismann's Germ-Plasm* I. i. 38, I shall..call the vital substance of the cell the 'formative plasm' or morphoplasm (Nägeli's '*trophoplasm'), in contrast to the idioplasm. [1899 *Allbutt's Syst. Med.* VI. 718 [The axis cylinder] is a prolongation of the achromatic amorphous substance, called also trophoplasma.] 1903 *Bot. Gaz.* May 340 Everything seems to point to the ooplasm as *trophoplasmic in character. 1885 GOODALE *Physiol. Bot.* (1892) 287 General Term.. *Trophoplast. Special Terms..anaplast, autoplast, chromoplast. 1889 *Science* 22 Nov. 355/1 The nucleus and other granules (the trophoplasts) within the cell...Each protoplast possesses the organs necessary for continuous transmission; the nucleus for new nuclei, the trophoplasts for new granules of all kinds. 1832 LINDLEY *Introd. Bot.* I. ii. 126 That part of the anther..which is called..the *trophopollen by Turpin. 1870 NICHOLSON *Man. Zool.* 26 The individual Campanularia consists of a series of nutritive zooids, collectively called the '*trophosome'. 1888 ROLLESTON & JACKSON *Anim. Life* 245 The Sea-fir..forms a fixed colony or *hydrosoma*...The hydrosome consists of a number of *hydranths* or nutritive zooids collectively forming the *trophosome* and connected to one another by a branching *cœnosarc*. 1819 LINDLEY tr. *Richard's Observ. Fruits & Seeds* 6, I substitute the name of *Trophosperm* for that of *Placenta*, which botanists have given to the internal part of the pericarp, on which the seeds are immediately attached. 1889 HUBRECHT (as above) 322 These two together [the trophoblast and the trophospongia], forming in Erinaceus a sphere which is shut off from the uterus lumen by the fusion of the lips of the decidua reflexa, should be indicated by the name of *trophosphere. *Ibid.*, It is to this cell-mass of which we have just traced the maternal origin, that I propose to give the name of *trophospongia. *Ibid.* 326 The topography of the *trophospongian region. 1897 C. B. DAVENPORT *Exper. Morphol.* I. § 3. 39 Chemotaxis is, therefore, in some cases, a response to the stimulus afforded by substances which can be employed by the organism as food; under which circumstances it can be called '*Trophotaxis'. 1891 *Cent. Dict.*, *Trophotropic. 1887 GARNSEY & BALFOUR tr. *De Bary's Fungi*, etc. ix. 449 *Trophotropism.—Vegetating plasmodia spread out on surfaces which yield little or no nutriment move towards bodies which contain nutrient substances as soon as they are offered to them. 1906 *Lancet* 27 Oct. 1161/2 The problem of digestion is intimately related to.. 'trophotropism', both positive and negative. 1900–13 DORLAND *Med. Dict.* (ed. 7), *Trophozoïte. 1909 *Cent. Dict. Suppl.*, Trophozoite. 1888 W. A. HERDMAN in *Encycl. Brit.* XXIII. 615/2 Nutritive forms (*trophozooids) which remain permanently attached to the nurse, and serve to provide it with food.

**Trophonian** (trofōu·niăn), *a.* [f. L. *Trophōnius*, Gr. Τροφώνιος, proper name (see below) + -AN.] Pertaining to Trophonius, the mythical builder of the original temple of Apollo at Delphi, who after his death was worshipped as a god, and had an oracle in a cave in Bœotia, which was said to affect those who entered with such awe that they never smiled again: hence *allusively*.

1792 in Morse *Amer. Geog.* (1794) I. 398 Two young ladies ..who had heroism enough to make the trophonian [*mispr.* trophimium] tour with us. 1796 BURKE *Regic. Peace* i. Wks. VIII. 109 There is great danger that they who enter smiling into this Trophonian cave, will come out of it sad and serious conspirators. 1896 GOSSE in *Contemp. Rev.* Jan. 87 His face had the solemn Trophonian pallor, the look of the man who has seen death in the cave.

**Trophy** (trōu·fi), *sb.* Forms: 6–7 trophe, -ee, -ey, -æ, (6 -ææ), 7 -ea, -ie, -ye, (tropee, -æe), 7– trophy. See also TROPÆUM. [a. F. *trophée* (15th c. in Hatz.-Darm.), ad. post-cl.L. *trophæum*, cl.L. *tropæum*, ad. Gr. τρόπαιον, neut. of τροπαῖος, f. τροπή turning, putting to flight, defeat.]

**1.** *Gr.* and *Rom. Antiq.* A structure erected (originally on the field of battle, later in any public place) as a memorial of a victory in war, consisting of arms or other spoils taken from the enemy, hung upon a tree, pillar, etc. and dedicated to some divinity. Hence applied to similar monuments or memorials in later times.

1550 T. NICHOLS *Thucydides* I. 36 The Athenians dyd make and set vp their Trophe or signe of victorye, pretending to haue had the better. 1638 JUNIUS *Paint. Ancients* 145 Religion..hindering the Rhodians to deface this monument, because dedicated tropæes might not be removed. 1697 DRYDEN *Æneid* VII. 254 Around the posts hung helmets, darts, and spears, And captive chariots, axes, shields, and bars, And broken beaks of ships, the trophies of their wars. 1700 PRIOR *Carmen Seculare* 369 Let every Sacred Pillar bear Trophies of Arms, and Monuments of War. 1776 GIBBON *Decl. & F.* ii. (1788) I. 45 Alexander erected the Macedonian trophies on the banks of the Hyphasis. *a* 1854 H. REED *Lect. Eng. Hist.* iv. (1855) 146 The banners of the ships of Spain hung out as trophies from the battlements of the Cathedral of St. Paul. 1881 JOWETT *Thucyd.* I. 159 The Athenians..raised a trophy on the place from which they had just sailed out to their victory.

**b.** *transf.* A painted or carved figure of such a memorial; by extension, an ornamental or symbolic group of any objects, or a representation of such a group in decorative art.

1634 SIR T. HERBERT *Trav.* 64 The Trophies of his Ormus Victory..painted in Gold..wherein are set downe..the assaults and massacres of the Ormusians. 1688 *Lond. Gaz.* No. 2363/4 A Steel Sword, the Hilt cut with Trophies, the Trophies black, the Ground inlaid with Gold. 1716 LADY M. W. MONTAGU *Let. to C'tess Mar* 14 Sept., Near the Empress was a gilded trophy wreathed with flowers. 1753 CHAMBERS *Cycl. Supp.*, *Trophy*, in architecture, an ornament which represents the trunk of a tree, charged.. with arms or military weapons. 1848 THACKERAY *Bk. Snobs* xxvi, His gorget, sash, and sabre of the Horse Marines, with his boot-hooks underneath in a trophy.

**2. a.** *transf.* Anything taken in war, or in hunting, etc.; a spoil, prize: esp. if kept or displayed as a memorial. Also *fig.*

1513 DOUGLAS *Æneis* XI. iv. 75 For all the Tuscane menȝe ..Greyt trophe and rich spulȝe hyddir bringis. 1599 B. JONSON *Cynthia's Rev.* I. ii, That trophæe of selfe-loue, and spoile of nature. 1612 DRAYTON *Poly-olb.* iv. 317 For a Trophy brought the Giants coat away, Made of the beards of Kings. 1681 FLAVEL *Right. Man's Ref.* x. 244 They are.. not left as a prey and trophy to their enemy. 1788 GIBBON *Decl. & F.* lxiii. (1846) III. 580 A defeat and a wound were the only trophies of his expedition. 1810 SCOTT *Lady of L.* I. xxvii, All around, the walls to grace, Hung trophies of the fight or chase. 1860 MAURY *Phys. Geog. Sea* (Low) xiv. § 586 It was upon this plateau that Brooke's sounding apparatus brought up its first trophies from the bottom of the sea. 1895 J. G. MILLAIS *Breath fr. Veldt* (1899) 322 Sable antelope, the heads of which are, to my thinking, the finest trophies that Africa produces.

**b.** *fig.* Anything serving as a token or evidence of victory, valour, power, skill, etc.; a monument, memorial.

1569 SPENSER *Vis. Bellay* xi, She raisde a Trophee ouer all the worlde. 1644 MILTON *Areop.* (Arb.) 31 Whereof this whole Discourse..will be a certaine testimony, if not a Trophey. 1661 SECRETARY NICHOLAS *Let.* 18 Nov. in *Remembrancia* (London, Town Clerk's Office), The officers of the Trained Bands of the City had been put to great expense and charges in providing themselves with trophies and other necessaries. 1675 TRAHERNE *Chr. Ethics* 397 Hands, hearts, and souls, our victories, And spoils, and trophies, our own joyes! 1750 GRAY *Elegy* 38 If Mem'ry o'er their Tomb no Trophies raise. 1847 EMERSON *Poems, Ode to Beauty* 89 The leafy dell, the city mart, Equal trophies of thine art. 1871 MACDUFF *Mem. Patmos* xxi. 292 The triumphs and trophies of intellect.

**3.** *attrib.* and *Comb.*, as *trophy-badge*, *-bearer*, *decoration* (see 1 b), *flag*, *-hunter*, *-hunting*, *-work*; **trophy-cress** = *trophywort*; **trophy-lock**, 'a lock of hair cut from the head of a slain enemy, used to adorn a weapon or shield' (*Cent. Dict.* 1891); **trophy-money, trophy-tax**, a tax formerly levied in each county, now only in the City of London, for incidental expenses connected with the militia: see quot. 1727–41, and cf. quot. 1661 in 2 b; **trophy-wort**, a book-name for the genus TROPÆOLUM.

1891 WESTERMARCK *Hist. Human Marr.* (1894) 172 Many ornaments are really nothing but *trophy-badges. 1614 T. WHITE *Martyrd. St. George* C iij b, Thou..the..name dost gaine Of *Trophee-bearer. 1888 *Cassell's Encycl. Dict.*, **Trophy-cress*, the genus Tropæolum. 1891 *Cent. Dict.* s.v. *Decoration*, **Trophy decoration*, decoration by means of groups of arms, musical instruments, scrolls, tools of painting and sculpture, and the like, or what may by extension be called trophies, especially in Italian decorative art. 1663 BUTLER *Hud.* I. II. 1121 The Squire in State..bore The *Trophee-Fiddle and the Case. 1898 G. MEREDITH *Odes Fr. Hist.* 78 To clasp his *trophy flag, and call him Saint. 1909 *Westm. Gaz.* 16 Apr. 3/3 He interweaves..many little incidents that would escape the notice of the mere *trophy-hunter. 1899 W. H. FURNESS *Folk Lore Borneo* 15 That savage love of *trophy-hunting which seems inborn in mankind. 1664 in J. Croft *Excerpta Ant.* (1797) 21 Item, paid for *Trophye Money, 3*l.* 8*s.* 8*d.* 1727–41 CHAMBERS *Cycl.*, *Trophy money*, a duty paid annually..towards providing harness, drums, colours, etc., for the militia. 1766 ENTICK *London* IV. 29 In 1682 a suit was commenced with the college..for trophy-money. 1897 *Outing* (U.S.) XXX. 227/1 The occasional sailor has no chance in the *trophy races. 1901 *Daily Chron.* 24 July 5/2 The '*Trophy Tax', or, to give it its full designation, the Trophy Tax Militia Rate..is peculiar to the City of London, and is a relic of the old train-band system. 1708 *New View Lond.* II. 491/2 A neat white marble monument, enricht with *Trophy work, an Urn, Cherub and Palm branches. 1866 *Treas. Bot.*, *Trophywort, *Tropæolum*.

Hence **Tro·phyless** *a.*, without a trophy.

1897 *19th Cent.* May 703 The disappointment at returning trophyless.

**Tro·phy**, *v.* [f. prec. sb.] *trans.* (chiefly *pass.*) †**a.** To transform into a trophy. *Obs. rare*—¹. **b.** To bestow a trophy upon, celebrate with a trophy. **c.** To adorn with a trophy or trophies; also *fig.* (See also TROPHIED.)

1599 B. JONSON *Cynthia's Rev.* v. xi, And so, swolne Niobe..was trophæed into stone. 1631 HEYWOOD *2nd Pt. Fair Maid of W.* I. i, If it prove as I have fashiond it, I shall be trophide ever. 1632 — *1st Pt. Iron Age* IV. Wks. 1874 III. 328 You beare your selfe more equall then you ought, With one so trophy'd. 1806 MOORE *Epist.* ix. 159 Heroes, trophied high In ancient fame. 1816 BYRON *Ch. Har.* III. xvii, Is the spot mark'd with no colossal bust? Nor column trophied for triumphal show? 1825 CAMPBELL *Poems, Stanzas Spanish Patriots* i, Looking on your graves, though trophied not, As holier hallow'd ground than priests could make the spot! 1847 R. W. HAMILTON *Disq. Sabbath* ii. (1848) 55 The Sabbath of the old covenant..descends to us trophied with holy illustrations.

**Tropic** (trǫ·pik), *sb.* and *a.*¹ Forms: 4 tropik, 6 -ycque(-we), -yk(e, 6–7 -ike, -ique, -icke, 6–8 -ick, 7– tropic. [ad. L. *tropicus*, a. Gr. τροπικός pertaining to the 'turning' of the sun at the solstice, tropical (hence as sb. (sc. κύκλος circle) the tropic); also, of the nature of a trope, figurative, f. τροπή turning. Cf. F. *tropique* (16th c.).] **A.** *sb.*

**I. 1.** *Astr.* †**a.** Each of the two solstitial points, the most northerly and southerly points of the ecliptic, at which the sun reaches his greatest distance north or south of the equator, and 'turns' or begins to move towards it again; also (*loosely*), each of the two signs (Cancer and Capricorn) at the beginning of which these points occur. *Obs.*

In quot. 1662 erroneously extended to include the equinoctial points.

*c* 1391 CHAUCER *Astrol.* I. § 17 This signe of cancre is cleped the tropik of Somer, of *tropos*, þat is to seyn Agaynward, for thanne by-gynneth the sonne to passe fro vs-ward. 1579 E. K. *Gloss. Spenser's Sheph. Cal.* Nov. 15 The sonne draweth low..toward his Tropick or returne. 1615 G. SANDYS *Trav.* 98 The Sunne performing his course in the winter Tropick. 1662 STANLEY *Hist. Chaldaic Philos.* (1701) 17/2 In Aries is the Spring Tropick, in Capricorn the Winter, in Cancer the Summer, in Libra the Autumnal.

**b.** Each of two circles of the celestial sphere (*tropic of* CANCER and *tropic of* CAPRICORN), parallel to the equinoctial or celestial equator, and distant about 23° 28′ north and south of it, touching the ecliptic at the solstitial points.

1503 *Kalender of Sheph.* i ij, The other two [circles] ar namyt tropycqwes, the oon of sommer the other of wynter. 1555 EDEN *Decades* 183 The soonne..remaynynge continually betwene the two tropykes of Cancer and Capricorne. 1561 — tr. *Cortez' Arte Nauig.* I. xv. 16 The Estiuall or sommer Tropyke. 1607 TOPSELL *Four-f. Beasts* (1658) 112 Other by the Dogs, do understand the two Tropicks, which are (as it were) the two porters of the Sun for the South and North. 1625 N. CARPENTER *Geog. Del.* I. vi. (1635) 144 The Tropicks are Parallels bounding the Suns greatest declination. 1658 WALLER *On Cromwell's Death* 21 Under the Tropick is our Language spoke. 1837 WHEWELL *Hist. Induct. Sc.* (1857) I. 114 Where the sun's path touches the tropics. 1868 LOCKYER *Elem. Astron.* iii. (1879) 65 At 23½° on either side of the equator are the Tropics.

**c.** *fig.* Turning-point; limit, boundary. (In quot. 1635 otherwise used: cf. 2 c.)

1635 QUARLES *Embl.* III. vii. (1718) 155 Our equinoctial hearts can never lie Secure, beneath the tropicks of that eye. *a* 1639 WOTTON *Charac. Kings Eng.* in *Reliq.* (1651) 166 States have their Conversions and Periods as well as Naturall Bodies, and we were come to our Tropique. 1670 EACHARD *Cont. Clergy* 54 It was a zodiacal mercy!..for Christ keeps within the tropicks; He goes not out of the pale of the church. 1844 N. PATERSON *Manse Garden* 63 Let rest and fatigue be your tropics and you will travel with unabated vigour over the undulating line of your ecliptic.

**2.** *Geog.* Each of two parallels of latitude on the earth's surface (corresponding to the celestial circles, 1 b, and called likewise *tropic of Cancer* and *tropic of Capricorn*), distant about 23° 28′ north and south of the equator, being the boundaries of the torrid zone.

1527 R. THORNE in Hakluyt *Voy.* (1589) 252 From the Tropickes to both the Poles. 1604 E. G[RIMSTONE] *D'Acosta's Hist. Indies* II. iv. 87 In Regions which lie without the Tropicks. *c* 1645 HOWELL *Lett.* (1688) III. 409 Our late Navigators..who use to cross the Equator and Tropiques so often. 1711 ADDISON *Spect.* No. 170 ¶ 13 It is a Misfortune for a Woman to be born between the Tropicks. *a* 1780 WATSON *Philip III* (1839) 175 Countries..on this side of the northern tropic. 1878 HUXLEY *Physiogr.* xx. 356 The boundaries of these zones are called tropics.

**b.** *pl.* With *def. art.*: The region between (and about) these parallels; the torrid zone and parts immediately adjacent.

1837 W. IRVING *Capt. Bonneville* III. 145 The Mississippi; whose rapid current traverses a succession of latitudes..in a few days..almost from the frozen regions to the tropics. 1854 EMERSON *Lett. & Soc. Aims, Resources* Wks. (Bohn) III. 203 The tropics are one vast garden. 1880 HAUGHTON *Phys. Geog.* iii. 130 The warm waters of the tropics are carried, bodily, into the temperate zone.

*Comb.* 1887 *Daily News* 7 Nov. 3/1 That pulmonary disease..generally..fatal to the tropic-born anthropoids.

**c.** *fig.* in allusion to the excessive heat or luxuriant growth of the tropics.

1641 J. JACKSON *True Evang. T.* I. 38 The sixt Persecution..did so scorch within the Tropicks of the Church, that many thousands suffered. 1893 *N. Y. New-Church Messenger* 19 Apr. 244 Mastodon-affections..swarming through the tropics of his soul.

**II.** †**3.** *pl.* [tr. L. *tropicī* (Athanasius, etc.).] Name for a sect who interpreted Scripture, or certain passages of Scripture, metaphorically. (Cf. TROPIST.) *Obs.*

1585–7 T. ROGERS *39 Art.* v. (1633) 23 Some affirme the holy Ghost to be but a meere creature, as did Arius,..the Tropickes, [etc.].

†**4.** *pl.* Tropical or metaphorical uses of words; tropes. *Obs.*

1697 tr. *Burgersdicius his Logic* I. xxvi. 104 The Change of the Word, from its proper Signification, as in the Tropicks.

**B.** *adj.*

**I. 1.** *Astr.* Connected with the sun's 'turning back' towards the equator at the solstices; pertaining to the tropics, or to either tropic (in sense A. 1 a or b): = TROPICAL 1. *Tropic circle* or *line* = A. 1 b; *tropic point* = A. 1 a. Now *rare* or *Obs.*

1551 RECORDE *Cast. Knowl.* (1556) 24 These other two cycles..are called the two Tropike cycles after the greeke deriuation. 1616 *Marlowe's Faust.* vi. Wks. (Rtldg.) 117/2 He views the clouds, the planets, and the stars, The Tropic Zones. 1667 MILTON *P. L.* x. 675 Som say the Sun Was bid turn Reines from th' Equinoctial Rode.. Up to the Tropic Crab. 1667 DRYDEN *Sir Martin Mar-all* v. i, I have seen your hurricanos and your calentures, and your ecliptics and your tropic lines. 1701 *Stanley's Hist. Philos.* Biog. bj, Stanley..thinks his Gnomon did only note the Tropick and Equinoctial Points.

†b. *fig.* or *allusively*. Of or pertaining to turning (in quot., in allusion to *Jas.* i. 17). *Obs.*

1677 GALE *Crt. Gentiles* II. IV. 258 It casts various shadows and causeth varietie of Seasons,..such is the ἀποσκίασμα or tropic shadow of the sun. But now the immutable God admits no such tropic shadows or variations.

2. *Geog.* Belonging to the tropics (in sense A. 2 or 2 b): = TROPICAL 2.

1799 WORDSW. *Ruth* vii, No dolphin ever was so gay Upon the tropic sea. 1806 MAURICE *Fall of Mogul* II. iv. 53 Relentless as the tropic whirlwind's rage. 1855 KINGSLEY *Westw. Ho!* xxv, The rapid tropic vegetation has reclaimed its old domains. 1875 BENNETT & DYER *Sachs' Bot.* 832 The vital conditions of all plants growing at a great elevation and in Arctic countries must be different from those growing in the lowlands of the Tropic and Temperate zones.

b. *fig.* = TROPICAL 2 c.

[1802 WORDSW. *Sonn.*, '*We had a female Passenger*' 10 Yet still her [a negro's] eyes retained their tropic fire.] 1887 *Daily News* 29 June 5/2 Spring completely lost its way..and it was winter,..till this tropic time came upon us unawares.

3. a. **Tropic bird**, any bird of the family *Phaethontidæ*, comprising sea-birds resembling terns, widely found in tropical regions, and characterized by webbed feet, rapid flight, and varied coloration.

1681 GREW *Musæum* I. IV. iii. 74 The Tropick Bird. So called because said never to be seen but between the Tropicks. 1756 P. BROWNE *Jamaica* 482 The Tropic Bird..breeds on the most desolate rocks and lonely places and is seldom seen near any inhabited shores. 1825 WATERTON *Wand. S. Amer.* II. (1903) 64 Sometimes..the tropic bird comes near enough to let you have a fair view of the long feathers in his tail. 1896 NEWTON *Dict. Birds* 990 The Yellow-billed Tropic-bird, *P[haethon] flavirostris*. *Ibid.* 991 The Red-tailed Tropic-bird, *P. rubricauda* or *phœnicurus*.

b. **Tropic crow**: see quot.

1781 LATHAM *Synopsis Birds* I. I. 384 Tropic [1800 SHAW, Tropical] Crow. Length twelve inches and a half..From O-wy-hee..in the South Seas.

c. **Tropic grape**, the gulf-weed: = SEA-GRAPE 6.

1850 MISS PRATT *Comm. Things Sea-side* ii. 111 The Sea-grape is an olive-green weed, with long slender leaves, and berries about as large as a pea, from which it derived its name of Tropic Grape. 1852 TH. ROSS *Humboldt's Trav.* I. iii. 129 To the north of the Cape Verd Islands we met with great masses of floating seaweeds. They were the tropic grape (*Fucus natans*), which grows..only from the equator to the fortieth degree of north and south latitude.

II. 4. *Biol.* [Properly the second element of GEOTROPIC, HELIOTROPIC, etc. used as an inclusive or generic term (cf. TROPISM).] Pertaining to, consisting in, or exhibiting tropism.

1903 T. H. MORGAN *Evol. & Adapt.* xi. 399 Another instinct, that appears to be due to a tropic response, is the definite time of day at which some marine animals deposit their eggs.

**Tro·pic**, *a.*[2] *Chem.* [Arbitrarily formed from ATROPIC: cf. TROPINE.] In *tropic acid*, an acid forming a constituent of atropine.

1881 WATTS *Dict. Chem.* VIII. 2062 *Tropic acid*, $C^9H^{10}O^3 = CH^2(OH).CH(C^6H^5).CO^2H$. This acid, one of the proximate constituents of atropine, has lately been prepared synthetically from atropic acid. 1882 *Nature* 2 Feb. 315/1 By decomposing atropine he obtained tropic acid and tropine, and by recombining these products he again formed atropine.

**Tropical** (trǫ·pikăl), *a.* [f. as TROPIC *a.*[1] + -AL. Cf. mod.F. *tropical*.]

1. *Astr.* Pertaining or relating to the tropics, or either tropic (in sense A. 1 a or b). Chiefly in *tropical year*, the interval between two successive passages of the sun through the same 'tropic' or solstitial point (or, equivalently, through the same equinoctial point); the natural year of the seasons, as reckoned from one (winter or summer) solstice or (vernal or autumnal) equinox to the next. So *tropical month*, the time taken by the moon in passing from either tropic (or either equinoctial point) to the same again.

1527 R. THORNE in Hakluyt *Voy.* (1589) 252 The quantitie of the earth vnder the Equinoctiall to both the Tropicall lines. 1594 BLUNDEVIL *Exerc.* III. I. xxxviii. (1636) 353 The Astronomicall yeere is either Tropicall or Syderall. 1662 STANLEY *Hist. Chaldaic Philos.* (1701) 17/2 Tropical [signs] are those to which when the Sun cometh he turneth back. 1715 tr. *Gregory's Astron.* (1726) I. 408 The Tropical Year is that space of time wherein the same Seasons of the Year return again. 1812 WOODHOUSE *Astron.* xxxi. 305 The tropical revolution of the Moon, or the revolution with respect to the equinoxes. 1834 *Nat. Philos.* III. *Astron.* i. 41/1 (Usef. Knowl. Soc.) The year from equinox to equinox is called the equinoctial year, or sometimes the tropical year. 1868 LOCKYER *Elem. Astron.* v. (1879) 203 The tropical month is the revolution of the moon with respect to the moveable equinox.

2. *Geog.* Pertaining to, occurring in, or inhabiting the tropics; belonging to the torrid zone.

1698 FROGER *Voy.* 3 At three o'clock in the morning we passed the tropick of Cancer;..and in the afternoon performed the ceremonies of Tropical baptism or duckings, which are commonly us'd by mariners in those places. 1699 DAMPIER *Voy.* II. I. ii. 33 Many reasons..beside the accidental ones from the make of the particular Countries, Tropical Winds, or the like. *a* 1700 SALMON (J.), The pine-apple is one of the tropical fruits. 1788 GIBBON *Decl. & F.* l. (1846) V. 2 The face of the desert..is scorched by the direct and intense rays of a tropical sun. 1851 CARPENTER *Man. Phys.* (ed. 2) 67 The highest temperature which the soil usually possesses in tropical climates, is about 126°. 1862 DANA *Man. Geol.* 615 Coral formations are most abundant in the tropical Pacific. 1880 HAUGHTON *Phys. Geog.* vi. 272 The second and third of the sub-orders are confined to the tropical forests of South America.

b. *Path.* Applied to diseases to which one is liable in tropical regions.

1828 WEBSTER, *Tropical*, 2. Incident to the tropics; as, tropical diseases. 1843 R. J. GRAVES *Syst. Clin. Med.* xi. 118 [Salivation] has been also very extensively recommended by army and navy surgeons, in the treatment of tropical fevers. 1893 A. DAVIDSON *Hygiene & Dis. Warm Climates* xvii. 613 Tropical Liver. 1905 *Daily Chron.* 9 Oct. 5/3 The notorious disease known in Germany as 'tropencholer', or tropical frenzy.

c. *fig.* Like the climate or growth of the tropics; very hot, ardent, or luxuriant.

1834 *Tait's Mag.* I. 383/1 Home he came, after an absence of fifty years, in a hissing hot fit of tropical rage. 1850 S. DOBELL *Roman* vi. Poet. Wks. (1875) 85 My fierce and tropical fancy, Hot with swift pulses. 1880 'OUIDA' *Moths* I. 174 We Russians have a passion for tropical houses. *Mod.* The heat was perfectly tropical.

3. *Zool.* (transf. from 1 or 2.) Used to describe the position of certain spines in the skeleton of some radiolarians: see quot.

1888 ROLLESTON & JACKSON *Anim. Life* 874 *note*, Imagine a globe with an axis of rotation, and five circles inscribed on it, an equatorial, two tropical and two polar. The twenty spines lie four in each of these circles, the equatorial and polar spines in the same meridian lines,..the tropical in meridian lines exactly intermediate.

4. Pertaining to, involving, or of the nature of a trope or tropes; metaphorical, figurative.

1567 MAPLET *Gr. Forest* 97 To sende ouer Owles to Athens. In Tropicall sense, ment of such as bestow largely vpon them that haue no neede. 1620 T. GRANGER *Div. Logike* 19 Whether the words bee plaine, and proper, or tropicall, and figuratiue. 1646 SIR T. BROWNE *Pseud. Ep.* III. iii. 111 A strict and literall acception of a loose and tropicall expression. 1725 WATTS *Logic* I. iv. § 7 They are used in a figurative or tropical Sense, when they are made to signify some things, which only bear either a Reference or a Resemblance to the primary Ideas of them. 1819 G. S. FABER *Dispensations* (1823) II. II. v. 190 The great sheet let down from heaven was as perfect a tropical hieroglyphic as any invented by the ingenuity of Moses. 1862 H. SPENCER *First Princ.* xv. (1875) 349 These [writings] had been partially differentiated into the kuriological or imitative, and the tropical or symbolic.

5. *Math.* ? Relating to the number of values of a function corresponding to one value of the variable.

1887 CAYLEY *Math. Papers* XII. 433 We wish to know whether *u* is a monotropic function of *z*. It will not be so if we have a tropical point,..such that [etc.].

**Tropicalian** (trǫpikē·liăn), *a. Zoogeog.* [f. mod.L. *Tropicalia* (f. Gr. τροπικός tropic + ἅλς sea) + -AN.] Belonging to the marine region called *Tropicalia*, comprising the seas between the isocrymes of 68° Fahr. on each side of the equator.

1888 *Proc. Biol. Soc. Washington* II. 34 (Cass. Supp.) Generic and specific modifications of the Arctalian and Tropicalian realms.

**Tropicalize** (trǫ·pikălaiz), *v.* [f. TROPICAL + -IZE.] *trans.* To make tropical; to give a tropical character to. Hence **Tro·picalized** *ppl. a.*

1885 LADY BRASSEY *The Trades* 125 Vegetation not unlike a patch of British fern suddenly transferred to a temperature of about fifty degrees above what it is accustomed to,—and thus, as it were 'tropicalised'. 1888 *Harper's Mag.* Sept. 616 The architecture is a tropicalized Swiss style.

**Tropically** (trǫ·pikăli), *adv.* [f. as prec. + -LY [2].] In a tropical manner.

1. In the way of a trope; metaphorically, figuratively.

1564 J. RASTELL *Confut. Jewell's Serm.* 140 The body of Christ is, onlye figuratiuelye,..tropicallie, imaginatiuelie, in the Sacrament. 1602 SHAKS. *Ham.* III. ii. 247 *King.* What do you call the Play? *Ham.* The Mouse-trap: Marry how? Tropically. 1646 SIR T. BROWNE *Pseud. Ep.* III. iii. 111 Spanish Mares, whose swiftnesse [is] tropically expressed from their generation by the wind. *a* 1703 BURKITT *On N. T.* Gal. v. 24 The work of mortification (called here tropically, a crucifixion). 1809 W. IRVING *Knickerb.* v. ix. (1849) 302 It is tropically observed by honest old Socrates, that heaven infuses into some men..a portion of intellectual gold. 1879 R. T. SMITH *St. Basil* 91 There are multitudes of expressions applied in Scripture to God, which we agree are to be tropically taken.

2. In a way characteristic of the tropics; with tropical heat, luxuriance, or violence.

1852 HAWTHORNE *Blithedale Rom.* xvii. (1885) 173 The sunshine lay tropically there. 1886 *Pall Mall G.* 10 June 9/1 The rain..continues, although not quite so tropically. 1896 *Academy* 11 July 27/1 Hume's tropically coloured account of what..he called 'the Irish rebellion'.

**Tropicopolitan** (trǫ pikoˌpǫ·lităn), *a. Nat. Hist.* [f. TROPIC, after COSMOPOLITAN.] Belonging to or inhabiting the whole of the tropics, or tropical regions generally.

1878 P. L. SCLATER in *19th Cent.* Dec. 1050 'Tropicopolitan' forms, by which I mean tropical forms that are found in the tropics of both hemispheres. 1879 A. R. WALLACE *ibid.* Feb. 254 The tropical land..which afforded the passage of the tropicopolitan forms from one continent to the other. 1895 C. DIXON in *Fortn. Rev.* Apr. 652 We have many tropicopolitan families that are confined absolutely to the great equatorial zone round the entire earth.

**Tropidial** (tropi·diăl), *a. Zool.* [f. Gr. τρόπις, τροπιδ- keel + -IAL.] Pertaining to the *tropis* or keel of a C-shaped sponge-spicule.

1887 SOLLAS in *Encycl. Brit.* XXII. 418/1 (*Sponges*) The pterocymba is subject to considerable modifications;..the pteres may be lamellar or ungual; additional lamellæ (tropidial pteres) may be produced by a lateral outgrowth of the keel.

**Tropidine** (trǫ·pidəin). *Chem.* [Arbitrary formation from TROPINE.] A colourless oily alkaloid obtained from tropine by the action of acids. So **Tropi·lidine**, a liquid hydrocarbon, $C_7H_8$, obtained by the dry distillation of tropine with quicklime (Webster, 1911).

1883 *Science* 11 May 401/2 When distilled with soda-lime, tropine is decomposed, giving methylamine and tropilidine ($C_7H_8$); and, when treated with fuming hydrochloric acid, a volatile base, tropidine ($C_8H_{13}N$), is formed. 1890 BILLINGS *Med. Dict.*, *Tropidine*, $C_8H_{13}N$, a liquid basic substance obtained from tropine by heating with strong hydrochloric acid in a sealed tube.

**Tropidosternal** (trǫpidoˌstə·ɹnăl), *a. Ornith.* [f. mod.L. *Tropidosterni* pl. (f. Gr. τρόπις, -ιδ- keel + στέρνον, L. *sternum* breast-bone) + -AL.] Belonging to the division *Tropidosterni* (= *Carinatæ*) of birds; having a keeled breast-bone.

In recent Dicts.

**Tropilidine**: see TROPIDINE.

**Tropine** (trōᵘ·pəin). *Chem.* [Arbitrarily formed from ATROPINE.] An alkaloid forming a constituent of atropine.

1881 WATTS *Dict. Chem.* VIII. 2062 *Tropine*, $C^8H^{15}NO$. This base, which Kraut obtained, together with atropic acid, by the action of baryta-water on atropine, may also be extracted..from the residues of the preparation of atropine.

**Troping** (trōᵘ·piŋ). [f. TROPE + -ING [1].] a. Figurative or metaphorical speech or conversation. b. The composition or use of tropes (sense 5).

1678 DRYDEN *Kind Keeper* v. i, Will you leave your Troping, and let me pass? 1907 J. M. MANLY in *Mod. Philol.* IV. 593 It was an age of troping. Tropes—that is, insertions in the authorized liturgy—were composed by the hundreds, and of all conceivable varieties.

‖ **Tropis** (trōᵘ·pis). *Zool.* Pl. **tropides** (trǫ·pidīz). [mod.L., a. Gr. τρόπις keel.] The 'keel' or middle part of a *cymba* or C-shaped sponge-spicule, between the *proræ* or 'prows'.

1887 SOLLAS in *Encycl. Brit.* XXII. 417/2 (*Sponges*) A truly C-shaped spicule...The back of the 'C' is the keel or *tropis*; the points are the prows or *proræ*.

**Tropism** (trǫ·piz'm). *Biol.* [The second element of HELIOTROPISM, GEOTROPISM, etc., used as an inclusive or generic term.] The turning of an organism, or a part of one, in a particular direction (either in the way of growth, bending, or locomotion) in response to some special external stimulus, as that of light (*phototropism*, *heliotropism*), heat (*thermotropism*), gravity (*geotropism*), etc.

1899 C. B. DAVENPORT *Morphology* II. 480 All cases of true tropism are cases of response to stimuli: such are chemotropism, hydrotropism, thigmotropism, traumatropism, rheotropism, geotropism, electrotropism, phototropism and thermotropism. 1909 J. W. JENKINSON *Experim. Embryol.* 273 The outgrowth and anastomoses of nerves, glands, ducts, the concrescence of layers may be tropisms of various sorts.

**Tropist** (trōᵘ·pist). *rare*—⁰. [f. as TROPE + -IST; cf. F. *tropiste* (Calvin, 1560).] a. A member of a sect who interpreted Scripture or some passage of Scripture in the way of trope or metaphor: see TROPIC *sb.* 3. b. One who deals in tropes or metaphors.

1727–41 CHAMBERS *Cycl.*, *Tropists*, or *Tropici*, the name of a sect...The reason of the name tropist was that they explained the scripture altogether by tropes and figures of speech...The Romanists also give the appellation tropists to those of the reformed religion, in regard of their construing the words of the eucharist figuratively. 1775 ASH, *Tropist*, one who deals in tropes, one who explains the scriptures by tropes and figures.

**Tropistic** (tropi·stik), *a. Biol.* [f. TROPISM: see -ISTIC.] Pertaining to or constituting tropism. Hence **Tropi·stically** *adv.* [see -ICALLY], in the way of tropism.

1910 F. KEEBLE *Plant-Anim.* ii. 41 We may use the term tropistic to describe the reactions of both fixed and free organisms to directive stimuli. *Ibid.* 52 Responding tropistically to unilateral light.

**Trople**, variant of TROPEL *Obs.*

**Tropo-**, combining form repr. Gr. τρόπος turning, etc. (see TROPE), occurring in a few modern technical terms. **Tropometer** (trǫpǫ·mītəɹ) [-METER], an instrument for measuring the angle of turning or torsion of some part of the body, as the eye-ball or a long bone. **Tropophil** (trǫ·pofil), **Tropophilous** (trǫpǫ·filəs) *adjs.* [Gr. -φιλος loving], applied to a plant adapted to a climate which is alternately moist and dry (or cold, the physiological effect of cold being similar to that of dryness); so **Tropophyte** (trǫ·pofəit) [Gr. φυτόν plant], a tropophilous plant; whence **Tropophytic** (-fi·tik) *a.* **Tropostereoscope** (trǫpoˌste·rīǫskoᵘp), a stereoscope with an arrangement for rotating the figures so as to bring them into some required position, in experiments on vision.

1881 *Athenæum* 11 June 787/1 The *tropometer, an instrument for measuring the angle of torsion of the humerus. 1902 I. B. BALFOUR in *Encycl. Brit.* XXV. 439/2 Parasitism

..occurs in..*tropophil woods of temperate regions, and alpine slopes. 1900 B. D. JACKSON *Gloss. Bot. Terms*, **Tropophilous*,..loving change of condition, as Tropophytes. 1903 tr. *Schimper's Plant-Geog.* I. i. 21 The vegetation of districts with climates alternately damp and dry or cold, is alternately of a hygrophilous and of a xerophilous character; it is therefore tropophilous. 1900 B. D. JACKSON *Gloss. Bot. Terms*, **Tropophyte*. 1903 tr. *Schimper's Plant-Geog.* I. i. 3 It appears..necessary to place in a third category all plants whose conditions of life are, according to the season of the year, alternately those of hygrophytes or of xerophytes. All such plants, including..the great majority of the plants composing the Central European flora, should be termed tropophytes. *Ibid.*, There are hygrophytic, xerophytic, and *tropophytic climates. 1901 TITCHENER *Exper. Psychol.* I. II. 272 Ludwig's *tropostereoscope..is..a refined form of the tube stereoscope.

† **Tro:pologe·tically**, *adv. Obs. rare*$^{-1}$. [Extended form of TROPOLOGICALLY, after *apologetically*.] = TROPOLOGICALLY, TROPICALLY I.

1652 URQUHART *Jewel* Wks. (1834) 292, I could have enlarged this discourse..tropologetically, by metonymical, ironical, metaphorical and synecdochical instruments of elocution.

**Tropologic** (trǫpǫlǫ·dʒik), *a.* [ad. late L. *tropologicus* (Jerome, *a* 400), = late Gr. τροπολογικός (*c* 1160), f. τρόπος trope: see -LOGIC. Cf. F. *tropologique* (Godef. *Compl.*).] = next (in either sense).

*c* 1380 WYCLIF *Sel. Wks.* II. 277 Þe þridde witt is tropologik, þat bitokeneþ witt of vertues. 1388 — *Gen. Prol. Bks. Proph.* 226 Moral ether tropologik [vndurstondyng of scripture] techith what we owen to do to fle vices, and kepe vertues. 1677 GALE *Crt. Gentiles* II. III. 153 These mystic Divines glorie in their Tropologic, Anagogic and Allegoric explication of Scripture: Neither is there any so plain, literal, or historic, but they have some tropologic or mystic sense for it. 1884 *Expositor* Jan. 45 The three traditional divisions of the mystic sense into allegoric, tropologic or moral, and anagogic or spiritual.

**Tropological** (trǫpǫlǫ·dʒikăl), *a.* [f. as prec. + -AL.] Belonging to or involving tropology.

**1.** Metaphorical, figurative: = TROPICAL 4.

1555 EDEN *Decades* 44 *margin*, Here nedeth sum tropologicall interpretour. 1621 BURTON *Anat. Mel.* III. iv. I. iii. (1628) 607 Tropological, allegorical expositions, to salve all appearances. 1862 NEALE *Hymns East. Ch.* 24 The ingenuity of some tropological applications.

**2.** Applied to a secondary sense or interpretation of Scripture, relating or applied to conduct or morals.

1528 TINDALE *Obed. Chr. Man* 129 They devide yᵉ scripture in to iiij senses, yᵉ literall, tropologicall, allegoricall, anagogicall. 1607 R. C[AREW] tr. *Estienne's World of Wonders* 255 To reduce all they haue to say, to certaine Allegoricall, Anagogicall, and Tropologicall senses. 1734 WATERLAND *Doctr. Trinity* vii. § 6. 438 Such a kind of Exercise I take many of those Allegorical Comments (Those especially of the Tropological kind) to have been. 1882–3 *Schaff's Encycl. Relig. Knowl.* I. 784 The moral, or tropological [sense of Scripture] teaches what to do.

**Tropolo·gically**, *adv.* [f. prec. + -LY ².] In a tropological manner (in either sense of the adj.).

1549 CHALONER *Erasm. Praise Folly* N iv b, Moralisyng the same bothe Allegorically, Tropologically, and Anegogically. 1678 CUDWORTH *Intell. Syst.* I. iv. § 32. 512 This was the General opinion concerning the Greekish Fables, that some of them were Physically, and some Tropologically Allegorical. 1730 WATERLAND *Script. Vind.* Pref. 18 The Law about the Sabbath..may be supposed..tropologically to denote the Rest of the Soul and its Cessation from Sin. 1888 SCHAFF *Hist. Chr. Ch.* VI. I. xxxii. 139 Jerusalem means..allegorically the good, tropologically virtue, anagogically reward.

**Tropologize** (trǫpǫ·lŏdʒəiz), *v. rare*$^{-1}$. [f. as TROPOLOGY + -IZE.] *trans.* To convert by a trope or metaphor; to use in a tropological sense.

1678 CUDWORTH *Intell. Syst.* I. iv. § 33. 520 If Athena or Minerva be tropologized into Prudence, then let the Pagans show what substantial essence it hath, or that it really subsists according to their tropology.

**Tropology** (trǫpǫ·lŏdʒi). [ad. late L. *tropologia* (Jerome, *a* 400), a. late Gr. τροπολογία (Justin Martyr, *a* 160), f. τρόπος trope: see -LOGY. Cf. F. *tropologie* (*a* 1300 in Godef. *Compl.*).]

**1.** 'A speaking by tropes' (Blount, 1656); the use of metaphor in speech or writing; figurative discourse.

1519 HORMAN *Vulg.* 98 b, The figuris of construction and locucion: and specially allygoris: and tropologies: & anagogies. 1613 PURCHAS *Pilgrimage* (1614) 88 Those, that by Allegories and Tropologies peruert and obscure the Historie of their Gods. 1678 [see TROPOLOGIZE]. 1873 F. HALL *Mod. Eng.* vi. 170 But, whether due to tropology, or to whatever other cause, multivocals, as conducing to brevity and expressiveness, are unwisely condemned, or deprecated, except where they entail ambiguity.

**2.** A moral discourse; a secondary sense or interpretation of Scripture relating to morals (cf. TROPOLOGICAL 2).

1583 FULKE *Defence* 47, I can not, following both the storie, and the tropologie or doctrine of maners, comprehend both briefly. 1706 PHILLIPS (ed. Kersey), *Tropology*,..a Moral Discourse tending to the Reformation of Manners. 1896 LINA ECKENSTEIN *Woman under Monast.* 113 The four-square pattern of ecclesiastical usage, namely according to the letter, allegory, tropology and anagogy.

**3.** A treatise on tropes or figures of speech.

*a* 1667 JER. TAYLOR *Serm.* Wks. 1831 IV. 160 Vocabularies, tropologies, and expositions of words and phrases. 1768 J. BROWN (*title*), Sacred Tropology.

**Tropometer** to **Tropostereoscope**: see TROPO-.

† **Troque** (trōuk). *Obs. rare.* [ad. L. *trochus*, a. Gr. τροχός: see TROCHE ², TROCHUS.] A hoop: = TROCHUS I.

1743 FRANCIS tr. *Hor.*, *Odes* III. xxiv. 58 More skill'd in.. The whirling troque, or law-forbidden dice. 1746 — *Art Poetry* 515 The bounding Ball, round Quoit, or whirling Troque.

**Tros, tross, trosse**: see TRUSS. **Trossers**: see TROUSERS. **Trost, Trosty**, obs. ff. TRUST, TRUSTY. **Trostell, -yle**, obs. ff. TRESTLE.

**Trot** (trǫt), *sb.*¹ Also 3–7 **trott**, 5–6 **trotte**, 5–7 **trote**. [a. F. *trot* (12th c. in Godef. *Compl.*), verbal sb. of *trotter* to TROT.]

**I. 1.** A gait of a quadruped, originally of a horse, between walking and running, in which the legs move in diagonal pairs almost together, so that in a slow trot there is always one foot at least on the ground, but in a fast trot one pair leaves the ground before the other reaches it, all four feet being thus momentarily off the ground at once; hence applied to a similar gait of a man (or other biped), between a walk and a run.

*a* 1300 *Cursor M.* 15872 (Cott.) His [Christ's] hend þai band and ledd him forth, A-trott and noght þe pas [2 *MSS.* a-pas, a pas]. 13.. *E. E. Allit. P.* B. 976 Trynande ay a hyȝe trot þat torne neuer dorsten. *c* 1386 CHAUCER *Can. Yeom. Prol.* & *T.* 22 His hat heeng at his bak doun by a laas For he hadde riden moore than trot [*v.rr.* trote, trotte]or paas. *c* 1425 *Cast. Persev.* 3100 in *Macro Plays* 169 Now dagge we hens a dogge trot. *a* 1547 SURREY *Æneid* IV. 957 Redouble gan her nurse Her steppes, forth on an aged womans trot. 1590 BARWICK *Disc. Weapons* 9 b, They retired a soft trote: their enemies..made after them with more speed. 1638 SIR T. HERBERT *Trav.* (ed. 2) 35 Our Chariot drawn by 2 Buffolls who by practise are nimble in their trot. 1737 BRACKEN *Farriery Impr.* (1757) II. Index s. v., A good Trot may be judged of by the Ear. 1755 JOHNSON, *Trot*, the jolting high pace of a horse. 1780 *Mirror* No. 92 A smart young man..passed by in his carriage at a brisk trot. 1818 SCOTT *Rob Roy* v, His [a fox's] drooping brush, his soiled appearance, and jaded trot, proclaimed his fate impending. 1835 ALISON *Hist. Europe* (1849–50) V. xxviii. § 43. 124 The pontoons arrived at a quick trot, from Dietikon. 1845 FORD *Handbk. Spain* I. 52 Their pace is the peculiar '*paso Castellano*', which is something more than a walk and less than a trot.

† **b.** An action of trotting; a journey or expedition on horseback. *Obs.*

*a* 1670 SPALDING *Troub. Chas. I* (1850) I. 186 The barronis ..rydis fra Turreff to New Abirdein,..Thay plunder the laird of Kermok...The covenanteris, heiring of this trot of Turref..began to hyde thair goodis. 1676 COTTON *Angler* II. ii. 22 I'le make as bold with your meat; for the Trot has got me a good stomach.

**c.** The sound of a horse, etc., trotting.

1858 CAPERN *Ball. & Songs* (1859) 138 The lime-team's trot, And milkmaid's carol..Are the chief sounds. 1882 'OUIDA' *In Maremma* I. 6 The trot of the chargers and the clash of the steel had passed into silence.

**d.** *transf.* and *fig.* *On the trot*, continually moving without intervals for rest; on the go.

*a* 1625 FLETCHER & MASS. *Custom of Country* IV. iv, Nor am I able to endure it longer,..I am at my trot already. 1646 JENKYN *Remora* 28 Shall we go a dull Asses trot heavenward? 1697 DRYDEN *Virg.* Ded. (1721) I. 20 The Virtuoso's Saddle, which will be sure to amble, when the World is upon the hardest Trott. 1822 W. IRVING *Braceb. Hall* (1823) I. xiv. 103 One of those who eat and growl, and keep the waiter on the trot. 1892 G. MEREDITH *Poet. Wks.* (1912) 454 Away on the trot of thy servitude start.

**2.** A trotting-race. *rare.*

1891 *Auckland Star* 1 Oct. 8/6 Spring Meeting...Handicap Maiden Trot, of 40sovs; second horse to receive 5sovs from stakes...Selling Trot...Pony Trot Handicap. 1893 *Scott. Leader* 12 June 1 Grand Handicap Trot—First, £10; Second, £3; Third, £2.

**3.** † *Irish trot* (obs.), *Turkey trot*, names of dances. Also † *shake a trot* (Sc. obs.).

1549 *Compl. Scot.* vi. 66 In the fyrst, thai dancit al cristyn mennis dance, the northt of scotland, huntis vp,..schaik a trot. 1652 *News fr. Lowe-Countr.* 7 The Scottish Jigg, the Irish Trot.

**4.** A toddling child; also, a small or young animal. *colloq.* Hence **Tro·ttie**, a little toddling child.

1854 THACKERAY *Newcomes* x, Ethel romped with the little children—the rosy little trots—and took them on her knees, and told them a thousand stories. 1895 SKELTON *Table-Talk* iv. 72 Black, hairy little trots..with their big bills and their big feet. 1905 *Contemp. Rev.* July 62 A practising school is maintained, partly of grave little trots from outside and partly of little boarders.

**5.** *U.S.* A literal translation of a text used by students; a 'crib'. Cf. HORSE *sb.* 13, PONY *sb.* 3. (*College slang.*) 1891 in *Cent. Dict.*

**II. 6.** *Fishing.* (Perhaps a different word: cf. TRAT.) A long-line lightly anchored or buoyed, with baited hooks hung by short lines or snoods a few feet apart; a trawl-line; also called a *trotline*; also, each of the short lines attached to this.

1858 [see *trot-line* in 7]. 1883 *Fisheries Exhib. Catal.* 10 Floating Trots and Spillers. 1884 *St. James's Gaz.* 18 Jan. 6/2 A 'trot' is a line some twenty yards long. 1886 R. C. LESLIE *Sea-painter's Log* x. 199 Much longer lines than the trots just described are used for flounders.

**III. 7.** *attrib.* and *Comb.* **trot-line** = sense 6; **trot-rope**, a rope securely pegged down at each end, on which runs a sliding ring to which a horse is tethered, enabling him to graze a strip the length of the rope (*Cent. Dict. Suppl.* 1909).

1858 in A. E. Lee *Hist. Columbus, Ohio* (1892) I. 146 Father went down to the river to examine a trotline.

**Trot** (trǫt), *sb.*² Forms: α. 4 **trate**, 4–6 **trat**, **tratte**; β. 6 **trott**, **trotte**, **trote**, (8 **trout**), 6– **trot**. [AF. *trote* occurs twice in Gower's French *Mirour de l'Omme*, ll. 8713 and 17900 ('la viele trote q'est jolie'), but the ME. instances have all *trat(e*, *tratte*, and the word has not been found in Continental French either as *trote* or *tratte*, so that the derivation is uncertain. It can hardly be connected with TROT *sb.*¹, or with OF. *baudetrot*, BAWDSTROT.] An old woman; usually disparaging: an old beldame, a hag.

α. *c* 1350 *Will. Palerne* 4769 Þat þo tvo trattes þat William wold haue traysted. *c* 1380 *Sir Ferumb.* 1370 Þan ful doun þat olde trate in-to þe salte see. *c* 1460 *Towneley Myst.* xvi. 394 Gett out of thise wonys! ye trattys, all at onys. 1513 DOUGLAS *Æneis* IV. xi. 114 Thus said Dido; and the tother, with that, Hichit on furth with slaw pase lyke ane trat. 1570 LEVINS *Manip.* 37/14 A tratte, *anus*.

β. 1530 PALSGR. 642/1 Se yonder olde trot howe she mumbleth, *auisez ceste vielle* [etc.]. 1596 SHAKS. *Tam. Shr.* I. ii. 79 Marrie him to a Puppet or an Aglet babie, or an old trot with ne're a tooth in her head. 1598 DRAYTON *Heroic. Ep.* xiii. 105 And call me, Beldam, Gib, Witch, Night-mare, Trot, With all despight that may a Woman spot. 1654 WHITLOCK *Zootomia* 78 An old Trot (that boasted of her Giftishnesse in Waterology). 1719 D'URFEY *Pills* V. 74 You are..A fulsome Trot and good for nought. *a* 1845 HOOD *Forget-me-nots* ii, Some strange, neglectful, gossiping old Trot. 1906 E. V. LUCAS *Listener's Lure* (1910) 282 Miss Graham got an old trot after a good deal of messing about.

**Trot** (trǫt), *v.* Forms: see TROT *sb.*¹; also 5 **tret**. [ME. a. OF. *troter* (12th c. in Hatz.-Darm.), F. *trotter* (Prov., Sp., Pg. *trotar*, It. *trottare*) to TROT. A med.L. deriv. *trottare* appears *c* 1150 in Thesaurus of Thomas.]

**I. 1.** *intr.* Of a horse, and occasionally other quadrupeds: To go at the gait called the trot (see TROT *sb.*¹ 1). Also said of a man.

*To trot all* (see ALL C. 4), *altogether* (ALTOGETHER B. 2), *high* (HIGH *adv.* 1 b), *large* (LARGE B. 6), *rough* (ROUGH *adv.* 1), *short* (SHORT C. 4); *to trot out*, to trot with extended action (opposed to *trot short*).

1362 LANGL. *P. Pl.* A. II. 135 Fauuel fette forþ Foles of þe beste, And sette..fals on a sysoures backe þat softly trotted. *c* 1386 CHAUCER *Merch. T.* 294 No man fynden shal Noon in this world, that trotteth [*v.r.* (*Petw. MS.*) treteþ] hool in al Ne man ne beest. *c* 1410 *Master of Game* (MS. Digby 182) iv, Somtyme þei [roe-deer] trotteth and goth a paas. 14.. *Beryn* 939 As hors þat evir trottid..It were hard to make hym aftir to ambill well. *c* 1450 *Merlin* 279 A Curroure trottynge on foote. 1553 T. WILSON *Rhet.* 61 Trotte sire and trotte damme, how should the fole amble? *c* 1566 *Merie Tales of Skelton* in *S.'s Wks.* (1843) I. p. lx, Hee was a litell olde fellowe, and woulde lye as fast as a horse woulde trotte. 1633 MARMION *Antiquary* I, You'll hardly find..beast that trots sound of all four: There will be some defect. 1674 *Lond. Gaz.* No. 882/4 A light gray Mare about fourteen hands high, five years old, trots altogether. 1675 *Ibid.* No. 959/4 A Brown Bay Nag,..Trots all. 1676 *Ibid.* No. 1107/4 Gray Mare,..trots rough. 1677 *Ibid.* No. 1222/4 A Sorrel Chesnut Gelding.., paces little, but trotteth high. 1706 Trot out [see SHORT C. 4]. 1856 MISS MULOCK *J. Halifax* ii, He took me on his back..and fairly trotted with me down the garden-walk. 1859 GEO. ELIOT *A. Bede* I. i, Gyp with his basket, trotting at his master's heels. 1883 H. CRAIG in *Harper's Mag.* Aug. 346/1 She trotted a mile in the unparalleled time of 2.10¼. 1897 *Daily Chron.* 23 Aug. 8/2, I trotted down the wicket very slowly.

**b.** *transf.* Of a rider, etc., or of a vehicle.

*c* 1386 CHAUCER *Wife's Prol.* 838 Amble, or trotte [*v. r.* trote], or pees, or go sit doun, Thou lettest oure disport. *a* 1450 *Le Morte Arth.* 3339 Arthur with knyghtis fully xiiij..With helme, sheld, And hauberke shene; Ryght so they trotted vppon þe grownde. 1599 SHAKS. *Hen. V*, III. vii. 86, I will trot to morrow a mile. *c* 1682 CLAVERHOUSE in 15*th Rep. Hist. MSS. Comm.* App. VIII. 270 The smith at Menegaff,..after whom the forces has troted so often. 1688 R. HOLME *Armoury* III. xix. (Roxb.) 186/2 Words of command about wheelings of Horsmen...Trot large, and wheele to the left. 1807 CRABBE *Par. Reg.* I. 487 Who trots to market on a steed so fine. 1833 *Regul. Instr. Cavalry* I. 66 '*Trot Out*'—Increase gradually to the trot of manœuvre, 8½ miles per hour. When steady, '*Trot Short*'—Collect the horses to the school pace again. 1833 T. HOOK *Parson's Dau.* I. iii, At Windsor..a royal coach may be often seen trotting about the town. 1913 *Times* 14 May 6/2 The Brigade was an imposing picture as it trotted past the King.

**c.** *transf.* and *fig.*

*c* 1430 *Pilgr. Lyf Manhode* III. xl. (1869) 157 Alwey j muste make the chyn trotte, and the throte gaape. 1600 SHAKS. *A. Y. L.* III. ii. 331 Time..trots hard with a yong maid, between the contract of her marriage, and the day it is solemnizd. 1612 DEKKER *If it be not good* Wks. 1873 III. 275 Vncle write that. *Oct.* Fast as my pen can trot. 1671 R. MACWARD *True Nonconf.* 273 Your loftie Pindarick.. doth trote more rudely, and lamely, then our hobling meeter. *a* 1758 RAMSAY *Generous Gentl.* iii, She lean'd upon a flow'ry brae, By which a burnie trotted. 1852 THACKERAY *Esmond* II. xi, We college poets trot..on very easy nags. 1893 SALTUS *Madam Sapphira* 31 A woman is never led astray. She trots, or gallops or bolts astray, but never is she led.

† **d.** In the alliterative phrases *trot and tremble*, *tremble and trot*. *Obs. rare.*

*c* 1425 *Cast. Persev.* 459 in *Macro Plays* 91 Now I sytte in my semly sale; I trotte & tremle in my trew trone. *c* 1485 *Digby Myst.* (1882) III. 555 A! how I tremyl and trott for ȝese tydynges!

**2.** *intr.* To go or move quickly; to go briskly or busily; to bustle; to run. Also *refl.*, and with *it.* Now *colloq.*, implying short, quick motion in a limited area. Cf. TODDLE *v.* 2 b.

Also *trans.* in *to trot one's terms*, at Durham University, to keep one's terms as a day-student: cf. TROTTER 2.

*c* **1416** HOCCLEVE *Balade to Henry V* 8 The scantnesse [of gold] Wole arte vs three to trotte vn-to Newgate. *c* **1440** *York Myst.* xxviii. 204 Do trottes on for that traytoure apas. **1530** PALSGR. 763/1, I have doone naught sythe syxe of the clocke in the mornyng but trotte aboute from place to place. *a* **1553** C. BANSLEY *Treat.* xii. (Percy Soc.) 5 Sponge up your vysage, olde bounsynge trotte, and tricke it wyth the beste, Tyll you tricke and trotte youre selfe to the devyls trounsynge neste. **1581** T. HOWELL *Deuises* E ij b, Wante makes the olde wyfe trot. *c* **1645** HOWELL *Lett.* (1753) 126 Som..find the Table ready laid; but som Must for their commons trot. *a* **1704** T. BROWN *Alsop's State of Conform.* Wks. 1711 IV. 116 If you'd have me trot it to the East-Indies,..'tis no sooner said, than done. **1774** C. KEITH *Farmer's Ha!* lx, Now lasses round the ingle trot, To make the brose. **1825** T. HOOK *Sayings* Ser. II. *Man of Many Fr.* (Colburn) 125, I will trot myself off for the moment, and be back immediately. **1863** MRS. C. CLARKE *Shaks. Char.* xvi. 402 She..will keep her husband trotting. **1883** *Durham Univ. Jrnl.* 17 Dec. 141 'To trot one's terms' was, we believe originally, a Dublin phrase.

†**3.** *trans.* **a.** To trot upon (something) (*rare*). **b.** To make, describe, or execute by trotting; to go through at a trot. **c.** To follow, traverse (a path) as if by trotting (*rare*). *Obs.*

**1599** SHAKS. *Hen. V*, III. vii. 16 My horse..boundes from the Earth..he trots the ayre. **1602** MARSTON *Antonio's Rev.* III. i. Wks. 1856 I. 104 The black jades of swart night trot foggy rings Bout heavens browe. **1612** *Two Noble K.* v. iv. 68 On this horse is Arcite Trotting the stones of Athens. **1633** FORD *'Tis Pity* I. ii, I have seen an ass and a mule trot the Spanish pavin with a better grace. **1638** SIR T. HERBERT *Trav.* 58 He..was..compell'd to trot the knotty path of inevitable destinie.

**4.** *trans.* To cause to trot; to lead or ride at the trot. Also *fig.*

**1592** WARNER *Alb. Eng.* VIII. xxxviii. (1612) 189 Whether that he trots, or turnes, or bounds his barded Steede. *a* **1628** G. CARLETON *Life B. Gilpin* (1636) 66 He commanded William Airy..to trott the horses up and downe. **1684** R. H. *School Recreat.* 21 Trot him about in your hand a good while; Then offer to mount. **1884** *Daily Chron.* 25 Oct. (Cassell's) The whips trotted the pack to Gravel-hill. **1886** *Sat. Rev.* 6 Mar. 315/1 The public..is being trotted up and down in front of Home Rule in the belief that, like a nervous horse, it can be familiarized with the alarming object.

**b.** *To trot out*: To lead out and show off the paces of (a horse); hence *fig.* to bring forward (a person, an opinion, etc.) for or as for inspection or approval; to exhibit, show off. *colloq.*

**1838** LYTTON *Alice* VII. iii, His guest, to be shown off.. and trotted out before all the rest of the company. **1841** SIR G. STEPHEN *Adv. Search Horse* (ed. 6) p. xxiv, A little cross-bred, vicious beast..was 'trotted out' before a circle of ladies and gentlemen, to be admired. *Ibid.* ii. 46 He is trotted out, admired, and purchased. **1848** THACKERAY *Bk. Snobs* xxv, She began to trot out scraps of French. **1884** *Manch. Exam.* 20 Aug. 5/1 The fine old historical commonplaces were trotted out.

**c.** To draw out (a person) in conversation so that he appears ridiculous; to make game of, make a butt of. Chiefly with *out*.

**1818** *Blackw. Mag.* III. 527 Menippus, accordingly, would fain trot Dr. Chalmers. **1848** THACKERAY *Van. Fair* xxxiv, You want to trot me out, but it's no go. **1888** BURGON *Lives 12 Gd. Men* II. x. 298 [He] trotted out his neighbour to his heart's content.

**d.** To conduct or escort (a person) *to* or *round* a place. *To trot out* (a woman), to walk out with, as a lover. *slang.*

**1888** 'J. S. WINTER' *Bootle's Childr.* xiv, I've trotted 'em out, all sorts of girls—but I never could..tie myself to any one of 'em. **1898** 'MERRIMAN' *Roden's Corner* vi. 60 Perhaps you'll trot us round the works. **1902** *Daily Chron.* 23 Aug. 6/7 He gave religious instruction..in his school, and on saints' days 'trotted' the children to church.

**e.** To jog (a child) on one's knee; to 'give a ride' to.

**1853** HAWTHORNE *Tanglewood Tales* (Chandos) 193 He had trotted him on his knee when a baby. **1887** AUG. J. E. WILSON *At Mercy of Tiberius* 79, I trotted her on my knee.

**II. 5.** *intr.* To fish with a trot-line. (Perhaps a different word: cf. TROT *sb.*[1] 6.) *dial.*

**1864** *Daily Tel.* 18 May, They are trawlers, trotters, dredgers, and shrimpers, and their fathers have trawled, trotted, dredged, and shrimped ever since Earl Godwin. **1884** *St. James's Gaz.* 18 Jan. 6/2 The eel-spearer..digging himself a good supply of bait, goes 'trotting' for flounders.

**Trot-cosy, -cosey, -cozy.** *Sc.* [app. f. TROT *v.* + COSY *a.*] A kind of cloak with a hood, worn when travelling in cold weather.

**1814** SCOTT *Wav.* xxix, At length the tall ungainly figure and ungracious visage of Ebenezer presented themselves. The upper part of his form..was shrouded in a large great-coat, belted over his under habiliments, and crested with a huge cowl of the same stuff, which, when drawn over the head and hat, completely overshadowed both, and being buttoned beneath the chin, was called a trot-cozy. **1818** — *Rob Roy* xxvi, He roared to Mattie to 'air his trot-cosey, to have his jackboots greased..and to see that his beast be corned, and a' his riding gear in order.' **1867** A. DAWSON *Rambling Recoll.* (1868) 31 Mr. More..—trotcosey enveloping his head.

†**Trotevale, -uale.** *Obs. rare.* Also trotouale, trotyuale. [Derivation unascertained. The word occurs 4 times in R. Brunne *Handlyng Synne*, and once in Map's *Body & Soul*; no OF. equivalents. In *Piers Plowman* B. XVIII. 142, C. XXI. 146, *waltrot, walterot* appears to have the same elements in reversed order: see Skeat's *Notes*, p. 407, where the word is discussed, and conjectures put forth, but with little success.] Idle tale-telling, vain talk.

*a* **1300** *Body & Soul* in *Map's Poems* (Camden) 337 Al ye maden troteuale [*printed* trotenale], that I haved seid biforn. **1303** R. BRUNNE *Handl. Synne* 48 Yn gamys, & festys, & at þe ale, Loue men to lestene troteuale [*v. rr.* trotouale, to telle trotyuale]. *Ibid.* 8080 Þenkeþ on þys tale, And takeþ hyt for no troteuale! *Ibid.* 5970. *Ibid.* 9244.

**Troth** (trōuþ, trǫþ), *sb. arch.* Forms: α. 2–5 trowþe, 3 (*Orm.*) trowwþe, 3–5 trouþe, 4–5 trowþ, trowthe, 4–6 trouthe, 4–6 (*Sc.* 4–) trowth, trouth, 5 trouþ, (trowith, -yth, 5–6 trougth, 6 trowgthe, trough). (Also 4 troutht, trout, troght, 4–6 trought(e, 6 trowht, trouht; 4 throwth, throut, 5 throuth, throughte.) β. 5 trothe, 6–7 troath, 6– troth. γ. 4 trawþe, trauþ(e, 5 trauthe, trawethe, 5–6 trawth(e. [Early ME. *trowþe, trouþe*, for OE. *tréowþ*, TRUTH, app. due to the shifting of *éo* to *eó*, with subsequent loss of the unaccented *e*. Cf. TROW *v.*, and the development of ME. and mod. *four* from OE. *féower*, and of ME. *fourti*, and *forty* from OE. *féowertig*. *Trowth, troth* were thus originally phonetic variants of OE. *tréowþ*, TRUTH, which hardly survived the 16th c. except as midland and northern dialect forms, and in special archaic locutions as 'to plight one's troth', 'wedded troth', 'by' or 'upon my troth', and in some combinations, as *trothless, troth-plighted*. Cf. also BETROTH. *Trawthe, trauth* are specially northern forms in which *aw, au* take the place of *ow, ou*. They are cited in the English Dialect Dictionary from Yorkshire.]

**I. 1.** Faithfulness, good faith, loyalty; honesty: = TRUTH *sb.* 1, 4. ? *Obs.*

α. *c* **1175** *Pater Noster* 42 in *Lamb. Hom.* 57 Mid al þis haue þu charite and soðfeste leaue and trowðe lef. *a* **1275** *Prov. Ælfred* 506 in *O. E. Misc.* 132 On him þu maist þe tresten, ȝif is trowþe deȝh. *c* **1325** *Spec. Gy Warw.* 1033 To serue hym [Christ] and hys moder dere In trowþe, loue, and in charite. **1340–70** *Alex. & Dind.* 910 For-þy vs keneþ our kinde to a-corde in trowþe. **1448** HEN. VI *Will* in Willis & Clark *Cambridge* (1886) I. 379 His high trought and feruent zele. **1474** CAXTON *Chesse* II. iv. (1883) 48 He knewe well the trouth of his felawe. *a* **1548** HALL *Chron.*, *Hen. VI* 164 Many thynges..declared the duke of Yorkes trought and innocencye in this case.

β. **1568** GRAFTON *Chron.* II. 766 The Lord Hastings, whose troth towarde the king no man doubted. **1620** J. WILKINSON *Courts Leet* 139, I shall sweare that I will bee true liege man and true faith and troth beare to our soveraigne lord the king. **1664** BUTLER *Hud.* II. ii. 227 These thinking they're obliged to Troth In Swearing, will not take an Oath. **1866** NEALE *Sequences & Hymns* 130 Wedded troth remains as firm, and wedded love as pure. **1905** C. WHITLEY in *Disraeli's Bentinck* Introd. 15 His..followers lacked either troth or cordiality.

**b.** *By* (rarely *upon*) *my troth*, as a form of asseveration. See also TRUTH 1 b.

α. *c* **1374** CHAUCER *Troylus* V. 1001 If þat I sholde of any Grek han rouþe, It shulde be youre seluen, by my trouþe. **14..** *Beryn* 116 Kit, how likith the? Be my trowith, wondir wele. *c* **1518** SKELTON *Magnyf.* 1669 Ye, by my trouthe, I shall waraunt you. **1564** in *Child-Marriages* 64 Bie my faith and trouth, I will marry the.

β. **1555** in Foxe *A. & M.* (1576) 1604/2 No, by my troth my Lord, we can do no good. **1599** SHAKS. *Much Ado* II. iii. 103 By my troth my Lord, I cannot tell what to think of it. **1704** SWIFT *Batt. Bks.* Misc. (1711) 236 By my Troth, said the Bee, the Comparison will amount to a very good Jest. **1820** COMBE *Consol.* II. (Chandos) 158 Nay, if you swear, Sir, by my troth, The Echo will repeat the oath. *a* **1839** PRAED *Everyday Char., Quince* 45 Old Quince averred, upon his troth, They were the ugliest beasts in Devon.

γ. **13..** *E. E. Allit. P.* B. 63 On hade boȝt hym a borȝ he sayde by his trawþe. *c* **1400** *Destr. Troy* 1749 And now is tyme, by my trauthe, to take it on hond.

**2.** One's faith as pledged or plighted in a solemn agreement or undertaking; one's plighted word; the act of pledging one's faith, a promise, covenant. Chiefly in phr. *to plight one's troth*, to pledge one's faith; to make a solemn promise or engagement; *spec.* to engage oneself to marry. = TRUTH 2.

α. *a* **1225** *Ancr. R.* 54 Þerefter of þen ilke weren trouðen tobrokene. *Ibid.* 310 *Pepigimus cum morte fedus*..we habbeð trouðe ipluht deaðe. **1303** R. BRUNNE *Handl. Synne* 8360–1 Trouþe þat men alle day breke,..fals trouþes, and fykyl,..are ȝyue mechyl. *c* **1386** CHAUCER *Frankl. T.* 746 Ye shul youre trouthe holden. *c* **1430–40** *Anturs of Arth.* 465 (Thornton MS.) Here my trouthe I ȝow plyghte, I salle feghte withe ȝone knyghte. *a* **1440** *Sir Eglam.* 246 'Ȝys', seyde the erle, 'here myn honde!' Hys trowthe to hym he strake. **1543–4** *Act* 35 *Hen. VIII*, c. 12 The.. Frenche King nothing regarding his honor, othe, trouthe, promyse, and fidelitie. **1552** HULOET, Plyght fayeth and trougth in matrimonye, *sponso*. **1564** in *Child-Marriages* 201 Therapon they plightid their trouthes together, and kissed together, and after dronk, and made mery.

β. *c* **1420** *Anturs of Arth.* xxxvi. (Ireland MS.), I wille countur with the knyȝte,..Ther-to my trothe y the plyȝte. **1515** *Acc. Ld. High Treas. Scot.* V. 36 Item, to David Cameroun for to pas to the day of troth, and erandis to the Lord Dakkir, to his expensis, xlijs. **1578** T. N. tr. *Conq. W. India* 7 She demaunded him as hir husband by faith and troth of hand. **1600** HOLLAND *Livy* XXI. vii. 397 They observed their troth and loyaltie with their allies. **1724** RAMSAY *Tea-t. Misc.* (1733) II. 149 Give me back my maiden-vow And give me back my troth. **1848** LYTTON *Harold* VI. i, Gryffyth will never keep troth with the English. **1872** YEATS *Techn. Hist. Comm.* 188 Betrothal rings, set with pearls and gems, were worn by maidens who had plighted their troth.

γ. *c* **1375** *Cursor M.* 3240 (Fairf.) Of þi trauþ I make þe free. *c* **1400** *Destr. Troy* 1749 And now [is] tyme, by my trauthe, to take it on hond. *Ibid.* 10110 Vntrew of his trawth trust neuer after. *c* **1420** *Avow. Arth.* xxx, Ther-to grawuntus the knyȝte, And truly his trauthe pliȝte.

†**3. a.** Faith, trust, confidence. (Cf. TRUTH 3 a.)

α. *c* **1200** ORMIN 4015 He wass Drihhtin swiþe lef Þurrh trowwþess rihhtwisnesse. *Ibid.* 18857 Hæþenn trowwþe on hæþenn Godd. *a* **1300** *Cursor M.* 2387 (Cott.) Abram þat o trouth was tru. **13..** *Ibid.* 18678 (Gött.) Þair mistrovth..Es strinthing of vr troght to-day. *a* **1400** *Religious Pieces fr. Thornton MS.* (1867) 10 Þe firste vertu es trouthe wharethurghe we trow anely in Godd...Trouthe es begynnynge of all gude dedis. *c* **1425** WYNTOUN *Cron.* VI. xviii. 2205 Makbeth aye In fantown fretis had gret fay, And trowth had in swylk fantasy.

γ. *c* **1375** *Cursor M.* 2525 (Fairf.) Abraham þat was in trauþe strange.

†**b.** Belief; *spec.* a form of religious belief, a creed. (Cf. TRUTH 3 b.) *Obs.*

*c* **1200** ORMIN 1347 Ȝiff þatt tu willt..Wiþþ fulle trowwþe lefenn Al þætt tatt wass bitacnedd tær. *Ibid.* 6953 Forrþi þatt teȝȝ þatt time ȝet unnderrstodenn littleswhatt Off all þe rihhte trowwþe. *a* **1340** HAMPOLE *Psalter* i. 6 Fals cristen men, þat has þe trouth of ihū crist withouten luf & goed werkes. **1340** — *Pr. Consc.* 4228 Þai lyved in fals trowthe. *c* **1375** *Lay Folks Mass Bk.* (MS. B.) 414 Þis is þo trouthe of holy kirk. *c* **1400** MAUNDEV. (Roxb.) xxxiv. 154 If all þai be of diuerse lawes and diuerse trowyngs, þai hafe sum gude poyntes of oure trowth. **1481** CAXTON *Myrr.* III. xii. 159 In this only veryte, he [Plato] preuyd the right trouthe, ffor he preued his power, his wisedom, and his goodnes.. that is the fader, the sone, and the holy goste.

**II.** †**4.** Truth, in various senses: see TRUTH 5–13.

α. *c* **1300** *Cursor M.* 22789 (Edin.) Of þis trowþe hard es trowþe to find. **13..** *Ibid.* 18710 (Cott.) He badd..his disciplis..Oueral þis werld his trouth to teche. *c* **1386** CHAUCER *Man of Law's T.* 532 He wolde enquere Depper in this, a trouthe for to lere. **1387** TREVISA *Higden* (Rolls) III. 221 God..is cause of al þing..and liȝt of soþnesse, and of trowþe [*v. rr.* trouthe, truthe], and welle of grace. **1390** GOWER *Conf.* III. 151 Hou so that the cause wende, The trouthe is schameles ate ende. *c* **1400** *Apol. Loll.* 13 In two maner of þing, is [a man] seid iust; first sympli, or after trowþ. ..In þe secound maner..onli in name. **14..** in *Babees Bk.* (1868) 332 Deame þee best in euery doute Tyl þe trouthe be tryed oute. **1422** tr. *Secreta Secret., Priv. Priv.* 211 He sholde bene sothefaste in worde and dedd, and lowe throuth abowe al thynge, and hate lesynge. **1436** *Pol. Poems* (Rolls) II. 204 Go furthe, libelle,..And pray my lordes the to take in grace.., if that not variaunce Thow haste fro troughte. **1470–85** MALORY *Arthur* I. iii. 38 Telle me the trouthe... Syre saide she I shalle telle you the trouthe...That is trouthe..as ye say. *a* **1533** LD. BERNERS *Huon* cxxxix. 521, I shall neuer haue ioye..tyll I maye knowe the trought. **1545** *Plumpton Corr.* (Camden) 250 Send forth your excuse ..with a letter of the trough of your sicknes. **1593** Q. ELIZ. *Boethius* V. pr. i. 103 Aristotle..hath defynd it [chance] in a neere reason to breefenes & trouth.

β. **1538** STARKEY *England* I. ii. 30 Thys ys of trothe. **1553** T. WILSON *Rhet.* (1580) 173 When perfite iudgement is wantyng, the trothe can not be knowne. **1600** HOLLAND *Livy* XXIV. xxx. 529 They reported other newes besides, as well lies as troths. **1663** COWLEY *Country Mouse* 56 Plainly, the troth to tell, the Sun was set.

γ. **13..** *E. E. Allit. P.* A. 494 For al is trawþe þat he con dresse, And he may do no þynk bot ryȝt. *Ibid.* B. 1490 Hit [the sacred candlestick] watz..wont..in temple of þe trauþe trwly to stonde. *c* **1420** *Sir Amadace* (Camden) xxix, Butte the trauthe fulle litulle thay wote. **1432–50** tr. *Higden* (Rolls) III. 221 The philosophres knowenge the trawthe of God profite moche to the cognicion of trawthe. **1504** *Plumpton Corr.* (Camden) p. lxiv, All that ys afore rehersed..we wyll..yf nede be, depely depose afore the kynge and hys counsell, that yt is matter of trawth.

**b.** *In troth* (arch.), †*of* (*a*) *troth* (obs.): truly, verily, indeed: = *in truth, of* (*a*) *truth* (TRUTH 13).

α. *a* **1380** *Pistill of Susan* 187 Heo was in trouþe, as we trowe, tristi and trewe. *c* **1475** *Partenay* 1568 Many merueles of trought cam ther ryght. **1508** FISHER *Penit. Ps.* xxxviii. Wks. (1876) 60 This of a trouth is a grete mysery wherof..Dauyd maketh his complaynte. **1546** J. HEYWOOD *Prov. & Epigr.* (1867) 50 But of trough I thought, better to haue then wishe. **1789** BURNS *To Dr. Blacklock* ii, I lippen'd to the chiel in trouth.

β. *a* **1566** R. EDWARDES *Damon & Pithias* (1571) Bj, Tell me of troth, Is not that great Wisdom as the world goth? **1607** SHAKS. *Cor.* I. iii. 118 In troth I thinke she would. **1660** R. COKE *Power & Subj.* 205 Divers sums of money (which in troath were the oblations and offerings). **1727** GAY *Begg. Op.* I. viii, A mighty likely speech in troth. **1756** FOOTE *Eng. fr. Paris* I. Wks. 1799 I. 98 In gude troth, not a mighty booty.

γ. **1432–50** tr. *Higden* (Rolls) II. 365 The faders of whom were not knowen in trawthe.

**c.** Also *ellipt.* or as *int.* = TRUTH 13 c. *arch.*

α. **1719** RAMSAY *To Arbuckle* 48 And trouth I think they're in the right on't. **1728** — *A Character* iv, And trowth the picture I have drawn Is very like. **1786** BURNS *Brigs of Ayr* 129 Fine Architecture, trowth, I needs must say't o't.

β. **1603** SHAKS. *Meas. for M.* III. ii. 60 Troth sir, shee hath eaten vp all her beefe, and she is her selfe in the tub. *a* **1627** MIDDLETON, etc. *Widow* II. i, Troth, and I would have my will then, if I were as you. **1741** RICHARDSON *Pamela* (1824) I. xxiii. 34 Troth, sir, said he,..I never knew her peer. **1843** LYTTON *Last Bar.* I. i, 'Troth', answered Master Heyford [etc.].

III. 5. *attrib.* and *Comb.*, as *troth-breaker*, *-breaking*, *-keeping*, *-kiss*, *-ring*; *troth-contracted*, *-like*, *-telling* adjs.

**1648** HERRICK *Hesper.*, *To His Mistresse* ii, Promise, and keep your vowes, Or vow ye never; Loves doctrine disallowes *Troth-breakers ever. **13..** *Cursor M.* 26234 (Cott.) Fals wijtnes and *trouth breking. **1464** *Paston Lett.* II. 159 Master Constantyn sewyd hym for feyth and trowth brekyng. **1633** FORD *Broken H.* II. iii, Intercourse of *troth-contracted loves. **1605** VERSTEGAN *Dec. Intell.* viii. (1628) 253 A mouth of *troth-keeping or loyaltie. **1844** MRS. BROWNING *Lay Brown Rosary* II. 64, I was betrothed that day; I wore a *troth-kiss on my lips, I could not give away. **1544** BETHAM *Precepts War* II. xl. K viij, Such other thynges are to be feyned, whyche appere *trouthlyke. **1856** MRS. BROWNING *Aur. Leigh* IX. 100, I had sooner cut My hand off (though 't were..promised a duke's *troth-ring). **1673** WYCHERLEY *Gentl. Dancing-Master* IV. i, The *troth-telling Trojan gentlewoman of old was ne'er believed till the town was taken.

**Troth,** *v.* *Obs.* or *arch.* [f. TROTH *sb.* or aphetic f. BETROTH *v.*] *trans.* To plight one's troth to; to engage in a contract, esp. of marriage: = BETROTH 1, 2, 4 a. Hence **Tro·thed** *ppl. a.*, **Tro·thing** *vbl. sb.* and *ppl. a.* (See also TRUTH *v.* 2.)

**1422** tr. *Secreta Secret.*, *Priv. Priv.* 190 A gentill-man of the contrey had hyr trouthid. **1565** COOPER *Thesaurus*, *Coemptio*,..a solemnitie of the ciuill lawe where the woman and man commyng together at a trothyng, as it were, bye one the other. **1567** DRANT *Horace*, *Epistles* II. ii. H iv, Too Orators..th' one was to the other, In mutuall prayse for both their gaynes a faste ytrothed brother. **1599** SHAKS. *Much Ado* III. i. 38 So saies the Prince, and my new trothed Lord. **1605** *Tryall Chev.* II. i. in Bullen *O. Pl.* III. 288, I scorne..to give answere to such a trothing question. **1893** F. THOMPSON *Love in Dian's Lap* I. Poems 4, I reach back through the days A trothed hand to the dead.

**Tro·thful,** *a. arch. rare.* [f. TROTH *sb.* + -FUL.] Full of 'troth' or loyalty, faithful, trusty; trustworthy, truthful.

*a* **1380** *Minor Poems fr. Vernon MS.* xxviii. 9 Heil trewe, trouþeful and tretable. **1861** LYTTON & FANE *Tannhäuser* 13 Trothful men..Aver he was the fairest-favour'd knight.

**Trothless** (trōu·þlės), *a.* [f. as prec. + -LESS.]

1. Destitute of 'troth' or loyalty; faithless, perfidious, disloyal. *arch.*

*a.* *c* **1200** ORMIN 188 He shall turrnenn þurrh hiss spell þe trowwþelæse leode. **1513** DOUGLAS *Æneis* IV. vii. 8 Thow trouthles wycht.

*β.* **1567** DRANT *Horace*, *Art Poetry* A iv, Let Ino still be sad, Ixie trothlesse, Io wandring. **1594** LODGE *Wounds Civil War* III. i. D iij b, The trustfull man that builds on trothles vowes. **1647** TRAPP *Comm. Matt.* viii. 32 [Drunkenness] making the understanding ignorant, the strong staggering, the trusty trothless. **1887** SWINBURNE *Locrine* I. i. 68 No coward indeed, but faithless, trothless.

†**2.** Destitute of truth; false, mendacious; incredible, untrustworthy. *Obs.*

*a.* **1390** GOWER *Conf.* III. 151 Bot what thing that is troutheles, It mai noght wel be schameles.

*β.* **1592** GREENE *Groat's W. Wit* (1874) 13 Trothlesse toungs of men. **1601** DEACON & WALKER *Answ. Darel* 60 To trauerse the trueth of their trothlesse tales. *Ibid.* 75 Will you leaue the law, and the testimonies, and trot after a blind and a trothlesse lad for the reuelation of these hidden truthes?

†**Tro·thly,** *adv.* *Obs.* *rare*$^{-1}$. In 5 **trouþly.** [f. as prec. + -LY [2].] Faithfully, loyally.

*c* **1425** *Cursor M.* 19950 (Trin.) Noon wol he awey cast þat trouþly [*v. r.* traistili] wol him loue & last.

**Troth-plight** (trōu·þ,pləit), *sb. arch.* Forms: see TROTH, TRUTH, PLIGHT *sb.*[1], *v.*[1] [f. TROTH *sb.* + PLIGHT *sb.*[1]] The act of plighting troth, or troth plighted; a solemn promise or engagement, esp. of marriage; betrothal.

[**13..** *Cursor M.* 28485 (Cott.) Broken..my trouth plight.] **1513** DOUGLAS *Æneis* x. xii. 82 A Greik,..That fugityve ..Had left hys spowsal trewth plycht oncompleit. **1570** FOXE *A. & M.* (ed. 2) 265/2 That all debtes, that were owyng through trouth plyght, should not be pledid in spirituall but in temporall court. **1611** SHAKS. *Wint. T.* I. ii. 278 A Name As ranke as any Flax-Wench, that puts to Before her troth-plight. **1818** SCOTT *Br. Lamm.* xix. [xx], The lovers going through an emblematic ceremony of their troth-plight...They broke betwixt them the thin broad-piece of gold. **1881** SWINBURNE *Mary Stuart* I. i. 52 To set again the seal on our past oaths And bind their trothplight faster than it is With one more witness.

*attrib.* **1550** *Reg. Gild Corp. Chr. York* (1872) 228 *note*, A trouth-plighte rynge. *a* **1652** BROME *Queenes Exch.* II. i, A very trothplight qualm.

**Tro·th-plight,** *pa. pple.* and *ppl. a. arch.* [f. as prec. + *plight*, pa. pple. of PLIGHT *v.*[1]] Engaged by a 'troth' or covenant, esp. of marriage; betrothed, affianced.

*c* **1330** R. BRUNNE *Chron.* (1810) 153 Whan þei were trouth plight, & purueied þe sposage. **1393** LANGL. *P. Pl.* C. VII. 208 Ich serued symme at þe style, And was his prentys yplyght [*v. r.* truþeplith]. **1491** CAXTON *Vitas Patr.* (W. de W. 1495) I. xlviii. 93 b/2 The doughter of a noble Romayne; whyche some tyme was fyaunced and trouthplyght in maryage to a noble man of Rome. **1513** DOUGLAS *Æneis* x. xii. 87 The purpour brycht, Quhilk of his trewth plycht lufe he bair in sing. **1599** SHAKS. *Hen. V*, II. i. 21 He is marryed to Nell Quickly, and certainly she did you wrong, for you were troth-plight to her. **1633** HEYWOOD *Eng. Trav.* III. Wks. 1874 IV. 57 Shee a Prostitute? Nay, and to him my troath plight, and my Friend. **1887** SWINBURNE *Locrine* I. ii. 33, I that was trothplight servant to thy sire. **1896** MORRIS *Poems by the Way* (1898) 119 There are troth-plight maids unwed.

**Troth-pli·ght,** *v. arch.* [f. as prec. + PLIGHT *v.*[1]] *trans.* To plight one's troth to; to engage, or engage oneself to, in order to marriage; to betroth, affiance: = TROTH *v.* †In quot. 1470-85, to plight one's troth, engage (*to do* something).

[**1303** R. BRUNNE *Handl. Synne* 8363 ȝyf þou a womman trouþe plyght.] *c* **1440** *Promp. Parv.* 504/1 Trutheplytyn (*K.*, *S.* truplytyn, *P.* trouthplityn), *affido*, C. F. **1470-85** MALORY *Arthur* VII. xxii. 247 And thenne they trouth-plyte eche other to loue, and neuer to faylle whyles their lyfe lasteth. **1494** FABYAN *Chron.* VII. 676 Fraunceys,..whose doughter..Maximylian had before trouth plyted for his lawfull wyfe. **1601** MUNDAY *Downfall Robt. Earl of Huntington* I. ii. A iv b, Marian, daughter to Lord Lacy, Is troth-plighted to wastfull Huntington. **1825** SCOTT *Betrothed* xxix, Not married, perhaps, but engaged—troth-plighted. **1878** SUSAN PHILLIPS *On Seaboard* 75 Hand in hand, Troth-plighted, we two heard the midnight chime.

So † **Tro·th-pli·ghting,** the action of plighting troth, engagement, betrothal: = TROTH-PLIGHT *sb.*

*c* **1440** *Jacob's Well* 52 Þow3 non othe be made, ne trewthe plyȝtyng, ne no fleschly knowyng, ne no wytnes be þere. *c* **1477** CAXTON *Jason* 127 The fyansailles and trouthplighting of Iason and Creusa. **1530** PALSGR. 283/1 Trouth plyghtyng, *fianceailles.*

**Tro·tlet.** *nonce-wd.* [f. TROT *sb.*[1] + -LET.] A diminutive trot.

**1879** STEVENSON *Trav. Cevennes* 38 A prick, and she broke forth into a gallant little trotlet that devoured the miles.

**Trottee** (trǫtī·). *nonce-wd.* [f. TROT *v.* + -EE.] One who is trotted out (see TROT *v.* 4 c).

**1818** *Blackw. Mag.* III. 527 There is something about the Doctor that all at once converts the trotter into the trottee. **1819** LOCKHART *Peter's Lett.* lxxi. III. 246, I had the good sense..to perceive the danger of the practice,..and..hope never to fill the roll either of Trotter or Trottee.

**Trotter** (trǫ·təɹ). [f. TROT *v.* + -ER [1]; cf. med.L. *trotārius* (Du Cange), OF. *trotier* (Godef.).]

1. A horse (or other quadruped) which trots; *spec.* a horse especially bred and trained to the trot.

**1381-2** [see 6]. **1391-2** *Earl Derby's Exped.* (Camden) 143 Pro duobus equis trotters cum duabus sellis per ipsum emptis. **1452** *Test. Ebor.* (Surtees) III. 137, j equi basii, trotter, x[s]. **1592** GREENE *Maiden's Dream* Wks. (Rtldg.) 279/1 His stable full of coursers.., Trotters whose manag'd looks would some affright. **1679** *Lond. Gaz.* No. 1412/4 A black brown Gelding about 15 hands,..a Trotter only. **1776** *Pennsylv. Even. Post* 26 Mar. 154/2 A Dark Brown Coloured Horse..a natural trotter. **1812** *Sporting Mag.* XXXIX. 31 A trotter constantly habituated to that pace. **1858** O. W. HOLMES *Aut. Breakf.-t.* ii, Compare the racer with the trotter. **1890** W. P. LETT in *Big Game N. Amer.* 88 The Caribou is the champion trotter of America. **1898** DOYLE *Trag. Korosko* v. 110 Most of them [camels] were beautiful creatures, true Arabian trotters.

b. A trotting-cart, a sulky.

**1902** *Times* 4 Apr. 9/6 He would come up in the morning in his 'trotter'.

2. One who moves or goes about briskly and constantly; see TROT *v.* 2.

*spec.* (*Univ. slang*) a tailor's assistant who goes round for orders; also, a tailor's, dressmaker's, or milliner's girl messenger; at *Dublin University*, one who goes to Dublin for a degree, without residence (cf. *term-trotter*, at Oxford: see TERM *sb.* 17); at *Durham University*, a day-student (cf. TROT *v.* 2).

**1562** J. HEYWOOD *Prov. & Epigr.* (1867) 140 Neede makth tholde wyfe trot: is she a trotter now? **1580** HOLLYBAND *Treas. Fr. Tong*, *Gaste-pavé*, a trotter vpon the pauements, a walker by the streets. **1605** *Tryall Chev.* II. i. in Bullen *O. Pl.* III. 288 And this trotter is my ryval and loves Thomasin. **1765** FOOTE *Commissary* I. Wks. 1799 II. 17 That eternal trotter after all the little draggle-tail'd girls of town. **1860** *Slang Dict.*, *Trotter*, a tailor's man who goes round for orders. *University.* **1883** *Durham Univ. Jrnl.* 17 Dec. 141 We suspect that the ingenious inventor of the name 'trotter' was well aware that the name had a ridiculous sound. **1897** *Daily News* 23 Feb. 3/1 She was a Trotter..she trotted to and fro between the East and the West, with patterns to match—silks, stuffs, and so on.

3. Usually *pl.* The feet of a quadruped, esp. those of sheep and pigs as used for food; also *humorously*, the feet of a human being.

(Quot. *c* 1358 doubtfully belongs here.)

[*c* **1358** in *Eng. Hist. Rev.* Oct. (1909) 742 Item in duro pisce frisc. v[d] o. Item in trotters viij[d].] **1522** SKELTON *Why not to Court* 908 The chefe of your fayre Myght stand nowe by potters, And suche as sell trotters. *c* **1550** LACY *Wyl Buck's Test.* (Halliw.) 58 For to make the Trotters of the Bucke. Take the foure fete, and skalde them [etc.]..and that ben the trotters. **1602** CAREW *Cornwall* I. 24 Not the dammes Foale, but the dames Trotters, be trusted vnto. **1630** *R. Johnson's Kingd. & Commw.* 174 He steales the sheepe; and gives the Trotters for Gods sake. *a* **1650** *Anc. Poems*, etc. (Percy Soc.) 164 Two calves' feet, and a bull's trotter. **1755** *Gentl. Mag.* XXV. Pref., Finding out that some bald pated drone of a monk laid up his useless trotters in the corner of his Abbey, about 500 years ago. **1775** ADAIR *Amer. Ind.* 309 They will fasten the paws and trotters of panthers, bears, and buffalos, to their feet and hands. **1851** MAYHEW *Lond. Labour* I. 158/2 For supper there is a sandwich, a meat pudding, or a 'trotter'. **1872** MARY JEWRY *Every-day Cookery* 72/2 Perfectly cleanse and blanch the trotters.

4. See quot.

**1864** *Daily Tel.* 18 May, 'The..trotters'—fishermen who ..trot for whelks to sell as bait to the North Sea cod-smacks.

5. One who trots another out in conversation: see TROT *v.* 4 c. **1818-19** [see TROTTEE].

6. *attrib.* and *Comb.*, as *trotter-bone*, *-girl* (see sense 2), †*-saddle*, *-stall*; **trotter-boiler**, one whose business is to treat the hoofs of animals by boiling; **trotter-cases**, *sb. pl.* boots or shoes (*slang*); **trotter-pie**: see quot.; **trotter skirt** (see also TROTTEUR), a short, neat walking skirt.

**1883** R. HALDANE *Workshop Receipts* Ser. II. 301/1 Some [glue-making materials] that come from the *trotter-boilers ..have been limed already. **1799** G. SMITH *Laboratory* II. 407 Take *trotter-bones; calcine and beat them to a fine powder, wherewith rub the spots on both sides. **1869** *Daily News* 23 Aug., The original floor..was laid with 'trotter bones',..closely packed and driven into the ground to the depth of from three to four inches. **1821** HOOD *Sent. Journ.* Wks. 1862 I. 34 A young gentleman in very tight *trotter-cases,..his feet gave evident signs of suffering. **1838** DICKENS *O. Twist* xviii, 'Japanning his trotter-cases'..rendered into plain English signifieth, cleaning his boots. **1903** *Westm. Gaz.* 10 Aug. 10/1 The streets of Soho are unusually quiet; the *trotter girl, with her bundle of coats or trousers, is almost a curiosity. *a* **1693** *Urquhart's Rabelais* III. xviii. 151 We were..eating a Bushel of *Trotter-pies [*orig.* goudiveaulx (see Cotgr.)]. **1381-2** *Durham Acc. Rolls* (Surtees) 592 Pro reparacione j *trottersadill. **1909** *Westm. Gaz.* 15 Feb. 5/3 A..gown..for roller skating or merely for walking [with] a *trotter skirt. **1595** *Eng. Tripe-wife* (1881) 148 Since I trotted from my *trotter stall, And figd about from neates feete neatly drest: I finde no pleasure nor content at all.

Hence **Tro·tteress** (*nonce-wd.*), a female trotter (in *globe-trotteress*: cf *globe-trotter* s.v. GLOBE *sb.* 10 b).

**1892** MARIANNE NORTH *Recoll. Happy Life* (ed. 2) II. 213 Lady A. joined our three pairs of hands and blessed us—'Three globe trotteresses all at once!'

‖ **Trotteur** (trotör), fem. **trotteuse** (trotö·z). [Fr.] = TROTTER: see *trotter skirt* (prec. 6).

**1904** *Daily Chron.* 6 Feb. 9/1 The short trotteuse costume is quite out of place at a wedding. *Ibid.* 20 Feb. 8/5 The trotteuse skirt..is being more and more worn. **1909** *Westm. Gaz.* 29 May 15/2 Seaside dresses..are short, and the pleated trotteur skirt can scarcely be improved upon. **1910** *Ibid.* 15 Apr. 5/3 The black and white check 'trotteur'.

**Trotting** (trǫ·tiŋ), *vbl. sb.* [f. TROT *v.* + -ING [1].] The action of the verb TROT in various senses; *spec.* in *U.S.*, a trotting-race.

**14..** *Beryn* 2402 Yeur rennyng & yeur trotting, in-to an esy pase I shall turn. **1470-85** MALORY *Arthur* III. xiii. 116 A lytel afore mydnyȝt they herd the trottynge of an hors. **1581** MULCASTER *Positions* xxiv. (1887) 98 Trotting ..shaketh the bodie to violently. **1646** SIR T. BROWNE *Pseud. Ep.* IV. vi. 193 Animalls..move *per latera*,..or *per diametrum*,..lifting the foot before, and the crosse foot behinde, which is succussation or trotting. **1787** 'G. GAMBADO' *Acad. Horsem.* Title-p., Instructions for Walking, Trotting, Cantering, Galloping. **1873** H. E. P. SPOFFORD *Pilot's Wife* in *Casquet Lit.* IV. 13/2 She and the nurse made such a racket.., with their shshshing and trotting and patting and stirring and sipping. **1882** *Standard* 26 Sept. 2/2 At Lynn and other parts of the Wash they [whelks] are caught by a mode of fishing designated 'trotting'. Green crabs are threaded together and let down into the water, and the whelk,..while sucking the meat out of the crabs, is easily drawn to the surface. **1883** F. M. CRAWFORD *Dr. Claudius* v, 'Do you have much racing in America?'..'Yes. Trotting. Ag'd nags in sulkies. See how fast they can go a mile.'

b. *attrib.*, as *trotting-match*, *-race*, *-sulky*, *-term* (see TROT *v.* 2), *-track*, *-turf.*

**1840** BLAINE *Encycl. Rur. Sports* § 1046 Formerly it was a maxim in trotting races, that weight did not form a considerable object. *Ibid.* § 1049 The distances of this trotting match were [etc.]. **1863** 'OUIDA' *Held in Bondage* (1870) 41 The certainty that Vane Steven's roan filly would lose the trotting-match. **1883** *Durham Univ. Jrnl.* 17 Dec. 141 I'm going to keep a trotting term. **1888** LIGHTHALL *Yng. Seigneur* 74 The horse-trader's trotting-sulky was standing at the door. **1893** *Outing* (U.S.) May 98/1 The perfect trotting track of the present time is built [etc.]. *Ibid.* 99/1 This early heroine of the trotting turf.

**Tro·tting,** *ppl. a.* [f. as prec. + -ING [2].] That trots, in various senses.

*Trotting butcher*, a butcher who goes his rounds on horseback. *Trotting seconds hand*, in a watch, a hand which registers the seconds on the minute-divisions of the dial, pausing on each.

*c* **1425** *Eng. Conq. Irel.* 88 Vnnethe he [Henry III] wold ryde any amblynge hors, bot myche trottynge hors, for to trauaylle hys body the more. **1480** in *Cely Papers* (1900) 55, I whowlde awise yow brynge hower aull yowr trottyng hors. **1523** FITZHERB. *Husb.* § 77 The .ix. propertyes of a foxe,..the .vii. to be shorte-trottynge. **1579** J. JONES *Preserv. Bodie & Soule* I. xv. 28 Blinde bittels, flattering fellowes, trotting trulles, and wilful murtherers. **1660** BLOUNT *Boscobel* 23 The valiant Earl of Cleveland (who being above 60 years of age had marched 21 dayes together upon a trotting horse). **1725** RAMSAY *Gentle Sheph.* I. ii. Prol., A trotting burnie wimpling through the ground. **1842** MRS. F. TROLLOPE *Visit to Italy* I. i. 2 Inferences..deduced by trotting travellers from the aspect of the scenes through which they passed. **1851** MAYHEW *Lond. Labour* I. 175/2 The trotting butcher is.. not likely to be succeeded by any in the same line, or.. 'ride' of business. **1888** BRYCE *Amer. Commw.* III. 528 *note*, The trotting horse is driven, not ridden. **1900** *Jeweller's Catal.*, The Nurse's Watch, with long trotting seconds hand for taking the beats of the pulse.

**Trottle**: see TRATTLE *sb.*[2]

‖ **Trottoir** (trotwār). [F. (16th c.), f. *trotter* to TROT + *-oir*, L. *-ōrium.*] A paved footway on each side of a street; a pavement. Also *attrib.*

**1804** *Edinb. Rev.* Jan. 337 A neat *trottoir* of flat stones runs before the doors. **1828** H. BEST *Italy as it is* 88 Milan is well paved, though there are no *trottoirs*, or foot passengers' pavements. **1832** MRS. F. TROLLOPE *Dom. Mann. Amer.* xxx. (1839) 293 The *trottoir* paving, in most of the streets, is extremely good, being of large flag stones, very superior to the bricks of Philadelphia. **1864** G. MUSGRAVE *Ten Days Fr. Parsonage* I. i. 22 Water-carts..irrigating.. the splashed..pedestrians on the trottoir.

Hence **Trottoired** *a.*, furnished with a trottoir.
**1858** MAYHEW *Upper Rhine* iv. (1860) 185 The streets..are mostly broad and trottoired.

**Trou, Trouage, Trouant**: see TROW, TREWAGE, TRUANT.

**Troubadour** (trū·bădūᵊɹ). [a. F. *troubadour* (16th c. in Godef. *Compl.*), ad. Prov. *trobador* (= Cat. *trobador*, Sp., Pg. *trovador*, It. *trovatore*), agent-n. f. Prov. *trobar*, Sp., Pg. *trovar*, It. *trovare*, F. *trouver* to find, invent, compose in verse; cf. TROUVÈRE.

The origin of the verb itself is questioned. As it exists in most of the Romanic langs., it is generally held to be late popular L. Diez explained it as formed by metathesis from L. *turbāre* to disturb, through the sense 'turn up'. Cf. for the form F. *troubler*, OF. *trubler*, from late L. **turbulāre*; see *Etymol. Wörterbuch* ed. 4, s.v.; cf. also the Neapol. *controvare* from L. *conturbāre*. Another conjecture in Du Cange would take the Romanic forms from med.L. *tropus*, TROPE *sb.* 5, a verse or versicle, whence **tropāre*. Both of these, and other conjectures, present difficulties.]

One of a class of lyric poets, living in southern France, eastern Spain, and northern Italy, from the 11th to the 13th centuries, who sang in Provençal (*langue d'oc*), chiefly of chivalry and gallantry, sometimes including wandering minstrels and jongleurs.

**1727–41** CHAMBERS *Cycl.* s.v., The poesy of the troubadours consisted in sonnets, pastorals, songs [etc.]. **1767** PERCY *Rel. Anc. Eng. Poetry* (ed. 2) I. p. xxvii, The Troubadours of Provence..are supposed to have led the way to the poets of Italy, France, and Spain. **1801** STRUTT *Sports & Past.* III. iii. 162 The troubadours brought with them into the north a new species of language called the Roman Language...It evidently originated from the Latin, and was the parent of the French tongue. **1833** LONGF. *Outre-Mer* Prose Wks. 1886 I. 94 The lyre of the Troubadour seems to have responded to the impulse of momentary feelings only,—to the touch of local and transitory circumstances. **1884** TENNYSON *Becket* Prol., I am a Troubadour, you know, and won the violet at Toulouse.

**b.** *transf.* One who composes or sings verses or ballads; also, a composer or writer in support of some cause or interest.

**1826** J. M. SHERER *Refl. Ramble Germany* Introd. 24 At the inn here I found a young German troubadour. He sung ballads for me, accompanying himself on the guitar. **1840** DICKENS *Old C. Shop* li, He's quite a Troubadour, you know. **1861** GOLDW. SMITH *Inaug. Lect.* 32 Novels and poems by the troubadours of the landed interest. **1869** B. TAYLOR *Byeways of Europe* I. 227 The Majorcans still have their troubadours, who are hired by languishing lovers to improvise strains.

**c.** *attrib.*

**1883** *Chambers' Encycl.* IX. 560/2 The extent of territory on which the troubadour poetry was cultivated—viz...France south of the Loire; Catalonia, Valencia, and Aragon in Spain; and part of Upper Italy. **1887** MISS R. H. BUSK *Folk-Songs Italy* 122 The influence of the troubadour songs of Provence is scarcely felt beyond the region of Piedmont in the songs of the people. **1898** LADY MARY LOYD tr. *Uzanne's Fashion in Paris* iii. 55 Towards the close of the [First] Empire, when troubadour fashions came in. **1902** CHAYTOR *Troubadours Dante* Introd. 19 The great feature of the troubadour love-poetry is the glorification of the married woman.

Hence **Trou·badourish** *a.*, pertaining to, or having the character or style of a troubadour, or of the poetry of the troubadours (whence **Trou·badourishly** *adv.*); **Trou·badourism,** the character, principles, or style of the troubadours; **Trou·badourist,** one who writes in the style or studies the productions of the troubadours (in quot. *attrib.*).

**1849** *Fraser's Mag.* XL. 448 'Effeminate and *troubadourish', I thought. **1864** PEARSON in *Spectator* 245/2 Blondel..maintained the honours of his troubadourish name by a patriotic Latin poem 'Complanctus Bonorum Gallicorum'. **1905** *Daily Chron.* 17 May 3/3 The troubadourish, unworldly, exquisite passionateness of it all. **1880** G. MEREDITH *Tragic Com.* xiii. (1892) 184 The pleading was not done *troubadourishly, in soft flute-notes. **1898** LADY MARY LOYD tr. *Uzanne's Fashion in Paris* Introd. 7 The stiff lines and starched manners of a sham *Troubadourism. **1901** *Daily Chron.* 18 Dec. 3/6 Tiptoft, whose..career..is entirely lacking in *troubadourist qualities, good or bad.

† **Trou·blable,** *a. Obs. rare*—¹. [f. TROUBLE *v.* + -ABLE.] Troublesome, grievous.

*c* **1374** CHAUCER *Boeth.* IV. met. ii. 92 (Camb. MS.) Trowblable [*Add. MS.* troublable] Ire þat arayseth in hym the floodes of trwblynges tormentith..hyr thowht.

† **Trou·blance.** *Obs.* Also 5 turbulaunce, turblaunce, 6 trublance, 7 trubellance. [a. OF. *trublance*, *troblance* (13th c. in Godef.), f. *trubler*, *trobler* to TROUBLE. With the earlier examples cf. the β-forms of TROUBLE; *turbulaunce* is conformed to L. *turbulentia*.] The action of troubling or state of being troubled; disturbance; trouble, sorrow, pain. (In later use only *Sc.*)

*c* **1400** LOVE *Bonavent. Mirr.* (1907) 287 With grete ioye.. of the blessed presence of her lorde; but..with grete drede and turbulaunce of his aweie passynge. *c* **1425** *Orolog. Sapient.* iv. in *Anglia* X. 353/44 The periles of turblaunce of þis noyous worlde. **15..** *Aberdeen Regr.* (Jam.), Conwickit for the trublance of him in wordis, calland him koffcaryll one the oppin gait. **1627** *Dumbarton Burgh Rec.* in J. Irving *Hist. Dumbartonshire* (1860) 475 The sd Rᵗ M'Cawlay..to pay unlaw, and find caution for trubellance in tyme coming. **1819** W. TENNANT *Papistry Storm'd* iv. (1827) 127 The tipsy sutors..wi' their iron grapples, grippit His flesh, and unto troublance nippit, Garrin' him scream.

**Trouble** (trʊ·b'l), *sb.* Forms: 3–7 truble, (3 trubuil), 4–6 troble, -el(l, -il(l, -yll, -ul, trowble, (5 thruble, trobbyll), 5–6 trubel, trubble, troubel(l, trowbel, (-ill, -yll, -ul(l), 4– trouble. β. 4–6 turble, -el, -ill, 5 torble, -el, tourbel. [ME. a. OF. *truble*, *turble* (12th c.), *torble*, *tourble*, *troble* (13th c.), F. *trouble* (15th c.), f. *tourbler*, *troubler* to TROUBLE.]

**1.** Disturbance of mind or feelings; worry, vexation; affliction; grief; perplexity; distress.

Now often also in lighter use, expressing any degree, however slight, of embarrassment or 'bother', or a condition of suffering some inconvenience or discomfort.

*c* **1230** *Hali Meid.* 29 Godes spuses þat ise swote eise wiðute swuch trubuil. *c* **1430** LYDG. *Min. Poems* (Percy Soc.) 14 Out of the lond he put awey alle trobelle, And made of newe oure joies to be dobelle. **1509** FISHER *Fun. Serm. C'tess Richmond* Wks. (1876) 299 The greuaunce trouble and vexacyon of the good persone hath gretter cause of pyte..than of the euyll persone. **1535** COVERDALE *Ps.* lxxxv[i]. 7 In the tyme of my trouble I call vpon the. **1611** BIBLE *Job* v. 7 Man is borne vnto trouble [*earlier vv.* labour, travail], as the sparkes flie vpward. **1667** MILTON *P. L.* v. 96 The trouble of thy thoughts..in sleep. **1719** DE FOE *Crusoe* II. vi, In trouble to be troubled Is to have your trouble doubled. **1818** SCOTT *Hrt. Midl.* xxiii, Her head was so carried with pain of body and trouble of mind. **1910** *Stage Year Bk.* 23 There are two services [of electricity] installed, to prevent trouble in case of a breakdown on the mains. *Mod.* The family were in great trouble on account of the death of the eldest son.

**b.** With *a* and *pl.* An instance of this; a misfortune, calamity; a distressing or vexatious circumstance, occurrence, or experience.

**1515** BARCLAY *Egloges* iv. (1570) C v/2 Graunt me a liuing sufficient..And voyde of troubles. **1560** DAUS tr. *Sleidane's Comm.* 208 The Ambassadors were in a pecke of troubles. *a* **1591** H. SMITH *Serm.* (1637) 244 Troubles come in an hundred wayes. **1602** SHAKS. *Ham.* III. i. 59 To take Armes against a Sea of troubles. **1612** BRINSLEY *Lud. Lit.* iii. (1627) 20 The trouble is this: that when as my children doe first enter into Latine, many of them will forget to reade English. **1861** PALEY *Æschylus* (ed. 2) *Choeph.* 683 *note*, At the very time when his troubles seemed at an end. **1863** READE *Hard Cash* I. 5 She was determined to share his every trouble.

**c.** *transf.* A thing or person that gives trouble; an occasion or cause of affliction or distress.

**1591** SAVILE *Tacitus, Hist.* IV. lxxvi. 228 The Germans.. were..a kinde of vnprofitable troubles of a campe. **1610** SHAKS. *Temp.* I. ii. 152 Alack, what trouble Was I then to you? **1611** BIBLE *Isa.* i. 14 Your appointed Feasts..are a trouble vnto me, I am weary to beare them. **1709** POPE *Ess. Crit.* 502 Then most our trouble still when most admir'd. **1859** TENNYSON *Geraint & Enid* 1619 The useful trouble of the rain.

† **d.** Harm, injury, offence. *Obs.*

**1463** ASHBY *Prisoner's Refl.* 255 Seyntes..That suffred trowbyll with out resystence. **1568** GRAFTON *Chron.* II. 281 The Fleminges did the French men great trouble.

**2.** Public disturbance, disorder, or confusion; with *a* and *pl.* an instance of this, a disturbance, an agitation.

[**1378** *Rolls of Parlt.* III. 43/1 Le Roialme en diverses parties est mys en grant troboill.] *c* **1400** *Apol. Loll.* 87 Mansleyng, þeft,..corrupcoun,..troubyl[l], periury. *c* **1435** *Chron. London* (Kingsford 1905) 85 To eschew Rebellion, dysobeyssaunce and Trouble. *c* **1460** FORTESCUE *Abs. & Lim. Mon.* xvii. (1885) 153 Whereoff hath comyn..mony gret trowbels and debates. **1550** LATIMER *Last Serm. bef. Edw. VI*, 105 It maketh troble and rebellion in the realme. **1651** HOBBES *Leviath.* II. xxx. 184 It is a hard matter to know who expecteth benefit from publique troubles. **1760–72** H. BROOKE *Fool of Qual.* i, [Then] the troubles happened; and Cromwell assumed the regency. **1855** MACAULAY *Hist. Eng.* xvi. IV. 105 They were to be allowed to exercise any profession which they had exercised before the troubles.

β. *c* **1440** *Promp. Parv.* 497/1 Torble, or torblynge.., *turbacio*. **1463** *Plumpton Corr.* (Camden) p. lxix, When any turble or enterprise was like to fall hurt or scaythe to the Kings people.

**3.** Pains or exertion, esp. in accomplishing or attempting something; care, toil, labour. Phr. *to put to* (*the*) *trouble*, *to take* (*the*) *trouble*.

**1577** B. GOOGE tr. *Heresbach's Husb.* 35 b, Lupines..This pulse requireth least trouble. **1662** J. DAVIES tr. *Olearius' Voy. Ambass.* 248 That trouble we had been at, put us all in a sweat. **1729** LAW *Serious C.* iii. (1732) 31 If it costs me no pains or trouble. **1840** MISS MITFORD in L'Estrange *Life* (1870) III. vii. 108 To be quit of the trouble and expense of the garden. **1856** *Titan Mag.* Dec. 525/1 He..did not care to put himself to the least trouble. **1866** DK. ARGYLL *Reign Law* vii. (1871) 366 Wherever we take the trouble to trace any..phenomenon through the sequences of cause and effect. **1912** *Oxford Mag.* 14 Nov. 78/1 To save themselves the trouble of thinking.

**4. a.** A disease, disorder, ailment; a morbid affection.

**1726** *Wodrow Corr.* (1843) III. 267 Riding..agrees much with my trouble which I am not altogether free of. **1897** *Allbutt's Syst. Med.* III. 882 Perityphlitis due to trouble in the cæcum. **1899** *Ibid.* VIII. 16 Writer's cramp and like troubles.

**b.** A woman's travail. (Also of an animal.) *dial.* or *euphem.*

*a* **1825** FORBY *Voc. E. Anglia* s.v., She is now in her trouble. **1877** H. SMART *Bound to Win* i, Calvert came..and told me Veturia [the mare] was getting very close upon her trouble. **1889** M. GRAY *Annesley* III. i. 95 He rode over the bleak downs to help Daniel Pink's wife in her trouble. **1896** A. LILBURN *Borderer* xxix. 219 Come now, my canny woman, you must try and drink this, or you'll never win through your trouble. **1901** M. E. FRANCIS *Pastorals Dorset* 162 When I'm over my trouble I'll come to see you.

**5.** In various other special applications, euphemistic, colloquial, dialectal, or vulgar. **a.** Unpleasant relations with the authorities, esp. such as involve arrest, summons before a magistrate, imprisonment, or punishment; e.g. *to bring oneself into trouble*, *to get into trouble*; *to be in trouble*, to be in jail (*slang*).

**1560** DAUS tr. *Sleidane's Comm.* 115 Lest they should both offend the Mayor, and bring themselues in trouble. *a* **1562** CAVENDISH *Wolsey* (1893) 266 This gentilman..who hathe byn late in troble in the Tower of London. **1837** J. D. LANG *New S. Wales* II. 34 His wife very soon got into trouble, as it is technically termed in the colony; i.e. into the commission of some crime or misdemeanour, which issues in ..flagellation, or imprisonment, or transportation, or death by the law. **1899** MARY JOHNSTON *Old Dominion* vii, My friend has been in trouble..He will not make the worse conspirator for that. *Mod.* Take care what you say, or you'll get into trouble.

**b.** Said of the condition of an unmarried woman with child.

**1891** T. HARDY *Tess* xxxi, On no account do you say a word of your Bygone Trouble to him...Many a woman—some of the Highest in the Land—have had a Trouble in their time. **1891** *Daily News* 26 Jan. 7/2 She said she consented to come to London to be married to the prisoner as she believed she was in trouble.

**c.** *U.S. colloq.* or *slang.* Public festivity; interruption or disturbance of ordinary work.

**1884** C. T. BUCKLAND *Sk. Social Life India* iii. 66 A day of rest comes in between each day of pleasure, or 'trouble' as the Yankees more rightly call it. **1897** FLANDRAU *Harvard Episodes* 313 That particular quarter..was not..the most decorous on Class Day. There is always more or less, what is technically known as 'trouble'..on Class Day afternoon.

**6.** *Mining.* A dislocation in a stratum; a fault (usually small).

**1672** SINCLAIR *Misc. Obs. Hydrostaticks* (1683) 267 That alteration..was not occasioned by any Gae, or trouble. *Ibid.* 276 Gae's, and Dykes..being the occasion of so much Trouble, in the working of Coal,..the Coal-hewers call them ordinarily by that name Trouble. **1789** BRAND *Hist. Newcastle* II. 680 *note*, Troubles [are] dikes of the smallest degree;..strata are generally altered by a trouble, from their regular site to a different position. **1859** R. HUNT *Guide Mus. Pract. Geol.* (ed. 2) 228 The effects of these movements will be visible in faults, troubles, dykes, throws, or heaves (as in different localities they are named).

**7.** *attrib.* and *Comb.*, as *trouble-bearer*, *-cup*, *-hunter*, *-maker*; *trouble-free*, *-giving*, *-haunted*, *-proof*, *-saving*, *-tost*, *-void* adjs. (See also TROUBLE *v.* 6.)

**1559** *Mirr. Mag.*, *Mortimers* xiv, Seldome ioye continueth trouble voyde. **1608** SYLVESTER *Du Bartas* II. iv. III. *Schism* 506 Art not thou hee that sow'st the Isaacian Plain With Trouble-Tares? **1648** HERRICK *Hesper.*, *Content, not Cates* 7 A little pipkin..Set on my table, trouble-free. **1807** WORDSW. *White Doe* VII. 151 All now was trouble-haunted ground. **1850** STRUTHERS *Poet. Wks.* II. 244 Quaff'd it must be, life's trouble-cup. **1850** TENNYSON *In Mem.* lxv, I lull a fancy trouble-tost. **1878** A. PAUL *Random Writ.* 202 We think ourselves giants and trouble-proof until it [illness] overtakes us. **1893** *Westm. Gaz.* 3 Feb. 1/3 A most trouble-giving class. **1909** *Daily Chron.* 14 Apr. 7/5 A laugh is the best trouble bearer.

Hence † **Trou·bleful** *a.*, full of trouble, troublesome (*obs.*); **Trou·bleless** *a.*, free from trouble.

**1588** J. HARVEY *Disc. Probl.* 71 To what end..haue they breathed out so loude, boisterous, and troublefull blasts? **1838** MARY HOWITT *Birds & Flowers*, *Birds* ii, In a troubleless delight!

† **Trou·ble,** *a. Obs.* Forms: 4–5 trouble, -el, -ele, trowble, (4 turble), 5 trobil, trobille, trowbul, *Sc.* trubill. [a. F. *trouble* (in 12th c. *truble*, *turble*, *troble*, 13th c. *tourble*, *troble*, *trouble*), according to Hatz.-Darm.:—late pop.L. **turbulum*, for cl.L. *turbidum*, whence *troubler* to TROUBLE. A genuine adjectival form, but perh. sometimes standing in Eng. for *troublé*, TROUBLY.]

**1.** Of water, wine, etc., Troubled, turbid, muddy, thick; of air, etc., Misty, murky, cloudy, not clear; in quot. *c* 1400¹, dim, dusky.

*a* **1327** *On Dreams* in *Rel. Ant.* I. 263 Water thikke ant trouble. *c* **1400** *Rom. Rose* 7116 As moche as..The sunne sourmounteth the mone, That troubler is, and chaungeth sone. *c* **1400** MAUNDEV. (1839) viii. 108 Þere is a welle that iiij. sithes in the ȝeer chaungeth his colour: somtyme grene, somtyme reed, somtyme cleer, & somtyme trouble [*Roxb.* trublee]. *Ibid.* xiv. 157 The gode dyamandes..ben of trouble colour. *c* **1450** *Merlin* 236 Thei loked towarde Lanneriur, and saugh the eyr trouble, and thikke of duste. **1482** WARKW. *Chron.* (Camden) 24 Whenne it betokenethe battayle it rennys foule and trouble watere [cf. quot. 1605 s. v. TROUBLY 1].

**2.** Disturbed, distressed, confused; marked by disturbance or confusion; troublous, restless, unquiet.

*c* **1374** CHAUCER *Boeth.* IV. pr. iv. 107 (Camb. MS.) Alle thingys semen to be confus and trowble [*Add. MS.* trouble] to vs men. *c* **1386** — *Clerk's T.* 409 With steirne face and with ful trouble cheere. *c* **1430** *Pilgr. Lyf Manhode* IV. xvii. (1869) 184 Þe anguishe þat so harde presseth troubel herte.

**3.** Turbulent, tempestuous, stormy, violent.

*c* **1374** CHAUCER *Boeth.* I. Met. vii. 19 (Camb. MS.) The trowble [*Add. MS.* trouble] wynde þat hyht Auster. *c* **1470** HENRY *Wallace* VII. 182 Trubbill weddyr makis schippis to droune. **1509** *Payne Evyll Marr.* 95 Like perilous Caribeis of the trouble see.

Hence **Trou·bleness**, troubledness, turbidity.

*c* **1380** Wyclif *Serm.* Sel. Wks. II. 333 Þe wynd of Goddis lawe shulde be cleer, ffor turblenes in þis wynde mut nedis turble mennis lif. **14..** *Beryn* 1417 Of hertis trobilnes I had nevir knowlech, but of al gladnes. **1482** *Monk of Evesham* (Arb.) 73 They sofryd greuys and varyante trowbulnes of the eyre.

**Trouble** (trɒ·b'l), *v.* Forms: see Trouble *sb.* [ME. a. OF. *trubler*, *trobler*, *torbler*, *tourbler*, *turbler* (11–14th c.), F. *troubler*:—late L. **turbulāre*, f. **turbulus* = cl.L. *turbidus* Turbid.]

**I. 1.** *trans.* To disturb, agitate, ruffle (water, air, etc.); *esp.* to stir up (water) so as to make it thick or muddy; to make (wine) thick by stirring up the lees; to make turbid, dim, or cloudy. Now *rare* or *arch.*

**1340** Hampole *Pr. Consc.* 4319 He sal trobel þe se when he wille, And pees it and make it be stille. **1382** Wyclif *Ezek.* xxxii. 2 Thou..trublist to gidre watris with thi feet. **1422** tr. *Secreta Secret., Priv. Priv.* 230 Tho that haue eyen discolourid and trowbelid. **1534** Tindale *John* v. 4 For an angell went doune..and troubled the water. *a***1550** in *Dunbar's Poems* (S.T.S.) 315 He trublit all the air. **1579** Gosson *Sch. Abuse* (Arb.) 56 The fishe Sepia can trouble the water. **1596** Shaks. *Tam. Shr.* v. ii. 141 Like a fountaine troubled, Muddie, ill seeming, thicke. **1660** Dryden *Astr. Red.* 272 As those lees, that trouble it, refine The agitated soul of generous wine. **1859** Gullick & Timbs *Paint.* 231 In the application of paint,..to avoid unnecessarily mixing, or, as it is called, 'troubling', 'saddening', or 'tormenting' the tints. **1878** Huxley *Physiogr.* 170 Its [the sea's] surface is ordinarily more or less troubled with waves.

†**b.** *intr.* for *pass.* Of water, to grow turbid; of the sun or sky, to grow dark, cloudy, or stormy; of a storm, to rage. Also *fig. Obs.*

**1390** Gower *Conf.* viii. 3009* But hou so that it trowble in their [=the air], The Sonne is evere briht and feir. *c* **1400** Maundev. (1839) v. 52 Put a drope of bawme in clere water ..& stere it wel;..And ȝif þat the bawme be fyn..the water schall neuere trouble. *c* **1400** *Destr. Troy* 7619 A thondir with a thicke Rayn thrublit in þe skewes. **1568** Grafton *Chron.* II. 885 The British affayres..began now againe to flow out and to trouble.

**2.** *trans.* To disturb, derange; to interfere with, interrupt; to hinder, mar. *Obs.* or *arch.*

*c* **1330** R. Brunne *Chron. Wace* (Rolls) 4764 (Petyt MS.) Þe feste was turbled & mirth aweye. *c* **1470** Henry *Wallace* viii. 1462 Your fredom we sall trowbill na ma. **1558** Knox *First Blast* (Arb.) 13 By her babling she troubled the hole assemblie. **1607** Shaks. *Cor.* v. vi. 129 Trouble not the peace. **1642** Jer. Taylor *Episc.* (1647) 195 Lucius..troubled the affayre by his interposing. **1713** Addison *Guardian* No. 99 ⁋4 Such who..might..trouble and pervert the course of justice. **1832** Tennyson *Lotos-Eaters* 119 And we should come like ghosts to trouble joy.

**II. 3.** To put into a state of (mental) agitation or disquiet; to disturb, distress, grieve, perplex.

*a* **1225** *Ancr. R.* 268 Þu nouhst nout sturien ne trublen þine heorte. **1340** *Ayenb.* 104 Wyþ-oute him to trobli, wyþ-oute him to chongi, wyþ-oute him remue ine none manere. **1382** Wyclif *John* xii. 27 Now my soule is troublid. *c* **1440** *Generydes* 54 Sore trobelyd in his mynde. **1526** Tindale *John* xiv. 1 Lett nott youre hertes be trubled. **1538** Starkey *England* i. i. 20 Let thys dyuersyte of sectys..no thyng trowbul vs at al. **1657** *North's Plutarch, Add. Lives* (1676) 8 Orators who do break their brains to utter good things, and never trouble their heads in the least to do them. **1715** De Foe *Fam. Instruct.* i. iii. (1841) I. 57 Husband, I believe something troubles thee. **1866** G. Macdonald *Ann. Q. Neighb.* xxiii. (1878) 417, I was troubled in my own mind. **1875** Jowett *Plato* (ed. 2) IV. 133 No such perplexity could ever trouble a modern metaphysician.

β. *c* **1380** Wyclif *Sel. Wks.* II. 328 And þerfore Petre biddiþ Cristen men, Be not turblid bi þer manas. *c* **1450** *St. Cuthbert* (Surtees) 2850 Turbyld in spirit he chaunged his mode.

†**b.** *intr.* for *pass.* To be disturbed or agitated; to be in or get into an unsettled state. *Obs. rare*$^{-1}$.

**1618** Bolton *Florus* iv. iii. (1636) 295 In the change of the government of the Romans,..the world troubled throughout, and the whole body of the Empire was turmoiled with all sorts of perils.

**4.** *trans.* To do harm or hurt to; to injure; to molest, oppress.

**1375** Barbour *Bruce* i. 479 And swa trowblyt the folk saw he, That he tharoff had gret pitte. *c* **1475** *Rauf Coilȝear* 136 For sa troublit with stormis was I neuer stad. **1526** Tindale *Matt.* xxvi. 10 Why trouble ye the woman? **1567** *Gude & Godlie B.* (S.T.S.) 107 The fleand dartis,..To trubill the, sall haif na mycht. **1667** Milton *P. L.* xii. 209 God looking forth will trouble all his Host And craze thir Chariot wheels. **1711** in *Nairne Peerage Evid.* (1874) 143 From all citing conveening judging fyning or otherwayes molesting and troubling the saids heritors tennents possessors and occupiers. **1855** Singleton *Virgil* I. 246 Swans..Whom, swooping from the region of the skies, Jove's bird was troubling. **1912** *Times* 19 Oct. 5/4 No individual..shall be proceeded against or troubled in his person or property.

*absol.* *c* **1570** R. Robinson *Gold. Mirr.* (Chetham Soc.) Introd. 7 Stormes that troubleth sore. **1611** Bible *Job* iii. 17 There the wicked cease from troubling.

**b.** Of disease or ailment: To cause bodily derangement, pain, or inconvenience to; to afflict; sometimes in weakened sense, to affect. (Often in *pass.* with *with*; also *fig.*)

*c* **1400** tr. *Secreta Secret., Gov. Lordsh.* 72 Þy stomak shal fille hym with euyl humours.., and þat shall trobbyl þy brayn with euyll fumosyte. *Ibid.* 80 Wyn þat ys takyn abundanly..lettys þe vnderstondynge,..troblys þe brayn. **1508** Dunbar *Poems* iv. 2, I..Am trublit now with gret seiknes. *a* **1548** Hall *Chron., Hen. IV*, 32 b, His pange so sore trobeled him that he lay as though al his vitall sprites had bene from him departed. **1595** Shaks. *John* v. iii. 3 This Feauer that hath troubled me so long, Lyes heauie on me. **1604** — *Oth.* iii. iii. 414 Being troubled with a raging tooth, I could not sleepe. **1684** Bunyan *Pilgr.* ii. 84 He said, That Mercy was a pretty Lass; but troubled with ill Conditions. **1751** Johnson *Rambler* No. 153 ⁋19 All whom I intreat to sing are troubled with colds. **1899** *Allbutt's Syst. Med.* VIII. 842 For many years he has had an ulcer..which troubles him.

**5.** To distress *with* something disagreeable and unwelcome; to vex, annoy; to tease, plague, worry, pester, bother. †Also *intr.* with *with* (obs.).

**1515** *Plumpton Corr.* (Camden) 213 If they may find any hole or colur therin, they will troble with me for the same. **1538** Audley in *Lett. Suppress. Monasteries* (Camden) 247 Thus I trobill you with my sutes. **1560** Daus tr. *Sleidane's Comm.* 23 b, [He] besecheth him and his adherentes to trouble the church no more. **1590** Shaks. *Com. Err.* iii. i. 62 Your towne is troubled with unruly boies. **1611** — *Wint. T.* ii. i. 1 Take the Boy to you: he so troubles me, 'Tis past enduring. **1794** Nelson in Nicolas *Disp.* (1845) I. 440, I made..thirteen scaling ladders,..for I think the Troops will be troubled in getting up the wall, 'because the earth is too loose. **1885** 'Mrs. Alexander' *Valerie's Fate* ii, 'He would trouble me no more.' 'Does he really trouble you, Valerie?' 'Yes, really. I am frightened and nervous when I go out.'

**b.** In lighter sense: To put to inconvenience, incommode: often used hyperbolically by way of courtesy: 'to give occasion of labour to: a word of civility or slight regard' (J.). Usu. const. *with*: also with *inf.* (esp. in a formula of polite or quasi-polite request), to give (one) the trouble *to do* something (cf. c, d).

**1516** Q. Margaret in Mrs. Wood *Lett. Illustr. Ladies* (1846) I. 221, I pray you send me word, for I will trouble you no more with my sending. **1612** Brinsley *Lud. Lit.* iii. (1627) 12 It seemeth to mee..unreasonable..that the Grammar Schooles should bee troubled with teaching A.B.C. **1669** Sturmy *Mariner's Mag.* i. 14 He will not be troubled with small Fractions..which breedeth no great error. **1708** Arbuthnot in *Lett. Eminent Persons* (1813) I. 180, I shall trouble you to give my services to my friends at Oxford. **1711** Steele *Spect.* No. 142 ⁋11, I will not trouble you with more Letters at this time. **1875** Jowett *Plato* (ed. 2) I. 294 Let me trouble you with one more question. *Mod.* May I trouble you to pass the mustard? I'll trouble you to wipe your feet the next time you come into the house.

**c.** With *for*: To pester with requests, ask importunately, importune; hence (usually) in lighter use, in a formula of polite request: to give (one) the trouble of passing or handing something.

**1516** Q. Margaret in Mrs. Wood *Lett. Illustr. Ladies* (1846) I. 221, I shall trouble you no more for no money. **1755** Johnson, *To Trouble*...9. (In low language.) To sue for a debt. **1844** Dickens *Mart. Chuz.* vi, The new pupil who 'troubled' Mr. Pecksniff for the loaf. **1894** H. Nisbet *Bush Girl's Rom.* 30 I'll trouble you, Shafton, for another of those good cigars.

**d.** *refl.* To take the trouble, take pains, exert oneself (*to do* something).

**1500–20** Dunbar *Poems* xx. 6 Trubill nevir thy self,.. Vthiris to rewill, that will not rewlit be. **1621** T. Williamson tr. *Goulart's Wise Vieillard* 49 Pilots.., without much troubling themselues, or stirring from their places, sit quietly at the sterne, and holding the Rudder,..doe cond and carry their Ships..to their vnlading port. **1845** R. Monckton Milnes in *Life* (1891) I. viii. 357 He had never troubled himself..to understand the question. **1855** Macaulay *Hist Eng.* xv. III. 581 The officer never troubles himself to ascertain whether the arms are in good order.

**e.** *intr.* for *refl.* = prec. sense. *mod. colloq.*

**1880** McCarthy *Own Times* III. xl. 206 He would have allowed reform to go its way for him, and never troubled. **1884** W. C. Smith *Kildrostan* 50 Do not trouble to bring back the boat.

**III. 6.** The verb-stem in comb., prefixed to sbs., forming sbs. with sense 'one who or that which troubles, disturbs, or mars the peace or enjoyment of'; as †*trouble-belly* (gutwort, *Globularia Alypum*), *trouble-cup*, *trouble-feast* (also attrib.), *trouble-house*, *trouble-mirth*, *trouble-rest*, *trouble-state*, *trouble-tomb*, *trouble-town*, *trouble-world*. (Mostly *rare* or *Obs.*)

**1668** Wilkins *Real Char.* 112 Guttwort, *Trouble-belly. *a* **1610** Healey *Theophrastus* (1636) 70 Then he railes on the Fidler as a *trouble-cup. **1603** Florio *Montaigne* iii. ix. (1632) 562 This *trouble-feast reason. **1630** Lennard tr. *Charron's Wisd.* (1658) 52 A little trouble-feast, a tedious and importunate parasite. **1691** tr. *Emilianne's Frauds Rom. Monks* (ed. 3) 226 The old Fryer was a *Turba Festa*, a meer Trouble-Feast to talk so at random. **1608** Dod & Cleaver *Expos. Prov.* xi–xii. 100 This unthrifty *trouble-house. **1643, 1690** [see *trouble-town*]. **1874** T. Hardy *Far fr. Madding Crowd* xxxv, 'Tis well to say 'Friend' outwardly, though you say 'Troublehouse' within. **1598** Sylvester *Du Bartas* ii. i. iii. *Furies* 328 Th' other Furie.. Foule, *trouble-rest. **1604** Daniel *Civ. Wars* iv. xxiv, Those faire bayts these *Trouble-States still vse. **1822** Lamb *Elia* Ser. ii. *Detached Th. Bks.*, They covered [Shakespeare's effigy] over with a coat of white paint...I think I see them..these sapient *trouble-tombs. **1619** J. Dyke *Counterpoison* 23 What breedeth these *trouble-townes but couetousnesse? **1643** Trapp *Comm. Gen.* xxxiv. 30 Many such trouble-houses and trouble-towns there are abroad. **1690** C. Nesse *O. & N. Test.* I. 319 Branding his sons with the black name of trouble-houses, and trouble-towns. **1663** *Flagellum or O. Cromwell* Pref., *Trouble-worlds. **1691** Wood *Ath. Oxon.* II. 101 John Lilbourne [was] naturally a great trouble-world.

**Troubled** (trɒ·b'ld), *ppl. a.* [f. prec. + -ed [1].]

**1.** Physically agitated; of the sea, sky, etc., stormy; of water, wine, etc., stirred up so as to diffuse the sediment, made thick or muddy, turbid.

*Troubled waters* (*fig.*), a state of agitation or disquiet.

**1388** Wyclif *Josh.* xiii. 2 The troblid flood that moistith Egipt. **1581** J. Walker in *Confer.* iv. (1584) F f iij, It is troubled water when we mingle our workes and righteousnes with Gods. **1611** Bible *Isa.* lvii. 20 The wicked are like the troubled sea, when it cannot rest, whose waters cast vp myre and dirt. **1632** Lithgow *Trav.* i. 12 The Riuer Tyber [is] of a troubled and muddy colour. **1796** Kirwan *Elem. Min.* (ed. 2) I. 334 Jargon...Heated to redness, and quenched in water, it becomes rifty, and troubled. **1855** Macaulay *Hist. Eng.* xx. IV. 535 The sky was dark and troubled. **1864** G. Musgrave *Ten Days Fr. Parsonage* II. iii. 98 An inadvertent inquiry would have brought us into troubled waters.

**2.** Disturbed; disquieted; disordered; agitated; afflicted. Also *absol.*

*a* **1325** *Prose Psalter* l. 18 [li. 17] Trubled gost is sacrifice to God. *c* **1450** Capgrave *Life St. Aug.* xv. 21 Augustine with a troubled mynde be-gan to loke up-on his felaw Alipius, and..cried: What suffir we? **1535** Coverdale *2 Esdras* xv. 8 The innocent bloude of the troubled crieth vnto me. **1611** Beaum. & Fl. *Philaster* iii. i, Medicine for a troubled mind. **1651** Hobbes *Leviath.* ii. xxiii. 126 Some private partie of a troubled State. **1728** Eliza Heywood tr. *Mme de Gomez's Belle A.* (1734) II. 31 Philosophy could give his troubled Thoughts but little ease. **1849** Macaulay *Hist. Eng.* vi. II. 127 The historian of this troubled reign. **1885** 'Mrs. Alexander' *At Bay* vii, I wandered about the old scenes like a troubled ghost. **1894** Hall Caine *Manxman* iii. xxi, She slept a troubled sleep.

**Troubledly** (trɒ·b'ldli), *adv. rare.* [f. prec. + -ly [2].] In a troubled or agitated manner; in quot. 1624, in a disorderly way, confusedly (*obs.*).

**1599** Nashe *Lenten Stuffe* 23 So troubledly bemudded with griefe and care. **1624** Bp. Hall *Art Divine Medit.* xvi, Our Meditation must proceed in due order; not troubledly, not preposterously. **1630** Lennard tr. *Charron's Wisd.* Pref. A ij a, He that carieth himselfe troubledly, disquietly, malcontent, fearing death, is not wise. **1891** H. C. Halliday *Someone must suffer* II. ii. 51 He answered troubledly.

**Troubledness** (trɒ·b'ldnės). *rare.* [f. as prec. + -ness.] The quality or condition of being troubled, disturbed, or disquieted; also, turbidity.

*c* **1530** *Judic. Urines* ii. xii. 40 b, That same thycknes & trublydnes. **1631** *Celestina* xx. 191 With so great importunity, and troublednesse of minde. *a* **1681** Wharton *Causes Earthquakes* Wks. (1683) 323 Putrefaction and Troubledness of the Waters of Pits and Wells.

†**Trou·blement.** *Obs. rare.* [a. F. *troublement*, f. *troubler* to Trouble: see -ment.] The act of troubling or condition of being troubled.

**1484** Caxton *Chivalry* 84 Ire is in courage troublement and remembraunce of wycked wil. *c* **1557** Abp. Parker *Ps.* xviii. L iv, They did preuent with troublement, the day of my great stresse.

**Troubler** (trɒ·blər). Forms: see Trouble *sb.*: also 4 -ere, 5–6 -ar(e. [ME. a. OF. *trobleor*, F. *troubleur* (13th c.), *tourbleur* (15th c.), f. *trobler*, etc.: see Trouble *v.*] One who or that which troubles (in any sense); a disturber; an oppressor.

**1382** Wyclif *Isa.* xix. 20 They shul crien to the Lord fro the face of the trublere. *c* **1440** *Promp. Parv.* 497/1 Torbelare, or he þat makythe debate, *turbator.* **1547–64** Bauldwin *Mor. Philos.* (Palfr.) 140 Conscience..is..an inward troubler or tormentor. **1594** Shaks. *Rich. III*, i. iii. 221 The troubler of the poore Worlds peace. **1624** Middleton *Game at Chess* i. i, Yon troubler of all Christian waters. **1710** Hume *Sacred Success.* (1716) 108 That troubler of the Church. **1869** Trollope *He knew*, etc. xxv. 195 That pernicious troubler of the peace of families.

**Troublesome** (trɒ·b'lsɒ̆m), *a.* Forms: see Trouble *sb.* [f. Trouble *sb.* + -some [1].] Full of, characterized by, or causing trouble.

†**1.** Full of disturbance or tumult; disturbed, disorderly, unsettled, troublous. *Obs.*

*a* **1548** Hall *Chron., Hen. IV*, 19 His painfull and busi wanderyng, his troblesome and vncertaine abidyng. **1553** in Hakluyt *Voy.* (1599) II. 111 There arose in the ship such a troublesome disturbance, that all the ship was in an vprore with weapons. **1560** Daus tr. *Sleidane's Comm.* 98 The state of Christendom was troublesome. **1687** Aldworth in *Magd. Coll. & Jas. II* (O.H.S.) 63 In troublesome times.

†**b.** Causing or inclined to cause disturbance; turbulent. *Obs.*

**1552** Huloet, Troublesome, or full of troublynge, or who troubleth muche, *vexabundus.* **1591** Savile *Tacitus, Hist.* i. lxvii. 37 His froward and troublesome disposition. **1687** H. Holden in *Magd. Coll. & Jas. II* (O.H.S.) 124 The Crowd..was very troublesome.

†**c.** Characterized by physical disturbance or agitation; stormy. *Obs.*

**1560** Daus tr. *Sleidane's Comm.* Pref. 2 b, In so many troublesome stormes, and tempestes full of pearil. **1610** Holland *Camden's Brit.* (1637) 697 It is a troublesome River and dangerous even in Summer time. **1623** Lisle *Ælfric on O. & N. Test.* Pref., A troublesome and tempestuous sea.

**2.** Full of trouble, affliction, or distress; troubled, sorrowful. *arch.*

**1552** *Bk. Com. Prayer, Public Baptism Infants*, That they..maye so passe the waues of thys troublesome world, that [etc.]. **1575–85** Abp. Sandys *Serm.* (Parker Soc.) 321 Heretics, by whom it [marriage] hath been not only misliked as troublesome, but utterly condemned as unclean. **1614** Raleigh *Hist. World* iv. vi. § 4. 281 So many Darts..as tooke away his..hopes, together with his troublesome life. **1734** Arbuthnot *Let. to Swift* 4 Oct., I am going out of this troublesome world. **1853** Lynch *Self-Improv.* ii. 43 Christianity is..plainly designed for a troublesome world.

†**b.** Troubled in mind, having trouble. *rare*$^{-1}$.

1596 DALRYMPLE tr. *Leslie's Hist. Scot.* v. (S.T.S.) I. 289 For the cleir cloudis to the dulfull was pleisant, and to the trublesum happie.

**3.** Giving trouble; causing annoyance; vexatious, distressing, worrying, bothering.

1573 G. HARVEY *Letter-bk.* (Camden) 4, I hope you wil haue me excusid thouh I be trubblesum to your waihtier affaiers. 1598 SHAKS. *Merry W.* I. i. 325 Ile rather be vnmannerly, then troublesome. 1604 E. G[RIMSTONE] *D'Acosta's Hist. Indies* II. xiii. 112 Why are not the nightes in summer at Peru, as hotte and troublesome as in Spaine? 1662 J. DAVIES tr. *Olearius' Voy. Ambass.* 97 This small mony..is troublesome in the telling and handling 1747 WESLEY *Prim. Physic* (1762) 84 If the Cough be very troublesome. 1839 THIRLWALL *Greece* xlv. VI. 33 If the barbarians were troublesome neighbours.

**4.** Involving labour or effort; toilsome, laborious, difficult; tiresome, wearisome, oppressive. Now *rare.*

1576 FLEMING *Panopl. Epist.* 243 An office of exceeding great authoritie, and maruellous troublesome. 1600 J. PORY tr. *Leo's Africa* v. 236 Their streetes either descend or ascend, which is verie troublesome to them that haue any busines in the towne. 1632 LITHGOW *Trav.* VI. 253 Leauing our troublesome way. 1780 *Mirror* No. 97 ⁋ 30 When I first got the multiplication-table by heart..it was a plaguy troublesome job. 1836–41 BRANDE *Chem.* (ed. 5) 485 Phosphorus may be purified by careful distillation, but the process is troublesome and dangerous.

†**b.** Painstaking, laborious. *Obs. rare.*

1818 MOORE *Mem.* (1853) II. 245 A most learned and troublesome practician.

**Troublesomely** (trɒ·b'lsɒ̆mli), *adv.* [f. prec. + -LY [2].] In a troublesome manner.

†**1.** In a disturbed or disorderly manner; confusedly. *Obs.*

1561 T. NORTON *Calvin's Inst.* IV. 25 They were wonte..to be present at the election..that nothyng should be troublesomly done. *a* 1699 R. GILPIN in Spurgeon *Treas. Dav.* Ps. cxix. 32 When the mind is so distracted..it acts troublesomely.

**2.** So as to cause trouble; annoyingly, distressingly, vexatiously; oppressively; tiresomely.

1591 PERCIVALL *Sp. Dict., Molestamente*, troublesomely. 1641 MILTON *Reform.* I. Wks. 1851 III. 4 [Peter] falling troublesomly upon the..alwise, and unexaminable intention of Christ. 1663 BOYLE *Usef. Exp. Nat. Philos.* II. v. xviii. 273 Wonderful cures..by the long use of this Decoction, notwithstanding its..troublesomely heating Quality. 1689 SHADWELL *Bury F.* I, More troublesomly ill-bred with his formality, than a high-shoo'd peasant with his roughness. 1870 W. CHAMBERS *Winter Mentone* iv. 54 Troublesomely cold and wet weather.

†**b.** In a condition of trouble or distress. *Obs.*

1625 K. LONG tr. *Barclay's Argenis* I. x x. 56 The night being troublesomely spent betweene hope and feare.

**Troublesomeness** (trɒ·b'lsɒ̆mnės). [f. as prec. + -NESS.] The quality or condition of being troublesome.

†**1.** Disturbed or unsettled state; confusion, disorderliness. *Obs.*

1561 T. NORTON *Calvin's Inst.* I. xv. (1634) 79 As though Reason also did not dissent from it selfe... But..that troublesomenesse proceedeth of the corruption of nature. 1655 FULLER *Ch. Hist.* III. iv. § 27 The troublesomness of the times. 1715 in Black *Hist. Brechin* (1867) 126 Taking into..consideration the troublesomeness of the times.

†**b.** Disposition to cause disturbance; turbulence. *Obs.*

1591 TURNBULL *Exp. Jas.* 167 b, Prosperous estate..which by brauling, contention and troublesomnes is hindered. 1657 in *Eng. Hist. Rev.* Oct. (1910) 727 Filled with passion and troublesomness of spirit.

†**c.** Physically disturbed or agitated state. *Obs.*

1648 HEXHAM II. s.v. *Zee*, The troublesomenesse, or the swelling of the Sea. 1652–62 HEYLIN *Cosmogr.* IV. (1682) 149 Exposed..to the troublesomeness of sudden tempests. 1658 ROWLAND *Moufet's Theat. Ins.* 953 By the troublesomenesse of the air they are dispersed hither and thither.

†**2.** Trouble, affliction, distress. *Obs.*

1561 T. NORTON *Calvin's Inst.* II. x. (1634) 202 He suffered much troublesomenesse by his childrens wives. 1604 T. WRIGHT *Passions* II. Pref. 47 Troublesomenesse or disquietnesse of the soule. *a* 1639 W. WHATELEY *Prototypes* II. xxvi. (1640) 44 To inflict disquietment and troublesomenesse upon men in their labour.

**3.** The quality of giving trouble; vexatiousness, annoying character; toilsomeness; oppressiveness.

1548 UDALL, etc. *Erasm. Par. Matt.* xii. 74 Offended with this importunitie and troublesumnes. 1608 D. T[UVIL] *Ess. Pol. & Mor.* 79 The troublesomnesse of labor. 1630 J. TAYLOR (Water P.) *Heaven's Blessing* Wks. III. 116/1 For the auoyding of the troublesomenesse of Boats and Wherries. 1764 HARMER *Observ.* I. i. 6 Even grammarians derive.. summer from a root which points out the troublesomeness of its heats. 1787 W. MARSHALL *Norfolk* I. 375 Many farmers ..dislike the noise and troublesomeness of these animals. 1881 MISS BRADDON *Asph.* i. 5 With the air of a sinner who gloried in her troublesomeness.

**Troubling** (trɒ·bliŋ), *vbl. sb.* [f. TROUBLE *v.* + -ING [1].] The action of the verb TROUBLE, or an instance of this (in various senses).

*c* 1340 HAMPOLE *Prose Tr.* 17 A fantasie caused of trubblyng of þe brayne. *c* 1374 [see TROUBLABLE]. *c* 1400 LOVE *Bonavent. Mirr.* (1907) 92 With moche noyse and turblynge prayer wil not wele and deuoutly be seide. *c* 1400 MAUNDEV. (Roxb.) vii. 23 Þer es na trubling of þe aer thurgh raynes. *c* 1440 *Jacob's Well* 97 Þe feend..louyth dyscord & trubelyng of pes. 1530 PALSGR. 283/1 Troublyng of ones mynde, *distraction.* 1611 BIBLE *John* v. 4 Whosoeuer then first after the troubling of the water stepped in, was made whole. 1617 MORYSON *Itin.* I. 208, I thinke they would not haue denied vs wine,..yet to auoide troubling of them, my selfe and my brother carried some flaggons of rich wine. 1842 PARNELL *Chem. Anal.* (1845) 44 A faint troubling in strong solutions. 1878 F. FERGUSON *Life Christ* xviii. 174 The medicinal properties..would be intensified at the time of the periodical natural troublings.

**Trou·bling,** *ppl. a.* [f. as prec. + -ING [2].] That troubles; causing trouble.

*a* 1325 *Prose Psalter* li[i]. 4 Þou louedest alle trubland wordes. 1552 HULOET, Troublynge, *angens.* *a* 1684 LEIGHTON *Comm. 1 Peter* v. 7 Wks. (1868) 291 The troubling cares of men. 1851 LYNCH *Sabbath Medit.* in *Lett. to Scattered* (1872) 157 A third troubling thought. 1871 HOWELLS *Wedd. Journ.* (1892) 66 They disposed of their troubling bags and packages.

†**Trou·blish,** *a. Obs. rare.* [f. TROUBLE *a.* + -ISH [1].] Somewhat 'troubled' or turbid.

*c* 1530 *Judic. Urines* II. iii. 18 Whye it is thyckysshe and trublysshe, is bycause that the humours..are all distempred.

**Troublous** (trɒ·bləs), *a.* Now only *literary* or *arch.* Forms: see TROUBLE *sb.*; also 5 -ose, -ows, (-es, -ys, 5–6 -is), 6 -us. [a. OF. *troubleus, -eux, torbleus* (12th c. in Godef.), f. *trouble* TROUBLE: see -OUS.]

†**1.** Of water or other liquid: Troubled, turbid, thick, muddy. *Obs.*

1495 *Trevisa's Barth. De P. R.* XVIII. xxxix. (W. de W.) cc vj/2 The horse..hath lykynge..to drynke trowblous [*MS.* troubly] and thycke water. 1527 ANDREW *Brunswyke's Distyll. Waters* B ij, Other lyquor..which ye wyl puryfye from all trowblous and vnclere substaunces. 1544 PHAER *Pestilence* (1553) L viij, Thick wyne and troubleous.

**2.** Characterized by trouble, agitation, or disturbance; disordered, disturbed, unsettled, confused.

*c* 1449 PECOCK *Repr.* III. vii. (Rolls) 318 Like troubelose tyme was in Ierusalem. 1555 BALE in Strype *Eccl. Mem.* (1721) III. App. xxxix. 107 The state of our Church..is troublous at this present. 1675 TRAHERNE *Chr. Ethics* 363 That troublous times are the seasons of honour, and that a warlike-field is the seed-plot of great and heroical actions. 1840 CARLYLE *Heroes* iv. (1858) 274 There are long troublous periods, before matters come to a settlement. 1878 BROWNING *La Saisiaz* 599 The millions..live their calm or troublous day.

**b.** Of persons or their attributes: Causing disturbance; turbulent, disorderly; restless, unquiet.

1450–1530 [implied in TROUBLOUSNESS]. *c* 1485 *Digby Myst.* (1882) III. 1611 Thow froward Kyng, trobelows and wood. 1550 LATIMER *Last Serm. bef. Edw. VI*, (1562) 115 They.. accused hym..that he was a sedicious fellow, and a troublous preacher. 1855 MOTLEY *Dutch Rep.* I. II. vi. 501 Troublous and adventurous spirits, men of broken fortunes..and boundless desires.

**c.** Of the sea, wind, etc.: Tempestuous, stormy, violent.

1482 *Cely Papers* (Camden) 123 Here was noon passage.. the wynd was so contrary and the see soo trublys. *a* 1548 HALL *Chron., Hen. VIII*, 48 The wynde was troblous and the wether foule. 1610 HOLLAND *Camden's Brit.* (1637) 305 The sea is..rough, and troublous. 1742 COLLINS *Ode Evening* 46 Winter yelling thro' the troublous air. 1855 SINGLETON *Virgil* I. 364 He hunts the storms, and swims through troublous clouds.

**3.** Causing trouble or grief; painful, grievous; vexatious, troublesome.

1463 ASHBY *Prisoner's Refl.* 250 With hys trowbelous hurt. 1465 MARG. PASTON in *P. Lett.* II. 211 I..trost..that ye shall overcome your enemys and your trobelows maters. 1535 COVERDALE *Ezek.* xiv. 21, I sende my foure troublous plages vpon Ierusalem: the swearde, honger, perlous beestes and pestilence. 1651 BIGGS *New Disp.* ⁋ 273 A difficulty of breathing, troublous to life. 1747 UPTON *New Canto Spenser's F. Q.* xxii, Bowers, that exclude the troublous Light. 1880 MCCARTHY *Own Times* IV. li. 79 Mr. Walpole took on himself the management of the Home Office, little knowing what a troublous business he had brought upon his shoulders.

†**b.** Expressing or indicating trouble or grief; sad, sorrowful. *Obs. rare.*

1535 COVERDALE *2 Kings* viii. 11 The man of God loked earnestly, & made a troublous countenaunce, & wepte. 1590 MARLOWE *2nd Pt. Tamburl.* IV. i, As when an herd of lusty Cimbrian bulls..Fill all the air with troublous bellowing.

Hence **Trou·blously** *adv.*; **Trou·blousness.**

1538 ELYOT, *Fluctuation*, *troublously, doubtfully. 1548 UDALL *Erasm. Par. Luke* xii. 106 To bee troubleously vexed with the care of suche thynges is a poynte..of mystrustfulnesse towardes god. 1573–80 BARET *Alv.* S 635 The sea riseth vp troubloúslie with great sourges, *vnda exæstuat vorticibus*, Virg. 1897 F. THOMPSON *New Poems* 6 Their orbs are troublously Over-gloomed. 1450–1530 *Myrr. our Ladye* 45 When goddes seruantes ar besy..in hys seruyce: they with theyre vanyte & *troubelousnes pulle downe theyre myndes. 1577 *St. Aug. Manual* (Longman) 37 Let the troubleousnesse of the flesh cease. 1846 H. W. TORRENS *Rem. Milit. Hist.* 179 His worst troublousness had something quiescent in it.

†**Troubly,** *a. Obs.* Forms: 4 trubli, -byly, 4–5 **troubli, trobli, -bly, trublee,** 4–6 **trowbly, trubly,** 4–7 **troubly,** 5 **trow-, trobely.** [f. TROUBLE *sb.* + -Y [1] or -LY [1]: cf. *cloudy, muddy.*]

**1.** = TROUBLE *a.* 1.

*c* 1380 WYCLIF *Serm.* Sel. Wks. I. 14 Þese fisheris of God shulden waishe þere nettis in þis ryuer, for Cristis prechours shulden..not medle wiþ mannis lawe, þat is trobly water. *c* 1400 Trublee [see TROUBLE *a.* 1]. 1422 tr. *Secreta Secret., Priv. Priv.* 229 Tho that bene Pale and trowbly y-colurid. 1450–80 tr. *Secreta Secret.* xlv. 28 The eyre wexith trobely. *c* 1530 *Judic. Urines* II. i. 11 b, *Rubeus & subrubeus color* with a thycke and a trowbly bodye, sheweth grete dysturblynge of the humours. *Ibid.* vii. 28 Trubly. 1605 STOW *Annals* 707 When it betokeneth battaile, [it] runneth foule, and troubly water; and when it betokeneth dearth or pestilence, it runneth cleare [cf. TROUBLE *a.* 1, q. 1482].

**2.** = TROUBLE *a.* 2.

*c* 1340 HAMPOLE *Prose Tr.* 31 Þe trubylyere þat þou hase bene owtwarde with actyfe werkes, the mare brynnande desyre þou sall hafe to Godd. *c* 1412 HOCCLEVE *De Reg. Princ.* 2 The restles bisynesse Which that this troubly world hath ay on honde. 1421 — *Compl.* 302 This troubly lyfe hathe all to longe enduryd. 14.. in *Hist. Coll. Citizen Lond.* (Camden) 188 He..passyde owte of thys wrecchyde and false trobely worlde.

**3.** = TROUBLE *a.* 3.

1398 TREVISA *Barth. De P. R.* XIII. xxii. (Bodl. MS.), Whanne þe see is aboue troublye and to hiȝe bi windes and stormes. ? *c* 1400 LYDG. *Æsop's Fab.* ii. 44 Þou..Sekest occasion by trobly violence Ayenst me. 1430–40 — *Bochas* IX. xxiii. (MS. Bodl. 263) lf. 427/2 Who may the furies of fortune appese Hir troubli wawes to make hem calm and pleyne? 1513 DOUGLAS *Æneis* IV. v. 133 He chasis the windis away, And trubly cluddis dividis in a thraw.

Hence †**Trou·bliness,** troubled or disturbed condition; turbidity.

*c* 1530 *Judic. Urines* II. iii. 18 Vryne..with a trublynes.. sheweth a wombe fluxe.

**Trouchman,** obs. form of TRUCHMAN.

**Trouch̄t,** obs. Sc. form of TROUGH.

**Troucit,** obs. Sc. f. *trussed*, pa. pple. of TRUSS *v.*

‖**Trou-de-loup** (trudəlu). *Mil.* [F., lit. 'wolf-hole, wolf-pit'.] In field fortification, a conical pit with a pointed stake fixed vertically in the centre, rows of which are dug before a work to hinder an enemy's approach. Usually *pl.* **trous-de-loup** (trudəlu).

1789 REES *Chambers' Cycl.*, *Trous-de-loup*,..are round holes, about six feet deep, and pointed at the bottom, with a stake placed in the middle. They are frequently dug round a redoubt. 1828 J. M. SPEARMAN *Brit. Gunner* (ed. 2) 400 Trous-de-loup...Diameter of the base, 4 feet 6 inches. Depth, 6 feet. Picket, 6 feet long. 1862 *Catal. Internat. Exhib.* II. XI. 14 This kind of obstacle would, on service, be found to occasion much more confusion than crows-feet, trous-de-loup, &c.

**Troue, Trouel,** obs. forms of TROW, TROWEL.

**Trough** (trǫf), *sb.* Forms: 1–2 troᵹ, (troh), 4 **trowȝ, trouȝ,** 4–6 **trowe,** 4–7 (8–9 *dial.*) **trow,** 5–6 **trogh, troghe,** *Sc.* **trouch** (also 9 *Sc. dial.*), 5–7 **troughe, trowgh, trowghe,** (5 **troȝ, troue, trowh, trowegh,** 6 **trouthe, troh, trogh, troght,** *Sc.* **troch** (also 9 *Sc. dial.*), **trowch, -t, truch, troich, troucht, troycht, troyt,** 7 **traught**), 5– **trough;** *β.* 6 **troffe, troofe,** 7 **trof, trofe, trouff;** *γ.* 5 **throwhe,** 6 **throuh,** *Sc.* **throch, -t,** 7 **through.** [Com. Teutonic: OE. *trog*, OFris. *trog*, OS. *trog* (MLG., LG., EFris. *trog*, MDu. *troch(-gh)*, Du. *trog*), OHG., MHG. *troc* (*trog*), Ger. *trog*, ON. *trog* (Sw. *tråg*, Da. *trug*, Norw. dial. *trog, trugh* (*traug, trau*) :—OTeut. **trugoᶻ*, Indo-Eur. **druko-*, deriv. of *dru*, TREE, wood, timber; primary meaning 'wooden vessel'.]

**1.** A narrow open box-like vessel, of V-shaped or curved section, made of wood, stone, metal, or earthenware, and often a fixture, to contain liquid; *esp.* a drinking-vessel for domestic animals; also, a tank or vat used for washing, kneading, brewing, tanning, fulling, and various other purposes. (Often with prefix, as *drinking-, hog-, horse-, kneading-, pig-, water-trough*, etc.: see the first element.)

*a.* *c* 725 *Corpus Gloss.* (O.E.T.) 425 *Canthera*, troᵹ. *a* 800 *Erfurt Gloss.* 1140 *Albeus* (*v*), *genus vasis*, troᵹ. *c* 950 *Lindisf. Gosp.* John xiii. 5 Soðða sende þatuæter in troᵹ and ongann geðoa foet ðara ðegna. *c* 1000 *Sax. Leechd.* II. 68 Do on troh hate stanas. *Ibid.* 326 ᵹecnua ealle wel, leᵹe on hatne stan on troᵹe, ᵹeot hwon wæteres on. 11.. *Rec. Gifts of Adeluuold* (963–84) in Birch *Cart. Sax.* III. 367, vi bidenfate & ii cuflas & þry troᵹas & lead & trefet. *c* 1325 *Gloss. W. de Bibbesw.* in Wright *Voc.* 155 *De un rastuer*, a douwribbe, *le auge*, a trow. 1382 WYCLIF *Gen.* xxiv. 20 She, heldynge out the water pot into the water trowis,..ȝaue to alle the camelis. *c* 1386 CHAUCER *Reeve's T.* 123 Thanne wil I be bynethe..And when he sawe þat the Mele falles doun In to the trough [*v. rr.* trogh, trow, troughe]. *c* 1410 *Master of Game* (MS. Digby 182) xxxiii, Þe trowegh fillede with clene water. *c* 1460 *Registr. Aberdon.* (Maitl. Cl.) II. 85 In brasina vnum plumbum cum cuppa que dicitur Masfate vel caldarium. et algeam que dicitur le trovch. 1485 *Naval Acc. Hen. VII* (1896) 51 Moldyng trowghes [for leaden shot]. *a* 1500 *Kyng & Hermit* 486 in Hazl. *E. P. P.* I. 32 Till two trowys he gan him lede; Off venyson there was many brede. 1502 ARNOLDE *Chron.* (1811) 188 Take iij. C. weight orchell drye grounde and doo it in a trouthe. 1535 *Aberdeen Regr.* XV. (Jam.), Ane troycht & tua aiking buyrdis. 1536 *Abstr. Protocols Town Clerks Glasgow* (1897) IV. 87 Ane lyme trowcht. 1546 *Inv. Ch. Goods* (Surtees No. 97) 132 One stone troght. ? *a* 1550 *Freiris of Berwyk* 210 in *Dunbar's Poems* (S.T.S.) 292 Hyd ȝou..Into ȝone troich... It held a boll of meill quhen that we buke. 1583 in Wadley *Bristol Wills* (1886) 234 My howse wᶜʰ I [a tanner] nowe dwell in wᵗʰ vates and trowes. 1632 in E. B. Jupp *Carpenters' Co.* (1848) 301 All manner of traughts for Bakers. 1710–11 SWIFT *Jrnl. to Stella* 25 Mar., We have let Guiscard be buried at last, after shewing him pickled in a trough this fortnight for two pence apiece. 1789 MRS. PIOZZI *Journ. France* I. 245 The old original trough at the corner of the road. 1815 J. SMITH *Panorama Sci. & Art* II. 534 In troughs of water mixed with fuller's earth. 1859 G. MEREDITH *Juggling Jerry* x, You shan't beg from the troughs and tubs.

*β.* 1545 JOYE *Exp. Dan.* iv. 56 The vnthrifty sone..at last was compelled to come to the hoggis troffe for hunger. 1574 N. DANIEL in Grosart *Spenser's Wks.* I. 422 A pulpitt, many swynes troofe better. 1620 *Inv.* in *Essex Rev.* (1907)

XVI. 206 A payer of Quarnes, a kneedinge trof, and shellves 2s. **1626** *Ibid.* (1906) XV. 67 One kneedinge trofe. **1688** R. HOLME *Armoury* III. xx. (Roxb.) 246/2 A Tallow Trough, and of some termed a Trouff, it is to let the Tallow in working drop or run into it.

γ. *c* **1440** *Promp. Parv.* 503/2 Throwhe, vessel (*K.*, *S.* trow, *P.* trough), *alveus.* *a* **1539** *Cartular. Abb. de Rievalle* (Surtees) 340 The Bruehouse vi kelynge throuhs of lede, ii coper vesselles. **1560** *Aberdeen Regr.* (1844) 329 Lawaris and throchtis of brass. *a* **1660** *Contemp. Hist. Irel.* (Ir. Archæol. Soc.) I. 254 Some..burned the through, broke the kievve, demolished the house.

**b.** A small vessel of similar shape used in chemistry, photography, microscopy, etc.

**1819** *Pantologia* s.v., In [operations with] gasses absorbable by water the trough must be filled..with mercury. **1826** Pneumatic trough [see PNEUMATIC 2]. **1827** FARADAY *Chem. Manip.* i. 20 The mercurial trough. **1831** BREWSTER *Nat. Magic* iv. (1833) 79 A trough having two of its sides parallel, and made of plate glass. **1853** W. GREGORY *Inorg. Chem.* (ed. 3) 68 Closing the tube with the finger, and inverting it, with the open end under water in a basin or trough.

**c.** *fig.* In contempt, A person who is a mere receptacle for liquor; a toper.

**1613** FLETCHER, etc. *Captain* IV. iii, This drunken trowgh has killed him. **1899** LUMSDEN *Edinb. Poems & Songs* 131 A thae trochs are drucken slochs.

**2.** In spec. uses: **a.** An oblong vessel containing the water in which a grindstone runs; also *transf.* the stone itself, or the place where it stands; a workman's compartment in a grindery.

**1725** T. THOMAS in *Portland Papers* VI. (Hist. MSS. Comm.) 144 Most of their wheels and troughs (as they call those places where these grindstones are). **1743** in H. S. Wyndham *Ann. Cov. Gard. Theatre* (1906) II. 312 A grindstone handle and trough. **1839** S. ROBERTS *Tom & Charles* in *Yorkshire Tales* 130 The building itself is generally the property of one person, but he lets off, to different grinders, what are denominated the Troughs, or the parts in which each grinding-stone is fixed. **1884** W. H. RIDEING in *Harper's Mag.* June 79/1 The lower part of the stones touches a long vessel containing water, and by a technical peculiarity each stone is called a 'trough'. **1892** *Labour Commission Gloss.* s.v., It is customary to speak of the trough not only as the actual vessel..but as..the portion of the room containing the trough. In this sense..local.

**b.** An oblong box with divisions serving as the cells of a voltaic battery; also short for *trough-battery.*

**1806** *Med. Jrnl.* XV. 150 Having constructed a very powerful Galvanic trough, I have tried its effects..with very satisfactory results. *Ibid.* 153 My trough contains about 1280 square inches of metallic surface; at first I did not use above four or five pair of plates. **1815** J. SMITH *Panorama Sci. & Art* II. 277 This apparatus..combines the principle of the battery with glasses and that of the common trough. **1866** R. M. FERGUSON *Electr.* § 79 The inner surface of the trough is coated with an insulating substance.

**c.** *Mining.* (*a*) An oblong tank in which ores are washed; a rocker or buddle; (*b*) A passage cut through a wall or pillar of coal: = THIRLING *vbl. sb.*[1] 2 (*Cent. Dict. Suppl.* 1909).

**1877** KNIGHT *Dict. Mech.*, *Trough*.., a frame, vat, buddle, or rocker in which ores or slimes are washed and sorted.

**d.** See quot.

**1877** KNIGHT *Dict. Mech.*, *Trough*,..the tray or vat containing the metallic solution used in electro-plating.

**e.** *Typog.* A metal-lined box in which stones, inking-rollers, and forms are washed.

**1891** in *Cent. Dict.* **1892** *Labour Commission Gloss.* s.v., A trough in the printing industry is a box, lined with lead, with pieces of wood laid across for stones to rest on; the water runs off from the stone into the trough.

**3.** †A small primitive boat; sometimes app. a canoe hollowed out of a solid block of wood (*obs.*); also locally applied to various kinds of boats or barges: see TROW *sb.*[2]

*c* **893** K. ÆLFRED *Oros.* II. v. § 6 He eft wæs biddende anes lytles troȝes æt anum earman men. **1531–2** *Act* 23 *Hen. VIII*, c. 12 § 1 Their troughes barges botes and other vessells passing..on the said River of Severne. **1555** R. TOMSON in Hakluyt *Voy.* (1600) III. 454 A great caue or ditch of water..where come euery morning at the break of the day twentie or thirtie Canoas, or troughes of the Indians. **1570** LEVINS *Manip.* 217/24 A Trough, bote, *linter.* **1574** R. EDEN tr. *Taisner's De Natura Magnetis* Ded., If none had proceeded further then the inuentions of our predecessors, we..had yet haue sayled in troughes or in boates. **1633** T. STAFFORD *Pac. Hib.* III. xvii. (1810) 658 No boats nor troughs to passe them over into Connaght. **1869** *Pall Mall G.* 21 Sept. 6 In Weymouth Bay..Four fishermen went out in a boat known as a 'trough', a little flat-bottomed craft, to fish for herrings.

**4.** A stone tomb or coffin. Cf. THROUGH *sb.*[1] 2. Now *dial.*

**1494** FABYAN *Chron.* VI. ccxiii. 230 In case that ye may kepe my body from tourment,..laye it in a troughe of stone, and hyll it with lede close and iuste [cf. quot. *c* 1400 s.v. THROUGH *sb.*[1] 2 β]. **1610** HOLLAND *Camden's Brit.* (1637) 486 A little trough or coffin, very cunningly and finely wrought of Marble. *a* **1682** SIR T. BROWNE *Tracts* ix. 155 In one of the Mounts..there were found three Troughs containing broken Bones. **1876** *Mid-Yorks. Gloss.*, *Trough*.., a coffin, of old shape; a stone cistern.

†**b.** App. confused with THROUGH *sb.*[1] 3, a flat grave-stone. *Obs.*

**1501** *Bury Wills* (Camden) 83 Also I wyll that the tabernacle of Seynt Jamys..and the troues of the auter ther by, be well and suffyciently peyntyd. **1588** *Knaresborough Wills* (Surtees) I. 163 My bodye to be buryed in Fuiston churche yeard under my grandfather trough.

**5.** A channel, pipe, or trunk for conveying water; a conduit; a gutter fixed under the eaves of a building; *Sc.* (*pl.*) the channel conducting the water to a mill-wheel. Now *dial.* (usually *trow*).

**1398** TREVISA *Barth. De P. R.* XVII. cxxi. (Tollem. MS.), Trowes and condites made of pine tre, and leyde deep under erþe dureþ many ȝeres. **1554** *Burgh Rec. Edinb.* (1871) II. 309 The beitting and mending of the fyve Commoun Mylnis, making of thair haill watter wallis, scheitts and trouchtis. **1555** W. WATREMAN *Fardle Facions* Pref. 10 By conduicte of pipes and troughes, and such other conueyance. **1678** PHILLIPS (ed. 4), *Trough*,..a hollow thing made of Boards, and lying open for the Conveyance of Water. **1792** A. YOUNG *Trav. France* 137 All the houses at Nancy have tin eave troughs and pipes. **1808–18** JAMIESON, *Trow*, the wooden spout in which water is carried to a mill-wheel. **1825** *Ibid.*, *Trows* s. pl., properly..the troughs which conduct the water to the mill-wheel. **1881** RAYMOND *Mining Gloss.*, *Trow*, a wooden channel for air or water. **1901** LAWSON *Remin. Dollar Acad.* 112 He washed himself..in the small lade or 'trows' which conveyed the water from the burn at the bleaching-green.

**6.** A hollow or valley resembling a trough; the bed or channel of a stream, or the depressed tract through which it flows; *spec.* in *Geol.* a basin-shaped depression, a syncline (longer than broad).

**1513** DOUGLAS *Æneis* IX. i. 76 Lyke as sum tyme Ganges, the flude Indane,..In hys deip trowch now flowis esely. **1719** HAMILTON *Ep. to Ramsay* 24 July xvii, Mony a lang and weary wimple, Like trough of Clyde. **1796** W. MARSHALL *W. England* II. 175 Mountain heights..partially severed by deep rich Vallies or 'Troughs'—as they are called. **1819** LOCKHART *Peter's Lett.* lxxiv. III. 299 The whole valley, or strath, or trough of the Clyde. **1854** MURCHISON *Siluria* viii. 155 These schists and limestones are overlain in the contiguous troughs by other rocks. **1862** W. CORY *Lett. & Jrnls.* (1897) 78 The long troughs of woodland where the deer and the streamlets wander. **1883** *Good Words* July 438/2 It is therefore a question how far the ocean troughs may have the antiquity assigned to them.

**b.** *Trough of the sea*, the hollow on the surface between two waves. Also *fig.*

*a* **1625** *Nomenclator Navalis* (Harl. MS. 2301), Ye *Trowgh of the Sea*..when wee lay a Shipp vnder the Sea, (..her broadeside to the Sea) wee saie shee lies in ye Trowgh of the Sea. **1699** DAMPIER *Voy.* II. III. 64 The ship by the mistake of him that con'd, broched to, and lay in the trough of the Sea. **1762–9** FALCONER *Shipwr.* II. 890 Still in the yawning trough the vessel reels, Ingulf'd beneath two fluctuating hills. **1856** MRS. STOWE *Dred* xvii, Tom..never is himself; always up on a wave, or down in the trough. **1886** FROUDE *Oceana* ii. 21 The engines stopped, the ship lay rolling in the trough of the sea broadside on to the waves.

**c.** *Meteorol.* A line or elongated region of lower barometric pressure between two regions of higher.

**1882** W. MARRIOTT in *Standard* 26 Dec. 7/4 At right angles to the path of a cyclone there is always a line running through the centre, called the trough, where the barometer reading is the lowest. **1887** R. ABERCROMBY *Weather* ii. (1888) 30 If we look at the barometer-trace at any one place, the 'ups' and 'downs' suggest the analogy of waves, so that the lowest part of a trace may be called a 'trough'. **1904** *Westm. Gaz.* 10 May 6/2 A long trough of low barometric pressure now lies over the southern parts of our islands.

**7.** *attrib.* and *Comb.*, as *trough form*, *frame*, *-meat*, *plate* (sense 2 b), *-sailing* (see sense 3), *-stone*; *trough-like*, *-shaped* adjs.; also **trough battery**, a voltaic battery consisting of a number of cells in a trough (sense 2 b); **trough-closet**: see quot.; **trough core**, *Geol.*: see quot.; **trough-current**, the current produced by a moving vessel; **trough fault**, *Geol.*: see quot.; **trough flooring**, steel troughing riveted together to form the floor of a bridge; **trough girder**, an iron girder shaped like a trough; **trough gutter**, a box-like channel for drainage; a rain-water pipe of this form; **trough-joint**, **trough limb**, *Geol.*: see quots.; **trough mercury**, the mercury used in a pneumatic trough; **trough roof**, *U.S.*: see quot.; **trough shell**, a mollusc of the family *Mactridæ*.

**1841** *Encycl. Brit.* (ed. 7) XXI. 665/2 A valuable modification of the '*couronne des tasses*', called the *trough battery. **1878** G. PRESCOTT *Sp. Telephone* 260 A trough battery of six cells. **1870** CORFIELD *Treatm. Sewage* 121 What are called *trough-closets have been erected in Liverpool. ..A long trough is placed below and behind the seats of a series of closets. **1911** *Encycl. Brit.* X. 598 The innermost strata in a fold constitute the 'core', arch-core, or *trough core. **1843** *Mech. Mag.* XXXVIII. 70/1 The *trough-current can only act against the front of the screw and the bevelled or slanting sides of the recess. **1883** GRESLEY *Gloss. Coal Mining*, **Trough fault*, a wedge-shaped fault, or, more correctly, a mass of rock, coal, &c., let down in between two faults. **1911** *Encycl. Brit.* IV. 538 The *trough flooring, 3/8 in. thick and 6 in. deep, is rivetted to the longitudinals. **1876** PREECE & SIVEWRIGHT *Telegraphy* 244 In the *trough form of battery this [short circuit] is caused by leakage. **1827** FARADAY *Chem. Manip.* xv. (1842) 318 A flap fixed to this end of the *trough frame, which..may be used when there is occasion. **1883** *Specif. Alnwick & Cornhill Railw.* 48 The superstructure is to consist of two wrought-iron *trough girders carrying the rails. **1856** BREES *Gloss. Terms*, **Trough gutter*, a sort of sunk or enclosed gutter, about 8 or 10 inches wide, and adopted with advantage in exposed situations. The wooden trunks employed as gutters for sheds and common buildings ..are also known by this name. **1865** PAGE *Handbk. Geol. Terms* (ed. 2), **Trough-joint*, the fissure or joint which frequently accompanies the abrupt bending of strata passing through the middle of the curvature. **1839** DE LA BECHE *Rep. Geol. Cornwall*, etc. iii. 43 These rocks rested in a *trough-like cavity extending east and west. **1869** TOZER *Highl. Turkey* II. 109 A trough-like depression between two ridges. **1911** *Encycl. Brit.* X. 598 In a fold of this kind we have an 'arch limb', a middle limb, and a floor or '*trough limb'. **1844** H. STEPHENS *Bk. Farm* II. 71 The whole have hay or *trough-meat..on wet or stormy nights. **1827** FARADAY *Chem. Manip.* xx. (1842) 554 These chemical cleansings of the *trough mercury are intended to destroy the disposition which exists in impure mercury to form films upon its surface. *Ibid.* xvii. (1842) 457 The wires are soldered to plates equal in size to those of the troughs,..though they may not touch the *trough plates. **1905** *U.S. Dept. Agric., Bureau Forestry* Bulletin lxi, **Trough roof*, a roof on a logging camp or barn, made of small logs split lengthwise, hollowed into troughs and laid from ridge pole to eaves. **1855** J. D. MACLAREN in *Mem.* vii. (1861) 134, I could almost resume the bathing and the *trough-sailing. **1871** NESBITT *Catal. Slade Coll. Glass* 77 A *trough-shaped spout. **1867** LOVELL *Edible Mollusks* 152 *Mactra solida*, Linnæus. *Trough shell. **1470–1** *Durham Acc. Rolls* (Surtees) 643 Pro nova factura unius le *Troughstane pro aqueductu in gardino. **1587** *Wills & Inv. N. C.* (Surtees) II. 157 In the brewhowsse. One brew lead..j maskefatte and a troghstone. **1854** MURCHISON *Siluria* xiii. 329 Yellow sandstones ..extensively used as..trough-stones.

Hence **Trou·ghful**, as much as a trough will hold; **Trou·ghster**, one who feeds at a trough, a pig; **Trou·ghwise** *adv.*, as or like a trough; **Troughy** (trǫ·fi) *a.*, characterized by troughs.

**1877** *Honourable Miss Ferrard* I. v. 128 A *troughful of buttermilk. **1891** *Daily News* 30 Oct. 5/6 Wheaten flour, which I distributed among them by troughfulls. **1892** G. MEREDITH *Ode to Comic Spirit* 19 The poor smoke Struck from a puff-ball, or the *troughster's grunt. **1551** ROBINSON tr. *More's Utop.* I. (1895) 31 The shyppes that they founde fyrste were made playne, flatte, and broade in the botome, *troughewyse. **1877** BEER *Prophet of Nineveh* I. iv. 58 She plunges heavy in the *troughy seas.

**Trough** (trǫf), *v.* [f. prec. sb.]

**1.** *trans.* †**a.** To furnish with a trough or troughs for irrigation or drainage. *dial. Obs.* **b.** *Geol.* To form into a trough or into the shape of a trough. **c.** To treat in some way in a trough; to stain, gauge, or mould in a trough.

**1668** *Demise of Coal Mine* (Arncliffe Hall MSS.), To carry a sough or watergate through the demised ground..and to leave the same trowed and scoured. **1839** MURCHISON *Silur. Syst.* I. xxix. 388 This spur reposes conformably on the Old Red Sandstone..being troughed between the latter and the ridge of Old Red Sandstone to the South of it. **1872** W. S. SYMONDS *Rec. Rocks* viii. 277 The Pilton rocks are rolled and troughed to a great extent about Ashford. **1881** GREENER *Gun* 254 The same method of troughing is required to brown them a dark brown. **1887** *Daily News* 20 May 3/2 Sword-bayonets..in store were re-tested,..being sprung round a curved block 2½ inches high,..troughed and gauged. **1905** *Daily Chron.* 25 July 4/4 Cottages which have unusual features..—concrete troughed between upright timbers.

**2.** *intr.* To feed at or as at a trough; to feed swinishly.

**1748** RICHARDSON *Clarissa* (1811) VIII. 168 What miry wallowers the generality of men of our class are in themselves, and constantly trough and sty with.

†**3.** *Mining.* Of a vein: To dip. *Obs. rare.*

**1747** HOOSON *Miner's Dict.* R ij, When Veins or Pipes take a chop up higher than ordinary into their proper Lids, whethersoever the Lids be Stone, Mixt-beds, &c., this is opposite to Troughing or Choping down.

Hence **Troughed** (trǫft) *ppl. a.*, **Troughing** (trǫ·fiŋ) *vbl. sb.* and *ppl. a.*

**1897** *Daily News* 31 Dec. 2/1 A rather lumbering looking 'troughing' machine automatically scours the edges with emery until the embryo sword-bayonet will just fit in flat into a gauge or 'trough'. **1898** G. MEREDITH *Odes Fr. Hist.*, *Napoleon* vi, Heap over heap [of horses and men] Right through the troughed black lines turned to bunches or shreds, or a fog.

**Trough**, obs. form of TROTH.

**Troughing** (trǫ·fiŋ), *sb.* [f. TROUGH *sb.* + -ING[1] 1 g.] Troughs collectively; provision of troughs; a set or system of troughs.

**1825** J. NICHOLSON *Operat. Mechanic* 85 The openings in the bottom of the troughing should be of iron. **1904** *Daily Chron.* 31 Dec. 6/7 On the walls of the tunnels 153 miles of troughing have been fixed to carry the cables.

**Trought(e**, obs. form of TROTH, TROUT.

**Trougth**, obs. form of TROTH.

**Trouker, Troukle**, obs. ff. TRUCKER, TRUCKLE.

**Troul**, obs. form of TRAWL, TROLL, TRULL.

**Trou-madam**: see TROLL-MADAM.

**Troump, -ar, -ate, -erie, -etter**, obs. ff. TRUMP, TRUMPER, TRUMPET, TRUMPERY, TRUMPETER.

**Trounce** (trauns), *v.*[1] Also 6–7 **trounse**, 7 **trownse, -ce.** [Of obscure origin; usually compared with OF. *troncer*, *troncher*, Cotgr. *troncir*, *tronchir* to cut, cut off a piece from, retrench, f. *tronce*, *tronche* stump or stock of wood (14th c. in Godef.): cf. *tronc* TRUNK, and *tronçon* TRUNCHEON. But the OF. and Eng. vbs. do not agree in sense. See also *Eng. Dial. Dict.*]

†**1.** *trans.* To trouble, afflict, distress; to discomfit, harass. *Obs.*

**1551** BIBLE *Judg.* iv. 15 But the Lorde trounsed [1611 discomfited] Sisara and all his charettes, and all hys hoste with the edge of ye swerde, before Barak. **1553** *Respublica* III. iii. 652 Lorde Ihese Christe whan he was I-pounst & I-pilate, Was ner zo I-trounst as we [ignoram people] have been of yeares Late. **1570** FOXE *A. & M.* (ed. 2) 408/2 If any do speake against them, he is miserablye tossed & trounsed for his labour. **1646** TRAPP *Comm. John* ii. 16 The churchwarden of Ipswich was much trounced and troubled in the High-commission. **1655** GURNALL *Chr. in Arm.* I. 111 Joseph's mistresse first tries to draw him to gratifie her lust; that string breaking, she hath another to trounce him and charge him.

†**b.** *intr. Obs. rare*⁻¹.

**1589** *Rare Triumphs Love & Fortune* IV. (Roxb.) 119 Oh, terrible tormentes that trounce in my toe!

**2.** To beat, thrash, belabour, cudgel; to beat by way of punishment, to flog.

**1568** *Hist. Jacob & Esau* II. ii. C ij, There was neuer none trounced as I shal trounce that elf. **1621** MOLLE *Camerar. Liv. Libr.* II. iv. 85 He tug'd and trownst his aduersarie. **1748** SMOLLETT *Rod. Rand.* xxii. (1804) 149 Flattered with the hopes of seeing a bailiff trounced. **1820** *Gentl. Mag.* XC. I. 412 The common provincial phrase of 'I'll trounce you', meaning to beat or bruise with a stick or fists. **1887** BESANT *The World went*, etc. xxi. 169 One after another, they were tied up..and soundly trounced.

**3.** To inflict chastisement upon; to punish; also, to get the better of, defeat.

**1657** HOWELL *Londinop.* 40 How Rich. the first trounced her for murthuring the Jews. *a* **1704** T. BROWN *Comm.-Place-Bk.* Wks. 1709 III. II. 136 The Gods Neptune and Apollo trounc'd Laomedon for cheating 'em of their Hire. **1833** MARRYAT *P. Simple* lxiv, We will set to and trounce that scoundrel of an uncle. **1859** J. R. GREEN *Lett.* I. (1901) 28 You honour a man..by condescending to an encounter, even though you trounce him. **1878** BROWNING *Poets Croisic* xlv, Who chides..the unchilded monarch shall be trounced For irreligion.

**b.** To punish by legal action or process; to indict, to sue at law. Now *dial.*

**1638** FORD *Fancies* IV. i, The court shall trounce thee. **1678** BUTLER *Hud.* III. iii. 683, I would so trounce her, and her Purse, I'd make her kneel for better or worse. **1681** DRYDEN *Spanish Fryar* IV. i, I'll trounce you for offering to corrupt my Honesty. *a* **1700** B. E. *Dict. Cant. Crew*, *Trounc'd*,.. Cast in Law. **1730–6** BAILEY (folio), *Trounce*, to sue at law. **1755** JOHNSON, *Trounce*, to punish by an indictment or information. **1818** MOORE *Fudge Fam. Paris* vi. 206 Who shall describe..Thy candour, when it falls to thee To help in trouncing for a libel? **1830** DE QUINCEY *Bentley* Wks. 1857 VII. 98 He 'trounced' Colbatch, who was sentenced to pay 3*s.* 6*d.*, together with 2*s.* 6*d.* arrears, and £20 costs. **1888** ELWORTHY *W. Somerset Word-bk.*, *Trounce*, to summon before a magistrate; to sue at law.

**4.** To assail or attack with rebuke or abuse; to censure; to scold severely.

**1607** R. C[AREW] tr. *Estienne's World of Wonders* 2 These learned Latin authors haue been trounced by these dangerously conceited and proud presumptuous censurers. **1673** MARVELL *Reh. Transp.* II. Wks. 1776 II. 261 Had not Mr. Killigrew foreseen that they must..fall to dirt of themselves, he would ere this..have trounced the author. **1865** *Star* 6 Jan., He deals chiefly with the best-named folly and trounces it most severely. **1894** BESANT *Equal Woman* 127 He very finely trounced the Public for daring to like these favourites.

Hence **Trounced** (traunst) *ppl. adj.*

**1898** *Blackw. Mag.* Oct. 469/1 The howling of trounced sailors.

**Trounce**, *v.*², a dialectal or quasi-dialectal variant of *traunce*, TRANCE *v.*²; also *trans.* in causal sense. Hence **Trouncing** *ppl. a.*

**1566** DRANT *Horace, Sat.* vi. D vj, In cytie, I must set vppon my golde bespangled mule, In deeper way, a trounsinge steede, whome vneth ought can rule. **1824** SCOTT *Redgauntlet* ch. xi, They behoved to trounce us away to be tried at Carlisle. **1824** MACTAGGART *Gallovid. Encycl.* 166 The Prince of Darkness trounces through the world in the form of a black dog. **1887** *Charity Organis. Rev.* Nov. 416 The young woman refused to pay, and trounced off to a..hospital.

**Trouncer** (trau·nsəɹ). [f. TROUNCE *v.*¹ + -ER¹.] One who trounces; *spec.* an odd man (see ODD A. 8 d); †on a man-of-war: see quot. 1867 (*obs.*).

*c* **1630** DR. TRIPLET in Aubrey *Brief Lives* (1898) I. 264 When this well trouss't trounser Into the school doth enter. **1867** SMYTH *Sailor's Word-bk.*, *Trouncer*, an old word for a waister. [*Ibid.*, *Waisters*..had little else of duty but hoisting and swabbing the decks.] **1896** BOOTH in *Westm. Gaz.* 26 Mar. 2/1 Brewhouse men, cellar men, yardmen, coopers, filings-makers, draymen, and trouncers. **1898** A. LANG in *Longm. Mag.* Nov. 92 My friend and constant 'trouncer'..has been pitching into me.

**Trounchen**, obs. form of TRUNCHEON.

**Trounchman**, obs. corrupt f. TRUCHMAN.

**Trouncing** (trau·nsiŋ), *vbl. sb.* [f. TROUNCE *v.*¹ + -ING¹.] The action of TROUNCE *v.*¹; a beating, thrashing; also *fig.* Also *attrib.*

*a* **1553** C. BANSLEY *Treat.* xii. (Percy Soc.) 5 Tyll you tricke and trotte youre selfe, to the devyls trounsynge neste. *c* **1580** JEFFERIE *Bugbears* Epil. in *Archiv Stud. Neu. Spr.* (1897), With rowsynges, with bownsynges, with trownsynges. **1803** R. ANDERSON *Cumberld. Ball.* 64 In a passion I flew, And gave her a trouncin. **1867** *Routledge's Ev. Boy's Ann.* Aug. 3 Cheltenham gave Marylebone a fine trouncing.

**Troune, Trounson, Troup, -e,** obs. ff. THRONE, TRUNCHEON, TROOP.

‖ **Troupe** (trūp). [F. (16th c.), = OF. *trope* (13th c.): see TROOP *sb.*] A company, band, troop; *esp.* a company of players, dancers, or the like.

**1825** *N. Y. Evening Post* 6 Dec. 2 The whole troupe were equally excellent. **1847** W. IRVING in *Life & Lett.* (1864) IV. 32, I have attended the opera..the troupe [is] very fair. **1906** E. V. LUCAS *Listener's Lure* (1910) 181 A troupe of jumping dogs.

**Troupial**, var. TROOPIAL. **Trous,** obs. f. TRUSS.

**Trous-de-loup**, pl. of TROU-DE-LOUP.

**Trouse** (traus), *sb.*¹ Now *dial.* Forms: 1 trus, 3–4 trous, 6–7 trousse, trowse, 5– trouse. [OE. *trus*, perh. a. OIcel. *tros* rubbish, fallen leaves and twigs, ON. and Norw. *tros*, Sw. *tr*å*s*, perh. in ablaut relation with *tras* twig, sprout: see TRASH *sb.*¹; but the ON. word is applied only to twigs, etc. used for burning.] Brushwood, cuttings from hedges or copses; = TRASH *sb.*¹ 1.

**978** *Charter Bp. Oswald* in Kemble *Cod. Dipl.* III. 169 Ðæt mylenstall and vi. æcras ðærto, and vi. foðra truses ælce ʒeare on Bloccanlea. **1293** *Anc. Deed* A. 9277 (P.R.O.), Dederunt..dicto Hamundo.., trous de alnetis et spinis ad claudendum schidstauid yord. *a* **1310** in Wright *Lyric P.* xxxix. 110 For hope of ys thornes to dutten is doren, He mot myd is twy-byl other trous make. **1458** *Anc. Deed* A. 7587 (P.R.O.), To take als moche wode & trouse vpone þe seid londe growyng as is sufficiaunt for closure of alle þe seid londes. **1523** FITZHERB. *Husb.* § 126 Lay thy small trouse or thornes, that thou hedgeste withal, ouer thy quickesettes. **1573** *Nottingham Rec.* IV. 149 Fellyng of trouse.. in the nere Coppy. **1600** HOLLAND *Livy* VI. x. 223 They provided themselves out of the fields of a number of faggots, of brushwood, and such like trousse, and so..filled up the ditches close to the wals. **1610** *Nottingham Rec.* IV. 301 To fetch any trowse or tinsell out of the same woodes. **1691** *Blount's Law Dict.* (ed. 2), *Tinet*,..Trouse, Brushwood and Thorns to make and repair Hedges. **1881** MISS JACKSON *Shropsh. Word-bk.* s.v., 'That rough trouse ool be rar' stuff fur breastin' the 'edge to keep the ship [*i. e.* sheep] out.'

Hence † **Trouse** *v. Obs.*, to cut brushwood (cf. TRASH *v.*³); † **Trou·sing** *vbl. sb.* (in quot. *attrib.*).

**1512** *Nottingham Rec.* IV. 454 A trowsyng ax. **1787** GROSE *Provinc. Gloss.* s.v., Trousing a hedge or faggot; trimming off the superfluous branches. *Warw.*

**Trouse** (trūz, trauz), *sb.*² Now *Hist.* and *arch.* [App. taken in 16th c. from Irish (and Sc. Gaelic) *triubhas*, recorded *c* 1500 (see quot.), orig. pronounced *trīv*ă*s* or *trīw*ă*s*, in mod. Irish pronunc. *trūs* (see TREWS). (The quot. of 1306, from its early date and late form, is doubtful, and may not belong to this word.) The 16th and 17th c. quots. here and under TREWS refer to it as worn by the Celts. It has been held to be derived from OF. *trousse* TRUSS, etc. q.v., but a careful examination of OF. literature by M. Antoine Thomas shows no trace of *trousse* in the sense assumed, which appears, later than in English, in Miège's *Dict.* 1679. The thing is said by Littré to have been worn (? in 17th c.) by young pages and by certain novices, and to survive in certain expressions, as *il avait quitté les trousses*, and *être aux trousses de l'ennemi*.

As to the ulterior history, Prof. Bergin of Dublin thinks well of the suggestion in Holder *Alt-celt. Sprachsch.* II. 1974, that the Celtic *triubhas* represents OF. *trebus* 'sorte de chaussure ou de chausse' (13th c., Godef.), from late L. *tubrācōs* 'tubrucos vocatos quod tibias braccasque tegant' (Isidore *Orig.* XIX. xxii. 30). 'Tubraci quod a braccis ad tibias usque perveniant', which appears later as *tribraci*. Miège *F. Dict.* (1679) has '*Trousses, sorte de chausses*, trunk-breeches'.]

**1.** Originally, A close-fitting article of attire for the buttocks and thighs (divided below so as to form a separate covering for each thigh), to the lower extremities of which stockings (when worn) were attached; *spec.* = TREWS. In later use drawers, or knee-breeches.

*a. sing.* **6 trowes, trwse, 7 trous, trouze, 7–8 trowze, 8 trowse, 6– trouse.**

[**1306** *Pleas of Crown (Irel.)* 34–5 *Edw. I*, m. 10 d, Vnum crannoc..vnus arcus cum sagittis..vna spartha (unum par) [so app.; MS. faint] s[o]tularium cum trues..precii vnius denarii et oboli. *c* **1500** in W. Stokes *Irish Glosses, Tract on L. Declen.* (1860) 12 Hee brace gl. *tribus*.]

**1578** in Sharp *Cov. Myst.* 37 Pd. for a trwse for Judas ijs. viijd. **1581** Trowes [see TREWS]. **1630** *Conceits, Clinches*, etc. (1860) 8 A jellous wife was like an Irish trouze, alwayes close to a mans tayle. **1633** *Spenser's State Irel.* 48 The leather quilted Iacke..for any occasion of suddaine service, ..to cover his trouse [*Add. MS.* thinn breeche] on horse-backe. **1676** WISEMAN *Chirurg. Treat.* I. xviii. 85 The Trowze being made, I saw it laced on...The lower part of the Trowze was tacked to a Cotton Stocking he put on that Leg. *c* **1730** BURT *Lett. N. Scotl.* xxii. (1818) II. 84 Few besides gentlemen wear the trowze, that is, the breeches and stockings all of one piece. **1746** Trowse [see TREWS]. **1775** F. GREGOR tr. *Fortescue De Laudibus* xxxv. 125 Nor do they [French common people] wear any Trowse, but from the Knees upwards; their Legs being exposed and naked. **1813** JAS. GRANT *Orig. Gael* (1814) 213 Strabo describes the clothing of the Gauls as consisting of..a sort of breeches, which covered the inferior members of the body, similar to the *triumhas* or trouse of the Gael. **1852** *Meanderings of Mem.* I. 86 The belted blouse Of velvet black, and closely-fitting trouse.

*β. pl.* **6–7 trouzes, 7 trousses, trooses, troosses, troozes, truzes, trusses, 7–8 trowzes, 7–9 trowses, 8 truses, 6– trouses.**

**1581** DERRICK *Image Irel.* II. E iij b, His skirtes be verie shorte, with pleates set thicke about, And Irishe trouzes more to put, their straunge protractours out. **1586** D. ROWLAND *Lazarillo* II. (1672) T iv, A Gentleman-Usher with handsom Trouses, a neat Doublet, a good Cloak, and a comely bonnet. **1601** HOLLAND *Pliny* VII. xliii. I. 177 In his youth he was a poore souldier, and served as a footman in his single trousses and grieves. **1612** R. DABORNE *Chr. turned Turke* 1409 S'hart, a French slop, these are none of the Iewes trouses. **1622** *Relat. Eng. Plantation* in Arber *Story Pilgrim Fathers* (1897) 453 They had most of them long hosen up to their groins, close made; and above their groins to their waist, another leather. They were altogether like the Irish trouses. **1625** B. JONSON *Staple of N.* I. i, Hee walks in his Gowne, wastcoate, and trouses, Expecting his Taylor. **1634** SIR T. HERBERT *Trav.* 146 Their [Persians'] breeches are like Irish troozes, hose and stockings sowed together. **1673** *Lond. Gaz.* No. 807/4 A Cook,..in a sad coloured Stuff Coat and Trowses. **1741** in *Scott. Hist. Rev.* Apr. (1905) 303 The prisoner was going to the field in truses, Contrary to orders. **1747** CARTE *Hist. Eng.* I. 20 The inhabitants of those provinces, who wore Braccæ, trowses striped and of various colours serving for both hose and breeches. **1834** PLANCHÉ *Brit. Costume* 234 The close hose, fitting exactly to the limbs, in fact, the Norman chausses, were..revived [Henry VIII] under the..name of trouses.

†**2.** (*pl.*) = TROUSERS 2. *Obs.*

**1679** V. ALSOP *Melius Inquir.* I. i. 60 The Papists..maliciously reproach the Scripture..when they call it..a Leaden Dagger, a pair of Seamans Trowzes, a movable Dyal. **1705** ELSTOB in *Hearne's Collect.* 30 Nov. (O.H.S.) I. 107 His trowzes wch with loops emboss'd he tyes. **1820** *Acc. Coronation Geo. IV*, The King's Trowses.

**3.** *Comb.*, as **trouse-like** *a.* or *adv.*

**1650** BULWER *Anthropomet.* Pref., Their colour'd thighs Trous-like being died black.

Hence †**Troused** *a. Obs. rare*⁻¹, wearing the trouse (cf. *kilted*, *plaided*).

**1612** DRAYTON *Poly-olb.* xviii. 638 The trowzed Irish led by their uniust Tyrone.

**Trouser** to **Trouser-wearer**: see TROUSERS.

**Trousering** (trau·zəriŋ). [f. TROUSER(S + -ING¹ 1 g.] Cloth suitable for making trousers; a species of this. Chiefly *pl.*

**1883** *Daily News* 24 Sept. 2/6 Worsted coatings and trouserings, fancy twills, diagonals, and other fabrics suitable for the leading markets. **1899** O. SEAMAN *In Cap & Bells* (1900) 46 We sit in sable Trouserings and Boots.

**Trousers** (trau·zəɹz), *sb. pl.* Forms: 7–8 **trossers, trowzers,** 7– **trowsers, trousers,** 8 **trouzers.** See also STROSSER. [An extended form of TROUSE *sb.*², cf. other words indicating a pair, as *tweezers*; perh. directly after DRAWERS.]

†**1.** = TROUSE *sb.*² 1, TREWS. *Obs.*

[**1599**: see STROSSER.] **1613** FLETCHER *Coxcomb* II. iii, I'le haue you flead and trossers made of thy skin to tumble in. **1633** T. STAFFORD *Pac. Hib.* I. xviii. (1821) 191 Cloathed in a simple mantle, and torne trowsers. **1676** WISEMAN *Chirurg. Treat.* I. xviii. 85 By laced Stockings and Trowzers the Swellings in his Legs and Thighs went off. **1752** C. STEWART in *Scots Mag.* (1753) 293/1 Stewart had on blue and white trowsers. **1776** GIBBON *Decl. & F.* xi. I. 315 The emperor Tetricus..as well as his son, whom he had created Augustus, was dressed in Gallic trowsers, a saffron tunic, and a robe of purple. **1778** LD. CARLISLE *Let.* 21 June in *15th Rep. Hist. MSS. Comm.* App. VI. 345 The gnats in this part of the river [Delaware] are as large as sparrows; I have armed myself against them by wearing trousers, which is the constant dress of this country. **1789** M. MADAN *Persius* (1795) 80 *note*, The bracca was a peculiar dress of the Medes, which like trowzers, reached from the loins to the ankles. **1834** PLANCHÉ *Brit. Costume* 8 They wore close trousers, which they called *bracæ*; these trousers, an article of apparel by which all barbaric nations seem to have been distinguished from the Romans, being made of their chequered cloth, called *breach* and *brycan*, and by the Irish, *breacan*.

**2.** A loose-fitting garment of cloth worn by men, covering the loins and legs to the ankles; sometimes said to have been worn over close-fitting breeches or pantaloons. (Also *a pair of trousers*.) Cf. TROUSE *sb.*² 2, PANTALOON 3 c.

In early use esp. worn by sailors, later by soldiers, and gradually becoming common from about 1820. Now distinguished from *breeches* chiefly by covering the whole leg, and by not being shaped so as to fit tightly: cf. BREECH.

**1681** *Lond. Gaz.* No. 1661/4 John Clarke, a stout Man,.. in..a pair of Buck skin Leather Breeches..(sometimes wearing Trousers over his Breeches) rid away on a Grey Gelding. **1718** OZELL tr. *Tournefort's Voy. Levant* I. Life 9 All he could afford himself was a Thrum-cap, Linen Trowzers, and a Pair of Wooden Shoes. **1731** *Gentl. Mag.* Nov. 474/2 Instead of Breeches, he proposes that the Ladies should wear Trowsers, which will be particularly convenient for those who have not handsome Legs. **1742** J. PARRY *True Anti-Pamela* 216 *note*, Trowzers are commonly worn by those that ride Post down into the North, and are very warm; at the same Time, they keep the Coat, Breeches, &c., very clean, by being wore over them. **1748** *Anson's Voy.* I. iii. 29 Orellana and his companions..having prepared their weapons, and thrown off their trouzers and the more cumbrous part of their dress, came all together on the quarter-deck. **1768** WALES in *Phil. Trans.* LX. 108 Breeches made of seal, or deer skin, much in the form of our seamens short trousers. **1772** COOK *Voy. S. Pole* I. ii. (1777) I. 20, I..gave to each man the fearnought jacket and trowsers allowed them by the Admiralty. **1786** *Gentl. Mag.* Sept. 814/1 Twenty-five boys belonging to the Marine Society, in new jackets and trowsers. **1814** WELLINGTON in Gurw. *Desp.* (1838) XI. 504, I beg leave to recommend that 20,000 shirts, 20,000 pairs of socks or stockings and 6,000 pairs of trousers should be sent out to Tarragona. **1869** E. A. PARKES *Pract. Hygiene* (ed. 3) 415 Shortly before or during the Peninsular war trousers were introduced.

**b.** The loose bag-like drawers or pantaloons worn by both sexes in Mohammedan countries.

**1775** R. CHANDLER *Trav. Asia M.* xix. 66 Their ladies wear..large trowsers or breeches, which reach to the ancle. **1810** E. D. CLARKE *Trav. Russia* (1839) 62/1 The dress of a Cossack girl is elegant; a silk tunic, with trousers fastened by a girdle of solid silver [etc.]. **1815** ELPHINSTONE *Acc. Caubul* (1842) II. 57 The Murwuts..are tall, fair men, and wear a pair of loose trowsers, something thrown over their shoulders, and a handkerchief tied round their heads. **1882** FLOYER *Unexpl. Baluchistan* 256 He had the ordinary white calico trowsers. **1913** D. BRAY *Life-Hist. Brahui* ii. 31 A girl should be put into trousers as soon as she is two, or at the most four.

**c.** White frilled or trimmed drawers reaching to the ankles (or nearly so), worn by women and girls, and young boys, about the second quarter of the 19th c.; pantalettes.

**1821** SHELLEY 15 Aug. in Ingpen *Life* (1909) II. xix. 900 She was prettily dressed in white muslin, and an apron of black silk, with trousers. **1838** DICKENS *Nich. Nick.* xiv, Her little girls..wore little white trousers with frills round the ancles. **1844** *Ladies' Hand-bk. Haberdashery* 56 Ladies' Wearing Apparel...Trowsers with Worked Bottoms. **1859** GEO. ELIOT *A. Bede* xii, His hearty affection for the Rector dated from the age of frocks and trousers. **1873** J. ASHBY-STERRY *Shuttlecock Papers* 95 Girls..in short frocks, frilled trousers, and broad blue sashes.

**3.** In *sing.* form **trouser**, in various senses. (See also attrib. and combinations in 4.)

[**1609**: see STROSSER.] **1702** ADDISON *Dial. Medals* i. Wks. 1766 III. 17 Of the old British Trowser. **1823** SCOTT *Quentin D.* Introd., All the rest was mustache, pelisse, and calico trowser. **1885** STEVENSON *Dynamiter* i. 2, I have scarcely a decent trouser in my wardrobe.

**b.** A single leg of a pair of trousers (in quots. *transf.*).

**1893** MARY CHOLMONDELEY *Diana Tempest* v, A little palm near had its one slender leg draped in an *impromptu* Turkish trouser, made out of an amber handkerchief. **1899** — *Red Pottage* ix, One melancholy Scotch fir embarrassed by its trouser of ivy.

**4.** *attrib.* and *Comb.* (more usually in sing. form *trouser*), as *trouser-brace* (BRACE *sb.*[2] 9 b), *-button, -finisher, -hem, -knee, -leg, -lining, -making, -pocket, -wearer*; *trouser-wearing* adj.; also **trouser-band**, the waistband of a pair of trousers; †**trouser breeches**, = sense 1; **trouser-press**, a contrivance for pressing the legs of trousers so as to produce a crease; **trouser-presser**, a workman engaged in ironing trousers; also = *trouser-press*; **trouser-stockings**, ? waterproof overalls or leggings used by fishermen; **trouser-strap**, a strap passing beneath the instep and attached at each end to the bottom of the trouser-leg; **trouser-stretcher**, a device for stretching trousers so as to take out any 'bagginess'.

**1892** ZANGWILL *Childr. Ghetto* I. 221 His blue bandana.. tied round his *trouser-band. **1896** A. MORRISON *Child of the Jago* 126 He gave a hitch to his trousers-band. **1875** BEDFORD *Sailor's Pocket Bk.* viii. (ed. 2) 286 The shoulder-strings..cross behind like *trouser-braces. **1762–71** H. WALPOLE *Vertue's Anecd. Paint.* (1786) II. 1 James..hated novelties. He..hunted in the most cumbrous and inconvenient of all dresses, a ruff and *trowser breeches. **1898** *Daily News* 22 Nov. 7/3 Stanley once characterised the Heligoland Treaty as follows: 'England received in exchange for a *trouser-button a new suit of clothes'. **1887** W. WESTALL *Her Two Millions* li, She was a *trousers finisher. **1896** MRS. CAFFYN *Quaker Grandmother* 251 John..flicked an atom of fluff off his *trouser-knee. **1849** CUPPLES *Green Hand* xiii. (1856) 130 One of his long *trowser-legs. **1901** G. DOUGLAS *House w. Green Shutters* 239 They stopped—their trouser-legs flapping behind them. **1909** ELIZ. L. BANKS *Myst. Fr. Farrington* 37 A strip of his *trousers-lining. **1906** *Daily News* 8 Mar. 6 Her work of *trousers-making yields her a good deal less than a penny an hour. **1856** GEO. ELIOT *Ess.* (1884) 106 His hands stuck in his *trouser-pockets. **1898** W. W. JACOBS *Sea Urchins, Money-changers* (1906) 223 The fare..rose slowly and felt in his trousers-pocket. **1905** H. A. VACHELL *The Hill* iii. 49 He possessed a *trouser-press. **1887** *Pall Mall G.* 4 Nov. 8/1 They had heard Allman, the *trousers-presser, say, 'Now, gentlemen, I'm going to talk sedition'. **1906** *Daily Chron.* 25 Apr. 8/2 The crease..savours of the automatic trousers-pressers,.. rather than of the hot iron of the tailor. **1883** *Fisheries Exhib. Catal.* 45 The *Trouser-Stockings..and Cork Jackets are indispensable adjuncts. **1841** *Civil Eng. & Arch. Jrnl.* IV. 176/2 Improved apparatus to be attached to trowsers, commonly called *trowser-straps. **1860** E. FALKENER *Dædalus, Mod. Art* ii. 202 German hobnailed boots and leather trouser-straps. **1897** MARY KINGSLEY *W. Africa* 590 Xenia, who is the one and only *trouser wearer in our band, spends fifty per cent. of the night on one leg struggling to get the other in or out of these garments. *c* **1820** HUGH BOURNE *Let.* in *N. & Q.* 9th ser. IX. 489/2 That *trousers-wearing, beer-drinking Clowes will never get to heaven.

Hence **Trou·ser** *v. slang, trans.* to put (money, etc.) into the trouser-pocket, to pocket; **Trou·serdom**, the realm of trousers; the wearing of trousers; **Trou·sered** (-əɹd) *a.*, wearing or dressed in trousers; also *fig.*; **Trou·serettes**, girls' 'knickerbockers'; **Trouse·rian** *a. nonce-wd.*, of or pertaining to trousers; **Trou·serless** *a.*, without trousers; wearing or having no trousers.

*c* **1890** G. H. KINGSLEY *Sport & Trav.* vi. (1900) 183 The sheriff *trousered the dollars! **1892** *Labour Commission Gloss.* s.v., To trouser is to put money into one's pocket, that is, to earn; a slang expression used by cabmen. **1882** *Pall Mall G.* 27 Oct. 2 The regeneration of feminine attire will never be compassed by the way of *trouserdom. **1789** M. MADAN *Persius* (1795) 81 The *trowzer'd Medes. **1825** COBBETT *Rur. Rides* (1885) I. 319 The tarred, and trowsered, and blue-and-buff crew whose very vicinage I..detest. **1878** STEVENSON *Inland Voy.* 49 My pipe..was..pretty well 'trousered', as they call it [cf. Fr. *culotter un pipe*]. **1895** L. DOUGALL *Question of Faith* 277 The roadside elms, trowsered to the ground with brush of branches. **1874** J. ASHBY-STERRY *Tiny Trav.* 284 Troublesome Twelve in..the frilliest of frilled *Trouserettes. **1896** *Godey's Mag.* Apr. 387/2 Bloomers, very short tunics, or trouserettes. ?*c* **1820** L. HUNT *Secret Existing Fashions* Ess. (1887) 276 Round comes the kindly *trouserian veil,..the legs retreat..into retirement. **1857** in Ld. Dufferin *Lett. High Lat.* vii. 124 Before I knew where I was, I found myself sitting on a chair, in my shirt, *trowserless.

**Trouss**, obs. f. TRUSS. **Troussage**, var. TRUSSAGE *Obs.* **Trousse**, obs. f. TRUCE, TRUSS.

‖ **Trousseau** (truso). Also 3 trusseau. [F. (13th c.), dim. f. *trousse* TRUSS *sb.*; cf. TRUSSELL.]

**1.** †**a.** A bundle; cf. TRUSSELL 1. *Obs.* **b.** A bunch of keys. *rare.* (perhaps only as Fr.)

*a* **1225** *Ancr. R.* 168 Noble men & gentile ne bereð nout packes, ne ne uareð nout itrussed mid trusseaus [*v.r.* trusses], ne mid purses... Trusseaus, & purses, baggen, & packes beoð alle eorðliche weolen, & worldliche renten. **1847** DE QUINCEY *Sp. Mil. Nun* § 5 There lay the total keys, in one massive *trousseau*, of that monastic fortress, impregnable even to armies from without.

**2.** A bride's outfit of clothes, house-linen, etc. Also *attrib.*

[**1817** LADY MORGAN *France* I. (1818) I. 27 An *armoire*.. held the bridal wardrobe, or rustic *trousseau*.] **1833** T. HOOK *Widow & Marquess* iv, The trousseau is ready, and the day fixed. **1855** MRS. GASKELL *North & S.* i, I have spared no expense in her trousseau. **1880** 'OUIDA' *Moths* III. 293 Claire has got the coffer for her doll's trousseau. **1896** *Westm. Gaz.* 28 Mar. 3/2, I have just seen some of the trousseau gowns of a much-talked-of April bride-elect.

**Troust**, abbrev. f. **trouest, trowest*: see TROW *v.*

**Trout** (traut), *sb.*[1] Forms: 1–2 truht, 3 troit, 4 trouȝt(e, trouhte, troȝte, 4–5 trote, 4–6 trute, trowte, 4–7 troute, 5 trowȝt(e, trowyt, troughte, trouth(e, troyte, (tryotht), 6–7 trowt, trought, (7 trowet, troot), 6– trout. [OE. *truht*, ad. late L. *tructus, tructa, truta, trutta*, etc. = Gr. τρώκτης gnawer, also the name of a sea-fish, f. τρώγειν to gnaw; the forms *troit, troute*, etc. correspond to OF. *troite, troute*, etc., F. *truite* (13th c.).]

**1.** A well-known freshwater fish of the genus *Salmo*, esp. *S. fario*, the common trout, inhabiting most rivers and lakes of the temperate or colder parts of the northern hemisphere; it is distinguished by numerous spots of red and black on its sides and head, and is greatly valued as a sporting fish and on account of its edible quality. See also 3.

† *Whole* or *sound as a trout*: cf. *sound as a roach* (ROACH *sb.*[1] 1 b). *Obs.*

*c* **1050** *Suppl. Ælfric's Voc.* in Wr.-Wülcker 180/37 *Tructa*, truht. *a* **1100** *Ags. Voc.* ibid. 319/15 *Tructa*, truht. **1290** in *Archæologia* XV. 354 Pro uno paner. gurnardi..pro iiij troites. *a* **1300** *Cursor M.* 11884 (Cott.) Bi þat þou þar-of cum vte þou sal be hale sum ani trute [*v.r.* troute]. **1375** BARBOUR *Bruce* II. 577 Gynnys, to tak geddis & salmonys, Trowtis, elys and als menovnys. **1387** TREVISA *Higden* (Rolls) I. 423 Perche and trouȝtis. *c* **1420** *Liber Cocorum* (1862) 50 Trowȝtes..Wele soþun and hakked. *a* **1450** *Fysshynge wyth an angle* (1883) 22 For þe Trowte. The trowyt ys a deyntet fyche and a fre bytyng. *c* **1518** SKELTON *Magnyf.* 1624, I am forthwith as hole as a troute. **1525** LD. BERNERS *Froiss.* II. cxiii. 325 Pastyes of samonde, troutes, and elys, wraped in towels. **1589** [? LYLY] *Pappe w. Hatchet* 3, I..will giue them line enough like a trowte. *a* **1616** BEAUM. & FL. *Scornf. Lady* III. ii, Leave off your tickling of young heirs like Trouts. **1635** SWAN *Spec. M.* (1670) 347 When we speak of one who is sound indeed, we say that he is sound as a Trout. *a* **1677** HALE *Prim. Orig. Man.* II. vii. 200 River-Fish, as Trouts..will alter their figure, some for the better and some for the worse, being put into Ponds. **1727–46** THOMSON *Summer* 253 They sportive wheel, or sailing down the stream Are snatched immediate by the quick-eyed trout. **1735** SOMERVILLE *Chase* IV. 371 The crimson-spotted Trout, the River's Pride, And Beauty of the Stream. **1790** SCOTT *Let. to W. Clerk* 3 Sept. in *Lockhart*, Two miles from an excellent water for trouts. **1839** DOUGLAS in *Proc. Berw. Nat. Club* I. 185 The trouts were scarcely covered in the small pools. **1860** GOSSE *Rom. Nat. Hist.* 6 The streams..where the trout displays his speckled side as he leaps from pool to pool. **1885** *Good Words* 255/2 He may guddle trouts in a stream.

**b.** *collective sing.* (in sporting use taking the place of the pl.).

**1602** CAREW *Cornwall* II. 105 b, The pond will moreouer keepe Shote, Seale, Trought, and Sammon, in seasonable plight, but not in their wonted reddish graine. **1609** in *Craven Gloss.* (1828), 33 pearch and troot from Mawater for my Ld. Judge. **1789** MRS. PIOZZI *Journ. France* I. 41 The trout..there have been over praised. **1849** JAMES *Woodman* ii, She was exceedingly fond of trout. **1875** W. MCILWRAITH *Guide Wigtownshire* 24 Pike and trout are to be had in the lochs.

**2.** Used as a name of various fish (chiefly *Salmonidæ*) resembling the trout in appearance or habits. Now *local.*

**1604** E. G[RIMSTONE] *D'Acosta's Hist. Indies* III. xv. 164, I have not seene any *Besugues* there, nor trowts. **1854** BADHAM *Halieut.* 313 Of salars caught in the Ribble, those of the first year are called smolts; those of the second year, sprods; those of the third, trouts. **1884** MATHER in *Century Mag.* Apr. 908/1 The name of 'trout' is also applied.. to a salt-water fish called 'squeteague'. **1891** G. H. KINGSLEY *Sport & Trav.* (1900) 456 Char, known to the natives [of Colorado] by the name of trout. **1897** *Outing* (U.S.) XXX. 217/2 In the South, he [the black bass] is commonly called 'trout'.

**3.** With defining prefix, as the name of various species of the genus *Salmo* (or of the allied genus *Salvelinus*), and occasionally of other genera.

**Bastard trout** (*U.S.*), a squeteague or weak-fish, *Cynoscion nothus*; **brook trout**, *Salmo fario*; in *U.S.*, *S. fontinalis*, or *S. irideus*, the rainbow trout; **brown trout**, *S. fario*; **Dolly Varden trout** (*U.S.*), *Salvelinus Malma*; **grey trout**, *Salmo trutta*; in *U.S.* the squeteague; **lake trout**, *S. ferox* (the great lake trout); in *U.S.*, (*a*) *S. confinis* (the North American lake trout), inhabiting the deepest waters of the great lakes; (*b*) = next; **Mackinaw** or **Namaycush trout**, *S. Namaycush*, of Lake Huron and Lake Superior; **rainbow trout**, *S. irideus*, a Californian species, now introduced in British trout-streams; **red-bellied trout**, the char, *S. salvelinus*; also *S.* or *Fario erythrogaster*, of the lakes of New York State and Pennsylvania; **red-spotted trout**, *S. fontinalis* or *S. salvelinus*; **rock trout**, *Chirus constellatus* (ROCK *sb.*[1] 9 d); † **skegger trout** = SKEGGER; **speckled trout**, *S. fontinalis*; **white trout**, (*a*) a variety of *S. fario*; (*b*) the weakfish (*Cynoscion nothus*). See also BULL-TROUT, SALMON-TROUT, SEA-TROUT.

**1661** LOVELL *Hist. Anim. & Min.* 228 Both the Salmon and gray trouts are very pleasant, and good for sound persons, but in agues they are not comparable to the Perch. **1668** CHARLETON *Onomast.* 163 *Trutta Lacustris*, the Lake-Trout. **1836** YARRELL *Brit. Fishes* II. 31 The Grey Trout. *Ibid.* 60 The Great Lake Trout of Loch Awe..was shortly noticed by Pennant..as a native of Ullswater Lake in Cumberland, and of Lough Neagh in Ireland. *Ibid.* 74 This species has been called a Red-bellied Trout. **1861** *Act* 24 & 25 *Vict.* c. 109 § 4 All migratory fish of the genus salmon,..that is to say, salmon..harvest cock, sea trout, white trout, sewin, buntling [etc.]. **1868** *Rep. U. S. Commissioner Agric.* (1869) 322 It is..rank folly to allow so great a delicacy as the speckled brook trout (*Salmo fontinalis*) to become extinct. *Ibid.* 330 The commission has..bred salmon, trout, lake trout (*Salmo toma*), and land-locked salmon (*S. Gloveri*). **1881** *Cassell's Nat. Hist.* V. 115 The Grey Trout (*Salmo Cambricus*). **1883** *Fisheries Exhib. Catal.* 204 Brook Trout, Lake Trout,.. Rainbow Trout, Rangeley Trout. **1884** GOODE, etc. *Nat. Hist. Aquatic Anim.* 468 According to the latest system..the second group [of the old genus *Salmo*] includes the Chars, or Red-spotted Trout, and the gray-spotted species known as Salmon Trout, or Lake Trout. These are assigned to the genus *Salvelinus*. *Ibid.* 504 The Dolly Varden Trout—*Salvelinus Malma*,.. known in the mountains as 'Lake Trout', 'Bull Trout', 'Speckled Trout', and 'Red-Spotted Trout'. **1884** *St. James's Gaz.* 23 Feb. 5/2 Like mice in a house, the little brook-trout are often almost under your feet. **1888** GOODE *Amer. Fishes* 120 The Silver Squeteague, *Cynoscion nothum*, called at Charleston the 'Bastard Trout'. The 'White Trout'..is caught with hook and line.

†**4.** *slang*, originally in the alliterative phrase *true* or *trusty trout*, a confidential friend or servant; so *humble trout*. *Obs.*

*c* **1661** *Roxb. Ball.* (1883) IV. 518, I was a trusty trout In all that I went about. **1682** *New News fr. Bedlam* 30 They are all very honest Fellows, true Trouts. **1688** SHADWELL *Sqr. Alsatia* I. i, Your humble Trout, good noble squire.

**5.** *attrib.* and *Comb.*, as *trout-angler, -angling, -brook, farm, -hole, -hook, -line, -net, ova, -preserve, -rod, -spawn, -spear, -stream, -worm*; objective and obj. gen., as *trout-breeder, -catcher, -fisher, -fishing, -pirate, -rearing, -tickler*; also *trout-coloured, -famous, -haunted* adjs.; *trout-like* adj.

**1538** ELYOT, *Fuscina*..a troute speare, an yele speare. **1555** [see EEL-SPEAR]. **1591** SYLVESTER *Du Bartas* I. vi. 653 Kennet, whose Trout-famous Drift..by Hungerford doth hasten. **1653** R. SANDERS *Physiogn.* 35 A greenish eye, a trout-nose, a great mouth. **1653** WALTON *Angler* v. 126, I shall tel you a little more of Trout fishing before I speak of the Salmon. *Ibid.* 128 In Hamp-shire..they use to catch Trouts in the night by the light of a Torch or straw, which when they have discovered, they strike with a Trout spear. **1668** WILKINS *Real Char.* 140 [These] may be stiled the Trout-kind. **1727** BAILEY vol. II, *Trout-coloured* (spoken of Horses) is White speckled with Spots of Black, Bay, or Sorrel, particularly about the Head and Neck. **1799** A. YOUNG *Agric. Lincoln.* 4 A narrow vale, through which runs a trout stream. **1807** W. IRVING *Salmag.* xi. 2 July (1855) 115 Trout-fishing was my uncle's favourite sport. **1839** T. C. HOFLAND *Brit. Angler's Man.* ii. (1841) 11 He [the peacock red worm] is a good trout-worm. **1845** J. COULTER *Adv. Pacific* vii. 78 They can be caught with small trout hooks, carefully baited. **1868** *Rep. U. S. Commissioner Agric.* (1869) 327, I hatched about five hundred thousand trout last season, and sold about five hundred thousand impregnated trout spawn. *Ibid.* 328 A fountain capable of filling constantly a two-inch pipe will sustain a trout preserve which may prove a source of pleasure and profit. *Ibid.* 337 Experimental and initiatory practice in trout-rearing is becoming common upon Long Island. **1883** W. E. NORRIS *No New Thing* I. i. 9 His gun, and a trout-rod, and some other things. **1884** JEFFERIES *Life of Fields* 199 The swan is a well-known trout-pirate. **1887** HISSEY *Holiday on Road* 7 By the side of a trout-haunted stream. **1894** *Field* 9 June 833/3 Fine trout given our society by Mr. A., the trout breeder. **1897** *Outing* (U.S.) XXX. 324/2 In this place one can..trace.. the trout-brook to its source. **1904** GALLICHAN *Fishing Spain* 185 The Portuguese peasant lads are expert trout-ticklers. **1904** *Pilot* Apr. 330/1 It is clear..that the really desirable *requies senectæ* will be afforded by a trout farm. **1906** *Westm. Gaz.* 28 Apr. 14/3 The appearance of the may-fly..is eagerly looked forward to every year by the trout-angler. **1910** H. T. SHERINGHAM in *Encycl. Brit.* II. 28/2 (*Angling*) Grayling injure a trout stream by devouring trout-ova and trout-food.

**b.** Special Combs.: **trout-fly**, (*a*) the may-fly; (*b*) an artificial fly for trout-fishing; **trout-louse**, a fish-louse parasitic on the trout, also called *sug*; **trout-perch**, the black bass (*local, U.S.*); also, a trout-like fish (*Percopsis guttatus*) of the rivers and Great Lakes of U.S., having the mouth and scales like those of a perch; **trout-spoon**, a small spoon-bait for trout-fishing (*Cent. Dict.* 1891); **trout-stone**, *Min.* (G. *forellenstein*) = TROCTOLITE.

**1744–50** W. ELLIS *Mod. Husbandm.* III. II. xiii. 84 The Caddis or *Trout Fly,..certainly the best natural Baits of all others for taking Trouts. **1787** BEST *Angling* (ed. 2) 109 They [salmon] will rise at anything gaudy, and where they are plenty, at Trout flies. **1888** GOODE *Amer. Fishes* 466 The young fish rise freely to trout-flies in rapid water. **1910** H. T. SHERINGHAM in *Encycl. Brit.* II. 28/2 Grayling will take most small trout-flies. **1653** WALTON *Angler* iii. 90 In winter..many of them have sticking on them Sugs, or *Trout lice, which is a kind of worm. **1883** *Century Mag.* July 376/2 A description of a Carolina bass was sent to Lacépède under the local name of trout, or *trout-perch.

who accordingly named it salmoides, meaning trout-like. **1892** *Trout-stone [see TROCTOLITE].

Hence **Trou·ted** *a.* [cf. F. *porcelaine truitée*], see quot.; **Trou·tful** *a.*, full of or abounding in trout; **Trou·tless** *a.*, without trout, devoid of trout (whence **Trou·tlessness**); **Trou·ty**, a troutlet.

**1783** JUSTAMOND tr. *Raynal's Hist. Indies* III. 153 The *trouted china, which no doubt is called so from the resemblance it bears to the scales of a trout. *a* **1661** FULLER *Worthies, Hants.* (1662) II. 1 Clear and fresh rivulets of *troutful water. **1891** ATKINSON *Moorland Par.* 197 Our troutful little stream of the Esk. **1865** KINGSLEY in *Life & Lett.* (1879) II. 180, I catch a trout now and then..so I am not left *troutless. **1904** GALLICHAN *Fishing Spain* 15 He maintains that the Bidasoa will be troutless in two years. **1879** *Daily News* 25 Nov. 5/2 Dynamite, disease, pollution of rivers, have destroyed their thousands since Thomas Stoddart wrote a sad song on the *troutlessness of Yarrow. **1848** *Fraser's Mag.* XXXVIII. 73 My wilfulness that bright day..was rewarded with a few *trouties.

† **Trout**, *sb.*[2] *dial. Obs.* Also 5 trowtt. [Of uncertain origin.] *pl.* (See quot. 1691.) So † **Trout** *v. Obs.*, to curdle, coagulate.

**1483** *Cath. Angl.* 395/1 To Trowtt, *coagulare.* Trowttis, *coagulum.* **1683** G. MERITON *Yorks. Dialogue* 402 (E.D.S.) Ile give um some Trouts, reach me hither th' Bowl. **1691** RAY *N. C. Words* 77 *Trouts*, Curds taken off the Whey when it is boiled: a Rustick word. In some places they call them Trotters.

**Trout**, obs. form of TROAT *v.*, TROTH.

**Trouter** (trau·təɹ). [f. TROUT *sb.*[1] + -ER[1].] One who fishes for trout; a trout-fisher.

**1830** HOWITT *Seasons* (1837) 122 Cloudy weather, a little windy, especially from the South, is in high favour with the trouter. **1854** *Fraser's Mag.* L. 397 However well a trouter may get on by keeping to the banks of his river, the salmon fisher can rarely be successful by fishing from dry land. **1887** *Macm. Mag.* June 107/1 Your dry-fly man is inclined to look upon the great mass of trouters..with something akin to complacent and patronizing compassion.

**Trouthe**, obs. form of TROTH, TROUGH.

**Trou·tiness.** [f. TROUTY *a.* + -NESS.] The condition or quality of being 'trouty'; speckledness, spottiness.

**1895** R. GRAHAM *Notes Menteith* v. 72 A..much patched coat of various shades of troutiness and stages of decay.

**Trouting** (trau·tiŋ). [f. TROUT *sb.*[1] + -ING[1].] Fishing for trout, trout-fishing.

*a* **1768** ERSKINE *Inst. Law Scot.* II. ix. § 13 Depriving him of the pleasure of trouting. **1827** SCOTT *Surg. Dau.* v, The game was plenty, and the trouting in the brook such as had been represented by advertisement.

**b.** *attrib.*

**1806** *Gazetteer Scotl.* (ed. 2) 558 Venny or Finny; a small rivulet of Angus-shire,..is a fine trouting-stream. **1833** J. RENNIE *Alph. Angling* 64 A trouting-rod is usually made from twelve to fifteen feet. **1883** *Fisheries Exhib. Catal.* (ed. 4) 176 Salmon Lines, Deep Sea Lines, Trouting Lines. **1896** *Westm. Gaz.* 16 Sept. 3/3 The one good trouting loch in Scotland is Loch Leven.

**c.** as *pres. pple.* (chiefly after *go*).

*a* **1845** HOOD *To I. Walton* 65 Sham flies to go trolling and trouting. **1866** ALGER *Solit. Nat. & Man* III. 181 The loneliness of Izaak Walton trouting in a secluded glen. **1899** *Q. Rev.* Jan. 88 At Villeneuve he goes trouting in the dark with the servant of the inn.

**Troutlet** (trau·tlėt). [f. as prec. + -LET.] A little or tiny trout. Also *attrib.*

**1829** HOOD *Eugene Aram* i, There were some that ran and some that leapt, Like troutlets in a pool. **1879** SENIOR *Trav. & Trout Antipodes* (1880) 121 By the 15th of June three thousand young salmon and fifty troutlet immigrants were swimming about, strong, contented, and merry. **1881** G. ALLEN *Vignettes fr. Nat., Mountain Tarn* 175 If ever a young Llyn Gwernant troutlet..leaps the cascades.

**Troutling** (trau·tliŋ). [f. as prec. + -LING[1].] = prec.

*a* **1739** JARVIS *Quix.* I. I. ii, If there be many troutlings,.. they will supply the place of one trout. **1856** 'STONEHENGE' *Brit. Sports* I. v. iii. §13 In using the Spinning-Tackle with the parr-tail or troutling as a bait, it is spun exactly as for trout. **1889** H. C. PENNELL *Fishing* 100 The catching and eating of half a dozen troutlings.

**Trouty**, *sb.*: see after TROUT *sb.*[1]

**Trouty** (trau·ti), *a.* [f. TROUT *sb.*[1] + -Y.] Full of, abounding in, or containing trout.

**1676** COTTON *Walton's Angler* II. ii. 17 Little inconsiderable Rivers, as Awber, Eroways, and the like, scarce worth naming, but Trouty too. **1831** *Blackw. Mag.* XXX. 965 Heavens! among the gravel what a trouty congregation! **1883** STEVENSON *Across the Plains* i. (1892) 74 Every trouty pool along that mountain river.

**b.** Speckled like a trout.

**1895** [implied in TROUTINESS].

‖ **Trouvaille** (truvā·ly'). [Fr., f. *trouver* to find.] A lucky find; a windfall.

[**1753** LADY LUXBOROUGH *Lett. to Shenstone* 12 Dec., I.. should else have stolen a word from the French and have said *une trouvaille.*] **1842** THACKERAY *Profess. Fitz-Boodle* i, The *plebs* have robbed us of that trade among others, nor, I confess, do I much grudge them their *trouvaille.* **1848** — *Van. Fair* xi, My dear, you are a perfect *trouvaille.* **1881** *Blackw. Mag.* Apr. 523 The trouvaille proved to be the first edition of Shakspere.

‖ **Trouvère** (truvę̄·r, -ẹ·r), **trouveur** (truvö̆r). [OF. *trovere, -eur, truveur* (12th c. in Godef.), F. *trouvère, trouveur* (= Prov. *trobaire*), f. *trouver*: cf. TROUBADOUR.] One of a school of poets who flourished in Northern France from the 11th to the 14th c., whose works are chiefly epic in character. They produced the *chansons de geste, fabliaux*, etc. Cf. TROUBADOUR.

**1795** SOUTHEY *Joan of Arc* IV. 175 Meantime the Trouveur struck the harp; he sung Of Lancelot Du Lake. **1833** LONGF. *Outre-Mer* Prose Wks. 1886 I. 94 The great mass of the poetry of the Trouvères is of a narrative or epic character. **1887** LOWELL *Old Eng. Dram.* (1892) 7 One French Miracle Play of the thirteenth century, by the trouvère Rutebeuf. **1889** DOYLE *Micah Clarke* 208 A king of bards and trouveurs.

**Trouwe, Trouzed**, obs. ff. TROW *v.*, TROUSED.

**Trove**: see TREASURE-TROVE. Also short for *treasure-trove*, in sense 'a valuable find'.

**1888** KIPLING *Plain Tales* xiii. 94 The value of her trove struck her, and she cast about for the best method of using it. **1901** — *Kim* i. 11 Delighted as a child at each new trove. **1909** G. W. YOUNG *Wind & Hill* Ded., A kingdom..More rich than childhood's fairy trove.

**Trove**, obs. Sc. and north. form of TURF.

**Trover** (trōᵘ·vəɹ). *Law.* [subst. use of OF. *trover* (11th c.), F. *trouver* pres. inf., to find.] The act of finding and assuming possession of any personal property; hence (in full, *action of trover*), an action at law to recover the value of personal property illegally converted by another to his own use.

Originally the action was brought for damages against one who had found and refused to give up the goods of the plaintiff on demand; this refusal constituted 'conversion' (CONVERSION 7); hence the action was called *trover and conversion.* Later, the finding became a legal fiction, and it is now only necessary to prove the ownership and detention of the goods.

**1594** WEST *2nd Pt. Symbol., Chancerie* § 148 They came to the handes and possession of your poore suppliant.. by way of trover. **1615, 1712, 1765** [see CONVERSION 7]. **1678** BUTLER *Hud.* III. iii. 648 Whether I should..bring my Action of Conversion And Trover for my Goods? **1749** FIELDING *Tom Jones* XII. iv, Some perhaps would have given nothing [for the pocket-book] and left the Fellow to his Action of Trover. **1848** ARNOULD *Mar. Insur.* I. iv. (1866) 195 The policy, when effected, becomes in law the property of the assured, who may maintain trover for it. **1876** LOWELL *Among my Bks.* Ser. II. 323 In this sense the author of a dictionary might bring an action of trover against every other author who used his words.

† **Tro·vy**, *int. Obs.* [?a. OF. *trové*, pa. pple. of *trover*, F. *trouver* to find.] ? A call in hawking.

*a* **1529** SKELTON *Ware the Hauke* 116 With troll, cytrace, and trouy, They ranged, hankin bouy.

† **Trow** (trōᵘ), *sb.*[1] *Obs. rare.* [f. TROW *v.* (cf. Norse, Sw., Dan. *tro*).]

**1.** Belief; faith, trust.

*c* **1300** *Cursor M.* 22722 (Edin.) Þai þat war in dred and dout, Þar-of wit trow [*v. rr.* trouth, trouþe] he broht þaim out. [**1883** G. STEPHENS *Bugge's Stud. N. Mythol.* 149 Teaching of the new trow by help of the old.]

**2.** Fancy, supposition.

**14..** *Beryn* 38 For they that loven so passyngly, such trowes þey have echone. *a* **1536** *Calisto & Melib.* A iv, Her lyttyll handis in meane maner this is no trow.

**3.** Faith as pledged, covenant: = TROTH *sb.* 2.

**1515** *Acc. Ld. High Treas. Scot.* V. 40 For keeping the day of trow. **1634** *Malory's Arthur* IX. viii. (1816) I. 375 Then sir Plenorius yielded him and his tower, and all his prisoners at his will; and then sir Launcelot received him, and took his trow [1470-85 trouthe].

**Trow** (trōᵘ, *locally* trōu, trau), *sb.*[2] *local.* [Dial. variant of TROUGH.] A name for various kinds of boats or barges: *spec.* **a.** Formerly, on the Severn, a large flat-bottomed sailing barge; **b.** in the south of Scotland and north of England, a double canoe or boat used in spearing salmon by torch-light (also *pl.* const. as *sing.*): see quot. 1825 (? *obs.*); **c.** on the south coast of England, a small flat-bottomed boat used in herring-fishing. **d.** *attrib.*, as *trow-fisher, -lock*; also TROWMAN.

*c* **1330** R. BRUNNE *Chron. Wace* (Rolls) 10218 Arthur.. gadered botes, chalans, & trowes. **1479** *Office Mayor of Bristol* in *Eng. Gilds* (1870) 424 Such as bryngeth whete to towne, as wele in trowys, as otherwyse, by lande and by watir. **1778** WESLEY *Wks.* (1872) XI. 144 Are there fewer trows or barges employed on rivers and canals? **1825** JAMIESON, *Trows*,..used in Roxb. and other southern shires, to denote two pieces of wood, each formed like the half or section of an ellipsis, fenced with upright boards, so as to prevent the entrance of water. These two are conjoined... An interstice is left between the two sections, so that the water is seen distinctly through it. This sort of vessel..is used..in night-fishing on rivers for salmon. **1835** 'STEPHEN OLIVER' *Rambles Northumb.* 154 'The trows'..used in spearing salmon in parts of the river where they cannot be taken with a net. The trows consist of..two narrow boats,..connected at the top by a piece of flat board. *Ibid.* 155 Some of the old trow-fishers here are of opinion [etc.]. **1838** SIMMS *Public Wks. Gt. Brit.* ii. 14 The trow-lock [in the Gloucester and Berkeley canal] is eighty-one feet six inches long. **1875** *Bristol Times* 17 June (E.D.D.), The Fanny was a ketch-rigged (two-masted) trow, of 120 tons,..and was used for trading purposes. **1888** ELWORTHY *W. Somerset Word-bk.* s. v., On the south coast about Sidmouth a small fishing-boat is a trow. **1899** *Daily News* 13 Feb. 7/3 The trow 'Flower of the Severn',..moored in the river, was carried away by the tide and wrecked.

† **Trow**, *sb.*[3] *Obs. rare.* Also trew. [a. OF. *trëud, trëu, trou*, etc. (Roland, 11th c.):—L. *tribūt-um* TRIBUTE.] = TREWAGE, toll.

*c* **1380** *Sir Ferumb.* 1732 ȝe mote furst..þe truwage make fyn þat to þis brigge longeþ..do tell me wat is þe trow. *Ibid.* 4471 Tel me, sire,..Of þys passage what ys þe trow? *Ibid.* 4477 My trew þay sayde þay wolde pay.

**Trow** (trou), *sb.*[4] *Orkney* and *Shetl.* [= Swed. *troll*: see TROLL *sb.*[2]] = TROLL *sb.*[2]

**1640** *Orkney Witch Trial* in *Abbotsford Cl. Misc.* I. 167 ȝe ansuered hir againe, that it was but the Trow that haid gripped her. **1643** *ibid.* 173 Knoweing that the said Thomas was lying seik in his hous, ȝe said that it was the sea trow or spirit that was lying vpoun him. **1701** BRAND *Descr. Orkney* etc. (1703) 115 They tell us that several such Creatures do appear to Fishers at Sea, particularly such as they call *Sea-Trowes.* **1822** SCOTT *Pirate* v, Other [magicians] dealt with spirits of a different and less odious class—the ancient dwarfs, called, in Zetland, Trows, or Drows, the modern fairies, and so forth. **1868** D. GORRIE *Summ. & Wint. Orkneys* v. 168 The trows, or drows...resembled the *daoine shith* of the Highlanders, in the malevolent feelings which they..entertained towards mankind. **1883** R. M. FERGUSSON *Rambling Sk. Far North* xvii. 121 It was an unlucky moment when a fisherman cast his eyes on a seatrow; panic and fear seized him.

**Trow** (trōᵘ), *v. arch.* Forms: *α.* 1 trúwian, 4 truu, 4–5 tru, 4–6 (8–9 *Sc.*) true. *β.* 1 tréowan, tréowian, 3 treowe, 3–6 (9 *Sc.*) trew, 4 ? *Sc.* treu. *γ.* 3–5 trowen, (3 (*Orm.*) trowwenn, 4 trouwe), 3–6 (8 *Sc.*) trou, 4–7 trowe, (4 *Sc.* throw, throu), 5 troue, 5–7 tro, (8 tro'), 5, 9 *Sc.* troo, 6–7 troe, troa, 4– trow. *δ.* (*north. dial.*) 4 trau, (tray), 4–5 traue, trawe, traw, (5 traywe). Pa. t. and pple. **trowed** (trōᵘd); also *pa. t.* 3–5 -ede, 4–6 *Sc.* -it, etc.; 4 troud, 4–6 trowd, 6 troude; *pa. pple.* 4 troud, troude, trod, trawet, 5 trawt; (4 (?) trowen). [OE. had more than one type: (1) OE. *trúwian*, f. *trúwa* sb. 'faith, belief' = OS. *trûon* (MLG. *truwe*), OHG. *trû(u)ên* (MHG. *trûen, truuen*, Ger. *trauen*), ON. *trúa* (Sw. and Norw. *tro*), Goth. *trauan*, OTeut. **trûwian*, from base *trū-*, orig. 'strong, firm, sure'; (2) OE. *tréowan, tréowian*, from *tréowe* 'faith, belief', with the ablaut grade **trēu(w)*; cf. OS. *tre(u)wa*, OWFris. *trouwa* (MLG., MDu., Du. *trouwen* to believe, trust, espouse). Of the two OE. forms, *trúwian* was the earlier and more usual; but its place was mainly taken in ME. by *trowen*, with its variants *traue, traw*, from *tréow(i)an*. In some of the ME. forms, *trúwian* and *tréow(i)an* appear to run together.]

† **1.** *trans.* (orig. *intr.* with *dat.*; cf. 2). To trust, have confidence in, believe (a person or thing).

*α.* *c* **897** K. ÆLFRED *Gregory's Past. C.* ix. 58 Swiðe eaðe mæg on smyltre sæ unȝelæred scipstiora ȝenoh ryhte stieran, ac se ȝelæreda hine ne truwað on ðære hreon sæ & on ðæm miclan stormum. **13..** *Cursor M.* 4366 (Cott.) And for he es traist o mi leute Of all his god he trues me. **1728** RAMSAY *Fables* xii. 12 His colour's green, If ane may true his ain twa een.

*β.* *Beowulf* (Z.) 1166 ȝehwylc hiora his ferhþe treowde, þæt he hæfde mod micel. *c* **888** K. ÆLFRED *Boeth.* xxxvii. § 2 Ymnað ealle endemes ða ðe hiora æringe trewað. *a* **1000** *Cædmon's Gen.* 2318 Ic eow treowiȝe ȝif ȝe þæt tacen ȝegað. *c* **1175** *12th c. Hom.* 136 ȝyf he þa bote deþ.. & on Gode trywiȝe. **1375** BARBOUR *Bruce* II. 326 He that will trew His fa, It sall him sum tyme rew.

*γ.* *c* **1250** *Gen. & Ex.* 1092 Loth hem warnede,..Oc he ne troweden him. *c* **1275** LAY. 3413 Wan hii þe troueþ alre best. **13..** *Cursor M.* 5212 (Gött.) Þis es þe soth, trou [*Cott.* tru] ȝe me. *c* **1400** MAUNDEV. (1839) xx. 221 And all be it that sum men wil not trow me, but holden it for fable. **1500–20** DUNBAR *Poems* xxxii. 40 The silly thing trowd him, allace! The lame gaif creddence to the tod. *c* **1600** MONTGOMERIE *Cherrie & Slae* 842 Suld not I trow my ain twa een? *a* **1829** *Parcy Reed* xviii. in Child *Ballads* VII. (1890) 26/2 The three false Halls of Girsonsfield, They'll never be trusted or trowed again.

*δ.* **13..** *Cursor M.* 5151 (Cott.) If þat þou noght traues me, ..come þi-self and se. *c* **1460** *Towneley Myst.* iii. 45 To those that wille hym trawe.

† **b.** *refl.* To trust oneself *to* a person. *Obs. rare.*

*α.* *c* **950** *Lindisf. Gosp.* John ii. 24 Se hælend ne lefde *vel* ne truȝude hine seolfne him *vel* ðæm, foreðon he uiste alle.

*γ.* **1388** WYCLIF *ibid.*, But Jhesus trowide not hym silf to hem, for he knewe alle men.

† **2.** *intr.* with prep. To believe *in* or *on*; to have confidence *in*; to trust *to*. *Obs.* or *rare arch.*

*α.* *c* **1000** ÆLFRIC *Saints' Lives* xxv. 446 Ða burhware.. truwodon to þam wealle. *c* **1300** *Cursor M.* 19883 (Edin.) Truis tu in god?

*β.* *c* **1000** *Ags. Ps.* (Th.) cxvii[i]. 8 God ys on Dryhten ȝeorne to þenceanne, þonne on mannan wese mod to treowianne.

*γ.* *c* **1205** LAY. 2351 He nom his enne hired mon þe he wel trowede on. *c* **1330** R. BRUNNE *Chron. Wace* (Rolls) 2855 Trowe til vs & oure consayl! **1340–70** *Alex. & Dind.* 829 ȝif alle þe lorus..Ben trewe to be trowen on & trysty to leue. **1375** BARBOUR *Bruce* I. 490 Gyff that ȝe will trow to me. *c* **1385** CHAUCER *L. G. W.* 1707 (*Lucrece*) It is no nede To trowyn on the word but on the dede. *c* **1400** tr. *Secreta Secret., Gov. Lordsh.* vi. 52 A trew discret man..to whom he may trowe to ordeyne þe besynesse of his godys. *c* **1449** PECOCK *Repr.* I. xviii. (Rolls) 102 Thei wolen not trowe to his teching. *c* **1460** *Towneley Myst.* xx. 434 Bot trow in god, that you has wroght. *c* **1470** HENRY *Wallace* II. 235 In Inglismen, allace, quhi suld we trow? **1522** *World & Child* C vij, The xij. artycles of the fayth That mankynde must on trowe. **1552** ABP. HAMILTON *Catech.* (1884) 14 We suld trow in the sonne of God. **1870** MORRIS *Earthly Par.* III. IV. 369 Vague tales, wherein I was well fain to trow.

*δ.* **13..** *Cursor M.* 13671 (Cott.) Traus [*Fairf.* trawes] þou in godd sun or nai?

† **b.** *trans.* To believe in (a doctrine, etc.). *Obs.*

**1340–70** *Alex. & Dind.* 841 Hit semeþ..Þat ȝe no giuen of no gome no none godus trowe. *c* **1380** WYCLIF *Wks.* (1880)

422 Oon article of bileue..is to trowe hooly chirche. *c* 1400 MAUNDEV. (Roxb.) xv. 66 Þe Sarzenes trowes þe incarnacioun. 1513 DOUGLAS *Æneis* vi. Prol. 81 We trow a God, regnand in personis thre.

**3.** *trans.* To believe (a statement, etc.); to give credence to, accept as true or trustworthy.

α. *a* 1300 *Cursor M.* 14708 (Cott.) Qua wil noght tru [*Gött.* trou, *Fairf.* traw, *Trin.* trowe] þat i tell.

β. *c* 1250 *Gen. & Ex.* 2037 Pvtifar trewið hise wiwes tale.

γ. *c* 1200 ORMIN Ded. 134, I wollde bliþeliȝ þatt all Engglisshe lede..shollde itt trowwenn. 1413 *Pilgr. Sowle* (Caxton) I. iii. (1859) 4 Such thynges wold I nought haue trowyd, yf I had nought seen it my self. 1450–80 tr. *Secreta Secret.* xvi. 14 Trowe not lightly alle that that men wille telle the. 1536 BELLENDEN *Cron. Scot.* (1821) II. 272 We may nocht trow ane wourd he sayis. 1605 SHAKS. *Lear* I. iv. 135 Speake lesse then thou knowest,..Learne more then thou trowest. 1816 SCOTT *Antiq.* xxi, I hae garr'd him trow mony a queer tale. *a* 1818 MACNEILL *Poems* (1844) 102 She trou'd ilka word that the fause loon did say. 1876 MORRIS *Sigurd* II. 79 Men trowed his every word.

δ. 13.. *E. E. Allit. P.* B. 662 Saré laȝez, Not trawande þe tale.

†**b.** with *obj.* and *compl.* To believe or suppose (a thing or person) to be (so and so); also with *compl. inf.* (*to be* .., or *to do* something). *Obs.*

γ. *a* 1275 *Prov. Ælfred* 164 in *O. E. Misc.* 113 For wanne he is lif alre beste trowen, þenne sal he letin lif his oȝene. *c* 1400 tr. *Secreta Secret., Gov. Lordsh.* xxix. 63 Yf þe nedys of a woman, drawe to þe to here þat þow trowys trewe, and þat þou demys good. *c* 1460 *Play Sacram.* 559, I trowe best we mak a crye. 1581 A. HALL *Iliad* IV. 69 Thou Agamemnon trowes Vs dastards and faint hearted folke. 1596 DALRYMPLE tr. *Leslie's Hist. Scot.* VIII. (S.T.S.) II. 59 The chanceller trowit al to be trew.

δ. 13.. *E. E. Allit. P.* A. 282, I trawed my perle don out of dawez. 1432–50 tr. *Higden* (Rolls) II. 121 Of whom somme men trawe that cite to have taken name.

†**c.** Phr. *To trow* (in passive sense): to be believed or thought (so and so). Also *at trow* (AT *prep.* 39), in quot. *a* 1340, worthy of belief, credible.

13.. *Cursor M.* 27126 (Cott.) And es he for a fule to trou [*Fairf.* traw]. *a* 1340 HAMPOLE *Psalter* xcii. 7 *Testimonia sua credibilia facta sunt nimis*..þi biddyngis ere mykil made at trow. 1596 SPENSER *F. Q.* v. ii. 34 How much it doth over-flowe, Or faile thereof, so much is more then iust to trowe.

**4.** with *obj. cl.* To believe, think, be of opinion, suppose, imagine; sometimes, to believe confidently, feel sure, be assured. † *Trow you what* .. (?) 'what do you think..?'

α. *c* 1000 *Ælfric's Past. Ep.* iii. in Thorpe *Ags. Laws* II. 364 Ic truwiȝe þeah þæt sum wurðe abrird þurh God. *a* 1818 MACNEILL *Poems* (1844) 96, I pree'd it aft as ye may true!

γ. *c* 1200 ORMIN 6946 Þeȝȝ munndenn trowwenn þatt te child Josæþess sune wære. 1362 LANGL. *P. Pl.* A. I. 133 Þis I trouwe beo treuþe! *a* 1400 *Prymer* (1891) 83 Trowest þou auȝt that a deed man schal lyue aȝen? 14.. *Cov. Corp. Christi Pl.* I. 883, I tro there wolbe a carefull syght. *c* 1470 HENRY *Wallace* II. 391, I trow thow be sum spy. 1526 TINDALE *Luke* xvii. 9 Doeth he thanke that servaunt be cause he did that which was commaunded vnto hym? I trowe not. 1533 BELLENDEN *Livy* III. v. (S.T.S.) 256 Þe hevynnis apperit birnand; The erde trymblit..; men trowis ane kow spak. 1588 SHAKS. *L. L. L.* v. ii. 279 Trow you what he call'd me? 1590 SPENSER *F. Q.* II. v. 13 And henceforth by this daies ensample trow, That hasty wroth, and heedlesse hazardry, Doe breede repentaunce late, and lasting infamy. 1613 SHAKS. *Hen. VIII*, I. i. 184 As I troa Which I doe well; for I am sure [etc.]. 1637–50 Row *Hist. Kirk* (Wodrow Soc.) 451, I used..to..cast up the whyte of my eyes, so that any bodie wold have trowed that I was blind. 1786 BURNS *A Dream* ii, The poets..Wad gar you trow ye ne'er do wrang. 1818 SCOTT *Rob Roy* iv, I trow he's a dealer in cattle. 1872 THIRLWALL *Rem.* (1878) III. 254 Can anything be more clearly proved..? I trow not.

δ. *c* 1400 *Destr. Troy* 3351 Ne trawes not, tru lady, þat I take wolde Thy ladyship to losse.

**b.** Parenthetically or at the end of a sentence (often merely expletive), as *I trow* (in assertions) = 'I suppose', 'I ween'; †also rarely in questions (where the sense is not clear).

α. 13.. *Cursor M.* 371 (Cott.) Þarfor scaples was it [I] tru [*Fairf.* traw].

γ. [1423 JAS. I *Kingis Q.* xi, Bot now, how trowe ȝe? suich a fantasye Fell me to mynd.] *c* 1491 *Chast. Goddes Chyld.* 35 Thyse wordes I trowe shall suffyse. 1549 LATIMER *Ploughers* (Arb.) 20 Who trowe you is a faythefull seruante? 1577 NORTHBROOKE *Dicing* (1843) 71 No man is so foolishe, I trowe, so to doe. 1598 SHAKS. *Merry W.* I. iv. 140 Who's there, I troa? 1676 MARVELL *Gen. Councils* Wks. (Grosart) IV. 138 Did not this Historian, trow you, deserve [etc.]? 1678 BUNYAN *Pilgr.* I. 174 But I tro, you will put some difference between Little-faith and the Kings Champion. 1748 RICHARDSON *Clarissa* (1811) IV. xxxv. 224 What is become of Lord M. I trow, that he writes not to me? 1798 COLERIDGE *Anc. Mar.* VII. iii, Why, this is strange, I trow! 1852 H. ROGERS *Ecl. Faith* (1853) 438 A sceptic is not to be startled by paradoxes, I trow.

†**c.** Also simply *trow* (ellipt. for *I trow* or *trow you*). *Obs.*

1553 *Respublica* IV. ii. 998 Was not he drownde, trowe, last yeare? 1601 B. JONSON *Ev. Man in Hum.* (Qo.) IV. i. I iv, Where are these villaines troe? 1620 SHELTON *Quix.* II. x. 57 And haue you euer seene her, trow? 1636 HEYWOOD *Challenge* I. Wks. 1874 V. 14 How came you by them tro? honestly? 1741 RICHARDSON *Pamela* I. 57 What could you have done to him, tro'?

†**5.** *intr.* or *absol.* To believe; to hold a belief; to have or exercise faith. *Obs.*

α. *c* 1300 *Cursor M.* 19530 (Edin.) Simon [Magus] lete als þoȝ he truwid, And baptizid him.

γ. *c* 1200 ORMIN 2820 & tu full æðiȝ wurrþenn arrt, Forr þatt tu mihhtesst trowwenn. *c* 1330 R. BRUNNE *Chron. Wace* (Rolls) 7358 He asked þenne how þey trowd, & what þer Godes name hight. *c* 1440 *York Myst.* xxx. 162 What man þat trowis and baptised be. 1573 TYRIE *Refut.* in *Cath. Tractates* (S.T.S.) 12 Befoir a thousand yeiris..wes thair peple of God that trowit as thai do.

†**6.** *trans.* To expect, hope. Usually with *inf.*; less commonly with *obj. cl.*; rarely with *simple obj.*

γ. 1340–70 *Alisaunder* 919 Þei trowed no tresoun untruly too haue. *c* 1470 HENRY *Wallace* IX. 1266 Fra Fyff was tynt, the war thai trowyt to speid. 1470–85 MALORY *Arthur* x. xii. 432 Shewe me the Knyght, & I trowe I shalle bere hym doune. 1575 *Durham Depos.* (Surtees) 301 She..was sore sike.., so that none of hir frendes trowed hir life. *c* 1600 MONTGOMERIE *Sonn.* xxviii. 11 Vhair sho [an ass] troude hir maister suld hir treit, They battound hir.

†**7.** To prove to be true; to vouch for; to verify; to ascertain. *Obs. rare.*

β. *a* 901 *Laws of Alfred* c. 33 ȝif he hine treowan [*v. r.* treowian] wille.

γ. *c* 1330 R. BRUNNE *Chron.* (1810) 258 Þe letter forth þei nam, to trowe þer sayng. *Ibid.* 339 Blissed be þou God,..Þi word is wele trod, I say it, bi William. 1603 *Philotus* iii, First try the treuth, then may ȝe trow, Gif I mynd to desaue.

**Trow**: see THROW *v.*[1], TREE, TROLL, TROUGH.

†**Trow·able**, *a. Obs.* [f. TROW *v.* + -ABLE.] That can be 'trowed' or believed; credible.

*a* 1340 HAMPOLE *Psalter* xcii. 7 Þi witnessyngis ere made trowabile ful mykil. *c* 1440 *Alphabet of Tales* 154 It is not trowable at he þat I hafe luffid so lang, att I sulde not be luffid of hym agayn. 1533 BELLENDEN *Livy* IV. viii. (S.T.S.) 75 It is als nocht trowabil þat sic exempil suld be Introducit be ane patriciane.

**Trowage**, variant of TREWAGE *Obs.*

**Trowan, -ande, -ane, -ant**, obs. ff. TRUANT.

**Trowandise, -yse**, etc., var. TRUANDISE *Obs.*

**Trowch**, obs. Sc. form of TROUGH.

**Trowe**, var. THROW *sb.*[1] *Obs.*; obs. f. TROW, TRUE.

**Trowean**, obs. form of TRUANT.

†**Trowed**, *ppl. a. Obs.* [f. TROW *v.* + -ED[1].] Believed to be such; supposed, reputed.

*c* 1410 LOVE *Bonavent. Mirr.* xv. (1908) 100 Joseph..his trowed fader.

**Trowel** (trau·ĕl), *sb.* Forms: 4–5 trowelle, 4–7 truel, 5 trowylle, 7 trewel, 5–8 trowell, 6 truell, 6–7 trewell, 8 trouel, 5– trowel; also 4 trulle, 5 troll(e, 7 trull, trule. [ME. *truel*, a. OF. *truele* (13th c.), F. *truelle* (14th c.), ad. vulgar or late L. *truella* (1163 in Du Cange), for cl.L. *trulla*, dim. of *trua* stirring-spoon, skimmer, ladle, whence the monosyllabic form.]

**1.** A tool consisting of a flat (or, less commonly, rounded) plate of metal or wood, of various shapes, attached to a short handle; used by masons, bricklayers, plasterers, and others for spreading, moulding, or smoothing mortar, cement, and the like.

*To lay it on with a trowel*, to express a thing coarsely or bluntly; now *spec.* to flatter excessively or grossly.

1344 *Pipe Roll* 18 *Edw. III*, m. 45 (P.R.O.) In..iiij. hamers, iiij. Trowellis, vj hirdellis pro lymeputtes..xxx. ladlis pro cemento fundendo. 1382 WYCLIF *Amos* vii. 7 Loo! the Lord stondynge on a wall teerid, or morterd, and in the hond of hym a truel [*v.r.* trulle] of masoun. 1398 TREVISA *Barth. De P. R.* II. iv. (Harl. MS. 614) lf. 8 b/1 Aungels..ben seen to haue trollis & hangynge plometis and mesuris & towles & werke men. *c* 1440 *Pallad. on Husb.* I. 415 The parget of thy wough be strong & bryght; The trewel first ful ofte hit most distreyne. 1533 ELYOT *Cast. Helthe* Pref. (1539) 1, I toke my penne in the stede of a truell. *c* 1570 *Pride & Lowl.* (1841) 32 A Bricklayer,..A trewell at his gyrdle weared he. 1600 SHAKS. *A. Y. L.* I. ii. 112 Well said, that was laid on with a trowell. 1693 EVELYN *De la Quint. Compl. Gard.* II. 110 The said Gum must be kept hot,..to be apply'd with a kind of Wooden Trule. 1719 *Free-thinker* No. 118 ¶ 8 Mr. Thornhill [cannot] paint the Cupolo of Paul's with a Trowel. 1836 THIRLWALL *Greece* III. xxii. 237 They supplied the place both of hods and trowels with their hands. 1887 RUSKIN *Præterita* II. x. 362 The instrument I finally decided to be the most difficult of management was the trowel.

**b.** A culinary ladle or slice of this shape. Cf. *trowel-slicer* in 2.

1773 *Lond. Chron.* 7 Sept. 248/3 Fish and pudding trowells. 1855 H. CLARKE *Dict.*, Fish-trowel.

**c.** A tool of this kind used in gardening, having a hollow, scoop-like, semi-cylindrical blade.

1796 C. MARSHALL *Garden.* iv. (1813) 52 Plants..are best put in by a small spade or trowel. 1846 J. BAXTER *Libr. Pract. Agric.* (ed. 4) II. 119 The compound is firmly pressed into the moulds with a gardener's trowel. 1855 DELAMER *Kitch. Gard.* (1861) 16 The English trowel is excellent for many purposes; but besides it, it will be found convenient to have one or two long, narrow ones.

**d.** An elastic flat steel instrument used in spreading the paint in the manufacture of oilcloth.

1881 [implied in TROWELLER].

**e.** See quot.

1892 GREENER *Breech Loader* 180 A properly-made trowel will load millions of cartridges before the holes become so worn that it has to be discarded. The author uses this counting trowel in loading all his cartridges.

**2.** *attrib.* and *Comb.*, as *trowel-handling*, *-planting*, *-slicer* (cf. 1 b); *trowel-shaped* adj.; **trowel-bayonet**, a bayonet resembling a mason's trowel, which may be used as a light entrenchment tool, or when detached from the rifle, as a hatchet (Knight *Dict. Mech.* 1877); **trowel-beak**, a bird, a Sumatran broadbill, *Corydon sumatranus* (*Cent. Dict.* 1891); **trowel-gauge**, an instrument for setting the nippers on a cotton-combing machine; **trowel-man**, one who uses a trowel; *spec.* a mason, bricklayer, or the like; also *fig.*

1902 THORNLEY *Cotton Combing Mach.* 151 In setting the nippers great assistance is rendered by the use of a *trowel gauge. 1887 RUSKIN *Præterita* II. x. 362 *note*, A piece of *trowel-handling as subtle as spreading the mortar under a brick. 1632 B. JONSON *Magn. Lady* II. vii, A hard-handed, and stiff ignorance, worthy a *Trewel, or a Hammer-man. 1737 *Salmon's Country Builder's Estimator* (ed. 2) 69 A Trowel-man and Labourer..can perform one Rod of rough Work in five Days 1756 *Monitor* No. 73 II. 203 It has been the general defect of English politicians to proceed without a plan; ignorant trowel-men in the service of the state. 1815 J. SMITH *Panorama Sci. & Art* II. 657, 7. Furrow planting. .. 8. Dibbling. .. 9. *Trowel planting. 1776 WITHERING *Brit. Plants* (1796) III. 573 [*Cochlearia danica*] All the leaves *trowel-shaped. 1897 MARY KINGSLEY *W. Africa* 454 Broad, trowel-shaped, almost triangular daggers. 1862 *Catal. Internat. Exhib., Brit.* II. No. 6504 A very large bread knife, and *trowel slicer.

Hence **Trow·elful**, as much as can be taken up on a trowel (also *fig.*).

1580 HOLLYBAND *Treas. Fr. Tong*, s. v. *Truellée*, A trowell full of plaster or morter. 1801 LD. MINTO *Let.* in *Edin. Rev.* Apr. (1896) 405 Cramming Nelson with trowelfuls of flattery. 1843 LD. COCKBURN *Circuit Journeys* (1883) 184 Not one trowelful of lime.

**Trowel** (trau·ĕl), *v.* [f. prec. sb.]

**1.** *trans.* To spread, smooth, or dress (a surface) with or as with a trowel; to form or mould with a trowel; in quot. *c* 1670, to coat thickly *with*.

*c* 1670 LD. ORRERY in *Daily Chron.* 12 June (1903) 3/3 The Women are never old, for the Wrinkles are well filled up by Paint,..the Women trowel themselves with red. 1703 MOXON *Mech. Exerc.* 249 They finish the Plastering..either by Trowelling and brishing it over with fair Water, or else by laying a thin Coat of fine stuff..and..Trowelling and brishing it. 1774 GOLDSM. *Nat. Hist.* VIII. IV. iii. 99 They [wasps] stick their load of paste on that part where they make their walls and partitions; they tread it close with their feet, and trowel it with their trunks. 1842 *Civil Eng. & Arch. Jrnl.* V. 337/2 After being properly trowelled, it is jointed to imitate stone.

**2.** To put, place, or move (something) with or as with a trowel; to lay on with a trowel, i. e. thickly or clumsily; often *fig.* of flattery or laudation.

1772 NUGENT tr. *Hist. Friar Gerund* I. 502 The good gentleman trowels on himself the plaister of praise without reserve. 1792 COLERIDGE *Lett., to G. Coleridge* 24 If ever hog's lard is pleasing it is when our superiors trowel it on. 1841 THACKERAY *Men & Pictures* 111 The skies are trowelled on; the light-vapouring distances are as thick as plum-pudding. 1898 HOLLINGSHEAD *Gaiety Chron.* i. 45 Mortar and cement were trowelled into their proper places.

Hence **Trow·elled** *ppl. a.*; *trowelled stucco*, stucco of the best description intended to be painted; **Trow·elling** *vbl. sb.*; also **Trow·eller**, one who uses a trowel.

1823 P. NICHOLSON *Pract. Build.* 375 *Trowelled-stucco is a very neat kind of work, much used in dining-rooms, vestibules, stair-cases, &c. 1913 *Daily News* 31 Mar. 6 The roof ..has a fall of 5 in. in 13 ft. and was simply left with a trowelled finish. 1611 COTGR., *Truelleur*, a *Troweller; a Plaisterer, or any one that workes with a Trowell. 1881 *Instr. Census Clerks* (1885) 80 Floor Cloth, Oil Cloth Manufacture...Oil Skin Maker, Dealer. Silk Oiler. Trowler. 1630 *R. Johnson's Kingd. & Commw.* 598 Their Painting is meere steyning or *trowelling in respect of ours.

**Trowell**, obs. form of TROLL *sb.*[1]

**Trowe maddam**, var. TROLL-MADAM *Obs.*

**Trowent, -tyze**: see TRUANT, TRUANDISE.

†**Trow·er.** *Obs. rare*[−1]. In 4 truer(e, trawere. [f. TROW *v.* + -ER[1].] A believer.

*c* 1300 *Cursor M.* 21092 (Edin.) Thomas..þat he ne moȝte noȝte tru wiþ here, Wiþ eie he was made lele truer [*v. rr* truere, trawere].

**Trowes**, obs. pl. of TREE; obs. f. TRUCE.

**Trowet, Trowht**, obs. forms of TROUT, TROTH.

**Trowie** (trou·i), *a. Orkney* and *Shetl.* [f. TROW *sb.*[4] + -IE, -Y.] Of or pertaining to the 'trows' or trolls; elfin; also, influenced by a 'trow'. So **Trow·ist** (*nonce-wd.*), a person credited with acquaintance with 'trows' and power to avert their influence.

1793 *Statist. Acc. Scotl.* VII. 396 Sponges are found upon the shore in great plenty, shaped like a man's hand, and called by the people Trowie Gloves. 1825 JAMIESON, *Trowie* adj., sickly, *Orkn.*..Shall we view this as signifying 'under the malign influence of the Trow, or daemon'? 1840 *New Statist. Acc. Scot.* (1845) XV. 142 (*Shetland*) When a cow or sheep happens to turn sick or die, it is firmly believed.. that the real animal has been taken away and something of a trowie breed substituted in its place. 1895 J. J. HALDANE BURGESS *Shetland Folklore* 99 He at once sent for an old woman who was celebrated as a 'trowist'. *Ibid.* 101 He.. found lying on the ground and half-hidden among the heather, a beautifully-wrought 'trowie' dart or arrow.

**Trowing** (trōᵘ·iŋ), *vbl. sb. Obs.* or *arch.* [f. TROW *v.* + -ING[1].] The action of the verb TROW; belief; faith, creed; opinion, notion, idea. † *To trowing*, to be believed, worthy of belief (cf. *to trow*, TROW *v.* 3 c).

*a* 1300 *Cursor M.* 25088 (Cott.) To haf wit santes communing; Þis es a pointe of vr truing [*Gött.* truyng, *Fairf.* trowing]. 1303 R. BRUNNE *Handl. Synne* 498 For whan þou trowyst yn a fals þyng Þe deuyl hyt shewyþ for þat trowyng. 1387 TREVISA *Higden* (Rolls) III. 401 Nectanabus seide þis sawe, and was a wicche, and þerfore it is nevere þe bettre to trowynge. *Ibid.* V. 89 So seiþ martilogie, þat is more to trowynge [L. *credendum*] þan cronicles of auctours þat beeþ nouȝt i-knowe. *Ibid.* VI. 195 It is nouȝt to trowynge [L. *opinandum*] þat þis Iohn is the Ermyte. c 1400 Maundev. (Roxb.) xxxiv. 154 Þai be of diuerse lawes and diuerse trowyngs. c 1449 Pecock *Repr.* I. i. (Rolls) 5 Thre trowingis or opinions ben causis..of manie..errouris. 1491 Caxton *Vitas Patr.* I. c. (W. de W. 1495) 131 b/2 By the thynges passed he had some trowynge of those that were to come. c 1570 in Redforde *Play Wit & Sc.* (Shaks. Soc.) 57 Ever in trowing and never in knowinge.

So † **Trow·ing** *ppl. a. Obs.*, believing; in first quot. as *sb.* one who believes.

a 1300 *Cursor M.* 18719 (Cott.) Þe truand [*Fairf.* trawande] and þe baptist bath þai sal be saue. c 1400 *Apol. Loll.* 61 Crist is end of þe lawe to riȝtfulnes to ilk man trowing. 1483 *Cath. Angl.* 394/2 Trowinge, *credulus*.

**Trowith**, obs. f. Troth. **Trowkle**, obs. f. Truckle. **Trowl**, obs. f. Trawl, Troll, Trull.

**Trowlesworthite** (trōu·lz,wə̄ɹþəit). *Min.* [f. the name of Trowlesworthy Tor, Devonshire, where found: see -ite[1].] An altered granite in which fluorite, orthoclase, and tourmaline have taken the place of the original quartz, feldspar, and mica.

1884 Bonney in *Q. Jrnl. Geol. Soc.* XL. 7 A rock-specimen exhibited by Mr. R. N. Worth,..and by him named Trowlesworthite. It consisted chiefly of reddish orthoclase, purple fluor, and black schorl, in intimate association with quartz, and was found..as a loose block on Trowlesworthy Tor.

**Trow·ling**. *Orkney* and *Shetl.* [f. Trow *sb.*[4] + -ling[1].] A young or infant 'trow' or troll.

1840 *New Statist. Acc. Scot.* (1845) XV. 142 (*Shetland*) Females newly confined must..be watched..lest they be carried off to perform the office of wet-nurse to some trowling of gentle blood.

**Trowly**, obs. Sc. form of Truly.

**Trowman** (trōu·mæn). *local.* [f. Trow *sb.*[2] + Man *sb.*[1]] The master or captain of a trow: see Trow *sb.*[2] a

1429 *Rolls of Parlt.* IV. 345/2 The owners..and the saide trowmen. 1505 *Sel. Cas. Crt. Star Chamber* (Selden Soc.) I. 220 During which xl yeris I occupyed vppon the seide Ryuer as a Trowman. 1641 J. Taylor (Water P.) *Last Voy.* B vij, Usually much abused by Trow-men. 1752 *Deed* in Miss Jackson *Shropsh. Word-bk.* s.v., This Indenture made ..Between John Rogers of the Town of Shrewsbury..Trowman and [etc.].

**Trown, Trownsciown, Trowple, Trowse, Trowth**: see Throne, Truncheon, Tropel, Trouse, Truss, Troth.

**Troy**[1] (troi). The name of an ancient city in Asia Minor, besieged and taken by the Greeks; in comb. *Troy-bane, -jousting*; **Troy-fair, Troy-town** (also simply † **Troy**), *fig.* a scene of disorder or confusion (now *dial.*).

a 1520 *Vox Populi* 522 in Hazl. *E. P. P.* III. 286 And Pauper he above satte In the seate of Habrahams lappe, And was taken from thys Troye, To lyve allwaye with God in ioye. 1606 Holland *Sueton.* 130 He represented besides, many Cirq-games, .. interposing .. the Troie-justing and Turnament. 1652 Benlowes *Theoph.* I. xii, Does Troy-bane Hellen..with Angels share? 1678 Otway *Friendship in F.* v. i, And for the Cittern, if ever Troy Town were a Tune, he master'd it upon that Instrument. 1870 *N. & Q.* 4th Ser. VI. 300/1 Troy Fair. I heard this phrase lately employed..to describe a time of household confusion. *Ibid.* 401 In this part of Devonshire a room with its furniture disarranged is said to be 'like Troy Town'. 1880 *W. Cornwall Gloss., Troy town*, a maze; a labyrinth of streets. 'I lost my way; 'twas a regular Troy town'.

**Troy**[2] (troi). Forms: 4–6 **troye**, 5 **troie**, 5– **troy**; also *Sc.* 5–7 **trois**, 6 **troiss, troyis,** (**troce**). [The received opinion is that it took its name from a weight used at the fair of Troyes in France, which is favoured by the Scottish forms, *trois, troiss, troyis.*] *Troy weight* († *weight of Troy*), also ellipt. *Troy*: The standard system of weights used for the precious metals and precious stones; formerly also for bread. Also attrib., *troy ounce, pound*, etc. (also *ounce troy, pound troy*, etc.). Cf. Tower pound.

The pound troy contains 5760 grains, and is divided into 12 ounces. Cf. Avoirdupois.

1390–1 *Earl Derby's Exped.* (Camden) 100 Pro j chargeour, iij diocis, et j sawcere, ponderis xx marc. de troye. 1423 *Rolls of Parlt.* IV. 256/2 Silver is bought atte pris of xxxii s. the pound of troie. 1458 Agnes Paston in *P. Lett.* I. 422 To do make me vj. sponys, of viij. ounce of troy wyght. 1488–91 *Acc. Ld. High Treas. Scot.* I. 168 The cunȝeing of fifty tua Trois pundis and ane halue vnce of brokin siluer. 1542 Recorde *Gr. Artes* (1575) 202 Of Ounces after Troye rate ..12 doe make 1 pounde. 1565 *Reg. Privy Council Scot.* I. 413 That thair be cunyeit ane penny of silver..of wecht ane unce, troce wecht. 1573 *Aberdeen Regr.* (1848) II. 10 A troiss pund of brass, pryce v. s. 1582 *Reg. Privy Council Scot.* III. 481 Quhilk [penny] suld wey ane quarter unce troyis wecht. 1641 in R. W. Cochran-Patrick *Rec. Coinage Scotl.* (1876) I. Introd. 32 The once trois of bullione. 1688 R. Holme *Armoury* III. 259/2 [By] Troy Weight..are Weighed ..Bread, and all manner of Corn and Grain. 1825 J. Nicholson *Operat. Mechanic* 759 Take an exact troy ounce of the ore. 1868 Rogers *Pol. Econ.* iii. (1876) 29 In the rough, it may be said that the cost of producing a pound Troy of gold is fifteen-and-a-half times as great as that of producing a pound Troy of silver.

**b.** *fig.* in allusion to the pound troy being less than the pound avoirdupois.

1599 Massinger, etc. *Old Law* IV. i, There was Cressid was Troy weight, and Nell was avoirdupois. 1647 Ward *Simp. Cobler* (1843) 38 Heads.., who will weigh Rules by Troyweight, and not by the old Haber-du-pois. 18.. J. Parker in W. Adamson *Life* i. (1902) 4 No namby-pamby speaker, weighing words in troy scales and mincing syllables as if afraid of them. 1906 *Daily Chron.* 21 Dec. 9/2 Years and years of troy-weight legislation have left unrectified the avoirdupois anomaly.

† **Troyan(e, -en(e**: see Trojan. Hence † **Troy·anish** (troi-) *a.* and *sb.* = Trojan. So † **Troy·ish** *a. Obs.*

c 893 K. Ælfred *Oros.* I. x. § 4 Pentesilia, sio on þæm *Troianiscan ȝefeohte mære ȝewearð. c 1205 Lay. 416 Þat Troynisce folc. *Ibid.* 809 Iherden hit Troynisce [c 1275 Troynisse]. c 1384 Chaucer *Ho. Fame* I. 201 Iuno..That hast y-hated al thy lyfe Alle the Troianysshe [*v. r.* Troyanyssh] bloode. 1412–20 Lydg. *Chron. Troy* III. 219 On Troyanysche grounde. a 900 tr. *Bæda's Eccl. Hist.* IV. xvi. (1890) 307 ȝelice þy *troiscan wæle. c 1205 Lay. 410 Ah he hefde muchele strengþe of meren his cunne, of þan Troyscen monnen.

**Troycht**, obs. Sc. f. Trough. **Troylebaston**, var. Trailbaston. **Troyne**, obs. f. Throne, Tron, trone. **Troyte**, obs. f. Troat, Trout *sb.*[1]; obs. Sc. f. Trough.

**Tru**, obs. form of Trow *v.*, Truce, True.

**Truage**, variant of Trewage *Obs.*

**Truan**, obs. form of Truant.

**Truancy** (trū·ănsi). Also **truantcy.** [f. Truant + -cy.] The action, or an act, of playing truant; truant conduct or practice.

1784 Mme. D'Arblay *Diary* 24 Apr., I had many flattering reproaches for my late truancy from these parties. 1858 Carlyle *Fredk. Gt.* VII. iii. (1872) II. 270 Suggesting to him idle truantcies or worse. 1905 W. B. Boulton *Life Gainsborough* 12 The boy..brought back..a collection of sketches as the result of the day's truancy.

† **Truandal.** *Obs. rare.* [OF. *truandaille*, f. *truand*, assemblage of beggars.] *pl.* Beggars; camp-followers.

1523 Ld. Berners *Froiss.* I. xvii. 7 b/2 They are all a horsbacke, without it be the truandals [orig. *la truandail*] and laggers of ye oost, who folow after a foote.

† **Truandise.** *Obs.* Forms: 3 **truw-**, 4 **treu-, trowandise, -is, truandis,** 4–5 **-ise,** 5 **trewaundise, trowandyse, -aundyse, -antyse, -entyze, truaundise, trwandyse, -aundise,** 5–6 **trewandise, -yse,** 6 **truantisse.** [a. OF. *truandise* (13th c. in Godef.), f. *truand* Truant (q. v.) + *-ise*, suffix :—L. *-itia*: see -ise[2].]

**1.** Fraudulent begging; vagabondage; roguery, knavery.

a 1225 *Ancr. R.* 330 Mid iseli truwandise heo hut [=hides] euer hire god, & scheaweð forð hire pouerte. c 1400 *Rom. Rose* 3954 Which han assailed hym to shende, And with her trowandyse to blynde. c 1430 *Pilgr. Lyf Manhode* III. xxiii. (1869) 148 Whan I make hem thus to bere the dish of trewaundise. 1547 *Bk. Marchauntes* c vij b, Thus can these fyne marchants by wyls [= wiles] and trewandise fructifie at the expence of other.

**2.** Idle or loitering ways or habits; idleness.

a 1300 *Cursor M.* 253 Þoo..Þat won..es to wast þair liif in trofel and truandis [*Gött.* trowandis, *Trin.* trewandise]. c 1400 *Rom. Rose* 6664 Seynt poule..bade thappostles forto wirche And wynnen her lyflode in that wise And hem defended truaundise. c 1440 *Jacob's Well* 104 Whanne þou ..in tyme of lernyng, ȝeuyst þe to trowaundyse.

**Truant** (trū·ănt), *sb.* (*a.*) Forms: α. 3– **truant,** 4 **-ont,** (*pl.* **-ons**), **truan,** 4–5 **truaunt,** 5 **truwaunt(e,** (**trwaunt**), **truaund,** 6 **-ande,** (**-ent**), 6–7 **truand.** β. 4–6 **trewaunt,** 5 **-aund(e,** 5–6 **-ante,** 6 **-ande,** (**trewnt**), 6–7 **trewant, -and,** 7 **treuant.** γ. 4–5 **trowaunt,** 5 **-ande,** (**-awnt, -ent, -ean, trovwont, trownt**), 5–6 **trowan(e,** 6 **-ant, trouant.** δ. *dial.* 8–9 **troant,** 9 **troan, trawn, trown.** See also Trivant. [ME. a. OF. *truant*, F. *truand* adj. (12th c. in Godef.), (now only) as sb. = Prov. *truan*, Sp. *truhan*, Pg. *truão*; prob. from a Celtic source (Thurneysen): cf. Welsh *truan* wretched, a wretch, Gael. *truaghan* wretched, *trudanach* vagabond.]

† **1.** One who begs without justification; a sturdy beggar; a vagabond; an idle rogue or knave. (Often a mere term of abuse.) *Obs.*

c 1290 *S. Eng. Leg.* I. 60/240 Manie heolden him [St. Francis] a truant. 1340 *Ayenb.* 174 Þe truont..þet sseweþ hare pouerte and hare ziknesse..uor to habbe þe elmesse. c 1425 tr. *Arderne's Treat. Fistula* 100 Ribaldez and trowans ..þat felawshypeþ þam by þe waiez to pilgrimez, þat þai may robbe þam of þair siluer. c 1489 Caxton *Sonnes of Aymon* xxii. 490 Now shall I be a goode trewaunt, for I can well aske brede whan me nedeth. 1526 *Pilgr. Perf.* (W. de W. 1531) 224 b, Obey your..rulers, although they be trewantes, that is to saye..though they..be not so good and vertuous as they sholde be. 1599 Shaks. *Much Ado* III. ii. 18 Hang him truant, there's no true drop of bloud in him to be truly toucht with loue. 1656 Blount *Glossogr.*, *Truand* (Fr.), a common beggar, a lazie rascal, a vagabond; a knave, a scowndrel. [1895 J. C. Beckwith tr. *Hugo's Notre Dame* II. vi. I. 147 Such law as you mete to the Truands (vagabonds and outlaws), the Truands mete to you.]

**2.** A lazy, idle person; *esp.* a boy who absents himself from school without leave; hence *fig.*, one who wanders from an appointed place or neglects his duty or business.

c 1449 Pecock *Repr.* II. xii. (Rolls) 219 Truauntis in the scole of God. a 1548 Hall *Chron., Hen. V* 61 b, I am not so loiteryng a truand as to forgette so good a lesson. 1591 Shaks. 1 *Hen. VI*, II. iv. 7. 1596 — 1 *Hen. IV*, v. i. 94, I haue a Truant beene to Chiualry. 1697 Dryden *Virg. Georg.* IV. 160 When the Swarms..loath their empty Hives, and idly stray,..take A timely Care to bring the Truants back. 1770 Goldsm. *Des. Vill.* 198 The village master..A man severe he was, .. I knew him well, and every truant knew. 1856 Kane *Arct. Expl.* I. xxix. 398 One of our dogs, a truant from Morton's team.

**b.** Phr. *To play truant*; also formerly † *to play the truant, -s* (obs.). Const. *from, to.*

1560 *Nice Wanton* Aij, Be ye not ashamed the treauandes to play? 1598 Shaks. *Merry W.* v. i. 27 Since I pluckt Geese, plaide Trewant, and whipt Top, I knew not what 'twas to be beaten, till lately. 1642 Rogers *Naaman* 93 That so they may shun this sharpe Schoolemaster by playing the trewants. 1834 Medwin *Angler in Wales* I. viii. 129, I was scarcely breeched when I used to play the truant. 1887 Bowen *Virg. Æneid* v. 845 Rest those brows, let wearied eyes play truant to toil.

**B.** *adj.* **1.** That is a truant, or plays truant; idle, lazy, loitering, *esp.* of a boy, staying from school without leave; hence, wandering, straying.

a 1550 *Hye Way to Spyttel Ho.* 43 in Hazl. *E. P. P.* IV. 24 These trewant beggers begging fro place to place. 1561 Awdelay *Frat. Vacab.* (1869) 13 A Trewand knaue that faineth himselfe sicke when he should woorke. 1615 A. Stafford *Heav. Dogge* 59 To behold an austere..Philosopher ..quake at the name of death, even as a treuant boy does at the name of his Tutor. 1784 Cowper *Task* I. 114 E'er since, a truant boy, I passed my bounds. 1791 E. Darwin *Bot. Gard.* I. 54 Down the steep slopes He led..The willing pathway, and the truant rill. 1793 (ed. 1) Wordsw. *Descr. Sketches* 49 Through her truant pathway's native charms. 1824 W. Irving *T. Trav.* I. II. vii. 259 This freak of fancy made me more truant from my studies than ever. 1869 Tozer *Highl. Turkey* I. 318 We recovered the truant saddle.

**b.** Characterized or marked by truancy or idleness; befitting a truant or idler.

1602 Shaks. *Ham.* I. ii. 169 But what in faith make you from Wittemberge? *Hor.* A truant disposition, good my Lord. 1649 Milton *Eikon.* xvi. 152 Wee are not..to distrust God in the removal of that Truant help to our Devotion, which by him was never appointed. 1803 Scott *Let. to G. Ellis* 25 May in *Lockhart*, My truant days spent in London having thrown me a little behind.

† **2.** Trivial, trite; idle, vain. *Obs. rare.*

a 1572 Knox *Hist. Ref.* III. Wks. 1848 II. 141 We should nott wonder albeit that the auld trowane verse be trew, *Patrem sequitur sua proles.* 1682 Oldham *8th Sat. Boileau Imit.* 49 So fam'd for many a truant jest On wiving.

**C.** *Comb.*, as *truant-like* adj.; **truant-inspector,** a school attendance officer; **truant-school,** an industrial school to which truant or other children may be sent by order of a magistrate.

1583 Melbancke *Philotimus* M j, A trewantlike barrister. 1628 Ford *Lover's Mel.* I. i, If my experience hath not, truant-like, Mispent the time..For bettering my mind. 1882 *Standard* 31 Aug. 2/4 Truant Schools have..been doing good work in checking truancy. 1891 E. Kinglake *Australian at H.* 22 Attendance officers, called truant inspectors, go and examine the books of the state schools periodically, and then visit the parents of those children who have not fulfilled the required conditions.

Hence **Tru·antness** (**truanness**), truancy.

1483 *Cath. Angl.* 394/2 Trowannes, *trutannitas.* 1658 J. Jones tr. *Ovid's Ibis* 52 Boys will excuse the fault of Treuantness by the sin of lying.

**Tru·ant,** *v.* Forms: see the sb. [ME. f. prec.: cf. obs. F. *truander* (12th c. in Godef. *Compl.*), f. *truand* Truant.]

† **1.** *intr.* To play the vagabond or rogue. *Obs.*

c 1400 *Rom. Rose* 6721 Somme maner crafte..Thurgh which without truaundyng He may..haue his lyuyng. c 1430 *Pilgr. Lyf Manhode* III. xxiii. (1869) 148 Wel thei kunne glooven maungepayn whan thei wolen trewande therwith. c 1440 *Promp. Parv.* 503/2 Trovwonton (*S.* trownton, *P.* trowantyn), *trutannizo*, Cath.

**2.** *intr.* To idle, play truant (esp. from school); to wander, stray. Also with *it.*

1580 Lyly *Euphues* (Arb.) 279 What made the Gods so often to trewant from Heauen? 1637 Heywood *Dial.* Wks. 1874 VI. 285, I must..truly study man, (A booke in which I yet have truanted). 1642 Fuller *Holy & Prof. St.* I. ix. 24 He will not truant it now in the afternoon. 1748 Richardson *Clarissa* (1811) V. i. 6 Her good angel is gone a journey: is truanting at least. 1879 M. Pattison *Milton* xii. 143 He returned with concentrated ardour to woo the muse, from whom he had so long truanted.

† **3.** *trans.* To waste or idle away (time); to spend in truanting. *Obs.*

1597 *1st Pt. Return fr. Parnass.* III. i. 1115 In trewantinge there time, wastinge whole years. 1638 Ford *Fancies* III. iii, I dare not be the author Of truanting the time. 1708 Ozell tr. *Boileau's Lutrin* III. 120 A heedless Troop of wanton Boys..In idle Pastime truanting the Day.

**b.** To play truant from. *dial.*

1899 Crockett *Kit Kennedy* xii. 95 Kit Kennedy,..Ye troaned the schule yesterday.

Hence **Tru·anting** *ppl. a.*

1634 Rainbow *Labour* (1635) 25, 't has given the truanting world a desired play-day.

**Tru·anting,** *vbl. sb.* [f. Truant *v.* + -ing[1].] The action of the verb Truant; an instance of this.

c 1400 [see Truant v. 1]. 1532 More *Confut. Tindale* Wks. 574/2 With three strypes for hys tarying and trewaunting by the way. 1630 Lennard tr. *Charron's Wisd.* III. xiv. § 12 (1670) 443 To save themselves from the rigour of the punishment, they have recourse to..false excuses,.. flights, truantings. 1884 Hunter & Whyte *My Ducats* xx. (1885) 286 The sense of truanting gave a..spice of excitement to his reflections.

**Truantism** (trū·ăntiz'm). [f. Truant *sb.* + -ism.] The practice of a truant; truancy.

1812 J. J. Henry *Camp. agst. Quebec* 13 His own education, though made by his truantisms..an incorrect one. 1875

G. Dawson *Shaks. Lect.* (1888) 117 He..neglected his studies with that persistent truantism some great men have been guilty of.

**Truantly** (trū·ăntli), *a.* and *adv.* Now *rare.* [f. as prec. + -LY 1, -LY 2.]

**A.** *adj.* Having the qualities of a truant; characteristic of or befitting a truant.

1579 Twyne *Phisicke agst. Fort.* I. cv. 131 b, You, like wilful and truently children, can neuer learne wisedome without whipping. 1651 Jer. Taylor *Serm. for Year* I. Ep. Ded. 5 The Spirit of a man is truantly, and trifling. 1690 C. Nesse *O. & N. Test.* I. 125 For his truantly tricks [he] is turned down into the lowest form.

**B.** *adv.* After the manner of a truant.

1822 Scott *Nigel* xxviii, Idle and truantly disposed.

**Truantness**: see after Truant *a.*

**Truantry** (trū·ăntri). Forms: 5 **trewaundrie, trwandrye, truantrye,** 6 **trewantrie,** 7– **truantry.** [a. F. *truanderie* (13th c. in Godef. *Compl.*), f. *truand* Truant: see -RY.]

†**1.** Fraudulent begging; knavery, roguery. *Obs.*

1426 Lydg. *De Guil. Pilgr.* 17828 Thys dyssh that I holde in myn hond, (In ffrenche callyd 'Coquynerye' And in ynglyssh 'Trwandrye'). c 1430 *Pilgr. Lyf Manhode* III. xxii. (1869) 147 This hand heere is cleped coquinerie; Trewaundrie bi name j cleyme it.

**2.** Idleness, truancy; the practice, or an act, of playing truant.

1481 Caxton *Reynard* iv. (Arb.) 8 Yf the scolers were not beten..and reprised of their truantrye, they shold neuer lerne. 1581 Mulcaster *Positions* xl. (1887) 225 In the maisters house..children may..be lesse subiect to loytering and trewantrie. 1685 Cotton tr. *Montaigne* I. 301 An understanding Tutor, who..knew discreetly to connive at this and other truantries. 1811 L. M. Hawkins *C'tess & Gertr.* I. 166 Her frequent..truantries from the place where she ought to have been. 1887 Stevenson *Mem. & Portraits* ii. 27 Infinite yawnings during lecture and unquenchable gusto in the delights of truantry.

**Tru·antship.** *rare.* [f. Truant *sb.* + -SHIP.] Truancy. **b.** with possessive, as a mock title.

a 1568 Ascham *Scholem.* I. (Arb.) 27 If the childe haue done his diligence, and vsed no trewandship. 1592 Nashe *Four Lett. Confut.* Wks. (Grosart) II. 264, I would teach thy old Trewantship the true vse of words.

† **Trub.** *Obs.* or *dial.* Also 8–9 **trubbe.** [app. short for *truffle*, OF. *truffe* (Sp., Pg. *trufa*), or for L. *tūber.*]

**1.** A truffle.

1668 Wilkins *Real Char.* II. iv. § 3. 70 Imperfect Herbs.. Without a Stem,..growing..in the ground, being esculent, ..Trubs, Trufle. 1673 Ray *Journ. Low C.* (1738) I. 346 A kind of subterraneous musheroom, which our herbarists English Trubs, or after the French name Trufles. 1693 Robinson in *Phil. Trans.* XVII. 825 Ludovicus Romanus.. affirms, That Thirty Camels Load of these Truffles or Trubs ..have been..sold at Damascus in two or three days. 1727–41 Chambers *Cycl.* s.v. *Truffles*, Bradley calls them underground edible mushrooms, or Spanish trubbes. 1860 Mayne *Expos. Lex.*, *Trubs*,..common name for the *Lycoperdon tuber.* 1866 *Treas. Bot.*, *Trubs*, or *Trubbes*, truffles.

**2.** 'A little squat woman' (Phillips 1706); also, 'a slut, sloven; a wanton; an opprobrious term' (*Eng. Dial. Dict.*). Also **Tru·bkin, Tru·b-tail.**

1625 Purchas *Pilgrims* IX. xvi. § 3. 1622 The Dogges.. satiate with the Womans flesh.., who was a short fat trubkin. 1706 Phillips (ed. Kersey), *Trub* or *Trub-tail*, a little squat Woman. 1746 *Exmoor Scolding* 104 (E.D.S.) Andra wou'd ha' had a Trub in tha.

**Trublance, Truble,** etc., obs. ff. Troublance, Trouble, etc.

† **Truble.** *Obs. rare.* [a. F. *truble* kind of net (13th c. in Littré).] A small net for catching fish in ponds and stews.

1600 Surflet *Countrie Farme* IV. xiii. 646 Taking..little fish with the shouenet, small net, called a truble and line. *Ibid.* xvi. 650 The gudgeon is taken with a hooke or the little net called a truble.

**Truce** (trūs), *sb.* Forms: α. *sing.* 4 **truwe,** 4–5 **trewe,** 5 **tru,** 5–6 **trew,** 5–7 **true.** β. *pl.* 3 **triwes, triws,** 4 **treus, treuwes,** *Sc.* **trowis,** 4–6 **trewes, trues,** 5 **trewys, triew(i)s, trieux, tryew(e)s, trowes, truwes, -ys, trwes, trwys, trux,** 5–6 **trews, treux,** 5 (5–7 *Sc.*) **trewis,** 6 **treuis, -ys; treuges.** γ. 5 **trewysse, truyse,** 5–6 **trewse, truxe,** 5–7 **truse,** 6 **trewice, -yce, treuce, trewce, trwce, trusse,** 7 **trousse,** 5– **truce.** [ME. *trewe* and *triewe*, mostly in pl. form *trewes* and *triewes*:—OE. *trēow* sb. masc. (fem. pl. *trēwa*), 'truth or fidelity to a promise, good faith, assurance of faith or truth, promise, engagement, covenant, league', = OEFris. *triuwe*, OWFris. and MDu. *trouwe* (Du. *trouw*), OS. *treuwa*, *triuwa*, OHG. *triuwa* (MHG. *triuwe*, Ger. *treue*) :—WGer. **trewwa*, Goth. *triggwa* 'covenant' (whence late L. and Romanic *tregua*, *treuga*, F. *trève*); also, in ablaut form, OE. *trūwa* sb. masc. and pl. *-an*; = ON. *trúa*, *trú*, Norw. *tru*, Sw. *trōa*: see True *a.* Already in OE. the pl. *trēwa* was often used in the sense of the sing.; this became still more frequent with the ME. pl. *trewes, triues, triwes, trues,* and finally this, as *trews, trewse, truse, truce,* became the received sing. (app. in reference to the pledges or engagements given by both parties), with a new pl. *truses*, *truces*, when required. Cf. *cherries*, *pease.* See also *trève* from French, and the rare *treuges* after MLat. *treugas.*]

**1.** A suspension of hostilities for a specified period between armies at war (formerly also between combatants in a private feud or quarrel); a temporary peace or cessation from arms; an armistice; also, an agreement or treaty effecting this.

*To* † *take*, † *cry*, *call* (*a*) *truce*, to make, call for a truce. *Flag of truce*: see Flag *sb.*[1] 1 b.

α. c 1330 R. Brunne *Chron.* (1810) 193 If þou pes wille ȝerne,..& trewe for seuen ȝere, I consent þertille. *Ibid.* 275 For þre days trewe þe Inglis him hete. c 1374 Chaucer *Troylus* IV. 1284–6 (1312–4) It is now a truwe..And er þat truwe is don I shal ben here. c 1400 *Destr. Troy* 7874 Then takyn was the true. *Ibid.* 8372 For a trew to be takon of a tyme short. 1494 Fabyan *Chron.* VI. clxxxi. 179 To requyre a trewe or trewse for .iii. monethes. 1575 Churchyard *Chippes* (1817) 91 But ere the heate, of this great skirmishe grew, The Dowager, with trumpet tooke a trew.

β. a 1225 *Ancr. R.* 286 He..brekeð þe triws, & awrekeð him of þe, oðer of him seoluen. 1297 R. Glouc. (Rolls) 10005 He .. triwes nom of saladin. c 1330 R. Brunne *Chron. Wace* (Rolls) 7843 Þorow trist of trues..þey sette a day of Parlement. c 1375 *Cursor M.* 26768 (Fairf.) As trewes þat is tane. 1387 Trevisa *Higden* (Rolls) II. 413 Whan Hector was i-buried, were trewes i-take for a ȝere. — VIII. 337 Trewes [*v. r.* truwes] were i-take bytwene þe kynges. 1442 *Rolls of Parlt.* V. 44/2 Ayenst þe fourme of trieux..betwixt.. England and Scotland had and concludyd. 1483 in Rymer *Foedera* (1711) XII. 174/1 By thies Presentis is made.. assured Treux and Abstinence of Werre for oon hool Yere. 1483 Caxton *Gold. Leg.* 306 b/1 The Crysten men tooke triews for thre dayes. 1496 *Act 12 Hen. VII*, c. 13 § 15 After the seid perfite peas be had and concluded, or such abstynence of Warre, Trux and Peax for a tyme be had and made. 1524 *Carew MSS.* (1867) I. 25 The patched and inhonorable treuges, which by inforcement of pure necessity be tolerated. 1596 Dalrymple tr. *Leslie's Hist. Scot.* I. (S.T.S.) I. 75 Trues ar bund, mariages ar maid with sum of the Inhabitouris.

γ. 14.. in *Wars Eng. in France* (1864) II. 526 The tyme that the last truxe was take betwene Herre the VI...and his aduersarie of Fraunce. c 1440 *Generydes* 5882 To graunt them truse for ij monethis day. c 1440 *Promp. Parv.* 503/2 Truwys, or truce of pees. 1483 *Cath. Angl.* 393/1 Trewysse, *inducie.* 1494 Trewse [see α]. 1538 Cromwell in Merriman *Life & Lett.* (1902) II. 124 To offer therfor a longer treux. 1552 Huloet, Trewice, *fœdus,..induciæ.* 1560 Daus tr. *Sleidane's Comm.* 41 Yt eyther a suer peace, or els a long treuce may be taken. 1613 Purchas *Pilgrimage* (1614) 634 They obserue three dayes in a week truce, when euery man may travell or barter safely. 1621 in Foster *Eng. Factories Ind.* (1906) 306 Truse taken betwene the Mogull and them. a 1780 Watson *Philip III* (1839) 145 To put a period to the miseries attendant upon war, by a peace or truce. 1875 Stubbs *Const. Hist.* II. xiv. 148 A truce which in the following November became a permanent peace.

**b.** Loosely or vaguely: Cessation or absence of hostilities (without limitation of time); peace.

1377 Langl. *P. Pl.* B. XVIII. 416 Trewes, quod treuth .. Clippe we in couenaunt, & vch of vs cusse other. 1456 Sir G. Haye *Law Arms* (S.T.S.) 164 Nocht brekand gude faith, and, namely, fra trewis be gevin our, and diffiaunce maid. 1535 Coverdale 1 *Macc.* vi. 49 The kynge toke truce with them that were in Bethsura. 1578 T. Norton *Calvin's Inst.* Table RRRR vj/1, I will put my couenaunt betwene me and thee: and betwene thy seede after thee..by an euerlasting truce. 1598 Sylvester *Du Bartas* II. ii. I. *Ark* 377 Behold the peacefull Dove Brings in her beak the Peace-branch, boading weal And truce with God.

†**c.** A document recording the terms of a truce. *Sc. Obs. rare.*

1502 *Acc. Ld. High Treas. Scot.* II. 350 To illumyn the trewis and the conjunct infeftment.

†**d.** *Sc. Law.* A suspension of judicial proceedings; a stay. *Obs.*

1609 Skene *Reg. Maj.* II. 112 And therfore this time is called *induciæ deliberatoriæ*, because..the pley ceases, and stayes: and trewis are taken betwixt the parties.

†**e.** *Day of truce*, a court held by the Wardens of the Marches (of England and Scotland), or the day appointed for this, on which a truce was observed. Also called *truce-day* (see 4).

1486–7 *Plumpton Corr.* (Camden) 56 Ye prepared yourselfe to have ridden with me to this day of trewe. 1564 *Reg. Privy Council Scot.* I. 282 Accustumat to serve and await upoun the wardane at all dayis of trew. 1863 S. S. Jones *Northumberland* 162 The days of Trews, or Warden Courts, had to be held frequently.

**f.** *Truce of God*, a suspension of hostilities between armies, or of private feuds, ordered by the Church during certain days and seasons in mediæval times. Hence *allusively.*

[a 867 in Mansi *Concilia* XV. 448 Pax vero illa quam treguam Dei dicimus, fideliter observetur.] 1727–41 Chambers *Cycl.*, *Truce of God, Treuga Dei*, is a phrase famous in the histories of the xith century, when the disorders and licences of private wars..obliged the bishops of France to forbid such violences within certain times, under canonical pains. 1828 Scott *F. M. Perth* xxxiv, The Church of Rome..had decided that during the holy season of Easter..the sword of war should be sheathed, and angry monarchs should respect the season termed the Truce of God. 1870 Lowell *Study Wind.* I. 20 It was Sunday, and I gave him the benefit of its gracious truce of God.

**2.** Figurative and allusive uses (from 1).

1560 Daus tr. *Sleidane's Comm.* 140 b, He would now take occasion to breake that treuce of Religion. 1590 Shaks. *Com. Err.* II. ii. 147 Keepe then faire league and truce with thy true bed. 1606 — *Tr. & Cr.* II. ii. 75 The Seas and Windes (old Wranglers) tooke a Truce. 1647 N. Bacon *Disc. Govt. Eng.* I. lxiv. (1739) 137 The King foresaw the storm, and thought it safest first to cry truce with the people. a 1711 Ken *Hymns Evang.* Poet. Wks. 1721 I. 52 But jealous Fears no Truce with Tyrants make. 1849 Macaulay *Hist. Eng.* ii. I. 159 Between the bigoted followers of Laud and the bigoted followers of Calvin there could be neither peace nor truce.

†**b.** *King's truce*: a cry for the discontinuance of a game. *Obs.*

1608 Day *Hum. out of Br.* IV. iii, *Hort.* What haue I catchd you? *Pa.* Kisse her and let her goe. *Host.* Kings truce till I breath a little.

**3.** Hence, Respite or intermission (more loosely, freedom or liberty) from something irksome, painful, or oppressive.

1567 Drant *Horace, Epistles* To Rdr., To take truce with myne other studyes,..and to become a sillye translator rythmical. 1598 J. Dickenson *Greene in Conc.* (1878) 160 Till death gaue truce to hir distresses. 1667 Milton *P. L.* II. 526 Where he may..find Truce to his restless thoughts. 1713 Swift *Imit. Hor.* I. vii. 130 Truce, good my lord, I beg a truce,..Your raillery is misapply'd. 1859–69 Heavysege *Saul* (ed. 3) 337 Let us dry these unavailing tears, And, with such truce to sorrow as we may, Wend each..his.. several road.

**b.** In interjectional phrase (*a*) *truce with*, now usually (*a*) *truce to*, enough of, have done with.

1700 Congreve *Way of World* II. v, Truce with your Similitudes: For I am as sick of 'em —. 1757 Mrs. Griffith *Lett. Henry and Frances* (1767) II. 150 But a truce with the subject, for I am determined to never mention it more. 1786 tr. *Beckford's Vathek* (1868) 90, I am going on affairs of emergency, a truce therefore to parade! 1835 Lytton *Rienzi* II. i, A truce to this light conversation. 1846 Browning *Soul's Trag.* I. 142 Truce with toying for this once! 1878 — *La Saisiaz* 249 Truce to such old sad contention.

**4.** *attrib.* and *Comb.* **a.** attrib., as *truce-day* († *true-day* = day of truce), *-flag*, *-note*, *-place* (*true-place*). **b.** objective, as *truce-bearer*, *-breaker*, *-maker*, *-taker*; *truce-breaking*, *-hating*, *-making*, *-taking* sbs. and adjs.

1853 Hickie tr. *Aristoph.* (1887) I. 11 This *truce-bearer would not so easily have escaped. 1534 Tindale 2 *Tim.* iii. 3 Vnkinde, *truce-breakers, stubborn. 1625 K. Long tr. *Barclay's Argenis* I. xx. 61 The Herald..rehearses a long prayer, containing many curses against Truce-breakers. 1592 Timme *Ten Eng. Lepers* vii. I j, A wilful *trucebreaking and perjurie. 1719 *Free-thinker* No. 110 ⁋ 1 An unjust, Truce-breaking Prince. 1587 Fleming *Contn. Holinshed* III. 1413/2 Slaine..by a Scot..as they met vpon a *true daie. 1610 Holland *Camden's Brit.* I. 403 In a tumult upon a True-day in the midle marches. 1876 T. Hardy *Ethelberta* (1890) 376 A little tufted white feather..like a *truce-flag between the blood of noble and vassal. 1591 Sylvester *Du Bartas* I. ii. 251 *Truce-hating Twins. 1552 Huloet, *Trewice maker, *synmachus.* 1523 Ld. Berners *Froiss.* I. clxii. 197 Without any peace or *trewse makynge. 1810 Scott *Lady of L.* VI. xxi, Clarion and trumpet..Rung forth a *truce-note. 1674 Blount *Glossogr.*, *† *True-place*, i.e. a place of Parley and Conference in Northumberland, antiently so called. 1483 *Cath. Angl.* 393/1 *Trews taker. 1533 *Acc. Ld. High Treas. Scot.* VI. 138 For keping of gude reule during the *trewis taking. 1581 Marbeck *Bk of Notes* 471 This tranquilitie of the sea..as a trewes taking in the Winter, called the Halcions daies.

**Truce** (trūs), *v.* Also 6 **truse.** Now *rare.* [f. prec. sb.]

**1.** *intr.* To make a truce.

1569 Stocker tr. *Diod. Sic.* III. v. 109 Who after that victorie, trused with the Aretians. 1731 Fielding *Mod. Husb.* II. xi, If you please, my lord, to truce with your proposals. 1893 E. L. Wakeman in *Columbus (Ohio) Dispatch* 25 May, The factions had attacked each other, retreated, parleyed, blarneyed, scorned, truced.

**2.** *trans.* To bring to an end by or as by means of a truce; to put an end to.

1618 Middleton *Peacemaker* Wks. (Bullen) VIII. 326 Spain..betwixt whom and England the ocean ran with blood.., nor ever truced her crimson effusion. 1706 T. Baker *Tunbr. Walks* II. i, We may truce the debate.

**Truceless** (trū·slės), *a.* [f. Truce *sb.* + -LESS.] That is without truce; unceasing in hostility; also *fig.*

1631 Fuller *David's Sin* v, With truceless war each other doth oppose. 1747 B. Sowden *Death Gardiner* in Doddridge *Life Col. Gardiner* App. ii. 198 Dissolv'd in truceless grief she lay. 1852 Ld. Cockburn *Jeffrey* I. 202 His whole session was one keen and truceless conflict. 1886 E. King in *Flaubert's Salammbô* p. xv, The truceless war between the Carthaginians and those barbarian mercenaries.

**Truceman,** obs. variant of Truchman.

**Truch,** obs. Sc. form of Trough; obs. f. Trush.

**Truche,** variant of Troke *v. Obs.*, to fail.

**Truchman** (trɒ·tʃmăn). Forms: 5 **tourcheman,** (6 **trooche-, truce-, trowch-, trounch-, trush-, treush-man,** *Sc.* **trwcheman, trunsche-**), 6–7 **truche-, trouch(e)-, (trunch-), treuch-,** 7 **trudgeman,** 6– **truchman.** [ad. med.L. *turchemannus*, F. *trucheman* (Cotgr. 1611), *truchement* = It. *turcimanno*, Sp. *trujaman*, ad. Arab. ترجمان *turjamān* (also *tarjumān*, *tarjamān*), interpreter, the same word which through Gr. and med.L. appears as Dragoman. The Arabic letter *jim* which is now generally *j* was orig. *g*, like Heb. *gimel*, the early form of the word being *targumān*, f. *targama* to translate: cf. Targum.] An interpreter.

1485 Caxton *Paris & V.* (1868) 77 Thenne sayd parys vnderstondeth he mouryshe and they sayd nay but..yf he wold speke to hym they should find tourchemen ynough. 1525 Ld. Berners *Froiss.* II. clxxi. [clxvii.] 503 They..toke a truchman that coulde speke Italyan, and commanded hym to go to the crysten host. **1575** GASCOIGNE *Flowers, Maske Visct. Mountacute* Wks. 1907 I. 85 He may your Trounchman bee, Your herald and ambassador. **1577** STANYHURST *Descr. Irel.* in Holinshed (1808) VI. 4 If a traveller of the Irish had..spoken Irish, they would command him..to..speake English, or els bring his trouchman with him. **1578** in Feuillerat *Revels Q. Eliz.* (1908) 287 Torche bearers with the troocheman. **1613** PURCHAS *Pilgrimage* v. xvii. (1614) 543 Suborning his Trudge-man..to poyson or murder him by the way. **1679** BLOUNT *Anc. Tenures* 17 Beneath Whittington in Shropshire, one Wrenoc ..held Lands by the service of being Latimer, that is, Trucheman or Interpreter, between the English and the Welshmen. **1888** DOUGHTY *Arabia Deserta* I. 175 Their truch-man in entering Moses' valley had paid out presents to the Howeytât sheykhs.

**b.** *fig.*

**1585** JAS. I *Vranie* 124 Poets..Dame Naturs trunchmen, heauens interprets trewe. **1637** SUCKLING *Aglaura* II. i, Our soules..will not need that duller truch-man Flesh. *a* **1649** DRUMM. OF HAWTH. *Cypress Grove* Wks. (1711) 126 Formed..to be the interpreter and trunchman of His creation. *a* **1680** BUTLER *Rem.* (1759) II. 405 He is a Truch-Man, that interprets between learned Writers and gentle Readers.

Hence † **Tru·chmanry** *Obs.*, the office or function of an interpreter; so † **Truch sprite** *nonce-wd.*, a spirit acting as interpreter or messenger; † **Tru·chwoman** *Obs.* [cf. *Mussulwoman*], a female interpreter.

**1573** in Feuillerat *Revels Q. Eliz.* (1908) 217 For the Tronchwoman's Heade and for vii Hatbandes for the men Maskers. **1582** STANYHURST *Æneis* IV. (Arb.) 107 Latelye toe mee posted from Ioue thee truch sprit, or herrald Of Gods. **1663** SIR G. MACKENZIE *Religio Stoici* 97 To teach that sensual croud, by the trunchmanrie of sense.

**Trucidation** (trūsidēⁱ·ʃən). *rare.* [ad. L. *trucīdātiōn-em*, n. of action f. *trucīdāre* to cut to pieces, kill cruelly, slaughter.] A cruel killing or murdering; in use *humorous*: slaughter.

**1623** COCKERAM, *Trucidation*, a cruell murder. [Whence in subsequent dicts.] **1883** STEVENSON *Lett.* (1901) I. 267, I loathe the snails: but from loathing to actual butchery, trucidation of multitudes, there is still a step that I hesitate to take.

**Truck** (trɒk), *sb.*[1] Also 6–7 **trucke**, 8–9 *Sc.* **troke, trock.** [a. F. *troque*, † *troq*, *troc* (16th c.), AF. *truke* (1364), f. *troquer*: see TRUCK *v.*[1]]

**1.** The action or practice of trucking; trading by exchange of commodities; barter. Often *in truck* (*for*, † *of*), *by truck for*.

[**1364** *Vintner's Co. Charter* in *Pat. Roll* 38 *Edw. III*, m. 44 (P.R.O.) Si mettent pris sur les vins par Truke ou par eschaunges.] **1553** in Hakluyt *Voy.* (1598) I. 228 No commutation or trucke to be made by any of the petie marchants, without the assent abouesaid. **1567** HAWKINS *Let. to Eliz.* 16 Sept. (St. Pap. Dom. XLIV. 7, P.R.O.) To..sell them [negroes] in the West Indyes in trvcke of golde peirels and Esmeraldes. **1625** PURCHAS *Pilgrims* x. i. 1674 The Moores gave them in trucke for them againe black Moores. **1667** in Magens *Insurances* (1755) II. 437 If..any ..shall buy, or get to themselves by Truck, or any other way, such Ship or Goods. **1747** *Gentl. Mag.* Apr. 173/2 Their trade is managed by truck, or bartering one commodity for another. **1861** *Sat. Rev.* 14 Dec. 609 The mind has organs and functions..ranging beyond the things of avoirdupois and truck.

**b.** *transf.* and *fig.*

**1741** tr. *D'Argens' Chinese Lett.* xxxix. 300 There's a Place at Moscow for the Truck and Barter of Images, and the Money given is in Proportion to the Size of the Figure. **1784** COWPER *Task* II. 741 Precedence went in truck, And he was competent whose purse was so. **1796** MRS. M. ROBINSON *Angelina* II. 128 My girl has money, my Lord has a title;—'tis a sort of truck, Sir Clifford.

**c.** with *a* and *pl.* (*a*) A traffic, trade. (*b*) An act of trading; a bargain or deal.

**1638** *Diary Citizen Exeter* (ed. Brushfield, 1901) 16 For 30 yards Canvas..for wch I set nothing bec[ause] taken in a truck. **1642** TASMAN *Jrnl.* in *Acc. Sev. Late Voy.* I. (1694) 134 They indeavoured to begin a Truck or Merchandize with the yacht. **1678** R. L'ESTRANGE *Seneca's Mor.* (1702) 47 This for That, is rather a Truck than a Benefit. **1749** CHESTERF. *Lett.* 14 Nov., Utility..established a truck of the little *agrémens* and pleasures of life. **1851** MAYHEW *Lond. Labour* I. 417/1 There's Paddy in the truck too; he makes a good thing.

**2.** The payment of wages otherwise than in money; the system or practice of such payment, the *truck system* (see 5); in quots. 1879, 1911, goods supplied in lieu of wages.

**1743** *Ir. Act* 17 *Geo. II*, c. 8 § 6 In case any person or persons..shall pay any such artificer, workman, servant or labourer..their wages, or other price agreed on, or any part thereof, either in goods or by way of truck, or in any other manner than in ready money. **1766** *Museum Rust.* VI. 420 The workmen alledged, that the clothiers..had..obliged them to take goods in truck, at exorbitant prices. **1879** *Cassell's Techn. Educ.* IV. 12/2 Wages are largely paid in truck, in defiance of the law. **1886** *Act* 49 & 50 *Vict.* c. 40 § 1 The provisions of the Acts relating to truck. **1911** *Daily News* 13 Oct. 3 She pays 2s. 9d. as well as a small amount of 'truck', worth a few pence, for getting the whole of her washing done by a washerwoman.

**3.** 'Traffic', intercourse, communication, dealings.

*a* **1625** FLETCHER *Chances* II. i, Hark ye Frederick, What truck betwixt my infant—? **1790** MORISON *Poems* 106 Nor does our blinded master see The trocks between the Clerk and she. **1809** J. SKINNER *Ep. to Capt. R. B.* xv, Ye and I have had a trock This forty year. **1866** *N. & Q.* 3rd Ser. IX. 400/1 [In Suffolk] A man who has left off courting a girl, says that he has 'no more truck along o' har'. **1894** *Blackw. Mag.* June 748 You would think he is a Christian to see the troke there is between that beast and my man.

**b.** *pl.* Small matters of business or work; odd jobs, errands, chores. *Sc. dial.*

**1808–18** JAMIESON s.v. *Troke, Troques*, or *trockies*, pl. Small pieces of business that require a good deal of stirring. **1894** 'IAN MACLAREN' *Bonnie Brier Bush, Lachlan Campbell* iii, A'll come for ye as sune as a' get..ma little trokes feenished.

†**4.** Commodities for barter. *Obs.*

**1555** EDEN *Decades* 281 The Tartars..bringe none other wares then truckes or droues of swyfte runnynge horses and clokes made of whyte feltes. **1621** in Foster *Eng. Factories Ind.* (1906) 233 The[y] would not geve 2s. a pece nether in money nor truck. **1688** CLAYTON in *Phil. Trans.* XVII. 792 They must carry all sort of Truck that trade thither, having one Commodity to pass off another. **1770** SIR J. BANKS *Jrnl.* (1896) 332 The boat with some truck was sent ashore..in hopes of purchasing some trifling refreshment for the sick.

**b.** Small articles of a miscellaneous character; sundries; stuff; chiefly in depreciative use: odds and ends; things of little value; trash, rubbish. (Rarely *pl.*) Also *fig.*

**1785** SHIRREFS *Poems* (1790) 250 Scales, compasses, and ither trocks. **1792** in *Hist. Broughton Place U. P. Ch.* (1872) 20 Your Priests wear bands an' pouther'd hair, An' sick vain troke. **1834** J. HALL *Kentucky* I. 221 Several bouncing girls..were clearing away the truck of the evening meal. **1840** R. H. DANA *Bef. Mast* xxx, Spent all his time in the bush and along the beach, picking up flowers and shells, and such truck. **1871** W. ALEXANDER *Johnny Gibb* i, Is their trock a' in noo, I won'er? **1890** L. C. D'OYLE *Notches* 67 What cooking utensils and other 'truck' we thought we needed. **1897** KIPLING *Captains Courageous* i, I can't smoke the truck the steward sells.

**c.** *U.S.* Market-garden produce; hence as a general term for culinary vegetables.

**1784** *Maryland Jrnl.* 14 Dec., Advt. (Thornton), A large Room..for his Customers to lodge in, and deposit their Market-truck. **1822** J. FLINT *Lett. Amer.* 264 Truck.. Culinary vegetables. **1870** S. LANIER *Nine fr. Eight* 2, I was drivin' my two-mule waggin, With a lot of truck for sale. **1885** *Blackw. Mag.* Sept. 330/1 He is laying out the back land in truck or early vegetables. **1902** *Ibid.* Apr. 498/1 'Truck' means briefly such things as can be grown for the Northern markets—cucumbers, cabbages, sweet potatoes, strawberries, tomatoes, &c.

**5.** *attrib.* and *Comb.*; in sense 2, as *truck act, law, principle, system*; in sense 4 c, *truck-farm, -farmer, -farming, -garden, -gardener, -gardening, -patch, -produce*; also **truck-economy**: see quot.; **truck-house**, in North America, a store-house for trading with Indians; also, any storage building (*Funk's Stand. Dict.* 1895); **truck-knight**, **-man**: see quots.; **truck-master**, (*a*) one who is in charge of a truck-house; (*b*) an employer who uses the truck system; **truck-shop**, a shop at which vouchers given instead of wages may be exchanged for goods, a tommy-shop; **truck-store** = prec.; also, a greengrocery shop (*local U.S.*).

**1889** R. T. ELY *Introd. Pol. Econ.* I. vii. 50 *Truck-economy is the term used to denote the period which precedes the use of money. **1866** *N. & Q.* 3rd Ser. IX. 323/1 A truck garden, a *truck farm, is a market-garden or farm. **1877** A. DOUAI *Better Times* (1884) 7 The *truck-farmers from Virginia down to Florida. **1885** *Blackw. Mag.* Sept. 331/1 The river-bluffs are admirably suited for *truck-farming. **1891** *N. Y. Weekly Witness* 22 Apr. 2/2 A distinction is made between truck-farming and what is known as market-gardening...Truck-farming is defined as the production of green vegetables on tracts remote from market. **1866** *Truck garden [see *truck farm*]. **1868** LOSSING *Hudson* 394 Numerous 'truck' gardens, from which the city draws vegetable supplies. **1889** L. H. BAILEY (*title*) The Horticulturist's Rule-Book. A Compendium of Useful Information for Fruit-Growers, *Truck-Gardeners, Florists, and Others. **1890** *Boston* (Mass.) *Jrnl.* 12 Apr. 2/4 During their two years' residence they have done all of their own work and *truck-gardening. **1731** *Massachusetts Stat.* 9 Nov., The Indians..have their dependance on this government for supplies..several *truck-houses having been erected..for that purpose. **1753** DOUGLASS *Brit. Settlem. N. Amer.* 228 Some place of Strength, Security, or Retreat for our Indian traders under the name of a Trading or Truck-House. **1625** F. MARKHAM *Bk. Hon.* II. viii. § 2 Dunghill or *Truck-Knights, whose Honors haue no other assent or scale to rise by, but onely their wealth and purchase trucking and bargaining with gold or other merchandise. **1914** *Daily News* 24 Mar. 6 For practical purposes the present *Truck Laws are a dead letter. **1864** WEBSTER, **Truckman*, 1. One who does business in the way of barter and exchange. **1694** *Massachusetts Stat.* 13 June, That all trade with the said Eastern Indians be managed and carried on at the charge of and with the public stock..by suitable *truck masters. **1767** T. HUTCHINSON *Hist. Mass.* II. iii. 318 The charge of trading houses, truckmasters, garrisons, and a vessel employed in transporting goods. **1906** *Daily Chron.* 22 June 5/2 The wool was given out, and the payment in tea or groceries for the manufactured article was made from the shop of a truck master. **1829** T. FLINT *G. Mason* iii. 33 A garden, or, as the people call it, a *truck patch, was also prepared. **1837** SYD. SMITH *2nd Let. Archd. Singleton* Wks. 1859 II. 285/1 Recommending the *truck principle to the Bishops, and offering to pay them in hassocks, cassocks, aprons, shovel-hats [etc.]. **1890** L. C. D'OYLE *Notches* 145 The proximity of the camp would ensure them a ready market for all '*truck' produce. **1845** DISRAELI *Sybil* III. i, The Butty generally keeps a Tommy or *Truck shop and pays the wages of his labourers in goods. **1886** *Appleton's Ann. Cycl.* 84/1 In Liége..employers compelled the labourers to purchase supplies from their *Truck stores, at prices from 50 to 90 per cent. above..retail rates. **1830** COBBETT *Rur. Rides* (1885) II. 352 In the iron country..the *truck or tommy system generally prevails. **1869** *Adam Smith's W. N.* I. x. II. I. 150 *note*, The truck system..is now uniformly illegal. **1740** DOUGLASS *Disc. Curr. Brit. Plant. Amer.* 4 All Commerce naturally is a *Truck Trade exchanging Commodities which we can spare (or their Value) for Goods we are in want of. **1794** *Gaz. U.S.A.* (Philad.) 6 Jan. (Thornton), It is a truck trade that is proposed.

**Truck** (trɒk), *sb.*[2] Also 7 **trucke.** [app. deriv. of L. *trochus* = Gr. τροχός: see TROCHUS, or short for TRUCKLE, a. AF. *trokle* :—L. *trochlea*.]

**1.** A small solid wooden wheel or roller; *spec.* *Naut.* one of those on which the carriages of ships' guns were formerly mounted.

**1611** FLORIO, *Rigolo*, a little wheele vsed vnder sleds. Gunners call it a trucke. **1627** CAPT. SMITH *Seaman's Gram.* xiv. 65 If for Sea she [gun carriage] haue Trucks, which are round intier peeces of wood like wheeles. **1727** A. HAMILTON *New Acc. E. Ind.* I. xxii. 269 Those Priests had erected a Scaffold on two Axle-trees, that had Trucks fitted for them like the Carriage of Ship Guns. **1860** *All Year Round* No. 67. 404 At another of the guns, a shot came in and took off the truck (or, as a shore-going person would say, 'the wheel'). **1883** [implied in *truck gun*, 4].

**2.** *Naut.* A circular or square cap of wood fixed on the head of a mast or flag-staff, usually with small holes or sheaves for halliards.

**1626** CAPT. SMITH *Accid. Yng. Seamen* 13 The maine top gallant sayle yeard, the trucke or flagge staffe. **1627** — *Seaman's Gram.* iv. 18 The Trucke is a square peece of wood at the top wherein you put the Flag-staffe. **1697** DAMPIER *Voy.* (1729) I. 414 At our Main-top-mast head, on the very top of the truck of the Spindle. **1774** *Westm. Mag.* II. 429 What surprise he declar'd at the Boy on the truck! **1840** R. H. DANA *Bef. Mast* viii. 18 We painted her, both inside and out, from the truck to the water's edge. **1899** F. T. BULLEN *Log Sea-waif* 192 The second mate..ordered me to go up and reeve the signal halliards in the mizzen truck.

**b.** One of the small wooden blocks through which the rope of a parrel is threaded to prevent its being frayed against the mast. **c.** See quot. *c* 1635. **d.** A similar block lashed to the shrouds to form a guide or fair-leader for running rigging.

*a* **1625** *Nomenclator Navalis* (Harl. MS. 2301) s.v., Those little round thinges of Wood which belong to the *Parrells*, are called *Trucks*. **1627** CAPT. SMITH *Seaman's Gram.* v. 20 Parrels are little round Balls called Trucks, and little peeces of wood called ribs, and ropes. *c* **1635** CAPT. N. BOTELER *Dial. Sea Services* iv. (1685) 236 When the Main-capstan is not able to purchase in the Cable..they use to take a Hawser, and open a Strond thereof, and so put in Nippers, (which are small Ropes with a small Truck at one end) and with them they bind fast this Hawser to the Cable. **1688** R. HOLME *Armoury* III. xv. (Roxb.) 42/1 The Trucks are the little round things of wood made with holes through, to turne vpon a rope as aforesaid. **1711** W. SUTHERLAND *Ship-build. Assist.* 135 Trucks for Shrouds—42.

**3.** A wheeled vehicle for carrying heavy weights; variously applied. **a.** A strong flat open trolley for carrying blocks of stone or the like; a lorry. **b.** A light two-wheeled hand-propelled vehicle; a hand-cart. **c.** An open railway wagon. **d.** A bogie truck; = BOGIE 2. **e.** A low barrow of various types, with one to four wheels; as that used on railway platforms for moving luggage, etc. **f.** A small barrow, with two stout low wheels and a projecting plate or lip in front, used for moving sacks or other heavy packages.

**1774** *Hull Dock Act* 46 Any truck or cart, sledge waggon, dray. **1815** *Chron.* in *Ann. Reg.* 47/2 A baker's boy was wheeling his truck of bread along the road. **1838** N. WOOD *Railroads* 209 Truck for the conveyance of general merchandise. **1843** *Proc. Inst. Civil Eng.* 99 A 'bogie' engine, having a four-wheeled truck to support one end of the boiler. **1844** DICKENS *Mart. Chuz.* ix, There were more trucks near Todgers's than you would suppose a whole city could ever need. **1866** R. M. BALLANTYNE *Shift. Winds* xxiv. (1881) 274 Porters are hurrying to and fro with luggage on trucks. **1888** F. HUME *Mme. Midas* I. v, Another truck was waiting to take it to the main shaft, from whence it went up to the puddlers.

**4.** *attrib.* and *Comb.*, as *truck-barrow, -boy, construction, -driver, -horse, -load, -man, -porter, -proprietor, -wagon, -wheel*; *truck-like* adj.; **truck-bolster**, the cross-beam of a bogie truck on which the weight of the carriage rests (*Cent. Dict.* 1891); **truck-gun**, a gun mounted on trucks (see sense 1); **truck-jack**: see quot.; **truck-light**, in the U.S. Navy, a mast-head signalling light; **truck-windlass**, a windlass mounted on a truck (*Funk's Stand. Dict.* 1895).

**1849** CRAIG, **Truck-barrow*, in Ropemaking, a sort of barrow with three wheels, used to take hauls of yarn from the yarn-house. **1900** *Engineering Mag.* XIX. 705 Castings keep coming in until there is a perfect wilderness of them piled about, through which the *truck-boy winds his tortuous way. **1901** *Daily News* 16 Jan. 6/5 Colossal expenditure on track improvements, *truck construction, and increased power of locomotives. **1907** *Ibid.* 17 Apr. 4 All sorts and conditions of people,..business men, *truck drivers, workgirls, policemen, Army men, everybody. **1883** *Ibid.* 31 Aug. 6/6 One of the old class of corvettes with *truck guns. **1894** S. FISKE *Holiday Stories* (1900) 21 What does it cost to keep a *truck-horse? **1877** KNIGHT *Dict. Mech.*, **Truck-jack*, a lifting-jack suspended from a truck-axle to lift logs or other objects so that they may be loaded on to a sled or other low-bodied vehicle. **18..** *Army & Navy Reg.* (U.S.A.) XXIV. 277 (Cent. Supp.) *Truck-light. **1895** *Daily News* 8 Apr. 6/4 The third-class passenger for a long time had to be content with a *truck-like carriage, with low sides, and seldom roofed. **1862** *Sat. Rev.* 18 Feb. 157 The great London firms have sent off many railway *truck-loads of their publications. **1787** M. Cutler in *Life*, etc. (1888) I. 306 By them.. licensing retailers, taverns, carters, *truckmen,.. are regulated. **1854** Emerson *Lett. & Soc. Aims, Eloquence* Wks. (Bohn) III. 192 Ought not the scholar to be able to convey his meaning in terms as..strong as the porter or truckman uses to convey his? **1901** *Scotsman* 11 Apr. 8/1 The truckman..delivered the gold from the Assay office to the steamship. **1897** *Outing* (U.S.) XXX. 351/2 At Baddeck our camping outfit was packed upon a *truck-wagon. **1825** J. Nicholson *Operat. Mechanic* 423 The motion given to the *truck-wheels of the spinning-machine. **1909** *Daily Chron.* 25 Sept. 7/6 Lad wanted for *truck work.

Hence **Tru·ckful**, as much as fills or loads a truck.

**1893** *Columbus (Ohio) Dispatch* 12 Oct., Cigars are pouring in by the truckful and the cigarettes are innumerable. **1900** *Daily News* 1 Aug. 6/6 The truckful of sick and wounded left at Bloemfontein Station.

**Truck** (trɒk), *v.*[1] Forms: 3 **trukie**, 5 **trukke**, 6–7 **trucke**, (7 **trucque**, 8 *Sc.* **troak**), 8–9 *Sc.* **troke**, **trock**, 9 *Sc.* **troque**, 6– **truck**. [ME. *trukie*, a. F. *troquer* to truck, shop, barter, exchange (Cotgr.), Norman-Picard form of OF. **trocher*, in med.L. *trocāre* (1257 in Cartulary, Hatz.-Darm.), Fr. has also verbal sb. *troc*, †*troq* barter, Pg. *troca* = Sp., Pg. *trocar*, It. *truccare* (Florio, 1598): of unknown origin: see suggestions in Diez.

In 13th c., and in *Promp. Parv.*, but rare before 1580.]

**1.** *trans.* To give in exchange *for* something else; to exchange (one thing) *for* another; also, to exchange (a thing) *with* a person (also *absol.*).

*a* **1225** *Ancr. R.* 408 Vndeore he makeð God, & to unwurð mid alle, þet for eni worldliche luue his luue trukie. *c* **1230** *Hali Meid.* 5 And trukie for a mon of lam þe heuenliche lauerd. **1598** Sylvester *Du Bartas* II. ii. II. *Babylon* 485 Trade..with hardy luck Doth words for words barter, exchange and truck. **1614** B. Jonson *Bart. Fair* II. vi, S'blood, how braue is he? in a garded coate? you were best trucke with him. *c* **1645** Howell *Lett.* (1650) II. 105 To truck the Latine for any other vulgar Language, is but an ill barter. **1698** Farquhar *Love & Bottle* I. i, What, slighted! despised! my honourable love trucked for a whore! **1706** E. Ward *Wooden World Diss.* (1708) 23 Let him truck Jackets with any of his Barge-men. **1819** Keats *K. Stephen* I. iii. 11, I would not truck this brilliant day To rule in Pylos with a Nestor's beard. **1827** Barrington *Pers. Sk.* II. 305 Revolutions have been effected..dynasties annihilated, and kings trucked, with as little confusion as the exchanging a gig horse.

**2.** To exchange (commodities) for profit; to barter. Const. *for* a thing, *with* a person.

*c* **1440** *Promp. Parv.* 503/2 Trukkon, roryn, or chaungyn, *cambio, campso*. **1588** Parke tr. *Mendoza's Hist. China* 329 They..brought with them many curious thinges..to truck for other thinges. **1650** Fuller *Pisgah* II. ii. 80 They kept swine to truck and barter with other nations. *c* **1660** D. North in R. North *Lives* (1826) II. 306 The seamen trucked some tobacco with them for their capeaks, or furred caps. **1774** *Phil. Trans.* LXIV. 380 For blanketing, fire-arms..and ammunition, they truck the greatest part of their furs. **1817–18** Cobbett *Resid. U. S.* (1822) 40 My own stock being gone, I have trucked turnips for apples. **1884** *St. James' Gaz.* 19 Dec. 4/1 When the smacksmen have no money he [the skipper] will tempt them to 'truck' the stores of their vessel.

*fig.* *c* **1645** Howell *Lett.* (1650) III. 3 Since we are both agred to truck Intelligence [etc.]. *a* **1774** Fergusson *Butter-fly in Street* 41 How cou'd you troke the mavis' note For 'penny pies all piping hot'? **1896** J. Lumsden *Poems* 171 A' the news the country offered Crinch for crinch they trockit thrang.

†**b.** To acquire by barter. *Obs. rare.*

**1553** S. Cabot *Ordinances* in Hakluyt *Voy.* (1589) 261 All wares and commodities trucked, bought or giuen to the companie. **1600** Hakluyt *Voy.* III. 326 Fiue or sixe pounds weight of siluer which he had trucked and traffiqued with Indians. **1631** J. Rous *Diary* (Camden) 67 Fish, either bought or trucked at Norwich.

**c.** To dispose of *to* a person by barter. ? *Obs.*

**1686** *Col. Rec. Pennsylv.* I. 187 Nicho. Skull hath sould and trucked to and with ye Indians severall quantities of Liquors. **1755** T. Prince *Ann. New Eng.* II. ii. (1826) 317 That no person give, sell, truck or send any Indian corn to any English out of this jurisdiction. **1819** Wiffen *Aonian Hours* (1820) 47 No selfish ministers,..for place, Truck to a crown their dignity of mind.

†**d.** To deal or traffic in (a commodity). *rare.*

**1715** Bentley *Serm.* x. 358 The very Sins of the Living, the Wages of Damnation, were negotiated and truck'd by the wicked Politic of Popery.

†**e.** To carry *about* for sale; to hawk, peddle.

**1681** R. Knox *Hist. Ceylon* IV. ix. 157 We shewed him.. the Cotton Yarn which we had trucked about the Country.

**3.** To barter away (what should be sacred or precious) *for* something unworthy; = Barter *v.* 2 b.

**1649** G. Daniel *Trinarch., Hen. V*, cccxxviii, The Painted Apple, for his part In Paradice; France truck't, for a faire face. **1706** De Foe *Jure Div.* v. 9 Liberty's too often truck'd for Gold. *a* **1726** W. Reeves *Serm.* (1729) 160 He will not..truck his religion for preferment. **1781** Cowper *Expost.* 374 Having trucked thy soul, brought home the fee. **1829** J. Sterling *Ess.*, etc. (1848) I. 124 Many of..the Spaniards..were willing to truck the independence of their country for the political benefits promised by the invaders.

**b.** *To truck away*: to dispose of by barter.

**1631** Sanderson *Serm., Ad Aulam* i. (1660) II. 6 For the obtaining whereof they truck away their precious souls. **1657** R. Ligon *Barbadoes* (1673) 119 His men..(for some Commodities useful to themselves) had truckt away the greatest part of his Bisket. **1796** Burke *Regic. Peace* iv. Wks. IX. 110 Some of our Kings have..trucked away, for foreign gold, the interests and glory of their crown.

**4.** *intr.* To trade by exchange of commodities; to barter. Const. *for* a thing *with* a person.

**1594** [see Trucking *vbl. sb.*[1]]. **1599** Hakluyt *Voy.* II. 227 Neither would they take money for their fruite but would trucke for olde shirtes or pieces of olde linnen breeches. **1623** Lisle *Ælfric on O. & N. Test.* To Rdr. 3 Wee liue here as on the great Bursse and Exchange of the World, trucquing and trading as it were by the Merchant Waters thereof. **1697** Dampier *Voy.* (1729) I. 41 Spaniards who lived there to truck with the Indians for gold. **1797** S. James *Narr. Voy.* 162 He would either sell them to him, or truck with him for any thing. **1854** R. G. Latham *Native Races Russian Emp.* 181 Chinese..tobacco, for which they truck with the Russians.

**5.** *intr. fig.* or in fig. context: To bargain or deal *for* a commodity, *with* a person; to negotiate; also to have dealings *in*, to trade; esp. of dealings of an underhand or improper character: to traffic.

**1615** Jackson *Creed* IV. III. vii. § 6 A city which is above, whose commodities cannot be purchased with gold or silver ..much less may we truck for them with our unclean worldly delights. **1640** in Rushw. *Hist. Coll.* III. (1692) I. 122 He hath most unworthily trucked and chaffered in the meanest of them. *a* **1656** Ussher *Ann.* vi. (1658) 500 [She] trucked with the army..and brought it over to her husband as her dowry. **1664** in Howell *State Trials* (1816) VI. 607 Here is Wild commits a robbery, you come and truck with Wild, and agree with him that Mr. Tryon shall let him go. *a* **1774** Fergusson *Election* Poems (1845) 43 Ye louns! that troke in doctors' stuff. **1824** Scott *St. Ronan's* xxxi, She must go on troking wi' the old carrier, as if there was no post-house in the neighbourhood. **1904** *Daily News* 7 Dec. 11 Private communities have no business to 'truck with' the State.

**b.** In weakened sense: To have dealings or intercourse *with*, to have to do *with*, be on familiar terms; †*spec.* of sexual intercourse. Now *dial.*

**1622** F. Markham *Bk. War* II. iv. 54 If he haue..the vnderstanding of other Languages he is an inestimable Iuell, for so he shall be able to trucke with strangers for the benefit of his Company. **1624** Massinger *Parl. Love* II. i, Truck with old ladies That nature hath given o'er. *a* **1658** Cleveland *Mixt Assembly* 86 If they two truck together, 'twill not be A Child-birth, but a Goal-delivery. *a* **1704** T. Brown *Sat. Quack* 95 Wrinkled witches, when they truck with hell. **1719** Hamilton *Ep. to Ramsay* 24 July v, To troke with thee I'd best forbear 't. **1787** W. Taylor *Poems* 132 Me..wuss me hae never Enbowr see, Nor wi' sic Lady trockit. **1815** Scott *Guy M.* xi, He held ower muckle troking and communing wi' that Meg Merrilies, wha was the maist notorious witch in a' Galloway. **1893–4** *Northumbld. Gloss.*, *Troke*, to truck, to negotiate with, to be on familiar terms.

**6.** *intr.* To walk about on petty business; to potter. *Sc.*

**1864** Gilfillan *Jrnl.* in Watson *Life* (1892) 384, I troked about Edinburgh for a day or two. **1871** W. Alexander *Johnny Gibb* xxxix, Tak' a girse parkie or twa, an' trock aboot amo' nowte beasts. **1892** Stevenson & L. Osbourne *Wrecker* vi, Going troking across a continent on a wild goose chase. **1894** Traikings and trokings [see *traiking* s.v. Traik *v.*].

**7.** *trans.* To pay (an employee) otherwise than in money; to pay or deal with on the truck system (with the implication of profiting by the transaction). Also *intr.*

**1871** A. S. Harvey in *Gd. Words* 610 A large proportion of the trade is in the hands of middlemen, called 'foggers', —those who truck being known as 'pettifoggers',—each of whom employs a certain number of nailmakers. *Ibid.* 614 He..works on,..trucked by the same merchant from boyhood to manhood, from manhood to old age. *Ibid.* 615 The very paupers used to be 'trucked', the inspectors..gave the paupers their relief in kind. **1879** Escott *England* I. 265, 25,000 hands are employed, and, speaking roughly, about 14,000 are trucked.

¶**8.** *intr.* = Truckle *v.* 2 a. *Obs. rare.*

**1665** *Surv. Aff. Netherl.* 174 Their Towns..ready to submit to any new Masters, rather than Truck under Amsterdam. **1674** Staveley *Rom. Horseleach* Ep. Ded., Amsterdam supplanted Antwerp,—Flanders trucked under Holland.

Hence **Tru·cking** *ppl. a.*, that trucks or barters.

**1776** Adam Smith *W. N.* I. ii. (1869) I. 16 This same trucking disposition..originally gives occasion to the division of labour. **1871** A. S. Harvey in *Gd. Words* 611 In the hosiery trade the trucking middlemen undersell the cash-paying masters.

**Truck**, *v.*[2] [f. Truck *sb.*[2]]

**1.** *trans.* To put on or into a truck; to convey by means of a truck or trucks.

**1809** [see *trucking* below]. **1864** *Pall Mall G.* 4 Sept. 10/2 At stations where cattle are trucked, special accommodation for trucking them quietly and carefully,..ought to be provided. **1865** *Ibid.* 29 Sept. 7/2 A farmer in Perthshire, having lost one or two animals from the plague, immediately trucked off the rest to London for the Monday morning's market. **1884** *West. Morn. News* 6 Aug. 1/2 Lots can be trucked..to any part of the West of England.

**2.** *intr.* To drive or take charge of a truck, to act as a truck-driver. *U.S. colloq.*

**1907** *Black Cat* June 3, I been truckin' fer you, or rather fer your father and uncle, eighteen years, and that's the first time any one's ever accused me of droppin' anything.

Hence **Tru·cking** *vbl. sb.*

**1809** R. Langford *Introd. Trade* 73 Wharfage and Shipping Marking £1 16*s.* 7*d.*, Trucking..£1 10*s.* **1891** *Echo* 10 Mar. 3/2 On the quays..the snow is a foot deep, and trucking from the sheds to the ship has been delayed. **1909** *Dundee Advertiser* 24 Nov. 7 Miners..have struck work owing to a difference with the management regarding the trucking of coal.

†**Truck**, *v.*[3] *Obs. rare*—[1]. [Cf. It. *truccare* 'to trudge, to skud, or pack away' (Florio, 1598).] *intr.* To trudge, tramp.

**1631** Brathwait *Whimzies, Wine-soaker* 102 If he..fall into a gravell-pit hee taxeth the citie for her governement, for leaving her cellar doores so wide open at that time a night. Yet on hee trucks, if he can mount the pit.

**Truck**, var. Trug[2] *Obs.*; dial. var. Troke *v.*

†**Truckage**[1]. *Obs. rare.* In 7 **truccage**. [f. Truck *v.*[1] + -age.] The action of trucking; exchange, barter.

**1641** Milton *Reform.* II. 15 If such Divine ministeries as these must..not passe to and fro..without the truccage of perishing Coine.

**Truckage**[2] (trɒ·kėdʒ). [f. Truck *sb.*[2] or *v.*[2] + -age.] Conveyance by truck or trucks, or the cost of this; also, supply of trucks collectively (cf. Tonnage *sb.* 5).

**1846** Worcester, *Truckage*,..expense of conveying by trucks. **1883** Joncas *Fisheries Canada* 28 (Fish. Exhib. Publ.) The erection and repairs of buildings, tin and iron work, boat-building, fuel-cutting, truckage, and other expenditure. **1901** *Daily Chron.* 11 Nov. 5/6 Unless a further amount of truckage can be allotted immediately, the inhabitants will have to go extremely short.

**Trucker**[1] (trɒ·kəɹ). [f. Truck *v.*[1] and *sb.*[1] + -er[1]. Cf. F. *troqueur* (17th c.).]

**1.** One who trucks or barters; a barterer, bargainer; *Sc.* an itinerant dealer, a pedlar; †also, as a term of reproach: a haggler, huckster, trafficker (*obs.*).

**1598** Florio, *Barattiere*,..a trucker, a marter, an exchanger. **1622** Mabbe tr. *Aleman's Guzman d'Alf.* II. 239 This silly foole was a kinde of trucker of commodities. **1632** Massinger *City Madam* III. i, I know them—swaggering, suburbian roarers, Sixpenny truckers. **1660** J. Lloyd *Prim. Episc.* 31 The sacrilegious truckers, which would have the reverend Clergy live upon their leavings and scraps. *c* **1790** in Ramsay *Scot. in 18th C.* (1888) II. xi. 323 *note*, Every year there came a set of *troquers* or *trockhers* (barterers, Fr. *troquer*) from Ireland with horse-loads of linen, which they bartered for the miner's old clothes. **1802** Joanna Baillie *Ethwald* II. I. iii, Come on, base trokers of your country's blood. **1816** Scott *Antiq.* iii, Brokers and trokers, those miscellaneous dealers in things rare and curious.

**2.** *U.S.* One who grows 'truck' or garden produce for market; a truck-gardener or truck-farmer.

**1868** *Norfolk* (Virginia) *Jrnl.*, The truckers in this neighborhood. **1882** *Philad. Even. Star* 2 May, Norfolk truckers are picking their strawberries. **1890** *Boston* (Mass.) *Jrnl.* 10 Apr. 2/4 Southern vegetables are looking very well and the truckers are hopeful.

**3.** *attrib.*, as *trucker-fashion*; also †**trucker-cloth**, ? cloth for trucking; cf. *trucking-cloth*.

**1536** *Somerset Medieval Wills* (Som. Rec. Soc.) 34 To my brother Edward a Trucker cloth. **1543** *Ibid.* 75 To John Burges my prentice, a trucker cloth. **1881** A. Watt in *Mod. Scott. Poets* III. 137 In true troker fashion, she ca'd at ilk dwellin'.

**Tru·cker**[2]. [f. Truck *sb.*[2] + -er[1].] A labourer who uses a truck.

**1878** F. S. Williams *Midl. Railw.* 640 No sooner is the train marshalled in its dock .. than the 'truckers' bring forward the goods to be loaded. **1895** *Westm. Gaz.* 30 May 5/3 Two wagonettes, in each of which thirty dock labourers had been driven from the East End at the expense of a lucky 'trucker'.

**Trucking** (trɒ·kiŋ), *vbl. sb.*[1] [f. Truck *v.*[1] + -ing[1].] The action of Truck *v.*[1]; exchanging, bartering, trafficking, bargaining; dealings, intercourse; also *spec.* the giving or receiving payment of wages in kind.

**1594** Carew *Huarte's Exam. Wits* xiii. (1616) 216 Manie ..by trafficking and trucking, within few dayes haue lost their principall. **1624** Massinger *Renegado* II. vi, Pray you, help me to some trucking With your last she-customer. **1661** *Colet's Serm. Conf. & Ref.* II. 27 Unloose your selves from the worldly bondage, from trucking with the world. **1705** Vanbrugh *Confed.* II. i, You like your neighbour's [wife] better...What a pity it is the law don't allow trucking. **1755** Ramsay *To Jas. Clerk* 11 To fend by troaking, buying, selling. **1818** Scott *Rob Roy* xxvi, He was here about some Jacobitical papistical troking in seventeen hundred and seven. **1830** Cobbett *Rur. Rides* (1885) II. 354 The workman..if he will have liquor,..must get it by trucking with the goods that he has got at the tommy shop. *a* **1867** Sir A. Alison *Autobiog.* (1883) I. ii. 30 Our..interchange of little purchases or troking as we called it.

**b.** *U.S.* The cultivation of 'truck' or vegetables.

**1897** *Philad. Jrnl. Fine Arts* June, About one half [of the grounds] is used for trucking and pasture purposes.

**c.** *attrib.* in sense 'used for truck or barter', as †*trucking-cloth, -house, stuff.*

**1675** in Hubbard *Narrative* I. (1865) 78 He or they..shall receive for their Pains, forty *Trucking-cloth Coats. **1632** *Rec. Crt. Assistants Mass. Bay* (1904) II. 23 There shalbe a *trucking howse..in euery plantacion whither the Indians may resorte to trade. **1648** B. Plantagenet *Descr. New Albion* 23 To reduce all their trading to five Ports or Pallisadoed trucking houses. **1755** T. Prince *Ann. New Eng.* II. ii. (1826) 395 There shall be a trucking house in every plantation. **1624** *Good News fr. New Eng.* in Arber *Pilgrim Fathers* (1897) 533 We were worn out of all manner of *trucking stuff, not having [therefore] any means left to help ourselves by trade.

**Trucking** *vbl. sb.*[2], see under Truck *v.*[2]

**Truckle** (trɒ·k'l), *sb.* Forms: 5 **trokel**, **-ill**, **trookyll**, **trokle**, *pl.* **trokleys**, 5–6 **trokell**, **trocle**, 6 **troukle**, **-cle**, **trowkle**, **truckill**, 7 **truckel**, **trukle**, **trickle** (also 9 *dial.*), 6– **truckle**. [= AF. *trocle, trokle*, ad. L. *trochlea* = Gr. τροχιλία, τροχιλέα, etc., sheaf of a pulley: see Trochlea.]

**1.** A small wheel with a groove in its circumference round which a cord passes; a pulley, a sheave.

1417 in *For. Acc.* 8 *Hen. V*, D/2, j apparaille ix pullifs vj Trokles. *Ibid.* G/1 Eiusdem Nauis j apparatu ix Pullifs vj Trocles j securi. 14.. *MS. Digby 233* lf. 221/2 Þanne drawe þei & wyndeþ vp þe lasse toure with ropes & trokelus. 1545 ELYOT, *Artemon*, a troukle wherby ropes dooe runne. It maye also be taken for any instrument that hath troucles. 1592 R. D. *Hypnerotomachia* 8 With what Cranes, winding beames, Trocles, round pullies, Capres. *a* 1693 *Urquhart's Rabelais* III. xvi. 132 A Truckle for a Pully. 1761 STERNE *Tr. Shandy* III. xx, A truckle for a pully. 1904 ANSTRUTHER THOMSON *Remin.* II. v. 135 They hoisted him and then let the truckle go with a run.

**2.** A small roller or wheel placed under or attached to a heavy object to facilitate moving it; a castor on a piece of furniture. Now *dial.*

1459 [see TRUCKLE-BED]. 1519 HORMAN *Vulg.* 244 b, This house may be remoued with trocles, & slyddis. 1617 HIERON *Wks.* (1619–20) II. 351 Thou which canst not goe alone, maist be allowed to goe by truckles, or as thou art led by anothers hand. 1655 tr. *Com. Hist. Francion* IX. 14 He showed them a great round chair very ancient, which had truckles under it to move withall. 1706 PHILLIPS (ed. Kersey), *Truckle*, a little running Wheel. 1837 *Penny Mag.* VI. 338 [A wooden horse] placed on a stand made moveable by truckles. 1888 ELWORTHY *W. Somerset Word-bk.*, *Truckle*, ..2. a caster. 'The very chairs 'ad a-got truckles to 'em'.

**3.** Short for TRUCKLE-BED.

1637 HEYWOOD *Royall King* III. vii, A close roome, with a standing bed in 't, and a truckle too. 1664 BUTLER *Hud.* II. ii. 40 With knocking loud and bauling, He rous'd the Squire, in Truckle lolling. 1707 PRIOR *Sat. Poets* 76 No Friend.. but trusting Landlady, Who stows you on hard Truckle, Garret high. 1826 SCOTT *Woodst.* xxi, His..attendant.. deposited himself on his truckle. 1851 W. ANDERSON *Rhymes* (1867) 143 (E.D.D.) A wee truckle filled wi' fusionless strae.

**4.** A low-wheeled car; a truck. Chiefly in Irish use.

1689 *Irish Procl.* 14 Sept., [Not] to..meddle with any of their horses, carts, truckels, or other their tacklings. 1751 R. PALTOCK *P. Wilkins* (1884) I. 118, I no sooner unloaded but down went I again with my cart, or truckle rather, to the lake, and brought from thence on it my other chest. 1807 P. GASS *Jrnl.* 240 Our waggons and truckles to transport the baggage and canoes. 1880 *Antrim & Down Gloss.*, *Truckle*, a small car, in common use before the introduction of the present farm-carts.

**5.** A small barrel-shaped cheese. *dial.*

*a* 1813 [see *truckle-cheese* in 6]. 1850 *Jrnl. R. Agric. Soc.* XI. II. 705 Besides these cheeses, some small ones are made, called 'truckles'. 1891 *Catal. Oxf. Agric. Show* 45 The best lot of Cheese not less than ½ cwt. (Truckles excepted). 1901 *Scotsman* 9 Oct. 10/2 For cheddar truckles.

**6.** *attrib.* and *Comb.*, as *truckle-car*, *-cheese* (= 5), *-wheel*. See also TRUCKLE-BED.

1748 MRS. DELANY *Life & Corr.* (1861) II. 491 *Truckle-car (what they [Irish] make use of for carrying goods) drawn by one horse and the wheels not three foot high. *a* 1813 in Ellis *Brand's Pop. Antiq.* I. 55 A piece of *Truckle Cheese. 1891 *Catal. Oxf. Agric. Show* 45 The best lot of 3 Loaf or other Truckle Cheese (not Stilton). 1533 *Lett. & Pap. Hen. VIII*, VI. 503, 4 carpenters..making of *truckill whelis. 1706 *Phil. Trans.* XXV. 2253 Near the one End..let a little Truckle-wheel..be fastened to the Rular by a Pin.

**Tru·ckle,** *v.* Also 8 *Sc.* **trockle.** [f. *truckle* in TRUCKLE-BED.]

†**1.** *intr.* To sleep in a truckle-bed. Const. *under* (*beneath*) the person occupying the high bed, or the high bed itself. Also *fig.* *Obs.*

1613 BEAUM. & FL. *Coxcomb* I. vi, I'll truckle here, boy; give me another pillow. 1655 R. BOREMAN *Mirr. Mercy & Judgm.* 21 Who had the custody of him at the house of master Foster, Keeper of the Prison, and truckled under him every night. 1657 HOWELL *Londinop.* 399 [St. Paul's] having a large Church..truckling, as one may say, under her Chancel. 1658 E. PHILLIPS *Gard. Tulips* 51 The Knight keeps to his Lady in the high bed, and never truckles. 1674 N. FAIRFAX *Bulk & Selv.* 21 Such a kind of somewhatkin, as truckles beneath the very tinyness of an half nothing.

**2.** *fig.* †**a.** To take a subordinate or inferior position; to be subservient, to submit, to give precedence. Const. *under*, *to*. *Obs.*

1667 PEPYS *Diary* 2 Sept., He will never..truckle under any body or any faction, but do just as his own reason and judgment directs. 1671 MARVELL *Corr.* Wks. (Grosart) II. 395 We truckle to France in all things, to the prejudice of our honour. 1681 EVELYN *Let. to Pepys* 5 Dec., in *Mem.* (1819) II. 216 Unlesse it be, that we designe to truckle under France. *a* 1704 T. BROWN *Praise Poverty* Wks. 1730 I. 92 Publick good is made to truckle to private gain. 1738 tr. *Guazzo's Art Conversation* 66 Where Sense imperious bears the Sway, Reason must truckle and obey.

**b.** To submit from an unworthy motive; to yield meanly or obsequiously; to act with servility. Const. *down*, *to* a person, *for* an object.

1680 C. NESSE *Church-Hist.* 285 His sordid spirit truckles and crouches. *a* 1715 EARL HALIFAX *Man of Hon.* Poems (1779) 226 Those that meanly truckle to your power. 1789 PARR *Tracts Warburton*, etc. 184 He was..too proud to truckle to a Superior. 1809 — *Char. Fox* Wks. 1828 IV. 111 Ambition..which..truckles for office by the barter of principle. 1842 THACKERAY *Miss Tickletoby* ix, These nobles..were the first to truckle down to him when he came to assert..his right. 1858 FROUDE *Hist. Eng.* III. xiv. 223 The short years which might have been his, had he..denied his faith and truckled to the time. 1885 R. L. & F. STEVENSON *Dynamiter* i, Doubtful people of all sorts and conditions begging and truckling for your notice.

**c.** To submit or give way timidly; in quot. 1840, to quail, cower, be daunted.

1837 CAMPBELL *Hybrias* i, With these I make..all around me truckle. 1840 DICKENS *Barn. Rudge* xxiii, Hugh truckled before the hidden meaning of these words. *a* 1845 HOOD *Jack Hall* xii, To my commands The strongest truckles.

†**3.** *trans.* To cause to truckle. *Obs. rare*⁻¹.

1687 *Good Advice* 9 They..compell men to truckle their tender Consciences to the Grandure and Dominion of their Doctors.

†**4.** *intr.* and *trans.* To move on truckles or castors; = TRUNDLE *v.* 3 a, b. *Obs.*

1656 [see TRUCKLING *ppl. a.*]. 1796 MME. D'ARBLAY *Camilla* III. xiii, Tables with two legs, and chairs without bottoms, were truckled from the middle to one end of the room.

¶ **5.** *intr.* To traffic, deal. = TRUCK *v.*[1] 5, 5 b. Const. *with*. *rare.*

1806 FELLOWES tr. *Milton's 2nd Defence* (1848) 293 Those money-changers..do not merely truckle with doves, but with the Dove itself, with the Spirit of the Most High. 1909 *Q. Rev.* July 284 He declined to truckle with any practices tending, as he thought, towards Rome.

**Truckle**, obs. form of TRICKLE *v.*

**Tru·ckle-bed.** [TRUCKLE *sb.* 2.] A low bed running on truckles or castors, usually pushed beneath a high or 'standing' bed when not in use; a trundle-bed. So **Truckle bedstead.**

1459 *Stat. Magd. Coll. Oxf.* xlv, Sint duo lecti principales, et duo lecti rotales, Trookyll beddys vulgariter nuncupati. 1531 in *Rec. St. Mary at Hill* 45 Item, an olde lytell couervng for a lytell Trokell bed. 1597 BP. HALL *Sat.* II. vi. 5 First that He lie vpon the Truckle-bed, Whiles his yong maister lieth ore his hed. 1598 SHAKS. *Merry W.* IV. v. 6 There's his Chamber, his House, his Castle, his standing-bed and truckle-bed. 1662 PEPYS *Diary* 1 May, To bed all alone, and my Will in the truckle bed. 1755 SMOLLETT *Quix.* (1803) IV. 273 Sancho slept that night in a truckle-bed, in the apartment of Don Quixote. 1807 SIR R. C. HOARE *Tour Irel.* 302 Numbers [of peasants]..have not a bedstead, nor even what is called a truckle bed frame. 1831 CARLYLE *Sart. Res.* I. iii, Wretchedness cowers into truckle-beds, or shivers hunger-stricken into its lair of straw. 1895 RIDER HAGGARD *Heart of World* vii, A few chairs, a rough washing-stand, and two truckle bedsteads of American make.

**Truckler** (trɒ·kləɹ). [f. TRUCKLE *v.* + -ER[1].] One who truckles (in sense 2 b of the verb).

1827 SCOTT *Napoleon* Introd., Wks. 1870 IX. 31 These trucklers to fortune. 1848 KINGSLEY *Saint's Trag.* III. iii, The wonder Of timid trucklers. 1872 GEO. ELIOT *Middlem.* xliv, I should be a base truckler if I allowed any consideration of personal comfort to hinder me.

**Truckling** (trɒ·kliŋ), *vbl. sb.* [f. TRUCKLE *v.* + -ING[1].] The action of the verb TRUCKLE; mean submission.

*c* 1665 MRS. HUTCHINSON *Mem. Col. Hutchinson* (1846) 475, I am free from any truckling with them. 1820 L. HUNT *Indicator* No. 55 (1822) II. 22 He had a grudge against Milton for what he called his trucklings about Pandæmonium. 1848 THACKERAY *Bk. Snobs* iii, The habit of truckling and cringing. 1888 BURGON *Lives 12 Gd. Men* I. ii. 140 The base truckling of an ungodly age, ever ready to surrender what is unpopular.

**Tru·ckling,** *ppl. a.* [f. as prec. + -ING[2].] That truckles; †that is subordinate or inferior (*obs.*); meanly submissive, servile.

1656 [see *standing-stool*, STANDING *vbl. sb.* 11]. 1665 TEMPLE *Let. to Ld. Arlington* Wks. 1731 II. 6 Their last Resourse, which is the Protection of France,..or else a perfect truckling Peace with England. 1701 SWIFT *Contests Nobles & Com. Athens & Rome* ii, A small truckling state, of no name or reputation. 1728 RAMSAY *Epist. to Burchet* v, The like of you..Should gar the trockling rogues look blue. 1796 BURKE *Regic. Peace* i. Wks. VIII. 87 In small truckling states a timely compromise with power has often been the means..of drawling out their puny existence. 1823 SCOTT *Peveril* xvii, Unworthy or truckling compliance with tenets which my heart disowns. 1868 FARRAR *Silence & V.* iii. (1875) 64 Our beloved English Church..may, even yet, be unable to escape..the Nemesis ..due to the sluggish impotence and truckling worldliness of her 18th Century.

Hence **Tru·cklingly** *adv.*, in a truckling manner.

1831 *Fraser's Mag.* III. 605 He would joyfully, thankfully, trucklingly accept it. 1857 *Tait's Mag.* XXIV. 30, I could conceive women..unhappy; but not meanly, timidly, trucklingly miserable.

**Trucks** (trɒks). *Obs.* exc. *Hist.* Also (? *erron.*) 7–8 **truck.** [ad. It. *trucco* (see below), Sp. *troco.*] An early form of billiards, in which an upright mark called the king was placed near one end of the table. Cf. TROLL-MADAM and TRUNK *sb.* 16.

[Cf. 1598 FLORIO, *Truccare*,..to play at billiards. *Trucco*, a kinde of play with balles vpon a table called billiards, but properly a kinde of game vsed in England with casting little bowles at a boord with thirteene holes in it.]

1671 SKINNER *Etymol.*, *Truck*, Biliers or Biliards. 1674 COTTON (*title*) The Compleat Gamester: or, Instructions how to play at Billiards, Trucks, Bowls, and Chess. 1688 R. HOLME *Armoury* III. 263/1 *Truck*, is an Italian Game, and is not very unlike Billiards, the Table..hath 3 holes at each end, besides the corner holes. 1736 AINSWORTH *Lat. Dict.*, Truck (the play), *ludus tudicularis*. 1801 STRUTT *Sports & Past.* IV. i. § 16 The Italian method of playing, known in England by the name of Trucks,..had its king at one end of the table.

**Truckster** (trɒ·kstəɹ). *rare.* [f. TRUCK *v.*[1] + -STER.] A base trafficker; cf. TRUCK *v.*[1] 3.

1868 TUCKERMAN *Collector* 83 Many a poet..has degenerated into a hack, a truckster, and a mercenary penman.

**Truculence** (trū·k-, trɒ·kiŭlĕns). [ad. L. *truculentia* savageness, ferocity, f. *truculentus* TRUCULENT: see -ENCE.] The condition or quality of being truculent; fierceness, savageness.

1727 BAILEY vol. II, *Truculence*, *Truculentness*, cruelty, savageness, sternness. 1877 D. M. WALLACE *Russia* vi. 83 The entire absence of obsequiousness or truculence in his manner. 1890 GLADSTONE *Sp. Ho. Comm.* 28 Nov., He sometimes accompanies the temperance of language with a truculence of action.

**Truculency** (trū·k-, trɒ·kiŭlĕnsi). [f. as prec.: see -ENCY.] = prec.

1569 J. SANFORD tr. *Agrippa's Van. Artes* 111 The truculencie of the Beare. 1630 BRATHWAIT *Eng. Gentlem.* (1641) 88 It was Saint Augustine's prayer unto God that he would root out of him all..truculencie. 1855 MILMAN *Lat. Chr.* XIV. iv. (1864) IX. 188 They have more of Juvenal..of his pitilessness, of his bitterness, it may be said of his truculency, than of Catullus. 1864 CARLYLE *Fredk. Gt.* XVII. v. IV. 556 Friedrich's First Campaign..will by no means check the Austrian truculencies.

**Truculent** (trū·k-, trɒ·kiŭlĕnt), *a.* [ad. L. *truculentus*, f. *trux* (*truc-em*) fierce, savage; cf. obs. F. *truculent* (Cotgr. 1611).]

**1.** Characterized by or exhibiting ferocity or cruelty; fierce, cruel, savage, barbarous.

*c* 1540 tr. *Pol. Verg. Eng. Hist.* (Camden) I. 105 Havinge attained libertie, [Britain] entered into moste truculent warrs. 1607 TOPSELL *Four-f. Beasts* (1658) 10 His aspect and countenance was fierce, truculent, and fearful. *Ibid.* 254 Many Horses by their seed and stones are made very fierce, truculent, and unruly. 1670 BAXTER *Cure Ch.-Div.* 4 It is the character of a truculent people..that they regard not the person of the old. 1722 WOLLASTON *Relig. Nat.* vi. 141 Convulsed and agonizing under the knife of some truculent villain. 1889 JESSOPP *Coming of Friars* i. 4 The truculent ruffianism that pretended to be animated by the crusading spirit.

**b.** Of speech or writing: Violent; rude; scathing; savage; harsh.

1850 MARSDEN *Early Purit.* (1853) 204 Pamphlets.. scarcely less truculent or less contemptuous of the Christian virtues. 1868 MILMAN *St. Paul's* xvii. 416 The broader and more truculent satire of Ulrich Hutten. 1872 MORLEY *Voltaire* iii. (ed. 2) 120 Voltaire is never either gross or truculent.

†**c.** *transf.* Of a disease: Destructive; deadly. *Obs. rare.*

1665 G. HARVEY *Advice agst. Plague* x, More or less truculent Plagues.

¶ **2.** (In catachrestic use, associated with TRUCK *sb.*[1], *v.*[1], TRUCKLE *v.*) Mean, base, mercenary.

1825 BENTHAM *Ration. Rew.* 62 A truculent exchange not only of truth, but of sincerity, for money. 1884 J. T. DAVIDSON *Talks Yng. Men* viii, The mean dastard [Ahab] sent back the truculent reply: 'My lord, O king, according to thy saying, I am thine, and all that I have'.

**3.** Comb., as *truculent-looking*.

1828 SCOTT *F. M. Perth* xvii, This ungainly and truculent-looking savage. 1866 HOWELLS *Venet. Life* viii, That truculent-looking craft.

So † **Trucule·ntal** *a.* *Obs. rare*⁻¹.

1593 G. HARVEY *Pierce's Super.* ***j, A glorious, and brauing Knight, That would be deem'd a truculental wight.

**Tru·culently** (see the adj.), *adv.* [f. TRUCULENT + -LY[2].] In a truculent manner; savagely.

1654 VILVAIN *Epit. Ess.* I. 86 Most truculently butchered. 1837 CARLYLE *Misc. Ess.*, *Diam. Neckl.* xiv. (1872) V. 186 How fares it with his Eminence..at times truculently stamping? 1868 M. E. G. DUFF *Pol. Surv.* 179 Often beaten..from the firm land, he always returned again, truculently fought again.

So **Tru·culentness** (*rare*⁻⁰) = TRUCULENCE.

1727 [see TRUCULENCE].

†**Tru·ddle,** obs. form of TREADLE.

1667 in Pettus *Fodinæ Reg.* (1670) 37 One large new Wheel, that carrieth three Pair of bellows, with Swords, Beams, Truddles.

**Trudge** (trɒdʒ), *v.*[1] Also 6 **tredge,** 6–7 (8–9 *dial.*) **tridge,** 7 **trug.** [Of obscure origin. Skeat suggests F. *trucher* to beg from laziness (in Oudin, 16th c.), but this does not agree in sense.]

**1.** *intr.* To walk laboriously, wearily, or without spirit, but steadily and persistently; 'to jog on; to march heavily on' (J.). Sometimes merely an undignified equivalent of 'walk', 'go on foot'.

1547 *Bk. Marchauntes* e j b, If the belles rynge in any place..for an obit, than oure gentyl gallants trudge apace. *c* 1550 in Strype *Mem. Cranmer* (1694) App. xlix. 138 Some of their carcases standith on the gates, And their heads..on London bridge, Therefore, ye Traytors, beware your pates, For yf ye be founde, the same way must ye tridge. 1573 TUSSER *Husb.* (1878) 21 Good husband he trudgeth, to bring in the gaines, Good huswife she drudgeth, refusing no paines. 1622 MABBE tr. *Aleman's Guzman d'Alf.* I. 219, I..trugg'd along with my sore legge. 1685 EVELYN *Mrs. Godolphin* (1888) 122 Wherever a certaine Lady goes,—I must trudge. 1709–10 STEELE *Tatler* No. 137 ¶ 3, I was the other Day trudging along Fleet street on Foot. 1795 WOLCOTT (P. Pindar) *Royal Visit Exeter* II. xi, Now trudg'd to aldermen and may'r, 'Squire Rolle. 1856 R. A. VAUGHAN *Mystics* (1860) II. XI. i. 216 From house to house he trudges in the snow, visiting poor widows. 1880 L. OLIPHANT *Gilead* i. 18 We were perpetually meeting them trudging behind their loaded mules.

**b.** Also with *it*.

1649 G. DANIEL *Trinarch.*, *Hen. V*, clxxxv, The Ragged Squad..will trudge it out And Combat all the world, if Harrie lead. 1787 *Minor* IV. i. 203 So my mentor and I trudged it on foot to Oxford. 1806 SURR *Winter in Lond.* I. 194 Give me your arm, we'll trudge it.

**c.** *spec.* To go away, be off, depart.

1547–64 BAULDWIN *Mor. Philos.* (Palfr.) 77 The cowardly ..souldier..betaketh him to his feete, & trudgeth away. 1562 *Jack Juggler* (1873) 50 Be tredging, or in faith you bere me a souse. 1573 *New Custom* I. ii, Hence out of my sight, away, packing, trudge. 1623–34 FLETCHER & MASS. *Lover's Progr.* I. ii, 'Tis time for me to trudge. 1824 SCOTT *Let. to Ld. Montagu* 14 Apr., in *Lockhart*, A dog of a banker has bought his house.., and I fear he must trudge.

**d.** *fig.*

**1573** TUSSER *Husb.* (1878) 177 If pennie for all thing be suffred to trudge, Trust long, not to pennie, to haue him thy drudge. **1575** R. B. *Appius & Virg.* B iij b, By beuty of Virginia, my wisdome all is trudged. **1683** KENNETT tr. *Erasm. on Folly* 54 Trudging after learning. **1763** JEFFERSON *Corr.* Wks. 1859 I. 185 All things here appear to me to trudge on in one and the same round. **1856** J. RICHARDSON *Recoll.* I. iv. 86 [The other masters at Eton] trudged leisurely on in the beaten track of school literature.

**2.** *trans.* **a.** To perform (a journey) or travel over (a distance) by trudging; to tramp; to trudge along or over.

**1635** PAGITT *Christianogr.* 190 They..are constrained to trudge no small journeyes, to begge their wages. **1884** BROWNING *Ferishtah, Two Camels* 37, I shall trudge The distance. **1886** HALL CAINE *Son of Hagar* III. iii, Drayton ..trudged the floor uneasily.

**b.** To trudge with (a burden); to drag *about.*

**1883** W. H. BISHOP in *Harper's Mag.* Mar. 504/2 A few old men trudge about their bake-ovens and water jars and strings of dried squash.

**3.** The vb.-stem used *advb.*: cf. TRAMP *v.*[1] 7.

**1904** MAX PEMBERTON *Red Morn* xx, Trudge, trudge, trudge upon the muddy path she went.

Hence **Tru·dging** *vbl. sb.* and *ppl. a.*; also **Tru·dger**, one who trudges.

*a* **1849** H. COLERIDGE *Poems* (1850) II. 379 Dear..To weary *trudger by the long black lake. **1896** *Blackw. Mag.* Feb. 224 The steadiest trudger along life's road. **1570** *Marr. Wit & Science* v. iii, Such *trudging and such toyle..was neuer seene. **1653** MILTON *Hirelings* Wks. 1851 V. 369 To save them the trudging of many miles thither. **1728** MORGAN *Algiers* I. Pref. 15 My Trudgings have been so misguided, by an Ignis Fatuus. **1828** P. CUNNINGHAM *N. S. Wales* (ed. 3) II. 197 After three hard weeks of toilsome trudging over rugged hills. **1584** R. SCOT *Discov. Witchcr.* XIV. viii. (1886) 310 He set forward on his journey a good trudging pase. **1716** GAY *Trivia* I. 118 The griping Broker..laughs at Honesty, and trudging Wits. **1848** DICKENS *Dombey* xviii, His trudging wife..loiters to see the company come out.

**Trudge,** *v.*[2]: see TRUDGEN.

**Trudge** (trʊdʒ), *sb.* [f. TRUDGE *v.*[1]]

**1.** A person who trudges; a trudger.

**1748** SMOLLETT *Rod. Rand.* xxx, Nor would he be a tennis-ball, nor a shuttle-cock, nor a trudge, nor a scullion. **1775** JEKYLL *Corr.* (1894) 22 Miss would have felt the absence of her fellow-trudge in clambering stiles and scrambling through hedges.

**2.** An act of trudging; a laborious or wearisome walk; a 'tramp'.

**1835** J. BROWN *Lett.* (1907) 32 You say nothing of your body and how it fared in your darkness trudge. **1871** L. STEPHEN *Playgr. Eur.* iv. 111. 257 We reached the mule track, and a steady trudge along it led us back.

†**3.** (Meaning uncertain: ?error for *thrutch.*)

**1579** LYLY *Euphues* (Arb.) 137 One thing said twice (as we say commonly) deserveth a trudge.

†**Trudge,** *a. Obs. rare*$^{-1}$. [f. as prec.] ? That trudges (as in service or attendance upon one).

**1602** F. HERING *Anat.* 14 Those old Suresbies and Trudge blew-coats, Antimony and Mercury Precipitate.

**Trudge-man,** obs. variant of TRUCHMAN.

**Trudgen** (trʊ·dʒən). Also *erron.* trudgeon. [f. proper name *Trudgen*: see below.] In full *trudgen stroke*: applied to a kind of hand-over-hand or double over-arm breast-stroke in swimming: so *trudgen swimmer.* Hence **Trudge** *v.*, *intr.* to swim with this stroke; whence **Tru·dger.**

**1893** *Westm. Gaz.* 3 Oct. 5/2 Thompson adopted the old-fashioned 'trudgeon' stroke in his spurt. **1902** J. A. JARVIS *Swimming* vi. 35 The best trudgen swimmers use a similar, though shorter leg kick, to that made when swimming over arm. *Ibid.*, I am firmly convinced that the present records at all distances will be wiped out, and fresh ones put in their place by 'trudgers'. **1904** RALPH THOMAS *Swimming* 40 Hand-over-hand or Indian stroke. In this each hand (or arm) is alternately raised above the surface of the water, thrust forward and brought sharply back under water to the loins. There are many varieties, one of which is called the trudgen. *Ibid.* 418 *note*, John Trudgen..in 1863..went to Buenos Ayres...While there he learnt 'to trudge' from the natives. **1905** *N. & Q.* 10th Ser. IV. 205/1 The trudgeon-stroke..appears to date from 1868, when it was popularized by a Mr. Trudgen.

**Trudgeon** (trʊ·dʒən). *rare*$^{-1}$. [App. nonce-wd. f. TRUDGE *v.*[1]] ? One who trudges; a toddling child.

**1814** W. IRVING in *Life & Lett.* (1864) I. 308 To take holiday and go to the country with his wife and little trudgeons.

**Trudger** [1], [2], see after TRUDGE *v.*[1], TRUDGEN.

**True** (trū), *a.* (*sb.*, *adv.*). Forms: *α.* 1 (ʒe)-tríewe), 1–3 tréowe, 1–4 trýwe, 3 treouwe, 3–4 triwe, 3–7 trewe, trew, 4–7 treu, 5 treewe, triew(e. *β.* 3 (*Orm.*) trowwe, 5 trowe, 5–6 trow; 5 traw. *γ.* 3–5 truwe, 4–5 trwe, 4–7 tru, 6 trw, 5– true. [OE. (strict WS. (*ge*)*tríewe*, commonly) *tréowe* (ME. also *truwe*) = OS. (*gi*)*trûui*, OEFris. *triuwe*, OWFris. *trouwe*, (MDu. (*ghe*)-*trûwe*, (*ghe*)*trouwe*, Du. *getrouw*), OHG. (*ga*)-*triuwu*, (Ger. *treu*), ON. *tryggr*, Goth. *triggws*; repr. WGer. **trewwj-*, lit. 'having or characterized by good faith', deriv. of the sb. which is represented by OE. *tréow, trúw*, OHG. *triuwa*, Goth. *triggwa* faith, covenant: see TRUCE.]

**1.** Of persons: Steadfast in adherence to a commander or friend, to a principle or cause, to one's promises, faith, etc.; firm in allegiance; faithful, loyal, constant, trusty. Somewhat *arch.*

*a* **1000** *St. Guthlac* 1269 (Gr.) Se wuldormaʒo..spræc..to his treowum ʒesiðe. *c* **1205** LAY. 8851 Mildeliche spæc þus þe treowe cniht Androgeus. *c* **1250** *Hymn Virg.* 2 in *Trin. Coll. Hom.* App. 257 þu ert leuedi swuþe treowe..þi loue is euer iliche neowe. **1303** R. BRUNNE *Handl. Synne* 2320 May y þan trust to þy sawe þat þou be now my trew felawe? **1388** WYCLIF *Luke* xvi. 10 He that is trewe in the leeste thing, is trewe also in the more. **1450–80** tr. *Secreta Secret.* 19 Kepe wel thi feith and thi word euermore..gret worshipe vnto hem þat so trewe are founden in here feith. **1476** *Surtees Misc.* (1888) 35 To all trewe Christen men. *a* **1533** LD. BERNERS *Huon* xcv. 307 Ye haue done as a trew subjet ought to do to his lorde. **1646** *Hamilton Papers* (Camden) 119 Your Grace's humblest truest seruant, R. Moray. **1821** SHELLEY *Bridal Song* i, Never smiled the inconstant moon On a pair so true. **1847** TENNYSON *Princess* IV. 80 Bright and fierce and fickle is the South, And dark and true and tender is the North.

**b.** *transf.* of personal attributes or actions. Somewhat *arch.*; often passing into sense 2 or 5.

*a* **800** [see TRUE-LOVE 1]. *c* **1200** ORMIN Introd. 69 Trigg & trowwe griþþ & friþþ. *c* **1275** *Passion our Lord* 45 in *O. E. Misc.* 38 Alle men he tauhte to holde treowe luue Erest to god almyhti. **13..** *Cursor M.* 4422 (Gött.) Ille es þe quit þi treu seruis. **1454** *Cal. Anc. Rec. Dublin* (1889) 281 That they shall do trewe execucion. *c* **1560** A. SCOTT *Poems* (S.T.S.) ix. 14 Ane trewar hairt may no man haif. **1667** MILTON *P. L.* III. 104 What proof could they have givn..Of true allegiance? **1832** TENNYSON *Miller's Dau.* 216 Round my true heart thine arms entwine.

**c.** Const. *to* (in early use with simple dative).

*Beowulf* (Z.) 1165 Æʒ-hwylc oðrum trywe. *c* **1200** ORMIN 6177 þin laferrd birrþ þe buhsumm beon & hold & trigg & trowwe. *c* **1350** *Will. Palerne* 596 And be tristy and trew to ʒow for euer-more. *c* **1400** *Trevisa's Higden* (Rolls) V. 447 (MS. γ) þanne doo as þou hast byhote, and be truwe [*v. r.* trewe] to hym þat so haþ þe i-holpe. *a* **1450** *Knt. de la Tour* (1906) 97, Y haue founde you..not true vnto me. **1583** MELBANCKE *Philotimus* E e j, I will bee as true to thee as the begger to his dishe. **1602** SHAKS. *Ham.* I. iii. 78 This aboue all; to thine owne selfe be true:..Thou canst not then be false to any man. **1678** WANLEY *Wond. Lit. World* v. ii. § 82. 472/2 A Prince more just and true to his word. *a* **1721** PRIOR *Song* 'Still, *Dorinda*' iv, To my vows I have been true. **1849** MACAULAY *Hist. Eng.* ii. I. 258 Hyde had been true to his Tory opinions. **1855** *Ibid.* xi. III. 1 True..to the cause of civil freedom.

**d.** *fig.* of things: Reliable; constant; † sure, secure (*obs.*).

*c* **1205** [see TRULY 1 b]. *c* **1330** R. BRUNNE *Chron.* (1810) 73 þe pes to ʒeme & gyue with lawes trewe als stele. *c* **1425** *Cursor M.* 59 (Trin.) For whenne þou wenest hit trewest [*v. r.* truyst] to be, þou shalt from hit or hit from þe. *a* **1733** BARTON BOOTH *Song*, '*Sweet are the charms of her I love*' ii, True as the Needle to the Pole, Or as the Dial to the Sun. **1791** COWPER *Iliad* VI. 60 Steel Of truest temper. **1872** DORA GREENWELL *Liber Hum.* (1875) 209 To the rock the root adheres, In every fibre true.

**2.** In more general sense: Honest, honourable, upright, virtuous, trustworthy (*arch.*); free from deceit, sincere, truthful (cf. 3 d); of actions, feelings, etc., sincere, unfeigned (now passing into or merged in 5). See also TRUEMAN.

*a* **1012** *Laws of Ethelred* III. c. 9 Buton he habbe twegra trywra manna ʒewitnesse. *c* **1200** *Vices & Virt.* 45 Be trewe mann and halt tin god. *a* **1225** *Ancr. R.* 2 þeos riwle is cherité of schir heorte and cleane inwit, and trewe bileaue. **1297** R. GLOUC. (Rolls) 859 Men triwest [*v. r.* trewest] we [*v. r.* me] seþ And best me mai to hom truste þat of lest wordes beþ. *c* **1380** WYCLIF *Eng. Wks.* (1880) 321 As lif of a trew plow man..is betere preyere to god þen preyere of any ordre þat god loueþ lesse. *c* **1385** CHAUCER *L. G. W.* 464 (*Balade*) A trewe man..Hath nat to parte with a theuys dede. **1446** LYDG. *Two Night. Poems* ii. 69 Triewe meanyng rooted so withynne, Fer from the conceyte of any maner synne. *c* **1460** FORTESCUE *Abs. & Lim. Mon.* xiii. (1885) 141, iij. or iiij. theves..haue sett apon vj. or vij. trewe men, and robbed hem all. **1484** CAXTON *Fables of Alfonce* ii, He is.. reputed..for a good man and trewe. **1599** SHAKS. *Much Ado* I. i. 27 There are no faces truer, then those that are so wash'd, how much better is it to weepe at ioy, then to ioy at weeping? **1611** BIBLE *Gen.* xlii. 11 We are true men: thy seruants are no spies. *c* **1614** SIR W. MURE *Dido & Æneas* I. 715 Her waxen heart, touch't with a trew remorse. **1710** ADDISON *Tatler* No. 250 ⁋ 8 Good Men and true for a Petty Jury. **1847** HELPS *Friends in C.* I. 8 A true man does not think what his hearers are feeling, but what he is saying. **1865** DICKENS *Mut. Fr.* III. v, Your own father has not a truer interest in you.

**3.** Of a statement or belief: Consistent with fact; agreeing with the reality; representing the thing as it is.

*c* **1205** LAY. 4443 Belin iħærde sugge þurh summe sæʒ treowe Of his broðer wifðinge. **1382** WYCLIF *John* xxi. 24 We witen, for [1388 that] his witnessing is trewe. **1393** LANGL. *P. Pl.* C. I. 100 Al þe world wot wel hit myʒte nat be trewe. *c* **1489** CAXTON *Sonnes of Aymon* xvii. 396 'Syr, wyte that charlemagne is come wyth his oost'...'Is it true?' said mawgis. *a* **1529** SKELTON *Dk. Albany* 4 These tidinges newe Whiche be as trewe As the gospell. *a* **1584** MONTGOMERIE *Cherrie & Slae* 1018, I..Thocht all thair tales was trew. **1608** WILLET *Hexapla Exod.* 839 The truer opinion. **1710** BINGHAM *Chr. Antiq.* XX. vii. § 10 The fact was too true, and the charge too well-grounded, to be denied of them all in general. **1759** JOHNSON *Rasselas* xlvii, The same proposition cannot be at once true and false. **1858** LARDNER *Handbk. Nat. Phil.*, etc. 16 This will be true, however shallow the vessel..and however narrow the tube.

**b.** Often in phr. *it is true* (also inverted, *true it is*), introducing a statement; also ellipt. or interjectionally, *true*, introducing or in reply to a statement; usually in concessive sense: = truly, verily, certainly, doubtless.

**1594** T. B. *La Primaud. Fr. Acad.* II. 13 True it is, that we haue now taken in hand a very long piece of worke. **1604** SHAKS. *Oth.* I. iii. 79 That I haue tane away this old mans Daughter, It is most true: true I haue married her. **1611** BIBLE *Dan.* iii. 24 They answered and said vnto the king: True, O king. **1724** DE FOE *Mem. Cavalier* (1840) 173 It is true, we were all but young in the War. **1784** COWPER *Task* III. 210 True; I am no proficient, I confess, In arts like yours. **1859** RUSKIN *Two Paths* i. § 1 It is true that the art which carves and colours the front of a Swiss cottage is not of any very exalted kind; yet [etc.].

**c.** *Come true*: to be verified or realized in actual experience; to be fulfilled. *Hold true*: see HOLD *v.* 23 c.

**1819** SHELLEY *Questions* 7 To patch up fragments of a dream, Part of which comes true. **1875** MORRIS *Æneid* VIII. 580 While yet my fear is unfulfilled, and hope may yet come true. **1879** M. J. GUEST *Lect. Hist. Eng.* xxi. 206 His prophecy had come true.

**d.** *transf.* Speaking truly, telling the truth; trustworthy in statement; veracious, truthful. (Not always distinguishable from 2.) Also *fig.*

*a* **1300** *Cursor M.* 6599 (Cott.) All er yee tru, þis es your saghes, Es nan of yow þat þis calf knaues. *c* **1440** *Promp. Parv.* 503/2 Truwe mann, or woman, *verax.* *c* **1460** *Towneley Myst.* vii. 77 That thay be traw of thare tong, And bere no fals witnes. **1526** TINDALE *Matt.* xxii. 16 Master, we knowe that thou arte true, and that thou teachest the waye of god trueli. **1611** BIBLE *Prov.* xiv. 25 A true witnesse deliuereth soules: but a deceitfull witnesse speaketh lyes. **1634** MILTON *Comus* 170 This way the noise was, if mine ear be true. **1697** DRYDEN *Virg. Past.* II. 33 If the Glass be true, With Daphnis I may vie. **1850** TENNYSON *In Mem.* lxxxv. 5 O true in word, and tried in deed.

**4.** Agreeing with a standard, pattern, or rule; exact, accurate, precise; correct, right.

*c* **1550** CHEKE *Matt.* x. 5 (1843) 46 An Apostol, if ye wold have yᵉ trutorn of yᵉ naam is as much to sai as a frosent. **1570** DEE *Math. Pref.* a iv b, Of the Variacion of the Compas, from true North. **1583** STUBBES *Anat. Abus.* II. (1882) 77 Such as can scarcely read true English. **1651** HOBBES *Leviath.* III. xxxv. 217 The truest Translation is the first. **1674** RAY *Collect. Words, Smelting Silver* 114 Where the furnace is come to a true temper of heat. *a* **1721** PRIOR *Protogenes & Apelles* 54 Apelles drew A Circle regularly true. **1782** COWPER *Gilpin* 72 He..hung a bottle on each side To make his balance true. **1822** IMISON *Sc. & Art* I. 98 Clocks and watches..so regulated as to measure true equal time. **1850** TENNYSON *In Mem.* xcvi. 8 One indeed I knew..Who touch'd a jarring lyre at first, But ever strove to make it true.

**b.** In more general sense: Of the right kind, such as it should be, proper. (Cf. 5.)

**1340–70** *Alex. & Dind.* 513 þat þou miht trystli trye þe treweste lawe...þat þou miht..þe beste lawe kenne. **1435** *Coventry Leet Bk.* 182 Yif the cardwiredrawer were..disseyued withe ontrewe wire..then wold he sey vnto the smythier..'Sir, amende your honde, or, in feithe, I wille no more bye of you'. And then the smythier, lest he lost his Custemers, wolde make true goode. *c* **1600** SHAKS. *Sonn.* lxii, Me thinkes no face so gratious is.., No shape so true. **1677** YARRANTON *Eng. Improv.* 51 The Land in this Mannor is sound, rich, dry, and good, and that is the true Land to bear Flax. *a* **1770** JORTIN *Serm.* (1771) II. i. 12 To place things in their true order. **1911** H. WACE *Proph. Jew. & Chr.* v. 92 Facts thus placed in their true bearings.

**c.** That is rightly or lawfully such; rightful, legitimate.

*c* **1400** *Destr. Troy* 5411 How Thelaphus tide to be treu kyng. **1593** SHAKS. 3 *Hen. VI*, I. ii. 23 An Oath is of no moment, being not tooke Before a true and lawfull Magistrate. **1681** DRYDEN *Abs. & Achit.* 921 The true successor from the court removed. **1790** BURKE *Fr. Rev.* 322 By the laws of nature the occupant and subduer of the soil is the true proprietor.

**d.** Accurately placed, fitted, or shaped; exact in position or form, as an instrument, a part of mechanism, or the like.

**1474** *Coventry Leet Bk.* 400 That his weyghtes be sised & sealed and true beme. **1551** RECORDE *Pathw. Knowl.* I. xxiv, More easyly..may you..make any suche line with a true ruler. **1664** BUTLER *Hud.* II. iii. 1019 I'll make them serve for perpendiculars As true as e'er were us'd by bricklayers. **1726** LEONI tr. *Alberti's Archit.* I. 38/2 We must use a Square Rule..of a very large Size, that our strait Lines may be the truer. **1875** *Carpentry & Join.* 43 A strip required to be cut and planed up perfectly true and even on its sides and ends. **1897** PEMBERTON *Compl. Cyclist* 87 A wheel which will remain perfectly true.

**e.** *True to*: consistent with, exactly agreeing with, 'faithful to' (cf. 1 c).

*a* **1735** ARBUTHNOT (J.), A translation nicely true to the original. **1840** DICKENS *Old C. Shop* i, Be true to your time in the morning. **1883** MORFILL *Slavonic Lit.* i. 15 The dialects of a language are truer to its spirit than its literary form. **1885** *Athenæum* 23 May 661/2 The incident is very true to life and graphically described.

**f.** Conformable to reality, natural: = *true to nature.*

**1870** HUXLEY *Lay Serm.* i. 1 That truest of fictions, 'The History of the Plague Year'. **1894** S. G. GREEN in *Sunday at H.* June 527, I do not object to fiction provided it be true.

**g.** Remaining constant to type; not subject to variation. (Cf. C. 3 b.)

**1839** DARWIN *Voy. Nat.* viii. (1873) 146 This breed is very true. **1859** — *Orig. Spec.* iv. (1860) 84 Can we wonder, then, that Nature's productions should be far 'truer' in character than man's productions?

**h.** Of the wind: Steady, constant, uniform in direction and force.

**1894** *Dundee Advertiser* 11 July 6/1 The Britannia was now 400 yards ahead...The wind was continuing true.

**5.** Real, genuine; rightly answering to the description; properly so called; not counterfeit, spurious, or imaginary; also, conforming or approaching to the ideal character of such.

1398 TREVISA *Barth. De P. R.* XVI. xlvii. (Bodl. MS.) lf. 176/2 Stones..þat bene fals..seme moste liche..to ham þat bene trew. [*c* 1440 *Promp. Parv.* 503/2 Trvwe, in belevynge, *catholicus.*] *c* 1470 HENRY *Wallace* I. 22 His forbearis..Of hale lynage, and trew lyne of Scotland. 1526 TINDALE 1 *John* ii. 8 The darknes is past, and the true lyght nowe shyneth. 1535 COVERDALE 1 *John* v. 20 This is the true God, and euerlastinge life. 1562 A. SCOTT *Poems* (S.T.S.) i. 21 Caus his trew Kirk be had in reuerence. 1589 PUTTENHAM *Eng. Poesie* I. xii. (Arb.) 43 Vntrue praise neuer giueth any true reputation. 1680 OTWAY *Orphan* I. i, The World has not A truer Soldier, or a better Subject. 1697 DRYDEN *Virg. Georg.* IV. 598 He turns agen To his true Shape. 1781 COWPER *Truth* 176 True Piety is cheerful as the day. 1828 SCOTT *F. M. Perth* ii, The best armourer that ever made sword, and the truest soldier that ever drew one. 1849 MACAULAY *Hist. Eng.* vi. II. 16 It was thought that the flocks..would soon return to the true fold. 1854 MOSELEY *Astron.* xx. (1874) 93 About the equinox the time of true noon precedes the time of mean noon. 1891 FARRAR *Darkn. & Dawn* liii, You may yet find the true criminals.

**b.** In scientific use: Conformable to the type, or to the accepted idea or character of the genus, class, or kind; properly or strictly so called.

1578 LYTE *Dodoens* III. lxviii. 408 True Maydenheare, Ladies heare, Venus heare. 1704 F. FULLER *Med. Gymn.* (1711) 201 The true skin, and all its innumerable Glands. 1741 MONRO *Anat. Bones* (ed. 3) 222 The Ribs are commonly divided into True and False. The True Costæ are the seven superior of each Side. 1809 *Med. Jrnl.* XXI. 274 In all cases of true hydrophobia. 1841 *Penny Cycl.* XXI. 415/1 The *Lanianæ*, or true Shrikes. 1855 PHILLIPS *Man. Geol.* 513 Masses of true granite. 1899 *Allbutt's Syst. Med.* VIII. 825 True nerve tumours are exceedingly rare.

**c.** *True bill* (in *Law*), a bill of indictment found by a Grand Jury to be supported by sufficient evidence to justify the hearing of a case: see BILL *sb.*[3] 4. Hence *allusively*, a true statement or charge (*true* being loosely taken in sense 3).

1591 LAMBARDE *Eiren.* IV. v. 484 An Enditement in their [Jurors'] finding of a Bill of accusation to be true. 1659 *Termes de la Ley* 135 b, *Indictment*..is a Bill..exhibited by way of accusation..and preferred unto Jurors, and by their verdict found presented to be true before a Judge. 1769 BLACKSTONE *Comm.* IV. xxiii. 305 If they [the grand jury] are satisfied of the truth of the accusation, they then endorse upon it, 'a true bill'; antiently, '*billa vera*'. The indictment is then said to be found. 1809 MALKIN *Gil Blas* IX. vi. (Rtldg.) 321 Him they taxed with the plotted massacre, and the bill was a true one. 1852 SMEDLEY *L. Arundel* lii, A true bill, by all that's unlucky!

**B.** *sb.* (absol. use of the adj.)

†**1.** A faithful, loyal, or trusty person; a 'true man'. *Obs.*

13.. *Gaw. & Gr. Knt.* 2354 Trwe mon [= must] trwe restore. *c* 1400 *Destr. Troy* 11976 A! traytor vntrew, how toke þou on honde þat trew to be-tray? *c* 1470 *Golagros & Gaw.* 356 Thus with trety ye cast yon trew vndre tyld.

†**b.** *spec.* Nickname for a member of the Protestant or Whig party in the 17th c.: cf. *true blue* (see BLUE *sb.* 8). *Obs.*

*a* 1734 NORTH *Exam.* II. v. § 68. (1740) 357 Most of the eminent Fanatics in England, with all their Trues and True-blues.

**2.** *The true*: That which is true; truth, reality.

1812 CRABBE *Tales* xi. 388 If sleep one moment closed the dismal view, Fancy her terrors built upon the true. 1874 GEO. ELIOT *Coll. Breakf. P.* 13 Yearning for that True Which has no qualities.

**3.** Accurate position or adjustment (in phr. *out of the true*): cf. sense 4 d above, and TRUTH *sb.* 6.

1890 W. J. GORDON *Foundry* 51 The bottom member would be out of the true as it expanded unequally.

**C.** *adv.*

**1.** Faithfully; †honestly; †confidently: = TRULY 1, 1 b, 2.

1303 R. BRUNNE *Handl. Synne* 1912 Þere ys no solas vndyr heuene..Þat shuld a man so moche glew As a gode womman þat loueþ trew. 13.. [see B. 1]. *a* 1425 *Cursor M.* 4913 (Trin.) Þing þat we truly bouȝt And so is oure trewe geten þing. *c* 1470 HENRY *Wallace* I. 86 Ressawide he was and trastyt werray trew. *c* 1555, 1633 [see *true-dealing, true-meaning*, in D. 2].

**2.** In accordance with fact; truthfully; rightly: = TRULY 3.

*a* 1300 *Cursor M.* 18420 (Cott.), I hight þe tru þat þou þis ilk dai sal be..in paradis wit me. *c* 1450 *Merlin* i. 7 The gode woman that spake with me seyde full trewe. 1526 TINDALE *John* xix. 35 He knoweth that he sayth true. 1638 BAKER tr. *Balzac's Lett.* (vol. II.) 142 Tell mee true, Did you not [etc.]? 1711 ADDISON *Spect.* No. 58 ⁋ 13 If he tells me true. 1883 *Athenæum* 17 Feb. 217/1 If report speak true.

**3.** Exactly, accurately, correctly: = TRULY 4.

1530 PALSGR. 698/2 *Sauf vostre grace*, or *saulue vostre grace*, for I fynde bothe, but *saulue* is trewer written. 1660 BLOOME *Archit.* A c, Sima being made true Square. 1687 A. LOVELL tr. *Thevenot's Trav.* I. 35 They shoot at a mark very true with a Bow and Arrow. 1765 WESLEY *Wks.* (1872) XIV. 335, I want the people called Methodists to sing true the tunes..in common use. 1835 SIR J. ROSS *Narr. 2nd Voy.* viii. 119 The wind had continued true north. 1850 LYNCH *Theo. Trin.* xii. 232 Thy love in ours is imaged true As skies in water clear.

**b.** In agreement with the ancestral type; without variation: in phr. *to breed true*. (Cf. A. 4 g.)

1859 DARWIN *Orig. Spec.* i. (1860) 19 Every race that breeds true. 1868 — *Anim. & Pl.* I. vii. 242 The Spanish breed has long been known to breed true.

**4.** Really, genuinely; authentically. (Cf. TRULY 5.)

*a* 1586, 1847 [see *true-felt, true-heroic*, in D. 2]. 1895 *Daily News* 17 Dec. 5/1 Miss Rushton does not say what paper or letter is true signed.

**D.** Combinations.

**1.** The adj. in comb.: **a.** parasynthetic, as *true-blooded, -breasted, -eyed, -paced, -souled, -spirited, -stamped* (having the true stamp, genuine), *-toned, -tongued* adjs.: see also TRUE-HEARTED; **b.** with other adjs., as *true-like, -seeming*; **c.** with sbs.: **true-metal** *a.*, like that of genuine metal; †**true-stitch**, a kind of embroidery exactly alike on both sides (*obs.*); **true-tongue**, one having a true tongue, a truthful person, truth-teller; †**true-wit** (**tru-witt**), a genuinely witty person, a real 'wit' (*obs.*).

1818 COBBETT *Pol. Reg.* XXXIII. 598 They are more *true-blooded. 1605 *1st Pt. Ieronimo* I. iii, O my *true brested father. 1883 MRS. PLUNKETT in *Harper's Mag.* Jan. 240/2 Some *true-eyed artist. 1588 FRAUNCE *Lawiers Log.* I. ii. 5 Plato..ascribeth truth to God and Gods children, leaving nothing but *truelike to mortall men. 1611 SHAKS. *Cymb.* I. vi. 166 He is one The *truest manner'd. 1868 J. H. BLUNT *Ref. Ch. Eng.* I. 449 This is the *true-metal ring of the Book of Common Prayer. 1648 HERRICK *Hesper.*, *Fare-well to Sack* 35 Before they sing Their *true-pac'd numbers. 1590 SPENSER *F. Q.* I. i. 38 The falsest twoo, And fittest for to forge *true-seeming lyes. 1824 MISS MITFORD *Village* Ser. I. (1863) 222 The equally apocryphal but still truer-seeming History of the Plague. 1854 GRACE GREENWOOD *Haps & Mishaps* 37 A *true-souled old man. 1684 OTWAY *Atheist* I. i, A dozen..jolly,* true-spirited..Friends. 1678 DRYDEN *All for Love* I. i, The..rugged Virtue Of an old *true-stampt Roman. 1598 B. JONSON *Case is Altered* II. iii, What, *true-stitch, sister! both your sides alike! 1664 F. HAWKINS *Youths Behav.* II. 7 True-Stitch, Sattin stitch, Queen-stitch [etc.]. 1907 *Daily Chron.* 21 Nov. 5/3 Her.. E flat rang out clear and perfect like a *true-toned bell. 1377 LANGL. *P. Pl.* B. III. 320 Thanne worth *trewe-tonge a tidy man þat tened me neuere. *c* 1369 CHAUCER *Dethe Blaunche* 927 Of eloquence was neuer founde So swete a sownynge facounde, Ne *trewer tonged. 1651 CHARLETON *Ephes. & Cimm. Matrons* II. (1668) 60 Transformed from an Ideot, a Bartholmew-Cokes, a Clown, to a Bon Esprit, a Virtuoso, a *Truwitt.

**2.** The adv. in comb.: **a.** with ppl. adjs., as *true-begotten, -dealing, -derived, -devoted, -disposing, -divining, -felt, -made, -meaning, -meant, -ringing, -run, -speaking, -spelling, -strung*; see also TRUE-BORN, -BRED; **b.** with other adjs., as *true-heroic, -noble, -sweet, -sublime*.

1596 SHAKS. *Merch. V.* II. ii. 36 O heauens, this is my *true begotten Father. 1708 MRS. CENTLIVRE *Busie Body* I. i, He ..scarce believes there's a true-begotten child in the city. *c* 1555 HARPSFIELD *Divorce Hen. VIII* (Camden) 94 Like an honest *true-dealing man. 1594 SHAKS. *Rich. III*, III. vii. 200 To draw forth your Noble Ancestrie..Vnto a Lineall *true deriued course. 1591 — *Two Gent.* II. vii. 9 A *true-deuoted Pilgrime is not weary To measure Kingdomes with his feeble steps. 1594 — *Rich. III*, IV. iv. 55 O vpright, iust, and *true-disposing God. 1588 — *Tit. A.* II. iii. 214 To proue thou hast a *true diuining heart. *a* 1586 SIDNEY *Arcadia* I. (1622) 40 Such tokens of *true-felt sorrow. 1847 TENNYSON *Princess* Concl., Why Not make her *true-heroic —true-sublime? 1598 DRAYTON *Heroic. Ep.*, *O. Tudor to Q. Cath.* 44 By Frances conquest, and by Englands oth, You are the *true made dowager of both. 1633 T. ADAMS *Exp. 2 Peter* ii. 18 A thief lighting into *true-meaning company. 1603 SHAKS. *Meas. for M.* I. iv. 55 Of an infinite distance From his *true meant designe. 1601 CHESTER *Love's Mart.*, *Poet. Ess.* Title-p., The *true-noble Knight. 1907 *Daily Chron.* 23 Feb. 3/2 These *true-ringing, rough-hewn epistles. 1893 *Bailey's Mag.* Oct. 273/1 Was the race a *true-run one? 1570–6 LAMBARDE *Peramb. Kent* (1826) 290 The opinion of any one *true speaking man. 1604 MIDDLETON *Father Hubburd's T.* Wks (Bullen) VIII. 53 A *true-spelling printer. 1598 SYLVESTER *Du Bartas* II. i. III. *Furies* 55 This mighty World did seem an Instrument *True-strung, well-tun'd. 1593–4 — *Profit Imprisonm.* 766 That this world's fained sweet..Should be preferr'd before these seeming-sowrs, that make us Taste many *true-sweet sweets. *c* 1600 SHAKS. *Sonn.* lxxxii, Thy *true telling friend. 1821 CLARE *Vill. Minstr.* (1823) I. 26 *True-thought legends.

**True**, *v.* [f. TRUE *a.*]

†**1.** *trans.* To prove true, verify. *Obs. rare*$^{-1}$.

1647 WARD *Simp. Cobler* (1843) 81 Easilier told than tryed or trued.

**2.** To make true, as a piece of mechanism or the like; to place, adjust, or shape accurately; to give the precise required form or position to; to make accurately or perfectly straight, level, round, smooth, sharp, etc. as required. Often with *up*.

1841 *Civil Eng. & Arch. Jrnl.* IV. 234/1 An apparatus for 'truing up' the wheels of carriages and engines on railways. 1875 KNIGHT *Dict. Mech.*, *Marble-finishing Machine*, one for truing and molding the edges of marble slabs for mantels, tables, etc. 1881 GREENER *Gun* 267 The common barrels are done at half the cost of the best..by grinding them without turning and trueing them in the lathe. 1888 HASLUCK *Model Engin. Handybk.* (1900) 84 The next thing is to true up the valve-face on the cylinder.

Hence **Tru·ing** *vbl. sb.* (also *attrib.*).

1851–4 TOMLINSON *Cycl. Arts* (1867) II. 40/1 The trueing of the lenses..being completed, the polishing is next proceeded with. 1877 KNIGHT *Dict. Mech.*, *Truing-tool*, a device for truing the face of a grindstone, or any other surface. 1897 PEMBERTON *Compl. Cyclist* iii. 82 [The 'jointless' rim] takes even less trueing than a good wood rim.

†**True**, variant of TREWE *Obs.*, tribute.

*c* 1330 R. BRUNNE *Chron. Wace* (Rolls) 5605 Þe true to Rome gyue he [Arviragus] nolde, For he dedeyned of hem to holde.

**True**, obs. form of TROW *v.*, TRUCE.

**True blue**: see BLUE *a.* 1 e, 6 b, *sb.* 8.

**True·-born**, *a.* Born of a true or pure stock; legitimately born; having the sterling qualities associated with such descent.

1591 SHAKS. 1 *Hen. VI*, II. iv. 27 Let him that is a true-borne Gentleman..From off this Bryer pluck a white Rose with me. 1593 — *Rich. II*, I. iii. 309 Though banish'd, yet a true-borne Englishman. 1645 FULLER *Gd. Th. in Bad T.* (1841) 54 He will acknowledge us to be no bastards, but his trueborn children. 1701 DE FOE (*title*) The True-Born Englishman. 1812 BYRON *Ch. Har.* II. lxxxiii, If Greece one true-born patriot still can boast.

**True·-bred**, *a.* **a.** Bred of a true or pure stock; of the true breed; thoroughbred. **b.** Having or manifesting true breeding or education.

1596 SHAKS. 1 *Hen. IV*, I. ii. 206, I know them to bee as true bred Cowards as euer turn'd backe. 1690 DRYDEN *Don Sebast.* I. i, He is a substantial true-bred beast. 1809 JEFFERSON *Writ.* (1830) IV. 126 True-bred shepherd's dogs. 1886 C. SCOTT *Sheep-Farming* 183 In a true-bred sheep the staple of the wool is of an equal length and texture on all parts of the body. 1911 W. P. KER *Eng. Lit., Mediaeval* viii. 210 He writes of it in true-bred language.

†**True·fast**, *a. Obs.* [OE. *tréowfæst*, f. *tréowe*, TRUE + *fæst*, FAST *a.*] Faithful. Hence †**True-fastness** *Obs.*, faithfulness.

*c* 950 *Lindisf. Gosp.* Matt. xxv. 21 Wel ðe la god ðegn and trewufæst. *a* 1000 *Ags. Ps.* (Th.) cx. 5 [cxi. 7] Wærun his bebodu ealle treowfæste. *c* 1175 *Lamb. Hom.* 89 Þa weren þer igedered wiðinne þere buruh of ierusalem trowfeste men of elchere þeode. *Ibid.* 99 Þe halie gast..onlihte ure mod ..mid gode dedan and trewfestnesse. 1532 *Thynne's Chaucer*, *Lydgate's Ball. our Lady* 78 O trustie turtle truefastest [*MSS.* trewest] of all true.

†**True·ful**, *a. Obs. rare.* In 4 treuful, 4–5 truful. [f. TRUE + -FUL.] Full of truth or loyalty, faithful. Hence †**True·fully** *adv. Obs.*, faithfully.

13.. *Cursor M.* 20628 (Cott.) All..bat þe seruis treufulli [*v. r.* trufully]. 1435 MISYN *Fire of Love* II. iii. 74 Truful lufe in mynde is risyn.

†**True·head.** *Obs. rare.* In 3 **trewehede**, (**trywede**), 4 **trewhede**, 5 **trowhede.** [f. OE. *tréowe*, TRUE + *-hede*, -HEAD.] Faithfulness, fidelity.

1297 R. GLOUC. (Rolls) 7370 He wolde þat alle men iseye is trewehede [*v. r.* trywede]. *c* 1375 *Cursor M.* 97 (Fairf.) Of hir godenes and hir trew hede.

**True-hearted** (trū·hāːɹtėd), *a.* Having a true heart; faithful, loyal; honest, sincere.

1471 MARG. PASTON in *P. Lett.* III. 30 Remembyr ho[w] keynd and true hartyd he hath ben to us to hys powre. 1535 COVERDALE *Ps.* xcvii. 11 A ioyfull gladnesse for soch as be true herted. 1608 CHAPMAN *Byron's Consp.* II. i, To be reputed a true harted subiect. 1760–72 H. BROOKE *Fool of Qual.* (1809) III. 21 His downright and true-hearted kindness to me. 1855 MACAULAY *Hist. Eng.* xviii. IV. 196 The son of one of the bravest and most truehearted of Scottish patriots.

Hence **True·-hea·rtedness.**

1608 HIERON *Wks.* I. 694 Encrease..loyalty and true-heartednesse in his subiects. 1858 LADY MORGAN *Autobiog.* (1859) 222 *note*, The same nobleness of soul,..the same single-mindedness, the same true-heartedness, were always present [in Ary-Scheffer].

**Truel**, obs. form of TROWEL.

**True-love** (trū·lɒv). Forms: 1 **tréowlufu**, 4–5 **trulofe**, 4–6 **trewelove, trewlove**, 5 **treulofe, trew-luf, -lufe**, *pl.* **-luffes, treue loue**, 6 **tru-, treulove**, 6– **true love**, 7– **truelove.** [f. OE. *tréowe*, TRUE + *lufu*, LOVE.]

**1.** Faithful love. Usually as two words (see TRUE *a.* 1 b), exc. *attrib.* (see 5).

*a* 800 CYNEWULF *Christ* 538 Wæs seo treow lufu, hat æt heortan. 1813 SCOTT *Trierm.* II. xvii, To plead their right, and true-love plight.

**2.** A faithful lover; one whose love is pledged; a sweetheart, beloved.

*c* 1385 CHAUCER *L. G. W.* 2542 (*Phillis*) This is he..That was his trewe loue In thought & dede. *c* 1460 *Quia amore langueo* 17 in *Pol. Rel. & L. Poems* (1866) 151, I am treulove that fals was neuer, My sistur, mannys soule, I loued hyr thus. *a* 1586 SIDNEY *Arcadia* Poems (Grosart) II. 128 My true-love hath my heart, and I haue his. ?16.. *Friar of Orders Gray*, I pray thee, tell to me If ever at yon holy shrine My true love thou didst see. ?17.. *Song*, '*Wala, wala, up the bank*' (Jam.), I leant my back unto an aik, I thought it was a trusty tree; But first it bow'd, and syne it brak, And sae did my true-love to me. 1871 PALGRAVE *Lyr. Poems* 73 My one true-love, My only.

†**3.** An ornament or figure symbolic of true love; a TRUE-LOVE KNOT. *Obs.*

13.. *Gaw. & Gr. Knt.* 612 Tortors & trulofez entayled so þyk. *c* 1420 *Anturs of Arth.* 354 (Thornton MS.) His mantylle..Trofelyte and trauerste wythe trewloues in trete. 1509 *Will* (MS. Prerog. Crt. Canterb.), Another standing Cupe gilt and enameled wt blew Trulovys in the botom. *a* 1550 *Image Hypocr.* I. 404 in *Skelton's Wks.* (1843) II. 419/1 Gay gloves..Wroughte with true loves. 1575 LANEHAM *Let.* (1871) 38 His napkin, edged with a blu lace, & marked with a truloue, a hart, and A.D. for Damian.

**4.** A name for the Herb Paris (*Paris quadrifolia*), the whorl of four leaves with the single flower or berry in the midst suggesting the figure of a true-love knot. Also † *herb true-love*, *true-love flower*, † **true-love grass**, four-leaved clover. Also, † the North American genus *Trillium* (*obs.*).

13.. *Test. Christi* 126 (Vernon MS.) in Herrig's *Archiv* LXXIX. 428 A foure-leued gras..Whon þeose four leues togeder ben set A trewe-loue men clepen hit. *c* 1386

CHAUCER *Miller's T.* 3692 Vnder his tonge a trewe loue he beer For ther-by wende he to ben gracious. *c* **1400** *Emare* 125 Portrayed þey wer wyth trewe-loue-flour. **1448** *Paston Lett.* IV. 17 Floweris of sylver on the bukkelis made of iiij. lyke a trewlove. **1578** LYTE *Dodoens* I. v. 10 The seede [of Hound's-tongue] is flat and rough, three or foure together like to a trueloue, or foure leaued grasse. **1597** GERARDE *Herbal* II. lxxxv. § 6. 329 One Berrie is also called herbe Trueloue, and herbe Paris. *a* **1674** ? HERRICK *Fairie Kings Diet* 4 The outside of his doublet was Made of the foure-leaued trueloue grass. **1760** LEE *Introd. Bot.* Tab. i, *Trillium*, Herb Truelove of Canada. **1838** MARY HOWITT *Birds & Fl.*, *Summer Woods* iv, There grows the four-leaved plant, 'true love', In some dusk woodland spot.

**5.** *attrib.* (usually in sense 1; in quot. *c* 1430, in sense 3). See also sense 4, and next.

*c* **1430** *Syr Gener.* (Roxb.) 173 Of trewloue werk wroght ful wele. **1593** SHAKS. *Rich. II*, v. i. 10 And wash him fresh againe with true-loue Teares. **1602** — *Ham.* IV. v. 39 Which bewept to the graue did go, With true-loue showres. **1818** SCOTT *Hrt. Midl.* xxxv, 'A sincere weel-wisher of mine, sir'..'O, I understand,'..—'a true-love affair'.

**True-love knot, true lover's knot.** Also † **true-love's knot** (*obs.*). A kind of knot, of a complicated and ornamental form (usually either a double-looped bow, or a knot formed of two loops intertwined), used as a symbol of true love; a figure of this. Also *fig.* or *allusively*.

*α.* **1495** *Will J. Rogers* (Somerset Ho.), Treue loue knottes. **1591** SHAKS. *Two Gent.* II. vii. 46 Ile knit it vp in silken strings, With twentie od-conceited true-loue knots. **1643** WITHER *Campo Musæ* 74 A Peace, that by a true-love-knot, shall knit Three Nations..into One. **1877** W. JONES *Finger-ring* 414 True-love knots were common [on rings].

*β.* **1530** PALSGR. 283/1 Treweloves knotte, *neu damours*. **1583** STUBBES *Anat. Abus.* I. (1877) 74 Sleeues..tyed with true-loues knottes (for so they call them). **1662** HIBBERT *Body Div.* II. 145 The Lords brother, tyed unto him with a true-loves-knot. **1664** BUTLER *Hud.* II. i. 566 I'll carve your name on Barks of Trees, With True-loves knots, and Flourishes.

*γ.* **1615** BRATHWAIT (*title*) Loves Labyrinth: or The true-Louers knot. **1679** LOGAN *Treat. Hon.* II. 177 Or, on a Cheveron, Gules, a true Lovers Knot of the first. **1865** DICKENS *Mut. Fr.* I. x, Splendid cake, covered with Cupids, silver, and true-lover's knots. **1906** *Lady* 12 July 82/1 Pretty but simple hair ornaments are true-lovers' knots of sequined gauze, very stiffly wired.

**Truely**, obs. form of TRULY.

† **True·man.** *Obs.* Forms: see TRUE *a.* [The phr. *true man* written as one word; cf. *oldman*, OLD MAN 1.] A faithful or trusty man; an honest man (as distinguished from a thief or other criminal).

**1297** R. GLOUC. (Rolls) 7274 Ac þe gode trywemen of þe lond wolde abbe ymad king..edgar aþeling. **1303** R. BRUNNE *Handl. Synne* 1337 Þys fals men..Þat, for hate, a trewman wyl endyte, And a þefe for syluer quyte. *c* **1400** *Destr. Troy* 11157 Wacchemen for to wale, wacches to kepe, Of trewmen in towres, for treason of other. **1583** MELBANCKE *Philotimus* Y ij, Thou art like a Thiefe, that thinkes euerye Tree a trueman. **1647** A. ROSS *Myst. Poet.* xiii. (1675) 326 Thieves..use to stand nearer the Altar of Occasion, than True-men many times do.

**Trueness** (trū·nės). Forms: see TRUE *a.* [OE. *tré(o)wnes*, f. *tréowe*, TRUE + -NESS.]

**I.** † **1.** Trust, confidence; object of trust. Only *OE.*

*c* **888** K. ÆLFRED *Boeth.* xlii. (1899) 149 Drihten ælmihtiȝa God,..þu eart min sceoppend, & min alesend,..min trewnes, & min tohopa.

† **2.** = TRUCE *sb.* 1. *Obs. rare.*

*a* **1400** *Siege of Troy* 1058 in *Archiv neu. Spr.* LXXII. 34 Þeo folk of Grece on heore side Beden Treowenes [*v. r.* truce] for to abyde.

**II.** The quality of being true; truth (in various senses).

**3.** Faithfulness, loyalty: = TRUTH 1.

*c* **1290** *Beket* 487 in *S. Eng. Leg.* I. 120 Wel þov wost þat ech of us..Trewenesse we þe sworen ase riȝt was. **1297** R. GLOUC. (Rolls) 738 Ac god þouȝte ȝut on hire vor hire triwenesse [*v. rr.* trewnesse, trewenesse, trunesse]. **1583** GOLDING *Calvin on Deut.* viii. 46 God shall..continue faithfull and his trewnesse shall be knowen. **1612** BACON *Ess.*, *Faction* (Arb.) 83 The euen carriage betweene two factions, proceedeth not alwaies of moderation, but of a truenesse to a mans selfe, with end to make vse of both. **1909** P. C. SIMPSON *Life Rainy* v. 111 A shrewd, hardheaded race..with ..not only trueness but deep tenderness of heart.

**4.** Conformity with fact or reality; verity: = TRUTH 5.

**1587** GOLDING *De Mornay* xxxiv. (1592) 550, I hope I haue now shewed the truenesse and substantialnesse of the Christian Religion, and the vanitie & wickednes of al other Religions. **1861** H. BONAR *God's Way of Peace* viii. (1868) 91 The trueness of the Father's testimony.

**5.** Conformity to a standard; accuracy, exactitude: = TRUTH 6.

**1594** BLUNDEVIL *Exerc.* v. (1636) 592 There were no way ..to be compared vnto it, neither for the truenesse, easinesse, nor readinesse of working thereby. **1805** LUCCOCK *Nat. Wool* 176 A far more valuable quality..which the woolgrower should observe..called the trueness of the hair.

**6.** Genuineness; reality, actuality: = TRUTH 7.

**1613** PURCHAS *Pilgrimage* IX. xv. (1614) 912 They make this ..one of the Markes of the truenesse and Catholicisme of their Church. **1622** MABBE tr. *Aleman's Guzman d'Alf.* II. (1623) 198 That seeing the truenesse of the stampe, she might be the sooner molded to entertaine the motion. **1833** CHALMERS *Const. Man* (1835) I. II. i. 151 The objective trueness of the things which are perceived.

**Truepenny** (trū·peni). *arch.* A trusty person, an honest fellow (compared to a coin of genuine metal); as *adj.* true, genuine. *colloq.*

**1589** *Hay any Work* A ij b, You haue shewed reuerende Martin to be truepenie in deede. **1595** *Eng. Tripe-wife* (1881) 152 Mother Messingham, the old true peny for trimming of a Tripe. **1602** SHAKS. *Ham.* I. v. 150 Art thou there truepenny? *a* **1825** FORBY *Voc. E. Anglia*, *True-penny*, s. Generally, 'Old True-penny',..hearty old fellow; staunch and trusty; true to his purpose or pledge.

*attrib.* **1906** *Westm. Gaz.* 26 May 4/2, I send you away to Spain With a catch in your ears from London, a truepenny pavement strain.

**Truer** (trū·əɹ). [f. TRUE *v.* + -ER [1].] An instrument for truing a piece of mechanism or the like.

**1877** KNIGHT *Dict. Mech.* s. v. *Truing-tool*, A grindstone-truer, for keeping the face in good shape.

**Truer**, compar. of TRUE *a.*: var. TROWER *Obs.*

**Trues**, obs. form of TRUCE.

† **True·ship.** *Obs.* Forms: see TRUE *a.* and -SHIP. [f. TRUE + -SHIP.] Faithfulness, fidelity.

*c* **1175** *Lamb. Hom.* 107 ȝif þe alde bið butan treuscipe. *a* **1225** *Ancr. R.* 8 Edmodnesse, & þolemodnesse, treoweschipe, & holding of ðe tene olde hesten. *a* **1250** *Owl & Night.* 1344, & mayde may luue cheose þat hire trevschipe ne forleose.

† **True-table**, app. an error for *trey-table*: see TREY *sb.* 3.

**1646** EVELYN *Diary* (1827) I. 384 There is also..a tavern, and a true-table.

**Trueth, Trufel**, obs. forms of TRUTH, TRIFLE.

† **Truff**, *sb.*[1] *Obs.* Forms: 4, 8 *Sc.* truf, 5–7 truffe, (6 *Sc. pl.* trufis), 7–8 truff. [a. F. *truffe* a truffle (1370 in Godef. *Compl.*), in OF. also figuratively *trufe* a cozening, cheating, etc. (1265 in Godef.) in which sense it is first recorded in English: see TRUFFLE.]

**1.** An idle tale or jest. Cf. TRIFLE *sb.* 1.

**1483** CAXTON *Gold. Leg.* 272 b/1 In the same errour Austyn fylle..and was broughte to byleue the truffes and Iapes. **1494** FABYAN *Chron.* VII. 440 The Scottis in despyte of yͤ Englysh men,..and also to theyr more derysyon made dyuerse truffys, roundys, & songys. **1513** DOUGLAS *Æneis* VIII. Prol. 170 Than wol I tene at I tuk to sic trufis [*ed.* 1553 truffuris] tent. **1611** SPEED *Hist. Gt. Brit.* IX. xii. § 29 Playing vpon the English with Truffes and Rounds.

**2.** A truffle. *rare.*

**1633** HART *Diet Diseased* I. xiii. 47 Those roots, commonly called Puffes, or Truffes. **1669** *Phil. Trans.* IV. 1013 Other odd things in Nature, as Truffs, Mushroms. **1672** EVELYN *Fr. Gard.* 260 Concerning Morilles and Truffs.

**Truff**, *sb.*[2] Local name for the bull-trout, *Salmo eriox*. Also *sea-truff*.

**1818** *Sporting Mag.* II. 158 What some call 'truffs', others sea-trout. **1865** COUCH *Brit. Fishes* IV. 211 Sea Trout. Grey Trout. Bull Trout. Sea Truff. Pugtrout. **1880** in Elworthy *W. Somerset Word-bk.* (1888) s.v., They've a-catcht a little truff, nort else.

† **Truff**, *v. Obs.* Forms: see TRUFF *sb.*[1] [ad. OF. *truffer*, *trufer* to mock, deride, gibe at (13th c.); cf. med.L. *trufare*, *truphare* to mock, It. *truffare* to cozen, cheat (Florio); see TRUPHANE.]

**1.** *trans.* To deceive, befool. Hence **Tru·ffing** *vbl. sb.*

*c* **1375** *Sc. Leg. Saints* i. 242 Sa cuth he deile with trufinge. **1657** C. BECK *Univ. Char.* L viij b, To truffe, *v.* gird.

**2.** *intr.* To trifle *with*.

**1485** CAXTON *Chas. Gt.* II. II. x. 119 Ye haue seen how he truffed wyth me.

**3.** *trans. Sc.* To obtain by deceit; to steal, pilfer.

**1720** A. PENNECUIK *Helicon* (ed. 2) 66 I've truf'd you a Ladies Shirt from the Hedge. **1721** RAMSAY *Lucky Spence* vi, Be sure to truff his pocket-book.

Hence † **Tru·ffer** [cf. OF. *trufeor*, *truffour* (*c* 1170 in Godef.)], one who 'truffs'; so † **Tru·ffery** [a. OF. *truf(f)erie* (*c* 1230 in Godef.)], a mockery, trifle, thing of no importance.

*c* **1450** *Mirour Saluacioun* 2225 The first two causes pilat helde bot a truferye. **1553** Truffuris [see TRUFF *sb.*[1] 1, quot. 1513]. **1728** RAMSAY *Fables* xvii. 8 The hand of this young foolish truffer.

**Truff**, Sc. form of TURF.

**Truffille**, obs. form of TRIFLE.

**Truffle** (trɒ·f'l, trū·f'l). Also 7–8 trufle, treuffle, 8 trouffle. [app. a derivative of Fr. *trufe*, *truffe* (1370 in Hatz.-Darm.), Comask. *treufol*, Genev. *trufola*, in same sense; of unsettled etymology. According to Diez and Hatz.-Darm., prob. repr. L. *tūber-*, supposed to have been altered at an early date to **tūfer-*, whence **tūfre*, *trūfe*, *tuffe*. The change of gender has been accounted for by supposing the neuter pl. *tūbera* to have been treated as a fem. sing. (cf. BIBLE, ARMS); according to Graff *tūbera* appears as a fem. sing. in some Ger. glossaries of the 9th c. A form without *r* is found in Swiss Romand and Languedoc *tufelle*, *tufeda*. Cf. also the Eng. contraction TRUB.

But this derivation is by no means certain; a longer form appears in It. *tartuffo*, Milanese *tartuffel*, Ven. *tartuf*, *tartufola*, Piemont *tartifla*, Rheto-Rumansch *tartufe*, Languedoc *tartifle*, Berry *tartrufle*. These mean 'potato', and have been explained by Miège as = *terræ tuber*; whence Ger. *kartoffel*, dial. *tartoffel*, Icel. *tartuflur* pl. potatoes. See the word in Diez, Scheler, and Littré.]

Any one of various underground fungi of the family *Tuberaceæ*; *spec.* an edible fungus of the genus *Tuber*, a native of Central and Southern Europe, esteemed as a delicacy; esp. *T. æstivum* or *cibarium*, the Common (English) Truffle, and *T. melanosporum*, the French Truffle, which have a black, warty exterior, and vary in size between that of a walnut and that of a large potato, which they more or less resemble in shape.

**1591** SPARRY tr. *Cattan's Geomancie* B ij, The Topas and the Truffle haue power of Chastity, and to subdue the flesh. **1644** EVELYN *Diary* 30 Sept., Here we supped.., having amongst other dainties, a dish of trufles, an earth nut found by an hogg train'd to it. **1691** RAY *Creation* II. (1692) 99 By tying a Cord to the hind-leg of a Pig, and driving him before them..observing where he stops and begins to root,..they are sure to find a Trufle. **1726** ARBUTHNOT *It cannot rain*, etc. 10 A Dog is an Ass to him [Peter the Wild Boy] for finding Trouffles. **1742** POPE *Dunc.* IV. 558 Thy Truffles, Perigord! thy Hams, Bayonne! **1847** THACKERAY *Mrs. Perkins's Ball* ¶ 17 Such a quantity of goose-liver and truffles. **1866** *Treas. Bot.* s.v., Applied generally, the name Truffle (or Trubs) comprises all the Fungi which belong to the natural orders *Hypogæi* and *Tuberacei*.

*fig.* **1897** *Literature* 20 Nov. 155/1 A thin, ancient-looking octavo,..rooted up with other literary truffles.

**b.** *attrib.* and *Comb.*, as *truffle-bed*, *-grower*, *-hunter*, *-hunting*, etc.; *truffle-like*, *-stuffed* adjs.; **truffle-beetle**, a beetle whose subterranean larvæ feed on the truffle; **truffle-dog**, **-pig**, a dog or pig trained to discover truffles; also *fig.*; **truffle-worm**, the larva of an insect infesting the truffle: see quots.

**1726** BRADLEY *Gardening* App. 38 No Herb or plant is ever seen to grow upon a Truffiery or *Truffle bed. **1885** F. WHYMPER in *Girl's Own Paper* Jan. 169/1 A trained hog, when it has discovered a truffle bed, is immovable. **1899** SHARP in *Cambr. Nat. Hist.* VI. v. 222 The larvae of the group Anisotomides are believed to be chiefly subterranean in habits; that of *A. cinnamomea* feeds on the truffle, and the beetle is known as the *truffle-beetle. **1874** LISLE CARR *Jud. Gwynne* I. iv. 114 As a *truffle-dog noses out the dainty objects of his search. **1899** HALE *Lowell & Friends* xiv. 254 The reader is not necessarily an authority in language. He is a scout or truffle-dog who brings the result of his exploration to the authorities. **1898** *Gard. Mag.* 3 Sept. 572/2 The Agricultural Society of the Department of the Lot awards prizes at its shows to *truffle growers. *a* **1793** G. WHITE *Observ. Veg.* in *Selborne*, etc. (1837) 487 A *truffle-hunter called on us, having in his pocket several large truffles found in this neighbourhood. **1885** F. WHYMPER in *Girl's Own Paper* Jan. 169/1 In Upper Provence a hog trained to *truffle-hunting is worth the equivalent of eight pounds sterling. **1898** P. MANSON *Trop. Diseases* xxxvii. 573 Moulded into *truffle-like masses. **1841** THACKERAY *Mem. Gormandising* Wks. 1900 XIII. 589 Fat *truffle-stuffed partridges. **1753** CHAMBERS *Cycl. Supp.*, **Truffle-worms*,..a species of fly-worm which is found in Truffles. **1888** *Cassell's Encycl. Dict.* s.v., A species of Leiodes deposits its ova in it, which in the pupa state feed upon the substance of the truffle; in this state they are called truffle-worms.

Hence **Truffled** (trɒ·f'ld) *a.*, cooked, garnished, or stuffed with truffles; † **Tru·ffiery**, a truffle-bed; **Truffle·sque** *a.* (*nonce-wd.*), resembling that of truffles; **Tru·ffling** *vbl. sb.*, gathering truffles.

**1837** M. DONOVAN *Dom. Econ.* II. 131 The liver and thighs of geese,..made into pies, and properly truffled,..are reckoned a most delicate article. **1902** ELINOR GLYN *Refl. Ambrosine* II. viii, Truffled partridge in aspic. **1726** *Truffiery [see *truffle-bed* above]. **1841** THACKERAY *Mem. Gormandising* Wks. 1900 XIII. 583 A *trufflesque odour was left in the room. *Ibid.* 588 Some faint trufflesque savour. **1859** *Times* 14 Feb. 5/5 Many of these..people [poor labourers in Wiltshire] live by *truffling and poaching, in the absence of farmer's employment.

**Truffle, trufle, truful**, obs. forms of TRIFLE.

**Trug** [1] (trɒg). *local.* Also 6–8 trugg. [? Dialectal variant of TROUGH.]

**1.** An old local measure for wheat, equal to two-thirds of a bushel. Also *attrib.*, **trug-corn**, **trug-wheat**: see quots.

[*c* **1350** in Blount *Law Dict.* (1670) s.v., Tres Trugge frumenti vel avenae faciunt 2 Bushels infra Prebendam de Hunderton in Ecclesia Heref.] **1670** BLOUNT *Law Dict.* s.v., At Lempster at this day the Vicar has Trug Corn allow'd him for Officiating at some Chappels of ease. **1676** COLES *Dict.*, *Trug*, three trugs make two bushels. **1866** *N. & Q.* 3rd Ser. X. 415/2 There is in the parish of Leominster, a payment of the nature of tithe, which is known as trug-wheat.

**2.** A shallow wooden tray or pan to hold milk; also a tray or hod for mortar; also (*northern dial.*), a wooden coal-box.

**1580, 1630** [implied in TRUGGER]. **1600** in W. F. Shaw *Mem. Eastry* (1870) 226 Item in the mylke house..two dowsin of bowles and Truggs. **1630** *Will W. Buncker* (C. C. Canterb. MS.), Two milke trugges [and] two milk boules. **1674** RAY *S. & E. C. Words* 77 *A Trug*, a tray for milk or the like, *Suss. Dial.* **1706** PHILLIPS (ed. Kersey), *Trugg*, (Country-Word) a Milk-Tray or such like Vessel, a Hod to carry Mortar in. **1847–78** HALLIWELL, *Ash-trug*, a coal-scuttle. *North.* **1878–81** *Cumberld. Gloss.*, *Trug*, a wooden coal-box.

**3.** A shallow oblong basket made of wooden strips with a handle from side to side, chiefly used for carrying fruit, vegetables, and the like; also *trug-basket*.

**1862** M. A. LOWER in *Athenæum* 30 Aug. 281 A trug-basket,..a vessel..almost peculiar to the county of Sussex. Some such trugs were sent to the Great Exhibition of 1851. **1882** *Ibid.* 26 Aug. 271/2 A Sussex trug..is a flat basket, not of wicker, but of flakes of sallow, braced with ash and furnished with a handle of the latter wood. **1909** *Spectator*

10 July 49/1 She descends with a huge wooden trug half filled with maize.

**Trug**[2]. *Obs.* exc. *dial.* Also 6–7 trugge, 7 truck. [? ad. It. *trucca* 'a fustian or rogish word for a trull, a whore, or a wench' (Florio); perh. cognate with TRUCK *sb.*[1]] A prostitute; a trull.

1592 GREENE *Upst. Courtier* G j, You Tom tapster.. haue your trugges to draw men on to villanie. 1620 tr. *Boccaccio's Decam.* VI. x. 18 b, One of the Hostesses Female attendants, a gross fat Trugge. 1631 BRATHWAIT *Whimzies* 139 Would you have a true survey of his family..? you shall finde them subsist of three heads: himselfe, his truck, and her misset. *a* 1700 B. E. *Dict. Cant. Crew*, *Trug*, a dirty Puzzel, an ord'nary sorry Woman. 1883 *Hampsh. Gloss.*, *Trug*, a trull, low female companion.

† **b.** A catamite. *Obs. rare.*

*c* 1608 HEALEY *Disc. new World* III. vii. § 2. 194 Euery other house keepes sale Trugges or Ganymedes. *a* 1630 J. TAYLOR (Water P.) *Bawd* Wks. II. 93/2 A cursed Catalogue of those veneriall caterpillars .. with the number of trugs which each of them kept.

Hence † **Tru·gging-house**, † **tru·gging-place**, a brothel.

1591 GREENE *Disc. Coosnage* Wks. (Grosart) X. 37 The whoore house, a Trugging place. 1592 — *Blacke Bkes. Messenger* Wks. (ed. Huth) XI. 12 This olde Letcher..had a haunt into Petticote Lane to a Trugging house there.

**Trug**, obs. form of TRUDGE.

† **Tru·gger.** *Obs.* [f. TRUG[1] (sense 2) + -ER[1].] A maker of trugs.

1580 *Reg. St. Alphage, Canterb.* (MS.), Sonne of John Harman, trugger. 1630 *Canterb. Marriage Licences* (MS.), Giles Reinold's of Great Chart, trugger.

† **Trugma·llion.** *Obs.* Also trugmullion. [f. TRUG[2]; cf. *tatterdemalion*, *rampallion*, etc.] = TRUG[2].

1715 tr. *C'tess D'Aunoy's Wks.* 414, I, cry'd the Charming King, I Marry such a Trugmullion as this! 1719 D'URFEY *Pills* V. 308 Tarpaulins, Trugmallions, Lords, Ladys.

**Truiff**, obs. Sc. form of TURF.

**Truikour**, obs. Sc. form of TRUCKER.

**Truing**: see TRUE *v.* **Truis**, variant of TREWS.

**Tru·ish**, *a. rare.* [f. TRUE *a.* + -ISH[1].] Somewhat true.

1659 GAUDEN *Tears Ch.* II. xvi. 198 Something that seems truish and newish. 1869 MRS. OLIPHANT *Hist. Sk. Reign Geo. II* (1879) I. 140 It was truish sentiment in its way.

**Truism** (trū·iz'm). Also 8 trueism. [f. TRUE *a.* + -ISM.] A self-evident truth, esp. one of slight importance; a statement so obviously true as not to require discussion.

1708 SWIFT *Remarks Bk.* vii. Wks. 1841 II. 190/2 The title of this chapter [is] a truism. 1757 MRS. GRIFFITH *Lett. Henry & Frances* (1767) I. 135, I have..often illustrated the latter part of this trueism. 1817 MALTHUS *Popul.* III. App. 338 Truisms..of the same kind as the assertion that man cannot live without food. 1880 L. STEPHEN *Pope* ii. 25 Maxims, some of which strike us as palpable truisms.

**b.** (without article) Truistic statement.

1812 SHELLEY *Let. to Eliz. Hitchener* 20 Jan., You..tell me truism when you egotize at all. 1861 MAX MÜLLER *Chips* (1880) I. xiii. 312 The fear of truism in our modern writers.

Hence **Truisma·tic** *a.* (*rare*—⁰) = next.

1860 WORCESTER cites *Edinb. Rev.*

**Truistic** (truˌi·stik), *a.* [f. TRUISM: see -ISTIC.] Having the character of a truism; trivially self-evident. (In quot. 1885, Dealing in or uttering truisms.)

1844 F. D. MAURICE in W. Ward *W. G. Ward & Oxford Movem.* (1889) 321 Merely truistic statements. 1885 *Pall Mall G.* 30 May 2/1 It is the fashion nowadays to be truistic. 1902 *Athenæum* 11 Jan. 52/3 To a trained psychologist this statement looks truistic and commonplace.

So **Trui·stical** *a.*, in same sense.

1858 *Brit. Q. Rev.* LVI. 444 While some are true, not to say truistical, others are as utterly false. 1906 *Hibbert Jrnl.* July 788 Quite obvious..in fact, almost suspiciously truistical.

† **Truit, truyt.** *Obs. rare.* [?] ? Wrong, injury.

*a* 1400 *Leg. Rood* viii. 41 Fouled is my fayre fruit, þat neuer dude tripet ne truit. *Ibid.* 480 Rihtful schul ryse to riche restyng, Truyt and tripet to helle shal sterue.

**Truke**, var. TROKE. **Trule**, obs. f. TROWEL.

† **Trule.** *Sc. Obs.* [Cf. TROLL *v.* to roll, trundle.] A game app. played with balls or bowls.

*c* 1508 DUNBAR *Poems* xiv. 22 Sa mony lordis, so mony naturall fulis, That better accordis to play thame at the trulis, Nor seiss the dulis that commonis dois sustene.

**Trull** (trɒl). Also 6 trowle, 6–7 trulle, trul, 7 troul. [= Ger. *trulle*, Swiss *trolle*, Swabian *trull.*]

**1.** A low prostitute or concubine; a drab, strumpet, trollop.

1519 *Interl. Four Elements* (Percy Soc.) 46, I shall apoynt you a trull of trust, Not a feyrer in this towne! 1591 GREENE *Disc. Coosnage* (1592) 15 These common truls..walke abroad ..as stales to draw men into hell. 1632 CHAPMAN & SHIRLEY *Ball* II. i, Have you as much left..as will Keep you and this old troul a fortnight longer? 1737 SWIFT *Proposal Badges to Beggars* Wks. 1761 III. 337 He and his trull, and his litter of brats. 1871 MORLEY *Crit. Misc.* 255 Coarse orgies with the trulls of Wapping.

*attrib.* 1898 G. EGERTON *Fantasias* 144 Singing a song of the trull forces of nature.

† **2.** A girl, lass, wench. *Obs.*

1560 INGELEND *Disob. Child* (Percy Soc.) 26 This mynion here, this myncing trull. 1573 TUSSER *Husb.* (1878) 85 Sow pease (good trull) the Moone past full. *a* 1600 J. WOOTTON *Jigge* in *Eng. Helicon* G vj, Heard to each Swaine, seen to each Trull.

**Trull, Trulle**, obs. ff. TROLL *v.*, TROWEL.

**Trullibub**, variant of TRILLIBUB.

† **Trulliza·tion.** *Obs. rare*—⁰. Also -iss-. [ad. L. *trullissātiōn-em* (n. of action f. *trullissāre* to plaster, f. *trulla* TROWEL), F. † *trullization*, *trullisation* (1691 in Hatz.-Darm.).] (See quots.)

1656 BLOUNT *Glossogr.*, *Trullissation* (*trullisatio*), a pargetting or plaistering with mortar or loam. 1727–41 CHAMBERS *Cycl.*, *Trullization*, in the ancient architecture, the art of laying on strata or layers of mortar, gypsum, or the like, with the trowel.

† **Tru·lly.** *Obs. rare.* [f. TRULL + -Y.] A trull.

1711 E. WARD *Quix.* I. 32 Poor Tinker-like, without a Trully, Must beat the dusty Road but dully.

**Truly** (trū·li), *adv.* (*sb.*) Forms: 1 tréowlíce, 3 treo-, treou-, trouliche, 3–6 treu-, trew-, etc., -lich(e, -ly, etc. (see TRUE *a.* and -LY[2]), 5 treoly, 5–6 trulye, 5–8 truely, 6–7 trulie, (7 trooly), 4– truly. [OE. *tréowlíce*, ME. *treulich*, etc., f. *tréow*, *treu*, TRUE: see -LY[2].] In a true manner (in various senses of the adj.).

**1.** Faithfully, loyally, constantly, with steadfast allegiance. *arch.*

*a* 1000 *Ags. Ps.* (Th.) xi. 6 [xii. 5] Ic do swyðe treowlice ymb hy. *c* 1205 LAY. 20000 Alle heo sworen þene að, Trouliche [*c* 1275 Treuliche] þat heo wolden Mid Arðure halden. 1297 R. GLOUC. (Rolls) 2070 Conan..bihet him to serui triweliche. *a* 1300 *Cursor M.* 81 (Cott.) Qua truly [*v.rr.* treuli, trewely] loues þis lemman, þis es þe loue bes neuer gan. 13.. *Ibid.* 1062 (Gött.) Rightwis [Abel] was, and goddes freind, And treuli gaf he him his tend. *c* 1380 WYCLIF *Sel. Wks.* III. 152 Hit were better þat lewid men diden to lordes þis offis..for better and lighter and treulier schulde hit be done. *c* 1400 *Brut* ccxli. 350 Alle þe conauntes..schulde be trewly kept. 1563 WINȜET *Four Scoir Thre Quest.* Wks. (S.T.S.) I. 121 The haill Kirk of God, professing trewlie Christ Iesus. 1611 SHAKS. *Cymb.* III. v. 110. 1852 M. ARNOLD *Second Best* 24 An impulse..To the words, 'Hope, Light, Persistence', Strongly sets and truly burns.

† **b.** With steadfast faith or assurance; confidently. In quot. *c* 1275, ? so as to be safe or trustworthy; securely (cf. TRUE *a.* 1 d). *Obs.*

*c* 1275 LAY. 11898 And wel he makede his castles Treuliche [*c* 1205 Treowe] and faste. *c* 1325 *Spec. Gy Warw.* 208 Þu shalt..bileue also And treuliche in þin herte do, Þat god had neuere biginning Ne neuere shal haue ending. *c* 1375 *Sc. Leg. Saints* i. (*Petrus*) 485 Gyf he liffis, he ma spek, and ga, ..And gyf he na may, trewis trewly þat ȝe se is all fantassy. *a* 1548 HALL *Chron.*, *Edw. IV* 202 b, Trustynge truely that all thynges were at a good poynt.

† **2.** Honestly, honourably, uprightly. *Obs.*

1362 LANGL. *P. Pl.* A. I. 155, 156 Bote ȝe liuen trewely and eke loue þe pore, And such good as God sent Treweliche parten. 1453 *Dunfermline Regr.* (Bann. Cl.) 340 To gife and to pay lelly and treuly but fraude or gille a hundreth pundis. 1530 PALSGR. 358, I holde with them that deale trewly. 1558 in Foxe *A. & M.* (1570) 2249/2, I am a poore woman and do liue by my hands, gettyng a peny truly.

**3.** In accordance with the fact; truthfully; correctly (in reference to a statement).

1303 R. BRUNNE *Handl. Synne* 2712 Trewely to swere hys oþe. *c* 1400 *Ywaine & Gaw.* 329 By that well hinges a bacyne..With a cheyne, trewly to tell. *a* 1548 HALL *Chron.*, *Hen. VIII* 228 b, The people thus instructed (or as I may trulier speake) deceiued. 1599 SHAKS. *Much Ado* I. i. 180 Tell me truely how thou lik'st her. *Ibid.* IV. i. 76 Bid her answer truly. 1607 — *Cor.* v. iv. 27. *a* 1718 PENN *Truth Rescued* II. Wks. 1726 I. 494 [Words] truliest apply'd to Himself. 1766 GOLDSM. *Vic. W.* xvii, An elegy that may truly be called tragical. 1875 JOWETT *Plato* (ed. 2) I. 88 Unable to decide which of you speaks truly.

**4.** In accordance with a rule or standard; exactly, accurately, precisely, correctly.

1375 in Horstm. *Altengl. Leg.* (1878) 138/2 Fro Moyses to Dauid kyng Fyue hondred & two [years],..To kounten riȝt trewely. 1486 *Bk. St. Albans*, *Her.* e v, Trulier they shal be blasit on this wyse. 1535 JOYE *Apol. Tindale* (Arb.) 20 Correcking a false Copie..that thei mought be the trewlyer printed agen. 1696 WHISTON *Th. Earth* II. (1722) 131 The little Planets about Jupiter move in Orbits truly Circular. 1787 BEST *Angling* (ed. 2) 10 A long rod is..of more use.. provided it is truly made. 1875 KNIGHT *Dict. Mech.* 593/2 To make the spindle run truly.

**b.** Rightly, justly, duly; as it ought to be, properly; often in phrase *well and truly.*

1417 *York Memo. Bk.* (Surtees) I. 182 Sufficiant recorde that he es wele and lely and treuly partyd fra thiens whare he come fra. 1531 TINDALE *Exp.* 1 *John* ii. (1537) 29 Wyl ye therfore worship saintes truely? 1596 DALRYMPLE tr. *Leslie's Hist. Scot.* VII. (S.T.S.) II. 47 Quhen he saw [them]..as tha war worthie, treulie tormented. *a* 1647 HABINGTON *Surv. Worc.* in *Worcs. Hist. Soc. Proc.* III. 535 After whose death it [some land] returned truely to the monastery. 1849 RUSKIN *Sev. Lamps* Introd. 4 Every action..is capable of a peculiar dignity..which we sometimes express by saying that it is truly done (as a line or tone is true).

**c.** Rightfully, legitimately. *Obs.* or merged in 5.

1605 SHAKS. *Macb.* v. ii. 26 To giue Obedience, where 'tis truly ow'd. 1611 — *Wint. T.* III. ii. 135 His innocent Babe truly begotten.

**d.** In accordance with nature, naturally.

1600 SHAKS. *A. Y. L.* III. iv. 55 If you will see a pageant truely plaid. 1884 CHURCH *Bacon* ix. 219 A sketch so truly and forcibly drawn.

**e.** Without cross-breeding; purely; also, without variation from the ancestral type.

1854 *Poultry Chron.* II. 63 Very fine truly-bred birds. 1859 DARWIN *Orig. Spec.* i. (1866) 17 The greyhound, bloodhound, [etc.] propagate their kind truly.

**5.** Genuinely, really, actually, in fact, in reality; sincerely, unfeignedly.

*c* 1380 WYCLIF *Wks.* (1880) 5 Men þat trewly dispisen synne. 1591 SHAKS. *Two Gent.* v. iv. 76, I doe as truely suffer, As ere I did commit. 1682 NORRIS *Hierocles* 35 So may we learn to know what we ourselves truly are. 1711 STEELE *Spect.* No. 79 ¶ 9 A Mind truly virtuous. 1857 MILLER *Elem. Chem.* (1862) III. 236 The view that they were truly alcohol radicles. 1874 MOTLEY *Barneveld* II. xviii. 276 Nothing could be more truly respectable. 1908 MISS FOWLER *Betw. Trent & Ancholme* 231 She truly believed..that he [her donkey] liked the thistles best.

**b.** Used to emphasize a statement (sometimes as a mere expletive): Indeed, forsooth, verily.

*c* 1205 LAY. 20720 Arður [etc.] þene wude al bileien..Treo uppen oðer Treoliche faste. *c* 1300 *Cursor M.* 23952 (Edin.) Of hir trewlik es al mi tale. *a* 1400–50 *Alexander* 2094 'Bot treuly, ser', quod þe duke, 'gret tresore me thinke At Alexander þe athill'. *c* 1470 HENRY *Wallace* III. 268 Ane awfull chyftane trewly he is ane. 1598 SHAKS. *Merry W.* I. i. 322 Truely I will not goe first: truely-la: I will not doe you that wrong. 1641 BROME *Jov. Crew* III. Wks. 1873 III. 399 Never in our lives trooly. 1781 COWPER *Truth* 521 Charge not a God with such outrageous wrong. Truly, not I. 1821 SCOTT *Kenilw.* xli, 'Is he dead?' 'Ay, truly is he'. 1869 RUSKIN *Q. of Air* iii. § 146 A wide freedom, truly!

† **c.** Hence as quasi-*sb.* in phr. *by* (*upon*) *my truly*, *in* (*good*) *truly*, used as a kind of oath or asseveration. (In quot. 1594, ? a person who uses 'truly' as an asseveration.) *colloq. Obs.*

1580 G. HARVEY *Two Lett.* Wks. (Grosart) I. 42 By my truely, I was neuer so scared in my lyfe. 1594 NASHE *Unfort. Trav.* Wks. (Grosart) V. 86 Hee..was one of those trecherous brother Trulies. 1604 WEBSTER *Westw. Hoe* II. i, Have you a new pen for me, master? for, by my truly, my old one is stark naught. 1672 WYCHERLEY *Love in Wood* I. i, Patience,..'tis a necessary virtue for a widow without a jointure, in truly. 1697 VANBRUGH *Relapse* v. v, Why, in good truly, as a body may say, he is but a slam. 1795 *Jemima* I. 110 Part, repeated Rosina, yes, by my truly must we.

**d.** In phr. *yours truly*, the most formal of the phrases used in subscribing a letter; hence humorously = 'myself'.

[1638 BAKER tr. *Balzac's Lett.* (vol. II.) 15 And with this I solemnly assure you that I truely am Sir Yrs &c.] 1788 BURNS *Let. to R. Brown* 24 Feb., Believe me to be, My dear Sir, yours most truly, R. B. 1817 SCOTT *Let. to Miss J. Baillie* 26 Sept., in *Lockhart*, Yours truly, W. S. 1849 THACKERAY *Pendennis* iii, Give the young one a glass,..and score it up to yours truly. 1850 DE MORGAN *Let. to Sir J. Herschel* 26 Mar. in *Mem.* vii. (1882) 209 Yours very truly, A. De Morgan.

**Trumbash**, var. TROMBASH. **Trumbe**, var. TROMBE *Obs.*; obs. Sc. f. TRUMP. **Trumbill, trumle**, obs. forms of TREMBLE.

† **Trume, trome,** *sb. Obs.* Forms: 1 truma; 3–4 trume, trome, (4 trun; cf. SHELTRON[1]). [OE. *truma*, app. a derivative of the adj. *trum* firm, strong, able to resist (neither *truma* nor *trum* appears outside English.)

Notwithstanding a suspicious likeness in form and sense to L. *turma* 'troop, squadron, crowd, throng', the OE. derivatives of *truma* (e.g. *getruma*, *antruma*, *trymman*, to TRIM, etc.) show it to be a native word.]

A body of persons, esp. of troops, etc. in battle array; a troop; a company, band; a crowd, multitude. Cf. THRUM *sb.*[1]

*c* 893 K. ÆLFRED *Oros.* v. xii. § 5 He hæfde eahta & eahtatiȝ coortana, þæt we nu truman hatað. *c* 1205 LAY. 26968 Rom-leoden ræsden to..Breken Bruttene trume. *c* 1230 *Hali Meid.* 21 Þat eadi trume of schimerinde meidenes. *c* 1300 *Havelok* 8 Hauelok was a ful god gome, He was ful god in euerie trome. *c* 1380 *Sir Ferumb.* 2372 Þe Ameral þyderward haþ him nome, To þᵉ feldeward þan ful riȝt; & wan he sawe þat huge trome, His herte anon gan lyȝte. *Ibid.* 5432 Wanne hire hostes were to-gadre y-come, Þanne was ther an huge trome, iij hundred þousent & mo.

† **Trume, trome,** *v. Obs. rare*—¹. [f. prec.] ? *intr.* To assemble in a troop.

? *a* 1400 *Morte Arth.* 3592 Nowe bownes the bolde kynge.. Gers trome and trusse, and trynes forth aftyre.

[**Trummelett**, misreading for TRAMMELET.]

**Trump** (trɒmp), *sb.*[1] Also 3–6 trompe, 6 (8–9 *arch.*) tromp, 4–5 troumpe, 4–7 trumpe, (5 trommpe, trumppe); β. 6 *Sc.* trum, trumme, trumb(e. [ME. a. F. *trompe* (12–13th c. in Hatz.-Darm.) = Prov. *tromba*, *trompa*, It. *tromba*; ulterior derivation uncertain.]

**1.** = TRUMPET *sb.* 1. *arch.* and *poet.*

1297 R. GLOUC. (Rolls) 8166 Of trompes & of tabors þe sarazins made þere So gret noyse. *a* 1300 *Cursor M.* 15011 (Cott.) Wit harp and pipe, and horn and trump. 1303 R. BRUNNE *Handl. Synne* 4770 As Dauyd seyþ yn þe sautere, ..Wurschepe God, yn troumpes, and sautre. *c* 1375 *Sc. Leg. Saints* xiv. (*Lucas*) 178 Þat þe angel his trumpe sal blav, And ger þame ryse þat lyis law. 1382 WYCLIF 1 *Cor.* xv. 52 In the laste trumpe; forsoth the trumpe schal synge. — 1 *Thess.* iv. 15 In the voys of archaungel, and in the trumpe of God. *c* 1440 *Alphabet of Tales* 306 He sett þis trompe to his mouthe & began to blaw. 1526 *Pilgr. Perf.* (W. de W. 1531) 214 b, The day of the sounde of the claryon & trumpe of god. 1622 DRAYTON *Poly-olb.* xix. 141 With their crooked trumps his Tritons Neptune sent. 1748 THOMSON *Cast. Indol.* I. xxviii, Withouten tromp was proclamation made. 1805 SCOTT *Last Minstr.* VI. xxxi, When louder yet, and yet more dread, Swells the high trump that wakes the dead! 1835 LYTTON *Rienzi* v. iii, Like a king in his pomp, To the blast of the tromp, And the roar of the mighty drum.

β. 15.. *Aberdeen Regr.* (Jam.), To play vpoune the trum nychtly, to convene the waich at ewin. 1549 *Acc. Ld. High Treas. Scot.* IX. 281 Foure Duchemen quha with thair trumbis playit before Ladye Barbara. *Ibid.* 283 For ane trumme..to convene hors and pyonaris.

**b.** = JEWS' HARP, JEWS' TRUMP. Now *Sc.* and *north. Ireland. Tongue of the trump*: see TONGUE *sb.* 14 c.

1549 *Compl. Scot.* vi. 65 The thrid [shepherd] playit on ane trump. 1670 NARBOROUGH *Jrnl.* in *Acc. Sev. Late Voy.* I. (1694) 63, I gave them a Hatchet and Knives, and Beads, and Toys, Trumps etc. 1774 [see JEWS' HARP]. 1830 SCOTT *Demonol.* 314 She played on a Jews harp called in Scotland a trump.

**c.** *Trump marine* = trumpet marine: see TRUMPET *sb.* 2 b.

1667 PEPYS *Diary* 24 Oct., We in to see..one Monsieur Prin play on the trump-marine, which he do beyond belief. 1863 THORNBURY *True as Steel* II. 164 Some blew hideous discord from the square-mouthed trump marine (a sort of bassoon). [An error.]

**d.** *transf.* in reference to a sound like that of a trumpet.

1809 W. IRVING *Knickerb.* IV. ii. (1861) 117 Wilhelmus Kieft..availed himself of that musical organ or trump which nature has implanted in the midst of a man's face. 1895 J. G. MILLAIS *Breath fr. Veldt* (1899) 26 At sunset their [cranes'] hoarse trumps may be heard as they wing their flight to some solitary spot.

**e.** *slang* or *vulgar*. The act of breaking wind audibly. 1903 in FARMER & HENLEY *Slang.*

† **2.** *transf.* One who plays a trump, a trumpeter.

13.. *Sir Beues* (A.) 3793 Þe trompes gonne here bemes blowe. 1473–4 *Acc. Ld. High Treas. Scot.* I. 14 Gevin to James sadillare for a sadill to the Kingis trompis.

† **3.** *transf.* A hollow tube or pipe; *spec.* (*a*) the convoluted windpipe of the crane; (*b*) the trunk of an elephant; the proboscis of an insect. *Obs. rare.*

*c* 1440 *Pallad. on Husb.* IX. 179 To ha made Trumpis of cley bi potters. *c* 1460 J. RUSSELL *Bk. Nurture* 431 The Crane..of hyre trompe in þe brest loke þat ye beware [in carving]. 1648 HEXHAM II, *Rotel ofte russel*, the Trumpe or Snout of an Elephant. 1750 *Phil. Trans.* XLVI. 545 So that it [the Bee] does not suck, but laps or licks with its rough Fang or Tromp, like a Dog.

**4.** *fig.* One who or that which proclaims, celebrates, or summons loudly like a trumpet; esp. in *trump of fame* and the like (cf. quot. *c* 1384 in TRUMP *v.*[1] 2). *arch.* and *poet.*

1531 ELYOT *Gov.* III. xix, Howe moche worthyar had he [Cato] bene to haue hadde Homere, the trumpe of his fame immortall, than Achilles. 1548 UDALL, etc. *Erasm. Par. Matt.* iv. 33 The trumpe of the voyce of the gospell. 1575 R. B. *Appius & Virg.* Prol., Who doth desire the trump of fame, to sound vnto the Skies. 1630 QUARLES *Funeral Elegies* xiii, When the latest breath of fame Shall want her Trumpe, to glorifie a name. 1741–2 GRAY *Agrippina* 122 Say we sound The trump of liberty. 1827 KEBLE *Chr. Y.*, *1st Sun. Adv.* i, Awake—again the Gospel-trump is blown.

**5.** *Comb.*, as *trump-like* adj., *trump-maker.*

1609 *Reg. Mag. Sig. Scot.* 57/2 Confectoris instrumentorum lusorialium lie trumpmaker. *c* 1611 CHAPMAN *Iliad* II. 419 A breast of brasse, a voyce Infract and trumplike.

**Trump** (trɒmp), *sb.*[2] Also 6 troumpe, 6–7 tromp(e, trumpe. [Corruption of TRIUMPH *sb.*, in senses 8, 8 b.]

**1.** A playing-card of that suit which for the time being ranks above the other three, so that any one such card can 'take' any card of another suit; *spec.* the card, usually that last turned up by the dealer, determining this suit; also, *pl.* (formerly also in *sing.*), the suit thus determined.

1529 LATIMER *1st Serm. on Card* in Foxe *A. & M.* (1563) 1302/2 Heartes is trumpe. — *2nd Serm.* ibid. 1306/1 Cast thy tromp vnto them both, and gather them all three together. 1575 *Gamm. Gurton* II. ii. B iv, There is 5 trumps beside the Queene. 1607 HEYWOOD *Wom. Kild w. Kindn.* Wks. 1874 II. 123 *Anne.* What's trumpes? *Wend.* Harts. 1656 EARL MONM. tr. *Boccalini's Advts. fr. Parnass.* I. ii. (1674) 4 Every the least Trump did take all the best Coat-Cards. 1779 WARNER in Jesse *Selwyn & Contemp.* (1844) IV. 254, I won the first trick and led a trump. 1849 HANNAY (*title*) Hearts are Trumps. 1885 PROCTOR *Whist* vii. 88 With good plain cards and five trumps you need never hesitate to lead trumps.

† **b.** An obsolete card-game, known also as ruff.

1529 LATIMER *1st Serm. on Card* in Foxe *A. & M.* (1563) 1303/1 There be many one that breaketh this carde,..and playeth there with oftentimes at the blinde trompe, wherby they be no winners but great losers. 1575 *Gamm. Gurton* II. ii. B iv, We be fast set at trumpe, man, hard by the fyre. 1598 FLORIO, *Trionfo*,..also a trump at cards, or the play called trump or ruff. 1688 R. HOLME *Armoury* III. xvi. (Roxb.) 72/1 Ruffe and Honors, and Whisk, which are generally amongst the Vulgar Termed Trump. 1798 *Sporting Mag.* XII. 299 Laws of the game of Trumps. [1807 DOUCE *Illustr. Shaks.* II. 96 The old card game of trump ..bore a very strong resemblance to our modern whist.]

**c.** An act of trumping; the taking of a trick with a trump card.

1853 LYTTON *My Novel* I. xii, Parson..mixes all the cards together again, and..groans,..'The cruelest trump!'

**2.** *fig.* and in *fig.* context. *To turn up trumps*, to turn out well or successfully (*mod. colloq.*).

1595 *Locrine* IV. ii, She..snatcht vp a fagot stick..and came furiously marching towards me,..thundering out.. Thou drunken knaue, where hast thou bin so long?..and so shee began to play knaues trumps. 1621 BURTON *Anat. Mel.* III. iii. I. ii. (1651) 602 They turned up trumpe, before the Cards were shuffled. 1641 HOLLIS in Rushw. *Hist. Coll.* III. (1692) I. 346 To be honest when every body else is honest, when Honesty is in fashion, and is Trump, as I may say, is nothing so meritorious. *a* 1734 NORTH *Exam.* III. vi. § 63 (1740) 470 The same Card was going to be Trump in the factious Game against King Charles II. 1862 W. W. COLLINS *No Name* IV. viii, Instances..of short courtships and speedy marriages, which have turned up trumps—I beg your pardon—which have turned out well, after all.

† **b.** *fig.* An obstruction, a hindrance: in phr. (*to cast*) *a trump in* (one's) *way. Obs.*

1529 LATIMER *1st Serm. on Card* in Foxe *A. & M.* (1563) 1302/2 We wil fyrst cast a trumpe in theyr way, and play with them at cardes who shall haue the better. *a* 1548 HALL *Chron.*, *Edw. V* 2 Euery one of these castes had been a troumpe in the duke of Gloucesters waye. 1577–87 HOLINSHED *Chron.* III. 855/2 He thought good first to send him some whither out of the waie, least he might cast a trumpe in his waie.

**c.** *To put* (one) *to* († *upon*) *his trump* or *trumps*: To oblige a card-player to play out his trumps; *fig.* 'to put to the last expedient' (J.).

1559 *Mirr. Mag.*, *Jack Cade* xx, Ere he took me, I put him to his trumpes. 1584 LYLY *Campaspe* III. iv, Doeth not your beauty put the painter to his trump? 1681 DRYDEN *Span. Friar* IV. i, We are now put upon our last trump. 1697 DAMPIER *Voy.* (1729) I. 526 The Wind..oft put us to our trumps to manage the Ship. 1751 R. PALTOCK *P. Wilkins* xiv. (1883) 46/2 The strangeness of her dress put me to my trumps, to conceive either what it was, or how it was put on. 1824 W. IRVING *T. Trav.* I. i. ii. 9 Whether such an unexpected accession of company..would not put the housekeeper to her trumps to accommodate them. 1907 W. JAMES *Pragmatism* iv. 142 A bit of danger or hardship puts us agreeably to our trumps.

**3.** *colloq.* as a term of hearty commendation: A person of surpassing excellence; a first-rate fellow; a 'brick'.

[1762 T. BRYDGES *Burlesque Homer* I. (1797) 37 But I, in spite of all his frumps, Shall make him know I'm king of trumps.] 1819 *Sporting Mag.* IV. 236 The Irish trump again got the throw. 1829 *Chron.* in *Ann. Reg.* 65/1 Girls of dissolute character..called out..'Good bye, Tom! God bless you, my trump!' 1837 DICKENS *Pickw.* xli, You're a trump. 1867 TROLLOPE *Chron. Barset* I. xv. 127 Nobody knows better than you what a trump I got in my wife. 1894 DU MAURIER *Trilby* II. 257 Taffy, what a regular downright old trump you are!

**4.** *attrib.* and *Comb.*, as *trump card* (also *fig.*), *lead*, *suit*; *trump-like* adj.; **trump signal**, at Whist, a call for trumps: see CALL *v.* 22 d (*Funk's Stand. Dict.*, 1895).

1822 BYRON *Juan* VIII. xxv, 'The best Intentions'..form all mankind's *trump-card. 1876 A. CAMPBELL-WALKER *Correct Card* (1880) 65 After the dealer has taken the trump card into his hand. 1884 *Times* (weekly ed.) 10 Oct. 9/3 The trump card which the Radicals played was the general remission of taxes. 1870 HARDY & WARE *Mod. Hoyle* 25 *Trump leads, without strength in trumps can only be justified [etc.]. 1836–9 DICKENS *Sk. Boz*, *Making a Night of it*, A certain *trump-like punctuality in turning up just in the very nick of time. 1861 *Macm. Mag.* Dec. 130 No trump is turned up, the *trump suit being determined in another way. 1862 'CAVENDISH' *Whist* (1879) 10 Any one may inquire what the trump suit is, at any time.

Hence **Tru·mpless** *a.* (*nonce-wd.*), having or containing no trumps.

1899 A. MAINWARING *Cut Cavendish* 51 'Chicane', i.e. a trumpless hand, counts twice the value of the trump suit.

† **Trump**, *sb.*[3] *Sc. Obs. rare.* [(?) Back-formation from TRUMPERY.] A thing of small value, a trifle; *pl.* goods of small value, trumpery.

1513 DOUGLAS *Æneis* V. xii. 47 From distructioun deliuer.. Thir sobir trumpis, and mene grayth of Troianis. *Ibid.* VIII. Prol. 107 Ten tendis ar a trump, bot gif he tak ma, Ane kinrik of paroch kyrkis cuppillit with commendis.

**Trump** (trɒmp), *v.*[1] Forms: see TRUMP *sb.*[1]; also 4 *Sc.* trwmp. [ME. a. OF. *tromper* (12th c. in Godef.), f. *trompe*, TRUMP *sb.*[1]]

**1.** *intr.* To blow or sound a trumpet: = TRUMPET *v.* 1. Also with *up.* ? *Obs.* or *arch.*

13.. *Coer de L.* 3892 They trumpyd, and her baners displaye. 13.. *Cursor M.* 21307 (Cott.) An..ringes.., dinnes þe toþer, trumpes þe thrid. 1375 BARBOUR *Bruce* VIII. 293 He left his amonystyng, And gert trumpe to þe assemble. *Ibid.* XII. 491 He gert trwmp vp to the assemble. 1377 LANGL. *P. Pl.* B. XIII. 230, I can noither tabre ne trompe, ne telle none gestes. *c* 1470 HARDING *Chron.* CCXXX. (MS. Lansd. 204 lf. 219 b), The kynge..trumped vp and home he rode in hy. 1513 DOUGLAS *Æneis* XI. viii. 17 Tharfor trump vp, blaw furth thyne eloquens. 1535 COVERDALE *2 Chron.* xiii. 15 The prestes tromped with the trompettes.

**b.** To give forth a trumpet-like sound; *spec.* to break wind audibly (*slang* or *vulgar*).

*c* 1425 WYNTOUN *Cron.* VI. ii. 176 In publik placis ay fra þat day Scho was behynde þan trumpande ay; Sa wes scho schamyt in ilk steid. 1552 HULOET, Trump or let a crackke, or fart, *crepo.* 1598 FLORIO, *Trombeggiare*,..to snort, to trump or bray as an asse. 1719 D'URFEY *Pills* I. 35 She who doth Trump, Through defect in her rump. 1798 R. CUMBERLAND *Aristoph. Clouds* ii, I too..under sufferance trump against your thunder:..my frights..Have pinch'd and cholick'd my poor bowels so. *a* 1845 [see *trumping* below].

**2.** *trans.* To proclaim, celebrate, or extol by, or as by, the sound of a trumpet: = TRUMPET *v.* 2 b. Now *rare* or *Obs.*

*c* 1384 CHAUCER *H. Fame* III. 539 Take forth thy trumpe, ..That is cleped sklaundre..For thou shalt trumpe alle the contrarie Of that they han don wel or fayre. 1422 tr. *Secreta Secret.*, *Priv. Priv.* 163 The trues [= truce] weryn trumped vp for that day. 1548 UDALL *Erasm. Par. Luke* iv. 52 That the fathers glorye may be..troumped abrode by the sonne. 1686 F. SPENCE tr. *Varillas' Ho. Medicis* 231 This infirmity ..trumpt him up the aversion of such people as knew not otherwise his merit. 1847 L. HUNT *Men, Women, & B.* II. i. 4 See also how Pope, and Swift, and others, trumped up Lord Bolingbroke for a philosopher!

¶ **3.** *intr.* To march or go (as at the sound of a trumpet). Cf. quots. 1375, *c* 1470 in sense 1. *Obs.*

1513 DOUGLAS *Æneis* XI. ix. 4 Eneas all his ost and haill army Hes rasyt, trumping to the town in hy. *Ibid.* xiii. 99 Bot this Orsilochus fled hyr in the feyld, And gan to trump with mony a turnyng went.

Hence **Tru·mping** *vbl. sb.* and *ppl. a.*

13.. *K. Alis.* 924 (Bodl. MS.), Þer was trumpyng & tabouryng. 1398 TREVISA *Barth. De P. R.* IX. xxvii. (Bodl. MS.) lf. 97 b, By trumpinge þe peple was icleped to þis feste þat hatte neomenia. 1631 P. FLETCHER *Sicelides* III. iv. F ij b, Thou bluebeard Neptune, and thou trumphing [*sic*] Triton. *a* 1845 HOOD *Schoolboy Joys & Griefs*, Six small Boys; Who ever and anon declare their joys, With trumping horns, and juvenile huzzas.

† **Trump**, *v.*[2] *Obs.* Also 4 *Sc.* trwmp, 6 trumpe, 6–7 tromp(e. [a. F. *tromper* (14th c.), of uncertain origin; perh. the same word as prec.: see Littré.] *trans.* To deceive, cheat.

In quot. 1629, perh. identified with TRUMP *v.*[3]

1375 BARBOUR *Bruce* XIX. 712 Than sall we all be at our will, And thai sall let thame trwmpit [*v.r.* trumpyt] Ill. 1513 DOUGLAS *Æneis* I. vi. 82 That fals man,..With wanhope trumpit the lele luwair. 1584 J. CARMICHAEL *Lett.* in *Wodrow Soc. Misc.* (1844) 415 To haif bein trompit with fair words. 1598 DALLINGTON *Meth. Trav.* E iij, They very wrongfully tromped the heires of Edward the third, of their enioying this Crowne of France. 1629 B. JONSON *New Inn* I. i, When she [Fortune] is pleas'd to trick or tromp mankind.

**Trump**, *v.*[3] [f. TRUMP *sb.*[2]

Appears first in figurative senses (2–3); in some early quots. it may have been confused with TRUMP *v.*[2]; but the sense-development is not quite clear.]

**I. 1.** *Cards.* **a.** *trans.* To put a trump upon; to take with a trump.

1598 FLORIO, *Trionfare*,..to trump at cards. 1680 COTTON *Gamester* xi. 87 A Card that is trumped by the follower, if the next player hath none of the former suit he must trump it again. 1778 C. JONES *Hoyle's Games Impr.* 58 If your Partner forces you to trump a Card early in the Deal. 1837 DICKENS *Pickw.* vi, Miller ought to have trumped the diamond. 1862 'CAVENDISH' *Whist* (1879) 70 You may sometimes discontinue a suit if you suspect it will be trumped.

**b.** *absol.* or *intr.* To play a trump; to take a trick with a trump. *Trump out*, to play out one's trumps.

1680 COTTON *Gamester* x. 82 You ought to have a special eye to what Cards are play'd out, that you may know..how to trump securely. 1746 HOYLE *Whist* (ed. 6) 15 Do not trump out. *Ibid.* 79 If your Partner calls.., you are to trump to him. 1862 'CAVENDISH' *Whist* (1879) 108 It is an advantage to trump when you are weak.

**2.** *fig.* or in fig. context: in quot. 1586, ? to 'put to one's trumps', to nonplus; now usually, to beat, to 'cap'.

1586 FERNE *Blaz. Gentrie* 190 If you be not trumped, in the blazonne of this coate, I care not to what I put you. *a* 1612 HARINGTON *Epigr.* IV. xii, An odious play, and yet in Court oft seen, A sawcy Knave, to trump both King and Queene. 1681 DRYDEN *Princess of Cleves* Prol. 35 But since they're at renouncing, 'tis our parts, To trump their diamonds, as they trump our hearts. 1860 THACKERAY *Lovel* iii, I trumped her old-world stories..with the latest ..intelligence. 1880 S. WALPOLE *Hist. Eng.* III. 296 The Liberals set themselves to trump his [Peel's] best cards.

**II.** † **3.** *Trump in* (one's) *way* (cf. TRUMP *sb.*[2] 2 b): **a.** *trans.* To cast in one's way as a hindrance or obstruction; in quot. 1553, to allege against one (cf. 5 b). *Obs.*

1553 BALE *Gardiner's De vera Obed.* H j b, And that, that is fondly layed to the husbandes charge after he is divorced, because he perfourmed not his promyse, that he ought not to haue made: shall that..be..earnestly tromped in my waye? 1583 GOLDING *Calvin on Deut.* vi. 34 To ouercome all that euer the deuill trumpeth in our way. 1607 *Schol. Disc. agst. Antichr.* I. iv. 178 Sathan is suffered to trompe hinderances in their way.

† **b.** *intr.* To get in one's way; to obstruct or impede one. *Obs.*

1570 FOXE *A. & M.* (ed. 2) 1146/2 But here now commeth Syr Thomas More trumpyng in our way. 1650 WELDON *Crt. Jas. I* 53 For all their setting their Cards..to their owne advantages.., there was one Knave in the Packe would cousen their designes, and Trump in their way.

† **4.** To impose or thrust (something) *upon* a person. *Obs.*

1694 LESLIE *Short Meth. w. Deists* (1699) 3 Authors have been Trump'd upon us, Interpolated and Corrupted. *a* 1704 T. BROWN *Dial. Dead, Reas. Oaths* Wks. 1711 IV. 96 There are abundance of ill-affected Men..that have trumped that unlucky Card upon the Dr. *a* 1716 SOUTH *Serm.* (1727) VI. 104 A sort of odd ill-natur'd Men, whom neither Hopes nor Fears..can prevail upon to have any..forlorn.. Kinswomen of any Lord or Grandee..trump'd upon them.

† **b.** *intr.* ? To impose *upon. Obs. rare.*

*a* 1716 SOUTH *Serm.* (1727) IV. 384 Fit for nothing but to be trumped and trampled upon, to be led by the Nose.

**5.** *Trump up* (trans.). † **a.** ? To put (one) off *with. Obs. rare*[—1].

1634 MASSINGER *Very Woman* II. iii, Hang honesty! Trump me not up with 'honesty'!

† **b.** To bring up, bring forward, allege. *Obs.*

1697 T. SMITH in *Lett. Lit. Men* (Camden) 252 When the Benedictine Monks were so busy to trump up old charters of exemption and priveleges. *a* 1704 T. BROWN *Laconics* Wks. 1711 IV. 14 The Cavaliers..us'd to trump up the 12th of the Romans upon the Parliament; the Parliament trump'd it upon the Army. 1710 PALMER *Proverbs* 333 Necessity is trump'd up for a plea. 1712 ADDISON *Spect.* No. 507 ¶ 2 To husband a lie, and trump it up in some extraordinary emergency. 1772 *Town & Country Mag.* 128 B[olland] trumped up an imaginary debt against him.

**c.** To get up or devise in an unscrupulous way; to forge, fabricate, invent.

1695 W. W. *Colbatch's New Lt. Chirurg. Put out* 64 His Pouder being..disgraced, he was obliged to trump up another Medicine to supply its Defect. 1726 C. D'ANVERS *Craftsman* No. 3 (1727) 22 They..forewarn us to beware of impostures trumpt up in imitation of their approved remedies. *a* 1774 TUCKER *Lt. Nat.* (1834) II. 328 Their very existence is mere hypothesis, trumped up to serve a turn. 1794 GODWIN *Cal. Williams* 277 If..those servants could trump up such accusations. 1809 MALKIN *Gil Blas* IV. vii. ¶ 16 You have trumped up a cock-and-bull story. 1885 HOWELLS *Silas Lapham* viii, She had not..courage to confess..why she had come, but trumped up an excuse.

Hence **Trumped** (trvmpt) *ppl. a.* (only in *trumped-up*, in sense 5 c).

1800 COLERIDGE *Wallenst.* II. iii, A trumped up Spanish story. 1878 Bosw. SMITH *Carthage* 302 Three hundred ..youths were thrown into prison..on a trumped-up charge.

**Trumper** [1] (trv·mpəɪ). Forms: 4 trompor, -er, trumpour, 4–5 trompour(e, 5 trumpowre, 5– trumper. [a. OF. *trompeor, -peur, -pour, trumpeur*, etc. (13th c.), f. *tromper*, TRUMP *v.*[1]]

†**1.** A trumpeter. *Obs.*

13.. *K. Alis.* 3426 For the noise of the taboures, And the trumpours [*Bodl. MS.* trumpes] and jangelours. *c* 1330 *King of Tars* 499 Trompors gunne heore bemes blowe. *a* 1440 *Sir Degrev.* 661 Trompers tromped to the mete. 14.. *Nom.* in Wr.-Wülcker 693/7 *Hec tubicina*, a trumper. *Ibid.* 696/30 *Hic tubicen*, a trumper. 1483 *Cath. Angl.* 395/2 A Trumper, *buccinator*.

**2.** *slang* or *vulgar*. (Cf. TRUMP *sb.*[1] 1 e, *v.*[1] 1 b.)

1836–48 B. D. WALSH *Aristoph., Clouds* 313.

†**Tru·mper** [2]. *Obs.* Forms: 5 trompour, -er, -eur, 6 trumpour, -ir, troumpar, 6– trumper. [a. F. *trompeur* (13–14th c. in Godef. *Compl.*), f. *tromper*, TRUMP *v.*[2]] A deceiver, impostor, cheat. (In quot. 1456 app. a trifler: cf. TRUMPERY.)

*a* 1450 *Knt. de la Tour* (1906) 33 He nis not so trewe a knight as we wende, for he is but a tromper and a iaper. 1456 SIR G. HAYE *Law Arms* (S.T.S.) 287 For syk maner of tromperyis, a prince sulde nocht juge na thole bataill to be. Bot he suld..punys sik trompouris, that..gage bataill for sik fule causis. 1560 ROLLAND *Seven Sag.* 37 Fy Trumpour that did sic ane deid. 1571 in Calderwood *Hist. Kirk* (Wodrow Soc.) III. 104 The most vile carion,..the greatest trumper in all Europ. 1603 *Philotus* l, How durst thow trumper sa bald To tant or tell, that he was ald?

**Trumpery** (trv·mpəri), *sb.* (*a.*) Forms: 5–6 trompery(e, (6 tromperey, troumperie, trumprie), 6–7 tromp-, trumperie, 6– trumpery. [a. F. *tromperie* (14th c. in Godef. *Compl.*), f. *tromper* TRUMP *v.*[2]: see -ERY 1.]

†**1.** Deceit, fraud, imposture, trickery. *Obs.*

1456 SIR G. HAYE *Law Arms* (S.T.S.) 226 Sa that thare be na trompery. *a* 1578 LINDESAY (Pitscottie) *Chron. Scot.* (S.T.S.) I. 141 They concordit alltogither in trumperie and fallsit. 1677 GALE *Crt. Gentiles* II. III. 78 Their Ethics were but false or..imperfect ideas of Vertues..their politics were but carnal and so false reasons of State..and therefore stiled in the Scripture tromperie, deceit, and lies. 1847 DISRAELI *Tancred* II. iv, Irish Papists denouncing the whole movement as fraud and trumpery.

*pl.* 1481 CAXTON *Godeffroy* clxiii. 241 His fayr wordes full of tromperyes and deceytes. 1598 DALLINGTON *Meth. Trav.* H j b, He left none of his trumperies and double dealings vnreuealed. 1646 SIR T. BROWNE *Pseud. Ep.* VII. xii. 362 He runnes into corners, exercising minor trumperies, and acting his deceits in Witches, Magicians, Diviners. 1687 R. L'ESTRANGE *Brief Hist. Times* I. 140 How was the Justice of the Nation, Abus'd, and Impos'd upon by the Trumperies of Confederacy.

**2.** 'Something of less value than it seems'; hence, 'something of no value; trifles' (J.); worthless stuff, trash, rubbish. (Usually *collective sing.*; also, now rarely, *pl.*) **a.** Applied to material objects (see also c, d, e).

1531 *Test. Ebor.* (Surtees) V. 324 A tub, a hogeshed wt other trumperie, viij d. 1611 SHAKS. *Wint. T.* IV. iv. 608, I haue sold all my Tromperie: not a counterfeit Stone, not a Ribbon, Glasse, Pomander, Browch..to keepe my Pack from fasting. 1789 MRS. PIOZZI *Journ. France*, etc. II. 353 A heap of trumpery fit to furnish out the shop of a Westminster pawnbroker. 1807 W. IRVING *Salmag.* vi. (1824) 90 An abundance of trumpery and rubbish, with which the house is encumbered,..every room, and closet, and corner, is crammed with three-legged chairs, clocks without hands, swords without scabbards [etc.].

*pl. a* 1618 RALEIGH *Invent. Shipping* 41 Silver, Cut works, Cambricks, and a world of other trumperyes. 1848 THACKERAY *Van. Fair* xliv, Drawers and cupboards crammed with the dirty relics and congregated trumperies of a couple of generations of Lady Crawleys.

**b.** Applied to abstract things, as beliefs, practices, discourse, writing, etc.: Nonsense, 'rubbish'.

1456 SIR G. HAYE *Law Arms* (S.T.S.) 287 For gif fulis.. be sa daft that thai wage bataill for lytill, evyn as to say.. that he dauncis or syngis better na he dois, or for syk maner of tromperyis. 1578 LYTE *Dodoens* III. lx. 401 The blacke spottes growing on the backside of the leaues [of 'male fern': cf. FERN-SEED]..some do gather thinking to worke wonders, but to say the trueth, it is nothing els but trumperie and superstition. 1693 DRYDEN *Juvenal* vi. 191 With all their Trumpery of Charms. 1726 DE FOE *Hist. Devil* I. ii. (1840) 23 All the metaphysical trumpery of the schools. 1846 D. JERROLD *Mrs. Caudle's Curt. Lect.* viii, I'd put an end to free-masonry and all such trumpery.

**c.** Applied contemptuously to religious practices, ceremonies, ornaments, etc. regarded as idle or superstitious. (Cf. TRINKET *sb.*[1] 3.) Now *rare* or merged in general sense.

1542–5 BRINKLOW *Lament.* 15 b, Pardons, and other of their tromperye, hath bene bought and solde. 1566 in Peacock *Eng. Ch. Furniture* (1866) 95 Banner clothes, crosse clothes, with the rest of the trash as vestments albes and such lik tromperie—wear defacid..by the said churchwardens. 1667 MILTON *P. L.* III. 475 Embryos, and Idiots, Eremits and Friers White, Black and Grey, with all thir trumperie. 1756 C. LUCAS *Ess. Waters* III. 12 This City is famed for ..reliques of saints, and such like holy trumpery. 1824 SOUTHEY *Bk. of Ch.* (1841) 267 St. Francis, St. Dominic, and their fellows, must dislodge with all their trumpery.

*pl.* 1548 *Luther's Art. Faith* Pref. A v, Our juglynge tromperies. 1625 PURCHAS *Pilgrims* IX. vii. § 1. 1487 Wearied with the trumperies of the Religion of Mahumet. 1704 J. PITTS *Acc. Mohammetans* vi. (1738) 55 They blame the Papists for having so many Trumperies in their Churches.

**d.** Showy but unsubstantial apparel; worthless finery.

1610 SHAKS. *Temp.* IV. i. 186 The trumpery in my house, goe bring it hither For stale to catch these theeues. 1801 MAR. EDGEWORTH *Out of Debt* iii, 'You have brought me to the gallows, and all for this trumpery', cried he, snatching her gaudy hat from her head. 1851 C. BRONTE in Mrs. Gaskell *Life* (1857) 364 It would be no shame for a person of my means to wear a cheaper thing;..if you..call it 'trumpery' so much the worse.

**e.** *Gardening.* Weeds or refuse, such as hinder the growth of valuable plants. *Obs.* exc. *dial.*

1669 WORLIDGE *Syst. Agric.* (1681) 214 Broom, Furze, Heath, and other suchlike trumpery, that delight only in barren Lands. 1707 MORTIMER *Husb.* (1721) II. 387 Finish your last Weeding, and cleanse your Garden of Trumpery. 1758 R. BROWN *Compl. Farmer* II. (1760) 30 It occasions its running to May-weed, and other trumpery. 1888 in ELWORTHY *W. Somerset Word-bk.*

**f.** Applied to a person, esp. a woman: cf. TRASH *sb.*[1] 4. ? *Obs.* exc. *dial.*

1738 SWIFT *Pol. Conversat.* iii. 195 For Want of Company, welcome Trumpery. 1766 GOLDSM. *Vic. W.* xxi, Out, I say; ..tramp, thou infamous strumpet...What! you trumpery, to come and take up an honest house without cross or coin to bless yourself with! 1852 MRS. STOWE *Uncle Tom's C.* xviii, Get out wid ye, ye trumpery—I won't have ye round!

**B.** *attrib.* or *adj.* Of little or no value; trifling, paltry, insignificant; worthless, rubbishy, trashy.

1576 FLEMING *Caius' Dogs* (1880) 16 A Hare..was seene.. playing with his former feete vppon a tabbaret...This is no trumpery tale, nor trifling toye. 1748 H. WALPOLE *Lett.* (1845) II. 229 Mr. Ashurst..has built a trumpery new house. 1781 — *Let. to W. Mason* 14 Apr., Dr. Johnson's 'Life of Pope'..is a most trumpery performance. 1810 SCOTT *Let. to Miss J. Baillie* 23 Nov., in *Lockhart*, I hope you will set some value upon this little trumpery brooch, because it is.. a Scotch harp, and set with Iona stones. 1865 M. ARNOLD *Ess. Crit.* viii. (1875) 323 The accents of a trumpery rhetorician. 1869 TROLLOPE *He knew*, etc. xvi, It seems a trumpery quarrel,—as to which should beg each other's pardon first.

Hence **Tru·mperiness.**

1868 A. K. H. BOYD *Less. Mid. Age* 271 How these things impress the lover of Gothic who dwells in a country of churches of inexpressible trumperiness and shabbiness!

**Trumpet** (trv·mpĕt), *sb.* Also 4–6 trompette, -et, trumpette, 5 trompett, troumpette, 6–7 trumpett; *Sc.* 5 trompat, troumpat(e, trumpate, 5–6 trumpat, 6 -ait. [a. F. *trompette* (14th c.), dim. f. *trompe*, TRUMP *sb.*[1]]

**1.** A musical wind-instrument (or one of a class of such) of bright, powerful, and penetrating tone, used from ancient times, especially for military or other signals, and in modern times also in the orchestra; it consists of a cylindrical or conical tube, usually of metal (anciently also of horn or wood), straight or curved (or bent upon itself), with a cup-shaped mouthpiece and a flaring bell.

The natural tones of the instrument are the series of harmonics produced by varying force of breath; in modern forms of it additional tones are obtained by means of slides, crooks, valves, or keys.

13.. *Coer de L.* 303 Trumpettes began for to blowe, Knyghtes justed in a rowe. 1390 GOWER *Conf.* III. 217 Ech of hem ek a trompette Bar in his other hond. *c* 1470 HENRY *Wallace* VIII. 1021 Thai within..defyit Wallace, And trumpattis blew with mony werlik soun. 1533 GAU *Richt Vay* (S.T.S.) 71 Our lord sal thane command ane archangel to blaw the trumpait of God. 1535 COVERDALE *Ezek.* xxxiii. 4 Yff a man now heare the noyse off the trompet & will not be warned. 1606 SHAKS. *Tr. & Cr.* I. iii. 213. 1638 SIR T. HERBERT *Trav.* (ed. 2) 135 In another [mosque] sleeps Sandant-Emyr-amahow..; with many moe, who are like to sleep till the Trumpet raise them. 1788 GIBBON *Decl. & F.* xli. (1869) II. 506 The general's trumpet gave the signal of departure. 1844 THIRLWALL *Greece* VIII. lxiv. 317 Before the games began, after silence had been bidden by the sound of the trumpet, proclamation was made by a herald. 1889 W. H. STONE in Grove *Dict. Mus.* IV. 181 The simple or Field Trumpet is merely a tube twice bent on itself, ending in a bell...The modern orchestral or slide Trumpet..is twice turned or curved, thus forming three lengths. *Ibid.* 182 It [the tempering of the notes] is quite impossible on the Valve Trumpet.

†**b.** Distinguished from *trump*, as being smaller.

*c* 1407 LYDG. *Reson & Sens.* 5589 And for folkys that lyst daunce Ther wer trumpes and trumpetes. *c* 1440 *Promp. Parv.* 504/1 Trumpet, or a lytylle trumpe, that clepythe to mete, or men togedur, *sistrum*.

**c.** *Feast of trumpets*, a Jewish festival observed at the beginning of the month Tisri, blowing of trumpets being a prominent part of the solemnities.

1560 BIBLE (Genev.) *Num.* xxix. (*heading*) 1 The feast of trumpets. 1611 *Ibid.*, The offering at the feast of Trumpets. 1903 W. BRIGHT *Age of Fathers* II. xxxiii. 192 Chrysostom was..indignant at the numbers that flocked to the festivals of 'Trumpets' or 'Tabernacles'.

**2.** Something of the nature of or resembling a trumpet. **a.** A reed-stop on the organ, of powerful tone resembling that of a trumpet.

1659 LEAK *Waterwks.* 31 To make Organs, or Trumpets of Organs, to Sound. 1660 *Specif. Organ* in Grove *Dict. Mus.* II. 591 Great Organ. 10 stops...10. Trumpet...Eccho Organ. 4 stops...19. Trumpet. 1688 in E. J. Hopkins *Organ* (1870) 453 Trumpett, of mettle. 1776 HAWKINS *Hist. Mus.* IV. I. x. 149 Of the stops of an organ, the most usual are the..Trumpet [etc.]. 1876 HILES *Catech. Organ* x. (1878) 70 *Trumpet, Tromba*, a striking reed stop of clear, penetrating tone.

**b.** *Trumpet marine, marine trumpet* [tr. Ital. *tromba marina*, F. *trompette marine*], a large obsolete musical instrument of the viol kind, played with a bow, and having a single thick string passing over a bridge fastened at one end only, the other vibrating against the body, and producing a tone like that of a trumpet.

1675 *Lond. Gaz.* No. 961/4 A Rare Concert of four Trumpets Marine, never heard of before in England. 1748 tr. *Molière's Le Bourg. Gent.* II. i, The Trumpet-Marine is an Instrument that pleases me, and is very harmonious. 1838 G. F. GRAHAM *Mus. Comp.* App. 78 In Europe, in the last century, the only remnant of the most ancient monochord was the tromba-marina (trumpet-marine).

**c.** A conical tube with a wide mouth, used for increasing the force and carrying power of the voice: = SPEAKING-TRUMPET. **d.** A similar apparatus for conveying sound to the ear of a partially deaf person: = EAR-TRUMPET, HEARING-TRUMPET.

1696 PHILLIPS (ed. 5), *A Speaking Trumpet*, a Trumpet about Eight Foot, and sometimes Six Foot long, straight and very wide at the end...It carries the Voice so as to be distinctly heard above a Mile. 1774 GOLDSM. *Retal.* 146 When they judged without skill, he was still hard of hearing; When they talked of their Raphaels, Correggios, and stuff, He shifted his trumpet, and only took snuff. 1849 CUPPLES *Green Hand* xiv, 'Stand by to let go the larboard anchor!' I sang out through the trumpet. 1883 S. C. HALL *Retrospect* II. 46 So deaf that a trumpet was constantly at her ear.

**3.** *fig.* A means or agent (real or imaginary) which proclaims, celebrates, or gives warning of something. *To blow one's own trumpet*, to sound one's own praises, boast, brag.

1447 BOKENHAM *Seyntys* (Roxb.) 35 Whan it was knowe.. And be the trumpet of fame aboute blowe. 1513 DOUGLAS *Æneis* I. Prol. 346 Venerable Chaucer, principall poet but peir, Hevinlie trumpat, horleige and reguleir. 1560 DAUS tr. *Sleidane's Comm.* 264 The decree of Wormes was the trompet of this warre. 1576 FLEMING *Panopl. Epist.* 59, I will..sound the trumpet of mine owne merites. 1644 MILTON *Areop.* (Arb.) 68 Why..was this Nation chos'n..that out of her..should be..sounded forth the first tidings and trumpet of Reformation to all Europ? 1783 WOLCOTT (P. Pindar) *Odes to R.A.'s* vi, Sound their own praise from their own penny trumpet. 1803–6 WORDSW. *Ode Intim. Immort.* 25 The cataracts blow their trumpets from the steep. 1902 ELIZ. L. BANKS *Newspaper Girl* 22 It was with a great flourish of newspaper trumpets that I started off.

**4.** *transf.* One who blows or plays on a trumpet; a trumpeter.

1390–1 *Earl Derby's Exp.* (Camden) 114 Dati a le Trumpet de dono domini ibidem, xxiiij s. viij d. *a* 1450 *Le Morte Arth.* 2723 The trompettis vppon the wallis went. 1560 DAUS tr. *Sleidane's Comm.* 225 b, The Duke of Brunswicke sendeth a trompet to Duke Moris, and desyreth a communication. 1617 MORYSON *Itin.* I. 106 Our guard of horse left vs, and their trumpet asked of euery man a gift in curtesie. 1752 J. LOUTHIAN *Form of Process* (ed. 2) 233 The Judges ..set out..for their respective Districts, attended with a Macer of Court and two Trumpets. 1855 MOTLEY *Dutch Rep.* I. ii. (1864) I. 178 Nevers sent a trumpet, after the battle, to the Duke of Savoy, for the purpose of negotiating concerning the prisoners.

**b.** *fig.* = TRUMPETER 2. Cf. 3 above.

1549 CHALONER *Erasm. Praise Folly* A ij, What..maie be ..better fittyng, than dame Foly to praise hir selfe, and be hir owne trumpet? 1577 *F. de L'isle's Leg.* G viij, Munkes and such other trumpets of sedition. 1595 SHAKS. *John* I. i. 27 So hence: be thou the trumpet of our wrath. 1709 STEELE *Tatler* No. 52 ¶ 4 He must in some Measure be the Trumpet of his Fame.

**5.** A sound like that of a trumpet; the loud cry of certain animals, esp. the elephant; the shrill hum of the gnat or mosquito.

1850 R. G. CUMMING *Hunter's Life S. Afr.* (1902) 86/2 He [the elephant] charged with a terrific trumpet. 1852 MUNDY *Our Antipodes* (1857) 195 The shrill scream of the heron, and the rough trumpet of the pelican. 1896 J. H. SKRINE in *Speaker* 25 July 98/2 The steed..neighed his trumpet. 1911 *Blackw. Mag.* Nov. 707/1 Suddenly there comes the well-known trumpet of the crane.

**6.** Something shaped like a trumpet.

* *natural.* **a.** = *trumpet-shell* (see 7); also called SEA-TRUMPET (1).

1668 CHARLETON *Onomast.* 180 *Buccinum*..the Trumpet. 1713 PETIVER *Aquat. Anim. Amboinæ* Tab. vii, *Buccinum Amboin. rarum, nubulis castaneis*: *Nobis*, Brown Amboina Trumpet. 1895 *Edin. Rev.* Oct. 355 Cuttles and squids.. crown-melons and fighting trumpets.

**b.** Applied to a plant having trumpet-shaped flowers; in quot. 1705 app. = *trumpet-daffodil* (see 7). Also *pl.* a name for a species of pitcher-plant, *Sarracenia flava* (cf. *trumpet-leaf* in 7). Also *gen.* a trumpet-shaped blossom or part of a blossom (as the tubular *corona* of a daffodil).

1705 tr. *Cowley's Plants* Wks. 1711 III. 344 Then a gay Flow'r for Shape the Trumpet nam'd. 1883 MRS. G. L.

BANKS *Forbidden to Marry* v, The white and rosy trumpets of the bindweed. **1884** MILLER *Plant-n.*, Trumpets, *Sarracenia flava.* **1904** *Daily Chron.* 8 Mar. 8/5 The White Queen [narcissus], a novelty with white perianth and trumpet of pale chrome.

** *artificial.* **c.** A funnel-shaped conductor in a spinning-machine, etc.; also called *trumpet-mouth* (see 7). **d.** The flaring mouth of an automatic coupling on a railway car. **e.** (See quot. 1877 [2].)

**1877** KNIGHT *Dict. Mech.*, *Trumpet*...4. (*Spinning.*) *a.* The funnel which leads a sliver to the cylinders of a drawing-machine, or which collects a number of combined rovings, and leads them to condensing cylinders. *b.* A funnel-shaped conductor used in many forms of thread-machines [etc.]...5. (*Railway.*) The flaring mouth of a railway-car draw-head which directs the entering coupling-link. **1877** G. F. MACLEAR *St. Mark* xii. (1879) 139 This treasury, according to the Rabbis, consisted of thirteen brazen chests, called 'trumpets', because the mouths..were wide at the top and narrow below.

**7.** *attrib.* and *Comb.* **a.** Simple attrib., as *trumpet-blare, -blast, -bray, -clang, -clangor, -flourish, music, -note, -peal, signal, -sound, stop* (= sense 2 a), *tone, -voice, -word.* **b.** Objective, as *trumpet-blowing* adj. and sb.; instrumental, as *trumpet-hung* adj. (cf. 6 b); parasynthetic and similative, as *trumpet-flowered, -loud, -toned, -voiced* adjs.; also *trumpet-like* adj. **c.** Special Combs.: **trumpet animalcule**, an infusorian of the genus *Stentor* or family *Stentoridæ*, so called from its shape; **trumpet-ash** = *trumpet-creeper* (Cent. Dict. 1891); **trumpet-banner**, a small banner attached to a trumpet, formerly used by heralds; **trumpet-bird** = TRUMPETER 5 b; **trumpet-call**, a call or summons sounded on a trumpet; also *fig.*; **trumpet-cheek**, a cheek inflated or distended as in blowing a trumpet; **trumpet-conch** = *trumpet-shell* (Cent. Dict. 1891); **trumpet creeper**, a climbing shrub of the genus *Tecoma* (N.O. *Bignoniaceæ*), *esp.* the common trumpet-flower, *T. radicans* (formerly *Bignonia radicans*), of the Southern U.S., with scarlet trumpet-shaped flowers; **trumpet daffodil**, a variety of daffodil with conspicuous 'trumpet' or tubular *corona* (cf. 6 b); **trumpet-fish**, name for various fishes with long tubular snout, *esp.* the bellows-fish or sea-snipe (*Centriscus scolopax*) and the tobacco-pipe fish (*Fistularia*); **trumpet-flower**, name for various plants with large or showy trumpet-shaped flowers, esp. of the genera *Tecoma* (see *trumpet-creeper* above) and *Bignonia*, also species of *Catalpa, Brunfelsia, Datura, Solandra*, etc.; **trumpet-fly** (see quot.); **trumpet-gall**, a small trumpet-shaped gall found on grape-vines in U.S. (*Cent. Dict.*); **trumpet-gourd**, a trumpet-shaped variety of the common gourd (*Lagenaria vulgaris*); **trumpet-grass** = *trumpet-weed*; **trumpet-guide** = sense 6 c (*Cent. Dict. Suppl.* 1909); **trumpet honeysuckle** (see HONEYSUCKLE 2); **trumpet hypha** (pl. **-hyphæ**), *Bot.* (see quot.); **trumpet-jasmine** = *trumpet-creeper* (Cent. Dict.); **trumpet-keck** (see KECK *sb.*); **trumpet lamp**, 'miner's term for a *Mueseler* or Belgian safety-lamp' (Gresley *Gloss. Coal Mining* 1883); **trumpet-leaf**, name for species of pitcher-plant (*Sarracenia*) with leaves resembling trumpets rather than pitchers; **trumpet-lily**, the white arum-lily (see ARUM b); also some species of *Lilium*; **trumpet-major**, the chief trumpeter of a band or regiment; **trumpet milkweed** = *trumpet-weed* (*c*); **trumpet-mouth**, the 'mouth' or expanded end of a trumpet, or something resembling this (in quot. 1835 = sense 6 c); **trumpet-mouthed** *a.*, (*a*) = *trumpet-tongued, -voiced*; (*b*) having a wide opening like the mouth of a trumpet; **trumpet narcissus** (cf. *trumpet daffodil* above); **trumpet-pipe**, (*a*) name for a particular pattern of musket; (*b*) a pipe of the trumpet-stop on an organ; **trumpet reed**, a West Indian species of reed, *Arundo occidentalis*; **trumpet-seaweed** = *trumpet-weed* (*a*); **trumpet-shaped** *a.*, of the shape of a trumpet; in *Nat. Hist.* tubular with one end dilated; **trumpet-shell**, a shell of the genus *Triton* or family *Tritonidæ* (see TRITON 2 a), or any other shell which can be blown like a trumpet; **trumpet-tongued** (-tvŋd) *a.*, 'having a tongue vociferous as a trumpet' (J.), loud-voiced; so **trumpet-tongue** *v.*, *trans.* to proclaim loudly; **trumpet-tree**, a West Indian and South American tree (*Cecropia peltata*, N.O. *Artocarpaceæ*), with hollow stem and branches which are used for wind-instruments; **trumpet-vine** = *trumpet-creeper*; **trumpet-weed**, (*a*) a large S. African seaweed, *Ecklonia buccinalis* = SEA-TRUMPET 3; (*b*) a N. American species of hemp-agrimony, *Eupatorium purpureum*, with hollow stems which children blow through like trumpets; (*c*) a N. American sp. of lettuce, *Lactuca canadensis*; **trumpet-wood** = *trumpet-tree.*

**1891** *Cent. Dict.*, *Trumpet-animalcule. **1895** L. WRIGHT *Pop. Handbk. Microscope* viii. 154 The largest animals of this type are the *Stentors* or Trumpet-Animalcules. **1503** *Acc. Gt. Wardrobe* in *Calr. Doc. rel. Scotl.* IV. 441 Item, vij *trumpetbaners pro v trumpetters et ij shakbotters. **1586** FERNE *Blaz. Gentrie* 161 The..French king, for want of a Hereald..was constrained to subbornate a vadelict, or common seruing man, with a trumpet banner..in steede of a better cote-armour of Fraunce. **1896** NEWTON *Dict. Birds* 992 Messrs. Sclater and Salvin in their *Nomenclator*..admit 6 species of *Trumpet-birds. **1865** KINGSLEY *Herew.* xv, The streets..rang with clank, and tramp, and *trumpet-blare. **1837** CARLYLE *Fr. Rev.* I. IV. ii, As it [the edict] sounds out..accompanied with*trumpet-blast. **1879** FARRAR *St. Paul* I. 582 Their faith had been as a trumpet-blast through all the Mediterranean coasts. **1856** *Mem. F. Perthes* II. xxiv. 362 The *trumpet-blowing angels. **1859** TENNYSON *Vivien* 416 Such a song, such fire for fame, Such trumpet-blowing in it. **1815** SCOTT *Waterloo* vii, Cannon-roar and *trumpet-bray. **1808** — *Marm.* I. xii, Loudly flourish'd the *trumpet-call. **1909** *Blackw. Mag.* Mar. 402/1 His name was still a trumpet-call. **1693** DRYDEN *Juvenal* iii. 64 The Minstrels of a Country Show..By *Trumpet-Cheeks and Bloated Faces known. **1808** SCOTT *Marm.* v. xxv, And voice of Scotland's law was sent In glorious *trumpet clang. **1597** SHAKS. 2 *Hen. IV*, v. v. 42 There roar'd the Sea: and *Trumpet Clangour sounds. **1857** A. GRAY *First Less. Bot.* (1866) 34 By these rootlets..the *Trumpet Creeper, the Ivy [etc.] fasten themselves firmly to walls. **1895** *Outing* (U.S.) XXVII. 220/1 Trumpet creepers, yellow as gold, and starry blue passion flowers. **1895** *Daily News* 25 Apr. 5/2 The great white and yellow *trumpet daffodils. **1668** WILKINS *Real Char.* 137 *Trumpet-fish. **1683–4** ROBINSON in *Phil. Trans.* XXIX. 479 The *Scolopax* or *Trombetta*, call'd by our Seamen the Bellows or Trumpet-Fish. **1871** KINGSLEY *At Last* vi, The good people of Trinidad believe that the fish which makes this noise is the trumpet-fish, or Fistularia. **1811** SCOTT *Vis. Don Roderick* lvi, Thrills the loud fife, the *trumpet-flourish pours. **1844** *Regul. & Ord. Army* 29 Trumpets sounding twice the Trumpet-flourish. **1731** MORTIMER in *Phil. Trans.* XXXVII. 175 *Bignonia Fraxini foliis, coccineo flore minore.* The *Trumpet-Flower. **1812** *New Bot. Gard.* I. 93 The Trumpet Flower, or Scarlet Jasmine. **1847** LONGF. *Ev.* II. ii. 80 The trumpet-flower and the grape-vine Hung their ladder of ropes aloft. **1857** HENFREY *Elem. Bot.* 353 The *Trumpet-flowered climbers form striking features of American forests. **1752** J. HILL *Hist. Anim.* 31 The blackish Œstrus, with a yellow breast...We call it the grey fly from it's colour, or the *trumpet fly from the noise it makes in the heats of summer. **1884** *De Candolle's Orig. Cultiv. Pl.* 245 The pilgrim's gourd,..the long-necked gourd, the *trumpet gourd, and the calabash. **1850** MISS PRATT *Comm. Things of Sea-side* II. 119 Thunberg..calls it [*sc.* the Sea-trumpet] the *Trumpet-grass. **1753** *Trumpet honey-suckle [see HONEYSUCKLE 2]. **1882** *Garden* 3 June 383/1 The North American Trumpet Honeysuckle..one seldom sees outside a greenhouse. **1870** MRS. WHITNEY *We Girls* xi, Its..splendid vista of *trumpet-hung bignonia vines. **1900** B. D. JACKSON *Gloss. Bot. Terms*, **Trumpet-hyphae*, tubes in Laminarieae having swollen portions with transverse septa (F. Oliver). **1884** MILLER *Plant-n.*, **Trumpet-leaf*, the genus *Sarracenia.* **1814** ANNE PLUMPTRE tr. *Langsdorff's Voy. & Trav.* II. 104 *Anas Glacialis*...The harmonious *trumpet-like noise of this bird distinguishes it from every other species of duck. **1825** *Green Ho. Comp.* I. 57 Tube-shaped or long trumpet-like flowers. **1862** SHIRLEY *Nugæ Crit.* i. 89 The shrill trumpet-like call of the wild swan. **1878** F. FERGUSON *Life Christ* 465 The thirteen trumpet-like boxes in which the gifts of the people were received. **1857** HENFREY *Elem. Bot.* 397 *Richardia africana* is the white-spathed '*Trumpet-lily' of our conservatories. **1884** MILLER *Plant-n.*, *Lilium eximium*, Transparent Trumpet Lily...[*L.*] *longiflorum*, Common Trumpet Lily. *Ibid.*, *Richardia* (*Calla*) *æthiopica*, Lily-of-the-Nile, Trumpet Lily, White Arum-Lily. **1857** G. W. THORNBURY *Songs Cavaliers & Roundh.* 56 Blow the organ *trumpet-loud. **1855** HYDE CLARKE, **Trumpet-major*, head trumpeter. **1902** *Westm. Gaz.* 26 May 8/2 There died at Shrewsbury yesterday Trumpet-Major Thomas Monks, who sounded the 'Charge' for the Heavy Brigade at Balaclava. **1835** URE *Philos. Manuf.* 153 A copper funnel, or *trumpet mouth, for conducting the sliver delivered by the second rollers. **1839** *Civil Eng. & Arch. Jrnl.* II. 231/2 The smoke pipe..having a wide, or trumpet mouth. **1899** R. MUNRO *Prehist. Scotl.* vi. 203 Its present mode of attachment to the trumpet-mouth is evidently modern. **1767** A. YOUNG *Farmer's Lett.* ii. 43 These are facts which speak *trumpet mouthed in favour of this..measure. **1895** *Daily News* 31 May 5/2 What Mr. Burns described as a trumpet-mouthed approach to the Houses of Parliament and Westminster Abbey. **1818** SCOTT *Br. Lamm.* xxiii[i], What had his memory to do with the degeneracy of the *trumpet music? **1904** *Daily Chron.* 8 Mar. 8/5 Weardale Perfection, an exquisite *trumpet narcissus. **1813** SCOTT *Trierm.* III. x, A wild and lonely *trumpet note. **1887** J. HUTCHISON *Lect. Philippians* i. 7 It is not a trumpet-note of defiance like the Epistle to the Galatians. **1804** J. GRAHAME *Sabbath*, etc. (1808) 56 The battle's *trumpet-peal. **1844** *Regul. & Ord. Army* 90 For long-fore or *trumpet-pipe. **1855** E. J. HOPKINS *Organ* xxii. 123 The tubes of the Trumpet-pipes are usually..of tin or metal,..occasionally..of zinc or wood. **1866** *Treas. Bot.* 963 *Trumpet [Reed], *Arundo occidentalis.* **1884** MILLER *Plant-n.*, *Ecklonia buccinalis*, Cape *Trumpet-Sea-weed, Horn-plant. **1767** ELLIS in *Phil. Trans.* LVII. 420 The figure of one of the *trumpet-shaped suckers highly magnified. **1861** BENTLEY *Man. Bot.* 446 Perennial boggy plants, with pitcher or trumpet-shaped leaves. **1887** RIDER HAGGARD *Jess* i, Long trumpet-shaped flowers. **1753** CHAMBERS *Cycl. Supp.*, *Trumpet-Shell, *Buccinum.* **1890** H. DRUMMOND in *Life* xv. (1899) 386 The great trumpet-shell, now rare [in Tongoa, New Hebrides]. **1864** ENGEL *Mus. Anc. Nat.* 98 *Trumpet signals are better fitted for transmitting orders to a great distance, than verbal messages through a speaking-trumpet. **1718** ROWE tr. *Lucan* 224 At once the warriors shouts and *Trumpet-sounds surprise. **1823** SCOTT *Quentin D.* xxi, Summoned together, by war-cry and trumpet-sound, to assist in repelling a desperate sally. **1795** MASON *Ch. Mus.* i. 64 Instead of using either the *Trumpet stop or the full organ, he will modulate on.. the more delicate and softer series of Pipes. **1876** HILES *Catech. Organ* x. (1878) 71 *Trompette Harmonique*, a Trumpet stop..made to overblow, by a strong and copious wind; they sound the octave, or the super octave above the usual note. **1841** T. H. WHITE *Fragm. Italy & Rhineland* 9 Well may they dread to waken its [the Bible's] *trumpet tones! **1854** J. S. C. ABBOTT *Napoleon* (1855) I. i. 25 Those *trumpet-toned proclamations which..electrified Europe. **1880** BURTON *Reign Q. Anne* I. i. 27 Friends can confide their thoughts..to each other without their being *trumpet-tongued by..unscrupulous parasites. **1605** SHAKS. *Macb.* I. vii. 19 His Vertues Will pleade like Angels, *Trumpet-tongu'd against The deepe damnation of his taking off. **1775** J. ADAMS in *Fam. Lett.* (1876) 52 It will plead..with more irresistible persuasion than angels trumpet-tongued. **1860** PUSEY *Min. Proph.* 453 That Day of the Lord..shall, trumpet-tongued, proclaim the holiness and justice of Almighty God. **1756** P. BROWNE *Jamaica* 111 The *Trumpet-Tree...The trunk and branches are hollow,..stopped from space to space with membranous septæ...The smaller branches..serve for wind instruments. **1871** KINGSLEY *At Last* v, A tall stick, thirty feet high, with a flat top of gigantic curly horse-chestnut leaves, which is a Trumpet-tree. **1717** *Petiveriana* III. 255 Scarlet *Trumpet-Vine. Makes a fine Arbour. **1818** BYRON *Ch. Har.* IV. xcviii, Yet Freedom! yet..Thy *trumpet-voice, though..dying, The loudest still the tempest leaves behind. **1902** *Athenæum* 4 Jan. 6/2 Howel Harris, the *trumpet-voiced revivalist. **1856** GRAY *Man. Bot.* (1860) 186 *Eupatorium purpureum* (..*Trumpet-Weed). **1866** *Treas. Bot.* 1179 *Trumpet-weed*, the name of a seaweed, *Ecklonia buccinalis*,..very common ..at the Cape of Good Hope...The stem of this seaweed, says Dr. Harvey, which is hollow in the upper portion, is when dried..used..as a siphon, and by the native herdsmen is formed into a trumpet for collecting the cattle in the evening...The name is also applied in America to *Eupatorium purpureum.* **1888** EGGLESTON *Graysons* xx, Shaded by the broad-leaved horse and trumpet weeds in the fence-row. **1836** LOUDON *Encycl. Plants* 826 *Cecropia.* From κεκραγω, to cry out, a sort of translation of the English word *trumpet-wood. This tree has the trunk and branches hollow every where...The leaves are large, peltate. **1827** G. DARLEY *Sylvia* 117 The wild reed breathes no *trumpet-word.

Hence **Tru·mpetless** *a.*, without a trumpet, without trumpeting; **Tru·mpetry**, trumpets collectively; trumpeting; **Tru·mpety** *a.* (*colloq.*), having the tone or style of a trumpet, blaring.

*a* **1711** KEN *Edmund* Poet. Wks. 1721 II. 321 It was impossible the Beast to rein, While *trumpetless the Pagans did remain. **1860** THACKERAY *Round. Papers* v, Cornhill..has witnessed every ninth of November..a prodigious annual pageant, chariot, progress, and flourish of *trumpetry. **1884** *Sat. Rev.* 14 June 778/1 The blare of modern trumpetry. **1822** *Examiner* 810/2 The music..was altogether too clanging and *trumpetty—the word is a good word. **1896** *Pall Mall G.* 8 Jan. 1/3 A good stirring military song with an inspiriting trumpety air.

**Tru·mpet**, *v.* [f. TRUMPET *sb.*; cf. F. *trompeter* (14th c. in Godef. *Compl.*).]

**1.** *intr.* To blow or sound a trumpet.

**1530** PALSGR. 763/1, I trompet, I blowe or sownde in a trumpet, *je sonne vne trompette.* **1535** COVERDALE 2 *Chron.* v. 13 As yᵉ one dyd trompet and synge. **1672** VILLIERS (Dk. Buckhm.) *Rehearsal* IV. i. (Arb.) 91 It [the Play] shall Drum, Trumpet, Shout and Battel, I gad, with any the most warlike Tragœdy we have. **1862** DICKENS *Somebody's Luggage* ii, Practising soldiers trumpeted and bugled. **1913** SIR H. JOHNSTON *Pioneers Australia* iv. 135 The seamen.. trumpeted back..in reply.

**b.** To emit a sound like that of a trumpet; used esp. in reference to the cry of an elephant when enraged or excited; also, to the musical piping of a mosquito or gnat when about to bite.

**1828** CAPT. MUNDY *Pen & Pencil Sk.* (1832) I. ii. 112 My elephant suddenly raised his trunk and trumpeted several times. **1860** GOSSE *Rom. Nat. Hist.* 258 He..drives off the alarmed animal trumpeting shrilly with rage and pain. **1872** DARWIN *Emotions* vi. 168 The keeper ordered the old and the young elephant to trumpet. **1900** *Pilot* 22 Sept. 357/2 Anopheles, a mosquito that does not trumpet.

**2.** *trans.* **a.** To sound on a trumpet; to utter with a sound like that of a trumpet.

**1729** YOUNG *Merchant* II. ix, She trumpets shrill her dread command. **1854** *Poultry Chron.* II. 84 An old..black cock, who could never utter the least sound without trumpeting a prolonged *finale.* **1875** BUCKLAND *Log-bk.* 355 He seems to have trumpeted the order. **1886** F. HARRISON *Choice Bks.* ii. 29 A passage of Homer, rolling along in the hexameter or trumpeted out by Pope.

**b.** *fig.* To announce or publish as by sound of trumpet; to proclaim, celebrate, or extol loudly; to noise abroad. Also with *forth.*

**1604** SHAKS. *Oth.* I. iii. 251 That I loue the Moore,..My.. storme of Fortunes, May trumpet to the world. **1608** — *Per.* I. i. 145 He must not liue to trumpet foorth my infamie. **1702** C. MATHER *Magn. Chr.* IV. I. (1852) 14 Commenius, the fame of whose worth hath been trumpetted as far as more than three languages could carry it. **1756** H. WALPOLE *Lett. to Mann* 23 Feb., They trumpeted the story all over the town. **1841** THACKERAY *Gt. Hoggarty Diam.* ix, This I state not to trumpet my own praises. **1856** DOVE *Logic Chr. Faith* III. iii. 148 Atheism may trumpet forth her astounding discovery.

**c.** To summon or denounce formally (cf. F. *trompeter*, and HORN *v.* 5), or to drive away, by sound of trumpet.

**1680** SIR R. SOUTHWELL in *Cal. Ormonde MSS.* IV. 579 The Duchess of Soissons is trumpetted, which is the manner of citation used in like cases...And if she appear not at the third trumpetting, her crimes and sentences will be pronounced. **1795** BURKE *Regic. Peace* iv. Wks. IX. 52 They drummed and trumpeted the wretches out of their Hall.

**Trumpeted** (trɒ·mpĕtĕd), *ppl. a.* and *a.* [f. TRUMPET *v.* and *sb.* + -ED.]

**I. 1.** Sounded on a trumpet; *fig.* celebrated as with a trumpet, greatly extolled or boasted of.

1611 Cotgr., *Trompetté*, trumpetted, or noised abroad; published, or proclaymed with sound of Trumpets. 1775 Mme. D'Arblay *Early Diary, Let. to Crisp* 19 Nov., Giving..his opinion in disfavour of so trumpeted a character. 1804 Larwood *No Gun Boats* 34 A complete Destruction of this trumpeted Flotilla. 1908 *Athenæum* 29 Aug. 236/1 Some of the most trumpeted names are..authors of no..consequence.

II. [f. the sb.] 2. Furnished with a trumpet (or something likened to one).

1841 L. Hunt *Seer* (1864) 4 The gnat,..airy, trumpeted, and plumed.

3. Formed like a trumpet; made with one end expanded; funnel-shaped.

1889 *Philos. Mag.* Aug. 95 Their [the wires'] ends were passed into two small trumpeted holes in a stout brass plate.

**Trumpeter** (trʊ·mpėtəɹ). Forms: 5–6 *Sc.* trumpatour(e, 6 trompetor, -etter, -atere, troumpetor, trumpetor, -ettor, -etour, -ettour, -ytar, -yter, -itour, 6–7 -etter, 6– trumpeter. [f. Trumpet *sb.* or *v.* + -er[1], or a. F. *trompeteur* (Palsgr. 1530), f. *trompeter* to Trumpet.]

1. One who sounds or plays upon a trumpet; *spec.* a soldier in a cavalry regiment who gives signals with a trumpet; also, one who has a similar function in a war-ship (? *obs.*); in quot. 1673, a herald.

1497 *Acc. Ld. High Treas. Scot.* (1877) I. 326 For their Pasche reward..to Thome Pringil and his brodir trumpatouris, xxviij s. 1533 *Ibid.* (1905) VI. 95 To Juliane and the laif of the trumpatouris in Dunbar. 1555 Eden *Decades* 117 The gouernour commaunded the trumpitour to blowe a retraite. 1581 Mulcaster *Positions* xv. (1887) 70 Trumpeters, and those that play vpon winde instruments. 1627 Capt. Smith *Seaman's Gram.* viii. 35 The Trumpeter is..to attend the Captaines command, and to sound either at his going a shore, or comming aboord, at the entertainment of strangers, also when you hale a ship, when you charge, boord, or enter. 1673 Temple *Let. to Dk. Florence* Wks. 1731 II. 291 A Trumpeter arrived from Holland, bringing full and entire Powers to the Ambassador of Spain, to treat here of a Peace. 1855 Macaulay *Hist. Eng.* xvi. III. 680 A trumpeter was sent to summon the place. *Ibid.* xxi. IV. 654 Keyes..had formerly been trumpeter of the corps.

2. *fig.* One who gives the signal for, proclaims, or extols something as by sound of trumpet.

1581 J. Hamilton in *Cath. Tract.* (S.T.S.) 84 Thir seditius trumpeters brocht hir maiestie in disdane of the peple. 1599 *Broughton's Let.* A ij, A clamorous trumpetor of his owne praises. 1793 Burke *Policy of Allies* Wks. VII. 198 Subordinate instruments and trumpeters of sedition. 1796 Grose *Dict. Vulgar T.* s. v., His trumpeter is dead, he is therefore forced to sound his own trumpet. 1869 Freeman *Norm. Conq.* (1875) III. xi. 33 Osbert, Prior of Westminster, the special trumpeter of Eadward's renown.

3. *Trumpeter's muscle*, †also simply *trumpeter* (obs.) = Buccinator.

1615 Crooke *Body of Man* 754 Muscles..common to the Cheekes and the Lippes are foure, two on either side called *Quadratus* and *Buccinator*, the square muscle and the Trumpeter. 1758 J. S. *Le Dran's Observ. Surg.* Dict. (1771) B b ij b, *Buccinator*, the..Muscle of the Cheek, called the Trumpeter's Muscle. 1875 Sir W. Turner in *Encycl. Brit.* I. 837/2 The buccinator..compresses the cheeks, and drives the air out of the cavity of the mouth as in playing a wind instrument; hence the name, 'trumpeter's muscle'.

4. Applied to a. a braying ass (*humorous*); b. a broken-winded horse: cf. Roarer[1] 2.

1638 Sir T. Herbert *Trav.* (ed. 2) 133 We joggd leasurely on upon our Portugall Trumpetters,..sometimes braying out. 1785 Grose *Dict. Vulgar T.* s. v., The King of Spain's trumpeter, a braying ass. 1844 Stephens *Bk. Farm* II. 227 There are many degrees of broken wind, which receive appellations according to the noise emitted by the horse; and on this account he is called a..trumpeter.

5. Name given to various birds, from their loud note suggesting the sound of a trumpet. a. A variety of domestic pigeon. b. Any species of the South American genus *Psophia* or family *Psophiidæ*, allied to the Cranes. †c. 'An obsolete name in Tasmania for the black Crow-Shrike, *Strepera fuliginosa*' (Morris *Austral Eng.*). d. = *trumpeter-swan*: see 7. e. (See quot. 1897.)

a. 1725 *Bradley's Fam. Dict.* s. v. *Pigeon*, Many sorts of pigeons, such as..Owls, Spots, Trumpeters. 1859 Darwin *Orig. Spec.* i. (1860) 21 The trumpeter and laugher, as their names express, utter a very different coo from the other breeds.

b. 1747 tr. *De la Condamine's Trav. S. Amer.* 87 The bird called Trompetero by the Spaniards..is the same with the Agami..the noise it occasionally makes..has earned it the title of trumpeter. 1843 *Penny Cycl.* XXV. 317/2 *Trumpeter*.., the vulgar name for *Psophia crepitans*. 1879 E. P. Wright *Anim. Life* 326 The Trumpeters, or *Psophiidæ*, are..found only in the Great Amazon Valley.

c. 1827 Hellyer in Bischoff *Van Diemen's L.* (1832) 177 We..occasionally heard the trumpeter or black magpie.

d. 1891 *Cent. Dict.*, *Trumpeter*...5. The trumpeter-swan. 1899 *Daily News* 4 May 8/2 The cry of the Trumpeter..is .far-reaching and sonorous, and like the note of a horn.

e. 1897 *Month* Apr. 417 The Canada goose, sometimes called, from its note, the 'trumpeter'.

6. a. = *trumpet-fish* (see Trumpet *sb.* 7). ? *Obs.* b. Any species of the genus *Latris*, comprising large food-fishes of Australia, Tasmania, and New Zealand: so called from the sound they utter when taken out of water.

1756 P. Browne *Jamaica* 441 The Trumpeter or Trumpet Fish..is frequent in the harbours of Jamaica. 1834 *Van Diemen's Land Ann.* 30 The most admired fish of the Island may be considered the Trumpeter. 1883 E. P. Ramsay *Food Fishes N. S. Wales* 13 (Fish. Exhib. Publ.) Among the best are the trumpeters (*Latris*), of which there are several species...The Hobart trumpeter (*L. hecateia*).. in a smoked and dried state forms an article of export from Tasmania to the other colonies. 1883 *Roy. Comm. Fisheries Tasmania* 35 (Morris) The bastard trumpeter (*Latris Forsteri*)..Scarcely inferior to the real trumpeter.

7. *attrib.*, esp. in names of certain birds and fishes (cf. 5, 6): **trumpeter hornbill**, an African bird of the genus *Bycanistes*; **trumpeter perch**, a small Australian food-fish, *Therapon cuvieri*; **trumpeter swan**, a large N. American species of swan, *Cygnus* (*Olor*) *buccinator*; **trumpeter whiting**, an Australian fish, *Sillago bassensis*.

1899 F. V. Kirby *Sport E. C. Africa* viii. 95 In the vicinity of this Kraal the great *trumpeter hornbill abounds, his hideous cries resounding through the dense forest. *Ibid.* xiii. 142, I..missed two shots..at a couple of lesser trumpeter hornbills (*Bycanistes buccinator*). 1669 Dryden *Tyrannic Love* iv. i, A *trumpeter-hornet to battle sounds loud. 1883 E. P. Ramsay *Food Fishes N. S. Wales* 13 (Fish. Exhib. Publ.) The *trumpeter perch (*Therapon cuvieri*), was formerly very numerous in Port Jackson...It is a small, delicious fish, and prettily striped. 1842 *Penny Cycl.* XXIII. 375/1 The *trumpeter swan, *Cygnus Buccinator.* 1874 J. W. Long *Amer. Wild-fowl* xxii. 227 The *cygnus buccinator*, or trumpeter swan, the largest of its kind, and most common to the valley of the Mississippi. 1882 Tenison-Woods *Fish N.S. Wales* 65 The *trumpeter whiting (*Sillago bassensis*).. the most common species in Brisbane.

**Trumpeting** (trʊ·mpėtiŋ), *vbl. sb.* [f. Trumpet *v.* + -ing[1].]

1. The action of the verb Trumpet. a. Blowing of a trumpet or trumpets; utterance of a sound like that of a trumpet.

1535 Coverdale 1 *Esdr.* v. 66 Then came the enemies..to knowe what that trompettynge and noyse of shawmes might be. 1843 B. Webb *Continental Ecclesiol.* 277 There was a great deal too much trumpeting and kettle-drumming in the orchestra. 1850 R. G. Cumming *Hunter's Life S. Afr.* (1902) 90/1 Crash came a second charge of elephants..accompanied by a trumpeting which caused our ears to tingle. 1861 J. Lamont *Seahorses* v. 74 The sonorous bellowing and trumpeting of a vast number of walruses. 1881 Miss Yonge *Lads & Lasses Langley* iii, The door..had..a trick of squeaking and trumpeting.

b. The action of proclaiming as by sound of trumpet.

1878 Bayne *Purit. Rev.* xi. 487 The Lords Spiritual..for all their trumpeting of the duty of passive obedience, reminded Charles of the limitations of his prerogative when he tried to show mercy to the Presbyterians. 1885 *Pall Mall G.* 7 May 3/2 There was a great deal of party trumpeting on both sides.

2. *Mining.* A channel or passage-way made in a shaft by a partition of brickwork, boarding, etc., for ventilation or other purpose.

1839 Ure *Dict. Arts* 985 There is a simple mode of conducting air from the pit bottom to the forehead of the mine, by cutting a ragglin, or trumpeting, as it is termed, in the side of the gallery.

So **Tru·mpeting** *ppl. a.* (in various senses: see the vb.).

1849 Cupples *Green Hand* xvi, Lifting his trunk..with a sharp trumpeting scream. 1852 Thackeray *Esmond* ii. iii, The Princess Anne..was proclaimed by trumpeting heralds ..from Westminster to Ludgate Hill. 1859 Tennyson *Elaine* 138 The tiny-trumpeting gnat can break our dream. 1880 G. Meredith *Tragic Com.* (1881) 12 His publication of a trumpeting book fell appallingly flat.

**Trumpetless** to **Trumpetry**: see after Trumpet *sb.*

†**Trumpettie·r.** *Obs.* [f. Trumpet + -ier, -eer.] = Trumpeter.

1609 Holland *Amm. Marcell.* 6 Having..heard the trumpettiers and cornettiers sound.

**Truncage** (trʊ·ŋkėdʒ). *Hist.* [ad. med.L. *truncāgium*, f. L. *truncus* Trunk: see -age.] The furnishing of a trunk of a tree for the king's hearth, as a condition of the tenure of certain lands, e. g. at Bamburgh.

[1212 *Exch. K. R., Knights' Fees* 2/2 m. 5 (P.R.O.) Thomas de Bedinhale..caritabit truncas ad castellum de Banburg. 1235 *Ibid.* 2/20 m. 4 Thomas de Bedenhal..facit truncagium castello de Bamburg' annuatim.] 1893 Bateson *Hist. Northumb.* I. 36 (*Bamburgh*) The truncage due to the castle from the several townships had by that time been commuted for the small sum of £4. 19s. 4½d.

**Truncal** (trʊ·ŋkăl), *a.* Also trunkal. [f. L. *trunc-us* Trunk + -al.] Pertaining to, or of the nature of, a trunk; situated in or affecting the trunk.

1847 Webster, *Truncal*, pertaining to the trunk or body. 1860 A. Phelps *Still Hour* xi. 67 A Christian's life, so conducted, must languish, as a tree does whose fibrous roots are stripped off, leaving only its truncal roots..for its nourishment. 1875 H. C. Wood *Therap.* (1879) 651 Internal trunkal inflammations, such as pneumonia and pleurisy.

**Truncate** (trʊ·ŋkeɪt), *a.* [ad. L. *truncāt-us*, pa. pple. of *truncāre*: see Truncate *v.*]

†1. Cut short, mutilated. *Obs.* (exc. as in 2).

1579–83 [implied in Truncately].

2. In scientific and technical use: = Truncated 2.

1716 E. Halley in *Phil. Trans.* XXIX. 408 Like truncate Cones or Cylinders. 1785 Martyn *Rousseau's Bot.* xxi. 305 The Tulip Tree..is remarkable for the shape of its leaves, having the middle lobe of the three truncate, or cut transversely at the end. 1826 Kirby & Sp. *Entomol.* IV. xlvi. 333 Elytra..Truncate...When they are shorter than the abdomen and transverse at the end. 1839 Darwin *Voy. Nat.* i. (1879) 2 Successive steps of tableland, interspersed with some truncate conical hills [i. e. kopjes]. 1872 Coues *N. Amer. Birds* 38 A rectrix broad to the very tip, and there cut squarely off, is truncate.

b. In combination with another adj. of form, as *truncate-turbinate*; = Truncato-.

1887 W. Phillips *Brit. Discomycetes* 354 Cups substipitate, truncate-turbinate.

**Truncate** (trʊ·ŋkeɪt), *v.* [f. L. *truncāt-*, ppl. stem of *truncāre*, f. *truncus* Trunk.] *trans.* To shorten or diminish by cutting off a part; to cut short; to maim, mutilate. Also *fig.*

1486, 1572 [implied in Truncated 1]. 1727 Bailey vol. II, *Truncate*, to cut shorter, to maim. 1755 Johnson *Dict.* Pref. ⁋ 70 The examples are too often injudiciously truncated. 1852 W. R. Williams *Relig. Progr.* iii. (1854) 53 It wrongs man by truncating his nature of conscience and immortality. 1911 *Athenæum* 16 Sept. 318/2 He..never wrote short stories, only truncated long ones.

b. In scientific and technical use: *spec.* in *Cryst.* to 'cut off' or replace (an edge or solid angle) by a plane face, esp. so as to make equal angles with the adjacent faces. Chiefly in *pa. pple.*: see Truncated 2.

1758 Reid tr. *Macquer's Chem.* I. 97 Pyramids..some of which..are obtuse as if truncated. 1830 Lyell *Princ. Geol.* I. 393 If this gulf were..choked up,..so that new explosions ..should truncate the cone once more. 1883 *Encycl. Brit.* XVI. 348/1 The faces of one hexagonal prism would truncate the lateral edges of the rhombohedron, while the faces of the other..would truncate its lateral solid angles.

Hence **Tru·ncating** *ppl. a.*, that truncates; *spec.* said of a plane that replaces an edge or solid angle.

1805–17 R. Jameson *Char. Min.* (ed. 3) 118 These new planes are named Truncating Planes, and the edges which they form with the other planes Truncating Edges. 1882 Ruskin *Bible of Amiens* iii. 95 These two truncating and guarding rivers.

**Truncated** (trʊ·ŋkeɪtėd), *ppl. a.* [f. L. *truncāt-us*, pa. pple. of *truncāre* (see prec.) + -ed[1] 2, or f. prec. + -ed[1].] Cut short (actually or apparently); having a part cut off, or of such a form as if a part were cut off.

1. *Her.* Of a cross or tree: Having the arms or boughs cut off, so as not to extend to the boundaries of the shield; couped. ? *Obs.*

1486 *Bk. St. Albans, Her.* C vj b, A cros truncatid, And hit is calde trunkatid for hit is made of ij treys the boys [= boughs] cut a Way. 1572 Bossewell *Armorie* ii. 95 b, These trees are truncated, that is to saie, ye boughes cut of from the body, and laide in the forme of a Saltier. The endes whereof may not touch the Angles of the shield.

2. In modern scientific and technical use. (Const. as *adj.* preceding the noun, or as *pa. pple.* following the noun.) a. *Geom.*, etc. Of a figure: Having one end cut off by a transverse line or plane; *esp.* of a cone or pyramid: Having the vertex cut off by a plane section, esp. one parallel to the base: thus *truncated cone* or *pyramid* = Frustum of a cone or pyramid.

1704 J. Harris *Lex. Techn.* I, *Truncated Pyramid* or *Cone*, is one whose top is cut off by a Plane parallel to its Base; and therefore the Figure of the truncated top must always be similar to the Base. 1827 Faraday *Chem. Manip.* ii. (1842) 26 Weights..constructed in sets, each weight.. having the form of a truncated cone. 1831 R. Knox *Cloquet's Anat.* 581 The Cartilages of the apertures of the Nose..represent an ellipse truncated posteriorly. 1840 Lardner *Geom.* 68 A trapezium is a truncated triangle. *Ibid.* 166 A figure formed by the section of a prism by a plane not parallel to its base is called a truncated prism. 1868 Lockyer *Guillemin's Heavens* (ed. 3) 73 The southern horn of the crescent was truncated.

b. *Cryst.* and *Solid Geom.* Of an edge or solid angle: Cut off or replaced by a plane face, esp. one equally inclined to the adjacent faces; also said of a solid figure having its edges or angles thus cut off.

1796 Kirwan *Elem. Min.* (ed. 2) I. 128 [Fluor] the angles or edges rarely truncated or bevilled. 1823 H. J. Brooke *Introd. Crystallogr.* 24 When an edge, or solid angle, is replaced by one plane, it is said to be *truncated*. When an edge is replaced by two planes, which respectively incline on the adjacent primary planes at equal angles, it is *bevilled*. 1863 Geo. Eliot *Romola* xxvi, The wide doorway, standing at the truncated angle of a great block..of houses. 1875 Bennett & Dyer *Sachs' Bot.* 51 The separate crystalloids are thin plates, single regular rhombs, often with truncated angles. 1891 *Cent. Dict.* s. v. *Truncate* v., Truncated cube, cuboctahedron, dodecahedron [etc.].

c. *Nat. Hist.* Appearing as if the tip or end were cut off transversely; terminating in a flat or broad edge or surface instead of a point.

1752 J. Hill *Hist. Anim.* 3 The Enchelis, with the head small, and the tail truncated. 1753 Chambers *Cycl. Supp.* s. v. *Leaf*, *Truncated Leaf*, that whose summit or point seems to have been cut off, or is terminated by a strait line in a transverse direction. 1816 Stephens in Shaw *Gen. Zool.* IX. ii. 236 Quills dusky black; the points..truncated. 1835 J. Duncan *Beetles* (Nat. Libr.) 184 The elytra are short and truncated at the extremity. 1899 *Allbutt's Syst. Med.* VIII. 774 These truncated hairs are of..importance for diagnosis.

d. So in *Architecture*, *Geology*, etc.

1723 Chambers tr. *Le Clerc's Treat. Archit.* I. 114 Pediments..supported by an Entablature truncated in the middle. 1727–41 Chambers *Cycl.* s. v. *Roof*, Sometimes it is truncated; that is, instead of terminating in a ridge or angle, it is cut square off at a certain heighth. 1829 Scott *Anne of G.* xi, A truncated column of marble, having its base sculptured with hieroglyphical imagery. 1830 Lyell *Princ. Geol.* (1872) I. ii. xxiii. 588 The summit of the loftiest peak is truncated. 1869 Boutell *Arms & Arm.* ii. (1874) 11 In some [Assyrian] examples, the raised upper crest-like part of the helm is seen to have been bent backwards and truncated.

**3.** Maimed, mutilated; also *fig.*

1731 Bailey, *Truncated*, cut shorter, maimed, mangled. 1791–1823 D'Israeli *Cur. Lit.* (1858) III. 181 All the Italian editions continued to be reprinted in the same truncated condition. 1845 R. W. Hamilton *Pop. Educ.* v. (ed. 2) 97 The truncated frame of man is without power of locomotion or external action. 1890 J. Stalker *Imago Christi* v. (1891) 104 It is a truncated and most imperfect friendship when this region is closed.

**Truncately** (trʊ·ŋkeⁱtli), *adv.* [f. Truncate *a.* + -ly$^{2}$.] In a truncate manner or form; in quots., in a mutilated form, with omission of something essential.

1579 Fulke *Heskins' Parl.* 62 Augustines wordes, not truncately and by peece meale rehearsed nor altered. 1583 — *Defence* Answ. to Pref. 62 The doctors you quote without iudgment fraudulently, falsly, truncately, and otherwise abusiuely.

**Truncation** (trʊŋkēⁱ·ʃən). [ad. late L. *truncātiōn-em*, n. of action f. L. *truncāre* to Truncate; cf. OF. *troncacion* (1495 in Godef.).]

**1.** The action of truncating; cutting short; maiming, mutilation. Also *fig.*

1579 Fulke *Heskins' Parl.* 262 The alteration, falsification, and truncation of Tertullians wordes. 1611 Cotgr., *Troncation*, a truncation, trunking, mutilation, cutting off. 1637 Prynne *Huntley's Breviate* 48 Decreeing judgment of death, or truncation of members. *a* 1682 Sir T. Browne *Tracts* xiii. (1684) 204 Singular inhumanities in Tortures.. The living truncation of the Turks. 1779–81 Johnson *L. P., Cowley* Wks. II. 69 In the Davideis are some..verses left imperfect..in imitation of Virgil, whom he supposes not to have intended to complete them: that this opinion is erroneous, may be probably concluded, because this truncation is imitated by no subsequent Roman Poet [etc.]. 1903 F. W. H. Myers *Hum. Personality* II. 301 If it [death] be..a sheer truncation of moral progress.

**2.** In scientific and technical use: The process of truncating, or condition of being truncated; diminution by or as by cutting off an end or point, so that the object terminates in a straight edge or plane surface instead; *spec.* in *Cryst.* replacement of an edge or solid angle by a plane face, esp. one equally inclined to the adjacent faces.

1796 Kirwan *Elem. Min.* (ed. 2) II. 203 White Lead Ore ..Occurs..crystalized in..prisms, or pyramids, with or without truncations. 1803 H. J. Brooke *Introd. Crystallogr.* 86 The rhomboid being converted into a six-sided prism by the truncation of all its solid angles, or of its terminal solid angles and its lateral edges. 1853 Kane *Grinnell Exp.* xlv. (1856) 416 The truncation of the muzzle..set their faces in almost perfect and human-like oval. 1861 W. Pole in *Macm. Mag.* III. 184/2 The corresponding facet..formed by the truncation of the lower..pyramid, is..called the collet. 1874 Lyell *Elem. Geol.* xxviii. 495 Similar..catastrophes have caused..the truncation..of some large cones in Java.

**b.** *transf.* The place or part where something is truncated.

1805–17 R. Jameson *Char. Min.* (ed. 3) 117 When we observe on a fundamental figure, in place of an edge or angle, a small plane, such a plane is denominated a Truncation. 1853 Phillips *Rivers Yorksh.* iv. 135 The 'High Peak'..is at the truncation of an interior range of hills. 1897 Hazlitt *Suppl. Coinage European Cont.* 29 This Portuguese piece has under the truncation of the bust the name of W. Wyon as the engraver.

**Truncato-** (trʊŋkēⁱ·to), combining form of L. *truncātus* Truncate, used with other adjs. of form in sense 'truncately'.

1852 Dana *Crust.* ii. 698 Abdomen..broad truncato-rotund at apex. 1891 *Cent. Dict.*, *Truncatosinuate*, in *entom.*, truncate, with a sinus or slight inward curve on the edge of the truncation.

**Truncator** (trʊ·ŋkeⁱtəɹ). *rare.* [a. L. *truncātor*, agent-n. f. *truncāre* to Truncate: see -or.] One who truncates; a mutilator.

1579 Fulke *Heskins' Parl.* 184 Heskins, the impudent falsifier, truncator,..peruerter,..of Augustine.

**Truncature** (trʊ·ŋkătiuɹ). Now *rare.* [f. Truncate *v.* + -ure.] = Truncation 2.

1828 Stark *Elem. Nat. Hist.* II. 56 Shell oval, oblong, or turreted;..columella smooth, straight, without truncature or widening at the base. 1854 Kelly & Tomlinson tr. *Arago's Astron.* 75 One horn of its [Mercury's] crescent is truncated; and it is this truncature that has enabled us to determine the period of its rotation. 1866 *Contemp. Rev.* July 452 Crystals are characterized by the truncatures of their angles, and the bevelment of their edges.

†**Trunch**, *sb. Obs. rare.* [ad. F. *tronche* fem. :—pop.L. **trunca* for *truncus* stump of a tree, Trunk (14th c. in Godef.).]

**1.** = Truncheon *sb.* 3.

1590 L. Lloyd *Diall Daies* Oct. 14 Tipstaves..with silver trunches and staves to go before.., and to keep the people in order.

**2.** A post, stake.

1622 W. Bradford *Relat. New Eng.* 12 Little trunches knockt into the ground, and small stickes laid over, on which they hung their Pots.

**Trunch** (trʊnʃ), *a.* Now *dial.* [app. shortened f. Truncheon *a.*; cf. L. *truncus* maimed, mutilated.] Short and thick. Also in comb. *trunch-made.* Cf. Truncheon *a.*

1683 *Lond. Gaz.* No. 1842/8 Lost.., a Black Gelding,.. a thick trunch Horse. *a* 1825 Forby *Voc. E. Anglia*, *Trunch, trunch-made*,..short and thick, compact and squab in figure.

Also **Trunched** (trʊnʃt), **Tru·nchy** *adjs.* in same sense (*U.S.*). *rare.* ? *Obs.*

1787 M. Cutler in *Life*, etc. (1888) I. 267, I saw a short, *trunched old man, in a plain Quaker dress. 1778 *Maryland Jrnl.* 21 July Advt. (Thornton), A thick, *trunchy fellow. 1789 *Ibid.* 21 Apr., A trunchy well-set bright-bay horse.

**Truncheon** (trʊ·nʃən), *sb.* Forms: 4 tronsoun, trounsoun, trunsoun, -ioune, *Sc.* trwnsown, 5 trounson; 4–5 tronchoun, -eoun, -en, 4–7 tronchon, 5–7 troncheon, 6–7 tronchion, (5 trounchen, tronchown, -yn, trenchoune, 6 tronchone, trenshon, 7 trouncheon); *Sc.* 4–5 trunschoun, 5 trunscyoune, 6 trownsciown, trunscheon, -e; 6–8 trunchion, 6– truncheon, (5–6 trunchoun, -on, -en, -in, -yn, -yne). [ME. a. OF. *trunçun, tronchon*, F. *tronçon* a piece cut or broken off, a stump (11th c. in Godef.), f. late L. type **trunciōn-em*, f. L. *truncus* Trunk.]

**1.** A piece broken or cut off, a fragment. Also *fig. Obs.* or *arch.*

13.. *Seuyn Sag.* (W.) 819 Of the adder he fond mani tronsoun. *a* 1450 *Le Morte Arth.* 3071 One hytte hym vpon the olde wounde With a tronchon of an ore. 1570 Levins *Manip.* 164/29 A Trenshon, *fragmentum.* 1587 Mascall *Govt. Cattle, Oxen* (1627) 18 Small trunchions of coleworts sod in sallet oyle and..brine. 1611 Cotgr., *Tronçonneur*,..a cutter of things into truncheons or lumpes. 1882 Stevenson *New Arab. Nts.* II. i. 7 A huge truncheon of wreck half buried in the sands. 1892 — *Across the Plains* 240 [They] set before him truncheons of tales upon their lighted theatre.

**b.** *spec.* A fragment of a spear or lance; a piece broken off from a spear. *Obs.* or *arch.*

13.. *Sir Beues* (A.) 827 On a tronsoun [*v.rr.* tronchen, tronchyn, tronchon, trunchyn] of is spere þat heued a stikede for to bere. 13.. *K. Alis.* 2149 (Bodl. MS.) Þe spere tobrast on two trunsoun. *Ibid.* 3740 A gentyl kniȝth..Had on hym many wounde And a trunchoun in his flaunche. *c* 1400 Maundev. (1839) xxii. 238 Þei breken here speres so rudely þat the tronchouns fleu in sprotes and peces all aboute the halle. 1470–85 Malory *Arthur* i. xxii. 69 He smote Gryflet ..and brake the spere that the troncheon stack in his body. 1596 Spenser *F. Q.* iv. iii. 12 Therewith asunder in the midst it brast, And in his hand nought but the troncheon left. 1697 Dryden *Æneid* xi. 16 His brazen buckler on the left was seen: Truncheons of shiver'd lances hung between. 1825 Scott *Talism.* xxviii, Sir Kenneth's lance..had wounded him deep in the bosom,..leaving the truncheon of the lance fixed in his wound.

**c.** The shaft of a spear. *Obs.* or *arch.*

13.. *K. Alis.* 2154 Alisaundre..him mette with speris egge; Through brunny and scheld, to the akedoun, He tobarst atwo his tronchon. 13.. *Guy Warw.* (A.) 3093 Þurch þe bodi he bar a trounsoun. 1600 Holland *Livy* xxxv. v. 801 Their captaines..laying about with their truncheons [L. *hastile*] upon the backs of them that so trembled for feare,..forced them againe into their ranks. 1805 Scott *Last Minstr.* i. xix, A fancied moss-trooper, the boy The truncheon of a spear bestrode.

**2.** A short thick staff; a club, a cudgel. *Obs.* or *arch.* exc. as in 3.

13.. *Sir Beues* (A.) 1428 At þe prisoun dore Beues fond A tronsoun, þat he tok in is hond. 14.. *Stockh. Med. MS.* ii. 709 in *Anglia* XVIII. 324 He beryth his spede, Lik a trwnsown or a pestell. *c* 1500 *Lancelot* 2890 O gret trownsciown In til his hond. 1593 Shaks. *2 Hen. VI*, iv. x. 52 Thy legge a sticke compared with this Truncheon. *c* 1618 Moryson *Itin.* iv. (1903) 449 A Castle of wood..which the Senatours Armed with tronchions did assault and take. 1682 N. O. tr. *Boileau's Lutrin* iii. 113 A Truncheon strong Confirms his staggering steps. 1725 Pope *Odyss.* xi. 707 Stern beasts in trains that by his truncheon fell. 1756 Mrs. Delany in *Life & Corr.* (1861) III. 451 You walk with your stick as with a truncheon, whilst we poor invalids make use of ours as a walking-staff.

**3.** A staff carried as a symbol of office, command, or authority; a marshal's baton; most freq. in modern usage, a short staff or club with which a police constable is armed.

1573 in Feuillerat *Revels Q. Eliz.* (1908) 203 A Trunchin for the dictator. 1603 Shaks. *Meas. for M.* ii. ii. 61 Not the Kings Crowne; nor the deputed sword, The Marshalls Truncheon, nor the Iudges Robe Become them with one halfe so good a grace As mercie does. 1728 Morgan *Algiers* I. iii. 43 An express Embassy, attended with an Ivory Truncheon and a Triumphal Robe. 1843 Lytton *Last Bar.* vii. iii, You are come..to take the command of the troops.., and into your hands, I resign this truncheon. 1855 Macaulay *Hist. Eng.* xiv. III. 412 For his religion [Schomberg] had resigned a splendid income, had laid down the truncheon of a Marshal of France. 1880 McCarthy *Own Times* IV. li. 82 Stones were thrown on the one side and truncheons used on the other.

†**b.** *fig.* Cf. Trunk *sb.* 1 b, quot. 1586. *Obs.*

1601 ?Marston *Pasquil & Kath.* iv. 115 For such a one to yoke her free sweet youth Vnto a Lowne,..A gilden Trunchion, fie! 'tis slauish vile.

**4.** †**a.** The stem or stock of a tree. *Obs. rare.*

*c* 1449 Pecock *Repr.* i. vi. (Rolls) 28 Tho bowis grewen out of stockis or tronchons, and the tronchons or schaftis grewen out of the roote.

**b.** A length cut from a plant, esp. one used for grafting or planting; a stout cutting. Now *rare.*

1572 Mascall *Plant. & Graff.* (1592) 17 An other way to set Mulberies.., cut..great Mulberie bowes or stockes, asunder in yᵉ bodie (with a saw) in troncheons a foot long or more,..make a..furrow in good earth well and deepe, so that ye may couer..your troncheons. 1664 Evelyn *Sylva* i. xviii. (1729) 86 [Alders] are propagated of Trunchions..the Trunchions being set as big as the Small of one's Leg. 1725 *Bradley's Fam. Dict.* s.v. *Lime tree*, The Truncheons make far better Coal for Gun-Powder, than that of Alder it self. *Ibid.* s.v. *Sallow*, When you Graft Sallow, take a Truncheon as big as your Wrist, of two Foot and an half long. 1855 Singleton *Virgil* I. 127 Neither wild truncheons on the olive graft.

†**5.** An intestinal worm, short and thick in form, parasitic in horses. *Obs.*

*c* 1440 *Promp. Parv.* 504/1 Trunchon, wyrme, *lumbricus.* 1530 Palsgr. 283/2 Trunchon a worme. 1565 Blundevil *Horsemanship* iv. xcvi. (1580) 43 In a Horses guts do breede three kinds of wormes:..The third be short and thicke, like the end of a mans little finger, and therefore be called Troncheons. *c* 1720 W. Gibson *Farrier's Guide* ii. xxxix. (1738) 142 Several Kinds of Vermin bred in the bodies of Horses, which go under the Denomination of Bots, Worms and Trunchions. 1748 tr. *Vegetius' Distempers Horses* 84 Another Drench for Worms, Botts and Truncheons.

†**6.** 'The solid part of a horse's tail, towards the croup' (Littré s.v. *Tronçon*). *Obs. rare*$^{-1}$.

1639 T. de Gray *Compl. Horsem.* 24 The hams dry, and straight, the trunchion small, long, well set on, and well couched.

¶**7.** Erroneously used for Truncheour, Trencher$^{1}$ 2 or 3. *Obs.*

1548 *Acc. Ld. High Treas. Scot.* IX. 167 For serving of his gracis tabill upoun tuelf sylver trunscheones. 1739 'R. Bull' tr. *Dedekindus' Grobianus* 131 Trojans their Tables ate, eat thou thy Truncheon.

**8.** *attrib.* and *Comb.*, as *truncheon-bearer, -fashion, officer, -sceptre*; **truncheon-snake** (see quot.); **truncheon-wise** *adv.*, in the manner or form of a truncheon.

1896 *Westm. Gaz.* 18 Feb. 5/2 Yesterday was a busy..day for *truncheon-bearers all over London. 1912 S. R. Driver in *Expositor* Jan. 35 Out of Machir came down truncheon-bearers. 1750 R. Pococke *Trav.* (1888) 71 A sceptre..in the *truncheon fashion, having a round head guarded with points. 1708 *Mem. Right Villanous John Hall* 11 Out jump Four *Trunchion Officers. 1814 *Sporting Mag.* XLIV. 147 Brandishing his *truncheon-sceptre. 1736 Mortimer in *Phil. Trans.* XXXIX. 254 *Vipera fusca*: The brown Viper in Virginia: In Carolina it is called the *Truncheon-Snake. 1572 Mascall *Plant. & Graff.* (1592) 43 Certaine.. trees..which in cutting the great branches ther of *truncheon wise, doe renew againe.

Hence **Tru·ncheoner, Tru·ncheonist** (*nonce-wds.*), one who bears a truncheon.

1613 Shaks. *Hen. VIII*, v. iv. 54, I..hit that Woman, who cryed out Clubbes, when I might see from farre, some forty Truncheoners [*Wks.* (ed. Johnson, 1765) truncheoneers] draw to her succour. 1854 *Tait's Mag.* XXI. 372 Circumscribed ..by 184 B and his co-truncheonists.

†**Truncheon**, *a. Obs. rare*$^{-1}$. [? attrib. use of Truncheon *sb.*] = Trunch *a.*

1611 Cotgr., *Retroussé*, thicke and short, druggellie, trunchion.

**Tru·ncheon**, *v.* Forms: see Truncheon *sb.* [a. F. *tronçonner* (12th c. in Godef.), f. *tronçon*, Truncheon *sb.*]

†**1.** *trans.* To reduce to 'truncheons' or fragments; to break in pieces; to shatter. Also *fig.*

*c* 1477 Caxton *Jason* 16 Thus began the bataylle..with speris that sone were tronchoned. *Ibid.* 35 b, She fill doune ..alle thurghe smyten and tronchoned with amerouse sorowe. *c* 1500 *Melusine* xxxvi. 286 The Saudan valyauntly smote geffray, & tronchoned hys spere vpon his shild.

†**b.** *spec.* To carve (an eel): the proper term for this. Cf. Tranch *v. Obs.*

1486 *Bk. St. Albans* F vij b, An Ele trounsoned. 1787 Best *Angling* (ed. 2) 169 *Trounchen an eel*, cut him up. 1853 Badham *Halieut.* 343 He gobbets trout, truncheons eel, fins chub, tusks barbel [etc.].

**2.** To beat with a truncheon, to baton.

1597 Shaks. *2 Hen. IV*, ii. iv. 154 If captaines were of my minde, they would trunchion you out, for taking their names vpon you. 1839 *Morn. Herald* 20 July, They are occasionally truncheoned by the police.

Hence **Tru·ncheoning** *vbl. sb.*

*c* 1477 Caxton *Jason* 15 b, Whan hit cam to the tronchoning of their speris.

**Truncheoned** (trʊ·nʃənd), *a.* [f. Truncheon *sb.* + -ed$^{2}$.] Furnished or armed with a truncheon.

1761 Goldsm. *Cit. W.* cix, The brickdust man took up as much room as the truncheoned hero. 1821 *Blackw. Mag.* X. 698 Truncheoned and uniformed as becomes a man of his military habits. 1839 *Morn. Herald* 11 July, The truncheoned police of the metropolis. 1883 Hall Caine *Cobwebs Crit.* vii. 202 A city-marshal broke his leg..while walking truncheoned from the Mansion House.

[**Truncheoneer**, a suggested reading for *truncheoner* (see after Truncheon *sb.*).]

†**Truncheour**, obs. form of Trencher$^{1}$.

1511–12 *Acc. Ld. High Treas. Scot.* IV. 321 To Johne Aitkyne, goldsmith,..to mak foure gret truncheouris.. threttein small truncheouris and five saltfattis.

†**Tru·nchfiddle.** *Obs. rare*$^{-1}$. [? f. Trunch *a.* + Fiddle *sb.*, or ? for **trunkfiddle*: cf. next and *trunk-wame* (Trunk *sb.* 18).] (?)

1589 *Hay any Work* 6 He might freely..florish with his 2. hand sword. O tis a sweete trunchfiddle.

†**Tru·nch-hole.** *Obs. rare*$^{-1}$. ? = *trunk-hole*: see Trunk *sb.* 18, and cf. sense 10 e.

1683 R. D. *State of Turkey* 153 The..crew..clapt an iron spike into the trunch-hole of the prow.

**Trunchman**, obs. corrupt f. Truchman.

**Trunchy**: see after Trunch *a.*

‖**Truncus** (trʊ·ŋkɒs). [L.: see Trunk.] **a.** *Anat.* The trunk or main stem of a vessel or nerve. **b.** *Zool.* The trunk or body of an animal, without the head, limbs, and tail; in *Entom.* the thorax. **c.** *Bot.* The trunk or stem of a tree.

1693 tr. *Blancard's Phys. Dict.* (ed. 2), *Truncus*, in general..that part of the great Artery and *Vena Cava*, which descends from the Heart..more especially..those Branches which are sent from the great Trunk to the *Viscera*. 1706 PHILLIPS (ed. Kersey), *Truncus*, (Lat.) the Stem or Stock of a Tree without the Boughs; a Body without a Head. 1875 HUXLEY & MARTIN *Elem. Biol.* (1883) 177 As the truncus becomes more and more distended, the longitudinal valve..tends more and more completely to shut off the openings of the pulmonary arteries.

**Trundle** (trɒ·nd'l), *sb.* Also 6–7 **trundel(l)**, 7 **trondle**, 8–9 *Sc.* **truntle**, 9 *dial.* **trunnel**, **-nle**. [A parallel form to TRENDLE, TRINDLE *sb.*]

**I.** Something that trundles or is trundled.

**1.** A small wheel, roller, or revolving disk; *esp.* a small but massive wheel adapted for supporting a heavy weight, as the wheel of a castor.

1564, 1602 [see TRUNDLE-BED β]. 1668 WILKINS *Real Char.* 257 Wheel, Truckle, Trundle. 1669 STURMY *Mariner's Mag.* II. vi. 68 Points, Halfs, and Quarters, which is on the two Trundles. 1833 J. HOLLAND *Manuf. Metal* II. 16 They are submitted to the buff, which is a trundle of wood covered with thick soft leather, and made to revolve rapidly.

**b.** *Organ-building.* In the draw-stop action, A roller with two arms by the rotation of which a slider is drawn or replaced.

1876–98 STAINER & BARRETT *Dict. Mus. Terms* 342 When the stop is pulled out, the arms *aa* draw the trace *b* from right to left, the end of the trundle *c* being attached to the trace is moved in a similar direction, whilst the other end of the trundle *d* moves in an opposite direction, and draws out the slider. 1881 W. E. DICKSON *Organ-Build.* x. 130 The connection of these horizontal draw-bars with the vertical levers will be effected by squares or bell-cranks of a form known as 'trundles'.

**2.** A device consisting of two disks turning on an axle, and connected by a series of parallel staves cylindrically arranged, which engage with the teeth of a cog-wheel; a lantern-wheel. In early use, each of such disks (= *trundle-head* (*a*): see 7). Also, each of the staves of this device.

1611 COTGR., *Lanterne à pagnons*, a paire of trundles, or trundle heads; that which is turned about by the cog wheele of a Mill. 1660 R. D'ACRES *Art Water-drawing* 13 Great wooden wheels with Coggs in them, working Trundles with round staves in them. 1764 J. FERGUSON *Lect.* iii. 35 A winch six inches long, fixt on the axis of a trundle of 8 staves or rounds. 1801 BOURNON in *Phil. Trans.* XCI. 186 They form a kind of indented cylinders, which have some resemblance to the trundle of a mill. 1829 *Nat. Philos.* I. *Mechanics* II. vii. 30 (Usef. Knowl. Soc.) The cylindrical teeth or bars of the lantern are called trundles or spindles. 1861 SMILES *Engineers* II. 125 He employed cast iron pinions, instead of the wooden trundles formerly used.

**3.** A low truck or carriage on small wheels. ? *Obs.*

1664 EVELYN *Sylva* (1679) 22 [In replanting a tree] You may weigh up, and place the whole weighty Clod upon a Trundle to be convey'd, and Replanted where you please. 1766 *Compl. Farmer*, *Trundle*, a sort of carriage with low wheels, for carrying heavy and cumbersome loads.

**4.** An embroiderer's quill of gold thread; in *Her.*, a charge representing this.

c 1828 BERRY *Encycl. Her.* I. Gloss., *Trundles*, quills of gold thread used by embroiderers, and borne by them in the Arms of their Company. 1894 *Parker's Gloss. Her.* 225 Embroiderers' Broaches, Trundles, and Quill...The Trundle represents a quill of gold thread, two of which are represented in the arms of the London company.

**II.** An act of trundling (*lit.* or *fig.*).

**5.** An act of trundling or rolling; an impulse that causes something to roll.

1893 Q. COUCH *Delect. Duchy* 95 They..gave the stone a trundle.

**6.** *fig.* A going along or away; a course; departure: in phr. *to run* or *take one's trundle*, to take one's course. *dial.*

1675 V. ALSOP *Anti-Sozzo* 388, I resolved he should run his Trundle. 1821 CLARE *Vill. Minstr.* I. 41 So take your trundle now, and good luck may ye see! *Ibid.* II. 97 Ye're each at once as free To take your trundle as ye us'd to be.

**III. 7.** *attrib.* and *Comb.* (in some cases perh. directly from the vb.): **trundle-head**, (*a*) each of the disks of a trundle (sense 2); (*b*) = sense 2; (*c*) *Naut.* (see quot. 1867); **trundle-shot**, a shot consisting of a bar of iron with sharpened ends and a ball of lead attached near each end so as to cause it to turn in its flight; **trundle-wheel** = sense 2. See also TRUNDLE-BED, -TAIL; also *trunnel-head*, *-hole* s. v. TRUNNEL.

1611 *Trundle heads [see 2]. 1766 *Compl. Farmer* s.v. *Madder*, The trundle-head, thirteen inches semi-diameter, furnished with eighteen rounds, each a foot long, and two inches diameter: the ends of this trundle-head are two inches and a half thick. 1867 SMYTH *Sailor's Word-bk.*, *Trundle-head*, the lower drum-head of a capstern, when it is double, and worked on one shaft both on an upper and lower deck. 1627 CAPT. SMITH *Seaman's Gram.* xiv. 67 *Trundle shot is ..a bolt of iron sixteene or eighteene inches in length; at both ends sharpe pointed, and about a handfull from each end a round broad bowle of lead. 1807 JOYCE *Sci. Dial.* xvii. (1846) 47 A small *trundle wheel made to work in the cogs. 1839 *Civil Eng. & Arch. Jrnl.* II. 357/2 A part of an ancient trundle wheel was found a few days ago in Chalmerston Moss.

**Tru·ndle,** *v.* Forms: see prec. [A parallel form to TRENDLE, TRINDLE *v.*; cf. OF. *trondeler* to fall rolling (Godef.), 'to trundle as a ball' (Cotgr. 1611).]

**I. 1. a.** *trans.* To cause to roll along upon a surface, as a ball, hoop, or other globular or circular object; to roll, bowl. Also *fig.*

1598 FLORIO, *Carrucolare*, to trundle or rowle. 1601 HOLLAND *Pliny* VIII. vii. I. 196 One Elephant did wonders:..hee caught from them their targuets and bucklers perforce, flung them aloft into the aire, which as they fell, turned round, as if they had beene trundeled by art. 1630 J. TAYLOR (Water P.) *Pennilesse Pilgr.* Wks. I. 122/2 There did we trundle down health after health. 1698 VANBRUGH *Æsop* III. i, I could tell my mother's pedigree before I could speak plain; which, to show you..the strength of my memory, I'll trundle you down in an instant. 1760–72 H. BROOKE *Fool of Qual.* (1809) III. 92 Various exercises.., such as wrestling.., and tossing or trundling leaden balls. 1798 COLERIDGE *Fears in Solit.* 114 Terms which we trundle smoothly o'er our tongues. 1824 MISS MITFORD *Village* Ser. I. (1863) 109 George Hearn, the little post-boy, trundling his hoop at full speed. 1832 COBBETT *Rur. Rides* (1885) II. 380 Sitting round a dirty board, with potatoes trundled out upon it, as the Irish do. 1901 R. ANDERSON *Hist. Kilsyth* vi. 50 [He] trundled an orange across the floor.

**b.** *intr.* To move along on a surface by revolving; to roll. Also *fig.*

1629 B. JONSON *New Inn* II. i, To be cropp'd..Close to his head to trundle on his pillow. a 1661 FULLER *Worthies, Cornw.* (1662) I. 201 His Round-Table,..the tale whereof hath Trundled so smoothly along for many ages. 1711 ADDISON *Spect.* No. 253 ¶ 10 A Description in Homer's Odyssey, where Sisyphus is represented lifting his Stone up the Hill..it is heaved up by several Spondees..and at last trundles down in a continual Line of Dactyls. 1840 DICKENS *Barn. Rudge* v, Occasionally a hat or wig..came spinning and trundling past him.

**c.** *Cricket.* (*trans.* or *absol.*) To bowl. *colloq.*

The ball was originally trundled along the ground.

1882 [see TRUNDLER b, *trundling* below].

**2.** *trans.* To cause to rotate; to twirl, spin, whirl (something held in the hand); *spec.* to twirl (a mop) so as to free it from water. Cf. ROLL *v.*[2] 5.

a 1756 [see *trundled* below]. 1787 COLMAN *Prose on Sev. Occas.* III. 277 While Footmen, women grown..Shall darn old hose, sweep rooms, and trundle mops. 1864 SIR F. PALGRAVE *Norm. & Eng.* IV. 60 Instead of trundling the theodolite they yoked the oxen. 1883 H. J. POWELL *Glass-making* 65 The English workman attains the same result by trundling the glass during reheating.

**b.** *intr.* for *pass.*

1782 [see *trundling* below].

**3.** *intr.* To move or run on a wheel or wheels. (Cf. ROLL *v.*[2] 11 c.)

1688 R. HOLME *Armoury* III. xiv. (Roxb.) 16/2 Such are termed Truckle beds, because they trundle under other beds. 1768 TUCKER *Lt. Nat.* (1834) I. 59 To see the wheelbarrow trundle. 1824 *Blackw. Mag.* IV. 95 The night coaches and mails were now trundling in. 1882 J. HAWTHORNE *Fort. Fool* I. xiv, Numbers of fine carriages..trundle up.

**b.** *trans.* To draw or push along on a wheel or wheels, as a wheelbarrow, vehicle, etc.

1825 SCOTT *Let.* 7 June, A light barouche..which two horses will trundle along like a bowl. 1862 SALA *Seven Sons* II. iii. 80 [He] was trundling a wheelbarrow full of sand. 1886 H. F. LESTER *Under two Fig Trees* 128 If nurse..was requested..to trundle the perambulator.

**4.** *trans.* To convey in a wheeled vehicle, to wheel.

1773 GOLDSM. *Stoops to Conq.* II. *ad fin.*, I'll clap a pair of horses to your chaise that shall trundle you off in a twinkling. 1842 J. WILSON *Chr. North* (1857) I. 142 The children are all trundled away out of the cottage. 1847–8 H. MILLER *First Impr.* ix. 156 As many bricks as an Irish labourer would trundle in a wheel-barrow. 1869 DICKENS *Lett.* (1880) II. 413 The Bath chairs trundling the dowagers about the streets.

**b.** *intr.* To go in a wheeled vehicle (in quot. 1909, on a bicycle or tricycle).

1840 DICKENS *Barn. Rudge* xxii, Mr. Tappertit trundled off with the chaise. 1909 *Spectator* 31 July 164/2 On my trusty 'Rover' I trundle down the brae.

**5.** *fig.* (*intr.*) To go, walk, or run easily or rapidly; to go away, 'be off'; also, to walk unsteadily or with a rolling gait.

1680 V. ALSOP *Mischief Impos.* iv. 27 Some may come [to their own Parish-church] out of custom, because they have used to trundle thither down the hill. 1700 CONGREVE *Way of World* I. ii, *Bet.* They are gone, sir, in great anger. *Peb.* Enough, let 'em trundle. a 1754 FIELDING *Fathers* IV. i, The next morning down trundled her and I to Dirty Park. 1820 LADY GRANVILLE *Lett.* 22 Aug., She..trundled out of the House. 1872 C. KING *Mountain. Sierra Nev.* x. 220 Sarah Jane rolled, I might almost say, trundled in.

**b.** *trans.* To carry or send off, turn out, dismiss.

1794 WOLCOTT (P. Pindar) *Dinah* 99 Wks. 1816 III. 315 Off were the couple trundled—man and maid. 1818 SCOTT *Br. Lamm.* xxi, The women..always contrived to trundle me out of favour before the honeymoon was over.

**II.** [back-formation from *trundle-bed.*]

†**6.** *intr.* To occupy a trundle-bed; = TRUCKLE *v.* 1. *Obs. rare*[−1].

c 1626 *Dick of Devon.* IV. i. in Bullen *O. Pl.* II. 61 You and your brother Manuell lay in the high Bed, and I trondling underneath.

Hence **Trundled** (trɒ·nd'ld) *ppl. a.*, **Tru·ndling** *vbl. sb.* and *ppl. a.*

a 1637 B. JONSON *Horace, Art Poetrie* 568 Who's unskilful at the coit, or ball, Or trundling wheele. 1674 N. FAIRFAX *Bulk & Selv.* 68 As a Coach may be so tickly set..as to give it self a trundling. a 1756 MRS. HAYWOOD *New Present* (1771) 256 The house-maid then, with a trundled mop, dries the floor very neatly. 1782 COWPER *Gilpin* 139 Just like unto a trundling mop. 1803 R. COUPER *Tourifications* xvi. II. 121 The extremity of this avenue was crossed by a fine little clear trundling rivulet. 1882 *Daily Tel.* 19 May, Making a slashing drive to the off for 4 from the same trundling. 1908 *Chron. Lond. Mission. Soc.* Mar. 47/2 Trundling carts threw up clouds of choking dust.

**Trundle**, obs. form of TREENAIL.

**Tru·ndle-bed.** Forms: α. 6 **trendyll-**, **trindle-**, **tryndle-**, **trindell-**; β. 6 **trundell-**, 6– **trundle-**; cf. TRENDLE, TRINDLE, TRUNDLE. [TRUNDLE *sb.* 1.] = TRUCKLE-BED.

α. 1542 *MS. Acc. St. John's Hosp., Canterb.*, For makyng a trendyll bed iiij[d]. 1560 DAUS tr. *Sleidane's Comm.* 232 He slept quietly in the trindle bed. 1599 *Nottingham Rec.* IV. 250, j. trindle bedd; one mattrice.

β. 1564 *Knaresborough Wills* (Surtees) I. 96, j trundell bedd. 1602 *2nd Pt. Return fr. Parnass.* II. vi. 979 When I was in Cambridge, and lay in a Trundlebed vnder my Tutor. 1667 PEPYS *Diary* 9 Oct., My wife and I in the high bed in our chamber, and Willet in the trundle-bed. 1727 DUDLEY in *Phil. Trans.* XXXIX. 68, I thought at first my Servants..were haling along a Trundle-bed. 1852 MRS. STOWE *Uncle Tom's C.* iv, Aunt Chloe..had been busy in pulling out a rude box of a trundle-bed.

So † **Tru·ndle be·dstead** *Obs.*

1590 in *Archæologia* XL. 326 Itm. a trundell bedsted and a boulster. 1686 in *Essex Rev.* (1906) XV. 173 One trundle beadsted.

**Trundler** (trɒ·ndləɹ). [f. TRUNDLE *v.* + -ER[1].] One who or that which trundles.

1648–60 HEXHAM *Dutch Dict.*, *Een Roller*, a Roler, or a Trundler. 1879 SALA *Paris herself again* (1880) I. xviii. 326 A friendly trundler of a Bath-chair..came to my assistance.

**b.** *Cricket.* A bowler. (See TRUNDLE *v.* 1 c.) *colloq.*

1882 *Daily Tel.* 27 May, Each trundler sent up five overs for one single run. 1895 *Westm. Gaz.* 1 Mar. 5/2 The two greatest Australian batsmen were seen playing the balls of England's two most famous trundlers.

**Trundle-tail.** *Obs.* or *arch.* Forms: 5 **tryndel-**, 6–8 **trundle-**, 6–9 **trindle-**, 7 **trondle-**, **trendle-**.

**1.** A dog with a curly tail; a low-bred dog, a cur. Also *attrib.*

1486 *Bk. St. Albans* F iv b, Myddyng dogges. Tryndeltayles, and Prikherid curris. 1599 NASHE *Lenten Stuffe* 29 A trundle-taile tike or shaugh or two. 1602 *2nd Pt. Return fr. Parnass.* II. v. 872 All kinde of dogges..trindle tailes, prick-eard curres, small Ladies puppies. 1605 SHAKS. *Lear* III. vi. 73 Hound or Spaniell,..Or Bobtaile tight, or Trondle taile. a 1639 WEBSTER *Appius & Virg.* III. iv, Amongst curs a trendle tale. 1820 SCOTT *Monast.* xxiv, The very brutes are degenerated..our hounds are turnspits and trindle-tails.

**b.** Applied contemptuously to a person.

1614 B. JONSON *Bart. Fair* II. v, Doe you sneere, you dogs-head, you Trendle tayle! 1632 ROWLEY *Woman Never Vexed* II. i. 18 How now my fine Trundletayles; My wodden Cosmographers. 1706 PHILLIPS (ed. Kersey), *Trundle-tail*, a Wench that runs fisking up and down with a draggled Tail.

**2.** (as two words) A curly tail (of a dog).

a 1625 FLETCHER *Love's Cure* III. iii, Like a poor cur, clapping his trindle tail Betwixt his legs. 1651 OGILBY *Æsop* (1665) 205 Rough with a trundle Tail, a Prick-ear'd Cur.

**Trunel**, obs. form of TREENAIL.

**Trunes(se, trunisse**, obs. ff. TRUENESS.

**Trunion**, variant of TRUNNION.

**Trunk** (trɒŋk), *sb.* Forms: 5–7 **tronk**, **tronke**, **troncke**, (7 **tronck**), 5–7 **trunke**, 6 **trounk**, **trounke**, (**tronque**, **troonke**, **trouncke**), 6–7 **truncke**, 6–8 **trunck**, 6– **trunk**. [a. F. *tronc* (12th c.), ad. L. *truncum*, acc. of *truncus* main stem or stock of a tree, the human body, a piece cut or broken off, etc. In branch III app. associated with TRUMP *sb.*[1], F. *trompe*. With IV cf. TRUNK-HOSE.]

**I.** The main part of something as distinguished from its appendages.

**1.** The main stem of a tree, as distinct from the roots and branches; the bole or stock.

1490 CAXTON *Eneydos* iv. 17 Eneas..hewe the troncke of a tree oute of the whiche yssued bloode. 1605 CAMDEN *Rem.* 161 A golden truncke of a tree. 1615 W. LAWSON *Country Housew. Gard.* (1626) 14 Cut away all his twigs..burying his trunck in the crust of the earth. 1697 DRYDEN *Virg. Georg.* III. 580 With Trunks of Elms and Oaks the Hearth they load. 1787 WINTER *Syst. Husb.* 103 The roots of trees grow in proportion to their trunks and branches. 1872 YEATS *Techn. Hist. Comm.* 21 These were formed from a single trunk of oak.

**b.** *fig.* or in fig. context.

1586 A. DAY *Eng. Secretary* I. (1625) 140 In stead of a louing and contented husband, to giue her a withered old Truncke. *Ibid.* II. 97 For his stature, a dwarffe; for his person, a trunke; for his qualities, a dog. 1603 SHAKS. *Meas. for M.* III. i. 72 You consenting too't, Would barke your honor from that trunke you beare, And leaue you naked. 1663 BP. PATRICK *Parab. Pilgr.* xv. (1687) 117 His endowments were divine;..yet blocks and trunks are wont now to lift up themselves higher in their own conceit than he could be tempted to do. 1839 H. ROGERS *Ess.* II. iii. 140 While the trunk of the language remains the same, the twigs and frailer branches are torn away by the storm. 1876 C. M. DAVIES *Unorth. Lond.* 81 Different offshoots which had from time to time separated themselves from the main trunk of Presbyterianism.

**c.** *transf.* The shaft of a column; also, the dado or die of a pedestal.

1563 SHUTE *Archit.* C ij b, Scapus,..being the troncke or body of the pillor. 1664 EVELYN tr. *Freart's Archit.* 124 [The Pedestal] is likewise called Truncus the Trunk..also

Abacus, Dado, Zocco, etc. 1727–41 in CHAMBERS *Cycl.* 1842–76 in GWILT *Encycl. Archit.* Gloss.

**2.** The human body, or that of an animal, without the head, or esp. without the head and limbs, or considered apart from these; in *Entom.* the thorax. Also *transf.* and *fig.*

1494 FABYAN *Chron.* VI. clxiii. 156 There was heddys, armys, leggys, and trunkys of dede mennys bodyes, lyinge as thycke as flowres growe in tyme of May. *Ibid.* VII. 495 His hed stryken of, & the trunke of his body hanged by chaynes vpon ye common gybet of Parys. 1541 R. COPLAND *Galyen's Terap.* 2 G ij, In diuiding ye tronke which is betwene the necke & the legges, is two great capacytees. 1593 SHAKS. 2 *Hen. VI*, IV. x. 90 There [will I] cut off thy most vngracious head;..Leauing thy trunke for Crowes to feed vpon. 1610 HOLLAND *Camden's Brit.* (1637) 336 His head smitten off, and the truncke of his body throwen into the fire. 1711 ADDISON *Spect.* No. 229 ⁋ 1 The Trunk of a Statue which has lost the Arms, Legs, and Head. 1715 ROWE *Lady Jane Gray* V. *ad fin.*, Blasted be the hand That struck my Guilford! Oh, his bleeding trunk Shall live in these distracted eyes for ever! 1804 ABERNETHY *Surg. Obs.* 26 The front, or back part of the trunk of the body. 1826 KIRBY & SP. *Entomol.* xxviii. III. 48 The second portion of the body is the Trunk, which is interposed between the head and abdomen. 1837 EMERSON *Address, Amer. Schol.* Wks. (Bohn) II. 175 The state of society is one in which the members have suffered amputation from the trunk. 1870 ROLLESTON *Anim. Life* 7 In the trunk [of the Rat] we observe that the spines of the dorsal vertebræ ..point backwards. 1913 *Times* 9 Aug. 4/1 A tendency to hairlessness on the trunk and limbs.

†**b.** *Her.* The head of a beast cut off immediately behind the horns or ears, i. e. caboched; cf. TRUNKED *ppl. a.*[1] 2. *Obs. rare*—[1].

1486 *Bk. St. Albans, Her.* b v, Tronkys be calde in armys any bestys hede or neck Ykytt chagikli [= jaggedly] a sonder.

†**3.** A dead body, a corpse; also, the body considered apart from the soul or life. *Obs.*

1588 SHAKS. *Tit. A.* V. iii. 152 Vnckle draw you neere, To shed obsequious teares vpon this Trunke. 1605 — *Lear* I. i. 180 If on the tenth day following, Thy banisht trunke be found in our Dominions. 1611 B. JONSON *Catiline* V. vi, His troops Couer'd that earth, they had fought on, with their trunkes. 1709 STEELE *Tatler* No. 83 ⁋ 3 This poor meagre Trunk of mine is a very ill Habitation for Love.

**4.** *Anat.* The main body or line of a blood-vessel, nerve, or similar structure, as distinct from its branches; also *transf.* the main line of a river, railway, telegraph or telephone, road or canal system; see *trunk-drainage, -glacier, -line*, etc. in 18. Also *fig.*

1615 CROOKE *Body of Man* 906 The lesser Trunke creepeth along the inside of the Legge..and in his progresse sprinkleth diuers surcles into the skine. 1707 FLOYER *Physic. Pulse-Watch* 352 The Arteries join'd on each side in the same Original Trunk. 1817 J. BRADBURY *Trav. Amer.* 246 Small rivers that fall immediately into the great trunk of the Mississippi. 1841–71 T. R. JONES *Anim. Kingd.* (ed. 4) 156 The ovigerous canals..uniting on each side of the body into two principal trunks. 1843 R. J. GRAVES *Syst. Clin. Med.* xxx. 396 Not only the nervous filaments.. may be affected, but also the main trunk of the nerve. 1876 GEO. ELIOT *Dan. Der.* xxviii, Like the main trunk of an exorbitant egoism.

**b.** *pl.* In Stock Exchange language, short for Grand Trunk Railway of Canada, or its stock.

1892 *Pall Mall G.* 9 Feb. 5/3 Trunks have risen, partly in sympathy with American, and also on a much better traffic than was expected. 1898 *Westm. Gaz.* 1 Dec. 8/1 A bull account in Trunks is always followed by a bad revenue statement.

†**5.** The scale of a map or plan; see SCALE *sb.*[3] 9. *Obs. rare.*

1561 EDEN *Arte Nauig.* III. ii. 58 This the Maryners call the truncke or scale of leaques. 1574 BOURNE *Regiment for Sea* xviii. (1577) 47 b, As you may see in measuring it by the trunke of your carde there. 1594 BLUNDEVIL *Exerc.* VII. xxviii. (1636) 692 To know the distance of places,..there is wont to be set downe in the Mariners Card, a scale, otherwise called by the Mariners a Trunk.

**II.** A chest, box, case, etc. (supposed to have been orig. made out of a tree-trunk).

†**6.** A chest, coffer, box. *Obs.* in *gen.* sense.

1462 *Mann. & Househ. Exp.* (Roxb.) 150 Item, payd ffor a new tronke ffor my lord whych was delyvared to Willyam off Wardrope x. s. 1494 FABYAN *Chron.* cxxxi. 113 He ordeyned a cheste, or trunke of clene syluer, to thentent yt all suche iuellys and ryche gyftes..shuld therein be kepte. 1591 GREENE *Art Conny Catch.* III. (1592) 34 At the beds feete stood a hansome truncke, wherein was very good linnen. *a* 1648 LD. HERBERT *Autobiog.* (1824) 190 Having the copies of all my dispatches in a great trunk in my House in London. 1687 A. LOVELL tr. *Thevenot's Trav.* I. 62 So curious and elaborate a Work might deserve a better Fate, than to lye moulding in the bottom of a Trunk. 1702 ADDISON *Dial. Medals* ii. (1726) 51 The little trunk she holds in her left hand is the *acerra*.., in which the frankincense was preserv'd. 1726 SHELVOCKE *Voy. round World* Pref. 17 No chests, boxes, or trunks, which shall be found in the ship when taken, shall be open'd.

**7.** A box, usually lined with paper or linen, and with a rounded top, for carrying clothes and other personal necessaries when travelling; originally covered with leather, now often of canvas, painted metal, etc. Cf. PORTMANTEAU 1.

1609 *Shuttleworths' Acc.* (Chetham Soc.) 181 To the porter, for the carridge of the gentlewomens truncke..xvd. 1662–3 PEPYS *Diary* 8 Jan., We were forced to send for a smith, to break open her trunk. 1709 STEELE & ADDISON *Tatler* No. 93 ⁋ 3 He had got his Trunk and his Books all packed up to be transported into Foreign Parts. 1773 GOLDSM. *Stoops to Conq.* II. i, I like to see their horses and trunks taken care of. 1841 THACKERAY *Gt. Hoggarty Diam.* viii, Away I went..with a couple of bran new suits from Von Stiltz's in my trunk. 1859 W. COLLINS *Q. of Hearts* iii, Ring the bell, and have your trunks packed.

**8.** A perforated floating box in which live fish are kept.

*c* 1440 *Promp. Parv.* 504/1 Trunke, for kepynge of fysche, *gurgustium.* 1450–1 *Abingdon Rolls* (Camden) 130 In factura j tronke pro piscibus custodiendis. 1540 in *Sel. Pleas Crt. Admiralty* (1894) I. 99 He toke the tronke in his hands and hallyd it up to the land and there put forth alle the fysh that was in the tronke into a basket. 1674 tr. *Scheffer's Lapland* 70 Fishes also, of which they have so great draughts, that they are forced to keep them in trunks and ponds. 1766 BLACKSTONE *Comm.* II. xxv. 393 If the pheasants escape from the mew, or the fishes from the trunk, ..they become *feræ naturæ* again. 1898 J. K. FOWLER *Rec. Old Times* 108 In the midst was a large shallow pond,..in which was kept an eel trunk, consisting of a strong iron-bound box about four feet long and two feet wide and deep, perforated with holes, and a lid fastened with lock and key. ..In this trunk or box were kept live eels, the trunk having a strong iron chain attached to it..; this enabled the trunk to be hauled up a sloping bank.

**b.** An open box or case (containing from 80 to 90 lb.) in which fresh fish are sold wholesale.

1883 S. PLIMSOLL in *19th Cent.* July 147 The box, which is called by many names, as 'van', 'machine', 'tank', 'trunk', &c. 1883 *Daily News* 27 July 7/1 Soles and such fish are sold in open boxes, without any covering whatever, called trunks. 1909 *Times* 12 Aug. 11/6 Two trunks of plaice made the remarkably high price of £3 10s. per trunk.

**c.** A net or trap for lobster-catching. *dial.*

1835 'S. OLIVER' *Rambles Northumbld.* v. 210 For catching lobsters the fishermen of Holy Island mostly use small hoop-nets, called by them trunks. 1867 SMYTH *Sailor's Word-bk.*, *Trunk*,..an iron hoop with a bag, used to catch crabs and lobsters.

**9.** *Mining.* A long shallow trough in which lead or tin ore is dressed.

1653 MANLOVE *Lead Mines* 273 (E.D.S.) The miner's Tearms..Fleaks, Knockings, Coestid, Trunks and Sparks of oar. 1839 DE LA BECHE *Rep. Geol. Cornw.* etc. xv. 579 The trunk was a pit ten feet long, three wide, and nine inches deep. 1839 URE *Dict. Arts* 1244 The rough is washed in buddles..the slimes in trunks. 1851 TAPPING *Manlove's Lead Mines* Gloss. s. v., The trunks are agitated with water, and thereby the metals separated from the base minerals.

**10.** A box-like passage for light, air, water, or solid objects, usually made of boards; a shaft, conduit; a chute. Now chiefly *techn.*

1610 NORTH *Plutarch* 1117 He was newly come from Trophonius truncke or hole. 1632 in E. B. Jupp *Carpenters' Co.* (1887) 301 Truncks for bringing in of light into mens howses..truncks for Jackewaights or conveyance of water. 1642 C. VERNON *Consid. Exch.* 42 Which Bill they..put..downe through a Trunke made for that purpose, into the Chamberlaines Court. 1747 HOOSON *Miner's Dict.* H j, As to..having the Trunks in the Roof of the Drift, that never does well. 1759 SMEATON in *Phil. Trans.* LI. 126 A trunk, for bringing the water upon the wheel, was fixed. 1861 R. WILLIS in Willis & Clark *Cambridge* (1886) III. 173 An opening or horizontal trunk through the rising seats, by which the solar ray may be directed upon the Lecture-table. 1886 *Act* 49 & 50 *Vict.* c. 38 § 6 Any bridge, waggon-way, or trunk for conveying minerals or other product from any mine or quarry. 1888 ELWORTHY *W. Somerset Word-bk.*, *Trunk*..a wooden tube much used in corn mills to convey grain or flour to or from the mills. Any wooden tube.

**b.** *spec.* A chute through which coal is emptied from the wagons into lighters, etc. *dial.*

1725 T. THOMAS in *Portland Papers* VI. (Hist. MSS. Comm.) 104 Those [steathes] that are covered with timber work are called trunks. 1893–4 *Northumbld. Gloss.*, *Trunk-staith*, a coal-spout at a shipping place. In former times a coal-staith was called a 'dyke', or trunk if a shoot or spout was used.

**c.** *Organ-building.* Short for *wind-trunk.*

1852 SEIDEL *Organ* 44 The principal canal..into which the wind passes from the bellows, is called the trunk.

**d.** In a steam-engine, A tubular piston-rod large enough to allow of the lateral movement of the connecting-rod when jointed directly to the piston.

1859 RANKINE *Steam Engine* (1861) 481 In large engines there are sometimes more than one piston rod and stuffing-box, and sometimes a tubular piston rod called a trunk.

**e.** *Naut.* A water-tight shaft passing through the decks of a vessel, for loading, coaling, etc.

1862 *Catal. Internat. Exhib.* II. XII. 2/1 The lower deck ..is made of iron, water-tight, and fitted with water-tight trunks, to communicate with the upper deck, so that access can be had at all times distinct from the other decks. 1877 W. H. WHITE *Man. Naval Archit.* i. 29 Where openings have to be made in a watertight deck or platform, either watertight covers must be fitted to the openings or water-tight trunks, carried to a sufficient height above the load-line, must be built around them.

**f.** See quot.

1877 KNIGHT *Dict. Mech.*, *Trunk* 5 (Hatting), the conduit, tube, or guiding-box which guides the air-currents and directs the fur fibers from the picker to the cone, in hat-body forming machines.

**g.** *Salt-making.* A box-like cover placed over an evaporating-pan.

1885 C. G. W. LOCK *Workshop Receipts* Ser. IV. 155 In ..Cheshire..the evaporating-pans are at times employed quite open and exposed to the sky, but nowadays they are mostly surrounded with sheds,..furnished with ventilating openings in the roof...On the Continent, all except the fine and butter-salt pans are generally covered in with wooden trunks, flat on top with sides converging upwards, thus forming an elongated truncated cone about 5 ft. high over the pan.

**h.** The water-tight case in which the centre-board of a sailing-boat works.

1894 *Westm. Gaz.* 20 Aug. 7/2 The centre board had not been lost, but had been jammed in the trunk and was held fast. 1897 *Outing* (U.S.) XXX. 228/2 The centerboard trunk is made long so that the board may be dropped at any desired point forward or aft.

**III.** A pipe or tube.

†**11.** A cylindrical case to contain or discharge explosives or combustibles; the barrel of a mortar, the case of a rocket, etc. *Obs.*

1548 *Privy Council Acts* (1890) II. 177, ij dosan of tronques for wild fyer. 1581 STYWARD *Mart. Discipl.* I. 12 To haue such gouernours as are..skilfull..in the making of trunkes, bawles, arrowes, and all other sortes of wilde fire. 1634 I. B. *Myst. Nat. & Art* 57 Fire-works..as Crackers, Trunks, etc. *a* 1660 *Contemp. Hist. Irel.* (Ir. Archæol. Soc.) I. 61 None could passe the same without eminent danger of fallinge under the fumie reache of that murtheringe troncke. *Ibid.* 102 Within the truncke some wilde fire in maner and forme of a bombe and granados. 1799 G. SMITH *Laboratory* I. 7 The cases, or trunks, of rockets.

†**12.** A pipe used as a speaking-tube or ear-trumpet. *Obs.*

1546 BALE *Eng. Votaries* I. (1550) 70 The roode spake these wordes, or else a knaue monke behynde hym in a truncke through the wall. 1589 PUTTENHAM *Eng. Poesie* III. xxv. (Arb.) 311 Not to heare but by a trunke put to his eare. 1631 SHIRLEY *Traitor* III. i, Ha! are there no trunks to convey secret voices? 1680 C. NESSE *Church-Hist.* 75 Which..did but pass through him as a trunk through which a man speaks. 1704 SWIFT *Battle of Bks.* Misc. (1711) 245 They whisper to each other thro a large hollow Trunk.

†**13.** A hollow tube from which a dart or pellet is shot by blowing; a blow-gun, a pea-shooter.

1553 EDEN *Treat. Newe Ind.* (Arb.) 20 They..blowe them [arrows] oute of a trunke as we doe pellets of claye. *a* 1652 BROME *New Acad.* IV. i, All my..tops, gigs, balls, cat and catsticks, pot guns, key guns, trunks, tillers, and all. 1755 B. MARTIN *Misc. Corr.* Oct. 170 Two youths..in the gallery of Covent-garden Play-house..shooting Peas thro' a Tin Trunk in the Faces of the Audience. 1801 STRUTT *Sports & Past.* IV. iv. § 1 A substitute for the gun,..a long hollow tube called a trunk.

†**14.** More fully *perspective trunk*: A telescope; cf. *trunk-glass, -spectacle* in 18.

1610 I. HEYDON in *Camden's Lett.* (1691) 130 With one of our ordinary Trunks I have told eleven stars in the Pleiades. 1620 B. JONSON *New World in Moon* Wks. (Rtldg.) 615/1 From the Moon!..Oh, by a trunk! I know it, a thing no bigger than a flute-case: a neighbour of mine, a spectacle-maker, has drawn the moon through it at the bore of a whistle. 1620 WOTTON *Let. to Bacon* in *Reliq.* (1651) 414 A long perspective-trunke with the convexe glasse fitted to the said hole [in a camera obscura], and the concave taken out at the other end.

**15.** The elongated proboscis of the elephant; also *transf.* the prolonged flexible snout of the tapir, etc.

*c* 1565 R. BAKER in Hakluyt *Voy.* (1589) 150 The Elephant ..With water fils his troonke right hie, and blowes it on the rest. 1613 PURCHAS *Pilgrimage* (1614) 816 There was another strange creature in Nicaragua..like a blacke Hogge, with ..a short truncke or snowt like an Elephant. 1687 A. LOVELL tr. *Thevenot's Trav.* III. 45 An Elephant..his Governour can make him do what he pleases with his Trunck. 1774 GOLDSM. *Nat. Hist.* (1776) IV. 273 Two tame elephants..that caress the indignant animal with their trunks. *c* 1850 *Arab. Nts.* (Rtldg.) 685 The trunks, ears, and other parts of these elephants, were painted red and other colours.

**b.** *slang.* The human nose.

*a* 1700 B. E. *Dict. Cant. Crew*, *Trunk*, a Nose. 1785 GROSE *Dict. Vulg. T.*, *Trunk*, a nose [in various phrases]. 1901 LAWSON *Remin. Dollar Acad.* 87 The deep bass rumbling sound, which was emitted from his trunk.

†**c.** The long pointed bill of the heron. *Obs. rare*—[1].

1575 TURBERV. *Falconrie* 160 A live hearon uppon the upper part of whose bill or truncke you must convey the joynt of a reed or cane.

**d.** The proboscis of some molluscs; also the proboscis of various insects. Now *rare* or *Obs.*

1661 LOVELL *Hist. Anim. & Min.* Introd., The Mollusca, ..some have acetabula, and two long trunks, which they use as anchors in storms. 1664 POWER *Exp. Philos.* I. 2 At his [the flea's] snout is fixed a Proboscis, or hollow trunk or probe. 1692 BENTLEY *Boyle Lect.* 125 Insects, which wound the tender buds with a long hollow trunk, and deposit an egg in the hole. 1805 PRISC. WAKEFIELD *Dom. Recreat.* i. (1806) 5 There is as great a variety in the trunks of insects as in their antennae.

†**16.** *pl.* Also *small trunks*: an old game: = TROLL-MADAM; cf. TRUCKS. *Obs.*

1607 *Christmas Prince* II. (1816) 45 Why say you not that Munday will bee drunke, Keepes all vnruly wakes, and playes at trunkes? 1611 COTGR., *Trou Madame*, the Game called Trunkes, or the Hole. 1621 BURTON *Anat. Mel.* II. ii. IV, The ordinary recreations which we haue in Winter..are Cardes, Tables,..the Philosophers game, small trunckes [etc.]. 1654 GAYTON *Pleas. Notes* IV. iv. 196 Billiards, Kettle-pins, Noddy-boards, Tables, Truncks, Shovell-boards, Fox and Geese, or the like. 1706 PHILLIPS (ed. Kersey), *Trunks*, a kind of Play otherwise call'd Troll-Madame and Pigeon-holes. 1854 MISS BAKER *Northampt. Gloss.*, *Nine-holes*, or *Trunks*, a game played with a long piece of wood or bridge with nine arches cut in it...Each player has two flattened balls, which he aims to bowl edge-ways under the arches; he scores the number marked over the arch he bowls through.

**IV. 17.** *pl.* †**a.** = TRUNK-HOSE. *Obs.*

1583 *Rates of Custome Ho.* F j, Truncks the dosen xii. s. 1610 B. JONSON *Alch.* III. iii, Sixe great slopps, Bigger then three Dutch hoighs, besides round trunkes. 1652 in *Verney Mem.* (1907) I. 490 There are Pages in trunks that ride behind the coches..cloath trunks billited or garded with velvet. **1672** *Lond. Gaz.* No. 656/4 His Trunks and Stockings are of grey Worsted.

**b.** Short breeches of silk or other thin material; in theatrical use, often worn over tights; in quot. 1896 applied to ordinary breeches or knickerbockers.

**1825** Hone *Every-day Bk.* I. 1463 Theatrical 'trunks', or short breeches. **1837** Dickens *Pickw.* xv, The appearance of Mr. Snodgrass in blue satin trunks and cloak, white silk tights and shoes, and Grecian helmet. **1874** R. Buchanan *Kitty Kemble* 86 A slim fairy prince in trunks and tights. **1896** Crockett *Grey Man* xvi, David had donned the trunks and laid by the bairn's kilts. **1906** N. Munro in *Blackw. Mag.* Dec. 802/1 A right smart Alick in short trunks.

**c.** *U.S.* Short tight-fitting drawers worn by swimmers and athletes.

**1883** *Pall Mall G.* 26 July 7/1 Captain Webb attempted his perilous feat of swimming the Niagara Rapids...He wore a pair of silk trunks. **1889** Gunter *That Frenchman* xi, Black-velvet trunks cover his [the wrestler's] hips and thighs. **1891** *Daily News* 30 May 5/5 The men are together in front of Harvard boathouse in caps, 'sweaters', trunks, and canvas shoes. **1894** Ralph in *Harper's Mag.* Aug. 341 Nude bathing will not be permitted...The use of tights or 'trunks' will not be allowed.

**V. 18.** *attrib.* and *Comb.*, as, in senses 1 and 2, *trunk-armour*, *-bark*, *-bone*, *-diameter*, *-muscle*, *-rib*, *-root*, *-scar*; in senses 4 and 4 b, *trunk-dealer*, *-drainage*, *exchange*, *-glacier*, *-jack* (Jack *sb.*[1] 15 d), *-line*, *-market* (Market *sb.* 1 d), *-road*, *-sewer*, *-sheath*, *stream*, *-telegraph*, *-telephone*, *-traffic*, *-train*, *-wire*; in senses 6 and 7, *trunk-boot* (Boot *sb.*[3] 4 c), *-buddle* (see quot.), *-castor*, *-check*, *-lid*, *-liner*, *-lock*, *-mail* (Mail *sb.*[2]), *-shop*; in sense 10 (c and d), *trunk-hole*, *-piston*, *-plunger*; in sense 15, *trunk-bearer*; *trunk-nosed* adj.; also **trunk-alarm**, an alarum which sounds when the trunk-lid is lifted (Knight *Dict. Mech.* 1877); **trunk-back** = *trunk-turtle* (*U.S.*); **trunk-band**, *Organ-building*, a shallow box in the horizontal bellows to which the wind-trunk is attached; also called *trunk-lining*; †**trunk-board**, a platform for a trunk or trunks at the back of a carriage; **trunk-brace**, a support or stay for a trunk-lid, to prevent it from falling again when raised (Knight); **trunk-cabin**, a ship's cabin partly above and partly below the upper deck; cf. sense 10 e and *trunk-deck* (*Cent. Dict.* 1891); **trunk-call**, a call from one telephone exchange to another; **trunk-case**, that part of a chrysalis case which covers the thorax; **trunk-deck**, the top of a hatchway trunk projecting above the deck, or a row of these joined so as to form a kind of raised deck (*Cent. Dict. Suppl.* 1909); **trunk dial**, a clock having a long case to accommodate the pendulum; **trunk-engine**, an engine having a tubular piston-rod; see sense 10 d; †**trunk-glass** = sense 14; **trunk-leg**, **-limb**, in Crustaceans, a leg attached to the thorax; **trunk-light**, a skylight placed over a trunk or shaft (*Cassell's Encycl. Dict.* 1888); **trunk-lining**, (*a*) = *trunk-band*; (*b*) material for lining trunks: cf. Trunk-maker; **trunk-machine**, a tube or shaft for the conveyance of cotton from one machine to another during the preparatory processes (*Cent. Dict. Suppl.* 1909); **trunk main**, a large pipe for the conveyance of water, etc. under pressure, as distinguished from the reticulation of smaller mains fed therefrom; †**trunk-manna**: see quot.; **trunk-nail**, a short nail with broad convex brass head used for ornamenting trunks and coffins (Knight); **trunk-nose**, the sea-elephant or elephant-seal (*Funk's Stand. Dict.* 1895); **trunk-rod**, a fishing-rod composed of short joints for convenience in packing (*U.S.*); †**trunk-saddle**, ? a packsaddle adapted for carrying a trunk or chest; †**trunk sleeve**, a full, puffed sleeve; cf. sense 17 a; so **trunk slops** (Slop *sb.*[1] 4); †**trunk-spectacle** = sense 14; **trunk-staithe**, a wharf at which coal is loaded into vessels by a trunk or shoot; **trunk-stay** = *trunk-brace* (Knight); **trunk-turtle**, the Leathery Turtle or Leather-back, *Dermatochelys* (*Sphargis*) *coriacea*, of warm seas, having a flexible leathery carapace with osseous deposits and several longitudinal ridges; **trunk-valve**, in a steam-engine, a D slide-valve long enough to cover direct steam-ports when placed near the end of the cylinder (*Cent. Dict. Suppl.* 1909); †**trunk-wame**, a fiddle (*dial.*); **trunk-way**: see quot.; **trunk-weed**, ? a species of sea-weed; †**trunk-work**, secret or clandestine action, as by means of a trunk. See also Trunk-fish, -maker.

**1854** Owen *Skel. & Teeth* in *Orr's Circ. Sc.* I. *Org. Nat.* 165 In these colossal armadillos..the *trunk-armour was in one immovable piece, covering the back and sides, and was not divided by bands. **1883** S. Garman *Rept. & Batrach. N. Amer.* Introd. 6 Sea Turtles are numerous off the coasts of Florida. '*Trunk-backs' or 'Leather-backs', *Sphargis*, are the largest. **1876** Stainer & Barrett *Dict. Mus. Terms*, *Organ Construction*, On it [the middle board] rests a strong ridge called the *trunk-band or lining, to which the wind trunks can be at any point joined. **1881** W. E. Dickson *Organ-Build.* vi. 73 A shallow box, say 4 inches deep, upon the middle board, of the same size as the top board. This is called a trunk-band, and is introduced to allow of fixing the wind-trunks. **1880** C. R. Markham *Peruv. Bark* 37 It [*Cinchona Condaminea*] once yielded great quantities of thick *trunk bark, but..is now almost exterminated. *Ibid.* 81 From the trunk-bark of a plant of this species [*Cinchona Calisaya*]..he obtained..5 per cent. of alkaloids. **1861** P. P. Carpenter in *Rep. Smithsonian Inst.* 1860, 174 The shell of the *Trunk-bearers may almost always be known by a notch or canal at the base. **1819** B. H. Latrobe *Jrnl.* (1905) 224 A girl of thirteen or fourteen years old sat up on the *trunk board behind. **1904** *Westm. Gaz.* 23 Sept. 7/3 A second skull..but no trace of *trunk bones can be found. **1794** W. Felton *Carriages* (1801) II. 54 The carriage..; an iron coach-box on a square *trunk-boot, raised on neat, carved blocks. **1839** Ure *Dict. Arts* 751 The *trunk buddle is..composed of two parts; of a cistern or box into which a stream of water flows, and of a large tank with a smooth level bottom. **1910** *Times* 19 Aug. 4/6 The telephone is still open, but..a message into the country usually involves a *trunk call. **1826** Kirby & Sp. *Entomol.* III. xxxi. 250 The *Trunk-case, divided into the thorax, or upper surface, extending from the head to the dorsal segments of the abdomen. **1877** Knight *Dict. Mech.*, *Trunk-caster. **1906** M. Nicholson *House of 1000 Candles* iii, I gave him my *trunk-checks. **1909** *Westm. Gaz.* 3 Mar. 9/1 *Trunk dealers received another disappointment in the traffic, which showed a decrease. **1884** F. J. Britten *Watch & Clockm.* 274 Generally *trunk dials have half seconds pendulums. **1909** *Chamb. Jrnl.* Sept. 561/2 The Rajah-tree..with a *trunk-diameter of six or eight feet. **1864** C. S. Read in W. White *Norfolk* 67 Some better system of *trunk drainage should be at once adopted. **1864** Webster, *Trunk-engine. **1867** Smyth *Sailor's Word-bk.*, *Trunk-engine*, a direct-acting steam-engine, in which the end of the connecting-rod is attached to the bottom of a hollow trunk, passing steam-tight through the cylinder cover. **1908** *Daily Chron.* 9 Dec. 1/4 Telephonists employed in *trunk exchanges. **1860** Tyndall *Glac.* I. xiv. 99 The medial moraine of the *trunk glacier. **1875** *Wond. Phys. World* I. ii. 55 To coalesce in one great trunk-glacier. **1613** M. Ridley *Magn. Bodies* 28 A thing worthy of better observation from the *Truncke-glasse. **1881** W. E. Dickson *Organ-Build.* v. 60 In one of these cheeks a *trunk-hole may have to be cut for the entrance of the wind. **1902** *Encycl. Brit.* XXX. 479/2 Of the corresponding pairs of appendages..three..may be all maxillipeds or may help to swell the number of *trunk-legs. **1858** Simmonds *Dict. Trade*, **Trunk-line*, the main line of a railway, separate from the branch lines or feeders. **1861** *Sat. Rev.* 7 Sept. 236 The trunk lines already in existence are substantially all that the country requires. **1888** B. F. C. Costelloe *Ch. Cath.* 19 Great trunk lines of liturgical tradition. **1905** *Daily Chron.* 4 Oct. 9/7 *Trunk Liner wanted; must be used to glue work. **1876** *Trunk-lining [see *trunk-band*]. **1907** *Times* 29 Mar. 6/2 Second-hand booksellers..know more about books, have a sounder judgment as to what is literature and what is trunk-lining. **1677** Moxon *Mech. Exerc.* ii. 21 Chest Locks, *Trunk Locks, Pad-locks, &c. **1771** Smollett *Humph. Cl.* 17 Apr., Tell Gwyllim that she forgot to pack up my flannels and wide shoes in the *trunk mail. **1820** Scott *Monast.* xv, I hope, a'gad, they have not forgotten my trunk-mails of apparel. **1663** Boyle *Usef. Exp. Nat. Philos.* II. iv. 101 The Calabrians..by Incisions obtain from the common Ash Tree..a sweet Juice, so like to the Manna..that the Natives call it in their Language, *Manna del corpo*, or *Trunk-manna. **1902** *Westm. Gaz.* 3 Apr. 9/1 A *Trunk market wit. **1907** *Ibid.* 25 Mar. 9/3 Just come into the Trunk market for a second. **1884** *Birmingham Daily Post* 23 Feb. 2/4 *Trunk moulding machine, 32 in. long, with dies complete. **1872** Humphry *Myology* 32 Where the fibres diverge from the *trunk-muscle. **1899** *Allbutt's Syst. Med.* VIII. 59 Rarely the spasm [of tetany] begins in the trunk muscles. **1900** Kipling in *Daily News* 9 Mar. 6/2 The temple wherein the 'tun-bellied', '*trunk-nosed' god Ganesha (the divine Elephant) receives his worshippers. **1888** Hasluck *Model Engin. Handybk.* (1900) 108 The feed-pump..is on the *trunk principle. **1885** Nicholson *Man. Zool.* (ed. 4) 495 The anterior *trunk-ribs [of the *Dinosauria*] were double-headed. **1861** Hughes *Tom Brown at Oxf.* xlvi, Englebourn was situated on no *trunk road. **1869** E. A. Parkes *Pract. Hygiene* (ed. 3) 398 In India, on some of the trunk roads there are regular halting grounds. **1890** R. S. Ferguson *Hist. Cumberld.* x. 149 The trunk-road itself passes Waverton. **1893** *Outing* (U.S.) XXII. 121/2 *Trunk rods made to pack in small space often have six or seven [joints]. **1671** Grew *Anat. Plants* iii. App. § 1 *Trunk-Roots are of two kinds:..those that vegetate by a direct descent...The other sort..shoot forth at right Angles with the Trunk. **1569** in *Richmond Wills* (Surtees) 219 In his owen stable..iiij hackney sadles..one *trouncke sadle. **1857** Gosse *Omphalos* xii. 364 The Palm and the Tree-fern show, in their *trunk-scars, evidences of organs which have completely died away and disappeared. **1899** *Daily News* 6 Dec. 6/6 We cannot possibly deal with local floodings..unless you give us the necessary additional *trunk sewers. **1893** A. S. Eccles *Sciatica* 15 The nerves of the *trunk-sheath have been stimulated by the cold impression. **1596** Shaks. *Tam. Shr.* iv. iii. 142 A loose bodied gowne..With a small compast cape..a *trunke sleeue. **1603** Florio *Montaigne* ii. xii. (1632) 301 They make trunk-sleeves of wyre and whale-bone bodies. **1606** Marston *Parasit.* iv. F iij b, A simple, country Ladie, wore gold buttons, trunck sleeues, and flaggon bracelets. **1592** Nashe *P. Penilesse* (ed. 2) 6 b, A paire of *trunke slops, sagging down like a Shoomakers wallet. **1613** M. Ridley *Magn. Bodies* 1 The foure attenders vpon Iupiter, lately discouered by the *trunke spectacle. **1625** N. Carpenter *Geog. Del.* i. iv. (1635) 79 Many [stars] haue lately beene discouered, by reason of the Trunk-spectacle lately found out. **1789** Brand *Hist. Newcastle* II. 256 *note*, When the waggons are emptied into a keel or vessel by a spout, it is called a *trunk staith. **1860** Tyndall *Glac.* i. xxi. 149 All the glaciers..are suddenly turned aside where they meet the great *trunk stream. *Ibid.* ii. x. 287 The width of the trunk stream is a little better than one-third of that of its tributaries. **1903** *Daily Chron.* 7 Oct. 7/1 An underground *trunk telegraph line to Scotland. **1909** *Westm. Gaz.* 17 Apr. 9/4 Sunday duty by females in the *trunk telephone department should be abolished. **1899** *Ibid.* 31 Aug. 4/3 It is no light task to make up a *trunk train in such satisfactory proportions. **1697** Dampier *Voy. round World* (1699) 103 There are 4 sorts of Sea-turtle, viz. the *Trunk-turtle, the Loggerhead, the Hawks-bill and the Green-turtle. **1735** Mortimer in *Phil. Trans.* XXXIX. 117 *Testudo Arcuata*: The Trunk-Turtle. **1827** Roberts *Voy. Centr. Amer.* 94 A trunk-turtle, a species of immense size and exceedingly fat. **16..** *Poems, Ballads*, etc. (Percy Soc.) 196, I pray who's this we've met with here, That tickles his *trunk weam?..If he'll play,..We'll dance you Jumping Joan. *a* **1825** Forby *Voc. E. Anglia*, **Trunk-way*, a water course through an arch of masonry, turned over a ditch before a gate. The name arose no doubt, from the trunks of trees used for the same purpose in ancient and simpler times. **1730** Capt. W. Wriglesworth *MS. Log-bk. of the 'Lyell'* 5 May, At 6 this morning Saw a bunch of *Trunk Weeds. **1897** *Daily News* 20 Jan. 10/4 The Postmaster-General..states that..efficient working of the *trunk wires is engaging his earnest attention. **1611** Shaks. *Wint. T.* iii. iii. 75 This has beene some staire-worke, some *Trunke-worke, some behinde-doore worke.

Hence **Tru·nkie** *Sc.*, a little trunk (sense 7).

**1728** Ramsay *Bob of Dunblane* i, Gang to the ground of ye'r trunkies, Busk ye braw.

† **Trunk**, *v.*[1] *Obs.* [ad. L. *truncāre*: see Truncate *v.*] *trans.* To cut a part off from; to cut short, truncate; to lop, clip, prune.

*c* **1440** *Pallad. on Husb.* iv. 86 Ek summe her aged vynes wole repare, And trunke hem of al hie abouen grounde. *a* **1550**–*c* **1828** [see Trunked *ppl. a.*[1] 2]. **1586** Ferne *Blaz. Gentrie* ii. 38 His coate-armor rased, his Sheeld reuersed, his Speare truncked, his spurres hewed from his heeles. **1611** [see Trunking *vbl. sb.*[1]]. **1688** R. Holme *Armoury* iii. xxii. (Roxb.) 274/1 Termes used by Tobacconists...Trunk it, is to make it in Order for the boxes.

**Trunk** (trʌŋk), *v.*[2] [f. Trunk *sb.*]

**1.** *trans.* To shut up as in a trunk; to imprison. *rare.*

**1608** Middleton *Fam. Love* ii. iv, I thought thou had'st been cabin'd in thy ship, Not trunk'd within my cruel guardian's house.

**2.** *Mining.* To dress (lead or tin ore) by agitating it in water; cf. Trunk *sb.* 9.

**1758** Borlase *Nat. Hist. Cornw.* 204 What runs off to the hindermost part of the pit..and..is slimy..must be trunked, buddled, and tozed, as the slimy tin. **1778** Pryce *Min. Cornub.* 238 In order to clear the earthy sordes from the slime or loobs, it may be trunked. **1839** De la Beche *Rep. Geol. Cornw.*, etc. xv. 579 In 1778 we find that the slime and tails, after having been allowed to dry, were trunked and framed. **1881** [see Trunking *vbl. sb.*[2]].

**3.** To cover or enclose with a casing; see quots.

**1838** *Civil Eng. & Arch. Jrnl.* I. 383/2 The road-way is then to be floored or trunked over with five courses of dry heathy sods. **1883** [see Trunking *vbl. sb.*[2] b].

**4.** Of an elephant: To pick *up*, pull, or pluck with the trunk. *nonce-use.*

**1901** *N. & Q.* 9th Ser. VII. 165/1 The elephants went past a garden with cabbages in it, and did not they trunk them up!

**Trunkal**, variant of Truncal.

**Tru·nk-bree:ches**, *sb. pl.* Now only *Hist.* = Trunk-hose.

**1662** Bagshaw in *Acc. Baxter's Suspension* 43 The Trunk-Breeches, and Wooden Daggers of our Ancestors. **1691** T. H[ale] *Acc. New Invent.* p. xlvi, To make the..writing of Politicks..grow as much out of Fashion as the garb of Trunk-breeches. **1735** Byrom *Jrnl. & Lit. Rem.* (1855) I. ii. 621 John..brought my trunk-breeches, which had been forgotten. **1755** Smollett *Quix.* (1803) IV. 108, I have, ever since I was born, longed to see father in laced trunk-breeches. **1809** W. Irving *Knickerb.* vi. v. (1849) 341 These were short fat men, wearing exceeding large trunk-breeches. **1850** *N. & Q.* 1st Ser. I. 489/1.

**Trunked** (trʌŋkt), *ppl. a.*[1] [f. Trunk *v.*[1] + -ed [1].]

†**1.** Cut short, truncated; lopped; mutilated. *Obs.* exc. as in 2.

**1551–2** in Feuillerat *Revels Edw. VI* (1914) 79 A payre of sleves trunked. **1559** W. Cunningham *Cosmogr. Glasse* 36 They be named Colures, or trunckid circles. **1586** J. Hooker *Hist. Irel.* in *Holinshed* II. 24/1 By reason they had beene so long couered,..buried vnder the sands, they stood as trunked and polled trees. **1590** Spenser *F. Q.* ii. v. 4 The sharpe steele..from the head the body sundred quight...The truncked beast fast bleeding did him fowly dight. **1594** ? Greene *Selimus* Wks. (Grosart) XIV. 249 My blood, Streaming in riuers from my tronked armes.

**2.** *Her.* (*a*) Having the extremities cut off smoothly: = Couped. (*b*) Of the head of a beast: Cut off close behind the horns; = Caboched.

*a* **1550** in Baring-Gould & Twigge *W. Armory* (1898) 4 A fesse trunked betweene 3 escalops sab. **1610** Bolton *Elem. Armories* 111 Of that maim'd, or truncked kinde, are this, and the like. **1610** Guillim *Heraldry* iii. iv. 95 Argent; two Billets Raguled, and Truncked, placed Saltirewaies. *Ibid.* xiv. 128 These horned beasts..haue also their heads borne Trunked [*ed.* 1638 *adds* Which of some Armorists is blazoned Cabossed]. **1766–84** Porny *Heraldry* (ed. 4) Gloss., *Trunked*.., is applied to Trees, &c. that are couped or cut off smooth. *c* **1828** Berry *Encycl. Her.* I. Gloss. s. v. *Trunk*, When the tree is borne couped of all its branches, and separated from its roots, it is then termed trunked. *Ibid.*, *Trunked*,..is likewise used in the same sense as *cabossed*, or *caboshed*, that is, showing only the head or face of a beast.

**Trunked** (trʌŋkt, *poet.* trʌ·ŋkėd), *a.* and *ppl. a.*[2] [In branch I, f. Trunk *sb.* + -ed [2]; in branch II, f. Trunk *v.*[2] (sense 2) + -ed [1].]

**I. 1.** Having a trunk, as a tree; usually in compounds, as *straight-trunked*, etc., for which see the first element.

1640 HOWELL *Dodona's Gr.* 48 Strong and well trunked Trees of all sorts. 1852 *Meanderings of Mem.* I. 132 The trunkèd forest's deep Where graces dance. 1905 HOLMAN-HUNT *Pre-Raphaelitism* II. 74 The trees were mightily trunked and limbed.

**b.** *Her.* Having the trunk of a tincture different from the rest of the tree.

1678 PHILLIPS (ed. 4), *Trunked*, in Heraldry Trees growing on a Stock, are said to be Trunked. *c* 1828 BERRY *Encycl. Her.* I. Gloss., *Trunked* is..said of a tree, the main stem of which is borne of a different tincture from the branches.

**2.** Having a trunk or proboscis; proboscidiferous.

*a* 1794 SIR W. JONES *Tales* (1807) 182 In vain their high-priz'd tusks they gnash'd; Their trunked heads my Geda mash'd. 1899 BEAZLEY & PRESTAGE *Disc. Guinea* (Hakl. Soc.) II. 337 The Proboscidians, or trunked Pachyderms. 1913 A. G. THACKER tr. *Buttel-Reepen's Man & Forerunners* ii. 15 Great trunked mammals, precursors of our modern elephants.

**3.** Wearing trunks (TRUNK *sb.* 17 a). *rare.*

1904 M. HEWLETT *Queen's Quair* I. vi, The Queen and her maids braved it as saucy young men, trunked, puffed, pointed, trussed and doubleted.

**II. 4.** *Mining.* Washed in a trunk (see TRUNK *sb.* 9, *v.*[2] 2).

1828 HENWOOD in *Trans. R. Geol. Soc. Cornwall* (1832) IV. 158 The operator..spreads on the jagging board from two to three quarts of the trunked slime.

**Tru·nk-fish.** Any fish of the genus *Ostracion* or family *Ostraciontidæ*, inhabiting tropical seas, and having the body of angular cross-section and covered with bony hexagonal plates; a coffer-fish.

1804 SHAW *Gen. Zool.* V. 420 Triquetral Trunk-fish. 1835 *Encycl. Brit.* (ed. 7) XII. 229/2 The horned trunk-fish, *Ostracion cornutus*, a native, like most of the genus, of the Indian and American seas. 1851 GOSSE *Nat. Hist., Fishes* 288 The Trunk-fishes..have the body angular, four or three-sided, covered with angular plates of solid bone soldered together, and forming a sort of inflexible box, with openings for the mouth, the fins, the tail, and the gill-aperture. 1876 GOODE *Fishes Bermudas* 23 The locomotion of the trunk-fishes is very peculiar.

**Trunkful** (trʌ·ŋkful). [f. TRUNK *sb.* + -FUL.] As much or as many as a trunk will hold.

1707 HEARNE *Collect.* 25 Oct. (O.H.S.) II. 65 A whole trunkful of papers. 1883 *Century Mag.* XXVI. 370 A trunkful of dresses fresh from Worth's. 1897 MARY KINGSLEY *W. Africa* xii. 259 Some [elephants] drew up trunkfuls of water and syringed themselves and each other.

**Tru·nk-hose.** Now only *Hist.* [f. TRUNK (*sb.* or *v.*[1]) + HOSE.

The sense of 'trunk' here, as in the later *trunk-breeches*, and the earlier TRUNK *sb.* 17, appears to be uncertain. Various suggestions have been made, e.g. that trunk refers to the trunk of the body, or that it is TRUNK *sb.* 13, 'a hollow tube or pipe'; or that it is = *truncate* or *truncated*, as being, as it were, cut short. Early explanations have not been found: the term may have been of vulgar origin.]

Full bag-like breeches covering the hips and upper thighs, and sometimes stuffed with wool or the like, worn in the 16th and early 17th c.

1637 HEYWOOD *Royall King* Epil. 9 Those Trunke-hose, which now the age doth scorn, Were all in fashion, and with frequence worne. 1694 LD. MOLESWORTH *Acc. Denmark* 162 In the habit of the North-Holland Boors, with great Trunk-hose, short Doublets. 1735 BYROM *Jrnl. & Lit. Rem.* (1855) I. II. 616 Put on my boots and coat and trunk-hose. 1907 *Verney Mem.* I. 53 His..trunk hose slashed and lined with dull red.

**b.** *attrib.*, in sense 'wearing trunk-hose'; hence, old-fashioned, out-of-date.

*a* 1643 W. CARTWRIGHT *Ordinary* II. i. (1651) 24 The trunck-hose Justices will try all means To bind you to the Peace. 1647 J. BERKENHEAD *Pref. Verses* in *Beaumont & Fletcher's Wks.* e j b, You Two thought fit To weare just Robes, and leave off Trunk-hose-Wit.

Hence † **Tru·nk-hosed** *a.*, wearing trunk-hose.

1621 FLETCHER *Wild Goose Chase* v. v, I would the trunk-hos'd woman would go with me. 1631 BRATHWAIT *Whimzies, Metall-man* 61 A Metall-man..that walking trunk-hos'd goblin.

† **Tru·nking,** *vbl. sb.*[1] *Obs.* [f. TRUNK *v.*[1] + -ING[1].] The action of TRUNK *v.*[1]; truncation.

1611 COTGR., *Troncation*, a truncation, trunking, mutilation, cutting off.

**Tru·nking,** *vbl. sb.*[2] [f. TRUNK *v.*[2] + -ING[1].] The action of TRUNK *v.*[2]: **a.** in sense 2; also *attrib.*

1838 *Civil Eng. & Arch. Jrnl.* I. 409/2 The engine was working..a trunking machine. 1839 DE LA BECHE *Rep. Geol. Cornw.*, etc. XV. 579 The trunking by machinery..was introduced at St. Ives, according to Mr. Henwood, about the year 1825. 1839 URE *Dict. Arts* 1245 The portion B is to be washed again in the trunking-box. 1881 RAYMOND *Mining Gloss.*, *Trunking* (Cornw.), separating slimes by means of a trunk. 1884 C. G. W. LOCK *Workshop Receipts* Ser. III. 53/1 A revolving 'trunking' apparatus.

**b.** in sense 3; also *concr.*

1838 *Civil Eng. & Arch. Jrnl.* I. 383/2 Perfect drainage and good trunking,..if these are not attained, roads constructed on bog will lose their shape, become ruinous, and soon go to decay. *Ibid.*, Upon this trunking is to be laid a soling. 1883 *Science* II. 99/1 A 'trunking' or wooden covering is then placed over them to protect them from snow and the feet of any one walking about the yard.

**Trunkless** (trʌ·ŋklės), *a.* [f. TRUNK *sb.* + -LESS.] Having no trunk; *esp.* without a body, or severed from the body, as a head.

1631 WEEVER *Anc. Fun. Mon.* 279 Their trunklesse faces. 1682 J. BANKS *Anna Bullen* v. i. 78 The Trunkless Head with darting Eyes beheld her. 1820 *Examiner* No. 630. 290/1 The exhibition of their trunkless heads. 1897 *Daily News* 18 Feb. 2/2 The woolly elephant is trunkless. 1897 *Naturalist* 243 A generation..that lops its oaks into trunkless brush-wood.

**Tru·nk-ma:ker.** One whose business is the making of trunks (TRUNK *sb.* 7); often with allusion to the use of the sheets of unsaleable books for trunk-linings.

*a* 1704 T. BROWN *Laconics* Wks. 1711 IV. 2 *The True-born Englishman* had dy'd silently among the Grocers and Trunk-makers, if the Libeller had not help'd off the Poet. *a* 1734 NORTH *Exam.* III. vii. § 38 (1740) 530 The Trunk-maker, who pretended to be the right Heir Male of the noble Family of the Piercies. 1764 G. WILLIAMS in Jesse *Selwyn & Contemp.* (1843) I. 321, I hear he has been a pamphleteer, though as yet only to the benefit of the trunk-maker and pastrycook. 1845 J. COULTER *Adv. Pacific* xiv. 211 The hitting of the stick is so very rapid, that it resembles nothing that I know of more accurately than a trunk-maker driving in his nails. 1890 *Globe* 1 July 7/2 'All round St. Paul's, not forgetting the trunkmaker's daughter'. By the trunkmaker was understood, in the latter part of the last and the former part of the present century, the depository for unsaleable books.

**Tru·nnel,** dial. form of TRUNDLE *sb.* Also in comb. **trunnel-head**, a circular plate or disk at the head of a coke-oven or in a furnace; **trunnel-hole**, the aperture or throat of a puddling furnace in which this disk works.

1868 JOYNSON *Metals* 16 The opening at the top of the furnace, called the throat or trunnel-hole. 18.. *Amer. Manuf.* LXII. 626 (Cent. Suppl.) The trunnel-head, or ring, is a much more important part of a coke oven than most people imagine.

**Trunnel, -ell,** variants of TREENAIL.

**Trunnion** (trʌ·nyən). Chiefly in *pl.* Also 7–9 **trunion**, 8 **tronion.** [ad. F. *trognon* core of fruit, stump, trunk of a tree (14th c. in Godef. *Compl.*); of uncertain origin.]

**1.** Each of a pair of opposite gudgeons on the sides of a cannon, upon which it is pivoted upon its carriage. (Disused in large modern guns.)

*a* 1625 *Nomenclator Navalis* (Harl. MS. 2301), *Trunnions* are those knobbs which come from the side of the Ordnance and doe beare them vpp vpon the Cheekes of the Carriages. 1690 J. MACKENZIE *Siege London-Derry* 17/1 The rest attending the Lord Kingston till they had broke the Trunnions, and nailed the heavier Guns. 1781 JUSTAMOND *Priv. Life Lewis XV*, III. 389 They broke off the trunnions of the canon. 1794 NELSON in Nicolas *Disp.* (1845) I. 430 The Agamemnon's two twenty-four pounders are both ruined: one split up to the rings; the other with the trunnion knocked so much off, that it is useless for shot. 1890 W. J. GORDON *Foundry* 26 One of the strangest of the very latest developments of modern gunnery is the abolition of the trunnions.

**b.** Each of any similar pair of opposite pins or pivots on which anything is supported; *spec.* in the oscillating steam-engine, a hollow gudgeon on each side of the cylinder, upon which it is pivoted, and through which the steam passes into and out of the cylinder; also, a single projecting pivot.

1727 *Bradley's Fam. Dict.* s.v. *Chimney*, They fit two Trunnions or Knobs to the Middle of this Swipe. 1831 J. HOLLAND *Manuf. Metal* I. 88 The centre of the pivots or trunnions on which it [the large metal helve] works. 1833 *Ibid.* II. 215 The bar-handle acting..upon a fulcrum or mouth-piece of solid iron, the top of which works against a trunnion under the middle of the press head. 1867 J. HOGG *Microsc.* I. ii. 82 The tripod-stand gives a firm support to the trunnions. 1873 W. S. MAYO *Never Again* xxii, This vessel I shall hang on trunnions, and keep in constant revolution while the glass is in a liquid state. 1895 *Model Steam Engine* 21 In a real engine, the centres on which the cylinders oscillate are called trunnions.

† **c.** *transf.* A pin or peg of wood; a treenail. *Obs. rare.*

1627 CAPT. SMITH *Seaman's Gram.* ii. 4 Those plankes are made fast with good Treenailes and Trunnions of well seasoned timber.

**2.** *attrib.* and *Comb.*, as *trunnion-hole, -joint, -lathe, -piece, -pin*; **trunnion-band**, the band on which the trunnions are fixed; **trunnion-box**, a metal case fixed over the trunnion to prevent the gun leaving the carriage; **trunnion-carriage**, the top carriage of a mortar (Webster, 1911); **trunnion-chain**, a chain for slinging a cannon by the trunnions (ibid.); **trunnion-cradle**, branching arms in certain gun-carriages, in the extremities of which the trunnions play (ibid.); **trunnion-ledge, -level**, a small ledge on the trunnion of a heavy gun, parallel with the axis, as a guide to the elevation or depression of the piece (*Cent. Dict. Suppl.* 1909); **trunnion-plate**, an iron plate on the cheek of a wooden gun-carriage, on which the trunnion plays; also, a strengthening shoulder reinforcing the trunnion (*Cent. Dict.* 1891); **trunnion-ring**, the raised band or moulding encircling a cannon a little in front of the trunnions; **trunnion-rule**, an instrument for determining the distance from the trunnions to the base-ring (*Cent. Dict. Suppl.*); **trunnion-sight**, a front sight placed on the trunnion-band; **trunnion-square**, an instrument for determining whether the trunnions are perpendicular to the axis of the gun; **trunnion-valve**, a steam-valve situated in or attached to the trunnion of an oscillating cylinder.

1812 WELLINGTON in Gurw. *Desp.* (1838) IX. 131 It is recommended by the officers of the artillery that they should be fitted with strong iron *trunnion boxes, to secure the guns. 1795 BURKE *Let. to Ld. Auckland* Wks. IX. p. xxii, Those planks of tough and hardy oak, that used for years to brave the buffets of the Bay of Biscay, are now turned, with their warped grain and empty *trunnion-holes, into very wretched pales. 1859 F. A. GRIFFITHS *Artill. Man.* Plate (1862) 112 Trunnion hole. 1876 ROUTLEDGE *Discov.* 14 The *trunnion joints are easily packed, so that no leakage takes place. 1877 KNIGHT *Dict. Mech.*, **Trunnion-lathe*, a machine-tool for turning off the trunnions of ordnance or oscillating steam-cylinders. 1859 F. A. GRIFFITHS *Artill. Man.* (1862) 190 The *trunnion piece is made from a solid forging, and after being bored and turned, is shrunk in its place on the gun. 1888 HASLUCK *Model Engin. Handybk.* (1900) 27 The upper hole..takes the trunnion or pin on which the cylinder oscillates. Fig. 13 shows this *trunnion pin. 1644 NYE *Gunnery* (1670) 42 The Base-ring, the *Trunnion-ring, or Rings. 1868 *Rep. to Govt. U.S. Munitions War* 81 The Whitworth gun..is manufactured of one material (except the trunnion-ring).

Hence **Tru·nnioned** *a.*, provided with trunnions (Webster, 1864); **Tru·nnionless** *a.*, having no trunnions.

1890 W. J. GORDON *Foundry* 26 A trunnionless gun has a curious crippled look about it.

† **Trunnion,** (?) perversion of TRIN-UNION or TRI-UNION, used as an asseveration or oath.

1577 *Misogonus* IV. ii, Gods trunnion, Alison, go thy wayes and fatch me hether my gose spitt.

**Trunsch(e)our, -owr,** obs. Sc. ff. TRENCHER.

**Truntle, Truont**: see TRUNDLE, TRUANT.

† **Truphane.** *Sc. Obs.* [app. ad. OF. *truf(f)ant* deceiver, f. *truf(f)er*, *trupher* to mock: see TRUFF *v.*, *truf(f)e*, TRUFF *sb.*[1] Or it might directly represent a med.L. **truf(f)ānus*, f. med.L. *truf(f)a*, *trupha* fraud, cheatery (Du Cange): cf. *pagānus*.] A deceiver, an impostor.

? *a* 1500 *Colkelbie Sow* 145 (Bann. MS.) A tyrant, a tormentour, A truphane, and a tratlour.

† **Trupt,** *int. Obs.* An exclamation expressing contempt. Cf. TPROT.

*c* 1380 *Sir Ferumb.* 1872 ȝea, trupt..y set noȝt by þy sawes.

**Trus,** obs. form of TRUSS.

† **Trusatile** (trū·sătil, -təil), *a. Obs. rare.* [ad. L. *trūsātil-is*, f. *trūsāt-*, ppl. stem of *trūsāre* to push strongly, freq. of *trūd-ĕre*: see -ATILE, and cf. *versatile*.] That may be pushed; worked or driven by pushing.

1715 tr. *Pancirollus' Rerum Mem.* II. xxii. 399 Mills, or Versatile, or Trusatile Engines..which were turn'd about either by Men or Beasts.

**Truse, Trush,** obs. forms of TRUCE, TRUSS.

**Trush** (trʌʃ). *local.* Also 7 **thruch,** 8 **truch, thurse, truss, trouss.** [A local form of *turse*, TRUSS *sb.*] A round cushion made of matted flags, for kneeling on in church.

1621 in *Archæol. Cant.* (1902) XXV. 18 She abused Sibil Martin in taking of her trush from her that she sat upon. 1695 KENNETT *Paroch. Antiq.* Gloss., *Basse*,..the round matted cushion of flags used for kneeling [upon] in churches .., in Kent a trush. 1699 *Churchw. Acc. Holy Cross, Canterb.*, Paid for a Thruch for yᵉ Minister, 00. 01. 06. 1709 *Ibid.*, Pd. for twelve Thurses, 00. 09 .00. 1734 *Ibid.*, Paide Tho. Strouts Bill for truches, 0. 12. 0. 1719–21 *Overseers' Acc. Holy Cross, Canterb.*, Pd Goody Arnell for 4 Trusses for har to Chilldren..00.03.09. 1887 *Kent Gloss.* s.v., In the old Churchwardens' Accounts for the parish of Eastry the entry frequently occurs 'To mending the trushes'; and the word is still occasionally used.

† **Trush-trash.** *Obs. rare*[—1]. [A reduplication of TRASH *sb.*[1]; cf. RIFF-RAFF.] = TRISH-TRASH.

1582 STANYHURST *Æneis* IV. (Arb.) 118, I purpose..toe put in fyre brands this Troian pedlerye trush trash.

**Trusion** (trū·ʒən). Now *rare* or *Obs.* [ad. med.L. *trūsiōn-em*, n. of action f. *trūdĕre* to push, thrust. In sense 1 app. short for *intrusion*.]

**1.** *Law.* Illegal entry; = INTRUSION 2.

*a* 1604 HANMER *Chron. Irel.* (1809) 349 It was agreed, that his wife should not be endowed, because that her husband had not entred by the King, but rather by trusion.

**2.** The action of pushing or thrusting.

1656 tr. *Hobbes' Elem. Philos.* (1839) 214 Pulsion;..when the motions of the movent and moved body begin both together..may be called trusion or thrusting and vection. 1678 CUDWORTH *Intell. Syst.* I. v. § 5. 888 As Engines and Machines move, by Trusion or Pulsion. 1729 DESAGULIERS in *Phil. Trans.* XXXVI. 132 If..the Point of Trusion be taken at C.

**Trusle,** obs. form of TRESTLE.

**Truss** (trʌs), *sb.* Forms: 3–8 **trusse,** (4–6 **trosse, trus,** 5 **truse,** *Sc.* **trois**), 9 (in sense 5) **tross,** 7– **truss.** *β. Sc.* 5 **turss,** 5–7 **turs,** 7 **turse, tirrs.** [a. F. *trousse*, OF. also *torse*, *trusse*, *tourse* (12–15th c. in Godef.), Prov. *trossa*, Sp. *troxa*, Pg. *trouxa*; according to Scheler and Hatz.-Darm. vbl. sb. from *trousser* to TRUSS.]

**1.** A collection of things bound together, or packed in a receptacle; a bundle, pack; † in quot. 1577–87 *collect.* baggage. Now chiefly *technical.*

12.. *Ancr. R.* 168 (MS. C.) Noble men & gentile..ne uareð nout itrussed mid trusses [*Cott. Nero* trusseaus], ne mid purses. 1390 GOWER *Conf.* III. 194 The paien rod upon an asse, And of his catell more and lasse With him a riche trusse he ladde. *c* 1400 *Rom. Rose* 4004 Undir his heed no pilowe was, But in the stede a trusse of gras. 1472 *Rental Bk. Cupar-Angus* (1879) I. 162 A turs of fresche ate fodder. 1562 BULLEYN *Bulwark, Dial. Soarnes & Chir.* 46 Knede it with a little Beane meale, and roule theim vp into a trosse. 1577–87 HOLINSHED *Chron.* (1807) II. 342 They spoiled the carriage and trusse of the said barons. 1622 MALYNES *Anc. Law-Merch.* 199 Commodities..packt vp in Bundels, Trusses, Cases, Coffers or Packes. 1712 TICKELL *Spect.* No. 410 ¶ 2 She..devoured a Trusse of Sallet.

*fig.* 1531 ELYOT *Gov.* I. xiv, Lerned men..whiche..haue..perused the great fardelles and trusses of the moste barbarouse autours, stuffed with innumerable gloses. 1878 VILLARI *Machiavelli* (1898) I. 3 The Commune was merely a truss of minor associations, badly bound together.

**b.** *spec.* A bundle of hay or straw; in technical use, of a definite weight, varying at different times and places: see below.

The *truss of hay* is usually a compact mass of hay, approximately cubical, cut from the stack, and tied; now generally, in England, of old hay, 56 lbs.; of new hay, 60 lbs.; *a truss of straw*, 36 lbs.

1483 in *Acta Audit.* (1839) 123*/2 Thre hundreth turss of hay. 1561 in *Reg. Mag. Sig. Scot. 1587* 401/1, 20 laid of cane peitis, ane turs of stray. 1608–9 *Shuttleworths' Acc.* (Chetham Soc.) 180 Towe trusses of haye, ijs. 1609 *Ibid.*, A trusse of strawe, vd. 1688 R. HOLME *Armoury* III. 73/1 A Truss of Hay, as much as can be tied together in an Hay Rope, for a Man to carry on his shoulder. 1727–41 CHAMBERS *Cycl.* s.v., A truss of hay is to contain fifty-six pounds,..thirty-six trusses make a load. In June and August the truss is to weigh sixty pounds. 1846 *J. Baxter's Libr. Pract. Agric.* (ed. 4) II. 63 Result.—On the acre sown with nitrate, 7 sacks 1 bushel of wheat, 50 trusses of straw. On the acre without manure, 6 sacks, 40 trusses of straw. 1862 MISS BRADDON *Lady Audley* x, A waggon laden with trusses of hay. 1866 ROGERS *Agric. & Prices* I. ii. 16 The hay was, as at present, cut into trusses.

† **c.** Applied to a person, in contempt or ridicule. *Obs. rare.*

1585 LUPTON *Thous. Notable Th.* (1675) 270 A Truss, a Rawbon, a Skeleton, a Doudy slut,..blinded by besotting lust, he admires all.

**2.** *Naut.* A tackle by which the centre of the yard was hauled back and secured to the mast; in mod. use extended to an iron fitting, consisting of a ring encircling the mast, with a goose-neck by which the yard is secured. Cf. *truss-parrel, -rope, -tackle* in 8. (The earliest use.)

1296 *Acc. Exch. K. R.* 5/20 m. 5 In vna Corda, et vnum par de Trusses Inuentis in domo Iohannis de Pytingtone. 1336–7 *Acc. Exch. K. R.* 19/31 m. 4 (P.R.O.) In diuersis cordis de Russhewale cum schiuis et Trussis pro vno rakke inde faciendo. *Ibid.* m. 5 In iiijor poleyns emptis ad eandem [galeam] pro trussis..xvj. d. 1420 in *For. Acc.* 3 *Hen. VI*, F/2 *dorso*, j. hauser pro Prialle ropes j. hauser pro trusses. 1582 N. LICHEFIELD tr. *Castanheda's Conq. E. Ind.* 71 Other some vering the trusses. *a* 1625 *Nomenclator Navalis* (Harl. MS. 2301), *Trusses* are Roapes which are made faste to the Parrell of the yardes and are vsed to two vses, one to bind fast the yarde to the Mast when shee rowles either a hull or at an Anchor; the other is to hale downe the Yards in a Storme, or Gust. 1704 J. HARRIS *Lex. Techn.* I, *Trusses*..belong to the Main-yard, Fore-yard and Missen. 1840 R. H. DANA *Bef. Mast* xxvi, Running trusses on the yards. 1841 — *Seaman's Man.* iv. 22 Lower yards are rigged now with iron trusses and quarter-blocks. 1867 SMYTH *Sailor's Word-bk.* s. v., The trusses or parrels of the lower yards serve to bind them to their masts, and are bowsed taut when the yards are trimmed, in order to arrest motion and friction. But the introduction of an iron goose-neck, centering and securing the yard well free of the mast, very much supersedes the use of trusses.

† **3. a.** A close-fitting body-garment or jacket formerly worn by men and women; cf. *trussing-bolster, trussing-coat*, s. v. TRUSSING *vbl. sb.* 3. *Obs.*

1563 FOXE *A. & M.* 1377/2 Mayster Ridley..sayd to his brother: it wer best for me to go in my trusse styll. No (quod his brother), it wyll put you to more payne: and the trusse wil dooe a poore manne good. 1585 HIGINS *Junius' Nomenclator* 164/2 *Strophium*, a womans breast trusse or stomacher. 1591 HARINGTON *Orl. Fur.* XXVI. lviii, She still did weare A slender trusse beneath her womans weed. 1612 DRAYTON *Poly-olb.* xii. 269 Puts off his Palmer's weede vnto his trusse, which bore The staines of ancient Armes.

† **b.** *pl.* Close-fitting breeches or drawers, covering the buttocks and tops of the thighs: = TROUSE[2].

1592 NASHE *P. Penilesse* Wks. (Grosart) II. 31 We..of the vesture of saluation make some of vs Babies and Apes coates, others straight trusses and Diuells breeches. 1598 FLORIO, *Cotigie*, leather hosen, or trusses such as our elders were woont to weare. 1631 SHIRLEY *Schoole Complement* I. i. C iij, *Gasp.* Canst be close? *Gor.* As..a paire of Trusses to an Irish mans buttockes.

**4.** A surgical appliance serving for support in cases of rupture, etc., now usually consisting of a pad with a belt or spring to produce equable pressure on the part.

1543 TRAHERON *Vigo's Chirurg.* (1586) 118 Let the spunge be bounde upon a trusse, made by a good artificer. 1552 HULOET, Trusse for a wrestler, or diseased body, *strigil.* 1580 HOLLYBAND *Treas. Fr. Tong, Vne Trousseure*,..a trusse as such as be broken do vse. 1601 HOLLAND *Pliny* XXVII. vii. II. 277 If wormewood be worne in a trusse to the bottome of the belly, it allayeth the swelling in the share. 1696 *Lond. Gaz.* No. 3227/4 He..wears a Truss, being bursten. 1876 GROSS *Dis. Bladder* 99 Compression of the perineum with a spring truss.

**5.** *Gardening.* A compact cluster or head of flowers growing upon one stalk.

1688 R. HOLME *Armoury* II. 70/2 These Auricula's..bear a great Truss of many flowers. 1859 DARWIN *Orig. Spec.* v. (1860) 145, I have recently observed, in some garden pelargoniums, that the central flower of the truss often loses the patches of darker colour in the two upper petals. 1885 H. O. FORBES *Nat. Wand. E. Archip.* 108 A shrubby species of Cassia bearing large trosses of bright golden flowers.

**6.** *Building*, etc. A framework of timber or iron, or both, so constructed as to form a firm support for a superincumbent weight, as that of a roof or bridge.

1654 in E. B. Jupp *Carpenters' Co.* (1887) 316 When any Chimney..shalbe sett vpon a trusse of timber That it be sett two foote 6 inches from the vpside of the trusse to the vpside of the floore. 1751 LABELYE *Westm. Br.* 87 The Wooden Trusses, or rather Arches under its Roof. 1840 *Civil Eng. & Arch. Jrnl.* III. 125/1 These bridges are built on piers far apart and formed of a truss..of continuous trellis work.

**b.** *Arch.* A projection from the face of a wall, often serving to support a cornice, etc.; a kind of large corbel or modillion.

1519 HORMAN *Vulg.* 241 Make me a trusse (*podium, suggestum, vel pulpitum*) standynge out vpon gargellys that I may se about. 1812 RICKMAN *Archit.* (1862) 11 A truss is a modillion enlarged, and placed flat against a wall, often used to support the cornice of doors and windows. *Ibid.*, A Console is an ornament like a truss carved on a key-stone.

**c.** *Ship-building.* (*a*) See quot. 1823. (*b*) See quot. *c* 1860; also called *truss-piece* (see 8).

1823 CRABB *Technol. Dict.*, *Truss* is also the name of short pieces of carved work fitted under the taffrail, in the same manner as the terms. *c* 1860 H. STUART *Seaman's Catech.* 70 The trusses are diagonal shores crossing each other, and resting against the abutments. 1874 THEARLE *Naval Archit.* 34 Besides these plate riders, a complementary set of diagonal wood internal frames, termed trusses, are fitted between the thick strakes or clamps under the orlop deck beams and the binding strake over the floor heads.

† **7.** Name of some game. Cf. TRUSS-A-FAIL. *Obs. rare*[−1].

1627 W. HAWKINS *Apollo Shroving* v. iv, The waues..play at trusse and at leapfrogge on one anothers backe.

**8.** *attrib.* and *Comb.* Of, pertaining to or constituting a truss, in sense 2, as *truss-line, -pendant, -pulley, -rope, -tackle* (see quots.); in sense 6, as *truss centre, frame, framing, girder, post, rib*; furnished with or supported by a truss or trusses, as *truss-bridge, -roof*; also *truss-maker*; *truss-bound, -galled* adjs.; **truss-band** *Naut.*, one of two iron bands by which an iron truss (sense 2) is fastened to the yard; **truss-beam**, a beam forming part of a truss; also a beam, or iron frame used as a beam, strengthened with a tie-rod or struts, so as to form a truss; † **truss-bed**, ? = *trussing bed* (see TRUSSING *vbl. sb.* 3); **truss-block**, a block between a beam and a tie-rod in a truss, serving to keep them apart (*Cent. Dict.* 1891); **truss-bolt**, a bolt or iron rod forming part of a truss (see quot.); **truss-hoop**, (*a*) *Naut.* (see quot. 1867); (*b*) *Coopering* = *trussing-hoop* (see TRUSSING *vbl. sb.* 3); **truss-parrel** *Naut.*, a parrel encircling a mast, forming part of or connected with a truss (sense 2); **truss-partition** (see quots.); **truss-piece** (see quot.); **truss-plank**, 'in a railway passenger-car, a wide piece of timber fastened on the inside of the car to the posts of the frame directly above the sills' (*Cent. Dict.*); **truss-rod**, a tie-rod forming part of a truss; **truss-work**, work consisting of trusses.

1909 *Cent. Dict. Suppl.* (lettering of figure s.v. *Truss*), *a*, truss; *b, b*, *truss-bands; *c*, truss-parrel. 1877 KNIGHT *Dict. Mech.*, **Truss-beam*, an iron frame serving as a beam, girder, or summer; a wooden beam or frame with a tie-rod to strengthen it against deflection. 1541 *Test. Ebor.* (Surtees) VI. 142 Towe *trusbeddes of the best. 1825 J. NICHOLSON *Operat. Mechanic* 563 Either with one king-bolt in the middle, or with a *truss-bolt at one-third of the length from each end. 1778 [W. MARSHALL] *Minutes Agric.* 16 Jan. an. 1776, To hinder the rats from harbouring in *truss-bound straw, and gnawing the bands. 1840 *Civil Eng. & Arch. Jrnl.* III. 125/2 Wood for small *truss bridges. 1735 J. PRICE *Stone Br. Thames* 7 A fram'd *Truss Center. 1874 THEARLE *Naval Archit.* 34 These *truss frames are the same thickness as the binding strakes, and are placed at an angle of 45 degrees in an opposite direction to the plate riders. 1825 J. NICHOLSON *Operat. Mechanic* 91 A large timber,..which is supported at its ends in the side walls, and has a *truss-framing applied to the back of it, like the framing of a roof. 1679 *Lond. Gaz.* No. 1410/4 A Cart Gelding *truss-gall'd on the sides. 1825 J. NICHOLSON *Operat. Mechanic* 569 When the flooring is to be very stiff and firm, it is necessary to introduce *truss girders. 1867 SMYTH *Sailor's Word-bk.*, **Truss-hoops*, [or] clasp-hoops for masts or spars..are open iron hoops, so made that their ends, being let into each other, may be well fastened by means of iron wedges or forelock keys. 1877 KNIGHT *Dict. Mech.*, *Truss-hoop*, one placed around a barrel to strain the staves into position. 1407 *Acc. Exch. K. R.* 44/11(1) m. 5 *dorso*, ij Bowelynes, ij Stetynges debiles, ij *Truslynes debiles. 1776 *Court & City Reg.* 167/1 *Truss-maker, Alexander Reid. 1824 WATT *Bibl. Brit.*, *Sheldrake, Timothy*..Truss-maker to the East India Company, and the Westminster Hospital. 1411 *Acc. Exch. K. R.* 44/17 m. 2 (P.R.O.) Vn Bowespret, vn Rakke, vn *trusp[ar]aille ..vn Canone de Ferre. 1485 *Naval Acc. Hen. VII* (1896) 39 Maine perells..j, Truss perells..j. 1823 P. NICHOLSON *Pract. Build.* 595 **Truss-partition*, one with a truss, generally consisting of a quadrangular frame, two braces, and two queen-posts, with a straining piece between the queen-posts, opposite the top of the braces. 1856 S. C. BREES *Gloss. Terms*, *Truss-partition*, a partition in which trussing is employed as well as the regular quartering. 1867 SMYTH *Sailor's Word-bk.*, **Truss-pendant*, that part of a rope-truss into which the truss-tackle blocks are seized. **Truss-pieces*, the fillings in between the frame compartments of the riders, in diagonal trussing. 1823 P. NICHOLSON *Pract. Build.* 231 **Truss-post*, any of the posts of a trussed roof. 1357 in *Pipe Roll* 32 *Edw. III*, m. 34/2, j. wyndingrope, j. ȝerderope, ij. *trusspoliues. 1417 in *For. Acc.* 8 *Hen. V*, G/1, j. slynge, iiij Trusse Polleys, j henge pulley. 1735 J. PRICE *Stone Br. Thames* 7, 7 Pair of these *Truss Ribs. 1873 J. RICHARDS *Wood-Working Factories* 8 The *truss rods are generally in the way of the belts,..in nearly all cases it is both better and cheaper to provide strength in the girders without trussing them. 1842–76 GWILT *Encycl. Archit.* Gloss., **Truss Roof*, a roof formed of a tiebeam, principal rafters, king post or queen post, and other necessary timbers to carry the purlins and common rafters, etc. 1336 *Exch. Acc.* 19/31 m. 4 (P.R.O.) Et in xx. petris cordi de canabo..pro duobus *Trusseropes inde faciendis. 1417 in *For. Acc.* 8 *Hen. V*, G/1 De..ij. Prialle ropes debilibus j. Trusse rope. 1569 in *Richmond Wills* (Surtees) 226 Two pare of trusse roips. 1867 SMYTH *Sailor's Word-bk.*, **Truss-tackle*, a gun-tackle purchase applied to the ends of the truss-pendants, to bowse them taut home to the mast. 1884 *Harper's Mag.* Nov. 826/2 A triple-arch roof supported by iron *truss-work.

† **Truss**, *a.* *Obs.* [attrib. use of prec. sb. in similative sense; cf. TRUSSED 1 b.] Of a thick rounded form, like a bundle or parcel; neatly and compactly framed; tight, compact; in quot. *a* 1722, shrunken, shrivelled.

1674 *Lond. Gaz.* No. 909/4 A truss well underlaid Horse. 1699 DAMPIER *Voy.* II. II. 62 The Tigre-Cat is about the bigness of a Bull-Dog, with short Legs, and a truss Body. 1709 *Lond. Gaz.* No. 4608/4 A truss well set Lad, about 16 years of Age. *a* 1722 LISLE *Husb.* (1752) 265, I..observed the cod [of the ox] to be truss. 1825 COBBETT *Rur. Rides* (1830) I. 85 A pretty, little, oldish, smart, truss, nice cockney-looking gentleman.

**Truss** (trʌs), *v.* Forms: 3–7 **trusse**, (3–6 **trosse**, 4–5 **tros(e)**, 4–5 **trus**, (**truse**, 5 **trush**, **trusshe**), 6 **trousse**, **trowse**, 6– **truss.** *β. Sc.* 4–6 **turss**, 5 **twrss**, 6 **turs**, **turse.** Pa. t. and pple. **trussed** (trʌst); also 5–7 **trust**, 6 **truste**; *β. Sc.* 4–6 **tursit**, 5 **-id**, **-ed**, 6 **turst.** [ad. F. *trousser*, in OF. also *trusser* (*Chanson Roland*, 11th c.), *trosser, torser, tourser* 'to trusse, tucke, packe up, to bind or gird up or in' (Cotgr.) = Pr. *trossar* (and med.L. *trossare*), OSp. *trossar*, Sp. *troxar*, Pg. *trouxar* (Diez), of disputed etymology; referred by Diez to the late L. ppl. stem *tort-* or *tors-* of L. *torquēre* to twist. But the sense in the mod. langs. presents difficulties, and other derivations have been conjectured; see Diez, Littré, Scheler, Hatz.-Darm.]

**1.** *trans.* To tie in a bundle, or stow away closely in a receptacle; to bundle, pack. Also with *up*. (With the stuff, or the bundle or receptacle, as obj.) Now *rare* or *Obs.*

*c* 1300 *Havelok* 2017 He wolden..trusse al þat he mihten fynde..in arke or in kiste. 13.. *Gaw. & Gr. Knt.* 1129 Þay ..Tyffen her takles, trussen her males. 1375 BARBOUR *Bruce* XVII. 859 He gert turss his geir. *c* 1386 CHAUCER *Prol.* 681 But hood..wered he noon, For it was trussed vp in his walet. *a* 1450 *Songs & Carols* (Warton Cl.) 43 Fowre and xx good arwys trusyd in a thrumme. *a* 1450 *Brut* 435 The Frensshe men..trussid hir packe and went her wey. *a* 1533 LD. BERNERS *Huon* lii. 173 They shall gyue me bothe gownes and mantelles, so that thou shalt haue myche a do to truss them in my male. 1557 N. T. (Genev.) *Acts* xxi. 15 We trussed vp our fardeles [1611 tooke vp our cariages] and went vp to Ierusalem. 1623 BINGHAM *Xenophon* 69 They trussed vp their baggage, and..marched forth. 1725 DE FOE *Voy. round World* (1840) 119 A bundle of plants, such as he had trussed up together. 1861 *Our Eng. Home* 105 Officers..whose duty it was to..truss the beds in sacks or hides.

**b.** *fig.* (See also TRUSSED 1 b.)

*c* 1394 *P. Pl. Crede* 618 Of þat blissinge..Þei may trussen her part in a terre powȝe! *c* 1425 *Cast. Persev.* 1637 in *Macro Plays* 125 Þat curteys qwene..in here was trussyd þe trinite. 1500–20 DUNBAR *Poems* xiii. 38 Sum in his toung his kyndnes tursis. 1579 E. K. in *Spenser's Sheph. Cal.* Ded., What in most English wryters vseth to be loose, ..in this Authour is well grounded, finely framed, and strongly trussed vp together. 1664 OWEN *Vind. Animad. Fiat Lux* i, Trussing up such a fardel of trifles and quibbles.

† **c.** To charge or burden with a bundle or pack, or a number of such; to load (a pack-horse, etc.); to lade (a ship). *Obs.*

*a* 1225 *Ancr. R.* 166 Noble men & gentile ne bereð nout packes, ne ne uareð nout itrussed mid trusseaus. 13.. *K. Alis.* 850 (Bodl. MS.) Þe..kniȝttes..trusseden her somers And lepen vpon her destrers. *c* 1400 *Destr. Troy* 12313 Tho shippes to shilde o þe shyre whaghes,..And tyrn hom to takle, & trusse for the sea. *a* 1533 LD. BERNERS *Huon* cxxx. 478 They..trussyd & wene wyttelyd theyr shyppes. 1570 LEVINS *Manip.* 193/28 To Trusse, *sarcinare.*

**d.** *Naut.* To furl (a sail). Also *absol.* (? *Obs.*)

*a* 1400 *Morte Arth.* 3655 The marynerse..Of theire termys they talke, how thay ware tydd, Towyne trvsselle one trete, trvssene vpe sailes. *c* 1400 [see TRUSSING *vbl. sb.* 1]. *c* 1515 *Cocke Lorell's B.* (Percy Soc.) 12 Some wounde at ye capstayne,..some dyde trusse and thrynge. 1594 GREENE & LODGE *Looking Gl.* G.'s Wks. (Rtldg.) 134 Our topsails up, we truss our spritsails in. 1867 SMYTH *Sailor's Word-bk.*, *Brails*, ropes..fastened to the outermost leech of the sail, in different places, to truss it close up as occasion requires. *Ibid.*, *Truss up*, *to*, to brail up a sail suddenly; to toss up a bunt.

† **e.** *trans.* and *intr.* To become shrunken and compact; cf. TRUSS *a.*, TRUSSED 1 b. *Obs. rare.*

1552 Huloet, Trusse vp as a cow or like best doth of milke, *subducere lac.* *Ibid.*, Trused vp as a bitch, or cow is of milke, *subductus.* Trussed vp, to be, of milche, *subducor.* 1693 [see Trussed *ppl. a.* 1 b].

†2. To pack up and carry away; to convey or take with one in a pack; to carry off. (In later use only *Sc.*) *Obs.*

*a* 1300 *Cursor M.* 4911 Ne haue we wit us trussed noght, Bot thing þat we ha lele boght. *c* 1400 Maundev. (Roxb.) viii. 30 Þam behoues also trusse þaire vitailles with þam thurgh þe forsaid desertes. 1422 tr. *Secreta Secret., Priv. Priv.* 162 Hare golde, Syluyr, armure, and Iowell with ham thay tursid. 1535 Stewart *Cron. Scot.* (Rolls) II. 342 Tha left na gude that tha mycht turs awa. 1567 *Gude & Godlie B.* (S.T.S.) 195 Preistis, keip no gold..Nor ȝit twa coittis with ȝow turs.

†3. *intr.* or *absol.* To pack up one's clothes, etc. in readiness for a journey: = Pack *v.*[1] 2 c. Also *fig.* *Obs.*

1297 R. Glouc. (Rolls) 9978 Vaste he [King Philip] let trossi, to france uor to drawe. *c* 1375 *Cursor M.* 21115 (Fairf.) Þai bad him trusse & make him boun. 1470–85 Malory *Arthur* xx. xviii. 829 They trussed and payd alle that wold aske hem, and holy an honderd knyghtes departed with sir launcelot. 1696–7 Evelyn *Let. to Bohun* 18 Jan., And so you have the history of a very old man... I..am now every day trussing up to be gon.

†4. *intr.* To take oneself off, be off, go away, depart: = Pack *v.*[1] 10 b; sometimes simply to go.

1362 Langl. *P. Pl.* A. ii. 194 Lyȝere..nas nouȝwher welcome..Bote ouur al i-hunted and hote to trusse. *c* 1440 *York Myst.* xxiii. 151 A! lord, late vs no forther trus. *c* 1518 Skelton *Magnyf.* 1774 As for all other, let them trusse and packe. 1592 Babington *Notes on Gen.* xii. § 10 She trusseth vp and away with him whither God should appoint. 1721 Ramsay *Richy & Sandy* 73 Let us truse and hame o'er bend.

†b. *refl.* in same sense: = Pack *v.* 10 a. *Obs.*

*a* 1400–50 *Alexander* 1143 And þen he trussys hym to tyre & þar hys tentes settes. *c* 1400 *Sowdone Bab.* 1707 Trusse the forth eke. *c* 1440 *Partonope* 3692 Therto eche man trusse hym home.

†c. *trans.* To 'send packing', drive off, put to flight. *Obs. rare.*

*c* 1475 *Partenay* 2154 The Brehaignons went out thaim Faste trussing [F. *destruisant*]. 1596 Dalrymple tr. *Leslie's Hist. Scot.* ix. (S.T.S.) II. 183 Al scotis..suld be turssed away to Scotland.

5. *trans.* To make fast to something with or as with a cord, band, or the like; to bind, tie, fasten; †also, to put on, gird on (clothing, etc.): cf. 6. Now *rare.*

*a* 1225 *Ancr. R.* 322 Ich chulle..trussen al þi schendfulnesse o þine owune necke. 13.. *K. Alis.* 5477 (Bodl. MS.) Þe kyng..dooþ on a Borel of a squyer,..And trusseþ a male hym bihynde. *c* 1400 *Destr. Troy* 5293 Teutra the true kyng was trust on a litter. 1575 R. B. *Appius & Virg.* E ij b, Goe trusse him to a tree. 1646 H. Lawrence *Comm. Angells* 113 They would..let him trusse on their armour. 1698 Fryer *Acc. E. India & P.* 20 Only a Clout..trust with a String about their Waists. 1813 Scott *Rokeby* v. xxxvi, Round his left arm his mantle truss'd, Received and foiled three lances' thrust.

b. *spec.* To tie the 'points' or laces with which the hose were fastened to the doublet. (With the hose, the points, or the person as obj.) Cf. 6. *Obs.* exc. *Hist.*

*c* 1460 J. Russell *Bk. Nurture* 898 Strike his hosyn vppewarde his legge..Þen trusse ye them vp strayte. *c* 1530 H. Rhodes *Bk. Nurture* in *Babees Bk.* (1868) 70 Help to araye him, trusse his poyntes, stryke vp his Hosen. 1598 B. Jonson *Ev. Man in Hum.* i. iii, *Steph.* Helpe to trusse me...He dos so vexe me—. *Bray.* You'll be worse vex'd, when you are truss'd...Best keepe vn-brac'd. 1632 Massinger *Maid of Hon.* i. i, In the time of trussing a point, he can undo Or make a man. 1822 Scott *Nigel* xvii, Let me have the honour of trussing you. Now, observe, I have left several of the points untied of set purpose. 1856 Doran *Knights & Days* ix. 139 Guy trussed his points, pulled up his hose.

6. To confine or enclose (the body, or some part of it) by something fastened closely round; to bind or tie up; to gird; to fasten up (the hair) with ribbon, pins, combs, etc.; to adjust and draw close the garments of (a person); hence contemptuously in reference to dress. Also with *up.* (Cf. 5 b.) ? *Obs.*

1340 [see Trussing *vbl. sb.* 1]. *c* 1440 *Promp. Parv.* 504/2 Trussyn, and byndyn, as menn done soore lymys, *fascio.* 1560 Bible (Genev.) *Jer.* i. 17 Trusse vp thy loynes. 1610 G. Fletcher *Christ's Vict.* i. lxv, Now she would sighing sit, ..in sack cloth trust. 1712 Budgell *Spect.* No. 277 ¶ 7 How ridiculously..we have all been trussed up..and how infinitely the French Dress excels ours. 1736 Ainsworth *Lat. Dict.* (1783) i, To truss up the hair of one's head, *caesariem, vel comam, in nodum colligere.* 1833 J. Holland *Manuf. Metal* II. 32 The combs used by the lower class of females for trussing their hair.

†b. To insert closely, to tuck. *Obs.*

1523 Ld. Berners *Froiss.* I. xvii. 18 Bitwene the saddyll and the pannell, they trusse a brode plate of metall. *a* 1550 in *Archæologia* IV. 313 To trusse the endes of the said sheete under every end of the bolster. 1638 Guillim *Heraldry* iii. xx. (ed. 3) 231 Fowles having long shankes doe (in their flight) stretch forth their legges..; but such as are short legged doe trusse their feet to the middest of their bodies. 1651 tr. *De-las-Coveras' Don Fenise* 114 This woman..trussing up her garment turned her legs into wings and fled.

7. To fasten up on a gallows or cross, to hang as a criminal; to 'string up'. (Chiefly with *up*) *arch.*

1536 *Remedy Sedition* B iij b, He was forthwith truste vppe. 1600 Holland *Livy* xxviii. xxxvii. 696 He commanded them to be roundly trussed up and crucified [*cruci affigi*]. 1618 Bolton *Florus* iii. xix. (1636) 234 He bound the remaynes of those strong theeves in chaines..and trussed them on gallowses. *a* 1721 Prior *Vicar of Bray & Sir T. Moor* 426 To be trussed up..as a Traytor. 1818 Scott *Hrt. Midl.* xxiii, If they must truss me, I will repent of nothing so much..as of the injury I have done my Lily. 1882 Stevenson *Fam. Stud. Men & Bks.*, *Villon* (1905) 162 How or when he died, whether decently in bed or trussed up to a gallows, remains a riddle.

†b. *intr.* for *pass.* To be hanged: cf. *to hang.*

1592 *Arden of Feversham* iii. vi, If thou beest tainted.. And come in question, surely, thou wilt trusse. 1601 F. Godwin *Bps. of Eng.* 275 The halter was..about the yoong mans necke and he euen ready to trusse.

8. To fasten the wings or legs of (a fowl or other animal) to the body with skewers or otherwise, in preparation for cooking.

[*c* 1450 *Two Cookery-bks.* 81 Take a kydde..fle him, and larde him, and trusse his legges in þe sides, and roste him.] 1704 Swift *Batt. Bks.* Misc. (1711) 266 As when a skilful Cook has truss'd a Brace of Woodcocks. 1796 Mrs. Glasse *Cookery* v. 90 Take a fat pig,..slit and truss him up like a lamb. 1846 *J. Baxter's Libr. Pract. Agric.* II. 221 The Higgler's method of Killing, Picking, and Trussing Fowls.

b. *transf.*

1899 *Allbutt's Syst. Med.* VIII. 9 The patient must.. make the shoulder blades meet by trussing back the elbows.

9 Of a bird of prey: To seize or clutch (the prey) in its talons; *spec.* to seize (the quarry) in the air and carry it off. *arch.* (and *Her.*) Also *fig.*

1567 Golding *Ovid's Met.* vi. (1593) 144 As when the scarefull erne With hooked talents trussing up a hare among the ferne, Hath laid her in his nest. 1575 Turberv. *Falconrie* 50 If shee strike hir or stoupe hir or trusse hir then suffer hir to kill it. 1590 Spenser *F. Q.* i. xi. 19 As hagard hauke.. His wearie pounces all in vaine doth spend To trusse the pray too heavy for his flight. 1649 G. Daniel *Trinarch., Hen. IV* ccxxxiv, A young Eagle..rather Chus'd..at Armed Cranes to flye; Or trusse a farr-seen Swan. 1667 Dryden *Maiden Queen* iii. i, So—at last he has truss'd his Quarry. 1742 Somerville *Field Sports* 210 The vigorous hawk.. Truss'd in mid-air bears down her captive prey. 1864 Boutell *Her. Hist. & Pop.* xvii. § 2 (ed. 3) 274 A cormorant trussing a fish all ppr. 1867 J. B. Rose tr. *Virgil's Æneid* 266 So stoops the bird of Jove..To truss the snowy swan or dusky hare. 1883 Harting *Perf. Bk. Kepinge Sparhawkes* Gloss. 49 *Truss*, to clutch the quarry in the air instead of striking it to the ground. 1910 Radcliffe in *Encycl. Brit.* X. 143/1 A hawk is said to 'truss' a bird when she catches it in the air, and comes to the ground with it in her talons.

*transf.* 1470–85 Malory *Arthur* xiv. vi. 649 The lyon took his lytel whelp and trussed hym, and bare hym there he came fro. 1855 Browning *Fra Lippo* 88 The wind doubled me up, and down I went. Old Aunt Lapaccia trussed me with one hand.

10. To tighten up (a bell) on its stock after it has worked loose. ? *Obs.*

1468–1540 [see Trussing *vbl. sb.* 1]. 1545 *Churchw. Acc. St. Dunstan's, Canterb.*, For yerone [iron] worke to trowse the bellys xij d. 1622–3 in Swayne *Sarum Churchw. Acc.* (1896) 175 For newe Trussinge the 2 3 4 and 5 bells, 5 s.

11. To compress the staves of (a cask) into the required shape and position by means of a *trussing-hoop* (see Trussing *vbl. sb.* 3).

1535 Coverdale *Jer.* xlviii. 12, I shall sende hir trussers to trusse her vp, to prepare and season hir vessels. 1688 R. Holme *Armoury* iii. 108/1 Trussing a Barrel, is putting it together from Boards or Staves within a Hoop. 1883 *Fisheries Exhib. Catal.* 83 Apparatus for heating casks before being trussed.

12. *Building*, etc. a. *Truss over*: see quot. ? *Obs.*

1703 T. N. *City & C. Purchaser* 109 Instead of Arching, they truss-over, or over-span, as they phrase it, i.e. they lay the end of one Brick about half way over the end of another, and so, till both sides meet within half a Bricks length, and then a bonding Brick at the top finishes the Arch. *Ibid.* 198 A kind of Bench,..upon which they lay the largest Stones, and so truss them over,..after the manner of Clamps for Bricks.

b. To support or strengthen with a Truss (*sb.* 6).

1823 [see Trussing *vbl. sb.* 1]. 1847 Smeaton *Builder's Man.* 77 It is not necessary to truss all the rafters in a roof. 1889 *Daily News* 15 July 6/3 This new safety ladder, securely trussed on springs and wheels.

†**Truss-a-fail.** *Obs. rare*⁻¹. App. the name of some game. Cf. Truss *sb.* 7.

*a* 1658 Cleveland *Model New Relig.* 9 Or do the Iuncto leap at truss-a-fail?

†**Tru·ssage.** *Obs.* Also 6 **troussage**, (**trosache**). [a. OF. *troussage* (14th c. in Godef.), f. F. *trousser* to Truss: see -age.] Articles 'trussed' or packed up, collectively; baggage; *spec.* booty carried off. Also *attrib.*

*c* 1500 *Melusine* xxi. 132 Who that myght flee, fledd toward theire folke that lede theyre proye, oxen, kyn & shep, swynes & othre troussage [orig. *troussages*]. 1527 *Acc. R. Gibson* in *Lett. & Pap. Hen. VIII* § 45 lf. 23 (P.R.O.), For trosache kasis. *a* 1548 Hall *Chron., Hen. VIII* 119 b, The Frenchmen were readye to depart with trussages and cariages.

**Trusse**, obs. form of Truce, Truss.

**Trussed** (trɒst), *ppl. a.* [f. Truss *v.* + -ed[1].]

1. Packed, tied up, etc. (see the vb.); in quot. 1904, with 'points' trussed (Truss *v.* 5 b). †*Trussed bed, bedstead*: cf. *trussing bed*, etc. (Trussing *vbl. sb.* 3).

*c* 1440 *Promp. Parv.* 504/1 Trussyd, of fardel,..*fardellatus, sarcinatus.* Trussyd vp, and bowndyn,..*fasciatus.* 1530 *Test. Ebor.* (Surtees) V. 297 A trust bed with a fedder bed. ? 1537 *Rutland MSS.* (1905) IV. 279 A truste bedsted for my Lord to cary to the Court, vij *s.* 1552 Huloet, Trussed, *suffarcinatus*...Trussed, beaten, layed, or stopped hard together, *stipatus.* 1578 Lyte *Dodoens* v. lxxx. 650 Clusters of many berries.. thicke set and trussed togither. 1890 Doyle *White Company* iii, His robe was much too long and loose..so that even with trussed-up skirts he could make little progress. 1904 M. Hewlett *Queen's Quair* i. vi, The Queen and her maids braved it as saucy young men, trunked, puffed, pointed, trussed and doubleted.

b. *fig.* Knit together, compactly framed or formed. (Usually const. as *pa. pple.*, often with *well* or other adv.) ? *Obs.*

1548 Elyot, *Compactilis*, that is well compacted and trussed togither, shorte and rounde. 1676 *Lond. Gaz.* No. 1080/4 A bay Nag,..short necked, well trussed. 1693 *Ibid.* No. 2916/4 She has lately had Puppies, and is not yet fully Truss'd.

c. *Cookery.* Of a fowl, etc.: see Truss *v.* 8. Also in *Her.*: see quot. *c* 1828.

1828 Scott *F. M. Perth* viii, 'It's all here', said the little man, expanding his breast like a trussed fowl. *c* 1828 Berry *Encycl. Her.* I. Gloss., *Trussed*, Close, or Complicated, are terms unnecessarily introduced into blazon when birds are borne with their wings closed to the body; which is ever implied when the contrary is not expressed. 1900 Mrs. Glyn *Visits Eliz.* (1906) 59 He does look like a trussed pigeon.

2. *Building*, etc. Furnished, supported, or strengthened with a truss or trusses.

1840 H. Spencer *Autobiog.* (1904) I. xi. 164 Experiments on trussed beams. 1853 Sir H. Douglas *Milit. Bridges* vii. (ed. 3) 307 On trussed and suspension bridges. 1873 Medley *Autumn Tour U. S. & Canada* ix. 146 Trussed girders are preferred [in bridge-building].

**Trussel, -ell**, obs. forms of Trestle.

†**Trussell.** *Obs.* Also 5 **trusselle**, 5–9 **trussel**; *Sc.* 6 **tursall**, 6–7 **tursell**. [a. OF. *troussel*, earlier *torsel*, *toursel*, mod.F. *trousseau*, dim. of *trousse*, vbl. sb. of *trousser*: see Truss.]

1. A bundle, package; in quot. *a* 1400, a furled sail. Cf. Trousseau.

? *a* 1400 [see Truss *v.* 1 d]. 1426 Lydg. *De Guil. Pilgr.* 2755 And at the gate for to se Trussellys, ffardellys, in that place. Or any marchaunt in may passe, He mvste vntrusse hem & vnbynde. *c* 1460 *Towneley Myst.* ii. 170 Lay downe thi trussell apon this hill.

2. The puncheon for making the impress on the upper side of the coin; cf. Pile *sb.*[4] 1.

[1300: see Pile *sb.*[4] 1.] 1473 *Chancery Enrolments, Durham* 3/49 m. 6 (P.R.O.) We..haue..licencid oure welbelouyd William Omorighe..to make graue and prynte ij dosene Trussellys and j dosene Standerdys for penys and iiij Standerdys and viij Trussellys for half penys. 1484 *Chancery Warr.* Ser. i. File 1531. No. 5767 (P.R.O.) Receptis..tribus standardis et novem trussellis ruptis..tria standarda et novem trussellos de novo fieri..faciatis. 1562–3–1605 [see Pile *sb.*[4] 1, Puncheon[1] 3]. 1611 Cotgr., *Trousseau*, a Trussell; the vpper yron, or mould, thats vsed in the stamping of coyne. 1817 Ruding *Ann. Coinage* I. 67, III. 24. 1876 Cochran-Patrick *Rec. Coinage Scotl.* I. Introd. 49 The 'flan' being placed on the 'pile', the 'trussell' was applied to the upper side of it by means of a twisted wand, or by the hand, and the moneyer then struck the end of the puncheon with the hammer until the impression was produced on the 'flan'.

**Trusser** (trɒ·səɹ). [f. Truss *v.* + -er[1].]

†1. A receptacle or appliance in or with which something is 'trussed'; a bundle, package; a bandage. *Obs.*

1519 Horman *Vulg.* 30 The bounche or botche.. can vnneth be bounde vp with a trussar. *a* 1548 Hall *Chron., Hen. VIII* 17 Byndyng of males and fardelles, trussyng of coffers and trussers.

2. One who or that which trusses, in various senses: see the verb. *spec.* a. One who trusses a cask. 1535 [see Truss *v.* 11].

b. A person employed in, or a machine for, trussing hay or straw.

1889 *Engineer* LXVII. 292 Hay and straw trussers. 1890 *Univ. Exhib. Guide* June 29/2 The Straw Trusser..was shown at work attached to the Steam Thrashing Machine. 1892 T. B. F. Eminson *Epidemic Pneumonia at Scotter* 49 The trussers..were engaged trussing the hay for sale.

c. A person employed in trussing poultry, etc.

1903 *Daily Chron.* 16 Sept. 8/6 Poultry.—Wanted a trusser for best-class work. 1906 *Daily News* 14 Dec. 7 The removal of this favourite bone by the trusser.

3. A plant that produces trusses of blossom: usually with qualifying adj. expressing the quality of the trusses.

1843 *Florist's Jrnl.* (1846) IV. 153 The flowers are extra-sized, and it is a very fine trusser. 1882 *Garden* 11 Mar. 160/3 This..red good Polyanthus..is a noble trusser.

†**Tru·ssery.** *Obs. rare*⁻¹. [f. Truss *sb.* + -ery.] Things 'trussed' or packed, baggage.

*a* 1548 Hall *Chron., Hen. VIII* 65 A great numbre of rascal & pedlers, & Iuellers..brought ouer..diuerse merchandise vncustomed, all vnder the coloure of the trussery of the Ambassadours.

**Trussing** (trɒ·siŋ), *vbl. sb.* [f. Truss *v.* + -ing[1].]

1. The action of the verb Truss, in various senses.

1340 *Ayenb.* 176 Ynoȝ þer is of ydelnesse aboute hire heaued, to kembe, to wesse, ine trossinge. *c* 1400 *Destr. Troy* 4653 All turnyt þaire tacle with trussyng of sailes. 1468–9 in Swayne *Sarum Churchw. Acc.* (1896) 11 Pro le trussyng magne campane ad thascum x d. 1540 *Churchw. Acc. St. Giles, Reading* 59 For trussing of the greate bell. 1615 Latham *Falconry* (1633) Explan. Words, *Trussing* is when a Hawke raiseth a fowle aloft, and so descendeth downe with it to the ground. 1670 Eachard *Cont. Clergy* 75 Let your loins be girded...There must be a holy girding and trussing up for heaven. 1694 R. L'Estrange *Fables* clxxvii.

(1714) 190 The Trussing up of Thieves is the Security of Honest Men. **1823** P. Nicholson *Pract. Builder* 124 To frame timbers, so that their external surfaces shall keep this position, is the business of trussing. **1852** Mrs. Stowe *Uncle Tom's C.* iv, Not a chicken, or turkey, or duck..but looked grave when they saw her approaching,..she was always meditating on trussing, stuffing, and roasting.

**2.** *concr.* The timber or other material forming a truss (Truss *sb.* 6); a work or structure consisting of trusses.

**1840** *Civil Eng. & Arch. Jrnl.* III. 43/1 A plan of the trussed foot-bridge..exhibiting the trussing and cast iron frames. **1890** W. J. Gordon *Foundry* 48 A platform of temporary girders..strengthened by supplementary trussing.

**3.** *attrib.* Adapted or used for 'trussing', packing, or tying up (*obs.* exc. *Hist.*), as *trussing chest, coffer, gear, mail, -needle, point, -thread*; adapted for being 'trussed' or packed up for 'travelling' (*obs.* exc. *Hist.*), as *trussing bed, bedstead, chalice*; used for trussing (in various senses of the verb), as (sense 1 d) *trussing-rope*, (sense 10) *-key, -nail*, (sense 11) *-hoop, -machine*, (sense 12 b) *-bar, -bolt, -piece, -rod*; also †**trussing-bolster**: see quot., and cf. Truss *sb.* 3 a; †**trussing-coat**, a padded jacket worn under armour.

**1843** *Penny Cycl.* XXV. 318/2 So long as it [the beam] retains this curvature the weight laid upon it must eventually press upon the *trussing-bars. **1398** *Will John of Gaunt* in Armitage Smith *Life* (1904) 426 Lits faitz pur mon corps, appelles en Engleterre *trussyng beddes. **1482** Marg. Paston in *P. Lett.* III. 286 A litel white bedde..for a trussyng bedde. **1572** in Whitaker *Hist. Craven* (1812) 327 One trussing bedd for the field. **1861** *Our Eng. Home* 105 Portable beds were often called 'trussing' beds. **1534** *Inv. Wardr. Kath. Arragon* in *Camden Misc.* (1855) 34 A lytille *trussinge bedsteede..withe two lether cases to trusse it in. **1910** E. R. Suffling *Eng. Ch. Brasses* 110 *Trussing-Bolster, a padded belt for equalising and taking the weight of the heavy cuirass. **1843** *Penny Cycl.* XXV. 319/2 Through these eyes were passed vertical bars or *trussing-bolts. **1440** in Peacock *Eng. Ch. Furniture* (1866) 182 My *trushing challis and my highest guilt chalis. **1540** *Act 32 Hen. VIII* c. 14 Item for a *trussyng cheste ii. s. *a* **1562** Cavendish *Wolsey* (1893) 257 Syttyng uppon a trussyng chest. **1884** *Leisure Hour* Apr. 233/1 Large trunks, used for general packing..were called trussing-chests. **1493** *Will of W. Oseney* (Somerset Ho.), A *trussing coat. **1387** Trevisa *Higden* (Rolls) VII. 385 His malys..his bouges and his *trussynge cofres. **1485** in *Ripon Ch. Acts* (Surtees) 368, ij trussyng coffers 3s...unum magnum trussyng mayle precii 2s. **1466** *Mann. & Househ. Exp.* (Roxb.) 367, I payd fore viij. heles [= ells] of kanas for *trosenge gere, xx.d. **1688** R. Holme *Armoury* III. 108/1 *Trussing Hoop, is a large strong Hoop..first put about the Barrel staves to draw them to their compass. **1621–2** in Swayne *Sarum Churchw. Acc.* (1896) 172, ix *trussinge keyes. **1877** Knight *Dict. Mech.*, **Trussing-machine*, one for drawing the truss-hoops upon casks. **1883** *Fisheries Exhib. Catal.* 83 Trussing machine and accumulator. **1485** *Trussyng mayle [see *trussing coffer* above]. **1621–2** in Swayne *Sarum Churchw. Acc.* (1896) 172 One Hundred of *Trussinge nayles 10d. **1846** Soyer *Cookery* 149 To try when done run a *trussing needle into them. **1823** P. Nicholson *Pract. Builder* 595 **Trussing-pieces*, such timbers in a roof as are in a state of compression. **1548** Elyot, *Strigmentum* ..it maie be vsed for a *trussyng pointe. **1843** *Penny Cycl.* XXV. 319/1 A formula for calculating the size of the iron *trussing-rods. **1420** in *For. Acc.* 3 *Hen. VI*, G/2 *dorso*, j haunser pro *trussynge rope. **1369–72** *Exch. Acc. K. R.* Bundle 178 No. 16 m. 4 (P.R.O.), lxiiij lb. fili pro cordis balistarum, lij lb. *trussyngthred, lj lb. di. trenchefyll.

† **Tru·ssure.** *Obs.* [a. OF. *trusseure* (Cotgr. *troussure, -eure*), med.L. **trossātūra*, f. *trossare* to Truss: see -ure.] ? = Truss *sb.* 2.

**1295** *Acc. Exch. K. R.* 5/8 m. 13 (P. R. O.) In j ancora et .j. Cable emptis de Hugone Kelinge. Et xxij. s. in Trussurs, Girdelinges [etc.] emptis de eodem.

**Trust** (trʌst), *sb.* Forms: *α.* 3–6 truste, 3– trust; *β.* 4–7 trost, 5 troste. See also Traist *sb.*, Trest *sb.*[1], Trist *sb.*[1] [Early ME. *trost(e, truste*, ad. ON. *traust* sb. neut.: see Trust *a.*]

**1.** Confidence in or reliance on some quality or attribute of a person or thing, or the truth of a statement. Const. *in* († *of, on, upon, to, unto*).

*α. a* **1225** *Ancr. R.* 274 Me haueð truste to Godes helpe þet euer is neih bute ȝif bileaue trukie. *a* **1240** *Ureisun* in *Cott. Hom.* 187 As mi trust is þer to hit beo mi lechunge. **13..** *Guy Warw.* (A.) 7242 He a lappe rent out anon Of his brini, þat alle his trust was on. **1484** Caxton *Fables of Auian* i, He is wel a fole that setteth his hope and truste in a woman. **1505** in *Mem. Hen. VII* (Rolls) 275 Don Fernando of Aragon hathe no confidens nor trust unto the Kynge of Romaynes. **1605** Stow *Ann.* 671 A staffe of reede, of the which there is no trust. **1611** Shaks. *Wint. T.* iv. iv. 607 Ha, ha, what a Foole Honestie is! and Trust (his sworne brother) a very simple Gentleman. **1729** Butler *Serm.* Wks. 1874 II. 189 To see and know and feel that our trust was not vain. **1823** Scott *Quentin D.* xiii, The honour and trust which were about to be reposed in him. **1860** Tyndall *Glac.* i. xix. 134 We had..to get round overhanging ledges, where our main trust was in our feet.

*β.* **1382** Wyclif *Prov.* iii. 5 Haue trost in the Lord, of al thin herte. — *Isa.* xxxi. 1 Hauende trost [1388 trist] vpon foure horsid carres. *c* **1440** *Promp. Parv.* 503/1 Troste, *confidencia, fiducia.* **1648** *Hamilton Papers* (Camden) 228 The trost reposid in me bi your Lordshipe.

**b.** *Take on* or *upon trust* († *receive, take up in trust, take up upon trust*), to accept or give credit to without investigation or evidence.

**1641** *Nicholas Papers* (Camden) 4 Being constrayned to take upp all my intelligence concerning Parliament affaires upon trust..from others. *c* **1645** Howell *Lett.* (1650) I. 67 Ey-witnesses of those things which other receive but in trust. *Ibid.* II. *The Vote* I ij b, Scribling Pamphletors..thrust Lame things upon the world, t'ane up in trust. **1662** Stillingfl. *Orig. Sacræ* i. iv. § 5 The story was taken upon trust by Herodotus, Pliny, and many others. **1797** Godwin *Enquirer* i. vi. 36 Active spirits..take..little upon trust. **1824** *Examiner* 353/1 That numerous body who take things on trust. **1869** J. Martineau *Ess.* II. 98 Take what is set before him on trust.

**c.** *transf.* with possessive: That in which one's confidence is put; an object of trust.

**1526** *Pilgr. Perf.* (W. de W. 1531) 8 b, Let hym be all your trust. **1560** Bible (Genev.) *Ps.* xl. 4 Blessed is the man, that maketh the Lord his trust. **1866** Bryant *Death Abraham Lincoln* i, The sword of power, a nation's trust.

**2.** Confident expectation of something; hope.

[*c* **1200**: see Trist *sb.*[1]] *c* **1400** *Destr. Troy* 8689 Þai had no hope of þere heale..all hor trust þan was tynt. **1523** Ld. Berners *Froiss.* I. xviii. 22 They were all the weeke, without heryng of any worde of the scottis, vpon trust they shulde repasse agayn..the same way. *a* **1548** Hall *Chron., Hen. IV* 28 This prince was sent thither, in trust of sauegard, in hope of refuge, and in trust of aide and comfort against his euill willers. **1667** Milton *P. L.* ii. 46 His trust was with th' Eternal to be deem'd Equal in strength. **1864** J. Martineau *Ess., Addr.*, etc. (1891) IV. 563 The trusts of eighteen centuries and the sighs and hopes of more.

**3.** Confidence in the ability and intention of a buyer to pay at a future time for goods supplied without present payment: = Credit *sb.* 9 a. Chiefly in phrases *on, upon,* † *of trust.*

**1573** Tusser *Husb.* (1878) 134 At first hand he buieth that paieth all doune..At third hand he buieth that buieth of trust. **1649** Bp. Hall *Cases Consc.* (1650) 26 Those who are able to pay downe ready money..know to expect a better pennyworth, then those that runne upon trust. **1681** in *New Mills Cloth Manuf.* (S.H.S.) Introd. 85 Cloath will be..delivered out to the merchants and after 12 moneths trust they will be paying [etc.]. **1758** Johnson *Idler* No. 26 ⁋ 8 My master lived on trust at an ale-house. **1829** Cobbett *Adv. Yng. Man* ii. 63 The man therefore who purchases on trust not only pays for the trust, but he also pays his due share of what the tradesman loses by trust.

*fig.* **1821** Byron *Sardan.* ii. i. 596, I am content To be beloved on trust for what I feel. **1865** Ruskin *Sesame* i. § 1, I had even intended to ask your attention for a little while on trust..until [etc.].

**4.** The quality of being trustworthy; fidelity, reliability; loyalty, trustiness. Now *rare.*

**1470–85** Malory *Arthur* xxi. v. 850 Comfort thyself..and doo as wel as thou mayst, for in me is no truste for to truste in. *c* **1489** Caxton *Sonnes of Aymon* vii. 166 There ys noo truste in hym And therfore I wyll kepe me from hym. **1590** Marlowe *Edw. II*, iii. ii, Our friend Levune, faithful and full of trust. **1592** Shaks. *Rom. & Jul.* iii. ii. 85 There's no trust, no faith, no honestie in men. **1620** May *Heir* iii. (1622) D iv, Well I beleeue thee wench, and will reward Thy trust in this. **1695** Prior *Ode Queen's Death* iv, Fair Albion shall, with faithful Trust, Her holy Queen's sad Reliques guard. **1821** Byron *Mar. Fal.* ii. i, You have done well.—I thank you for that trust.

**5. a.** The condition of having confidence reposed in one, or of being entrusted *with* something; esp. in the phrases *in trust, to* one's *trust, under trust.*

*a* **1548** Hall *Chron., Edw. V* 11, I dare putte no persone earthely in truste with his kepyng, but my selfe onely. **1577** Hanmer *Anc. Eccl. Hist., Socrates* i. xxvi, He putteth the priest..in trust with his testament. **1609** Skene *Reg. Maj.* ii. 131 Murther..of our Soveraine Lords lieges, quhere the persone slaine is vnder the trust, credit, assurance, and power of the slayer, is treason and lese majestie. [*Margin*] Slauchter vnder trust. **1611** Bible 1 *Thess.* ii. 4 As we were allowed of God to bee put in trust with the Gospel. — 1 *Tim.* vi. 20 O Timothie, keepe that which is committed to thy trust. **1675** tr. *Camden's Hist. Eliz.* ii. (1688) 174 Such Letters I should never have committed to Barker's Trust. **1817** W. Selwyn *Law Nisi Prius* (ed. 4) II. 821 A devisee or executor in trust, who has acted, may be examined as a witness in support of the will. **1818** Scott *Br. Lamm.* xvii, The celebrated case of Sir Coolie Condiddle of Condiddle, who was tried for theft under trust.

**b.** The obligation or responsibility imposed on one in whom confidence is placed or authority is vested, or who has given an undertaking of fidelity.

**1535** Coverdale *Micah* vii. 20 Thou shalt kepe thy trust with Iacob, and thy mercy for Abraham, like as thou hast sworne vnto oure fathers longe agoo. *a* **1548** Hall *Chron., Rich. III* 27 The man..beynge hindered and kepte vnder by sir Richarde Ratcliffe and sir Willyam Catesbye, which ..kept him by secrete driftes out of al secrete trust. *a* **1661** Fuller *Worthies* (1840) I. 402 His youth spent in some military employments of good trust. **1770** *Junius Lett.* xxxvii. (1820) 182 Until parliament itself betrays its trust, by contributing to establish new principles of government. **1784** J. Brown *Hist. Brit. Ch.* (1820) II. vi. 289 Bringing them into places of power and trust. **1849** Macaulay *Hist. Eng.* vii. II. 236 Grave apprehensions that, if Roman Catholics were made capable of public trust, great evils would ensue. **1907** *Verney Mem.* I. 72 A breach of trust.

**c.** The condition of that which is entrusted to some one. Only in phrase *in* († *on*) *trust.*

**1425** W. Paston in *P. Lett.* I. 20 The whiche procuracie and appelle I shal sende to yowr persone,..with moneye onward, on trust. **1596** Spenser *F. Q.* v. iv. 2 To knights of great emprise The charge of Justice given was in trust, That they might execute her iudgements wise. **1608** Shaks. *Per.* i. iii. 13 His sealed Commission, left in trust with mee. **1664** Butler *Hud.* ii. i. 507 To make over In trust your fortune to your Lover. **1827** Jarman *J. J. Powell's Devises* (ed. 3) II. 17 A gift to a college, in trust for another charitable object. **1858** O. W. Holmes *Aut. Breakf.-t.* ii. (1891) 49 Put not your trust in money, but put your money in trust.

**d.** (with *pl.*) A duty or office, also a thing or person, entrusted to one.

**1643** Chas. I *Treaty at Oxford* Wks. 1662 II. 282 Those Trusts which the Law of the Land hath settled in the Crown alone. **1684** *Scanderbeg Rediv.* iii. 32 It was not fit two such great Trusts, as Marshal and General should both be managed by one Person. **1750** Johnson *Rambler* No. 71 ⁋ 14 The few moments remaining are to be considered as the last trust of heaven. **1822–34** *Good's Study Med.* (ed. 4) II. 463 The digestive powers, or some of them, do not perform their trust as they should do. **1844** G. N. Briggs in *Massachusetts Acts* 363 Public offices are public trusts, created for the benefit of the whole people, and not for the benefit of those who may fill them. **1898** Sophia M. Palmer in Ld. Selborne *Mem.* I. p. v. (*Notice*) These Memorials are a Trust.

**6.** *Law.* The confidence reposed in a person in whom the legal ownership of property is vested to hold or use for the benefit of another; hence, an estate committed to the charge of trustees; also *transf.* a trustee; a body of persons appointed as trustees; in quot. 1712, the position or relation of a trustee.

**1442** *Rolls of Parlt.* V. 57/1 The seid Feffees haue no title ner interest therynne, but only upon trust, and to his use, to execute his will. **1455** *Ibid.* 295/1 Londes or Tenementes of which we were enfeoffed by them of trust, in which we had never title..but onely by the feoffement made by us in trust. **1544** tr. *Littleton's Tenures* (1574) 96 b, If a manne enfeoffe another in hys lande vppon truste. **1628** Coke *On Litt.* 272 b, An Vse is a Trust or Confidence reposed in some other. **1712** Steele *Spect.* No. 402 ⁋ 3, I am in a Trust relating to this Lady's Fortune. **1797** Mrs. A. M. Bennett *Beggar Girl* (1813) II. 96 Both Mr. Frazer and doctor Cameron were trusts to a will made a few years back. **1828** Hood *Kilmansegg, Marriage*, It tipp'd the post-boy and paid the trust. **1873** *Iron* 3 May 493/1 The trustees of the Submarine Cables Trust.

**7.** *Commerce.* **a.** See quot.

**1882–93** Bithell *Counting-ho. Dict.* s. v., The 'Trusts' instituted in the City.., such as the 'Foreign and Colonial Securities Trust' [etc.]; in all these instances, a certain capital is subscribed..which is placed in the hands of trustees to be invested.

**b.** A body of producers or traders in some class of business, organized to reduce or defeat competition, lessen expenses, and control production and distribution for their common advantage; *spec.* such a combination of commercial or industrial companies, with a central governing body of trustees which holds a majority or the whole of the stock of each of the combining firms, thus having a controlling vote in the conduct and operation of each. Cf. *trust-certificate* in 8 b.

**1887** *Pall Mall G.* 2 Nov. 6/1 A high customs tariff offers a special temptation to indulge in corners, pools, and trusts. *Ibid.* 16 Nov. 12/1 A distillers' 'trust' has been formed..in order to regulate the production and price of spirits, and another large section of the trade have combined to curtail the production. **1888** Bryce *Amer. Commw.* III. 415 Those anomalous giants called Trusts,—groups of individuals and corporations concerned in one branch of trade or manufacture, which are placed under the irresponsible management of a small knot of persons, who, through their command of all the main producing or distributing agencies, intend and expect to dominate the market. *a* **1890** in G. B. Shaw *Fabian Ess. Socialism* 94 A trust is defined..as a combination to destroy competition and to restrain trade. **1894** W. T. Stead *If Christ came to Chicago* 191 The Gas Trust is as arbitrary as any Persian satrap in its dealings with the citizens.

**8.** *attrib.* and *Comb.*, as *trust-betrayer, -breaker*; *trust-breaking, -winning* adjs.; also in sense 6, *trust-beneficiary, -estate, -fund, -gift, -money, -right*; in sense 7 b, *trust-maker, -regulation, -share*; *trust-bolstering, -controlled, -ridden* adjs.

**1675** Cotton *Scoffer Scoft* 28 And like a treacherous Trust-breaker, Lewdly embezzel'd your Exchequer. **1766** Blackstone *Comm.* II. xx. 337 They now consider a trust-estate..as equivalent to the legal ownership. **1776** Adam Smith *W. N.* ii. iii. (1869) I. 341 The..allotment..of this fund ..is not always guarded by any..trust-right or deed of mortmain. **1802–12** Bentham *Ration. Judic. Evid.* (1827) II. 114 The hypocritical and trust-breaking humanity of judges. **1827** Jarman *J. J. Powell's Devises* (ed. 3) II. 99 He gave several pecuniary legacies out of his said trust monies and personal estate. **1855** Dickens *Dorrit* ii. x, Plunderers, forgers, and trust-betrayers of many sorts. **1872** Talmage *Serm.* 291 The heroes of this country are fast getting to be those who have most skill in swallowing 'trust-funds'. **1880** Muirhead *Gaius* Digest 495 A request to heir, legatee, or even a trust-beneficiary, to give effect to the truster's wishes. *Ibid.* ii. § 271 A legacy cannot be charged upon a legatee, but a trust-gift may. **1881** M. A. Lewis *Two Pretty G.* II. 201 All the more trust-winning, solid qualities. **1892** *Daily News* 21 Dec. 7/3 Trust shares received a smart shock. Banks are reported unwilling lenders on some trust securities. **1896** S. Plimsoll in *Westm. Gaz.* 3 June (1898) 7/1, I would rather than see our English shopkeepers and manufacturers dragged..to a similar position, see those trust-makers one and all hanging from lamp-posts. **1901** Sir C. Furness *Ibid.* 22 Feb. 6/2 An object-lesson..as to the trust-bolstering effect of the tariff. **1901** *Spectator* 20 July 77/2 The Trustmakers are seeking monopoly. **1902** *Daily Chron.* 26 Apr. 5/1 Weep as you think of these Trust-ridden isles! **1902** *Westm. Gaz.* 28 Aug. 1/3 The striking fact is that President Roosevelt should have thrown himself into the Anti-Trust or Trust-regulation movement. *Ibid.* 5 Nov. 5/1 The whole of the share capital will stand in the names of five voting trustees...These voting trustees will issue voting trust share certificates which will be negotiable and will entitle the holders of them to all dividends declared upon the shares, but all voting powers upon the shares are reserved to the voting trustees. **1908** *Ibid.* 5 Nov. 2/1 All 'articles entering into competition with Trust-controlled products'.

**b.** Special combs.: **trust-certificate** (in full *trust-share certificate*), a negotiable certificate issued by the controlling board of a trust (sense 7 b), which entitles the holder to all dividends declared upon the surrendered shares which it represents, but gives him no voting power; **trust company**, a company formed (originally in *U.S.*) for the purpose of exercising the functions of a trustee, with which other financial activities were later combined; **trust deed**, a deed of conveyance by which a trust (sense 6) is created, and its conditions set out; **trust-investment**, the investment of trust-money; a security sanctioned by law as one in which trustees may invest trust-money; †**trust-man**, a trustee; **trust-manager**, under the Education Act of 1902, one of the four managers of a voluntary elementary school appointed by the trustees; †**trust-road**, a road administered by a turnpike trust; **trust-stock**, a high-class stock in which trust-funds are or may legally be invested; trustee-stock.

**1891** *Cent. Dict.* s.v. *Trust*, *Trust certificate. **1904** *Q. Rev.* Jan. 187 The original stock-holders received trust-certificates. **1834** *Congress Debates* 14 Jan. 2392 In New York, a *trust company, incorporated only two or three years since, has now three or four millions in deposite. **1913** *Times* 9 Aug. 17/6 The movements in trust companies' stocks were in the upward direction. **1846** WORCESTER (citing HILLIARD), *Trust-deed. **1880** A. MCKAY *Hist. Kilmarnock* (ed. 4) 321 Then follows a digest of the trust-deed. **1897** *Westm. Gaz.* 7 Oct. 7/3 The stock is a *trust investment stock. **1867** R. S. HAWKER *Footpr. in Far Cornw.* (1903) 151 Twenty acres of woodland copse..were bought and conveyed by..Dame Thomasine Gull, to feoffees and *trust-men. **1902** *Westm. Gaz.* 17 July 6/2 A board of management consisting of a number of *trust managers not exceeding four appointed as provided by this Act, and..two appointed [etc.]. **1821** GALT *Ann. Parish* x, The toll or *trust-road was set a-going. **1858** LD. ST. LEONARDS *Handy-Bk. Prop. Law* xxi. 166 One trustee sold the *trust-stock and gave the money to his co-trustee..to invest. **1898** *Daily News* 28 May 10/1 A few trust stocks have improved.

† **Trust**, *a. Obs.* Also 3–5 trost, 5 truste. See also TRAIST *a.*, TREST *a.*, TRIST *a.*[1] [Early ME. *trust* (*ū* or *ŭ*), app. :—OE. **trust* (*ū* or *ŭ*) (not recorded, evidently not WSax.), simple grade of which ON. *traustr* 'strong, firm, secure, trusty', is an ablaut grade (*trust, treust, traust*); thence ME. *trust* and *trost*; the rare *trist* was app. assimilated to TRIST *v.*]

**1.** Confident, safe, secure, sure.

*c* **1200** [implied in TRUSTLY 1]. **12..** *Ancr. R.* 66 To sum gostliche monne þat ȝe beoð strusti uppen [*MS. Titus*, þat ȝe arn trust on]. *a* **1425** *Cursor M.* 2573 (Trin.) Be trust in þis þat I þe hiȝt. *Ibid.* 11161 Be truste & in no deewrynes.

**2.** Faithful, trusty; reliable, sound.

*c* **1440** *Jacob's Well* 212 ȝif þou selle a crokyd hors for a clene, a ruynous howse for trust hows.

*β. c* **1330** R. BRUNNE *Chron.* (1810) 60 His sonnes boþe tille him war trost als stele. ? **13..** *Adultery* 102 in Herrig's *Archiv* LXXIX. 420 Sche was..bothe trost & trewe. **1389** in *Eng. Gilds* (1870) 46 An Aldirman..; and foure skeuaynes, trost men and trewe. *c* **1425** *Cast. Persev.* 477 in *Macro Plays* 91 If he wyl be trost & trye, he schal be kyng.

**Trust** (trɒst), *v.* Also 3–5 trusten, (5 trusty), 5–6 truste, 5– trust; *β.* 4–5 troste(n, (4 trosti). Pa. t. and pple. **trusted**, († **trust**). See also TRAIST *v.*, TREST *v.*, TRIST *v.* [Early ME. ad. ON. *treysta*, assimilated in ME. to TRUST, *trost*, *a.* and *sb.* Cf. Sw. *tröst* comfort, *trösta* to comfort, console, Norw. *trøste sig til* to confide in; OS. *trôstan*, MLG. *trôsten*, Du. *troosten*, OHG. *trôsten*, Ger. *trösten* (with the sense to comfort (cf. L. *fortis* strong), cheer, encourage): see TRUST *a.*]

**1.** *intr.* To have faith or confidence; to place reliance; to confide. Const. *in*, *to* († *of*, *on*, *upon*).

*a* **1225** *Leg. Kath.* 503 Þeo þ[e] ham makieð..& alle þ[e] on ham trusteð [*v.r.* trusten]. *a* **1240** *Lofsong* in *Cott. Hom.* 213 Þeo hwile ðet ich truste uppo mon þu..lettest me al iwurden wið þeo þet ich truste uppon. **1297** R. GLOUC. (Rolls) 9606 So muche he truste on him, þat in is warde he let do Henri is eldoste sone. *a* **1425** *Cursor M.* 4962 (Trin.) In oþere helpe me truste I nouȝt. *a* **1500** *Sir Beues* (Pynson) 3270 Moche he trusted in Arundel. **1560** ABP. PARKER *Let. to Bp. Grindal* 18 Nov., Trusting of your lordship's good diligence herein. **1638** *Hamilton Papers* (Camden) 9, I trust in God to keipe them a sunder. **1656** H. PHILLIPS *Purch. Patt.* (1676) 3 Though the man..have the repute of an honest man, yet trust not too much upon that. **1706** E. WARD *Wooden World Diss.* (1708) 50 He trusts much more to the Sun, for his Guide, than to the Creator of it. **1791** CHARLOTTE SMITH *Celestina* (ed. 2) III. 22 She trusted on the long tried, the long assured tenderness of her lover. **1860** TYNDALL *Glac.* I. xvi. 112 Each had to trust to himself.

*β. c* **1330** R. BRUNNE *Chron.* (1810) 45 Bliþely tille Inglond wild he com..If he myght on þam troste. *c* **1394** *P. Pl. Crede* 350 Þei ben certayne men & syker on to trosten. *c* **1440** *Promp. Parv.* 503/1 Troston, *confido*.

**2.** *trans.* To have faith or confidence in; to rely or depend upon.

*c* **1374** CHAUCER *Anel. & Arc.* 91 She him trustith aboue eche creature. **1491** *Act 7 Hen. VII*, c. 22 *Preamble*, Ye may send John Aleyne of Pole whom ye trust and y also. **1560** DAUS tr. *Sleidane's Comm.* 165 b, He woulde not retourne to his Prince, for that he trusted hym no more. **1572** *Satir. Poems Reform.* xxxiv. 24 For Lordis and Lairdes ar nather Just Nor ȝit the communis to be trust. **1687** A. LOVELL tr. *Thevenot's Trav.* I. 74 He desired the command of a Ship, but they would not trust him so much. **1756** C. SMART tr. *Horace, Sat.* II. iv. (1826) II. 133 The mushrooms, that grow in meadows, are of the best kind: all others are dangerously trusted. **1827** SCOTT *Highl. Widow* iv, He has trusted me, and I will trust him. **1874** RUSKIN *Fors Clav.* xxxvii. 17, I cannot trust other people, without perpetual looking after them.

*β.* **1382** WYCLIF *Isa.* xxxvi. 4 What is this trist, that thou trostest? *c* **1394** *P. Pl. Crede* 237 For sich a certeyn man syker wold y trosten. *c* **1400** *Apol. Loll.* 45 If þei lofid & trostid Him aboue þe wark of þer hondis.

**b.** Imperative, used sarcastically or ironically to express one's assurance that a person will or will not do something. *colloq.* (Cf. CATCH *v.* 40.)

**1834** L. RITCHIE *Wand. by Seine* 67 If a woman is in danger from the rain, whose umbrella..is at her service? The Frenchman's? Trust him! **1902** R. BAGOT *Donna Diana* vi, Trust a religious old maid for scenting out love!

**3.** To have faith or confidence *that* something desired is, or will be, the case; also const. with *infin.* or *for*; to hope.

**1482** *Cely Papers* (Camden) 124 Howr mother and whe ar in good heyll, thankyd be God, and so we truste that ȝe be. *c* **1500** *New Not-br. Mayd* xxxix, Trustying to shewe..That men have an yll use..women to blame. **1518** HEN. VIII in *State Papers* I. 1, I trust the Quene my Wyfe be with chylde. **1603** SHAKS. *Meas. for M.* III. i. 271, I trust it will grow to a most prosperous perfection. *a* **1648** LD. HERBERT *Hen. VIII* (1683) 466 We should not trust to obtain at their [Saints'] hands that which is to be had only of God. **1781** BURKE *Corr.* (1844) II. 445, I trust that these things are wholly repugnant to my nature, and inconsistent with my principles. **1857** T. MOORE *Handbk. Brit. Ferns* (ed. 3) Pref., The author..trusts for a continuance of similar communications. **1880** SWINBURNE *Stud. Shaks.* 307 He trusted to establish the secret history and import of each.

*β.* **1389** in *Eng. Gilds* (1870) 53 Oure godes [we] han dispent..; no catelle kepende,—trostende, as children, withe ȝiftes to ben amendyd. **1451** CAPGRAVE *Life St. Gilbert* 90 Trostand for þis obediens to receyue sumtyme þe mor mede.

† **b.** with simple object: To hope for, look for. *Obs. rare*$^{-1}$.

**1523** LD. BERNERS *Froiss.* I. cxlvi. 174 We truste in hym somoche gentylnesse, that by the grace of god his purpose shall chaung.

**4.** To give credence to, believe (a statement); to rely upon the veracity or evidence of (a person, etc.).

?*a* **1366** CHAUCER *Rom. Rose* 649 So faire it was, that, trusteth wel, It semede a place espiritueel. **1586** A. DAY *Eng. Secretary* II. (1625) 26 Trust me I am vnused to these deuices. **1632** LITHGOW *Trav.* III. 85 Trust me, I told..at one time, and within my sight, some 67. Villages. **1697** DRYDEN *Virg. Georg.* III. 601 'Twas thus with Fleeces milky white (if we May trust Report,) Pan God of Arcady Did bribe thee Cynthia. *a* **1806** BP. HORSLEY *Serm.* (1816) III. xlii. 262 Every man implicitly trusts his bodily senses concerning external objects placed at a convenient distance. **1871** FREEMAN *Norm. Conq.* IV. xviii. 286 If the tale is to be trusted, the ford must be looked for in the hilly country.

*β.* **1399** LANGL. *Rich. Redeles* I. 102 Ffor trostiþ rith treuly..All þat þey moued..Was to be sure of hem-self. *c* **1440** *Generydes* 1624 Troste me wele it goo not as ye wene.

**5.** To commit the safety of (something) with confidence *to* a place, etc., *to* or *with* a person; to entrust; to place or allow (a person or thing) to be *in* a place or condition, or *to do* some action, with expectation of safety, or without fear of the consequences.

**1340** *Ayenb.* 241 Þanne þe angel zayde to lot..'ne trost þe naȝt ine þe stede þet þou hest ylete'. *c* **1440** *York Myst.* xxxii. 322 As touchyng þis money..Tite truste it tille oure tresorie. **1596** SHAKS. *Merch. V.* I. i. 42 My ventures are not in one bottome trusted. **1617** MORYSON *Itin.* III. 1 Neither would I aduise Angelica..to trust her self alone..to the protection of wandering Knights. **1667** MILTON *P. L.* XII. 133 Not wandring poor, but trusting all his wealth With God. **1748** *Anson's Voy.* II. xi. 254 The Spaniards never trust the silver without an armed force to protect it. **1781** GIBBON *Decl. & F.* xxii. (1869) I. 626 He trusted the event to valour and to fortune. **1819** SCOTT *Ivanhoe* xxv, The Jewish maiden will rather trust her soul with God, than her honour to the Templar! **1908** R. BAGOT *A. Cuthbert* vi, Afraid to trust herself to a retort, [she] walked out of the room.

**6.** To invest *with* a charge; to confide or entrust something to the care or disposal of.

**1548** UDALL, etc. *Erasm. Par. Matt.* xxiv. 96 The mayster hauynge a tryall of his trustines, wyll be bolde to truste hym with greater thynges. **1598** SHAKS. *Merry W.* II. ii. 316, I will rather trust a Fleming with my butter,..then my wife with her selfe. **1651** HOBBES *Leviath.* II. xix. 98 To keep those that had trusted him with the Government [etc.]. **1718** *Free-thinker* No. 16 ¶ 4 They should never trust him with a Lighted Candle again. **1789** J. MOORE *Zeluco* (1797) II. lxviii. 189 She was still afraid to trust her voice with words. **1828** SCOTT *F. M. Perth* vii, Let us meet at the East Port; ..if it is your pleasure..to trust us with the matter. **1884** CHURCH *Bacon* ix. 223 English seemed to him too homely to express the hopes of the world, too unstable to be trusted with them.

**7.** To give (a person) credit *for* goods supplied; † to supply *with* goods on credit (*obs.*); also, † to supply (goods) to a person on credit (*obs.*): see CREDIT *sb.* 9 a.

**1530** PALSGR. 763/2, I truste a dettoure..No man wyll trust me, except I have redye money. **1541** *Act 33 Hen. VIII*, c. 15 Straungers..vsed to credite and truste the pore inhabitauntes..which..had not redy money to pay in hand. **1648** CROMWELL *Lett.* 25 Nov., Without money the stubborn townspeople will not trust them for the worth of a penny. **1678** in Fountainhall *Decis.* (1759) I. 7 The prices of such..goods as were trusted by him. *a* **1687** PETTY *Pol. Arith.* (1690) 113 Any Tradesman of good Reputation worth 500*l.* will be trusted with above 1000*l.* worth of Commodities. **1775** *Pennsylvania Even. Post* 13 July 301/2 All persons are forbid to trust my Wife Sarah, as I will pay no debts of her contracting after this date.

**b.** *absol.* or *intr.*

**1718** *Free-thinker* No. 152 ¶ 5 My Dealing being in the Retail Way, I trusted little. **1818** SCOTT *Br. Lamm.* xii, The brewster's wife—she had trusted long, and the bill was aye scored up.

† **8.** *trans.* To place (a person) in trust *with* property; to make a trustee of. *Obs. rare*$^{-1}$.

**1670** *Act 22 Chas. II*, c. 12 § 2 All such persons that are or shall be enfeoffed or trusted with any such Lands shall lett them to farme [etc.].

Hence **Tru·sted** *ppl. a.*; whence **Tru·stedly** *adv.* (*rare*).

**1450** W. LOMNER in *Four C. Eng. Lett.* (1880) 3 The queche spynner he sente with certyn letters to certyn of his trustid men. **1784** COWPER *Task* III. 650 Ere he gives The beds the trusted treasure of their seeds. **1816** SOUTHEY *Lay Laureate* lxxviii, Shall she not then diffuse the word of Heaven Through all the regions of her trusted reign? **1856** RUSKIN *Mod. Paint.* IV. v. xi. § 9 The gateless path turns trustedly aside. **1875** JOWETT *Plato* (ed. 2) I. 467 Within the circle of his own most trusted friends.

**Trust**, obs. f. *trussed*, pa. t. and pple. of TRUSS *v.*

**Trustable** (trɒ·stăb'l), *a.* (In 7 -ible.) [f. TRUST *v.* + -ABLE.] That may be trusted, trustworthy.

**1606** *Sir G. Goosecappe* I. ii. in Bullen *O. Pl.* III. 14 We might have tickled the vanity out an howre longer, if my watch be trustible. **1884** EDNA LYALL *We Two* viii, At least one trustable, sympathetic person had been with her mother at the last. *Ibid.*, Jesus Christ..is the most perfectly loveable and trustable Being I know. **1900** A. BLACK *Evening & Morn.* iii. 83 They are trusting all that men have found to be trustable.

**Trustee** (trɒstī·), *sb.* Also 7 *Sc.* trustie. [f. TRUST *v.* + -EE [1].]

**1.** One who is trusted, or to whom something is entrusted; a person in whom confidence is put. *rare. Obs.*, or merged in 3.

**1647** R. STAPYLTON *Juvenal* xiii. 249 It was the custome, when any person trusting would put his trustee to his oath, to bring him into the temple, and to make him sweare. **1652** J. WRIGHT tr. *Camus' Nat. Paradox* I. 9 It was to change her child, in case shee were brought to bed of a girle, Cleorite (her Trustee) took the business upon her. **1671** [R. MACWARD] *True Nonconf.* 132 Suppose..the exact fidelity of the one trustie, to be notourly known. **1824** BENTHAM *Bk. Fallacies* Wks. 1843 II. 413 In every public trust, the legislator should, for the purpose of prevention, suppose the trustee disposed to break the trust in every imaginable way in which it would be possible for him to reap..any personal advantage.

**2.** *Law. spec.* One to whom property is entrusted to be administered for the benefit of another; often *loosely*, one of a number of persons appointed to manage the affairs of an institution; also a member of the controlling body of a trust (TRUST *sb.* 7 b).

**1653** W. RAMESEY *Astrol. Restored* IV. xiv. 331 Scribes and Secretaries shall suffer detriment, and..Trustees [etc.]. **1686** tr. *Chardin's Trav. Persia* 386 The fourscore Pounds have bin since converted to other uses, through the Covetousness of the Trustees. **1695–6** *Act 7 & 8 Will. III*, c. 30 § 40 One Annuity..payable out of the Profittes..unto the most Noble Barbara Dutchesse of Cleveland or to her Trustees. **1782** PRIESTLEY *Corrupt. Chr.* II. x. 243 A clergyman could not..be..trustee to a child. **1818** CRUISE *Digest* (ed. 2) VI. 333 Sir R. Worsley being seised in fee of the premises in question, devised them to trustees, upon trust that they should stand seised thereof to the use of his grandson. **1846** MCCULLOCH *Acc. Brit. Empire* (1854) II. 53 By these Acts the administration of all matters relating to the roads is vested in trustees. **1891** E. PEACOCK *N. Brendon* I. 295, I am trustee for her property. **1902** *Fabian News* XII. 38/2 Any attempt of a trustee of a corporation or trust to make a secret profit out of his position..should be punished.

**b.** In *U.S.* by extension, One in whose hands the property of a debtor is attached in a *trustee process* (see 4 and quots.).

[Cf. **1758** *Stat. Massachusetts* (1814) 614 Be it..enacted, that where no goods or effects of such absent or absconding person in the hands of his attorney, factor, agent or trustee, ..can be come at so as to be attached [etc.]. **1794** *Stat. Massachusetts* c. 65 § 1 The goods, effects and credits of the principal, in the hands and possession of his trustee or trustees,..shall stand bound and be held to satisfy such judgment as the plaintiff shall recover against the principal.] **1811** W. C. WHITE *Compend. Laws Massachusetts* 1268 In this state there is a process given by statute..whereby a creditor may attach any property or credits of his debtor in the hands of a third person. This third person is called in the English law, the *garnishee*: in our law he is called the *trustee*. **1864** in WEBSTER.

**3.** *transf.* One who is held responsible for the preservation and administration of anything.

**1655** JER. TAYLOR *Unum Necess.* ix. § 4. 620 The Trustees and Stewards of the mysteries of God. **1682** DRYDEN *Medal* Ep. Whigs ¶ 2 You are not the trustees of the public liberty. **1746–7** HERVEY *Medit.* (1767) I. 10 These dumb Monitors..had received a Charge to preserve their Names, and were the remaining Trustees of their Memory. **1897** T. F. BAYARD in *Daily News* 3 Mar. 10/4 The recognised trustees of the world's advancement and civilization.

**4.** *attrib.* and *Comb.*, as *trustee investor*, *meeting*; also **trustee bank** (in full **trustee savings bank**): see SAVINGS BANK; so **trustee banker**; **trustee investment**: see *trustee stock*; **trustee process**, in *U.S.*, a judicial process by which the goods, effects, and credits (but not the real estate) of a debtor may be attached while in the hands of a third person; in Eng. Law called *foreign attachment*; **trustee security**, **trustee stock** = *trust-stock* (TRUST *sb.* 8 b).

1898 *Westm. Gaz.* 9 Nov. 10/1 At that time [1861] there were 638 *trustee banks in existence. 1903 *Ibid.* 11 Mar. 5/1 As for the great *trustee bankers, they are not in the least affected. 1895 *Daily News* 30 Dec. 2/2 'A gilt-edge security' or 'quite a *trustee investment'. 1906 *Westm. Gaz.* 17 Sept. 3/2 Neither of these advantages affects the private or *trustee investor. 1820 SCOTT *Monast.* Introd. Ep., The laird..had to attend *trustee meetings, and lieutenancy meetings,..and what not. 1811 W. C. WHITE *Compend. Laws Massachusetts* 1268 In what cases, and against whom, a *trustee process will lie. 18.. *Laws Massachusetts* (Bartlett), The suit may be commenced by the process of foreign attachment, or trustee process. 1860 in BARTLETT *Dict. Amer.* s. v. 1898 *Westm. Gaz.* 18 Nov. 8/1 The new capital required will be raised jointly..and will be a *trustee security. 1901 *Ibid.* 29 Aug. 7/1 The failure of the issue.. to be classed as a *Trustee stock.

Hence **Trustee·ism** (*nonce-wd.*), the system of vesting (church) patronage in trustees.

1889 A. H. DRYSDALE *Hist. Presbyt. Eng.* 511 The evils of both family patronage and trusteeism. 1889 *Tablet* 30 Nov. 878 A system of lay trusteeism.

**Trustee** (trɒstī·), *v.* [f. prec. sb.]

1. a. *trans.* To place (a person or his property) in the hands of a trustee or trustees. b. *intr.* To act as a trustee. *nonce-uses.*

1818 *Blackw. Mag.* III. 518 In my younger days, country gentlemen..made a shift to continue in the management of their own affairs..; but now the prevailing fashion, or rather passion is to get Trusteed with all possible expedition. 1909 *Ibid.* Sept. 413/2 Trusteeing is an unprofitable business.

2. *U.S.* a. To appoint (a person) trustee in the *trustee process* (see prec. 4), in order to restrain a debtor from collecting moneys due to him. b. To attach (effects of a debtor) in the hands of a third person.

1883 HOWELLS *Woman's Reason* I. ix. 164 You don't say you never was *trusteed* before? *Ibid.* 165 When they sent in their bill,..I didn't believe they'd really go so far as to trustee me. *Ibid.*, I presume they'll be trusteein' all of you. I shall have to pay it now. 1898 *Westm. Gaz.* 14 June 7/1 Yesterday his options were hastily closed, and his cash wheat trusteed.

Hence **Trustee·d** *ppl. a.* (in quot. *absol.*), **Trustee·ing** *vbl. sb.*

1818 *Blackw. Mag.* III. 518 The trusteed..secures all the pleasure, as well as the profit,..entirely to himself. 1883 HOWELLS *Woman's Reason* I. ix. 166 Do you think she liked your coming out about that trusteeing?

**Trusteeship** (trɒstī·ʃip). [f. TRUSTEE *sb.* + -SHIP.] The office or function of a trustee; also, a body of trustees.

1730–6 BAILEY (folio), *Trustee-ship*, the office of a trustee. 1748 RICHARDSON *Clarissa* (1811) IV. vii. 36 To settle and give up my trusteeship is one of the principal motives of my leaving these parts. 1831 DISRAELI *Yng. Duke* III. vii, I have just had a note from Challoner, preliminary, I suppose, to my trusteeship. 1883 H. P. SPOFFORD in *Harper's Mag.* Aug. 459/2 He gave his wife the trusteeship of his diet. 1885 SIR J. PEARSON in *Law Times Rep.* LI. 902/1 The will contained a direction that any vacancy in the trusteeship should be filled up within a year. 1912 *Times* 19 Dec. 16/3 Directorates and voting trusteeships of various large banks, financial institutions, and corporations.

† **Trusten**, *v. Obs.* exc. *dial.* [irreg. f. TRUST *v.* + -EN [5].] = TRUST *v.* (Cf. TRISTEN.)

13.. *Metr. Hom.* (Vernon MS.) in Herrig's *Archiv* LVII. 288 Trustneþ not in ȝor wyues Ne in ȝour children. 13.. *Propr. Sanct.* ibid. LXXXI. 312/164 Tresur of seluer and of golde, He may not passe to heuene þen, Whil he trustneþ vppon hem. 1382 WYCLIF *Eph.* iii. 12 In whom we han trust and nyȝ comynge, in trustnynge [1388 tristenyng] by the feith of him. 1861 GEO. ELIOT *Silas M.* xvi, All as we've got to do is to trusten. 1895 [T. PINNOCK] *T. Brown's Black Country Ann.* (E.D.D.), If he trespasses on my ground, he knows what he's got to trusten to.

**Truster** (trɒ·stəɹ). Also *technically* 7 -or. [f. TRUST *v.* + -ER [1].] One who trusts, confides, or relies; one who believes or credits; one who gives credit, a creditor.

1537 *Orig. & Sprynge Sectes* 42 Onely they yt be earnest trusters & beleuers in God are Christen men. 1602 SHAKS. *Ham.* I. ii. 172 Nor shall you doe mine eare that violence, To make it truster of your owne report Against your selfe. 1607 — *Timon* IV. i. 10 Bankrupts..out with your Kniues, And cut your Trusters throates. 1649 W. BALL *Power of Kings* 5 It is against Reason..that such Trustees or Stewards should derive no Power from the People their Trustors. 1800 A. SWANSTON *Serm. & Lect.* I. 181 The trusters have been put to the severest trials. 1870 SPURGEON *Treas. Dav.* Ps. xl. 3 Through grace [they] shall receive faith and become trusters in Jehovah.

b. *Sc. Law. spec.* One who puts property in trust; correlative to TRUSTEE 2.

1675 in W. M. Morison *Dict. Decis.* (1807) 16173. 1741 *Ibid.* 16201 Where a trust does not arise from any deed or disposition of the truster, but from the voluntary interposition of the trustee [etc.]. 1838 W. BELL *Dict. Law Scot.* 1010 Where the truster had conveyed his whole estate, heritable and moveable, to trustees,..it was held [etc.]. 1885 *Law Rep.* 10 App. Cas. 452 The truster had a very large amount of personalty in Scotland.

**Trustful** (trɒ·stfŭl), *a.* [f. TRUST *sb.* + -FUL 1.]

† 1. Trustworthy, trusty, faithful. *Obs.*

1580 SIDNEY *Ps.* VII. i, O Lord, my God, Thou art my trustfull stay. 1582 STANYHURST *Æneis* I. (Arb.) 40 His gyde was trustful Achates. 1674 N. FAIRFAX *Bulk & Selv.* 189 The same most trustful witness that tells us when the world began [etc.].

2. Full of or exercising trust; trusting, confiding.

1832 [implied in TRUSTFULNESS]. 1834 LYTTON *Pompeii* III. iv, They went in their trustful thoughts far down the stream of time. 1850 TENNYSON *In Mem.* cix, The child would twine A trustful hand, unask'd, in thine. 1897 MARY KINGSLEY *W. Africa* xiv. 311, I am not of a trustful disposition.

Hence **Tru·stfully** *adv.*, in a trustful manner.

1846 WORCESTER cites *Monthly Rev.* 1856 R. A. VAUGHAN *Mystics* (1860) I. VI. v. 314 *note*, Sorrow and joy, pain and pleasure, are trustfully accepted as alike coming from the hand of Love.

**Trustfulness** (trɒ·stfŭlnės). [f. prec. + -NESS.] The quality of being trustful or confiding.

1832 LYTTON *Eugene A.* III. iii, There was a remarkable trustfulness in Madeline's disposition. 1864 DICKENS *Lett.* (1880) II. 213 Trustfulness is at the bottom of all social institutions. 1896 DK. ARGYLL *Philos. Belief* 411 A reasonable trustfulness in our fellow-men is..recognized as a virtue.

**Trustible**, obs. form of TRUSTABLE.

**Trustify** (trɒ·stifəi), *v. Commercial slang.* [f. TRUST *sb.* + -[I]FY.] *trans.* To make into a trust; to form a trust of or in (a business): see TRUST *sb.* 7 b. Only in *pa. pple.* and *ppl. a.* **Tru·stified.** So **Trustifica·tion**, the formation of a trust.

1902 *Daily Chron.* 7 Jan. 3/1 Great American manufacturing concerns not yet trustified. 1902 *Fabian News* XII. 38/2 A somewhat novel danger in the trustification of industry. 1902 R. DONALD in *Westm. Gaz.* 12 June 1/3 Investors and speculators in the trustified interests. 1902 *Daily Record & Mail* 22 Feb. 4 More than half the capital, means of production, and distribution in the United States, are 'trustified' in one form or another.

**Trustihood** (trɒ·stihud). [f. TRUSTY *a.* + -HOOD; cf. *hardihood.*] The quality or condition of being trusty, trustiness.

1823 *Blackw. Mag.* XIII. 37 All are types of spotless purity, of maiden modesty, and trustyhood.

**Trustily** (trɒ·stili), *adv.* Also 5 trostili, -yly. [f. TRUSTY *a.* + -LY [2].] In a trusty manner.

† 1. With trust or confidence; trustfully, confidently, hopefully, boldly. *Obs.*

*c* 1350 *Will. Palerne* 3904 Þan turned þei titli aȝen & trustili gon fiȝt. 1382 WYCLIF *1 Sam.* xii. 11 He delyuerde ȝow fro the hoond of ȝoure enemyes bi enuyroun; and ȝe han dwellid trustily. *c* 1450 LOVELICH *Grail* l. 537 Trostily I beleve forsothe That God for my gilte nys not wrothe. 1485 CAXTON *Chas. Gt.* III. i. vi. 212 He shold come to hym peasybly & trustyly, with a fewe peple. 1573 TUSSER *Husb.* (1878) 17 To learne how foe to pacifie, But trust him not too trustilie. 1579 J. JONES *Preserv. Bodie & Soule* Ep. Ded. 4 Faith by the Charitie doth trustily water.

2. With fidelity or loyalty; faithfully.

*c* 1425 *Cast. Persev.* 635 in *Macro Plays* 96 Serue hym at honde Bothe nyth & day. *Voluptas.* Trostyly, lord, redy. 1583 GOLDING *Calvin on Deut.* Pref. 7 All such as behaue not themselues trustilie towards their neighbours. 1639 HORN & ROB. *Gate Lang. Unl.* lvi. § 607 [Trustees] who, if they deale trustily..., make inventories. 1823 SCOTT *Quentin D.* xii, He would have borne a letter trustily enough.

† 3. Truly, assuredly, certainly. *Obs.*

*a* 1425 *Langland's P. Pl.* C. IV. 498 (MS. F.) Trustilich [*v. r.* tristilich] a teonful text. *c* 1450 LOVELICH *Grail* liii. 262 For the I schal don More,..Trustylich, Symew, As I the Seye.

**Trustiness** (trɒ·stinės). [f. as prec. + -NESS.] The quality of being trusty.

† 1. Trustfulness, faith, confidence. *Obs.*

*c* 1557 ABP. PARKER *Ps.* xxxiii. 79 Extend O Lord thy gentlenesse, As we in thee have trustinesse. 1685 BAXTER *Paraphr. N. T.*, *Gal.* v. 23 The Fruits of the Spirit..are Love to God and Men,..Trustiness and trusting God.

2. Fidelity, faithfulness, loyalty, trustworthiness.

1530 PALSGR. 283/2 Trustynesse, *fealte.* 1542 UDALL *Erasm. Apoph.* 329 b, Not so muche as any one poincte of diligence..or yet of trustynesse. 1592 tr. *Junius on Rev.* xv. 12 The girdle of gold was a sign of sincerity and trustines in taking in charge the commandments of God. 1652 LOVEDAY tr. *Calprenede's Cassandra* I. 41 Two servants, of whose trustinesse I was well assured. 1822 SCOTT *Nigel* viii, Her character for trustiness remained..unimpeached. 1868 G. STEPHENS *Runic Mon.* I. 259 Prof. Bugge was convinced of the intelligence and trustiness of the finder.

**Trusting** (trɒ·stiŋ), *vbl. sb.* [f. TRUST *v.* + -ING [1].] The action of the verb TRUST.

*c* 1440 *Jacob's Well* 288 Trustynge settyth a mannys herte faste in goodnes. 1526 *Pilgr. Perf.* (W. de W. 1531) 8 So moche trustynge in the cerimonyes of theyr lawe. 1573 TUSSER *Husb.* (1878) 106 Ill huswife..Through trusting of others hath this for hir fees. 1607 HIERON *Wks.* I. 301 There should be..a trusting to Him, an expecting saluation by His meanes. *a* 1771 GRAY *Dante* 17 Betray'd By trusting, and by Treachery slain. 1855 SINGLETON *Virgil* I. 22 There is no safe trusting to the bank.

**Tru·sting,** *ppl. a.* [f. as prec. + -ING [2].] That trusts: see the verb.

*c* 1450 [implied in TRUSTINGLY]. 1545 ELYOT, *Fretus*, of *fruor*, trustyng. 1693 *Humours Town* 27 Believing Vintners, Tailors, Sempstresses, and the rest of the trusting Shopkeepers. 1707 PRIOR *Sat. Poets* 75 You've no Friend left, but trusting Landlady. 1790 HAN. MORE *Relig. Fash. World* (1791) 108 Unsuspecting goodness, and trusting honesty. 1816 BYRON *Parisina* v, She must lay her conscious head A husband's trusting heart beside. 1866 G. MACDONALD *Ann. Q. Neighb.* xxviii, He was of a kindly, gentle, trusting nature.

Hence **Tru·stingly** *adv.*, in a trusting manner; **Tru·stingness,** the quality of being trusting or trustful; trustfulness.

*c* 1450 tr. *De Imitatione* III. viii. 75 He..lasse *trustingly thynkyth or felyth of me þan it behoueþ. 1849 *Fraser's Mag.* XL. 645 Most firmly and trustingly do I believe. 1883 CON. F. WOOLSON *For the Major* iv, The person one loves becomes..trustingly dependent like a..child, upon one's.. care. 1820 L. HUNT *Indicator* No. 49 (1822) I. 386 Clearness of blood, freshness of perception, and *trustingness of heart. 1852 THACKERAY *Esmond* III. viii, Sure there is no bound to the trustingness of women.

**Trustle**, variant of TRESTLE.

**Trustless** (trɒ·stlės), *a.* [f. TRUST *sb.* + -LESS.]

1. Not to be trusted or relied upon; unfaithful, unreliable, treacherous, untrustworthy.

*c* 1530 H. RHODES *Bk. Nurture* 711 in *Babees Bk.* (1868) 101 To catche ech trustlesse traytor, see thou faythfull doe remayne. 1578 T. PROCTOR *Gorg. Gallery* B ij, A sternles ship amidst the trustles Seaes. 1603 FLORIO *Montaigne* II. xii. (1632) 320 A trustles and not to be beleeved voice. 1688–9 LADY R. RUSSELL *Lett.* (1819) II. 18 An unkind and trustless world it has been to us. 1797 ANNA SEWARD *Lett.* (1811) IV. 356 A melancholy instance of the trustless flattery of youth and prosperity. 1828 E. IRVING *Last Days* 81 Every juvenile delinquent,..every trustless servant. 1858 H. SPENCER *Ess.* I. 308 We are constantly obliged to act out our inferences, trustless as they may be.

2. Having no trust or confidence; unbelieving, distrustful.

1598 YONG *Diana* 114, I was..so trustles and misconceiuing of my selfe, that I thought [etc.]. 1619 SIR J. SEMPILL *Sacrilege Handled* 81 Trustles Thomas must first put his finger in his side, and then beleeue. 1838 ELIZA COOK *Lines written at Midnight* x, I've learned to look With trustless eye on all and each. 1882 J. WALKER *Jaunt to Auld Reekie*, etc. 27 This trustless mammon-serving age.

Hence **Tru·stlessness,** untrustworthy character, faithlessness; distrustfulness.

1825 LD. COCKBURN *Mem.* (1856) 324 Disclosing the trustlessness of town Councils..in their protected abuse of power. 1909 R. LAW *Tests Life* ix. 178 The sin and folly, the trustlessness and ingratitude of his children.

† **Tru·stly,** *adv. Obs.* [f. TRUST *a.* + -LY [2].]

1. = TRUSTILY 1.

*c* 1200 *Trin. Coll. Hom.* 9 On swilch liflode we muȝen trustliche abiden ure louerd ihesu cristes tocume. *c* 1220 *Bestiary* 634 in *O. E. Misc.* 20 A tre he [the elephant] sekeð ..and leneð him trostlike ðer-bi. 1382 WYCLIF *Isa.* xiv. 30 And pore men trostly [Vulg. *fiducialiter*] shul resten. *a* 1400 HYLTON *Scala Perf.* (W. de W. 1494) I. xliv, Aske only salvacion bi vertue of this precious passion mekely and trustly, and wythoute dowte thou shal haue it. *c* 1440 *Promp. Parv.* 503/1 Trostly, or sekyrly, *confidenter.*

2. Certainly, surely; = TRUSTILY 3.

*c* 1320 R. BRUNNE *Medit.* 1107 Beeþ of gode cumfort, for trustly y say, We shullen hym se. 1426 LYDG. *De Guil. Pilgr.* 14831 And trustly..I am hys douhter.

**Trustor**: see TRUSTER.

**Trustworthy** (trɒ·st,wɒ̄:ɹði), *a.* [f. TRUST *sb.* + WORTHY *a.*] Worthy of trust or confidence; reliable.

1808 [implied in TRUSTWORTHINESS]. 1829 LYTTON *Devereux* VI. iii, Anselmo..was a trustworthy man. 1855 MACAULAY *Hist. Eng.* xiv. III. 442 The most trustworthy comment on the text of the Gospels and Epistles is to be found in the practice of the primitive Christians. 1874 RUSKIN *Fors Clav.* IV. xliii. 139 Whatever is set down in *Fors* for you is assuredly true,...trustworthy to the uttermost,—however strange. 1889 GRETTON *Memory's Harkb.* 313 Because he trusted them, they proved themselves trustworthy.

Hence **Tru·stwo:rthily** *adv.*, **Tru·stwo:rthiness.**

1851–9 MALLET in *Man. Sci. Enq.* 355 Alterations of level may be *trustworthily evidenced by changes of depth or run of water. 1870 *Daily News* 14 Dec., I am trustworthily informed that [etc.]. 1893 W. C. WILKINSON in Barrows *Parl. Relig.* II. 1247 The religion that can trustworthily offer to save. 1808 *Edin. Rev.* July 478 The cardinal virtue .. of historic composition,—*trustworthiness. 1879 *Cassell's Techn. Educ.* IV. 399/2 The trustworthiness of mild steel. 1885 CLODD *Myths & Dr.* I. vii. 115 Criticism is testing without fear or favour the trustworthiness of records of the past.

**Trusty** (trɒ·sti), *a.* (*sb.*) Also 3–5 trusti, 5–7 -ie, 6 -ye; 5 trosty. [f. TRUST *a.* + -Y [1].]

1. Characterized by trust; having faith, confidence, or assurance; trustful, confident. Now *rare.*

*a* 1225 *Ancr. R.* 334 Ȝif þu ert to trusti, & holdest God to nesche uorto awreken sunne. *c* 1230 *Hali Meid.* 45 Ne beo þu nawt tu trusti ane to þi meidenhad. *a* 1425 *Cursor M.* 3272 (Trin.) Lord .. graunte me .. Trusti to be of my preyere. *c* 1460 METHAM *Wks.* (E.E.T.S.) 90 Yf sqwyche lynys..pase thorw the tryangyl or by the tryangyl, yt sygnyfyith a trosty persone and a louyng. 1541 WYATT *Let.* Wks. (1861) p. xxiv, If in these matters I have presumed to be trusty more than I was trusted, surely the zeal of the King's service drove me to it. 1616 R. C. *Times' Whistle*, etc. (E.E.T.S.) 115 He wilbe..Apt to deceive even his most trusty friend. 1908 *Times* 28 July 4/1 A very intimate and trusty friendship sprang up between them.

2. Characterized by faithfulness or reliability; that may be trusted or relied upon; trustworthy.

In letters of the sovereign to subjects, *Our trusty and well-beloved* takes the place of L. *dilecto et fideli nostro*, before the names of the addressees. Privy Councillors are addressed as Right trusty and well-beloved.

*a* 1310 in Wright *Lyric P.* xv. (Percy Soc.) 47 Trusti kyng ant trewe in trone. 1432 LD. SCROPE in *Plumpton Corr.* (Camden) p. xxxvi, Trusty & wellbeloved, I greet you wel. *c* 1440 *Promp. Parv.* 503/1 Trosty, sekyr, *fidus, fidelis.* 1511–12 *Act* 3 *Hen. VIII*, c. 23 § 3 Billes signed..with the hande of the Kinges trusty servaunt John Heron. 1577 B. GOOGE *Heresbach's Husb.* III. (1586) 114 The Horse ..the trustiest beast that we vse in our seruice. 1615 W. LAWSON *Country Housew. Gard.* (1626) 17 Euery Gardiner is not trusty to sell you good fruit. 1674 [see RIGHT *adv.* 9 c]. 1726 SWIFT *Gulliver* I. vii, A trusty servant. 1803 in *Nairne Peerage Evid.* (1874) 113 Our right trusty and welbeloved George baron Keith. 1838 THIRLWALL *Greece* II. xvi. 369 He..sent a trusty messenger to Xerxes, to claim the merit of this service. 1877 J. D. CHAMBERS

*Div. Worship* 230 It should be carried to the mill by a trusty person.

**b.** *transf.* and *fig.* of things.

1596 SPENSER *F. Q.* VI. vii. 25 His trustie sword, the servant of his might. 1697 DRYDEN *Æneid* VII. 886 The neighing steeds are to the chariots tied, The trusty weapon sits on ev'ry side. 1706 E. WARD *Wooden World Diss.* (1708) 73 One of the most trusty Timbers of the Common-wealth. 1782 COWPER *Gilpin* 63 My leathern belt..In which I bear my trusty sword. 1890 R. BRIDGES *Elegy*, Poems (1912) 239 Her trusty window open wide.

**B.** *sb.* One who (or that which) is trusty; a trustworthy person; *spec.* in *U.S.*, a well-conducted convict to whom special privileges are granted.

1573 TUSSER *Husb.* (1878) 62 Get trustie to tend them [cattle], not lubberlie squire. *Ibid.* 124 Reape corne by the day,..By great is the cheaper, if trustie were reaper. 1756 TOLDERVY *Hist. 2 Orphans* II. 140 Why gentlemen, [answered the landlord], your old trusty there, parts with his money, and cries for it again. 1889 *Century Mag.* Jan. 448/1 The 'trusties' are often domesticated upon ranches near the town. 1892 *Pall Mall G.* 15 Nov. 2/3 Martin left his camp in charge of various captains—generally assisted by 'trusties', that is, well-behaved convicts, who were found to be the cruellest taskmasters.

**b.** *local Irish.* A great coat.

1804 MAR. EDGEWORTH *Limerick Gloves* vii, 'There was a sort of a frieze trusty'. 'A trusty!' said Mr. Hill, 'what is that, pray?' 'A big coat, sure, plase your honour'. 1837-8 J. KEEGAN *Leg. & Poems* (1907) 4 He thrust his hands into the ample pockets of his 'trusty', which was closely buttoned round his waist. 1846 *Ibid.* 365 He opened his white frieze trusty.

† **Trut**, *int. Obs.* An ejaculation of contempt.

c 1330 R. BRUNNE *Chron.* (1810) 317 A foule herlote him slowe, trut for his renoun. c 1440 *Promp. Parv.* 505/1 Trut, or ptrot, skornefulle word (*S.*, *A.*, thprut), *vath.*

**Truth** (trūþ), *sb.* Forms: *α.* 1 **triewþ, treowþ, trywþ,** 2 **treothe,** 2–3 **treouþe,** 2–4 **trewþe,** 2–5 **treuthe,** 3 **treowthe, treoþe,** (**treweðe**), 3–5 **treuþe,** 4 **treuþ,** (**tryuþe, trewepe, -ethe, trewht,** *Sc.* **treutht, trewcht,** 4–5 *Sc.* **trewtht**), 4–6 **trewth(e,** 4–7 **treuth,** 5 **trewþ,** (**treut, truyt, þreuth, treweth,** 6 **trewith, -ythe, troeuth, treugth**). *β.* 3–4 **trewþe,** 4 **truþ,** 4–7 **truthe,** (5 **truwþe, trwth**), 6–7 **trueth,** 4– **truth.** [OE. *triewþ, tréowþ, trýwþ*, ME. *trewþe, treuþ(e*, f. OE. *triewe* adj., TRUE: see -TH[1]. Cf. OHG. *triuwida*, ON. *tryggð*.

The *β*-forms perh. show a different ablaut grade, *u* beside *eu, eo*, whence OE. *trúwa, trúa*, faith, good faith (see TRUCE), *trúwian* to TROW, trust, confide, and ON. *trúr* true; but, as *trūþ* does not appear before the 13th c., when *u* and *eu* (*ew*) in other words had phonetically fallen together, it is possible that ME. *truthe* really comes from OE. *treowþe*. See also TROTH.]

**I.** The quality of being true (and allied senses).

**1.** The character of being, or disposition to be, true to a person, principle, cause, etc.; faithfulness, fidelity, loyalty, constancy, steadfast allegiance. (See also TROTH 1.) Now *rare* or *arch.*

*α.* c 893 K. ÆLFRED *Oros.* v. ii. § 6 Þær dydon þeah Romane lytla triewþa. c 1000 ÆLFRIC *On Old Test.* (Gr.) 1 Heora ȝemynd þurhwunað..for..heora trywðe wið god. c 1200 *Vices & Virtues* 103 For ðare gode trewðe ðe ðu him bere. c 1290 *S. Eng. Leg.* I. 98/203 Bi þe treuþe þat i schal to Mahon. c 1390 CHAUCER *Compl. Damours* 7 On hir,.. Which hath on me no mercy ne no rewthe That love hir best, but sleeth me for my trewthe. c 1470 HENRY *Wallace* III. 274, I knaw he will do mekill for his kyne; Gentryss and trewtht ay restis him within. c 1560 A. SCOTT *Poems* (S.T.S.) xxvi. 33 Thay wald be rewit, and hes no rewth;.. Thay wald be trowit, and hes no trewth.

*β.* 1530 PALSGR. 283/2 Truthe, *uerite, loialte.* 1568 GRAFTON *Chron.* II. 729 The king had alwayes known his truth and fidelitie towarde the crowne of Fraunce. 1611 SHAKS. *Cymb.* v. v. 107 Briefely dye their ioyes, That place them on the truth of Gyrles, and Boyes. 1719 *Free-thinker* No. 137. ⁋6 Lucius..preserving still his Truth to Marcia. 1800 COLERIDGE *Christabel* II. 78 Alas! they had been friends in youth; But whispering tongues can poison truth. 1860 RUSKIN *Mod. Paint.* V. IX. xii. 345 Truth to himself; that is to say, the resolution to do his duty by his art.

† **b.** *By my truth*, as an asseveration. (Cf. TROTH 1 b.) *Obs.*

13.. *Guy Warw.* (A.) 405 Bi mi trewþe y schal þe swere, Schal y mi fader þe tiding bere. 1563 in *Child-Marriages* 59 [He] promysed, bie his faith and treuth, that [etc.]. 1605 CAMDEN *Rem.* 222 By my trueth, wife (quoth he) [etc.].

† **2.** One's faith or loyalty as pledged in a promise or agreement; a solemn engagement or promise, a covenant: = TROTH 2. *Obs.*

*α.* c 1000 ÆLFRIC *Exod.* vi. 5 Ic ȝemunde minra treowþa þe ic Abrahame behet. 1154 *O. E. Chron.* an. 1137 Hi hadden him manred maked & athes suoren, ac hi nan treuthe ne heolden. alle he wæron forsworen & here treothes forloren. c 1205 LAY. 10631 Heo sworen..& treoðen heo plihten [c 1275 treuþe him plihte]. 1297 R. GLOUC. (Rolls) 3584 Þis luþer saxons abbeþ gret dedeyn Vor to holde me treuþe. a 1330 *Otuel* 311 Selpe me gode.., Eiþer oþer his trewþe pliȝte, Vppon morwen for to fiȝte. c 1400 *Laud Troy Bk.* 877 My trewthe .I. layd, To do al as thow hast sayd. 1460 CAPGRAVE *Chron.* (Rolls) 182 He cursed the Kyng of Scottis for brekyng of his treuth, whech he had mad to the Englisch Kyng. a 1572 KNOX *Hist. Ref.* Wks. 1846 I. 183 To the end, that under treuth thei mycht eyther gett the Castell betrayed, or elles some principall men.. tackin at unwarres.

*β.* c 1450 METHAM *Wks.* (E.E.T.S.) 42/1114 To serue yow be-ffore alle odyr my truth I plyght. ?16.. *Young Beichan* xiii. in Child *Ballads* II. (1884) 470 I'll give thee the truth of my right hand, The truth of it I'll freely gie.

† **b.** *spec.* in reference to marriage; also, in quot. a 1300, betrothal. *Obs.*

*α.* c 1275 LAY. 2251 Locrin was on foreward Hire habbe to wife And he hire hafde treouþe i-pliþt.

*β.* a 1300 *K. Horn* 674 Muchel was þe ruþe þat was at þare truþe. c 1440 *Gesta Rom.* xii. 37 (Harl. MS.) The maide saide, she wold consent; and þer they pliȝt hire truthe.

† **3. a.** Faith, trust, confidence. (Cf. TROTH 3 a.) *Obs.*

*α.* a 1300 *Cursor M.* 14072 (Cott.) Þi mikel treuth Has þe saued. 1375 BARBOUR *Bruce* IV. 223 (Cambr. MS.) He wes fule,..That gaf treuth [*Edin. MS.* throuth; *ed.* 1620 traist] to that Creature.

*β.* 13.. *Cursor M.* 21406 Thoru þair stedfast truth in dright. 1677 MARVELL *Corr.* Wks. (Grosart) II. 552 You shall not repent any truth you repose in me.

† **b.** Belief; a formula of belief, a creed. (Cf. TROTH 3 b.) *Obs.*

13.. *Cursor M.* 4246 (Gött.) Putyfar..held ioseph in mensk and lare Al þou þair treuthes sundri ware. 1456 SIR G. HAYE *Law Arms* (S.T.S.) 8 The hard hertis, and untrewe treuth of the pagans. 1500-20 DUNBAR *Poems* ix. 57 The Articulis of Trewth,—in God to trow,..And in his haly blissit Sone, Jesu.

**4.** Disposition to speak or act truly or without deceit; truthfulness, veracity, sincerity; formerly sometimes in wider sense: Honesty, uprightness, righteousness, virtue, integrity.

*α.* 13.. *Cursor M.* 13891 (Cott.) Þat neuer leigh, ne neuer sale, For wijt and treuth he has ai hale. 1377 LANGL. *P. Pl.* B. XII. 284 Trewth þat trespassed neuere ne transuersed aȝeines his lawe, But lyueth as his lawe techeth. c 1400 *Non-Cycle Myst. Plays, Pride of Life* 330 Dred of God is al ago And treut is go to ground. *Ibid.* 334 And truyt is don of dau. 1500-20 DUNBAR *Poems* xii. 30 Fredome returnis in wrechitness, And trewth returnis in dowbilness. 1535 COVERDALE *Ps.* cxviii. [cxix.] 30, I haue chosen the waye of treuth. a 1657 SIR W. MURE *Sonn.* i. 12 Extold by treuth of thy most loyall word.

*β.* 13.. *Cursor M.* 9661 (Cott.) Dom þan com foluand in hi, And Iuged þam in sothfast truth. 1568 GRAFTON *Chron.* II. 775 [They] lacked eyther wit or truth. 1592 SHAKS. *Ven. & Ad.* 804 Loue is all truth, lust full of forged lies. 1596 — *Merch. V.* IV. i. 214 Malice beares downe truth. 1611 BIBLE *Ps.* li. 6 Thou desirest trueth in the inward parts. 1680 BURNET *Rochester* (1692) 55 Truth is a Rational Natures acting in conformity to itself in all things. 1750 GRAY *Elegy* 69 The struggling pangs of conscious truth to hide. 1802 MAR. EDGEWORTH *Moral T.* (1816) I. iii. 16 Do you doubt my truth? 1852 MRS. STOWE *Uncle Tom's C.* xx, 'La, there an't any such thing as truth in that limb', said Rosa, looking indignantly at Topsy.

**II. 5.** Conformity with fact; agreement with reality; accuracy, correctness, verity (of statement or thought).

*α.* 1570 LEVINS *Manip.* 96/5 Trewth, *veritas.* Vntruth, *error.*

*β.* 1596 DALRYMPLE tr. *Leslie's Hist. Scot.* x. (S.T.S.) II. 422 Tha declair the truth of the Catholick religioune. 1600 SHAKS. *A. Y. L.* v. iv. 124 If there be truth in sight, you are my daughter. 1628 PRYNNE *Cens. Cozens* 65, I haue here sufficiently euidenced the trueth of this Assertion. 1718 PRIOR *Solomon* Pref., In this case Probability must atone for the want of Truth. a 1829 J. YOUNG *Lect. Intell. Philos.* xxxviii. (1835) 382 Truth is the agreement of our ideas and words with the nature of things. 1849 JAMES *Woodman* vii, There is some truth in what you say.

**b.** Agreement with the thing represented, in art or literature; accuracy of delineation or representation; the quality of being 'true to life'. Also, in *Arch.*, absence of deceit, pretence, or counterfeit, e. g. of imitation of stone in paint or plaster.

1828 DUPPA *Trav. Italy*, etc. 105 The interior of the two houses of Pansa and Sallust..restored..with great apparent truth. 1840 *C. O. Müller's Hist. Lit. Greece* xi. § 7. 135 These pictures..had a striking truth. 1890 C. H. MOORE *Gothic Archit.* viii. 286 In truth and skill of modelling even the sculptures of Chartres and St. Denis..surpass these of Wells.

**6.** Agreement with a standard or rule; accuracy, correctness; *spec.* accuracy of position or adjustment; often in phrase *out of truth.*

1669 STURMY *Mariner's Mag.* v. i. 2 This Instrument will come to the Truth, as well as a Needle of greater charge. 1707 MORTIMER *Husb.* 43 To make them [ploughs]..go true depends much upon the truth of the Iron-work. 1825 J. NICHOLSON *Operat. Mechanic* 590 Otherwise the door, when put together, will be out of truth. 1854 *Poultry Chron.* I. 609 The best fowls..as to truth of feather, condition, and general character. 1862 *Catal. Internat. Exhib., Brit.* II. No. 5831, The friction..allows the wheels to rotate with perfect truth and freedom.

**7.** Genuineness, reality, actual existence.

1599 SHAKS. *Hen. V*, IV. iii. 14 Thou art fram'd of the firme truth of valour. 1603 — *Meas. for M.* III. i. 166 She (hauing the truth of honour in her). 1842 TENNYSON *Morte D'Arthur* 291 On to dawn, when dreams Begin to feel the truth and stir of day. 1844 MRS. BROWNING *Lost Bower* xlvii, The golden-hearted daisies Witnessed..To the truth of things,.. And I woke to Nature's real.

**III.** Something that is true.

**8.** True statement or account; that which is in accordance with the fact: chiefly in phr. *to say, speak*, or *tell the truth* (also *arch.* without *the*), to speak truly, to report the matter as it really is (see also SAY *v.*[1] 11, SPEAK *v.* 23, TELL *v.* 18). Cf. sense 11, from which this is not always distinguishable.

Prov. *Tell* (*say, speak*) *the truth and shame the devil*: see SHAME *v.* 4 d.

*α.* 1362 LANGL. *P. Pl.* A. I. 133 Þis I trouwe beo treuþe! hose con teche þe betere, Loke þou suffre him to seye. c 1400 *Destr. Troy* 2338 Yf ye wilne for to witte how hit worthe shulde, I shall telle you the trewthe. c 1440 *Jacob's Well* 152 Þerfore, levyth ȝoure lesynges, & spekyth trewthe.

*β.* 1548 PATTEN *Exped. Scotl.* Pref. a v, An Epigram.., the whiche I had, or rather (to saie truth and shame the deuel, for out it wool) I stale..from a frende of myne. 1576 GASCOIGNE *Philomene* xcviii, Truth is truth, and muste be tolde. 1610 SHAKS. *Temp.* II. i. 137 The truth you speake doth lacke some gentlenesse, And time to speake it in. 1610 HOLLAND *Camden's Brit.* (1637) 632 A man to say truth well skilled in antiquities. 1735-8 BOLINGBROKE *Parties* Ded. 18 Truth may sometimes offend. 1823 BYRON *Juan* XIV. ci, Truth is always strange; Stranger than fiction. 1869 LOWELL *Lett.* (1894) II. 42 Tell us the truth as much as you like,..but tell it in a friendly way.

**b.** *loosely.* Mental apprehension of truth (in sense 10); knowledge.

1644 MILTON *Educ.* Wks. (1847) 98/1 Assertions, the knowledge and the use of which cannot but be a great furtherance..to the enlargement of truth. 1843 LOWELL *Glance behind Curtain* Poems (1844) 176 Men..Made wiser by the steady growth of truth.

**9.** True religious belief or doctrine; orthodoxy. Often with *the*, denoting a particular form of belief or teaching held by the speaker to be the true one; esp. in Quaker language. Cf. also sense 10.

*α.* c 1375 *Sc. Leg. Saints* i. (*Petrus*) 607 Twa knychttis.. þe quhilk petir..Conuertit...And fra thay þe treutht had tane [etc.]. 1562 WINȜET *Cert. Tract.* iii. Wks. (S.T.S.) I. 25, I can espy na thing thairin abhorring fra the treuth. 1567 *Gude & Godlie B.* (S.T.S.) 8 Heir him that preiche the word of treuth.

*β.* 1387 TREVISA *Higden* (Rolls) VII. 205 Þere is no verrey martirdom bot it be by meynteninge of truþe [*v.r.* truwþe]. 1556 OLDE *Antichrist* 9 b, Fauourers of the gospelles truthe. 1655 MILTON *Sonn. Massacher Piemont* 3 Them who kept thy truth so pure of old When all our Fathers worship't Stocks and Stones. 1662 in *Extr. S. P. rel. Friends* II. (1911) 144 It is ordered that there be a Collectione this month for the seruis of the truth. 1710 O. SANSOM *Acc. Life* 40 The Friend was declaring the Truth, when the Priest..came in. 1795 MACKNIGHT *Epist.* (1820) III. 147 The inspired writers often call'd the Gospel Revelation, The Truth. 1893 A. BIRRELL *Res Judicatæ* 134 The Church became a Living Witness to the Truth.

**b.** Conduct in accordance with the divine standard; spirituality of life and behaviour. (Cf. sense 4.)

*α.* 1382 WYCLIF *John* iii. 21 He that doth treuthe, cometh to the liȝt, that his workis be schewid, for thei ben don in God. — 1 *John* i. 6 If we shulen seie, for [1388 that] we han felauschip with him, and we wandren in derknessis, we liȝen, and we don not treuthe. — 2 *John* 4, I ioyede ful miche, for I foond of thi sones goynge in treuthe, as we receyueden maundement of the fadir.

*β.* 1526 TINDALE *John* iii. 21 He that doth the trueth [1534 TINDALE, *Geneva*, doth truth; CRANMER, 1611 trueth] commeth to the light.

**10.** That which is true, real, or actual (in a general or abstract sense); reality; *spec.* in religious use, spiritual reality as the subject of revelation or object of faith (often not distinguishable from 9).

*α.* c 1380 WYCLIF *Serm.* Sel. Wks. I. 13 Crist is a corner stoon, and groundiþ al treuþe. 1382 — *John* viii. 32 ȝe schulen knowe the treuthe, and the treuthe schal delyuere ȝou [1388 make you fre]. *Ibid.* xiv. 6, I am weye, treuthe, and lyf. 1458 in Parker *Dom. Archit.* III. 44 Now God geve us grace to folowe treuthe even That we may have a place in the blysse of heven. 1560 DAUS tr. *Sleidane's Comm.* 31 The trewth, will, and commaundement of the heauenly Father must be accomplished.

*β.* 1547-64 BAULDWIN *Mor. Philos.* (Palfr.) 145 Forasmuch as God is the trueth, & that truth is God, hee that departeth from the one departeth from the other. 1646 SIR T. BROWNE *Pseud. Ep.* I. v. 18 In knowledge there is no slender difficulty,..truth..wise men say doth lye in a well. 1785 REID *Intell. Powers* 277 The light of truth..fills my mind. 1819 KEATS *Ode Grecian Urn* 49 Beauty is truth, truth beauty. 1855 BREWSTER *Newton* II. xxiv. 340 Truth has no greater enemy than its unwise defenders. 1895 H. R. REYNOLDS in *Expositor* Jan. 75 God's thought is our most conclusive definition of truth. 1895 VERN. LEE in *Contemp. Rev.* Mar. 346 Truth is perceived by flashes.

**b.** Personified; *spec.* each of the two goddesses of truth in ancient Egyptian mythology.

*α.* 1362 LANGL. *P. Pl.* A. I. 12 Þis Tour & þis Toft..treuþe is þer-inne,..he is Fader of Fei, þat formed ow alle.

*β.* 1553 BALE *Gardiner's De vera Obed.* H j b, I..am compelled to take my wyfe Truthe to me. 1644 MILTON *Areop.* (Arb.) 74 So Truth be in the field, we do injuriously by licencing and prohibiting to misdoubt her strength. Let her and Falshood grapple. 1858 WILKINSON in Rawlinson *Herodotus* II. lviii. II. 101 *note*, The sacred beetle of the sun, overshadowed by the wings of two figures of the goddess Thmei, or 'Truth'. 1910 MRS. H. M. TIRARD *Bk. of Dead* v. 125 The weighing of the soul takes place in the great hall of the two truths in the Heliopolis of the nether-world. The two goddesses of truth at the eastern and western ends of the hall.

**11.** The fact or facts; the actual state of the case; the matter or circumstance as it really is. (Cf. sense 8.)

*α.* c 1450 *Mankind* 831 in *Macro Plays* 31 The prowerbe seyth 'þe trewth tryith þe sylfe'.

*β.* 1340-70 *Alex. & Dind.* 275 Of þat þou senteste, sire king, to say þe truthe Of al þe lore of our lif..haue vs exkused, For we ne konne þe nouht kenne our costomus alle. c 1537 DE BENESE *Measuryng Lande* X iv, They make the square therof muche lesse than the truthe. 1606 SHAKS. *Ant. & Cl.* IV. xiv. 126 She sent you word she was dead: But fearing since how it might worke, hath sent Me to proclaime the truth. 1691 T. H[ALE] *Acc. New Invent.* 52 The said Commissioners are to report to this Board the Truth of the Fact. 1748 HARTLEY *Observ. Man* I. ii. 202 We judge the Distances to be less than the Truth. 1908 R. BAGOT *A. Cuthbert* xxvii, 362 If he does not know, he more than suspects the truth.

**b.** The real thing, as distinguished from an imitation; the genuine article; the reality corresponding to a type or symbol, the antitype. Now *rare* or *Obs.*

**1531** *Acc. Ld. High Treas. Scot.* VI. 20 Item, for romaney buge to lyne the samyn goune, all truth..xiij li. ix s. *a* **1653** Gouge *Comm. Heb.* ix. 23 (1655) 390 His body was the truth of the Tabernacle:..His mediation the truth of the incense: ..He the truth of most types. **1774** Goldsm. *Nat. Hist.* (1776) V. 270 [The parrot's] voice..is more like a man's than that of any other [bird]; the raven is too hoarse, and the jay and magpie too shrill, to resemble the truth.

**c.** ? Actual property or nature (*of* something). *rare.*

**1552** *Bk. Com. Prayer, Communion* Rubric (*ad fin.*), It is against the truthe of Christes true naturall body, to be in mo places then in one, at one tyme.

**12.** with *a* and *pl.* A true statement or proposition; a point of true belief, a true doctrine; a fixed or established principle; a verified fact; a reality.

*α.* *c* **1380** Wyclif *Wks.* (1880) 94 Prelatis constreynen men of symple vnderstondyng..to assente to here dampnacion of treuþes of goddis lawe.

*β.* *c* **1380** Wyclif *Wks.* (1880) 293 þe creature þat telliþ hem a truþe in name of god. **1613** Jackson *Creed* I. 42 Some notable truth, whose beleefe did concerne vs. **1615** G. Sandys *Trav.* 60 The truths of religion are many times above reason, but never against it. **1646** Sir T. Browne *Pseud. Ep.* IV. xii. 210 That women are menstruant, and men pubescent, at the year of twice seven, is accounted a punctual truth. **1758** S. Hayward *Serm.* i. 3 This is not a fancy, ..but is a truth built upon divine testimony. **1858** O. W. Holmes *Aut. Breakf.-t.* iii, Leave your friend to learn unpleasant truths from his enemies. **1876** G. Macdonald *T. Wingfold* xiii, Something at the root of all facts—namely, truths, or eternal laws of being.

**IV. 13.** Phrases. (See also 6, 8.) *In truth, of a truth* (arch.), † *of truth*, † *for a truth* (obs.): in fact, as a fact; truly, verily, really, indeed: mostly used to strengthen or emphasize a statement.

*α.* **14..** *Why I can't be a Nun* 191 in *E. E. P.* (1862) 143 Hyt was a howse of nunes in trewthe,..But not welle gouernede, and þat was rowthe. *a* **1548** Hall *Chron., Edw. IV* 226 And for a treugth at thys season there was mortal warre betwene king Lewes and the duke of Borgoyne. *c* **1560** A. Scott *Poems* (S.T.S.) ii. 2 The grit Debait and Turnament Off trewth no toung can tell.

*β.* **1526** Tindale *Matt.* xiv. 33 Of a truth thou arte the sonne of God. **1647** Clarendon *Hist. Reb.* I. § 67 They did in truth desire it. **1727** De Foe *Syst. Magic* I. iii. (1840) 84 These people pretend to blame him, whereas in truth they ought only to blame themselves. **1795** Burke *Corr.* (1844) IV. 327 In truth, all these distempers pass my skill. **1873** 'Ouida' *Pascarèl* I. 57 Of a truth I loved you. **1884** Pae *Eustace* 6 It was in truth a scene of great beauty.

† **b.** *Of (a) truth* (predicatively): True; actually or really so. *Obs. rare.*

*c* **1566** J. Alday tr. *Boaystuau's Theat. World* I j b, It is of a truth, that the Priests of the Heathen..were chosen [etc.]. **1590** Webbe *Trav.* Epist. (Arb.) 13 In this booke there is nothing mentioned..but that which is of truth: and what mine own Eies haue perfectly seene.

**c.** *ellipt.* or as *int. Truth!* either as an expression of assent (cf. True *a.* 3 b), or as intensive (= *in truth*). Cf. Troth *sb.* 4 c. *arch.*

**1534** Tindale *Matt.* xv. 27 She answered and sayde: truthe Lorde: neverthclesse the whelpes eate of the crommes. **1568** Grafton *Chron.* II. 69 Truth said he, my predecessors..were much both better and greater than I. **1854** Tennyson *Geraint & Enid* 289 Arms? truth! I know not.

**V. 14.** Combinations. **a.** attrib., as *truth-breach, -gold, -light, -world, -worship.* **b.** instrumental, as *truth-dictated, -filled, -led, -shod, -tried, -writ.* **c.** objective and obj. gen., as *truth-finder, -hunter, -lover, -seeker, -speaker, -teller, -unraveller; truth-bearing, -bringing, -denying, -desiring, -loving, -painting, -passing, -perplexing, -revealing, -saying, -seeking, -speaking, -telling*, etc., sbs. and adjs. See also Truthlike.

**1847** Cdl. Wiseman *Ess., Unreality Anglican Belief* (1853) II. 394 Such vivid, *truth-bearing phrase. **1597** Beard *Theatre God's Judgem.* (1612) 279 A grieuous crime of disloyaltie and *truth-breach. **1895** Church *Pascal Serm.* xix. 319 Imagination is at once the most misleading and the most *truth-bringing of mental powers. **1895** Sayce *Egypt of Hebr. & Herod.* 94 Ameni the *truth-declaring name. **1850** O. Winslow *Inner Life* iv. 119 *Truth-denying,..soul-destroying error. **1871** E. F. Burr *Ad Fidem* vi. 92 A *truth-desiring spirit. **1830** Gen. P. Thompson *Exerc.* (1842) I. 278 The noxious and *truth-destroying practice of oath-taking. *a* **1770** Chatterton *On Mr. Alcock* Poet. Wks. (1886) 107 In *truth-dictated lays. *a* **1847** Eliza Cook *Poems* II. Pref. 7 Many a brave, *truth-filled mind. **1749** Fielding *Tom Jones* vi. i, The *truth-finder, and the gold-finder. **1839** Bailey *Festus* xix. (1848) 211 Some grains of *truth-gold. **1892** A. Birrell *Res Judicatæ* (1893) 157 The anxious *truth-hunter. **1839** Bailey *Festus* vi. (1848) 61 *Truth-led in Time's darkest hour. **1853** Reade *Chr. Johnstone* vi, We'll fight for nature-light, *truth-light, and sun-light. **1852** Tennyson *Ode Death Wellington* 189 *Truth-lover was our English Duke. **1856** *N. Brit. Rev.* XXVI. 16 Reasonable and *truth-loving men. **1612** Selden *Illustr. Drayton's Poly-olb.* i. 16 *Truth-passing reports of Poeticall Bards. **1735-6** Thomson *Liberty* v. 610 *Truth-perplexing metaphysick wits. **1600** Fairfax *Tasso* v. lxvi, Ere *truth-reuealing time..Bewraid her act. **1895** Jas. Kidd *Moral. & Relig.* x. 426 Truth-revealing teaching. **1552** Huloet, *Trought sayinge, or spekinge, or tellyng, *ueridicentia, ueriloquentia.* **1864** Bowen *Logic* vii. (1870) 225 The inductive *truth-seeker. **1852** Robertson *Serm.* Ser. III. xvi. 207 He is responsible..for the way in which he arrived at them [opinions]—whether in a slothful and selfish, or in an honest and *truth-seeking manner. **1876** Blackie *Songs Relig. & Life* 130 A *truth-shod Christian brotherhood. **1552** Huloet, *Trought speker, *ueridicus.* **1711** Pope *Let. to Jas. Craggs* 19 July, Their Method of Revenge on the Truth-Speaker is to attack his Reputation. **1552** *Truth-speaking (*sb.*) [see *truth-saying*]. **1856** S. J. Rigaud *Serm. Inspir. Script.* i. 20 According to that general law of truth-speaking, which exacts not that a statement should be verbally correct, but that it should convey a true impression. **1552** Huloet, *Trought speking, or sayinge, *ueridicus.* **1872** Tennyson *Gareth & Lyn.* 415 Bounteous, merciful, Truth-speaking, brave. **1552** Huloet, *Trought teller, and trought speker. *c* **1586** C'tess Pembroke *Ps.* ci. v, For truth-tellers I will search the land. **1852** Tennyson *Ode Death Wellington* 188 Truth-teller was our England's Alfred named. **1552** *Truth-telling (*sb.*) [see *truth-saying*]. **1803** Mary Charlton *Wife & Mistress* IV. 278 His system of truth-telling. **1847** Helps *Friends in C.* I. i. 8 Truth-telling in its highest sense requires a well-balanced mind. **1756** C. Smart tr. *Horace, Sat.* I. iv. (1826) II. 43 When *truth-telling Bacchus opens the secrets of his heart. **1908** R. Bagot *A. Cuthbert* viii, Impressions..confirmed by the truth-telling light of day. **1784** Cowper *Task* III. 56 The calm of *truth-tried love. **1850** Bushnell *God in Christ* 59 Whosoever..would have the *truth-world overhang him as an empyrean of stars. **1879** Geo. Eliot *Theo. Such* iii. 55 This sort of *truth-worship.

**Truth,** *v.* [f. prec. sb., in various independent senses.]

† **1.** *trans.* To believe, trust. *Obs.*

? *a* **1300** *Prayer to Virgin* 24 in *O. E. Misc.* 196 Wil ich neuer eft more Lauedi for þine sake treuþen feondes lore.

† **2. a.** *intr.* To plight one's troth; to enter into an engagement of marriage. **b.** *trans.* To betroth, affiance: = Troth *v. Obs.*

*c* **1315** Shoreham I. 1660 ȝyf an oþer treuþeþ seþe Wyþ word of þat hys nouþe. *c* **1330** *Arth. & Merl.* (Kölbing) 8639 þer treuþed Arthour Gwenore, his quen. *c* **1412** Hoccleve *De Reg. Princ.* 3690 She truthede was to Indibal.

† **3.** *trans.* To name or call truly; to describe with truth as. *Obs. nonce-use.*

**1638** Ford *Fancies* II. ii, The ancients Who chatted of the golden age, feign'd trifles. Had they dreamt this, they would have truth'd it heav'n.

† **4.** *intr.* with *it*: To speak or deal truly (nonce-rendering of Gr. ἀληθεύειν in Eph. iv. 15). *Obs.*

**1648** T. Hill *Serm. Truth & Love* 22 Truthing it in love, which were an admirable motto for saints. **1656** S. Winter *Serm.* Ep. Ded., I have without gall..managed this controversie, truthing it in love.

**5.** *trans.* To bring to 'truth' (Truth *sb.* 6), adjust accurately: = True *v.* 2.

**1881** J. W. Warman in *Eng. Mechanic* No. 874. 368/1 It permits of the removal of such Rails for any truthing which they may require.

Hence **Tru·thing** *vbl. sb.*, † **a.** the action of plighting troth, contract of marriage (*obs.*); **b.** (see sense 5).

*c* **1315** Shoreham I. 1665 Bote ȝef þer folȝede þat treuþyng A ferst flesch ymone. *Ibid.* 1759 And ȝef þer hys condicioun Yset atter treuþynge.

† **Tru·thable,** *a. Obs. rare*⁻¹. [f. Truth *sb.* + -able.] = True *a.* 4; correct.

*a* **1593** Nashe in G. Harvey *Pierce's Super.* 180 Truthable and eligible English.

**Truthful** (trū·þfŭl), *a.* [f. Truth *sb.* + -ful.]

**1.** Of statements, etc.: Full of truth; sincere. (Now only as *transf.* from 2.)

**1596** R. L[inche] *Diella* xiii, My truthfull pleadings will not cause you rue. *Mod.* A perfectly honest and truthful statement.

**2.** Of persons (or their attributes): Disposed to tell, or habitually telling, the truth; free from deceitfulness; veracious. (In quot. 1787, Telling the truth, correct in statement.) Also *fig.* Giving true information, not deceptive (cf. 3).

**1787** Berington *Abeill.* Pref. 16, I profess to be as accurate as I can, and as truthful as the character of my records will allow. **1816** Scott *Antiq.* xx, What my poverty takes awa frae the weight o' my counsel, grey hairs and a truthfu' heart should add it twenty times. **1860** W. G. Ward *Nat. & Grace* I. 109 He has given us faculties, which are truthful and not mendacious. **1865** Max Müller *Chips* (1880) I. i. 16 In order to discover truth, we must be truthful ourselves. **1866** Reade *G. Gaunt* (ed. 2) III. 39 Before he got into this mess he was a singularly truthful person; but now a lie was nothing to him.

**3.** Of ideas, artistic representation, etc.: Characterized by truth; corresponding with fact or reality; true, accurate, exact.

**1859** [implied in Truthfulness]. **1868** E. Edwards *Ralegh* I. x. 163 For a long period, the truthful knowledge of what Spaniards had really achieved was slight. **1871** *Routledge's Ev. Boy's Ann., Suppl.* June 9 A beautifully executed and truthful portrait. **1885** Swinburne *Misc.* (1886) 294 There is none left..whose bright and sweet invention is so fruitful, so truthful, or so delightful as Mrs. Molesworth's.

**Truthfully** (trū·þfŭli), *adv.* [f. prec. + -ly [2].] In a truthful manner; with truth, truly.

**1846** in Worcester. **1871** H. Ainsworth *Tower Hill* III. xix, One question more,..By answering it truthfully, thou may'st escape the rack. **1892** Swinburne *Stud. Prose & Poetry* (1894) 226 What has been said of Lamb's or of Landor's ..briefest..notes may as truthfully be said of Hugo's.

**Truthfulness** (trū·þfŭlnės). [f. as prec. + -ness.] The quality of being truthful.

**1.** Disposition to tell the truth; veracity.

**1843** Miall in *Nonconf.* III. 1 Soundness of principles, and ..truthfulness of spirit. *a* **1873** Wilberforce *Ch. & Empires* (1874) 110 Any..writer..who..commands belief by his accuracy and truthfulness.

**2.** Accuracy in representing the reality; freedom from pretence or counterfeit, as in a work of art or literature.

**1859** Geo. Eliot *A. Bede* xvii, It is for this rare, precious quality of truthfulness that I delight in many Dutch paintings. **1874** Green *Short Hist.* vi. § 5. 324 No words could paint with so terrible a truthfulness the spirit of the New Monarchy. **1886** C. E. Pascoe *Lond. of To-day* xlii. (ed. 3) 362 English work, and especially as applied to furniture, used to have a character for truthfulness, simplicity, solidity, and comfort.

† **Tru·thhead.** *Obs.* In 4 **treuth-hede, treuthede, truthhede, trouth-hedd,** 5 **trewþehede, trouþhede.** [f. Truth, Troth + -head.] Faithfulness, loyalty.

*a* **1300** *Cursor M.* 97 (Cott.) Of hir godnes and hir treuthede [*v.rr.* trouth-hedd, trouþhede]. *Ibid.* 4423 For þi leute and þi truthhede [*v.r.* treuth-hede]. **14..** *R. Gloucester's Chron.* (Rolls) 7370 Uor he wolde þat alle men schulde se his trewþehede [*Cott. MS.* trewehede].

**Tru·thify,** *v. nonce-wd.* [f. Truth + -(i)fy.] *intr.* To act according to truth; to deal truly. (Cf. Truth *v.* 4.)

**1647** Trapp *Comm. Eph.* iv. 15 Speaking the truth, or, Doing the truth, as the Vulgar hath it. Truthifying, or following the truth, as one rendereth it. **1689** M. Sylvester *Serm. Heb.* x. 24-5 (1690) 334 b, This is indeed..to truthifie in Love, if I may make an English Word to express the valor of the Greek Word, ἀληθεύοντες ἐν ἀγάπῃ.

**Truthiness**: see Truthy.

**Truthless** (trū·þlės), *a.* Forms: see Truth. [f. Truth *sb.* + -less.] Destitute of truth (in various senses).

† **1.** Lacking faith; distrustful. (In quot. app. *absol.* as *sb.*) *Obs. rare*⁻¹.

*c* **1200** *Trin. Coll. Hom.* 73 Ten þing..leten men of here scrifte,..shamfestnesse, drede, ortrowe, trewðeleas [app. gloss on 'ortrowe'].

**2.** Faithless, unfaithful, perfidious. *Obs.* or *arch.*

**1567** *Satir. Poems Reform.* iv. 84 Off Tygeris quholpis,.. Ane treuthles troup hes drewin me to this end. *a* **1600** *Flodden F.* II. (1664) 15 And turn such truthless guest to teen.

**3.** Untruthful, mendacious; making false statements, 'false'.

**1567** *Satir. Poems Reform.* iv. 41 My truethles toung my honoure defylit. **1605** Camden *Rem.* (1637) 251 He prooved a truthlesse Prophet. **1888** *Gd. Words* Oct. 682 The truthless look, the shuffling gait, The mind that darkly schemes.

**4.** Having no truth in it, as a statement, etc.; void of truth; untrue, false.

**1610** Holland *Camden's Brit.* I. 9 These opinions are altogether truthlesse. **1660** *Trial Regic.* (1679) 235, I hope ..that what I have said..is not Truthless but of Weight. **1850** *Tait's Mag.* XVII. 715/1 Senseless and truthless clamour. **1911** *Contemp. Rev.* Nov. 666 Idolaters of truthless imaginations.

Hence **Tru·thlessness.**

**1854** *Tait's Mag.* XXI. 494 Representatives of the wit and truthlessness of our age. **1900** Morley *Cromwell* II. v. 184 The letters disclosed his truthlessness.

**Truthlike** (trū·þləik), *a.* [f. as prec. + -like.] Like or resembling truth or the truth; † likely to be true, probable (quot. 1657).

**1567** Drant *Horace, Art Poetry* A iv, If thou feyne, feyne then the things as truthlyke as you maye. **1570** Foxe *A. & M.* (ed. 2) 124/1 They seme more legendlike, then truthlike. **1657** Earl Monm. tr. *Paruta's Pol. Disc.* 78 To seek out the truest, or at least, the most truthlike causes thereof. **1894** J. T. Fowler *Adamnan* Introd. 25 It.. mentions certain incidents in a remarkably naïve and truthlike manner.

Hence **Tru·thlikeness,** likeness to truth, verisimilitude.

*a* **1586** Sidney *Arcadia* III. (1622) 241 He knew..how few there be that can discerne betweene trueth and truthlikenesse, betweene shewes and substance. **1865** W. Kay *Crisis Hupfeldiana* 81 The results may have such simplicity, truthlikeness, and internal concinnity as may make us accept them. **1904** *Westm. Gaz.* 29 Aug. 3/1 The actor regards the part as farcical, for he pushes it..beyond truth-likeness.

† **Tru·thly,** *adv. Obs. rare*⁻¹. [irreg. f. as prec. + -ly [2].] In accordance with truth; honestly, without deceit.

**1493** *Acta Dom. Conc.* (1839) 313 Aithir of þe sadis partiis has subscriuit þis write with þar avne handis,..leilie or trewthelie, but fraud or gile.

**Truth-plight**: see Troth-plight.

**Truthsman** (trū·þsmæ̆n). *nonce-wd.* [f. *truth's*, gen. of Truth *sb.* + Man *sb.*[1]] A man of truth; a man characterized by or devoted to truth.

**1844** Miall *Ethics Nonconf.* (1847) 54 He stands before the world..as a truthsman.

**Truthy** (trū·þi), *a. rare* or *dial.* [f. as prec. + -y.] Characterized by truth; truthful, true. Hence **Tru·thiness,** truthfulness, faithfulness.

*c* **1800** J. H. Colls *Theodore* I, You..are afraid Theodore your sweetheart shouldn't prove truthy. **1824** J. J. Gurney in Braithwaite *Mem.* (1854) I. 242 Everyone who knows her is aware of her truthiness. **1848** *Fraser's Mag.* XXXVII. 404 Descriptions of country life and truthy touches of native manners. **1851** Sir F. Palgrave *Norm. & Eng.* I. 601 Regino was truthy and honest.

† **Tru·tinate,** *v. Obs.* [f. L. *trutināt-*, ppl. stem of *trutināre*, f. *trutina* = Gr. τρυτάνη balance, pair of scales: see -ate [3].] *trans.* To weigh in the balances; also *fig.* to weigh mentally, consider, estimate. So † **Tru·tinate** *ppl. a.* [ad. L. *tru-*

*inātus*, pa. pple.], weighed; *fig.* considered, estimated (usually const. as pple.); † **Trutination**, the action of weighing; *fig.* consideration, estimation; † **Tru·tine** [ad. L. *trutina* = Gr. τρυτάνη], a balance; *fig.* in *trutine of Hermes* (see quots.).

**1528** *St. Papers Hen. VIII*, VII. 123 Howe to discerne enserche and *trutynate the true from the false. **1638** WHITING *Albino & Bellama* 10 Madam, sayes he, be pleas'd to trutinate, And wisely weigh your servants gracefull voyce. **1657** TOMLINSON *Renou's Disp.* 136 To be trutinated by just weight and measure. **1528** *St. Papers Hen. VIII*, VII. 124 So weighty a cause well *trutinate and expended..by the jugement of..the most excellent clerks and doctours. **1570** FOXE *A. & M.* (ed. 2) 1127/2 Humaine fragilitie suffereth not all things to bee pondered, trutinate, and weyed in iust balaunce. **1610** W. FOLKINGHAM *Art of Survey* I. i. 1 The view and trutinate intimation of a subiect, from Center to Circumference. **1633** B. C. *Puritanism* I. 22 The lesser sinne, and the greatest are alike..in Gods iust *trutination and weighing of them. **1646** SIR T. BROWNE *Pseud. Ep.* IV. vii. 196 In regard of the scale or decision of trutination. **1647** LILLY *Chr. Astrol.* xcviii. 501 The first way..of rectifying a Nativity..was by the *Trutine or Scrutiny of Hermes. **1696** PHILLIPS (ed. 5), *Trutine of Hermes*, an artificial method of rectifying a Nativity, by finding out the Day of Conception, and the place of the Moon at that time. **1819** JAS. WILSON *Compl. Dict. Astrol.*, *Rectification*, the method of bringing a nativity to its true time... Beside the animoder of Ptolemy, we have the trutine of Hermes, the methods of Argol, Morin, Kepler, &c., &c.

**Truttaceous** (trʊtēɪ·ʃəs), *a. Ichth.* [f. mod.L. *truttāceus* (Willughby *a* 1672), f. late L. *trutta* TROUT: see -ACEOUS.] Related to the trout.

**1753** CHAMBERS *Cycl. Suppl.*, *Salmo*, the salmon... It is distinguished from other fish of the truttaceous kind by these characters. *Ibid.* s. v., The truttaceous fishes are divided into two tribes.

**Truttle**, variant of TRATTLE *sb.*[2]

**Truu**, obs. f. TROW *v.* **Truwage**, var. TREWAGE *Obs.* **Truwandise, -aund, -aunt**: see TRUANDISE, TRUANT. **Truwe, truwes, -ys**, obs. ff. TRUCE. **Truwitt**: see *true-wit* s. v. TRUE D. 1. **Trux, truxe**, obs. ff. TRUCE. **Truys, -yse, Truyt**, obs. ff. TRUCE, TRUTH. **Trw**, obs. f. TRUE. **Trwandrye, Trwandyse, Trwaunt**, see TRUANTRY, TRUANDISE, TRUANT. **Trwce**, obs. f. TRUCE. **Trwcheman**, obs. Sc. f. TRUCHMAN, dragoman. **Trwe, Trwes, trwys**, obs. ff. TRUE, TRUCE.

**Try** (trəi), *sb.* [f. TRY *v.*]

I. An act of trying, etc

† **1.** *Naut.* In phrase *At try*, *a-try* (see A-TRY), the position of a vessel lying-to in a storm; see TRY *v.* 17. *Obs.*

*α.* **1556** W. TOWRSON in Hakluyt *Voy.* (1589) 98 All the night [wee] laye at trie with much raine and foule weather. *a* **1618** RALEIGH *Royal Navy* 12 We are forced to lye at trye with our maine Course and Missen. **1627** CAPT. SMITH *Seaman's Gram.* ix. 40 A storme let vs lie at Trie with our maine course, that is, to hale the tacke aboord, the sheat close aft, the boling set vp, and the helme tied close aboord. **1694** MOTTEUX *Rabelais* v. xviii. 80 Let us go and lye at Trie with our main Course.

*β.* **1558-89** A. JENKINSON *Voy. & Trav.* (Hakl. Soc.) I. 96 There arose another great storme..and we lay a trie, being driuen farre into the sea. **1611-1867** [see A-TRY]. **1676** WOOD *Jrnl.* in *Acc. Sev. Late Voy.* I. (1694) 173 We lay a try under a Main-sail. **1729** CAPT. W. WRIGLESWORTH *MS. Log-bk. of the 'Lyell'* 22 Dec., At 5 Reefed our Courses, furled the Fore Sail, brought to, and lay a try under Main Sail.

† **2.** A trial, a test. *Obs. rare.*

**1607** SHAKS. *Timon* v. i. 11 Then this breaking of his, Ha's beene but a Try for his Friends?

**3.** *Joinery.* The condition of being 'tried' to a perfect level; cf. TRY *v.* 8.

**1678** MOXON *Mech. Exerc.* iv. 65 If your work be hollow in the middle, you must Plain both the Bearing sides thinner, till they come to a Try with the middle.

**4.** An attempt, endeavour, effort. Chiefly *colloq.*

**1832** FROUDE in *Rem.* (1838) I. 322 Versification is out of my line, else I should have had a try at it. **1848** MRS. GASKELL *M. Barton* xxvii, Don't give it up..let's have a try for him. **1890** *Pall Mall G.* 30 July 2/2 The Emperor.. succeeded at the first try.

**b.** *Rugby Football.* The right of attempting to kick a goal, obtained by carrying the ball behind the goal-line and touching it on the ground. Cf. *touch-down* (TOUCH- 2).

**1845** *Rules Footb. Rugby School* § 5 *Try at goal*...The ball when punted must be within, when caught without, the line of goal. **1880** *Times* 12 Nov. 4/5 The efforts of a worsted side..to gain the goal or the 'try' which is required to make the match a tie. **1893** *Ibid.* 18 Dec. 10/3 The North were victors by two goals and two tries to three tries.

II. An instrument for trying.

† **5.** A sieve or sifting screen. *Obs.*

*c* **1475** *Pict. Voc.* in Wr.-Wülcker 808/14 *Panducsator cum suis implementis*...*Hec falanga*, a try. **1603** HOLLAND *Plutarch's Mor.* 86 They will not passe thorough the holes of the sieve, ruddle, or trie, if they be narrow. **1644** G. PLATTES in *Hartlib's Legacy* (1655) 201 Mingling Corn with great Beans, exceeding hard dryed on a Kiln, which may be separated easily with a wire Trie. **1804** DUNCUMB *Hist. Hereford.* Gloss., *Try*, a wire screen for cleansing wheat from the chaff.

† **6.** = TRYSAIL. *Obs. rare*$^{-1}$.

**1665-6** *Adm. Crt. Exam.* 22 Mar. 66 A maine course or try.

† **Try, trie**, *a. Obs.* Forms: 3-5 trie, 4 tri, triȝe, 4-6 trye, 5, 7 try. [ME. *trie*, etc., prob. a. OF. *trié*, pa. pple. of *trier* to pick out, cull, select (see TRY *v.*), or OF. *trie* sb. choice, 'élite', used attrib.]

**1.** Choice, excellent, good; = TRIED *ppl. a.* 2.

*a* **1300** *Sat. People Kildare* xiv. in *E. E. P.* (1862) 155 Worþ hit wer þat he wer king þat ditid þis trie þing. *c* **1315** SHOREHAM i. 1575 By-tuixe god and holy folk Loue hys wel trye and ryche. **1377** LANGL. *P. Pl.* B. I. 135 Treuthe is tresore þe triest [*v. rr.* trieste, tryest, triȝest] on erþe. *c* **1425** *Cast. Persev.* 536 in *Macro Plays* 93 He schal be serwaunt good & try. **1596** SPENSER *F. Q.* v. ii. 26 Those hands of gold,..those feete of silver trye.

**2.** *Joinery.* Quite true, correctly wrought: cf. TRY *sb.* 3, *v.* 8.

**1678** MOXON *Mech. Exerc.* vi. 101 If they can see light between the edge of the Rule and their Work: If they cannot they conclude their Work is Try, and well wrought.

Hence † **Try·ly, triely** *adv. Obs.*, choicely, excellently, finely.

*c* **1350** *Will. Palerne* 1228 Triliche was he a-tired in ful tristy armes. *Ibid.* 3198 Tvo baþes were boun by a litel while, & a-tired tryli to trusty trewe lordes. **1377** LANGL. *P. Pl.* B. Prol. 14, I seigh a toure on a toft trielich ymaked.

**Try** (trəi), *v.* Forms: 4-6 tri, 4-7 trie, trye, (4 treye, trei), 5- try. Pa. t. and pple. **tried** (trəid); also 4 (*pa. t.*) **triȝed**, (*pa. pple.*) **triȝede, i-triȝed, -et, ytried, ytryed**, 5 **y-tryid**; 4-5 **treid, tryyd**, 4-6 **tryede**, 4-7 **tryde**, 4-9 **tryed**, 5 (**tryude**), **triet, tryet** (also 6 *Sc.*), 5-6 **tryid**, 6-7 **tride, tryd**, *Sc.* **tryit**, 7 **tri'd**, 7-8 **try'd**. [a. OFr. *trie-r* (12th c., Benoit *Ducs de Norm.* II. 11518 Le tort del dreit Trier e conoistre e sevrer (to sift and know and sever the wrong from the right) = Pr., Cat. *triar*, also med.L. *triāre* (from Prov. or Fr.) to sift or pick out. The legal use appears to have been developed in Anglo-French, where it is known *c* 1280; there is no trace of this use in continental French. The origin of the Fr. and Prov. word is unknown.

The conjecture of Frisch, mentioned by Diez and by Skeat, that it represents a late L. *trītāre to grind out, thresh out, freq. of *terĕre*, is incompatible with the Provençal form. Another conjecture is that it was a transposed form of *tirer* 'to draw, extract', in a specific sense; but evidence is wanting.]

**1.** *trans.* To separate (one thing) from another or others; to set apart; to distinguish. Often with *out*. *Obs.* or *arch.*

*c* **1330** R. BRUNNE *Chron. Wace* (Rolls) 13260 Þey turnde ageyn, And tryde þe Bretons fro ilk Romeyn. **1413** *26 Pol. Poems* xii. 69 Til trouþe be fro treson tryed, Shal neuere be pes in regyon. *c* **1515** *Cocke Lorells B.* 13 With this man was a lusty company, For all raskyllers fro them they dyde trye. *a* **1548** HALL *Chron.*, *Hen. VII* 54 b, He [Henry VII] espyed and tried oute suche as he knewe..to beare no good wyll..towarde his person. **1592** WARNER *Alb. Eng.* VII. xxxvii. (1612) 180 For what is it but reason that humaine from brutish tries? [**1847** BUSHNELL *Chr. Nurt.* I. i. (1861) 11 Human children still living a mixed life, trying out the good and evil of the world.]

† **b.** To pick out, choose, select; *pa. pple.* (quot. 1340-70), selected, choice (cf. TRIED 2).

[**1292** BRITTON II. xxvii. § 5 Face le viscounte trier xii. prodeshommes.] **1340-70** *Alisaunder* 1233 For too keepe in that kith cumlich & riche All his tresour ytryed. *c* **1440** *Pallad. on Husb.* IV. 727 The kiyn also this tyme hit is to trie; Do chese hem that be chested huge & hie. *c* **1440** *Promp. Parv.* 502/2 Tryin [*v. r.* tryyn], *eligo, preeligo.* **1481** *Coventry Leet Bk.* 484 See that the seid persones so be [= by] you to be tried oute & chosen.

† **2.** To separate the good part of a thing from the rest, esp. by sifting or straining; hence, to sift or strain. Usually with *out*. *Obs.*

**1382** [see TRIED 1]. *c* **1420** ? LYDG. *Assembly of Gods* 2071 Try out the corne clene from the chaff. *c* **1430** *Two Cookery-bks.* 11 Take ȝolkys of eyroun y-tryid fro þe whyte. **14..** *Noble Bk. Cookry* (Napier 1882) 90 Put it to gedur with a crust of bred and try it through a strener. **1548** UDALL *Erasm. Par.* Pref. 10 The boulter tryeth out the branne. **1581** W. STAFFORD *Exam. Compl.* ii. (1876) 51 What neede they..to trie out the sandes of the ryuers of Tagus in Spaine, Pactolus in Asia, and Ganges in India, to get..small sparkes of gold. **1657** C. BECK *Univ. Char.* L viij, To trye, or fine from the dreggs. **1790** W. MARSHALL *Midl. Co.* (1796) II. Gloss. (E.D.S.), *Try*, v. to skreen.

† **b.** *gen.* To take or get *out*, to extract; also, in extended sense, To put *into*, insert. *Obs. rare.*

*c* **1440** *Pallad. on Husb.* II. 165 Impedymentis, rootis out thou trie. *Ibid.* 263 Aysell and wyne eke oute of hem men trie, As oute of peres. *Ibid.* III. 639 Wild asperages rootes many trie Into erthe ytilde. *Ibid.* XII. 94 The boones..in askes moolde Thay mynge, and it thai into skeppes trie.

† **3.** *spec.* To separate (metal) from the ore or dross by melting; to refine, purify by fire; also, to remove (the dross or impurity) from metal by fire. Usually with *out*. Also *fig.* *Obs.*

**13..** [see TRIED 1]. **1524** in *Acts Parlt. Scotl.* (1875) XII. 41/1 Þe gold gais furth of þe sammyn [realm] in greit quantite becaus it is tryit to ane hieare price and valoure in vþir realmis. **1535** COVERDALE *Zech.* xiii. 9, I..will clense them, as the syluer is clensed: Yee and trye them, like as golde is tryed. **1539** BIBLE (Great) *Ps.* xxvi. 2 Examen me, o Lord, & proue me: trie out my reynes and my hert. **1545** ELYOT, *Chalcites*, a stone..wherof brasse is tried. **1555** *Inv. Ch. Goods* (Surtees No. 97) 152 So moche refuse and baggaige tried out, by meane of the melting of the said plate. **1572** *Pat. Roll 14 Eliz.* XII. m. 22 (P.R.O.) Thomas Smyth ..hath..founde out and put in vse a newe and certene arte to trye out and make of yron verye true perfytt and good copper. **1596** SHAKS. *Merch. V.* II. ix. 63 The fier seauen times tried this, Seauen times tried that iud[g]ement is, That did neuer choose amis. **1686** W. HARRIS tr. *Lemery's Course Chym.* Introd. (ed. 3) 44 Coppels are porous vessels made in form of a cup to be used for the trying and purifying of Gold and Silver.

**4.** To extract (oil) from blubber or fat by heat; to melt down (blubber, etc.), to obtain the oil; to render; also, to extract (wax) from a honey-comb. Usually with *out*.

**1582** in W. H. Turner *Select. Rec. Oxford* (1880) 423 No chaundeler shall..trie or melt any tallowe w[th]in the walles. **1610** BARROUGH *Meth. Physick* III. lxii. (1639) 198 Oile tried out of wooll in sheeps flanks or necks. **1630** J. LEVETT *Ord. Bees* (1634) 51 After what manner doe you deale with your Combes to try out the waxe. **1852** MUNDY *Our Antipodes* viii. (1855) 195 A dead whale was..'tried out' by some speculating fisherman. **1867** SMYTH *Sailor's Word-bk.*, *To try down*, to boil out the oil from blubber at sea in whalers. **1883** SIR A. SHEA *Newfound. Fisheries* 10 (Fish. Exhib. Publ.) The fat is then cut up..and tried out by steam.

**b.** *intr.* for *pass.* *U.S.A.*

**1891** *Cent. Dict.* s. v., Grease tries out of a ham in cooking; ..the perspiration is trying out of him.

† **5.** To ascertain, find out (something doubtful, obscure, or secret) by search or examination; to sift out. Usually *to try out*. *Obs.*

[Cf. *c* **1300-25** N. BOZON *Contes Moral.* (1889) 9 La cause [of the attraction of the loadstone] ne peut estre triée.] *c* **1325** *Metr. Hom.* 56 Yef we wil the sothe treye, Gon we til dom of our Leuedye. **1430-40** LYDG. *Bochas* I. viii. (MS. Bodl. 263) lf. 36/1 But folke that list off daunger hem discharge..Til the trouthe be tried out in deed. **1567** *Satir. Poems Reform.* iii. 92 Tresoun to try sho was that tyme maist stout But sho is slak to try this tresoun out. **1584** COGAN *Haven Health* (1636) 9 By this meanes doth Galen trie out the time most fit for exercise. **1675** tr *Camden's Hist. Eliz.* I. (1688) 129 They all agreed on this, that Lidington..should first try the Queens mind. *a* **1761** LAW *Comf. Weary Pilgr.* (1809) 52 This therefore may serve as a touchstone wherby every one may try the truth of his state.

† **b.** With material object. *Obs. rare*$^{-1}$.

**1539** POLLARD, etc. in *St. Papers Hen. VIII* (1830) I. 619 We have dayly fownde and tryede oute bothe money and plate, hyde and muryde up in walls, vauttis and other secrette placis.

**c.** To ascertain the truth or right of (a matter, a quarrel, etc.) by test or endeavour; with *out*, to thrash or fight out; to determine. Now *rare*.

**1542** UDALL *Erasm. Apoph.* 163 b, To trye y[e] mater w[t] dynte of swearde. **1545** ELYOT, *Disceptare armis*, to trye by battayle. **1654** R. CODRINGTON tr. *Justine* XI. 298 He was enforced by them to try it out in battel with them. **1703** POPE *Thebais* 490 The rushing winds..With equal rage their airy quarrel try, And win by turns the Kingdoms of the sky. **1857** TROLLOPE *Barchester T.* xxiii, Mr. Arabin said that he would try the question out with Mrs. Bold.

**6.** *Law.* To examine and determine (a cause or question) judicially; to determine the guilt or otherwise of (an accused person) by consideration of the evidence; to sit in judgement on; to judge. Also *fig.* † Also *intr.* with *of* (quot. *c* 1330). (Prob. the earliest sense recorded in English.)

**a.** To try a cause or question.

[**1292** BRITTON I. v. § 8 Et si n'i eynt mie asez, si soint les chalengs triez. Et si les chalengs soint trovez verrays [etc.].] *a* **1300** *Cursor M.* 9686 (Cott.) Al þat þai striue a-mang þam thre, Thoru pes it agh at tried be. *c* **1330** R. BRUNNE *Chron.* (1810) 313 The wisest of þe clergie, with erles & barouns Togider went to trie of þer peticions. **1467** in *Eng. Gilds* (1870) 401 To trye it by xij. men aftur the lawe in suche case provided. **1562** *Aberdeen Kirk Sess. Rec.* (Spald. Cl.) 4 To trye, discusse, and examyn all faltis and offencis..off the haill inhabitantis off the burgh. *a* **1631** DONNE *Poems* (1650) 103 This will be tryed to morrow. **1755** W. DUNCAN *Cicero's Sel. Orations* x. (1816) 307 He.. may desire to know what crime it is that is trying. **1770** C. JENNER *Placid Man* VI. iv, Whilst the..cause had been trying at Mrs. Stapleton's fire-side [etc.]. **1815** SCOTT *Guy M.* xxxiii, It was tried in the Inner-house afore the Feifteen. **1892** SIR A. KEKEWICH in *Law Times Rep.* LXVII. 139/1, I have to try the case before me according to those cases. **1895** *Daily News* 4 Nov. 4/6 Mr. Justice Mathew, who tried the action,..had granted the injunction.

**b.** To try a person.

**1538** ELYOT, *Interrogari legibus*, to be tried by examination, that they had offended against the lawis. **1603** SHAKS. *Meas. for M.* II. i. 21 The Iury..May in the sworne-twelue haue a thiefe, or two Guiltier then him they try. **1674** in *Verney Mem.* (1907) II. 317 Judg Torner's son, who was tryed for his life last November for killing a man. **1797** MRS. RADCLIFFE *Italian* xvi, You must be tried before you are condemned. **1849** CUPPLES *Green Hand* ix, A gang o' Spanish pirates I saw tried for their lives. **1875** JOWETT *Plato* (ed. 2) V. 450 Let him who dares to smite an elder be tried for assault.

**7.** To test the strength, goodness, value, truth, or other quality of; to put to the proof, test, prove.

**13..** *E. E. Allit. P.* A. 311 To leue no tale be true to tryȝe, Bot þat hys one skyl may dem. **1362** LANGL. *P. Pl.* A. I. 183 Whan alle tresouris arn triȝede [B3 I-triȝed] treuþe is þe beste. **1422** tr. *Secreta Secret.*, *Priv. Priv.* 188 No word Sholde out-Passe, but yf hit were triet wyth reyson. *a* **1536** TINDALE *Expos. Matt.* vi. (1550) 65 b, Excepte a man be proued and tried it cannot be knowen..that he is righteous. **1602** SHAKS. *Ham.* I. iii. 62 The friends thou hast, and their adoption tride, Grapple them to thy Soule, with hoopes of Steele. **1825** T. HOOK *Sayings* Ser. II. *Man of Many Fr.* (Colburn) 157 Jumping and bumping himself about in Colonel Arden's new carriage in order to try the springs. **1881** FROUDE *Short Stud.* (1883) IV. II. v. 230 He..had determined to try every fact..by the strict rules of inductive science.

**b.** To examine (a person) for the purpose of

testing his qualifications: cf. TRIAL *sb.*[1] 6, TRIER 5. *Obs.* or *Hist.*

1636 in J. Bulloch *Pynours* (1887) 70 In cais any persone.. desyr to be admittit a laborar at the Shoir..they must first be tryit be the watter Baillie. 1654 *Clarke Papers* (Camden) III. 15 Those that sitte at Whitehall to try Ministers.

†**c.** *To try out*: to reject after trial; in quot., to dismiss (a challenged juryman): cf. TRIER 2.

1542-3 *Act 34 & 35 Hen. VIII*, c. 26 § 46 If..the residue of the saide Iurye make defaulte or be tryed out.

**d.** *To try a door, window*, etc., to ascertain by attempting to open it whether it is fastened or locked.

1844 DICKENS *Chimes* I. 2 The night-wind..trying, with its unseen hand, the windows and the doors; and seeking out some crevice by which to enter. 1889 GUNTER *That Frenchman* iv, Maurice..closes the door behind him, trying it to be sure the spring lock has worked.

**8.** *Joinery*. To bring (a piece of timber) to a perfectly flat surface by repeatedly testing it and planing off the projecting parts; to plane with the trying-plane; also *to try up*; also, to test the straightness of (a planed surface) or the correspondence of (adjoining surfaces); also *intr.* (of a surface) to prove accurate or straight when tested.

1593 FALE *Dialling* 2 Prepare a piece of very good wood, try it perfectly on both sides to an equall thicknesse. 1678 MOXON *Mech. Exerc.* iv. 60 To lay Boards..flat against, whiles they are Trying or Plaining. *Ibid.* v. 78 Try it again, as before, and if you find it Try all the way, you may..go over it again. 1679 *Ibid.* ix. 156 Try one side flat,..and both the edges straight. 1683 *Ibid., Printing* x. ¶ 2 All its Sides are tryed square to one another. 1776 G. SEMPLE *Building in Water* 85 After your Work is tried up or even put together. 1828 ADCOCK *Builders' Pocket-Bk.* 52 Swedish deals .., if tried up square at night they will be crooked in the morning.

**9.** *Try on*: to test the fit or style of (a garment) by putting it on. Also *absol.*

1693 CONGREVE *Old Bach.* IV. viii, The daughters only tore two pair of kid-leather gloves, with trying 'em on. 1804 MAR. EDGEWORTH *Pop. T., The Will* ii, Miss Barton was trying on her dress. 1848 THACKERAY *Van. Fair* xiii, He.. tried a new coat in Pall Mall. 1883 *Harper's Mag.* Feb. 446/1 She must go at once and 'try on!' It is a special order.

**10.** To subject to a severe test or strain; to strain the endurance or patience of, put to straits, afflict.

1539 BIBLE (Great) *Hebr.* xi. 36 Other were tried wt mockynges & scourgynges, moreouer, wt bondes & presonment. [Cf. 3.] 1545 ASCHAM *Toxoph.* (Arb.) 156 A syde wynde tryeth an archer and good gere verye muche. 1702 R. NELSON in *Pepys' Diary*, etc. (1879) VI. 257 If the Providence of God thinks fit to try you with the want of both. 1824 BYRON *Juan* XVI. l, Her temper had been tried So much. 1825 B'NESS BUNSEN in Hare *Life* (1879) I. vii. 248 She has been tried in life more hardly than anybody whose..history I ever yet heard. 1859 MACAULAY in Trevelyan *Life & Lett.* (1876) II. xv. 470 This malady tries me severely. 1905 ELIN. GLYN *Viciss. Evangeline* 142 You look very pale, child—the journey has tried you probably.

**11.** To test the effect or operation of; to use, apply, or practise tentatively or by way of experiment; to experiment with. *Try an experiment*: to make an experiment; to do something in order to see what will come of it, or whether it produces the expected result.

*To try conclusions, try a fall, try masteries*: see the sbs. 1545 *Primer Hen. VIII* (1546) 126 Try not the lawe with thy seruaunt. 1573 TUSSER *Husb.* (1878) 24 He that of wilfulnes trieth the law, Shall striue for a coxcome, and thriue as a daw. 1625 BACON *Ess., Innovations* (Arb.) 527 It is good also, not to try Experiments in States. 1676 LADY CHAWORTH in *12th Rep. Hist. MSS. Comm.* App. v. 29 Lady Portsmouth continues sicke, and some say she will try the French ayre, others the Bath watters. 1701 in *Lett. Lit. Men* (Camden) 302, I wish you would try Smith and Walford for Cowper's Anatomy, and the Philosophical Transactions. 1702 *Eng. Theophrast.* 170 Those that will be trying masteries with their superiors. 1863 W. C. BALDWIN *Afr. Hunting* vii. 246, I have tried fishing to-day, as I dare not fire a shot for fear of frightening the elephants. 1875 JEVONS *Money* (1878) 246 The United States government tried a similar experiment.

**b.** To experiment upon (*with* something); to test the effect of something upon.

1784 COWPER in *Gentl. Mag.* LIV. I. 413/1 By..trying him with a variety of herbs [I] restored him to perfect health.

**c.** *absol.* or *intr.* To make experiment; † in quot. ? to practise.

1573 TUSSER *Husb.* (1878) 60 Dank ling forgot will quickly rot. Here learne and trie to turne it and drie.

**d.** *To try* (*one's*) *hand*, to attempt to do something for the first time; to test one's ability or aptitude *at* something.

1711 SHAFTESB. *Charac.* I. i. (1737) I. 156 Who will willingly be the first to try our Hand. 1768 TUCKER *Lt. Nat.* (1834) I. 384 Why should I be debarred the liberty of trying my hand as well as another? 1809 W. IRVING *Knickerb.* v. iii. (1849) 271 He determined to try his hand at negotiation. 1896 *N. York Weekly Witness* 30 Dec. 13/1 He prayed to be permitted to try his hand at spellbinding.

**12.** To endeavour to ascertain by experiment or effort; to attempt to find out; sometimes nearly = sense 11. **a.** with simple obj. (usually *fortune, luck*, or the like.)

1573 [see FORTUNE *sb.* 3 c]. 1601 R. JOHNSON *Kingd. & Commw.* (1603) 59 If he had but thirtie thousand good footemen..he could willingly haue found in his hart to trie his fortune with this enemie. 1741 S. SPEED in *Buccleuch MSS.* (Hist. MSS. Comm.) I. 398 We shall go to Jamaica, ..and try our luck once more. 1838 DE MORGAN *Ess. Probabilities* i. 21 They think they are *trying their luck*, as the phrase is. 1849 MACAULAY *Hist. Eng.* vii. II. 202 He tried the effects of frowns and menaces. 1885 'MRS. ALEXANDER' *At Bay* x, I have not yet been accepted. I have not even tried my chance. 1902 A. E. W. MASON *Four Feathers* viii, If he tried his luck with Miss Eustace.

**b.** with indirect interrogative clause (*how, if, what, whether*, etc.).

1596 SHAKS. *Tam. Shr.* I. ii. 17 Ile trie how you can Sol, Fa, and sing it. *c* 1643 LD. HERBERT *Autobiog.* (1824) 20 Many ships scattering themselves to try whether they could obtain a prize. 1680 MOXON *Mech. Exerc.* xii. 208 Try how the Centers are pitcht, by Treading the Treddle lightly down. *a* 1700 in *Cath. Rec. Soc. Publ.* (1911) IX. 341 To trie what effects her Maiestys example might have on others. 1819 in *Shelley Mem.* (1859) 126 Let you and I try if we cannot be as punctual and businesslike as the best of them.

**13.** To show or find to be so by test or experience; to prove, demonstrate. (With simple obj., obj. cl., inf., or obj. and compl.) Now *rare* or *Obs.*

*c* 1412 [see TRIED 3]. *c* 1500 in I. S. Leadam *Star Chamb. Cases* (1903) 101 He wold not take oon peny of him Except his right were tryed good. *a* 1553 UDALL *Royster D.* v. i. (Arb.) 79 She may hir selfe discharge and trie hir honestie. 1589 *Whip for Ape* A 2, Sometimes his choppes doo walke in poynts too hie, Wherein the Ape himselfe a Woodcocke tries. 1592 SHAKS. *Rom. & Jul.* IV. iii. 29 He hath still beene tried a holy man. 1642 *Declar. Lords & Comm.* 2 Sept. 5 Fasting and Prayer having bin often tryed to be very effectuall. 1892 J. KENT *Racing Life Ld. G. Cavendish Bentinck* 47 Lord George Cavendish tried Godolphin to be a good horse.

†**14.** To have experience of; to undergo, go through. *Obs.*

1579 LYLY *Euphues* (Arb.) 84 The quiet life which I haue tryed being a mayden. 1625 GILL *Sacr. Philos.* Pref., That treatise tryed the common fortune of all bookes; some slighted..others condemned it. 1667 MILTON *P. L.* IX. 860 Never more Mean I to trie what rash untri'd I sought, The paine of absence from thy sight. 1738 GRAY *Propertius* II. v. 39 Or if, alas! it be my Fate to try Another Love.

**15.** To test one's ability to deal with (something); to attempt to do, perform, or accomplish (an action); to venture upon, to essay. *To try over*, to go through (a performance, etc.) experimentally.

*c* 1315 SHOREHAM I. 1290 Nou ich habbe of þe ferste yteld, Þat oþer wyl ich trye. 1500-20 DUNBAR *Poems* xxvii. 1 Nixt that a turnament wes tryid That lang befoir in hell wes cryid. 1607 WALKINGTON *Opt. Glass* 83 b, This little barke.., which neuer tryed the foming maine beforne. 1638 JUNIUS *Paint. Ancients* 12 All kind of worke seemeth to be hard before we doe try it. 1812 J. WILSON *Isle of Palms* II. 489 The boat hath left the lonesome rock And tries the wave again. 1870 LOWELL *Among my Bks.* Ser. I. 176 Fancy a parody of Shakespeare...You might as well try it with the Venus of Melos. *Mod.* I should like to try it over first.

**b.** *Try it on* (with play on sense 9): to attempt an imposition; to endeavour to outwit or get the better of some one (usu. const. *with*); *spec.* in *Thieves Cant*, to live by thieving. *slang.*

1811 *Lex. Balatr., Try on*, to endeavour. To live by thieving. Coves who try it on; professed thieves. 1812 *Sporting Mag.* XXXIX. 284 Witness agreed to try it on again although he considered himself in danger. 1848 THACKERAY *Van. Fair* xxxiv, No jokes, old boy: no trying it on me. 1903 FARMER & HENLEY *Slang* s. v., *To try it on*, to seek to outwit, get the better of, fleece, cheat... *To try it on a dog* = to experiment at another's expense or risk. 1912 *Oxf. & Camb. Rev.* Nov. 14 If he tries it on, the audience..is ready to convince him of his mistake.

**16.** *intr.* To make an effort, endeavour, attempt. (With *inf.*, or *absol.*)

1638 [implied in TRIAL *sb.*[1] 8]. 1697 DRYDEN *Virg. Georg.* III. 355 To repair his Strength he tries: Hardning his Limbs with painful Exercise. 1738 GRAY *Propertius* iii. 23 While to retain the envious Lawn she tries. 1847 MARRYAT *Childr. N. Forest* iv, You will have to try and try again. 1895 *Pall Mall G.* 7 Oct. 1/3 England..has tried her best to head him off the path down which he seems determined to rush. 18.. *Pop. Melody*, If at first you don't succeed, Try, try, try again.

**b.** Followed by *and* and a co-ordinated verb (instead of *to* with inf.) expressing the action attempted. *colloq.* Cf. AND B. 10.

1686 J. S[ERGEANT] *Hist. Monast. Convent* 9 They try and express their love to God by their thankfulness to him. 1802 H. MARTIN *Helen of Glenross* II. 143 Frances retired, to try and procure a little rest. 1819, 1878 [see AND B. 10]. 1855 in Coleridge *Mem. Keble* (1869) II. 425, I have something to write to you on that matter, which I shall try and put on another piece of paper. 1883 L. OLIPHANT *Altiora Peto* I. 251 He had good reason to think that Sark was likely to try and back out.

**c.** Const. with preposition. *Try for*, to attempt to obtain or find (an object), or to reach (a place). *Try at*, to make an attempt upon, endeavour to get at; to attempt to do or accomplish.

1534 in I. S. Leadam *Sel. Cas. Crt. Requests* (Selden Soc.) 43 Your sayd humble subgett is a very powre man and nott able to trye for his sayd libertie..by the ordre of the comen lawe. 1653 *Caldwell Papers* (Maitl. Cl.) I. 108 Quhen he went to search and try for the lard's hors yt was stollen. 1763 [see FOR *prep.* 12]. 1794 CHARLOTTE SMITH *Wand. Warwick* 195 Xaviera..seemed, by an effort of resolution, to try at conquering her confusion. 1816 TUCKEY *Narr. Exped. R. Zaire* i. (1818) 10 The sea being much discoloured, we tried for soundings, but did not get bottom with 120 fathoms of line. 1913 *Illustr. Lond. News* 16 Aug. 266/2 On three occasions he made some show of trying for a degree, and between times attended as few lectures as he could.

**d.** *intr.* and *trans.* To search a place in order to find something, esp. game, or its scent. *colloq.*

1810 *Sporting Mag.* XXXVI. 233 He bid the other defendants try across the Six Acres. 1821 CLARE *Vill. Minstr.* I. 125 Bees in every peep did try. 1827 G. A. MCCALL *Lett. fr. Frontiers* (1868) 178 The Colonel had directed Maximo to bring..all..appliances for hunting the green turtle; and the latter..was thus early in motion to 'try' after turtle. 1909 *Toilers of Deep* Oct. 246/1 Frequently they 'try a piece', as fishing parlance has it.

**e.** *intr. Try back*: to go back (*lit.* or *fig.*) so as to cover ground afresh where something has previously been missed; to 'hark back'.

1816 KNOX & JEBB *Corr.* II. 273 At college, I was obliged to try back in mathematics. Through daily life, I am obliged to try back in minor morals. 1857 HUGHES *Tom Brown* I. vii, They tried back slowly and sorrowfully, and found the lane. 1863 WHYTE MELVILLE *Gladiators* 233 Like a hound..now trying back with untiring perseverance. 1874 R. TYRWHITT *Sketch. Club* 3 To get people to see when their work won't do, and to try back and attempt simpler things.

**f.** *trans.* To attempt or solicit (a woman); to endeavour to seduce; also of a stallion, to attempt to cover (a mare).

1713 LADY M. W. MONTAGU *Lady's Resolve*, In part she is to blame that has been try'd; He comes too near, that comes to be deny'd. 1811 *Sporting Mag.* XXXVIII. 212 The horse took as much pains to try the mare as any stallion.

†**17.** *Naut. intr.* Of a vessel: To lie to. (See quot. 1867.) Also, *to try a-hull. Obs.*

The meaning in first quot. is doubtful.

[1533 J. HEYWOOD *Play Wether* (1903) 572 The see..Where shyppes by meane of wynd try from port to porte.] 1556 in Hakluyt *Voy.* (1598) I. 277 When the barke had way, we cut the hawser, and so gate the sea to our friend, and tryed out al that day with our maine corse. 1610 SHAKS. *Temp.* I. i. 37 Downe with the top-Mast: yare, lower, lower, bring her to Try with Maine-course. 1725 H. DE SAUMAREZ in *Phil. Trans.* XXXIII. 427 We had hard Gales..and a distracted Sea, insomuch that we try'd under a double reef'd Mainsail, great Part of the Time. 1773 *Life N. Frowde* 122 We were obliged..to ly too, and let the Ship drive with the Tempest, and at length, to try a Hull. 1867 SMYTH *Sailor's Word-bk., Try*, or Lie-to in a Gale, is by a judicious balance of canvas, to keep a ship's bow to the sea, and..prevent her rolling to windward in the trough of a sea.

**Try-**, the verb-stem in combination.

**1.** with sbs., forming sbs. denoting appliances, etc. for trying (in various senses of the verb): **try-cock**, 'a gauge-cock' (Webster 1864); **try-gun**, a model gun with an adjustable stock (see quot.); **try-house**, a building for 'trying' or extracting oil from blubber, etc.; **try-pit**, a testing pit for trying new engines; **try-plane**, a trying-plane (Knight *Dict. Mech.* 1877); **try-pot**, a pot for 'trying' oil from blubber; **try rule** (see quot.); **try-square**, a carpenter's square for laying off short perpendiculars; **try-stick**, a stick used in fitting leather work; **try-works**, the apparatus used for 'trying' oil from blubber. See also TRYSAIL.

1892 GREENER *Breech-Loader* 95 The '*try gun'..permits of the stock being altered to any length, bend, cast-off, and shape of the butt, and is of use in fitting a sportsman who needs a gun of special build. 1891 *Cent. Dict.*, *Try-house. 1895 *Century Mag.* Aug. 575/1 To come up the crooked road..past the try-house. 1896 KIPLING *Seven Seas, M'Andrews' Hymn* 44 Mill, forge, an' *try-pit taught them [ship's engines] that. 1836 *Uncle Philip's Convers. Whale Fishery* 267 [They] cut the blubber, before it is thrown into the *try-pots. 1875 TEMPLE & SHELDON *Hist. Northfield, Mass.* 159 In those days, no frames were set out by the square rule, but by what they called the *try rule,..i.e. the sills, posts and beams were framed and tried, and the braces were laid on to mark their bevels and length. 1877 KNIGHT *Dict. Mech.*, **Try-square*..consists of a thin blade of steel ..let into a wooden piece..and securely fastened at right angles. 1901 *J. Black's Illustr. Carp. & Build., Home Handicr.* 19 The transverse lines..drawn with the pencil.. can afterwards be corrected with the try square. 1888 FARR & THRUPP *Coach Trimming* iii. 39 He should neatly join on the back and side pieces, making use of *try-sticks..to secure their right appliance. *c* 1825 CHOYCE *Log of Jack Tar* (1891) 198 A native trying to steal a brass cock from the *try-works. 1898 F. T. BULLEN *Cruise 'Cachalot'* 11 Her deck was flush fore and aft, the only obstructions being the brick-built 'try-works' in the waist.

**2.** with advbs., forming sbs. derived from adverbial combinations of the verb: **try-on** (TRY *v.* 15 b, 9), (*a*) (*slang*) an attempt, *esp.* an attempt at imposition or deceit; also *transf.* the subject of an attempt; (*b*) the act of trying on a garment; **try-out** (*U.S. slang* or *colloq.*), a selective trial.

1874 *Siliad* 57 The flagitious claims—Call them, or damages, '*tries-on', or shams. 1885 *Law Times Rep.* LIII. 479/2 This was a try-on, on the part of the solicitors which ought not to be allowed. 1905 *Daily News* 28 Oct. 6 Garments must be cut to fit without successive try-ons. 1906 *Tyer* VI. 171 One girl represented the Athena Club in the debaters' *tryout, and won a place as an inter-collegiate debater.

**Tryable, Tryacle**, obs. ff. TRIABLE, TREACLE. **Tryangle, -gyl**, obs. ff. TRIANGLE. **Tryb, trybe**, obs. ff. TRIBE. **Tryce**, obs. f. TRICE. **Trycherye, Trychor, -our**: see TREACHERY, TREACHER. **Tryde**, obs. f. *tried*: see TRY *v.* **Trydle**, obs. f. TREADLE. **Trye**, var. TRAY *sb.*[1]; obs. f. TREY, TRY. **Tryefull, Tryen, Tryer, Tryews**, obs. ff. TRIFLE, TREEN, TRIER, TRUCE. **Tryfetrafe**: see TRIFF-TRAFF. **Tryfoly, -foyle**, obs. ff. TREFOIL. **Tryget, -our**, var. TREGET, -OUR *Obs.*

‖ **Trygon** (trəi·gǫn). [L. *trȳgōn* (Pliny), a. Gr. τρυγών a dove, also the fish.] A fish with a sharp spine in its tail, a sting-ray.

[1706 PHILLIPS (ed. Kersey), *Trygon*, the Turtle-Dove.] 1749 G. WEST tr. *Odes of Pindar* (1753) I. 258 And by my Dart the Lord of Ithaca, Not by the pois'nous Trygon's Bone expir'd. 1774 GOLDSM. *Nat. Hist.* VI. 260 Circe armed her son with a spear headed with the spine of the trygon.

**Trygon, Tryhumphe,** obs. ff. TRIGON, TRIUMPH.

**Trying** (trəi·iŋ), *vbl. sb.* [f. TRY *v.* + -ING [1].] The action of the verb TRY, in various senses.

*c* 1440 *Promp. Parv.* 502/2 Tryynge, *eleccio, preeleccio, examinacio.* 1447 *Ordinaunce of Exchequer* 35 c. 62 (6) A iij, To the mayster for laboure of redynge endosynge and tryenge of peticyons and fynes. 1535 COVERDALE *Ecclus.* xvi. 22 The tryenge out of men is in the fulfillynge. 1630 *R. Johnson's Kingd. & Commw.* 216 They know not the use of trying of Mettals. 1669 STURMY *Mariner's Mag.* I. ii. 17 It is better spooning before the Sea, than trying or hulling. 1819 *Sporting Mag.* V. 123 All the frolic, fun,.. gammon, and trying-it-on are depicted. 1898 F. T. BULLEN *Cruise 'Cachalot'* 95 The whole work of cutting in and trying out was got through without a single accident.

**b.** *attrib.*, as **trying-plane**, a long heavy plane used after the jack-plane for the accurate squaring of timber; **trying-pot**, a pot for 'trying' out oil; **trying-square** = *try-square* (see TRY- 1).

1579 [see SQUARE *sb.* 2]. 1815 J. SMITH *Panorama Sc. & Art* I. 109 The trying-plane is made use of to produce a higher degree of regularity and smoothness. 1823 P. NICHOLSON *Pract. Build.* 244 The Trying-Plane..is used to regulate and smooth, to a higher degree, the surface of a piece of stuff that has already been reduced to its intended form by means of the jack-plane. 1882 F. M. CRAWFORD *Mr. Isaacs* iii, The only way to arrive at any conclusion is by a sort of trying-on process. 1885 C. F. HOLDER *Marvels Anim. Life* 177 The trying-pots were taken to a small inlet.

**Trying** (trəi·iŋ), *ppl. a.* [f. TRY *v.* + -ING [2].] That tries. **1.** That tests severely; that is a trial; hard to bear or endure; severe, distressing, painful; that tries one's endurance or patience.

1718 HICKES & NELSON *J. Kettlewell* II. xv. 98 For the Security of the Church..in such a Trying Time. 1798 *Monthly Mag.* Mar. 183 Sudden vicissitudes of temperature must be exceedingly trying to delicate constitutions. 1825 HONE *Every-day Bk.* I. 652 The month of May is..a 'trying' month, to persons..ailing. 1907 J. H. PATTERSON *Man-Eaters of Tsavo* xvi. 175 She was so..exhausted by her trying march..that she was scarcely able to speak.

**2.** Attempting, endeavouring, striving. *rare.*

1577 GRANGE *Golden Aphrod.*, etc. O iij, This got I say my trying tongue, whiche tolde hyr many a lye. 1836 MRS. BROWNING *Poet's Vow* IV. iv, The old eyes searching ..The young ones..To read their look if sound forsook The trying, trembling breath. 1841 [implied in *tryingly*].

Hence **Try·ingly** *adv.*, in a trying manner or degree; in the way of attempt or endeavour (*rare*); distressingly, painfully; **Try·ingness**, trying or distressing quality or character.

1841 *Tait's Mag.* VIII. 109 The small hand put out so tryingly. 1859 CORNWALLIS *New World* I. 359 The climate..is..at times rather tryingly warm. 1885 *My Wife's Niece* II. xi, An attitude which showed so freely and tryingly the lines of her figure. 1897 MARY KINGSLEY *W. Africa* xxv. 569 To walk through, give me kokos for good all-round tryingness, particularly when they are wet.

**Tryist,** obs. form of TRYST.

† **Trylle,** *v. Obs. rare*—[1]. [app. = MDu., early mod.Du. *drillen, trillen* to tremble, shiver (Plantijn, Kilian). Cf. TRILL *v.*[4]] *intr.* To tremble.

13.. *E. E. Allit. P.* A. 78 As bornyst syluer þe lef onslydez, Þat þike con trylle on vcha tynde.

‖ **Tryma** (trəi·mă). *Bot.* [mod.L. (Necker), ad. Gr. τρῦμα or τρυμή hole, f. τρύειν to rub down, wear out.] A fruit resembling a drupe, but formed from an originally compound ovary, and having an ultimately dehiscent fleshy or fibrous exocarp, as the walnut and coco-nut; a kind of drupaceous nut.

1857 HENFREY *Elem. Bot.* § 280. 1861 BENTLEY *Man. Bot.* 321 The Tryma..differs but little from the ordinary drupe, except in being formed from an originally compound ovary. 1900 JACKSON *Gloss. Bot. Terms*, *Tryma*.., Necker's term for a drupaceous nut with dehiscent exocarp, as the walnut.

**Trymble, trym(m)le,** etc., obs. ff. TREMBLE.

**Trymebote, trymle bote:** see TRIMBOAT.

**Tryndall, -dell, -dle,** etc., obs. ff. TRINDLE.

**Tryndle bed, -tayle,** obs. ff. TRUNDLE-BED, -TAIL. **Tryne,** obs. f. TRAIN, TREEN, TRINE.

**Trynitee, -tie, Trynle, Trynsch, Trynter,** obs. ff. TRINITY, TRINDLE, TRENCH, THRINTER.

**Tryor, Tryoumffe,** obs. ff. TRIER, TRIUMPH.

**Tryp,** var. TRIPE [2] *Obs.*, velvet.

**Trypan** (tri·păn). [Short for TRYPANOSOMA.] In **trypan red** [rendering Ger. *trypanrot*], a drug used in cases of trypanosomiasis.

1905 *Brit. Med. Jrnl.* 27 May 1140 The treatment of trypan red in various trypanosomic diseases. 1907 *Daily News* 31 Aug. 4 According to 'The Hospital', the correct name for trypan red, which is now used in cases of trypanosomiasis, is 'sodium-ortho-benzidine-mono-sulphoacid-diazo-b-2-naphthylamine-3.6-sulphoacid'!

**Try:pano,ly·tic,** *a.* [f. TRYPANO(SOMA) + Gr. λυτικός loosing, dissolving.] Tending to, or connected with the destruction of trypanosomes.

1907 *Nature* 31 Oct. 680/1 The causes of trypanolytic crises and relapses.

‖ **Trypanosoma** (tri:pănǫ,sōu·mă). *Zool.* [mod.L. f. Gr. τρύπανον borer + σῶμα body.] A genus of flagellate infusorial protozoa, species of which are parasitic in the blood of man and other animals, causing specific diseases, such as sleeping-sickness; an infusorian of this genus. Hence **Try:panoso·macide** [L. *-cīda*, -CIDE 1], a substance having the property of destroying trypanosomes; **Trypanosomal** (-sōu·măl), **-somatic** (-somæ·tik), **-somatous** (-sōu·mătəs) *adjs.*, of, pertaining to, or caused by trypanosomes; ‖ **Try:pano,somato·sis** [mod.L.: see -OSIS] = *trypanosomiasis*; **Try·pano,some** (-sōum) [a. F. *trypanosome* (Gruby, 1843)], an infusorian of the genus *Trypanosoma*; ‖ **Trypanosomiasis** (-soməi·ăsis), pl. **-ases** (-ăsīz) [mod.L., after *elephantiasis*, etc.; but the etymological pronunciation would be -i,ī·sis], a disease produced by infection with trypanosomes; **Trypanosomic** (-sōu·mik) *a.* = *trypanosomal* (in quot. 1906, infected with trypanosomes).

[1843 GRUBY in *Comptes Rendus* XVII. 1134 (*title*) Recherches et observations sur une nouvelle espèce d'hémato-zoaire, **Trypanosoma sanguinis*. Les travaux des physiologistes modernes ont fait connaître l'existence de parasites vivants dans le sang des animaux. *Ibid.* 1135 Je propose de nommer cet hématozoaire *Trypanosome*.] 1880 KENT *Infusoria* I. 218 *Trypanosoma*...Occurring in the blood of Amphibia, and within the intestinal viscera of domestic poultry. 1898 P. MANSON *Trop. Diseases* v. 102 [Sir David] Bruce's notable work on the tsetse fly as a medium in diffusing the trypanosoma of 'fly disease'. 1903 *Daily Chron.* 20 Nov. 5/2 A fly had been found to convey the newly-discovered blood-parasite of tropical countries, called the trypanosoma. 1903 *Times* 7 Nov. 12/1 The search for what must, we suppose, be styled a *trypanosomacide. 1904 *Brit. Med. Jrnl.* 17 Sept. 644 Prowazek..finds similar *trypanosomal forms which also assume resting forms. 1908 *Lancet* 2 May 1285/2 Trypanosomal infection. 1904 *Science* 22 July 112/2 The cultivation of the organisms causing *trypanosomatic diseases. 1903 *Lancet* 4 Apr. 945/2 [The chimpanzee] suffers from ankylostomiasis, filariasis, and *trypanosomatosis. 1891 *Cent. Dict.*, **Trypanosomatous*. 1903 *Daily Record & Mail* 16 Apr. 5 Although we found the parasite in none of the natives..we did find a *trypanasome in each of two horses belonging to the commandant. 1908 *Athenæum* 21 Nov. 651/3 Prof. E. A. Minchin exhibited a series of drawings of trypanosomes obtained from British freshwater fishes. 1902 *Westm. Gaz.* 21 Aug. 5/2 An..expedition to West Africa..left..to-day...They go to French Senegal,.. into the interior to investigate the tropical disease known as *trypanosomiasis. 1912 *Nature* 21 Nov. 338/2 The progress ..of our knowledge with regard to the trypanosomiases of animals and human beings in Africa. 1905 *Brit. Med. Jrnl.* 27 May 1140 The heavy loss among horses and cattle ..from various *trypanosomic diseases. *Ibid.* [see TRYPAN]. 1906 *Jrnl. Med. Research* July 125 This water is then inoculated with the otherwise sterile trypanosomic blood.

**Trypet,** obs. f. TRIPPET [1]. **Trypit:** see TRIPE [2].

**Trypograph** (tri·pŏgraf). [f. Gr. τρῦπα hole, τρυπᾶν to perforate + -GRAPH.] A kind of printing done by means of a paper stencil made by writing with a stylus on paper placed over a finely roughened steel surface so as to produce minute perforations. So **Trypogra·phic** *a.*, of the nature of, pertaining to, or made by such printing.

1883 R. HALDANE *Workshop Receipts* Ser. II. 191/2 This kind of printing is called 'trypograph'...Calico receives the trypographic impression admirably.

**Tryppe,** obs. form of TRIP, TRIPE [1].

**Tryppgette,** obs. form of TREBUCHET.

**Trypsin** (tri·psin). *Physiol. Chem.* [app. for **tripsin*, f. Gr. τρῖψις rubbing (because first obtained by rubbing down the pancreas with glycerin) + -IN [1].] The chief digestive ferment of the pancreatic juice, which converts proteins into peptones. Hence **Trypsi·nogen** (-dʒən) [-GEN 1], a granular substance occurring in the pancreas, from which trypsin is formed; **Try·psogen** [abbrev. of prec.], (*a*) = *trypsinogen*; (*b*) a drug prepared from trypsin and other ferments with gold and arsenic bromides, used in diabetes, etc. (Dorland).

1876 FOSTER *Phys.* II. i. (1879) 233 The digestive powers of the [pancreatic] juice..depend..on the presence of a ferment, to which the name *trypsin has been given. 1907 *Westm. Gaz.* 12 Dec. 12/2 The new treatment of cancer by the pancreatic ferments, trypsin and amylopsin.. suggested by Dr. Beard. 1890 BILLINGS *Med. Dict.*, *Trypsinogen. 1900 *Lancet* 27 Oct. 1187/1 The fact observed by Heidenhain of the continuous formation and storing up trypsinogen in the pancreas, and its subsequent transformation into trypsin during the culmen of gastric digestion, proved that the former substance .. enjoyed an origin quite independent of all influence outside the pancreas. 1907 H. W. BETTMANN in *Med. Record* 3 Aug. 171 The intestinal juice contains two other ferments .., enterokinase, and erepsin. The former activates the pancreatic juice by transforming trypsinogen into trypsin. 1883 *Science* I. 372/1 The absence of oxygen from the blood has led to a reconversion of trypsin into *trypsogen.

**Tryptic** (tri·ptik), *a.* [f. TRYPSIN, after *pepsin, peptic.*] Pertaining to or of the nature of trypsin. So **Tryptogen** (tri·ptodʒen), **-gene** (-dʒīn) [-GEN 1], a producer of trypsin; **Tryptone** (tri·ptoun) [after *peptone*], a peptone formed by the action of trypsin upon a protein; **Try·ptophan** (-fæn) [Gr. φαίνειν to appear], a nitrogenous substance formed by decomposition of peptones in tryptic digestion.

1888 ROLLESTON & JACKSON *Anim. Life* 196 Common Starfish...The cells in the caeca form enterochlorophyll, and *tryptic, peptic, and diastatic ferments. 1901 *Athenæum* 7 Dec. 778/3 It seems probable..that proteolytic digestion in plants is always tryptic. 1900 *Lancet* 27 Oct. 1187/1 The hypothesis of Schiff as to the manner in which the spleen acts as a *tryptogene. 1890 BILLINGS *Med. Dict.*, *Tryptone. 1901 *Athenæum* 7 Dec. 778/3 Among these final products of tryptic digestion there is a substance termed *tryptophan, which has the property of giving a pink or violet colour on the addition of chlorine-water. 1902 *Daily Chron.* 22 Nov. 6/6 Decomposing the proteid molecule into non-proteid nitrogenous substances, such as leucin and tryptophane.

**Trysail** (trəi·sē̆il, trəi·s'l). *Naut.* Also 9 **trey-, tray-, trice-, tri-.** [f. TRY *sb.* + SAIL.] A small fore-and-aft sail, set with a gaff, and sometimes with a boom, on the fore- or mainmast, or on a small supplementary mast abaft either of these. Also *attrib.*, as *trysail gaff, mast, mizen, sheet.*

1769 FALCONER *Dict. Marine* (1789) M m iv, When the sloops of war are rigged as snows, they are furnished with a horse, which answers the purpose of the try-sail-mast, the fore part of the sail being attached by rings to the said horse. 1794 *Rigging & Seamanship* I. 83 A trysail, used instead of a mizen,.. is extended towards the stern, and..fastened by hoops round a small mast, called a trysail mast, fixed near the aft-side of the main-mast in a block of wood in the quarter deck. 1810 J. H. MOORE *Pract. Navigator* 290 Trey-sail. A small sail used by brigs and cutters in blowing weather. 1832 J. GUY *Pocket Cycl.* 402 A small mast, reaching up into the maintop, to which a tricesail mizen is attached. 1840 R. H. DANA *Bef. Mast* iv. 16 We..hauled up the mainsail and trysail. *Ibid.* ix. 22 Trysail gaff [see GAFF *sb.*[1] 2]. 1850 L. HUNT *Autobiog.* II. xvii. 259 We saw her..lying-to under trysails.

**Tryschor,** variant of TREACHER *Obs.*

**Trysselle,** obs. form of TRESTLE.

‖ **Tryssil, trysil.** Also **trysle, trysel(l, trissle.** [Said to be native name among the Arawak Indians.] Name in British Guiana for a timber-tree, *Pentaclethra filamentosa.*

1862 *List Contrib. fr. Brit. Guiana to Lond. Exhib.*, Arrara, or Tryssil (*Pentaclethra filamentosa*, Benth.). Used for furniture and staves. 1878 *Woods Brit. Guiana collected by M. McTurk for local & Paris Internat. Exhib.* 1 Kooroo-balli or Trysil, from the Moraballi Creek, Essequebo River..is a dark close-grained wood suitable for making furniture. 1881 *Rep. Crown Surveyor Brit. Guiana for 1880* 24 Trysell. A beautiful light brown wood, close-grained and hard. 1912 C. W. ANDERSON *Forests Brit. Guiana* 23 Trysil or Koro-balli.

**Tryst** (trəist), *sb.* Chiefly *Sc.* before 19th c. Also 4–5 **triste,** 4–9 **trist,** (6 **treste, tryist**), 6–9 **tryste.** [Originally the same word as *triste*, TRIST *sb.*[1] (in which the *i* was in ME. long or short). The sense seems to be generalized from that of 'appointed station in hunting': cf. TRIST *sb.*[2] and the OF. and med.L. words there mentioned. The sense sometimes corresponds to some extent with that of TRUCE.]

**1.** A mutual appointment, agreement, engagement, covenant. Now *rare* or *Obs.* exc. as in 2.

*c* 1375 *Sc. Leg. Saints* xxvi. (*Nycholas*) 236 Þai sailyt.. Quhare-to þare tryst wes mad[e], And þare þe quhet delieuryt hale. 1570 *Satir. Poems Reform.* xix. 90 Hudge is ȝour fais..With Ithand trystis contractand vp new bandis To bring ȝow to schame and confusioun. 1635 JACKSON *Creed* VIII. xii. § 9 A captaine..being surprised by the subtilty of his enemy, whom hee had trusted too farre upon a tryste of parly. *a* 1670 SPALDING *Troub. Chas. I* (1851) II. 205 Johne Forbes of Leslie brak tryst appointit to haue satled the samen. 1715 PENNECUIK *Tweeddale* App. 36 Thus clos'd our Trist, all was Miscarried, And Bonnie Maggie's still Unmarried. 1871 WADDELL *Ps. in Scottis* lxxiv. 20 Hae min' o' the tryst ye made.

**2.** *spec.* An appointment or engagement to meet at a specified time and place. Chiefly in phrases, as *to make,* † *set tryst*; *to hold, keep tryst*; *to break,* † *crack tryst*; *to bide tryst*, to wait at the appointed place for the person with whom the appointment is made. Also *fig.*

Only Sc. till 19th c.

1375 BARBOUR *Bruce* VII. 235 The kyng..richt toward the houss is gane Quhar he set trist to mete his men. *c* 1470 HENRY *Wallace* VI. 865 In Ruglen kyrk the tryst than haiff thai set. 1500–20 DUNBAR *Poems* lxxxiii. 13 Ȝe keipit tryst so winder weill. 1546 *St. Papers Hen. VIII*, V. 561 Yar is ane trist be twin ye Lord of Loichenwer and Herell of Cassellis on Frydye nest to cum in Glasquhow. 1629 Z. BOYD *Last Battell* 1257 The Salmons.. in their season returne to the place where they were spawned:..and for no rubs in the way will they be moued to cracke their tryst. 1818 SCOTT *Rob Roy* xxi, 'You walk late, sir', said I..'I bide tryste', was the reply. 1853 C. BRONTË *Villette* xii, To keep tryste with the rising moon. 1878 SUSAN PHILLIPS *On Seaboard* 214 She stood..keeping her tryst at the stile. 1881 W. R. SMITH *Old Test. Jew. Ch.* 232 The place where Jehovah has promised to hold tryst with His people.

**3.** An appointed meeting or assembly: = RENDEZVOUS 5. In quot. 1681 *fig.* 'a [divinely appointed] concurrence of circumstances or events' (Jam.): cf. TRYST *v.* 4, 5.

*c* 1425 WYNTOUN *Cron.* IX. xvi. 1670 In Marche a day of trew was set..Schir Dauid Lorde de Lyndissay Was at þat tryst þat ilka day. 1456 SIR G. HAYE *Law Arms* (S.T.S.) 181 Ane Inglis lord.. cummys till a tryst to lordis of Fraunce. 1524 *St. Papers Hen. VIII*, IV. 279 The saide

Erle..hath appointed trestes and metingges with thErle of Angwisshe and his frendes. *c* 1560 A. SCOTT *Poems* (S.T.S.) xxxiv. 75 ȝe trane þame to ane tryst. 1681 R. FLEMING *Fulfilling Script.* I. (1726) 148 Acknowledging a divine hand ..where all did thus meet together in a solemn tryst to accomplish that peoples ruin. ?*a* 1700 *Lord's Marie* i. in Cromek *Rem. Nithsdale Song* (1810) 6 An' she has put on her net-silk hose, An' awa to the tryste has gane. 1859 G. MEREDITH *R. Feverel* xxi, Their tryst in the wood.

†**b.** An appointed journey. *Obs. rare.*

1768 Ross *Helenore* I. 65 Gin we reach na' our tryst's end gin night.

**4.** An appointed place of meeting: = RENDEZVOUS 2.

1375 BARBOUR *Bruce* VII. 230 And syne..richt toward his trist is gane. *c* 1450 HOLLAND *Howlat* 307 Thai..Walis wyslie the wayis,..Quhill thai approche to the Pape..At the forsaid trist quhar the trete tellis. 1844 MRS. BROWNING *Brown Rosary* I. v, 'Now where is Onora?'..'At the tryst with her lover'.

**5.** An appointed time; in quot. 1864, an appointed period or term. *rare. ? Obs.*

*c* 1470 HENRY *Wallace* IV. 731 At the set trist he entrit in the toune. 1827 HONE *Every-day Bk.* II. 164 The time agreed on..for playing it [i.e. a curling-match] is called the *tryst.* 1864 SIR F. PALGRAVE *Norm. & Eng.* IV. 620 In the year 1100, the end of Robert's tryste, when the term would be concluded.

**6.** An appointed gathering for buying and selling; a market or fair, esp. for cattle. *Sc.* and *north. Eng.*

1776 NIMMO *Hist. Stirling.* iii. (1817) 62 The two great annual markets for black cattle, called the Trysts of Falkirk. ?*a* 1800 *Thomas the Rhymer* I. xviii. in Scott *Minstr. Scot. Bord.*, I neither dought to buy nor sell, At fair or tryst where I may be. 1808 SCOTT in Lockhart *Life* i, The master and servant set off to purchase a stock of sheep at Whitsun-Tryste, a fair held..near Wooler in Northumberland. 1884 Q. VICTORIA *More Leaves* 46 We met many droves of cattle on the road, as it was the day for the tryst at Castleton.

**7.** *attrib.*, as **tryst-place**, a trysting-place; **tryst-stone**, 'a stone anciently erected for marking out a rendezvous' (Jam.); **tryst-word**, a password or watchword.

1795 *Statist. Acc. Scot.* XVI. 512 The tryst-stanes are commonly on high ground. They are placed perpendicularly in rows, not unfrequently in a circular direction. 1851 MRS. BROWNING *Casa Guidi Windows* I. 618 Thy favourite stone's elected right As tryst-place for thy Tuscans. 1896 R. REID in *N. York Scot. American* Oct., The tryst-word seemed 'Kirkbride'.

**Tryst** (trəist), *v.* Orig. and chiefly *Sc.* [f. TRYST *sb.*]

**1.** *intr.* To make an agreement *to do* something, *with* a person; *esp.* to fix or arrange time and place of meeting *with* some one.

*c* 1375 *Sc. Leg. Saints* xxx. (*Theodera*) 334 Scho kepyt þe trist..And with hyr brocht þe man in hy, Quhare scho tristit priuely. *c* 1475 *Rauf Coilȝear* 797 To the Montane he maid hem full boun, Quhair he had trystit to meit Schir Rolland. 1678 SIR G. MACKENZIE *Crim. Laws Scot.* I. xx. § 3 (1699) 108 Whosoever intercommuns with Thieves ..or Trysts with them any manner of way. 1725 RAMSAY *Gentle Sheph.* v. i, As she had trysted, I met wi'er this night. 1899 CROCKETT *Kit Kennedy* xxxiii, Kit..had trysted with the 'Orra Man' to meet him at the smiddy.

**2.** *trans.* To engage (a person) to meet one at a given place and time; to appoint or agree to meet. In quot. 1643, loosely used as = meet.

1643 *Declar. Com., Reb. Irel.* 60 It was my good fortune ..to trist a Barke come from the Isle of Man. 1766 A. NICOL *Poems* 43 He trysted me one evening fair, Among the groves to take the air. 1893 STEVENSON *Catriona* xiii, I am trysted with your cousin Charlie; I have passed my word.

**b.** With advb. extension: To invite or entice to a place, or to a distance.

*a* 1800 in Kinloch *Anc. Scott. Ballads* (1827) 157, I trysted her Unto yon shade o' broom. 1894 LATTO *Tam. Bodkin* xxiii, Trystin' me awa on that eventfu' pilgrimage.

**c.** To engage (a person) to do something: to appoint, agree upon, arrange, fix (a task). Only in *pa. pple.*

1897 [see *trysted* below]. 1899 CROCKETT *Kit Kennedy* viii. He was trysted to give what help he could to the herd.. in lambing time.

**3.** To appoint, fix (a time, occurrence, etc.).

1586 *Reg. Privy Council Scot.* IV. 63 Upoun the XI day of Marche..as the day tryistit and appointit be the said Williame Ker. 1716 *Wodrow Corr.* (1843) II. 120 Had not God tristed the flight of the rebels just at that time.

**b.** To bespeak; to arrange for, or order in advance; to engage.

1825 JAMIESON s. v., 'I trystit my furniture to be hame' on such a day. 1834 LATTO *Tam. Bodkin* xxiv, I had trystit a chaise an' pair frae the Fleein' Horse.

**4.** To visit *with* good or evil; of an experience: to come upon, befall; 'used in relation to a divine ordination' (Jam.).

1645 R. BAILLIE *Lett.* (1841) II. 314 That this should have trysted the enemie at that tyme and place..is evidentlie God's hand. *a* 1679 SOMERVILLE *Mem. Somervilles* (1815) II. 351 Untill Divyne Justice trysted them with some crosse dispensatione. 1681 R. FLEMING *Fulfilling Script.* Ep. to Rdr. (1726) 6 The most eminent and honourable service of the church doth usually tryst her in a low and suffering condition. 1816 SCOTT *Old Mort.* xl[i], Sair she's been trysted wi' misfortunes.

†**b.** To fix upon. *Obs. rare*—[1].

1700 SIR A. BALFOUR *Lett.* 254 They go at the Rate of an Ordinary Horse trot, & as they go will trist the stones to step upon, which lye confusedly here and there, as exactly as if they were a paire of stairs.

†**5.** *intr.* To coincide in time *with*; to fall *together*, concur. Also *trans.* in causal sense (quot. 1681). *Obs.*

1676 W. Row *Contn. Blair's Autobiog.* ix. (1848) 134 His stroke trysting with the public burden. 1681 R. FLEMING *Fulfilling Script.* I. (1726) 148 What a marvelous concurrence of providence..was in this judgment, the besieging of Jerusalem by the Romans, trysted with the very time of the passover [etc.]. 1730 T. BOSTON *Mem.* iv. (1899) 39 That discouragement and the spring-season trysting together, there was a notable breach made in my health.

**6.** *intr.* To keep tryst; to meet at the appointed time and place.

*a* 1842 CUNNINGHAM in *Casquet of Lit.* (1886) V. 303 There flows the stream I've trysted through, when it was wild in flood. 1898 *Westm. Gaz.* 7 Dec. 11/2 When the Cottesmore trysted at Somerby on Saturday.

†**7.** *intr.* To treat or negotiate *with. Obs.*

1637 RUTHERFORD *Let. to Lady Kilconquhair* 8 Aug., You came to this life about a necessary and weighty business, to tryst with Christ anent your precious soul. 1637–50 [see TRYSTING *vbl. sb.* 1]. 1639 LD. WARISTON *Diary* (S.H.S.) 351 We trysted on al day with the Commissioner, bot could settle nothing. *a* 1670 SPALDING *Troub. Chas. I* (1850) I. 176 Thay raisit ane army and cam to Innervrie, quhilk he could not resist, nor whome fra he could onnawayis flie, be sea or land, [and he] wes forsit to tryst and give his band, no doubt to thair contentment.

Hence **Try·sted**, **Try·sting** *ppl. adjs.*

1793 BURNS *Mary Morison* i, It is the wish'd, the trysted hour! 1878 T. HARDY *Return of Native* I. ix, The conversation of the trysting pair could not be overheard. 1897 CROCKETT *Lad's Love* xxix, That his shepherd..is shirking his trysted labour.

**Tryst(e**, obs. f. TREST; var. TRIST *Obs.*

**Trystel, -ell(e**, obs. forms of TRESTLE.

†**Try·stell.** *Obs. rare.* [f. TRYST *sb.*] = TRYST *sb.*; *trystell-tree*, a tree where a tryst is arranged (cf. TRYSTY).

*c* 1500 *Gest Robyn Hode* IV. 274 in Child *Ball.* III. 69/2 Welcome be thou, gentyll knyght, Under my trystell-tre.

**Tryster** (trəi·stəɹ). [f. TRYST *v.* + -ER[1].] One who trysts. **a.** 'A person who convenes others, .. fixing the time and place of meeting' (Jam.). **b.** One who appoints to meet another. **c.** One who attends a tryst or appointed meeting.

1655 R. BAILLIE *Lett.* (1842) III. 279 We had drawne up ane overture,..according to the Assemblie's late overture for union, and by the hands of the trysters..sent it into their meeting. 1810 CROMEK *Rem. Nithsdale Song* Introd. 21 The old cottars (the trysters of other years) are mostly dead in good old age. 1878 T. HARDY *Return of Native* I. ix, The expected trysters did not appear.

**Tryster, -ere**, variants of TRISTRE *Obs.*

**Trysting** (trəi·stiŋ), *vbl. sb.* [f. TRYST *v.*]

**1.** The action of the verb TRYST, q.v.; a tryst. *Under trysting* = under tryst or agreement.

1633 W. STRUTHER *True Happiness* 79 Since he keepeth both time and place of trysting, let us not be so ingrate as not to meet with him. 1637–50 Row *Hist. Kirk* (Wodrow Soc.) 514 After some trysting, and intermediat parleying. 1640 R. BAILLIE *Lett.* (1841) I. 276 A declaration..that our trysting there [in London] was no submission to the Inglish Parliament. *a* 1670 SPALDING *Troub. Chas. I* (1851) II. 337 The committee of Estaites..directit him..to hold the Marques wnder trysting whill thay sould raiss wp forces to go vpone him. 1832 MRS. CARLYLE in *Lett. & Mem.* (1903) I. 42, I was fatigued enough by the journey home; still more by the trysting that awaited me here.

**2.** *attrib.*, as *trysting day, ground, place, stile, thorn, tree*, etc.

1842 MACAULAY *Horatius* i, By the Nine Gods he swore it, And named a *trysting day. 1838 J. P. KENNEDY *Rob of Bowl* xx, The customary..*trysting ground for personal combats. 1898 MAX MÜLLER *Auld Lang Syne* 195 [In] the Thirty Years' War we find Anhalt the constant trysting ground of the two parties. 1633 W. STRUTHER *True Happiness* 115 Wee come to the Sanctuarie..the Lords *trysting place. *a* 1665 W. GUTHRIE *Chr. Gt. Interest* II. viii. (1724) 223 A fit Trysting-place for God and Men to meet into. 1805 SCOTT *Eve St. John* xliii, At our trysting place, for a certain space, I must wander to and fro. 1867 FREEMAN *Norm. Conq.* I. v. 426 Those who had horses seem to have reached the same trysting-place by land. 1858 CAPERN *Ball. & Songs* (1859) 100 Meet me..by the *trysting stile. 1793 BURNS *Soldier's Return* iii, I pass'd the mill and *trysting thorn, Where Nancy aft I courted. 1802 SCOTT *Reiver's Wedding* 50 When he came to Falsehope glen, Beneath the *trysting-tree. 1806 *Chron.* in *Ann. Reg.* (1808) 385/2 A hurricane..destroyed the famous elm tree, which had existed for ages, on the banks of the Teviot, and was known by the name of the *Trysting Tree.* 1872 HOLLAND *Marb. Proph.* 45, I await her in the dewy gloom Of the old trysting tree.

**Trystor**, variant of TRISTRE *Obs.*

†**Try·sty**, *a. Obs. rare.* [f. TRYST *sb.* + -Y.] Of or pertaining to a tryst: only in *trysty tree* = trysting tree: see TRYSTING *vbl. sb.* 2.

15.. *Adam Bel* 380 in Hazl. *E. P. P.* II. 154 When they came to Inglys wode, Under theyr trysty tre. *Ibid.* 392.

**Trysty**, var. TRISTY *Obs.* **Tryton, Tryumph, -wmph**, obs. ff. TRITON, TRIUMPH. **Tryuþe, Tryvette, Trywage, Trywede**: see TRUTH, TRIVET, TREWAGE, TRUEHEAD. **Tryys, -st, -ste**, var. TRICE *sb.*[1] *Obs.*

**Tsabaism, Tsabian**, var. SABAISM, SABIAN.

**Tsaing**: see TSINE.

‖ **Tsamba** (tsæ·mbă). [Tibetan.] An article of food made from barley-meal, extensively used in Tibet and adjacent parts.

1858 SIMMONDS *Dict. Trade, Tsamba*, a Tartar [properly Tibetan] name for the meal of barley. 1891 W. W. ROCKHILL *Land of Lamas* iii. 129 They cultivate the soil sufficiently to raise what barley is needed to make tsamba. 1908 *Athenæum* 13 June 721/3 The native food..in the Tibetan districts *tsamba* (barley meal mixed with yak butter)..was plain and uninviting. 1909 *Bible in the World* Sept. 268/2 After tea and *tsamba* I retired to the roof.

**Tsar** (tsāɹ) [Russ. царь], the now prevalent spelling of CZAR, q. v. for etymology and history. (Also **Tzar.**) Hence **Tsa·rate, Tsa·rdom, Tsare·vitch, Tsare·vna, Tsaritsa**, etc.: see CZARATE, CZARDOM, etc. So **Tsarist** (tsā·rist), an adherent or maintainer of Tsarism; **Tsarlet** (tsā·ɹlėt), a petty Tsar.

*a* 1670 [S. COLLINS] *Pres. St. Russia* (1671) 55 By the Grace of God We the Great Lord *Tzar, and Great Duke Alexei, [etc.] ..Tzar of Cazan, Tzar of Astrachan, Tsar of Siberia [etc.]. 1802–3 tr. *Pallas' Trav.* (1812) I. 229 Heraclius, the Tzar of Georgia. 1810 E. D. CLARKE *Trav. Russia*, etc. (1839) 29/1 The connection which subsisted between the tsars of Muscovy and the emperors of Constantinople. 1890–93 [see CZAR]. 1863 *Tsarate [see CZARATE]. 1877 D. M. WALLACE *Russia* xvii. 270 When the Grand Princes of Moscow brought the other principalities under their power, and formed them into the *Tsardom of Muscovy. 1901 *Fortn. Rev.* June 1034 Some..doubt as to the future of the Tzardom. 1906 KROPOTKIN *Mem. Revolutionist* (1908) II. ix. 143 The *Tsarevich..began to scold the officer. 1890 *Tsarevna [see CZAREVNA]. 1799 W. TOOKE *View Russian Emp.* I. 10 He caused to be inserted in all the *tzarian titles, the words: of all..Russia. 1905 *Daily Chron.* 21 Aug. 5/6 The ideal of Tsarian authority. 1895 *Blackw. Mag.* Feb. 312/1 The trial of those accused of *Tsaricide. 1891 *Tsarina [see CZARINA]. 1904 *Longm. Mag.* Oct. 204 If his *Tsarish Grace should..find himself in danger. 1882 C. HAMLIN in *Chicago Advance* 9 Mar., That cold-hearted cruelty which *Tsarism has engendered. 1902 *Daily Chron.* 4 June 8/2 Tolstoy's last pamphlet..is hostile to Socialism, and favourable to Tsarism. 1907 *Contemp. Rev.* Feb. 202 The tide of *Tsarist Power has passed over the steppes. 1833 R. PINKERTON *Russia* 300 The Tzar..performed a pilgrimage..accompanied by his *Tzaritza. 1890 Tsaritsa [see CZARITZA]. 1889 *Fortn. Rev.* XLVI. 285 This frightful régime of innumerable *Tsarlets. 1905 DILLON in *Contemp. Rev.* Aug. 280 They are sharers of autocratic absolutism, provincial tsarlets.

‖ **Tsatlee** (tsæ·tˌlī). [Cantonese, corresp. to Pekinese *Ch'i Li* 'seven miles': named after a locality in the Chekiang province, where it is produced.] A very superior kind of white native-reeled raw silk, produced for the foreign market.

1848 S. W. WILLIAMS *Middle Kingd.* xv. II. 123 The raw silk is an article of sale; the sorts usually known in the Canton market are tsatle, taysaam, and Canton raw silk. 1858 SIMMONDS *Dict. Trade, Tsat-lie, Tseh-li*, a species of China silk obtained in Nankin and the Northern parts of the empire, superior to the Canton kinds. 1913 *Times* 27 June 24 The silk of China comprises, white, yellow, and wild silk. Of these raw white silk (the tsatlee of the European market) is the most important.

**Tsch-**, German spelling of CH- (= tʃ).

‖ **Tschaike**, app. a form of CAÏQUE.

1790 *Naval Chron.* IV. 452 One chebec,..one tschaike,.. were destroyed.

**Tscheffkinite** (tʃe·fkinəit). *Min.* Also **tschev-**, and (after Ger. spelling) **tschewkinite.** [See quot. 1868 and -ITE[1].] A rare mineral, a silicate containing titanium, iron, and the metals of the cerium group, occurring in velvet-black masses.

1850 ANSTED *Elem. Geol., Min.* etc. 443 Tschewkinite, silicate and titanate of cerium, lanthanum, and didymium, with oxide of iron. 1868 DANA *Min.* (ed. 5) 387–8 Tscheffkinite...*Tschewkinit.* G. Rose, Reis. Ural, ii. 1839...From the Ilmen Mountains in the Urals; only a few specimens have been found... Named after the Russian general, Tschevkin [Tshefkin].

**Tschermigite** (tʃɜ̄·ɹmigəit). *Min.* [See def. and -ITE[1].] A name for ammonia alum (see ALUM 2), esp. as occurring native in brown coal at Tschermig in Bohemia.

1868 DANA *Min.* (ed. 5) 651–2 Tschermigite. Ammonia Alum. This salt is manufactured from the waste of gas works, and used extensively in place of potash alum.

‖ **Tschibouque**, variant of CHIBOUK.

1845 E. FITZGERALD *Lett.* (1889) I. 150 Now the bores are those who have smoked tschibouques with a Peshaw!

‖ **Tschoadar**, obs. variant of CHOBDAR.

1687 A. LOVELL tr. *Thevenot's Trav.* I. 25 The Tschoadar, who carries his Yagmourluk or Cloak for rain.

‖ **Tserin**, var. DZEREN, *dseren.*

1893 LYDEKKER *Horns & Hoofs* iv. 182 The tserin [*mispr.* tseain], or Mongolian gazelle (*Gazella* [or *Procapra*] *gutturosa*) of the desert regions of portions of Mongolia.

**Tsessabi, -ebe, -eby**, variants of SASSABY.

‖ **Tsetse** (tse·tsi). Also **tzetse, tzetze**, (*erron.* **tse**). [Sechwana (i. e. Bechuana language) *tsetse.*] A dipterous insect (*Glossina morsitans*, of the family *Tabanidæ*), abundant in parts of tropical and southern Africa; its bite is often fatal to horses and other domestic animals. Also applied to other species of *Glossina*. More fully *tsetse-fly.*

1849 E. E. NAPIER *Excurs. S. Africa* II. 396 [Gordon Cumming's] horses were killed either by lions or horse sickness, and the fly called 'tzetse'. All his oxen were killed by this insect. 1850 R. G. CUMMING *Hunter's Life S. Afr.* (1902) 139/2 Four [horses] that are bitten with 'tsetse', and must die in a week or two. 1865 — *Last Jrnls.* i. (1873) 15 The people..say there are no tsetse flies. 1889 L. V. SHELDON *S. Africa* 94 The Tse fly stings their horses. [1895

J. Brown *Secwana Dict.*, *Tsetse*, a fly destructive to cattle.] **1898** [see Trypanosoma]. **1904** *Brit. Med. Jrnl.* 20 Aug. 368 Sleeping sickness is conveyed, at least in Uganda, by that species of tsetse fly we know as *Glossina palpalis*.

**Tshekh** (tʃeχ), variant of Czech, Bohemian.

† **Tsia**, variant of *tcha*, Chia *Obs.*, tea.

**1662** J. Davies tr. *Mandelslo's Trav.* 183 A little Pot for Tsia or The..; another greater Tsia Pot. **1712** tr. *Pomet's Hist. Drugs* I. 85 The, or Tsia, is a very little Leaf, which is brought dry'd from China.

Hence **Tsio·logy** (*nonce-wd.*), a scientific dissertation on tea.

**1827** (*title*) Tsiology: Discourse on Tea, Tea Making, History of East India Co., &c.

**Tsigane**, etc.: see Tzigane.

**Tsine** (tsain). Also **tsaing** (saiŋ). [translit. Burmese *saing*.] A species of wild ox (*Bos sondaicus*) found in Burma and the Malay archipelago; also called *banteng*.

**1898** *Zoologist* Jan. 1 Tsine are certainly kittle cattle. **1900** Pollok & Thom *Sports Burma* iii. 102 During my long residence in Lower Burma..I killed but five tsine. *Ibid.*, Tsaing or Tsine. *Ibid.* 342 There were numerous signs of *Bos sondaicus*, the banting or tsine, as well as gaur about. **1903** *Sat. Rev.* 18 Apr. 481/1 The gaur, the gayal, the tsine or banting..might be acclimatised.

**T square**: see T 3 b.

**Tu**, obs. f. Thou *pers. pron.*, To *prep.*, Two.

**Tua, Tuaine**, obs. Sc. ff. Two, Twain.

**Tuae**, Sc. dial. form of Tway, two.

**Tualy**, obs. form of Towel.

‖ **Tuan** (tū·ăn). Also touan. Native name in Australia for the Flying Squirrel or Flying Phalanger (genus *Belideus*).

**1846** G. H. Haydon *Five Y. Exper. Australia Felix* iii. 57 The flying squirrel, or tuan, is much sought after for its fine fur. **1859** H. Kingsley *G. Hamlyn* xxxi, The Touan, the little grey flying squirrel, only begins to fly about at night.

‖ **Tuant** (tüañ), *a. Obs. rare.* [Fr., = killing, pres. pple. of *tuer* to slay, kill.] Of language or words: Cutting, biting, keen, trenchant.

**1672** Villiers (Dk. Buckhm.) *Rehearsal* iv. i. (Arb.) 99 Ay, I gad, but is not that *tuant* now, ha? is it not *tuant*? **1672** Marvell *Reh. Transp.* i. 17 To say Mr. Bayes is more civil than to say Villain and Caitiff, though these indeed are more tuant. **1673** [R. Leigh] *Transp. Reh.* 13. **1673** Hickeringill *Greg. F. Greyb.* 142 This harangue tuant and clean. **1706** Phillips (ed. Kersey) s. v., *A Tuant Jest*, i. e. a tart, biting Jest.

**Tuarn, Tuart**: see Tew-iron, Tooart.

‖ **Tuatara** (tūatā·ra). Also (*erron.*) **tuatera, -tura**. [Maori, f. *tua* on the back + *tara* spine (Webster, 1911).] A large lizard, *Sphenodon punctatum* or *Hatteria punctata*, dark bronze green in colour with white or yellowish specks, and having a dorsal row of yellow spines, formerly common in New Zealand: see quot. 1911.

[**1820** *Gram. & Voc. N. Zealand* 218 (Morris) *Túa tára*, a species of lizard.] **1890** *Catal. N. Zealand Exhib.* (ibid.), The Tuatara is the largest existing New Zealand reptile. It..is placed..in a separate order (*Rhyncocephalina*). **1911** C. de Thierry in *United Empire* Mar. 183 One of the peculiar animals from which scientists have estimated the probable age of New Zealand is the tuatara, a small lizard about a foot in length and of a dark bronze colour. It is extinct on the mainland but is still to be found on the shores of the outlying islands. **1914** *Chamb. Jrnl.* Nov. 750/2 The extraordinary characteristic of the tuatara is its capacity for perfect rest, and its apparent power of existing without food or water.

‖ **Tuath** (tū·ăh). *Irish Hist.* [Ir. *tūath* people, cognate with OE. *þéod*, Goth. *þiuda*, OTeut. **þeudô*, Indo-Eur. **teutā*; ME. Thede, q. v.] A 'tribe' or 'people' in Ireland; hence, the territory or district of a tribe, in which sense written in 16th c. *toghe*, Toughe, q. v.

**1873** W. K. Sullivan in *O'Curry's Anc. Irish* I. Introd. 79 The term *Tuath* was..applied to the people occupying a district which had a complete political and legal administration, a chief or *Rig*, and could bring into the field a battalion of seven hundred men. The word was also applied however to a larger division, consisting of three or four, or even more *Tuaths*, called a *Mór Tuath*, or great *Tuath*,.. associated together for certain legal and legislative purposes. **1877** W. F. Skene *Celtic Scotl.* II. ii. x. 460 Before letters were introduced..each tuath, or tribe, had probably its own variety of the common speech. **1898** J. Heron *Celtic Ch.* 14 A group of families from a common ancestry made a sept; a still larger group was called a clann..; while a tribe or tuath consisted of several of such clanns, septs, and families. *Ibid.* 16 There were in Ireland one hundred and eighty four tuaths or tribal territories.

**Tuay**, obs. Sc. form of Tway, two.

**Tuayl**, obs. form of Towel.

**Tub** (tʌb), *sb.* Forms: 4–7 **tubbe**, 5–6 **tobbe**, 5–7 **tob**, 6 **toubbe, tube, toob** (also 9 *dial.*), 6–7 **tubb**, 6– **tub**. [ME. *tubbe* = MDu., MLG. *tubbe*, *tobbe*, Du. and MFl. *tobbe*, Flem. *tubbe* (*ü*), *tibbe*, WFris. *tobbe*, LG., and EFris. *tubbe*.]

**1.** An open wooden vessel, wide in proportion to its height, usually formed of staves and hoops, of cylindrical or slightly concave form, with a flat bottom.

Often with defining word indicating its special use, as *alms-tub, bath-t., butter-t., kneading-t., wash-t.*, etc.: see these words. Also loosely applied to a butt, barrel, or cask.

*c* **1386** Chaucer *Miller's T.* 435 He gooth and geteth hym a knedyng trogh, And after that a tubbe and a kymelyn. **1392–3** *Earl Derby's Exp.* (Camden) 224 Pro vasis ligneis.. viz. tubbes, trowes, boketes et basketes. **1481–90** *Howard Househ. Bks.* (Roxb.) 228 Item, for a lok for the almes tobbe, ij. d. **1496** *Nottingham Rec.* III. 296 For v. tobys. **1509–10** *Rec. St. Mary at Hill* 269 Paid to a Coper for hopyng of the Tobbys and þe Barelles that longith to the Chirche xvj d. **1526** *Dunmow Churchw. Acc.* lf. 5 b (MS.) Payde for a toob and ii. bokks to fett watter, viij*d*. **1531** *Lett. & Pap. Hen. VIII*, V. 180 For morter toubbis, cowlis, water buckettes,..etc. **1557** in *Lanc. & Chesh. Wills* (1884) 64, iiij Tubbs to salte fleshe in. **1561** Hollybush *Hom. Apoth.* 3 b, Bath his fete in a depe tob. **1573** Tusser *Husb.* (1878) 58 Take tub for a season, take sack for a shift. **1645** Bp. Hall *Remedy Discontent.* xvi. 86 Here doe I see a Cynick housed in his Tub, scorning all wealth and state. **1829** Lytton *Devereux* iii. iv, Diogenes in his tub. **1838** Dickens *Nich. Nick.* ii, A distorted fir-tree, planted..in a tub.

*fig.* **1693** *Humours Town* 2 Coop'd up..like a Cinic, in thy Tub of a Study.

† **b.** A sweating-tub formerly used in the treatment of venereal disease; hence, the use of this; see quots. and cf. *tub-fast* in 10; also called (*mother*) *Cornelius' tub*, and allusively *powdering-tub. Obs.*

**1594** Nashe *Unfort. Trav.* 17 Mother Cornelius tub why it was like hell, he that came into it, neuer came out of it. **1599** [see Powdering-tub 2]. **1603** Shaks. *Meas. for M.* iii. ii. 60 *Luc.* How doth..thy Mistris? Procures she still? Ha? *Clo.* Troth sir, shee hath eaten vp all her beefe, and she is her selfe in the tub. **1608** Armin *Nest Ninn.* E iv b, Where they should study in priuate with Diogenes in his Cell, they are with Cornelius in his tub. **1676** Wiseman *Chirurg. Treat.* viii. ii. 13 Tub and Chair were the old way of sweating, but [etc.]. **1688** R. Holme *Armoury* iii. 421/2 He beareth Argent, a Doctors Tub, (otherwise called a Cleansing Tub), Sable; Hooped, Or.

**c.** *Gold-mining.* A puddling tub.

**1859, 1869** [see Puddling *vbl. sb.* 4, Puddle *v.* 6]. **1864** Rogers *New Rush* ii. 47 Miners' tubs and cradles, left to chance, On the resistless torrent's surface dance. **1884** T. Bracken *Lays of Maori* 154 The music of the puddling mill, the cradle, and the tub.

**d.** Used as a measure of capacity, varying with the commodity it contained: see quots.

**1706** Phillips (ed. Kersey), *Tub of Tea*, the Quantity of about 60 Pounds: of Camphire from 56 to 86 Pounds: of Vermilion from 3 to 4 Hundred Weight. **1858** Simmonds *Dict. Trade* s.v., The tub of butter must contain at least 84 lbs.; the tub of camphor is 130 Dutch lbs.

**e.** A small cask or keg of spirit, containing about four gallons. (A smugglers' term.)

**1835** Marryat *Three Cutters* ii, I made three seizures, besides sweeping up those thirty-seven tubs. **1869** R. M. Ballantyne *Deep Down* xiv. 180 They do say that the boatsmen [coast-guards] are informed about the toobs. **1884** J. C. Egerton *Sussex Folk & Ways* v. 65 This cottage..has ..been as full of tubs from top to bottom as ever it could hold.

**f.** *vulgar colloq.* Applied to a corpulent person.

**1897** Flandrau *Harvard Episodes* 316 With a moon-faced tub of a woman I'd never seen before,..hanging on to me.

**2.** A bathing-tub, bath-tub (of any shape); *colloq.* or *jocularly*, a bath; hence, the action or practice of taking a bath, esp. on rising.

[**1594** Plat *Jewell-ho.* iii. 94 The room would be close wherin you place your bathing tub.] **1849** *Knife & Fork* 11 They..have an hereditary aversion for the Saturday tub. **1861** Hughes *Tom Brown at Oxf.* iii, A great splashing in an inner room stopped..and Drysdale's voice shouted out that he was in his tub. **1865** 'C. Bede' *Rook's Gard.*, etc. 251 It must have been prior to the date of the institution of the tub. **1893** A. Lang *St. Andrews* i. 15 *note*, George Wishart astonished his contemporaries by taking cold tubs.

**3.** Applied to a slow clumsy ship, esp. one which is too broad in proportion to its length; often *humorous* or *contemptuous*; also, a short, broad boat; *spec.* a stout roomy boat used for rowing practice, as distinguished from a racing-boat; cf. *tub-gig, tub-pair* (see 10), Tub *v.* 4.

*a* **1618** Raleigh *Invent. Shipping* 9 In Cæsars time, the French Brittains..had very untoward Tubs in which they made Warre against him. **1675** Hobbes *Odyssey* (1677) 54 And now my child at sea is in a tub. **1809** W. Irving *Knickerb.* ii. iv. (1861) 52 Here the rapid tide..seizing on the gallant tub.., hurried it forward with a velocity unparalleled in a Dutch boat, navigated by Dutchmen. **1827** *Blackw. Mag.* XXI. 398 One was four feet broader, another was as much shorter than the Victory, and they were in comparison all Tubs. **1841** J. T. Hewlett *Parish Clerk* III. 4 No lighter boat, except the little tubs used for rowing off from the beach, could be obtained. **1853** 'C. Bede' *Verdant Green* x, He next day..made his first essay in a 'tub'. **1901** D. B. Hall & Ld. A. Osborne *Sunshine & Surf* iv, His old tub of a vessel..was known from one end of the Pacific to the other.

**4.** Applied contemptuously or jocularly to a pulpit, esp. of a nonconformist preacher: cf. Tub-preacher, -thumper.

**1643** Owen *Duty of Pastors & People* viii, Must a master of a family cease praying in his family,..for fear of being counted a preacher in a tub? **1680** Dryden *Prol. to University of Oxford* 13 Jack Presbyter shall here erect his throne, Knock out a tub with preaching once a day. **1710** Hearne *Collect.* (O.H.S.) II. 351 A huge Bonfire was made, and the Tub in wch he used to hold forth was plac'd on ye top of the Pile. **1728** Pope *Dunc.* ii. 2 A gorgeous seat, that far out-shone Henley's gilt tub, or Flecknо's Irish throne. **1891** *Spectator* 5 Dec. 804/2 Let the pulpit speak, and the tub too—there will still be too much sleep.

**5.** *Coal-mining.* 'Originally a mining bucket, now specially applied to the open-topped box of wood or iron, mounted on wheels, in which coal is brought from the face to the surface. It has supplanted the old 'corf', which was a basket carried on a tram. The tram and tub are now, in most cases, a single structure' (Heslop *Northumb. Gloss.* 1894). Cf. Corf 2, Tram *sb.*[2] 2.

**1851** Greenwell *Coal-trade Terms Northumb. & Durh.* 54 *Tub*, an open-topped box of wood or iron, attached to a tram, and used in conveying coals from the working places to the surface. **1859** R. Hunt *Guide Mus. Pract. Geol.* (ed. 2) 222 Cages [in coal mines] are attached to the wire rope, and these move in guides in the pit. The *tub* (8 cwt.) is placed in those [cages], and when drawn to the surface placed in the *teaming cradles*. **1893** *Athenæum* 21 Oct. 551/3 The old-fashioned 'tub' in the cut 'A Coal Mine' will hardly be recognized by the present generation of pitmen.., who, though they still use the word, no longer know the thing, which has been replaced by small trucks which run on rails into the cage. **1894** Heslop (as above), The tub, containing twenty-four pecks [is] three feet in length, thirty inches in width, and twenty-six in depth.

**b.** The lining of a pit-shaft.

**1839** [implied in *tub-plank* in 10]. **1855** *Orr's Circ. Sc.*, *Inorg. Nat.* 237 In all cases, the foundation of a permanent tub should rest on a water-tight stratum. **1860** Weale *Dict. Terms* (ed. 2), *Tub*, a cast-iron cylinder put in the shaft instead of bricking. **1877** Knight *Dict. Mech.*, *Tub*,..a casing of wood or of cast-iron sections..lining a shaft.

**6.** † **a.** On the early railways vulgarly applied to an open truck or a seatless carriage. *Obs.*

**1886** H. S. Brown *Autobiog.* vii. (1887) 30 We called it a 'stand up' and it also went by the name of 'a tub'. **1890** *N. & Q.* 7th Ser. IX. 470/2 At the time when the railway between Nottingham and Grantham was opened forty years ago, carriages of the lowest class,.. third or fourth, were something like [what] cattle-trucks are now, and were known colloquially as 'tubs'.

† **b.** A covered carriage or conveyance. *Obs.*

**c.** ? = *tub-gig* (*a*) (see 10).

**1889** *John Bull* 2 Mar. 142/2 Tubs we ca' the covered carriages, tubs wasn't known in these parts. **1911** F. Harrison *Autobiog. Mem.* II. xxiv. 73 It was the age of 'tubs' and they often took Jane Brice, my mother and Ellinor Abraham..as sitters.

**7.** *Naut.* See quot.

**1867** Smyth *Sailor's Word-bk.*, *Tubs, Topsail-halliard*, circular framed racks in which the topsail-halliards are coiled clear for running.

**8.** A local name of the gurnard, esp. the sapphirine gurnard, *Trigla hirundo*. Also *tub-fish* (see 10).

Couch takes this as a contraction of Cornish *tubbot, -ut*.

**1602** Carew *Cornwall* 32 Of flat [fish there are] Brets, Turbets, Dories,..Tub, Breame &c. **1836** Yarrell *Brit. Fishes* I. 42 From West bay to the Land's End, where the Gurnards are called Tubs, Tubfish and, in reference to colour, Red Tubs. **1861** *Act* 24 & 25 *Vict.* c. 109 § 4 All migratory fish of the genus salmon,.. salmon,.. buntling, guiniad, tubs, yellow fin, sprod, herling,.. or .. any other local name. **1863** *Rep. Sea Fisheries Comm.* (1865) II. 404/2 A tub..is a large specimen of the gurnet...Hake and tubs are the most we catch.

**9.** In proverbial phrases: † **a.** *A tale of a tub*, an apocryphal tale; a 'cock and bull' story. *Obs.* **b.** (*To throw out*) *a tub to the whale*, to create a diversion, esp. in order to escape a threatened danger. **c.** *Every tub must* (or *let every tub*) *stand on its own bottom*: cf. Bottom *sb.* 11 b.

**a. 1532** More *Confut. Tindale* Wks. 371/2 Consider the places & his wordes together, & ye shal find al his processe therin a fayre tale of a Tub. *Ibid.* [see Tale *sb.* 5 b]. **1562** J. Heywood *Prov. & Epigr.* (1867) 144 A tale of a tub, thy tales taste all of ale. **1631** Lenton *Charac.* F ix b, Oft-times hee goes but to the next Tauerne, and then very discreetly brings her home a tale of a Tubbe. **1709** O. Dykes *Eng. Prov. & Refl.* (ed. 2) 57 If one talks of Chalk, another will talk of Cheese still, or tell a Tale of a Tub. **1724** [see Tale *sb.* 5 b].

**b. 1704** Swift *T. Tub* Author's Pref. 14 Sea-men have a Custom when they meet a Whale, to fling him out an empty Tub,..to divert him from laying violent Hands upon the Ship. ..It was decreed, that in order to prevent these Leviathans from tossing and sporting with the Commonwealth (which of it self is too apt to fluctuate) they should be diverted..by a Tale of a Tub. **1728–31** *Lett. fr. Fog's Jrnl.* (1732) II. 73 It has been common to throw out something to divert and amuse the People, such as a Plot, a Conspiracy, or an Enquiry about Nothing,..which Method of Proceeding, by a very apt Metaphor, is call'd Throwing out the Tub. **1748** Richardson *Clarissa* (1810) III. vii. 54. **1768** Earl Malmesbury *Diaries & Corr.* I. 23 We find it a mere tub to amuse the whale. **1826** J. Doyle *Ess. Cath. Claims* 248 Some tub for a whale of prejudice to knash its teeth against. **1912** *Nation* 29 June 465/2 He throws a tub to the High Church whale.

**c.** *c* **1730–6** Bailey (folio) s. v., Every Tub must stand upon it's own Bottom. **1772** Graves *Spir. Quix.* (1820) I. 171. **1885** 'H. Conway' *Fam. Affair* xxix, I think it's better to let every tub stand on its own bottom.

**10.** *attrib.* and *Comb.*, as *tub-bath, -boat, -ear* (Ear *sb.*[1] 8), *-eight* (Eight B. 2 b), *-end, -hoop* (in quot. *transf.*), *-kennel, -life, -plank, -plant, -pulpit, -timber, -washing*; objective, as *tub-buyer, -carrier, -filler, -maker*; in sense 4, as *tub-lecture, -meeter, -minister, -orator*; also *tub-bellied, -brained, -cooperíng, -keeping, -like, -shaped* adjs.; also **tub-butter**, butter packed in tubs for keeping or export; **tub-camphor**, camphor imported in tubs (from Japan); **tub-cart** = *tub-gig* (*a*); **tub-chair**, a deep semicircular chair resembling a tub; **tub-dress**, a dress of washing material: cf. *tub-frock*; **tub-drubber** = Tub-thumper; **tub-engine**, a contrivance for raising water by means of a chain of tubs or the like; **tub-fake** (Fake *sb.*[1]), the coiled tow-line in the line-tub of a whale-boat (*Cent. Dict.* 1891 cites J. W. Collins); † **tub-fast**, abstinence during treatment in the sweating-tub: cf. 1 b; **tub-fish** = sense 8; **tub-frock** = *tub-dress*; **tub-gardening**, cultivation of plants or trees in tubs; **tub-gig**, (*a*) a deep low-hung gig with rounded corners and seats facing inwards; a governess car; (*b*) = *tub-pair*; **tub-gin** = *tub-engine*; †**tub-hunter**, a parasite, a sponger; **tub-loader**, *Coal-mining*: see quot.; **tub-oar**, the oar next the line-tub in a whale-boat; so **tub-oarsman**, one who attends to the running of the line when in use (*Cent. Dict.* 1891); **tub-pair**, a pair-oared practice boat (*College slang*); **tub-plot**, cf. *Meal-tub Plot* (MEAL *sb.*[1] 3 b); **tub-race**, a race in which the competitors use tubs instead of boats; **tub-saw**, a cylindrical saw; **tub-size** *v. trans.* to size (paper) in a tub or vat; to hand-size, as distinguished from *engine-size*; **tub-skirt**, **tub-suit**: cf. *tub-dress*; **tub-sugar**, sugar packed in chests and covered with fine clay (*Cent. Dict.* 1891); †**tub-tail**, a farthingale or hooped skirt; one who wears this (*contemptuous*); **tub-trimmer**, ?a cooper; in quot. *fig.*; **tub-wheel**, (*a*) the wheel of a colliery 'tub'; (*b*) a horizontal water-wheel with spiral floats; = DANAIDE; (*c*) a rotating drum in which hides are washed (*Funk's Stand. Dict.* 1895); **tub-woman**, a woman who carries a tub or tubs; also a woman suggesting a tub in figure. See also TUBMAN, TUB-PREACHER, TUB-THUMPER, etc.

1896 *Allbutt's Syst. Med.* I. 850 Each patient receives a *tub-bath of twenty minutes at 70° every third hour. 1846 *J. Baxter's Libr. Pract. Agric.* (ed. 4) II. 263 Before the South-down sheep were improved, they were very flat on the ribs, and *tub-bellied. 1883 *Brit. Q. Rev.* July 108 Crossing the narrow water-way in one of the heavy *tub-boats of the country. 1634 W. WOOD *New Eng. Prosp.* To Rdr., Many a *tub-brain'd Cynicke, who because any thing ..is too large for the straite hoopes of his apprehension, he peremptorily concludes it is a lye. 1829 S. SHAW *Hist. Staffordsh. Potteries* iv. 105 The common people of the district at the present day, call Irish **Tub* Butter, Pot Butter. 1880 *Spons' Encycl. Manuf.* 574 Japanese camphor..is also known as 'Dutch', or '*tub' camphor,..from its being imported to Europe in tubs covered with matting, each placed within a second tub. 1899 BARING-GOULD *Bk. of West* II. 275 The '*tub-carriers', who conveyed the kegs on their backs. 1906 *Daily Chron.* 26 Sept. 4/4 Three little girls.. clambering and pushing their way into the *tub-cart. 1839 MRS. CARLYLE *Lett., to Mrs. Welsh* 7 Apr. (1903) I. 76 Carlyle in his grey plaid suit, and his *tub-chair. 1847 — *Lett.* (1883) II. 20 In a tub-chair—a little live bundle of flannel shawls. 1818 SCOTT *Br. Lamm.* xii, The devil's in the pedling *tub-coopering carle! 1909 *Philad. Public Ledger* 24 June 5/1 (*Advt.*) Women's and Misses' Stylish *Tub Dresses. *a* 1704 T. BROWN *Wks.* (1730) IV. 199 Faith and Reason.., as has been judiciously observ'd by the fam'd *Tub-drubber of Covent Garden, can never be brought to set their Horses together. 1533 *MS. Rawl. D.* 776 lf. 170 For ij *Tubb Eares of woode sett on the same tubbe. 1901 *Daily News* 22 Feb. 5/1 The boats used in these novice races are clinker built...They are outrigged, but have fixed seats. At Oxford and Cambridge they are generically known as '*tub' eights. 1542 *Richmond Wills* (Surtees) 30 Two trowes, and a bowtyn ton, and a *tube ende. 1702 T. SAVERY *Miner's Friend* 55 Your *Tub-Engines, or Chain-Pumps, may draw forth the Water. 1607 SHAKS. *Timon* IV. iii. 85 Bring downe Rose-cheekt youth to the *Tubfast, and the Diet. 1820 SCORESBY *Acc. Arctic Reg.* II. 176 A man, designated '*tub-filler', with a ladle of copper, was employed in filling a hogshead with chopped blubber. 1668 WILKINS *Real Char.* II. v. § 3. 136 *Tub-fish, *Piper*. 1769 PENNANT *Zool.* III. 233 The Red Gurnard..agrees in its general appearance with the tub fish. 1888 GOODE *Amer. Fishes* 304 The Tub-fish, *T[rigla] hirundo*, is of frequent occurrence on the west coast of Scotland. 1909 *Westm. Gaz.* 1 Feb. 5/2 What we have for some time now called '*tub frocks' are certainly the best for the South. 1904 *Daily News* 9 Aug. 5 A most fascinating article, entitled '*Tub-Gardening'. 1836 SIR G. HEAD *Home Tour* 433, I pursued my journey to Whitehaven, in a covered car, or '*tub-gig', for which vehicle the title of the 'conveyance' is generally applied. 1884 FROUDE *Carlyle, Life in Lond.* xi. I. 316 The brothers went in a steamer from Liverpool to Bangor, and thence to Llanberis, again in a 'tub-gig', or Welsh car. 1888 WOODGATE *Boating* 72 Lessons in a tub-gig are the best remedies for this fault. 1702 T. SAVERY *Miner's Friend* 21 As easily learn'd as their driving of a Horse in a *Tub-Gin. *Ibid.* 57 My Engine..will clear an old work..as readily as your Tub-Gins or Chain-Pumps. 1892 *Pall Mall G.* 24 Oct. 2/3 Hoops, or (as they were called in Queen Anne's time, when they reached their maximum proportions) *tub-hoops. 1600 *Dr. Dodypoll* III. i. in Bullen *O. Pl.* III. 125 You are a sweet smell-feast, Doctor; that I see. Ile [have] no such *tub-hunters use my house. 1900 *Speaker* 10 Feb. 506/1 The *tub-keeping philosopher .. with the Psalmist crying 'All men are liars'. 1908 RHYS DAVIDS *Early Buddhism* i. 7 When he [Diogenes] lived, like a dog, in his *tub-kennel. 1709 O. DYKES *Eng. Prov. & Refl.* (ed. 2) 56 From a Pulpit-Harangue, to a *Tub-Lecture of extemporary Zeal. 1857 RUSKIN *Pol. Econ. Art* i. 2 People who..lived in tubs, and used gravely to maintain the superiority of *tub-life to town-life. 1867 *Morn. Star* 12 Apr., The miserable *pompes à incendies* that do duty in their own streets [Paris]..these weak *tublike structures. 1895 W. WRIGHT *Palmyra & Zenobia* xxix. 371 The tublike turban of the Druzes. 1891 *Labour Commission Gloss.*, **Tub Loaders*, men who hew at night-time and on other occasions, while the pit is not drawing coals, and fill the empty tubs left in the pit. 1719 D'URFEY *Pills* I. 153 The Tories, and the *Tub-meeters, That roosted near Leadenhall. 1661 GAUDEN *Hooker's Eccl. Pol.* Ded. 4 Those club-masters and *tub-ministers, who sought..to overthrow the ancient and goodly fabric of this church and kingdom. 1849 BRONTE *Shirley* viii, 'The Rev. Moses Barraclough: t' *tub orator'...'Ah!' said the Rector..'He's a tailor by trade'. 1870 *Daily News* 11 Feb., The president..had Messrs. Moss, Burgess, Payne, Baker, Mirehouse, and Lewis out in '*tub' pairs, a mode of improvement which has been generally found very beneficial to the individual members of the crew. 1839 URE *Dict. Arts* 973 The upper ends of the first set of *tub-planks being cut square and level all round, the second spiking crib..is fixed. 1801 JEFFERSON *Writ.* (1830) III. 455 The poor arts of *tub-plots, &c. were repeated till the designs of the party became suspected. *a* 1791 WESLEY *Wks.* (1872) VIII. 332 Let there be no..*tub-pulpit, but a square projection, with a long seat behind. 1903 SIR W. J. FARRAR in *Mem. Abp. Temple* (1906) I. vi. 86, I don't think Temple joined in the attempted *tub-race. 1874 KNIGHT *Dict. Mech.*, *Cylindrical Saw* .. is variously called a *tub-saw, drum-saw, barrel-saw. 1888 F. G. LEE in *Archæologia* LI. 363 A circular *tub-shaped font. 1880 J. DUNBAR *Pract. Papermaker* 55 **Tub-sizing*, preparation of the gelatine. 1887 *Harper's Mag.* June 124/2 If paper is to be 'tub-sized' as well as 'engine-sized', an animal size..is mixed with dissolved alum and placed in a tub or vat, through which the web of paper is run after leaving the first set of driers. 1909 *Philad. Public Ledger* 24 June 7/7 (*Advt.*) '*Tub' Skirts..Nice quality linen in white, tan & blue. 1595 GOSSON *Quippes Upst. Gentlew.* 161 in Hazl. *E. P. P.* IV. 257 Therefore *tubtailes all may rue, That they came from so vile a crue. 1591 *Knaresb. Wills* (Surtees) I. 173 All the *tubbe tymber thatt I have hewene. 1589 *Hay any Work* Title-p., An vnskilfull and a deceytfull *tubtrimmer. 1886 C. SCOTT *Sheep-Farming* 133 *Tub-washing is sometimes more convenient for small flocks. 1851 GREENWELL *Coal-trade Terms Northumb. & Durh.* 7 The small diameter of the *tub wheels. 1858 SIMMONDS *Dict. Trade*, *Tub-wheel*, a peculiar kind of wheel to a water-mill. 1660 *Okie's Lament.* 33 A Fat *Tub-woman was my Goddesse great of War. 1727 CAPT. S. BRUNT *Voy. to Cackl.* 34 They carried two Pails a-piece with a Yoke, like our Tub-women.

**Tub** (tɒb), *v.* [f. prec. sb.]

**1.** *trans.* To bathe or wash in a tub or bath. *colloq.*

1610 B. JONSON *Alch.* IV. iii, In your *bathada* You shall be sok'd, and strok'd, and tub'd, and rub'd. 1883 G. H. BOUGHTON in *Harper's Mag.* Apr. 700/1 She was 'tubbing' the two babies.

**b.** *intr.* To wash oneself in a tub or bath; to take a tub or bath, esp. on rising. *colloq.*

1867 *Pall Mall G.* No. 708. 1722/2 Gentlemen who didn't tub of a morning. 1885 C. H. EDEN *G. Donnington* ii, It was necessary..to tub and dress by the feeble flame of a single candle.

**2.** *trans.* To line (a pit-shaft) with a water-tight casing of timber, masonry, or iron; to dam *back* (water) in a shaft or tunnel in this way; to shut *off* (watery strata or seams) from the shaft with tubbing.

1812 J. HODGSON in J. Raine *Mem.* (1857) I. 94 The low-main coal is kept perfectly dry by tubbing the watery seams with a circular casing of oak wood. 1839 URE *Dict. Arts* 972 When several fathoms of the strata must be tubbed, in order to stop up the water-flow. 1862 *Chamb. Jrnl.* 5 Apr. 217/1 The shaft..is built round with brick at the top and bottom, while the rest of the way is 'tubbed' with long planks placed perpendicularly round the sides. 1865 JEVONS *Coal-Question* (1866) 68 When this flood of water.. had been 'tubbed back'. 1881 SANDS *Sk. Tranent* i. 17 The Coal Company offered to 'tub' or line the faulty pit with iron plates. 1884 tr. *Lotze's Logic* viii. 359 Men who are tubbing a well with masonry.

**3.** To put or pack in a tub; to plant in a tub.

1828 T. HOOK *Hum. Wks., Fashionable Parties* (1873) 322 Drawing rooms at ninety-six, and half-a-score sickly orange-trees tubbed on the top of a staircase. 1889 *Daily News* 29 June 6/3 As soon as the grower finds it won't pay him to send all his strawberries to market for table use, he begins to pick them and tub them, and sell them by the ton to the jam maker.

**b.** To soak (bricks) in a tub before setting or laying them.

1913 *Daily News* 31 Mar. 6 The walls..were built in cement mortar and the bricks properly tubbed.

**4.** *trans.* and *intr.* To coach (oarsmen) in a 'tub'; to practise rowing in a 'tub' (TUB *sb.* 3). *Rowing slang.*

1882 *Society* 18 Nov. 7/2 'Tubbing' vigorously, with the ..intention of putting on a boat for the Lent races. 1883 in *Standard* 17 Jan. 3/7 An hour and a half was then spent in tubbing the men. 1887 *Daily News* 28 Jan. 3/6 Proceedings commenced..by Mr. Orde tubbing the [men] in the gig pair.

Hence **Tubbed** (tɒbd) *ppl. a.*

1882 SALA *Amer. Revis.* (1885) 250 Our pickled or 'tubbed' pork. 1890 J. HATTON *By Order of Czar* III. iii, A court-yard..gay with tubbed laurel and tented tables.

‖ **Tuba**[1] (tiū·bă). [L. and It. *tuba*.]

**1.** (*pl.* tubæ.) The straight bronze war-trumpet of the ancient Romans.

1882 *Athenæum* 8 Apr. 452/1 Two other musicians blow long straight trumpets, exactly like the Roman *tuba*. 1890 E. B. CUSTER *Following Guidon* Pref. 9 The tuba..was a kind of straight bronze clarion, about thirty-nine inches long.

**2.** *Mus.* (*pl.* tubas.) A bass wind-instrument of the sax-horn family; a sax-tuba or bombardon; cf. SAX-HORN; also, one who plays this instrument.

1852 *Crystal Palace* 285/1 The Sax-horns in alto, soprano, tenor, tuba, bass, &c. 1888 *Pall Mall G.* 10 Dec. 4/2 Three trombones and a tuba have..a free run for their money. 1889 *Ibid.* 13 July 3/1 In 'Otello' Verdi..has written important parts for piccolo, cor anglais, bass clarinet, a third bassoon, two cornets, and a tuba. 1889 W. H. STONE in Grove *Dict. Mus.* IV. 184/1 Tubas are made in many keys, in F in Germany, in E♭ and B♭ in this country. 1909 *Punch* 20 Jan. 38/2 A..nonagenarian with a voice like a bass tuba.

**b.** An 8-foot high-pressure reed-stop in an organ.

1876 HILES *Catech. Organ* x. (1878) 72 Tuba, Tuba Mirabilis, Ophicleide—a Trumpet stop (striking reed) of large scale and on a high pressure of wind. 1889 SIR J. STAINER in Grove *Dict. Mus.* IV. 184/1 The Tuba is not solely used as a Solo stop. 1907 *Westm. Gaz.* 24 Aug. 15/3 The organ ..soared and swelled.., a crash of trumpet and tuba that left a vibrant humming in the air.

‖ **Tuba**[2] (tū·ba). Also **tooba.** [Arab. (in *Koran* xiii. 28) طوبى *ṭūbah*, supposed to be a. Aramaic *ṭūbā* beatitude, Heb. טובה *ṭobah*. Some commentators suppose a tree to be meant, the opinion cited by Sale, and adopted in the quots.] A mythical tree growing in the Mohammedan paradise: see quots. Also *tuba-tree*.

1817 MOORE *Lalla R., Paradise & Peri* 622 My feast is now of the Tooba Tree, Whose scent is the breath of Eternity! 1833 A. CRICHTON *Hist. Arabia* I. vii. 317 The Tooba, or tree of happiness, so large that the fleetest horse could not gallop in a hundred years from one end of its shadow to the other. 1875 EMERSON *Lett. & Soc. Aims* viii. 206 In [a Persian] poem the soul is figured as the Phoenix alighting on Tuba, the tree of Life. 1894 W. R. THAYER *Poems* 26 The odors of blooming tuba-trees Thro' the gardens steal.

‖ **Tuba**[3] (tuba·, tū·ba). [Malay توبا *tūba*.]

**1.** In the Malay archipelago, the Philippines, etc., the name of species of *Dalbergia* from the roots of which an intoxicating juice is extracted; also, the juice itself, which is used as a fish-poison. Also applied to the berry of *Anamirta Cocculus* (known as *cocculus indicus*), and to the fruits of *Jatropha Curcas* and *Croton Tiglium*, used for the same purpose. Also *attrib.*

[1894 DENNYS *Dict. Malaya* 416 *Tuba*, the name of a creeping plant (dalbergia) the root of which..is used to stupefy fish for the purpose of capture.] 1895 SWETTENHAM *Malay Sk.* 225 The water is poisoned with the juice of the tuba root. 1898 *Blackw. Mag.* Mar. 414/1 This is how we fished with the tuba six years ago. 1899 W. H. FURNESS *Folk Lore Borneo* 27 The people go Tuba fishing, poisoning the stream with the juice of the Tuba root.

**2.** The fermented sap of the unopened flower-buds of various palms, esp. the coco-nut and Palmyra palms; palm-wine; also, the alcoholic liquor distilled from this; arrack.

1902 W. E. SAFFORD in *Amer. Anthropologist* 728 He climbed a coconut-tree..and brought in a bamboo joint full of tuba, delicious as cider just beginning to turn sharp. 1912 *Contemp. Rev.* Apr. 560 Long tumblers of pink tuba.

**Tubage** (tiū·bėdʒ). [= F. *tubage* (Littré, 1874), f. *tube* TUBE: see -AGE.]

**1.** *Surg.* The introduction of a tube into a cavity or canal; *esp.* intubation of the larynx.

1880 M. MACKENZIE *Dis. Throat & Nose* I. 181, I must here briefly refer to the subject of catheterism and 'tubage' of the larynx. 1886 in *Trans. Amer. Pediatric Soc.* (1897) IX. 29 [In 1886 O'Dwyer predicted] that at no distant day tracheotomy would be entirely superseded by 'tubage of the larynx'. 1896 [see INTUBATION].

**b.** *Ordnance.* The insertion of an inner tube or lining in the bore of a cannon; also, the process of shrinking an outer tube on an inner bore.

1882 *Rep. of Chief of U. S. Ordnance* 244 (Cent. D.) The present short steel tube has been the result of the essays in the tubage of guns.

**2.** Tubes collectively; tubing; a system of tubes; in quot., in a tubular boiler.

1896 *Daily News* 20 Apr. 5/1 When the fires are at work, the slender tubage heaves and throbs, and through it scurries the river of steam-generating water.

**Tubal** (tiū·băl), *a.* [f. L. *tub-us* TUBE + -AL.]

**1.** Of, pertaining to, or of the nature of a tube; consisting of tubes; tubular. *rare.*

1735–6 H. BROOKE *Univ. Beauty* IV. 126 Its wanton floods the tubal system lave. 1899 *Allbutt's Syst. Med.* VI. 46 In the early tubal form of the heart, the auricles are placed below..the ventricles.

**2.** *Anat.* and *Path.* Pertaining to, occurring in, or affecting the Fallopian tube, as *tubal dropsy*, *pregnancy*, the bronchial tubes, as *tubal cough*, *respiration*, or the renal tubules, as *tubal nephritis*.

1822–34 *Good's Study Med.* (ed. 4) IV. 181 *Eccyesis Tubalis*, Tubal Exfetation. 1857 BULLOCK *Cazeaux' Midwif.* 244 Having been once deposited in the tubal canal, the ovule traverses its whole length, and falls into the uterine cavity. *Ibid.* 246 Tubal Pregnancy..is the most frequent of all the varieties of extra-uterine pregnancy. 1857 DUNGLISON *Med. Lex.* s.v. *Murmur, Respiratory*, The respiration, perceived over the trachea and bronchia in health, is called *tracheal* or *bronchial* or *tubal*,..according to the situation in which it is heard. 1860 MAYNE *Expos. Lex.*, *Tubal Cough*, see *Bronchial Cough*. 1873 T. H. GREEN *Introd. Pathol.* (ed. 2) 276 Tubal nephritis..is one of those morbid processes which constitute Bright's disease. 1890 BILLINGS *Med. Dict.* s.v., *T[ubal] dropsy*, hydrosalpinx.

**Tubar** (tiū·băɹ), *a.* [f. as prec. + -AR[1]: cf. F. *tubaire*.] Of the form of a tube; tubular.

1887 SOLLAS in *Encycl. Brit.* XXII. 418/1 Articulate and inarticulate tubar skeletons of calcispongès.

**Tubate** (tiū·beᵻt), *a. Bot. rare.* [ad. mod.L. *tubātus*, f. L. *tubus* TUBE: see -ATE[2].] Formed into a tube; having a tube or tubes; tubal, tubular.

1866 in *Treas. Bot.*

**Tubbal** (tɒ·băl). Also **tubble.** [? dial. var. of TWIBILL.] Local name of the common mattock, or of a special form (see quot. 1902); in Cornwall, a miner's tool of similar form (= TUBBER[2]).

1847–78 HALLIWELL, *Tubble*, a mattock. *Devon.* 1880 *W. Cornwall Gloss.*, *Tubbal*, a miner's tool. 1902 *Rep. Provinc.* Aug. (E.D.D.), *Tubbal*, usually a heavy mattock.

with a small axe-head, used for grubbing or rooting. Also a very common name for the common mattock.

**Tubber**[1] (tʊ·bəɹ). [f. TUB *sb.* or *v.* + -ER[1].] **a.** One who makes tubs, a cooper. **b.** One who lives in a tub, a cynic like Diogenes. **c.** A rowing man who is 'coached' in a 'tub' (*nonce-use*). **d.** One who tubs: see TUB *v.* 1 b.

**1825** BROCKETT *N. C. Words, Tubber*, a cooper, a maker of tubs. **1883** *Almondbury & Huddersfield Gloss., Tubber*, a cooper. **1891** *Blackw. Mag.* Mar. 374 A concession to Diogenes and other tubbers. **1894** *Sporting Life* 28 Feb. 6/2 Shortly after four o'clock tubbing practice was begun... Lewis and Kerrison were the third set of tubbers taken out.

**Tu·bber**[2]. *local.* [Cf. TUBBAL, TWIBILL.] A tool used in Cornish mines: = BEELE[2].

**1671** *Phil. Trans.* VI. 2104 The Instruments commonly used in Mines, that serve for ripping the Loads.. A Beele or Cornish Tubber (i. e. double points) of 8 l. or 10 l. weight, sharped at both ends, well steeled and holed in the middle. **1753** CHAMBERS *Cycl. Supp., Tubber-Men* are the people who work with this tool,..called in other places *beel-men*.

**Tu·bbiness.** [f. TUBBY + -NESS.] Tubby quality or condition.

**1881** *Daily News* 29 Dec. 6/4 Fishing smacks...Stoutly built..and somewhat inclined to tubbiness. **1906** H. G. WELLS *Days of Comet* (1907) 130 Its long skirts accentuated the tubbiness of his body, the shortness of his legs. **1910** *Sat. Rev.* 18 June 785/2 Arpeggio passages..opulent and satisfying without any suspicion of tubbiness.

**Tubbing** (tʊ·biŋ), *vbl. sb.* [f. TUB *v.* (or *sb.*) + -ING[1].] The action of TUB *v.*

**1. a.** † Treatment in the sweating-tub: see TUB *sb.* 1 b. **b.** Washing or bathing in a tub or bath.

**1657** G. STARKEY *Nature's Explic.* To Rdr. 9 Salivation in the Lues or Tubbing is a dotage. *a* **1845** HOOD *Black Job* xiii, In spite of all the tubbing, rubbing, scrubbing..The blacks..were as black as ever! **1894** BOASE *Exeter Coll.* (O.H.S.) p. clxii, The quite modern institution of tubbing in the mornings.

**2.** The lining of a pit-shaft or tunnel with a watertight casing: see TUB *v.* 2; *concr.* the casing of timber, masonry, or metal sections used for this.

**1839** URE *Dict. Arts* 969 The pit..must..be sunk through the quicksand by means of tubbing. **1851** GREENWELL *Coal-trade Terms Northumb. & Durh.* 55 At present, tubbing is put in in metal segments. **1855** *Orr's Circ. Sc., Inorg. Nat.* 237 There are several kinds of stopping out water, or tubbing, as it is called...Stone tubbing,.. Plank tubbing,..Solid wood tubbing,..and Metal tubbing. **1862** SMILES *Engineers* III. 297 The skilful casing of the shaft with segments of cast-iron—a process called 'tubbing'.

**b.** *attrib.*, as *tubbing-deal, -plate, -wedge.*

**1839** URE *Dict. Arts* 973 The tubbing deals..must now be fixed. **1883** GRESLEY *Gloss. Terms Coal Mining, Tubbing plates*, cast-iron segments forming portion of a ring of tubbing... *Tubbing wedges*, small wooden wedges of pitch pine..hammered in between the joints of tubbing plates.., thus stopping back every drop of water from the shaft. **1886** J. BARROWMAN *Sc. Mining Terms* 68 *Tubbing-deals*, deals put behind tubbing in a shaft.

**3.** Rowing in a 'tub'; training for a boat-race in a 'tub': see TUB *sb.* 3, *v.* 4.

**1884** *Pall Mall G.* 11 Jan. 10/2 Operations on the Cam commenced yesterday with 'tubbing'. **1904** *Daily News* 23 Mar. 11/2 The Dark Blues did some tubbing work first.

**Tubbish** (tʊ·biʃ), *a.* [f. TUB *sb.* + -ISH[1].] Somewhat tubby; resembling a tub.

**1565** GOLDING *Ovid's Met.* IV. (1593) 91 Of tubbish timbrels ..a hoarse and jarring sound. **1785** WOLCOTT (P. Pindar) *Odes Roy. Acad.* iv. 11 Men whose heads are rather tubbish, Or, drum-like, better form'd for sound than sense. **1836–7** DICKENS *Sk. Boz, Charac.* vii, He was a short, round, large-faced, tubbish sort of man.

**Tubble**: see TUBBAL.

‖ **Tubboe** (tʊ·bǒ). Also **tubba.** [? native word in W. Africa.] Each of the excrescences or sores in framboesia; also in *pl.* = FRAMBŒSIA, YAWS.

**1769** E. BANCROFT *Guiana* 387 The infectious matter.. produces subcutaneous sores, which are called Tubboes. **1822–34** *Good's Study Med.* (ed. 4) II. 432 When the tumours point from the soles of the feet, they cannot press through the thickness of the skin, and hence form imperfectly, and produce highly elevated calluses, which are called tubba or crab-yaws. **1898** SIR P. MANSON *Trop. Diseases* xxvii. 428 'Tubboes', 'tubba', 'crabs', 'crappox', 'crabes' are expressions applied to the painful manifestations on the soles of the feet [in yaws]. Forms of chronic dermatitis on hands and feet are 'dartres', 'tubboe', 'crabs', dry 'tubboes'.

**Tubby** (tʊ·bi), *a.* [f. TUB *sb.* + -Y.] Resembling or suggesting a tub.

**1.** Tub-shaped, tub-like; of rounded outline, and stout or broad in proportion to the length; of a person, corpulent.

**1835** ANSTER tr. *Faustus* II. v. (1887) 269 Come, short-horned, thick Devils, tubby, stubby. **1859** SALA *Tw. round Clock* (1861) 14 They are mostly square and squat in rigging, and somewhat tubby in build. **1885** *Pall Mall G.* 9 June 2/2 In 1690..he [Stradivarius] began to improve his model, bringing it flatter, the great secret of the true violin as opposed to the old tubby model. **1891** KIPLING *Plain Tales fr. Hills* vii. 54 Fat Captains and tubby Majors. **1905** *Westm. Gaz.* 21 Mar. 4/2 Driving a tubby [motor] car.

**2.** Sounding like a tub when struck; dull or wooden in sound. (Said of stringed instruments.)

**1806–7** J. BERESFORD *Miseries Hum. Life* (ed. 3) XVI. 90 The dead, lumpish, tubby tones of the fourth and fifth strings of the guittar. **1883** HAWEIS *My Musical Life* (1884) I. 95 He [the violin] goes 'tubby' (a term used to express a dull vibration).

**Tube** (tiūb), *sb.* [a. F. *tube* (1460 in Godef. *Compl.*), ad. L. *tub-us.*] **I.** Artificial.

**1.** A hollow body, usually cylindrical, and long in proportion to its diameter, of wood, metal, glass, or other material, used to convey or contain a liquid or fluid, or for other purposes; a pipe.

A more recent and more generic term than *pipe*, in which the form of the thing is chiefly considered, and thus used in reference to many things to which *pipe* is not applied, *pipe* being an older term retained for tubes used for the passage of liquids, smoke, air, or gas, while *tube* is applied to most recent inventions; but the distinction is often arbitrary, depending on the custom of the workshops.

**1658** PHILLIPS, *Tube*,..any long pipe through which water or other liquid substance is conveyed. **1660** BOYLE *New Exp. Phys. Mech.* i. 33 The Mercury in the [barometric] Tube fell down lower, about three inches, at the top of the Mountain then at the bottom. **1690** LOCKE *Hum. Und.* II. iv. § 3 When the Sucker in a Pump is drawn, the space it filled in the Tube is certainly the same, whether any other body follows the motion of the Sucker or no. **1837** GORING & PRITCHARD *Microgr.* 206 [In] a solar microscope..B, the tube containing the condensing lens. **1846** GREENER *Sc. Gunnery* 288 Lateral pressure on the sides of the tube of the gun. **1861** N. A. WOODS *Pr. Wales in Canada & U.S.* 122 The whole Tube [of a tubular bridge] was first actually built in England and sent out piece meal.

**b.** = TUBING, material of a tubular form.

**1823** J. BADCOCK *Dom. Amusem.* 78 Some feet or yards.. of that more pliable composition tube, employed by the makers of beer engines. **1893** J. A. HODGES *Elem. Photogr.* (1907) 87 A piece of india rubber tube.

**2.** In specific applications usually indicated by context. **a.** A glass or other tube used in chemistry; *esp.* = TEST-TUBE. *Tube of safety* = *safety-tube* (SAFETY 10).

**1800** tr. *Lagrange's Chem.* I. 60 Melt the phosphorus in boiling water, and apply to it one of the ends of the tube, while you hold the other in your mouth. **1807** T. THOMSON *Chem.* (ed. 3) II. 207 A tube of safety is a tube open at its upper end, and having its lower end plunged in water. **1827** FARADAY *Chem. Manip.* i. (1842) 21 Glass tubes of various sizes closed at one end. *Ibid.* xiv. 307 The best tubes are those made of Bohemian potash glass, and used by Liebig in his analyses of organic bodies.

**b.** A tubular surgical instrument; a cannula; an intubation-tube.

**1803** *Med. Jrnl.* IX. 7 The tube is to be passed downwards until it again reaches the substance to be extracted. **1857** DUNGLISON *Med. Lex., Tube, Œsophageal*, stomach tube... *Rectal tube*, defecation tube. **1877** KNIGHT *Dict. Mech.* s. v., (*Surgical tubes*) *a.* An esophageal tube, capable of being passed into the stomach. *b.* An elastic gum tube passed *per anum* into the colon...*c.* A tracheal tube. **1902** *Brit. Med. Jrnl.* 3 July, Owing to the depth of the wound two drainage tubes were introduced at the time of operation.

**c.** A fire-tube or water-tube in a steam-boiler; a boiler-tube.

**1833** N. ARNOTT *Physics* (ed. 5) II. 32 In a long waggon-shaped boiler the tubes..should be made flat and broad enough to reach from side to side. **1903** *Daily Chron.* 7 Jan. 7/2 In the fire-tube or cylindrical boiler the fire and smoke went through the tubes, and in the water-tube the fire was outside the tubes and the water passed through them.

**d.** A small collapsible cylinder of tin or lead used to hold semi-liquid substances, as oil-colours.

**1841** RAND *Patent Specif.* No. 8863 Their contents may easily be squeezed out by collapsing the said tubes or cases. **1877** KNIGHT *Dict. Mech.* 2643/1 Collapsible tin tubes for artists' colors. **1881** [see *tube-colour* in 12 b].

**e.** In wool or worsted spinning: cf. *tube yarn* in 12 b, and TUBE *v.* 2.

**1884** *West. Morn. News* 5 Sept. 7/4 The foreign yarn trade keeps pretty brisk, particularly in lustre wefts, and similar yarns on the tube.

**f.** (See quot.)

**1877** KNIGHT *Dict. Mech., Tube*,..4. the barrel of a chain-pump.

**3.** An optical instrument of tubular form, *esp.* a telescope: more fully *optic tube.* Now *arch.*

**1651** [see OPTIC A. 4]. **1668** PEPYS *Diary* 4 Dec., Wrote a letter at the Board, by the help of a tube, to Lord Brouncker. **1668–9** *Ibid.* 14 Mar., My eyes being very bad, and..I forced to find a way to use by turns with my tube, one after another. *a* **1718** PRIOR *Solomon* III. 470 Of his fair Deeds a distant View I took; But turn'd the Tube upon his Faults to look. **1781** COWPER *Charity* 387 Some grave optician.. finds that though his tubes assist the sight, They cannot give it. **1807** J. BARLOW *Columb.* VII. 386 On the tall decks, their curious chiefs explore, With optic tube, our camp-encumber'd shore. **1867** G. GILFILLAN *Night* iv. 116 To the silent tube in Herschel's hand A hundred suns spring up.

†**4.** Applied to a tobacco-pipe. *poet. Obs. rare.*

**1736** I. H. BROWNE *Pipe of Tobacco* Poems (1768) 117 Little tube of mighty pow'r, Charmer of an idle hour. **1784** COWPER *Task* V. 55 With pressure of his thumb To adjust the fragrant charge of a short tube, That fumes beneath his nose.

†**5.** A cannon; also a rifle or hand-gun. *poet.*

**1762** FALCONER *Ode Dk. of York* 138 The ships their horrid tubes display, Tier over tier. **1801** *Sporting Mag.* XVII. 148 With curious skill the deathful tube is made. **1816** BYRON *Siege of Cor.* iii, To point the tube, the lance to wield.

**b.** A small pipe introduced through the vent, formerly used in firing cannon; a *friction-tube, quill-tube*, or *priming-tube.*

**1797** *Encycl. Brit.* (ed. 3) VIII. 230/2 Firing it [gunpowder] with tubes, introduced at a vent bored through the button and breech of the gun, of different lengths, so as to reach the different parts of the powder. **1828** WEBSTER, *Tube*, in artillery, an instrument of tin, used in quick firing. **1867** SMYTH *Sailor's Word-bk., Tubes*, for guns, a kind of portable priming, for insertion into the vent,—of various patterns.

**c.** The inner cylinder of a built-up gun, upon which the outer case is shrunk. Cf. TUBAGE 1 b.

**1895** in *Funk's Stand. Dict.*

**6. a.** A musical wind-instrument, a pipe. *poet. rare.* **b.** The main cylinder of a wind-instrument (*Cent. Dict.* 1891).

**1820** KEATS *Hyperion* I. 206 Solemn tubes, Blown by the serious Zephyrs, gave of sweet And wandering sounds, slow-breathed melodies.

**7. a.** A pneumatic dispatch-tube.

**1860** *Once a Week* 28 July 130/2 Written messages are sucked through tubes...We hear a whistle; this is to give notice that a despatch is about to be put into the tube at Mincing Lane, two-thirds of a mile distant. **1861, 1874** [see DISPATCH *sb.* 12]. **1866, 1894** [implied in *tube-journey, tube-room*: see 12]. **1905** *Daily Chron.* 27 May 4/3 From Whiteley's 6,194 parcels were dispatched in five hours, of which 78 per cent. could have been sent by tube.

**b.** The cylindrical tunnel in which an underground electric railway runs; also short for *tube-railway. colloq.*

*Twopenny Tube*, the Central London Railway, opened in 1900: see TWOPENNY.

**1900** H. D. BROWNE in *Londoner* 30 June (*heading*), The Twopenny Tube. **1900** *Punch* 4 July 7/1. **1901** *Lancet* 2 Nov. 1209/2 A good portion of the air must be driven backwards and forwards unchanged in the tube. **1902** *Westm. Gaz.* 24 Oct. 2/3 When the phrase 'the twopenny tube' came into existence..a similar electric 'tube' had been in regular running for close upon ten years. **1905** RIDER HAGGARD in *Gardener's Year* May 165 The first part of my journey.. was by Tube.

**8.** *Physics.* A tubular figure conceived as being formed by lines of force or action passing through every point of a closed curve; as *tube of flow* (see FLOW *sb.*[1] 1 b), *tube of force, tube of induction.*

**1878** W. K. CLIFFORD *Dynamic* 199 If we take a small closed curve, and draw lines of flow through all points on it, the tubular surface traced out by these lines is called a tube of flow. **1881** [see FLOW *sb.*[1] 1 b]. **1885** WATSON & BURBURY *Math. The. Electr. & Magn.* I. 104 The portions of any surfaces in an electric field intercepted by the same tube of force are called corresponding surfaces,..the algebraic sum of the electricities included in the tube in its passage from any one surface to any other. **1902** SLOANE *Stand. Electr. Dict., Tubes of Force*, aggregations of lines of force, either electrostatic or magnetic. They generally have a truncated, conical or pyramidal shape and are not hollow. Every cross-section contains the same number of lines.

**II.** Natural.

**9.** *Anat.* and *Zool.* A hollow cylindrical vessel or organ in the animal body; a canal, duct, passage, or pipe, as in the circulatory, alimentary, respiratory, reproductive, or excretory systems; often preceded by a defining word, as *alimentary, bronchial, Eustachian, Fallopian, intestinal tube*, etc.: see these words.

[cf. **1598** FLORIO, *Tubo*,..the pipe wherethrough the marrow of the backe bone runneth. **1611** COTGR., *Tube*, a Conduit-pipe; also, the hollow of the back-bone, or the pipe through which the marrow thereof doth runne.] **1661** BLOUNT *Glossogr.* (ed. 2). **1696** PHILLIPS (ed. 5), *Fallopian Tubes*, two slender Passages proceeding from the Womb. **1741**, **1755** Eustachian tube [see EUSTACHIAN]. **1809** *Med. Jrnl.* XXI. 400 The œsophagus..that animated tube. **1826** KIRBY & SP. *Entomol.* IV. xli. 128 Connected by a slender tube with each mandible in spiders is a vessel with spiral folds, which seems properly to belong to this head. **1831** J. DAVIES *Man. Mat. Med.* 374 Its passage in the intestinal tube is attended with the same phenomena. **1904** *Brit. Med. Jrnl.* 10 Sept. 584 The main depôts of lymphocytes.. are round the hollow tubes of the body.

**b.** One of the siphons of a mollusc.

**1839** DARWIN *Voy. Nat.* i. (1852) 8 It [cuttle-fish] could..take good aim by directing the tube or siphon on the under side of its body.

**10.** A hollow cylindrical channel in a plant; *spec.* in *Bot.* the lower united portion of a gamopetalous corolla or gamosepalous calyx; also, a united circle of stamens.

*a* **1704** LOCKE *Elem. Nat. Philos.* ix. (1754) 34 This [juice] is convey'd by the stalk up into the branches, and leaves, through little, and in some plants, imperceptible tubes. **1760** J. LEE *Introd. Bot.* I. iii. (1765) 7 Monopetalous [corolla].. consists of two Parts, viz. the Tube, or lower Part, which is usually Tube-shaped; and the Limb, or upper Part. **1776** WITHERING *Brit. Plants* (1796) IV. 310 Tubes white, brownish with age. **1807** J. E. SMITH *Phys. Bot.* 394 *Syngenesia.* Stamens united by their Anthers into a tube, rarely by their Filaments also. **1884** BOWER & SCOTT *De Bary's Phaner.* 187 The laticiferous tubes permeate the whole body of the plant, in most cases as a continuous system.

**11.** Applied to other tubular or cylindrical objects or formations of natural origin.

**1831** *Literary Gaz.* 15 Jan. 44/2 Lightning Tubes—In the neighbourhood of the old castle of Remstein..there have been found this summer very firm and long vitreous tubes. **1860** TYNDALL *Glac.* II. xxv. 362 The tube in fact resembled a vast organ-pipe. **1865, 1884** [see FULGURITE]. **1878** HUXLEY *Physiogr.* 190 The molten matter..thus forms a hard stony tube lining the volcanic chimney.

**III. 12.** *attrib.* and *Comb.*, as *tube attendant, -holder, -room, system, trade, -vase, -wall, -work, -worker*; *tube-rolling* sb. and adj.; *tube-eyed, -like, -shaped* adjs.; in sense 2 a, as *tube-apparatus, -atmolyser, -bath, -chemistry, -furnace, -receiver, -retort*; in sense 7 b, as *tube bill* (BILL *sb.*[3] 3), *conductor, mileage, railway, -route, station, -train, traveller, tunnel.*

1827 FARADAY *Chem. Manip.* xiv. (1842) 315 Sulphur may be combined with platina, and phosphorus with lime, in a *tube apparatus. 1873 WATTS *Fownes' Chem.* (ed. 11) 126 Atmolysis is best exhibited by means of an instrument called the *tube-atmolyser. 1908 *Daily Chron.* 15 Feb. 1/7 A *tube attendant at the G.P.O. 1827 FARADAY *Chem. Manip.* xvi. (1842) 400 *Tube-baths for the conveyance of limited temperatures either by the intermedium of water, solutions, or metals. 1902 *Westm. Gaz.* 5 Nov. 11/1 The County Council has found itself unable to frame a *Tube Bill. 1827 FARADAY *Chem. Manip.* vii. (1842) 225 Processes of this kind will be described and illustrated in Section xvi. on *Tube Chemistry. 1909 *Westm. Gaz.* 18 Feb. 9/4 *Tube conductor's shocking death. 1792 SOUTHEY *To Contemplation* v, I..watch'd the *tube-eyed snail Creep o'er his long moon-glittering trail. 1827 FARADAY *Chem. Manip.* xiv. (1842) 309 Placing two bricks edgeways, across a loose square grate,..makes an excellent *tube-furnace. *Ibid.* xix. 505 The tube furnace..is an excellent instrument for softening considerable lengths of tubes. 1897 *Westm. Gaz.* 16 Dec. 3/1 A cigar *tube-holder that prevents the odoriferous tube from spoiling his pocket. 1905 *Brit. Med. Jrnl.* 16 Sept. 618 The tube-holder is graduated so that the tube may be easily moved a distance of 2½ inches. 1866 GEO. ELIOT *F. Holt* Introd., The *tube-journey can never lend much to picture and narrative. 1847–9 *Todd's Cycl. Anat.* IV. 27/1 Animals whose *tube-like bodies are prolonged deeply into the common mass. 1898 P. MANSON *Trop. Diseases* xviii. 291 Sometimes tube-like pieces, evidently rings of mucous membrane..are discharged. 1902 *Westm. Gaz.* 21 Apr. 10/1 The '*tube' mileage in London. 1900 *Daily News* 3 Dec. 5/2 One of the most useful of the new *tube railways. 1906 CHARL. MANSFIELD *Girl & Gods* vi, The warm stench from the Tube railway assailed her nostrils. 1827 FARADAY *Chem. Manip.* xxiv. (1842) 644 Make some closed tubes,..some *tube receivers..and other useful apparatus. *Ibid.* xix. 510 *Tube retorts..are made by first closing the end of a piece of tube, and then [etc.]. 1908 *Westm. Gaz.* 13 Aug. 8/1 *Tube-rolling..at 1s. 6d. per 1,000. 1894 *Daily News* 22 Feb. 2/1 About 30 feet of *tube-room on ground floor and contents severely damaged by fire. 1901 *Brit. Med. Jrnl.* 9 Mar. 591/2 The lines of *tube-route being chosen with a view to supplementing and completing the means of communication from the suburbs. 1760 J. LEE *Introd. Bot.* I. iii. (1765) 7 The..lower Part..is usually *Tube-shaped. 1825 *Greenhouse Comp.* I. 56 *Erica aurea*, tube-shaped yellow flowers on plants nearly 2 feet high. 1913 *Daily News* 28 Jan. 6 The trains that roar in and out of a *tube station. 1908 *Installation News* II. 92/2 The *tube system [of electric wiring]. 1900 *Westm. Gaz.* 8 Jan. 9/1 Severe competition in the *tube trade. 1901 *Daily News* 15 June 4/7 Journeying to and from the scenes of their labour in *tube-trains. 1903 *Westm. Gaz.* 4 July 3/2 Thousands of *Tube travellers. 1910 *Daily Chron.* 19 Feb. 3/4 Macdonald..ran to the end of the train and jumped into the *tube tunnel. 1870 MRS. WHITNEY *We Girls* iii, They were so pretty to put in..little *tube-vases. 1857 GOSSE *Creation* 226 The margin of the *tube-wall. 1890 *Daily News* 9 Jan. 2/8 The advance applies to gas, water, and steam tubes, and all the *tube works of England and Scotland are affected. 1896 *N. Brit. Daily Mail* 8 July 2 The pensioner..is a Coatbridge man, having wrought as a *tube-worker in the burgh.

**b.** Special Combs.: **tube-bearing** *a.*, bearing a tube; *spec.* in *Entom.* having a tubular ovipositor, tubuliferous (*Cent. Dict.* 1891); **tube-board**, a board above the reeds in a reed-organ in which are the tubes or sound-channels to which the wind passes from the reeds; **tube-breather** (distinguished from *gill-breather*), an animal which breathes through tubes, tracheæ, or spiracles; **tube-brush**, a wire brush for cleaning out boiler-tubes or flues; also, a slender brush for cleaning the flexible tube of a feeding-bottle; **tube-budding**, budding by means of a cylindrical ring of bark; **tube-case**, in a steam-engine, the chamber containing the tubes of a surface-condenser; **tube-cast**, a cast of a kidney tubule excreted in the urine in Bright's disease; **tube-chime**, a chime of tubular 'bells'; **tube-clamp**, a grab for seizing and lifting well-tubes (Knight *Dict. Mech.* 1877); **tube-cleaner**, a tool or other device for cleaning boiler-tubes, etc. (*ibid.*); **tube-clip**, tongs for holding heated test-tubes; also a clamp or clip for gripping a pipe (*ibid.*); **tube-cock**, a valve operated by compressing an elastic tube fitted into the supply pipe (*ibid.*); **tube-colour**, paint packed in a collapsible tube; **tube-compass**, compasses with tubular telescopic legs (Knight); **tube-condenser**, (*a*) a bent glass tube with a stopper at each end through which a smaller tube is passed; (*b*) in a steam-engine, a condenser in which the cooling surface consists of tubes; **tube-coral**, organ-pipe coral (see CORAL *sb.*[1] 1 b), or its polyp; **tube-culture**, culture of a microbe in a test-tube; **tube-cutter**, a tool for cutting off metal pipes, a pipe-cutter; so **tube-cutting**; **tube-door**, a door in the smoke-box of a steam-engine, giving access to the flues (Knight); **tube-drawing**, the making of metal tubes by drawing roughly shaped cylinders through gauged holes or over a triblet; also withdrawal of boiler-tubes for inspection or repair; so **tube-drawer**; **tube-expander, -fastener**, a tool for fixing the ends of boiler-tubes in the *tube-plate* by expanding their ends against the holes in the plate (Knight); **tube-ferrule**, a ring or thimble forced into the end of a boiler-tube to fix it in the tube-plate (*ibid.*); **tube-filter**, in a tube-well, a strainer to prevent gravel from choking the pump (*ibid.*); **tube-firing**, ? the use of a torpedo-tube; **tube-flower**, a tropical verbenaceous plant, *Clerodendron Siphonanthus*, in which the corolla is funnel-shaped with a very long tube (*Treas. Bot.* 1866); **tube-flue**, a fire-tube in a steam-boiler; **tube-foot**, one of the numerous ambulacral tubes of an echinoderm; **tube-former**, a machine for making small tubes; **tube-frame**, a *tube roving-frame*; **tube-funnel**, a glass funnel prolonged at the bottom into a tube, a funnel-tube; **tube-germination**, the production of a germ-tube in the germination of a spore; **tube-head** = *tube-plate* (Webster, 1911); **tube-hearted** *a.*, having a series of pulsating sinuses instead of a heart, as the Amphioxus (*Cent. Dict.* 1891); **tube-ignition**, in the internal combustion engine, ignition of the charge by a hot tube; **tube-machine**, a tube-drawing machine; **tube-maker**, (*a*) one who makes tubing; (*b*) a tube-dwelling spider or annelid; so **tube-making**; †**tube-marine**, rendering It. *tuba* (*tromba*) *marina*, the trumpet marine: see TRUMPET *sb.* 2 b; **tube-medusa**, a medusa with an internal system of tubes; a siphonophore; **tube-mill**, (*a*) a tube-making establishment or machine; (*b*) a mill for pulverizing ore, etc., which is placed in a revolving cylinder with loose flints or pebbles; **tube-nosed** *a.*, tubinarial (*Cent. Dict.*); **tube-packing**, packing to prevent water reaching the tube of an oil-well (Knight); **tube-plate**, the plate in which the ends of the boiler-tubes are set; **tube-plug**, a plug or stopper for boiler-tubes in case of leakage (Knight); **tube-pouch**, a pouch for priming-tubes (Webster, 1864); **tube roving-frame, roving-machine**, a roving-frame having revolving horizontal cylinders instead of conical cans; **tube-saw**, a cylindrical saw (Webster, 1911); **tube-scaler, -scraper** = *tube-cleaner* (Knight); **tube-sheet** = *tube-plate*; **tube-shell**, a bivalve mollusc of the family *Tubicolæ* or *Gastrochænidæ*, distinguished by having a shelly tube inclosing the siphons, in addition to the ordinary valves of the shell; **tube-shutter**, a shutter closing the outer end of a submerged torpedo-tube (Webster, 1911); **tube-spinner** = *tube-weaver*; **tube-stopper** = *tube-plug*; **tube-surface**, the heating or cooling surface comprised in the tubes of a boiler or condenser (*Funk's Stand. Dict.* 1895); **tube-valve**, a tubular valve; **tube-vice (-vise)**, a pipe-vice (Knight); **tube-weaver**, a spider which spins a tubular nest or lair; **tube-well**, an iron pipe with a solid steel point, and with lateral perforations towards the point, which is driven into the earth until a water-bearing stratum is reached, when a suction pump is applied to the upper end; **tube-worm**, a tubicolous worm; a pipe-worm; **tube-wrench**, a wrench for gripping pipes or tubes, a pipe-wrench; **tube yarn**, yarn passed through a tube in the process of manufacture.

1880 A. J. HIPKINS in *Encycl. Brit.* XI. 483/2 The channels, the resonators above the reeds [in the American organ] exactly correspond with the reeds, and are collectively known as the '*tube-board'. 1889 *Cent. Dict.* s.v. *Gill-breather*, *Tube-breather. 1877 KNIGHT *Dict. Mech.* s.v., Stillwell's *tube-brush,..may be operated by pulling and pushing from the respective ends of the tubes. 1842 LOUDON *Suburban Hort.* 307 Sometimes the stock is shortened, and the ring put on its upper extremity, when it is called flute-budding, or terminal *tube-budding. 1890 D. K. CLARK *Steam Engine* II. 683 The water is driven through the *tube-case by two centrifugal pumps in each engine-room. 1873 T. H. GREEN *Introd. Pathol.* (ed. 2) 69 *Tube casts..are for the most part hyaline and finely granular. 1888 FAGGE & PYE-SMITH *Princ. Med.* (1891) II. 154 Tube-casts comparable with those which occur in the urine in Bright's disease. 1887 *Pall Mall G.* 20 June 3/2 *Tube chimes for church towers—an English invention. 1881 BOUVIER tr. *Delamardelle & Goupil's Painting on China* 1 Thanks to the ingenious invention of *Tube Colours. 1877 KNIGHT *Dict. Mech.*, *Tube-condenser. 1890 D. K. CLARK *Steam Engine* II. 641 The exhaust steam is condensed to the extent of two-thirds in a tube-condenser overhead. 1876 PAGE *Adv. Text-bk. Geol.* xiv. 245 Among the zoophytes we have cup-corals, star-corals, *tube-corals. 1886 H. M. BIGGS tr. *Hueppe's Methods Bacteriol. Invest.* 143 The changes in such a *tube-culture after the inoculation with the bacteria vary considerably. 1901 WATERHOUSE *Conduit Wiring* 43 In all conduit work a certain amount of *tube cutting is necessary. 1858 SIMMONDS *Dict. Trade*, *Tube-drawer, a maker of metal piping. 1897 *Daily News* 7 May 7/4 Consumers of iron—engineers' ironfounders, bridge-builders, rolling-stock manufacturers, and tube-drawers. 1835 URE *Philos. Manuf.* 61 The foundations of kindred works, such as..*tube-drawing apparatus. 1901 *Scotsman* 13 Mar. 9/8 The crews however practised *tube-firing. 1888 ROLLESTON & JACKSON *Anim. Life* 551 The *tube feet are either partially or completely retractile. 1837 *Penny Cycl.* VIII. 96/1 The *tube frame..Instead of cans,..is provided with revolving horizontal cylinders...The rove which it produces has no twist. 1903 *Motor. Ann.* 220 *Tube-ignition is satisfactory for a fixed engine. 1891 *Cent. Dict.*, *Tube-machine. 1901 WATERHOUSE *Conduit Wiring* 8 This strip..is passed through a tube machine from which it emerges as a perfectly smooth and regular tube. 1888 *Cassell's Encycl. Dict.*, *Tube-makers, the Tubicolæ. 1890 *Daily News* 6 Oct. 2/5 Tube makers have this week advanced their discounts 5 per cent. 1898 *Westm. Gaz.* 9 Mar. 8/2 The amalgamation of all the big *tube-making concerns in Scotland. 1694 W. HOLDER *Harmony* (1731) 152 The *Tube-Marine, or Sea-Trumpet..fully expresseth the Trumpet. 1860 WRAXALL *Life in Sea* x. 243 Among the *Tube Medusæ is also classed the pleasing Velella. 1909 *Westm. Gaz.* 1 June 9/3 The addition of eighty stamps and three *tube mills at the Nourse Mines. 1864 WEBSTER, *Tube-plate. 1875 BEDFORD *Sailor's Pocket Bk.* v. (ed. 2) 211 Leaks about tubes and tube-plates are most frequently caused by forced steaming. 1839 URE *Dict. Arts* 355 The Bobbin and Fly frame is now the great roving machine of the cotton manufacture; to which may be added, for coarse spinning, the *tube roving frame. *Ibid.* 354 The cotton sliver receives a twist..in the bobbin and fly frame, or..in the *tube-roving machine. 1877 KNIGHT *Dict. Mech.*, *Tube-sheet. 1903 *Daily Chron.* 20 Jan. 6/3 The boiler tubes getting choked up..through the tubes leaking in the back tube sheet. 1861 P. P. CARPENTER in *Rep. Smithsonian Instit.* 1860, 249 Family Gastrochænidæ. (*Tube-Shells). 1884 KNIGHT *Dict. Mech., Supp.*, *Tube-valve. 1899 *Daily News* 16 Jan. 7/3 The tube-valve that set those massive hydraulic triggers free. 1885 H. C. MCCOOK *Tenants Old Farm* 233 The arbor vitæ hedge, where numbers of the speckled *Tubeweaver (*Agalena nævia*) yearly spin their broad snares. 1877 KNIGHT *Dict. Mech.*, *Tube-well. 1885 *Daily News* 7 Feb. 3/2 Pack saddles for mules, and tube-wells. 1819 *Pantologia*, *Sipunculus*, *tube-worm. 1891 *Daily News* 2 Oct. 2/6 Single yarns, *tube yarns, and mohair yarns.

Hence **Tu·beful**, as much as a tube will hold; **Tu·beless** *a.*, having no tube or tubes.

1897 G. C. BATEMAN *Vivarium* vii. 292 One or more *tubefuls [*printed* tubesful] of meat can be inserted into the gullet of each Reptile. 1855 *Chamb. Jrnl.* III. 206 Huyghens made his observations with a *tubeless telescope. 1898 *Cycling* 71 The Fleuss or 'Tubeless Tyre'.

**Tube**, *v.* [f. prec. sb.; cf. F. *tuber* (1489 in Littré).]

**1.** *trans.* To furnish or fit with a tube or tubes; to insert a tube in.

1828 WEBSTER, *Tube v.*, to furnish with a tube; as, to tube a well. 1840 *Civil Eng. & Arch. Jrnl.* III. 27/1 This..shaft ..should be properly tubed with cast or sheet iron. 1867 *N. Syd. Soc. Bienn. Retrosp. Med. & Surg.* 1865–6, 247 The ease with which 'tubing' the larynx can be accomplished. 1886 H. S. BROWN *Autobiog.* x. (1887) 57, I was engaged.. in tubing boilers.

**2.** To pass through or enclose in a tube; cf. *tube yarn* (TUBE *sb.* 12 b).

1863–98 LUCE *Seamanship* App. A. 461 A recent improvement in the spinner tubes the yarn, rendering it smoother and..leaving little to be desired in the manufacture of rope.

**3.** *intr.* To travel by tube railway; also *to tube it. colloq.*

1902 *Daily Chron.* 31 Oct. 5/1 Yet my cherished hope was this—That under our Metropolis From end to end I'd tube it. 1907 *Ibid.* 1 June 5/5 Shoppers can 'tube' to the West-end.

**Tubed** (tiūbd), *ppl. a.* [f. TUBE *v.* or *sb.* + -ED.] Made or furnished with, consisting of, or having a tube or tubes; resembling a tube; tubular.

1816 WORDSW. *Ode Day Thanksg.* x. 12 While the tubed engine [i.e. organ] feels the inspiring blast And has begun— its clouds of sound to cast Forth. 1848 *Jrnl. R. Agric. Soc.* IX. II. 372 The larch presents a tubed decayed heart. 1860 WRAXALL *Life in Sea* x. 241 Among the strangest of existing animals are the Tubed Jelly Fish, or Siphonophoræ. 1875 HOWELLS *Foregone Concl.* 105 Mrs. Veevain began to look at the sketch through her tubed hand.

‖**Tuber**[1]. *Obs.* Pl. **tuberes**. [L. *tuber* masc. (the fruit), fem. (the tree).] A kind of apple, or the tree on which it grows.

*c* 1440 *Pallad. on Husb.* II. 393 Now tuberis in quyncis me may graffe. 1546 LANGLEY *Pol. Verg. De Invent.* III. ii. 65 b, Zizypha and Tuberes two kyndes of apple trees. 1658 tr. *Porta's Nat. Magic* IV. vii. 124 Medlars, and the fruit Tuber may be shut up in pitchers, so to be preserved.

**Tuber**[2] (tiū·bəɪ). [a. L. *tūber* neut., a hump, swelling, pl. *tūbera*.]

**1.** *Bot.* An underground structure consisting of a solid thickened portion or outgrowth of a stem or rhizome, of a more or less rounded form, and bearing 'eyes' or buds from which new plants may arise; a familiar example is the potato. Also applied to other underground structures resembling this but of different origin, as in tuberous roots.

1668 WILKINS *Real Char.* 90 Tuberous roots; consisting of one single tuber, or of several. 1704 [see b]. 1822 J. FLINT *Lett. Amer.* 57 The potato crops are better.., the plants are more vigorous, and the tubers much larger. 1870 HOOKER *Stud. Flora* 352 Orchis. Tubers globose ovoid or palmate. 1880 GRAY *Struct. Bot.* iii. § 3 (ed. 6) 59 A Tuber may be..characterized as a short thickened rhizoma on a slender base, or a rootstock some portion of which..is thickened by the deposition of nourishing matter.

‖**b.** A genus of underground discomycetous fungi, comprising the truffles.

[1693 *Phil. Trans.* XVII. 824 The *Tubera Terræ*..observ'd lately at Rushton in Northamptonshire..are indeed the true French *Truffles*, the Italian *Tartuffi*. 1699 EVELYN *Acetaria* 42 Trufles, Pig-Nuts, and other subterraneous *Tubera*.] 1704 J. HARRIS *Lex. Techn.* I, *Tuber*, properly, is a subterraneous Mushroom, or a Truffle; but by Botanick Writers, is often used to signifie the round turgid Roots of some Plants: which they call Tuberose, or Knobby Roots.

**2.** A rounded swelling or protuberant part in the animal body. **a.** *Path.* A morbid swelling or enlargement, as of a gland, etc.

1706 PHILLIPS (ed. Kersey), *Tuber*,..a Swelling or Bunch

in a Man's Body. 1834 *Good's Study Med.* (ed. 4) IV. 233 Those who are constitutionally predisposed to a production of tubers and tubercles. 1888 Fagge & Pye-Smith *Princ. Med.* (ed. 2) I. 96 In a solid organ it [i.e. a tumour] may form a rounded mass, which is called a nodule or tuber.

b. *Anat.* A rounded projecting part or structure; a tuberosity.

Chiefly as Latin, with pl. *tubera*: often with defining word, as the specific name of such a structure: e.g. *tuber cinereum*, a conical projection at the base of the brain; *tuber cochleæ* or *tympani*, the promontory of the tympanum.

1741 Monro *Anat.* (ed. 3) 209 The Tuber is afterwards added in the Manner that other Epiphyses are. 1857 Dunglison *Med. Lex.*, *Tuber cinereum*, a grayish tubercle, seen at the base of the brain behind the commissure of the optic nerves. 1866 Huxley *Preh. Rem. Caithn.* 110 Norwegians are remarkable for the length of their skulls, and the very general development of an occipital tuber, or probole.

3. *gen.* A rounded projection, protuberance. *rare.*

1888 Doughty *Arabia Deserta* I. 32 We..came where in a torrent bed are laid bare certain great tubers of the lime rock underlying.

**Tuberaceous** (tiūbərēⁱ·ʃəs), *a. Bot.* [f. mod.L. *Tūberāceī* (masc. pl.), *-āceæ* (fem. pl.), f. *Tūber*: see prec. 1 b and -ACEOUS.] Belonging to the order *Tuberaceæ* or *Tuberacei* of discomycetous fungi, typified by the genus *Tuber*.

1909 in *Cent. Dict. Suppl.*

†**Tu·berant**, *a. Obs. rare*$^{-1}$. [ad. late L. *tūberānt-em* (Appuleius), f. *tūber*, TUBER²: see -ANT.] Swelling out, protruding, protuberant.

1668 Culpepper & Cole *Barthol. Anat.* I. xiv. 33 The tuberant or bossie part of the Liver.

**Tuberated** (tiū·bəreⁱtėd), *a.* [f. L. *tūberāt-us* covered with tubers or knobs, f. *tūber*, TUBER²: see -ED.] Having a tuber or rounded swelling; in *Her.* applied to a serpent borne with the middle part twisted in a close knot.

c 1828 Berry *Encycl. Her.* I. Gloss., *Tuberated*, gibbous, knotted, or swelled out, as the middle part of the serpent.

**Tuberation** (tiūbərēⁱ·ʃən). *rare*$^{-1}$. [f. as prec. + -ATION.] Formation or production of a tuber or tubers.

1727 Bailey vol. II, *Tuberation*, a swelling. 1902 *Times* 19 Sept. 6/3 The excessive tuberation which potatoes brought under cultivation acquire.

**Tubercle** (tiū·bəɹk'l). [ad. L. *tūberculum* small swelling, boil, pimple, dim. of *tūber*, TUBER². Cf. obs. F. *tubercle* (Cotgr., 1611).] A small tuber or body resembling a tuber.

1. *Anat.* and *Zool.* A small rounded projection or protuberance, as on a bone, or on the surface of the body in various animals.

Often with defining word, as the specific name of such a structure: e.g. *conoid, cuneiform, genial, laminated, madreporic, optic, scalene* (etc.) *tubercle*: see the adjs.

1578 Banister *Hist. Man* I. 17 To this Tubercle they ['bones' of the larynx] are inarticulated and knit. 1747 *Gentl. Mag.* Mar. 122/2 These creatures have several rows of tubercles on their bodies. 1846 Brittan tr. *Malgaigne's Man. Oper. Surg.* 133 A more or less projecting tubercle on the first rib, which gives attachment to the anterior scalenus. 1880 Barwell *Aneurism* iii. 29 Chassaignac's tubercle, the transverse process of the fifth cervical vertebra.

2. *Path.* A small firm rounded swelling or nodule on the surface of the body or in a part or organ; *spec.* a mass of granulation-cells characteristic of *tuberculosis*; *transf.* the disease tuberculosis.

*Miliary tubercle*: see MILIARY 1.

1661 Lovell *Hist. Anim. & Min.* 355 The tubercles of the lungs. 1710 T. Fuller *Pharm. Extemp.* 52 A Balsamick Decoction..dissipates Crude Tubercles. 1804 Abernethy *Surg. Obs. Tumours* 149 The ulcerated surface may heal, and leave an indurated knob or tubercle in the affected part. 1818 *Art Preserv. Feet* 3 The corn is technically termed 'clavus pedum', and considered as a tubercle without organization, proceeding from the substance of the epidermis, and originating in the tightness of shoes or boots. 1859 J. Tomes *Dental Surg.* (1873) 51 Tubercle does not appear to interfere with the progress of dentition. 1876 Bristowe *The. & Pract. Med.* (1878) 67 It is a..characteristic of tubercle that its specific cells very rapidly fall into degeneration.

3. *Bot.* a. A small tuber, or a root-growth resembling a tuber, as in many orchids. b. A small wart-like swelling or protuberance on a plant.

1727–41 Chambers *Cycl.*, *Tuber*, or *Tubercle*, in botany, a kind of round turgid root. 1756–7 tr. *Keysler's Trav.* (1760) IV. 349 A particular species..has large prickles growing on round tubercles. 1807 J. E. Smith *Phys. Bot.* 498 Fucus,..whose seeds are collected together in tubercles or swellings, of various forms and sizes. 1880 Gray *Struct. Bot.* iii. § 3 (ed. 6) 60 Tubercles..are of a mixed..character between tubers and tuberous roots.

4. *attrib.* and *Comb.*, as *tubercle-like, -infected* adjs.; **tubercle-bacillus**, the species of bacillus which causes tuberculosis (also *attrib.*).

1866 Tate *Brit. Mollusks* iv. 165 A tubercle-like tooth [in a shell]. 1891 *Cent. Dict.* s.v. *Tubercle*, Tubercle-bacillus. 1897 *Daily News* 1 Apr. 3/4 Both assume the so-called tubercle-bacillus tint. 1898 *Westm. Gaz.* 3 Nov. 9/2 If the Council can prevent the sale of tubercle-infected milk. 1913 *Times* 6 Aug. 8/4 Microscopical examination of milk and tubercle bacillus by analytical methods.

**Tubercled** (tiū·bəɹk'ld), *a. Nat. Hist.* and *Path.* [f. prec. + -ED².] Furnished or affected with tubercles; tuberculate.

1755 *Gentl. Mag.* Sept. 391/1 The grain..is green and tubercled. 1819 Turton *Conchol. Dict.* 43 *Haliotis.* Sea-ear. *Haliotis tuberculata.* Tubercled Sea-ear. 1829 Loudon *Encycl. Plants* (1836) 410 The smaller melon thistle..is tubercled all over. 1864 Webster s.v., A tubercled lung.

**Tubercular** (tiubɜ̄·ɹkiŭlăɹ), *a.* [ad. mod.L. **tūberculār-is*, f. L. *tūbercul-um* TUBERCLE + -AR.]

1. *Nat. Hist.*, etc. a. Of the nature or form of a tubercle; consisting of or constituting a tubercle. b. Having or covered with tubercles, tuberculate.

1817 Kirby & Sp. *Entomol.* xxii. (1818) II. 279 A subcutaneous larva belonging to the same order,..moves also by tubercular legs. 1860 Mayne *Expos. Lex.*, *Tubercular*, having tubercles; tubercled; tuberculate. 1877 Huxley *Anat. Inv. Anim.* v. 231 The surface of the elytron is covered with..tubercular prominences. 1880 Günther *Fishes* 176 The young are smooth and the old have a tubercular skin.

2. *Path.* Of, pertaining to, caused or characterized by, or affected with tubercles.

1799– [see b]. 1864 H. Spencer *Princ. Biol.* II. ii. 152 Tubercular matter, making its appearance at particular points, collects more and more round those points. 1897 *Allbutt's Syst. Med.* II. 47 Symptomatology — Nodular Leprosy—'Tuberculated', 'tubercular', 'tuberculous', 'nodular-dermal', 'dermal', 'cutaneous', 'hypertrophic' leprosy. 1899 *Ibid.* VIII. 805 Tubercular syphilide. ..The term 'tubercular' used above refers solely to the gross infiltration of the skin causing raised nodules, and has..no relation to the tubercle bacillus.

b. *spec.* In reference to tuberculosis or the tubercle-bacillus; now technically replaced by TUBERCULOUS, q. v.

But as the discovery of the bacillus was made known only in 1882, the earlier examples of the word, though actually descriptive of results of the action of the bacillus, did not refer to it, but merely to the presence of tubercles.

1799 *Med. Jrnl.* II. 267, I have had..three cases of confirmed tubercular consumption. 1834 J. Forbes *Laennec's Dis. Chest* (ed. 4) 297 A portion of the pulmonary tissue..impregnated with grey tubercular matter. 1876 Bristowe *The. & Pract. Med.* (1878) 68 A..tendency of organs to become tubercular. 1898 *Westm. Gaz.* 10 Nov. 8/2 He did not recommend..the removal of every tubercular cow from our dairies and cow-sheds.

Hence **Tube·rcularize** *v.*, *trans.* to make tubercular; to infect with tubercles, *spec.* with tuberculosis, = TUBERCULIZE; whence **Tube:rculariza·tion**; **Tube·rcularly** *adv.*, by means of tubercles, in quot. *spec.* of tuberculosis.

1843 F. H. Ramadge *Curability of Consumption* (1850) 55 The more this tissue is expanded, the less susceptibility does it retain of fresh tubercularization. 1889 *Science* 13 Sept. 177/1 Spittoons..should never be emptied on dung-heaps, [or] on garden-soil (where they may tubercularize fowl). 1889 *Pop. Sci. Monthly* Dec. 260 Having found a characteristic ..bacillus in all tubercularly altered organs.

**Tuberculate** (tiubɜ̄·ɹkiŭlět), *a. Nat. Hist.* and *Path.* [ad. mod.L. *tūberculātus*, f. L. *tūbercul-um* TUBERCLE: see -ATE².] Furnished or affected with tubercles; tubercled.

1785 Martyn *Rousseau's Bot.* xxxii. (1794) 497 The Tuberculate [Lichens], consisting of a crust adhering closely to the bark of trees, or stones, above which roundish tubercles rise a little. 1834 *Good's Study Med.* (ed. 4) IV. 454 A thick, rugose, livid, tuberculate..skin. 1875 C. C. Blake *Zool.* 27 The molar teeth are usually tuberculate. 1887 W. Phillips *Brit. Discomycetes* 57 The tuberculate sporidia are frequently furnished with thread-like appendages at the extremities.

b. In comb. with another adj. (in *Bot.*), as *tuberculate-hispid*, hispid or rough with tubercles.

1821 W. P. C. Barton *Flora N. Amer.* I. 102 Petioles and stem tuberculate-hispid.

**Tuberculated** (tiubɜ̄·ɹkiŭleⁱtėd), *a.* [f. as prec. + -ED.] = prec. a. *Nat. Hist.*

1771 Pennant in *Phil. Trans.* LXI. 272 The whole circumference of the back bounded by a tuberculated rib. 1784 André *ibid.* LXXIV. 274 Let us..recollect the tuberculated teeth in the thorn-back. 1845 Lindley *Sch. Bot.* vi. (1858) 83 Receptacle conical, toothed, tuberculated. 1861 Bentley *Man. Bot.* 129 When some of the divisions of a root become enlarged so as to form more or less rounded or egg-shaped expansions.., the root is said to be tuberculated, and each enlargement is called a tubercle.

b. *Path.* (also *transf.* characterized by tubercles).

1797 M. Baillie *Morb. Anat.* (1807) 221 The formation of the common tuberculated liver. 1804 Abernethy *Surg. Obs. Tumours* (1816) 51 Tuberculated Sarcoma..consists of an aggregation of small, firm, roundish tumours,..connected together by a kind of cellular substance. 1822–7 Good *Study Med.* (1829) II. 489 A tuberculated state of the lungs. 1829 *Ibid.* III. 428 The palms of the hands [in leprosy] were seldom tuberculated. 1854 F. H. Ramadge *Curability of Consumption* (1861) Pref. 11 All..might be tuberculated, and yet not one of them die of consumption.

Hence **Tube·rculatedly** *adv.*

1822 J. Parkinson *Outl. Oryctol.* 220 With transverse tuberculatedly scabrous ribs.

**Tuberculation** (tiubɜ̄ɹkiŭlēⁱ·ʃən). [f. L. *tūbercul-um* TUBERCLE + -ATION.]

1. *Nat. Hist.* Formation of tubercles; *concr.* a growth or set of tubercles.

1835–6 *Todd's Cycl. Anat.* I. 778/1 Branchiae..covered with a multitude of small tuberculations. 1880 Huxley *Crayfish* vi. 294 The tuberculation of the carapace and limbs.

2. *Path.* Formation of tubercles as a symptom of disease; tubercular or tuberculous affection.

1861 T. J. Graham *Pract. Med.* 300 A confirmatory sign of tuberculation of the lungs. 1899 *Allbutt's Syst. Med.* VIII. 795 The erythematous lupus may be distinguished from lupus vulgaris..by the absence of tuberculation.

**Tuberculato-** (tiubɜ̄ɹkiŭlēⁱ·to), combining form of mod.L. *tūberculātus* TUBERCULATE, used in *Nat. Hist.* prefixed to adjs., expressing a form or structure with tuberculations, as *tuberculato-gibbous, -nodose, -radiate, -spinous.*

1822 J. Parkinson *Outl. Oryctol.* 220 Longitudinal tuberculato-nodose ribs. 1846 Dana *Zooph.* (1848) 284 Corallum lamello-radiate above, tuberculato-radiate below. *Ibid.* 495 Lobes short,..often tuberculato-gibbous. 1852 — *Crust.* I. 88 Carapax..sparsely tuberculato-spinous.

**Tubercule** (tiū·bəɹkiul). [a. F. *tubercule* (Paré, 16th c.), ad. L. *tūbercul-um* TUBERCLE.] = TUBERCLE, in various senses.

1678 Phillips (ed. 4), *Tuberculs*, in Chiromancy are those ..protuberant parts under the Fingers,..otherwise called *Montes.* 1727–41 Chambers *Cycl.*, *Tubercules, Tubercles*, little tumors which suppurate and discharge pus; often found in the lungs. 1760 J. Lee *Introd. Bot.* III. v. (1765) 183 *Scabrous, rugged*; when the Disk is covered with Tubercules. 1835 Lindley *Introd. Bot.* I. ii. (ed 2) 87 The roots of many plants are often fleshy, and composed of lobes, which appear to serve as reservoirs of nutriment. In Orchis the tubercules are often palmated. 1842 H. Miller *O. R. Sandst.* viii. (ed. 2) 170 The inner sides of the pincers are armed with..tubercules. 1901 *Scotsman* 2 Mar. 10/1 Death ..of tubercule of the lungs.

Hence **Tu·berculed** *a.*, tubercled, tuberculate.

1858 Geikie *Hist. Boulder* vii. 117 Ornamented by long rows of tuberculed lines.

**Tuberculide** (tiubɜ̄·ɹkiŭləid). *Path.* Also -id. [ad. mod.L. *tūberculīdēs*, f. L. *tūbercul-um* TUBERCLE.] A general term for any skin lesion of a tuberculous nature.

1900 *Lancet* 18 Aug. 534/1 True tuberculosis of the skin was asymmetrical, but the tuberculides were strikingly symmetrical. 1900–13 Dorland *Med. Dict.*, Tuberculid, tuberculide.

**Tuberculiferous** (tiubɜ̄ɹkiŭli·fĕrəs), *a.* [f. L. *tūbercul-um* TUBERCLE + -I)FEROUS.] Bearing tubercles.

1822 J. Parkinson *Outl. Oryctol.* 224 Distant tuberculiferous ribs on the larger valve; tubercles fornicated. 1846 Dana *Zooph.* (1848) 140 Sides naked above, below tuberculiferous and tubercles perforate.

**Tuberculiform** (tiubɜ̄·ɹkiŭlifǭɹm), *a.* [f. as prec. + -FORM.] Having the form of a tubercle.

1817 Kirby & Sp. *Entomol.* xxii. (1818) II. 277 Apodous larvæ..that move by means of fleshy tuberculiform..prominences. 1846 Dana *Zooph.* (1848) 153 The body is covered with large tuberculiform suckers. 1885 H. O. Forbes *Nat. Wand. E. Archip.* II. App. 120 At the hinder part..are several strong tuberculiform eminences and prominences.

**Tuberculin** (tiubɜ̄·ɹkiŭlin). *Med.* Also *erron.* -ine. [f. L. *tūberculum* TUBERCLE + -IN¹.] A liquid prepared from cultures of tubercle-bacillus, originally by Dr. Koch of Berlin in 1890, or any one of various later modifications of this, used by hypodermic injection as a remedy, or (now esp.) as a test, for tuberculosis.

1891 *Daily News* 12 Feb. 6/5 Dr. Koch's lymph has received the name of 'tuberculine'. 1893 *Times* 19 Dec. 3/2 'Tuberculin'..has been employed as an aid to the diagnosis of tuberculosis. 1896 *Westm. Gaz.* 10 Mar. 4/1 At the Balneological Congress,..Dr. Kaatzer spoke very highly of the value of tuberculin in phthisis. .. Professor Liebreich asserted that the cure of lupus by tuberculin was more apparent than real. 1899 *Syd. Soc. Lex.*, *Tuberculin*, Koch's lymph..consisting of ptomaines of the tubercle bacilli.

Hence **Tube·rculinize** *v.*, *trans.* to treat with tuberculin; whence **Tube:rculiniza·tion** (Dorland).

1895 *Buck's Handbk. Med. Sc.* IX. 900/2 Comparing..the condition of the various organs of the tuberculinized with that of the same in healthy animals. 1899 in *Syd. Soc. Lex.*

**Tuberculization** (tiubɜ̄ɹkiŭləizēⁱ·ʃən). [f. next + -ATION; cf. F. *tuberculisation* (Littré).] The action or process of tuberculizing; infection with or formation of tubercle.

1843 R. J. Graves *Syst. Clin. Med.* xxii. 277 Tuberculization commences suddenly and proceeds rapidly. 1847–9 *Todd's Cycl. Anat.* IV. 108/1 Tuberculization of the bronchial glands. 1899 *Allbutt's Syst. Med.* VI. 103 The gray pneumonia attending tuberculisation.

**Tuberculize** (tiubɜ̄·ɹkiŭləiz), *v.* [f. L. *tūbercul-um* TUBERCLE + -IZE; cf. F. *tuberculiser* (Littré).] a. *trans.* To affect or infect with tubercle or tuberculosis; to make tuberculous; also, 'to treat with tuberculin' (Dorland *Med. Dict.* 1913). b. *intr.* To become tuberculous. Hence **Tube·rculized** *ppl. a.*

1847–9 *Todd's Cycl. Anat.* IV. 106/2 Tuberculized pulmonary substance. 1863 Aitken *Sc. & Pract. Med.* (1866) II. 191 These cells tuberculize, or undergo the tuberculous metamorphosis. 1897 D. N. Kinsman in *Columbus* (Ohio) *Dispatch* 20 Feb., As soon as a person is known to be tuberculized. 1901 *Lancet* 9 Nov. 1252/1, I hold..that a scrofulous person is not, and need not be, a tuberculised person.

**Tuberculo-** (tiubɜ̄·ɹkiŭlo), combining form of L. *tūbercul-um* TUBERCLE, properly used adverbially; also attrib. or objectively (instead of the regular *tuberculi-*: see -O), in several technical terms, chiefly of pathology and medicine. **Tube·rculoce:le** (-sīl) [Gr. κήλη tumour], 'tuberculous disease of the testicle' (Dorland *Med. Dict.* 1900–13). **Tube·rculoci:de** (-səid) [irreg. for **tuberculicide*: see -CIDE], any preparation which destroys the tubercle-bacillus; hence **Tube·r-**

**culoci·din** [-IN [1]], an albumose obtained from tuberculin, used as a tuberculicide. ‖ **Tube:rculo-de·rma** [Gr. δέρμα skin], tuberculosis of the skin (*Cent. Dict. Suppl.* 1909). **Tube:rculo-fi·broid** *a.*, 'characterized by tubercle that has undergone a fibroid degeneration' (Dorland). **Tube:rculo-opso·nic** *a.*, relating to the opsonin of the tubercle-bacillus. **Tube:rculopho·bia** [-PHOBIA], a morbid dread of tuberculosis. **Tube:rculopla·smin,** a solution of the protoplasm of tubercle-bacilli. **Tube:rculosecto·rial** *a., Zool.* [SECTORIAL *a.*[2]], applied to a type of molar teeth having high conical tubercles or cusps adapted for cutting. **Tube:rculo-squa·mous** *a.* [SQUAMOUS], characterized by tubercles and scales. **Tube:rculo-the·rapy** [Gr. θεραπεία nurture, medical treatment], 'treatment of tuberculous patients by feeding with the raw flesh of animals affected by tuberculosis' (Dorland). **Tube:rculoto·xin,** 'any toxin of the tubercle bacillus' (*ibid.*). **Tube:rculotro·pic** *a.* [? after *heliotropic*, etc.: cf. TROPIC *a.*[1] 4], having the property of combining chemically with the tubercle-bacillus.

*c* 1900 *Buck's Handbk. Med. Sc.* I. 461 *Tuberculocide. **1892** *Pall Mall G.* 23 July 5/1 An experiment..on twelve more or less tuberculous persons with the so-called *tuberculocidin, which is a modification of Professor Koch's remedy, invented by Professor Klebs, of Zurich. **1895** *Buck's Handbk. Med. Sc.* IX. 903/1 Tuberculin yields about two and a half per cent. of tuberculocidin. **1898** *Allbutt's Syst. Med.* V. 255 Sir A. Clark..describes two main forms [of pneumoconiosis] as..the *tuberculo-fibroid and fibro-tuberculous. **1907** *Med. Record* 14 Dec. 987 In one of these [cases] the *tuberculo-opsonic index was from normal to 0·7 below normal. **1901** *Lancet* 27 July 192/1 *Tuberculophobia must not be produced, the patient must not be made a pariah. *c* 1900 *Buck's Handbk. Med. Sc.* I. 692 *Tuberculoplasmin. **1893** *Proc. Zool. Soc.* 28 Feb. 197 The..*tuberculo-sectorial type of inferior molars. **1879** *St. George's Hosp. Rep.* IX. 592 Rupial sore; *tuberculo-squamous eruption. **1909** *Cent. Dict. Suppl.*, *Tuberculotropic.

**Tuberculoid** (tiubə̄·ɹkiŭloid), *a. Zool.* [f. L. *tūbercul-um* TUBERCLE + -OID.] = TUBERCULIFORM.

**1891** in *Cent. Dict.*

**Tuberculome** (tiubə̄·ɹkiŭlōum). *Path.* [ad. mod.L. *tūberculōma*, f. *tūbercul-um* TUBERCLE, after *sarcoma*, etc.] A tumour or abscess caused by the tubercle-bacillus.

**1903** *Nature* 5 Mar. 431/2 If the tuberculous abscess or tuberculome is not too large, a cure may be effected by a simple washing with an antiseptic liquid.

**Tuberculose** (tiubə̄·ɹkiŭlōus), *a.* [f. L. type **tūberculōs-us*, f. *tūbercul-um* TUBERCLE: see -OSE.] = TUBERCULOUS 2, TUBERCULATE.

**1752** J. HILL *Hist. Anim.* 249 The green Turdus..is a very beautiful fish;..it is not unfrequently..almost entire black, and sometimes spotted or tuberculose. **1854** WOODWARD *Mollusca* II. 191 Doris Bilamellata:..Back elevated, tuberculose. **1900** in B. D. JACKSON *Gloss. Bot. Terms.*

**Tuberculosed** (tiubə̄·ɹkiŭlōuzd), *a. Path.* [f. TUBERCULOS-IS + -ED [2].] Affected with tuberculosis; rendered tuberculous.

**1888** *Med. News* 25 Aug. 216 We must distinguish those forms in which the tuberculosed lymphatic glands are separated in chains. **1897** *Daily News* 22 Apr. 3/1 Methods..for dealing with tuberculosed meat. **1899** H. STUART *Lochs & Loch Fishing* I. iv. 34 They contained the bacilli of consumption, and were, in a word, tuberculosed or consumptive fish.

‖ **Tuberculosis** (tiubə̄ɹkiŭlōu·sis). *Path.* [mod.L., f. *tūbercul-um* TUBERCLE: see -OSIS.] *Originally*, Any disease characterized by the formation of tubercles; now, since the discovery by Koch in 1882 of the tubercle-bacillus, *spec.* restricted to disease caused by this bacillus in any of the bodily tissues; examples are pulmonary consumption or phthisis (tuberculosis of the lungs), and scrofula (tuberculosis of the lymphatic glands). Also *attrib.*

**1860** TANNER *Pregnancy* ii. 48 Many females with a tendency to tuberculosis having a copious watery catamenial flow. **1873** T. H. GREEN *Introd. Pathol.* (ed. 2) 203 Acute tuberculosis is..a general infective disease,..characterized..by..numerous minute nodular lesions..in the various organs and tissues. **1877** ROBERTS *Handbk. Med.* (ed. 3) I. 267 Looking upon tuberculosis as a constitutional disease, it has almost universally been regarded as having a hereditary origin. *attrib.* **1898** *Westm. Gaz.* 13 June 10/1 The provision of sanatoria for poor tuberculosis patients. **1899** Q. VICTORIA in *Daily News* 27 May 7/6, I beg your Excellency to express in my name to the Lung Tuberculosis Congress my best thanks for the good wishes tendered to me. **1913** *Times* 6 Aug. 8/4 Milk containing tuberculosis bacilli.

**Tuberculo·so-**, combining form of L. type **tūberculōsus* TUBERCULOUS, in combination with an adj. of form, as *tuberculoso-subramose.*

**1846** DANA *Zooph.* (1848) 497 Either convoluted-foliate, or tuberculoso-subramose.

**Tuberculous** (tiubə̄·ɹkiŭləs), *a.* [ad. L. type **tūberculōs-us*, f. *tūbercul-um* TUBERCLE: see -OUS; cf. F. *tuberculeux* (1812 in Hatz.-Darm.).]

**1.** *Path.* Pertaining to or produced by tubercles; consisting of or of the nature of tubercles; affected with tubercles.

**1747** tr. *Astruc's Fevers* 129 Though the..tuberculous ulcers may seem to be healed, yet they frequently return. *a* **1834** R. CARSWELL *Pathol. Anat., Tubercle* (1838) a iv b, I have never found these [scrofulous] glands..exempt from the presence of tuberculous matter. **1897** [see TUBERCULAR 2].

**b.** Since 1882, almost always used *spec.* in reference to the tubercle-bacillus or to tuberculosis, and thus technically distinguished from *tubercular* in the general sense: see TUBERCULAR 2, 2 b.

**1891** *Dublin Rev.* Jan. 162 The new remedy can only act on living tuberculous tissue. **1897** *Allbutt's Syst. Med.* II. 17 Guinea-pigs inoculated subcutaneously..by virulent tuberculous material. **1899** *Ibid.* VII. 466 Tuberculous meningitis is an acute disease depending on the invasion of the cerebral pia mater by the tubercle bacillus. **1903** *Times* 7 Mar. 15/2 The eating of tuberculous pork. **1913** *Ibid.* 13 Aug. 3/2 A steady increase in the use of hospitals for the tuberculous sick.

**2.** *Nat. Hist.* Full of or covered with tubercles; tuberculate, tubercular. (Now disused.)

**1828** WEBSTER, *Tubercular, Tuberculous*,..full of knobs or pimples. **1833** *Penny Cycl.* I. 114/2 The three first molars are pointed and trenchant, and the other four tuberculous. **1846** DANA *Zooph.* (1848) 502 Surface tuberculous, with the tubercles subconical.

‖ **Tuberculum** (tiubə̄·ɹkiŭlŏm). Pl. **tubercula.** [L. dim. of *tūber*, TUBER [2].] = TUBERCLE (in various senses).

**1693** tr. *Blancard's Phys. Dict.* (ed. 2), *Tubercula*, the same that *Phymata*. **1721** BAILEY, *Tubercula*, (among Surgeons) little Swellings or Pushes. **1857** DUNGLISON *Med. Lex.*, *Tuberculum Cinereum*, 'Ash-coloured tubercle', a mass of cineritious substance at the top of the calamus scriptorius [in the medulla oblongata]. **1872** NICHOLSON *Palæont.* 350 The ribs have distinct capitula and tubercula.

**Tuberiferous** (tiūbəri·fĕrəs), *a. Bot.* [f. L. *tūber*, TUBER [2] + -I)FEROUS.] Producing or bearing tubers.

**1846** WORCESTER cites GRAY. **1847** W. E. STEELE *Field Bot.* 174 *Melantheæ.* Mostly bulbiferous or tuberiferous plants, possessing highly poisonous, acrid, and narcotic properties. **1881** BENTHAM in *Jrnl. Linn. Soc.* XVIII. 347 Their rhizome is..more or less tuberiferous.

**Tuberiform** (tiū·bərifǭɹm), *a. Nat. Hist.* and *Path.* [f. L. type **tūberiform-is*: see TUBER [2] and -FORM.] Having the form of a tuber; also characterized, as a disease, by growths of this form.

**1822** J. PARKINSON *Outl. Oryctol.* 61* A free, carnose, tuberiform polypifer. **1834** COOPER *Good's Study Med.* (ed. 4) II. 555 *note*, Tuberiform melanosis. **1854** JONES & SIEV. *Pathol. Anat.* (1874) 141 A globular tumour, with a smooth or somewhat tuberiform surface. **1899** *Allbutt's Syst. Med.* VI. 106 Another variety [of malignant pleural growth] is the tuberiform.

**Tuberin** (tiū·bərin). *Org. Chem.* [f. TUBER [2] + -IN [1].] A globulin occurring in potato-tubers.

**1900** C. F. LANGWORTHY in *Year-bk. U. S. Dept. Agric.* 340 The potato contains two proteids, a globulin, to which the name 'tuberin' is given, and a proteose.

**Tuberless** (tiū·bəɹlės), *a.* [f. as prec. + -LESS.] Destitute of tubers; not bearing tubers.

**1851** *B'ham & Midl. Gard. Mag.* Dec. 217 Finding..that the plant [*Tropæolum Deckerianum*] was tuberless, I came to the conclusion that it must be an annual.

**Tu·bero-**, combining form of TUBER [2], as in **tu·bero-cy·stic,** having or forming a tuberous cyst.

**1879** *St. George's Hosp. Rep.* IX. 433 Tubero-cystic tumour of the ovary.

†**Tuberon, -e** [ad. Pg. *tubarão*], obs. forms of TIBURON, a large shark.

[**1521** PETER MARTYR *De nuper repertis insulis* 9 Piscis vorax qui Tuberon vocatur.] **1555, 1579** [see TIBURON]. **1599** NASHE *Lenten Stuffe* (1871) 76 A shark or tuberon, that lay gaping for the flying fish. **1665** SIR T. HERBERT *Trav.* (1677) 6 When..men swim in the bearing Ocean, the greedy Hayen called Tuberon or Shark..pursue them. **1784–5** *Chron.* in *Ann. Reg.* 241/1 The dog-fish, or tuberone of Josselyn, never exceeds three feet and a half in length.

**Tuberose** (tiū·bərōus, *often incorrectly* tiū·bɪ-rōuz), *sb.* Also 7 **tuberuse, -euse, (tuber-rose).** [ad. L. *tūberōsa*, the specific name of the plant (see below), fem. of *tūberōsus* (see next); corrupted by popular etymology into a disyllable, as if f. *tube + rose*, and so most commonly pronounced. (In the obs. forms *tuberuse, -euse*, a. F. *tubéreuse*, ad. L. *tūberōsa.*)] A liliaceous plant, *Polianthes tuberosa*, with creamy white, funnel-shaped, very fragrant flowers, and a tuberous root; a native of the East Indies, cultivated in southern Europe and the southern U.S., and in northern parts as a greenhouse plant.

**1664** EVELYN *Kal. Hort.* 200 Now take out your Indian Tuberoses, parting the Off-sets. *Ibid.* 208 Tuber-rose. **1691** *Lond. Gaz.* No. 2654/4 There are lately brought from Italy several Orange and Limon Trees,..Onions of Tubereuse. *a* **1718** PRIOR *Solomon* I. 80 The smelling Tub'rose and Junquele declare, The stronger Impulse of an Evening Air. *a* **1763** SHENSTONE *Ode to Sir R. Lyttelton* xiii, So would some tuberose delight, That struck the pilgrim's wondering sight. **1820** SHELLEY *Sensit. Plant* I. x, The jessamine faint, and the sweet tuberose. **1873** MRS. H. KING *Disciples, Ugo Bassi* II. (1877) 66 In the cool shadow heaps of tuberose Lay by the fountains in the market-place.

**b.** A perfume extracted from the flowers of this.

**1682** MRS. BEHN *City Heiress* 22 Sprinkle my Handkercher with Tuberuse. **1867** AUG. J. E. WILSON *Vashti* xix, Stooping to pick it [a handkerchief] up, he inhaled the delicate, tenacious perfume of tube-rose.

**Tuberose** (tiū·bərōus), *a.* [ad. L. *tūberōs-us*, f. *tūber*, TUBER [2]: see -OSE [1].] = TUBEROUS.

**1704** [see TUBER [2] 1 b]. **1796** KIRWAN *Elem. Min.* (ed. 2) II. 259 Indurated [Calx of Arsenic]...Found Massive, or Stalactitic with a tuberose or botryoidal surface. **1815** J. SMITH *Panorama Sc. & Art* II. 670 A tuberose root, as exemplified in the turnip and carrot. **1878** H. M. STANLEY *Dark Cont.* I. xv. 381 The tuberose muscles of the flanks. **1898** SIR P. MANSON *Trop. Diseases* xxxvii. 574 Vincent..found it [i.e. the parasite of mycetoma] in the unbroken tuberose swellings under the skin. *Comb.* **1806** GALPINE *Brit. Bot.* § 77 *Symphytum..tuberosum*, tuberose-rooted.

**Tuberosity** (tiūbərǫ·sĭti). [a. F. *tuberosité* (Paré, *c* 1550), f. late L. *tūberōsitās*, f. *tūberōs-us* TUBEROSE + -ITY.]

**1.** The quality or condition of being tuberous; bulging; gibbosity. Now *rare* or *Obs.*

**1541** R. COPLAND *Guydon's Quest. Chirurg.* Q iv b, Hardnes and tuberosyte of the ioyntes outwarde. **1610** GUILLIM *Heraldry* II. vi. 63 A bow, which being bent hath a moderate bowing voide of excess of tuberositie.

**2.** *concr.* A tuberous formation or part; a swelling, protuberance, prominence. **a.** *Anat.* and *Zool.*: *esp.* a large irregular projection of a bone, usually serving for attachment of a muscle.

**1611** COTGR., *Condyle*, the tuberiositie, out-swelling, roundnesse, or knots, of the thigh, knee, ankle, elbow, or knuckle-bones. **1741** MONRO *Anat.* (ed. 3) 134 The internal posterior Part of the Tuberosity and Alveoli of the Teeth. **1852** TH. ROSS *Humboldt's Trav.* I. i. 27 The brownish tuberosities of its body. **1870** ROLLESTON *Anim. Life* 13 The great triangular tuberosity of the humerus.

**b.** *generally.* A swelling, a swollen mass.

**1611** COTGR., *Tuberositez*, tuberosities, swellings;..knobs; knots. **1831** CARLYLE *Sart. Res.* I. v, Whether he flow gracefully out in folded mantles;..swell-out in starched ruffs, buckram stuffings, and monstrous tuberosities; or [etc.]. *Ibid.* III. vi, I sojourned in that monstrous tuberosity of Civilised Life, the Capital of England.

**Tuberous** (tiū·bərəs), *a.* [ad. F. *tubéreux, -euse* (Paré, *c* 1550), ad. L. *tūberōsus*, f. *tūber*, TUBER [2]: see -OUS.]

**1.** *Anat., Zool.*, etc. Of the form of, or constituting, a tuber or rounded projection; covered with such projections; knobbed, knobby. Now *rare.*

**1650** BULWER *Anthropomet.* iii. 63 This forehead is..neither globous nor tuberous as the forehead of women. **1678** RAY *Willughby's Ornith.* II. xv. § 2. 182 A broad circle of naked, tuberous, white flesh compasses the Eyes, as in the Carriers. **1804** SHAW *Gen. Zool.* V. 208 Tuberous Carp...Carp with thirteen rays in the anal fin, and slightly tuberous body.

**2.** *Path.* Affected with tubers or morbid swellings; of the nature of such a swelling; characterized, as a disease, by such swellings.

**1656** BLOUNT *Glossogr.*, *Tuberous*, full of bunches, swellings, wennes or knots. **1762** R. GUY *Pract. Obs. Cancers* 150 The tuberous Vessels were rather fuller than ordinary. **1834** COOPER *Good's Study Med.* (ed. 4) I. 353 The origin of vascular tuberous growths. **1900** J. HUTCHINSON in *Arch. Surg.* XI. 73 His face was covered with tuberous acne.

**3.** *Bot.* **a.** Of the nature of a tuber; chiefly in *tuberous root*, (*a*) a tuber, or an underground stem bearing tubers (see TUBER [2] 1); (*b*) more strictly, a true root (usually one of a cluster) thickened so as to resemble a tuber, but bearing no buds; as in the lesser celandine and the dahlia.

**1668** Tuberous roots [see TUBER [2] 1]. **1730** MARTYN in *Phil. Trans.* XXXVI. 385 Their Roots are either bulbous, tuberous, or consisting of thick, fleshy Fibres. **1776** WITHERING *Brit. Plants* (1796) IV. 346 *Peziza tuberosa*...Stem growing at the base to a blackish fungous tuberous substance. **1807** J. E. SMITH *Phys. Bot.* 140 The knobs of genuine tuberous roots, like the potatoe, are studded with them [buds]. **1872** OLIVER *Elem. Bot.* I. vii. 66 When the branches or fibres of a root become thickened in this way, as..in the Garden Dahlia, the root is said to be tuberous.

**b.** Of a plant: Producing or bearing tubers; tuberous-rooted.

**1664** EVELYN *Kal. Hort.* Sept. (1729) 218 Tuberous Indian Jacinth. **1786** ABERCROMBIE *Gard. Assist.* 51 Bulbous and tuberous irises. **1861** MISS PRATT *Flower. Pl.* IV. 55 Tuberous Comfrey. *Ibid.* VI. 56 Tuberous Fox-tail.

**4.** *Comb.* **Tuberous-rooted** *a.*, having a tuberous root (in either sense: see 3 a).

**1721** MORTIMER *Husb.* II. 226 Irises are both bulbous and tuberous Rooted. **1808** KNIGHT in *Phil. Trans.* XCIX. 174 Such tuberous rooted plants as the potatoe. **1914** *Daily Mail* 31 Jan. 9/2 The planting of tuberous-rooted anemones and ranunculuses.

Hence **Tu·berously** *adv.*; **Tu·berousness.**

**1681** GREW *Musæum* III. I. i. 255 The tuberousness of the Bone in some places. **1847–9** *Todd's Cycl. Anat.* IV. 133/2 This disease produces..irregular tuberousness of the hand. *a* **1891** *Bull. of Ill. State Laboratory* II. 28 (Cent. D.) Tuberously.

**Tubful** (tʊ·bful). [f. TUB *sb.* + -FUL.] As much as a tub will hold.

**1788** LD. AUCKLAND *Corr.* etc. (1861) II. 71 We have a large tubful brought to us every morning. **1812** SIR J. SINCLAIR *Syst. Husb. Scot.* II. 72 The rain is pouring on in tubfuls. **1894** J. MENZIES *Our Town* xx. 211 A gudewife had come to her door with a tubful of soapsuds.

**Tubi-** (tiūbi), combining form of L. *tubus* TUBE, in modern scientific terms, chiefly zoological. **Tubicolar** (tiubi·kŏlăɪ), **Tubicolous** (tiubi·kŏləs) *adjs.* [mod.L. *tubicola*, f. *colĕre* to cultivate, inhabit], inhabiting a tube; applied to annelids and rotifers that secrete tubular cases, spiders that spin tubular webs (cf. *tubitelar*), and molluscs with shelly tubes (cf. TUBE-*shell*, *tubivalve*); so **Tubicole** (tiū·bikǭul) *a.* = prec.; *sb.* a tubicolar annelid or mollusc. **Tu·bicorn** [L. *cornū* horn], *sb.* a hollow-horned ruminant; *adj.* hollow-horned, as a ruminant; also **Tubico·rnous** *a.* **Tubifacient** (-fēⁱ·ʃiĕnt) *a.* [L. *facient-em* making], making a tube for habitation, as a tubicolous annelid, etc. **Tu·bifer** [L. *-fer* bearing], an animal bearing a tube, as a tubicolous annelid; so **Tubi·ferous** (-fĕrəs) *a.*, bearing a tube or tubes. **Tubiflorous** (-flōᵊ·rəs) *a.*, *Bot.* [L. *flōs, flōr-* flower], having tubular flowers or florets, as the division *Tubifloræ* of composite plants (= TUBULIFLOROUS). **Tu·biform** *a.*, having the form of a tube; tube-shaped, tubular. **Tubilingual** (-li·ŋgwăl) *a.* [L. *lingua* tongue], belonging to the division *Tubilingues* of passerine birds, having long extensile tubular tongues used for sucking up honey. **Tubinarial** (-nēᵊ·riăl), **Tubinarine** (-nēᵊ·rəin) *adjs.* [L. *nāris* nostril], belonging to the order *Tubinārēs* (Illiger, 1811) of water-birds, comprising the albatrosses and petrels, having nostrils of tubular form. **Tubiparous** (tiubi·pärəs) *a.* [-PAROUS], producing a tube; applied to certain glands in tubicolous annelids, supposed to secrete the substance which forms the tube. **Tu·bipore** (-pōᵊɹ) *sb.*, a member of the genus *Tubipora*, family *Tubiporidæ*, or order *Tubiporaceæ*, of alcyonarians (the organ-pipe corals), in which each polyp has a tubular corallet opening by a pore; *adj.* belonging to or having the characters of this genus, family, or order; in quot., containing or formed of fossil tubipores; so **Tu:biporacean** (-porēⁱ·ʃiăn), **-poraceous** (-porēⁱ·ʃəs) *adjs.*, belonging to the order *Tubiporaceæ*; **Tubi·porid**, a coral of the family *Tubiporidæ*; **Tubi·porite** [-ITE[1] 2 a], a fossil tubipore; **Tubi·poroid** *a.* [-OID], resembling or allied to the genus *Tubipora*; **Tubi·porous** *a.* = *tubipore* adj. **Tubitelar** (-tī·lăɹ) *a.* [L. *tēla* web], belonging to the division *Tubitelæ* or *Tubitelariæ* of spiders, which spin tubular webs; so **Tu:bitelarian** (-tīlēᵊ·riăn) *a.* = prec.; *sb.* a spider of this division (*Cent. Dict.* 1891). **Tu·bivalve,** *sb.* a bivalve mollusc having a shelly tube in addition to the valves of the shell; a tube-shell; *adj.* having such a tube.

1835–6 *Todd's Cycl. Anat.* I. 619/1 A common marine *tubicolar worm. 1877 HUXLEY *Anat. Inv. Anim.* v. 238 The tubicolar Annelids possess neither proboscis nor teeth. 1842 BRANDE *Dict. Sc.* etc., **Tubicoles, Tubicola*, the name of an order of Annelidans, comprehending those which live in tubes..; also the name of a family of.. Mollusks, including those which have a tubular calcareous sheath in addition to the two shelly valves. 1864 WEBSTER, *Tubicole*,.. one of an order of annelides most of which live in shelly tubes. 1891 *Cent. Dict.*, Tubicole, *a.* and *n.* 1870 H. SPENCER *Princ. Psychol.* (ed. 2) I. I. i. 6 The *tubicolous Annelids. 1881 E. R. LANKESTER in *Jrnl. Microsc. Sc.* Jan. 123 The proximal region of the stomach..was infested by a remarkable little free swimming, yet tubicolous Rotifer. 1842 BRANDE *Dict. Sc.* etc., **Tubicorns, Tubicornia*,.. Ruminants comprehending those in which the horns are composed of a horny axis covered with a horny sheath. 1891 *Cent. Dict.*, *Tubicorn*,..*a.* hollow-horned, as a ruminant. 1864 WEBSTER, *Tubicornous. 1891 *Cent. Dict.*, *Tubifacient. 1899 in *Syd. Soc. Lex.* 1842 BRANDE *Dict. Sc.* etc., **Tubifers, Tubifera*, the name given by Lamarck to an order of the class *Polypi*,..whose surface is..covered with retractile hollow tubes. 1860 MAYNE *Expos. Lex.*, *Tubiferus*,..bearing tubes: *tubiferous. 1888 ROLLESTON & JACKSON *Anim. Life* 246 A Cyclostomatous Polyzoan,.. which with its aggregated calcareous cells presents an appearance not unlike that of a small *tubiflorous flower belonging to a plant of the order *Compositae*. 1745 NEEDHAM *Microsc. Disc.* Introd. 6 The Barnacle..a small *tubiform Animal,..adhering in Clusters to Rocks. 1880 GÜNTHER *Fishes* 57 A pair of small tubiform bones, the turbinals. 1891 *Cent. Dict.*, *Tubilingual. 1882 W. A. FORBES in *Rep. Challenger Exped., Zool.* IV. 64 One branch of this stock has since become greatly modified in the *Tubinarial direction. 1895 *Funk's Stand. Dict.*, *Tubinarine. 1890 *Q. Jrnl. Microsc. Sc.* June 186 *note*, Such thoracic nephridia in other sedentary annelids have been called '*tubiparous glands' by Claparède and others. 1800 HATCHETT in *Phil. Trans.* XC. 333 In the interstices of the *Tubipore. 1846 DANA *Zooph.* iv. (1848) 68 In the Tubipores, the polyps form, by their secretions, parallel tubes. 1876 PAGE *Adv. Text-bk. Geol.* xviii. 353 The tubipore cherts and flints of the mountain limestone. 1895 *Funk's Stand. Dict.*, *Tubiporid. 1828 WEBSTER, **Tubiporite*. 1895 *Funk's Stand. Dict.*, *Tubiporoid. 1848 SMART, **Tubiporous*, pertaining to, or resembling tubipores. 1882 OGILVIE, **Tubivalve*, an annelid [*sic*: *read* mollusc] of the order Tubicolidæ. 1891 *Cent. Dict.*, Tubivalve *n.* and *a.*

† **Tubi·cinate,** *v. Obs. rare*⁻⁰. [f. med.L. *tubicināt-*, ppl. stem of *tubicināre*, f. L. *tubicen* trumpeter, f. *tuba* trumpet + *canĕre* to sing, play.] (See quot.) So † **Tubicina·tion** (*obs. rare*⁻⁰).

1656 BLOUNT *Glossogr.*, *Tubicinate*.., to sound the Trumpet. 1658 PHILLIPS, *Tubicination*,..a sounding of a Trumpet, Pipe, or Cornet.

**Tubing** (tiū·biŋ), *vbl. sb.* [f. TUBE *v.* or *sb.* + -ING[1].] The action of furnishing with a tube or tubes; also *concr.* tubes collectively, or as a material; a length or piece of tube. Also *attrib.*

1845 I. FARRELL *Archimedean Railw.* 8 This rail is made of iron tubing. 1854 J. SCOFFERN in *Orr's Circ. Sc., Chem.* 350 India-rubber tubing can be obtained. 1881 RAYMOND *Mining Gloss.*, *Tubing*, lining a deep bore-hole by driving down iron tubes. 1886 J. BARROWMAN *Sc. Mining Terms* 69 *Tubing*, sheet-iron lining of a bore-hole. 1909 *Installation News* III. 112/1 Any carpenter could locate the weak spots in tubing work.

**Tubman, tub-man** (tɒ·bmăn). [f. TUB *sb.* + MAN *sb.*[1]]

†**1.** = TUB-PREACHER. *Obs.*

1642 P. BLAND *Royall Position* 9 No Conventicling Tubman should have made my words his text. *a* 1643 LD. FALKLAND, etc. *Infallibility* (1646) 97 The meanest Seducer may doe mischiefe, as we finde by the effects of the Tubmen. 1651 JANE Εικων Ακλαστος 213 Tubmen whose prayers not only want salt, but are besmeared with prophanes.

**2.** † **a.** ? A maker of tubs, a cooper. *Obs.* **b.** At Christ's Hospital, formerly, one who had charge of the latrine tubs; now, a lavatory attendant.

1677 (*title*) A Caution to Married Couples..how a man having beat his wife, murthered a Tub-man that endeavoured to stop him from killing her. 1723 *Lond. Gaz.* No. 6196/7 John Thumwood,..Tub-man. *c* 1865 *Skit Christ's Hospital*, Has she a round of butter'd toast to give to tubman Joe?

**3.** A barrister in the Court of Exchequer whose place was beside the tub used as a measure of capacity in excise cases; the position conferred the right of precedence in motions, except over the 'postman' and in Crown business. Cf. POSTMAN[3]. *Obs.* exc. *Hist.*

1768 BLACKSTONE *Comm.* III. iii. 28 *note*, In the court of exchequer two of the most experienced barristers called the *post*-man and the *tub*-man..have also a precedence in motions. 1841 MEESON & WELSBY *Rep.* VII. 188 The Attorney-General moved in this case. The Postman and Tubman claimed pre-audience; but upon the Attorney-General's stating that it was the Queen's business in which he moved, the Court decided that he was entitled to be heard before the Postman and Tubman. 1882 *Daily News* 15 Dec. 2/1 With the appointment of Mr. Anstie as a Queen's Counsel, the ancient office of tubman to the Exchequer disappears. 1886 [see POSTMAN[3]].

† **Tu·bnell.** *Obs. rare*⁻¹. [app. irreg. dim. of TUB *sb.*, or arbitrary alteration of TURNEL.] A small tub.

1688 R. HOLME *Armoury* III. xiv. (Roxb.) 18/1 This containing half a Barrell of water or something lesse, is called a Tub; if lesse a Tubnell, that is vulgarly a Turnell.

**Tubo-** (tiū̆bo), used in certain cases as combining form of L. *tubus* TUBE (instead of the usual Latin form TUBI-: see -O) in several terms of zoology, anatomy, etc. **a.** *Zool.* in adjs. denoting a combination of tubular with some other form, as *tu:bo-labe·llate, -na·riform.* **b.** *Anat.*, etc. in terms relating to the Fallopian (rarely, the Eustachian) tube in connexion with some other part; chiefly adjs., as *tu:bo-abdo·minal* (pertaining to or occurring in the Fallopian tube and the abdomen), *-ligame·ntous, -ova·rian, -peritone·al, -u·terine, -vagi·nal*; *tu:bo-ty·mpanal* (pertaining to the Eustachian tube and the tympanum); rarely sbs., as *tu:bo-ovario·tomy* (excision of the Fallopian tube and ovary).

1846 DANA *Zooph.* (1848) 432 The nariform calicle is tubular at base—tubo-nariform. *Ibid.* 444 Corallum having the calicles tubo-labellate. 1857 BULLOCK *Cazeaux' Midwif.* 245 Tubo-ovarian Pregnancy. *Ibid.* 246 Tubo-abdominal Pregnancy. 1889 J. M. DUNCAN *Lect. Dis. Women* viii. (ed. 4) 243 An interstitial pregnancy may become tubo-uterine. 1900–13 DORLAND *Med. Dict.*, *Tuboligamentous*, pertaining to an oviduct and a broad ligament. *Tubo-ovarial, tubo-ovarian,.. Tubo-ovariotomy,.. Tuboperitoneal Tubotympanal,.. Tubovaginal.*

**Tu·b-prea:cher.** [See TUB *sb.* 4.] One who preaches from a 'tub' (TUB *sb.* 4); a dissenting preacher or minister (*contemptuous*). So **Tu·b-prea:ching** *sb.* and *a.*

1643 *xiv Art. of Treason exhib. I. Pennington* 5 Stephan Evans, alias Prince of Morocco, Knight of the Burning Pestle, Salter, and Tub-preacher, on Snow Hill. 1661 J. DAVIES *Civ. Warres* xxxii. 52 Tub-Preachings and Conventicle-Lectures were listened to as to Oracles. *a* 1670 HACKET *Abp. Williams* II. (1693) 165 Your lawful Ministers..to whom ..you do not resort,..but to Tub-preachers in Conventicles. 1719 D'URFEY *Pills* IV. 14 The Tub-preaching Saint was so zealous a Blade. 1899 S. R. GARDINER *Cromwell* 48 Those who looked down with scorn on the vagaries of the tub-preacher.

† **Tu-brugge.** *Obs. rare.* Also 3 tobrugge, 4 tuybrugge. [The second part is the ME. *brugge*, BRIDGE; the first is uncertain; perh. a deriv. of OE. *togian* or *tēon* to draw (see TOW *v.*[1], TEE *v.*[1]): cf. Ger. *zugbrücke*, MHG. *zogebrucke*, drawbridge.] A drawbridge.

1297 R. GLOUC. (Rolls) 11257 Þe castel brugge..he barnde fram þen ende To þe tobrugge [*v.r.* tuybrugge] along. *Ibid.* 11595 Þe tu brugge [*v.r.* tun brugge] hii drowe vp.

† **Tu·bster.** *Obs.* [f. TUB *sb.* + -STER.] A tub-preacher. (*Contemptuous.*)

1681 T. FLATMAN *Heraclitus Ridens* No. 45 (1713) II. 34 A certain Dissenting Tubster, who told his Audience, he would..divide the Observations he should make from his Text, into forty eight Particulars. 1682 *Ibid.* No. 82. 248 Why, if we should lay down,..the Tubsters would appoint a solemn Day of Thanksgiving among themselves. 1700 T. BROWN *Amusem. Ser. & Com.* 121 He, says the Tubster, that would be Rich.., must play the Thief or the Cheat.

**Tu·b-thu:mper.**

**1.** A speaker or preacher who for emphasis thumps the pulpit; a violent or declamatory preacher or orator; a ranter.

1662 H. FOULIS *Hist. Plots Pretended Saints* 80 Tub-thumpers..a sort of people more antick in their Devotions than Don Buscos Fencing-Master. 1720–1 *Lett. fr. Mist's Jrnl.* (1722) II. 225 An honest Presbyterian Tub-thumper, who has lost his Voice with bawling to his Flock. 1864 *Athenæum* 27 Aug. 267/3 Preachers, humorous tub-thumpers. 1908 *Daily Chron.* 3 Nov. 5/7 It would reduce the M.P... to the position of a Temperance tub-thumper.

**2.** A cooper. *humorous dial.*

1872 HARTLEY *Yorks. Ditties* Ser. I. 98 At last au set up as tub-thumper. 1880 L. J. JENNINGS *Rambles* 110 'A tub-thumper?'..'Ay Mister—what you call a cooper.'

So **Tu·b-thu:mping** *sb.* and *a.*

1888 *Contemp. Rev.* Aug. 253 Very modest gifts, belonging to what may be called the tub-thumping school of oratory. 1894 *Westm. Gaz.* 22 Aug. 1/2 What we demand is not a display of tub-thumping at the fag-end of a Session,..but a deliberate plan of campaign, carefully thought out and doggedly pursued. 1909 *Times* 21 Mar., A democratic election, with all its tub-thumping and unreasoning passion and sheer noise.

**Tubular** (tiū·biŭlăɹ), *a.* [f. L. *tubul-us* a small tube, a pipe + -AR; cf. F. *tubulaire* (1771 in *Dict. Trévoux*).]

**1.** Having the form of a tube or pipe; constituting or consisting of a tube; cylindrical, hollow, and open at one or both ends; tube-shaped.

*Tubular bridge*, a bridge formed of a great tube or hollow beam, usually of wrought iron, through which the roadway passes.

1673 GREW *Anat. Trunks* I. iv. § 15 The Pins being also conceived to be Tubular. 1827 FARADAY *Chem. Manip.* xvi. (1842) 405 These tubular vessels may be supported with facility..upon the table across two or three pieces of glass. 1850 E. CLARK (*title*) The Britannia and Conway Tubular Bridges. 1872 YEATS *Techn. Hist. Comm.* 243 The idea of tubular bricks is not new, for they were used by the Romans.

**b.** *Bot.*: *esp.* applied to a flower or floret consisting mainly of a tube, with small or inconspicuous limb; *spec.* to such florets in a composite flower (opp. to LIGULATE).

1776 J. LEE *Introd. Bot.* Explan. Terms 396 *Tubulosa*, Florets that are all tubular and equal. 1807 J. E. SMITH *Phys. Bot.* 457 Flowers..with united tubular anthers. 1877–84 F. E. HULME *Wild Fl.* p. vii, Primrose,—Calyx tubular, five-toothed. 1880 GRAY *Struct. Bot.* vi. § 5 (ed. 6) 248 '*Tubular*..strictly..denotes a gamophyllous perianth with limb inconspicuous..as in Trumpet Honeysuckle.

**c.** *Zool.* and *Anat.*

1794 SULLIVAN *View Nat.* II. 175 Those of the coral class, of a ramified and tubular form. 1802 BINGLEY *Anim. Biog.* (1813) I. 46 The tongue..in several [insects]..is fleshy and tubular. 1872 COUES *N. Amer. Birds* 29 Rounded nostrils may have a raised border or rim; when this is prolonged they are called tubular.

**2.** Relating to, or performed by means of, a tube.

*a* 1716 R. COTES *Lect.* (1738) A vj, Experiments for the most part tubular.

**3.** Constructed with or consisting of a number of tubes; as a *tubular boiler* (see also TUBULOUS 2 b and cf. *tubular-flued*).

1804 TROUGHTON in *Nicholson's Philos. Jrnl.* Dec. 225 (*title*) Description of a Tubular Pendulum. *Ibid.* 228 The first pendulum which I made of the tubular kind, had only three steel wires, and one tube above the bob. 1819 *Pantologia* s. v. *Pendulum*, We may date the invention of the tubular pendulum..about the year 1775. 1825 J. NICHOLSON *Operat. Mechanic* 527 Troughton's tubular-pendulum ..is constructed of an exterior tube of brass,..within which is another tube, and five brass wires in its belly. 1858 SIMMONDS *Dict. Trade*, *Tubular-boiler*, a boiler consisting of tubes. 1862 *Catal. Internat. Exhib., Brit.* II. No. 6132 Metallic tubular bedsteads. 1877 KNIGHT *Dict. Mech.*, *Tubular Boiler*, a name properly applicable to a steam-boiler in which the water circulates in pipes,..the fire encircling them.

**4. a.** *Path.* (See quot.) ? *Obs.*

1822–7 GOOD *Study Med.* (1829) I. 287 Diarrhœa Tubularis. Tubular Looseness. The dejections consisting more or less of membrane-like tubes, whitish, viscous, and inodorous. *Ibid.* V. 49 Tubular diarrhœa.

**b.** *Phys.* and *Path.* Applied to a high-pitched respiratory murmur, like the sound made by blowing through a tube, heard normally over the trachea and bronchial tubes, and in diseased conditions over the lung.

1834 J. FORBES *Laennec's Dis. Chest* (ed. 4) 119 The stethoscope detected..no other respiratory sound, but that of a dry respiration, evidently tubular or bronchial. 1898 *Allbutt's Syst. Med.* V. 205 The breath-sounds are tubular or cavernous—the term 'tubular' is used here as synonymous with bronchial.

**5.** *Comb.*, as *tubular-shaped*; *esp.* in *Bot.* with another adj., denoting a combination of tubular with another form, as *tubular-campanulate, -urceolate*; **tubular-flued,** having tubular flues.

1815 J. SMITH *Panorama Sc. & Art* II. 825 In a proper cylindrical, almost tubular-shaped vessel, two feet high. 1840 *Encycl. Brit.* (ed. 7) XX. 674/2 These tubular-flued boilers are at the present day extensively used. 1847 W. E. STEELE *Field Bot.* 118 [*Erica*] *Mediterranea*. Cor[olla] tubular-urceolate. 1870 HOOKER *Stud. Flora* 379 Polygonatum...Perianth tubular-campanulate.

Hence **Tubularity** (-æ·rĭti), the quality of being tubular, tubular form of structure; **Tu·bularly** *adv.*, in a tubular manner, so as to form a tube.

1746 DA COSTA in *Phil. Trans.* XLIV. 402 Such different Effects as Solidity and Tubularity. 1856 R. SHIELD *Pract. Hints Moths & Butterfl.* 74 In tubularly rolled leaves of honeysuckle we shall find the larvæ. 1890 *Manch. Exam.* 20 June, The special advantage of tubularity in bells seems to be that they are only heard in the immediate neighbourhood.

**Tubularian** (tiūbiulēᵊ·riăn), *a.* and *sb. Zool.* [f. mod.L. *Tubulāria* (in Linnæus, 1755, f. *tubulus* TUBULE) + -AN.] **a.** *adj.* Belonging to the Linnæan genus *Tubularia*, the group *Tubulariæ*, or the family *Tubulariidæ*, of gymnoblastic Hydrozoa, in which the polyps are of tubular form, protected by a perisarc, with naked hydranths. **b.** *sb.* A tubularian hydroid. Also **Tubularidan** (-æ·ridăn) *a.* and *sb.* in same sense (*Cent. Dict.* 1891).

1859 *Todd's Cycl. Anat.* V. 296/2 In the Tubularian Polyp the canal is modified. 1864 WEBSTER, *Tubularian*,..one of a family of polypoid acalephs, having simple or branched horny tubes, and terminating above in polyp-like extremities. 1883 *Science* I. 196/2 The Anthomedusæ (e.g., *Margelis*), from the tubularian hydroids. 1888 ROLLESTON & JACKSON *Anim. Life* 247 A Campanularian differs from a Tubularian in three important respects.

**Tubulary** (tiū·biulări), *sb. Zool.* [ad. mod.L. *Tubulāria*: see prec.] †**a.** ? A tubular species of coral. *Obs.* **b.** = TUBULARIAN *sb.*

1708 *Phil. Trans.* XXVI. 79 *Tubularia*, The Tubulary, or Lesser Pipe-shell. [1753 CHAMBERS *Cycl. Supp.*, *Tubularia Fossilis*,..a species of coral found very often fossile in Germany and Italy, and composed of a great number of tubes.] 1876 *Beneden's Anim. Parasites* iv. 84 The tubulary observed by Gwyn Jeffreys..perhaps belongs to the same species.

†**Tu·bulary,** *a. Obs.* [f. as TUBULAR: see -ARY [2].] = TUBULAR.

1673 *Phil. Trans.* VIII. 6133 Lignous, consisting of Tubulary vessels. 1673 GREW *Anat. Trunks* I. iv. § 10 Sometimes the Pith is hollow or Tubulary. 1754 ELLIS in *Phil. Trans.* XLVIII. 506 That genus of corallines which I have called tubulary.

**Tubulate** (tiū·biulĕt), *a. Nat. Hist.* [ad. L. *tubulāt-us*, f. *tubul-us* TUBULE: see -ATE [2].] Formed into or like a tube; tubular.

1753 CHAMBERS *Cycl. Supp.* App. s.v. *Petal*, The tubulate bell-fashioned flowers. 1760 J. LEE *Introd. Bot.* II. xxii. (1765) 124 Syngenesia...Characters of the Florets...Corolla ..is either *tubulate*..; *ligulate* [etc.]. 1846 DANA *Zooph.* (1848) 151 A few tubulate pores over the surface. 1872 NICHOLSON *Palæont.* 74 The group of the Tubulate Corals is now much reduced in numbers.

**Tubulate** (tiū·biuleɪt), *v.* [f. as prec.: see -ATE [3]; cf. *tubulation*.] *trans.* **a.** To form into a tube. **b.** 'To furnish with a tube' (*Cent. D.* 1891).

1802 W. TAYLOR in *Monthly Mag.* XIII. 207 A wooden cullender..the orifices of which have in the center a wire or skewer, which tubulates the extruded dough [macaroni].

**Tubulated** (tiū·biuleɪtĕd), *a.* [f. L. *tubulāt-us* TUBULATE *a.* + -ED [1].]

**1.** Furnished with a tube; *esp.* of a retort or receiver: Having a short tube with a stopper (*tubulature* or *tubulure*), through which substances can be introduced.

1663 BOYLE *Usef. Exp. Nat. Philos.* II. v. vii. 173 This kinde of Vessel is inferior to those tubulated Retorts. 1758 REID tr. *Macquer's Chym.* I. 176 Some retorts are also made with an opening on their upper side, like that of tubulated glass alembics,..closed..with a glass stopple. 1831 BREWSTER *Nat. Magic* xiii. (1833) 343 To expose nitrate of ammonia in a tubulated glass retort to the heat of an Argand's lamp.

**2.** Formed into, or like, a tube; longitudinally perforated; tubular.

1713 DERHAM *Phys. Theol.* IX. i. 437 The Teeth are tubulated, for the Conveyance..of the Poyson into the Wound. 1753 CHAMBERS *Cycl. Supp.* s.v. *Tubulated Flower*, The tubulated floscules generally compose the disk [of *Compositæ*], and the ligulated ones the radius of the compound flowers. 1774 PRINGLE *Torpedo* 28 Those singular tubulated organs of the torpedo consist..of many bodies of a prismatic form. 1859 SEMPLE *Diphtheria* 96 Some slender and tubulated fragments of false membranes, mixed with mucus, were expelled.

So **Tubulation** (-ēɪ·ʃən) [ad. L. *tubulātiōn-em*, n. of action f. *tubul-us*, TUBULE, as if from **tubulāre*], the process of making or becoming tubular; **Tubulature** (tiū·biulătiuɹ) [see -URE], the tube of a tubulated retort: = TUBULURE.

1656 BLOUNT *Glossogr.*, *Tubilation* [*ed.* 1674 *Tubulation*] (*tubulatio*), a making hollow like pipes. 1827 FARADAY *Chem. Manip.* vii. (1842) 201 The tubulature is safest when it is not much thicker than the retort at the part where they join, but should thicken upwards. 1855 *Q. Jrnl. Chem. Soc.* VII. 98 The liquid..was placed in a retort with a thermometer in the tubulature. 1866 *Reader* No. 163. 154/1 Pseudopodial tubulation.

**Tubule** (tiū·biul). [ad. L. *tubul-us*, dim. of *tubus* TUBE; cf. F. *tubule* (Cotgr.).] A small tube; a minute tubular structure in an animal or plant body, as the *Malpighian* or *uriniferous tubules* of the kidney, the *dentinal tubules* of the teeth, etc.

1677 tr. *Groeneveldt's Treat. Stone* 19 The stone growing in the tubule or pelvis of the kidney. 1699 J. WOODWARD in *Phil. Trans.* XXI. 211 Reduced to single Corpuscles, all fit to enter the Tubules and Vessels of Plants. 1867 J. HOGG *Microsc.* II. i. 333 Contrivances to enable the tubules of the woody tissues to discharge their contents. 1869 HUXLEY *Phys.* xii. 322 The chief constituent of a tooth is dentine... It presents innumerable, minute, parallel, wavy tubules... The wider ends of these tubules open into the pulp cavity.

Hence **Tu·bulet** [-ET], a minute tubule.

1826 KIRBY & SP. *Entomol.* III. xxxiii. 363 *Tubulus* (the Tubulet), The tube or retractile base of the *Rostellum*. *Siphunculus* (the Siphuncle), the real instrument of suction, which when unemployed is retracted within the tubulet.

**Tubuli-** (tiū·biuli), combining form of mod.L. *tubulus* TUBULE, in several scientific terms. **Tu·bulibra·nch** (-bræŋk), **Tu:bulibra·nchian** *Zool.*, *sb.* a member of the *Tubulibranchiata*, branchiate gastropod molluscs with tubular shells, in Cuvier's classification; *adj.* = next. **Tu:bulibra·nchiate,** *adj.* belonging to the *Tubulibranchiata*; *sb.* = prec. **Tu·bulico:le,** *Zool.* [L. *-cola* inhabitant], *sb.* a member of the *Tubulicolæ* in Cuvier's classification, a tubularian; *adj.* inhabiting a tubule; belonging to the *Tubulicolæ*. **Tu:bulide·ntate** *a.*, *Zool.* [L. *dentātus* toothed], belonging to the *Tubulidentāta*, a group of edentates having compound teeth traversed by parallel vertical tubules. **Tubuli·ferous** *a.*, *Nat. Hist.* [-FEROUS], bearing tubules; *spec.* having a tubular ovipositor, as the females of certain insects. **Tu:buliflo·ral, -flo·rous** *adjs.*, *Bot.* [L. *flōs*, *flōr-em* flower], belonging to the division *Tubulifloræ* of Composite plants, having either all the florets, or those of the disk, tubular. **Tu·bulifo:rm** *a*, having the form of a tubule, tubular. **Tu·bulipo:re,** *Zool.* [L. *porus* PORE], a polyzoan of the genus *Tubuli·pora* or family *Tubulipo·ridæ*, having tubular calcareous calicles; also **Tubuli·porid** (*Funk's Stand. Dict.* 1895). **Tubuli·poroid** *a.* [see -OID], resembling, or having the characters of, the family *Tubuliporidæ* (*Cent. Dict.* 1891).

1855 T. WILLIAMS in *Ann. & Mag. Nat. Hist.* Ser. II. XVI. 408 The two preceding *Tubulibranchs. *Ibid.* 407 The *Tubulibranchiate genera. 1842 BRANDE *Dict. Sc.* etc., *Tubulibranchians... **Tubulicoles*, a name applied by Cuvier to a family of Polypes. 1822 J. PARKINSON *Outl. Oryctol.* 40 With *tubuliferous lobes. 1852 *Zoologist* X. 3405 They were certainly tubuliferous and not merely membranous appendages. 1882 M. T. MASTERS in *Jrnl. Bot.* XI. 39 The *Tubulifloral division of the Composites. 1891 *Cent. Dict.*, *Tubuliflorous. 1796 KIRWAN *Elem. Min.* (ed. 2) I. 30 **Tubuliform*, slender cylinders. 1877 HUXLEY *Anat. Inv. Anim.* vii. 381 Glands..divisible into five different kinds (aciniform, ampullate, aggregate, tubuliform, and tuberous). 1864 WEBSTER, *Tubulipore.

†**Tu·bulite.** *Obs.* [ad. mod.L. *tubulītēs*, introduced by Gesner, *Tractat. Physic. de Petrificatis*, 1758.] A fossil or petrifaction of a tube or tubular shell occupied by an animal.

Gesner specified the tubular shell of the ship-worm, a lamellibranch mollusc, the coiled tube of a *Serpula*, the tubular shell of a *Dentalium*, all then regarded as 'worms'. But as these were the shells of different animals, the word was not permanently used.

1799 KIRWAN *Geol. Ess.* 236 Common marlites..frequently [contain] shells, or petrifactions, ammonites, pectinites, tubulites. 1834 BOASE *Primary Geol.* 372 Those secondary strata, which contain tubulites and similar fossils.

**Tubulo-** (tiū·biulo), used as combining form of mod.L. *tubulus* TUBULE, instead of the usual TUBULI-, either before a word of Greek derivation, or in adverbial relation to an adj. (see -O); occurring in a few recent scientific terms. **Tu·bulocy:st** (-sist), 'any cystic dilatation of an obsolete canal or functionless duct' (Dorland *Med. Dict.* 1900–13). **Tu·bulode·rmoid,** 'a dermoid tumor due to the persistence of a fetal tube' (*ibid.*). **Tu:bulo-ra·cemose** (-ræsīmōᵘs) *a.*, 'both tubular and racemose, as, a *tubuloracemose* gland' (*ibid.*). **Tu:bulosa·ccular** *a.*, 'both tubular and saccular' (*ibid.*). **Tu:bulostri·ate** *a.*, 'having the surface striated with hollow ribs, as some brachiopod and molluscan shells' (*Cent. Dict. Suppl.* 1909).

c 1900 *Buck's Handbk. Med. Sc.* VII. 10 Tubulosaccular.

**Tubulose** (tiū·biulōus), *a.* [ad. mod.L. *tubulōs-us*, f. L. *tubulus* TUBULE.]

**1.** = next, 1. Now *rare*.

1713 J. PETIVER in *Phil. Trans.* XXVIII. 203 Small tubulose Scarlet Flowers. 1752 J. HILL *Hist. Anim.* 268 The Trigla, with a bifid rostrum, and tubulose nostrils. 1826 KIRBY & SP. *Entomol.* IV. xlvi. 312 Tongue..Tubulose... When it..is long and tubular, and capable of inflation.

**2.** *Palæont.* Belonging to the *Tubulosa*, a group of palæozoic corals characterized by tubular thecæ.

1891 in *Cent. Dict.*

**Tubulous** (tiū·biuləs), *a.* [ad. mod.L. *tubulōs-us*; cf. F. *tubuleux* (1771 in *Dict. Trévoux*).]

**1.** Having the form of a tube; = TUBULAR 1.

1664 POWER *Exp. Philos.* I. 4 The stings in all Bees are hollow and tubulous. 1755 *Gentl. Mag.* Jan. 8/2 The flower is red and tubulous. 1826 SAMOUELLE *Direct. Collect. Insects & Crust.* 23 A very short tubulous haustellum.

**2.** Containing or composed of tubes: = TUBULAR 3. **a.** *Bot.* (See quot.) *rare*[−0].

1864 WEBSTER, *Tubulose*, *Tubulous*...2. Containing small tubes; composed wholly of tubulous florets; as, a tubulous compound flower.

**b.** Of a steam boiler: Having either fire-tubes or water-tubes.

1860 *Illustr. Lond. News* 5 May 422/3 Safety-boilers (Tubulous)..are now made with water fire-box. 1892 *Spectator* 19 Mar. 386/1 The tubulous boiler [for ships]..is growing in favour both in France and America.

Hence **Tu·bulously** *adv.*, in a tubulous form; **Tu·bulousness** (Bailey, 1727, vol. II).

1818 T. NUTTALL *Genera N. Amer. Plants* II. 80 Spatha tubulously cucullate.

**Tubulure** (tiū·biuliuɹ). [a. F. *tubulure* (Baumé, 1773), f. L. *tubul-us* TUBULE: see -URE.] A short tube, or projecting opening for the insertion of a tube, in a retort or receiver. (Cf. TUBULATED 1.)

1800 tr. *Lagrange's Chem.* I. 55 Put iron filings into a jar with two tubulures,..pour into the jar through the second tubulure diluted sulphuric acid. *Ibid.* 85 Fit to one of the tubulures of the bottle another tube. 1863 TYNDALL *Heat* i. 24 This glass bulb has three tubulures. 1883 R. HALDANE *Workshop Receipts* Ser. II. 46/1 The water enters the apparatus by the tubulure.

‖**Tubulus** (tiū·biulŭs). Pl. **tubuli** (-əi). [dim. of L. *tubus* TUBE.]

**1.** = TUBULE; in *Entom.* a tubular ovipositor.

[1681 tr. *Willis' Rem. Med. Wks.* Vocab., *Tubuli*, small little pipes, the veins and very small arteries, or little hollow parts of the bowels so called. 1704 J. HARRIS *Lex. Techn.* I, *Tubuli Lactiferi*, certain Lactiferous..Pipes..through which [the milk] flows to the Nipples.] 1826 KIRBY & SP. *Entomol.* III. xxxiii. 390 *Tubulus*. A tubular ovipositor, consisting of several pieces often retractile within each other, like the tubes of a telescope. 1878 T. BRYANT *Pract. Surg.* I. 565 The tubuli serving to convey nutrition from the pulp to the periphery.

**2.** = TUBULURE.

c 1900 *Buck's Handbk. Med. Sc.* IV. 784 A small tubulated receiver, from the *tubulus* of which a tube..is in air-tight communication.

**Tuca(n**: see TUSA. **Tucan**, var. TOUCAN.

**Tucatuca, -tucu**: see TUCUTUCU.

†**Tucet.** *Obs. rare*[−1]. [ad. L. *tūcētum*, *tuccētum* 'a kind of sausage or haggis' (Lewis and Short); cf. It. *tocchetti* 'minced meate, shread, sliced, or cut in collops' (Florio 1598), dim. f. *tocco* piece, scrap, collop.] A collop; a small piece of meat.

1653 JER. TAYLOR *Serm. for Year* I. xvi. 212 The pulse and the leeks, Lavinian sausages, and the Cisalpine tucets or gobbets of condited buls flesh [cf. *Schol. Persii* (Du Cange) Tucetum, bubula condita apud Gallos Cisalpinos condimentis crassis oblita et macerata].

**Tuch**, obs. f. TUSH *int.*

†**Tuch, tuche,** obs. ff. TOUCH (in quots. in sense 6 of TOUCH *sb.*, touchstone).

1591 HARINGTON *Orl. Fur.* XLII. lxviii, The Porch was all of Porpherie and Tuch. a 1647 HABINGTON *Surv. Worc.* in *Worc. Hist. Soc. Proc.* II. 410 Noble monuments..formed of Tuche, Marble, Alabaster and Rauns.

**Tuchet,** Sc. var. TEWHIT, the lapwing.

**Tucht,** obs. Sc. f. TOUGH. **Tucia**: see TUTTY.

**Tuck** (tʊk), *sb.*[1] Forms: 4–7 tucke, 9 *Sc.* towk, 6– tuck. [f. TUCK *v.*[1], in various senses.]

**1.** A fold or pleat in drapery; †in quot. 1613, a plait of the hair (*obs.*); now *spec.* a flattened fold (or one of several parallel folds) in a garment, secured by stitching, either to shorten the article or for ornamentation.

1387–8 T. USK *Test. Love* I. v. (Skeat) l. 132 That no iangling may greue the lest tucke of thy hemmes. 1591 PERCIVALL *Sp. Dict.*, *Alforza de vestido*, a plaite in a garment, a tucke. 1613 CHAPMAN *Maske Inns Court* A iv, Her tresses in tucks, braided with siluer. 1824 MACTAGGART *Gallovid. Encycl.*, *Towk*, a take up in ladies' clothing. 1861 *Gloucestershire Chron.* 21 Sept., 'What do you do when you have outgrown your clothes?' You throw them aside, don't you?' 'Oh, no', replied the little girl, 'we let out the tucks'. 1882 CAULFEILD & SAWARD *Dict. Needlework*, *Tucks*..are parallel folds of material, lying..on any article of dress,..either for shortening a garment, or for the purpose of ornamentation.

**2.** The gathering of the ends of the bottom planks of a ship under the stern; that part of the hull where the bottom planks are collected and terminated by the *tuck-rail* (see 8).

a 1625 *Nomenclator Navalis* (Harl. MS. 2301), *Ye Tuck*, the word is significant for it is (as you would saie) the verie gathering vp of the Ships quarter, vnder water. a 1687 PETTY *Treat. Naval Philos.* I. i, The..Stern-post, and Dead-rising up the Tuck. 1709 *Lond. Gaz.* No. 4510/7 The Hoy Burthen 9 or 10 Tun,..Moon shap'd in her Sleir, with a square Tuck. 1833 MARRYAT *P. Simple* xxvii, He's built like a Dutch schuyt, great breadth of beam, and very square tuck. c 1850 *Rudim. Navig.* (Weale) 157 The *tuck*, the aft-part of the ship where the ends of the planks of the bottom are terminated by the tuck-rail.

**3.** *Fishing.* Short for TUCK-NET.

1602 CAREW *Cornwall* I. 30 The Tucke..is narrower meashed, and..with a long bunt in the midst. 1865 COUCH *Fishes Brit. Islands* IV. 91 To take up the fish [pilchards]..the principal sean is left undisturbed, while the volyer passes within the enclosure and lays its sean, termed the Tuck, round the former on the inner side; and then the latter is drawn together so as gradually to contract the space and raise the fish to the surface.

**4.** A pluck, twitch, pull, tug; in quot. 1648 referring to the 'tucking' of freshmen at Oxford: see TUCK *v.*[1] 4 b. Now only *dial.*

1648 WOOD *Life* 15 Feb. (O.H.S.) I. 139 Nothing was given him but salted drink..with tucks to boot. 1805 A. SCOTT *Poems* 105 (Jam.) Whan thou had fairly pass'd the clips, An' a' the taylor's tukes an' nips. 1887 *Suppl. to Jamieson*, *Took*, *touk*, *towk*, a tug, pluck, pull: 'He gied her sleeve a bit took'.

**5.** The thrusting in of the ends or edges of anything so as to secure them in position. Also with *in.*

1852 MRS. STOWE *Uncle Tom's C.* xiii, She ever and anon came to the bedside, and smoothed and arranged something about the bed-clothes, and gave a tuck here and there. 1865 DICKENS *Mut. Fr.* III. ii, The sentinel smartly giving his rolled shirt-sleeves an extra tuck on the shoulders. **1900** *Daily Mail* 5 Feb. 7/1 The guimpe or tiny tuck-in chemisette.

**b.** A flap on one cover of a book, which folds over and is tucked in a band or the like on the other cover, serving to keep the book closed.

**1880** *Print. Trades Jrnl.* No. 32. 30 A double tuck, rendering a clasp of any description unnecessary. **1893** [see *tuck-cover* in 8].

**6.** *slang.* Usually *tuck-out* (also *tuck-in*): A hearty meal; esp. in school use, a feast of delicacies, a 'blow-out'.

**1823** in *Spirit Pub. Jrnls.* 232 He, being inclined for a tuck out, repaired where he was likely to meet with oysters. **1836** E. Howard *R. Reefer* xxxviii, Tell my steward to give them a good tuck-out and a glass of grog. **1844** J. T. Hewlett *Parsons & W.* xv, We meant to save all our money for the tuck. **1856** F. E. Paget *Owlet Owlst.* 172, I was at the dessert; and a jolly good tuck I had, besides. **1886** T. Hardy *Mayor Casterbr.* ix, We will have a solid, staunch tuck-in.

**b.** Food, eatables; *esp.* delicacies, as sweet-stuff, pastry, jam, etc. (*school slang*). Cf. Tucker *sb.* 6.

**1857** Hughes *Tom Brown* ii. v, The Slogger looks rather sodden, as if he didn't take much exercise and ate too much tuck. **1860** Tylor *Anahuac* viii. (1861) 210 Ten or twelve of these little bowls on the table, each with a different kind of 'tuck' in it. **1899** E. Phillpotts *Human Boy* iv. ii. 93 [He spoke] regretfully, as though he was being robbed of tuck.

**c.** A hearty appetite for food. *dial.*

**1838** Holloway *Dict. Provincialisms* s. v., 'He has a pretty good Tuck of his own', means that a man is a great eater. *Hants. Sussex.* **1847–78** Halliwell, *Tuck* (1) to eat. Also, an appetite.

**7.** Phrases. †**a.** *Ducks and tucks* (of uncertain meaning). *Obs.*

**1598** Barckley *Felic. Man* (1631) 621 Covet not to win estimation..by..Frierly ducks, and such like Italian and Spanish tricks and tuckes. **1609** Sir E. Hoby *Let. to T. H[iggons]* 106 *margin*, Leaue your ducks and your tuckes, and your apish toies, and serue God in spirit and truth.

**b.** *Nip and tuck*: see Nip *sb.*[1] 6.

**8.** *attrib.* and *Comb.* (some f. the verb-stem): **tuck-basket**, a basket used in dipping the fish from the tuck-net; **tuck-boat**, in seine-fishing, a boat which carries the tuck-net; **tuck-cover** (see 5 b); **tuck-creaser, tuck-folder**, an attachment in a sewing-machine which marks the line of, or folds down, the next tuck in readiness for stitching (Knight *Dict. Mech.* 1877); †**tuck-hole**, a hole in a ploughshare by means of which it is hooked to the beam (cf. Tuck *v.*[1] 8, quot. 1733); **tuck-hunter**, one in search of a feast; **tuck-joint**, a joint in tuck-pointing (see Tuck-point); **tuck-marker** = *tuck-creaser*; **tuck-plate**, in an iron ship, a curved plate of the hull at the point where the stern-post is bolted to the transom-frame: cf. sense 2; **tuck-rail**: see quot.; **tuck-seine** = Tuck-net. Also Tuck-mill, -net, -point, -shop.

**1883** *Fisheries Exhib. Catal.* (ed. 4) 127 *Tuck basket for taking fish out of seine. **1855** J. R. Leifchild *Cornwall Mines* 15 The '*tuck' boat then makes the inner circuit of the 'seine', the smaller net being dropped overboard as she goes. **1893** *Westm. Gaz.* 24 June 7/2 With *tuck cover (like pocket-book), and flap and pencil. **1805** R. W. Dickson *Pract. Agric.* I. Pl. v. 40 Heel to *tuck hole of share—2 ft. 6½ in...Tuck hole to point of share—8½ in. **1840** A. Bunn *Stage* I. xii. 295 Nothing can stop the mouth of a *tuck-hunter. **1879** *Cassell's Techn. Educ.* iv. 226 Rough arches ..finished off with..a '*tuck joint'. This consists in marking the divisions by a neatly raised line of fine white plaster. **1877** Knight *Dict. Mech.*, **Tuck-marker*, ..also known as a tuck-creaser, for making a crease on goods as a guide for width in making the next fold. **c 1850** *Rudim. Navig.* (Weale) 157 **Tuck-rail*, the rail which..forms a rabbet for the purpose of caulking the butt ends of the planks of the bottom [see sense 2]. **1825** *Encycl. Lond.* XX. 435/1 [In pilchard fishing] three boats belong to each sean; the first and largest is called the sean-boat...The next boat is called the vollier (follower).., and carries another sean, called the *tuck-sean, which is about 100 fathoms long, and 18 deep...The third boat is called the lurker. **1874** [see Seine *sb.*[1] β].

**Tuck** (tɒk), *sb.*[2] *arch.* and *dial.* Chiefly *Sc.* (tʊk). Forms: 5 **tuk**, 6 **tuicke**, 6–9 **touk**, 8 **tuke**, 8–9 **took**, 6– **tuck**. [f. Tuck *v.*[2]: cf. Pr. *toco*, It. *tocco* 'a stroke or knock, also a stroke of a bell or clocke', f. *toccare* 'to touch, hit, to smite, strike' (Florio).]

†**1.** A blast of a trumpet. *Obs. rare*—[1].

**c 1400** *Destr. Troy* 7107 With the tuk of a trump, all his tore knightes He assemblit full sone.

**2.** A blow, a stroke, a tap; esp. in *tuck of drum*.

**a 1500** *Battle of Harlaw* xv. in *Sel. Coll. Sc. Ballads* (1790) III. 17 With trumpets and with tuicke of drum. **1513** Douglas *Æneis* viii. iv. 119 Hercules it smyttis wyth a mychty touk Apon the richt half, for to mak it jouk. **1640–1** *Kirkcudbr. War-Comm. Min. Bk.* (1855) 23 Within eight days efter intimatione be maid thairof, aither at the severall merkat crocess, or by touk of drume, or by advertisement. **1710** Ruddiman *Douglas' Æneis* Gloss., *Touk*, stroak, blow, ..a touch, pull; as *to take a touk of any thing*, i.e. have a touch at it. **1761** in *St. Andrews Citizen* 21 Mar. (1903), Published through the city by took of drum. **1818** Scott *Hrt Midl.* xii, An open convocation of the king's lieges.. by touk of drum. **1891** *N. W. Devon Gloss.*, *Tuck*, a blow.

**b.** *fig.* or allusively.

**1825** Carlyle *Schiller* App. (1845) 259 Schubart was happy to evacuate Munich without tuck of drum. **1878** Stevenson *Inland Voy.* 85 Wherever death..sounds his own potent tuck upon the cannons.

†**3.** (?) A kiss. *Obs. rare.*

**1611** Cotgr., *Bouquer*, to take, or giue a tucke, or kisse.

**Tuck** (tɒk), *sb.*[3] *arch.* Forms: 6 **toke, tocke, touke,** *Sc.* **towk**, 6–7 **tucke**, (7 **took, touk, tuke**), 7– **tuck**. [app. ad. F. *estoc* in same sense, in OF. and Norm. dial. *étoc* = Pr. *estoc*, It. *stocco*, ad. Ger. *stock* stick.] A slender, pointed, straight, thrusting sword; a rapier. Also *transf.* and *fig.*

**1508** *Acc. Ld. High Treas. Scot.* IV. 122 Item for gilting and grathing of the lang towk,.. iiij li. **1525** *Rutland MSS.* (1905) IV. 267 For the delyverance of a toke to my Lorde, xxd. **c 1526** *Harl. MS. 4217* lf. 10 A longe Tocke iij square, the hafte of siluer. **1553** *Will of H. Cornish* (MS.), A gilte saddell..a touke, a dagger, stirropes spurres and a handgoune. **1566** Drant *Horace, Sat.* i. A j b, The Tucke, the targe, the sheilde. **1625** Darcie *Hist. Eliz.* iii. 223 To fight..in Duels, with a Rapier called a Tucke, onely for the thrust. **1647–8** Cotterell *Davila's Hist. Fr.* (1678) 25 Running him into the Visor with his Tuck. **1683** Sir J. Turner *Pallas Armata* 176 Long Rapiers and Touks. **1688** R. Holme *Armoury* iii. 91/2 A Tuck [is] a four square Blade. **a 1699** Lady Halkett *Autobiog.* (1875) 63 Run through the body with a tuke. **1707** J. Stevens tr. *Quevedo's Com. Wks.* (1709) 176 My Sword..was a stiff Tuck. **1770** Langhorne *Plutarch* (1879) II. 880/1 He appeared with a tuck, such as is used by robbers. **1826** Scott *Woodst.* i, He wore..a tuck, as it was then called, or rapier. **1885** *Harper's Mag.* Mar. 656/1 The..'tuck' or 'rapier' has been refined into the *épée* or duelling sword.

**b.** *attrib.* and *Comb.*, as *tuck-sheath*; **tuck-cane**, a cane in which a tuck or rapier is carried, serving as a sheath; a sword-cane; **tuck-fish**: see quot.; **tuck-stick** = *tuck-cane.*

**1700** S. L. tr. *Fryke's Voy. E. Ind.* 160, I had a *tuck Cane in my hand. **1785** Trusler *Mod. Times* II. 18, I.. never went out afterwards, but with a tuck cane and a brace of pistols loaded. **1681** Grew *Musæum* i. v. i. 86 The Head of the *Tuck-Fish...The Snout is not so flat as in the Rapier-fish, but thicker and rounder, more like a Tuck, from whence I take leave to name it. **1506–7** *Acc. Ld. High Treas. Scot.* III. 250 Tua *towk schethis. **1765** *Lond. Chron.* 19 Dec. 588 The master run the apprentice through the body with a *tuck-stick, which killed him.

**Tuck** (tɒk), *v.*[1] Forms: *α.* 1 **túcian, túcigan**; 3–5 **tuke**, 4 **touk**, 5 **touke**, 5–6 **toke**, 7 *Sc.* **towk.** *β.* 5 **tokke**, 5–6 **tukke, tuk**, 6–7 **tucke**, 5– **tuck.** [The forms of this verb fall into two distinct groups; the development of the senses also offers difficulties. The *α*-forms (with long vowel or diphthong) belong to senses 1 and 2 and the earlier quots. under 3; the *β*-forms (with short vowel) to the rest of sense 3 and all the other senses, beginning in 14th c. in senses 4, 7, and occurring in 15th c. in sense 6 (and in one or two later instances in sense 2). The latter appear to correspond to MLG. *tucken, tocken* to draw, pull sharply or forcibly, MDu. *tocken, tucken*, OHG. *zocchôn, zucchen* to move or remove with a jerk, snatch away, pluck, pull, mod.Ger. *zucken* to jerk, tuck, tug, *das schwert zücken*, to draw the sword. The shortening of the *ū* in OE. *túcian*, early ME. *tuke*, etc. to *u* (ɒ) in *tuck* is notable, but is paralleled by that of OE. *súcan* to Suck; cf. also Duck *v.* from ME. *dūke(n).*]

†**1.** *trans.* To afflict by way of punishment; to punish, chastise; to ill-treat, torment. *Obs.*

**c 888** K. Ælfred *Boeth.* xxxviii. § 7 Lustlice hi woldon lætan þa rican hi tucian æfter hiora agnum willan. **a 1000** *Boeth. Metr.* xxiv. 60 Unrihtwise eorðan cyningas..ðe þis werige folc wyrst tuciað. **c 1000** Ælfric *Judg.* xv. 8 He.. heora fela ofsloh and to sceame tucode. **c 1000** — *Saints' Lives* xxiii. 715 Swingan and to ealre sorȝe tuciȝan. **c 1200** *Trin. Coll. Hom.* 21 His heued [was] heled mid þornene crune and on fele wise [he was] rewliche tuked. **a 1225** *Ancr. R.* 366 He..was..so scheomeliche ituked. **c 1230** *Hali Meid.* 17 Leccherie..tukeð hire [maidenhood] al to wundre & þreat to don hire schome.

†**b.** *intr. Obs.*

**a 1250** *Owl & Night.* 63 Þu tukest wroþe & vuele Hwar þu myht ouer smale vowele.

†**2.** *fig.* To reprove, check, rebuke, find fault with; to upbraid, reproach. *Obs.*

In quot. 1584 with *up* (but sense doubtful).

**a 1225** *Leg. Kath.* 550 Ha tukeð ure godes to balewe & to bismere. **a 1225** *Ancr. R.* 316 Þet is tocne of hatunge þet men tukeð to wundre þet þing þet me hateð swuðe. **1584** B. R. tr. *Herodotus* ii. 99 The vassals hauing ended their speeche, Protheus turned hymselfe to Alexander, and tucked hym vp with thys rounde tale. **1600** in *Maitland Club Misc.* (1843) III. 102 Towking outragious countenance. **1616** *Orkney Witch Trial* in Rogers *Soc. Life Scot.* (1886) III. 298 She haid tuckit him and given him mony injurious wordis. **1651** R. Baillie *Lett. & Jrnls.* (1841) III. 163 His brother Adam Wilson towks him, calling him a fool and bidding him desist.

**3.** To dress or finish (cloth) after it comes from the weaver, esp. to stretch on tenters; cf. Tucker *sb.* 1; also *intr.* to work as a tucker. Now *local.*

*α.* [**1273**: implied in Tucker *sb.* 1.] **1377** Langl. *P. Pl.* B. xv. 447 Cloth þat cometh fro þe weuyng is nouȝt comly to were, Tyl it is fulled vnder fote or in fullyng stokkes, Wasshen wel with water and with taseles cracched, Ytouked, and ytented. **1459** in *10th Rep. Hist. MSS. Comm.* App. v. 300 It was ordayned that no woman sholde touke in no manere place aforstrete within the saide citie. **1467–8** *Rolls of Parlt.* V. 621/2 Yef..the seid Cloth [were] toked and fulled within this your Reame, your Highnes shuld have the Custume and Awnage for the same. **1513–14** *Act* 5 *Hen. VIII*, c. 2 Noo person make noo such Clothys..to sell without that he be whan he is rawe redy to be tokyd of the brede of a yerde and half quarter.

*β.* **1621** in Harding *Hist. Tiverton* (1817) II. 181 Not.. white weavers or tuckers that make white kersies, but.. such as weave and tuck upon coloured mixed kerseys. **1780** A. Young *Tour Irel.* II. 34 A mill for milling, tucking, &c. broad cloths. **1837** Whittock, etc. *Bk. Trades* (1842) 255 After the process of fulling and dyeing, the dressed cloths are..pricked on the tenter hooks and stretched to their utmost bearing...This is considered as *tucking*, in the west of England. **1882** Jago *Cornw. Gloss.*, *Tucking*, working in a fulling-mill.

**4.** † To tug at; to snatch, pluck, pull; to gather (herbs, fruit, etc.) (*obs.*); now *spec.* to pluck or pull the loose hay from the sides of (a new rick) (*dial.*).

**13..** *K. Alis.* 2305 (Bodl. MS.), Als he hit [his weapon] tukked [*v.r.* toggid], out to habbe, Philot hym ȝaf anothere dabbe. **1625** T. Godwin *Moses & Aaron* iii. iii. 125 They held it vnlawfull, to roste an apple, to tucke an herbe, to climbe a tree, to kill or catch a flea. **1658** tr. *Porta's Nat. Magic* iv. xi. 136 You must tuck them off the Tree with your hand. *Ibid.* [see Tucker *sb.* 2]. **1794** P. Foot *Agric. Middlesex* 57 The hay-farmer pays great attention to have the stack well tucked and thatched. **1888** Elworthy *W. Somerset Word-bk.* s.v., Now, Bob, don't bethink thy vingers, tuck'n in tight, mind—i. e. pull it out until you get to the solid mass.

†**b.** See quot. 1647. *Obs.*

**c 1640** Shaftesb. in *Remin. Oxford* (O.H.S.) 37, I caused that ill custom of tucking freshmen [at Oxford] to be left off. **1647** Wood *Life* Dec. (O.H.S.) I. 134 If any of the freshmen came off dull, or not cleverly, some of the forward or pragmaticall seniors would 'tuck' them, that is, set the nail of their thumb to their chin, just under the lower lipp, and by the help of their other fingers under the chin, they would give him a mark, which sometimes would produce blood.

**5.** *Fishing.* To take the fish from (the seine) by means of a *tuck-net*; also with the fish as object.

**1786** *Act* 26 *Geo. III*, c. 26 § 11 (Cod fishing) It shall not be lawful..to use..any Sean or Net..for the Purpose of catching Cod Fish by hauling such Sean or Net on Shore, or tucking such Sean or Net into any Boat or Boats, the Scale or Mesh of which said Sean or Net shall be less in Dimension than Four Inches. **1857** *Morning Chron.* 28 Aug. (Cassell's), 185 hogsheads [of pilchards] were tucked on Sunday. **1866** *Standard* 3 Oct. 3/4 All these [i. e. seines] have enclosed fish, which are being tucked, and many thousands of hogsheads are expected to be landed. **1879** *Encycl. Brit.* IX. 254/2 'Tucking' the fish..is performed with the tuck-sean,..and as it is hauled in, the foot of the bunt is raised so as to bring the fish to the surface, whence they are dipped out in large baskets and put into attendant boats to be carried on shore.

**6.** To pull or gather up in a fold or folds; to fold or turn up; *esp.* to gird up (a garment, etc.). Usually const. *up.*

**c 1440** *Promp. Parv.* 504/2 Tukkyn vp, or stykkyn vp (*K.* tuckyn or stychyn up clothis), .. *suffarcino.* **1513** Douglas *Æneis* v. x. 21 Thair haris all war tukkit wp on thar croun. **1523** Fitzherb. *Husb.* § 151 Theyr cotes be so syde [=long] that they be fayne to tucke them vp whan they ryde. **1590** Spenser *F. Q.* iii. ix. 21 Her well-plighted frock, which she did won To tucke about her short when she did ryde. **1687** A. Lovell tr. *Thevenot's Trav.* i. 156 They are tuck'd aside, that the Diamonds may not be covered. **1756** Mrs. Calderwood in *Coltness Collect.* (Maitl. Cl.) 218 All the Capucines..were marching in sixes and sevens with their gowns tucked up, great fat carles. **1835–6** *Todd's Cycl. Anat.* I. 479/1 The intestines are.. tucked up into folds and sacs. **1840** Dickens *Old C. Shop* iii, He tucked up his sleeves and squared his elbows. **1880** 'Ouida' *Moths* I. 77 The stout north countrywoman tucked up her petticoats, and began to climb up the steep path with a will. **1885** *Cornh. Mag.* Mar. 283 Priests sitting with their legs tucked up tailor-wise, in the attitude of Buddha.

**b.** To put a tuck or tucks in; to shorten or ornament with tucks.

**1626** *Vestry Bks.* (Surtees) 181 Item for tuckeinge up the surples, xij d. **1709** [see Tucked *ppl. a.* 1]. **1873** Eliz. Phelps *Trotty's Wedding Tour* 126 She tucked the pantalets, darned the stockings.

**7.** To pull or gather up and confine the loose garments of; to gird (a person) *up.* Chiefly in *pa. pple.* Now *rare.*

**c 1385** Chaucer *L. G. W.* 982 (*Dido*) Saw ȝe..Onye of myne susteryn..I-tukkid [*v. r.* Itucked] vp with arwis in hire cas? **c 1386** — *Sompn. T.* 29 With scrippe and tipped staf, ytukked [*v.rr.* tucked, tukked, tokked] hye In euery hous, he gan to poure and prye. **c 1440** *Generydes* 4397 Tokkyd vppe she [the queen] was well fro the grounde. **c 1450** in Aungier *Syon* (1840) 342 Some of the brethren tukke the mynysters..in the begynnyng of masse, and also tuk the confessour whan he taketh the cope aboute the ende of the same masse. **1483** Caxton *Gold. Leg.* 160/2 A pylgrym tucked and made redy for to goo hastely ouer see. **1558** Phaer *Æneid* i. Bj, Tukt she was that naked was her knee. **1566** Drant *Horace, Sat.* viii. D viij b, Bare foote, hyr lockes about her heade, ytuckde in pukishe frocke. **1727** [see Tucked *ppl. a.* 1]. **a 1801** Bloomfield *Rural T., Rich. & Kate* xi, Who, snug tuck't up, walk'd slow behind. **1841** Orderson *Creol.* ix. 96 She was..'tucked up', in the indecorous manner of those days.

**b.** To shorten or short-coat (an infant). Usually with *up. dial.*

**1888** Elworthy *W. Somerset Word-bk.* s.v., I was a-frightened to zee the cheel a-tuck'd up a'ready. **1901** E. Phillpotts *Striking Hours* 135 Afore I was tucked-up, or, as you might say, 'short-coated', her went..down to Cornwall. **a 1905** in *Eng. Dial. Dict.* s.v., Tuck it in May, Tuck it away.

**c.** *fig.* To cramp or hamper by lack of space, time, or means. See also Tucked *ppl. a.* 2 c.

**1886** *Field* 13 Feb. 179/3 They [fox-hunters] have been

playing the old game of skirting, eventually to find themselves fairly tucked up by wire-fencing. **1887** [see TUCKED *ppl. a.* 2 c]. **1890** 'R. BOLDREWOOD' *Col. Reformer* xxvii, In England you have your bad seasons..; and the poor man..gets tucked up a bit.

**8.** To thrust or put away (an object) into a close place where it is snugly held or concealed.

**1587** TURBERV. *Trag. T.* (1837) 195 Shee tuckt it [the head] in her apron close. **1621–3** MIDDLETON & ROWLEY *Changeling* IV. i, Folio forty-five, here 'tis, The leaf tuck'd down upon it. **1710** STEELE *Tatler* No. 164 ⁋ 6, To carry Pistols about me, which I have always tuck'd within my Girdle. **1733** W. ELLIS *Chiltern & Vale Farm.* 321 The Sharr also is tuck'd up to the Beam by an Iron-hook. **1781** COWPER *Truth* 147 The shivering urchin..Carries her Bible tucked beneath his arm. **1861** GEO. ELIOT *Silas M.* i, Finding the well-known bag, empty, tucked behind the chest of drawers. **1874** BURNAND *My time* xxxii. 329 He tucked his wife's arm under his own. **1912** W. B. SELBIE *Nonconformity* xii. 225 The little old meeting-houses tucked away in back streets gave place to large and commodious buildings.

**9.** To thrust in the edge or end of (anything pendent or loose) so as to retain or confine it; now *esp.* to turn in the edges of (bed-coverings or the like) under the bed or its occupant. With various advbs., esp. *in*, *up*.

**1635** QUARLES *Embl.* III. ix. 37 Snares tuck thy bed. **1697** DAMPIER *Voy.* I. xii. 327 They gather it in their Hands,.. tucking in the twisted part between their Waste and the edge of the Petticoat, which keeps it close. **1746** JAMESON in A. McKAY *Hist. Kilmarnock* (1880) 83 Tucking his shirt under the waistcoat, that it might not obstruct the blow. **1843** SIR C. SCUDAMORE *Med. Visit Gräfenberg* 102 Early in the morning, the bed-clothes were tucked up tight about him, so as to retain the animal heat. **1852** THACKERAY *Esmond* III. iii, A nymph that can tuck my bed-clothes up. **1905** ELIN. GLYN *Viciss. Evang.* 169 Mr. Carruthers .. tucked his sable rug round me.

**b.** With the person as object. Also *fig.*

**1692** LOCKE *Educ.* § 22 To have his Maid tuck him in warm. **1739** 'R. BULL' tr. *Dedekindus' Grobianus* 225 The Muse would willingly..tuck you in, and then put out the Light. **1809** MALKIN *Gil Blas* VII. xvi. ⁋4 The nurse forced me under the bedclothes again, and tucked me up. **1854** EMERSON *Lett. & Soc. Aims, Resources* Wks. (Bohn) III. 199 Nature keeps the lakes warm by tucking them up under a blanket of ice.

**c.** *intr.* To draw together, contract, pucker.

**1797** *Encycl. Brit.* (ed. 3) XVIII. 102/2 When an ulcer becomes foul,..the edges of it, in process of time, tuck in. **1899** *Allbutt's Syst. Med.* VI. 834 Another symptom..is a tucking-up of one or both of the upper lids.

**10.** *slang.* **a.** *trans.* To consume, swallow (food or drink); to 'put away', 'put out of sight'.

**1784** R. BAGE *Barham Downs* I. 191 We will dine together; tuck up a bottle or two of claret. **1833** MARRYAT *P. Simple* xi, Now that I've cured you, you'll be tucking all that into your own little breadbasket. *a* **1845** BARHAM *Ingol. Leg.*, *House-warming*, The strawberries.. Which our Grandmother's Uncle tuck'd in like a pig. **1861** HOLLAND *Less. Life* xii. 144 Let's go over and see if we can't tuck away some of that grub.

**b.** *intr.* To feed heartily or greedily; esp. with *in*, *into*.

**1810** [see TUCKING *vbl. sb.*[1] 4]. **1838** DICKENS *Nich. Nick.* xxxix, If you'll just let little Wackford tuck into something fat. **1860** THACKERAY *Round. Papers* vii, There is Rasherwell 'tucking' away in the coffee-room. **1887** EDNA LYALL *Knight-Errant* xv. (1889) 129 Always in at dinner-time and to be found at odd hours tucking in.

†**c.** *trans.* To distend with food; to fill *out*. *Obs. rare*[−1].

**1824** in *Spirit Pub. Jrnls.* (1825) 304 He had been 'Taking his ease in his inn',..and feeling himself comfortably tucked out, he wished to bolt.

**11.** *slang.* To hang (a criminal); usually with *up*.

*a* **1700** B. E. *Dict. Cant. Crew*, *Tuck't*, Hang'd. **1738** tr. *Guazzo's Art Conversation* 231, I expect..to see him tucked up to a Gibbet. **1755** H. WALPOLE *Lett.* (1846) III. 142 Poor Fanny! I always thought she would play till she would be forced to tuck herself up! **1825–9** MRS. SHERWOOD *Lady of Manor* V. xxix. 100, I wish some one had tucked him up before he had made acquaintance with this house.

**b.** To hang (a bell) high in the stock.

**1860** BECKETT *Clocks, Watches*, etc. (ed. 4) 424 A large bell may be tolled easily by one man, if it is properly hung, though not if it is 'tucked up in the stock'.

**12.** = TUCK-POINT *v.*

**1803** *Usef. Proj.* in *Ann. Reg.* 829/2 Tucking and pointing all stone and brick works that require proof against water and damp.

**Tuck** (tɒk), *v.*[2] Now *dial.* Chiefly *Sc.* (tʊk). Forms: 4–5 **tukke**, 5 **tuke**, 5–7 **touk**, 6 **tuik**, 7 **touck**, **-e**, **towke**, 9 **took**, **towk**, 7– **tuck**. [a. ONF. *toker*, *toquer*, *touker* (*a* 1400 in Godef. *Compl.*) to touch, strike, northern form of *toucher* to TOUCH, = Prov., Sp., Pg. *tocar*, It. *toccare* 'to touch, hit, to smite, strike' (Florio): cf. also TOCSIN.]

**1.** *trans.* and *intr.* To touch (*rare*); to beat the drum; also *intr.* of a drum: To sound.

**13..** *E. E. Allit. P.* B. 1414, & ay þe nakeryn noyse, notes of pipes, Tymbres & tabornes, tukket [*MS.* tulket] among. *a* **1400–50** *Alexander* 2427 Þe Tebies tukkid [*MSS.* tulkid, -yd] vs with tene, a-tired þam in armes. *a* **1500** *Battle of Harlaw* xviii. in *Sel. Coll. Sc. Ballads* (1790) III. 17 The trumpet sounds, The dandring drums aloud did tuik. **1629** *Reg. Privy Council Scot.* Ser. II. III. 5 The said James.. caused ring the kirk bell and towke thair drwm. **1642** *Burgh Rec. Glasgow* 12 Feb. (1876) 437 Ordains the drummers to touk throughe the toun. *a* **1670** SPALDING *Troub. Chas. I* (1850) I. 202 Trvmpettis soundis and drumis tovkis. **1887** *Suppl. to Jamieson*, *Took*, *touk*, *towk*, to strike, beat, blow, tuck; as, 'to took the drum'.

†**2.** *trans.* To sound a blast on (a trumpet); to blow *up*. *Obs. rare.*

*a* **1400–50** *Alexander* 773 With þat þai tuke vp [*v.r.* tukkyn vp] þaire trompes.

**3.** *intr.* Of the wind: To blow in gusts. *dial.*

**1833** D. M'KAY in *Rec. & Bards Angus & Mearns* (1897) 301, I have wondered full oft as it [the hurricane] tookit and blew, If ever its sughin was leerie to you. **1893** *Wiltshire Gloss.* s.v., 'The wind is so tucking to-day', i. e. gusty, veering.

†**Tuck, tucka, tucke,** obs. ff. TOQUE, in sense of 'a kerchief worn on the head', or 'a turban'.

**1505** in *Facsimiles Nat. MSS.* I. (1865) 92 And as to hir forehed, the heighte or the breid therof, we cowde not perfectly diserne, for the maner of the wereynge of the kerches or tuckas in that contry ys suche that a man can nott welle Iuge hit. **1553** A. JENKINSON *Voy. & Trav.* (Hakl. Soc.) I. 3 Vpon his head a goodly white tuck, containing in length by estimation fifteene yards. **1582** N. LICHEFIELD tr. *Castanheda's Conq. E. Ind.* I. iv. 14 Vpon their heads they weare a certeine kinde of tucks or kerchiefe somewhat wrought with silke and gold thrid.

†**Tu·ckage.** *Obs. rare*[−1]. [f. TUCK *v.*[1] + -AGE.] Tucking, cloth-dressing.

**1612** STURTEVANT *Metallica* 46 Winde water milnes..for tuckeage, and fulleage of wollen cloath.

**Tuckahoe** (tɒ·kăhō). *U.S.* Forms: 7 **tockwough, tockawhough, -waugh,** 8 **tuccaho,** 8–9 **tuckahoo,** 7– **tuckahoe.** [ad. Powhatan or Virginian (N. Amer. Indian) *tockawhoughe*, app. cognate with Mohegan *tquogh*, Shawnee *tukwhah*. Webster (1911) compares Natick *petukqunneg* cake of bread, f. *petukqui* round, Cree *pitikwaw* made round.]

**1.** A name applied by North American Indians (esp. of Virginia) to edible roots of various plants: see *Report of Smithsonian Inst.* 1881, pp. 687–701.

**1612** CAPT. SMITH *Map Virginia* 22 In Iune, Iulie, and August they feede vpon the rootes of *Tockwough* [printed *-nough*], berries, fish and greene wheat. **1612** *Proc. Virginia* 87 in *Capt. Smith's Wks.* (Arb.) 155 Others would gather as much *Tockwough* roots in a day as would make them bread a weeke. **1662** *Laws of Virginia* cxxxvi. 77 The poor Indians, whom, the seating of the English, hath forced from their wonted Conveniences of..gathering Tuckahoe, Cortenions, and other Wild-Fruits. **1671** OGILBY *Amer.* 196 Their peculiar roots are the tockawaugh, good to eat [etc.].

**a.** Among these are or were the thick and starchy root-stocks of certain araceous plants, particularly *Peltandra undulata* or *Virginica* (formerly *Arum Virginicum*), the Arrow Arum, and *Orontium aquaticum*, the Golden-Club.

**1613** PURCHAS *Pilgrimage* VIII. v. 635 [The aborigines of Virginia] haue two rootes;..the other called Tockawhough, growing like a flagge, of the greatnesse and tast of a Potato, which passeth a fierie purgation before they may eate it, being poison whiles it is raw. **1705** BEVERLEY *Virginia* III. iv. (1722) 153 A tuberous Root they call Tuckahoe, which while crude is of a very hot and virulent Quality: But they can manage..to make Bread of it. **1770** J. R. FORSTER *Kalm's Trav. N. Amer.* (1772) I. 225 To judge by these qualities the Tuckahoo was very likely be the Arum Virginicum.

**b.** Now app. restricted to an underground tuber-like production (*Pachyma Cocos*, Fries, *Lycoperdon solidum*, Clayton), prob. the sclerotium of some fungus, parasitic on tree-roots in the southern parts of North America, the affinities of which are uncertain. Also called *Indian bread*, *Indian loaf*, *Indian head*, and *tuckahoe truffle*.

**1731** CATESBY *Nat. Hist. Carolina*, etc. p. x, Indians also eat the earth nuts which they call tuccaho. **1782** T. JEFFERSON *Notes State Virginia* (1787) 58 Tuckahoe. *Lycoperdon tuber.* **1816** in *Massachusetts Spy* 23 Oct. (Thornton), The name of Tuckahoe..has also been applied to the Troffle. **1866** *Treas. Bot.*, *Tuckahoo*,..a curious tuberous production,..has been referred by Fries to the genus *Pachyma*.

**2.** A nickname for the lowlands of Virginia; also for an inhabitant of this district. *local U. S.*

**1817** J. K. PAULDING *Lett. fr. South* I. x. 112 The people [west of the Blue Ridge] call those east of the mountain Tuckahoes, and their country Old Virginia. **1835** *Lett. Virginia Springs* (Philad.) 16–17 (Thornton) [The Blue Ridge] divides the Ancient Dominion into two nations, called Tuckahoes and Quo'hees; the former inhabiting the lowland. **1848–60** BARTLETT *Dict. Amer.* s. v., Tuckahoe is often applied to an inhabitant of Lower Virginia, and to the poor land in that portion of the State.

**Tucked** (tɒkt), *ppl. a.* [f. TUCK *v.*[1] (and *sb.*[1]) in various senses + -ED.]

**1.** Gathered or girded *up*, arranged in tucks or folds; † of a person: having the clothes girded up (*obs.*); shortened or ornamented with tucks; thrust or doubled in; poked *in* or *away* so as to be retained in position; enveloped, covered snugly *up*.

**1530** PALSGR. 327/2 Tucked up as ones clothes is, *rebroucé*. **1582** STANYHURST *Æneis* III. (Arb.) 75, I knew theire tucktlocks. **1709** STEELE *Tatler* No. 30 ⁋ 9 With blue and red Stockings in Morning; tuck'd Cravats, and Nightcap Wigs. **1727** SWIFT *City Shower* 37 The tuck'd-up semstress walks with hasty strides. **1823** SCOTT *Quentin D.* xxii, The butcher ..was distinguished by his tucked-up sleeves. **1883** 'SYLVIA' *Lady's Guide Dressmaking* 107, 4 tucked flannel petticoats. **1913** *Play Pictorial* No. 131. p. vi/1 A prettily tucked chemisette of soft French net.

**2.** *Tucked up* (of a dog or horse): having the flanks drawn in from hunger, malnutrition, or fatigue; hence, tired out, exhausted. Cf. TUCKER *v.*, *tuckered*. *slang* and *dial.*

**1845** YOUATT *Dog* ii. 18 They generally are very thin,.. with sharp-pointed ears, deep chest, and tucked-up flanks. **1888** ELWORTHY *W. Somerset Word-bk.*, *Tucked up*, applied to animals, especially horses after hard riding—looking thin. Th' old mare's a bit a-tucked up. **1891** KIPLING *Light that Failed* iii. 43 'You're looking tucked up', he concluded.

**b.** Said of a bell that is hung high in the stock.

**1874** BECKETT *Clocks, Watches*, etc. (ed. 6) 366 It is difficult to set a much tucked-up bell tolling, though easy to keep it up afterwards.

**c.** Hampered or cramped for lack of space, time, means, etc. *colloq.*

**1887** BURY & HILLIER *Cycling* iv. 189 A closely built fifty-eight inch racer will be noticeably too short in the reach for him, and he will feel that he is what cyclists call 'tucked up', 'cramped', or 'going short'. **1889** *N. W. Linc. Gloss.* s.v., We're terrible tucked up e' this little hoose...Oats is ripenin' that fast we shall be tucked up for time to get 'em afoore thaay begins to shak. **1891** *Cent. Dict.* s.v., At Billiards the player is said to be tucked-up when his ball lies close under the cushion.

**3.** *Naut.* (in combination): Having a tuck (TUCK *sb.*[1] 2) of a specified shape.

**1867** SMYTH *Sailor's Word-bk.* s. v. *Tuck*, The fir frigates of 1812–14 had flat, square transoms similar to boats, or heart-shaped. Hence our square-tucked frigates, brigs, &c.

**Tucker** (tɒ·kəɹ), *sb.* Forms: 4 **toukere**, 5 **tokker,** (**toucher**), **towkere**, 5–6 **towker, touker, toker,** (6 **towcker, toukar, toocker, tooker, tukkar**), 6– **tucker.** [f. TUCK *v.*[1] + -ER[1].]

**1.** One whose occupation is the fulling and dressing of cloth; a fuller; a cloth-finisher. *Obs.* exc. *dial.* Perh. originally one who burled or teased the cloth.

*Tucker's earth*, fuller's earth.

[**1273** *Hundred Rolls, Dorset*, Roger le Tukere. **13..** *Fine Rolls*, Nicholas le Tokere.] **1388** WYCLIF 2 *Kings* xviii. 17 The water cundijt of the hiȝere cisterne,..in the weie of the fullere, [*gloss*] ethir toukere [1382 the fullers feeld]. *c* **1475** *Pol. Poems* (Rolls) II. 285 A ordynaunce..for spynners, carders, wevers, also, Ffor toukers, dyers, and schermyn. **1496** *Somerset Medieval Wills* (1901) 344 To my wevers and tokers thorow the towne xij d a pece. **1506** *Will of Abadam* (Somerset Ho.), Tucker's schers. **1545** ELYOT, *Gnafos*, a tesyll, whiche toukars do vse. **1603** HOLLAND *Plutarch's Mor.* 1231 [Crœsus] caught one of the nobles, ..and within a fullers mill all to beclawed and mangled him with tuckers cards and burling combs. **1610** W. FOLKINGHAM *Art of Survey* I. ii. 4 Tuckers or Fullers Earth. **1615** BRATHWAIT *Strappado* (1878) 174 Where errant pedlers, mercinarie slaues, Tinkers and Tookers and such idle knaues. **1636** in E. Owen *Catal. MSS. relating to Wales in Brit. Mus.* (1908) 724 Ground for the erection of .. tentors or tucker's rackes. **1745** *De Foe's Eng. Tradesman* xx. (1841) I. 193 Cloth-workers, tuckers, and merchants. **1837** WHITTOCK, etc. *Bk. Trades* (1842) 253 Wool could not be spun without being combed in oil; nor would it take the dye when woven, unless divested of the oil. This is the proper business of the Fuller;..provincially called, the *Tucker*. **1888** ELWORTHY *W. Somerset Word-bk.*, *Tucker*, one who mills, or fulls and finishes cloth...Probably the entire finishing of the cloth, from the time it left the weaver, was performed by the tucker at the tucking-mills.

†**2.** An instrument for tucking or plucking; *pair of tuckers*, tweezers. *Obs. rare*[−1].

**1658** tr. *Porta's Nat. Magic* IV. x. 133 Tuck away the dry, and withered, and rotten grapes with a pair of tuckers.

**3.** A piece of lace or the like, worn by women within or around the top of the bodice in the 17–18th c.; a frill of lace worn round the neck. *Best bib and tucker*: see BIB *sb.*[1] b.

**1688** R. HOLME *Armoury* III. 17/1 A Pinner or Tucker, is a narrow piece of Cloth..which compasseth the top of a Womans Gown about the Neck part. **1710** LADY GRISELL BAILLIE *Househ. Bk.* (1911) 204 For musline for night cloathes, ruffles, tuckers, etc. £3. 4. 0. **1793** J. WILLIAMS *Life Ld. Barrymore* 67 The Butcher's Lady thinks, that living in style, is manifested in putting on her best bib and tucker on holidays. **1847** C. BRONTE *J. Eyre* vii, Some of the girls have two clean tuckers in the week;..the rules limit them to one. **1875** [see BIB *sb.*[1] b]. **1881** E. F. POYNTER *Among Hills* I. 150 Pulling out her white tucker round her white throat.

**4.** One who tucks; in quot. in sense 9.

**1796** *Grose's Dict. Vulg. T.* (ed. 3) s.v. *Tucked up*, A tucker up to an old bachelor or widower; a supposed mistress.

**5.** *Needlework.* One who makes or 'runs' tucks; the device in a sewing-machine which does this.

**1905** *Daily Chron.* 11 Aug. 10/7 Machinists..,shirts and blouses; also a few vacancies for tuckers.

**6.** [f. TUCK *sb.*[1] 6 or *v.*[1] 10.] The daily supply of food of a gold-digger or station-hand; rations, meals; also, food generally, victuals: = TUCK *sb.*[1] 6 b. *To earn* or *make one's tucker*, to earn merely enough to pay for one's keep. *Australian slang.*

**1858** *Morn. Chron.* 31 Aug. (Farmer), Diggers, who have great difficulty in making their tucker at digging. **1874** G. WALCH *Head over Heels* 73 For want of more nourishing tucker, I believe they'd have eaten him. **1883** A. FORBES in *Contemp. Rev.* Oct. 606 A peer's son who is earning his 'tucker' as a station cook in New Zealand. **1898** M. DAVITT *Life & Progr. Australia* xl. 275 A pound of a week, including lodgings and 'tucker'.

*attrib.* **1890** 'R. BOLDREWOOD' *Miner's Right* iv, Cyrus and Joe will go splitting or fencing..to pay the tucker-bill. **1902** H. LAWSON *Children of Bush* 88 There's some women that can never see a tucker-bag, even if you hold it right under their noses. **1902** *Westm. Gaz.* 30 July 2/1 Weird dishes in which every ingredient in the 'tucker box' struggles for mastery. **1904** *Daily Chron.* 21 Mar. 5/5 It is no time to be mealy-mouthed when capitalists..want slave workers at tucker wages.

**Tucker** (tʊ·kəɹ), *v. New Eng. colloq.* [f. Tuck *v.*[1]; cf. Tucked *ppl. a.* 2.] *trans.* To tire, to weary; usually *tucker out*; esp. in pa. pple. *tuckered out*, worn out, exhausted. Hence **Tu·cker** *sb.*, the state of being tired out (*Cent. Dict.* 1891).

*c* **1840** *Story of Bee Tree* (Bartlett), I'm clear tuckered out with these young ones. **1853** *Turnover* vi. 59 Set us to runnin', an' I could tucker him. **1862** Lowell *Biglow P.*, *Mason & Slidell* 12 Hard work is good an' wholesome, past all doubt; But 't ain't so, ef the mind gits tuckered out. **1879** Howells *L. Aroostook* xxiii, She's tired to death—quite tuckered, you know. **1890** S. W. Baker *Wild Beasts* I. 378 The old bear got regularly tuckered-out.

**Tucket** [1] (tʊ·kėt). *arch.* Also 7 **tucquet**. [Connected with Tuck *sb.*[2]; cf. Toccata, also OF. *touchet* blow, stroke (*c* 1500 in Godef. *Compl.*).] A flourish on a trumpet; a signal for marching used by cavalry troops. (Cf. Sennet [1].) Also *fig.*

**1593** Shaks. *Rich. II*, i. iii. 26 (*Stage direct.*) Tucket. Enter Hereford, and Harold [Herald; the lists at Coventry]. **1599** — *Hen. V*, iv. ii. 35 Then let the Trumpets sound The Tucket Sonuance, and the Note to mount. **1601** — *All's Well* iii. v, (*Stage direct.*) A Tucket afarre off. Enter old Widdow of Florence [etc.]. **1605** *1st Pt. Ieronimo* i. v, (*Stage direct.*) A Tucket within. *King.* How now, what means this trumpets sound? **1623** Webster *Devil's Law-Case* v. vi, (*Stage direct.*) Two tuckets by several trumpets. **1625** Markham *Soldier's Accid.* 61 The fourth [sound or signal given by the trumpet] is, Tucquet, or March; Which being hearde simplie of it selfe..Commands nothing but Marching after the Leader. **1889** W. B. Squire in Grove *Dict. Mus.* IV. 184. **1891** G. Meredith *One of our Conq.* 242 A tucket of herald newspapers told the world of Victor's returning to his London.

**Tucket** [2] (tʊ·kėt). *local U.S.* [Origin obscure; perh. ad. F. *toquet*, dim. of *toque* cap.] A small ear of Indian corn in the unripe milky stage.

**1874** J. T. Trowbridge *Coupon Bonds* etc. 253 He had made, during the day, frequent deposits of green corn, of the diminutive species called *tucket*. **1889** Farmer *Americanisms*, *Tucket*, the young green ear of Indian corn. Gathered when soft, and cooked in milk.

[**Tucket**, erron. f. Tucet, a steak, a collop.]

**Tuck-in**, act of feasting: see Tuck *sb.*[1] 6.

**Tu·cking**, *vbl. sb.*[1] [f. Tuck *v.*[1] + -ing [1].]

† **1.** The fulling and dressing of cloth. *Obs.*

**1467–8** [see Tucking-mill]. **1530** in Weaver *Wells Wills* (1890) 24 All that belongyth to my crafte of tokynge and sherynge. *c* **1640** J. Smyth *Lives Berkeleys* (1883) I. 167 The..charges in the wholl manufactory..in..Tuckinge, shearinge, dying, dressinge and the like.

**2.** *Fishing.* The taking of fish from the seine with the tuck-net.

**1847** *Zoologist* V. 1706 On tucking, all the fish were discovered to be dead. **1888** *Argosy* 279 To get the fish [pilchards] out of the seine is the next operation..this is called tucking, and it is carried on by means of a small net or tuck net.

**3.** The gathering or girding up of one's garments; *concr.* the part or fold so gathered; also, the putting of tucks in a garment; *concr.* a tuck, or tucks collectively.

*c* **1440** *Promp. Parv.* 504/2 Tukkynge vp (of clothys, or stykkynge..), *suffarci(naci)o*. **1713** *Guardian* No. 10 ⁋ 7 The taking and tucking up of gowns. **1880** *Plain Hints Needle-work* 22 Tucking..is used both as ornament, and for elongation when the material has shrunk. **1893** *Athenæum* 7 Oct. 498/1 A higher tucking of the picturesque and flowing robes.

**4.** The action of putting anything away so that it is snugly covered or concealed, or of thrusting in something, as a bed-covering, so as to confine it at the end or edge; hence (*slang*) *tucking in*, hearty or greedy feeding; also *concr.*

**1810** *Splendid Follies* I. 186 Tom Sponge now began cramming unmercifully, exclaiming every three mouthfuls, 'Rare tucking in, Sir William'. **1833** Macaulay *Ess.*, *Walpole* (1897) 272 Whose vast volume of wig and infinite length of riband had figured at the dressing or at the tucking up of Louis the Fourteenth. **1874** J. Brown *Lett.* in *Recoll.* (1893) 65 This tucking [of the leg of a fowl under its wing]..was due to the force automatic. **1876** Besant & Rice *Gold. Butterfly* (1877) 196 They gave themselves unreservedly to 'tucking in'. **1884** Roe *Nat. Ser. Story* vi, High winds and frosty nights prompted to careful covering and tucking away.

**5.** *attrib.*, as **tucking-bush**, the dwarf juniper, *Juniperus nana*; **tucking-comb**, a comb confining the hair; **tucking-gauge**: see quot.; †**tucking-girdle**, a girdle worn with the alb, which is drawn through it until the skirt is of the proper length; **tucking-maund**, a tuck-basket (Tuck *sb.*[1] 8); † **tucking-shear(s**, shears used in cloth-finishing; † **tucking-stock**, a fulling-stock or fulling-mill. See also Tucking-mill.

**1890** W. P. Lett in *Big Game N. Amer.* 88 Large patches of '*tucking-bushes', or dwarf juniper, which grow about breast-high, with strong branches stiffly interlaced. **1895** S. B. Kennedy in *Outing* (U.S.) XXVII. 11/2 He stopped and held up a gold-tipped *tucking comb. **1877** Knight *Dict. Mech.*, **Tucking-gage*, an attachment for marking tucks at a determinate distance ready for the next line of sewing. **1487–8** *Rec. St. Mary at Hill* 131 Item, for a dossen *tuckyng gyrdilles, x d. **1490–1** in Swayne *Sarum Churchw. Acc.* (1896) 37 For tukkynge girdillis for Awbis, iiij d. **1499–1500** *Ibid.* 51 For a dossyn Tokynggirdels for the Vestre, xij d. **1530** Palsgr. 283/2 Tuckyng gyrdell [*printed* kyrdell], *saincture a ecourter* [printed *ecourser*]. **1896** *Gd. Words* Jan. 18/1 The '*tucking-maund' is..a somewhat shallow basket, through which water may readily escape, but mackerel cannot. **1478** *Croscombe Churchw. Acc.* (Som. Rec. Soc.) 6 A *tokyng shere. **1533** in Weaver *Wells Wills* (1890) 102 My son Thomas..ii pere of tokyne sherys. **1778** *Eng. Gazetteer* (ed. 2) s.v. *Staverton*, Staverton, Wilts, on the Avon,..has 4 *tucking-stocks and 2 grist-mills.

† **Tu·cking**, *vbl. sb.*[2] *Obs.* or *arch.* [f. Tuck *v.*[2] + -ing [1].] Touching; beating of a drum.

*c* **1485** *Digby Myst.* (1882) iii. 969 Whan he towcheyd it with his toukkyng, þey brast as ony glase, and rofe asonder, as it byn with thondor. **1632** Lithgow *Trav.* vii. 316 Singing, touching of kettle Drummes, sounding of Trumpets, and other ostentations of ioy.

**Tu·cking-mill.** [f. Tucking *vbl. sb.*[1] + Mill *sb.*[1]] See quot. 1888. (A West of England term.)

**1467–8** *Rolls of Parlt.* V. 587/1 A Water Mille 11 Tokyng Milles and Medowes, Pastures and Wodes. **1555** *Act 2 & 3 Phil. & Mary* c. 11 § 4 No..Weaver..shall..kepe or have any Tucking Mill. **1617** Sir R. Boyle *Diary* in *Lismore Papers* (1886) I. 176, I made him a new lease of thowld Tucking myll. **1796** W. Marshall *W. England* I. Gloss. (E.D.S.) *Tucking-mill*, fulling-mill. **1810** J. T. *Risdon's Surv. Devon* p. xxiv, The traces of ruined tucking mills, as they were provincially called,..denote the former extent of the manufactory. **1888** Elworthy *W. Somerset Word-bk.*, *Tucking-mill*,..fuller's stocks, or beaters for milling cloth. The term is also applied to the building and machinery as a whole.

**Tuck-mill** (tʊ·kmil). Now *rare*. [f. Tuck *v.*[1] + Mill *sb.*[1]] = prec. (Chiefly West of England.)

*c* **1640** J. Smyth *Hundred of Berkeley* (1885) 4 The multitude of Tuckmills, and fullinge mills which heere abound. **1733** P. Lindsay *Interest Scot.* 108 Where-ever there is a Conveniency of a River for Tuck-mills near the Woollcountries, they may be made. **1780** A. Young *Tour Irel.* II. 35 To this mill is since added..two tuck-mills. **1812** J. Smyth *Pract. of Customs* (1821) 324 All Manufactures made of Wool, which are milled in a Tuck Mill, or other machine, whether twilled or plain, as Coatings, Cassimeres, Kerseys, Druggets, German Serges, Ratteens, and such like. **1884** *St. James' Gaz.* 9 Sept. 6/2 A walk..past the scutching-mills for flax and the old tuck-mill.

**Tu·ck-net.** [f. Tuck *v.*[1] 5.] A smaller net used within the great seine to gather and bring the fish to the surface. Also **Tu·ckner**, the small boat which carries the tuck-net.

**1520** *Lett. & Pap. Hen. VIII*, XIX. 196 (P.R.O.) Vnum rethe vocatum a Tucknett..de precio .xxvj. s. viij. d. **1580** in *Sussex Archæol. Collect.* (1849) II. 43 [The fishermen proceeded to set down their ancient fishing customs under certain heads, called fares,..such as those used in] Tucknett Fare, Shotnett Fare, [etc.]. **1848** C. A. Johns *Week at Lizard* 52 The seine is then moored, and..a smaller boat..passes within the circle of floating corks and lets down a small net, called a tuck-net. **1849** *Sussex Archæol. Collect.* II. 43 The boats used in Tucknett fare were called tuckners, ..they were 'used between Februarye and Aprill to goe to sea uppon the coaste for playce', of the burden of three ton or thereabouts. **1907** *Victoria Hist. Sussex* II. 265/2 'Tucknett fare' lasted from February to April, small boats called 'tuckners' of about 3 tons plying during that season for plaice.

**Tuck-out** (*slang*), a 'feed', feast: see Tuck *sb.*[1] 6.

**Tu·ck-point**, *v.* [f. Tuck *sb.*[1] + Point *v.*[1]] To point or fill up the joints of (brickwork) with coloured mortar, grooved with a narrow groove, which is filled with fine white lime putty, allowed to project slightly. Hence **Tuck-pointer, -pointing.**

**1881** Tuck pointing [see Pointing *vbl. sb.*[1] 5]. **1893** *Law Times* XCV. 5/2 Any kind of brickwork, tuckpointing, or plastering that may have been contracted for..under the original contract. **1901** *Daily Chron.* 2 Sept. 9/6 Bricklayer and tuck pointer, good, wants Work. **1902** J. Hebb in *N. & Q.* 9th Ser. X. 193/1 The brickwork..has been coloured and tuck-pointed.

**Tu·ck-shop.** *slang.* [f. Tuck *sb.*[1] (sense 6 b).] A pastry-cook's shop for the sale of pastry, sweets, fruit, and the like, chiefly to schoolboys.

**1857** Hughes *Tom Brown* i. vi, Come along down to Sally Harrowell's; that's our School-house tuck-shop—she bakes such stunning murphies. **1861** Thackeray *Round. Papers* xvi. 378 We share our toffy; go halves at the tuck-shop; do each other's exercises. **1885** Mozley *Remin.* I. 410 The five years I was at Charterhouse [1820–5] I never once went near the tuck-shop.

‖ **Tucktoo** (tʊktū·). [Echoic: = Burmese *tokté* (Yule), *taukte*, from the animal's cry.] Name in Burma for a large house lizard.

**1896** *Athenæum* 19 Dec. 870/1 The larger house lizard, which she calls the tucktoo. **1901** J. W. Payne in *Bulwark* Nov. 260/1 In many a village you can see and hear the children with mock gravity keeping time to the tucktoo. *Ibid.*, By day and by night he will tell you his name—'Tuck-too! Tuck-too!' And though he speaks often, it's always the same—'Tuck-too!'

**Tucky** (tʊ·ki), *a. rare*—[1]. [f. Tuck *sb.*[1] + -y.] Characterized by tucks; wearing tucked garments.

**1748** *Ballad* in Mitchell *Hist. Montrose* viii. (1866) 75 His curling wigs And his fine tucky lady.

**Tucotuco**: see Tucutucu.

‖ **Tucum** (tū·kǒm). Also **tocon, tocum, tokaun.** [ad. Tupi *tucumá*: see next.] Name for several Brazilian palms of the genera *Astrocaryum* and *Bactris*, esp. *Astrocaryum vulgare*, from the young leaves of which the natives obtain a fibre which they make into cordage, nets, hats, etc.; also, the fibre itself. Also *attrib.*, as *tucum-fibre, -oil, -thread.*

[**1658** Piso *De Ind. Re Nat. et Med.* 128.] **1810** Southey *Brazil* I. vii. 205 They used a plant called tocon for the string. **1824** tr. *Spix & Martius' Trav. Brazil* II. 248 Strings of the fibres of palm leaves (tucum). **1874** tr. *Captivity H. Stade* (Hakl. Soc.) 128 Long leaves which they call tokauns. **1901** Nery *Amazon* 180 The tucum is the fibre of a great palm, *Astrocaryum vulgare*.

‖ **Tucuma** (tū·kumă). [Tupi *tucumá*, the native name.] A Brazilian palm, *Astrocaryum Tucuma*, which produces a fleshy fruit used by the natives as food, and a fibre like that of tucum. Also *tūcuma palm.*

**1824** tr. *Spix & Martius' Trav. Brazil* II. 248 *note*, The tucuma palm and others of the same genus. **1853** Wallace *Palm Trees Amazon* 107–8. **1901** Nery *Amazon* 363 The men wore rings of tucuma, *Astrocaryum tucuma*.

‖ **Tucutucu** (tū·kuˌtū·ku). Also **tucutuco, tucotuco, tucatuca, tucatucu.** [Native name, imitating the grunting sound made by the animal when in its burrow.] A rat-like burrowing rodent of the genus *Ctenomys*, esp. *C. magellanica* and *C. brasiliensis*; found in Patagonia and La Plata. Also, the sound made by this animal. Also *attrib.*

**1833** Darwin *Jrnl. Beagle* iii. (1845) 50–1 The tucutucos appear, to a certain degree, to be gregarious...They are nocturnal in their habits...This animal is universally known by a very peculiar noise which it makes when beneath the ground...The name Tucutuco is given in imitation of the sound...When angry or frightened they uttered the tucutuco. **1839** Fitz-Roy *Voy. Beagle* II. 313 The 'tucutuco', a little animal like a small rabbit. **1880** Lady F. Dixie *Across Patagonia* ix. 112 Putting his foot in an unusually deep tuca-tuca hole, my little horse comes with a crash upon his head. **1899** *Daily News* 4 May 4/3 Patagonia was always noted for its strange ground game, as armadillos and tucotucos. **1904** *Times, Lit. Suppl.* 11 Nov. 347/2 They rode northwards towards the Andes..knee-deep mud and tucutucu country (earth undermined by prairie rat) were common everywhere.

† **Tud**, var. *tid*, obs. pa. pple. of Tide *v.*[1]

*c* **1400** *Laud Troy Bk.* 3804 Off al the harme that we him dud Hadde now not this harme tud.

† **Tudder, tuder.** *Obs.* [OE. *túddor, túdor* neut.; of uncertain origin. Cf. Tidder *v.*[1]] Progeny, offspring.

*c* **897** K. Ælfred *Gregory's Past. C.* xv. 97 Ðonne mæᵹ he cennan mid ðam ðæt tuder ryhtes ᵹeðohtes. *a* **1000** *Ags. Gloss.* in Wr.-Wülcker 238/5 *Foetus*, *i. fructus*, *partus*, *filius*, tudder, *soboles*. *c* **1000** Ælfric *Saints' Lives* xxxiii. 314 He þa..feoll and cwæð Eufrosina cristes bryd and haliᵹra manna tuddor ne beo þu forgitende þinra efenþeowa. *c* **1000** *Sax. Leechd.* I. 166 Sona hyt þæt tuddur ut asendeþ. *c* **1050** *Gloss.* in Wr.-Wülcker 467/24 *Propago*, tudor oððe cyn. *c* **1200** *Trin. Coll. Hom.* 177 Deor and fishshes and fuᵹeles and here tuder.

**-tude** (tiud), *suffix*, repr. L. *-tūdo, -tūdin-em* (F. *-tude*), a suffix of abstract nouns, chiefly from adjs., as *altitūdo* height, f. *altus* high, *fortitūdo* bravery, f. *fortis* brave, *hebetūdo* bluntness, f. *hebes* blunt, less commonly from participles, as *consuētūdo* custom, f. *consuētus* accustomed, *habitūdo* habit, f. *habitus* held, or verbs, as *valētūdo* health, f. *valēre* to be well; occurring in many words derived from Latin either directly, as *altitude, hebetude, latitude, longitude, magnitude*, or through French, as *amplitude, aptitude, attitude, consuetude, fortitude, habitude, plenitude, solitude*, etc., or formed (in F. or Eng.) on Latin analogies, as *debilitude, decrepitude, exactitude*, or occasionally irregularly, as *dispiritude, torpitude.*

**Tu·del**, *v. rare.* [app. repr. Ger. *dudeln, tudeln*, 'to perform badly on a musical instrument'; cf. also Toodle *v.*] *intr.* A depreciative or humorous expression for 'to play on a musical instrument'. Hence **Tu·deler** [cf. Ger. *dudler* bad player or singer]. So **Tu·dle** *adv.* or *int.*, an imitation of the sound of a flute or similar instrument (cf. *toodle-toodle* s.v. Toodle *v.*).

**1814** Mme. D'Arblay *Wanderer* II. 109 Give her as much of your tudeling as will come to this...By then, she'll be able to twiddle over them wires by herself. *Ibid.* 110 He called her his pretty tudeler. **1834** J. Downing *Life & Writ.* 23 The fifes and the bugles..went tudle, tudle, tudle, tudle.

**Tuder**: see Tidder *v.*[1], Tudder.

**Tudesque** (tiude·sk), *a. rare.* [a. F. *tudesque*, It. *tedesco*:—med.L. *theotisc-us, theodiscus*, esp. in *lingua Theotisca, Theodisca, Theudisca* the German language: see Tedesco, Theodisc, Dutch, Teutonic.] German, esp. said of the language.

**1801** Ranken *Hist. France* I. i. iv. 409 His native tongue was the German or Tudesque. **1833** Longf. *Outre-Mer* Prose Wks. 1886 I. 92 When at length the old Tudesque language..had given place to the Langue d'Oil.

† **Tudi·culate**, *v. Obs. rare*—[0]. [f. L. *tudiculāre*, f. *tudicula*, dim. of *tudes* mallet, f. root *tud-* of *tundĕre* to pound: see -ate [3].] (See quot.) So † **Tudicula·tion** (*obs. rare*—[0]).

**1623** Cockeram, *Tudiculate*, to pound, to bruise. **1656** Blount *Glossogr.*, *Tudiculate*, to pound or bruise; to work as Smiths do with a hammer. **1658** Phillips, *Tudiculation*, (Lat.) a bruising or pounding with Smiths hammers.

**Tudle**: see Tudel *v.*

**Tudor** (tiū·dǫɹ), *a.* [attrib. use of the surname *Tudor* (in Welsh *Tewdwr*): see below.]

**1.** Belonging to the line of English sovereigns (from Henry VII to Elizabeth) descended from Owen Tudor, who married Catherine, the widowed queen of Henry V.

1779 *Mirror* No. 18 ¶9 In England,..the high prerogative exerted by the Princes of the Tudor race. 1906 *Q. Rev.* July 56 A Tudor dynasty held the throne.

**2.** Applied to the style of architecture (the latest form of Perpendicular) which prevailed in England during the reigns of the Tudors; belonging to or characteristic of this.

*Tudor arch*, the flattened form of arch characteristic of the Tudor style. *Tudor flower*, an upright stalked trefoil ornament used in long rows on cornices, etc. in Tudor architecture. *Tudor rose*, a conventional figure of a rose adopted as a badge by Henry VII, occurring in architectural and other decoration in the Tudor period; in *Her.* figured as a combination of a red and a white rose (either a smaller rose set upon a larger, or a single rose with the two tinctures divided quarterly).

1815 J. SMITH *Panorama Sc. & Art* I. 131 [An arch] of four centres, commonly called the Tudor arch. 1842 TENNYSON *Edwin Morris* 11 A Tudor-chimnied bulk Of mellow brickwork. 1848 RICKMAN *Archit.* 212 What has been called the Tudor flower, an ornament used instead of battlement, as an upper finish. 1860 WEALE *Dict. Terms* s. v. *Tudor Badges*, [Henry VII] assumed the Tudor rose, or the red rose charged with the white, as emblematical of his united claims to the throne. 1880 MISS BRADDON *Just as I am* ii, It was a Tudor house.

So **Tudoresque** (-e·sk) *a.*, characteristic of the Tudors or the Tudor period; in or resembling the Tudor style, in architecture or art.

1847 HELPS *Friends in C.* I. v. 81 Those Protestant proceedings, which we may rather hope were Tudoresque than Protestant. 1881 OAKEY *Build. Home* 101 An old sixteenth-century Tudoresque house. 1893 *Athenæum* 20 May 635/1 We have the Tudoresque, the Caroline, the Restoration, and other styles [of book-plates].

†**Tue.** *Obs.* [? a. F. *tue* kill.] A hunting cry.

1602 CAREW *Cornwall* I. 22 The Captaine hunters, discouering his sallies by their Espyals doe lay their souldier-like Hounds, his borne enemies, in ambush betweene him [the Fox] and home, and so with *Har* and *Tue* pursue him to the death.

**Tue**, short for TUE-IRON, TEW-IRON.

1883 CRANE *Smithy & Forge* 10 In its centre a thick projecting iron nozzle, perforated to allow of the wind for the blast. This is termed the Tue.

**Tue**, var. TEW *sb.*[1], *v.*[1], *v.*[2]

**Tuech(e, tueiche**, obs. Sc. ff. TOUCH.

**Tuechit**, obs. Sc. form of TEWHIT, lapwing.

**Tuedian** (twī·diăn), *a. Geol.* Also **Twedian.** [f. med.L. *Tueda* the river Tweed + -IAN.] An epithet applied by Geo. Tate in 1856 to the lowest beds of the Carboniferous series, as developed in and near the valley of the Tweed.

1856 R. EMBLETON in *Proc. Berw. Nat. Club* III. No. 7. 219 These beds form the lowest portion of the Carboniferous formation, lying below the Productal and Encrinal Mountain Limestone of Northumberland, and might properly be designated as the Tuedian group... Specimens of these fossils were exhibited by Mr. Tate. 1859 TATE *ibid.* IV. No. 3. 151 In 1856, I applied this name [Tuedian] to a series of beds, lying below the Mountain Limestone, which are largely developed on the Tweed. 1876 PAGE *Adv. Text-bk. Geol.* xiv. 240 The term Calciferous sandstones..is sometimes employed, as well as the more strictly local one of Twedian beds. 1882 G. A. LEBOUR in *Proc. Berw. Nat. Club* IX. No. 3. 527 This great division..has been..split into two members, the *Bernician* above,..and the *Tuedian* below, the equivalent of the Calciferous Sandstone Series and part of the Upper Old Red Sandstone of Scotland.

**Tuefall, -fold**, erron. forms of TO-FALL *sb.*

1664 in *Northumb. Gloss.* (1894), Recd. of Mark Hobson for a year's rent for a Tuefold, 2s. 6d. 1846 WORCESTER, Tuefall; hence in later Dicts.

**Tuei, tueie**, obs. ff. TWAY, two. **Tueil, Tueill**, obs. ff. TOWEL, TWILL. **Tue iron**, var. TEW-IRON.

1862 *Catal. Internat. Exhib., Brit.* II. No. 6182, Tue irons, tin goods, wire of all kinds.

**Tueit**, obs. Sc. f. TWIT. **Tuel, tuell(e**: see TEWEL, TOWEL, TWELVE. **Tuelf, Tuelfed, tuelft, tuelt**, etc., obs. ff. TWELVE, TWELFTH.

**Tuen, Tuene**, var. TEE *v.*[1], TEEN *v.*[1] *Obs.*

**Tuentende, -tiand(e, -tieth, -tiþe**, obs. ff. TWENTIETH. **Tuenti, -tie, -ty, -tye**, obs. ff. TWENTY. **Tuer**, obs. f. TUYERE.

**Tuesday** (tiū·zdeⁱ). Forms: α. 1–2 **Tiwesdæȝ**, 3 **Tiwesday, -dai, Tywesdaiȝ**, 3–5 **Tywesday**, 4 **Tues-, Tewisdai**, 4–6 **Twysday**, 5 **Tywys-, Tyvys-, Tewys-, Towes-**, 5–6 **Tewisday**, 6 **Tewes-, Tuis-, Twis-, Teyus-, Teudins-, Tewsday**, 6–7 **Twesdaie**, 7 **Twesday**, 6– **Tuesday**. β. 3 **Tisdæi, -dei**, 4 **Tisday**; *Sc.* 4–6 **Tysday**, 5–9 **Tyesday**, 6–7 **Tyisday**, 8 **Tiseday.** [OE. *Tīwesdæg*; = OFris. *tīes-, tīsdei, -di*; OHG. *zīestag*, MHG. *zīstag* (Ger. dial. *zīstig*); ON. *týsdagr, týrsdagr* (Norw. *tys-, tisdag*, Sw. and early Da. *tisdag*, Da. *tirsdag*. ME. and Sc. *tīesdæi, tȳsday*); f. genitive of OE. *Tīw* = ON. *Týr*, OHG. *Zīo*, name of an ancient Teutonic deity, identified with the Roman Mars; whence *Tīwesdæg*, etc., rendering late L. *dies Martis*, It. *Martedì*, F. *Mardi*. *Týr, Tīw*:—OTeut. **Tīwaz* was cognate with L. *deus*, Gr. genit. *διός*, OIr. *dia*, cf. Skr. *dyāus*.

Another form appears in MLG. *dīnstag*, whence mod. Ger. *Dienstag* (Swab. *zienstig, zeinstig*), Du. *Dinsdag*, MDu. *Ding(e)stag, dinse(n)dach*, of which the first component appears to be *ding, þing*, 'public assembly', but is thought to be *Thinxus*, a synonym of the name of the war-god preserved in a Latin inscription.]

The third day of the week.

c 1050 *Byrhtferth's Handboc* in *Anglia* VIII. 321 Tiwesdæges of martie. a 1123 *O. E. Chron.* an. 1104 On þam Tiwæs dæȝe þær æfter. c 1205 LAY. 13936 Þene Sunne heo ȝiuen sonedæi, Monenen..monedæi, Tidea heo ȝeuen tisdæi [c 1275 (l. 13924) tisdei]. c 1290 *Beket* 1147 in *S. Eng. Leg.* I. 139 An alle soulene dai, þene tywesdaiȝ [*v. r.* Tuesdai]. c 1375 *Sc. Leg. Saints* xl. (*Ninian*) 734 Of witsone owke þe twysday. 1375 BARBOUR *Bruce* xv. 101 Quhill the tysday in pask-owk. c 1450 *Merlin* xiv. 205 It be-fill on a tewisday. a 1500 *Bale's Chron.* in *Six Town Chron.* (1911) 143 Þis was upon a towesday. 1530 PALSGR. 178 *Mardy*, tuesday. a 1572 KNOX *Hist. Ref.* II. Wks. 1846 I. 350 The nixt day..(whiche was Tyisday, the 13 of Junij). 1587 F. JAMES in *Collect.* (O.H.S.) I. 199 From Twesdaie till Satterdaie. 1607 *Reg. Mag. Sig. Scot.* 729/1 Upon Tyisday befoir the feist of Pasche. 1691 J. WILSON *Belphegor* II. iv, I shall be married a Tuesday next. 17.. *Runaway Bride* in Herd *Coll. Sc. Poems* (1776) II. 87 The bridal-day was set, On Tiseday for to be. 1848 THACKERAY *Van. Fair* xviii, We must have a party...Shall I say Tuesday fortnight? 1912 C. MURRAY in *The Odd Volume* 21 A towmond come Tyesday, the lassies been wad.

*attrib.* 1473 WARKW. *Chron.* (Camden) 21 Kynge Henry ..was putt to dethe..on a tywesday nyght. 1596 SHAKS. 1 *Hen. IV*, I. ii. 40 A Purse of Gold most resolutely snatch'd on Monday night, and most dissolutely spent on Tuesday morning. 1622 BOYS *Wks.* 787 A Tuesday breakfast..a Fridayes drinking.

**Tuesite** (tiu,ĭ·səit). *Min.* [f. L. *Tuesa* the Spey, mistaken by Camden for the Tweed + -ITE[1].] An indurated variety of lithomarge of a milk-white colour.

1837 THOMSON in *Proc. Berw. Nat. Club* I. No. 5. 157 Fracture earthy,..soiling the fingers;..tuesite and gypsum. 1868 DANA *Min.* (ed. 5) 474 *Tuesite* of Thomson is a lithomarge from Scotland, used sometimes for slate pencils;.. color milk-white.

**Tueþyng**, obs. f. TITHING. **Tuewhite**, obs. Sc. f. TEWHIT, lapwing. **Tuey, Tueye, Tueyne**: see TWAY, TWIE, TWAIN.

**Tuf**, obs. f. TOUGH; var. TUFF.

**Tufa** (tū·fă, tiū·fă). *Geol.* Also 8–9 **tuffa**, 9 **tufo, tupha.** [a. It. *tufa, tufo*:—L. *tōfus, tōphus*: see TOPHUS; cf. TUFF *sb.*]

**1.** A generic name for porous stones, formed of pulverulent matter consolidated and often stratified. (See Note s. v. TUFF *sb.* 1.)

1777 G. FORSTER *Voy. round World* I. 586 The stone of which the statue itself is formed..being nothing but the red tufa which covers the whole island. 1789 J. WILLIAMS *Nat. Hist. Min. Kingd.* II. 382 There are great quantities of the concreted substance called tufa in many parts of Scotland. 1849 DANA *Geol.* iii. (1850) 241 The tufa is very friable, yielding easily to the fingers.

*spec.* **a.** *Calcareous tufa*: 'a porous or vesicular carbonate of lime, generally deposited near the sources and along the courses of calcareous springs' (Page *Geol. Terms*, 1865). Cf. TUFF *sb.* 1 a.

1811 PINKERTON *Petralogy* I. 518 *note*, At Bionnay there are houses built of a calcareous tufa, containing fragments of lime-spar, limestone, and slate. *Ibid.* II. 374 *note*, This [*tufo*] is the Italian and classical orthography. *Tufa* may be reserved for depositions merely aqueous. 1839 G. ROBERTS *Dict. Geol.*, *Tufa*, or *Calcareous Tufa*.., a friable earthy deposit from calcareous springs. The more solid form is *travertin*. 1865 LIVINGSTONE *Zambesi* xi. 222 In the vicinity of the erupted rocks we usually meet soft calcareous tufa. 1867 ANSTED in Brande & Cox *Dict. Sc.* etc., *Tufa* [is] a name applied in Italy to certain porous loose rocks... Volcanic Tufa is the material under which Pompeii was buried...Calcareous Tufa when consolidated passes into Travertine.

**b.** *Volcanic tufa*: see TUFF *sb.* 1 b.

1770 HAMILTON in *Phil. Trans.* LXI. 7 The Italians distinguish it by the name of tufa, and it is in general use for building. 1772 *Nat. Hist.* in *Ann. Reg.* 79/2 What is called here Tuffa..is the same that covers Herculaneum, and that composes most of the high grounds about Naples; it is..a mixture of small pumice stones, ashes, and fragments of lava, ..hardened into a sort of stone. 1778 *Phil. Trans.* LXVIII. 2 The walls were..of a tuffa exactly resembling that of Naples and its environs. 1794 SULLIVAN *View Nat.* I. 84 The..mass through which the catacombs are excavated are all indurated tufa. 1811 PINKERTON *Petralogy* II. 374 Brochant.. supposes that they become volcanic tufo. 1838 *Murray's Hand Bk. N. Germ.* 239/1 Composed..of tufa and scoriæ, exactly similar to that found on Vesuvius. 1862 DANA *Man. Geol.* I. 685 When rain or moisture from any source descends with the cinders, the mass forms tufa,—a stratified, somewhat earthy, granular..rock, of gray, yellowish-brown, and brownish colors. 1866 LAWRENCE tr. *Cotta's Rocks Class.* (1878) 89 Tufa is now principally used to denote an earthy compound of volcanic products of the most various kind.

**2.** *attrib.* and *Comb.*, as *tufa cement, grotto, quarry, rock, stone, wall*; *tufa-like, -paved* adjs.

1839 W. CHAMBERS *Tour Holland* etc. 55/1 Andernach is an ancient walled town, and the seat of a considerable export trade in oven stones and *tufa cement. 1910 *19th Cent.* Feb. 365 The piers were formed of *tufa-like Caux stone. 1905 R. BAGOT *Passport* i, The steep, *tufa-paved street. 1891 FARRAR *Darkn. & Dawn* xxiv, The overhanging sides of the *tufa quarry. 1820 T. S. HUGHES *Trav. Sicily* II. xv. 368 Some workmen were excavating a wine vault in the *tufa-rock. 1861 J. H. BENNET *Winter Medit.* I. viii. (1875) 229 The island [Capri] is of limestone—a healthier geological formation than the soft tufa rock of Naples. 1793 *Trans. Soc. Arts* (ed. 2) V. 222 A *Tufa stone, found on the rocky banks of the Rhine. 1894 *Daily News* 22 Sept. 6/2 The columns..are generally of grey tufa-stone. 1877 J. NORTHCOTE *Catacombs* I. iii. 45 He strengthened the friable *tufa walls of some of the galleries..by..arches of brick and stone work.

**Tufaceous** (*tu-*, tiufē·ʃəs), *a.* [f. prec. + -ACEOUS.] Having the nature or texture of tufa; consisting of tufa.

(Chiefly used of non-volcanic formations: cf. TUFFACEOUS.)

1811 PINKERTON *Petralogy* I. 518 Wallerius would perhaps have called it a tufaceous limestone. 1851 WOODWARD *Mollusca* 142 The tufaceous deposits of petrifying wells. 1876 PAGE *Adv. Text-bk. Geol.* vii. 131 The tufaceous accumulations round the craters of..volcanoes.

**Tufall, Tufan**, obs. ff. TO-FALL, TYPHOON.

**Tufat**, dial. var. TEWHIT, lapwing.

**Tuff** (tɒf), *sb. Geol.* Forms: 6 **tuph**, 7–8 (9 *dial.*) **tuft**, (8 **tufft**), 7– **tuff**, (9 **tuf**). [ad. 16th c. F. *tufe, tuffe*, (R. Estienne) *tuf*, Cotgr. *tuf, tuffe*, ad. It. *tufo* 'a kind of soft, crumbling, or mouldring stone to build withall' (Florio):—L. *tōfus*, TOPHUS, q.v. The change of gender in obs. F. *tuffe* (= *tufa*) has not been explained. *Tuft* follows the better known TUFT *sb.* (where also the *t* is an addition).]

**1.** Any light porous cellular rock; = TUFA. (But there is a recent tendency to differentiate *tuff* from TUFA, and restrict it to 'volcanic tuff'.)

**a.** *Calcareous* (or *calc*) *tuff*: see TUFA 1 a and quot. 1816.

1569 STOCKER tr. *Diod. Sic.* II. xliv. 99/2 With their axes and hatchets they cut thereof as a man shoulde do on a Tuph or softe Stone. 1603 [see *tuff stone* in 2]. 1744 PLATT in *Phil. Trans.* XLIII. 266 A rocky petrified Substance,..by the Miners called Tuft. 1785 BARKER *ibid.* LXXV. 353 *note*, Tuft is a stone formed by the deposit left by water passing through beds of sticks, roots, vegetables, &c. of which there is a large stratum at Matlock Bath. 1816 ACCUM *Chem. Tests* (1818) 166 When these waters suddenly lose the excess of carbonic acid..essential to the solution of the lime, there is an irregular precipitation; hence those tender calcareous cellular stones, and calcareous spongy tuffs. 1839 URE *Dict. Arts* 771 Calcareous tuf consists of similar incrustations made by petrifying rivulets running over mud, sand, vegetable remains, etc. 1843 PORTLOCK *Geol.* 213 As calc tuff, it [carbonate of lime] is of very frequent occurrence throughout the primary and secondary district. 1881 RAYMOND *Mining Gloss.*, *Tuff* or *Tufa*, a soft sandstone or calcareous deposit.

(*b*) 1893–4 HESLOP *Northumbld. Gloss.*, *Tuft*, a bed of fine-grained, siliceous stone, like ganister, which occurs in the carboniferous series below the Great Limestone. It is also known as *water sill*.

**b.** *Volcanic tuff*, a tuff produced by the consolidation of volcanic ashes and other erupted material.

1815 W. PHILLIPS *Outlines Mineralogy & Geol.* (1818) 187 Pumice, obsidian or volcanic glass, slime called volcanic tuff,..are also the products of volcanic eruptions. 1839 DARWIN *Voy. Nat.* xvii. (1852) 373 Craters, composed of the soft and yielding tuff. 1841 TRIMMER *Pract. Geol.* 173 Aqueous lavas, which, as they consolidate, form rocks of an earthy appearance, known by the name of volcanic tuff or tufa. 1850 ANSTED *Elem. Geol., Min.* etc. Gloss., *Tufa, Tuff*, an Italian name for a variety of volcanic rock of earthy texture, ..made up..of fragments of volcanic ashes. 1881 JUDD *Volcanoes* v. 117 The tuffs covering the city of Pompeii consist of numerous thin layers of lapilli and volcanic dust. 1914 *Brit. Mus. Return* 229 Volcanic lapilli and palagonite-tuff from Monte Brazil, Terceira, Azores.

**c.** *Trap-tuff*: see quot.

1833–4 J. PHILLIPS *Geol.* in *Encycl. Metrop.* (1845) VI. 768/1 Aggregations of the disintegrated..materials of trap rocks are generally known under the vague name of trap tuff and compared with volcanic tuff.

**2.** *attrib.* and *Comb.*, as *tuff bed, block, cone, crater, mountain, stone* [F. *pierre de tuffe* (Cotgr.)], *tuff-wacke*; *tuff-like* adj.

1854 HOOKER *Himal. Jrnls.* I. ii. 44 Enormous *tuff beds are deposited on the sandstone. 1864 J. HUNT tr. *Vogt's Lect. Man* x. 262 In these *tuff blocks, in the vicinity of the town of Puy, are found the mammoth and the rhinoceros with a bony nasal septum. 1881 JUDD *Volcanoes* 118 Finely-stratified *tuff-cones. 1839 DARWIN *Voy. Nat.* xvii. (1845) 376 To the south of the broken *tuff-crater. 1880 *Academy* 20 Nov. 370 They [certain Chinese rocks] exhibit *tuff-like characters. 1861 E. T. HOLLAND in *Peaks, Passes & Gl.* Ser. II. I. 9 A high range of *tuff mountains. 1603 OWEN *Pembrokeshire* (1892) 80 There is *Tuff Stone found in the Mountaine over Newport. c 1640 J. SMYTH *Lives Berkeleys* (1883) I. 309 Fetching..the Tuft stone from Dursley by land. 1802 *Brookes' Gazetteer* (ed. 12) s. v. *Lugano*, Most of the houses are built of tufstone. 1822–7 GOOD *Study Med.* (1829) I. 61 Tufa or tuffwacke, as Schmeisser calls it, and tarras, which are compounds of iron, alumine, silex, and carbonate of lime. 1847 LEITCH tr. *C. O. Müller's Anc. Art* § 271. (1850) 303 Pozzolana (an earthy tuff-wack).

†**Tuff**, *v. Obs. rare.* [Echoic.: cf. PUFF.] *intr.* To make a short explosive sound with the breath. So **Tuff** *int.*, an imitation of such a sound.

1553 *Respublica* I. iii. 247 *Avarice.* What saie ye? *Inso.* Hake. *Adul.* Tuff. *Op.* Hem. *Ibid.* III. iv. 774 *Adul.* But looke, who cometh yonder, puffing and tuffing? ..*Avar.*..Where have ye lost your breath? 1598 FLORIO, *Sbuffante*..panting, breathing, tuffing as a cat, chafing. a 1821 KEATS in *Critic* 9 Feb. (1895) 104/1, I for a moment whiles was prisoner ta'en And rifled, tuff!

**Tuff**, obs. form of TOUGH, TUFT.

**Tuffaceous** (tɒfē·ʃəs), *a.* [f. TUFF *sb.* + -ACEOUS.] 'Having the properties of or composed of volcanic tuff' (*Cent. Dict. Suppl.* 1909); distinguished from *tufaceous* in the specific sense.

1882 GEIKIE *Textbk. Geol.* II. II. vi. 164 Tuffs passing gradually into shale, limestone, sandstone, &c. The intermediate varieties have been called *ashy shale, tuffaceous shale*, or *shaley tuff*, &c.

**Tuffall, Tuffe**, obs. ff. TO-FALL, TOUGH, TUFT.

**Tuffet** (tɒ·fėt). ? *Obs.* exc. *dial.* [f. *tuff*, F.

*touffe* (see TUFT *sb.*) with suffix-exchange dim. **-ET** for **-EL** in OF. *touffel*.]

**1.** = TUFT *sb.* 1, 1 b.

**1553** *Respublica* III. vi. 928 The goddesse occasyon.. weareth a greate long tuffet of heare beefore, and behinde hathe not one heare. **1578** LYTE *Dodoens* I. lxxiii. 108 At the toppe of the stalkes groweth blewish floures in thicke tuffets. *a* **1691** BOYLE *Hist. Air* (1692) 178 Emerging from the ground like tuffets of rushes. **1899** P. ROBINSON in *Contemp. Rev.* June 844 [A blackcap] standing between two 'tuffets' of bloom.

**2.** A hillock, mound: = TUFT *sb.* 3 b.

**1877** BLACKMORE *Erema* II. xxxiv. 193 Here were six little grassy tuffets.

**3.** ? A hassock or footstool.

(Doubtful: perh. due to misunderstanding of the nursery rime, which may belong to sense 2.)

?**18..** *Nursery Rime*, Little Miss Muffet sat on a tuffet, Eating of curds and whey. [Cf. BUFFET [1].] **1895** BENSON in *Contemp. Rev.* July 125 Miss Moffat..hastily got up from the tuffet—which turned out to be a three-legged stool. **1904** *Westm. Gaz.* 22 Dec. 1/3 Mamie..gave him a tuffet for his narrow feet.

Hence † **Tu·ffetwise** *adv.* [-WISE], in the manner or form of a tuffet or tuft.

**1578** LYTE *Dodoens* II. lvi. 217 The stalke is of a foote and half long: at which groweth a great sort of floures tuffetwise.

**Tuffie**: see TUFTY. **Tuffin**, obs. f. TYPHOON.

**Tuffing** (tʊ·fiŋ). *rare.* [f. *tuff*, TUFT + -ING[1].]

†**1.** Caulking material; oakum. *Obs.*

**1513** DOUGLAS *Æneis* v. xii. 31 The tuffing kendillis betuixt the plankis wak.

**2.** *Bell-ringing* (also **tuftin**). The tufts of wool woven into a bell-rope to give a grip for the hand: = SALLY *sb.*[2] 2.

**1869** TROYTE *Change Ringing* i. 2 The 'hand stroke' blow will be the one on which he pulls the 'sallie', or tuffing on the rope. **1897** F. T. JANE *Lordship* vi. 66 The tuftin being worn, she hurt a man's hands a good deal on the sally, and had mainly to be rung on the back-stroke.

**Tuffle** (tʊ·f'l), *v. dial.* [app. onomatopœic: cf. TIFFLE *v.*[2]]

**1.** *trans.* To put into disorder, ruffle, rumple; to entangle, ravel; = TIFFLE *v.*[2]

**1777** *Horæ Subsecivæ* 431 (E.D.D.). *a* **1810** in Cromek *Rem. Nithsdale Song* 67 An' what has tuffled yere gowden locks..?

**2.** To bind up (flax) in loose sheaves.

**1799** A. YOUNG *Agric. Lincoln* 164 (*Flax cultivation*) Tuffle it; that is making it in a loose sheaf, open at bottom.

**Tuffon, -oon**, obs. ff. TYPHOON.

**Tuff-tafata**, etc.: see TUFTAFFETA.

**Tufit**, dial. var. TEWHIT, lapwing. **Tufo**: see TUFA.

**Tuft** (tʊft), *sb.* Also 5 **toft, tofte**, 5–7 **tufft**, 6 **tufte**; 6–7 **tuffe**, 7–8 **tuff**. [The derivation presents many difficulties. Supposed to represent F. *touffe* (in OF. also *toffe*, *tofe*), generally referred to L. *tūfa*, 'a kind of helmet crest', or 'a kind of military standard' (in Vegetius, 386), appearing in Byzantine Greek as τοῦφα (see Du Cange). By some held to be ult. of German origin, ? ad. OLG. *top* or OHG. *zopf*. The final *t* is evidently an Eng. addition: cf. *carafe*, vulg. *craft*; also *cliff*, *clift*; *draff*, *draft*; *graff*, *graft*, and vulgar *paragraft*, *telegraft*.

The difficulties of this derivation are that F. *touffe* is not the normal repr. of L. *tūfa*, but points to **tuffa*, whereas the long *ū* of *tūfa* is supported by the Greek and by Beda's *tuuf*; also that *tūfa*, *touffe*, answer phonetically neither to Low nor High German. Cf. Pr. *chuf*, It. *ciuffo*, a tuft or lock of hair, ad. Ger. *zopf*. Beside these, the final *t* in the Eng. word is of minor difficulty.]

**1.** A bunch (natural or artificial) of small things, usually soft and flexible, as hairs, feathers, etc., fixed or attached at the base.

[*a* **731** BEDA *Eccl. Hist.* II. xvi, Illud genus uexilli, quod Romani tufam, Angli uero appellant tuuf. (Hence in Henry of Huntingdon: see Du Cange.)]

*c* **1386** CHAUCER *Prol.* 555 (Harl.) Vpon þe cop right of his nose he hade A werte and þer on stood a tuft [*v. r.* toft(e)] of heres. **1463** in *Bury Wills* (Camden) 36 A peyre of bedys ..with a knoppe, othir wyse callyd a tufft, of blak sylke. **1585** T. WASHINGTON tr. *Nicholay's Voy.* III. iii. 73 b, The rest of the haires..they doe cut away.., except a tuffe of haire on the top of their head. *Ibid.* v. 78 Great tufts of feathers vpon their heads. **1664** H. MORE *Myst. Iniq.* 273 A tuft of seven bristles. **1727** [DORRINGTON] *Philip Quarll* 193 A small Tuff of Hair on each Shoulder and Hip. **1794** W. FELTON *Carriages* (1801) I. 141 The quilting of the cloth with small ornaments, called tufts, also gives a richness to the lining. **1842** TENNYSON *Lancelot & Guinevere* iii, A light-green tuft of plumes she bore Closed in a golden ring **1845** GREGORY *Outl. Chem.* II. 345 Salicylic acid crystallises in tufts of slender prisms.

**b.** *Bot.*, etc. A cluster of short-stalked leaves or flowers growing from a common point, of stems growing from a common root, etc.; an umbel or fascicle; also, a clump of small herbs growing closely together.

Formerly applied more widely, e. g. to the receptacle of a composite flower, or to a compact seed-vessel.

†*London tuft*, an old name for Sweet William: see LONDON. See also CANDYTUFT.

**1523** FITZHERB. *Husb.* § 70 Beastes alone, nor horses aloone, nor shepe alone,..wyll not eate a pasture euen, but leaue many tuftes and hygh grasse. **1530** PALSGR. 283/2 Tufte of grasse, *monceau de herbe*. **1578** LYTE *Dodoens* I. x. 18 The ..common Tansie hath a blackishe stalke..diuided..into many single braunches, at the end wherof are round tuftes, bearing yellow floures like small round buttons. **1620** VENNER *Via Recta* vii. 159 The round tufts or heads which conteine the seede. **1645–50** BOATE *Irel. Nat. Hist.* (1860) 93 Hassocky-bogs..are very thick overspread with little Tufts or Ilets..consisting of reeds, rushes [etc.]. **1727** P. BLAIR *Pharmaco-Bot.* v. 235 Tufts or Umbels of pentapetalous yellow Flowers. *Ibid.* 236 Dispos'd in small Umbells or Tuffs. **1824** W. IRVING *T. Trav.* IV. (1848) 278 Tom had long been picking his way cautiously through this treacherous forest; stepping from tuft to tuft of rushes and roots. **1853** MISS YONGE *Heir of Redclyffe* xxx, A tuft of deep purple, the beautiful Alpine saxifrage. **1861** BENTLEY *Man. Bot.* 137 All the leaves of that branch may be brought in contact at their base, in which case they form a tuft or fascicle. **1908** [MISS FOWLER] *Betw. Trent & Ancholme* 89 The Robin's favourite tuft on the top of the Cedar-tree.

**2.** A small tufted patch of hair on the head or chin; a lock; an imperial (IMPERIAL B. 8).

**1601** DENT *Pathw. Heaven* (1831) 37 What say you then to these—long locks, fore tufts, shag hair, and all these new fashions? *c* **1610** *Women Saints* 160 No..friselled tuffes, borrowed to deceiue. **1654** tr. *Martini's Conq. China* 33 In the hinder part of their Heads they leave a Tuff, which being curiously woven and plated, they let hang down. **1711** HEARNE *Collect.* (O.H.S.) III. 150 On his [Chaucer's] Chin 2 thin forked Tuffs. **1831** SCOTT *Ct. Robt.* ii, One of the soldiers..who showed the shaven head and the single tuft of a Mussulman. **1840** THACKERAY *Shabby-genteel Story* v, The stylish tuft on his chin.

**3.** A small group of trees or bushes; a clump. (Cf. TOFT 4, which perh. belongs here.)

**1555** EDEN *Decades* 352 Vppon the innermoste necke to the landewarde, is a tufte of trees. **1611** SHAKS. *Wint. T.* IV. i. 34 Behind the tuft of Pines I met them. **1667** MILTON *P. L.* VII. 327 With high Woods the Hills were crownd, With tufts the vallies and each fountain side. **1778** *Eng. Gazetteer* (ed. 2) s. v. *Tottenham*, A circular tuft of elms..called the Seven Sisters. **1879** S. C. BARTLETT *Egypt to Pal.* xi. 239 Land..more or less sprinkled with tufts of desert shrubs.

†**b.** A grassy hillock, a small knoll or mound. (Cf. TOFT 3.) *Obs. rare.*

**1651** HOWELL *Venice* 32 The Adriatic Sea..spreading himself..towards the Continent of Italie, leaves som green tuffs or tombs of Earth uncoverd.

**4.** (*a*) *Anat.* A small cluster or plexus of capillary blood-vessels, as the *Malpighian tufts* of the kidney; a glomerule. (*b*) *Zool. Branchial* or *respiratory tuft*: a cluster of tentacles having a respiratory function, in some tubicolous worms.

**1841–71** T. R. JONES *Anim. Kingd.* (ed. 4) 277 The respiratory tufts..attached to the anterior extremity of the creature..form most elegant arborescent appendages, generally tinted with brilliant colours. **1848** [see MALPIGHIAN [1]]. **1873** T. H. GREEN *Introd. Pathol.* (ed. 2) 68 The tufts of vessels which form the Malpighian bodies.

†**5.** A crest, as of a bird. *Obs.*

**1598** FLORIO, *Capelletto*, a little tuffe vpon a peacocks head. **1706** PHILLIPS (ed. Kersey), *Tuft*, a lock of Hair,..also the Crest of a Bird.

†**b.** *fig.* Head, chief, top. *Obs. nonce-use.*

**1625** B. JONSON *Staple of N.* II. v, He is..my Chiefe, the Point, Tip, Top, and Tuft of all our family.

†**6.** A turban. *Obs.*

**1585** HIGINS *Junius' Nomencl.* 165/1 *Tiara*, a Turkish tuffe, such as the Turkes weare..on their head. **1621** AINSWORTH *Annot. Pentat., Exod.* xxviii. 39. (1639) 117 Miter..signifieth a thing wrapped about the head. Such as the Tuffe which..is worne in the Easterne Countries.

**7.** An ornamental tassel on a cap; *spec.* the gold tassel formerly worn by titled undergraduates at Oxford and Cambridge (see quot. 1894).

Originally, at Oxford, a distinction of the sons of those peers who had a vote in the House of Lords, after 1861 of all peers and their eldest sons; since 1870 made optional.

**1670** G. H. *Hist. Cardinals* I. III. 71 That invention of Bishops and Prelates to wear Green Tufts in their Caps. *a* **1704** T. BROWN *Contn. Quaker's Serm.* Wks. 1709 III. II. 3 Let not a Cap be seen among us, with an Idolatrous Tuff upon it. **1770** LANGHORNE *Plutarch* (1851) I. 336/2 As he was sacrificing the tuft of his cap fell off. **1861** HUGHES *Tom Brown at Oxf.* viii, Men..all in tufts or gentlemen-commoners' caps. **1894** *Westm. Gaz.* 5 Mar. 3/1 Lord Rosebery..was one of the last undergraduates of Christ Church who wore the gold tassel, known by the name of 'tuft', which was the distinguishing mark of noblemen and the sons of noblemen.

**b.** *transf.* in *University slang*, One who wears a tuft; a titled undergraduate.

**1755** [see TUFT-HUNTER]. **1789** *Loiterer* No. 11. 6 A Tuft (when once suffered to get away from you) is scarcely ever recovered again. **1840** THACKERAY *Shabby-genteel Story* ii, The lad went to Oxford,..frequented the best society, followed with a kind of proud obsequiousness all the tufts of the university **1847** JOWETT *Let.* 10 Mar., in *Life & Lett.* (1897) I. 158 Dufferin of Christ Church..seems a most excellent tuft. **1884** *Weekly Register* 18 Oct. 503/2 One don is much like another, to a lively young tuft who keeps beagles.

**8.** *attrib.* and *Comb.* **a.** *attrib.*: †**tuft gilly-flower**, a kind of gillyflower (? = pink) growing in tufts; †**tuft mockado** (see MOCKADO 1, 1 b, and cf. TUFTAFFETA); also *attrib.*

[In both these, *tuft* may be, not the sb., but = *tuffed*, TUFTED: cf. quot. 1587 s. v. MOCKADO.]

**1573** TUSSER *Husb.* (1878) 96 Herbes..for windowes and pots..*Tuft gilleflowers. **1579** *Tuft mockado [see MOCKADO 1]. **1589** R. HARVEY *Pl. Perc.* (1590) 8, I will nicke-name no bodie: I am none of these tuft mockadoo mak-a-dooes. **1599** NASHE *Lenten Stuffe* 25 Penning a discourse of Tuftmockados. **1847–78** HALLIWELL, *Tuft-mockado*, a mixed stuff made to imitate tufted taffeta, or velvet.

**b.** *Comb.* as **tuft-topped** adj.; **tuft-gill**, a tuft-gilled fish, a lophobranch (*Cent. Dict.*); **tuft-gilled** *a.*, having tufted gills, as the order *Cirribranchiata* of molluscs (tooth-shells), or *Lophobranchii* of fishes (see LOPHOBRANCHIATE). See also TUFT-HUNTER.

**1840** LUNDIE *Mission. Life in Samoa* xiii. (1846) 79 Tall tuft-topped cocoa-nut trees. **1861** P. P. CARPENTER in *Rep. Smithsonian Instit.* 1860, 222 Order *Cirrobranchiata*. (Tuft-gilled Crawlers).

**Tuft**, *v.* Forms: see prec. [f. prec. sb.]

**I. 1.** *trans.* To furnish with a tuft or tufts.

**1535** in *Archæologia* IX. 251 A pair of upper stockis of purple veluette embroidered with golde and tuffed with cameryke. **1573** in Feuillerat *Revels Q. Eliz.* (1908) 210 For Tufting vi lardge kirtells of greene Sattin with golde sarcenet. **1630** J. TAYLOR (Water P.) *Trav.* Wks. III. 98/1 She's ring'd, she's braceleted, she's richly tuff'd. **1728–46** THOMSON *Spring* 914 Solemn oaks, that tuft the swelling mounts. **1743** J. DAVIDSON *Æneid* VIII. 264 Caps tufted with wool. **1833** T. HOOK *Parson's Dau.* III. ix, The officers of a crack Hussar regiment..tipped and tufted. **1850** TENNYSON *In Mem.* cxxviii. 20 To make old bareness picturesque And tuft with grass a feudal tower.

**b.** *Upholstery.* To draw together the two surfaces of (a cushion or the like) by a thread passed through at regular intervals producing depressions, which are then usually ornamented with tufts or buttons.

**1884** [implied in *tufting-button*: see TUFTING *vbl. sb.* 3]. **1891** in *Cent. Dict.*

**2.** *intr.* To form a tuft or tufts; to grow in tufts.

**1598** SYLVESTER *Du Bartas* II. i. II. *Imposture* 397 Among the dark shade of those tufting arbors. **1629** PARKINSON *Paradisus* 317 Tufting close vpon the ground, like vnto the common Thrift. **1794** G. ADAMS *Nat. & Exp. Philos.* III. xxxiv. 408 A sea of cotton, tufting here and there by the action of the air in the undisturbed parts of the clouds.

**3.** *trans.* To form into a tuft. *rare*[—1]. (Cf. TUFTED 2.)

**1860** HAWTHORNE *Marb. Faun* viii, What weeds cluster and tuft themselves on the cornices of ruins.

**II. 4.** *trans.* To beat (a covert) in stag-hunting. Also *absol.*

**1590** COKAINE *Treat. Hunting* C iv b, You may begin to tuft for a Bucke. **1612** DRAYTON *Poly-olb.* xiii. 113 When with his hounds The laboring Hunter tufts the thicke vnbarbed grounds Where harbor'd is the Hart. **1870** BLAINE *Encycl. Rur. Sports* (ed. 3) § 1813 Tufting of deer. As deer frequently herd in copses, woods, and brakes, it is usual to *tuft* (hunt) a covert with a couple or two of steady old hounds, called tufters. **1908** *Q. Rev.* July 90 The lonely ridges of the Brendon hills are 'tufted' for a 'warrantable' deer.

**b.** To dislodge (the game) by 'tufting'; also *fig.*

*a* **1640** JACKSON *Creed* x. xxiv. § 4 The..meaning of the learned moderator hath been by his followers..so meanly tufted, and so unskilfully hunted after. **1909** QUILLER COUCH *True Tilda* xxi, They had tufted him [a stag] out of the wood.

**Tuft**, obs. form of TOFT, TUFF.

**Tuftaffeta, -taffety** (tʊf,tæ·fĕtă, -tæ·fĕti). *Obs.* or *arch.* Forms (with hyphen, or as one word, or as two words): 6–7 **tuft-**, **tufte-**; 6–9 **tuf-**, 7 **tuffe-**, 7–8 **tuff-**, (8 ? **tiff-**): see TAFFETA, TAFFETY. [f. *tuff*, TUFT *sb.* + TAFFETA, TAFFETY.]

**1.** A kind of taffeta with a pile or nap arranged in tufts.

**1572** in *Rep. MSS. Ld. Middleton* (1911) 422 For vi yardes of tufte taffyta at xij s. the yarde. **1593** DONNE *Sat.* iv. 33 His Ierkin..had been Velvet, but 'twas now (so much ground was seen) Become tufftaffaty. **1635** CRANLEY *Amanda* 76 What shall I doe with rich Tuftafaties? **1735** POPE *Donne's Sat.* iv. 42 The suit..Was velvet in the youth of good queen Bess, But mere tuff-taffety what now remain'd. **1899** MARY JOHNSTON *By Order of Company* iii, He..hitched forward his cloak of sky-blue tuftaffeta with an air.

**2.** *transf.* A person wearing tuftaffeta.

**1613** BEAUM. & FL. *Coxcomb* v. i, Such an old Tuff-taffity that knows not.

**3.** *attrib.* **a.** Made of tuftaffeta.

**1587** *Lanc. Wills* (Chetham Soc.) III. 34 My blacke tuf. tafata hosen. **1611** MIDDLETON & DEKKER *Roaring Girle* E iij b, Any coacht veluet cappe or tuftaffety iacket. *c* **1618** MORYSON *Itin.* IV. (1903) 96, I did see her apparrelled once in a Tuft taffety gowne and an other tyme in a purple Taffety gowne. **1629** B. JONSON *New Inn* II. i, I'll help to fit her With a tuft-taffeta cloak.

**b.** Clothed in tuftaffeta; luxuriously dressed; hence *fig.* Cf. TAFFETA B. 2.

**1598** E. GILPIN *Skial.* (1878) 49, I smile at thy Atturneys silken pride, Tufttaffeta state. **1612** *Proc. Virginia* ii. 13 in *Capt. Smith's Wks.* (Arb.) 97 We daily feasted with.. fish, fowle, and diverse sorts of wild beasts as fat as we could eat them: so that none of our Tuftaffaty humorists desired to goe for England. **1614** B JONSON *Bart. Fair* IV. iii, Such as you are..with your tuft-taffata hanches. [**1829** H. MURRAY *N. Amer.* I. iv. 212 A plot which had arisen among what he [Smith] oddly calls the 'tuftaffety' part of the colony, to break up and return to England.]

**c.** *Tuftaffeta cream*: a very soft or smooth kind of cream; velvet cream.

**1661** HAN. WOOLLEY *Ladies Direct.* 98 To make the Tuff-Taffete Cream. **1773** GOLDSM. *Stoops to Conq.* II. i, A shaking pudding, and a dish of tiff—taff—taffety cream. *Hast.* Confound your made dishes.

**Tufted** (tʊ·ftĕd), *a.* [f. TUFT *sb.* and *v.* + -ED.]

**1.** Having or adorned with a tuft or tufts. **a.** Adorned with tufts or clumps of trees or bushes.

**1606** SYLVESTER *Du Bartas* II. iv. II. *Magnif.* 1106 The tufted tops of sacred Libanon. 1779 *Mirror* No. 43 ⁋ 3 A stream..circled round a tufted plain, and formed a little lake in front of a village. 1810 Scott *Lady of L.* i. xiii, Tall rocks and tufted knolls. 1883 R. Bridges *Prometheus* 148 The cones And needles of the fir..are strewn upon the tufted floor.

**b.** Adorned with tufts of some fabric, as a garment, or with a natural tuft, as the tail or other part of an animal.

1651 in *Verney Mem.* (1907) I. 480, 2 Tufted Holland Wastcoates. 1662 *Irish Stat.* (1765) II. 411 Linnen cloth or canvas called stript or tufted canvas. 1709 Steele *Tatler* No. 45 ⁋ 5 A young Gentleman who sat next me..in a tufted Gown. 1774 Goldsm. *Nat. Hist.* (1776) III. 291 The tail long, and tufted at the point..like the lion. 1815 Kirby & Sp. *Entomol.* iii. (1818) I. 63 Head..adorned with elegantly tufted antennæ. 1877 Knight *Dict. Mech.*, *Tufted fabric*, a fabric in which tufts are set, as in the old form of Turkish and Persian carpets.

**c.** *Her.* Having the tuft (of the tail) of a specified tincture.

1761 *Brit. Mag.* II. 13 An antelope,..gules;..chained, armed, crested, tufted, and hoofed, or. 1864 Boutell *Her. Hist. & Pop.* xvii. § 3. (ed. 3) 281 An unicorn arg., armed, maned and tufted or.

**d.** Of a bird: Having a tuft of feathers upon the head; crested: *esp.* in *Ornith.* as the epithet of a particular species.

1768 Pennant *Zool.* II. 458 The Tufted Duck. 1770 M. Bruce in *Life*, etc. xii. (1914) 176 From her low nest the tufted lark upsprings. 1785 Pennant *Arct. Zool.* II. 432 Tufted Auk. 1807 Col. Hawker *Diary* (1893) I. 6, I saw 5 tufted ducks. 1833 Tennyson *New-Year's Eve* v, The tufted plover [will] pipe along the fallow lea. 1883 *Fisheries Exhib. Catal.* (ed. 4) 134 Tufted Cormorant or 'Shag'.

**2.** Formed into or forming a tuft; growing in a tuft or tufts; clustered.

1632 Milton *L'Allegro* 78 Towers and Battlements.. Boosom'd high in tufted Trees. 1637 — *Lycidas* 143 The tufted Crow-toe, and pale Gessamine. 1740 Somerville *Hobbinol* i. 101 The tufted Cowslips breathe their faint Perfume. 1807 Wordsw. *Wh. Doe* vii. 142 A hut, by tufted trees defended. 1853 Chr. G. Rossetti *Poems* (1904) 152/2 The stream shines silver in the tufted grass.

**3.** *Nat. Hist.* (esp. as the epithet of a particular species or variety: see quots. See also 1 d.) **a.** *Bot.* Bearing flowers in tufts or fascicles. **b.** *Bot.* and *Zool.* Growing in tufts, cæspitose.

1629 Tufted Colombines [see Columbine *sb.*[2] 3]. 1707 Mortimer *Husb.* (1721) II. 216 Cowslips are of various kinds..: The double green ones, the single green, the tufted, ..&c. 1805 R. W. Dickson *Pract. Agric.* II. 895 The Tufted Vetch..might..be useful..as a green fodder. 1857 Miss Pratt *Flower. Pl.* IV. 237 *L[ysimachia] thyrsiflora* (Tufted Loosestrife). 1872 Nicholson *Palæont.* 95 The corallum is cæspitose, or tufted. *Mod.* Tufted violas of many colours.

**4.** *Comb.*, as *tufted-eared, -necked* adjs.

1811 Shaw *Gen. Zool.* VIII. 236 Tufted Eared Creeper. *Ibid.* 345 Tufted-necked Humming-bird.

Hence **Tu·ftedness,** the quality of being tufted; in quot. *concr.* a tufted structure.

1665 Hooke *Microgr.* xlvi. 196 A seeming tuftedness or brushy part on each side.

**Tufter** (tʊ·ftəɹ). *Stag-hunting.* [f. Tuft *v.* 4 + -er[1].] A hound trained to drive the deer out of cover.

1856 'Stonehenge' *Brit. Sports* i. ii. ii. § 2. (ed. 2) 109 Men, called 'harbourers', with hounds trained for the purpose, called 'tufters', undertake the task. 1868 *Daily News* 2 Sept., The tufters..soon roused two fine stags. 1884 Jefferies *Red Deer* iii, When the tufters enter the woods—that is, the hounds detached from the pack to force the deer to break cover.

**Tu·ft-hu:nter.** [f. Tuft *sb.* + Hunter.] One who meanly or obsequiously courts the acquaintance of persons of rank and title (originally at the universities: see Tuft *sb.* 7, 7 b); a toady, sycophant.

1755 *Connoisseur* No. 97 ⁋ 1, I remember to have heard a cousin of mine,..formerly at Cambridge,..mentioning a sect of Philosophers, distinguished by the rest of the collegians under the appellation of Tuft-Hunters. These were..the followers (literally speaking) of the fellow-commoners, noblemen, and other rich students. 1855 Thackeray *Newcomes* xlv, Some..accused him of being a tuft-hunter, and flatterer of the aristocracy. *a* 1884 M. Pattison *Mem.* (1885) 4 My father was too proud to be a tuft-hunter.

So **Tu·ft-hu:nted** *a.*, sought after by tuft-hunters; **Tu·ft-hu:nting** *sb.*, the practice of a tuft-hunter; *adj.* that is, or is characteristic of, a tuft-hunter.

1849 Thackeray *On Friendship* Wks. 1901 VI. 625 His old acquaintances..set the *Tufthunted down as the Tufthunter. 1894 Du Maurier *Trilby* II. 95 Little Billee was no tuft-hunter, he was the tuft-hunted. 1789 *Loiterer* No. 11. 6 The diversion of *tuft-hunting..has been so long.. practised in this place [Oxford]. 1848 Thackeray *Bk. Snobs* xix, Tuft-hunting is snobbish. 1829 [H. Best] *Pers. & Lit. Mem.* 101 He made no disgraceful *tuft-hunting distinctions in favour of noblemen or gentlemen commoners. 1856 R. A. Vaughan *Mystics* (1860) II. 208 A tuft-hunting sort of Quietism.

**Tuftily** (tʊ·ftili), *adv.* [f. Tufty + -ly[2].] In a tufty manner; so as to form tufts.

1859 *Jrnl. R. Agric. Soc.* XX. i. 259 It [grass] grows tuftily.

**Tuftin** (*Bell-ringing*): see Tuffing 2.

**Tufting** (tʊ·ftiŋ), *vbl. sb.* [f. Tuft *v.* + -ing[1].] The action of the verb Tuft, or the result of this.

**1.** Adornment with a tuft or tufts.

1554–5 in Feuillerat *Revels Q. Mary* (1914) 175, vj yardes of red gold sarcenet..for the tuftinge of the wemens hedpeces. 1558 *Ibid.*, *Q. Eliz.* (1908) 24 Spente in pullinges oute, tuftinges, tyringes [etc.].

**b.** *concr.* Tufts collectively; a mass of tufts.

1791 Gilpin *Forest Scenery* i. 243 Sun-shine striking a wood..and reposing on the tuftings of a clump. 1894 R. Bridges *Shorter Poems* v. xvi. (1912) 317 The fir-trees.. wave aloft..their blue-green tuftings.

**2.** *Stag-hunting.* The action of beating a covert to dislodge the deer. Also *attrib.*

1862 C. P. Collyns *Chase Wild Red Deer* iv. 82 What I have said will sufficiently indicate what the object of *tufting* is. 1883 *Standard* 10 Aug. 2/1 Tufting is not a popular form of passing the time on an opening day. 1884 Jefferies *Red Deer* vii. 118 The hounds..are called the 'tufters';..drawing the cover is called 'tufting'.

**3.** *Comb.* **Tufting-button,** one of the buttons used in 'tufting' a cushion, etc. (see Tuft *v.* 1 b).

1884 Forney *Car-Builder's Dict.* (Cent. Dict.).

**Tu·fting,** *ppl. a.* [f. as prec. + -ing[2].] That tufts: see the vb. 1598 [see Tuft *v.* 2].

**Tu·ftlet.** [f. Tuft *sb.* + -let.] A little tuft.

1892 J. Mather *Poems* 129 Tuftlets brown Of rush and bracken.

**Tufty** (tʊ·fti), *a.* Also 7 **tuffie.** [f. Tuft *sb.* + -y.]

**1.** Full of or abounding in tufts; covered or adorned with tufts: **a.** of hair, thread, or the like.

1641 Best *Farm. Bks.* (Surtees) 6 Signes of a good Ewe. ..Her buttocke broade and large, and shewing tufty and thicke of wooll. 1716 M. Davies *Athen. Brit.* II. 241 His black Thread-bare Coat..of a tufty and rusty Hue. 1848 *Fraser's Mag.* XXXVII. 404 Shaven round his head, so as to leave a tufty patch at top.

**b.** Of foliage, herbage, or blossoms.

1638 Brathwait *Barnabees Jrnl.* iii. (1818) 133 Vallies.. Deckt with tufty woods. 1796 An. Seward *Hoyle Lake* in *New Ann. Reg.* 158 Dry are the tufty downs, diffusive spread O'er the light surface of the sandy mound. 1869 Blackmore *Lorna D.* lix, Here the ground lay jagged and shaggy, wrought up with high tufts of reed...This tufty, flaggy ground..will not hold impressions. 1903 *Academy* 25 July 94/2 Yarrow and the tufty melilot.

**c.** Covered with tufts or clumps of trees. *rare*—[1].

1612 Drayton *Poly-olb.* xvii. 388 About the neighbouring woods..in the tufty Frith, and in the mossy Fell.

**2.** Forming a tuft or tufts; consisting of or growing in tufts.

1611 Cotgr., *Touffu*.., tuffie [1632 Sherwood, Tuftie or tuffie], thicke growing, thicke of boughs, growing close together. 1613–16 W. Browne *Brit. Past.* i. v. 310 An humble dale, Where tufty daizies nod at every gale. 1776 *Phil. Trans.* LXVI. 100 Islands are overspread with a short, tufty, round grass. 1889 *Standard* 24 Apr., They are all distinguished by frizzly hair, more or less tufty.

**Tug** (tʊg), *sb.* Forms: see Tug *v.*; also 5 **teug.** [f. Tug *v.*]

**1.** An act or the action of tugging; a forcible or violent pull; a severe strain or drag.

1500–20 Dunbar *Poems* xxxiii. 81 The tarsall gaif him tug for tug. 1635 Quarles *Embl.* iv. iii. 28 The idle vessell slides that watry lay, Without the blast, or tug, of wind, or Oare. 1697 Dryden *Æneid* ix. 759 Downward by the feet he drew The trembling dastard: at the tug he falls. 1754 Mrs. Delany in *Life & Corr.* (1861) III. 307 Lady Harriet had a tooth drawn by Rutter,..and he gave three tugs before he got it out! 1815 *Hist. J. Decastro* IV. 111 The door stuck to the posts so fast that I was forced to take three or four good tugs at it before it would come open. 1886 Fenn *Master of Cerem.* xiv, Morton felt a tug at his line.

**2.** † Labour, toil (*obs. rare*); *esp.* a determined effort to accomplish or attain something; a hard try; a struggle; a 'go'.

1504 *Plumpton Corr.* (Camden) 191 It ryseth on my owne mynd to give over grett tuggs of husbandry which I had, and take me to lesse charge. 1673 Ld. Conway in *Essex Papers* (Camden) I. 141, I shall yet have a tug for the M[r] of the Ordnance place. 1764 *Mem. G. Psalmanazar* 84, I ..found it a very hard tug to keep up my credit. 1856 Bryant *Autumn Woods* xii, The vain low strife That makes men mad—the tug for wealth and power.

**3.** A strenuous contest between two forces or persons.

1660 Gower in *5th Rep. Hist. MSS. Comm.* (1876) 204/1 The only tug is between Episcopacy and Presbytery. 1830 Scott *Demonol.* i. 11 Amid the mortal tug of combat. 1868 Freeman *Norm. Conq.* II. viii. 269 On this day..William began that career of..good fortune in the mere tug of battle. 1897 *Westm. Gaz.* 8 Dec. 2/3 The tug of will between the overbearing Kaiser and his hitherto subservient people.

**b.** *Tug of war.* (*a*) The decisive contest; the real struggle or tussle; a severe contest for supremacy. (*b*) An athletic contest between two teams who haul at the opposite ends of a rope, each trying to drag the other over a line marked between them. Also *attrib.*

1677 N. Lee *Alex. Gt.* iv. ii, When Greeks joined Greeks, then was the tug of war. 1822 Byron *Juan* viii. li, At last [the mob] takes to weapons..Then comes 'the tug of war'. 1876 *World* V. No. 108. 13 The tug of war..was the most popular item in Saturday's entertainment. 1893 E. H. Barker *Wand. Southern Waters* 263 He [the devil] therefore lost no time in entering upon a tug-of-war with the saintly interloper. 1902 *Westm. Gaz.* 6 June 7/1 Their tug-of-war team pulled over two teams of British Tommies.

**4.** In harness: **a.** (Chiefly *pl.*) A pair of short chains attached to the hames, by which the collar is connected with the shafts. **b.** A trace. **c.** A short strap sewn on various parts of the harness and serving to keep it in position; also (*pl.*) the loops of the back-strap which support the shafts. **d.** A metal stud or pin on the shaft to prevent it running too far forward through the loops of the back-strap. **e.** See quot. 1844. **Also** *locally* applied to other parts of harness: see quot. 1888.

[*c* 1250 *MS. Barlow 49* (2) lf. 16 In carucis..emendandis... In iugis et tuggis ad idem emptis ix. d.] 1417–18 in *Archæol. Jrnl.* (1881) XXXVIII. 78 Item in vij Teugys, xij d. 1481–3 *Acc. Exch. K. R.* File 496 No. 26 Tuggis et hamis. 1497 *Naval Acc. Hen. VII* (1896) 96 Tugges for horsharnesse, ij baskettes. 1562 Bulleyn *Bulwark, Dial. Soarnes & Chir.* 7 b, Banishe them from Chyrurgi, commende them to the Carte. To the flaile and the rake, the trace and the togge. 1589 Puttenham *Eng. Poesie* iii. xxiii. (Arb.) 281 Which word tugge..signifieth the pull or draught of the oxen or horses, and therefore the leathers that beare the chiefe stresse of the draught, the cartars call them tugges. 1786 Burns *To Auld Mare* xi, Thou was a noble fittie-lan', As e'er in tug or tow was drawn! 1794 W. Felton *Carriages* (1801) II. x. 134 Tugs to hold up the traces. *Ibid.* 135 The hipstrap..buckles to the tugs of the breeching to hold it up. *Ibid.* 147 In the middle [of each of a pair of hames] other loops are hung, to which the tugs for the draught are fixed. 1808–18 Jamieson, *Tug*, raw-hide, of which formerly plough-traces were made. 1844 Stephens *Bk. Farm* II. 695 The pace of the old horse should be subdued..by the rein and tug; which the short reins are called, that pass from the head of one horse to the collar of the other. 1862 *Catal. Internat. Exhib., Brit.* II. No. 4708, The collars, hames, and tugs are suited to give the horse the least fatigue in drawing the vehicle. 1888 Elworthy *W. Somerset Word-bk.*, *Tug*,..the hook or other iron on the carriage, or on the whipple-tree, to which the trace is attached...The end of the leather trace at the part where it is attached to the vehicle...A loose loop buckled round the shaft, to which (when used) is fastened the kicking-strap.

**f.** *Mining.* The iron hoop of a corf or hoisting bucket.

1858 Simmonds *Dict. Trade*, *Tug*,..a hoop of iron to hold a tackle. 1877 in Knight *Dict. Mech.* 1881 Raymond *Mining Gloss.*, *Tug* (Derb.), the iron hook of a hoisting bucket, to which the tacklers are attached.

**5.** A timber-wagon. *south.* and *east. dial.*

1706 Phillips (ed. Kersey), *Tug*,..a Country-Word for a Waggon to carry Timber. 1724 De Foe *Tour Gt. Brit.* I. 59, I have seen one tree on a carriage which they call here [Lewes] a tug, drawn by two and twenty oxen. 1791 Gilpin *Forest Scenery* i. 116 A sort of wain, which in that deep country [Sussex], is expressively called a tugg. 1829 Hor. Smith *New Forest* I. i. 3 A timber-wain, in Hampshire called a tug.

**6.** A small, stoutly built, and powerful steamer used to tow other vessels; a tug-boat.

1817 *Chron.* in *Ann. Reg.* 101 This vessel,..appropriately named the Tug, is meant to track ten other vessels...The utility of the Tug is not confined to tracking. 1840 *Evid. Hull Docks Comm.* 73 You use the tug to tow them from the harbour. 1908 [Miss Fowler] *Betw. Trent & Ancholme* 12 The smoke of a tug drawing vessels.

**7.** Phrases. † *To hold tug*, (also *hold a tug*), *to hold one tug*, to keep one strenuously occupied, or fully engaged; *in tug*, † *upon a tug*, in conflict or contest (*with*).

1577 Grange *Golden Aphrod.* I iv, Whiche twoo pretie poyntes [for discussion] helde them tugge with hard holde vntill..aboute dinner tyme. 1659 *Burton's Diary* (1828) IV. 317 The debate held such tug that it was moved to adjourn. 1667 Wood *Life* 18 July (O.H.S.) II. 113 There was work enough..that would hold him tugg for a whole yeare. 1672 *Westminster Drollery* ii. 94 No Tankerd, Flaggon, Bottle, nor Jugg..so well can hold Tugg. 1681 R. L'Estrange *Apol. Prot.* iv. i. 99 The Popes were at that time upon a Tugg with the Emperor. 1700 Motteux *Quix.* i. iv. iv. II. 398 The Barber held tugg with her till the Curate advis'd him to return it. 1791 Gouv. Morris in Sparks *Life & Writ.* (1832) I. 355 Lafayette will hold a good tug, being as cunning as any body. 1849 C. Brontë *Shirley* xx, She had seen from the window Tartar in full tug with two carriers' dogs.

**8.** *attrib.* and *Comb.*: in sense 6, as *tug-boat* (whence *tug-boatman*), *-captain, -man, -master, -owner, -service, -steamer, -traffic*; also *tug-like* adj.; **tug-buckle,** a trace-buckle; **tug-carrier,** each of a pair of loops through which the tugs or traces pass (Knight *Dict. Mech.* 1877); **tug-chain,** a chain trace; also a short chain by which a leather trace is attached to the splinter-bar (*Funk's Stand. Dict.* 1895); **tug-hole**: cf. sense 4 f; **tug-hook,** a hook on the hame to which the trace is attached; **tug-iron**: see quot.; **tug-plate**: see quot.; † **tug-rope,** a trace of rope; **tug-slide,** a tongueless trace-buckle: cf. Slide *sb.* 6; **tug-spring,** a spring connexion for traces to reduce the strain of starting a load; **tug-strap,** a leather trace; **tug-whiting,** a whiting caught by a hand-line (*Sc.*). See also Tugwithe.

1832 Babbage *Econ. Manuf.* vi. (ed. 3) 44 A kind of *tug-boat for vessels which have occasion to ascend the rapid. 1860 *Merc. Marine Mag.* VII. 73 One ship was..waiting to be towed out by the tugboat. 1891 *Daily News* 3 Feb. 3/5 The tug-boatmen who struck on Friday at Liverpool were still out yesterday. 1851 Mayhew *Lond. Labour* I. 359 His foreman..says to me, 'Give that *tug-buckle a file'. 1862 *Catal. Internat. Exhib., Brit.* II. No. 4686 Set of carriage harness, with improved tug buckles. 1897 *Westm. Gaz.* 26 May 4/3 A *tug captain from Limehouse was called by the police. 1797 J. Curr *Coal Viewer* 18 Should the corves be made to draw by conductors, the chains..from the center of the *tug hole to the center of the ring that connects them, should measure 22½ inches. 1417–18 in *Archæol. Jrnl.* (1881) XXXVIII. 78 Item in *Teughookys, vij d. 1844 W. Barnes *Poems Rur. Life* Gloss., **Tugiron of shafts*, an iron on the shafts [of a wagon] to hitch the traces to. 1890

'R. BOLDREWOOD' *Col. Reformer* (1891) 155 Energetic people have certain advantages. Their *tuglike, unremitting habit of doing something keeps the machine going. **1891** *Scott. Leader* 24 Jan. 6 Over 80 per cent. of the *tugmen at Liverpool have joined the Sailors' Union. **1896** *Pall Mall Mag.* Nov. 386 The responsibilities and anxieties of a *tug-master. **1901** *Westm. Gaz.* 26 Aug. 5/2 They were *tug-owners, and worked the ferry between Hobbs's Point and the Neyland Ordnance Stores. **1794** W. FELTON *Carriages* (1801) II. Gloss., **Tug Plate*, a plate, fixed on the shafts, in which the tugs of a one horse harness is placed. **1417–18** in *Archæol. Jrnl.* (1881) XXXVIII. 78 Item in cordis vocatis *Teugropis, viij$^{d}$. **1877** KNIGHT *Dict. Mech.*, *Tug-slide..*Tug-spring. **1861** *Wheat & Tares* 252 *Tug steamers flashed hither and thither, panting and groaning with their heavy train of stone-laden barges. **1882** *Cassell's Encycl. Dict.* s. v. *Breast-strap*, The breast-collar ..at its rear ends receives the *tug-straps. **1906** *Daily Tel.* 1 Feb., The Thames and London Rowing Clubs..have never complained of the general, business *tug-traffic. *a* **1670** SPALDING *Troub. Chas. I* (1851) II. 174 About this tyme [1642], sum *tug-quhytinges [were] takin.

**Tug** (tɒg), *v.* Forms: 3 toggen, 4–6 togge; (6 tog, toug), 4–7 tugge, 5–8 (9 *dial.*) tugg; 5– tug. [Early ME. *togg-en*, intensive from weak grade of **teuhan, tauh, tugum*, OE. *téo(ha)n, téah, tugon, togen*: see TEE *v.*[1]]

†**1.** *intr.* To pull sportively, struggle amorously. *Obs. rare.*

*a* **1225** *Ancr. R.* 424 Heo ne schulen cussen nenne mon,.. ne toggen mid him, ne pleien. *a* **1225** *St. Marher.* 14 Wið plohe speche sputte to mare, swa longe þat ha tollið togederes ant toggið.

**2.** To contend, strive in opposition. Now *rare.*

**14..** *Tourn. Tottenham* 199 in Hazl. *E. P. P.* III. 91 Thus thai tuggut and thei ruggut til hit was nyȝt. *a* **1550** *Dr. Doubble Ale* 148 ibid. III. 311 The sexton and he truly Did tog by the eares earnestly. **1598** *Mucedorus* Epil. 28 Let us tugge, till one the mastrie winne. **1657** *Burton's Diary* (1828) II. 255, I..came away, and left them tugging upon that debate. **1693** DRYDEN *Love Triumph.* I. i, Fierce Ramirez, the Castilian king, Who tugged for empire with our warlike son. **1701** J. SAGE *Vind. Cyprianic Age* Wks. 1847 II. 45, I have dared to tug a little with Gilbert Rule. **1807** J. BARLOW *Columb.* III. 602 Man tugs with man, and clubs with axes play. **1872** LE FANU *In a Glass Darkly* III. 116 All her energies seemed strained to suppress a fit, with which she was then breathlessly tugging.

†**b.** *Tug it out*, to decide a matter by contest or debate; to 'have it out'; also, to go through with a thing to the end. *Obs.*

**1624** HEYWOOD *Captives* I. ii. in Bullen *O. Pl.* IV, We'll tugge it out by the teeth. **1648** in *Verney Mem.* (1907) I. 411 My Lord is resolved to go aboard this night and to tugge it out with any wind. **1655** FULLER *Ch. Hist.* II. iii. § 1 This tough old man, being 70. yeares of age, took a Journey to Rome, there to tugg it out with his Adversaries. **1673** HICKERINGILL *Greg. F. Greyb.* 319 The great courage of Cæsar reviv'd the poor spirited man and made him tug it out.

**3.** *intr.* To toil, labour, struggle; to go toilsomely, advance laboriously.

**1619** VISCT. DONCASTER in *Eng. & Germ.* (Camden) 46, I came..to Cologne..put myselfe into the boate..tugged up the river in five days to Francfort. **1634** RAINBOW *Labour* 40 All for which you tugge thus diligently, shall perish. **1691** WOOD *Ath. Oxon.* II. 238 He was..deprived of all the Church lands..notwithstanding he tugged hard to keep some. **1719** WATTS *Hymn*, '*My drowsy pow'rs, why sleep ye so*' ii, The little ants for one poor grain Labour, and tug, and strive. **1860** HOLLAND *Miss Gilbert* vi, To tug and tug all their lives to get money together. **1911** E. SIDGWICK *Le Gentleman* x, He had..tugged up one great boulevard.. and down another.

†**b.** *trans.* To acquire by toil or exertion. *rare.*

**1649** G. DANIEL *Trinarch., Hen. V* cccxciii, The Soldier tumbles what the owner Tugg'd.

**c.** To carry or convey (something ponderous) with difficulty or exertion; to lug, drag. *colloq.*

**1710** STEELE *Tatler* No. 231 ⁋ 2 [He] then says to his Wife, Child, prithee take up the Saddle; which she readily did, and tugged it Home.

**4.** *trans.* To pull at with force; to strain or haul at.

**13..** *K. Alis.* 2305 He hit toggid [*Bodl. MS.* tukked] out to habbe. *a* **1375** *Lay Folks' Mass Bk.* App. iv. 314 Wiþ his teeþ he gon hit togge. *c* **1440** *Promp. Parv.* 495/2 Toggyn, or drawyn.., *tractulo.* **1513** MORE *Rich. III* (1883) 85 His here in despite torn and togged lyke a cur dogge. **1671** MILTON *Samson* 1650 Those two massie Pillars ..He tugg'd, he shook, till down they came. **1697** DRYDEN *Virg. Past.* III. 153 In vain the Milk-maid tugs an empty Teat. **1711** GAY *Rural Sports* I. 154 He greedily sucks in the twining bait, And tugs and nibbles the fallacious meat. **1855** MACAULAY *Hist. Eng.* xvi. III. 649 Each oar was tugged by five or six slaves.

†**b.** To pull about roughly; to touse, to maul.

**1493** *Festivall* (W. de W. 1515) 102 b, His neyghbours..all to-bette this man & drewe hym and tugged hym in the worst maner that they coude. **1577–87** HOLINSHED *Chron.* III. 1029/1 He himselfe was cruellie tugged and cast into a dich. **1600** HOLLAND *Livy* VI. xvi. 227 Suffer ye your Knight and Defender, to be thus tugged, misused, and evill entreated by his adversaries? **1605** SHAKS. *Macb.* III. i. 112 And I..So wearie with Disasters, tugg'd with Fortune. **1611** SPEED *Hist. Gt. Brit.* IX. xix. § 59 The slaine body of the vsurping Tyrant, all tugged, and torne.

**c.** To get into some condition by tugging. *rare.*

**1548** UDALL, etc. *Erasm. Par. Mark* i. 15 Tugged and haled into sondrye pieces.

†**d.** *intr.* for *pass. Obs. rare.*

**1568** *Satir. Poems Reform.* xlviii. 40 It [cloth] tuggis in hoilis, and gais abbreid.

†**e.** *fig. Tug out*, to go through with a struggle to the end; to drag out. *Obs. rare*$^{-1}$.

**1631** WEEVER *Anc. Fun. Mon.* 617 Hauing beene Earle of Oxford full fifty yeares; a long time to tugge out, in the troublesome raignes of so many kings.

**5.** To move by pulling forcibly; to pull with great exertion or difficulty; to drag, haul. Also *fig.*

*c* **1320** R. BRUNNE *Medit.* 441 Some tugge [*v.r.* tugge him], sum drawe [*v.r.* drawe him] fro ce to ce. **1406** HOCCLEVE *Misrule* 197 Ther the bootmen took vp-on me keep..With hem was I I-tugged to and fro. **1526** *Pilgr. Perf.* (W. de W. 1531) 97 b, With all abieccyon haled and tugged from place to place. **1659** *Burton's Diary* (1828) IV. 308 The debate was thus tugged to and again till one o'clock. **1715** J. CHAPPELOW *Rt. way Rich* (1717) 142 Often sin tuggs him down. **1730** POPE *Let. to Gay* 11 Sept., I am tugg'd back to the world and its regards too often. **1840** MACAULAY *Ess., Clive* (1887) 547 Fifty pieces of ordnance of the largest size, each tugged by a long team of white oxen. **1877** W. R. COOPER *Egypt. Obelisks* viii. (1878) 35 Three hundred rowers tugged the huge trireme with its ponderous burden across the waters of the Mediterranean.

**6.** *intr.* To pull with great effort or force; to drag, haul. Often with *at.*

**1303** R. BRUNNE *Handl. Synne* 9286 With hys teþe he gan to drawe, And harde for to tugge and gnawe. **1500–20** DUNBAR *Poems* xxxiii. 69 And evir the cuschettis at him tuggit, The rukis him rent, the ravynis him druggit. *c* **1613** MIDDLETON *No Wit like Woman's* II. iii, The streams of fortune, 'gainst which he tugs in vain. **1698** FRYER *Acc. E. India & P.* 51 The Men tugged stoutly at their Paddles. *a* **1721** PRIOR *Dial. betw. Locke & Montaigne* 381 If you are always tugging at your Purse Strings, you may chance to break them. **1791** COWPER *Iliad* XII. 485 Sarpedon..with both hands Tugg'd, and down fell the battlement entire. **1852** MRS. STOWE *Uncle Tom's C.* xvii, Tugging at her pocket to get out the package.

**b.** In phrase *to tug at the (an) oar*, to row as a galley-slave; hence *fig.* to toil unremittingly; to labour in a subordinate capacity; to do the drudgery. Cf. OAR *sb.* 1 b.

**1612** DEKKER *If it be not good* Wks. 1873 III. 265 Hels drudge, her Gally-slaue. I ha' wore My flesh to th' bones.. at the Oare Tugging. *a* **1680** BUTLER *Rem.* (1759) I. 295 We must sit here..and tug at the Oar, while they steer which way they please. *a* **1764** LLOYD *Author's Apol.* 21 Oh! 'Tis a service irksome more Than tugging at the slavish oar. **1875** MCLAREN *Serm.* Ser. II. viii. 145 Kept him tugging away all his life at the oar, administering the affairs of a Kingdom.

**c.** *transf.* and *fig.*

**1706** E. WARD *Wooden World Diss.* (1708) 103 Tugging at a large Rummer of Rhenish and Sugar. **1833** L. RITCHIE *Wand. by Loire* 79 How many recollections tugged at his heart as he went on! **1860** EMERSON *Cond. Life, Consid.* Wks. (Bohn) II. 426 All sensible people are selfish, and nature is tugging at every contract to make the terms of it fair.

**d.** The verb-stem used adverbially.

**1849** CUPPLES *Green Hand* viii, Tug came both Mrs. Brady's hands through his hair.

**7.** *trans.* [f. TUG *sb.* 6.] To tow by means of a steam-tug.

**1839** J. M. W. TURNER (*title of painting*), The Fighting Téméraire Tugged to her Last Berth to be Broken Up.

**Tugger** (tɒ·gəɪ). [f. TUG *v.* + -ER [1].] One who tugs or pulls with force; *spec.* one who pulls in a tug-of-war (*colloq.*).

**1611** COTGR., *Tireur*, a drawer, puller,..tugger. *a* **1624** BP. M. SMITH *Serm.* (1632) 243 Being vnequally yoked with a tugger. **1909** *Athenæum* 13 Mar. 315/1 The strain from without slackened, and..the victorious tuggers fell on their backs.

**Tugging** (tɒ·giŋ), *vbl. sb.* [f. TUG *v.* + -ING [1].] The action of TUG *v.* in various senses.

*a* **1225** *Ancr. R.* 204 Hwonne þe schil & te heorte..hunten þer efter, mid wouhinge, mid togginge, oðer mid eni tollunge. *c* **1440** *Promp. Parv.* 495/2 Toggynge, or strogelynge.., *colluctacio.* ? *a* **1500** *Chester Pl.* vii. 210 For thy teeth here is good tugging. **1551** T. WILSON *Logike* (1580) 60 In all whiche matchyng and touggyng together, this would bee obserued, that [etc.]. **1660** MILTON *Free Commw.* Wks. 1851 V. 441 An endless tugging between Petition of Right and Royal Prerogative. **1742** FIELDING *Jos. Andrews* III. vi, Being roused by these Tuggings, he constantly awaked. **1866** MRS. GASKELL *Wives & Dau.* i, After some tugging, she opened the casement.

**Tu·gging**, *ppl. a.* [f. as prec. + -ING [2].] That tugs, in various senses.

*c* **1440** *Promp. Parv.* 495/2 Toggynge (*A.* or) drawynge, *attractulus.* **1611** COTGR., *Roulier*,..a lustie, tugging Iade. **1642** ROGERS *Naaman* 149 Oh! it is a tugging crying sinne. **1657** *Burton's Diary* (1828) II. 270 The Bill for the Excise was read the third time, and after..a great and tugging debate thereupon, the Bill passed. **1865** *Cornh. Mag.* May 584, I should like a little more quiet talk with you, without this tugging brute for a third.

Hence **Tu·ggingly** *adv.*, with tugging.

**1731** BAILEY, *Tuggingly*, difficultly.

†**Tu·ggle**, *v. Obs.* Forms: 5 tuggel, tugle, *Sc.* tuggill, 6 tuggle. [app. a freq. of TUG *v.*; see -LE 3; cf. FORTOGGLE *v.*, TOGGLE *v.*[2], also Du. *tokkelen* from *tokken.*]

**1.** *trans.* To pull about roughly; to drag about. Cf. TUG *v.* 4 b.

[Cf. *a* **1225** *Ancr. R.* 424 Heo ne schulen..toggen [*v.r.* toggle] mid him, ne pleien. *a* **1300** *Cursor M.* 24606 (Edin.) Fortuglid [*Cott.* Fortoglid, *Gött.* Fortugild] þus wit trai and ten.] *c* **1440** *Bone Flor.* 1938 He was so tuggelde in a toyle. *c* **1470** *Golagros & Gaw.* 34 Tuglit and travalit thus trew men can tyre. *c* **1475** *Rauf Coilȝear* 521 Thair is mony toun man to tuggill is full teuch. *a* **1585** MONTGOMERIE *Flyting* 362 Tousled and tuggled with towne tykes.

**2.** *intr.* To struggle, labour: = TUG *v.* 3.

**1650** TRAPP *Comm. Num.* vi. 4 He that would not toll the bell, must not tuggle with the rope. **1768** ROSS *Helenore* I. 38 Tuggling an' struggling how to get him free.

† **Tugh**, obs. variant of TOUGH.

*a* **1660** *Contemp. Hist. Irel.* (Ir. Archæol. Soc.) I. 151 The waies from thence to Sligo 20 miles, verie roughe, sliperie and tugh for artilerie or wagons.

† **Tug-net.** *Sc. Obs.* [? f. TUG *sb.* or *v.* + NET.] ? A fishing-net that is drawn or tugged, not fixed; a drag-net. (Cf. also *draw-net.*)

**1584** *Reg. Mag. Sig. Scot.* 232/1 Ad locum et aquam de Spay ubi rete piscationis vulgo tugnettis fisching dicti Rob. solebant piscare. **1607** *Ibid.* 686/1 Salmonum piscariam et lie tug-net tam rubrorum piscium et lie scaill-fische quam aliorum. **1611** *Ibid.* 170/1. **1603** in *Inform. Dk. Gordon v. Earls Murray & Fife* 2 The said Marquis's tugnet to be used by him within the bounds used and wont. **1760** *Ibid.* 1 A tugnet-fishing in the mouth of the river, or a fishing with a larger kind of net, such as is used for fishing in the sea and mouths of rivers.

† **Tu·gury, ti·gurye.** *Obs. rare.* Also 5 tygurie, -ye, te-, tugurry. [ad. L. *tugurium, tigurium* a hut, cot, peasant's cottage. Cf. F. *tugure, tugurion* (Cotgr.).] A hut, cot, cell.

**1412–20** LYDG. *Chron. Troy* II. 8660 From storm & reyn hem silf[e] for to saue, þei deuised oþer habitacles, Tegurries [*ed.* **1555** tigurves] & smale receptacles To schroude hem in. *c* **1440** *Promp. Parv.* 505/1 Tugurry, schudde, *tugurrium.* **1483** CAXTON *Gold. Leg.* (1498) 11 b/1 O blessyd tygurie or lytyl hous. **1491** — *Vitas Patr.* (1495) 11 They [hermits] were unyed in charytee in theyr tyguryes or celles.

† **Tu·gwithe, tu·gwithy.** *Obs.* In 6 togwith, -whythe, -wethe, togewith, 6–8 tugwith; 6 tugwithie, -wydie, -wedie, tough wethie. [f. TUG *sb.* or *v.* + WITHE, WITHY.] A withe formerly used to attach the swingle-tree to the head of the plough or to the harrow or cart.

**1523** FITZHERB. *Husb.* § 15 A swyngletre to holde the tresses abrode, and a togewith to be bytwene the swyngletre and the harowe. **1536** in *Archæologia* XLIII. 240 Temys and togwhythys for ij horses. **1565** *Richmond Wills* (Surtees) 169 Inventory..a tugwydie. **1572** *Ibid.* 152, ij payre of clammers, one foit eche, with togwethes, xx$^{d}$. **1570** LEVINS *Manip.* 150/33 Ye Tugwith, *traha, helcinum.* **1747** HOOSON *Miner's Dict.*, *Tugwith*, a writhen Hassel Rod..fastened with the small end to the Spindle, then brought over the Turntree at one end of it, and made fast to the Spindle again.

**Tuh** (tŭh), *int. rare.* An ejaculation expressing disgust or disdain. Cf. POOH.

**1607** *Puritan* II. i. 179 Purgatory? tuh; that word deserues to bee spit vpon.

**Tuhseeldar**, var. TAHSILDAR.

† **Tuht** (*ü*), obs. form of TIGHT *sb.*[1] (OE. *tyht*), discipline, training, breeding; conduct; usage. Also † **Tuhtle** in same sense.

*c* **1205** LAY. 2419 To Corinee hine sende..þat he hine sculde wel i-teon & tuhten [*printed* tuhlen; *c* 1275 manscipe] him teachen. *Ibid.* 2720 Hire tuhtlen weren gode. *Ibid.* 24675 For þere ilke tuhtle Cnihtes weoren ohte.

**Tuhte** (pa. t.), **tuhten**: see TIGHT *v.*[1] *Obs.*

‖ **Tui** (tū·i). [Maori name.] A New Zealand bird, *Prosthematodera novæ-zelandiæ*: = PARSON-BIRD 1, MOCKING-BIRD 2 f.

**1835** [see MOCKING-BIRD 2 f]. **1857, 1866** [se PARSON-BIRD 1]. **1869** G. H. KINGSLEY *Sport & Trav.* iv. (1900) 64 Singing birds, some like the New Zealand tui. **1884** BRACKEN *Lays Maori* 101, I hear the swell Of Nature's psalms through tree and bush, From tui, blackbird, finch and thrush. **1908** *Auckland Weekly News* 17 Dec. 50/1 It is only occasionally that the silence is broken by the liquid notes of the tui and the bell-bird.

**Tuicche**, obs. f. TWITCH. **Tuich, tuiche**, obs. Sc. ff. TOUCH, TOUGH. **Tuig**, obs. Sc. f. TWIG. **Tuik**, Sc. f. *took*, pa. t. of TAKE *v.* **Tuil, -ll**, obs. ff. TEWEL, TUILYIE, TWILL.

**Tuille, tuile** (twīl). Forms: 5–7 toile, 7 toyle, 9 tuille, tuile. [a. F. *tuile*, OF. *tieule*, in 15th c. *teuille*, L. *tēgula* TILE, plaque.] In mediæval armour, One of two or more plates of steel hanging below, or forming the lowest part of, the tasses, and covering the front of the thighs.

*c* **1400** *Destr. Troy* 6420 Ector..come..þere the corse lay, Wold haue Robbit the Renke of his riche wede With the ton hond in the toile tyrnyt it offe. *a* **1470** TIPTOFT in Segar *Hon. Mil. & Civ.* III. li. (1602) 189 Who so hitteth the Toyle three times, shall haue no prize. **1688** R. HOLME *Armoury* III. xix. (Roxb.) 180/2. **1834** PLANCHÉ *Brit. Costume* 195 *Tuiles*, plates depending from the taces or skirt of the armour in front, over an apron of chain-mail, are first visible at this period [that of Henry VI]. **1869** BOUTELL *Arms & Arm.* viii. (1874) 147 Over the flanks, on each side of the figure, to the faudes or taces was appended a plate, or small shield, or *gardefaude* (in England called a *tuille*), which would cover the front of the thigh.

† **Tuillet**, obs. form of TOILET.

**1673** *Lady's Call.* II. i. § 15 For more worthy uses then those of the comb, the tuillets, and the glass.

**Tuillette, tuilette** (twīle·t). [dim. of TUILLE: see -ETTE.] A small tuille.

**1869** BOUTELL *Arms & Arm.* x. (1874) 205 [In the effigy of Richard Beauchamp, Earl of Warwick] besides two large tuilles, there are two smaller ones or *tuillettes.* **1882** *Athenæum* 26 Aug. 278/3 Tuilettes are..generally later than 1406.

**Tuilyie, tulyie, tulie** (tü·lʸi, tü·li), *sb. Sc.* Forms: 4–6 tulȝe, tolȝe, 5 tuyl, toilȝe, (tulyhe, tohile, tohyle), 5–6 tulye, 6 tuilȝe (-ze), tuylȝe, -ȝhe, tuill, tule, toulȝe, 6–7 tuilye; 5–6 tuilyie, 6–9 tulyie, -ȝie (-zie), 8 tuilie, toolie, 7–9

**tuilȝie** (-zie), 8–9 tooly, 9 tully. [ad. OF. *tooil, touil, tueil*, contention, f. OF. *toillier*: see next and Toil *v.*[1] For the forms cf. *brulyie, fulȝie, spulȝe, ulye*. The forms in *-ie, -ye* are app. taken from the vb.] A quarrel, brawl, fight; a noisy contest, dispute: = Toil *sb.*[1] 1.

(In quot. *c* 1425 vaguely used. In Hawick it was formerly usual in time of frost to have a slide of a quarter of a mile long down the centre of the steep street called the Loan, on which long files of sliders came down at a thundering pace: this was famous as the '*Yokit tuilie*' or '*Yoke o' tuilie*'.)

*c* **1425** Wyntoun *Cron.* v. xii. 3943 (Wemyss MS.) It may be callit vnhonest tulȝe [*v.rr.* tuyl, tohyle, tolȝe, tule, tuylȝe, tuylȝhe] To se þe quyk þe dede dispulȝe Quhen he is woundit in his schete. *a* **1500** *Peebles to Play* xix, Sevin-sum, that the tulye maid, Lay gruffling in the stokks. **1557** *Peebles Burgh Rec.* (1872) 242 Gif ony suddand tulye happyng within the tovne. **1609** Skene *Reg. Maj.* I. 142 Na man quha is given to tuilzies or strife, sall presume to beare ane knife with ane poynt, within the Portes..of our Gild. **1728** Ramsay *Advice to Mr.* —— 38 And, smiling, ca' her little foolie, Syne with a kiss evite a toolie. **1814** Scott *Wav.* lxiii, Killed that same night in the tuilzie. **1886** Masson *Edinb. Sk.* 25 Edinburgh was famous for its tulzies or causeway fights between noblemen and lairds.

**b.** without article: Quarrelling, contention, strife; trouble, turmoil.

**1550** *Records of Elgin* (New Spald. Cl. 1903) I. 106 Burges that beis convict for tuilze sall pay for the first tuilze viii s. **1572** *Satir. Poems Reform.* xxxiv. 59 In Scotland had not bene sic tuill, Gif this had bene þe common reull. **1785** Burns *To W. Simpson* xxxi, But tho' dull-prose folk Latin splatter In logic tulzie, I hope we Bardies ken some better Than mind sic brulzie.

**c.** Also Tulyie-mulyie.

**1819** W. Tennant *Papistry Storm'd* (1827) 4 In mony a fecht and tulzie-mulzie. *Ibid.* 196 In hideous tulyie-mulyie.

**Tui·lyie, tu·lyie, tu·lie,** *v. Sc.* Forms: see prec. sb.; also 6 teulie. [a. OF. *tooillier, toillier, touillier*: see prec. and Toil *v.*[1]]

†**1.** *trans.* To harass; to quarrel with, assail contentiously, assault. *Obs.*

**1375** (MS. 1487) Barbour *Bruce* iv. 152 (Camb. MS.) Þai on twa halfis war assalit; Within with fyre, þat þame sa brulȝeit, Without with folk þat þaim sa tulȝeit [*Edinb. MS.* (1489) broilȝit, toilȝit]. *c* **1425** Wyntoun *Cron.* vi. xv. 1477 (Wemyss MS.) Fell tyrandis, þat had delite Possessionis and pilgrymage to tulȝe. **1595** in *Maitl. Cl. Misc.* I. 70 To have followit Thomas McNair, and to have teuliit him in the porche of Govane kirk.

**2.** *intr.* To quarrel, fight, contend. Hence **Tui·lyieing** *vbl. sb.* and *ppl. a.*

**1444** *Aberdeen Regr.* (1844) I. 12 Conuicte thrise for barganyng and tulyheing. **1565** *Reg. Privy Council Scot.* I. 333 Ony Scottismen that fechtis, tulyeis, or drawis bluid. **1725** Ramsay *Gentle Sheph.* I. ii, Sic wee tots toolying at your knee;..to be made o', and obtain a kiss. **1818** Scott *Rob Roy* xxvi, That they suld let folk tuilzie in their yards. **1862** Hislop *Prov. Scot.* 27 A toolying tike comes limping hame. **1895** Crockett *Men of Moss-Hags* 55 Let there be no more tullying and brawling.

**Tuilyier** (tü·lʸiəɹ). *Sc.* Forms: 5 tuilyeour, -your, (tulyhour), 6 tulȝear, -ȝeour (-zeour), -yeour, tuilyair, -ȝour, -ȝeour (7 -zeour), 7 tuilȝier. [ME. *tuilȝeour*, agent-n. from *tuilȝie* Tuilyie *v.*: see -our.] A quarrelsome person, a brawler. Also in comb. **tuilyier-like** *a.*, quarrelsome.

**1444** *Aberdeen Regr.* (1844) I. 12 A common tulyhour and rebellour. *c* **1480** Henryson *Test. Cres.* 194 Lyk to ane bair quhetting his tuskis kene Richt tuilyour-lyk. **1535** Stewart *Cron. Scot.* (Rolls) III. 440 Semdill[is]..Ane mydding tulzear in ane battell bydar. **1583** *Burgh Rec. Edinb.* (1882) IV. 295 Tuilyairs and trubleris of the quyett estaitt of this burgh. **1650** in Butler *Ch. & Parish Abernethy* xxv. (1897) 389 Fighters and tuilȝiers to satisfy publicly by sitting on a seat in face of the congregation.

**Tui·lyiesome,** *a. Sc.* [f. Tuilyie + -some.] Quarrelsome, contentious. Hence **Tui·lȝiesomeness.**

**1599** Jas. I. Βασιλ. Δωρον (1682) 84 Tuilyesome weapons in the Court, betokens confusion in the Countrey. **1808** Jamieson s.v., 'Tuilyiesum dogs cum happing hame'. S. Prov.

**Tuim** (tüm), Sc. var. Toom *a.*, empty.

**Tuin, tuine, tuinne,** obs. ff. Tune, Twin.

**Tuiron, Tuis, tuise:** see Tew-iron, Twice.

**Tuisday,** obs. form of Tuesday.

**Tuism** (tiū·iz'm). *rare.* [f. L. *tū* thou + -ism, after *egoism, egotism*.] A form of expression involving the use of the pronoun *thou*, or implying reference to a second person; also, in *Ethics*, primary regard to the interests of another person or persons (opp. to Egoism 2, Egotism 2); in *Philos.*, 'the doctrine that all thought is addressed to a second person, or to one's future self as a second person' (*Cent. Dict.* 1891; cf. Egoism 1).

**1796** Coleridge *Watchman* 9 Mar. 38 Omitting the long preambles..and the whole parade of egotisms and tuisms: we shall select from one such speech [etc.]. **1809–10** — *Friend* (1818) I. iv. 36 For one piece of egotism that presents itself under its own honest bare face of 'I myself I', there are fifty that steal out in the mask of tuisms and ille-isms. **1824** Byron *Juan* xvi. xiii, To hail her with the apostrophe—'O thou!' Of amatory egotism the Tuism. **1884** J. Rae *Contemp. Socialism* 124 Feuerbach's peculiar ethical principle.. has been well termed Tuism, to distinguish it from Egoism.

Hence **Tui·stic** *a.* [see -istic], of the nature of tuism.

**1880** H. Bradshaw in *Life* (1888) 292 You should..avoid.. the tuistic form of letter.

†**Tuit,** obs. form of Tewhit.

**1570** Levins *Manip.* 149/35 A Tuit, lapwing, *vpupa.*

**Tuitch,** obs. Sc. form of Touch.

**Tuition** (tiu,i·ʃən). Forms: 5–6 tuicion, tuission, etc. (with *y* for either *i*, and *-one, -oun(e,* for *-on*), 6 tuytion, -tyon, tuityon, 6–7 -tione, 5– tuition. [a. AF. *tuycioun*, obs. F. *tuition* (Cotgr., 1611), OF. *tuicion, -ssion, -tion* (1335 in Godef.), ad. L. *tuitio* guard, guardianship, n. of action from L. *tuērī* to look to, look after.]

†**1.** The action of looking after or taking care of, or condition of being taken care of; safe-keeping, protection, defence, custody, care, tutelage. *Obs.*

[**1292** Britton I. xvii. § 2 Et si il reconusent felonie..et prient tuycioun del eglise [*transl.* and beg the protection of the church].] **1436** *Libel Eng. Policy* in *Pol. Poems* (Rolls) II. 204 There glorified in reste wyth his tuicione, The deité to see wyth fulle fruicione. **1462** Edw. IV in Ellis *Orig. Lett.* Ser. II. I. 129 For the tuicion and defence of this owr Realme. **1557** *Order of Hospitalls* F vij, Which [copy] he shall haue vnder the Auditors hands, in his own tuition. *c* **1575** J. Hooker *Life Sir P. Carew* (1857) 276, I commit your Lordeship to the tuission of the Almightie. **1611** Broughton *Require Agreement* 53 A jest..that Diana ..was so busie about Alexanders birth, that she forgot the tuition of her owne Temple. **1693** Stair *Inst. Law Scot.* (ed. 2) I. vi. § 1 There is a Duty of Tuition, and Protection of Orphans. **1790** Burke *Fr. Rev.* 352 Liberty without wisdom, and without virtue..is folly, vice, and madness, without tuition or restraint.

†**b.** *spec.* The position of a guardian or Tutor in relation to a ward; guardianship. *Obs.*

**1494** Fabyan *Chron.* v. ci. 75 Clodomyrus was slayne, leuyng..iii. sonnes..whiche.iii. sonnes Clotilde toke to her tuyssion & guydynge. **1568** *Hist. Jacob & Esau* I. ii. Aiv, They were brought vp bothe vnder one tuition. **1643** Prynne *Sov. Power Parl.* App. 21 They chose Eudo,..to be King.. till Charles should come to his lawfull age, whom they put under Eudo his tuition. **1690** Locke *Govt.* II. vi. § 67 That [power] which the Father hath, in the Right of Tuition, during Minority.

†**c.** *concr.* A defence, fortification. *Obs. rare*—[1].

**1513** *Life Hen. V* (1911) 109 This Towne was fortified wth innumerable tuytions and defences.

**2.** The action or business of teaching a pupil or pupils; the function of a tutor or instructor (see Tutor); teaching, instruction.

**1582** in *Campion's Wks.* (1909) Introd. 26 Allowance for Thomas Sisley and Thomas Campion at Cambridge beginning at cristmas 1582. First, eche of them for thir diete weakely ijs. vjd.: in the whole yere..xiij. li. Item, thir tuition yerely xlv.s. for eche. **1650** Sir R. Boyle *Diary* in *Lismore Papers* (1886) I. 235, vli that he gave the ffrenchman and his wyffe for their first quarters tuicon of my children. **1781** Gibbon *Decl. & F.* xix. II. 129 They pursued their studies..under the tuition of the most skilful masters. **1807** Southey *H. K. White* 3 One of the ushers, when he came to receive the money due for tuition. **1845** E. Holmes *Mozart* 7 Obliged to devote every hour that he could spare ..to tuition on the violin and clavier.

**b.** *attrib.*, as *tuition-fee, -money.*

**1867** Aug. J. E. Wilson *Vashti* viii, In future I shall not advance one cent of my tuition-money.

Hence **Tui·tional** *a.*, pertaining or relating to tuition; of a school, supported by tuition-fees; **Tui·tionary** *a.*, pertaining to tuition.

**1847** Bushnell *Chr. Nurt.* II. i. (1861) 229 *Tuitional and regulative influences that come after. **1892** E. F. Williams in *Chicago Advance* 24 Nov., What are called 'Daughter Schools', or the 'Higher Girls' Schools' [in Germany],..are for the most part tuitional schools. **1906** *United Free Ch. Mag.* July 6/1 The tuitional side of missionary work. **1879** M. C. Tyler *Hist. Amer. Lit.* xiii. II. 93 The clerical profession..to develop the other learned professions—the legal, medical, and *tuitionary.

**Tuitive** (tiū·itiv), *a. rare.* [f. L. *tuit-*, ppl. stem of *tu-ērī*: see prec.]

**1.** Giving tuition or instruction.

**1776** *Adv. Corkscrew* ii. 17 His tutor resolved not to swerve from the general rule of these tuitive companions, but let his pupil indulge in every extravagance.

**2.** Acquired by instruction as opposed to *intuitive* or innate (Intuitive 3 c). *rare.*

**1784** *New Spectator* No. 22. 1 A man without an innate idea would be incapable of acquiring any.—Without intuitive knowledge he could have no tuitive.

**Tuix,** obs. form of Twixt.

**Tuk,** obs. pa. t. of Take *v.*; obs. f. Tuck.

†**Tuke, tewke.** *Obs.* Also 6 tuyke. [Etymology uncertain. (See Prof. Weekley in *N. & Q.* 11th Ser. III. 130.) Connexion suggested with F. *teugue, tuque*, in Boyer *Fr.-Eng. Dict.* 1702 '*tuque*, a tarpaulin, or tarpawling', Lescallier *Vocab. des Termes de Marine* 1777 has '*toile de tugue*, a canvas covering for the poop of a frigate'. According to Jal *Gloss. Nautique*, related to L. *tēgula* tiling, subseq. a canvas awning: but in Eng. applied to the material.] Canvas, such as is used for an awning or canopy; but also applied to a finer fabric.

**1477** *Lanc. Wills* (1884) 2, vij yardes Cane Tuke price the yarde vd..iiij yardes of fustian Tuke, price ye yarde xijd. **1481–90** *Howard Househ. Bks.* (Roxb.) 416 Item, iiij. yardes of tewke rossett, price vj. s. viij. d. **1494** in Rogers *Agric. & Prices* (1882) III. 560 (Oxford), 1 piece of Tewke for Tergates..@ 1/3. **1496** *Ibid.*, 3 yds Tewke 3/4. **1521** *MS. Will*, A gowne watteryd tuyke. **1527** *MS. Inv. Goods T. Cromwell* (P.R.O.), ij jerkyns of blacke saten lyned with tuke. **1530** Palsgr. 280/1 Tewke to make purses of, *trelis.* **1552–3** *Inv. Ch. Goods Staffs.* in *Ann. Lichfield* (1863) IV. 75 One canopye of tewke,..iij crosse clothes, ij of sarsnet, and the other of tewke. **1586** *Rates of Custome* F j, Tukes the peece viij. s.

**Tuke,** obs. pa. t. of Take *v.*; obs. Sc. f. Tuck.

**Tukkar, Tukne,** obs. ff. Tucker, Token.

**Tul,** obs. or dial. f. Till *prep.* and *conj.*

**Tula** (tū·lă). In full **tula metal**: Niello made at Tula in Russia. Also *attrib.*, as *tula-work.*

**1839** Ure *Dict. Arts* 1259 Tula Metal, is an alloy of silver, copper, and lead. **1884** Knight *Dict. Mech., Suppl., Tula*, the Russian niello silver. **1891** *Cent. Dict., Tula-work.*

**Tulasi**: see Tulsi. **Tulat,** obs. Sc. f. Toilet.

**Tulban, -bent,** obs. ff. Turban.

**Tulce,** obs. form of Tulsi.

**Tulchan** (tʊ·lχăn). *Sc.* Forms: 6 tulchen, 6–9 -in, 9 -ane, 8– tulchan. [a. Gaelic *tulchan*, app. local variant of *tulachan* 'little hillock', applied locally to a device used to induce a cow to give her milk: still so called in the Outer Hebrides, and in Moidart in Inverness-shire, and prob. more widely in the 16th c.

The cow is allowed to sniff at the skin of her own calf, which may be stuffed with straw or hay, but is often merely spread over the bottom of a creel or a small heap or hump of earth or turf, whence app. the name 'little hillock'. The etymology given in Highland Society's Dict., 1828, is erroneous.]

**1.** *lit.* A calf's skin set under a cow to make her yield her milk freely: see above.

*a* **1578**–*a* **1651** [see 2] **1785** *Jrnl. fr. London to Portsmouth* 2 Flae him belly-flaught, his skin wad mak' a gallant tulchin for you. **1808–18** Jamieson, *Tulchane, -in*...2. A bag or budget, generally of the skin of an animal. **1866** Livingstone *Last Jrnls.* (1873) I. ii. 51 The cattle of Africa.. never give their milk without the presence of the calf or its stuffed skin, the 'tulchan'.

**2.** *Hist.* Hence *attrib.*, applied in derision to the titular bishops appointed in Scotland immediately after the Reformation, in whose names the revenues of the sees were drawn by the lay barons.

*a* **1578** Lindesay (Pitscottie) *Chron. Scot.* (S.T.S.) II. 282 The tulchen, to wit ane feinȝeit counterfeitt bischope...The kingis lordis that obtenit thair beneficeis culd find na way to have proffeit thairof without thay had ane tulchen lyk as the kow had or scho wald gif milk, ane calfis skin stoppit with stra. **1583** *Leg. Bp. St. Androis* Pref. 61 Albeit they be now Tulchin bischops stylit. *a* **1651** Calderwood *Hist. Kirk* (1678) 55 The Bishops, admitted according to this new order, were called in jest, Tulchane Bishops. A Tulchane is a calf's skin stuffed full with straw, to cause the cow give milk. **1703** D. Williamson *Serm. bef. Gen. Assemb. Edin.* 43 Then were imposed the Tulchan, or meer nominal Bishops, who by simoniacal Contracts allowed the great men to enjoy the Revenues of the Church. **1859** J. J. Marshall *Hist. Scott. Eccles. & Civ. Affairs* x. 211 The Episcopacy thus introduced has always gone under the name of the Tulchan or Titular Episcopacy.

*transf.* **1884** Dunckley in *Contemp. Rev.* July 7 Henceforth the Khedive was to be a mere 'tulchan' ruler.

‖**Tule** (tū·le). *U.S.* Also **tula.** [ad. Aztec *tullin*, the final *n* being dropped by the Spaniards as in *Guatemala, Jalapa*, etc.] Either of two species of bulrush (*Scirpus lacustris* var. *occidentalis*, and *S. Tatora*) abundant in low lands along riversides in California; hence, a thicket of this, or a flat tract of land in which it grows.

**1856** Olmsted *Journ. Texas* iii. 149 Windowless cabins of stakes, plastered with mud and roofed with river-grass or 'tula'. **1882** *Harper's Mag.* Nov. 876 The tules or rushes rise high above our heads, and..are infested with a dangerous breed of wild hogs. **1893** A. F. Battelle in *Chicago Advance* 2 Feb., Because of the tall rushes that grow there the land is called the tule. The tule is always low and level. **1894** O. Wister in *Harper's Mag.* Sept. 520 That dug-out with side-thatch and roofing of tule.

**b.** *attrib.*, as *tule farm, hut, land, marsh, root, swamp*; **tule wren**, a kind of marsh wren (*Telmatodytes* or *Cistothorus palustris*, var. *paludicola*) which frequents the tules of California.

**1850** B. Taylor *Eldorado* vii. (1862) 73 The hazy air, made more dense by the smoke of the burning tule marshes. **1883** Stevenson *Silverado Sq.* 2 Across the cornlands and thick tule swamps of Sacramento Valley. **1890** Gunter *Miss Nobody* iv, The baked leaves of century plant, acorns, and tule roots. **1891** A. Welcker *Wild West* 64 A cabin on a swampy tule farm.

**Tule,** obs. f. Tool, Tuilyie; var. Tuly *Obs.*

†**Tulet,** obs. Sc. f. Toilet, wrapper.

**1541** *Acc. Ld. High Treas. Scot.* VIII. 22 For ane tulet to thir clathis quhilkis wer deliverit be Thomas Arthuir to the Kingis grace.

**Tuliban, Tulie,** obs. ff. Turban, Till *v.*[1]

**Tulip** (tiū·lip). [Formerly *tulipa, tulippa*, also *tulipant, -pan* = F. *tulipan, tulipe*, It. *tulipano*, Sp. *tulipan*, Pg. *tulipa, -ippa*, mod.L. *tulīpa*; early mod.Du. and Ger. *tulpe*, Du. *tulp*, Da. *tulipan*, Sw. *tulpan*; all from *tul(i)band*, vulgar Turkish pronunciation of Persian دلبند *dulband* 'turban', which the expanded flower of the tulip is thought to resemble: cf. Turban.]

**1.** A bulbous plant of the genus *Tulipa* (N.O. *Liliaceæ*), esp. the species *T. Gesneriana*, introduced from Turkey into Western Europe in the 16th c., and since extensively cultivated in very numerous varieties, blooming in spring, with broad bell-shaped or cup-shaped, usually erect, showy flowers, of various colours and markings; also, the flower itself.

The first mention of it by a Western European is by Busbek (*c* 1554), the Emperor's ambassador, on the way from Adrianople to Constantinople, where 'ingens ubique florum copia offerebatur, narcissorum, hyacinthorum, et eorum quos Turcae tulipan vocant'. It was grown by the Fuggers at Augsburg, where it was seen and described by Gesner in 1561. It was introduced successively in Vienna, Mechlin, France, and England; it is mentioned by Lyte in his transl. of Dodoneus.

α. **1578** LYTE *Dodoens* II. lii. 212 Of Tulpia, or Tulipa... The great Tulpia, or rather Tulipa. *Ibid.* 213 The greater Tulipa is brought from Grece, and the Countrie about Constantinople...The greater is called both *Tulpia*, and *Tulpian*, and of some *Tulipa*, which is a Turkie name or worde, we may call it Lillynarcissus. **1582** in Hakluyt *Voy.* (1599) II. 165 Now within these foure yeeres there haue bene brought into England from Vienna..diuers kinds of flowers called Tulipas. **1597** GERARDE *Herbal* I. lxxvii. 116 Tulipa, or the Dalmatian cap, is a strang and forraine flower. [*Ibid.* 117 After [the Tulipa of Bolonia] hath beene some fewe daies floured, the points and brims of the flower turne backward, like a Dalmatian or Turkes cap, called *Tulipan, Tolepan, Turban*, and *Turfan*, whereof it tooke his name.] **1621** BURTON *Anat. Mel.* III. ii. IV. i, As a tulipant to the sun (which our herbalists call Narcissus) when it shines is..a glorious flower exposing itself. **1629** PARKINSON *Paradisus* II. viii. 46 The early Tulipa (and so all other Tulipas) springeth out of the ground with his leaues folded one within another. *Ibid.* 66 We call it in English the Turkes Cap, but most vsually Tulipa.

β. **1615** G. SANDYS *Trav.* I. 57 You cannot stirre abroad but you shall be presented by the Deruises and Ianizaries, with tulips and trifles. **1633** JOHNSON *Gerarde's Herbal* I. lxxxvii. 139 The bloud-red Tulip with a yellow bottome. *Ibid.* 140 *Tulipa purpurea*. The purple Tulip. *Tulipa rubra amethistina*. The bright red Tulip. **1758** JOHNSON *Idler* No. 30 ⁋ 5 Another searches the world for tulips. **1842** TENNYSON *Gard. Dau.* 189 A Dutch love For tulips. **1872** YEATS *Techn. Hist. Comm.* 228 Tulips were introduced from Constantinople, and first bloomed in the beautiful grounds of Heinrich Herwart, in 1559.

**b.** Applied, usually with defining word, to species of this, and various plants more or less resembling it, or their flowers; also to the flowers of the TULIP-TREE; in S. Africa, to a poisonous herb also called *tulip-grass* (see 5).

**African tulip,** the genus *Hæmanthus* (N. O. *Amaryllidaceæ*). **Butterfly tulip,** the genus *Calochortus* of California, also called *mariposa-lily*. **Cape tulip,** name for several S. African plants: (*a*) various species of *Homeria* (= *tulip-grass*: see 5); (*b*) *Melanthium uniflorum* (*Bæometra columellaris*); (*c*) Red Cape tulip, *Hæmanthus coccineus*. **Chequered tulip, Drooping tulip** = *wild tulip*, (*b*). **Native tulip,** of Australia (see quot. 1898, and TULIP-TREE 2 a). **Parrot tulip** (see PARROT *sb.* 4). **Wild tulip,** (*a*) *Tulipa sylvestris*, a rare and doubtful native of Britain, with fragrant yellow flowers; (*b*) a name for the wild fritillary, *Fritillaria Meleagris*; (*c*) in California, = *butterfly tulip*.

**1759** MILLER *Gard. Dict.* (ed. 7) s.v. *Tulip-tree*, The Flowers..[have] six Petals,..which form a Sort of Bell-shaped Flower, from whence the Inhabitants of North America gave it the Title of Tulip. **1760** J. LEE *Introd. Bot.* App. 330 African Tulip, *Hæmanthus*...Chequer'd Tulip, *Fritillaria*. **1850** PAPPE *Floræ Capensis Med. Prodr.* 26 *Moræa collina*, Thbg. (known to almost every child in the colony as the *Cape Tulip*), not for its therapeutical use, but for its obnoxiousness. **1861** MISS PRATT *Flower. Pl.* V. 276 Wild Tulip..has a much smaller blossom than the cultivated species,..its colour within is bright yellow, and externally yellowish-green. [**1863** W. C. BALDWIN *Afr. Hunting* vi. 144 Donker, my best ox is dead, having got at a poisonous kind of grass, called by the Dutch tulp.] **1884** MILLER *Plant-n.*, Cape Tulip, *Melanthium uniflorum* (*Tulipa Breyiana*). —, Red Cape, *Hæmanthus coccineus*...Drooping T., *Fritillaria Meleagris*. *Ibid.*, *Calochortus*, Butterfly-Tulip,.. Mariposa Lily,..Wild Tulip, of California. **1885** RIDER HAGGARD *K. Solomon's Mines* iv, The other three [oxen] died from eating the poisonous herb called 'tulip'. **1898** MORRIS *Austral Eng.*, *Telopea*,..the genus containing..the *Waratah*...The name has been corrupted popularly into *Tulip*, and the flower is often called the *Native Tulip*. **1908** *Westm. Gaz.* 14 May 12/1 A field..covered with the purple blossoms of the 'tulip', as the villagers call it [the fritillary].

**2.** *fig.* A showy person or thing, or one greatly admired.

**1647** COWLEY *Mistress, Beauty* iii, Beauty, thou active passive Ill!..Thou Tulip, who thy Stock in Paint dost waste. **1672** *Mede's Wks.* Life p. xlii, Such Fellow-commoners who came to the University only to see it and to be seen..he call'd The University-Tulips, that made a Gaudy shew for a while. **1701** CIBBER *Love makes Man* v. ii, My little Blossom! my Gilliflower! my Rose! my Pink! my Tulip! **1837** THACKERAY *Ravenswing* i, Morgiana was a tulip among women, and the tulip fanciers all came flocking round her.

**b.** *slang. My tulip*, 'my fine fellow'.

**3.** A bell-shaped outward swell in the muzzle of a gun, now generally disused.

**1884** [implied in *tulip choke*]. **1889** *Engineer* Oct. 314 Breech-loading guns,..gradually tapering from a diameter of 4 ft. 7 in. at the breech to 17 in. near the muzzle, which possesses what artillerists call a tulip or 'swell'.

**4.** *slang.* A bishop's mitre, or a figure of one.

**1879** A. R. ASHWELL *Bp. Wilberforce* I. iii. 66 *note*, I heard one of the low fellows..say 'No, It's not a Tulip', meaning that there was no mitre on the panel [of the carriage].

**5.** *attrib.* and *Comb.*, as *tulip-bed, -bulb, -fancier, -glass, -grower, -leaf, -mania; tulip-fancying, -like, -shaped, -tinted* adjs.; **tulip-apple,** a variety of apple with bright-coloured fruit; **tulip choke** (cf. sense 3 and CHOKE *sb.*[1] 4); **tulip ear,** of a dog: see quot. 1877; so **tulip-eared** *a.*; **tulip-grass,** a name for several S. African poisonous herbs of the genus *Homeria* (N.O. *Iridaceæ*); **tulip-laurel,** ? a species of *Magnolia*; **tulip poplar** = TULIP-TREE 1 (see POPLAR 2); **tulip-poppy,** a Mexican papaveraceous plant, *Hunnemannia fumariæfolia*, with flowers like those of *Eschscholtzia*; **tulip-root,** (*a*) the 'root' or bulb of a tulip; (*b*) a disease of oats, characterized by a swelling at the base of the stem, caused by a minute nematoid worm; **tulip-shell,** (*a*) a bivalve of the genus *Tellina*; (*b*) any gastropod of the family *Fasciolariadæ*, as *Fasciolaria tulipa*. Also TULIP-TREE, -WOOD.

**1842** LOUDON *Suburban Hort.* 529 The tree is still more beautiful when covered with fruit, especially with such as are highly-coloured, such as the red Astrachan, the *tulip-apple, &c. **1664** EVELYN *Kal. Hort.* June (1729) 208 Take up your *Tulip Bulbs. **1884** BURGESS *Sporting Fire Arms* 4 The sketches show the ordinary choke and the *tulip choke. **1877** G. STABLES *Pract. Kennel Guide* iii. (ed. 3) 36 *Tulip-ear.—Partly pricked, and drooping at the tip. *Ibid.* vii. § 3 81 [Ears of Skye Terrier] may be pricked, or tulip. **1837** *Tulip fanciers [see 2]. **1826** SCOTT *Woodst.* xxxiii, A *tulip-fancying fellow,..intended for a Dutch gardener. **1760** J. LEE *Introd. Bot.* App. 330 *Tulip-flower, *Bignonia*. **1755** *Gentl. Mag.* Sept. 416/1 Several lacrymatories have also been dug up, some are of glass,..and some are of burnt earth, like our *tulip-glasses. **1900** *Blackw. Mag.* Apr. 574/1 He has eaten *tulip-grass. **1882** *Pall Mall G.* 18 Oct. 4 A Dutch *tulip-grower. **1766** W. STORK *Acc. East Florida* 47 The magnolia, *tulip-laurel, tupelow-tree, are all beautiful. *a* **1718** PRIOR *Alma* I. 381 But *Tulip-leaves, and Limon-peel Help only to adorn the meal. *c* **1711** PETIVER *Gazophyl.* IX. Tab. 85 Red *Tulip-like Flowers. **1839** *Penny Cycl.* XIV. 314/1 The extravagances of those visited by the *tulip mania. **1683** *Lond. Gaz.* No. 1810/4 Lost.., a Gold Pendulum Watch,..with..a Steel Chain, and *Tulip Pillars. **1868** *Rep. U. S. Comm. Agric.* (1869) 99 *Endecatomus rugosus*..has been also taken under the bark of *tulip poplars. **1909** *Cent. Dict. Suppl.*, *Hunnemannia*..contains a single Mexican species, *H. fumariæfolia*, now somewhat cultivated under the name *tulip-poppy. **1728-46** THOMSON *Spring* 538 Then comes the *tulip race, where Beauty plays Her idle freaks. **1711** ADDISON *Spect.* No. 108 ⁋ 3 He carries a *Tulip-root in his Pocket. **1875** *Encycl. Brit.* I. 360/2 The oat frequently suffers much from a disease called 'segging' or 'tulip root'. **1833** LOUDON *Encycl. Archit.* § 190 Ornamental *tulip-shaped chimney-pots. **1835** KIRBY *Hab. & Inst. Anim.* I. viii. 265 The *tulip-shell (Tellina) when it walks,..opens and shuts its valves. **1861** P. P. CARPENTER in *Rep. Smithsonian Instit.* 1860, 180 Family *Fasciolariadæ*. (Tulip-shells and Mitres).

Hence (or from mod.L. *tulipa*) **Tulipi·ferous** *a.* [-FEROUS], bearing flowers like tulips, as the tulip-tree; **Tu·lipine,** *Chem.*, a poisonous stimulant alkaloid obtained from the garden tulip; **Tu·lipist,** a person devoted to the cultivation of tulips; **Tu:lipoma·nia** [-MANIA], a craze for tulips, as that which prevailed in Holland in the 17th c.; **Tu:lipoma·niac,** one affected with tulipomania; **Tu·lipy** *a.*, abounding in tulips; † *sb.* a tulip.

**1786** J. ABERCROMBIE *Arrangem.* in *Gard. Assist.* 38/1 *Tulipiferous, or common tulip bearing [Tulip tree]. **1909** *Cent. Dict. Suppl.*, *Tulipine. **1913** DORLAND *Med. Dict.*, Tulipin. **1658** SIR T. BROWNE *Hydriot.* Ded., The Ingenuous delight of *Tulipists. **1710** ADDISON *Tatler* No. 218 ⁋ 7 A Person of good Sense, had not his Head been touched with..the..*Tulippomania. **1842** *Chamb. Jrnl.* 12 Feb. 32/3 When the Tulipomania infected Holland, and single roots were sold for many hundred pounds. **1842** *Blackw. Mag.* LI. 426 The prices of these roots..are enough..to delight the cupidity of a Dutch *tulipo-maniac. *a* **1849** J. C. MANGAN *Poems* (1859) 322 Shaarmal's *tulipy dell. *c* **1626** W. BOSWORTH *Arcadius & Sepha* I. 882 That blood with wat'ry eye Which leaves her breast to turn t' a *tulippy.

**Tulipan, -pant,** obs. ff. TULIP, TURBAN.

† **Tulipa·nted,** *a. Obs. rare.* [f. *tulipant*, early form of TURBAN + -ED [2].] = TURBANED.

**1634** SIR T. HERBERT *Trav.* 206 They [Chinese] are tulipanted about their heads.

**Tu·lip-tree.**

**1.** A large N. American tree, *Liriodendron Tulipifera* (N.O. *Magnoliaceæ*), bearing flowers resembling large tulips, of a greenish colour variegated with yellow and orange; also called *tulip poplar, saddle-tree* (from the shape of its peculiar truncated leaves), and *whitewood*.

**1705** BEVERLEY *Virginia* II. iv. § 18 (1722) 123 The large Tulip-Tree, which we call a Poplar. **1800** *Med. Jrnl.* IV. 376 The leaves and roots of the tulip-tree,..recommended as an useful bitter. **1857** GOSSE *Omphalos* vii. 165 This noble Tulip-tree.., a giant of this primeval forest.

**b.** Applied to other trees with tulip-like flowers, as species of *Magnolia*, and the mountain mahoe (*Paritium elatum* or *Hibiscus elatus*, N.O. *Malvaceæ*) of the West Indies.

**1751** J. HILL *Hist. Plants* 487 The great-flowered Magnolia, the Laurel-leaved Tulip-tree. **1884** MILLER *Plant-n.*, Tulip-tree, Chinese, *Magnolia fuscata*.

**2.** Applied in Australia to two proteaceous trees with brilliantly coloured flowers: **a.** A Victorian and Tasmanian species of Waratah, *Telopea orcades*, also called *native tulip* (see TULIP 1 b); **b.** *Stenocarpus cunninghami*, of Queensland.

**1830** *Hobart Town Almanack* 66 (Morris) That magnificent shrub called warratah or tulip-tree, and its beautiful scarlet flowers. **1835** ROSS *Hobart Town Almanack* 110 The generic name [*Telopea*]..has been corrupted into tulip tree, to which it bears not the least resemblance. **1866** *Treas. Bot.*, Tulip-tree, Queensland, *Stenocarpus Cunninghami*. **1898** MORRIS *Austral English*, *Tulip-tree*. The name is given, in Australia, to *Stenocarpus cunninghamii*,..on account of the brilliancy of its bright-red flowers.

**Tu·lip-wood.**

**a.** The wood of the tulip-tree (see prec. 1), a light ornamental wood used by cabinet-makers, etc. **b.** A name for various coloured and striped woods, or the trees producing them, as *Physocalymma floribundum* of Brazil, *Homoiceltis* (*Aphananthe*) *philippinensis*, and species of *Owenia* and *Harpullia*, of Australia. (Also *attrib.*)

**1843** HOLTZAPFFEL *Turning* I. ii. 20 Some of the hardest foreign woods, as king-wood, tulip-wood,..are rarely sound in the center. **1845** J. O. BALFOUR *Sketch N. S. Wales* ii. 39 The tulip wood, with its variegated flowers, and delightful perfume, grows in abundance. **1866** *Treas. Bot.* 882 The beautifully striped rose-coloured wood imported from Brazil, and called Tulip-wood by our cabinet-makers,..is the produce of *P*[*hysocalymma*] *floribundum*. **1884** MILLER *Plant-n.*, *Harpulia Hillii* and *H. pendula*, Tulip-wood, of Queensland. **1891** *Cent. Dict.* s.v. *Owenia*, *O*[*wenia*] *cerasifera* and *O. venosa* are in Queensland called respectively *sweet* and *sour plum*. Both have hard wood, that of the latter highly coloured.., used in cabinet-making and wheelwrights' work. *O. venosa* is called *tulip-wood*. **1898** MORRIS *Austral Eng.*, *Tulip-wood*. The name is given, in Australia, to *Aphnanthe philipinensis*, Planch., N. O. *Urticaceæ*, and to the timber of *Harpullia pendula*, Planch. [Moreton Bay tulip-wood], N. O. *Sapindaceæ*. It is, further, a synonym for the Emu-Apple [*Owenia acidula*, called also Native Nectarine and Native Quince]. **1906** *Times* 8 Feb. 7/6 A Dutch kingwood and tulipwood secretaire cabinet.

† **Tulk, tolk,** *sb. Obs.* [Generally identified with ON. *túlkr* interpreter, spokesman (cf. ON. *túlka* vb.: see next), Da., Sw. *tolk* = MLG. *tolk, tollik*, Du. *tolk* translator, MHG. *tolc, tolke*, ad. Lith. *tulkas*, Lett. *tulks*, OSl. *tl*[ŭ]*k*[ŭ] interpreter: cf. Russ. *tolk*[ŭ] sense, meaning, talk. But nothing has been found to connect the ME. sense, common in alliterative verse, with these.] A man.

**13..** *E. E. Allit. P.* B. 498 Tyl þay had tyþyng fro þe tolke þat tyned hem þer-inne. *Ibid.* 1262 Er he to þe tempple tee wyth his tulkkes alle. **13..** *Gaw. & Gr. Knt.* 3 Þe tulk þat þe trammes of tresoun þer wroȝt, Watz tried for his tricherie. *a* **1400-50** *Alexander* 752 Alexander.. turnyd hym þan to þis tulke & talkez þir wordez. *c* **1400** *Destr. Troy* 5790 Prothenor, the prise kyng, & proud Archelaus, Mony tolke of þe Troiens tyrnyt to dethe. *Ibid.* 6115 Mony abill knyghtes,..Of þe tulkys of troy, tidé men all.

† **Tulk,** *v. Obs. rare*[—1]. [app. a. ON. *túlka* to interpret, plead one's cause, be the spokesman: cf. prec.] *intr.* To utter sound, to sound.

**13..** *E. E. Allit. P.* B. 1414 And ay þe nakeryn noyse, notes of pipes, Tymbres & tabornes, tulket among.

**Tull,** obs. or dial. f. TILL *prep.* and *conj.*

‖ **Tulle** (tül, tul). [F. *tulle* (1812 in Hatz.-Darm.), 'named from Tulle, chief town of the department of Corrèze, where the fabric was first manufactured' (Littré).] A fine silk bobbin-net used for women's dresses, veils, hats, etc.

*c* **1818** MRS. CAREY *Tour France* xv. (1823) 310 This imitation is of silk, called tulle, from the name of the town where it is principally made. **1868** *Morn. Star* 7 Mar., Her Royal Highness..wore..a petticoat of white tulle over rich glacé silk. **1888** 'J. S. WINTER' *Bootle's Childr.* ix, The effect of the sweeping train, the shower of *tulle* which fell from the golden coronet of her hair.

*attrib.* **1859** *Habits Gd. Society* iv. (new ed.) 183 A beautiful tulle dress. **1900** EL. GLYN *Visits Eliz.* (1906) 54, I wore the white silk and my pink tulle hat.

**Tulle,** var. TILL *v.*[3] *Obs.*; obs. f. TOLL *v.*[1]

**Tullibee** (tʊ·libī). Also **tulibbi.** [ad. N. Amer. Indian (Cree and Odjibway) *too-nie-bee*.] A species of whitefish (*Coregonus tullibee*) found in the Great Lakes of N. America.

[**1822** in Morse *Rep. Indian Affairs* App. 31 A fish called by the savages 'Too-nie-bee', and by the English and French 'Telibees', not equal to, but greatly resembling, the white fish.] **1888** GOODE *Amer. Fishes* 93 Tautog, chogset,.. tullibee..are among the best. **1906** *Blackw. Mag.* Mar. 394/1 The tulibbis..often sold as fresh water herring..are only fit to eat in winter.

**Tullipant,** obs. form of TURBAN.

‖ **Tulsi** (tū·lsī). *E. Ind.* Also 7 **tulce,** 9 **tulsee, toolsee, -si, -sy.** [Hindī *tūlsī* :—Skr. *tulasī*.] A species of basil (*Ocimum sanctum*), sacred to Vishnu, cultivated by the Hindus as a sacred plant. Also *attrib.*

**1698** FRYER *Acc. E. India & P.* 199 Having a little place or two built up a Foot Square of Mud, where they plant Calaminth, or (by them called) Tulce, which they worship every Morning. **1813** J. FORBES *Oriental Mem.* III. 62 A garden and fountain with an altar of Tulsee, the sacred plant of the Brahmins. **1834** [A. PRINSEP] *Baboo* II. iii. 44 They..would laugh at the holy Toolsee-leaf, and Ganges water. **1866** *Treas. Bot.*, *Toolsi, Tulasi*, Indian names for species of Basil. **1895** R. W. FRAZER *Silent Gods, Pearl of Temple* (1896) 46 The short square pillar..with sacred Tulsī plant growing on its summit.

‖ **Tulwar** (tʊ·lwāɹ). Also **talwar.** [Hindī *talwār* (also *tarwār*).] An (Indian) sabre.

**1834** [A. PRINSEP] *Baboo* I. viii. 125 With my tulwar unsheathed on my arm, I moved to the edge of the tope. **1861** HUGHES *Tom Brown at Oxf.* xliv, I just caught the flash of his tulwar, and thought it was all up. **1892** J. PAYN *Mod. Whittington* I. 195 The tulwar of the Rajah of Bundlecumbad: the scabbard he described as a triumph of Eastern decoration.

† **Tu·ly,** *a.* (*sb.*) *Obs.* Forms: 4 tuli, tule, tuely, twily, 4–5 tuly, 4–6 tewly, 5 toly. [app. from a place-name. The quots. from *Gaw. & Gr. Knt.* suggest connexion with Toulouse.] An attribute of silk, tapestry, etc. of a rich red colour; perh. orig. applied to such fabrics imported from Toulouse. Also *absol.* Any fabric described as 'tuly'.

**1321** in Legg & Hope *Inv. Ch. Ch. Canterb.* (1902) 52 Casula..de rubeo sindone de tuly cum rosis brudato. *Ibid.* 55 Capa..de Rubeo panno de Tuly. **13..** *Coer de L.* 67 Her ropes wer off tuely sylk, Al so whyt as ony mylk. **13..** *Gaw. & Gr. Knt.* 568 Fyrst a tule tapit, tyȝt ouer þe flet. *Ibid.* 858 Tapytez tyȝt to þe woȝe, of tuly & tars. [Cf. 77 A selure..Of tryed Tolouse, of Tars tapites.] **1523** SKELTON *Garl. Laurel* 798 Reche me that skane of tewly sylk.

**b.** *transf.* Of a deep red colour, like that of 'tuly' silk; *absol.* or as *sb.* the red colour of this.

**1398** TREVISA *Barth. De P. R.* XVI. lxxxi. (Tollem. MS.) Ofte it gendreþ semely coloure and feyre, as tewly reed and stibium. *a* **1400–50** *Alexander* 4335 Nouthire to toly ne to taunde transmitte we na vebbis, To vermylion ne violett ne variant littis. **14..** *MS. Sloane 73* lf. 200 Resseit..for to make bokerham tuly or tuly þred. *c* **1440** *Promp. Parv.* 505/2 Tuly, colowre, *puniceus*.

**Tuly,** obs. f. TEWLY *a.*, sickly. **Tulye,** obs. f. TILL *v.*[1] **Tulye, -yie, -ȝe, -ȝie**: see TUILYIE. **Tulyhour,** obs. f. TUILYIER.

**Tum** (tʊm), *v.*[1] *north. dial.* [Origin not ascertained.] *trans.* To card (wool), esp. for the first time, in preparation for the finer cards. Also, to mix wool of different colours. Hence **Tu·mming** *vbl. sb.*, the action or process of doing this; *concr.* coarse cardings of wool; also **Tu·mmer**: see quots. 1877, 1884.

**1615** MARKHAM *Eng. Housew.* iii. 88 After your wooll is oild..you shall then tumme it; which is, you shall..card it ouer againe vpon your Stocke cards: And then those cardings which you strike off are called tummings. *Ibid.*, After your Wooll is thus mixed oiled and tummed, you shall then Spinne it vpon great Wooll wheeles. **1691** RAY *N. C. Words* 77 To *Tum* Wooll; to mix Wooll of divers colours. **1703** THORESBY *Let. to Ray* Gloss. (E.D.S.) *Tooming*, wool taken off the cards. **1788** W. MARSHALL *Yorksh.* II. Gloss. (E.D.S.) *Tum, v.*, to card wool roughly, to prepare it for the finer cards. **1822** *Lonsdale Mag.* Jan. 13/1, I thought my father had a neater method of mixing the black and white wool, in tumming. **1877** *Encycl. Brit.* VI. 494/2 The carding engines [in cotton-manufacture] are often made with two main cylinders and a connecting cylinder called the tummer. **1878–81** *Cumberld. Gloss.*, *Tummins*, rough cardings of wool. **1879** *Ibid.* Suppl., *Toom, tum*, to tease wool. **1884** R. MARSDEN *Cotton Spinning* (1891) 129 In these cards there are two large cylinders, the first being stripped by a doffer cylinder called a slow tummer.

**Tum** (tʊm), *sb.* and *v.*[2] [Echoic; more usual in reduplicated form TUM-TUM.] An imitation of the sound made by plucking a tense string, as in a musical instrument, or by striking a drum, or the like. Also as vb. *trans.* and *intr.* to produce this sound; hence **Tu·mming** *vbl. sb.*

*c* **1830** *Negro Song*, Don't ye 'ear de banjo tum? **1882** ELWES tr. *Capello & Ivens' Benguella to Yacca* II. iv. 77 The echoes..repeating the tumming of the drums. **1911** *Daily News* 23 June 3 The monotonous tum to which the dancers keep time for weeks together.

**Tum,** obs. form of TOOM *a.*

**Tumain,** obs. form of TOMAN[1], Persian coin.

**Tumasha,** var. TAMASHA.

**1863** TREVELYAN *Compet. Wallah* (1866) 104 He had invited all the English residents to a grand tumasha at his camp.

‖ **Tumata-kuru** (tūmätăkuru). Also tumatu-, tomata-kuru, -guru, tumatagowry, toomatoogooroo. [Maori.] A spiny, spreading New Zealand shrub, *Discaria Toumatou*, N.O. *Rhamnaceæ*, the thorns of which were used by the Maori in tattooing. Also called New Zealand Hawthorn, Wild Irishman, and corruptly MATAGOURI.

**1859** J. T. THOMSON in *Otago Gaz.* 22 Sept. 264 (Morris) Much over-run with the scrub called 'tomata-guru'. **1883** J. HECTOR *Handbk. N. Zealand* 131 Tumatakuru, Wild Irishman. A bush or small tree with spreading branches. ..The spines were used by the Maoris for tatooing. **1898** MORRIS *Austral Eng.*, *Tumata-kuru*..Tumatagowry, or Matagory is the Southern corruption of contractors, labourers, and others.

† **Tumb,** *v.* *Obs. rare.* Also 4 tombe. [OE. *tumbian* (see TUMBLE *v.*) = ON. *tumba*, OHG. *tūmôn* (from OLG.).] *intr.* To tumble, to perform saltatory feats; to dance.

*c* **1000** *Ags. Gosp.* Matt. xiv. 6 Ða on herodes ȝebyrd-dæȝe tumbude [*Hatton MS.* tumbede; Vulg. *saltavit*] þære herodiadiscan dohtor inneode & tumbode [*Hatt. MS.* tumbede; Vulg. *saltasset*]. **1387** TREVISA *Higden* (Rolls) IV. 365 Þe eorþe swelowede þe wenche þat tomblede [*MSS. α and γ* tombede (which represents Trevisa's own s.w. form)].

**Tumb, Tumbaga,** obs. ff. TOMB, TOMBAC.

‖ **Tumbak, tumbaki** (tʊmbā·k, -bā·kī). Also tumbek, -i, toumbeki, toombak, (tumbki). [a. Arabic تنباك *tunbā·k*, ad. F. *tabac* tobacco.] Name in Turkey for a coarse kind of tobacco imported from Persia; Shiraz tobacco.

**1836** LANE *Mod. Egypt.* I. v. 167 A particular kind of tobacco, called *toombak*, from Persia, is used in the water-pipe. **1858** SIMMONDS *Dict. Trade*, *Toumbeki*, a Turkish name for Schiraz tobacco. **1882** O'DONOVAN *Merv Oasis* I. v. 80 A handful of *tumbaki*, a coarse kind of tobacco used in these regions, is thrown in, and the smoker..inhales the fumes of the tobacco, mingled with air. **1891** *Kew Bulletin* 77 Tumbeki. **1897** *Daily News* 31 Dec. 3/6 Lazily smoking a narghilé charged with fragrant Persian tumbki.

**Tumbe,** obs. form of TOMB.

† **Tumbester.** *Obs.* Also 4–5 tombester(e, tumbestere, 5 -istere. [Feminine of OE. *tumbere* tumbler, dancer, acrobat: see -STER. Cf. OF. *tumberesse, tumeresse* (f. *tomber* to fall), in same sense (13th c. in Godef.).] A female tumbler or dancer. See also TUMBLESTER.

*c* **1386** CHAUCER *Pard. T.* 15 (Ellesm.) And right anon thanne comen Tombesteres [*Cambr.* Tumbesteris; *Corp.*, *Petw.*, *Lansd.* tombl-] Fetys and smale and yonge frutesteres. **1387** TREVISA *Higden* (Rolls) IV. 15 In Grees was no man grettre þan Alisaundre; noþeles Perdica, a tombester [*MS. β and Caxton* tomblestres; HIGDEN *saltatricis*] sone, was his successour, and nouȝt his owne sone. **1387–8** T. USK *Test. Love* II. ii. (Skeat) l. 118 Perdicas..was of no kinges blod, his dame was a tombystere. **14..** *MS. Harl. 2398* lf. 8 Herodias douȝter, þat was a tumbestere, and tumblede by fore him and oþer grete lordes. *c* **1430** *Pilgr. Lyf Manhode* IV. ix. (1869) 180, I hatte jolyfnesse, þe lyghte, þe tumbistere, þe rennere, þe fonne, þe lepere.

**Tumble** (tʊ·mb'l), *sb.* [f. next.] An act of tumbling; the condition of being tumbled.

**1.** An act of acrobatic tumbling; an acrobatic feat. *rare.*

**1824** LANDOR *Imag. Conv.*, *Gen. Lascy & Curate Merino* II. 75 A tumble of heels over head, a feat performed by beggar-boys on the roads. **1825** J. NEAL *Bro. Jonathan* I. ii. 28 A few hearty tumbles, all alone.

**2.** An accidental fall; also, the falling of a stream.

**1716** LADY M. W. MONTAGU *Let. to C'tess Mar* 21 Nov., In case of a tumble, it was utterly impossible to come alive to the bottom. **1749** FIELDING *Tom Jones* XII. viii, The landlord..became perfectly well acquainted with the tumble of Sophia from her horse. **1860** TYNDALL *Glac.* I. xvi. 116 The end..was always a plunge and tumble in the deeper snow. **1871** R. ELLIS *Catullus* lxviii. 60 As hill-born brook ..O'er his moss-grown crags leaps with a tumble a-down. **1880** MISS BIRD *Japan* I. 101 Mountains..noisy with the dash and tumble of a thousand streams.

**b.** *fig.* A fall, downfall.

**1728** VANBR. & CIB. *Prov. Husb.* II. i, The Demoivre Baronet had a bloody Tumble [at cards]. **1765** G. WILLIAMS in Jesse *Selwyn & Contemp.* (1843) I. 404 Pembroke gave him such a tumble the other night, by telling him Mr. Pitt would no more trust him than his postilion, that [etc.]. **1833** T. HOOK *Parson's Dau.* III. x, Our unlooked-for tumble [from high estate]. **1886** *Pall Mall G.* 8 Oct. 11/2 There will be a terrible tumble in the price of American oil in Europe. **1893** STEVENSON *Catriona* xxvi, Here were all my dreams come to a sad tumble.

**c.** In phrase ROUGH-AND-TUMBLE, q. v.

**3.** Tumbled condition; disorder, confusion, disturbance; a confused or tangled heap.

**1634** JACKSON *Creed* VII. xxxii. § 4 Some authority in all this tumble did still remain in the tribe of Judah. **1641** LAUD *Wks.* (1853) VI. 88 After much tumble, a major part of the votes made choice of me. **1755** H. WALPOLE *Lett.* (1846) III. 129, I could not expect that any drawing could give a full idea of the..masterly tumble of the feathers [of Walpole's eagle]. **1762–71** — *Vertue's Anecd. Paint.* (1786) I. x. 138 Rubens was never greater than in landscape; the tumble of his rocks and trees [etc.] show a variety of genius. **1869** BLACKMORE *Lorna D.* xxxi, Glad..that his story might get out of the tumble which all our talk had made in it. **1903** *Westm. Gaz.* 21 Mar. 5/1 The moorhen..swimming out from the overhanging tumble of bush and bramble.

**Tumble** (tʊ·mb'l), *v.* Also 4–5 tumbel, 4–6 tumbil, 4–7 tomble, 5 towmble, tumbell, -bill (also 6 *Sc.*), 5–6 tombel, toumble, 6 toomble; *Sc.* 4 twmmyll, 4–6 tummyll, tumle, 6 tummill, *north. dial.* tomyll, 8–9 tummle. [ME. *tumbel*, etc. = MLG., LG., mod.Ger. (*sich*) *tummeln*, EFris. *tummeln*, early mod.Du. (Kilian) *tommelen*, *tummelen*, Fris. *tommelje*, Da. *tumle*, Sw. *tumla* to tumble down, (*refl.*) to roll oneself, turn round, also OHG. *tumalôn*, mod.Ger. *tummeln* to bustle, hurry, make haste. By the side of these, OHG. had, with long *ū*, *tûmalôn*, mod.Ger. *taumeln* to be giddy, reel, stagger, tumble, Du. *tuimelen*, earlier *tuymelen* (Kilian), to tumble, fall. The forms with short and long *u* were originally variants, formed as frequentatives or diminutives of OHG. *tumôn*, OE. *tumbian*, TUMB; in mod.Ger. they have become differentiated in sense as well as in form. From an OLG. *tumben*, *tummen*, came OF. *tumer*, *tumber*, *tomber* to fall, which has prob. influenced the Eng. sense of *tumble*. The ME. spelling *tomb-* was merely graphic: see O (the letter).]

**I. 1.** *intr.* † To dance with posturing, balancing, contortions, and the like (*obs.*); to perform as an acrobat; *esp.* to execute leaps, springs, somersaults, and similar feats.

*a* **1300** *Cursor M.* 13140 (Gött.) His broþer doghtir..Balid wele and tumblid [*v.rr.* tumbel, tumble, tomblyng] wid al. **1303** R. BRUNNE *Handl. Synne* 2820 Eroud swore To here þat tumbled yn þe flore, þat [etc.]. *a* **1350** *St. Thomas* 40 in Horstm. *Altengl. Leg.* (1881) 20 A woman was þore in þe hall þat tumbild fast bifor þam all. **1530** PALSGR. 763/2, I tumble, as a tombler dothe, *je tumbe*...This felowe can tomble well. **1604** E. G[RIMSTONE] *D'Acosta's Hist. Indies* VI. xxviii. 493 Their great agilitie, in leaping, vaulting and tumbling. **1768** JOHNSON in *Boswell* (1906) I. 343 A man who is paid for tumbling upon his hands. **1840** DICKENS *Old C. Shop* v, The boy..having a natural taste for tumbling, was now standing on his head.

**2.** *intr.* To roll about on the ground, or in the water or air; to wallow; also to throw oneself about in a restless way on a bed or couch; to toss. Also *fig.*

**14..** *26 Pol. Poems* xxv. 223 The pyt of hell..Where synful soules tumble and raue. **1549** COVERDALE, etc. *Erasm. Par. Eph.* Prol., Yf thou..wylt tomble and walowe styll in wylful ignoraunce, and errour. **1606** SHAKS. *Ant. & Cl.* I. iv. 17 Let us grant it is not Amisse to tumble on the bed of Ptolomy. **1608** — *Per.* II. i. 27, I saw the Porpas how he bounst and tumbled. *a* **1684** LEIGHTON *Wks.* (1835) I. 116 Shall they then, who are purified..return to live among the swine, and tumble with them in the puddle? **1745** P. THOMAS *Jrnl. Anson's Voy.* 20 Seals..leaping and tumbling in the Water. **1819** BYRON *Juan* II. cxxxviii, Haidée.. sadly toss'd and tumbled, And started from her sleep. **1840** DICKENS *Barn. Rudge* v, He was very restless.., and for some hours tossed and tumbled.

† **b.** *refl.* in same sense. *Obs.*

**1577** B. GOOGE *Heresbach's Husb.* III. (1586) 122 A place meete for their wallowing, wherein..they may tumble themselues. **1616** SURFL. & MARKH. *Country Farme* 75 The Goose..doth loue to swim, and to coole, plunge, and tumble her selfe euerie day. **1661** LOVELL *Hist. Anim. & Min.* 95 When hungry they tumble themselves in red earth, and so lie as if dead.., and when the birds of prey come to feed on them, they suddainly take them.

**c.** *intr.* *spec.* of a pigeon: To throw itself over backwards during its flight; cf. TUMBLER 4; in gunnery, of a projectile, to turn end over end in its flight.

**1698** FRYER *Acc. E. India & P.* 116 Pigeons tumbling in the Air. **1735** J. MOORE *Columbarium* 40 When they are up at their Pitch, the better Sort seldom or never tumble. **1868** DARWIN *Anim. & Pl.* I. v. 151 The common English Tumblers have exactly the same habits as the Persian Tumbler, but tumble better. **1906** *Westm. Gaz.* 4 Oct. 5/3 Erosion..not sufficiently serious to..affect the flight of the projectiles, none of which were observed to 'tumble'.

**II. 3.** *intr.* To fall; *esp.* to fall in a helpless way, as from stumbling or violence; to be precipitated, fall headlong; also said of a stream falling in a cataract.

**13..** *K. Alis.* 2465 (Bodl. MS.) Men miȝtten sen..Heuedes tumblen guttes drawe Many body ouerþrowe. *c* **1330** R. BRUNNE *Chron.* (1810) 70 He stombled at a nayle, Into þe waise..he tombled top ouer taile. **1470–85** MALORY *Arthur* X. lvi. 507 He tombled doune of his hors in a swoune. **1560** DAUS tr. *Sleidane's Comm.* 323 b, They..tomble of the bridge into the Rhine. **1610** G. FLETCHER *Christ's Tri.* I. xlix, From heav'n it tumbled to the deep. **1687** A. LOVELL tr. *Thevenot's Trav.* II. 74 One of the gang tumbled off of his Mule, and had almost broken his Neck. **1697** DRYDEN *Æneid* VIII. 317 The fix'd foundations of the rock Gave way; ..Tumbling it chok'd the flood. **1796** MORSE *Amer. Geog.* I. 449 In passing through this hilly country, it tumbles over many falls. **1855** MACAULAY *Hist. Eng.* xiv. III. 401 He opened the barrel; and from among a heap of shells out tumbled a stout halter. **1878** HUXLEY *Physiogr.* 132 Fragments of rock..tumble down into the stream.

**b.** *intr.* To fall prone, fall to the ground; often const. *down*, *over*. Also, to stumble by tripping *over* an object.

*c* **1350** *Will. Palerne* 3388 But our on [= unless one of us] titly tumbel trowe me neuer after. *Ibid.* 3866 He tit ouer his hors tayl tombled ded to þerþe. **1375** BARBOUR *Bruce* XIII. 29 Thar mycht man..se tummyll knychtis and stedis. *c* **1489** CAXTON *Sonnes of Aymon* xxii. 478 Suche a stroke ..that he made him tomble over & over at his fete. **1732** LEDIARD *Sethos* II. IX. 325 The force..only made him tumble the sooner. **1843** BORROW *Bible in Spain* xxiv. (Pelh. Libr.) 167 The mule of the peasant tumbled prostrate.

**c.** *intr.* Of a building or structure: To fall in ruins or fragments; to collapse. Also *fig.*

*a* **1400–50** *Alexander* 552 All þe erd euyn ouer sa egirly schakis, þat teldis, templis, & touris tomble on hepis. *a* **1539** *Cartular. Abb. de Rievalle* (Surtees) 337 A steple tomylled down The tymber all to brokyn. *a* **1682** SIR T. BROWNE *Tracts* ix. (1683) 156 Obelisks have their term, and Pyramids will tumble. **1820** BELZONI *Egypt & Nubia* III. 385 There are a great number of houses, half tumbled down. **1880** MISS BRADDON *Just as I am* xix, We should tumble to pieces without you.

**d.** *intr.* To fall rapidly in value, amount, or price: said esp. of stocks. *Commercial slang.*

**1886** *Pall Mall G.* 8 Nov. 2/1 Rents had tumbled from 18 to 30 per cent., were likely to tumble still more. **1895** *Daily News* 21 Dec. 5/4 As stock after stock tumbled the shouting became a prolonged roar.

**4.** *trans.* To cause to fall suddenly or violently; to throw or cast down.

**1375** BARBOUR *Bruce* VI. 255 He tumlit doun on þaim þe stane. *c* **1489** CAXTON *Sonnes of Aymon* xxiii. 496 Whan bayarde was thus tombled in the ryver, he sanke vnto the botome of it. *a* **1533** LD. BERNERS *Huon* clix. 611 With all his strengthe he tombelyd Barnarde ouer the bourde into the water. **1588** SHAKS. *Tit. A.* II. iii. 176 Oh ..tumble me into some loathsome pit. **1623** R. CARPENTER *Conscionable Christian* 72 Let Romish Jezebel..not be spared, tumble her out at window. **1774** GOLDSM. *Nat. Hist.* (1776) III. 68 It [the chamois] drives at the hunter with its head, and often tumbles him down the neighbouring precipice. **1889** GRETTON *Memory's Harkb.* 36 He collared one of the men, and tumbled him over the balusters.

*fig.* **1549** COVERDALE, etc. *Erasm. Par. 1 Pet.* II God forbydde that I..shoulde be tombled backe agayne to this worldes delices. **1663** BP. PATRICK *Parab. Pilgr.* xi. (1687) 65 They tumbled themselves into an Abysse of misery and woe irrecoverable. **1812** BYRON *Ch. Har.* I. lii, He whose nod Has tumbled feebler despots from their sway. **1848** THACKERAY

*Van. Fair* xxxv, It is she who has tumbled my hopes and all my pride down.

**b.** To cause to fall prostrate; to overthrow.

*c* 1400 *Destr. Troy* 7243 Achilles..Mony Troiens ouertyrnyt, tumblit to dethe. 1534 More *Treat. Passion* Wks. 1294/2 Thys fierce furious kynge..was with the waues of the water..ouer throwen and tumbled downe..and wretchedlye drowned. 1625 T. Godwin *Moses & Aaron* v. vii. 246 One of the witnesses tumbled him by a stroke vpon the loynes. 1700 Dryden *Pal. & Arc.* iii. 653 King Lycurgus..was tumbled on the plain. 1837–8 J. Keegan *Leg. & Poems* (1907) 59 Come boys, have at him,..now's the time to tumble him. 1895 *Outing* (U.S.) XXVII. 219/2, I now had him [the bull] in plain view, broadside on, and tumbled him in his tracks.

**c.** To throw down and destroy (a structure); to overthrow, demolish, reduce to ruins. Also *fig.*

1375 Barbour *Bruce* xx. 452 Þe towris euerilkane And vallis gert he tummyll doune. *c* 1400 *Destr. Troy* 4877, I put not vnpossible ȝon place for to take..And all the toures of the toun tumbell to ground. 1596 Shaks. 1 *Hen. IV*, iii. i. 32 Vnruly Winde..which..tombles downe Steeples, and mosse-growne Towers. 1696 Brookhouse *Temple Open.* Pref. A iv, To undermine the Foundation, and to tumble down the whole Frame. 1809 W. Irving *Knickerb.* vi. ix. (1849) 375 The noblest monuments which pride has ever reared..the hand of time will shortly tumble into ruins. 1875 Whitney *Life Lang.* ii. 30 Some antagonist or successor, perhaps,..tumbles into ruins the whole magnificent structure of fancied truth.

**5.** To cause to fall in a confused heap; to throw *down, in, out*, etc. without order or regularity; to mix *up* in confusion, jumble *together*. Also *fig.*

1562 in W. H. Turner *Select. Rec. Oxford* (1880) 291 To be shaked and tombled together [in balloting]. 1601 ? Marston *Pasquil & Kath.* (1878) i. 133 And after death..We all together shall be tumbled vp, into one bagge. 1663 Gerbier *Counsel* 26 Car-men turne or tumble down their Bricks. 1787 Sir J. Hawkins *Life Johnson* 99 He would not suffer any one to approach, except the compositor or Cave's boy for matter, which, as fast as he composed it, he tumbled out at the door. 1821 Lamb *Elia* Ser. i. *Mackery End*, She was tumbled early..into a spacious closet of good old English reading. 1869 Tozer *Highl. Turkey* I. 312 He tumbled on to my plate..half a dishful of mulberries.

**6.** To propel or drive headlong, or with a falling, stumbling, or rolling movement; to precipitate; to throw or thrust roughly or forcibly; to toss, pitch, bundle. Also *fig.*

1509 Hawes *Past. Pleas.* xiv. (Percy Soc.) 52 O thoughtful herte, tombled all aboute Upon the se of stormy ignoraunce. 1553 T. Wilson *Rhet.* (1580) 109 We..tell one thyng after an other, from tyme to tyme, not tomblyng one tale in an others necke. 1595 Shaks. *John* iii. iv. 176 A little snow, tumbled about, Anon becomes a Mountaine. 1684 Bunyan *Pilgr.* ii. 23 They were greatly tumbled up and down in their minds, and knew not what to do. 1757 Smollett *Reprisal* i. i, To be tossed and tumbled about like a football. 1760–72 H. Brooke *Fool of Qual.* (1809) III. 87, I was bound.., and then tumbled with kicks..along the deck. 1818 Scott *Hrt. Midl.* v, Effie used to help me to tumble the bundles o' barkened leather up and down. 1840 Carlyle *Heroes* iii. 171 He [Shakspere]..tumbles and tosses him [his butt] in all sorts of horse-play.

*refl.* 1548 Udall *Erasm. Par. Luke* iii. 47 No manne should presse or toumble himselfe into suche an high office. 1884 Tennyson *Becket* i. i, The hog hath tumbled himself into some corner.

**7.** *intr.* To move or pass with a motion as if falling or stumbling; to move precipitately; to proceed hastily, without order or premeditation; to bowl, bundle, roll, rush. Also *fig.* Now *colloq.*

1590 Greene *Orl. Fur.* Wks. (Rtldg.) 92 When I take my truncheon in my fist, A sceptre then comes tumbling in my thoughts. 1590 Spenser *F. Q.* ii. xi. 18 A great water flood, ..tombling low From the high mountaines. 1683 Bunyan *Greatness of Soul* Wks. (ed. Offor) I. 141 What was the cause..? Why, their profits came tumbling in. 1712 Steele *Spect.* No. 552 ⁋1, I was tumbling about the town the other day in a hackney-coach. 1798 *Hull Advertiser* 10 Nov. 1/4 We..have been tumbling about in very bad weather. 1832 Marryat *N. Forster* xxii, Tumble up smartly, my lads. 1843 Lever *J. Hinton* xiii, Tumble into bed, and go to sleep as fast as you can. 1850 Smedley *F. Fairlegh* i, Hastily tumbling into my clothes,..I rushed down-stairs.

**8.** *trans.* To turn over as in examination or search; hence *fig.* to examine cursorily. Now *rare.*

1597 Morley *Introd. Mus.* Pref., What labour it was to tomble, tosse, and search so manie bookes. 1633 G. Herbert *Temple, Ch. Porch* xxv, Look in thy chest;..And tumble up and down what thou find'st there. 1652 Cotterell *Cassandra* iii. (1676) 49 Tumbling over a thousand several designs in his head. 1737 [S. Berington] *G. di Lucca's Mem.* To Rdr. (1738) 12 The Custom-House Officers at Marseilles..tumbled over his Effects at a very rude Rate. 1823 Byron *Juan* xiii. cii, The elderly walk'd through the library, And tumbled books.

**9.** To handle roughly or indelicately; to touse, tousle; to upset the arrangement of (anything neat or orderly); to disorder, rumple; to disarrange by tossing: e. g. to tumble bedclothes, a bed, or dress.

1602 Shaks. *Ham.* iv. v. 62 Quoth she before you tumbled me, You promis'd me to Wed. 1698 Vanbrugh *Prov. Wife* v. iii, To deliver up her fair body, to be tumbled and mumbled by..Heartfree. 1715 Lady M. W. Montagu *Town Eclogues, Tuesday*, Her night-cloaths tumbled with resistless grace. 1716 B. Church *Hist. Philip's War* (1867) II. 24 The ground being much tumbled with them. *a* 1732 Gay *Rehearsal at Goatham* i, How frightfully he hath tumbled me. 1825 Scott *Talism.* ix, Lay me the couch more fairly, it is tumbled like a stormy sea.

**10.** *intr. fig.* or in *fig.* context; *esp.* To come by chance, stumble, blunder *into, on, upon.*

1565 T. Stapleton *Fortr. Faith* 56 b, A sorte of Christians, called papistes, which were tombled themselues in idolatry, blindnesse, and superstition. 1632 Lithgow *Trav.* i. 38 [We] tumbled in by chance, *Alla capello Ruosso.* 1706 E. Ward *Wooden World Diss.* (1708) 90 If he had not tumbl'd into a Ship, he had long ago dropt from the Gallows. 1874 Lisle Carr *Jud. Gwynne* I. ii. 47 After hunting for you everywhere..here I tumble on you amidst the howling wilderness of Furrowshire. 1903 Morley *Gladstone* I. 428 The impossible parliament had tumbled into a great war.

**b.** *fig.* To understand something not clearly expressed; to perceive or apprehend a hidden design or signal. Const. *to. slang.*

1851 Mayhew *Lond. Labour* I. 15/1 The high words in a tragedy we call jaw-breakers, and say we can't tumble to that barrikin. 1889 *Opelousas* (Louisiana) *Democrat* 4 Feb. 3/4 The clerk smiled rather wickedly..but I didn't tumble worth a cent. 1889 H. O'Reilly *50 Yrs. on Trail* 375, I didn't tumble to this for a long time.

**c.** To fall in with, agree *to*; to take a liking or fancy *to. slang.*

1887 E. J. Goodman *Too Curious* xvii, He did not like the idea at first; but..he tumbled to it at last. 1892 *Daily News* 21 Apr. 2/1 But the British public, in the slang of the day, 'tumbles' to a man who refuses anything good.

**III. 11.** *intr.* Of the sides of a ship: To incline or slope inwards, to contract above the point of extreme breadth; to batter. Usually *tumble home.* Opposed to Flare *v.* 4 a. Also *transf.*

*a* 1687 Petty *Treat. Naval Philos.* i. ii, Let the supernatant sides of a Ship so much tumble..as that the said sides may remain perpendicular when the Ship stoops. 1711 W. Sutherland *Shipbuild. Assist.* 165 Tumbling home; when the Ship-side declines from a Perpendicular upwards, or, as some call it, houses in. 1761 H. Walpole *Let. to G. Montagu* 28 Apr., Old Newcastle, whose teeth are tumbled out, and his mouth tumbled in. 1848 T. White *Ship Build.* 39 The upper works usually incline towards the middle line, or as it is termed 'tumble home'.

**12.** *trans. Carpentry.* See quot.

1823 P. Nicholson *Pract. Build.* 120 Tumbling in a Joist, is to frame a joist between two timbers, of which the sides, which ought to be vertical or square to the upper edges, are oblique to these edges. 1856 Brees *Gloss. Terms* s.v., The purlines are sometimes tumbled in..between the sides of the principals of a roof.

**13.** *Mech.* To mix, cleanse, or polish in a tumbling-box. Cf. Tumbler 13 e.

1884 Wahl *Galvanoplastic Manip.* 529 (Cent. D.) Small castings can be tumbled and thus deprived of much of their adhering scale and sand.

**Tumble-,** the verb-stem in combination:

**1.** with substantives: **tumble-bug** = *tumble-dung*; **tumble-car, -cart**: see quots.; **tumble-dung**, name in *U.S.* for a scarabæid beetle which rolls up balls of dung, in which it deposits its eggs and in which the larvæ go through their transformations; a dung-beetle; also *attrib.*; **tumble fruit**, fallen fruit, windfalls; **tumble-rose**, a species of the parrot-fish, *Scarus cæruleus*, found on the Atlantic coast from southern U.S. to Brazil (*Cent. Dict. Suppl.* 1909); †**tumble-turd** = *tumble-dung*; **tumble-weed**, name in *U.S.* for various plants which form a globular bush which in late summer is broken off and rolled about by the wind; a rolling weed (Rolling *ppl. a.* 6).

1848 Lowell *Biglow Papers* Ser. i. ii. 62 *note*, *Tumblebug. 1868 *Rep. U. S. Commissioner Agric.* (1869) 86 The best known and most common beetle of this family in this country is the Canton lævis, usually termed the tumble-bug. 1794 Bailey & Culley *Agric. Cumberld.* 31 We suppose they had the name of *tumble carrs, from the axle being made fast in the wheels, and the whole turning or tumbling round together. 1887 *Suppl. to Jamieson* s.v., The *tumble-cart, tumbler, or car, continued in use in the upland districts till the beginning of the present century. 1775 R. Twiss *Trav. Portugal & Sp.* 247 The beetle, known by the name of *tumble-dung. 1798 in *Spirit Pub. Jrnls.* (1799) II. 355 The *scarabæus carnifex*, or tumble-dung-beetle. 1880 *New Virginians* I. 103 The humble rusty-black 'tumbledung'. 1891 *B'ham Weekly Post* 8 Aug. 4/7 Babies, like *tumble fruit, everywhere. 1754 Catesby *Carolina* II. App., The *Tumble Turds. *Scarabæus pillularis Americanus. Scarabæus carnifex*, L. 1887 *Amer. Nat.* Oct. 930 *Amarantus albus*, the common *tumble-weed.

**2.** with adverbs: **tumble home**, in a ship, = *tumbling home* (Tumbling *vbl. sb.* b); **tumble-over**, *sb.* an act of falling over; *concr.* a toy so weighted that it always takes a position of equilibrium; also *attrib.* inclined to fall down, rickety, tottering; **tumble-up**, ? a tumbler having a very heavy base which tends to keep it erect. See also Tumble-down.

1833 T. Richardson *Merc. Marine Archit.* 13 Giving only six inches *tumble home of the topside. 1874 Thearle *Naval Archit.* 60 When the ship has considerable beam, the breadth of the channel is kept within reasonable limits by giving a 'tumble home' to the top-sides. 1883 Black *Shandon Bells* xxx, But the gable of the house is a *leetle* *tumble-over, isn't it? 1895 *Outing* (U. S.) XXVI. 380/1 Those lead-weighted, pith 'tumble-overs', with which we played when children. 1899 *Allbutt's Syst. Med.* VI. 51 He was suddenly seized with intense darting pain in the region of the heart..accompanied by a sensation of 'tumble over' of the organ. 1891 *Sale Catal. Glass Wks. Stourbridge*, Seventy-one *tumble-ups.

**Tumbled** (tʊ·mb'ld), *ppl. a.* [f. Tumble *v.* + -ed [1].] That has tumbled or fallen; that has been thrown, tossed, or pitched *down, together*, etc.; also, tousled, disordered, rumpled.

1649 G. Daniel *Trinarch., Hen. V* cclxxxvii, Stand Harrie, ..Whose tumbled Character, tooke from the Life, Has but resemblance. 1727 Pope, etc. *Art of Sinking* 79 If he looks upon a tempest, he shall have an image of a tumbled bed. 1815 Scott *Guy M.* xxxvii, [A preacher with] no gown, not even that of Geneva, a tumbled band [etc.]. 1857 Dufferin *Lett. High Lat.* (ed. 3) 7 An amphitheatre of tumbled porphyry hills. 1872 Black *Adv. Phaeton* xiv, Bell was seated on a bit of tumbled pillar. 1891 tr. *Didon's Jesus Christ* I. iii. vii. 388 The old basalt walls of the tumbled-down houses..are still to be distinguished. 1895 Zangwill *Master* 443 Poets with lack-lustre visages and tumbled hair. 1907 *Daily Chron.* 11 Nov. 4/4 We read in these tumbled-together books the progress of a nation through all its stages.

**Tu·mble-down,** *a.* (*sb.*) [the phrase *tumble down* used attrib. or as sb.] †**a.** Of a horse: That falls down habitually. *Obs. rare*$^{-1}$.

1791 'G. Gambado' *Ann. Horsem.* i. (1809) 67 The Noble Puzzle for Tumble down Horses.

**b.** That is in a tumbling condition; falling or fallen into ruin; dilapidated, ruinous.

1818 Scott *Br. Lamm.* xxi, His old tumble-down tower yonder. 1859 Geo. Eliot *A. Bede* ii, The parsonage here's a tumble-down place, sir, not fit for gentry to live in. 1898 *N. & Q.* 9th Ser. II. 124 One of the grimiest and most tumbledown of the many dilapidated craft.

**c.** *absol.* as *sb.* A tumble-down house. *rare.*

1866 Howells *Venet. Life* vii, The tumble-down is patched up and sold at rates astonishing to innocent strangers who come from countries in good repair, where the tumble-down is worth nothing.

**Tumbler** (tʊ·mbləɹ). [f. Tumble *v.* + -er [1].]

**1.** One who performs feats of agility and strength, somersaults, leaps, and gymnastics; an acrobat.

*a* 1340 Hampole *Psalter* xxxix. 6 Hoppynge & daunceynge of tumblers and herlotis. *c* 1380 Wyclif *Sel. Wks.* III. 352 Mynystrel or joȝelour, tumbler and harlot. *c* 1440 *Promp. Parv.* 506/1 Tumlare (*P.* tumblar), *volutator* (S. *volutatrix*). 1581 Pettie *Guazzo's Civ. Conv.* ii. (1586) 57 b, Certaine vearses like us verie well,..when we heare some tumbler or dauncer sing them to the Harpe. 1614 Raleigh *Hist. World* v. vi. § 7 A tricke of climing vpon mens heads, somewhat after the manner of our tumblers. 1840 Dickens *Old C. Shop* xl, Kit faced about on the ladder like some dexterous tumbler. 1874 Blackie *Self-Cult.* 16 Dexterous riders and expert tumblers in the circus.

**2.** A dog like a small greyhound, formerly used to catch rabbits; a lurcher. So called from its action in taking its quarry: see quots. *Obs.* exc. *Hist.*

1519 Horman *Vulg.* 277 Tumblers, houndes, that can goo an huntynge by them selfe: brynge home theyr praye. 1576 Fleming tr. *Caius' Dogs* (1880) 11 This sorte of Dogges..we ..call Tvmblers, because in hunting they turne and tumble, winding their bodyes about in circle wise...He..so prouideth ..that the selly simple Conny is debarred quite from his hole. 1646 Sir T. Browne *Pseud. Ep.* iv. v. 187 Men observe that the eye of a Tumbler is biggest not constantly in one, but in the bearing side. 1688 R. Holme *Armoury* ii. 185/1 The Tumbler, or Lurcher is..in shape like the Grey-hound. 1766 Pennant *Zool.* (1768) I. 54 The *Vertagus*, or Tumbler,..took its prey by mere subtility. 1847–78 Halliwell, *Tumbler*, a dog formerly employed for taking rabbits. This it effected by tumbling itself about in a careless manner till within reach of the prey, and then seizing it by a sudden spring. 1897 *Q. Rev.* Jan. 141 Dogs are no longer trained as 'Norfolk tumblers', to attract the rabbits on the warrens by their quaint antics.

†**b.** *transf.* applied to a person; *spec.* one who allures or inveigles persons into the hands of swindlers (*slang*). *Obs.*

1601 B. Jonson *Poetaster* i. ii, Away, setter, away. Yet, stay, my little tumbler. *a* 1700 B. E. *Dict. Cant. Crew*, *Tumbler*,..one that Decoys, or draws others into Play. 1785 Grose *Dict. Vulg. T.*, *Tumbler*,..a sharper employed to draw in pigeons to game.

†**c.** The six of trumps in the game of gleek. *Obs.*

1680 [see Towser *sb.* b]. 1688 R. Holme *Armoury* iii. xvi. (Roxb.) 73/2 Tumbler, is the sixth of the trumps.

†**3.** A name of the porpoise. *Obs.*

1671 Marten *Voy. Spitzbergen* in *Acc. Sev. Late Voy.* ii. (1694) 125 They are not Sword-fish, nor of the same kind we call Tumblers. 1808–12 J. Walker *Ess. Nat. Hist.* 532 *Delphinus Phocaena*...Porpesse...Scot. Pellock. Tumbler.

**4.** A variety of domestic pigeon characterized by the habit or faculty of turning over and over backwards during its flight.

1678 Ray *Willughby's Ornith.* ii. xv. § 2. 182 Pigeons... *Tumblers*..are small, and of divers colours. They have strange motions, turning themselves backward over their Heads, and shew like footbals in the Air. 1859 Darwin *Orig. Spec.* i. (1878) 16 The common tumbler has the singular inherited habit of flying at a great height in a compact flock, and tumbling in the air head over heels.

**5.** One who tumbles or falls. *nonce-use.*

1904 *Daily Chron.* 1 Mar. 6/3 It was real hockey..; when a collision brought a tumble, the tumbler took the accident like a lady.

**6.** A drinking cup, originally having a rounded or pointed bottom, so that it could not be set down until emptied; often of silver or gold; now, a tapering cylindrical, or barrel-shaped, glass cup without a handle or foot, having a heavy flat bottom.

1664 Pepys *Diary* 20 Oct., Thence home, taking two silver tumblers home, which I have bought. 1689 *Lond. Gaz.* No. 2485/4 A Gold Tumbler of 100*l.* value. 1698 B. Bullivant in *Phil. Trans.* XX. 168, I put a Straw for a Perch into a Venice Glass Tumbler. 1779 Black in *Phil. Trans.* LXXIII. *305 A common tumbler or water-glass. 1842 S. Lover *Handy Andy* iii, I thought there was no tumbler but a tumbler for punch. 1865 Lubbock *Preh. Times* 136 Rings of pottery..evidently intended to serve as supports for these earthenware tumblers. **1876** W. F. COLLIER *Tales O. Eng. Life* 79 The guests were supplied with tumblers, or glass vessels, which, being rounded at the base, could not stand upright, and must, therefore, be emptied at a draught. **1886** G. R. SIMS *Ring o' Bells*, etc. I. Introd. 1 The tumblers were rattled upon the table.

**b.** The contents of a tumbler; a tumblerful.

**1831** J. DAVIES *Manual Mat. Med.* 150 From two to five tumblers, pure or mixed with any other drink, every morning. **1873** BLACK *Pr. Thule* v, Mackenzie mixed another tumbler of toddy.

**c.** A toy, usually representing a grotesque squatting figure, having the centre of gravity low and the base rounded so as to continue rocking when touched; cf. MANDARIN 1 b. *rare.*

**1851** MAYHEW *Lond. Labour* (1861) II. 504/1 Her legs tucked up mysteriously under her gown into a round ball, so that her figure resembled in shape the plaster tumblers sold by the Italians.

**7.** = TUMBREL [1] 3, 3 b; cf. *tumbler-cart* in 14. *slang* and *dial.*

**1673** R. HEAD *Canting Acad.* 16 (Flaugg'd at the Tumbler) whipt at the Carts-arse. **1692** LUTTRELL *Brief Rel.* (1857) II. 534 They had on board 200 horses for the artillery,..40 feild pieces, 80 tumblers. *a* **1700** [see SHOVE *v.* 10]. **1757** WASHINGTON *Lett.* Writ. 1889 I. 490 Choose me..as much thread as is necessary,..and send them up by John who comes down with a Tumbler for that purpose. **1799** ROBERTSON *Agric. Perth* 92 The shafts had two pins that embraced the axle and made these awkward wheels tumble along; from which circumstance they were named tumblers. *a* **1814** RAMSAY *Scot. & Scotsm. in 18th C.* (1888) II. x. 199 Tumblers, a trifling species of carts which have for ages been used about Alloa for transporting coals to the shore. **1815** SCOTT *Guy M.* viii, Small carts or tumblers, as they were called in that country.

**8.** *Geol.* A detached mass of rock; a rolled stone or boulder. Now only *dial.*

**1789** MILLS in *Phil. Trans.* LXXX. 77 On the surface are tumblers of red granite, and some few of lava. *Ibid.* 80 The bottom of the glen is covered with large tumblers of lava. **1799** KIRWAN *Geol. Ess.* i. 209 That [sandstone]..must also be primary, though it contains tumblers (*caillous roulés*). **1876** H. B. WOODWARD *Geol. Eng. & Wales* x. 305 *note*, In the eastern part of North Wales the boulders are called 'Granite tumblers'. **1894** *Northumbld. Gloss.*, *Tumbler*, *Tumler*, a boulder, a detached block of stone.

**9.** With capital *T*: A *Dunker* or *Tunker* (see DUNKER [1]): in allusion to their method of baptism. *U.S.*

**1796** MORSE *Amer. Geog.* I. 281 They are also called Tumblers, from the manner in which they perform baptism, which is by putting the person, while kneeling, head first under water, so as to resemble the motion of the body in the action of tumbling.

†**10.** One who tumbles or tosses things into confusion or disorder; a muddler; one who turns something over confusedly. *Obs. rare.*

**1580** HOLLYBAND *Treas. Fr. Tong*, *Brouilleur, ou qui Brouille*, a tumbler together, a slubberer. **1694** MOTTEUX *Rabelais* IV. lxiv. (1737) 260 Tumblers of Beads, Mumblers of *Ave Marias.*

†**11.** A class of street ruffians; see quot., and cf. MOHOCK. *Obs.*

**1712** STEELE *Spect.* No. 324 ⁋ 1 The Mohock Club...A third sort are the Tumblers, whose office it is to set Women on their Heads. **1878** LECKY *Eng. in 18th C.* (1883) I. 482.

**12. a.** = *Tumble-dung* (see TUMBLE-). **b.** The aquatic larva of the mosquito or other species of the *Culicidæ*: see quot. 1858–63. *U.S.*

**1807–8** W. IRVING *Salmag.* xv. (1824) 282 The aspiring politician may be compared to that indefatigable insect, called the tumbler,..which..forms a little ball, which it rolls laboriously along. **1858–63** RIPLEY & DANA *Amer. Cycl.* VIII. 51 (Cassell's) They are..called tumblers from the manner in which they roll over and over in the water.

**13.** In mechanical applications.

**a.** In a gun-lock, a pivoted plate through which the mainspring acts on the hammer, and in the notches of which the sear engages.

**1624** *Althorp MS.* in Simpkinson *Washingtons* (1860) App. 58 For a new tumbler for a muskit locke 00 00 06. **1688** R. HOLME *Armoury* III. xviii. (Roxb.) 135/1 The seuerall parts of a Fire lock and a match lock, and wheele lock...The Tumbler. **1833** J. HOLLAND *Manuf. Metal* II. 117 In consequence of the firm locking of the sear in the Tumbler, the gun cannot possibly go off. **1862** *Catal. Internat. Exhib.* II. XI. 24 The cock works in a slot in the middle of the stock; there is no tumbler. **1871** 'STONEHENGE' *Brit. Sports* I. I. ii. § 1 Occasionally, in central-fire guns, the tumbler itself is made to propel the striker.

**b.** In a roasting-jack, a pawl or catch which allows a barrel to revolve in one direction independently of a wheel centred on the same axle, but which takes the wheel with it when it revolves in the other direction.

**1677** MOXON *Mech. Exerc.* iii. 47 The Tumbler is so placed ..that while the Jack line is winding up upon the Barrel its round britch passes forwards by all the Crosses of the Main wheel,..But when the Barrel is turned the contrary way,.. the Tumbler..thrusts the Main Wheel about with [it]. **1688** R. HOLME *Armoury* III. 323/1 [Of a jack] The Tumbler, the Center whereof moveth upon the Center Pin.

**c.** In a lock: †A pivoted piece through which the pressure of a spring was transmitted to the tail of the bolt, tending to keep it pushed forwards (*obs.*); now, a pivoted piece kept in position by a spring, with projections which drop into notches in the bolt and hold it until lifted by the proper key.

**1677** MOXON *Mech. Exerc.* ii. 28 The Tumbler..is a long piece of Iron,..and it hath an Hook returning at the other end of it, to fall into the breech of the Bolt, and by the spring H forces the Bolt forwards. **1792** *Trans. Soc. Arts* (ed. 2) III. 166 The tumbler and tail of the latch or spring bolt. **1833** J. HOLLAND *Manuf. Metal* II. 277 Mr. Kemp ..published in 1816, a lock, the interior security of which consists in the adaptation of tumblers or sliders. **1911** J. WARD *Roman Era in Brit.* xiii. 238 The lock had both wards and tumblers.

**d.** *Naut.* App. a sleeve or cap fitted on a mast, with a hook, ring, or swivel to afford means of attachment, etc.; see also quot. 1877.

**1867** SMYTH *Sailor's Word-bk.*, *Tumbler*,..a contrivance to avoid the necessity of having copper nailed on the mast to prevent a gaff from chafing it. **1877** KNIGHT *Dict. Mech.*, *Tumbler* (Nautical), one of the movable pins with which the cathead-stopper and shank-painter are respectively engaged. **1882** NARES *Seamanship* (ed. 6) 9 There is a tumbler on each cap to connect the conductors of the two masts together. *Ibid.* 121 A..derrick..working on a swivel tumbler on the mast.

**e.** A revolving barrel, or a barrel with a rotating paddle, used in tanning skins; also, a tumbling-box.

**1857** *Encycl. Brit.* (ed. 8) XIII. 310/2 They [lamb-skins] are first fed with alum and salt in a drum or tumbler made like a huge churn. **1877** KNIGHT *Dict. Mech.*, *Tumbler*,..a vertically rotating case for cleaning castings placed within it. **1883** R. HALDANE *Workshop Receipts* Ser. II. 367/2 After leaving the press, they [the skins] are put into a 'tumbler', or revolving barrel. **1891** SADTLER *Hand-bk. Industr. Org. Chem.* x. (1900) 329 The tanning was formerly done with sumach and gambier, either in revolving paddle 'tumblers'..or according to the English method.

**f.** Each of the stickers of a *tumbler-coupler* in an organ (see 14).

**1881** W. E. DICKSON *Organ-Build.* xii. 154 A slender bridge, having as many notches as keys in the manual, and fitted with short stickers called tumblers.

**g.** *Coal-mining.* A tipper; cf. *tumbling tom* (TUMBLING-).

**1883** GRESLEY *Coal-mining Gloss.*, *Tumbler*, (S[cotland]), see *Tipper.* **1886** J. BARROWMAN *Sc. Mining Terms* 69 *Tumbler*, tipping apparatus for tubs or waggons.

**h.** In a clock or watch: see quot.

**1884** F. J. BRITTEN *Watch & Clockm.* 110 [A] Tumbler [is] a revolving finger that in striking clocks and repeating watches moves the rack one tooth for each blow struck.

**i.** In some looms, each of the levers from which the heddles are suspended.

**1891** in *Cent. Dict.*

**14.** *attrib.* and *Comb.*, as *tumbler bitch*, *-brush* (sense 6), *fancier*, *-glass*, *lock*, *-maker*, *movement* (cf. *tumbler-coupler*), *pigeon*, *-pin*, *-pivot*, *-screw*; *tumbler-shaped* adj.; **tumbler-bearing**, a bearing which automatically falls out of position to make way for a gear travelling upon the shaft which it supports; **tumbler-beds**, *pl.*, a local name for the loose crumbly upper portion of the carboniferous limestone; **tumbler-cart** = sense 7; **tumbler closet**: see quot.; **tumbler-coupler**, a unison manual coupler in an organ in which the connexion between each two keys is made by a short sticker (see 13 f) which turns over at an angle when not in use; **tumbler-cup**, a cup with a rounded bottom: cf. sense 6; **tumbler dog** = sense 2 (*obs.*); also, a catch or detent in a padlock which retains the hasp (Forney *Car-Builder's Dict.* 1884); **tumbler-drum**, = sense 13 e; **tumbler-holder**, a metal frame in which a tumbler of drink is served (Knight *Dict. Mech.* 1877); **tumbler-music**, music produced with tumblers or 'musical glasses'; **tumbler-punch**: see quot.; **tumbler-stand**, a tray on which tumblers are automatically rinsed (Knight); **tumbler switch**, an electric switch operated by pushing over a small spring tumbler or thumb-piece; **tumbler-tank**, a flushing cistern having two compartments, one of which when filled tilts the other into the position for filling and empties itself (*Cent. Dict.* 1891); **tumbler-washer**, a stand with jets of water for rinsing tumblers (Knight).

**1901** *J. Black's Carp. & Build.*, *Scaffolding* 60 We have power transmitted with square shaft, with *tumbler bearings bolted to the walls of a building. **1821** W. FORSTER *Section of Strata* (ed. 2) 103 About sixteen feet of the upper part of [the Great Limestone] is called the *Tumbler Beds. **1680** *Lond. Gaz.* No. 1481/4 Lost ..a white *Tumbler Bitch with yellow ears. **1877** KNIGHT *Dict. Mech.*, *Tumbler-brush. **1880** D. MURRAY *Old Cardross* 38 The only wheeled vehicles known prior to that time [*c* 1763] were *tumbler carts, which were simply sledges mounted on small wheels..made solid..united by a wooden axle, and all turning round together. **1888** *Q. Rev.* July 38 Sledges were used.., more recently tumbler carts with solid wheels, mere slabs of timber. **1870** CORFIELD *Treatm. Sewage* 123 The '*Tumbler' closet...In this there is..a trough running under the privy-seats..; the water trickles into a swinging basin at the upper end, which is so constructed that it capsizes when full and washes out the contents of the trough into the drain. **1876–98** STAINER & BARRETT *Dict. Mus. Terms* 342/2 The *tumbler coupler is now almost obsolete. **1900** *Westm. Gaz.* 7 Mar. 1/3 A pair of *tumbler cups, 1698, 10oz. **1908** *Ibid.* 27 Mar. 8/1 A Georgian plain tumbler-cup,..weighing 4oz. 13dwt. **1675** *Lond. Gaz.* No. 1022/4 Lost..a white *Tumbler Dog, both Ears spotted with red. **1883** R. HALDANE *Workshop Receipts* Ser. II. 373/1 The skins are either trodden in it with the feet, or put into a *tumbler-drum. **1854** *Poultry Chron.* II. 276/1 The Almond *Tumbler fancier, whose 'little wonders' cannot feed their own young! **1831** BREWSTER *Nat. Magic* viii. (1833) 194 Stretch a thin sheet of wet paper..over the mouth of a *tumbler-glass with a footstalk. **1844** J. T. HEWLETT *Parsons & W.* xi, A tumbler-glass of iced punch. **1833** LOUDON *Encycl. Archit.* § 1585, 3-inch brass *tumbler lock and key on each door. **1881** YOUNG *Ev. Man his own Mechanic* § 1488 A lock of better and more complicated construction..called a tumbler lock. **1902** *Westm. Gaz.* 29 Mar. 9/1 Under the present rule the *tumbler-makers must keep on working just as long as the fancy glass makers continue to work. **1881** C. A. EDWARDS *Organs* 112 The means provided to effect this coupling was called the '*tumbler' movement. **1893** F. F. MOORE *I Forbid Banns* (1899) 150 She thought the *tumbler-music very interesting. **1688** R. HOLME *Armoury* II. 244/2 The *Tumbler Pigeon is small and of diverse colours. **1890** *Science-Gossip* XXVI. 215/2 A tumbler-pigeon hatched out a Minorca chicken, a hen having laid in the pigeon-box. **1853** URE *Dict. Arts* II. 251 The lock outside,..*a*, the plate; *b*, the cock; *c*, the *tumbler-pin. **1881** GREENER *Gun* 264 The tumbler-pin is first turned out, and by means of a wire punch inserted in the hole, the tumbler is knocked away from both hammers and lock-plate. **1892** — *Breech Loader* 116 Knock in the *tumbler-pivot half-way. **1877** KNIGHT *Dict. Mech.*, **Tumbler-punch*.., a small two-bladed punch used for pushing the arbor of the tumbler, the band-springs, etc., from their seats, in taking a gun apart. **1856** 'STONEHENGE' *Brit. Sports* I. I. ii. (ed. 2) 19/1 The various parts of the lock [of a gun] are..5th, the *tumbler-screw, which fastens the tumbler and cock together. **1862** *Catal. Internat. Exhib.* II. XI. 16 The loop upon each barrel receiving the end of a steel *tumbler-shaped bolt. **1907** *Installation News* Apr. 16/1 A new form of *tumbler Switch.

**Tumblerful** (tʊ·mbləɹful). [f. prec. + -FUL.] The quantity that fills a tumbler.

**1831** J. DAVIES *Manual Mat. Med.* 94 From four to five tumblerfulls every morning. **1857** *G. Bird's Urin. Deposits* (ed. 5) 171 The use of a small tumblerful of this water on rising in the morning. **1897** *Allbutt's Syst. Med.* III. 419 Several tumblerfuls of lukewarm or warm water.

† **Tu·mblester.** *Obs.* Forms: 4–5 **tomblester**, **-stre**, **tomblister(e**, 5 **tumbelyster.** [Feminine of TUMBLER: see -STER, and the parallel form TUMBESTER.] A female tumbler or dancer; a dancing-girl.

*c* **1386** CHAUCER *Pard. T.* 15 (Lansd. MS.) And riht anone þan come tomblesters [so *Petw.*; *Corpus* tomblisteres] Fetis and smal and ȝonge fruytsters. **14..** *Voc.* in Wr.-Wülcker 616/47 *Tornatrix*, a tumbelyster. **1844** JAMES *Agincourt* I. 233 Who ever heard of King before who troubled his nobility about minstrels and tomblesteres? **1850** — *Old Oak Chest* I. 125 To make the contortions of their 'saltimbanks' and 'tomblesteres' act as a sort of argument or introduction to what was to follow.

**Tumblification** (tʊ·mblifikēⁱ·ʃən). *humorous.* [irreg. f. TUMBLE *v.* + -FICATION.] Tumbling, falling, or tossing; *esp.* the pitching and rolling of a ship in a storm.

**1833** M. SCOTT *Tom Cringle* xi. (1859) 250 Then another Tumblification of the whole party. **1881** CLARK RUSSELL *Ocean Free Lance* II. iv. 169 The tumblification was sometimes so furious that we had to hold on with our hands to save ourselves. **1890** *Chamb. Jrnl.* 14 June 371 The jerky, feverish, staggering, tumblefication of the wreck.

**Tumbling** (tʊ·mbliŋ), *vbl. sb.* [f. as prec. + -ING [1].] The action of TUMBLE *v.* in various senses.

*a* **1425** *Cursor M.* 13195 (Trin.) In euel tyme bigan she tomblyng To make his heed of be brouȝt. *c* **1440** *Promp. Parv.* 506/1 Tumlynge, *volutacio.* **1523** FITZHERB. *Husb.* § 102 It apperethe by stampynge of the horse or tomblynge. *c* **1580** JEFFERIE *Bugbears* Epil., Song ii. in *Archiv Stud. Neu. Spr.* (1897), With joomblynges, with foomblynges, with toomblynges. **1611** COTGR., *Basteleuse*, a woman that makes a profession of Jugling, Tumbling, and such other idle, or base exercises. **1660** BURNEY *Κέρδ. Δῶρον* (1661) 30 The tumblings of the Leviathan in the Seas. **1687** FOUNTAINHALL *Decis.* (1759) I. 440 Physicians attested the employment of tumbling would kill her. *a* **1774** TUCKER *Lt. Nat.* (1834) II. 456 Lucretius..granted that the atoms,..after infinite tumblings and tossings about, would fall into their former situation. **1870** LOWELL *Study Wind.* 2 We can explain the odd tumbling of rooks in the air.

**b.** *Tumbling home*: the inward inclination of the upper part of a ship's sides; opposed to FLARE *sb.*[1] 4; see TUMBLE *v.* 11. Also *tumbling-in.*

**1664** E. BUSHNELL *Compl. Shipwright* 11 Then set off the Tumbling Home, at the Height of the two first Haanses. **1769** FALCONER *Dict. Marine* (1789), *Encabanement*, the tumbling-home of a ship's side from the lower-deck-beam upwards, to the gunnel. **1832** *Encycl. Amer.* XI. 367/2 Nothing can be urged in favor of tumbling in..but that it brings the guns nearer the centre. *c* **1850** *Rudim. Navig.* (Weale) 157 The topsides of three-decked ships have the greatest tumbling-home, for the purpose of clearing the upper works from the smoke and fire of the lower guns.

**Tu·mbling,** *ppl. a.* [f. as prec. + -ING [2].] That tumbles, in various senses of the verb; falling; tossing; rolling headlong; also *fig.*

*c* **1374** CHAUCER *Boeth.* III. pr. ix. 67 (Camb. MS.) Trowesthow þat ther be any thing in thise erthely mortal towmblynge thinges? **1509** HAWES *Past. Pleas.* (Percy Soc.) 131 Stere well the frayle tombling barge. *c* **1620** Z. BOYD *Zion's Flowers* (1855) 109 Where tumbling billowes bath the very sky. **1638** JUNIUS *Paint. Ancients* 306 A tumbling and wallowing horse. **1760–72** H. BROOKE *Fool of Qual.* (1809) II. 128 All that I owed came like a tumbling house upon me. **1837** W. IRVING *Capt. Bonneville* II. ix. 130 Down the ravine of a tumbling stream, the commencement of some future river. **1873** BLACK *Pr. Thule* vi, This tumbling mass of dark stones standing high over the green hollows.

Hence **Tu·mblingly** *adv.*, in a tumbling manner.

**1620** THOMAS *Lat. Dict.*, *Volutatim*,..rollingly, tumblingly. tossingly.

**Tumbling-.** The vbl. sb. and ppl. adj. in combinations and special collocations, as *tumbling boy, girl, -ground, lass, -trick*; also **tumbling-barrel** = *tumbling-box*; **tumbling-bay**, an outfall from a river, canal, or reservoir; a weir; also, the pool into which the water falls from this; **tumbling bob**, a weighted lever or arm in machinery, which when moved to a certain point falls and produces some motion; **tumbling-box**, a rotating drum in which small articles (usually of metal) are cleaned and polished by attrition; also used in dissolving and mixing paints, varnishes, etc.; **tumbling car**, a tumbrel; † **tumbling cast**, a somersault; a fall, overthrow; **tumbling crank**: see quot.; **tumbling gear**, a gear with one or more idle wheels on a swinging frame for producing reverse motion; † **tumbling glass**, a tumbler; **tumbling joint**: see quot.; **tumbling metre**, cf. *tumbling verse*; **tumbling-mill**, a tumbling-box or set of these (*Cent. Dict. Supp.* 1909); **tumbling-room**, space for tumbling; *spec.* a room in which a tumbling-box is set up; **tumbling shaft**, a revolving shaft carrying cams producing intermittent motion; **tumbling-star**, an iron ball with projecting spikes which is put into the tumbling-box to stir up the polishing or abrading medium (*Cent. Dict. Supp.* 1909); **tumbling stone**, a loose stone embedded in clay; a boulder: = TUMBLER 8; **tumbling tom**, in Coal-mining: see quot. 1883; also *Sc.* (*tumbling Tam*), a thick heavy halfpenny of George III's reign; **tumbling-trough**, in sulphuric acid manufacture, a receptacle which pours nitric acid from each of its two balancing chambers in turn (*Cent. Dict.* 1891); **tumbling verse**, a kind of irregular anapæstic verse: see quot.; **tumbling water-cracker**, a kind of aquatic firework; **tumbling weight** = *tumbling bob*; **tumbling-wheel**, a revolving chamber in which small wooden objects are smoothed by attrition; cf. *tumbling-box*.

1724 *Jrnl. Ho. Comm.* XX. 382 The water is to be divided by an overfall or *tumbling bay. 1795 J. PHILLIPS *Hist. Inland Navig.* Add. 90 To preserve the water of the same river, a tumbling bay is to be erected. 1847 ADDISON *Law of Contracts* II. i. § 1. (1883) 244 The lessee of a water-mill ..has no right to alter the height of the tumbling-bay. 1891 A. J. FOSTER *Ouse* 136 A fine large 'tumbling bay', as the pools below the sluices are sometimes called. 1824 R. STUART *Hist. Steam Engine* 73 A weight or *tumbling bob, or Y piece, to give the necessary momentum to the movement of the injection-cock lever. 1877 KNIGHT *Dict. Mech.*, **Tumbling-box*, .. a cylindrical or barrel-shaped vessel .. mounted on an axis so as to be revolved by a winch or pulley. Called also *rumble, rolling barrel.* 1840 DICKENS *Old C. Shop* xi, He sent an express to the wharf for the *tumbling boy. 1881 *Daily News* 2 June 5 The little tumbling boy and his oppressors. 1811 in *Chamb. Jrnl.* 11 Jan. (1845) 31/2 The chief part..was brought from the sand-beds of Esk in *tumbling cars. 1530 PALSGR. 179 *Sombresault*, a *tumblyng caste. 1677 NEEDHAM *2nd Pacquet Adv.* 31 They are for a Tumbling-Cast to the present rulers of Church and State. 1886 J. BARROWMAN *Sc. Mining Terms* 69 **Tumbling-crank*, a crank on the end of the pumping shaft for giving reciprocating motion. 1793 *Trans. Soc. Arts* (ed. 2) V. 202 The common *Tumbling Geer, as used in the Fire Engine. 1896 K. LEASK *H. Miller* ii. 39 A *tumbling-girl who had been sold by her parents to a travelling mountebank. 1803 *MS. Diary* in *N. & Q.* 8th Ser. (1893) III. 168/1 Had a few friends to dine, tried my new *tumbling-glasses; very successful, all got drunk early. 1861 *Sat. Rev.* 14 Dec. 604 A field is lent for a circus or a *tumbling-ground for an acrobat. 1844 STEPHENS *Bk. Farm* III. 981 The English hay-tedding machine..having a series of revolving rakes... The rakes are attached to the wheels by a *tumbling-joint,..when any undue resistance is opposed to a rake..the rake falls back till the obstruction has been passed. 1687 FOUNTAINHALL *Decis.* (1759) I. 439 Reid the Mountebank pursues Scot of Harden..for stealing away from him a little girl, called the *Tumbling-Lassie, that danced upon his stage. 1847 *Proc. Philol. Soc.* III. 103 When this licence is taken frequently the metre becomes of that species..called ..'*tumbling metres'. 1860 G. MEREDITH *Evan Harrington* viii, No *tumbling-room for the wine, eh? 1901 *Trans. Amer. Inst. Electr. Engin.* 562 (Cent. Supp.). *c* 1790 IMISON *Sch. Art* I. 36 It [the universal joint] is of great use in cotton mills, where the *tumbling shafts are continued to a great distance from the moving power. 1857 J. ROBERTSON in Charteris *Life* xii. (1863) 338 There are many sloughs and *tumbling stones on the road. 1881 *Borings & Sinkings* II. 2 (E.D.D.) Strong blue clay with large tumbling stones. 1826 GALT *Last of Lairds* iv, I gave him a whole penny—twa new bawbees, gude weight, for it was then the days o' the *tumbling Tams. 1883 GRESLEY *Coal-Mining Gloss.*, *Tumbling Toms*, tippers that turn completely over. 1596 SHAKS. *Tam. Shr.* Induct. ii. 140 Is it not a Comontie, a Christmas gambold, or a *tumbling tricke? 1673 HICKERINGILL *Greg. F. Greyb.* 302 They coming not to church to see tumbling tricks and hocus juglings. 1585 JAS. I *Ess. Poesie* (Arb.) 63 Thir hes twa short, and ane lang throuch all the lyne, quhen they keip ordour: albeit the maist pairt of thame be out of ordour, and keipis na kynde nor reule of Flowing, and for that cause are callit *Tumbling verse. 1799 G. SMITH *Laboratory* I. 24 Charges for *Tumbling Water-crackers. Mealed powder.., nitre.., and charcoal. [Cf. 21 Water-crackers, which turn in the water.] 1903 *Nature* 19 Nov. 68/1 Barney's illustration of the Dudley Castle engine (erected in 1712) was made in 1719, and contains the plug-frame and *tumbling-weight device... It is possible that the tumbling-weight had just been added for actuating the steam-valve.

**Tumbly** (tʊ·mbli), *a. rare.* [f. TUMBLE *v.* + -Y.] Ready to tumble; tumble-down, ruinous.

*c* 1855 SIR E. BURNE-JONES in Mackail *Life Morris* (1899) I. 51 They were tumbly old buildings.

**Tumboora**, var. TAMBOURA, musical instrument.

**Tumbrel**[1], **tumbril** (tʊ·mbrĕl, -ĭl). Forms: 4 **tombrel**, 4–5 **tumberell, tumrelle**, 5 **tomberel, tomerel, tumrel**, 5–7 **tumbrell**, 6 **-e, tumrell, tomberell, -brill**, 6–8 **-brell**, 7 **-bril**, 8 **tumbral**, 9 *dial.* **tumril**, 6– **tumbrel, -il**; also 6–7 **timbrell**. [ad. med.L. *tumb(e)rellum* (Du Cange), *-ellus*, OF. *tumb-, tomberel, tummerel, tumerel, -il*, etc., fall, chute, tip-cart, dung-cart, trebuchet (13th c. in Godef.), mod.F. *tombereau* 'a Tumbrell or Dung-cart' (Cotgr.), a tipcart for carting and shooting dung, sand, stones, etc., f. *tomber* to let fall, tumble out. (No record in French of its use in punishment.)]

**1.** An instrument of punishment, the nature and operation of which in early times is uncertain; from 16th c. usually identified with CUCKING-STOOL, q. v. See also THEW *sb.*[2], TREBUCHET 4.

For full account of the word, with additional quots., see Dr. Brushfield's article quoted below.

[1223 *Bracton's Note Bk.* (1887) III. 504 Et Radulfus questitus quando leuauit tumberellum et per quod warantum, dicit quod de nouo et ea occasione quod habet tumberellum in quodam manerio suo in comitatu Essexie, et bene putauit quod per libertatem illam illum leuare potuit. Et quia nulla fuit mencio in carta Dom. Regis de tali libertate, consideratum est quod tumberellus prosternatur et Radulfus in misericordia. 1266–7 *Judicium Pillorie* in *Stat. Realm* (1810) I. 201/1 Si aliquis senescallus vel ballivus..remiserit judicium pillorie vel tumbrelli adjudicatum.] 1313–14 *Eyre of Kent* (Selden Soc.) III. 182 Cely qvad amendes dassisse de payn et de servoise il ad pillori et tombrel [*v.rr.* turmberell, turmelle]. 1494 FABYAN *Chron.* VII. 345 Syr Hughe.. punysshed the bakers for lacke of syze by the tumberell [1568 GRAFTON tomberell] where before tymes they were punysshed by the pyllery. *Ibid.* 385 Myllers for stelyng of corne to be chastysed by y^e^ tumbrell. 1538 ELYOT, *Numellæ*, a tumbrelle, wherein menne be punysshed, hauyng their heedes and fete put into it. 1581 LAMBARDE *Eiren.* I. xii. (1588) 67 Setting on the Pillorie or Cucking stoole, which in old time was called the Tumbrell. 1607 COWELL *Interpr.*, *Cucking stoole*..is an engine inuented for the punishment of scolds and vnquiet women, called in auncient time a tumbrell... Kitchin, where he saith, that euery one hauing view of Frankpledge, ought to haue a pillorie and a tumbrell, seemeth by a tumbrell to meane the same thing [i.e. a cucking-stool]. *a* 1634 COKE *On Litt.* III. ci. (1648) 219 Those that have been adjudged to the Pillory, or Tumbrell, are so infamous [as not to be admitted to give evidence]. 1688 Ducking Tumbrel [see DUCKING-STOOL]. 1857–9 T. N. BRUSHFIELD *Obs. Punishments* II. *Cucking Stool* (1861) 5 In the Statutes, manorial claims, and law books, [the cucking stool] is usually alluded to as a *tumbrel* or *trebuchet*. *Ibid.* 9 From the 15th c., the identity of the meaning of the two terms [*cucking stool* and *tumbrel*] is easily proved.

† **2.** A counterpoise beam for raising a well-bucket. *Obs. rare.*

*c* 1475 *Pict. Voc.* in Wr.-Wülcker 799/36 *Nomina Aquarum*...*Hoc tolumen*, a tumrelle. 1483 *Cath. Angl.* 396/1 A Tumrelle of A wele,..*ciconia, tollinum.*

**3.** A cart so constructed that the body tilts backwards to empty out the load; *esp.* a dung-cart.

*c* 1440 *Promp. Parv.* 496/2 Tomerel, donge cart. *Ibid.* 506/1 Tumrel, donge carte, *fimaria, titubatorium.* 1481–90 *Howard Househ. Bks.* (Roxb.) 174 Item, Gante is owing for another day with his tomberel. 1494 FABYAN *Chron.* VII. 495 He was..sette in a tumbrell, & therunto fastenyd with chaynes of iren, and so conueyed, bareheded, with dynne and crye, thorough the hyghe stretes of Parys tyll he came vnto the bysshoppes palays. 1620 MARKHAM *Farew. Husb.* (1625) 69 Any clay earth..you shall carry it in tumbrels or carriages to the new plowed ground. 1632 *Foxe's A. & M.* III. *Contin.* 69/1 The dead bodies..were conueyed in tumbrils out of the citie. 1700 DRYDEN *Cock & Fox* 251 My corps is in a tumbril laid; among The filth and ordure, and enclos'd with dung. 1856 R. A. VAUGHAN *Mystics* (1860) I. 281 He sees..the emissaries of the Pope..dragged through the streets in a scavenger's tumbril. 1901 *Essex Weekly News* 8 Mar. 3/3 The frequent tipping of the tumbril.

† **b.** app. *transf.* to a lumbering cart. *Obs.*

Cf. also TUMBLER 7.

1597–8 BP. HALL *Sat.* V. iv. 14 A Friezeland trotter halfe-yarde deepe To drag his tumbrell through the staring Cheape. 1699 GARTH *Dispens.* V. 57 Haspt in a Tombril, awkwardly you've shin'd With one fat Slave before, and none behind. 1709 STEELE *Tatler* No. 51 ¶ 1 He sometimes rode in an open Tumbril, of less Size than ordinary, to show the Largeness of his Limbs. 1800 WEEMS *Washington* vi. (1877) 44 And he assisted him in a tumbril or little cart.

**c.** *fig.* Applied to a person or his gorge.

1601 WEEVER *Mirr. Mart.* E iij b, But by misfortune t'was the Abbots land Whereas we lay; so by his priuie spies The fat-backt tumbrell soone did vnderstand. 1630 J. TAYLOR (Water P.) *Laugh & be fat* Wks. II. 72/1 Thou mightst relate At thy returne, their manners liues and law, Belcht from the tumbrell of thy gorged maw.

† **4.** *transf.* A flat-bottomed boat or barge; cf. *tumbrel boat* in 7; also *fig.* applied to a person loaded with drink. *Obs.*

1468 *Medulla Gram.* in *Cath. Angl.* 396 *note*, *Cimbula*, a tomerel [cf. *c* 1050 *Gloss.* in Wr.-Wülcker 379/16 *Cimbula*, lytlum scipe]. *a* 1625 FLETCHER *Woman's Prize* III. ii, There rid (like a Dutch hoy) the Tumbrel. When she had got her Ballast..How fain [etc.] 1676 ETHEREDGE *Man of Mode* III. ii, Have you taken notice of the gallegh I brought over? ..'Tis as easily known from an English Tumbril, as an Inns of Court-man is from one of us. 1700 CONGREVE *Way of World* IV. ii, Good lack! what shall I do with this beastly tumbril [a drunken man]?

**5.** *Mil.* A two-wheeled covered cart which carries ammunition, tools, or sometimes money for an army.

1715 *Lond. Gaz.* No. 5383/3 We have..carried off..Tombrels with Ammunition. 1803 WELLESLEY in Owen *Desp.* (1877) 393 Sixty-four tumbrils, completely laden with ammunition, together with three tumbrils of money. 1859 JEPHSON *Brittany* xvi. 267 In our Artillery the guns are..drawn by horses, and the men sit on the ammunition-tumbrels.

**6.** A square rack for holding fodder in the open field or yard. *dial.*

1635 BP. J. WILLIAMS *Articles Eng. Linc.* A iv, Tumbrels, or other things in your church-yard, to fodder cattell in. 1840 *Boston Advert.* 30 June 3/4 We went together into the crew, and found some eggs under a tumbril. 1870 *Daily News* 6 Dec., A small quantity of linseed cake, crushed fine, scattered upon the top of the provender, as it is placed in the tumbrils.

**7.** *attrib.* and *Comb.*, as *tumbrel boat, cart, load, post* (sense 6), *-slop* (cf. 3 b); *tumbrel-shaped* adj.

1688 R. HOLME *Armoury* III. xv. (Roxb.) 26/1 A *Tumbrell boate, or flat bottomed boate or Turnell boate. 1852 WIGGINS *Embanking* 101 The application of chalk rubbish, i.e. soft chalk, to the land, after the rate of at least ten *tumbril cart-loads per acre. 1764 *Museum Rust.* III. lxiii. 292, I have mentioned a *tumbrel-load to be thirty bushels, and a waggon-load to be but two tumbrels. 1821 *Bill* in *N. W. Linc. Gloss.* (1877) s.v., 12 *tumprill posts at 1^s^. 3^d^. 1598 B. JONSON *Ev. Man in Hum.* II. ii, I'le goe neere to fill that huge *tumbrel-slop of yours, with somewhat, an I have good luck. 1826 HOR. SMITH *Tor Hill* (1838) II. 270 That French tumbril-slop is transcendant. 1776 *Evelyn's Sylva* I. ii. 43 The water might fall..like drops of rain; which I should much prefer before the barrels and *tumbral way.

† **Tumbrel**[2]. *Obs. rare*[—1]. In 3 **tumberel**. [app. deriv. of OF. *tumber, tomber* to tumble; cf. TUMBLER 3, the porpoise (*obs.*), the young cod-fish (*Eng. Dial. Dict.*).] A kind of fish.

*c* 1300 *Havelok* 757 Keling he tok, and tumberel, Hering, and þe makerel, þe butte, þe schulle, þe þornbake.

**Tumbrel(le**, obs. forms of TIMBREL *sb.*[1]

**Tume**, obs. Sc. form of TOOM, empty.

**Tumefacient** (tiūmĭfēⁱ·ʃiĕnt), *a. rare*[—1]. [ad. L. *tumefacient-em*, pr. pple. of *tumefac-ĕre* to tumefy.] Tumefying, swelling. (In quot. *humorously pedantic.*)

1885 B. HARTE *By Shore & Sedge, Sarah Walker* 45 The infant..had grown unctuous and tumefacient under the kisses.

† **Tumefa·cted**, *a. Obs. rare.* [f. L. *tumefact-us*, pa. pple. of *tumefac-ĕre* to tumefy + -ED[1].] = TUMEFIED, swollen.

1597 A. M. tr. *Guillemeau's Fr. Chirurg.* 44 b/2 This ligature is very commodiouse in tumefacted Legges. 1599 — tr. *Gabelhouer's Bk. Physicke* 238/2 When as the privityes..are tumefactede, or swollene.

**Tumefaction** (tiūmĭfæ·kʃən). [a. F. *tumefaction* (16th c. in Godef. *Compl.*), f. L. *tumefac-ĕre* to tumefy: see -TION.]

**1.** The action or process of tumefying, or state of being tumefied; swelling; swollen condition: **a.** as a morbid affection of some part of the body.

1597 A. M. tr. *Guillemeau's Fr. Chirurg.* 14/2 Throughe the tumefactione which therof ensueth. 1689 MOYLE *Sea Chyrurg.* III. iv. 108 A Tumifaction of the inward Tunicle of the Ribbs, called Plura. 1737 BRACKEN *Farriery Impr.* (1757) II. 268 An Inflammation and Tumefaction of these Kernels. 1872 COHEN *Dis. Throat* 93 Tumefaction of the tonsils.

**b.** in general. *rare.*

1665–6 *Phil. Trans.* I. 287 The Progressive motion, which he fansieth to follow upon this Tumefaction. 1686 GOAD *Celest. Bodies* II. vii. 249 Tumefaction is inseparable from a troubled Sea. 1837 HERSCHEL in Babbage *Bridgew. Treat.* App. I. 237 Granting the heat, there is no difficulty in deducing expansions, disruptions, tumefactions, &c.

**2.** *concr.* A swollen part; a swelling, a tumour.

1802 PALEY *Nat. Theol.* ix. § 4 (ed. 2) 138 The muscles which move the toes..gracefully..disposed in the calf of the leg, instead of forming an unwieldy tumefaction in the foot itself. 1854 MARION HARLAND *Alone* xiv, She beheld reflected in the mirror, a tumefaction of the cheek, nearly closing one eye.

**Tumefied** (tiū·mĭfəid), *ppl. a.* (erron. **tumi-**.) [f. next + -ED[1], repr. L. *tumefactus*, pa. pple. of *tumefacĕre.*] Caused to swell, swollen. (Const. as *pa. pple.* or *ppl. adj.*) **a.** said of a bodily part thus morbidly affected.

1597 LOWE *Chirurg.* (1634) 71 The signes of resolution are lightnesse or ease of the member tumified, diminution of dolour [etc.]. 1691 HOWE *Carnality Relig. Contention* Wks. (1846) 211 This angry, tumefied, proud flesh. 1748 *Phil. Trans.* XLV. 412 The Eye was inflamed, and the Lids tumefied. 1762 *Gentl. Mag.* 250 A tumefied tendon. 1847 YOUATT *Horse* xii. 258 The parotids are a little tumefied.

**b.** generally. *rare.*

1651 BIGGS *New Disp.* ¶ 248 Tumified gumme. 1796 KIRWAN *Elem. Min.* (ed. 2) I. 314 Melted..into a spongy,.. tumefied semitransparent mass. 1815 J. SMITH *Panorama Sc. & Art* II. 726 Where a figure..is fore-shortened, the drapery must appear more tumefied.

**c.** *fig.* 'Inflated' or 'puffed up' with pride or the like. *rare.*

1677 GILPIN *Demonol.* (1867) 114 Yet were they so tumefied with the apprehensions of their privileges. 1680 BAXTER *Cath. Commun.* Pref. A iij, The Crimes of a few tumified Sectarian Soldiers. 1892 G. HAKE *Mem. Eighty Y.* 118 Tumid young men rigged out in newest apparel...None of these tumefied gentlemen ever walked in a hurry.

**Tumefy** (tiū·mĭfəi), *v.* (erron. **tumi-**). [= F. *tumé̆fi-er*, ad. L. type **tumeficāre* (cf. L. *tume-*

*facĕre*), f. L. *tumē-re* to swell: see -FY, and cf. *stupefy*, *rubefy*.]

**1.** *trans.* To cause to swell; to swell, make tumid.

1597 [see prec. a]. 1656 BLOUNT *Glossogr.*, *Tumefie*.., to make to swell, or puff up. 1686 [see *tumefying* below]. 1718 J. CHAMBERLAYNE *Relig. Philos.* (1730) I. xi. § 15 The Sucker, tumified with Water, is thrust into the Tube. 1822–7 GOOD *Study Med.* (1829) III. 132 Like the Athenian plague ..it commenced in the head, inflamed the eyes, and tumefied the face.

**b.** *fig.* To 'swell'; to make too bulky; to 'puff up', as with pride; to make turgid or bombastic.

1674 JEAKE *Arith.* (1696) 89 Being not willing to spare so much time, or tumefie these Papers. 1677 [see prec. c]. 1837 J. MORIER *A. Allnutt* iv. 21 Having tumefied himself and his possessions by all the pomp and circumstance of two shields, and..a variety of heraldic insignia. 18.. DE QUINCEY (Webster 1864), To swell, tumefy, stiffen, not the diction only, but the tenor of the thought.

**2.** *intr.* To swell, swell up, become tumid.

1615 [see *tumefying* below]. 1689 MOYLE *Sea Chyrurg.* II. vii. 51 The wound..will be apt to Tumifie. 1811 PINKERTON *Petralogy* II. 286 Where the air..has most liberty to escape, it will tumify, burst through the liquid mass, and form cellular lava. 1822–7 GOOD *Study Med.* (1829) I. 102 The tongue tumefies; the throat becomes sore. 1883 R. HALDANE *Workshop Receipts* Ser. II. 304/2 The solid sheet glue, while drying.., tumefied and became very porous.

Hence **Tu·mefying** *vbl. sb.* and *ppl. a.*

1615 CROOKE *Body of Man* 79 Although there be no outward tumifying..to be seene. 1686 GOAD *Celest. Bodies* II. vii. 249 Its tumefying influence.

**Tumen**, obs. form of TOMAN [1].

**Tumerous**, obs. f. TIMOROUS, TUMOROUS.

**Tumescence** (tiume·sĕns). [f. next, corresp. to a Latin type **tumēscentia*.] A becoming tumid, swelling up; a tendency to tumidity; also *concr.* a tumid part, a swelling.

1859 R. F. BURTON *Centr. Afr.* in *Jrnl. Geog. Soc.* XXIX. 321 Tumescence..appears to characterize the human as it does the vegetable productions of Inner Africa. 1874 NASMYTH & CARPENTER *Moon* Contents p. xiii, Scrope's Hypothesis of Terrestrial Tumescences. 1901–6 H. ELLIS in Westermarck *Orig. & Devel. Moral Ideas* xl. (1908) II. 374 Erethistic excitement which produces sexual tumescence.

**Tumescent** (tiume·sĕnt), *a.* [f. L. *tumēscent-em*, pr. pple. of *tumēscĕre* to begin to swell, become tumid, inceptive of *tumēre* to swell.] Becoming tumid, swelling; somewhat tumid; also *fig.*

1882 ADAMSON in *Mind* Apr. 281 The style is of a vapid and somewhat tumescent character. 1899 *Allbutt's Syst. Med.* VIII. 479 Heat..will make the lesions red and tumescent. 1899 BARING-GOULD *Bk. of West* v, Tumescent undergarments.

**Tumfie**, var. TUMPHY.

**Tumid** (tiū·mid), *a.* Also 6 -yde. [ad. L. *tumid-us*, f. *tumē-re* to swell: see -ID [1].]

**1.** Swollen; characterized by swelling. **a.** Morbidly affected with swelling, as a part of the body.

1541 R. COPLAND *Galyen's Terap.* 2 F j, Varyce (that is to say a tumyde vayne). 1650 BULWER *Anthropomet.* 178 Making..the Belly tumid. 1784 JOHNSON *Let. to Mrs. Thrale* 12 Jan., My thighs grow very tumid. 1878 T. BRYANT *Pract. Surg.* I. 32 Ulcers..distinguished by their livid colour and irregular tumid border.

**b.** Of a swollen or protuberant form; swelling, bulging; in quot. 1659, swollen or puffed out with the wind. In later use chiefly *Nat. Hist.*

1621 G. SANDYS *Ovid's Met.* XI. (1626) 221 Who, with the Father of the tumid Maine, Indues a mortall shape. 1659 T. PECKE *Parnassi Puerp.* 132 Tumid Sail-cloaths gratifi'd our Sight. 1819 STEPHENS in Shaw *Gen. Zool.* XI. I. 1 The upper mandible with a soft and tumid membrane at its base. 1828 J. E. SMITH *Eng. Flora* II. 97 Styles short and close in the flower;..their bases tumid.

**2.** *fig.* esp. of language or literary style: 'Swelling', inflated, turgid, bombastic.

1648 BOYLE *Seraph. Love* xx. (1700) 126 Such expressions may seem somewhat tumid and aspiring. 1760 JORTIN *Erasmus* II. 200 A puerile performance, in a poetical, tumid, and idolatrous style. 1809 BYRON *Bards & Rev.* xiv, Turgid ode and tumid stanza. 1877 SYMONDS *Renaissance in Italy* v. 272 His Greek style is at the same time tame and tumid.

**b.** 'Big', pregnant, teeming. *rare.*

1840 DE QUINCEY *Style* III. Wks. 1860 XI. 252 It is tumid with revolutionary life. 1850 BLACKIE *Æschylus* I. Pref. 6 Greek..is a language..tumid with luxuriant growth and overgrowth.

Hence **Tu·midly** *adv.*, in a tumid manner (*lit.* and *fig.*); **Tu·midness**, tumidity.

1688 BOYLE *Final Causes Nat. Things*, *Vitiated Sight* 259 Her eyes did not always retain the same measure of tumidness. 1822 J. PARKINSON *Outl. Oryctol.* 164 A multilocular, tumidly discoidal and elliptically spiral shell. 1864 CARLYLE *Fredk. Gt.* XVI. v. (1872) VI. 184 Remarks..of dim tumidly insignificant character.

**Tumidity** (tiumi·dĭti). [ad. late L. *tumiditās*, f. *tumidus* TUMID.] The quality or condition of being tumid; swollenness. **a.** *lit.*; also *concr.* a swelling.

1721 BAILEY, *Tumidity*, swelling. 1828 MACAULAY *Dryden* Wks. 1898 VII. 152 No more than the tumidity of a muscle resembles the tumidity of a boil. 1873 A. W. WARD tr. *Curtius' Hist. Greece* I. I. i. 24 Every muscle, every sinew, is developed into full play,..there is no trace of tumidity or of inert matter. 1897 *Allbutt's Syst. Med.* III. 476 Windy tumidities and occasionally phantom tumours arise.

**b.** *fig.* in reference to language: see TUMID 2.

1791 BOSWELL *Johnson* an. 1784 (1816) IV. 433 [A passage] blown up into such tumidity, as to be truly ludicrous. 1883 R. BROWN in *Fortn. Rev.* 1 Sept. 380 Their periods turned with Johnsonian tumidity. 1895 *Q. Rev.* Oct. 336 Aeschylus, grandiose at times almost to tumidity.

**Tummer**: see TUM *v.*[1]

**Tummock** (tɒ·mək). *dial.* Also (*Sc.*) tammock, tummack. [app. f. Gaelic *tom* hillock + -OCK; cf. TUMP *sb.*] A hillock, mound, knoll.

1789 D. DAVIDSON *Seasons* 5 Twa 'herds..straught down on tammocks clap Their nether ends, and talk their unco's o'er. 1855 KINGSLEY *Westw. Ho.* xiv, Your ghost may sit there on a grass tummock, and tell your beads. 1901 A. TROTTER *E. Galloway Sk.* 32/1 Wandering among its hills and 'tummacks', its singing spouts and burns.

**Tummon**, obs. form of TOMAN [1].

**Tumorous** (tiū·mŏrəs), *a.* Also 7 tumerous, -ourous. [ad. L. *tumōrōsus*, f. *tumor* TUMOUR; cf. OF. *tumoreux* (*c* 1400 in Godef.).]

†**1.** Characterized by tumour or swelling; swollen, protuberant, bulging, tumid. *Obs.* exc. as in b.

1547 BOORDE *Brev. Health* cccxliv. 111 b, A venemous humour which is tumorous. 1601 B. JONSON *Poetaster* v. iii, That should purge His braine, and stomack of those tumorous heates. 1678 CUDWORTH *Intell. Syst.* I. v. § 3. 30 Besides this Outside Bulky Extension, and Tumourous Magnitude, there must be another kind of Entity [cf. quot. 1678 s.v. TUMOUR 2].

**b.** Pertaining to or of the nature of a (morbid) tumour; affected with tumours.

1863 SALA *Capt. Dangerous* II. ii. 78 It began to swell.. to a most alarming size and tumorous discoloration. 1884 J. TAIT *Mind in Matter* (1892) 80 Other influences..may produce tumourous growths. 1890 H. M. STANLEY in *Times* 6 May, There are trees prematurely aged and blanched, others were tumorous.

†**2.** *fig.* **a.** Swelling with pride or passion; vainglorious, puffed up, haughty. *Obs.*

1603 DRAYTON *Bar. Wars* III. lxxxi, To ease the anguish of her tumorous Spleene. *a* 1639 WOTTON *Panegyrick Chas. I* in *Reliq.* (1652) 147 He had no austerity of behaviour, nothing outwardly tumerous. 1676 SPARROW *Caution agst. False Doctr.* 8 The same tumorous vain-glory.

†**b.** Of language, style, or demeanour: Inflated, bombastic, turgid: = TUMID 2. *Obs.*

1636 B. JONSON *Discov.* Wks. (Rtldg.) 759/1 These styles vary..: for that which is high and lofty, declaring excellent matter, becomes vast and tumorous, speaking of petty and inferior things. *a* 1639 WOTTON *Charac. Will. I*, Sublime and almost Tumorous in His Looks and Gestures. *a* 1652 A. WILSON *Jas. I* (1653) 285 Some tumorous Discourses.

**Tumour, tumor** (tiū·məɹ). [a. L. *tumor*, *-ōrem*, swollen state, a swelling, f. *tum-ēre* to swell; cf. OF. *tumour* (14th c. in Godef. *Compl.*).]

†**1.** The action, or an act, of swelling; distension, increase of bulk; swollen condition. *Obs.*

1541 R. COPLAND *Galyen's Terap.* 2 A iv, The..flesshe.. whan with the euyl qualyte it hath tumour agaynst nature. 1609 HOLLAND *Amm. Marcell.* XXV. iv. 267 The tumor of his veines and arteries stopped his spirits. 1671 R. BOHUN *Wind* (Contents), The suddain tumours in the Lake of Geneva. 1693 EVELYN *De la Quint. Compl. Gard.*, *Refl. Agric.* xix. 72 This Distension or Tumor of such tyed Branches.

**2.** *concr.* A part rising above or projecting beyond the general level or surface; a swollen part or object; a swelling. Now *rare* or *Obs.* exc. as in 3.

In quot. 1678 applied to anything having bulk, i. e. occupying space.

1601 HOLLAND *Pliny* VIII. xlv. I. 225 [The cattle] of Caria.. are illfavoured to be seen, having between their necks & shoulders a tumor or swelling hanging over. 1647 H. MORE *Song of Soul* Notes 151/2 The tumour [of water] at B is bigger then that at A. 1678 CUDWORTH *Intell. Syst.* I. v. § 3. 780 There are..two kinds of Substances in the universe; the first corporeal,..are nothing but ὄγκοι, bulks, or tumours, devoid of all self-active power; the second incorporeal..are ἄογκοι δυνάμεις, substantial powers. 1692 BENTLEY *Boyle Lect.* 111 A like ferment makes notable tumours and ventricles. 1847 W. E. STEELE *Field Bot.* 13 Style..thickened beneath its branches, and often fringed at the tumour.

**3.** An abnormal or morbid swelling or enlargement in any part of the body of an animal or plant; an excrescence; a tumefaction. Now usually in restricted sense: see b.

[1541: cf. 1.] 1597 HOOKER *Eccl. Pol.* v. lxxii. § 18 To helpe the tumors which alwaies fulnes breedeth. *a* 1601 ? MARSTON *Pasquil & Kath.* II. 61 The gowt causeth a great tumour in a mans legs. 1692 BENTLEY *Boyle Lect.* iv. 136 Tumors and Excrescences of Plants..made by such Insects. 1758 GOOCH *Cases Surg.* 17 A Species of tumor called by the common people the Mumps. 1874 LUBBOCK *Orig. & Met. Ins.* i. 10 To produce a tumour or gall.

**b.** *spec.* A permanent circumscribed morbid swelling, consisting in a new growth of tissue, without inflammation.

*Phantom tumour*: see PHANTOM 8.

1804 ABERNETHY *Surg. Obs.* 6, I shall restrict the surgical signification of the word 'Tumour' to such swellings as arise from some new production. 1807–26 S. COOPER *First Lines Surg.* (ed. 5) 428 The tumour being removed, the surgeon should examine the interior of the wound... He should also examine the surface of every scirrhous tumour, immediately it is taken out. 1870 MAUDSLEY *Body & Mind* 184 Certain colloid tumours have the structure of the umbilical cord. 1878 T. BRYANT *Pract. Surg.* (1879) II. 28 Tumours of the pharynx or tonsils are occasionally met with.

†**4.** *fig.* **a.** 'Swelling' of passion, pride, or the like; the condition of being 'puffed up'; haughtiness, arrogance, vain-glory; inflated pride or conceit. *Obs.*

1600 HEYWOOD *1st Pt. Edw. IV* Wks. 1874 I. 5 If you resist this tumour of her will. 1636 WOTTON *Let. to Q. of Bohemia* in *Reliq.* (1651) 394 There is in him no tumour, no sowrenesse,..but a quiet mind. 1751 JOHNSON *Rambler* No. 98 ⁋ 11 The tumour of insolence, or petulance of contempt. 1778 SIR J. REYNOLDS *Disc.* viii. (1876) 444 The tumour of this presumptuous loftiness.

†**b.** Turgidity of language, style, or deportment; affected grandeur; bombast: = TUMIDITY b. *Obs.*

*a* 1639 WOTTON *Parallel Essex & Buckhm.* (1641) 8 His Stile was..rich of praise [1651 phrase],..and so farre from Tumor that it rather wanted a little Elevation. 1652 J. HALL *Height of Eloquence* p. v, It appears one of the nicest cautions in all Speech to beware of Tumour. 1751 JOHNSON *Rambler* No. 105 ⁋ 4 A slow pace, and tumour of dignity. 1840 DE QUINCEY *Style* I. Wks. 1860 XI. 204 Better to be flippant, than by a revolting habit of tumour and perplexity [etc.].

†**c.** Something vain or empty; a 'bubble'. *Obs.*

1629 MASSINGER *Picture* I. i, Nor is it in me mere desire of fame..that puts on my armour: Such airy tumours take not me. 1662 *Royal Trade of Fishing* 15, I present you with no Chimeraes or tumors, toyes to please Children.

**5.** *attrib.* and *Comb.*, as *tumour-cell*, *-formation*, *growth*, *-mass*, *symptom*, etc.; *tumour-like* adj.

1880 BARWELL *Aneurism* 116 Tumor symptoms on the left side of the chest. 1889 J. M. DUNCAN *Clin. Lect. Dis. Women* ii. (ed. 4) 5 A rounded soft, tumour-like mass. 1898 J. HUTCHINSON in *Arch. Surg.* IX. No. 36. 295 Multiple Fractures..with Tumour Growths.

Hence † **Tumoured, tumored** (tiū·məɹd) *a.*, *obs.*, affected with tumour or swelling, swollen (*lit.* and *fig.*): const. as *adj.* or *pa. pple.*

1635 HEYWOOD *Hierarch.* VI. 362 By his poys'nous draught which life expel'd I might behold his legs tumor'd and swell'd. 1639 JUNIUS *Sin Stigm.* 50 Such an one..seldome unbuttons his tumored breast. 1647 TRAPP *Comm. Matt.* xix. 23 The greatest wealth..tumoured up with the greatest swelth of rebellion.

**Tump** (tɒmp), *sb. local.* Also 6 tumpe, 7 toompe, tomp. [Not found before end of 16th c.; chiefly a western and w. midl. word; see *Eng. Dial. Dict.*; origin obscure.

Also in Welsh *twmp* (cf. Buttington Tump in Montgomeryshire); but this may be from English. Welsh has also *Twmpath* (in Mabinogion *twympath*), 'a clump or tuft of rough grass, a barrow or tumulus', etc., with which cf. *tumpet* in *Eng. Dial. Dict.*]

**1.** A hillock, mound; a mole-hill, or ant-hill; a barrow, tumulus.

1589 NASHE *Martins Months M.* 53 They brought him vnawares to a dunghill, taking it for a tumpe, since a Tombe might not be had. 1603 OWEN *Pembrokeshire* (1892) 84 *note*, No traces remained..but highe and rounde toompes of earth. *Ibid.* 283 Tomps of erth. 1664 EVELYN *Pomona* vi. (1729) 71 To raise Tumps, or temporary Banks in the midst of an Inclosure. 1763 J. HUTCHINS in *Mem. W. Stukeley* (Surtees) II. 133 On the top of the hill..are small tumps. 1829 E. JESSE *Jrnl. Nat.* 313 Cutting up anthills, or tumps, as we call them. 1881 FREEMAN in *Life & Lett.* (1895) II. 245 A few tumps so old that you can tell nothing about them. 1891 *Kelly's P. O. Guide Herefordsh.* 1 Tump is a peculiar term for barrow hills in the western shires..the Tumps at Bolston, Horne Lacy, and Hope Mansel.

**2.** A clump of trees or shrubs; a clump of grass, esp. one forming a dry spot in a bog or fen.

1802 G. MONTAGU *Ornith. Dict.* N iij, The nest..is placed on a tump or dry spot. 1869 BLACKMORE *Lorna D.* xxxi, He..looked ahead of him, from behind a tump of whortles. 1880 — *Mary Anerley* xvii, Every tump of wiry grass.

**3.** A heap of anything; a hay-cock or rick; a heap of stones.

Also a store-heap of potatoes, turnips, etc., covered with straw and earth (*Eng. Dial. Dict.*).

1892 *Stratford-on-Avon Herald* 5 Aug. 4/2 To sell by Auction,..Tump of Old Hay about 2 tons. 1905 *Daily News* 24 Jan. 6 A tump of rubbish.

Hence **Tu·mpy** *a.*, of ground: humpy, hummocky.

1825 in *Eng. Dial. Dict.* 1847–78 in HALLIWELL.

**Tump**, *v.*[1] *local.* [f. prec. sb.] To make a 'tump' or mound about the root of a tree. Also, to store roots in a tump (*E.D.D.*). Hence **Tu·mping** *vbl. sb.*

1721 BAILEY, *Tumping*, a sort of Fencing for Trees. 1725 *Bradley's Fam. Dict.* s. v. *Paling*, This Method is.. more chargeable than Tumping.., but much more durable. *Ibid.*, *Tumping*, a sort of Fencing in Fields, when a Tree is set..no deeper than to make it stand, tho' all the Roots be not cover'd, till the Tump or Mould be raised about it. 1727 BAILEY vol. II, To *Tump*, to fence trees.

**Tump**, *v.*[2] *U.S.* [Origin obscure: cf. TUMP-LINE.] *trans.* To drag or carry by means of a tump-line.

1855 HALIBURTON *Nat. & Hum. Nat.* I. 268 A man passed the..barrack-gate, tumping (which means..hauling) an immense bull-moose on a sled. 1860 BARTLETT *Dict. Amer.*, *To Tump.* Probably an Indian word...'We tumped the deer to our cabin'. (Maine.)

**Tumphy** (tɒ·mfi). *Sc.* Also tumfie. [Cf. SUMPH, in same sense.] **a.** A stupid person, a blockhead. **b.** *Coal-mining.* (See quot. 1886.)

1795 A. WILSON *The Spouter* in *Poems & Lit. Prose* (1876) II. 331 The puir unfort'nate tumphy. 1823 GALT *Entail* III. iv. 41 Neither you nor that unreverent and misleart tumphy your wife. 1886 J. BARROWMAN *Sc. Mining Terms* 69 *Tumphy*, coaly fire-clay. 1890 J. SERVICE *Thir Notandums* i. 3, I hear that tumfie o' a lassock nickerin' an' lauchin' in the kitchen.

**Tu·mp-line.** *local U.S.* [Origin obscure: cf. TUMP *v.*[2]] See quots.

1860 BARTLETT *Dict. Amer.*, *Tumpline*, a strap placed across the forehead to assist a man in carrying a pack on his back. Used in Maine, where the custom was borrowed from the Indians. 1890 W. J. GORDON *Foundry* 114 Bundles.. secured by the leather strap or 'tump' line, are slung across the chest or forehead. 1904 S. E. WHITE *Forest* xiii, The carrying we did with the universal tump-line. It passes across the top of the head. The weight should rest on the small of the back just above the hips.

**Tum-tum** (tʌ·mˌtʌ·m), *sb.*[1] and *adv.* Also in various extended forms, as **tum-a-tum, tum-ti-tum**, etc. An imitation of the sound of a stringed instrument or instruments, esp. when monotonously played; strumming; a monotonous air. Also *attrib.*

1859 *Habits Gd. Society* xiii. 344 A..nightmare of 'tum-tum-tiddy-tum', and waltzes *à deux temps*. 1884 *Pall Mall G.* 4 July 4/1 The thrum-thrum, ting-ting, tum-a-tum-tum of their banjoes. 1886 *Overland Monthly* Dec. 612/2 Tum! tum-ti-tum! tum! went the guitar. 1887 *Pall Mall G.* 31 Oct. 5/1 'Florid' accompaniments consisting of tum tum in the bass and scales like pianoforte finger studies in the treble. 1894 BARING-GOULD *Kitty Alone* III. 79 All the harmonies in thirds and fifths, and a solemn tum-tum bass.

So **Tum-tum** *v.*, *intr.* to play monotonously (or make a similar sound), to strum; hence **Tum-tu·mmer, Tum-tu·mming** *vbl. sb.* and *ppl. a.*

1866 A. G. MIDDLETON *Earnest* (1867) 5 The lubras..tum-tummed on bits of stick. 1879 BARING-GOULD *Germany* II. 87 Nothing better in the musical line than pretty tum-tumming. 1892 D. SLADEN *Japs at Home* ii, A 'tum-tumming' noise is kept up. 1898 *Westm. Gaz.* 20 Apr. 3/2 Mr. Cookson..the tootler and tumtummer on old themes.

**Tum-tum**, *sb.*[2] *Anglo-Indian.* [Derivation unascertained.] A dog-cart.

1863 TREVELYAN *Compet. Wallah* vi. (1864) 139 We..started off..in two tumtums, or dog-carts. 1908 *Ch. Mission. Gleaner* 1 Oct. 150/1 Our low two-wheeled tum-tum.. bumping and jolting along the track of dry grass.

**Tum-tum**, *sb.*[3] *W. Indies.* [Derivation uncertain; perh. from the thumping sound made.] A West-Indian dish: see quot.

1833 CARMICHAEL *W. Indies* I. vii. 183 They often have tum-tum—made of plantains boiled quite soft, and beat in a wooden mortar,—it is eaten like a potatoe pudding. 1860 in BARTLETT *Dict. Amer.*

**Tumular** (tiū·miŭlăɹ), *a.* [f. L. *tumul-us* (see TUMULUS) + -AR[1].] Pertaining to or consisting of a mound or tumulus.

1828 WEBSTER, *Tumular*, consisting in a heap; formed or being in a heap or hillock. 1851 D. WILSON *Preh. Ann.* (1863) II. IV. iv. 306 The disturbance of this tumular cemetery.

**Tumulary** (tiū·miŭlări), *a.* [f. as prec. + -ARY[2]: cf. F. *tumulaire* (1835 in *Dict. Acad.*).]

1. Pertaining to or placed over a tomb; sepulchral.

1758 *Monthly Rev.* 160 Adapted to the..tumulary style. 1834 L. RITCHIE *Wand. by Seine* 97 On some prostrate tumulary stone. 1869 MRS. PALLISER *Brittany* 194 The pavement [of the church] is covered with tumulary stones.

2. = TUMULAR.

18.. W. H. RUSSELL (Ogilvie), Bounded by red tumulary cliffs.

†**Tu·mulate**, *ppl. a. Obs.* Also 5 -ylat, 6 -ylate, -ulat. [f. L. *tumulāt-us*, pa. pple. of *tumulāre* to bury, f. *tumulus*: see TUMULUS and -ATE[2].] Buried, entombed. (Const. as *pa. pple.*)

1455 *Rolls of Parlt.* V. 308/1 The..Erle,..is..tumylat and restyng within the Priory. 1513 BRADSHAW *St. Werburge* II. 659 The body of Saynt Oswalde..she translate..to Gloucetur, there to be tumulate. *c* 1536 in Ellis *Orig. Lett.* Ser. III. III. 18 Many of them be there tumulate and buryed.

**Tumulate** (tiū·miŭleɪt), *v. rare.* [f. ppl. stem of L. *tumulāre* to bury: see prec. and -ATE[3].] *trans.* To bury, entomb.

1623 COCKERAM, *Tumulate*, to enterre, to bury. 1656 in BLOUNT *Glossogr.* 1866 J. B. ROSE tr. *Ovid's Fasti* III. 592 Dido despondent, on the funeral pyre,..Consumed, inurned, and tumulated.

[**Tumulate**, *v.* (in J. with quot. from Boyle, and in Richardson and later Dicts. with quot. from Wilkins), error for TUMULTUATE.]

**Tumulation** (tiūmiŭleɪ·ʃən). *rare.* [f. L. *tumulā-re* to bury + -TION.] Burying, interment; *spec.* interment in a tumulus or grave-mound.

1623 COCKERAM, *Tumulation*, a burying or enterring. 1827 J. ANDERSON *Ess. St. Soc. & Knowl. Highl.* 138 Burning before tumulation seems to have succeeded simple interment.

**Tumuli**, pl. of TUMULUS.

†**Tu·mulose**, *a. Obs. rare*—°. [ad. L. *tumulōs-us* (Sallust), f. *tumulus*, TUMULUS: see -OSE.] (See quot.) Hence †**Tumulo·sity** (*obs. rare*—°).

1727 BAILEY vol. II, *Tumulose* (*tumulōsus*, L.), full of little Hills or Knops. *Tumulosity* (*tumulōsitās*), Hilliness.

**Tumulous** (tiū·miŭləs), *a. rare.* [f. L. *tumul-us*, TUMULUS + -OUS: cf. prec.] **a.** = prec. (*rare*—°). **b.** Forming a tumulus; tumular.

1828 WEBSTER, *Tumulous*, full of hills. 1897 *Daily News* 21 Sept. 8/3 Parcels built up in tumulous columns, which rise from the floor nearly up to the ceiling.

**Tumult** (tiū·mʌlt), *sb.* Also 5–6 -te. [ad. L. *tumultus* (*u*-stem), f. *tumēre* to swell: cf. F. *tumulte* (12th c. in Godef. *Compl.*; in OF. also *temulte*, 1201 in Hatz.-Darm.).]

1. Commotion of a multitude, usually with confused speech or uproar; public disturbance; disorderly or riotous proceeding.

1412–20 LYDG. *Chron. Troy* II. 5235 Al tumulte stinted, and silence Was þoruȝ þe pres, to ȝif hym audyence. 1562 *Reg. Privy Council Scot.* I. 209 Ane seditious persone and rasar of tumult. 1615 G. SANDYS *Trav.* 8 To avoid occasions of tumult. *a* 1718 PRIOR *Henry & Emma* 332 When the loud Tumult speaks the Battel nigh. 1838 LYTTON *Leila* II. i, The tumult of the Camp was to him but a holiday exhibition.

**b.** (with *pl.*) An instance of this; a popular commotion or disturbance; a riot, an insurrection.

1560 DAUS tr. *Sleidane's Comm.* 22 b, It is like to styre vp suche tumultes in Germany. 1641 EVELYN *Diary* 8 Oct., The late tumults in Belgia. 1775 JOHNSON *Tax. no Tyr.* 68 The tumults of a conflagration. 1838 THIRLWALL *Greece* II. xii. 155 A tumult..in which the populace set fire to Milo's house.

†**c.** *transf.* A disorderly crowd, a mob. *rare.*

1628 GAULE *Pract. The.* (1629) 189 The Tumult shall know [that, etc.]. 1648 *Eikon Bas.* vi. 38 To see the barbarous rudenesse of those Tumults who resolved they would take the boldnesse to demand any thing.

2. *gen.* Commotion, agitation, disturbance; disorderly or noisy movement or action. Also *pl.*

1580 SIDNEY *Ps.* XXXV. viii, Oh! on my soul let not these tumults hitt. 1591 SHAKS. *1 Hen. VI*, I. iv. 98 It Thunders and Lightens...What tumult's in the Heauens? 1662 CHARLETON *Myst. Vintners* (1675) 178 The tumult will..be recomposed, the liquor refined. 1781 COWPER *Retirement* 176 Some..are averse to noise And hate the tumult half the world enjoys. 1844 DISRAELI *Coningsby* I. iii, His heart beat with tumult. 1846 TRENCH *Mirac.* vi. (1862) 190 The fiercest tumult of the elements allays itself at last.

3. *fig.* Great disturbance or agitation of mind or feeling; confused and violent emotion.

[1595 SHAKS. *John* IV. ii. 247 Hostilitie, and ciuill tumult reignes Betweene my conscience and my Cosins death.] 1663 BP. PATRICK *Parab. Pilgr.* xxxi. (1687) 378 Such contrary passions..I cannot overcome..without suffering a great tumult and disorder. 1711 ADDISON *Spect.* No. 164 ¶1 A long Tumult of Passions which naturally rise in a Lover's Heart. 1777 BURKE *Corr.* (1844) II. 199 The wild tumult of joy that the news..caused. 1844 THIRLWALL *Greece* VIII. lx. 31 A tumult of grief and indignation.

**Tu·mult**, *v.* [f. prec.]

1. *intr.* To make a tumult, commotion, or disturbance; to raise an insurrection, to riot. ? *Obs.*

1570 LEVINS *Manip.* 187/42 To Tumulte, *tumultuare.* 1616 HAYWARD *Sanct. Troub. Soul* II. To Rdr. ¶2 The sensuall powers did tumult, and breake loose. 1653 MILTON *Paraphr. Ps. ii.* 1 Why do the Gentiles tumult..? 1699 R. L'ESTRANGE *Erasm. Colloq.* (1725) 248 Monks run up and down,..the Rabble tumult; Erasmus writes Colloquies. 1864 [see *tumulting* below].

2. *trans.* To put into tumult; to agitate violently.

1819 'B. CORNWALL' *Dram. Scenes, Rape Proserpine* i, My heart..seems tumulted By some delicious passion. *a* 1851 MOIR *To wounded Ptarmigan* iv, The snorting whale..In its anger tumults ocean.

Hence **Tu·multing** *vbl. sb.*; also †**Tu·multer**, one who stirs up a tumult, a rioter (*obs.*).

1584 HORSEY *Trav.* (Hakl. Soc.) App. 270 To subdue the *tumulters and mainteine quietnes. 1670 MILTON *Hist. Eng.* II. Wks. (1847) 497/1 He..punished the tumulters. 1658 CROMWELL *Sp.* 4 Feb. in Carlyle *Lett. & Sp.* (1871) V. 130 To stir up the people of this town into a *tumulting. 1864 CARLYLE *Fredk. Gt.* XVII. ii. IV. 519 Tired of..fighting and tumulting.

**Tumultuarily** (tiumʌ·ltiuˌărili), *adv.* [f. TUMULTUARY + -LY[2].] In a tumultuary manner.

1. Hastily and without order; irregularly, confusedly, unsystematically, at random.

1590 SIR J. SMYTH *Disc. Weapons* Ded. 5 Ciuill warres,.. maintained..tumultuarilie..by spoyle, sedition, passion, and faction. 1613–18 DANIEL *Coll. Hist. Eng.* (1626) 5 The ..souldiers..tumultuarilie proclaimed Emperour one Marcus. 1676 EVELYN in Aubrey *Nat. Hist. Surrey* (1719) I. Pref. 9, I have set things down tumultuarily, as they came into my..thoughts. 1695 H. DODWELL *Def. Vind. Deprived Bps.* 1 More hastily and tumultuarily laid together.

2. With tumult or disturbance; tumultuously.

1609 DANIEL *Civ. Wars* I. xii. *margin*, Stephen..contendes with Maude the Empresse for the succession, and raigned tumultuarily 18 yeares and 10 monethes. 1647 JER. TAYLOR *Lib. Proph.* Ep. Ded. 20 Arrius behav'd himselfe so seditiously and tumultuarily. 1682 T. FLATMAN *Heraclitus Ridens* No. 74 (1713) II. 203 Those so tumultuarily assembled and so outragious.

So **Tumu·ltuariness**, the quality of being tumultuary; in quots., disposition to tumult.

1648 *Eikon Bas.* xvii. 148 The tumultuariness of People. 1653 GAUDEN *Hierasp.* 24 Tumultuariness, faction, and sedition.

**Tumultuarious** (tiumʌltiuˌēə·riəs), *a. rare*—[1]. [f. as next + -OUS.] = next, 2.

1895 E. F. M. BENECKE tr. *Comparetti's Virgil in Mid. Ages* xiv, Neither a tumultuarious improvisation nor a frigid versification.

**Tumultuary** (tiumʌ·ltiuˌări), *a.* (*sb.*) [ad. L. *tumultuāri-us* of or belonging to hurry or tumult, raised hastily (as troops), f. *tumultus* TUMULT: see -ARY[1]; cf. F. *tumultuaire.*]

1. Of troops: Gathered hastily and promiscuously, without order or system; irregular, undisciplined. Also of warfare, etc. carried on by such troops, or in an irregular way.

1590 SIR J. SMYTH *Disc. Weapons* Ded. 2 b, The tumultuarie and disordered wars of the Lowe Countries. 1600 HOLLAND *Livy* VIII. ii. 289 A tumultuarie armie in great hast levied..out of all quarters. 1759 ROBERTSON *Hist. Scot.* (1817) I. II. 396 With tumultuary..violence, they fell upon the churches. 1841 ELPHINSTONE *Hist. Ind.* II. VII. iv. 165 A tumultuary attack, which was repelled by the garrison.

2. Hurriedly done; irregular, disorderly, confused; haphazard, unsystematic, random.

1609 HOLLAND *Amm. Marcell.* 245 In hast and in tumultuarie manner. 1613–18 DANIEL *Coll. Hist. Eng.* (1626) 22 Content with a tumultuarie learning. *a* 1638 MEDE *Wks.* (1672) 772 So tumultuary and confused a Discourse. 1771 MACPHERSON *Introd. Hist. Gt. Brit.* 235 Their resolutions must..have been tumultuary and precipitate. 1843 CHURCH *St. Anselm & Hen. I*, ¶4 The tumultuary beginnings of society. 1879 FARRAR *St. Paul* I. 501 Ashamed of their tumultuary injustice.

†**b.** Of a person: Acting, writing, or speaking hastily and at random; unsystematic, disorderly. *Obs.*

1618 BOLTON *Florus* To Rdr., With merematicall Stadius, Florus is but a tumultuary author. 1644 BULWER *Chiron.* Præłud., Those upstart and tumultuarie Oratours. 1648 *Eikon Bas.* vi. 40 Whatever tumultuary Patrons shall project.

3. Disposed to, marked by, or of the nature of tumult; tumultuous, turbulent.

1650 HOWELL *Giraffi's Rev. Naples* I. 42 Against the will of a tumultuary people. 1661 GLANVILL *Van. Dogm.* 13 The tumultuary disorders of our passions. 1664 POWER *Exp. Philos.* Pref., The..tumultuary motion of the Atoms. 1705 tr. *Bosman's Guinea* 229 This confused Tumultuary Noise. 1834 *Tait's Mag.* I. 404/1 The reign of Governor King..was a tumultuary period. 1876 GEO. ELIOT *Dan. Der.* VIII. lviii, Struggling with a tumultuary crowd of thoughts.

**B.** *sb.* in *pl.* Tumultuary forces: see 1.

1654 EARL MONM. tr. *Bentivoglio's Warrs Flanders* 76 The Tumultuaries expecting..better progress. 1830 JAMES *Darnley* xxxiv, The leader of the tumultuaries.

**Tumultuate** (tiumʌ·ltiuˌeɪt), *v.* Now *rare.* [f. ppl. stem of L. *tumultuārī* to make a bustle or disturbance: see -ATE[3].]

1. *intr.* To stir up a tumult; to make a disturbance or commotion; to become or be tumultuous, turbulent, agitated, or restless.

1611 [see *tumultuating* below]. 1616 JAS. I *Sp. Star-Chamb.* 20 June 35 Acquiesce in the Iudgement, and doe not tumultuate against it. 1671 R. BOHUN *Wind* 27 Noise of Winds, that..tumultuate. *a* 1734 NORTH *Exam.* I. ii. § 44. (1740) 51 To afflict the poor People..to make them restless and apt to tumultuate. 1860 W. ARNOT *Laws fr. Heaven* 268 The dread of evil and the desire of good tumultuate and struggle for the mastery in a human breast.

2. *trans.* To excite to tumult, put into a state of tumult, make tumultuous; to disorder or disturb violently.

1616 JAS. I *Sp. Star-Chamb.* 20 June 44 Tumultuating the countrey. 1661 R. L'ESTRANGE *Interest Mistaken* Ded. 2 Their Ayme being to Tumultuate the People. 1768 [W. DONALDSON] *Life Sir B. Sapskull* II. Ded. 3 The street.. was tumultuated with the loud roar of..raps, perpetually thundering at my..door! 1820 *Blackw. Mag.* VII. 316 The feelings that tumultuate the heart of a father.

Hence **Tumu·ltuating** *vbl. sb.* and *ppl. a.*

1611 SPEED *Hist. Gt. Brit.* IX. viii. (1623) 574 Hauing let loose many tumultuating Spirits. 1642 HALES *Gold. Rem.*, *Tract on Schism* (1673) 5 Ecclesiastical stories.., of which the greatest [part] consists of factionating and tumultuating of great and potent Bishops. 1815 J. LOVE *Lett.* (1840) 367 Whatever be the tumultuating of flesh and blood. 1854 MAR. HARLAND *Alone* xxxi, Tumultuating passions were stilled into a calm, delicious ecstasy.

**Tumultuation** (tiumʌltiuˌēɪ·ʃən). Now *rare.* [ad. L. *tumultuātiōn-em*, n. of action from *tumultuārī*: see prec. and -ATION. Cf. OF. *tumultuation* (13th c.).] The action of making a tumult; a condition of tumult; commotion, disturbance, agitation.

*c* 1475 *Harl. Contn. Higden* (Rolls) VIII. 454 A grete tumultuacion and murmur..amonge the peple. 1559 KENNEDY *Let. to Willock* in *Wodrow Soc. Misc.* (1844) 270, I desire nolder tumultuatioun, cummyr, nor stryfe. 1631 R. H. *Arraignm. Whole Creature* xviii. 326 The tumultuations.. of our inordinate affections. 1786 G. FRAZER *Dove's Flight to Thicket* 71 The wicked have great tumultuations in their minds. 1883 J. PARKER *Tyne Ch.* 109 The tumultuations of His tabernacle.

**Tumultuous** (tiumʌ·ltiuˌəs), *a.* Also 6 -eous, 7 -ious. [ad. OF. *tumultuous*, F. *tumultueux*, ad. L. *tumultuōs-us* full of tumult, bustle, or confusion: f. *tumultu-s* TUMULT: see -OUS.]

1. Full of tumult or commotion; marked by confusion and uproar; disorderly and noisy; violent and clamorous; turbulent.

*a* 1548 HALL *Chron.*, *Edw. IV* 223 Suche, as in the last tumulteous busines, toke part with .. Fauconbrige. 1553 BRENDE *Q. Curtius* X. 210 b, They..disturbed his tale with their tumultuous crye. 1638 SIR T. HERBERT *Trav.* (ed. 2) 274 After 30 yeeres tumultuous reigne. 1739 WESLEY *Wks.* (1830) I. 214, I do indeed go out into the highways and hedges, but not in a tumultuous manner. 1807 WORDSW. *White Doe* II. 62 Tumultuous noises filled the hall. 1840 HAWTHORNE *Biog. Sk. Sir W. Pepperrell* (1879) 193 The tumultuous advance of the conquering army. 1881 JOWETT *Thucyd.* I. 160 Embarking in tumultuous haste.

†**b.** Tending to excite tumult; seditious. *Obs.*

1619 [implied in TUMULTUOUSNESS]. 1623 COCKERAM, *Tumultuous*, seditious, full of trouble. 1651 HOBBES *Leviath.* II. xxii. 122 An unlawfull, and tumultuous designe. 1679 LUTTRELL *Brief Rel.* (1857) I. 27 Tumultuous and seditious petitions.

†**c.** Causing tumult; disturbing, disquieting. *Obs. rare.*

1604 R. CAWDREY *Table Alph.*, *Tumultuous*, troublous, disturbing or disquieting. 1614 RALEIGH *Hist. World* IV. vi. § 3 The tumultuous newes of Lysimachus his victories.

**2.** Making a tumult or commotion; acting in a disorderly and noisy way; turbulent, riotous.

**1576** FLEMING *Panopl. Epist.* 49 He might..fortifie, with his ayde,..those tumultuous villaines. **1635** JACKSON *Creed* VIII. xvii. § 6 The promised Prince of peace..should not be sought amongst the tumultuous hosts of warre. *a* **1718** PRIOR *1st Hymn Callimachus* 59 The fierce Curetes..trod tumultuous Their Mystic Dance. **1868** E. EDWARDS *Ralegh* I. xxi. 471 His house was beset by a tumultuous crowd.

**3.** Of physical actions or agents: Marked by disorderly commotion; acting or moving irregularly and violently; confusedly agitated; tempestuous.

**1667** MILTON *P. L.* II. 936 The strong rebuff of som tumultuous cloud Instinct with Fire. **1794** G. ADAMS *Nat. & Exp. Philos.* I. ix. 335 A sudden and very tumultuous ebullition ensued. **1843** R. J. GRAVES *Syst. Clin. Med.* ix. 104 The action of the heart tumultuous. **1856** KANE *Arct. Expl.* I. ix. 97 A roaring and tumultuous river. **1870** MORRIS *Earthly Par.* (1871) IV. 124 The far-off rooks' sweet tumultuous voice.

**4.** *fig.* of, or in reference to, emotion or thought.

**1667** MILTON *P. L.* IV. 16 His dire attempt, which nigh the birth Now rowling, boiles in his tumultuous brest. **1719** DE FOE *Crusoe* (1840) II. iii. 57 He..found his thoughts tumultuous. **1772** PRIESTLEY *Inst. Relig.* (1782) II. 102 Tumultuous joy. **1822–56** DE QUINCEY *Confess.* Wks. 1897 III. 446 A tumultuous dream.

**Tumu·ltuously,** *adv.* [f. prec. + -LY [2].] In a tumultuous manner; with tumult or commotion; with confusion and uproar; riotously.

**1548** UDALL, etc. *Erasm. Par. Matt.* xii. 53 b, He shall not do this tumultuously or violently. For he shall not chide, nor..crye oute. **1617** MORYSON *Itin.* III. 27 If they tumultiously revenge thy wrong. *a* **1768** ABP. SECKER *Serm.* (1771) V. xviii. 431 Death..suddenly and tumultuously inflicted. **1834** L. RITCHIE *Wand. by Seine* 166 The clang of innumerable church-bells comes tumultuously on the breeze. **1857** MILLER *Elem. Chem.* (1862) III. 118 The reaction..is apt to become tumultuously violent.

†**b.** Seditiously: cf. prec. 1 b. *Obs.*

**1682** *Addr. Lond. Freemen* in *Lond. Gaz.* No. 1738/2 Being Popishly and Tumultuously Inclined.

†**c.** Hurriedly and irregularly; in a hurry, without order or system: cf. TUMULTUARILY 1. *Obs.*

**1597** HOOKER *Eccl. Pol.* v. lxxvi. § 6 They attempted tumultuously they saw not what. **1726** LEONI tr. *Alberti's Archit.* II. 8/2 The Wall of Athens..was built so tumultuously that they even threw into it some of the Statues.

**Tumu·ltuousness.** [f. as prec. + -NESS.] The quality or state of being tumultuous or disturbed; †in quot. 1619, seditiousness (*obs.*).

**1619** HIERON *Wks.* II. 442 Swaggering, and tumultuousnesse, and carelesnesse. **1647** TRAPP *Comm. Matt.* iv. 19 The world is compared to the sea, for its .. tumultuousness. **1822** DE QUINCEY *Confess.* 39 The tumultuousness of my dreams. **1899** *Allbutt's Syst. Med.* VII. 159 The tumultuousness of the movements.

‖**Tumulus** (tiū·miŭlŏs). Pl. **tumuli** (-ləi). [Derivative (? dim.) from root *tum-* of *tumē-re* to swell, *tumor*, etc.] An ancient sepulchral mound, a barrow (BARROW *sb.*[1] 3).

[**1398** TREVISA *Barth. De P. R.* XIV. xlv. (Bodl. MS.), A downe [is] lower þan an hille..and hatte *tumulus*, as it were swelling londe.] **1686** PLOT *Staffordsh.* 403 Not the only signe of Roman tumuli. **1765** J. BARTRAM *Jrnl.* 26 Dec., in W. Stork *Acc. E. Florida* (1766) 7 A middling sized Indian tumulus. **1794** SULLIVAN *View Nat.* IV. 393 The tumuli, and the other repositories of the dead,..discovered in the.. deserts of the north. **1853** FELTON *Fam. Lett.* xxx. (1865) 264 Leonidas and his Three Hundred..lie beneath yonder tumulus. **1863** LYELL *Antiq. Man* 15 Tumuli of the stone period.

**Tumyde**, obs. form of TUMID.

**Tun** (tʊn), *sb.* Forms: *α.* 1–7 **tunne**, 4 **toun**, 4–5 **towne**, 4–6 **toune**, 4, 7–8 **tunn**, 5–6 **towne**, 5–7 **tune**, *Sc.* **twn(e**, 6 **tounne**, 4– **tun**. *β.* 3–7 **tonne**, 5–6 **tonn**, **tone**, 5–8 **ton**, 6 **toon**. See also TON [1]. [OE. *tunne*, wk. fem., ME. *tunne*, later *tonne*; cogn. with OFris. *tunne*, *tonne*, OLG. **tunna* (MLG., LG. *tunne* (*tünne*)), MDu. *tonne* (Du. *ton*), OHG. *tunna* (MHG. *tunne*, Ger. *tonne*); late ON. *tunna* (Sw. *tunna*, mod.Norw. *tunna*, *tynna*, MDu. *tunde*, Da. *tønde*); also med.L. *tunna* (9th c. in Cassel Gloss.), OF. *tonne*, Pr. *tona* (in other Rom. langs. only in derivative forms: see TONNEL, TUNNEL); also MIr., Ir. and Gael. *tunna*. Origin uncertain: app. not orig. Latin or Romanic.

As the OHG. retains initial *t* it must have been adopted (from LG. or med.L.) after the HG. sound shifting, i.e. after 700. Some suggest a Celtic source, viz. OIr. *toun* hide, skin, so that the original sense would be 'wine-skin'; but the MIr. *tunna* looks like an adopted word. At present it can only be said that the word appears to be as old or older in the LG. group of langs., including OE., than anywhere else; its occurrence in the Corpus Gloss *c* 725 is app. the earliest trace of the word in any lang. The later ME. spelling *tonne* was perh. after F., but prob. largely due to the scribal fashion of writing *o* for *u*, in contiguity to *m*, *n*, *v*, etc., as in *son*, *tongue*, *honey*, *come*, *some*, *above*, *love*, etc. From *c* 1688 the two forms *tun* and *ton* have been differentiated in use: see TON.[1]]

**1.** A large cask or barrel, usually for liquids, esp. wine, ale, or beer, or for various provisions. Now less common than *cask*.

*α.* *c* **725** *Corpus Gloss.* (Hessels) C 945 *Cuba*, tunne. **791–6** in Birch *Cart. Sax.* I. 380 Twa tunnan fulle hlutres aloð. *c* **1205** LAY. 14957 Rouuenne eode to are tunne þer wes idon in þes kinges deoreste win. *c* **1325** *Gloss. W. de Bibbesw.* in Wright *Voc.* 160 Cerveyse en tonne [*gloss* a toune]. **1387** TREVISA *Higden* (Rolls) III. 309 He [Diogenes] torned þe mouth of his toun toward þe souþ in colde tyme and toward þe norþ in somer tyme. *c* **1425** *Voc.* in Wr.-Wülcker 658/20 *Hoc dolium*, townne. *c* **1475** *Pict. Voc.* ibid. 770/36 *Hoc dolium*, a tune. *a* **1529** SKELTON *El. Rummyng* 194 In the ale tunnes. **1644** EVELYN *Diary* 6 June, The Abbot's Palace, where we were shew'd a vast Tun (as big as that at Heidelberg). **1717** PRIOR *Alma* III. 426 L'Avare..Strikes not the present Tun, for fear The Vintage should be bad next Year. **1819** KEATS *Lamia* II. 188 Wine Came from the gloomy tun.

*β.* **1340** *Ayenb.* 35 Tonnen mid wyn. *c* **1400** *Laud Troy Bk.* 4677 Grete tonnes ful of flour. *c* **1440** *Gesta Rom.* lxi. 252 (Harl. MS.) Do gete me..a ler tonne. **1562** J. HEYWOOD *Prov. & Epigr.* (1867) 158 He hath fed till he is as full as a toon. **1577** B. GOOGE *Heresbach's Husb.* 11 Tonnes..for Wine; Beere..and suche like.

†**b.** A large vessel in general; a tub or vat; a chest. *Obs.*

*α.* *c* **1205** LAY. 6079 Heo makeden ane tunne of golde and of ȝimme. *a* **1225** *St. Marher.* 17 Salomon the wise..bitunde us in ane tunne. *a* **1300** *Cursor M.* 21042 (Cott.) Þat Imperur wend [John] to mat In a tun was welland hat. *a* **1400–50** *Alexander* 1807 He tellis quyche a tunne of tresoure he hauys. **1577** B. GOOGE *Heresbach's Husb.* 11 Wherefore serueth that great Tounne? To water the Barly in. **1599** SHAKS. *Hen. V*, I. ii. 255. **1601** HOLLAND *Pliny* III. vi. I. 61 Earthen vessels, as tunnes and such like.

*β.* *c* **1290** *S. Eng. Leg.* I. 401/315 Þis tormentores nomen þis guode kniȝht and is sones and is wif, And duden heom in ane tonne of bras,..Gret fuyr huy þare-aboute maden. *c* **1330** R. BRUNNE *Chron. Wace* (Rolls) 2246 Tonnes of bras wiþ queynte þynges þat make þe water euere hot. *a* **1450** MYRC *Festial* 31 Domician..send aftyr Ion, and made put hym yn a brasyn tonne full of oyle. *c* **1450** *Brut* ccxliv. 374 Yn scorne & despite he [the Dauphin] sent to hym [Henry V] a tonne fulle of teneys-ballis. **1567** *Wills & Inv. N. C.* (Surtees) I. 266 A tonning tubb, a tonn for bread.

**c.** *Brewing.* A mashing-vat (*mash-tun*) or fermenting-vat (*gyle-tun*).

**1713** [see *mash-tun* s. v. MASH *sb.*[1] 5]. **1743** [see *gyle-tun* s. v. GYLE 4]. **1815** J. SMITH *Panorama Sc. & Art* II. 569 The mash-tun is shallow in proportion to its diameter... When the mashing is completed, the tun is covered, to prevent the escape of heat. **1830** M. DONOVAN *Dom. Econ.* I. 221 He urges it to a tumultuous effervescence,..threatening the overflow of the tun.

**d.** *fig.* or in figurative allusion.

*α.* **1447** BOKENHAM *Seyntys* (Roxb.) 58 Of annes wombe sprange ye oyle tunne Of gracyous helthe to alle that beth seke. **1596** SHAKS. 1 *Hen. IV*, II. iv. 493 A Deuill..in the likenesse of a fat old Man; a Tunne of Man is thy Companion. **1603** KNOLLES *Hist. Turks* (1638) 148 In Iupiter's court no man might drinke of the tun of blisse, but that he must taste also of the tun of wo. *a* **1704** T. BROWN *Walk round London* (1709) 25 Such a Tun of Female Fat [a very fat woman]. **1909** *Remin. Lady Wake* xv. 168 His enormous tun of a body.

*β.* **1340** *Ayenb.* 247 In-to þe greate tauerne, huer þe tonne is betake, þet is ine þe liue eurelestinde. *c* **1485** *Digby Myst.* (1882) I. 515 Tonne of tranquylyte, to yeve hem drynke that han thrustyd sore. **1513** DOUGLAS *Æneis* I. Prol. 59 All man purches drink at thi sugurat tone.

**2.** A cask of definite capacity; hence, a measure of capacity for wine and other liquids (formerly also for other commodities), usually equivalent to 2 pipes or 4 hogsheads, containing 252 old wine-gallons.

*α.* *c* **1440** *Jacob's Well* 47 He hadde a vyneȝerd, þe whiche, ȝere be ȝere, bare hym x. tunne of wyn. and euery ȝere he payed þe tenthe tunne of wyn to tythe. **1504** *Acc. Ld. High Treas. Scot.* II. 277 For xx twn of plaistir. **1535** in Weaver *Wells Wills* (1890) 90 A tunne of leade or the value thereof. **1583** *Rates of Custome Ho.* Hj, What number of all kinde of dry French wares make a Tun.. Wol cardes,..Two C. dosen. Playing cardes,..Fiftie groce. Canuas..ii. M. vi. c. elles. **1655** *Acts Parlt. Scotl.* VI. II. 829/1 Two Buts, two Pipes, four Hogsheads.., six Tierces, three Punchions.., and eight Quarter-Casks, shal be accounted..for a Tun. **1674** *Reg. Privy Council Scot.* Ser. III. IV. 275 Importation of brandie upon payment of ten lib. sterling per tune for custome. **1778** PENNANT *Tour Wales* (1883) I. 54 The well..is found to fling out about twenty one tuns of water in a minute. **1898** F. T. BULLEN *Cruise Cachalot* 33 At the rate of £40 per tun or £4 per barrel.

*β.* *c* **1400** *Gamelyn* 316 Fyue tonne of wyn. **1526** TINDALE *Luke* xvi. 6 A hondred tonnes of oyle. **1654** GRAHAM *Glencairn's Exp.* in *Misc. Scot.* (1819) IV. 69 She was loaded with near forty tons of French wine. **1793** NELSON in Nicolas *Disp.* (1845) I 352 Five hundred tons of Wine.

†**b.** *Tun of gold*: 100,000 guilders, florins, etc. [transl. the corresponding use of *tonne* in G., obs. Du., etc.] *Obs.*

**1603** KNOLLES *Hist. Turks* (1621) 1052 Promising..to lend him a tunne of gold to pay them their wages. **1666** *Lond. Gaz.* No. 28/2 Holland and Zealand..are like to carry it in favour to the East-India Company, upon payment to be made by them of 12 Tuns of Gold, as they count here, that is, about 120000 *l.* sterling. **1680** C. NESSE *Church Hist.* 501 To let about nine tun of gold go yearly hence to Rome. **1683** *Lond. Gaz.* No. 1789/1 The King [of Sweden]..demanded of them a Supply of 16 Tun of Gold, that is 16 hundred thousand Florins.

**3.** A measure of capacity or weight: see TON [1] 3, 4.

**4.** 'A chimney, esp. the upper part above the roof of a house; a chimney-pot' (*Eng. Dial. Dict.*). Now *dial.*

**1463** *Bury Wills* (Camden) 20 My newe hous with the iij. tunnys of chemeneyis. **1596** HARINGTON *Metam. Ajax* 89 The tuns..drawing up the aire as a chimney doth smoke. **1859** PARKER *Dom. Archit.* III. ii. 37 *note*, Chimney shafts are still called tuns in some districts. **1905** in *Eng. Dial. Dict.* in various dialects of south and S.W.

†**5.** Name of a prison in Cornhill, London. *Obs.*

*a* **1500** in Arnolde *Chron.* (1811) 92 Sette in the tonne in Cornhyll for his dishoneste. **1533** *Fabyan's Chron.* VII. 64 b/2 This yere..certayne persones of London brake vp the tunne [*so edd.* 1542, 1559; *ed.* 1516 towre] in the warde of Cornhyll. **1598** STOW *Surv.* (1603) 189 The Tunne upon Cornehill, because the same was builded somewhat in fashion of a Tunne standing on the one ende.

**6.** A kind of cup or small drinking vessel.

**1555** in Hakluyt *Voy.* (1599) I. 263 A great chamber, where stood many small tunnes, pailes, bowles, and pots of siluer, ..all parsel gilt. **1634** BRERETON *Trav.* (Chetham Soc.) 6 The young children, girls, walked all the Sabbath in the afternoon, with cups or tuns in their hands. [The name is still applied at Magdalen College, Oxford, to silver drinking cups, holding a third of a quart, some of which are dated 1657 and 1663.]

**7.** †**a.** *Sea tun*, a name for a seal (the animal). *Obs.*

**1601** HOLLAND *Pliny* XXXII. xi. II. 451 Sea Men and Women,..Sea Tuns or Pipes. **1672** JOSSELYN *New Eng. Rarities* 31 A Catalogue of Fish,..Sea Tun.

**b.** *Conch.* = *tun-shell*: see 8.

**1837** [see *partridge-tun* s. v. PARTRIDGE 5]. **1861** P. P. CARPENTER in *Rep. Smithsonian Instit.* 1860, 184 The Tuns are nearly related to the Helmets, both in animal and shell.

**8.** *attrib.* and *Comb.*, as *tun* †*board*, *hole*, *hoop*, *stave*; *tun-like*; **tun-back**, name of a breed of pigs; **tun-butt** (in quot. applied *fig.* to a very corpulent person); † **tun form**, *Geom.* the form of a tun; an ellipsoid or similar figure; **tun-glass**, ? a barrel-shaped drinking-glass; † **tun-great** *a.*, as thick as a tun or cask; † **tun-grown** *a.*, grown as big as a tun, very corpulent; † **tun-gutted** *a.* = TUN-BELLIED; **tun liquor** (see quot.); **tun-man**, a man who attends to a tun (1 c) in brewing; **tun-pail**, a kind of funnel used in brewing (cf. TUN-DISH); **tun-room**, a room in a brewery in which a tun (1 c) is kept; **tun-shell**, *Conch.* a shell of the genus *Dolium* (*Cent. Dict.* 1891); † **tun-silver** (*Sc. Obs.*), a duty levied upon casks of merchandise; **tun-tub**, = sense 1 c. See also TUN-BELLIED, etc.; also *tun tight* (*ton tight*) s. v. TIGHT *a.* 14.

**1778** [W. MARSHALL] *Minutes Agric.* 15 Oct. an. 1776, A fine farrow of the large black-spotted *tun-backs. **1558** in Feuillerat *Revels Q. Eliz.* (1908) 99 For furnysshinge of *tunbborde and other parties of the banketinge howse at westmynster. **1829** CLAPPERTON *Jrnl. Africa* iv. 112 A walking *tun-butt for a queen! **1551** RECORDE *Pathw. Knowl.* I. Defin., If it be lyke..a circle pressed in length, and bothe endes lyke bygge, then is it called a *tunne forme. *a* **1843** SOUTHEY *Comm.-pl. Bk.* IV. 575 Always a *tun-glass standing by him. *c* **1386** CHAUCER *Knt.'s T.* 1136 Euery pyler..Was *tonne greet. **1628** PRYNNE *Brief Survay* 71 Like so many Epicures, or *Tonne-growne Abbylubbers. **1607** *Lingua* III. ii. E iv, *Tun-gutted drones. **1657** AUSTEN *Fruit Trees* I. 77 Take Clay and lay it round about the *Tunne hole. **1510** in *10th Rep. Hist. MSS. Comm.* App. v. 394 Towe *toune hopis for a penye. **1498** *Aberdeen Regr.* (1844) 426 Tunnys and vyther gudis *tunlyk. *a* **1813** A. WILSON *Prayer to Love* Poet. Wks. (1846) 168 Cits with tun-like bellies, Melted down almost to jellies. **1853** URE *Dict. Arts* I. 57 The mother liquor of the 'rock alum' is called '*tun liquor'. **1743** *Lond. & Country Brew.* III. (ed. 2) 221 The *Tun-man..ambitious to supplant the Workman Brewer. **1833** LOUDON *Encycl. Archit.* § 1318 Racking-can, *tun-pail. **1870** J. FLEET in *Eng. Mech.* 18 Feb. 561/1 Insert a tunpail and strainer. **1826** *Art Brewing* (ed. 2) 40 In cold weather keep the *tun-room closed. **1600** *Reg. Mag. Sig. Scot.* 377/2 Levare..doliorum pecunias (*lie* *tun-silver). **1398** TREVISA *Barth. De P. R.* XIX. cxxviii. (1495) 934 Bordes and *tonne staues. **1842** J. AITON *Domest. Econ.* (1857) 330 A *tun-tub..to put the ale into to work, the mash-tub, as we shall see, serving as a tun-tub for the small beer.

**Tun,** *v.* Forms: see prec. sb. [f. prec.]

**1.** *trans.* To put into or store in a tun or tuns. Often with *up*, more rarely *in*; also *absol.*

*α.* *c* **1430** *Pilgr. Lyf Manhode* III. xliii. (1869) 158 Þe fonelle..aualeth and tunneth þe wyn. *c* **1440** *Promp. Parv.* 506/1 Tunnon, or put drynke or other thynge yn a tunne. *a* **1533** LD. BERNERS *Gold. Bk. M. Aurel.* (1546) C c ij, Whan the newe wine is tunned. **1638** *MS. Min. Archdeaconry of Essex* lf. 18 b, He did brew on a Satterday and tunne vpon the Sunday morneing. **1696** *Phil. Trans.* XIX. 274 When they [Figs] were pulled off and Tunned up, to be sent beyond Seas. **1766** ENTICK *London* (1776) I. 410 Merchandize.., to be packed, tunned, piped, barrelled. **1843** *Jrnl. R. Agric. Soc.* IV. II. 489 To carry and tun the cider.

*β.* **1426** LYDG. *De Guil. Pilgr.* 12987 Thys phonel Wyth wych my wynes I vp tonne. **1477** J. PASTON in *P. Lett.* III. 175, I shall do tonnen in to your place a doseyn ale. **1580** HOLLYBAND *Treas. Fr. Tong*, *Entonner*, to tonne wine, or poure it into tonnes.

**b.** *fig.* To put or store as in a cask; *spec.* to drink to excess, to swill oneself with. Also *absol.*

*α.* **1589** NASHE *Anat. Absurd.* 20 These Bussards thinke knowledge a burthen, tapping it before they haue halfe tunde it. **1595** R. HASLETON *Strange & Wonderf. Things* in Arb. *Garner* VIII. 384 Pouring water through a cane which was in my mouth..until they had tunned in such quantity as was not tolerable. **1628** FELTHAM *Resolves* II. [I.] lxxxiv. 241 Whose delights are only to tunne in. **1761** STERNE *Tr. Shandy* III. xx, They [brain-cells] might continue to be injected and tunn'd into. **1841** *Fraser's Mag.* XXV. 514 He used to tun down beer..during dinner.

*β.* **1597–8** BP. HALL *Sat.* v. ii. 101 The swolne bezell.. That tonnes in gallons to his bursten panch.

**c.** (See quot.)

**1781** P. BECKFORD *Hunting* (1802) 337 Poachers..catch the young foxes in trenches dug at the mouth of the hole, which I believe they call tunning them.

**2.** To fill as, or like, a tun or cask. ? *Obs.*

**1635** QUARLES *Embl.* II. x. 6 A Cask, that seems as full, as faire; But meerely tunn'd with Ayre. **1664** COTTON *Scarron.* I. 104 Tunning themselves with Ale, and Beer.

**3.** app. *intr.* Of young rabbits: To become corpulent or 'pot-bellied'.

**1741** *Compl. Fam.-Piece* III. 510 Ground Malt helps to recover the young ones when tunned. [Cf. TUNNING 2.]

Hence **Tunned** (tʊnd) *ppl. a.*

**1671** GREW *Anat. Plants* i. § 32 The said Aperture being that..to the Sap, which..the Bung-hole of the Barrel, is to the new tunn'd Liquor.

**Tun,** obs. form of TON [1], TOWN.

‖ **Tuna** [1] (tū·na). Also 7–8 in anglicized form tune. [According to Humboldt, taken from Haytian into Spanish: see quot. 1852.] = INDIAN FIG 1, PRICKLY PEAR; esp. *Opuntia Tuna*, a tall-growing species found in Central America and the West Indies, and introduced elsewhere.

**1555** EDEN *Decades* (Arb.) 228 Wyld plantes..which I haue not seene but in the Ilande of Hispaniola...These they caule *Tunas*. They growe of a thistle full of thornes, and brynge foorth a frute muche lyke vnto great fygges. **1614** PURCHAS *Pilgrimage* VIII. vii. (ed. 2) 774 A kind of fruit called Tune, of the bignes of an egge, black and of good tast. **a 1715** TATE tr. *Cowley's Plants* v. C.'s Wks. 1721 III. 411 The Tuna to the Indian-Fig a kin, (The Glory of Tlascalla) next came in. **1760–72** tr. *Juan & Ulloa's Voy.* (ed. 3) I. 325 The leaf of the tuna being broad, flat, and prickly. [**1852** TH. ROSS *Humboldt's Trav.* I. 328 The following are Haytian words, in their real form, which have passed into the Castilian language since the end of the 15th century... *Tuna.*] **1866** *Treas. Bot.* 818 Tuna is a Spanish-American name given to several Opuntias, but botanists have adopted it as the..name of a single species, *O. Tuna*, a native.. from Quito to Mexico and the West Indies.

*attrib.* **1911** *Dundee Advertiser* 12 Apr. 12/1 San Luis Potosi has long been the great *tuna cheese market of Mexico...The cheese is made by simply boiling and straining the tuna pulp until the proper consistency is reached. **1748** *Earthquake of Peru* iii. 210 These they call Higas de Tuna, or *Tuna Figs. **1912** R. B. C. GRAHAM in *Eng. Rev.* May 229 The great trumpet-shaped and dark red fleshy *tuna flowers.

‖ **Tuna** [2] (tū·na). [Spanish American: perh. related to L. *thunnus, tunnus*, tunny, cf. med.L. *tunnina* 'thunnus falsus' false tunny (Du Cange).] Name in California for the tunny. Cf. TON [4].

**1900** *Westm. Gaz.* 29 June 8/1 The tuna, one of the gamest fighting fish for its size in the sea. **1901** *Field* 23 Nov. 812/2 There is no doubt whatever as to the identity of the horse mackerel of the Gulf of St. Lawrence, the tuna of Catalina, and the thon, thuna, or tunny of the Mediterranean.

‖ **Tuna** [3] (tū·na). [Maori name.] The common species of eel found in New Zealand.

**1895** *Funk's Standard Dict.*, *Tuna*, the common eel..of New Zealand. **1898** MORRIS *Austral Eng.* s.v. *Eel*, New Zealand Eels...Tuna E[el], *Anguilla aucklandii.*

**Tunable, tuneable** (tiū·năb'l), *a.* [f. TUNE *sb.* or *v.* + -ABLE: cf. *comfortable.*]

**1.** Tuneful, musical, melodious, harmonious, sweet-sounding. *arch.* **a.** Of music, musical instruments, the singing voice, etc.

*c* **1500** *Proverbs* in *Antiq. Rep.* (1809) IV. 407 In tunabill tewnys he hathe non experyment. *c* **1525** in Herrig *Archiv Neu. Spr.* (1908) CXX. 423 The songe of hym selff, yet nevyrtheles, Ys trew and tvnabyle, & syng yt as yt ys. *c* **1581** LODGE *Repl. Gosson's Sch. Abuse* (Shaks. Soc.) 20 The tunable voyces of men. **1598** FLORIO, *Simphonia*,..a tunable singing without iarring. **1658** R. FRANCK *North. Mem.* (1821) 250 The birds..beat the ambient air with their tunable notes. **1700** J. BROME *Trav. Eng.* etc. ii. (1707) 52 A Chapel..in which there is placed a tunable Organ. **1820** H. MATTHEWS *Diary of Invalid* (ed. 2) 34 Airs not at all tuneable to an English ear. **1890** W. MORRIS in *Eng. Illustr. Mag.* July 757 The noise though it was great was tuneable.

**b.** *spec.* Of a peal of bells: in first 2 quots., well-tuned, in tune.

**1510–11** *Rec. St. Mary at Hill* 274 To go and see wheþer Smythes bell wer Tewneabill or nat. **1581** in *Rep. Hist. MSS. Comm., Var. Coll.* (1907) IV. 91 Such of the sayd bells as be not tuneable at this present. **1631** WEEVER *Anc. Fun. Mon.* 226 A tunable ring of fiue bels vpon the same. **1778** G. WHITE *Selborne* lxxx, The notes of a hunting horn, a tunable ring of bells. **1844** PALEY *Church Restorers* 33 The Tower contained a tunable ring of eight new bells.

**c.** Of speech or the speaking voice, or other sounds.

**1579** FULKE *Heskins' Parl.* 21 A well tunable sound of the waues reboundeth. **1589** PUTTENHAM *Eng. Poesie* I. v. (Arb.) 26 Without any rime or tunable concord in th'end of their verses. **1661** H. D. *Disc. Liturgies* 82 A tunable and distinct pronouncing of the words. **1709** STEELE & SWIFT *Tatler* No. 70 ¶7 What a secret Force there is in the Accents of a tunable Voice! **1836** S. ROGERS *From Euripides* 7 As tuneable as harp of many strings.

**d.** *fig.* Harmonious, concordant; pleasant-sounding (quot. 1639); well-strung (quot. 1691).

**1561** DAUS tr. *Bullinger on Apoc.* (1573) 68 b, A continuall holdyng on and tunable agrement in praysing God. **1639** FULLER *Holy War* v. vii. (1840) 253 This counsel, harsh at first, grew tunable in the ears of the Hospitallers. **1691** NORRIS *Pract. Disc.* 327 He that is blessed with the strongest and most tunable Constitution. **1854** EMERSON *Lett. & Soc. Aims, Quot. & Orig.* Wks. (Bohn) III. 214 It [the Bible] has been played upon by the devotion of thousands of years until every word and particle is..tunable.

† **e.** with *to*: In tune with, accordant to (*lit.* and *fig.*). *Obs.*

**1584** LODGE *Hist. Forbonius & Prisc.* (Shaks. Soc.) 85 Making his lute tunable to the straine of his voice. **1688** W. BATES *Harm. Div. Attrib.* v. (ed. 3) 87 His Heart might be made tunable to the Hearts of the afflicted.

**2.** Capable of being tuned. *rare*—⁰.

**1706** PHILLIPS (ed. Kersey), *Tunable*, that may be tuned, or put in Tune; agreeable to the Rules of Musick. **1828** in WEBSTER. [Hence in later Dicts.]

**Tunableness, tune-** (tiū·năb'lnės). [f. prec. + -NESS.] The quality of being tunable; tunefulness, harmoniousness, sweetness of sound.

**1561** T. HOBY tr. *Castiglione's Courtyer* I. I iij, The tunablenes of musicke is a very great refreshing of..griefs. **1694** W. WOTTON *Anc. & Mod. Learn.* (1697) 27 That derived Language actually has a Sweetness and Tunableness in its Composition. **1727** J. SPENCE *Ess. on Pope's Odyss.* 15 A general tuneableness in the Verse will carry a Man on strangely. **1887** *Athenæum* 26 Mar. 411/2 There is a certain lilt and tuneableness about some of these songs.

**b.** *fig.* Harmony, concord.

**1569** GOLDING *Heminges Post.* Ded. 21 All the degrees of the realme being setled in a most sweete tunablenesse.

**Tunably, tuneably** (tiū·năbli), *adv.* [f. as prec. + -LY [2].] In a tunable manner; tunefully, musically, harmoniously.

**1586** W. WEBBE *Eng. Poetrie* (Arb.) 38 He sang fine ditties ..tunably to their Musick notes. **1644** FEATLY *Gentle Lash* 9 The more to praise God, and sing more tuneably and delightfully. **a 1668** LASSELS *Voy. Italy* (1698) II. 199 Pan also plays on his mouth-organ tuneably. **1834** H. AINSWORTH *Rookwood* III. iv, They can sing..most tuneably.

**Tunack, tunake,** obs. forms of TUNIC.

‖ **Tunal** (tūna·l). [Sp., f. TUNA [1] + *-al* (cf. CHAPARRAL).] A grove or thicket of tunas: see TUNA [1]. (Also erron. used for *tuna.*)

**1613** PURCHAS *Pilgrimage* VIII. x. 661 That they should goe seeke out a Tunal in the Lake, which grew out of a stone. **1666** J. DAVIES *Hist. Caribby Isles* 62 A kind of Tunal, on which there have been seen certain little Worms in colour like a Ruby, which dye Linen..a very fair and lively Scarlet-colour. **1722** D. COXE *Descr. Carolina* 85 This noble ingredient for dying is produc'd by a tree or shrub call'd the tunal or tuna. **1857** KINGSLEY *Two Y. Ago* II. 104 Mexicans among tunals of cactus and agave.

**Tun-bellied** (tʊ·n,be:lid), *a.* Having a belly rounded like a tun; pot-bellied, corpulent.

**1550** LEVER *Serm.* (Arb.) 119 Fyfty tunne belyed Monckes geuen to glotony fylled theyr pawnches. **1683** KENNETT tr. *Erasm. on Folly* 134, I prefer the opinion of the good old tun-bellied Divines. **1760** FAWKES tr. *Anacreon, Ode* xxxviii. 17 *note*, Silenus was..represented by a little, flat-nosed, bald, fat, tun-bellied, old drunken Fellow. **1866** *Cornh. Mag.* May 636 A crew of useless tunbellied gourmands.

So **Tu·n-belly,** a belly like a tun, a big round belly.

*a* **1704** T. BROWN *Lett. Ser. & Com., To Men* Wks. 1709 III. 120 The presumptuous Wretch that should think irreverently of a double Chin, and a Tun-Belly.

‖ **Tunc, tunk.** *Welsh Hist.* Also 4 tung, 7–8 tuncke. [ad. Welsh *twng, twnc* (pl. *ty(n)geu*); perh. connected with *tyng-u* to swear.] A kind of customary rent or payment (analogous to the 'chief-rents' or 'quit-rents' of English Real Property Law), issuing out of certain lands in North Wales, and still payable in respect of Crown Lands.

Commonly explained as the money-commutation paid in lieu of the *gwestva* (in Latin *cena*), an entertainment due or tribute-in-kind rendered to the lord of the cymwd or prince, in respect of the free maenols of the cymwds (see COMMOT). Hence translated by Seebohm as 'food-rent'. As to the derivation, the conjecture has been offered that an oath was originally required of inability to render the *gwestva* in kind, before the tunc-pound was accepted instead.

**1311** *Inq. P. M.* (C.) *Edw. II*, File 22. m. 23 (P.R.O.) Idem Comes..habuit lx. s., tam de liberis quam de natiuis, pro quadam custuma que vocatur Tung. **1334** in Vinogradoff *Survey of Denbigh* (1914) 7 Quelibet istarum xj. gavellarum reddit de Tung' per annum xij d. et pro pastu familie Principis per annum ij. s. v. d. q. **1658** in W. M. Myddelton *Chirk Castle Acc.* (1908) 73 Tuncke rent for the same lands for yeare ended at Michelmas 1657. **1793** *Jrnls. Ho. Comm.* 28 Mar. 558/2 The Sheriffs of the County of Flint..are charged with an Annual Rent called The Tuncke Rent, payable in small Sums, or Rents, for divers Tenures..in the said County. *Ibid.* 560/1 The Nature and Original of the Tunck Rent, called also *Porthan Keys*, cannot now be traced or explained. **1895** SEEBOHM *Tribal Syst. Wales* vi. § 4 (1904) 154 In the Extents the food-rents of the free tribesmen were found to be commuted into definite money payments made under the name of *tunc*. **1914** MISS M. NEILSON in Vinogradoff *Survey of Denbigh* Introd. 59 The tunk-pound in the Venedotian code is due from the maenol. *Ibid.*, In the Denbigh Survey the tunk is a definite money charge on all Welsh customary tenants, free and *nativi*.

**Tund** (tʊnd), *v.* [ad. L. *tund-ĕre* to beat.]

**1.** *Winchester School slang. trans.* To beat with a stick, esp. an ash rod, by way of punishment. Hence **Tu·nded** *ppl. a.*, **Tu·nding** *vbl. sb.*; also **Tu·nder,** one who 'tunds'.

**1871** *Echo* 11 Apr. 1 He may be 'tunded', in which case he has to stand upon a table, that the præfect may the more conveniently cut into the calves of his legs with an apple twig. **1872** *Punch* 23 Nov. 210/1 'Tunding'..is a brutality, in the way of chastisement, inflicted by the big lads on the little ones at Winchester School. **1876** LD. SHERBROOKE in *Life & Lett.* (1893) I. 12 To put a stick into the hand of a boy of sixteen and allow him to use it upon his schoolfellows ..is neither fair on the tunder nor the tunded. **1884** *Times* 13 Feb. 11/4 The clamour aroused by the celebrated 'tunding' case [at Winchester].

**2.** *gen.* To beat, thump (*trans.* and *intr.*).

**1885** BURTON *Arab. Nts.* (1887) III. 44 All the apes were wroth with the plucked ape..and tunded him the more. **1895** *Brit. Weekly* 29 June 131 If he had..but command of the racial tom-tom, it seems to him that he would tund upon it in honour of that great man. **1904** *Speaker* 28 May 206 Louder than the Sea-surge tunds the Harbour-bar.

† **Tu·nder** [1]. *Obs. rare.* Also tundor. (app.) A funnel: cf. TUNNEL *sb.* 3, TUNNER 1.

**1343–4** *Pipe Roll* 18 *Edw. III*, m. 45 (P.R.O.), j tunder et j skopa pro aqua in eisdem doliis infundenda. **1344** *Acc. Exch. K. R.* 492/26. m. 2 Pro uno Tundor et uno skopo pro aqua infundenda in dolia.

**Tunder** [2]: see TUND *v.* 1.

**Tunder, -dyr,** obs. or dial. ff. TINDER.

**Tun-dish, tundish** (tʊ·n,diʃ). Now *local.* [f. TUN *sb.* + DISH *sb.*] A wooden dish or shallow vessel with a tube at the bottom fitting into the bung-hole of a tun or cask, forming a kind of funnel used in brewing; hence *gen.* = FUNNEL *sb.* [1] 1.

**1388–9** *Abingdon Acc.* (Camden) 57, iij scale, j tundys. **1573** in *Rep. MSS. Ld. Middleton* (1911) 437 Making..a forme and a tundishe for the buttrye. **1603** SHAKS. *Meas. for M.* III. ii. 182 For filling a bottle with a Tunne-dish. **1756** MATTHEWS in *Phil. Trans.* XLIX. 549 These pits..growing gradually narrower to a center, in shape of a funnel or tun-dish. **1795** SIR J. DALRYMPLE *Let. to Admiralty* 3 The froth, that is, the Yeast, is prevented by a tun-dish from running over. **1892** GREENER *Breech-Loader* 176 The shot must be poured in through a tundish, and preferably counted with the 'Greener Shot Counter', or weighed to measure.

‖ **Tundra** (tu·ndră, tʊ·n-). Also toondra, toundra. [a. Lap. *tundra.*] One of the vast, nearly level, treeless regions which make up the greater part of the north of Russia, resembling the *steppes* farther south, but with arctic climate and vegetation. Also applied to similar regions in Siberia and Alaska.

**1841** *Penny Cycl.* XXI. 458/1 The most northern part of Siberia is a low plain, called the Tundra. The surface is nearly a dead level, and quite destitute of trees. **1861** H. MACMILLAN *Footnotes fr. Page Nat.* 93 In the vast sandy plains called by the Laplanders tundra, which border on the Arctic ocean. **1889** G. F. WRIGHT *Ice Age in N. Amer.* 32 Much of the region north of St. Elias, Alaska, is now covered with tundra.

*attrib.* **1894** *Outing* (U. S.) XXIII. 388/1 In the far northwest, the vast tundra plains, bordering upon the Arctic Ocean. **1894** *Daily News* 24 July 5/4 Russian traders and inhabitants of the polar tundra zone. **1901** H. SEEBOHM *Birds Siberia* xiv. 119 A swampy, hummocky strip of tundra land.

**Tundun**: see TURNDUN.

**Tune** (tiūn), *sb.* Forms: (4 tun), 4– tune; also 5 tuyn(e, (tyune, teone), twn(e, 5–6 tewne, toyn(e, 6 *Sc.* tuin, tone, toon, 6–7 *Sc.* toone; cf. also TONE *sb.* [A peculiar phonetic variant of TONE *sb.*, appearing first in 14th c.: the Sc. *toon, tuin* (= tön, tün) show the normal Sc. representative of ME. *ō*, as in *muin, suin, duin, shuin* (shoes).]

† **1.** A (musical) sound or tone; *esp.* the sound of the voice: = TONE *sb.* 1. *Obs.*

**1387** TREVISA *Higden* (Rolls) I. 355 Þey makeþ wel mery armonye and melody wiþ wel þicke tunes [CAXTON tewnes], werbeles, and nootes. *c* **1400** *Laud Troy Bk.* 14292 He tolde him of the deth of Brunes; Then were mad hidus tuynes Off many a gentil damysel. **1413** *Pilgr. Sowle* (Caxton) v. i. (1859) 72 There was no tune of musik that ther was forgeten. **1435** MISYN *Fire of Love* II. iii. 73 Emonge aungels twnys it has a acceptabyll melody. *c* **1450** *Songs & Carols* (E.E.T.S.) 89/53 Thus seyth þis byrde, in tyunes gay. **1508** FISHER *Penit. Ps.* xxxviii. Wks. (E.E.T.S.) I. 71 In the whiche swete soundes we shall here so grete plente & dyuersite of tunes as euer was herde before. **1560** INGELEND *Disob. Child* C ij, Her tonge and her tune is very shryll. **1573–80** BARET *Alv.* T 415 The tune of the Harpe, *canor lyræ*. Ouid. **1592** SHAKS. *Ven. & Ad.* 431 Melodious discord, heauenly tune harsh sounding. *a* **1600** MONTGOMERIE *Misc. Poems* vi. 31 Lamenting toons best lyks me for relief. *c* **1600** SHAKS. *Sonn.* cxli, Nor are mine eares with thy toungs tune delighted. *c* **1614** SIR W. MURE *Dido & Æneas* III. 20 And als the light-envying owl, alone, With tragick toones her smarte and sorrow shew. **1706** PRIOR *Ode to Queen* 9 High as their Trumpets Tune His Lyre he strung. **1819** KEATS *Isabella* iv, Lorenzo, if thy lips breathe not love's tune. *a* **1849** HOR. SMITH *Addr. Mummy* ii, Thou hast a tongue: come, let us hear its tune.

**b.** Applied to a special affected or peculiar intonation in speaking: cf. 2, and TONE *sb.* 5 c.

**1783** BLAIR *Lect. Rhet.* xxxiii. II. 214 If any one, in Public Speaking, shall have formed to himself a certain melody or tune, which requires rest and pauses of its own, distinct from those of the sense, he has..contracted one of the worst habits into which a Public Speaker can fall.

**2.** A rhythmical succession of musical tones produced by (or composed for) an instrument or voice; an air, melody (with or without the harmony which accompanies it). Now the leading sense. (Not in TONE *sb.*)

**1387** TREVISA *Higden* (Rolls) III. 207 By the sleuþe of þe manere of tunes [*orig.* modorum tarditate]. **1491** *Cartular. St. Nicholai Aberdon.* (New Spald. Cl.) I. 256 Chaplannis yat kepis nocht ye Seculorum and twne gewin yame be ye chantour. **1500–20** DUNBAR *Poems* lxxxii. 29 Ȝour commone menstrallis hes no tone, Bot 'Now the day dawis', and 'Into Joun'. **1535** COVERDALE *Ezek.* xxxiii. 32 As a balet yᵗ hath a swete tune, and is pleasaunt to synge. **1591** SHAKS. *Two Gent.* I. ii. 82 Best sing it to the tune of *Light o' Loue*. *a* **1600** MONTGOMERIE *Misc. Poems* xlviii. 94 Vp uent our saillis, tauntit to the huins; The trumpets soundit tuentie mirrie tuins. **1697** DRYDEN *Virg. Past.* IX. 62 The Tune I still retain, but not the Words. **1717** LADY M. W. MONTAGU *Let. to Pope* 1 Apr., The tunes are extremely gay and lively. **1798** COLERIDGE *Anc. Mar.* v. 81 A hidden brook In the leafy month of June, That to the sleeping woods all night Singeth a quiet tune. **1828** SCOTT *F. M. Perth* x, The tune, ..played upon a viol, was gay and sprightly in the commencement. *Proverb.* He who pays the piper, calls the tune.

**b.** *spec.* A musical setting of a hymn or psalm, usually in four-part harmony, intended for use in public worship; a hymn-tune.

*c* 1450 CAPGRAVE *Life St. Aug.* xix. 27 Ambrose mad hem to be sunge delectabily with consent of dyuers tewnys whech had not be used þere be-for. 1567 *Gude & Godlie B.* (S.T.S.) 7 Heir followis the Catechisme put in meter, to be sung with the tone [*edd.* 1578, *etc.* tune]. 1795 MASON *Ch. Mus.* iii. 195 Adapted, if not originally written, to one particular Melody or Tune. 1833 T. HOOK *Parson's Dau.* I. i, Which [house-clock] strikes every hour, chimes the quarters, and plays Rule Britannia and the Hundreth Psalm tune two hundred and fifty times in the four and twenty hours. 1908 [MISS FOWLER] *Betw. Trent & Ancholme* 50 The tune ('Oxford') was brought by our grandfather from thence.

†**c.** Applied to the mediæval ecclesiastical modes (*the eight tunes*): see MODE *sb.* 1 a (*b*), and cf. TONE *sb.* 3 b. *Obs.*

1597 MORLEY *Introd. Mus.* 147 The churchmen for keeping their Keyes haue deuised certaine notes commonlie called the eight tunes, so that according to the tune which is to be obserued,..if it beginne in such a key, it may end in such and such others. *Annot., The eight tunes*...The tunes (which are also called *modi musici*) the practitioners do define, to be a rule whereby the melodie of euerie song is directed.

**d.** (In full, *act-tune*.) A piece of music played between the acts of a play. Cf. ENTR'ACTE b.

1889 W. H. HUSK in Grove *Dict. Mus.* s. v. *Tune*, In the latter half of the 17th century and first quarter of the 18th century act-tunes were composed specially for every play...But act-tunes, now styled 'Entr'actes', have been occasionally composed in modern times. 1891 *Cent. Dict.*, *Tune*...4. Same as *entr'acte*. Sometimes called *act-tune*.

**e.** *The tune the* (*old*) *cow died of*: humorously applied to a grotesque or unmusical succession of sounds, or a tedious ill-played piece of music.

Supposed to refer to an 'old ballad' in which a piper who had nothing else to give his cow 'took his pipe and played a tune, and bade the cow consider'. See *N. & Q.* 11th Ser. XI. 309.

1836 LADY GRANVILLE *Lett.* (1894) II. 218 The tune the old cow died of throughout, grunts and groans of instruments.

**3.** The state of being in the proper pitch; correct intonation in singing, or in instrumental music; agreement in pitch, unison, or harmony (*with* something): mostly in phr. *in* or *out of tune*; cf. TONE *sb.* 2 b, c. Also, simply, the pitch of a musical note (quot. 1694, *obs.*).

*c* 1440 *Jacob's Well* 82 Whanne an harpe is weel sett in tewne. 1450–1530 *Myrr. our Ladye* 56 That all the notes be songe, as they are in youre bokes, eche of them in theyr owne tewne. 1483 *Cath. Angl.* 396/1 Oute of Tune, *dissonus*,..*discors*. 1530 RASTELL *Bk. Purgat.* II. xviii, When hys harpe is out of tune. *a* 1548 HALL *Chron., Hen. VII* 3 To set all the strynges in a monacorde and tune. 1602 SHAKS. *Ham.* III. i. 166 Like sweet Bels iangled out of tune [*2nd Qo.* time], and harsh. 1617–18 in Swayne *Sarum Churchw. Acc.* (1896) 167 For keeping the Organ in tune. 1694 W. HOLDER *Harmony* ii. (1731) 5 The Tune of a Note..is constituted by the Measure and Proportion of Vibrations of the sonorous Body. 1707 WATTS *Hymn*, '*Let others boast how strong they be*' iii, Strange that a harp of thousand strings Should keep in tune so long! 1773 *Phil. Trans.* LXIII. 268 The B flat of the spinnet..was perfectly in tune with the great bell of St. Paul's. 1884 TENNYSON *Becket* Prol. 16 My voice is harsh here, not in tune.

**b.** *fig.* in phr. *in tune, out of tune*, in or out of order or proper condition; in or out of harmony *with* some person or thing. (See also 4, and cf. TONE *sb.* 2 c.)

1535 STEWART *Cron. Scot.* (Rolls) II. 390 On euerie syde thair wes richt mony slane, Or tha culd weill be put in tune agane. 1579 TOMSON *Calvin's Serm. Tim.* 280/2 How many occasions are there to bring vs out of tune? 1605 ROWLANDS *Hell's Broke Loose* 21 If Siluer in my Pockets do not ring, All's out of tune with mee in eu'ry thing. 1638 W. MOUNTAGU in *Buccleuch MSS.* (Hist. MSS. Comm.) I. 282 Fire-locks..are not mendable when out of tune. *c* 1680 BEVERIDGE *Serm.* (1729) I. 332 If our bodies be out of tune so are our minds too. 1737 BRACKEN *Farriery Impr.* (1757) II. 100 If you have a Horse in good Tune and Order. 1887 RIDER HAGGARD *Jess* xi, Bessie's mind was not quite in tune with the profundities of that learned journal.

**c.** *Phren.* The faculty of perception of musical pitch, and thus of melody and harmony.

1860 MAYNE *Expos. Lex., Tune. Phrenol.*, a faculty (its organ at the lateral part of the forehead immediately above Number and Order) giving the perception of harmony and melody.

**d.** *transf.* Harmony or accordance in respect of vibrations other than those of sound; *spec.* between the transmitter and receiver in wireless telegraphy.

1909 *Westm. Gaz.* 29 Apr. 5/3 You see, we must have a commercial or general 'tune', and when that is known any person installing the same 'tune' can intercept the messages. ..No one could intercept messages in such a case unless they had instruments of the same 'tune'. 1911 WEBSTER s. v., To place the receiver of a system of wireless telegraphy in tune with the transmitter so as to respond to impulses given out by the latter.

†**4.** Style, manner, or 'tone' (of discourse or writing). *Obs.* (Cf. TONE 5 d.)

1537 CROMWELL in Merriman *Life & Lett.* (1902) II. 74, I must nedes now..write unto you in an other tune. 1610 HOLLAND *Camden's Brit.* (1637) 107 Missive letters..in this tune; To Ætius thrice Consul, the grones of Britans.

**b.** *To change one's tune, sing another tune* (etc.): *fig.* to change one's tone, speak in a different strain. (Often directly *fig.* from 1 or 2.)

1524 *St. Papers Hen. VIII*, VI. 349 Percace the said Frenche King wolde by this tyme have spoken of an other toyne. ? *a* 1800 *Wedding Robin Hood & Lit. John* ii. in Child *Ballads* (1886) IV. 422 O gin I live and bruik my life, I'll gar ye change your tune. 1890 [see SING *v.*[1] 10 a].

**5.** *fig.* Frame of mind, temper, mood, disposition, humour; cf. TONE 8.

1599 SHAKS. *Much Ado* III. iv. 41 *Hero.* How now? do you speake in the sick tune? *Beat.* I am out of all other tune, me thinkes. 1605 — *Lear* IV. iii. 41 (Qo.) [Lear] some time in his better tune remembers, What we are come about. 1647 T. CALVERT *Heart Salve for Wounded Soul* 33 This is the tone and tune of men in distress. *a* 1691 FLAVEL *Sea Deliverances* (1754) 165 Our fancies were out of tune to be pleasant with anything. 1785 BURNS *Holy Fair* xxvi, They're a' in famous tune For crack that day. 1833 MOORE *Mem.* (1854) VI. 335 Being in but bad tune for a fête.

**6.** *Phrases. To the tune of* (*fig.* from 2): †**a.** According to the gist of, in accordance with (*obs.*). **b.** To the amount or sum of. So *to some tune* (to a considerable extent), etc.

1607 HIERON *Wks.* I. 405 Singing nothing but to the tune of Judas 'What will ye give me?' 1692 R. L'ESTRANGE *Fables* ccclvi. (1694) 372 This came to the Bishop's Ear, who presently sent for the Curate, Rattled him to some Tune. 1714 R. FIDDES *Pract. Disc.* II. 95 This is exactly to the tune of the old popular objection. 1716 M. DAVIES *Athen. Brit.* II. 296 To Libel the Bishop..by exhibiting Articles against him to the Tune of 56. 1722 DE FOE *Col. Jack* (1840) 113 To go over..into Flanders, to be knocked on the head at the tune of 3s. 6d. a week. 1797 *Wonderf. Advant. Lottery* (Cheap Repos. Tr.) 8, I had demands on me yesterday to the tune of 300 l. 1809 MALKIN *Gil Blas* VII. xvi. ¶ 13 Other articles were much to the same tune. 1874 *Punch* 22 Aug. 76/2 A defaulter to the imposing tune of £10,000. 1883 *Manch. Exam.* 24 Nov. 5/1 His peasant countrymen..have been spoiled and pilled, and whipt to every tune.

**7.** *Comb.*, as *tune-grinder, -hummer, -maker, -phrase, -tinkler, -weaving*; *tune-composed, -led, -skilled* adjs.

1606 SYLVESTER *Du Bartas* II. iv. II. *Magnif.* 898 Their Tune-skill'd feet in so true Time doe fall. 1756 COWPER *Connoisseur* No. 138 ¶ 4 The Whistlers or Tune-hummers, who never articulate at all. 1795 WOLCOTT (P. Pindar) *Frogmore Fête* Wks. 1812 III. 315 Musicians and racers, tune-grinders and dancers. 1816 J. GILCHRIST *Philos. Etym.* 234 A tune-composed style. 1898 T. HARDY *Wessex Poems* 118 She trod the flags with tune-led feet. 1901 *Palestine Exploration Fund Q. Statem.* Oct. 420 One tune-phrase, repeated to every line, serves for a whole song.

**Tune,** *v.* [f. TUNE *sb.*]

**I. 1.** *trans.* To adjust the tones of (a musical instrument) to a standard of pitch; to bring into condition for producing the required sounds correctly; to put in tune. Also *absol.*

1505 *Tower of Doctrine* xxvi. in *Percy's Reliq.*, With goodly pypes, in their mouthes ituned. 1513 BRADSHAW *St. Werburge* I. 1696 A synguler mynstrell..Toyned his instrument in pleasaunte armony. 1530 PALSGR. 763/2, I pray you, tune my virgynalles. 1567 *Triall Treas.* (1850) 16, I must tune my pipes first of all by drinking. 1584 GREENE *Anat. Fort.* Wks. (Grosart) III. 187, I thought..that where fortune once tuned, in the strings could neuer be founde anie discord. 1597 *1st Pt. Return fr. Parnass.* V. i. 1978 Letts tune our instruments. 1638 in Willis & Clark *Cambridge* (1886) II. 142 Mr Dallam for tuneing the Organ. 1681 DRYDEN *Span. Friar* II. i. 21 Tune your Harps Ye Angels to that sound. 1871 TYNDALL *Fragm. Sc.* (1879) I. iii. 81 These two tuning-forks are tuned absolutely alike.

**b.** To adapt (the voice, song, etc.) to a particular tone, or to the expression of a particular feeling or subject; to modify or modulate the tones of, according to the purpose in view.

†In 1688, to adapt (a song) to a particular instrument (*obs.*).

1596 SPENSER *F. Q.* VI. x. 7 Nymphes and Faeries..to the waters fall tuning their accents fit. *c* 1630 MILTON *Passion* 8 For now to sorrow must I tune my song. 1688 R. HOLME *Armoury* III. 201/2 Odes [are] Songs Tuned to the Lute, or other Instrument. 1702 POPE *Sappho* 8 Love..tun'd my heart to Elegies of woe. 1751 *Transl. & Paraphr. Ch. Scot.* XLIII. iv, His presence fills each heart with joy: tunes every mouth to sing. 1852 MISS YONGE *Cameos* I. xxxiii. 282 The bards tuned their songs to recall the indignities of Islington.

**c.** *transf.* To adapt, put into accordance, or make responsive, in respect of some physical quality or condition; e. g. an organ or organism in relation to a particular stimulus, or the transmitter and receiver in wireless telegraphy.

1887 LOCKYER *Chem. Sun* vii. 87 Ears are tuned to hear different sounds. 1900 *Daily News* 6 Sept. 2/4 'Tapping' the messages is quite impossible, the transmitter and receiver being so 'tuned' or synchronized to each other that no message can be received except by the instrument for which it is intended. 1904 *Electr. World & Engin.* 11 June 1120 The distance between the transmitter and receiver was varied from two meters to twenty meters. No effort was made to 'tune' the circuits.

**d.** *transf.* To set (a machine, etc.) in order for accurate working; to adjust. *local.* (Cf. TUNER 2 b.) See also 8 c, and TUNING 1 c.

1814 W. NICHOLSON in Trotter *E. Galloway Sk.* (1901) 44/1, I wot a pleugh he weel could tune. 1891 [see TUNING *vbl. sb.* 1 c]. *c* 1904 in *Eng. Dial. Dict.* s. v., He tunes his own loom (w. Yks.).

**2.** *fig.* To 'put in tune' (with various shades of meaning). **a.** To bring into a proper or desirable condition; to give a special tone or character (esp. of a good kind) to.

1530 RASTELL *Bk. Purgat.* II. xviii, Curyng & tunyng his body. 1639 FULLER *Holy War* II. xviii. (1647) 68 All his life was religiously tuned. *c* 1811 FUSELI in *Lect. Paint.* V. (1848) 461 Violent foreshortening, set off and tuned by magic light and shade. 1866 G. MACDONALD *Ann. Q. Neighb.* xiii, The place..tuned me to a solemn mood.

**b.** To bring into accord or harmony; to attune. Also *intr.* for *refl.* to attune itself, to harmonize (quot. 1653).

1590 MARLOWE *Edw. II*, IV. ii, Thou art deceiv'd,..To think that we can yet be tun'd together. 1653 HOLCROFT *Procopius* IV. 137 Mens judgements ever thus tune to that which pleases their wills. *a* 1711 KEN *Hymnotheo* Poet. Wks. 1721 III. 310 They both were tun'd with equal Sympathy.

**c.** To put into a proper condition for producing some effect; to adapt to a particular purpose; *esp.* to make subservient to one's own ends.

1581 PETTIE *Guazzo's Civ. Conv.* III. (1586) 168 b, The maister is troubled to tune his new seruaunts to his fancie. 1636 W. SCOT *Apol. Narr.* (1846) 93 Mr. Thomas Buchanan tuned and tutored him as he saw it fitting. *a* 1722 FOUNTAINHALL *Decis.* (1759) I. 184 A Scots Council is instantly called, who..fly very high, as they had been tuned. 1868 J. H. BLUNT *Ref. Ch. Eng.* I. 161 The most effective way, except the pulpit, of tuning public opinion. 1882 *Ibid.* II. 483 The pulpits were industriously tuned by means of lecturers.

**3.** *intr.* To give forth a musical sound; to sound; to sing.

*c* 1500 *Proverbs* in *Antiq. Rep.* (1809) IV. 407 A Shawme makithe a swete sounde, for he tunythe the basse. *c* 1580–1627 [implied in TUNER 1]. 1760–72 [see TUNING *vbl. sb.* 2]. 1906 *Westm. Gaz.* 10 Nov. 14/2 Last week..I heard a blackbird tuning. 1907 GALSWORTHY *Country Ho.* I. i, Like a breeze tuning through the frigid silence of a fog.

**b.** with *to*: To sing or sound in tune with (*intr.* of 1 b).

1627 DRAYTON *Quest of Cynthia* xxxiv, Tuning to the waters fall, The small Birds sang to her. 1755 JOHNSON, *Tune*, to form one sound to another.

**c.** To utter inarticulate musical notes or melody; to hum. *dial.*

1755 JOHNSON, *To Tune*, v.n...2. To utter with the voice inarticulate harmony. 1848 A. B. EVANS *Leicester. Words* s.v., My children could tune before they could speak. 1882 in OGILVIE.

**4.** *trans.* To utter or express (something) musically, to sing; to celebrate in music. *poet.* or *arch.*

1593 SHAKS. *Lucr.* 1107 The little birds that tune their mornings ioy. 1667 MILTON *P. L.* V. 196 Fountains and yee that warble, as ye flow, Melodious murmurs, warbling tune his praise. 1678 DRYDEN & LEE *Œdipus* I. i, Rouze up ye Thebans; tune your Io Pæans! 1697 DRYDEN *Virg. Georg.* II. 542 To Bacchus..let us tune our Lays. 1791 BURNS *Lament for Glencairn* ii, As he tuned his doleful sang. *a* 1814 A. BURN in *Mem.* iii. (1816) 135 Tuning a hymn of thanksgiving to her praise.

†**b.** To set or start the tune for (a hymn, etc. in public worship), as a precentor. *Obs.*

1667 PEPYS *Diary* 21 Apr., The organ, which is handsome, and tunes the psalm. 1679 *Marriage Chas. II* 10 The Cardinal tun'd the *Te deum*, which was sung with musick. 1895 J. BROWN *Pilgr. Fathers* xi. 349 The 'tuning the psalm' as it was called was left to some member of the congregation who volunteered the performance.

**5.** To produce music from, to play upon (an instrument), esp. the lyre. *poet.*

1701 ADDISON *Epil. to Granville's Brit. Enchant.* Wks. 1721 I. 142 When Orpheus tun'd his lyre..Rivers forgot to run, and winds to blow. 1746 FRANCIS tr. *Horace, Epist.* I. iii. 16 To tune to Theban Sounds the Roman Lyres.

**II.** With adverbs.

**6. Tune in.** *intr.* To strike into a chorus; to interpose in a conversation.

1912 *World* 7 May 680/1 The..Passenger is preparing to continue the cross-examination, when an old lady carrying a long broom tunes in.

**7. Tune off.** *intr.* To get out of 'tune' or adjustment.

1703 T. N. *City & C. Purchaser* (1736), *Raking-Work*, that which (..in Mouldings, etc.) is to be join'd by Mitering exactly, to prevent the Work tuneing off, as Workmen call it, after 'tis put together.

**8. Tune up. a.** *trans.* and *intr.* To raise one's voice (in song or otherwise), to sing out (cf. 3).

1701 STANHOPE *St. Aug. Medit.* xxvi. 54 Let us tune our Voices up with theirs. 1763 T. SMITH *Jrnl.* (1849) 274 The robin and spring birds begin to tune up. 1895 J. G. MILLAIS *Breath fr. Veldt* (1899) 202, I have heard an old cow tune up in like manner.

**b.** *trans.* To bring (an instrument) up to the proper pitch, to put in tune (= 1); also *absol.*; also *fig.* (cf. 2).

*a* 1718 PENN *Maxims* Wks. 1726 I. 830 We are too apt to awaken and tune up their [Children's] Passions by the Example of our own. 1776 GRAVES *Euphrosyne* I. 224 Each Cockney that tunes up his lyre. 1902 VIOLET JACOB *Sheep-Stealers* x, The band began to tune up, and a general feeling of expectation pervaded the building.

**c.** To put (a machine, a racing vessel, etc.) into the most efficient working order (cf. 1 d).

1901 *Daily Chron.* 24 Aug. 5/7 The..captain will keep all hands at work tuning her [a yacht] up until she is able to show all the speed she has in her. 1908 *Westm. Gaz.* 31 Dec. 4/2 The art of tuning up a car is understood by very few amateurs, who..are satisfied with results which could be improved upon.

† **Tune** (*ü*), early ME. form of *tyne*, TINE *v.*[1] (OE. *týnan*), to close, shut; to fence or enclose.

*c* 1175 *Lamb. Hom.* 49 Þe mon þe tuneð his eren in halie chirche toȝeines godes laȝe. *Ibid.*, Þe put ne tuneð noht..his muð ouer us bute we tunen ure muð. *a* 1225 *Ancr. R.* 80 Vuel speche; þat ȝe þertoȝeines tunen ower earen. 1605 VERSTEGAN *Dec. Intell.* ix. (1628) 295 His Cote or house was fenced or tuned about.

**Tune**, anglicized form of TUNA [1].

**Tuneable**, etc.: see TUNABLE, etc.

**Tuned** (tiūnd, *poet.* tiū·nėd), *ppl. a.* [f. TUNE *v.* (and *sb.*) + -ED.] Put in tune, sounded musically, etc. (see the verb): usually with qualifying word (in which case sometimes from the sb. = having a specified 'tune' or tone); also with adv.

**1579** W. WILKINSON *Confut. Familye of Loue* 26 b, Straunge doctrine and new tuned opinions. *c* **1586** C'TESS PEMBROKE *Ps.* LVII. vi, To spread thy praise With tuned laies. **1598** *Mucedorus* Induct. 6 Sound foorth Bellonas siluer tuned strings. **1662** PLAYFORD *Skill Mus.* (1674) 58 The Dorick Mood consisted of sober slow Tun'd Notes. **1746–7** HERVEY *Medit., Tombs* (1767) I. 37 Their Inclinations were nicely-tuned Unisons, and all their conversation was Harmony. **1908** *Daily Report* 31 Aug. 9/1 The professional rider on a specially tuned-up machine [motor].

**Tuneful** (tiū·nfŭl), *a.* [f. TUNE *sb.* + -FUL.]

**1.** Full of 'tune' or musical sound; musical, sweet-sounding.

**1598** MARSTON *Sco. Villanie, Ad rithmum* (1599) 194 In tunefull numbers keeping musicks time. **1697** PRIOR *Sat. Mod. Translators* 120 The just Measure of a tuneful Dance. *a* **1764** LLOYD *Actor* Poet. Wks. 1774 I. 22 The tuneful voice, the eye that spoke the mind. **1814** SCOTT *Ld. of Isles* IV. xi, His bright and brief career is o'er, And mute his tuneful strains. **1843** JAMES *Forest Days* iii, It was a time of year when the whole world was tuneful.

**2.** Producing or yielding musical sounds; making melody; performing or skilled in music; musical (as a person, instrument, etc.).

**1591** SPENSER *Teares of Muses* 27 The trembling streames ..were by them right tunefull taught to beare A Bases part amongst their consorts oft. **1606** SYLVESTER *Du Bartas* II. iv. I. *Trophies* 416 With his tunefull Lyre, Expels th' ill Spirit which doth the body tyre. **1671** MILTON *P. R.* II. 290 With chaunt of tuneful Birds resounding loud. **1693** YALDEN *Ode to Congreve* v, From tuneful Chaucer's down to thy own Dryden's Muse. **1704** PRIOR *Let. to Despreaux* 18 When thy young Muse invok'd the tuneful Nine. **1805** SCOTT *Last Minstr.* I. Introd. i, For, well-a-day! their date was fled, His tuneful brethren all were dead. **1878** H. S. LEIGH *Town Garland* 10, I listen, contented and calm, to a band Of the tuneful Teutonics who favour the Strand.

**3.** Relating or adapted to music.

**1697** DRYDEN *Virg. Past.* IX. 44 A Member of the tuneful trade. **1762–77** SIR W. JONES *Arcadia* Poems (1777) 105 Ev'n Pan thy tuneful skill confess'd. **1842** WHITTIER *Raphael* xviii, Think ye the notes of holy song On Milton's tuneful ear have died?

Hence **Tu·nefully** *adv.*, in a tuneful manner, with sweet sound, musically; **Tu·nefulness**, tuneful or musical quality.

**1638–56** COWLEY *Davideis* I. 476 Storehouse of all Proportions! single Quire! Which first God's Breath did tunefully inspire! **1798** WORDSW. *Peter Bell* Prol. xv, How tunefully the forests ring! **1882** OGILVIE, Tunefulness. **1893** L. S. KEYSER in *Chicago Advance* 3 Aug., A song sparrow .. taking the bays for real tunefulness from every rival.

**Tuneless** (tiū·nlės), *a.* [f. as prec. + -LESS.]

**1.** Having no sweetness of tone; untuneful, unmusical, unmelodious, harsh-sounding.

**1594** SPENSER *Amoretti* xliv, Then Orpheus with his harp theyr strife did bar.. But, when in hand my tunelesse harp I take, Then doe I more augment my foes despight. **1656** COWLEY *Misc., Swallow* 3 Foolish Prater, what dost thou.. With thy tuneless Serenade? **1759** [H. DALRYMPLE] *Woodstock: an Elegy* (1761) 16 His tuneless numbers hardly now survive. **1870** MORRIS *Earthly Par.* II. III. 47 The music of her voice Made the birds' song seem tuneless noise.

**2.** Giving no 'tune' or sound; not making music; songless; silent.

**1728** W. STARRAT *Epist.* 48 in *Ramsay's Poems* (1877) II. 275 What tuneless heart-strings wadna twang, When love and beauty animate the sang? **1774** GOLDSM. *Nat. Hist.* IV. ii. (1824) II. 337 The Field-fare and the Red-wing..With us..are insipid tuneless birds, flying in flocks. **1821** BYRON *Juan* III. *Isles of Greece* v, The heroic lay is tuneless now. **1868** GEO. ELIOT *Sp. Gipsy* 227 As tuneless as a bag of wool.

**3.** Without musical knowledge or skill. *rare.*

**1821** BYRON *Juan* IV. lxxxvii, An ignorant, noteless timeless, tuneless fellow.

Hence **Tu·nelessly** *adv.*, **Tu·nelessness**.

**1881** M. ARNOLD in *Macm. Mag.* Mar. 370 The slovenliness and tunelessness of much of Byron's production. **1905** Q. COUCH *Shining Ferry* II. xii, Mr. Sam spoke tunelessly.

**Tuner** (tiū·nəɹ). [f. TUNE *v.* + -ER [1].] One who or that which tunes.

**1.** One who produces or utters musical sounds; a player or singer. *arch.*

*c* **1580** LODGE *Reply Gosson's Sch. Abuse* (Hunter. Cl.) 26 A doleful tuner. **1627** DRAYTON *Sheph. Sirena* 200 Our mournefull Philomell, that rarest Tuner.

**b.** One who gives a particular (vocal) tone to something. *rare*[−1].

**1592** SHAKS. *Rom. & Jul.* II. iv. 30 The Pox of such antique lisping affecting phantacies, these new tuners of accent.

**2.** One who tunes a musical instrument; *spec.* whose occupation is to tune pianos or organs. Also *fig.*

**1801** BUSBY *Dict. Mus., Tuner*, one whose profession it is to rectify the false sounds of musical instruments. **1842** MRS. BROWNING *Grk. Chr. Poets* etc. 128 Lord Surrey passes as the tuner of our English. **1872** SPURGEON *Treas. Dav.* Ps. lix. Introd. III. 74 Affliction is the tuner of the harps of sanctified songsters. **1883** GODDEN in *Knowledge* 25 May 315/2 This [interval] is so equally dispersed by good tuners as to be almost imperceptible.

**b.** A workman employed to 'tune' a loom: see TUNE *v.* 1 d.

**1885** *Scotsman* 26 Aug. 3/6 Tweed Trade—Wanted..An assistant power-loom tuner. **1888** *Engineering* 20 Jan. 69 Mules and looms..in the charge of men known as 'tuners'.

**c.** An adjustable flap or opening in a flue-pipe of an organ, by means of which it is tuned (cf. *tuning-hole* s.v. TUNING 4).

**1891** in *Cent. Dict.*

**Tunesome** (tiū·nsŏm), *a. rare*[−1]. [f. TUNE *sb.* + -SOME.] Having 'tune' or melody; tuneful.

**1890** *Sat. Rev.* 26 Apr. 514/2 These pieces are..tunesome and original.

**Tunful** (tʊ·nful). [f. TUN *sb.* + -FUL 2.] As much as fills a tun.

**1562** TURNER *Baths* 4 Manye..carye great tunnfulls of it awaye, and drinke it in theyr houses. *a* **1592** GREENE *Vision* Wks. (Grosart) XII. 203 But for euery dram of mirth, they leaue behinde..a Tunfull of infecting mischiefs. **1819** SHELLEY *Cyclops* 197 You may drink a tunful if you will.

**Tung**: see TUNC. **Tung, tunge,** obs. ff. TONGUE.

**Tungah**, var. TANGA, an Indian (etc.) coin.

**Tung-oil**: see WOOD-OIL.

**Tungstate** (tʊ·ŋstēt). *Chem.* [f. TUNGST(IC + -ATE [4].] A salt of tungstic acid.

**1800** tr. *Lagrange's Chem.* I. 371 The other is known by mineralogists, under the name of *wolfram*..this is the tungstate of iron. **1839** DE LA BECHE *Rep. Geol. Cornwall*, etc. xv. 584 Except when mixed with wolfram, or the tungstate of iron and manganese. **1897** *Allbutt's Syst. Med.* IV. 596 One patient..recovered..while taking tungstate of soda.

**Tungsten** (tʊ·ŋsten). [a. Sw. *tungsten*, f. *tung* heavy + *sten* stone.]

†**1.** *Min.* = SCHEELITE, native calcium tungstate. *Obs.*

**1770** ENGESTROM tr. *Cronstedt's Syst. Min.* 201 *Ferrum calciforme terrâ quâdam incognitâ intime mixtum.* The Tungsten of the Swedes. **1786** BEDDOES *Chem. Ess. Scheele* 285 Lapis Ponderosus, or Tungsten...It is probable that the constituent parts of this..have been hitherto unknown. **1799** *Med. Jrnl.* I. 239 Tungsten...Scheele..affirmed that it consisted of calcareous earth, united to a peculiar acid. **1822** IMISON *Sc. & Art* II. 120 A mineral called *Tungsten* or ponderous stone, affords a peculiar metal.

**2.** *Chem.* (Formerly also in L. form **tungstenum**, as in other names of metals.) A heavy, steel-grey, ductile, very infusible metal, contained in the above mineral and in WOLFRAM (iron and manganese tungstate) and other minerals; used for wire in incandescent electric lamps. Symbol W (= *wolframium*); atomic weight 184 (O = 16).

**1796** HATCHETT in *Phil. Trans.* LXXXVI. 291 The yellow oxyde of tungsten by ignition becomes blue or black. **1812** DAVY *Chem. Philos.* 427 Tungstenum is obtained from a mineral known by the name of *wolfram*. **1836–41** BRANDE *Man. Chem.* (ed. 5) 921 Tungsten..which has also been called *Scheelium* and *Wolframium*, was first obtained by Messrs. de Luyart [in 1783], from the *tungstic acid* previously discovered by Scheele, in 1781. **1862** *London Rev.* 16 Aug. 154 Tungsten added to steel communicates a most intense hardness to it, and renders it also very fine-grained. **1911** *Daily News* 22 Aug. 2 Tungsten may be converted into strong ductile form and drawn into a wire only one thousandth of an inch in diameter. **1912** *Ann. Rep. Chem. Soc.* IX. 69 Tungsten melts at 3100°±60°.

**3.** *attrib.*, as *tungsten lamp, -steel, wire.*

**1862** *London Rev.* 16 Aug. 154 The alloy..is now becoming rather celebrated under the name of wolfram- or tungsten-steel. **1909** *Installation News* II. 171/2 The Tungsten lamp will not withstand over running to any great extent. **1911** *Encycl. Brit.* XVI. 669/2 The zirconium and tungsten wire lamps are equal to or surpass the tantalum lamp.

Hence †**Tu·ngstenane**, Davy's proposed name for a chloride of tungsten: see -ANE [2]; **Tungste·nic**, †**Tungste·nical**, **Tungsteni·tic**, *adjs.*, of, pertaining to, or containing tungsten, tungstic; **Tungsteni·ferous** *a.* [-FEROUS] yielding tungsten.

**1812** DAVY *Chem. Philos.* 429 *Tungstenane. **1796** KIRWAN *Elem. Min.* (ed. 2) I. 131 The *tungstenic acid..assumes a blue colour when heated to redness. *Ibid.* 133 An ore of *tungstenical substance. *Ibid.* II. 316 *Tungstenitic Calx, with Iron and Manganese, or Iron singly. Wolfram.

**Tungstenite** (tʊ·ŋstĕnəit). *Min.* [f. TUNGSTEN + -ITE [1].]

†**1.** = TUNGSTEN 2. *Obs.*

**1796** KIRWAN *Elem. Min.* (ed. 2) II. 308 Tungstenite... This substance is capable of existing in three states. That of a Regulus, which I call Tungstenite. *Ibid.*, Tungstenite. ..Hitherto it has been produced only in very minute Globules, being more difficultly reducible to a Metallic State than Manganese or Uranite.

**2.** = TUNGSTEN 1.

**1894** MUIR & MORLEY *Watts' Dict. Chem.* IV. 797 *Tungstenite*, or *scheelite* (tungstate of Ca[lcium])..occur in various localities.

**Tungstic** (tʊ·ŋstik), *a. Chem.* [f. TUNGST(EN + -IC 1 b.] Pertaining to or formed from tungsten; applied to compounds in which tungsten combines as a hexad (see -IC 1 b), as *tungstic acid*, $H_2O.WO_3$ (formerly = *t. oxide*), *tungstic chloride*, $WCl_6$, *tungstic oxide*, $WO_3$; also to minerals containing tungsten, as *tungstic ochre* (see OCHRE *sb.* 2), native tungstic oxide, also called **Tu·ngstite**.

**1796** HATCHETT in *Phil. Trans.* LXXXVI. 286 In 1790, Mr. Heyer..made some experiments on this ore [molybdate of lead], from which he inferred that it was composed of lead, combined with the tungstic acid. **1836–41** BRANDE *Man. Chem.* (ed. 5) 923 The *Nitro-tungstate of Potassa* is the salt originally described by Scheele [1781] as tungstic acid. **1868** WATTS *Dict. Chem.* V. 915 *Tungstic compounds*, ..in which tungsten is hexatomic. **1868** DANA *Min.* (ed. 5) 186 Tungstite.

**Tu·ngsto-**, combining form from TUNGSTEN, used in the names of compound acids (and their salts) containing the oxides of tungsten and another element, as *tungstobo·ric* and *tungstosili·cic acids*, whose salts are *tungstobo·rates* and *tungstosi·licates*.

**1868** WATTS *Dict. Chem.* V. 915 Tungstosilicic acids. *Ibid.* 917 The tungstosilicates are obtained by saturating the acid with carbonates. **1883** *Science* I. 489/2 Tungstoboric acid proves to be a convenient reagent for characterizing the alkaloids and peptones. *Ibid.*, Cadmic tungstoborate.

**Tungstous** (tʊ·ŋstəs), *a. Chem.* [f. TUNGST(EN + -OUS c.] Applied to compounds in which tungsten combines as a tetrad, as *tungstous chloride*, $WCl_4$, *tungstous oxide*, $WO_2$. (Cf. TUNGSTIC.)

**1860** in MAYNE *Expos. Lex.* **1868** WATTS *Dict. Chem.* V. 898 Tungsten forms two classes of compounds, in one of which it is tetratomic, and in the other hexatomic: Tungstous Chloride, $WCl^4$; Tungstous Oxide, $WO^2$.

‖ **Tu·ngua**, a West Indian name of the CHIGOE.

**1815** KIRBY & SP. *Entomol.* iv. (1818) I. 103 The celebrated Chigoe or Jiggers, called also.. Tungua. **1861** MAYHEW *Lond. Labour* III. 35 The most annoying species, however, is..a native of the tropical latitudes, variously named in the West Indies, chigoe, jigger, nigua, tungua, pique.

**Tunhoof** (tʊ·nhūf). Now *dial.* Forms: 1 tunhófe, 4 tunhowe, -hoo, 5–6 tunhove, 6 tune-, 7 tunnehoofe, 8– tunhoof. [f. TUN *sb.* + OE. *hófe*, HOVE *sb.*[1]: see ALE-HOOF.] The herb Ground Ivy (*Nepeta Glechoma*).

*c* **1000** *Sax. Leechd.* II. 344 Wyrc gode earsealfe..tunhofe niþoweard, celeþonian leaf garleac, cropleac, do on win. **14..** *Stockh. Med. MS.* II. 406 in *Anglia* XVIII. 317 Anoþer herbe is callyd soo [ground-ivy] þat we callyn tunhoo. *c* **1440** *Promp. Parv.* 506/1 Tunhove, herbe (*K.* tunhowe, *S.* thomyhow, *A.* thonnhowe), *edera terrestris.* **1597** GERARDE *Herbal* I. ccc. 705 In English ground Iuie, Alehoof,..Tunehoofe, and Cats foote. **1640** PARKINSON *Theatr. Bot.* v. xciii. 677 Gill creepe by the ground, Catsfoote, Haymaides, and Alehoofe most generally, or Tunnehoofe, because the countrey people use it much in their Ale. **1869** *Gd. Words* Mar. Supp. 4, I used to gather in armfuls primroses,..and strong-scented tunhoof.

**Tunic** (tiū·nik). Forms: 1 tunece, (tonica), 1–2 tunice, 2 tuneke; 6 tunake, 7 -ike, 7–8 tunick, tunique (also 9 as Fr.), 7– tunic. [ad. F. *tunique* or its source L. *tunica* (whence also Pr., Sp., Pg. *tunica*, It. *tonica, tonaca, tunica*, OE. *tunece*, OHG. *tûnihha*).]

**1.** A garment resembling a shirt or gown, worn by both sexes among the Greeks and Romans; in OE. and mediæval times, a body-garment or coat over which a loose mantle or cloak was worn.

Now worn on ceremonial occasions by princes and nobles.

[*c* **893** K. ÆLFRED *Oros.* v. x. § 3 Eft hie him sendon ane tunecan ongean. *c* **975** *Rushw. Gosp.* Matt. xxiv. 18 Seþe on londæ sy ne cerraþ he eft to nimene his tunican [*c* **1000** *Ags. Gosp.* tunecan, *c* **1160** *Hatton* tuneken; Vulg. *tunicam*]. **1603** *Cerem. Coronat. Jas I* (1685) 3 There is then also to be delivered to his Majesty the *Tunica*, or Shirt of red Silk.] **1609** BIBLE (Douay) *Lev.* viii. 7 (*Comm.*) A Tunike, or long robe downe to the foote. **1666** EVELYN *Diary* 30 Oct., To London to our office, and now had I on the vest and surcoat and tunic as 'twas call'd, after his Ma[ty] had brought the whole Court to it. *a* **1678** MARVELL *Royal Resolutions* Wks. (Grosart) I. 434 I'll have a fine tunick, a sash, and a vest. **1725** POPE *Odyss.* x. 647 The goddess with a radiant tunick drest My limbs. **1768** STERNE *Sent. Journ., The Monk, Calais*, He [a Franciscan] gave a slight glance with his eye downwards upon the sleeve of his tunick. **1835** LYTTON *Rienzi* i, His garb..consisted of the long loose gown and the plain tunic, both of dark-grey serge.

**2.** *Eccl.* = TUNICLE 2. Only *Hist.*

**1696** PHILLIPS (ed. 5), *Tunic*,..a Church Ornament among the Romanists, worn by the Deacons that serve the Priest or Bishop at the Altar. **1764** in J. H. Harting *Hist. Sardinian Chapel* (1905) 23 Two tunics, with a stole, two maniples of taffeta. **1844** [see DALMATIC B.]. **1877** J. D. CHAMBERS *Div. Worship* 54 The Subdeacon was invested with the Tunic by the Bishop at his ordination.

**3.** In modern costume. **a.** A close, usually plain body-coat; now *spec.* that forming part of the uniform of soldiers and policemen.

**1667** PEPYS *Diary* 20 Oct., Put on my new tunique of velvett; which is very plain, but good. **1668** *Ibid.* 17 May, Put on my new stuff-suit,..the bands of my vest and tunique laced with silk lace, of the colour of my suit. **1868** *Regul. & Ord. Army* § 607 Medals are only to be worn with the tunic.

**b.** A garment worn by women, consisting of a bodice and an upper skirt, belted or drawn in at (or fitted to) the waist, worn over and displaying a longer skirt. (In very recent use, applied to the upper skirt alone.) Also, a kind of belted frock or smock worn by children.

Now often in Fr. form *tunique* (tünī·k).

**1762** STERNE *Tr. Shandy* VI. xviii, The child looks extremely well..in his vests and tunicks. **1800** *Hull Advertiser* 4 Oct. 3/3 Paris fashions..tuniques of black crape are coming into wear. **1803** *Times* 15 Jan., The short tunics of last year, which were called Mamelukes, are in great esteem this year under the name of Jewess Tunics. ? **1838** *First Year of Silken Reign* 230 (Cent. D.) Her Majesty wore a white satin petticoat, over which was a silver llama tunic, trimmed with silver and white blonde lace. **1883** *Truth* 31 May 768/2 Tabs..appear on tunics, polonaises, bodices, and sleeves. **1899** *Westm. Gaz.* 19 Jan. 3/2 It has consented to sport something tapering away over the back, which it has called its tunique. **1909** *Daily Graphic* 20 Oct. 13/1 A noticeable feature in these dresses is the tight-fitting tunic which runs to the knees.

**4.** *transf.* **a.** *Anat.* A membranous sheath enveloping or lining an organ of the body; a 'coat'.
1661 Blount *Glossogr.* (ed. 2), *Tunick*..a skin or coat that covers the eye, whereof there are four sorts. 1678 *Phil. Trans.* XII. 976 The inner Tunick of the Nose. 1725 *Bradley's Fam. Dict.* s.v. *Appetite*, When the Stomach proves empty, the acid Liquor begins to work upon its internal Tunick. 1826 Kirby & Sp. *Entomol.* IV. xxxvii. 7 Besides these is an exterior and an interior tunic. 1880 M. C. Drysdale in *Med. Temp. Jrnl.* Oct. 9 The tunics of the capillaries.

**b.** The integument of a part or organ in a plant; *spec.* in *Bot.* any loose membranous skin not formed from the epidermis; also, each layer or coating of a tunicate bulb.
1760 J. Lee *Introd. Bot.* I. vi. (1765) 14 A Seed..is a Rudiment of a new Vegetable..covered with a bladdery Coat or Tunic. 1830 Lindley *Nat. Syst. Bot.* 155 The long loose tunic of the seed is intended to act at first as a buoy, to float the seed upon the surface of the water. 1832 *Veg. Subst. Food* 295 The tunics of the onion.

**5.** *attrib.* and *Comb.*
1828 *Souvenir* II. 79/2 A Tunique pelisse robe of white jaconet muslin. 1832 G. Clarke *Pompeii* II. xiii. 317 Tunic-pallium displayed. 1835 *Court Mag.* VI. p. i/1 The shirt is trimmed in the tunic style. 1860 Russell *Diary India* II. ix. 174 Thus, with an able-bodied aborigen holding on by my tunic-tails behind, I parachuted down. 1900 *Daily News* 12 Dec. 7/3 The skirt is in the tunic form now fashionable.

Hence **Tu·nic-hood** (*nonce-wd.*), the condition of one who wears a tunic; **Tunicked** (tiū·nikt) *a.*, wearing a tunic: usually as second element in a compound; **Tu·nicless** *a.*, without a tunic.
1756 C. Smart tr. *Horace, Epist.* I. vii. (1826) II. 211 Vulteius..selling brokery-goods to the tunicked populace. 1859 Sala *Tw. round Clock* (1861) 155 Still in a state of tunic-hood, I remember a very tall, handsome gentleman, with a crimson velvet under-waistcoat. 1876 A. J. Evans *Through Bosnia* ii. 77 Croat men, white tunicked and white breeked. 1893 R. K. Douglas *Chinese Stories* 218 A larger band of red-tunicked men. 1899 *Westm. Gaz.* 21 Sept. 2/1 The King wears a long tunic-like garment..and a cloak. 1904 *Daily News* 30 Sept. 7 He pulled me, tunicless, out, giving me my sword and revolver.

† **Tu·nical**, *a. Obs. rare.* [f. L. *tunica* Tunic + -al.] Of, pertaining to, or of the nature of a tunic.
1805 *Med. Jrnl.* XIV. 299 Different from pericardium, dura mater, or any other yielding tunical covering.

**Tunicary** (tiū·nikări), *a.* and *sb.* [f. as prec. + -ary[1].]
**A.** *adj.* Of or pertaining to a tunic or membrane.
1900–13 in Dorland *Med. Dict.* 1901 *Jrnl. Exper. Med.* 15 Jan. 343 (Cent. D. Suppl.) The tunicary hernia of the jejunum..still lay entirely on one side of the mesentery.
**B.** *sb. Zool.* A member of the *Tunicata*; a tunicated mollusc.
1835 Kirby *Hab. & Inst. Anim.* I. vii. 218 The Tunicaries ..form part of the headless Molluscans of Cuvier and belong to the section of them that have no shells. 1851 Woodward *Mollusca* I. iii. 11 The tunicary cements itself to rock or sea-weed. 1872 Nicholson *Palæont.* 30 The entire class of the Tunicaries presents no hard structures.

‖ **Tunicata** (tiūnikēⁱ·tă), *sb. pl. Zool.* [mod. L., neut. pl. of *tunicātus* (sc. *animālia*) coated, Tunicate.] A division of animals, now regarded as a sub-phylum of the *Chordata*; also called *Urochorda*: see next, B.
1828 Stark *Elem. Nat. Hist.* II. 115 Class III.—Tunicata. Gelatinous or coriaceous biforous, bituminated animals, isolated, in groups, or often joined together in a common mass. 1851 Richardson *Geol.* viii. (1855) 230 The Tunicata have no shell, and are enclosed in an elastic muscular sac, with two openings. 1855 H. Spencer *Princ. Psychol.* (1872) I. I. i. 10 Humble Mollusks, like the fixed Tunicata.

**Tunicate** (tiū·nikēⁱt), *a.* and *sb.* [ad. L. *tunicāt-us*, pa. pple. of *tunicāre*: see next.]
**A.** *adj.* Having or enclosed in a tunic or covering; *spec. Bot.* having or consisting of a series of concentric layers, as a bulb; *Entom.* sheathed in or issuing from one another, as the joints of antennæ; *Zool.* having a tunic or mantle; belonging to the *Tunicata*.
1760 J. Lee *Introd. Bot.* III. ix. (1765) 195 A tunicate Bulb, when it consists of many Tunics or Coats. 1825 *Greenhouse Comp.* I. 237 Tunicate bulbs..may be increased by cutting off the upper part of the bulb horizontally. 1826 Kirby & Sp. *Entomol.* IV. xlvi. 323 Tunicate Knob (*Capitulum tunicatum*). When the laminæ, at least on one side, appear to inosculate or to be imbedded in each other. 1847 *Nat. Encycl.* I. 752 It embraces..the conchiferous and tunicate mollusks. 1875 *Zoologist* X. 4313 Sponges, Anemones, and Tunicate Mollusca.

**B.** *sb.* One of a class of marine animals, formerly regarded as molluscs, but now classified as a degenerate branch of *Chordata*, comprising the ascidians and allied forms, characterized by a pouch-like body enclosed in a tough leathery integument, with a single or double aperture through which the water enters and leaves the pharynx.
1848 Smart Suppl., *Tunicates*, or *Tunicaries*, an order of acephalous mollusks having a soft outer covering or mantle; otherwise called Ascidians. 1863 E. V. Neale *Anal. Th. & Nat.* 177 The Tunicates, a class of creatures with a fleshy centre and tough leathery skin. 1877 Huxley *Anat. Inv. Anim.* x. 600 All the fixed Tunicates present two, more or less closely approximated, apertures. 1889 Geddes & Thomson *Evol. Sex* v. § 2 Among the sea-squirts or tunicates, the reproductive organs are frequently ductless.

† **Tu·nicate**, *v. Obs. rare*⁻⁰. [f. L. *tunicāt-*, ppl. stem of *tunicāre* to clothe with a tunic, cover with a skin, peel, etc., f. *tunica* Tunic.]
1623 Cockeram, *Tunicate*, to cloake or hide a thing.

**Tunicated** (tiū·nikēⁱtĕd), *a.* [f. as Tunicate *a.* + -ed[1].] † **a.** Clad in a coat or tunic (*obs. rare*⁻⁰). **b.** = Tunicate *a.*
1623 Cockeram II, One Wearing a Coate, *tunicated.* 1744 J. Wilson *Synopsis Brit. Pl.* 256 Garlick..hath a bulbous tunicated root. 1760 J. Lee *Introd. Bot.* II. xxxi. (1765) 152 *Iris*, with a tunicated Bulb. 1828 J. E. Smith *Eng. Flora* II. 1 Chenopodium. Seed lenticular, tunicated, superior. 1840 F. D. Bennett *Whaling Voy.* II. 322 Fishes, shell-fish, and tunicated molluscs have their luminous matter deposited beneath a dense integument. 1861 Bentley *Man. Bot.* (1870) 110 There are two kinds of bulbs commonly distinguished by botanists, the tunicated, and the scaly.

**Tunicin** (tiū·nisin). *Chem.* [f. Tunic + -in[1].] A kind of animal cellulose, $C_6H_{10}O_5$, or chitin, occurring in the mantles of tunicates.
1862 Miller *Elem. Chem.* (ed. 2) III. 781 Berthelot calls it [chitin] tunicin, from its entering into the composition of the envelope of some of the tunicate mollusks. 1876 tr. *Schützenberger's Ferment.* 147 Derived..from the decomposition of a substance analogous to tunicin or chitin.

**Tunicle** (tiū·nik'l). Forms: 4– tunicle, 4–6 -ycle, 5–7 -acle, (5–6 -akyl, -ekil, -ek(k)el(l), -yk(k)il(l), -ycale, tuinicle, twynykil, tunnycall); 4–5 tonacle, (5 -ecle, -icle, -ycle, -ykyl, -ykle, -akle, -ucle, 6 -aculle); (5 tenekylle, -ucle, 6 -acull, tin-, tynacle, -akle, tynnacle, *Sc.* -akil, -akyl, -akel). [ad. L. *tunicula* dim. of *tunica* Tunic.
But it may also represent OF. *tunikle* for *tunike* (cf. *bouticle, dalmaticle, triacle*: see M. Antoine Thomas in *Romania* XXXIX. 231.)]

† **1.** A small tunic; also *fig.* a wrapping, covering, integument. *Obs.*
1377 Langl. *P. Pl.* B. xv. 163 As gladde of a goune of a graye russet As of a tunicle of tarse or of a trye scarlet. *a* 1400–50 *Alexander* 1547 Doctours & deuynours..tyrett all in tonacles of tartaren webbys. 14.. *Nom.* in Wr.-Wülcker 721/28 *Hec tunicula*, a tunakyl. 1656 Blount *Glossogr.*, *Tunicle*.., a little jacket or coat. 1678 Cudworth *Intell. Syst.* I. v. 789 The Chaldaick Philosophers bestow upon the Soul, Two Interiour Tunicles or Vestments. 1744 Berkeley *Siris* § 171 This tunicle of the soul, whether it be called pure æther, or luciform vehicle, or animal spirit.

**2.** *Eccl.* A vestment resembling the dalmatic, worn by subdeacons over the alb (and also by bishops between the alb and the dalmatic) at celebrations of the Eucharist.
*c* 1425 Wyntoun *Cron.* IX. v. 595 A prestis westment alhaille, Withe tunakyl [*v.r.* tynnakyllis] and dalmatyk. 1495 in *Somerset Medieval Wills* (1901) 330, 2 Tenucles with the hole appurtenances. 1502 *Acc. Ld. High Treas. Scot.* II. 288 To the woman that maid the frenȝeis for tunycales.., xs. 1536 *Reg. Riches* in *Antiq. Sarisb.* (1771) 197 Ten Chesibles..with dyvers Albs and Tunicles. 1548–9 (Mar.) *Bk. Com. Prayer, Communion* (Rubric), Albes with tunacles. 1583 Fulke *Defence* iv. 132 If the word Deacon, be taken for such an one, as at a popish masse standeth in a disguised tunicle, holding a patten. 1849 Rock *Ch. of Fathers* I. v. (1903) I. 315 The sleeves of the tunicle were neither so wide nor so long, nor did its skirts reach quite so far down as those of the dalmatic. 1877 J. D. Chambers *Div. Worship* 54 The Tunicle of the Subdeacon and Dalmatic of the Deacon are nearly identical.

† **b.** One vested in a tunicle; a subdeacon or 'clerk'. *Obs.*
1554 *Ludlow Churchw. Acc.* (Camden) 56 Item, paid for a tonaculle to cary hally water.

† **3.** A membrane enclosing a bodily organ, part of a plant, etc.; = Tunic 4. *Obs.* (or *rare arch.*)
1398 Trevisa *Barth. De P. R.* v. v. (1495) g iv/2, The glasy humour..kepyth the humour cristalyn [of the eye] fro touchyng and sharpnes of tunycles. 1543 Traheron *Vigo's Chirurg.* I. ix. 8 The tunicles or rymes of the arteries ben of harder substaunce than the tunicles proceeding from the veynes. 1601 Holland *Pliny* XIII. iv. I. 387 Some of these stones be..covered with many skins or pellicles, and others with fewer: ye shall have in this Date, those tunicles thicke and grosse; in that, thinner and more fine. 1725 Sloane *Jamaica* II. 313 The stomach had a very thick inward tunicle. 1912 *Nation* 5 Oct. 13/1 Our modern doctors apparently leave the tunicles of the brain unpurged.

Hence **Tu·nicled** *a. nonce-wd.*, enclosed in or as in a tunicle.
1652 A. Wilson *Pref. Verses* in Benlowes *Theoph.*, The distances of every Sphere Which in full Orbs do move, tunicled so That the lesse Spheres within the greater go.

**Tunie, Tunill**, obs. ff. Tunny, Tunnel.

**Tuning** (tiū·niŋ), *vbl. sb.* [f. Tune *v.* + -ing[1].] The action of the verb Tune.

**1.** The action or process of putting an instrument in tune; a system according to which this is done (cf. Temperament 10).
1554–5 *Burgh Rec. Edinb.* (1871) II. 358 Item, to Sir Johne Fietie,..for tonying of the organis at Sanct Geillis day.. xxiijˢ. 1615 G. Sandys *Trav.* 72 The foolish Musitians.. spent so much time in unseasonable tuning. 1655 in *12th Rep. Hist. MSS. Comm.* App. v. 5 The polyphon is an instrument of so different a stringing and tuning that [etc.]. 1787 *Thompson's Pat.* in *6th Rep. Dep. Kpr. Pub. Rec.* II. 176 A perfect and compleat Machine or Instrument..for the more easy and expeditious tuning of Harpsichords, Piano Forts, Spinnets [etc.]. 1910 Tovey in *Encycl. Brit.* III. 129/2 (*Bach*) With the object of stimulating tuning by 'equal temperament' instead of sacrificing the euphony of remoter keys to that of the more usual ones.

**b.** *fig.*: see Tune *v.* 2.
1654 Whitlock *Zootomia* 342 The Soule needs not more a well organiz'd Body, to exercise it Functions with spritely Vigor,..than that Soule, and those Organs need the Tunings of Education. 1711 Shaftesb. *Charac.* (1737) II. 95 It might be agreeable..to enquire thus into the different tunings of the passions. 1868 J. H. Blunt *Ref. Ch. Eng.* I. 273 Such a 'tuning' of pulpits and official houses..has been succeeded..by the influence of the press.

**c.** *transf.*: see Tune *v.* 1 c, d.
1863 E. FitzGerald *Lett.* (1889) I. 290 Yesterday we gave her what they call 'a tuning' in a rather heavy swell round Orford Ness. 1891 *Labour Commission Gloss.*, *Tuning*, a term used in Yorkshire synonymous with the term 'tackling ..; it means repairing, &c. a loom when it breaks down and keeping it generally in order.

**2.** The action of uttering musical sounds.
1609 Douland *Ornith. Microl.* B ij b, Musicke..is a knowledge of Tuning, which consists in sound and Song. 1610 Attersoll *Hist. Balak* (*N. & Q.* 9th Ser. IV. 104/1) Many vse in their teaching..knocking of the Pulpit..fidling with the fingers, tuning with the voice. 1760–72 H. Brooke *Fool of Qual.* (1809) III. 158 Sentimental and rapturous tunings that rise up..from eternity to eternity.

† **b.** The setting or determination of pitch in singing; the exercising of the voice in the correct pitch of the notes of the scale. *Obs.*
1597 Morley *Introd. Mus.* Pref., Any of but meane capacitie, so they can but truely sing their tunings, which we commonly call the sixe notes. 1662 Playford *Skill Mus.* I. xi. (1674) 42 The Tuning of the Voice in all the Notes.

**3.** With *up*: see Tune *v.* 8.
1902 *Westm. Gaz.* 24 Oct. 3/1 These chapters, however, form but a preliminary tuning-up,..and the first vigorous note is struck in the fourth chapter, 'Dissent and Defoe'. 1908 *Ibid.* 14 May 10/1 A new place had been provided for 'tuning-up'..a long way from plaintiffs' houses.

**4.** *attrib.* and *Comb.* (all in sense 1): **tuning-board**, in the organ, a piece of wood screwed to one side of the top of an open wood pipe for tuning it; **tuning-cone**, a hollow cone of wood or metal used for tuning the metal flue-pipes of an organ; **tuning-crook**, (*a*) an implement used in tuning the reed-pipes of an organ; (*b*) in brass wind-instruments, = Crook *sb.* 8 a; **tuning-funnel** = *tuning-cone*; **tuning-hammer**, a tuning-key for a piano, properly one with a double wooden head like that of a hammer, used for driving in the wrest-pins when new strings are fitted in; **tuning-hole**, in the organ, an opening near the top of a flue-pipe, adjustable by a flap (see Tuner 2 c) so as to alter the pitch; **tuning-horn**, = *tuning-cone*; **tuning-key**, a key (Key *sb.*[1] 13 (*b*)) used for turning the wrest-pins in tuning a stringed instrument, as a piano or harp; **tuning-knife**, a long piece of steel used in tuning the reed-pipes of an organ (also called *reed-knife*); **tuning-lever**, = *tuning-key*; **tuning-peg, -pin**, one of the pegs round which the strings of a stringed instrument are passed, and by turning which they are tuned; a wrest-pin; **tuning-screw**, a screw used in tuning a musical instrument; **tuning-slide**, a slide in a metal wind-instrument, used to bring it into tune with other instruments in an orchestra; **tuning-wire**, in the organ, a bent wire in a reed-pipe, used in tuning; **tuning-wrench**, = *tuning-key*.
1852 Seidel *Organ* 149 Open wood pipes have at their aperture a small board, called a *tuning-board. 1881 Broadhouse *Mus. Acoustics* 405 An organ-pipe is..slightly sharpened by pressing out the edges of its open end, as by the '*tuning cone'. 1852 Seidel *Organ* 28 The screw-key (now used in tuning the reed-pipes instead of the *tuning-crook) is an invention of our own time. *Ibid.* 149 With some open pewter pipes the *tuning-funnels cannot be used. 1801 Busby *Dict. Mus.*, *Tuning-hammer. 1805 E. Thunder *Specif. Patent* No. 2811. 2 The top..is flattened to receive the tuning hammer. 1860 *All Year Round* No. 68. 430 The *tuning-key of David's harp, which was shown at Erfurt. 1889 A. J. Hipkins in Grove *Dict. Mus.* IV. 189/2 The old way of tuning pianos by the Tuning Hammer (or a *Tuning Lever) remains in vogue. 1842 S. Lover *Handy Andy* xv, Having adjusted the blue ribbon over her shoulder, and twisted the *tuning-pegs, and thrummed upon the wires for some time. 1877 Knight *Dict. Mech.*, *Tuning-pin. 1896 A. J. Hipkins *Pianoforte* 13 The Wrest-plank..is the plank or block in which the wrest or tuning-pins are inserted. 1872 Ellacombe *Ch. Bells Devon* etc. 208 There was in the *tuning room a peal of eight bells. 1852 Seidel *Organ* 153 Some organ-builders provide reed-pipes with a *tuning-screw instead of a tuning-crook. 1876–98 Stainer & Barrett *Dict. Mus. Terms* 345/1 A reed-pipe consists of a *boot, block, reed, tongue, wedge, *tuning wire,* and *tube.*

**Tu·ning-fork.**

**1.** A small steel instrument (invented in 1711 by John Shore) consisting of a stem with two stout flat prongs which on being caused to vibrate produce a definite musical note of constant pitch, thus serving as a standard for tuning musical instruments and in acoustical investigations, etc.
1799 Young in *Phil. Trans.* XC. 134 The fundamental note was found to be one-sixth of a tone higher than the respective octave of a tuning-fork marked C. 1862 *Catal. Internat. Exhib., Brit.* II. No. 3403 Chromatic tuning-forks. 1878 G. B. Prescott *Sp. Telephone* (1879) 51 Vibrating a tuning fork in front of the mouth.

**2.** An instrument used for turning the pins in tuning a pianoforte. 1877 in Knight *Dict. Mech.*

**Tunique**, obs. and Fr. form of TUNIC.

**Tunist** (tiū·nist). *rare.* [f. TUNE *v.* + -IST.] = TUNER 2.

18.. SEDLEY TAYLOR *Science of Music* 132 (Cent. Dict.).

**Tunk**: see TUNG. **Tunker**: see DUNKER[1].

**Tun-moot.** *Hist.* [repr. OE. *túngemót*, f. *tún*, TOWN + *gemót* meeting: see MOOT *sb.*[1]] A public meeting of the town or village community.

**1881** GREEN *Making of Eng.* iv. 193 *note*, There is no ground for believing that the 'tun-moot' was a judicial court. Its work was the ordering of the village life and the village industry.

**Tunn(e, Tunnage**, obs. ff. TON, TUN, TONNAGE.

**Tunnel** (tʊ·nĕl), *sb.* Forms: 5–7 tonel, 6 -ell, 6–7 tonnel, -ell, tunell, 6–8 tunnell, (7 tunill), 6– tunnel; see also TONNEL. [a. OF. *tonel* masc., in mod.F. *tonneau* tun, cask, and the fem. derivative *tonnelle*, to which the early Eng. in sense 1 corresponds. The sense of 'tube, pipe, opening' and its extensions are of Eng. development, and for that of 'subterranean passage' *tunnel* has been adopted in mod.F. (in *Dict. Acad.* 1878) from English.]

**1.** A net for catching partridges or water-fowl, having a pipe-like passage with a wide opening, and narrowing towards the end; a tunnel-net. ? *Obs.*

*c* **1440** *Promp. Parv.* 496/2 Tonel, to take byrdys, *obvolutorium*. **1538** *York Wills* (Surtees) VI. 85 To Brian Lelome all my partrike nettes called a tonnell. **1611** COTGR., *Tonnelle*, a Tunnell, or staulking horse for Partridges. **1616** SURFL. & MARKH. *Country Farme* 731 To take Partridges with the Tonnell, or Tombrell, there must a man be placed behind a Cow or a Horse, of wood, or of osier, painted in.. the fashion of a Cow or a Horse. **1710** *Act* 9 *Anne* c. 27 § 5 The pernicious Practice of driving and taking [Wild Fowl] with Hayes Tunnells and other Nets in the Fens. **1822** *Sporting Mag.* IX. 177 A tunnel..(a net used in taking game).

**b.** 'The funnel-shaped conductor leading from the *heart* to the pound in a pound-net' (Knight *Dict. Mech.* Suppl. 1884).

†**2.** The shaft or flue of a chimney. *Obs.*

**1508** STANBRIDGE *Vulgaria* (W. de W.) A vj b, *Infumibulum*, the tonell [*printed* towell] of the chymnaye. **1510** — *Vocab.* (W. de W.) B ij b, *Infunibulum*, a tunnell of a chymney. **1530** PALSGR. 282/1 Tonnell [283/2 Tunnell] of a chymney, *tuyau*. **1595** in *Archæologia* LXIV. 374 Opening yᵉ tunnel in yᵉ low bakt mete house. **1680** AUBREY *Lives, Bacon* (1898) I. 78 The tunnells of the chimneys were carried into the middle of the howse. *c* **1710** CELIA FIENNES *Diary* (1888) 4 The Chimney is just under the window and the Tunnells runnes upon each side. **1818** SCOTT *Rob Roy* v, The fire..roared, blazed, and ascended, half in smoke, half in flame, up a huge tunnel, with an opening wide enough to accommodate a stone seat within its ample vault.

†**b.** A pipe or tube in general. Now *rare.*

**1545** RAYNOLD *Byrth Mankynde* 144 Let the woman set her selfe..on a couar made for the nonce with a tunnel or cundyte. **1601** HOLLAND *Pliny* XVII. xxi. I. 528 Let them passe..through..an earthen pipe or tunnell. **1615** G. SANDYS *Trav.* 248 It [the island Volcano] had three tunnels whereat it evaporated fire. **1642** ROGERS *Naaman* (1662) 3 By and with them [miracles] as by Tunnels, the influence, power and authority of truth might enter and prevaile. **1890** [see TUNNELLED 1 b].

†**c.** *fig. pl.* Applied to the nostrils (as a passage for tobacco-smoke). *Obs. humorous nonce-use.*

**1598** B. JONSON *Ev. Man in Hum.* I. iii, He dos take this same filthy roguish tabacco,..it would doe a man good to see the fume come forth at 's tonnells!

**3.** A funnel. *Obs.* exc. *dial.*

*a* **1529** SKELTON *El. Rummyng* 403 Another..brought a pottel pycher, A tonnel, and a bottell. **1530** PALSGR. 282/1 Tonnell to fyll wyne with, *antonnoyr*. **1601** HOLLAND *Pliny* XXX. vi. II. 381 Given in drink and swallowed downe by a pipe or tunill. **1662** R. MATHEW *Unl. Alch.* lxxxix. 157 Be careful that..it fit thy Funnel or Tunnel. **1719** D'URFEY *Pills* (1872) III. 251 For the Bottle, you cannot well fill it, Without a Tunnel. **1802** PALEY *Nat. Theol.* xv. (ed. 2) 286 Cocks, pipes, tunnels, for transferring the cyder from one vessel to another. *a* **1825** FORBY *Voc. E. Anglia*, *Tunnel*, s. a funnel,..in constant use. **1863** MRS. TOOGOOD *Yorks. Dial.* (MS.), Pour the wine thro the tunnel into the bottle.

**4.** A subterranean passage; a road-way excavated under ground, esp. under a hill or mountain, or beneath the bed of a river: now most commonly on a railway; also in earliest use on a canal, in a mine, etc. (The chief current sense.)

**1782** PENNANT *Journey* 52 The most southern tunnel, as it is called, is at Hermitage. **1790** JANE SNOW in *A. C. Bower's Diaries & Corr.* (1903) 105 We went through what they call a Tunnel—a passage through the Earth for the convenience of carrying Coals by Water: it is two miles and a half long, fifteen feet wide, the same high. **1792** A. YOUNG *Trav. France* 366 At Orgon the canal de Boisgelin..is a noble work, but unfinished; it passes here in a tunnel four hundred and forty yards through a mountain. **1792** J. PHILLIPS *Hist. Inland Navig.* xiv. 363 The celebrated tunnel through Harecastle-hill, Staffordshire, was cut under the direction of ..Mr. Brindley [in 1766]. **1798** *Monthly Mag.* July 74 A cylindrical tunnel under the Thames from Gravesend to Tilbury. **1861** *Sat. Rev.* 23 Nov. 540 The projectors of a tunnel thirty miles long under the Channel. **1872** RAYMOND *Statist. Mines & Mining* 15 The vein has been attacked by various tunnels and shafts.

**b.** An arched drain. *dial.*

**1828** *Craven Gloss.*, *Tunnel*, an arched drain.

**c.** A working-hole in the wall of a glass-furnace.

**1839** URE *Dict. Arts* 587 Two principal openings of the furnace...These are called tunnels. They are destined for the introduction of the pots and the fuel.

**d.** *transf.* The burrow of an animal.

**1873** TRISTRAM *Moab* vii. 124 The burrows of the mole-rat, which does duty, in the making of runs and molehills, for the common mole, but excavates much larger tunnels. **1886** BURROUGHS *Signs & Seasons* (1895) 179 Through the tunnel of the meadow mouse the water rushes as through a pipe.

**e.** A canal in an animal body resembling a tunnel, as that of the organ of Corti in the internal ear.

**1882** *Syd. Soc. Lex.*, *Corti, organ of*, a papillary-looking structure, stretching along the whole length of the canalis cochlearis...It is a sort of tunnel, composed of closely lying arches, the arches of Corti. **1898** P. MANSON *Trop. Diseases* xxxiv. 525 The septa between the tunnels may break down and a considerable cavity be thus produced.

**5.** *attrib.* and *Comb.*, as *tunnel-borer*, *-boring*, *darkness*, *-drain*, *excavation*, *-maker*, *-mouth*, *-passage*, *-way*, *-worker*, *-workman*; *tunnel-like*, *-shaped* adjs.; **tunnel-anæmia**, = *tunnel-disease* (*a*) (Dorland *Med. Dict.* 1900–13); **tunnel-disease**, a disease incident to workers in tunnels, mines, etc.; *spec.* (*a*) a form of anæmia caused by an intestinal parasite, the *tunnel-worm* (*Dochmius duodenalis* or *Ankylostoma duodenale*); (*b*) = CAISSON-*disease*; † **tunnel dish**, ? a funnel (= sense 3; cf. TUN-DISH); **tunnel-head**, (*a*) the top of a shaft- or blast-furnace; (*b*) the point to which the construction of a tunnel has progressed; **tunnel-hole**, 'the throat of a blast-furnace' (*Cent. Dict.* 1891); **tunnel-kiln** (see quot.); **tunnel-man**, a workman employed in making a tunnel; **tunnel-net**, = sense 1; also a similar net for fishing; **tunnel-pit**, **-shaft**, a shaft sunk to the level of a tunnel; **tunnel-sickness**, = *tunnel-disease*; **tunnel-vault**, = *barrel-vault* (see BARREL *sb.* 11); **tunnel-weaver**, a spider that weaves a tunnel-like underground web; **tunnel-worm**, the parasitic nematode worm (see *tunnel-disease*) which causes *tunnel-anæmia*.

**1877** KNIGHT *Dict. Mech.*, **Tunnel-borer*, a ram, operated by compressed air, for making excavations through rock. **1899** CAGNEY tr. *Jaksch's Clin. Diagn.* vi. (ed. 4) 228 Where a severe form of anæmia occurs in labourers..especially.. brick-burners, miners, and tunnel-borers. **1909** *Westm. Gaz.* 29 Dec. 5/4 No Swiss are employed..because they have enough other work and do not care particularly for such employment as *tunnel-boring. **1877** RAYMOND *Statist. Mines & Mining* 123 Rich placer-mines formerly existed in many of the gulches, and several *tunnel-claims in the gravel-hills gave excellent profits. **1839–48** BAILEY *Festus* xxi. 273 Without God all things are in *tunnel darkness. **1887** *19th Cent.* Aug. 149 Italians who died from cholera in digging the Suez Canal, or from '*tunnel-disease' in the St. Gothard Tunnel. **1898** P. MANSON *Trop. Diseases* xxxvi. 537 In Europe it [i.e. ankylostomiasis] is sometimes known as 'miner's anæmia' or 'tunnel disease',..in allusion to the notorious Saint Gothard epidemic. **1610** *Althorp MS.* in Simpkinson *Washingtons* (1860) App. p. vii, Itm *tunnell dishes. **1840** MARRYAT *Olla Podr.* III. 317 A long *tunnel drain. **1877** RAYMOND *Statist. Mines & Mining* 190 A *tunnel drive at the Dutchman Mine, to reach the ledge about 225 feet below the outcrop. **1843** HT. MARTINEAU *Hill & Valley* 79 They saw the filler at the *tunnel-head pouring in at the doors the materials that were furnished by the kilns. **1905** *Daily News* 24 Feb. 6 In the St. Gothard Tunnel there was much disease due to the imperfect sanitation and ventilation at the tunnel-head. **1889** H. DRUMMOND *Trop. Africa* vi. 133 As the Esquimaux heap up snow, building it into the low *tunnel-huts in which they live. **1828** WEBSTER, **Tunnel-kiln*, a lime-kiln in which coal is burnt, as distinguished from a flame-kiln, in which wood or peat is used. **1885** *Fortnight in Waggonette* 51, I know no part of our complex system that requires more constant and careful attention than the *tunnel-like way to the machinery within us. **1894** SMILES *J. Wedgwood* x. 95 He had known him as a..*tunnel-maker. **1897** *Daily News* 25 Sept. 7/1 Average daily wages earned..., *tunnel-men, 9s. 10d. **1877** RAYMOND *Statist. Mines & Mining* 125 The scenes of extensive *tunnel-mining. **1908** *Daily Chron.* 19 Aug. 1/7 Turning his head towards the *tunnel-mouth. **1721** BRADLEY *Philos. Acc. Wks. Nat.* 131 The Figure of a *Tunnel-Net, disposed for catching all kind of Flies that come into it. **1828** WEBSTER, *Tunnel-net*, a net with a wide mouth at one end and narrow at the other. **1840** [see TUNNEL *v.* 1 b]. **1883** G. C. DAVIES *Norfolk Broads* xxii. (1884) 165 The 'tunnel net'..is a bow-net 8 or 10 feet long, the extreme end of which is stretched out and tied to a stake. **1908** SIR H. JOHNSTON *Grenfell & Congo* II. xxvi. 736 The *tunnel-passage goes straight to the river. **1688** R. HOLME *Armoury* III. xx. (Roxb.) 232 The *Tunell pipe by which the water may be poured in. **1828** WEBSTER, **Tunnel-pit*, a shaft sunk from the top of the ground to the level of an intended tunnel, for drawing up the earth and stones. **1882** *Rep. to Ho. Repr. Prec. Met. U. S.* 638 *Tunnel-running is expensive, and where the depth..is not supposed to exceed 150 feet, a vertical prospect shaft is often sunk. **1858** SIMMONDS *Dict. Trade*, **Tunnel-shaft*. **1826** KIRBY & SP. *Entomol.* III. xxx. 147 When retracted, they form a *tunnel-shaped cavity, varying in depth. **1903** *Strand Mag.* July 98/2 Hundreds ..had perished in the darkness and heat of the terrible '*tunnel sickness'. **1870** MRS. WHITNEY *We Girls* ix. Gathers and gores, *tunnel-skirts and barrel-skirts and paniers. **1883** *Century Mag.* Oct. 823/2 A *tunnel-way for passengers connects the whole. **1911** *Daily News* 1 Apr. 4 All *tunnel-workers in Switzerland being of this nationality [Italian]. **1843** HT. MARTINEAU *Hill & Valley* 36 The *tunnel-workmen were..going to dinner. **1895** *Funk's Standard Dict.*, **Tunnel-worm*, an anchylostome. **1906** *Scott. Rev.* 29 Mar. 338/1 Acute anæmia due to the bite of the so-called tunnel-worm.

Hence **Tu·nnelism**, the theory or practice of tunnelling; **Tu·nnelist**, one who constructs a tunnel (in quot. 1871 *transf.* a burrowing animal); **Tu·nnellite**, one in favour of a proposed submarine tunnel between England and France; **Tu·nnelly** *a.*, resembling a tunnel.

**1799** C. CLARKE *Obs. Tunnel Thames* 23 *note*, A complete system of Tunnellism. *Ibid.* 14 The Tunnelist and his Friends. **1871** A. STEWART *Nether Lochaber* xxiii. (1883) 138 The velvet coated tunnelists live on worms and insect larvae. **1874** LADY HERBERT tr. *Hübner's Ramble* I. xi. (1878) 169 Having passed through the tunnelly trunk of one of these trees and the interior of the other [Big Trees of Mariposa]. **1882** *Sat. Rev.* 4 Mar. 261/1 The Tunnellites.. can say nothing but that their opponents are panic-mongers.

**Tu·nnel,** *v.* [f. prec. sb. Cf. F. *tonneler* to net partridges.]

**1.** † **a.** *trans.* ? To furnish with a tunnel-net, or a tubular passage resembling one. *Obs. rare*⁻¹.

**1577** B. GOOGE *Heresbach's Husb.* IV. (1586) 169 b, The windowes must be so placed..hauing a hole of sufficient widenesse ouer against them, well netted and tunnelled, in such sort as the Pigions may easely flee out and in at.

**b.** To catch (partridges) with a tunnel-net. Also *absol.*

**1687** [see TUNNELLING *vbl. sb.* 1]. **1718** *Free-thinker* No. 49 ₱ 8 A Poacher..has writ to a Friend to send him a Dozen of Second-hand Hoops into the Countrey, which by the Addition of a Cabbage-Net, will serve to Tunnel Partridges. **1840** BLAINE *Encycl. Rur. Sports* VII. iv. § 2623 By tunnelling them [partridges], that is, by taking them in what is called a tunnel net.

†**2.** To pour *in* through a funnel. *Obs.*

**1664** POWER *Exp. Philos.* I. 94 You may alter the height of the Mercurial Cylinder, as you do rudely or cautiously tunnel in the Quicksilver into the Tube.

†**3.** To form into, or like, a tube or pipe. *Obs.*

**1713** DERHAM *Phys.-Theol.* IV. xiii. (1727) 232 With what prodigious Subtilty do some foreign Birds..plat and weave the fibrous Parts of Vegetables together, and curiously tunnel them, and commodiously form them into Nests. *Ibid.* 235 *note*, These little Houses look coarse, and shew no great Artifice outwardly; but are well tunnelled, and made within with a hard tough Paste.

†**b.** (In earlier use.) To line a shaft or pit with tubbing: see TUB *v.* 2. *Obs.*

**1686** [see TUNNELLING 2 b].

**4.** *intr.* To make a tunnel; to excavate a passage under ground, or through some body or substance.

**1795** [see TUNNELLING *vbl. sb.* 3]. **1839** J. STERLING *Ess.*, etc. (1848) I. 322 As some great earth-monster, Johnson tunnels under ground, and heaves out rocks and tons of soil. **1887** *Century Mag.* Dec. 250/1 Then [I] began to tunnel into the huge bank of snow. **1889** *Nature* 11 Apr. 600/2 This had to be tunnelled through before an inch of progress could be made. **1897** *Allbutt's Syst. Med.* IV. 418 Below, the abscess has..tunnelled along the psoas muscle.

**b.** *trans.* To excavate, as a tunnel; to make (one's way) by boring or excavating. Also *fig.*

**1856** KANE *Arct. Expl.* II. xxi. 208 The stream, which tunnels its way out near the glacier-foot. **1856–1898** [see TUNNELLED 3]. **1884** J. TAIT *Mind in Matter* (1892) 114 In tunnelling out a theory of thought-production Mr. Spencer's light grows dim and expires.

**c.** To make a tunnel through; to perforate with or as with a tunnel.

**1865** RUSKIN *Sesame* i. § 35 You have tunnelled the cliffs of Lucerne by Tell's chapel. **1910** *Blackw. Mag.* Jan. 33/2 The cover warped and tunnelled by white ants. **1913** *Times* 6 Aug. 7/4 A more formidable rival to the plan of tunnelling the Channel is that of instituting a ferry service from Dover to Calais.

**Tunnelled, -eled** (tʊ·nĕld), *ppl. a.* [f. TUNNEL *v.* (and *sb.*) + -ED.]

†**1.** Formed like a pipe or tube. *Obs.*

**1713** DERHAM *Phys.-Theol.* IV. xiii. (1727) 234 *note*, The Phalænæ-Tribe..inhabit the tunnelled, convolved Leaves.

**b.** Perforated with a tube.

**1890** BILLINGS *Nat. Med. Dict.*, *Tunnelled*, term applied to sounds or other instruments having a short tube or tunnel, through which a fine bougie..passes.

**c.** Enclosed in a tunnel-like cavity.

**1901** *Westm. Gaz.* 13 May 5/3 A double-funnelled lifeboat, with a tunnelled screw, which will enable her to go in safety into shallow waters and amongst rocks, was launched at Harwich on Saturday.

†**2.** Having a tunnel (sense 2), as a chimney.

**1818** SCOTT *Br. Lamm.* x, The soot..showered down the huge tunnelled chimneys.

**3.** Excavated as, or by, a tunnel; formed by tunnelling.

**1856** KANE *Arct. Expl.* I. xxix. 380 An expansion of the tunnelled entrance made an appendage of..two feet more. **1861** WILSON & GEIKIE *Mem. E. Forbes* viii. 206 The caves and tunnelled caverns worn out by the Atlantic breakers. **1879** JAS. GRANT in *Cassell's Techn. Educ.* v. 286 A tunnelled staircase led to the roof. **1898** P. MANSON *Trop. Diseases* xxxiv. 525 In the latter [the brain] it [the distomum Ringesi] forms a sort of tunnelled tumour.

**Tunneller, -eler** (tʊ·nĕlə). [f. TUNNEL *v.* + -ER[1].]

**1.** One who catches birds with a tunnel-net. ? *Obs.*

**1611** COTGR., *Tonnelleur*, a Tunneller; a Taker of Partridges with a tunnell. **1706** PHILLIPS (ed. Kersey), *Tunnel*.., a sort of Net to catch Partridges. *Tunneller*, one that goes a Fowling with such a Net.

**2.** One who excavates a tunnel; *transf.* a burrowing animal.

**1860** P. P. CARPENTER in *Rep. Smithsonian Instit.* 1859, 213 Our little tunneler [*Gastrochæna*, a bivalve mollusc] sets to work with all the ardor of youth. **1871** PROCTOR *Light*

*Sc.* 153 Tunnellers from one end have sometimes..failed to meet those from the other.

**Tunnelling, -eling** (tʊ·nĕliŋ), *vbl. sb.* [f. TUNNEL *v.* (and *sb.*) + -ING[1].]

I. The action of TUNNEL *v.*

1. The use of a tunnel-net to catch birds.

1687 *Roy. Proclam.* 30 July in *Lond. Gaz.* No. 2267/1 That henceforward none presume,..to Kill or Destroy any Hare, Partridge [etc.] by Hunting, Hawking,..Tunnelling, Gins, or any way whatsoever. 1796 ANSTEY *Pleader's Guide* (1803) 129 Acts 'gainst tunneling and snaring. 1819 *Sporting Mag.* IV. 208 It is neither very dark nor very light, in tunnelling for partridges.

2. The work or process of making a tunnel; excavation of, or by, a tunnel.

1810 J. T. in *Risdon's Surv. Devon* p. xxix, This is the Tavistock canal, which is..attended with the grand operations of tunnelling. 1871 PROCTOR *Light Sc.* 153 Any inaccuracy in the direction of the two tunnellings would have been fatal to the success of the work.

*attrib.* 1812 SIR R. WILSON *Diary* in *Life* (1862) I. 377 The excavations are certainly some of nature's most surprising tunnelling achievements. 1871 *Daily News* 25 Apr., A new tunnelling machine..was exhibited at the meeting of the British Association last year.

†b. The lining of a shaft or pit with tubbing.

1686 PLOT *Staffordsh.* ii. 98 The Art of tunnelling much used in Cheshire to keep out the freshes.

II. 3. *concr.* Work of the nature of a tunnel; subterranean excavation for a canal, road, or railway; a tunnel, or tunnels collectively.

1795 J. PHILLIPS *Hist. Inland Navig.* Add. 131 Another navigable cut.., principally tunneling, will shorten the line four miles. 1798 *Monthly Mag.* July 74, 900 yards of tunneling. 1894 *Daily News* 22 Jan. 4/8 One of the fat, pink, repulsive-looking grubs, coiled up in one of the wide tunnellings that have ruined the tree.

†**Tunner** (tʊ·nəɹ). *Obs.* exc. *dial.* Forms: 4 tonour, 5 -owre, tunnowre, 6 tuner, 6– tunner. [f. TUN *sb.* or *v.* + -ER[1].]

1. An instrument for tunning liquor; a funnel.

1337 in Riley *Memorials* (1868) 200 [One iron spit, 3*d.*; one frying-pan, 1*d.* one] tonour, 1*d.* *c* 1440 *Promp. Parv.* 496/2 Tonowre, or fonel, *infusorium*. *Ibid.*, Tunnowre, *idem quod* tonowre. 1552–3 in *Midl. Counties Hist. Coll.* I. 233 A cherne a tuner a hopp iiij kytts. 1888 ELWORTHY *W. Somerset Word-bk.*, *Tunner*, a wooden funnel. 'Urn down, Jack, to farm' Perry's and borry he's tunner.

†2. One who tuns liquor. *Obs.*

1598 STOW *Surv.* 192 The successors of those Vintners.. were all incorporated by the name of wine tunners.

So **Tu·nnery,** a place in which liquor is tunned.

1796 MORSE *Amer. Geog.* II. 444 The tunnery, fishery, and salt produce a good revenue. 1869 W. MOLYNEUX *Burton on Trent* 250 [The cask] is thence transmitted to the tunnery to be refilled.

**Tunnified** (tʊ·nifəid), *ppl. a. humorous nonce-wd.* [f. TUN *sb.* + -I)FY + -ED[1].] Grown as big as a tun; very corpulent. (Cf. TUN-BELLIED.)

1806 R. CUMBERLAND *Memoirs* (1807) II. 72 Scarcely able to support himself on his tottering legs, now miserably tunnified.

**Tunning** (tʊ·niŋ), *vbl. sb.* [f. TUN *v.* + -ING[1].] The action of the verb TUN.

1. Putting into or storing in a tun or tuns. Also with *up*.

14.. [see *tunning-dish* in 3]. *a* 1529 SKELTON *El. Rummyng* 130 Wyth all theyr myght runnynge..To haue of her tunnynge. 1577 HARRISON *England* II. vi. in *Holinshed* I. 95/1 The bere..is commonlye of a yeare olde (or..of two yeres tunning or more). 1669 WORLIDGE *Syst. Agric.* vii. § 12. 120 The best Vessels for the tunning up of Cider. 1766 *Compl. Farmer* s. v. *Cyder*, At first tunning they do not fill their hogsheads to the bung, but leave an empty space to receive a pailful of fresh cyder from the press. 1822 IMISON *Sc. & Art* II. 159 It is mixed with yeast..in order to excite the vinous fermentation. This process is called tunning.

2. Of rabbits: see TUN *v.* 3.

1741 *Compl. Fam.-Piece* III. 510 The main Art of keeping these Creatures, is to preserve them from Tunning, or being Pot-belly'd.

3. *attrib.* Used in or for tunning liquor, as *tunning cask, tub, vessel*; †**tunning dish,** = TUN-DISH; †**tunning mell,** ?a 'mell' or mallet used to knock in the bung of a tun or cask.

1891 *Cent. Dict.*, **Tunning-cask*, a cask in which fermented ale is stored when racked off. 14.. *Voc.* in Wr.-Wülcker 574/15 *Colum*, a colyndore, or a *tunnyng dysch. 1611 COTGR., *Sibille*, a tunning and tasting dish in the time of Vintage. 1688 R. HOLME *Armoury* III. 320/1 A Tunning Dish, some term it a Fulling or Filling Dish; for by the help of it Liquor is poured into Vessels with small holes. 1362–3 *Durham Acc. Rolls* (Surtees) 565 In j *Tunnyngmell et ij duzayns de ciphis ligneis empt. ij d. ob. 1567 *Wills & Inv. N. C.* (Surtees) I. 266 A *tonning tubb, a tonn for bread. 1504 *Bury Wills* (Camden) 101 All brewyng ledys,..brasse bruyng vessels, *tonnyng vessells.

†**Tunnis,** *a. Her. Obs.* = TENNÉ. (? error.)

1625 MARKHAM *Souldiers Accid.* 31 Proper Colours, as Blacke, Blew, Red, Greene, Purple, Tunnis, and Ermine. *Ibid.* 32 Tunnis, or Tawnie, signifieth Merit, or desert, and a foe to Ingratitude. 1661 PEACHAM *Compl. Gent.* (ed. 3) 156.

†**Tu·nnish,** *a. Obs. rare*[−1]. In 6 tonnish. [f. TUN *sb.* + -ISH[1].] Somewhat like a tun or cask; very corpulent.

*a* 1529 SKELTON *El. Rummyng* 99 She is a tonnish gyb.

**Tunny** (tʊ·ni). Forms: 6 tuny(e, thunie, tunnye, 6–7 tony, tonny, tunnie, 7 tonnie, tunie, tunney, thinnye, 8–9 thunny, 7– tunny. [ad. F. *thon* (14th c.), ad. Pr. *ton*, or It. *tonno*, L. *thunnus* (*thynnus*), ad. Gr. *θύννος*, in same sense; the termination *-ie*, *-y* seems to be only English, perh. orig. diminutive, as in *Johnnie*.] A scombroid fish of the genus *Orcynus*, esp. the common tunny, *O. thynnus*, which has been fished from ancient times in the Mediterranean and Atlantic; it is one of the largest of food-fishes, often reaching a length of ten feet.

1530 PALSGR. 282/1 Tonny. 1555 EDEN *Decades* 202 The Tunnye which is a great and good fysshe. 1556 WITHALS *Dict.* (1568) 8 b/2 A tony, *thinnus*. 1565–73 COOPER *Thesaurus, Auxumae*, the yong fish, comming of the spawne of Thunie. 1591 HARINGTON *Orl. Fur.* VI. xxxvi, The Dolphin strong, the Tunny good of tast, The Mullet, Sturgeon, Samon (princely fish). 1601 HOLLAND *Pliny* IX. xv. I. 242 The Tunies are exceeding great fishes: we have seene some of them to weigh fifteen talents, and the taile to be two cubits broad and a span. 1617 MORYSON *Itin.* III. 47 The fish called a Thinnye of Calcedonia. 1760–72 tr. *Juan & Ulloa's Voy.* (ed. 3) II. 308 We now..saw the Tunny and a great many flying-fish. 1781 GIBBON *Decl. & F.* xvii. II. 10 *note*, Among a variety of different species, the Pelamides, a sort of Thunnies, were the most celebrated. 1834 *Nat. Philos.* III. *Phys. Geog.* 50/2 (U.K.S.) Tunnies..migrate.. every year from the Atlantic Ocean to the Mediterranean.

b. *attrib.* and *Comb.*, as *tunny fish* (= tunny), *-fisher, -fishery, -net*; *tunny-faced* adj.

1901 *19th Cent.* Oct. 641 The stupid or *tunny-faced man. 1552 HULOET, *Tunye fyshe when it exceadeth not a foote in length, *limaria*. 1620 J. MASON *New-found-land* 5, I haue also seene Tonnie fish in Newland. 1796 MORSE *Amer. Geog.* II. 428 The fisheries on the coast of Sardinia produce upwards of 60000 scudi in the article of tunny-fish. 1889 C. EDWARDES *Sardinia* 350 A veteran *tunny-fisher. 1765 SMOLLETT *Trav.* (1766) II. xxxix. 225 Pliny says it [Antibes] was famous for its *tunny-fishery. 1901 *19th Cent.* Oct. 645 Steaming out in our little launch to the fixed *tunny-nets.

Hence **Tu·nnyhood** (*nonce-wd.* after *manhood*), the state of a full-grown tunny.

1853 BADHAM *Halieut.* 193 An unfortunate habit of squinting acquired by the young cordylas, and not corrected by the parents as their offspring advanced to thunnyhood.

**Tuno,** variant of TUNU.

†**Tu·nsion.** *Obs.* Also 6 tonsion. [n. of action on L. type **tunsio*, from *tundĕre* to beat.] The action, or an act, of beating or striking.

*c* 1440 *Alphabet of Tales* 390 Þan þe monkis with all þer hertis prayed for hym, & did of þer clothis & bete þer selfe for hym, & made tunsions on þer breste. 1526 *Pilgr. Perf.* (W. de W. 1531) 60 b, But if thou fynde the gylty, gyue a tonsion on thy brest. 1532 MORE *Confut. Tindale* Wks. 350/1 He diuers times repeted those wordes with tunsions and knockinges vppon his brest.

†**Tu·nster.** *Sc. Obs. rare.* [f. TUN *v.* + -STER.] ?An officer who superintended the tunning of liquor.

1610 in J. Davidson *Inverurie* vi. (1878) 195 Appointit taisters tunsters of aill within the bruch. *Ibid.*, Who evere refuses to gif lawful obedience to the tunsters or Bailis.

‖**Tunu** (tū·nu). Also tuno, toonu. [Carib name in Honduras.] A Central American tree, *Castilloa Tunu*, Hemsley (N.O. *Artocarpaceæ*), which yields a non-elastic caoutchouc called *tunu gum* (or *tunu*). (Other species produce rubber.)

1883 D. MORRIS *Colony Brit. Honduras* 74 Next to cacao, the most interesting plant found wild in the forests of British Honduras is the indiarubber-tree, called by the natives 'Toonu'. 1886 SIR J. D. HOOKER in *Trans. Linnean Soc.* Ser. II. II. 209 Three forms or species of Castilloa..two of these are named Ule.., the third is named Tunu, and said to yield a gutta-percha. 1894 *Outing* (U.S.) XXIII. 354/1 On the smooth bamboo lie thick piles of tuno-bark blankets. *Ibid.* 356/2 Tuno gum, with which wicked huleros are wont to adulterate their rubber.

**Tuny** (tiū·ni), *a. colloq.* Also tuney. [f. TUNE *sb.* + -Y.] Characterized by 'tune' or melody; melodious: sometimes depreciative.

1885 *Graphic* 21 Feb. 190/3 Oh, Mozart!..So very tune-y, isn't he? 1887 *Twin Soul* vii, Music that is not 'tuny' is not to my taste.

Hence **Tu·niness.**

1905 *Athenæum* 5 Aug. 169/3 Patrick Hannay..has a pretty, if thin, tunefulness (we might rather say tuniness). 1909 *Daily Chron.* 8 June 4/7 Italian music..has shape, form, symmetry, in its tuniness.

**Tuo,** obs. form of TWO. **Tuoche, tuouche,** obs. ff. TOUCH. **Tuo-name**: see TO-NAME.

**Tup** (tʊp), *sb.* Forms: 4 tope, *Sc.* toupe, 4–6 tupe, 5–7 tuppe, (6 tuepe, touppe, towpe), 6–7 tup, 6, 8–9 *Sc.* tip, 6– tup; 8–9 *Sc.* and *north. dial.* tuip (tüp), teep, teap, toop. [Origin unknown; chiefly Sc. and north. Eng. App. etymologically *tōp*, which would regularly give *toop* (tūp) in north. Eng., and (tüp) or (tö̆p) in Sc.: cf. *bóc*, *bōk*, *book*, Sc. *buik*. (Skeat suggests that it may be a transferred use of Norw. and Sw. *tupp* 'cock', said to be the same word as TOP *sb*[1].)]

1. A male sheep; a ram.

13.. *Ballad Scot. Wars* xxvii. in Ritson *Anc. Songs & Ball.* (1877) 38 A Toupe sal stande agayn ay Bare. *c* 1340 [see *tup-head* in 2]. *a* 1400–50 *Alexander* 5566 Þai ware hedously hoge & horned as Tupis. *c* 1440 *Pallad. on Husb.* VIII. 77 The tuppe is chosun fair of altitude Ywombe[d] side. 1510 STANBRIDGE *Vocab.* (W. de W.) C v b, *Aries*, a tup or a ram. 1570 LEVINS *Manip.* 140/18 A Tip, shepe, *aries*. 1590 *Shuttleworths' Acc.* (Chetham Soc.) 58 A touppe iij[s] viij[d]. *Ibid.* 61 Seven towpes. 1594 *Ibid.* 118 Three tupes. 1600 *Ibid.* 123 Towe old tupps. 1653 GATAKER *Vind. Annot. Jer.* 61 To run ful but, as rams, or tups, use to do, one against another. 1771 *Usef. Proj.* in *Ann. Reg.* 107/1 He sells no tups, but lets them at from 5 guineas to 30 guineas for the season. 1804 SCOTT *Let. to Ellis* 19 May, in *Lockhart*, Long sheep, and short sheep, and tups, and gimmers, and hogs, and dinmonts, had made a perfect sheepfold of my understanding. 1903 *Times* 12 Feb. 12/4 Heavy sheep 7½d. to 8d.; ewes and tups 6d. to 7d.

b. *transf.* Applied to a person.

1652 SHIRLEY *Honoria & Mam.* III. i, Cuckolds' sconce, Or haven, to which all the tups strike sail. 1694 MOTTEUX *Rabelais* IV. viii, The Ship being clear'd of Dingdong and his Tups. 1785 GROSE *Dict. Vulg. T.*, *Tup*, a ram; figuratively a cuckold. 1815 SCOTT *Guy M.* xxxvi, 'He 'll be a Teviotdale tup, tat ane', said the chairman, 'tat's for keeping ta crown o' ta causeway tat gate'. 1880 EBEN. SMITH *Verses* 68 Douce old tups.

c. *transf.* (*a*) A pavier's mallet. (*b*) The head of a forge-hammer or steam-hammer. (*c*) The falling weight of a pile-engine.

1848 'TOM TREDDLEHOYLE' *Bairnsla Foak's Ann.* 46 (E.D.D.) Little undersized munkeys, not much heigher than tups at thay knock boolders daan we i't street. 1873 *Iron* 5 Apr. 356/1 A 45-cwt. double-acting Nasmyth's steam hammer, with wrought iron tup. 1884 *Building News* 15 Aug. 242/3 Ram, tup, monkey, are names variously given by workmen to the block..which is let fall upon the head of the pile. 1907 *Daily Chron.* 22 Mar. 9/5 The heavy 'tup' comes down smack! on the bar.

2. *attrib.* and *Comb.*, as *tup-breeder, -head, -horn* (in quot. *attrib.*), *-mutton, -seller*; *tup-headed*, adj.; also **tup-eild, -eill** *a. Sc.* [EILD, GELD, YELD *adjs.*], of a ewe: barren; **tup fair,** a fair or annual market mainly for the sale of rams; **tup-hog,** a male lamb from its weaning till its first shearing; **tup-lamb,** a he-lamb; **tup-man,** one who keeps and supplies rams for breeding purposes; **tup running**: see quot.; **tup society,** a sheep-breeding association; **tup-yeld, -yield** *a.* = *tup-eild*.

1831 *Sutherland Farm Rep.* 82 in *Libr. Usef. Knowl.*, *Husb.* III, In order to suit the market, the *tup-breeders preserved only the finest of their young store. 1823 *Farmer's Mag.* 278 At the lambing time..there were found 99 *tup-eild ewes and gimmers. 1844 STEPHENS *Bk. Farm* II. 38 If she has failed being in lamb she is said to be a tup-eill gimmer. *c* 1340 *Peter & Paul* 248 in Horstm. *Altengl. Leg.* (1881) 79/1 When þe heuede was smiten awaie, A *tope-heued on þe erde laie. 1816 SCOTT *Antiq.* vi, Did you ever hear such an old *tup-headed ass? 1591 *Vestry Bks.* (Surtees) 30 Shepe remainynge in this parishe...At North Pittington a *tuppe hogge. 1844 STEPHENS *Bk. Farm* II. 38 After a lamb has been weaned, until the first fleece is shorn from its back..a female is called a *ewe-hogg*, a male a *tup-hogg*. 1718 RAMSAY *Christ's Kirk Gr.* III. iii, Twa *toop-horn-spoons down Maggie lays. *a* 1722 LISLE *Husb.* (1757) 313 They used..to cut their *tup-lambs early within six weeks old. 1782 BURNS *Death Poor Mailie* 43 My poor toop-lamb, my son an' heir. 1844 STEPHENS *Bk. Farm* II. 613 Tup-lambs are allowed to retain their full tails until a year old, in order to strengthen the back. 1790 W. MARSHALL *Midl. C.* I. 429 Getting Rams, to be let out again to inferior *tupmen, as ram-getters. 1844 STEPHENS *Bk. Farm* II. 100 *Tup-mutton..is always hard, of disagreeable flavour, and in autumn not eatable. 1785 GROSE *Dict. Vulg. T.*, **Tup running*,..in Derbyshire, a ram whose tail is well soaped and greased is turned out to the multitude, any one that can take him by the tail and hold him fast is to have him for his own. 1831 *Sutherland Farm Rep.* 82 in *Libr. Usef. Knowl.*, *Husb.* III, To the surprise of the *tup-sellers..nothing could be sold [at the fair] but tups of coarse quality. 1799 A. YOUNG *Agric. Lincoln.* 309 In 1796 there was a new *Tup Society established at Lincoln, for the encouragement of breeding. 1825 JAMIESON, **Tup-yield*, *tup-eild*, adj.

**Tup** (tʊp), *v.* [f. prec. sb.]

1. *trans.* Of the ram: To copulate with (the ewe); also *transf.*

1604 SHAKS. *Oth.* I. i. 89 An old blacke Ram Is tupping your white Ewe. 1641 BEST *Farm. Bks.* (Surtees) 28 Those that have theire ewes tupped betimes. 1694 MOTTEUX *Rabelais* V. (1737) 222 They will not be ridden, tupp'd, and ramm'd. 1844 STEPHENS *Bk. Farm* III. 1108 Most of the ewes will be tupped during the second week the tup is amongst them. 1861 *Times* 16 Oct., Ewes are tupped on grass, have hay on the winter pasture in case of deep snow, lamb in the same field, and are also fattened off on grass.

b. To beget (a lamb); in quot. *pass.*

1721 KELLY *Scot. Prov.* 307 The Lamb where it's tipped, and the Ewe where she's clipped. A proverbial Rule about Tythes; signifying that the Lamb shall pay Tythes in the Place where the Ewe was when she took the Ram, but the old Sheep where they were shorn.

c. To put (ewes) to the ram. *dial.*

1799 A. YOUNG *Agric. Lincoln.* 318 Mr. Skipwith of Alesby tups 1400 ewes. *Ibid.* 337 Little farmers, who tup under 60 ewes.

2. *intr.* a. Of the ewe: To admit the ram. b. Of the ram: To copulate. Also *transf.*

1549 CHALONER *Erasm. Praise Folly* F ij b, These old women..will euer yet haue this prouerbe (lyfe is lyfe) in their mouthes, still plaie the wantons, and still be tuppyng. 1614 C. BROOKE *Eglogues* F vj b, Whiles thy Rams do Tup, thy Ewes do twyn. 1641 BEST *Farm. Bks.* (Surtees) 3 The tuppes goinge allwayes with them, some of the ewes will tuppe sooner, and some later. 1721 KELLY *Scot. Prov.* 306 Tip when you will, you shall Lamb with the Leave [= lave].

†3. *trans.* To furnish with horns like a ram's; cf. HORN *v.* 2. *Obs. rare*[−1].

1608 DAY *Law Trickes* I. i. A iv, She was my wife and by her meanes, my head Was fayrely tupt, and you will buy a Lanthorne: Bespeake my sconce, tis ready hornd and all.

4. *trans.* and *intr.* 'To but like a ram' (J.).

1654 [see *tupping* vbl. sb. below]. 1847–78 in HALLIWELL. 1876 *Mid-Yorks. Gloss.*, *Tup*,..to butt.

Hence **Tupped** (tɒpt) *ppl. a.*, **Tu·pping** *vbl. sb.* (also *attrib.*).

**1654** GAYTON *Pleas. Notes* III. iv. 89 Ramms taken for Gyants,..the Wethers bels for Drumms, and their taile clouts, their colours, their tupping and rutting for the maine Battalia. **1799** A. YOUNG *Agric. Lincoln.* 318 Never give turnips to tupped ewes. **1844** STEPHENS *Bk. Farm* II. 599 A shepherd..has attentively observed the tupping, and marked the reckoning of every ewe. **1886** C. SCOTT *Sheep-Farming* 80 The ewes will have been marked at tupping-time for each week's lambing.

‖ **Tupaia** (tupai·ă). *Zool.* [mod.L., ad. Malay توفي *tūpai* squirrel, in توفي تانه *tūpai tāna* ground-squirrel.] A genus of insectivorous mammals, typical of the family *Tupaiidæ*, including the Banxring, *Tupaia peguana*, of Burma and Pegu, and the Tana tupai, *Tupaia tana*, of Borneo, etc. (sometimes erroneously called the *Tana*).

**1820** SIR T. S. RAFFLES in *Linnæan Trans.* (1822) XIII. 256 Tupaia...Snout elongated...Habit and tail of a Squirrel. *Ibid.* 257 Tupaia Tana. **1824** HORSFIELD *Zool. Res. Java* s.v. *Tupaia*, The Bangsring fell under my observation during an early period of my researches in Java. **1847** CARPENTER *Zool.* § 179 The last family..*Tupaidae*, at present contains only one genus, the *Tupaia* or *Banxring*..of which only three species are known. **1868** OWEN *Vertebr. Anim.* III. xxx. 428 The Tupaias and some of the snouted-shrews.

‖ **Tupak-grass** (tū·păk grɑs). [f. the Maori name + GRASS *sb.*[1]] A New Zealand grassy sedge, *Carex appressa*.

**1884** MILLER *Plant-n.*, *Carex appressa*, Otago Tupak-grass. **1901** A. TROTTER *E. Galloway Sk.* 319/2 He advocated a plan for making tracts of sand productive by planting them with Tupac grass.

‖ **Tupakihi.** [Maori.] A small tree of New Zealand, *Coriaria ruscifolia*; = TOOT *sb.*[5]

**1867** E. SAUTER tr. *Hochstetter's N. Zealand* vii. 139 *note*, The Toot-plant, Tutu or Tupakihi of the Maoris (*Coriaria sarmentosa*, Forst. = *C. ruscifolia*, L.). **1883** J. HECTOR *Handbk. N. Zealand* 131 Tupakihi, Tree Tutu.

**Tupe**, obs. form of TUP.

† **Tupee**, obs. var. TOUPEE.

**1751** ELIZA HEYWOOD *Betsy Thoughtless* II. 163 A fine fellow, with his tupee wig, and laced waistcoat.

‖ **Tupelo** (tū·pėlo). Also 8 tupelow, 9 tupeloo, tupola. [N. Amer. Ind.] Native name of trees of the North American genus *Nyssa* (N.O. *Alangiaceæ* or *Nyssaceæ*), large trees growing in swamps or on river banks in the southern states; esp. *N. villosa* or *multiflora* (also called Black or Sour Gum, and Pepperidge), and the large tupelo or tupelo gum (*N. uniflora*), which produces a light tough timber. Also *attrib.*, as *tupelo-gum*, *-swamp*, *-tree*; **tupelo-tent**, a surgical tent made of the spongy wood of the root of the tupelo.

**1730** MORTIMER in *Phil. Trans.* XXXVI. 431 The Tupelo Tree. *Ibid.* 434 The Water Tupelo. **1756** P. COLLINSON in Darlington *Mem.* (1849) 202 Billy's drawing and painting of the Tupelo, is fine. **1765** in W. Stork *Acc. East Florida* (1766) 79 The low lands are partly cypress and tupelow swamps. **1816** W. DARBY *Descr. Louisiana* iv. 62 The tupeloo is known in Louisiana by the popular name of olive. **1864** LOWELL *Fireside Trav.* 42 Maple, and the rarer tupelo with downward limbs. **1865** PARKMAN *Champlain* ix. (1875) 305 The garnet hue of the young oaks, the bonfire blaze of the tupelo at the water's edge. **1885** in *Milnor* (Dakota) *Free Press* 25 Apr. 5/5 The tupelo-gum and the willow-oak are timbers that are destined to a commercial value never until recently dreamed of. **1900** W. D. HOWELLS in *Scribner's Mag.* Sept. 367/2 He wished to show me a tupelo-tree.

**Tuph, Tupha**, obs. ff. TUFF, TUFA. **Tuphan**, obs. var. TYPHOON. **Tuphlo-**: see TYPHLO-.

**Tuphramancy**, error for TEPHROMANCY.

‖ **Tupi** (tū·pī). A native language widely spoken in Brazil, which has yielded various names of animals, plants, etc. Also **Tu·pian.**

**1882** *Athenæum* 9 Sept. 341/2 The widely diffused Tupi language, spoken throughout a great part of Brazil.

‖ **Tupik** (tū·pik). Also **topek.** [Eskimo of Alaska.] A hut or tent of skins used by Eskimo as a summer residence.

**1898** *Geogr. Jrnl.* Nov. 499 These people [Eskimo], who live in *tupiks* (tents or huts of skin) in summer, and in *igloos*, partly excavated, partly stone-built dwellings, in winter. **1900** *Scribner's Mag.* Sept. 297/2 There were three or four tupiks, or sealskin tents, pitched upon the turf at the foot of the talus.

‖ **Tupina·mbis.** [mod.L., said to have been coined by Lamarck, perh. f. TUPI.] A genus of South American lizards.

Misapplied by Geoffrey to the Egyptian Monitor (*Varanus Niloticus*), whence app. Lytton's use, quot. 1863.

**1839** *Penny Cycl.* XV. 332/1 Cuvier divides them [the Monitors] into two groups, and Fitzinger into three, under the names of *Tupinambis*, *Varanus*, and *Psammosaurus*. **1863** LD. LYTTON *Ring Amasis* II. II. i, The museum..presented a very respectable arrangement of gems, scarabaei, sphinxes, stuffed crocodiles, and tupinambes.

**Tuppat**, obs. Sc. f. TIPPET.

† **Tuppee**, obs. var. TOUPEE.

**1778** B'NESS DE BODE *Lett.* 27 Jan. (1900) 10 A dwarf man with an immense *tuppée*.

**Tuppence, -pens**: see TWOPENCE.

**Tuppe·rian**, *a.* and *sb.* **a.** *adj.* Of, belonging to, or in the style of Martin F. Tupper's Proverbial Philosophy (1838–42). **b.** *sb.* An admirer of Tupper. So **Tu·pperish** *a.*, **Tu·pperism**, **Tu·pperize** *v.*

**1858** O. W. HOLMES *Aut. Breakf.-t.* xi. (1891) 271 Whether I dipped them from the ocean of Tupperian wisdom,..I cannot say. **1866** *Reader* No. 168. 271/3 Tupperian pretentiousness and moralizations. **1869** BARING-GOULD *Orig. Relig. Belief* (1878) II. xx. 380 Truth must be Tupperish—allow me the word,—or public opinion will not tolerate it. **1870** *Observer* 13 Nov., Tupperising in deerskin breeches is not an intellectual frolic that we can contemplate with patience. **1905** *Daily Chron.* 20 June 3/3 Our fathers found entertainment and even worldly wisdom in the Tupperisms of yesterday.

‖ **Tupsee** (tɒ·psī). *E. Indies.* Also tupsy, -ey, and more etymologically spelt *tăpsī*. [a. Hindī *tapsī*, more fully *tapsī machh* :—Skr. *tapasya matsya*, i. e. fish produced from heat, or in the spring season *Phalguna* (Feb. and March) when the mango blossoms.] A fish of the genus *Polynemus*, allied to the mullet, 8 or 9 inches long, found in the Ganges and Irawadi; a variety from the estuaries of the Hooghli is considered a great delicacy at Calcutta. Also called MANGO-*fish*.

**1839** CANTOR in *Proc. Zool. Soc.* July 116 The species best known is the *Polynemus risua*, Hamilton; *Pol. longifilis*, Cuvier; the Tupsee or Mango Fish of the Anglo-Indians. **1858** SIMMONDS *Dict. Trade*, *Mango-fish*,..esteemed as a delicacy in India, where it is also called the Tupsee. *Ibid.*, Tupsee, Tupsey.

**Tupsiturvie**, obs. form of TOPSY-TURVY.

**Tupto-ing** (tiū·ptoˌiŋ), *pres. pple. nonce-wd.* In quot. tuptowing. [f. Gr. τύπτω, 1st pers. pres. ind. of τύπτειν (as the verb commonly learned first) + -ING[2].] Conjugating τύπτω; 'grinding' at Greek (and Latin) verbs.

[**1762** STERNE *Tr. Shandy* V. xlii, Seven long years..τυπτω-ing it, at Greek and Latin.] **1824** SCOTT *Redgauntlet* ch. xiv, Jack Hadaway..was 'tuptowing' away with a dozen of wretched boys.

**Tuque** (tiūk, tūk). *Canadian.* [a. Canadian Fr., f. F. *toque*, TOQUE.] A knitted stocking-cap tapered and closed at both ends, one end being tucked into the other to form the cap; formerly the characteristic winter head-dress of the Canadian 'habitant'; now chiefly worn as part of a toboggan or snow-shoe club costume.

**1871** W. G. BEERS in *Scribner's Monthly* Sept. 454/2 The snow-shoe clubs have adopted the tuque. **1887** *Cornh. Mag.* Mar. 267 The real head-dress of the snowshoer being the knitted woollen *tuque*, a bag-shaped cap,..suggesting..the headgear of the Royal Artillery. **1894** *Outing* (U.S.) XXIII. 358 The Snow Shoer's Song. Tighten the tuque, and girdle the sash, Lads and lasses, the snow shoes lash. **1909** *Westm. Gaz.* 23 Feb. 8/3 Their uniforms were blanket costumes, with tuques, mocassins and snowshoes.

**Tuquheit**, Sc. dial. var. TEWHIT, lapwing.

**1553** *Burgh Rec. Edinb.* II. 185 The best tuquheit iij. d.

‖ **Tu quoque** (tiūkwōu·kwī). [L., lit. 'thou also', = Eng. slang 'you're another!'] An argument which consists in retorting a charge upon one's accuser. Also *attrib.*

[**1614** J. COOKE (*title*) Greenes Tu quoque, Or, The Cittie Gallant. *Ibid.* E ij b, *Rash*...M. Bubble, God saue you. *Bub.* Tu quoque Sir. *Ibid.* G j b, *Bub*...I want the *Bone Ioure*, and the *Tu quoques*, Which yonder Gentleman has.] **1671** SHADWELL *Humorist* II. 28 Nay Sir, I say nothing, Mum is the Italian *tu quoque* word. **1838** LYTTON *Alice* III. iv, No man knew better the rhetorical effect of the *tu quoque* form of argument. **1874** J. O. DYKES *Relations Kingd. to World* II. 107 The tu quoque rejoinder, 'Physician heal thyself', is in its place here. *a* **1903** 'MERRIMAN' *Last Hope* v, I leave myself open to a *tu quoque*, I know.

**Turacin** (tiū°·răsin). *Chem.* [f. mod.L. *Turac-us* TOURACO + -IN[1].] A crimson animal pigment, found by Professor A. H. Church in the wing-feathers of about 26 species of birds of the genera *Turacus*, *Gallirex*, and *Musophaga*, confined to the Æthiopic region of Central Africa; closely allied to hæmoglobin, but free from iron, and containing over 7 per cent. of copper.

**1868** A. H. CHURCH in *Student & Intell. Observ.* I. 161 Turacine, a new animal pigment containing copper. **1869** — in *Phil. Trans.* CLIX. 627 Researches on Turacin. **1885** *Riverside Nat. Hist.* (1888) IV. 5 Another red [pigment], turacin, causes the magnificent red on the wings of the Musophagidæ.

**Turaco, -ko, -koo**, var. TOURACO.

**Turacoverdin** (tiū°:răkoˌvɜ·ɹdin). *Chem.* [f. as TURACIN; cf. *biliverdin*.] A green colouring-matter occurring in the feathers of some Touracos.

**1885** *Riverside Nat. Hist.* (1888) IV. 5 A really green pigment has only been found in the touracos—hence the name turacoverdin. **1892** A. H. CHURCH in *Phil. Trans.* CLXXXIII. 512 Dr. C. F. W. Krukenberg..has described a green colouring matter obtained from the green feathers of *Turacus corythaix*, and of other plantain-eaters, by the employment of a 2 per cent. caustic soda-solution as the solvent. He calls this pigment 'turacoverdin', and..states that it contains 'much iron, but no great quantity of copper and manganese'.

**Turanian** (tiurē¹·niăn), *sb.* and *a.* [f. Pers. توران *Turān*, name of the realm beyond the Oxus, used by Firdusi *c* 1000 in opposition to *Irān* or Persia. In 1840 Pott (Ersch & Gruber II. xviii. 1) contrasts *Turan* with *arisch* (Aryan).]

**A.** *sb.*

**1.** A member of any of the races speaking the 'Turanian' or Ural-Altaic languages: see B.

**1777** J. RICHARDSON *Dict. Persian*, etc., Dissert. p. xxx/2 The Tartars, Scythians, or Turanians. **1854** BUNSEN *Christianity* IV. 26 The native religion of the Turanian is Shamanism. **1861** HULME tr. *Moquin-Tandon* I. v. 32 Turanians: Physiognomy: Mongol. Language: Agglutinate. Area: Mongolia, Mantshuria. **1888** G. SMITH *S. Hislop* vii. (1889) 182 Brahmanism assimilated to itself the cults of the Turanians and Sudras.

**2.** The so-called Turanian languages collectively.

**1908** *Christian Express* 1 Apr. 59/1 He states that in Bantu, as in Turanian (by-the-bye, we would be thankful to know what is Turanian) there is a regular phonetic interchange k=p=b=f=d!

**B.** *adj.*

**1.** Applied loosely to a group or supposed 'family' of languages, originally applied to all or nearly all of Asiatic origin that are neither Aryan nor Semitic; in later use nearly = URAL-ALTAIC.

**1854** BUNSEN *Christianity* VI. 64 All the languages of Asia and Europe which are neither Semitic nor Arian. I ventured in 1847 to write all these under the name Turanian. **1860** FARRAR *Orig. Lang.* 199 Languages which belong to neither of these two..families have been classed together under the name of the Turanian, Nomadic, or Allophylian family. **1865** — *Chapt. Lang.* 29 Various sporadic families, which some would call Turanian. **1892** WHITNEY *Max Müller* 49 The old 'Turanian' aggregation, which..has for a generation been a stumbling-block in the way of science.

**2.** Applied to the peoples speaking these languages.

**1859** MAX MÜLLER *Sc. Lang.* (1861) I. 276 The name Turanian is used in opposition to Aryan and is applied to the nomadic races of Asia as opposed to the agricultural or Aryan races. **1874** BANCROFT *Footpr. Time* i. 30 Turanian means 'outside', or 'barbarian'. **1890** J. G. FRAZER *Gold. Bough* (1913) I. iv. 179 The Magyars belong to the great Turanian family of mankind.

‖ **Turani·ra, tourane·ro.** [Native name in Guiana.] A small tree of Brazil and Guiana, *Humirium floribundum*, the wood of which, **turanira-wood**, is used for rafters; its bark is greatly esteemed as a perfume, and when wounded a fragrant yellow balsam, termed in Brazil balsam of Umiri, flows from it. See also quot. 1884.

**1862** *List Contrib. Brit. Guiana to Lond. Exhib.* in Veness *El Dorado* (1866) App. 136 Turanira, Touranero, or Bastard Bully-tree (*Humirium floribundum*, Mart.). Used for framing timber, spokes, &c. **1884** MILLER *Plant-n.*, *Turanira-wood*, the wood of *Bumelia retusa*.

**Turat**, obs. Sc. form of TURRET.

**Turb** (tɜ̄ɹb). *Obs.* exc. *Hist.* Forms: 4–6 **turbe**, 5–6, 9 **tourbe**, 7–9 **turb.** [a. F. *tourbe*, OF. *torbe* (11th c. in Hatz.-Darm.) also *turbe*, ad. L. *turba* crowd.] A crowd, swarm, heap; a troop; also, a group or clump of trees.

*c* **1330** R. BRUNNE *Chron.* (1810) 188 In þe secund turbe was maister Coradyn. *c* **1480** *St. Ursula* vii, This holy turbe to Colen made theyr retourne. *c* **1489** CAXTON *Blanchardyn* xlix. 191 They came so fast by and by, And by so grete tourbes and hepes, that [etc.]. **1509** WATSON *Ship of Fools* xx. (1517) F ij, A grete turbe of foles fleeth to our shyppe. **1618** DEKKER *Owles Almanack* 21 Every heddge and quick-set, every knot, and turb of trees. **1694** MOTTEUX *Rabelais* v. (1737) 230 When the Turb is once accumulate. [**1886** *Punch* 20 Mar. 144 His front by nasiterge occult To serve from muscan turb his vult.] **1900** A. LANG *Hist. Scot.* I. vi. 149 John Knox or Bothwell would come to his trial at the head of an armed tourbe, or gathering of partisans.

**Turban** (tɜ̄·ɹbăn), *sb.* Forms: α. 6 **tolipane, -epan, tolliban, tulbant, (tal-), 6–7 tuliban, tolibant, -e, tulipan, 7 tulipant, -e, tullipant, -band, tul-, (tel-)-bent, dulipan, tulban**; β. 6 **torbant, turribant, turbanto, 6–9 turbant, -band, (6–7 -bante, -bent, 7 -bond, -bat)**; γ. 7 **turben, -bine, -bane, 6– turban.** [Altered form of Pers. دلبند *dulbănd* or دولبند *dōlbănd*, in vulgar Turkish pronounced *tulbant*, *tul(i)pant*, *toli-*, whence OIt. *tolipante*, *tolipano*, mod.It., Sp., Pg. *turbante*; obs. F. *tolliban* (15th c.), *tulban*, *turbant* (Cotgr.), F. *turban*; early mod.Du. *turbant* (Kilian), Du. *tulband*, Ger., Da., Sw. *turban*. It is not clear in which language the change of *tul-* to *tur-* took place; it may have been in S.W. India, or in Portuguese; we find it first in Hickock's translation of Cesar Frederick, who cites it from the Portuguese Indies. *Tulipant*, *turbant*, were the most usual English forms in 17th c.; *turban* was used by Johnson and Gibbon. See also TULIP, which goes back to the same word.]

**1.** A head-dress of Moslem origin worn by men of Eastern nations, consisting of a cap round which is wound a long piece of linen, cotton, or silk.

(In quot. 1561, the tarboosh or fez as distinct from its wrapping.)

α. **1561** A. JENKINSON *Voy.* (Hakl. Soc.) I. 132 Upon his head was a tolipane with a sharpe end standing upwards halfe a yard long, of riche cloth of golde, wrapped about with a piece of India silke of twentie yards long, wrought with golde, and on the left side of his tolipane stood a plume of feathers. **1585** T. WASHINGTON tr. *Nicholay's Voy.* III. xx. 108 Kinsemen of Mahomet..doe weare a green Tulbant. *Ibid.* IV. iv. 116 Their custome is to weare a Talbant high topped before. **1588** in Hakluyt *Voy.* (1600) III. 821 Died linen cloth folded vp like vnto a Turkes Tuliban. **1589** PUTTEN-

HAM *Eng. Poesie* III. xxiv. (Arb.) 291 The Turke and Persian to weare great tolibants of ten, fifteene, and twentie elles of linnen a peece vpon their heads. **1596** DANETT tr. *Comines* (1614) 296 They were not vppon their head such a great roule of linnen as the Turkes doe, called Tolliban. **1597** GERARDE *Herbal* 117 Tulipan, Tolepan [see TULIP 1]. **1600** J. PORY tr. *Leo's Africa* III. 160 On their heads they weare a blacke dulipan. **1603** KNOLLES *Hist. Turks* (1621) 201 Upon his tombe lieth..a little Turkish tulipant, much differing from those great turbants which the Turks now weare. **1613** PURCHAS *Pilgrimage* III. xi. 255 With a great Tullipant on his head. *Ibid.* xiv. 267 These weare greene Tulipans, which colour none else may weare, and that onely on their head. **1617** MORYSON *Itin.* III. 174 A round globe, which in their tongue is called a Tulbent. **1652** H. L'ESTRANGE *Amer. no Jewes* 57 A Cap of linnen somewhat full like a Turk's Turband or Tulliband. **1653** GREAVES *Seraglio* 129 The name of the stuff (as we call ours lawn, cambrick, holland, &c.) is *Telbent*; whence we (falsly) call that which a Turk wears a Turbant, using the name of the stuff for the thing made up. **1662** J. DAVIES tr. *Olearius' Voy. Ambass.* 314 The Coeffure of the Men, which they call Mendils, and the Turks, Tulbans, or Turbants, is made of Cotton cloath, or some silk Stuff,..of several Colours. [**1686** tr. *Chardin's Coronat. Solyman* 40 A *Dhul-bandt* (which our Writers.. erroneously call a Turbant).] **1688** R. HOLME *Armoury* IV. xi. (Roxb.) 440/2 In Egypt the great Sultan used a Tulipant or Turbat made of three score or more elles of thin stuffe diuersely folded.

*β.* **1588** T. HICKOCK tr. *Frederick's Voy.* 5 The *Torbants* are made in Diu. **1596** SPENSER *F. Q.* IV. xi. 28 Old Cybele,.. Wearing a Diademe embattild wide With hundred turrets, like a Turribant. **1598** R. HAYDOCKE tr. *Lomazzo* II. 124 Some of them beare blewe turbantes;..the Iewes beare them yeallow. **1599** HAKLUYT *Voy.* II. 168 With their turbents very white and cleane. **1607** R. C[AREW] tr. *Estienne's World of Wonders* 235 A Turkish turbant [*margin* or tolibante]. **1611** SHAKS. *Cymb.* III. iii. 6 The Gates of Monarches Are Arch'd so high, that Giants may iet through And keepe their impious Turbonds on. **1652** Turband, **1653–86** Turbant, **1688** Turbat [see *a.*]. **1697** DAMPIER *Voy.* I. xv. 427 They wear no Hat, Cap, nor Turbat, nor any thing to keep off the Sun. **1710** ADDISON *Tatler* No. 161 ¶9 Ignorance with a Turband upon her Head. **1735** JOHNSON *Lobo's Abyssinia, Voy.* v. 30 He [the King]..with a Turbant on his Head, to which were fastned some Rings. **1839** MONTEITH in *Madras Jrnl. Lit. & Sc.* X. 162 Dressed in their blue clothes and white turbands.

*γ.* **1597** GERARDE *Herbal* 117 Turban, Turfan [see TULIP 1]. **1623** COCKERAM, *Turbine*, a thing of linnen which the Turks weare on their heads. **1624** BEDELL *Lett.* iii. 78 There were also Turkish Turbanes, and Diadems of diuers fashions. **1687** A. LOVELL tr. *Thevenot's Trav.* III. 37 The turban worn in the Indies is commonly little. **1755** JOHNSON, Turban, turbant, turband. **1774** GOLDSM. *Nat. Hist.* (1776) II. 77 The size of the head is encreased by a great variety of bandages, formed into a turban. **1788** GIBBON *Decl. & F.* lvii. V. 667 His ample turban was fashioned in the shape of a crown. **1803** *Med. Jrnl.* X. 281 Oriental travellers, who exchange their hat for the turban, experience it to be a much cooler and more agreeable covering.

**b.** As the symbol of Mohammedanism, or of those who profess it.

**1610** MARCELLINE *Triumphs Jas. I* 74 Go generous Race, go gather Laurels..chase the Turbants from those Provinces. **1660** INGELO *Bentiv. & Ur.* II. (1682) 55 Their Emperour commanded only the Turbants to be beaten. **1693** *Mem. Cnt. Teckely* I. 13 The Turk..does not force the Transylvanians to take up the Turban. **1753** HANWAY *Trav.* (1762) II. v. iii. 139 As he refused to wear the turbant, his younger brother..offered himself in his stead. **1812** BYRON *Ch. Har.* II. lxxix, Though turbans now pollute Sophia's shrine, And Greece her very altars eyes in vain. **1878** VILLARI *Machiavelli* (1898) I. iii. 160, I was better fitted for the turban than the cowl.

**c.** A figure or representation of a turban, e. g. on Moslem funeral monuments. Also in *Her.*

**1687** A. LOVELL tr. *Thevenot's Trav.* I. 224 Five great Sepulchres, in one whereof a Basha is Interred, having his Turban cut in Marble, at one end of his Tomb. **1717** LADY M. W. MONTAGU *Let. to Abbé Conti* 29 May, They set up a pillar with a carved turbant on the top of it. **1720** STRYPE *Stow's Surv.* (1754) II. v. xiv. 320/2 A Turk..upon his Head a Turbant, Argent..with a Tassel upon the Top, Gules. **1766** PORNY *Elem. Her.* (1787) 214 The Great-Turk bears over his arms a Turband..under two Coronets,..and the uppermost is surmounted with Crescents. **1844** E. WARBURTON *Crescent & Cross* (1846) II. xvii. 249 A cemetery, whose sculptured turbans showed that the neighbouring village was Moslem. **1876** [see TURBANED b].

**d.** Applied to the head-dress of the ancient Jewish high priest.

**1624** BP. HALL *Imprese of God* I. Wks. 442 An honourable Motto; such as was written vpon the מצנפת, the Turbant, of the High priest; Holinesse to the Lord. **1885** BIBLE (R.V.) *Exod.* xxviii. 37 Upon the forefront of the mitre [*marg.* turban].

**e.** *transf.* and *fig.* Applied to a head-dress, or a head of hair, likened to a turban.

**1609** B. JONSON *Sil. Wom.* I. i, A huge turbant of nightcaps on his head, buckled over his eares. **1609** BP. W. BARLOW *Answ. Nameless Cath.* 161 Obedience to Princes makes not for the Popes Triple Turbant. **1727** A. HAMILTON *New Acc. E. Ind.* I. xiii. 152 A sanctified Rascal of 7 Foot high,..with a large Turband of his own Hair wreathed about his Head. **1827** STEUART *Planter's G.* (1828) 429 The woolly head of the Negro; who, without that light and natural turban, would [etc.].

**f.** Erroneously supposed to be worn by women of Eastern nations and Jewesses.

**1805–6** CAMPBELL *Turkish Lady* vii, 'Captive! could the brightest jewel From my turban set thee free?' 'Lady, no!' **1819** SCOTT *Ivanhoe* viii, Her [Rebecca's] form..was shewn to advantage by a sort of Eastern dress,..Her turban of yellow silk suited well with the darkness of her complexion. **1835** *Ladies' Cabinet* Nov. 337 The Jewish style of *coiffure*, as copied from the daughters of Israel in their days of splendour, will be decidedly fashionable. We have seen already some turbans *à l'Israelite*,..that have been ordered by *élegantes* of high fashion.

**g.** *Cookery.* (See quot. 1911: perh. only as Fr.)

**1846** SOYER *Cookery* 514 *Turban de Meringues glacé.* Make a turban as directed in the last..fill the turban, at the moment of serving [etc.]. **1911** WEBSTER, *Turban* .. 5. *Cookery.* A drum-shaped case for entrées, fillets, etc.

**2.** A head-dress made to resemble or suggest the oriental turban, worn by ladies in Europe and America during the late 18th and the earlier part of the 19th c., and temporarily revived in 1908. Cf. *turban-fold* in 8.

**1776** *Lady's Mag.* Mar. 118/1 Ladies'..Hair..very..high ..Turbans more the taste than caps. **1796** MME. D'ARBLAY *Camilla* III. 325 Assuring her [the cap] was grown so old-fashioned, that not a lady's maid..would now be seen in it, she offered to pin her up a turban. **1823** LADY BLESSINGTON *Sk. & Fragm.* 59 Went to the Opera: wore my tissue turban. **1835** *Ladies' Cabinet* Mar. 199 Hats and turbans are equally fashionable for ladies who do not dance. **1838** DISRAELI *Corr. w. Sister* (1886) 96 She was most becomingly dressed in a white turban of a very *recherché* construction. **1908** *Paris Fashions* 15 Feb. 6/2 The large 'de Stael' turbans, such as are seen in old pictures, are being worn at the theatre.

**b.** A style of hair-dressing for women.

**1909** *Daily Graphic* 13 Oct. 13/3 The up-to-date turban.. is in a loose wave wound round with a plain strand of smooth hair. *Ibid.*, The turban coiffure. *Ibid.* 25 Oct. 13/3 The Revived Turban. Hair draped round head in turban fashion.

**3.** A bright-coloured cloth worn as a head-dress by negroes (esp. women) in the West Indies and southern U.S.

**1839** DARWIN *Voy. Nat.* i. (1879) 4 Their black skins and snow-white linen being set off by coloured turbans and large shawls. **1852** MRS. STOWE *Uncle Tom's C.* xx, Miss Ophelia found Topsy with her very best scarlet India Canton crape shawl wound round her head for a turban. **1852** THACKERAY *Esmond* III. iii, A..negro..with a bird of paradise in his turban.

**4.** Name for a small brimless hat, or round cap with closely turned up brim, worn, chiefly by women and children, since about 1850.

**1862** [implied in *turban-hat* in 8]. **1865** MELTON *Hints on Hats* 53 The boating-hat of straw; the 'turban', or 'pork-pie'; the fishing-cap, [etc.].

**5.** *Zool.* A name for certain species of echinoderms, esp. the genus *Cidaris*.

**1713** PETIVER *Aquat. Anim. Amboinæ* Tab. viii, *Echinus S. Diadema Turcarum*...Turks Turband. **1837** *Penny Cycl.* IX. 262/1 Fossil Echini...Subspheroidal species, more elevated than wide..(The Turbans). Example, *Cidaris imperialis*.

**6. a.** The spire or whorl of a twisted univalve shell. *rare.* **b.** A mollusc of the genus *Turbo*.

Taken to represent L. *turbo*; but confounded with *turban*.

**1681** GREW *Musæum* I. vi. i. 125 A Shell like the Oriental, with a Knobed Turban or Whirle. **1685** *Phil. Trans.* XV. 1019 Fig. 3[d]. Represents the Shell in its true bigness,..there are six or seven spiral lines or Rounds in the Turban. **1815** W. WOOD *Gen. Conchol.* I. *Dict. Terms* 60 All the whirls, or spires, of a Univalve, taken collectively, are called the turban. **1819** W. TURTON *Conchol. Dict.* 198 *Turbo petræus.* Rock Turban.

**7.** Florist's name for cultivated varieties of *Ranunculus*; more fully *Turk's turban*.

**1760** J. LEE *Introd. Bot.* App. 330 Turk's Turban, *Ranunculus*. **1882** *Standard* 6 Nov. 1/8, 25 Ranunculi, scarlet turban. 25 Ranunculi, mixed turban.

**8.** *attrib.* and *Comb.*, as *turban-cap, -cloth, encrinite, -flower, -fold*, †*grout-head, hat, -roll, style, -wisp*; *turban-crested, -crowned, -like, -shaped*, adjs.; **turban-eye**, a pillared eye, found in the males of some May-flies; **turban gourd**, a variety of *Cucurbita maxima*: cf. *turban squash*; **turban-lily**, the Siberian *Lilium Pomponium*, bearing deep-red spotted flowers and edible bulbs; **turban-shell** = 5, 6 b; **turban squash**, a variety of squash or pumpkin in which the fleshy receptacle does not extend over the ovary, which therefore protrudes so as to resemble a turban (Webster, 1911); **turban-stone**, a Moslem tombstone, a pillar having at the head the carved representation of a turban: cf. 1 c; **turban swathe**, in hair-dressing: cf. 2 b; **turban-top**, ? the Bishop's Mitre mushroom, *Helvella Mitra*; **turban toque**: see quot.

**1900** *Westm. Gaz.* 15 Feb. 3/2 All toques, and especially those of tulle, had more or less the *turban build. **1881** 'RITA' *Lady Coquette* iii, She's got a *turban-cap to match it. **1900** S. WEYMAN *Sophia* x, Sir Hervey's turban-cap and embroidered gown. **1877** J. T. BEER *Proph. Nineveh* i. 17 My leather wallet and best *turban cloth. **1894** MRS. DYAN *All in a Man's K.* i, The General's carriage, with its *turban-crested servants. **1822** J. PARKINSON *Outl. Oryctol.* 174 The vertebral column of the *turban Encrinite. **1907** *Nature* 4 Apr. 541/2 These *turban-eyes are restricted to the males of these may-flies, which seek the females during flight in the gloaming. **1841** BROWNING *Pippa Passes* Introd. 93 Fairies watch unroll Such *turban-flowers. **1898** *Daily News* 31 May 6/4 *Turban folds of tulle are worn in the evening..at the opera. In one instance the turban was in palest blue. **1884** *De Candolle's Orig. Cultiv. Pl.* 250 The principal varieties of *Cucurbita maxima* are the great yellow gourd,..the Spanish, the *turban gourd. **1599** NASHE *Lenten Stuffe* 39 Those *Turbanto grout-heads, that hang all men by the throates on Iron hookes. **1862** *Eng. Wom. Dom. Mag.* IV. 237/1 The velvet *Turban Hats that are being worn by little boys. **1862** MISS YONGE *C'tess Kate* ix, Sylvia's face was exposed by a little turban hat. **1909** *Daily Graphic* 20 Oct. 13/3 A swathed turban hat of pale blue velvet. **1900** *Dundee Advertiser* 16 Apr. 4 Stalwart Zouaves..in their richly embroidered jackets, wide trousers, and quaint *turban-like headgear. **1884** MILLER *Plant-n.* 78 *Turban Lily, *Lilium Pomponium*. **1762** *Lond. Chron.* XI. 167/3 The present *Turband Roll, which is now wore round the Mecklenburgh caps. **1776** WITHERING *Brit. Plants* (1796) IV. 181 Fungi. Agaricus..convex hemispherical,..at length *turban-shaped and viscid. **1897** *Allbutt's Syst. Med.* IV. 738 The epiglottis..becoming enormously swollen and turban-shaped. **1753** CHAMBERS *Cycl. Supp.*, *Turban-Shell, *Cidaris*,..the name of a genus of the echinodermata. **1895** *Funk's Stand. Dict.*, *Turban-shell*, a gastropod of the genus *Turbo*, or its shell. **1872** J. FERGUSSON *Rude Stone Mon.* x. 404 A headstone which, if it is not the *turban-stone that is usually found in Turkish tombs of modern date, is most singularly like it. **1909** *Punch* 10 Nov. 326/1 Women are in revolt against the '*turban' style of coiffure. **1912** *Daily News* 13 Aug. 5 The imported '*Turban swathe' has had a very short run. **1828** WEBSTER, *Turban-top*, a plant of the genus Helvella; a kind of fungus or mushroom. *Cyc.* **1897** *Westm. Gaz.* 18 Feb. 3/1 The *turban toque,..in form pertaining to the fez, is just encircled with twisted tulles and finished by some one note of height. **1899** *Westm. Gaz.* 2 Dec. 2/1 He.. could doze in a tree like a crow (the *turban-wisp passed round his body and tied to a branch steadied him from falling).

Hence **Turbane·sque** *a.*, having the appearance of a turban; **Turbane·tte**, a diminutive turban; **Tu·rbanless** *a.*, without or destitute of a turban; **Tu·rbanwise** *adv.*, in the manner of a turban.

**1840** BROWNING *Sordello* I. 708 He Partook the poppy's red effrontery, Till Autumn spoiled their fleering quite with rain, And, turbanless, a coarse, brown, rattling crane Lay bare. **1882** O'DONOVAN *Merv Oasis* xiii. (1884) 142 Not turban-wise, but rather as if it were applied as a bandage for some cranial injury. **1890** JESSOPP *Trials Country Parson* 64 Do you mean..that you will persist in sporting that emasculated felt turbanette? **1891** STEVENSON *South Seas* (1908) III. iii. 221 The hair is worn turban-wise in a frizzled bush. **1893** *Nat. Observer* 25 Feb. 361/1 Caps, too—Greek, Byzantine, turbanesque—are popular vanities.

**Turban** (tɜ̄·ɹbăn), *v.* [f. prec. sb.] *trans.* To envelop as or with a turban; also, to wind a cloth round (a cap).

**1822** MILMAN *Belshazzar* 108 The wreaths, like mist, That turban thy dusk brow. **1851** G. W. CURTIS *Nile Notes* xxv. 111 Long men and short, bald and grisly, capped and turbaned variously. **1860** TYNDALL *Glac.* I. xvi. 109 Clouds turbaned the head of the giant [mountain], and hid it from our view. **1876** A. ARNOLD in *Contemp. Rev.* June 48 They wear skull-caps of felt, turbaned with cotton.

**Turbaned** (tɜ̄·ɹbănd), *a.* [f. TURBAN *sb.* + -ED.[2]] Wearing a turban.

**1591** JAS. I *Lepanto* 10 Circumsised Turband Turkes. **1604** SHAKS. *Oth.* v. ii. 353 A malignant, and a Turbond-Turke Beate a Venetian. *a* **1649** DRUMM. OF HAWTH. *Poems* 170 Though turban'd Princes for a Badge her weare. **1802** SOUTHEY *La Caba* 67 Moor! turbaned misbeliever! renegade! Circumcised traitor! **1817** SCOTT *Harold* III. vi, The turban'd race of Termagaunt. **1895** W. WRIGHT *Palmyra & Zenobia* xxv. 296 The old green-turbaned keeper of the Mosque.

**b.** Of a Moslem tombstone: Surmounted by a carved turban.

**1835** WILLIS *Pencillings* II. xlvi. 60 Its small dark cemetery of cypressed and turbaned head-stones. **1876** A. J. EVANS *Through Bosnia* iii. 93 A Turkish graveyard, with the usual turbaned tombstones—some of the turbans of majestic height.

**Turbarian** (tɜɹbēᵊ·riăn), *a. Geol.* [f. med.L. *turbāria* peat-bog + -AN.] Of or pertaining to peat-bogs; denoting a subdivision of the Pleistocene or glacial period, during which extensive deposits of peat were formed in Northern Europe and Asia.

**1895** J. GEIKIE in *Jrnl. Geol.* (Chicago) III. 251 'Lower Turbarian' Fifth glacial epoch. *Ibid.* 252 'Upper Turbarian' Sixth glacial epoch.

**Turbary** (tɜ̄·ɹbări). Forms: 4–6 **turbarye**, (5 **turbere**), 5–7 **turbarie**, (6 **to(u)rberie**), 8 **turbery**, 6– **turbary**. [a. AF. *turberie* (Britton), a. OF. *turb-, torb-, tourberie* (12–13th c. in Godef.), med.L. *turbāria*, f. OF. *tourbe* (Swiss *turbe*), med.L. *turba*, ad. LG. *turf* or *turv*: see TURF.]

**1.** Land, or a piece of land, where turf or peat may be dug for fuel; a peat-bog or peat-moss.

[**1292** BRITTON II. xxix. § 3 Mes si turberie, ou bruere, ou herbage, ou pesson,..soit tenu en commun par entre parceners ou veisins, et acun face exces [etc.]. **1314–15** *Rolls of Parlt.* I. 313/2 A fower tourbes en la tourberie denz lour Commune pasture.] **1363** *Cockersand Chartul.* (Chetham Soc.) I. 64 They may..delfe theyr turves in yᵉ mosse and turbarye in Gayrstang. **1455** *Rolls of Parlt.* V. 311/2, cc acres of Turbarie in the marshe of Holand. **1571** *Lanc. Wills* (Chetham Soc.) II. 244 My mosse and turbarie commonly called Toft Mosse. **1583** *Shuttleworths' Acc.* (ibid.) 15 For turbery and paustere. *Ibid.*, For his tourberie and pausture. *Ibid.*, For his torberie and pastre. **1607** NORDEN *Surv. Dial.* II. 66 Woodsales, sales of heath, flags, and Turbarie. **1765** *Act 5 Geo. III* c. 26 *Preamble*, Moors, marshes, turbarys, waters,..commons, and other commodities. **1832** LYELL *Princ. Geol.* II. 215 In a turbary on the estate of the Earl of Moira, in Ireland, a human body was dug up,..covered with eleven feet of moss. **1865** LUBBOCK *Preh. Times* i. (1869) 19 This sword was discovered in a turbary..in a large boat, which had evidently been sunk.

†**b.** *transf.* The substance obtained from or forming a turbary; peat. *Obs.*

*c* **1440** *Jacob's Well* 38 In tythyng of wyn,..of flex, of hemp, of turbarye & fewall, of frute of treen. **1798** *Trans. Soc. Arts* XVI. 241 The soil consists chiefly of about twelve inches of turbary, and under that, gravel or stone.

**2.** *Law.* In full *common of turbary*: The right to cut turf or peat for fuel on a common or on another person's land.

**1567** *Lanc. Wills* (Chetham Soc.) II. 84 Concerning turbarye and sute of Court. **1622** CALLIS *Stat. Sewers* (1647) 106 Common of Pischary, Turbary, or of Pasture in great Fens, Marishes and Wastes, may be charged..for their Commons. **1641** *Termes de la Ley* 209 Turbary is an interest of digging turfes upon a common. **1798** J. MIDDLETON *View Agric. Middlesex* 103 The value of the commons ..including..pasturage, locality of situation, and the barbarous custom of turbary. **1807** VANCOUVER *Agric. Devon* (1813) 294 The parishioners have a right of turbary on these moors, by which they have been much injured. **1884** *Times* (weekly ed.) 19 Sept. 6/4 Each infinitesimal right of grazing or turbary had to be surveyed, examined into.

**3.** *attrib.* and *Comb.*

**1850** MANTELL in *Q. Jrnl. Geol. Soc.* VI. 327 The so-called 'turbary deposit', whence bones of the Moa..have been obtained. **1896** *N. Brit. Daily Mail* 8 June 4 The clauses relating to purchase, turbary rights, and other matters. **1896** *Speaker* 18 July 58/2 The turbary and sea-wrack clause will have the most important effects.

**Turbat, -batt,** obs. ff. TURBAN, TURBOT.

† **Turbation** (tɒɹbēⁱ·ʃən). *Obs.* [a. OF. *turbacioun* (14th c. in Godef.), ad. L. *turbātio, -ōnem*, from *turbāre* to disturb.] Confusion, disorder, disturbance; perturbation, agitation of mind.

*c* **1400** *Sc. Trojan War* II. 117 In the tyme of turbacions. *c* **1450** tr. *De Imitatione* III. xxv. 96 A liȝt turbacion shuld not so sone springe in me. **1480** CAXTON *Chron. Eng.* v. (1520) 61 b/2 There was then turbacyon in the chyrche for stryfe and heretykes. *c* **1530** *Judic. Urines* II. ii. 12 b, Turbacyon and distemperaunse of the humours in the body. **1642** T. HODGES *Glimpse Gods Glory* 38 It intimates a turbation of minde.

‖ **Turbeh** (tu·rbe(þ)). Also **turbé.** [Turkish, a. Arab. تربة *turbah* tomb, sepulchre.] A small mosque-like building erected over the tomb of a Moslem, esp. a person of sanctity or rank.

**1687** A. LOVELL tr. *Thevenot's Trav.* I. 22 At the back of this Mosque there is a Turbe, where are the bodies of Sultan Achmet and his children. **1853** LAYARD *Nineveh & Babylon* ii. 24 In the midst..rose here and there a conical *turbeh* of beautiful shape, covered with exquisite tracery. **1906** W. M. RAMSAY in *Expositor* Nov. 463 When it [the building] is little more than a mausoleum, it is called a turbe.

**Turbel,** obs. form of TROUBLE.

**Turbellarian** (tɒɹbelēᵊ·riăn), *a.* and *sb. Zool.* [f. mod.L. *Turbellāria*, neuter pl. (f. L. *turbella* a little crowd, a bustle, stir, dim. of *turba* crowd) + -AN.] **a.** *adj.* Of or belonging to the *Turbellaria*, a class of worms inhabiting fresh or salt water or damp earth, having the body covered with vibratile cilia producing minute whirls in the water. **b.** *sb.* A worm of this class; a whirl-worm.

**1879** E. P. WRIGHT *Anim. Life* 580 Rhynchocœla. These are the flat worms. To one section thereof would belong the Turbellarian and Nemertean worms. **1883** *Science* I. 433/1 The form and armature of the tail resemble those of many turbellarians.

So **Turbellariform** (-ēᵊ·rifɒɹm) *a.*, having the form of a turbellarian.

**1877** HUXLEY *Anat. Inv. Anim.* xii. 675 The Tunicate *Pharyngopneusta*, with their caudate larvæ, may be supposed to stand in the same relation to the Turbellariform *Pharyngopneusta*, as the *Trematoda*, with their cercariform larvæ, to the *Turbellaria*.

‖ **Turben.** *Obs. rare.* [L. *turben*, by-form of *turbo, turbin-em*: see TURBO.] The spire or whorl of a twisted shell.

**1669** *Phil. Trans.* IV. 1012 This Turben or Conical figure [of a snail shell] is well neare a quarter of an inch.

**Turben, Turbentyne,** obs. ff. TURBAN, TURPENTINE.

**Turbescency** (tɒ̄ɹbe·sĕnsi). *rare.* [f. assumed L. *turbescĕre to grow turbid: see -ENCY. Cf. *putrescency*.] The condition of becoming turbid.

**1834** *Fraser's Mag.* X. 569 The sudden turbescency of water is generally attributed to rains.

**Turbet,** obs. form of TURBIT, TURBOT.

**Turbeth**: see TURPETH.

**Turbid** (tɒ̄·ɹbid), *a.* [ad. L. *turbid-us* full of confusion or disorder; troubled, muddy; perplexed, violent, etc.; f. *turba* crowd, disturbance.]

**1.** Of liquid: Thick or opaque with suspended matter; not clear; cloudy, muddy.

**1626** BACON *Sylva* § 306 Though the Lees doe make the Liquour turbide, yet they refine the Spirits. *a* **1701** MAUNDRELL *Journ. Jerus.* (1732) 4 It's Waters are turbid and very unwholesome. **1800** tr. *Lagrange's Chem.* II. 375 At the end of some time this water becomes turbid, putrifies, and emits an ammoniacal odour. **1896** *Q. Rev.* Apr. 498 Gases ..acted upon them [the X rays] as turbid media, stopping them by vague diffusion, as milky water stops light.

**b.** Of air, smoke, clouds, etc.: Thick, dense; dark.

**1705** J. PHILIPS *Blenheim* 145 Horrible Flames, and turbid streaming Clouds Of Smoak sulphureous. **1807** J. BARLOW *Columb.* III. 21 The nations, temper'd to the turbid air, Breathe deadly strife. **1811** PINKERTON *Petralogy* II. 330 The sun rose above the horizon, turbid at first and dimmed by mists. **1829** *Chapters Phys. Sc.* 267 Whether the sky be clear and serene, or cloudy and turbid, whether it snows or rains. *a* **1831** A. KNOX *Rem.* I. 7 Turbid wreaths, Sullying joy's gilded ceilings.

**c.** *fig.* or in figurative language.

**1752** WARBURTON *Serm. 1 John iv. 20* Wks. 1788 V. 45 Benevolence, arising from this source, at first runs thick and turbid. **1800** WELLESLEY in Owen *Desp.* (1877) 732 It is not the nature of these inestimable blessings to spring from a turbid source. **1810** CRABBE *Borough* xxiii. 144 Each feature in the face, Pinched through neglect or turbid by disgrace. **1876** MERIVALE *Rom. Triumvirates* vi. 121 The readers and thinkers of the day..withdrew more and more from the turbid sphere of political action.

**2.** *fig.* Characterized by or producing confusion or obscurity of thought, feeling, etc.; mentally confused, perplexed, muddled; disturbed, troubled.

*c* **1645** HOWELL *Lett.* (1650) II. xxx. 44, I had divers fits of melancholy, and such turbid intervalls that use to attend close prisoners, who for the most part have no other companions, but confus'd troops of wandring cogitations. **1663** COWLEY *Ess. in Verse & Prose, Of Greatness*, Senecio was a man of a turbid and confused wit. **1684** HOWE *Redeemer's Tears* Wks. 1862 II. 316 No grief, sorrow or sighing, which are all fled away; as there can be no other turbid passion of any kind. *a* **1688** CUDWORTH *Immut. Mor.* (1731) 90 The Perceptions of which..are confused, indistinct, turbid and encumbred Cogitations. **1744** HARRIS *Three Treat.* III. II. (1765) 245 This turbid, this fickle, fleeting Period. **1820** BYRON *Mar. Fal.* II. i. 487 Your sleep for many nights has been so turbid. **1839** STONEHOUSE *Axholme* 207 Wesley's mind seems at this time to have been in a turbid and restless state. **1866** GEO. ELIOT *F. Holt* xxx, A grimy man in a flannel shirt, hatless and with turbid red hair. **1896** *Edin. Rev.* Apr. 332 The turbid utterances and twisted language of Carlyle.

**3.** *Comb.*, as *turbid-looking*.

**1899** *Allbutt's Syst. Med.* VI. 911 The latter membrane is turbid-looking and thickened.

**Turbidity** (tɒɹbi·dĭti). [ad. med.L. *turbiditās* (Albertus Magnus, *c* 1255), f. L. *turbidus* TURBID: see -ITY.] = TURBIDNESS.

**1782** KIRWAN in *Phil. Trans.* LXXX. 215 Dr. Priestley, in a similar experiment, did not observe this turbidity. **1845** G. E. DAY tr. *Simon's Anim. Chem.* I. 323 The serum..exhibited a remarkable milk-white turbidity. **1862** TYNDALL *Mountaineer.* iii. 25 No mist or turbidity interferes with the sharpness of the outlines. **1868** VISCT. STRANGFORD *Select.* (1869) II. 306 A dense circumfluous atmosphere of intellectual turbidity, of ignorance, of gross superstition. **1888** RUTLEY *Rock-Forming Min.* 127 Any turbidity or milkiness which a crystal may exhibit.

**Turbidly** (tɒ̄·ɹbidli), *adv. rare.* [f. TURBID + -LY [2].] In a turbid or troubled manner.

**1728** YOUNG *Vind. Providence* 21 A Person of small Merit is anxiously jealous of Imputations on his Honour, because he knows his Title is weak; one of great Merit turbidly resents them, because he knows his Title is strong. *a* **1861** MRS. BROWNING *Musical Instr.* ii, The limpid water turbidly ran. **1874** SYMONDS *Italy & Gr.* (1898) I. xiv. 305 The gondolas moved turbidly upon the face of the waters.

**Turbidness** (tɒ̄·ɹbidnĕs). [f. as prec. + -NESS.] The quality or condition of being turbid; thickness of a fluid; cloudiness; also *fig.*

**1676** *Phil. Trans.* XI. 614 It will mixe..without turbidness and without coagulation. **1772** JACKSON *ibid.* LXIII. 5 Instead of clarifying beer, [it] increased both its tenacity and turbidness. **1800** W. SAUNDERS *Min. Waters* iv. 278 Lime water produces a turbidness when added to the fresh water. **1807** *Med. Jrnl.* XVII. 194 On examining the anterior chamber [of the eye], all the turbidness had disappeared. **1906** E. A. ABBOTT *Silanus* xxxv. 352 Trouble of soul does not mean confusion or turbidness of soul.

† **Tu·rbidous,** *a. Obs. rare.* [f. L. *turbid-us* TURBID + -OUS.] = TURBID.

**1628** HOBBES *Thucyd.* (1822) 130 The stream of the river is swift, broad and turbidous.

**Turbill, Turbillion, -billoun,** obs. forms of TROUBLE, TOURBILLION.

**Turbinaceous** (tɒɹbinēⁱ·ʃəs), *a.*[1] *rare.* [f. L. *turbo, turbin-em*: see TURBO and -ACEOUS.] Resembling the gastropod genus *Turbo*; top-shaped.

**1842** *Penny Cycl.* XXII. 53/1 *Siphonostomata..Turbinella*...Turbinaceous and spiny species.

† **Turbina·ceous,** *a.*[2] *Obs.* [Erroneous formation for *turbaceous f. med.L. *turba* turf, peat, as if f. L. *turbo, turbin-* (cf. prec.).] Pertaining to peat; peaty; flavoured with peat-smoke.

**1824** SCOTT *St. Ronan's* xiii, The real turbinacious flavour [of the whisky] no sooner reached the nose of the Captain than the beverage was turned down his throat.

‖ **Turbinage** (türbinaʒ). *Sugar manuf.* [F. (Littré), f. *turbine*, TURBINE: see -AGE.] Separation of the sugar crystals from the molasses by centrifugal filters or turbines. Cf. TURBINE 1 c.

**1911** in WEBSTER.

**Turbinal** (tɒ̄·ɹbinăl), *a.* and *sb.* [f. L. *turbo, turbin-em* (see TURBO) + -AL.] **A.** *adj.* Turbinated, top-shaped; in *Anat.* = TURBINATE *a.*: cf. B.

**1584** R. SCOT *Discov. Witchcr.* XIII. xix. (1886) 258 Experiments..in diverse sorts of glasses;..the columnarie, the pyramidate or piked, the turbinall. **1883** *Science* I. 233/1 The arrangement of the turbinal bones in the fissiped carnivores. **1903** *Brit. Med. Jrnl.* 18 Apr. 910 No swelling as yet of turbinal bodies or septal mucous membrane.

**B.** *sb. Anat.* A turbinal or turbinate bone; the ethmo-, the maxillo-, or the spheno-turbinal.

**1848** OWEN *Archetype & Homol. Vertebr. Skel.* i. 13 'Turbinal'..is a substitute for the phrase 'os turbinatum inferius' and its synonym 'os spongiosum inferius'. *Ibid.* ii. 114 The Turbinal or nose-capsule. **1854** — *Skel. & Teeth* in *Orr's Circ. Sc.* I. *Org. Nat.* 179 An ossified part of the capsule of the organ of smell, 'turbinal'. *Ibid.* 251 The superior turbinals extend..below into the presphenoidal sinus. **1871** HUXLEY *Anat. Vertebr. Anim.* v. 237 Forming the floor of the front part of the nasal chamber, on each side, is a large concavo-convex bone, which..protects the nasal gland, and is commonly termed a turbinal, though, if it be a membrane bone, it does not truly correspond with the turbinals of the higher Vertebrata.

**Turbinate** (tɒ̄·ɹbinĕt), *a.* and *sb.* [ad. L. *turbināt-us*, f. *turbo, turbin-*: see TURBO and -ATE [2].]

**A.** *adj. Nat. Hist.* Resembling a spinning-top in shape; of a mollusc, having a spiral shell; in *Bot. spec.* inversely conical; having a narrow tapering base and broad rounded apex; in *Anat.* applied to the scroll-like spongy bones of the nasal fossæ in the higher vertebrates.

**1661** LOVELL *Hist. Anim. & Min.* Introd., Fishes, which are..testaceous, and..turbinate, which are either involute, as the Nautilus,..murex,..or orbicular, as the Welke. *a* **1706** EVELYN *Sylva* (1776) II. i. § 1 [The larch tribe] Easily raised of the kernels and nuts, which may be gotten out of their polysperm and turbinate cones. **1750** G. HUGHES *Barbadoes* 283 The largest, as well as the most beautiful of the turbinate kind. **1760** J. LEE *Introd. Bot.* III. xxii. (1765) 229 The *Pericarpium* is..turbinate, Top-shaped, when it tapers towards the Base. **1828** STARK *Elem. Nat. Hist.* II. 24 *C[onus] Hebræus*, Lin. Shell turbinate, coronate, white..the spire convex, obtuse. **1840** G. V. ELLIS *Anat.* 244 Three convoluted portions of bone named spongy or turbinate bones, which project into the cavity. **1870** HOOKER *Stud. Flora* 366 *Leucojum æstivum*..Fruit turbinate.

**b.** In combination, modifying another adj., as *turbinate-lentiform, -truncate.*

**1887** W. PHILLIPS *Brit. Discomycetes* 355 *Tympanis Fraxini*,..cups subsessile, turbinate-truncate, shining, black.

**B.** *sb.* **a.** A turbinate shell. **b.** A turbinate bone.

**1802–3** tr. *Pallas' Trav.* (1812) I. 70 A multitude of turbinates of the large kind, and especially whole strata, full of small striped turbinates. **1872** MIVART *Elem. Anat.* 84 That part of it immediately below the cribriform plate is called the upper spongy bone, or superior turbinate, or turbinal. **1903** *Detroit Med. Jrnl.* 733 (Cent. D. Suppl.) Cases of asthma treated by removal of the middle turbinate.

† **Tu·rbinate,** *v. Obs. rare.* [f. L. *turbo, turbin-* (see TURBO) + -ATE [3].] **a.** *trans.* To fashion like a top; to make top-shaped. **b.** *intr.* To turn or whirl like a top or a whirlwind.

**1721** BAILEY, *Turbinate*, to fashion like a Top, to sharpen at one End. **1791** BURKE *French Affairs* Wks. VII. 41 The Russian Government is..liable to be subverted by military seditions,..and sometimes by headlong rebellions of the people, such as the turbinating movement of Pugatchef.

**Turbinated** (tɒ̄·ɹbinēⁱtĕd), *a.* [f. as TURBINATE *a.* + -ED [1].]

**1.** Top-shaped, top-like; *spec.* in *Nat. Hist.* whorled, = TURBINATE *a.*

**1615** CROOKE *Body of Man* 215 It is equall, smooth, and turbinated, that is, broad at the basis or bottom, and growing smaller. **1668** WILKINS *Real Char.* 122 Turbinated; consisting of a cone-like cavity, rouled up in a spiral. *a* **1706** EVELYN *Sylva* II. i. (1776) 274 The Wild or Bastard-Pine and Teda..bearing a turbinated cone. **1759** JOHNSON *Idler* No. 56 ¶ 6 An irregular contortion of a turbinated shell. **1800** *Phil. Trans.* XC. 434 The turbinated bones are in the same relative situation to the other parts of the skull as in quadrupeds. **1835** LINDLEY *Introd. Bot.* (1848) I. 387 [The placenta] its form is now turbinated. **1840** E. WILSON *Anat. Vade M.* (1842) 38 The inferior Turbinated or spongy Bone is a thin layer of loose and spongy bone, slightly curled upon itself, and projected inwards from the inner wall of the Nares. **1884** M. MACKENZIE *Dis. Throat & Nose* II. 233 There are always three turbinated bones, and frequently a fourth.

† **2.** Of motion: Like that of a top; gyrating, rotary, whirling. *Obs.*

**1665** HOOKE *Microgr.* lx. 246 [Gravitation] does not depend upon the diurnal or turbinated motion of the Earth. **1692** BENTLEY *Boyle Lect.* iv. 125 Let Mechanism here..produce a spiral and turbinated motion of the whole moved Body without an external director.

**Turbination** (tɒɹbinēⁱ·ʃən). [ad. L. *turbinātiōn-em* a pointing in the form of a cone, f. *turbināt-us* TURBINATE *a.*: see -ATION.]

**1.** † The action of making top-shaped (*obs.*); top-like or turbinate form; formation of a whorl.

**1623** COCKERAM, *Turbination*, the fashioning of a thing like a top or gigge. **1656** in BLOUNT *Glossogr.* **1834** McMURTRIE *Cuvier's Anim. Kingd.* 257 Their shells are very open,..most of them without the slightest turbination.

† **2.** The action of spinning or whirling round like a top. *Obs.*

**1665** HOOKE *Microgr.* lx. 246 Then certainly the turbination cannot be the cause of the attraction of the Earth. *a* **1680** ALLESTREE *Serm., Matt. xi. 28* (1684) II. 124 They have a most perfect acquiescency in that their turbination.

**Turbinato-** (tɒɹbinēⁱ·to), combining form from L. *turbinātus* TURBINATE *a.*; qualifying adjs. used in natural history, as *turbinato-concave, -cylindrical, -globose, -stipitate.*

**1846** DANA *Zooph.* (1848) 384 Turbinato-cylindrical, four and a half lines broad at top. **1846** BERKELEY in *Proc. Berw. Nat. Club* II. No. 14. 190 Cup..turbinato-stipitate. **1887** W. PHILLIPS *Brit. Discomycetes* 195 *Mollisia versicolor*..at first globose, then turbinato-concave. *Ibid.* 236 *Lachnella caulicola*...Cups gregarious, stipitate, turbinato-globose, then hemispherical.

**Turbine** (tɒ̄·ɹbin). [a. F. *turbine*, ad. L. *turbo, turbin-em*: see TURBO.]

**1.** Originally applied to a wheel revolving on a vertical axis, and driven by a column of water falling into its interior, and escaping by pipes, channels, or apertures, so arranged as to press by reaction on the periphery of the wheel, and cause it to revolve in the direction opposite to that of the escaping water. Now applied to any kind of machine in which this principle (sometimes combined with that of direct impact) is used or developed; the modifications and developments are very numerous, many of these being of highly complicated structure, in which neither the horizontality of the wheel nor the motive power is retained.

[1824 BURDIN in *Bull. Soc. Encouragem.* July 256 Machines rotatoires à grande vitesse nommées turbines hydrauliques.] 1842 *Civil Eng. & Arch. Jrnl.* V. 266/1 The mechanical construction of the Turbine is..given, and its action..described. 1861 O. W. HOLMES *Voice of Loyal North* 33 'Tis hard..To see the rusting turbines stand Before the emptied flumes. 1861 RANKINE *Steam Engine* 189. 1881 W. C. UNWIN in *Encycl. Brit.* XII. 524/2 The Scotch turbine.. differs in no essential respect from the older form of reaction wheel. 1884 *Athenæum* 16 Aug. 212/2 A well-constructed water-wheel or turbine can..be worked with far greater economy than steam. 1897 *Spectator* 4 Sept., There are at Niagara single turbines which produce 5000 horse-power.

**b.** More fully *steam-turbine*: A steam motor in which rotatory motion is produced by steam impinging directly upon a series of vanes upon the circumference of a revolving cylinder or disk (or, in some types, acting and reacting alternately on moving and stationary elements).

1900 *Engineer* 2 Feb. 127/3 The main applications of the De Laval steam turbine are:—(1) Turbine motors, driving machinery direct by means of belts or ropes; (2) Turbine dynamos, the dynamos being placed on the second motion shafts or a prolongation of the same; (3) turbine pumps..and (4) turbine exhaust and pressure fans or ventilators. 1900 *N. Brit. Daily Mail* 30 Jan. 4 That is the whole secret of the turbine. In the modern application of it the steam blows upon the shaft and the shaft turns, and by an ingenious application of blades the steam which enters the first turbine when it leaves the boiler at a pressure of 225 lbs. to the square inch is utilised till the value of the last pound is all used up. 1905 *Westm. Gaz.* 16 Mar. 10/1 The dynamo is coupled directly to a Parsons turbine, which has introduced great changes and great economies in the driving of huge electrical plants.

**c.** A centrifugal separator used in sugar manufacture.

1873 BESANT & RICE *Little Girl* II. x. 116 The sweet, rich smell of the sugar; the huge vats of seething, foaming juice, and the whirling turbines.

**2.** *attrib.* and *Comb.*, as *turbine dynamo, dynamometer, engine, machinery, mill, motor, shaft, top, (water) wheel*; *turbine-driven, -engined, -like, -propelled*, adjs.; driven by a steam-turbine, as *turbine boat, destroyer, steamer, yacht*, etc.; **turbine-alternator, -generator**: see TURBO-; **turbine-pump**, a turbine water wheel used to raise water by being driven by external power in the direction opposite to that in which it turns when used as a motor.

1904 *Longm. Mag.* Jan. 215 The *Revolution*..the first American-built *turbine boat. 1900 *Engineer* 8 June 595/3 The Elswick *turbine destroyer, which made 36·88 knots on trial. *Ibid.* 22 June 645/2 This will be the largest *turbine-driven generating set ever built. 1901 *Westm. Gaz.* 19 June 4/3 The adaptability of the turbine-driven steamship for passenger traffic was tested on the Clyde yesterday. 1900 *Turbine dynamo [see 1 b]. 1900 *Engineer* 16 Feb. 170/1 The *turbine engines are similar to those of the Turbinia. 1901 *Scotsman* 20 Sept. 4/4 The new turbine engines.. were built to secure a speed of 35 knots. 1902 *Daily Chron.* 12 Nov. 7/2 At the present time there is only one *turbine-engined war-vessel in the world. This is H.M.S. Velox. 1904 *Longm. Mag.* Jan. 214 Two new cross-channel steamers ..are turbine-engined. 1906 J. W. THURSO *Mod. Turbine Pract.* etc. 147 Of great importance in connection with *turbine governors is the time of closing. 1907 *Westm. Gaz.* 11 Nov. 6/3 The many advantages of this special type of engine [six-cylinder motor] are its smooth, *turbine-like motion. 1900 *Engineer* 2 Nov. 444/3 *Turbine machinery occupying less space than the present cramped-up reciprocating engines. 1904 *Daily Chron.* 3 June 6/6 It has yet to be proved that turbine machinery is suitable for the propulsion of cargo vessels where speed is not a great requisite. 1900 *Engineer* 2 Feb. 127/3 A steam consumption as low as 13·9 lb. of steam per brake horse-power on a 300 horse-power steam *turbine motor. 1901 *Ibid.* 11 Jan. 45/1 The first absolute decision to adopt the *turbine principle in a large passenger vessel. 1906 *Westm. Gaz.* 3 May 6/3 Only their fast vessels would be *turbine-propelled. 1901 *Engineer* 11 Jan. 45/1 *Turbine propulsion for a new Clyde passenger steamer. 1900 *Turbine pump [see 1 b]. 1887 D. A. LOW *Machine Draw.* (1892) 120 Bearing for a *turbine shaft. 1900 *Engineer* 2 Feb. 127/3 The pinion on the turbine shaft gears into two wheels on opposite sides. 1904 *Longm. Mag.* Jan. 214 The first Transatlantic *turbine steamer. 1906 STEVENS & HOBART *Steam Turbine Engin.* 12 At high speeds the *turbine vessels excel in economy. 1860 EMERSON *Cond. Life, Worship* Wks. (Bohn) II. 396 There is faith in chemistry, in meat and wine, in..*turbine-wheels,..but not in divine causes.

Hence **Tu·rbined** *a.*, having or propelled by a turbine or turbines (Webster, 1911); **Tu·rbiner**, a turbine-driven vessel.

1905 *St. John (N. Brunswick) Daily Sun* 3 Apr. 1/1 Turbiner Victorian will dock this morning.

**Turbinectomy** (tɜːbine·ktŏmi). *Surg.* [f. TURBIN(AL + Gr. ἐκτομή excision.] Excision of a turbinal bone or bones.

1900–13 in DORLAND *Med. Dict.* 1901 *Lancet* 16 Nov. 1321/2 For short operations, such as..turbinectomy,..gas is sometimes sufficient.

**Turbinelloid** (tɜːbine·loid), *a. Zool.* [f. mod.L. *Turbinella* (f. *turbin-em*: see TURBO) + -OID.] Resembling or having the characters of the *Turbinellidæ*, a family of large marine gastropods having a pyriform shell with transverse columellar folds.

In recent Dicts.

† **Turbineous** (tɜːbi·niəs), *a. Obs. rare.* [f. L. *turbine-us* (f. *turbo*: see TURBO) + -OUS.] Of the nature of a whirlwind.

1656 BLOUNT *Glossogr.*, *Turbineous* (*turbineus*), of or belonging to a storm and blustering winde, whirling round. 1675 E. WILSON *Spadacrene Dunelm.* 26 The mighty Tempests and turbinious Winds.

**Turbiner**: see after TURBINE.

‖ **Turbines** (tɜ̄·ɹbiniz), pl. of TURBO, a genus of gastropod molluscs, q. v.

Perh. sometimes used as pl. of *turbine*, in sense of TURBO.

**Turbiniform** (tɜːbi·nifǫɹm), *a. Nat. Hist.* [ad. mod.L. *turbiniform-is*, f. L. *turbin-em*: see TURBO and -FORM.] Top-shaped, turbinate; also, having the form of the genus *Turbo* of gastropods; turbinoid, spiral.

1826 KIRBY & SP. *Entomol.* IV. xlvi. 265 Turbiniform (*Turbiniformis*). Whose vertical section is turbinate, and horizontal circular. Ex. *Antennæ* of *Aleochara socialis*. 1856 WOODWARD *Mollusca* III. 463 Vitrinella...Shell minute, hyaline, turbiniform, umbilicated.

**Turbinite** (tɜ̄·ɹbinəit). [ad. mod.L. *turbinīt-ēs*, or a. F. *turbinite*, f. L. *turbin-em*: see TURBO and -ITE [1].] A fossil turbinate shell. Also **Turbite**.

1828 WEBSTER, *Turbinite, Turbite.* 1852 TH. ROSS *Humboldt's Trav.* I. vi. 204 Some beds are almost unmixed with petrifactions, but .. the cardites, the turbinites, the ostracites, and shells of small dimension, are found.

**Turbinoid** (tɜ̄·ɹbinoid), *a. Zool.* [f. L. *turbin-em* (see TURBO) + -OID.] Resembling the genus *Turbo* or family *Turbinidæ* of gastropod molluscs (esp. those of tropical and subtropical seas) characterized by a thick top-shaped shell with a rounded opening closed by a calcareous operculum.

1861 P. P. CARPENTER in *Rep. Smithsonian Instit.* 1860, 213 Fossils of Turbinoid form. 1879 W. B. CARPENTER in *Encycl. Brit.* IX. 379/2 The type of the second group is the almost universally diffused *Rotalia*, in which the chambers are disposed in a turbinoid spire.

**Turbinotomy** (tɜːbinǫ·tŏmi). *Surg.* [f. TURBIN(AL + Gr. τομή cutting.] Incision of the turbinal bone. So **Turbinotome** (tɜːbi·nŏtōum), an instrument for performing this operation (Dorland *Med. Dict.* 1900–13).

1895 T. C. JONES in *Brit. Med. Jrnl.* II. 1289 Turbinotomy in cases of deafness and tinnitus aurium.

**Turbit** (tɜ̄·ɹbit). Also 8 -et. [app. f. L. *turbo* a top, from its figure; cf. TURBOT.] A small fancy variety of the domestic pigeon, distinguished by its stout rounded build, a short beak, the ruffle or frill on its neck and breast, and a small crest. Also *attrib.*

1688 R. HOLME *Armoury* II. 244/2 The Turbit Pigeon, or Cortbeck. 1725 *Bradley's Fam. Dict.* s.v. *Pigeon*, Many Sorts of Pigeons, such as Carriers,..Jacobins, Turbits, Helmets, [etc.]. 1859 DARWIN *Orig. Spec.* i. (1878) 16 The turbit has a short and conical beak, with a line of reversed feathers down the breast. 1896 *Westm. Gaz.* 17 Feb. 2/1 He has a strain of the turbit pigeon in him, while all the rest are just the common wild Blue Rock sort.

Hence **Turbiteen** (tɜːbitī·n), an oriental frilled variety of domestic pigeon resembling the turbit, and said to be derived from it. Also *attrib.*

1876 H. P. CARIDIA in R. Fulton *Bk. Pigeons* 317 The Turbiteens. These are the present Oriental Turbits, which twenty-five years ago were marked as the present British Turbits. 1885 *Bazaar* 30 Mar. 1265/1 Handsome chequered turbiteen cock.

**Turbite**: see under TURBINITE. **Turbith**: see TURPETH. **Turblaunce**, var. TROUBLANCE *Obs.* **Turble**, obs. f. TROUBLE.

**Turbo** (tɜ̄·ɹbo). [a. L. *turbo* (also *turben*), *turbin-em* a whirlwind or tornado, a spinning-top, a reel or spindle, a whirl, twirl, twist, revolution.]

† **1.** A whirlwind, a tornado. *Obs. rare.*

1677 PLOT *Oxfordsh.* 5 Those that have sailed to the Indies can inform them what force Hurricane's and Turbo's have.

‖ **2.** (mod.L., pl. *turbines* (-nīz).) A genus of gastropod molluscs, typical of the family *Turbinidæ*, having a regularly turbinate or whorled shell, with a rounded aperture and a calcareous operculum; also loosely, any member of the *Turbinidæ*; any turbinate or wreathed shell.

1661 LOVELL *Hist. Anim. & Min.* Introd., The turbines are great, eared, tuberous. 1760–72 tr. *Juan & Ulloa's Voy.* (ed. 3) I. 168 This species of turbines, the juice of which is also used in dying cotton threads. 1779 MRS. DELANY in *Life & Corr.* Ser. II. (1862) II. 475 She has found at her grotto some shells,..and found on Bunster a left-handed tooth'd turbo. 1837 *Encycl. Brit.* (ed. 7) XV. 347/2 A rigorous examination of the turbines of British writers. 1884 G. ALLEN in *Pall Mall G.* 26 Sept. 4/1 The objects inside the bower [of the Australian bower-bird] comprise a large and very handsome marine shell,..a pale blue turbo; a purplish pink cowrie.

**3.** *Mech.* = TURBINE: cf. next. *colloq.*

1904 *Electr. World & Engin.* 30 July 165I Oil coolers are erected in the basement below the turbos, through which the lubricating oil is passed, and cooled by means of a cold water circulation.

**Turbo-** (tɜ̄·ɹbo), a verbal element repr. TURBINE, in compounds forming the names of various machines driven by and directly coupled to a turbine, or which are themselves turbines, the second element being the name of the machine so driven or coupled; thus = TURBINE in comb.; as *turbo-alternator, -dynamo, -generator, -machine, -motor, -pump, -unit, -ventilator.*

1900 *Engineer* 2 Nov. 444/3 Tests..on two *turbo alternators of 1000 kilowatts per hour nominal output. 1902 SLOANE *Stand. Electr. Dict.* App., *Turbo-alternator*, an alternating current dynamo coupled direct to a high-speed steam turbine. 1904 *Electr. World & Engin.* 19 Mar. 558 Electrical and mechanical difficulties which arise in the design of *turbo-dynamos (dynamo-electric generators directly connected to steam-turbines). 1904 *Ibid.* 21 May 945 Each of the..*turbo-electric units is of the vertical type. 1903 *Ibid.* 25 July 147 Two groups of *turbo-exciters, of 110 h. p. each. 1902 SLOANE *Stand. Electr. Dict.* App., **Turbo-generator*, a generator coupled or geared to a high-speed steam turbine, and on the same base with it. 1911 *Evolution of Parsons Steam Turbine* 30 This turbo-generator worked for many years. 1903 *Sci. Amer., Supp.* 26 Sept. 23185 Steam-turbines are .. analogous to hydraulic turbines, and form part of the general class which the author [Professor Rateau] will call '*turbo-machines'. 1900 *Westm. Gaz.* 7 Sept. 6/1 A torpedo-destroyer..driven through the water at the rate of forty-three miles an hour by the use of the *turbo-motor instead of reciprocating engines. 1903 *Electr. World & Engin.* 4 July 17 Prof. Rateau has installed *turbo-ventilators giving a pressure of half an atmosphere, and *turbo-pumps with a lift of several hundred metres.

**Turbot** (tɜ̄·ɹbət). Forms: 3–8 turbut, 4–5 -bote, 4–7 -butt, 5 -bott, 6 -butte, 6–7 -bat, 7 *Sc.* -batt, 6–8 -bet, 7, 9 -bit, 4– **turbot**. [a. OF. *tourbout* (12th c. in Hatz.-Darm.), *torbout*, AF. *turbut*, MDu. *turbot, terbot, tarbot*; of uncertain origin; perh. a deriv. of L. *turbo* spinning top (also in med.L. 'turbot'), referring to its shape; but the termination of the F. word is unexplained.]

**1.** A large flat fish (*Rhombus maximus* or *Psetta maxima*), having a wide scaleless body covered with conical bony tubercles, with the eyes normally on the left side, found on the European coasts and much esteemed as food.

*c* 1300 *Havelok* 754 He tok þe sturgiun, and þe qual, And þe turbut, and lax with-al. 1307–8 *Durham Acc. Rolls* (Surtees) 4 In j turbote, iiij s. ij d. 1377 *Ibid.* 46 In j Turbutt et j leyng emp. in villa, xs. vj d. 14.. *Nom.* in Wr.-Wülcker 704/36 (*Nomina piscium*) *Hic turbo, -[i]nis*, a turbott. *c* 1450 *Two Cookery-bks.* 112 Nym luys, turbot, and elys & gobete hem in mosselys. 1502–3 *Rec. St. Mary at Hill* 248 Payd for di. a turbutt xx d. 1570 LEVINS *Manip.* 93/24 A Turbet, fish, *rhombus, i.* *Ibid.* 195/28 Turbutte, fish, *chalchis, rhombus, i.* 1596 DALRYMPLE tr. *Leslie's Hist. Scot.* (S.T.S.) I. 41 Turbat, ffluik, and plase fluik. 1655 MOUFET & BENNET *Health's Improv.* (1746) 266 Turbots.. were in old time counted so good and delicate, that this Proverb grew upon them, *Nihil ad Rhombum*; that is to say, *What is all this in comparison of a Turbot.* 1728 YOUNG *Love Fame* III. 74 The salmon is refus'd, the turbot bought. 1771 SMOLLETT *Humph. Cl.* 5 June, My uncle..asked him to dinner, and treated him with a fine turbot. 1836 YARRELL *Brit. Fishes* II. 238 Reversed Turbots..that is, Turbots having the eyes and dark colour on the right side instead of the left, are also occasionally brought to market. 1870 YEATS *Nat. Hist. Comm.* 324 The English markets..are supplied chiefly with Dutch turbot.

**2.** Applied to other fish more or less resembling the turbot.

**a.** In north of Eng. and parts of Scotland, the halibut. **b.** In U. S., any of various large flat fishes, as the diamond flounder of California (*Hypopsetta guttulata*), or the spotted flounder of the Pacific coast (*Bothus maculatus*). **c.** In New Zealand, *Ammotretis guntheri*, also called *lemon-sole* (Morris). **d.** Locally, any of various species of *Balistes*, the file-fishes and trigger-fishes (*Cent. Dict.* 1891).

1555 EDEN *Decades* 200 Certeyne other fysshes: as soles, mackerelles, turbuttes [in W. Indies]. 1598 HAKLUYT *Voy.* I. 104 They gaue vnto vs a great fresh turbut. 1601 HOLLAND *Pliny* IX. xx. I. 247 In a Turbot the right side turneth upward, and in a Plaice the left. 1674 RAY *Collect. Words, Fishes* s. v., What in the [South] they call the Halibut in the North they call the Turbot;..in some parts of the West of England they call the Turbot Bret and the Halibut Turbot. 1794 *Statist. Acc. Scot.* XII. 171 *note*, The fish..are cod, ling, skate, mackerel, hollybut, here called turbot. 1810 P. NEILL *List Fishes* 11 (Jam.) Holibut...In our [Edinburgh] market ..named the turbot; the proper turbot..getting another name, that of rawnfleuk. 1883 *Chambers' Encycl.* IX. 581/2 The American or Spotted Turbot (*Rhombus maculatus*)..is common on the coasts of New England and New York. 1885 LADY BRASSEY *The Trades* 302 There were fish here [Jamaica] called turbot—not the least like our turbot, but of bright ultramarine and azure blue.

**3.** *attrib.* and *Comb.*, as *turbot-boat, -fish, -fisher, -fishery, -kettle, -line*, † *-sprout* (SPROUT *sb.*[2]); *turbot-like* adj.

1845 GOSSE *Ocean* ii. (1849) 82 *Turbot-boat off Scarborough. 1611 COTGR., *Turbot*, the *Turbot fish. 1845 GOSSE *Ocean* ii. (1849) 82 Even the practised eye of the *turbot-fisher..fails to detect a fish when thus concealed. 1765 *Museum Rust.* IV. 238 The *turbot-fishery off the British coasts. 1846 SOYER *Cookery* 85 Put the whole of the turtle..into a large *turbot kettle. 1611 COTGR., *Barbuë*,.. a kind of lesse Turbot, or *Turbot-like fish, called by some, a Dab, or Sandling. 1763 *Chron.* in *Ann. Reg.* 162/1 A complete sett of *turbot-lines. 1324–5 *Durham Acc. Rolls* (Surtees) 14 In..xij *torbotes sproutes, xvj Lopsters. 1430 *Ibid.* 61 In..j Turbotspreute [*printed* -sprente].

† **Turbulacioun, -aunce**, obs. var. TRIBULATION, TROUBLANCE.

*c* 1430 LYDG. *Min. Poems* (Percy Soc.) 251 My socoure and refuge, Geyn every tempest and turbulacioun.

**Turbulence** (tɜ̄·ɹbiŭlĕns). Also 7 -ance. [ad.

L. *turbulentia*, f. *turbulentus* TURBULENT: see -ENCE: cf. F. *turbulance*, *-ence* (14th c. in Hatz.-Darm.), perh. the immediate source.] The state or quality of being turbulent; violent commotion, agitation, or disturbance; disorderly or tumultuous character or conduct; with *a* and *pl.*, an instance of this.

**1598** FLORIO, *Torbolenza*, turbulence, disturbance. **1606** SHAKS. *Tr. & Cr.* v. iii. 11, I haue dreampt Of bloody turbulence. **1639** in *Kirkcudbr. War-Comm. Min. Bk.* etc. (1855) 231 Whatsomever tumilts and turbulances that shall happen to fall out. **1777** ROBERTSON *Hist. Amer.* II. v. 4 The turbulence of youth .. gradually subsided. **1845** M. PATTISON *Ess.* (1889) I. 18 It required all the personal influence of the king to check the turbulence of his irritated followers. **1853** J. H. NEWMAN *Hist. Sk.* (1873) III. I. i. 5 A temporary retreat from the turbulence of ecclesiastical politics.

**b.** Of natural conditions: Stormy or tempestuous state or action; violence.

**1726–46** THOMSON *Winter* 56 Congregated clouds, And all the vapoury turbulence of heaven. **1748** *Anson's Voy.* I. viii. 82 The turbulence of the weather. **1820** SCORESBY *Acc. Arctic Reg.* I. 301 Capable of resisting the turbulence of the ocean. **1862** GOULBURN *Pers. Relig.* III. vii. 205 Think of Him as calm .. amidst the most furious agitations and turbulences of nature.

**Turbulency** (tǝ̄·ɹbiŭlĕnsi). Now *rare.* [f. as prec.: see next and -ENCY.] Turbulent state, disturbed condition.

**1607** *Puritan* I. ii. 61, I .. for my part wish a Turbulency in the world. *c* **1645** HOWELL *Lett.* vi. 80 Since the turbulency of these times, the same moderation shines in you. **1671** MILTON *P. R.* IV. 462 Like turbulencies in the affairs of men, .. They oft fore-signifie and threaten ill. **1694** SALMON *Bate's Dispens.* (1713) 512/1 Where there is need of quieting the Turbulency and Effervescency of the Humours. **1734** tr. *Rollin's Anc. Hist.* XVI. ii. (1827) VI. 349 Endeavour to calm the turbulency of their minds. **1831** POE *Bells* iii, What a tale of terror their turbulency tells!

**Turbulent** (tǝ̄·ɹbiŭlĕnt), *a.* [ad. L. *turbulent-us* full of disturbance or commotion, restless, f. *turba* crowd, *turbāre* to disturb, agitate: cf. *corpulent*, *truculent*. So F. *turbulent* (12–13th c.).]

**1.** Of persons, their attributes and actions: Causing disturbance or commotion; disposed or inclined to disorder; tumultuous; unruly; violent.

**1538** COVERDALE *N. T.* Ded., These turbulent and stormy assaultes of the wicked. **1593** G. HARVEY *Pierce's Super.* 98 That execrable Seruetus, or other turbulent rebells in Religion. **1602** SHAKS. *Ham.* III. i. 4 Grating so harshly all his dayes of quiet With turbulent and dangerous Lunacy. *a* **1780** WATSON *Philip III*, III. (1793) I. 289 The danger to which he was exposed from their turbulent ambition. **1846** TRENCH *Mirac.* vi. (1862) 188 He expelled from the house the crowd of turbulent mourners. **1856** EMERSON *Eng. Traits, Char.* Wks. (Bohn) II. 59 They stoutly carry into every nook and corner of the earth their turbulent sense.

†**b.** Of things: Having a disturbing effect; tending to produce disturbance or trouble. *Obs.*

**1625** BACON *Ess., Innovations* (Arb.) 527 A Froward Retention of Custome, is as turbulent a Thing, as an Innouation. **1625** K. LONG tr. *Barclay's Argenis* II. xvii. 121 Such, whose angry and turbulent Planets have indued them with a more violent disposition. **1671** MILTON *Samson* 522 Nor envied them the grape Whose heads that turbulent liquor fills with fumes.

**c.** Violent in action or effect.

**1656** RIDGLEY *Pract. Physick* 65 The cause is a Narcotick vapour, but it is turbulent also. **1874** GARROD & BAXTER *Mat. Med.* (1880) 440 When the heart is turbulent in its action, then the sedative remedies which act upon this organ are indicated; .. a turbulent cardiac condition is often combined with a very imperfect flow of blood through its cavities.

**2.** Characterized by violent disturbance or commotion; violently disturbed or agitated; disorderly, troubled. **a.** Of weather, the sea, etc.: Stormy, tempestuous.

**1573** G. HARVEY *Letter-bk.* (Camden) 34 After thes turbulent raging tempests I hope verrely for caulm and faier wether. **1608** SHAKS. *Per.* III. ii. 4 T'as been a turbulent and stormie night. *a* **1687** PETTY *Pol. Arith.* (1690) 20 One sort of Vessels for the turbulent Sea, another for Inland Waters. **1770** G. WHITE *Selborne* xxix. 80 Last month we had such a series of cold turbulent weather. **1860** TYNDALL *Glac.* I. xiv. 94 Our way sometimes lay .. across turbulent brooks. **1864** A. McKAY *Hist. Kilmarnock* 261 The swollen waters bore upon their turbulent bosoms planks, trees, [etc.].

**b.** Of a state of mind or thought, social or political affairs, etc.

**1609** DANIEL *Civ. Wars* I. 9 [He] making the succession doubtfull, rent This new-got State, and left it turbulent. **1667** MILTON *P. L.* IX. 1126 Thir inward State of Mind, calme Region once And full of Peace, now tost and turbulent. **1788** GIBBON *Decl. & F.* xxxix. (1869) II. 433 The reign of the usurper was short and turbulent. **1848** DICKENS *Dombey* lix, However turbulent his thoughts, .. that was all past now. **1849** MACAULAY *Hist. Eng.* iv. I. 455 In the City of London, lately so turbulent, scarcely a murmur was heard.

Hence **Tu·rbulently** *adv.*, in a turbulent manner; with much commotion, tumultuously, violently; **Tu·rbulentness**, *rare* = TURBULENCE.

**1602** WARNER *Alb. Eng.* Epit. (1612) 392 The aforesaid intermitted Controuersie .. hence-forth turbulently and Tragically proceeded. **1609** W. SCLATER *Threefold Preserv.* (1610) Ep. Ded., I know not what show of turbulentnesse they can accuse me of. **1655** FULLER *Ch. Hist.* XI. i. § 11 This meeting .. proceeded turbulently, and suspiciously. **1746** SMART *Ode St. Cecilia's Day* vi, In sorrow's tempest turbulently tost. **1863** W. C. BALDWIN *Afr. Hunting* ix. 397 The gorge [at Victoria Falls] cannot be more than a hundred yards wide, and at the bottom the river rolls turbulently boiling.

†**Tu·rbulous**, *a.* *Obs. rare.* Also 6 **tourbulus.** [f. L. *turbul-entus* TURBULENT + -OUS: cf. OF. *torbleus* TROUBLOUS.] = TURBULENT, TROUBLOUS 2.

**1527** HACKET *Let. to Wolsey* (MS. Cott. Galba B. xiv. 91), That [we] may cheyse the best for owr own parte and for t[he] welt and comodyte of all the tourbulus Cristynd[om]. **1579** J. STUBBES in *Harington's Nugæ Ant.* (1804) I. 151 A miserable turbulous wretch, seekinge to interrupt her peace. **1676** W. ROW *Contn. Blair's Autobiog.* xii. (1848) 582 Turbulous and seditious.

**Turbyll**, obs. form of TROUBLE.

**Turc**, obs. f. TURK. **Turcais, -cas, -e, -casse, turches, -is, -ois**: see TURKIS, TURQUOISE.

**Turchine**, var. TURKIN *Obs.*, blue cloth.

†**Tu·rcian**, *a.* *Obs.* = next.

**1576** FOXE *A. & M.* 3/1 Ottomannus the first Turcian Emperour.

†**Tu·rcic**, *a.* *Obs. rare.* [f. med.L. *Turc-us* TURK + -IC.] Of Turkey, Turkish. So †**Tu·rcical** *a.* *Obs. rare*, Turkish, Turk-like.

**1600** W. WATSON *Decacordon* (1602) 331 Their [the Jesuits'] intended gouernment is most Antichristian, Tartarian, Turcicall and Tyrannicall. **1661** LOVELL *Hist. Anim. & Min.* Introd., Pulveratricious domestick, as the Cock and hen, Patavine, Turcick, Persick, .. Indian, and Guinie.

† **Turciman**, obs. var. TRUCHMAN.

**1562** J. SHUTE tr. *Cambini's Turk. Wars* 68 b, A notable matter, which was declared vnto me .. (by a Persian ..) hauing for my turciman a citizen of ours named Iohn Cerini.

†**Turcism** (tǝ̄·ɹsiz'm). *Obs.* See also TURKISM. [f. med.L. *Turc-us* TURK + -ISM.] The religion or system of the Turks; Mohammedanism.

**1566** in Neal *Hist. Purit.* (1732) I. 233 Turcism stood upon as good ground as Popery. **1582** MUNDAY *Breefe & True Rep. Exec. Traytours* 122, I think .. if any Prince fal by infidelity into Turscisme, Atheisme, Paganisme or any such lyke, that the Pope hath auchoritie to depose such a Prince. **1607** R. C[AREW] tr. *Estienne's World of Wonders* 75 If a man would haue a perfect .. religion .., he must compound it of Christian religion, Iudaizm, and Turcizm. **1621–31** LAUD *Sev. Serm.* (1847) 13 Heathenism, and Turcism, and Judaism, and Heresy, and Superstition, and Schism. **1721** STRYPE *Eccl. Mem.* I. xxxv. 271 He grounds his .. discourse upon the probability of the fall of Turcism.

**b.** Turkish principles and practice.

**1581** ALLEN *Apol.* 29 b, Greekes and Hungarians infected with Turcisme. **1613** ZOUCH *Dove* 29 Illyricum whilst Turcisme it oreflowes, Feeles not her billowes, nor respects her blowes. *a* **1643** LD. FALKLAND, etc. *Infallibility* (1646) 109 The very using of this violence is a prime piece of Turcisme. **1705** STANHOPE *Paraphr.* III. 324 The Parts of the Christian Church once most conspicuous and flourishing .. have long since been overrun with Turcism and Barbarity.

**Turcize**: see TURKIZE.

**Turco** (tǝ̄·ɹko). [a. Sp., Pg., and It. *turco* TURK.]

**1.** A Chilian bird, *Hylactes megapodius*, related to and resembling the TAPACULO.

**1839** DARWIN *Voy. Nat.* xii. (1873) 270 The former, called by the Chilenos 'el Turco', is as large as a fieldfare .. The Turco is not uncommon. **1896** NEWTON *Dict. Birds* 947 The 'Turco', .. *Hylactes megapodius*, is larger, with greatly developed feet and claws.

**2.** A Turk or Moor (in S. America).

**1909** *Bible in World* Aug. 242/2 The Arabic Version is needed by the so-called Turcos, who settle chiefly in North Brazil.

**3.** One of a body of native Algerian light infantry in the French army; a Zouave soldier. Also *attrib.* or *adj.*

**1860** CAPT. S. OSBORN in *Once a Week* 7 July 35/1 A small breadth of blue water stayed the charge of the Tartar cutthroat of the olden day, as we trust it may do the *pas accéléré* of the more modern Zouaves or Turcos. **1898** *Edin. Rev.* Apr. 344 The Turco battalion was constantly engaged. *Ibid.* 345 A battalion of Turcos. **1902** R. W. CHAMBERS *Maids of Paradise* v, A Turco soldier came into the room.

**Turco-, Turko-** (tǝ̄·ɹko), combining form repr. med.L. *Turcus* or TURK. **a.** Used with adjs. or sbs. denoting other peoples or countries, signifying 'Turkish and ..' or 'Turkishly ..', as *Turco-Bulgarian*, *-Byzantine*, *-Egyptian*, *-Italian*, etc.

**1813** A. BRUCE *Life Alex. Morus* ii. 27 The iniquity of that Turcopopish government. **1813** *Q. Rev.* Oct. 256/2 Turcotartarian. **1865** *Reader* No. 107. 33/3 Hungarian and Turcotartaric dialects. **1884** *Graphic* 4 Oct. 360/3 The style is Turco-Byzantine—the beginning of the end. **1897** *Westm. Gaz.* 25 Sept. 2/2 Other Greek statesmen .. were also enamoured of the idea of a Turko-Greek alliance. **1903** *Daily Chron.* 28 May 6/1 On my arrival I found the Turkish and Turco-Albanian population of the town calm. **1909** *Westm. Gaz.* 13 July 1/3 In order to gain the confidence of the Turco-Cretans.

**b.** in other derivatives, as **Turco·logist** (*nonce-wd.*), one who is versed in Turkish history, literature, language, or art; **Turcoma·nia**, a rage for Turkish manners or customs; excessive favour for Turkish policy, etc.; **Tu·rcophil, -e** *a.*, tending to favour Turkey or the Turks; *sb.* one who favours Turkey; hence **Turco·philism**; **Tu·rcophobe**, one who has a morbid fear or dislike of the Turks; so **Turco·phobist.**

**1881** A. VÁMBÉRY in *Athenæum* 31 Dec. 888/2 *Turcologists will be always thankful for his edition of the Cumanian glossary. **1834** *Ayesha* I. i. 9 He had been bitten by the *turcomania to such a degree, that [etc.]. **1876** *Times* 16 June, *Turcophile. **1880** *Manch. Guard.* 3 Nov., They are Turcophiles, but they would very much like to see a sequestration of Turkish revenues for their own advantage. **1895** *Eclectic Mag.* Oct. 566 A Turkophil Bulgaria might come .. to mean a great autonomous .. Balkan Kingdom. **1903** *Speaker* 10 Oct. 28/2 His wonderful achievement in destroying the great Turcophil tradition. **1880** *Daily News* 7 Oct. 4/6 Their conduct is not to be ascribed to what they call *Turcophilism—meaning .. affection for the Turk. **1896** *Westm. Gaz.* 14 May 2/2 His kindness .. should convince the sternest *Turkophobe. **1877** J. BAKER *Turkey* Pref. 4 Another resident of .. long standing, but a *Turcophobist.

**Turcois**, obs. form of TURQUOISE.

**Turcoman** (tǝ̄·ɹkomæ̆n). Also 7 **Turcomane, Turkeman,** 9 **Toorkoman, Turkoman**; *β.* 7 **Turcman,** 7– **Turkman.** See also TURKMAN. [a. Pers. تركمان *turkumān* 'one like or resembling a Turk', f. ترك TURK + ماندن *mān-dan* to resemble: applied to the Turkish nomads. Hence med.L. *Turcomannus*, F. *tourcouman*. In English sometimes made into *Turkman*, and the second element treated as MAN, as in *Chinaman*, etc., with pl. *Turkmen*: cf. *Mussulman*.]

**1.** A member of a branch of the Turkish race, consisting of a number of tribes inhabiting the region lying east of the Caspian Sea and about the Sea of Aral, formerly known as Turkestan or Independent Tartary (now annexed by Russia) and parts of Persia and Afghanistan; mainly nomadic and pastoral, and notorious for their predatory habits.

**1600** J. PORY tr. *Leo's Africa* IX. 337 Camels are gentle and domesticall beasts, and .. are vsed in Asia by the Tartars, the Curdians, the Dalemians, and the Turcomans. **1625** PURCHAS *Pilgrims* II. IX. iv. § 2. 1427 The noble Kingdome of Armenia, called now Turcomania, because of the Turcomanes a people that came out of Scythia .. who live as Shepheards in their Tents. **1632** LITHGOW *Trav.* V. 196 Poore miserable people called Turcomani, liuing in Tents. **1854** CHURCH *Misc. Writ.* (1891) I. 288 The traveller in Asia Minor comes from time to time upon encampments of Turkomans.

*β.* **1683** T. SMITH *Acc. Prusa* in *Misc. Cur.* (1708) III. 73 The Turkmans, (for so they are peculiarly called, as if they were the true Descendents of the Old Turks or Scythians,) .. have no fixt Residence any where, but Travel with their Families and Cattle from Place to Place, carrying their Wives and Children upon Camels. **1686** tr. *Chardin's Coronat. Solyman* 123 A great number of Turkmans or Shepherds. *Ibid.* 124 These People our Modern Authors call Turcomans, which are properly Turks. **1823** BYRON *Island* II. xix, Sublime tobacco! which from east to west Cheers the tar's labour or the Turkman's rest. **1897** RAMSAY *Every Day Life Turkey* iii. 96 These people are Turkmans and their customs are different from those of other Moslems. **1906** — in *Contemp. Rev.* July 11 The Byzantine historians, who distinguish these Turkmen or Nomads .. from the Turks.

**b.** The Turkish language of this people.

**1798** *Brit. Critic* XI. 37 The Turkish language, .. that corrupt jargon; a strange harsh mixture of the vernacular Turcoman, Arabic, and Persian.

**2.** A Turcoman horse: see quot. 1831.

**1831** YOUATT *Horse* ii. 17 The Toorkoman horse. Turkistan .. has been celebrated from very early times, for producing a pure and valuable breed of horses. They are called Toorkomans. They are said to be preferable even to the pure Persians, for service. **1884** O'DONOVAN *Merv* xxiv. 270 They are generally .. a mixture of Arab and Turcoman blood, but thoroughbred Turcomans are also .. for sale. **1905** *Statesman* (Calcutta) 23 Aug. 2/3 For Sale—Pair of Handsome Red spotted Cream Turcomans (ponies).

**3.** A kind of textile material; cf. *Turcoman carpet* in 4.

**1885** E. W. LIGHTNER in *Harper's Mag.* Mar. 531/2 An autograph *portière* with alternate stripes of 'crazy patchwork' embroidered on crimson turcoman.

**4.** *attrib.* or as *adj.* Of or pertaining to this people, their language, or the region they inhabit. **Turcoman carpet** or **rug**, a soft, rich-coloured carpet made by the Turcomans.

**1613** PURCHAS *Pilgrimage* (1614) 44 Some also attribute the Turkes or Turkeman Nation to this name and Authour. **1687** A. LOVELL tr. *Thevenot's Trav.* II. 44 A score of Turcoman Horsemen, armed with Muskets and Lances. **1798** *Brit. Critic* XI. 34 The Turcoman nymphs there spoken of, are not, by any means, the damsels of the country we now denominate Turkey. **1842** J. B. FRASER *Mesopot. & Assyria* xv. 366 Of hares there are two kinds; the Turkoman variety, which haunts the plains, and that of the desert, with long hair and ears. **1859** *Blackw. Mag.* Oct. 428/1 The Arab and Turcoman women go unveiled. **1901** SKRINE *Sir W. W. Hunter* xxi. 450 The feats of Alexander are still told with bated breath in the Turkoman nomad's tent. **1911** B. HOLLAND *Life Dk. Devonshire* I. xiv. 321 Some new advance across the Turcoman steppes.

**Turcopole** (tǝ̄·ɹkopōul). *Hist.* [ad. med.L. *Turcopōlus* (Orderic. Vital.) *-pūlus* (Matt. Paris), *Turcoplus* (Roger Hoveden), in Byzantine Gr. Τουρκόπουλοι or -πουλα, according to Albert Aq. (in Du Cange) f. Τουρκο- Turk + πῶλος foal, young animal, in late Gr. 'child', L. *pullus* young animal, applied to children of a Turkish or Saracen father and Greek mother. So OF. *turcople*.] A light-armed soldier of the Order of St. John of Jerusalem.

[**1852** SIR J. TAAFFE *Hist. Order St. John* I. I. iii. 191 Of *Turcopili* we read in old chronicles they were light cavalry, but on other occasions they had cuirasses. There were a corps of them kept by the Emperor of Constantinople.] **1896** *Dict. Nat. Biog.* XLVII. 336/2 He [John Rawson] was appointed [in 1527] turcopolier or commander of the turcopoles or light infantry of the order.

**Turcopolier** (tǝ̄·ɹkǫ̆pǫ̆lī·ǝɹ). *Hist.* Forms: 5

**turkepler, twrkepler, 6 turkeplyer, Turkeiplier, Turcuplyar, 6–7 Turcoplier, 8– Turcopolier.** [ad. med.L. *turcopolerius* (Statutes of Order Hospitallers, xix. 7), also *-ārius*, f. *Turcopolus*: see prec. In F. *Turcopolier*, OF. *turcoplier*, *Turcupler*: see -IER 2.] The commander of the turcopoles or light-armed soldiers of the order of St. John of Jerusalem (later of Rhodes, and Malta).

**1481** *Cely Papers* (Camden) 60 My loorde and the turkepler goys to the Rodys togyddyr. *Ibid.* 63 Twrkepler. **1527** SIR R. WESTON *Let. to Wolsey* 12 Apr., The Turkeplyer hath evermore bene wont to succede the master of Sainct Johns in his rome. *a* **1548** HALL *Chron., Hen. VIII* 204 The Lorde Master appoynted the Prior of Rome and the Turcuplyar of England to be Capitaynes of this enterprise. *Ibid.*, The Turkeiplier with .vi. English knyghtes were appoynted to defende the Molle or Peere at the hauen mouthe. **1599** HAKLUYT *Voy.* II. I. 83 Sir Iohn Bourgh Turcoplier of England, chiefe captaine of the succours of the sayd posterne of England. *a* **1648** LD. HERBERT *Hen. VIII* (1649) 461 They never attained higher dignity then the Turcoplier or Captains place. **1709** STRYPE *Ann. Ref.* I. xxii. 231 Shelly..went..to Malta, to establish his office and dignity of Turcopolier for the English nation. **1788** tr. *Bisani's Pict. Tour Europe*, etc. 20 The different Nations of which the Order is composed..have each of them chiefs, who are here called Piliers...The Pilier of Germany is Grand Chancellor; and that of England, Turcopolier, or General of Infantry. **1887** DOWDEN *Shelley* I. 1 Sir Richard as English Grand Prior enjoying the eminent title of Turcopolier.

**Turd** (tɒ̄ɹd). Not now in polite use. Forms: 1, 3–6 **tord**, (3 **tort**), 4–6 **toord**, 6 **toorde**, 5–6 **torde**, 5–7 **turde**, 6 **tourd**, **-e**, **towrde**, *Sc.* **tuird**, 5– **turd**. [OE. *tord*, = MDu., MFl. *torde, tort*, (whence also early mod.Du. *tort-wevel* (Kilian), OE. *tord-wifel*, ON. *tord-ýfill*, OSw. *tord-öfvil*, Sw. *tordyfvel*, Norw. *tordivel, -yvel*, dung-beetle, sharn-bug), prob. :—IndoEur. **drtó-*, pa. pple. of **der-* to tear, split. See Falk and Torp *Etymol. Wbch.* s.v. *Torbist*. Cf. also *tirdle, trottle*, TRATTLE, TREDDLE.]

**1.** A lump or piece of excrement; also, excrement, ordure.

*c* **1000** *Sax. Leechd.* II. 62 Swines tord. *Ibid.* 322 Culfran tord. *Ibid.* 330 Niwe horses tord. *a* **1250**, **13..** [see b]. **1382** WYCLIF *Zeph.* i. 17 The blood of hem shal be shed out as erthe, and the bodyes of hem as tordis. **1388** — *Isa.* v. 25 The deed bodies of hem weren maad as a toord [1382 drit] in the myddis of stretis. *c* **1400** *Lanfranc's Cyrurg.* 194 Sprynge þeron poudre maad of tapsia,..& tordis of a culuere. **1483** *Cath. Angl.* 189/2 An Horse turde, *donarium*. **1553** BALE *Vocacyon* 45 Yet will a toorde be but a stinkinge toorde, both in smele and syght, pepper him and bawme him ..as wele as they can. **1651** C. CARTWRIGHT *Cert. Relig.* I. 91 No marvel that he [Luther] is so taxed for his stincking repetition of turds and dunghils. *c* **1720** W. GIBSON *Farrier's Dispens.* ix. (1734) 232 Turd and all manner of filth. **1761** *Brit. Mag.* II. 63 Thatch your house with t—d, and you'll have more teachers than reachers.

**b.** As a type of worthlessness or vileness.

*a* **1250** *Owl & Night.* 1686 A tord [*v.r.* tort] ne yeue ic for eu alle. **13..** *Guy Warw.* (A.) 3704 Þou nart nouȝt worþ a tord. **1382** WYCLIF *Phil.* iii. 8 Alle thingis..I deme as toordis, that I wynne Crist. *c* **1450** *Debate Carpenter's Tools* 110 in Hazlitt *E. P. P.* I. 83 Thou arte not worth a tord. **1619–20** *Archdeaconry of Essex Minutes* lf. 265 (MS.) He did demaunde rent of one who holdeth some land which was given ..for the poore of the same parishe, who bid a turde for him and a turde for them.

**c.** In coarse abuse; also applied to a person as a term of execration or contempt.

*c* **1450** *Mankind* 127 in *Macro Plays* 6. *a* **1518** SKELTON *Magnyf.* 397 Do away, I say, the deuylles torde! **1598** E. GILPIN *Skial.* (1878) 37 The foul-mouthd knave wil call thee goodman Tord. **1614** B. JONSON *Bart. Fair* I. iv, Good Master Hornet, turd i' your teeth, hold you your tongue.

**2.** *attrib.* and *Comb.*, as *turd-monger*; also *turd-coloured, -faced* adjs; **turd-bird**, local name for species of Skua (*Stercorarius*).

**1550** BALE *Apol.* 112 That torde monger, whych dysdaynynge my precious preceptes, presenteth me with his vile dirty donge. *a* **1585** POLWART *Flyting w. Montgomerie* 787 Tuirdfacit, ay chaisit, almaist fyld for ane theif! *a* **1704** T. BROWN *Walk round Lond., Thames* Wks. 1709 III. III. 59 Out you nasty T—d colour'd dog. **18..** ATKINSON *Provinc. Names Birds* (MS.), *Turd-bird*, a provincial name for Richardson's Skua.

**Turdiform** (tɒ̄·ɹdifǭɹm), *a.* *Ornith.* [ad. mod. L. *turdiform-is*, f. L. *turdus* thrush: see -FORM.] Having the form or appearance of a thrush; thrush-like. So **Turdine** (tɒ̄·ɹdəin) *a.* [-INE[1]], belonging to the sub-family *Turdinæ* of true thrushes; **Tu·rdoid** *a.* [ad. F. *turdoïde* (Temminck, 1823)], akin to a thrush; *spec.* belonging to the family *Turdidæ*.

**1874** A. R. WALLACE in *Ibis* Oct. 409 Typical or Turdoid Passeres. Wing with 10 primaries. **1890** *Field* 12 Apr. 517/3 The three leading forms of Turdine families, viz., Thrushes, Warblers, and Flycatchers, are well characterized.

†**Turdion.** *Obs. rare.* Also 6 **turgion.** [a. F. *tordion*, OF. *tourdion, -eon*, deriv. of *tord-re* to twist.] A lively dance, said to be of the nature of a galliard; 'a round' (Cotgrave).

**1531** ELYOT *Gov.* I. xx, We haue nowe base daunsis, bargenettes, pauions, turgions, and roundes. **1549** *Compl. Scot.* vi. 66 Base dansis, pauuans, galȝardis, turdions, braulis and branglis, buffons, vitht mony vthir lycht dancis.

**Turdy** (tɒ̄·ɹdi), *a.* [f. TURD + -Y.] Full of, befouled, or defiled with ordure; † of or pertaining to excrement, fæcal (*obs.*).

*c* **1600** *Timon* I. iv. 11 *G.* Bloudy. *P.* Nay, rather, turdy. **1605** B. JONSON *Volpone* II. ii. **1611** COTGR., *Stercorin*.. Excrementall, turdie. **1668** CULPEPPER & COLE *Barthol. Anat.* I. ii. 26 The *Fermentum stercoreum* or turdie Leaven, which turns the Excrements of the Chyle into plain Turds.

**Ture**, obs. or dial. form of TURF *sb.*[1]

**Tureen** (tərī·n, tiurī·n). Forms: *α.* 8 **terrene, terene**, 8–9 **terrine**, 9 **tereen**; *β.* 8 **turen(n)e, -ein, turrene**, 8– **tureen.** [a. F. *terrine* a large circular flat-bottomed earthenware dish, as a milk-pan, in OF. *therine* (1412 in Godef. *Compl.*), fem. of OF. *terrin* of earth, earthen :—pop. L. **terrīn-us*, f. *terra* earth. In English first spelt etymologically *terrene, terrine*, and later corrupted to *turein, tureen*, from phonetic equivalence of *terr-* and *tur-*, and then perh. conformed to the place-name *Turin*.] A deep earthenware or plated vessel (usually oval) with a lid, from which soup is served. Also a smaller vessel of similar shape for sauce or gravy.

*α.* **1706** PHILLIPS (ed. Kersey), *Terrine* (Fr.), an Earthen Pan. **1708** W. KING *Cookery* 298 In their gilt plate all delicates were seen And what was earth before became a rich terrene. **1745–6** MRS. DELANY in *Life & Corr.* (1861) II. 416 Did I write you word we had got a new terene? The.. chasing is mighty well done: it holds six quarts, and has a very light look. **1760** H. WALPOLE *Lett. to Montagu* cxx, The house is..loaded with terreens, philigree, figures, and every thing upon earth. **1779** FORREST *Voy. N. Guinea* 244 The contents of the small terrenes were put into eight large ones, consequently jumbled together; but, fish with fish, and fowl with fowl. **1865** ELIZA METEYARD *J. Wedgwood* I. 227 Ordinary jugs, globular teapots, circular terrines, and other articles. [*Note.*] The old term..the one preferred and always used by Josiah Wedgwood.

*β.* **1752** G. WHITE *Acc. Bk.* in *Selborne* etc. (1877) II. 323 A round China-turene. **1761** *Ann. Reg.* 242 First service, .. turrenes, fish, venison, etc. **1769** *De Foe's Tour Gt. Brit.* (ed. 7) I. i. 2 They have already made large Quantities of Tea-Cups, Saucers, Plates, Dishes, Tureins. **1771** GOLDSM. *Haunch of Venison* 82 At the bottom was tripe, in a swinging tureen. **1776** *Pennsylvania Even. Post* 27 Apr. 212/1 Blue and white and enamelled sauce Turennes, 2 sizes. **1910** *Civ. Serv. Supply Assoc. Catal.* 1427 Dinner Services, 61 pieces, ..2 Sauce Tureens and Stands, 1 Soup Tureen and Stand.

Hence †**Turee·ner**, a dish of various meats, etc. baked in a closed pot or tureen: cf. HOT-POT 2; **Turee·nful**, as much as a tureen contains.

**1728** E. SMITH *Compl. Housewife* 101 To make a Tureiner. Take a China Pot or Bowl, and fill it [with]..Beef steaks.. Veal steaks..Forc'd meat..Chickens, Pigeons,..Rabbets ..; Season..every Thing as you put it in..: Then put in a quart of Gravy,..and cover it close with a Lid of Puff-paste. ..Eight hours will bake it. **1883** 'ANNIE THOMAS' *Mod. Housewife* 58 The making of one tureenful of soup. **1895** KIPLING *Wee Willie Winkie* (1896) 3 Shovelling down his ice by tureenfuls.

**Tureile, turel**, var. TOURELLE *Obs.*

**Turet, -ette**, obs. forms of TURRET.

**Turf** (tɒ̄ɹf), *sb.*[1] Forms: 1– **turf**; also 4–7 **turfe**, 4–5 **torf**, 4 (8–9 *dial.*) **turff**, 6–7 **turffe**, (5 **turfh**, 6 **turph, tourffe, torve, towrve**, 6–7 **turue, turve**, 7 **turfth, terf, turph**); 6 **toure**, *Sc.* 6– **turr**, (8–9 **toor, ture**, 9 **tour, -e**, etc.). *Pl.* 1 **tyrf**; 3–6 **turues (v)**, (4–5 **-uys**, 6 *Sc.* **-uis**), 4–7 **torues (v)**, (4–5 **toruys**), 6– **turves** (*Sc.* 6 **tirvis**); 5– **turfs** (6 **tyrfes**, 6–7 *Sc.* **turreffis, turres, -is**). *β.* 6 **troffe**, 7 **truffe**, 7–9 **truff**; *pl.* *Sc.* 6–7 **truiffis**, 6–8 **troves, -is.** [OE. *turf* fem. cons. stem (gen.-dat. sing. and nom.-acc. pl. *tyrf*): Common Teut. (with variation of gender and declension); cf. OFris. *turf* (EFris. *turf*); OS. *turf*, (MDu. *torf, turf*, Du. *turf*), MLG., LG. *torf* (whence mod.Ger. *torf* peat); OHG. *zurba, zurf* 'terra avulsa, cespes', sod; ON. *torf* (Norw. *torv*, Sw. *torf*, Da. *tørv*) :—OTeut. **turb-*, from Indo Eur. **drbh*: cf. Skr. *darbhá* tuft of grass, f. *drbh* to make into tufts, string together. From the Teut. came also med.L. *turba* (cf. TURBARY), F. *tourbe* (1200), It. *torba*, Sp. *turba*.]

**1.** A slab pared from the surface of the soil with the grass and herbage growing on it; a sod of grass, with the roots and earth adhering. Also, in early quots., a small portion of the sward *in situ*.

*c* **725** *Corpus Gloss.* (O.E.T.) 452 *Cespites* (pl.), tyrb. *a* **1000** *Prose Life Guthlac* xv. (1848) 64 Hi þa [flaxan] ȝehyddon under anre tyrf. *c* **1000** *Sax. Leechd.* I. 290 Ðeos wyrt..of anre tyrf maneȝa boȝas asendeþ. *c* **1122** *O. E. Chron.* an. 189 Þa ȝewrohte he [Seuerus] weall mid turfum, & bred weall ðær on ufon fram sæ to sæ. *c* **1205** LAY. 15395 Vortigerne þe king Bi-tæhte heom al þis lond þ ne bilæfde him an heonde a turf of londe. *a* **1250** *Owl & Night.* 1167 Hervore hit is þat me þe suneþ & þe totorueþ & tobuneþ Mid staue & stone & turf & clute. *a* **1300** *Cursor M.* 16762 + 120 (Cott.) War-on he miȝt dee fayre, Ne a torf of herd erth. *c* **1386** CHAUCER *Merch. T.* 991 A bench of turues [*v.rr.* turves, torues] fressh and grene. *c* **1482** J. KAY tr. *Caoursin's Siege of Rhodes* (1870) F ii They made certayn dyches..and couered theym with grene bowes, and afterward they putted erthe and turues uppon the same. **1550** BALE *Eng. Votaries* II. 57 b, His owne clergye wold scarsely suffer hym to be buryed about the church vndre turfes or soddes of the grasse. **1551** ROBINSON tr. *More's Utop.* I. (1895) 29 Vpon a benche coueryd wyth grene torues, we satte downe. **1691** NORRIS *Pract. Disc.* 252 There are some..that..will readily part with the great Reversion of another World for a Turf of Ground in present Possession. **1776** WITHERING *Brit. Plants* (1796) II. 509 In a turf containing 6 plants the roots were all distinct. **1832** *Planting* 53 in *Libr. Usef. Knowl., Husb.* III, The coping consisted of a row of turfs laid with the grass side upwards. **1851** GLENNY *Handbk. Fl. Gard.* 40 The compost in which it should be grown is loam from rotted turves.

**b.** *collect.*, as a substance or material.

**1565** STAPLETON tr. *Bede's Hist. Ch. Eng.* 16 A trench and a rampaire of turue and timber, thyck fenced with bulwarkes and turrets. **1598** BARRET *Theor. Warres* III. ii. 132 A number of other places fortified with earth and turfe onely. **1774** M. MACKENZIE *Maritime Surv.* 66 Cause Turrets, or Signals, of Stone or Turf, to be built. **1821** BYRON *Cain* III. i, They to me are so much turf And stone.

†**c.** A clod of earth. Also *fig.* cf. CLOD *sb.* 4. *Obs.*

**1607** MARSTON *What you will* II. i, He is a turfe that will be slave to man. **1674** ABP. LEIGHTON in *Lauderdale Papers* (Camden) III. 76 Those pains and distempers that hang about this litle crazy turf of earth y[t] I carry.

†**d.** A sod cut from the turf of an estate, etc., as a token or symbol of possession. Also in phrase *turf and twig*. *Obs.*

**1585** in H. Hall *Soc. Eliz. Age* (1886) 239 Delyvered lyke possession..by a turffe cutt there. **1613** R. HARCOURT *Voy. Guiana* 42, I tooke possession of the land, by turfe and twig. **1643** TRAPP *Comm. Gen.* xiv. 23 The most High God, possessour of heaven and earth, who hath sent me with this bread and wine, as by turfe and twig, as by an earnest, and a little for the whole, to give thee possession of both.

**2.** *collect. sing.* The covering of grass and other plants, with its matted roots, forming the surface of grass land; the greensward; growing grass. Also *fig.*

*c* **890** tr. *Bæda's Hist.* v. vi. (1890) 400 Sum stan ðære eorðan ȝelic mid ðinre tyrf bewriȝen. *a* **1000** *Gloss.* in Wr.-Wülcker 236/18 *Feraces glebas*, þa wæstmbære tyrf. *Ibid.* 240/27 *Florei cespitis*, blowendre tyrf. **1387** TREVISA *Higden* (Rolls) II. 15 Vnder þe torf of þe lond is good marl i-founde. **1600** SHAKS. *A. Y. L.* III. iv. 52 The Shepheard..Who you saw sitting by me on the Turph. **1634** MILTON *Comus* 280 They left me weary on a grassie terf. **1721** BRADLEY *Philos. Acc. Wks. Nat.* 4 The first Stratum immediately under the Turff, a yellowish Clay. **1838** LYTTON *Alice* I. i, The first few flowers and fresh turf of the reviving Spring. **1895** G. W. SMALLEY *Stud. Men* 144 Sunny glades clothed in rough turf.

**b.** as a substance or material.

**1601** HOLLAND *Pliny* XVII. xiv. 518 To preserve it [the graft] with turfe and mosse against the injurie of rain and cold. **1632** LITHGOW *Trav.* x. 429 These Fabrickes are.. erected in a singular Frame of Smoake-torne straw, greene long prick'd truff [*ed.* **1682** turff], and Raine-dropping watles. **1706** HEARNE *Collect.* 12 Apr. (O.H.S.) I. 223 The..Garden..he order'd to be cover'd with Green Turff. **1874** J. D. HEATH *Croquet Player* 87 If the subsoil be poor, the turf should not be placed directly on it, but on a layer of good earth some inches thick.

**3.** A slab or block of peat dug for use as fuel.

But in many districts *turfs* are distinguished from *peats*, as being pared from a dry surface, containing roots of grass and recent herbage, and being lighter coloured, while *peats* are usually dug from a 'moss' or bog, and consist chiefly of long-decayed and compressed vegetable matter, black or dark brown, formed from Sphagnum and other mosses.

*c* **1300** *Havelok* 939 He bar þe turues, he bar þe star, Þe wode fro the brigge he bar. **1363** *Cockersand Chartul.* (Chetham Soc.) I. 64 To delfe turvez and carye at theyr wylle in y[e] mosse of Gayrstang. **1398** TREVISA *Barth. De P. R.* xv. lviii. (Bodl. MS.) Myres and mores in þe whiche þei diggeþ turues and makeþ fuyre þereof in stede of wode. **1506** *Reg. Mag. Sig. Scot.* I. 623/2 Licentiam ad capiendum genestam, petas et glebas, viz. *le hadir, petis et turffis*. **1536** *Act* 28 *Hen. VIII* in Bolton *Stat. Irel.* (1621) 77 The third part of all the tythe torves. **1557** *Peebles Burgh Rec.* (1872) 235 Castand tirvis..without licence. **1592** *Reg. Mag. Sig. Scot.* 755/1 Turris. **1604** *Urie Court-bk.* (1892) 4 Fewaill.. syik as petteis, turris, or haidder. **1637** *Reg. Mag. Sig. Scot.* 237/2 Cum..libertate lucrandi *lie peittis plodis* et *truffis* in maresia sua. **1709** LADY GRISELL BAILLIE *Househ. Bk.* (1911) 77 For 8 darg troves casting at 6 pence per day. **17..** *Old Song* in Jamieson s.v. *Tour*, O! is my toor a' shorn, he said, Or is my toors a' won? **1809** *Med. Jrnl.* XXI. 7 Turfs or peat, dug for fuel in the fenny parts of Cambridgshire. **1822** C. W. WYNN in Dk. Buckhm. *Mem. Crt. Geo. IV* (1859) I. 275 There are considerable apprehension in Ireland of distress from the utter failure of the potatoes,..and of the turves which they were prevented by the wet from cutting.

**b.** *collect.* as a substance; peat.

**1510** in *10th Rep. Hist. MSS. Comm.* App. v. 394 Anny man to bring in wode, troffe, or vattil. **1573** TUSSER *Husb.* (1878) 133 Er winter preuenteth,..get home with thy wood, ..both timber and furzen, the turfe and the cole. **1610** HOLLAND *Camden's Brit.* (1637) 500 Abundance of turfe gotten for fewell. **1725** *Bradley's Fam. Dict.* s.v. *Turfing Spade*, In some Counties they call that *Turf*, which in others they name *Peat*, which is dug out of Fenny and Moorish Grounds. **1796** MORSE *Amer. Geog.* I. 523 There is said to be coal on Raritan river,..and turf in Bethlehem. **1818** SCOTT *Rob Roy* xxvii, Swamps, green with treacherous verdure, or sable with turf, or, as they call them in Scotland, peat-bogs. **1866** ROGERS *Agric. & Prices* I. ii. 12 All tenants had right of pasture, and sometimes of turf. **1878** HUXLEY *Physiogr.* 233 Accumulations of partially decomposed vegetable matter form the substance known as peat or turf.

**4.** *The turf* (often with capital T): The grassy track or course over which horse-racing takes place; hence, the institution, action, or practice of horse-racing; the racing world.

**1755** *Gentl. Mag.* Apr. 153/1 If you are a true sportsman, and have the honour of the turf at heart. **1771** P. PARSONS *Newmarket* I. p. ii, The heroes of the Turf. **1785** GROSE *Dict. Vulg. Tongue*, *Man of the turf*, a horse racer, or jockey. **1803–5** W. PICK *Turf Reg.* (title-p.), All the Horses ..that have appeared on the British and Irish Turfs as Racers. **1838** LYTTON *Alice* III. v, Have you any horses on the turf? **1849** MACAULAY *Hist. Eng.* iii. I. 315 Already.. there was among our nobility and gentry a passion for the amusements of the turf.

**5.** *attrib.* and *Comb.* **a.** simple attrib., as *turf-*

*ashes, -back* (BACK *sb.*²), *-bed, -bog, -cart, -charcoal, -fire, -fuel, -ground, -heap, -hole, -house, -land, -moor, -moss, -nook, -pit, -pool, -rick, -shears, -shed, -smoke, -stack, -wain*; made, built, or consisting of turf, as *turf-cabin, -dike, -hedge* (Webster, 1828), *-hut, -monument, -roof, -seat, -walk, -wall*; also in sense 4, as *turf affair, -associate, -guide, horse, -market, parlance, phrase, -racing, -writer*; b. obj. and obj. gen., as *turf-digger, -getter, -graver, -worker*; *turf-boring, -cutting, -forming, -getting, -graving* sbs. and adjs.; c. instrumental, etc., as *turf-bound, -built, -clad, -covered, -grown, -laid, -like, -roofed, -spread, -theekit* (*Sc.*, = thatched) adjs.

**1825** T. HOOK *Sayings* Ser. II. *Man of Many Fr.* (Colburn) 195 The man to whose guidance I have committed all my *turf affairs. **1763** *Museum Rust.* I. 221 One sort of ashes, which are on all accounts valuable; I mean peat or *turf-ashes. **1818** SCOTT *Rob Roy* xxviii, I boldly entered the house; ..narrowly escaping breaking my shins over a *turf-back and a salting-tub. **1811** W. R. SPENCER *Poems* 137 This *turf-bed with flow'rs Ever crown'd. **1685** W. KING in *Phil. Trans.* XV. 950, I chiefly impute the red, or *turf Bog to it [moss, called in the north of Ireland *old wives' tow*]. **1767** BUSH *Hibernia Cur.* (1769) 76 By the natives it [peat] is called turf..and from thence they are usually called turf bogs. **1816** KIRBY & SP. *Entomol.* xxiii. (1818) II. 368 The common *turf-boring crane-fly (*T[ipula] oleracea*, L.)..moves over the grass with her body in a vertical position. **1787** WINTER *Syst. Husb.* 219 Harrowing loosens the hardened, *turf-bound soil. *a* **1748** J. WARTON *Ode to Fancy* 5 My footsteps to thy temple guide, To offer at thy *turf-built shrine. **1803** LEYDEN *Scenes of Inf.* III. 364 On Yeta's banks the vagrant gypsies place Their turf-built cots; a sun-burnt swarthy race. **1865** ALEX. SMITH *Summ. Skye* v. 103 His school-house was a *turf-cabin. **1557** in *Lanc. & Chesh. Wills* (1884) 61 Implements of husbandrye..ij *torve cartes. **1839** *Civil Eng. & Arch. Jrnl.* II. 145/2 The iron founders..might probably.. be supplied with *turf-charcoal. **1782** V. KNOX *Ess.* xciii. II. 45 The *turf-clad heap of mould which covers the poor man's grave. **1828** WEBSTER, *Turf-covered. **1898** F. DAVIS *Rom.-Brit. City Silchester* 21 Over the turf-covered area, denudation is not inoperative. **1868** *Rep. U. S. Commissioner Agric.* (1869) 154 *Turf-cutting field. **1882** F. POLLOCK in *Macm. Mag.* XLVI. 362 It is subject..to rights of turf-cutting. **1851** MANTELL *Petrifact.* iii. § 5. 308 A spade used by *turf-diggers. **1863** KINGSLEY *Water Bab.* v. 193 They liked better to brew potheen..shoot each other from behind *turf-dykes. **1818** LADY MORGAN *Autobiog.* (1859) 88 All my Irish *turf-fire habits came strong upon me. **1880** HAUGHTON *Phys. Geog.* vi. 301 Its meadows are clothed with *turf-forming grasses. **1838** *Civil Eng. & Arch. Jrnl.* I. 383/2 *Turf fuel is also used most extensively in working the steam engine in many districts of Ireland. **1751** *Phil. Trans.* XLVII. 221, I..have made all possible inquiry from the shepherds, *turf-getters, &c. **1884** *Cheshire Gloss.* s. v. *Turf*, *Turf-getting is a peculiar industry carried on at most of the larger peat bogs, and notably at Lindow Common near Wilmslow. **1483** *Cath. Angl.* 397/1 A *Turfe grauer, *glebarius, turbarius*. *a* **1905** in *Eng. Dial. Dict.* s. v., (N. Yorks.) We cut turves wiv a turf-greeaver. **1411** *Rolls of Parlt.* III. 650/1 Certein Commune of Pasture, and *Turf-gravyng, the whiche the said Lord the Roos claymes. **1599** NASHE *Lenten Stuffe* 8 As stable as clod-mould, or *turffe ground. **1893** PATER *Wks.* (1901) VIII. 147 They went through the endless, lonely, *turf-grown tracts. **1868** YATES *Rock Ahead* I. vi, Ruff, Bell, Bailey, and other leading *turf-guides. **1862** BORROW *Wild Wales* lxxxviii. (1911) 453 *Turf-heaps..are in abundance in the vicinity. **1851** — *Lavengro* xii, He had some difficulty in getting there on account of the *turf-holes in the bog. *c* **1802** S. CHIFNEY *Genius Genuine* (title-p.), Why the *Turf Horses Degenerate. **1569** in *Lanc. & Chesh. Wills* (1884) 35 The haybarne and two bayes of the *turfehowse next the halle. **1865** ALEX. SMITH *Summ. Skye* v. 101 We passed a colony of *turf-huts. **1806** J. GRAHAME *Birds Scot.*, etc. 141 Still shall the *turf-laid seat invite Thy weary limbs. *a* **1625** SIR H. FINCH *Law* (1636) 286 Likewise an assise is giuen for common of *Turue land, fishing, and such like. **1756-7** tr. *Keysler's Trav.* (1760) III. 315 That ashes, coals, bones, potsherds, trees, &c. are frequently found in the turf-lands or marshes in Holland and Friesland. **1910** *Westm. Gaz.* 19 Mar. 10/2 Hard at work in converting the barren surface into turf-land. **1841** LEVER *C. O'Malley* xxx, A brown, scruffy, *turf-like face. **1884** H. SMART *From Post to Finish* ix, One of the wiliest speculators in the *turf market. **1695** J. EDWARDS *Perfect. Script.* 286 There are many of these *turf-monuments on Salisbury plain. **1834-5** J. PHILLIPS *Geol.* in *Encycl. Metrop.* VI. 595/2 The *turf or peat moors,..which occur in low ground toward the estuaries of rivers. **1583-4** *Shuttleworths' Acc.* (Chetham Soc.) 17 For workinge at the *tourffe mosse [= bog] nene dayes xiij$^d$ ob. **1840** A. LAING *Wayside Flowers* (1878) 37 The *truff neuk is toom o' its eenin' supply. **1884** *Marshall's Tennis Cuts* 148 It is only played by what in *Turf-parlance we should call 'crocks', or gentlemen who are not physically capable of taking part in any other outdoor amusement. *Ibid.* 141 From first to last Owen à Biscoe simply cantered away (to use a *turf phrase) from his antagonist. **1678** *Massacre in Ireland* 4 Thousands ..were drowned, cast into Ditches, Bogs, and *Turf-pits. **1764** *Museum Rust.* II. cvi. 355 The pits, or *turf-pools as they are commonly called. **1828** *Sporting Mag.* XXII. 235 His happiness was road-racing, as it is now *turf-racing. **1869** BLACKMORE *Lorna D.* iv, A dozen men, who seemed to come out of a *turf-rick. **1871** W. MORRIS in Mackail *Life* (1899) I. 247 Close by the sea lay the many gables (black wood with green *turf-roofs). **1842** I. WILLIAMS *Baptistery* II. xxxii. (1874) 188 With each her Saviour deigns to dwell E'en in the *turf-roof'd cell. **1818** SCOTT *Hrt. Midl.* xviii, The old man was seated on the deas, or *turf-seat, at the end of his cottage. **1822** LOUDON *Encycl. Gard.* § 617 *Turf-Shears..,for cutting the tops of box-edgings and the tufts of grass at the roots of shrubs. **1912** *Daily News* 4 Oct. 6 The peat..has been stacked by now in rick or *turf-shed ready for the winter's burning. **1815** SCOTT *Guy M.* xxvi, Fish, dried in the *turf smoke of their cabins, or shealings. **1743** LADY GRISELL BAILLIE *Househ. Bk.* (1911) 279 That the *Turf Stack be not tred down. **1881** *Mod. Scott. Poets* III. 75 Thy *turf-theekit roof. **1902** CORNISH *Naturalist Thames* 181 Half wild banks, and *turfwalk stretches for nearly a mile among the fields. **1911** J. WARD *Rom. Era in Brit.* iii. 70 No trace of a *turf-wall has been found. **1589** *Shuttleworths' Acc.* (Chetham Soc.) 52 For dryvinge a *turffe-wane a fortenyghte, xvj$^d$. **1865** *Daily Tel.* 1 Nov. 5/1 'Warning off' intruders, whether defaulting betters, or *turf-writers whose criticisms were displeasing.

**d.** Special combs.: **turf-accountant**, a book-maker in horse-racing; **turf-ant**, a small yellow European ant (*Formica flava*, or *Lasius flavus*), living in dry heathy turf; **turf-boy** (see quots.); **turf-cake**, a tea-cake baked in a covered pan among the ashes of a peat-fire; **turf-cutter**, one who is employed in cutting or digging peat; also, a *turf-spade*; also, a paring-plough or *turf-plough*; **turf-drain**, a drain in which the channel is covered by turves placed over it; a sod-drain; so **turf-draining**; † **turf-graft** [GRAFT *sb.*³], the right to dig turf for fuel; also, a place where turf is dug, a turbary; **turf-hog**: see quot.; **turf-knife**, a cutting blade set upright in a curved handle, which is pushed along to mark out turves, lines of ditches, etc. (Ogilvie, 1882); **turf-man**, a devotee of the turf, a racing man; †**turf-penny**, a rent or due paid for turbary; **turf-plough**, a plough for paring off the surface to destroy weeds and grubs preparatory to deep ploughing (Knight *Dict. Mech.* 1877); **turf-spade**, a spade for cutting turf or peats; also, a turfing-iron; **turf-spanker**, name for a kind of croquet mallet: see quot.; **turf-stick**, a stick from a turbary or peat-bog; **turf-tie**: see TYE; **turf-time**, the season for digging turf, usually between hay-time and harvest; **turf-worm**, the sod-worm (SOD *sb.*¹ 5).

**1915** *Scots Pictorial* 27 Mar. p. iv, The time when the standing and stability of all *turf accountants are put to the test. **1816** KIRBY & SP. *Entomol.* (1818) II. 94 The little *turf-ants (*F[ormica] cæspitum*, L.) carry their recruits uncoiled. **1905** *Blackw. Mag.* Jan. 58 There was the *turf boy whose duty it was to fill the turf-boxes. **1906** SOMERVILLE & ROSS *Irish Yesterdays* 71 In those days the turf-boy was an institution...All day they plied bare-foot between the turf-house and the various fuel-depôts of the house with baskets. **1863** MRS. GASKELL *Sylvia's L.* iii, Neither cream nor finest wheaten flour was wanting for '*turf-cakes' and 'singing-hinnies'. **1817-18** COBBETT *Resid. U. S.* (1822) 129 The surface of the land is taken off to a depth of two or three inches... In England, this operation is performed with a *turf-cutter, and by hand. **1844** in Whitelaw *Bk. Scot. Song* (1875) 228, I promised to rove With the turf-cutter's daughter. **1860** G. H. K. in *Vac. Tour.* 164 The turf-cutter left her divots unturned. **1805** R. W. DICKSON *Pract. Agric.* I. Plate xlviii. 332 Fig. 1. Represents a shouldered *turf-drain. *c* **1830** *Glouc. Farm Rep.* 26 in *Libr. Usef. Knowl., Husb.* III, *Turf-draining answers well, where the turf is strong enough to bear ramming. **1313** *Yorkshire Deeds* (Yorks. Archæol. Soc.) II. 18 [His common of pasture with] le *turff graft [from either moor]. **1483** *Cath. Angl.* 396/2 Turfe grafte, *turbarium*. **1773** *Holme-on-Sp. Moor Inclos. Act* 2 Which privilege of selling turves is called Turf-Graft. **1880** DAWKINS *Early Man* viii. 261 The third group consists of the short-horned ox, the *turf-hog, and the goat, which escaped from the servitude of man and reverted to a wild state. **1818** *Sporting Mag.* II. 214, I never was a *turfman, and am only a spectator. **1881** *Scribner's Mag.* XXII. 642 The form which turfmen love to see in a horse which they have backed heavily. **1282** *Inquis. P. M.* (*C.*) *Edw. I*, File 31. m. 3 (P.R.O.) Coterii et bondi reddunt per annum de consuetudine que vocatur *Turfpeny et grundpeni xlviij s. x d. **1477-8** *Durham Acc. Rolls* (Surtees) 95 Pro j *Turfspade, viijd. **1824** LOUDON *Encycl. Gard.* 2101 The turf-spade or turfing iron is employed to separate the individual turves. **1868** ATKINSON *Cleveland Gloss.*, *Turf-spade, turf-spit*, the implement or tool used in graving Turves,..a triangular cutting instrument with one upright side, to sever the Turf sideways as well as from the subsoil. **1874** J. D. HEATH *Croquet-Player* 25 The bottom of the cylindrical head..is sliced off, so that the part of the mallet that rests on the ground is quite flat. This '*turf-spanker' ..met with some opposition at first. **1843** *Florist's Jrnl.* (1846) IV. 86 A mixture of loam and peat, with all the *turf-sticks, etc. contained in it, should be well chopped with the spade and mixed with some rich garden mould. **1912** *Daily News* 28 Feb. 4 Every Dartmoor farmer has his *turf-tie lying somewhere near his farm in a hollow between the tors. **1594** *Shuttleworths' Acc.* (Chetham Soc.) 90 He is to be hired for haytyme, *turvetyme and harvest.

† **Turf, tyrf,** *sb.*² Forms: 5-6 tyrf(e, turfe, turff(e; *pl.* 6 **turves**: see also TARF, TARVE. [f. root of TIRVE *v.*² to turn, roll back.] The turn-over, turn-up, or facing of a cap, hood, sleeve, etc.; a cock (of a cap, etc.). Also *attrib.*

*c* **1440** *Promp. Parv.* 494/2 Tyrf, or tyrvynge vp on an hoode or sleue (*K.* tyrfe or turnynge vp aȝen, *S.* tyrwynge of an hoode, *A.* tyrvyng of an hood, etc., *P.* tyrfte or turnynge vp agayne), *resolucio* (H., S. *revolucio*). **1522** in *Archæologia* XXV. 460 Item..for a black bonett w$^t$ a dobill turffe y$^t$ was dressyd w$^t$ velvett vj s. viij d. **1530** PALSGR. 281/2 Tyrfe of a cappe or suche lyke, *rebras*. *Ibid.* 284/1 Turfe. **1546-7** in Feuillerat *Revels Edw. VI* (1914) 6 For making of one doble turff Cappe of vellett. **1547** *Ibid.* 10, xij hedpeces to the same Rounde of clothe of Syluer the Turffes of Crymsin Tilsent bownde with yolowe Satten. *a* **1548** HALL *Chron.*, *Hen. VIII* 235 Euery man..garnyshed their bassenetes with turues lyke cappes of sylke. **1587** FLEMING *Contn. Holinshed* III. 947/1.

**Turf,** *v.*¹ Also 5-7 turve. [f. TURF *sb.*¹]

**1.** *trans.* To cover with turf; to lay with turf.

*c* **1430** LYDG. *Min. Poems* (Percy Soc.) 181 Alle the aleis were made playne with sond, The benches turued with newe turvis grene. *a* **1500** *Flower & Leaf* 51 A plesaunt herber.. That benched was, and [al] with turves new Freshly turved. **1644** G. PLATTES in *Hartlib's Legacy* (1655) 187 Barley..had cover'd the ground so full, that it was as if it were even turfed with the Corn. *a* **1774** TUCKER *Lt. Nat.* (1834) I. 299 After you have new turfed the banks. **1882** CON. F. WOOLSON *Anne* 118 Graves are made and turfed over.

**b.** *transf.* To place or lay under the turf; to cover with turf, or as turf does; to bury; also *intr.* with *it*, to die and be buried.

**1628** [see TURFED *ppl. a.*]. **1763** COWPER *Let.* in Nichols *Lit. Anecd. 18th C.* (1814) VIII. 563 That you may not think I have turfed it, to speak in the Newmarket phrase..I send you this letter. **1844** J. T. HEWLETT *Parsons & W.* xxxii, Until the governor was turfed. **1859** TENNYSON *Merl. & Vivien* 655 As vast a mound As after furious battle turfs the slain. **1888** G. MEREDITH *Question Whither* i, You who sadly turf us, Believe not that all living seed Must flower above the surface.

**2.** To dig up or excavate for turf or peat.

**1780** INGENHOUSZ in *Phil. Trans.* LXX. 372 Draining a large meer..which was turfed out in former ages. **1878** J. DAVIDSON *Inverurie* 352 They protected the burgh muir from being indiscriminately turfed.

**3.** *intr.* To get turf or peat for fuel. *dial.*

**1876** *Whitby Gloss.* s.v. *Turf-spit*, 'We're turfing', getting our turves for a winter supply. **1896** BARING-GOULD *Dartmoor Idylls* v. 131 Her wants to take the washing..and the turving out o' my hands.

† **Turf,** *v.*² Variant of TIRVE *v.*² (sense 2 c): cf. TURF *sb.*² *Obs.*

**1592** GREENE *Def. Conny Catch.* (1859) 60 A beaver hatte turft with velvet, so quaintly as if he had been some Espagnolo trickt up. **1611** BEAUM. & FL. *Philaster* IV. i, Marry, the steward would have had the velvet head [of the deer].. to turf his hat withal.

**Tu·rfage.** *rare.* [f. TURF *sb.*¹ + -AGE; cf. *herbage, leafage.*] Turf collectively, sward.

**1899** CROCKETT *Kit Kennedy* liii, A little short slope of bare gray turfage.

**Tu·rfdom.** *rare.* [f. TURF *sb.*¹ 4 + -DOM.] The votaries of the turf; the racing community.

**1864** *Daily Tel.* 20 Sept., Gentlemen of high standing who are very useful to the rising turfdom of this country.

† **Tu·rfed,** *a. Obs.* Also 6 turft. [f. TURF *sb.*² + -ED ². See also *tarfed* s. v. TARF.] Provided, adorned, or turned up with a facing, as a cap, a sleeve, etc.

**1526** *Lett. & Pap. Hen. VIII*, IV. 846 A black Milan bonnet, double turfed,..A black single turfed bonnet, with 11½ pair of small aglets. **1547** in Feuillerat *Revels Edw. VI* (1914) 21 One Capp doble turft of grene satten. **1586** *Rates of Customs* Bj, Caps double turfed called cockred caps the dosen xxxiiij.s.

**Turfed** (tɔ̄ɹft), *ppl. a.* [f. TURF *v.*¹ + -ED ¹.] Overlaid or covered with turf.

**1628** FELTHAM *Resolves* II. [I.] xxv. 81 Degenerate Man! that hauing so often experimented his Iugling, wilt yet beleeue his fictions, and his turfed Mines. **1649** BLITHE *Eng. Improv. Impr.* (1653) 61 For although I differ from many.. about this denshiring their thin turved Lands, that are pure from roots, twitch, or moss. **1741** RICHARDSON *Pamela* I. 157 The turfed Slope of the fine Fish-pond. **1862** M. HOPKINS *Hawaii* 152 Between the parallel walls, there are turfed spaces terminating suddenly in faults or breaks of some thirty feet depth. **1896** *Edin. Rev.* July 166 Turfed seats with brick fronts appear to be usual.

† **Turfel,** *a. Obs. rare*⁻¹. In 6 turfill. [Deriv. of TIRVE *v.*²; cf. TURFED *a.*] Of a hat: Furnished with a turn or cock.

**1558** *Richmond Wills* (Surtees) 126 Inventory 21 January, 1 Mary. In ye Shoppe. Inprimis, xxxj feltts, ij turfill hatts, ij ruggid hatts.

**Turfen** (tɔ̄·ɹf'n), *a.* [f. TURF *sb.*¹ + -EN ⁴.] Made of or covered with turf; turfy.

**1778** [W. MARSHALL] *Minutes Agric., Digest* 115 A turfen hut might screen us from the tempest. **1824** *Blackw. Mag.* XVI. 582 He pluck'd them from the branches, scattering them Wide o'er the turfen floor. **1849** *Zoologist* VII. 2338 A kind of earthen or turfen wall. **1903** N. MUNRO in *Blackw. Mag.* Jan. 87/2 Sea scents and the odours of turfen fires.

†**Tu·rfer.** *Obs. rare*⁻⁰. [f. TURF *sb.*¹ + -ER: cf. med.L. *turbārius.*] One who enjoys common of turbary. So † **Tu·rfery** *dial.* = TURBARY.

*c* **1440** *Promp. Parv.* 507/2 Turvare, *glebarius*. **1769** *Public Advertiser* 2 June 3/4 Right of Pasturage and Turfery on the..Commons of Sunning-Hill and Wingfield.

**Turfing** (tɔ̄·ɹfiŋ), *vbl. sb.* [f. TURF *v.*¹ or *sb.*¹ + -ING ¹.] The action of TURF *v.*¹ Also *attrib.* **turfing-iron**, a tool for raising turf; **turfing-spade**, a spade used in digging peat, a peat-spade.

**1649** BLITHE *Eng. Improv. Impr.* (1653) 69 [Figure of] The Turving Spade. **1677** PLOT *Oxfordsh.* 249 To be pared off the ground with a turfing Spade. **1725** *Bradley's Fam. Dict.*, *Turf*, or *Green Turf*, Earth cover'd with small and very short Grass; its done two ways either by sowing or Turfing. **1842** LOUDON *Suburban Hort.* 173 Take a piece of turf four feet by four feet, shaped out with the edging-iron, and taken up with the turfing or floating spade. **1852** G.W. JOHNSON *Gard. Dict.* 898/1 The Turfing Iron is for raising or peeling off the turves from the soil. **1896** [see TURF *v.*¹ 3].

**Turfite** (tɔ̄·ɹfəit). [f. TURF *sb.*¹ + -ITE ¹ 1 b.] A votary or frequenter of the turf; a racing man. Also *attrib.*

**1846** G. J. DOW (*title*) Calculus, the turfite's computer. **1847** *Illustr. Lond. News* 2 Oct. 219/2 Mr. Pedley, a professional turfite, won the Derby. **1870** *Sat. Rev.* 26 Feb. 275/1 Bankrupt Dukes, spendthrift and profligate Lordlings, turfite peers. **1910** GOLDW. SMITH *Remin.* xi. 180 A patron ..with a good deal of the turfite in his character.

**Turfless** (tɒ̄·ɹflės), *a.* [f. TURF *sb.*[1] + -LESS.] Devoid of turf, bare.

*a* 1743 SAVAGE *Public Spirit* 44 Turfless, leafless, and unculturd plains. 1816 BYRON *Pr. of Chillon* vii, The flat and turfless earth above The being we so much did love. 1897 *Blackw. Mag.* Mar. 338 The graveyard with its turfless mounds of red earth.

**Turfy** (tɒ̄·ɹfi), *a.* Forms: see TURF *sb.*[1] [f. TURF *sb.*[1] + -Y.]

**1.** Covered with or consisting of turf; grassy; turfen; in quot. 1733, of arable land: full of weeds and roots, not 'clean'.

1552 HULOET, Turffie, or of turfe, *cespitius, a.* 1610 SHAKS. *Temp.* IV. i. 62 Thy Turphie-Mountaines, where liue nibling Sheepe. 1685 POMFRET *Cruelty & Lust* 149 When Charion saw me from his turfy bed. 1718 ROWE tr. *Lucan* 137 Each to his turphy Table bids his Guest. 1733 TULL *Horse-Hoeing Husb.* xi. 136 The Third Crop made that Land so Foul and Turffy, that 'twas forc'd to lie for a Fallow. 1818 MISS MITFORD in L'Estrange *Life* (1870) II. ii. 23 A turfy, almost inaccessible hill, called Finchamstead Ridges. 1869 TOZER *Highl. Turkey* II. 185 We made our way along a turfy level to the city.

**2.** Of the nature of or abounding in turf or peat; peaty.

1660 H. MORE *Myst. Godl.* VI. vii. 231 For what of the Earth is not combustible? The exteriour turfy part is ordinary fewel. *a* 1661 FULLER *Worthies, Lanc.* (1662) II. 107 They pierce the Turffie ground, and under it meet with a black and deadish water. 1776 WITHERING *Brit. Plants* (1796) II. 362 *Alisma ranunculoides*.. Lesser Thrumwort. Wet turfy bogs... Boggy meadows, common. Bungay, Suffolk. 1842 LOUDON *Suburban Hort.* 509 He uses turfy loam two parts, thoroughly decomposed dung two parts, leaf mould two parts, and very sandy turfy peat two parts. 1870 HOOKER *Stud. Flora* 302 *Centunculus minimus*... Wet turfy and sandy places, local.

**3.** Pertaining to or characteristic of the turf; suggestive of horse-racing; horsy.

1844 DICKENS *Mart. Chuz.* xxvi, It was an easy, horse-fleshy, turfy sort of thing to do. 1868 YATES *Rock Ahead* II. vii, The man has an air of turfey, horsey life. 1885 'MRS. ALEXANDER' *At Bay* ii, The talk became.. of the Turf—turfy.

Hence **Tu·rfiness,** turfy character, horsiness.

1905 *Daily Chron.* 22 June 4/4 Each American newcomer feels.. at first horribly out of it in this world of universal turfyness.

† **Turgeman,** obs. f. TRUCHMAN, an interpreter: cf. METURGEMAN.

1670 COVEL in *Early Voy. Levant* (Hakl. Soc.) 109 A Greek (who had been in England some time to learn our language, in order to be a Turgeman). 1864 PUSEY *Lect. Daniel* i. 41 The Turgeman was not to be under 50; his was one of the most honourable offices in the Synagogue.

† **Tu·rgence.** *Obs.* [f. TURGENT: see -ENCE.] The action of swelling or becoming swollen.

1671 R. BOHUN *Wind* 34 Suddain turgences of the river Severn.

**Turgency** (tɒ̄·ɹdʒĕnsi). Now *rare* or *Obs.* [f. TURGENT: see -ENCY.]

**1.** The condition or quality of swelling or being turgent; a swollen or turgid state.

1650 H. BROOKE *Conserv. Health* 49 A Turgency of Humors. 1684 tr. *Bonet's Merc. Compit.* XIX. 776 The Patients feel a certain sense of turgency in that part. 1713 DERHAM *Phys.-Theol.* IV. ii. 108 Nature repaired the watery Humour again, the Eyes returned to their former Turgency. 1794 G. ADAMS *Nat. & Exp. Philos.* (1806) IV. xlix. 349 This excessive mobility of parts.. of the most rigid bodies.. implies a great turgency of their substance with some very active fluid.

**2.** *fig.* **a.** An inflated or bombastic style of language.

1654 HAMMOND *Answ. Animadv. Ignat.* iii. § 2. 54 This double objection against turgencie of style and barbarousnesse of words. 1660 H. MORE *Myst. Godl.* I. v. 14 Their Tongues are swelled with greater tumor and turgency of speech.

**b.** An insurrectionary condition or movement.

1660 T. M. *C. Walker's Hist. Independ.* IV. Ded., Yet is it necessary that the history of such turgencies in the State should be communicated, that posterity may hereafter see.. the certain punishment of Treason.

**Turgent** (tɒ̄·ɹdʒĕnt), *a.* Now *rare* or *Obs.* [ad. L. *turgĕnt-em*, pr. pple. of *turgēre* to swell out, be swollen or inflated: see -ENT.]

**1.** Physically swelling or swollen; distended, turgid.

*c* 1440 *Pallad. on Husb.* IV. 601 The turgent trunke let scarifie, That humour effluent out of it hie. 1657 *Physical Dict., Turgent*,.. usually spoken of the humors of the body when they are in combustion and violent motion. 1664 POWER *Exp. Philos.* I. 59 When [the eyes] are preternaturally distended in an Ophthalmia, and so grow turgent and conspicuous. 1684 tr. *Bonet's Merc. Compit.* XIV. 478 An Asthmatical Woman, whose Lungs [were] turgent with Serum. *a* 1722 LISLE *Husb.* (1752) 332 The cow's.. teats will be turgent and spring forth. 1730–46 THOMSON *Autumn* 693 While Perfection breathes White o'er the turgent film [of the grape] the living dew.

**2.** *fig.* Swollen or inflated with pride or conceit; bumptious; also, using inflated language.

1621 BURTON *Anat. Mel.* II. iii. VII, Good men doe not alwaies finde grace and favour, least they should be puffed vp with turgent titles, growe insolent and prowd. 1654 HAMMOND *Answ. Animadv. Ignat.* iii. § 2. 54 All must be rejected.. which hath any of this turgent style, or these barbarous words in it. 1681 H. MORE *Exp. Dan.* App. iii. 303 This Title were too big and turgent for any private Church.

**Turgesce** (tɒdʒe·s), *v. rare.* [ad. L. *turgēscĕre*, inceptive of *turgēre*: see prec. and -ESCE.] *intr.* To begin to swell, to become turgid or inflated.

1864 in WEBSTER; and in later Dicts.

**Turgescence** (tɒdʒe·sĕns). [ad. med. or mod.L. *turgēscentia*: see next and -ENCE. So mod.F. *turgescence* (1752).]

**1.** The action or condition of swelling up; the fact or state of being swollen.

1631 JORDEN *Nat. Bathes* xiv. (1632) 106 Animals haue their set times when their spermatick spirits are in turgescence. 1737 BRACKEN *Farriery Impr.* (1763) 47 Any Turgescence or Swelling of the Blood-Vessels. 1843 R. J. GRAVES *Syst. Clin. Med.* ix. 98 That turgescence of the cerebral vessels which precedes apoplectic seizures. 1875 BENNETT & DYER *Sachs' Bot.* 634 The pressure caused by the tension and turgescence of the tissues.

**2.** *fig.* **a.** Progressive swelling or increase. **b.** Inflation, pomposity, bombast.

1806 W. TAYLOR in *Ann. Rev.* IV. 244 The turgescence of effort travelling at every hitch from head to tail. 1813—in *Monthly Rev.* LXX. 451 A marked tendency to affectation, to turgescence.

**Turgescency** (tɒdʒe·sĕnsi). [ad. med. or mod. L. *turgēscentia* (Blancard *a* 1693), f. *turgēscent-em*, pr. pple. of *turgēscĕre*: see above and -ENCY.] The quality or state of being turgescent; swelling or swollen condition.

1666 J. SMITH *Old Age* (1676) 117 Inflation, and Turgescency of the Seminary vessels. 1721 QUINCY *Hodges' Hist. Acc. Plague Lond.* 157 A Turgescency or Distemperature of Humours. 1860 *Encycl. Brit.* (ed. 8) XXI. 973/2 The turgescency and relaxation of the organs that perform the offices of feet. *fig.* 1710 *Brit. Apollo* II. No. 109. 2/2 It.. proceeds from a certain Turgescency of Soul.

**Turgescent** (tɒdʒe·sĕnt), *a.* [ad. L. *turgēscent-em*: see prec. and -ENT.] Becoming swollen; swelling, growing bigger.

1727 BAILEY vol. II, *Turgescent*, swelling or growing big. 1755 in JOHNSON. 1822–7 GOOD *Study Med.* (1829) I. 378 A turgescent, and especially a varicose state of the internal hemorrhoidal vessels. 1831 T. L. PEACOCK *Crotchet Castle* 6 Arms, three empty bladders, turgescent, to show how opinions are formed. 1857 BULLOCK *Cazeaux' Midwif.* 83 The nipple is more projecting, turgescent, and sensitive. 1891 F. DARWIN in *Nature* 27 Aug. 408/1 In a growing shoot the turgescent pith stretches the cortex.

**Turgescible** (tɒdʒe·sib'l), *a.* [f. L. *turgēsc-ĕre*: see above and -IBLE.] Capable of swelling up.

1886 *Med. News* 21 Aug. 214 Similar but less extensive turgescible tissue exists in other portions of the nasal mucous membrane.

**Turgid** (tɒ̄·ɹdʒid), *a.* [ad. L. *turgid-us* swollen, inflated, f. *turgēre* to swell: see -ID [1].]

**1.** Swollen, distended, puffed out.

1620 VENNER *Via Recta* iv. 82 You shall commonly see them.. to haue turgid, and strouting-out bellies. 1660 BOYLE *New Exp. Phys. Mech.* v. 52 A Bladder, but moderately fill'd with Air and strongly ty'd, being.. held near the Fire, ..grew exceedingly turgid and hard. 1669 J. ROSE *Eng. Vineyard* (1675) 33 Proud and turgid buds. 1674 GREW *Anat. Trunks* II. i. § 15 The Bladders.. being swelled up and turgid with Sap. 1776 WITHERING *Brit. Plants* (1796) III. 618 *Anthyllis*. Cup swoln and turgid; inclosing the legumen. 1797 M. BAILLIE *Morb. Anat.* (1807) 456 The veins of the pia mater have been found turgid with blood. 1846 ELLIS *Elgin Marb.* I. 102 Turgid muscles of the breast. 1860 MAURY *Phys. Geog. Sea* (Low) xi. § 523 This condensation is followed by a turgid intumescence.

*fig.* 1692 BENTLEY *Boyle Lect.* ix. 329 Their Imaginations turgid and pregnant with the glorious Ideas. 1697 EVELYN *Numism.* iii. 82 That turgid Vanity and gross Adulation.

**2.** *fig.* in reference to language: Inflated, grandiloquent, pompous, bombastic.

1725 WATTS *Logic* II. iii. III. § 6 Some.. have a violent and turgid manner both of talking and thinking. 1762 FOOTE *Orators* II. Wks. 1799 I. 219 The frothy, the turgid, the calm, and the clamorous [declaimers]. 1781 GIBBON *Decl. & F.* xvii. II. 40 The advocates, who filled the Forum with the sound of their turgid and loquacious rhetoric. 1856 R. A. VAUGHAN *Mystics* (1860) I. 97 His verbose and turgid style, too, is destitute of all genuine feeling.

**Turgidity** (tɒdʒi·dĭti). [f. L. *turgid-us* (see prec.) + -ITY.]

**1.** The state of being turgid or swollen.

1732 ARBUTHNOT *Rules of Diet* iii. in *Aliments*, etc. 363 Weakness, Wateryness and Turgidity of the eyes. 1820 JEFFERSON *Writ.* (1830) IV. 323 The tendency to turgidity may proceed from debility alone. 1854 JONES & SIEV. *Pathol. Anat.* (1874) 255 Turgidity of the blood-vessels. 1875 BENNETT & DYER *Sachs' Bot.* 700 By *Turgidity* we understand the hydrostatic pressure which the water absorbed by endosmose exercises equally on all sides on the cell-wall.

**2.** *fig.* Inflation of language; grandiloquence, pomposity, bombast; also with *a* and *pl.* an example of this.

1756–82 J. WARTON *Ess. Pope* (ed. 4) I. iii. 103 Obscurity or turgidity, and a false grandeur of diction. 1788 *Lond. Mag.* 247 They appear to abound with turgidities, and, if they can be called splendid, to dazzle by their splendour. 1827 HARE *Guesses* Ser. I. (1847) 62 The empty turgidity of Dryden. 1903 *Edin. Rev.* Apr. 320 We are willing to forget the latter turgidities [of a poem].

**Turgidly** (tɒ̄·ɹdʒidli), *adv.* [f. TURGID + -LY [2].] In a turgid, inflated, or swollen manner; in turgid style or language.

1668 H. MORE *Div. Dial.* II. xviii. 282 A kind of Lunacy .. that reigns thus turgidly in Cuphophron's copious Harangue. 1846 DANA *Zooph.* (1848) 344 Interstices .. usually throughout turgidly elevated. 1910 *Spectator* 29 Oct. 696/2 He.. puts turgidly and obscurely what could far better have been expressed in homely idioms.

**Tu·rgidness.** [f. as prec. + -NESS.] The quality of being turgid; = TURGIDITY.

1757 WARBURTON *Lett. to Hurd* 15 Jan. (1809) 227 The turgidness of a young scribbler. 1817 COLERIDGE *Biog. Lit.* i. 2 A general turgidness of diction, and a profusion of new-coined double epithets. 1864 BURTON *Scot Abr.* II. i. 43 That strange flighty turgidness of style which Urquhart had caught by working so much on Rabelais.

† **Tu·rgidous,** *a. Obs. rare.* [f. as TURGID + -OUS.] = TURGID.

1601 B. JONSON *Poetaster* v. iii, Barmy froth, puffy, inflate, turgidous, and ventositous are come vp.

**Turgion**: see TURDION.

**Turgite** (tɒ̄·ɹdʒəit). *Min.* [Named by Hermann 1845, from the Turginsk mine, Ural Mtns., where found: see -ITE [1].] A hydrous sesquioxide of iron, allied to limonite but containing less water.

1850 ANSTED *Elem. Geol., Min.* etc. § 454 Brown hæmatite. Under this .. we include.. Limonite,.. Turgite, Iron ochre, and others. 1888 RUTLEY *Rock-Forming Min.* 122 Turgite.. also gives a red streak.

† **Turgman,** obs. f. TRUCHMAN, interpreter.

1615 BEDWELL *Arab. Trudg.* O j, *Tørgman*, Trudgman, ταργούμενος, δραγούμενος, in the latter Greeke writers, signifieth, an interpretor.

**Turgo·meter.** [irreg. f. L. *turgēre* to swell + -[O]METER.] A measurer of turgidity.

1885 W. GARDINER in *Proc. Roy. Soc.* XXXIX. 232 The plastoid may be regarded as a turgometer, since it indicates the state of turgidity of the cell.

**Turgor** (tɒ̄·ɹgǫɹ). *Physiol.* and *Bot.* [a. post-cl. L. *turgor* (Martianus Capella), f. *turgēre* to swell: cf. *horror, terror*, etc.] **a.** The normal swollen condition of the capillaries and smaller blood-vessels. **b.** A state of turgidity and consequent rigidity in a cell, as that caused by the absorption of fluid.

1876 tr. *Wagner's Gen. Pathol.* 178 Lymphatics are the chief regulators of the turgor of the tissues. 1882 *Nature* 12 Jan. 258/2 The second phase of the.. variation is probably dependent on the diminution of turgor of the excited cells. 1882 *Quain's Med. Dict.* 328/1 With the cessation of the circulation and vital turgor, the skin becomes ashy pale, and the tissues lose their elasticity.

† **Turify,** obs. f. THURIFY.

*c* 1400 MAUNDEV. (Roxb.) xix. 87 Þai bring.. incense and oþer thinges swete smelland for to turify þat ymage.

**Turion** (tiū°·riǫn). *Bot.* [= F. *turion* (15th c.), ad. L. *turio*, pl. **turiōnēs**, formerly also in Eng. use.] A young shoot rising from the ground, produced from a subterranean bud: see quot. 1894.

[1693 tr. *Blancard's Phys. Dict.* (ed. 2), *Turiones*, the tender Tops of Trees, that grow yearly. 1704 J. HARRIS *Lex. Techn.* I, *Turiones*, amongst Botanick Writers, are the first young tender shoots or tops which any Plants do annually put forth of the Ground.] 1725 *Bradley's Fam. Dict.* s. v. *Sallet*, The gentle Turiones and Tops [of Blite] may be eaten like Asparagus. 1880 GRAY *Struct. Bot.* iii. § 2. (ed. 6) 41 In the Turions, or subterranean budding shoots of.. perennial herbs. 1894 OLIVER tr. *Kerner's Nat. Hist. Plants* I. 624 The scale-leaves.. developed on subterranean shoots, especially on bulbs, rhizomes, and turions, differ considerably... By turion.. is meant a bud originating laterally on underground stem-structures and developing in the summer into a shoot which rises above the ground.

Hence **Turioni·ferous** *a.*, producing turions.

1828 in WEBSTER (citing BARTON). 1900 in B. D. JACKSON *Gloss. Bot. Terms.*

**Turit,** obs. Sc. form of TURRET.

**Turk** [1] (tɒ̄ɹk). Also 4–7 **Turke,** 5 **turque,** 7 **Turc;** 9 **Toork** (sense 1). [= F. *Turc*, fem. *turque*, It., Sp., Pg. *Turco, -a*, med.L. *Turcus, -a*, Byz. Gr. Τοῦρκος, Pers. (and Arab.) ترك *turk.* A national name of unknown origin. Possibly the same as the Chinese equivalent *Tu-kin*, applied to a division of the Hiong-nu (identified by Deguigne with the Huns), who occupied the country south of the Altaian mountains *c* 177 B.C. (In Persian dicts. ترك *turk* is explained as 'A Turk, a beautiful youth, a barbarian, a robber', but the last three definitions are only applications of the national name, not explanations of its original meaning.)]

**1.** *Ethnology.* Pl. *Turks.* The name of a numerous and widely spread family of the human race, occupying from prehistoric times large parts of Central Asia, and speaking a language and dialects belonging to the TURKIC branch of the Ural-Altaic (Finno-Tartar, or Turanian) linguistic family (a primary family of co-ordinate rank with the Indo-European or Aryan, and Semitic). Within this linguistic family the Turks are usually held to stand between the Ugrians and Mongols, having closest relationship to the latter group. The form *Toork* or *Tourk* (after Persian) is used by some (esp. in India) in this wide sense.

From their original home in Central Asia, chiefly from Turkestan, hordes of Turks at various times assailed and conquered other lands. Of these, the best known in the West were those calling themselves, after famous leaders, Seljûk and Osmānli respectively. The former overthrew the Abbasides, or first Mohammedan caliphs of Baghdad, and founded the Seljûk dynasty in their room; the latter, after embracing Islām, and receiving much Persian and Arab culture, arose on the ruins of the Seljûk empire in A.D. 1300 and became the ancestors of the Osmanli or Ottoman Turks in Asia and south-eastern Europe (see sense 2).

Probably the name *Turk* appears in English first in connexion with the Third Crusade, 1187–1192. The Turks of that date were Seljúks, not Ottomans. Saladin, the antagonist of Richard I., was a Kurd, originally in the service of the Seljúks. In the wider sense 1, the name is of comparatively late use in English and the European langs. generally, the Turks of Central Asia being unknown in Western Europe.

**1500–20** DUNBAR *Poems* xxxiii. 5 Me thocht a Turk of Tartary Come throw the boundis of Barbary And lay forloppin in Lumbardy. **1545** ASCHAM *Toxoph.* I. (Arb.) 80 After them the Turkes hauing an other name, but yet the same people, borne in Scythia. **1815** ELPHINSTONE *Acc. Caubul* (1842) I. 417 The Kuzzilbaushes are members of that colony of Toorks which now predominates in Persia. I call them by this name (which is usually given them at Caubul). ..They speak Persian, and among themselves Toorkee. *Ibid.* II. 185 That great division of the human race which is known in Asia by the name of Toork, and which, with the Moguls and Manshoors, compose what we call the Tartar nation. Each of these divisions has its separate language, and that of the Toorks is widely diffused throughout the west of Asia. *a* **1833** SIR J. MALCOLM *Life & Corr.* (1856) I. vi. 91 We were now threatened with an invasion of Toorks and Tartars. **1843** *Penny Cycl.* XXV. 395/1 The Turks-Osmanlis are a branch of the Turks in the larger meaning of the word. *Ibid.*, We cannot precisely ascertain when the Turks (..in the larger meaning of the word) first appeared in Europe. *Ibid.*, The Káyi,..the most illustrious of all [the Turkish tribes], because the Turks-Osmanlis descend from them. **1877** FREEMAN *Ottoman Power in Europe* vii. 286 It is..in the Anatolian peninsula only, that the Turk is really at home. The Ottoman is hardly at home even there; but the Turk, the representative of the earlier and better Turkish races, is at home. **1888** *Encycl. Brit.* XXIII. 658/2 The use of the name 'Turks' has never been limited in a clear and definite way from the time of the Byzantine authors to the present day. To the former, as also to the Arabs, it has a collective sense like Scythians or Huns. *Ibid.*, The Kirghiz..are considered as the typical Turks of the present day, and are described..as being midway between the Mongol and the Caucasian. **1899** J. T. BEALBY in *Times Gazetteer* 1613/2 Thirty years later [than 1017] the Turks—not the Ottomans (Osmanlis), but their predecessors, the Seljuks — invaded the Byzantine Empire for the first time.

**2.** *Politics.* A member of the dominant race of the Ottoman empire; in earlier times, a Seljúk; since 1300, an Osmanli or Ottoman; one who is, or considers himself, a descendant of the Osmanlis or other Turks. Sometimes (now rarely), any subject of the Grand Turk or Turkish Sultan; but usually restricted to Mohammedans. Pl. *The Turks*, the Ottomans, the Turkish people.

**13..** *Coer de L.* 5003 Thre thousand Turkes com, with bost, Betwen Jakes and his hoost. *c* **1375** *Sc. Leg. Saints* xxvi. (*Nycholas*) 591 Lang tyme eftyre with gret were, þe turkis thru iniquite distroyt þe towne of myrre [Myra]. *c* **1400** MAUNDEV. (1839) iv. 26 [Rodes] was wont to be clept Collos; and so callen it the Turkes ȝit. *Ibid.* xiii. 145 But a gret man þat he [the Greek Emperour] sente for to kepe the contree aȝenst the Turkes vsurped the lond & helde it to him self, & cleped him Emperour of Trapazond. *c* **1489** CAXTON *Sonnes of Aymon* xiv. 348 We shall werre styll on goddys enmyes as ben turques & sarrasins. **1517** TORKINGTON *Pilgr.* (1884) 23 We war receyvyd by the Turkys and Sarrasyns. **1547** in Feuillerat *Revels Edw. VI* (1914) 11 Hedpeces to the same, turkes ffasshyon of blewe Red & yolowe sarcenet. **1599** DALLAM in *Early Voy. Levant* (Hakl. Soc.) 79 My drugaman..was a Turke, but a Cornish man borne. **1634** *Cal. St. Papers, Dom.* 31 May (1864) 44 Complaints out of the west country of divers outrages lately committed in those parts by Turks and pirates. **1644** EVELYN *Diary* 7 Oct., One Turke he much favor'd, who waited on him in his cabin. *a* **1658** J. DURHAM *Exp. Rev.* v. ii. (1680) 275 To redeem so many of them from the bondage of the Turks. **1673** RAY *Journ. Low C.* 140 The Turcs at our being there [Vienna] having taken Neuhausel. **1696** PHILLIPS (ed. 5), *Turk*, a Subject of the Grand Signiors, who is also call'd the Great Turk. **1801** *Med. Jrnl.* V. 352 The debt which England and all Europe had contracted with the Turks for the inoculation of the Small-pox. **1847** MRS. A. KERR tr. *Ranke's Hist. Servia* 24 The Servians, the Bosnians..and the Albanians, once more stood united against the Osmanlis. But the Turks were stronger than all these nations combined. **1888** *Encycl. Brit.* XXIII. 658/2 At the present day we are wont to restrict the name to the Osmanli Turks, though they themselves refuse to be called Turks, having..ceased to be such in becoming imbued with Arabo-Persian culture. On the other hand when we speak of Uigurs and Tatars, we mean tribes who style themselves Turks and really are such.

**b.** *The Turk*, comprehensively or collectively: the Turks; the Turkish power; also, the Turkish Sultan, the Grand Turk.

*c* **1482** J. KAY tr. *Caoursin's Siege of Rhodes* ⁋ 3 In what tyme that thees thynges were thought and counseyled in Constantynople among the turke and his counseyle. **1561** *New Calendar* 17 Jan. in *Prayer-bk. Q. Eliz.* (1890) 194 The good Prince Scanderbeg.., a scourge to the Turke. **1581** ALLEN *Apol.* 18 b, Christians of al sortes,..and al other vnder the Turke. **1591** SHAKS. 1 *Hen. VI*, IV. vii. 73 The Turke that two and fiftie Kingdomes hath, Writes not so tedious a Stile as this. **1605** — *Lear* III. iv. 94. **1735** POPE *Prol. Sat.* 198 Should such a man, too fond to rule alone, Bear, like the Turk, no brother near the throne. **1896** *N. Brit. Daily Mail* 17 June 4 The unfortunate lands over which the Turk now exercises his baleful sway. **1898** *Daily News* 7 Sept. 5/4 The Dervishes..animated by an implacable hatred of 'The Turk', which is a comprehensive phrase applied to Egyptians and Englishmen alike.

**c.** *The Grand* or *Great Turk*, the Ottoman Sultan. Cf. *the Great Khan, the Great Mogul.*

*c* **1482** J. KAY tr. *Caoursin's Siege of Rhodes* ⁋ 6 The turkes ..saydyn that theyr lord the gret Turke was dede. **1503** *Lett. Rich. III & Hen. VII* (Rolls) I. 210 He said that the Grete Turke feared not the pope. **1563** *Homilies* II. *Place of Prayer* II. (1859) 348 The Enemie of our Lord Christ, the great Turke. **1615** BEDWELL *Arab. Trudg.* N iv. s. v. *Sultan*, For thus they now call the Great Turke,..The Souldan of Stamboli. **1689** *Andros Tracts* I. 165 They were as Arbitrary as the great Turk. **1846** HUXLEY in *Life* (1900) I. ii. 26, I am in a very fair way, and would snap my fingers at the Grand Turk. **1853** C. BRONTE *Villette* iii, He was more than the Grand Turk in her estimation.

†**d.** Applied vaguely to Saracens. *Obs.*

**13..** *Coer de L.* 4971 Thre thousand Turkes com at the last, With bowe Turkeys, and arweblaste.

**e.** *Young Turks*, a name given in the 20th century to the Ottomans who tried to rejuvenate the Turkish empire, and bring it more into line with European ideas: opposed to *Old Turks* who were against such ideals. (See also sense 4.)

**1908** *Daily News* 5 Aug. 4/7 Will the glorification of the 'Young Turk' kill this expression as one of reproach to be used in the nursery? **1909** [see *Turkdom* below].

**3.** Often used as = Moslem or Mohammedan.

(The Turks being to Christian nations the typical Moslem power from *c* 1300.)

*a* **1548** HALL *Chron., Edw. IV* 233 He..hated hym more then a Panym or a Turke. **1548–9** (Mar.) *Bk. Com. Prayer, Collect Gd. Friday*, Haue mercy upon all Jewes, Turkes, Infidels, and heretikes. *c* **1645** HOWELL *Lett.* (1650) II. 16 No Jew is capable to be a Turk but he must be first an Abdula a Christian. **1697** COLLIER *Ess. Mor. Subj.* II. 137 He is a Christian at Rome, a Heathen at Japan, and a Turk at Constantinople. **1725** WATTS *Logic* I. vi. § 10 A divine distributes [mankind] into Turks, Heathens, Jews, or Christians.

**b.** In *to turn Turk, become Turk*, and similar phrases. (But also used in senses 2 and 4.)

**1592** KYD *Sol. & Pers.* III. v, What say these prisoners? will they turne Turke, or no? **1602** SHAKS. *Ham.* III. ii. 287 If the rest of my Fortunes turne Turke with me. **1615** G. SANDYS *Trav.* I. 54 No Iew can turne Turke, untill he first turne Christian. **1629** J. M. tr. *Fonseca's Dev. Contempl.* 403 The Souldier, he will turne Turke vpon point either of profit, or of honor. **1632** LITHGOW *Trav.* IV. 141 [He] turnd Turke, and was circumcised. **1687** A. LOVELL tr. *Thevenot's Trav.* I. 42 Many are persuaded, that when a Jew turns Turk, he must first become Christian, which is very false. **1737** [S. BERINGTON] *G. di Lucca's Mem.* (1738) 282 He offered to turn Turk if they would spare him.

**4.** *transf.* Applied to any one having qualities attributed to the Turks; a cruel, rigorous, or tyrannical man; any one behaving as a barbarian or savage; one who treats his wife hardly; a bad-tempered or unmanageable man. Often, with alliterative qualification, *terrible Turk. Young* or *little Turk*, an unmanageable or violent child or youth.

**1536** *Exhort. North* 56 in Furniv. *Ballads fr. MSS.* I. 306 Thes Sothorne turkes pervertyng owre lawe. **1579** LYLY *Euphues* (Arb.) 42 Was neuer any Impe so wicked and barbarous, any Turke so vyle and brutishe. *a* **1700** B. E. *Dict. Cant. Crew, Turk*, any cruel hard-hearted Man. *a* **1845** HOOD *Lay Real Life* v, Who said my mother was a Turk, And took me home—and made me work, But managed half my meals to shirk? My Aunt. **1847** HELPS *Friends in C.* Ser. I. vii. 114 Why you Mahometan, you Turk of a lawyer—would you do away with all the higher things of courtesy, tenderness for the weaker [etc.]? **1854** *N. & Q.* 1st Ser. IX. 451/1 We often hear of people bad to manage being 'regular Turks'. **1862** *Spectator* 6 Dec. 1363/1 The new generation of Greeks have a real passion for education; without it they say a man is a 'Turk', that last epithet of opprobrium. **1863** FRITH in *Autobiog. & Remin.* (1887) I. xxiv. 351 As to Prince William of Prussia, of all the little Turks he is one of the worst. **1874** SIR W. W. HUNTER in *Life* xiii. (1901) 228 Mr. Lyall is a terrible Turk at keeping his wife up to her social duties. **1875** ANNE MOZLEY *Ess. fr. Blackwood* 217 A bad temper does seem often favourable to health. The man who has been a Turk all his life lives long to plague all about him. **1891** G. MEREDITH *One of our Conq.* xxix, The tastes of the civilized man—a creature that is not clean-washed of the Turk in him. **1904** *Police Magistrate* in *Daily News* 26 Nov. 9/2 'You are a young Turk, and a bad Turk, too;..I think I ought to send you to a reformatory school.' **1908** [see 2 e].

†**5. a.** A human figure at which to practise shooting. **b.** A hideous image to frighten children; a bugbear. *Obs.*

**1569** in *Camden's Hist. Eliz.* (1717) Pref. 29 The shotinge with the brode arrowe, the shotinge at the twelve skore prick, the shotinge at the Turke. **1598** FLORIO, *Manduco*, a disguised or vglie picture vsed in shewes to make children afraid,..a turke, or a bug-beare. **1608** [see PRICK *sb.* 10 b]. **1616** *Manifest. Abp. Spalato's Motives* App. iii. 7 All the rest were but painted posts, and Turkes of ten pence, to fill and adorne the shooting-field. **1631** J. BURGES *Answ. Rejoined* 182 The Replier hath set vp a man of cloutes of his owne making, and then shootes at a Turke, as boyes doe.

**6. a.** A Turkish or Turkey horse. †**b.** A Turkish sword or sabre, a scimitar (*obs.*).

**1623** MARKHAM *Cheap Husb.* I. iii. (ed. 3) 42 The best Stallion to beget horses for the warres is the Courser, the Iennet, or the Turke. **1638** WHITING *Hist. Albino & B.* 108 He forthwith unsheathd his trusty Turke, Cald forth that blood which in his veines did lurk. **1831** YOUATT *Horse* iii. 29 Charles II sent his master of the horse to the Levant, to purchase brood mares and stallions. These were principally Barbs and Turks.

**7.** *attrib.* or *adj.* = TURKISH; also in *comb.*, as *Turk-like* adj. and adv., *-ruled, -worked* adjs. Also in possessive in names of plants, etc., as TURK'S CAP, TURK'S HEAD, *Turk's knife, Turk's turban.*

?*a* **1366** CHAUCER *Rom. Rose* 923 In his honde holdyng Turke bowes two, fulle wel deuysed had he. **1534** *Acc. Ld. High Treas. Scot.* VI. 193, iij quarteris of taphety turke, price of the elne xiiij s. **1683** R. HOLME *Armoury* III. xiv. (Roxb.) 3/2 These are called Turks knives because they turne vpward in the back towards the end, or point of the blade. **1708** *Lond. Gaz.* No. 4435/4 To be sold.., a true Turk Stalion about 15 Hands high. **1760** J. LEE *Introd. Bot.* App. (1788) 353 Turk's Turban, *Ranunculus.* *a* **1791** GROSE *Olio, Grumbler* xi. (1796) 44 The best parlour..was furnished with Turk-worked chairs. **1850** BROWNING *Christmas Eve* xviii, Or Turk-like brandishing a scimetar. **1857** LIVINGSTONE *Trav.* Introd. 5 Adopting the Turk-like philosophy of this Scotchman! **1873** W. CORY *Lett. & Jrnls.* (1897) 328 Frankified Turk-ruled Egyptians.

Hence **Tu·rkdom**, the realm or domain of the Turks; Turkey. *Young T.*, the party of Young Turks.

**1900** *Eng. Hist. Rev.* Jan. 150 For fifty years the whole of Turkdom was then more or less effectively administered by Chinese proconsuls. **1909** VAMBÉRY in *19th Cent.* Mar. 371 The whole Turkish nation, with very few exceptions, belongs to Young Turkdom. Every one who feels Turkish and speaks Turkish is a Young Turk.

**Turk** [2]. [ad. F. *turc*; origin and history uncertain. As early as 1688 associated in French with the national name *turc* TURK; but Littré and Hatz.-Darm. treat it as a distinct word.

Boyceau de la Baraudière *Tr. du Jardin* 58 (1688) has 'Les poiriers de bon chrestien en sont sur tous autres endommagez, et c'est pourquoy on a nommé ce ver Turc.' But the American *Little Turk* is said to be named from the crescent-shaped punctures made in the fruit by the female.]

The larva of an insect (perh. of the fruit-bark beetle, *Scolytus rugulosus*) dreaded for the destruction it does to pear-trees by mining under the bark; also, the larva of the cockchafer (Littré). According to *Century Dict.*, the plum-weevil or plum-curculio, *Conotrachelus nenuphar*, which is very destructive to fruit-trees generally, is known as the *Turk* or *Little Turk.*

**1712** J. JAMES tr. *Le Blond's Gardening* 173 The great Enemies to Trees, are..Snails, Tons, Turks, and abundance of Worms. *Ibid.* 176 Turks are certain white Worms that get into Trees and eat Holes in them, running betwixt the Bark and the Stem. **1815** KIRBY & SP. *Entomol.* vi. (1818) I. 213 Their ravages have long been known in Germany under the name of Wurm trökniss (decay caused by worms); and in the old liturgies of that country the animal itself is formally mentioned under its vulgar appellation, 'The Turk'.

**Turkas, -ass, -eis(e**: see TURKESS(E, TURKIS, TURQUOISE.

†**Turkein.** *Obs. rare.* Also tour-. [a. OF. **turcain*:—L. type *Turcān-us*, f. *Turcus* Turk.] = TURK [1].

*a* **1330** *Otuel* 1380 A turkein þat was ful of prude. *Ibid.* 1392 He smot þe tourkein oppon þe hood.

† **Tu·rken,** *v. Obs. rare.* Also 6 turquen, turkin. [Etymology uncertain. Taken by Skeat as a deriv. of F. *torquer* to twist, 'to writhe, wreath, wind in, wrap about' (Cotgr.), ad. L. *torquēre* to twist; but there are difficulties both of form and of sense; see TURKESS(E, TURKISH *v.*

Possibly f. TURK [1] + -EN [5], referring to the action of the Turks in transforming Christian churches into mosques, or from the Koran being regarded as a transformation or perversion of the Bible.)]

*trans.* = TURKESS(E *v.* 2.

**1575** GASCOIGNE *Making of Verse* in *Steele Gl.* etc. (Arb.) 37 This poeticall licence is a shrewde fellow,..it maketh wordes longer, shorter, of mo sillables, of fewer, newer, older ..and to conclude it turkeneth all things at pleasure, for example, *ydone* for *done.* **1575** — *Poesies, Ep. to Rev. Divines* Wks. 1907 I. 7 You shall find it now in this second imprinting so turquened and turned, so clensed from all unclenly wordes. **1587** GOLDING *De Mornay* xxiii. (1592) 353 They turkining themselues as much as they can into Gods, that is to say into Angels of light, to beguile our sence and imagination with strange vanities. *Ibid.* xxiv. 368 If they chaunce to stumble vpon some good saying for maners or for the life of man, they turkin it a thousand waies to make it seem good for thir purpose. **1607** T. ROGERS *39 Art.* Pref. § 28 Not either Articles of his owne, lately deuised; or the old newly turkened: but the very Articles agreed vpon by the Archbishops and Bishops.

**Turkery** (tɜ̄·ɹkəri). [f. TURK [1] + -ERY: cf. *popery, foolery.*] †**a.** The Turkish religion or practice; Mohammedanism (*obs.*). **b.** 'Turks' collectively.

**1585** W. WHITAKER *Answ. Rainolds* 360, I thinke it flat Atheisme and Turkery to denie that Christ was borne of a virgine. **1678** MARVELL *Growth Popery* 4 Either open Judaism, or plain Turkery, or honest Paganism. **1709** STRYPE *Ann. Ref.* I. lvi. 576 A religion of their devising worse than Turkery. **1878** FREEMAN in *Life & Lett.* (1895) II. 164 The whole accursed den of Jewry and Turkery, clubs, rookeries, and all.

**Turkes, -ese, -esse,** var. TURKIS, TURQUOISE.

†**Turke·sco,** *a. Obs. rare.* [a. It. *turchesco*, = obs. F. *turquesque* (Cotgr.).] = TURKISH.

**1584** W. BARRET in Hakluyt *Voy.* (1599) II. I. 272 The said danine is of siluer, hauing the Turkesco stampe on both sides, and 2 and a halfe of these make a Saie,..in value as the Saie of Aleppo.

**Turkese,** var. TURKEYS *Obs.*

**Turkess** (tɜ̄·ɹkes). *nonce-wd.* [f. TURK [1] + -ESS.] A female Turk; the consort of the Turkish Sultan.

**1586** MARLOWE *1st Pt. Tamburl.* III. iii, Disdainful Turkess, and unreverend boss. *Ibid.*, Bind them both, and one lead in the Turk; The Turkess let my love's maid lead away.

† **Turkess(e, -eis(e, -is(s,** *v. Obs.* Forms: 6 torcasse, torkes, -esse, turkiss, -ise, 6–7 turkess(e, 7 turkeise, turquese, turkis(s, turkize, turcase, turches. [Derivation uncertain: evi-

dently related to TURKEN, and, like that verb, referred by some to F. *torquer*, ad. L. *torquēre* to twist; but there are difficulties both of form and sense, and possibly both *turken* and *turkesse* were Eng. formations from TURK and TURKEYS, Turkish; at least, they were often associated with these words, this verb being actually in 17th c. spelt *turkize*; cf. also TURKISH *v.* in same sense. (There is no trace of any OF. verb *torquir*, *torquiss-ant*.)]

**1.** *trans.* To transform or alter for the worse; to wrest, twist, distort, pervert.

**1521** FISHER *Serm. agst. Luther* Wks. (E.E.T.S.) I. 341 Many of [these heretics]..had the propre fayth [*ed.* 1556 feate] to wrye and to torcasse the scryptures. *a* **1603** T. CARTWRIGHT *Confut. Rhem. N. T.* (1618) 245 The body of Christ is a more pretious thing then hee will suffer to be turkessed and transformed after that sort. **1612** SIR R. NAUNTON in *Buccleuch MSS.* (Hist. MSS. Comm.) I. 118 My mediation..was, I know not how, turquesed into a reprobate sense with Sir H. Nevill. **1612** T. TAYLOR *Comm. Titus* ii. 1. (1619) 336 Some sentence of Scripture..must be turkist, and mishapen out of his natiue simplicitie. **1648** *Petit. Eastern Assoc.* 5 Those..which are so audacious as to turcase the revealed, and sealed Standard of our salvation ..to the mishapen models of their intoxicated phansies.

**2.** To alter the form or appearance of; to change, modify, refashion (not necessarily for the worse).

**1530** PALSGR. 759/1, I torkes, I alter the shappe of a thyng, *je contourne*, and *je transmue*. He hath torkessed his house quyte a newe. *c* **1577** G. HARVEY *Marginalia* (1913) 141 Erasmus three cheefist Paper bookes..His Similes.. Apothegges..Prouerbs, newly turkissed by diuers. **1593** ABP. BANCROFT *Surv. Discipl.* i. 6 He taketh the said sentence out of Esay (somewhat turkised) for his poesie aswell as the rest. *a* **1610** HEALEY *Theophrastus* (1636) 21 Hee trimmeth himselfe often: he..changeth and Turkizeth his cloathes. **1613** PURCHAS *Pilgrimage* I. iii. (1614) 298 The Turkes, when they turkeised it [St. Sophia], threw downe the Altars, turned the Bells into great Ordinance [etc.]. **1639** HORN & ROB. *Gate Lang. Unl.* xlvii. § 505 He that makes cast-cloathes new of old (trimmeth up, new turkizeth), and exposeth them to sale, is a broker. *a* **1650** P. FLETCHER *Father's Test.* (1670) 108 So curiously painted..and turchest in new fashions.

Hence †**Turkessing, -ising**, *vbl. sb. Obs.*

**1612** T. TAYLOR *Comm. Titus* i. 5 (1619) 84 Adding, detracting, or depraving his institutions by a restless turkising of them. **1673** *Jackson's Wks.* III. *Creed* x. xxxi. Notes 133 An Alteration, Change, or Turning. Or if these be thought Terms too good, Let it be called a Turkizing of Sensitives.

**Turkey**[1] (tɒ̄·ɹki). Also 5 torke, 6–7 **Turkie**, 6–8 **Turky**, (5–7 **Turkye**, 6 **torkey**, **Turquey**, **Turkeye**, 7 **Tyrkye**). [= F. *Turquie*, med.L. *Turchia*, *Turquia*, f. *Turc*, *Turc-us*, TURK[1]: cf. *Germān-us*, *Germānia*, *Germany*; *Indus*, *India*.]

**1.** The land of the Turks, 'Turkey in Asia' and 'Turkey in Europe'; formerly sometimes Turkestan or Tartary.

*c* **1369** CHAUCER *Dethe Blaunche* 1026 Ne sende men in-to Walakye,..To Alisaundre, ne in-to Turkye. *c* **1485** *Digby Myst.* (1882) III. 1435 Þer is þe lond of torke. **1500–20** DUNBAR *Poems* xxxiii. 61 A fedrem on he tuke..in Turky for to fle. **1570** LEVINS *Manip.* 98/45 Turkie, *Tartaria*. **1626** BACON *Sylva* § 49 Rice is in Turky..most fed upon. **1719** W. WOOD *Surv. Trade* 180 The Turkey Company ..have Factories and Houses in Turkey. **1892** *Chamb. Encycl.* X. 329 Turkey or the Ottoman Empire comprises the wide but heterogeneous territories really or nominally subject to the Osmânli sultan, in Europe, Asia, and Africa.

† **2.** Short for **a.** TURKEY STONE, the turquoise; **b.** *Turkey horse* (cf. TURKI); **c.** *Turkey leather*.

**a.** **1487** *Ann. Barber-Surgeons Lond.* (1890) 530, I bequeath to my mother my golde ringe which hath in it a stone called a Turkey. **1509** HAWES *Past. Pleas.* xxxviii. (Percy Soc.) 197 Of the mervaylous rofe set full of rubyes, And tynst with saphers and many turkeys. **1577** E. HOGAN in Hakluyt *Voy.* (1589) 158 A short dagger set with 200 stones, rubies, and turkies. **1587** GREENE *Tritameron* Wks. (Grosart) III. 59 The Turkie hauing lost his color is of no value. **1592** *Wills & Inv. N.C.* (Surtees) II. 204 To my daughter Gee my Turkey ringe. **1595** *Ibid.* 168 My goulde ringe wherein my turkie is. **1615** G. SANDYS *Trav.* 221 They haue [in Cyprus] .. diuerse kinds of precious stones of inferiour value, amongst which the emerald, and the turky. *c* **1618** MORYSON *Itin.* IV. IV. i. (1903) 335 Three ringes on his fingers, a Dyamond, a Turky, and a Ruby. **1680** MORDEN *Geog. Rect.* (1685) 358 There are Mines of..divers Kinds of precious Stones, viz. the Emerald and the Turky.

**b.** **1678** *Extracts Govt. Rec. Fort St. George* 6 Mar. (Yule), Four horses bought for the Company—One young Arab, One old Turkey [etc.].

**c.** **1715** *Hearne's Collect.* (O.H.S.) V. 66 One in large paper, bound in Turkey. **1721** RAMSAY *Conclusion* 4 Dear, vent'rous book..In gilded Turkey clad. **1835** *J. R. Smith's Catal. Bks.* Nov. 8/2 Life of the Famous Comedian, Joe Hayns,..in old turkey, very scarce.

**3.** *attrib.* and *Comb.* **a.** Simple *attrib.*; now mostly superseded by TURKISH, except in particular connexions, as in *Turkey Company*, *merchant*.

*a* **1518** SKELTON *Magnyf.* 1480 Porcenya, the prowde prouoste of Turky lande. **1543** *Rutland MSS.* (1905) IV. 346, v long table carpettes of Turky makyng, j fote carpet of Turky makyng. *a* **1548** HALL *Chron.*, *Hen. VIII* 6 b, Appareled after Turkey fashion. **1585** T. WASHINGTON tr. *Nicholay's Voy.* IV. xiii. 126 b, A fair Turkie horse. *Ibid.* xvi. 130 b, [They] are not permitted to print the Turkie or Arabian tongue. **1651** HOWELL *Venice* 134 They had taken some Turky Vessells in the Venetian Seas. **1690** CHILD *Disc. Trade* (1698) 118 The Turkey-Company do maintain an Ambassador and two Consuls. **1817** BYRON *Beppo* xcvii, He..pass'd for a true Turkey-merchant. **1845** DISRAELI *Sybil* II. vi, A couple of centuries ago, a Turkey Merchant was the great creator of wealth.

**b.** In names of things of actual or supposed Turkish or Levantine origin, as *Turkey apricot*, *gall*, *myrrh*, *parsley*, *plum*, *sponge*, *tobacco*, *wood*; of Turkish workmanship or manufacture, or made in imitation of this, as *Turkey bow*, *coverlet*, *cushion*, *garter*, *grogram*, *morocco*, *opium*, *satin*, *slipper*, *tapestry*, *towel*.

**1696** LANGFORD *Fruit Trees* 140 Amongst Apricocks..the *Turkey is much commended. **1731–59** MILLER *Gard. Dict.* s. v. *Armeniaca*, The Turkey Apricot is yet larger..and of a globular Figure; the Fruit turns to a deeper Colour. **1572** in Feuillerat *Revels Q. Eliz.* (1908) 157 One *Turky Bowe and iii arrowes. **1578** *Ibid.* 292, vii Turkie Bowes at XII[d] the peece. **1585** T. WASHINGTON tr. *Nicholay's Voy.* II. v. 35 *Turkie couerlettes. **1596** SHAKS. *Tam. Shr.* II. i. 355 Fine Linnen, *Turky cushions bost with pearle. **1684** in *Archæol. Cambr.*, *Orig. Doc.* (1877) 8 Turky cushions. **1874** FLÜCKIGER & HANBURY *Pharmacographia* 536 *Gallæ Halepenses*, *Gallæ Turcicæ*; Galls, Nutgalls, Oak Galls, Aleppo or *Turkey Galls. **1650** in *Verney Mem.* (1907) I. 469 A paire of Scarlet silk stockings, with a paire of *Turkey garters to them. **1603–4** BP. W. BARLOW *Confer. Hampton Crt.* P ij, These are Cartwrightes Schollers, Scismatikes,..; you may know them by their Turkie gownes, and silke *Turky Grogorum. **1819** REES *Cycl.*, *Turkey Opium. **1890** BILLINGS *Med. Dict.*, *Turkey opium*, the official opium of the pharmacopœias, produced in Asia Minor, and shipped from Turkish ports. **1690** in *Thanes of Cawdor* (Spald. Club) 353 Ane unce of *Turkie persell. **1577** B. GOOGE *Heresbach's Husb.* II. (1586) 88 Quinces, Pomegranates, and *Turkie Plomes. **1664** EVELYN *Kal. Hort.* (1729) 214 Plums..Great Anthony, Turkey-Plum [etc.]. **1545** *Rates of Customs* C viij, *Turky satten the pece. **1551** SIR J. WILLIAMS *Accompte* (Abbotsf. Cl. 1836) 51 A cope..with an orpheres of redde Turquey satten. **1760** W. J. MICKLE *Song*, '*There's nae Luck aboot the House*' iv, My *Turkey slippers maun gae on, My stockings pearly blue. *c* **1645** HOWELL *Lett.* vi. 41 The wrong-side of a *Turky Tapistry. **1812** J. SMYTH *Pract. of Customs* (1821) 260 *Turkey Tobacco may be imported in small packages within any hogshead. **1545** ASCHAM *Toxoph.* (Arb.) 123 Steles be made of dyuerse woodes, as Brasell, *Turkie wood, Fusticke, Sugercheste, Hardbeame, Byrche.

**c.** Special combs., as **Turkey alder**, *Alnus oblongata* Willd.; † **Turkey balm**, *Dracocephalum Moldavica* Linn.; **Turkey bean**, ? the scarlet runner, *Phaseolus multiflorus*; **Turkey berry**, the fruit of species of *Rhamnus*, used in dyeing; cf. *Persian berries*; see also TURKEY[2] 6; **Turkey blue**, a dye: see quot.; **Turkey chair**, (*a*) a chair of Turkish make; (*b*) the sphenoid bone (of the horse); also *Turkey-chair bone*; **Turkey colour**: see quot.; **Turkey corn**, an old name for Indian corn; **Turkey cress, earth**: see quots.; **Turkey fig**, the common fig, *Ficus carica*; in Australia, the Indian fig or prickly pear, *Opuntia*; **Turkey gilliflower**, the French and the African marigold; †**Turkey gown**; †**Turkey gruel**, app. a contemptuous description of coffee; **Turkey gum**: see quot.; †**Turkey hirse** = *Turkey millet*; **Turkey hone** = TURKEY STONE 2; **Turkey leather**, leather tawed with oil, the hair side not being removed until after the tawing; hence **Turkey-leathered** *a.*, bound in Turkey leather; **Turkey** †**mill, millet**, *Sorghum vulgare*: see MILLET 2; **Turkey oak**, the mossy-cup oak of southern Europe, *Quercus Cerris*; **Turkey rhubarb**, medicinal RHUBARB (1): see quot. 1866; **Turkey slate** = TURKEY STONE 2 (Ogilvie 1882); †**Turkey stool**: cf. *Turkey chair* (*a*); **Turkey twill**: see quot. 1904. See also TURKEY CARPET, T. RED, T. STONE, T. WHEAT, T. WORK.

**1822** *Hortus Angl.* II. 468 *A*[*lnus*] *Oblongata.* *Turkey Alder. Leaves elliptic, bluntish, glutinous. **1688** R. HOLME *Armoury* II. 72/1 The *Turky Balm have the flowers growing on the top of the branch spire-like. **1690** in *Thanes of Cawdor* (Spald. Club) 353 Half pd. of *Turkie benes. **1806** SOUTHEY *Let. to W. Taylor* (*Pearson's Catal.* (1900) 76) My acorn will continue to grow when his Turkey bean shall have withered. **1841** *Penny Cycl.* XIX. 445/1 The berries of several species of Rhamnus..under the name of French, *Turkey, and Persian berries. **1815** J. SMITH *Panorama Sc. & Art* II. 541 To dye Silk Blue...For the *Turkey blue, which is the deepest, a very strong archil bath is first used. **1683** SNAPE *Anat. Horse* III. viii. 122 The Bone called the *Turkey chair. [Cf. *Ibid.* v. iv. 204 The Sphenoides, or Wedge-like Bone..hath several Processes, of which..the internal are four, standing out like four feet of a Table or Chair, which..form the *Sella Turcica*.] *Ibid.* III. ix. 124 Near the side of the Turky-chair-bone they are inoculated with the second or greater branches of the fifth pair. **1684** in *Archæol. Cambr.*, *Orig. Doc.* (1877) 7 In the greate Parlour..twelve turky chaires one table and Carpett. **1661** PEACHAM *Compl. Gent* (ed. 3) 156 *Turkie colour, *i.e.* Venice blew, or as others will have it, red. [Cf. **1611** COTGR., *Couleur Turquine*, a right blue, or Venice blue. *Ibid.* s. v. *Turc*, *Couleur Turque*, azure.] **1597** GERARDE *Herbal* I. liv. 74 Of *Turkie cornes there be diuers sorts. **1611** COTGR., *Mays*,..Turkie corne, Turkie wheat. **1865** WEDGWOOD *Dict. Eng. Etymol.* s. v., It is singular that a bird which came from America should have been considered as a Turkey fowl, but the same is the case with maize, which was called Turkey corn or Turkey wheat, Fr. *bled de Turquie*. **1633** *Gerarde's Herbal* II. xxiv. 274 *Turkie cresses .. is iudged to be the *Arabis* or *Draba* of the Ancients. **1748** J. HILL *Hist. Fossils* 14 Friable greyish red Bole, called *Turky Earth. **1866** *Treas. Bot.* 492/1 *Turkey figs are imported from Smyrna. **1888** *Antipodean Notes* 12 The 'Turkey fig' [in Adelaide] is about four times the size of a well-grown English fig. **1578** LYTE *Dodoens* II. xxv. 176 Of *Turkie or Aphrican Gilofers. We do call this floure Turkie Gillofers, and French Marygoldes. **1558** in Feuillerat *Revels Q. Eliz.* (1908) 20, vi longe streighte *turkye gounes of redd cloth. **1603–4** BP. W. BARLOW *Confer. Hampton Crt.* ii. 27 They [Puritan divines] appeared before his Maiestie in Turky gownes, not in their Scholastical habites, sorting to their degrees. **1705** E. WARD *Hud. Reviv.* II. III. 54 Some sucking Smoak from Indian Fuel, And others sipping *Turky Gruel. **1890** BILLINGS *Med. Dict.*, **Turkey gum*, the generic name applied to the various species of Egyptian gums. **1597** GERARDE *Herbal* I. lv. 77 [Millet] is called..Turkie Mill or *Turkie Hirsse. **1796** KIRWAN *Elem. Min.* (ed. 2) I. 238 Novaculite. *Turkey hone. **1839** URE *Dict. Arts* 1141 Whet-slate, or Turkey hone, is a slaty rock, containing a great proportion of quartz. **1843** *Penny Cycl.* XXV. 410/2 Turkey-hone..was first brought to Europe from the Levant. **1655–6** WOOD *Life* Mar. (O.H.S.) I. 200 A very fair copie of them [sermons] bound in blew *Turkey-leather. **1821** SCOTT *Kenilw.* v, A small dagger..which hung in his turkey-leather sword-belt. **1843** *Penny Cycl.* XXV. 408/1 The so-called Turkey leather is made in England. **1710** *Lond. Gaz.* No. 4521/4 A small *Turkey Leather'd Bible. **1597** *Turkey mill [see *Turkey hirse*]. **1597** GERARDE *Herbal* I. lv. 77 *Tvrkie Millet is a stranger in England. **1640** PARKINSON *Theat. Bot.* 1137. **1819** *Pantologia*, *Quercus cerris*, *Turkey oak...South of Europe. **1842** J. B. FRASER *Mesopot. & Assyria* xv. 353 The forest-trees are for the most part the following:—.. *Quercus cerris*..Turkey oak. **1789** *Trans. Soc. Arts* I. 94 Commonly sold in the shops under the name of *Turkey or Russian Rhubarb. **1866** *Treas. Bot.* 971/2 What is known ..as the best Turkey Rhubarb in reality comes from China through Russia...It was formerly imported from Natolia, whence the name Turkey Rhubarb. **1640** *Inv.* in Nicholson *Hist. & Trad. Tales* (1843) 267 A *Turky stule and a rich work stule. **1904** *Woollen Draper's Terms* in *Tailor & Cutter* 480/1 **Turkey Twill*, a soft make of cotton twill, usually red, but by no means confined to that colour. **1912** D. CRAWFORD *Thinking Black* xiv. 271 Four cut-throats, with red turkey-twill turbans.

Hence (*nonce-words*) **Tu·rkeydom**, the realm or empire of the Turks; †**Turkeyed** (tɒ̄·ɹkid), *a.* [-ED[2]], Turkish, Turk-like, Turkified; **Tu·rkeyism**, belief in Turkey, Turkish political sympathies.

**1849** THACKERAY *Pendennis* liii, We will cut off all the heads in Christendom or *Turkeydom rather than that. **1600** O. E. *Repl. Libel* III. Pref. 1 His owne friendes charge him with *Turkeied machiauelisme. **1877** GLADSTONE in *Daily News* 13 Nov. 6 This distinguished man, who represents what I have called *Turkeyism, in his speech at the Guildhall drops entirely the 'integrity' of the Turkish empire.

**Turkey**[2] (tɒ̄·ɹki). Also 6–7 **turkie**, 6–8 **turky.** Pl. **turkeys**, formerly **turkies.** [Short for TURKEY-COCK, -HEN, app. applied orig. to the Guinea-fowl, a native of Africa, with which the American turkey was at first confounded: see TURKEY-COCK.]

†**1.** The Guinea-fowl. *Obs.*

[**1552–1601**: see TURKEY-COCK 2, TURKEY-HEN 1.] **1655** MOUFET & BENNET *Health's Improv.* (1746) 166 They were first brought from Numidia into Turky, and thence to Europe, whereupon they were called Turkies.

**2.** In current use: A well-known large gallinaceous bird of the Linnæan genus *Meleagris*, the species of which are all American; esp. *M. gallopāvo*, which was found domesticated in Mexico at the discovery of that country in 1518, and was soon after introduced into Europe, and is now valued as a table fowl in all civilized lands.

Two races of this, which have been variously regarded as sub-species or species, are found wild, of which one, the Northern wild turkey, which has been variously distinguished as *americana*, *sylvestris*, and *fera*, is a native of the eastern half of the continent, from parts of Canada and the Missouri region to Texas, where it is succeeded by *M. mexicana*, the Mexican wild turkey. As in the case of many long-domesticated animals, it is doubtful from which of these wild types the domestic turkey has arisen, but the fact that the latter was domesticated in Mexico, and that the northern race shows less adaptability to domestication, favours the opinion that *M. mexicana* was the source. Some however hold that there may have been two domestic breeds, represented in England by the Norfolk and the Cambridgeshire breeds, or that at least mixture with *americana* has taken place. Another species, *M. ocellata*, which inhabits Guatemala, is smaller and much more beautiful; it has not been tamed.

(The first two quotations app. belong to this sense.)

**1555** in Dugdale *Orig. Jurid.* xlviii. (1666) 135 Turkies 2. rated at 4[s]. a piece..00. 08. 00. **1573** TUSSER *Husb.* (1878) 89 Runciuall pease..more tender and greater they wex, If peacock and turkey leaue iobbing their bex. **1596** SHAKS. 1 *Hen. IV*, II. i. 29 The Turkies in my Pannier are quite starued. **1616** CAPT. SMITH *Descr. New Eng.* 29 Teale, Meawes, Guls, Turkies, Diue-doppers. **1634** W. WOOD *New Eng. Prosp.* (1865) 32 The Turkey is a very large Bird, of a blacke colour, yet white in flesh. **1643** BAKER *Chron.* (1660) 317 About [1524], it happened that divers things were newly brought into England, whereupon this Rhyme was made: 'Turkeys, Carps, Hoppes, Piccarell, and Beer, Came into England all in one year'. **1698** FRYER *Acc. E. India & P.* 116 Others [Pigeons] walked on the Ground, with their Breasts bearing out, and the Feathers of their Tails spreading like Turkies. *a* **1705** PRIOR *Ladle* 74 Fat Turkeys gobbling at the Door. **1766** PENNANT *Zool.* (1768) I. 213 The Turky was unknown to the antient naturalists, and even to the old world before the discovery of America. **1805** SOUTHEY *Madoc* II. xi, The loud turkey's voice Is heralding the dawn. **1860** TYLOR *Anahuac* ix. (1861) 228 The turkey, which was introduced into Europe from Mexico, was called 'huexolotl' from the gobbling noise it makes. **1886** RUSKIN *Præterita* I. iv. 115 Civilities at Christmas, in the way of turkeys and boxes of raisins.

**b.** *Wild turkey*, the wild original of the domestic fowl; commonly applied to the North American bird: see above and sense 3.

**1613** PURCHAS *Pilgrimage* (1614) 762 They haue Eagles, Haukes, wilde Turkeys and other Fowle. **1624** CAPT. SMITH *Virginia* II. 27 Wild Turkies are as bigge as our tame. **1707** MORTIMER *Husb.* (1721) I. 260, I knew a Gentleman that had a Hen-Turkey of the wild kind from Virginia; of which, and an English Cock, he raised a very fine Breed. **1830** 'B. MOUBRAY' *Domest. Poultry* x. (ed. 6) 81 There is a sameness of colour in the wild turkey, and the original stock seems to have been black, domestication generally inducing a variety of colours. **1849** D. J. BROWNE *Amer. Poultry Yd.* (1855) 138 Two species only are known to naturalists, namely, the common wild turkey, (*Meleagris gallopavo*,) of North America, the origin of our domestic stock, and the Honduras turkey, (*M. ocellata*).

**c.** The flesh of this bird, esp. the domestic turkey, as food.

**1573** TUSSER *Husb.* (1878) 70 Christmas husbandlie fare.. shred pies of the best,..and turkey well drest. **1840** BARHAM *Ingol. Leg., St. Nicholas*, The lay-brothers bring To the board a magnificent turkey and chine. The turkey and chine..are done to a nicety. **1886** W. J. TUCKER *E. Europe* 122 Cold turkey and ham, or roast chicken. How I hate that turkey! It's so vulgar too; almost as vulgar as goose.

**d.** *U.S.* and *Canada.* Allusively, in colloquial or dialect phrases, etc.

*To say* or *talk turkey*, to talk agreeably or affably, to say pleasant things; *to talk turkey*, to use high-flown language; hence *absol.* language of this character; *not to say* (*pea-*) *turkey*, to say nothing at all, 'not to say a word' (about something); *to walk turkey*, to strut or swagger; of a ship, to pitch and roll. (See Bartlett *Dict. Amer.*, and Thornton *American Glossary*.)

**1846** J. W. ABERT in *Congress Documents* XXX. 502 The Indian replied, 'You never once said turkey to me'. **1851** *Adv. Capt. Suggs* 122 (Thornton) He won't get a chance to say turkey to a good lookin gall to-day. *a* **1860** MCCLINTOCK *Beedle's Marriage* (Bartlett), I was plaguy apt to talk turkey always when I got sociable, if it was only out of politeness. **1888** *San Francisco Weekly Examiner* 22 Mar. (Farmer *Amer.*), The north wind commenced to make the Yaquina walk turkey, standing her up on either end alternately. **1888** *Washington Critic* (ibid.), 'What.. does locum tenens mean, Tim?'..'Why, that's turkey for *pro tem.*, of course'. **1909** *Dialect Notes* (U.S.) III. 356 (Thornton) She never said pea-turkey to me about it.

**3.** Applied with qualification to other birds: A local name of the Bustard; now usually applied to the Australian Bustard, also called *Native*, *Plain*, or *Wild Turkey* (*Eupodotis* (*Otis*) *australis*); in Australia also, the *Brush-* or *Wattled Turkey* and the *Scrub-turkey*: see these words; in America, *Colorado* or *Water-turkey*, names for native species of Ibis; *Water-turkey*, the Darter or Snake-bird (*Plotus anhinga*); in South Africa, the Bald Ibis (*Gerontius calvus*).

**1847, 1852** Brush-turkey [see BRUSH *sb.*[1] 4]. **1848** Native turkey [see NATIVE *a.* 13 c]. *c* **1868** G. PRYME in *Autobiog. Recoll.* xxvi. (1870) 386, I have seen Bustards,..which the natives called *Wild Turkey*,..flying over the Gogmagog Hills. **1872** C. H. EDEN *Queensland* iv. 122 The plain turkey or bustard (*Otis Australasianus*),..the male weighing from eighteen to twenty-five pounds. **1872** Scrub-turkey [see SCRUB *sb.*[1] 6 c]. *a* **1889** RIPLEY & DANA *Amer. Cycl.* V. 692 This bird [*Plotus anhinga*] is a constant resident in Florida, and the lower parts of Louisiana, Alabama, and Georgia...In these localities it bears the various names of water crow, Grecian lady, water turkey, and cormorant.

†**4.** *Angling.* Short for *turkey-fly* (see 6). *Obs.*

**1799** G. SMITH *Laboratory* II. 301 The Turkey, or March-fly. Body, brown foal's hair [etc.].

**5.** *transf.* in lumbering: see quots. *U.S.*

**1893** *Scribner's Mag.* June 715/2 With his 'time' in his pocket and his 'turkey', a two-bushel bag in which he carries his belongings, strung over his shoulder, the shanty boy starts..for town. **1905** *Logging Terms* (U. S. Dept. Agric., Forestry, Bulletin lxi.), *Turkey*, a bag containing a lumberjack's outfit. To 'histe the turkey' is to take one's personal belongings and leave camp.

**6.** *attrib.* and *Comb.*, as *turkey-butcher*, *-chick* (also fig.), *-coop*, *-drumstick* (in quot. *attrib.*), *-feather*, *-gobbler*, *-hunt*, *-hunter*, *-pie*, *-poult*, *-shooter*, *-wing*; *turkey-like* adj.; **turkey-apple**, local name of *Cratægus induta*, a small tree of Arkansas, bearing small reddish berries (*Cent. Dict. Supp.* 1909); **turkey-back**, a large variety of the yellowshank, *Totanus melanoleucus*; **turkey-beard**, also **turkey's beard**, a North American herb, *Xerophyllum asphodeloides*, N.O. *Liliaceæ*, having a tuft of wiry root-leaves, and an erect stem with a raceme of white flowers; **turkey-berry**, (*a*) *Solanum mammosum* and *S. torvum* of the West Indies; (*b*) the fruit of a W. Indian tree, *Cordia Collococca* (*turkey-berry tree*); see also TURKEY[1] 3 c; **turkey-bird**, local name of the wryneck, and of the turnstone; **turkey-blossom**, W. Indian name of *Tribulus cistoides*; **turkey-buzzard**, an American carrion vulture, *Cathartes aura*, so called from its bare reddish head and neck and dark plumage; the John Crow of Jamaica; also *fig.*; in W. Africa, the Vulturine Pie, *Picathartes gymnocephalus*; **turkey-call**, the gobbling sound characteristic of the turkey-cock; also (*b*) an instrument for imitating this, used to decoy the wild turkey; **turkey-corn**, *Dicentra* (*Dielytra*) *canadensis* of eastern N. America, having yellow tubers like grains of maize; also called *squirrel-corn*; see also TURKEY[1] 3 c; **turkey-dog**, a dog trained to hunt the wild turkey; **turkey-egg**, the egg of the turkey; also (*pl.*) the common fritillary (*local*); **turkey-fat ore**, local name for a variety of smithsonite (carbonate of zinc) coloured yellow by greenockite (*Cent. Dict.* 1891); **turkey-feather fucus, laver**, peacock's-tail seaweed, *Padina pavonia*; **turkey-flower** = *turkey-blossom*; †**turkey-fly**, a kind of angler's fly: cf. sense 4; **turkey-foot** [from the shape of the spike], local name for North American grasses of the genus *Andropogon*; **turkey-gnat**, a small black fly of the genus *Simulium* which infests poultry in southern and western N. America; **turkey-grass**, goose-grass or cleavers (*Galium Aparine*); **turkey-louse**, a feather-eating parasite, as *Goniodes stylifer*, infesting turkeys (*Cent. Dict.*, and *Supp.*); **turkey-merchant** (*slang*): see quots.; cf. TURKEY[1] 3 a; **turkey-oak**, *Quercus Catesbæi*, of south-eastern N. America; also, the American 'Spanish' oak, *Q. falcata*; **turkey-pea** (*wild-turkey pea*) = *turkey-corn*; also applied to the hoary pea, *Tephrosia virginiana*; **turkey-pen** (*U. S.*), a pen for trapping wild turkeys; **turkey-shoot**, a shooting-match in which the mark is a live turkey, or its head only; †**turkey-tomb**, a turkey-pie (*humorous*); **turkey-trot**, a kind of ball-room dance recently introduced from U.S.; **turkey-vulture** = *turkey-buzzard*; **turkey-yelper**, a decoy call: = *turkey-call* (*b*). See also TURKEY-COCK, -HEN.

**1888** G. TRUMBULL *Names Birds* 168 At Salem, Mass., the larger birds of the species [*Totanus melanoleucus*] have long been distinguished from the others under the name of **Turkey-back*. **1884** MILLER *Plant-n.*, *Turkey's-beard, *Xerophyllum asphodeloides*. *Ibid.*, *Turkey-berry, *Solanum mammosum* and *S. torvum*. **1819** *Pantologia* s.v. *Cordia*,..*C. collococca*,..of Jamaica..the clammy-cherry, or *turky-berry tree. **1858** HOGG *Veg. Kingd.* 538 Turkey and other poultry feed on the fruit of *C*[*ordia*] *collococca*, called Turkey-berry Tree and..Clammy Cherry. **1885** SWAINSON *Provinc. Names Birds* 104 Wryneck (*Jynx torquilla*),.. *Turkey bird. Because it erects and ruffles the feathers of its neck when disturbed. **1894** SCOTT WILLCOX *Egg Collector's Handy Dict.*, *Turkey-bird*,..Turnstone, *Strepsilas interpres*. **1849** CRAIG, **Turkey-blossom*, the name given in Jamaica to the plant *Tribulus terrestris*. **1849** D. J. BROWNE *Amer. Poultry Yd.* (1858) 165 There are *turkey butchers of whom you may buy the half or a quarter of a bird. **1672** JOSSELYN *New Eng. Rarities* 12 The *Turkie Buzzard, a kind of Kite, but as big as a Turkie, brown of colour, and very good meat. **1839** DARWIN *Voy. Nat.* iii. 68 The turkey-buzzard (*Vultur aura*)..is found wherever the country is moderately damp, from Cape Horn to North America. **1897** MARY KINGSLEY *W. Africa* 23 One of the chief features of Free Town are the jack crows...*Picathartes gymnocephalus*. To the white people who live in daily contact with them they are turkey-buzzards; to the natives, Yubu. **1873** *Forest & Stream* 2 Oct. 123/1 A *turkey-call is easily imitated by using the hollow bone of the leg or wing of the same. **1555** in Dugdale *Orig. Jurid.* xlviii. (1666) 135 *Turky-Chicks 4. rated at iiij[s] a piece. oo. 16. oo. **1664** BUTLER *Hud.* II. III. 150 Putting Knavish tricks Upon Green-Geese, and Turkey-Chicks. **1833** MARRYAT *P. Simple* xxvii, The geese and *turkey-coops are divided off into apartments for four sows. **1884** MILLER *Plant-n.*, *Turkey-corn, *Corydalis formosa*. **1895** *Outing* (U. S.) XXVII. 231/1 This setter..was an excellent *turkey dog. **1860** O. W. HOLMES *Prof. Breakf.-t.* ii, The *turkey-drumstick style of organization. **1718** LADY M. W. MONTAGU *Let. to C'tess of Mar* 10 Mar., A fine coloured emerald, as big as a *turkey-egg. **1624** CAPT. SMITH *Virginia* II. 30 We haue seene some vse mantels made of *Turky feathers. **1767** ELLIS in *Phil. Trans.* LVII. 407 It is well known by the name of *Turky-feather Fucus,..*Fucus Pavonius*. **1866** *Treas. Bot.*, **Turkey-feather laver*, the common name of *Padina pavonia*. **1843** *Penny Cycl.* XXVII. 830/2 *T*[*ribulus*] *cistoides*..is abundant about Kingston in Jamaica, where it is called *turkey-flower...Fowls are said to be fond of this plant. **1676** COTTON *Angler* II. vii. 63 The first flie we take notice of..is call'd the *Turky-flie. **1899** D. SHARP in *Cambr. Nat. Hist.* VI. vii. 477 In North America the.. *Turkey-gnats attack a variety of mammals and birds. **1879** J. BURROUGHS *Locusts & W. Honey* 46 The *turkey-gobbler and the rooster. **1874** EDITH WADDY *Year Wild Fl.* 62 Goosegrass, *Turkey-grass, Cleavers,..names..familiar to all..for the Bedstraw. **1827** J. F. COOPER *Prairie* I. iii. 46 Dreaming of a *turkey hunt. **1895** *Outing* (U. S.) XXVII. 231/1 Nearly every negro man and boy on the plantation came up to have a look at the famous *turkey hunter. **1855** *Poultry Chron.* III. 67 Large *turkey-like bird, native of Mexico. *a* **1700** B. E. *Dict. Cant. Crew*, **Turky-Merchants*, drivers of Turkies. **1785** GROSE *Dict. Vulg. T.*, *Turkey merchant*, a poulterer. **1717** *Petiveriana* III. 206 *Turkey Oak. From a small Acorn it bears which the Wild Turkeys feed on. **1884** MILLER *Plant-n.*, *Turkey-pea, Wild, *Corydalis formosa*. **1602** *2nd Pt. Return fr. Parnass.* II. vi. 982, I inuited the hungry slaue..to the canuasing of a *Turkey Pye. **1694** *Turkey-poots [see TURKEY-COCK 3]. **1769** MRS. RAFFALD *Eng. Housekpr.* (1778) 373 Ducklings, Turkey Poults, Plovers. *a* **1809** ANNA SEWARD *Lett.* (1811) I. 113 A Turkey-poot casting about with a pitiful poked-out neck, for its lost companion. **1849** D. J. BROWNE *Amer. Poultry Yd.* (1855) 165 To eat turkey poults is a wasteful piece of luxury. **1869** T. W. HIGGINSON *Army Life* 11 Some steady old *turkey-shooter hit the mark. **1622** FLETCHER *Beggar's Bush* IV. iv, Fat capons..And *turkey-tombs, such honourable monuments. **1912** *Nation* 22 June 427/1 The Lord's prayer, followed by the '*Turkey trot'. **1913** G. GROSSMITH in *Daily Graphic* 12 May 9/1 Adventurous persons will see the Turkey trot or Tango as they are danced in a cabaret, but not as danced in a Paris ball-room. **1846** in *Congress Documents* XLI. 405 Amongst the birds [we have] the *turkey vulture. **1908** *Daily Chron.* 18 Aug. 5/4 They are about the size of large barn-door fowls, with red heads (hence their name 'turkey vultures'). **1888** *Century Mag.* XXXVI. 760/2 *Turkey-wing fans and fans of peacock feathers. **1895** *Outing* (U. S.) XXVII. 231/2 Matt drew from his pocket a '*turkey-yelper' and began to call.

**Tu·rkey ca·rpet.** [f. TURKEY[1] + CARPET.] A carpet manufactured in or imported from Turkey, or of a style in imitation of this; made in one piece of richly-coloured wools, without any imitative pattern, on a foundation of flax, hemp, or other material, and having a deep pile, cut so as to resemble velvet.

**1546** *Acts Privy Council* 9 Oct. (1890) I. 537, vij chestes of Spanisshe velvettes, one fardell of Turkey carpettes. **1552** in J. O. Payne *St. Paul's Cathedr. time Edw. VI* (1893) 24 One Turkeye carpett for the Communyon table. **1688** in Willis & Clark *Cambridge* (1886) II. 219 A long Turkey Carpet in the Meeting roome. **1751** JOHNSON *Rambler* No. 112 ⁋ 10 She spilt her coffee on a Turkey carpet. **1836** W. IRVING *Astoria* I. xviii. 305 The prairies..were gaily painted with innumerable flowers, exhibiting the motley confusion of colours of a Turkey carpet. **1894** FENN *In Alpine Valley* I. 3 The thick Turkey carpet.

Hence **Turkey-ca·rpeted** *a.*, furnished with a Turkey carpet; **Turkey carpeting**, the material of Turkey carpets.

**1843** *Penny Cycl.* XXVII. 181/1 Fustians are..a kind of cotton velvet, as Turkey carpeting is a woollen velvet. **1849** DICKENS *Dav. Copp.* xx, A snug private apartment, red-curtained and Turkey-carpeted.

**Turkey-cock** (tɜ·ɹki kɒ:k). Also 6–7 Turkicock(e. [f. TURKEY[1] + COCK *sb.*[1] In the 16th c. synonymous with *Guinea-cock* or *Guinea-fowl*, an African bird known to the ancients (the μελεαγρίς of Aristotle, *meleagris* of Varro and Pliny), the American bird being at first identified with or treated as a species of this. The African bird is believed to have been so called as originally imported through the Turkish dominions; it was called *Guinea-fowl* when brought by the Portuguese from Guinea in West Africa. After the two birds were distinguished and the names differentiated, *turkey* was erroneously retained for the American bird, instead of the African. From the same imperfect knowledge and confusion *Meleagris*, the ancient name of the African fowl, was unfortunately adopted by Linnæus as the generic name of the American bird.]

†**1.** Of doubtful meaning (? = sense 2 or 3): in quot. 1555 perh. the Curassow. *Obs.*

**1541** *Constitutio T. Cranmeri* in Wilkins *Concilia* (1737) III. 862 It was also provided, that of the greater fyshes or fowles there should be but one in a dishe, as crane, swan, turkeycocke, hadocke, pyke, tench. **1555** EDEN *Decades* 79 The inhabitantes of Paria..gaue them also a greate multitude of theyr peacockes [L. *pavones*]. [*margin*] Paria. Peacockes whiche wee caule Turkye cockes. **1561** in Rogers *Agric. & Prices* III. 195/4 Oxford...Turkey Cocks 2 @ 5/-. **1579** E. HAKE *Newes Powles Churchyarde* iv. D ij b, He must prouide..Both Peacock, Crane, and Turkicock. **1599** HAKLUYT *Voy.* II. 165 In time of Memory things haue bene brought in that were not here before, as..the Turky cocks and hennes about fifty yeres past.

†**2.** The male of the Guinea-fowl, *Numida meleagris*: cf. TURKEY[2] 1, TURKEY-HEN 1. *Obs.*

**1577** B. GOOGE tr. *Heresbach's Husb.* (1586) 12 b, Here I keepe Geese, Duckes, Peacocks, Turkicockes, and other poultry. **1601** HOLLAND *Pliny* XI. xxxvii. I. 331 The Ginnie or Turkie Cockes and Hens.

**3.** The male of the turkey.

**1578** T. N[ICHOLAS] tr. *Conq. W. India* 38 They ..brought bread and fruite and eyght Turkie Cockes. **1588** PARKE tr. *Mendoza's Hist. China* vi. 322 You shall buy there [in Mexico]..a whole sheepe for foure rials, and two hennes, such as you haue in Spaine for one riall, and of Ginny hennes, otherwise called Turkey cockes, and in Spanish *Pauos*, you shall haue an hundred thousande..for a riall and a halfe of plate a peece. **1592** *Shuttleworths' Acc.* (Chetham) 73 A turkye coke and a hene iij[s]. **1599** SHAKS. *Hen. V*, v. i. 15 *Gower.* Why heere hee comes, swelling like a Turky-cock. *Flu.* 'Tis no matter for his swellings, nor his Turky-cocks, God plesse you aunchient Pistoll. **1616** R. C. *Times' Whistle* iii. 1095 And swell in big lookes like some turkie cocke. **1668** CHARLETON *Onomast.* 72 *Gallopavo*..the Turky-Cock. **1694** MOTTEUX *Rabelais* IV. lix. (1737) 243 Hortolans. Turkey-Cocks, Hen-Turkeys, and Turkey-poots. **1727** SOMERVILLE *Bowling-green* 58 No turkey-cock appears with better grace, His garments black, vermilion paints his face. **1727** SWIFT *Country Post* Wks. 1755 III. I. 176 An old turkey-cock attacked a maid in a red petticoat, and she retired with great precipitation. **1760** EDWARDS in *Phil. Trans.* LI. 836 Whether this bird be produced from a turkey-hen and a cock-pheasant, or from a turkey-cock and hen-pheasant, no one knows. **1833** MARRYAT *P. Simple* xxxiv, The idea..mantled the blood in my cheeks till I was as red as a turkey-cock. **1855** *Poultry Chron.* III. 149/2 Turkey Cock and one Hen.

**b.** *fig.* and *allusively*. Also *attrib.*

**1601** SHAKS. *Twel. N.* II. v. 36 Contemplation makes a rare Turkey Cocke of him, how he iets vnder his aduanc'd plumes. **1650** B. *Discolliminium* 2 Which makes him write with such a Turky-Cocks quill, too..censoriously. *a* **1849** J. C. MANGAN *Poems* (1859) 428 Thy snub nose..And thy turkey-cock air.

**Turkey-hen.** [Cf. TURKEY-COCK.]

†**1.** The guinea-hen. *Obs.*

**1552** ELYOT, *Meleagrides*, byrdes, whiche we doo call hennes of Genny, or Turkie hennes. **1578** LYTE *Dodoens* II. lii. 214 Called..*Flos Meleagris*..from a kinde of birde..whose feathers be speckled..not with Violet speckes, but with white and blacke spots, lyke to the feathers of the Turkie or Ginny hen, which is called *Meleagris auis*: some do also cal this flower *Fritillaria*. 1601 HOLLAND *Pliny* I. 296 The Ginnie or Turkey hens in a part of Africke called Numidia, be in great request.

2. The female of the turkey.

1555 EDEN *Decades* 158 They [of Yucatan] brought..eyght of their hennes beynge as bygge as peacockes, of brownyshe colour, and not inferiour to peacockes in pleasaunte tast. [*margin*] Turky hens. 1580 HOLLYBAND *Treas. Fr. Tong*, *Poule d'Inde*, a Turkie henne. 1592 *Shuttleworths' Acc.* (Chetham) 72 Towe turkes and onne turkie henne vijs. 1760 [see TURKEY-COCK 3]. 1844 STEPHENS *Bk. Farm* II. 710 When a turkey-hen is seen disposed to lay, a nest should be made for her in the hatching-house.

**Turkey red.** [TURKEY [1].] A brilliant and permanent red colour produced on cotton goods, essentially a madder red in combination with oil or fat, with an aluminous mordant. Also called *Adrianople* or *Levant red*. Also *attrib.*

1789 *Trans. Soc. Arts* I. 19 Dying Turkey red. 1799 *Med. Jrnl.* I. 168 A whole month's labour is scarcely sufficient to terminate the different operations thought necessary to obtain the fine Turkey red, called Adrianople. 1799 *Monthly Rev.* XXX. 561 The art of dyeing cotton scarlet, or turkey-red, was imported into France by Greek families. 1801 *Encycl. Brit.* Suppl. II. 393/2 Turkey-Red, Levant-Red and Adrianople-Red, the names indifferently given to that beautiful red dye which distinguishes the cotton manufactured in the Ottoman empire. 1815 J. SMITH *Panorama Sc. & Art* II. 545 P. J. Papillon established a dyehouse at Glasgow, for giving to cotton-yarn that beautiful colour known by the name of Turkey or Adrianople red. 1838 T. THOMSON *Chem. Org. Bodies* 396 The first Turkey-red work in Great Britain was established about 50 years ago in Glasgow by M. Papillon. 1844 G. DODD *Textile Manuf.* ii. 74 About a century ago some Greek dyers were invited to settle in France, where they introduced the art of Turkey-red dyeing. 1862 *Catal. Internat. Exhib., Brit.* II. No. 4329 Turkey red goods. *Ibid.* No. 4340 Turkey red plain and printed cottons. 1877 O'NEILL in *Encycl. Brit.* VII. 576/1. 1899 *Westm. Gaz.* 10 Aug. 2/1 Before the days of Turkey-red-dyeing and calico-printing. *Ibid.* 2 Dec. 9/1 It is a turkey-red dyeing firm.

b. Cotton cloth of this colour.

1880 J. DUNBAR *Pract. Papermaker* 72 For pink blottings furnish two thirds of white cottons and one third of turkey reds. 1882 CAULFEILD & SAWARD *Dict. Needlework* 503 *Turkey Red*, a cotton cambric, of a bright scarlet colour of indelible dye,..originally imported from Turkey.

†**Turkeys, Turkese**, *a. Obs.* Also 5–6 **Turkes**, 6 **Turcas, Turkys.** [a. OF. *turqueis, -queze*, mod.F. *turquois* Turkish (= It. *turchese*, Pr., OSp. *turques*): see -ESE.] = TURKISH.

13.. *Coer de L.* 4972 Thre thousand Turkes com at the last, With bowe Turkeys, and arweblaste. 14.. *Sir Beues* (M.) 767 With Bowes turkes and arablaste. *Ibid.* 3706 They shott dartys with bows turkeys. 1513 DOUGLAS *Æneis* XI. xiii. 11 Apon hir schulder the gyltin bow Turcas. 1517 TORKINGTON *Pilgr.* (1884) 23 Jherusalem—And Rama thane beyng turkys. 1530 PALSGR. 284/1 Turkes bowe, *arc turquoys*.

**Turkeys**, obs. form of TURQUOISE.

**Turkey stone.** [TURKEY [1].]

1. = TURQUOISE.

1607 TOPSELL *Four-f. Beasts* (1658) 5 Mammonets are lesse than an Ape:..his stones greenish blew, like a Turkey stone. 1611 COTGR., *Couleur Turquine*,..the colour of the Turkie stone. 1667–8 PEPYS *Diary* 18 Feb., She shows me her ring of a Turky-stone, set with little sparks of dyamonds. *a* 1668 LASSELS *Voy. Italy* (1698) II. 239 They shewed us a cup or dish..all of one Turky-stone entire. 1710 STEELE *Tatler* No. 245 ⁋ 2 Another [ring] of Turkey Stone. 1820 LADY GRANVILLE *Lett.* (1894) I. 188 A beautiful ring, a turkey stone set in gold. 1877 W. JONES *Finger-ring* 158 The turquoise, turkise, or turkey-stone having, from remote periods, been supposed to possess talismanic properties.

2. A hard, fine-grained, siliceous rock imported from the Levant for whetstones; novaculite; a whetstone made of this. Also *attrib.*

1816 CLEAVELAND *Min.* 364 The Novaculite is employed in the arts under the names of hone, oil-stone, Turkey stone, and whetstone. 1840 *Civil Eng. & Arch. Jrnl.* III. 421/1 A scraping tool..carefully sharpened on a Turkey stone. 1867 J. HOGG *Microsc.* I. iii. 210 Polish..on a hone of Turkey-stone kept wet with water. 1875 SIR T. SEATON *Fret Cutting* 3 Oil-stones are sold by weight, Turkey-stone being the dearest, and also by far the best. *Ibid.* 117 A Turkey-stone slip will polish them.

**Turkey wheat.** [TURKEY [1].] The cereal Maize, called also †*Guinea corn* and *Indian corn.*

1598 FLORIO, *Brena*, a kind of ginnie or turkie wheate. 1611 COTGR., *Mays*, Turkie corne, Turkie wheat. 1674 JOSSELYN *Voy. New Eng.* 73 Maze, otherwise called Turkie-wheat, or rather Indian-wheat, because it came first from thence. 1704 tr. *Lemery's Treat. Foods* 71 (D.) There grows in several parts of Africa, Asia, and America, a kind of corn called Mays, and such as we commonly name Turkey wheat. 1777 ROBERTSON *Hist. Amer.* (1796) II. IV. 102 Maize, well-known in Europe by the name of Turkey or Indian Wheat. 1883 PARKMAN *Discov. Gt. West* ii. 13 The ordinary food is Indian corn, or Turkey wheat as they call it in France.

**Tu·rkey work.** [TURKEY [1].] Turkish tapestry work, or an imitation of this. Also *attrib.* Hence **Turkey-worked** *a.*

1537 *Wills & Inv. N. C.* (Surtees) 101 The carpet of turkey warke. 1608 [TOFTE] *Ariosto's Sat.* III. (1611) 30, I..vnder rugs, as much safe quiet hold, As vnder Turky workes, Arras or gold. 1687 A. LOVELL tr. *Thevenot's Trav.* I. 143 Fine ones are made at Caire, and are called Turkie-work Carpets. 1697 VANBRUGH *Relapse* III. iii, Set all the Turkey-work chairs in their places. 1714 *Fr. Bk. of Rates* 83 Turkey-work English, for Chairs. 1748 RICHARDSON *Clarissa* VI. 157 Four old turkey-worked chairs, bursten-bottomed, the stuffing staring out. 1751 JOHNSON *Rambler* No. 84 ⁋ 8 A large screen, which I had undertaken to adorn with turkey-work against winter, made very slow advances.

**Turki** (tʊ·rki), *a.* (*sb.*) Also 8 **toorkay**, 8–9 **toorkee, toorky.** [a. Pers. تركى *turkī*, deriv. of ترك Turk, applied to language and race: cf. *Shirāzī, Panjābī, Hindūstānī*, etc.] Turkish; belonging to the typical Turkic languages, *East* and *West Turki*, and to the peoples speaking them. **b.** *sb.* A member of the Turkish race; also, a Turkish horse.

1782 *India Gaz.* 2 Mar. (Y.), To be disposed of..a Buggy, ..a pair of uncommonly beautiful spotted Toorkays. 1800 *Misc. Tr.* in *Asiat. Ann. Reg.* 189/1 A Toorky horse which I generally rode. 1841 ELPHINSTONE *Hist. Ind.* II. i, The Tūrki slaves, who rose to sovereignty throughout Asia, and ..furnished a succession of rulers to India. 1888 *Encycl. Brit.* XXIV. 1/2 Corrupt Turki dialects spoken by Tatarized Finn populations from the Altai to the Urals. 1907 *Blackw. Mag.* May 661/2 The Turki can holloa. *Ibid.* June 807/1 He had a Turki interpreter.

**Turkic** (tʊ̄·ɹkik), *a.* [f. TURK [1] + -IC.] Name of one of the branches of the Ural-Altaic or Turanian family of languages, which comprises the Samoyedic, Finnic, Ugric, Turkic, Mongolic, and Tungusic; the Turkic branch comprises Eastern Turki or Uigur (including Jagatai and Turconian), West Turki or Seljúk and Osmanli, Kazan Tartar, Kirghiz, Nogai, Yakut, etc., the languages of the Turks (in the wide sense); also applied to the peoples using these: cf. TURKISH, TARTAR *sb.*[2], and TURCIC.

1859 DWIGHT *Mod. Philol.* 124 The Turkic [languages]. 1863 C. L. BRACE *Races Old World* xi. 86 Another Turanian tribe are the Khazars, probably Finnic, though with Turkic mixture. They appear in Europe between the seventh and tenth century,..between the Caspian and the Dnieper. They are followed by the Pechenegs, a Turkic tribe, who occupy Bessarabia, Cherson, and part of Taurida, in the tenth and eleventh centuries. 1875–6 RAWLINSON *Orig. Nat.* I. i. (1878) 4 The Muscovite and Turkic hordes are becoming scarce distinguishable from other Europeans. 1878 *N. Amer. Rev.* CXXVI. 557 The Magyars received the knowledge of southern products and of agriculture from their Turkic neighbors. 1892 S. LAING *Hum. Orig.* iii. (1894) 86 Various Turkic and Mongolian dialects.

**Turkies**, obs. pl. of TURKEY; obs. f. TURQUOISE.

**Turkify** (tʊ̄·ɹkifəi), *v.* In 7 **Turkefy.** [f. TURK [1] + -I)FY.] *trans.* To render Turkish. Hence **Turkifica·tion**, a rendering Turkish.

1682 MRS. BEHN *False Count* Wks. 1724 III. 150, I hope the Jade will be Turkefied with a vengeance. 1813 T. MOORE *Interc. Lett.* ii. (ed. 2) 9 With sashes, turbans, and pabouches..And all things fitting and expedient To turkify our gracious R–g–nt. 1911 *Contemp. Rev.* July 11 They believed that every institution ought to be Turkified. *Ibid.* 12 The desire for Turkification.

†**Turkin,** *a.* and *sb. Obs.* In 5 **-kyn**, 7 **-chine.** [a. F. *turquin, turquine* (1471 in Hatz.-Darm.), = It. *turchino, -ina*, 'blue, azure, watchet' (Florio), dim. of *turco* Turk. See TURQUIN.] **a.** *adj.* Light blue. **b.** *sb.* A kind of light blue cloth.

1483 *Act 1 Rich. III* c. 8 § 18 Provided alwey that this Acte..extende not..to the makynge..of eny clothe called Vervise, otherwise called Plounkettes Turkyns or Celestrines, with broade Lists. [Cf. 1611 COTGR., *Couleur Turquine*, a right blue, or Venice blue; the colour of the Turkie stone. *Ibid.* s. v. *Turc, Couleur Turque*, Azure, Sky-colour, the colour of a Turkeis-stone (betweene a blue, and an Azure).] *c* 1618 MORYSON *Itin.* (1903) 441 The Dukes [= doge's] officers,..50 in nomber, attyred in Turchine gownes.

**Turkin**, var. TURKEN *v. Obs.*

**Turkis, turkes, -esse** (tʊ̄·ɹkės). Chiefly, now only, *Sc. dial.* Forms: 4 **thourkeys**, *Sc.* 5–6 **turkas**, 6 **turkass, turkes, turcase, turcas**, 7 **turkesse**, 9 **turkis.** [ad. OF. *turcaise, -quaise, -queise, turquoise* (14–15th c.), *terquoise, truquaise, trucoise*, mod.F. *tricoises*, fem. pl. of *turcois, -queis, -quois* Turkish; prop. *tenailles turquoises*, Turkish nippers.] A pair of smith's pincers; pincers or nippers generally; forceps.

1390–1 *Earl Derby's Exped.* (Camden) 35 Pro j pare de thourkeys, xij d. *c* 1470 HENRY *Wallace* VI. 411 He gert a smyth, with his turkas rycht thar, Pow out his eyne. 1503–4 *Acc. Ld. High Treas. Scot.* II. 419 Ane turcas to tak out teith. 1513 DOUGLAS *Æneis* VIII. vii. 185 Wyth the grippand turkas [*v. r.* turkes] oft also The glowand lump thai turnit to and fro. 1591 *News fr. Scot.* (1820) 33 His nailes upon all his fingers were riven and pulled off with an instrument called in Scottich a Turkas, which in England we call a pair of pincers. 1629 Z. BOYD *Last Battle* 534 Like a tooth in the jaw, the deeper roote it hath, the more paine it causeth, when it is drawing out with the Turkesse. 1871 W. ALEXANDER *Johnny Gibb* xxvii. (1873) 162 There's yersel', 't kens nae mair aboot the prencipels o' the struggle nor that turkis i' the smith's sheein [= shoeing] box.

**Turkis(e**, obs. or arch. ff. TURQUOISE.

**Turkise**, var. TURKESS(E *v. Obs.*

**Turkish** (tʊ̄·ɹkiʃ), *a.* (*sb.*) [f. TURK [1] + -ISH [1]; the usual adj. from *Turk, Turkey*, taking the place of the earlier TURKEYS from French.]

1. Of, pertaining or belonging to the Turks or to Turkey; now commonly = Ottoman.

1545 ASCHAM *Toxoph.* I. (Arb.) 81 Surely no Turkyshe power can ouerthrowe vs, if Turkysshe lyfe do not cast vs downe before. 1546 P. ASHTON tr. *Jovius* (*title*) A shorte treatise vpon the Turkes Chronicles;..The begynnyng of the turkysshe empyre. The lyues of al the Turkyshe Emperours. 1552–3 *Inv. Ch. Goods, Staffs.* in *Ann. Lichfield* (1863) IV. 44 Itm: a cope of turkishe saten. *a* 1568 ASCHAM *Scholem.* I. (Arb.) 61 This opinion is not French, but plaine Turckishe. 1585 T. WASHINGTON tr. *Nicholay's Voy.* I. xvii. 19 b, To weare armes against the Turkish nation. *Ibid.* III. ii. 71 To learne the turkish language. 1604 SHAKS. *Oth.* I. iii. 8 Yet do they all confirme A Turkish Fleete, and bearing vp to Cyprus. *a* 1658 J. DURHAM *Exp. Rev.* IX. ii. (1680) 385 The first Turkish Government being by four Souldans. 1732 BERKELEY *Alciphr.* V. § 18 Free-thinkers, who at present applaud Turkish maxims and manners. 1842 PRICHARD *Nat. Hist. Man* 209 The Turkish tribes have been often erroneously termed Tartars. 1870 DICKENS *E. Drood* iii, 'I want to go to the Lumps-of-Delight shop.' 'To the ——?' 'A Turkish sweetmeat, sir.' 1896 A. MACKAY *Hist. Fife & Kinross* ii. 32 His Arab charger with his Turkish trappings was led to the high altar.

b. Like or resembling the Turks or their character; cruel, savage, barbarous.

1600 W. WATSON *Decacordon* (1602) 242 Turkish, Iesuitish, Puritanian, and barbarous designements. *Ibid.* 246 There is no mischiefe or villany, which they [Jesuits] will not attempt, to further their most sauage and Turkish designements. 1603 DEKKER *Wonderfull Yeare* F iij b, They seeme by their turkish and barberous actions to belieue that there is no felicitie after this life. 1648 LD. ORMOND in Milton *Observ. Art. Peace* Wks. (1847) 259/1 To constitute an elective kingdom..then..to establish a perfect Turkish tyranny. *a* 1700 B. E. *Dict. Cant. Crew*, *Turkish Treatment*, very sharp or ill dealing in Business.

2. In special collocations. **a. Turkish bath**: a hot bath introduced from the East and now extensively used, inducing copious perspiration, followed by soaping, washing, shampooing, massage, and cooling. Also *attrib.*

1644 DIGBY *Nat. Bodies* xxvii. § 2. 243 The Turkish bathes ..that seemeth chilly cold att his returne; which appeared melting hoat att his going in. 1867 F. W. NEWMAN in *Mem.* ix. (1909) 200 Turkish-bath keepers find it [smallpox] a most tractable disease. 1876 BRISTOWE *The. & Pract. Med.* (1878) 745 For diaphoretic purposes we must not forget the value of the hot bath, the vapour bath, and the Turkish bath. 1908 *Daily Chron.* 5 Oct. 5/7 The Turkish bath conditions in which London has been living for the past few days were not so pronounced, and a drier heat seems to have taken the place of the vapour.

b. *Turkish bean, cock, hen, horse, red, stone, wheat*: see TURKEY [1] 3 a, 3 c, TURKEY-COCK, etc.; **Turkish delight**, a favourite sweetmeat of tough consistence, of Turkish origin; **Turkish music, rug**: see quots.; **Turkish stitch**, a kind of stitch used in Turkish and other Oriental embroideries. **Turkish towel**: see quot. 1882.

1894 E. EGGLESTON in *Century Mag.* Apr. 849 The beans ..found here were called '*Turkish-beans' by the first Dutch and Swedish writers on America. 1849 D. J. BROWNE *Amer. Poultry Yd.* (1855) 51 Aldrovandi [1599–1603] in describing a *Turkish cock and two *Turkish hens, says: 'The cock, whose likeness we now give, is called the Turkish cock'. 1870 *Turkish delight [cf. quot. from Dickens in 1]. 1901 F. HUME *Golden Wang-ho* x, The thrusting forward of the Turkish delight box. *a* 1648 LD. HERBERT *Henry VIII* (1683) 184 He got hastily upon a *Turkish and swift Horse. 1889 GROVE *Dict. Mus.* IV. 191 **Turkish Music*.., the accepted name for the noisy percussion instruments—big-drum, cymbals, triangle—in the orchestra. 1900 *Jrnl. Soc. Dyers* XVI. 4 Dyeing in Adrianople or *Turkish Red. 1901 ROSA B. HOLT *Rugs* ii. (Chicago) 52 *Turkish Rugs includes all those rugs that are manufactured within the Turkish Empire, whether [by] Kurds or Circassians or Christians;..Turkish rugs are not so finely woven as Persian. *c* 1890 TH. DE DILLMONT *Encycl. Needlewk.* 94 Triangular two-sided *Turkish stitch worked diagonally. *Ibid.* 96 Triangular two-sided Turkish stitch worked horizontally. *Ibid.* 115 The triangular Turkish stitch..is particularly effective when combined with other kinds of embroidery. 1577 tr. *Bullinger's Decades* (1592) 737 His bodie..was like the *Turkish or Iasper stone. 1862 *Catal. Internat. Exhib., Brit.* II. No. 3648 Royal *Turkish towels. 1882 CAULFEILD & SAWARD *Dict. Needlework* 504 *Turkish Towels*..are cotton cloths, having a long nap, cut or uncut. 1670 COVEL in *Early Voy. Levant* (Hakl. Soc.) 120 They make some [bread] of pure good wheat,..some of what we call *Turkish wheat. 1894 *Century Mag.* Apr. 849 Henry Hudson..called the maize 'Turkish wheat'.

**B.** *sb.* **1.** The Turkish or Turk's language.

1718 LADY M. W. MONTAGU *Let. to Lady Rich* 16 Mar., In Pera they speak Turkish, Greek, Hebrew, Armenian, Arabic, Persian, Russian [etc.]. 1753 [see RUSS *sb.* 2]. 1888 *Encycl. Brit.* XXIII. 662/1 The relative pronoun has been borrowed from the Persian in many dialects; it is absent in the original Turkish.

2. *ellipt.* for *Turkish fashion, people*, etc.; also *colloq.* for *Turkish delight, Turkish tobacco*, etc.

*a* 1674 MILTON *Hist. Mosc.* i. Wks. 1738 II. 132 The rest.. ride with a short Stirrup after the Turkish. 1898 *Century Mag.* Feb. 558/1 The best 'Turkish' [*sc.* tobacco] the town provided. 1901 F. HUME *Golden Wang-ho* x, Feeling for another lump of 'Turkish' [*sc.* delight].

Hence †**Tu·rkisher**, a Turk; cf. *Britisher*. *Obs.*

1607 R. C[AREW] tr. *Estienne's World of Wonders* 13, I soone perceiued that it was my onely course to preuent these turkishers, by being mine owne interpreter.

†**Tu·rkish**, *v. Obs.* [app. f. TURKISH *a.*: cf. TURKESS(E *v.*] *trans.* To transform, esp. for the worse; to pervert; to turn into something different.

1560 DAUS tr. *Sleidane's Comm.* 142 b, He [Cardinal Poole] sayeth how the Turkyshed seede is sowen abroade in England and in Germany, signifiyng the doctrine that is contrary to the byshop of Rome. 1596 HARINGTON *Ulysses upon Ajax* (1814) 62 Away with this serious talk, let us turkish this text into a merrier colour. 1607 R. C[AREW] tr.

*Estienne's World of Wonders* 19 Turkishing the storie, or (to speak more properly) turning it into a meere fable.

**Tu·rkishly,** *adv.* [f. TURKISH *a.* + -LY [2].] In a Turkish way or manner.

**1611** SPEED *Hist. Gt. Brit.* IX. ix. § 29 Seeing the Great Emperour Fredericke..so Turkishly in his absence deposed from his owne Empire by the Pope. **1662** J. SPARROW tr. *Behme's Rem. Wks., 2nd Apol. Tylcken* 56 They live Turkishly, and more then Turkishly or Heathenishly. **1828** SOUTHEY in *Q. Rev.* Oct. 556 The Pope himself, if he were Turkishly inclined.

So **Tu·rkishness,** Turkish quality or conduct; addiction to what is Turkish.

**1545** ASCHAM *Toxoph.* I. (Arb.) 81 A more Turkishnesse and more beastlye blynde barbarousnesse. **1701** J. SAGE *Wks.* (1847) II. 52 The Turkishness of the Government whether in Church or State I do confess. **1814** SOUTHEY *Lett.* (1856) II. 382 The Turkishness of the writer is sometimes very comical. **1897** *Westm. Gaz.* 24 Aug. 1/3 The Turkishness of the Turk might make him restive under England's controlling advice.

**Turkism** (tɜ̄·ɹkiz'm). [f. TURK [1] + -ISM.]

†**1.** Mohammedanism; = TURCISM. *Obs.*

**1595** J. KING *Queen's Day Serm.* in *On Jonas* (1618) 704 So much of Christendom at this day buried in the very bowels of Turkisme & infidelity. **1645** E. CALAMY *Indictment agst. Eng.* 33 An illimited toleration of all Religions, even of Turkisme, Iudaisme, &c. **1660** F. BROOKE tr. *Le Blanc's Trav.* 8 Resolved to leave Turkisme, and become a Christian again.

**2.** = TURCISM b.

**1877** GLADSTONE in *Echo* 28 Sept., The professors of Turkism..declared that the people of England had changed their minds.

**Turkize** (tɜ̄·ɹkəiz), *v.* Also 6–9 **turkise,** 7 **turkeise;** 9 **turcise** (tɜ̄·ɹsəiz). [f. TURK [1] + -IZE.]

**1.** *trans.* To render Turkish.

**1599** in *Archpriest Controv.* (Camden) I. 220 All three words of one significacion, viz. turkized atheism. **1625** PURCHAS *Pilgrims* II. vi. Pref. 1464 A halfe-turkised Christian with divers Turkes following immediatly after. **1911** *Q. Rev.* Apr. 471 The 'Turcising' of the Ottoman Empire which is one of the objects of the Young Turk party.

**2.** *intr.* To play the Turk; † to tyrannize *over*.

**1599** in *Archpriest Controv.* (Camden) I. 97 Blackwell, y[t] will turkise over vs to vrge our consent by violent force. **1600** W. WATSON *Decacordon* (1602) 169 The Iesuits..would Turkize ouer vs in that shamelesse manner. **1612** T. JAMES *Jesuits' Downf.* 2 They vse to turkize over men in a shameful maner, nay, it were better to liue vnder the Turke. **1862** CUNNINGHAM *Hist. Theol.* (1864) I. xx. 629 A book..called 'Calvinus Turcisans' or Calvin Turkising,—that is teaching the doctrine of the Turks or Mohometans.

**Turkize,** var. TURKESS(E *v. Obs.*

**Tu·rkman.** [Altered from TURCOMAN.]

†**1.** = TURK [1]. *Obs. rare.*

**1481** CAXTON *Godeffroy* cl. 222 They sente to the admyrals of the turkes...The turkmans acorded wel to this werk.

**2.** = TURCOMAN, q. v.

**Turko-**: see TURCO-. **Turkois,** obs. f. TURQUOISE. **Turkoman**: see TURCOMAN.

**Turk's cap.** [TURK [1].]

†**1.** Early name for the tulip. *Obs.*

**1597** GERARDE *Herbal* I. lxxvii. § 14. 120 It is called..after the Turkish name Tulipa, or it may be called Dalmatian Cap, or the Turkes Cap. **1629** PARKINSON *Paradisus* Table 12 The Turkes Cap, that is, the *Tulipa*.

**2.** The Martagon lily; also *Turk's-cap lily.* **American Turk's-cap lily,** *Lilium superbum.*

**1672** JOSSELYN *New Eng. Rarities* 54 Turning up their Leaves like the Martigon, or Turks Cap. **1778** MILNE *Bot. Dict.* (ed. 2) 130 Martagon lilly..having its petals rowled or turned backwards in form of a Turkish turbant; from which ..the flower is generally known by the name of Turk's-cap. **1791** *Gentl. Mag.* July 619/1 The Martagon or Turk's-cap Lily. **1884** MILLER *Plant-n., Lilium superbum,* Great American Turk's-Cap Lily, Swamp Lily. **1899** WARNER *Capt. Locusts* 5 A couple of blossoms of the crimson Turk's-cap lily. **1906** EARL SELBORNE *Pers. & Pol. Mem.* II. xxxii. 268 A cream-coloured Turk's-cap and several kinds of white lilies.

**3.** The Melon-thistle, *Cactus Melocactus*: see quot. 1866; also *Turk's-cap Cactus, Turk's head.*

**1829** LOUDON *Encycl. Plants* (1836) 410 C[actus] melocactus, the great melon thistle or Turk's cap. **1866** *Treas. Bot.* 733/2 *Melocactus communis,* the Turk's-cap Cactus, so called from the flowering portion on the top of the plant being of a cylindrical form and red colour like a fez cap.

**4.** A local name for the common aconite (*Aconitum Napellus*).

**1854** MISS BAKER *Northampt. Gloss.,* Turk's cap. *Ibid.* 129 *Pope's-Ode,* the garden Monk's-hood or Turk's-cap. *Aconitum napellus.*

**5.** A variety of the great pumpkin, *Cucurbita maxima.* **1891** in *Cent. Dict.*

**6.** *Cookery.* A form of mould. Cf. TURBAN *sb.* 1 g.

**1859** F. S. COOPER *Ironmongers' Catal.* 178 Jelly and Cake Moulds...Turk's Cap.

**Turk's head.** [TURK [1].]

†**1.** The Melon-thistle; = TURK'S CAP 3; also called *Englishman's head, pope's head. Obs.*

**1725** SLOANE *Jamaica* II. 159 Turks head. This has a great many..roots,..which send up a very strange plant, or masse. **1760** J. LEE *Introd. Bot.* App. 330 Turk's Head, *Cactus.*

**2.** *Naut.* An ornamental knot resembling a turban.

**1833** MARRYAT *P. Simple* vi, Whether something should not be fitted with a *mouse* or only a *Turk's head.* **c 1860** H. STUART *Seaman's Catech.* 5 The train tackles are fitted with a Turk's head on the standing part. **1909** *Blackw. Mag.* Apr. 536/2 He could work a Turk's head, cover a manrope, or point a lashing for the cabin table.

**3.** A round long-handled broom or brush; also called *pope's head.*

**1859** F. S. COOPER *Ironmongers' Catal.* 34 Turks' Heads. **1889** HUXLEY in *19th Cent.* XX. 102 Phyllis, gracefully wielding her long-handled 'Turk's head'.

**4.** (See quot.) ? *Obs.*

**1853** URE *Dict. Arts* I. 345 This colour is generally known by the name of *solitaire bistre,* and sometimes turks-head.

**5.** A round pan for baking cake, having a conical core in the centre. **1891** in *Cent. Dict.*

**6.** *attrib.* and *Comb.,* as *Turk's-head besom, broom, brush* (= 3); **Turk's-head grass,** *Lagurus ovatus,* having a rounded inflorescence; hare's-tail grass.

**1851** *Regul. R. Engineers* xix. 95 The bore must be well brushed out..with a Turks-head brush. **1853** LYTTON *My Novel* x. xx, Dick was all for sweeping away other cobwebs, ..he saw a great Turk's-head besom poked up at his own. **1882** *Garden* 14 Jan. 28/3 *Lagurus ovatus* (the Turk's-head Grass) is one of the most distinct kinds, as well as one of the best for keeping purposes. **1910** *Chron. Lond. Mission. Soc.* Mar. 44/1 What looks more like a turks-head broom than anything else.

**Turky, Turkyn**: see TURKEY, TURKIN.

**Turle,** obs. form of TIRL *sb.*[1] and *v.*[3]

†**Turlehyde,** var. THURLHEAD (= THIRLEPOLL).

**1766** W. HARRIS *Hist. Dublin* xi. 265 About the 24[th] of June [1331] a prodigious number of large sea fish, called Turlehydes, were brought into the bay of Dublin, and cast on Shore at the Mouth of the river Dodder.

†**Turlery, Turlery ginke**: see TERLERIE.

**1593** G. HARVEY *Pierce's Super.* 158 Where [can be found] such a Turlery-ginkes of conceit, or such a gibbihorse of pastime as Straunge Newes?

**Turlough** (tɜ·ɹlou̯χ). [ad. Ir., Gael. *turloch* a brook, ground covered with water in winter and dry in summer, f. *tur* whole, absolute, entire + *loch* lake, pool.] (See quots.)

**1685** *Phil. Trans.* XV. 958 As to those places we call Turloughs, *quasi Terreni lacus,* or land-lakes; they answer the name very well, being lakes one part of the year of considerable depth; and very smooth fields the rest. **1861** *Zoologist* XIX. 7617 Serving .. as water-courses for the 'buried' rivers which give rise to the sink-holes and turloughs for which the district of the Burren is famous. **1878** KINAHAN *Geol. Irel.* xix. 325 When the water during floods rises in the [shallow hollows], it overflows the adjoining lands, forming the turloughs, which are usually lakes in winter and callows in summer.

†**Tu·rlupin.** *Obs. rare.* [In sense 1, = OF. *turlupin,* in med.L. *turlupīn-us* (14th c., Du Cange), of unknown origin. In later F. in other senses: see below, also Littré and Hatz.-Darm.]

**1.** A name given to a sect of heretics in the 14th c., who are said to have maintained that one ought not to be ashamed of anything that is natural.

**1639** FULLER *Holy War* III. xix. (1840) 149 Turlupins; that is, dwellers with wolves..being forced to flee into woods. **1804** RANKEN *Hist. France* III. ii. § 1. 198 We shall not trace their [the Waldenses'] progress under the new names of Wickliffites, Lollards, Turlupins, Bohemians, etc. in other countries. **1882–3** *Schaff's Encycl. Relig. Knowl.* III. 2407/2 Gregory XI in 1373 urged the king of France to support the Dominicans against the Turlupins. **1910** *Encycl. Brit.* XIV. 592/2 [A woman, Jeanne Daubenton] being the head of a sect called the Turlupins. The Turlupins reappeared in 1421 at Arras and Douai and were persecuted in a similar way.

¶**2.** By Urquhart taken to render F. *tirelupin* in Rabelais, said by Duchat to be a name given in 1372 to a certain people who imitated Cynics, and lived on *lupins* which they gathered (*tiraient*) in the fields.

Cotgrave and Littré (who spells *tirelopin*) treat this as a separate word. Cotgr. has '*Tirelupin,* a catch-bit, or captious companion; a scowndrell, or scuruie fellow'; '*Turlupin,* a grub, mushrome, start-up, new-nothing, man of no value'. Urquhart applied Cotgrave's explanation of *turlupin* to *tirelupin.*

**1653** URQUHART *Rabelais* I. Prol., So saith a Turlupin or a new start-up grub of my books, but a turd for him. [RABELAIS Aultant en dict ung Tirelupin de mes livres: mais bren pour luy.]

[Mod. F. has *turlupin* in the sense 'buffoon, merry-andrew' (from the name assumed by an actor in French farce *a* 1630), hence 'a sorry jester, a low punster', and *turlupinade* a low pun or word-play. Cf. obs. Ital. *turlupino* (Douce) = '*turluru* a foole, a gull, a ninnie, a patch' (Florio).]

**Turm** (tɜɹm). [a. OF. *turme, torme* (15th c. in Godef.), ad. L. *turma* a troop, squadron.] A body or band of people, *esp.* a troop of horsemen; *spec.* a troop of thirty or thirty-two horsemen (= L. *turma*).

**1483** CAXTON *Gold. Leg.* 47 b/1 Iacob was sore aferde thenne and devyded his companye in to tweyne turmes. **c 1520** BARCLAY *Jugurth* (1557) 41 One bande or cohorte of Lumbardes and twoo turmes, that is to saye three score Thraciens. **1533** BELLENDEN *Livy* II. xx. (S.T.S.) I. 210 But dout þai had gevin bakkis, war nocht marcus fabius..come on ane spedy horss, with ane certane turmys of horsmen. **1671** MILTON *P. R.* IV. 66 Legions and Cohorts, turmes of horse and wings. **1800–24** CAMPBELL *Dead Eagle* 18 Rome array'd her turms And cohorts for the conquest of the world.

**Turmagant, Turmalin(e, Turmat**: see TERMAGANT, TOURMALINE, TURNIP.

†**Turmatur.** *Obs. rare.* App. corruption of TORMENTOR.

**c 1440** *Alphabet of Tales* 404 We rede of Saynt Pawle þat ..when þe turmaturs smate of his head [etc.]...When þe turmatur was gone, þis Ploattyll mett hym & axkid hym whare he had done hur maister Pawle.

**Turment,** etc., obs. ff. TORMENT, etc.

**Turmeric** (tɜ̄·ɹmərik), *sb.* (*a.*) Forms: 6 **tarmaret, tormarith, -marthe, tormerik, -yke, turmirick,** 6–7 **turmericke** (7 **turn-merick, turmerocke, -ack, termarcke, tarmanick, tarmaluk**), 7–9 **turmerick,** 8– **turmeric.** [Origin obscure. The English forms vary greatly, but *tarmaret, tormarith* resemble a recorded F. *terre mérite* and med. or mod.L. *terra merita* 'deserving or deserved earth', a name which the powder is said by Littré to have borne in commerce. The reason and origin of this L. and F. appellation are obscure; but in English the final *t* appears (by scribal error, or phonetic differentiation, or influence of such words as *arsenic*) to have become *c* or *k,* with the second *r* sometimes changed to *l* or *n.* Some have suggested a corruption of the Persian-Arabic name *kurkum* 'saffron', whence L., F., and Sp. *curcuma*; but the change seems too unlikely. The application of the name in Eng. to Tormentil arose apparently from some real or fancied similarity of properties or uses.

(Littré has s. v. *Curcuma* 'safran des Indes et curcuma, dite *terre-mérite,* quand elle est réduite en poudre'. Hatz.-Darm. have also, s. v. *Curcuma,* Du Pinet, 16th c. in Delbœuf *Recueil* 'La curcuma ou terra merita des apothicaires'.)]

**1.** The aromatic and pungent root-stock of an East Indian plant (see 2), or the powder made of this, the chief ingredient in curry powder, used also in dyeing yellow, and as a chemical test, and in the East as a condiment and medicinally; also called *curcuma* (CURCUMA b).

**1545** *Rates of Custome* c vj b, Tarmaret the C. pounde xl s. **1577** *Richmond Wills* (Surtees) 269 Spicknell, turmirick, and galingall ij[s]. **1586** *Rates of Custome* F j, Tormarith the c, contayning v. xx. xii. pound, iij. l. vj. s. viij. d. **1607** TOPSELL *Four-f. Beasts* (1658) 300 Take..of Ale a quart, and put thereunto of Saffron, Turmerick, of each half an ounce [for the Yellows (Jaundice) in the horse]. **1614** MARKHAM *Cheap Husb.* I. (1668) Table, *Turn-merick* is a yellow Simple, of strong savour, to be bought at the Apothecaries. **1621** *Shuttleworths' Acc.* (Chetham Soc.) 248 Longe peper graines and turmerocke. **1685** *Minute Bk. New Mills Cloth Manuf.* (S.H.S.) 97 Dye stuffs..tarmanick, logwood, woad. **1694** in Dunbar *Soc. Life Moray* (1865) 148 Ane kinkine tarmaluk, for dying. **1791** HAMILTON *Berthollet's Dyeing* II. II. III. iv. 185 Neither fustic nor turmeric gives a permanent colour. **1805** W. SAUNDERS *Min. Waters* iv. 117 The yellow of turmeric is not altered, shewing therefore the absence of an alkali. **1812** J. SMYTH *Pract. of Customs* (1821) 264 Turmerick..with alum, communicates a beautiful but perishable yellow dye to woollen cloth, cotton, or linen. It is also used as a drug. **1851** RICHARDSON *Geol.* v. (1855) 84 Alkalis..change to a reddish brown the yellow colour of paper stained with turmeric.

**b.** applied to other products: † by English herbalists to the root of Tormentil (in obs. F. *souchet de bois,* as distinct from *souchet d'Inde,* Indian galingale, curcuma) (Cotgr.); also, the root-stock of *Sanguinaria canadensis,* having medicinal qualities.

*African turmeric,* the fleshy underground stems of a species of *Canna,* cultivated in Sierra Leone and used for dyeing yellow. *Indian turmeric* (of N. America), the yellow root of *Hydrastis canadensis,* occasionally used in dyeing and medicinally. See also quot. 1898.

**1538** TURNER *Libellus, Heptaphillon,* officinis bistorta, & tormentilla, nostratibus Tormentyll & Tormeryke dicitur. **1548** — *Names of Herbes* 87 *Tormentilla,* .. in englishe Tormentil, or Tormerik. **1857** DUNGLISON *Med. Lex.,* Turmeric, *Curcuma longa, Sanguinaria Canadensis.* **1888** *Encycl. Brit.* XXIII. 662/2 In Sierra Leone a kind of turmeric is obtained from a species of *Canna.* **1890** BILLINGS *Med. Dict.,* Indian turmeric, *Hydrastis canadensis.* **1898** MORRIS *Austral Eng., Turmeric,* i. q. *Stinkwood* (q. v.); also applied occasionally to *Hakea dactyloides,* N.O. *Proteaceæ.* [*Ibid., Stinkwood,*..in Tasmania,..the timber of *Zieria smithii,* Andr., N. O. *Rutaceæ.*]

**2.** The plant *Curcuma longa,* N.O. *Zingiberaceæ.*

**1601** HOLLAND *Pliny* XXI. xviii. II. 101 Cyperus..is counted to have a depilatorie vertue for to fech off haire. [*Margin*] This Cyperis is taken to be Curcuma, or Terramerita, called therupon corruptly, Turmericke. **1671** SALMON *Syn. Med.* III. xxii. 397 Curcuma, κυπάρισσος ἰνδικὸς, Turmerick, the root opens the Gall, .. cures the Jaundies. **1785** MARTYN *Rousseau's Bot.* xi. (1794) 118 This order contains several interesting plants, such as .. turmerick. **1840** F. D. BENNETT *Whaling Voy.* I. 42 Tobacco and turmeric grow wild in great abundance.

**3.** *attrib.* and *Comb.,* as *turmeric crop, plant, powder, root, test-paper, water*; *turmeric-faced* adj.; **turmeric-oil** = TURMEROL; **turmeric paper,** unsized paper tinged with a solution of turmeric, used as a test for alkalis; **turmeric pudding,** a pudding coloured with turmeric; **turmeric-tree,** *Zieria Smithii* (*Acronychia Baueri*), the stinkwood of Tasmania, a tree having bright yellow inner bark.

**1912** THURSTON *Omens & Superst. S. India* vii. 206 A human sacrifice, which was intended to give a rich colour to the *turmeric crop. **1840** HOOD *Up the Rhine* 48 That *turmeric-faced Yankee is my evil genius. **1809** PEARSON in *Phil. Trans.* XCIX. 316 The presence of an alkali I could in no instance perceive, by means of the usual tests, namely, *turmeric paper, litmus paper [etc.]. **1826** HENRY *Elem. Chem.* II. 522 Turmeric paper and tincture are changed to a reddish brown by alkalis...Turmeric paper..however..is turned brown by muriatic acid gas and strong acids in general.

1857 *G. Bird's Urin. Deposits* (ed. 5) 288 The urine was clear, alkaline, turning turmeric paper brown. 1837 *Penny Cycl.* VIII. 233/2 *Curcuma longa*, the *Turmerick plant. 1866 *Treas. Bot.* 1250/2 The ground ginger of the shops is adulterated with sago-meal,..mustard husks, and *turmeric powder. *a* 1704 T. BROWN *Walk round Lond., Thames* Wks. 1709 III. III. 59 To make his Countenance shine like a *Turmerick Pudding. 1843 *Penny Cycl.* XXV. 416/2 *Turmeric root. 1868 WATTS *Dict. Chem.* V. 919 The root of *Canna speciosa*,..in West Africa, is said to be exactly similar to East Indian turmeric-root, in taste, smell, and chemical reactions. 1880 J. DUNBAR *Pract. Papermaker* 70 *Turmeric test paper. 1866 *Treas. Bot.* 1249/2 One [species of Zieria] common at Illawarra, and there called *Turmeric-tree, has a very yellow inner bark, suitable for dyeing. 1913 FRAZER *Gold. Bough* I. II. vi. 68 Smeared with *turmeric water, they all bathe and return home.

**B.** *adj. Chem.* Obtained from turmeric: in *turmeric acid*, an acid, $C_{11}H_{14}O_2$, formed by the oxidation of turmerol.

**Turmerol** (tɜ̄·ɹmərǫl). *Chem.* [f. TURMER-IC + -OL 3.] (See quot.)

1890 BILLINGS *Med. Dict.*, *Turmerol*, $C_{19}H_{28}O$, an aromatic volatile product obtained by Jackson and Menke (1882–83) from turmeric.

**Turmoil** (tɜ̄·ɹmoil), *sb.* Forms: see TURMOIL *v.* [See TURMOIL *v.*] A state of agitation or commotion; disturbance, tumult; trouble, disquiet.

1526 *Pilgr. Perf.* (W. de W. 1531) 75 Where..the mynde is full of vayne cogitacyons and turmoyle of worldly desyres. 1555 EDEN *Decades* 144 In all the turmoyles and tragicall affayres of the Ocean, nothynge hath so muche displeased me as the couetousnes of this man. 1596 DALRYMPLE tr. *Leslie's Hist. Scot.* II. (S.T.S.) I. 138 Nathir in al this truble and Tormoyle of the Scottis was the Pechtis frie of truble. 1698 FRYER *Acc. E. India & P.* 2 What makes these Seas in such a constant Turmoil? 1792 V. KNOX *Serm.* xix. 412 The noise of business, as it is called, or the jarring turmoil which avarice occasions. 1838 THIRLWALL *Greece* II. xv. 251 For four years longer Asia was still kept in restless turmoil. 1872 JENKINSON *Guide Eng. Lakes* (1879) 259 Relics of bygone ages of turmoil and border warfare. 1888 BRYCE *Amer. Commw.* I. vii. 90 The presidential election ..throws the country for several months into a state of turmoil.

†**b.** Harassing labour, toil. *Obs. rare.*

1568 GRAFTON *Chron.* II. 915 Myning and digging tynne and mettall oute of the grounde both daye and night with great turmoile and laboure. 1591 SHAKS. *Two Gent.* II. vii. 37 And there Ile rest, as after much turmoile, A blessed soule doth in Elizium.

**Turmoil** (tɜ̄·ɹmoil), *v.* Also 6 tour-, tor-, 6–7 -moile, -moyle, 7 -moyl. [Found along with TURMOIL *sb.* early in 16th c.; origin unascertained. There is no corresp. word in French, but some have conjectured a connexion with OF. *tremouille* (Cotgr.), in 17th c. *tremuye*, mod.F. *trémie de moulin* mill-hopper, in reference to its constant motion to and fro. The sb. is app. from the verb. In sense 3 app. associated with *moil*.]

**1.** *trans.* To agitate, disquiet, disturb; to throw into commotion and confusion; to trouble, harass, worry, torment. Often *to toss and turmoil*. Now somewhat *rare*.

1530 TINDALE *Gen.* Pref. A iij, I was so turmoyled in the contre where I was that I coude no lenger there dwell. 1530 — *Answ. to More* III. xiii, The matter in the meane tyme is turmoyled and tossed among them-selues. 1552 LATIMER *Serm., Luke ii. 6, 7* (1584) 279 b, Heritickes do wrongfully violate, tosse, and turmoyle the scriptures of God. *a* 1586 SIDNEY *Arcadia* (1622) 372 Yet of all other were Zelmanes braines most turmoyled, troubled with loue both actiue and passiue. 1610 HOLLAND *Camden's Brit.* II. 39 After hee had beene tormoiled with many troubles. 1637 DRYDEN *Æneid* I. 381 Haughty Juno, who, with endless broils Earth, seas, and heav'n, and Jove himself, turmoils. 1746–7 MRS. DELANY in *Life & Corr.* (1862) II. 454 Mr. Stanley and twenty fiddle faddles have turmoiled me all the morning. 1862 *Zoologist* XX. 8151 Mr. Beilby.. could not be turmoiled with disputes of any kind. 1894 W. WALKER *Hist. Congregat. Ch. U.S.* 53 The quarrel which was to turmoil the early Amsterdam life of this little communion had its beginnings in London.

**b.** To disorder or distress physically. *arch.*

1542 *Lam. & Piteous Treat.* in *Harl. Misc.* (Malh.) I. 241 Our shippes of warre, rydyng alongest the coste, were woondrefully turmoyled. 1561 T. HOBY tr. *Castiglione's Courtyer* II. (1577) M vij b, A great throng of people caryed him to the ynne aboue grounde, all tourmoyled and without his cappe. 1601 DOLMAN *La Primaud. Fr. Acad.* (1618) III. 746 The seas are much turmoiled with tempests. *a* 1610 HEALEY *Theophrastus* (1636) 41 Hee will tosse, turmoile, and ransacke euery corner of the house. 1657 TRAPP *Comm. Ps.* lxxvii. 17 The Lord..so troubled and turmoiled them with stormy tempests. 1867 J. B. ROSE tr. *Virgil's Æneid* 145 Aeolus..let loose his slaves And on your ocean empire turmoiled waves.

†**c.** *refl. Obs.*

*c* 1511 COLET *Serm. Conf. & Ref.* B viij, Religious men.. nat to turmoile them selfe in busynes, nother secular nor other. 1530 *Proper Dyaloge* 194 in Roy *Rede me*, etc. (Arb.) 139 We tourmoyle oure selfes nyght and daye..For to maynteyne the clargyes facciones. 1611 A. STAFFORD *Niobe* 202 Hee hath turmoiled himselfe through-out all the six Ages of the world. 1651 *C. Love's Case* 53 How doth he here toyl and turmoyl himself to salve the honor of his Conscience. 1720 MRS. MANLEY *Power of Love* (1741) 76 After turmoiling himself for some Hours, he saw the Stone was cast, and that it was in vain now to repine.

†**d.** With advb. extension: *fig.* To drive or throw roughly or without ceremony. *Obs.*

1588 G. D. *Brief Discov. Dr. Allen's Sedit. Drifts* 112 They were imprisoned, tossed, and turmoyled from place to place. 1596 SPENSER *F. Q.* IV. ix. 39 But thus turmoild from one to other stowre I wast my life. 1602 *Contention betw. Liberality & Prodigality* IV. i. D iij b, I haue bin turmoyled From post to piller.

†**2.** *intr.* To be or live in turmoil, agitation, or commotion; to move agitatedly or restlessly. *Obs.*

*c* 1540 tr. *Pol. Verg. Eng. Hist.* (Camden) I. 186 Then Eugenius the viij. Fergusius the iij. bothe continuallie weltered and turmoyled in fillthie vices. 1548 RECORDE *Urin. Physick* ii. (1651) 4 If the way by any means be stopped, then the water turmoileth and laboureth. 1560 DAUS tr. *Sleidane's Comm.* 134 Nowe that God hathe made a restraynte, he rageth and tourmoyleth. 1618 G. STRODE *Anat. Mortalitie* 9 Sicke men which turmoile and tosse from one side of the bed vnto the other. 1681 in *Lond. Gaz.* No. 1640/6 Continual overflows of violent Misrule.. turmoiling to a common Chaos.

**3.** *intr.* To toil, drudge; cf. MOIL *v.* 3. Now *dial.*

*a* 1548 HALL *Chron., Hen. VII* 41 Cornyshmen..gate their lyuyng hardly..bothe daye and night labouryng and turmoylyng. 1598 BARCKLEY *Felic. Man* VI. (1603) 574 What doe men but digge and turmoile in the earth? 1652 C. B. STAPYLTON *Herodian* xx. 171 To stop the flame both Rich and poor Turmoile, Some carry hooks, some water Conduits turne. 1684 N. S. *Crit. Enq. Edit. Bible* iv. 22 A person that had very much and long turmoil'd in these studies. *c* 1755 MURPHY *Apprentice* I. i, I have been turmoiling for the fellow all the days of my life. 1759 SARAH FIELDING *C'tess of Dellwyn* I. 53 That [mind] which is burthened with many Griefs, and at the same time is turmoiling and bustling. 1840 PUSEY tr. *Confess. August.* III. vi. 11 Toiling and turmoiling through want of Truth. 1901 F. E. TAYLOR *Folk-Sp. S. Lanc.* s.v., He has for t' turmoil hard for his bread.

Hence **Tu·rmoiled, Tu·rmoiling** *ppl. adjs.*

1550 BALE *Apol.* 33 A doctryne..for turmoylynge Thomistes. *c* 1555 HARPSFIELD *Divorce Hen. VIII* (Camden) 221 The tossing, turmoyling, tempestuous sea. 1570–6 LAMBARDE *Peramb. Kent* (1596) 429 In the time of the turmoiled King Ethelred, the whole fleete of the Danish army lay at roade..before Greenewiche. 1671 F. PHILLIPS *Reg. Necess.* 141 A turmoiled impoverished, and over burdened Debtor. 1676 E. BURY *Medit.* 322 Turmoiling thoughts, how he shall pay his rent, discharge his debts. 1735 SEWEL *Dutch Dict.*, *Raasbol*, a Turmoiling fellow. 1823 SCOTT *Quentin D.* v, Quentin..endeavoured to compose his turmoiled and scattered thoughts. 1866 J. B. ROSE tr. *Ovid's Met.* 332 The turmoiled waters gurgitate the crew.

**Turmoiler** (tɜ̄·ɹmoiləɹ). *rare.* [f. TURMOIL *v.* + -ER [1].] One who turmoils; a disquieter.

1591 PERCIVALL *Sp. Dict.*, *Rebolvedor*, an ouerturner, a turmoiler, a disquieter. 1906 W. WALKER *Calvin* xii. 335 He was an intentional turmoiler of the public peace.

**Turmoiling** (tɜ̄·ɹmoiliŋ), *vbl. sb.* [f. TURMOIL *v.* + -ING [1].] The action of the verb TURMOIL; commotion, agitation, disquietude; also, toiling, severe labour.

1550 LATIMER *Serm. Stamford* (1562) 102 b, I was once in examination before fiue or sixe Bishops, where I had much turmoyling. 1550 BALE *Eng. Votaries* II. M iv, To rehearce yͤ turmoilinges of Pope Calixte yͤ second. 1578 LYTE *Dodoens* III. xxxiv. 365 It rayseth vp great windinesse, blastinges, tormoyling and ouerturning the whole body. 1691 WOOD *Ath. Oxon.* II. 205 After a great deal of moyling, turmoyling, perfidiousness, and I know not what, he laid down his head and died. 1863 COWDEN CLARKE *Shaks. Char.* xi. 291 Amidst the turmoiling and common-places of every-day action.

†**Turmoilous**, *a. Obs. rare.* [f. TURMOIL *sb.* + -OUS.] Full of turmoil or tumult; disturbed, troublous. So **Tu·rmoily** *a. rare*, in same sense.

1553 EDEN *Treat. Newe Ind.* (Arb.) 10 Settynge foorth Christes true Relygion in those turmoylous dayes. 1877 MARY MOHL in Simpson *Lett. & Recoll.* (1887) 360 This country is in a great turmoily state.

**Turmyntyne**, obs. corrupt f. TURPENTINE.

**Turn** (tɜ̄ɹn), *sb.* Forms: 3– turn; also 3–7 turne, 4–6 torn, torne, 4–7 tourne, 5–7 tourn, 6 terne. [Partly a. AF. **torn, turn, tourn*, = OF. *tor, tour*, F. *tour* (= Pr. *torn, tor*, Cat. *torn*, Sp., Pg., It. *torno*) :—L. *torn-us* (acc. *-um*), a. Gr. τόρνος turning-lathe. Cf. for the form, F. *jour*, AF. *jorn* :—L. *diurn-um*. In English, partly treated as n. of action from TURN *v.* (So OF. *torne, tourne*, fr. *tourner* vb.) See also TOUR *sb.* from the later French form.]

**I.** Rotation, and connected senses. (Cf. TURN *v.* I, II.)

**1.** The action of turning about an axis or centre, as a wheel; rotation, revolution. Now *rare.*

*c* 1250 *Gen. & Ex.* 79 On walkenes turn wid dai and niȝt Of foure and twenti time riȝt. *c* 1400 *Rom. Rose* 5470 Froward Fortune..,Whanne high estatis she doth reverse, And maketh hem to tumble doune Off hir whele, with sodeyn tourne. 1500–20 DUNBAR *Poems* xxiv. 8 Fortoun sa fast hir quheill dois cary; Na tyme bot turne can [*v.r.* in turning can it] tak rest. *c* 1680 HICKERINGILL *Hist. Whiggism* II. Wks. 1716 I. 111 Fortune's-wheel..is always..upon the Turn. 1879 J. MARTINEAU *Hours Th.* (1880) II. i. 6 You may expect a prize from the turn of a lottery.

**2.** An act of turning; a movement of rotation (total or partial); *esp.* a single revolution, as of a wheel.

1481 CAXTON *Myrr.* III. viii. 148 The sonne..gooth euery yere aboute the heuen one torne. 1596 DAVIES *Orchestra* lxxi, A gallant daunce,..With loftie turnes and capriols. 1665 BOYLE *Occas. Refl.* I. vi, The Giddy turns of Fortune's Wheel. 1687 A. LOVELL tr. *Thevenot's Trav.* I. 35 He darts his Zagaye..with a turn of hand that doubles the force of it. 1759 SMEATON in *Phil. Trans.* LI. 157 The turns of the sails in a given time will be as the square of the velocity of the wind. 1849 CLOUGH *Dipsychus* II. ii. 32 And hear the soft turns of the oar! 1872 RUSKIN *Fors Clav.* (1896) I. xix. 370 In a few turns of the hands of the..clock.

**b.** (*Roasted, done*, etc.) *to a turn*, i.e. exactly to the proper degree, precisely right: orig. in reference to the turns of the spit.

1780 MACKENZIE *Mirror* No. 93 ¶ 12 The beef was roasted to a turn. 1864 D. G. MITCHELL *Sev. Stor.* 11 The chops were done to a turn.

**c.** *Turn of the scale(s*, the slight advantage given to the buyer by which the article sold overbalances the weight and brings down the scale-pan. Hence, a very slight degree or amount, a very little (just enough to *turn the scale*: see TURN *v.* 58).

In quot. 1888 *the turn of a hair* = a close chance, a 'narrow shave'. But cf. *not to turn a hair*, in HAIR *sb.* 8 n.

1888 *Century Mag.* May 127/1 It was the turn of a hair that they hadn't buried him alive. 1890 'R. BOLDREWOOD' *Col. Reformer* (1891) 218 All that's a turn too good for making slaughter-yard bacon, does for the Chinamen.

**3.** A brain-disease of sheep and cattle, caused by a hydatid, and characterized by giddiness: = GID [1]. Also *transf.* a beast affected with this (quot. 1658).

1523 FITZHERB. *Husb.* § 62 *heading*, The turne, and remedy therfore. 1651 *Manchester Crt. Leet Rec.* (1887) IV. 51 Sellinge a beast..yett had the turne. 1658 *Ibid.* 243 Sellinge parte of a Turne which was not Markettable. 1718 BP. HUTCHINSON *Witchcraft* ix. (1720) 162 Twirl like a Calf that hath the Turn. 1805 R. W. DICKSON *Pract. Agric.* II. 1168 The Turn or Giddy is a disorder with which these animals [sheep] are often seized.

**4.** A movement round something, a twist; *spec. Naut.* an act of passing a rope once round a mast or other object.

1743 BULKELEY & CUMMINS *Voy. S. Seas* 115 All Hands haul'd, took a Turn round the Main-Mast, and went aft. 1881 WHITEHEAD *Hops* 35 The young bines only take short turns, and cannot lay hold of supports which are stout at the base. 1882 NARES *Seamanship* (ed. 6) 256 The blocks ..act like a sailor's 'turn and a half'.

**5.** *Mus.* A melodic ornament consisting of a group of three (four, or five) notes, viz. the principal note (*on* which it is performed) and the notes one degree above and below it.

In the *common* or *direct turn*, the note above precedes, and that below follows, the principal note; in the *inverted turn* or *back-turn*, the note below precedes and that above follows; in either case, the principal note is repeated at the end, and sometimes also precedes. *Turn of a shake*: see quot. 1881 s.v. SHAKE *sb.*[1] 5.

1801 BUSBY *Dict. Mus.* 1818 — *Gram. Mus.* 143 Full, or Double Turn. Partial Turn. Inverted Turn. 1868 BROWNING *Ring & Bk.* I. 1210 Clavecinist debarred his instrument, He yet thrums—shirking neither turn nor trill,.. on dumb table-edge.

**6.** The condition of being, or direction in which something is, twisted or convoluted; hence, a portion or 'length' of something of a convoluted or twisted form, corresponding to one whole revolution; a (single) coil or twist; a round (of coiled rope, etc.).

1669 RAY in *Phil. Trans.* IV. 1011 Observations Concerning the odd Turn of some Shell-snailes..The Turn of the wreaths is from the right hand to the left. 1678 *Lond. Gaz.* No. 1269/4 A dapple gray Mare,..a feather under the mane, two turns in the forehead. 1774 GOLDSM. *Nat. Hist.* (1776) VII. 32 Its convolutions are more numerous. The garden snail has but five turns at the most; in the sea snail the convolutions are sometimes..ten. 1827 D. JOHNSON *Ind. Field Sports* 83 Wound round with a few turns of fine silk. 1884 HIGGS *Magn. & Dynamo-Electr. Machines* 214 We can..calculate the length..of the turns wound on a magnetic core, if we divide the length of the coil by the number of turns.

**7.** Something that turns or spins round; a rotatory apparatus or contrivance. **a.** A lathe; now only applied to a watchmaker's lathe, also called *a pair of turns*. **b.** A spinning-wheel, windlass, or the like; in quot. 1578, a top. ?*Obs.* exc. *dial.* **c.** = TURN-TABLE 2.

**a.** 1483 *Cath. Angl.* 397/2 A Turne of a turnour, *tornus*. 1580 HOLLYBAND *Treas. Fr. Tong*, *Vn tour*.., a turne, as *boule faite au tour*, a boule made at the turne. 1668 *Phil. Trans.* III. 795 An Artist, that polishes Optick-Glasses on a Turn. 1884 F. J. BRITTEN *Watch & Clockm.* 202 The wheel..is put in a pair of turns. *Ibid.* 205 The hollows of small pinions are often polished in the turns.

**b.** *c* 1564 in Noake *Worc. Relics* (1877) 10 A spynynge turne and a spolynge turne. 1578 LYTE *Dodoens* VI. vi. 664 Almost like to a little Turne or Peare, brode beneath, and narrow aboue. 1675 *Phil. Trans.* X. 452 It shot off the Turne at the mouth of the Pit. 1688 R. HOLME *Armoury* III. 342/1 An Engine called a Turne, or the Turne Engine.. by which great Weights are lifted up. 1870 R. S. HAWKER *Footpr. Far Cornw.* 88 The mother stood by her turn or wheel, and span.

**c.** *a* 1668 LASSELS *Voy. Italy* (1670) II. 71 A grate..where ..infants are put into a squar hole of a Turne, and so turned in by night. 1808 LADY JERNINGHAM *Lett.* (1896) I. 321 Her victuals were put in a turn, like at a Convent.

**II.** Change of direction or course, and connected senses. (Cf. TURN *v.* III, IV, V.)

**8.** An act of turning or facing another way; a change of direction or posture.

1412–20 LYDG. *Chron. Troy* IV. 3273 Fortunys variaunce, ..And sodeyn torn of hir false visage. 1606 SHAKS. *Ant. & Cl.* II. v. 59 He's bound vnto Octauia. *Cleo.* For what good turne? *Mes.* For the best turne i' th' bed. 1754 RICHARDSON *Grandison* (1810) IV. xxxii. 237 Her..half-saucy turns upon him. 1827 SCOTT *Surg. Dau.* xiv, Shooting a glance at his

..companion by a turn of the eye. **1847** TENNYSON *Princess* IV. 375 She..made a sudden turn As if to speak.

**b.** 'A step off the ladder at the gallows' (J.); hanging. Cf. TURN *v.* 73 d. Now *rare* or *Obs.*

**1631** WEEVER *Anc. Fun. Mon.* 49 What man will venture a turne at the Gallows, for a little small siluer chalice?

**c.** Change of position (by a rotatory movement) of something inanimate, as a die when thrown.

**1801** STRUTT *Sports & Past.* Introd. iii. 4 Stake their liberty upon the turn of the dice. **1802** MAR. EDGEWORTH *Moral T.* (1816) I. xi. 89 Few people chose to venture a hundred guineas upon the turn of a straw. **1809** MALKIN *Gil Blas* v. i. ⁋ 29 Florence and her dowry therefore were lost..by a turn of the dice.

**9.** *Printing.* A reversal of type in composing; also *concr.* a type turned face downwards so as to produce a square black mark on the proof, in place of a missing letter.

**1888** J. H. HESSELS in *Encycl. Brit.* XXIII. 693/1 The whole of the last reference-line is put in upside down...A 'turn' of this magnitude could hardly have occurred [etc.].

**10.** An act (or, rarely, the action) of turning aside from one's course; deflection, deviation; a roundabout course, a detour. Also *fig.*

*a* **1300** *Cursor M.* 4323 (Cott.) Qua folus lang, wit-outen turn, Oft his fote sal find a spurn. *c* **1410** *Master of Game* (MS. Digby 182) xxx, Þen he shulde make a longe turne and vmbicaste aboute by somme wayes, or by pathes. *c* **1530** LD. BERNERS *Arth. Lyt. Bryt.* (1814) 327 And some behelde the hye tournes & tournynges of the sakers & gerfawcons. **1685–6** STILLINGFL. *Serm.* (1698) III. i. 13 True Repentance is the turn of the whole Soul from the Love, as well as the Practice of Sin. **1689–90** TEMPLE *Ess. Heroic Virt.* Wks. 1731 I. 222 The Arians..made easy Turns to the Mahometan Doctrines, that professed Christ to have been so great and so divine a Prophet. **1874** WHYTE MELVILLE *Uncle John* xxiii, To follow him through the many turns and windings of his wearisome..chase. **1892** GREENER *Breech Loader* 231 The woodcock..is one of the most difficult birds to bag;..its turn to right and left being most erratic.

**b.** in phr. *at every turn*: usually *fig.* at every change of circumstance (cf. 18); hence, on every occasion, constantly, continually.

(Cf. quot. 1579 in TURNING *vbl. sb.* 4 b.)

**1590** SHAKS. *Mids. N.* III. i. 114 Ile leade you about a Round, Through bogge, through bush, through brake,..And neigh, and barke, and grunt,..Like horse, hound, hog,..at euery turne. *c* **1685** SOUTH *Serm., Will for Deed* (1715) 377 One or both..being used by Men, almost at every Turn, to elude the Precept. **1735** BERKELEY *Reasons* etc. § 2 Wks. 1871 III. 340 Should he at every turn say such uncouth things. **1876** TREVELYAN *Life & Lett. Macaulay* II. ix. 131 Compelled to disgust his supporters at every turn. **1907** *Blackw. Mag.* Apr. 48 Palaces of rusticated stone meet us at every turn.

**11.** A place or point at which a road, river, or the like turns, or turns off; a curved or bent part of anything; a bend, curve, or angle.

**1412–20** LYDG. *Chron. Troy* I. 1367 Thoruȝ many halle and many riche tour, By many tourn and many diuerse way. **1513** DOUGLAS *Æneis* IX. vii. 26 The horsmen than prekis, and fast furth sprentis To weil beknawin pethis, and turnys [and] wentis. **1688** R. HOLME *Armoury* IV. xi. (Roxb.) 438/2 Annoynted..in..the breast, betweene the shoulders, in the Joynts, and turne of the Armes. **1768** STERNE *Sent. Journ., Pulse* (1778) I. 163 There are two turns; and be so good as to take the second. **1816** BYRON *Ch. Har.* III. lv. Song iv, The river nobly..flows,..And all its thousand turns disclose Some fresher beauty. **1856** KANE *Arct. Expl.* I. xxiii. 286 They..walked around the turn of the cape.

**b, c.** *Mining.* (See quots.)

**b. 1681** T. HOUGHTON *Rara Avis* Gloss. (E.D.S.), *Turn*, a pit sunk in some part of a drift; if the mine be deep, there is many of these turns, one below another. **1824** MANDER *Derbysh. Miner's Gloss.* s. v., Eight, ten, or twelve fathoms is [a depth] common for a Turn; and note, that a vein which is wrought ninety or a hundred fathoms must have divers Turns. **c. 1851** GREENWELL *Coal-trade Terms Northumb. & Durh.* 55 *Turns*, curved plates, made of cast metal, used at a branch-off tramway in the workings. **1886** J. BARROWMAN *Sc. Mining Terms* 69 *Turn*,..the arrangement of rails, sleepers and pulleys at a curve on a haulage road.

**12.** *Arch.* The curved flank or haunch of an arch, between the key-stone and the foot. ? *Obs.*

**1726** LEONI tr. *Alberti's Archit.* I. 53/2 An Arch is..a conjunction..of wedges, whereof some..are call'd the foot.., those in the middle above, the Key.., and those on the sides.., the Turn, or Ribs of the Arch.

**13.** The act of turning so as to face about or go in the opposite direction; reversal of position or course; turning back. *On the turn*, in or close upon the act of turning, at the turning-point. Also *fig.* esp. in *turn of the tide*, etc. (cf. TIDE *sb.* 9).

**1669** R. FLEMING *Fulfill. Script.* (1801) I. 302 Antichrist should be at his height and his kingdom upon the turn. **1690** C. NESSE *O. & N. Test.* I. 271 The half-turn, from West to North. *Ibid.*, The whole turn from West to East. *Ibid.*, The round turn from sin to Christ. **1782** MISS BURNEY *Cecilia* VII. v, Whether we shall go on, or take a turn back? **1796** — *Camilla* V. 540 Such turns in the tide of fortune. **1862** R. H. PATTERSON *Ess. Hist. & Art* 329 Fine Art is at a low ebb. But..the tide is on the turn.

**14.** *Coursing.* The act of suddenly turning, as a hare when closely pursued, and making off more or less in the opposite direction, or at least at a considerable angle from the direction of pursuit. Usually in phr. *to give the hare* (etc.) *a turn*, said of the hound.

**1575** TURBERV. *Venerie* 246 A Cote is when a Greyhounde goeth endways by his fellow and giueth the Hare a turne (which is called setting a Hare aboute). **1670** NARBOROUGH *Jrnl.* in *Acc. Sev. Late Voy.* I. (1694) 30 A Greyhound..gave Chase to one of them, and at last gave her a turn. **1834** T. THACKER *Courser's Comp.* I. 183 A turn to be reckoned one point; but if the hare turn not, as it were round, she only wrenches...A wrench is when she strikes off..at about a right angle. **1856** 'STONEHENGE' *Brit. Sports* I. III. viii. 212/1 It is a Turn if the hare is forced more than 45 degrees, and one point is to be scored.

†**15.** A journey, expedition, tour, course. *Obs.*

*c* **1400** *St. Alexius* (Laud 622) 341 He took his tourne From Rome. **1570** LEVINS *Manip.* 191/13 Turne,..*cursus.* **1665** CHAS. II in Julia Cartwright *Henrietta of Orleans* (1894) 224, I am goeing to make a little turne into dorset sheere for 8 or 9 dayes. **1734** H. WALPOLE *Let.* Oct., in *10th Rep. Hist. MSS. Comm.* App. I. 254 His design to take a turn into England.

**b.** A sheriff's tour, or court: see TOURN.

†**c.** *Venery.* Pairing of roe-deer. *Obs.*

**1486** *Bk. St. Albans* E iv b, Then shall the Roobucke gendre with the Roo..Then is he calde a Roobucke goyng in his turne. **1610** GUILLIM *Heraldry* III. xiv. (1660) 166 You shall sey Roe goeth to his Tourne.

**16.** An act of walking or pacing around or about a limited area, as a park, garden, or sequence of streets; a short walk (or ride) forth and back, esp. by a different route; a stroll.

*a* **1591** H. SMITH *Wks.* (1866) I. 185 Go now and walk in thy galleries, fetch one turn more before thou be turned out of door. **1610** SHAKS. *Temp.* IV. i. 162 A turne or two Ile walke To still my beating minde. **1710** STEELE *Tatler* No. 160 ⁋ 2, I took several Turns about my Chamber. **1715** *Lond. Gaz.* No. 5336/1 He..has..taken a Turn on Horse-back on the Isle. **1823** SCOTT *Quentin D.* Introd., This circumstance of explanation and remark..occupied us during two or three turns upon the long terrace. **1867** TROLLOPE *Chron. Barset* xlvii, I will take a turn round the garden.

**b.** *Knitting.* See quot.

**1893** ELIZ. ROSEVEAR *Text-bk. Needlework*, etc. 406 A Turn is used for two rows in the same stitches backwards and forwards.

**III.** Change in general. (See also sense 36.) Cf. TURN *v.* VI.

**17.** The action, or an act, of turning or changing; change, alteration, modification; in quot. 1901, change of colour. *rare* exc. as in next sense. *On the turn*, turning sour, as food; of the weather or the season, changing.

**1597** HOOKER *Eccl. Pol.* V. xxxviii. § 1 An admirable facilitie which musique hath to expresse..the turnes and varieties of all passions. **1726** LEONI tr. *Alberti's Archit.* I. 3/2 Sudden Turns and Changes in the Air, from Hot to Cold, and from Cold to Hot. *c* **1850** *Arab. Nights* (Rtldg.) 251 One..would fain have given a turn to these melancholy ideas by singing a little air to her lute. **1901** L. MALET *Sir R. Calmady* III. ii, The turn of the leaf was very brilliant.

**18.** *spec.* A change in affairs, conditions, or circumstances; vicissitude; revolution; *esp.* a change for better or worse, or the like, at a crisis; hence, sometimes, the time at which such a change takes place. (Often *fig.* from or associated with 10.)

**1607** SHAKS. *Cor.* IV. iv. 12 Oh World, thy slippery turnes! Friends now fast sworn..shall within this houre..breake out To bitterest Enmity. **1622** BACON *Hen. VII* 217 The State of Christendome might by this late Accident haue a turne. **1725** B. HIGGONS *Rem. Burnet* I. Hist. Wks. 1736 II. 71 Why the Republicans..made so little Opposition to a Turn of State [the Restoration] which must infallibly be their Ruin. **1781** GIBBON *Decl. & F.* xviii. II. 120 The engagement ..was maintained with various and singular turns of fortune. **1842** TENNYSON *Two Voices* 55 Some turn this sickness yet might take. **1859** G. MEREDITH *R. Feverel* xxv, In the turn of the year. **1892** W. RAMAGE *Last Words* 65 Two turns are possible in a crisis: the issue may be favourable or fatal.

**b.** *Turn of life*: a name for the time, or symptoms, of cessation of menstruation: = *change of life* (CHANGE *sb.* 3 d).

**1834** COOPER *Good's Study Med.* (ed. 4) IV. 54 *note*, When menstruation is about to cease, the period is called 'the change or turn of life'. **1860** MAYNE *Expos. Lex., Turn of Life*, popular term for the constitutional disturbance frequently attendant on the cessation of the catamenia.

**19.** A momentary shock caused by sudden alarm, fright, or the like. *colloq.* (Cf. 25 b.)

**1846** DICKENS *Cricket on Hearth* ii, What a hard-hearted monster you must be, John, not to have said so, at once, and saved me such a turn! **1860** GEO. ELIOT *Mill on Fl.* I. vii, Mrs. Tulliver gave a little scream as she saw her, and felt such a 'turn' that she dropt the large gravy-spoon into the dish. **1886** BESANT *Children of Gibeon* II. xix, It was only a dream...But it gave me a terrible turn.

**IV.** Senses denoting actions of various kinds.

†**20.** A movement, device, or trick, by which a wrestler attempts to throw his antagonist: = F. *tour.*

*a* **1225** *Ancr. R.* 280 He iseih hu ueole þe grimme wrastlare of helle breid up on his hupe, & werp, mid þe haunche turn, into golnesse. *c* **1325** *Metr. Hom.* 83 Bot sinful man gers him [the devil] oft schurne, And castis him wit his awen turne. *c* **1400** *Gamelyn* 244 Of all the tornes that he cowthe he schewed him but oon, And caste him on the lefte syde that three ribbes to-brak. **1562** J. HEYWOOD *Prov. & Epigr.* (1867) 162 He is cast in his owne turne, that is likly And yet in all turnes he turnth wonders quikly.

**21.** A subtle device of any kind; a trick, wile, artifice, stratagem. ? *Obs.*

*a* **1225** *Ancr. R.* 78 Vre strencðe..aȝein þes deofles turnes & his fondunges. *c* **1380** *Sir Ferumb.* 796 Y warne þe of a torn..Y leuede ȝond on a buchyment sarasyns wonder fale. *a* **1533** LD. BERNERS *Huon* lxiv. 221, I thynke to playe hym a tourne. **1697** VANBRUGH *Relapse* v. iii, Come, no equivocations, no Roman turns upon us. **1720** WATERLAND *Eight Serm.* Pref. 30 The unlearned Reader..may be easily imposed upon by little Turns, and Fallacies. **1735** H. WALPOLE *Let.* 9 Sept., in *10th Rep. Hist. MSS. Comm.* App. I. 259 A variety of artifices and turns.

†**22.** An act, deed, proceeding; a deed of valour, feat, exploit. *Obs.*

**13..** *E. E. Allit. P.* B. 192 In þe creatores cort com neuer more, Ne neuer see hym with syȝt for such sour tournez. **1415** HOCCLEVE *To Sir J. Oldcastle* ii, Was no knyghtly turn no where, Ne no manhode shewid in no wyse, But Oldcastel wolde, his thankes, be there. **1590** *Reg. Privy Council Scot.* IV. 560 He had done greitar turnis nor to ding oute all thair harnis.

**23.** An act of good or ill will, or that does good or harm to another; a service: almost always with qualifying word, as *good turn*, a benefit; *bad, evil, ill*, † *shrewd turn*, an injury. Cf. *to do the turn* in 30 b (*c*).

**13..** *Cursor M.* 4330 (Cott.) Sco [Potiphar's wife] waited him wit a werr turn. *c* **1386** CHAUCER *Pard. T.* 487 Hadde I nat doon a freendes torn to thee? *c* **1440** *Alphabet of Tales* lviii. 43, I hafe yit in my mynde a little gude turn at þou did me. *Ibid.* xcvii. 72 Thow hase done me ane ill turn. **1526** *Pilgr. Perf.* (W. de W. 1531) 98 Wysshe hym a shrewde turne, or saye, I wolde the deuyll had hym. **1546** J. HEYWOOD *Prov.* (1867) 34 One good tourne askth an other. **1647** H. MORE *Cupid's Conflict* xlv, He..Requiteth evil turns with hearty love. **1654** H. L'ESTRANGE *Chas. I* (1655) 15 One good turn deserves another. **1724** DE FOE *Mem. Cavalier* (1840) 242 Ready..to do us any ill turn. **1886** G. R. SIMS *Ring o' Bells*, etc. vii. 198, I did the lass a bad turn when I took her away.

**24.** A stroke or spell of work; a piece of work; a task, job. *Sc.* ? *Obs.* exc. in *hand's turn* (see HAND *sb.* 59).

*c* **1375** *Sc. Leg. Saints* xxx. (*Theodera*) 121 Of sorcery scho cuth do, And as scho mycht did turne and chare. **1572** *Satir. Poems Reform.* xxxii. 35 Thay..brocht thair butter and egges To Edinburgh Croce, and did na vther turne. **1609** SKENE *Reg. Maj.* II. xli. 36 b, The over-lord sall doe all the turnis and affairs perteining to the heire. **1791** J. LEARMONT *Poems* 331 My turns are lying to do.

**25.** A spell or bout of action, a 'go'; *spec.* a spell of wrestling; hence, a contest (quot. 1829). Now often associated with sense 28.

*c* **1380** *Sir Ferumb.* 335 Þov hast y dremed of venesoun; þov mostest drynke a torn. *a* **1400–50** *Alexander* 2276, I walde..now wrastyll a turne. ? *a* **1500** *Chester Pl.* vii. 246 A turne to take have I tight with my maistores. **1653** *Clarke Papers* (Camden) III. 9 Yesterday wee had another turne in the House. **1829** SCOTT *Anne of G.* xxv, We have seen.. so many turns betwixt York and Lancaster. **1877** SPURGEON *Serm.* XXIII. 643 You young people, I like to see you run, and I am glad to take a turn at it myself. **1882** FURNIVALL in *E. E. Wills* Ded. 8 Since I first saw the Boxes and their contents at Doctors' Commons,..I always meant to have a turn at them.

**b.** An attack of illness, faintness, or the like; also, a fit of passion or excitement. (Cf. 19.)

**1775** ABIGAIL ADAMS in *Fam. Lett.* (1876) 97 Jonathan is the only one..in the family who has not had a turn of the disorder. **1859** TENNYSON *Merl. & Vivien* 519 Not so much from wickedness, As some wild turn of anger, or a mood Of overstrain'd affection. **1913** EDITH WHARTON *Custom of Country* I. ii, Her mother..sat in a drooping attitude, her head sunk on her breast, as she did when she had one of her 'turns' [of palpitation].

**c.** *pl.* A name for monthly courses or catamenia.

**1857** DUNGLISON *Med. Lex., Turns*, menses.

†**26.** An event, circumstance, occurrence, hap. (Not always clearly distinguishable from 18.) In quot. 1719, a series or course of events (cf. 25). *Obs.* or merged in other senses.

**1579** TOMSON *Calvin's Serm. Tim.* 853/1 Beside the losse of our time, there is a worse turne followeth it, and more deadly. **1596** SPENSER *F. Q.* VI. x. 18 The shepheard..broke his bag-pipe quight, And made great mone for that unhappy turne. **1708** MRS. CENTLIVRE *Busie Body* v. i, Pox on 't, this is an unlucky Turn. What shall I say? **1719** DE FOE *Crusoe* (1840) II. xiii. 268 To bring this long turn of our affairs to a conclusion.

**V.** Occasion, etc.

†**27.** The occasion or time at which something happens. (Cf. 18, 26.) *Obs.*

**13..** *Cursor M.* 19445 (Cott.) He sagh him croised þat ilk turn þat he for staning suld not skurn. *c* **1330** R. BRUNNE *Chron.* (1810) 154 Richard at þat turne gaf him a faire Juelle.

**28.** The time for action or proceeding of any kind which comes round to each individual of a series in succession; (each or any one's) recurring occasion of action, etc. in a series of acts done, or to be done, by (or to) a number in rotation. (Often in adverbial phrases: see below.)

*c* **1393** CHAUCER *Scogan* 42 Tak euery man his torn as for his tyme. **1586** B. YOUNG *Guazzo's Civ. Conv.* IV. 188 It came to L. Iohns turne to drinke. **1593** SHAKS. 3 *Hen. VI*, II. ii. 105 Then 'twas my turne to fly, and now 'tis thine. **1642** DENHAM *Sophy* Prol. 10 His turne will come, to laugh at you agen. **1697** COLLIER *Ess.* II. *Envy* 113 Every one has a fair Turn to be as Great as he pleases. **1719** YOUNG *Paraphr. Job* 5 Wks. 1757 I. 204 At length misfortunes take their turn to reign, And ills on ills succeed. **1778** C. JONES *Hoyle's Games Impr.* 79 If..the last Player plays out of his Turn. **1849** MACAULAY *Hist. Eng.* ix. II. 553 It was Northumberland's turn to perform this duty. **1885** *Manch. Exam.* 12 Feb. 5/3 The manufacturers have had their share [of protection]; now it is the turn of the corn growers and cattle breeders.

**b.** Phrases. (*a*) *By turns* (also † *by turn*), one after another in regular succession; successively, in rotation. (*b*) *In turn, in turns*, each in due succession: = (*a*). (*In turn* is also used rhetorically like *in one's turn*: see *c*.) (*c*) *In one's turn*, in one's due order in the series. (Often also used rhetorically to indicate an act duly or naturally following a similar act on the part of another, but without the notion of pre-arranged succession.) (*d*) *Turn about, turn and turn about* (also rarely *turn and turn*): *advb.* in turn, by turns, alternately († sometimes preceded by possessive: cf. *c*); *adj.* performed in turn, mutual, reciprocal (*rare*); *sb.* the action of doing something in turn; alternate or successive turns at doing something.

(*a*). **1538** Elyot, *Vicissatim*, by tymes, by tournes. *Vicissim*, by tourne, nowe one, nowe an nother. **1585** T. Washington tr. *Nicholay's Voy.* iii. iv. 76 [They] by change and turnes..keepe watch. **1667** Milton *P. L.* ii. 598 The damn'd..feel by turns the bitter change Of fierce extreams. **1712** Steele *Spect.* No. 508 ¶ 3 He is by turns outrageous, peevish, froward and jovial. *a* **1839** Praed *Poems* (1864) II. 13 He aped each folly of the throng, Was all by turns and nothing long. *c* **1850** *Arab. Nights* (Rtldg.) 326 They slept only by turns, in order to guard against wild beasts.

(*b*). **1586** A. Day *Eng. Secretary* ii. (1625) 59 The next and last in turne, are those letters familiar. **1688** Prior *Ode* v, Why does each consenting Sign With prudent Harmony combine In Turns to move? **1832** Tennyson *Palace of Art*, '*I send you here a sort of allegory*' 14 He that shuts Love out, in turn shall be Shut out from Love. **1883** Fenn *Middy & Ensign* xxxv, They would take it in turns to sleep. **1908** [Miss Fowler] *Betw. Trent & Ancholme* 303 The daughters in turn riding on pillion-seat.

(*c*). **1573–80** Baret *Alv.* T 430 By course, or euerie man in his turne, *alternis*. **1710** W. King *Heathen Gods & Heroes* xi. (1722) 44 Argus..had a hundred Eyes, two of which sleeping in their Turns, the rest continu'd waking. **1781** Cowper *Charity* 74 To see the oppressor in his turn oppressed. **1861** M. Pattison *Ess.* (1889) I. 47 A committee ..in which every Hanse town was in its turn represented, according to a fixed cycle. **1864** Bryce *Holy Rom. Emp.* viii. (1875) 143 Germany became in her turn the instructress of the neighbouring tribes.

(*d*). **1650** Earl Monm. tr. *Senault's Man bec. Guilty* 357 Being weary of obeying, they fain would command their turn about. **1709** T. Robinson *Vind. Mosaick Syst.* 94 The Cock..Sitting upon the Eggs his turn about. **1802** H. Martin *Helen of Glenross* II. 14 To complete the turn-about good offices, Frances can marry your cast-off Sedley. **1821** Scott *Kenilw.* xv, Fit to sit low at the board, carve turn about with the chaplain. **1833** T. Hook *Widow & Marquess* vii, Turn-about is all fair play. **1834** [S. Smith] *Lett. J. Downing* xxvii. (1835) 176 When one gets drunk, tother keeps sober, and so they take turn and turn about. **1840** E. E. Napier *Scenes & Sports For. Lands* II. v. 174 We took it turn and turn to send out [etc.]. **1848** Mrs. Gaskell *M. Barton* ix. (1882) 23/2 We took it turn and turn about to sit up and rock th' babby.

**29.** *spec.* **a.** The time during which one workman or body of workmen is at work in alternation with another or others; a shift. (Cf. 24.)

**1793** Smeaton *Edystone L.* § 230, I proposed to visit each company..once in each company's turn, if wind and weather should permit. **1883** Gresley *Gloss. Coal-mining, Turn*, the hours during which coals, &c., are being raised from the mine. **1897** *Worc. County Express* 3 Apr., In the turn's work, six hours, Potts would have been able to make 1½ dozen shades.

**b.** *Theatr.* 'A public appearance on the stage, preceding or following others' (Farmer *Slang*); an item in a variety entertainment; also *transf.* applied to the performer.

**1890** *Even. News & Post* 9 June 1/7 The wire-walking of Mme. Zuila and her little girl..furnishes a clever and interesting turn. **1905** *Daily News* 15 July 8 An animal 'turn' new to England will be seen at the Palace Theatre..Kern and his Mimic Dog have been drawing crowded houses..in Paris. **1907** *Times* 30 Jan 6/6 Under the barring clause the gentleman, who is not a big turn, did not appear.

**30.** Requirement, need, exigency; purpose, use, convenience. *arch.* (Chiefly in special phrases; see below.)

**1573** Tusser *Husb.* (1878) 33/1 To serue to burne for many a turne. **1602** *Life T. Cromwell* ii. iii, We hardly shall finde such a one as he, To fit our turnes. **1659** Hammond *On Ps.* xviii. 5 Annot. 99 Ropes or cords are proper for that turne. **1788** Jefferson *Writ.* (1859) II. 354 Such persons as his turn and time might render desirable. **1881** Mrs. Riddell *A. Spenceley* I. 285 You will answer my turn..as well as another.

**b.** Phrases. (*a*) *To serve one's turn*: to answer one's purpose or requirement; to suffice for or satisfy a need; to be useful or helpful in an emergency; to suit, answer, serve, avail, 'do'. Also in passive. So: † (*b*) *To serve a* (*this, that*, etc.) *turn* (*obs.*). (*c*) *To serve the turn*; also † *to do the turn* (cf. 23). † (*d*) *To serve turn*; also with inf. = to serve *to do* something (*obs.*). † (*e*) *To serve* or *do the turn of*, to serve the purpose of, do instead of (*obs.*). (*f*) *To serve one's* (*one's own*, or *a*) *turn* (said of the person): to compass one's own purpose; to consult one's own need. (Cf. (*a*).) † Also with *by, on, upon*: to operate by or upon another in order to gain one's end; to make use of for one's own purposes. † (*g*) *For one's turn*: (suitable) for one's requirement or purpose (*obs.*).

(*a*). **1540** Palsgr. *Acolastus* ii. iii. L iij b, Loke thou serue my tourne, what so euer I saye [orig. *Fac uerbis meis subseruias*]. **1576** Gascoigne *Steel Gl.* Wks. 1910 II. 159 Let not the Mercer pul thee by the sleeve For sutes of silke, when cloth may serve thy turne. **1647** N. Bacon *Disc. Govt. Eng.* i. xvi. (1739) 32 The turns both of Pope and King were competently served. **1742** Fielding *Jos. Andrews* i. xiv, Nothing would serve the fellow's turn but tea. *a* **1859** Macaulay *Hist. Eng.* xxiii. V. 72 Pipes he could not obtain; but a cow's horn perforated served his turn.

(*b*). **1577** B. Googe *Heresbach's Husb.* i. (1586) 10 It serueth other turnes beside. **1586** in *Eng. Hist. Rev.* Jan. (1914) 117 The lord chauncellor should have a serjant at armes.. and hathe none,..his gentleman ussher sarvethe that torne. *a* **1628** Preston *New Covt.* (1634) 17 All the fish in the Sea should be..little enough to serve such a turne. **1687** Dryden *Hind & P.* iii. 65, I serv'd a turn, and then was cast away.

(*c*). **1551** in Feuillerat *Revels Edw. VI* (1914) 57 Furnysshed of suche thinges..as yourself shall thyncke convenient to serue the turne. **1591** Shaks. *Two Gent.* iii. i. 131 A cloake as long as thine will serue the turne? **1594** J. Melvill *Diary* (Wodrow Soc.) 318 The forces that war reposit on to do the turn. **1669** Sturmy *Mariner's Mag.* Advt. C iij b, Where the Fear of God is not, no Art can serve the turn. **1731** Miller *Gard. Dict.* s.v. *Wine*, A little Yeast,..or even a little new Wine may serve the Turn. **1768** Ross *Helenore* ii. 79 Nor will sick aff setts do the turn wi' me.

(*d*). *a* **1638** Mede *Wks.* (1672) 68 To say the Ark was brought thither upon this occasion, will not serve turn. **1667** Poole *Dial. betw. Protest. & Papist* (1735) 91 This may serve Turn, to let you see, that I had Warrant to say, that [etc.]. **1700** Tyrrell *Hist. Eng.* II. 847 When the Lyon's Skin alone would not serve turn, he knew how to make it out with that of the Fox.

(*e*). **1577** B. Googe *Heresbach's Husb.* ii. 49 b, Some Pompe is to be made, or Kettell, Myll, or such like, as may serue the turne of a naturall streame. *a* **1653** Binning *Serm.* (1845) 605 Imputed righteousness comes in as a covering over the man's nakedness, and doth the turn of perfect inherent holiness. **1818** Scott *Br. Lamm.* ix, As if there werena men eneugh in the castle, or as if I couldna serve the turn of ony o' them that are out o' the gate.

(*f*). **1581** Mulcaster *Positions* v. (1887) 32 Necessitie caught hold of it, to serue her owne tourne. **1583** Golding *Calvin on Deut.* iii. 13 Although Iethro was an heathen man: yet did God serue his owne turne by him [orig. *Dieu s'est servi de luy*] in this behalfe. **1604** Shaks. *Oth.* i. i. 42, I follow him to serue my turne vpon him. **1664** Butler *Hud.* ii. ii. 123 If the Dev'l, to serve his turn, Can tell Truth. **1697** Bentley *Phal.* (1699) 114 Changing a plain Reading against the Authority of three MSS,..purely to serve a turn. **1759** Bp. Hurd *Moral Dial.* iv. 154 A parade of courage, put on to serve a turn, and keep her people in spirits. **1855** Macaulay *Hist. Eng.* xii. III. 208 Those slanderers who had accused him of affecting zeal for religious liberty merely in order to serve a turn.

(*g*). **1579** W. Wilkinson *Confut. Familye of Loue* 38 b, To judge, if that..shalbe for their turne or no. **1625** Ussher in *Lett. Lit. Men* (Camden) 132 For my turne he is altogether unfit. **1719** De Foe *Crusoe* (1840) II. xii. 256 When.. I could find a ship for my turn. **1773** *Life N. Frowde* 25, I am not a Man for their turn.

**VI.** Various other abstract senses, of later development.

**31.** Style, character, quality; *esp.* style of language, arrangement of words in a sentence. (Cf. Turn *v.* 5 b.)

**1601** B. Jonson *Poetaster* iii. i, Doubtlesse this gallants tongue has a good turne when hee sleeps. **1692** Dryden *St. Euremont's Ess.* Pref. 6 A Purity of Language, and a beautiful turn of Words, so little understood by modern Writers. **1697** Bentley *Phal.* (1699) 158 It has not the Turn and Composition of a Greek Name. **1718** *Free-thinker* No. 80 ¶ 3 Her Turn of Wit was gentle, polite, and insinuating. **1825** Mrs. Sherwood *Yng. Forester* i. 5 Such a turn of behaviour as enabled him to conceal much roguery under a smooth appearance. **1869** Gladstone *Juv. Mundi* i. 15 A careful comparison..between the Odyssey and Iliad, and of a number of particulars of turn and manner.

**32.** (with *a* and *pl.*) A modification of phraseology for a particular effect, or as a grace or embellishment; a special point or detail of style or expression (in literary work, or *transf.* in art, etc.).

**1693** Dryden *Juvenal* Ded. (1697) 84 Had I time, I cou'd enlarge on the beautiful Turns of Words and Thoughts; which are as requisite in this, as in Heroique Poetry. **1705** Addison *Italy, Ferrara* 121 There is a Turn in the Third Verse that we lose by not knowing the Circumstances. **1738** Earl of Oxford in *Portland Papers* (Hist. MSS. Comm.) VI. 178 The dress of this person..gives a turn and life to the other figures...He is leading her up and has one foot upon the step, which gives a fine turn. **1868** M. E. G. Duff *Pol. Surv.* 4 His felicitous turns of expression.

**33.** Form, make, mould, cast (of a material object). Cf. Turn *v.* 5 a. ? *Obs.*

**1702** Addison *Dial. Medals* ii. (1726) 84 The Roman poets, in their descriptions of a beautiful man, so often mentioning the Turn of his Neck and Arms. **1709** Steele *Tatler* No. 75 ¶ 8 The Turn of Faces he meets as soon as he passes Cheapside-Conduit. **1748** *Anson's Voy.* iii. iii. 325 For.. rollers..the body of the coco-nut tree was..useful;..its smoothness and circular turn..fitted it for the purpose.

**34.** Natural inclination, disposition, bent; aptitude, capacity for something. Usually const. *for* (rarely *to*), or with defining adj. (Cf. Turn *v.* 5 c.)

**1702** Rowe *Tamerl.* Ded., That happy Turn which your Lordship has to Business. **1736** Butler *Anal.* Introd. 6 A person of such a Turn of Mind. **1749** Wesley *Acc. School at Kingswood* 3 They..learn, (those who have a Turn for it) to make Verses. *a* **1763** W. King *Lit. & Polit. Anecd.* (1819) 67 Ladies..who have a fine understanding and a turn to poetry. **1812** Sir H. Davy *Chem. Philos.* 15 He [Roger Bacon] was a man of a truly philosophical turn, desirous of investigating nature. **1821** Scott *Kenilw.* xi, But Flibbertigibbet..hath that about him which may redeem his turn for mischievous frolic. **1844** Alb. Smith *Adv. Mr. Ledbury* i, Mr. Ledbury was of an inquiring turn of mind. **1854** Milman *Lat. Chr.* iv. i. (1864) II. 190 The rude and simple Arab had..no turn to or comprehension of metaphysical subtlety. **1871** Napheys *Prev. & Cure Dis.* i. ii. 58 Persons of a dyspeptic turn.

**b.** *transf.* That to which (the age or time) is disposed. (Cf. *the fashion, the rage.*) *rare*⁻¹.

**1709** Swift *Advanc. Relig.* Wks. 1755 II. i. 114 This is not to be accomplished [but] by introducing religion as much as possible to be the turn and fashion of the age.

† **c.** ? Aptitude, talent. *Obs. rare*⁻¹.

**1721** Cibber *Refusal* i. (1777) 19 Honest Witling is not to be put out of humour, I see. *Gran.* No, faith, nor out of countenance. *Wit.* Not I, faith..; and a man of turn may say any thing to me.

† **d.** A particular element of the disposition; a characteristic; in quot. 1745, a characteristic act.

**1729** Law *Serious C.* vi. (1732) 84 Some turn of mind, which every good Christian is called upon to renounce. **1745** P. Thomas *Jrnl. Anson's Voy.* 313 A true French Turn, and not unlike old Lewis le Grand's singing Te Deum for being defeated. **1764** Sterne in Traill *Life* (1882) 85 This amiable turn of his character.

**e.** *Turn of speed*, capacity for speed, ability to run or go fast.

**1867** in Sir M. G. Gerard *Leaves fr. Diaries* iii. 65 Showing an unexpected turn of speed. **1894** Astley *50 Y. my Life* I. 35, I discovered that I possessed a fair turn of speed.

**35.** Direction, tendency, drift, trend. (Cf. Turn *v.* 26, 28.)

**1704** M. Henry *Commun. Comp.* iv. Wks. 1853 I. 312/1 If this blessed turn be given to the bent of my soul. **1719** De Foe *Crusoe* (1840) II. vi. 143 Providence gave a..happy turn to all this. **1736** Butler *Anal.* ii. vii. 355, I know no pretence for saying the general turn of them [prophecies] is capable of any other [application]. **1815** Scott *Guy M.* xxxii, 'What turn did your conversation take?' said Glossin. **1845** J. Coulter *Adv. in Pacific* xiii. 180 Four days after, I discovered what gave my thoughts a new turn.

**36.** A change from the original intention; a particular construction or interpretation put upon something: usually with *give*.

**1710** Palmer *Proverbs* 141 His best actions [are] thrown by and lessen'd by false turns. **1749** Fielding *Tom Jones* vii. v, For heaven's sake, sir,..do not give so cruel a turn to my silence. **1796** Jane Austen *Pride & Prej.* x, You are giving it a turn which that gentleman did by no means intend. **1850** Mrs. Jameson *Leg. Monast. Ord.* (1863) 85 The turn which they have given to the story differs altogether from what I conceive to be the real significance.

**VII.** Various technical senses.

**37.** A measure of various commodities, etc. (? the quantity dealt with at one 'turn' or stroke of work: cf. 24).

**a.** A quantity or measure by which some fish are sold: of loose haddocks it is ten stone or 140 lbs.: see also quot. 1674. **b.** (See quot.) **c.** A load of wood or other commodity; also in *Logging*: see quot. 1905. **d.** *Fur trade.* A bundle of sixty skins. **e.** *Mining.* The number of cars filled by a miner during his turn or shift (cf. 29 a).

**a. 1674** Jeake *Arith.* (1696) 66 Soles. In 1 Turn 4. **1882** *Daily News* 9 Mar. 2/8 Plaice, 30s. per turn. **1895** *Times* 7 Jan. 3/5 Haddocks,..25s. to 30s. per turn.

**b. 1805** R. W. Dickson *Pract. Agric.* II. 923 Turn of Water.—As much as can be distributed at a single operation by the management of the hatches within the reach of the labourers employed.

**c.** *c* **1888** J. C. Harris in *Harper's Mag.* Apr. 704/2 Sometimes he would bring a 'turn' of wood, sometimes a bag of meal or potatoes. **1893** *Daily News* 9 Jan. 5/7 Another has slipped while carrying a 'turn' of deal upon his shoulders. **1905** *Terms Forestry & Logging* (U.S. Dep. Agric., Forestry, Bulletin No. 61), *Turn*,..two or more logs coupled together end to end for hauling.

**d. 1891** in *Cent. Dict.* **1897** *19th Cent.* Nov. 737 A turn means sixty skins and the rate of pay is 11d per turn.

**38.** The amount of some commodity turned out or produced: = Turn-out 9.

**1875** R. F. Martin tr. *Havrez' Winding Mach.* 9 The steel cages..had worked for four years, with a daily 'turn' of 637 tons (coal and dirt together).

**39.** *Comm.* (in full, *turn of the market*): A change in price, or the difference between the buying and selling prices, of a stock or commodity; the profit made by this.

**1882** Bithell *Counting-Ho. Dict.*, *Turn of the Market*. The 'turn of the market', or the 'jobbers' turn', is the difference between the two prices quoted in the official lists for stocks, shares, &c...Consols are quoted 99¾ to ⅞, and it means that the jobber, when asked the price of Consols at that moment, was prepared to give 99¾ for them, or to sell them at 99⅞. The difference between the two is the compensation to the jobber. **1885** *Pall Mall G.* 23 May 5/2 Brokers coming together without paying exorbitant 'turns' to the middleman—that is, the jobber. **1897** *Daily News* 28 June 2/7 Tows, hemps, and flaxes are also the turn dearer. **1913** Edith Wharton *Custom of Country* ii. xi, In consequence of a lucky 'turn' in the Street.

**VIII.** Collocations and Combinations.

**40.** With adverbs, forming sb. phrases corresponding to the adverbial combinations of the verb (see Turn *v.* VIII): as *turn in*, an act of turning in. (Most commonly with hyphen or as one word; see Turn-, Turnabout, etc.)

**1833** T. Hook *Parson's Dau.* iii. i, Now for..a glass of grog, and then for a turn in.

**41.** *attrib.* and *Comb.*, as *turn-claimer* (see quot.), † *turn-keeping* sb. and adj., *turn movement*. *Turn toll*: see Toll *sb.*[1] 2 h. See also Turn-serving.

**1610** Holland *Camden's Brit.* i. 195 A rocke about whose foote the tides turne-keeping play. **1708** *Constit. Watermen's Co.* xxxiii. 38 The Country-Watermen shall have equal Privilege and Turn keeping with the Towns-men. **1892** *Labour Commission* Gloss., *Turn-claimers*, the persons occupied in a coal-mine who possess the privilege of claiming a 'ben'., that is a tub to fill in turn. **1908** *Installation News* II. 14 The switch has a turn movement worked from the outside.

**Turn** (tɜːn), *v.* Forms: *α.* 1 tyrnan, 3 tuyrne; 3 teorne, 3–5 terne, 5 tern. *β.* 1 turnian, 3 (*Orm.*) turrnenn, (3–4 teurne), 3–7 turne, 4-6 *Sc.* twrn(e, 4- turn; 3-6 torne, 4-6 tourne, 4-7 torn. [OE. *tyrnan* and *turnian*, both ad. L. *tornāre* to turn in a lathe, round off, f. *torn-us* a lathe, a turner's wheel = Gr. τόρνος a carpenter's tool to draw circles with, compasses, whence τορνεύειν to turn, work with a lathe; perhaps reinforced in ME. by OF. *torner, turner, tourner*, F. *tourner*, Pic. *torner*, Prov., Sp. *tornar*, It. *tornare*, all :—L. *tornāre*; cf. OHG. *turnen*, Icel. *turna* to turn (*turnera* to tilt, joust, Norw. dial. *tunna* to swing, whirl), ad. F. *tourner*.

On the twofold representation of L. *tornāre* in OE. see Pogatscher *Latein. u. Roman. Lehnworte im Altenglischen*, §§ 9, 159, 271; he shows that the umlauted *tyrnan* must have already existed *c*600.

The pa. pple. in Southern Eng. in the 12-13th c. had commonly the prefix *i-, y-, i-tyrnd, i-turned*, and the pa. t. was freq. *i-turnde*; there is also one instance of the infinitive *i-turnen* in the earlier text of Layamon, but no known instance in OE. of a compound *getyrnan or *geturnian; these ME. forms with *i-, y-* have therefore been included here.]

*General arrangement of senses.* I. To rotate or revolve, and derived uses: 1-3. II. To form or shape by rotation, and derived uses: 4-5. III. To change or reverse position: * Senses denoting change of position: 6-9; ** Senses denoting reversal of position: 10-12. IV. To change or reverse course or direction: * denoting change of course or direction: 13-18; ** denoting reversal of course or direction: 19-21. V. Senses allied to III and IV, but referring specially to direction or destination: 22-34. VI. To change, alter: * general senses: 35-43; ** specific senses: 44-47. VII. Phrases, * with sb.: 48-60; ** with adj. or advb. phrase: 61-63; *** with another verb: 64. VIII. In comb. with adverbs (*turn about, again, aside, in, out, up*, etc.): 65-80. (Combinations formed on the vb.-stem are given in a separate article, TURN-, or as Main words.)

I. To rotate or revolve, and derived senses.

**1.** *trans.* To cause to move round on an axis or about a centre; to cause to rotate or revolve, as a wheel.

See also *turn about*, 65 c; *turn round*, 78 d.

*c* 1000 ÆLFRIC *Saints' Lives* xiv. 93 Þa tyrndon þa hæðenan hetelice þæt hweowl. *a* 1300 *Cursor M.* 23719 (Cott.) Dame fortune turnes [*Gött.* ternes] þan hir quele And castes vs dun vntil a wele. *c* 1440 *Promp. Parv.* 507/2 Turnon forthe, *idem quod* trolle [502/2 Tryllyn, or trollyn, *volvo*]. 1599 SHAKS. *Much Ado* II. i. 261 She would haue made Hercules haue turnd spit. 1687 A. LOVELL tr. *Thevenot's Trav.* II. 38 There were two Boys.., one turning a wheel by the handle, to grind the Coffee, and the other boyling it. 1781 COWPER *Retirement* 334 Waters turning busy mills. 1852 THACKERAY *Esmond* III. ix, Preparing paste, and turning rolling-pins.

**b.** To cause to move round, or (usually) partly round, in this way, esp. for opening or closing something: as a key, tap, door-handle, screw, etc.

*a* 1300 *Cursor M.* 16906 (Cott.) Þe prince o preistes..sperd it wit a mikel stan, To turn i-nogh had tuent [?twenty]. 1382 WYCLIF *Prov.* xxvi. 14 As a dore is turned in his heeng. 1593 SHAKS. *Rich. II*, v. iii. 36 Giue me leaue, that I may turne the key, That no man enter. 1655 [see COCK *sb.*[1] 12]. *a* 1715 BURNET *Own Time* (1823) I. 401 He..turned all the cocks that were then open, and stopped the water. 1880 P. GREG *Errant* III. xi. 158 The lamp was turned very low. [Cf. 71 g.] 1890 FENN *Double Knot* III. xiv. 192 She softly turned the handle of the door.

**c.** To perform by revolving, as a somersault.

1860 [see SOMERSAULT]. 1863 [see COACH-WHEEL 3]. 1864 [see CART-WHEEL 3]. 1881 [see CATHERINE WHEEL 4].

**2.** *intr.* To move round on an axis or about a centre; to rotate, revolve, whirl, spin, as a wheel; to move partly round in this way, as a door or the like upon hinges, a key, a weathercock, etc.

See also *turn about*, 65 a; *t. round*, 78 a.

*c* 1000 *Sax. Leechd.* III. 270 Se firmamentum went on ðam twam steorran, swa swa hweoȝel tyrnð on eaxe. *c* 1330 R. BRUNNE *Chron. Wace* (Rolls) 1453 Nykeres..brynge schipmen..To som swelw to turne or steke. *c* 1435 *Torr. Portugal* 188 They tornyd xxxii tymys, In armys walloyng fast. 1560 BIBLE (Genev.) *Prov.* xxvi. 14 As the dore turneth vpon his henges. 1589 PUTTENHAM *Eng. Poesie* II. xi. (Arb.) 111 The Roundell or Spheare is..most voluble and apt to turne. 1698 KEILL *Exam. Th. Earth* (1734) 109 Jupiter ..turns round his own Axis in..ten hours. 1796 MME. D'ARBLAY *Camilla* I. 259 A little boy..turning head over heels. 1843 MACAULAY *Horatius* lxix, The kid turns on the spit. 1890 MRS. LAFFAN *Louis Draycott* III. ii, The key turned and grated in the lock.

**b.** *fig.* To revolve (as time, etc.). In later use said chiefly of the head or brain: To have a sensation as of whirling; to be affected with giddiness; to reel, swim, be in a whirl. (Cf. 45 c, 78 a.)

*c* 1000 ÆLFRIC *Hom.* (Th.) I. 514 Þa arleasan turniað on ymbhwyrfte. *c* 1200 ORMIN 3641 All þiss middellærdess þing Aȝȝ turrneþþ her & wharrfeþþ..swa summ þe wheol. *c* 1230, 1398 [see TURNING *vbl. sb.* 1 b]. *c* 1400 *Destr. Troy* 9400 The tyme of the tru turnyde to end. 1605 SHAKS. *Lear* IV. vi. 23 How fearefull..And dizie 'tis, to cast ones eyes so low...Ile looke no more, Least my braine turne. 1853 M. ARNOLD *Requiescat* 9 Her life was turning, turning, In mazes of heat and sound. 1892 STEVENSON & L. OSBOURNE *Wrecker* vi. 93, I looked at the handbill and my head turned.

**3.** *Turn on* or *upon* (fig.): **a.** To hinge upon, depend on, have as the centre or pivot of movement or action.

1661 J. STEPHENS *Procurations* 26 They that turn upon this hinge, I mean that receive Procurations upon the ground of Custome. 1712 SWIFT *Conduct of Allies* ¶ 35 Great Events often turn upon very small Circumstances. 1823 *Examiner* 268/2 The plot..turns upon the secret marriage of Claudio. 1892 *Sat. Rev.* 2 Jan. 2/2 The contest..is to turn on Home Rule.

**b.** To have as its subject, be about or concerned with, relate to: usually said of conversation or debate.

App. orig. a development of prec. sense, but often associated with other senses: cf. 28.

1711 ADDISON *Spect.* No. 119 ¶ 7 As the two Points of Good Breeding, which I have..insisted upon, regard Behaviour and Conversation, there is a third which turns upon Dress. 1729 BUTLER *Serm.* Wks. 1874 II. 49 That the conversation might turn upon somewhat instructive. 1879 M. PATTISON *Milton* xiii. 203 The Dutch drama turns entirely on the revolt of the angels. 1884 *Manch. Exam.* 26 May 4/7 The debate..did not turn upon any..practical proposition.

II. To form or shape by rotation, and derived senses.

**4.** *trans.* To shape, esp. into a rounded form, by cutting with a chisel or similar tool while rotating in a lathe; to form, work, or make by means of a lathe. Also *absol.* to work with a lathe.

*c* 1305 *Land Cockayne* 68 in *E. E. P.* (1862) 158 Þe pilers of þat cloistre alle Beþ i-turned of cristale. 1341-2 *Ely Sacr. Rolls* (1907) II. 117 In le turning xxx bases pro columpnis. *c* 1440 *Promp. Parv.* 507/2 Turnon, or throwe treyne [*S.* trene] vessel, *torno.* 1504 in *Bury Wills* (Camden) 101, I wyll that my sonne..shall haue..also ij cheyres, on turnyd and the other closse. 1600 J. PORY tr. *Leo's Africa* v. 253 Such as turne wooden vessels. 1756 MRS. CALDERWOOD in *Coltness Collect.* (Maitl. Club) 212 A famous turner.., he turns things in ivory that would exceed beleif. 1833 J. HOLLAND *Manuf. Metal* II. 140 In turning..metals ..and even wood, much depends upon the proper management of the tools. 1858 RAMSAY *Remin.* iv. (1870) 80 He.. taught us to saw, and to plane, and to turn.

**b.** *Building.* To form, construct, build (an arched or vaulted structure).

1703 MOXON *Mech. Exerc.* 256 You may turn Arches over those insufficient places,..and..Arches inversed, or upside down. 1720 W. STUKELEY *Mem. & Corr.* (Surtees) I. 32 At this time [1706-7]..the great arch of boards was made to turn the Cupola of St. Pauls. 1828 ELMES *Metrop. Improv.* 88 The arches for the coal-cellars [were] turned.

**c.** *Cookery.* To pare off the rind or peel of (an orange, lemon, etc.) round and round in a long narrow thin strip; to stone (an olive) in this way.

1706 PHILLIPS (ed. Kersey), *Turning* (among Confectioners) a..manner of paring..Oranges and Lemons when the.. Rind..is par'd off very thin and narrow..; turning it [the knife] round about the Fruit, so as the Peel may be extended to a very great length. 1846 SOYER *Cookery* 43 Turning or peeling mushrooms is an art that practice alone can attain. 1904 *Daily Chron.* 6 June 8/5 Soak the olives in cold water.., drain thoroughly and proceed to 'turn' them...This means to peel them very evenly..so that it unfolds..in one strip, which will close up again..without the stone in the centre when done.

**d.** *Knitting* and *Lace-making.* To make in a curved form: see quots.

1882 CAULFEILD & SAWARD *Dict. Needlework* 504/1 *Turn Heel*—See Knitting Stockings. *Ibid.* 504/2 *To Turn a Scallop*: work across to the inside..but instead of completing the edge, work back with the same pair of Bobbins [etc.]...Repeat until the scallop has been rounded. 1902 R. BAGOT *Donna Diana* viii. 93 She was always knitting, and appeared to be in a perpetual state of turning the heel of a stocking.

**5.** *fig.* To shape, form, or fashion artistically or gracefully: **a.** a material object: usually into a rounded form, as if shaped on a lathe. Chiefly in *pa. pple.*

1616 B. JONSON *Devil an Ass* II. vi, This smooth, round, And well torn'd chin. 1695 BLACKMORE *Pr. Arthur* IV. 88 He turn'd their Orbs, and polish'd all the Stars. 1711 STEELE *Spect.* No. 2 ¶ 5 His Person is well turn'd. 1847 L. HUNT *Men, Women, & B.* I. xiv. 273 The hand long, delicate, and well turned. 1855 THACKERAY in *Yates' Recoll.* (1884) I. 280 The T of the signature..is [not] near so elegant as my ordinary T's are;..my attention was drawn off just as I was turning it.

**b.** a piece of literary work, a tune, a compliment, etc.

1636 B. JONSON *Discov.* Wks. (Rtldg.) 762/2 Cast not away the quills..; but bring all to the forge and file again; torn it anew. 1687 A. LOVELL tr. *Thevenot's Trav.* I. C j b, The Reader..is not to expect that the Language should be so Accurate, nor the Style so well turned, as [etc.]. 1791 BOSWELL *Johnson* an. 1754, Some studied compliments, so finely turned, that [etc.]. 1849 THACKERAY *Pendennis* ix, If I could turn a tune,..I should sing. 1850 W. IRVING *Goldsmith* xv. 178 Turning a couplet.

†**c.** *pa. pple.* Of a person (or the mind, etc.): Naturally adapted, fitted, or 'cut out' for some pursuit. *Obs.*

1671 TEMPLE *Let. to de Witt* Wks. 1731 II. 247, I find I am better turned for making a good Gard'ner. 1723 in *Eng. Hist. Rev.* Jan. (1912) 56 *note*, A head the most turned for business of any I have known. 1728 SWIFT *Jrnl. Mod. Lady* 36 By nature turn'd to play the rake. 1767 *Woman of Fashion* I. 41 A Genius like her's, is little turn'd to Business.

III. To change or reverse position.

* *Senses denoting change of position.*

**6.** *intr.* To move or shift (by a rotary motion, or through an angle) so as to change one's posture or position; *esp.* to shift the body (as on an axis) from side to side; to twist or writhe about.

*To make a person turn in his grave*: see GRAVE *sb.*[1] 1 d.

*c* 1000 ÆLFRIC *Hom.* (Th.) II. 508 He ealle ȝefæstnode heora fet to eorðan...Hi tyrndon mid bodiȝe, ȝebiȝedum sceancum. *c* 1205 LAY. 4586 Scipen þer sunken...In þa teonfulle sæ Torneden sæiles. *c* 1394 *P. Pl. Crede* 543 But he lepe vp on heiȝ,..& þi name lakke Wiþ proude wordes... And turne as a tyrant þat turmenteþ him-selue [etc.]. 1500-20 DUNBAR *Poems* lxix. 11, I walk [= wake], I turne, sleip may I nocht. *a* 1700 DRYDEN (J.), I turn'd, and try'd each corner of my bed, To find if sleep were there, but sleep was lost. 1827 SCOTT *Chron. Canongate* v, Turning to the other side to enjoy his slumbers. 1881 MRS. LYNN LINTON *My Love* II. v. 92 It is enough to make your poor father turn in his grave. 1888 [see GRAVE *sb.*[1] 1 d].

**b.** To move circularly or as on a pivot, so as to face all ways successively, or so as ultimately to face in the opposite direction. (Cf. 2, 10.)

1500-20 DUNBAR *Poems* lxvi. 43 On thair conscience..May turne aucht oxin and ane wane. 1644 EVELYN *Diary* 8 Feb., Capable of containing an hundred coaches to turne commodiously. 1893 *Chamb. Jrnl.* 28 Jan. 50/2 She veered as if she would turn within her own length.

**c.** Said of the scale or beam of a balance, or of the balance itself: To move up or down from the horizontal position. (Cf. 49, 58.)

1596 SHAKS. *Merch. V.* IV. i. 330 If the scale doe turne But in the estimation of a hayre. 1654 tr. *Scudery's Curia Pol.* 59 To weigh in the Scales and not discern how the Beam turnes. 1827 FARADAY *Chem. Manip.* ii. (1842) 25 Another balance..turning with about one-half or one-third of a grain.

**7.** *trans.* To alter the position or posture of (an object) by moving it through an angle; to move (a thing or person) into a different posture.

1377 LANGL. *P. Pl.* B. XVII. 183 Vnfolden or folden, my fuste & myn paume, Al is but an hande [= one hand] how so I torne it. *c* 1440 *Promp. Parv.* 507/1 Turnon a thynge, *verto, verso.* 1578 BANISTER *Hist. Man* v. 65 Some partes of the skinne are wholly immoueable, and resistant to turne. 1644 S. KEM *Messengers Prepar.* 22 He speaks too late.. for a reprieve, when the ladder is turned. 1711 ADDISON *Spect.* No. 120 ¶ 14 When she [a hen] has laid her Eggs.., what Care does she take in turning them frequently! 1720 WATTS *Moral Songs, Sluggard* i, As the door on its hinges, so he on his bed Turns his sides, and his shoulders, and his heavy head. 1843 R. J. GRAVES *Syst. Clin. Med.* ix. 100 He cannot be lifted up or even turned in bed, without having a tendency to faint. 1885 'MRS. ALEXANDER' *At Bay* iv, He took up a paper-knife, which he turned restlessly to and fro.

**b.** *refl.* = senses 6, 6 b. *Obs.* or *arch.*

13.. *Sir Beues* (A.) 4414 Þat lane was so narw..He ne Arondel, is stede, Ne miȝte him terne. *c* 1385 CHAUCER *L. G. W.* Prol. 144 Vpon the braunches..In hire delyt, they turned hem ful ofte. 1509 HAWES *Past. Pleas.* xvi. (Percy Soc.) 75, I myght not lye styll; On every syde I tourned me ful ofte.

**8.** *fig.* To consider in different aspects; to revolve in the mind. (See also *turn over*, 77 e.)

1725 [see *turn about*, 65 e]. 1825 T. HOOK *Sayings* Ser. II. *Sutherl.* (Colburn) 54 Turn these things in your mind. 1891 *Strand Mag.* II. 483/2, I pondered over it, and turned it every way in my mind.

**9.** To give a curved or crooked form to; to bend or twist; † to fold (quot. 1303); † to form by twisting, to plait (quot. 1665); to bend or twist *round* something so as to encircle it (quot. 1821); to form by bending (quot. 1827[2]). (Cf. *turn down*, 71 a.)

1303 R. BRUNNE *Handl. Synne* 1153 [He] bade hym take A sak.. And.. turne hyt tweyfolde..And ley hyt on hys fadyr for colde. 14.. *Sloane MS.* 1986 lf. 19 b, Wyspes drawen out at fote and syde, Wele wrethyn and turnyd. 1665 HOOKE *Microgr.* xxvii. 149 Let all the sides of this Box be turned of Basket-work. 1821 SCOTT *Kenilw.* xiv, A bonnet ..encircled with a gold chain turned three times round it. 1827 — *Surg. Dau.* xiv, His mustaches were turned and curled. 1827 FARADAY *Chem. Manip.* xiv. (1842) 307 Those [tubes] which are turned or bent, and soldered with gold, will not bear the high temperature.

**b.** *spec.* To bend back (the edge of a sharp instrument) so as to make it useless for cutting; to blunt in this way. *To turn edge*, to have the edge thus bent, to become blunt. Also *fig.*

*a* 1568 ASCHAM *Scholem.* (Arb.) 32 Quicke wittes are..like ouer sharpe tooles, whose edges be verie soone turned. 1593 SHAKS. 2 *Hen. VI*, II. i. 180 This Newes I thinke hath turn'd your Weapons edge. 1639 FULLER *Holy War* v. iii. (1647) 234 However at this time they might turn edge, they had formerly been true blades for his Holinesse. 1673-4 GREW *Anat. Trunks* II. vii. § 3 It turns not the edge of their Knives. 1714 FIDDES *Pract. Disc.* II. 82 A difficulty sufficient to turn the edge of the finest wit. 1879 J. C. SHAIRP *Burns* viii. 193 When the caustic wit is beginning to get too biting, the edge of it is turned by a touch of kindlier humour.

**c.** *To turn* (a person) *round one's* (*little*) *finger*, a proverbial phrase denoting that one can 'do what one likes' with him. (Cf. *turn and wind*, 64 b.)

1855 [see FINGER *sb.* 3 a]. 1861 HUGHES *Tom Brown at Oxf.* xxv. (1889) 244, I am sure one could turn him round one's finger.

**d.** *intr.* for *pass.* To assume a curved form, to bend; to become blunted by bending. (See also *turn again*, 66 e.)

[1579: see *turn again*, 66 e.] 1815 J. SMITH *Panorama Sc. & Art* I. 4 If..it be too soft,..the edge will turn or bend.

** *Senses denoting reversal of position.*

**10.** *trans.* To reverse the position or posture of; to move into the contrary position, so that the upper side becomes the under (= *turn* UPSIDE DOWN), or the front the back; to invert.

See also *turn about*, 65 d; *turn over*, 77 a; *turn round*, 78 e. *To turne turtle*: see TURTLE *sb.*[2] 2.

*c* **1200** *Trin. Coll. Hom.* 103 Wi list þu turnd [orig. L. *pronus*] on þe eorðe? aris. *c* **1440** *Douce MS. 55* lf. 15 b, Folde vppe the cake .. & turne it onys in the panne. **1533** J. HEYWOOD *Johan* A iv b, It were tyme for to tourne The pye, for ywys it doth borne. **1577** B. GOOGE tr. *Heresbach's Husb.* 46 The grasse being cutte, must be well tedded and turned. **1687** A. LOVELL tr. *Thevenot's Trav.* I. 268 They turn a half minute Sand-Glass. **1706** PHILLIPS s.v. *Literal Fault*, When a Letter is.. transpos'd or turn'd. **1773** BOSWELL *Tour Hebrides* 3 Oct., When he turned his cup at Aberbrothick, where we drank tea. **1868** MISS YONGE *Pupils of St. John* vii. 97 He turned his horse, and was about to flee. **1875** RUSKIN *Fors Clav.* V. liii. 117 Her.. fine legerdemain in turning pancakes.

†**b.** *fig.* To invert the order of, to reverse; to convert (a proposition). *Obs.*

*a* **1569** KINGESMYLL *Godly Advise* (1580) 20 Christe tourned Water into Wine. Turne not his miracle, make not, I meane, water of wine. **1654** Z. COKE *Logick* 114 These.. are not to be turned; Christ is a vine; Bread is Christs body.

**11.** *spec.* **a.** To reverse (a leaf of a book) in order to read (or write) on the other side (or on the next leaf); to do this with the leaves of (a book) in succession, to read or search through. (See also *turn over*, 77 b, and LEAF *sb.* 7 b.)

In quot. *c* 1830, to find and open at the place in (the service-books) for the organist and choir; cf. *turn up*, 80 h.

*c* **1275** LAY. 46 Laweman þes bokes bi[h]eolde An þe leues tornde [*c* 1205 wende]. **1377** LANGL. *P. Pl.* B. III. 337 Had she loked þat oþer half and þe lef torned. **1526** *Pilgr. Perf.* (W. de W. 1531) 167 Handes.. redy to turne theyr boke. **1599** DAVIES *Immort. Soul* Introd. xiv, When we have all the learned Volumes turn'd. **1688** PENTON *Guard. Instruct.* (1877) 67 Able to read Greek, and turn the Lexicon upon occasion. *c* **1830** G. ELVEY in *Bumpus's Cathedrals, Canterbury* (1906) 36 Going down.. to turn the books for the service one morning. *Mod.* I had just turned the leaf of my diary and begun to write on the other side.

**b.** To reverse the position of the turf, or of the soil, in ploughing or digging, so as to bring the under parts to the surface. Also *absol.*

In quot. 1844, to bring (seed) *under* by doing this. See also *turn in*, 72 b; *turn over*, 77 c; *turn up*, 80 f.

*c* **1477** CAXTON *Jason* 81 Thou shalt yoke hem and make hem to tourne foure rodd of londe. **1523** FITZHERB. *Husb.* § 4 Howe these plowes shulde be tempered, to plowe and turne clene. **1697** DRYDEN *Virg. Georg.* III. 138 Starting, with a bound He turns the Turf, and shakes the solid Ground. **1799** HT. LEE *Canterb. T.*, *Old Woman's T.* (ed. 2) I. 392 The earth has been newly turned. **1825** *Mirror* V. 278/2 He.. when turning peats walked.. fearlessly among the Hags of Lochar Moss. **1844** *Jrnl. R. Agric. Soc.* V. I. 62 The seed being sown on the surface, and turned under by a shallow furrow with the plough. **1892** *Sat. Rev.* 11 June 671/1 The first sod of the.. Railway was turned on Tuesday.

**c.** To reverse (a garment, etc.) so that the inner side becomes the outer, to turn inside out; hence, to alter or remake by putting the inner side outward.

**1483**, **1552** [implied in TURNED *ppl. a.* 6 c]. **1557** [implied in TURNCOAT]. **1576**– [see COAT *sb.* 13]. **1596** SHAKS. *Tam. Shr.* III. ii. 44 A paire of olde breeches thrice turn'd. **1680** V. ALSOP *Mischief Impos.* Ep. Ded., Like an old Livery new turn'd and fresh trim'd up. **1834** MRS. CARLYLE *Lett.* (1883) I. 10, I am now turning my pelisse. **1893** *Illustr. Sport. & Dram. News* 11 Feb. 774/2 A way of turning an old frock. (See also *turn one's coat* 51.)

**12.** To cause (the stomach) to reject or revolt against the food (also *transf.* and *fig.*, as in quots. 1749, 1818); *to turn the stomach of*, to nauseate, to disgust extremely.

**1622** MABBE tr. *Aleman's Guzman d'Alf.* II. 355, I may not giue it a worse word, for feare of turning thy stomake. **1738** POPE *Epil. Sat.* II. 182 This filthy simile.. Quite turns my stomach. **1749** FIELDING *Tom Jones* I. i, The one provokes .. the most languid appetite, the other turns and palls that which is.. keenest. **1818** BYRON *Ch. Har.* IV. lxxvi, The daily drug which turn'd My sickening memory. **1892** *Temple Bar Mag.* Sept. 35 Questions that would turn the stomach of a school inspector.

**b.** *intr.* Of the stomach: To be affected with nausea.

**1719** DE FOE *Crusoe* (1840) II. iv. 78 Their stomachs turned at this sight. *c* **1850** *Arab. Nts.* (Rtldg.) 159 He was obliged to take it out of his mouth again, for his stomach turned against it.

**IV.** To change or reverse course.

* *Senses denoting change of course or direction.*

**13.** *trans.* To alter the course of; to cause to go another way; to divert, deflect. (In quot. *c* 1200 *refl.* = 16.)

See also *turn aside*, 67 a; *turn off*, 73 f. *Turn house* (Mining): see quot. 1778, and cf. HOUSE *sb.*[1] 7 c.

*c* **1200** ORMIN 6568 Þatt ta þreo kingess turrndenn hemm Ut off þe rihhte wezze, & forenn till Herode. *c* **1205** LAY. 4092 He turnde his fare & ferd feorh riht to Wales. **1303** R. BRUNNE *Handl. Synne* 4624 As a shyppe þat ys turned with þe roþer. *c* **1330** — *Chron. Wace* (Rolls) 8165 Do scope þis water, & turn þe borne. **1596** SHAKS. 1 *Hen. IV*, III. i. 136 You shall haue Trent turn'd. *a* **1648** LD. HERBERT *Autobiog.* (1824) 66 His Rod over the left Ear of his Horse, which he is to use for turning him every way. *a* **1680** CHARNOCK *Attrib. God* (1834) II. 67 You.. see a.. flight of birds.. turn wing another way. **1778** PRYCE *Min. Cornub.* 99 If they are working or driving from east to west,.. and perceive the Lode is gone,.. they.. turn house as they call it, or, in other words, they drive north or south. **1794** *Act for inclosing South Kelsey* 12 Such.. Path so stopped up or turned. **1821** CLARE *Vill. Minstr.* II. 48 They turn'd the winding rivulet's course.

**b.** To check the course of; to cause to go aside or retreat (cf. 19); to throw off, keep out (wet).

*c* **1620** SANDERSON *Serm.* (1689) 204 Like an unruly colt..; no ground will hold him, no fence turn him. *a* **1658** CLEVELAND *Inund. Trent* 60 We whose unliquor'd Hides will turn no wet. **1821** CLARE *Vill. Minstr.* I. 51 Spreading thorns that turn'd a summer shower. **1843** MACAULAY *Horatius* xliv, With shield and blade Horatius Right deftly turned the blow. **1891** *Eng. Illustr. Mag.* IX. 153 The snapping of a dry stick is not sufficient to turn the tiger.

**14.** *fig.* To divert or deflect from a course of action, purpose, thought, etc.; to alter the course of (something immaterial); †sometimes (with mixture of sense 34), to pervert, misapply (*obs.*).

See also *turn aside*, 67 a; *turn off*, 73 f.

*c* **1200** ORMIN 14240 Swa to turrnenn all þe boc Till þezzre gredizznesse. *a* **1225** *Leg. Kath.* 1514 Ne mei me nowðer teone ne tintreohe turnen From mi leofmonnes luue. *a* **1340** HAMPOLE *Psalter* xvii. 41, I sall noght be turnyd fra þat entent. **1474** CAXTON *Chesse* III. iii. (1883) 95 How torne they the lawe and statutes at their pleasir. **1591** SHAKS. 1 *Hen. VI*, v. iv. 59 Will nothing turne your vnrelenting hearts? **1622** FLETCHER & MASSINGER *Prophetess* III. iii, It is not in thy power to turn this destiny. **1687** DRYDEN *Hind & P.* III. 34 She turn'd the talk. **1766** GOLDSM. *Vic. W.* xxviii, No submission can turn our severe master. **1859** JEPHSON *Brittany* xvi. 273, I.. turned the conversation to something else. **1888** BRYCE *Amer. Commw.* I. v. 55 These thirty six votes turned the election. [Cf. 49, 58.]

†**b.** To mislead, beguile, cheat. *Obs. rare*—[1].

*c* **1386** CHAUCER *Can. Yeom. Prol. & T.* 618 Hym to bigile he thoghte.. Til he had terned hym, he koude nat blynne.

†**c.** *refl.* To change one's course of action. *Obs.*

**1535** COVERDALE *Josh.* xxiv. 20 Yf ye forsake the Lorde,.. then shall the Lorde turne him, and do you euell. — *Ps.* xc. 13 Turne the agayne (o Lorde) at the last, and be gracious vnto thy seruauntes.

**15.** †**a.** To transfer, hand over. (Cf. *turn over*, 77 h.) Also *intr.* in passive sense. *Obs.*

*c* **1200** *Trin. Coll. Hom.* 185 He dude his wille þar-offe, swo ich wile mine, nu hit [property] is to me iturnd. *c* **1290** *Beket* 243 in *S. Eng. Leg.* I. 113 Þis holi Man was i-torned fram þe office of holi churche To a gret office of þe worlde. **1387** TREVISA *Higden* (Rolls) VII. 301 Þe abbot was i-chaunged and i-torned [orig. L. *translatus est*] to his owne abbay in Normandie. **1400** in *Ancestor* July (1904) 14 Yef it so be that Sir Nicholl deye.. I wil that the fornseyd place wyth alle the portenans torne to Anneys Nook myn servant. **1535** COVERDALE 1 *Chron.* xi. [x.] 14 Therfore slewe he him, & turned the kyngdome vnto Dauid. — *Lam.* v. 2 Oure enheritaunce is turned to the straungers.

**b.** 'To keep passing in a course of exchange or traffick' (J.); to cause (money or commodities) to circulate.

See also *turn over*, 77 i. *To turn the penny, to turn an honest penny*: see PENNY 9 k, HONEST *a.* 4 b.

**1605** B. JONSON *Volpone* I. i, I turne no moneys, in the publike banke. **1673** TEMPLE *Ess. Adv. Trade Irel.* in *Misc.* (1680) 119 Hide, Tallow, Butter.. yield the readiest Money of any [commodities] that are turned in this Kingdom. **1863** D. G. MITCHELL *Farm Edgewood* 214 The shopkeeper, who turns his capital three or four times in a year.

**16.** *intr.* To change one's course, so as to go in a different direction; to deviate.

See also *turn aside*, 67 b; *t. away*, 68 f; *t. down*, 71 h; *t. in*, 72 e; *t. off*, 73 k; *t. up*, 80 t.

**13..** *Sir Beues* (A.) 3669 Out of þe way ȝhe gan terne Ase ȝhe wolde do hire dedes derne. **1375** BARBOUR *Bruce* III. 106 Quhen þai þe king.. Saw sua behind his mengne rid, And saw him torne sa mony tid. **1579** GOSSON *Sch. Abuse* (Arb.) 41 Hee runnes farre that neuer turnes. **1645** EVELYN *Diary* 21 Feb., Turning a little down we came to another piazza. **1797** MRS. RADCLIFFE *Italian* i, As they turned into the Strada di Toledo he had nearly lost them. **1827** SCOTT *Highl. Widow* v, He.. turned from the road, and descended the path towards the hut. **1894** BARING-GOULD *Kitty Alone* II. 164, I shall turn to the left, and leave the road. *fig.* **1613** PURCHAS *Pilgrimage* (1614) 292 Imminent miserie,.. (they say) together with the almes, turneth from them to the poore man. **1697** DRYDEN *Æneid* Ded., Ess. (ed. Ker) II. 202 Virgil.. turns short on the sudden into some similitude, which diverts.. your attention from the main subject.

**b.** *Naut.* To beat to windward; to tack.

**1569** SIR J. HAWKINS *Voy.* (Hakl. Soc.) 37 With contrary windes blowing, whereby for feare of the shore we were faine to hale off to haue ankerhold, sometimes a whole day and a night turning vp and downe. **1633** T. JAMES *Voy.* 93 We turned amongst this Ice, staying the Ship. **1706** *Lond. Gaz.* No. 4215/3 The Wind being at North-East, they turned all that day.., but could not fetch Torbay. **1835** MARRYAT *Pirate* xvi, The sloop of war.. continued to turn to windward. **1867** SMYTH *Sailor's Word-bk.*, *Turn to windward, to*, to gain on the wind by alternate tacking.

†**c.** *Turn about* (something); to walk or travel round, circumambulate. *Obs.*

**1585** T. WASHINGTON tr. *Nicholay's Voy.* III. xxi. 110 b, They goe turning seuen times about a fouresquare towre. **1642** TASMAN *Jrnl.* in *Acc. Sev. Late Voy.* I. (1694) 135 In turning about this Island there appeared very few Men.

**d.** Of the wind: To shift, so as to blow from a different quarter.

**1610** HOLLAND *Camden's Brit.* (1637) 587 Unlesse the winde turne from West into the South. **1702** MARWOOD *Diary* in *Cath. Rec. Soc. Publ.* VII. 121 After Noon the Wind turned, and it rayned a little.

**e.** Of a road, path, line, etc.: To change direction, as at a bend or curve; also, to branch off at an angle from the main road or line.

**1535** COVERDALE *Josh.* xix. 34 Their border.. goeth out vnto Iordane, and turneth westwarde to Asnoth Thabor. **1821** SCOTT *Kenilw.* xiii, Following the smith down a lane which turned to the left hand towards the river. **1892** *Harper's Mag.* May 907/2 Railways turn and curve through the valleys.

**17.** *trans.* To bend one's course so as to get to the other side of; to go or pass round (a corner, etc.). See also CORNER *sb.*[1] 2 b.

**1687–1877** [see CORNER *sb.*[1] 2 b]. **1743** P. FRANCIS tr. *Hor. Odes* I. i. 6 To turn with kindling wheels the goal. **1820** BELZONI *Egypt & Nubia* III. 318 With the expectation, that on turning the next angle, I should have the glorious sight. **1855** MACAULAY *Hist. Eng.* xx. IV. 493 Before Columbus had crossed the Atlantic, before Gama had turned the Cape.

**b.** *Mil.* To get round (an enemy's position, etc.); also *fig.* See also *turn flank*, 55.

**1845–6** TRENCH *Huls. Lect.* Ser. II. i. 152 Not so much anxiously defending our own position as confidently turning theirs. **1861** MILL *Utilit.* v. 84 These are difficulties;.. and many devices have been invented to turn rather than to overcome them. **1892** *Black & White* 19 Mar. 371/2 The skill of the attack in turning the Russian defences.

**18.** To pass, get beyond (a particular age, time, or amount).

**1789** MRS. PIOZZI *Journ. France* I. 90 Let a man once turn sixty.. and his natural heirs are sure of him. **1844** W. H. MAXWELL *Sports & Adv. Scotl.* xxxvii. (1855) 290, I had turned my fourteenth year. **1893** *Illustr. Sport. & Dram. News* 10 June 524/3 It had turned a quarter past one. **1899** *Q. Rev.* Jan. 194 The vast 'Coleccion de documentos inéditos' is turning the hundred in the numbering of its volumes.

**b.** *pa. pple.* (in active sense) with or (now more usually in England) without *of*: Having passed (a particular age or time); more than, past.

**1700** CONGREVE *Way of World* III. viii, I hear he is turn'd of forty. **1703** FARQUHAR *Inconstant* I. i, *D.* Sirrah, What's a Clock? *P.* Turn'd of Eleven, Sir. **1789** MRS. PIOZZI *Journ. France* I. 21 The little knot of unmarried females turned fifty. **1890** FENN *Double Knot* I. i. 84 I'm nineteen, ..and you are turned twenty. **1892** *Harper's Mag.* Aug. 450/2, I was young then—only just turned of two-and-twenty. And now,.. I am turned of forty-five!

** *Senses denoting reversal of course or direction.*

**19.** *trans.* To reverse the course of; to cause to go in the opposite direction; = *turn back*, 69 a. Also *fig.*

*Turn the dice* (quot. *a* 1700), to reverse the luck.

**13..** *Cursor M.* 20713 (Cott.) Feres, gon we son onan, And turn we þis processiun. **1664** HOWARD & DRYDEN *Ind. Queen* II. ii, Till this strange man had power to turn the tide, And carry conquest unto any side. *a* **1700** DRYDEN *Cock & Fox* 754 But see how Fortune can confound the Wise, And when they least expect it, turn the Dice.

**20.** *intr.* To reverse one's, or its, course; to begin to go, or to tend, in the opposite direction; to be reversed: = *turn back*, 69 e. (*lit.* and *fig.*)

*c* **1205** LAY. 7547 He.. turnde to flæme [*c* **1275** tornde to flende]. *a* **1400** *Cato's Morals* 170 in *Cursor M.* p. 1671 Quen þi hap turnis baft, and logh þou lise. **1593** SHAKS. *Lucr.* 646 My vncontrolled tide Turnes not, but swels the higher by this let. **1689** *Lond. Gaz.* No. 2518/3 About four in the Afternoon the Tide turn'd. **1827** DISRAELI *Viv. Grey* v. xiv, Stocks fell.., the exchange turned, money became scarce. **1867** J. B. ROSE tr. *Virgil's Æneid* 337 Before a woman do ye turn and flee? **1885** MALET *Col. Enderby's Wife* III. iv, I fancied.. the luck would turn.

†**21.** *intr.* To go or come back; to return. (See also *turn again*, 66 b.) *Obs.*

*a* **1300** *Cursor M.* 11526 (Cott.) Þai had in wil þat ilk night To torn be herods. *c* **1385** CHAUCER *L. G. W.* 1619 (*Hypsipyle & Medea*) So that ȝe schal nat die But turnyn sound hom to ȝoure tessalye. *c* **1420** *Anturs of Arth.* 284 Turne þou to tuskayne. **1594** SHAKS. *Rich. III*, IV. iv. 184 Ere from this warre thou turne a Conqueror.

†**b.** Of property: To return *to* the former possessor; to revert. (See also *turn again*, 66 c.) *Obs.*

**1500** *Reg. Mag. Sig. Scot.* 537 Landis.. To be haldin to the said Patrik and hys airis maill.., the quhilkis failyeand turnand to me.. and my airis.

†**c.** *trans.* To give or send back; to return. *Obs.*

**1593** SHAKS. *Rich. II*, IV. i. 39, I will turne thy falshood to thy hart, Where it was forged, with my Rapiers point. **1637** B. JONSON *Sad Sheph.* I. ii, She'll turn us thanks.

**V.** Senses allied to III and IV, but referring specially to direction or destination.

**22.** **a.** *trans.* To change the direction of; to direct another way, or different ways alternately (esp. the eyes or face); sometimes, to avert (= *turn away*, 68 a); also, to cause to face in the opposite direction (= *turn round*, 78 e).

*a* **1300** *Cursor M.* 4311 (Cott.) Fleand turn þou noght þin ei. *c* **1300** *St. Margarete* 128 Þe justise.. nolde loke þerto Ac bihuld abac & tournde his eȝen. *c* **1450** MYRC *Par. Pr.* 63 Tuynde [*v. r.* Turne] þyn ye þat thow ne se The cursede worldes vanyte. *c* **1460** *Towneley Myst.* iii. 336 For Iak nor for gille wille I turne my face Tille I haue.. spon a space on my rok. **1697** DRYDEN *Virg. Georg.* III. 353 Often he turns his Eyes, and.. Surveys the pleasing Kingdoms. **1842** TENNYSON *Walking to Mail* 38 Jack, turn the horses' heads and home again. **1842** — *Day Dream* Prol. 17 Turn your face, Nor look with that too-earnest eye.

**b.** *refl.* To change one's position (or course) so as to face (or go) another way: = c. *arch.*

**13..** *Cursor M.* 17288+224 (Cott.) Scho tourned hir and saȝe our lord stand nere. *c* **1400** *Destr. Troy* 11000 Turnes yow full tyte, & taries a while. **1592** SHAKS. *Rom. & Jul.* I. i. 74 Turne thee Benuolio, looke vpon thy death. **1849** M. ARNOLD *Sick King in Bokhara* 127 Turning him quickly to go in.

**c.** *intr.* To change one's position so as to face in the contrary, or a different, direction; to face about.

*Right turn!*, *Left turn!*, as military words of command = turn (through a right angle) to the right, to the left;

*Right about turn!* = turn (by a movement to the right) so as to face in the opposite direction (see RIGHT ABOUT).

*c* **1275** LAY. 26576 Þo tornden hii sone.. And ech his sweord swiþe droh. **1388** WYCLIF *John* i. 38 Jhesu turnede, and say hem suynge hym. *a* **1533** LD. BERNERS *Huon* lix. 205 Whan they aprochyd nere, Huon sodenly tournyd. **1606** SHAKS. *Tr. & Cr.* v. vii. 33 Turne slaue and fight. **1667** MILTON *P. L.* VIII. 507 Seeing me, she turn'd. **1780** C. SIMEON in Carus *Life* (1847) 19 Turning at the Creed, [I] saw the table covered. **1844** DICKENS *Mart. Chuz.* ii, He.. turned upon his heel, and walked out. **1890** A. GISSING *Vill. Hampden* II. iv. 72 He recognised her figure, but never turned to look behind.

**23.** With reference chiefly to the new direction taken. (See also uses with adverbs in VIII.) **a.** *trans.* To direct, present, point (towards or away from some specified person or thing, or in some specified direction).

*c* **1205** LAY. 20658 Turnden [*c* **1275** tornde] heo heore ordes, Stikeden & sloȝen Al þat heo neh comen. *c* **1230** *Hali Meid.* 17 Þu most turne þe rug [= back]. *a* **1330** *Roland & V.* 341 An image..Stode on a roche..Þe face of him was turned souþe riȝt. *c* **1425** WYNTOUN *Cron.* v. xiv. 5608 Be þe takyn þat þat ymage Had turnyt fra Romule his wissage. *a* **1533** LD. BERNERS *Huon* lxxxii. 254 He tournyd his face to her warde. **1583** MELBANCKE *Philotimus* H j b, You are so wetherwise, turninge your tayle into euery wynde. **1667** MILTON *P. L.* IX. 527 His gentle dumb expression turn'd at length The Eye of Eve to mark his play. *a* **1700** DRYDEN *Ovid's Met.* XIII. *Acis, Pol. & Galatea* 111 Plums, to tempt you, turn their glossy side. **1756** MRS. CALDERWOOD in *Coltness Collect.* (Maitl. Cl.) 205 The armies upon which the eyes of all Europe are turned. **1823** SCOTT *Quentin D.* xxxvi, D'Hymbercourt turned two culverins on the gate. **1880** L. STEPHEN *Pope* vi. 157 A soured man prefers to turn his worst side outwards.

**b.** *refl.* = next sense. *arch.* (See also e.)

*c* **1375** *Sc. Leg. Saints* xviii. (*Egipciane*) 265, I ma nocht me turne to þe. *c* **1400** MAUNDEV. (Roxb.) xvi. 72 When a man turnez him to þe este. **1548–9** (Mar.) *Bk. Com. Prayer, Communion* (Rubric), Then the priest shall turne hym to the people. **1596** SHAKS. *Merch. V.* III. ii. 138 Turne you where your Lady is. **1725** POPE *Odyss.* III. 603 The Monarch turns him to his royal guest. **1812** CARY *Dante, Paradise* XXII. 2 To the guardian of my steps I turn'd me.

**c.** *intr.* To change one's position so as to face towards or away from some specified person or thing; to direct oneself; to face (with implied change of direction). See also e.

*c* **1325** *Spec. Gy Warw.* 435 For toward hem he wole turne Boþe wraþful and eke sterne. *c* **1425** *Cursor M.* 11711 (Trin.) Iesu turned to þat tre. **1593** SHAKS. 3 *Hen. VI*, I. i. 189 Turne this way Henry, and regard them not. **1602** HARINGTON *Nugæ Ant.* (ed. Park 1804) I. 321 To turne askante from her condition withe tearlesse eyes. **1754** GRAY *Poesy* 37 Where'er she turns the Graces homage pay. **18..** T. MOORE *Irish Melodies*, '*She is far from the land*' i, But coldly she turns from their gaze, and weeps. **1890** A. GISSING *Vill. Hampden* II. xiii. 273 All faces turned towards him as he rose.

† **d.** (without the notion of change.) To have a specified direction or aspect; to face. *Obs. rare.*

**1535** COVERDALE *Ezek.* xliii. 1 He brought me to ye dore, that turneth towarde the east. **1604** E. G[RIMSTONE] *D'Acosta's Hist. Indies* III. xxi. 188 In places whereas the land..turnes from the shadow of the mountaines.

**e.** In *not to know which way to turn* (or *turn oneself* arch.), and similar phrases, the sense is partly *lit.* and partly *fig.* (= what course to take, what to do: cf. 28 c).

*c* **1400** *Brut* xxxix. 146 He hade so miche to done wiþ þe Erl Randulf..& wiþ Hugh Bigot..þat he ne wist whider to turne. **1526** TINDALE *Luke* xxi. 25 They shall not tell which waye to turne them selves. **1669** STURMY *Mariner's Mag.* Advt. C iij b, We have been at our wits end, and knew not which way in the World to turn our selves. **1719** DE FOE *Crusoe* (1840) II. x. 219 They knew not which way to turn themselves. **1825** WATERTON *Wand. S. Amer.* III. iii. 270 There is a vast deal of knowledge to be picked up..whichever way we turn ourselves. **1885** SIR W. V. FIELD in *Law Times Rep.* LII. 651/1 She did not know which way to turn to find means.

**24. a.** *trans.* To direct in the way of movement; to set going in a particular direction; to bend the course of.

*a* **1300** *Cursor M.* 13476 (Cott.) If þai..turn ham [= home] þair wai, Bi þe wai son faile sal þai. *a* **1548** HALL *Chron.*, *Hen. V* 49 In whiche..just quarel al good persons shal rather set bothe theyr feete forwarde, then once to turne theyr one heale backward. **1692** PRIOR *Ode in Imit. Horace* x, Where-e'er old Rhine his fruitful Water turns. **1891** *New Rev.* Oct. 347 He then turned his steps towards the south.

**b.** *refl.* = next sense. *arch.*

*a* **1240** *Sawles Warde* in *Cott. Hom.* 257 Al þat hird.. turneð ham treowliliche to wit hare lauerd. *a* **1300** *Cursor M.* 2391 (Cott.) Abram turned him to þe south. *c* **1482** J. KAY tr. *Caoursin's Siege of Rhodes* P 7 And thenne they tourned theyme in the see toward Rhodes. **1700** S. L. tr. *Fryke's Voy. E. Ind.* 306 We turned our selves to a River. **1867** J. B. ROSE tr. *Virgil's Æneid* 342 Turn thee hither, turn thee.

**c.** *intr.* To direct one's course; to set oneself to go in a particular direction: usually with implied change of course (cf. 16); sometimes almost synonymous with 'go' or 'come', with special reference to destination.

*c* **1200** ORMIN 6596, & tatt te kingess turrndenn efft Till þeȝȝre rihhte weȝȝe. *c* **1290** *S. Eng. Leg.* I. 25/54 Þat he scholde after þis lijf tuyrne into þulke blis. *c* **1380** *Sir Ferumb.* 3545 Þay..in-to þe paleys þan tornde. *c* **1470** *Golagros & Gaw.* 2 The king turnit on ane tyde towart Tuskane. *a* **1631** DONNE *Poems* (1650) 58 Turne thou ghost that way, and let me turne this. **1653** WALTON *Angler* i. 38, I thought we had wanted three miles of the thatcht House ..but now we are at it, we'l turn into it. **1893** *Cornh. Mag.* Nov. 474 Thither their footsteps turn.

**25.** *trans.* To cause or command to go; to send, drive; *esp.* (with qualifying adv. or advb. phrase) to send or order away, dismiss.

See also *turn away*, 68 c; *t. off*, 73 b; *t. out*, 75 c, e. In quot. 1903 app. short for *turn loose* (61 b).

**1526** TINDALE *Heb.* xi. 34 [They] turned to flyght the armees of the alientes. **1545** ASCHAM *Toxoph.* I. (Arb.) 88 Where they turned with so fewe Archers so many Frenchemen to flight. **1586** A. DAY *Eng. Secretary* II. (1625) 118 They are turned at the last quite forth by the elbowes. **1600** SHAKS. *A. Y. L.* III. i. 18 Push him out of dores.. turne him going. *a* **1649** WINTHROP *New Eng.* (1853) II. 267 A vessel..was fallen into the hands of D'Aulnay, who had made prize of her, and turned the men upon an island. **1782** MISS BURNEY *Cecilia* VII. ix, You will not..turn me from your door. **1891** L. KEITH *Halletts* II. ii. 37 He would turn me adrift without the smallest consideration. **1903** A. ADAMS *Log Cowboy* xiii, Five six-shooters were turned into the ceiling.

**b.** *spec.* To drive or put forth (beasts) to pasture. (See also *t. out*, 75 d.) Also in *fig.* or *allusive* use (= prec. sense).

**1602** *2nd Pt. Return fr. Parnass.* I. ii. 268 Clap a lock on their feete, and turne them to commons. **1646** J. LILBURNE *Unhappy Game Scotch & Eng.* 12 When the King hath got all, he'll turne our brethren to grasse. **1765** *Museum Rust.* IV. 183 Let the grass take head for about..three weeks, before you turn your sheep upon it. **1825** SCOTT *Betrothed* x, It's like old Raoul and I will be turned to grass with the lord's old chargers. **1847** *Jrnl. R. Agric. Soc.* VIII. I. 35 The privilege of turning stock into the park.

**c.** To put, cast, or convey into a receptacle or the like; now esp. by inverting the containing vessel (cf. 10), or diverting into a new channel (cf. 13).

In quot. 1598 *turn into* = 'put into' (a different dress), with mixture of sense 'change' (branch VI).

**1594** SHAKS. *Rich. III*, I. ii. 261 But first Ile turne yon Fellow in [= into] his Graue. **1598** — *Merry W.* v. v. 214, I knew of your purpose: turn'd my daughter into white. **1844** *Jrnl. R. Agric. Soc.* V. I. 107 The sewers..may be cleansed by turning some water into them out of a large pond. **1901** ALLDRIDGE *Sherbro* ii. 15 A common method to detect bad kernels is to turn them into great casks containing water.

**d.** *intr.* for *pass.*

**1801** *Naval Chron.* VI. 76 At the top of the tide she turned off the stocks.

**26.** *fig. trans.* To direct or set (thought, desire, speech, action, etc.) towards (or away from) something. Usually const. *to*, rarely *on*, *upon*.

† In quot. 1659, to direct, refer (a person) *to* something (cf. 28 d).

*c* **1200** *Trin. Coll. Hom.* 59 We and ure heldrene habbæð ben turnd fro him [God] eure siððen þe deuel com on neddre liche to adam. *a* **1225** *Ancr. R.* 52 Eue biheold o þen uorbodene eppele,..& turnde hire lust þer toward, & nom & et þerof. **1297** R. GLOUC. (Rolls) 6824 Þe luþer men of denemarch..To hor olde luþerhede iturnd adde hor þoȝt. *c* **1325** *Metr. Hom.* Prol. 32 An unkind man es he, That turnes alle his thoht fra the. *c* **1386** CHAUCER *Miller's T.* 6 Al his fantasye Was turned for to lerne Astrologye. **1483** CAXTON *G. de la Tour* F ij b, Moche merueylled the neyghbours how she had turned her herte to loue suche a pryour. **1560** DAUS tr. *Sleidane's Comm.* 420 b, Turning his talke to him. **1659** H. THORNDIKE *Wks.* (1846) II. 504 Those who..turn simple..Christians to that translation. **1727** SWIFT *What passed in Lond.* Wks. 1755 III. I. 183 His mind was wholly turned upon spiritual matters. **1823** SCOTT *Quentin D.* xi, He turned his thoughts from this subject of reflection. **1863** A. BLOMFIELD *Mem. Bp. Blomfield* II. iii. 90 He could turn the whole force of his mind at a moment's notice on any subject. **1883** STEVENSON *Treas. Isl.* IV. xviii, We..turned our attention to poor Tom.

**b.** To cause or induce (a person, etc.) to take a particular course; to direct the course of (events, etc.). *arch.*

*c* **1386** CHAUCER *Knt.'s T.* 380 Wel hath ffortune y-turned thee the dys. **1390** GOWER *Conf.* III. 73 The kinge he torneth at his wille, And makth him forto dreme. *c* **1400** *Destr. Troy* 2943 Throgh which treason betydes, & ternes vmqwhile Bolde men to batell and biker with hond. **1611** SHAKS. *Wint. T.* III. i. 15 Great Apollo Turne all to th' best.

**27.** *refl.* To direct one's mind, will, attention, etc. to or from a person or thing: = 28, 28 b, 28 c. Now *rare* or *arch.*

*c* **1200** *Trin. Coll. Hom.* 61 Turneð ȝiu to me, and ich wile turnen me to ȝiu. *c* **1200** *Ormin* 6586 He þatt turrneþþ himm fra Crist..Forrleoseþþ sawless soþe lihht. *c* **1375** *Sc. Leg. Saints* xli. (*Agnes*) 242 Men sal..twrne þaim to þe cristine fay. **1535** COVERDALE *Exod.* xxxii. 12 O turne the from the fearcenesse of thy wrath. **1539** BIBLE (Great) *Ps.* xxv. 16 Turne the vnto me, and haue mercy vpon me. **1551** ROBINSON tr. *More's Utop.* I. (1895) 87 Ynough for hym, yea, and more then he can well turne hym to. **1832** *Examiner* 92/1 They were compelled to turn themselves to other employments.

**28.** *intr.* To direct one's mind, desire, or will to or from some person, thing, or action.

*c* **1200** *Trin. Coll. Hom.* 61 We turnen ofte to him, and fro him. *c* **1315** SHOREHAM *Poems* I. 122 Þaȝ he torni to senne aȝen. *c* **1475** *Partenay* 518 Vnto my purpos torn shall I therfore. **1539** BIBLE (Great) *Exod.* xxxii. 12 Turne from thy fearse wrath. **1567** *Gude & Godlie B.* (S. T. S.) 173 Turnand till Goddis infinite. **1690** LOCKE *Hum. Und.* II. i. § 8 Ideas..make not deep Impressions..till the Understanding turn inwards upon it self, and reflect on its own Operations. **1764** GOLDSM. *Trav.* 8 Where'er I roam,..My heart untravell'd fondly turns to thee. **1891** M. MAARTENS *Old Maid's Love* II. iii. 46 She turned from the thought of scandal with impatience.

**b.** *spec.* To direct one's attention *to* a different subject; to begin to speak or think of something else.

*c* **1374** CHAUCER *Troylus* II. 639 (688) Now lat vs stynte of Troylus.., and late vs tourne [*v.rr.* torne, turne] faste Vnto Criseyde. *c* **1375** *Sc. Leg. Saints* xxi. (*Clement*) 622 Off þis matere now no mare I tel, Bot to þe story twrne I sel Of sancte clement. **1836** W. IRVING *Astoria* III. lvi. 188 It is with a feeling of momentary relief we turn to something of a more pleasing complexion. **1880** L. STEPHEN *Pope* ii. 43 Let us now turn from the poems to the author's personal career.

**c.** To direct one's attention *to* something practically; to apply oneself *to* or take up an occupation or pursuit.

**1667** MILTON *P. L.* v. 630 Forthwith from dance to sweet repast they turn. **1842** TENNYSON *Locksley Hall* 99 What is that which I should turn to..? Every door is barr'd with gold, and opens but to golden keys. **1891** *Sat. Rev.* 26 Dec. 730/1 He turned next to log-splitting.

**d.** *Turn to*: to refer to, look up, consult (a book, list, table, etc.).

**1631** COTTON (*title*) A Complete Concordance..By helpe whereof any passage of holy Scripture may bee readily turned unto. **1693** LOCKE *Educ.* § 172 Helvicus's Tables may be..turned to on all occasions. **1850** *Jrnl. R. Agric. Soc.* XI. II. 400 To their reports the reader must turn for accurate information. **1886** K. S. MACQUOID *Sir J. Appleby* II. viii. 111 He took up a local paper and turned to the list of visitors.

**e.** To resort, betake oneself, have recourse *to* (a person, etc.); to appeal *to* for help or support.

**1821** CLARE *Vill. Minstr.* II. 80 He turns to heaven to witness what he feels. **1869** A. W. WARD tr. *Curtius' Hist. Greece* II. III. iii. 472 The Milesians were unable to maintain themselves in Priene and turned to Athens. **1890** CLARK RUSSELL *Ocean Trag.* I. i. 20 You are the one man..that I should turn to in such a time. **1912** *Jrnl. Friends' Hist. Soc.* IX. 204 Once more we have to turn to a German writer for information.

† **f.** To tend, have a tendency *to* something. *Obs.*

**1340–70** *Alex. & Dind.* 365 Tale tende we non þat turneþ to harme. *Ibid.* 469 When we tenden any tale þat turneþ to bourde. **1583** *Leg. Bp. St. Androis* 976 Whairto it turnes I can not tell.

† **29.** *trans.* To induce or persuade to adopt a (different) religious faith (usually with implication of its truth or excellence), or a religious or godly (instead of an irreligious or ungodly) life; to convert; less commonly in bad sense, to pervert (cf. 14). *Obs.* or merged in other senses. **a.** Const. *to*, *into*; *from.*

*c* **1200** ORMIN 169 He shall turrnenn mikell flocc..till þe rihhte læfe. *c* **1205** LAY. 12734 Heo þencheð..to..turne to heðenesse þa hæȝe & þa læsse. **1297** R. GLOUC. (Rolls) 4956 Seint birin þe bissop..Þat in to þis lond..ysend was. To turne þe king of west sex, kingilf, to cristendom. *a* **1375** *Joseph Arim.* 11 In þe nome of þe fader Ioseph him folewede, And hedde I-turned to þe feyþ fifti with him-seluen. *c* **1380** *Antecrist* in Todd *3 Treat. Wyclif* 122 Þei shal.. bowe a wey from trewþe and ben turned in to fables. *c* **1380** WYCLIF *Sel. Wks.* III. 107 We scholde nouȝt tarye to be yturned to God. *c* **1440** *Promp. Parv.* 507/2 Turne, to badnesse, *perverto.* **1513** MORE *Rich. III* (1641) 14 But if grace turne him to wisedome. **1579** W. WILKINSON *Confut. Familye of Loue, Brief Descr.* iij b, Who sought to peruert and turne from the truth xii godly Christians.

**b.** *simply.*

*c* **1305** *St. Swithin* 10 in *E. E. P.* (1862) 43 Seint berin her bi weste wende And turnde þe king kenewold as oure louerd him grace sende. **1377** LANGL. *P. Pl.* B. xv. 540 Many miracles he wrouȝte man for to turne. **1539** BIBLE (Great) *Jer.* xxxi. 19 As soone as thou turnest me, I shall reforme my selfe. *c* **1592** MARLOWE *Jew of Malta* IV. i, Why, brother, you converted Abigail.. One [friar] turn'd my daughter, therefore he shall die. **1692** LOCKE *Toleration* ii. Wks. 1727 II. 266 The two Reynold's (..one a Protestant, the other a Papist) who upon the exchange of Papers between them, were both turn'd.

**30.** *intr.* To adopt a different (esp. the true) religion, or a godly life; to be converted. **a.** Const. *to.* (Now merged in sense 28.)

*a* **1225** *St. Marher.* 22 Turnden þa þurh þis to criste swiðe monie. *c* **1300** *Cursor M.* 22119 (Edinb.) If þai wil noȝte turne til his lare, He sal taim sla wiþoutin spare. **1387** TREVISA *Higden* (Rolls) VI. 335 Þe kyng of Bulgares and his men tornede to Cristes fey and bileve. [*c* **1410** *Hampole's Psalter* lxxxvi. 3 (MS. U²) Þai resceyf sinfull men that will torune [? tourne] to me. *c* **1590** MARLOWE *Faust.* v. 8 Abjure this magic, turn to God again. **1891** *Temple Bar* Dec. 599 It is never too late to turn to God.]

**b.** *simply.* To be converted; to repent. *arch.*

*c* **1300** *Cursor M.* 19013 (Edinb.) Þis wordis herd, þair hertis gan turne, alsua for þaire misdedis murne. **13..** *Ibid.* 16762+148 (Cott.) Mony þat stode & saȝe..Torned & wore baptized. **1526** TINDALE *Matt.* xviii. 3 Except ye tourne and become as children. **1679** *Estabi. Test* 45 So would they say to all Protestants,..Turn, or burn. **1876** W. ARNOT *Anchor of Soul* 333 If..the lost shall turn, they will get life in the Lord.

**c.** To go over to another side or party; to revolt, desert. Const. *to.* *arch.*

**1297** R. GLOUC. (Rolls) 9891 Richard þe kinges sone,.. Aȝen is fader turnde to þe king of france alas! **13..** *Cursor M.* 15137 (Cott.) All þis werld es turnand Til him. *c* **1470** HENRY *Wallace* I. 110 Erle Patrik than..Till our fa turnd, and harmyng did ws mast. **1593** SHAKS. 3 *Hen. VI*, I. i. 151 All will reuolt from me, and turne to him. **18..** J. FORBES *Battle of Corichie* ix. in A. Whitwell *Bk. Sc. Ball.* (1857) 556 Whan the haf o' the Gordones desertit, An' turnit wi' Murray in a crack.

**31.** *trans.* To direct or bring to bear in the way of

(active) opposition; to retort or cause to recoil *upon*; to proceed to use *against*.

1297 [see *turn one's hand*, 56 a]. 1538 CROMWELL in Merriman *Life & Lett.* (1902) II. 125 By this meane their owne craft..shalbe torned into their owne neckes. *a* 1641 BP. MOUNTAGU *Acts & Mon.* iii. (1642) 184 To wrest his weapon out of his hands, and turne it upon himselfe. 1687 ATTERBURY *Answ. Consid. Spirit Luther* 48 Luther's Conscience.. turn's these very reasonings upon him. 1839 YEOWELL *Anc. Brit. Ch.* x. (1847) 107 Her cruel masters turned their ruthless hands against every thing and person that had a religious character. 1855 *Jrnl. R. Agric. Soc.* XVI. II. 569 He has sufficient security that the disclosure will not be turned against himself.

**b.** To direct *against* in feeling; to make antagonistic; to imbue with hatred or dislike.

1831 *Examiner* 722/2 The hearts of the poor were turned in bitterness against the rich. 1881 MRS. LYNN LINTON *My Love* xi, Not even Papa could turn me against Cyril.

**32.** *intr.* To recoil *upon*; to fall *upon* with disastrous effect; to have an adverse tendency or result. Now *rare* or *Obs.*, or merged in next.

1377 LANGL. *P. Pl.* B. XVIII. 359 Now bygynneth þi gyle ageyne þe to tourne. *c* 1380 WYCLIF *Sel. Wks.* III. 351 Certis synne of siche children turneþ into heed of þer fadir. 1550 J. COKE *Eng. & Fr. Heralds* § 71 (1877) 80 Thus your bostes, syr heralde, turne upon your heles. 1625 BACON *Ess., Empire* (Arb.) 305 The destruction of Demetrius, Sonne to Philip the Second of Macedon, turned vpon the Father, who died of Repentance. 1660 *Trial Regic.* 24 *Court.* There is nothing you can say, but Guilty, or Not guilty. All other discourses turn upon your self. *a* 1715 BURNET *Own Time* (1823) I. II. 430 (an. 1667) The Dutch war had turned so fatally on the king. 1881 GARDINER & MULLINGER *Stud. Eng. Hist.* I. viii. 153 It turns upon those who attempt it, as the Florentine people turned upon Savonarola.

**33.** *intr.* To change one's position in order to attack or resist some one; to take up an attitude of opposition; to oppose oneself; with *on* or *upon*, to assail suddenly or violently (in act or word); with *against*, usually implying a change from previous friendliness. See also *turn again*, 66 d; *turn round*, 78 c.

13.. in *Pol. Songs* (Camden) 189 Hue turnden hem aȝeynes with suerd ant with launce. 1477 EARL RIVERS (Caxton) *Dictes* 72 Be not gladde of the euill fortune of another, for thou knowest not howe the worlde may tourne ayenst the. 1596 SHAKS. 1 *Hen. IV*, II. iv. 297 Should I turne vpon the true Prince? 1625 BACON *Ess., Friendship* (Arb.) 169 Pompey turned vpon him againe, and .. bad him be quiet. 1804 A. DUNCAN *Mariner's Chron.* II. 241 At this place, Mr. Hamilton met with a large seal, or sea-lion, and fired a brace of balls into him, upon which the animal turned upon him open-mouthed. 1854 THACKERAY *Rose & Ring* iii, These people who are following you will be the first to turn against you. 1865 KINGSLEY *Herew.* xxxii, The king turned on his courtiers, glad to ease his own conscience by cursing them. 1887 F. W. ROBINSON *In Bad Hands* I. 33 The impudence of some people..would make a worm turn. 1892 *Black & White* 12 Mar. 327/2 His adulators of yesterday are prepared to turn and rend him.

**34.** *trans.* To apply *to* some use or purpose; to make use of, employ.

See also *turn one's hand to*, 56 b; *turn to account*, 62 b. † In quot. *a* 1225, to dedicate *to* a saint.

*a* 1225 *Ancr. R.* 18 To þeo halewen þet ȝe habbeð to þurh luue iturnd ower weouedes. 1398 *Munim. de Melros* (Bann. Cl.) 489 To be distreignede..and in[to] þaire profite to be turnide. 1445 in *Charters rel. Glasgow* (1906) 440 A certane sowm..beforehand..payit be the said Davy and in myne use turnit. 1605 BACON *Adv. Learn.* I. ii. § 1 Virgil, turning his pen to the advantage of his country. 1711 ADDISON *Spect.* No. 251 ¶ 2, I..would willingly turn my Head to any thing for an honest Livelihood. 1821 SCOTT *Kenilw.* vi, I trust that what I have spoken..will not be turned to my ruin. 1873 MRS. OLIPHANT *Innocent* II. iii. 33 An old house..which she had turned to a great many uses.

**b.** To set (a person) to some work or employment; in quot. 1781 *Naut.* = *turn up*, 80 r.

1781 ARCHER in *Naval Chron.* XI. 283 Turn all hands! make sail! 1869 HUGHES *Alfred Gt.* xii. 139 The whole manhood of the kingdom might have been..turned upon this work. 1892 *Blackw. Mag.* CLI. 204/2 To turn the whole country on a deserter, and so take him dead or alive.

**VI.** To change, alter.

* *General senses.*

**35.** *trans.* To change, transmute; to alter, make different, or substitute something else (of the same kind) for. Now *rare* or *Obs.* exc. as in 37, 40 or associated with other senses: cf. *turn colour*, 52.

† *Turn sides* (quot. 1736), to change sides, go over from one side to the other.

*c* 1230 *Hali Meid.* 9 Godd ne schop hit neauer swuch, Ah Adam & eue turnden hit to beo swuch þurh hare sunne. *a* 1300 *Cursor M.* 10434 (Cott.) Mend þi mode and turn þi chere. *c* 1400 MAUNDEV. (1839) viii. 86 An Aungel helde Jacob stille, & turned his name, & cleped him Israel. *c* 1470 *Golagros & Gaw.* 1066 Schir Gawane tretit the knight to turn his entent. *c* 1489 CAXTON *Sonnes of Aymon* vii. 170 Whan the barons sawe reynawde & bayarde so torned, they began to laughe. 1566 DRANT *Horace, Sat.* viii. F vj b, But pleasure hath lyke Circes cuppes yturnde them from their Kynde. 1596 SHAKS. *Merch. V.* III. ii. 249 Some deere friend dead, else nothing in the world Could turne so much the constitution Of any constant man. 1607 TOPSELL *Four-f. Beasts* (1658) 340 Orus writeth, that there is a Fish of this name which turneth sex. 1736 LEDIARD *Life Marlborough* II. 524 Their good Fortune..may, hereafter, turn Sides. 1892 *Temple Bar Mag.* Jan. 144 Suddenly she turned the subject. *Ibid.* Apr. 485 They .. turned their dresses and their opinions.

**36.** *intr.* To undergo change or alteration; to become different, to change; in quot. 1599, to be fickle or inconstant. *rare* (exc. as in 38, 39).

*c* 1175 *Lamb. Hom.* 91 Þa þet folc þis iherde, þa iturn[d]e heore mod. *c* 1275 LAY. 3069 His euhe [= hue] torne[d] and.. Bicom alse a blac cloþ. 14.. *Sir Beues* (MS. C.) 1283+47 Al his þouȝt bygan to tern. 1474 CAXTON *Chesse* III. iii. (1883) 98 Whan fortune torneth and perishith ther abideth not to hym one frende. 1599 SHAKS. *Passionate Pilgr.* vii, She bad loue last, and yet she fell a turning. 1732 POPE *Ep. Bathurst* 379 Things change their titles, as our manners turn. 1894 PARRY *Stud. Gt. Composers, Schubert* 226 How to make the form turn and vary.

**37.** *trans.* with *into* or *to*: To change, transform, or convert into; to cause to become (something else).

*c* 1175 *Lamb. Hom.* 97 Petrus wes fixere [= fisher] þene iturnde þe ilcan godes gast to apostle. *c* 1200 *Trin. Coll. Hom.* 45 Þanne is here foshipe turnd al to frendshipe. *c* 1275 *Passion of our Lord* 10 in *O. E. Misc.* 37 He..turnde water to wyne. *a* 1350 HAMPOLE *Poems* Wks. 1895 I. 78 Ihesu es lufe þat lastes ay:..Ihesu þe nyght turnes to þe day, þe dawyng in til spryng. 1413 *Pilgr. Sowle* (Caxton 1483) IV. xxviii. 73 The floure is forfaded and al the beaute therof torned to nouȝt. 1484 CAXTON *Fables of Alfonce* xi, The goddes..haue torned my daughter in to this catte. *a* 1569 [see 10 b]. 1631 WEEVER *Anc. Fun. Mon.* 433 This religious house is now turned into an Hospitall. 1765 GRAY *Shakespeare* 11 May not honey's self be turn'd to gall? 1853 J. H. NEWMAN *Hist. Sk.* (1873) II. I. ii. 63 A river overflows and turns a fruitful plain into a marsh.

**b.** To change into, cause to become of (a specified nature, form, or aspect).

1390 GOWER *Conf.* II. 326 Echon of hem..Was torned into a briddes kinde. *c* 1400 MAUNDEV. (Roxb.) iv. 13 He schall turne þat damysell in to hir riȝt schappe. 1644 MILTON *Areop.* (Arb.) 75 She turns herself into all shapes. 1651 HOBBES *Leviath.* II. xxv. 132 Then is the Counsell turned into the nature of a Command.

**c.** *transf.* To exchange for; to get something else instead of; also, to substitute something else for. Cf. CONVERT *v.* 15.

*c* 1449 PECOCK *Repr.* v. xiv. (Rolls) 557 Eer than he haue turnede or chaungid the iewelis into money. *c* 1537 DE BENESE *Measurynge Lande* F iv b, Ye must turne the perches in to pence. *c* 1593 *Trag. Rich. II*, II. iii. 23 My iewells and my plaite are turnd to coyne. 1697 DRYDEN *Virg. Past.* VII. 51 Thy Marble Statue shall be turn'd to Gold. 1827 JARMAN *Powell's Devises* (ed. 3) II. 97 He laid some stress upon the fact of the real estate being turned into personal. 1855 *Jrnl. R. Agric. Soc.* XVI. II. 557 [They] turned their little stock into Cash.

†**d.** With inverse construction: To form by change *out of*. *Obs. nonce-use.*

1526 *Pilgr. Perf.* (W. de W. 1531) 180 Whiche worde Aue was turned out of Eua, & made Aue, & that not without great mistery.

**38.** *intr.* with *into* or *to*: To change into; to be changed, transformed, or converted into; to become.

*c* 1250 *Long Life* 3 in *O. E. Misc.* 156 Fair weder turneð ofte into reine. 1393 LANGL. *P. Pl.* C. XIV. 19 Al hus sorwe to solas þorgh þat songe turnede. *c* 1400 *Brut* cc. 228 Þe sonne þo turnede into blode. 1526 *Pilgr. Perf.* (W. de W. 1531) 93 Lest our Ire turne to enuy, and our enuy to hate. 1660 BOYLE *New Exp. Phys. Mech.* xxxvii. 312 Water turning from perspicuous to white. 1764 GOLDSM. *Trav.* 86 These rocks, by custom, turn to beds of down. 1892 *Monthly Packet* May 532 The monkeys did not turn into men, the men turned into monkeys.

**b.** To change into, become of (a specified nature, form, or aspect).

1678 J. PHILLIPS *Tavernier's Trav.* II. xxii. 155 The milk will turn to the colour of an Apostemated matter. 1856 *Jrnl. R. Agric. Soc.* XVII. II. 482 Black cattle have been observed to turn..to a dun colour.

**39.** *intr.* with *compl.* To change so as to be, to become. **a.** with *adj. compl.* (in quot. 1303 with *advb. phr.*).

1303 R. BRUNNE *Handl. Synne* 6584 With wykked man, þou turnest as he. 1450 *Paston Lett.* I. 158 Therwith he turned pale colour. *a* 1548 HALL *Chron., Hen. VI* 103 Saiyng: that God was turned Englishe, and the devill would not helpe Fraunce. 1592 SHAKS. *Rom. & Jul.* I. ii. 48 Turne giddie, and be holpe by backward turning. 1626 BACON *Sylva* § 851 Cygnets from Gray turne White. 1758 R. BROWN *Compl. Farmer* (1759) 111 When..the stalk begins to die, and to turn brown. 1818 SCOTT *Br. Lamm.* xxii, 'It is my mother!' said Lucy, turning as pale as ashes, and clasping her hands together. 1861 *Jrnl. R. Agric. Soc.* XXII. I. 48 The milk is apt to turn sour. 1888 'J. S. WINTER' *Bootle's Childr.* viii, Lassie turned very white, and gasped for breath.

**b.** with *sb. compl.* (most commonly without article).

1596 SHAKS. *Merch. V.* III. i. 82 Vnlesse the diuell himselfe turne Iew. 1660 FULLER *Mixt Contempl.* (1841) 172 The remedy turned the malady of the land. 1758 S. HAYWARD *Serm.* xvii. 531 A mother must turn monster if she does not love her babe. 1853 LYTTON *My Novel* v. ix, Did not you turn..a common stage-player, sir? 1879 DOWDEN *Southey* vi. 178 Under such strokes a courageous heart may turn coward. 1879 MINTO *Defoe* x. 170 He had seen Whig turn Tory and Tory turn Whig.

**c.** *Turn after* (of offspring): to become or grow like, to 'take after' (the parent).

1848 *Jrnl. R. Agric. Soc.* IX. II. 256 Where one parent is sound and the other diseased the progeny may turn after the former; but then it is just as likely to turn after the latter.

**40.** *trans.* with *compl.* (usually *adj.*) To change so as to make...; to make (so) by alteration; to render.

1607 SHAKS. *Timon* IV. iii. 499 It almost turnes my dangerous Nature wilde. 1732 POPE *Ep. Cobham* 163 That gay Free-thinker,..What turns him now a stupid silent dunce? 1821 CLARE *Vill. Minstr.* I. 23 His fears would turn him chill. 1849 *Jrnl. R. Agric. Soc.* X. I. 177 It turns the fibre black. 1904 WEYMAN *Abbess of Vlaye* xiv, With a..shock of the mind that turned her hot.

†**41. a.** *trans.* To change so as to bring *into* some specified condition: e. g. *to turn into madness* = to cause to become mad, to make mad. *Obs.*

In quot. *c* 1400, to set *on fire*; in quot. 1470–85 *torned vnto helpyng* (?) = brought into a condition of recovery, 'getting better'.

1382 WYCLIF *Mark* iii. 21 Thei seiden, for he is turnyd in to wodenesse. *c* 1400 *Destr. Troy* 7112 The Troiens þaire tore shippis hade turnyt on fyre. 1470–85 MALORY *Arthur* XIII. xiii. 631 He asked syr Melyas how it stood with him. Thenne he sayd he was torned vnto helpyng, god be thanked. 1608 TOPSELL *Serpents* (1658) 701 Dionysius,..being turned by Juno into madnesse.

†**b.** *intr.* To get *into* some specified condition: e. g. *to turn into ire* = to become angry. *Obs.*

*c* 1400 *Destr. Troy* 12252 Þen Thelamon was tenfull, & turnyt into yre.

**42.** *trans.* with *into* or *to*: To make the subject of (praise, mockery, etc.); now chiefly in phr. *to turn* (a thing) *into ridicule* (see RIDICULE *sb.*[1] 3 b).

1387 TREVISA *Higden* (Rolls) IV. 143 He wolde torne [*v.r.* teurne] hit to bourde and to lawȝhynge. 1533 GAU *Richt Vay* (S. T. S.) 13 Thay that..twrnis the halie writ to lichtlines and scorne. 1601 SHAKS. *Twel. N.* II. v. 223 It cannot but turn him into a notable contempt. 1611 — *Cymb.* IV. i. 23 Her Father..may..be a little angry..: but my Mother..shall turne all into my commendations. 1673–1784 [see RIDICULE *sb.*[1] 3 b]. 1891 E. & D. GERARD *Sensitive Pl.* I. II. vii. 276 Does any one turn the true poet..into ridicule?

†**43.** *intr.* with *to*: To lead to as a consequence; to become the cause or occasion of; to result in, bring about. (See also *turn to account*, 62 a.) *Obs.* or merged in other senses.

*c* 1200 ORMIN Ded. 18 Þu þohhtesst tatt itt mihhte wel Till mikell frame turrnenn. *c* 1205 LAY. 25574 Let þu mi sweuen To selþen iturnen. 1297 R. GLOUC. (Rolls) 7711 Þe vnriȝt ido to poueremen to such mesaunture turnde. *c* 1350 *Will. Palerne* 254 Perauenture þurth goddis grace to gode may it turne. 1422 tr. *Secreta Secret., Priv. Priv.* xxxvii. 194 Yef hit shold torn to pereill of the child. 1560 DAUS tr. *Sleidane's Comm.* 42 Fearynge lest this broile..would tourne to his vtter destruction. 1631 GOUGE *God's Arrows* III. § 93. 355 Their plots turned to their owne damage. *a* 1774 GOLDSM. *Surv. Exp. Philos.* (1776) II. 147 To deduce any general theory that shall turn to public benefit.

†**b.** *To turn* (a person) *to* (something): to result in or bring about for the person; to put him to (trouble, etc.); to be for his (advantage, etc.). *Obs.*

Orig. *intr.* with dative of person; afterwards taken as *trans.* with the person as direct object.

*c* 1200 ORMIN Ded. 150 Ȝiff þeȝȝ all forrwerrpenn itt, Itt turrneþþ hemm till sinne. *c* 1230 *Hali Meid.* 7 Serue Godd ane, & alle þinge schulen þe turnen to gode. 13.. *Guy Warw.* (A.) 898 Wiþ him he wald iusti, It turned him to vilani [*Caius MS.* And therof hym befelle grete vilanye]. 1463 in *Acts Parlt. Scot.* (1874) XII. 28/2 That occupatioun & vse þat I sal haue of þe said landis..sal turn ȝou na ȝoure successowris in na preiudice. 1523 LD. BERNERS *Froiss.* I. cccxlii. 537 It shall tourne hym to moche blame. *Ibid.* ccccxxxvi. 767 He was as thanne xl. dayes iourney from thens, but..he rode it in fourtene dayes..whiche tourned to hym [*prob.* = hym to] a great valyantnesse. [*Orig.* On luy doit tourner a bonne voulenté et vaillance.] 1593 SHAKS. 3 *Hen. VI*, v. vi. 16 All the trouble thou hast turn'd me to. 1607 — *Cor.* III. i. 284 A word or two, The which shall turne you to no further harme, Then so much losse of time. 1610 — *Temp.* I. ii. 64 O my heart bleedes To thinke oth' teene that I haue turn'd you to.

** *Specific senses.*

**44.** *trans.* To change from one language or form of expression to another; to translate or paraphrase; to render. Also *absol.*

*c* 1200 ORMIN Ded. 129, & tærfore hafe icc turrnedd itt Inntill Ennglisshe spæche. *a* 1225 *Juliana* 2 Þat is of latin iturnd into englisch. *a* 1300 *Cursor M.* 21108 (Cott.) Godspell he turnd in tung of ind. 14.. *Minor Poems fr. Vernon MS.* (E.E.T.S.) I. App. 407 This romance turned [a] Munk of sallay out of a frenche romance. 1548 TURNER *Names of Herbes* (1881) 62 Picea is called in greeke as Theodore Gaza turneth, pitys. 1605 CAMDEN *Rem.* (1637) 86 Others untruely turne it [Robert] Red-beard. 1700 DRYDEN *Fables* Pref., Ess. (ed. Ker) II. 248, I..resolved to put their merits to the trial, by turning some of the *Canterbury Tales* into our language, as it is now refined. 1711 ADDISON *Spect.* No. 39 ¶ 6 If the Writer laid down the whole Contexture of his Dialogue in plain English, before he turned it into Blank Verse. 1735 POPE *Prol. Sat.* 180 The Bard.. Who turns a Persian tale for half a Crown. 1879 M. PATTISON *Milton* vii. 90 In 1648 he turned nine psalms, and..in 1653, 'did into verse' eight more.

**b.** To alter the phrasing of (a sentence); to word differently, give another turn to.

1593 SHAKS. *Lucr.* 1539 She..turn'd it thus, it cannot be, I find, But such a face should beare a wicked mind. 1869 BROWNING *Ring & Bk.* XII. 651 How he dares reprehend both high and low! Else had he turned the sentence 'God is true And every man a liar–save the Pope'. 1895 NORTH & HILLARD *Latin Prose Comp.* (1901) 24 The English has to be turned; *e.g.* 'The Greeks, having captured Troy, burnt it', cannot go straight into Latin, because Latin has no Perfect Participle Active.

**45.** To disturb or overthrow the mental balance of; to impair the power of judgement of; to make mad or crazy, distract, dement, infatuate.

**a.** with the brain or head as obj.

*c* 1340 HAMPOLE *Prose Tr.* 17 He..ouertrauells by ymaginacions his wittes, and by vndiscrete trauellynge turnes þe braynes in his heuede. 1601 R. JOHNSON *Kingd. & Commw.* (1603) 167 The Arabians..delight in sower milke, or Cosmus, a kind of charmed-sower-mares milke verie forcible to turne the braine. **1683** *Apol. Prot. France* iv. 40 The Prince's head was a little turned. **1719** De Foe *Crusoe* (1840) II. i. 8 My head was..turned with..whimsies. **1816** Scott *Bl. Dwarf* v, Your plays and romances have positively turned your brain. **1861** Hughes *Tom Brown at Oxf.* xxxv, You have been making serious love to Patty, and have turned the poor girl's head.

† **b.** with the person as obj. *Obs.*

*c* **1400** *Destr. Troy* 3272 All tourniet with tene,..Wailyng & weping. **1560** Daus tr. *Sleidane's Comm.* 136 b, Albeit they did not chaunge him wholy,..yet did they turne him & confounde him. **1709** Hearne *Collect.* (O.H.S.) II. 300 It quite turn'd him, and destroy'd his Memory.

**c.** *intr.* for *pass.* of the head. *rare.* (Cf. 2 b.)

**1852** M. Arnold *Second Best* 8 So many books thou readest,..That thy poor head almost turns. **1885** 'Mrs. Alexander' *At Bay* xi, I trust the poor man's head hasn't turned with all his troubles.

**46.** *trans.* To make sour, taint (milk or fermented liquor); † in early use, to coagulate, curdle. Also *fig.*

**1548** Elyot, *Coagulum*..a courde or creame, the ruen of a beaste, wherewith mylke is tourned. **1563** Hyll *Art Garden.* (1593) 164 A Hogshead..of white wine Lees, not yet turned and sowr. **1670** Dryden *2nd Pt. Conq. of Granada* iii. i, Love..'Tis soon made sour, and turn'd by jealousy. **1722** De Foe *Col. Jack* (1840) 138 This..turned the very blood within my veins. **1887** M. B. Edwards *Next of Kin Wanted* II. x. 130 A thunderstorm to-night might turn the syllabub.

**b.** *intr.* To become sour or tainted, as milk or fermented liquor; †in early use, To become curdled. Also *transf.* and *fig.*

**1577** B. Googe *Heresbach's Husb.* 147 Some vse to put into the bottome of the payles, the greene kernelles of the Pine apple, and milking into them, doo cause it so to turne. **1594** Lyly *Moth. Bomb.* ii. v, If it thunder, though all the Ale and Beere in the towne turne, it will be constant. **1623** Massinger *Bondman* i. iii, The blood turns! **1727** *Bradley's Fam. Dict.* s.v. *Chocolate,* If you would have Milk Chocolate, take as much Milk as you do Water,..and take care it does not turn. **1839** Ure *Dict. Arts* 602 A thunderstorm sometimes destroys the coagulating power in the whole laminæ at once; or causes the glue to turn on the nets, in the language of the manufacturer.

**47.** *intr.* To change colour, become of a different colour (as ripening fruit, fading leaves, hair in old age): = *turn colour*, 52.

† *Turn upon*, to verge upon or shade off into (a different colour). *Obs.*

**1578** Lyte *Dodoens* iii. lxxix. 428 In the middle of the sayde flowers are many smal hearie threddes..turning vpon yellowe. **1888** Howells *Annie Kilburn* iv, When her hair had begun to turn. **1892** *Daily News* 8 Nov. 6/2 No two trees turn alike; in every group each member wears his own livery. **1893** *Argosy* Jan. 71 Really some ripe strawberries?..Ours are not turning yet.

**b.** *trans.* To change the colour of.

**1791** Hamilton *Berthollet's Dyeing* II. ii. iii. ix. 233 The silk being distributed on the rods.., lemon-juice..is poured into the bath, till it is of a fine cherry colour. This is called turning (*virer*) the bath. **1867** Adelaide Sartoris *Week Fr. Country Ho.* i. 17 Poplars, already turned by the season.

**VII.** Phrases.

* *with sb. obj.*

(For *turn* Cat *in pan*, *t. a* Hair, *t. the* (or *a new*) Leaf, *t. the* Penny, *t. the* Tables, *t.* Tippet, *t.* Turtle, *t.* Wind, see the sbs.)

**48. Turn the** (or **one's**) **back:** to turn away, go away; *turn the back upon*, to depart from, abandon: see Back *sb.*[1] 24 g.

*c* **1330** R. Brunne *Chron. Wace* (Rolls) 8486 When þey wer sondred, þey tur[n]d þe bak. *c* **1400–1866** [see Back *sb.*[1] 24 g]. **1581** Earl Morton in *Calr. Scott. Pap.* VI. 14, I was purposed to have..turned my backe upon Scotland while I had sene further.

**49. Turn the balance** or **beam:** to preponderate: = *turn the scale*, 58.

**1590** Shaks. *Mids. N.* v. i. 324 A Mote [ed. 1623 Moth] wil turne the ballance, which Piramus which Thisby is the better. **1602** — *Ham.* iv. v. 157 Thy madnesse shall be payed by waight, Till our Scale turnes the beame. **1722** Wollaston *Relig. Nat.* iii. 59 When there is nothing in the opposite Scale..this [probability] in the course of nature must turn the beam. **1892** *Eng. Illustr. Mag.* X. 36 A straw will often suffice to turn the balance.

**50. Turn bridle:** to turn one's horse and ride back; to retreat, as a rider. (In first quot. *fig.*)

**1579** Tomson *Calvin's Serm. Tim.* 731/2 If there bee but one man that turneth backe the bridle [orig. *qui aura tourné bride*], wee seeme to seeke such occasions to become wicked and lewde. **1653** Holcroft *Procopius, Pers. Wars* ii. 60 The Persians..drave them out of the fastnesses, and then turn'd bridle. **1825** Scott *Betrothed* xiii, Were I you, my Lady Eveline,..I would turn bridle yet; for this old dungeon seems little likely to afford food or shelter to Christian folk. **1892** *Black & White* 9 Jan. 47/1 We turned bridle and trotted back.

**51. Turn one's coat:** to change one's principles or party: see Coat *sb.* 13, and cf. Turncoat.

**1565** Shacklock *Hatchet of Heresyes* 74 Howe many tymes Melancthon hath turned his cote in this one opinion. **1577** Grange *Golden Aphrod.*, etc. O iij b, Now must I turne my coate and cleaue vnto my God, Desiring pardon for my crime. **1655** Fuller *Ch. Hist* ix. vii. § 24 That all the Protestants would either turn their Coats, Copies, arms, or fly away. **1819** Scott *Leg. Montrose* xvii, Sir John Urrie, a soldier.., who had already changed sides twice during the Civil War, and was destined to turn his coat a third time before it was ended.

**52. Turn** (**one's**) **colour:** to change colour, become of a different colour; of a person, to become pale or red in the face (now *rare*).

[**1450**: cf. 39a.] **1602** Shaks. *Ham.* ii. ii. 542 Looke where he ha's not turn'd his colour, and ha's teares in's eyes. **1720** Mrs. Manley *Power of Love* (1741) VI. 346 She turned colour, and was much surprized to see so great a Company. **1899** *Tit-Bits* 19 Aug. 420/2 [These] buttons..do not turn colour. *Mod.* The fruit is beginning to turn colour.

**53. Turn a deaf ear:** to refuse to listen: cf. Ear *sb.*[1] 3 d.

**1663** Bp. Patrick *Parab. Pilgr.* xviii. (1687) 176 Turn a deaf ear to him, and do not go along with him. **1793** R. Hall *Apol. Freed. Press* 45 They..turn a deaf ear to their complaints. **1855** Dickens *Dorrit* ii. xxiii, Affery..turned a deaf ear to all adjuration.

**54. Turn edge:** see 9 b.

**55. Turn..flank:** *Mil.* to get round an enemy's flank so as to make an attack in flank or in rear (cf. 17 b); hence *fig.* to 'get round', circumvent, or outwit a person.

**1813** Wellington in Gurw. *Desp.* (1839) X. 596 Sir Lowry Cole..retired..because his right flank was turned. **1841–4** Emerson *Ess., Circles* Wks. (Bohn) I. 128 There is not a piece of science, but its flank may be turned to-morrow. **1844** H. H. Wilson *Brit. India* ii. ii. II. 45 Detaching.. seven companies to turn the left flank of the position.

**56. Turn one's hand. a.** To make an attack *upon*: cf. 31. *arch.*

**1297** R. Glouc. (Rolls) 6070 Suan þe duc of denemarch, bigan to turne is hond. & after þat he adde destrued þe souþhalf of þis lond, He wende & robbede al þis lond al þe norþ side. **1382** Wyclif *2 Sam.* xxiv. 17, I biseche, be thin hoond turned aȝens me, and aȝens the hows of my fader. **1839** [see sense 31]. **1877** *Queen's Printers' Bible-Aids* 134 David..entreating him [God] to spare the innocent people, and to turn his hand upon himself.

**b.** with *to*: To apply oneself to, set to work at, take up as an occupation: cf. 34.

**1703** Steele *Tender Husb.* ii. i, A good Servant should turn his Hand to every thing in a Family. **1856** *Jrnl. R. Agric. Soc.* XVII. ii. 358 [He] can turn his own hand to the plough when wanted. **1867** Smiles *Huguenots Eng.* ii. (1880) 22 [He] was ready to turn his hand to anything that might enable him to earn a living.

**57. Turn head:** to turn and face an enemy; to show a bold opposing front: the opposite of *turn tail*. Cf. Head *sb.* 29. ? *Obs.*

**1596** Shaks. *1 Hen. IV*, iii. ii. 102 He..Turnes head against the Lyons armed Iawes. **1677** N. Cox *Gentl. Recreat.* (ed. 2) 17 When Deer..turn head against the Hounds, we say, they Bay. **1724** De Foe *Mem. Cavalier* i. 125 Twas to no Purpose to turn Head, no Man would stand by us.

**58. Turn the scale:** to cause one scale of a balance to descend: said of an additional weight, usually a slight or just sufficient one; hence *fig.* to preponderate so as to determine the success or superiority of one of two opposing parties or sides.

**1603** Shaks. *Meas. for M.* iv. ii. 32 You waigh equallie: a feather will turne the Scale. **1697** Dryden *Æneid* x. 736 A single Soul's too light to turn the Scale. **1814** [see Scale *sb.*[1] 4]. **1874** Stubbs *Const. Hist.* I. x. 311 The scale was turned in favour of strong measures by the voice of the native troops.

**b.** with *at*, in lit. sense: To weigh slightly more than.

**1889** J. K. Jerome *Three Men in Boat* 283 He had weighed it carefully..and it turned the scale at thirty-four pounds. **1892** *Photogr. Ann.* II. 883 A case containing a ¼-plate camera..turning the scale at 6 lbs.

**59. Turn tail. a.** (orig. in *Falconry*) To turn the back and flee; to run away, retreat: see Tail *sb.*[1] 11 d.

**1575** Turberv. *Falconrie* 126 Most commonly if a yong hawke be let flee at olde game shee will turne tayle. *a* **1586–1719** [see Tail *sb.*[1] 11 d]. **1841** Capt. B. Hall *Patchwork* II. vii. 139 As soon as my companion turned tail..I was compelled..to run for it likewise. **1891** Gwen. D. Galton *La Fenton* v, He turned tail and fled.

**b.** with *on* or *upon*: To abandon, forsake.

**1624** Quarles *Job* v. 4 As a Truant-Scholler..turnes speedy tayle Upon his tedious booke. **1807** [see Tail *sb.*[1] 11 d]. **1852** James *Agnes Sorel* (1860) I. 14 [They] have turned tail upon their former faith.

† **c.** To turn in opposition or defiance: in proverbial phrase (see quots., and cf. 33, 66 d). *Obs.*

**1611** Middleton & Dekker *Roaring Girle* D.'s Wks. 1873 III. 158 Tread vpon a worme they say twill turne taile. **1641** G. Raleigh *Albania* 28 There is not the least Worme, but being trodden upon will turne taile.

† **60. Turn one's tale:** to tell a different story, 'change one's tune'. *Obs.*

**1535** Coverdale *Ecclus.* xxvii. 23 Whan thou art present, he shal..prayse thy wordes: but at the last he shall turne his tayle [1560 tale] and slaunder thy sayenge. **1678** Bunyan *Pilgr.* i. 13 Then they all turned their tales, and began to deride poor Christian behind his back.

** *with compl. adj. or adv. phr.* (*prep.* + *sb.*, *etc.*)

(See also In and out 2, *inside out* (Inside A. 4), *top over tail* (Top *sb.*[1] 24 d), Topsy-turvy, Upside down, *out of* (or *at*) Window, *the* Wrong *side out*.)

**61. Turn loose.** *trans.* To set free (an animal) and allow to go loose; *transf.* and *fig.* to free from restraint and allow to go where, or do as, one will; to leave to oneself or one's own devices.

**1598** Shaks. *Merry W.* ii. i. 190 If hee should intend this voyage toward my wife, I would turne her loose to him. **1679** Dryden *Tr. & Cr.* i. ii, He's the ablest man for judgment in all Troy; you may turn him loose, i' faith. **1765** *Treat. Dom. Pigeons* 77 He braces a letter under the wings of a Pigeon,..and..turns it loose. **1892** *Sat. Rev.* 9 Jan. 40/2 They are turned loose to graze on the succulent grasses.

**b.** To discharge, fire off (a bullet, or a firearm); also (*humorously*) *fig. intr.* with *on*, to speak to, address (cf. *open fire*, Fire *sb.* 14). *U.S.*

**1874** J. W. Long *Amer. Wild Fowl* xxvi. 269 When they are coming to your decoys down-wind..as they double back to alight, 'turn it loose' at the middle of the cluster. **1903** A. Adams *Log Cowboy* x, The chief could not speak a word of English..; when I turned loose on him in Spanish, he.. signed back to his band. *Ibid.* xiii, Somebody..turned his gun loose into the air.

**62. Turn to account.** † **a.** *intr.* To result in profit or advantage (cf. 43 and Account *sb.* 5); to be profitable, to 'pay'; also with dat. of person (prob. often taken as direct object: cf. 43 b). *Obs.*

**1675** G. R. tr. *Le Grand's Man without Passion* 227 Sometimes troubles turn us to account. *a* **1677** Barrow *Serm.* Wks. 1716 I. 10 Any of us may..throughly compass and carry it on; which will exceedingly turn to accompt. *a* **1692** Pollexfen *Disc. Trade* (1697) 20 Bullion or Coyn will turn them to a better Account. **1700** Wallis in *Collect.* (O.H.S.) I. 326 It may turn to good account. **1727** Swift *Modest Prop.* Wks. 1755 II. ii. 61 They will not yield above three pounds..which cannot turn to account either to the parents or kingdom. **1743** Pococke *Descr. East* I. 134 Of late the West India coffee..has sold so cheap, that it does not turn to account to send it to England.

**b.** *trans.* To make use of for one's advantage or profit (cf. 34); to employ profitably.

**1826** B'ness Bunsen in Hare *Life* (1879) I. vii. 267 Whether I shall ever find time..to turn to account the instructions of Neukomm. **1870** Tyndall *Notes Lect. Electr.* § 20 Others have turned to account mechanically the attraction exerted by electro-magnetic cores on bars of iron. **1878** L. Stephen *Johnson* i. 11 He could at least turn his talents to account.

**63. Turn to bay:** to turn and defend oneself, as a hunted animal at bay (see Bay *sb.*[4] 3); also *fig.*

**1810** Scott *Lady of L.* i. viii, The Stag must turn to bay, Where that rude rampart barred the way. **1832** Macaulay *Armada* 25 So glared he when at Agincourt in wrath he turned to bay. **1849** — *Hist. Eng.* vi. II. 137 The colonists turned to bay with the stubborn hardihood of their race.

*** *with another verb.*

† **64. Turn and wind** (in specific uses). *Obs.*

**a.** *intr.* and *refl.* To turn this way and that; to go or move in a winding course.

*a* **1300** *Cursor M.* 6540 (Cott.) He ne wist queþer it bettur war To turn or winde him forþar mare. **1634** Sir T. Herbert *Trav.* 20 In Mæanders [the dancers] turne and winde themselues. **1676** D'Urfey *Mad. Fickle* iv. ii, Turn and wind Like Foxes in a storme. *c* **1680** Beveridge *Serm.* (1729) I. 462 We see how all things wind and turn and work together, till they accomplish the end for which they were designed. **1824** Scott *Redgauntlet* Let. iv, A tall man, well mounted on a strong black horse, which he caused to turn and wind like a bird in the air.

† **b.** *trans.* To turn this way and that, as a rider his horse; *fig.* to manage according to one's pleasure, to do what one will with. (Cf. 9 c.)

**1596** Shaks. *1 Hen. IV*, iv. i. 109 To turne and winde a fierie Pegasus. **1606** *Sir G. Goosecappe* i. iv. in Bullen *O. Pl.* III. 26 Wee will turne her, and winde her, and make her so plyant, that we will drawe her thorugh a wedding ring yfaith. **1673** Milton *True Relig.* Wks. 1851 V. 414 An ordinary Protestant, well read in the Bible, may turn and wind their Doctors.

† **c.** To put in circulation, circulate, cause to pass in exchange: = *turn over*, 77 i. (Cf. 15 b.) *Obs.*

**1598** Grenewey *Tacitus' Ann.* iv. iv. (1622) 93 By turning and winding base merchandise in Affrica and Sicilia, he gayned his liuing. **1686** tr. *Chardin's Coronat. Solyman* 92 All the money that we turn and wind is the Kings.

**VIII.** In combination with adverbs.

**65. Turn about.** (See also simple senses and About *adv.*) * *intr.* † **a.** To move circularly on an axis; to rotate, revolve: = *turn round*, 78 a. *Obs.*

*c* **1000** *Sax. Leechd.* III. 254 Seo firmamentum tyrnþ symle onbutan us under þyssere eorðan & bufan .. & ealle ða steorran þe hyre on fæste synd turniað onbutan mid hyre. *a* **1300** *Holy Rode* 379 in *Leg. Rood* 48 Þer-aboute he let do Þe fourme of sonne and mone and of sterres also Scyne as it hem-sulf were and turne aboute vaste. **1539** Bible (Great) *Prov.* xxvi. 14 Lyke as the dore turneth aboute vpon the thresholde. **1609** Bible (Douay) *Numb.* xxviii. 14 Through al monethes, that succede one another as the yeare turneth about.

**b.** To reverse one's position or course; to turn so as to face or go in the opposite direction: = *turn round*, 78 b. Now *rare.*

**1303** [see Turning *vbl. sb.* 4]. **13..** *Sir Beues* (A.) 4070 'Fro whanne komeþ þis fair deistrer?..Which is þe kroupe? terne about!' Aboute he ternde þe deistrer. **1526** Tindale *John* i. 38 Jesus turned about, and sawe them folowe. **1676** Dryden *Aureng-z.* v. i, The Morning, as mistaken, turns about, And all her early fires again go out. **1719** De Foe *Crusoe* (1840) I. xx. 358 They began to retire, and turn about. **1804** *Man in Moon* 191, I turned about and went to sleep again. **1868** Morris *Earthly Par., Man born to be King* 250 He..turned about and left him there.

** *trans.* † **c.** To cause to rotate or revolve: = sense 1. *Obs.*

**1483** Caxton *G. de la Tour* F viij, [They] made hym to tourne aboute a mylle as a blynde hors. **1579** Tomson *Calvin's Serm. Tim.* 348/1 They..doe but turne about the pot. **1669** Sturmy *Mariner's Mag.* i. 34 The other Foot [of the compasses] being turned about, will..touch the Line AG.

**d.** To alter or reverse the position of; to put into a different, or the opposite, position (by a rotatory motion): = *turn round*, 78 e; *refl.* = b. Now *rare* or *Obs.*

*a* **1300** *Cursor M.* 15951 (Cott.) Jesus þan turnd him about. *c* **1300** *Ibid.* 23223 (Edinb.) Quil þou moht turn þin hand about. **13..** [see b]. *c* **1550** *Song Sir A. Barton* iii. in *Surtees Misc.* (1888) 65 King Henry was stout, and turnd hime about. **1590** SPENSER *F. Q.* II. iii. 42 So [she] turned her about, and fled. **1826** F. REYNOLDS *Life & Times* I. 174 Give me only time to turn myself about, and something must soon turn up trumps. [Cf. 78 b, note.]

**e.** To turn this way and that; to move or push about; also *fig.* = *turn over*, 77 e.

**1598** SHAKS. *Merry W.* v. v. 108 Pinch him, and burne him, and turne him about. **1610** — *Temp.* II. ii. 118 'Prethee doe not turne me about, my stomacke is not constant. **1725** WATTS *Logic* II. iv. § 3 Turn these Ideas about in your Mind.

**66. Turn again.** (See also simple senses and AGAIN *adv.*) * *intr.* † **a.** To face round the other way (usually in order to go back): = *turn back*, 69 e. *arch.*

*a* **1300** *Cursor M.* 12594 (Cott.) At þe vte-cuming o þe yatte He turnd again. *c* **1400** MAUNDEV. (Roxb.) iv. 13 Scho turned agayne with a hidous crie. **1678** [see AGAIN A. 1 b]. **1818** SCOTT *Rob Roy* xxi, Few turned again to take some minutes' voluntary exercise.

† **b.** To return, go back (= sense 21). *Obs.*

*c* **1200** *Trin. Coll. Hom.* 87 Ihc wile turnen agen to mine huse. **1340** HAMPOLE *Pr. Consc.* 7241 Alle þase þat tylle helle wendes.. Salle never after turne ogayne. *c* **1386** CHAUCER *Clerk's T.* 872 Naked out of my fadres hous, quod she, I cam and naked moot I turne agayn. *c* **1420** *Anturs of Arth.* 292 Ther salle.. Ane torne home a-3ayne [*v. r.* ye shullene turne ayene] for that tydynge. *c* **1511** *1st Eng. Bk. Amer.* (Arb.) Introd. 33/1 To tourne ageyne unto there owne lande. **1535** COVERDALE *Ruth* i. 11 But Naemi sayde: Turne agayne my doughters, why wolde ye go with me? **1612** R. JOHNSON *Song Sir Richard Whittington* v. in *Crown-Garl. Gould. Roses* B v b, London bells sweetly rung... Euermore sounding so, turne againe Whittington: For thou in time shalt grow, Lord Maior of London. **1640** SHIRLEY *Constant Maid* II. ii, Six bells in every steeple, And let them all go to the city tune,—*Turn again, Whittington.* **1667** PEPYS *Diary* 2 Sept., I took a coach and went homewards; but then turned again, and to White Hall.

† **c.** *fig.* To return to a former condition (or possessor: cf. 21 b); to revert. *Obs.* (or merged in other senses).

**1303** R. BRUNNE *Handl. Synne* 5232 To leue hys synne.. And turne a3en to lyfe and grace. *c* **1400** MAUNDEV. (Roxb.) iv. 12 Þan sall scho turne agayne to hir awen kynde and be a womman. *c* **1450** *Godstow Reg.* 198 Aftur þe deceasse of þe foreseyde..þe foreseyde mansyon with hys pertinences shulde turne holly & fully a-geyne to þe foreseyde abbas & couent. **1600** SHAKS. *A. Y. L.* II. vii. 162 His bigge manly voice, Turning againe toward childish trebble, pipes And whistles in his sound. **1697** DRYDEN *Virg. Georg.* IV. 597 Till..he turns agen To his true Shape.

† **d.** To turn in opposition or defiance; in quot. 1393, to recoil *on*; cf. 32, 33. *Obs.*

*c* **1330** *Arth. & Merl.* (Kölbing) 6871 Þe Sarrazins turned o3en On king Vrien. **1393** LANGL. *P. Pl.* C. xxi. 402 Now by-gynneþ thi gyle a-gayn on þe turne. *a* **1548** HALL *Chron., Edw. IV* 199 What worme is touched, and will not once turne again? **1641** in *Verney Mem.* (1907) I. 199 A worme will turne agayne if it be trod on.

† **e.** Of an edge: To bend back so as to become blunted: = sense 9 d. *Obs.*

**1579** SPENSER *Sheph. Cal.* Feb. 203 The Axes edge did oft turne againe.

** *trans.* † **f.** *refl.* = a, b. *Obs.*

*c* **1275** *Passion of our Lord* 653 in *O. E. Misc.* 55 Hi turnden heom ayeyn..to iherusalem. **13..** *Cursor M.* 12608 (Gött.) Ioseph and mari þaim turned againe To sek him. *c* **1420** *Chron. Vilod.* 1739 When þe messagers seyen herre so stedfaste..þey tur[n]den hem a3eyne. **1539** BIBLE (Great) *Ps.* xc. 13 Turne the agayne (O Lorde) at the last, and be gracious.

† **g.** *trans.* To cause to turn back (in various senses); to avert (cf. 13 b); to drive back, repel (cf. 19, 25); to convert (= 29). *Obs.*

*c* **1380** WYCLIF *Wks.* (1880) 288 To turnen a3en þis þondir þat it persiþ no3t. **1387** TREVISA *Higden* (Rolls) V. 233 By his witte and sleiþe þe Hunnes were i-torned a3en. **1483** *Cath. Angl.* 397/1 To Turne agayn to gudnes,..*conuertere.*

**67. Turn aside:** see simple senses and ASIDE *adv.* **a.** *trans.*: cf. 13, 14. In quot. 13.. *refl.* (= b); cf. 7 b.

**13..** *Coer de L.* 355 The baroun turnyd hym asyde. **1535** COVERDALE *Isa.* xliv. 20 Folishnesse of herte hath turned them a syde. *a* **1648** LD. HERBERT *Autobiog.* (1824) 114 Lieutenant Prichard.. taking me by the shoulder, turned me aside. **1718** *Free-thinker* No. 62 ¶ 14 The Gods were beseeched to turn aside the Event. **1892** *Cornh. Mag.* May 478 He had never been turned aside from the execution of his purpose.

**b.** *intr.*: cf. 6, 16, 28.

**1535** COVERDALE *Deut.* v. 32 Turne not asyde nether to ye right hande ner to the lefte. **1560** BIBLE (Genev.) *Exod.* iii. 3, I wil turne aside now, and se this great sight. — *Ps.* xl. 4 Blessed is the man, that..regardeth not the proude, nor suche as turne aside to lies. **1606** SHAKS. *Ant. & Cl.* I. iii. 76, I prythee turne aside, and weepe for her. **1844** LD. BROUGHAM *A. Lunel* (1872) I. xiv. 282 The Baron turned not aside from his argument. **1891** *Temple Bar Mag.* Dec. 581 He turned aside and crept in at the open door.

**68. Turn away.** (See simple senses and AWAY *adv.*) * *trans.* **a.** To avert (one's face, etc.); in quot. 1827, to place so as to be directed away from something (cf. 23 d).

*c* **1175** *Lamb. Hom.* 53 Swa sone se hi beoð iturnd awey from heom. *c* **1380** WYCLIF *Wks.* (1880) 8 His preiere is cursid..þat turneþ a-wey his eris. **1382** — *Ps.* xii[i]. 1 Lord..hou longe thou turnest awei thi face fro me? **1588** SHAKS. *L. L. L.* v. ii. 148 Each turne away his face. **1782** COWPER *Anti-thelyphthora* 87 She saw,—and turn'd her rosy cheek away. **1827** FARADAY *Chem. Manip.* xv. (1842) 327 In filling the fresh jar with water, its mouth is to be turned away from the gas jars. **1889** FRANCES M. PEARD *Paul's Sister* v, She..turned away her head.

**b.** *fig.* To divert; to avert (calamity, etc.): cf. 14, 26; in quot. 1848 = *turn off*, 73 g.

**1382** WYCLIF *Ps.* liii[i]. 7 [5] Turne awei euelis to myn enemys. — *Isa.* xliii. 13, I shal werchen, and who shal turnen awei it? *c* **1591** in *Lett. Lit. Men* (Camden) 79 To turne awaie the peoples likinge from him. **1658** *Whole Duty Man* v. 112 Deprecation,.. when we pray to God to turn away some evil from us. **1848** THACKERAY *Bk. Snobs* xxvi, Which question Lady Hawbuck turned away with a sudden query regarding her..daughters.

**c.** To send away, dismiss; *spec.* to dismiss from service; † in quot. *c* 1400, ? to take away, carry off. (Cf. 25.)

*c* **1400** *Destr. Troy* 8553 He was takon full tite & turnyt away. **1598** SHAKS. *Merry W.* I. iii. 4, I must turne away some of my followers. *a* **1654** SELDEN *Table-T.* (Arb.) 63 The Master of the House may turn away all his Servants. **1793** *Regal Rambler* 17 The footman..was turned away without wages or warning. **1866** MRS. GASKELL *Wives & Dau.* xxiii, He has turned away all the men off the new works. **1901** W. R. H. TROWBRIDGE *Lett. Mother to Eliz.* vii, We were lucky to get rooms.., for they are turning people away.

**d.** *refl.* = e, f. *Obs.* or *arch.*

**1375** BARBOUR *Bruce* I. 167 [He] turnyt him in wreth away. **1382** WYCLIF *Ezek.* xviii. 24 If a iust man shal turne hym awei fro his ri3twisness.

** *intr.* **e.** To turn so as to face away from some person or thing; to avert one's face; also *fig.*: cf. 22 c, 23 c, 28.

*a* **1300** *Floriz & Bl.* 744 Al wepinge he turnde away. **1470–85** MALORY *Arthur* XIII. viii. 623 The kyng tourned awey and myghte not speke for wepynge. **1593** SHAKS. *2 Hen. VI*, III. ii. 74 What, dost thou turne away, and hide thy face? **1840** DICKENS *Barn. Rudge* xxii, 'Oh, very well—if you're in a huff', cried Miggs, turning away. **1865** RUSKIN *Sesame* ii. § 91 Instead of trying to do this, you turn away from it.

**f.** To leave the straight course, deviate; to be averted: cf. 16. *Obs.* or *arch.*

**1535** COVERDALE *Ezek.* xviii. 24 Yf the rightuous turne awaye from his rightuousnes. **1611** BIBLE *Gen.* xxvii. 45 Vntill thy brothers anger turne away from thee.

† **g.** To go away, depart; to vanish. (Cf. 24 c.) *Obs. rare.*

**1340** HAMPOLE *Pr. Consc.* 516 Naked,..I cam Hyder,.. And naked I sal turne away. *c* **1425** *Cursor M.* 22472 (Trin.) Whenne alle þinge shul turne away.

**69. Turn back.** (See simple senses and BACK *adv.*) * *trans.* **a.** To reverse the course of, drive back, cause to retreat: cf. 19.

**1535** COVERDALE *Jer.* xxi. 4, I will turne backe the weapens ..wherwith ye fight agaynst the kinge of Babilon. **1872** MORLEY *Voltaire* vi. (1886) 314 The man who turned the tide back. **1880** R. MACKENZIE *19th Cent.* III. ix. 448 To arrest and turn back the mightiest power.

† **b.** To send or give back, return: cf. 21 c. *Obs.*

**1597** SHAKS. *2 Hen. IV*, I. i. 34 Sir Iohn Vmfreuill turn'd me backe With ioyfull tydings. **1606** — *Tr. & Cr.* II. ii. 69 We turne not backe the Silkes vpon the Merchant When we haue spoyl'd them. **1672** VILLIERS (Dk. Buckhm.) *Rehearsal* II. iii. (Arb.) 55 These insolent Raskals have turn'd 'em all back upon my hands again.

**c.** To reverse the direction of; to direct backwards: cf. 22 a, 23 a.

In quot. 1845, to expose by reversing: = *turn over*, 77 c.

**1663** BP. PATRICK *Parab. Pilgr.* xxxiv. (1687) 417 They heard the noise of an horses heels behind them. Which causing them to turn their eyes back [etc.]. **1825** SCOTT *Talism.* ii, It were better..to turn back thy horse's head towards the camp of thy people. **1845** *Jrnl. R. Agric. Soc.* VI. II. 344 Both heaps [of potatoes] have now been turned back, and none are diseased.

**d.** To fold or double back or over (part of a garment, etc.). Also in *pa. pple.* with *with* = *turned up with*: see 80 e.

**1869** H. S. LEIGH *Carols of Cockayne* 166 He turn'd back his cuffs, and he put back his hair. **1913** *Play Pictorial* No. 130. 18/2 A gown of green paon broché crêpe de chine, draped ..with tulle,..turned back with handsome cream guipure.

** *intr.* **e.** To reverse one's position so as to face (and, usually, go) in the opposite direction; to turn and go back: cf. 20, 22 c, 23 c, 24 c.

**1535** COVERDALE *Ps.* cxiii[i]. 5 What ayled the..thou Iordan that thou turnedst backe? **1592** SHAKS. *Rom. & Jul.* II. i. 2 Can I goe forward when my heart is here? Turne backe dull earth, and find thy Center out. **1816** SCOTT *Antiq.* vii, 'Turn back! turn back!' exclaimed the vagrant. **1843** MACAULAY *Horatius* lii, He..thrice came on in fury, And thrice turned back in dread. **1886** MRS. LYNN LINTON *P. Carew* xxv, He had put his hand to the plough, and he was not the man to turn back.

† **f.** To come or go back, return: cf. 21. *Obs.*

*c* **1600** SHAKS. *Sonn.* cxliii. 11 Turne back to me. **1611** BIBLE *2 Kings* i. 5 When the messengers turned backe vnto him, he said.., Why are ye now turned backe? **1660** F. BROOKE tr. *Le Blanc's Trav.* 37 We turned back again into Persia.

†**70. Turn by.** *trans.* To set aside, reject (a candidate): cf. BY *adv.* 2. (Also with *by* as prep.: cf. BY *prep.* 16 c.) *Obs.*

**1705** HEARNE *Collect.* 7 Dec. (O.H.S.) I. 119 When he stood for orders [he] was turn'd by for Deficiency. [**1709** *Ibid.* II. 294 Reasons..not reckon'd as sufficient for turning Mr. Littleton by his Degree.] **1803** J. ADAMS in *Harvard Grad. Mag.* IX. 349, I was in a great fright, and expected to be turned by.

**71. Turn down.** (See simple senses and DOWN *adv.*) * *trans.* **a.** To fold or double down; to bend downwards: cf. 9.

**1601** SHAKS. *Jul. C.* IV. iii. 273 Is not the Leafe turn'd downe Where I left reading? **1793** SMEATON *Edystone L.* § 273 The cramps..were turned down at each end. **1828** [H. BEST] *Italy as it is* 128 The beds..were all, in the housewife's phrase, turned down. **1841** THACKERAY *Gt. Hoggarty Diam.* vii, Nothing could make him..refrain from wearing his collars turned down.

**b.** To turn upside down, to invert; to turn (a card) face downwards: cf. 10.

**1763** *Brit. Mag.* IV. 117 Sometimes she turns down my cup herself, after the first dish, because..tea is nervous. **1859** FITZGERALD *Omar* lxxv, Turn down an empty Glass! **1890** FENN *Double Knot* III. viii. 115 The played cards were solemnly turned down.

**c.** To put down, send to a lower position (as in a class at school; also *fig.*): cf. 25. ? *Obs.*

**1581** J. BELL *Haddon's Answ. Osor.* 69 You beyng ignoraunt what difference is betwixt an affirmative, & a negative proposition, must be turned doune agayne behinde the Schoolehouse doore. **1693** DRYDEN *Examen Poeticum* Ded., Ess. (Ker) II. 3 Julius Scaliger would needs turn down Homer and abdicate him.

**d.** *U.S. slang.* To rebuke, snub, 'put down'; to reject, refuse to accept.

**1891** *Cent. Dict.* s.v., *To turn down*..(*c*) to snub; suppress. (Slang, U.S.) **1897** *Boston* (Mass.) *Jrnl.* 14 Jan. 7/6 Secretary Olney was turned down by the Senate..in his effort to have the vote on the extradition treaties..reconsidered. **1900** *Montreal Gaz.* 3 Mar. 2/7 [Denmark] turns down America's offer. **1913** EDITH WHARTON *Custom of Country* II. xvi, The Ararat investigation had been..quashed, ..and Elmer Moffatt 'turned down'.

**e.** *colloq.* To drink down, 'toss off' (? *obs.*); also in *Brewing*, to put (liquor) into a vat to ferment. (Cf. 25 c.)

**1760–72** H. BROOKE *Fool of Qual.* (1809) III. 150 Asking for a flask of champaign, [he] turned it down without taking it once from his head. **1826** *Art Brewing* (ed. 2) 109 Turned down 28 barrels of liquor, at 158 deg. **1844** W. H. MAXWELL *Sports & Adv. Scotl.* xxxvi. (1855) 289 We turned down a second tumbler.

**f.** *Sporting*, etc. To put (game, etc.) in a place to stock it.

**1891** *Field* 26 Dec. 963/3 Foxes..are turned down in order that the supply may be kept up. **1892** *Ibid.* 19 Nov. 793/3, I would urge all farmers to turn down some Indian game cocks in their yards.

**g.** To lower (a lamp, gas) by turning the handle or stop-cock: cf. 1 b.

**1868** MISS BRADDON *Dead Sea Fr.* xix, Love's torch.. flames anew before we turn it down for ever. **1892** *Harper's Mag.* LXXXIV. 283/2 She..turned the lamps down low.

** *intr.* **h.** To bend one's course downwards (with change of direction); to turn aside and go down: cf. 16.

*c* **1595** CAPT. WYATT *R. Dudley's Voy. W. Ind.* (Hakl. Soc.) 29 Commaundinge him that they shoulde..turne downe unto the other carvell. **1833** T. HOOK *Parson's Dau.* I. i, Opposite the limekilns, as you turn down to the Duke's Head, near the turnpike. **1887** P. M'NEILL *Blawearie* 88 Long before the men in general began to turn down, he had every box in the pit-bottom filled.

**i.** To bend downwards: cf. 9 d.

**1885** MALET *Col. Enderby's Wife* III. ii, The corners of his mouth began to turn down in an ominous fashion.

**72. Turn in.** (See simple senses and IN *adv.*) * *trans.* **a.** To send, drive, put, or take in: cf. 25, 25 b, 25 c. † In quot. *c* 1300 *refl.* = e below.

*c* **1300** *St. Brandan* 472 Ther cam out a grislich wi3t..Thurf suart and berning al his e3en upe hem he caste, And turnde him in anon. **1607** TOPSELL *Four-f. Beasts* (1658) 373 He turned in amongst them some of his foresaid children. **1762** in W. WING *Ann. Steeple Aston* (1875) 63 No horse or sheep to be turn'd in under the penalty of twenty shillings..for each offence. **1891** F. W. ROBINSON *Her Love & His Life* IV. x, You will turn in the cash by wholesale.

**b.** *Agric.* To bury or cover (weeds, stubble, manure) by turning the soil over them in digging or ploughing; to dig or plough into the ground. Also with the ground as obj. (Cf. 11 b, 25 c.)

**1563** HYLL *Art Garden.* (1593) 3 The Gardens..should be .. both well digged and turned in with dung. **1577** B. GOOGE *Heresbach's Husb.* 22 In the Spring the ground being mellowe..the weedes are then best turned in. **1864** *Jrnl. R. Agric. Soc.* XXV. II. 526 Not to turn in the wheat-stubble much before Christmas. *Ibid.* 528 The clover-lands that I have just turned in for roots. **1866** *Ibid.* Ser. II. II. I. 170 Loamy land is ploughed a second time before winter, and the manure turned in.

**c.** To bend or fold inwards: cf. 9. Also *Naut.*: see quot. 1867.

**1572** in Feuillerat *Revels Q. Eliz.* (1908) 159 White Rownde plates turnde in with a crest. **1721** SWIFT *George-Nim-Dan-Dean's Answ.* 18 Thus a wise tailor is not pinching, But turns at every seam an inch in. **1776** WITHERING *Brit. Plants* (1796) IV. 201 Pileus pale yellow,..edge turned in, 1½ to 2 inches over. **1867** SMYTH *Sailor's Word-bk.*, *Turn in a dead eye* or *heart*, *to*, to seize the end of a shroud or stay, &c., securely round it.

**d.** To cause to point or face inwards: cf. 7, 23 a.

**1851** MAYHEW *Lond. Labour* (1861) III. 200/2, I gives 'em.. the bandy jig, that's dancing with my toes turned in. **1865** *Morn. Star* 27 Jan., To turn the tallies in. That is to put the tallies against the wall, so that they should not be seen. **1870** *Daily News* 19 July 6 Go-ahead, a good mare..turns in her toes a little.

** *intr.* **e.** To turn aside and go in (to a place, house, room, etc.): cf. 16, 24 c.

**1535** COVERDALE *Judg.* iv. 18 Iael wente forth to mete Sissera, & sayde..: Turne in my lorde. **1658** GURNALL *Chr. in Arm.* verse 14. III. ix. 257 Even they sometimes turne in at the fairest signe. **1888** MISS TYTLER *Blackhall Ghosts* II

xv. 23 Hearing your stable clock strike as I turned in at your gate.

**f.** (orig. *Naut.*) To go to bed. *colloq.*

**1695** CONGREVE *Love for L.* III. xv, *Mrs. F.* I believe it's late. *B.*...An you think so, you had best go to Bed...I mean to toss a Can..afore I turn in. **1837** T. HOOK *Jack Brag* xiii, Jack 'turned in', as the sailors say. **1891** N. GOULD *Double Event* 218 It's late..and quite time we turned in.

**g.** To change its course and go inwards; †of an eruption, to disappear (opp. to *break out*).

*a* **1776** R. JAMES *Dissert. Fevers* (1778) 29 Small-pox.. which turned in the seventh day of the eruption and went off in the most desirable manner. **1862** PYCROFT *Cricket Tutor* 35 Spinning bowling is always liable to turn in or break away contrary to all expectation.

**h.** To have an inward direction, point inwards: as, 'his toes turn in'. (Cf. 23 c, d.)

**73. Turn off.** (See simple senses and OFF *adv.*) * *trans.* **a.** To strip off, peel off. Also *intr.* for *pass.* (Cf. 4 c.) ? *Obs.*

**1737** BRACKEN *Farriery Impr.* (1756) I. 108 The Crystalline ..becomes White, and turns off in..Laminae..like unto the Coats of an Onion. *Ibid.* 109 We cut this..thin Membrane, and turn off..one or more of the Laminae of the Crystalline Humour.

**b.** To dismiss, send away; *spec.* to discharge from service or employment: cf. *turn away*, 68 c.

In quot. 1841, = *turn loose* (61).

**1564** HARDING *Answ. Welles Chalenge* xi. 128 If any deuout person require to be partetaker with the priest,..he is not tourned of, but with all gentlenes admitted. **1601** SHAKS. *All's Well* v. iii. 220 You that haue turn'd off a first so noble wife. **1676** EARL ESSEX in *Essex Papers* (Camden) II. 73 It not being reasonable to turne off an old servant without some provision. **1768** GOLDSM. *Good-n. Man* I, Pay him his wages and turn him off. **1841** *Jrnl. R. Agric. Soc.* II. II. 152 His unshod cattle..were turned off to regale themselves upon the neighbouring waste. **1892** *Temple Bar Mag.* Mar. 321 A packer had been turned off for carelessness.

†**c.** To give over, resign, consign (*to*). *Obs.*

**1667** *Decay Chr. Piety* (J.), We are not so wholly turned off to that reversion, as to have no supplies for the present. **1674** *Govt. Tongue* x. 185 The murmurer seems to be turn'd off to the company of those doleful Creatures..which were to inhabit the ruines of Babylon.

**d.** To hang (on a gallows): orig. *to turn off the ladder* (cf. 7, and LADDER *sb.* 1 b). Now *rare* or *Obs.*

[**1594** NASHE *Unfort. Trav.* Wks. (Grosart) V. 185 A fidler cannot turne his pin so soone, as he would turn a man of the ladder.] **1680** C. NESSE *Church Hist.* 143 His own mule ..as it were, turns him off the ladder..he turns himself off when he had tyed his halter. **1715** J. CHAPPELOW *Right Way Rich* (1717) 64 The executioner has him upon the ladder.. and turns him off in an instant. **1840** THACKERAY *Catherine* viii, I've seen a many men turned off.

**e.** *humorously* (? *fig.* from prec.). To marry, join in marriage. (Cf. *to tie the knot.*)

**1759** H. WALPOLE *Let. to G. Montagu* 16 May, Lord Weymouth is to be married on Tuesday, or, as he said himself, to be turned off. **1833** MARRYAT *P. Simple* xxxix, They will be turned off next Friday, and I only wish you were here to dance at the weddings. **1891** S. MOSTYN *Curatica* 157, I sent a reply..wishing her every happiness and consenting 'to turn her off'.

**f.** To deflect, divert (*lit.* and *fig.*): cf. 13, 14.

**1716** ADDISON *Freeholder* No. 34 ⁋ 6 To turn off the Thoughts of the People from busying themselves in Matters of State. **1719** DE FOE *Crusoe* (1840) II. vi. 151 He turned off the discourse to the rest. **1736** LEDIARD *Life Marlborough* III. 75 To turn off the Waters of the River..which made the Inundations. **1846** H. G. ROBINSON *Odes Horace* II. xvii, Had Faunus not turn'd off the stroke.

**g.** *spec.* To give a different turn to; to divert attention from, or alter the effect of (a remark, etc.).

**1744** OZELL tr. *Brantome's Sp. Rhodomontades* 18 He turn'd it off with a Laugh, which was only Teeth outwards. **1836** G. GISSING *Isabel Clarendon* viii, Ada seemed about to rise, but turned it off in an arrangement of her dress. **1892** *Blackw. Mag.* CLI. 88/2 That's all very fine; ..you may turn it off in that way, but the fact remains.

**h.** To stop the flow of (water, gas, electric current, etc.) by turning a tap or the like (cf. 1 b), or by closing a sluice; to shut off; to turn out (a light). Also with the tap, etc. as obj.

**1850** *Jrnl. R. Agric. Soc.* XI. I. 199 The waste steam..may be..turned on or off by a cock. **1886** *Law Times Rep.* LIII. 676/1 The gas is turned off at eleven o'clock. **1891** L. KEITH *Lost Illusion* II. xiv. 101 She did not turn the gas off at the meter. **1892** *Black & White* 23 Jan. 116/2 The electric lights..were turned off. **1892** *Monthly Packet* Dec. 656 When the water is running away one must hurry up and turn off the tap.

**i.** To complete and get off one's hands; to produce (with skill or facility): = *turn out*, 75 j.

In quot. 1897, to accomplish (a distance) swiftly.

[**1684** *New Hampshire Prov. Papers* (1867) I. 521 The actions go on, and are turned off hand apace, twelve at a clap.] **1840** DICKENS *Barn. Rudge* xxxix, 'When I [the hangman] look at that hand and remember the helegant bits of work it has turned off.' [With play on sense d.] **1855** *Poultry Chron.* III. 160 The hens were..square short-legged birds, likely to turn off some good chickens. **1879** M. PATTISON *Milton* ix. 108 Turning off 300 pages of fluent Latin. **1897** *Outing* (U.S.) XXX. 242/2 We [cyclists] rode on through Harrisonburg and turned off the twenty-five miles to..Staunton.

**j.** To turn the soil so as to form (a furrow); in quot. 1858, to round off (a corner) in ploughing.

**1842** *Jrnl. R. Agric. Soc.* III. I. 11 Admiring..its [the Scotch plough's] apparent facility in cleaving and turning off the furrow. **1858** *Ibid.* XIX. II. 277 One plough goes and turns off the corners.

** *intr.* (See also a.) **k.** To turn away or aside from the direct road; to deviate; also *transf.* of a road or path, to branch off: cf. 16, 16 e.

**1687** NORRIS *Misc.*, *To his Muse* iv, Where with noise the waters creep Turn off with Care, for treacherous rocks are nigh. **1742** POPE *Dunc.* IV. 525 The vulgar herd turn off to roll with Hogs. **1776** *Pennsylv. Even. Post* 27 June 320/2 A road that turns off on the left hand. **1820** W. IRVING *Sketch Bk.* (1859) 11 He turned off, through a gate, into some ornamented grounds. **1892** *Leisure Hour* Jan. 188/1, I took a wrong turning, or kept straight on when I ought to have turned off.

**l.** To fall off in quality, 'go off', change for the worse; to wither and fall off; also, of food, etc.: to become sour or bad. Also with *compl. adj.*

**1797** *Monthly Mag.* III. 489 The Rye-Grass and Clovers are expected..to turn off light. **1813** JANE AUSTEN *Lett.* (1884) II. 202 The day turned off..and we came home in some rain. **1846** *Jrnl. R. Agric. Soc.* VII. II. 380 My ash-leaf potatoes..looked healthy; they, however, turned off sickly in June...The Shaw[s]..were short in the haulm, and turned off by the middle of July. **1889** *Devonsh. Provinc.* in *Eng. Dial. Dict.* s. v., I think the chutney's turned off, sir.

**74. Turn on. a.** *trans.* To induce a flow of (water, steam, gas, electric current) by turning a tap or stop-cock (cf. 1 b), or by opening a sluice; also with the tap, etc. as obj.; also *intr.* for *pass.* (quot. 1890); also *fig.*

**1833** HT. MARTINEAU *Loom & Lugger* I. i. 10 He turned on the gas in his back room to an unusual brightness. **1846** *Jrnl. R. Agric. Soc.* VII. II. 403 The steam being turned on. **1874** MICKLETHWAITE *Mod. Par. Churches* 186 Having certain jets [of gas] turned on at full. **1890** MRS. HUNGERFORD *Born Coquette* xiii, A moon..warranted to last for eight hours and to turn on at any moment. **1891** *Review of Rev.* 14 Nov. 523/2 The electric lamp that glows..when the current is turned on. **1892** *Blackw. Mag.* CLI. 79/2 A sluice might be turned on to flood a certain meadow. **1892** *Black & White* 21 May 674/2 A woman who turned on her smiles as we do the electric light.

**b.** To set (a person) *to do* something; to employ: cf. 34 b. *colloq.*

**1893** *Chamb. Jrnl.* 8 July 419/2 Ainsworth had turned him on to assist him in 'doing' the theatres.

**75. Turn out.** (See simple senses and OUT *adv.*) * *trans.* †**a.** ? To change from one's normal condition, to 'put out'; or ? to divert from one's course. *Obs. rare*⁻¹.

*c* **1320** *Cast. Love* 1211 In wonhope weore his disciples.. Ac þou weore studefast..Ne miȝte þe no þing tornen out.

**b.** To put or take out by a rotary movement (in quot. 1892, on a lathe); †to bore or gouge out.

**13..** *Erasmus* in Horstm. *Altengl. Leg.* (1878) 202 Þe turmentours .. turnyng oute his ien withe wymbles. **1892** *Photogr. Ann.* II. 286 Extending frame and reversing back mitred, keyed and glued up; the front turned out for circular disc.

**c.** To cause to go or come out; to drive out or forth, to expel; also (*trans.* of o), to fetch or summon out (quots. 1867, 1903). Cf. 25.

**1546** J. HEYWOOD *Prov.* (1867) 82 He turnde hir out at doores. **1611** BEAUM. & FL. *Knt. Burning Pest.* III. v, Open the doore, and turne me out those mangy companions. **1672** VILLIERS (Dk. Buckhm.) *Rehearsal* II. iv. (Arb.) 61 If they heard us whisper, they'l turn us out. **1832** *Examiner* 418/1 If he ever turned out a tenant for voting against him. **1867** SMYTH *Sailor's Word-bk.*, *Turn out the guard!* the order for the marines of the guard to fall in, on the quarter-deck, in order to receive a superior officer. **1894** BARING-GOULD *Queen of L.* I. viii. 86 'Turn him out!' was shouted from the further side of the hall. **1903** BOSW. SMITH in *19th Cent.* Mar. 436 One raven..managed more than once to 'turn out' the guard, who thought they were summoned by the sentinel.

**d.** To drive or put out (beasts) to pasture or to the open, or (pheasants, etc.) into a covert: cf. 25 b.

**1560** DAUS tr. *Sleidane's Comm.* 360 b, The cattel which the townes men daily turned out into the pasture. **1679** J. GOODMAN *Penit. Pard.* II. iv. (1713) 229 He hath now, like Nebuchadnezzar, been turned out to grass. **1802** G. MONTAGU *Ornith. Dict.* (1831) 424 Lord Caernarvon..turned out several [ring pheasants] at his seat at Highclere. **1853** *Jrnl. R. Agric. Soc.* XIV. I. 64 The colts were turned out on the open commons.

**e.** To dismiss or eject from office or employment.

**1588** J. UDALL *Diotrephes* (Arb.) 16 Neither will the Churche euer be in quiet vntill you be all turned out. **1667** in *10th Rep. Hist. MSS. Comm.* App. v. 41 The..Captain hath..turned out some of his said Company that have refused to compound for lesse than the King's pay. **1708** *Constit. Watermen's Co.* xviii, If any..of the Rulers or Auditors shall happen to dye, or be turned out for Corruption. **1885** 'MRS. ALEXANDER' *At Bay* ii, I am very sorry he lost the election...It was the radical mining people that turned him out. **1892** *Sat. Rev.* 17 Dec. 705/2 They will seize 'the first occasion' to turn the Government out.

**f.** To put (things) out of a house, room, or receptacle; to empty out by sloping or inverting the containing vessel.

**1666** in *Verney Mem.* (1907) II. 255 My hous is not yet burnt, but all I have turn'd out. **1827** FARADAY *Chem. Manip.* xvi. (1842) 420 The small quantity of fluid remaining..is to be turned out, by inclining the tube. **1892** *Blackw. Mag.* CLI. 190/1, I shall turn out all your furniture.

**g.** (*transf.* from f.) To clear (a receptacle or room) of its contents; to empty (usually for the sake of examining or re-arranging the contents).

**1809** MALKIN *Gil Blas* VII. xi. ⁋ 6 The enraged marquis.. turning her whole house out at window. **1862** MRS. H. WOOD *Mrs. Hallib.* I. xxi, She turned out his pockets. **1887** E. F. BYRRNE *Heir without Heritage* III. iii. 66, I will go to my room..and turn my drawers out. **1894** HALL CAINE *Manxman* 211 She overhauled the linen; turned out every room twice a week.

**h.** To put or throw (land) out of cultivation.

**1856** OLMSTED *Slave States* 373 The greater part, even of these once rich low lands, that had been in cultivation, were now 'turned out', and covered..with..broom-sedge and brushwood.

**i.** To put out, extinguish (a lamp, gas) by turning a tap or the like.

**1884** *Punch* 27 Dec. 310/2 Then the gas was turned out. **1905** ELIN. GLYN *Viciss. Evangeline* 237 She..was turning out the light.

**j.** To finish making and get off one's hands; to dispose of as a finished product; to produce (usually implying rapidity, facility, or skill): = 73 i.

[**1757** W. THOMPSON *R. N. Advoc.* 47 Casks would..be turn'd out of their Hands, fit for the several Purposes.] **1847** L. HUNT *Men, Women, & B.* II. vi. 86 Books were books in those days, not batches, by the baker's dozen, turned out every morning. **1878** BESANT & RICE *Celia's Arb.* xv, No place..could..turn out more splendid ships' figure-heads. **1878** L. STEPHEN *Johnson* ii. 16 A man who turned out books as a bricklayer turns out houses or a tailor coats. **1913** E. H. D. SEWELL in *Daily Graphic* 26 Mar. 14/2 La Touche..is one of the best half-backs Sedbergh has ever turned out.

**k.** To equip, 'rig out', 'get up'.

**1812** [implied in TURN-OUT *sb.* 7]. **1833** [see TURNED *ppl. a.* 8]. **1886** C. E. PASCOE *Lond. of To-day* xli. (ed. 3) 354 At either of these places the visitor may be sure of being turned out 'one of the best-dressed men in London'. **1892** *Pictorial World* 4 June 12/1 Coaches were fewer..but they were better 'turned out'.

**l.** To refer to, look up: = *turn up*, 80 h. *rare.*

**1834** *Tracts for Times* No. 29. 8 To turn out for him the texts he had referred to. **1895** RASHDALL *Universities* II. 329 Turning out the word..in the indices of..chroniclers.

**m.** To alter the position of so as to bring it to the outside. (In quot. with figurative allusion.)

**1605** SHAKS. *Lear* IV. ii. 9 He..told me I had turn'd the wrong side out.

**n.** To direct or cause to point outwards.

**1697** J. LEWIS *Mem. Dk. Glocester* (1789) 12 Turning out his toes. **1813** PRICHARD *Phys. Hist. Man.* (1837) II. 138 The lips are thick without being turned out. **1892** *Illustr. Sport. & Dram. News* 5 Nov. 270/3 Do not reject a nag, though he may turn out his toes a little.

** *intr.* **o.** To turn aside and go out; to go away, depart, 'clear out'; to go forth, sally forth (usually with the notion of some compelling force, or of leaving a place of safety or comfort for one of danger or discomfort).

**1473** WARKW. *Chron.* (Camden) 18 A prest that turnyd oute at his messe and the sacrament in his handys, whanne Kynge Edwarde came with his swerde into the chirche. **1649** BAXTER *Saints' R.* III. x. § 4 If there be but one gap open..how ready are we to..turn out at it? **1700** T. BROWN *Amusem. Ser. & Com.* 21 Turn out there you Country Put, says a Bully with a Sword two Yards long. **1763** C. JOHNSTON *Reverie* II. 9 To run into danger with delight, turning out to a man, at the first mention of the matter. **1811** *Regul. & Ord. Army* 15 The Line turns out without arms whenever any part of the Royal Family..comes along the Front of the Camp. **1889** JESSOPP *Coming of Friars* ii. 86 When the Friars came into a village,..the whole population would turn out to listen.

**p.** To get out of bed. (Cf. 72 f.) *colloq.*

**1805** W. IRVING in *Life & Lett.* (1864) I. 154 The next morning on turning out, I had the first glimpse of old England. **1837** MARRYAT *Dog-fiend* vi, 'Turn out', said Dick. *c* **1847** in R. C. Winthrop *Rem. For. Trav.* (1894) 14 (*attributed to Dk. Wellington*) When a man begins to turn at all in bed, it is time for him to turn out.

**q.** To leave one's abode and betake oneself to some outside occupation.

**1793** [EARL DUNDONALD] *Descr. Estate of Culross* 42 He had two sons..ready to turn out in the sea line. **1888** 'R. BOLDREWOOD' *Robbery Under Arms* xxii, What lay we're going upon and whether we're all greed in our mind to turn out. **1891** L. KEITH *Halletts* x, She may have to turn out and be a governess.

**r.** To abandon one's work; to go out on strike.

**1806** [implied in TURN-OUT *sb.* 2]. **1825** *Examiner* 79/1 The journeymen spinners..have turned out for an advance of wages. **1871** W. PHILLIPS *Labor Question* 17 He becomes a railway conductor. If that doesn't suit him, he turns out, and becomes the agent of an insurance office. **1885** *Manch. Exam.* 23 June 5/1 It is expected that the whole of the operatives will turn out against the reduction.

**s.** To bend or be directed outwards. (*intr.* of n.)

**1676** WISEMAN *Chirurg. Treat.* VII. x. 498 The Ancle-bone is apt to turn out on either side, by .. Relaxation of the Tendons. **1807-26** [see TURNING *vbl. sb.* 12]. *Mod.* His toes turn out.

**t.** (*a*) To come about in the end or issue; to result, eventuate.

Now always with adv., advb. phr., or *as*; †also *absol.* (*obs. rare*: nearly = *turn up*, 80 v).

**1735** WALPOLE *Let.* 19 Oct. in *10th Rep. Hist. MSS. Comm.* App. I. 264 As things have fortunately turn'd out. **1786** MRS. A. M. BENNETT *Juvenile Indiscr.* III. 85 Who knows what may turn out? **1830** B'NESS BUNSEN in Hare *Life* (1879) I. ix. 353 Our expedition up Vesuvius turned out very well. **1891** *Law Times* XC. 460/2 A speculator.. whose transactions..had turned out disastrously to himself.

(*b*) with *compl.* To come to be, become ultimately (and so be found or known to be).

**1744** M. BISHOP *Life & Adv.* 98 She has turned out a very undutiful Child. **1769** LADY MARY COKE *Jrnl.* 13 May (1892) III. 70 The day has turned out better then I expected it. **1875** JOWETT *Plato* (ed. 2) I. 140 Why then do the sons of good fathers often turn out ill? **1883** W. E. NORRIS *No New Thing* vii, What a pretty girl Nellie..has turned out!

(*c*) To be ultimately found or known, to prove *to be* (without implication of becoming).

Const. usually with inf.; also with simple compl. (cf. *b*).

**1790** PALEY *Horæ Paul.* ii. § 1 We have that time turning out, upon examination, to be in all the same. *a* **1859** DE QUINCEY *Autobiog. Sk.* vii. Wks. 1863 XIV. 205 *note*, These propositions, not..seeming to be true and turning out false, but..wearing an air of falsehood and turning out true. **1859** THACKERAY *Virgin.* xxi, That he should turn out to be the son of my old schoolfellow. **1893** SIR R. BALL *Story of Sun* 81 The result turns out to be considerably less. **1907** J. H. PATTERSON *Man-Eaters of Tsavo* App. I. 331 His photograph..unfortunately turned out a failure. *Mod.* He pretended to be destitute, but turns out to have had £200 in the bank.

**76. Turn out of.** (See simple senses and OUT OF.) **a.** *trans.* To drive, send, or put out of (a place), or dismiss from (a position or office), forcibly or peremptorily; to expel or eject from; † formerly more widely, to put or take out of in any way; *fig.* to bring out of, deliver from; to dissuade from.

*c* **1300** *Havelok* 154 He [= they]..preyden cristes hore, Þat he wolde turnen him [Athelwold] Vt of þat yuel. *c* **1430** in *Hymns Virg.* 108 ȝif þei talke of tales vn-trewe, Þou torn hem out of þat entent. **1562** *Child-Marriages* 104 The said Roger turnid the said mare out of the Close. **1610** HOLLAND *Camden's Brit.* (1637) 518 His dead Corps was..turned out of his grave. **1690** E. GEE *Jesuit's Memorial* Introd. 2 He was..turned out of his Fellowship. **1818** SCOTT *Hrt. Midl.* viii, The tenants..were not actually turned out of doors among the snow wreaths. **1890** F. M. CRAWFORD *Cigarette-maker's Rom.* v, He turned me out of the house.

† **b.** To do out of, deprive or strip of. *Obs.*

**1545** ASCHAM *Toxoph.* I. (Arb.) 88 They..turned so many out of theyr Iackes. **1560** DAUS tr. *Sleidane's Comm.* 56 To torne you out of your weapons.

**c.** To put or empty out of (a vessel) by inverting it.

**1791** *Gentl. Mag.* Jan. 25/1 Like a pudding turned out of a bason.

**d.** *intr.* To get out of, leave, quit. (Cf. 75 o, p.)

**1860** DICKENS *Uncomm. Trav.* x, My last special feat was turning out of bed at two, after a hard day. **1892** *Chamb. Jrnl.* 1 Oct. 638/1 Five is an early hour to turn out of bed.

**77. Turn over.** (See simple senses and OVER *adv.*) * *trans.* **a.** To turn (something) from its position on to one side, or from one side to the other, or upside down; to invert, reverse; to knock over, overturn, upset; *refl.* (now *rare*) = j below. Cf. senses 7, 10, and OVER *adv.* 4 b, c.

*c* **1375** *Cursor M.* 8611 (Fairf.) Þe toþer womman childe ho hent..Ho turned hir ouer wiþ hit in arme. *a* **1635** SIBBES *Confer. Christ & Mary* (1656) 12 We must..turn over every stone,—use all kind of means, till we find him. **1710** ADDISON *Tatler* No. 243 ¶ 3 He turned himself over hastily in his Bed. **1897** *Boston* (Mass.) *Jrnl.* 4 Jan. 1/2 The 'Blue Goose' saloon, which is situated in the middle of the river, was turned over by the flood. *Mod.* Turn the patient over on his right side (or, on his face).

**b.** To reverse (a leaf, or the successive leaves, of a book) in order to read (or write) on further; to read or search through, peruse (a book) by doing this. Cf. 11 a.

*To turn over a new leaf* (fig.): see LEAF *sb.* 7 b.

**1551** ROBINSON tr. *More's Utop.* I. (1895) 84 If I, sely man, should..wylle them to turne ouer the leafe, and learne a newe lesson. **1635** in Foster *Crt. Min. E. India Co.* (1907) 16 The Company were surprized..when the Voyages were turned over. **1711** STEELE *Spect.* No. 75 ¶ 2 Turning over the Leaves, she reads alternately, and speaks. **1821** SCOTT *Kenilw.* xxii, The countess..turning over such rare volumes as would now make the fortune of twenty retail booksellers. **1885** 'MRS. ALEXANDER' *At Bay* ii, 'I must read it again,' said Glynn,..as he turned over the pages.

**c.** To reverse or shift (soil, hay, etc.) so as to expose the under parts, or different parts successively: cf. 11 b.

**1737** BRACKEN *Farriery Impr.* (1756) I. 25 The same ground has not been turned over for a Hundred Years. **1842** *Jrnl. R. Agric. Soc.* III. I. 43 The trench-plough.. turns over from 10 to 18 inches of clean soil. **1862** *Ibid.* XXIII. 51 Turn over and lighten up the hay.

**d.** To reverse and shift successively (papers or other articles lying flat in a heap) for the purpose of examining those that are beneath.

**1798** S. & HT. LEE *Canterb. T., Yng. Lady's T.* II. 405 In turning over his papers.., Sir Edward laid his hand on the will. **1887** E. F. BYRRNE *Heir without Heritage* III. iii. 66 She..began to turn over the linen and examine it.

**e.** *fig.* To agitate or revolve *in the mind*, go through and examine mentally, consider and reconsider: cf. 8.

**1821** W. IRVING *Sketch Bk., Royal Poet*, After closing the volume, he turns its contents over in his mind. **1850** *Tait's Mag.* XVII. 118/1 The rumour induces us to turn over again this question. **1902** VIOLET JACOB *Sheep-Stealers* x, Turning over in his mind what possible pretext he could invent for an early visit.

**f.** To turn off the ladder in hanging: = 73 d.

**1678** BUTLER *Hud.* III. II. 598 As Criminals condemn'd to suffer, Are blinded first, and then turn'd over. **1702** [see TURNING *vbl. sb.* 12]. **1882** J. TAYLOR *Sc. Covenanters* 37 Just before he was turned over, the..intrepid sufferer lifted the napkin from his face and exclaimed, [etc.].

† **g.** To drink off, swallow at one draught: cf. 71 e. *Obs.*

**1796** *Hist. Ned Evans* I. 115 He turned over a full bumper to the toast.

**h.** To transfer, hand over, make over, deliver, commit (*to*); *spec.* to transfer (an apprentice) to another master, (a sailor) to another ship (cf. TURN-OVER *sb.* 2); in quot. 1632 ², to convert to a different use.

**1552** HULOET, Turne ouer, *transuerto.* *a* **1586** SIDNEY *Arcadia* I. (1629) 63 He excusing himselfe, and turning ouer the fault to fortune. **1632** LITHGOW *Trav.* III. 91 [He] was turned ouer to the new Captaine for fiue yeares more. *Ibid.* VI. 273 That house..is turned ouer for a shelterage to sheepe. **1744** M. BISHOP *Life & Adv.* 41 Our Ship was condemned, and the Men turned over, some on board the *Breda*, and some to the *Ipswich*. **1795** *Lupton's Thous. Notable Th.* XIV. 254 The chamberlain of London attends.. to enrol and turn over apprentices. **1890** MRS. H. WOOD *House of Halliwell* i, She would..turn over to her all the sewing.

**i.** *Comm.* To pass or hand over in the way of exchange; to employ in business, to invest and realize; to sell or dispose of goods to the amount of (a specified sum). Cf. 15 b.

**1611** L. BARRY *Ram-Alley* I. B iv b, Some hundred bookes ..I haue Turnd ouer..But that is nothing for a studient. Or a Stationer: they turne them ouer too. **1863** FAWCETT *Pol. Econ.* II. (1876) 260 Their capital is not unfrequently turned over ten times in the course of the year. **1890** *Spectator* 6 Sept., His land can produce corn but once a year, and he cannot 'turn over' his capital so invested. **1893** *Gd. Words* Mar. 187/1 Thousands of dollars were being turned over hourly.

** *intr.* **j.** To turn on to one side, or from one side to the other, or upside down; to reverse itself; to be upset, fall over, capsize; to roll about. Cf. a, and sense 6.

**1660** [implied in TURN-OVER *sb.* 1]. **1845** J. COULTER *Adv. in Pacific* vii. 87 [The whale] died, and turned over in a few minutes. **1892** *Illustr. Sport. & Dram. News* 17 Dec. 486/1 They cannot turn over if pushed, but must right themselves immediately. **1895** MRS. B. M. CROKER *Village T.* (1896) 88, I had watched the big rohu turning lazily over in the river. **1899** *Tit-Bits* 28 Oct. 97/3 Turn over and go to sleep.

**k.** To be transferred, to shift. (Cf. h.) *rare.*

**1851** *Jrnl. R. Agric. Soc.* XII. I. 287 The embankment has been made on that portion which is not liable to 'turn over' [*i. e.* be shifted by the tide].

**78. Turn round.** (See simple senses and ROUND *adv.*) * *intr.* **a.** To move round on an axis or centre; to revolve, rotate. Also *fig.* of the brain or head, to be affected with giddiness. Cf. 2, 2 b.

*c* **1400** *Destr. Troy* 453 Hir Ene as a trendull turned full rounde, First on hir fader, .. And sethyn on þat semely. *c* **1500** [see ROUND *adv.* 6]. **1596** SHAKS. *Tam. Shr.* V. ii. 20 He that is giddie thinks the world turns round. **1676** MARVELL *Mr. Smirke* 11 As it fares with those whose Brain turnes round. **1687** A. LOVELL tr. *Thevenot's Trav.* I. 54 Making a leap,..they fall a turning round with their naked feet. **1710** SWIFT *Jrnl. to Stella* 31 Oct., I had a fit of giddiness: the room turned round for about a minute. **1824** SCOTT *St. Ronan's* xxxvi, The strangeness of the news ..made Mowbray's head turn round.

**b.** To turn so as to face in the opposite direction; to reverse one's position or course; to face about; to turn from one side to the other. Cf. 6, 22 c.

Also *fig.* in such phrases as *to give one time to turn round*, i.e. to get into the proper position or condition for doing something required.

**1591** [see TURNING *vbl. sb.* 12]. **1787** 'G. GAMBADO' *Acad. Horsemen* (1809) 38 If his horse has stopt and turned round five thousand times with him. **1830** *Debates in Congress* 29 Mar. App. 105 Payment is..suffered to lie occasionally until the bank can turn round. **1856** SIR B. BRODIE *Psychol. Inq.* I. iv. 137 We see persons turn round in their sleep. **1886** *Lesterre Durant* vi, She turned round to where her brother stood.

**c.** *fig.* To change to the opposite opinion, state of mind, etc.; *esp.* to change from a friendly to a hostile attitude; with *on* or *upon*, to assail suddenly, esp. in words (cf. 33).

**1822** *Examiner* 427/1 The Alderman being absent, our schemer turns round, and personates the Alderman. **1863** KINGSLEY *Water Bab.* v, Now he turned round and abused it. **1891** *Law Times* XCI. 405/2 [They] cannot turn round on the executors and blame them.

** *trans.* **d.** To cause to revolve or rotate (cf. 1); also, to cause to face in all directions successively.

*c* **1633** MILTON *Arcades* 66 Those that hold the vital shears, And turn the Adamantine spindle round. **1731** POPE *Ep. Burlington* 135 In Books, not Authors, curious is my Lord; To all their dated Backs he turns you round. **1823** H. J. BROOKE *Introd. Crystallogr.* 28 If we now turn round the circle with its attached crystal. **1857** TENNYSON *Geraint & Enid* 740 The maiden..robed herself, Helped by the mother's careful hand and eye, ..Who, after, turn'd her daughter round, and said, She never yet had seen her half so fair.

**e.** To put into the opposite position or direction, to reverse (*lit.* and *fig.*): cf. 10, 10 b.

**1858** J. MARTINEAU *Stud. Chr.* 40 The Prophets, whom we shall very imperfectly understand, if we suppose them mere historians, for whom God had turned round time the other way. **1887** *Times* (weekly ed.) 11 Nov. 4/3 He has.. turned it right round and made it say exactly the opposite of what it does say.

**f.** To cause to face in a different direction; *refl.* = b above (*arch.*). Also *fig.* to induce (a person) to take an opposite course or view (quot. 1860).

**1628** FELTHAM *Resolves* II. [I.] xxxii. 101 That Philosopher ..turn'd him round, and vanisht. *a* **1765** [see ROUND *adv.* 8]. **1782** COWPER *Gilpin* 51 Turning round his head, he saw Three customers come in. **1850** TENNYSON *In Mem.* xliv. 14 If such a dreamy touch should fall, O turn thee round, resolve the doubt. **1860** GEO. ELIOT *Mill on Fl.* III. viii. The utter impossibility of ever turning Mr. Tulliver round .., or getting him to hear reason.

**79. Turn to.** **a.** *intr.* To apply oneself to some task or occupation; to set to work. Cf. 28 c.

**1813** SOUTHEY *March to Moscow* vi, But the Russians stoutly they turned-to Upon the road to Moscow. **1840** R. H. DANA *Bef. Mast* iii, The watch..'turning to' at daybreak and washing down, scrubbing, and swabbing the decks. **1893** *Chamb. Jrnl.* 8 July 421/1 She..would turn to again and earn a living.

**b.** *trans.* To set (a person) to work. Cf. 34 b.

**1840** R. H. DANA *Bef. Mast* xii. 27 We were turned-to upon the rigging.

**80. Turn up.** (See simple senses and UP *adv.*) * *trans.* **a.** To direct or bend upwards (also *fig.*); in *pa. pple.* often denoting the form of a projecting part or border of something; in quot. 1707, to have (such a part) bent or directed upwards. Cf. 9.

In *Bookbinding*, to flatten the back of (a book) with trindles, in preparation for cutting the front edge: see TRINDLE *sb.* 4.

*c* **1510** MORE *Picus* B v, He exhorted them to turne vp theyr myndes to loue God. *a* **1548** HALL *Chron., Hen. VIII* 6 b, Bootes with pykes turned vp. **1607** SHARPHAM *Fleire* V. (1610) H ij, A Puritane [damn'd] for saying Grace without turning vp the white of his eyes. **1623** GOUGE *Serm. Extent God's Provid.* § 15 A red cap, over a white linnen one turned up about the brimmes. **1707** MORTIMER *Husb.* (1721) I. 259 A sort of Duck that turns up the Bill more than the common kind. **1819** SCOTT *Leg. Montrose* Introd., The right side of his head a little turned up, the better to catch..the clergyman's voice. **1877** [see TURNING *vbl. sb.* 12]. **1888** MISS TYTLER *Blackhall Ghosts* II. xv. 72 He even..turned up the collar of his morning coat.

**b.** esp. in phr. *to turn up one's nose* (as an expression of contempt): usually *fig.* (*turn up one's nose at* = despise, scorn).

**1779** MME. D'ARBLAY *Diary* 20 Oct., Mr. Thrale..turned up his nose with an expression of contempt. **1836** MARRYAT *Midsh. Easy* xxiv, Miss Julia, who turned up her nose at a midshipman.

**c.** To turn upside down, invert (now esp. in order to examine what is beneath); † to overthrow, demolish; *fig.* to upset, throw into disorder (*obs.*). Cf. 10.

*a* **1548** HALL *Chron., Hen. VI* 137 b, No doubt, but kyng Charles, and the whole publique wealthe of Fraunce, had been turned vp, and cleane ouerthrowen. **1581** A. HALL *Iliad* IV. 71 You should haue seene them [the walls of Thebes] torne, & turned vp from the rout. **1592** SHAKS. *Rom. & Jul.* I. v. 29 Turne the Tables vp. **1664** EVELYN *Kal. Hort.* (1729) 191 Turn up your Bee-hives, and sprinkle them. **1843** MIALL in *Nonconf.* III. 209 Men who turn up words that they may see the ideas that lie under them. **1848** THACKERAY *Van. Fair* vii, The chairs are turned up heads and tails along the walls.

**d.** To fold over (a garment or part of one) so as to shorten it; also *transf.* with the person as obj.

**1611** COTGR., *Rebrasser*, to turne, fould, or tucke vp, the sleeues, &c. **1662** J. DAVIES tr. *Olearius' Voy. Ambass.* 375 They turn up their sleeves above the Elbow. **1836** [see TURNED 8]. **1896** HARE *Story my Life* I. ii. 136 If any of the children behaved ill during the service, they were turned up and soundly whipped then and there.

**e.** In *pa. pple.* of a garment: Having the border turned or folded over and covered *with* some ornamental material. † In quot. 1573 app. *transf.* to decorate, adorn.

**1537** *Test. Ebor.* (Surtees) VI. 72 My mariage gowne of russet damaske, with the sleves turne[d] upe with russet velvet. **1573** TUSSER *Husb.* (1878) 100 [Plants] to turn vp their house, and to furnish their pot. **1714** *Lond. Gaz.* No. 5270/7 A..Cap of Crimson Velvet, turn'd up with Ermine. **1850** *Tait's Mag.* XVII. 749/1 A green blouse turned up with red.

**f.** To turn (soil, etc.) so as to bring up the under parts to the surface, as by digging or ploughing, or with the snout or paws, as an animal (cf. 11 b); to dig or plough up; also, to bring to the surface (something buried) by digging, etc.

**1563** *Homilies* II. *Rogation Week* IV. (1640) 235 They doe wickedly, which doe turne up the ancient terris of the fields. **1577** B. GOOGE *Heresbach's Husb.* 44 Take heede of Swyne, that spoyle and turne vp the grounde ilfauoredly. *a* **1613** J. DENNYS *Secr. Angling* II. xlvii, Yealow bobs turnd vp before the Plough. **1667** MILTON *P. L.* VII. 213 The vast.. Abyss Outrageous as a Sea,..Up from the bottom turn'd by furious windes. **1774** GOLDSM. *Nat. Hist.* (1776) VI. 226 The neck is furnished with very strong muscles, which enable it the readier to turn up the sand. **1833** JAS. DAVIDSON *Brit. & Rom. Rem. Axminster* 27 A man digging a hole for a gate-post,..turned up a golden ornament. **1843** *Jrnl. R. Agric. Soc.* IV. II. 116 Turn up the earth with a trowel.

**g.** To turn (a card) face upwards; *esp.* to do this in dealing to determine the trump suit (cf. TURN-UP *sb.* 3).

**1611** SHAKS. *Cymb.* II. iii. 2 The most coldest that euer turn'd vp Ace. **1709** *Brit. Apollo* II. No. 18. 2/2 D...turns up the last Card for Trump. **1891** *Field* 28 Nov. 842/3 The card turned up by the second hand is the king.

**h.** To find in a book, a set of papers, etc. some passage or document; to look up, refer to. (With the book, etc., or the passage, as obj.) Cf. 11 a, 77 b.

'In the Durham Cathedral Choir *to turn up* means to look out and place ready the music for the organist and singers' (Canon J. T. Fowler).

**1710** STEELE *Tatler* No. 179 ¶ 11 When I turn up some Masterly Writer to my Imagination. **1818** SCOTT *Hrt. Midl.* xxxi, She then turned up the ritual. **1892** *Illustr.*

*Sport. & Dram. News* 7 May 267/2, I have not time now to turn up my old notes on the subject. *Mod.* Turn up the article in the Encyclopædia.

**i.** To lay (a person or animal) on the back; to turn belly upwards; hence, to kill.

In quot. 1850 causal of y below.

**1740** tr. *De Mouhy's Fort. Country-Maid* (1741) I. 62 Go your ways, or I'll turn you up as I would a Hare. **1832** Col. Hawker *Diary* (1893) II. 46, I turned up two [geese] with the first barrel, and the other with the second. **1844** Stephens *Bk. Farm* II. 95 You will have to turn him up, as it is termed; that is, the sheep is set upon his rump with his back down and his hind-feet pointing upwards and outwards. **1850** Scoresby *Cheever's Whalem. Adv.* xiv. (1859) 212 After Captain Hosmer had succeeded in 'turning up' his whale.

**j.** *To turn up one's heels* (or *toes*), to die; *to turn up* (a person's) *heels*, to lay low, kill: see Heel *sb.*[1] 23, Toe *sb.* 5 j.

**k.** To turn the stomach of (see 12); to nauseate; also *fig.*

**1892** *Chamb. Jrnl.* 11 June 375/2 Men who have never known what sea-sickness is..get thoroughly 'turned up' with the awful motion and vibration.

†**l.** To roll up, twist up in a wrapper. *Obs. rare.*

**1701** *Lond. Gaz.* No. 3741/4 A painted Fan..turned up in a white Paper.

**m.** To turn the handle or tap of (a lamp or gas-jet) so as to raise the wick, or increase the flow of gas, and thus make it burn more brightly.

**1889** *Repent. P. Wentworth* II. v. 105 He..turned up his reading lamp. **1893** Kipling *Many Invent.* 102 Turn up the gas a little, I want to go on reading.

†**n.** ? To excite, rouse. *Obs. rare.*

**1579** Gosson *Sch. Abuse* (Arb.) 63, I shall please the wise, though the malicious turne vpp their gall.

**o.** To set free, turn loose; to discharge or release (a prisoner). Cf. 25. Now only *slang*.

**1653** H. More *Antid. Ath.* iii. ii. § 2 The Horse.. for his unserviceableness.. was fain to be turned up loose in the pasture. **1715** *Lond. Gaz.* No. 5368/4 Which said..Gelding was turned up by the said Rogues. **1812** J. H. Vaux *Flash Dict.* s.v., A person acquitted by a jury, or discharged by a magistrate..is said to be turned up. **1904** Maj. A. Griffiths *50 Y. Public Service* xxiii. 354 They are not brothers, only brother convicts, who 'did time' together.., were 'turned up' together.

**p.** To give up, renounce, abandon, cast off, discard, 'throw up'. Now only *slang*.

**1621** Burton *Anat. Mel.* iii. iv. ii. i. (1651) 685 He.. married wives, and turned them up as he thought fit. **1643** Trapp *Comm. Gen.* xii. 1 Many follow God..as a dog doth his master, till he meet with carrion; and then turn him up. **1885** *Punch* 13 June, So turn up the job,..And leave it to me! **1893** *Illustr. Sport. & Dram. News* 10 June 532/3 After one disastrous round..I intimated to the champion my intention to turn it up.

**q.** *Naut.* To cause to appear above the horizon; to come in sight of: = Raise *v.*[1] 23 a. Also *transf.*

**1698** Fryer *Acc. E. India & P.* 82, I was sent to Surat. In a week's time we turned it up. **1859** Sala *Tw. round Clock* (1861) 25 Keep struggling; and..you will eventually turn up Printing House Square.

**r.** *Naut.* To summon (the crew) on deck.

**1805** in Nicolas *Nelson's Disp.* (1846) VII. 164 *note*, Ceased firing and turned the hands up to clear the wreck. **1835** Marryat *Pirate* ix, 'Turn the hands up',..said the captain.

** *intr.* **s.** To bend or point upwards; to have an upward direction: cf. 9 d.

**1608** Topsell *Serpents* (1658) 675 The tail is very long, at the end and turning up like a Vipers tail. **1710** Steele *Tatler* No. 245 ⁋ 2 Nose very broad at bottom, and turning up at the end. **1827** Faraday *Chem. Manip.* xvi. (1842) 417 The apparatus delivering gas should always be made to turn up at the end.

**t.** To turn aside and go up; to make one's way up: cf. 16.

*c* **1350** *Will. Palerne* 2906 Sche went..to þe castel, & turned vp to þe heiȝest tour. *c* **1450** in Aungier *Syon* (1840) 334 Alle seruyse ended..they schal echone turne up in to ther stalles, and say..knelynge fyftene Aues. **1760–72** H. Brooke *Fool of Qual.* (1809) III. 60, I turned up to a sorry kind of inn.

**u.** *Naut.* To beat up to windward; to tack. Also with *it*. Cf. 16 b.

**1569** [see 16 b]. *a* **1647** Pett in *Archæologia* (1796) XII. 227 We weighed and turned up with the wind at South-west as high as Lambeth. **1682** W. Hedges *Diary* (Hakl. Soc.) I. 31 We.. bore down about 2 or 3 miles to 2 sloops which could not turn it up to us. **1701** Cunningham in *Phil. Trans.* XXIII. 1201 We were forced to turn it up against Wind and Current all the way. **1711** Littleton *Let.* 13 Aug. in *Lond. Gaz.* No. 4906/3 We turn'd up to Windward as far as Donna Maria Bay. **1745** P. Thomas *Jrnl. Anson's Voy.* 178 We had run three or four Leagues too far to Leeward, which we now had to turn up.

**v.** (often *intr.* for *refl.* or *pass.* of various *trans.* senses.) To make its (or one's) appearance; to present itself (or oneself) casually or unexpectedly; to occur, appear, be discovered or encountered (as if exposed by turning something over, by turning face upwards, by turning the leaves of a book, etc.).

**1704** N. N. tr. *Boccalini's Advts. fr. Parnass.* I. 255 Hoping a Card might turn up to better their Fortunes. **1715** M. Davies *Athen. Brit.* I. 202 He open'd the New Testament at a venture, and pray'd that such a Place might turn up as might comfort him in his last moments. **1755** *Monitor* No. 10. I. 82 They must watch.. the.. occasions, which in the whirl of time will turn up. **1809** Malkin *Gil Blas* x. vi. ⁋ 2 It seems incredible that Raphael should turn up in such a guise! **1824** Whewell in *Life* (1881) 97 Leaving directions to have the thing sent after me if it should turn up. **1827** *Examiner* 731/2 When..a flat cries 'head'.., a 'tail' is sure to turn up. **1849** Dickens *Dav. Copp.* xi, 'And then', said Mr. Micawber,..'I shall, please Heaven, begin to be beforehand with the world,..if—in short, if anything turns up'. **1889** W. E. Norris *Miss Shafto* 170 You didn't expect me to turn up here, did you?

**w.** with *compl.* To appear or present itself in a specified character; to be found to be: nearly = *turn out*, 75 t (*b*), (*c*).

*To turn up rough*, to become angry or quarrelsome (cf. *cut up rough*, Cut *v.* 59 l). *To turn up trumps*, to turn out favourably (see Trump *sb.*[2] 2).

**1756** *Monitor* No. 39. I. 374 A great deal of waste land and timber.., which by care and cultivation, must in time turn up a great thing. **1785** Grose *Dict. Vulg. T.* s.v. *Trump*, Something may turn up trumps, something lucky may happen. **1831** *Examiner* 534/1 A lottery ticket which has turned up a prize. **1872** *Judy* 29 May 59/2 (Farmer) Have the ornaments [= handcuffs] handy, in case he should turn up rough. **1890** J. Hatton *Order of Czar* II. ii. xiii. 159 Nitrates have turned up trumps.

**x.** Of soil (*intr.* for *pass.* of f, with qualifying phr. or compl.).

**1855** *Jrnl. R. Agric. Soc.* XVI. i. 176 Such soils turn up as a fine mould. *Ibid.* 197 The soil..will turn up raw and stubborn. **1858** *Ibid.* XIX. i. 186 It [a soil] is all exceedingly sticky when wet, and, if ploughed in that state, turns up in large masses, which as they dry become hard as rock.

**y.** 'To turn belly upward: said of a dying whale' (*Cent. Dict.* 1891). Cf. quots. 1850 in i, and 1845 in 77 j (*turn over*).

**z.** *slang.* To throw up or abandon one's work. (Cf. o, p.)

**1904** Maj. A. Griffiths *50 Y. Public Service* xiii. 173 Smith..'turned up' one day, in other words refused to labour on the works.

*** *trans.*, and *intr.* (for *refl.*), of doubtful sense: app. to prostitute; to prostitute oneself. *Obs.*

**1670** Dryden *1st Pt. Conq. Granada* Epil. 12 Fame is false to all that keep her long; And turns up to the fop that's brisk and young. **1678** Butler *Hud.* iii. i. 824 Prepost'rously would have all women Turn'd up to all the world in common. **1682** Dryden *Abs. & Achit.* ii. 383 'Tis a leading card to make a whore To prove her mother had turned up before. [Cf. Turn-up *sb.* 1.]

**Turn-**, the verb-stem in combination with a sb., adv., or adj., forming sbs. and adjs., in the sense 'that turns or is turned', 'for turning', in various uses of the verb. The more important compounds are entered as Main words: see Turncoat, Turnkey, Turn-out, Turnpike, Turnspit, Turnstone, etc.; those of less importance follow here. **Turn-away**, †(*a*) one who turns away; a deserter, forsaker (*obs.*); (*b*) the act of turning people away from a place of assembly already full; also *transf.*; **turn-bat**, in *Metallurgy*: see quot.; **turn-beam**, the drum of a windlass; **turn-bench**, a small portable lathe used by watchmakers, etc.; **turn-bolt**, †(*a*) a wrench or spanner; (*b*) a bolt that rotates, as to unlock a mechanism; **turn-boat**, a boat used as a turn-mark in yacht-racing; †**turn-bout** [Bout *adv.*[2]] = Turn-buckle 1; **turn-bridge**, a bridge turning horizontally on a pivot; a swing-bridge; **turn-button**, a small bar pivoted near its centre, so that when turned its end engages with a catch, the edge of a door, or the like; **turn-cap**, (*a*) (also **turn-cap lily**), *Lilium Martagon*; (*b*) a revolving cowl; **turn-crowned** *a.*, having the feathers on the crown reversed, as some varieties of the domestic pigeon: cf. *turn-pate*; **turn-file**: see quot.; †**turn-frame** = Turn-table 1; **turn-furrow**, the mould-board of a plough; **turn-gate** = Turnstile; **turn-hole**, an eddy or whirlpool; **turn-in** *a. rare*, that turns or folds in; **turn-lathe**, a turning-lathe; **turn-mark**, a buoy or boat round which yachts turn in racing; **turn-net**: see quot.; **turn-off** *a.*, that is turned off, or turns off; that is taken or got off by turning or screwing; *sb.* that which is turned off; in quot., the quantity of any product finished and disposed of; †**turn-pate**, a crested pigeon: cf. *turn-crowned*; **turn-penny**, a person who is intent on profit (cf. Turn *v.* 15 b); **turn-pin**, (*a*) a pin that turns, or on which something turns; a pivot; (*b*) a conical plug for stopping or enlarging the end of a pipe; **turn-plate**, †(*a*) a curved plate-rail; (*b*) = Turn-table 1; **turn-plough**, a plough with a mould-board, which turns over the furrow-slice, as distinct from a shovel-plough (*Cent. Dict.*, *Supp.* 1909); †**turn-point**, turning-point; in quot., the sun's 'turning-point': see Tropic *sb.* 1 a; †**turn-poke**, in cock-fighting, a game-cock of the largest breed; = Shake-bag 1; **turn-rail** = Turn-table 1; also, a point or switch for directing railway vehicles from one line to another; **turn-row**, the space at the side of a field in which the horses turn in ploughing, used as a path (*U.S.*); **turn-saw**, a narrow saw for cutting curves (= *turning-saw*, Turning *vbl. sb.* 13); **turn-scale** *a.*, that (merely) turns the scale: cf. Make-weight 2; **turn-screw**, a screw-driver; also, a wrench; **turn-shoe**, a shoe that is made inside out and then turned: see quots.; a pump; **turn-side**, a disease of cattle, also affecting the dog, resembling the gid in sheep: cf. Turn-sick *sb.*, Turnabout b; **turn-skin** (rendering L. *versipellis*), one who turns or changes his skin; *spec.* one who can turn into a wolf at will, a were-wolf; †**turn-stair**, a winding staircase; **turn-stick**, a tourniquet consisting of a bandage tightened by twisting a stick or bar passed through it; **turn-stitch**, in knitting, = *purl-stitch* (Purl *sb.*[1] 5); in lace-making: see quot. 1882[2]; **turn-stool**, a stool with a revolving seat; †**turn-tale** *Rhet.* = Apostrophe[1] 1; †**turn-tippet**, a turncoat, a renegade: see Tippet *sb.* 1 e; **turn-to**, a tussle, a set-to; also, a beginning or setting to work (in quot. *attrib.*); †**turn-tool**, a turning lathe; **turn-tree** = *turn-beam*; **turn-trencher**, a game of forfeits in which a trencher or the like is spun; more commonly *turn the trencher*; **turn-under**, the curving in of a carriage-body towards the bottom; †**turn-wheel**, ? a boy employed to turn a lathe or rope-wheel; †**turn-wicket**, a kissing-gate.

**1688** Bunyan *Jerus. Sinner Saved* (1886) 42 Witness those *turn-aways from God that you also read of in Jeremiah. **1858** Dickens *Let.* 11 Aug., Wherever I read twice the turn-away is invariably on the second occasion. **1867** *Ibid.* (1880) II. 277 We had an enormous turn-away last night, and do not doubt about having a cram to-night. **1881** Raymond *Mining Gloss.*, **Turn-bat*, a wooden stick used in turning the tongs which hold a bloom under the hammer. **1909** in *Cent. Dict. Suppl.* **1679** *Phil. Collect.* XII. 7 The *turn-beam which hangs over the shaft has been thrown off its frame by the force of it [explosion]. **1828** Webster s.v. *Jig-pin*, A pin used by miners to hold the turn-beams, and prevent them from turning. **1680** Moxon *Mech. Exerc.* xiii. 225 An Iron Lathe called a *Turn-Bench..When they use it they screw it in the Chaps of a Vice. **1688** R. Holme *Armoury* iii. 359/2 To work small work in Metal..a Turn-Bench. **1895** *Model Steam Engine* 94 Turn Bench..a miniature lathe, used for small turning, and to which the.. circular motion is imparted by a catgut bow. **1896** *Daily News* 29 June 7/1 Ailsa rapidly gained.., and at the *turn-boat she had reduced the gap between her and Britannia to five minutes. **1569** in *Richmond Wills* (Surtees) 226 Inventorium..a *torne boltte: a peate sledd..etc. **1898** *Daily News* 9 May 3/1 The Lee Turnbolt Rifle..is easily kept in order by a soldier or sportsman. **1703** T. N. *City & C. Purchaser* 100 Smiths..ask'd me 6*d.* per Pound for Casements..with *Turn-bouts (or Turn-buckles, as some call'd 'em) or Cock-spurs, and Pull-backs at the Hind-side to pull them to with. **1767** S. Paterson *Another Trav.* I. 109 Their draw bridges, ..*turn-bridges, as the bars of turnpikes. **1861** Smiles *Engineers* II. 361 The turnbridges which he introduced upon his canals, instead of the old drawbridges. **1849** Noad *Electricity* ix. (ed. 3) 419 The rings are secured in the circular rabbett of the square piece of wood..by small *turn buttons. **1893** J. A. Hodges *Elem. Photogr.* (1907) 33 Two turn-buttons, screwed to the window frame, will keep the frame in position. **1688** R. Holme *Armoury* ii. 65/2 The Mountain Lilly Imperial,..by Florists called Martagon Imperial, but by common People the *Turn-Cap. **1842** G. Francis *Dict. Arts*, *Turn-Cap*, a chimney top, which turns round with the wind. **1908** [Miss Fowler] *Betw. Trent & Ancholme* 14 The little bright scarlet or 'Turn-cap' Lily. **1765** *Treat. Dom. Pigeons* 134 The Trumpeter..very feather-footed and leg'd, *turn-crown'd like the nun. **1859** Darwin *Orig. Spec.* v. (1872) 127 The parent rock-pigeon was not feather-footed or turn-crowned. **1877** Knight *Dict. Mech.*, **Turn-file*, a burnisher used in throwing up slight burs on the edges of the comb-maker's files, the teeth of which are originally made by the file and not by the chisel. **1789** Brand *Hist. Newcastle* II. 256 *note*, Waggons, after being emptied, are brought round into the road or waggon-way by a *turn-frame. **1837** *Flemish Husb.* 15 in *Libr. Usef. Knowl.*, *Husb.* III, The sole is a kind of sledge, formed by the end of the share towards the heel, and the lower edge of the *turn-furrow. **1905** *Pall Mall G.* 29 May 2/2 Some belated visitor hurrying to leave the gardens by one of the *turngates. **1851** Newland *The Erne* 352, I.. gaffed him out of the great boiling *turnhole below. **1894** *Outing* (U. S.) XXIV. 249/2 Under the seat..of the car was a sort of turn-up or *turn-in bunk, with a comfortable hair-mattress. **1665–6** *Phil. Trans.* I. 71 The contrivance of Signor Campani for making Great Optick-Glasses, by the means of a *Turn-lath. **1896** *Daily News* 29 June 7/1 Britannia closed on the leaders and had the *turn mark first. **1883** G. C. Davies *Norfolk Broads* xxxvi. (1884) 278 The '*turn-net'..This was a long drag-net, having a pocket at one end. This end was fixed to the bank, and the other paid out so as to enclose a space of water, and then drawn ashore, when the fish were driven into the pocket. **1688** R. Holme *Armoury* iii. xviii. (Roxb.) 135/1 A *Turn off screwed barrell is a barrell of two peeces and screwed together iust at the height of the charge. *Ibid.*, Turn off vnscrewed, is when the barrell is in two peeces as foresaid and the top part bored round. **1889** *Daily News* 5 Aug. 11/3 The turnoff from looms is very limited, prices very steady. Bleached and finished stocks are very small. **1611** Cotgr. s.v. *Hupé*, *Pigeons hupez*, copped, or crested Pigeons, called about London, *Turne-pats. [**1824** Scott *Redgauntlet* xii, That's always the way with old *Turnpenny,..he cares for nothing of the trade but the profit.] **1872** De Morgan *Budget of Paradoxes* 83 Some observant turn-penny might construct such a treatise as this from the third book. **1862** *Catal. Internat. Exhib.* II. xi. 16 The centre of the breech-piece being cut away, all the strain acts upon the attaching of the *turnpin. **1877** Knight *Dict. Mech.*, *Turn-pin*, a plug for stopping the flow from the open end of a pipe. A tube-stopper. **1797** J. Curr *Coal Viewer* 25 Plain *turn plates. Used for going round a turn. **1838**

*Civil Eng. & Arch. Jrnl.* I. 164/2 The shed for the engines and the coaches is erected—the necessary turnplates fixed. **1587** GOLDING *De Mornay* vii. (1592) 86 The Sunne maketh there his naturall course in the Zodiacke between the two Tropickes or *Turnepointes. **1615** MARKHAM *Pleas. Princes* (1635) 42 The huge Cocke (which we call the *turne-Pocke). **1773** PEGGE in *Archæologia* (1775) III. 142 What our sportsmen call Shakebags, or Turn-pokes. **1793** SMEATON *Edystone L.* § 167 *note*, The carriage being turned a quarter round upon the Turnpike, or *Turnrail. **1801** W. COXE *Monmouthshire* xxiv. II. 231 At the junction of two roads.., moveable rails, called turn rails, are occasionally used, which are fastened with screws.., and may be pushed sideways. **1838** SIMMS *Publ. Wks. Gt. Brit.* 49 The turn-rails to be twelve feet diameter..the table to be hung on a centre pivot. **1888** *Atlantic Monthly* May 677/1 All adown the *turn-row between the ranks of corn. **1875** *Carpentry & Join.* 16 For cutting out curved or circular pieces,..the sweep saw or *turn saw..comes into..use. **1841** *L'pool Mercury* 11 June 196/2 The majority..was only a *turn-scale one; but it was expected to be on the other side. **1801** *Sporting Mag.* XVII. 148 Be the spare flint, and ready *turn-screw there. **1837** *Civil Eng. & Architect's Jrnl.* I. 29/1 The fourth was screwed into the bed of the river..by a curious windlass, and lengthening turn-screw, worked by forty men. **1889** HENTY *With Lee in Virginia* (1890) 176 By a strong turn-screw a bar could be removed in five minutes. **1886** *Encycl. Brit.* XXI. 830/2 The making of '*turn shoes' embraces all work in which there is only one thin flexible sole which is sewed to the upper while outside in and turned over when completed. *Mod. Advt.*, The shoe is made inside out and then turned. 'Turn shoes' they are called in some parts of the country. **1845** YOUATT *Dog* vi. 118 *Turnside, or Giddiness..a singular disease prevalent among cattle, but only occasionally seen in the dog. **1831** A. H. in *Will. & Werwolf* (1832) 6 That notion has become so inveterate, that a *turnskin (*versipellis*) is become a common term of reproach. **1861** T. L. PEACOCK *Gryll Gr.* xxxiv, I felt that he was a turnskin, and I could never after taste bread with him. **1871** TYLOR *Prim. Cult.* I. iii. 77 Men who are versipelles or turnskins have the actual faculty of jumping out of their skins, to become for a time wolves. **1616** SURFL. & MARKH. *Country Farme* 17 Vnder, or vpon the side of your *turne-stayres,..your Farmer shall haue a way into the Gardens. **1813** J. THOMSON *Lect. Inflam.* 259 The *turn-stick is still a very useful instrument,..but its place in operation is now generally supplied by the screw tourniquet. **1882** CAULFEILD & SAWARD *Dict. Needlework* 286/2 **Turn-Stitch*, another name for Purl. *Ibid.* 504/2 *Turn Stitch.* Also known as Turning Stitch, used [in lace-making]..at the end of a row..is made with a Cloth Stitch and a half-Cloth Stitch as follows: Work a Cloth Stitch, give each pair of Bobbins one Twist to the left, put the middle left hand Bobbin over the middle right; lift the two pairs with each hand. **1893** ELIZ. ROSEVEAR *Text-bk. Needlework*, etc. 405 Purl, Pearl, Seam, Rib, and Turn Stitch all mean the same thing. **1890** S. W. BAKER *Wild Beasts* I. 153 The watcher will sit upon a low *turn stool, that will enable him to rest in comfort. **1589** PUTTENHAM *Eng. Poesie* III. xix. (Arb.) 244 *Apostrophe*, or the *turnetale. **1558** CRANMER *Confut. Unwritten Verities* Pref. C ij *margin*, The priestes for the most part wer double faced, *turne tippettes and flattere[r]s. **1562** PILKINGTON *Expos. Abdyas* Pref. 14 All turntippets that turn with the worlde, and kepe their livings still, should have no office in Christs Church. **1893** HUXLEY *Evol. & Ethics* 7 A *turn-to with a giant. **1909** *Chron. Lond. Mission. Soc.* Aug. 150/2 This nine o'clock 'turn-to' whistle is also the signal for a girls' muster. **1665** *Phil. Trans.* I. 2 Campani..pretends to have found a way to work great Optick Glasses with a *Turne-tool, without any mould. **1653** MANLOVE *Lead-mines* 268 (E.D.S.) Crosses, Holes, Hange-benches, *Turntree, and Coes. **1747** HOOSON *Miner's Dict.* E ij, If he once set on his Stoce and Turntree, and falls to drawing. **1829** *Glover's Hist. Derby* I. 74 The spindles of a turn-tree, or rope-barrel, for winding up ore in small tubs. **1837** HOWITT *Rur. Life* II. ii. (1862) 101 The old games of blindman's-buff, *turn-trencher and forfeits..pursued in the evening firelight. **1891** *Cent. Dict.*, *Turn-under. **1903** *Westm. Gaz.* 16 Nov. 4/2 The back panel in particular is conspicuously attractive, by reason of..the 'big turn-under' from top to bottom, the very large side-sweep. **1672–3** in Welch *Hist. Pewterers' Co.* (1902) II. 145 [Richard Heath was summoned..for setting his] *Turn Wheel to work on yᵉ mistery [by employing him to pour saudware and open a mould. A 'turn-wheel' was an unskilled labourer, usually a lad]. **1816** T. PARKER *Ess. Turnpike Gate* 18 The three posts in front of the *turn-wicket should be sawed into octagons.

**Turnable** (tǭ·ɹnăb'l), *a. rare.* [f. TURN *v.* + -ABLE.] That may be turned.

**1483** *Cath. Angl.* 397/1 Turneabylle, *conuertibilis, tropicus, versilis, versatilis.* **1603** FLORIO *Montaigne* III. iii. (1632) 458 A wit so turneable for all things alike. **1611** COTGR. s.v. *Flechir*, *Facile à flechir*, gentle, pliant, flexible, tractable, turnable. **1820** *Examiner* No. 612. 1/2 Something laudable, or at least complimentable,—something turnable into a little grace and acknowledgment.

**Turnabout** (tǭ·ɹnˌăbaut). Also with hyphen. [f. the verbal phr. *turn about* (TURN *v.* 65). See also TURN *sb.* 40, and *turn-bout* (TURN-).] The action or an act of turning about; one who or that which does this. **a.** The act of turning so as to face the other way. Also *fig.*

**1833** *Regul. Instr. Cavalry* I. 48 By a turn-about the dressing is changed. **1878** BROWNING *Poets Croisic* cxxxviii, A moment's horror; then quick turn-about On high-heeled shoe. **1897** *Westm. Gaz.* 25 Mar. 1/2 The strange turn-about in the attitude of some zealous people towards Russia.

†**b.** A disease causing cattle to turn round and round; gid. Also *turn-about sickness*, vertigo. *Obs.*

**1598** SYLVESTER *Du Bartas* II. i. III. *Furies* 610 The Turn-about and Murrain trouble Cattell. **1611** COTGR., s.v. *Tournement*, *Tournement de teste*, the turne-about sicknesse; a giddinesse, or dizzinesse.

†**c.** A winding; a 'maze'. *Obs.*

*a* **1603** T. CARTWRIGHT *Confut. Rhem. N. T.* (1618) 604 The Iesuites ignorant of their owne mystery of iniquity, and strangers as it were in the giddy turn-about of their owne Cloisters.

†**d.** One who turns about or alters things; an innovator. *Obs.*

*a* **1670** HACKET *Abp. Williams* II. (1693) 36 Our modern Turn-abouts cannot evince us, but that we feel we are best affected, when the great Mysteries of Christ are celebrated upon Anniversary Festivals.

†**e.** A double-barrelled gun. *Obs.* †**f.** A turnstile. *Obs.* **g.** A small steamer having the deadwood cut away astern, and an additional rudder fitted in the space thus made, to facilitate quick turning; also *attrib.* **h.** *U.S.* A 'giant's stride' or merry-go-round.

**1801** *Sporting Mag.* XVII. 159 A kind of double gun, known by the name of Turnabout. **1805** R. W. DICKSON *Pract. Agric.* I. 144 The *turn-about* or w[h]irlout gate is only necessary where a frequency of passage is required. **1885** *Pall Mall G.* 22 June 3/1 The folly which led them [the Admiralty] to use a swift and finely lined turnabout, built by White, of Cowes, to carry cabbages and potatoes on board the vessels lying in Portsmouth Harbour. **1889** *Harper's Mag.* Sept. 560/1 The high swings and the turnabouts; the tests of the strength of limb and lung. **1894** W. H. WHITE *Man. Nav. Archit.* xviii. (ed. 3) 652 In a considerable number of small vessels and torpedo-boats an arrangement of balanced rudders has been fitted...This arrangement ..is known as the 'turn-about' system. *Ibid.* 699 A second [gun-boat]..identical..except that the after deadwood had been cut away, and the 'turn-about' system applied.

**Turnado**, obs. form of TORNADO.

**Turnagain** (tǭ·ɹnˌăgen, -ăgēⁱn), *sb.* (*a.*) [f. the verbal phr. *turn again* (TURN *v.* 66).]

†**1.** A turning again or about; a revolution; a winding or deviation. *Obs.*

**1545** RAYNOLD *Byrth Mankynde* I. x. (1634) 34 The.. vaines infinitely intricate and writhed with a thousand revolutions or turnagaines. **1587** GOLDING *De Mornay* xxv. (1592) 380 Moyses in leading the people of Israell through so many turnagaines.

†**b.** That which turns back an advance. *Obs.*

**1630** *R. Johnson's Kingd. & Commw.* 43 Mountaines are natures bulwarkes..; the Retreats they are of the oppressed, the scornes and turne-againes of victorious Armies. **1642** ROGERS *Naaman* 252 Why then fall there out so many turnagaines in the lives of the best?

**2.** A device in the bobbin-net machine.

**1832** BABBAGE *Econ. Manuf.* xxxiii. (ed. 3) 349 An improvement in a particular part of such machines, called a turn-again.

**3.** = ANTISTROPHE.

**1871** BROWNING *Balaust.* 214 Sing them a strophe, with the turn-again, Down to the verse that ends all, proverb-like.

†**4.** *attrib.* or as *adj.* in **turn-again alley, lane,** a blind alley, a cul-de-sac; also, a winding or crooked lane. *Obs.*

**1531** TINDALE *Expos. 1 John* Prol. (1537) 5 It is become a turne-agayne lane unto them, which they can not go thorow. **1624** HEYWOOD *Gunaik.* v. 256 A turne-againe-lane, that had no passage through. *c* **1730** BURT *Lett. N. Scotl.* (1818) I. 56 [In Scotland] A little court or turn-again alley, is a closs. **1807** *Antiq. Rep.* I. 346 It was Friar Richard's ill fate to take into a turn-again lane, that had no passage through.

**Turnament**, obs. f. TOURNAMENT, TORMENT.

†**Turnas**, obs. var. TOURNOIS, coin of Tours.

**1617** MORYSON *Itin.* I. 292 At Naples..ten quatrines make one sequin, three quatrines one turnas.

**Turnay**: see TOURNEY.

**Turnback** (tǭ·ɹnbæk), *sb.* and *a.* [f. the verbal phr. *turn back* (TURN *v.* 69).] One who or that which turns back or is turned back. **a.** *sb.* (*a*) One who faint-heartedly retreats, or gives up an enterprise. (*b*) That part of anything which is folded back. **b.** *attrib.* or *adj.* That is folded back.

**1847–78** HALLIWELL, *Turnback*, a coward. **1879** *Unif. Regul.* in *Navy List* July (1882) 489/2 Stand-up collar, with a white turn-back on each side of the collar. **1881** A. C. GRANT *Bush-Life Queensland* II. 232 The unfavourable reports of these turnbacks were.. little heeded. **1900** *Westm. Gaz.* 29 Nov. 2/2 A little more protection round the throat than a turn-back collar can afford. **1909** *Daily Graphic* 19 Oct. 17/3 The little turn-back brim in a Dutch baby bonnet. *Ibid.* 20 Oct. 13/1 The tight-fitting tunic.. ends in a turnback fold of the material.

**Turnbroach** (tǭ·ɹnbrōᵘtʃ). *arch.* [f. TURN *v.* + BROACH *sb.*] = TURNSPIT 2, 3. Also *attrib.* or *adj.*

**14..** *Voc.* in Wr.-Wülcker 619/1 *Verugirus*, a turnebroche. *c* **1430** LYDG. *Min. Poems* (Percy Soc.) 52 A turne-broche, a boy for hogge at Ware, With loury face, noddyng and slombryng. *a* **1548** HALL *Chron.*, *Hen. VII* 10 b, This Lambert..was made the kynges faulkener, after that he had been a turne broche..in the kynges kytchyn. **1596** NASHE *Saffron Walden* 127 Downe his throate I will thrust this turnbroach comparison. **1610** W. FOLKINGHAM *Art of Survey* I. xiii. 45 Fulling-mils, Shere-mils, Turne-broach-milles, Oyle-mills, Barke-mills. **1682** N. O. *Boileau's Lutrin* II. 112 A Bastard-brat rather of some Turn-broch. **1795** *Commons Jrnls.* L. 525, 5 Boys in the Kitchen. Scowerer..Soil Carrier..3 Turnbroaches. **1822** SCOTT *Nigel* xxxi, A turnbroche, or deputy scullion.

**Turn-broacher**, erroneous f. TURNBROACH.

**Tu·rn-bu·ckle.** [f. TURN *v.* + BUCKLE *sb.*]

**1.** A catch or fastening for window casements, shutters, etc., consisting of a thin flat bar pivoted so that it falls by its weight into a slit or groove.

**1703** Turn-buckle [see *turn-bout*, TURN-]. **1717** *Inventory of Goods* (MS.), One Glass Window, One Casemᵗ with a Turnbuckle. **1859** F. A. GRIFFITHS *Artill. Man.* (1862) 184 Turnbuckles, small..6.

**2.** A coupling with internal screw threads for connecting metal rods lengthwise or for regulating their length or tension; *transf.* a device for coupling electric wires (*Funk's Stand. Dict.*, 1895).

**1877** KNIGHT *Dict. Mech.*, *Turn-buckle*, ..(*Nautical*), a link used for setting up and tightening the iron rods employed as stays for the smoke-stack. **1895** *Outing* (U. S.) XXVI. 44 Deadeyes and lanyards are fast giving way before the advance of the turnbuckle.

**Turncoat** (tǭ·ɹnkoᵘt), *sb.* and *a.* [f. TURN *v.* + COAT *sb.* lit. one who turns his coat; cf. TURN *v.* 51.]

**A.** *sb.* One who changes his principles or party; a renegade; an apostate.

**1557** WOODMAN in Foxe *A. & M.* (1570) 2193/2, I will beleue none of you all, for you be turne coates, and chaungelinges, and be wauering minded. **1579** FULKE *Confut. Sanders* 688 It sheweth what turne coates they were, which changed as euerie prince was affected. *a* **1632** G. HERBERT *Outlandish Prov.* § 929 Wine is a turne-coate (first a friend, then an enemy). **1777** MME. D'ARBLAY *Early Diary*, I am afraid Mrs. Wall is a turn-coat. **1855** MACAULAY *Hist. Eng.* xv. III. 567 The Tory who voted for those motions would run a great risk of being pointed at as a turncoat by the..Cavaliers.

†**b.** *transf.* applied to anything that changes in appearance or colour. Also *turn-coat-coloured.*

**1567** MAPLET *Gr. Forest* 11 This is a maruellous turncote, for that it doth conforme it self to all settes and dispositions of the Ayre. *Ibid.* 12 b, Kaman the stone may well be called a turncote, for that it is nowe blacke, now white, now shamefast & blushing. **1608** TOPSELL *Serpents* (1658) 672 Of a changeable colour, betwixt white, green, brown and yellow, for which occasion some have called it *versicolor Chamæleon*, that is, a turn-coat-coloured Chamæleon.

**c.** A coat renovated by being turned; in quot. *fig.*

**1726** GAY in *Swift's Lett.* (1766) II. 65 Next week I shall have a new coat, and new buttons, for the birth-day, though ..a turn-coat might have been more for my advantage.

**B.** *adj.* Of, pertaining to, or that is a turncoat.

**1571** GOLDING *Calvin on Ps.* lviii. 5 Hee peynteth out more expressely theire turnecote craftynesse. **1624** MIDDLETON *Game at Chess* II. ii, Yond greasy turncoat gormandising prelate. **1706** HEARNE *Collect.* 3 Nov. (O.H.S.) I. 302 An old, rich,..turn-coat Dʳ. **1796** WOLCOTT (P. Pindar) *Satire* Wks. 1812 III. 400 Turncoat Windham to no party true. **1876** LOWELL *Among my Bks.* Ser. II. 40 We have heard that the Commedia was..the revengeful satire of a disappointed Ghibelline, nay, worse, of a turncoat Guelph.

Hence (*nonce-wds.*) **Tu·rncoat** *v.*, *intr.* to play the turncoat, to change sides; **Tu·rncoated** *a.*, having the coat turned; **Tu·rncoatery, Tu·rncoating** *vbl. sb.*, **Tu·rncoatism,** the action or practice of a turncoat.

**1892** *Pall Mall G.* 4 July 3/1 Whichever way I've voted, One or the other's sure to swear that I've *turn-coated. *c* **1645** HOWELL *Lett.* (1650) III. xxi. 33 Translations are but as *turn-coated things at best, specially among languages that have advantages one of the other. **1841** HAMPDEN in *Some Mem.* (1871) 132 Apologising for his *turn-coaterie, saying, that those who now brought in the new Government would as soon turn them out if they came forward with the proposal of a fixed duty. **1624** BP. MOUNTAGU *Immed. Addr.* A j b, To take notice of his dealing,..in his *turne-coating from side to side. **1889** W. ROBERTS in *N. & Q.* 7th Ser. VII. 41/1 The most barefaced and flagrant *turncoatism.

**Tu·rncock.** [f. TURN *v.* + COCK *sb.*[1]]

†**1.** A stop-cock of which the plug is turned to open or close it. *Obs.*

**1702** SAVERY *Miner's Friend* 42 At every Floor there may be a turn-cock with a Skrew. **1755** HALES in *Phil. Trans.* XLIX. 320 When, by means of a turn-cock, a gallon of water was two minutes in running, then the heat was 140.

**2.** A water-works official entrusted with the turning on of the water from the mains to supply-pipes, etc.

**1711** in Halliwell *Acc. Collect. Bills*, etc. (1852) 27 Christmas Boxes,..Turncock, 2*s.* 6*d.* **1791** 'G. GAMBADO' *Ann. Horsem.* xvii. (1809) 139 No Turncocks to be found—all the Water at a stop. **1863** DICKENS *Uncomm. Trav.* xxi, A meditative turncock..gives the fire-plug a disparaging wrench. **1875** RUSKIN *Fors Clav.* V. 56 The turncock..turned and turned till a fountain sprang up in the middle of the street.

**Tu·rn-down,** *a.* and *sb.* [f. the verbal phr. *turn down* (TURN *v.* 71).]

**A.** *adj.* **1.** That turns down or may be turned down; esp. said of a collar worn with the upper part turned down over the neck-band; *turn-down bed*, a folding bed.

**1840** MARRYAT *Poor Jack* xlvi, He wore..a turn-down collar. *a* **1860** ALB. SMITH *Lond. Med. Student* (1861) 86 The faithful Mary..has long since retired to rest in the turn-down bedstead of the back kitchen. **1884** *Marshall's Tennis Cuts* 104 A pretty shape which..admits of a tie being passed under the turn-down corners.

**2.** *Electr. spec.* designating an incandescent lamp of which one small filament only is used when little light is wanted. **1911** in WEBSTER.

**B.** *sb.* **1.** The turned-down part of anything; also, an article of dress that is worn turned down; *spec.* a turn-down collar (see A. 1).

**1849** ALB. SMITH *Pottleton Leg.* iv, Her other hand.. hidden beneath the turn-down of the thin worn sheet. **1865** LEVER *Luttrell* xxxii. 232, I showed him the turn-down, only the turn-down, of your note. **1896** *Punch* 8 Aug. 64/1 When he's out of Jackets and Turn-downs, and gets into Tails and Stick-ups! **1903** *Blackw. Mag.* Mar. 372/1 Heather stockings with loud-patterned 'turn-downs'.

**2.** The action of turning down (see TURN *v.* 71 d).

**1902** *Speaker* 23 Aug. 550/2, I look back on that period of sour welcome and curt turn-down with feelings I cannot express.

‖ **Tu·rndun, tu·ndun.** [Native Australian of the Kurnai tribe in Gippsland.
Originally written *tŭrndŭn* by Howitt (see quot. 1880), who however employs the spelling *tundun* in his *Native Tribes S.E. Austr.* (1904) 493.]

A flattish, fish-shaped piece of wood fastened by one end to a thong, which when whirled round makes a peculiar penetrating roaring sound; a bull-roarer.

**1880** FISON & HOWITT *Kamilaroi & Kurnai* 197 About a week after the boys have run away.., the old men go out and make certain wooden instruments called tŭrndŭn. **1883** *Cornh. Mag.* Jan. 84 This object, called Turndun by the Australians, is a very early savage invention, probably discovered and applied to religious purposes in various.. centres, and retained from the age of savagery in the mystic rites of Greeks and perhaps of Romans. **1887** *Athenæum* 1 Oct. 430 The living Australian savage as he twirls the turndun, bedaubs himself with clay. **1898** A. LANG *Making Relig.* v. 91 Many other races use the bull-roarer, turndun, or *rhombos*.

†**Turne,** *a. Obs. rare*⁻¹. [Cf. OE. *torn* anger.] ? Hot-tempered, irritable.

*c* **1375** *Sc. Leg. Saints* xl. (*Ninian*) 1242 For men hurt communly Ar mar turne & mare angry..þane he þat has his lymmys al.

**Turned** (tɔ̄ɹnd), *ppl. a.* [f. TURN *v.* + -ED¹.] In various senses corresponding to those of the verb, q. v.; those chiefly in use are given here.

**1.** Moved round on an axis, rotated: see TURN *v.* I.

**1552** HULOET, Turned, or dryuen aboute wyth the handes as a mustarde querne is, *trusatilis.* **1606** MARSTON *Parasit.* II. D iv, Beware legge-ringes And the turnd key on thee.

**2.** Wrought in a lathe; shaped or rounded with a lathe: see TURN *v.* 4.

*c* **1440** *Promp. Parv.* 507/1 Turnyd vessel, or other thynge, ..*toreuma.* **1501** *Maldon, Essex, Crt. Rolls* Bundle 60, No. 7, 1 tabill, ii trestellis,..a turned cheyr. **1556** in Willis & Clark *Cambridge* (1886) II. 564 Thende of the partitions to be with turned pillers. **1681** GREW *Musæum* III. I. ii. 271 It looks like some sort of Turn'd-Work. *c* **1790** IMISON *Sch. Art* I. 221 A small turn'd handle..to screw on or off at pleasure. **1792** BELKNAP *Hist. New Hampsh.* III. 112 [Poplar] is used..for some kinds of turned work. **1838** DICKENS *Nich. Nick.* x, Chairs, with turned legs.

**b.** *Turned shells* (Zool.), a name for the family *Actæonidæ* or *Tornatellidæ* of gastropods.

**1891** in *Cent. Dict.*

**3.** (With advs., as *well*, etc.) Shaped, formed, fashioned: see TURN *v.* 5.

*a* **1637** B. JONSON *Underwoods* xii. 68 The race Of Shakespeare's mind and manners brightly shines In his well torned, and true filed lines. **1699** VANBRUGH *False Friend* II. i, See, here he comes..a pretty turn'd fellow. **1710** *Lond. Gaz.* No. 4689/4 A strong well turned little Mare. **1837** CARLYLE *Fr. Rev.* III. III. iv, In sweetly turned periods. **1874** L. STEPHEN *Hours in Libr.* (1892) I. iii. 123 So many exquisitely turned compliments.

**4.** Bent or twisted: see TURN *v.* 9.

**1585** *Durham Wills* (Surtees) II. 111 A eireon wayne, a turned teame. **1703** T. N. *City & C. Purchaser* 193 They call it Turn'd-lead, when the Came has pass'd through the Vice, and is thereby made with a Groove on each side to go on upon the Glass. *Mod.* The knife has a turned edge, and won't cut.

**5.** Moved into a different posture or direction (*lit.* or *fig.*); diverted, deflected, etc.: see TURN *v.* 7, 13, 14, 22, etc.

*c* **1586** C'TESS PEMBROKE *Ps.* LXXVII. iv, With turned thought, A new I fell to thinck Upon the auncient tymes. **1621** BP. HALL *Heaven upon Earth* § 4 The galled soule.. after many tossed and turned sides, complaines of..vnabated torment. **1847** TENNYSON *Princ.* I. 65 He chew'd The thrice-turn'd cud of wrath.

**b.** *Turned of* (an age, etc.): see TURN *v.* 18 b.

**6.** †**a.** Opposite, contrary, adverse. *Obs. rare*⁻¹.

*a* **1325** *MS. Rawl. B.* 520 lf. 64 For partie torned [*MS. Rawl. B.* 820 lf. 139 Pro parte aduerssa].

**b.** Reversed so as to be upside down; inverted (see TURN *v.* 10); *spec.* in *Printing*, of a type placed or letter printed upside down.

**1513** DOUGLAS *Æneis* VIII. vi. 114 The housis war lik a turnit barge. **1638–56** COWLEY *Davideis* I. lix, Numbers which still encrease more high and wide From One, the root of their turn'd Pyramide. **1771** LUCKOMBE *Hist. Print.* 443 The Article of marking turned letters tries a Corrector's skill. **1826** WELLINGTON in *Croker Papers* (1884) I. xi. 330 They..lay sprawling and kicking like..turned turtles. **1877** SWEET *Handbk. Phonetics* § 45 The narrow back unrounded vowels are indicated by the 'turned' letters of the corresponding wides...(ɔ) is assumed to be a turned (o).

**c.** Reversed or altered so as to be inside out, as a garment (see TURN *v.* 11 c); also of a shoe (see quot. 1882).

**1483** *Cath. Angl.* 397/2 A Turnyd cloth, *interpola.* **1552** HULOET, Turned garmente whose wronge side is turned vpwarde, *tra[n]slata uestis.* *a* **1643** CARTWRIGHT *On Dram. Poems Fletcher* in *Comedies*, etc. (1651) 8 Old fashioned wit! which walked..In turned hose. **1765** W. GORDON *Gen. Counting-ho.* 317, 12 doz. turned pumps for men [cf. *turn-shoe*, TURN-]. **1819** *Metropolis* I. 120 A turned coat,..and a wig turned inside out, were spoken of. **1837** THACKERAY *Ravenswing* iv, Professionals with turned frocks. **1882** *Worc. Exhib. Catal.* iii. 30 Turned work [in shoemaking] (so called from being made inside out and afterwards turned).

**7.** That has turned sour or become tainted, as milk; †curdled (*obs.*): see TURN *v.* 46.

**1548** UDALL *Erasm. Par. Luke* vi. 72 b, The olde soure turned wine of Moses lawe. **1556** WITHALS *Dict.* (1568) 49 b/1 Turned milke or sower, *oxia gala.* **1665** NEEDHAM *Med. Medicinæ* 408 Curdled or Turnd Milk. **1903** N. MUNRO in *Blackw. Mag.* 237/1 Curdling like turned cream.

**8.** With adverbs, as *turned-back, -down, -in, -out, -up*: see TURN *v.* VIII.

**1861** *Eng. Wom. Dom. Mag.* III. 263 A..crêpe sleeve, with a *turned-back cuff in Brussels lace. **1889** HENTY *With Lee in Virginia* (1890) 17 There was no mistaking the expression of its [the horse's] turned-back eye. **1840** THACKERAY *Shabby-genteel Story* ii, A dirty *turned-down shirt-collar. **1900** *Law Rep.* App. Cas. 404 At the *turned-in end of the hook. **1833** T. HOOK *Widow & Marquess* xii, The best *turned-out equipage that rattled through its streets. **1621** G. SANDYS *Ovid's Met.* v. (1626) 92 As he did roule His *turn'd-vp eyes. **1686** *Lond. Gaz.* No. 2131/4 A little..white Bitch, with a turned-up Nose. **1836** *Penny Cycl.* VI. 444/1 The turned-up edges of the mantle. **1904** BUDGE *3rd & 4th Egypt. Rooms Brit. Mus.* 226 A pair of gazelle skin sandals, with turned up toes.

**Turneke,** obs. f. TOURNIQUET.

**Turnel**¹ (tɔ̄·ɹnĕl). *Obs.* exc. *dial.* Also 5 -elle, 6 -yll(e, 6–7 -ell, 7 tournell, 7–9 turnil. [Derivative of TURN *v.*: cf. OF. *tornel, tournel*, that which turns, in various spec. applications.]

**1.** A ring turning on a swivel, a terret.

**1469** in *Househ. Ord.* (1790) 97 The maister of the horses.. for sadelles, harnesse, horse-houses, wateringe-bridles, halters, turnelles, pastrons. **1607** MARKHAM *Caval.* IV. ix. 41 This peece of leather you shall buckle about your horses farre fore-leg,..also when it is buckled on you must so place it, that a strong tournell of iron being cunningly fastned within the leather, may stand iust behind his leg.

**2.** The windlass over a well.

**1578** *Nottingham Rec.* IV. 179 Mendyng of the turnyll of the welle. **1599** *Ibid.* 251 One bucket, one turnell, and a rope.

**3.** The catch or fastening of a casement: = TURN-BUCKLE 1.

**1696** *Rector's Bk. Clayworth* (1910) 118 The Thief came in at yᵉ Casemᵗ window, in wᶜʰ he broke a Quarry to get in his hand to turn yᵉ Turnil.

**4.** (See quots.)

**1621** MARKHAM *Prev. Hunger* xi. 115 Certaine toyes made of long Goose feathers in the manner of shettlecocks and with little small turnells of wood running in broad and flat Swan quilles made round like a small hoope, and so with longer strings fastened to the Poale will with any small winde or ayre whatsoeuer, twirle and flicker in the ayre. **1905** *Eng. Dial. Dict.*, *Turnil*, a small, round lump of coal.

**Turnel**² (tɔ̄·ɹnĕl). *Obs.* exc. *dial.* [Etymology doubtful.] A tub; *esp.* a shallow oval tub. Also *attrib.* **turnel boat**: see quot. 1688².

**1688** R. HOLME *Armoury* III. xiv. (Roxb.) 11/2 He beareth Gules, a Tub, or Turnell, with handles Argent, Hooped.. also termed a Netting or washing Turnell, because in such washer women and Laundresses use to wash their linnens. *Ibid.* xv. 26/1 A Tumbrell boate, or flat bottomed boate, or Turnell boate...This kind of boate is for the conveying of cowes or horses. **1875** *Auctioneer's Catal.* in Miss Jackson *Shropsh. Word-bk.* (1879), Salting turnel. **1886** *Cheshire Gloss.*, *Turnel*...Large ones are used for scalding pigs and are called 'pig turnels'. Smaller ones are used for various purposes, such as putting under a cheese press; kneading bread, salting meat, etc.

**Turnell, -elle,** var. TOURNELLE, *Obs.*, turret.

**Turnement,** obs. f. TORMENT, TOURNAMENT.

**Turnep,** obs. f. TURNIP.

**Turner**¹ (tɔ̄·ɹnəɹ). Forms: 4 tourner(e, 4–5 tornere, 5 turnere; 5 turnor, -owre, 5–6 -our, tornour; 5 turnare, 5–6 torner, 6 -ar, turnar, 5– turner. [a. OF. *tornere* (nom.) :–L. *tornātor*, and *torneor* (acc.), F. *tourneur* :–L. *tornatōr-em*, agent-n. from *tornāre* to turn in a lathe; in later senses f. TURN *v.* + -ER¹.]

**I. 1.** One who turns or fashions objects of wood, metal, bone, etc., on a lathe. Also *fig.*

*c* **1400** *Destr. Troy* 1586 Taliours, Telers, Turners of vessells. **1415** in *York Myst.* Introd. 25 Tielmakers, Milners,..Turnours,..Bollers. *c* **1440** *Promp. Parv.* 507/2 Turnowre, *tornator.* **1485** *Naval Acc. Hen. VII* (1896) 22 William Parken of London Turnor for iij dd shodde shovilles ..xvˢ. **1507–8** *Durham Acc. Rolls* (Surtees) 104 Le Tornour pro CCC parapsidum et CCC discorum ligneorum, vijs. **1530** PALSGR. 284/1 Turnar a maker of bolles and dysshes, *torneur.* **1551** RECORDE *Cast. Knowl.* (1556) 111 Euery common turner can..know yᵗ a little altering of the one side, maketh the boul to run biasse waies. **1552** HULOET, Turnours whele or instrument, *tornus.* **1578** LYTE *Dodoens* I. lxviii. 99 Horse tayle..stemmes..their roughnesse is such, that Turners..do vse them to polish.. and smoth their workes. **1685** BOYLE *Effects of Mot.* ii. 7, I have caused a skilfull Turner to turn for me an oblong piece of Iron. **1709** STEELE *Tatler* No. 3 ¶ 5 Advice to the Poets; that is to say, to the Turners of Verse, as he calls 'em. **1776** *Pennsylvania Even. Post* 23 Mar. 149/1 A Turner of Brass is likewise wanted. **1838** DICKENS *Nich. Nick.* xiv, One Mr. Kenwigs, a turner in ivory. **1892** *Labour Commission Gloss.* s.v., When a turner himself holds the tool which cuts the iron or other material he is turning, he is termed a hand tool turner.

**b.** A potter; *esp.* one who finishes and smooths the ware before it is fired.

**1601** HOLLAND *Pliny* xxxv. xii. II. 553 That kind [of earthenware] that is wrought by turners craft with the wheele. *Ibid.* xxxvi. xxii. 592 A stone, which they use to hew hollow, and by turners craft make vessels for the kitchin. **1790** in *Guide Mus. Pract. Geol.* (1859) 98 About 90 painters .. and about 200 throwers, turners, &c., were employed. **1853** URE *Dict. Arts* II. 455 When the 'thrown ware' is sufficiently dry, it is transferred to the hands of the 'turner'. **1881** *Porcelain Works, Worcester* 20 The turner..finishes the edge and foot, and if necessary the outside surface. **1892** *Labour Commission Gloss.*, *Turners*, potters who shape pottery ware upon a lathe.

**II.** One who or that which turns, in various other senses of the verb.

**2.** In general senses: see TURN *v.*

*c* **1440** *Promp. Parv.* 507/1 Turnare, or he that turnythe a spete or other lyke, *versor.* **1491** in *York Myst.* Introd. 39 Tixt-wryters, luminers, noters, turners, and florisschers. **1527** *Luton Trin. Guild* (1906) 188 Item payd to a xjᵗⁱˢ turners of spyttis xvij d. **1546** BP. GARDINER *Declar. Art. Joye* 55 b, I affirme yᵉ same iustification that was then taught, and yow be the turners. **1552** HULOET, Turnour of one out of the ryght waye, *obuaricator.* **1593** *Rites of Durham* (Surtees 1903) 3 Which wheele did burst in peices and caught the turners of the said wheele and..rent them in peices. **1697** BENTLEY *Phal.* (1699) 422 If I really were such a Turner of Index's and Lexicons. **1702** DENNIS *Monument* xxxiii, Nor sordid Turner of his Gold for Gain. **1730** SAVERY in *Phil. Trans.* XXXVI. 338 The whole may be made to turn with one's Hand, either with a Crank.., or with a Turner like that of a Grinding-stone. **1861** *Times* 1 June, Several winnowing machines and one hay turner are damaged. **1868** MORRIS *Earthly Par.* (1870) I. II. 588 An accursed race, Who with the turner of all hearts once strove. **1878** *N. Amer. Rev.* CXXVII. 490 He is a turner of night into day. **1893** W. B. YEATS *Celtic Twilight* (1902) 24 Villages of fishermen and turners of the earth.

**b.** With adverbs: cf. TURN *v.* VIII.

**1653** WATERHOUSE *Apol. Learn.* 245 Perswaders, and turners away of the people from obedience. **1681** MACWARD *Contendings* (1723) 89 Such Backdrawers, and Turners-aside with the Workers of Iniquity. **1892** *Sat. Rev.* 13 Aug. 205/2 To the idle turner-over, perhaps the most remarkable thing is the frequency of the phrase 'no information'.

†**3.** A translator. *Obs. rare.*

**1387** TREVISA *Higden* (Rolls) II. 237 Þe seuenty torneres [CAXTON turneres] and Isidre also..seiþ two þowsand ȝere seuen hondred and two and fourty. *Ibid.* 245 Þey beeþ specialliche i-cleped þe Seuenty tourneris [*v. r.* turneres], for þey torned Holy Writte out of Ebrew in to Grewe. *c* **1425** *Saints' Lives, Apol.* in *Anglia* VIII. 195/31 Þe turner of þis englysshe.

**4.** In shirt-making: see quot.

**1884** E. SIMCOX in *19th Cent.* June 1041 A preparer of collars and wristbands, known as a 'tacker and turner'.

†**5.** A variety of fancy pigeon. See quot. 1735. *Obs.*

**1688** R. HOLME *Armoury* II. 244/2 Of Pigeons...Turners having a tuft turning down backwards from the Head. **1735** MOORE *Columbarium* 50 *Columba Circumagens*, The Turner ..in many Respects like the Finnikin, except that when it ..plays to the Female it turns only one Way, whereas the other turns both. [**1854** MEALL *Moubray's Poultry* 280 The *Turner* is also mentioned...However, if they ever existed, there are certainly none such known now. **1867** TEGETMEIER *Pigeons* xxii. 175.]

**6.** In the Newfoundland seal-fishery, a seal which is between the immature and mature stages of development; a three-year old seal. Also attrib. *turner-harp, -hood* (see HARP *sb.*¹ 7, HOOD *sb.* 6).

**1891** in *Cent. Dict.*

**7.** A small piece of fire-clay on which a watch-dial is held and turned while in the enamelling oven. **1891** in *Cent. Dict.*

**III. 8.** A member of one of the gymnastic societies instituted in Germany by F. L. Jahn (1778–1852); cf. TURNING *vbl. sb.* 4 d.

[In this sense a. G. *turner*, f. *turnen* to perform gymnastic exercises, an adoption (by Jahn) of F. *tourner*.]

**1860** in WORCESTER citing ADLER. **1860** BARTLETT *Dict. Amer.*, *Turner* (Germ.), a gymnast. **1865** *Pall Mall G.* 31 May 9 The late meeting of German turners in Paris. *Ibid.*, The turners who had come from Germany. **1888** *U.S. Newspaper* 17 Aug., The red and white flags of the turners may be seen.

**Tu·rner**². *Hist.* Also 7 turno(u)r. [Etymology not ascertained: perh. an alteration of TOURNOIS, as the coin has considerable resemblance to the double tournois of copper current in France in the 17th cent.; cf. the Irish TURNEYS.] A small copper coin, current in Scotland in the 17th c., called also a twopenny piece or bodle, valued (when pure) at one-sixth of an English penny. See also TURNOVER.

They were originally coined by the Earl of Stirling *c* 1623. Counterfeits were also fabricated by gipsies: see quots.

**1631** *Act Privy Council* in Cochran-Patrick *Rec. Coinage Scot.* (1876) II. 28 It is our pleasure that yow giue order ..for calling in of the copper money callit Turnours. **1635** BRERETON *Trav.* (Chetham Soc.) 188 Coins current in Scotland—In Copper, Turners 6 to one penny English or 12 Scottish. **1640** *Records of Elgin* (New Spald. Cl.) I. 266 Geving..thrie dolloris in siluer and receaving back..sex dolloris in turnoris for the samyn. **1642** in Row *Hist. Kirk* (Wodrow Soc.) p. xviii, Four pund weght of turnoris. *Ibid.* p. xix, Four markis of turnouris quhilk was gottin out of the Coinze-house. *a* **1670** SPALDING *Troub. Chas. I* (1850) I. 235 King Charles turnouris, stricken be the Erll of Striviling,..wes, be proclamatioun..cryit doun fra tua penneis to ane penny; King James turnouris to pas for tua penneis, becauss thay war no less worth; and the kaird turnouris simpliciter dischargeit as falss cungzie. **1786** CARDONNEL *Numism. Scot.* 34 After 1660, we hear of two pennies, bodles, and turners. **1842** *Penny Cycl.* XXIII. 60/1 s.v. *Stirling, Wm. Earl of*, He obtained the privilege of coining for Scotland a sort of base copper-money, called 'turners'. **1882** FRANCISQUE-MICHEL *Scot. Lang.* vi. 123 Charles I..continued the coinage of the turner. The name was revived and applied to a similar piece coined after the Restoration, in the beginning of Charles II's reign. **1893** *Antiquary* Mar. 105 Coins found in St. Queran's Well 1869. Scottish..Charles II., Turners and Half Turners.

**Turneraceous** (tɔ̄ɹnərēⁱ·ʃəs), *a. Bot.* [f. mod.L. *Turnerāce-æ* (f. *Turnera*, the typical genus, named after William Turner, the herbalist) + -OUS.] Of or pertaining to the *Turneraceæ*, a small order of tropical herbs and undershrubs, mainly American and African, having yellowish or blue axillary flowers and alternate leaves.

1895 in *Funk's Standard Dict.*

**Tu·rnerad.** *Bot.* [f. mod.L. *Turner-a*: see prec.] *pl.* Lindley's name for the *Turneraceæ.*

1846 LINDLEY *Veget. Kingd.* 347 The forked styles of Turnerads are very peculiar.

**Turneresque** (-e·sk), *a.* [f. the name of J. M. W. *Turner* (1775–1851), landscape painter + -ESQUE.] Partaking of the character of the pictures of Turner.

1851 RUSKIN *Stones Ven.* I. App. xi. 369 The peculiarly Turneresque characters of the earlier pictures. 1862 MISS BRADDON *Lady Audley* xv, A water-coloured sketch of an impossibly beautiful Italian peasant, in an impossibly Turneresque atmosphere. 1877 *Contemp. Rev.* Feb. 351 The Turneresque splendour of sunset in a great city.

So **Turne·rian** *a.*, characteristic of or resembling the work of Turner; **Tu·rnerism**, the manner or school of Turner; **Tu·rnerize** *v.*, *trans.* to render Turnerian.

1889 RUSKIN *Præterita* III. ii. 90 Turnerian mist effects of morning, and Turnerian sunsets at evening. 1893 W. G. COLLINGWOOD *Ruskin* (1911) II. i. 79 The father was more or less converted to Turnerism and lined his walls with Turner drawings. 1903 *Daily Chron.* 3 July 3/2 'Blackwood'..foretold that the pictorial world would never be Turnerised.

**Turnerite** (tʊ̄·rnərəit). *Min.* [f. the name of C. H. Turner + -ITE[1].] A variety of monazite, occurring in yellow or brown crystals.

1823 A. LEVY in *Ann. Philos.* V. 242 Mr. Heuland has proposed to me to call it *Turnerite*, from the name of the gentleman in whose collection it was first noticed as a distinct species. 1850 ANSTED *Elem. Geol., Min.* etc. § 441 Turnerite; Aluminate of lime and magnesia. 1868 DANA *Min.* (ed. 5) 540 Turnerite is isomorphous with monazite, and like it in cleavage and color...It is known only in rare crystals...Lustre adamantine; color yellow or brown.

**Turnery** (tʊ̄·rnəri). Also 7 tourn-. [f. TURNER[1] + -Y.]

**1.** The art of the turner; the fashioning of objects or designs by means of a lathe.

1662 J. BARGRAVE *Pope Alex. VII* (1867) 126 A very artificial anatomy of a human eye, with all its films or tunicles, by way of turnery in ivory and horn. 1783 JUSTAMOND tr. *Raynal's Hist. Indies* IV. 449 This wood is very fit for works of turnery. 1842 LOUDON *Suburban Hort.* 545 The wood [of the pear] is light, smooth, and compact, and much used in turnery. 1882 HASLUCK in *Mechanical World* 4 Mar. 138/1 Numerous objects of turnery lying on the bench.

**2.** Collectively: Turner's work; objects fashioned on the lathe; turnery ware. † Also with *a* and *pl.*

1644 EVELYN *Diary* 22 Oct., In another roome are such rare tourneries in ivory as are not to be described for their curiosity. 1761 H. WALPOLE *Let. to G. Montagu* 20 Aug., [Some old chairs] the backs, arms, and legs loaded with turnery. 1881 YOUNG *Ev. Man his own Mechanic* § 41 The Birch..is used..for making wheels, casks, tubs, and turnery.

**3.** A place where turning is done; a turner's workshop.

1863 P. BARRY *Dockyard Econ.* 271 Boiler shop, erecting shop, turnery, foundry, forge, &c. 1878 F. S. WILLIAMS *Midl. Railw.* 649 The light turnery or fitting shop. 1888 *Pall Mall G.* 6 June 2/1 In the shell turnery, shrapnel, Palliser, and other projectiles of divers weight and pattern, were shown us.

**4.** *attrib.* and *Comb.*, as *turnery-room, ware, warehouse, work.*

1895 *Jrnl. R. Instit. Brit. Archit.* May 490 The shaft may in itself be elaborately enriched with *turnery forms. 1756–7 tr. *Keysler's Trav.* (1760) III. 294 In the *turnery-room are all kinds of lathes and instruments for turning. 1670 CAPT. J. SMITH *Eng. Improv. Reviv'd* 195 This Timber is..very good for Hoops and Hoppoles, *Turnery ware and Joyners. 1717 *Petiveriana* III. 218 They make Mortars, Pestles, and other Turnery Ware of it. 1788 AIKIN *Eng. Delineated* 269 Tunbridge..is famous for its elegant turnery ware. 1855 *Times* in *N. & Q.* 11th Ser. XI. 325/2 To be seen at Wyatt's toy and *turnery warehouse. *a* 1734 NORTH *Lives* (1826) II. 336 Ivory wrought most exquisitely;..for *turnery work in that it is so small and crooked as is admirable. 1859 W. S. COLEMAN *Woodlands* (1862) 81 The heart-wood of the Yew is..the finest of all native woods for purposes of cabinet-making and turnery-work.

**Turnesall**, obs. form of TURNSOLE.

† **Turnet.** *Obs. rare.* [var. of, or error for, *turret* TORRET; cf. obs. F. *tournet* 'a small turning rundle, or ring, in the mouth of a Bit' (Cotgr.).] = TORRET c.

1543 *Act* 1 *Rich. III* 1483, c. 12 § 2 Laton nayles with yron chaunkes, turnettes [*so in some later edd.*; *Record ed. and Anglo-F.* turrettes], hangyng candelstyckes.

**Turney**, dial. var. TORNEY, attorney.

1807 R. ANDERSON *Cumbld. Ball., Kit Craffet* v, When onie neybor was fash'd by the turnies. 1886, 1895 in *Eng. Dial Dict.* s. v. *Torney.*

**Turney**, obs. f. TOURNEY *sb.* and *v.*

† **Tu·rneys.** *Obs. rare*[−1]. [Prob. the same as TOURNOIS. Cf. TURNER[2].] A 'black money' or base coin, made in Ireland in the 14th c.

1339 in Rymer *Foedera* (1708) V. 113 Dato nobis intelligi quod quidam, Homines Hibernici, quandam Nigram Monetam, vocatam Turneys, in partibus Hiberniæ fabricari fecerunt.

**Turneys**, obs. var. TOURNOIS.

† **Turngi·ddy,** *a.* and *sb. Obs. rare.* [f. TURN *v.* to rotate + GIDDY *a.* Cf. TURN-SICK *a.*] **a.** *adj.* Giddy as from turning round; dizzy; affected with vertigo. **b.** *sb.* Giddiness, dizziness. Hence † **Turngi·ddiness** *Obs. rare.* = b.

Perh. a western dial. word, as the first quot. is from the work of Nicholas of Hereford.

1382 *Wycliffite Bible* Isa. xix. 14 The Lord mengde in his myddel the spirit of turnegidy [Vulg. *vertiginis*]. 1398 TREVISA *Barth. De P. R.* XVII. cviii. (Tollem. MS.), Yf he eteþ many þerof, it bredeþ heedache and makeþ hem turnegedy [orig. *capiti vertiginem inferunt*]. *Ibid.* VII. xl. (Add. MS. 27944 lf. 90 b/2) Þe mouþ is soure with mystringe of ʒʒen and tur[n]gidinesse [orig. *vertigine*] & wiþ oþir wel yuel signes.

† **Turngrece, turngree.** Chiefly *Sc. Obs.* [f. TURN *v.* + GRECE, GREE *sb.*[1]] A winding stair, as in a turret, etc. Also *attrib.*

*c* 1470 HENRY *Wallace* IX. 511 Richard Wallace the turngreys [*ed.* 1570 Turngrece] weill has seyn; He folowit fast apon the portar keyn,..Tuk wp the port, and leit in all the layff. 1483 *Cath. Angl.* 397/2 A Turne grece, *troclea.* 1506–7 *Acc. Ld. High Treas. Scot.* III. 366 Item for ane lok to the turngree dur in the Abbay, xiiij d. 1535 COVERDALE 1 *Kings* vi. 8 They might go vp to the myddest stacion by a turne grese. 1554 *Burgh Rec. Edinb.* (1871) II. 296 To Thomas Hallis servand for paittelling and deichting of all the steppis of the turngryss of the tolbuith, viij[d]. 1600 *Reg. Mag. Sig. Scot.* 353/1 De cellario sub inferiore gradu lie turnegres tenementi quondam M. Thome Marjoribankis.

**Turnicimorphic** (tʊ̄ːnisimǭ·ɹfik), *a. Ornith.* [f. mod.L. *Turnicimorphæ* (f. *Turnix* + Gr. μορφή form) + -IC.] Resembling, or having the structure or characters of, the *Turnicimorphæ*, in Huxley's classification the group of birds akin in form to the genus *Turnix.* In recent Dicts.

**Turnicine** (tʊ̄·ɹnisəin), *a. Ornith.* [f. mod.L. *Turnic-, Turnix*, TURNIX + -INE[1].] Belonging to the *Turnicidæ*, a family of birds of which the turnix or hemipod is the type.

1891 in *Cent. Dict.*

**Turning** (tʊ̄·ɹniŋ), *vbl. sb.* [f. TURN *v.* + -ING[1].] The action of the verb TURN, in various senses (also concretely).

The earliest examples occur in senses 1 b (*c* 1230) and 4 (1303).

**1.** Movement about an axis or centre; rotation, revolution.

1387–8 T. USK *Test. Love* I. v. (Skeat) l. 64 Olde doinges and by many turninges of yeres used. 1390 GOWER *Conf.* I. 8 After the tornynge of the whiel. 1538 ELYOT, *Reuolutio*, ..a reuolucion or tournynge of celestiall bodyes or spheres. 1615 G. SANDYS *Trav.* 55 An Order of Monkes,.. called Dervises, whom I haue often seene to dance..; dances that consist of continuall turnings. 1802 PALEY *Nat. Theol.* xx. (ed. 2) 376 As the turning of a weather-board or tin cap upon the top of a chimney. 1821 SCOTT *Kenilw.* xxix, I mind it not the turning of a key. 1868 MISS BRADDON *Dead Sea Fr.* viii, An earthly river..instrumental in the turning of paper-mills.

**b.** A sensation as of rotation; 'whirling', giddiness, vertigo.

*c* 1230 *Hali Meid.* 35 Of breines turnunge þin heaued [schal] ake. 1398 TREVISA *Barth De P. R.* XVI. lxii. (Add. MS. 27944) lf. 202/2 It schal seme..þat þe hous schulde falle anone and þat semynge is by moeuynge þat comeþ by tornynge of þe brayne.

**2.** The action of shaping or working something on a lathe; the art of shaping things by means of a lathe; the work of a turner.

*c* 1440 *Promp. Parv.* 507/1 Turnynge, or throwynge of treyn vessel..*tornatura.* 1620 in Swayne *Sarum Churchw. Acc.* (1896) 171 Turninge of Banisters and pendantes. 1680 MOXON *Mech. Exerc.* xi. 194 In Turning, all Irregularities must be wrought smooth down. 1726 LEONI tr. *Alberti's Archit.* I. 25/1 Workmen lay their Timber under water.., especially such as they design for turning. 1873 J. RICHARDS *Wood-working Factories* 158 Turning is an..important branch of wood work.

**b.** *pl.* (*concr.*) Chips or shavings *of* some substance produced by turning in a lathe.

1800 HENRY *Epit. Chem.* (1808) 64 A small ball formed of turnings of zinc. 1812 SIR H. DAVY *Chem. Philos.* 322 If iron turnings be heated to whiteness in a curved gun-barrel, and potash be melted and made slowly to come in contact with the turnings,..potassium will be formed. 1868 JOYNSON *Metals* 115 To make an iron cement..mix..112 lbs. of clean cast-iron borings or turnings, with 8 oz. of sal ammoniac.

**3.** *fig.* Shaping, moulding, fashioning (of literary work, etc.).

1586 W. WEBBE *Eng. Poetrie* (Arb.) 65 Such are the turning of verses: the infolding of wordes. 1858 LONGF. *M. Standish* II. 90 You are an elegant scholar, Having.. skill in the turning of phrases.

**4.** The action, or an act, of changing posture or direction by moving as on a pivot; movement so as to face or point in a different, or in some particular, direction. Also *fig.*

1303 R. BRUNNE *Handl. Synne* 8875 Whan we turnede aboute On a womman myn ʒʒe ys y-caste... Þe dekene loked at þe nexte turnyng, She was a-wey, he sagh no þyng. *c* 1489 CAXTON *Sonnes of Aymon* iii. 114, & at this tornyng that he thus made he slewe Esmenfray. 1545 ASCHAM *Toxoph.* I. (Arb.) 89 A weake smithe..wyl wyth a lipe and turnyng of his arme, take vp a barre of yron. *c* 1618 MORYSON *Itin.* IV. v. i. (1903) 440 The Crossings, Bowings, turnings of the body to the Alter. 1631 WIDDOWES *Nat. Philos.* 53 Griefe is his [Delight's] contrary, which is a turning from the hurtfull object. 1738 SWIFT *Pol. Conversat.* Introd. 17 Turnings of the Head, and motions of the Hands. 1825 COLERIDGE *Aids Refl.* (1884) 271 A turning of the thoughts exclusively to the so-called physical attributes. 1845 J. COULTER *Adv. Pacific* ix. 116 The seal cannot quickly turn, so you may..finish him..with a..sharp axe..; but be careful to watch his turning on you.

† **b.** Phr. *Turning of a hand* = moment, instant (see HAND *sb.* 60 f). So *turning of a straw. Obs.* (Cf. quot. *c* 1425 for *turning about*, in 12 below.)

1579 TOMSON *Calvin's Serm. Tim.* 239/1 Ye Christians are at euery turning of an hand, at the pits side. 1600 HOLLAND *Livy* XXI. xiv. 401 Anniball..assailed the cittie, and wan it in the turning of an hand. 1679 J. GOODMAN *Penit. Pard.* II. v. (1713) 236 In the turning of an hand a lewd and flagitious person starts up a great saint. 1755 SMOLLETT *Quix.* (1803) IV. 224 Two thousand copies, that will fetch six rials a-piece in the turning of a straw.

**c.** *Obstet.* (See quot. 1857.)

1857 DUNGLISON *Med. Lex.*, *Turning..Versio Fœtûs*, the operation of bringing down the feet, or some part of the lower extremity, when the presentation of the child is such that it cannot be delivered by the natural efforts. 1899 *Allbutt's Syst. Med.* VII. 737 A labour necessitating the use of instruments or of turning.

**d.** The practice of gymnastics according to the system of F. L. Jahn: cf. TURNER[1] 8.

1888 *U. S. Newspaper* 17 Aug., Turning began at 10 o'clock.

**5.** Reversal, inversion: as of soil, or other substance or object, for exposure to air; of a leaf of a book in reading; of an hour-glass; of a garment; of words in a sentence.

1536 *MS. Rawl. D.* 780 lf. 73 In the turnyng of tymbre in the tymber yard. 1538 ELYOT Addit. Gg iij b/1 *Anastrophe*, a tournynge out of a commune order, as, *Italiam contra*, for *contra Italiam.* 1551 in Feuillerat *Revels Edw. VI* (1914) 53 The layenge abroade eyringe turnynge soinge mendinge ..foldinge and layeng vp of the same. 1551 T. WILSON *Logike* (1580) 29 When I intreated of the conversion, or tournyng of Propositions. 1562 J. HEYWOOD *Prov. & Epigr.* (1867) 137 He hath turned his typpet an honest turnyng. 1573 TUSSER *Husb.* (1878) 56 By oft turning [of wheat] ye seeme to refresh it. 1581 *Confer.* III. (1584) Pj, After a little turning, he sayde, This is not the booke that I meant. 1726 SHELVOCKE *Voy. round World* 137 At the turning of every glass ..we beat 3 ruffs on the drum. *c* 1830 *Glouc. Farm. Rep.* 14 in *Libr. Usef. Knowl., Husb.* III, It will be ready to carry in four or five days, with one turning. 1842 LOUDON *Suburban Hort.* 57 Peat..reduced..to a fine mould..by exposure to the air, and repeated turnings. 1844 MRS. BROWNING *Wine of Cyprus* ix, Betwixt the folio's turnings, Solemn flowed the rhythmic Greek.

**b.** A row of hay turned with the rake; a windrow. *local.*

1795 *Scots Mag.* LVII. 304/2 [The hay] is again made into small rows called turnings. 1834 *Brit. Husb.* I. 491 It is turned with the rake-head, and is before noon raked into small rows, called 'turnings';..and in the evening of the same day, the rows are made into small 'hay-cocks'.

**6.** The action of bending or folding over, or condition of being folded over; a part of something folded over, a fold; in quot. 1660, a curl, a volute.

1631 WEEVER *Anc. Fun. Mon.* 581 The forme of a Rose..: and in the turnings of the leaues this Inscription. 1660 BLOOME *Archit.* Ej, The middle Voluta hath a Circle.. of one part, but the corner turning hath two parts. 1894 *Daily News* 18 Sept. 6/4 Providing deep hems and turnings ..for the days when the garments will be all too short.

**7.** A change in the direction of movement or course; deflection, deviation; winding, tortuous course. Also *fig.*

1426 LYDG. *De Guil. Pilgr.* 8666 Lyk a corde..Wythinne yt tourneth ofte aboute,.. For cordys be sayd..Off offte tournynges in an herte. 1585 T. WASHINGTON tr. *Nicholay's Voy.* IV. xxv. 140 b, [The] riuers by the turning in their course haue made..many..yles. 1587 HARMAR tr. *Beza's Serm.* i. 11 The diuers turnings and windings, by the which men wander and goe astray. 1617 MORYSON *Itin.* I. 244 The Mountaine..was very high, but the way easie, with many turnings about the Mountaine. 1719 D'URFEY *Pills* (1872) VI. 102 For 'tis of the making of Dunstable way, Plain without turning. 1751 LABELYE *Westm. Br.* 25 This Bridge was built without turning of..the River.

**b.** *fig.* of verse or melody; in quot. *a* 1830, a refrain.

1579 SPENSER *Sheph. Cal., Aug.* 194 How I admire ech turning of thy verse. 1662 PLAYFORD *Skill Mus.* I. xi. (1674) 39 Those long Windings and Turnings of the Voice. *a* 1830 *Yng. Musgrave* xi. in Child *Ballads* II. 249/2 And aye the turning o the tune 'Away, Musgrave, awa!'

**8.** A place or point where a road, path, etc. turns, or turns off. Also *fig.*

*c* 1384 CHAUCER *H. Fame* I. 182 In a forest..At a turnynge of a went How Creusa was y-loste allas. *c* 1440 *Promp. Parv.* 507/1 Turnynge, of dyuerse weyys, *diverticulum.* 1596 SHAKS. *Merch. V.* II. ii. 43 Turne vpon your right hand at the next turning, but at the next turning of all on your left. 1600 HAKLUYT *Voy.* III. 300 We discouered 32 Islands..hauing many turnings and windings betweene them, making many faire harboroughs and chanels. 1624 BP. MOUNTAGU *Immed. Addr.* 125 God..knoweth the secrets, discouereth the boughts and turnings of the heart. 1771 SMOLLETT *Humph. Cl.* 26 June, At the turning of a lane, that led to a village,..a couple of robbers a-horseback suddenly appeared. 1778– [see LANE *sb.* 1 b]. 1864 BURTON *Scot Abr.* II. i. 110 About the turning of the 17th into the 18th century. 1866 G. MACDONALD *Ann. Quiet Neighb.* vii. (1878) 121, I had not gone down more than three turnings [of the stairs].

**9.** Reversal of movement or course; † return, going back (*obs.*).

*c* 1440 *Gesta Rom.* lxiv. 276 (Harl. MS.) In hire turnyng hom fro chirch. 1806 SCOTT *Let. to Earl Dalkeith* 11 Feb. in *Lockhart*, I abhor even the shadow of changing or turning with the tide. 1857 J. W. CROKER in *C. Papers*

1 Feb. (1884) I. 83, I..never saw..so..complete a turning of the tide of victory.

**10.** *fig.* Conversion; perversion; desertion to another side (quot. 1665). *arch.*

**1340** HAMPOLE *Pr. Consc.* 4111 Thurgh his turnyng fra gode til ille. **1434** MISYN *Mending Life* 105 Of conuersyon or holy turnynge. **1532** MORE *Confut. Tindale* Wks. 819/2 The turnyng to them selfe or to Lucifer was in it selfe a tourning from God. *a* **1555** BRADFORD in Coverdale *Lett. Mart.* (1564) 262 [The Lord] hath no pleasure in the death of a sinner: he rather wold our conversion and turning. **1665** MANLEY *Grotius' Low C. Warres* 544 More..that among all these Turnings, would yet remain faithful to their Parties.

**11.** Change; vicissitude; alteration.

**1548** ELYOT, *Volubilitas*,..the turnyng of any thyng. **1617** HIERON *Wks.* II. 264 An abuse of Gods goodnesse, and a turning of His graces into wantonnesse. **1659** HAMMOND *On Ps.* lxix. 22 Annot. 342 Safe from the turnings of the World. **1689** in *Acts Parlt. Scot.* (1875) XII. 71/1 The clause anent the turneing of this meetting into a parliament.

**12.** With adverbs, corresponding to adverbial combinations of the verb in various senses (see TURN *v.* VIII), as *turning about, again, away, back, down, in* (also *attrib.*), *out* (also *attrib.*), *over, round, up* (also *concr.* a part turned up).

*c* **1425** *Cursor M.* 23223 (Trin.) In *turnyng of þin honde aboute. **1570** DEE *Math. Pref.* Civ b, Two Wheles.., whose turnynges about in one and the same tyme [etc.]. **1663** BP. PATRICK *Parab. Pilgr.* xvii. (1687) 150 The converting and turning about of our minds and hearts to the original of our Being. *c* **1400** *Brut* clxiii. 182 Þere was so miche presse of peple at the *turnyng aȝeyne. **1382** WYCLIF *Prov.* i. 32 The *turning awei of litle childer [**1611** the turning away of the simple] shal slen hem. **1552** HULOET, *Turnyng backe, *vide in* reuolucion. **1703** MOXON *Mech. Exerc.* 233 The end of an Iron Axis turned Square down, and again turned Square to the first *turning down. **1837** MRS. SHERWOOD *H. Milner* III. xv, A turning-down which contained the signature..of the epistle. **1808** *Lady's Econ. Assist.* 5 The patterns are drawn, allowing for *turning in. **1877** KNIGHT *Dict. Mech.*, *Turning-in*, the process of strapping a dead-eye, that is, bending a rope tightly around it in the score. **1901** *Daily Express* 21 Mar. 6/5 The crew had gathered about the forecastle to smoke their turning-in pipe. **1711** SWIFT *Jrnl. to Stella* 22 May, This man has grown by persecutions, *turnings out, and stabbing. **1807–26** S. COOPER *First Lines Surg.* (ed. 8) 325 Ectropium. A turning out of the eyelids is so named. **1894** ELIZ. L. BANKS *Camp. Curiosity* 29 You must turn out a room...On turning-out day, you must shake the rug, and scrub up the floor. **1702** C. MATHER *Magn. Chr.* VI. v. App. 38 It prov'd her own Father that was to be hang'd, at whose *Turning over, she thus cry'd out. **1842** LOUDON *Suburban Hort.* 131 Picks.. combine the operation of perforating with that of separating, breaking, loosening, and turning over. **1856** *Jrnl. R. Agric. Soc.* XVII. I. 119 There is a quicker turning over of the farmer's capital. **1899** *Allbutt's Syst. Med.* VIII. 173 The heart executes an asymmetry of movement which gives rise to a sensation popularly known as turning over. **1591** PERCIVALL *Sp. Dict.*, *Buelta*, a returne, turning away, *turning round, *reditus, conuersio, auersio.* **1690** NORRIS *Beatitudes* (1692) 159 The swiftest turnings round of a Globe look like standing still. **1628** EARLE *Microcosm.*, *Shee Precise Hypocrite* (Arb.) 63 Her deuotion at the Church is much in the *turning vp of her eye. **1648** HEXHAM *Dutch Dict.* 11 *Schoenen met tuyten*, Shoes with turnings up. **1683** MOXON *Mech. Exerc.*, *Printing* xxii. ¶ 1 He leaves no wrinckles in the turnings up [of the paper lining] against the sides of the Box. **1712** J. JAMES tr. *Le Blond's Gardening* 166 Tillings, or second Turnings up of the Ground. **1844** STEPHENS *Bk. Farm* II. 95 The turning up of a fat sheep. **1877** KNIGHT *Dict. Mech.*, *Turning-up* (*Bookbinding*), taking the round out of the back, while the fore edge is cut.

**13.** *attrib.* and *Comb.*, as (in sense 2) *turning-carrier, -chisel, -gauge, -gouge, -lathe, -tool*; also **turning-engine**, (*a*) a lathe (Knight *Dict. Mech.* 1877); (*b*) a small engine for turning over a large one slowly for inspection or adjustment (*Cent. Dict.* Suppl. 1909); **turning-glass** (see quot.); **turning-loom**, a lathe; **turning-machine, -mill, -piece** (see quots.); **turning-pin** = *turn-pin* (*a*) (see TURN-); also *attrib.*; **turning-plate**, (*a*) = *turn-plate* (*a*): see TURN-; (*b*) (see quot. 1877); **turning-rest**, a rest for a turning-tool, attached to a lathe, as a slide-rest (*Cent. Dict.* 1891); **turning-saw**, a saw with a narrow blade adapted for cutting in a curve, as a bow-saw, compass-saw, keyhole-saw, etc.; **turning-steel**, a smooth round bar of steel used to turn the edge of a cutting instrument so as to give it a flanged form (*Cent. Dict.* 1891); †**turning-tree**, a gallows (cf. TURN *v.* 73 d, 77 f). See also next, 7, and TURNING-EVIL, -POINT.

**1877** KNIGHT *Dict. Mech.*, **Turning-carrier*, a device for holding metallic work while being turned in the foot-lathe. *Ibid.*, **Turning-chisel*, a chisel used by turners for finishing work after being roughed out by the gouge. **1881** DICKSON *Organ Build.* i. 6 The usual turning-chisels and gouges. **1877** KNIGHT *Dict. Mech.*, **Turning-gage*, an instrument to assist in setting over the tail-stock of the lathe, so that a given taper in a given length of work may be obtained. **1902** *Census Bulletin* 216, 28 June 64 (Cent. Dict. Suppl.) After the negative [in half-tone engraving] is developed the film is stripped from the plate, reversed, and placed on another, called a *turning-glass, thus becoming a positive. **1877** KNIGHT *Dict. Mech.* s.v. *Turning-tools*, [description of figure] *n*, *turning-gouge. **1794** *Rigging & Seamanship* I. 152 **Turning-lathe*, a well known machine for turning. **1840** *Civil Eng. & Arch. Jrnl.* III. 175/2 An improved expanding mandrel for turning-lathes. **1879** R. S. BALL in *Cassell's Techn. Educ.* VII. 60 The turning-lathe..enables us to produce with perfect accuracy any surface of revolution. *a* **1805** A. CARLYLE *Autobiog.* (1860) 96 He said he would order his son.., who was a more powerful master of the *turning-loom than he was, to turn me a nice snuff-box or egg-cup. **1877** KNIGHT *Dict. Mech.*, **Turning-machine*, one for turning boot-legs after the seams have been sewn and rolled. **Turning-mill*, a form of horizontal lathe or boring-mill. **1823** P. NICHOLSON *Pract. Build.* 595 **Turning-piece*, a board with a circular edge, for turning a thin brick arch upon. **1591** PERCIVALL *Sp. Dict.*, *Vira*, a *turning pin, a shaft, *verticulum, subscus, sagitta.* **1875** W. MCILWRAITH *Guide Wigtownshire* 43 This quern-stone.. has three turning-pin holes in it. **1797** CURR *Coal Viewer* 28 These *turning plates [in a cast iron rail road]. **1877** KNIGHT *Dict. Mech.*, *Turning-plate*, a circular plate above the front axle, where the bed moves upon it as the carriage turns from its direct course; a *fifth-wheel.* **1725** W. HALFPENNY *Sound Building* 24 With a narrow *Turning-Saw cut directly thro' the Arch-Line. **1825** J. NICHOLSON *Operat. Mechanic* 584 A compass-saw, .. a key-hole-saw. Both of these..are called turning-saws, and have their plates thin and narrow towards their bottoms, and each succeeding tooth finer. **1680** MOXON *Mech. Exerc.* x. 192 These Gouges (and..other *Turning Tools). *a* **1548** HALL *Chron.*, *Hen. VIII*, 224 b, She and her husband..were.. hanged at the foresayd *turnyng tree.

**Tu·rning,** *ppl. a.* [f. as prec. + -ING [2].] That turns, in various senses of the verb.

**1.** That moves round, or so as to face another way; rotating, revolving, etc. (See also 7.)

**1558** KNOX *First Blast* (Arb.) 19 The turning wether cocke. **1629** MILTON *Ode Nativity*, *Hymn* iii, Peace.. came softly sliding Down through the turning sphear. **1700** PRIOR *Carmen Seculare* xxxiii, Practise them now to curb the turning Steed.

**2.** Changing direction of movement or course; winding, sinuous; branching off, as a road or path.

**1495** *Trevisa's Barth. De P. R.* XVII. clxxiii. (W. de W.) 715 Of Thus set a fyr comyth a good smellynge smoke:..full meuable and tornynge and crokyd wyth many bendynges and wrynklynges. **1552** HULOET, Turnyng or wyndyng manye wayes lyke an eale, or snake, *tortuosus.* **1573–80** BARET *Alv.* T 439 A little lane, or turning path going out of the great or high waie, *diuerticulum.* **1590** GREENE *Orl. Fur.* Wks. (Rtldg.) 96/2 And Rhodanus..flew with calm alongst his turning bounds. **1867** TROLLOPE *Chron. Barset* II. liii. 98 Near a corner, where a turning path made an angle in the iron rails. **1879** STEVENSON *Trav. Cevennes* (1892) 163 A deep turning gully in the hills.

**3.** *Mil.* That turns an enemy's position.

**1877** *Daily News* 30 Nov. 5/7 The cavalry of the turning column had captured their whole camp. **1912** COL. H. S. MASSY in *Standard* 20 Sept. 7/2 Direct general attacks are not anticipated, but wide turning movements..will be the chief aim.

**4.** Reversing its course; beginning to go back.

In quot. 1601 as rendering of Gr. τροπικός (see TROPIC).

**1601** DOLMAN *La Primaud. Fr. Acad.* (1618) III. 686 These circles are nominated Tropickes, that is, turning or conuertiue. **1857** W. A. BUTLER *Serm.* iv. 98 Turning with the turning tide.

**5.** Changing, changeful, variable. *Obs.* or *arch.*

*c* **1450** *Songs, Carols*, etc. (E.E.T.S.) 78/202 Love..vertu, ..Which dowble Fortune may neuer tak þe fro: Than mayst þou boldly desire her tornyng chance. **1599** SHAKS. *Hen. V*, III. vi. 35 Fortune..is painted..with a Wheele, to signifie..that shee is turning and inconstant.

**6.** With adverb (cf. TURN *v.* VIII), as *turning-up.*

**1591** PERCIVALL *Sp. Dict.*, *Tornatiles*, turning vp, *aduncus.* **1841** MRS. GREY *Lit. Wife* xxix, I won't let them come into this room, with all their sneers, and turning-up noses.

**7.** In combinations or special collocations: **turning-beam**, an axle-tree (cf. *turn-beam*, TURN-); **turning-box**, a kind of turn-table; **turning bridge**, = *turn-bridge* (see TURN-); †**turning platform**, = TURN-TABLE I; **turning plough**, = *turn-plough* (see TURN-); †**turning-stile** = TURNSTILE; **turning-table** = TURN-TABLE; †**turning-wheel**, (*a*) a turnstile or similar device; (*b*) an apparatus consisting of a rapidly revolving wheel (see quot.).

**1766** *Compl. Farmer* s.v. *Madder*, Another axle-tree, or *turning-beam,..ten inches square near the trundle-head, and fourteen inches diameter in its octogonal part. **1611** COTGR., *Tour*,..the open *turning box in the wall of a Nunnerie, whereby the sisters..receiue in, and deliuer out, commodities. **1809** MALKIN *Gil Blas* I. xiv. ¶ 2, I besought the attendant at the turning-box to tell the lady. **1840** *Evid. Hull Docks Comm.* 39 *Q.* Are those bridges all draw-bridges? *A.* Yes, draw or *turning bridges. **1825** TREDGOLD *Railroads & Carriages* 121 *Turning platforms for changing the direction of a carriage. **1868** *Rep. U. S. Commissioner Agric.* (1869) 414 The field was plowed with a *turning plow, followed in the same furrow with a long bull-tongue plow. **1611** COTGR., *Tour*,..a Turnepike, or *Turning-stile. **1839** *Civil Eng. & Arch. Jrnl.* II. 202/2 Some method of turning..trains more efficiently than the common *turning-table. **1843** BORROW *Bible in Spain* vi. 39 A kind of window occupied by a turning table, at which articles were received into the convent, and delivered out. **1671** WOODHEAD *St. Teresa* II. 274 [Knocks] given by some Body at the *turning-wheel of the Vestry. **1734** tr. *Rollin's Anc. Hist.* (1827) VI. xv. vi. 91 They warded off..the darts..by the assistance of turning-wheels.

Hence **Tu·rningness,** *rare* (in quot. *fig.* tortuous character, as opp. to 'straightforwardness').

*a* **1586** SIDNEY *Arcadia* II. (1622) 135 So had nature formed him, and the exercise of craft conformed him to all turningnesse of sleights.

†**Tu·rning-evil.** *Obs.* [f. TURNING *vbl. sb.* + EVIL *sb.*[1] 7.] = TURN-SICK *sb.* 2.

**1614** MARKHAM *Cheap Husb.* 47 Of the diseases in the head, as the Sturdie, or turning-euill. **1663** BOYLE *Usef. Exp. Nat. Philos.* II. v. xii. 234 Oxen, and such-like Cattle, are troubled with that Disease .. called The turning Evil, or Sturdy. [**1704** *Dict. Rust.* s.v. **1725** *Family Dict.* s.v.]

**Tu·rning-point.** [f. TURNING *vbl. sb.* + POINT *sb.*]

**1.** *lit.* A point at which something turns, or changes its direction of motion, etc.; *spec.* a maximum or minimum point on a graph, where it begins to tend downwards or upwards.

**1856** STANLEY *Sinai & Pal.* xii. 400 Near what may be called the turning-point of its course, where its spacious stream is diverted..by the chain of Amanus.

**2.** *fig.* A point at which a decisive change of any kind takes place; a critical point, crisis. (The usual sense.)

**1851** RUSKIN *Arrows of Chace* (1880) I. 86, I believe these young artists to be..at a turning-point, from which they may either sink into nothingness or rise to very real greatness. **1874** PARKER *Illustr. Goth. Archit.* I. iii. 92 At this principal turning-point in the history of architecture. **1885** *Athenæum* 23 May 669/1 The turning-point from summer to autumnal weather. **1887** J. C. MORISON *Service of Man* 8 One of those turning-points in the evolution of thought which mark the close of an old epoch.

**3.** *Surveying.* A subsidiary bench-mark whose height above datum is determined during the operation of finding, by differential levelling, the difference of level of two permanent bench-marks.

So called because the graduated staff on which the height is read off is at this point turned round so as to be read from the permanent (or the next subsidiary) bench-mark.

**1891** in *Cent. Dict.*

**Turnip** (tɒ̄·rnip), *sb.* Also 6–7 **turnepe**, (**-eppe, -op**), 6–9 **turnep**, (7 **turnepp, turnup, turneupp, turneip, turnoop**); *dial.* **turmit, -at, -ut, tormit, tummit**, etc. [In 16–17th c. *turnepe*, in 16–19th c. *turnep*, from *c* 1782 *turnip*; the second element being NEEP, *nepe*, or *nep*, OE. *nǣp*, ad. L. *nāpus* navew, turnip (mentioned by Columella and Pliny); the first element is uncertain, but is generally supposed to be F. *tour* or Eng. TURN, referring to its rounded shape. There is no kindred name in other langs., except when evidently from Eng., as in Welsh and Irish.]

**1.** The fleshy, globular or spheroidal root of a biennial cruciferous plant, *Brassica Rapa*, **var.** *depressa*, having toothed, somewhat hairy leaves, and yellow flowers, cultivated from ancient times as a culinary vegetable, and for feeding sheep and cattle; also, the plant itself, of which the young shoots (*turnip-tops*) are frequently boiled as greens.

**1533** ELYOT *Cast. Helthe* (1539) 25 Turnepes beinge welle boyled in water, and after with fatte fleshe, norysheth moche. **1562** TURNER *Herbal* II. 113 The great round rape, called commonly a turnepe, groweth in very great plenty in all Germany. **1601** HOLLAND *Pliny* XVIII. xiii. I. 571 The best Husbandmen..give order, That the ground for Turneps [L. *napum*] should have five tilthes. **1629** PARKINSON *Paradisus* 508 There are diuers sorts of Turneps, as white, yellow, and red. **1672** *Court-bk. Barony of Urie* (1892) 92 Some people..did steall furth thereof turnepes and carrottis and uther rootis. **1759** in *Q. Jrnl. Economics* (1907) Nov. 78 In case of Wet Weather while the Sheep are at turneps they are to have the Liberty of Great Oxenden. **1764** in W. Wing *Ann. Steeple Aston* (1875) 63 Agreed at vestry to sow Sandhill turnoops this next year. **1782** BARKER in *Phil. Trans.* LXXII. 282 A wet week in the middle did not greatly hurt the hay, and was very good for the turnips. **1839** COL. HAWKER *Diary* (1893) II. 168, I brought home 18 prime partridges and I lost another in the high turnips. **1863** ROBSON *Bards of Tyne* 315 We hev taties and turmits like Rosemary toppin.

† **b.** *spec.* The spheroidal root itself. *Obs. rare.*

**1578** LYTE *Dodoens* V. xxxiii. 593 There is another kinde of Turnep or Rape...His rootes or Turneppes are not white but red. **1765** J. W. BAKER in *Museum Rust.* V. 265 When the sheep have eaten all the leaves, and begin to eat the butts or turneps of this plant [turnip-cabbage], they will not rot as turnips do, when wounded.

**c.** app. = *turnip-lantern*: see 4 b.

**1766** LADY MARY COKE *Jrnl.* 30 Sept. (1889) I. 64, I told Lucy unless She cou'd produce more light I must go. She said She wou'd send for two turnips; 'twas all She cou'd do.

**2.** Applied, usually with defining word, to other species or varieties of *Brassica*; as **Cabbage-t.** or **Hungarian t.**, the turnip-rooted Cabbage or Kohlrabi (*B. oleracea gongylodes*); **French t.** (*a*) the rape, *B. Napus* or *B. campestris*; (*b*) a variety of *B. Napus*, extensively cultivated in France and Germany, and much used as a flavouring for soups; **Swedish t.**, *B. campestris Rutabaga*; **Teltow t.** = *French t.* (*b*); **Wild t.**, the rape; see also b; **Yellow t.**, a yellow variety of the common turnip.

**1548** TURNER *Names Herbs* (E.D.S.) 55 Napus...I haue hearde sume cal it in englishe a turnepe, and other some a naued or nauet. **1562** — *Herbal* II. 112 b, Rapum..is called in English of them of the South countre, turnepe, of other countre men a rape. **1597** GERARDE *Herbal* II. ii. 179 There be three sorts of wilde Turneps. *Ibid.*, Wilde Turneps or Rapes, haue long, broad, and rough leaues like those of Turneps. *Ibid.* 180 Wilde Turneps or Rapes, do grow of themselues in fallow fields. **1600** HAKLUYT *Voy.* (1810) III. 288 We sowed it part with Naueaus or small Turneps. **1707** MORTIMER *Husb.* (1721) I. 157 Yellow Turneps..are commonly sown in Gardens, but are of very great advantage to be sown in Fields, not only for the use of the Kitchen, but for Food for Cattle in Winter. **1731–3** MILLER *Gard. Dict.* (ed. 2), *Napus*, the Navew or French Turnip. **1760** J. LEE

*Introd. Bot.* App. 330 Turnep, French, *Brassica.* c **1791** *Encycl. Brit.* (ed. 3) VIII. 761/1 The ruta baga, or Swedish turnip, is a plant from which great expectations have been formed. **1796** C. MARSHALL *Garden.* xv. (1813) 261 The most common [turneps] are the white sorts; but the yellow and red are worthy of trial. *Ibid.* 262 The cabbage turnep is of two kinds: one apples above ground, and the other in it. **1858** HOGG *Veg. Kingd.* 67 *B. napus* is the..Rape or Coleseed...There is a variety of this, called by the French *Chou Navette*, and by us French Turnip (*B. n. esculenta*), which is employed in flavouring all foreign soups. **1866** *Treas. Bot.* 167/2 The Teltow Turnip, or 'Navet de Berlin petit' of the French (*B. Napus var.*), is very different from any of our cultivated varieties of Turnip, its root being long and spindle-shaped.

**b.** Applied to plants of other genera having roots or tubers like those of the turnip, as *Indian t., Lion's t., Prairie t.*: see these words; also *St. Anthony's t.*, the bulbous buttercup, *Ranunculus bulbosus*; *Wild t.* = *Indian t.* (in both uses).

**1597** GERARDE *Herbal* II. iv. 182 Lyons Turnep [*Leontice Leontopetalum*] is of force to digest. **1856** A. GRAY *Man. Bot.* (1860) 94 *Psoralea esculenta*,..the Indian Turnip,..used as food by the aborigines. *Ibid.* 427 *Arisæma triphyllum*, Indian Turnip. **1866** *Treas. Bot.* 176/1 *B[ryonia] dioica*, the Common Bryony...The root is used..as a purgative; but it is unsafe from its uncertain and sometimes violent action, whence the French call it Devil's-turnip. **1894** GIBSON in *Harper's Mag.* 565 The wild arum of Great Britain..the foreign counterpart of our well known jack-in-the-pulpit, or Indian turnip.

**3. a.** In slang phrases, sometimes with pun on *turn-up*. See quots.

a **1596** *Sir T. More* II. ii, Come, come; wele tickle ther turnips, wele butter ther boxes. Shall strangers rule the roste? **1812** J. H. VAUX *Flash Dict.*, *Turnips*, to give any body turnips signifies to turn him or her up, and the party so turned up, is said to have knap'd turnips. **1845** FORD *Handbk. Spain* I. 27 *note*, This gourd forms a favourite metaphor in common parlance: '*le ha dado Calabazas*', she has refused him; it is the 'giving cold turnips' of Suffolk.

**b.** Slang term for an old-fashioned thick silver watch.

**1840** E. FITZGERALD *Lett.* (1889) I. 59 An old turnip of a watch..on the table beside her. **1853** 'C. BEDE' *Verdant Green* I. vi, His mechanical turnip showed him that he had no time to lose. **1903** A. ADAMS *Log Cowboy* xv. 234 My turnip says it's eight o'clock now.

**c.** Humorously applied to a person: cf. *turnip-head, -headed* in 4.

**1837** DICKENS *Pickw.* xxxiii, 'But now', continued Sam, 'now I find what a reg'lar soft-headed, inkred'lous turnip I must ha' been'.

**4.** *attrib.* and *Comb.* **a.** simple attrib., as *turnip-cart, crop, -culture, -drill, -farmer, -field, -husbandry, -leaf, -pit, plot, -root, -seed, -trough*, etc.; also allusively, *turnip-head, -heart, -pate, -watch*; in names of things made of turnips, or in which the turnip is a principal ingredient, as *turnip-bread, pasty, pie, poultice*; objective and obj. genitive, as *turnip-chopper, -cutter, -grower, -hoer, -picker, -puller, -pulper, -slicer, -sower, -thinner* (freq. as names of machines); *turnip-bearing, -cutting, -eating, -hacking, -sowing, -thinning*, sbs. and adjs.; instrumental, parasynthetic, similative, etc., as *turnip-feeding*; *turnip-fed, -headed, -leaved, -like, -pointed, -rooted, -shaped, -stalked, -stemmed, -tailed* adjs.

**1812** W. TENNANT *Anster F.* I. viii, Anster's *turnip-bearing vales. **1693** S. DALE in *Phil. Trans.* XVII. 970 Of this *Turnep-Bread (for so they call it) I have both seen and tasted. **1763** *Museum Rust.* (ed. 2) I. 106, I baked my turnep-bread rather longer than the other. **1832** *Veg. Subst. Food* 236 In .. 1629 and 1630 .. good .. wholesome bread was made of boiled turnips,..kneaded with..wheaten flour,..called turnip-bread. **1664** BUTLER *Hud.* II. *Heroic. Ep. Sidrophel* 20 A Wheel-barrow, or *Turnip Cart. **1837** *Brit. Husb.* II. 246 The roots are commonly cut into pieces by an instrument called the '*turnip-chopper'. **1844** STEPHENS *Bk. Farm* II. 119 Much better instruments will be found in the two hand turnip-choppers. **1801** *Farmer's Mag.* Jan. 107 The *turnip crop is probably the best..ever remembered. *Ibid.* Aug. 279 The soil..is not..of that stiff sort adapted to beans or wheat, but abundantly free, so as to be well adapted to *turnip-culture. **1837** *Flemish Husb.* 89 in *Libr. Usef. Knowl., Husb.* III, The roots were cut by a machine something like our *turnip-cutters. **1879** J. WRIGHTSON in *Cassell's Techn. Educ.* IV. 108/2, 1 bushel of swedes, cut small in a .. turnip-cutter. **1854** MARY HOWITT *Pict. Calend. Seasons* 17 There was a noise of straw-cutting and *turnip-cutting. **1733** TULL *Horse-Hoeing Husb.* xxii. 328 The spring of the *Turnep-Drill being so very thin [etc.]. **1805** R. W. DICKSON *Pract. Agric.* I. 17 Turnip-Drill..for sowing turnips on the tops of one-bout ridges. **1856** MORTON *Cycl. Agric.* II. 1026 The proper width of a turnip drill in Scotland seems..to be..twenty-seven inches. a **1668** DAVENANT *Vacation in Lond.* Wks. (1673) 291 All these on hoof now trudge from Town, To cheat poor *Turnip-eating Clown. **1733** TULL *Horse-Hoeing Husb.* x. 103 If Turneps be sown in June,..the most experienc'd *Turnep-Farmers, will have no more than Thirty to a square Perch left in Hand-hoeing. **1805** R. W. DICKSON *Pract. Agric.* I. Plate x. 40 A Scuffler employed..in putting in grain crops on *turnip-fed lands after one ploughing. **1812** SIR J. SINCLAIR *Syst. Husb. Scot.* I. 354 If straw be economically applied in littering turnip-fed stock [etc.]. a **1722** LISLE *Husb.* (1757) 329 *Turnip-feeding was apt to breed wind in the sheep. **1773** *Gentl. Mag.* Dec. 618/2 In his distress he frequented a *turnep-field. **1812** SIR J. SINCLAIR *Syst. Husb. Scot.* I. 39 Sheep-flakes, or hurdles, a sort of portable fence, well known to every *turnip grower. **1883** T. HARDY in *Longm. Mag.* July 267 A farm-woman's occupation is often '*turnip-hacking'—that is, picking out from the land the stumps of turnips which have been eaten off by the sheep. **1898** J. ARCH *Story of Life* xiii. 322 The *turnip-headed farmer turned his back upon us. c **1620** FLETCHER & MASSINGER *Trag. Barnavelt* II. ii, We are strong enough to curb 'em. But we have *turnop hearts. **1791** W. H. MARSHALL *W. England* (1796) II. 283 Any woman..will, in one full season become a sufficient *Turnep hoer. **1886** T. HARDY *Mayor of Casterbr.* i, A turnip-hoer with his hoe on his shoulder. **1733** TULL *Horse-Hoeing Husb.* x. 102 The greatest Inconvenience, which has been observ'd in the *Turnep-Husbandry, is when they are Fed off late in the Spring. **1848** HEPBURN in *Proc. Berw. Nat. Club* II. No. 6. 272 Turnip husbandry, and the cultivation of red clover, were introduced about 1740. **1766** J. W. BAKER in *Compl. Farmer* s.v. *Turnep*, The upper side of the *turnip leaf, in its infant state, is very smooth, and on that part the flies always lodge. c **1711** PETIVER *Gazophyl.* Dec. ix. Tab. 81 *Turnep-leaved Cape Dandelion. **1766** *Museum Rust.* VI. 46 By this..production of the *turnep-like knob, together with its being perennial, this species of cabbage is distinguished from all others. **1905** *Daily Chron.* 14 July 4/7 In Cornwall the fisherman home from sea, in the intervals of blowing the fire, blows himself out with *turnip pasty. **1813** *Columbian Centinel* (Boston) 1 Sept. 1/2, I cannot protect every man's *turnip patch. a **1700** B. E. *Dict. Cant. Crew*, **Turnep-pate*, White or Fair-hair'd. **1844** STEPHENS *Bk. Farm* II. 40 The shells..were picked out of the ground with..a *turnip-picker. **1835** W. HOWITT in L'Estrange *Friendships Miss Mitford* (1882) I. 267 A *turnip-pie fit in size to set on Arthur's own round table. **1899** CROCKETT *Kit Kennedy* xxx, Kit only lifted the lantern and made for the *turnip-pits. **1670** WOOD *Life* 2 June (O.H.S.) II. 194 Buried..in her garden..under a *turnip plot. **1887** *Amer. Naturalist* XXI. 435 *Turnip-pointed red [beet]. **1735** BURDON *Pocket Farrier* 29 The *Turnip Poultice will infallibly cure it. **1606** G. W[OODCOCKE] *Lives Emperors* in *Hist. Ivstine* L l v b, It rained wheat, *Turnup-rootes, and pease in Slesia, which much comforted the poore people, in the extreamity of famine. **1733** TULL *Horse-Hoeing Husb.* I. 5 A large Root..which..might have..extended near as far as the Turnep Roots did. **1727** *Bradley's Fam. Dict.* s.v. *Cyclamen*, The German Cyclamens are rather *Turnep-rooted Plants than Bulbs. **1769** *Chron.* in *Ann. Reg.* 65/2 A premium for the cultivating..of..the turnip-rooted cabbage. **1842** LOUDON *Suburban Hort.* 651 The Red Beet...The turnip-rooted is an early variety with the roots round. **1580** HOLLYBAND *Treas. Fr. Tong, De la Navette*, *turnop seed. **1621** *Shuttleworths' Acc.* (Chetham Soc.) 250 Turneppe seede, iiij[d]. **1833** *Ridgemont Farm Rep.* 155 in *Libr. Usef. Knowl., Husb.* III, It was drilled with turnip-seed upon a limestone soil. **1788** *Trans. Soc. Arts* VI. 231 A Model of a Cabbage and *Turnep Slicer. **1844** STEPHENS *Bk. Farm* II. 41 The .. better plan of serving turnips to sheep..is to cut them into small pieces with a turnip-slicer into troughs conveniently placed for use. **1889** H. M. B. REID *Galloway Folk* 42 A brand-new gaudily painted *turnip-sower. **1765** J. W. BAKER in *Museum Rust.* V. 270, I could not accomplish my *turnip-sowing earlier. **1786** ABERCROMBIE *Arr.* in *Gard. Assist.* p. vi, *Turnep-stalked, with the turnep above ground. **1844** STEPHENS *Bk. Farm* II. 29 The *turnip-stemmed cabbage or kholrabi. *Ibid.* 11 Fig. 213 represents the form of the *turnip-store. **1875** *Encycl. Brit.* I. 321/2 *Turnip-Thinners...A class of machines has been brought out, of which Huckvale's turnip-thinner may be named as a type. **1905** *Contemp. Rev.* July 97, [I] went down the cart-track to the *turnip-thinning. **1844** STEPHENS *Bk. Farm* II. 41 A simple form of *turnip-trough. **1898** *Tit-Bits* 25 June 245/2 Consulting his..*turnip watch to see if his daughters' train was due. **1886** C. SCOTT *Sheep-Farming* 77 A bad *turnip year.

**b.** Special combinations: **turnip-aphid, -aphis**, the plant-louse of the turnip, *Aphis rapæ*; **turnip-beetle**, the *turnip-flea*; **turnip-cabbage**, the turnip-stemmed cabbage or KOHLRABI; **turnip-flea** (also **turnip flea-beetle**), a minute shiny black leaping beetle, *Haltica nemorum*, which feeds on the young leaves of the turnip and other crucifers; its larva mines in the full-grown leaf; **turnip-flowerbeetle**: see quot.; **turnip-fly**, (*a*) = *turnip-flea*; (*b*) the turnip-sawfly, a hymenopterous insect, *Athalia centifoliæ*, the larva of which (*turnip-nigger*) feeds on turnip-leaves; (*c*) a dipterous insect, *Anthomyia radicum*, whose larva lives in the root of the turnip; **turnip-gall weevil**: see quot.; **turnip-ghost**, a simulated ghost or apparition of which the head is formed by a turnip-lantern; **turnip-grass**, *Panicum bulbosum*, used as hay in Texas, Arizona, and Mexico, the stems of which have a bulbous base (*Cent. Dict. Supp.* 1909); **turnip-greens** = *turnip-tops*; **turnip-jack** = *turnip-flea*; **turnip-land** = *turnip-soil*; **turnip-lantern**, the hollowed rind of a turnip employed as a lantern; also as a term of abuse (*Eng. Dial. Dict.*); **turnip leaf-miner**, ? the larva of the turnip-flea; **turnip-louse** = *turnip-aphis* (*Cent. Dict. Supp.*); **turnip-maggot**, the larva of *Anthomyia radicum* (*turnip-fly* c) (*Cent. Dict.*); **turnip-mutton**, the flesh of *turnip-sheep*; **turnip-nigger**, the black larva of *Athalia centifoliæ* (*turnip-fly* b); **turnip-oats**, a crop of oats succeeding turnips; **turnip-parsnip**, a turnip-rooted parsnip; so **turnip-radish**; **turnip-saw-fly** = *turnip-fly* b; **turnip-sheep**, sheep that have been fed on turnips; **turnip-shell**, a shell of the family *Turbinellidæ*, esp. of the genus *Rapa* (*Cent. Dict.*): **turnip-sick** *a.*, of land: exhausted by successive crops of turnips; **turnip-soil**, soil suitable or used for turnip-culture; **turnip-system**, a system of crop-rotation based on turnip-culture; **turnip-top** (usu. *pl.*), the sprouting leaves of the second year's growth of the turnip, used as a vegetable; **turnip-tray**, a hurdle used for penning sheep on turnip-land; **turnip-wheat**, cf. *turnip-oats*; **turnip-wood**, Australian rosewood, *Synoum glandulosum* (N.O. *Meliaceæ*), or its timber, which smells like turnips; see also quot. 1898.

**1891** *Cent. Dict.*, *Turnip-aphid... Also *turnip-aphis. **1908** *Westm. Gaz.* 30 May 7/3 The corn-aphis, hop-aphis, turnip-aphis, bean-aphis. **1816** KIRBY & SP. *Entomol.* xxiii. (1818) II. 312 When the *turnip-beetle (*Haltica oleracea*, F.) walks, its antennæ are alternately elevated and depressed. **1882** *Garden* 25 Mar. 198/1 The Turnip fly (or, as the well-known insect should more properly be called, the Turnip beetle or flea). **1765** *Ann. Reg.* II. 146/2 The *turnep-cabbage is so called, because the stalk, after rising to some distance from the ground .. swells suddenly into a roundish knob. **1842** LOUDON *Suburban Hort.* 627 The Turnip-cabbage, or turnip borecole,..is a dwarf-growing plant, with the stem swelled out so as to resemble a turnip above ground, but of a delicate green colour. **1867** BRANDE & COX *Dict. Sc.*, etc. III. 881/2 The *turnip-flea belongs to a genus..of minute Coleopterous insects, of the section Tetramera, and family Galerucidæ. **1843** *Zoologist* I. 371 The valuable Sweedish turnip [has] put forth its second pair of leaves, and just escaped the ravages of the turnip flea beetle. **1882** *Garden* 25 Mar. 198/2 The *Turnip flower beetle..a very small, flat, bronzy green beetle. **1733** TULL *Horse-Hoeing Husb.* xxiv. 391 By the shallow or deep [seed sown], the *Turnep-Fly is generally disappointed. **1765** J. W. BAKER in *Museum Rust.* V. 277, I discovered last season three distinct species of the turnip fly..one of them is black; it seems to hop like a flea. **1771** [see DOLPHIN 7]. **1813** SIR H. DAVY *Agric. Chem.* (1814) 217 The turnip fly..fixes itself upon the seed leaves of the turnip at the time that they are beginning to perform their functions. **1879** E. P. WRIGHT *Anim. Life* 498 One of the best-known species [of *Tetramera*] is the so-called Turnip-fly (*Haltica nemorum*). **1844** STEPHENS *Bk. Farm* III. 781 The *Curculio plurostigma*, the *Turnip-gall weevil. **1863** KINGSLEY *Water-Bab.* viii. (1864) 349 Out popped *turnip-ghosts and magic-lanthorns and pasteboard bogies. **1858** GLENNY *Gard. Every-day Bk.* 247/2 They may give a few *Turnip-greens when they are very useful. **1873** *Routledge's Yng. Gentl. Mag.* Mar. 229/1 The young and tender leaves, which are popularly called 'turnip-greens'. **1801** *Farmer's Mag.* Apr. 238 Almost every acre of *turnip-land has been sown with wheat, as fast as the grounds were cleared. **1844** E. FITZGERALD *Lett.* (1894) I. 163 You have seen a *turnip-lantern, perhaps. **1844** STEPHENS *Bk. Farm* III. 778 A class of insects called *turnip-leaf miners. a **1722** LISLE *Husb.* (1757) 335 Several butchers .. agreed..that *turnip-mutton would be waterish. **1893** *Daily News* 20 Apr. 6/2 The sparrow,..that brazen little thief who affects to despise wireworm, *turnip nigger, and gooseberry grub, but has the keenest of keen eyes for blossoming peas and delicate young wheat. c **1800** T. BLACKADDER in *Proc. Berw. Nat. Club* II. No. 12. 101 Your queys and stots, Hae trampled a' my *turnip oats. **1786** ABERCROMBIE *Gard. Assist.* 81 *Turnep-radish—sow the small white Italian sort. **1844** STEPHENS *Bk. Farm* III. 772 The *turnip saw-fly, *Athalia spinarum*,..is denominated a *saw*-fly, from the use and appearance of the instrument with which it deposits its eggs. *Ibid.* II. 48 *Turnip-sheep are thus easily obtained at fairs in autumn. **1880** JEFFERIES *Gt. Estate* i. 6 Some of the land is getting '*turnip-sick', the roots come stringy and small and useless. **1812** SIR J. SINCLAIR *Syst. Husb. Scot.* I. 34 This ought more especially to be attended to upon all *turnip soils. **1844** STEPHENS *Bk. Farm* I. 330 No kind of soil affords so dry and comfortable a lair to sheep on turnips, and on this account it is distinguished as 'turnip-soil'. **1805** R. W. DICKSON *Pract. Agric.* I. 540 Another sort of this grain that may probably be cultivated to advantage in particular cases, as where the *turnip system is much practised. **1710** SWIFT *City Shower* 63 Dead Cats and *Turnip-Tops come tumbling down the Flood. **1848** C. C. CLIFFORD *Aristoph., Frogs* 22 Don't beat him with a leek or turnip-top. **1886** C. SCOTT *Sheep-Farming* 44 Turnip-tops contain a considerable amount of nutritive matter. **1805** R. W. DICKSON *Pract. Agric.* II. 672 Sheep-penns or *turnip-trays made and fixed in such a way as to constitute a sort of moveable trough. **1807** VANCOUVER *Agric. Devon* (1813) 164 This stubble as well as that of the lay and *turnip wheat is frequently refreshed with..dung. **1891** *Cent. Dict.*, *Turnip-wood, .. *Synoum glandulosum*. **1898** MORRIS *Austral Eng.*, *Turnip-wood*, the timbers of the trees *Akania hillii*,..N.O. *Sapindaceæ*, and *Dysoxylon Muelleri*..N.O. *Meliaceæ*, from their white and red colours respectively.

Hence **Turnipo·logy** (*nonce-wd.*), contemptuous term for phrenology; whence **Turnipo·logist**; **Tu·rnipy** *a.*, like, or like that of, a turnip; pertaining to or connected with turnips; tasting of turnips.

**1824** J. WILSON in *Blackw. Mag.* XV. 711 Bad novels, which no human creature above the calibre of a *Turnipologist would now endure three pages of. *Ibid.* 150 The system..I mean *Turnipology. **1826** SCOTT *Jrnl.* 29 Dec., The son..tampers with phrenology...There is a certain kind of cleverish men..who are attached to that same turnipology. **1792–5** AIKIN *Even. at Home* xxiii. (1805) V. 70 The reason why *turnipy milk and butter have such a strong taste. **1818** *Sporting Mag.* II. 229 His constitution is inclined to the turnippy sort, and .. he will not stand through those lengthened..combats. **1853** *Jrnl. R. Agric. Soc.* XIV. I. 72 Disagreeable turnipy flavour. **1873** MISS BROUGHTON *Nancy* I. 70 My acquaintance is confined to half-a-dozen turnipy squires and their wives.

**Tu·rnip**, *v.* [f. prec. sb.]

**1.** *trans.* To plant or crop (land) with turnips.

**1789** *Trans. Soc. Arts* (ed. 2) II. 63 Was the ground turneped three years? **1854** *Jrnl. R. Agric. Soc.* XV. II. 420 The land is given to couch if not turniped often.

**2.** To feed or fatten (sheep) on turnips.

**1799** A. YOUNG *Agric. Lincoln* 320 Shearling wethers; turniped by many, and sold in the wool. **1847** *Jrnl. R. Agric. Soc.* VIII. II. 430 Those [sheep] in good condition, and off the best farms, are bought for turnipping. **1868** *Ibid.* Ser. II. IV. II. 350 Not a few 'Penrith hoggs' are turniped in Dumfries.

‖ **Turnix** (tɜ̄·ɹniks). *Ornith.* [mod.L. (Bonnaterre, 1790), app. shortened from L. *coturnix* quail.] A genus of quail-like birds (also called *Hemipodius*: see HEMIPOD); the bush-quails.

**1819** STEPHENS in Shaw *Gen. Zool.* XI. 388 Black-fronted Turnix...Turnix with the forehead with three fasciæ. *Ibid.* 389 Black-necked Turnix. **1869** GILLMORE tr. *Figuier's Rept. & Birds* (1870) 392 The Turnix are [*sic*] closely allied to the Quails.

**Turnkey** (tɜ̄·ɹnkī). [f. TURN *v.* + KEY *sb.*]

**1.** One who has charge of the keys of a prison; a jailer, *esp.* a subordinate; also *transf.*

**1654** H. L'ESTRANGE *Chas. I* (1655) 106 Mr. Atturney was turn-key, *pro tempore*, and let them in single at one door. **1680** C. NESSE *Church Hist.* 31 God..vouchsaf'd to be Noah's turnkey. **1791** BOSWELL *Johnson* an. 1780 (1848) 649/1 Mr. Akerman..ordered the outer turnkey upon no account to open the gate. **1864** MRS. CARLYLE *Lett.* (1883) III. 232 He bowed to the judge, and walked away with the turnkey. **1878** SPURGEON *Treas. Dav.* Ps. cv. 20 When God means to enlarge his prisoners, kings become his turnkeys.

**2. a.** ? A burglar's implement for turning from the outside a key left in the door. ? *Obs.* **b.** A tooth-key, formerly used in dentistry; a tooth-wrest.

**1803** *Sporting Mag.* XXII. 126 A Bow-street officer found a little loose powder, a turnkey, and some other trifling articles. **1877** KNIGHT *Dict. Mech.*, *Turnkey*, an instrument to extract teeth; not much used now.

† **Tu·rnkind**, *sb.* and *v. Obs.* In 6 tornekynde. [f. TURN *v.* 35 + KIND *sb.* 3.] A nonce rendering of *transubstantiation*, *transubstantiate*.

**1548** GESTE *Pr. Masse* B ij, Nowe to transubstantiatyon, or tornekynde. *Ibid.* B v b, What can be more effectually & expresselye spoken agaynste tornekynde, then thys the rehersed Englysshed sentence of Augustyne? *Ibid.* B vij b, Yf say they yᵉ bred nature were not tornekynded vnto christes body: why dyd he name it hys bodye? *Ibid.* C j b, Some of our catholiques do contend yᵗ the sayd tornekinding must be nedes granted as right certayn & godly.

**Turnor, -our,** obs. ff. TURNER, TOURNEYER.

† **Turnour.** *Obs. rare*⁻¹. [irreg. ad. OF. *tourneure* TOURNURE.] A piece of turned work.

**1382** WYCLIF 1 *Kings* vi. 18 With cedre al the hows with ynforth was clothid, hauynge his turnours, and his iunctions forgid.

**Turn-out** (tɜ̄·ɹn,aut), *sb.* (*a.*) [f. the verbal phr. *turn out* (TURN *v.* 75).]

**1.** A turning out or getting out (of bed, etc.); hence, a call to duty, esp. during one's period of rest; *spec. Mil.* a signal to rise (? *obs.*).

**1688** R. HOLME *Armoury* III. xix. (Roxb.) 154/2 The seuerall Beates or points of warre are these...13. A Turn out. **1815** SCOTT *Guy M.* xxxix, Is he always fit for duty upon a sudden turn-out? **1848** THACKERAY *Van. Fair* xxx, The bugles were sounding the turn-out. **1873** *Routledge's Yng. Gentl. Mag.* July 482/1 A sudden turn-out during his watch below.

**2.** A withdrawal of workmen from their place of employment by common consent; a strike.

**1806** *Docum. Hist. Amer. Industr. Soc.* (1910) III. 74 In a little time there came a turn-out to raise the wages...They would grant me no quarters at all, but I must turn out. **1834** HT. MARTINEAU *Moral* II. 55 To show how tremendous is the waste of capital in a turn-out. **1835** URE *Philos. Manuf.* 283, I have had several turn-outs, and have heard of many more, but never heard of a turn-out for short time. **1837** WHITTOCK, etc. *Bk. Trades* (1842) 430 A..turn out which proved instructively unavailing, and was utterly disastrous to their funds. **1898** W. WHITE *Jrnls.* 15 Much discussion in shop, relative to the turn-out; refused to join.

**b.** One of a body of strikers.

**1826** *Examiner* 663/2 Skirmishes..between the turn-outs and those whom they call 'knobsticks'. **1842** R. OASTLER *Fleet Papers* II. 286 The failure of 'the Strike' will be attributable..to divisions in the camp of the 'turn-outs'. **1848** MRS. GASKELL *M. Barton* xxi, One of the poor, maddened turn-outs.

**3.** Those who turn out or assemble for any purpose; an assemblage, muster; also, a turning out or assembling of persons.

**1816** CHALMERS *Let.* in *Life* (1851) II. 78, I met with several people here, and had a turn out of population from several of the houses. **1819** *Sporting Mag.* V. 54 The circumstances..account..for the small turn-out of sportsmen. **1843** LE FEVRE *Life Trav. Phys.* III. II. x. 5 Compared with the turn-out in Hyde Park in the season, it sinks into insignificance. **1880** *Antrim & Down Gloss.*, *The Hurries*, a term for the Irish Rebellion of 1798. Called also the *Turn-out*. **1901** *Scotsman* 1 Mar. 8/1 The turnout was much larger than might have been expected.

**4.** A loop-line or siding in a railway or tramway; also, in a narrow road, a part wider than the rest, or a short side road, to enable vehicles to pass one another; a similar place in a canal.

**1824** T. G. CUMMING *Rail & Tram Roads* 16 A pointer, fixed at the intersection between the principal rail and the turn out,..to open the way into the turn out, and shut that along the road. **1826** *Act 7 Geo. IV*, c. 49 § 38 Passing-places or turn-outs, for the purpose of enabling waggons, carts, and other carriages drawn along the said [L'pool and Manch.] railway or tram road to pass each other. **1898** *Westm. Gaz.* 31 May 6/3 A canal..with locks at each end, and suitable turnouts.

**5.** A place where animals may be turned out to graze.

**1895** *Queenslander* 7 Dec. 1090 There was not a turnout for a carrier from Westwood to Tambo, a distance of fully 300 miles,..the marsupials having cleared the pasture off the face of the country. **1901** *19th Cent.* July 59 The cottager could get fuel..with a turn-out for a cow, pig,..donkey and geese.

**6.** A turning or clearing out; a clearance, emptying.

**1856** MISS YONGE *Daisy Chain* xiv, You must make interest with Margaret for the turn-out of my pocket to-morrow. **1857** HUGHES *Tom Brown* II. iii, A regular turn-out of the den.

**7.** The manner in which anything is turned out or equipped; style of equipment; 'get-up'; also *concr.* equipment, outfit, array.

**1812** COL. HAWKER *Diary* (1893) I. 46 Their 'turns-out' of horses and harness are beggarly. **1825** *Sporting Mag.* XV. 355 The turn-out of himself and his horse is 'quite the thing'. **1859** JEPHSON *Brittany* x. 171 On a holiday..the whole turn-out would be much more dressy. **1883** *Harper's Mag.* Aug. 378/2 The parishioners coming to mass in their best turn-outs. **1901** *Scotsman* 1 Mar. 8/1 The significant feature of their turn out, however, was that they carried, not the cavalry carbine, but the infantry service rifle.

**b.** *Tea and turn out* (cf. TEA *sb.* 4), tea and something with it; tea and accompaniments.

**1806** *Francis Lett.* (1901) II. 638 We brought the Irish custom of suppers into fashion,..for last year they only gave tea and turn out. **1830** H. ANGELO *Remin.* II. 184 This was not tea and turn out, but tea and walk up stairs. **1858** RAMSAY *Remin.* v. (1870) 120, I hope you will sport it..at your first tea and turn out.

**8.** A driving equipage; a carriage with its horse or horses, and other adjuncts. Also *transf.*

**1817** LADY MORGAN *France* (1818) I. 258 No man..founds his celebrity..upon the superior excellence and appointment of his turn-out. **1842** THACKERAY *Sultan Stork* Wks. 1900 V. 750 Egad! what a neat turn-out of a barge! **1856** KANE *Arct. Expl.* I. xvii. 211 Quite a neat turn-out of sledge and dogs. **1891** 'J. S. WINTER' *Mrs. Bob* 19 The sort of coachman that you get in London with a turn-out from the job-master's. **1895** *Daily News* 13 July 5/4 A special prize will be given for the best turn-out of donkey and barrow.

**9.** The quantity of anything turned out or produced in an industry, etc.; the total product; output.

**1879** *Spons' Encycl. Manuf.* I. 10 If a large turn-out is necessary, carbonization may be effected in twelve or thirteen hours. **1884** LD. BRAMWELL in *Law Rep.* 9 App. Cases 203 The actual turnout was over one million a year.

**B.** *attrib.* or as *adj.* That turns out, or is turned out, in various senses.

**1899** *Westm. Gaz.* 11 Feb. 7/1 A slashed velvet jacket with a Manx turn-out collar. **1908** *Daily Chron.* 9 Jan. 7/2 The 'turn-out' switch rings electric bells in every room in the building [fire station]. **1909** *Toilers of Deep* Sept. 225/1 As we are working on 'turn out' tides, we must be up betimes to embark on the outward turn...The men turn out ..at one o'clock in the morning.

**Turn-over** (tɜ̄·ɹn,ōu:vəɹ), *sb.* and *a.* [f. the verbal phr. *turn over* (TURN *v.* 77).]

**A.** *sb.* **1.** The action of turning over, in various senses: see quots.; *spec.* in *Polit. slang*, a transference of votes from one party to another.

**1660** F. BROOKE tr. *Le Blanc's Trav.* 365 Dancers on the rope, standing with their head down, and feet up, with a thousand Turn-overs, and Gamboles. **1825** J. NEAL *Bro. Jonathan* II. 62 The turn-over proved quite a relief to the company. **1868** A. K. H. BOYD *Less. Mid. Age* 279 The music was good, after the choir got themselves settled to their work. But if I were Dean of Wells, there should be a thorough turn-over. **1895** G. W. E. RUSSELL in *Forum* (N. Y.) Oct. 160 No very sweeping change of opinion—no very considerable turnover of votes.

**2.** An apprentice whose indentures are transferred to another master on the retirement or failure of his original one; also, the action or process of turning over an apprentice. Now *dial.*

**1631** HEYWOOD *1st Pt. Fair Maid of West* II. i. Wks. 1874 II. 276 *Bess.* Your olde Master..hath turn'd over your yeares to me. *Clem.* Right forsooth: before he was a Vintner, hee was a shoo-maker, and left two or three turne-overs more besides my selfe. **1666** in *Eng. Gilds* (1870) Introd. 161 *note*, Supernumerary Apprentices and Turn-overs, which have increased the number [of printers] almost to twice as many. **1708** *Constit. Waterman's Co.* xii. 24 Every Apprentice, whose Master and Mistress shall happen to dye..shall..apply himself to the Rulers,..and..be by them..turned over to some other able and fit Master or Mistress,..by Indorsing such Turn-over upon his Indenture of Apprentiship. **1886** T. FROST *Remin. Country Journalist* v. (1888) 52 A 'turn-over', that is, an apprentice who, after serving a portion of his term, is transferred to another employer.

**3.** Any thing or part which is turned or folded over. † **a.** ? In a cork shoe, a welt which is turned over the insole; also a shoe with such a welt. *Obs.* **b.** The flap of an envelope; a leaf of a book, etc. **c.** An article that begins in the last column of a newspaper page and continues overleaf.

**1611** COTGR., *Bord*,..the welt, or turneouer of a corke shoe. **1630** in Welford *Hist. Newcastle* (1887) III. 298 Stall rooms—of Mark Milbank, for himself for a turnover, 3ˢ. **1829** *Yng. Lady's Bk.* 338 A very small bit of wax may be dropped beneath the turn-over of the letter. *Ibid.* 340 These envelopes..resemble a sort of pocket; the ends are closed, and the turn-over is sealed in the usual way, after the enclosure is inserted. **1842** S. LOVER *Handy Andy* ii, He caught some words that were on the last turn-over of the sheet. **1883** (*title*) 'Turnovers' from 'The Globe'. **1899** ROBERTSON *Kipling Guide Bk.* 52 'Turn-overs', so called from the sketch ('turning over' to the second page) by Mr. Kipling.

**4. a.** A linen band or the like worn round the neck and turned down; a turn-down collar or neck-band.

**1716–20** *Lett. fr. Mist's Jrnl.* (1722) I. 204 Curious Linnen, made up into very fine Turnovers, Necks, and Ruffles. **1802** JAMES *Milit. Dict.*, *Turnover*, a piece of white linen which is worn by the soldiers belonging to the British cavalry over their stocks, about half an inch deep. Three turnovers per annum are ordered to be provided. **1825** HONE *Every-day Bk.* I. 158 The 'turnovers' worn by the beaux of those days [1770] with 'ruffles'.

**b.** *local.* A small shawl worn by women.

**1891** QUILLER COUCH *Noughts & Crosses, Gifts F. Hmkoff* 206 She wore a violet turnover.

**5.** A kind of tart in which the fruit is laid on one half of the rolled out paste, and the other half turned over it; a child's sweetmeat resembling this. Also *attrib.* as *turn-over shop.*

**1798** *Sporting Mag.* XI. 176 An old woman..preparing her turnovers, commonly called apple-pies. **1825** S. R. in Hone *Every-day Bk.* I. 1291 Our 'tart' and 'turn-over' shop. **1847** in HALLIWELL. **1882** *Gd. Words* 606 Venison pasties and apple turnovers and runlets of ale. **1892** *Star* 24 Dec. 3/2 There were sweets called turnovers, in which were coins of various values.

**6.** The total amount of business done in a given time; also, the amount of goods produced and disposed of by a manufacturer; also, the 'turning over' of the capital involved in a business; also, the net profit derived from a business in a given time.

**1879** ESCOTT *England* I. 391 On this large turn-over the gross profit averages 8½ per cent. **1880** *Daily News* 10 Dec. 5/7 The Blarney mills make a great 'turn over' of tweed. **1883** BLOOMFIELD *Fisheries Irel.* 13 (Fish. Exhib. Publ.) The great trading motto of low price and large and quick turn overs. **1894** *Brit. Jrnl. Photogr.* XLI. 5 The cost of production, unless very carefully managed, runs the turnover very close.

**B.** *adj.* That turns or is turned over, as *turn-over apprentice, collar, hand, lip, majority*: cf. senses above; **turnover boiler, concern, gear**: see quots.; **turnover rake**, a hay-rake which, when full, turns over and deposits its collection; **turnover-table**, a table with hinged top: see quot.; also a table with a sliding panel prepared for use as a draught-board or the like when reversed (*Cent. Dict.* 1891).

**1849** CRAIG, *Turnover-table*, a sort of small table, the top of which..may be turned over perpendicularly when out of use, thus occupying less room. **1859** *Autobiog. Beggar Boy* 113 There was no opening for a turnover apprentice. **1864** WEBSTER s. v., A turn-over collar. **1874** F. G. LEE *Man. Cleric.* 7 The Chalice should never have turn-over lips. **1877** KNIGHT *Dict. Mech.*, *Turn-over Boiler*, a form of boiler in which the flues were turned over the fire-box or furnace. *Ibid.*, *Turn-over Gear*,..an application of machinery for hauling up logs from the saw-mill to the log-carriage, or turning the log on the carriage after slabbing one side. **1883** *Daily News* 20 July 6/1 Messrs. Riches and Watts's turn-over gathering rake. **1892** *Labour Commission Gloss.*, *Turn-over Concerns*, mills and machinery..turned over to a limited liability company. **1913** *Daily Graphic* 24 Mar. 13/1 Nearly all the women were wearing low turn-over collars in colour, with flowing Quartier Latin ties.

† **Turnover,** erroneous for *turnour*, TURNER².

**1640** *Burgh Rec. Glasgow* (1876) I. 422 Thretie dollours and ane halfe of good dollours, and alevine and ane halfe of turnovers, quhilk sall be put in the touns commoune chist to bee applayed *ad pios usus.* **1679** R. CAMERON in Herkless *Life* (1896) 111 For suffering, that man will confine in the breadth of a turnover that that he will suffer for.

**Turnpike** (tɜ̄·ɹnpəik), *sb.* Forms: see TURN *v.* and PICK *sb.*¹, PIKE *sb.*¹; also 5–7 *Sc.* **-pik**, 6 *Sc.* **-pek**, 7 *Sc.* **-pecke, -pyck**; 7–8 **turn(e)-peg.** [f. TURN- + PICK *sb.*¹, PIKE *sb.*¹]

**I. 1.** *Hist.* A spiked barrier fixed in or across a road or passage, as a defence against sudden attack, esp. of men on horseback.

It does not appear certain how this was originally constructed, or how it acted; later writers identify it with the CHEVAL DE FRISE (see quotations 1704–1716), but the other senses suggest that in older use the axis was vertical.

*c* **1420** *Siege of Rouen* in *Collect. Lond. Cit.* (Camden) 17 He made a dyche of grete coste, Pyght with stakys that wolde perysce, With turnepykys, and with many an hers. *c* **1425** WYNTOUN *Cron.* VIII. 5716 Þan a staf tuk Wate of Curry, And set vndyr þe portculyce, Þat cum down it mycht on na wise. Syne þe crelis and cilis wiþe all Apon þe turnpik [*v.rr.* turnepike, -pyk] let he fal. And ane þan blew a horne in hy. **1477** *Paston Lett.* III. 203 My lord hath do brokyn all the passages excep Newham bryge, weche is wached, and the turne pyke shette every nyght. **1543** WALLOP in *St. Papers Hen. VIII*, IX. 454 There was 2 horsemen of Mr. Bowlmers companey taken, which went over at Marguyson, notwithstanding the turnpike, being then there sett on with certen horsemen of Bullen, were constrayned to take the ryver, where as it is saied never any hath passed. **1545** ASCHAM *Toxoph.* (Arb.) 88 At the Turne pike besyde Hammes where they turned with so fewe Archers, so many Frenchemen to flight. **1577–87** HOLINSHED *Chron.* (1807) III. 103 A large trench..pight full of sharpe stakes, with a great rampire fensed with bulworks, and turnepikes. **1642** *Relat. Action bef. Cirencester* 4 Each end of the high street..was secured against Horse with strong slaght-boomes which our men call Turne-pikes. **1644** in Rushw. *Hist. Coll.* III. II. 739 They had no Drawbridge but only a Turnpyke. **1704** J. HARRIS *Lex. Techn.* I, *Turn-Pikes* in the Art of War, are Spars of Wood of 12 or 14 Foot long, and about 6 Inches diameter in a sexangular Form: They are bored with holes..six Inches one from another, but to go by turns from each side, the Pickets that are driven into the hole[s], are 6 or 5 Foot long, pointed with

Iron. **1711** *Milit. & Sea Dict.* (ed. 4), *Chevaux de Frise*,.. the same as Turnpikes,..one being the French, the other the English Name, yet both indifferently now used in England, and the French rather the most. **1716** Perry *St. Russia* 47 The Czar having disposed his Army behind a Line of Chevaux de Frize, or Turn-pikes shod with Iron,..maintain'd so regular and strong a fire, that [etc.]. **1724** De Foe *Mem. Cavalier* I. 108 Coming up to the Turn-pike, I found it defended by 200 Musqueteers.

† **b.** *transf.* and *fig.* in various applications. *Obs.*

*a* **1616** Beaumont *Antiplatonic* v, Love stormes his lips, and takes the fortresse in, For all the bristled turn-pikes of his chin. **1641** G. H. *Wit's Recreat.* X vj, He hath such subtile turnes and nookes, Such turne-pegs, mazes, tenter-hookes. **1661** Feltham *Resolves* II. xxix. (ed. 8) 241 It makes a man a Turn-pike, that will be sure to prick you, which side soever you come on. **1661** K. W. *Conf. Charac., Covetous Usurer* (1860) 74 That Fryday face of his, whose rowsey whiskers and brischy turn-pikes make him resemble some shaggy meteor, or some borish Turk. **1665** Hooke *Microgr.* l. 205 Each of these legs were bestuck..with multitudes of small hairs, or (if we respect the proportion they bore to the bigness of the leg) turnpikes. **1679** V. Alsop *Melius Inquir.* I. i. 77 He that..shall thrust other men upon the turn-pikes of sin, and force them to act against their light.

† **2.** A horizontal cross of timber turning on a vertical pin, set up to exclude horse-traffic from a foot-way; a turnstile. *Obs.*

**1547** in J. R. Boyle *Hedon* (1875) App. 135 For makynge on hoppe to the tornepyke, iiij.d. **1600** W. Kemp *Nine Days' Wonder* D j, The Cittizens [of Norwich] had caused all the turne-pikes to be taken vp..that I might not be hindred. **1626** B. Jonson *Staple of N.* III. i, I moue vpon my axell, like a turne-pike. **1684–5** in Willis & Clark *Cambridge* (1886) II. 642 Painting the barrs and Turnepikes in the entrance to the New walke. **1755** Johnson, *Turnpike*,..a cross of two bars armed with pikes at the end, and turning on a pin, fixed to hinder horses from entering.

† **3.** A barrier across a water-course or stream; a water-gate, allowing the water to flow, but obstructing cattle; also, a lock on a navigable stream. Also *turnpike-lock* (see 9). *Obs.*

**1623–4** *Act* 21 *Jas. I*, c. 32 § 1 To open prepare or make all Weares and Lockes or Turnepickes fitt for the said Passage. *Ibid.*, To make and erect any Wharfes Lockes or Turnepickes or Pennes for Water. **1677** Plot *Oxfordsh.* 233 Where the declivity of the Channel, and fall of water is so great, that few barges could live in the passage of them, there we have Turn-pikes. **1702** *Act* 1 *Anne* St. II. c. 11 § 2 Altering the said Wharfs Sluces Wears Sasses Locks Turnpikes or Pens for Water or Passages. **1751** *Act* 24 *Geo. II*, c. 8 § 2 Tenants or Occupiers of all Locks, Weirs, Bucks, Winches, Turnpikes, Dams, Flood-Gates.

**4.** A barrier (orig. of the nature of a turnpike in sense 2, later a gate or gates) placed across a road to stop passage till the toll is paid; a toll-gate. Cf. Turnstile. Now chiefly *Hist.*

*a* **1678** [see b]. **1695–6** *Act* 7 & 8 *Will. III*, c. 9 § 4 The Place for collecting the said Toll to be in some convenient Place upon the said Highway..by setting up a Turnpike or otherwise. **1705** *Lond. Gaz.* No. 4125/4 Whoever..gives Notice to Mr. John Baker, Keeper of the Turn-Pipe [*sic*] aforesaid,..shall have a Guinea Reward. **1723** Mandeville *Fab. Bees* (1725) I. 365 A poor Traveller that at every Ten Miles end is stop'd by a Turnpike. **1771** Smollett *Humph. Cl.* 26 June, Considering the tax we pay for turnpikes, the roads of this country constitute a most intolerable grievance. **1806** *Chron.* 23 Feb., in *Ann. Reg.* (1808) 375/2 Close to Oxford-street turnpike. **1829** *Chapters Phys. Sc.* 58 The weighing-machine is formed of a combination of levers..and is commonly used at turnpikes in weighing waggons, to ascertain that they are not loaded beyond what is allowed by law to the breadth of their wheels. **1845** McCulloch *Taxation* Introd. (1852) 33 Turnpikes being erected only on the principal roads, the old plan for keeping up cross or parish roads [by statute labour, or at the cost of the parish] was not affected by their institution. **1885** *Act* 48 & 49 *Vict.* c. 37 § 5 The provisions now in force respecting turnpikes and tolls [etc.]..shall continue in force until Parliament otherwise provides.

**b.** *transf.* and *fig.*

*a* **1678** Marvell *Growth Popery* 11 It will suffer no man to pass without paying at their Turn-pikes. **1730** Fielding *Rape upon Rape* II. ii. 16 The Laws are Turnpikes, only made to stop People who walk on Foot. **1745** *Season. Adv. Protest.* 38 A Tax to the Priests, for suffering them to pass the Turnpike of Purgatory. **1765** Foote *Commissary* II. i, He capers through a whole region of turnpegs. **1807** Opie in *Lect. Paint.* ii. (1848) 271 The possessors..had..been often denied the usual road to eminence:..they defrauded the turnpike, and conducted their silent march another way.

**c.** *dial.* A wire snare set by a poacher across a hare's or rabbit's run.

**1879** Jefferies *Amateur Poacher* ii. 29 The blacksmith started the idea of putting up a 'turnpike',—i.e. a wire.

**5.** Elliptical for Turnpike road; also *fig.*

**1748** De Foe *Tour Gt. Brit.* II. 178 The Road is by this means so continually torn, that it is one of the worst Turnpikes round about London. **1756** *Demi-Rep* 10 You may ride the turnpike to her heart. **1796** Burke *Regic. Peace* i. Wks. VIII. 124 There is a Minister from Denmark at Paris..We sent through this turnpike to demand a passport. **1802** *Debates in U. S. Congress* 25 Feb. (1850) 759 As plain as a turnpike. **1861** Geo. Eliot *Silas M.* i, [Raveloe] was nestled in a snug well-wooded hollow, quite an hour's journey on horseback from any turnpike. **1875** W. McIlwraith *Guide Wigtownshire* 77 Here the turnpike winds along a terrace hewn from the hillside.

**b.** Short for *turnpike trust* (see 9) or the like.

**1728** Vanbr. & Cib. *Prov. Husb.* I. i, He won't sit long enough to give his Vote for a Turn-pike. **1773** *Observ. State Poor* 105 The roads of our nation are its standing opprobrium, the complaint and the jest of foreigners. The few, which under the direction of turnpikes, are justly exempted from this general censure or ridicule, only serve to facilitate the conveyance of provision to the capital.

† **6.** A turn-table on a railway. *Obs.*

**1793** Smeaton *Edystone L.* § 167 *note*, The carriage being turned a quarter round upon the Turnpike, or Turnrail.

**7.** *U.S.* A small cake used to raise bread: see quots. ? *local.*

**1850** Susan Warner *Wide, Wide World* xiv, I am scalding this meal with it to make turnpikes. **1850** *Knickerbocker Mag.* (N. Y.) July 83 (Thornton) Some little yellow cakes, called turnpikes, and used, I believe, for some purpose or other in baking bread.

**II. 8.** *Sc.* A staircase which winds round a central axis; a spiral or winding stair; later applied to other forms of staircase: cf. *turnpike stair, staircase* in 9.

**1501** Douglas *Pal. Hon.* III. xvii, A palice..with mony royall towris,..Pinnakillis, fyellis, turnpekkis mony one, Gilt birneist torris,..Skarsment, reprise, corbell, and battellingis. **1516** *Acc. Ld. High Treas. Scot.* V. 78 For the makin of ane turnpek in the palis of the Abbay Halyrudhous. **1546** Lyndesay in *St. Papers Hen. VIII*, V. 560 Normond Leslie and his cumpanye met hym [Cdl. Beaton] in þe turnpyk þer off, and slew hym. **1552** *Acc. Ld. High Treas. Scot.* X. 91 Item, foure lokkis put in the ȝett, ȝard ȝett, and durris of the tway turnpykis of my lord governouris lugeing of the Kirk of Feild..iij li. *c* **1590** J. Stewart *Poems* (S.T.S.) II. 55/93 Butt and ben he bends from bour to bour, Vp turnpyks, turats, And from tour to tour. **1600** *Gowrie Conspir.* in *Harl. Misc.* (Malh.) II. 343 The Earle of Gowrie and his seruants made them for another way vp a quyet turnpyke, which..was onlie then left open, as appeared for that purpose. **1643** in A. Maxwell *Hist. Old Dundee* (1884) 213 [The Council] concludit that the turne-pyk upon the steeple be presently repaired. **1730** *Mem. Capt. Creichton* in *Swift's Wks.* (1869) 534/2 Steele suddenly opening the door, fired a blunderbuss down at the two dragoons as they were coming up the stairs; but the bullets, grazing against the side of the turnpike, only wounded and did not kill them. **1818** Scott *Rob Roy* xxii, The turnkey, who..led me up a 'turnpike' (so the Scotch call a winding stair). **1899** Crockett *Black Douglas* (1900) 106 He was upon the last step of the turnpike and at the entrance of the corridor.

**III. 9.** *attrib.* and *Comb.* (chiefly in sense 4), as *turnpike act, bridge, -house, -keeper, -man, -people, -system, trust*; in sense 8, as *turnpike foot, head, stair, staircase*; also **turnpike cake**: see sense 7; **turnpike-free** *a.*, free from tolls for passage; **turnpike gate**, † (*a*) a gate or door at the foot of a turnpike stair (*Sc.*); † (*b*) = sense 1; (*c*) = sense 4; † **turnpike-lock** = sense 3; **turnpike meeting**, a meeting of a turnpike trust; **turnpike sailor**, a beggar in the guise of a distressed sailor. See also Turnpike road.

**1794** Donaldson *Agric. Carse of Gowrie* 32 Making another application to parliament, and in a short time a *turnpike act was procured, in which these, and other particular roads in the county, were included. **1841** *Penny Cycl.* XX. 29/1 The inefficiency of the system of maintenance by parish and statute labour was proved before the passing of the first Turnpike Act in 1653. **1903** *Law Rep.* 1 K. B. 407 A bicycle is not a carriage for the purposes of a turnpike Act. **1840** *Act* 3 & 4 *Vict.* c. 88 § 1 That no Toll shall be demanded or taken on any *Turnpike..Bridge for any Horse, or Police Van, Carriage or Cart,..in the Service of the Police. **1850** Susan Warner *Wide, Wide World* xiv, Cakes, child, cakes!—*turnpike cakes—what I raise the bread with. **1565** in Hay Fleming *Reform. in Scot.* (1910) Append. M. 610 In the chalmer at the *turne pyk fuit. **1903** J. K. Jerome *Tea T. Talk* (ed Tauchn.) 112 The world's highroads run *turnpike-free from pole to pole. **1513** *Acc. Ld. High Treas. Scot.* IV. 526 To the..smyth for viij score of square hedit nalis to the *turnepyk yett of the nethir toure. **1688** R. Holme *Armoury* III. xvi. (Roxb.) 88/1 A Turne pike...Some terme it a Turnepike Gate. **1806** *Chron.* 19 Feb., in *Ann. Reg.* (1808) 371/2 A boy riding on a cart, drove against a turnpike-gate. **1840** Dickens *Barn. Rudge* iii, The horse stopped until the turnpike gate was opened. **1889** Gretton *Memory's Harkb.* 115 The wheelers..knocked against the turnpike-gate-post in passing through. **1623** *Reg. Mag. Sig. Scot.* 151/1 Infra *lie turnpyke* ejusdem cameram *lie *turnpyke-heid*, occidentalem..et mediam cameram. **1774** Nicholson in *Phil. Trans.* LXIV. 351 These appearances continued till I reached the *turnpike-house. **1806** *Chron.* 15 May, in *Ann. Reg.* (1808) 405/1 The toll-table, against the turnpike house, at Whalley. **1863** Dickens *Uncomm. Trav.* xxii, The Turnpike-house was all overgrown with ivy; and the Turnpike-keeper, unable to get a living out of the tolls, plied the trade of a cobbler. **1738** *Gentl. Mag.* May 247/2 From the Respect he was treated with by the *Turnpike-keeper, I perceived..that he was..some Person of Distinction. **1771** *Act* 11 *Geo. III*, c. 45 § 8 Making *Turnpike Locks on the Sides of the present Locks. **1769** Earl March in Jesse *Selwyn & Contemp.* (1843) II. 366, I wrote you a note with a pencil upon the road, which a *turnpike-man promised to send to you. **1782** Cowper *Gilpin* 119 In a trice the turnpike-men Their gates wide open threw. **1876** Blackmore *Cripps* xxxii, He would rather have a row with three turnpike-men than presume to speak to a gentleman. **1764** Foote *Mayor of G.* I. i, After twenty years attendance at *turnpike-meetings. **1858** Dickens *Holly Tree Inn* i, Even *turnpike people have children. **1851** Mayhew *Lond. Labour* I. 415/2, I became a *turnpike sailor,..and went out as one of the Shallow Brigade. **1884** Clark Russell in *Longm. Mag.* III. 563 The roadway was filled with a crowd of grimy fellows, turnpike sailors, loafing scarecrows. **1730** *Mem. Capt. Creichton* in *Swift's Wks.* (1869) 534/1 The dragoons..went up a pair of *turnpike stairs. **1779** Arnot *Hist. Edin.* 246 *note*, A turnpike stair is the term used..over all Scotland, to denote a stair, of which the steps are built in a spiral form, like a screen winding round the same axis. **1805** Forsyth *Beauties Scotl.* II. 309 A small turnpike-stair, built in the wall. **1818** Scott *Hrt. Midl.* xxvi, A half-circular turret,..bartizan'd on the top, served as a case for a narrow turnpike-stair. **1888** Stevenson *Black Arrow* IV. iv, The authors..had clattered down a turnpike stair and decamped. **1800** W. F. Baylay *Northern Tour* 267 (MS.) A beautiful *turnpike staircase here..the roof of it winding like a snail cap. **1801** *Farmer's Mag.* Apr. 158 The defective principles, adopted when the *turnpike system was first introduced, are completely avoided. **1895** *Westm. Gaz.* 28 Oct., The last of the turnpike system. ..The turnpike gates, which will enjoy the honour of thus being last in the field, belong to that portion of the Shrewsbury and Holyhead-road which traverses the island of Anglesea, the trust for which was continued by a special Act of Parliament until November 1, 1895. **1843** *Penny Cycl.* XXV. 429/1 *Turnpike trusts. Turnpike-roads are.. highways placed..under the management of trustees or commissioners.

Hence **Tu·rnpike** *v.*, *trans.* to erect turnpikes on (a road); to make into a turnpike road; **Turnpiker**, one who frequents the turnpike or turnpike road; hence (*a*) a foot-traveller; (*b*) = *turnpike sailor* (see 9 above).

**1806** Webster, **Turnpike*,..to form or erect a turnpike. **1825** *Amer. St. Papers, Post-office* (1834) 137 The road from Elkton to Staunton has been turnpiked. **1903** H. T. Crofton *Old Moss Side* 6 The lane was but little altered even after Acts are passed in 1749 and 1793 for turnpiking and improving it. **1812** *Boston Gaz.* 27 Aug. (Thornton), The heroes, who were to have mounted the heights of Abram, are yet in the garb of *turnpikers, unaccoutred and undisciplined. **1896** Clark Russell *What Cheer!* xi. 189 When it came to lee shores and frightful cliffs resounding the thunder of the tempest of the Atlantic..the turnpikers bent their backs and pulled with a will.

**Tu·rnpike road.** A road on which turnpikes are or were erected for the collection of tolls; hence, a main road or highway, formerly maintained by a toll levied on cattle and wheeled vehicles. Also *fig.*

**1745** Wesley *Wks.* (1830) I. 485 Turnpike roads were not known in that part of England till some years after. **1776** Adam Smith *W. N.* I. xi. I. (1869) I. 156 Some of the counties in the neighbourhood of London petitioned the Parliament against the extension of the turnpike roads into the remoter counties. **1845** McCulloch *Taxation* Introd. (1852) 33 It was not..till after the peace of Paris, in 1763, that turnpike-roads began to be extended to all parts of the kingdom. *Ibid.* II. x. 377 It has..been proposed to abolish tolls, as being essentially partial and unfair, and to raise a fund for constructing and repairing turnpike roads by a tax on property assessed and collected in the same way..as the rate for cross and parish roads. **1875** W. S. Hayward *Love agst. World* 16 After an hour's ride, by cross-country lanes and by-paths, they struck into the turnpike road.

**Turn-rice, -rise,** var. Turnwrest.

**Turn-serving** (tɔ̄·ɹnsɔ̄ːɹviŋ), *sb.* and *a.* [f. Turn *sb.* 30 + Serving *vbl. sb.* and *ppl. a.*] **a.** *sb.* The action or practice of serving one's own turn; the promotion of one's private interest; self-seeking; an instance of this. **b.** *adj.* That serves its own turn; promoting one's own ends. So † **Tu·rn-served** *a.*, that has served his own turn (*obs.*); **Tu·rn-se:rver**, one whose motive is his own interest. Cf. Time-server, etc.

**1613** Chapman *Masque Inns of Court* Plays 1873 III. 109 The sight of an attendant for reward is abominable in the eyes of a *turne-seru'd Politician. **1611** Speed *Hist. Gt. Brit.* IX. xvi. (1623) 839 A deceitfull man, a *turne-server. **1710** *Answ. to Bp. of Oxford's Sp.* 18 The Memory of all Time and Turn-Servers will be forgotten. **1611** Speed *Hist. Gt. Brit.* IX. xi. § 62 His name was abased to all sorts of *turne-seruings. **1616** Bacon *Let. to Sir G. Villiers* 12 Aug., Though now, since Choice goeth better both in Church and Common-wealth, yet Money, and Turn-Serving, and Cunning Canvises, and Importunity, prevail too much. **1584** Powel *Lloyd's Cambria* 278 Let people take heede how they build upon *turne-seruing freendship. **1842** G. S. Faber *Prov. Lett.* (1844) II. 189 A mere temporary and turn-serving appeal to Antiquity.

**Turn-sick** (tɔ̄·ɹnsik), *a.* and *sb.* *Obs.* exc. *dial.* Also 5–6 -seke, 6 -sycke, -sicke. [f. Turn *v.* + Sick *a.*]

† **A.** *adj.* Affected with vertigo; giddy; dizzy.

*c* **1440** *Promp. Parv.* 507/1 Turnseke, *vertiginosus.* **1534** Whitinton *Tullyes Offices* I. (1540) 49 We here tell of Lysander of Lacedemony, a turnesycke person and a man that myght abyde all paynes. **1626** Bacon *Sylva* § 795 If a Man see another turn swiftly, and long; Or if he look upon Wheels that turne, Himselfe waxeth Turne-sick. **1657** J. Watts *Dipper Sprinkled* 6 Running round in a ring until you be turn-sick and giddy-headed.

*fig.* *a* **1603** T. Cartwright *Confut. Rhem. N. T.* (1618) 179 You are fallen out with your selues, and turne-sick with the maze of your own inuentions. *Ibid.* 382 These turnesick Iesuites make their note cleane contrary to the text. *a* **1617** Bayne *On Eph.* (1658) 104 An escape of a turn-sick brain blinded with wilfulness. **1664** J. C. *Praxis Lat. Syntax* 130 Divers teachers, so giddy turn-sick.

† **b.** *Turn-sick giddiness*, vertigo. *Obs.*

**1577** B. Googe *Heresbach's Husb.* IV. (1586) 192 The water of this hearbe..helpeth the turnesicke giddinesse of the heade.

**B.** *sb.* † **1. a.** Vertigo, swimming in the head; also, staggers in the horse. *Obs.*

*c* **1450** in *Vicary's Anat.* (1888) App. ix. 229 Be-hynde þe eres er twa vayns þat er gude to be opynd for turnseke and for scall, & alsso for euyll sight. **1565** Blundevil *Horsemanship* IV. xvi. (1580) 8 In the ventricles or celles of the braine..do breede the turnesicke, or staggers. **1592** in *Vicary's Anat.* (1888) App. ix. 228 If thowe lett blode of thoo, His syght shall neuer fale, And heles of torne-seke, and of scale.

**2.** A disease caused by an encysted worm in the brain of the sheep; the gid or sturdy. *dial.* Cf. Turn *sb.* 3.

**1834** Youatt *Cattle* 294 The sheep is subject to a disease strangely termed *turnsick*, in which the animal goes round and round. **1837** — *Sheep* 391 The turnsick is not so frequent as it used to be thirty or forty years ago. **1844** STEPHENS *Bk. Farm* III. 877 There is a disease in sheep called sturdy or turnsick. **1870** ROLLESTON *Anim. Life* 136 The cause of the disease commonly known as the 'sturdy', 'gid', 'staggers', or 'turn-sick'.

Hence † **Turnsickness** = B. 1. *Obs.*

**1559** MORWYNG *Evonym.* 137 The headache, fallinge sicknesse, swindle or turnsicknes.

† **Turnsilver.** *Obs. rare*$^{-1}$. [? f. TURN *sb.* or *v.* + SILVER *sb.*] A local payment of uncertain nature.

**1578** in Whellan *Hist. Cumb. & Westm.* (1860) 208/2 [From the inquisition taken in 1578, we learn the following particulars... The tenants of Ulterside pay yearly]..for cornage, 4 s. 6 d.; for seawake, 7 d.; for turnsilver, 1 s. 3 d.

**Turnsole** (tʊ̄·ɹnsōul). Forms: 4 turnisoll, 4–8 turnesole, (5–6 turne-, 7 turnsoyle, turn(e)-soil(e), 6 turnesoll, -sell, -sall, -saule, turnsale, -sowell, tornsole, -sell, -salle, tornesall(e, -sol(e, -solt, tournesoll, -sole, -soule, 6–7 turnsall, 7 -soll, -soule, 7–8 turnesol, 8 tournsol, 6–9 turnsol, 5- turnsole. [a. F. *tournesol* (14th c. in Littré), prob. ad. older Prov. *tournasol* (now *tournosol*) = Sp. and Pg. *tornasol*, It. *tornasole*, f. Romanic *tornare* to TURN + L. *sōl* the sun.

In F., as in Eng., first recorded as the name of the colouring matter derived from one of the plants bearing the name. In mod. Sp., Pg., and It. chiefly used in sense 2 b.]

**1.** A violet-blue or purple colouring matter, obtained from the plant *Crozophora tinctoria* (see 2 a), formerly much used for colouring jellies, confectionery, wines, etc., and later as a pigment. (See also quots. 1712 and 1830.)

Coarse linen rags are steeped in the juice, and then dried and exposed in vats over an ammoniacal mixture; hence the designation † *turnsole in rags* = F. *tournesol en drapeau*.

**1375** *Exch. Rolls Scotl.* II. 507 Computat per empcionem de iij libris alkynet, j libra de turnisoll, et j libra de savndre. **1392** *Earl Derby's Exp.* (Camden) 154 Pro iij lb. turnesole ad xiiij d. *c* **1440** *Anc. Cookery* in *Househ. Ord.* (1790) 437 Colour hit with turnesole, or with ynde, or with alkenet, or saunders, or saffron. **1513** *Bk. Kervynge* in *Babees Bk.* (1868) 268 Tornsole is holsome for reed wyne colourynge. **1573** *Art of Limming* 4 To make azure and bize sadder, take good blewe tournesoll and wet it in gumme water. **1606** PEACHAM *Art of Drawing* I. xxiii. (1612) 86 The sorts of Red are these. Vermilion. Synaper lake... Red lead. Roset. Turnsoile [etc.]. *Ibid.* 88 Turnesoile is made of old linnen ragges died:..it is good to shadow carnations, and all yealowes. **1615** MARKHAM *Eng. Housew.* II. ii. 70 If you will haue [the jelly] coloured, then put in a little Tournesall. **1616–61** HOLYDAY *Persius* 308 The armorists indeed slight your common purple made of grocer's turnesol, a mixture of vermilion and blew bysse, or cynnaber, or the colour of violets. **1688** [see 2 a]. **1712** tr. *Pomet's Hist. Drugs* v. 93/2 Tornesol or Turnsole in Rags, is made of Linnen Cloth dyed at Constantinople, with Cocheneal and some Acids. The Cotton Turnsole, call'd Portugal or Spanish Wool, is made from Cotton that is..dyed in Spain or Portugal with Mestich Cochineal. Both Sorts are made use of to colour Liquors, Fruits and Gellies. There is another Kind of Turnsole that is made with Rags dipp'd in a red Tincture, prepar'd with the Juice of the Berry, and a little acid Liquor. **1783** *Phil. Trans.* LXXIII. 39 Acids possess the property of changing the juice of turnsol, or infusion of litmus, red. **1830** LINDLEY *Nat. Syst. Bot.* 103 The preparation called Turnsol,..chiefly obtained from Crozophora (Croton) tinctoria, is to be procured equally abundantly from many other plants of the order [Euphorbiaceæ]. **1866** *Treas. Bot.* 352/1 *C*[*rozophora*] *tinctoria*..is cultivated in the South of France for the sake of a dye which is obtained from it. This dye is called Turnsole, and is obtained by grinding the plants..to a pulp in a mill, when they yield about half their weight of a dark green coloured juice, which becomes purple by exposure to the air or under the influence of ammonia.

*fig.* **1599** *Broughton's Let.* xi. 38 Coloured with the Turnsalue of your Phantasticall braine.

**b.** *transf.* = LITMUS.

So F. *tournesol* and *tournesol en pain*.

**1839** URE *Dict. Arts* 53 The lichen which produces archil is subjected to another preparation, to make turnsole (litmus). This article is made in Holland. **1842** BRANDE *Dict. Sc.* etc. 671/1 *Litmus*..a blue pigment obtained from the lichen *Rocella*..it is often called *turnsol*, and yields the dye called *archil*.

**2.** A plant of which the flowers or leaves turn so as to follow the sun; a heliotrope. **a.** An annual euphorbiaceous plant, *Crozophora tinctoria*, the *Small Tornesol* of Lyte's Herbal, found wild by the Mediterranean, and cultivated in the south of France for its colouring juice (see 1).

In earlier botanical use called *Croton tinctorium* (or *-ius*), *Ricinoides* (Tournefort), and (after Pliny) *Heliotropium tricoccum*.

**1578** LYTE *Dodoens* I. xli. 61 With the seede of the smal Tornesoll..they die and stayne old linnen cloutes and ragges into a purple colour,..wherewithall in this countrey men vse to colour gellies, wynes, fine Confections, and Comfittes. **1688** R. HOLME *Armoury* II. 91/1 Turnsole, at the leaves comes forth three berries..which have within them a juice, or moisture of a purple colour of which that Turn-sole is made; sold by the Drugists. **1728** CHAMBERS *Cycl.*, *Tornesol*, *Tournesol*, or *Turnsol*, called also *Heliotrope*, and *Sunflower*, and by the Botanists *Ricinoides*. *Ibid.*, The *tournsol* being no Plant of their [i.e. Dutch] Growth. **1756** C. LUCAS *Ess. Waters* I. 21 Blews obtained from..archil, tournsol, &c. have their colors exalted or preserved by alcalies.

**b.** The plant *Heliotropium europæum*, the *Great Tornesol* of Lyte's Herbal; sometimes used by modern botanists as a name for the genus *Heliotropium*.

**1578** LYTE *Dodoens* I. xli. 60 The great Tornesol hath straight round stalkes, couered with a white hearie cotton... The floures be white, at the toppe of the stalke, growing thicke togither in rewes. **1603** B. JONSON *Jas. I's Entertainm.* Wks. (Rtldg.) 528/2 Agrypnia, or Vigilance, in yellow,..her chaplet of Heliotropium, or turnsole. **1707** *Curios. in Husb. & Gard.* 142 The Famous Plant, call'd Heliotrope, Turn-Sole, or Sun-Flower. **1731** MILLER *Gard. Dict.* s.v. *Heliotropium*, The great Turnsole of Dioscorides. *Ibid.*, Blue American Turnsole, with Clary Leaves. *a* **1832** BENTHAM *Deontol.* i. (1834) I. 20 Let the moralist regard the great Deontological law, as steadily as the Turnsole looks upon the sun. **1866** *Treas. Bot.* 576/2 The Heliotrope or Turnsole, is a large genus of *Ehretiaceæ*...They are herbs or undershrubs found chiefly in tropical and subtropical regions, but a few species reach Europe, and one, *H*[*eliotropium*] *europæum*, is distributed over..southern and central Europe. **1887** MOLONEY *Forestry W. Afr.* 388 Indian Turnsole (*Heliotropium indicum*, L.).—Small annual.

**c.** Formerly applied to the Sunflower; also to the Sun-spurge or Wartwort, *Euphorbia helioscopia*.

**1725** *Family Dict.* s.v. *Sunflower*, It's named *Turn-Sol* by the Italians and French. *Ibid.*, Between which [trees], at three Foot distance one from the other, our Turn-Sols may be planted. **1804** MALKIN *Scen. etc. S. Wales* 606 Turnsoles,..though beautiful, are never planted on graves, because they are not sweet-scented. **1863–79** PRIOR *Pop. Names Brit. Plants*, *Turnsole* or *Tornsole*, a name erroneously given in some old works to the wartwort.

**3.** *attrib.*, as *turnsole paper*, *rag*, *tincture*.

**1733** SHAW *Chem. Lect.* xi. (1755) 210 We put four Ounces of what is commonly called Turnsol Rags into an earthen Vessel. **1753** *Chambers' Cycl.* Supp. s.v. *Turnesol*, The plant that afforded the Turnesol colour. *Ibid.*, The true Turnesol plant here described. **1797** PEARSON in *Phil. Trans.* LXXXVIII. 35 It reddened turnsole paper and tincture. **1836** J. M. GULLY *Magendie's Formul.* (ed. 2) 191 The solution in question reddened turnsol paper.

**Turnspit** (tʊ̄·ɹnspit). [f. TURN *v.* + SPIT *sb.*; cf. TURNBROACH.]

**1.** A dog kept to turn the roasting-spit by running within a kind of tread-wheel connected with it; a *turnspit dog*. Also *fig.*

**1576** FLEMING tr. *Caius' Dogs* (1880) 35 A certaine dogge ..when any meate is to bee roasted they go into a wheele.. turning rounde about with the waight of their bodies...Whom the popular sort herevpon call Turnespets. *a* **1619** FLETCHER *Mad Lover* III. ii, Get thee to school again, and talk of turnspits. **1793** [E. D. CLARKE] *Tour S. Eng.* iv. 215 Dogs are universally used, in this part of the world, as turnspits. **1801** COL. G. HANGER *Life* II. 246 These turnspits, who, in the metaphysical wheel, turn the spit of conjecture. **1863** JESSE in Chambers *Bk. Days* 8 Apr. I. 490/1 His two turnspits..were long-bodied, crook-legged, and ugly dogs.

**2.** A boy or man whose office was to turn the spit. Also used as a term of contempt.

**1607** *Puritan* I. ii. 3 As hot as a turn-spit. **1683** *Roxb. Ball.* (1885) V. 455 Fat Turnspit Frank,..Whom we despise, in time may rise to be Jester to King Perkin. **1723** SWIFT *French Dog* Wks. 1755 IV. I. 36 A turn-spit in the royal kitchen. **1802–12** BENTHAM *Ration. Judic. Evid.* (1827) II. 139 The King's turnspit used to be a member of parliament. **1809** MALKIN *Gil Blas* II. i. ¶ 5 Leonarda..passed for a very decent plain cook; but a mere turnspit to dame Jacintha. **1869** BLACKMORE *Lorna D.* v, All good people..knowing his kitchen range to be cold, no longer would play turnspit.

**3.** A roasting-jack. *rare.*

**1606** CHAPMAN *Gent. Usher* III. i, Euen as in a turne-spit calld a Iacke..the great wheeles, Turning but softly, make the lesse to whirre. **1858** SIMMONDS *Dict. Trade*, *Turnspit*, a clock-work machine for cooking.

**4.** *attrib.*, as *turnspit-boy*, *cur*, *dog*, *-jack*, *terrier*.

**1820** SCOTT *Monast.* xiv, A little dirty *turnspit-boy. **1603** HARSNET *Pop. Impost.* xxii. 145 Moved..as a Wheele is by a *turnspit curre, that is put into it. **1625** N. CARPENTER *Geog. Del.* I. iv. (1635) 81 *Turne-spit-dogs labouring in their wheeles. *a* **1704** T. BROWN *Laconics* Wks. 1711 IV. 14 Seeing one of the Turn-spit Dogs bask himself in the Sun. **1845** YOUATT *Dog* ii. 18 Colonel Sykes says..among the pariahs is frequently found the turnspit-dog. **1674** PETTY *Disc. Dupl. Proportion* 39 In any good *Turnspit-Jack,..a quadruple weight makes double Velocity. **1857** HUGHES *Tom Brown* I. iii, Toby the *turnspit terrier.

**Turnstile** (tʊ̄·ɹnstəil). [f. TURN *v.* + STILE *sb.*] A gateway formed of four radiating arms of timber or iron at right angles to each other, revolving horizontally on a fixed vertical post, set up in a passage or entrance, originally to exclude any but foot-passengers; now often to prevent the passage of more than one person at a time at a place where fees, fares, or tickets are collected, or where it is desired to count those passing.

*a* **1643** CARTWRIGHT *Lady Errant* I. v, Double forked Like a turn-stile, or some such engin. **1650** B. *Discolliminium* 48, I can devise none fitter then Weather-cocks and a Turne-stile. **1716** GAY *Trivia* III. 108 Where twirling turnstiles intercept the way, The thwarting passenger shall force them round. **1818** LEIGH *New Pict. Lond.* 313 The kind of iron turn-stiles, which admit of only one person passing at a time. **1861** *All Year Round* 29 June 324 The railway station is full, the voluminous gowns are jamming up the ticket collectors' turnstiles. **1890** *Spectator* 31 May 756 Sixty thousand passed the turnstiles of the Zoological Gardens.

*fig.* **1852** JERDAN *Autobiog.* II. xxi. 296 Bills..were frequently only turnstiles opening into paths of difficulty.

**b.** *attrib.*

**1688** R. HOLME *Armoury* III. 336/2 A Turning Hatch, or Turnstyle gate. **1877** KNIGHT *Dict. Mech.* s.v., A turnstile counter for omnibuses and cars is described in English patent No. 2189, of 1854. *Turnstile-register*,..for registering the number of persons who pass through a turnstile. **1896** *Daily News* 21 Aug. 3/5 Turnstile attendant at the Crystal Palace.

**Turnstone** (tʊ̄·ɹnstōun). [f. TURN *v.* + STONE *sb.*] A limicoline bird (*Strepsilas interpres*) of about the size of the snipe, widely distributed in the Old and New Worlds, which turns over stones to get at the crustacea and other small animals to be found under them.

**1674** RAY *Words*, *Water Fowl* 91 *The Turn-stone*:..Cinclus Turneri. This bird we observed on the coast of Cornwall: it is lesser then a Plover, and somewhat bigger then a Black-bird. **1678** RAY *Willughby's Ornith.* III. v. 311 The Turn-stone, or Sea-Dottrel. **1731** MORTIMER in *Phil. Trans.* XXXVII. 176 The Turn-Stone or Sea-Dottrel..is a Native both of England and America. **1802** MONTAGU *Ornith. Dict.* s.v., The Turnstone is subject to great variety in respect to the markings about the head and neck. **1862** ANSTED *Channel Isl.* 207 The turnstone is found about the neighbourhood of Herm throughout the year. **1904** *Blackw. Mag.* Feb. 250/2 The turnstones..breed in Alaska.

**Turn-table** (tʊ̄·ɹntēⁱb'l). [f. TURN *v.* + TABLE *sb.*]

**1.** On a railway: A revolving platform turning on a central pivot, laid with rails connecting with adjacent tracks, for turning railway vehicles; a turn-plate.

**1835** *Massachusetts Stat.* 4 Apr., To unite any rail-road or rail-roads..by turn-tables or otherwise. **1838** N. WOOD *Railroads* (ed. 3) 186 On each of these lines..circular turntables are placed, upon which the carriages are run. **1854** *John Bull* 2 Sept. 558/2 An engine having been accidentally put in motion while on the turn table, ran over a side wall, and rested on end in the street below.

**2.** A revolving platform, table, stand, or disk of various kinds: see quots.; *spec.* (*a*) a rotating disk on which microscope slides are held for tracing the circular cement cells in which specimens are placed for examination; (*b*) see quot. 1889; (*c*) a turning device allowing a photographic camera to rotate on the stand or tripod; (*d*) a rotating plate-glass show stand used in shop-windows (*Funk's Stand. Dict.* 1895).

**1865** *Morn. Star* 2 Sept., The burial board..determined on placing a stand, or what is called a 'turn-table', in the church, and also one in the chapel [for use at funerals]. **1867** J. HOGG *Microsc.* I. iii. 254 The little box contains:—Shadbolts turn-table, brass table [etc.]. **1887** T. A. TROLLOPE *What I remember* II. xv. 279 His food..is passed in to him by a little turntable made in the wall. **1889** WELCH *Text Bk. Naval Archit.* v. 79 The four heavy guns are carried on revolving turntables in two fixed armoured redoubts or barbettes. **1892** *Photogr. Ann.* II. p. cxci, A special form of Turntable is fixed to the Camera, to which the legs may be quickly attached...The centre of the Turntable is cut away.

**3.** *attrib.*, as *turn-table ladder*, *stack*.

**1893** *Nation* (N. Y.) 13 July 28/3 At the Columbian Fair there is a turn-table stack of official publications. **1912** *Times* 19 Dec. 12/6 A horsed escape, a fire engine, a turntable ladder, and ten men turned out from the Theobald's-road fire station.

**Tu·rn-tail,** *sb.* and *a.* [f. the verbal phr. *turn tail* (TURN *v.* 59).]

**A.** *sb.* **1.** One who turns tail; one who abandons or forsakes his former associates or principles; also, a coward. Now *rare*.

**1621** BRATHWAIT *Nat. Embassie*, etc. (1877) 301 Thou art the rich mans claw-backe,..Go turne-taile go. *a* **1670** SPALDING *Troub. Chas. I* (1850) I. 206 Mony covenanteris proveit turne-taillis throw plane feir, and cam most willinglie into him. **1819** LINGARD *Hist. Eng.* I. xix. III. 136 *note*, Under the penalty of culvertage (culvert, a turn-tail) that is perpetual slavery.

† **2.** A variety of domestic pigeon. *Obs.*

**1741** *Compl. Fam.-Piece* III. 512 The Croppers are valuable for their Swell...The Turn-tails for their turning them up almost to their Back.

**B.** *adj.* That turns tail.

**1861** GEO. ELIOT *Silas M.* vi, I aren't a turn-tail cur.

**Turn-up** (tʊ̄·ɹn,ʊp), *sb.* and *a.* [f. the verbal phr. *turn up* (TURN *v.* 80).]

**A.** *sb.* † **1.** See quot., and cf. *turn up*, TURN *v.* 80***. *Obs. rare*$^{-1}$.

**1612** *Benvenuto's Passenger* I. iv. 315 They are whores, harlots, trulls, baggages, bayards, turne-vps, curtesanes.

**2.** The turned up part of anything, esp. of a garment.

**1688** R. HOLME *Armoury* IV. iv. (Roxb.) 295/2 A pilgrims hat of St. James,..on the turne-vp, two staves in salter debrused with an Escalop shell Or. *Ibid.* v. 307/1, I haue obserued that sleeues both in coates and crests haue had their Turn-vps of diuerse fashions. **1764** FOOTE *Patron* I. 5 He found the turn-up of her nose too exactly resemble the bust of the princess Popæa. **1901** *Daily Record* 21 Dec. 4 They..have velvet collars, narrow turn-ups at the cuffs, and are well shaped to the waist. **1902** ELIZ. L. BANKS *Newspaper Girl* 230 A hat..that'd suit you to a T! It's exactly made for you, turn-up on the side and all!

**3.** The turning up of a particular card or die in games of chance; the card or die turned up; hence *fig.*, a mere chance, a 'toss-up'; a result which is purely a matter of chance; also, an unexpected appearance or phenomenon.

**1810** *Sporting Mag.* XXXVI. 265 He..recorded turns up of all the chances. **1820** W. IRVING *Sketch Bk.*, *Stratford* (1865) 327 It is often a turn-up of a die, in the gambling freaks of fate, whether a natural genius shall turn out a great rogue or a great poet. **1844** J. T. Hewlett *Parsons & W.* vi, What the 'turn-up' would be I knew no more than a card-player, who has just had the pack cut to him. **1870** Hardy & Ware *Mod. Hoyle, Cribbage* 79 If the turn up should also be of the same suit, you count one extra. **1884** J. Burroughs in *Century Mag.* XXVII. 926 The type of men of which Emerson and Carlyle are the most pronounced ..examples..are comparatively a new turn-up in literature.

**b.** *spec.* in Racing: see quot. 1873.

**1873** *Slang Dict., Turn up*,..an unexpected slice of luck. Among sporting men bookmakers are said to have a turn up when an unbacked horse wins. **1895** *Westm. Gaz.* 10 Sept. 7/2 With such a moderate field nobody will be surprised if the result is a 'turn-up' as astonishing as was the victory of Throstle last year. **1900** *Ibid.* 15 May 8/1 The Jubilee Handicap on Saturday ended in a tremendous turn-up for the fielders.

**4.** A boxing contest; hence, *loosely*, a fight, a set-to, esp. with the fists; also, a tussle, struggle; a disturbance, row.

**1810** *Sporting Mag.* XXXVI. 195 The next amusement was a turn-up betwixt Crib and Richman. **1827** Scott *Two Drovers* ii, We must have a turn-up, or we shall be the talk of the countryside... Come, stand forward like a man. *c* **1874** G. H. Kingsley *Sport & Trav.* vi. (1900) 160 Campbell, however, had a turn-up with a grizzly. **1891** Sarah J. Duncan *Amer. Girl in Lond.* 78 The why and the wherefore of all this turn-up.

**B.** *attrib.* or *adj.* That is turned up, or turns up, in various senses.

**1685** *Lond. Gaz.* No. 2032/4 A small Spaniel Lap Dog.., with..a short turn-up Nose. *c* **1690** *Roxb. Ball.* (1895) VIII. 17 Turn-up stockings they constantly wear. **1767** in *Daily Chron.* 19 Nov. (1908) 4/7 You may sit in their Royal presence, not in pews, but in turn-up seats on the side of them. **1800** *Hull Advertiser* 19 Apr. 3/2 An infant..was smothered..with the bed-clothes of a turn-up bedstead. **1809** Malkin *Gil Blas* xi. ii. (Rtldg.) 397 The sharp-pointed, turn-up chin of a pantaloon. **1821** Lamb *Elia* Ser. i. *Mrs. Battle on Whist*, She would not take advantage of the turn-up knave. **1848** Rickman *Archit.* 211 Stalls with turn-up seats and benches. **1874** Burnand *My Time* xix. 166 It was neatly furnished, with a small table, a turn-up bedstead, etc. **1909** *Daily Graphic* 20 Oct. 13/1 The hat with the turn-up brim.

†**Turnway**[1]. *Rhet. Obs. rare*[−1]. [f. Turn *v.* + Way *adv.* away, after Gr. ἀποστροφή.] = Apostrophe[1] 1.

**1589** Puttenham *Eng. Poesie* iii. xix. (Arb.) 245 When we haue runne a long race in our tale..we do sodainly flye out and either speake or exclaime at some other person or thing, and therefore the Greekes call such figure (as we do) the turnway or turnetale.

**Turnway**[2] (tǭ·ɹnwēi). [f. Turn *sb.* + Way *sb.*] A system or method of turns; in quot. *attrib.*

**1897** Webb *Indust. Democ.* I. ii. ix. 437 The 'turnway' societies of the Thames watermen, for regulating the 'turns', or order in which the men plying at any particular 'stairs' serve the passengers who present themselves.

**Turnwrest** (tǭ·ɹnrest), *a.* (*sb.*) Also 8–9 **turn-wrist**, **-rise**, 9 **-rice**. [f. Turn- + Wrest *sb.* (See also Reest *sb.*)] *Turnwrest plough*, a plough in which the mould-board may be shifted from one side to the other at the end of each furrow, so that the furrow-slice is always thrown the same way; a one-way plough.

In the 18th cent. freq. called the *Kentish plough*.

**1653** Blithe *Eng. Improv. Impr.* ii. xxix. (ed. 3) 203 There is another double Wheeled-plough, & it is called the Turn wrest plough, which of all ploughs that ever I saw, surpasseth for weight and clumsiness. **1766** *Museum Rust.* VI. 129 He had made one, which he called a turn-rise plough. **1794** A. Pringle *Agric. Westmorland* 34 The turn-wrist plough is about to be introduced into the county. **1812** Sir J. Sinclair *Syst. Husb. Scot.* i. 156 A plough with a shifting mould-board, usually called a turn-wrest plough, admits of ploughing both backwards and forwards. **1846** Davis in *Jrnl. R. Agric. Soc.* VII. ii. 526 This I accomplished with a monster turn-rice plough made for the purpose. **1856** Morton *Cyclop. Agric.* II. 628–30 [Various forms described]. **1884** *W. Sussex Gaz.* 25 Sept., Strong turnwrist, round, snap, and strike furrow ploughs.

*transf.* **1844** Stephens *Bk. Farm* II. 624 The mountain turn-wrist snow-plough.

**b.** *ellipt.* as *sb.* Also *attrib.*

**1778** [W. Marshall] *Minutes Agric.* 25 Oct. an. 1775, A Turn-wrist is obviously preferable to a fixed-wrist, for cross-plowing. **1846** Clarke in *Jrnl. R. Agric. Soc.* VII. ii. 512 The old Kentish turn-wrest. **1902** *Westm. Gaz.* 7 Nov. 7/2 In the North Kent Agricultural Association's ploughing match..the variety of ploughs to be seen was surprising. The old wooden turnrise type was well to the fore.

† **Turny** (tǭ·ɹni), *a. Obs. rare.* [f. Turn *sb.* 3 + -y.] Of an ox, etc.: Affected with the turn.

**1651** *Manch. Crt. Leet Rec.* (1887) IV. 51 Thomas Peele [presented] for sellinge a leane turney beast.

† **Turon.** *Obs. rare.* [ad. med.L. *Turonia* or *Turonī*: see next.] The city of Tours; used *attrib.* = next, b.

Freq. in Trevisa's *Higden* as the name of the city.

**1568** Grafton *Chron.* II. 136 He..solde him his title that he had in Normandy, Gascoyne and Guyan... Taking for the same title three hundreth thousande of small Turon money.

† **Turoneis, Turoneys,** *sb.* and *a. Obs* [ad. med.L. *Turonensis* (f. *Turonēs*, later *Turonī*, *Turonii*, a people of ancient Gaul, whence Tours on the Loire took its name), with ending assimilated to OF. *torneis* (F. *tournois* Tournois *a.*).] **a.** *sb. pl.* The people or citizens of Tours. **b.** *adj.* Of or pertaining to Tours; = Tournois.

The sing. form *Turoney* employed by Trevisa is irregular. Both Trevisa and the anonymous translator of Higden also employ the Latin ending *-ens(e*.

**1387** Trevisa *Higden* (Rolls) VI. 259 He sette and pighte a lettre of gold of þe wight of an hondred pound of Turoneys [*v.rr.* Turoneyes, -eies]. *Ibid.*, He schal not spende at his comencement passynge þre þowsand of grootes turonens [*v.r.* turoneies]. Þe groot turoney is somwhat lasse worþy þan an Englische groote, ffor.. I have i-fonge in chaunge enlevene grotes turoneys for a duket.. But þere is double manere of money of turoneis [*v.r.* turoneies], more and lasse [etc.].

**Turonian** (tiurōu·niăn), *a. Geol.* [= F. *turonien*, f. L. *Turonēs*: see prec. and -ian.] Denoting a subdivision of the Cretaceous or Chalk period and series of strata, answering to the 'Lower White Chalk without flints' of English geologists.

**1850** Ansted *Elem. Geol., Min.* etc., Index, Turonian formation. [*Ibid.* § 792 These beds are represented in France by the lower members of the 'Terrain turonien', which exhibit nearly the same peculiarities as in England, though to a somewhat greater extent.] **1885** Geikie *Text Bk. Geol.* vi. ii. iii. § 2 (ed. 2) 820 The Cretaceous system of Europe has been subdivided as follows:—Upper.. Danian, Senonian, Turonian, Cenomanian, Gault. Lower.. Neocomian.

† **Turow**, ? var. of *thorow*, Through *sb.*[1] 2.

**1533** in Weaver *Wells Wills* (1890) 139 To be buryd in holy turow.

**Turpel, -pele, -pell**, var. Tirpeil *Obs.*

**Turpentine** (tǭ·ɹpĕntəin), *sb.* Forms: *α.* 5–6 **terebentine, -yne** (see also Terebinthine); *β.* 4–5 **terb-,** 5 **turbentyne**; *γ.* 5–6 **terpentin, turpentyne,** 6 **-tyn,** 7 **terpentine,** 6– **turpentine**; *δ.* 5 **turmyntyne,** 6 **termenteyne.** [In 14–15th c. *terebentyne, terbentyne*, a. OF. *tere-, terbentine*, ad. L. *terebentina* or *terebinthina* (*rēsīna*): see Terebinthina, -ine. Already *a* 1400, OF. had *tourbentine* (in R. Estienne 1550, *turbentine*); so Eng. *turbentyn* and *turpentine.* The 15–16th c. variant *termenteyne* curiously approaches the earlier Gr. τερμινθίνη (ῥητίνη) terebinthine resin, turpentine.]

**1.** A term applied originally (as in Gr. and Lat.) to the semifluid resin of the terebinth tree, *Pistacia Terebinthus* (Chian or Cyprian turpentine); now chiefly to the various oleoresins which exude from coniferous trees, consisting of more or less viscid solutions of resin in a volatile oil.

*α.* [**1398** Trevisa *Barth. De P. R.* xvii. clxiv. (Bodl. MS.) lf. 232/1 Therebintus..is a tre þat sweteþ rosine..and þe rosine þereof hatte Therebentina.] *c* **1425** tr. *Arderne's Treat. Fistula* 31 Putte to of terebentyne als moche as sufficeþ.. moue it strongly wiþ a spature vnto þat þe terebentyne be dronken in. **1541** R. Copland *Guydon's Formul.* X j b, Fomentacyon with oyle and terebentyne medled & warmed. **1597** A. M. tr. *Guillemeau's Fr. Chirurg.* 42 b/2 Made of Oyle of Egges and of Venetiane Terebentine.

*β.* **1322** in *Wardr. Acc. 16 Edw. II* 23/20 Terbentyn 7[d] þe lb. *c* **1400** Maundev. (1839) v. 51 A gome, þat men clepen Turbentyne. *c* **1425** tr. *Arderne's Treat. Fistula* 32 Terbentyne. **1460–70** *Bk. Quintessence* ii. 25 Wiþ frank-encense, mirre, and rosyn, terbentyn and rewe.

*γ.* *c* **1400** Maundev. (Roxb.) vii. 26 A maner of gumme, þat es called Turpentyne. **1576** Baker *Jewell of Health* 128 Turpentine, which is a lycour dystilled and gotten of the Fyrre tree. **1580** Hollyband *Treas. Fr. Tong, Térébinthine*, turpentyne. **1601** Holland *Pliny* xv. xii. I. 465 In Syria they use to plucke the barke from the Terebinth, yea, and they pill the boughs and roots too for Terpentine. **1673** Grew *Anat. Trunks* i. ii. § 18 Out of these Vessels all the clear Turpentine, that drops from the Tree, doth issue. **1718** Quincy *Compl. Disp.* 125 Common Turpentine..is procured from the Larch-Tree. **1813** Sir H. Davy *Agric. Chem.* iii. (1814) 97 When a portion of the bark is removed from a fir tree in Spring a matter exudes which is called turpentine. **1875** H. C. Wood *Therap.* (1879) 131 Turpentine is remarkable for having the property of absorbing oxygen and converting it into ozone.

*δ.* **1448–9** in Willis & Clark *Cambridge* (1886) I. 403, j lb et di. de Turmyntyne. **1502** Arnolde *Chron.* 35/2 Kark of termenteyne, xij d.

**b.** With qualification, indicating different varieties. See quot. 1831.

**1577** Frampton *Joyful News* 45 Adde therto three Ounces of Venise Turpentine. **1634** Peacham *Gentl. Exerc.* i. xxvii. 98 Temper it with Spanish Turpentine. **1728** Chambers *Cycl.* s.v. [Various kinds described.] **1744** Berkeley *Siris* § 20 The Strasburgh turpentine..is procured from the knots of the silver fir. *Ibid.*, Venice turpentine, which is got by piercing the larch tree. **1831** J. Davies *Manual Mat. Med.* 191 The principal kinds of turpentine are—the American Turpentine, furnished abundantly by the *Pinus palustris*, Lin., *P. australis*, Michaux, a tree growing principally in the southern states; the Common Turpentine, *Terebinthina communis*, obtained from the *Pinus sylvestris* and *P. rubra*, Lin.;..the Bordeaux Turpentine, *Terebinthina picea*, from the *P. maritima*, Lin., Bordeaux pine; the Strasbourg Turpentine, *Terebinthina abietina*, from the *P. picea*,..silver fir tree; the Venice Turpentine, *Terebinthina laricea*, from.. *P. larix*, Lin., white larch; and..Canada or Fir Balsam, *Terebinthina canadensis*,..furnished by the *P. balsamea*, American silver fir. *c* **1865** Letheby in *Circ. Sc.* I. 106/1 The oleo-resin is imported into this country under the names of common turpentine, Bordeaux t..., Strasburg t..., and Venice t.

**c.** *pl.* Varieties of turpentine.

**1605** Timme *Quersit.* iii. 184 After one manner, hony,.. after another, turpentines and gummes (as mastic, euphorb[i]um, styrax, and such like)..are to be distilled. **1718** Quincy *Compl. Disp.* 7 Of Turpentines, Gums, and all of that Tribe. **1843** *Penny Cycl.* XXV. 432/1 As turpentines have a very disagreeable taste, it is customary to form them into pills or boluses. **1874** Garrod & Baxter *Mat. Med.* (1880) 366 Canada balsam resembles the other turpentines in its action, but it is not often given as a medicine.

**d.** = *Oil of turpentine*: see 3. *To talk turpentine* (colloq.), to discuss painting.

**1876** Bristowe *The. & Pract. Med.* (1878) 607 Among the remedies..recommended [for scurvy] are perchloride of iron, acetate of lead, arsenic, digitalis, turpentine. **1891** Kipling *Light that Failed* vii. 118, I was told that all the world was interested in my work, and everybody at Kami's talked turpentine.

**2.** † **a.** The fruit of the terebinth tree. *Obs.* **b.** A terebinth tree; = Terebinthine B. 1, Turpentine tree 1. Also, any tree that yields turpentine, as the larch.

**1562** Turner *Herbal* ii. 115 The fruite [of Sumach] is lyke vnto small clusters of grapes of the bignes of a turpentine. **1577** B. Googe *Heresbach's Husb.* (1586) 72 b, The cherie refuseth not the companie of the Peach, nor the Turpentine, nor they his. **1601** Chester *Love's Mart.* (N. Shaks. Soc.) 96 The Turpentine that sweet iuyce doth deplore. **1615** G. Sandys *Trav.* 90 Cypresse trees and Turpentine, with divers others. **1885** 'Wanderer' *Beauteous Terrorist* 29 There 'mid giant turpentines Groups of climbing, clustering vines. **1898** Morris *Austral Eng.*, *Turpentine, Brush*, name given to two trees—*Metrosideros leptopetala*,.. and *Rhodamnia trinervia*,.. both N. O. *Myrtaceæ*.

**3. Oil of turpentine** (also vulgarly known as *spirit of t.*), a volatile oil, contained in the wood, bark, leaves, and other parts of coniferous trees, and usually prepared by distilling crude turpentine. There are many varieties according to the source, which, though all having the same formula, $C_{10}H_{16}$, vary in their physical and, more especially, their optical properties.

**1597** A. M. tr. *Guillemeau's Fr. Chirurg.* 30/2 Hott oyle of Terpentin. **1660** Boyle *New Exp. Phys. Mech.* xxiv. 188 Common Oyl or Spirit (for in the Shops..the same Liquor is promiscuously call'd by either name) of Turpentine. **1728** Chambers *Cycl.* s.v. *Turpentine*, What is commonly sold under the name of Oil of Turpentine, or Etherial Oil, is only a Distillation of the Rosin called Galipot, fresh from the Tree. **1791** Hamilton tr. *Berthollet's Dyeing* I. i. i. i. 6 The oil of turpentine..has a considerable refracting power. **1859** Gullick & Timbs *Paint.* 208 The rectified oil, improperly called Spirit of turpentine, is now most commonly employed. Its great use among house painters, under the cant name of 'turps', is to thin and assist the drying of oil paints. **1875** H. C. Wood *Therap.* (1879) 501 Oil of turpentine is never employed to increase the flow of urine.

**4.** *attrib.* and *Comb.*, as *turpentine ball*, *business*, *clyster*, *distiller*, *epithem*, *fomentation*, *liniment*, *odour*, *pill*, *smell*, *stupe*, *varnish*; 'pertaining to the production of turpentine or the cultivation of turpentine trees', as *turpentine camp*, *district*, *farm*, *farmer*, *orchard*, *region*, *wood*; instrumental, as *turpentine-anointed*, *-filled* adjs.; **turpentine bucket**: see quot.; **turpentine camphor**, a name sometimes given to the solid mono-hydrochlorate, sometimes to the solid hydrates of turpentine oil; **turpentine gall-nut**, an excrescence formed by the puncture of an insect on the branches of the terebinth-tree; **turpentine gum**, American Thus (*sb.*) (*Cent. Dict. Supp.* 1909); **turpentine hack**, a tool for hacking the bark of pine trees, to cause the turpentine to exude (Knight *Dict. Mech.* 1877); **turpentine moth**, a leaf-roller moth of the genus *Retinia*, of which the larvæ bore into the twigs of conifers (*Cent. Dict.* 1891); **turpentine oil** = *oil of turpentine*; **turpentine ointment**, an ointment of which turpentine oil is a principal ingredient (*ibid.*); † **turpentine rod**, a rod of a terebinth tree; **turpentine shrub**, a name of the Prairie Burdock, *Silphium terebinthinaceum*, a tall herbaceous plant with bright yellow flowers, a native of North America cultivated in European gardens since 1765 (*Cassell's Encycl. Dict.* 1888); **Turpentine State** (U.S.): see quot.; **turpentine still**, an apparatus for distilling turpentine from pine wood or spirit from turpentine (Knight *Dict. Mech.* 1877); **turpentine vessel**, in a coniferous tree, one of the tubes formed in the interstices of tissue, into which turpentine or like secretion naturally drains during the growth of the plant; **turpentine weed** = *turpentine shrub*. See also Turpentine tree.

**1861** Knight *Pop. Hist. Eng.* VII. xvii. 309 Robespierre ..sets fire to the *turpentine-anointed images. **1844** A. Page *Suppl. to Kirby's Suffolk Trav.* 141 A *turpentine ball.. which they set on fire. **1877** Knight *Dict. Mech.*, **Turpentine-bucket*, a cup or vessel to catch crude turpentine as it exudes from the tree. **1856** Olmsted *Slave States* 338 There are very large forests of [*Pinus Palustris*] in North and South Carolina, Georgia, and Alabama; and the *turpentine business is carried on..in all these States. **1901** *Westm. Gaz.* 16 Mar. 4/1 A *turpentine camp in Baldwin County, Alabama. **1857** Miller *Elem. Chem.* III. 452 *Turpentine camphor..($C_{20}H_{16}$, 4 HO). **1694** Salmon *Bate's Dispens.* iii. viii. (1713) 708/2 *Enema Terebinthinatum*, A *Turpentine Clyster. **1858** Simmonds *Dict. Trade*, **Turpentine and Tar Distiller*, a refiner of these substances. **1901** *Westm. Gaz.* 4 May 5/2 The *turpentine district along the St. John's River has been completely wiped out. **1843** R. J. Graves *Syst. Clin. Med.* x. 107 *note*,

A warm *turpentine epithem should be placed upon this region 1867 H. LATHAM *Black & White* 124 The paths which lead among the *turpentine farms. 1856 OLMSTED *Slave States* 350 The majority of what I have termed *turpentine-farmers—..the small proprietors of the long-leafed pine forest land. 1887 FENN *Dick o' the Fens* ii, They were the roots of *turpentine-filled pines. 1879 *St. George's Hosp. Rep.* IX. 319 Great tenderness over the lower half of the abdomen. *Turpentine fomentations were applied. 1860 MAYNE *Expos. Lex.*, **Turpentine Liniment*,..a preparation ..of yellow basilicon ointment diluted with turpentine. 1830 LINDLEY *Nat. Syst. Bot.* 127 A copious flow of limpid oil of a pungent *turpentine odour. 1868 WATTS *Dict. Chem.* V. 920 The diversities of character exhibited by *turpentine-oils..relate chiefly to the specific gravity, boiling-point, and optical rotatory power. 1884 C. S. SARGENT *Rep. Forests N. Amer.* 518 Their owners oftener .. employing them [negroes in N. Carolina] in *turpentine orchards than in the cotton-fields. 1622 DEKKER & MASSINGER *Virgin Mart.* III. Wks. 1873 IV. 52 One gave me *turpentine pils. 1856 OLMSTED *Slave States* 325, I was now..in the *Turpentine region of North Carolina. 1632 LITHGOW *Trav.* (1906) 230 A *Turpentine rod brought from Jordan and given to King James. 1887 MOLONEY *Forestry W. Afr.* 372 The plant has a strong *turpentine smell. 1859 BARTLETT *Dict. Amer.*, **Turpentine State*, the State of North Carolina, so called from the quantity of turpentine obtained from its pine forests. 1877 ROBERTS *Handbk. Med.* (ed. 3) I. 130 Occasionally *turpentine-stupes or sinapisms are needed in order to give relief. 1815 J. SMITH *Panorama Sc. & Art* II. 791 It dries as well as any other *turpentine-varnish, and when dry it appears to be as durable as any other solution of copal. 1868 WATTS *Dict. Chem.* V. 925 *Turpentine-varnishes*, solutions of resins in oil of turpentine. 1673-4 GREW *Anat. Trunks* I. ii. § 20 The..*Turpentine-Vessels of Pine are likewise remarkably bigger..than the Milk-Vessels themselves. 1861 BENTLEY *Man. Bot.* 55 In the Coniferæ they.. have..been termed turpentine vessels. 1866 *Treas. Bot.* 1059/1 The plant [*Silphium laciniatum*] is also known as the..*Turpentine-weed. 1885 F. WHYMPER in *Girl's Own Paper* Jan. 171/1 The compass plant—..known, also, as the ..turpentine weed—is a vigorous perennial. 1892 *Pall Mall G.* 15 Nov. 2/3 The Florida convicts..were mostly put to work in the *turpentine woods.

**Tu·rpentine**, *v.* [f. prec. sb.] *trans.* To treat, rub, or smear with turpentine or turpentine oil. Hence **Tu·rpentined** *ppl. a.* So **Tu·rpentining** *vbl. sb.*, the process of obtaining crude turpentine from living pine-trees (*Cent. Dict. Supp.* 1909).

1759 *N. Jersey Archives* XX. 374 Stolen..A Battoe.. painted with Spanish Brown in the Inside, and the Outsides turpentined. 1789 WOLCOTT (P. Pindar) *Subj. for Painters* 110 Fir'd like turpentin'd poor roasting rats. 1836 DICKENS *Sk. Boz, Old Lady*, The table-covers are never taken off, except when the leaves are turpentined and bees'-waxed. 1893 *Spons' Mechanics' Own Bk.* (ed. 4) 433 Put in others with the second marbling colour, also on a turpentined feather.

**Tu·rpentine tree.**

**1.** *orig.* The Terebinth, *Pistacia Terebinthus* (N. O. *Anacardiaceæ*), the source of Chian or Cyprian turpentine.

1562 TURNER *Herbal* II. 29 Amongest other rosynes, it of ye turpentinetre is best. *Ibid.* 151, I call it Turpentine tre, because Turpentine cometh oute of it. 1615 G. SANDYS *Trav.* 176 Some two miles from the City..there groweth a Turpentine-tree yet flourishing. 1726 LEONI *Alberti's Archit.* II. 6/2 The Turpentine-tree near Hebron, which was reported to have stood from the creation of the world to the days of Josephus. 1728 BRADLEY *Dict. Bot.* s.v. *Terebinthus*, The Broader-leav'd Turpentine-Tree. *Ibid.*, The Narrow-leav'd Turpentine-Tree. 1869 H. SNOW *Theocritus, Epigr.* i. Notes (1873) 214 The terebinth or turpentine-tree (*Pistachia Terebinthus*), is often mentioned in the Bible, under the names of oak or terebinth.

**2.** Any tree yielding turpentine, esp. species of pine and fir, as the Larch, *Abies Larix*, which yields Venice turpentine; *Bursera gummifera* (N. O. *Amyridaceæ*), of the West Indies; in Australia, species of *Eucalyptus*, *Syncarpia*, and *Tristania*; in New Zealand, the Tarata (Morris).

1726 LEONI *Alberti's Archit.* I. 26/2, I do not know any Wood that is to be preferr'd to the Larch, or Turpentine Tree. 1818 OXLEY *Jrnls. Two Exped. N. S. Wales* (1820) 331 The timber was chiefly..stringy bark, turpentine tree, and forest oak. 1866 *Treas. Bot.*, Turpentine-tree, *Pistacia Terebinthus*; also *Bursera gummifera*. —, Australian, *Tristania albicans*. 1889 J. H. MAIDEN *Usef. Native Plants Australia* 493 *Eucalyptus microcorys*..North of Port Jackson it bears the name of 'Turpentine Tree', and 'Forest Mahogany'. *Ibid.* 523 *Eucalyptus Stuartiana*.. frequently called 'Turpentine Tree', or 'Peppermint Tree'.

**Turpentinic** (-ti·nik), *a. Chem.* [f. TURPENTINE *sb.* + -IC.] In *turpentinic acid*, a synonym of TEREBIC *acid*.

1868 WATTS *Dict. Chem.* V. 724 Discovered by Bromeis, who called it turpentinic acid.

**Tu·rpentinous**, *a. rare.* [f. TURPENTINE *sb.* + -OUS.] Of the nature of turpentine.

1909 *Eng. Rev.* Jan. 311 Powder 'em and get a little tar and turpentinous smell in..woodpacking for hot baths.

**Tu·rpentiny**, *a.* [f. as prec. + -Y.] Containing turpentine; having the smell or other properties of turpentine; smeared with turpentine.

1735 *Dict. Polygraph.* I. Sij, The best wood for this purpose,..provided it be not turpentiny. 1866 *Treas. Bot.* 718/2 Manna of Briançon, a turpentiny saccharine exudation from the larch. 1894 DU MAURIER *Trilby* III. (1901) 44/2 Clasping his painty turpentiny hand. 1906 *Macm. Mag.* Sept. 809, I should have..got my fingers all sticky and turpentiney.

**Turpeth, turbith** (tɒ̄·ɹpeþ, -biþ). Forms: *α.* 5 **turbyte**, 5–8 **-bit**, 6 **torbith**, **turbythe**, *pl.* **-bithes**, 7–9 **turbeth**, 6– **turbith**; *β.* 7– **turpith**, **-peth**. [a. OF. *turbit*, *-ith*, *turpet* (F. *turbith*) or ad. med.L. *turbith(um*, *turpethum*, *turpetum*, ad. Pers. and Arab. تربد *turbid*, *-bed*, whence also Pg., Sp. *turbit*. *Turbith* was the preponderant Eng. form to the 18th c., till assimilated to med.L. *turpethum*.]

**1.** A cathartic drug prepared from the root of East Indian jalap, *Ipomœa Turpethum*, an Indian and Australian plant; also, the plant itself, or its root.

† *Garganic Turbith*: see quot. 1760.

*α.* *c* 1400 *Lanfranc's Cirurg.* 180 He mote ofte purge fleume with turbit. 1460–70 *Bk. Quintessence* 16 Þo laxatyues þat purgen flewme & viscous humouris, as a litil of euforbie, or turbit, or sambucy. 1545 *Rates of Custom-ho.* C vj b, Torbith the pounde, xij d. 1567 MAPLET *Gr. Forest* 63 Tvrbit whose Leafe is like the Laurell, groweth in Ægypt ..It is giuen to purge fleume. 1652 CULPEPPER *Eng. Physic.* (1809) 261 For choler, rhubarb; for phlegm, turbith; for watery humours, scammony. 1760 J. LEE *Introd. Bot.* App. 330 Garganic Turbith, *Thapsia*. *Ibid.*, Indian Turbith, or of the Shops, *Convolvulus*. 1785 MARTYN *Rousseau's Bot.* xvi. (1794) 185 This genus contains several remarkable plants; as..Turpethum or Turbith.

*β.* 1658 ROWLAND *Moufet's Theat. Ins.* 1119 The Turpeth drives them from their nests. 1758 J. S. *Le Dran's Observ. Surg.* (1771) A a iv b, Turpeth, Hermodactyles, Polypody of the Oak. 1905 H. D. ROLLESTON *Dis. Liver* 262 Turpeth, the Ipomœa turpethum of the Colonial and Indian Pharmacopœias, is recommended in 20 grain doses.

**b.** *Montpellier Turpeth*, common name for *Globularia alypum*, the decoction of the leaves of which acts as an active but gentle purgative.

1860 in MAYNE *Expos. Lex.*

**2.** *Turpeth* or *turbith mineral* (MINERAL *a.* 4): basic sulphate of mercury ($HgSO_4 . 2HgO$), obtained as a lemon-yellow powder from the normal sulphate by washing with hot water.

It has emetic, cathartic, and sternutatory properties, but is no longer used internally.

*α.* 1616 BULLOKAR *Eng. Expos.*, *Turbith minerall*, a certaine red powder..which is vsed against the French disease. 1669 W. SIMPSON *Hydrol. Chym.* 60 Dissolving quicksilver in oyl of vitriol, according to what is done in making turbith mineral. 1685 BOYLE *Enq. Notion Nat.* vi. 233 A patient, who..could not be brought to salivate, neither by the gentler ways, nor by turbith-mineral and other harsher medicines. 1758 REID tr. *Macquer's Chym.* I. 402 Wash this yellow matter in five or six warm waters, and it will be what is called in medicine Turbith mineral; that is, a combination of the Vitriolic Acid with Mercury, five or six grains whereof is a violent purgative, and also an emetick; qualities which it possesses in common with the vegetable Turbith, whose name it hath therefore taken. 1849 D. CAMPBELL *Inorg. Chem.* 236 This yellow powder is a subsulphate [of mercury] ($3HgO, SO_3$), and is known as turbeth mineral. 1874 GARROD & BAXTER *Mat. Med.* (1880) 110 The yellow subsulphate above mentioned, under the name of Turbith Mineral, has been employed as an errhine.

*β.* 1716 M. DAVIES *Athen. Brit.* II. 352 Turpith Mineral, made of Hydrargyry and Oyl of Vitriol. 1815 J. SMITH *Panorama Sc. & Art* II. 795 King's yellow, turpith mineral, and Dutch pink, all form very bright yellows. 1868 WATTS *Dict. Chem.* V. 925 *Turpeth* or *turbith mineral*, an old name for basic mercuric sulphate, $HgSO_4 . 2HgO$. 1899 *Allbutt's Syst. Med.* VIII. 516 Native mercurous sulphate (turpeth mineral) is much used in France.

**†3.** *ellipt.* = prec. sense. *Obs.*

*Black turpeth*: see quot. 1895.

*α.* 1658 PHILLIPS, *Turbith*,..a red Mineral, which being beaten to powder, is used in physick. 1675 *Phil. Trans.* X. 299 Mercury..having been..reduced into water, turbith and ashes. 1707 *Curios. in Husb. & Gard.* 325 Olaus..tormented some Quicksilver..into Water, Turbith and Ashes.

*β.* 1678 PHILLIPS (ed. 4), *Turpith*, a Chymical preparation of Mercury, and the Oyl of Vitriol, whereby the Mercury is precipitated into a sweetnesse. 1800 *Phil. Trans.* XC. 215 Not only the pure red oxide, but the red nitrous oxide, and turpeth, may be substituted. 1895 *Funk's Standard Dict.* s.v., *Black turpeth*, black mercurous acid: old name.

**4.** *attrib.*, as *t. plant*, *root*, *vomit.*

1773 T. PERCIVAL *Ess.* II. 163 The powerful effects of Turpeth vomits in white swellings of the joints. 1860 MAYNE *Expos. Lex.*, *Turbeth Plant*, common name for the *Convolvulus turpethum*. 1868 WATTS *Dict. Chem.* V. 925 *Turpeth* or *turbith root*.

**Turpethic** (tɒɹpe·þik), *a. Chem.* [f. mod.L. *turpeth-um* TURPETH + -IC.] Of or pertaining to turpeth or turbith; in *turpethic acid*, $C_{34}H_{60}O_{18}$, produced by the action of bases on turpethin. So **Turpethin** (tɒ̄·ɹpeþin), *Chem.* [see -IN [1]], a brownish-yellow purgative resin, $C_{34}H_{56}O_{16}$, obtained from turpeth- or turbith-root; **Turpetho·lic** *a.*, in *turpetholic acid*, $C_{16}H_{32}O_4$, a derivative of turpethin, crystallizing in a mass of slender microscopic needles having an irritant taste; hence **Turpe·tholate**, a salt of turpetholic acid.

1868 WATTS *Dict. Chem.* V. 926 When turpethin is dissolved in warm baryta-water, the baryta removed [etc.], turpethic acid remains as an amorphous yellowish mass. *Ibid.*, Under the influence of mineral acids, it [turpethin] is re-dissolved into glucose and turpetholic acid. *Ibid.*, Turpetholate of Sodium, $C_{16}H_{31}NaO_4$.

**Turpeyl**, var. TIRPEIL *Obs.*, fear.

**Turph, -y**, obs. ff. TURF, TURFY.

**Tu·rpid**, *a. rare.* [irreg. f. L. *turp-is* ugly, unsightly, foul, disgraceful + -ID, after *torpid*, etc.] Base, filthy, worthless. Hence **Tu·rpidly** *adv.*

1623 COCKERAM, *Turpid*, filthy. 1866 J. B. ROSE tr. *Virg. Georg.* II. 60 But fruit degenerates,—its flavour lost, The turpid grapes are left to birds or frost. 1867 — *Æneid* 44 Smitten with turpid fear. 1866 — tr. *Ovid's Fasti* VI. 623 The female crew..Turned turpidly and fled.

**† Tu·rpie**, *a. Obs. rare.* [f. L. *turpi-s* ugly, foul; in quot. after the L. phrase *turpe lucrum* (see FILTHY *a.* 4 b).] Filthy.

1632 NASHE *Quaternio* 90 How the nostrils savour nothing more than turpie lucre.

**Tu·rpify**, *v. rare.* [ad. L. *turpificāre* (recorded only in pa. pple. *turpificātus*) to make filthy, foul, or bad, f. L. *turpi-s* + *-ficāre*: see prec. and -FY.] *trans.* To make foul or filthy; to befoul, besmirch.

*a* 1586 SIDNEY *Wanstead Play* Wks. (1629) 620 O [that] a woman..should thus turpifie the reputation of my doctrine, with the superscription of a foole.

**† Turpin.** *Obs. rare.* A fanciful name for, or appellation of, the hare.

*a* 1325 *Names of Hare* in *Rel. Ant.* I. 133 He shal saien on oreisoun In þe worshipe of þe hare..The scotewine, the skikart, The turpin, the tirart.

**† Turpin**, obs. abbreviated f. TURPENTINE.

1688 R. HOLME *Armoury* II. 80/1 The Turpin, or Turpentine Tree [hath] the leaves smooth, four on a side.

**Turpinite** (tɒ̄·ɹpinəit). [a. F. *turpinite*, f. Turpin, name of the inventor + -ITE [1].] An explosive, used in making shells.

1895 *Daily Chron.* 6 Dec. 6/1 'Turpinite', a comprehensive word coined in honour of a string of episodes bearing upon the new methods of putting a stop to war by the prospective destruction of all cities.

**Turpith**: see TURPETH.

**Turpitude** (tɒ̄·ɹpitiud). Also 5 **turpytude.** [a. F. *turpitude* (*a* 1417 in Godef. *Compl.*), or directly ad. L. *turpitūdo*, f. *turpi-s* base: see -TUDE.]

**1.** Base or shameful character; baseness, vileness; depravity, wickedness.

1490 CAXTON *Eneydos* xxii. 83 In sygne of vengaunce of the dethe of hys fader, And turpytude dyshonest of clytemnestra his moder. 1589 PUTTENHAM *Eng. Poesie* III. xxiv. (Arb.) 295 All maner of conceites that stirre vp any vehement passion in a man, doo it by some turpitude or euill and vndecency that is in them. 1606 SHAKS. *Ant. & Cl.* IV. vi. 33 How would'st thou haue payed My better seruice, when my turpitude Thou dost so Crowne with Gold. 1659 HAMMOND *On Ps.* cxix. 137–8 Paraphr. 609 Those which have a natural turpitude and indispensable sinfulnesse in them! *a* 1711 KEN *Preparatives* Poet. Wks. 1721 III. 25 Some for their Turpitude had Shame, And Terrors of infernal Flame. 1794 LD. AUCKLAND *Corr.* (1862) III. 261 Indignation and horror at the infatuated turpitude of some of the allied powers. 1849 MACAULAY *Hist. Eng.* iii. I. 402 The artists corrupted the spectators, and the spectators the artists, till the turpitude of the drama became such as must astonish all who are not aware that extreme relaxation is the natural effect of extreme restraint. 1879 *Temple Bar Mag.* Oct. 172 A career great from the historical importance of the period.. but inglorious and almost without a parallel in recent times for moral turpitude and unscrupulous self-seeking.

**b.** With *a* and *pl.* An instance of this.

1597 J. PAYNE *Royal Exch.* 28 Every Christian ought.. to lament to se suche turpitudes. 1607 COKE *Charge at Norwich Assizes* 5 Partialitie in a Judge is a Turpitude, which doth soyle and stayne all the Actions done by him. 1810 BENTHAM *Packing* (1821) 71 A picture in which all deformities and turpitudes are plaistered over with the most brilliant colours. 1833 CHALMERS *Const. Man* (1835) I. iii. 157 Temptation to a turpitude or a crime. 1913 *19th Cent.* Aug. 393 The minor offences and turpitudes which are condemned in the court of conscience.

**† c.** Rendering L. *turpitudo* of the Vulgate: 'nakedness'; 'shame'. *Obs. rare.*

1570 FOXE *A. & M.* 157/2 The holy lawe of God forbiddeth to reueale the turpitude of thy blood or kyndred. *Ibid.*, Thou shalt not reueale the turpitude of thy father.

**† 2.** in *lit.* sense: Foulness, offensiveness, unsightliness. *Obs. rare.*

1684 tr. *Bonet's Merc. Compit.* XIX. 719 This Medicin helps notably any cutaneous turpitude whatsoever.

**Turple**, var. TORPLE.

**Turps** (tɒ̄ɹps). [Colloq. (workmen's or painters') abbreviation of TURPENTINE; the final *-s* appears to be collective.] Oil of turpentine.

1823 P. NICHOLSON *Pract. Build.* 411 Oil of Turpentine, or Turps, is made from the resin of that name, which is obtained from all larch and fir-trees. 1867 F. FRANCIS *Angling* xiv. (1880) 506 Cut up some white indiarubber..dissolve it in turps. 1894 *Brit. Jrnl. Photogr.* XLI. 5 Not soluble in either benzole, turps, or xylol.

**Turque**, obs. f. TURK. **Turquen**, var. TURKEN *v. Obs.* **Turques**, var. TURKIS *v. Obs.*

**† Turque·sque.** *Obs. rare.* [a. obs. F. *turquesque* (= It. *turchesco*) Turkish.] *pl.* ? Turkish cloths or carpets.

1594 BLUNDEVIL *Exerc.* V. IV. (1597) 259 b, The chiefe marchandizes that come from this countrie [Turkey] to other Prouinces are..Veluets, Damaske, Grograins, Turquesques and Wood.

**† Turquet** [1]. *Obs. rare*$^{-1}$. [app. f. *Turque*, TURK + -ET; cf. F. *turquet* 'petit chien, d'origine turque, à nez camus et à poil ras' (16–17th c. in Hatz.-Darm.).] But *Turquets* may be a misprint for *Turques*.] A player dressed up to resemble a Turk.

1625 BACON *Ess.*, *Masques* (Arb.) 540 Anti-masques..haue been commonly of Fooles, Satyres, Baboones, Wilde-Men, Antiques, Beasts, Sprites, Witches, Ethiopes, Pigmies, Turquets,..and the like.

**† Turquet** [2]. *Obs. rare*$^{-1}$. [a. F. *turquet*, now = maize, but given by Cotgr. as a var. of *turguet* spelt.] ? Spelt.

The passage is translated from a French source, and the rendering *starch-corn* is perh. derived from Cotgrave.

1725 *Family Dict.* II. s.v. *Stone*, A Remedy for the Stone and Gravel is, to take the Herb Turquet or Storch-Corn [*sic*], dry it and reduce it to Powder.

† **Turquin.** *Obs. rare.* [a. F. *turquin* (= Sp. and Pg. *turqui*), ad. It. *turchino* (med.L. *turchīnus*) blue, f. *Turco* Turk.

Different reasons are assigned for the use of the adj. to designate 'blue'. In sense 1 the meaning of 'Turkish' may be preserved.]

**1.** A dark-green pumpkin.

After obs. F. *pompon Turquin* (Cotgr.).

1616 SURFL. & MARKH. *Country Farme* 193 Some of them are called Turquins, as those which haue a verie greene colour, and drawing somewhat toward a blacke.

**2.** A bluish-grey or slate-coloured marble.

1811 PINKERTON *Petralogy* I. 412 A singular marble is still known to be found at Sitifi, in the north of Africa, being the proper turquin, because, like the turquois, it is supposed to be brought from a country subject to the Turks. It is of a bluish grey, or slate colour, with spots of siderite or hornblende.

**Turquoise** (tǝ̄·ɹkoi·z, tǝ̄·ɹkoiz, *arch.* tǝ̄ɹkī·z, tǝ̄·ɹkiz), *sb.* (*a.*) Forms: see below. [In 15–16th c. *turkeis*, *-keys*, a. OF. *turqueise*, *-quaise*, later *turquoise*, fem. of *turqueis*, *-quais*, *turquois* adj. Turkish, in full *pierre turquoise*, i.e. 'Turkish stone' (cf. Marco Polo c. xxxiv 'pierres qui s'appellent *turquesses*') = Pr., Sp. *turquesa*, Pg. *turqueza*, It. *turchese*, med.L. (*lapis*) *turchēsius* or *turkēsius*; = MDu. *turcoys*, *turckois*, Du. *turkoois*, MHG. *turkîs*, *-koys*, etc., mod.Ger. *türkis*, *türkiss*, Da. *turkis*, *tyrkis*, Sw. *turkos*. So named as coming from Turkestan, where first found, or through the Turkish dominions: cf. also med.L. *turchīnus*, It. *turchino*, F. *turquin* blue, azure. The earliest Eng. form was the OF. and AF. *turkeis*; this by vowel-progression became *turkē·se*, *-ī·se*, and by stress-shift, as in other Teutonic languages, *tu·rkes*, *-as*, *-is*; but these forms began before 1600 to be displaced by adoption of the French spelling *turquoise*, *turkois*. Ben Jonson stresses *tu·rkise*, Dr. Johnson *tu·rkois*, *-koise*, Milton and Tennyson *tu·rkis*. Walker and Smart (1846) pronounce *turkī·z*, Cent. Dict. and Funk's Stand. *tǝrkoi·z*, *tǝrkī·z*, Webster 1911 *turkoi·z* or *tu·rkwoiz*.]

**I. 1.** A precious stone found in Persia (*the true* or *oriental turquoise*), much prized as a gem, of a sky-blue to apple-green colour, almost opaque or sometimes translucent, consisting of hydrous phosphate of aluminium.

*α.* 4–7 **turkeis**, 5–7 **turkeys**, 6 **turkeies**, **turquays**, **turkese**, **turkies**, 7 **turcais**, **torqueis**, **turquies**, **-quize**, **turchis**; 6– **turkis**, 7– **turkise** (both now *archaic*).

1398 TREVISA *Barth. De P. R.* XVI. xcvi. (Bodl. MS.) lf. 183 b/2 De Turtogis. Turtogis that hatte Turkeis also is a ȝelow white stone and haþ þat name of the contrey of Turkeis. Þis stone kepeþ and saueþ þe siȝt and bredeþ gladnes and comforte. 1463 in *Bury Wills* (Camden) 36, I beqwethe to the said Dame Margarete a doubyl ryng departyd of gold with a ruby and a turkeys. 1503 HAWES *Examp. Virt.* iv. 5 Of vertuous turkeys there was a cheyr. *c* 1530 *Crt. of Love* xii, There lacked than, nor emerald so grene, Balais, Turkeis, ne thing to my devise. 1545 *Test. Ebor.* (Surtees) VI. 226 A rynge of golde with a turquays. 1596 SHAKS. *Merch. V.* III. i. 126 Out vpon her,..it was my Turkies, I had it of Leah when I was a Batcheler. 1599 HAKLUYT *Voy.* II. I. 306 Orient perles & great Turkeses. 1603 B. JONSON *Sejanus* I. i, True as turkise in the deare lords ring. 1608 WILLET *Hexapla Exod.* 642 It is more like to be the turkeis..the turcais is of a blewish metalline colour. 1616 BULLOKAR *Eng. Expos.*, *Turkise*, a precious stone of a silke blew colour. 1634 MILTON *Comus* 894 The azurn sheen Of Turkis blew and Emrauld green. 1648 GAGE *West Ind.* 71 Bracelets of Turkises and of gold likewise. 1688 R. HOLME *Armoury* II. 40/2 The Turches or Turky stone..some call it Eranus, others Turcois or Torqueis. 1694 STRYPE *Abp. Cranmer* III. i. 308 They seized..a good Turkeys and a Diamond. 1857 TENNYSON *Geraint & Enid* 661 The turf was rich in plots that look'd Each like a garnet or a turkis in it. 1877 W. JONES *Finger-ring* 158 The turquoise, turkise, or turkey-stone having..been supposed to possess talismanic properties. *a* 1913 S. VINES *Hotel* 16 in *Oxford Poetry* 154 Sapphires and amethysts and wicked Turkises.

*β.* 5–6 **turkes**, 5–7 **turques**, (5 **torcas**, 5–6 *Sc.* **turcas**, 6 **turkas**, **torchas**, **turcasse**, **tourques**, **turquez**, **toorkes**, **turquesse**, **turkesse**), 6–7 **turches**.

1478 *Croscombe Churchw. Acc.* (Som. Rec. Soc.) 6 A ryng gold with a torcas. 1483 *Acc. Ld. High Treas. Scot.* I. 81 Item, a ryng with a turcas. 1511–12 *Ibid.* IV. 331 Ane ruby, ane turkas. 1501 *Bury Wills* (Camden) 91 A ryng of gold wt a toorkes set in. *a* 1512 FABYAN *Will* in *Chron.* Pref. 7 A ryng of gold, sett wt a turques, a dyamaunt, and a ruby. 1518 *Test. Ebor.* (Surtees) V. 8 A rynge of golde with a stone in hit callede a turkes. 1527 *Ibid.* 244 Unum annulum cum le torchas. 1530 PALSGR. 282/1 Tourques a precious stone, *tourquois*. 1551 T. WILSON *Logike* (1580) 4 *Lapis*, a stone, comprehendeth in it self, a Saphire, a Rubbie, a Christall, a Turkas. 1553 — *Rhet.* 209 No Diamonde, no Saphire, no Rubie, no Christall: no Turcasse, no Emerode. 1555 EDEN *Decades* 235 Turquesses are founde in Exer a place of Siech Ismael. 1567 MAPLET *Gr. Forest* 23 The Turches or Turcois, is of the common sort called Eranus...It is called a Turches for that it is onely found in Turkland or amongst the Turkes. 1599 *Warn. Faire Wom.* I. 217 You wear a pretty turkesse there, methinks. 1601 CHESTER *Love's Mart.* (N. Shaks. Soc.) 107 The Turches being worne in a Ring. 1653 GREAVES *Seraglio* 15 A Basen and Ewer of massive gold, set with Rubies and Turkesses. 1688 [see *α*].

*γ.* 6 **turkoise**, 6–7 **turquoys**, **turcoyse**, **turquoies**, 6–8 **turcois**, 7–8 **turcoise**, (**turchois**), 7–9 **turkois**, (8 **torquois**, **turkquoise**, 9 **tourquois**), 6– **turquoise**, **-ois**.

1567 Turcois [see *β*]. 1601 HOLLAND *Pliny* XXXVII. viii. II. 619 The best Turquois is that which approcheth nearest to the grasse green of an Emeraud. 1607 Turchois, 1631 Turcois [see b]. 1646 SIR T. BROWNE *Pseud. Ep.* II. i. (1686) 42 Crystall..will receive impression from Steel, in a manner like the Turchois. *a* 1658 CLEVELAND *Common Place* Wks. (1677) 166 The Compassionate Turcoise confesseth the Sickness of his Wearer by changing colour. 1668 WILKINS *Real Char.* II. iii. 63 Turkois. 1676 *Phil. Trans.* XI. 755 Turkoises are no where found but in Persia. 1679 *Lond. Gaz.* No. 1418/4 Lost..a Ring with a large Turquoies of the Old Rock, very good colour. 1747 MORTIMER in *Phil. Trans.* XLIV. 429 This Stone has received its..Name of Turchesia, and Turquoise, from its being most commonly brought from Turky. 1859 GEO. ELIOT *A. Bede* v, The small brown hand ..is laden with pearls, diamonds, and turquoises.

**b.** In *collect. sing.*, esp. as a substance.

1607 *Lingua* IV. iv, Orient Pearles, and sparkling Diamonds: Beset at the end with Emeraulds and Turchois. 1631 WIDDOWES *Nat. Philos.* 28 Turcois is darke, of a skie colour, and greenish. 1836 T. THOMSON *Min., Geol.* etc. I. 230 Tourquois seems to have been known to the ancients. 1857 WOOD *Comm. Objects Sea Shore* 64 They..are blue and bright as turquoise, to which jewel they bear some resemblance. 1882 'OUIDA' *Maremma* I. 62 The Ligurian sea, blue as turquoise. 1884 BROWNING *Ferishtah*, *Melon-seller* 35 Ferishtah..passed..To Nishapur, that Elburz looks above—Where they dig turquoise.

**2.** More fully **turquoise stone**: see also TURKEY STONE, *Turkish stone* (TURKISH *a.* 2 b). Now *rare*.

1556 *N. C. Wills* (Surtees 1908) 240 One ring of golde with a turkeys stone in it. 1600 HAKLUYT *Voy.* (1810) III. 440 In the gates..there are many Turques-stones. *c* 1610 in *Heriot's Mem.* App. VII. (1822) 215 A ring sett with 5 little Turkis stones. 1673 RAY *Journ. Low C.*, *Florence* 333 An entire image made of one Turchois stone. 1796 MORSE *Amer. Geog.* II. 568 Persia contains mines of..above all, turquoise stones. 1831 LD. HOUGHTON *Mem. Many Scenes* (1844) 75 This heaven..With richer, but less brilliant, hue, Built up of turkis-stone.

**3.** As name for a colour (short for *turquoise blue*): see 6 b.

1853 KANE *Grinnell Exp.* viii. (1856) 61 The blue and white were mixed in a pale turkois. 1860 W. G. CLARK in *Vac. Tour.* 42 A cave with a floor of liquid turquoise. 1876 MISS BROUGHTON *Joan* I. xix, Looking out through the open windows at the absolute turquoise of the heavens. 1878 MISS J. J. YOUNG *Ceram. Art* (1879) 41 The Chinese value one piece..for the depth of its turquoise. 1881 *Porcelain Works, Worcester* 35 To the admirers of colour, the Persian turquoise, Imperial yellow,..and other enamels present an interesting series.

**4.** Lapidaries' name for odontolite: see quot. 1839; also called *bone-turquoise* and *occidental turquoise*.

1796 KIRWAN *Elem. Min.* (ed. 2) II. 154 Turquoise is ivory tinged by the blue Calx of Copper. 1819 Odontolite Turquoise [see *odontolite* (ODONTO-)]. 1839 URE *Dict. Arts*, etc. 744 A totally different kind of turquois, called *bone turquois*, which seems to be phosphate of lime coloured with oxide of copper. 1868 DANA *Min.* (ed. 5) 580 *Turquoise de vieille roche* (in distinction from Odontolite, or *T. de nouvelle roche*, called also Occidental Turquois).

**b.** (See quot.)

1840 *Penny Cycl.* XVIII. 472/2 s.v. *Pottery*, These mixtures give a fine white body for ornaments...A body called turquoise has been manufactured to a great extent for a few years past...When glazed, it has the peculiar milky tint of the gem after which it has been named.

**II.** *attrib.* and *Comb.*

**5. a.** Simple attrib. 'of turquoise': as *turquoise bead*, *colour*, *enamel*, *gem*, *mine*, *miner*, *treasure*, *work*, *working*.

1662 MERRETT tr. *Neri's Art of Glass* 56 This [sea] salt so calcin'd, keep to make a Blew or Turcois colour. 1753 *Chambers' Cycl.* App. s.v. *Turcois*, The pale blue of the natural turcois gem. *Ibid.*, Turcois enamel. 1765 *Phil. Trans.* LV. 21 Copper..gives the torquois colour to white glass. 1826 KIRBY & SP. *Entomol.* III. xxx. 177 Three blue tubercles, like..little turquois beads. 1849 M. ARNOLD *Strayed Reveller* 195 Their wealth..Of gold and ivory, Of turquoise-earth and amethyst. 1876 BIRCH *Rede Lect. Egypt* 20 Magarah and its turquoise treasures had been lost. 1877 W. R. COOPER *Egypt. Obelisks* iv. (1878) 16 The copper and turquoise miners of the Wady Magari. 1882 *Rep. to Ho. Repr. Prec. Met. U. S.* 323 Many ancient turquois workings are found in the neighborhood. 1896 GEORG. M. STISTED *True Life of Sir R. F. Burton* xv. 377 The Land of Midian is still wealthy; turquoise mines exist. 1906 *Outlook* 30 June 881/2 [In common, doubtless, with the Sinai Bedawys, the Egyptians worshipped the Goddess of the Turquoise. *Ibid.*] That..the worship of the Turquoise goddess [was] non-Egyptian in nature. 1908 *Ch. Times* 20 Mar. 392/2 Turquoise and Indian Work for..Zenana Mission.

**b.** In sense 'set or adorned with a turquoise or turquoises, or composed of turquoises', as *turquoise ear-ring*, *locket*, *ring*.

1808 SCOTT *Marm.* v. x, The fair Queen of France Sent him a Turquois ring. 1868 LD. HOUGHTON *Select. fr. Wks.* 60 And turkis-lockets, that no churl Hath fashioned out mechanic-wise. 1896 GEORG. M. STISTED *True Life Sir R. F. Burton* vii. 164 A red sausage-shaped cushion strung with turquoise rings. 1901 *Westm. Gaz.* 28 Dec. 1/3 The girl with turquoise eyes and turquoise earrings.

**c.** Instrumental, similative, etc., as *turquoise-coloured*, *-encrusted*, *-hued*, *-like*, *-studded*, *-tinted* adjs.; **turquoise-berry**, a liliaceous Tasmanian herb, *Drymophila cyanocarpa*, bearing white flowers and blue pendulous berries.

1864 *Daily Tel.* 26 Sept., The turquoise-like water, too, sparkled in the light of the declining day. 1881 *Athenæum* 4 June 754 A pure turquoise-coloured sky. 1893 J. ASHBY-STERRY *Naughty Girl* xii, A coquettish turquoise-hued teagown. 1898 MORRIS *Austral Eng.* 426/2 *Solomon's Seal*, ..the Tasmanian name for *Drymophila cyanocarpa*,..also called Turquoise Berry. 1899 *Edin. Rev.* Jan. 35 The turquoise-tinted feathers of the Kingfisher. 1906 *Daily Chron.* 23 Mar. 8/1 Her strings of Orient pearls, her turquoise-encrusted heart-lockets. 1906 *Westm. Gaz.* 24 Nov. 7/2 A gossamer turquoise-coloured scarf, lightly thrown across her shoulders. 1909 *Daily Chron.* 15 July 4/5 Neck ornament in the form of a turquoise studded serpent.

**6.** As *adj.* Of the colour of the turquoise; turquoise-blue.

1573 G. HARVEY *Letter-bk.* (Camden) 125 An alabaster neck, a turcois eie. 1844 LADY G. FULLERTON *Ellen Middleton* (1854) II. xiv. 149 The cordon bleu [bird], with his turquoise breast. 1882 MRS. B. M. CROKER *Proper Pride* xi, Rising here and there against the turquoise sky were palms. 1891 E. ROPER *By Track & Trail* x. 138 Pools of lovely turquoise water. 1901 [see 5 b]. 1909 LE QUEUX *House of Shadows* xviii, Her pretty gown of turquoise chiffon.

**b.** With adj. or sb. of colour.

1799 G. SMITH *Laboratory* I. 122 A Turcoise blue enamel. 1828 STARK *Elem. Nat. Hist.* I. 279 Wings with from 8 to 10 spots of turquoise blue, bordered with orange. 1863 MISS BRADDON *Eleanor's Vict.* III. viii. 108 The turquoise-blue eyes shone with a feverish light. 1877 BLACK *Green Past.* xii, Beds of turquoise-blue forget-me-nots. 1883 *Truth* 31 May 769/2 A train and corsage of turquoise blue satin. 1886 KIPLING *Departm. Ditties*, *Delilah* viii, The wasteful sunset faded out in turkis-green and gold. 1890 *Daily News* 15 July 5/6 One of the..ladies who wore the beautiful turquoise blue that has been a specialty of this season.

**Turr**, *v. Obs.* or *dial.* Also 5 **turre**. [Origin unascertained.] *intr.* and *trans.* To butt, as a ram; to push *down* by butting. Hence **Turr** *sb. dial.*

*a* 1400–50 *Alexander* 5567 Neddirs..hedously hoge & horned as Tupis þai turred doun of his tulkis & with þar tyndis sloȝe. 1483 *Cath. Angl.* 398/1 To Turre, *arietare*, *est enim Arietum & aliorum animalium*. 1886 CUNLIFFE *Rochdale Gloss.* 93 *Turr*, to butt with the head. A beast possessing this vicious habit is said to have 'th turr ith head'.

**Turr**, Sc. form of TURF.

† **Turrell.** *Obs.* [Derivation uncertain: perh. ad. OF. **tourel* (not recorded, but cf. *touret* 'instrument servant à percer', 15th c. in Godef.), or obs. F. *tarelle*, *terelle* auger (Cotgr.), surviving in Picard *térelle*.] A cooper's auger.

1611 COTGR., *Barroir*, a Turrell; th' Oager wherewith Coopers make holes for the barre-pinnes of a peece of caske. *Ibid.*, *Tirefond de tonnelier*, a Coopers Turrell; the Auger wherewith he boreth holes. *Ibid.*, *Ville*..the long oagar tearmed by our Coopers, a Turrell. [Hence in Sherwood, Littleton, Kersey, Bailey, etc.]

**Turrene**, obs. form of TUREEN.

**Turret** (tʊ·rėt), *sb.*[1] Forms: *α.* 4–6 **turet**, 5 **-ete** (6 *pl.* **-ettes**, *Sc.* **-ettis**, **-etis**), 5–6 *Sc.* **-at(e** (*pl.* **-atis**, **-attis**), 6 **turryt**, **-ite**, *Sc.* **turit**, **turrat**, 6–8 **turrit**, 7 *Sc.* **turrett**, 5– **turret** (*pl.* 4–6 **-ettes**, *Sc.* 5 **-ettis**, 6 **-etis**). *β.* 4–5 (7–8 *Hist.*) **touret**, 5–6 **-ette** (*pl. Sc.* **-ettis**), **tourrett** (*pl.* **-ettes**), **towrette** (*pl.* **-ettis**, **-ys**), 6–7 **towret**, 8 **tourett**. *γ.* 4–5 **toret**, 5–8 **torret** (5 *pl.* **torettes**, **-is**, **torrettes**). *δ.* 6 **territ**, 6–7 **-et**, **-ett** (*pl.* **-ettes**), 7 **tirritt**. [ME. *turet*, *toret*, *tourette*, a. OF. *torete*, *tourete* (12th c. in Godef.), later *tourette* (still in 17th c.), dim. of *tur*, *tor*, *tour* fem., TOWER; cf. mod. It. *torretta*, dim. of *torre*:—L. *turris* (to the influence of which the current spelling *turret* may be due).

The slightly earlier *toret*, *torret*, occurring in the *S. Eng. Leg.* I. 300/15 and in R. Glouc. (Rolls) 3625 in the sense of 'summit' of a hill, is app. not identical with this word, but ad. OF. *turet* (still in Artois dial.), var. of *turel* (later and now dial. *tureau*) eminence, hill.]

**1.** A small or subordinate tower, usually one forming part of a larger structure; *esp.* a rounded addition to an angle of a building, sometimes commencing at some height above the ground, and freq. containing a spiral staircase.

*α.* 13.. *Guy Warw.* (A.) 7306+xxi. 1 To a turet sir Gij is went, And biheld þat firmament. *c* 1470 *Golagros & Gaw.* 42 Ane ciete..With torris and turatis. *c* 1470 HENRY *Wallace* VIII. 1014 A ryoll sted..With turrettis fayr. 1555 WATREMAN *Fardle of Facions* I. vi. 89 The gentlemen..haue neither cities nor townes, but Turrettes builte vpon the waters side. 1610 HOLLAND *Camden's Brit.* (1637) 37 An Elephant with a turret upon his backe. *Ibid.* 40 He raised an high turret, out of which..there might blaze all night long, lights and fires for the better direction of ships at sea. 1644 EVELYN *Diary* 17 Nov., Another wall full of small turrets. 1765 FOOTE *Commissary* III. (1782) 48 The large brick house..with a turrit at top. 1824 W. IRVING *T. Trav.* I. iii. 17 He perceived the turrets of an ancient chateau rising out of the trees of its walled park. 1861 M. PATTISON *Ess.* (1889) I. 45 Thick walls and turrets at the angles gave the whole the aspect..of a fortress.

*transf.* 1671 *Phil. Trans.* VI. 2265 By a new Earth-quake the Top or Turret of Mount Ætna..fell in.

*β.* 13.. *Coer de L.* 3969 The Sarezynes, armyd, forth lepe Upon the walles the toun to kepe, Stout in touret, and in hurdys. *c* 1400 *Rom. Rose* 4164 He hired hem to make a tour...And rounde environ eek were set Ful many a riche and fair touret. **1481** CAXTON *Godeffroy* ccvii. 303 They were so pour and so greued of tayllages and excises, that vnnethe they had among them alle wherof to repayre two towrettys. **1545** JOYE *Exp. Dan.* i. 13 It was dowble walled with many highe and strong towrets. **1633** *Stow's Surv.* 7/1 The wals of [London], which were sore decayed, and destitute of Towres and Towrets, to be repaired. **1736** McURE *Hist. Glasgow* 256 The Town-house or Tolbooth.. has Four large Touretts on the Corners thereof.

γ. *a* **1400–50** *Alexander* 1418 (Ashm.) Sum..Tilt torettis [*v.r.* torrettes] doun, toures on hepis. *c* **1400** *Gamelyn* 329 In a litel toret his brother lay i-steke. *c* **1440** *Promp. Parv.* 497/1 Toret, lytylle towre, *turricula.* **1648** J. RAYMOND *Il Mercurio Italico* 129 An ancient Torret, built halfe of solid Marble.

δ. *a* **1600** *Hymn, 'Hierusalem my happie home'* viii. in Julian *Dict. Hymnology* (1907) 580/2 Thy terrettes and thy pinacles. *c* **1618** MORYSON *Itin.* (1903) 335 Germany aboundes with Copper, wherewith many Cittyes have Terretts steeples and whole Churches Covered. **1643** MRS. THORNTON *Autobiog.* (Surtees) 33 The window sudainly shutt with such a force the whole tirritt shooke.

**b.** In *Heraldry*: see quots.

**1766–87** PORNY *Heraldry* Gloss., *Turret*, a small Tower. *Turreted*, having Turrets on the top. *c* **1828** BERRY *Encycl. Her.* I. Gloss., *Turret*, a small tower on the top of another. **1868** CUSSANS *Her.* vii. (1882) 123 *Turret*: a small tower commonly set upon a Castle. **1894** *Parker's Gloss. Her.* s. v. *Tower*, The tower is..frequently represented as bearing three smaller towers or turrets, and then it is blazoned *triple towered*, or triple turretted...The..turret is sometimes used alone, separate from the tower, and can only be represented as a smaller tower.

† **c.** *fig.* Highest point or position, height, acme. *Obs.*

**1593** *Tell-Troth's N. Y. Gift* (1876) 36 We thinke we are neuer at the territ of delight. **1614** RALEIGH *Hist. World* I. (1634) 111 Jupiter, whom the Greekes have seated in the top and highest Turret of their Divinitie. **1680** T. LAWSON *Mite into Treasury* 11 Mounted to the Terret of Philosophick Elevations, and to the Zenith of Scholastick Notions.

**2.** *Mil.* † **a.** = TOWER *sb.*[1] 5 a. *Obs. rare*$^{-1}$.

**1563** GOLDING *Cæsar* II. (1565) 62 When they saw..the mount raysed and a turret a buylding a farre of,..they began to laugh at it.

**b.** A low flat armour-plated tower, commonly cylindrical or conical, on a ship of war or a fort, made to contain a gun and gunners, and usually to revolve horizontally.

**1862** CAPT. P. COLES in *Times* 5 Nov., I obtained permission ..to substitute in the 'Prince Albert' three turrets, each carrying one 300-pounder. **1869** SIR E. J. REED *Iron-Clad Ships* Introd. 16 The 'Monarch'..with 25-ton guns mounted in turrets. **1887** *Spectator* 30 July 1019/1 The 'Inflexible'..with four 80-ton guns in her turrets. **1889** WELCH *Text Bk. Naval Archit.* xiv. 143 The plan of placing the guns in revolving towers or turrets. **1897** H. W. WILSON in *United Service Mag.* July 351 The distinction between turret and barbette is this; the turret is an armoured shelter revolving with the gun; the barbette an armoured shelter inside which the gun revolves on a turn-table.

**3.** Applied to various things resembling a small tower. † **a.** A high head-dress formerly worn by women (*obs.*). † **b.** A tall chimney on a lamp (*obs.*). **c.** A raised central portion in the roof of a railway passenger carriage (*U. S.*).

**1473–4** *Acc. Ld. High Treas. Scot.* I. 29, 1½ elne of satyne for turatis to the Quene. **1578** *Inv. Roy. Wardr.* (1815) 231 Ane hude and ane turit of quheit velvot. **1626** BACON *Sylva* § 373 Take a Turreted Lampe of Tinne,..The Height of the Turret being thrice as much, as the length of the lower part, whereupon the Lampe standeth. **1875** KNIGHT *Dict. Mech.*, *Turret*..3. (*Railway*.) The elevated central portion of a passenger-car, whose top forms an upper story of the roof, and whose sides are glazed for light and pierced for ventilation.

**4.** An attachment to a lathe, drill, or similar machine, consisting of a round or polygonal block with sockets for various dies or cutting tools, and capable of being rotated (cf. 2 b) so as to present the required tool to the work.

**1875** [see *turret-lathe* in 5].

**5.** *attrib.* and *Comb.*, as (sense 1) *turret-bell, -bridge, -chamber, -clock, -door, -roof, -room, -stair, -top*; *turret-like, -shaped, -topped* adjs.; (sense 2 b) *turret armour, -gun, -gunner*; *turret-turning* adj.; also **turret-crown**, a turreted crown (see TURRETED 2 a); **turret-deck**: see quot. 1909 (also *attrib.*); **turret head** = sense 4; **turret-lathe**, a lathe fitted with a turret (sense 4); **turret-shell** = TURRITELLID; **turret-ship**, a ship of war with a turret (sense 2 b); **turret-spider**, a spider that constructs a turret-like nest, as the N. American *Lycosa arenaria*; **turret-vessel** = *turret-ship*; **turret window** = *tower-window* (TOWER *sb.*[1] 10).

**1889** WELCH *Text Bk. Naval Archit.* xiv. 144 The side and *turret armour was made up of two thicknesses. *c* **1800** R. CUMBERLAND *John De Lancaster* (1809) III. 3 The *turret-bell gave the signal of an arrival. *c* **1470** HENRY *Wallace* VII. 990 Schir Jhon the Grayme, and Ramsay..The *turat bryg segyt. **1819** SCOTT *Ivanhoe* xx[i]v, A step was heard on the stair, and the door of the *turret chamber slowly opened. **1821** — *Kenilw.* xviii, Immured for day and night in a desolate turret-chamber. *c* **1820** S. ROGERS *Italy* (1839) 52 An hour and more, by the old *turret-clock. **1884** F. J. BRITTEN *Watch & Clockm.* 84 De Vick..made for Charles V of France the first turret clock of which we have reliable record. **1667** MILTON *P. L.* IX. 525 Oft he [the serpent] bowd His *turret Crest. **1886** CONDER *Syrian Stone-Lore* vii. (1896) 235 Jerusalem herself, with *turret-crown, appears on another [coin]. **1904** *Westm. Gaz.* 10 Oct. 9/1 Rules for the construction of *turret-deck steamers. **1909** *Cent. Dict. Supp.* s. v. *Deck*, In a special British design of cargo-steamer,..the side, instead of meeting the main deck rectangularly, is rounded off so as to make a continuous curved surface with the deck. Inboard of this the side is again curved up. The space between the sides at the top is covered by a narrow deck called the turret-deck. **1825** SCOTT *Betrothed* iii, The form of the huge and substantial Fleming at length issued from the *turret-door. **1875** KNIGHT *Dict. Mech.*, **Turret-gun*, one specially adapted for use in revolving turrets of vessels. **1870** *Daily News* 27 Sept., The *turret-gunner stands with his head through a hole in the roof of the turret. **1884** KNIGHT *Dict. Mech.* Supp., **Turret Head*, the revolving head of a bolt cutter. **1875** *Ibid.*, **Turret-lathe*.., a screw-cutting lathe having a slide provided with a polygonal block or turret, having apertures in each face for receiving dies which are secured therein by set-screws. **1711** SHAFTESB. *Charac.* (1738) II. 253 Like.. old reverend Cybele,..on her head a *turret-like attire. **1813** SCOTT *Rokeby* I. i, The warder..Hears, upon *turret-roof and wall, By fits the plashing rain-drop fall. **1822** — *Pirate* xxxi, A great banqueting-hall, communicating with several large rounds, or projecting *turret-rooms. **1844** MARG. FULLER *Wom. 19th C.* (1862) 362 Two vast towers of rock with *turret-shaped tops. **1859–62** SIR J. RICHARDSON, etc. *Mus. Nat. Hist.* (1868) II. 339 The family of *Turret or Screw shells (*Turritellidæ*). **1862** CAPT. P. COLES in *Times* 22 Nov., [The idea] that broadside ships can..effectively work these ponderous guns against *turret ships. **1880** *Daily News* 18 Dec., The trials of the eighty-ton guns on board the turret ship *Inflexible.* **1883** *Science* 13 July 43/2 A species of ground spider..known as the *turret spider. **1819** SCOTT *Ivanhoe* xx[i]v, Slowly and with difficulty she descended the *turret stair. **1886** WILLIS & CLARK *Cambridge* II. 573 An external turret-stair on the north side. **1866** *Capt. Coles & the Admiralty* 9 Captain Coles is not the inventor of the *turret system at all..the turret itself belongs to Ericsson. *c* **1800** R. CUMBERLAND *John De Lancaster* (1809) III. 115 The whole Castle garrison [turned out] from their sky-chambers on the *turret tops. **1892** E. REEVES *Homeward Bound* 271 The outside walls..are of the plain, one story, level, *turret-topped..style. **1889** WELCH *Text Bk. Naval Archit.* xiv. 143 The parts immediately underneath turrets must be protected by armour in order to shield the *turret-turning gear. **1862** CAPT. P. COLES in *Times* 5 Nov., A sea-going *turret vessel. **1870** O. H. STOKES in *Eng. Mech.* 7 Jan. 396/3 In a turret vessel, the whole of the deck, 'exclusive of that part which is occupied by the turrets', is exposed to the fire of the enemy. **1603** *Rites of Durham* (Surtees 1903) App. 110, 3 white *turrett wyndowes. **1823** SCOTT *Quentin D.* iv, Little turret-windows,..the lattice.. half open to admit the air.

**Turret,** *sb.*[2] var. TORRET.

**Tu·rret,** *v.* [f. TURRET *sb.*[1]] *trans.* To furnish, fortify, or adorn with or as with a turret or turrets. Usually in *pa. pple.*: see also next.

**1450** in *Charters &c. Edinb.* (1871) 71 To..wall, toure, turate, and uther wais to strengthen oure foresaid Burgh. *a* **1548** HALL *Chron., Hen. VIII*, 36 The citee..was strong, wel walled, and turryted with good Bulwarkes & defenses. **1636** DAVENANT *Platonick Lovers* I, Since yonder building on the Mount, And that large Marble square was turretted, The house lookes pleasant. **1818** SCOTT *Hrt. Midl.* xxxvi, The Thames, here turreted with villas and there garlanded with forests. **1843** S. C. HALL *Ireland* III. 180 A keep or castle turreted at the angles.

**Turreted** (tʊ·rĕtĕd), *a.* [f. TURRET *sb.*[1] or *v.*]

**1.** Furnished with or having a turret or turrets.

*a* **1550** [see TRIPLE *a.* C. a]. **1552** HULOET, Turretted or made full of turrettes, *turritus.* **1794** MRS. RADCLIFFE *Myst. Udolpho* vi, The one [avenue] leading to the turreted chateau. **1826** DISRAELI *Viv. Grey* II. iv, Over the gateway there rose a turreted tower. **1863** GEO. ELIOT *Romola* xxvi, It was a grand moment for those who were stationed on turreted roofs.

**2.** Furnished with something resembling a turret: cf. TURRET *sb.*[1] 2, 3. **a.** Of artificial things; *spec.* applied to a figure of a crown with battlements, or of a head (or person) wearing such a crown.

**1610** HOLLAND *Camden's Brit.* (1637) 801 The Goddesse Syria..with a turreted crown on her head. **1626** [see TURRET *sb.*[1] 3]. **1824** MISS MITFORD *Village* Ser. I. (1863) 120 No bonnet could hold the turreted cap. **1837** WHEWELL *Hist. Induct. Sc.* (1857) I. 189 Turretted ships. **1872** HEAD *Sel. Grk. Coins in Electrotype Brit. Mus.* 37 Head of Kybele.., wearing turreted crown. *Ibid.* 42 Turreted female figure, city of Antioch, seated..on rock.

**b.** Of natural objects; *spec.* of a shell with a long spire: = TURRITED.

**1826** KIRBY & SP. *Entomol.* IV. xlvi. 306 Turreted... When the head is producted into a kind of columnar recurved turret or rostrum, in the sides of which, towards the end, the eyes are fixed. **1828** STARK *Elem. Nat. Hist.* II. 30 Terebra,..Shell elongated, turreted, acuminate. **1872** NICHOLSON *Palæont.* 62 In other cases, the shell becomes turreted or top-shaped, in consequence of the coils of the spiral passing obliquely round a central axis. **1875** C. C. BLAKE *Zool.* 254 In the Pyramidellidæ the shell is spiral and turreted.

**Tu·rreting,** *vbl. sb.* [f. as prec. + -ING[1].] The action of furnishing with turrets; *concr.* turrets collectively.

**1847** CHR. G. ROSSETTI *Dead City* xxiv, Where..Rose a palace for a king; Golden was the turreting.

**Tu·rretry.** *nonce-wd.* [f. TURRET *sb.*[1] + -RY.] Turrets collectively.

**1824** GALT *Rothelan* II. xv, All the mysterious castles and turretry of Christendom.

**Turribant,** obs. form of TURBAN.

**Turricle** (tʊ·rik'l). *rare*$^{-1}$. [ad. L. *turricula*, dim. of *turris* tower.] A small tower, turret.

**1884** J. PAYNE *Tales fr. Arabic* II. 36 *note*, *Nawous*, a sort of overground well or turricle of masonry.

**Turricular** (tʊri·kiŭlăɹ), *a. rare*$^{-1}$. [f. L. *turricula* (see prec.) + -AR.] Having the form of or resembling a turret.

**1661** FELTHAM *Resolves* II. liii. (ed. 8) 293 In their Turricular Chariots.

**Turriculated** (tʊri·kiŭleitĕd), *ppl. a.* [f. as prec. + -ATE + -ED.] Furnished with a turret or turrets, turreted: *spec.* in *Conch.* = TURRETED 2 b, TURRITED. Also **Turriculate** (tʊri·kiŭlĕt) *a.*

**1822** J. PARKINSON *Outl. Oryctol.* 155 A longish turriculated univalve. *Ibid.* 250 The multilocular turriculated shells of the genus *Turriculites.* **1834** McMURTRIE *Cuvier's Anim. Kingd.* 255 A shell with a turriculated spire. **1843** *Penny Cycl.* XXVI. 444/2 *Mitra*...Turriculate species, with large spiral whorls, the aperture effuse anteriorly.

**Turri·ferous,** *a. rare*$^{-0}$. [f. L. *turrifer* (Ovid) + -OUS.] = TURRIGEROUS.

**1656** BLOUNT *Glossogr.* [copying Cooper], *Turriferous*.., that beares a Tower.

**Turriform** (tʊ·rifǭɹm), *a. rare*$^{-1}$. [f. L. *turri-s* tower + -FORM.] Tower-shaped.

**1875** C. C. BLAKE *Zool.* 254 The Staircase Shell has a spiral turriform operculum.

**Turri·gerous,** *a. rare*$^{-1}$. [f. L. *turriger*, f. *turris* tower: see -GEROUS.] Carrying a tower or 'castle'.

**1713** DERHAM *Phys.-Theol.* 398 We admire, saith he [*sc.* Pliny *Nat. Hist.* XI. 2], the turrigerous Shoulders of Elephants.

**Turrilite** (tʊ·rilǝit). *Palæont.* [ad. mod.L. *Turrilitēs* (Lamarck, 1801), f. L. *turris* tower + Gr. λίθος stone: see -LITE.] A fossil cephalopod belonging or related to the genus *Turrilites*, allied to the ammonites, but having a long spiral (turreted) shell, found in the Cretaceous formations.

**1828** WEBSTER, *Turrilite*, the fossil remains of a spiral multilocular shell. **1842** H. MILLER *O. R. Sandst.* viii. (ed. 2) 187 The..turrilites and sea-urchins of the Cretaceous group. **1850** ANSTED *Elem. Geol., Min.* etc., Gloss., *Turrilite*, an extinct genus of chambered shells, resembling an Ammonite wound into a turbinated form.

Hence **Turriliticone** (tʊrili·tikoun) [CONE *sb.*[1]], a fossil shell resembling and allied to the turrilites, found in the Upper Cretaceous formations (*Cent. Dict. Suppl.* 1909).

† **Turrion,** var. TORRION *Obs.*, a large tower.

**1599** HAKLUYT *Voy.* II. 108 Foure principall bulwarkes, and bitweene them turrions. *Ibid.* 123 The Turrion of the Arsenall.

**Turrited** (tʊ·rǝitĕd), *a.* [f. L. *turrīt-us* towered (f. *turris* tower) + -ED.] = TURRETED 2; *spec.* of a shell, having a long spire resembling a tower or turret: = TURRETED 2 b. Also **Tu·rrite** *a.*

**1758** SWINTON in *Phil. Trans.* L. 794 All these coins present..a turrited head and a branch of palm. **1835** KIRBY *Hab. & Inst. Anim.* I. ix. 276 The shells of some [Tracheli-pods] are what are called turrited or long and slender, with spiral whorls. **1856** W. CLARK *Van der Hoeven's Zool.* I. 798 Pyramidella...Shell turrite. **1863** P. P. CARPENTER in *Rep. Brit. Assoc.* I. 662 '*Columbella*' *carinata*...Small, turrited, smooth, with stout posterior keel.

**Turritellid** (tʊrite·lid). *Zool.* [ad. mod.L. *Turritellid-æ* pl., f. *Turritella* (Lamarck, 1799), name of the typical genus, f. *turris* tower; see -ID[3].] A gastropod of the family *Turritellidæ*, characterized by long turreted shells with spiral striations; a screw-shell. So **Turrite·lloid** *a.* [-OID], resembling a screw-shell; having the characters of the *Turritellidæ*.

**1860** P. P. CARPENTER in *Rep. Smithsonian Instit.* 1859, 206 The Turritelloid worm-shells. **1861** *Ibid.* 1860, 210 The shells of *Siphonium*, though spiral at birth, have no Turritelloid portion. **1895** *Funk's Standard Dict.*, Turritellid.

† **Tu·rrulet.** *Obs. rare*$^{-1}$. [dim. formation from L. *turris* tower; cf. *rivulet*.] = TURRET *sb.*[1] 1.

*c* **1620** T. ROBINSON *Mary Magd.* 49 A turrulet tooke vp each angles shade, .. The battelments of smoothest Iett were made.

**Turs, turse, turss,** obs. Sc. ff. TRUSS.

† **Tursable,** *a. Sc. Obs.* [f. *turs*, TRUSS *v.* + -ABLE.] Capable of being packed up and carried off; portable; see TRUSS *v.* 2.

*a* **1670** SPALDING *Troub. Chas. I* (1850) I. 283 The laird.. displenishis the place, left nothing tursabill within. [**1897** RAMPINI *Hist. Moray & Nairn* iv. 186.]

† **Tu·rsion.** *Obs. rare.* [ad. L. *tursio, -ōnem* (Pliny).] A porpoise.

**1655** MOUFET & BENNET *Health's Improv.* (1746) 257 Porpoises, Tursions, or Sea-hogs, are..never good till they be fat. **1661** LOVELL *Hist. Anim. & Min.* 217 Porpaise...Tursions, or Sea-hoggs are fatter than Dolphins. [**1706** PHILLIPS (ed. Kersey), *Tursio* or *Tyrsio*, a Sea-fish like a Dolphin, which some take for a Sturgeon, and others for a Porpoise.]

**Tursk,** var. TORSK, fish.

**Turskill.** *Sc. dial.* [var. of TUSKAR, prob. after Gael. *tairisgil*.] A kind of spade for cutting peat.

**1812** J. HENDERSON *Agric. Surv. Caithn.* xv. 234 When the peat-moss is not more than from one to two feet deep, the peat is cut perpendicularly, by a spade, called a *turskill.*

**Turtle** (tɔ̄·ɹt'l), *sb.*[1] Now *rare* or *arch.* Forms: 1 turtla, 1– turtle, 3 (*Orm.*) turrtle, 3–5 turtul, 4 tortle, 4–5 turtill, 4–6 -il, (5 -yl, -yle, -ylle, 5–6 -yll), (5 turckell), 5 tyrtle, 6 tyrtyll, turtell. [OE. *turtla* masc., *turtle* fem. = OHG. *turtulo* masc., *turtula* fem. (Du. *tortel* fem.): either dim.

or dissimilated form of L. *turtur* TURTUR with *r–l* for *r–r* (cf. Sp. and It. *tortola*, It. *tortora*). For other Germanic forms see TURTLE-DOVE.]

**1.** = TURTLE-DOVE 1. (Often mentioned as a type of conjugal affection and constancy: cf. 2.)

*c* **1000** *Ags. Ps.* (Th.) lxxxiii[i]. 3 Him eac spedlice spearuwa hus begyteð, and tidlice turtle nistlað. *c* **1000** *Ags. Gosp.* Luke ii. 24 Twa turtlan oððe twegen culfran briddas. *c* **1200** *Trin. Coll. Hom.* 49 Turtle ne wile habbe no make bute on and after þat non..Þe bitocninge þat is imene turtlen and duues...Eiðer turtles and duues habbet sorinesse for song. *c* **1200** ORMIN 7588 Twe33enn cullfre briddess.. Oþþr.. twe33en turrtless. **1382** WYCLIF *Ps.* lxxxiii. 4 [lxxxiv. 3] Forsothe the sparowe fonde to hym an hous; and the turtil a nest. *c* **1400** tr. *Secreta Secret., Gov. Lordsh.* ciii. 104 Pytous as turtyll. **1483** CAXTON *Gold. Leg.* 373/2 Lyke a turtle that allone without make waylleth and wepeth. *a* **1548** HALL *Chron., Hen. VI* 118 As louyng to him, as the Turtle to her make. **1611** SHAKS. *Wint. T.* IV. iv. 154 Your hand (my Perdita:) so Turtles paire That neuer meane to part. **1670** G. H. *Hist. Cardinals* I. III. 91 A Mass is sung, and his Holiness presented with two young Turtles. **1713** STEELE *Guard.* No. 22. ▸ 2 [She] kept a pair of turtles cooing in her chamber. **1802** MONTAGU *Ornith. Dict.* s.v. *Dove-turtle*, The Turtle visits the southern parts of England in the spring. **1851** MAYHEW *Lond. Labour* (1861) III. 64 His pigeon-cote.. is no longer stocked with carriers,.. jacobins,..turtles. **1860** CHR. G. ROSSETTI *O. & N. Year Ditties* iii, Turtle calleth turtle in Heaven's May.

**b.** *Greenland turtle, Sea-turtle*, names for the Black Guillemot: see GREENLAND 1, SEA-TURTLE[1].

**2.** *fig.* Applied to a person, as a term of endearment, etc. (cf. DOVE *sb.* 2 d), or (esp.) to lovers or married folk, in allusion to the turtle-dove's affection for its mate.

**14..** LYDG. *Balade Commend. Our Lady* 78 O trusty turtle, trewest of al trewe. *c* **1440** *Gesta Rom.* lxix. 312 (Harl. MS.), I shal be turtill in your absence þat hadde lost hire make. *a* **1548** HALL *Chron., Hen. VII* 20 b, Hym that ..watched, howe to..steale thys turtle oute of her mewe and lodgynge. **1588** SHAKS. *L. L. L.* IV. iii. 211 *Berow.* Will these Turtles be gone? *Kin.* Hence sirs, away. **1693** *Humours Town* 24 The Fool..concludes her the most constant pretty cooing Turtle in the Nation. **1717** LADY M. W. MONTAGU *Let. to Pope* 1 Apr., Several couple of true turtles ..saying soft things to one another. **1865** E. W. BENSON in *Life* (1899) I. vi. 232, I am a solitary Turtle (Dove, not Reptile) just now, my wife being at Rugby.

**3.** *attrib.* and *Comb.*, as *turtle love, pigeon, wing*; *turtle-billing, -footed, -haunted, -like, -winged* adjs.; †**turtle-bird**, the young of the turtle-dove.

**1598** B. JONSON *Ev. Man in Hum.* I. iv, The happy state of *Turtle-billing lovers. *c* **1200** *Trin. Coll. Hom.* 47 Gif hie was riche wimman, a lomb, gif hie was bitwene two, two *turtle briddes, gif hie was poure, two duue briddes. **1599** B. JONSON *Ev. Man out of Hum.* Epil., Let..The throat of War be stopt.., And *turtle-footed Peace dance fairy rings About her court. **1624** — *Sun's Darling* v. i. **1873** T. L. KINGSBURY *Comm. Song Sol.* iii, The *turtle-haunted groves. *a* **1586** SIDNEY *Arcadia* IV. (1629) 415 Lamenting..such as the *turtle-like loue is wont to make for the euer ouer-soone losse of her onely loued make. **1669** DRYDEN *Tyrannic Love* III. i, Then, turtle-like, I'll to my mate repair. **1608** TOPSELL *Serpents* (1658) 784 Such faithfull dealing, uprightnesse of conscience, and *Turtle love. **1819** STEPHENS in Shaw *Gen. Zool.* XI. 72 *Turtle Pigeon, *Columba Turtur*...Pigeon with the tail-feathers white at their tips, the back griseous, the breast vinaceous, a black spot on the sides of the neck, with white stripes, the abdomen white. **1629** MILTON *Nativity, Hymn* iii, Peace..With *Turtle wing the amorous clouds dividing. **1821** R. S. HAWKER *Cornish Ballads*, etc. (1908) 249 As on turtle-wings the moments fleet. **1745** AKENSIDE *Ode on Lyric Poetry* 18 While *turtle-wing'd the laughing hours.. Lead youth, and love, and harmless joy.

Hence (*nonce-wds.*) **Tu·rtlish** (tu·rtleish) *a.*, having the character or qualities of a turtle-dove; **Tu·rtlize** (tu·rtleize) *v.*, *trans.* to turn into or make like a turtle-dove.

**1855** *Fraser's Mag.* LI. 229 The most *turtleish of doves. **1798** SOUTHEY *Lett.* (1856) I. 59, I am softened, *turtleised, yea, a very lamb!

**Turtle** (tɔ̄·ɹt'l), *sb.*[2] Also 7 tortel. [app. a corruption, by English sailors, of the earlier *tortue*, or the French original of this (see TORTOISE), assimilated to the known word TURTLE *sb.*[1]]

**1.** Any species of marine tortoise; also extended to various other tortoises. (Pl. *turtles*, collectively usually *turtle*.)

As to the varying application of the names *tortoise* and *turtle*, see the note to sense 1 of the former word.

With defining words, applied to various species, as *box-turtle* (Box *sb.*[2] 24), DIAMOND-BACKED *t.*, HAWK'S-BILL *t.*, LAND *t.*, LEATHER-*t.*, *loggerhead t.* (LOGGERHEAD 6 a), MUD *t.*, PAINTED *t.*, SEA-TURTLE[2], SNAPPING-*t.*, SOFT-SHELLED *t.*, TRUNK-*t.* (see these words); **alligator-turtle**, the snapping-turtle, also called *alligator tortoise* (ALLIGATOR 3); **bastard turtle**, *Thalassochelys kempi*; **chicken-turtle**, *Chrysemys reticulata*, also called *chicken-tortoise*; **greaved turtle**, any species of the genus *Podocnemis*; **green turtle**, various species of *Chelonia*, having green shells, as *C. midas* of the W. Indies and *C. virgata* of the Pacific, both much esteemed as food; **horned turtle**, an extinct turtle of the genus *Miolania*, having projections at the back of the skull like the 'horned toad'.

**1657** *North's Plutarch, Add. Lives* 90 He took a Shipboard..fourty Parrots, many Tortels, and many other Animals strange to our World. **1657** R. LIGON *Barbadoes* (1673) 4 The Loggerhead Turtle,..the Hawks bill Turtle... A third kind called the Green Turtle,..far excelling the other two, in wholesomness, and Rareness of taste. **1689** *Relat. Sufferings H. Pitman* 22 We walked along the sea shore to watch for tortoise or turtle. **1712** E. COOKE *Voy. S. Sea* 13 Sea Tortoises, or, as the Sea-men call them, Turtle. **1719** DE FOE *Crusoe* I. 101, June 17. I spent in cooking the Turtle; I found in her threescore Eggs. **1745** P. THOMAS *Jrnl. Anson's Voy.* 105 Great Quantity of Tortoises, or, as the Seamen call them, Turtles. **1785** *Jackson's Oxford Jrnl.* 16 July, Dressing a very fine lively Chicken Turtle.. supplied.. at 6/- per quart or 10/6 the Tureen. **1792** MAR. RIDDELL *Voy. Madeira* 63 Four species of turtle are found on the shores of this island—the green-turtle, the hawk's-bill,..the logger-head, and the land-tortoise. **1839–40** W. IRVING *Wolfert's R.* v. (1855) 75 The island abounded with turtle, and great quantities of their eggs were to be found among the rocks. **1870** YEATS *Nat. Hist. Comm.* 114 Turtles abound in the enclosed seas of Central America.

**b.** The flesh of various species of turtle used as food; also short for *turtle-soup*. (See also MOCK TURTLE.)

Often mentioned or alluded to as a feature of civic banquets.

**1755** *World* No. 123 ▸ 3 Of all the improvements in the modern kitchen, there are none that can bear a comparison with the introduction of Turtle. **1780** T. DAVIES *Mem. Garrick* (1781) II. xxxviii. 122 High seasoned venison, delicious turtle, and excellent claret. **1848** THACKERAY *Van. Fair* xxvii, He..had dined on horse-flesh and turtle with equal relish. **1859** *Habits Gd. Society* xi. 310 A light soup is better than a thick one,..turtle is only fit for an alderman.

†**c.** Short for *turtle-dinner* or *turtle-feast*. *Obs.*

**1771** SMOLLETT *Humph. Cl.* 30 Apr., I..have almost prevailed upon uncle to give him a small turtle at the Bear. **1785** A. C. BOWER *Diaries & Corr.* 16 Sept. (1903) 29 Tuesday next the good people at Dulish intend giving a Turtle and the Misses have prevailed on their Mother to add a little Hop in the Evening by way of helping Digestion. **1788** *Ibid.* 49 We were at Whatcombe Tuesday—a large party and a turtle.

**2.** *To turn turtle.* **a.** *lit.* To catch turtle by throwing them on their backs.

**1689** *Relat. Sufferings H. Pitman* 20 They going ashore on the Main to turn Turtle, were set upon by the Indians. **1861** DU CHAILLU *Equat. Afr.* iv. 25 Turtle frequent the shores, and are 'turned' in considerable numbers. **1867** SMYTH *Sailor's Word-bk.*, *To turn a turtle*, to take the animal by seizing a flipper, and throwing him on his back, which renders him quite helpless.

**b.** *fig.* (in earlier use *to turn the turtle.*) To turn over, capsize, be upset.

**1842** MARRYAT *Perc. Keene* xxiii, But 'turning the turtle' is not making a quick passage, except to the other world. **1843** — *M. Violet* xli, The canoe turned the turtle with them. **1860** *All Year Round* No. 66. 384 If the wind catches that 'ere, she'll turn turtle at once. **1896** *Daily News* 2 July 9/1 An engine and two trucks had turned turtle on the embankment.

†**3.** *American turtle*: = TORPEDO *sb.* 2. *Obs.*

**1775–83** THACHER *Milit. Jrnl.* (1823) 75 A singular machine invented for destroying the British Shipping by explosion. ..American Turtle or Torpedo.

**4.** *Typog.* A curved bed in which types or stereotypes are secured, and which is mounted on one of the cylinders of a rotary printing-press: so called from a fancied resemblance of the bed to the back of a turtle.

**1860** *Ure's Dict. Arts* (ed. 5) III. 540 An American [printing] machine, the invention of R. Hoe and Company...Each page is locked up upon a detached segment of the large cylinder, called by the compositors a 'turtle'. **1875** KNIGHT *Dict. Mech.* 1797/2 The type is secured in *turtles*, or the stereotype is bent to the curve of the cylinder.

**5.** *attrib.* and *Comb.*, as *turtle-catcher, -chase, -dinner, -eater, -egg, -feast, -fishery, -fishing, -skeleton, -soup*; **turtle-corral** = *turtle-crawl* (*a*); **turtle cowry**, a large species of cowry, *Cypræa testudinaria*; **turtle-crab**, a minute species of crab parasitic upon turtles and other marine animals; **turtle-crawl**, (*a*) [CRAWL *sb.*[2]] an enclosure in which turtles are kept; (*b*) [CRAWL *sb.*[1]] 'the track of a turtle to and from its nest' (*Cent. Dict.* 1891); **turtle-deck** = TURTLE-BACK 1; **turtle-egging**, the gathering of turtles' eggs (*Cent. Dict.* 1891); **turtle-frolic** (*colloq.*), a turtle-feast; **turtle-grass**, name for two marine plants with long narrow grass-like leaves: (*a*) *Thalassia testudinum*, of the W. Indies, etc.; (*b*) the grass-wrack, *Zostera marina*; **turtle-head**, a N. American scrophulariaceous plant, *Chelone glabra*, allied to *Pentstemon*, so called from the shape of the flower; **turtle-insect**, a widely-distributed species of scale-insect, *Coccus* (*Lecanium*) *hesperidum*; **turtle-kraal** = *turtle-crawl* (*a*); **turtle-net**, a net for catching turtle; **turtle-peg**, a prong fastened to a pole or cord used for harpooning turtles (= PEG *sb.*[1] 8 a); hence **turtle-pegger**, one who uses a turtle-peg to catch turtles; **turtle-pegging**, the catching of turtles with a turtle-peg; **turtle-press**, a printing-press in which a 'turtle' (sense 4) is (or was) used; **turtle-shell**, (*a*) the shell of a turtle; the material of this, tortoise-shell; (*b*) = *turtle-cowry*; **turtle-stone** = SEPTARIUM 2 (from the markings on section resembling those of a tortoise-shell); **turtle-twine**, twine for making turtle-nets.

**1726** G. ROBERTS *Four Yrs. Voy.* 5 There might be some *Turtle-catchers here since the last Turtle Season. **1815** J. CAMPBELL *Trav. S. Afr.* xlii. 501 We were detained till noon next day..for the turtle catchers. **1860** WRAXALL *Life in Sea* iv. 90 A picturesque description of such a *Turtle-chase on Ascension Island. **1838** *Penny Cycl.* XI. 362/1 *Nautilograpsus minutus*.. *Turtle-Crab, Browne;.. M. Milne Edwards..sees no sufficient reason for distinguishing this species from *Grapsus testudinum*, Roux. **1833** M. SCOTT *Tom Cringle* xvi. (1859) 420 The *Turtle Crawls filled with beautiful clear water. **1903** *Daily Mail* 9 Sept. 5/3 A turtle crawl in Kingston, where over two hundred turtles were confined awaiting shipment,..was broken up by the force of the sea during the cyclone in Jamaica. **1889** *Cent. Dict.* s.v. *Deck*, The **turtle-deck* or *turtle-backed deck*..is a convex deck extending a short distance aft from the stem of an ocean steamer to shed the water in a head sea; in many ..steamships..there is a similar arrangement on the stern. **1908** *Daily Chron.* 15 May 8/6 The engines of the launch were not running... Mr. Moody and Mr. Smith stood on the turtle deck at the bow. **1805** in *Edin. Rev.* July 357 Who freely give two guineas for a *turtle dinner at the tavern. *a* **1774** TUCKER *Lt. Nat.* (1834) II. 430 Your *turtle eaters, city feast hunters, and persons who live in a continual round of pleasures. **1760** GARRICK *Prol. to Murphy's Desert Isl.* 22 Keep *turtle-eating Aldermen awake. **1860** WRAXALL *Life in Sea* iv. 87 Our two soldiers..stopped..to dig *turtle eggs out of the sand. **1753** H. WALPOLE *Lett.* (1846) III. 12 Knightly..has been entertaining all the parishes round with a *turtle-feast. **1760** LYTTLETON *Dial. Dead* xix. 204 A Turtle feast is a Novelty to me. **1767** GOLDSM. *Ess., Let. Common-council-man*, The mayor and aldermen ..celebrating the royal nuptials by a magnificent turtle feast. **1793** LD. H. SPENCER in *Ld. Auckland's Corr.* (1862) III. 112 Count Bernstorff gave us a turtle-feast at his château. **1848** THACKERAY *Van. Fair* xli, An alderman coming from a turtle feast will not step out of his carriage to steal a leg of mutton. *Ibid.* xx, A parcel of *turtle-fed tradesmen. **1834** *Tait's Mag.* I. 390/2 Your *turtle-feeding Aldermen. **1707** SLOANE *Jamaica* I. Introd. 87 The *Turtle-fishery.. thought..to be ours by right...The *Turtle-fishing.. pretended to by the French of the Island Tortugas. **1904** *Westm. Gaz.* 12 Apr. 9/2 The crews of the six Caymans turtle-fishing vessels..were seized.. by the Nicaraguan Government for alleged fishing in territorial waters. **1787** M. CUTLER in *Life*, etc. (1888) I. 205, I received a polite invitation from Governor Brown..to join them in a *Turtle frolic. **1886** BYNNER *A. Surriage* xv, There was a turtle-frolic at Cambridge. **1735** MORTIMER in *Phil. Trans.* XXXIX. 116 *Alga marina, gramineo angustissimo folio*. ..*Turtle-Grass: It grows at the Bottom of the Sea in shallow Water. **1756** P. BROWNE *Jamaica* 71 The small grassy-leaf'd Alga or Turtle-grass. **1871** KINGSLEY *At Last* vi, Manatis..coming in..to browse on mangrove shoots and turtle-grass. **1884** MILLER *Plant-n.*, *Thalassia testudinum*, Manatee-grass, Turtle-grass. *Ibid.*, *Zostera marina*, Bell-ware,.. Grass Wrack.., Turtle-grass. **1857** GRAY *First Less. Bot.* (1866) 94 The fifth stamen.. appears in the.. *Turtlehead as a sort of filament without any anther. **1896** E. G. LODEMAN *Spraying of Plants* I. i. 10 Corrosive sublimate..dissolved in..spirits, and..added to the water.. possesses the power of destroying the brown *turtle (scale) insect, white scaly coccus, pine bug [etc.]. **1885** LADY BRASSEY *The Trades* 353 What they call a '*turtle-kraal', consisting of a large tank, in which were a number of turtle. **1898** *Allbutt's Syst. Med.* V. 295 He sits..*turtle-like, with his neck dropped into his chest. **1906** *Westm. Gaz.* 20 June 8/2 A great turtle-like head, with large eyes. **1794** *Turtle-nets [see *turtle-twine*]. **1839** CAPT. WILSON in *Mag. Nat. Hist.* Oct. 519 They had got a large saw-fish entangled in their turtle-net. **1828** WEBSTER, **Turtle-shell*, a shell, a beautiful species of Murex; also, tortoise-shell. **1845** J. COULTER *Adv. Pacific* x. 126 Round it [*sc.* the hut] were scattered a number of terrapin and turtle shells. **1860** WRAXALL *Life in Sea* iv. 88 Hundreds of *Turtle skeletons lying about. **1763** SMOLLETT *Trav.* xi. (1766) I. 190 As for the *turtle-soupe, it is a good restorative. **1846** A. SOYER *Syst. Cookery* 85 Turtle Soup. This soup, the delight of civic corporations,..has been, and perhaps ever will be, the leading article of English cookery. *Ibid.* 87 Clear Turtle Soup. **1851** DE LA BECHE *Geol. Observer* 687 Those commonly known as septaria and *turtle stones. **1859** R. HUNT *Guide Mus. Pract. Geol.* (ed. 2) 32 Good specimens of septaria or turtle stone from the Oxford clay. **1766** W. GORDON *Gen. Counting-ho.* 386, 3 cwt. 2 qrs. 18 lb. *turtle twine. **1794** *Rigging & Seamanship* I. 65 Turtle-twine, for turtle-nets, is made of good bar hemp.

Hence **Tu·rtledom**, a collective name for those who eat turtle (i. e. *spec.* London aldermen), or for their practices, methods, etc.; **Tu·rtly** *a.*, addicted to or habitually eating turtle. (Cf. 1 b.)

**1893** *Punch* 4 Mar. 102/1 *Turtledom feareth what Turtledom deems The perils of—Unification! **1894** WOOLACOTT (*title*) The Curse of Turtledom: an Exposé of the Methods and Extravagant Expenditure of the Livery Companies. **1900** *Daily News* 26 Nov. 4/1 They appeal as much to the epicure of turtledom as to the vegetarian. **1868** *Cosmopolitan* 25 July 334 We doubt..if the most **turtly* Alderman out can beat in legal acumen Monsieur le Juge de Paix de la Nièvre.

†**Tu·rtle**, *v.*[1] *Obs.* [f. TURTLE *sb.*[1]] *intr.* To play the turtle, behave like a turtle-dove (cf. TURTLE *sb.*[1], 1, 2). Also with *it*.

**1701** J. PRINCE *Worthies of Devon* 338 He left..a Widow ..to Turtle it after him, as he had done before. **1754** SHEBBEARE *Marriage Act* xxv. I. 148, I..am convinced how foolish all this Stuff called Love, Fidelity, Billing and Turtling in England is.

**Tu·rtle**, *v.*[2] Chiefly *nonce-wd.* [f. TURTLE *sb.*[2]; in sense 2 a back-formation (or inference) from TURTLER, TURTLING.]

**1.** *trans.* To make mock turtle of.

*a* **1756** MRS. HAYWOOD *New Present* (1771) 149 To turtle a Calf's Head.

**2.** *intr.* To catch or 'fish' for turtle.

In recent Dicts.

**3.** *trans.* To turn over: cf. *to turn turtle* (TURTLE *sb.*[2] 2 b).

**1896** *Daily News* 3 Aug. 4/7 She [the boat] turtled herself right again.

**4.** To stretch (the neck) forward like a turtle.

**1909** *Daily Chron.* 30 Dec. 9/5 Nothing makes a woman look more awkward than to 'turtle' the neck.

**Turtle-back.** [TURTLE *sb.*²]

**1.** An arched structure over the deck of a steamer at the bow, and often also at the stern, to protect it from damage by a heavy sea.

**1881** *Standard* 30 Aug. 2/3 Erections for the purposes of shelter, such as turtle-backs, open at one end. **1882** *Ibid.* 14 Aug. 2/4 Covering these are a fine promenade deck amidships and a turtle-back forward. **1886** *Times* 20 Apr. 10/2 He went beneath the turtle-back. **1897** KIPLING *Captains Courageous* i, The second-saloon deck at the stern..was finished in a turtle-back.

**2.** *Archæol.* A roughly chipped stone implement, having one or both faces slightly convex. Also *attrib.*

**1890** W. H. HOLMES in *Amer. Anthrop.* Jan. 14 The familiar turtle-back or one-faced stone, the double turtle-back or two-faced stone. **1912** S. H. WARREN in *Man* XII. 205 The present writer also has a Levallois, or 'turtle-back' core, which he found in the Lea Valley in 1896.

**3.** The back of a turtle.

**1905** *Westm. Gaz.* 4 Apr. 3/2 The legends of the peopling of the islands are interesting...Some make the passage on turtle-back; others go afloat on rafts of cocoa-nut shells.

**4.** *attrib.*, as *turtle-back core* (see 2); **turtle-back scale** = *turtle-insect* (see TURTLE *sb.*² 5).

**1909** in *Cent. Dict. Suppl.* s.v. *Scale.*

Hence **Tu·rtle-ba·cked** *a.*, having a back like a turtle's; furnished with a turtle-back (sense 1).

**1889** [see *turtle-deck*, TURTLE *sb.*² 5]. **1891** *Chambers' Encycl.* VII. 421/2 An armoured turtle-backed deck which extends throughout the length of the ship. **1908** *Blackw. Mag.* Jan. 51/1, I can see..a turtle-backed affair pushing out from the advanced trench.

**Turtle-dove** (tɜ̄·ɹt'lˌdɒv). Forms: see TURTLE *sb.*¹ and DOVE. [f. TURTLE *sb.*¹ + DOVE: cf. Da. *turteldue* (Sw. *turturdufva*), Du. *tortelduyf* (Kilian *-duyve*), MLG. *torteldûve*, G. *turteltaube* (MHG. *turtel-*, *türteltûbe*, OHG. *turtel-*, *turtil(i)-*, *turtula-tûba*).]

**1.** A dove of the genus *Turtur*, esp. the common European species *T. communis*, noted for its graceful form, harmonious colouring, and affection for its mate: = TURTLE *sb.*¹ 1.

Also applied to *T. risorius*, the Barbary dove, and locally to doves of other genera, as the N. American *Zenaidura carolinensis*, and the Australian *Stictopelia cuneata*.

*a* **1300** *Cursor M.* 11304 (Cott.) To offer turtuls doues [*v.rr.* turtill dovis, turtil douues, turtur doufes] tua. *c* **1420** ? LYDG. *Assembly of Gods* 820 A turtyldoue he bare an hygh for hys crest. *c* **1530** *Crt. of Love* 234 Anelida, true as turtill-dove. **1616** SURFL. & MARKH. *Country Farme* 83 Of all these fore-named kinds of Birds, there is none more apt to tame than the Turtle doues. **1742** BLAIR *Grave* 532 The shrill-tongu'd Shrew, Meek as the Turtle-Dove, forgets her Chiding. **1802** MONTAGU *Ornith. Dict.* G 6 b, Spotted-necked Turtle-dove. **1834** PRINGLE *Afr. Sk.* ix. 308 The turtle dove (*Columba risoria*) cooing amorously in every mimosa brake. **1909** *Westm. Gaz.* 17 July 14/3 The turtle-dove, which we see so frequently in the fanciers' shops,..is not the common turtle-dove of this country, but the Collared or Barbary dove.

†**b.** *Sea turtle-dove*, the Black Guillemot or Dovekie: = SEA-TURTLE ¹. *Obs.*

**1753** [see DOVE *sb.* 1 c].

**2.** *fig.* applied to a person: cf. TURTLE *sb.*¹ 2.

**1535** COVERDALE *Ps.* lxxiii[i]. 19 O delyuer not the soule of thy turtle doue vnto the beestes. **1575** JUD. SMITH *Misticall Deuise* A iij b, My darling and my harts desyre, my onely Turtle Doue. *a* **1800** *Fause Foodrage* xxii. in Child *Ballads* II. 299, I shall learn your turtle-dow As well to write and read. **1856** MISS MULOCK *J. Halifax* xix, I am not interested in old turtle-doves.

Hence **Tu·rtle-do·veism, Tu·rtle-do·very,** *nonce-wds.*

**1850** LD. LYTTON in *Life* (1906) I. ii. 25 Only just married, and in a state of turtle-doveism. **1886** K. S. MACQUOID *Sir J. Appleby* iii, Half afraid I might be considered an intruder in such a turtle-dovery [the abode of a newly married couple].

**Turtler** (tɜ̄·ɹtləɹ). [f. TURTLE *sb.*² + -ER ¹.]

**1.** A person, or a vessel, engaged in turtling; a turtle-catcher.

**1697** DAMPIER *Voy.* (1729) I. 395 The Jamaica Turtlers have such [nets]. **1707** SLOANE *Jamaica* I. p. lvi, The Turtlers who furnish the island with Turtle, may be reckoned among the trading ships. **1831** JANE PORTER *Sir E. Seaward's Narr.* II. 91 The turtlers returned with twenty-six. **1898** *Blackw. Mag.* July 62/2 He had made acquaintance..with Florida wreckers, Tortuga turtlers, and Labrador eggers.

**2.** A seller of turtle.

**1740** *New Hist. Jamaica* vii. 180 No Butcher or Turtler shall sell any Meat or Turtle by Retail.

**Turtlet** (tɜ̄·ɹtlėt). [dim. of TURTLE *sb.*²: see -ET, -LET.] A small or young turtle.

**1831** TRELAWNY *Adv. Younger Son* II. 31 When, off Ceylon, I picked up that pretty little turtlet. **1899** *Nat. Science* Sept. 224 The turtlets show a greater percentage of abnormalities in the carapace than the older individuals.

**Turtling** (tɜ̄·ɹtliŋ). [f. TURTLE *sb.*² + -ING ¹.] The action or occupation of 'fishing' for or catching turtle. Also *attrib.*, and as *pres. pple.* (as if from TURTLE *v.*²).

**1669** *Admiralty Crt. Exam.* 77 19 Aug., Intended to goe ..with the ship to the Island of Kiamanas to make a turtling voyage. **1726** G. ROBERTS *Four Yrs. Voy.* 19, I sent my Boat ashore, to see..if any People were there a Turtling. **1810** *Sporting Mag.* XXXV. 287 The French fishermen come there turtling. **1889** H. H. ROMILLY *Verandah N. Guinea* 184 A turtling trip. *Ibid.* 189 The turtling was not very successful.

**Turtois, turtu,** obs. forms of TORTOISE.

†**Turtur.** *Obs.* Forms: 1, 4–5 turtur, (3 *gen.* turtres), 4–7 turture, 5–6 -our, 6 -or. [In OE. direct from L.; cf. OHG. *turtur* (Notker), OIcel. *turturi*. In ME. partly a. OF. *turtre, tortre, tourtre, tourte*, mod.F. *tourtre*; = Pr. *tortre*, It. *tortore, -ora*, OSp. *tortora* (Sp. *tortola*); all representing L. *turtur-em, turtur*, app. an echoic name, imitating the cooing of the dove.] = TURTLE *sb.*¹

*c* **825** *Vesp. Psalter* lxxxiii. 4 [lxxxiv. 3] Speara ȝemoeted him hus & turtur nest hwer ȝesettað briddas his. *c* **950** *Lindisf. Gosp.* Luke ii. 24 þætte sealdon..tuoe turturas *vel* tuoȝe birdas culfras. **971** *Blickl. Hom.* 23 Tweȝen culfran briddas..& tweȝen turturan ȝemæccan. *c* **1220** *Bestiary* 694 In boke is ðe turtres lif Writen o rime. *c* **1375** *Sc. Leg. Saints* xxiv. (*Alexis*) 231 þane scho sad,..þat but mak ay suld scho dwel As turtur. **1382** WYCLIF *Luke* ii. 24 A peyre of turtris [1388 turturis]. **1398** TREVISA *Barth. De P. R.* XII. xxxv. (Bodl. MS.), The Turture is a semple bridde. *c* **1440** *Pallad. on Husb.* I. 556 With whete & milk in this thi turturs fede. *c* **1450** HOLLAND *Howlat* 127 The Turtour trewest, Ferme, faithfull and fast. **1500–20** DUNBAR *Poems* lxxiv. 37 Swete gentill turtour, quhair is ȝour pete went? **1508** — *Tua Mariit Wemen* 262 And be as turtoris in your talk,..Be dragonis baitht and dowis, ay in double forme. **1649** JER. TAYLOR *Gt. Exemp.* I. Ad Sect. v. 81 The turtures ..being an oblation.

*attrib.* *c* **1425** *Cursor M.* 11304 (Trin.) And elles who þat myȝte not so Shulde offer turtur doufes two.

**Tu·r-tu·rring,** *vbl. sb.* [Echoic.] An imitation of the cooing of a dove, used to designate the action or sound.

**1896** *Q. Rev.* July 73 The 'tur-turring' of the turtledove, the 'coo' of the queest..tell of the shade.

†**Tu·rvary.** *Obs.*⁻¹ [ad. med.L. *turvāria*, var. of *turbāria*.] = TURBARY 2.

**1651** G. W. tr. *Cowel's Inst.* II. ii. 72 Fishing, digging of Turfes,..called Piscaryes, Turvaryes [orig. *turuariam*].

**Turve, Turved, Turves, Turving:** see TURF *sb.*¹ and ², *v.*¹, TURFING.

†**Turver.** *Obs.*⁻¹ In 5 -are. [f. *turv-* TURF *sb.*¹ or *turve* TURF *v.*¹] A turf-cutter.

*c* **1440** *Promp. Parv.* 507/2 Turvare, *glebarius*.

**Turveydrop** (tɜ̄·ɹvidrǫp). The surname of a character in Dickens's *Bleak House* (1852), who poses as a perfect model of deportment; allusively, a person who does this. Hence (*colloq.* and *journalistic*) **Tu·rveydropdom; Turveydro·pian** *a.*

**1876** J. WEISS *Wit, Hum. & Shaks.* iii. 101 Malvolio's conceit is Turveydropian and runs to deportment. **1877** W. H. RUSSELL *Prince of Wales' Tour* iv. 117 The maintenance of that staid deportment which the Oriental Turveydrop considers the best proof of high State and regal dignity. **1889** *Catholic News* 3 Aug. 5/1 She..deported herself so as to delight a Turveydrop's heart. **1892** *Pall Mall G.* 21 June 2/1 He showed himself a past master in deportment and might be envied by Court Chamberlains, Gold Sticks, Masters of Ceremonies, and the whole of Turveydropdom. **1897** *N. B. Daily Mail* 31 May 4 They pose in the deprecatory attitude, and become [a] sort of 'Turveydrops' in Church politics. **1899** *Longm. Mag.* Apr. 337 Those Turveydropian maxims on deportment and dress.

**Tusa**: see TUZA.

**Tuscan** (tɒ·skăn), *a.* and *sb.* Also 6 **Tuskan(e, Thuscane, 6–7 Tuscane, 6–8 Thuscan; 6 Toscane, Thoscan, -kan, 7 Toscan.** [= F. *Tuscan, -ane*, It. *Toscano*, ad. late L. *Tuscān-us* of or belonging to the *Tuscī* or *Thuscī*, a people of ancient Italy (called also *Etruscī* Etruscans), pl. of *Tuscus* adj. and sb., an ethnic name.]

**A.** *adj.* **a.** In reference to ancient times = ETRUSCAN *a.* **b.** Of or pertaining to Tuscany, formerly a grand duchy, having Florence as its capital; now a part of the kingdom of Italy, nearly corresponding to the ancient Etruria.

**a. 1513** DOUGLAS *Æneis* XI. xii. 3 The Tuscane Dukis and horsmen. **1552** HULOET, Tuskan tongue or language. **1587** W. FOWLER *Wks.* (S.T.S.) I. 100 Also Horatius that did alone defend the bridge aganis the Thoskan force. **1600** HOLLAND *Pliny* IX. 340 He was taught the Tuscane learning and knowledge. **1649** OGILBY *Virg. Georg.* I. (1684) 72 Great Vesta, Romulus, and Patriot Gods, Who guard Imperial Rome, and Tuscan Floods. **1706** SMITH in Hearne *Collect.* 14 Dec. (O.H.S.) I. 312 The old Thuscan language. **1843** MACAULAY *Horatius* xxxv, The Tuscan army, Right glorious to behold.

**b. 1588** KYD *Househ. Phil.* Wks. (1901) 263 Therefore was it well sayde of that Thoscan Poet [Petrarch]. **1728** CHAMBERS *Cycl.* s.v. *Italian*, The Tuscan is usually preferred to the other Dialects. **1841** W. SPALDING *Italy & It. Isl.* II. 171 All the Tuscan towns yield in interest to the classic city [Florence] which became their chief. **1841–4** EMERSON *Ess.*, *Art* Wks (Bohn) I. 149 The pictures of the Tuscan and Venetian Masters. **1886** PATER *Appreciations* (1890) 158 The delicate..sculpture of the early Tuscan school

**c.** *Arch.* Name of the simplest and rudest of the five classical orders of architecture; allied to the Doric (of which it is by many considered a simpler form), but devoid of all ornament; belonging to this order, as *a Tuscan pillar.*

**1563** SHUTE *Archit.* C iv, I haue more at large spoken of this matter in the ending of the Tuscan piller. **1624** WOTTON *Archit.* I. in *Reliq.* (1651) 228 The Tuscan is a plain, massie, rurall Pillar, resembling some sturdy well-limb'd Labourer, homely clad. *Ibid.* 230 The Tuscan is of all the rudest Pillar, and his Principall Character Simplicity. **1728** CHAMBERS *Cycl.* s.v., Of all the Orders, the Tuscan is the most easily executed; as having neither Triglyphs nor Dentils, nor Modillions to confine its Intercolumns. **1801** RANKEN *Hist. France* I. I. v. 446 The Tuscan was more robust and unadorned than any of these orders [Doric, Ionian, and Corinthian]. **1851** RUSKIN *Stones Venice* I. App. vii. 359 Another order, called Tuscan (which is no order at all, but a spoiled Doric).

**d.** Applied to a method of plaiting the fine wheaten straw grown in Tuscany for hats, bonnets, etc.; also to the golden yellow colour of this. Cf. LEGHORN 1.

**1834** MCCULLOCH *Dict. Comm.* (ed. 2) 629 The Tuscan plait ..largely imported, and made up into bonnets in this country. **1842** *Penny Cycl.* XXIII. 222/2 Men..employed in drabbets and Tuscan plait at Haverhill [Suffolk]. **1882** CAULFEILD & SAWARD *Dict. Needlework* 504 *Tuscan straw work*, finely plaited straw of wheat, having a delicate and slender stalk, and golden hue; growing in Tuscany, and manufactured into circular 'flats', for hat and bonnet. **1887** *Daily News* 11 Jan. 3/1 Tiring of that novelty the public called for other colours, and tuscan, apricot, coffee, and beige followed in quick succession.

**B.** *sb.* **a.** = ETRUSCAN *sb.* **b.** A native or inhabitant of mediæval or modern Tuscany.

**a. 1387** TREVISA *Higden* (Rolls) II. 435 Eneas afterward was kyng of eiþer kyngdom of Latyns and of Tuscans. *Ibid.* III. 159 He ouercame þe Vulces..and made pees wiþ Tuscans. *c* **1425** WYNTOUN *Cron.* IV. 149 He knyt hym to þe Tuskanys, And warrayide wiþe þaim þe Romanys. **1533** BELLENDEN *Livy* I. xx. (S.T.S.) 117 King tarquyne..renewit þe bond of confederacion with tuskanis. **1600** HOLLAND *Livy* IX. 340 The Romanes having slaine many thousands of the Tuscanes, gained thirtie eight ensignes of the field. **1770** LANGHORNE *Plutarch* (1851) I. 158/2 The Gauls expelled the Tuscans. **1843** MACAULAY *Horatius* xliii, He eyed the flinching Tuscans, And scorn was in his eye.

**b. 1633** MASSINGER *Guardian* II. v, The lusty girl of France, the sober German,.. The Roman libertine, and sprightful Tuscan.

**c.** The language of Tuscany, regarded as the classical form of Italian.

**1568** (*title*) The Fearfull Fansies of the Florentine Couper: Written in Toscane, by Iohn Baptista Gelli..and..translated into English by W. B[arker]. **1671** J. GAILHARD *Pres. St. Italy* (ed. 2) 173 The right Italian language, or Toscan, as they usually call it, is very Sententious. **1817** BYRON *Beppo* xxxi, He knew..French and Tuscan. **1906** *Hibbert Jrnl.* Apr. 583 Their language is the purest Tuscan of the golden age of the Italian Vernacular.

**C.** *Comb.*, as *Tuscan-coloured* adj. (of the colour of Tuscan straw: see A. d), *-like* adj. or adv.; †**Tuscan-top,** applied sarcastically to a style of hair-dressing.

**1581** PETTIE *Guazzo's Civ. Conv.* II. (1586) 65 If it be lawfull for me to write Tuscane like, why..not..likewise..to speake Tuscane like? **1601** B. JONSON *Poetaster* III. i, These high gable-ends, these tuscane-tops. **1905** *Westm. Gaz.* 8 Mar. 8/2 Such a hat would be very dainty in a..Tuscan-coloured straw with Saxe blue ribbon velvet.

Hence † **Tusca·nic** *a.* [ad. L. *Tuscānic-us*] = sense A. c; **Tu·scanish** *a.* = sense A. b; **Tu·scanism,** Tuscan style or character; a Tuscan idiom or phrase; **Tu·scanize** *v.*, (*a*) *intr.* to become Tuscan; (*b*) *trans.* to make Tuscan; (*c*) *intr.* to speak in the Italian of Florence or Tuscany.

**1601** HOLLAND *Pliny* XXXVI. xxiii. II. 595 Such pillars as beare in compasse.., as much as..the sixt part of the height, be called Dorique:..such as have a seventh part, be *Tuscanique. **1580** G. HARVEY *Let. to Spenser* Wks. (Grosart) I. 84 Not a looke but [is] *Tuscanish alwayes. *Ibid.*, Since Galateo came in, and *Tuscanisme gan vsurpe. **1593** — *Pierce's Super.* ibid. II. 19 The glory of our English Eloquence, and our vulgar Tuscanisme (if I may so terme it). **1596** NASHE *Saffron Walden* Wks. (Grosart) III. 90 He would needs crosse the seas to fetch home two penniworth of Tuscanisme. **1906** *Athenæum* 2 June 664/3 The Tuscanism 'si domanda'. *a* **1618** SYLVESTER *Epistles* vii. 13 When every thing now *Tuskanizeth so, That nothing is the same it is in show. **1768** BARETTI *Mann. & Cust. Italy* I. 161 His language is the most nauseous medley..taken from several of the Italian dialects, and tuscanized in a most ridiculous manner. **1905** *Athenæum* 8 Apr. 431/1 The Genoese who blames his Tuscanizing friend for saying 'arimmetica' in place of *aritemetica*.

**Tusche,** obs. Sc. f. TISSUE; obs. f. TUSH.

† **Tuscle.** *Obs.* Forms: 1, 4 tuxl, 6 tussle, tuscle. [OE. *tuscel, *tuxl*, derivative of *tusc, tux*, TUSK *sb.*¹] = TUSK *sb.*¹ 1.

*c* **1000** *Sax. Leechd.* II. 104 Wið onfealle ȝefoh fóx asleah of cucum þone tuxl. *a* **1400** *Octouian* 929 Twey tuxlys out of hys mouth set, As of a bore. **1600** F. WALKER *Sp. Mandeville* 10 b, This man..was borne..with all the teeth and tussles which he nowe hath. *Ibid.* 25 b, Her teeth and tussles ..began to bud and growe out anew. *Ibid.* 149 A wilde Boare, with two great tuscles shooting aboue foure spans out of his mouth.

**Tush** (tɒʃ), *sb.*¹ Forms: *α.* 1 tusc, 4 tussche, 4–6 tusche, 5 tusshe, 6– tush. *β.* 4 tossche, 5 tosch(e, toyssh, 6 (9 *dial.*) tosh. [ME. *tus(s)ch, tos(s)ch*, normal representatives of OE. *tusc* (see TUSK *sb.*¹); partly specialized in use.]

**1.** = TUSK *sb.*¹ 1. Now chiefly *arch.* or *dial.*

*α.* *c* **725** *Corpus Gloss.* G. 62 *Genuino*, tusc. *c* **1050** in Wr.-Wülcker 489 *Genuinis*, tuscum. **13..** *Seuyn Sages* (W.) 914 The tusches in the tre he smit. **13..** *Gaw. & Gr. Knt.* 1573 [The boar] Whettez his whyte tuschez. **1398** TREVISA *Barth. De P. R.* XVIII. xxxi. (Bodl. MS.), Beestes wiþ teeþ and tussches in aiþer iowe haue none hornes. *c* **1410** *Master of Game* (MS. Digby 82) v, Men beyonde þe see calleth þe neither tusshes of þe boore his armes, or elles his files,..also þei calleth his tusshes aboue gres. **1576** TURBERV. *Venerie* 150 Amonge the reste they have foure [teeth],..and we call them Tuskes or Tusches. **1621** G. SANDYS *Ovid's Met.* VIII. (1626) 157 His tushes equall those Of Indian Elephants. **1672** JOSSELYN *New Eng. Rarities* 97 Morse, or Sea Horse, having a great Head, .. armed with Tushes as white as Ivory. **1737** STACKHOUSE *Hist. Bible* (1767) VI. VI. iii. 77 The whale has neither teeth nor tushes. **1843** KINGSLEY *Saint's Trag.* II. viii. 299 He is an old boar, and honest; he wears his tushes outside, for a warning to all men.

*β.* **13..** *Seuyn Sages* (W.) 911 The bor..wette his tossches and his fet. *c* **1440** *Promp. Parv.* 497/2 Tosche, longe tothe (*Winch. MS.* tosch; *Pynson* toyssh), *colomellus, culmus.* *a* **1563** BECON *Humble Supplic.* Wks. III. 22 Whose teeth ar like to y^e^ venomous toshes of y^e^ rampyng lyon. **1823–78** in dial. glossaries (E. Anglia, Northumb., Cumb.).

**b.** *spec.* A canine tooth, esp. of a horse: cf. TUSK *sb.*[1] 1 b.

**1607** MARKHAM *Caval.* I. iv. (1617) 28 At fiue yeares olde he changes his tushes. **1610** — *Masterp.* II. clxvii. 477 The [horse's] tush will be white, small, short, and sharp. *c* **1720** W. GIBSON *Farrier's Guide* I. vi. (1738) 86 The canini or Dog teeth, which in Horses are called the Tushes. **1766** PENNANT *Zool.* (1768) I. 107 The Hedge hog... In each jaw are two sharp pointed cutting teeth: in the upper jaw are on each side four tushes, and five grinders: in the lower.. three tushes..and..four grinders. **1850** SMEDLEY *F. Fairlegh* xl, Rising five and six..tush well up in one, and nicely through in the other.

**c.** A stunted tusk in some Indian elephants.

**1859** TENNENT *Ceylon* II. VIII. i. 274 Not one elephant in a hundred is found with tusks in Ceylon... Nearly all, however, have those stunted processes which are called tushes, about ten or twelve inches in length and one or two in diameter. **1859** *All Year Round* No. 32. 129 All the untusked elephants of Ceylon have 'tushes',..which they use in snapping off small branches. **1878** J. GIBSON in *Encycl. Brit.* VIII. 125/1 The male [Ceylon elephant]..generally has a pair of upper incisors, known as 'tushes', about a foot long, and one or two inches in diameter. **1900** POLLOK & THOM *Sports Burma* ii. 35 The result of the cross-breed is that you get large males with very poor tusks, but still tusks, as distinct from tushes.

**2.** In a plough: = FIN *sb.* 3 b. *Obs.* exc. *dial.*

**1649** BLITHE *Eng. Improv. Impr.* (1653) 193 The Tush or Phin of the Share will whelm the more being set down to the work which is the Levell or bottom of the head. **1787** GROSE *Provinc. Gloss., Tush,* the wing of a ploughshare. *Glouc.* **1894** *S. E. Worc. Gloss., Tush,* (1) the broad part of a plough-share.

**3.** *Arch.* (See quot. and cf. TUSS.)

**1905** BOND *Gothic Archit.* 366 There may still be seen the 'tushes'; i. e. the projecting courses on which the heads of the flying buttresses were to rest.

Hence **Tushed** (tʊʃt) *a.*, having a tush or tushes; tusked.

*c* **1440** *Promp. Parv.* 497/2 Toschyd, or tuskyd (*P.* toysshyd), *colomellatus.* **1649** BLITHE *Eng. Improv. Impr.* (1653) 29 Plow thy Land a thin broad furrow,..or rather flay it, or take off thy Skin or Turf with a very broad whinged or tushed share. *c* **1828** [see TUSKED *a.* b].

†**Tush,** *sb.*[2] *Obs. rare.* [Variant of TUSK *sb.*[2]; for the form cf. prec.] A tuft.

**1570** LEVINS *Manip.* 193/39–41 A Tushe of heyres, *crinetum.* A Tushe of thornes, *dumetum.* A Tushe of trees, *arboretum.*

**Tush** (tʊʃ), *int.* (*sb.*[3]) *arch.* Forms: 5 tussch, tysche, 6 tusche, tusshe, tushe, tuch, 6– tush. [A natural utterance: cf. TWISH.] An exclamation of impatient contempt or disparagement.

*c* **1440** *York Myst.* xxxiii. 121 3a, tussch! for youre tales, þai touche not entente. *c* **1450** *Mankind* 783 in *Macro Plays* 29 Tysche! a flyes weynge! *c* **1520** SKELTON *Magnyf.* 591 Tushe! holde your pece. **1535** COVERDALE *Jer.* v. 11 Tush, there shall no miszfortune come vpon vs. **1602** SHAKS. *Ham.* I. i. 29 Tush, tush, 'twill not appeare. **1678** BUNYAN *Pilgr.* I. 251 Tush, said Obstinate, away with your book. **1791** COWPER *Iliad* II. 290 But tush,—Achilles lacks Himself the spirit of a man. **1837** HAWTHORNE *Twice-told T.* (1851) II. i. 16 Tush! we have nothing to fear. **1891** FARRAR *Darkn. & Dawn* xlv, Tush, Cæsar! be a man. Sweep aside these flies. Poison them both.

**B.** *sb.* as a name for this utterance: esp. in phr. †*to make a tush at* (or *of*), to scoff at, to pooh-pooh (*obs.*).

**1600** HOLLAND *Livy* VI. xxxviii. 244 When the Tribunes.. made but a tush therat. **1628** EARLE *Microcosm., Worlds wise Man* (Arb.) 61 His tush is greatest at Religion. **1632** LITHGOW *Trav.* (1906) p. xxii, A tush for that snarling Crew. *a* **1643** J. SHUTE *Judgement & Mercy* (1645) 128 People.. that make a tush of the Devills power. **1883** R. L. STEVENSON *Lett.* (1901) I. vi. 272 These tushes Are wearisome.

Hence **Tush** *v.*, *intr.* to say 'tush!', to scoff or express impatience *at*: also *trans.* to dismiss with 'tush!' (*nonce-use*); whence **Tu·shing** *vbl. sb.*; also **Tu·sher,** one who 'tushes'; **Tu·shery,** used by R. L. Stevenson for a conventional style of romance characterized by excessive use of affected archaisms such as 'tush!'.

**1548** UDALL *Erasm. Par. Luke* vi. 78 Thou makest muche tushyng, and many exceptions. **1555** HARPSFIELD in Bonner *Homilies* 30 b, [He] doth thou hym or tushe at hym. **1597** J. PAYNE *Royal Exch.* 11 To make men laughe at there tushinge and scoffinge of religiouse matters. **1679** J. BROWN *Life of Faith* (1824) II. xxii. 428 People become hardened in their sins..tushing at all threatenings. **1819** SCOTT *Ivanhoe* xl[i]v, Cedric tushed and pshawed more than once at the message. **1883** R. L. STEVENSON *Lett.* (1901) I. vi. 270 Every tusher tushes me so free that may I be tushed if the whole thing be worth a tush. **1883** — *Let. to Colvin* Oct. (1899) I. 285 It's great sport to write tushery. **1907** *Academy* 26 Jan. 96/1 This is what R. L. S. called 'tushery'. Luckily..for those who write tushery there is an enormous reading public that does not care a fig for Life. **1908** *Times* 9 Dec. 14/4 We overheard..an occasional pishing and tushing.

**Tushwe,** obs. form of TISSUE.

†**Tu·shy,** *a. Obs.* [f. TUSH *sb.*[1] + -Y.] Having tushes; = TUSKY.

**1430–40** LYDG. *Bochas* I. i. (MS. Bodl. 263) 10 Thei stood ..in daunger and in dreed Off cruel beestis, tigres and leouns, Off tusshi booris. *c* **1557** ABP. PARKER *Ps.* lxxx. 233 The tushy bore..doth route it up to stoure.

**Tusk** (tʊsk), *sb.*[1] Forms: *α.* 1–4 tux (1 twux), 3–7 tuske, 7– tusk. *β.* 4–5 tosk, *pl.* toskes. [OE. *tux* (whence by metathesis ME. *tusk, tosk*), normal and common variant of the rare OE. *tusc* (whence TUSH *sb.*[1]), = OFris. *tusk, tusch, tosch* (mod. WFris. *tosk*, NFris. *tosk, toske*, LG. of East Friesland *tûsk*); in OEFris. the mutated plural form *tesch* also occurs. There are no certain cognates outside of the Anglo-Frisian area; in mod. WFris. *tosk* has entirely displaced the OFris. *tôth* tooth.

On the supposition that the stem is that of Goth. *tunþ-us* tooth (with *-sko* suffix), it has been assumed that the OE. forms had a long vowel (*túsc, túx*), but of this there is no clear evidence. It is also very doubtful whether the second element in the ON. mythical name *Rata-toskr* or *-tǫskr* (a squirrel) can be definitely identified with this word.]

**1.** A long pointed tooth; *esp.* a tooth specially developed so as to project beyond the mouth, as in the elephant, wild boar, and various other animals.

A tusk is most frequently a development of a canine tooth, as in the boar and walrus; but it may be an incisor, as in the elephant and narwhal.

*a* **900** *Laws Ælfred* c. 49 Monnes tux bið xv. scill. weorð. ?*a* **950** *Prose Guthlac* v (Vercelli MS.), Heora teð wæron horses tuxum [*v.r.* twuxan] gelice. *c* **1000** *Sax. Leechd.* I. 370 Hundes tux gebærned & smale gegniden. *a* **1225** *Ancr. R.* 280 Þe wilde bor..is al kareleas of his tuxes. *a* **1225** *Juliana* 68 As an burst bar þat grunde his tuskes. *a* **1300** *E. E. Psalter* lvii. 6 [lviii. 6] Toskes of liouns lauerd breke sal ma. **13..** *Sir Beues* (A.) 742 A wilde bor..Wiþ his toskes he al to-schok. *a* **1340** HAMPOLE *Psalter* lvii. 6 Tuskis of lyons breke sall lord. *a* **1400–50** *Alexander* 4114 Þai..Tuke out þe tuskis & þe tethe [of elephants]. *c* **1470** HENRYSON *Mor. Fab.* 1184 Wks. (S.T.S.) II. 88 3e, Schir Wolf,..with 3our Tuskis rauenous Hes slane [etc.]. **1555** EDEN *Decades* 354 These great teeth or tuskes [of the elephant] growe in the vpper iaw downewarde. **1601** R. JOHNSON *Kingd. & Commw.* (1603) 203 To their tusks were fastened long and broad swords, to cut in sunder whatsoeuer stoode in their way. **1697** DRYDEN *Virg. Georg.* III. 387 Boars whet their Tusks. **1841–71** T. R. JONES *Anim. Kingd.* (ed. 4) 828 In the Male Narwal..from the intermaxillary bone of the left side of the face there projects a single tusk of great strength, which sometimes attains the length of eight or ten feet. **1851** D. WILSON *Preh. Ann.* (1863) II. III. iii. 101 Several very large tusks of boars or wolves. **1868** OWEN *Vertebr. Anim.* III. xxix. 369 Teeth..of uninterrupted growth, are called 'tusks'; such..are the incisors of the elephant, narwhal, dinotherium, and dugong, the canines of the boar, walrus, and hippopotamus. **1907** J. H. PATTERSON *Man-Eaters of Tsavo* ii. 23 The unfortunate jemadar's head had been left intact, save for the holes made by the lion's tusks on seizing him.

**b.** Applied *spec.* to the permanent canine teeth of a horse. More commonly called *tush.*

**1808** *Compl. Grazier* Introd. (ed. 3) 19 Twenty-four grinders,..four tushes or tusks, and twelve foreteeth. **1854** OWEN *Skel. & Teeth* in *Orr's Circ. Sc.* I. *Org. Nat.* 285 The permanent canine, or 'tusk', next follows; its appearance indicates the age of four years.

**c.** Used in contempt for human teeth.

[Cf. quot. 1614 s. v. TUSK *v.*[1] 2.] **1632** LITHGOW *Trav.* x. 446 He hath the longest Tuskes that euer stroke at Table.

**2.** A projecting part or object resembling the tusk of an animal. **a.** *Carpentry.* A bevel or sloping shoulder on a tenon, for additional strength.

**1679** MOXON *Mech. Exerc.* viii. 140 They cut a Tusk on the upper side of the Tennant, and let that Tusk into the upper side of the Girders. **1688** R. HOLME *Armoury* III. 110/2 *Tusk,* is a Bevel shoulder made to strengthen the Tennant of a Joyst. **1825** J. NICHOLSON *Operat. Mechanic* 566 In introducing binding joists,..it is necessary, in order to make the tenons sufficiently strong, to have a shorter bearing tenon attached to the principal tenon, with a sloping shoulder above, called a tusk, which term is likewise applied to this tenon, called the tusk tenon.

**b.** In miscellaneous uses.

**1823** BYRON *Juan* VII. lxiii, I've vow'd .. that shortly plough or harrow Shall pass o'er what was Ismail, and its tusk Be unimpeded by the proudest mosque. **1871** G. MACDONALD *Songs Days & Nights, Winter Days* IV. ii, Down tusks of ice one drop will go. **1908** *19th Cent.* Jan. 128 From the base of this tusk of land the grand river front of new Khartoum stretches.

**c.** In a lock, 'A sharp projecting point or claw which forms a means of engagement or attachment' (Knight *Dict. Mech.* 1875).

**d.** Short for *tusk-shell*: see 3.

In recent Dicts.

**3.** *attrib.* and *Comb.*, as *tusk-hunter, -mark; tusk-carrying, -like* adjs.; **tusk-shell** = TOOTH-SHELL; **tusk tenon,** a tenon made with a tusk (see 2 a); **tusk vase,** a vase made of an elephant's tusk, or in imitation of one so made.

**1898** *Daily News* 28 Apr. 6/1 Mr. Neumann brought many a procession of *tusk-carrying Zanzibaris to Mombasa... Carriers of the heaviest tusks are given the post of honour—the van. **1902** *Q. Rev.* Oct. 418 The *tusk-hunter will not be able to shoot his two elephants in..Kassola. **1876** HUXLEY in *Nature* 11 May 33/2 The male horse has a *tusk-like tooth, or canine. **1909** STACPOOLE *Pools of Silence* xvii, Above the *tusk marks..could be seen the rubbing mark where great shoulders had scratched themselves. **1861** P. P. CARPENTER in *Rep. Smithsonian Instit.* 1860, 222 Family *Dentaliadæ.* (*Tusk-Shells.) **1825** *Tusk tenon [see 2 a].

Hence **Tu·skish** *a.*, resembling a tusk; **Tu·skwise** *adv.*, in the manner of a tusk.

**1653** R. SANDERS *Physiogn.* 253 The teeth tuskish-like long. **1844** MRS. BROWNING *Drama of Exile* Wks. 1850 I. 72 Ye would perish,—beast by beast Devouring,—tree by tree, with strangling roots And trunks set tuskwise.

**Tusk,** *sb.*[2] *Obs.* exc. *dial.* [Of obscure origin; agrees in sense with TUSSOCK, which is found in use 20 years later. The variant *tush* (see TUSH *sb.*[2]) is common to this and TUSK *sb.*[1], but it is doubtful if there is any real connexion between the words.] A tuft (of hair); also, of rushes, grass, etc.

**1530** PALSGR. 284/1 Tuske of heer, *monceau de cheueulx.* **1565–73** COOPER *Thesaurus* s.v. *Cirrus, Cirratus,* that hath his heare..growing in tuskes and lockes. **1577** B. GOOGE *Heresbach's Husb.* II. (1586) 67 b, With a yellow hearie tuske in the midst. **1598** W. PHILLIP *Linschoten* xxxix. (Hakl. Soc.) I. 262 They weare onely a tuske of haire on the toppes of their heades. **1611** MARKHAM *Country Content.* I. iv. (1668) 26 Grounds that are all tusks of rushes, short ling, bramble bushes, or such like. **1851** STERNBERG *Dial. Northampt., Tusk,* a tuft of grass or weeds.

**Tusk,** *v.*[1] [f. TUSK *sb.*[1]]

†**1.** *trans.* The technical expression for: To carve (a barbel). *Obs.*

Perh. suggested by the tusk-like appearance of the two pairs of cirri depending from the upper jaw.

**1486** *Bk. St. Albans* F vij b, A Barbill tuskyd. **1513** *Bk. Keruynge* in *Babees Bk.* (1868) 265 Tuske that barbell. [**1787** BEST *Angling* (ed. 2) 169 *Tusk a barbel,* cut him up. **1853** *Fraser's Mag.* XLVIII. 694 The reader will remember when he puts the slice into a fish, that he gobbets trout, truncheons eel, fins chub, tusks barbel (etc.).]

**2.** *intr.* † **a.** ? To show the teeth. *Obs.*

**1614** B. JONSON *Bart. Fair* II. iii, Vapours? Neuer tuske, nor twirle your dibble... You shall not fright me with your Lyon-chap, Sir, nor your tuskes. **1616** — *Epigr.* cvii, Nay, now you puffe, tuske, and draw vp your chin, Twirle the poore chain you run a feasting in.

**b.** To use, or thrust with, the tusks; of a horse, to pull roughly with the teeth *at.*

**1825** JAMIESON, *To Tusk at,* to pluck or pull roughly; as when a horse tears hay from a stack, *Fife.* **1893** KIPLING *Many Invent.* 204 They were rooting and tusking among the young Sal.

**3.** *trans.* To root or dig *up*, or to tear *off* with the tusks; to wound with the tusk.

**1629** DEKKER *Londons Tempe* Wks. 1873 IV. 120, I could (to swell my trayne) beckon the Rhine, (But the wilde boare has tusked up his vine). **1818** KEATS *Endym.* II. 474 My poor mistress went..mad, When the boar tusked him. **1909** STACPOOLE *Pools of Silence* xvii, A tree..showed half its bark ripped off, tusked off by some old bull elephant. *Ibid.* xix, The screams of men trodden under foot or tusked to pieces.

**4.** To furnish with tusks; to project from or adorn like tusks.

**1896** KIPLING *Seven Seas, Merchantmen,* We've ratched beyond the Crossets That tusk the Southern Pole.

†**Tusk,** *v.*[2] *Obs. rare*[−1]. [app. f. TUSK *sb.*[2]: cf. in the same sense TUFT *v.* 4.] *trans.* ? To beat the bushes in (a wood) in order to rouse the game.

**1592** LYLY *Gallathea* II. i, You were best..make them tuske these Woodes, whilst we stande with our bowes.

**Tusk,** var. TORSK, fish.

**Tuskan,** obs. f. TUSCAN.

**Tuskar** (tʊ·skăɹ). Also **tusker**; **tuysker, twiscar.** [ad. ON. *torfskeri* (Fær. *torvskeri*), f. *torf* turf + *skera* to cut, shear. Hence also Sc. Gael. *toirsgein* (*-sgian*, assimilated to *sgian* knife), *tairisgein, tairisgil* (cf. TURSKILL).] An implement for cutting peats used in Orkney and Shetland: see quots.

**1808–18** JAMIESON, *Tusker,* an instrument made of iron, with a wooden handle, for casting peats, *Orkn.* **1809** EDMONDSTON *Zetl. Isl.* I. v. 177 The peats are cut with an instrument called a tuysker, which resembles a narrow spade, having a sharp plate of iron, called the feather, about seven inches long, projecting from the bottom on its left hand side, and it determines the form and size of the peat. **1822** HIBBERT *Shetl. Isl.* 430 An ancient Scandinavian implement of husbandry is used for casting the peats, named a tuskar. **1822** SCOTT *Pirate* xii, His thoughts were..engrossed in the deficiencies of the one-stilted plough; of the 'twiscar', with which they dig peats. **1883** *Chamb. Jrnl.* 211 Here he cuts his peats.., using..a spadelike instrument called a tusker. **1884** RAMPINI *Shetl. & Shetlanders* ii. 86 His archaic implements of agriculture—his tuskar or peat spade. **1900** J. GUNN *Orkney Bk.* 297 The flaying-spade and the tuskar are not mere toys, nor is 'taking out' the newly-cut peats a holiday task.

**Tusked** (tʊskt, *poet.* tʊ·skĕd), *a.* [f. TUSK *sb.*[1] + -ED [2].] Having tusks; armed with tusks.

*c* **1386** CHAUCER *Frankl. T.* 526 Biforn hym stant brawen of the tusked [*v.r.* tuxed] swyn. **1513** DOUGLAS *Æneis* VII. Prol. 82 Fed tuskit baris, and fat swyne. **1555** EDEN *Decades* 355 Of the Indian elephantes, only the males haue tuskes. But of them of Ethiopia and Lybia, both kyndes are tusked. **1656** COWLEY *Anacreontiques, Beauty,* Some with hard Hoofs, or forked claws, And some with Horns, or tusked jaws. **1681** GREW *Musæum* I. 27 As to those Beasts [wild boar] no one was horned and tusked too. **1860** WRAXALL *Life in Sea* ii. 44 A young animal [walrus], not yet tusked,..continued the attack. **1906** A. NOYES *Drake* III. in *Blackw. Mag.* May 622 Weird troops of tusked sea-lions.

**b.** *Her.* Having the tusks of a specified tincture different from that of the rest of the body.

**1766–87** PORNY *Heraldry* v. (ed. 4) 162 Gules, an Elephant statant Argent, tusked Or. *c* **1828** BERRY *Encycl. Her.* I.

Gloss., *Tusked*, or *Tushed*, .. is said of a boar, tyger, or elephant, when their tusks are borne of a different tincture to that of the body. **1864** BOUTELL *Her. Hist. & Pop.* xvii. § 3 (ed. 3) 281 Two boars arg., bristled, tusked, and unguled or.

**Tusker** (tʊ·skəɹ). [f. as prec. + -ER 1.] A beast having tusks, esp. an elephant or wild boar.

**1859** TENNENT *Ceylon* II. VIII. i. 280 Some natives,.. attracted by a noise in the jungle, witnessed a combat between a tusker and one without tusks. **1865** LIVINGSTONE *Zambesi* ix. 188 The tusker, fearing less, keeps his trunk down. **1887** E. GILLIAT *Forest Outlaws* 238 He..would fare forth in quest of a stag, a fox, or even a tusker [wild boar]. **1893** SELOUS *Trav. S. E. Africa* 372 About twenty elephants.., but no good tuskers.

**Tusker**, var. TUSKAR.

† **Tu·sking.** *Obs. rare.* [f. TUSK *sb.*2 + -ING 1.] = TUFTING *vbl. sb.* 1.

**1558** in Feuillerat *Revels Q. Eliz.* (1908) 93 Spente in attyres of hedpeces gerdells tuskynges pullinges owte and other garniture.

**Tuskless** (tʊ·skˌlės), *a.* [f. TUSK *sb.*1 + -LESS.] Having no tusks.

**1859** TENNENT *Ceylon* II. VIII. i. 281 The tuskless elephant. **1879** PRYER *Let.* 22 Nov. in J. Hatton *New Ceylon* iii. (1881) 72 Two of the elephants (tuskless) ran off, but the third faced about. **1895** *Chamb. Jrnl.* XII. 726/2 Apparently it is the male elephant that is usually found tuskless in Ceylon. **1907** *Spectator* 5 Jan. 11/1 Tuskless swine will grout up ground, if it be not too hard, almost as fast as the tusked boar.

**Tusky** (tʊ·ski), *a.* [f. as prec. + -Y.] Characterized by tusks; tusked: chiefly as a poetic epithet of the wild boar.

**1620** SHELTON *Quix.* II. xxxiv. 228 The Tuskie Boare was laid along, with many iauelins points. **1697** DRYDEN *Virg. Past.* x. 89 On Mountain tops to chace the tusky Boar. *a* **1763** SHENSTONE *Elegies* xx. 61 For them our tusky elephant expires. **1853** KANE *Grinnell Exp.* xx. (1856) 160 That marine pachyderm, the tusky walrus.

**b.** Having projections like tusks.

**1830** GALT *Lawrie T.* VI. x, The banks, ragged and tusky with fallen trees, were in few places accessible.

**Tusmose, tussemose**: see TUZZY-MUZZY.

**Tuss.** *dial.* or *Obs.* [Northern var. of TUSK *sb.*1] *Arch.* One of a series of stones or bricks forming a projecting course for the attachment of an additional structure. Cf. TUSH *sb.*1 3 and TOOTHING *vbl. sb.* 2 b.

**1412** in Raine *Catterick Church, Yorks.* (1834) 9 And the forsaide Richarde sall putte oute tusses for the makyng of a Reuestery. *Ibid.* 10 And also forsaide Richarde salle schote out tusses in the west ende for makyng of a stepill. **1834** RAINE *note*, This..term..implies the projecting stones left in..masonry..by which a contemplated building might in due time be attached...Such..stones..are still in the north of England not unfrequently called *tusses*, a corruption of *tusks*.

**Tussac, -ack**: see TUSSOCK.

**Tussah, -eh**, var. TUSSER, TUSSORE.

**Tussal** (tʊ·săl), *a. rare*—0. [f. L. *tuss-is* cough + -AL.] Of or pertaining to a cough.

**1890** BILLINGS *Med. Dict.*, *Tussal*, pertaining to cough. **1900–13** in DORLAND *Med. Dict.*

**Tusseeldar**, var. TAHSILDAR.

**Tusser** (tʊ·səɹ), **tussore** (tʊ·soəɹ). Also 7 **tussre, tessar, tessur,** 9 **tasar, tassar, tussar, tussur**; 8–9 **tusseh, tussah, tusha.** [ad. Hindī (and Urdū) *tasar* (tʊ·sʊɾ):—Skr. *tasara* (also *trasara*) shuttle, 'perhaps from the form of the cocoon' (Yule & Burnell).

Of the various spellings of this word the type *tussar, -er, -ur* represents most exactly the Hindī original. The forms *tussah, -eh*, though frequently employed in works dealing specially with India, are erroneous and due to some misunderstanding. The prevailing form in ordinary use is now *tussore* (prob. after Indian place-names such as *Mysore*), to which the incorrect pronunciation (tʊ̆sōᵊɹ) is frequently given.]

**1.** A coarse brown silk (furnished by *Antheræa mylitta* and other species of silkworm) made in and imported from India. Also *ellipt.* a dress made of this.

*α.* **1619** in Foster *Eng. Factories Ind.* (1906) 112 A kind of Bengala stuff of silke..called tessar. **1620** *Ibid.* 198 Quilts of 'Sutgonge'.. lined .. partly with taffeta and partly with 'tessur'. **1620** (Oct. 6) *Factory Rec., Patna* I. (India Office MS. Rec.), Wee have finished our provisiones for this yeare..12 courge of Tussres. **1810** in Milburn *Oriental Comm.* (1825) 263 Duty on..Tusha, 5 annas per seer of 80 Sic. wt. **1827** D. JOHNSON *Ind. Field Sports* 165 A coarse kind of silk known by the name of tussar, is produced there in large quantities. **1845** STOCQUELER *Handbk. Brit. India* (1854) 196 A lighter silk, termed tusser, much used..for room-punkahs,..gentlemen's blouses and ladies' morning-dresses. **1873** BLOCHMANN tr. *Aīn-i-Akbarī* I. 94 (Y.) Tassar, per piece..½ to 2 Rupees. **1876** COBB *Silk* in *Brit. Manuf. Industr.* V. 171 The silks now generally recognized as tussahs,..are a description of wild silk [etc.]. **1884** *Health Exhib. Catal.* p. xliii, Illustrations of silk culture, especially tussur.

*β.* **1876** BESANT & RICE *Gold. Butterfly* III. 132 You think it is silk,..and I believe they call it Indian tussore. **1884** G. ALLEN *Philistia* I. 58 A perfect fright in my shabby old Indian tussore. **1893** F. F. MOORE *I Forbid Banns* (1899) 120 Wearing a costume that..must have cost fifty guineas, while my daughters..are compelled to put up with the plainest of Tussores!

**b.** More fully *tusser* or *tussore silk*.

*α.* **1796** M. ATKINSON in *Trans. Linn. Soc.* (1804) VII. 41 A specimen of Bughy Tusseh silk. **1838** M. MARTIN *East India* II I. iv. 157 The chief use to which the tree..is.. applied is to rear the Tasar silk. **1867** PITT-RIVERS *Evol. Culture, Prim. Warfare* I. (1906) 62 *note*, The *Saturnia mylitta* is the caterpillar from which the Tusseh-silk is obtained. **1884** *Health Exhib. Catal.* 148/2 Tussah Silk, Corah Silk, Chuddahs.

*β.* **1882** CAULFEILD & SAWARD *Dict. Needlework* 504 Tussore silks..are of Indian manufacture. **1896** *Daily News* 26 May 6/4 The wild silks of India, known in commerce as 'Tussore silk', of which ladies' dresses and various articles are made.

**2.** A silkworm which yields tusser silk: = *tusser-worm* (see 3).

**1796** M. ATKINSON in *Trans. Linn. Soc.* (1804) VII. 41 There are none of the Palma Christi species of Tusseh to be had here.

**3.** *attrib.* and *Comb.*, as *tusser cloth, dress, parasol, stuff*; *tusser-coloured* adj.; **tusser-moth,** any moth of which the larva (*tusser-worm*) yields tusser, as the Indian *Antheræa mylitta* and the Chinese *A. pernyi*; **tusser-(silk)worm,** any silkworm yielding tusser; the larva of a tussermoth.

*α.* **1903** *New Reformer* I. 414 The varieties are that of the well-known Tassar..woven into the common *Tassar cloth, so highly esteemed all over the world for light clothing. **1802** ROXBURGH in *Trans. Linn. Soc.* (1804) VII. 34 A most durable, coarse, dark-coloured silk, commonly called Tusseh-silk, which is woven into a kind of cloth called *Tusseh doot'hies [DHOTI]. **1834** T. BROWN *Bk. Butterfl. & Moths* (ed. 2) I. Pref., That splendid insect, the *Tusseh Moth of Bengal. **1876** *Sat. Rev.* 14 Oct. 468/1 The work of the *Tussur silk-weavers. **1796** M. ATKINSON in *Trans. Linn. Soc.* (1804) VII. 41 There is another variation of the *Tusseh silk-worm in the hills near Bauglipore. **1837** HELFER in *Jrnl. Asiatic Soc. Bengal* VI. 42 The Tusseh Silkworm.. is the most common in use of the native silkworms. **1620** in Foster *Eng. Factories India* (1906) 197 *Tusser stufes of Bengala, of halfe silke, halfe cotten. **1813** W. MILBURN *Oriental Comm.* (1825) 303 There are two other kinds of worms which produce silk in Bengal, viz. the *Tusseh and Arrindy worms. **1878** T. WARDLE *Monogr. on Tusser & other Silks India* 3 Silk produced by the Tasar, Tusser or Tussore worm. **1890** 'R. BOLDREWOOD' *Col. Reformer* (1891) 336 Augusta's dust-coloured *tusser wrap.

*β.* **1887** *Daily News* 20 July 6/1 A *tussore-coloured lace dress. **1896** 'H. S. MERRIMAN' *Flotsam* iv. 46 Cool brown *tussore dresses, embroidered in white. **1881** MISS BRADDON *Asphodel* I. 54 Under her big *tussore parasol.

† **Tusserd**(e. *Obs. rare.* (?)

**1496** *Naval Acc. Hen. VII* (1896) 164, iij quarters of a c of Tusserdes iijs & a lode of grenewode xvjd.

**Tusshe,** obs. form of TUSH.

† **Tu·ssicate,** *v. Obs. rare*—1. [f. L. *tussic-us* afflicted with *tussis* a cough: see -ATE 3.] *intr.* To cough. Also **Tussicular** (tʊsi·kiŭlăɹ) *a.* [ad. L. *tussiculāris*, f. *tussicula*, dim. of *tussis* cough]; **Tussicula·tion**: see quots.

**1598** BASTARD *Chrestol.* I. xv. 11 Phisition Mirus talkes of saliuation,..Who doth ingurgitate, who tussicate. **1857** DUNGLISON *Med. Lex.*, *Tussicular*, relating to a cough, or to a slight cough. **1890** BILLINGS *Med. Dict.*, *Tussiculation*, slight, frequent, dry cough.

‖ **Tussilago** (tʊsilē·go). *Bot.* Also formerly, in French and anglicized form, 6 **tussyllage,** 7 **tussilage.** [L. (Pliny), f. *tussis* cough, from its use for curing coughs.] A genus of composite plants, including the coltsfoot, *T. Farfara*.

Formerly also including the butterbur (*T. Petasites*, now *Petasites vulgaris*).

**1510** STANBRIDGE *Vocabula* (W. de W.) D ij b, *Tussilego*, tussyllage. **1657** TOMLINSON *Renou's Disp.* 499 This syrupe is denominated from Tussilage. **1706** PHILLIPS (ed. Kersey), *Tussilago*, the Herb Foal's-foot, or Colts-foot, good for a Cough. **1712** in *Roses of Kilravock* (Spald. Cl.) 399 Debtor to A. Paterson, chyr-apothecarie..for tussilago-flower, maidenhair,..etc. **1741** *Compl. Fam.-Piece* I. i. 70 Put to it 3 Leaves of good Tussilago. **1786** ABERCROMBIE *Arr.* in *Gard. Assist.* 68 (Petasites) butterburr, or greater tussilago.

**Tussimussie,** obs. f. TUZZY-MUZZY, nosegay.

**Tussive** (tʊ·siv), *a.* [f. L. *tussi-s* cough + -IVE.] Pertaining to or caused by cough.

**1857** DUNGLISON *Med. Lex.*, *Tussive*, belonging or relating to cough:—as tussive vibration; the vibration of the parietes of the chest, caused by coughing. **1862** H. W. FULLER *Dis. Lungs* 22 Tussive fremitus and rhonchal fremitus..possess little value as indications of disease. **1899** *Allbutt's Syst. Med.* VI. 87 Vocal or tussive vibrations and sounds from the main air-tubes.

**Tussle** (tʊ·s'l), *sb.* Forms: see TUSSLE *v.* [f. TUSSLE *v.* Rare in literary use before 19th c.] A vigorous or disorderly conflict; a severe struggle, a hard contest; a scuffle. **a.** in physical sense; † in quot. 1629, an assault (*obs.*).

**1629** in Picton *L'pool Munic. Rec.* (1883) I. 232 Wee present Hugh Houghton for a tusle upon Mr. Ballive Chantrell. **1749** FIELDING *Tom Jones* IX. iv, I hate to see two people bear ill-will to one another, after they have had a tussel. **1818** SCOTT *Hrt. Midl.* li, It is some comfort, when one has had a sair tussle..that it is in a fair leddy's service. **1848** CLOUGH *Bothie* I. 146 Where the life and the strength came out in the tug and the tussle. **1851** BORROW *Lavengro* lxxxii. (1893) 318, I put myself into a posture which I deemed the best both for offence and defence, and the tuzzle commenced. **1862** SMILES *Engineers* III. 31 There was a terrible tussle and worrying between the dogs.

**b.** in figurative sense: *esp.* a sharp and determined contention or dispute.

**1857** DICKENS *Lett.* (1880) II. 23, I hope you have seen my tussle with the 'Edinburgh' [Review]. **1883** C. F. ADAMS *College Fetich* 11 An experience in the tussle of life. **1884** *Pall Mall G.* 17 July 2/1 The prospect of a tussle with the Peers.

**Tussle** (tʊ·s'l), *v.* Forms: 5 **tussill,** 6–7 **tusle,** 6–9 **tussel,** 8–9 **tustle,** 9 **tussell, tussle, tuzzle.** [Orig. app. Sc. and northern; prob. dim. or freq. of TOUSE *v.*: cf. TOUSLE, in north. dial. *toozle.*]

**1.** *trans.* To pull or push about roughly, to hustle; to struggle or contend roughly with, to engage in a tussle with. Now *rare.*

*c* **1470** HENRYSON *Mor. Fab.* IX. (*Wolf & Fox*) xvii, I trow, ye haif bene tussillit with sum tyke. **1573** G. HARVEY *Letter-bk.* (Camden) 18 Sum of them..hath baitid and tuslid and chasid me. **1706** PHILLIPS (ed. Kersey), To *Tustle*, to rumple, ruffle, or touze. **1775** S. J. PRATT *Liberal Opin.* lxxii. (1783) III. 34 The maid opened the door..and then we tussel'd her against the door-post. **1858** CARLYLE *Fredk. Gt.* VII. vi. (1872) II. 318 His Majesty hustled and tussled the unfortunate Crown-Prince.

**2.** *intr.* To struggle or contend in a vigorous and determined way; to wrestle confusedly; to scuffle.

**a.** in physical sense.

**1638** in Picton *L'pool Munic. Rec.* (1883) I. 232 Wee present ..Iane Ireland and Elizabeth Ireland for tusling and scolding one uppon another. **1719** D'URFEY *Pills* III. 322 These sons of him That hurls the bolt trisulcate..Did tustle with red-ey'd pole-cat. **1836** MARRYAT *Japhet* xxvi, I tussled with the man until my coat and shirt were torn. **1852** *Fraser's Mag.* XLVI. 95 When..fairly hooked, he shakes his head, tuzzles a little at the line, and..slips away.

**b.** in fig. use.

**1862** H. MARRYAT *Year in Sweden* I. 425 The Catholics tustled with the Reformed clergy for the pulpit. **1864** *John Greswold* I. 187 That..bitter thought..tussles hard with ones fortitude. **1897** *N. Y. Voice* 18 Mar. 8/2 The new tariff bill with which the extra session of Congress will tussle and pass, is said to be in the main a restoration of the McKinley tariff of 1890.

Hence **Tu·ssling** *vbl. sb.* and *ppl. a.*; also †**Tu·sslement,** an act of tussling, an assault (*obs.*).

**1597** *Salford Portmote Rec.* (1902) 3 Adam Pilkington and Isabell Traves made an affraye or tusselment. **1844** KINGLAKE *Eöthen* xxvii. (1878) 352 Forest trees, tall and stately..yet lead a tussling life of it below. **1858** CARLYLE *Fredk. Gt.* III. xvi. (1872) I. 240 The innumerable sanguinary tusselings of this War.

**Tussle,** var. TUSCLE *Obs.*, tusk.

**Tussock** (tʊ·sək), *sb.* Forms: 6–7 **tussocke,** (6 **thussocke**), 7–9 **tussuck,** 8– **tussock,** (9 **-ack, -ac, -ick**). [perh. an altered form of TUSK *sb.*2 (which is known in 1530), assimilated to diminutives in -OCK; but the actual relation of the two forms, as well as their ulterior history, is obscure.]

**1.** A tuft or bunch of hair. Now *rare* (cf. sense 3).

**1550** LATIMER *Last Serm. bef. Edw. VI* (1584) 107 b, If they would keepe it [hair]..as they ought to doe, there should not any such Thussockes nor Tuftes be seene. *Ibid.*, These Thussockes that are layd out now a dayes, there is no mention made in Scriptures, because they were not vsed in scripture tyme. They were not yet come to be so farre out of order, as to lay out suche Thussockes and Tuftes. **1550** CROWLEY *Epigr.* 1303 If theyr hayre wyl not take colour, then must they by newe, And laye it oute in tussockis: this thynge is to true. **1893** CROCKETT *Stickit Minister* (1894) 10 Bushy tussocks of grey eyebrow.

**2.** A tuft, clump, or matted growth, forming a small hillock, of grass, sedge, or the like; formerly also, a tuft or bunch of leaves, thorns, etc.

**1607** MARKHAM *Caval.* VI. iv. (1617) 12 If there bee any tussockes of long grasse, rushes, or dead fogge. **1681** GREW *Musæum* II. I. ii. 186 The Fruit [Prickle Apple] is remarkable for the several Tussucks or Bunches of Thorns wherewith it is armed. **1783** C. BRYANT *Flora Diæt.* (1787) 84 It hath a creeping root, from which comes forth a tussuck of long slender leaves. **1829** LOUDON *Encycl. Plants* (1836) 59 A[ira] cæspitosa is common in marsh-meadows, and occasions those excrescences called tussocks or hassocks which interrupt the progress of the scythe. **1883** *Century Mag.* XXVI. 925 Obliged to pick his way through an unusually soft marsh, springing from tussock to tussock. **1898** *Dublin Rev.* Jan. 166 Hills..overgrown with prickly plants forming rounded tussocks.

**3.** Short for *tussock-moth* or *caterpillar*: see 5.

**1819** G. SAMOUELLE *Entomol. Compend.* 247 Lar[ia] pudibunda (pale tussock)...Lar. fascelina (dark tussock). **1911** G. H. CARPENTER in *Encycl. Brit.* XVI. 472/2 The larvae.. are very hairy, and often carry dense tufts on some of their segments; hence the name of 'tussocks' frequently applied to them.

**4.** Short for TUSSOCK-GRASS. Also in *pl.*

**1832** C. M. GOODRIDGE *Voy. South Seas* 34 The Johnnys build their nests..among the long grass, generally termed Tussick. **1869** LADY BARKER *Station Life N. Zealand* iv. (1874) 25 Tussocks, the tall native grass, has the colour and appearance of hay. **1886** BRITTEN & HOLLAND *Eng. Plant-n.*, Tussocks, *Agrostis vulgaris*, and *A. alba*.—Glou[cester].

**5.** *attrib.* and *Comb.*, as (in sense 'covered with or consisting of tussock-grass') *tussock-bog, ground, mound*; **tussock-caterpillar,** the larva of the *tussock-moth*; **tussock-moth,** one of various kinds of moth, as those of the genus *Orgyia*, the larvæ of which have long tufts of hairs; **tussock-sedge,** a species of sedge, *Carex stricta*, growing in thick clumps. See also TUSSOCK-GRASS.

**1847** SIR J. C. ROSS *Voy. S. Seas* II. 262 A *Tussock-bog (for so a tract of land covered with this grass is called). **1843** J. D. HOOKER in *Gard. Chron.* 4 Mar. 131/1 These heaps, or tussacks, grow generally apart, but within a few feet of one another,..so that, in walking among them, you are quite hidden from view, and the whole *Tussac ground is a perfect labyrinth. **1826** KIRBY & SP. *Entomol.* III. xxx. 176 In the larva of *Tussock moths (*Laria pudibunda, fascelina*, etc.) the hairs are collected into tufts. **1887** *Amer. Naturalist*

XXI. 581 The white-marked tussock-moth, and the fall web-worm are the insects discussed. **1901** *Westm. Gaz.* 6 Sept. 10/2 The New York city parks have lately been invaded by a great army of caterpillars. The cause of all the trouble is the tussock moth. **1825** WADDELL *Voy.* 57 They differ from the king penguin..in having nests, which are sometimes in the sides of *tussac mounds. **1884** MILLER *Plant-n.*, *Carex stricta*, Greater Tufted Sedge, *Tussock Sedge.

Hence **Tu·ssocked** (-əkt) *a.*, covered with or formed into tussocks; planted, covered, etc. with tussock-grass; **Tu·ssocker** (*slang*): see quot.; **Tu·ssocky** *a.*, abounding in or forming tussocks.

**1796** MORSE *Amer. Geog.* I. 540 The marshes..are banked, drained, *tussocked, ploughed, and harrowed. **1832** C. M. GOODRIDGE *Voy. South Seas* 29 Our domicile..comfortable, in comparison to our boat tussicked up. **1892** *Times* 27 Dec. 10/1 Sunlight filters through..to promote the growth of the tussocked grass. **1889** V. PYKE *Wild Will Enderby* x. 148 A 'sun-downer' or '*tussocker'..is..one who loiters about till dusk, and then makes for the nearest station or hut, to beg for shelter and food. **1805** R. W. DICKSON *Pract. Agric.* II. 920 The grass [is liable]..to become *tussocky, or rise in large tufts. **1853** *Spring Lapl.* 54 We saw..rough tussocky meadows. **1880** SEEBOHM *Siberia in Europe* 180 The tussocky ridges between the little bogs. **1908** *Daily Chron.* 24 Dec. 1/3 A girl who has..a piece of his tussocky brown hair in a little locket on her breast.

**Tu·ssock-gra:ss.** Also tussac, -ack.

**1.** One or other of several grasses of the Southern Hemisphere; esp. (*a*) *Poa flabellata* (formerly *Dactylis cæspitosa*), a tall-growing valuable grass of the Falkland Islands and Patagonia; (*b*) *Lomandra longifolia* of Australia (N.O. *Juncaceæ*); (*c*) various New Zealand species of *Arundo* and *Poa*.

**1842** *Guernsey Star* Sept., The splendid Tussack Grass is the..glory of the Falkland Islands. Every animal there feeds upon it..and fattens in a short time...The blades are about six foot long, and from 200 to 300 shoots spring from one plant. **1845** LINDLEY *Veg. Kingd.* (1846) 113 Attention has lately been directed to the Tussac-grass of the Falklands, *Festuca flabellata*, a species forming tufts 5 or 6 feet high. **1866** *Treas. Bot.* 550 Tussac or Tussock [Grass], *Dactylis cæspitosa*. **1878** J. BULLER *N. Zealand* I. Introd. 9 It is generally..covered with either forest, tall fern or tussock-grass. **1880** BUCHANAN *Grasses N. Zealand* Tab. xxvii & xxviii, *Arundo conspicua*..*A. fulvida*, plumed tussac grass. **1884** 'R. BOLDREWOOD' *Melbourne Mem.* v. 38 The roof was neatly thatched with the tall, strong tussock-grass. **1906** CHEESMAN *N. Zealand Flora* 908 *Poa caespitosa*, Tussock grass.

**2.** The tufted hair-grass, *Aira cæspitosa*, or other native grass growing in tussocks.

**1860** G. H. K. in *Vac. Tour.* 117 Her cozy lair, amongst the sweet bog myrtle and warm tussock grass. *Ibid.* 134 The splashy moor, too wet to grow heather,..covered with tufts of coarse tussock grass. **1861** MISS PRATT *Flower. Pl.* VI. 73 Tufted Hair-grass..is commonly known..by the name of Hassock or Tussack-grass.

**Tussore, tussur**: see TUSSER.

† **Tu·ssy.** *Obs. rare.* [? Derivative of a simple **tus* or **tusse*, in *tus(se)mose*: see TUZZY-MUZZY.] A cluster, posy, or knot of flowers or leaves; an ornament of silver or gold of this form, forming a buckle or the like.

**1541** *Will E. Myllar* (Somerset Ho.), My blacke rybbonde with the hookes & a Tussy of syluer. **1633** J. DONE *Hist. Septuagint* 49 The Master Goldsmiths had laboured a Girdle of Flowers, and Tussies of all Fruits.

**Tussyllage, Tustle**: see TUSSILAGO, TUSSLE.

**Tut** (tʊt), *sb.*[1] Also 6, 8 tutt, 7 tit, toyte, 8–9 toit. [There is perh. more than one word here. Of the origin nothing has been ascertained.]

**1.** Each of a number of objects set up as 'bases' in rounders or similar games; also (in *pl.*), a kind of stool-ball in which the player at each base must move to the next base each time the ball is struck; also called *tut-ball*; also the game of rounders. *local.*

**1519** in *Priory of Hexham* (Surtees) II. 157 Ludi inhonesti, prout pili-ludus pedalis, et manualis, viz. tuttes, et handballa c Pennyston. *c* **1572** GASCOIGNE *Fruites of Warre* xciv, Yet haue I shot at maister Bellums butte And throwen his ball although I toucht no tutte, I haue percase as deeply dealt the dole As he that hit the marke and gat the gole. **1665** CLARKE *Phraseol. Puerilis* 141 (Halliw.). **1777** *Horæ Subsecivæ* (MS.) 443 (E.D.D.) *Tut*, a sort of stool ball much practised about the Easter holidays, particularly at Exeter. **1877** *Holderness Gloss.*, *Tut-ball*,..a very ancient game,..elsewhere called stool-ball. **1883** JACKSON & BURNE *Shropsh. Folk-Lore* 524 Tut-ball...One of the players in the den..hit back the ball with the palm of the hand, and immediately ran to one of three brick-bats, called 'tuts'—which were set up at equal distances.

**2.** *western dial.* 'A small seat or hassock made of straw; a cushion or hassock for kneeling upon' (*Eng. Dial. Dict.*).

**1553** BRADFORD *Serm. Repent.* (1574) F j, Oh hard harts that we haue, which make tuts for syn. **1637** *Churchw. Acc. Cheddle* (Davies), Paid for a tut for him that drawes the bellowes of the orgaines to sit upon. **1637–8** *Hartland (Devon) Church Acc.* in Chope *Hartland Gloss.* s.v. *Toyte*, Paid John Couch for a toyte for Mr. Churton to kneele upon 4 d. **1647–8** *Ibid.*, Paid for a tit for the minister 2 d. **1751–2** *E. Budleigh Churchw. Acc.* in *Rep. Devonsh. Provinc.* July (1902) (E.D.D.), For three tutts for the parson, 1 s. **1786** *Pilton Churchw. Acc.* in *Notes & Gleanings* (Exeter) II. 37/2 Pd for a Toit for the Minister's Dusk [*sic*].

**b** *transf.* as a butchers' term: = CUSHION *sb.* 4 a.

**1856** *Farmer's Mag.* Jan. 55 Wide fore-quarter..not quite matched by..the hind-quarters, the flank and tut being rather deficient.

† **3.** The orb borne as an emblem of sovereignty. *Obs. rare*—0.

**1674** BLOUNT *Glossogr.* (ed. 4), *Tut*,..a globe or ball, with a golden cross on it, anciently carried by Emperours and Kings. **1706** PHILLIPS (ed. Kersey), *Tut*, or *Mound*, an Imperial Ensign of a Golden Globe, with a Cross on it.

**Tut** (tʊt), *sb.*[2] *local.* Also 8 tote, tet-. [Origin unascertained.] Orig. in the Cornish tin-mines, now also in Derbysh. lead-mining: in the phrase *upon tut* (also *by the tut*), and *attrib.* as *tut-bargain*, *-man*, *-work* (also as vb.), *-worker*, *-working*, *-workman*: denoting a system of payment by measurement or by the piece, adopted in paying for work which brings no immediate returns, as distinct from TRIBUTE 3; hence, work of this character; dead-work.

**1778** PRYCE *Min. Cornub.* 180 [Under certain conditions] they set it to be sunk, driven, stoped, or cut down upon Tut; and in such case the Miners take what they term a Tut-bargain; that is, a piece or part of unmeasured ground, by the lump, for such price as can be agreed upon. *Ibid.* 184 The great inconvenience that attends this Tut-work or bargains by the lump or by the fathom, is, that if the ground proves hard and chargeable in the working, the labourer has no ability to go through with it. **1790** GROSE *Provinc. Gloss.* (ed. 2) s.v., To do work by the tut, or tote; to undertake it by the great. *West.* **1832** BABBAGE *Econ. Manuf.* xxvi. (ed. 3) 252 Tutwork..consists in sinking shafts, driving levels, and making excavations. **1839** DE LA BECHE *Rep. Geol. Cornw.* etc. xv. 567 Persons performing the work under the captains in the various parts of mines may..be divided into tributers, tutworkmen, and labourers. **1855** J. R. LEIFCHILD *Cornwall Mines* 147 The tutworkers, or tutmen, can readily judge of the hardness of the ground to be excavated. *Ibid.* 152 Dolcoath miners,..blasting and breaking, tut-working and tributing. *Ibid.* 175 Details of Expenses... Tutwork Bargains. **1874** J. H. COLLINS *Metal Mining* 40 Shafts are sunk and levels driven, in Cornwall and elsewhere, at a fixed rate per lineal fathom...This form of bargain is called tutwork. **1906** G. R. LEWIS in *Victoria Co. Hist., Cornw.* I. 568/2 The workmen..are, either tribute, tut, or daymen,..the tut worker contracting, at a certain rate for the sinking of shafts and..driving of levels.

**b.** Also in agricultural work (in s.w. counties).

**1800** SIR J. CALL in *Commun. to Board of Agric.* II. 482 Labourers and mechanics, who, instead of living with their employers,..have..undertaken tet-work, or worked for daily hire. **1854** *Jrnl. R. Agric. Soc.* XV. II. 401 The [Dorset] labourers are paid by 'tut' work, the dung-put fillers being paid by the square yard, and the spreaders and ploughmen by the acre. **1865** *Daily Tel.* 16 Nov. 3/5 He had had only one week of tut-work since harvest, when he earned 1s. extra. Mr. Bartlett..admitted that,..when he worked by the day, he gave him only 8s. a week, but he let him have his thatching and other tut-work, including hedging.

**Tut** (tʊt), *int.* (*sb.*[3]). Also 6 tutt, -e, 9 *Sc.* tuts. β. 9 *Sc.* toot, tout; toots. [A natural utterance; the spelling *tut* sometimes represents the palatal click (also spelt TCHICK, TCK). Cf. also *hut tut*, *hoot toot*, *hout tout* s.v. HOOT *int.*] An ejaculation (often reduplicated) expressing impatience or dissatisfaction with a statement, notion, or proceeding, or contemptuously dismissing it. (The Sc. *toot, toots*, expresses mild expostulation.)

*a* **1529** SKELTON *Caudatos Anglos* 27 Shake thy tayle, Scot, lyke a cur, For thou beggest at euery mannes dur: Tut, Scot, I sey, Go shake thy dog, hey! **1536** in Strype *Eccl. Mem.* (1721) I. xxxvi. 282 [He said, to what she had spoken, as it seems, in her own defence] Tut, tut, tut [and shaking his head three or four times]. *a* **1553** UDALL *Royster D.* I. ii. (Arb.) 14 Tut I owe nought. **1580** LUPTON *Sivqila* 18 Alteration (quoth you) tutte, it is wonderful. **1591** *Troub. Raigne K. John* (1611) 67 Tut, tut, my mercie serues to maime my selfe. **1599** PORTER *Angry Wom. Abingd.* (Percy Soc.) 57 Tut, tell not me of your impatience. **1601** SHAKS. *Jul. C.* v. i. 7 Tut, I am in their bosomes, and I know Wherefore they do it. **1773** GOLDSM. *Stoops to Conq.* v. i, I come,..once more, to ask pardon...Tut, boy, a trifle. **1826** J. WILSON *Noct. Ambr.* Wks. 1855 I. 200 *North.* I wish you would review these four volumes...*Shepherd.* Tuts! What's the use o' reviewin? **1859** THACKERAY *Virgin.* xc, Tut, tut!..let us hear no more of this nonsense! **1865** 'LEWIS CARROLL' *Alice's Adv.* ix, 'Tut, tut, child!' said the Duchess. 'Everything's got a moral, if only you can find it.'

β. **1805** MCINDOE *Poems* 71 Guillie said, toots, We'll have that there's no doubts. **1818** (Oct.) SCOTT in Lockhart *Life* xlii, He..rebuked the Captain with 'Toots, Adam! toots, Adam!' **1835** CARRICK *Laird of Logan* (1841) 137 Toot, man, haud your tongue. **1896–99** in *Eng. Dial. Dict.*

**b.** *sb.* The (or an) utterance of this exclamation, or a sound resembling this.

**1676** MACE *Musicks Mon.* 109 The Tut, is a Grace,..is a sudden taking away the Sound of any Note..in such a manner, as it will seem to cry Tut. **1894** DONOVAN *With Wilson in Matabeleland* 229 The incessant 'tut-tut-tut' of the Maxims. *Ibid.* 232 Each 'tut-tut' represents a bullet, at the rate of two to three hundred a minute. **1906** *Daily Chron.* 16 Jan. 6/7 There should be fixed stopping places [for motor-busses]...They would save many Balfourian 'Tut-tuts'.

Hence **Tut** *v. intr.*, to utter the exclamation 'tut'.

**1832** CARRICK in *Whistlebinkie* (1890) I. 99 Toots, sic nonsense. You may toots awa, but it's true sense, Mem. **1849** LYTTON *Caxtons* VIII. iii, In another moment the member of Parliament had forgotten the statist, and was pishing and tutting over the *Globe* or the *Sun*. **1873** MISS BRADDON *Str. & Pilgr.* III. x, The doctors had simpered at her, and tut-tuted, and patted her gently on the head. **1894** HALL CAINE *Manxman* v. ii, He laughed and tut-tutted.

† **Tut**, obs. var. *tit*, TEAT.

**1702** S. PARKER tr. *Cicero's De Finibus* III. 168 Parts of the Body..such as have no manifest Use, but serve only to beautifie, as the Peacock's Tail,..the Tuts and Beard of a Man [orig. *viris mammæ atque barba*].

† **Tut**, app. a var. of TOUTE *Obs.*, buttocks.

**13..** *Cursor M.* 28003 (Cott.) If þou..has bituix hir scankes gan, Or tirid or [? *read* hir] tut or skirt uptan.

† **Tu·tage.** *Obs. rare*—1. [f. L. *tūt-*, ppl. stem of *tuērī* to protect: see -AGE.] An object of protection or tutelage; (one's) care or charge.

**1593** DRAYTON *Eclogues* iii. 74 Apollo..Whose Tutage and especiall care I wish her still to bee.

† **Tu·tament.** *Obs. rare*—1. [ad. L. *tūtāmentum* defence, protection, f. *tūtārī* to protect: see -MENT.] A means of defence; a safeguard.

**1609** J. DAVIES *Holy Roode* (1878) 19 This holy Crosse is the true Tutament, Protecting all ensheltered by the same.

**Tutaneg**: see TUTENAG.

‖ **Tutang.** Also 7 tutan. [Chinese, f. *tu* to direct + *t'ang* hall; the latter is used as a kind of suffix in many Chinese titles.] One of several designations applied familiarly to a Chinese viceroy.

**1613** PURCHAS *Pilgrimage* IV. xvi. 369 These all are in subiection vnto the Tutan or Vice-roy of the Prouince. **1638** SIR T. HERBERT *Trav.* (ed. 2) 337 The whole Empire [China] is divided into fifteene great Provinces: governed by so many Quon-fu and Lausiæ; who have their Tutans, and Chyans, or Deputies under them. **1705** ROWE *Biter* II. i, I will put you into the Hands of the *Tutang*, which is,.. according to English Expression, the Constable of Croydon.

**Tutania** (tiutēⁱ·niă). [f. *Tutin*, name of the inventor or maker.] An earlier name for Britannia-metal.

**1790** RICHARDSON *Chem. Princ. Metallic Arts* 168 Tutania—8 oz brass; 2 lbs regulus of antimony, and 7 oz tin. **1825** J. NICHOLSON *Operat. Mechanic* 708 Tutania, or Britannia Metal...4 oz. of plate brass, and 4 oz. of tin; when in fusion, add 4 oz. of bismuth, and 4 oz. of regulus of antimony. **1842** G. FRANCIS *Dict. Arts*, etc., *Tutania*, or *Britannia Metal*...For the German tutania take 2 drachms of copper, 1 ounce regulus of antimony, and 12 ounces of tin. **1875** KNIGHT *Dict. Mech.*, *Spanish Tutania*, an alloy composed of 24 parts tin, 2 antimony, and 1 steel.

† **Tutch.** *Sc. Obs. rare*—1. See quot.

Perhaps an error for *cutches* (COACH *sb.*).

**1643** *Sc. Act Chas. I* (1870) VI. 16/2 That the parliament wald appoynt tuo pinnaces or tutches for convyeing diligence betuixt them & this Kingdome.

**Tutch, tutche, -ie**, obs. ff. TOUCH, TOUCHY.

**Tute**, obs. form of TEAT, TOOT *v.*[2]

† **Tu·tel**, *sb. Obs. rare.* [app. a derivative (with -EL[1]) of *tūte*, not recorded in Eng. but occurring in MDu. and MLG. and surviving as Du. *tuit*, WFris. *tute*, *tût*, LG. *tûte*, *tüte*, etc., spout, lip (of a can), pouting or protruding mouth, etc. (Sw. and Norw. *tut*, Da. *tud*, spout, are from LG.) The equivalent formation *tutel*, *tûtel* occurs in WFris. in transferred senses.] The mouth with the lips protruded in the act of whispering. (Cf. next.)

*a* **1225** *Ancr. R.* 74 Þe veond of helle mid his ferd went þurh þe tutel þ is euer open into þe heorte. *Ibid.* 80 Ne blowe ȝe hire [*sc.* hope] nout ut mid maðelinde muðe, ne mid ȝeoniinde tuteles. *Ibid.*, 212, & te deouel leieð his tutel adun to his earen, & tuteleð him al þet he euer wule.

† **Tutel, totel**, *v. Obs.* Forms: 3–5 tutel, 5 totel, -il, -yl, -ul. [ME. *tutel* (from early 13th c.), *totel* (*c* 1400), app. from the variant stems *tūt-* (see prec.) and *tōt-* (see TOOT *v.*[1]), the former of which occurs in the same sense in older Flemish *tuyten* (*in de oore*, Kilian), Du. dial. *tuiten*, WFris. *tûtsje* to whisper.] *intr.* and *trans.* To whisper. Hence † **Tutelinde** *ppl. a.*, † **Tuteling, toteling** *vbl. sb.*, whispering. (See also TUTELER.)

*a* **1225** *Ancr. R.* 106 Þu, uor þe luue of him..dute [= close] þinne tutelinde muð mit þine lippen. *Ibid.* 212 [see TUTEL *sb.*]. *Ibid.* 422 Þe ueond beot hire his werc þet ine Godes werke ne wurcheð: and he tuteleð anonrihtes touward hire. *c* **1440** *Promp. Parv.* 498/1 Totelon talys (..*S.* totylyn tale in onys ere), *susurro*. Totelynge, *susurrium*.

**Tutel**, obs. var. TOOTLE *v.*

**Tutelage** (tiū·tĕlėdʒ). Also 7 tutillage, 8 tutilage. [f. L. *tūtēla* watching, keeping, guardianship (f. *tūt-*, ppl. stem of *tuērī* to watch) + -AGE.]

**1.** The office or function of a guardian; protection, care, guardianship, patronage; governorship of a ward. Also *fig.*

**1605** SYLVESTER *Du Bartas* II. i. IV. *Handie-crafts* Ded., To beare againe..The noble Pasport of thy Tutelage, To salue her still from sullen Enuies wound. **1612** DRAYTON *Poly-olb.* iii. 217 That Citie..The Tutilage whereof..Some to Minerua gaue, and some to Hercules. **1689** *Def. Liberty agst. Tyrants* 29 A slave, or one that is under tutillage. **1777** PRIESTLEY *Disc. Philos. Necess.* 205 It came forth under my tutilage and kind protection. **1832** tr. *Sismondi's Ital. Rep.* iii. 60 Reigning under the pope's tutelage over the Two Sicilies only. **1879** DIXON *Windsor* I. xviii. 187 Under the tutelage of a patron saint.

**b.** Instruction, tuition.

**1857** H. MILLER *Test. Rocks* vi. 221 The dog acquires, under his tutelage, the virtues of fidelity..and affection. **1857** KINGSLEY *Two Y. Ago* (1877) 243 Under whose tutelage he had learnt to smoke..assiduously. **1863** HOLLAND *Lett. Joneses* xvii. 447 Under the tutelage of several different masters.

**2.** The condition of being under protection or guardianship.

1650 R. Stapylton *Strada's Low C. Warres* iv. 87 On his Christening day they delivered him in tutelage to the Prince Electour Augustus. 1792 V. Knox *Serm.* xiv. 309 Pleasure ..during the period of tutelage, engaged only a part of her votary's attention. 1878 Miss Braddon *Open Verd.* ii, At seventeen, when he was in his state of tutelage.

**Tutelar** (tiū·tĭlăɹ), *a.* and *sb.* Also 7 **tutelare.** [ad. L. *tūtēlār-is*, f. *tūtēla*: see prec. and -ar [1].]

**A.** *adj.* = Tutelary *a.*

1600 E. Blount *Hosp. Incur. Fooles* A iv, I coniure..the Gods Tutelar, that they will vndertake the tuition..of this new Hospitall. 1606 Holland *Sueton.* 51 The Tutelare Images of crosse-wayes called *Lares Compitales.* *a* 1661 Fuller *Worthies, Surrey* (1840) III. 215 He [Hammond] was the tutelar angel, to keep many a poor royalist from famishing. 1777 G. Forster *Voy. round World* I. 3 Reflecting on the tutelar guidance of Divine Providence. 1884 Tennyson *Becket* v. iii, All the tutelar Saints of Canterbury.

**B.** *sb.* One who is tutelar; a tutelar deity, angel, or saint. Also *transf.* and *fig.*

1603 Holland *Plutarch's Mor.* 1232 Minerva Poliuchos, that is to say, Tutelar and protectresse of the city. 1648 tr. *Senault's Paraphr. Job* 319 That Angel which hath been chosen out of a thousand to be their Tutelar. 1655 Fuller *Ch. Hist.* vi. iv. § 13 Were Judgment consulted with, Luke should be Tutelar to Physicians as his proper calling. *a* 1680 Butler *Rem.* (1759) I. 238 Dame Fortune some Men's tutelar Takes charge of them without their Care. 1702 H. Dodwell *Apol.* § 22 in S. Parker *Cicero's De Finibus*, Those who had brought themselves under the Dominion of ill Spirits by deserting their good Tutelars. *a* 1849 H. Coleridge *Ess.* (1851) II. 87 Ringlets that have been twisted with irons—to be the tutelars of hoops and earrings. 1890 E. Johnson *Rise of Christendom* 361 A religious congregation settled there to honour him as tutelar.

Hence **Tu·telarship** (*nonce-wd.*), the position or function of a tutelar.

1875 J. Hawthorne in *Contemp. Rev.* Nov. 925, I resigned my deputy-tutelarship perforce, and retired.

**Tutelary** (tiū·tĭlări), *a.* and *sb.* Also 7 **tutilary.** [ad. L. *tūtēlāri-us* a guardian, f. as prec: see -ary [1]. So F. *tutélaire.*]

**A.** *adj.* **1.** Of supernatural powers: Having the position of protector, guardian, or patron; *esp.* protecting or watching over a particular person, place, or thing.

1611 in *10th Rep. Hist. MSS. Comm.* App. i. 529 A Spanish governor, who adoreth them [Jesuits] as his tutelary gods. 1643 Sir T. Browne *Relig. Med.* i. § 33, I could easily beleeve, that..particular persons have their Tutelary and Guardian Angels. 1741 Middleton *Cicero* I. v. 400 That tutelary Minerva. 1794 Sullivan *View Nat.* I. xxiii. 316 Fountains and springs..watched over and guarded by tutelary divinities. 1806 R. Fellowes tr. *Milton's 2nd Defence* 290 The patron and tutelary genius of liberty. 1860 Motley *Netherl.* (1868) I. vi. 314 A little republic..suddenly bereft of its tutelary saint. 1908 Bigg *Orig. Chr.* i. (1909) 14 The Lares,..the little tutelary gods, who watched over the prosperity of the home.

**2.** *transf.* Of or pertaining to protection or a protector or guardian; protective.

1651 G. W. tr. *Cowel's Inst.* 203 Obligations..arise from implyed Contracts many wayes: As for transacting businesse Tutelary. 1692 Dryden *St. Euremont's Ess.* 2 They acknowledged a particular Care and Protection from its Tutelary Vertue. 1721 Prior *Predestination* 306 My Voice and heart I lift To ask th' Almighty's Tutelary Care. 1853 Grote *Greece* ii. lxxxv. XI. 198 The conduct of Timoleon and Æschylus..was in the highest degree tutelary to Corinth. 1879 Gladstone *Glean.* I. i. 30 Great acts of tutelary friendship.

**B.** *sb.* = Tutelar *sb.*

(In quot. 1866 used as almost = tutor; cf. Tutelage 1 b.)

1652 Gaule *Magastrom.* 177 The tutilaries of kingdoms, nations, &c. 1654 Z. Coke *Logick* a j, It is Janitrix Scientiarum; the Tutelary and Guardian of all. 1657–83 Evelyn *Hist. Relig.* (1850) II. 279 They have tutelaries for every trade. 1866 De Morgan in *Athenæum* 27 Oct. 535/1 My spiritual tutelary..referred the difficulty to the Almighty. 1908 S. A. Cook *Relig. Anc. Palestine* vi. 67 The status of a local tutelary was affected when commercial intercourse widened the horizon of both the traveller and the native.

† **Tutele.** *Obs.* Also 6 **tutell,** 6–7 **tutle,** 7 *Sc.* **tutill.** [a. OF. (also mod.F.) *tutelle* protection (14th c. in Godef. = Pr., Sp., It. *tutela*), or ad. L. *tūtēla*: see Tutelage.] Guardianship, protection; care of a ward; = Tutelage.

*c* 1420 Lydg. *Ball. our Lady* 57 in *Minor P.* (1911) I. 257 Of alle Cristen protectrix and tutele..To hem þat erryn, the path of her sequele. 1517 in *Acts Parlt. Scotl.* (1875) XII. 38/1 ȝe have sa usit ȝoure self tuiching the said tutele and regiment of oure soveran Lorde [etc.]. 1528 Roy *Rede Me* (Arb.) 24 The preservacion and tutell of the innocent and simple. 1579 *Sc. Acts Jas. VI* (1814) III. 158/2 Nwrist and brocht vp within our said Castell of strivelling vndir his tutele and gouuernance. 1602 E. Bruce in *Corr. Jas. VI* (Camden) 46 Her nerrast kinsman..sould be inwest in the tutill and administration of her state. 1622 in *Buccleuch MSS.* (Hist. MSS. Comm.) I. 210 He seeks not that the children should remain under the tutle of women. 1651 Howell *Venice* 20 They have the tutele of Pupills and Orphans when ther is no Gardian nominated in the Will of the Testator.

Hence † **Tuteleship** *Obs.*, the office or function of a guardian.

1557 N. T. (Genev.) *Gal.* iv. 1 *note*, The Churche of Israel was vnder the Lawe as the pupil subiect to his tutor, euen vnto the tyme of Christ.., and then her tutelshyp ended. 1580 Hollyband *Treas. Fr. Tong, Clientelle*, tutleship or custodie, keping. *a* 1656 Ussher *Ann.* vi. (1658) 377 The patronage and tutele-ship of the Minor.

† **Tuteler, toteler.** *Obs.* Forms: see Tutel *v.*; also 5 **tutlar, -er.** [f. Tutel *v.* + -er [1].] A whisperer, gossip, tale-bearer.

*c* 1385 Chaucer *L. G. W.* 353 (*Balade*) Ffor in ȝoure court is manye a losenger And manye a queynte totulour [*v. rr.* totelere, toteler, tutelere] acusour. *a* 1400 *Langland's P. Pl.* B. xx. 297 (MS. Camb. Dd. I. 17) Alle taletellers and tutelers. *c* 1400 *MS. Bibl. Reg.* 17 *B. xvii.* lf. 100 b, Be rightful. Be no totiler. *c* 1400 *Song Roland* 226 Yet will tutlers in toun talk bound [etc.]. *c* 1440 *Promp. Parv.* 498/1 Totelare, *susurro.* *c* 1470 Henryson *Poems* (S.T.S.) III. 142 (Maitl. MS.) Fals Tutlaris [*Bann. MS.* titlaris] now growis vp full rank. *Ibid.* 143 Giff þe tutelar [*Bann. MS.* tittillaris] so in his eir do roun. *a* 1500 *Colkelbie Sow* 128 (Bann. MS.) A tuttivillus, a tutlar, And a fanyeit flatterar.

**Tute-mowitt**: see Tut-mouthed.

**Tutenag** (tiū·tĕnæg). Forms: 7 (**tintenagall**), **tutunaga; tutunac, tutanag, -eg, tuthinag(e,** 8 **tutanague,** (**tuten-, tutanaque**), **tutteneg,** 9 **tuthenag, tutenage,** 7– **tutenag, tutenague;** also 7 (**teutenage**), **totaneg,** 8 **tootanag, toothenague, -aque, toothanegg** (**tooth and egg**), **tootnague** (Yule). [a. Marāṭhī *tuttināg* (Tamil *tuttunāgam*, Telugu *tuttunāgamu*), derived (according to native writers) fr. Skr. *tuttha-* blue vitriol, sulphate of copper + *nāga* tin or lead. Hence also Pg. *tutanaga, tutenaga*, F. *toutenague* (1723 in Hatz.-Darm.). The early forms in *tint-* used by Eng., Du., and French writers are difficult to account for.] A whitish alloy of copper, zinc, and nickel, with a little iron, silver, or arsenic, resembling German silver; said to have been originally imported from China; also used loosely in the Indian trade for zinc.

1622 in Foster *Eng. Factories in India* (1908) II. 135 Tintenagall [*sic*] not yet paid for. 1668 in J. F. Davis *Chinese* ii. (1836) I. 47 China commodities, as tutanag, silk, raw and wrought. 1679 in *Notes & Extr. Govt. Rec. Fort St. George* 31 Oct. (Y.), Dacca is not a good market for Gold, Copper, Lead, Tin, or Tutenague. 1681 Grew *Musæum* App. 386 *Teutenage.* A sort of Speltar...Hereof ..Vessels are made in Japan, wherein their Thea is brought over. 1684 W. Hedges *Diary* (Hakl. Soc.) I. 148 All the Copper and Tutenag which he sold them. 1687 A. Lovell tr. *Thevenot's Trav.* iii. 46 A certain Metal called *Tutunac*, that looks like Tin, but is much more lovely and fine, and is often taken for Silver. 1698 Fryer *Acc. E. India & P.* 86 To China for Sugar, Tea, Porcelane, Laccared Ware, Quicksilver, Tuthinag and Copper. *Ibid.* 264 Tuthinage brought from the South-Seas answers in all respects. 1699 Dampier *Voy.* II. i. 173 The product of the Country.., besides Rice and other eatables, is Tutaneg, a sort of Tin. 1711 C. Lockyer *Trade in India* v. 129 Tutanaque is a kind of course Tin in Oblong Pieces five or six to a Pecull. 1727 A. Hamilton *New Acc. E. Ind.* II. l. 223 The subterraneous Grounds were stored with Minerals, as Copper, Quick-silver, Allom, Toothenague, &c. *Ibid.* 233, 80 Chests of Japon Copper, and some Toothenague that I had weighed off at Canton. 1751 *Narr. Trans. Brit. Squadrons E. Indies* 20 From Malacca they bring a Metal very like Tin, call'd Toothanegg, and made much Use of for Alloy with Silver in Coining at all the European Settlements. 1754 Smeaton in *Phil. Trans.* XLVIII. 613 The semi-metallic substance call'd Zink, spelter, or tootanag. 1773 Jos. Wright *Let.* in Bemrose *Life* iv. (1885) 27 Four pillar Candlesticks called Tooth & Egg, to be cleaned as silver. 1782–3 W. F. Martyn *Geog. Mag.* I. 459 Tin, thus hardened, is the metal now well known in Europe by the name of tutanaque. 1806 *Naval Chron.* XV. 465 Ballasted with tuthenag or zinc. 1815 W. Phillips *Outl. Min. & Geol.* (1818) 46 With zinc and iron, copper forms tutenag. 1836 J. F. Davis *Chinese* I. viii. 316 Teapots..made of tutenague externally, covering earthenware on the inside. 1843 *Penny Cycl.* XXV. 446/1 *Tutenag*..is white, resembling silver...Dr. Fyfe found it to consist of—Copper 40·4, Zinc 25·4, Nickel 31·6, Iron 2·6. 1885 *Horological Jrnl.* Nov. 45/1 *note*, Tutenage, called Chinese copper..; in India, a name given to pure zinc or spelter.

*attrib.* 1699 J. Ovington *Ess. Tea* 11 Tea is brought over in round totaneg canisters. 1715 *Lond. Gaz.* No. 5394/4 Spanish Snuff, in Tutteneg Pots.

† **Tuther,** obs. Sc. f. Tother, the other.

1539 in *Abst. Protocols Town Clerks of Glasgow* (1897) IV. 113 The messis to be said..the tane half..the tane day, and the remanent of thame the tuther day.

**Tuþing,** early ME. f. Tithing.

**Tut-hoo,** var. of Tattoo *sb.*[3], Indian pony.

**Tutia, tutie**: see Tutty [1].

**Tutill, -age**: see Tutele, Tutelage.

**Tutiorist** (tiū·ʃiŏrist). *R. C. Theol.* [f. L. *tūtior* safer, comp. of *tūtus* safe + -ist.] One who holds that in cases of conscience the course of greater moral safety should be chosen. Cf. Rigorist 2 and Laxist. Also *attrib.* So **Tu·tiorism,** the doctrine of the Tutiorists; a less strict form of Rigorism.

1845 Gladstone *Glean.* (1879) VII. 192 There is also in the Latin Church a rigid school of those who pass by the name of Tutiorists. These hold that even such likelihood is insufficient, and that certainty is required as a warrant for our acts. 1885 *Catholic Dict.* (ed. 3) 602/2 The Rigorists, or Tutiorists..held that we must always take the safer way, always sacrifice our freedom, however small the probability that our freedom is restrained by the law. *Ibid.* 603/2 We cannot see that Probabiliorism is logical and consistent,..the arguments adduced by its advocates really tend to Tutiorism. 1906 *Ch. Times* 2 Mar. 291 Hence the prevailing 'tutiorist' tone [in the Lower House of Convocation].

**Tutivillar, -villus, Tutlar, -er, Tutle**: see Titiviller, Titivil, Tuteler, Tutele.

† **Tu·tlyng,** *vbl. sb. Obs. rare*—[1]. Also 5 **tutilling.** [f. OF. *tuteler, tutuler* (Godef.; Walloon *tûteler*), freq. of *tuter* to blow a horn, related to the Germanic forms cited s. v. Toot *v.*[2]] A blowing (of a horn).

1375 Barbour *Bruce* xix. 604 A tutlyng [*MS. E.* tutilling, *ed. Hart* (1616) towting] of his horne herd thai.

**Tut-mouthed,** *a. rare.* Now *Sc. dial.* Also 6 *Sc.* **tute-mowitt,** 9 **tuit-moot.** [f. *tute*, Toot *v.*[1] to protrude, stick out + Mouth *sb.* + -ed [2]. Cf. older Flem. *tuyt-muyl* 'broncus, brochus' (Kilian).] Having protruding lips; also, having a projecting under jaw. So **Tut-mouth** (*Sc.* **tuit mow**).

*a.* 1500–20 Dunbar *Poems* liv. 6 Quhou fain wald I descrywe perfytt, My ladye with the mekle lippis. Quhou scho is tute mowitt lyk an aip. *a* 1585 Polwart *Flyting w. Montgomerie* 755 (Harl. MS.) Tout mowe [*v. rr.* tait, tuit mow, cruik mow] woodie sow, sone bowe, or I wand thee. 1893 W. Gregor in *Dunbar's Poems* (S.T.S.) III. 286 *Tute mowitt*..still in use in parts of the North as a word of contempt, as, 'He's a tuit-moot smatchit'.

*β.* 1538 Elyot, *Bronchi*, they whyche haue their mouthe and tethe standyng farre out, tut mouthed. 1601 Holland *Pliny* xi. xxxvii. I. 336 The Lips: some men there be that put them far out, by reason that they are gag-toothed or tut-mouthed. 1616 Bullokar *Eng. Exp.*, *Tutmouthed*, he that hath the chin and nether iaw sticking out farther than the vpper.

**Tutoiement**: see under Tutoyer.

**Tutor** (tiū·tŏɹ), *sb.* Also 4–7 **tutour,** 5–6 **-oure,** (5 **-owre,** 5–7 **-ur,** 6 *Sc.* **toutour**); 6 **tutar,** *Sc.* **tuttar,** 6–8 **tuter**). [a. OF., AF. *tutour* (mod. F. *tuteur* = Sp., Pg. *tutor*, It. *tutore*), or a. L. *tūtor* watcher, protector, f. *tuērī* to watch, guard.]

† **1.** A guardian, custodian, keeper; a protector, defender. *Obs.*

1377 Langl. *P. Pl.* B. i. 56 Kynde witte be wardeyne ȝowre welthe to kepe, And tutour of ȝoure tresore and take it ȝow at nede. 1425 *Ord. Whittington's Alms-house* in Entick *London* (1766) IV. 354 To be one principal, which shal pas al other in power..and be called tutor. *Ibid.*, The seid tutour. *c* 1425 *Found. St. Bartholomews* (E.E.T.S.) 16 The kynge..behestid hym-self to be a tutur and defensur of hym and of hys. *c* 1440 *Promp. Parv.* 507/2 Tutowre, *tutor.* 1530 Palsgr. 284/1 Tutar, *tuteur.* 1562 Pilkington *Expos. Abdyas* 85 The poore oppressed people, whom God takes in to his custodie to be their tutor. 1570 Levins *Manip.* 77/14 A Túter, *tutor.* 1602 *Narcissus* (1893) 276 O thou which hast thy staffe to bee thy tutor.

**2.** One who has the custody of a ward; a guardian.

† **a.** in *gen.* sense. *Obs.*

1382 Wyclif *Gal.* iv. 2 How moche tyme the eyr is litil.. he is vndir tutouris and actouris. 1413 *Pilgr. Sowle* (Caxton) iv. xxxviii. (1859) 64 They leden the kynge at theyr owne lust,..as tutours, and couratours. 1526 Tindale *Gal.* iv. 2 The heyre as longe as he ys a chylde..is vnder tuters and governers. *c* 1550 Becon *Catech.* vi. Wks. 1564 I. 533 b, The honor that the chyldren owe to their parents and tutors. 1560 Daus tr. *Sleidane's Comm.* 175 The tutours..sent ambassadours to the Turke to commend the childe vnto hym. 1615 *North Riding Rec.* (1884) II. 109 [Taking away] a woman childe under eleven yeares of age from..her grandfather and lawfull tutor. 1616 Bullokar *Eng. Expos.*, *Tutour*, a defender, he that hath charge to bring vp a childe. 1642 Fuller *Holy & Prof. St.* v. xviii. 432 That interest which carefull tutours claim in those whose protection they tender. 1690 Locke *Govt.* ii. vi. § 59 If the Father..hath not provided a Tutor, to govern his Son, during his Minority..the Law takes care to do it.

**b.** *spec.* in *Rom.* and *Sc. Law*: The guardian and representative, and administrator of the estate, of a person legally incapable, failing the father.

*Tutor dative, t. nominate, t. optive, t. testamentar*: see these adjs. *Tutor-at-law, of law*, or *-legitim*, the nearest male relative on the father's side, who becomes guardian in the absence or failure of the tutor nominate.

1387 Trevisa *Higden* (Rolls) IV. 197 Pompeus..hymself fleigh to þe..kyng of Egipt, and axede help of hym, for he was assigned hym by þe senatoures to be his tutor and his wardeyn. 1432–50 tr. *Higden* (Rolls) IV. 75 Ptholomeus begynnenge to reigne the v[the] yere of his age, legates of Alexandrye preyede the Romanes thei wolde be tutores of þat childe, and defende the realme of Egipte. 1521 in *Acts Parlt. Scotl.* (1875) XII. 39/1 Þe Richt Illustre prince Duke of Albany Tutoure of Law to our said Soverane Lord [James V]. 1536 Bellenden *Cron. Scot.* (1821) I. 34 He was left tutour-testamenter be thair fader. 1546 [see Testamentar]. 1575 [see Dative *a.* 4]. 1597 Hooker *Eccl. Pol.* v. lxxiii. § 5 In ancient times all women which had not Husbands or Fathers to gouerne them, had their Tutors. 1681 [see Nominate B. 2]. 1765 Blackstone *Comm.* I. xvii. 448 The guardian with us performs the office both of the *tutor* and *curator* of the Roman laws;..according to the language of the court of chancery, the *tutor* was the committee of the person, the *curator* the committee of the estate. *a* 1768 Erskine *Inst. Law Scot.* i. vii. § 8 (1773) 117 In default of tutors-legitim, there is place for tutors-dative. 1826 G. J. Bell *Comm. Laws Scot.* (ed. 5) I. 133 Tutors may effectually grant deeds of ordinary administration of their pupil's estate. 1880 Muirhead *Ulpian* xi. § 3 Those are tutors-at-law, *legitimi*, who derive their office from some *lex.*

**c.** Formerly in Scotland used as a designation with the name of the estate of which the 'tutor' had charge. Now *Hist.*

1529 *Reg. Privy Seal Scot.* II. 53/1 Ane lettre maid to William Makclellane, tutour of Bomby, his airis and assignais [etc.]. *a* 1578 Lindesay (Pitscottie) *Chron. Scot.* (S.T.S.) I. 89 Ane callit Makclalene..quha was tutour of bombie for the tyme [in 1452]. *a* 1670 Spalding *Troub. Chas. I* (1850) I. 27 The Erll of Sutherland..with the tutour of Duffus and some seruandis followit. 1808 Scott *Autobiog.* in *Lockhart* i, Beardie became..Tutor of Raeburn..that is, guardian to his infant nephew.

**3.** One employed in the supervision and instruction of a youth in a private household. Also, one engaged to travel abroad with one or more pupils, a *travelling* or *foreign tutor*.

**1398** TREVISA *Barth. De P. R.* VI. v. (Bodl. MS.) lf. 36/2 Þe child [that] knowith goode and yuel is .. isette to lore vndur tutours. **1494** FABYAN *Chron.* cxxvii. 107 Clothayre, consyderynge the frowardnesse of .. his sone Dagobert, assigned to hym a tutoure or lerner of worldlye and knyghtlye maners. **1531** ELYOT *Gov.* I. xvi, Diuers maners of exercises. ..All these ought he that is a tutor to a noble man to haue in remembrance. **1622** GATAKER *Spirituall Watch* (ed. 2) 74 Two home-bred Tutors..that God hath set ouer each of vs, Shame and Feare, the shame of sinne, and the feare of wrath. **1699** LOCKE *Educ.* (ed. 4) § 167 Passionate words or blows from the Tutor fill the Child's Mind with Terror and Affrightment. **1701** tr. *Le Clerc's Prim. Fathers* (1702) 22 Aristobulus, a Peripatetick, who is said to have been Tutor to Ptolemy Philometer. *a* **1743** SAVAGE *Author to Let* Wks. 1777 II. 274 Few foreign tutors understand the dead languages. **1815** ELPHINSTONE *Acc. Caubul* (1842) I. 285 Some subsist by teaching and practising the law; others teach schools, or are tutors to the sons of rich men. **1822** SHELLEY *Triumph of Life* 261 The tutor and his pupil, whom Dominion Followed as tame as vulture in a chain.

**4.** In the Universities of Oxford, Cambridge, and Dublin: A graduate (most often the fellow of a college), to whom the special supervision of an undergraduate (called his pupil) is assigned.

The word was first used of those who stood in this relation to undergraduate members of colleges or halls, not on the foundation, and were responsible to the hall or college for their pupils' payments (= *creancers*: cf. CREANCER 2). By Wykeham's Statutes for New Coll., Oxf., imitated at King's Coll., Camb., and Magdalen Coll., Oxf., each junior foundationer was assigned to the special charge of a senior called his *informator*. Both these offices appear to have been merged later in the tutor. Naturally the tutor looked after his pupils' studies also, and this came to be the main part of his duties, esp. at Oxford. *Tutores* are also found at Louvain in 1476 supervising the studies of the *scholares* (Rashdall *Universities of Eur.* (1895) II. 766).

*c* **1610** in *Brasenose Coll. Quatercent. Monogr.* (1909) II. II. xi. 14 Tradesmen..inveagle young Gentlemen into new and chargeable fashions contrary to the desires of their parents and the directions of their Tutors. *a* **1648** LD. HERBERT *Autobiog.* (1824) 42 As if they meant to proceed Masters of Art and Doctors in some Science, for which purpose their tutors commonly spend much time in teaching them the subtilities of Logic. **1653** *Register of Visitors Univ. Oxford* (1881) 359 That noe man be admitted to the office of a Tutor in any Colledge or Hall that is not first approved of by the respective Head of such Colledge or Hall and the Visitors of the University. *Ibid.* 360 That all persons of whatever quality soever, untill they be admitted to the Degree of Bachelor of Arts..doe live under the care, tuition, and instruction of approved Tutors. **1696** PHILLIPS (ed. 5) s. v., A Tutour in the University, is one that takes care to teach and instruct the Youth that are sent thither from inferior Schools; and the Scholar so taught, is call'd the Tutour's Pupil. **1864** J. H. NEWMAN *Apol.* i.(1904) 7/2, I gave up that office in 1826, when I became Tutor of my College. **1884** C. DICKENS *Dict. Cambr.* 124/2 The Tutor ..generally acts as agent for the College in all business transactions with its members...The Tutor himself does not necessarily lecture or teach. Private Tutors are called Coaches. **1884** J. B. MULLINGER *Univ. Cambr. from 1535*, 396 The Cambridge system by which the expenditure of the student is supervised to a certain extent by the tutor was in operation as early as the sixteenth century. **1886** WILLIS & CLARK *Cambridge* I. Introd. 91 In the [Latin] statutes of .. Clare Hall [1551]..we meet for the first time at Cambridge with the term *tutor*, in the modern sense, namely, a fellow of the college who is to be responsible for his pupil's expenses, to explain to him what he has to do and to learn, and..is to be treated by him with filial obedience and respect. **1887** *Q. Rev.* Oct. 403 By the middle of the sixteenth century, the modern system of admitting students not on the foundation was fully established; and, as a natural result, the office of 'tutor' in the present meaning of the term then first appears. **1895** RASHDALL *Universities of Eur.* II. 515 It seems probable that before the middle of the fifteenth century the teaching of Undergraduates..was mainly in the hands of Tutors in the Colleges, or Principals and their assistant Regents or non-graduate Lectors in the Halls. *Note*, The word used both at New College [*c* 1400] and Magdalen [1479] is *Informator*. At Brasenose College [founded 1509] the word *Tutor* occurs for the first time, but only in reference to the Fellow who is to be responsible for a Commoner.

**b.** In U.S. universities and colleges: 'A teacher subordinate to a professor, usually appointed for a year or a term of years' (*Cent. Dict.*).

**1828** WEBSTER s. v., Tutors are graduates selected by the governors or trustees, for the instruction of undergraduates. ..They are usually officers of the institution, who have a share, with the president and professors, in the government of the students.

**c.** *Private tutor* (at the English Universities): A person engaged by students to assist them in their studies and preparation for the examinations, but not appointed or recognized by the University or College. Also, a person who makes it his business to prepare students for professional examinations apart from the universities, as *an army tutor, a law tutor*.

**1827** LYTTON *Falkland* I. 15, I was sent to a private tutor. **1840** *Encycl. Brit.* (ed. 7) XXI. 498/1 Although recognised neither by the universities, nor by any particular college, a very numerous class has long existed both at Oxford and Cambridge, who, under the denomination of *Private Tutors*, superintend and assist the studies of individuals. **1884** C. DICKENS [see 4].

**5.** In some English public schools: **a.** A senior boy appointed to help a junior in his studies. Now only at Winchester.

**1689** A. HILL *Life Barrow* B.'s Wks. 1687 I. a 2, Removing [from the Charterhouse] to Felsted..he quickly made so great a progress in Learning..that his Master appointed him a little Tutour to the Lord Viscount Fairfax. **1898** SARGEAUNT *Ann. Westminster* vii. 123 The very name of 'little tutor' familiar in the schools of the seventeenth century is now wholly forgotten...The 'little tutor' was paid for his services and might thus gather a small purse against the time when he should go to the University. **1901** *Winchester Coll. Notions* 130 The ten Senior Praefects in College are called Tutors.

**b.** A master charged with the special supervision of a particular boy.

**1861** J. T. COLERIDGE *Publ. Sch. Educ.* 37 [At Eton] Every Master therefore but the Head Master is also a Tutor and every boy must have his Tutor...Every exercise the pupil does is first submitted to the Tutor for inspection and correction and then carried into school. **1901** *Winchester Coll. Notions* 130 College Tutor formerly had to correct the composition of College men, but now he helps College Juniors with their work.

**6.** *transf.* As the name of an instruction book in any subject.

**1665** MOXON (*title*) A Tutor to Astronomy and Geography. **1776** *Pennsylvania Even. Post* 15 June 299/2 Just published, ..a complete Tutor for the Fife. *Mod.* An Easy French Tutor. Hémy's Pianoforte Tutor.

**7.** *attrib.* and *Comb.*, as *tutor-companion, -confessor, -farmer, -room*; *tutor-sick* adj.

**1771** SMOLLETT *Humph. Clinker* 8 Aug., I was tutor-sick at Alma Mater. **1844** STEPHENS *Bk. Farm* I. 96 The tutor-farmer should be provided with such a plan to give to each of his pupils. **1899** C. K. PAUL *Mem.* 247 My tutor days are not satisfactory in the retrospect. **1901** *Westm. Gaz.* 8 May 2/1 The tutor-confessor was instantly turned out. **1903** *Daily Chron.* 20 Mar. 6/1 Dr. Jüttner, the tutor-companion, who holds that youth should be allowed to revel in the sunshine. **1906** *Mem. Abp. Temple* I. 155 The power of the tutor-rooms had over-asserted itself.

**Tutor** (tiū·tǫ̈ɹ), *v.* [f. TUTOR *sb.*]

**1.** *trans.* To act the part of a tutor towards; to give special or individual instruction to; to teach, instruct (*in* a subject).

**1592** WARNER *Alb. Eng.* VII. xxxvii. (1612) 186 The last of our three Phaetons was tuter'd of a Fryer. **1621** in Foster *Eng. Factories Ind.* (1906) 241 [An accusation of having said] that our hopefull Prince Charles was tutored in the Papist religion. **1740** J. DUPRÉ *Conform. Anc. & Mod. Cerem.* 39 An Old Capuchin tutoring a Novice. **1814** CHALMERS *Evid. Chr. Revel.* x. 292 His mind is not yet tutored to the philosophy of the subject. **1867** MACFARREN *Harmony* vi. (1876) 221 Their ear being thus tutored. **1903** *Times, Lit. Suppl.* 2 Oct. 280/1 He was sent away to be tutored in English rectories, whence he proceeded to University College, London.

*absol.* **1892** *Nation* (N. Y.) 11 Aug. 116/2 Graduate..of experience wishes to tutor for the September examinations.

**b.** With extension: To get (a quality or the like) *out* or *in* by instruction or discipline. *rare.*

**1646** J. HALL *Poems* 64 Let not wealth tutor out Our spirits with her gout.

**2.** To instruct under discipline; to subject to discipline, control, or correction; to school; also to admonish or reprove.

**1592** SHAKS. *Rom. & Jul.* III. i. 33 Didst thou not fall out with a taylor for wearing his new doublet before Easter, with another for tying his new shooes with olde riband, and yet thou wilt tuter me from quarelling? **1641** MILTON *Ch. Govt.* i. Wks. 1851 III. 100 If men were but as good to discipline themselves, as some are to tutor their Horses and Hawks. **1645** — *Tetrach.* Wks. 1738 I. 240 The Fanatic boldness of this age, that dares tutor Christ to be more strict than he thought fit. **1667** DRYDEN & DK. NEWCASTLE *Sir Martin Mar-all* I. i, Saucy rascal, avoid my sight; must you tutor me? **1711** SHAFTESB. *Charac., Wit & Hum.* I. iii, The World however it may be taught will not be tutor'd. **1837** CARLYLE *Fr. Rev.* III. I. i, France is roused! Long have ye been lecturing and tutoring this poor Nation. **1850** MAURICE *Mor. & Met. Philos.* (1854) I. 9 Seneca..had tutored himself to endure personal injuries without indulging in anger. **1882** STEVENSON *Fam. Stud. Men & B., Thoreau* (1905) 115 Thoreau had plenty of humour till he tutored himself out of it.

**3.** To instruct (a person) in a course of action, to tell (one) what to do or say; often in sinister sense: to sophisticate or tamper with (a witness or his evidence).

**1757** J. LIND *Lett. Navy* ii. 77 Notwithstanding all the care that had been taken to manage and tutor his evidence. **1767** J. WINGRAVE *Narr. Cruelties Eliz. Brownrigg* 6 After tutoring the girl..what answer to make, and what behaviour to follow. **1826** C. BUTLER *Vind. Rom. Cath. Ch.* 126 Emissaries were employed, witnesses tutored, ..and even torture applied to procure evidence. **1850** MERIVALE *Rom. Emp.* (1865) III. xxiii. 67 The populace, tutored ..or bribed for the purpose, offered him the high priesthood.

†**4.** To take care or charge of. *Obs. rare.*

**1682** A. PEDEN in *Life* x. (1902) 209 Our blessed second Adam hath our Stock in guiding and he tutors it better.

Hence **Tu·tored** *ppl. a.*, **Tu·toring** *vbl. sb.*

**1589** R. HARVEY *Pl. Perc.* (1860) 25 A little tutoring in Diuinitie, and the reuersion of a benefice,..where his godfathers commendatorie letters may preuaile. **1601** WEEVER *Mirr. Mart.* F ij b, His Tutor'd pen..would..still repaire the ruin of my name. **1707** in Hearne *Collect.* 13 June (O.H.S.) II. 20 They must by the Tutoring of Plato maintain the same Doctrine. **1805** *Chron.* in *Ann. Reg.* (1807) XLVII. 475/2 His exhibition consisted of tutored birds. A number of little birds..formed themselves into ranks, like a company of soldiers. **1887** SAINTSBURY *Hist. Elizab. Lit.* viii. (1890) 299 [He] died possessed of landed property..(an unusual result of tutoring). **1889** BOSW. SMITH *Life Ld. Lawrence* viii. (1911) 124 The little prince..flung himself back..with a tutored obstinacy which was not to be shaken.

**Tutorage** (tiū·tǫ̈rėdʒ). Also 7 **tutridge, tutaradge.** [f. TUTOR *sb.* + -AGE.]

**1.** The office, authority, or action of a tutor or guardian; tutorship, guardianship, custody; tutorial control, direction, or supervision; instruction.

**1617** MORYSON *Itin.* III. 217 By the Law of Saxony, Tutorage belongs onely to the Kinsmen, by the Fathers side. **1657** R. LIGON *Barbadoes* 23, I wanted no tutridge, in the learning this mystery. **1711** SHAFTESB. *Charac., Misc.* IV. i, The Tutorage of Fancy and Pleasure. **1716** PRIDEAUX *Connex. O. & N. Test.* I. IV. (1718) 168 Under the discipline and tutorage of that prophet. **1801** STRUTT *Sports & Past.* I. i. § 2 These qualities..were natural to them, and not the effect of tutorage. **1837** LOCKHART *Scott* I. iii. 91 He was placed ..under the domestic tutorage of Mr. James French.

**b.** *spec.* at a university; also, the charge for or cost of this.

**1638** EARL OF CORK *Diary* in *Lismore Papers* Ser. I. (1886) V. 64 Whose expences..for three yeares, for diett, and tutaradge, and aparell, I paid. **1721** AMHERST *Terræ Fil.* App. (1726) 322 He has, ever since his admission into Baliol, constantly paid the same tutorage, which other scholars do. **1733** *Oxford Act* I. 7 Fifty Pounds with which I should have paid off my old Score, my Battles, my Tutorage, my Taylor [etc.]. **1775** A. BURNABY *Trav.* 55 The expence to a student for room-rent, commons, and tutorage. **1835** DE QUINCEY in *Tait's Mag.* II. 367 The next item..is that which in college bills is expressed by the word Tutorage.

**c.** A tutor's post, a tutorship.

**1796** LAMB *Let. to Coleridge* in *Mem.* i, Concerning the tutorage, is not the salary low? **1833** CARLYLE *Misc. Ess., Diderot* (1872) V. 40 He has reconciled Brothers, sought out Tutorages.

†**2.** The condition of being under authority or control; = TUTELAGE 2. *Obs. rare.*

**1651** BAXTER *Inf. Bapt.* 28 He hath redeemed us from our bondage and tutorage. **1751** JOHNSON *Rambler* No. 147 ¶4 Banqueting upon my own perfections, and longing in secret to escape from tutorage. **1768** TUCKER *Lt. Nat.* (1834) I. 596 Conceited pertness teaches the new-loosened school-boy ..thy scorn of tutorage and control.

**Tu·tordom.** *nonce-wd.* [f. TUTOR *sb.* + -DOM.] The occupation of a tutor; tutorship.

**1840** *Blackw. Mag.* XLVIII. 124 He then betook himself ..to tutordom and secretaryship.

**Tutorer** (tiū·tǫ̈rəɹ). *rare.* Also 8 **tuterour.** [f. TUTOR *v.* + -ER[1].] One who tutors; an instructor, tutor.

**1702** BLACKWELL *Compleat Tutor* 1 The English Fencing-Master: or, the Compleat Tuterour of the Small Sword. **1824** in *Spirit Pub. Jrnls.* (1825) 213 Of these patriarchal tutorers was Mr. Larry O'Larrop. **1841** J. T. HEWLETT *Parish Clerk* I. 144 The next time the tutorer went out for a drive.

**Tutoress** (tiū·tǫ̈rės). Also 7 **tutoresse.** [f. TUTOR *sb.* + -ESS; cf. TUTRESS.] A female tutor.

**a.** An instructress, a governess. Also *fig.*

**1614** RALEIGH *Hist. World* II. (1634) 456 Jezebel had cunning enough to be his Tutoresse. **1675** HAN. WOOLLEY *Gentlewom. Comp.* 4 A Gentlewoman every way accomplisht for a Tutoress to young Ladies. **1741** RICHARDSON *Pamela* II. 125, I hope, from her good Example, and your friendship,..in time to be half as good as my Tutoress. **1781** H. DOWNMAN tr. *Voltaire's Dram. Wks.* I. 238 School'd by adversity, Great tutoress of mankind. **1830** *Examiner* 822/1 Let her trust to these, and not to any tutoress in acting. **1848** THACKERAY *Van. Fair* xii, Love was Miss Amelia Sedley's last tutoress, and it was amazing what progress our young lady made under that popular teacher. **1888** *Pall Mall Gaz.* 20 Jan. 14/1 University tutoresses promise to be numerous within the next few years.

**b.** A female guardian.

**1759** *Chron.* in *Ann. Reg.* 59/1 The king..and the Princess ..are appointed honorary tutor and tutoress to her children.

**Tutorhood** (tiū·tǫ̈ɹhud). *rare.* [f. TUTOR *sb.* + -HOOD.] The condition or office of a tutor, tutorship; also, † a society or body of tutors.

**1752** H. WALPOLE *Lett.* (1845) II. 455 Storms gathering in the tutorhood [of Prince George]. *a* **1797** — *Mem. Geo. II* (1847) I. x. 298 The dissensions in the tutorhood had been carried so high. **1882** H. C. MERIVALE *Faucit of B.* I. i. v. 91 Faucit.., after six years of tutorhood,..had made up his mind to leave the place and the life.

**Tutorial** (tiutōᵊ·riăl), *a.* [f. L. *tūtōri-us* (f. *tūtor*, TUTOR) + -AL.] Of or pertaining to a tutor.

**1.** *Rom.* and *Sc. Law.* Of or pertaining to a legal guardian; cf. TUTOR 2 b.

**1742** KAMES *Decis. Crt. Sess. 1730–52* (1799) 44 After the Major's death, tutorial inventories were made up of his estate. *a* **1768** ERSKINE *Inst. Law Scot.* I. vii. § 32 (1773) 131 The defender does not..insist for any balance that may be due by the tutor upon his tutorial accounts. **1880** MUIRHEAD *Gaius* III. § 107 Provided that, where tutorial authorization is required, his tutor has intervened.

**b.** Protecting, defensive. *nonce-use.*

**1898** *Blackw. Mag.* Oct. 536/2 Stones..held in their place by diverse-running lines of Bricks..tutorial bricks till the adobe coping is reached.

**2.** Of or pertaining to a teacher or instructor; *esp.* pertaining to a college tutor.

**1822** MACAULAY in *Life & Lett.* (1883) I. ii. 110, I begin my tutorial labours to-morrow. **1858** GOLDW. SMITH in *Oxford Ess.* 265 The tutorial system was aroused from its lethargy, and the number of tutors and lectures was increased. **1881** *Nature* 28 Apr. 614/1 Their tutorial and laboratory courses of instruction. **1886** F. POLLARD in *Antiquary* Feb. 53/2 Colleges to be closed, and professorial and tutorial duties to be entirely suspended. **1906** *Times* 23 June 6/3 A tutorial Fellow will be appointed at Pembroke College early in Michaelmas term.

Hence **Tuto·rially** *adv.*, in a tutorial manner; as or by a tutor; by way of tuition.

1818–60 WHATELY *Commpl. Bk.* (1864) 34 Rough and awkward,..and of course tutorially pedantic. 1891 *Academy* 31 Jan. 102/2 (Advert.) His duties will be to assist the Professor..and to direct tutorially the English work of the Normal Students.

**Tutoriate** (tiutōᵊ·riĕt). *rare.* [f. L. *tūtōri-us* (see prec.) + -ATE¹: cf. *professoriate.*] A body of tutors; the tutorial staff of a college.

1858 GOLDW. SMITH in *Oxford Ess.* 281 The tutoriate will also be generally feeble in lay subjects, because the rule of celibacy will continue to drive from College all but clerical fellows.

**Tutorify** (tiū·tŏrifəi), *v. nonce-wd.* [f. TUTOR *sb.* + -(I)FY.] *trans.* To make or render tutorial.

1826 WHEWELL in Todhunter *Acc. Writ.* (1876) II. 77, I do not see why you should suppose I am so thoroughly tutorified.

**Tu·torism.** [f. as prec. + -ISM.] The sphere or duty of a tutor.

1855 CLOUGH *Poems*, etc. (1869) I. 94 Working away in the thoroughly terrestrial element of College tutorism.

**Tutorize** (tiū·tŏrəiz), *v.* [f. as prec. + -IZE.] **a.** *intr.* To act as a tutor; to play the tutor. (Also with *it.*) **b.** *trans.* To be tutor to; to instruct as a tutor.

1611 COTGR., *Preceptorizer*, to teach, instruct, tutorize it. 1839 F. W. FABER *Lett.* (1869) 77, I have been tutorized in the Breviary by a very nice priest. 1861 *Wheat & Tares* 3 You are coming with us to Westborough,..to tutorise Robert? 1873 HELPS *Anim. & Mast.* vi. (1875) 145 He would tutorize a poor Sizar without receiving any payment. 1899 H. G. GRAHAM *Soc. Life Scotl. in 18th C.* IX. § 5. II. 116 For £5 a year, 'with board and washing', they tutorised the children.

Hence **Tu·torizing** *vbl. sb.*; also **Tutoriza·tion**, tutoring, tuition.

1837 WHEWELL in Todhunter *Acc. Writ.* (1876) II. 263 Operations in the way of tutorizing and the like. 1842 G. S. FABER *Prov. Lett.* (1844) I. 18 He..will not be long in perceiving, under good Romish Tutorisation, that [etc.]. 1844 *Q. Rev.* June 78 Mr. Wm. Scott..was very willing to have his brother's assistance in the tutorizing at University, for which John no doubt had remuneration.

**Tutorless** (tiū·tŏlĕs), *a.* [f. as prec. + -LESS.] Having no tutor or guardian.

1618 J. RAWLINSON in Spurgeon *Treas. Dav.* Ps. lv. 6 As a husbandless widow, as a tutorless orphan. 1896 HARE *Story my Life* I. v. 397 Left tutorless just when I was going up to Oxford.

**Tutorly** (tiū·tŏəli), *a. rare.* [f. as prec. + -LY¹: cf. *fatherly.*] Befitting or pertaining properly to a tutor; like a tutor; dictatorial, pedagogic.

1611 COTGR. s.v. *Bonnet, Prendre le bonnet*,..to take on him the gouernment of himselfe; to waiue all tutorly Iurisdiction. *a* 1734 NORTH *Exam.* III. vi. § 42. (1740) 453 The Earl..was grown so infirm, peevish and forgetful, as also not a little tutorly, in his Majesty's Affairs. 1879 G. MEREDITH *Egoist* I. vi. 88 He was..indulgent, almost frolicsome, in contradistinction to Mr. Whitford's tutorly sharpness.

**Tutorship** (tiū·tɔːiʃip). [f. as prec. + -SHIP.] †**1.** The office of guardian or protector; guardianship. *Obs.*

1559 AYLMER *Harborowe* L j, In the ciuill lawe, the tutorshippe endith in the males at .14. yeares of age. 1579 J. STUBBES *Gaping Gulf* D j, Putting it in the hands of the father, who vnder colour of some tutorship to hys daughter, will haue her into Fraunce. 1586 *Acts Privy Counc.* (N.S.) 66 Douglas..desireth to haue the tutorshippe and keeping of the idiot with the goodes, leases [etc.]. 1629 WADSWORTH *Pilgr.* vi. 52 My Father continued in his tutorship of the Infant vntill he..dyed. 1665 SIR T. HERBERT *Trav.* (1677) 75 Anno 1610...The Prince (under tutorship of Mortesachan) was sent Viceroy to Guzurat.

**2.** The position or office of an instructor or teacher.

1581 MULCASTER *Positions* xxxvii. (1887) 155 So long as the child shalbe either vnder maistership in schole, or tutorship in colledge. 1796 MME. D'ARBLAY *Camilla* I. 105 An entire discontinuance of all pupilage and tutorship. 1841 W. SPALDING *Italy & It. Isl.* I. 140 Seneca, whose tutorship of Nero, and his murder by that wicked prince, are familiar to every one. 1856 MISS YONGE *Daisy Chain* xxi, Norman..had undertaken the tutorship of two school-boys for the holidays. 1893 W. G. COLLINGWOOD *Ruskin* iii. 34 He was now growing out of his mother's tutorship.

**Tutory** (tiū·tŏri). Also 5 **tutry**, 6 **tutoury.** [f. TUTOR: see -ORY¹. The form *tutry* is ad. OF. *tutrie, tuterie*, from *tuteur.*]

**1.** Guardianship, charge, protection; *spec.* the custody of a ward. *Obs.* exc. in *Law.*

*Tutory-at-law, tutory dative*, etc.: cf. *tutor-at-law*, etc. (TUTOR *sb.* 2 b).

*c* 1400 *Sc. Trojan War* II. 1624 Þir two sonnes, quhen þai war ȝing, War gevin in tutory and keping To king Teuteus. 1456 SIR G. HAYE *Law Arms* (S.T.S.) 264 Gif a man war our ȝong, within elde of tutry. 1596 DALRYMPLE tr. *Leslie's Hist. Scot.* VIII. (S.T.S.) II. 65 Alexander Ogiluie,..in quhais tutorie was Johne Ogiluie, his oy. 1614 in Ramsay *Bamff Charters* (1915) 175 To exerce the said office of tutorie to the weill of the saidis bairnis. 1643 *Ibid.* 262 Borrowing of money..be the tutour befoir the expyreing of his tutorie. 1754 Tutory dative [see DATIVE *a.* 4 c]. *a* 1768 ERSKINE *Inst. Law Scot.* I. vii. § 1 Tutory..is a power and faculty to govern the person, and to manage the estate, of a pupil. 1838 W. BELL *Dict. Law Scot.* 1018 The tutory may..expire by the tutor's renunciation made on reasonable cause. 1880 MUIRHEAD *Ulpian* xi. § 9 A tutory-at-law is lost by *capitis deminutio.*

*attrib.* *a* 1768 ERSKINE *Inst. Law Scot.* I. vii. § 32 (1773) 131 All purchases made by the tutor,.. till settling the tutory-accounts.

†**2.** Tuition, instruction. *Obs. rare.*

1692 A. PITCAIRN *Assembly* V. i. (1766) 62 The Tutory of Mr. Salathiel, who is as profess'd an Enemy to poor Priscian ..as he is to King James. 1764 REID *Inquiry* vi. § 24 Reason and reflection must superadd their tutory in order to produce a Rousseau, a Bacon, or a Newton.

‖**Tutoy·er**, *v.* Also 7 **tutay**, 9 **tutoy**, (9 **tutoyé**). [a. and ad. F. *tutoyer* (tütwaye), f. the sing. pronoun *tu, toi, te*, as used in speaking to a person instead of the pl. *vous*: see Littré.] *trans.* To use the singular pronoun *tu, toi, te* ('thou' and 'thee') to; to 'thou' (any one); to treat as an intimate; to address with familiarity, or as an inferior in rank or order. Also *intr.*

1697 J. DENNIS *Plot & no Plot* II. 24 There is an air of greatness in Tutaying men. 1819 *Hermit in London* III. 159 They [nobles] often tutoyered the leading favourite. 1840 CAROLINE FOX *Jrnls. & Lett.* vi. (1882) 53 He..promised to *tutoyer* us as long as we liked, but not to answer to *thee.* 1852 MRS. BROWNING *Lett.* 7 Apr. (1897) II. 63 The Greek in Greek costume who tutoyéd her, and she kissed her. 1861 T. HEYWOOD *S. Lancs. Dial.* in *Chetham Misc.* III. 9 Tutoying still pervades South Lancashire. 1865 KINGSLEY *Herew.* xvi, He was growing warm, and began to tutoyer Hereward. 1895 *Edin. Rev.* Oct. 386 Freron thought he perceived.. that 'tutoying' might be displeasing to him,..so he instantly substituted 'vous'.

Hence ‖**Tutoiement** (tütwaman̆), the action of addressing in this way; 'thouing'.

1817 LADY MORGAN *France* I. (1818) I. 72 The *tutoiement* universal in France, in all the intercourse of friendship and intimacy, is always used among the peasants, except to their superiors. 1879 *Scribner's Mag.* XIX. 97/1 It was not merely the *tutoiement* that struck him as saucy. 1898 *Daily News* 18 Apr. 4/5 M. Aulard and M. Sigismond Lacroix read ..papers, the one on the 'tutoiement', or use of the pronouns 'thee' and 'thou' during the Revolution.

**Tutress** (tiū·trĕs). Also 6–7 **tutresse**, 7 **tuteresse**, 8–9 **tut'ress.** [ad. OF. *tutreisse, tuteresse* (14th c. in Godef.), or f. L. *tūtrix* TUTRIX by change of ending.] **a.** = TUTORESS a.

1599 *Warn. Faire Wom.* I. 317 My tutress, Drury, gave me charge to speak. 1624 HEYWOOD *Gunaik.* VII. 344 A fit tuteresse for such an apt and forward pupill. 1664 BUTLER *Hud.* II. i. 812 Whipping, that's Virtues Governess, Tutress of Arts and Sciences. 1751 *Female Foundling* I. 20 Ah my dear Tutress, my dear Tutress, I cried out. 1796 MME. D'ARBLAY *Camilla* I. 98 To [her], however, she was but nominally a tutress. 1801 *Sporting Mag.* XVII. 42 Not many months since She was thought a fit Tut'ress for Statesman or Prince. 1871 M. COLLINS *Mrq. & Merch.* iv, Amy Gray became tutress to Mowbray's unmanageable daughter. 1886 *Pall Mall G.* 10 Feb. 4/2 Rouen, Geneva, and Pisa..have been tutresses of all I know.

**b.** = TUTORESS b.

1653 H. COGAN tr. *Pinto's Trav.* liii. (1663) 209, I.., a poor woman, Governess, and Tutress of my Son, an Orphan. *a* 1693 *Urquhart's Rabelais* III. xxxi. 262 The Goddess of Wisdom, Tutress, and Guardianess of such as are.. studious. 1747 R. KEITH in *Buccleuch MSS.* (Hist. MSS. Comm.) I. 413 If the Prince should die.., the Princess his spouse should be tutress to the child..during the nonage.

†**Tutrice.** *Obs. rare.* [a. OF. *tutrice* (14th c. in Littré), or ad. L. *tūtrīcem*, acc. of *tūtrix* (see next).] A tutoress.

1490 CAXTON *Eneydos* xxiii. 85 Theire maistres, theire tutryce and techer. 1514 JAS. V *Let.* in *Munim. Burgh Irvine* i. (1890) 33 Oure dearest moder, tutrice testamentar & governour.

†**Tutrix** (tiū·triks). *Obs.* [a. L. *tūtrix*, fem. of *tūtor* TUTOR. Cf. prec. and TUTRESS, TUTORESS.] A female tutor. **a.** A female guardian. **b.** An instructress, a governess. *rare.*

1515 in *Archæologia* XLVII. 303 Suffre me as tutrix of the yong king. 1546 *Reg. Privy Council Scot.* I. 50 Tutrix testamentar to hir barnes and said umquhile Hew. 1590 SWINBURNE *Testaments* 97 By the ciuill lawe a woman (the mother and grand-mother excepted) can not bee assigned tutrix. 1652 W. HARTLEY *Infant-Baptism* 10 Those pupils she became tutrix to. 1659 A. HAY *Diary* (S.H.S. 1901) 209 That the Lady subscryve her renunciation..in her name as tutrix. 1680 DALGARNO *Deaf & Dumb Man's Tutor* v. 49 A pratling Nurse is a better Tutrix to her foster-child. 1702–3 in Tindal tr. *Rapin's Hist. Eng.* (1745) IV. XXVI. 596/1 A Tutrix or Regent, during the minority of her supposed brother.

Hence †**Tu·trixship**, the office of tutrix. *Obs. rare*⁻¹.

1520 Q. MARGARET in Ellis *Orig. Lett.* Ser. II. I. 276 The recoveryng of my..Trutrixship of the Kyng my Soon.

**Tutsan** (tɒ·tsăn). Forms: α. 5 **totsane, toutsayne**, 6 **totsan, tutsane**, 6– **tutsan**, 7 **tutesain**; β. 6 **tutson, -sone, -som, -some.** [app. of F. or Anglo-F. origin. But the mod.F. *toute-saine* is not in Cotgr. (who gives *tutsan*, perh. from Lyte), and is known to Hatz.-Darm. only from 1762, when it appears in the Dict. of the Académie, whereas the name is found in Eng. *c* 1400–50.]

A name applied to various plants on account of their alleged healing virtues; formerly to Agnus Castus, and, in French, to Sanicle (Hatz.-Darm.); now, in Eng., to a shrubby species of St. John's-wort, *Hypericum Androsæmum*, with strongly aromatic foliage and berry-like fruit; formerly esteemed as a vulnerary. Also called PARK-LEAVES.

α. *a* 1400–50 *Stockh. Med. MS.* 157 Totsane or parkleuys: *agnus castus.* 14.. *Voc.* in Wr.-Wülcker 562/24 *Agnus castus*,..toutsayne. 1548 TURNER *Names of Herbes* 13 *Androsaemon.* Androsaemon is the herbe (as I dooe gesse) whiche we call totsan, and the Poticaries falsly cal *Agnus castus.* 1552 ELYOT (ed. Cooper), *Androsæmon*, an hearbe called sainct Johns woort, or rather Tutsane, and groweth in gardeyns, and no where els. 1578 LYTE *Dodoens* I. xlv. 66 Tutsan so called in French and in English. 1597 GERARDE *Herbal* II. clii. 435 The leaues laide vpon broken shins,.. healeth them, and many other hurtes and griefes, whereof it tooke his name Tout saine, or Tutsane,..healing all things. 1612 DRAYTON *Poly-olb.* xiii. 206 The yarrow,..The healing Tutsan then and Plantan for a sore. 1614 MARKHAM *Cheap Husb.* I. Table A v, *Agnus Castus*, of some called *Tutesaine*, is an hearbe with reddish leaues, and sinewie like Plantaine. 1640 PARKINSON *Theat. Bot.* v. lii. 575 *Androsæmum Matthioli.* Matthiolus his Tutsan. This Tutsan (for other English name I know not well, what it may haue, unlesse you would call it a great S. Iohns wort, because it is so like it). 1731 MILLER *Gard. Dict.* s.v. *Androsæmum*, Tutsan or Park-leaves. This Plant grows wild in many Parts of England. 1785 MARTYN *Rousseau's Bot.* xxv. (1794) 374 Garden Tutsan is evidently of this genus (*Hypericum*). 1859 R. THOMPSON *Gard. Assist.* (1878) 649 Hypericum Androsæmum, tutsan, sweet amber.

β. 1552 ELYOT (ed. Cooper), *Ascyrum*, the herbe, which of some is called Peter worte: other would haue it to be Tutson. *Ibid.*, *Cruciata*, of some is taken for the herbe called Tutsome. 1575 TURBERVILE *Venerie* 232 Take a handfull of Tutsome, a handfull of Rewe [etc.].

**b.** *attrib.* and *Comb.*

1804 CHARLOTTE SMITH *Conversations*, etc. I. 172 The Apocynum, or tutsan leaved dog's bane. 1872 H. KINGSLEY *Hornby Mills* I. 6 The golden Tutsan St John's wort lit up the darkness of the shrubbery.

‖**Tutti** (tu·tti). *Mus.* [It. *tutto* sing., *tutti* pl. all:—L. *tōtus, tōtī.*] In concerted music, a direction that all the performers are to take part; also, a passage or movement rendered by all the performers together; also *attrib.*

1724 *Short Explic. For. Wds. in Mus. Bks.*, *Tutti*, or *Tutto*,..signifies All, or All together,..in Musick of several Parts,..signifying that..all the several Parts are to perform together. 1833 *Penny Cycl.* I. 74/1 Except in the *tutti* parts (*i.e.*, those portions of the concerto in which the principal instrument rests). 1839 LONGF. *Hyperion* IV. iv, A surfeit of music; tuttis, finales, choruses, must be performed. 1884 *Leeds Mercury* Weekly Supp. 15 Nov. 1/6 Her solo passages were very pleasing, but the tutti music was wanting in tone and point.

**Tutty** (tɒ·ti), *sb.*¹ Forms: α. 4–7 **tutie**, (6 **thutie**), 5–8 **tuty**, (5 **tutye, tuthye**); β. in Latinized form 6–9 **tutia**, (6 **tucia**, 7 **tussia**); γ. 6– **tutty**, (7 **tuttie, tutti**). [a. F. *tutie* (13th c. in Wr.-Wülcker 559/13) = Sp. *tutia, atutia*, Pg. and med.L. *tutia* (erron. *tucia*); a. Arab. توتيا *tūtiyā* oxide of zinc (marked as a foreign word in Arabic lists, perh. Persian). Vullers compares the Sanskrit *tuttha* blue vitriol, used as an eye-ointment, and this is favoured by the statement of Ibn Baitar that the best *tūtiyā* comes from India.] A crude oxide of zinc found adhering in grey or brownish flakes to the flues of furnaces in which brass is melted (cf. POMPHOLYX); also occurring in some countries as a native mineral; formerly used medically, chiefly in astringent ointments and lotions, and now as a polishing powder. Also *attrib.* as *tutty ointment, powder.*

α. *c* 1400 *Lanfranc's Cirurg.* 95 Anoynte þe wounde.. with þis oynement of rasis & tutie [*v.rr.* tutye, tuthye]. *c* 1400 tr. *Secreta Secret., Gov. Lordsh.* lxxxvii. 95 Stones, Margarites, Corale, Tuty, and alany, and swylk lyk. 1541 R. COPLAND *Galyen's Terap.* 2 H j b, Pampholix commonly called thutie. *c* 1550 H. LLOYD *Treas. Health* (1585) ¶ ij, Tuty doth dry and clear the eyes, more than all medycynes. 1601 HOLLAND *Pliny* XXX. viii. II. 384 The tried grease of unwashed wooll, (whereunto some adde Tutie and oile of Roses). 1610 B. JONSON *Alch.* II. iii. 398 Your marchesite, your tutie, your magnesia. [1656–1706 in BLOUNT and PHILLIPS.]

β. 1543 TRAHERON *Vigo's Chirurg.* 107 b/1 Let the sayd thynges be boyled togyther, excepte the tutia. 1581 STYWARD *Mart. Discipl.* I. 12 They ought to haue.. greate store of.. Tarre, Campher, Waxe, Tucia, Ars-nicke. 1615 MARKHAM *Eng. Housew.* (1660) 17 Take two drams of prepared Tussia. 1652 CULPEPPER *Eng. Physic.* (1656) 308 For Distillations of Rhewms in the Eyes, especially if it be used with Tutia. 1678 R. R[USSELL] *Geber* III. II. i. iv. 149 Tutia is the fume of White Bodies. 1727–41 [see γ].

γ. 1547 BOORDE *Brev. Health* ccv. 71 To bedwarde anoynt the eyes divers tymes with Tutty. 1605 TIMME *Quersit.* III. 179 Infuse tuttie and lytharge, of each two ounces. 1682 WHELER *Journ. Greece* III. 223, I was shewed a dried Herb ..whereof the Powder is made, we commonly call Tutti. 1727–41 CHAMBERS *Cycl.*, *Tutty, Tutia*, or *Lapis Tutiæ*... Tutty is now brought chiefly from Germany. Anciently it came from Alexandria. 1731 FIELDING *Grubstreet Opera* II. iv, Your bills for tutty and rotten-stone, when you us'd nothing but poor whiting. 1812 J. SMYTH *Pract. of Customs* (1821) 119 The better sorts of Tutty..are in semi-cylindrical concave pieces, like the bark of a tree; ponderous, and somewhat sonorous. 1868 WATTS *Dict. Chem.* V. 1073 An impure oxide, sold under the name of *tutty*, is obtained from the furnaces in which brass is melted. 1883 *Chambers' Encycl.*, Tutty-powder. 1890 *Cent. Dict.* s.v. *Ointment*, Tutty ointment.

**Tutty** (tɒ·ti), *sb.*² Now *dial.* Forms: 6 **tuttay, -ey**, 7 **-ie, titty**, 9 *dial.* **totty, tutto**, 7– **tutty** (also in comb. 9 **tutti-**). [Origin obscure: perh. orig. a nursery or children's word. Cf. TUSSY, TUZZY-MUZZY.] A nosegay, a posy; a tuft or bunch of flowers.

1578 LYTE *Dodoens* III. xxii. 344 At the highest of the stalkes groweth white flowers..ioyning one to another lyke a tuttay, or little nosegaye. *Ibid.* VI. xvi. 677 Two kindes of Heath, one..bearing his flowers in tutteys or tuftes. 1599 MINSHEU *Span. Dict.*, A Tuttie, nosegay, or poesie, *ramil-*

*tête de florés.* c **1613** T. Campion *Bk. Ayres* I. i. '*Jack & Joan they think no ill*' iii, She can wreathes and tuttyes make. **1664** [see Tuzzy-muzzy]. **1706** Phillips (ed. Kersey), *Tutty* or *Tuzzimuzzy*, an old Word for a Nosegay. *a* **1800** Pegge *Suppl. Grose, Tutty*, and *Titty*, a nosegay. *Somersetsh.* **1825** J. Jennings *Obs. Dial. W. Eng.* 128 When spreng, adresst in tutties, Calls all tha birds abroad. **1904** *19th Cent.* Sept. 233, I had a tutty—a nosegay,..zix times zo big as the biggest picklen cabbage.

**b.** *Comb.*: **tutty men, tuttimen** *pl.*, at Hungerford, tithingmen who collect contributions on Hock Tuesday, carrying a **tutty-pole**, wreathed with flowers and ribbons; **tutty-more**: see quot. 1873.

**1873** Williams & Jones *Somerset Gloss.*, *Tutty*, flower. *Tutty-more*, flower-root. **1893** *Wilts Gloss.* s.v. *Totty*, At Hungerford the tything-men are known as Tutti-men, and carry Tutti-poles, or wands wreathed with flowers. **1904** *Daily News* 13 Apr. 11 The tutti-men sallied forth, armed with staves, adorned with handsome bouquets.

† **Tu·tty,** *a.*[1] *Obs. rare.* [Of obscure origin; cf. the dial. verb *tut*, to be uneven in length or height.] Of ground: Uneven, hummocky. Also in comb. *tutty-nosed*, ? snub-nosed.

**1607** Markham *Caval.* III. (1617) 29 If the ground bee tuttie, and full of false treading (which we call broken swarth)..then he must gather vp his body round and close. **1681** T. Flatman *Heraclitus Ridens* No. 39 (1713) I. 255 It is a little Tutty-nos'd yappeting Sprite; the Good Old Cause's Lap-Dog.

**Tutty** (tʊ·ti), *a.*[2] *dial.* [Of obscure origin: cf. Teety, tetty.] Irritable, testy, peevish.

**1809** T. Batchelor *Anal. Eng. Lang.* 145 *Tutty*, ill-tempered, sullen. **1848** A. B. Evans *Leicestersh. Words, Tutty*, touchy. **1855** [see Teety]. **1902** Baring-Gould *Nebo the Nailer* vii, He's that tutty, if not minded at wunce.

‖ **Tutu** (tū·tu). [Maori.] A New Zealand shrub yielding shining black juicy berries, containing poisonous seeds; = Toot *sb.*[5] Also *attrib.*

**1857** [see Toot *sb.*[5]]. **1861** C. C. Bowen *Poems* 57 And flax and fern and tutu grew In wild luxuriance round. **1867** [see Tupakihi]. **1884** A. Cox *Recoll.* 258 Footpaths..fringed with tutu bushes. **1889** G. P. Williams & W. P. Reeves *Colonial Couplets* 20 (Morris) The troublesome process.. Which old settlers are wont to call 'eating your tutu'.

‖ **Tutulus** (tiū·tiŭlɒs). *Archæol.* [L. *tutulus.*] A Roman head-dress formed by plaiting the hair in a cone above the forehead, worn esp. by the Flamen and his wife.

**1753** Chambers *Cycl. Supp.*, *Tutulus*, among the Romans, a manner of dressing the hair, by gathering it up on the forehead into the form of a tower... *Tutulus* likewise signified a woollen cap with a high top. **1816** J. Dallaway *Statuary & Sculpt.* vi. 321 The head-dress is that of the wife of a pontifex,..the tutulus or top of the hair is rolled with a lace round the crown of the head. **1891** Farrar *Darkn. & Dawn* xxvi, Domitia Lepida, whose *tutulus*, or conical head-dress, it was the exclusive task of a slave-maiden to adorn.

**Tutunac, Tuty, -ye,** obs. ff. Tutenag, Tutty.

**Tuuei, Tuueine, Tuuelf, Tuuiȝes,** obs. ff. Tway, Twain, Twelve, Twice.

**Tuum,** 'thine': see phr. *meum and tuum* s.v. Meum [1].

**Tuwel,** obs. form of Tewel.

**Tu-whit** (tuhwi·t), *v.* [See next.] *intr.* To hoot as an owl.

**1902** A. Lang in *Longm. Mag.* Dec. 99 He heard the owls towhitting and towhooing from the wood.

**Tu-whit, tu-whoo** (tuhwi·t tuhwū·), *int.* (*sb.*). Also 6–9 **to-, too-, -who, -hoo**; 9 **towhoo towhoo**; etc. [Imitative.] An imitation of the call of an owl. See also prec. and next.

**1588** Shaks. *L. L. L.* v. ii. 928 Then nightly sings the staring Owle Tu-whit to-who. A merrie note. **1594** Lyly *Moth. Bomb.* III. iv, To whit to whoo, the Owle does cry. **1607** *Barley-Breake* (1877) 9 Too whit, too whoo, cries out the broad-fac'd Owle. **1797** Coleridge *Christabel* I. 3 The owls have awakened the crowing cock; Tu—whit!——Tu—whoo!

**b.** *sb.* The utterance of this cry; the hoot of an owl; also, the use of the expression in literature.

**1830** Tennyson *2nd Song to Owl* i, Thy tuwhits are lull'd I wot, Thy tuwhoos of yesternight. *Ibid.* ii, With a lengthen'd loud halloo, Tuwhoo, tuwhit, tuwhit, tuwhoo-o-o. **1862** Borrow *Wild Wales* liii, What resemblance does Shakespear's to-whit-to-whoo bear to the cry of the owl? none whatever.

**c.** Hence as a name for the owl. *nonce-use.*

**1604** Terilo *Fr. Bacon's Proph.* (Percy Soc.) 8 And olde to whit to whoo Did watch the winter night.

**Tu-whoo** (tuhwū·), *int.* (*sb.*). Also **to-who(o, too-hoo.** [Cf. prec.] Imitation of the call of an owl.

**1797** Coleridge *Christabel* I. Concl. 31–2 From cliff and tower, tu—whoo! tu—whoo! Tu—whoo! tu—whoo! from wood and fell! **1853** Hickie tr. *Aristoph.* (1872) II. 425 The owls, which are constantly crying 'to-who'. **1862** Borrow *Wild Wales* liii, The owl..who cried Too-hoo-hoo. **1868** Tennyson *Last Tourn.* 346 Tuwhoo! do ye see it? do ye see the star? **1899** E. J. Chapman *Drama Two Lives, Canadian Summer-night* 69 The owl's weird cry.. With its long too-hoo! too-hoo! **1906** *Essex Rev.* XV. 54 The White or Barn owl cries 'Tu-which', and the Brown owl 'Tu-whoo', or 'Hoohoo; hoo, hoo, hoo, Hoo-hoo'.

**b.** *sb.* The owl's cry.

**1830** [see prec. b]. **1889** *Hilman's Handbk. Chepstow & Wye* (ed. 4) App. 125 Unless fair Philomel is silenced by the too-whoo of the prowling owl.

Hence **Tu-whoo·** *v. intr.*, to utter the cry *tu-whoo*; to hoot as an owl. Hence **Tu-whoo·ing** *vbl. sb.* Also **Tu-whoot** *v.*

**1843** Thackeray *Bluebeard's Ghost* Wks. 1908 VI. 363 An owl was too-whooing from the church tower. *Ibid.*, The toowhooing of the owl. **1893** Baring-Gould *Cheap Jack Z.* xxxvii, A barn-owl..to-whooed in its terror. **1912** *Blackw. Mag.* Mar. 374/1 An owl tu-whooted to us from the trefoiled arch.

**Tuwyte,** obs. dial. form of Tewhit, the lapwing.

**Tuxl**: see Tuscle. **Tuycion, -oun,** obs. ff. Tuition. **Tuye,** var. Twie *adv. Obs.*, twice.

**Tuyegge,** obs. f. Twig *sb.*

**Tuyere** (twīə̆ɹ, twəiəɹ, ‖tüiyēr, tüyēr). Forms: (4 tuer, toyer, toyere). *α.* 7 **twire-**, 9 **twyer(e, twyére, twyeer.** *β.* 8–9 **tweer,** 9 **twear.** *γ.* 9 **tuyer(e, tuyère; tewer, tewyre.** [The common current spelling of the word already entered in the forms Tew-iron and Tow-iren, and taken as ad. OF. *toiere* (1389 in Godef. *Compl.*), *tuyere, tuhiere, touyere* (1459), mod.F. *tuyère*. The remarkable gap between the 14th cent. instances and modern usage is partly filled by the occurrence of Twire-pipe in the 17th cent.] The nozzle through which the blast is forced into a forge or furnace.

[**1350–1** in *Archæologia* LXIV. 158 Item in ij tuers ferri emptis ij. s. viij. d. *Ibid.* 159 Item in xxvj egyn faciendis pro tuers vj s. vj d., pro ege iij d. **1354** *Ibid.* 150 Liberabuntur..in fabrica predicta..unum angire [? andire = and-iron] precii viij d. duo toyers precii xij d. *Ibid.* 163 In emendacione iij toyeres xij d.]

**1781** More *Iron Scoria* in *Phil. Trans.* LXXII. 51 *note*, The Tweer is that opening through which the air is driven by the bellows into the body of the furnace. **1839** *Civil Eng. & Arch. Jrnl.* II. 233/2 The 'Twyer' (or aperture by which the blast is admitted) of a cupola or furnace for melting cast iron. **1839** *Penny Cycl.* XIII. 33/1 The three tubes leading to this hearth..which are called *tuyeres*, are used for introducing the blast of air. **1859** R. Hunt *Guide Mus. Pract. Geol.* (ed. 2) 229 The use of hot blast at the tuyères. **1862** *Catal. Internat. Exhib.* II. x. 1 The horizontality of the lines of equal temperature from the tuyères upwards. **1864** *Q. Jrnl. Sc.* I. 492 The twyers are in the upper part of the boshes, and the blast is directed downwards. **1877** Raymond *Statist. Mines & Mining* p. viii, With the view of diminishing the waste of heat, it is customary to run the water through tuyeres and jacket just fast enough to keep it almost boiling. **1881** Young *Ev. Man his own Mechanic* § 1419 A short pipe or tuyere..acting as the nozzle of an ordinary pair of bellows. **1892** *Labour Commission Gloss.*, *Twear*, the pipe which conveys the hot blast into the furnace..surrounded by a large pipe, through which passes a constant flow of cold water to keep the twear cool. **1900** *Archæologia* LVII. 119 A blast of air from a bellows was admitted to the furnace through a pipe or twyer.

**b.** *attrib.* and *Comb.*, as *tuyere hole, opening, -pipe*; **tuyere arch**, in a blast furnace, an arch through which a tuyere is admitted (*Cent. Dict.* 1891); **tuyere-box**, in a converter or the like, a detachable chamber with a number of tuyeres; **tuyere coil**, a water-pipe coiled about the tuyere for cooling (Knight *Dict. Mech., Suppl.* 1884); **tuyere-house**, ? a recess in the wall of a furnace where the blast is admitted: cf. House *sb.* 7 c; **tuyere-plate**: see quot.

**1861** Fairbairn *Iron* 155 The *tuyere-box..is so arranged as to be easily detached. Two or more of these tuyere-boxes are provided, so that on the removal of one set of tuyeres, another box and tuyeres may be in readiness. **1836–41** Brande *Chem.* (ed. 5) 762 The expansion of the boshes; but as this is more than four feet above the *tuyere hole, the blast must be delivered with great velocity. **1879** G. Gladstone in *Cassell's Techn. Educ.* IV. 145/1 The blast..is let on through the twyer-hole. **1861** Fairbairn *Iron* 50 The number of blowpipe nozzles to each furnace varies..; the usual number is three, one for each of the *tuyere-houses. **1882** *Rep. to Ho. Repr. Prec. Met. U. S.* 580 Water..flows also around the *tuyere openings. **1674** *Twire-pipe [see Twire-pipe 2]. **1840** *Civil Eng. & Arch. Jrnl.* III. 297/2 A second layer of charcoal..is thereafter laid..under the twyére pipe. **1881** Raymond *Mining Gloss.*, *Bloomary*, a forge for making wrought iron...The sides are iron plated,.. the *tuyere-plate (through which the tuyere passes) at one side.

**Tuyis,** obs. Sc. f. Twice. **Tuyke,** var. Tuke, *Obs.* **Tuyl, tuylȝe,** obs. ff. Tuilyie. **Tuyn, tuyne, tuynne,** obs. ff. Twin, Twine. **Tuynde, tuyne,** obs. ff. Tine *v.*[1]

† **Tuyre,** app. erron. f. Tirve *v.*[2]

**13..** *E. E. Allit. P.* B. 1234 Ȝet nolde neuer Nabugo þis ilke note leue, Er he hade tuyred þis toun & torne hit to grounde.

**Tuyrne,** obs. f. Tew-iron: cf. Tuyere.

**Tuys, tuyse, tuyss, Tuyssion, -yon, Tuyx,** obs. ff. Twice, Tuition, Twixt.

**Tuz, tuzz** (tʊz). [Perhaps identical with **tus* in Tussy and *tus(se)mose*: see Tuzzy-muzzy. But it may be related to Touse *sb.* 2, a tousled mass (of hair).] A tuft of hair; in quot. applied to whiskers; *dial.* a knot of wool or hair.

**1693** Dryden *Persius* iv. 90 With odorous Oyl thy head and hair are sleek; And then thou kemb'st the Tuzzes on thy Cheek. **1847–78** Halliwell, *Tuz*, a knot of wool or hair. *Leic.*

**Tuza** (tū·ză). Also **tuça** (*erron.* **tuca**). [a. Sp. *tuza*, ad. Mexican *tuçan* or *tozan*, the native name.] A Mexican pocket-gopher or pouched rat: a rodent, formerly supposed to be a kind of mole.

[**1651** Hernandez *Hist. Anim. & Min. Novae Hisp.* I. xxiv. 7 De Tucan, seu Talparum Indicarum quodam genere.] **1787** Cullen tr. *Clavigero's Mexico* II. 321 Tuza, not Tucan as Count de Buffon writes, in Mexican tozan, a quadruped of Mexico of the mole kind but larger and more beautiful. **1895** C. H. Merriam in *U. S. Dept. Agric., N. Amer. Fauna* No. 8. 112 The *tuza* series [of *Geomys*] inhabits the South Atlantic and Gulf States south of the Savannah River and east of the Mississippi...The members of the *tuza* series agree among themselves and differ from the remaining forms of the genus *Geomys* in having longer and more naked tails, and in numerous cranial characters.

**Tuzzle,** variant of Tussle.

**Tuzzy** (tʊ·zi). [See Tuz and next, and cf. Tussy.] (See quot.)

**1890** *Sci. Amer.* 1 Mar. 131/3 A ball of horsehair, such as is used by copper plate printers to assist in freeing their hands from ink (they call it a 'tuzzy').

**Tuzzy-muzzy** (tʊ·zi₁mʊ·zi), *sb.* (*a.*) *Obs.* exc. *dial.* Forms: *α.* 5 **tusmose, tussemose,** 7 **tussimussie**; *β.* 7 **tuzzimussie,** 6–8 **tuzzie-, tuzzi-, -muzzie, -muzzy,** 8–9 **tuzzy-muzzy.** [app. a kind of reduplicated or riming jingle on Tussy. The early form *tus-* or *tussemose*, with the transitional *tussimussie*, suggest the existence of **tus* or **tusse* in the sense 'cluster or knot of flowers', whence Tussy.] † A bunch or posy of flowers, a nosegay; a garland of flowers. Also *fig. Obs.*

*α.* c **1440** *Promp. Parv.* 494/2 Tyte tust, or tusmose of flowrys or othyr herbys (*S.* tytetuste or tussemose), *olfactorium.* **1629** Parkinson *Paradisus* 281 A delicate Tussimussie, as they call it, or Nosegay.

*β.* **1585** J. Higins *Junius' Nomencl.* 113/2 *Seruia*, a nosegay: a tuzziemuzzie: a sweete posie. **1587** Golding *De Mornay* xxiii. (1592) 342 [Apollo] commaunded..to remoue the tuzzimuzzies of flowers from his feete. **1598** Florio, *Serta*..a circlet or garland or wreath, a tuzzie-muzzie. **1620** Thomas *Lat. Dict.*, *Sertum*,..a nosegay, a tuzzimussie. **1629** Symmer *Spir. Posie* Ep. A ij b, Then shall this Tuzzimuzzie have its wished and expected smell. **1664** Gouldman *Copious Dictionary* (1669) s. v. *Tuttie*, A Tuttie, nosegay, posie or tuzziemuzzie, *fasciculus*. **1706** [see Tutty *sb.*[2]].

**b.** *dial.* As popular name of particular plants or flowers (see quots.); also, a bur.

**1842** Phelps *Collect. Glouc.* 281 *Tuzzy muzzy*, a burr. **1886** Britten & Holland *Eng. Plant-n.*, Tuzzy muzzy, *Muscari comosum... Norf*[*olk*]. **1890** *Gloucester Gloss.* Supp., *Tuzzy-muzzy*, old man's beard; Clematis Vitalba.

**c.** *transf.* See quots. *slang.*

**1711** E. Ward *Quix.* I. 70 And Salt as Lot's Wife's Tuzzy-muzzy. **1721** Bailey, *Tuzzimuzzy*,..a jocular Name for the *Pudendum Muliebre.* [Hence in Halliwell, and in later Dicts.]

**B.** *adj.* Dishevelled, ragged; fuzzy. *dial.*

**1847–78** Halliwell, *Tuzzimuzzy*, rough; ragged; dishevelled.

**Twa,** OE. and Sc. form of Two.

**Twachel,** var. Twatchel.

**Twachylle,** obs. f. Twitchel [1], passage.

**Twaddell** (twǫ·d'l). Also **Twaddel, Twaddle.** [Short for *Twaddell's hydrometer*, from the name of the inventor.] A form of hydrometer or hydrometric scale in which 200 degrees correspond to a unit of specific gravity, that of distilled water being denoted by zero. Also *attrib.*

**1860** O'Neill *Chem. Calico Print.* etc. 11 To obtain the value of any degree of Twaddle, it must be multiplied by five, and the product added to 1,000. *Ibid.* 12 The specific gravity and the Twaddle value of a degree of Beaumé. **1873** E. Spon *Workshop Receipts* Ser. I. 30/1 A hot solution of nitro-sulphate of iron, 5° Twaddle, 150° Fahrenheit.

† **Twa·dding,** *adv. Obs. rare*$^{-1}$. [Of obscure origin: cf. Twagger.] Abundantly (fat).

**1657** G. Thornley *Daphnis & Chloe* 175 Nor had the Wolf raven'd away so much as one [goat], and they were all more twadding fat then the very sheep.

**Twaddle** (twǫ·d'l), *sb.* (*a.*) [Origin obscure: not found *a* 1780; perh. an alteration of the earlier Twattle (known as *vb.* from 1573, as *sb.* from 1639; in *twittle-twattle* from c 1550).]

**1.** Senseless, silly, or trifling talk or writing; empty verbosity; dull and trashy statement or discourse; empty commonplace; prosy nonsense.

**1782** in *Mrs. Delany's Life & Corr.* Ser. II. (1862) III. 125 Fanny Burney has taken possession of the ear of those who found their amusement in reading her twaddle (that piece of old fashioned slang I should not have dared to write or utter, within hearing of my dear mother). **1825** Scott *Jrnl.* 29 Nov., A letter..quoting the twaddle of some old woman. **1851** Thackeray *Eng. Hum.* v, Pouring out endless volumes of sentimental twaddle. **1878** M. C. Jackson *Chaperon's Cares* II. xii. 145 The odious small-talk and twaddle he was compelled to hear. *Ibid.* xx. 243 No need to talk a lot of twaddle and nonsense to a woman with brains. **1906** Sir F. Treves *Highways Dorset* xviii. 291 He was guided by personal..experience, and not by the twaddle of theorists.

**b.** In extended sense: Something trashy or worthless; rubbish.

**1786** *Lounger* (1787) II. 197 The Ton of London is mere Twaddle,..the only right Ton is to be found in Paris. **1842** Barham *Ingol. Leg.* Ser. II. *Babes in Wood*, Greek and Latin old twaddle I call!

† **2.** (See quots. and Bore *sb.*[2] 1.) *Obs. slang.*

**1785** *European Mag.* Dec. 473/2 The favourite phrases fall, and are no more, The Rage, the Thing, the Twaddle, and the Bore. **1785** Grose *Dict. Vulg. Tongue* Pref. 2 The fashionable words, or favourite expressions of the day,.. vanish without leaving a trace behind, such were the late fashionable words, a Bore and a Twaddle, among the great vulgar. **1796** *Ibid.* (ed. 3), *Twaddle*, perplexity, confusion, or anything else: a fashionable term that for a while succeeded that of *bore*.

†**3.** A person who talks or writes twaddle; a twaddler. *Obs.*

**1802** Mrs. J. West *Infidel Father* II. 100 [He] acknowledged himself to be..bored by detestable twaddles. **1813** Moore *Post-bag* ii. 29 He thinks..the imagination..Could only enter in the noddles Of dull and ledger-keeping twaddles. **1830** Macaulay *Ess., R. Montgomery's Poems* (1887) 142 A respectable and pious gentleman, whose principal fault is that he is something of a twaddle. *a* **1838** C. Morris *Lyra Urban.* (1840) II. 187, I fear I'm becoming a twaddle.

**4.** *attrib.* or *adj.* Of the nature of twaddle; empty and prosy; in quot. 1830, feeble.

**1830** Col. Hawker *Diary* (1893) II. 20 The difference between the twaddle and the vigorous in shooting. **1845** Carlyle *Cromwell* (1871) V. 114 High Art paintings, gilt frames, and twaddle criticisms. **1865** Trollope *Belton Est.* v, I hate the twaddle talk of love. **1889** Gretton *Memory's Harkb.* 219 Twaddle truisms instead of vital truths.

Hence (*nonce-wds.*) **Twa·ddledom**, the realm of twaddle, the habit of uttering twaddle; **Twa·ddleize** *v., trans.* to reduce to twaddle; **Twa·ddlesome** *a.*, full of or addicted to twaddle.

**1837** *Tait's Mag.* IV. 454 The *twaddledom of old age. **1850** *Ibid.* XVII. 547/1 Dulling his [Burns's] humour, prosefying his poetry, and *twaddleising his vigour. **1865** *Pall Mall G.* 11 Nov. 10 A grim villain immensely stupid, and.. a virtuous duke immensely *twaddlesome.

**Twaddle**, var. Twaddell.

**Twa·ddle**, *v.*[1] [f. Twaddle *sb.*; or perh. altered, like it, from Twattle *v.*]

**1.** *intr.* To utter twaddle; to talk or write in a silly, empty, or trashy style.

**1825** J. Wilson *Noct. Ambr.* Wks. 1855 I. 15 Pope..beats them hollow. Catch him twaddling. **1831** Scott *Jrnl.* 14 Feb., I am afraid I am twaddling. **1862** Thackeray *Round. Papers, Dessein's*, 'What is that old fellow twaddlin' about?' cries Brummel.

**2.** *trans.* To utter as twaddle, or in a trashy and prosy way.

**1837** Prescott in Ticknor *Life* (1864) 271 *note*, They twaddle out their humour as if they were afraid of its biting too hard. **1850** Carlyle *Latter-d. Pamph.* viii. (1872) 273 You are not bound to..twaddle pretended raptures. **1900** *Westm. Gaz.* 19 Jan. 7/1 Instead of twaddling out platitudes.

**b.** with *away*: To spend or pass in empty talk.

**1826** Scott *Jrnl.* 11 Apr., We twaddled away the evening well enough.

†**Twa·ddle**, *v.*[2] *Obs. rare*$^{-1}$. [Cf. prec. and Twiddle *v.*[1]] *intr.* To trifle or play *with*.

**1797** Mrs. M. Robinson *Walsingham* IV. 3, I hate twaddling with other people's happiness.

**Twa·ddle**, *v.*[3] Chiefly *dial.* [Cf. Waddle *v.*, and dial. *quaddle* in similar sense.] *intr.* 'To walk with a feeble, uncertain gait' (*E. D. D.*). So **Twaddle-toed** *a.*

**1823** in *Spirit Pub. Jrnls.* 43 The unfortunate gentleman had walked, or rather twaddled to the office in a pair of loose slippers. **1907** *Daily News* 20 Mar. 6 Greenfinches.. have an unmistakable twaddle-toed walk that..makes them look like parrots.

**Twaddler** (twǫ·dlər). Also **twadler**. [f. Twaddle *sb.* or *v.*[1] + -er[1].] One who twaddles; one who talks or writes twaddle.

**1787** Duke of Rutland in *14th Rep. Hist. MSS. Comm.* App. i. 395 Pray be particularly attentive to them (even tho' they be twaddlers). **1837** Dickens *Pickw.* li, A laugh at the style of this ungrammatical twaddler. **1882** Miss Braddon *Mt. Royal* x, One of your sickly, sentimental twaddlers.

**Twaddling** (twǫ·dliŋ), *ppl. a.* [f. Twaddle *sb.* or *v.*[1] + -ing[2].]

**1.** Having the character of twaddle; empty and prosy; rubbishy.

**1804** *Edin. Rev.* Jan. 448 And this *twaddling* stuff is supposed to be spoken by John of Gaunt! **1832** Lady Granville *Lett.* 8 Sept. (1894) II. 132 Dearest sis, what a twaddling letter this is. **1858** *Ecclesiologist* XIX. 38 The twaddling derivation of Pointed architecture from interlacing boughs. **1859** Geo. Eliot *A. Bede* v, It's a volume of poems,..most of them seem to be twaddling stuff.

**b.** Petty, paltry, trifling, insignificant: = Twattling *ppl. a.* 3. *rare*$^{-1}$.

**1852** W. C. Baldwin *Afr. Hunting* 12 Jan. (1863) 8 A little twaddling weapon.

**2.** Uttering or addicted to talking twaddle.

**1826** F. Reynolds *Life & Times* II. 92 [I] heard an old twaddling special pleader. **1862** Shirley *Nugæ Crit.* xi. 470 The position..assumed..by twaddling doctrinaires, and political pedants.

**Twaddly** (twǫ·dli), *a.* [f. Twaddle *sb.* + -y.] Characterized by, or of the nature of, twaddle.

**1841** *Fraser's Mag.* XXIII. 273 [The dialogue] sounds rather twaddly. **1879** Miss Braddon *Clov. Foot* xxx, When a mother gets to the elderly and twaddly age,.. one can't feel poetical about her.

**Twae**, Sc. dial. form of Two.

**Twafald, twae-**, obs. and Sc. ff. Twofold.

†**Twag**. *Cant. Obs.* (See quot.)

**1592** Greene *Conny-Catching* iii. C, Their word for knowing ech other, as is said, was *Quest*, and this villaines comfortable newes to them, was *Twag*, signifying he had sped.

**Twagger** (twæ·gər). *dial.* [Cf. Quag *v.*[1] and Twadding *adv.*] A (? big or fat) lamb.

**1599** Peele *Arraignm. Paris* i. i, I have brought a twagger for the nones, A bunting lamb;..my cunning much I miss, If ever Pan felt fatter lamb than this. *c* **1900** in *Eng. Dial. Dict.* (West Sussex).

†**Twail, twayle**. *Obs. rare*$^{-1}$. [app. a. F. *toile* (*d'araignée*) spider's web :—L. *tēla* web, cloth.] A spider's web.

**1608** Topsell *Serpents* 273 They [spiders] labour to, and doe prouide Gainst winds and things that break their twayles [*ed.* 1658 twails] That bands from tacklings may not slyde When greater strength doth them assayle.

**Twaile**, obs. form of Towel.

**Twain** (twēⁱn), *numeral a.* and *sb. arch.* Forms: 1 twœʒen, tueʒen, 1–2 tweʒen, twæʒen, 2 tweiʒen, 2–3 tweien, 3 tweyen; 2–5 twein, 3–5 tweyne, tweine, twene, (4 tweiyne, tuueine), 4–5 tweyn, 5 tweyne; 4 tuayn, tuain, 4–6 twayne (5 tueyne, thwayne), 5–6 twayn, 6 *Sc.* twane, 6–7 twaine, (7 *Sc.* tuaine), 6– twain. [The modern representative of OE. *twéʒen*, the nom. and acc. masc. of the numeral of which the fem. and neuter *twá, tú*, remain as Two (q. v.). It corresponds to OFris. *twêne, twên* (mod.Fris. dial. *tween, twein, twain*), OS. *twêna, twêne*, OHG. and MHG. *zwêne* (archaic Ger. *zween*). In ME. *twain* ceased to be confined to the masc., and became merely a secondary form of *two*, used esp. when the numeral followed the sb. Its use in the Bible of 1611 and in the Marriage Service, and its value as a rime-word, have contributed to its retention as an archaic and poetic synonym of *two*. See also the apocopate form Tway; and, for the inflexions, Two.]

**A.** Illustration of Forms.

*c* **725** *Corpus Gloss.* (O.E.T.) 1510 *Passus*, faeðm *vel* tueʒen stridi. *a* **800** *Casket* 1 in *O. E. Texts* 127 Twœʒen ʒibroþæra, fœddæ hiæ uylif in Romæcæstri. *a* **900** *O. E. Chron.* an. 822 Her tueʒen [*Laud MS.* twæʒen] aldormen wurdon ofslæʒene. *c* **1000** Ælfric *Gen.* xlii. 37 Ic hæbbe tweʒen suna. *c* **1160** *Hatton Gosp.* Matt. xviii. 20 Ðær tweiʒen [*Ags. G.* tweʒen] oððe þreo synden on minen namen ʒegadered. *c* **1175** *12th c. Hom.* (Bodley) 86 Tweʒen þisseræ dæle habbæð deor & nyten. *c* **1175** *Lamb. Hom.* 41 Heo tweien eoden et sume time in to helle. *Ibid.* 85 He haueð.. þa twein peneʒes. *c* **1200** *Trin. Coll. Hom.* 5 Tweien oðer tocumes of ure helende. *c* **1290** *S. Eng. Leg.* I. 276/168 Tweyen faire wommen. *a* **1325** *MS. Rawl. B.* 520 lf. 81 Noȝt..bi tuueine assoines a sullen sollemnen suuche ane assoine. *c* **1380** Wyclif *Sel. Wks.* III. 194 And þei schullen be tweiyne in o flesch. *c* **1385** Chaucer *L. G. W.* 1963 (*Ariadne*) It was longynge to the doughteren tweyne. **1387** Trevisa *Higden* (Rolls) VIII. 151 By twene [*v. r.* tweye] burgeys of Londoun. *c* **1400** *Gamelyn* 734 (Harl. MS.) To his tweyne bretheren anon-right he cam. **1423** Jas. I *Kingis Q.* xlii, With..wommen tueyne. *c* **1425** *Cursor M.* 523 (Trin.) [Þe] heed wiþynne haþ eȝen tweyn [*Cott., Gött.* tuin; *F.* twyn; *rime* certeyn]. *c* **1440** *Generydes* 155 It was be twix them thwayne. *c* **1450** *Godstow Reg.* 193 Rent, to be paid..at twayne termes in the yere. **1503** Dunbar *Thistle & Rose* 172 Haill, Roiss, both reid and quhyt,..of michty cullouris twane. **1511–12** *Act* 3 *Hen. VIII*, c. 23 § 5 Lettres..to twayn of his honourable Counseillours. **1542** Udall *Erasm. Apoph.* 165 The vertues..of bothe twain. **1548** Forrest *Pleas. Poesye* 61 b, Wee shall deuyde it into lessons twayne. **1675** Hobbes *Odyssey* iv. 470 But of the Princes lost are only twain. **1784** Cowper *Task* i. 77 The soft settee..received, United yet divided, twain at once. **1897** May Kendall in *Longm. Mag.* Aug. 340 Forth went.. Soldiers twain.

*β.* Abnormal genitive pl.: *her tweyners* = of them two. (After *alleris, altheris, botheris*: see All D. 4, Both A. 4 b.)

*c* **1450** *Cov. Myst.* (Shaks. Soc.) 125 And of her tweyners metyng Here gynnyth the proces.

**B.** Signification. = Two. **I.** *adj.*

**1.** In concord with a sb., etc. **a.** Preceding the sb. Now *rare*.

*c* **725**– [see A.]. *c* **1205** Lay. 8144 Þeos tweien cnihtes. *Ibid.* 12255 Twene ibroðeren. *c* **1380** Wyclif *Sel. Wks.* III. 310 Whanne tweyne horis stryvede whos was þe child. **1382** *Ibid.* 512 A þousand and tweyn hundrid ȝeer. **1432–50** tr. *Higden* (Rolls) I. 167 There be tweyne Mauritanyes, that firste is Mauritany Cesariense, whiche hathe at the este of hit Numidia. *a* **1450** *Knt. de la Tour* (1906) 162 It might be proued..by tweyn witnessis. *c* **1460** *Wisdom* 1077 in *Macro Plays* 71 In twayn myghtys of my soule I the offendyde. **1554** Cdl. Pole in *Eng. Hist. Rev.* July (1913) 528, I have recevyd twayne yowr lettres. **1870** R. Buchanan *Bk. Orm* iv. 89 Thy blue eyes twain stars. **1871** F. W. Newman *Iliad* xiii. 201 The twain full arm'd Aiantes.

**b.** *poet.* Following the sb.

Chiefly for the sake of a rime.

**13..** *Cursor M.* 4032 Þir breþer tuain þam tok to red. *c* **1330** R. Brunne *Chron.* (1810) 106 Godefrey of Louayn, ..Bi messengers tuayn sent to kyng Henry, For his douhter Adelayn. *c* **1386** Chaucer *Frankl. T.* 334 Let this flod enduren yeres twaine. *c* **1440** *R. Gloucester's Chron.* 1099 Þo adde king lud..ȝonge sones tueie [*MS.* δ tweyne]. *c* **1440** *Pallad. on Husb.* i. 671 On cok for hennys tweyne. **1513** Bradshaw *St. Werburge* i. 174 Whylom dyuyded in sondry kyngdomes twayne. *c* **1560** A. Scott *Poems* (S.T.S.) xxiii. 26 Hir bricht fair ene twane. **1700** Dryden *Cock & Fox* 717 The trembling widow, and her daughters twain. **1724** Swift *To Delany* Wks. 1755 IV. i. 46 Where we find the members twain. **1782** Cowper *Gilpin* 123 The bottles twain ..Were shatter'd at a blow. **1843** Neale *Hymns for Sick* (1863) 42 He loved the sisters twain. **1846** Keble *Lyra Innoc.* (1873) 147 Five loaves hath he, And fishes twain. **1860** Longf. *Wayside Inn, Saga K. Olaf* iv. 23 She had given the ring to her goldsmiths twain, Who smiled, as they handed it back again. **1871** R. Ellis *Catullus* lxxviii. 1, Brothers twain has Gallus.

**2.** Absolutely with ellipsis of sb., or following a pronoun or pronominal adjective.

*c* **1000** *Ags. Gosp.* Matt. xviii. 20 ʒyf tweʒen of eow ʒeþwæriað..be ælcum þinge. *c* **1160**, *c* **1175** [see A.]. *c* **1275** *Passion of Our Lord* 243 in *O. E. Misc.* 44 Þer arysen tweyne and bigunne to speke. *c* **1350** *Will. Palerne* 2507 Se what sorwe he suffres to saue vs tweine! **1401** *Pol. Poems* (Rolls) II. 27 What betokeneth that ye goe tweine and tweine togither? **1470–85** Malory *Arthur* ii. x. 87 Of the tweyne he had leuer kyng Lotte had be slayne than kynge Arthur. **1526** *Pilgr. Perf.* (W. de W. 1531) 143, I shall wryte a worde or twayne. **1596** *Edward III*, iv. v. 82 Which of these twaine is greater infamie? **1610** Shaks. *Temp.* i. ii. 438 All his Lords, the Duke of Millaine And his braue sonne, being twaine. **1657** Howell *Londinop.* 322 They had six..Meeting places,..twain in Bridge Street,.. twain in Old Fish Street, and twain in Stock-Fishmonger Row. **1824** Scott *Redgauntlet* Let. vii, We will pray him ..to tarry a day or twain. **1847** Tennyson *Princ.* vii. 271 These twain..Sit side by side. **1881** — *Cup* ii. i. 37 That the world may know You twain are reconciled.

**b.** *In* († *on*) *twain*: into two parts or pieces, in two, asunder.

**1398** Trevisa *Barth. De P. R.* iii. ix. (1495) 54 The vertue of apprehendynge..is departed in tweyne. **1415** *E. E. Wills* (1882) 23 Y wolle hit be parted on tweyne. *c* **1430** *Hymns Virg.* (1867) 58 Or þei be fulli partide on tweyne. *c* **1440** *Generydes* 2632 With that stroke he brake his sheld on twayn. **1509** Hawes *Past. Pleas.* xxxviii. (Percy Soc.) 197, I have thought long Sithen the time that we parted in twayne. **1598** *Mucedorus* ii. iv. 77 To cut in twaine the twisted thread. **1697** Dryden *Virg. Georg.* iv. 202 Cold Winter split the Rocks in twain. **1798** Soph. Lee *Canterb. T., Yng. Lady's T.* II. 145 The marble fountain..was cloven in twain. *a* **1862** Buckle *Misc. Wks.* (1872) I. 84 The nation was..severed in twain by..religious faction.

**3.** With special connotations. (Cf. One III.) **a.** Separate, parted asunder; disunited, estranged, at variance. (Only in predicate.)

*c* **1600** Shaks. *Sonn.* xxxvi, We two must be twaine, Although our vndeuided loues are one. **1611** Sir W. Mure *Misc. Poems* iv. 28 Ȝit in a breist sall both our herts no more at all be tuaine. **1619** Drayton *Idea* ix, Reason and I (you must conceive) are twaine. **1671** Milton *Samson* 929 Thou and I long since are twain. **1844** Talfourd *Athenian Capt.* iv. i, Henceforth we are twain.

**b.** Consisting of two parts or elements; double, twofold. *rare*.

**1398** Trevisa *Barth. De P. R.* v. i. (1495) f viij/2 A chylde borne, yᵗ was tweyne in yᵉ ouer partye & one in the nether partye. **1870** Morris *Earthly Par.* III. iv. 132 Hope and shame, Twain help,..unto her spirit came.

**II.** *sb.*

†**1.** The abstract number two. *Obs.*

**1398** Trevisa *Barth. De P. R.* xix. cxxiii. (1495) mm iij b/1 Superfluus is the nombre yᵗ hath partyes that maketh a greter nombre than itself:..one, tweyne, thre [etc.]. *c* **1425** *Craft of Nombrynge* (E.E.T.S.) 9 Þou mayst not draw sex out of 2. But þou mayst draw 2 out of sex. And þou maiste draw twene out of twene. *c* **1483** Caxton *Dialogues* x. 51/6 *Ung, deux, trois*, one, tweyne, thre.

**2.** A group of two; a pair, couple.

**1607** Topsell *Four-f. Beasts* (1658) 555 Horns which some men guess to be of the Unicorns..because they are found several, never by twains. **1610** Shaks. *Temp.* iv. i. 104 To blesse this twaine, that they may prosperous be. **1816** Byron *Let. to Moore* 24 Dec., You received my other twain of letters. **1843** S. Bamford *Homely Rhymes* etc. (1864) 71 The twain of young lovers have tarried behind.

**3.** *pl.* Twins. *dial.*

**1580** Hollyband *Treas. Fr. Tong*, *Besson*, twaines. **1897** J. Hammond *Cornish Parish* ix. 199, I remark in 1699 three entries of 'twains' out of 76 births. *Ibid.* xix. 344 Instead of 'twins', [we say] 'two twains'.

**III.** *Comb.*: **twain-cloud**, a name for the cumulostratus; †**twain-edged** *a.* = Two-edged.

**1382** Wyclif *Heb.* iv. 12 The word of God is..more able for to perse than al tweyne eggid swerd. **1823** T. Forster *Res. Atmospheric Phenomena* i. § 7. (ed. 3) 20 Of the Cumulostratus or Twaincloud. **1844** Stephens *Bk. Farm* I. 246 Why..the heaped stratus [should be called] the twain-cloud is by no means obvious, unless..[as] being composed of two clouds,..but, on the same principle, the cirro-cumulus, and the cirro-stratus and the cumulo-stratus may be termed twain-clouds.

†**Twain**, *v. Obs.* [f. Twain *a.* or *sb.*] *trans.* To part or divide in twain; to put apart, separate.

**13..** *E. E. Allit. P.* A. 251 Fro we in twynne wern towen & twayned, I haf ben a Ioylez Iuelere. **15..** *Chester Pl.* (Shaks. Soc.) I. 20 (Add. MS.) Nowe will I make the firmamente,..For to be a devidente To twayne [*Harl. MS. 2124* twyne] the watters. *Ibid.* II. 151 My people of Jewes he wulde twayne. ? **17..** *Clerk Saunders* xii. in Child *Ballads* (1886) II. 159 It wear great sin this twa to twain. **1878** B. Taylor *Deukalion* iii. vi, Who twains What once was one. **1900** Crockett *Joan Sw. Hand* xxxix, You may slay my husband, but he is mine still. You cannot twain our souls.

**b.** *intr.* for *refl.* or *pass.* To separate.

**15..** *Chester Pl.* (Shaks. Soc.) I. 18 (Add. MS.) Lightnes and darcknes, I byde you tweyne [*Harl. MS. 2124* twyn; *rimes* begin, myn, in].

**Twait**, var. of Thwait(e; obs. f. Twat.

**Twait, twaite** (twēⁱt). *local.* Forms: 7 tweat, thwait, 9 twayt, thwaite, 8– twait, twaite. [Origin not ascertained.] A European species of shad, *Alosa finta*. Also attrib. *twait shad*.

**1613** J. Dennys *Secr. Angling* ii. xlii, The Shad..The Bocher sweet, the pleasant Flounder thin, The Peele, the Tweat, the Botling, and the rest. *c* **1640** J. Smyth *Lives Berkeleys* (1885) III. 319, 53. sorts of sea fish...The turbut, Lamprey, Lamperne, Shad, tweat. **1688** R. Holme *Armoury* ii. 325/1 The Shad, Thwait, Plaice, and Flou[n]der have the greatest love for Salt, or Brackish Waters, which ebb and flow. **1769** Pennant *Zool.* III. 298 The variety [of the Shad] called near Gloucester the Twaite. **1882** *Standard* 2 Mar. 2/8 Two species which ascend certain streams..about the month of May—..the Twait shad and the Allice shad. **1904** GALLICHAN *Fishing Spain* 168 The two kinds of shad of our coast are known as the twaite and the allice.

**Twal(l, twalf,** Sc. and obs. ff. TWELVE. **Twalicht,** obs. Sc. f. TWILIGHT. **Twalt, Twalue**: see TWELFTH, TWELVE. **Twancle,** obs. f. TWANGLE *v.* **Twane,** obs. Sc. pa. t. of TWINE *v.*[1]; obs. f. TWAIN.

**Twang** (twæŋ), *sb.*[1] Also 6 **twange, twangue.** [Echoic: the *tw-* element expresses the sound or noise of the twitching or plucking, the *-ang* element the ringing or resonance.]

**1.** A vocal imitation of the resonant sound produced when a tense string is sharply plucked or suddenly released; used as interjection or adverb, e.g. *to cry twang, twang goes the bow.* Also extended, †*twangledom twang* (*obs.*). Cf. TANG *sb.*[2] b.

*a* **1553** UDALL *Royster D.* II. i. (Arb.) 32 Then vp to our lute at midnight, twangledome twang, Then twang with our sonets, and twang with our dumps. **1596** NASHE *Saffron-Walden* Wks. (Grosart) III. 101 He..made Powles Churchyard resound, or crie twang againe, with foure notable famous Letters. **1600** DEKKER *Shoemaker's Holiday* III. iv, Ile fill your bellies with good cheare til they crie twang. *c* **1720** PRIOR *Advice of Venus* 4 Twang goes the bow, my Girls, have at your hearts. *a* **1741** *Robin Hood & Ranger* ix. in Child *Ballads* (1888) III. 153/1 He made his broad weapon cry twang. **1881** BESANT & RICE *Chapl. of Fleet* II. 80 Twang, twang, twang, went the fiddles.

**b.** A sound of the above character; also, any sharp ringing sound resembling this. In quot. 1565 *fig.*

**1565** T. STAPLETON *Fortr. Faith* 8 To go to the matter alleaged directly without idle twanges. **1567** DRANT *Horace, Art Poetry* B iij, With twang of harp to stir the stones. **1594** NASHE *Unfort. Trav.* Wks. (Grosart) V. 159 None of them could make the cord come aloft with a twange halfe like him. *c* **1611** CHAPMAN *Iliad* IV. 143 The sinew forged string Did giue a mightie twang; and forth, the eager shaft did sing. **1728** POPE *Dunc.* II. 254 So swells each wind-pipe; ass intones to ass, Harmonic twang of leather, horn, and brass. **1779** WARNER in Jesse *Selwyn & Contemp.* (1844) IV. 133 The last twang of the postman's bell. **1804** J. GRAHAME *Sabbath* (1808) 65 The buzz..of moss-entangled bee, That, soon as loosed, booms with full twang away. **1853** KANE *Grinnell Exp.* xxiv. (1856) 196 The twang of a bow-string. **1858** R. S. SURTEES *Ask Mamma* li, A twang of the horn. *fig.* **1663** COWLEY *Cutter Coleman St.* v. xiii, There should ha' been..a lusty Cudgeling [at the end of the farce] to make it come off smartly, with a Twang at the Tail.

**c.** *transf.* and *fig.* Ringing sound or tone.

**1646** G. DANIEL *Poems* Wks. (Grosart) I. 89 When to the Twang of meeter, Poesie Shall fall to Sordid Groomes. *a* **1680** BUTLER *Elephant in Moon* II. 181 Transported with the Twang Of his own Elocution. **1714** R. FIDDES *Pract. Disc.* II. 345 Great things have been done by the mere twang of two or three good words. **1825** T. HOOK *Sayings* Ser. II. *Passion & Princ.* ix. III. 168 His father-in-law..had just pitched his voice to the true poetical twang.

**2. a.** The modification of vocal sound by its passage through the nose; nasal intonation, as formerly attributed to the Puritans; now esp. as characterizing the pronunciation of an individual, a country, or locality. More fully *nasal twang, twang of the nose.*

**1661** SOUTH *Serm., Tit.* ii. 15 (1715) I. 201 To make..incoherent Stuff (seasoned with Twang and Tautology) pass for high Rhetorick, and moving Preaching. **1663** BUTLER *Hud.* I. III. 1157 To find in lines of Beard and Face, The Physiognomy of Grace; And by the sound and twang of Nose, If all be sound within disclose. **1704** SWIFT *Mech. Operat. Spirit* Misc. (1711) 300 By this Method the Twang of the Nose becomes perfectly to resemble the Snuffle of the Bagpipe. **1784** COWPER *Task* II. 436 Odious as the nasal twang Heard at conventicle. **1839** SYD. SMITH *Mem. & Lett.* (1855) II. ccccxv, She..has the true Kentucky twang through the nose, converting that promontory into an organ of speech. **1877** SWEET *Handbk. Phonetics* 8 Many speakers pronounce all their vowels with imperfect closure of the nose passage, which gives their pronunciation the so-called 'nasal twang'. **1902** R. BAGOT *Donna Diana* ii, A wealthy American widow, the owner of a pronounced twang.

**b.** A distinctive manner of pronunciation or intonation differing from that usual, or regarded as the standard, in a country; esp. one associated with a particular district or locality.

In some of the earlier instances the fig. notion of 'a smack' is perhaps intended: cf. TWANG *sb.*[2] 2.

**1697** BENTLEY *Phal.* (1699) 313 Phalaris..must needs, for that reason, have a twang of their Dialect. **1705** ELSTOB in Hearne *Collect.* 30 Nov. (O.H.S.) I. 109 I'll make you Master of ye Gallick Twang. **1706** PHILLIPS (ed. Kersey), *Twang*,..an ill sound in one's Pronunciation. **1707** FARQUHAR *Beaux Strat.* III. ii, You talk very good English, but you have a mighty Twang of the Foreigner. **1725** tr. *Dupin's Eccl. Hist. 17th C.* I. II. iii. 35 His Italian has a twang of the Country in which he liv'd. **1736** DRAKE *Eboracum* I. vii. 242 The broad open accent, and twang, of the more northern [people]. **1781** MME. D'ARBLAY *Diary* Aug., The Hibernian twang of his pronunciation. **1822** SCOTT *Nigel* ii, His voice had a twang in it. **1852** THACKERAY *Esmond* III. v, A grating voice that had an Irish twang. *Ibid.* viii, This family..spoke French with the twang which the Flemings use. **1855** BAIN *Senses & Int.* III. ii. § 19 (1864) 485 By 'accent' I understand that indescribable accompaniment with the voice, termed also 'twang' or 'brogue'..which constitutes the indelible distinction between English, Irish, Scotch, Americans, French, &c. **1867** MISS BRADDON *Aur. Floyd* xxx, They talked with an honest northern twang. **1883** *Gd. Words* 12 You must not be too near them, or you will hear the Cockney twang.

**3.** *transf.* A ringing or resounding blow. Cf. TWANK *v. rare.*

**1712** STEELE *Spect.* No. 504 ¶ 1 These can slap you on the back unawares,..ask you how you do with a twang on your shoulders. **1843** LYTTON *Last Bar.* I. i, The leathern gauntlet that protected the arm from the painful twang of the string.

**4.** *transf.* A sharp pluck or twitch; a tweak; also, the effect of this: a twinge, a sharp pang. Now *dial.*

**1720** *Lett. Lond. Jrnl.* (1721) 29 A Kick in the Breech, or a Twang by the Nose. **1723** RAMSAY *Fair Assembly* xvi, 'T wad gi'e your hearts a twang! **1728** — *To G. Drummond* ix, Few twangs of guilt they feel. **1789** BURNS *To the Toothache* i, Your venom'd stang, That shoots my tortur'd gums alang; And thro' my lugs gies monie a twang. **1825** BROCKETT *N. C. Words, Twang*, a quick pull, a tweak—also pain. **1852** *Tomlinson's Cycl. Usef. Arts* (1866) I. 836/1 He then..gives repeated and sudden twangs to the string [in bowing furs for hats].

**Twang,** *sb.*[2] [Alteration of TANG *sb.*[1]; but often confused or associated with TWANG *sb.*[1]]

**1.** A penetrating or persisting taste, flavour, or odour, usually disagreeable: = TANG *sb.*[1] 5.

**1611** COTGR., *Deboire*, an after taste, ill smacke, or twang, which an vnsauorie thing leaues behind in the mouth. **1670** W. SIMPSON *Hydrol. Ess.* 69 The brackishness and sulphureous twang of the lee of kelp. **1768** TUCKER *Lt. Nat.* (1834) I. 468 Though the liquor was not at all impaired thereby..it might get some twang of the vessel. **1809** *Med. Jrnl.* XXI. 476 Its smell is alliaceous, mixed with another twang..still less grateful. **1859** F. E. PAGET *Curate of Cumberworth* 242, I particularly dislike a twang of onion. **1891** T. HARDY *Tess* xxii, A customer..complained that the butter had a twang.

**b.** *A tongue with a twang*: see TANG *sb.*[1] 5 c.

**1667** DRYDEN & DAVENANT *Tempest* II. i, She had a tongue with a twang.

**2.** *fig.* A trace or suggestion of some specified origin, quality, or the like; a 'smack', touch, tinge; a taint; = TANG *sb.*[1] 6.

**1633** MASSINGER *Guardian* v. iv, This is neither begging, borrowing, nor robbery; Yet it hath a twang of all of them. **1678** DRYDEN *Limberham* II. i, A twang of the mother; but I love to graff on such a crab-tree. **1702** *Eng. Theophrast.* 331 The Fondness or Indifference that Philosophers express'd for Life, was but a particular Twang of the Love of themselves. **1826** SCOTT *Jrnl.* 2 May, Yesterday had a twang of frost in it. **1855** HAWTHORNE *Eng. Note-bks.* (1870) I. 284 This position of tutor to a young Englishman..has an ugly twang of upper servitude.

**†3.** A tooth; *esp.* a canine tooth, a fang. Cf. TANG *sb.*[1] 2 b. *Obs.*

**1677** PLOT *Oxfordsh.* 276 Rapine with her fiery eyes, grinning teeth, sharp twangs, her hand imbrewed in blood. **1682** *Lond. Gaz.* No. 1782/4 Lost..,two Land Spaniels, a Dog and Bitch,..the ends of the two upper Twangs of the Dog cut off.

**†Twang,** *sb.*[3] *Obs.* [Of obscure origin.] *Huddle and twang*, a term of contempt for a person. Cf. CUM-TWANG, HUDDLE *sb.* 3.

Differently, and perh. improperly, applied in quot. 1591.

**1579** LYLY *Euphues* (Arb.) 106 Though Curio be olde huddle and twang, *ipse*, he, yet Euphues had rather shrinke in the wetting than wast in the wearing. **1591** FLORIO *2nd Fruites* 41 Who lets his wife goe to euerie feaste..Shall haue..of his best wife a twang with a huddle. **1600** *1st Pt. Sir J. Oldcastle* I. ii. 161 If euer woolfe were cloathed in sheepes coate, Then I am he,—olde huddle and twang, yfaith.

**Twang,** *v.*[1] [Echoic. Goes with TWANG *sb.*[1]]

**I.** Of sound.

**1.** *intr.* To give forth a ringing note, as a tense string or a stringed instrument when plucked; to clang. Said also of the sound produced. Also *fig.*

† *To go off twanging*, to be a great success. *Obs.*

**1567** [see TWANGING *ppl. a.*]. **1570** LEVINS *Manip.* 23/47 To Twangue, *resonare.* **1607** R. TURNER *Nosce Te* F iij, Now noses twang, guts grone. **1621** G. SANDYS *Ovid's Met.* VI. (1626) 114 This said, the bow-string twangs. **1626** MASSINGER *Rom. Actor* II. i, Had he died, As I resolve to do,..It [a play] had gone off twanging. *a* **1700** DRYDEN *Iliad* I. 70 His bow twanged, and his arrows rattled as they flew. **1728** W. STARRAT *Epist.* 48 in *Ramsay's Poems* (1877) II. 275 What tuneless heart-strings wadna twang When love and beauty animate the sang? **1812** H. & J. SMITH *Rej. Addr., Theatre* 27 Winds the French-horn, and twangs the tingling harp. **1840** R. H. DANA *Bef. Mast* xviii. 50 We found the violin and guitar screaming and twanging away under the piazza. **1862** MRS. H. WOOD *Mrs. Hallib.* II. v, [She] burst in at the door, with a violence that made its bell twang and tinkle.

**2.** *trans.* To cause to make a ringing note, as by plucking or twitching a tense string or strings of a bow or of a musical instrument; hence, to play on (an instrument). Also *fig.*

**1579–80** NORTH *Plutarch* (1595) 949 The Scythians, when they are disposed to drink drunk together, do diuerse times twang the strings of their bowes. **1652** BENLOWES *Theoph.* III. i, Muse, twang the powerful harp, and brush each String. **1788** R. CUMBERLAND *Aristoph., Clouds* viii, He would not sit twanging the lute, not he. **1855** THACKERAY *Newcomes* xxxi, Musicians came and twanged guitars to her. **1864** ENGEL *Mus. Anc. Nat.* 45 The strings are of lamb's gut, and are twanged with two small plectra. **1910** J. MACINTOSH in *Ayrshire Poets* 139 Hoar Winter twangs his trump in vain.

**†b.** *To twang one's nose*, to blow the nose loudly (see also 6). *Obs.*

**1748** RICHARDSON *Clarissa* V. 343 The mother twang'd her damn'd nose. **1810** S. GREEN *Reformist* I. 202 Percival felt for his handkerchief, twanged his nose.

**3.** *intr.* To produce a ringing note by or as by plucking a string or stringed instrument; hence (in depreciative sense) to play *on* a stringed instrument. *To twang* (*all*) *upon one string, the same string*: cf. HARP *v.* 2.

**1594** LYLY *Moth. Bomb.* III. iv, I wish'd for a noyse Of crack-halter Boyes, On those hempen strings to be twanging. **1624** GEE *New Shreds O. Snare* 18 The plots of their Comedies twang all vpon one string. **1671** H. FOULIS *Hist. Rom. Treasons* (1681) 88 Both twang upon the same string. **1840** R. H. DANA *Bef. Mast* xxvii. 92 The musicians were still there,..scraping and twanging away. **1885** *Chr. World* 15 Jan. 38/5 They took to twanging away on what seemed an inferior kind of guitar.

**†b.** In the phrases *the worst that, as good as, ever twanged. Obs.*

**1542** UDALL *Erasm. Apoph.* 110 b, A minstrel..ye wurste that euer twanged. **1579** GOSSON *Sch. Abuse* (Arb.) 24 His skill is showne too make his Scholer as good as euer twangde. **1678** RAY *Prov.* (ed. 2) 285 As good as ever twang'd. **1681** W. ROBERTSON *Phraseol. Gen.* (1693) 486 The worst that ever twang'd; He has all the ill qualities that you can name.

**4.** *trans.* To play (a melody or the like) on a stringed instrument; to sound forth on a twanging instrument. Also said of the instrument or its strings.

**1542** UDALL *Erasm. Apoph.* 207 Paris with his harpe did nothyng but twang fonde fansies of daliaunce and lasciuiousnesse. **1577** STANYHURST *Descr. Irel.* viii. in *Holinshed* I. 28/2 When the harper twangeth or singeth a song, all the company must be whist, or else he chafeth like a cutpurse, by reason his harmony is not had in better price. **1582** — *Æneis* I. (Arb.) 41 Curled Iöppas Twanged on his harp golden, what he whillon learned of Atlas. **1809** W. IRVING *Knickerb.* IV. iii. (1820) 240 His sturdy trumpeter..twanging his trumpet in the face of the whole world. **1842** THACKERAY *Fitz-Boodle's Conf., Ottilia* ii, She twanged off a rattling piece of Liszt. **1851** H. D. WOLFF *Madrilenia* (1853) 111 Three guitar players, hired for the occasion, twanged a variety of airs. **1872** BLACK *Adv. Phaeton* xiv, The cords of the guitar twanged out a few notes.

**†5.** Of a speaker: **a.** *trans.* To utter with a sharp ringing tone; = TANG *v.*[2] 2. *Obs. rare.*

**1601** SHAKS. *Twel. N.* III. iv. 198 A terrible oath, with a swaggering accent sharpely twang'd off.

**†b.** *intr.* To speak. *Obs. rare.*

**1601** B. JONSON *Poetaster* I. ii, The tongue of the oracle neuer twang'd truer. *Ibid.* v. iii, Thou twang'st right, little Horace.

**6.** *intr.* To speak with a nasal intonation or twang. Also *trans.* with *nose* (cf. 2 b). *rare.*

**1615** [see TWANGING *vbl. sb.*]. **1826** SCOTT *Woodst.* v, With yonder Puritanic, Round-headed soldiers..I..twanged my nose and turned up my eyes. **1844** WILLIS *Lady Jane* I. 238 Nasal Smith and Jones Will twang as usual in 'the better sphere'.

**b.** *trans.* To utter or pronounce with a nasal or other twang.

**1748** RICHARDSON *Clarissa* (1810) IV. xxviii. 154 [She] Twanged out a heigh-ho through her nose. **1754** J. SHEBBEARE *Matrimony* (1766) I. 17 The Master of the Family..twangs the Dictates of the Gospel through his Nose all Sunday. **1836** T. HOOK *G. Gurney* I. 155 Hearing Miss Crab..twang out the following. **1851** THACKERAY *Eng. Hum.* ii. (1858) 69 The Cicerone twangs his moral. **1864** *Daily Tel.* 29 July, A purer Whitechapel accent..than that with which a damsel with a dulcimer twanged out a nasal-guttural lyric. **1893** SALTUS *Madam Sapphira* 191 'Now Becky,' twanged the ponderous person, 'what is your name?'

**II.** Of the action (without special reference to the sound).

**7.** *trans.* To pull or pluck (the string of a bow), so as to shoot.

**1600** FAIRFAX *Tasso* VII. ciii, But from his quiuer huge a shaft he hent, And set it in his mightie bowe new bent, Twanged the string, out flew the quarell long. **1715–20** POPE *Iliad* I. 67 He twang'd his deadly bow, And hissing fly the feather'd fates below. **1890** C. MARTYN *W. Phillips* 236 Those [wits] twanged their bow-strings and sped their arrows of ridicule at so plain a target. **1891** E. FIELD *Bk. Western Verse* 25 He twanged his bow.

**b.** Used with reference to the bow (see BOW *sb.*[1] 13) employed in hat-making; also with the material as obj.

**1882** FLOYER *Unexpl. Baluchistan* 326 A boy 'twanging' wool with a bow, and reducing it to a coarse fluff. **1886** *Cheshire Gloss.* s. v. *Bow*, To 'twang the bow' was formerly considered a very skilful branch of hat manufacturing.

**8.** *trans.* To discharge (an arrow) with a twang of the bow-string; to let fly (an arrow). In quot. 1751 *absol.* Also *fig.*

**1751** SMOLLETT *Per. Pic.* lxxxvii, She..twanged off with the appellations of b—— and w——. **1807** W. IRVING *Salmag.* viii. (1824) 124 To be shot by the first lady's eye that can twang an arrow. **1833** MRS. BROWNING *Prometh. Bound* Poems 1850 I. 172 Where Scythia's shepherd peoples dwell aloft,..And twang the rapid arrow past the bow. **1847** TENNYSON *Princ.* II. 380 A thousand baby loves Fly twanging headless arrows at the hearts. **1862** THACKERAY *Philip* xi, This..may not have been the precise long bow which George Firmin..pulled; but..he twanged a famous lie out. **1863** *Reader* 31 Oct. 502 An athletic man..has twanged an arrow from his box against some object.

**b.** *intr.* Of an arrow: To leave the bow-string with a twang.

**1795** COLERIDGE *Lines in Manner of Spenser* iv, When twanged an arrow from Love's mystic string. **1831** JAMES *Phil. Augustus* I. v. The missile twanged away from the string.

**†9.** *intr.* To pluck, twitch *at. Obs. rare*—[1].

*a* **1678** MARVELL *Appleton House* 648 At my lines the fishes twang.

**Twang,** *v.*[2] [f. TWANG *sb.*[2], or alteration of TANG *v.*[1]]

†**1.** *trans.* To furnish with a tang or point; in quot. *fig.*; cf. TANG *v.*[1] 2. *Obs. rare.*

**1678** DRYDEN & LEE *Œdipus* v. i, With her thundring Voice she menac'd high, And every Accent twang'd with smarting Sorrow.

**2.** To cause (a sharp object) to pierce through something; to thrust *through*. *rare.*

**1821** CLARE *Vill. Minstr.* I. 155 How deep was the sorrow .., Like a bramble-thorn twang'd through her heart!

**3.** *intr.* To have a twang or 'smack' of something specified; to savour *of*. *rare*⁻¹.

**1821** SCOTT *Kenilw.* iv, Your speech twangs too much of the old stamp.

†**Twangdi·llo.** *Obs. rare.* Also **twangdillow.** [f. TWANG *sb.*[1] or *v.*[1] with a Sp. or It. adjunct; a more correct form than TRANGDILLIO.] The twanging of a stringed musical instrument.

**1762** COLLINS *Misc.* viii. (Farmer) The twangdillows of poor Crowdero in a country fair. **1794** J. COURTENAY *Manners*, etc. *France & Italy* 89 Music..the seed of the plague, by twang-dillo destroys.

**Twanger** (twæ·ŋəɹ). [f. TWANG *v.*[1] + -ER [1].] One who or that which twangs. **a.** One who plays a twanging instrument. **b.** Anything very large or fine of its kind; a whacker. *slang.*

**1598** FLORIO, *Tempêlla*, a fiddle, a croud, or kit. Also a great swaggring twanger. **1631** HAUSTED *Rival Friends* I. iii, You euerlasting Twanger [boy with a lute]—Auoyd. **1677** W. HUGHES *Man of Sin* III. iii. 59 Well,..Doth it not ring aloud like a Twanger, that the Angels should ring Bells in Heaven unto the honour of the Trinity? **1877** *N. W. Linc. Gloss.*, *Twanger*, a barefaced lie. **1889** *Ibid.* (ed. 2) s. v., Them to'nups e' th' foherteen aacre is twangers.

**Twa·nging,** *vbl. sb.* [f. TWANG *v.*[1] + -ING [1].] The action of TWANG *v.*[1] in various senses.

**1615** BRATHWAIT *Strappado, Poem to Cottoneers* 204 Bradford..Stile it I might Banberry of the North..Famous for twanging, Ale, Zeale, Cakes and Cheese. **1788** GIBBON *Decl. & F.* xli. (1869) II. 505 *note*, The twanging of the bow. **1831** CARLYLE *Misc.* (1857) II. 284 Twanging of the true Poetic Lyre. **1832** TENNYSON *Kate* i, Kate hath an unbridled tongue, Clear as the twanging of a harp. **1836** T. HOOK *G. Gurney* I. 81 The loud twanging of an elderly gentleman's nose, who was fast asleep. **1904** *19th Cent.* Apr. 633 The drawn, nasal twangings of the Samisen.

**Twa·nging,** *ppl. a.* [f. as prec. + -ING [2].] That twangs, in senses of the verb.

**1567** DRANT *Horace, Art Poet.* A vij, With the twanginge instrumente the singers voyce did matche. **1697** DRYDEN *Æneid* v. 688 To shew An archer's art, and boast his twanging bow. **1784** COWPER *Task* IV. 1 Hark! 'tis the twanging horn. **1856** KANE *Arct. Expl.* I. vii. 69 The sharp twanging snap of a cord. **1905** G. THORNE *Lost Cause* xi, The twanging accent of the United States, the guttural German, the purring, spitting Russian.

†**b.** *colloq.* Exceptionally fine or good. Cf. *stunning*, *ripping*, etc. *Obs.*

**1609** B. JONSON *Sil. Wom.* v. iii, O 'twill be full and twanging!

Hence **Twa·ngingly** *adv.*, in a twanging manner, with a twang; *fig.* successfully, with éclat (*arch.*).

**1825** SCOTT *Jrnl.* 22 Dec., I wrote six of my close pages [of the *Life of Napoleon*] yesterday,..I think it comes off twangingly. The story is so very interesting in itself. **1825** — *Talism.* xxvi, I like these rattling rolling Alexandrines; methinks they come more twangingly off to the music than that briefer measure.

**Twangle** (twæ·ŋg'l), *sb.* [Cf. TWANGLE *v.*] A twangling sound; a continuous or repeated resonant sound, usually lighter or thinner than a twang; a jingle.

**1812** COLMAN *Lady of Wreck* II. xxvi, Loud, on the heath, a twangle rush'd That rung out Supper..From the crack'd bell. **1873** *All Year Round* 18 Oct. 590/1 What gives that thin twangle to the sound? **1883** G. W. CABLE in *Century Mag.* XXVII. 55 That sight touched the pathetic chord of his heart with a rude twangle.

**Twangle** (twæ·ŋg'l), *v.* Also 6 **twancle**, 9 *dial.* **twankle** (*Eng. Dial. Dict.*). [dim. and freq. of TWANG *v.*[1] (see -LE), describing a resonant sound of the nature of a twang, but thinner and continuous or repeated. Used with contemptuous force.]

**1.** *intr.* Of a stringed instrument or one who plays it: To twang lightly and continuously or frequently; to jingle.

**1558** PHAER *Æneid* VI. Rij b, Rimes thei sown And Orpheus among them stands, as priest in trayling gown. And twancling makes them tune. **1576–1610** [see TWANGLING *ppl. a.*]. **1823** SCOTT *Peveril* xxii, The coxcomb is twangling it on the lute. **1824** *Blackw. Mag.* XV. 160 The guitar..is twangling on every side. **1868** TENNYSON *Last Tourn.* 251 He twangled on his harp.

**2.** *trans.* To twang (a stringed instrument) lightly; to play upon in a petty or trifling manner. Also to play (a melody) in this way. Also *fig.*

**1607** [see *twangling* vbl. sb.]. **1829** SCOTT *Anne of G.* xxx, The King looked after him, with some wonder at this want of breeding,..and then again began to twangle his viol. **1840** THACKERAY *Shabby Genteel Story* ii, The young Andrea bears up gaily..; twangles his guitar. **1874** RUSKIN *Fors Clav.* xlvii. 259 To..find you a barrel-organ, or a harmonium, to twangle psalm-tunes on.

Hence **Twa·ngling** *vbl. sb.*; also **Twa·ngler**, one who twangles.

**1594** LYLY *Moth. Bomb.* v. iii, What a mischiefe make the twanglers [fiddlers] here? **1607** HIERON *Wks.* I. 104 Not the twangling of religion vpon the tongue, but the practise of holinesse in the life. **1825** SCOTT *Betrothed* xxi, Such twangling of harps as would be enough to frighten our walls from their foundations. **1871** RUSKIN *Fors Clav.* vi. 17 He supposed David's 'twangling upon the harp' would have been unsatisfactory to modern taste. **1879** E. ARNOLD *Lt. Asia* I. (1881) 7 Beaters of drum, and twanglers of the wire. **1881** RUSKIN in Mather *Life* (1897) 102 A twangler or scratcher on keys or cat-gut. **1891** FARRAR *Darkn. & Dawn* lxiii, Vindex..described Nero as a wretched twangler on the harp.

**Twa·ngling,** *ppl. a.* [f. TWANGLE *v.* + -ING [2].] That twangles.

**1576** FLEMING *Panopl. Epist.* 239 A tuneable sounde vpon twangling stringes. **1596** SHAKS. *Tam. Shr.* II. i. 159 While she did call me Rascall, Fidler, And twangling lacke. **1610** — *Temp.* III. ii. 146 Sometimes a thousand twangling Instruments Will hum about mine eares. **1831** SCOTT *Cast. Dang.* viii, Far less has it [my life] allowed me leisure for such twangling follies. **1831** — *Ct. Robt.* iii, Some one .. who could contribute to his pleasure, instead of a twangling, squalling infant. **1867** *Athenæum* No. 2062. 587/2 Little twangling musical-box.

†**Twa·ngo,** *int. Obs. nonce-wd.* [An affected form of TWANG *sb.*[1]; app. after It. or Sp. words in *-o.*] = TWANG *sb.*[1] 1.

**1617** RICH *Irish Hubbub* (1623) 24 Hee..giues the cup a phillip, to make it cry *Twango.*

**Twangy** (twæ·ŋi), *a.* [f. TWANG *sb.*[1] and [2] + -Y.] Having a twang (in various senses). In quot. 1887, having a tang (TANG *sb.*[1] 5).

**1887** *Sat. Rev.* 8 Jan. 48 Worse..than any other cheese, being, as a rule, either tasteless or else twangy. **1893** E. H. BARKER *Wand. Southern Waters* 126 It [the American voice] becomes less twangy and harsh a little farther South. **1905** *Blackw. Mag.* Mar. 387/2 Hendriks showed off..on the twangy piano.

Hence **Twa·nginess**, twanging quality. *rare.*

**1870** BLACK *Kilmeny* xxvi, The twanginess of the guitar.

**Twank** (twæŋk), *v. dial.* [Echoic; expressing a sound that begins like a twang, but is abruptly cut short, such as is produced by striking a body with small resonance.] **a.** *intr.* To twang with short and sharp effect. **b.** *trans.* To strike with the open palm, to spank. Hence **Twa·nking** *vbl. sb.* and *ppl. a.*; also **Twa·nker** = TWANGER b.

**1711** ADDISON *Spect.* No. 251 ⁋4 Disturbing a whole Street for an Hour together, with the Twanking of a Brass-Kettle or a Frying-Pan. **1821** CLARE *Vill. Minstr.* I. 90 While distant thresher's swingle drops With sharp and hollow-twanking raps. *a* **1825** FORBY *Voc. E. Anglia*, *Twank, v.*..2. To give a smart slap with the flat of the hand, on the breech, or other fleshy part. **1828** *Craven Gloss.*, *Twanker*, a large bulky person; any thing large. **1905** *Daily Chron.* 16 June 6/5 When she tried to escape Mrs. Lewthwaite gave her a 'twanking'.

**Twankay** (twæ·ŋke). Also **twanky.** [ad. Chinese *Tong* (or *Taung*) *-kē* (or *-kei*), dialect form of *Tun-ki* or *Tun-chi*, the name of two streams (and a town) in An-hui and Chi-kiang, China. Authorities differ as to which of these is the real source of the tea; S. Ball refers it generally to the 'district' of Tuon Ky (Twan-kay) in the province of Kiang Nan.] A variety of green tea (in full *Twankay tea*), properly that from the place so called (see above), but also applied to blends of this with other growths.

A full account is given by S. Ball (1848) in the work cited below, pp. 235–240.

**1840** J. T. HEWLETT *P. Priggins* xiv, Our conversation over the twanky and brown Georges..chiefly related to college and university matters. **1843** THACKERAY *Wks.* (1886) XXIII. 60 We'll have a roaring pot of twankay. **1857** A. MAYHEW *Paved with Gold* III. xviii, He didn't want to sit drinking hot grog with the old boy. He infinitely preferred cold Twankay, with the young damsel. **1864** W. WOOD *Few Words about Tea* 7 The Green Tea-leaf is made up into six different shapes, called by us..Twankay, Hyson-Skin, Hyson, Young Hyson, Imperial and Gunpowder.

*attrib.* **1848** S. BALL *Cultiv. & Manuf. Tea in China* 235 A tendency to Twankay flavour. *Ibid.* 240 The first gathering of common Twankay shrubs.

**b.** *slang.* (See quot.)

**1900** F. ADAMS in *N. & Q.* 9th Ser. VI. 163/1 A friend mentions 'twankay', properly denoting a kind of green tea, as a name by which gin is frequently called.

**Twankle,** dial. var. or parallel f. TWANGLE.

**Twantie,** obs. Sc. form of TWENTY. **Tward,** obs. form of TOWARD. **Twart(e,** obs. ff. THWART.

**'Twas** (twǫz), abbreviation of *it was*, formerly common colloquially and in literature, now poetic or archaic, and dialectal. Cf. 'TIS, and see IT A. γ.

**1604** SHAKS. *Oth.* III. iii. 158 'Twas mine, 'tis his, and has bin slaue to thousands. **1693** J. BYROM *Let. to Aubrey* 15 Nov., in *Lett. Eminent Persons* (1813) II. I. 167 'Twas then commonly said. **1741** RICHARDSON *Pamela* I. 175 'Twas a Thing to be lamented. **1859** FITZGERALD *Omar* xlii, He bid me taste of it; and 'twas—the Grape!

†**Twat.** *low. Obs.* Also 8 **twait.** [Of obscure origin.] (See quot. 1727.)

Erroneously used (after quot. 1660) by Browning *Pippa Passes* IV. ii. 96 under the impression that it denoted some part of a nun's attire.

**1656** R. FLETCHER tr. *Martial* II. xliv. 104. **1660** *Vanity of Vanities* 50 They talk't of his having a Cardinalls Hat, They'd send him as soon an Old Nuns Twat. *a* **1704** T. BROWN *Sober Slip in Dark* Wks. 1711 IV. 182 A dang'rous Street, Where Stones and Twaits in frosty Winters meet. **1719** D'URFEY *Pills* III. 307. **1727** BAILEY vol. II, Twat, *pudendum muliebre.* *Twat-scowerer*, a Surgeon or Doctor. *E. Ward.*

†**Twat,** an error for TROAT *v.*

**1686** BLOME *Gentl. Recr.* II. 76 A Hart Belloweth, a Buck Groaneth or Twateth.

**Twatchel** (twæ·tʃĕl). *arch.* Also 7–8 **twachel.** [Related to *twæcce* in OE. *angol-twæcce*, ANGLE-TWITCH, -TOUCH, earthworm. Cf. TOUCHANGLE, TWEYANGLE.] A name for the earthworm.

Added in the 3rd ed. of Walton's Angler, and thence in subsequent books on fishing.

**1661** WALTON *Angler* v. (ed. 3) 92 The twachel or lobworm, (which of all other is the most excellent bait for a Salmon). **1681** CHETHAM *Angler's Vade-m.* iv. § 2 (1689) 30 Dew-worm, Garden-worm, Lob-worm or Twatchel are all but one Worm, although called in different Places by all the said Names. **1787** BEST *Angling* (ed. 2) 16 The Lob-worm, Dew-worm, Garden-worm, Twatchel or Treachet. **1865** A. S. MOFFAT *Secr. Angling* viii. 164 The Lob, Dew, Twatchel, or Garden Worm.

†**Twa·tter-light.** *Obs. rare.* [Cf. TWITTER-LIGHT.] Twilight.

**1606** *Wily Beguiled* (1623) E iij, *Mother Midnight.* What mak'st thou heere this twatter light?

**Twattle** (twǫ·t'l), *sb.*[1] Now *dial.* [The vb. and sb. (known in 1573 and *a* 1639 respectively) were perh. altered from TATTLE; the earliest appearance of *twattle* yet recorded being in the reduplicated TWITTLE-TWATTLE (1556), app. from TITTLE-TATTLE (evidenced *a* 1529).

The group of words *tittle*, *tittle-tattle*, *twittle*, *twattle*, *twittle-twattle*, and *twaddle*, being primarily colloquial and largely echoic, is prob. far from fully represented in written remains, so that dated evidence for the chronological order of these shows many lacunæ; the important data are that *tittle*, to whisper, is known from 1399, and *tattle* (in *tattler*) from *c* 1450, and that *tittle-tattle*, *twittle-twattle*, *twattle*, and *twaddle*, and their derivatives, appear successively later. No reason for the suggested change of *tattle* to *twattle* has been found, but the passage of *twattle* into *twaddle* seems certain.]

Idle talk, chatter, babble. Also in comb. **twattle-basket**, a chatterbox.

Passing in later use into the sense of TWADDLE *sb.*

*a* **1639** W. WHATELEY *Prototypes* I. xix. (1640) 234 Being men of tongue,..their chiefe employment is twattle. **1650** B. *Discolliminium* 47 It is pity any honest man should lose his life for want of a game at Twattle. [*Cf. above* I cannot hold my tongue for my life.] **1687** MIÈGE *Gt. Fr. Dict.* II, Twattle-basket,..*un caseur.* **1699** T. BROWN *Let. to Dr. Brown at Tunbridge* Wks. 1711 IV. 133 The empty Twattle of these silly..Country Projectors. **1715** tr. *C'tess D'Aunoy's Wks.* 462 Hold thy Peace, Twattle-basket. **1720** DE FOE *Apparition in 1665* Wks. 1841 XIX. 259 In the midst of our twattle. **1824** COBBETT *Weekly Reg.* L. 12 June 674 Men who have no cant, no evangelical twattle. **1876–** in dialect glossaries (Yorksh., E. Anglia).

†**Twattle** (twǫ·t'l), *sb.*[2] (*a.*) *Obs.* [Origin obscure. The sb. can hardly be related to TWATTLE *v.* or *sb.*[1]] A pygmy, a dwarf. Also *attrib.* or as *adj.*

**1598** FLORIO, *Pigméo*, a pigmey, a kinde of little man like a dwarfe, a dandiprat, a twattle, or an elfe. **1611** COTGR., *Nain*, a dwarfe, or dandiprat, an elfe, or twattle; one thats no higher then three horse-loaues. *a* **1693** *Urquhart's Rabelais* III. xviii. 144 They shew him the short and twattle [F. *petits*] Verses that were written [lines of 4 syllables].

**Twa·ttle,** *v. Obs.* exc. *dial.* [See TWATTLE *sb.*[1]]

**1.** *intr.* To talk idly or trivially; to chatter, babble, tattle, prate.

In later use passing into sense of TWADDLE *v.*[1]

**1573, 1586** [see TWATTLING *ppl. a.* 1, *vbl. sb.*]. **1596** NASHE *Saffron-Walden* Wks. (Grosart) III. 204 In that he twatleth, it had bin better to haue confuted Martin by Reuerend Cooper than such leuitie. *a* **1620** J. DYKE *Sel. Serm.* (1640) 34 Talking and twatling with other idle persons. **1685** J. DUNTON *Lett. fr. New-Eng.* (1867) 7 By that time I could move my Tongue, it would be twattling of Forreign Countrys. *a* **1800** PEGGE *Suppl. Grose*, *Twattle*, to prattle and tell idle tales. *Lanc.* **1833** SARAH AUSTIN *Charac. Goethe* I. 118 He [Mephistopheles] argues, dogmatizes, and twattles right and left. **1845** S. JUDD *Margaret* II. ii, How I twattled, skurried! **1877–** in dialect glossaries (Yorksh., E. Anglia, Cornw.).

**b.** *trans.* To utter or tell idly.

**1577** STANYHURST *Descr. Irel.* vi. in *Holinshed* I. 20/2 Such fables [are] twitled, such vntrue reportes twatled. **1582** — *Æneis* II. (Arb.) 46 No gloasing fabil I twattle. *Ibid.* IV. 101 As true tales vaynelye toe twattle. **1660** *Charac. Italy* 10 He [the Pope]..causeth whatsoever he parrot[s], or if you will have it Anagrammatically praterlike twattles, to pass for Bullion, and current. *a* **1688** VILLIERS (Dk. Buckhm.) *Chances* Wks. (1714) 149, I heard her grave Conductress twattle something as they went along.

**c.** with *prep.* To bring or get by chattering or gossiping.

**1692** R. L'ESTRANGE *Fables* cclxxvii. (1715) II. 266 Are you not a fine Gossiping Lady..to twattle your Husband thus out of his Life and Fortune?

**2.** *intr.* To sound, make a noise. (See also TWATTLING *ppl. a.* 2.) *vulgar.*

**1664** COTTON *Scarron.* I. 15 The Winds burst out with such a rattle, As he had broke the strings that twattle.

**3.** *trans.* To pat, fondle, make much of. *dial.*

Perh. not the same word.

**1790** GROSE *Provinc. Gloss.* (ed. 2), *Twattle*, to pat, to make much of, as horses, cows, dogs. *North.* **1825** BROCKETT *N. C. Words*, *Twattle*, to pat, to make much of, to fondle.

**Twattler** (twǫ·tləɹ). *Obs.* exc. *dial.* [f. prec. + -ER [1].] One who 'twattles'; a chatterer, babbler, tattler.

**1577** STANYHURST *Descr. Irel.* vi. in *Holinshed* I. 22/1 Let vs..leaue lying for varlettes, .. chatting for twatlers. **1679** J. SMITH *Narr. Pop. Plot* 21 Aspersed by..publick Scriblers, as well as by Coffee-house Twatlers. **1685** BAXTER *Paraphr. N. T., 1 Tim.* v. 14, 15 To speak evil of the Church, as if it were a Society of idle twatlers. **1818** COBBETT *Pol. Reg.* XXXIII. 515 As to the resources of the nation, what do these twatlers mean?

**Twa·ttling,** *vbl. sb. Obs.* exc. *dial.* [f. as prec. + -ING[1].] The action of the verb TWATTLE; idle talking, chattering.

**1586** J. HOOKER *Hist. Irel.* in *Holinshed* II. 83/1 The continuall twatling of fliring clawbacks in their eares. **1634** W. WHATELEY *Redempt. Time* 15 When one talkes toyes or trifles, .. such twatling cuts out the heart of good time. **1653** W. RAMESEY *Astrol. Rej.* 176 Addicted to twatling and prating. *a* **1745** SWIFT *To Dr. Sheridan* 14 Dec., You keep such a twattling with you and your bottling.

**Twa·ttling,** *ppl. a. Obs.* exc. *dial.* [f. as prec. + -ING[2].]

**1.** That 'twattles'; chattering, babbling, prating. (Said of the person, or of the talk.)

**1573** TWYNE *Æneid* XI. H h iv, Persist, And thoundre out thy twatling talke, as longe as thou shalt list. **1647** LILLY *Chr. Astrol.* cxxxiv. 594 She is..a twatling huswife, making discord where-ever she comes. **1702** *Eng. Theophrast.* 165 It is not for every Twatling Gossip.

**2.** Sounding, making a noise. *vulgar.*

*Twattling strings*, a vulgar expression for the *sphincter ani.* **1611** FLORIO, *Naccare*, drom-slades...Also vsed for twatling fartes. **1654** GAYTON *Pleas. Notes* III. iii. 83 Her Base Violl went..with great danger of breaking her twatling-strings. **1739** 'R. BULL' tr. *Dedekindus' Grobianus* 268 Her twattling Strings, with Laughter overcome, No more contract the Passage of the Bum.

†**3.** Petty, trifling, paltry: = TWADDLING *a.* 1 b. *Obs. rare*[—1]. [Perh. related to TWATTLE *sb.*[2]]

**1651** *Miller of Mansf.* 20 You feed us with twatling dishes so small.

**Tway** (twēi), *numeral a.* Now *arch.* Forms: see below. [Apocopate form of OE. *twēgen*, ME. *tweyen*, TWAIN, the final *n* being normally dropped. OE. *twēge* seems not to be recorded in WSax., but it occurs in Anglian in Rushw. Gospel Gl., and in the late Hatton Gosp. before a consonant, and is the ordinary form in Old Northumbrian (varying in Lindisfarne Gl. as *twoege, tuoge, tueg, tuoe, twoe, tue*; Rit. Dunelm. has *tvoegi, twoego*). These forms are not rigidly confined to the masc. From the OE. *twēge* (or by similar apocopation of ME. *tweyen, tweien*) came ME. *tweye, twei(e, twey* in Midld. and South Eng., *twai, tway* in North. and North-Midld. But *tway* in Scotch from *c* 1500 may also be only a variant spelling of the later *twae* from *twā*, TWO: the Sc. forms have therefore been separated as γ. Even as an archaism the form is now rarely employed.]

**A.** Illustration of Forms.

α. 1 **twóeʒe, tuéʒe** (**tuóʒe, tuéʒ, twé, tué**), 1–2 **twéʒe, twǣʒe,** 3 **tueye, tueie, tuei,** 2–5 **twei,** 3–5 **tweie, tweye,** 3–7 **twey,** 4 **tweiȝe, tweyȝe, tuuei**; 3 **twie,** 4–5 **twy.**

*a* **950** *Rituale Dunelm.* (Surtees) 113 Ðerh hvnd seofontiʒ tvoeʒi boec aldes & nives ʒicyðnisses. *c* **950** *Lindisf. Gosp.* Mark vi. 41 Fif hlafo & tue fiscas. — Luke ii. 24 Tuoe turturas *vel* tuoʒe birdas culfras [*Rushw.* twoeʒe t. *vel* twoeʒe birdas culfra]. *c* **975** *Rushw. Gosp.* John ii. 6 Nimende syndriʒe sestras twoeʒe *vel* ðria. *c* **1160** *Hatton Gosp.* Matt. xxvi. 37 He ʒenam petrum & zebedeus tweʒe sunes [*Ags. G.* tweʒen suna]. *c* **1175** *12th c. Hom.* (Bodley) 98 Twæʒe men herbiforen þis festen festen. *c* **1200** *Trin. Coll. Hom.* 207 Þe gostliche rode..haueð twei names, *cordis contritio et proximi compassio.* *c* **1275** *Passion of Our Lord* 438 in *O. E. Misc.* 49 Hi nome twey þeoues. *c* **1275** LAY. 10670 Hii..sende twie [*c* 1205 tweien] eorles. *c* **1290** *S. Eng. Leg.* I. 10/317 Þe tweie croiz..þat þe þeoues on i-hanguede were. **1297** R. GLOUC. (Rolls) 731 And ȝef is tueie doȝtren half, & half him sulf non. *Ibid.* 6322 Bi tuene þis tueye kinges. *a* **1325** *MS. Rawl. B. 520* lf. 65 b, Tuuei writes of wuche comez tuueine assoines. *c* **1325** *Spec. Gy Warw.* 785 Tweye manere shame..Þat on goþ to dampnacioun; þat oþer, to sauuacioun. **1387** TREVISA *Higden* (Rolls) VI. 5 Bytwene þe tweie [*MS.* γ twy] riveres. *c* **1400** *R. Gloucester's Chron.* 754 (MS. α) Þeos tweiȝe kinges. *c* **1449** PECOCK *Repr.* I. ii. (Rolls) 8 A sillogisme is mad of twey proposiciouns dryuyng out of hem the thridde proposicioun.

β. *north.* and *midl. Eng.* 3–4 **tuai,** 4 **tuay,** 4–7 (8– *arch.*) **tway** (6 **twaye**).

*a* **1300** *Cursor M.* 12699 (Cott.) Of hir war born god childer tuai [*rime* sai; *F.* tway; *Tr.* twey, *rime* sey]. *c* **1330** *Arth. & Merl.* (Kölbing) 4788 He hadde strengþe of kniȝtes tvay. **13..** *Cursor M.* 21756 (Gött.) Þe bodi [is] of element[s] tuis tuay [*Cott.* tuai; *F.* twies tway, *rime* I say]. **1559** *Mirr. Mag., Ld. Hastings* li, Vniudgd hangth yet the case betwixt them twaye [*rime* saye]. **1579** SPENSER *Sheph. Cal.* May 18 We tway bene men of elder witt. **1611** *Coryat's Crudities, Panegyr. Verses* d viij b, Tom is..the Greeker of the tway [*rime* say]. **1742** SHENSTONE *Schoolmistress* 51 For sceptre she does wield Tway birchen sprays. **1865** Tway [see B. 1 b].

γ. *Sc.* 4–7 **tway,** 6–7 **tuay.**

*c* **1375** *Sc. Leg. Saints* xxii. (*Laurentius*) 512 Þai tuk þe cors..Þai tway it bare. *c* **1470** HENRY *Wallace* IX. 801 Mycht we get ane or tway [*rime* way]. **1513** DOUGLAS *Æneis* I. vi. 17 Amyd the wod his modir met thame tway [*rime* array]. **1537** *Registr. Aberdon.* (Maitl. Cl.) I. 413 Tway pennies for ilk barne absent. **1549** *Ibid.* 438 For þe tuay part of þe mylne. **1570** *Satir. Poems Reform.* xvii. 105 That schot, allace! yis realme hes shot in tway [*rime* away]. *a* **1584** MONTGOMERIE *Cherrie & Slae* 460 Ane foule in hand, or tway [*rime* day]. *a* **1600** — *Misc. Poems* (S.T.S. 1887) i. 12 A turne in tyme is ay worth other tuay [*rime* auay.] **1615** SIR W. MURE *Misc. Poems* viii. 44 Reflecting only on ws tuay [*rime* away].

**B.** Signification. = Two.

**1.** In concord with a sb. **a.** Preceding the sb.

*a* **950** Tvoeʒi boec; *c* **950** Tuoʒe birdas; *c* **1160** Tweʒe sunes; *c* **1200** Twei names [see A. α above]. *c* **1275** *Passion of Our Lord* 645 in *O. E. Misc.* 55 Þer stoden twei veyre men. **1297** R. GLOUC. (Rolls) 312 Tweie dawes hii wende in þe see. *Ibid.* 1806 Tueie [*v. r.* twei] emperours of rome, Dioclician &..maximian. **1303** R. BRUNNE *Handl. Synne* 11264 To pray..saueþ man on twey partys. **1362** LANGL. *P. Pl.* A. v. 109 He was bitel-brouwed, with twei blered eiȝen. *c* **1380** WYCLIF *Sel. Wks.* III. 188 Oure Lord..spekiþ..of tweie matrimoneys. *c* **1394** *P. Pl. Crede* 439 A litell childe ..And tweyne of tweie ȝeres olde. *a* **1425** *Cursor M.* 19419 (Trin.) Tweye witenes had þei hem purueide. *c* **1450** *Godstow Reg.* 191 An hundred shillyngis..at twey termes in the yere. *c* **1570** *Marr. Wit & Science* IV. iv. D iv b, *Ignoraunce.* Choulde geue twaye pence to see it and tway pence moore. **1573** TYRIE *Refut.* in *Cath. Tractates* (S.T.S.) 17 The kirk is vniuersall, and..it hes continewall successioun of pastoures: quhilk tuay markis did neuer..aggrie to onie..congregatioun of heretikes. *a* **1586** SIDNEY *Arcadia, Geron & Mastix* 20 'Tis now full tway score Of yeares..since I good Mastix knew. **1712** PRIOR *Erle Robert's Mice* 1 Tway Mice..Batten beside Erle Robert's Table.

**b.** Following the sb. *poet.*

*c* **1205** LAY. 26235 Þa cleopede he eorles tweie. *c* **1275** *Moral Ode* 225 in *O. E. Misc.* 66 Hunger and þurst, vuele tweye [*earlier MSS.* twa, two] ivere. **13..** *K. Alis.* 7254 (Laud MS.) He knew þoo barouns tweye [*rime* cuntreye]. *c* **1320** R. BRUNNE *Medit.* 50 Þe soper was dyȝt..By dyscyplys seuenty and twey. *c* **1400** *Rom. Rose* 1744 Thanne toke I with myn hondis tweie The arowe. *c* **1440** *Pallad. on Husb.* VIII. 161 Vppon feet but tway. **1543** GRAFTON *Harding's Chron.* Ded. xii, The Scottish kyng, sending foorth heraldes tway. **1559** *Mirr. Mag., Dk. Buckhm.* xxviii, Downthrow we strayt his sellie nephewes twaye. **1865** S. EVANS *Bro. Fabian* 58 Now..shut mine eyen tway.

†**c.** *Tway part* (Sc.), two-thirds (= *twa part*: see TWO B. I. 1 c). *Obs.*

**1531** *Acc. Ld. High Treas. Scotl.* (1905) VI. 18 For tway elnis and ane tway-part elne gray weluet. **1549** *Registr. Aberdon.* (Maitl. Cl.) I. 438 With brew hous and tuay part of þe myln of þe said toune.

**2.** Absolutely with ellipsis of sb., or following a pronoun or pronominal adj.

**1297** R. GLOUC. (Rolls) 4071 Sibile þe sage sede..Þat þer ssolde of brutayne þre men be ybore þat ssolde winne þe aumperye of rome; of þe tueye ydo it is,..& þou art þe þridde. **13..** *Cursor M.* 635 (Gött.) Naked war þai bath tway [*Tr.* þei boþe tweyn]. *c* **1350** *Will. Palerne* 2147 To take hem tweie. *a* **1450** *Knt. de la Tour* (1906) 153 Y shalle saie of euery astate an ensaumple or twey. *a* **1553** UDALL *Royster D.* IV. i. (Arb.) 59, I haue a message or tway. *a* **1586** SIDNEY *Arcadia* III. *Geron & Histor* 91 Betwixt vs tway We beare our double yoke. **1642** H. MORE *Song of Soul* I. I. xxxiii, When Hattubus old..did tie them tway With nuptiall charm.

**b.** In genitive after possess. pron.

**1476** J. PASTON in *P. Lett.* III. 155 Ther tweys dysposysyon [= the disposition of them two].

**c.** as *sb.* A pair, couple.

? *a* **1800** *Lord Livingston* ix. in Child *Ballads* (1892) VIII. 432 They were a comely tway.

**3.** *In* (*into*) *tway*: into two parts or pieces, in two.

*c* **1375** *Cursor M.* 20556 (Fairf.) For ferde hir hert sulde brast in-twai. **1558** *Lydgate's Bochas* IX. xxxv. 36 b, The lyues threde for to breke in tway [*Bodl. MS.* tweyne]. **1567** *Gude & Godlie B.* (S.T.S.) 195 Cut ȝour typpet in to tway. **1590** SPENSER *F. Q.* I. vii. 27 Which..almost rent her tender hart in tway.

**4.** *Comb.*, as *tway-coned, -edged, -footed, -handed* adjs.; † **tway-biting** *a.*, 'biting' or cutting two ways, two-edged; † **tway-fold** *adv.* = TWIFOLD, TWOFOLD; † **tway-like** *a.*: see quot. and cf. TWILEKE; † **tway-toothed** *a.*, having two rows of teeth. See also TWAYBLADE.

**1382** WYCLIF *Prov.* v. 4 The tunge of hir sharp as a *twei bitende swerd. **1872** BLACKIE *Lays Highl.* 105 Fare-thee-well, thou *tway-coned Cruachan. **1545** JOYE *Exp. Dan.* i. B iij b, With the *twei edged swearde. **1303** R. BRUNNE *Handl. Synne* 1153 Þys olde man..bade hym take A sak.. And..turne hyt *tweyfolde. *c* **1386** CHAUCER *Can. Yeom. Prol. & T.* 13 (Ellesm.) A male tweyfoold [*v. r.* twyfold] vp on his croper lay. **1398** TREVISA *Barth. De P. R.* v. liv. (Bodl. MS.) lf. 28/1 Þe feete of foules and of *twey footed beestes. **1552** *Acc. Ld. High Treas. Scotl.* X. 82 *Tway handit sword. **1551** RECORDE *Pathw. Knowl.* I. Defin. B iij, An other distinction of the names of triangles, according to their sides, whiche other be all equal..other els two sydes bee equall and the thyrd vnequall, which the Greekes call *Isosceles*,..and in english *tweyleke may they be called. **1387** TREVISA *Higden* (Rolls) VI. 405 Wormes þat were *tweie [*v. r.* twy] toþed [*L. bidentati*] and i-liche to wontes.. ete þe brede corne.

**Twayblade** (twē¹·blēⁱd). Also 8 **twyblade.** [f. TWAY two + BLADE leaf. Cf. *twa-, two-blade(s)*, s. v. TWO *a.* IV. 2.] **a.** An orchidaceous plant of the genus *Listera*, characterized by two nearly opposite broad leaves springing from the stem; esp. the Common Twayblade, *L. ovata*, and Mountain or Heart-leaved T., *L. cordata.* **b.** Applied to N. American species of another orchidaceous genus *Liparis*, with two leaves springing from the root.

**a.** **1578** LYTE *Dodoens* II. lvii. 224 The Twayblade or Doubleleaf delighteth..in moyst..places. **1597** GERARDE *Herbal* II. lxxxiii. 326 Of Twayblade, or herbe Bifoile. **1668** WILKINS *Real Char.* II. iv. 78 That [herb] which hath only two leaves...Tway-blade. **1728** BRADLEY *Dict. Bot.*, *Ophris*, sive *Bifolium*, in English, Twyblade. **1778** LIGHTFOOT *Flora Scot.* (1789) I. 524 *Ophrys ovata.* Great Twayblade... *Ophrys cordata.* Little Twayblade. **1785** MARTYN *Rousseau's Bot.* xxvii. (1794) 419 Common Twayblade, or Twyblade,..is frequent in woods. **1859** MISS YONGE *Hist. Sir Thos. Thumb* iv. 21 He was no larger than the green lip of the tway-blade blossom. **1882** *Cornh. Mag.* Jan. 33 The twayblade and the parsley-piert are..descended from bright-hued ancestors. **1884** MILLER *Plant-n.*, Tway-blade, American, *Listera convallarioides.* **1905** *Longm. Mag.* Jan. 253 The rare mountain twayblade.

**b.** **1846–50** A. WOOD *Class-bk. Bot.* 530 *Liparis liliifolia*... Tway-blade. **1884** MILLER *Plant-n.*, Tway-blade, Green-flowered, *Liparis Loeselii.* —, Purple-flowered, *Liparis liliifolia.*

**Twayle, twaylle,** obs. ff. TOWEL; var. TWAIL.

**Twayn, twayne,** obs. ff. TWAIN.

**Twch,** obs. Sc. f. TOUGH.

**Tweag, tweague,** obs. or dial. ff. TWEAK *sb.*[1], *v.*

**Tweak** (twīk), *sb.*[1] Also 8 **tweague,** 8–9 **tweag.** [f. TWEAK *v.*]

**1.** An act of tweaking; a sharp wringing pull; a twitch, a pluck.

**1609** B. JONSON *Sil. Wom.* IV. v, Hee will..make you beare a blow, ouer the mouth,..tweakes by the nose, *sans numbre.* **1716** ADDISON *Drummer* V. i, He has given my shoulder such a cursed tweak. **1738** *Common Sense* II. 106 They may be drawn out of their Sockets with a moderate Tweag. **1809** W. IRVING *Knickerb.* VI. vii. (1861) 216 [He] was courteously dismissed with a tweak of the nose, to assist him in recollecting his message. **1847** C. BRONTË *J. Eyre* xxiv, A severe tweak of the ear. **1883** *Mag. of Art* June 309/2 Tweaks and slaps and pinches.

†**2.** *fig.* **a.** In phrase *in a tweak*, in a state of excitement or agitation, in a 'taking'. *Obs.*

*a* **1700** B. E. *Dict. Cant. Crew*, *Tweak*, *in a Tweak*, in a heavy taking,..very angry. **1706** PHILLIPS (ed. Kersey), *Tweag* or *Tweak*, Perplexity, Trouble; as To be in a sad Tweak. **1712** ARBUTHNOT *John Bull* III. vi, This put the old fellow in a rare tweag [*ed.* **1755** tweague]! **1755** JOHNSON, *Tweague, Tweak*, perplexity; ludicrous distress. A low word. **1779** WARNER in Jesse *Selwyn & Contemp.* (1844) IV. 12 What a tweague and a taking you would be in. **1841** HARTSHORNE *Salopia Antiqua* 602 'To be in a tweag' is a phrase of long standing, and not peculiarly dialectical.

**b.** *dial.* See quots.

**1881** MISS JACKSON *Shropsh. Word-bk.*, *Tweak*, a sharp, severe attack of illness—'a pinch'. **1886** DARLINGTON *S. Chesh. Gloss.*, *Tweak*,..a sharp, severe pain.

†**Tweak,** *sb.*[2] *Obs. slang.* Also 7 **tweake.** [? from TWEAK *sb.*[1] or *v.*] A harlot; 'also, a whoremonger' (Halliwell).

**1617** MIDDLETON & ROWLEY *Fair Quarrel* IV. iv, Your tweaks are like your mermaids, they have sweet voices to entice the passengers. **1631** BRATHWAIT *Whimzies, Char. Painter* 134 Hee sometimes playes the witty satyrist, and displayes light tweakes in loose roabes. **1638** — *Barnabees Jrnl.* I. D v, An apt one To be Tweake unto a Captaine. *Ibid.* III. R vij, From the bushes neare the Lane there Rush'd a Tweake in gesture flanting. **1719** D'URFEY *Pills* (1872) III. 146 If any man here be in bodily fear, Of a Wolf, a Wife, or a Tweak.

**Tweak** (twīk), *v.* Also 7 **tweake**; β. 7–8 (9 *dial.*) **tweag,** 8 **tweague.** [Of obscure origin: cf. TWICK *v.*]

**1.** *trans.* To seize and pull sharply with a twisting movement; to pull at with a jerk; to twitch, wring, pluck; *esp.* to pull (a person) *by* the nose (or a person's nose) as a mark of contempt or insult; †to press (the lips) *together* so as to pinch.

α. **1601** HOLLAND *Pliny* XI. xxiv. I. 324 These Spiders hunt also after the yong Lizards:..they catch hold and tweake both their lips together, and so bite and pinch them. **1602** SHAKS. *Ham.* II. ii. 601 Who calles me Villaine?..Tweakes me by th' Nose? giues me the Lye i' th' Throate..? **1663** BUTLER *Hud.* I. II. 974 To rouze him..He tweak'd his Nose, with gentle Thump Knock'd on his Breast. **1748** SMOLLETT *R. Random* xxvi, He seized me by the nose, which he tweaked so unmercifully, that I roared with anguish. **1795** WOLCOT (P. Pindar) *Hair Powder* Wks. 1812 III. 305 With hot pincers tweak each nose and ear! **1816** SCOTT *Old Mort.* iv, I will tweak thy proboscis or nose. **1826** F. REYNOLDS *Life & Times* I. 111 [He] tweaked our crabbed oppressor by the nose. **1858** BAILEY *Age* 148 He'd have tweaked your head clean off your shoulders. **1913** *Blackw. Mag.* June 796/1 She tweaked the coiffure of her much-enduring parent into position.

β. **1685** CROWNE *Sir C. Nice* III. Dram. Wks. 1874 III. 296 I'll not only libel him, but tweag him by the nose, kick him, cudgel him. **1738** *Common Sense* II. 106 They are all tweag'd into a Degree of Insensibility, which may incapacitate them for smelling a Fox. **1755** J. SHEBBEARE *Lydia* (1769) II. 139 Sweetwood stretched forth his hand and tweaged his nose. **1841** HARTSHORNE *Salopia Antiqua* 602. **1876** *Mid-Yorks. Gloss.*, *Tweag*.., to tweak.

†**2.** *fig.* (See quot., and cf. TWEAK *sb.*[1] 2 a.) *Obs.*

**1721** BAILEY, *To Tweag, To Tweak* (*tweken*, Du. to pinch), to put into a Fret or Perplexity. [Not in Johnson.]

**3.** *slang.* To hit with a missile from a catapult. Cf. TWEAKER.

**1898** KIPLING *Stalky* in *Windsor Mag.* Dec. 35 Corkran, through the roof, scientifically 'tweaked' a frisky heifer on the nose.

Hence **Tweaked** *ppl. a.*, **Twea·king** *vbl. sb.*

**1609** B. JONSON *Sil. Wom.* IV. v, Good, Sir John, leaue tweaking, you'll blow his nose off. **1894** H. SPENCER in *Life Mrs. Lynn Linton* xxi. (1901) 311 To return to the tweaking of the nose above indicated. **1900** *Daily News* 15 Nov. 6/1 This tweaked-up eyebrow..carries the idea of evil to the modern audience.

**Tweaker** (twī·kəɹ). *slang.* Also **tweeker.** [f. TWEAK *v.* + -ER[1].] A catapult.

**1884** C. H. *Her World* vii. 30 Every now and then taking aim with his 'tweeker'..at the said person below. **1897** *Badminton Mag.* Apr. 459 A few shot from a 'tweaker,' commonly called a catapult.

**Tweamen,** variant of TWEME *v. Obs.*

**Twear,** var. of TUYERE. **Tweaser-, Tweat,**

obs. ff. TWEEZER-, TWAIT, shad. **Twech, tweche,** obs. Sc. ff. TOUCH. **Twechell,** obs. f. TWITCHEL[1], narrow passage.

† **Twe·ddle,** *v. Sc. Obs.* [app. a back-formation from next.] (See quot.)

1808 JAMIESON, *To tweddle, tweel,* to work cloth in such a manner, that the woof appears to cross the warp vertically.

† **Twe·ddling.** *Sc. Obs. rare.* Forms: 6 **twedlyne,** 6–7 **tuidling,** 8 **tweedling,** 9 **tweddlin, -len.** [Of obscure origin: not a normal variant of Sc. *tweeling*, but app. a parallel formation to it.] = TWILLING.

1541 *Aberdeen Regr.* XVII. (Jam.), Ane sark of small twedlyne. 1595 *Compt Bk. D. Wedderburne* (S.H.S.) 47 Item..xxvj ellis tuidling. 1658 *Records of Elgin* (1903) I. 305 Tailyors within the said burghe shall neither buy nor sell any merchandice except so much plaiding, harne, lining, tuidling, stenting, bleached or unbleached. 1747 in *Nairne Peerage Evid.* (1874) 80 Sixteen pair tweedling sheets att one pound three shillings four pence. 1808 JAMIESON, *Tweddlin*, cloth that is tweeled, used also as an adj., as *tweddlen sheets*, sheets of cloth wrought as described above.

**Twedian,** var. TUEDIAN.

† **Twee,** *sb.*[1] *Obs.* Also 8 **twey-**; 7 *pl.* **tweeze.** [Aphetic f. *etwee* ETUI.] = TWEEZE.

1690 *Songs Costume* (Percy Soc.) 196 [We also see] Tweeze As rich and costly as all these. 1747 HOADLY *Susp. Husb.* II. ii, Sure I have not dropt my Twee. 1749 in *6th Rep. Dep. Kpr.* App. II. 123 Small perspective Glasses with Mathematical and other Instruments and Twees, in one and the same case. 1767 *Poetry* in *Ann. Reg.* 236 Seals, rings, 'twees, bodkins.

*attrib.* 1782 MISS BURNEY *Cecilia* v. ix, What has he left behind him? a twey-case, I suppose, and a bit of a hat won't go on a man's head.

**Twee** (twī), *sb.*[2] (*int.*) Variously extended, as **twee-we-we, twee-twee-twee, twee-ee.** [Echoic.] An imitation of the sound of a horn, and also of the notes of some birds: see quots.

1708 MOTTEUX in *Muses Mercury* Jan. 11 With a Twee-we-we, Twee-we-we, think it no Scorn, Cits, Souldiers, and Courtiers, give way to the Horn. 1880 A. B. TODD *Poet. Wks.* (1907) 258 A little wren its twee-twee-twee let fall. 1909 *Daily News* 21 June 4 Only the greenfinch's tireless 'twee-ee' was to be heard.

**Tweed** (twīd). [A trade name originating in an accidental misreading of *tweel*, Sc. form of TWILL (or a misunderstanding of an abbreviated *tweeled* TWILLED *a.*[1]), helped by association with the River Tweed.

The form appears to have originated in or about 1831, but published statements are not quite in accord as to the circumstances which gave rise to it. The more important of these accounts are to be found in Jas. Locke's *Tweed & Don* (1860) 37, in a paper by D. Watson in *Trans. Hawick Archæol. Soc.* (1868) 14, and in A. Barlow's *Weaving* (1878) 49. Barlow and others attribute the misreading of the word to Jas. Locke himself (who was a London merchant), but Locke in his own book does not claim to have been the originator of the name, which had become fully current by 1850.]

A twilled woollen cloth of somewhat rough surface, and of great variety of texture, originally and still chiefly made in the south of Scotland (usually of two or more colours combined in the same yarn); inferior kinds are made of wool with a mixture of shoddy or cotton. In *pl.*, cloths or garments of this kind.

1847 MCCULLOCH *Acc. Brit. Empire* (ed. 3) I. 667 Narrow cloths, of various kinds, known by the name of Tweeds,.. are extensively produced at Galashiels and Jedburgh, but especially at the former. They used, also, to be produced in considerable quantities at Hawick. 1859 JEPHSON *Brittany* i. 5 A suit of stout grey tweed. 1859 SALA *Tw. round Clock* (1861) 91 Lank office-boys, in..corduroys and tweeds too short, and jackets..too short for them. 1869 C. GIBBON *R. Gray* iv, Garments of rough home-spun tweed. 1882 CAULFEILD & SAWARD *Dict. Needlework* 505 *Tweed*, a woollen cloth woven of short lengths of wool, and lightly felted and milled, the yarn being dyed before woven. It is soft, durable, and flexible. 1894 FENN *In Alpine Valley* I. 186 We do look disreputable enough in our rough tweeds.

**b.** *attrib.* and *Comb.*, as *tweed cap, cloth, clothes, finisher, mill, suit, trousering, -weaving*; *tweed-clad, -covered, -suited* adjs.

1851 *Catal. Gt. Exhib.* III. 495/1 Specimens of Scotch tweed trouserings. *Ibid.* 497/2 Striped and Tweed cloth. 1864 *Fraser's Mag.* Apr. 494 A young gentleman in tweed suit and wideawake. 1865 ALEX. SMITH *Summ. Skye* i. 37 Tweed-clad tourists are everywhere. 1877 MAR. M. GRANT *Sun-Maid* i, His tweed-stalking-cap was drawn over his eyes. 1888 *Daily News* 26 Sept. 7/1 A tweed finisher, employed at Dunsdale mill. 1890 E. WARREN *Laughing Eyes* 61 Tweed-suited monthly-return-ticket visitors.

**Tweedle** (twī·d'l), *v.* [app. echoic: cf. TEEDLE, TOODLE, TWIDDLE *v.*[2] In sense 2, app. influenced by WHEEDLE.]

**1.** *intr.* Of a musical instrument or one who plays it: To produce a succession of shrill modulated sounds; also, to play triflingly or carelessly *upon* an instrument; of a bird, etc., to whistle or pipe with modulations of tone.

1684 'PHILO PATER' *Observ. Reproved* 2 The Replyer is only an Instrument of the Faction, the Club blows the Bag-pipes, and he Tweedles. 1728 MRS. DELANY in *Life & Corr.* (1861) I. 182 Yesterday I dined at the Percivals, and tweedled away upon a lovely harpsichord. 1795 COWPER *Pairing Time Anticipated* 38 Dick heard, and tweedling, ogling, bridling, .. Attested, glad, his approbation. 1835 BECKFORD *Recoll.* vii. 107 A pair of flutes most nauseously tweedled upon by two..young monks.

**2.** *trans.* To bring into some place or condition by or as by playing on an instrument in this way; to entice by or as by music; to wheedle, cajole.

*a* 1719 ADDISON (J.), A fiddler brought in with him a body of lusty young fellows, whom he had tweedled into the service. 1740 SOMERVILLE *Hobbinol* I. 149 Touch The trembling Chords,..and the fond yielding Maid Is tweedled into Love. *a* 1763 SHENSTONE *Ess.* (1765) 216 Why should he be esteemed devout..when he is tweedled into zeal by the dron pipe of an organ? 1896 OLIVE SCHREINER *Afr. Farm* I. xii, Wheedle her, tweedle her, teedle her, but don't let her make sure of you.

**Tweedle-** (twī·d'l), the stem of TWEEDLE *v.*, employed in combination with other elements (see below) to denote the action of the verb, or a high-pitched musical sound; chiefly in the humorous phrase **Tweedledum and tweedledee,** in the earliest example used in reference to two rival musicians (whence the *fig.* sense: see b); *tweedledee and tweedledum* (also *tweedle-dum*), used to suggest the contrast or combination of the sounds of high- and low-pitched musical instruments; hence in quot. 1792 *attrib.* = musical (*obs.*); *tweedle-dee, tweedle-dum*, a high-, or a low-pitched instrument, or one who plays it; in quots. 1785, 1806, 1826, a fiddler (*obs.*); *tweedle-tweedle*, the action or practice of tweedling; music, harmony (*obs.*).

1725 BYROM *Handel & Bononcini* Poems 1773 I. 344 Strange all this Difference should be, 'Twixt Tweedle-dum and Tweedle-dee! 1769 *Trinculo's Trip* 47 Squeeking fife and rumbling drum, Tweedle dee—and tweedle dum. 1785 BURNS *Jolly Beggars* Recit. vi, He taks the fiddler by the beard, And draws a roosty rapier—.. Wi' ghastly ee, poor tweedle-dee Upon his hunkers bended. 1786 WOLCOTT (P. Pindar) *Bozzy & Piozzi* 70 Great in the noble art of tweedle-tweedle. 1792 — *Odes Condol.* i. 61 No longer on the tweedle-dum account..Those Men of Taste and Music joyful greet. 1804 J. COLLINS (*title*) Scripscrapologia; or Collins's Doggerel Dish of All Sorts. Consisting of Songs.. which may be sung without..the ravishing Accompaniments of Tweedle-dum or Tweedle-dee. 1805 MRS. GRANT in Campbell *Mem. & Corr.* (1844) I. 59 Two hours of tweedle-dum and tweedle-dee were too much for me. 1806 LAMB *Let. to Manning* 5 Dec., Mary and I are to sit next the orchestra in the pit, next the tweedledees. 1826 F. REYNOLDS *Life & Times* II. 288 Two ordinary violin players..quarrelled..to such a pitch, that each tweedle-dum offered the opposing tweedle-dee, to play him for his whole year's salary.

**b.** *fig.*, usually in phrase *tweedledee and tweedledum*, two things or parties the difference between which is held to be insignificant. Also *attrib.*

1851 THACKERAY *Eng. Hum.* v. (1876) 304 Swift could not see the difference between tweedle-dee and tweedle-dum. 1871 MRS. BROOKFIELD *Influence* I. 76 Do you believe in tweedledee or in tweedledum? 1882 MISS BRADDON *Mt. Royal* II. x. 218 To the ears of Mopsy and Dopsy it was all tweedledum, and tweedledee. 1885 *Spectator* 24 Jan. 119/2 By no effort of the mind can we separate tweedle-dum and tweedle-dee. 1886 *Pall Mall G.* 29 Sept. 2/2 The general public need have no special objection to half-pay officers and local Bumbles spending their superfluous time and money in Tweedledum and Tweedledee quarrels. 1889 *Spectator* 14 Dec. 850 The political instinct..which leads Lord Randolph ..to discover a Tory Tweedledee for the Radical Tweedle-dum. 1911 *Chr. Endeavour Times* 10 Aug. 724/1 A..war of words over tweedledees of subtle doctrinal differences and tweedledums of Church polity.

Hence **Tweedle-dee·** *v. intr.*, to play or sing in a high-pitched tone; also, to play idly; to tweedle.

1837 CARLYLE *Fr. Rev.* III. I. vi, While right-arms here grew weary of slaying, right-arms there were twiddledeeing on melodious catgut. 1873 W. MORRIS in Mackail *Life* (1899) I. 299 A sandy-haired German tenor tweedledeeing over the unspeakable woes of Sigurd!

**Tweedle,** var. TWIDDLE *v.*[1]

**Tweedling,** var. TWEDDLING *Obs.*

**Tweel,** etc.: see TWILL, etc.

**'Tween,** † **tween** (twīn), *prep.* Forms: 4 **tuene,** 5 **twene, twen, twyn,** 6 **tweene,** 7 **'tweene,** 8– **'tween.** Aphetic form of ATWEEN, BETWEEN.

13.. *Cursor M.* 9363 (Gött.) Tuene þaim fayre acord es nane. 13.. *Guy Warw.* (A.) 4482 Þemperour cleped Herhaud him to, & aresound him tvene hem tvo. *c* 1420 ? LYDG. *Assembly of Gods* 16 Twene slepyng and wakyng he bad me aryse. 1430–40 — *Bochas* I. xiv. (MS. Bodl. 263) 62/1 Thus atwen yre and twen affeccion She heeld hir longe. 1443 *Pol. Poems* (Rolls) II. 214 God send us pees twen Ynglond and Ffraunce! 1447 BOKENHAM *Seyntys* (Roxb.) 20 Of alle thyngys lord thou art juge Twyn hym and me. 1581 A. HALL *Iliad* x. 178 Hie noise tweene them is trold. 1605 SHAKS. *Lear* I. ii. 12 A whole tribe of Fops Got 'tweene a sleepe, and wake. 1783 BURNS *Rigs o' Barley* i, The time flew by, wi' tentless heed, Till 'tween the late and early. 1806 SCOTT *Wandering Willie* vii, But oh, how we doubt when there's distance 'tween lovers.

**b.** In Combinations (cf. BETWEEN *adv.* 4): **'tween-brain**: see quot.; **'tween doffer,** a doffer intermediate between two others; **'tween-watch,** ? = DOG-WATCH. Also 'TWEEN-DECKS.

1821 CLARE *Vill. Minstr.* etc. (1823) I. 205 As 'tween-light hangs the eve. 1825 J. NICHOLSON *Operat. Mechanic* 391 A small intervening cylinder, called the 'tween doffer, which carries it to the third main cylinder. 1890 BILLINGS *Nat. Med. Dict.*, *'Tween-brain*, portion of brain between the hemispheres and the corpora quadrigemina:..proposed as an equivalent for the German Zwischen-hirn, the second of the five vesicles of the embryonic brain. 1899 W. CHURCHILL *R. Carvel* xx, Many and many the 'tween-watch have I passed in a coil of rope in the tops.

**'Tween-decks** (twī·n,deks). The usual sailors' abbreviation of BETWEEN-DECKS *sb.*

1816 TUCKEY *Narr. Exped. R. Zaire* ii. (1818) 64 At night our visitors were satisfied with a sail in the 'tween-decks. 1829 MARRYAT *F. Mildmay* ii, Another ladder..brought us to the 'tween-decks. 1892 *Labour Commission Gloss.*, *'Tween Decks*,..used to denote the inside deck immediately below the main or upper deck.

**Tweeny** (twī·ni). *local.* Also **tweeney, -ie.** [f. 'TWEEN + -Y.] A maid-servant who assists both the cook and the housemaid; a between-maid. Also *tweeny girl, -maid.*

1888 in *N. & Q.* 7th ser. VI. 458/1 A few years back.. Being in want of a girl to ease both the cook and the housemaid..[a] neighbour..replied..'You want a tweenie'. 1904 *Daily News* 18 Apr. 8 A certain useful section of the servant class, who..were known as 'tweenies'. 1906 *Daily Record & Mail* 17 Dec. 4 We may learn tone from our valets, courtesy from our cooks, and tact from our tweeny girls.

**Tweer,** var. TUYERE, TWIRE.

**Twees, -e, -es**: see TWEEZE.

**Tweet** (twīt), *sb.* and *int.* [Echoic.] An imitation of the note of a small bird. Also repeated.

Cf. *tueit* in the *Compl. Scot.* (1549) vi. 39.

1845 *Zoologist* III. 1063 Its usual note is monosyllabic, and like tweet, tweet, tweet. 1851 G. MEREDITH *S.-W.-Wind in Woodland* 8 A chirp or tweet, That utters fear or anxious love. 1897 A. H. REA in *Bards Angus & Mearns* 378, I heard the skylark singing gay, The tweet o' tiny wren. 1900 *Westm. Gaz.* 3 Dec. 10/1 'Wheet, tweet, tweet', .. they [quails] called in the meadows. 1910 *Blackw. Mag.* Feb. 286/1 The 'tweet tweet' of the snipe.

Hence **Tweet** *v. trans.*, to utter in this way, to twitter; also *transf.*

1851 G. MEREDITH *Pastorals* v, The little bird..Tweets to its mate a tiny loving note. 1891 S. MOSTYN *Curatica* 63 'Oh', tweet-tweets a tiny diaconal pullet, 'how splendid!' 1902 *Westm. Gaz.* 8 Oct. 8/2 The tweet-tweeting chicks make as much noise in their way as the crowing cockerels.

**Tweet,** dial. var. THWITE *v.*, to cut.

† **Tweetle,** *v.* By-form or altered form of TWEEDLE. Hence **Twee·tling** *vbl. sb.*, fiddling.

1749 J. COLLIER in Bamford *Dial. S. Lanc.* (1854) 72 He's gone Who lov'd the tweetling-trade. 1912 C. MURRAY *Hamewith* 5 He wheepled on 't at morning an' he tweetled on 't at nicht.

† **Tweeze.** *Obs.* Also *pl.* **tweeses, twizes, twises**; rare in *sing.* [Aphetic f. *etweese* (1657) = *etuys, etuis*, pl. of ETUI, ETWEE. See also TWEE[1].

The form-history in Eng. is not quite clear, but app. the plural form *etuis, etwees* was taken also as sing. and spelt *etweese*, and this aphetized to *tweese*.]

A case of small instruments, an etui; also *pl.* instruments kept or carried about in a small case. Occas. *a pair* (= set) *of tweezes.*

1622 MABBE tr. *Aleman's Guzman d'Alf.* II. (1623) 130 Whether shee would buy a very fine paire of twizes which we..had cut from another gentlewomans girdle.. having ground and whet them..and fitted them with a case. 1623–4 MIDDLETON & ROWLEY *Span. Gipsy* II. i, Take anything.., purses, knives, handkerchers, rosaries, tweezes, any toy. 1632 SHERWOOD s. v. *Tweese*, A Surgeons tweese (or box of instruments). [cf. 1611 COTGR., *Pennarol de Chirurgien*, a Chirurgians Case or Ettuy; the box wherein he carries his Instruments.] 1638 FORD *Fancies* I. ii, I will..break the teeth of thy combs, poison thy camphire-balls,..be-tallow thy tweezes. *c* 1645 HOWELL *Lett.* I. xvii. 32, I send you..the French Bever and Tweeses you writ for. 1665 BOYLE *Occas. Refl.* IV. xv. (1848) 255 Drawing a little Penknife out of a pair of Twises I then chanced to have about me. 1672 *Descr. Lake Geneva* in *Misc. Cur.* (1708) III. 409 There are found..Knives, and Needles as thick as Bodkins of tweeses. 1681 W. ROBERTSON *Phraseol. Gen.* (1693) 206 A barber's tweese, or case of instruments.

**Twee·zer,** *sb.* Also 8 **tweeser.** [f. TWEEZE, or *twees, tweeze* pl. of TWEE[1]. Also, in mod. use, a back-formation from TWEEZERS.]

† **1.** A case of small instruments; an etui, a tweezer-case. *Obs.*

1654 GAYTON *Pleas. Notes* III. vii. 111 His signe..is as attractive as..his Plaister-box (if he be a Chyron too) or if not, as his Tweezer. 1745 *Gentl. Mag.* Jan. 34/2 They admired my tweeser, and the trinkets in it. 1746 ELIZA HEYWOOD *Female Spect.* No. 22. (1748) IV. 187 Her maid.. went privately away in the night, taking with her..her watch, tweezer, a diamond solitaire, and several other trinkets.

**2.** = TWEEZERS 2; also *attrib.* formed like tweezers.

1904 H. G. WELLS *Food of Gods* I. iv. 105 His hand upon the tweezer of his balance weights. 1909 *Westm. Gaz.* 18 Nov. 4/2 Vertical springs in front and half-'tweezer' cross-springs in the rear.

**Twee·zer,** *v.* [f. TWEEZERS: cf. prec. 2.] *intr.* To use tweezers; *trans.* to pull out with tweezers; also to pinch or pluck with or as with tweezers. Hence **Twee·zering** *vbl. sb.*

1806 W. TAYLOR in Robberds *Mem.* (1843) II. 146 There is less micrology, less tweezering at trifles, in his erudition. 1848 in *Q. Rev.* Mar. 446 A hero..who when he has '*tweezered* out the slender blossom of manhood that lives on his lip and cheek', passes well for a tall young lady. 1911 *Blackw. Mag.* July 48/2 If he halted he was tweezered into activity again.

**Twee·zer-case.** Also 7 **tueser-,** 8 **tweaser-, twiser-, twitzer-.** [f. TWEEZER(S) + CASE *sb.*[2]] A case in which tweezers and other small instruments are carried; an etui or 'tweeze'.

1686 *Lond. Gaz.* No. 2122/4 A round Tueser Case of Tortoise-shell. 1707 J. STEVENS tr. *Quevedo's Com. Wks.* (1709) 229 We..lay as close..as Herrings in a Barrel, or Tools in a Tweezer-Case. 1709–10 STEELE *Tatler* No. 142 ⁋ 5 His Tweezer-Cases are incomparable: You shall have one not much bigger than your Finger, with 17 several Instruments in it. 1712 ARBUTHNOT *John Bull* III. i, Ladies, hung about with toys and trinkets, twiser cases [etc.]. 1755 SMOLLETT *Quix.* (1803) IV. 85 My lady..pulled out a large pin, or rather, ..a bodkin, from her tweezer-case. 1899 R. WHITEING *5 John St.* xvii. 177 Writing pads, tweezer cases, shaving sets.

**Tweezers** (twīˑzəɹz), *sb. pl.* Also 7 **twizers, twezers, tweesers.** [An extended form of *tweezes*, pl. of TWEEZE (cf. TROUSE *sb.*² and TROUSERS). See also TWEEZER *sb.*]

†**1.** A set or case of small instruments. Also *a pair* (= set) *of tweezers*. *Obs. rare.*

1654 DOROTHY OSBORNE *Lett. to Sir W. Temple* (1888) 223 Did not you say once you knew where good French tweezers were to be had? Pray send me a pair; they shall cut no love. 1662 PEPYS *Diary* 20 June, Bought me a pair of tweezers, cost me 14/-. 1686 tr. *Chardin's Trav. Persia* 122 Ribbands, Paper, Needles, Twizers, Knives and Scissars. 1688 R. L'ESTRANGE *Brief Hist. Times* III. 121 A Present of Twezers, and a Case of Knives to Father Sweetman at Madrid. 1742 MRS. DELANY in *Life & Corr.* (1861) II. 173 They much admired my tweezers and the trinkets that were in them.

**2.** Small pincers or nippers (orig. as included in the contents of an etui) used for plucking out hairs from the face or for grasping minute objects. Also *a pair of tweezers*.

1654 GAYTON *Pleas. Notes* III. vii. 110 If he had but spirit enough to have drawne, the very sight of his Tweezers would have put the Don to the Roares. *Ibid.* III. xii. 156 Mr. Barber with his Razor or his Tweezers, could not be so expeditious. *a* 1704 T. BROWN *Lett. to Gent. & Ladies* Wks. 1709 III. II. 122 His Eye-brows are fair, but over large,..I mean, when the Tweezers have not play'd their Part. 1796 MORSE *Amer. Geog.* II. 489 They pluck up the hairs..by the roots with tweezers. 1821 BYRON *Juan* V. lxxx, With some small aid from scissars, paint, and tweezers, He look'd in almost all respects a maid. 1863 LYELL *Antiq. Man* ii. 28 In it were found..a pair of tweezers in bronze. 1904 *Mission Field* June 71 Tweezers were used by the Indian men to pull out every hair that grew on their faces.

**b.** *transf.* in various senses.

1654 GAYTON *Pleas. Notes* II. ii. 40 Until these unpar'd nailes, these sharp and tearing tweesers I fasten on his face. 1889 *Science-Gossip* XXV. 118 That the use of the 'tweezers', borne by the ear-wig at the end of the abdomen, was considered somewhat obscure.

**Twei, tweie,** obs. ff. TWAY. **Tweich,** obs. Sc. form of TOUCH. **Tweien, twein, tweine,** obs. ff. TWAIN. **Tweies, tweis,** obs. ff. TWICE. **Twelf, twelfe, twelff,** obs. ff. TWELFTH, TWELVE.

**Twelfth** (twelfþ), *a.* and *sb.* Forms: see below. [OE. *twelfta*, = OFris. *twilifta*, *twel(e)fta* (WFris. *toalfte*, *-de*), MDu. *twal(e)fde*, *twael(e)fde*, *twel(e)fde* (Du. *twaalfde*), OS. **twelifto* (MLG. *twelf-*, *twalf-*, *twolfde*, LG. *twölfte*, etc.), OHG. *zwelifto*, *-lefto* (MHG. *zwelfte*, Ger. *zwölfte*), ON. *tólfti*, *-te*, (Norw. *tolvte*, dial. *tolte*, Sw. *tolfte*, Da. *tolvte*), Goth. **twalifta*: f. OE. *twelf* TWELVE. In southern ME. (14th c.), *twelft* became *twelfth*, after *fourth*, etc., but *twelft*, *twelt*, *twalt* remain in various dialects: see -TH ² and Note to TENTH.]

**A.** *adj.*

**1.** The ordinal numeral corresponding to the cardinal TWELVE; last of twelve; that comes next after the eleventh. **a.** In concord with a sb. expressed.

α. 1 **twelfta,** 1–6 **-te,** 2–3 (*Orm.*) **twellfte,** 3 **tweolfte, tuelfte,** (4 **tuelfd, -fed**), 4 (*Sc.* -6) **tuelft,** 4–7 (9 *dial.*) **twelft,** (4–5 **tuelfete**), 6 *Sc.* **tuelfet, tuelt,** 6 *Sc.* (9 *dial.*) **twelt, twalt.**

*a* 900 *O. E. Martyrol.* Dec. 216 On þam twelftan monðe. *c* 1000 *Sax. Leechd.* III. 190 Mona se twelfta on eallum weorcum nytlic ys. *c* 1200 ORMIN 11063 Þe twellfte daȝȝ. 1297 R. GLOUC. (Rolls) 8606 Þe tuelfte [*v.r.* (*a* 1400) tuelf] ȝer temese moni toun aseincte. *a* 1300 *Cursor M.* 22653 (Cott.) Þe twelft [*v.rr.* tuelft, twelþe] signe. *c* 1400 *Rule St. Benet* vii. 15 Saint benet spekis in þis sentence Of þe telfete [? tuelfete] maner o mekenes. 1513 DOUGLAS *Æneis* XII. Prol. 306, I..my pen furth tuike, Syne thus begouth of Virgill the twelt buike. 1535 STEWART *Cron. Scot.* (Rolls) III. 16 The tuelt ȝeir..of his ring. 1596 DALRYMPLE tr. *Leslie's Hist. Scot.* III. xxix. (S.T.S.) I. 180 The twelfte ȝeir of his regne. *Ibid.* VI. xcii. 332 The tuelfet ȝeir of his rigne. 1621 *N. Riding Rec.* (1894) 87 The twelft day of February.

β. 4 **twelfþe, tuelfthe,** 5 **twellifth, -yfth,** 6 **twelfyth, -veth,** 6– **twelfth,** (9 **twelvth**); also 4 **tweolthe,** 4–5 **twelþe,** 5 **twelthe, twolthe.**

13.. *K. Alis.* 6403 On tweolthe nyght. *c* 1380 Twelþe [see b]. 1387 TREVISA *Higden* (Rolls) V. 145 Þe twelfþe [*ed. Caxton* twellyfth] ȝere he was i-made cathecuminus. *c* 1420 *Chron. Vilod.* 4451 In þe twolthe ȝere of his regnynge. 1530 PALSGR. 372/1 *Douziesme*, twelfyth. 1564 HARDING *Answ. to Jewel's Challenge* (1565) 180 b, The twelfth councell of Toledo. 1820 CHALMERS *Congregat. Serm.* (1838) II. 189 The 31st verse of the 12th chapter. 1830 W. TAYLOR *Hist. Surv. Germ. Poetry* II. 4 The twelvth section. 1884 *Athenæum* 10 May, A star of the twelfth magnitude.

γ. (Chiefly *Sc.*) 4–5 **tuelf,** 4–7 **twelf,** 5–7 **twelfe,** 7 **twelff.**

*c* 1375 Twelf [see b]. *a* 1400 Tuelf [see quot. 1297 in α]. 1587 FLEMING *Contn. Holinshed* III. 1369/1 On the twelfe daie of Februarie. 1640 in P. H. Waddell *Old Kirk Chron.* (1893) 16 The twelff day of October. 1653 W. RAMESEY *Astrol. Restored* 4 His twelfe chapter.

**b.** With sb. understood, usually from context; also *spec.* with ellipsis of *day* (of the month), or *chapter* (of a book of Scripture).

*a* 1000 *Andreas* 665 (Gr.) He wæs twelfta sylf. *c* 1200 ORMIN 11063 Itt iss þe þrittennde daȝȝ Fra ȝoldaȝȝ, nohht te twellfte. ? *a* 1300 *Shires & Hundreds Eng.* in *O. E. Misc.* 146 Þe teonþe on wirecestre, þe eollefte on hereforde, þe tweolfte on lycchesfeld..Her beoþ xv. bispryche. *c* 1375 *Sc. Leg. Saints* xii. (*Mathias*) 355 Sa tuk þai hyme for þe twelf to be. *c* 1380 *Sir Ferumb.* 2846, Y me self was þe twelþe. 1558 *Lydgate's Bochas* IX. xiv. 26 The twelft [*Bodl. MS.* twelue] in nombre. 1562 WINȜET *Last Blast* Wks. (S.T.S.) I. 39 Sen the twelft of Marche. 1600 ABP. ABBOT *Exp. Jonah* 176 In the twelfth of the Revelation. 1611 BIBLE I *Kings* xix. 19 Elisha..was plowing with twelue yoke of oxen before him, and hee with the twelfth. 1867 'OUIDA' *Cecil Castlemaine's Gage*, etc. 345 We soon made up..to the Norwich girls for the loss of the Twelfth [Lancers]. 1887 BOWEN *Virg. Eclogues* VIII. 39 Years I had finished eleven, the twelfth was beginning.

**c.** *ellipt.* The 12th of August, on which grouse-shooting legally begins.

1868 *Field* 8 Aug. 105/3 Many seasons have come and gone since the first Twelfth that I remember. 1895 *Times* (Weekly ed.) 16 Aug. 657/2 In Derbyshire the 'Twelfth' opened delightfully.

**2.** *Twelfth part*, any one of twelve equal parts into which a whole may be divided.

1590 in *Reg. Mag. Sig. Scot. 1595*, 120/1 Reddendo 2 bollas 2 firlotas 2 peccas 2 mensuras vocatas twelf-pairtis farine avenatice. 1724 SWIFT *Drapier's Lett.* i. Wks. 1755 V. II. 23 The twelfth part of a half-penny will do him no more service. 1878 J. DAVIDSON *Inverurie* v. 184 The owners of Twelfth Parts had their lands divided..periodically by lot.

†**3.** *Twelfth whist*, whist with only twelve cards in each hand. *Obs.*

1752 H. WALPOLE *Let. to R. Nugent* (in *N. & Q.* 9th Ser. IV. 538/2), Amusing my selfe..at a game of 12th whist.

**B.** *sb.*

**1.** A twelfth part: see A. 2.

1557 RECORDE *Whetst.* B ij b, *Sesquiduodecima*, 13 to 12.. a tweleuth more. 1696 LOCKE *Lower. Interest* (ed. 2) 136 Supposing..5s. or a Crown, were to weigh an Ounce.. whereof one twelfth were Copper, and eleven twelfths Silver. 1712 J. JAMES tr. *Le Blond's Gardening* 197 Five Twelfths of an Inch thick. 1792 A. YOUNG *Trav. France* 537 No such thing was ever known in any part of France..as a tenth: it was always a twelfth, or a thirteenth, or even a twentieth of the produce. 1812 SIR H. DAVY *Chem. Philos.* 419 From a third to a twelfth of zinc is used. 1812 WOODHOUSE *Astron.* xxxv. 347 Expressed in twelvths of that diameter. 1897 *Westm. Gaz.* 20 Apr. 3/1 A decrease of a twelfth since 1894.

**b.** *spec.* A twelfth part of rents or movables granted or levied by way of tax.

1884 DOWALL *Hist. Taxation* I. IV. iv. 77 The use of grants of fractional parts of moveables was continued..in 1296 a twelfth and eighth..were granted. *Ibid.* 81 The grants made..were..in 1318 a twelfth from demesne.

**2.** *Mus.* **a.** A note twelve diatonic degrees above or below a given note (both notes being counted); the octave of a fifth; hence (usually) the interval, or consonance, between two such notes. **b.** An organ-stop sounding a twelfth above the normal pitch.

1597 MORLEY *Introd. Mus.* 70 Those notes which are distant from them eight notes, as from a fift, a twelfe..from Gamvt to D la sol re is a twelfe. 1613 *Organ Specif. Worcester Cathedral*, The particulars of the great organ.. 1 twelfth of mettal. 1797 *Encycl. Brit.* (ed. 3) XII. 511 Note E, The chord formed with the twelfth and seventeenth major united with the principal sound. 1891 PROUT *Counterpoint* (ed. 2) 74 The thirds above it now give the inversion in the twelfth.

†**3.** Short for TWELFTH-DAY. (Cf. TWELFTH-EVE(N.) *Obs.*

1472 SIR J. PASTON in *P. Lett.* III. 33, I have my pardon, ..for comfort whereoffe I have been the marier thys Crystmesse,..be ffor Twelthe I come to my Lorde Archebysshope.

**C.** *Comb.*: **twelfth-century** *a.*, of or belonging to the century from 1101 to 1200.

1867 FURNIVALL in *Percy Folio* I. 403 A twelfth-century writer.

**Twelfth-cake.** [Short for *Twelfth-night* or *Twelfth-tide cake*: cf. TWELFTH B. 3.] A large cake used at the festivities of Twelfth-night, usually frosted and otherwise ornamented, and with a bean (see BEAN 6 b) or coin introduced to determine the 'king' or 'queen' of the feast.

1774 in Brand *Pop. Antiq.* (1777) 206, I did not return till I had been present at drawing King and Queen, and eaten a Slice of the Twelfth Cake. 1826 HONE *Every-Day Bk.* [55 A citation by Brand represents the..Twelfth-night-cake to have been composed of flour, honey, ginger, and pepper.] 56 In France, the Twelfth-cake is plain, with a bean; the drawer of the slice containing the bean is king or queen. 1876 G. MEREDITH *Beauch. Career* xxix, A ricketty ornament like that you see on a confectioner's twelfth-cake.

*attrib.* 1837 [MISS MAITLAND] *Lett. fr. Madras* (1843) 54 A queer kind of sprig made of rice and beads, like a twelfth-cake ornament. 1838 *Civil Eng. & Arch. Jrnl.* I. 337/1 The house at Kenwood is quite in the twelfth-cake style—patched all over with panels of filagree work.

**Twelfth-day.** Forms: see TWELFTH and DAY. The twelfth day after Christmas; the sixth of January, on which the festival of the Epiphany is celebrated; formerly observed as the closing day of the Christmas festivities. (Cf. *the twelve days* s. v. TWELVE *adj.* 1 c.)

[*c* 900 tr. *Bæda's Hist.* IV. xix. 318 Æt Pentecosten & þy twelftan deȝe ofer ȝeochol.] *c* 1000 *Ags. Gosp.* Matt. ii. 1 *rubric*, Ðys sceal on twelftan dæȝ. *a* 1100 [see TWELFTH-EVE(N]. *c* 1200 ORMIN 11047 Jesu Crist wass fullhtnedd Rihht o þatt daȝȝ..Þatt twellfte daȝȝ iss nemmnedd. 1389 in *Eng. Gilds* (1870) 117 Ye sonunday next after ye twelft day. 1455 E. CLERE in *Paston Lett.* I. 315 On the morow after Tweltheday. 1553 BECON *Reliques of Rome* (1563) 75 b, The feastful day of the Epiphanye commonly called Twelfday. 1585 T. WASHINGTON tr. *Nicholay's Voy.* IV. xix. 133 b, They do not celebrate the natiuitie of..Christ, but on the twelfth day, vse great feasts and solemnitie. 1662 J. DAVIES tr. *Olearius' Voy. Ambass.* 211 *margin*, The Armenians blesse the Water on Twelf-day. 1689–90 WOOD *Life* Jan. (O.H.S.) III. 320 A great flood about Oxon before 12th day. 1725 H. BOURNE *Antiq. Vulg.* xvii, The Twelfth-Day it self is one of the greatest of the Twelve. 1863 *Chambers' Bk. Days* I. 61/1 January 6. This day, called Twelfth-day..and Epiphany..is a festival of the Church.

*attrib.* 1913 *19th Cent.* Aug. 320 He had promised the children a twelfth-day cake.

†**Twelfth-eve(n.** *Obs.* The eve of Twelfth-day; Twelfth-night.

*c* 1000 *Ags. Gosp.* Matt. ii. 19 *rubric*, Ðys sceal on twelftan æfen. *a* 1100 *O. E. Chron.* an. 1065 (MS. C.) Eadward.. forðferde on twelftan æfen, & hyne man bebyrigde on twelftan dæiȝ. 1538 *MS. Acc. St. John's Hosp., Canterb.*, Rec. vpon twelfte euen iijs vd. 1582 in Feuillerat *Revels Q. Eliz.* (1908) 349 At wyndesor at Twelf Eve at night. 1634–5 LAUD *Diary* 5 Jan., Monday night, being Twelfth-eve.

**Tweˑlfthic.** *Math.* [f. TWELFTH + -IC, after *quartic*, etc.] A quantic of the twelfth degree.

1882 DURFEE in *Amer. Jrnl. Math.* V. 45 (*heading*) Tables of the Symmetric Functions of the Twelfthic.

**Twelfthly** (tweˑlfþli), *adv.* [f. TWELFTH *a.*] In the twelfth place; as the twelfth in a series.

*c* 1532 DU WES *Introd. Fr.* in *Palsgr.* 929. *a* 1642 SIR W. MONSON *Naval Tracts* III. (1704) 322/1 Twelfthly, They should make quarterly Payments. 1644 PRYNNE & WALKER *Fiennes's Trial* 82 Twelfely, Might not every Governour and Generall upon this pretence deliver up any Fort? 1693 J. EDWARDS *Author. O. & N. Test.* 181 Twelfthly, we read in several authors [etc.].

**Tweˑlfth-night.** Forms: see TWELFTH and NIGHT. The evening before Twelfth-day, formerly observed as a time of merry-making. Also *attrib.*

*c* 900 *O. E. Chron.* an. 878 Her hiene bestæl se here on midne winter ofer tuelftan niht to Cippanhamme. 13.. *K. Alis.* (Laud MS.) 6388 Of þat cite comen..þe kynges thre, Þat foloweden goddis sterre..In cristemasse, on þe tweleuþ niȝth. 1601 SHAKS. (*title*) Twelfe Night, Or what you will. 1649 MILTON *Eikon.* Pref., Wks. 1851 III. 333 Quaint Emblems..begg'd from the olde Pageantry of some Twelfe-nights entertainment. 1764 *Chron.* in *Ann. Reg.* 45/1 The ancient custom of public hazard playing at court on twelfth night. 1826 Twelfth-night-cake [see TWELFTH-CAKE]. 1854 THACKERAY *Rose & Ring* Prel. (1866) 3 Twelfth-Night characters—those funny painted pictures of the King, the Queen, the Lover, the Lady, the Dandy, the Captain, and so on—with which our young ones are wont to recreate themselves at this festive time. 1863 *Chambers' Bk. Days* I. 64/1 In the last century, Twelfth-Night cards represented ministers, maids of honour, and other attendants of a court.

†**Tweˑlfthtide.** *Obs.* Forms: 6 **twelfe tyde,** 6–7 **twelftide, twelfetide** (in 7 also with hyphen), 6–8 **twelftyde,** (7 **twelvetide**). (*Twelfth-tide* occurs app. only in modernized editions.) [See TIDE *sb.* 4 b, 6.] The season including Twelfth-night and Twelfth-day; the season of Epiphany: formerly the concluding part of the Christmas holidays.

1530 PALSGR. 283/2 Twelftyde, *la typhayne.* 1561 T. NORTON *Calvin's Inst.* IV. xix. 159 That there be no mariages celebrate..from Aduent to Twelftide. 1632 MASSINGER & FIELD *Fatal Dowry* II. ii, As if he had come this Christmas ..To see his friends, and returned after twelf-tide. 1656 FINETT *For. Ambass.* 48 A mask prepared for twelftyde. 1687 *Lond. Gaz.* No. 2301/3 It will not be before Twelvetide.

*attrib.* 1639 S. DU VERGER tr. *Camus' Admir. Events* 64 Like a right Twelfetide King. 1648 HERRICK *New-yeares Gift to Sir S. Steward* 17 Of twelf-tide cakes, of pease, and beanes, Wherewith ye make those merry sceanes, When as ye chuse your king and queen.

† **Twell,** obs. form of TOWEL.

1422–3 *Abingdon Rolls* (Camden) 92 In twellis emptis pro Refectorio xjs.

**Twell,** obs. form of TWELVE.

**Twelt, twelth,** obs. or dial. Sc. ff. TWELFTH.

†**Tweˑlter aithe.** *Orkney* and *Shetland*. [ad. (after Sc. *twelt* TWELFTH *a.*) ON. *tylftar-eiðr*, f. *tylft* a body of twelve, a dozen + *eiðr* oath: cf. SAXTER AITHE.] An oath of twelve compurgators.

1603 *Lawting Court* 21 July, in Peterkin *Notes Orkney & Zetl.* (1822) App. 35 Ordainted to quit himsel of theft by the twelter-aith, because the stowth is great.

**Twelve** (twelv), *numeral a.* and *sb.* Forms: see below. [Comm. Teutonic: OE. *twelf*, (also *tuelf*, and in Lindisf. gl. *tuoelf*), = OFris. *twelef*, *twilif*, *twelf* (OWFris. *tolef*, WFris. *toalf*); MDu. *twalef*, *twaelf*, *twelef*, *twelf* (Du. *twaalf*); OS. *twelif*, *twilif*, *twulif* (MLG. *twelf*, *twolf*, *twalf*, LG. *twölf*); OHG. *zwelif*, MHG. *zwelif*, *zwelf*, Ger. *zwölf*, ON. *tólf*, (Sw. *tolf*, Norw., Da. *tolv*), Goth. *twalif* :—OTeut. **twalibi-*, f. *twa* two + *lib-* or *lif-*, of uncertain origin, but generally considered to belong to the same root as OTeut. **liban* to LEAVE (q. v.), and thus to denote 'two left or remaining over (ten)'; cf. Eleven. Analogous formations to *eleven* and *twelve* are the Lith. *vënū'lika* 11, *dvýlika* 12, in which the second element, Lith. *-lika*, has also the meaning of 'left over'. All other Indo-Eur. langs. have or had forms composed of 'two' + 'ten', like the numbers 13 to 19; cf. L. *duōdecim*, Gr. δώδεκα, Skr. *dwādaçan*.

As an adj. standing before a sb. OE. *twelf* was as a rule indeclinable; in other positions it was usually declined, nom.-acc. *twelfe*, gen. *twelfa*, dat. & prep. *twelfum*, but exceptions on both sides are found in OE., esp. in Northumbrian, and in ME. *twelfe*, and at length *twelve*, became the form in all positions. Reduction to *tuoel* occurs once in Lindisf. Gl., and in ME. and mod. dialects *twell*, *twall* are frequent.]

**A.** Illustration of Forms.

α. 1–7 **twelf,** (1–6 **tuelf,** 1 **tuoelf**) 2–3 **tweolf,** (*Orm.*) **twellf,** 3 **tueolf, twælf, twealf, twalf,** 3–4 **twolf,** 5 **twellif, -yf,** *Sc.* **tuelff** (6 **twelef**), 6–7 *Sc.* **twelff.**

c 888 K. Ælfred *Boeth.* xxxiv. § 10 De..on twelf monðum ʒewexð. 971 *Blickl. Hom.* 15 Hælend ʒenam his twelf þeʒnas. c 1000 *Ags. Gosp.* Matt. x. 5 Das twelf se hælynd sende. c 1020 *Rule St. Benet* (Logeman) 40 þæt ne siȝ læs twelf sealma. c 1175 *Lamb. Hom.* 141 þa fouwer [walmes] weren ideled a twelue, for þa twelf kunreden sculden þer mide heore þurst kelen. c 1200 Ormin 8900 Off twellf winnterr elde. c 1205 Lay. 1617 His tueolf iferen [c 1275 his twelue iueres]. *Ibid.* 25441 þer comen þa twalf [c 1275 twealf] iueren. *Ibid.* 25971 Twælf [c 1275 twealf] swine. c 1330 R. Brunne *Chron. Wace* (Rolls) 8232 Twolf ȝer old. 1375 Barbour *Bruce* x. 547 A schort leddir..I trow of tuelf fut. c 1470 *Golagros & Gaw.* 411 Tuelf crovnit kingis. 1567 *Gude & Godlie B.* (S.T.S.) 3 The twelf Artícklis of our Faith. 1588 A. King tr. *Canisius' Catech.* I. G vij, The cowrse of the moone, quhilk do change twelff tymes in the yere.

β. 1 **twelfe** (**tuelfe,** etc.), 2–3 (*Orm.*) **twellfe,** 3–7 **twelfe,** 5 **tuelfe.**

a 900 *Fate Apostles* 4 Twelfe wæron dædum domfæste. c 950 *Lindisf. Gosp.* Matt. x. 5 Das tuelfe [*Rushw.* twælfe] sende ðe hælend. c 1200 Ormin 956, & off þa twellfe namess ec þatt wærenn don þæronne. a 1400–50 *Alexander* 1079 Fyftene Burghes, And..xij grym waters [*Dubl. MS.* twelfe gret waters]. 1483 *Cath. Angl.* 398/2 Twelfe, *duodecim. Ibid.*, Twelfe ȝere space. 1552 Huloet, Twelfe together, *duodeni.* 1603 Owen *Pembrokeshire* v. (1892) 42 Ten or twelfe yeeres of age.

γ. 2–7 **twelue,** 3 **twælue, twalue,** 3–5 **twelwe,** 3–6 **twolue,** 4 **tuelue** (7 **twellue**), 4– **twelve.**

c 1175 Twelue [see α]. c 1250 *Gen. & Ex.* 663 Twelwe and sexti men. c 1275 *Passion our Lord* 42 in *O. E. Misc.* 38 He ches hym twolue yuere myd him vor to lede. c 1275 Twelue [see quot. c 1205 in α]. 1387 Trevisa *Higden* (Rolls) III. 401 Whanne Alisaundre was twelve ȝere olde. c 1440 *Promp. Parv.* 504/2 Twelwe, *duodecim.* 1535 Coverd. *Matt.* xix. 28 Ye..shal syt also vpon twolue seates. 1607 Shaks. *Cor.* iv. v. 128 Thou hast beate mee out Twelue seuerall times.

δ. 4 **tuel,** 4–7 **twel;** *Sc.* 6 **twoll,** 6–7 **twell,** 6–9 **twall,** 7 **tuel**(**l,** 8–9 **twal.**

c 1400 *Trevisa's Higden* (Rolls) III. 23 He regned in al twelve [*MS.* γ twel] ȝere. 1500–20 Dunbar *Poems* xxviii. 1 Betuix twell houris and ellevin. 1588 A. King tr. *Canisius' Catech.* ii. 3 The somme off our faith..quhilk ye twoll apostlis compylit..callit the creid, quhilk yai..dewyddit in twoll articlis. 1599 in *Maitl. Cl. Misc.* III. 341 The space of twell dayis. 1639 Ld. Wariston *Diary* (S.H.S.) 329 At tuel hours. 1785 Twal [see B. I. 2 b]. 1837 R. Nicoll *Poems* (1843) 106 Twal corporation feasts within the year.

**B.** Signification.

The cardinal number composed of ten and two; represented by the symbols 12 or xii.

**I.** *adj.* **1.** In concord with a sb. expressed.

(*a*) Preceding the sb.

*Beowulf* (Z.) 147, .xii. wintra tid. 971 [see A. α]. c 1050 *Byrhtferth's Handboc* in *Anglia* (1885) VIII. 298 On þisum daʒum beoð ʒesette twelf monðas. 1297 R. Glouc. (Rolls) 431 þis folc..departede hor ost in tuelf [*v.rr.* twolf, twelue] parties. c 1330 R. Brunne *Chron. Wace* (Rolls) 13534 þey were..set In twolue batailles. 1420–2 Lydg. *Siege Thebes* 3540 I-braunched out vpon twelue trees. 1526 Tindale *Acts* vii. 8 And Isaac begat Iacob, and Iacob the twelve patriarkes. 1584 Powel *Lloyd's Cambria* 53 He choose out of that companie..twelue men. 1638 Brome *Antipodes* iii. ii, Twelve Hymnes, For the twelve Sessions. 1750 tr. *Leonardus's Mirr. Stones* 80 There are twelve species of it. a 1774 Goldsm. *Hist. Greece* I. 30 At twelve years old the boys were removed into another class. 1847 Grote *Greece* ii. xix. III. 390 The division of the day into twelve parts.

(*b*) Following the sb. (Chiefly for rime.)

a 1000 *Sal. & Sat.* 15 (Gr.) Mine suna twelfe. a 1300 *Cursor M.* 174 (Cott.) Iesu crist him selue Ches til him apostels tuelue. *Ibid.* 29063 Crist..Spekand to his aposteles tueluen. c 1374 Chaucer *Troylus* ii. 59 (108) Herof ben þere maked bokes twelue. c 1386 — *Prol.* 527 But cristes lore, and hise Apostles twelue He taughte, but first he folwed it hym selue. 1390 Gower *Conf.* I. 181 The Souldan hise hostages sende..of Princes Sones tuelve.

**b.** As multiplier before a higher numeral (*hundred, thousand*, etc.). *Twelve score*, twelve twenties, two hundred and forty; † also *ellipt.* for *twelve score yards*, a common range for a shot in archery; hence *attrib.* in *twelve score prick* (see Prick *sb.* 10 b).

c 1205 Lay. 25443 Twelf [c 1275 Twealf] þusend cnihtes. c 1290 *S. Eng. Leg.* I. 66/450 He deide tweolf hundred ȝer ..Aftur ore louerdes burtyme. 1297 R. Glouc. (Rolls) 10121 In tuelf hundred ȝer of grace & þe secunde ȝere. c 1425 Wyntoun *Cron.* viii. 2011 Twelf hundir nynti ȝhere and sewyn Fra Crist was borne. [c 1470 Henry *Wallace* vi. 107 Tuelff hundreth ȝeer, tharto nynte and sewyn.] 1552 Huloet, Twelue hundreth thousande *sestertia.* 1653 H. Cogan tr. *Pinto's Trav.* ix. 28 Eleven or twelve thousand staves hardened in the fire. 1726 Swift *Gulliver* ii. vii, A gallery of twelve hundred feet long.

a 1300 *Cursor M.* 2168 (Cott.) Ragan..[lived] Twelue scor o yeires. 1550–3 *Decaye of Eng.* A v, Twelf score persons in Oxfordshire. 1569–1620 [see Prick *sb.* 10 b]. 1597 Shaks. *2 Hen. IV*, iii. ii. 52 Hee would haue clapt in the Clowt at Twelue-score. a 1700 Dryden *Theocritus, Epithal. Helen & Menelaus* 39 Twelvescore viragos of the Spartan race. 1753 Chambers *Cycl. Supp.* s.v. *Coursing*, When a hare is put up,..let her run twelve-score yards or thereabouts, before the greyhounds are slip'd at her.

**c.** In special collocations, as *the twelve* Apostles, *twelve labours* (of Hercules, q.v.), *twelve* Signs (of the zodiac, also †Tokens), *Twelve* Tables, *twelve* Tribes (of Israel): see these words; also † *the twelve days*, i. e. those immediately following Christmas (cf. Twelfth-day); † *the twelve men*, a body of twelve men having some special function, as a jury, a select vestry, etc.

c 975 *Rushw. Gosp.* Matt. x. 2 þara *twelf apostola noma [*Ags. Gosp.* naman] sindun þas. c 1175 *Lamb. Hom.* 75 þet rihte ileue setten þe twelue apostles on write. 1377 Langl. *P. Pl.* A. xi. 25 He þat..con tellen of Tobie and þe Twelue Apostles. 1890 *Science-Gossip* XXVI. 10/2 Among the most curious birds of Queensland are those known familiarly as the 'Twelve Apostles', from the circumstance that they are always seen in flocks of exactly twelve. [1600 Nashe *Summer's Last Will* Wks. (Grosart) VI. 156 To feede the poore *twelue dayes, & let them starue all the yeare after.] 1693 Sir T. P. Blount *Nat. Hist.* 132 Tobacco. In the Twelve-Days they begin to Sow their Seed. 1725 H. Bourne *Antiq. Vulg.* xvii. (*heading*), The Wickedness of observing the Twelve Days after the common Way. a 1577 Sir T. Smith *Commw. Eng.* (1633) 110 They which either condemne or acquite the man..are not called Judges but the *twelve men. 1607 *Henley-in-Arden Rolls* (MS.) 22 Oct., Henleye. Agreementes & paines bie the Tweluemenne as followeth made at the Couurte holden ther the 22 daye of october. 1608 in *N. & Q.* 8th Ser. XI. 201/1 Paines laid at the great courte at Sheffelde..by the twelue men of the sooke of Ecclesfelde. 1672 *Cowell's Interpr.*, *Twelve Men*,..otherwise called the Jury or Enquest, is a number of twelve persons [etc.]. 1744 in J. Hammond *Cornw. Parish* (1897) vi. 80 [It was resolved] that every Principall Inhabitant..under the denomination of a twelve-man shall be an acting Manager and Trustee [of the Workhouse]. 1886 *Johns Hopkins Univ. Stud.* Ser. iv. i. 55 The patentees are said to have been called the 'Twelve Men' or Duzine, and to have had both legislative and judicial powers in town affairs. 1390 Gower *Conf.* III. 108 Ther ben *signes tuelve, Whiche have her cercles be hemselve Compassed in the zodiaque. 1509 Hawes *Past. Pleas.* xxii. (Percy Soc.) 105 In the xii. signes them selfe to domify. a 1585 Montgomerie *Flyting* 421 Be the poles, and the planets, and the signes all twell. c 1000 *Ags. Man. Astron.* in *Pop. Treat. Sc.* (1841) 7 Under ælc þæra *twelf tacna. 1535 Coverdale *2 Kings* xxiii. 5 Them that brent incense..to the Sonne, and the Mone, and the twolue tokens.

**2.** *absol.* with ellipsis of sb., preceded by a pronoun or demonstrative, or as predicate.

a 900, c 950 [see A. β]. c 1000 [see A. α]. c 1000 *Ags. Gosp.* Mark xiv. 20 þa sæde he him, An of eow twelfum me sylð. c 1205 Lay. 25275 þas twælfe heore wai ferden. *Ibid.* 26206 For aȝan þine tweie Heo habbeoð twælue [c 1275 twalue]. 1382 Wyclif *Gen.* xxxv. 22 The sones of Jacob weren twelue. — *2 Sam.* ii. 15 Twelue of the children of Dauid. 1535 Coverdale *Josh.* xxi. 40 All the cities of the children of Merari..were twolue. 1646 J. Benbrigge *Vsura Accom.* 5 A Banke of Recovery..herein Twelve were given for the use of an Hundred per annum.

*spec.* **b.** with ellipsis of *hours* (of the day: cf. *twelve hours* in III. c.); also *twelve o'clock.*

*To strike twelve the first time* (or *all at once*), *fig.* to display all one's capacities in one's first performance.

c 1482 J. Kay tr. *Caoursin's Siege of Rhodes* (1870) ¶ 11 All the nyght frou twelfe the clocke unto v in the daye. 1605 Shaks. *Macb.* ii. i. 3 *Fleance.* The Moone is downe: I have not heard the Clock. *Banq.* And she goes downe at Twelve. 1638 Sanderson *Serm.* (1681) II. 129 If a man should vow he would never eat till all the clocks in the city should strike twelve together. 1665 in *Extr. S. P. rel. Friends* iii. (1912) 237 Betweene eleauen and twelue A clocke. 1709 Prior *Hans Carvel* 33 She..was wak'd at Ten;..At Twelve She rose. 1785 Burns *Dr. Hornbook* xxxi, Some wee, short hour ayont the twal. 1818 Scott *Rob Roy* xxii, D'ye think I wad hae come out at twal o'clock at night? 1832 Tennyson *Death Old Year* v, The light burns low: 'Tis nearly twelve o'clock. 1847 Emerson *Eng. Traits* xix. (1856) 310 Their best parts were slowly revealed; ..they did not strike twelve the first time. 1862 Miss Braddon *Lady Audley* xxiii, The clock struck twelve. 1894 J. A. Noble in *Academy* 10 Feb. 119/3 There are some writers who, to use a homely colloquialism, strike twelve all at once: their first achievement..tells us all about them.

**c.** with ellipsis of *years* (of age).

1607 Shaks. *Cor.* iv. v. 135 We would muster all From twelue, to seuentie. 1646 J. Hall *Horæ Vac.* 75 Unlesse an inclination be very discoverable [in a child], it cannot be perceived till after Twelve. 1818 Byron *Juan* i. l, At twelve he was a..quiet boy.

**d.** *The twelve* (spec.): applied to various bodies of twelve men having some special office, as the twelve apostles, a select vestry consisting of twelve parishioners, etc.; also, the books of the twelve 'minor prophets' in the Old Testament.

c 950 *Lindisf. Gosp.* John vi. 71 An of ðæm tuelfum. 1382 Wyclif *John* xx. 24 Thomas, oon of the twelue..was not with hem. 1526 Tindale *Luke* ix. 1 Then called he the xij. to gether, and gave them power and auctorite over all devyls. c 1605 *Acc. Bk. W. Wray* in *Antiquary* XXXII. 213 A great contention betwixt the xij as they tearmed theymselves and the commonaltie of Rippon about the election of the wakeman. 1635 *Vestry Bks.* (Surtees) 97 It was agreed by the twell of the parish of Pettingtone there should be a ceasment of six penns a pound. 1843 Macaulay *Regillus* xxxvii, Manlius, eldest of the Twelve Who kept the Golden Shield. 1882 Farrar *Early Chr.* II. 484 St. John was the last survivor of the Twelve. 1898 J. Robertson *Poetry & Relig. Ps.* iii. 52 The Twelve minor prophets.. perhaps the very first notice we have of them in history is a reference to them as a collection, known as 'the twelve'. 1909 Sir W. M. Ramsay in *Expositor* July 14 The duties.. discharged by the Twelve in the original congregation.

**3.** Used for the ordinal Twelfth; in quot. 1682 *Twelve eve* = Twelfth-eve (Twelfth C). *Obs.* (exc. after the sb. in such expressions as *page twelve, chapter twelve*, etc.).

See also Twelfth A. 1 γ; some of the quots. there may properly belong here.

1430–40 Lydg. *Bochas* ix. xiv. (MS. Bodl. 263) 419/2 The twelue in noumbre Callid Pope Iohn. 1586 W. Webbe *Eng. Poetrie* (Arb.) 62 Transpose anie of those feete..and make short either the two, foure, sixe, eight, tenne, twelue sillable, and it will..fall out very absurdly. 1660 Bloome *Archit.* B c, Within that twelve part. 1682 Piers *Descr. W. Meath* (1770) 124 On Twelve Eve in Christmas.

**II.** *sb.* (with plural *twelves*).

**1.** The abstract number.

c 1425 *Craft of Nombrynge* (E.E.T.S.) 9 Cast 6 to 6, & þere-of wil arise twelue. 1571 Digges *Pantom.* i. xii, Multiplie the distance..by 12. 1875 Todhunter *Algebra* (ed. 7) xxix. § 440 The number ten has only two divisors.., the number twelve has four...On this account twelve would have been more convenient than ten as a radix. *Mod.* Five twelves make sixty.

**2.** A set or group of twelve persons or things; *esp.* a company of twelve players forming a 'side' at some game.

1573 *Satir. Poems Reform.* xlii. 289 Amang Christis awin twelf..Ane tratour was. 1887 *Cornh. Mag.* Mar. 258 A 'twelve' of Irish players [at Lacrosse]. 1898 G. Meredith *Odes Fr. Hist.* 70 The rosed and starred Revolving Twelves [i.e. hours of the days and nights]. 1910 *Westm. Gaz.* 28 June 12/2 Both the University twelves were playing last week.

**3. a.** A thing or person distinguished by the number twelve, usually as being the twelfth in a series; also *number twelve* (see Number *sb.* 5). **b.** A shoe, glove, etc. of size twelve (in quot. 1607 allusively).

1607 Tourneur *Rev. Trag.* v. i, Courtiers haue feete a' th' nines and tongues a' th' twellues. 1652 *Proposals for regul. Law* in *Harl. Misc.* VI. 294 That there may be a distinction made between clerks of the children's threes, and stagers of the long twelves. 1855 Browning *Master Hugues of Saxe-Gotha* vii, Your masterpiece, hard number twelve.

**4.** A thing characterized in some way by the number twelve; *e.g.* a twelve-pounder, or a twelve-bore, gun (see III.), a candle weighing twelve to the pound, etc.

1804 Capt. Maitland in *Naval Chron.* XI. 409 A Ship Privateer, carrying sixteen twelves and sixes. 1895 *Outing* (U.S.) XXVII. 64/1 The opinion of sportsmen has changed during recent years, and twelves have steadily grown in favor.

**5.** (Only in *pl.*) **a.** A sheet of a book folded into twelve leaves (usually in phr. *in twelves*). (Cf. Twelvemo.)

1670 in S. Lennard tr. *Charron's Wisd.* Advert. Bks., Ovid Metamorphosis, in Verse, by George Sandys, in twelves. 1675 *Clavel's Gen. Catal. Bks.* 19 Divinity in large Twelves. *Ibid.* 30 Physick in small Twelves. 1683 Moxon *Mech. Exerc.*, *Printing* xxii. ¶ 4 If the Form be..Twelves, he sets also under the Fifth Page Signature 3, and under the Seventh Page Signature 4. 1766 *Public Advertiser* 20 May, Saturday will be published..in two volumes in twelves,..the second edition of The Vicar of Wakefield. 1792 *Advt. Perry's New Fr. Eng. Dict.*, To be comprised in 750 Pages, in large Pocket Twelves. 1882 J. Southward *Pract. Printing* xiii. 121 Twelves, or duodecimo, is a sheet folded into twelve leaves, making twenty-four pages. It is written 12mo. *Ibid.* 124 Long Twelves is a twelvemo the pages of which read across the broad way.

**b.** *transf.* A book (or books) of which each sheet is folded into twelve leaves.

1683 Moxon *Mech. Exerc.*, *Printing* xxii. ¶ 7 There are four Volumns in use that are differently Imposed, viz. Folio, Quarto, Octavo and Twelves. *Ibid.*, The other Volumns, viz. Sixteens, Twenty-fours, Thirty-two's, are but the Octavo's and Twelves doubled, or twice doubled. 1716 M. Davies *Athen. Brit.* III. 9 In a very small twelves of 36 sides in Print, call'd, *The Marrow of Prayer.* 1786 Cowper *Gratitude* 27 This moveable structure of shelves,..charged with octavos and twelves. 1809 Byron *Bards & Rev.* viii, And Little's lyrics shine in hot-press'd twelves. c 1888 A. Lang *Rowfant Books* ii, 'Dear, dumpy twelves', to fill the nooks.

**c.** *attrib.*

1755 *Connoisseur* No. 71 ¶ 6 Though contracted into the small space of a twelves volume. *Ibid.* No. 93 ¶ 10 The Twelves edition of the Connoisseur will be published on Tuesday the 25th of this instant November. 1771 Luckombe *Hist. Printing* 110 He printed a small twelves volume with the following title.

**III.** Combinations:

**a.** with sbs. forming adjs. in sense 'of, pertaining to, having, containing, measuring, weighing, costing, or in some way connected with, twelve of the things named', as *twelve-button, -candle, -feet, -foot, -head, -hole, -horse* (*-power*), *-inch, -mile, -pint, -pound, -shilling, -stone, -thread.* **b.** with sbs. + -ed², forming parasynthetic adjs. in sense 'having or characterized by twelve of the things named', as *twelve-banded, -footed, -fruited, -gated, -legged,*

*-oared, -rayed, -sided, -starred, -stranded, -towered.* **c.** Special Combs.: **twelve-bore** *a.* (of a gun), having a bore corresponding to the diameter of spherical bullets of twelve to the pound; *sb.*, a twelve-bore gun; **twelve-divided** *a.*, divided into twelve parts; **twelve-eight** (usually $\frac{12}{8}$), *Mus.*, denoting a 'time' or rhythm with twelve quavers in a bar, distributed in threes, the bar thus containing four beats; **twelve-gauge** = *twelve-bore*; **twelve-hour** *a.*, (*a*) *Sc.* (*twal-hour*) of or pertaining to twelve o'clock (noon); (*b*) turning once in twelve hours, as a wheel in a clock or watch; (*c*) consisting of twelve hours, as a working day; **twelve hours** (*Sc.*), twelve o'clock in the day, midday (also *attrib.*); a meal or refreshment taken at noon; **twelve-point sphere**, *Geom.*, a sphere passing through twelve special points in connexion with a tetrahedron, analogous to the *nine-point circle* of a triangle; **twelve-pounder**, a cannon which discharges shot weighing twelve pounds; † **twelve-tide** = TWELFTHTIDE (*obs.*); **twelve-yearly** *a.*, occurring every twelve years.

**1781** PENNANT *Hist. Quad.* II. 501 *Twelve-banded A[rmadillo]. **1859** 'STONEHENGE' *Shot-gun* 243 A good muzzle-loading gun of *twelve-bore, with a charge of..1¼ ounces of shot. **1892** GREENER *Breech-Loader* 132 The best all-round gun for sporting purposes is the 12-bore with 30-inch barrels. **1886** KIPLING *Departm. Ditties* (1888) 42 *Twelve-button gloves. *c* **1865** LETHEBY in *Circ. Sc.* I. 124/2, 26,000 cubic feet of *twelve-candle gas. **1904** *Westm. Gaz.* 15 Dec. 12/1 The Japanese material consists of a sharp strong warp of *twelve-cut yarn, with soft weft. **1864** TENNYSON *Aylmer's F.* 759 Sent like the *twelve-divided concubine To inflame the tribes. **1884** *Pall Mall G.* 8 Sept. 4/1 A..prelude in the key of A major, *twelve-eight time. **1792** in Picton *L'pool Munic. Rec.* (1886) II. 267 A *twelve feet figure executed in..green Bronze. **1898** *Review of Rev.* Feb. 178/2 A twelve-foot basswood Canadian Canoe. **1611** COTGR., *Charrée*,..a little *twelue-footed water-worme, much hunted after by Trowtes. **1872** O. W. HOLMES *Poet Breakf.-t.* i. (1885) 34 Yon *twelve-fruited tree. **1911** RAMSAY in *Expositor* Mar. 224 The *twelve-gated celestial city with its twelve-towered gates. **1859** 'STONEHENGE' *Shot-gun* 173 A gun of *12 gauge carries a ball weighing the twelfth part of a pound avoirdupois. **1894** *Outing* (U.S.) XXIII. 393/2, I carried a twelve-gauge and Srû his nondescript weapon. **1891** FARRAR *Darkn. & Dawn* li, Ishmael ben Phabi, High Priest of the Jews, on whose ephod has hung the *twelve-gemmed oracle. **1798** *Hull Advertiser* 6 Oct. 2/1 Damaged St. Petersburg *Twelve-Head Flax. **1834** MCCULLOCH *Dict. Commerce* 581 [The Petersburgh and Narva flax..come to us in bundles of 12, 9, and 6 heads. *Ibid.*] Charges at Petersburgh on 12 Head Flax, per ton. **1765** *Museum Rust.* IV. xxiii. 107 Cloth..made..of Narva *twelve-headed flax. **1903** *Westm. Gaz.* 16 Jan. 2/1 The wall that used to be the confine of the old *twelve-hole green. *Ibid.* 16 May 7/2 The car..was a *twelve-horse-power Gladiator. **1791** J. LEARMONT *Poems* 67 The Sun now frae the *twal hour point Had nearly skifftit twa hours yont. **1825** J. NICHOLSON *Operat. Mechanic* 491 The twelve-hour wheel turns the minute index. **1909** *Westm. Gaz.* 12 Aug. 6/3 The employers refuse to grant them the twelve-hour day. **1500–20** DUNBAR *Poems* xxviii. 1 Betuix *twell houris and ellevin. **1599** in *Spottisw. Miscell.* (1845) II. 279 She furnished drink to him until twelve hours (at noon). **1637** RUTHERFORD *Letters* 14 Mar. (1664) cxvii. 224 Our moon-light is better then their twelve-hours-sun. **1844** JAS. BALLANTINE *Miller of Deanhaugh* ii. 30 Was it to be expected..that such friends could meet..in the middle of a winter day, and separate without their 'twal hours'? **1876** S. R. WHITEHEAD *Daft Davie* 189 She sat down and took her twal-hours (noon meal). **1611** COTGR. s. v. *Royal, Pied Royal*..the ordinarie *twelue-ynch foot. **1882** *Rep. to Ho. Repr. Prec. Met. U. S.* 275 A 12-inch vein of high-grade ore was met in a cross-cut. **1839** T. MITCHELL *Aristoph., Frogs 42 note*, A laugh, such as the *twelve-labour demigod alone could give. **1656** *New Almanack* (ed. 2) 7 That triple-headed and so consequently *twelve legged curre. **1896** BADEN-POWELL *Matabele Campaign* xv. 116 A *twelve-mile ride next morning. **1815** SCOTT *Guy M.* xvi, I saw his boat..fly across the lake like a *twelve-oared barge. **1891** *Daily News* 17 Nov. 3/7 The pulling race for 12-oared cutters. **1785** BURNS *Address to Deil* x, An' dawtit, *twal-pint Hawkie's gaen As yell's the Bill. **1670** EACHARD *Cont. Clergy* 107 The service ..is read by some ten or *twelve-pound-man [who] has but just skil enough to reade the lessons with twice conning over. **1862** *Catal. Internat. Exhib., Brit. Div.* II. No. 2612 The average ranges obtained..with a 12-lb. shot. **1800** *Misc. Tr.* in *Asiat. Ann. Reg.* 24/2 A lucky ball from a *twelve-pounder. **1876** BANCROFT *Hist. U. S.* III. ix. 425 The 'Inflexible'..carried eighteen or twenty twelve-pounders and ten smaller guns. **1855** KINGSLEY *Glaucus* (1878) 167 The *twelve-rayed sun-star (Solaster papposa) with his rich scarlet armour. **1811** *Regul. & Ord. Army* 153 Good marketable Wheat, and well dressed through a *Twelve-Shilling seamed Cloth. **1831** BREWSTER *Optics* xxx. (1838) 250 This mineral, which crystallises in six and *twelve-sided prisms [etc.]. **1876** RUSKIN *St. Mark's Rest* ii. § 19 A twelve-sided figure. **1839** BAILEY *Festus* xix. (1848) 216 Like her who wears in Heaven the *twelve-starred crown. **1882** F. M. CRAWFORD *Mr. Isaacs* ii, Able to carry a *twelve-stone man. **1890** 'R. BOLDREWOOD' *Col. Reformer* (1891) 243 The properly-wielded *twelve-stranded intimidator [*i.e.* whip]. **1797** *Encycl. Brit.* (ed. 3) XVII. 433/2 Reef and head holes of large sails have grommets of *twelve thread line. **1557** TUSSER *100 Points Husb.* xlv, While *twelue tide doe last. **1568–70** *Darrell Papers* in H. Hall *Soc. Eliz. Age* (1886) App. ii. 242 Seven night at the lest after twelve-tide last. **1911** *Twelve-towered [see *twelve-gated*]. **1906** C. A. SHERRING *West. Tibet* xiv. 283 Every twelfth year, when there is a..*twelve-yearly fair.

**Twelvefold** (twe·lvfōuld), *a.* and *adv.* [f. TWELVE + -FOLD. Cf. OE. *twelf-feald* adj.]

**A.** *adj.* **a.** Twelve times as great or as much. **b.** Composed of twelve parts or divisions, or (in quot. 1854) of twelve kinds.

**1557** RECORDE *Whetst.* B ij, *Duodecupla*, 12 to 1:..Twelue-fold. *c* **1586** C'TESS PEMBROKE *Ps.* LXXVIII. xxii, The twelve-fold race of godly Israell. **1854** CHR. G. ROSSETTI *Paradise* iv, The Tree of Life..with its twelvefold fruits.

**B.** *adv.* Twelve times in amount.

**1660** R. COKE *Power & Subj.* 150 First fruits shall be paid upon the mass of S. Martin; he who shall not then pay them, shall forfeit forty shillings, and pay twelvefold the value of the fruits. **1910** *19th Cent.* Feb. 373 In Queensland the amount of sugar grown by white labour has increased twelvefold.

**Twelvemo** (twe·lvmo), English reading of the abbreviation 12mo or XIImo for DUODECIMO. Also *attrib.*

**1819** 'R. RABELAIS' *Abeillard & Heloisa* 56 We stew them down for twelvemo use. **1835** J. HANNETT *Bibliopegia* I. 12 The twelvemo also presents us with the eighteens, after the sheet is cut into three divisions. **1888** JACOBI *Printers' Vocab.*, *Twelvemo*, a sheet of paper folded into twelve leaves, written thus—12 mo. Also called 'duodecimo'. **1914** *Chambers' Jrnl.* Jan. 7/2 Another French book..is a twelvemo volume.

**Twelvemonth** (twe·lvmʌnþ). Forms: see TWELVE and MONTH; also 4 **tuelfmoth**; *β.* 4 **tuelmoneth, -monþ, -moth, twelmoneþ**, 4–6 **twelmunth**, 5 **-monyth, twolmonthe**, 5–6 **twelmoneth(e, -month(e, -mond(e**, (6 **-motte**); *γ.* 5 **towlmonyth**, 6 **tolmonth, -mont**, *Sc.* **-mount, -mond, -mowth, towmound**, 8 *Sc.* **towmond, -month**, 8–9 *Sc.* **towmont**. [f. OE. *twelf* TWELVE + *mónað* pl., MONTH. The *γ*-forms, however, are app. ad. ON. *tólfmánuðr*, of similar formation.]

**1.** A period of twelve months; a year.

[**1038** *Charter of Harold Harefoot* in Kemble *Cod. Dipl.* IV. 56 Wel neh twelf monað. *a* **1131** *O. E. Chron.* an. 1128 Wær it tweolf monð oððe mare. *a* **1225** *Ancr. R.* 218 Iðe uormeste tweolf moneð þet heo bigon ancre lif.] *c* **1275** *Passion our Lord* 86 in *O. E. Misc.* 39 Heore muchele feste Of alle þe twelfmoneþ þat wes þe alre meste. *a* **1300** *Cursor M.* 1917 A tuelfmoth [*v.rr.* twelf-monþe, tuelmoneth, tweluemoneþ] was gan. **1377** LANGL. *P. Pl.* B. XIII. 337 A feure, þat taketh me al a twelf-moneth. **1470–85** MALORY *Arthur* VII. xix. 242 A twelue moneth will soone be done. **1588** SHAKS. *L. L. L.* v. ii. 837 A tweluemonth and a day. **1640** BROME *Antipodes* I. vii, He has not drunke so deepe a draught this twelvmonth. **1766** BLACKSTONE *Comm.* II. ix. 141 A lease for 'twelve months' is only for forty eight weeks; but if it be for '*a* twelvemonth' in the singular number, it is good for the whole year. **1876** BANCROFT *Hist. U. S.* IV. xv. 420 Not a twelve-month passed away without a massacre of the pioneers.

*β.* [*c* **1305** *11000 Virgins* in *E. E. P.* (1862) 68 Tuelmonþ & elleue wyke.] **13..** *Cursor M.* 1919 (Gött.) A tuelmoneth was gan. *c* **1400** *Destr. Troy* 13230 A twelmond & two wekes. [*c* **1420** *Chron. Vilod.* 3148 Þe whyche was twolmonthe seke in þe palsy.] **1421** *Coventry Leet Bk.* 24 At the fourthe trespas to forswer the fredom of this Cite a twelmonyth & a day. **1573** G. HARVEY *Letter-bk.* (Camden) 12 The putting on of mi hat at problem, which I did not twelmunth nethir.

*γ.* **1477** MARG. PASTON in *P. Lett.* III. 215 He was not gladder of no thyng that he harde thys towlmonyth. **1535** *St. Papers Hen. VIII*, II. 287 He would not haue come in this tolmont, at the least. **1596** in *Spalding Club Misc.* I. 85, I sall giwe breid to my bairnis this towmound. **1726** RAMSAY *Verses on Last Leaf* ii, Thrice fifty and sax towmonds neat. *a* **1774** FERGUSSON *Election* Poems (1845) 42 For towmonths twa their saul is lent. **1785** BURNS *Cottar's Sat. Night* xi, 'T was a towmond auld, sin' lint was i' the bell. **1818** SCOTT *Hrt. Midl.* xxxix. [xl], There will be less scathe amang us; mine owsen hae been reckan this towmont.

**b.** Following and qualifying a date, in such phrases as *that day* (*† a*) *twelvemonth, Michaelmas was a twelvemonth, Easter come twelvemonth*: = a year before or after... (see BE *v.* 20, COME *v.* 35 b).

*c* **1290** *S. Eng. Leg.* I. 178/15 In þat dai a twelf monþe ore louerd..turnde water to win. *c* **1400** tr. *Higden* (Rolls) VII. 521 (MS. *β*) This day a twelve monthe the same houre whanne y schal dye, he schal dye. **1430–1** *Rolls of Parlt.* IV. 368 To been arezed and paied be the Fest of Ester come tuelfemonethe next. **1473–4** *Acc. Ld. High Treas. Scot.* I. 63 For schone..fra Michelmes wes a tuelfmoneth to the xxiiij day of Nouember last bipast. **1545** in Leadam *Court Requests* (Selden Soc.) 187 Abowte our Ladys day in Lent was a Twelmonethe. **1586** *Burgh Rec. Edinb.* (1882) IV. 464 The pest wer in the town as it wes this tyme tolmowth. **1667** in *Verney Mem.* (1907) II. 260 [They will pay no rent] till Christmas come twelvemonth. **1674** *Essex Papers* (Camden) I. 182 Discharging ye Twelvemonths Arrear..ye paymt of wch ought to have begun at Christmass last was twelvemonth. **1712** ADDISON *Spect.* No. 435 ⁋ 3 When I was at my Friend Sir Roger de Coverley's about this time Twelvemonth. **1715** RAMSAY *Christ's Kirk Gr.* II. iii, Till this time towmond. **1802** ANNA SEWARD *Lett.* (1811) VI. 22 The added weakness entailed upon me by the yet unrecovered accident of spring-twelvemonth.

**2.** *Twelvemonth('s mind*: a commemoration of a deceased person by celebration of masses, etc. a year after (or annually on the anniversary of) the day of his death or funeral. Cf. MONTH'S MIND. *Obs.* exc. *Hist.*

**1428** *E. E. Wills* (1882) 82 Y wolle þat myne executours, vij yere after my decesse, holdyn twelf monthes mynde. **1538** *MS. Acc. St. John's Hosp., Canterb.*, For wast of tapers att ye twelmonths mynde iiij d. **1572** R. H. tr. *Lavaterus' Ghostes* (1596) 211 Rites instituted by the Commandement of wandring soules, as Masses for the dead, vigils, prayers, and twelvemonths minds. **1829** HEATH *Grocers' Comp.* (1869) 232 A solemn obiit anniversary, or twelve months mind.

**3.** *attrib.* (In quot. 1536 referring to the 'twelvemonth's mind': see 2.)

*a* **1300** *Cursor M.* 7339 (Cott.) Þai wit-in a tuel-moth stage, War put vte o þair heritage. **13..** *Ibid.* 21038 (Gött.) Þar he was in a tuelfmoth quile. **1536** *Test. Ebor.* (Surtees) VI. 53 At the daye of my berelay, at my vij daye, and at my twelve moneth daye. **1897** MARY KINGSLEY *W. Africa* 649 Engaging for twelve-month terms of work.

Hence † **Twe·lvemonthing**, *a.* (of a beast) twelve months old; *sb.* a beast, as a calf or colt, twelve months old; = YEARLING; **Twe·lvemonthly** *adv.*, every twelve months, yearly, annually.

**1551** in *Longm. Mag.* Apr. (1905) 531, viii twelmonthyng bullocks..a twelmonting maire colt. **1600** in W. F. Shaw *Mem. Eastry* (1870) 226 Item vij kine iij towyering beasts and fower twelve monthings. **1686** PLOT *Staffordsh.* 261 A Cow-calf..had another..3 weeks and some odd days, before she was a Twelve-monthing. **1847–8** H. MILLER *First Impr.* x. (1857) 167 Six thousand loads of the young pole-wood..being used twelvemonthly.

**Twelvepence** (twe·lvpĕns). **a.** A sum of money equal to twelve pennies (now *rare*). † **b.** A coin of this value, a shilling (*obs.*). Also formerly abbreviated xij d.

*c* **1380** WYCLIF *Sel. Wks.* III. 301 Men of lawe and jurours han non conscience to forswere hem for twel pens and her dyner. **1563** *Child-Marriages* 60 Apon Midsomer even last, the said Thomas send a Token, videlicet a xijd. to the said Eleine. **1568** *Satir. Poems Reform.* xlviii. 58 Ȝour court-men heir hes maid my claith deir, And raisd it twell-pennis of the ell. **1622** BACON *Hen. VII* 216 The Recoinage of Groats and Halfe-groats now Twelve-pences and Six-pences. **1665** in De Foe *Plague* (1840) 41 Every of the said chirurgeons shall have twelvepence a body searched by them. **1864** BURTON *Scot Abr.* II. ii. 183 We..dined..very well for twelvepence a man.

**Twelvepenny** (twe·lvpĕni), *a.* (*sb.*) Now *rare.*

**1.** Of the value of, or amounting to, twelvepence. † *Twelvepenny piece*, a shilling (*obs.*).

**1594** BLUNDEVIL *Exerc.* I. vii. (1636) 21, 7 twelue-penny peeces of silver. **1710** ADDISON *Tatler* No. 249 ⁋ 1 The Adventures that this Twelvepenny-Piece has been engaged in. **1712** PRIDEAUX *Direct. Ch.-wardens* (ed. 4) 99 Done for the base Lucre of a Six-penny or Twelve-penny Fee.

**2.** Costing or priced at twelvepence; for or in connexion with which a shilling is paid or payable.

**1609** DEKKER *Gvlls Horne-bk.* Proœm B j b, When at a new play you take vp the twelue-penny roome, next the stage. **1609** B. JONSON *Sil. Wom.* II. v, At the tweluepeny ordinary. **1678** DRYDEN *All for Love* Pref. b iv, This Rhyming Judge of the Twelve-penny Gallery. **1712** *Lond. Gaz.* No. 4988/3 The Twelvepeny Stamps prescrib'd by Law for Ale-house-Licenses. **1726** SWIFT *Gulliver* II. iii, A bit of bread..as big as two twelve-penny loaves. **1728** MORGAN *Algiers* I. Pref. 15 A twelve-penny Pamphlet would contain full as much. **1814** SHIRREFF *Agric. Shetl. Isl.* 21 Rent is paid by the merk of land,..an indefinite quantity..of ground; merks being divided into different classes, such as sixpenny, ninepenny, and twelvepenny merks.

**3.** That may be hired for twelvepence; paying, or receiving, twelvepence.

**1614** B. JONSON *Bart. Fair* v. vi, Thou Esquire of Dames, Madams and twelue-penny Ladies. **1620** MELTON *Astrolog.* 31 The twelve-penny Hirelings make artificiall Lightning. **1683** BUNYAN *Greatn. Soul* Wks. 1853 I. 132 More vigilant in dealing with a twelvepenny customer than they will be with Christ. **1707** *Lond. Gaz.* No. 4296/3 The Out-Pensioners (commonly called the Twelve-Penny Pensioners).

**4.** *fig.* Of small value, paltry, insignificant.

**1603** in Fuller *Ch. Hist.* (1655) x. i. § 24 *ad fin.*, That men be not excommunicated for trifles, and twelve-peny matters.

**B.** *sb. Sc.* (in form *twalpenny*). A twelvepenny piece, a shilling (Scots): see SHILLING 1 b. Hence *twalpenny worth* = twelve pennyworth.

**1786** BURNS *Twa Dogs* 115 An' whyles twalpennie worth o' nappy Can mak the bodies unco happy. **1816** SCOTT *Antiq.* Advt., Perhaps a Scottish 'twalpenny', or English penny, which was expended in snuff or whisky.

† **Twe·lver.** *Obs. slang.* [f. TWELVE + -ER[1].] A coin worth twelve pence.

*a* **1700** B. E. *Dict. Cant. Crew, Twelver*, a Shilling. **1725** in *New Cant. Dict.* **1732** *Tricks of Town* 15 Coachmen.. demanding t'other Twelver or Tester above their Fare.

**Twelvetide**, obs. var. TWELFTHTIDE.

**Twelye**, obs. form of TWILLY *sb.*[1]

† **Tweme**, *v. Obs.* Forms: 1 **twǽman**, 3 **twemen, tweamin, tweamen.** [OE. *twǽman*, f. an extension of the stem of *twá*, TWO.] *trans.* To divide into two parts, separate (*lit.* and *fig.*).

[*c* **893**, *a* **1225**: see TO-TWEME.] *a* **1023** WULFSTAN *Hom.* I. (Napier) 272 Þæt we..ne lætan us deofol dwelian ne twæman. *c* **1050** *Byrhtferth's Handboc* in *Anglia* VIII. 334 Þys taken [dyple] ȝesetton þa ealdan writeras on ciriclicum bocum, þæt hiȝ twæmdon oððe ætywdon þa ȝewitnyssa haliȝra ȝewrita. *c* **1205** LAY. 2948 Ic wlle..twemen mine bearnen. *a* **1225** *St. Marher.* 5 Ne mei unc nowðer lif ne deað tweamin atwa. *a* **1240** *Sawles Warde* in *Cott. Hom.* 265 Hwet mei tweamen us from godd ant halden us þeonne.

† **Twen**, obs. form of TOWEN *a.*

**1612** in *Antiquary* Jan. (1906) 28/1 Thirtie paire of Twen Sheets,..sixe dozen of table napkins, thone halfe flexen, and thother halfe Twen.

**Twen, twene**, obs. ff. TWAIN, 'TWEEN, TWIN *v.*[1]

**Twenter**, obs. form of TWINTER.

**Twentieth** (twe·ntiĕþ), *a.* and *sb.* Forms: 1 **twentiȝoþa** (**-teoȝoþa, -tuȝoþa**), **twentiȝþa**

(-teȝþa), 3 **tuentiþe, twentide, 3–4 twentiþe, 4 tuuentiþe, 5 twentythe,** (**-tyd, 6 tuentieth**), **6–7 twentith, -teth, 6- twentieth**; *β.* **4 tuentende, tuentiand(e**; *γ.* **4 twentiest, 5 twentyest.** [OE. *twentigoða*, etc. (see above), f. *twentig* TWENTY + *-oða* (see -TH ²); becoming in ME. *twentiþe*, *-ythe*, from 16th c. *twentieth*. Northern ME. had also *twentende*, *twentiand(e*, with the Norse ordinal suffix *-andi*, *-ende*; cf. ON. *tuttugandi*, Norw. *tjugande*, Sw. *tjugonde*, MDa. *tjugende*, Da. *tyvende*. The other WGer. langs. have forms with the superlative suffix *-ōst-*, as OFris. *twinti-*, *twintegosta* (WFris. *tweintichste*), MDu. *twintechste*, Du., MLG., LG. *twintigste*, OHG. *zweinzugôsto*, (MHG. *zweinzigeste*, Ger. *zwanzigste*), also mod. Icel. *tuttugasti*; a similar form *twentiest* appears in 14–15th c. southern Eng.: cf. Caxton's *thirtiest* for THIRTIETH.]

**A.** *adj.*

**1.** The ordinal numeral corresponding to the cardinal TWENTY; last of twenty; next after the nineteenth. **a.** in concord with a sb. expressed.

†*Twentieth penny*, one penny in every twenty: cf. THIRD B. I. 4, and sense 2 below.

**a 900** *O. E. Martyrol.* 20 Mar., On þone twenteȝðan dæȝ þæs monðes bið se þridda woroldе dæȝ. **c 1000** *Sax. Leechd.* III. 194 Mona se twentiȝoþa. **c 1250** *Gen. & Ex.* 3641 On ðat oðer twentide dai, of ðe oðer moned taȝte he wei. **1297** R. GLOUC. (Rolls) 9036 In þe tuentiþe ȝer of is kinedom. **1387** TREVISA *Higden* (Rolls) VIII. 255 Kyng Henry hadde þe twentiþe peny of lewed men['s] catel. **c 1470** HENRY *Wallace* XI. 376 Xix thai war, and Craufurd,..The twentyd man, the nowmer to fullfill. **1530** PALSGR. 372/2 *Vingtiesme*, twenteth. **1564** HARDING *Answ. Jewell's Chalenge* (1565) 96 b, [This] Origen sheweth..in the twentith homilie vpon Josue. **1643** BAKER *Chron.* (1653) 395 In this twentieth yeer..Sir Piers Butler..was created Earle of Osory. **1779** *Mirror* No. 57. ¶ 6 Soon after my twentieth year my father died. **1818** FRERE *Monks & Giants* III. xi, The festivals.. That every twentieth century come in season. **1894** S. WEYMAN *Under Red Robe* vii, I was pondering for the twentieth time what step I should take next.

*β.* **c 1330** R. BRUNNE *Chron.* (1810) 309 Whan it wer.. stabled & sette, To gyue þe penie tuentende þe Kyng. **13..** *Cursor M.* 10999 (Cott.) Þe four and tuentiand night.

*γ.* **1398** TREVISA *Barth. De P. R.* XIX. cxxxi. (1495) nn iij/2 Siliqua is the twentiest parte of Solidus. **1480** CAXTON *Contn. Higden* (Rolls) VIII. 523 The two and twentyest day. **1483** — *Gold. Leg.* 334 b/1 The one and twentyest Chapytre.

**b.** with ellipsis of sb., usually to be supplied from context; also *spec.* of *day* (of the month), occas. of *year*.

**1643** BAKER *Chron.* (1653) 533 The twentieth of September, seven of the..Conspirators..were condemned. **a 1700** in *Cath. Rec. Soc. Publ.* IX. 337 In the 20th of her age. **1704** N. N. tr. *Boccalini's Advts. fr. Parnass.* III. 157 Yesterday..being the Twentieth of this Instant. **1749** F. SMITH *Voy. Disc.* II. 31 The Interim, between the twentieth and twenty-eighth was filled. **1782** in J. H. Harting *Hist. Sardin. Chapel* (1905) 25 On the 20th of April, 1782, on Easter Eve, this year. **1902** J. K. MANN *Hist. Popes* I. I. 245 In the sixth century, as in the twentieth.

**c.** with numerals below ten, forming ordinals of those between twenty and thirty: *one-and-twentieth*, *two-and-twentieth*, etc. (also † *twentieth* (*and*) *one*, etc., obs. rare); now mostly superseded by *twenty-first*, *twenty-second*, etc.

**a 900** *O. E. Martyrol.* 22 Jan., On þone twa & twentiȝðan dæȝ þæs monðes. **c 1000** *Sax. Leechd.* III. 194 Mona se an & twentiȝoða. **c 1290** *S. Eng. Leg.* I. 53/221 In þe on an twentiþe ȝere. **a 1325** *MS. Rawl. B. 520* lf. 50 b, Þe ȝere of his regne þe ȝette ant tuuentiþe. **c 1420** *Chron. Vilod.* 3086 In Septembre þe won & twentythe day. **1536** WRIOTHESLEY *Chron.* (Camden) I. 53 The twentith tow daie of Julie. **1596** DALRYMPLE tr. *Leslie's Hist. Scot.* II. xviii. (S.T.S.) I. 157 The tuentieth and ane ȝeir eftir the deith of his vnkle. **1631** MILTON *Sonn., On having arrived at Age of 23*, 2 How soon hath Time..Stoln on his wing my three and twentith yeer! **1719** DE FOE *Crusoe* I. 231 The four and twentieth Year.

**d.** *Comb.*

**1898** (*title*) The Twentieth Century New Testament. Part I. **1903** G. MATHESON *Repr. Men Bible* 201 Our interest in the narrative is a twentieth-century interest.

**2.** *Twentieth part*: any one of twenty equal parts into which a whole may be divided.

**c 1350** *Will. Palerne* 5354 No tong miȝt telle þe twentiþe parte. **1611** COTGR., *Vintain*, a twentieth; or a twentieth part of. **1710** SWIFT *Mem. to Mr. Harley* ¶ 7 The twentieth parts are 12*d.* in 1 *l.* paid annually out of all ecclesiastical benefices. **1848** DICKENS *Dombey* xxxvii, Not a twentieth part of the affection that you have for Florence. **1911** *Act 1 & 2 Geo. V*, c. 16 § 2 (1) (*a*) The yearly value..being taken to be one-twentieth part of the capital value.

**B.** *sb.*

**1.** A twentieth part: see A. 2.

**c 1330** R. BRUNNE *Chron.* (1810) 145 Þe tende suld be nouht, no þe tuen[ten]de non make. **1611** [see A. 2]. **1719** W. WOOD *Surv. Trade* 345 Crown Pieces..one Twentieth lighter. *Ibid.*, Nineteen twentieths of a Crown. **1792** A. YOUNG *Trav. France* 537 No such thing was known in any part of France..as a tenth: it was always a twelfth, or a thirteenth, or even a twentieth of the produce. **1815** J. SMITH *Panorama Sc. & Art* II. 218 The balls should not be more than one-twentieth of an inch in diameter.

**2.** *Mus.* A note twenty diatonic degrees above or below a given note (both notes being reckoned), or the interval between two such notes (equal to two octaves and a sixth). So *two and twentieth*: see TWO.

**1609** DOULAND *Ornith. Microl.* 79 Others are tripled, to wit,..a twentieth, which is equall to a sixt, and a thirteenth, and so forth.

**Twenty** (twe·nti), *numeral a.* and *sb.* Forms: 1 **twentiȝ,** (**tuentiȝ, tuoentiȝ, twoeȝentiȝ**), 2–6 **twenti,** 3 (*Orm.*) **twenntiȝ,** 3–6 **tuenty,** 4–5 **tuenti,** (4 **tuent**), 5–7 **twentie,** 6 **tuentie, twentye,** (*Sc.* **twantie,** *Sc. dial.* **twinti, twenti, tuonti, toontie**) 4– **twenty.** [OE. *twentiȝ*, f. *twen-* two + *-tig* (= Goth. *tigus*, ON. *tigr* decade: see -TY ²): = OFris. *twintich*, *-ech*, *tweintich*, *-tig* (WFris. *tweintich*, NFris. *twuntich*), OS. *twentig* or *twēntig*, MDu. *twintich* (Du. *twintig*), MLG. *twentig*, *twintig* (LG. *twintig*); OHG. *zweinzug*, *-uc*, *-och* (MHG. *zweinzec*, *-ic*, *zwênzic*, *-ig*, Ger. *zwanzig*); the first element is variously explained as a nom. plur. (OE. *twēgen*) and as a dative form. Cf. also ON. *tuttugu*, *-ogu* (Norw. *tjuge*, *tjug*, Sw. *tjugo*, MDa. *tiuge*, Da. *tyve*), and Goth. *twai-tigjus* (two decades).

Like the other cardinals in -TY, in OE. orig. a neuter sb. followed by a genitive plural: e. g.

**c 893** K. ÆLFRED *Oros.* I. i. 18 Næfde he þeah ma ðonne twentiȝ hryðera, & twentiȝ sceapa, & twentiȝ swyna. **971** *Blickl. Hom.* 231 Onbid her seofon & twentiȝ nihta. **c 1000** ÆLFRIC *Gen.* xxxi. 38 Wæs ic..mid þe nu twentiȝ wintra. *Ibid.* xxxii. 14 Twentiȝ buccena..and twentiȝ rammena.]

The cardinal number equal to twice ten: represented by the symbols 20 or XX (formerly sometimes xxti = L. *viginti*).

**A.** *adj.* **1.** In concord with a sb. expressed (or in OE. in plural form with implied sb.).

**a 900** *Elene* 830 (Gr.) On twentiȝum [*MS.* xx] fotmælum. **c 1000** ÆLFRIC *Numb.* xi. 19 Næs to anum dæȝe, ne to twam, ..ne to tynum, ne to twentiȝum [daȝum]. **a 1225** *Leg. Kath.* 2502 Twenti dahene ȝong [= journey]. **c 1330** R. BRUNNE *Chron.* (1810) 282 Wele tuenti ȝere. **1478** W. PASTON in *P. Lett.* III. 237 He seythe ye be xxtis. in hys dette. **1583** STOCKER *Civ. Warres Lowe C.* II. 48 A great multitude of people, who come twentie mile of to this goodly feast. **1637** *Decree Star Chamb.* § 15 in Milton *Areop.* (Arb.) 16 There shall be but Twentie Master Printers allowed to haue the vse of one Presse. **1758** R. BROWN *Compl. Farmer* (1759) 71 A hen sits twenty days. **1853** J. H. NEWMAN *Hist. Sk.* (1873) II. I. ii. 75 In the course of twenty years a new generation would arise.

**b.** Combined with the numerals below ten (*one* to *nine*) to express the numbers between twenty and thirty; formerly (and still occasionally) *one and twenty*, *two and twenty*, etc. (rarely *twenty and one*, etc.); now commonly *twenty-one*, *twenty-two*, etc.; similarly with the ordinals from *first* to *ninth*, forming the ordinals corresponding to the above (*twenty-first*, *twenty-second*, etc.), in modern use substituted for the earlier *one-and-twentieth*, *two-and-twentieth*, etc. (see TWENTIETH A. 1 c).

**c 893** K. ÆLFRED *Oros.* VI. ii. 256 Þara twa & twentiȝra monna þe he him to fultume hæfde acoren. **a 1131** *O. E. Chron.* an. 1124 Þes kinges cnihtes..namen..fif and twenti oðre cnihtes. **1297** R. GLOUC. (Rolls) 1532 Vif & twenti ȝer. **a 1400–50** *Alexander* 3930 Aȝt & tuenti men of armes. **1526** *Proclam.* 5 Nov. (*Pat. Roll* 18 *Hen. VIII*, II. m. 2 d), The Soueraygne..shalbe curraunt..for twenty two shillynges and sixe pens. **1596** DALRYMPLE tr. *Leslie's Hist. Scot.* II. xvi. (S.T.S.) I. 150 Four and tuentie cubites hich. **1604** E. G[RIMSTONE] *D'Acosta's Hist. Indies* III. xviii. 177, I haue gone ouer twenty and seauen riuers vpon that coast. **1777** ROBERTSON *Hist. Amer.* (1783) I. II. 163 In the parallel of twenty-two degrees of latitude. **1794** STEDMAN *Surinam* (1813) II. xxv. 224 What he called his Silver-feast, being the twenty-fifth anniversary of his marriage. **1820** SOUTHEY *Wesley* I. 53 More than four-and-twenty pounds. **1857** MILLER *Elem. Chem.* (1862) III. 204 Allowing the..mixture to stand for twenty-four hours.

**c.** As multiplier before a numeral, usually a higher one, as † *twenty hundred* obs. (= two thousand), *twenty thousand*, etc. (often hyperbolically: cf. d). So *twenty-one thousand*, etc.

**c 950** *Lindisf. Gosp.* Luke xiv. 31 Mið tuoentiȝum ðusendum [*Rushw.* twoeȝentiȝum ðusenda] cymeð to him. **c 1000** *Ags. Gosp.* ibid., Aȝen þone þe him aȝen cymð mid twentiȝum þusendum. **c 1205** LAY. 26824 Twenti hundred cnihten. **1377** LANGL. *P. Pl.* B. XVI. 10, I wolde trauaille..þis tree to se twenty hundreth myle. **c 1386** CHAUCER *Manciple's T.* 65 Yet hath this brid by twenty thousand foold Leuere in a fforest..Goon ete wormes. **1500–20** DUNBAR *Poems* l. 16 Off the Glen Quhettane twenti scoir He drawe as oxin him befoir. **1592** SHAKS. *Ven. & Ad.* 775 If loue haue lent you twentie thousand tongues. **1847** TENNYSON *Princess* IV. 83, I would pipe and trill, And cheep and twitter twenty million loves. *Mod.* Twenty thousand pounds sterling. Twenty million dollars.

**d.** Used vaguely or hyperbolically for a large number.

† *A twenty devil way*: see DEVIL *sb.* 19.

**c 1470** *Golagros & Gaw.* 970 His scheild he chopit hym fra In twenty pecis and ma. **1513** DOUGLAS *Æneis* I. Prol. 260 A twenty devill mot fall his werk at anis. **1592** SHAKS. *Ven. & Ad.* 575 Were beautie vnder twentie locks kept fast. **1622** BACON *Hen. VII* 228 Vpon Twentie respects hee could not haue beene the Man. **1748** RICHARDSON *Clarissa* II. xxviii. 164, I only came..to sit and talk of twenty and twenty fond things, as I used to do. **1848** BUCKLEY *Iliad* 412 Not even if they should place ten-fold and twenty-times such ransoms.

**2.** With ellipsis of sb. (which may usually be supplied from the context). So *twenty-one*, *twenty-first*, etc. †*And twenty*, used as an intensive.

**c 961** ÆTHELWOLD *Rule St. Benet* xxii. 47 (Gr.) [Let them sleep] tynum and twentiȝum on anum inne ætgædere. [**c 1000** ÆLFRIC *Gen.* xviii. 31 God cwæð: Ne do ic hit, ȝif þær beoð twentiȝ.] **c 1205** LAY. 3387 We mine fader habbet vnderfon mid þirtti cnihten,..Do we awai þane twenti. **13..** *Cursor M.* 16906 (Cott.) A mikel stan, to turn i-nogh had tuent [*rime* monument]. **1535** COVERD. *Gen.* xviii. 31 Peraduenture there might be twentie founde therin. **1601** SHAKS. *Twel. N.* II. iii. 52 In delay there lies no plentie, Then come kisse me sweet and twentie: Youths a stuffe will not endure. **1605** ROWLEY *When you see me*, etc. D ij, Godyegodnight and twentie syr. **1607** MIDDLETON *Five Gallants* I. i, As in one pie twenty may dip their sippits. **1735** JOHNSON *Lobo's Abyssinia, Descr.* xii. 115 The ordinary Dose is six of these Rinds, and I had devour'd twenty. **1897** MARY KINGSLEY *W. Africa* 550 The first man to reach the summit was Sir Richard Burton...He went up, as did the succeeding twenty-five (mostly Germans) from Babundi. **1902** O. WISTER *Virginian* xxiii, His thermometer..registered twenty below zero.

**b.** *spec.* with ellipsis of *years* (of age); so *twenty-one*, etc.

**1773** GOLDSM. *Stoops to Conq.* III, What will repair beauty at forty, will certainly improve it at twenty. **1836–9** DICKENS *Sk. Boz, Steam Excursion*, He..was smart, spoffish, and eight-and-twenty. **1849** E. B. EASTWICK *Dry Leaves* 83 A young man of twenty. **1898** MRS. B. M. CROKER *Peggy of Bartons* xxix, I shall be twenty-one in April.

**c.** The ordinals *twenty-first*, *twenty-second*, etc. are ordinarily used with ellipsis of *day* (of the month), also *year* (of a reign).

**1669** F. VERNON *Let.* 19 June in Lang *Valet's Trag.*, etc. (1903) 51 My last of the 26th Currt. **1711** *Lond. Gaz.* No. 4902/2 The King..was to embark on the Twenty-seventh. **1777** ROBERTSON *Hist. Amer.* (1783) I. II. 141 He set sail..on the twenty-fifth of September. **1879** E. WATERTON *Pietas Mariana Brit.* 78 In the twenty-second of Henry the Seventh. **1886** STEVENSON *Kidnapped* xxvi, The house.. where we slept the twenty-first of the month.

**d.** *The twenty* (at Rugby School): see quot. **a 1894**. *The Twenty-four*, a body of 24 men having some special office (at various times and places: see quots.).

**1440** in Glew *Hist. Walsall* (1856) 105 The Masters..shall not make gift or graunt of eny donacion of eny Chantrey.. withoute the assent of the xxiiij. **1736** DRAKE *Eboracum* I. vi. 184 These citizens are commonly called by the name of the twenty four; though they may be more or less than that number. **1857** HUGHES *Tom Brown* II. viii, How well I remember the day we were put out of the twenty [into the sixth form]. **1890** GROSS *Gild Merch.* II. 347 The governing body is no longer [after 1622] called 'the twenty-four'.. but simply the 'probi homines'. **a 1894** C. H. PEARSON in Stebbing *Life* (1900) 23 Scholarship at Rugby was picked up in the Twenty, a sort of lower sixth.

**e.** Phr. † *Twenty in the hundred*, a 20 per cent. rate of interest on loans; *transf.* a usurer. *Twenty to one*, twenty chances to one; an expression of very strong probability.

**1591** SHAKS. *Two Gent.* I. i. 72 Twenty to one then, he is ship'd already. **1602** B. JONSON *Poetaster* (Qo.) III. i, Thou art an honest twenty in the hundred. *Mod.* Ellington won the Derby in 1856 at 20 to 1.

**3.** Used for the ordinal TWENTIETH; so *twenty-one* (*one and twenty*) for *twenty-first*, etc. Now only after a sb. in such collocations as *chapter twenty*, *verse twenty-one*, etc.

**a 1100** *O. E. Chron.* (Laud MS.) an. 1086 On þam an & twentiȝan ȝeare þæs þe Willelm weolde & stihte Engle land. **1297** R. GLOUC. (Rolls) 7105 In þe ȝer of is kinedom tuenty & tuo. **c 1375** *Sc. Leg. Saints* xviii. (*Egipciane*) 208 One [=on] þe twenty day At þe sexte oure. **c 1380** WYCLIF *Last Age Ch.* in Todd *3 Treat.* p. xxxv, As Dauiþ seiþ, þe on and twenty Salme. **1544** tr. *Littleton's Tenures* (1574) 73 Thoughe the horse..bee not the twentye parte woorth in value of the summe of money. **1567** *Gude & Godlie B.* 2 The ten commandementis..in Exodus the twentie Chapter.

**B.** *sb.* (with plural *twenties*).

**1.** The abstract number 20; a symbol representing this. So *twenty-one*, etc.

**c 1425** *Craft of Nombryng* (E.E.T.S.) 22 Take 12 out of twenty, and þere schal leue 8. **1688** R. HOLME *Armoury* III. 141/1 Country People..reckon..their numbers..by..Scores or Twenty's. **1725** WATTS *Logic* II. v. § 5 Some Things.. almost as certain..as that..five Twenties make a Hundred. **1845** *Encycl. Metrop.* I. 384 The numeral language is constructed in conformity with the Phœnician numerals, proceeding by twenties as far as 100. *Mod.* Twenty is an even number. A twenty is printed thus: xx, 20.

**b.** A person or thing distinguished by this number, usually as the twentieth in a series; so *twenty-one*, *twenty-two*, etc.

**1888** H. MORTEM *Sk. Hospital Life* 18, I..heard her ask.. 'Who is "Twenty-two"?'—one of the detestable habits of the place being to call you by the number of your bed.

**2.** A group or set of twenty persons or things. So (rarely) *a twenty-five*, etc.

**1637** GILLESPIE *Eng. Pop. Cerem.* IV. vi. 26 Many societies conveened to the eating of the Paschall Supper by Twenties. **1725** SWIFT *Upright Judge* iii. Wks. 1755 IV. I. 64 My grand-dame had gallants by twenties. **1878** *Athletic World* 6 Dec. 430/1 The game lasting two twenties. **1879** BROWNING *Ned Bratts* 34 A twenty-five were tried, rank puritans caught at prayer In a cow-house.

**b.** Something equivalent to twenty of some unit, *e.g.* a twenty-pound bank-note.

**1850** *Househ. Words* 21 Sept. 620/1 There were two twenties, were there not?

**c.** A sheet (of a book) folded into 20 leaves (4 × 5), or each leaf of such a sheet. (Cf. TWENTYMO.)

**1771** LUCKOMBE *Hist. Printing* 418 A Sheet of Twenties. **1824** J. JOHNSON *Typogr.* II. vii. 172 [*headed* *28] A Half Sheet of Twenties.

**3.** Something characterized in some way by the number twenty. So the compound numerals, as *twenty-four* (a flower-pot of which there are 24 in a 'cast', etc.). See also (in special senses) TWENTY-FIVE, TWENTY-FOUR.

**1842** LOUDON *Suburban Hort.* 515 Those that have the strongest roots re-pot into twenty-fours. **1851** GLENNY *Handbk. Fl. Gard.* 251 In June, the potted ones will bear shifting to a size twenty-four. **1895** *Daily News* 22 Feb. 4/6 From twenties to twenty-fours, that is, from cotton with twenty hanks in the pound to the finer sort of cotton with twenty-four hanks in the pound.

**4.** *pl.* The numbers from 20 to 29; the years in a century or of one's life, or the degrees of any scale (e.g. of a thermometer) so numbered.

**1874** MISS MULOCK *My Mother & I* xiv. 301 In their twenties girls feel differently from what they do in their teens. **1886** *Athenæum* 16 Oct. 495/2 Little Claude Ramsay..in his twenties is always thinking about 'the draught'. **1886** SEELEY *Short Hist. Napoleon* 262 Had Louis XV died in childhood..there would certainly have been in the twenties a war of the French Succession. **1893** LOUISA TWINING *Recoll.* 242 A temperature in the twenties for some days. **1893** GEORGIANA HILL *Hist. Eng. Dress* II. 235 Arrayed in the costume of the twenties. **1894** *Voice* (N.Y.) 22 Feb., In age I judged them to be near the middle of the twenties.

**5.** *attrib.* (and *ellipt.*) as in *twenty* (*twenty-two*, etc.) *port*, port wine of the year 1820 (1822, etc.).

**1860** *All Year Round* No. 54. 87 Acquainted with 'Twenty port, and comet vintages. **1891** S. MOSTYN *Curatica* 10 Mostyn likes the 22 Port very much.

**C.** Combinations.

**a.** Adjs. or attrib. phrases formed by *twenty* with a sb. (= measuring, containing, weighing, etc. twenty of the things named), as *twenty-centimetre*, *-cubit*, *-foot* († *twenty-foot worm*, a centipede), *-grain*, *-gun*, *-inch*, *-knot*, *-man*, *-mark*, *-mile*, *-minute*, *-penny*, *-plume* (applied to a small species of moth, *Alucita polydactyla*), *-pound*, *-round*, *-shilling*, *-yard*, *-year*; so with compound numerals, as *twenty-five-foot*; *twenty-four-carat*, *-feet*, *-hour*, *-thread*; *twenty-one-inch*; *twenty-thousand-ton*; *twenty-two-mile*, etc. Also *twenty-bore*, *twenty-two-gauge*, etc. (of a gun: cf. *twelve-bore* s.v. TWELVE III. c). **b.** Parasynthetic sbs. (see -ER[1] 1), as *twenty-footer*, *-knotter*, *-pointer*, *-pounder*; so with the compound numerals, as *twenty-eight* (*-four*, *-six*, *-thousand*, etc.) *-pounder*, *twenty-one-gunner*, etc. **c.** Parasynthetic adjs., as *twenty-breeched*, *-coloured*.

**1892** GREENER *Breech-Loader* 43 The *20-bore has been strenuously advocated by writers in the sporting papers, but there are very few sold. **1908** *Outlook* 29 Aug. 280/1 The light twelve-bores now built especially for ladies' use..weigh no more than sixteen- or even twenty-bore guns of average weight. **1819** SCOTT *Leg. Montrose* ii, A soldier of honour shall be dragged..before a base mechanical burgomaster,..as if he were one of their own mean, amphibious, *twenty-breeched boors. **1904** *Daily Chron.* 28 May 5/4, *20-centimetre guns. **1600** FAIRFAX *Tasso* XVI. xxiv, Nor golden Iris so bendes in the aire Her *twentie colour'd bow. **1877** TENNYSON *Harold* III. i, Golden cherubim With *twenty-cubit wings. **1684** J. PETER *Siege Vienna* 109 *Twenty eight pounders. **1897** *Outing* (U.S.) XXX. 355/2 Two twenty-seven-footers,..*Rocky John*, as the Commodore's *twenty-five-foot craft was dubbed. *c* **1475** *Pict. Voc.* in Wr.-Wülcker 766/28 *Hic multipes*, a *tuentifot-wurme. **1910** *Encycl. Brit.* X. 258/1 Several large feeding-drains were dug, including the Forty Foot,..the Sixteen Foot river,..and the Twenty Foot river. **1899** *Daily News* 18 Nov. 4/5 A twenty-foot snake..had a quarrel with a fourteen-foot snake. The fourteen-footer was eating a chicken, which the *twenty-footer coveted. **1900** SARAH GRAND *Babs* lxxxi, A regular *twenty-four carat cad—without alloy. **1825** J. NICHOLSON *Operat. Mechanic* 82 The superior velocity of the *24 feet wheel. **1908** *Westm. Gaz.* 25 May 5/2 The *twenty-four-hour trip across the country. *c* **1850** *Rudim. Navig.* (Weale) 135, *24, 30, and 40-penny nails. **1825** J. NEAL *Bro. Jonathan* III. 380 A few *twenty four pound shot. **1684** J. PETER *Siege Vienna* 108 *Twenty four pounder. **1769** FALCONER *Dict. Marine* (1789) I iv, A piece that discharges a ball of twenty-four pounds, is called a twenty-four-pounder. **1903** *Daily Chron.* 30 May 5/1 A light rod and *24-thread line. **1890** *Anthony's Photogr. Bull.* III. 40 A *twenty-grain solution of gelatine. **1757** J. LIND *Lett. Navy* i. 34 Captains of *20, 40, and 50 gun ships. **1849** NOAD *Electricity* 92 A *twenty-inch cylinder electrical machine. **1903** *Daily Chron.* 3 July 8/2 The *twenty-knot wind blowing here to-day. **1898** *Harper's Mag.* XCVI. 830 They [ships] are to be *twenty-knotters. **1905** *Daily Chron.* 24 July 7/1 A member of the English *twenty-man team. **1788** J. SKINNER *Eccl. Hist. Scot.* II. 588 These itinerant preachers were..called the '*Twenty Merk Men'. **1908** *Daily Chron.* 4 Aug. 1/2 The Kaiser..rewarded him with a twenty mark piece. **1902** *Ibid.* 10 May 10/1 Come down to the country and take *twenty-mile walks. **1905** *Westm. Gaz.* 4 Aug. 6/3 Districts within the twenty-mile radius of London. **1898** *Ibid.* 27 July 1/1 The *twenty-minute sitting [of the House of Lords]. **1900** *Daily Chron.* 31 Aug. 5/1 The Gaekwar is a '*twenty-one gunner'—one of the three Indian Princes who alone are entitled to the royal salute. **1794** W. HUTCHINSON *Hist. Cumberld.* I. 175 *note*, 3l. a year customary rent..with a *twenty-penny fine. **1908** *Westm. Gaz.* 11 Sept. 10/1 Some remarkably fine heads have been secured in Highland deer forests...A *twenty-pointer was killed by Lord Burton..fifteen years ago. **1761–2** HUME *Hist. Eng.* (1806) III. 800 The small proprietors, or *twenty-pound men. **1822** GALT *Provost* xxx, I received a twenty-pound note. **1861** W. F. COLLIER *Hist. Eng. Lit.* 403 A silver-scaled *twenty-pounder [salmon]. **1891** S. C. SCRIVENER *Our Fields & Cities* 39 Persons paying rates on twenty pounds...These twenty-pounders. **1899** *Daily News* 12 Jan. 7/5 A *twenty-round glove fight. **1797** *Chron.* 4 Mar., in *Ann. Reg.* 14/1 *Twenty shilling Notes were issued by the Bank of England. **1855** MACAULAY *Hist. Eng.* xxii. IV. 698 The ministers at one time resolved to issue twentyshilling bills..for the payment of the troops. **1684** J. PETER *Siege Vienna* 109 *Twenty six pounders. **1756** *Connoisseur* No. 121 ¶ 6 A careful old gentleman came..to marry his son, and was recommended..to a *twenty thousand pounder. **1909** *Daily Chron.* 25 Sept. 5/5 The nineteen or *twenty-thousand ton Dreadnoughts. **1840** BLAINE *Encycl. Rur. Sports* § 2430 The higher the number of bullets [to the pound], the smaller is the caliber...Mr. Joseph Manton..recommends two-feet-eight and *twenty-two gauge as a general sporting length and bore of gun-barrel. **1902** *Westm. Gaz.* 7 Nov. 2/1 A *twenty-two-mile bridge across the Great Salt Lake. **1903** *Ibid.* 23 Oct. 3/1 You practically never see a *twenty-yard putt go ten yards off the line of the hole. **1902** *Ibid.* 2 Sept. 8/2 Rated..heavily upon the *twenty-year endowment plan.

**Twenty-eight.** [TWENTY A. 1 b, 2.] *Twenty-eight Parrakeet*, a name for the yellow-collared Parrakeet of Australia (*Platycercus semitorquatus*), from its note.

**1848** J. GOULD *Birds Australia* V. pl. 19 Yellow-collared Parrakeet...It often utters a note, which from its resemblance to those words has procured for it the appellation of 'twenty-eight' Parrakeet from the colonists.

See also TWENTY C.

**Twenty-five.** [TWENTY A. 1 b.]

**1.** *Rugby Football.* The line drawn across the ground twenty-five yards from each goal; also, the space enclosed by this.

**1877** *Field* 24 Feb. 220/2 They were completely penned in their own twenty-five. **1889** *Pauline* VIII. 36 The play was constantly in our opponents' twenty-five.

**2.** *Cards* (also *twenty-fives*): A variety of SPOIL-FIVE, in which the 'game' or winning score is twenty-five: cf. FORTY-FIVE b, JINK *sb.*[1] 2.

**1894** 'HOFFMANN' *Card & Table Games* (1898) 248 A player making all five tricks is said to make a 'jink', and wins the game, whether at twenty-five or forty-five. **1904** *Longm. Mag.* June 142 They produced an old pack of cards and played twentyfives.

See also TWENTY C.

**Twentyfold** (twe·ntifōuld), *a.*, *adv.*, and *v.* [f. TWENTY + -FOLD. Cf. OE. *twentigfeald.*]

**A.** *adj.* Twenty times as many or as great; multiplied by twenty; twenty times repeated.

**1610** HOLLAND *Camden's Brit.* (1637) 679 Rye with twenty fold encrease. **1653** T. C. in Blithe *Eng. Improv. Impr.* To Capt. W. B. Cvj, To raise from one to ten, yea Twentyfold. **1855** MILMAN *Lat. Chr.* XIV. iii. (1864) IX. 160 The interminable process of twentyfold assertion, twentyfold objection, twentyfold conclusion. **1897** P. WARUNG *Tales Old Regime* 207 Even in the twenty-fold perjurer and the thrice condemned murderer.

**B.** *adv.* Twenty times (in amount); twenty times as much.

**1872** TENNYSON *Gareth & Lyn.* 970 The savour of thy kitchen came upon me A little faintlier: but the wind hath changed: I scent it twentyfold. **1905** *Standard* 3 Mar. 2/5 After..heavy rains,..the volume of water..was twentyfold as great.

† **C.** *vb.* To multiply by twenty. *Obs. rare*—[0].

**1611** FLORIO, *Ventiplicare*, to twentyfold.

**Twenty-four.** [TWENTY A. 1 b.]

**1.** A sheet folded into 24 leaves; a form of type for printing a sheet to be so folded (quot. 1683); a book in which the sheets are thus folded. (Always in *pl.*; usually in phr. *in twenty-fours.*)

**1673** *Term Catal.* 6 May, Valerii Maximi dictorum factorumque memorabilium Libri IX. In Twenty-fours. **1683** MOXON *Mech. Exerc.*, *Printing* xxiv. ¶ 15 Any Form Imposed like Twelves, as Twenty fours. **1688** R. HOLME *Armoury* III. xv. (Roxb.) 23/2 Other bookes..whether they be..octavo's, sixteens or twentyfoures. **1715** M. DAVIES *Athen. Brit.* I. 11 Bound in Twelves, Sixteens, or Twenty-fours. **1771** LUCKOMBE *Hist. Print.* 419 A Sheet of Twenty-fours, with Two Signatures. *Ibid.* 420 A Half Sheet of Long Twenty-fours.

**2.** A period of 24 hours; a day. *nonce-use.*

**1735** BERKELEY *Querist* § 125 To pass the twenty-fours with tolerable ease.

See also TWENTY A. 2 d, B. 3, C.

**Twentyfou·rmo.** [English reading of 24mo or xxivmo, used as abbreviation of L. *vicesimo quarto*, after 12mo = *duodecimo*, etc.] The size of a book in which each sheet is folded into 24 leaves. So **Twe·ntymo** [= 20mo or xxmo, for L. *vicesimo*], the size of a book in which each sheet is folded into 20 leaves.

**1841** SAVAGE *Dict. Print.* 798 *Twenty-Fourmo*, a sheet of paper folded into twenty-four leaves, forty-eight pages, is termed twenty-fourmo. *Twentymo*, a sheet of paper folded into twenty leaves, forty pages, is termed twentymo. **1901** EGGLESTON *Transit Civiliz.* iii. 128 The sizes and shapes..running all the way to twenty-fourmos.

**Twenty-second.** *Mus.* [TWENTY A. 1 b.] A note 22 diatonic degrees distant from a given note, or the interval between two such notes (equal to three octaves); hence, an organ-stop formerly used, sounding three octaves above the normal pitch (more commonly called *two-and-twentieth*: see TWO B. I. 3 a).

*c* **1700** in Grove *Dict. Mus.* II. 595/1 Great Organ. 1. Open Diapason, .. 13. Tierce. 14. Larigot. 15. Twenty-second.

**Twentysome**: see -SOME *suffix*[2].

† **Tweon**, *v. Obs.* [OE. *twéonian* (with variant *twýnian*), f. *twéon* doubt, a derivative from the same root as TWO.] *intr.* To be doubtful, to doubt; to debate.

*c* **897** K. ÆLFRED *Gregory's Past. C.* xvi. 102 ȝif hie ðonne ȝit ðær tweonað, gongen ðonne to ðæm halȝum ȝewritum. *c* **1000** *Ags. Gosp.* Matt. xxviii. 17 Witodlice sume hiȝ tweonedon. *c* **1160** *Hatton Gosp.* Mark xi. 23 Swa hwilc swa..on his heorte ne tweoneð. *c* **1175** *Lamb. Hom.* 109 ȝunge monnan mei tweonian hweðer hi moten alibban. *c* **1205** LAY. 907 Þa wile þe heo tweoneden þus Clepede Membricius. *Ibid.* 25741 Þæ cnihtes þa tweoneden To whaþere heo faren mihten.

**Twere**, variant of TUYERE.

**'twere** (twēɹ, twəɹ), also **twer**, abbreviation of *it were* (= it would be), formerly common, now poetic or archaic: see IT.

**1605** SHAKS. *Macb.* I. vii. 1 If it were done,..then 'twer well, It were done quickly. **1607** — *Cor.* IV. iv. 15 Friends ..who Twin (as 'twere) in Loue, Vnseparable. **1614** GORGES *Lucan* x. 448 Thus doubtfull musing whether tweare Fitter to die or basely feare. **1808** [see IT A. γ]. **1832** TENNYSON *To J. S.* 66 'Twere better I should cease.

**Twerle**, obs. f. TWIRL *sb.* **Twesdaie, -day**, obs. ff. TUESDAY. **Twesel**, var. TWISEL *v. Obs.*

**Twey, tweye**: see TWAY, TWIE.

† **Tweyangle.** *Obs. rare*—[1]. App. synonym (or error) for TOUCHANGLE, ANGLE-TWITCH.

**14..** *Stockh. Med. MS.* II. 409 in *Anglia* XVIII. 317 [If] wermys, tweyanglys be name, [be] Mad to powdyr.

**Twey-case**: see TWEE[1]. **Tweyen, tweyn, tweyne**, obs. ff. TWAIN, TWINE. **Tweyfold, Tweyleke**: see TWAY 4. **Tweys, tweyss**, obs. ff. TWICE. **Tweyst**, obs. dial. f. TWIST. **Twezers**, obs. f. TWEEZERS.

**Twhart, twhert**, obs. ff. THWART.

**Twhite, twhyte**, obs. ff. THWITE.

**Twi-, twy-** (twəi), *prefix.* [OE. *twi-* = OFris. *twi-*, MLG. *twi-*, MDu. *twe-*, Du. *twee-*, OHG. *zwi-*, Ger. *zwie-*, ON. *tví-*, Norw., Sw., Da. *tve-*; cognate with Skr. *dvi-*, Gr. δι-, L. *bi-*, Lith. *dvi-*, from root akin to Skr. *dwau*, *dwē*, Gr. δύο, L. *duo*, Two. In OE. the regular comb. form expressing *two*, sometimes *twice*.]

**a.** In parasynthetic comb. with sb. + -ED[2], forming adjs. with the sense 'having two..', 'two..-ed', as *twi-* (or *twy-*)*arched*, *-clustered*, *-coloured*, *-eared*, *-faced*, *-flamed*, *-gated*, *-headed*, *-linked*, *-mouthed*, *-natured*, *-necked*, *-peaked*, *-pointed*, *-shaped* (see also *twi-banked*, etc. in e); also with sb. simply, in the same sense, as *twi-top* adj. (see also *twiform* in e). **b.** With adj. or pple. in sense 'in two ways or respects, doubly', as *twi-* (*twy-*) *streaming*, *-yoked*. **c.** With sb. in sense 'twofold, double', as *twi-circle*, *-reason* (see also *twi-car*, etc. in e). **d.** In sense 'twice' or 'a second time', as *twi-*(*twy-*)*born* adj. (see also *twichild* in e). **e.** Special Combs.: **twi-banked** *a.*, having two banks of oars; **twi-car**, used by W. Morris to represent Gr. δίφρος chariot (properly 'the chariot-board, on which two could stand', L. & Sc.); **twichild** (**twy-**) (*obs.* exc. *dial.*), one who is 'twice a child', an old man in his second childhood; also, (one's) second childhood; also as *adj.*; **twifoil** (**twy-**), *Her.* = DUFOIL; **twi-forked** (**twy-**) *a.*, divided in two like a fork, bifurcate; **twiform**, **-formed** (**twy-**) *adjs.*, having a double form; formed of two (esp. different or incongruous) parts (in quot. 1703, having some part double); **twi-life** (*nonce-wd.* after *twilight*), a life marked by indistinct perception or consciousness; **twi-minded** *a.*, ? having two minds or thoughts (about something); considering (it) in two ways or aspects; **twy-prong**, a two-pronged fork; **twi-thought** (*nonce-wd.* after *twilight*), an indistinct or vague thought; † **twi-wifing**, bigamy. See also TWIBILL, TWIBIT, TWIFALLOW, TWIFOLD, TWILIGHT, TWIREDE, TWISPECHE.

**1903** *Westm. Gaz.* 22 Aug. 2/1 A *twi-arched bridge of stone. **1875** MORRIS *Æneid* VIII. 79 Two *twi-banked keels. **1908** G. MURRAY *Euripides' Hippolytus* 30 That Mother fair Of *Twy-born Bacchus. **1887** MORRIS *Odyss.* XV. 75 But abide till I bring to thy *twi-car the gifts. *c* **1580** JEFFERIE *Bugbears* I. iii. 69 in *Archiv Stud. Neu. Spr.* (1897) XCVIII. 313 O my *twichild and my babye! **1656** W. D. tr. *Comenius' Gate Lat. Unl.* § 199 Old men are said to grow children again, and to bee twichilde. **1829** SOUTHEY *Oliver Newman* vi, Encumber'd with a twichild man. **1889** GISSING *Both of this Parish* xxiii. II. 175, I thought it was but a deception o' my twichild, for I be getting aged. **1895** F. THOMPSON *Sister Songs* 13 In *twi-circle o'er the grass. *a* **1834** COLERIDGE *The Pang more sharp* ii, Babe..From its *twy-cluster'd hiding-place of snow. **1903** *Academy* 18 July 56/1 A *twi-coloured thread, red and white. **1904** FARRER *Garden Asia* 270 Little twy-coloured bubbles. **1879** BUTCHER & LANG *Odyssey* 359 A..*twy-eared chalice of gold. **1635** QUARLES *Embl.* V. xiv. 40 Wry-mouth'd disdaine,..And *twy-fac'd Fraud. **1875** MORRIS *Æneid* XII. 198 Twi-faced Janus. **1822** T. G. WAINEWRIGHT *Ess. & Crit.* (1880) 298 The *twi-flamed torch. **1688** *Twyfoile [see DUFOIL]. *c* **1828** BERRY *Encycl. Her.* I. Gloss., Twyfoil or Dufoil.

**1891** *Cent. Dict.*, Twifoil. **1635** QUARLES *Embl.* II. xiii. 10 Her flaming head, *Twy-forked with death. **1639** G. DANIEL *Ecclus.* xxvii. 60 A Twi-forkt Iavelin doth divide his heart. **1658** BROMHALL *Treat. Specters* IV. 258 Ioves twy-forked lightning. **1738** *Gentl. Mag.* VIII. 375/1 Twi-fork'd Malvern with his tow'ring height. **1812** CARY *Dante, Purg.* XXXII. 95 The wain..Bound to the *twyform beast. **1907** F. THOMPSON *Ode Setting Sun*, Thou twi-form deity. **1607** J. DAVIES *Summa Totalis* H iij, This huge *twy-form'd Fabrick. **1703** T. N. *City & C. Purchaser* 7 Twiform'd Creatures, as..a Serpent with a Head at each end; the Spread Eagle with 2 Heads. **1852** KINGSLEY *Andromeda* 58 Twyformed, many-handed, terrible, shapeless. **1887** BOWEN *Æneid* VI. 25 Twiformed Minotaur, two bodies combined. **1573** TWYNE *Æneid* X. D d j, In parliment house they sat *twigated wyde. **1895** *Month* June 237 Illustrations of the eagle both single and *twi-headed. **1889** LOWELL in *Atlantic Monthly* LXIV. 146 This illusion..That witches us to hear and see As in a *twi-life what it will. **1875** MORRIS *Æneid* XII. 375 His *twilinked coat of mail. **1883** G. MEREDITH *Earth & Man* xliv, *Twi-minded of him, as the waxing tree, Or dated leaf. **1875** MORRIS *Æneid* IX. 617 To hear the flute's *twi-mouthed song. **1868** TENNYSON *Lucretius* 194 A satyr,..but him I proved impossible; *Twy-natured is no nature. **1879** F. W. H. MYERS in *19th Cent.* June 959 That strange antithesis in the 'twy-natured' French. **1840** BROWNING *Sordello* IV. 388 The Kaiser's ominous sign-mark..The crowned, grim, *twy-necked eagle. **1906** *Edin. Rev.* Apr. 319 A *twy-peaked monticule. **1623** LISLE *Ælfric on O. & N. Test.* Ded. 1 *Twi-pointed Pernas hill. **1840** BROWNING *Sordello* III. 1019 That's no *twy-prong, but a pastoral cross. **1884** — *Ferishtah, Camel-Driver* 51 This red-hot twy-prong. **1632** B. JONSON *Magn. Lady* III. v, You shall pardon me For a *twi-reason of State. **1907** F. THOMPSON *New Poems, Hermes* 188 Behold, with rod *twy-serpented Hermes, the prophet. **1875** MORRIS *Æneid* VI. 286 *Twi-shaped Scyllas. **1794** COLERIDGE *Relig. Musings* 204 Property..*twy-streaming fount, Whence Vice and Virtue flow, honey and gall. **1885** G. MEREDITH *Diana* xxiv, Diana saw herself through the haze she conjured up. 'Am I worse than other women?' was a piercing *twi-thought. **1622** WITHER *Fair Virtue* E ij, The *twy-top Hill, Where the Poets learne their skill. *c* **1250** *Gen. & Ex.* 450 Bigamie..On engleis tale, *twie-wifing. **1875** MORRIS *Æneid* XII. 164 With *twiyoked horses white.

**Twibill, twybill** (twəi·bil, † twi·b'l). *arch.* and *dial.* Forms: 1 twibile, 1–4 twybile (4 -byle); 1, 4– twibill, 1, 6– twibill (6 -bylle); 1, 4– twybill, 4–6 -bil, -byl(l(e, 6 -bille; 4 twybel(l, 5–6 twyble, 6 twible, *Sc.* twibbil, 7 twibble; 6–7 twyvel(l, 8 twivil(l: see also TUBBAL, TUBBER², and *two-bill* (Two B. IV. 2). [OE. *twibil*, *-bill* neut., and *twibile* masc., f. TWI- + BILL *sb.*¹ and *sb.*²]

†**1.** A kind of ax with two cutting edges; formerly used for cutting mortises. *Obs.*

*a* **1000** *Prose Life Guthlac* xii. (1848) 56 He..ʒenam sum twibil, and mid þan þry men to deaðe ofsloh. *a* **1000** *Ags. Gloss.* in Wr.-Wülcker 194/35 *Bipennis securis*, twilafte æx, *uel* twibile. **1295** *Acc. Exch. K. R.* 5/8 m. 9 (P.R.O.) Et iiij. d...in .j. Twybile emendando. *a* **1310** in Wright *Lyric P.* xxxix. 110 He mot myd is twybyl other trous make. *a* **1340** HAMPOLE *Psalter* lxxiii. 7 Wiþ bradaxis þai share down þe ʒates of it..in brade axe and twybile [Vulg. *in securi et ascia*] þai kest it down. **14..** *Tundale's Vis.* (Wagner) 722 Summe had twybyll, brodax and nawger. *c* **1440** *Promp. Parv.* 505/1 Twybyl, wryhtys instrument..*bisacuta, biceps*. **1500** *Ortus Vocab.*, *Bisacuta*, a twybyll. *c* **1500** *Debate Carpenter's Tools* 13 in Hazl. *E. P. P.* I. 80 ʒe, ʒe, seyd the twybylle, Thou spekes euer ageyne skylle. **1548** *Elyot's Dict.*, *Bipennis*, a twybill, wherwith carpenters doo make their mortayses. **1587** *Will of Arraie* (Somerset Ho.), Two wombells and a Twyvell. **1656** BLOUNT *Glossogr.*, *Twibil* (Belg. *Tweebill*), an instrument used by Carpenters to make mortise-holes. **1686** PLOT *Staffordsh.* 168 Grinding-stones..for thicker edg'd tooles, such as Axes, Hatchets, Chisells, Adds, Twy-bills, &c.

*attrib.* **1641** *Wit's Recreat.* § 583 'Twill make a good ship-anchor, when he lackes. It is his gimlet, and his twibill axe.

**2.** A mattock; also a similar tool used in mining, a tubbal. Now *local*.

*c* **1440** *Pallad. on Husb.* I. 1153 The mattok, twyble [*v. r.* twibil], picoys. *c* **1440** *Promp. Parv.* 505/1 Twybyl, or mattoke, *marra*,..*ligo*. **1555** PHAER *Æneid* II. E iv, The plowmen with their axes strong..and twibles tall. **1577** B. GOOGE *Heresbach's Husb.* (1586) 11 b, Iron hookes, Iron forkes, Twybilles, Dongforkes. **1612** DRAYTON *Poly-olb.* XVIII. 77 She learn'd the churlish ax and twybill to prepare, To steel the coulter's edge. **1687** TAUBMAN *London's Tri.* 7 Miners..bearing Spades, Pickaxes, Twibbles and Crows, fit to sink Shafts, and make Addits. **1898** *N. & Q.* 9th Ser. I. 243/2 [Given as a Devonshire name for 'a two-billed pick'.]

**b.** A reaping-hook used in cutting beans and peas; a pea-hook. *dial.*

**1763** *Museum Rust.* I. lxii. 263 The regularity with which these beans are sown, makes it much easier to cut them with the twibil and hink, than if they were sown at random. *Ibid.* lxiii. 266 Each labourer had in his right hand a cutting instrument called a twibil, and in his left a sort of hook called a hink. **1796** J. BOYS *Agric. Kent* 91 It [canary seed] is cut in the harvest..with a hook, called a twibil, and a hink. **1887** *Kentish Gloss.*, *Twibil* (twei·bil), a hook for cutting beans.

†**c.** See quot. *Obs. rare*⁻⁰.

**1706** PHILLIPS (ed. Kersey), *Twivill*, an Iron-Tool us'd by Paviers.

**3.** A double-bladed battle-ax or bill. *poet. arch.*

In quot. 1678 app. a halberd carried by a constable of the watch.

**1558** PHAER *Æneid* II. E ij, Him self in hand..a twyble great doth bryng. **1565** GOLDING *Ovid's Met.* IV. 28 Lycurgus with his twibill sharpe. *c* **1611** CHAPMAN *Iliad* XV. 656 Sharpe axes, twibils, two-hand swords, and speares with two heads borne, Were then the weapons. **1678** *Jovialists Coronat.* 3 in *Loyal Garland* D viij, If..a Halberdly train, Or a Constable chance to rebel, And would with his twyvels maliciously swell And against the Kings party raise Arms. **1834** PLANCHÉ *Brit. Costume* 31 They [Anglo-Saxons] had also axes with long handles which they called bills,..and the double-axe or *bipennis* (twy-bill). **1865** KINGSLEY *Herew.* xix, A little fair-haired man..who heaved up a long twybill, or double axe. **1876** MORRIS *Sigurd* I. 68 He bore a mighty twi-bill as he waded the fight-sheaves through.

†**Twibit.** *Obs. rare.* In 5 twybyte, 6 -byt, twibytte. [f. TWI- + BIT *sb.*¹ 5.] = TWIBILL.

**14..** *MS. Lansd.* 560 fol. 45 *Bipennis*, twybyte. **1510** STANBRIDGE *Vocabula* (W. de W.) B iv b, *Bipennis*, a twybyt. **1560** BECON *Jewel of Joy* Wks. II. 26 b, Is not my word lyke fire,..and lyke a twibytte cleauynge the rocke of stonne?

**Twice** (twəis), *adv.* (*sb.*, *a.*) Forms: 2 twiʒes, 3 (*Orm.*) twiʒʒess, twiʒess, 4 twiʒes, tuuiʒes; 2–5 twies, 4 twyese, tweis, 4–5 twyys, tweies, 4–6 twyes, twys, *Sc.* twyss, 4 (7 *Sc.*) tuis, 4–7 twyse, twise, 5 tweys, 5 (6 *Sc.*) twyis, tuyse, 5–6 twis, *Sc.* tuys(s, 6 *Sc.* twyiss, tweyss, tuyss, tuise, 7 twyce, 5– twice; 6 twyst, 7 twist, 9 *dial.* twyste, twiste, twicet. [Late OE. *twiʒes*, f. *twiʒe*, TWIE + advb. genitive ending *-es*; cf. *ǽnes*, *ānes* ONCE, *þriges* THRICE.

*Twees*, given by Kilian as a Du. and Fris. word, may be a similar formation, but Da. dial. *tøs*, *tøse* is a reduced form of MDa. *tøsser*, ON. *tvisvar*.]

In all senses now the regular substitute for the phrase *two times*: see Two B. I. 1 d.

**1.** Two (successive) times; on two occasions.

*c* **1122** *O. E. Chron.* (Laud MS.) an. 1120 Ðises ʒeares com þet leoht to Sepulchrum Dni..twiʒes. *a* **1175** *Cott. Hom.* 227 Þat cild his twies acenned. *c* **1200** ORMIN Ded. 104, & tatt he loke wel þatt he An bocstaff write twiʒʒess, Eʒʒwhær þær itt uppo þiss boc Iss writenn o þatt wise. *Ibid.* 16635 Niss nan mann..Þatt muʒhe Godess riche sen Butt he be borenn twiʒess. **13..** *Cursor M.* 27912 (Cott. Galba) Als gude war men to ett twise. *a* **1325** *MS. Rawl. B.* 520 lf. 54 Tuuiʒes in þe ʒere. *c* **1330** R. BRUNNE *Chron. Wace* (Rolls) 4704 Þe Bretons..had wonnen of Cesar twys. *c* **1350** *Will. Palerne* 3721 It a-louted lowe to vs twiʒes. *c* **1375** *Lay Folks Mass Bk.* (MS. B.) 309 In excelsis he neuens twyese. **1377** LANGL. *P. Pl.* B. v. 421, I nam nouʒte shryuen..tweies in two ʒere. *a* **1400-50** *Alexander* 1605 'Ay mott he leue, ay mot he leue', quod ilke a lede twyse. **14..** *R. Gloucester's Chron.* (Rolls) 9018 (MS. β) He smote him tweys on þe heuede. *c* **1449** PECOCK *Repr.* IV. vii. (Rolls) 462 If he hadde be twies weddid..Eny man tweies weddid. **1473–4** *Acc. Ld. High Treas. Scot.* I. 47 Passand twis to Sanctandrois and anys to Dunbare. **1508** DUNBAR *Tua Mariit Wemen* 303, I wes tuyse maryit. **1526** TINDALE *Luke* xviii. 12, I fast twyse in the weke. **1549** *Acc. Ld. High Treas. Scot.* IX. 280 To the furroure for tuys lynyng of ane goun. **1563–7** BUCHANAN *Reform. St. Andros* Wks. (1892) 11 At iij howris ryng twyiss. **1596** SHAKS. *Merch. V.* IV. i. 69 Wouldst thou haue a Serpent sting thee twice? **1612** in *2nd Rep. Rec. Irel.* 264 Twist or thrist a week. **1774** GOLDSM. *Nat. Hist.* (1776) V. 350 The swallow..sometimes breeds twice a year. **1839** T. MITCHELL *Aristoph.*, *Frogs* 145 *note*, [Cinesias] is alluded to twice more in the present play. **1868** LOCKYER *Elem. Astron.* III. xxxiii. (1879) 195 The sun crosses the equator twice a year at the equinoxes. **1888** EGGLESTON *Graysons* i. 15, I wouldn't look at her twiste.

**b.** Strengthened by *over* (OVER *adv.* 13 a).

**1648** BP. HALL *Serm. Higham* Rem. Wks. (1660) Z j b, The justice of God never punished the same sin twise over. **1711** ADDISON *Spect.* No. 72 ¶ 11 The Senior Member has outlived the whole Club twice over. **1721** RAMSAY *Richy & Sandy* 6 This aught days twice o'er tell'd. **1893** *Times* 29 Apr. 11/3 To tax the owners of property twice over in respect of the same thing.

**c.** Contextually: A second time; for the second time.

**13..** *Sir Beues* (A.) 4256 Now is ʒhe þer twies quene. **1382** WYCLIF *Phil.* iv. 16 To Tessalonyk ʒe senten oonis and twyes [TINDALE, CRANMER, *Geneva*, once and afterwarde agayne]. *a* **1450** *Knt. de la Tour* (1906) 85 The kynge sente vnto her onis, tuyes, thries. *c* **1475** *Rauf Coilʒear* 148 Now is twyse..me think thow hes forʒet. **1501** DOUGLAS *Pal. Hon.* I. 388 And now this time is twyis. **1582** T. WATSON *Centurie of Loue* lxxxv, I at last, Am now twise free. **1602** SHAKS. *Ham.* II. ii. 403 That great Baby..is not yet out of his swathing clouts. *Rosin.* Happily he's the second time come to them: for they say, an old man is twice a childe. **1633** BP. HALL *Occas. Medit.* (1851) 112 The old word is, that 'An old man is twice a child'; but I say, happy is he, that is thus a child always.

**d.** In phr. *once or twice*, *twice or thrice*, used indefinitely: a few times.

*a* **1225**–*c* **1450** [see ONCE 8 a]. *c* **1400** MAUNDEV. (1839) xxv. 261 Ones or twyes in the Woke. *c* **1400** tr. *Secreta Secret.*, *Gov. Lordsh.* xix. 58 Do noght þat ofte, but twyes or thryes yn þe ʒeer. **1526** *Pilgr. Perf.* (W. de W. 1531) 173 b, Not onely ones or twyse he hath hurted me. **1711** ADDISON *Spect.* No. 120 ¶ 1 He has caught me twice or thrice looking after a Bird's Nest. **1750** GRAY *Long Story* 125 He once or twice had pen'd a sonnet.

**e.** *To think twice*: to consider a matter a second time (before deciding or acting); to deliberate.

**1877** SPURGEON *Serm.* XXIII. 56 Do not think twice about it..but say 'No'. **1890** *Spectator* 27 Dec. 932/1 He may..think twice before he formally undertakes so unremunerative a struggle. **1910** [see THINK *v.* 5 b].

**2.** Expressing multiplication by two: Two times in number, amount, or value.

**a.** with a numeral, or a sb. or sb. phr. expressing quantity: Two times as much as; double of.

**1308** *Song* in Ritson *Anc. Songs & Ball.* (1877) 61 Tak twies ten ifere That wol be tuenti fulle. **1377** LANGL. *P. Pl.* B. XIII. 270 In þe date of owre dryʒte..A þousande and thre hondreth tweis thretty & ten. *c* **1425** *Craft of Nombrynge* (E.E.T.S.) 28 Yf þat þou wold wete qwat is twyes 40. **1593** in T. Morris *Provosts of Methven* (1875) 82 For the haill space of twyss nynetene ʒeiris. **1697** DAMPIER *Voy.* I. xv. 408 Any Stranger..must be a great Favourite to get a pair of Shoes of them [Chinese women], tho he give twice their value. **1743** FRANCIS tr. *Hor.*, *Odes* V. ix. 19 Twice a thousand Gauls aloud proclaim..great Cæsar's name. **1824** ARNOLD *Let.* in Stanley *Life & Corr.* (1844) I. 69, I am twice the man for labour that I have been..for the last year or two. **1826** HENRY *Elem. Chem.* II. 373 These crystals..require..between twice and three times their weight of water at 60°. **1875** JOWETT *Plato* (ed. 2) I. 475 Two is twice one.

**b.** In a twofold degree; two times as much; doubly.

Usually with *as* (†*so* obs.); more rarely with comparative, or (rhetorically) with an adj. of quality.

[*c* **1394** *P. Pl. Crede* 178 Mo þan twenty and two twyes y-noumbred.] **1398** TREVISA *Barth. De P. R.* XIX. cxxv. (1495) mm iv/1 A nombre that hyght Multiplex conteyneth yᵉ lesse nombre twyes or thryes or foure tymes. *c* **1460** *Towneley Myst.* viii. 320 We shall þem bond twyse as fast. **1500-20** DUNBAR *Poems* xvi. 9 Sum gevis for twyiss als gud agane. **1542** UDALL *Erasm. Apoph.* 303 A newe hous..twys so good & double so faire. **1583** STUBBES *Anat. Abus.* II. (1882) 63 Twise vnhappy be those parents that thinke any moneth, day or houre, infortunate for their children to be borne in. **1601** DOLMAN *La Primaud. Fr. Acad.* (1618) III. 728 The fire is twise more subtile then the aire. *a* **1774** GOLDSM. *Surv. Exp. Philos.* (1776) I. 238 If..the wedge be twice as long..the driver will cleave his wood with twice greater force. **1825** T. HOOK *Sayings* Ser. II. *Sutherl.* (Colburn) 9 Which..makes beauty doubly winning, and talent twice bewitching. **1885** 'MRS. ALEXANDER' *Valerie's Fate* iv, I am nearly as old as you are, and I know twice as much of the world.

**3.** quasi-*sb.*, preceded by a preposition or demonstrative: Two times. (Cf. ONCE 9.) **a.** with preposition; esp. *at twice*, on two occasions, in two distinct operations (somewhat *rare*); † *by twice*, twofold, doubly (*obs. Sc.*).

**1494** *Acc. Ld. High Treas. Scot.* I. 248 For a rape to the locke at twys,..brokyne wyth towen of the tymmyr. ? *a* **1500** *Wycket* (1828) p. xii, Whether is the body of the lorde made at once or at twyse. **1560** WHITEHORNE *Ord. Souldiours* (1573) 33 b, A ladle..that will take so muche pouder up at twise or thrise. *a* **1600** MONTGOMERIE *Sonn.* lxii. 5 My trumpets tone is terribler be tuyis [*rimes* wyse, lyis] Nor ʒon couhorne. **1664** J. WILSON *Projectors* IV, As many Citizens and their Wives at once, as the great Bed at Ware, will hold at twice. **1791** H. WALPOLE *Let. to Miss Berry* 29 Jan., I have written this at twice. **1860** GEO. ELIOT *Mill on Fl.* III. iii, 'Did Mr. Tulliver let you have the money all at once?'..'No; at twice.'

**b.** with demonstrative word or phrase. *rare*.

**1872** BAGEHOT *Eng. Constit.* (1878) 100 We reject your Bill for this once or these twice, or even these thrice. **1907** T. COBB in *Story-Teller* 93/1 Judging by Lady Kitty's demeanour the last twice they had met.

**4.** quasi-*adj.* Performed, occurring, given, etc. twice; doing something (implied by the sb.) twice.

Chiefly with verbal sb. or agent-n., the vb. in which is implicitly qualified by *twice*.

**1577** B. GOOGE *Heresbach's Husb.* 28 Sommer Barley [is to be sowed] in March or April, after twyse plowing. **1624** CAPT. SMITH *Virginia* 239 We heard of the twice returne of the Paragon. **1683** *Life & Death Ld. Shaftesbury* in *Select. fr. Harl. Misc.* (1793) 458 His twice Imprisonment in the Tower. **1876** FREEMAN *Hist. Sk.* 83 The twice pilgrim. **1894** MRS. H. WARD *Marcella* I. i. 6 Twice meat was forbidden and twice pudding allowed.

**5.** In combination with pples., forming compound adjs., as *twice-baked*, *-bearing*, *-blowing*, *-boiled*, *-conquered*, *-dipped*, *-dyed*, *-given*, *-married*, *-refined*, *-roasted*, *-shelled*, *-sworn*, *-turned* (see also TWICE-BORN, -LAID, -TOLD); rarely with other adjs., as *twice-foul*, *-mortal*; also † **twice-childish** *a.* in one's 'second childhood' (cf. quot. 1602 in 1 c); **twice-stabbed** *a. Entom.*, having two red marks suggesting stabs on the wing-cases, as the twice-stabbed ladybird, *Chilocorus bivulnerus* (*Cent. Dict.* 1891); † **twice-writhen**, Turner's rendering of med.L. *bistorta*, BISTORT.

**1542** *Reg. Mag. Sig. Scot.* 616/2 Tuyse schelit meill. **1568** TURNER *Herbal* III. 12 It [Bistort] may be called..twise-writhen. **1591** SYLVESTER *Du Bartas* I. iv. 304 The twice-foul Raven. **1592** HOOKER *Eccl. Pol.* Pref. ii. § 5 These twice-sworne men. **1598** SYLVESTER *Du Bartas* II. i. I. *Eden* 224 The passage of twice-childish age. **1642** FULLER *Holy & Prof. St.* V. xi. 405 Such as take themselves to be twice-refined. **1700** T. BROWN *Amusem. Ser. & Com.* x. 125 That unpalatable Ragoust, called in Latin *Cramben Biscoctum*, and in plain English, Twice-boil'd Cabbage. **1705** POPE *Jan. & May* 110 Twicemarry'd dames. **1742** YOUNG *Nt. Th.* IV. 765 Faith..dying, tenfold terror gives to death, And dips in venom his twice-mortal sting. **1743** FRANCIS tr. *Hor.*, *Odes* II. xvi. 42 The twice-dyed purple. *c* **1820** S. ROGERS *Italy, Pæstum* 89 Paestum's twice-blowing roses. **1842** LOUDON *Suburban Hort.* 568 The twice-bearing red [raspberry]. **1846** H. G. ROBINSON *Odes of Horace* II. xvi, And wool with Afric's dye..Twice-dipp'd. **1851** H. MELVILLE *Whale* xxvi. 125 As hard as twice-baked biscuits.

Hence **Twice** *v.* (*nonce-wd.* or *slang*), *trans.* to make twice as much, to double; to do twice as much as.

*a* **1636** FITZ-GEFFRAY *Compassion towards Capt.* ii. (1637) 33 Twice your gift by timely giving it. **1890** 'R. BOLDREWOOD' *Col. Reformer* (1891) 304 We can 'twice' you over and over.

**Twi·ce-born,** *a.*

**1.** Born twice: esp. in classical mythology as an epithet of Bacchus (also *absol.*).

**14..** W. PARIS *Cristine* 323 in Horstm. *Altengl. Leg.* (1878) 187 As twys borne childe that were righte yonge, Twys in credelle rokkede to be. **1608** SYLVESTER *Du Bartas* II. iv. III. *Schisme* 909 The twice-born Preacher to the Ninivite. **1697** CREECH *Manilius* II. 49 How twice-born Bacchus burst the Thunderer's Thigh. **1866** J. B. ROSE tr. *Ovid's Met.* 78 The twice-born whom with milk they feed.

**2.** An epithet of the three higher castes of Hindus: see CASTE 2. Also *absol.*

**1794** SIR W. JONES *Inst. Hindu Law* ii. § 169 The first birth is from a natural mother; the second, from the ligation of the zone; the third, from the due performance of the sacrifice; such are the births of him, who is usually called twice born, according to the text of the Véda. **1841** ELPHINSTONE *Hist. Ind.* I. I. iv. 79 Every Bramin, and, perhaps, every twice-born man, must bathe daily. **1877** J. E. CARPENTER tr. *Tiele's Outl. Hist. Relig.* iv. § 75. 120 The members of the three highest castes are all..*dvijâ's*, or twice-born. **1908** *Westm. Gaz.* 7 Dec. 11/1 He was a Hindu of the caste of 'The Twice Born', or 'Regenerates'.

**3.** *Theol.* That has experienced the second birth; born again, regenerate. Also *absol.*

**1849** F. W. NEWMAN *The Soul* iii. § 2 (ed. 2) 140 God has two families of children on this earth; the once born and the twice born. **1875** E. WHITE *Life in Christ* II. xi. (1878) 122 Regeneration, and .. the spiritual union of the twice-born with the..Lord. **1902** W. JAMES *Varieties Relig. Exper.* viii. 166 The sick souls, who must be twice-born in order to be happy.

**Twice-laid**, *a.* [See LAY *v.*[1] 37.] Of rope: Made from the yarns of old rope. Also *absol.* = twice-laid rope.

**1592–3** *Act 35 Eliz.* c. 8 (*heading*) An Acte for the auoiding of deceite vsed in making and selling of twicelayed Cordage. **1669** *St. Papers, Dom.* 280 A cable, and some twice-laid stuff. **1748** *Anson's Voy.* II. ii. 135 Working up all our junk and old shrouds, to make twice-laid cordage. **1796** NELSON in Nicolas *Disp.* (1846) VII. p. lxix, What [rope] is sent us is the worst I ever saw. The twice-laid we make on board is far preferable. *c* **1860** H. STUART *Seaman's Catech.* 56 Nippers are usually made of twice-laid rope.

**b.** *Naut. slang.* (See quot.)

**1867** SMYTH *Sailor's Word-bk.*, *Twice-laid*.., a sea-dish made of the salt-fish left from yesterday's dinner, and beaten up with potatoes or yams.

**Twicer** (twəi·səɹ). *colloq.* or *slang.* [f. TWICE.]

**1.** One who does something twice; *esp.* one who attends church (in quot. 1679, one who conducts public worship) twice on a Sunday.

**1679** V. ALSOP *Mel. Inquirend.* II. i. 170 What if a thousand or two more of Ministers were silenced..? What if Lectures were proscribed, private Conferences interdicted, and your Twicers suspended? **1902** *Onlooker's Note-Bk.* xxiii. 180 In his [Gladstone's] view every respectable person should be a 'Twice-er'. **1904** *Times, Lit. Supp.* 4 Mar. 68/1 The prodigious proportion of absentees from church or chapel and the small number of 'twicers'.

**b.** *Printers' slang.* (See quot.)

**1888** JACOBI *Printers' Vocab.*, *Twicer*, a term of contempt for a man who professes to work both at case and press.

**2.** Something of twice the usual force or value.

**1857** A. MAYHEW *Paved w. Gold* III. xiv, He expressed his delight by exclaiming, 'Here's a start! a reg'lar twicer!'

**Twice-told**, *a.* (*adv.*) [See TELL *v.* 21, 2.]

**1.** Counted or reckoned twice; twice as much as, twice (in amount). (Usually following the word or phrase qualified.) † In quot. 1579 advb. = in a twofold degree, doubly.

**1430–40** LYDG. *Bochas* I. xiv. (MS. Bodl. 263) 64/1 Vpon my fyngirs fyue twies told I hadde ryngis. **1579** TOMSON *Calvin's Serm. Tim.* 472/2 We see also yᵗ we are guiltie twise tolde. **1678** BUNYAN *Pilgr.* I. 195 An hundred times, twice told. **1742** YOUNG *Nt. Th.* IV. 66 Twice-told the period spent on stubborn Troy, Court-favour, yet untaken, I besiege.

**2.** Narrated or related twice.

**1595** SHAKS. *John* III. iv. 108 Life is as tedious as a twice-told tale. **1725** POPE *Odyssey* XII. 538 What so tedious as a twice-told tale? **1826** F. REYNOLDS *Life & Times* I. 94, I will now merely state, (to avoid a twice told tale,) that we arrived. **1837** HAWTHORNE (*title*) Twice-Told Tales.

**Twich, twiche,** obs. ff. TOUCH, TOUGH, TWITCH.

**Twicher,** obs. f. TWITCHER.

**Twick** (twik), *v. Obs.* exc. *dial.* Also 5 **twyk** (**twykkyn**). [OE. *twiccian* = OHG. *zwëcchôn* (rare). In ME. almost entirely displaced by the related *twicchen* TWITCH *v.*[1], but still surviving in south-western dial.] *trans.* and *absol.* To pull sharply or suddenly; to twitch.

*a* **1000** *Lat. & Ags. Gloss.* in Wr.-Wülcker 199/38 *Carpere, arripere*, twiccian. *c* **1000** *Sax. Leechd.* II. 196/13 Teoh him þa loccas & wringe þa earan & þone wangbeard twiccige. *c* **1000** *Malchus* in *Shrine* (Cockayne) 41 þa gesaeh ic micelne æmettena heap..& sume hio twiccedan þa grasu mid hiora muðe. *c* **1440** *Promp. Parv.* 505/1 Twykkyn, or sum-what drawyn (*K.* twychyn), *tractulo*. *c* **1440** *Pallad. on Husb.* VI. 26 Whil that me may..With fyngres lightly twyk hem [leaves] from the tre. **1825** JENNINGS *Obs. Dial. W. Eng.* 78 *To Twick*, to twist or jerk suddenly. **1837–91** in Somerset and Devon glossaries.

**Twiddle** (twi·d'l), *sb.* [f. TWIDDLE *v.*[1]] An act of twiddling; a twirl or twist; also, a curl, a twirled mark or sign. (In quot. 1774, applied to a 'grace' in music.)

**1774** T. TWINING in *Recreat. & Stud.* (1882) 30 Purcell, with all his old curls and twiddles, is perfection to him. **1849** THACKERAY *Dinners* Wks. 1901 VI. 646 The coaxing twiddle which they give to the ties of their white chokers. **1893** *Spectator* 28 Jan. 101/2, 'e' for 'æ' is just as much a contraction as 'r' with a twiddle for 'rum'. **1903** *Daily Chron.* 11 Dec. 7/2 A curious-looking diagram..with a few spots or twiddles on the light part of it.

**Twiddle** (twi·d'l), *v.*[1] Also 6 **twydle**, 9 **tweedle.** [App. onomatopœic, intended to combine the idea of *twirl* or *twist* with that of trifling action, as in *fiddle, piddle*. Both verb and sb. (see prec.) are very rare before the 19th c.]

**1.** *intr.* To be busy about trifles; to trifle; also *to twiddle with* or *at* = sense 2.

*c* **1540** J. REDFORD *Mor. Play Wit & Sc.* (Shaks. Soc.) 18 As for her syngyng, pypyng, and fydlyng, What unthryftynes therin is twydlyng? *a* **1825** FORBY *Voc. E. Anglia*, *Twiddle*,..to be busy and bestow seeming pains about the merest trifles..'What are you twiddling about there?' **1848** THACKERAY *Van. Fair* xxxii, Even in the midst of his terror he began mechanically to twiddle with his hair. **1865** LE FANU *Guy Dev.* ii, The Baronet twiddled at his whisker ..in the glass. **1874** CARPENTER *Ment. Phys.* I. viii. (1879) 373 The hands..may often be seen unconsciously stealing upwards to 'twiddle' with their watch-keys.

**2.** *trans.* To cause to rotate lightly or delicately; to turn (anything) about, esp. with the fingers; to twirl; to play with idly or absently; also, to adjust or bring into some place or condition by twirling or handling lightly.

**1676** WISEMAN *Chirurg. Treat.* III. ii. 220 With my fingers upon the Stupe I pressed close upon it, and twiddled it in first one side, then the other. **1814** L. HUNT *Feast of Poets* 6 He fell twiddling a sunbeam as I may my pen. **1824** BEDDOES *Let.* Feb., in *Poems* (1851) p. xxx, The sign of a fellow tweedling a mask in his fingers. **1840** MRS. F. TROLLOPE *Widow Married* xiv, The quilling of her tulle.. twiddling it into becoming shape. **1851** D. JERROLD *St. Giles* xvii. 182 He twiddled the reins between his fingers. **1860** THACKERAY *Round. Papers, Tunbridge Toys* 62, I.. amused myself with twiddling round the moveable calendar. **1886** G. ALLEN *Maimie's Sake* xii, With one hand twiddling his watch-chain nervously.

**b.** *fig.* To twist, twirl, in various senses. Also *Sc.*, to diddle or do (one) *out of* something.

**1825** JAMIESON s.v., 'He tried to twiddle me out of my money.' **1885** *Times* 12 Dec. 5 After being twiddled between the thumbs of two Conferences. **1891** *Sheffield Gloss.* Supp. s.v. *Tweedle*, 'I can tweedle him round my thumb.' **1898** *Daily News* 11 Nov. 3/4 They can twiddle the facts about so that you don't know where you are. **1901** 'R. CONNOR' *Man fr. Glengarry* xi, Bella just twiddled her father round her finger.

**c.** *To twiddle one's thumbs*, or *fingers*, to keep turning them idly around each other; *fig.* to have nothing to do, to be idle.

**1846** D. JERROLD *Mrs. Caudle* xxii, You'd have all the world do nothing half its time but twiddle its thumbs. **1849** CUPPLES *Green Hand* ii, The..cotton-grower twiddled his thumbs and looked modestly down on the deck. **1883** STEVENSON *Lett.* (1901) I. vi. 284, I have to twiddle my fingers and play patience. **1904** *Times* 15 June 4/1 We didn't twiddle our thumbs much that week.

**3.** *intr.* To move in a twirling manner; to turn about in a light or trifling way.

**1812** W. TENNANT *Anster F.* IV. lv, Five hundred fingers ..Play twiddling up and down on hole and bore. **1844** THACKERAY *Contrib. to Punch* Wks. 1901 VI. 56 A few wretched little vessels are twiddling up and down. **1848** — *Bk. Snobs* xxiv, She..made a majestic curtesy, during which all the bugles in her awful head-dress began to twiddle and quiver. **1876** SMILES *Sc. Natur.* xiii. (ed. 4) 261 Away went the bird, twiddling and straddling. **1887** *Suppl. to Jamieson*, *Tweedle*, to work in a trifling, careless, or slovenly manner. **1907** MRS. FR. CAMPBELL *Sheph. of Stars* 146 [The donkey's] very ears twiddled with laughter.

Hence **Twi·ddling** *ppl. a.*, that twiddles; twirling; also, trifling, paltry; also **Twi·ddler**, one who or that which twiddles; in quot. 1904, a twirling delivery of the ball at Cricket, a 'twister'; **Twi·ddly** *a.*, characterized by twiddling.

**1844** THACKERAY *Little Trav.* i, A lady in a little twiddling Parisian hat and feather. **1848** Mustachio-twiddler [see MUSTACHIO 3]. **1851** J. COLQUHOUN *Moor & Loch* (1880) I. 70 There is..the uncertainty whether the next point may be the red, or the 'jetty, heath-cock', or whether a twiddling snipe may spring. **1862** H. MARRYAT *Year in Sweden* I. 81 The wishiwashy lady with little twiddling curls round her face. **1862** G. MEREDITH *Modern Love* xxxiv, Time leers between, above his twiddling thumbs. **1904** *Daily Chron.* 29 June 4/1 Reputable batsmen going out to Jephson's twiddlers. **1906** *Westm. Gaz.* 19 Apr. 4/2 In your cradle safely nestling,..All your twiddly fingers wrestling With the toe-toes on your feet.

**Twi·ddle**, *v.*[2] [Imitative, or modification of TWEEDLE *v.* after prec.] *intr.* To twitter or warble; to play triflingly on an instrument; to talk in a trifling or inept manner.

**1863** J. R. WISE *New Forest* App. I. 287/2 The robins are twiddling,..which fact is said to be a sign of rain. **1873** C. KEENE *Let.* in G. S. Layard *Life* vii. (1892) 150 You have the great advantage of having already twiddled on the flute. **1893** *Nat. Observer* 4 Mar. 386/2 The mob that twiddles of Ibsen will to-morrow shout of the morals of sculpture.

**Twi·ddle-twa·ddle.** [Reduplication of TWADDLE *sb.*: cf. TWITTLE-TWATTLE.] Mere twaddle or foolish chatter. Also *attrib.*

**1798** CHARLOTTE SMITH *Yng. Philos.* I. 164 Then my Aunt will come with her tendernesses, and her tears, and twiddle twaddle ways of dear niecing and sweet girling me. **1868** J. GREENWOOD in *Morn. Star* 8 June, His schoolmaster.. gave him to learn twiddle-twaddle rubbish, without the least flavour in it! **1886** *Pall Mall G.* 31 Aug. 11/2 Mann ..reserved the hottest passages of his fiery speech for denunciations of the 'twiddle-twaddle of trade unionism'.

**Twiddling** (twi·dliŋ), *vbl. sb.* [f. TWIDDLE *v.*[1] + -ING[1].] The action of the verb TWIDDLE; twirling; trifling.

*Twiddling line* (*Naut.*), a light line formerly used to steady or secure the wheel; now, a line attached to the compass-box, by which the card may be jerked free when caught.

**1847** THACKERAY *Sk. Lond.* (1891) 166 A chin-tuft is a cheap enjoyment.., and the twiddling it about..a harmless amusement. **1867** SMYTH *Sailor's Word-bk.*, *Twiddling-line*, a piece of small rope ornamentally fitted and used for steadying the steering-wheel when required: no longer used. **1882** NARES *Seamanship* (ed. 6) 195 The rudder.. must be secured..with the twiddling lines. **1890** *Daily News* 3 Nov. 3/1 Jerry builders and draughtsmen, with their mindless twiddlings in stone and brick. **1906** *Spectator* 6 Jan. 10/2 That dance..interspersed with meaningless bowings, scrapings, and twiddlings in odd corners.

† **Twiddling string.** *Obs. rare*⁻¹. Cf. *twattling string*, TWATTLING *ppl. a.* 2.

**1594** GREENE & LODGE *Looking-gl.* I. iii, For indeed, sir, she is a woman that hath her twidling strings broke.

† **Twie, twye,** *adv. Obs.* Forms: 1 **twiʒea, twiʒa** (**tuiʒa, -ʒo**), **twia,** 1–2 **twiʒe,** 3 **tuye, tweiʒe, tueie, twi,** 3–5 **twie,** 4 **twiʒe, twyʒe, tueye, tuey, twy,** 4–5 **tweye,** 5 **twey, twye.** β. 2 **twiʒen,** 3 **twien, tweien.** [OE. *twiʒa*, etc. (also *twiwa, tuwa*, etc.) = OFris. *twia, tuiia*, OS. *tuuio* (MLG. *twie, twige*), adv. f. stem *twi-*, TWI-: cf. the etym. note to THRIE, THRYE *adv.*] = TWICE.

*a* **900** tr. *Bæda's Eccl. Hist.* IV. iv. 278 (Tanner MS.), þætte twiʒea on ʒere seonoð ʒesomnode. *c* **950** *Lindisf. Gosp.* Lk. xviii. 12 Ic fæsto tuiʒo [*Rushw.* twiʒe] in wico. *c* **1000** *Sax. Leechd.* I. 320 Eac, ys..sæd, þæt heo on ʒeare twiʒea blowe. *c* **1050** *Byrhtferth's Handboc* in *Anglia* (1885) VIII. 303 Twia seofon beoð feowertyne. *c* **1160** *Hatton Gosp.* Mk. xiv. 72 Ær se coc creowe twiʒe. *a* **1225** *Ancr. R.* 34 And so al þene psalm vt, mid Gloria Patri, ..twie. *c* **1275** LAY. 8325 Twi þou hauest beon ouer-come. **1297** R. GLOUC. (Rolls) 4556 King arþure was anguisous.. þat þe luþer traytour adde ofscaped so tuye [*v. rr.* twyʒe, tweye]. *Ibid.* 6646 Is [= his] stepmoder..þat quene adde ybe tueie [*v.r.* twyʒe]. *a* **1325** *Adam & Eve* 272 in Horstm. *Altengl. Leg.* (1878) 142 Now he haþ ygiled þe tvie. *c* **1375** *Cursor M.* 13627 (Fairf.) Quy quarto sulde I tel ʒou mare Twy or thry I talde ʒou are. *a* **1450** MYRC *Par. Pr.* 119 Folowe thow not þe chylde twye.

β. *c* **1175** *Lamb. Hom.* 37 Mon scal beon twiʒen awesscen of his sunne. *c* **1205** LAY. 8325 Twien [*c* 1275 Twi] þu hafuest ibeon ouer-cummen.

**Twies,** obs. form of TWICE.

† **Twifa·llow, twy-,** *v. Obs.* [f. TWI- + FALLOW *v.*[2]] *trans.* To fallow twice; to fallow a second time; to plough up (land) a second time in the course of its lying fallow. Hence † **Twifallowing** *vbl. sb.*; also **Twifallow** *sb.*

**1557** TUSSER *100 Points Husb.* lxxviii, In May at the furdest, twy fallow thy lande. **1573** — *Husb.* (1878) 114 Twifallow once ended, get tumbrell and man, And compas that fallow as soone as ye can. **1577** B. GOOGE *Heresbach's Husb.* I. (1586) 22 b, For some seede, you must not only twyfallowe and threefallowe your ground, but also fourefallow it. **1610** FOLKINGHAM *Art of Survey* I. xi. 43 Orders and seasons for fallowing, twifallowing, trifallowing and seed-furre. **1707** MORTIMER *Husb.* (1721) I. 155 The Land being fallowed in May, must be twy-fallowed in June. **1725** *Bradley's Fam. Dict.* s.v. *Plough*, The Times of the second plowing is about June, it bears the Name of Twy-fallowing. *Ibid.* s.v. *Barley*, Some at the Time of Twy-fallowing in June make the Land very fine. **1733** MILLER *Gard. Dict.* s.v. *Rapa*, The Land ..should be ploughed in May, and twy-fallow'd in June. **1890** *Glouc. Gloss.*, *Twy-fallow*, the second ploughing.

**Twifold, twyfold** (twəi·fōuld), *a.* and *adv. arch.* Forms: 1 **twyfeald** (**twiefeald, -fald, twiʒfeald, tweofeald**), 1–3 **twifeald,** 3 **twifald, -feld,** 4–5 **tweyfold(e,** 5–6 **twifolde,** 3– **twifold,** 5– **twyfold,** 7, 9 **twy-fold.** [OE. *twifeald, twyfeald*: = OFris. *twifald*, OHG. *zwifalt* (MHG. *zwivalt*), ON. *tvífaldr* (Norw. dial. *tvifald*): see TWI- and -FOLD, and cf. TWOFOLD.]

**A.** *adj.*

**1.** Twofold, double.

*c* **890** tr. *Bæda's Hist.* I. x. [xiii.] (1890) 48 Betwih him twam we þus tweofealdne deað þrowiað, oððe sticode beoð oððe on sæ adruncene. *c* **897** K. ÆLFRED *Gregory's Past. C.* xxxv. 238 Hu hefiʒ ðæt twyfealde [*v.r.* twiefalde] ʒeswinc bið. *c* **1200** ORMIN 4997 þatt fulle lufe..birrþ ben..Twifald ..; Forr þe birrþ lufenn Godd & mann. *c* **1220** *Bestiary* 424 in *O. E. Misc.* 14 Twifold forbisne in ðis der..we muʒen finden her. **1583** MELBANCKE *Philotimus* Q j, Her twifolde murther committed on her selfe and Telamon. **1623** LISLE *Ælfric on O. & N. Test.* Gen. B j, Adam..begat of his wife a twifold race of children. **1812** CARY *Dante, Purg.* XXXI. 122 Within those orbs the twyfold being shone. **1912** *Eng. Rev.* Apr. 1 Queen of the Shadows, Maid and Wife, Twifold in essence, as in life.

† **2.** *fig.* **a.** Double-dealing, deceitful, insincere: = DOUBLE *a.* 5. **b.** Double-minded, irresolute. *Obs.*

*c* **897** K. ÆLFRED *Gregory's Past. C.* xxxv. 244 Hwæt tacniað ðonne ða hean hwammas buton unclænu & twyfeald [*v.r.* twiefeald] mod? *c* **1200** *Vices & Virt.* 15 Bute he bie rihtwis and naht twifeald. *c* **1200** *Trin. Coll. Hom.* 187 Ðe twifealde man is unstedefast on alle his spechen, twifold oðer manifold is þe man þe nis stedefast.

**B.** *adv.*

**1.** In two parts or divisions; (folded) double.

**1591** PERCIVALL *Sp. Dict.*, *Doblegar* to double, to bend twifold.

**2.** In two ways or respects, doubly.

*a* **1619** FLETCHER, etc. *Q. Corinth* IV. i, Your T beard.. twifold doth express the enamour'd Courtier.

**Twifold,** *v. rare. arch.* [f. TWI- + FOLD *v.*[1]; cf. OE. *twifildan* to double.] *trans.* To fold in two; to bend double.

1875 MORRIS *Æneid* XII. 927 Then falleth..Turnus with his hampered knee twifolded with the wound.

¶ *trans.* and *intr.* [perh. f. TWIFOLD *a.*] (Sense uncertain; rendering L. *distinguere*, itself app. a mistranslation, in two passages of the Vulgate.) *Obs.*

*a* 1300 *E. E. Psalter* lxv[i]. 14 Mi hotes..Whilk twi-falded mi lippes. *Ibid.* cv[i]. 33 For þai gremed gast of him swa, And he twi-falded [*v.r.* twifolded] in his lippes.

† **Twifoldly**, *adv. Obs.* [OE. *twyfealdlice*, f. *twifeald*, TWIFOLD *a.* + *-lice*, -LY [2].] Twofold, doubly, to twice the amount.

*c* 1000 *Ags. Gosp.* Matt. xxiii. 15 Ȝe ȝedoð hyne helle bearn twyfealdlicor þonne eow. *c* 1000 ÆLFRIC *Exod.* xvi. 22 On þam sixtum dæȝe hiȝ gaderodon twyfealdlice. *c* 1200 *Trin. Coll. Hom.* 169 Ure drihten ȝiald twifoldliche iob, þat þe deuel him hadde binumen.

**Twig** (twig), *sb.*[1] Forms: 1–2, 4–7 twigge (1 tuigge, tuicg-), 4–6 twyggə (4 *pl.* tuygges, tuyeggəs); 2, 4 twige, 4 tvige, 6 twike; 4–5 tuyg, 4–6 twyg, 6–7 twygg, 5– twig (6 *Sc.* tuig, 7 twigg). [Northern OE. *twigge* fem. (pl. *twiggo*), obscurely related to OE. *twig* neut. (pl. *twigu*), later also *twi*. Neither *twigge* nor *twig* correspond exactly to the usual Continental forms having the same sense, viz. WFris. *twiich*, *twige* (NFris. *twich*), Du. *twijg* (Kilian *twijgh*), MLG. *twîch* (LG. *twîg*), OHG. *zwîg* (MHG. *zwîg-*, *zwîc*, G. *zweig*), but the Da. dial. forms *tveg*, *tvege*, may be more closely akin to *twigge* or to the ME. variant *twige*. All the types appear to be variant formations from the stem TWI-.]

**1.** A slender shoot issuing from a branch or stem.

*c* 950 *Lindisf. Gosp.* Mk. xi. 8 Oðero..ða twiggo *vel* ða telȝo..rendon of ðæm trewum. *Ibid.* xiii. 28 Mið-ðy..telȝe *vel* twigge his..nesc bið. *c* 1175 *Lamb. Hom.* 5 Heo stiȝen uppe on þe godes cunnes treowe & nomen þa twigga & þa blostme. *Ibid.* 149 Hwenne he..for his sunne swingeð him mid smele twige. 13.. *Guy Warw.* (A.) 2542 Wiþ þat come Gij.., a smal tvige in his hond bereinde Of oliue. 1340 [see b]. *c* 1384 CHAUCER *H. Fame* III. 846 Al thys hous..Was made of twigges [*v.rr.* twygges, twigys] falwe, rede, And grene eke. 1398 TREVISA *Barth. De P. R.* XVII. i. (Bodl. MS.) A tre haþ..outeward..þerinde twigges leues blossomes and fruyte. 1415 HOCCLEVE *To Sir J. Oldcastle* 471 A smal twig or rod. 1509 BARCLAY *Shyp of Folys* (1570) 13 A little twigge plyaunt is by kinde, A bigger branche is harde to bowe or winde. *a* 1552 LELAND *Itin.* (1711) V. 75 Hole Trees..without Twike or Bow. 1596 DALRYMPLE tr. *Leslie's Hist. Scot.* (S.T.S.) I. 39 Capercalȝe..lyues of only the tuigs or tendir branches of this [fir] trie. 1637 J. TAYLOR (Water P.) *Drinke & Welcome* D j b, My Muse doth..likea Squirrell skip, from twigge to twigge. 1732 POPE *Ep. Cobham* 150 Just as the Twig is bent, the Tree's inclin'd. 1784 COWPER *Task* I. 484 These..love life, and cling to it, as he That overhangs a torrent, to a twig. 1851 CARPENTER *Man. Phys.* (ed. 2) 107 Fibrine..may be obtained..by whipping fresh blood with a bundle of twigs. 1906 *Times, Lit. Supp.* 23 Mar. 99/2 The snap of a twig..gave the alarm.

**b.** *transf.* and *fig.*, and in fig. context.

*To hop the twig* (slang): see HOP *v.* 6 a.

*c* 950 *Lindisf. Gosp.* John xv. 5 Ic am þe wintreo, ȝie ða tuiggo [L. *palmites*] sint. 1340 *Ayenb.* 22 Þe uerþe tuyg of þe ilke boȝe [of pride]..is yelpingge. *Ibid.* 41 Þe zixte boȝ of auarice is symonye..And þes boȝ heþ manie tuygges. *c* 1386 CHAUCER *Pars. T.* ¶ 315 Euerich of thise chief synnes hath hise braunches and hise twigges. 1535 COVERDALE *Isa.* ix. 14 The Lorde shal rote out of Israel both heade and tale, braunch and twygge in one daye. 1553 *Respublica* I. iii. 339 *Adul.* Doe but whistle for me, and I comme foorth with-all. *Avar.*..I love suche a towarde twygg. *a* 1623 FLETCHER *Love's Cure* II. ii, Traiterous brat,..impious twig Of that old stock, dew'd with my kinsman's gore. 1678 in *Trial E. Coleman* 100 They would not you should have any Twigg to hold by to deceive you. 1764 LD. HALIFAX *Let.* 11 Mar., in *10th Rep. Hist. MSS. Comm.* App. I. 363, I was willing to keep Hold of any Twig of Hope that was left me. 1827 G. HIGGINS *Celtic Druids* 24 [The Irish] characters were called twigs and branch-letters..from their shape.

† **c.** *collect.* as the material for basket-making. *Obs. rare.*

*c* 1440 *Pallad. on Husb.* III. 209 Let make a skeppe of twygge. 1661 *Rec. Basketmakers Co.* (1911) 114 Paid an officer for seizing 10,000 of twigg at Bull Wharfe. 00. 05. 00.

**2.** *spec.* **a.** Short for LIME-TWIG (*obs.*); also, in *pl.*, the twigs forming a birch-rod.

1601 SHAKS. *All's Well* III. vi. 115, I must go looke my twigges, He shall be caught. [1603 — *Meas. for M.* I. iii. 24 Fond Fathers, Hauing bound vp the threatning twigs of birch, Onely to sticke it in their childrens sight, For terror, not to vse.] 1622 BP. HALL *Contempl.*, *O. T.* XVII. iii, Wise Salomon..laies insensible twigs for so foule an offender. 1736 *Gentl. Mag.* Nov. 679/2 Ye awful twigs!..Long may ye..far from my posteriors keep your sway! 1896 MAX PEMBERTON *Purit. Wife* iii, I had smarted often at the switch of his twigs.

**b.** *dial.* (*a*) A stout stick. (*b*) A divining-rod (cf. ROD *sb.*[1] 3 c). *To work the twig*, to use the divining-rod.

1842 B. BRIERLEY *Lanc. Tales & Sk.* 87 [He] could not see that his 'twig' would stand any chance against a bayonet. 18.. in T. Allan *Tyneside Songs* (1872) 201 Aw danced a jig an' swung my twig. 1883 *Folk-Lore Jrnl.* I. 28 At one spot the 'twig' was so violently affected that it flew out of his hands. 1883 A. LANG *Custom & Myth* (1884) 180 'To work the twig' is rural English for the craft of Dousterswivel in the *Antiquary*. 1894 [see DOWSE *v.*].

**3.** *transf. Anat.* A small ramification of a blood-vessel or nerve.

1683 A. SNAPE *Anat. Horse* I. ix. (1686) 18 The Stomachal Arteries are twigs from the Coeliacal branch of the *Arteria magna*. *Ibid.* xvi. 33 A Twig of the Splenic Artery opens into this Vein. 1691 RAY *Creation* II. (1692) 14 Particular Branches send forth some twigs to the neighbouring Muscles. 1741 MONRO *Anat. Nerves* (ed. 3) 80 A Twig of the Ophthalmick Branch of the fifth Pair of Nerves. 1831 R. KNOX *Cloquet's Anat.* 684 This artery gives numerous twigs to the pectoralis major. 1875 HUXLEY in *Encycl. Brit.* I. 766/1 The pulmonary artery gives twigs to the stomach.

**4.** *Pottery.* 'A thin strip of plastic clay used in modelling a pottery vessel, especially in the imitation basketwork common in Leeds pottery' (*Cent. Dict.* 1891).

**5.** *attrib.* and *Comb.* **a.** attrib. (usually = 'made of twigs'), as *twig-basket*, *-broom*, *charcoal*, *corf*, *-cutter*, †*head* (? HEAD *sb.* 5), *-hurdle*, *ware*. **b.** instrumental, similative, etc., as *twig-formed*, *-green*, *-like*, *-limed*, *-strewn*, *-suspended*, *-wrought*, adjs. **c.** Spec. Comb.: **twig-ait**: see quot.; **twig-beetle**, **-borer** (*U.S.*), names for various small beetles which bore into the twigs of trees (*Cent. Dict.* & *Supp.* 1891–1909); **twig-blight** (*U.S.*), a disease of the apple and quince, caused by *Micrococcus amylovorus*: see *pear-blight* a, PEAR *sb.* 5 (*Cent. Dict.* 1889); †**twig-bottle**, a bottle with a wicker envelope; **twig-bug** (*U.S.*) = *twig insect*; **twig-climber**: see quot.; **twig-gall**, an abnormal enlargement of a twig, due to the action of insects, fungi, or bacteria; **twig-girdler** (*U.S.*), an American beetle, *Oncideres cingulatus*, which deposits its eggs in the tips of twigs, which it then girdles below the eggs (*Cent. Dict.* 1891); **twig insect**, the stick-insect or 'walking-stick'; **twig-pruner** (*U.S.*), an American beetle of the genus *Elaphidion*, which burrows in twigs of oak and hickory (*Cent. Dict.*); **twig-rune**, a runic inscription with characters of twig-like form; **twig-rush**, a tall marsh-plant, *Cladium Mariscus*, N.O. *Cyperaceæ*, having very long narrow rigid leaves.

1867 SMYTH *Sailor's Word-bk.*, *Twig-ait, a river island where osiers grow. 1748 tr. *Vegetius' Distemp. Horses* 173 A close-wrought *Twig-basket must be put upon him. 1695 *Lond. Gaz.* No. 3085/3 Captain Bonnamy..took a French Ship of 40 Tuns, laden with Burstones and *Twig Bottles. 1863 HAWTHORNE *Our Old Home* (1879) 187 *Twig-brooms, beehives,..things that are commonly sold at a rural fair. 1895 *Westm. Gaz.* 31 Aug. 3/2 These latter doors are over a foot in thickness, each bearing a lining of twelve inches of '*twig charcoal'. 1900 B. D. JACKSON *Gloss. Bot. Terms*, **Twig Climbers*, Schenck's term for certain Brazilian lianes, the young leafy lateral branches being sensitive..in contact with their supports. 1797 J. CURR *Coal Viewer* 8 The basket or *twig corf..cannot..be introduced in the southern parts. 1911 *Contemp. Rev.*, *Lit. Suppl.* June 9 The chisel, the gouge..the sickle, the *twig-cutter, the scythe. 1806 J. GRAHAME *Birds Scot.*, etc. 75 The Raven's *twig-formed house. 1900 B. D. JACKSON *Gloss. Bot. Terms*, **Twig-Gall*, a morbid growth ascribed to the action of bacteria. 1892 *Daily News* 17 Dec. 5/7 The material is *twig-green velvet shot with gold. 1572 in Feuillerat *Revels Q. Eliz.* (1908) 156 Strigges of bay Leaves for *twig heades. 1726 S. LOWE *Lat. Gram.* Suppl. 15 *Gerrae*, *twig-hurdles, gabions. 1882 A. WILSON in *Nature Stud.* 37 The so-called 'stick insects', or 'walking twigs', ..the *Phasmidæ* of the naturalist...The bodies of these '*twig insects'..are represented by mere lines. 1898 *Pop. Sc. Monthly* LIII. 762 Curious plants with *twiglike leaves seem..provided against too great loss by transpiration. 1905 *Westm. Gaz.* 23 June 4/1 The twig-like attitudes assumed by some caterpillars and other insects. 1657 BILLINGSLY *Brachy-Martyrol.* xvi. 55 A third Is taken captive like a *twiglim'd bird. 1868 G. STEPHENS *Runic Mon.* I. 84 *Twig-runes occur on both Old-Northern and Scandinavian..runic monuments. 1836 J. T. MACKAY *Flora Hibern.* I. 324 *Cladium Mariscus*, Br. Prickly *Twig-rush. 1848 C. A. JOHNS *Week at Lizard* 311 *Cladium Mariscus*, Twig-rush, abounds in the higher parts of the stream. 1900 *Blackw. Mag.* Mar. 392/1 Bare and *twig-strewn circles in which the argus-pheasants strut. 1826 KIRBY & SP. *Entomol.* III. xxix. 96 The eggs of the tailor bird in its *twig-suspended nest. 1829 S. SHAW *Stafford. Potteries* vii. 173 A Lady's work-basket, which he was led to consider..as *twig or willow ware, and was..surprised, to find it of cane coloured pottery. 1855 SINGLETON *Virgil* I. 80 Celeus' furniture, *twig-wrought And mean.

Hence **Twi·gless** *a.*, destitute of twigs; **Twi·glet, -ling**, a little twig; **Twi·gsome** *a.*, twiggy.

1839 *Fraser's Mag.* XX. 345 A birch-tree, entirely boughless, branchless, and twigless. 1849 J. A. CARLYLE tr. *Dante's Inferno* 146 If thou breakest off any twiglet from one of these plants. 1860 DICKENS in *All Year Round* No. 50. 558 The twigsome trees by the wayside (which, I suppose, never will grow leafy, for they never did). 1882 *Garden* 18 Mar. 181/2 Slender twiglets of this semi-weeping Spruce. 1907 *Westm. Gaz* 19 Oct. 6/1 As pliant twigling to the rigid oak.

**Twig**, *sb.*[2] Now *dial.* [f. TWIG *v.*[3] 2.] A pull; a twitch; a tug; a draught.

*a* 1800 *Laird of Wariston* vi. in Child *Ballads* VII. (1890) 31/2 The nurice she knet the knot,..The lady did gie it a twig, Till it began to wicker. 1808 JAMIESON, *Twig*, a quick pull, a twitch. 1818 *Naval Chron.* XXXIX. 65 He was taken in tow by *A Friend*,..which twig to windward..will..enable him to round the Cape. 1825 J. NEAL *Bro. Jonathan* I. 54 A 'twig o' cider' a piece.

**Twig**, *sb.*[3] *slang.* ? *Obs.* [Origin unascertained.] Style, fashion; also condition, state, fettle; esp. in the phrases *in* (*prime*, *good*) *twig*. **b.** *Out of twig* [cf. TWIG *v.*[4]], out of knowledge or recognition: see quot. 1812.

1811 *Lexicon Balatr.* s. v., *In twig*, handsome; stilish. The cove is togged in twig; the fellow is dressed in the fashion. 1812 J. H. VAUX *Flash Dict.* s.v., Any thing accomplished cleverly, or as it should be, is said to be done in twig, in good twig, or in prime twig. *Ibid.*, *Out of twig*, to put yourself out of twig is to disguise your dress and appearance, to avoid being recognised..; a man reduced by poverty to wear a shabby dress is said by his acquaintance to be out of twig; to put any article out of twig, as a stolen coat, cloak, &c. is to alter it in such a way that it cannot be identified. 1828 *Sporting Mag.* XXII. 77 Palemon was not in the twig I should like to see a horse of mine if about to start for such a stake. 1834 H. AINSWORTH *Rookwood* III. v, With my strummel faked in the newest twig. 1840 DICKENS *Barn. Rudge* xi, You're in twig to-night I see. 1842 S. LOVER *Handy Andy* xvii, Going to the ball in proper twig.

**Twig**, *v.*[1] *Obs.* or *dial.* [f. TWIG *sb.*[1]]

**1.** *trans.* To beat with or as with a twig; *fig.* to reprove. ? *Obs.*

1550 BALE *Apol.* 142 Not one kynge hath bene in Englande sens the conquest, but they haue twygged hym one way or other, and had theyr false flynges at him. 1553 *Respublica* V. viii. 1630 *Insol.* I will whippe youe for this, ye peasaunte lowte. *Adul.* And twygge youe. 1570 LEVINS *Manip.* 119/4 To Twig, *verberare*. *a* 1825 FORBY *Voc. E. Anglia*, *Twig*, to give such..correction as may be inflicted with a twig...To give somewhat sharp, but not angry and severe reproof. 1826 MOORE *Mem.* (1854) V. 118 Only for my knowing Lord Holland (said Southey) I would have twigged him for that.

† **2.** To trim, prune (a tree). *Obs. rare.*

1570 LEVINS *Manip.* 119/5 To Twygge, *putare viburna*.

† **3.** To bind with twigs or withes. *Obs. rare.*

1688 R. HOLME *Armoury* III. 108/1 Twigging a Hoop [of a barrel], is binding the two ends together with cloven Twiggs of Withy, or Osier Twiggs.

**Twig**, *v.*[2] *Obs.* or *dial.* [Of obscure origin: cf. next.] *intr.* To do anything vigorously or strenuously. Hence **Twi·gging** *vbl. sb.* and *ppl. a.*

1573 TWYNE *Æneid* XI. I i iv b, Lyke a fawcon that..at a twyggynge doue vnto the cloudes swyft winge doth make. *Ibid.* XII. Ll iij, The bird of mightie Ioue..a shole of foules she did pursue And twigginge forth apace fast on her flight the Egle flue. 1573 TUSSER *Husb.* (1878) 81 The lamb of such twinners for breeders go take, For twinlings be twiggers, encrease for to bring, Though som for their twigging Peccantem may sing. 1828 *Craven Gloss.*, *Twig*,..to do any thing strenuously, to work with might and main.

**Twig**, *v.*[3] Now *dial.* [Of obscure origin; perh. merely an imitative word of the same type as TWICK, *tweag* TWEAK, and TUG.]

† **1.** *trans.* See quot. *Obs. slang.*

1725 *New Cant. Dict.*, *To Twig*, to disingage, to sunder, to snap, to break off. *To twig the Darbies*, to knock off the Irons.

**2.** To pull, pluck, twitch.

1755 J. SHEBBEARE *Lydia* (1769) II. 49 Write,..or Frank shall twig your nose from your face. 1790 D. MORISON *Poems* 78 Let rantin billys twig the string, An' for the tither mutchkin ring. 1864 *Reader* 23 Jan. 105 To stretch strings on pegs and to twig them with thumb or with plectrum was one of the earliest of human amusements. 1867 SMYTH *Sailor's Work-bk.*, *Twig*, *to*, to pull upon a bowline.

Hence **Twi·gging** *ppl. a.*

1864 *Reader* 23 Jan. 105 The genus stringed-instrument consists of three species, which may be defined, to use the vernacular, as the twigging, the hammering, and the scraping.

**Twig**, *v.*[4] *slang* or *colloq.* [Origin unascertained.]

**1.** *trans.* **a.** To watch; to look at; to inspect.

1764 FOOTE *Mayor of G.* II. Wks. 1799 I. 180 Now, twig him; now, mind him: mark how he hawls his muscles about. 1824 SCOTT *St. Ronan's* iv, 'Twig the old connoisseur', said the squire to the knight. 1837 DICKENS *Pickw.* xx, 'They're a twiggin' of you, sir', whispered Mr. Weller. 1841 J. T. HEWLETT *Parish Clerk* I. 173 Oblige me by twigging that trio. 1876 A. J. EVANS *Through Bosnia* iii. 89 A motley assemblage..'twigged us' at their leisure.

**b.** To become aware of by seeing; to perceive, discern, catch sight of; to recognize.

1796 J. G. HOLMAN *Abroad & at Home* III. ii, He twigs me. He knows Dicky here in his real and masquerade character both. 1801 M. G. LEWIS *Tales Wonder*, *Sailor's T.* ii, With strange surprise and fear, Jack Tackle's ghost I twigg'd. 1825 LADY GRANVILLE *Lett.* 30 Jan. (1894) I. 339 They have twigged me. 1860 *Hunting Grounds Old World* Ser. I. xii. (ed. 2) 189 The leader, whom at last I twigged lying down and chewing the cud. 1879 F. POLLOK *Sport Brit. Burmah* I. 191, I twigged the tigress creeping away in front of us.

**2.** *fig.* To understand, comprehend.

1815 *Zeluca* III. 144 You twig me—eh? 1821 LADY GRANVILLE *Lett.* (1894) I. 208 York roared again [at the jokes], Clarence was dull and did not twig them. 1852 R. S. SURTEES *Sponge's Sp. Tour* xxvii. 166, I twigged what you were after, and kept him up in talk. 1897 'TIVOLI' (H. W. Bleakley) *Short Innings* ix, Make a howler or two, or else he'll twig you've cribbed.

**b.** *intr.*

1833 M. SCOTT *Tom Cringle* xiii. (1859) 311 The Captain twigged and smiled. 1845 DISRAELI *Sybil* III. x, 'I twig', said Mick. 1893 LELAND *Mem.* I. 197, I twig; it's all right; I'll keep your secret.

**Twigged** (twigd), *a.* [f. TWIG *sb.*[1] or *v.*[1]]

**1.** Furnished with or bearing twigs.

1640 PARKINSON *Theatr. Bot.* 483 Hard and hoary twigged stalks. 1725 *Family Dict.*, *Ivy*,..a Shrub or Tree whose twigged Branches raise and extend themselves by creeping and sticking to Walls and Trees.

† **2.** Made of twigs or wickerwork. *Obs. rare*[−1].

1643 *Farington Papers* (Chetham Soc.) 99 One twiged cheare.

**Twiggen** (twi·g'n), *a. arch.* [f. TWIG *sb.*[1] +

-EN.] a. Made of twigs or wickerwork; also, having a wickerwork covering. b. Arising from burning twigs or brushwood.

1549 COVERDALE, etc. *Erasm. Par. Acts* vii. 29 A twiggen basket or hamper. 1588 *Lanc. Wills* (Chetham Soc.) III. 136 A twiggen cheare xijd. 1604 SHAKS. *Oth.* II. iii. 152 Ile beate the Knaue into a Twiggen-Bottle [*Qq.* wicker bottle]. 1681 GREW *Musæum* IV. iii. 372 The Sides and Rim sewed together after the manner of Twiggen-Work. 1747 CARTE *Hist. Eng.* I. 44 Those twiggen machines..filled in every part or member with the miserable wretches destined to be burnt by way of sacrifice. 1826 HOR. SMITH *Tor Hill* (1838) I. 94 What, neighbour Stiles, pawn thy wedding ring to fill the twiggen-bottle! 1875 MORRIS *Æneid* VII. 463 When with a mighty roar the twiggen flame [L. *flamma virgea*] goes up about the hollow side of brass.

† **Twi·gger.** *Obs.* [app. f. TWIG *v.*2 + -ER 1.] A vigorous prolific breeder: orig. said of a ewe; hence *slang*, an unchaste or lascivious person; *esp.* a strumpet, a harlot.

1573 [see TWIG *v.*2]. 1594 MARLOWE & NASHE *Dido* IV. v, Go, you wag! You'll be a twigger when you come to age. *c* 1613 MIDDLETON *No Wit like Wom.* IV. i, The mother of her was a good twigger. 1694 MOTTEUX *Rabelais* V. *Pantagr. Prognost.* v, Those whom Venus is said to Rule, as Punks, Jills, Flirts,..Whipsters, Twiggers, Harlots, Kept-wenches..will be famous this Year.

**Twiggy** (twi·gi), *a.* [f. TWIG *sb.*1 + -Y.]

1. Like a twig; slender, as a shoot or branch; also, † made of twigs or wickerwork (*obs.*).

1562 TURNER *Herbal* II. 40 b, Lithospermon..hath..diuerse twyggy braunches. 1597 GERARDE *Herbal* III. cxxix. 1330 These [trees]..do cast their branches and twiggie tendrels vnto the earth, where they likewise take hold and roote. 1664 EVELYN *Sylva* xix. 42 Oziers..yielding more limber, and flexible twigs for Baskets, Flaskets, Hampers, Chairs, Hurdles, Stages, Bands, &c...; In fine, for all Wicker and Twiggy Works. 1713 J. PETIVER in *Phil. Trans.* XXVIII. 35 This seems to differ..in having more twiggy Branches. 1721 BAILEY, *Wanded Chair*, a Wicker or Twiggy-Chair. 1800 *Misc. Tr.* in *Asiat. Ann. Reg.* 267/2 A slender twiggy climbing plant on the mountains. 1896 G. ALLEN in *Longm. Mag.* Nov. 45 The netted willow..sends up twiggy shoots from a prostrate stem.

2. Full of or abounding in twigs; bushy, shrubby.

1600 SURFLET *Countrie Farme* VII. xxiv. 844 A hart passing through a thick and twiggie woode. 1728 CHAMBERS *Cycl.* s.v. *Root*, *Sarmentous*, i.e. twiggy, or branching. 1881 *Encycl. Brit.* XII. 274/2 For the slender twiggy sorts [of pear-trees] the fan form is to be preferred. 1882 *Garden* 14 Jan. 19/3 Masses of twiggy growth at the bottom.

† **Twight**, obs. variant of QUITE *adv.*

*c* 1400 *Song Roland* 40 Mahoun And margat he will for-sak twight.

† **Twight**, obs. pa. t. and pple. of TWITCH *v.*1

In the following quots. the form appears to be erroneously used for *touched* (pa. t.) and for *touch* or *twitch* (inf.).

1558 PHAER *Æneid* IV. K j b, Whan first the bowres of Affrike land with wingid feete he twight [L. *tetigit*]. 1559 *Mirr. Mag., Collingbourne* xxiv, No bit nor reyne his tender iawes may twight. 1573 TWYNE *Æneid* XI. K k ij b, Arowehead doth twight The bowhand.

**Twight**, obs. form of TWIT *v.*

**Twik**, obs. f. TWICK *v.*; obs. Sc. pa. t. of TAKE *v.*

**Twike**, obs. f. TWIG *sb.*1

**Twile**, obs. form of TWILL *sb.*1

† **Twile**, obs. abbreviation of *it will.*

*a* 1660 *Contemp. Hist. Irel.* (Ir. Archæol. Soc.) I. 274, I beleeue twile be otherwise don.

† **Twi·leke**, var. *twey-leke*: see TWAY 4. *Obs.*

1551 RECORDE *Pathw. Knowl.* I. Def., Further more it may be yt they haue neuer a one syde equall to another, and they be in iij kyndes also distinct lyke the twilekes.

**Twilet, twilight**, obs. ff. TOILET.

**Twilight** (twəi·ləit), *sb.* Forms: 5 **twyliȝt, -lyghte, twye lyghte, 6 twie light, twylyght,** *Sc.* **twa licht, lycht, 6–8 twylight, 6– twilight;** also 6–8 with hyphen. [ME., f. TWI- + LIGHT *sb.*, corresponding to WFris. *twieljocht*, Du. *tweelicht* (from 16th c.), LG. *twilecht*, G. *zwielicht.* The rare form TWILIGHTING is recorded a little earlier. The exact force of *twi-* here is doubtful: cf. in same sense MHG. *zwischenliecht* 'tweenlight', and LG. *twēdustern, twēdunkern*, lit. 'twi-dark'.]

1. The light diffused by the reflection of the sun's rays from the atmosphere before sunrise, and after sunset; the period during which this prevails between daylight and darkness. a. Generally.

*c* 1440 *Promp. Parv.* 505/1 Twylyghte, be-twyx þe day and þe nyghte, or nyghte and þe day, *hesperus.* 1555 EDEN *Decades* 32 At the beginnynge of the euenyng twilight..in the morninge twylight. *a* 1600 HOOKER *2nd Serm. upon Jude* § 33 He must haue darknes for a vision, hee must stumble at noone daies, as at the twi-light. 1617 MORYSON *Itin.* I. 113 It [the grotto of Posilippo] hath no light in the middest, but like twilight,..in the twilight of morning and euening passengers vse torches. 1661 BOYLE *Style of Script.* (1675) 99 Faith and the Twilight seeming to agree in this Property, that a mixture of Darkness is requisite to both. 1698 FRYER *Acc. E. India & P.* 55 There is little or no Twilight, as there is nearer the Poles. 1796 MORSE *Amer. Geog.* I. 52 The twilight is that faint light which opens the morning by little and little in the east, before the sun rises; and gradually shuts in the evening in the west, after the sun is set. 1815 J. SMITH *Panorama Sc. & Art* I. 544 The atmosphere reflecting and refracting the sun's light, forms a twilight at the distance of even 18 degrees.

b. *spec.* Most commonly applied to the evening twilight, from sunset to dark night. *Second twilight*: see quot. 1883.

1412–20 LYDG. *Chron. Troy* I. 2733 In þe twyliȝt whan þe day gan fade. 1509 HAWES *Past. Pleas.* ii. (Percy Soc.) 14 In the fayre twylight, I sate me downe for to rest me all nyght. 1588 A. KING tr. *Canisius' Catech.* i vij, Ye quantitie of ye day brake and twa licht (for ye ane is æquall to ye vther) of euerie day. 1667 MILTON *P. L.* IV. 598 Now came still Eevning on, and Twilight gray Had in her sober Liverie all things clad. *a* 1700 DRYDEN *Cock & Fox* 214 When the sun was down, They just arrived by twilight at a town. 1793–6 COLERIDGE *Lines on Autumnal Evening* 63 When Twilight stole across the fading vale. 1836 W. IRVING *Astoria* xlviii. III. 99 A chasm that looked dark and frightful in the gathering twilight. 1883 *Chambers' Encycl.* IX. 604/1 A curious phenomenon, known as the afterglow, or second twilight, often seen in the Nubian desert, is referred by Sir John Herschel to a second reflection of solar light in the atmosphere.

c. Morning twilight, which lasts from daybreak to sunrise.

*c* 1440 *Promp. Parv.* 505/1 Twye lyghte, be-fore the day, *diluculum.* 1609 DANIEL *Civ. Wars* VIII. xiv, Upon the twi-light of that day..ere they had full light. 1617 MORYSON *Itin.* I. 240 By twilight of the morning we set sayle from Joppa. 1709 STANHOPE *Paraphr.* IV. 349 The Law and the Prophets, like the Glimmerings of the Twi-light, dawned first. 1727–46 THOMSON *Summer* 637 At once the bright-effulgent sun, Rising direct, swift chases from the sky The short-lived twilight. 1845 BROWNING *How they brought the Good News* iii, 'Twas moonset at starting; but while we drew near Lokeren, the cocks crew and twilight dawned clear. 1863 GEO. ELIOT *Romola* ii, [She] was weary after her labour in the morning twilight.

2. *transf.* A dim light resembling twilight; partial illumination.

1667 MILTON *P. L.* I. 597 As when the Sun..In dim Eclips disastrous twilight sheds. 1709 STEELE *Tatler* No. 8 ¶ 6 A Sable Cloud over-shadowed the whole Land...A Twilight began by Degrees to enlighten the Hemisphere. 1768 STERNE *Sent. Journ., Captive*, I..look'd through the twilight of his grated door. 1819 KEATS *Eve St. Agnes* xxix, The faded moon Made a dim, silver twilight. 1858 HAWTHORNE *Fr. & It. Note-Bks.* I. 264 The church..had a grand effect in its tinted twilight. 1872 BLACK *Adv. Phaeton* xxx, The soft green twilight of an avenue of trees.

3. *fig.* a. An intermediate condition or period; a condition before or after full development.

*Twilight of the gods* [transl. of Icel. *ragna rökkr*, altered from the original *ragna rök*, the history or judgement of the gods], in *Scandinavian mythol.* the destruction of the gods and of the world in conflict with the powers of evil.

*c* 1600 SHAKS. *Sonn.* lxxiii, In me thou seest the twi-light of such day, As after Sun-set fadeth in the West. 1679 C. NESSE *Antichrist* 144 As if the twilight of the church in her minority and nonage..exceeded the noon-day of the gospel-church. 1682 DRYDEN *Relig. Laici* Pref., Wks. (Globe) 186 The twilight of Revelation, after the sun of it was set in the race of Noah. 1768 GRAY *Desc. Odin* (note), Lok is the evil Being, who continues in chains till the Twilight of the Gods approaches. 1820 BYRON *Mar. Fal.* I. ii. 315 At my hour Of twilight little light of life remains. 1821 SCOTT *Kenilw.* xii, He is ever in a sort of twilight, that is neither sleeping nor waking. 1877 SPARROW *Serm.* xix. 251 Voltaire was..in the habit of saying that he lived in the twilight of Christianity; meaning thereby, that its sun would soon go down.

b. esp. in reference to imperfect mental illumination or perception.

1610 HOLLAND *Camden's Brit., Irel.* II. 89, I am out of all hope in so great darknesse to discover any twy-light of the truth. 1648 BOYLE *Seraph. Love* (1700) 167 The dim Twilight of Human Intellects in this Life. 1722 WOLLASTON *Relig. Nat.* iii. 54 Thus blind ignorance was succeeded by a twilight of 'Sense'. 1838 PRESCOTT *Ferd. & Is.* (1846) III. xiv. 127 A shadowy twilight of romance enveloped every object. 1869 TOZER *Highl. Turkey* II. 307 The minor deities ..live in a dim twilight of popular belief.

4. *attrib.* or as *adj.* a. Of, pertaining to, or resembling twilight; seen or done in the twilight.

*Twilight arc, arch,* or *curve*, the outline of the earth's shadow, which rises in the east as the sun sets, forming an arch which divides the twilight or shaded portion of the sky from that which is lighted by the direct rays of the sun. *Twilight parallel*, the small circle of the celestial sphere, parallel to and 18 degrees below the horizon, at the sun's crossing which evening twilight ceases or morning twilight begins (Webster, 1911).

*c* 1633 MILTON *Arcades* 99 Nymphs and Shepherds..Trip no more in twilight ranks. 1754 GRAY *Poesy* 56 The muse has broke the twilight-gloom. 1762–9 FALCONER *Shipwr.* I. 721 Now Morn advanced Whitening with orient beam the twilight sky. 1794 MRS. RADCLIFFE *Myst. Udolpho* xxxiv, Twilight shade and darkness veil the scene. 1812 BYRON *Ch. Har.* II. lx, When the lingering twilight hour was past. 1837 LYTTON *E. Maltrav.* I. viii, That twilight shower had given a racy and vigorous sweetness to the air. 1855 BAIN *Senses & Int.* III. ii. § 10 (1864) 472 There is a point of twilight dimness when objects begin to be doubtful. 1856 KANE *Arct. Expl.* I. xv. 169 It is either all day here, or all night, or a twilight mixture of both.

b. *fig.* Having an intermediate character.

1730 T. BOSTON *Mem.* vii. (1899) 136 The two days before I had a twilight frame, it being neither day nor night with me. 1825 WATERTON *Wand. S. Amer.* III. i. 211 A kind of twilight state of health, neither ill nor..well.

c. Lighted as by twilight; dim, obscure, shadowy; also *fig.* of early times.

1629 MILTON *Hymn Nativity* xx, The Nimphs in twilight shade of tangled thickets mourn. 1632 — *Il Penseroso* 133 Arched walks of twilight groves And shadows brown..Of pine. 1810 SCOTT *Lady of Lake* VI. Concl., In twilight copse the glow-worm lights her spark. 1863 HAWTHORNE *Our Old Home* (1879) 77 Warwick,..founded by King Cymbeline in the twilight ages. 1873 BLACK *Pr. Thule* viii, Some dim twilight recess—far in among the perilous rocks. 1887 BOWEN *Virg. Æneid* IV. 25 Down to the twilight world and the gloom where the buried rest.

d. *fig.* Of the nature of or pertaining to imperfect mental light.

*a* 1677 BARROW *Serm. Acts ii. 38* Wks. 1686 III. 531 Philosophy may yield some twilight glimmerings thereof. 1774 FLETCHER *Salvation by Grace* Wks. 1795 IV. 65 Our short-sightedness and twilight knowledge do not alter the nature of things. 1818 SCOTT *Hrt. Midl.* xxix. [xxx], A doubtful, uncertain, and twilight sort of rationality.

5. In combination with participle or adj., as *twilight-enfolded, -hidden, -like, -loving, -seeming, -tinctured* adjs.

1891 C. JAMES *Rom. Rigmarole* 88 Looking out at the soft *twilight-enfolded square. *a* 1882 ROSSETTI *Ho. Life* iv, Thy *twilight-hidden glimmering visage lies. 1839 BAILEY *Festus* xix. (1848) 202 A state Of *twilight-like existence. 1745 WARTON *Pleas. Melanch.* 267 The *twilight-loving bat. 1821 SCOTT *Kenilw.* vi, Two silver lamps..diffused a ..*twilight-seeming shimmer. 1777 WARTON *Ode Hamlet* 5 Morning's *twilight-tinctur'd beam.

Hence **Twi·light** *v. trans.*, to light imperfectly or dimly; **Twi·lighted** *a.*, partly illuminated; = TWILIT; **Twi·lightless** *a.*, having no twilight; **Twi·lighty** *a.*, resembling twilight.

1866 HOWELLS *Venet. Life* 149 Cavernous recesses..*twilighted by twinkling altar-lamps. 1880 P. GREG *Errant* I. xvi. 245 A room..lighted or rather twilighted by a window looking out on a back court. 1865 ALEX. SMITH *Summ. Skye* I. 314 A *twilighted shepherd at watch. 1868 MRS. WHITNEY *P. Strong* xvi, Warm twilighted evenings. 1886 MRS. F. CADDY *Footsteps Jeanne D'Arc* 226 Centuries, which..we have been until lately accustomed to consider as twilighted ages. 1892 M. DODS *Gosp. John* II. 94 The sudden night of the Eastern *twilightless sunset had fallen. 1856 MAYHEW *Rhine* 250 The soft *twilighty tone of more ancient piles. 1892 E. F. BENSON *Rubicon* I. 69 That grey shawl is very twilighty.

† **Twilighting.** *Obs. rare.* In 4 **twyliȝtynge,** 5 **-light-.** [f. TWI- + LIGHTING *vbl. sb.*2.] = TWILIGHT *sb.* 1 b.

1387 TREVISA *Higden* (Rolls) VII. 97 In þe twyliȝtynge of þe nyȝt he deide. 1483 *Cath. Angl.* 398/2 Þe Twylightynge, *vespere.*

**Twilit** (twəi·lit), *ppl. a.* [pa. pple. of TWILIGHT *v.*] Lit by or as by twilight.

1869 MISS BRADDON *Lady's Mile* xviii, Within the twilit painting-room. 1887 STEVENSON *Merry Men, Will o' Mill* 79 He was like someone lying in twilit, formless, preëxistence. 1900 'H. S. MERRIMAN' *Isle of Unrest* xvi, In the gloom of the twilit church.

**Twill** (twil), **tweel** (twīl), *sb.*1 Forms: α. 4 **twyle**, 6 **twile**; 4–5 **twyll** (6 **tywell**), 4–6 **twylle** (6 **tywlle, tylle**), 5– **twill** (7 **tuill**). β. 4 **twel**, 6 **tweal-**, 7 *Sc.* **tueill, tueile**, 8– (orig. *Sc.*) **tweel.** [Northern and Sc. forms of *twĭlle* TWILLY *sb.*1, with normal dropping of the final *-e*, and (esp. in Sc.) lengthening of original *ĭ* to *ē* in the stem-syllable: cf. the Sc. forms of the verbs *swill, till.*] A woven fabric characterized by parallel diagonal ridges or ribs, produced by causing the weft threads to pass over one and under two or more threads of the warp, instead of over and under in regular succession, as in plain weaving.

In quot. 1670, a twilled cloth used as a covering for a bed or mattress.

α. 1329 *Acc. Chamberl. Scotl.* (1771) 7 Sexaginta et decem ulnarum de twyll. 1330 in Dalrymple *Ann. Scot.* (1797) III. 356 De 70 ulnis de twylle. *c* 1330 *Durham Acc. Rolls* (Surtees) 519 In ij pec. de Twyle pro saccis faciendis. 1335–6 *Ibid.* 529 In ij peciis panni de Twyll pro saccis. 1465 *Reg. Gild Co. Chr. York* (1872) 294 Una mappa de twill, cont. viij ulnas. 1511 *Knaresborough Wills* (Surtees) I. 2, j mensale de le twile. 1552 *Inv. Ch. Goods* (Surtees No. 97) 10 One vestment of read twill. 1583 *Shuttleworths' Acc.* (Chetham Soc.) 12 Fivffe and tynty yardes of tywlle to be sakes. 1586 *Ibid.* 29 Sixtene yardes of tylle to be scakes. *Ibid.* 34 Sixtene yardes of tywell for to be sackes. 1670 COVEL in *Early Voy. Levant* (Hakl. Soc.) 115 All that lay on twills and bedsteads were sorely bitten with little bugs. 1674 JEAKE *Arith.* (1696) 65 In 1 Hundred of Tiking and Twill of Scotland, 120 Ells. *a* 1825 FORBY *Voc. E. Anglia*, *Twill*, a sort of coarse linen cloth, of which loose frocks, trowsers, &c. are made for working men. 1851–4 *Tomlinson's Cycl. Usef. Arts* (1867) II. 856/1 Twills are distinguished by the number of leaves required in weaving them, as a three-leaf twill. 1889 *Anthony's Photogr. Bull.* II. 310 A large piece of black twill, or other opaque material.

β. 1371 *Durham Acc. Rolls* (Surtees) 130, iiij manutergia de Twel. [1571: see TWILLED *a.*1] 1647 *Caldwell Pap.* (Maitl. Cl.) I. 99, 4 elnes of Northland tueill at 14ss ye elne. *a* 1724 in Ramsay *Tea-t. Misc.* (1733) I. 29 (*Maggie's Tocher*) Ye shall hae twa good pocks That anes were o' the tweel. 1815 SCOTT *Guy M.* xxvi, As gude a tweel as ever cam aff a pirn. 1824 *Blackw. Mag.* XV. 220 Manchester tweel, or by whatever more proper denomination..a white waistcoat may be characterized.

b. The, or a, method or process of weaving this fabric (also *fig.*); also the ribbed appearance or diagonal pattern of the material so woven.

*c* 1779 in J. Skinner *Misc. Poet.* (1809) 185 Some pawky chiel, That..seems to understand the tweel O' rustic rhyme. 1839 URE *Dict. Arts* 373 Crape..is woven with any crossing or tweel. *Ibid.* 1231 The first is the regular or run tweel, which..interweaves the warp and woof only at every fifth interval. 1843 *Penny Cycl.* XXVII. 178/1 When..in addition to a twill, the weaver has to produce..any kind of figure. 1892 *Labour Commission Gloss.*, *Twill*, the pattern of a piece running diagonally from left to right.

c. *attrib.* and *Comb.*, as *twill bolster, calico, cloth, -heddle, hem, overall*; *twill-wove* adj.; **twill set**: see quot.

1656 *Melrose Regality Rec.* (S.H.S.) 185 A *tueile bolster.

**1904** *Woollen Draper's Terms* in *Tailor & Cutt.* 4 Aug. 480/1 **Twill Calico*, a rather heavy calico with a twill pattern on it. **1839** URE *Dict. Arts* 1236 For such a pattern .., two sets of common *tweel-heddles, moved in the ordinary way,..are sufficient. **1897** MARY KINGSLEY *W. Africa* 420 My favourite coloured cloth, bright pink, with a cardinal *twill hem round it. **1909** *Cent. Dict.* Supp. s.v. *Set*$^1$, **Twill set*, one of the three methods of inserting wire into the foundation of card-clothing. **1880** *Plain Hints Needle-work* 109 Strong twilled flannel with closely *twill-wove self-edge..used for petticoats.

**Twill** (twil), *sb.*$^2$, dial. var. QUILL *sb.*$^1$

**1664** POWER *Exp. Philos.* I. 8 You may plainly see the twills by which they [feathers] stick to the wings. **1691** RAY *N. C. Words* (E.D.S.), *Twill*,..a spoole... In the South they call it winding of quills. **1788** W. MARSHALL *Yorksh.* II. Gloss. (E.D.S.), *Twill*, a quill. **1825** BROCKETT *N. C. Words*, *Twill*, a quill; either for a pen, or on which to wind yarn. **1855** ROBINSON *Whitby Gloss.*

**Twill** (twil), **tweel** (twīl), *v.*$^1$ [f. TWILL *sb.*$^1$ or TWILLED *a.*$^1$] *trans.* To weave so as to produce diagonal ridges on the surface of the cloth.

**1808–18** JAMIESON, *To..tweel*, v. a., to work cloth in such a manner, that the woof appears to cross the warp vertically. **1828** *Craven Gloss.*, *Twill*, to weave in a particular manner. **1839** URE *Dict. Arts* 1231 Florentine silks are tweeled with sixteen leaves. **1870** ROCK *Text. Fabr.* vii. (1876) 73 Fustian ..with a warp of linen thread and a woof of thick cotton, so twilled and cut that it showed on one side a thick but low pile.

**Twill**, *v.*$^2$, dial. var. QUILL *v.*; cf. TWILL *sb.*$^2$

**1848** THACKERAY *Van. Fair* xvi, The great fat pin-cushion lined with pink inside, and twilled like a lady's night-cap.

† **Twill**, obs. form of TEWEL.

**1611** FLORIO, *Budello dritto*, the twill, the longaon or straight gut. **1659** in TORRIANO.

**Twilled** (twild), **tweeled** (twīld), *a.*$^1$ [f. TWILL *sb.*$^1$ and *v.*$^1$ + -ED.] Woven with a twill; having diagonal lines or ridges on the surface.

*c* **1423** in Raine *Abps. York* (Rolls) III. 306, j fethirbed de panno vocato twylled. **1536** *Test. Ebor.* (Surtees) VI. 53 A long twilte towell. **1536** *Wills & Inv. N. C.* (Surtees) III. 141 Two dossyn napkyns, one twilled towell. **1571** *Ibid.* I. 360, vj twealed bord clothes short and long. **1666** in *Maitl. Club Misc.* (1840) II. 539 Another greene tuilled night cap. **1805** *Trans. Soc. Arts* XXIII. 249 Any web, twilled, striped, checked or plain. **1824** HOGG *Tales & Sk.* (1837) V. 206 (*Mem. Fanatic*) His coat..is tweeled, milled, and thicker than a carpet. **1831** G. R. PORTER *Silk Manuf.* 236 Tweeled or twilled cloth is a description of figure weaving. **1857** MILLER *Elem. Chem.* (1862) III. 87 A filtering apparatus consisting of tubes of twilled cotton.

† **Twilled**, *a.*$^2$ *Obs.*

Origin and meaning uncertain: numerous conjectures have been offered by commentators, but none has met with general acceptance. Cf. PIONED.

**1610** SHAKS. *Temp.* IV. i. 64 Thy bankes with pioned, and twilled brims Which spungie Aprill at thy hest betrims.

**Twillet**, obs. form of TOILET.

**Twilley**: see TWILLY *sb.*$^2$

**Twilling** (twi·liŋ), **tweeling** (twī·liŋ). [f. TWILL *sb.*$^1$ or *v.*$^1$ + -ING$^1$.] A twilled fabric or texture; also, the process of producing this. Also, *attrib.* **twilling-bar**, a device in the twilling-machine; **twilling-hook**, one of the hooks for lifting the warp-threads in a twilling-machine; **twilling-machine**, a modification of the Jacquard loom.

**1839** URE *Dict. Arts* 385 Damask belongs to that species of texture which is distinguished by practical men by the name of tweeling. **1880** *Plain Hints Needlework* 122 The regularity of the parallel lines is broken in various ways, in fanciful twillings. **1894** T. W. FOX *Mechanism Weaving* VI. 168 The advantage of a twilling machine over an ordinary Jacquard. *Ibid.* 171 When [the] barrel is pegged to produce the desired pattern, twilling bars..will turn two or more griffe blades vertical, and push corresponding twilling hooks over slanting blades.

† **Twillock**, obs. var. WILLOCK.

**1620** J. MASON *New-found-land* 4 Teales, Twillockes, excellent wilde Duckes.

† **Twilly** (twi·li), *a.* and *sb.*$^1$ *Obs.* Also 4 **tywele, twyle**, 7 **twylle**; 5 **twelye**, 6 **twyley**, 7 **twylly(e**. [OE. *twili* (= OHG. *zwilīh*), formed after L. *bilix* from *twi-* TWI-: cf. THRILI *a.* The ME. var. *twile* is parallel to *thrile*, the reduced form of *thrili*, and is the source of the northern TWILL *sb.*$^1$] **a.** *adj.* Twilled. **b.** *sb.* A twilled cloth. Also *attrib.*

*c* **875** *Erfurt Gloss.* (Sweet) 1151 *Biplex*, *duplex*, tuili. *a* **900** *Leiden Gloss.* 157 *Bilex*, t[u]ili. **1310** *Acc. Exors. of Bp. of Exeter* (1874) 4, j capa de samitrico tywele linita sindone yndico. **1375** in Boys *Hist. Sandwich* (1792) 556/2 De chescun twylecloth de la lb...ij d. **1440** in G. P. Scrope *Castle Combe* (1852) 230, ij. borde cloths, one of twelye. **1552** *Berksh. Ch. Goods* (1879) 11 One other Coope lyke unto twillye the border of woursted. **1560** *Will of Salmon* (Somerset Ho.) A Twyley cloth to lay upon her bed. **1600** HOLLAND *Livy* VII. xiv. 258 The mules sumpters should bee taken off their backes, leaving onely two course twillies or coverings upon them. **1601** — *Pliny* IX. lix. I. 269 His companion..latcheth them in a course twillie or couering. **1602** *Inv.* in *Collect. Archæol.* (1863) II. 98 Twyllye canvasses. *Ibid.*, One twylle. *Ibid.* 101 A doble twyllye. **1631** *Patent Specif.* No. 54. 2 All such kersy seves, otherwise twilly seves or haire seves. **1714** *Fr. Bk. of Rates* 152 Four Livres..for every Piece of Boucassines, Twillis Fustians, Bazins, and Bombasins

**Twilly** (twi·li), *sb.*$^2$ Also **twilley**. [Altered f. *willy*, WILLOW.] A willowing machine: = DEVIL *sb.* 8 a; also called *twilly-devil*. Hence **Twi·lly** *v. trans.* to willow.

**1858** SIMMONDS *Dict. Trade*, *Twilly*, a common name for the willying machine. **1859** TOMLINSON *Illustr. Usef. Arts* 19/1 Supposing the wool to be dyed, it is passed through the willy, or twilly—resembling the willow of the cotton manufacture. **1860** — *Usef. Arts* Ser. I. 37 The *willy*, or *shakewilly*, as it is called in Yorkshire, and *twilly* in Gloucestershire. **1869** *Eng. Mech.* 19 Nov. 240/2 The best machine for pulling flocks is called a 'twilly'. **1894** C. VICKERMAN *Woollen Spinning* viii. 117 This is the first operation after the wool is dyed, and is known by a variety of names, as teasing, willeying, willowing, and twilleying.

**Twilt** (also 6 **twylt**), obs. and dial. f. QUILT *sb.*$^1$, *v.*$^1$ and *v.*$^3$. (See also TWILLED *a.*$^1$)

**1477** [see QUILT *sb.*$^1$ 1]. **1538** in *Bury Wills* (Camden) 134, I wyll the bed, and the twylt couerlyt..be solde. **1593** [see QUILT *v.*$^1$ 2 *transf.*]. **1594** [see QUILTED *ppl. a.* 1]. **1715** PENNECUIK *City & Country Mouse* 34 The City-Mouse then plac't his Country-Guest, On a Rich Purple-Twilt to grace his Feast. **1790** GROSE *Provinc. Gloss.* (ed. 2), *Twilt*, a quilt or bed-cover. *North.* **1813** DUFF *Poems* (1816) 56 Blankets, sheets, and stripit tykin'; Twilts an' cov'rins to your likin'. **1818** SCOTT *Br. Lamm.* xxv[i], Beds of state, twilts, pands and testors, napery and broidered wark. *a* **1825** FORBY *Voc. E. Anglia*, *Twilt*,..a quilt; here as well as in the North. *Twilt*...1. To quilt...2. To beat. An expressive word, inasmuch as it is implied that weals are left, like the stripes or ridges in quilted work.

**Twin** (twin), *a.* and *sb.* Forms: 1 *adj.* **twinn**, (*sb. pl.* **ȝetwinnas**, 3 **itwinnes**), 3–6 **twynne**, 3–7 **twinne**, 4 **tuine**, *Sc.* **twene**, 4–5 **tuynne**, 4–5 (6 *Sc.*) **twyne**, 4 (6 *Sc.*) **tuin, tuinne, tuyne**, 4–7 **twyn**, 5–7 **twine**, 6 **twynn**, 7 **twinn**, 3– **twin**. [OE. *twinn* adj. (rare), *getwinn* adj. and sb., f. the stem of TWI-. Cf. OFris. *twina*, *twine* (NFris. *twēne*, *twāne*) two together, ON. *tvinnr*, *tvennr* double, (pl.) two, two pairs of, Norw. *tvinne*, *tvenne*, Da. *tvende* two. In northern ME. perhaps partly or mainly from ON.: cf. THRIN *a.*]

**A.** *adj.*

† **1.** Consisting of two; twofold, double. *Obs.* (exc. as in 4).

*c* **1000** in Napier *O. E. Glosses* I. 1836 *Gemina*, .i. *duppla*, twinnum. *Ibid.* 2605–6 *Geminis concentibus*, twinnum sangum. *c* **1200** ORMIN 7737–9 Ȝho brohhte twinne lac, Forr..her iss twinne lufe sett Bitwenenn menn onn eorþe; Forr uss birrþ lufenn Godd & mann. *c* **1250** *Gen. & Ex.* 485 [Lamech sinned in] Twin-wifing ant twin manslaȝt. **1357** *Lay Folks Catech.* 508 This is principaly done opon twyn wise. *c* **1400** *Rule St. Benet* (Prose) 5 Of twine maner at lere his discipilis..at serue god: baþe in word and dede.

† **2.** Two; a pair of...; the two, both. *Obs.*

*c* **1250** *Gen. & Ex.* 3248 Ðe water up-stod..On twinne half. *Ibid.* 4020 Heft haueð he mad her .vii. alter, And on ilc brend eft twin der. *a* **1300** *Cursor M.* 523 (Cott.) His heued with in has eien tuin. *Ibid.* 5235 Ioseph had þan suns tuin, Manassen and effraim. *Ibid.* 9136 His eild was fourti yeir and tuin. *Ibid.* 21750 Þe laghes tuin sal þou find sua.

**3.** (attrib. use of B. 1.) Born at the same birth, as two children or animals, or one of such. See also TWIN-BROTHER, -SISTER.

**1590** SHAKS. *Com. Err.* v. i. 350 He, and I, And the twin Dromio. *a* **1722** LISLE *Husb.* (1757) 313 A..twin-lamb. **1751** WARBURTON *Pope's Ep. Burlington* 117 *note*, These groves..can express themselves only like twin-ideots by nods. **1822** T. MITCHELL *Aristoph.* II. 191 By the twin-gods I vow. **1847** W. C. L. MARTIN *The Ox* 40/2 Every twin female..is not necessarily barren, even when the other calf is a male.

**4.** Forming a pair or couple; two closely associated, connected, or related, and (usually) alike or equal. (In quot. 1601 said of one thing cut in half; in quot. 1776 *loosely* of more than two.)

In this sense, and in senses b, d, and 5, often hyphened to the noun (cf. the combinations under C), or occasionally written as one word with it.

**1591** SYLVESTER *Du Bartas* I. ii. 64 Th' Elements, twin-twins (two sons, two daughters) To wit, the Fire, the Aire; the Earth, and Waters. **1601** SHAKS. *Twel. N.* v. i. 230 An apple cleft in two, is not more twin Then these two creatures. **1614** SYLVESTER *Litt. Bartas* 617 Those twin-Princes [the sun and moon]..Began their Kingdoms over day and night. **1673** [R. LEIGH] *Transp. Reh.* 131 Therefore are the twin-diseases deservedly associated. **1743** FRANCIS tr. *Hor.*, *Odes* III. xxix. 96 Perhaps some kinder gale, While the twin stars appear, shall fill my joyful sail. **1765** *Museum Rust.* IV. 20 When you meet with twin fruit, take off the least of them with all possible care not to shake the other. **1776** MICKLE tr. *Camoens' Lusiad* 163 The seven twin-mountains tremble at the sound. **1809–10** COLERIDGE *Friend* I. xv. (1865) 207 These twin truths, or rather..this one great truth considered in its two principal bearings. **1835** URE *Philos. Manuf.* 117 The leather must..be pierced with twin holes for each double tooth. **1875** KNIGHT *Dict. Mech.*, *Twin-screws*, a pair of screw-propellers on separate shaft[s], and having right-handed and left-handed twists respectively. **1898** J. T. FOWLER *Durham Cath.* 38 Twin shafts of Purbeck marble.

**b.** Composed of, or having, two similar and equal (or closely connected or related) parts or constituents; consisting of two joined in one.

*Twin boat, steam-engine, valve*: see quots. *c* 1816, 1875. *Twin crystal*: = B. 3 b. *Twin earthquake*: see quot. 1906.

**1585** JAS. I *Ess. Poesie* (Arb.) 35 Let Christ both God and man your Twinrock [orig. *croupe iumelle*] be. *a* **1661** FULLER *Worthies, Kent* (1662) II. 86 An Ingenuous Yeoman in this County..hath two Ploughs fastened together so finely, that he plougheth two furrows at once, one under another,.. this device of a Twinne-Plough. **1805–16** R. JAMESON *Char. Min.* (ed. 2) 220 A crystal..composed of two halves of one..crystal, of which the one-half appears to be turned round. Example, Twin-crystal of felspar. *c* **1816** REES *Cycl.* s.v. *Steam-Engine*, In 1811 and 1812 two steam-boats were built..as ferry-boats for crossing the Hudson river. These boats are what are called twin-boats; each of them being two complete hulls united by a deck or bridge. **1826** KIRBY & SP. *Entomol.* IV. xlvi. 288 Double Ocellus (*Ocellus geminatus*). When two ocelli are included in the same circle or spot...Twin Ocellus (*Ocellus didymus*). When such ocelli join each other. **1848** RICKMAN *Archit.* 152 They may be called twin-windows, consisting of two single lights coupled together. **1875** KNIGHT *Dict. Mech.* 2667 A large twin channel steamer..has lately been put upon the Dover and Calais ferry. *Ibid.* 2668 *Twin Steam-engine*,..a duplex engine; one in which two engines, complete in their parts, are associated in a single effort. *Ibid.*, *Twin-valve*, a form of valve attached to the discharge outlet of a pump..used for making a double connection, one with the steam-boiler ..and the other..for conducting water wherever desired. **1906** *19th Cent.* Mar. 465 To earthquakes of this description the name of 'twin' has been given, because the double shock is due to two distinct impulses resulting from a single generative effort. **1910** THOMPSON tr. *Aristotle's Hist. Anim.* 562 In some twin eggs a thin partition of white intervenes to prevent the yolks mixing.

**c.** *Nat. Hist.* Growing or occurring in pairs; geminate.

**1812** *New Bot. Gard.* I. 26 The anthers twin and erect. **1830** LINDLEY *Nat. Syst. Bot.* 130 Seeds solitary or twin. **1891** *Cent. Dict.*, *Twin*..I. *a*...6. In *entom.*, geminate: applied to spots, punctures, spines, etc., which are close together in pairs.

**d.** Pertaining to two (persons or things) in close connexion.

**1827** SOUTHEY *Devil's Walk* v, Such a twin-likeness there was in the pair. **1870** MORRIS *Earthly Par.* II. III. 174 Their twinlife seemed so piteous.

**5.** Forming one of a pair or couple; closely associated with or related to another.

**1605** CHAPMAN *All Fools* III. i, Here comes the twyn-Courtier his companion. **1781** COWPER *Hope* 102 Yesterday's face twin image of to-day. **1835** LYTTON *Rienzi* III. iii, True sentiment..is twin with melancholy. **1842** LOUDON *Suburban Hort.* Introd. 1 Having in a twin volume treated of Gardening as an Art of Design and Taste. **1868** HELPS *Realmah* viii. (1869) 217 Her soul was a twin-soul to his.

**B.** *sb.*

**1.** *pl.* Two children or young brought forth at one birth.

[*a* **900** *O. E. Martyrol.* 17 Jan. 24 Seo cierece..is neah Lingona byriȝ, þa man nemneð æt *sanctos geminos*, æt þæm halȝum ȝetwinnum. *a* **1000** in Cockayne *Shrine* (1864) 92 Hi wæron ȝetwinnas. *c* **1205** LAY. 12256 Twene ibroðeren itwinnes heo weoren.] *c* **1290** *S. Eng. Leg.* I. 322/5 Twynnes boþe huy were. **1388** WYCLIF *Song Sol.* vii. 3 Thi twei teetis ben as twei kidis, twynnes of a capret. **1514** BARCLAY *Cyt. & Uplondyshm.* (Percy Soc.) 10 So yere by yere two twynnes forthe she brought. **1573** TUSSER *Husb.* (1878) 74 Keepe twinnes for breed. **1607** TOPSELL *Four-f. Beasts* (1658) 86 They conceive and bring forth for the most part twins, or two at a time. **1793** HOLCROFT *Lavater's Physiogn.* xxix. 140, I have known twins not to be distinguished from each other, between whose minds there was not the least similarity. **1847** W. C. L. MARTIN *The Ox* 40/2 The cow..produces..sometimes..twins, and very rarely three. **1852** MRS. STOWE *Uncle Tom's C.* xix, My brother and I were twins.

**b.** *sing.* One of two children or young brought forth at a birth; with possessive or *of* = twin brother or sister.

*c* **1440** *Promp. Parv.* 505/2 Twynne, or twynlynge.., *gemellus*,..*geminus*. **1530** PALSGR. 283/2 Twyn, *jumeau*. *a* **1658** CLEVELAND *King's Ret. fr. Scotl.* 19 The divided Dam Runs to the Summons of her hungry Lamb; But when the Twin cryes halves, she quits the first. **1824** BYRON *Def. Transf.* I. ii. 81, I saw your Romulus..Slay his own twin. **1899** *Westm. Gaz.* 4 Mar. 2/1 It's not me..but Hilda, and she's my twin. **1912** KEITH *Human Body* viii. 116 All of these 'acardiac' or 'parasitic' fœtuses are never born alone; they are the twin of a normal child.

**c.** *Astron.* (*pl.*) The zodiacal constellation and sign GEMINI.

**1413** *Pilgr. Sowle* (Caxton 1483) v. x. 100 The signe of gemini that ben cleped twynnes or doubles. **1561** B. GOOGE *Palingenius' Zodiac of Life* Pref. ¶ j b, Saturne..with a backward course he ranne from out the twinnes apace. **1669** STURMY *Mariner's Mag.* VI. 95 Here in the zodiack begins The Ram, the Bull, the loving Twins. **1727–46** THOMSON *Summer* 43 When now no more the alternate Twins are fired, And Cancer reddens with the solar blaze. **1868** LOCKYER *Guillemin's Heavens* II. I. (ed. 3) 315 Part of the constellation of the Twins.

**d.** *dial.* (*pl.*) Applied to three children born at one birth; triplets.

**1606** *Transcr. Regrs. Cosmus Bleane in Kent* (MS.), Was Baptyzed three Twines, John, Sara, and Margeret, the sonne and daughters of Liby Strydwicke. **1631–2** *Canterbury Transcr., Kingsdown* (MS.), Two (of three twinnes) to wit daughters of Christopher Bacheler..were buried. **1646** *Inscr. Blyton Church, Lincs*, Hadassah Tabitha Cephas Twins of Robt. and Elizabeth Drury.

**e.** *With twins* (strengthening of *with child*, CHILD *sb.* 17 c (*b*)), *fig.* greatly longing. *rare*$^{-1}$.

**1768** GARRICK *Let.* June in *Burke's Corr.* (1844) I. 156 Hearing what a sweet place you have,..I am with twins till I am well delivered at Gregories.

**2.** *fig.* **a.** *pl.* Two persons or things intimately associated, connected, or related (esp. in origin, or from the beginning), or, as in quot. 1784, closely resembling or agreeing with each other; two forming a pair or couple. (In quot. *a* 1600 *loosely* applied to more than two.)

Applied by Puttenham (quot. 1589) to the figure HENDIADYS.

**1589** PUTTENHAM *Eng. Poesie* III. xvi. (Arb.) 188 Another manner of speach when ye will seeme to make two of one.., which therefore we call the figure of Twynnes, the Greekes *Endiadis*. *a* **1591** H. SMITH *Serm.* (1637) 395 Sinnes and excuses are twinnes born at a birth. *a* 1600 MONTGOMERIE *Sonn.* viii. 9 Come, troup of tuinis, about his temple tuyn ȝour laurell leivis. 1612 *Two Noble K.* II. ii. 21 Never Shall we two exercise, like Twyns of honour, Our Armes again. 1784 COWPER *Task* IV. 738 Two were never found Twins at all points. 1820 SHELLEY *Ode to Liberty* xiii, Twins of a single destiny!

**b.** *sing.* One of two thus related; in early use sometimes = mate, companion; now usually with *of, to*, or possessive: something closely connected with or resembling the other thing mentioned; a fellow, counterpart.

1540 HYRDE tr. *Vives' Instr. Chr. Wom.* (1592) N iij, A woman..with whom he shall live a twin. 1616 LANE *Contn. Sqr.'s T.* XI. 190 Hee..shall have his landes, and her to wifelie twinn. 1697 BENTLEY *Phal.* (1699) 249 Another consequence the very twin to that which went before. 1819 BYRON *Juan* II. clxxii, All who joy would win Must share it—Happiness was born a twin. 1822–7 GOOD *Study Med.* (1829) IV. 11 The great sympathetic..nerve..meets its twin from the opposite side. 1867 MAURICE *Patriarchs & Lawg.* viii. (1877) 168 Love would be seen to be the eternal twin of Truth. 1908 O. SEAMAN *Salvage, Sweet Uses Obesity* vii, Her bed, as a matter of course, is A twin of the wonder of Ware.

**3.** A pair of twin children or young; also *fig.* or *gen.* a pair, couple, brace. *Obs.* exc. *dial.*

1569 in *Spenser's Poet. Wks.* (1910) I. 494, I saw the roote in hie disdaine Sende forth againe a twinne of forked trees. 1607 TOPSELL *Four-f. Beasts* (1658) 195 Commonly they are brought forth in twins. 1635 A. STAFFORD *Fem. Glory* (1869) 80 Her Soul was delivered of a twinne of Vows. 1817 J. NICHOLS *Illustr. Lit. Hist. 18th C.* II. 657 [He] was born in December, 1744..and was one of a twin. 1901 M. E. FRANCIS *Past. Dorset* 142 'The twin', a fine healthy pair of four-year-old boys.

**b.** *Cryst.* A composite crystal consisting of two (usually equal and similar) crystals united in reversed positions with respect to each other, either by juxtaposition, embedding, or interpenetration. (Also extended to composite crystals consisting of more than two.)

1845 *Encycl. Metrop.* XVI. 364/2 Twinning on an octahedral face is seen in the apposition twin of Spinel. 1868 DANA *Min.* (ed. 5) 354 Orthoclase...Twins..right- or left-handed...A twin of 4 crystals...A twin of 3 crystals. 1895 STORY-MASKELYNE *Crystallogr.* vi. § 156 The two individuals may present a mere contact at a common surface.., the juxtaposed twin..: or there may be an interlocking of the crystals,..as in the..embedded twin of orthoclase..: or again, there may be a complete mutual interpenetration.., as in..an interpenetrant twin of galena...In the case of polysynthetic twins several or almost innumerable hemitropic individual crystals may be combined. *Ibid.* vii. § 193 Simple twins composed of two individuals, and..complex twins formed by repeated twinning.

**c.** *local.* An agricultural implement with two rows of teeth, for breaking up ploughed land and clearing it of weeds.

1847 in HALLIWELL. 1859 *Jrnl. R. Agric. Soc.* XX. I. 216 A pair of 'twins', or heavy drag-harrows. 1881 MISS JACKSON *Shropsh. Word-bk.*, *Twins*,..for breaking the clods and uprooting the weeds of ploughed land, preparatory to the harrows going on...The implement..is either single or double, and in the latter case is spoken of as 'a pair of twins', the several parts being coupled together.

†**4.** *In twin* (also contr. *itwin*), *on twin*: in or into two parts or divisions; in twain, in two, apart, asunder. (Cf. ATWIN *advb. phr.*[1]) Chiefly *northern. Obs.*

*a* 1300 *Cursor M.* 3968 (Cott.) For doute he delt þam in tuin. *Ibid.* 6269 He sagh þe see it drau in tuin. 13.. *E. E. Allit. P.* A. 251 Fro we in twynne wern towen & twayned, I haf ben a Ioylez Iuelere. *Ibid.* B. 1047 Quen hit is brused oþer broken, oþer byten in twynne. 1375 BARBOUR *Bruce* VIII. 175 Sa fer..that thai War in-twyn a bow-draucht & mar. *c* 1400 *Gamelyn* 317, I wil not þis companye parten on twyne. *c* 1400 *Destr. Troy* 6581 Anoþer..he nolpit to ground, Shent of þo shalkes, shudrit hom itwyn. *c* 1450 *Bk. Curtasye* 735 in *Babees Bk.* (1868) 324 Þe smalle lofe he cuttis euen in twynne. *c* 1480 *Lyt. Childr. Lyt. Bk.* 24 ibid. 18 Kerue not thy brede to thynne, Ne breke hit not on twynne. 1535 STEWART *Cron. Scot.* (Rolls) III. 226 Quhilk causit him stand..fra him..rycht far in tuyn.

†**b.** Hence (or from TWIN *v.*[1]) *twin* is used for 'parting, separation'. *Obs. rare*$^{-1}$.

*a* 1300 *Cursor M.* 24285 (Edin.) Ik am wit þe With outen twin [*Cott., Gött.* tuin] and ai sal be Fra nu for euirmar.

**C.** Combinations. **a.** with sbs., forming adjs. in sense 'having or characterized by twin ...s, i.e. a pair of (the things named)', as *twin-cylinder, -light, -power, -roller, -wire.* **b.** with sb. + -ED[2], forming parasynthetic adjs. in same sense, as *twin-balled, -forked, -headed, -hued, -leaved, -named, -peaked, -spiked, -striped, -towered, -towned, -wheeled.* **c.** objective, etc., as *twin-bearing* adj., *-getter, -killing*; *twin-like* adj. and adv. **d.** adverbial ('as a twin or twins'), as *twin-begot, -existent* adjs.; *twin-slumber* vb. **e.** Special Combs.: **twin-axis** (*Cryst.*), the axis of twinning in a twin crystal, i.e. the line about which either of the constituent crystals would have to revolve to come into the position of the other; **twin-barren**, a barren female calf twin with a male, a freemartin; **twinberry**, *U.S.*, a name for *Gaultheria procumbens* (also called *checkerberry, partridge-berry*, or *wintergreen*), or its fruit; **twin-birth**, the birth of twins; a pair born or produced as twins, or one of such in relation to the other (usually *fig.*); **twin-face** (*Cryst.*), a face in a twin crystal perpendicular to the *twin-axis*; **twinflower**, an American name for *Linnæa*, from the flowers being produced in pairs; †**twin-kin** *a.* [KIN *sb.*[1] 6 b], of two kinds, twofold, double; **twin-law**, *Cryst.* the law or principle of twinning of a twin crystal; **twin-leaf**, a name for the N. American herb *Jeffersonia diphylla*, the leaves being divided each into two leaflets; **twin-pair**, a pair of things precisely similar and equal; *attrib.* in **twin-pair sheet** (*Geom.*), that part of the surface of a cone of the third or higher degree which meets the concentric sphere in two equal and similar closed curves; **twin-plane** (*Cryst.*), a plane perpendicular to the *twin-axis* of a twin crystal; **twin-screw**, *a.* having twin screws; *spec.* of a steamer, having two screw propellers on separate shafts, which turn in opposite directions so as to counteract the tendency to lateral vibration; also *ellipt.* as *sb.* a twin-screw steamer; **twin-spot** *a.*, having twin spots; used in collectors' names of various moths having pairs of spots upon the wings; **twin-stock**, a beehive containing two colonies.

1855 *Orr's Circle Sci., Crystall.* 469 The axis about which the crystals are supposed to revolve is called the *twin axis, and the plane to which it is perpendicular the twin plane. 1608 SYLVESTER *Du Bartas* II. iv. IV. *Decay* 1165 With sharp bodkins bore they out his eyes:..an end-less night Be-clouds for ever his *twin-balled sight. 1778 [W. MARSHALL] *Minutes Agric., Digest* 40 English Beasts of Agricultural Labour..*Twin-Barrens. 1788 BURNS *Let.* 25 May, Wks. 1879 V. 125 A certain girl's prolific, *twin-bearing merit. 1865 SWINBURNE *Atalanta* 1261 Jason, and Dryas *twin-begot with war. 1836 MRS. TRAILL *Backw. Canada* xiv. 248 This plant is also called winter-green, or *twin-berry. 1868 *Rep. U. S. Comm. Agric.* (1869) 178 Among them [small fruits] may be noted red and black currants,..twin-berries [etc.]. 1807 COLERIDGE *To Wordsworth* 13 Of smiles spontaneous, and mysterious fear, The first-born they of Reason and *twin-birth. 1837 LOCKHART *Scott* xxv, The quarto of Rokeby was followed..by the small volume which had been designed for a twin-birth. 1850 MRS. JAMESON *Leg. Monast. Ord.* (1863) 227 The portentous twin-birth of the two great mendicant communities. 1912 KEITH *Human Body* viii. 113 Twins are common; in Ireland a twin birth has a frequency of one in seventy-two, in England about one in seventy-five. 1884 KNIGHT *Dict. Mech.* Suppl., *Twin Cylinder Steam Engine. 1907 *Daily Chron.* 24 May 9/3 The International Motor Cycle Tourist Trophy Race. .. Twenty-two single-cylinder and seven twin-cylinder machines have been entered. 1860 DORA GREENWELL *Patience of Hope* 75 Two principles..within contrariety, *twin-existent,..the desire for unity, and the..love of truth. 1878 GURNEY *Crystallogr.* 99 When the twin axis is perpendicular to a possible face this is called the *twin face. 1836 MRS. TRAILL *Backw. Canada* xiv. 238 The Americans call this honeysuckle '*twinflower'. 1845 S. JUDD *Margaret* I. xiv, Beds of purple twin-flower. 1776 WITHERING *Brit. Plants* (1796) II. 441 Ceratophyllum submersum...Leaves forked...Specimens from Paris had the leaves *twin-forked. 1837 YOUATT *Sheep* xv. 508 Certain rams..have the credit of being *twin-getters. 1872 BROWNING *Fifine* xi, The *Twin-headed Babe, and Human Nondescript! 1906 G. G. COULTON *Pearl* 43 *Twin-hued topaz. 1895 *Pall Mall G.* 13 Nov. 2/3 If *twin-killing is more reprehensible than drunkenness. 1897 MARY KINGSLEY *W. Africa* 473 This twin-killing is a widely diffused custom among the Negro tribes. 13.. *Cursor M.* 512 (Cott.) Þat kyng of craft Wald mensked be wyth *tuinkyn scaft. *Ibid.* 27677 Þaa dedes þat man mai Vnderstand on tuin-kyn wai. 1895 STORY-MASKELYNE *Crystallogr.* vi. § 162 The *twin-law..appears to permit of considerable divergence from precision in the relative orientation of the crystals subject to it. *Ibid.* vii. § 281 The twin-laws governing the union of rhombohedral crystals. 1912 *Return Brit. Museum* 196 Quartz, group of twinned crystals (Japanese twin-law) from New Mexico. 1845–50 MRS. LINCOLN *Lect. Bot.* App. 115/2 *Twin-leaf. 1857 GRAY *First Less. Bot.* (1866) 133 In Jeffersonia or Twin-leaf. 1861 MISS PRATT *Flower. Pl.* V. 272 *Scilla bifolia* (*Twin-leaved Squill). 1862 *Catal. Internat. Exhib., Brit.* II. No. 6720, *Twin-light window, with tracery. 1599 NASHE *Lenten Stuffe* Wks. (Grosart) V. 226 A *twinlike image of it. 1631 BRATHWAIT *Whimzies, Ballad-monger* 18 It would doe a mans heart good to see how twinne-like hee and his songman couple. 1816 SOUTHEY *Poet's Pilgr.* Proem ix, The playmate of her infancy, Her twin-like comrade. 1614 SYLVESTER *Bethulia's Rescue* VI. 48 *Twin-nam'd Ister, and Seaven-mouthed Nile. 1820 BYRON *Mar. Fal.* I. ii. 574 Twin-named from the apostles John and Paul. 1904 W. M. RAMSAY *Lett. to Seven Ch.* xvii. 213 A large..part of ancient Ephesus..can be seen only by ascending to the top of the *twin-peaked Pion. 1855 *Twin-plane [see *Twin-axis* above]. 1875 KNIGHT *Dict. Mech.*, **Twin-power Press*, one in which the power is brought upon two objects in alternation, as in some machines where the punch and shears are in the same frame. 1835 URE *Philos. Manuf.* 118 The *twin-roller mechanism, which was perfected..by Arkwright. 1864 *Athenæum* 24 Sept. 410/3 Small *twin screw boats. 1884 *Health Exhib. Catal.* 94/1 Patent Twin-screw Bath Fittings. 1891 KIPLING *Light that Failed* vii. 123 'It's a steamer', he said,—'a twin-screw steamer, by the beat'. 1897 *Daily News* 17 Feb. 2/7 They had increased their staff of steamboats by adding the twin-screw Connemara. 1850 S. DOBELL *Roman* vii, The foemen, Good and Ill, *twin-slumber in the womb of Fate. 1861 MISS PRATT *Flower. Pl.* VI. 133 *Twin-spiked Cord-grass. 1819 G. SAMOUELLE *Entomol. Compend.* 423 *Geometra quadrifasciaria.* The large *Twin-spot. —— *didymaria.* The Twin-spot Carpet. 1884 PHIN *Dict. Apiculture* 73 **Twin-stock*, a word that has been borrowed from the German. It signifies a hive containing two colonies. 1819 SAMOUELLE *Entomol. Compend.* 423 *Geometra costostrigata.* The *twin-striped Pinion. 1886 MRS. F. CADDY *Footsteps Jeanne D'Arc* 108 A *twin-towered church. 1878 *Archæol. Cantiana* XII. 331 The port for London was the *twin-towned port of Rutupiae. 1904 *Windsor Mag.* Jan. 245/1 A *twin-wheeled machine like the tricycle. 1892 *Daily News* 26 May 6/5 The New Telephone Company...The new exchange will be on the *twin-wire or metallic circuit system.

Hence (*nonce-wds.*) **Twi·nfold** *a.*, twofold, with the two parts or elements in close connexion; **Twi·nhood, Twi·nism, Twi·nness** = TWINSHIP; **Twi·nity** [after *trinity*], a group of two in intimate union, two in one; **Twi·nly** *a.*, characteristic of or befitting a twin (brother or sister).

1842 TENNYSON in *Mem.* (1897) I. viii. 200 Its [the heart's] *twinfold necessity, Capacious both of Friendship and of Love. 1871 BP. WILBERFORCE *Let.* in *Life* (1882) III. xiv. 387 That mystery of *twin-hood which seems to reach into the spirit world. 1796 BURNEY *Mem. Metastasio* III. 92 My fond *twinism has suggested to me, that you pass the chief part of your time in the open air. 1879 BARING-GOULD *Germany* I. 201 (tr. Schiller) Herder and his wife..form together a sort of sacred *twinity. 1889 J. VEITCH *Knowing & Being* i. 22 This may be called a unity; it is rather, if we might invent a term suited to the new and marvellous conception, ..an unparalleled and unbegotten twinity. 1796 BURNEY *Mem. Metastasio* III. 98 Accepting of your *twinly offer. *Ibid.* 259, I am, with usual twinly kindness, yours most faithfully. 1909 *Mod. Lang. Rev.* Jan. 197 The resemblance of the scheme of the play [*Twelfth Night*], with the wonderful likeness of Viola and Sebastian, to that of the *Comedy of Errors*, with the *twinness of the Antipholi.

**Twin,** *v.*[1] *Obs.* exc. *Sc.* Forms: see prec.; cf. also TWINE *v.*[2] [ME. *twinnen*, f. TWIN *a.* or *sb.* For the development of the senses cf. TWIN *sb.* 4.]

**1.** *trans.* To put asunder (*properly* two things or persons, or one *from* the other); to separate, disjoin, disunite, sunder, sever, part, divide; †to deliver, set free; *fig.* to distinguish.

*a* 1225 *Ancr. R.* 254 Euerichon to dealed [*MS. T.* itwinned] from oðer. *c* 1230 *Hali Meid.* 13 Engel & meiden beon euening in uertu of meidenhades mihte þah eadinesse ham twinni ȝette & to-tweame. *a* 1300 *Cursor M.* 390 (Cott.) For to tuin dai fra night. *Ibid.* 7948 Þi hus..Sal neuer tuind [*v. rr.* tuinned, twynned] be fra suord. *Ibid.* 22912 Nan es..þat can Tuin þat erth þat com o man Fra þat erth þat es bredd o best. *c* 1400 LOVE *Bonavent. Mirr.* (1907) 252 Our bodily felauschip is twynned, and now moste I nedes be departed fro the. *c* 1450 *St. Cuthbert* (Surtees) 6704 Twede fra scotlande bernyce twynnes. *c* 1460 *Towneley Myst.* i. 11 Oone god in persons thre, Which may neuer twynnyd be. *Ibid.* ii. 325 With cheke bon,..Shal I the and thi life twyn. *Ibid.* vii. 12 From hell he will theym twyn. 1513 DOUGLAS *Æneis* VI. vii. 11 From the sweit lyf twynnit vntymusly. 1637 [see 2]. 1686 G. STUART *Joco-Serious Disc.* 58 Then out he drew a gully knife With that he twinned me and my life. 1826– in dial. glossaries (Chesh., Lanc., Northumb.). 1832 MOTHERWELL *Poems* 184 The waves and cruel wars hae twinn'd My winsome luve frae me. 1855 *Fraser's Mag.* LI. 95 Ah, my cruel cruel stepdame, who hath twinn'd our love for aye.

†**b.** To divide or share; to part with. *Obs. rare.*

*c* 1330 R. BRUNNE *Chron.* (1810) 86 Þing þat a man wynnes, It is told purchase, whedir he it hold or tuynnes. 1790 SHIRREFS *Poems* 74 Narrow's the saul wha winna twin his gear To..help the poor!

**c.** To deprive *of.*

1722 RAMSAY *Three Bonnets* I. 180 His [Samson's] strength, O' which she twinn'd him at the length. *a* 1800 *Fine Flowers in Valley* in Child *Ballads* (1882) I. 220/1 She's taen out her little pen-knife, And twinnd the sweet babe o its life. 1887 SERVICE *Dr. Duguid* xvi. 103 It was just like the twinnin' him o' his vera life to part wi a plack.

**2.** *intr.* **a.** Of two persons or things: To go asunder; to separate, part.

*a* 1225 *Ancr. R.* 396 Leoue ureond beoð sorie hwon heo schulen twinnen. 1340 HAMPOLE *Pr. Consc.* 1823 When þe body and þe saule salle twyn. *c* 1410 *Master of Game* (MS. Digby 182) xxv, And or þei twynne þei moste acorde where þe metynge shall be on þe morowe. ? *a* 1500 *Chester Pl.* (E.E.T.S.) i. 271 Lightenes, darkenes, I byd yow twyn. 1567 *Gude & Godlie B.* (S.T.S.) 60 How suld we twin [*ed.* 1621 twine] that na man can depart? 1637 RUTHERFORD *Lett.* (1862) I. 209 We should never twin again, except heaven twinned and sundered us. 1790 *Scots Songs* I. 77 We twa will never twin.

†**b.** To depart, go away (also in weakened sense, to go, proceed); to escape, get free. *Obs.*

*c* 1375 *Sc. Leg. Saints* iv. (*Jacobus*) 375 Out of þis warld þat we ma twene But schame, det, or dedly syne. *c* 1386 CHAUCER *Prol.* 835 Now draweth cut er þat we ferrer twynne He which þat hath the shorteste shal bigynne. — *Monk's T.* 15 O Lucifer...Now artow sathanas, þat mayst nat twynne Out of miserie, in which þat thou art falle. *c* 1400 LYDG. *Flour of Curtesye* 256 And if you liste I dyed, I wolde assente, As ever twinne I quik out of this lynde! *c* 1422 HOCCLEVE *Learn to Die* 183, I keepe nat þat y shal hennes twyne [*rime* synne]. *a* 1600 MONTGOMERIE *Devot. Poems* v. 22 Or thou be sommound by vncerten death,..Sen tym is precious tak it or ȝe tuin.

†**c.** With *from*: To separate oneself from; to part from, take leave of; to depart from, leave, forsake, renounce. *Obs.*

*a* 1300 *Cursor M.* 23182 (Edin.) Fra þat dai forþe..Sal neuir fra bodi sauil tuin. *c* 1375 *Sc. Leg. Saints* xxxiv. (*Pelagia*) 182 Men but nombre..haf I Gert..fra god twyn. *c* 1386 CHAUCER *Pard. Prol.* 102 Yet kan I maken oother folk to twynne From Auarice. 1406 HOCCLEVE *Misrule* 42 Whan fro thee twynned shee. *c* 1430 LYDG. *Min. Poems* (Percy Soc.) 247 Thy feet embracyng fro whiche I shal nat twynne, Mercy requeeryng. 1430–40 — *Bochas* I. xiv. (MS. Bodl. 263) 62/1 Whan the sperit shal fro the body twynne.

**d.** With *with*: To part with; to take leave of; to deprive oneself of, give up.

*a* 1400–50 *Alexander* 2750 He..takis þam of his tresoure

& twynnes with þaim faire. **1486** *Bk. St. Albans* E iij b, When he [the hare] is female and kyndelis hym with in In .iij. degrees he hem berith or he with hem twyn. **1591** R. BRUCE *Serm.* (Wodrow Soc.) 207 No heart..can twin with the thing that it loveth, without exceeding sorrow. **1629** SIR W. MURE *True Crucifixe* Introd. 38 As crucified to sinne Readie for Him, with each thing els to twinne Wee labour should. **1721** RAMSAY *Katy's Answer* iii, He's unco sweer To twin wi' his gear.

†**e.** To break asunder; to burst or cleave in twain. *Obs.*

*c* **1450** *Cov. Myst.* (Shaks. Soc.) 326 Myn herte with peyn is pressyd, For sorwe myn hert doth twynne. **1513** BRADSHAW *St. Werburge* II. 706 For whiche the citezens..Were sore disconsolate, like for to twyn.

**Twin,** *v.*[2] [f. TWIN *a.* and *sb.*]

**1.** *intr.* To bring forth two children or young at a birth; to bear twins.

**1573** [see TWINNING *vbl. sb.*[2] 1]. **1587** HARRISON *England* III. i. in *Holinshed* I. 219/2 Kine..now and then twin. **1614** C. BROOKE *Eglogues* (1772) 99 Whiles thy rams do tup, thy ewes do twyn. **1659** HEYLIN *Examen Hist.* I. 108 The world had..never increased to such vast multitudes in so short a time, if Eve had not twinned at least at every birth. **1817** KEATINGE *Trav.* II. 187 The ewes of this country rarely twin. **1874** T. HARDY *Madding Crowd* xv. (1889) 111 Two more ewes have twinned.

**b.** *trans.* To conceive or bring forth as twins, or as a twin *with* another.

**1607** [see TWINNED *ppl. a.* 1]. **1621** G. SANDYS *Ovid's Met.* IX. (1626) 176 From each seuer'd head Each of her hundred necks two fiercer bred: More strong by twinning heires. **1760–72** H. BROOKE *Fool of Qual.* (1809) IV. 138, I have..a sister, twinned with me in the womb.

**c.** *intr.* in passive sense: To be born at the same birth *with*; to be the twin brother or sister of another. ? *Obs.*

**1604** SHAKS. *Oth.* II. iii. 212 Though he had twinn'd with me, both at a birth. **1701** WATTS *Horæ Lyr.*, *Indian Philos.* ix, Might I but see That gentle nymph that twinn'd with me. **1790** *Bystander* 308 If a brother..who had twinned with him should dare [etc.].

**2.** *trans.* To couple, join, unite, combine (two things or persons) closely or intimately. *lit.* and *fig.*

*c* **1394** *P. Pl. Crede* 496 Here y touche þis two, twynnen hem I þenke. **1611** BIBLE *Exod.* xxvi. 24 They shall be coupled [*marg.* twinned] together beneath. **1616** B. JONSON *Masque Ld. Haddington* Wks. 941 That twins their hearts; and doth, of two, make one. **1667** MILTON *P. L.* XII. 85 True Libertie..alwayes with right Reason dwells Twinn'd, and from her hath no dividual being. **1725** W. HALFPENNY *Sound Building* 22 To form a Centre so, that the Mason.. shall twin their Arches thereon. **1847** TENNYSON *Princ.* I. 56 Still we moved Together, twinn'd as horse's ear and eye.

**b.** *intr.* To be coupled; to join, combine, unite; to be parallel or equal, to agree. *rare.*

**1621** [see TWINNING *ppl. a.*]. **1638** G. SANDYS *Paraphr. Div. Poems, Job* xxxvii. 48 O how inscrutable! his equitie Twins with his Power. **1652** BENLOWES *Theoph.* x. lxxvi, Wealth twins with fear.

**c.** *Cryst.* (*trans.*) To unite (two crystals) according to some definite law so as to form a twin crystal (see TWIN *sb.* 3 b). Only in passive, and in vbl. sb. (TWINNING *vbl. sb.*[2] 2).

**1845** [see TWIN *sb.* 3 b]. **1883** *Encycl. Brit.* XVI. 363/2 Occasionally a simple form is twinned with a more complex one, as in chabasite. **1895** STORY-MASKELYNE *Crystallogr.* vii. § 193 Crystals twinned on an octahedron-face. *Ibid.* § 194 Two crystals twinned round an axis.

**3.** *trans.* To be, or furnish, a 'twin' or counterpart to; to match, parallel.

**1605** *1st Pt. Ieronimo* II. ii. 14 A suit iust of Andreas cullers, Proportiond in all parts—nay, twins his own. **1869** *Good Words* 1 Mar. 176 Thou hast no mate To..twin those matchless heights. **1873** LOWELL *Graves Eng. Soldiers Concord* 32 O'erhead the balanced hen-hawk slides, Twinned in the river's heaven below.

**4.** *Agric.* To break up or clear (land) with a 'twin' (TWIN *sb.* 3 c). *local.*

**1841** HARTSHORNE *Salopia Antiq.* Gloss., Twinning to tak away the scutch. **1859** *Jrnl. R. Agric. Soc.* XX. I. 217 Some of the turnip-soil, broken up and then 'twinned'.

**Twin-born,** *a.* Born a twin or twins; born at the same birth, as two, or one of two. Usually *fig.*

**1599** SHAKS. *Hen. V*, IV. i. 251 Let vs our Liues, our Soules,..our Sinnes, lay on the King:..O hard Condition, Twin-borne with Greatnesse. **1610** HEALEY *St. Aug. Citie of God* 122 Him that misliked the fellowship of his owne twin-borne brother. *c* **1647** MILTON *Sonnet* xii. 6 As when those Hinds..Raild at Latona's twin-born progenie. **1753** HANWAY *Trav.* (1762) I. III. xxx. 134 Ingratitude..is twin-born with pride. **1781** COWPER *Expost.* 634 Wisdom and Goodness are twin-born. **1855** BAILEY *Mystic*, etc. (ed. 2) 103 Twin-born passions.

**Twin-brother.** (Also as two words.) [TWIN *a.* 3.] A brother born at the same birth, as one of twins. Also *fig.* something closely related to or resembling the other thing mentioned.

**1598** SHAKS. *Merry W.* II. i. 74 Heere's the twyn-brother of thy Letter: but let thine inherit first, for I protest mine neuer shall. **1727** SWIFT *Wonder of Wonders* Wks. 1755 II. II. 51 He hath..a twin-brother, who lives over against him. **1829** LYTTON *Devereux* I. iii, My twin brother, Gerald, was a tall, strong, handsome boy. **1850** TENNYSON *In Mem.* lxviii, Sleep, Death's twin-brother.

**Twinch, twinck(e,** obs. forms of TWINK.

†**Twind** (twaind), *v. Obs.* Also **twinde, twynd;** *pa. t.* and *pple.* **twound.** [Variant of TWINE *v.*[1], perh. after the pa. t. and pple. *twined*, or by assimilation to WIND *v.*]

**1.** *trans.* To twist, twine, wind, turn.

**1548** THOMAS *Ital. Dict.* (1550), *Imbarbugliare*, to tangle, twynde, encombre. *a* **1562** G. CAVENDISH *Poems*, etc. (1825) II. 93 The spyndells end alredy is at the ground, The thred ontwynned cannot more be twound. **1590** FENNE *Fruits* F f j, In token of her last farewell her head towards me she twound [*rime* bound]. **1606** MARSTON *Sophonisba* III. i, Syphax with his dagger twound about her haire, drags in Sophonisba. **1610** MARKHAM *Masterp.* II. clvii. 464 Take a tampin of horse haire twound together. **1616** SURFL. & MARKH. *Country Farme* 130 The Rider euer obseruing..to make the Colt goe straight forth-right, and by no meanes to turne or twynd him about anie way. *Ibid.* 154 When the Brambles begin to shoot forth, to interlace them and twynd them bought-wise about the blacke Thornes. **1659** TORRIANO, *Torcere*, to wrap, to twinde in [**1598** FLORIO, winde in].

**2.** *intr.* To become entangled or knotted; to twist, twine, wind.

**1575** TURBERV. *Falconrie* 175 The falcon bating this way and that way she shall neuer twinde nor tangle bicause the ring followeth hir still. **1575** GASCOIGNE *Flowers, Dan Barth.* Tri. i. 19 The gentle slippe, which could both twist and twind. *c* **1626** W. BOSWORTH *Arcadius & Sepha* I. 955 She turn'd To Ivy, whence it still is twinding found.

**3.** Of an arrow: To part *from* the bow. *rare*$^{-1}$. (Cf. TWINE *v.*[1] 7 b.)

**1592** WYRLEY *Armorie, Ld. Chandos* 50 As the arrow from the bow doth twind [*rime* behind] He flieth towards the enimies field.

Hence **Twi·nding** *vbl. sb.*, **Twound** *ppl. a.*

**1600** W. WATSON *Decacordon* (1602) 35 Their dissimulation,..sophistication, winding, twinding, and doubling. *Ibid.* 335 [The hawk] flew a foule flight in windings, twindings, and girdings ouer all. **1610** MARKHAM *Masterp.* II. xviii. 245 Hard new twound hemp. **1616** SURFL. & MARKH. *Country Farme* 663 The making of naues for waggons or cart-wheeles, for which..the more knottie and twound they are, a great deale the fitter they are for that purpose.

**Twindle** (twi·nd'l), *sb.* Now *dial.* Also 6 **twyndle, -del,** 9 **twinnel.** [app. for **twinnle*, dim. of TWIN *sb.*: see -LE. Cf. OHG. *zwinal*, *-el*, *zwenel* (adj.), twin.] = TWIN *sb.* I.

**1526** R. WHYTFORD *Martiloge* 45 A woman..with her two chylder twyndles. **1529** RASTELL *Pastyme* (1811) 12 Romulus and Remus, bredyrne and twyndels. **1642** in Collins *Kirkburton Regrs.* (1887) I. 237 Thomas and Elizabeth children of Thomas Hepworth beinge twindles. **1674** LOWE *Lanc. Diary* (1876) 43 Ffriday was buried a twindle of John Leyland...lordsday was buryed the other twindle of John Leylands. *a* **1800** PEGGE *Suppl. Grose*, *Twindles*, twins. Lanc. **1882** *Lanc. Gloss.*, *Twindles*, twins.

**b.** *attrib.* = TWIN *a.* 4 b.

**1636** W. SAMPSON *Vow-Breaker* H ij, I dream'd my husband, when he came first a woing, cam i' the liknes of a Kentish twindle Pippen; that is, just as if two stones grew together.

Hence **Twindle** (twinnel) *v.*, *intr.* to bring forth twins: = TWIN *v.*[2] I.

**1845** THORNBER *Penny Stone* (1886) 14 Mother Cowburne has twinnelled.

**Twine** (twəin), *sb.*[1] (*a.*) Forms: 1 **tuiȝin, tuuin, tuin,** 1–3 **twin,** 4–5, (7) **twyn,** 4–7 **twyne,** (5 **tuyne,** 6 **twhyne, twind),** 6– **twine.** [OE. *twin* (also early *twiȝin*) = Du. and Flem. *twijn* (in Kilian also *tweyn*), related to TWINE *v.*[1], and ultimately from the stem of TWI-. Cf. ON. and Icel. *tvinni* (Norw. dial. *tvinne*, Da. *tvinde*, dial. *twin*, *twen*, NFris. *twin*), Du. *tweern*, MLG. *twern*, MHG. and G. *zwirn* in the same sense.]

**1.** Thread or string composed of two or more yarns or strands twisted together; now *spec.* string or strong thread, made of hemp, cotton, or other fibre, used for sewing coarse materials (as canvas or sacking), tying packages, netting, and the like; with *a* and *pl.* a piece or kind of this.

In OE. found only as a rendering of L. *byssus*, *bissus*, prob. through association of this with *bis* twice. In mod. English use chiefly technical or commercial, but in Scotland and U. S. common as a general synonym of *string*.

*c* **725** *Corpus Gloss.* (O.E.T.) 343 *Byssum*, tuin. *a* **800** *Erfurt Gloss.* 138 *Byssum*, tuiȝin. *c* **897** K. ÆLFRED *Gregory's Past. C.* xiv. 83 Ðæt hræȝl..of twispunnenum twine linenum. *Ibid.* 87 Ðæt scyle beon twiðræwen twin on ðæm masseȝierelan. *c* **1000** *Ags. Gosp.* Luke xvi. 19 He wæs ȝescrydd mid purpuran & mid twine. *c* **1205** LAY. 14220 Nes þe þwong noht swiðe bræd, Buten swulc a twines þræd. *c* **1385** CHAUCER *L. G. W.* 2016 (*Ariadne*), By a clewe of twyn [*v. r.* twyne] as he hath gon..he may returne a-non. **14..** HOCCLEVE *Ad beatam Virginem* 71 His sotil snares, and cacchynge twyn. *c* **1425** tr. *Arderne's Treat. Fistula* 23 A fourfold þrede of silk white or of strong lyne or tuyne. **1481–90** *Howard Househ. Bks.* (Roxb.) 63 Paid for marlyn twyn xvj. d. *c* **1500** *New Not-br. Mayd* 297 in Hazl. *E. P. P.* II. 284 Shetis clene, to lye betwene, made of thred and twyne. **1512–13** *Durham Acc. Rolls* (Surtees) 106 Pro vj li. lez sayll twyne..xviij$^{d}$. **1592** R. D. *Hypnerotom.* 17 b, A spindle ful of twind. **1614** GORGES *Lucan* VIII. 346 A twine, That strangle may this throate of mine. **1692** *Capt. Smith's Seaman's Gram.* II. xxxi. 150 The Cases..must be Armed about with strong Twine or Cord. **1719** DE FOE *Crusoe* (Globe) 20 A Parcel of Twine or Thread. *Ibid.* 578 We had Twine or Packthread. **1791** COWPER *Odyss.* x. 30 The winds, ..so bound With silver twine that not a breath escaped. **1806–7** J. BERESFORD *Miseries Hum. Life* (1826) III. xii, No garters, except twine, which you are at last obliged to use. **1827** D. JOHNSON *Ind. Field Sports* 42 To these cords a small twine or silk thread is fixed. **1862** *Catal. Internat. Exhib., Brit.* II. No. 3659, Cotton twines run 30 per cent. longer length than hemp, same weight. **1867** SMYTH *Sailor's Word-bk.* s.v., Irish twine or thumb-line, like nettles, is worked by the fingers from fine yarns drawn from bolt-rope. **1871** C. GIBBON *Lack of Gold* vi, He had a bundle of twine between his teeth.

**b.** *transf.* and *fig.* in various applications.

**1557** *Tottell's Misc.* (Arb.) 165 Of her vntrue professed loue so feble is the twine. **1567** DRANT *Horace, Epistles* II. i. G vij, Our toyle..in making of our poems..By drawing them so featly forth and with so cleane a twyne. **1595** MARKHAM *Sir R. Grinvile* cxxiii, Behold a goddesse shall my lifes twine breake. **1614** SYLVESTER *Bethulia's Rescue* II. 279 That sacred Twine Which Man to Man, and Man to God doth joyn. **1615** HIERON *Wks.* I. 595 An holy twine, artificially made vp..of three seuerall threeds..for the fastning of the soule of a Christian to his God. **1667** DRYDEN *Secret Love* III. i, Destiny..Spinn's all their fortunes in a silken twine. **1728–46** THOMSON *Spring* 210 The dissolving clouds Form..thy showery prism; And..unfold The various twine of light. *a* **1763** SHENSTONE *Elegies* xviii. 58 Rob'd in the Gallic loom's extraneous twine. **1895** CROCKETT *Men of Moss-Hags* xxv. 187 It liketh us to go to our King's court through the crash of battle rather than through the hank of the hangman's twine.

**2.** A twined or twisted object or part. **a.** A twining or trailing stem or spray of a plant.

**1579** SPENSER *Sheph. Cal.* Oct. 111 My temples..girt in girlonds of wild Yuie twine. **1590** — *F. Q.* I. vi. 14 With an yuie twine his waste is girt about. **1652** CULPEPPER *Eng. Physic.* 35 The root..with many long twines or branches growing from it. *a* **1678** MARVELL *Appleton Ho.* 609 Bind me, ye woodbines, in your 'twines. **1908** *Blackw. Mag.* Oct. 536 Golden clusters from the twine depend.

**b.** A fold; a coil; a convolution; a twist or turn in the course of anything.

**1600** FAIRFAX *Tasso* XVIII. c, That glorious ensigne, with a thousand twines. **1629** MILTON *Nativity* 226 Typhon huge ending in snaky twine. **1649** G. DANIEL *Trinarch.* To Rdr. 191 A trayterous spider in the Twine Of her owne Thred. **1814** SCOTT *Ld. of Isles* VI. xiii, A diadem of gold..And clasp'd within its glittering twine Was seen the glove of Argentine. **1870** E. PEACOCK *Ralf Skirl.* I. 22 As full of twines as a sheep-track.

**c.** A tangle, knot, snarl. In quots. *fig.*

**1865** J. THOMSON *Art* I. i, Such subtle knots and twines! **1869** BROWNING *Ring & Bk.* VIII. 778 So multiplied were reasons *pro* and *con*, Delicate, intertwisted and obscure, That Law refused loan of a finger-tip To unravel, re-adjust the hopeless twine.

**3.** The action or an act of twining. **a.** An embrace, a clasping. Now *rare* or *Obs.*

**1602** MARSTON *Antonio's Rev.* I. iv. Wks. 1856 I. 84 Clipping the strumpet with luxurious twines. **1607** BEAUMONT *Woman Hater* II. i, The twyns of Adders, and of Scorpions..will seem to me More tickling than those claspes, which men adore. **1697** DRYDEN *Virg. Georg.* II. 301 Aspiring Vines, Embracing Husband Elms in am'rous twines. **1759** W. MASON *Caractacus* Poems 1830 II. 78 In undulating twine, The foaming snakes prolific join. *a* **1839** L. E. LANDON *Poems* (1844) I. 34 The lattice..Half hidden by a bridal twine Of jasmine with the emerald vine.

**b.** *poet.* in various applications: see quots.

**1615** CHAPMAN *Odyss.* x. 306 As she some web wrought; or her spindles twine She cherisht with her song. **1652** J. RAMSEY in *Fletcher's Wild Goose Chase* Pref. Verses a ij, Till to his watry Center he [*sc.* the river] hath got By wrigling twines, subtile as Fletcher's plot. **1880** BROWNING *Dram. Idyls, Pan & Luna* 51 Vain each twist and twine Those lithe limbs try.

**c.** A turn of fortune, a vicissitude.

**1768** ROSS *Helenore* III. 124 A' that's past By unko twines, has fa'en sae well.

† **4.** as *adj.* Made by twining or twisting; twisted; spun. *Obs. rare.* (See also TWINE THREAD.)

**1513** DOUGLAS *Æneis* IV. x. 102 The god..biddis smyte the twyne cabill in tuay. **1583** *Durham Wills* (Surtees) II. 78, ij pair of twine roppes.

†**b.** Of a line: Forming a spiral; helical. *Obs. rare*$^{-1}$.

**1551** RECORDE *Pathw. Knowl.* I. Defin., A twine or twist line..goeth as a wreyth about some other bodie.

**5.** *attrib.* and *Comb.*, as *twine-ball* (BALL *sb.*[1] 10 c), *-box*, *colour*, *-cord*, *-maker*, *net*, *netting*, *-reel*, *-tone*; *twine-coloured*, *-like*, *-toned* adjs.; *twine-making*, *-twisting* adjs. and sbs.; also **twine-binder,** a binder which ties the sheaves with twine (cf. *wire-binder*); so **twine-binding** *a.*; **twine-bush,** an Australian shrub, *Hakea flexilis*, N.O. *Proteaceæ* (*Cent. Dict.* 1889, s. v. *Hakea*); **twine cloth,** fine cotton shirting, calico; **twine-cutter**: see quot.; **twine-grass,** the Tufted Vetch (*Vicia Cracca*), or the Hairy Vetch (*V. hirsuta*); **twine-holder, twine-machine,** † **twine-masking** [cf. MASK *sb.*[1]], **twine-reeler**: see quots.; **twine-spinner,** one who spins twine; so **twine-spinning; twine-wheel,** in a spinning-machine, a wheel through which the twisting motion is given. See also TWINE THREAD.

**1889** *Pall Mall G.* 26 Dec. 5/3 Freethinkers who imagine themselves able to sound with their penny *twine-balls the ocean of immensity. **1902** *Sci. Amer. Supp.* 20 Dec. 22546/3 A practical *twine binder. *Ibid.*, He established *twine binding machines as the grain harvesters of the time. **1907** *Westm. Gaz.* 1 Aug. 2/1 In the tinsmiths' shop..*twine-boxes, boxes for stamping-pads, and similar articles, are turned out. **1815** *Roy. Milit. Chron.* June *Advt.*, The New Imperial *Twine Cloth..for family use and for Sheeting. **1882** *Daily News* 3 June 3/1 Lace in the prevalent *twine colour. **1897** *Westm. Gaz.* 25 Mar. 3/2 Nile green and *twine-coloured lace. **1712** STEELE *Spect.* No. 444 ¶ 4 A *Twine-Cord, strained with two Nails at each End, over his Window. **1862** *Catal. Internat. Exhib., Brit.* II. No. 3800 Twine cord and line. **1875** KNIGHT *Dict. Mech.*, **Twine-cutter*, a blade or knife on a table, stand, or counter, to cut twine when tying packages. **1744–50** W. ELLIS *Mod. Husbandm.* VI. II. 48 (E.D.S.) Wild thetch or *twine-grass. **1875** KNIGHT *Dict. Mech.*, **Twine-holder*, a box or case to hold a ball of twine on a counter. **1817** COLERIDGE *Biog. Lit.* 82 Lank, black, *twine-like hair. **1875** KNIGHT *Dict. Mech.*, **Twine-machine*, a spinning-machine for small hempen or cotton string. **1815** SIMOND *Tour Gt. Brit.* II. 79 A number of *twine-makers. **1904** *Daily News* 18 May 5 At eleven I started *twine-making. **1615** E. S. *Britain's Buss* B iij, The 7 deepinges of each net are to be sowed, each to other, altogether, with a small thred called, *Twine Masking. **1855** *Poultry Chron.* II. 574 One tarred *Twine Net, 9 feet long, by 9 wide. **1854** *Ibid.* I. 228 New *twine netting..one yard wide, 1½d. per yard. **1858** SIMMONDS *Dict. Trade*, **Twine-reel*, a shop reel or box for holding string. *Ibid.*, **Twine-reeler*, a mule-doubler; a string-twister. **1723** *Lond. Gaz.* No. 6128/4 Foulk Wyatt,..*Twine-spinner or Ropemaker. **1896** *Daily News* 14 Nov. 7/6 A retired twine spinner. **1808** *Pict. London* 235 Rope-making and *twine-spinning. **1900** *Westm. Gaz.* 22 Mar. 3/1 *Twine-toned lawn...To get that *twine-tone,..one must either tint one's white collar with tea or coffee or [etc.]. **1897** *Daily News* 1 June 1/1 *Twine twisting and polishing mills for making the yarns into twines and thread. **1884** W. S. B. McLAREN *Spinning* viii. 159 The driving power comes.. through all the *twine wheels, to the front roller.

Hence **Twi·neless** *a.*, destitute of twine.

**1909** A. REID *Kirriemuir* ii. 12 They were the laddies' 'strings' in an almost twineless age.

†**Twine,** *sb.*[2] *Obs. nonce-wd.* [app. f. TWI- after TRINE (cf. *twinity*, s.v. TWIN *a.* and *sb.*).] Division, separation, disunion.

**1606** SYLVESTER *Du Bartas* II. iv. II. *Magnif.* 1338 Th' Vnity dwels in God, i' th' Fiend the Twine.

†**Twine,** app. an error for TUNNY.

The form is prob. due to mere copying of a misprint.

**1601** CHESTER *Love's M.* (1878) 100 Here swimmes the Shad..The Twine, the Trout, the Scallop, and the Whiting. [Cf. 1589 RIDER *Bibl. Schol.* 1724 A fish called a Twinne.. *Pelamys*; *ed.* 1617 II. Thinnie; *ed.* 1640 Thunny.]

**Twine** (twəin), *v.*[1] Forms: 4–7 **twyne**, 4 (9 *dial.*) **tweyne**, 4–5 **twyn**, 6 *Sc.* **tuyn**, 6– **twine**. *Pa. t.* and *pple.* **twined**; also *pa. t.* 6 *Sc.* **twane**; *pa. pple.* 4 **twynnen**, 6 **twon**, 7 **twone**. See also TWIND *v.* [ME. *twīnen*, = WFris. *twine*, *twynje*, Du. *twijnen* (in Kilian also *tweynen*), related to TWINE *sb.*[1] Cf. Icel., Norw., Sw. *tvinna*, Da. *tvinde* (NFris. *twinne*, etc.), and Du. *tweernen*, MLG. *twernen*, MHG. and G. *zwirnen* (OHG. *zwirnên*), to twist (thread).]

**I.** *trans.* **1.** To twist (two or more strands or filaments) together so as to form a thread or cord; to twist (one thread, etc.) *with* another; to form (thread or cord) by twisting or spinning; to spin (yarn, etc.) into thread or cord; also generally, to combine or make compact by twisting.

*c* **1275** LAY. 14220 Nas þe þwang noht brod Bote ase hit were a twined þred [*c* 1205 a twines þræd]. **13..** *Gaw. & Gr. Knt.* 191 Þe tayl & his toppyng [were] twynnen of a sute & bounden boþe wyth a bande. **1377** LANGL. *P. Pl.* B. XVII. 204 To a torche or a tapre þe trinitee is lykned; As wex and a weke were twyned [*v. rr.* tweyned, twynnyd] togideres. **14..** *Tundale's Vis.* (Wagner) 1885 The cordes.. were alle wyth silver twynned [*rime* shynned]. **1447** BOKENHAM *Seyntys* (Roxb.) 8 My fatal threed..Wych lachesys hath twynyd ful yerys fyfty. *c* **1470** HENRYSON *Mor. Fab.* VIII. (*Preach. Swallow*) xxx, His wyfe it span, and twynit [*Bann. MS.* twane] it in to threid. **1523** FITZHERB. *Husb.* § 25 Make a lyttell rope..and twyne it as harde together bytwen your handes as ye canne, and soo beynge hard twon,..cut it. **1599** HAKLUYT *Voy.* II. II. 91 They..do curiously keame their dainty locks..and, hauing twined and bound them vp, they couer them with calles. **1681** in *New Mills Cloth Manuf.* (S.H.S.) Introd. 86 [Wool] to be carded spunn twisted and twyned for listing to the cloaths made. **1697** DRYDEN *Virg. Georg.* I. 357 Let him..twine The Sallow Twigs to tye the stragling Vine. **1803** R. ANDERSON *Cumberld. Ball.* 55, I mind..at her wheel, How she'd tweyne the slow thread. **1855** KINGSLEY *Westw. Ho!* xxv, We'll twine a double strong halter for the Captain. **1899** RIDER HAGGARD *Swallow* xi, To twine little threads into a rope.

**b.** *fig.*

**14..** *Beryn* 686 Þe Nyȝtyngale, His amerous notis, lo, how he twyneth smale! [Cf. OUT-TWINE *v.*, quot. *a* 1400]. **1430–40** LYDG. *Bochas* I. xi. (MS. Bodl. 263) 52/2 Whan Antropos our lyuys threed hath twyned. **1612** *Two Noble K.* II. ii. 70 Our fortunes Were twyn'd together. **1651** N. BACON *Disc. Govt. Eng.* II. xxvii. (1739) 128 By Oath, which to make sure, was treble twined. **1670** DRYDEN *1st Pt. Conq. Granada* IV. ii, My clue of Life is twin'd with Ozmyn's Thred. **1827** SCOTT *Highl. Widow* i, If I persisted in twisting the discourse one way while Donald was twining it another, I should make his objection, like a hempen-cord, ..the tougher. **1833** LAMB *Elia* Ser. II. Pref. (1865) 236 To imply and twine with his own identity the griefs and affections of another. **1871** R. H. HUTTON *Ess.* (1877) I. 77 So closely twined are the threads of human faith and scepticism.

**c.** *transf.* To form by interlacing; to weave, to wreathe.

**1612** DRAYTON *Poly-olb.* xv. 139 The Naiads..some dainty Chaplets twine. **1697** DRYDEN *Virg. Æneid* VIII. 365 A double wreath Evander twin'd. **1709** PRIOR *Love & Friendship* 51 I'll twine fresh Garlands for Alexis' Brows. **1817** MOORE *Lalla R.* (1824) 311 Oh! twine that wreath for me tonight. **1858** W. T. MATSON *Armiger* iv. Poems 59 Mourning garlands twined of many a bloom Of doleful hue.

**d.** *transf.* To interlace, entwine.

**1679** S. LEE in *Row's 'Emmanuel'* Pref., Pray for the mantle..of Elijah, for the love of John, and the zeal of Paul, to twine hands together. *a* **1701** MAUNDRELL *Journ. Jerus.*, *Euphrates* (1732) 2 Two Syrens..twining their fishy Tails together. **1870** MRS. RIDDELL *Austin Friars* ii, She only sat still, with her fingers twined together. **1880** *Blackw. Mag.* Feb. 218 Reata..sat twining her fingers together in silence.

**2.** To cause (one thing) to encircle or embrace another; to twist, wreathe, clasp, or wrap (a thing) *about* or *around* another; also, to insert (one thing) *in* or *into* another with a twisting or sinuous movement (also *fig.*).

*c* **1585** MONTGOMERIE *Sonn.* viii. 9 About his temple tuyn ȝour laurell leivis with palmis perfytly plet. **1602** MARSTON *Antonio's Rev.* II. i. Wks. 1856 I. 89, I have but newly twone my arme in the curld locks Of snakie vengeance. **1607** SHAKS. *Cor.* IV. v. 112 Let me twine Mine armes about that body. **1613** PURCHAS *Pilgrimage* (1614) 513 In many places he insinuates himselfe within the Land by Gulfes or Bayes, twining his louing armes about some whole countries. **1617** MORYSON *Itin.* I. 239 Long bracelets of peeces of gold twined about his arme. **1789** E. DARWIN *Bot. Gard.*, *Loves Plants* II. 180 Round the white circlet in relievo bold, A Serpent twines his scaly length. **1820** W. IRVING *Sketch Bk.* I. 38 (*The Wife*) The vine, which has long twined its graceful foliage about the oak. **1838** SPARKS *Biog.* IX. 27 The only garment they possess is a blanket elegantly twined about them. **1853** ROCK *Ch. of Fathers* III. II. 25 'Tropes'.. twined and threaded into the words of the daily service. **1862** MISS BRADDON *Lady Audley* xxxii, My lady twined her fingers in her amber curls. **1890** R. BRIDGES *Shorter Poems* (1912) 298, I feel thy being twine Her graces over me. **1901** ALLDRIDGE *Sherbro* xxi. 220 The stem [of the pipe]..formed separately by twining a strip of clay round a thin stick of palm cane.

**b.** *refl.*

**1543** TRAHERON *Vigo's Chirurg.* Interpr., *Vitis alba*..twyneth it self aboute brambles, wyth hys tendrelles, as a vine byndeth it selfe to trees. **1662** J. DAVIES tr. *Olearius' Voy. Ambass.* 10 One end of the rope..twin'd itself about one of the Rocks. **1796** MORSE *Amer. Geog.* I. 220 They [Snakes] have sometimes twined themselves round the bodies of children, squeezing them till they die. **1823** LAMB *Elia* Ser. II. *Poor Relations*, Awful ideas..twined themselves about his presence. **1852** ROBERTSON *Serm.* Ser. III. xvii. 216 Round which the heart's best affections have twined themselves.

**3.** To enfold, wreathe, or encircle (one thing) *with* another; also of a plant, wreath, etc.: to clasp, encircle, enwrap. Also *fig.*

**1602** MARSTON *Antonio's Rev.* III. iii. Wks. 1856 I. 111 Maist thou be twined with the softst embrace Of clere eternitie. **1712–14** POPE *Rape Lock* III. 161 Let wreaths of triumph now my temples twine. **1790** W. WRIGHTE *Grotesque Archit.* 3 Branches of trees twined round with ivy. **1819** WIFFEN *Aonian Hours* (1820) 102 The weed of ruin darkly twines Her marble walls. **1848** LYTTON *Harold* I. i, Boys, with their May-gads (peeled willow wands twined with cowslips). **1876** LOWELL *Among my Bks.* Ser. II. 127 Twining the bare stem of old tradition with graceful sentiment.

**4. a.** To turn (something) *about, away, round,* etc.; to twist or wring. Now *dial.*

**1598** B. JONSON *Ev. Man in Hum.* I. v, O, twine your body more about, that you may fall to a more sweet, comely, gentleman-like guard. **1600** FAIRFAX *Tasso* XVII. lvii, From the waste shore their steps at last they twinde. *Ibid.* XX. cxxviii, She shrikes, and twines away her sdeignefull eies, From his sweete face. *a* **1655** J. NAYLOR *Answ. Perfect Pharisee* 12 You wrest and twine the Scriptures. **1901** F. E. TAYLOR *Folk-Speech S. Lanc.* s.v. (E.D.D.), Iv aw catch him, aw'll twoine his neck reawnd.

**b.** To get *off*, or *out*, by twisting. Now *dial.*

**1600** FAIRFAX *Tasso* XI. xliii, He..from the wound the reed out twinde, But left the iron in his flesh behinde. **1705** S. WESLEY in Quiller Couch *Hetty Wesley* (1913) I. ix. 87 The iron latch of my door was twined off. **1885** *Ballads & Poems Glasgow Club* 213 Twine out his lugs, root out his tongue.

**II.** *intr.* **5.** To wind or twist (*about, over,* or *round* something); almost always of a plant: to grow in a twisting or spiral manner; *spec.* to become twisted or wreathed together in growing; to grow in spiral convolutions. Also *fig.*

**13..** *E. E. Allit. P.* B. 1691 Faxe fyltered,..Þat schad fro his schulderes..& twenty-folde twynande hit to his tos raȝt. **1567** MAPLET *Gr. Forest* 64 b, It [woodbine] twineth like a threede or line, about other herbes and fruits. **1592** SHAKS. *Ven. & Ad.* 873 Some [bushes] twin'd about her thigh to make her stay. **1647** CRASHAW *Panegyr. Dk. York's Birth* 38 For whose manly brow Both laurels twine into one wreath. *a* **1652** J. SMITH *Sel. Disc.* i. 7 Like the wanton ivy..it will twine about our judgments and understandings. **1697** DRYDEN *Virg. Past.* VIII. 17 Amidst thy Laurels let this Ivy twine. *a* **1748** THOMSON *Happy Man* 9 For whom the cooling shade in summer twines. **1810** SCOTT *Lady of L.* I. xxvi, Where Ellen's hand had taught to twine The ivy and Idæan vine. **1831** JAMES *Phil. Augustus* I. ii, A thousand shrubs and flowers twined..over them. **1875** McLAREN *Serm.* Ser. II. viii. 136 His heart and will twined ..round the fragments. **1875** BENNETT & DYER *Sachs' Bot.* 772 Only a few plants twine to the right..the greater number twine to the left. **1879** TENNYSON *Lover's T.* I. 128 The light soul twines and mingles with the growths Of vigorous early days.

†**b.** To become entangled or complicated. *Obs. rare.*

**1658** OSBORN *Adv. Son* Wks. (1673) 220 Whilst one is unraveling, another twines.

†**6. a.** Of a weapon: To twist or turn aside. *Obs.*

*c* **1400** *Rowland & Otuel* 557 Þe Sarazene..hit hym on þe hede..And nere þe swerde twynede hade, His life þer hade he lefede.

†**b.** Of timber: To be contorted or irregular in formation. *Obs. rare.*

**1601** HOLLAND *Pliny* XVI. xxxviii. I. 486 If a man lay his eare close to one end of a beame or peece of timber, he shall heare the knocke or pricke that is made but with a penknife at the other end...By this meanes also a man shall find when the timber doth twine. *Ibid.* XVI. xl. 490 Because it twineth and casteth not, it is passing good for hinges and hookes, for sawne bords, for ledges in dores and gates.

**7.** To extend or proceed in a winding manner; to bend, incline circuitously; to wind about, meander; of a serpent, etc., to crawl sinuously (also *refl.*).

**1553** [see TWINING *vbl. sb.*]. **1601** HOLLAND *Pliny* VI. xvii. I. 124 Streight forth, as farre as to that place where India beginneth to twine and bend toward the Indian sea. **1610** HOLLAND *Camden's Brit.*, *Irel.* II. 117 The shore, as it twineth backe from hence Southerly. **1674** JOSSELYN *Voy. New Eng.* 2 The 28th we twined into the Downs. *c* **1710** CELIA FIENNES *Diary* (1888) 291 The river runns twineing about. *a* **1774** TUCKER *Lt. Nat.* (1834) II. 464, I have been forced to twist and twine over a great deal more ground than had otherwise been needful. **1831** SCOTT *Ct. Robt.* ix, The snake..twines himself through the grass. **1857** GOSSE *Omphalos* ii. 40 Sea-worms twined over the mud. **1902** BUCHAN *Watcher by Threshold* 267 The little brown river ..twined to the sea. **1913** *Daily News* 28 Mar. 6 A highway..twining through a wilderness.

†**b.** To turn away. *Obs. rare.*

**1600** FAIRFAX *Tasso* XVIII. xxxiii, But yet the knight, wise, warie, not vnkind, Drew foorth his sword and from her carelesse twind. **1614** W. BROWNE *Shepherd's Pipe* B vj b, He twyned thence, and home to his countree.

†**c.** To bend, bow, or sink *down*. *Obs.*[−1]

**1600** FAIRFAX *Tasso* XX. xliii, Right on the front he gaue that Ladie kinde A blow, so huge,..That out of sense and feeling, downe she twinde.

**8.** To contort the body; to writhe, wriggle, squirm. Now *dial.*

**1666** BUNYAN *Grace Abounding* § 166 Thus did I wind, and twine, and shrink under the burthen that was upon me. **1680** V. ALSOP *Mischief Impos.* iii. 19 When men are pincht with plain Scripture, they use to twist and twine and turn themselves into all shapes to get out of their streights. **1734** tr. *Rollin's Anc. Hist.* (1827) I. 75 The antagonists tumbling and twining with each other. **1837** MRS. PALMER *Devonshire Dial.* II. 17 I'd twack thee till I made thee twine like an angletwitch. **1877** MRS. M. TROTTER *Gall. Gossip* 290 The wean twining and kicking.

**Twine,** *v.*[2] *Sc.* [Later form of TWIN *v.*[1], prob. by misunderstanding of ambiguous spellings under the influence of TWINE *v.*[1]] *intr.* and *trans.* To separate, part, etc.; = TWIN *v.*[1] in various uses.

It is doubtful whether an inf. *twyne* is to be assumed for the ME. examples of the pa. t. *twynde* cited below; in other cases the form is shown by rimes or other evidence to be a mere variant of TWIN *v.*[1] The spelling *twin'd* is ambiguous, and may represent either *twined* or *twinned*.

[*c* **1450** *St. Cuthbert* (Surtees) 6305 In partyes he it twynde, Ȝit sulde he..within a while Aboute his nek it fynde. *a* **1500** *New Nut-brown Maid* 303 in Hazlitt *E. P. P.* III. 13 And I am twynde Out of his mynde, Ryght as a banysshed man.] **1621** [see quot. 1567 s.v. TWIN *v.*[1] 2 a]. **1728** RAMSAY *Robt., Richy, & Sandy* 57 Twin'd of its nourishment it lifeless lay. **1795** BURNS *Destr. Woods Drumlanrig* v, What ruefu' chance Has twin'd ye o' your stately trees? ?*a* **1800** *Bob Norice* vi. in Child *Ballads* (1886) II. 267/2 To twyne him o his wife. **1886** STEVENSON *Kidnapped* xviii, 'You and me must twine', I said...'I will hardly twine from ye, David, without some kind of reason for the same', said Alan. **1894** R. REID in *Poets of Dumfriesshire* x. (1910) 303 Cauld maun his heart be, twined o' its joys. **1895** CROCKETT *Men of Moss-Hags* 31 What cause is guid that twines a woman frae her ain man?

**Twined** (twəind), *ppl. a.* [f. TWINE *v.*[1] + -ED[1].] That has been twined, in various senses of the verb; twisted, plaited, curled, coiled, wreathed, etc.

*c* **1275** [see TWINE *v.*[1] 1]. **1510** STANBRIDGE *Vocabula* (W. de W.) C ij, *Filum contortum*, twyned threde. **1513** DOUGLAS *Æneis* VII. vii. 88 The round top of tre, Hit with the twynit quhyp, dois quherle. **1535** COVERDALE *Judg.* xvi. 9 He brake the roapes in sunder, euen as a twyned threde breaketh, whan it hath catched the heate of the fyre. **1539** BIBLE (Great) *Exod.* xxvi. 36 An hangynge.. of yelow sylke, purple, scarlet, & white twined silk. **1565** JEWEL *Repl. Harding* (1611) 66 The substance of all that he hath alleged hitherto, hangeth only by a twined threed. **1568** *Satir. Poems Reform.* xlviii. 35 Off all thir thre hewis I haif left clewis,..Tuynit and small. **1576** FLEMING *Panopl. Epist.* 310 One hanges himselfe..with a twyned haulter. **1611** COTGR., *Espée Romaine*, certaine twined, and retorted haires on a horse;..by some called, a feather. **1668** CULPEPPER & COLE *Barthol. Anat.* I. xi. 25 [It] spreds it self upon the Colon like a twined worm. **1799** *Hull Advertiser* 23 Feb. 3/2, 500 millfuls of twined yarn. **1851** MRS. BROWNING *Casa Guidi Wind.* II. 509 Priestcraft burns out, the twinèd linen blazes. **1900** CROCKETT *Black Douglas* I The twined May-pole had not yet been taken down.

**Twiner** (twəi·nəɹ). [f. TWINE *v.*[1] + -ER[1].]

**1.** One who or that which twines; *esp.* one who or a machine which twines or spins thread: see quot. 1891.

**1611** COTGR., *Retordeur*, a twister, twiner; a wrester, a retorter. **1708** SEWEL II, *Twynder*, a twiner, throster. **1864** JEFFREY *Hist. Roxburghshire* IV. ii. 117 In 1810 the twiner was invented by William Johnstone, Galashiels. **1885** *Pall Mall G.* 7 Oct. 7/2 The Huddersfield operative cotton twiners, after being out on strike..resumed work yesterday. **1891** *Labour Commission Gloss.*, *Twiners*, operative spinners who double yarn which has been spun by the common spinners.

**2.** A plant of twining habit.

**1830** LINDLEY *Nat. Syst. Bot.* 32 Schizandra is scarcely a twiner. **1859** DARWIN *Orig. Spec.* vii. (1880) 198 Plants became twiners..by the increase of a tendency to slight and irregular revolving movements. **1885** GOODALE *Physiol. Bot.* (1892) 405 Twiners are distinguished from proper climbers by the absence of any special organs, other than the stem itself for grasping supports.

†**Twine thread.** *Obs.* [f. TWINE *sb.*[1] + THREAD *sb.* Cf. Flem. *twijndraad* (in Kilian *tweyndraed*).] A twisted or double-spun thread; also *collectively*, cord, twine.

**1530** PALSGR. 283/2 Twynethrede, *fil reteurs.* **1560** DAUS tr. *Sleidane's Comm.* 63 b, A sworde dependynge ouer your neckes by a twhyne threde. **1607** TOPSELL *Four-f. Beasts* (1658) 488 A twine thread will not hold stretching in the presence (I mean in comparison) of a silk thread. **1654** FULLER *Comm. Ruth* (1868) 169, I have seen the twine-thread of a cordial friend hold. **1706** E. WARD *Wooden World Diss.* (1708) 76 The Boatswain... His Bamboo,..tip'd with simple Twine-thread.

**Twing,** *sb.* Now *dial.* Also 7 **twyng.** [Of obscure origin.] A small red spider supposed to be injurious to cattle; cf. TAINT *sb.* C. 3.

**1608** TOPSELL *Serpents* (1658) 770 There is to be found in Harvest-time amongst Pease, Beans, and other sorts of pulse, ..certain small Spiders called *Kantharidessi Eikela*..of a very red and fiery colour, such as we Englishmen call Twinges, by eating or licking up of which, both Oxen and other Beasts do many times die. **1658** ROWLAND *Moufet's Theat. Ins.* 1060 Small Phalangia..like to beetles, of a flame-red colour; such are those the English call Twyngs. **1878** *Cumberland Gloss.*, *Twing*, a small scarlet-coloured insect, said by the superstitious to occasion fatal illness to cattle.

† **Twing,** *v.*: see TWINGE *v.*[2]

**Twinge** (twindʒ), *sb.* Forms: 6 **twynge, twynche, 7 twindge, (twing), 7– twinge.** [f. TWINGE *v.*[1]]

†**1.** An act of tweaking or pinching; a tweak or pinch. Also *fig.* *Obs.*

**1548** UDALL *Erasm. Par. Luke* Prol. 15 Nipped my hert also with a litell twynge. *c* **1550** *Pryde & Abuse Women* 200 in Hazl. *E. P. P.* IV. 243 Rubbe a galde horse on thee backe, And he wyll kicke and wynse; And so wyll wanton wylyons When they have anye snaper or twynche. **1611** COTGR., *Strette*, a pinch, nip, wrinche, twindge. *Ibid.*, *Tire*, a..ierke, twang, twing. *a* **1625** FLETCHER *Nice Valour* III. ii, For the twindge by th' nose, 'Tis certainly unsightly. **1692** R. L'ESTRANGE *Fables* ccxciii. I. 255, I wonder..how you can Fawn thus upon a Master that gives you so many Blows, and Twinges by the Ears. [**1869** BROWNING *Ring & Bk.* IX. 146 Gently thou joggest by a twinge the wit.]

**2.** A sharp pinching or wringing pain; often, a momentary local pain; esp. applied to that of gout and rheumatism.

**1608** MIDDLETON *Mad World* II. vii, You feel as it were a twinge? **1639** in *Verney Mem.* (1907) I. 220 Crewell twinges [of gout]. **1787** WOLCOTT (P. Pindar) *Instr. Laureat* Wks. 1812 I. 497 They've felt a pain in all their Toes And often at the twinges started. **1824** LADY GRANVILLE *Lett.* 21 Mar. (1894) I. 267 Your..letter..soothed and comforted me during my sharpest twinges [of toothache]. **1827** *Edin. Weekly Jrnl.* 28 Feb., I can agree with Lord Ogleby as to his rheumatism, and say, 'There's a twinge'. **1831** BREWSTER *Nat. Magic* iii. (1833) 48 The account of any person having suffered severe pain..produces acute twinges of pain in the corresponding parts of her person. *a* **1839** PRAED *Poems* (1864) II. 77 When the twinge comes shooting through you. **1863** GEO. ELIOT *Romola* vii, The gout..gave him such severe twinges. **1880** L. STEPHEN *Pope* iv. 88 Philosophers capable of rheumatic twinges.

**b.** *transf.* A 'nip' of cold, etc.

**1888** E. GERARD *Land beyond Forest* lv. 360 Alternate twinges of cold and heat.

**3.** *fig.* A sharp mental pain; a pang of shame, remorse, sorrow, or the like; a prick of conscience; in quot. *a* 1745, a stimulating prick.

**1622** MABBE tr. *Aleman's Guzman d'Alf.* I. 19 Her feigned pangs cease[d], and those truer ones of loue beganne to manifest themselues, giuing other kinde of twinges. **1681** DRYDEN *Spanish Fryar* IV. i, The Wickedness of this old Villain..gives me a twinge for my own Sin. *a* **1745** SWIFT *Serm.* viii. Wks. 1841 II. 157/2 The poorer sort..have no twinges of ambition. **1780** COWPER *Table Talk* 425 Conscience will have twinges now and then. **1800** WEEMS *Washington* xv. (1877) 223 This could not save poor Jack from the twinges of envy. **1834** L. RITCHIE *Wand. by Seine* 168 The sudden clang of a church-bell arrests us, like a twinge of remorse. **1861** HUGHES *Tom Brown at Oxf.* viii. (1889) 69 It cost the Vicar some twinges of conscience to persuade him. **1874** L. STEPHEN *Hours in Library* (1892) II. iii. 91 Burke's politics gave him some severe twinges.

**4.** A twist, a turn. *lit.* and *fig.* *rare.*

**1860** HOLLAND *Miss Gilbert* ii. 38 'Easy!' exclaimed Arthur, a half-contemptuous twinge in his lip. **1875** J. MORISON in *Expositor* I. 124 Grotius gave the expression a most unnatural twinge.

**5.** *dial.* An earwig.

**1790** GROSE *Provinc. Gloss.* (ed. 2), *Twinge*, or *Twitch*, an earwig. *North.* **1828** *Craven Gloss.* **1863** MRS. TOOGOOD *Yorks. Dial.* (MS.).

**Twinge** (twindʒ), *v.*[1] Forms: 1 **twengan** (twæng-), 3 **twenge,** 3–4 **tuenge,** 5 **twynch,** 7 **twindge,** 7– **twinge.** [OE. *twengan*, of obscure etymology; there is no evidence of connexion with Continental forms from the stem *þwing-* denoting 'to constrain, oppress, etc.']

**1.** *trans.* To pinch, wring, tweak, twitch. Also *intr.* (quot. 1858). *Obs.* exc. *dial.*

*c* **1000** in *Techmer's Internat. Zeitschr.* II. 124/23 Twenge hine siððan mid þara swiþran hande. *Ibid.* 125/19 Wænd þinne scytefinger adune and twængc hine mid þinum twam fingrum. *a* **1250** *Owl & Night.* 156 Þu hauest clyures swiþe stronge Þu twengest þar mid so doþ a tonge. *Ibid.* 1114 An holeh stoc hwar þu þe mist hude Þat me ne twenge þine hude. *c* **1305** *St. Dunstan* 81 in *E. E. P.* (1862) 36 Þe deuel he bente by þe nose: He tuengde and schok hire bi þe nose. **1440** J. SHIRLEY *Dethe K. James* (1818) 26 The tourmentours..withe hookid ynstrumentes of yryne,..pynchid and twynchid his theghis, his legges,..and over all his body. **1607** BEAUMONT *Woman Hater* II. i, I doe use to tear their hair, to kick them, and twindge their noses, if they be not carefull in avoiding me. **1611** BEAUM. & FL. *King & no K.* v. i, Thus twinge your nose, thus kick, thus tread upon you. **1628** A. LEIGHTON *Zion's Plea* x. (1842) 195 There are too many flesh-flies, who..twinge and bite such as do deal faithfully with Princes. **1630** B. JONSON *New Inn* I. i, To..twinge three or four buttons From off my lady's gown. **1678** BUTLER *Hud.* III. i. 1155 Twindging him by th' Ears or Nose. **1858** KINGSLEY *Winter-Gard.* in *Misc.* I. 146 That flock of long-tailed tit-mice, which were twinging and pecking about the fir-cones.

**2.** † To cause to smart or tingle; to irritate (*obs.*); to affect (the body or mind) with a twinge or sharp pain; to prick (the conscience).

**1647** [see *twinging* below.] **1666** BUNYAN *Grace Ab.* § 184 Nothing did twinge my Conscience like this. **1674** N. FAIRFAX *Bulk & Selv.* 114 A willingness to be rid of those gallers that twinge the brain of the stiff maintainer of this. **1686** F. SPENCE tr. *Varillas' Ho. Medicis* 431 Leo.. twing'd him sometimes with severe corrections. **1727** GAY *Fables* I. xxxi. 7 As, twing'd with pain, he pensive sits, And raves, and prays, and swears by fits. **1780** S. J. PRATT *Emma Corbett* (ed. 4) II. 71 His old aches would twinge him a little. **1785** E. PERRONET *Occas. Verses, Acrostic* 203 His mission..Like that dumb brute's, that twing'd a prophet's ear. **1801** MAR. EDGEWORTH *Out of Debt* i, If any of his father's old notions of economy by chance twinged his conscience. **1815** SCOTT *Paul's Lett.* (1839) 173 The Bishop of Ghent..has found his conscience alarmingly twinged. **1893** D. C. MURRAY *Time's Revenges* II. xxviii. 208 The old wound twinged him.

**b.** *intr.* To experience a twinge or smart.

**1640** GLAPTHORNE *Wit in Constable* IV, To have your nose Twinge if ours' chance to itch. **1757** E. PERRONET *Mitre* IV. xiii, Shudder ye sires—twinge ev'ry ear. **1850** SIR A. AGNEW in McCrie *Mem.* viii. (1852) 199 Reflection arising and conscience twinging. **1868** [see *twinging* below].

Hence **Twinging** (twi·ndʒiŋ) *vbl. sb.*[1] and *ppl. a.*; also **Twinger** (twi·ndʒəɪ), one who or that which twinges.

**1608** DAY *Law Trickes* II. C ij, One Tristella..a twindger, a meere Horsleach, one that will suck out the braines of his treasurie. **1621** B. JONSON *Gipsies Metam.* Wks. (Rtldg.) 625/2 There's an old twinger Can shew ye the ginger. **1647** SPRIGGE *Anglia Rediv.* Address (1854) p. vii, Twinging convulsions. **1659** TATHAM *London's Triumph* 14 Ginger, That Nose tosting twinger. **1682** BUNYAN *Greatness of Soul* Wks. (ed. Offor) I. 120 Despair, which is the most twinging stripe of hell. **1816** J. WILSON *City of Plague* II. iii. 219 Felt you no little twinging of remorse? **1868** GEO. ELIOT *Sp. Gipsy* I. (1908) 27, I've a twinging knee. **1906** *Daily Chron.* 29 Mar. 6/4 How would he wear..with a twingeing tooth and an influenza cold?

† **Twinge,** *v.*[2] *Obs. rare.* [Perh. intended as a fig. use of prec., but prob. originating in some misunderstanding of earlier glosses. The strong pa. pple. *twungen* is app. less original than the weak form *twinged.*] *trans.* To oppress, afflict, persecute. Hence **Twinging** *vbl. sb.*[2]

*a* **1300** *E. E. Psalter* xvi. 10 [xvii. 9] Hile me..Fra face ofe wicked þat twinged me swa. *Ibid.* xvii. 21 [xviii. 18] Þai forcome me in daie of twinginge. *Ibid.* xxxvii[i]. 8, I am twinged, and meked for vnquerte [*MS. H.* I am meked and twungen smert]. *Ibid.* xli. 13 [xlii. 9] Wharfore murned in I go, Whil þat twinges me þe fo?

**Twingle** (twi·ŋg'l), *v. rare.* Now *dial.* [Prob. imitative.] *intr.* To twist, twine, wriggle, writhe.

*c* **1645** HOWELL *Lett.* II. lv, German mothers..put..into a cup of Rhenish..somtimes a little living Eel, which twingling in the wine while the child is drinking so scares him, that many com to abhor..wine all their lives after. **1813** W. BEATTIE *Fruits Time Parings* (1873) 4 A lingle, To swing the roast; They had nae jack, but this could twingle Wi' little cost. **1880** *W. Cornw. Gloss.*, *Twingle*, to wriggle; to writhe.

**Twingle,** obs. variant of TWINKLE.

**Twingle-twangle** (twiŋg'l,twæ·ŋg'l). [Reduplication of TWANGLE.] A representation of the continuous sounds of a harp or the like. Also as *vb.*

**1634** FORD *Perkin Warbeck* III. ii, Discord of bells pipes and tabours Hodgepodge of Scotch and Irish twingle twangles. **1791** BURNS *Let. to A. Alison* 14 Feb., The twingle twangle of a Jew's harp. **1900** CROCKETT *Black Douglas* 327 When he had..finished cocking his viol and twingle-twangling it to his satisfaction.

**Twing twang** (twiŋ,twæŋ). *rare.* [Reduplication of TWANG.] A representation of the sound of the harp, or other such instrument.

**1761** H. WALPOLE *Let. to C'tess Ailesbury* 20 July, All the guitars are untuned;..she must take some David or other to teach her the new twing twang, twing twing twang. **1762** STERNE *Tr. Shandy* V. xv, Ptr...r..r..ing,—twing,—twang, —prut,—trut; 'tis a cursed bad fiddle. **1800–1** SOUTHEY *Thalaba* Pref. to ed. 4, The regular Jew's harp twing-twang, of what has been foolishly called heroic measure.

**Twining** (twəɪ·niŋ), *vbl. sb.* [f. TWINE *v.*[1] + -ING[1].] The action of the verb TWINE; twisting, spinning, winding, embracing, writhing.

**1398** TREVISA *Barth. De P. R.* XVII. cxlii[i]. (Bodl. MS.) lf. 227 b/1 Smal [weþies]..beþ made stronge wiþ ..windinge as þrede is wt twynynge. *c* **1440** *Promp. Parv.* 505/1 Twynynge (or wyn(d)ynge, of threde..), *tortura.* **1553** T. WILSON *Rhet.* (1580) 101 A priuie twinyng, or close crepyng in, to win fauour.., called insinuation. *a* **1639** WEBSTER *Appius & Virginia* IV. ii, The rude twinings of a lecherous judge. *a* **1703** POMFRET *Poet. Wks.* (1833) 21 Love to one centre every twining brought. **1841** EMERSON *Lect., Man the Reformer* Wks. (Bohn) II. 238 Inextricable seem to be the twinings and tendrils of this evil. **1872** G. B. CHEEVER *Lect. Pilgr. Progr.* ii. 44 The twinings and wrestlings, the strivings and agonies of Bunyan's spirit. **1875** BENNETT & DYER *Sachs's Bot.* 772 The Twining of Climbing Plants...Twining is a consequence of unequal growth, of a revolving nutation.

*attrib.* **1648** HEXHAM II, *Een Twern ofte twijn-molen*, a Twinning-mill.

**Twining** (twəɪ·niŋ), *ppl. a.* [f. as prec. + -ING[2].] That twines, in various senses; twisting, winding, coiling, writhing, etc.; *spec.* of a plant: growing spirally round a support.

*a* **1593** MARLOWE in *Eng. Parnassus* (1600) 480 The Eglantine and Rose..As kind companions in one union grows, Folding their twining armes. **1664** POWER *Exp. Philos.* I. 8 The twining tendrils of the Vine. **1669** PENN *No Cross* vii. § 4 A Crooked, Twining, Twisting Serpent. **1735** SOMERVILLE *Chase* IV. 153 Spare not thou The twining whip, but ply his bleeding Sides. **1824** MISS L. M. HAWKINS *Annaline* II. 213 The thick forest [was] decorated with twining plants. **1861** BENTLEY *Man. Bot.* (1870) 100 If such stems twist round other bodies in a spiral manner they are said to be twining.

Hence **Twi·ningly** *adv.*, in a twining manner.

**1731** BAILEY, *Twiningly*, twistingly.

**Twink** (twiŋk), *sb.*[1] Forms: 5 **twynk,** 5–6 **twynke,** 6–7 **twinke,** 7 **twinck(e,** 7 **twinch,** 6– **twink.** [f. TWINK *v.*[1]]

**1.** A winking of the eye; *transf.* the time taken by this; a twinkling; now always in phrase *in a twink*; formerly *at, in, with* (*a* or *the*) *twink of an eye*; also *with a twink*; *in the twink of a bedstick*: cf. BEDSTAFF.

**14..** *Cov. Corp. Chr. Plays* I. 506 Myne enmyis to vanquese ..And with a twynke of myn iee not won to be lafte alyve. **1471** RIPLEY *Comp. Alch.* Pref. ii. in Ashm. *Theatr. Chem. Brit.* (1652) 127 In twynke of an Eye most sodenly. **1556** J. HEYWOOD *Spider & F.* lii. A a iv. (*heading*), Wherat with twynke of an iye (as it were) the head spider..hath builded a strong castell in that copweb. *Ibid.* xci. Oo iv b, Change (by chance) brought him (at twinke of an iye) From twig top of the tree, at the rote to lie. **1561** NORTON & SACKV. *Gorboduc* IV. ii. (Shaks. Soc.) 142 A pereles prince..Euen with a twinke a censeles stocke I sawe. **1596** SHAKS. *Tam. Shr.* II. i. 312 Kisse on kisse Shee vi'd so fast, protesting oath on oath, That in a twinke she won me to her loue. **1607** R. C[AREW] tr. *Estienne's World of Wonders* I. xxiv. 194 The poore gentlewoman..speaking not a word, gaue him a twinch with a weeping eye. **1715** NELSON tr. *à Kempis' Chr. Exerc.* III. xxv. 173 As lightning in the Twink of an eye, so do all the Kingdoms and Times of the World pass away. **1754** SHEBBEARE *Matrimony* (1766) II. 121 I'll cut it less in a Twink. **1756** TOLDERVY *Hist. 2 Orphans* I. 71, I can tell you in the twink of a bedstick. **1833** NYREN *Yng. Cricketer's Tutor* (1902) 93 The confident old bowler..thought to settle his business in a twink. **1898** WATTS-DUNTON *Aylwin* III. i, She's got the real witch's eye, and can do you a mischief in a twink, if she likes. **1902** BARRIE *Little White Bird* xiii. 135 Night passes in a twink.

*transf.* **1904** R. J. FARRER *Garden Asia* 276 With the merest twink of some nerve, sending prone his brawny opponent.

**2.** A twinkle or sparkle. *rare.*

**1830** [implied in *twinkless*: see below]. **1870** J. W. BOULDING *Catalina* 8 Saw ye not a strange twink in her eye?

Hence **Twi·nkless** *a.*, without a twink or twinkle.

**1830** R. MONTGOMERY *Satan* II. 121 When weary stars grow twinkless, and depart.

**Twink** (twiŋk), *sb.*[2] [Echoic; cf. PINK *sb.*[6], SPINK *sb.*[1] I.] A local name for the chaffinch.

**1816** STEPHENS in Shaw *Gen. Zool.* IX. II. 444 It [Chaffinch] is called by various names in this country, such as..Horsefinch, Pink, Twink, Spink, &c. **1829** [see PINK *sb.*[6]]. **1881** MISS JACKSON *Shropsh. Word-bk.*, *Twink*, the Chaffinch.

**Twink** (twiŋk), *v.*[1] Forms: see TWINK *sb.*[1] [ME. *twinken* (= MHG. and G. *zwinken* to wink), repr. the simple stem from which TWINKLE *v.*[1] is formed.]

† **1.** *intr.* To wink, to blink. *Obs.*

*c* **1400** *Gamelyn* 453 Whan I twynke [*v. r.* twynk] on the, loke for to goon. *c* **1440** *Promp. Parv.* 505/2 Twynkyn, wythe the eye.., *conniveo.* **1600** J. LANE *Tom Tel-troth* 262 Some winke, some twinke, some blinke, some stare. *a* **1652** BROME *Covent-Garden* III. i. Wks. 1873 II. 47, I will ..set mine eye against his, that he shall not twink, but I'le perceive it. **1681** W. ROBERTSON *Phraseol. Gen.* (1693) 567 To wink or twink with the eye, *nictare.*

**2.** To twinkle, sparkle.

**1637** N. WHITING *Albino & Bellama* 3 The curled tapers of the Firmament Did cease to twinke. **1795** *Cicely of Raby* I. 195 The last star had twinked in the west, ere we had gone half our journey. **1856** AIRD *Poet. Wks.* 194 The wings of birds Twink with illumination. **1884** BROWNING *Ferishtah, Cherries* 80 Like yon blue twinkle, twinks thine eye, my Love. **1896** C. K. PAUL tr. *Huysman's En Route* iv. 54 Durtal faintly saw..stars twinking in the air.

Hence **Twi·nking** *vbl. sb.*

**1519** HORMAN *Vulg.* 27 Ouermoche twyngynge [*sic*] of the yie betoketh vnstedfastnesse. **1627** MAY *Lucan* VI. 863 The eyes with twincking hard Are op'd.

**Twink** (twiŋk), *v.*[2] ? *Obs. rare.* [Echoic; cf. TINK, TWANK.] *intr.* To make a light clear abrupt ringing sound; to clink, chink. Also of a bird (*intr.* and *trans.*), to utter, or utter with, a shrill metallic note.

*a* **1529** SKELTON *Col. Cloute* 493 And wrest vp my harpe With sharpe twynkyng trebelles, Agaynst all suche rebelles. **1615** CHAPMAN *Odyss.* XXI. 548 A swallow..Twinks out her scatter'd voice in accents shrill. **1674** FLAVEL *Medit. Birds* ii. in *Husb. Spiritualized* App. 238 A whole quire of Birds chirping and twinking together.

**Twink,** *v.*[3] Now *dial.* [Of obscure origin: cf. TWANK *v.*] *trans.* To chastise. Hence **Twinka·tion** (*nonce-wd.*).

**1747** ELIZ. CARTER *Lett.* (1808) 132, I have been called away ten times, and shall be twinked if I do not leave you. **1748** *Ibid.* 164, I..wrote a twinkation to Mr. Richardson about it, to which I received so civil an answer that I knew not how to be angry. **1892** HEWETT *Peas. Sp. Devon* 138 I'll twink thee purty tight vur that, sure's a gun!

**Twinkle** (twi·ŋk'l), *sb.* Forms: see Twinkle *v.*[1] [f. Twinkle *v.*[1]]

**1.** A winking of the eye; a wink, blink; also, a momentary glance (in quot. 1593, of the mind); cf. Blink *sb.*[2] 2. ? *Obs.*

1548 Thomas *Ital. Gram.* (1567), *Cennare*, a nodde or twyncle with the eye. 1593 Q. Eliz. tr. *Boethius* v. pr. iv. 112 Vnderstanding..orderly by one twynkell of the mynde, all ouerlookith. 1594 Spenser *Amoretti* xvi, One of those archers..Ayming his arrow..suddenly, with twincle of her eye, The Damzell broke his misintended dart. 1660 tr. *Amyraldus' Treat. conc. Relig.* ii. i. 143, I do not conceive an honest man can consent so much as with one twinkle of his eye to such abominations. 1709 Steele *Tatler* No. 22 ⁋ 1 Her true Lover,..his Heart..waiting for a second Twincle of her Eye. 1818 Scott *Hrt. Midl.* xiv, An occasional convulsive sigh, or twinkle of the eyelid.

**b.** *transf.* A slight tremulous movement; a twitch, a flicker, a quiver.

1733 Cheyne *Eng. Malady* ii. xiii. § 1 (1734) 246 Now and then an uncertain Twitch or Twinkle in the Pulse. 1862 Carlyle *Fredk. Gt.* xi. ix. (1872) IV. 106 The slightest twinkle of Fleury's eyelashes would be duly speeded to Voltaire.

**2.** The time it takes to wink; = Twinkling *vbl. sb.*[1] 3; now only in phrase *in a twinkle, in the twinkle of an eye.*

*c* 1592 Marlowe *Jew of Malta* iv. iv, Vanish, and return in a twinkle. 1644 Digby *Nat. Soul* x. § 8. 429 That twinkle or moment, in which she becometh an..inhabitant of the next world. 1679 Dryden *Troilus & Cr.* iii. ii, Hast not slept to night? wou'd a not (a naughty Man) let it sleep one twinkle? 1681 Otway *Soldier's Fort.* iv. i, I'll..be with you in a Twinkle. 1903 *Pilot* 17 Oct. 373/1 The reduction of the military service to two years..ought to be done in a twinkle. 1905 Elinor Glyn *Viciss. Evangeline* 166 In the twinkle of an eye we were rolling..to Willis's.

**3.** An intermittent or transient shining; a sparkle, a scintillation; also, a faint or momentary gleam; a glimmer.

1663 J. Heath *Eng. Chron.* (1691) 76 The King..caused the Twinkles of his Eyes to be put out..by burning Glasses. 1718 Pope *Let. to Lady M. W. Montagu* 1 Sept., In the very twinkle of one eye of it [your body] there is more wit,.. than [etc.]. 1748 Thomson *Cast. Indol.* i. 617 He had a roguish twinkle in his eye. 1818 Scott *Rob Roy* xvii, As the benighted sailor descries the first distant twinkle of the lighthouse which marks his course. 1825 — *Talism.* iii, A twinkle in the star of thy nativity, which promises for thee something that is good and gracious. 1858 Carlyle *Fredk. Gt.* iii. i. (1872) I. 141 A certain twinkle of mirth in the serious eyes. 1860 Mayhew *Upper Rhine* i. § 1. 15 Nor is it possible to catch sight of even so much as a twinkle of the fire.

**b.** *transf.* and *fig.*

1864 Burton *Scot Abr.* II. ii. 169 The broad accent..and its sly twinkles of humour. 1885 G. Meredith *Diana* xxxiii, Was there a twinkle of probability in the story? 1893 L. S. Keyser in *Chicago Advance* 3 Aug., The twinkle of wings, the twitter of voices.

**Twinkle** (twi·ŋk'l), *v.*[1] Forms: 1 **twinclian**, 4–6 **twinkel, twynkle, twyncle,** (4 **twyngle,** *Sc.* **twinkil,** 4–5 **twynkel,** 5 **-kele, -kyl,** 5–6 *Sc.* **-kil,** 6 **-kell, twinckel),** 4–8 **twincle,** 6–8 **twinckle, (twingle),** 4– **twinkle.** [OE. *twinclian*, freq. of **twincan*: see Twink *v.*[1] and -le 3.]

**1.** *intr.* To shine with rapidly intermittent light; to emit tremulous radiance; to sparkle; to glitter; † to shine dimly, to glimmer; to flicker (*obs.*).

*c* 888 K. Ælfred *Boeth.* xxxv. § 3 Ic hire [the door] grapode ymbutan þæt ðe ic þæt lytle leoht ȝeseah twinclian. *c* 897 — *Gregory's Past. C.* xiv. 86 Se spearca ðara godra weorca, þe her twinclað [*v.r.* tuinclað] beforan monnum. *c* 1386 Chaucer *Prol.* 267 Hise eyen twynkled..As doon the sterres in the frosty nyght. 1423 Jas. I *Kingis Q.* i, Heigh In the hevynnis figure circulere The rody sterres twynklyng as the fyre. 1551 Recorde *Cast. Knowl.* (1556) 8 The Fixed starres doo twinkle, and not the Planetes. 1582 Stanyhurst *Æneis* ii. (Arb.) 69 Thee twylight twinckled [L. *consumta nocte*]. 1658 tr. *Porta's Nat. Magic* xiii. 306 When the Iron is sparkling red hot..that it twinkles. 1678 Cudworth *Intell. Syst.* i. i. § 37. 46 The Flame of a new lighted Candle is [not] the same with that Flame that twinkles last in the socket. 1740 Somerville *Hobbinol* i. 145 His single Eye Twinkles with Joy. 1784 Cowper *Task* vi. 251 The green blade that twinkles in the sun. 1818 Scott *Rob Roy* i, The tear twinkled in his dark eye. 1855 Macaulay *Hist. Eng.* xiii. III. 364 A solitary light which twinkled through the darkness. 1863 W. C. Baldwin *Afr. Hunting* vii. 283 His large black diamond eyes..used to twinkle like stars.

*transf.* 1850 Kingsley *Alt. Locke* xxiv, He twinkled, and winked, and chuckled. 1871 'M. Legrand' *Cambr. Freshm.* xvii, A smile twinkled in his eyes. 1889 Barrie *Window in Thrums* xix. 177 Jess twinkled gleefully over tales of sweethearting.

**b.** *trans.* To emit (radiance, flashes, or beams) rapidly and intermittently; to communicate (a message or signal) in this way.

*a* 1547 Surrey *Paraphr. Ps.* viii. Wks. (1815) 85 Thou mad'st..each one of the wand'ring stars to twinkle sparkles bright. 1632 J. Hayward tr. *Biondi's Eromena* 185 The minde..twinkled forth sparkles that argued great flames of excellencies. 1857 G. Meredith *Farina* viii. 134 A broad fire that twinkled branchy beams through an east hill-orchard. 1894 Mrs. Dyan *All in a Man's K.* (1899) 162 Not one bright star to twinkle hope and light to him. 1899 *Westm. Gaz.* 4 Aug. 7/3 The challenge-word..was twinkled..by the luminous dots and dashes from her masthead.

† **c.** To vary in twinkling. *Obs. rare*⁻¹.

1665 Hooke *Microgr.* lviii. 218 The Starrs neer the Horizon, are twinkled with several colours.

**d.** *poet.* To guide or light *to* some place by twinkling.

1690 Dryden *Don Sebastian* iv. i, The star of love That twinkles you to fair Almeyda's bed. 1818 Keats *Endymion* iv. 719 Those eyes..Shall be my grief, or twinkle me to pleasure.

**2.** *intr.* To close and open the eye or eyes quickly (voluntarily or involuntarily); to make a signal by this means; to wink, blink; also said of the eye or eyes. *Obs.* or *arch.*

*a* 1300 [see Twinkling *vbl. sb.*[1] 2]. *c* 1374 Chaucer *Boeth.* ii. pr. iii. 26 (Camb. MS.) She hath now twyncled [*v.r.* twynkeled] fyrst vp on the with wyckede eye. *c* 1375 *Sc. Leg. Saints* xxviii. (*Margarete*) 595, & þis merwale alsone cane be As man mycht twinkil with his e. 1382 Wyclif *Prov.* vi. 13 He twincleth [1388 bekeneth] with the eȝen. *c* 1440 *Bone Flor.* 1750 He twynkylde wyth hys eye, As who seyth, holde the stylle. 1513 Douglas *Æneis* iv. xii. 96 With ene rolling, and twynkilling wp full fane, Assayis scho to spy the hevinis lycht. 1608 Topsell *Serpents* (1653) 684 They have but one eye-lid, and that groweth from the neather part of the cheek, which by reason of their eyes never twinckleth. *a* 1625 Fletcher *Woman Pleas'd* iv. i, I saw the wench that twir'd and twinkled at thee The other day. 1653 R. Sanders *Physiogn.* 173 Beware of those who, when they speak to thee, twinkle. 1686 *Lond. Gaz.* No. 2103/4 He is about 17 years old,..near sighted, twinkling with his eyes. 1753 Richardson *Grandison* (1754) II. x. 64 We hemm'd, handkerchief'd, twinkled. 1772 *Test Filial Duty* I. 128 He did so simper and twinckle, and was so gallant, that [etc.]. 1784 R. Bage *Barham Downs* II. 309 The old Justice twinkles, hems, coughs, and chuckles. 1815 Scott *Guy M.* lv, He was observed to twinkle with his eyelids. 1825 — *Betrothed* xxxi, Ere an eye could twinkle, his right knee was on the croupe of the Constable's horse.

**b.** *trans.* with the eyes, eyelids, etc., as obj.

1591 Percivall *Sp. Dict.*, *Parpadear*, to twinkle the eies. 1846 Landor *Imag. Conv.*, *Pope Leo xii & Gigi* Wks. I. 347/1 Her little kid ran after the soldier..twinkling its ears and rubbing them between its legs. 1851 Hawthorne *Ho. Sev. Gables* xiv, Phœbe took leave of the desolate couple;..twinkling her eyelids to shake off a dewdrop.

**3.** *intr.* To move to and fro, or in and out, with rapid alternation; to appear and disappear in quick succession; to flutter, flit, flicker.

In quot. 1799–1805 said of a space filled with moving objects; in quot. 1849 *trans.* (cf. 2 b).

1616 [see Twinkling *ppl. a.* 2]. 1642 in P. H. Hore *Hist. Wexford* (1900) I. 303 A man might see them through the smoake of the gunpowder run twinckling like the moates in the sun. 1799–1805 Wordsw. *Prelude* vii. 691 The open space ..twinkles, is alive With heads. 1849 Saxe *Poems, Rape Lock* xix, [She] twinkled a foot in the polka's twirl. 1852 M. W. Savage *R. Medlicott* v. ii, I love to see the fans fluttering, the ankles twinkling, the bouquets waving. 1863 Kingsley *Water Bab.* i. 39 Her feet twinkled past each other so fast, that you could not see which was foremost.

**Twinkle** (twi·ŋk'l), *v.*[2] *rare.* Forms: 4 **twynkel,** 6 **twynkle,** 6– **twinkle.** [Echoic; cf. Tinkle *v.*[1]] *intr.* = Tinkle *v.*[1] 2, 3. Hence **Twi·nkling** *vbl. sb.*

13.. *K. Alis.* 2572 Mury is the twynkelyng [*Laud MS.* touchyng] of the harpour. 1523 Skelton *Garl. Laurel* 687 There Cintheus sat twynklyng vpon his harpe stringis. 1575 Laneham *Let.* (1871) 61 My wanton warblz, my running, my tyming, my tuning, and my twynkling. 1683 Pettus *Fleta Min.* i. (1686) 48 When the Grains of such two tryals have twinkled, fresh and clean, then take the Copper out of the oven. 1907 H. Wyndham *Flare of Footlights* i, An electric bell twinkled warningly.., and there was a general move towards the stalls and circle.

**Twinkledum** (twi·ŋk'ldǒm). An imitation of the sound of the guitar.

1681 Dryden *Spanish Fryar* i. ii, A Serenade of Twinckledum Twinckledum under my Windows.

**Twinkler** (twi·ŋklər). [f. Twinkle *v.*[1] + -er [1].] One who or that which twinkles.

† **1.** One who winks; a winker. *Obs. rare*⁻¹.

1382 Wyclif *Ecclus.* xxvii. 25 The twynclere with the eȝe forgeth wicke thingus.

**2.** Anything which emits intermittent, transient, or faint radiance; sometimes applied to eyes.

1591 Sylvester *Du Bartas* i. iv. 574 The Hoasts of th' upper Twinklers bright. 1654 Gayton *Pleas. Notes* ii. v. 56 His Dulcinea's twinclers enlarged to the full breadth of Queen Proserpines sawcers. 1708 Mrs. Centlivre *Busie Body* v. i, A consenting Look with those pretty Twinklers. 1747 Richardson *Clarissa* I. xxvii. 170 Such a sun in a family where there are none but faint twinklers. 1802 Mrs. E. Parsons *Myst. Visit* I. 18 The small twinkler held by the servant..is perfectly sufficient. 1813 Shelley *Q. Mab* ix. 223 Such tiny twinklers as the planet orbs. 1837 Marryat *Dog-fiend* xvii, Be plased..and not be staring at me, following me up and down..with those twinklers of yours. 1868 Lockyer *Guillemin's Heavens* xvii. 244 Enceladus, and coy Mimas, faintest of twinklers, are caught by Herschel's giant mirrors.

**Twinkling** (twi·ŋkliŋ), *vbl. sb.*[1] [f. Twinkle *v.*[1] + -ing [1].] The action of Twinkle *v.*[1]

**1.** The action of shining with tremulous or faint radiance; scintillation; † glimmering. Also *transf.* and *fig.*

1398 Trevisa *Barth. De P. R.* xvi. xxxvii. (Bodl. MS.) lf. 174 b/2 In twinkelinge and in liȝt [electrum] schyneþ more clere þan oþer metal. 1477 Norton *Ord. Alch.* v. in Ashm. *Theatr. Chem. Brit.* (1652) 64 Twinckling and glittering as in *Magnetia* is. 1551 Recorde *Cast. Knowl.* (1556) 8 Many men do make a difference of them by twinkelinge, affirming that the Fixed starres doo twinkle, and not the Planetes. 1635 Swan *Spec. M.* vii. § 3 (1643) 325 The twinkling of the starres is the vibration or trembling of their light. 1796 Morse *Amer. Geog.* I. 36 There is only a dim twinkling of twilight for an hour or two in the middle of the day. 1806 Wordsw. *Sonn., To Sleep*, O gentle Sleep! do they belong to thee, These twinklings of oblivion? 1815 Scott *Guy M.* xxvi, These [salmon] the party in the boat detected by the slightest indications; the twinkling of a fin, the rising of an air-bell. 1853 Herschel *Pop. Lect. Sc.* vii. § 117 (1873) 336 The twinkling or scintillation of the stars partakes..of the nature of a phænomenon of diffraction. 1879 Butcher & Lang *Odyssey* viii. 123 Odysseus gazed at the twinklings of the feet.

**2.** The action or an act of winking; nictitation; also *fig.* *Obs.* exc. as in 3.

*a* 1300 in *Minor Poems fr. Vernon MS.* (E.E.T.S.) 519/1 Þoruȝ twinklingues of heore eyȝen Heore soules beon alle for lore. 1398 Trevisa *Barth. De P. R.* xv. (Bodl. MS.) lf. 111 b/2 Liȝtnynge..comeþ oute of his moder as þe twinkelinge of an yȝe. *c* 1440 *Promp. Parv.* 505/2 Twynkelynge, of the eye, *conniventia*. 1530 Palsgr. 283/2 Twynclyng of an eye, *cilement, clin doeil*. 1601 Holland *Pliny* xxxii. x, An ague..accompanied with head-ach and much twinkling or inordinat palpitation of the eyes. 1609 Bible (Douay) *Isa.* iii. 16 The daughters of Sion..have walked with stretched out necke, and went with twinglings of eies. 1632 Lithgow *Trav.* x. 458 Being euery second or third day attended with the twinckling of an eye, and my sustenance agreeable to my attendance, my body grew exceeding debile and infirme. 1649 Jer. Taylor *Gt. Exemp.* ii. Disc. ix. 122 The first motions,..the twincklings of the eye as the Philosophers call them. 1691 Ray *Creation* ii. (1692) 145 The Eyes in squinting, the Eye-lids in twinkling. 1800 Wellington in Gurw. *Desp.* (1837) I. 252 He can extricate himself by the twinkling of an eye if he wishes it. 1822–7 Good *Study Med.* (1829) IV. 462 Twinkling or winking of the eyes is performed every minute without our thinking of it.

**3.** The time taken in winking the eye; a very brief period; a moment, an instant. Chiefly in phrases: see b, c, d.

1303 [see b.]. *c* 1374 Chaucer *Compl. Mars* 222 Her Ioy ..Ne lasteth not the twynkelyng of an eye. 1535 Coverdale *Ps.* xxix. [xxx.] 5 His wrath endureth but the twinckling of an eye. 1557 Traheron *Expos. John* i. H j b, He shewed not him selfe the twinckling of an eye, and so vanished awaie. 1644 Digby *Nat. Soul* ix. § 10. 421 He scorneth for this little twinckling of his life, to take any present paines.. to auoyde being ill. 1841 Lane *Arab. Nts.* I. ii. 114, I will never quit thee for the twinkling of an eye.

**b.** *In the twinkling of an eye*, in an instant; formerly also † *in (a), with (a* or *the) twinkling of an eye* (in quot. 1390 *of a look*) (*obs.*).

1303 R. Brunne *Handl. Synne* 9179 Yn twynkelyng of an ye, Yn-to þe cherche gun þey flye. *a* 1310 in Wright *Lyric P.* xxxvii. 106 In a twynglyng of an eȝe. *a* 1340 Hampole *Psalter* lxxii. 19 In þe twinkeling of an eigh ꝭai fal downe. *a* 1380 *Minor Poems fr. Vernon MS.* (E.E.T.S.) 673 Wiþ a twynklyng of an eiȝe. 1390 Gower *Conf.* I. 144 In a twinklinge of a lok His mannes forme aȝein he tok. 1483 Caxton *Cato* E v b, In the twynklyng of an eye. *c* 1489 — *Sonnes of Aymon* xxviii. 588 The corps..was broughte in to the carte agayne wyth the twynkelyng of an eye. 1508 Dunbar *Gold. Targe* 235 In twynkling of ane eye to schip thai went. 1567 *Gude & Godlie B.* (S.T.S.) 27 With twingling [*v.r.* twinkling] of ane eye anone, God sall the tak. 1599 Hakluyt *Voy.* (1903) IV. 250 In the very twinckling of an eye, both shippe and men were all cast away. 1792 Burke *Corr.* (1844) IV. 11 This clergy would lose,..in the twinkling of an eye, the little remains of influence which they yet retain. 1847 L. Hunt *Men, Women, & B.* II. iv. 52 A book, a picture, a memory, puts us, in the twinkling of an eye, in the midst of the most enchanting solitudes. 1904 *Times* 7 Sept. 7/4 Events..transformed Japan..in the twinkling of an eye ..into a modern State.

**c.** *In a twinkling* († *at a, in the twinkling*).

1582 Stanyhurst *Æneis* i. (Arb.) 22 At a twinckling thee swelling surges he calmed. 1609 *Ev. Woman in Hum.* i. i. in Bullen *O. Pl.* IV, Heere and there in the twinckling. 1610 B. Jonson *Alch.* v. v, An old Hargubuzier..Could prime his poulder, and give fire and hit, All in a twinckling. 1673 Dryden *Marr. à la Mode* ii. i, I'll..be with you again in a twinkling. 1760–72 H. Brooke *Fool of Qual.* (1809) III. 151 The liquor was out of sight in a twinkling. 1807 W. Irving *Salmag.* xiii. (1824) 224 The stoutest line-of-battle ship ..may be..decomposed in a twinkling. 1883 E. Pennell-Elmhirst *Cream Leicestersh.* 182 In a twinkling the pack is half a field away.

**d.** With (usually humorous) substitution: see quots.

1660, 1676 [see Bedstaff]. 1681 T. Flatman *Heraclitus Ridens* No. 40 (1713) II. 9 This Letter would alone have done it in the twinkling of a Broomstick. 1695 Congreve *Love for L.* ii. v, I have known an astrologer made a cuckold in the twinkling of a star. *a* 1704 T. Brown *Declam. Adverts* Wks. 1730 I. 40 All Thessaly had in the twinkling of a Shoeing-horn been certainly undermin'd by Lobsters. 1709 *Brit. Apollo* II. No. 57. 2/2 I'll do it in the twinkling of a Bedstaff. 1819 *Blackw. Mag.* V. 718 He went off in the twinkling of a bed post. 1821 *Ibid.* IX. 134 In the twinkling of a fan. 1853 Reade *Peg Woff.* iv. 106 You can..master a play in the twinkling of a tea-cup.

**4.** *attrib.*

*c* 1620 Z. Boyd *Zion's Flowers* (1855) 68 In a twinkling trice To goe to work.

**Twinkling,** *vbl. sb.*[2]: see Twinkle *v.*[2]

**Twinkling** (twi·ŋkliŋ), *ppl. a.* [f. Twinkle *v.*[1] + -ing [2].] That twinkles.

**1.** Shining tremulously (or † faintly); sparkling, scintillating; † glimmering; flickering (*obs.*).

1508 Dunbar *Gold. Targe* 31 All the lake as lamp did leme of licht, Quhilk schadovit all about wyth twynkling glemis. 1567 *Satir. Poems Reform.* iii. 58 Browis brent and twinkland Cristell eine. 1591 Shaks. *Two Gent.* ii. vi. 9 At first I did adore a twinkling Starre. 1683 Norris *Poems* (ed. Grosart) 58 Some twinkling stars give feeble light. 1765 Beattie *Judgm. Paris* cxvi, Till the morn Spangle with twinkling dew the flowery waste. 1821–30 Ld. Cockburn *Mem.* iv. (1874) 191 A bulky man with..twinkling eyes. 1829 Scott *Anne of G.* xviii, The windows exhibited here and there a twinkling gleam.

**2.** *transf.* Appearing and disappearing with rapid alternation; producing an effect as of tremulous light by rapid vibratory movement; tremulous, fluttering, quivering. Also *fig.*

**1616** CAPT. SMITH *Descr. New Eng.* 29 The twinkling mountaine of Aucociso. **1791** COWPER *Odyss.* VIII. 324 Ulysses wonder-fixt, The ceaseless play of twinkling feet admired. **1814** SOUTHEY *Roderick* XVI. 11 The lark..On twinkling pinions poised. **1816** CHALMERS *Let.* in *Life* (1851) II. 41 We were looking back on the twinkling rapidity of the months and the weeks which have already gone. **1889** GREGORY SMITH *Fra Angelico*, etc. (ed. 2) 90 The little twinkling feet which sped so fast and free.

†**3.** Winking, blinking. *Obs.*

**1740** SOMERVILLE *Hobbinol* III. 201 To point the holy Leer, by just Degrees To close the twingling Eye. **1742** RICHARDSON *Pamela* III. 332, I often endeavoured, by a twinkling Motion, to disperse the gathering Water, before it had formed itself into Drops too big to be restrained.

**4.** *Comb.*, as *twinkling-eyed*, *-footed* adjs.

**1871** HOWELLS *Wedd. Journ.* (1892) 308 Devotees of the twinkling-footed burlesque.. living the life of strolling players. **1904** *Daily Chron.* 13 July 8/2 A sunburnt, healthy-looking twinkling-eyed scamp of thirteen years.

Hence **Twi·nklingly** *adv.*, in a twinkling manner.

**1561** T. NORTON *Calvin's Inst.* II. 143 They shewed it.. twincklingly shining a farre of. **1657** J. SERGEANT *Schism Dispach't* 528 This Authority of the Pope in England twinklingly went out and in again. **1850** *Chamb. Jrnl.* XIV. 16 The glittering grains..leapt twinklingly.

**Twinkly** (twi·ŋkli), *a.* [f. TWINKLE *sb.* or *v.*[1] + -Y.] Characterized by twinkling.

**1884** *St. James's Gaz.* 21 June 5/1 The most twinkly star of contemporary journalism. **1903** *Daily Record & Mail* 5 Aug. 4 A twinkly humour about the lips.

†**Twi·nkum twa·nkum.** *Obs. rare.* A refrain of a song, expressing careless jollity.

**1728** GAY *Polly* I. Air x. (1777) 23 Old oaks can defy the thunder's roar, And I can stand woman's tongue—that's more. With a twinkum, twankum, &c.

†**Twinlepi,** *a. Obs. rare*[—1]. [f. TWIN *a.*, after ONLEPY.] Twofold, double.

*a* **1400-50** *Alexander* 5013 Þus be twinlepi tongis [*sc.* Greek and Indian] tell þai oure wirdis.

†**Twinlight,** obs. pseudo-archaism for TWILIGHT.

*c* **1532** *Remedie of Love* xliv, The night approched in the twinlight.

**Twinling** (twi·nliŋ). Now *dial.* Forms: see TWIN; also 4-6 -lyng(e, -linge, 5 -lenge, 8 -lin; 5 twyndyllyng. [ME., f. TWIN *a.* and *sb.* + -LING[1]. Cf. in the same sense Norw. dial. *tvinnling*, MSw. and MDa. *tvinling*, NFris. *twen-, twanling*, MLG. *twenneling*, MHG. *zwinlinch, zwineling*, (OHG. *zwiniling*); also the reduced or variant forms Da., Sw., Norw. *tvilling*, WFris. *twielling* (*twilling*), MDu. *twilinc*, *twēlinc* (Du. *tweeling*), MLG. *twēlinc*, MHG. *zwillinc* (G. *zwilling*).] = TWIN *sb.* I.

*a* **1300** *Cursor M.* 3445 (Cott.) Now sco bredes tua for ane, Tuinlinges [*v. rr.* tuynlinges, tuynlynges, twinlynges]. **1382** WYCLIF *Song Sol.* iv. 5 Thi two tetes as two ȝunge capretes, twynlingus of the capret. *c* **1430** *Chev. Assigne* 27 Se ȝe þe ȝonder pore womman, how þat she is pyned With twynlenges two. **1483** *Cath. Angl.* 399/1 A Twynlynge (*A.* Twyndyllyng), *gemellus*. **1573** TUSSER *Husb.* (1878) 81 Twinlings be twiggers. *a* **1625** SIR H. FINCH *Law* (1636) 334 Two being found heires by one and the same title, whether twinlings.. or diuerse men..found heires to the same auncestour. **1710** HILMAN *Tusser Redivivus* (1744) 8 In some part of Norfolk and Lincolnshire they will keep none but Twinlins.

**b.** *attrib.* = TWIN *a.* 3.

**1573** TWYNE *Æneid.* XII. L l ij, A priest..A younglings yelt of brestled sow, and twynlinge sheepe vntwight Bringes forth, and hales the beastes vnto the altars.

**Twinned** (twind, *poet.* twi·nèd), *ppl. a.* [f. TWIN *sb.* or *v.*[2] + -ED[1].]

**1.** Born two at one birth; twin.

**1607** SHAKS. *Timon* IV. iii. 3 Twin'd Brothers of one wombe. **1611** — *Wint. T.* I. ii. 67 We were as twyn'd lambs, that did frisk i' th' sun. **1621** G. SANDYS *Ovid's Met.* VIII. (1626) 157 The twin'd Tyndarides. [**1905** GARNETT *Shaks.* 33.]

**2.** Intimately joined or united, as two things; coupled (usually also implying close similarity).

**1611** SHAKS. *Cymb.* I. vi. 35 The twinn'd Stones Vpon the number'd Beach. **1641** SIR E. DERING *4 Sp. conc. Laud*, etc. i. 2 Two twinned Nations, united together under one regall head. **1872** SIR A. DE VERE *Leg. St. Patrick* (Cassell) 26 The sun had set; But still those summits twinned,.. Laughed with his latest beam.

**b.** *Cryst.* United, as two crystals, or consisting of two crystals united, so as to form a 'twin': see TWIN *sb.* 3 b.

**1879** RUTLEY *Study Rocks* x. 98 A group of three twinned crystals of triclinic felspar. **1895** STORY-MASKELYNE *Crystallogr.* vii. § 192 Cubic System. Twinned Forms. **1912** *Brit. Museum Return* 194 Tilasite, a large twinned crystal.

**Twinner** (twi·nəɹ). *rare.* [f. TWIN *v.*[2] + -ER[1].] An animal that brings forth twins.

**1573** TUSSER *Husb.* (1878) 81 The lamb of such twinners for breeders go take.

**Twinning** (twi·niŋ), *vbl. sb.*[1] *Obs.* exc. *Sc.* [f. TWIN *v.*[1] + -ING[1].] The action of TWIN *v.*[1]; parting, separation.

*a* **1225** *Ancr. R.* 396 Þe soule luueð þet bodi..& þet is eðcene iðe twinnunge. *c* **1374** CHAUCER *Troylus* IV. 1303 Þe twynnynge of vs twayne Wol vs dishese and cruwellyche anoye. *c* **1425** tr. *Arderne's Treat. Fistula* 58 Cleuyng or twynnyng, þat is called rixis. **1591** R. BRUCE *Serm.* (Wodrow Soc.) 206 Death is a violent twinning and rugging sundrie of..the soul and the bodie.

**Twi·nning,** *vbl. sb.*[2] [f. TWIN *v.*[2] + -ING[1].] The action of TWIN *v.*[2]

**1.** Production of two children or young at a birth; bearing of twins.

**1573** TUSSER *Husb.* (1878) 81 Ewes yeerly by twinning rich maisters doo make. **1822-9** GOOD *Study Med.* (ed. 3) V. 226 In Congruous Twinning, or ordinary twin cases, in which there is no disparity of size between the two. **1883** DUNCAN in *Brit. Med. Jrnl.* I. 497 In the mare, twinning is a far rarer event than in woman and the cow.

**2.** Coupling, close union or combination; *spec.* in *Cryst.* the union of two crystals so as to form a twin crystal (see TWIN *sb.* 3 b).

**1845** [see TWIN *sb.* 3 b]. **1879** RUTLEY *Study Rocks* x. 87 This twinning is frequently..many times repeated in the felspars. **1898** *Naturalist* 176 A zonal structure as well as twinning—both on the pericline and albite plans.

**3.** *attrib.*, as **twinning-axis, -law, -plane,** *Cryst.* = *twin-axis, -law, -plane* (see TWIN C.); **twinning-machine, -saw,** names of apparatus for cutting two combs from a single piece of material.

**1875** KNIGHT *Dict. Mech.*, *Twinning-machine*, a machine for cutting two combs (twins) from the single piece... *Twinning-saw*. **1883** *Science* I. 331/2 The twinning plane is parallel to the ortho-pinacoid.

**Twi·nning,** *ppl. a. rare.* [f. as prec. + -ING[2].] That twins (see TWIN *v.*[2]); in quot., joining, becoming united.

**1621** G. SANDYS *Ovid's Met.* XI. (1626) 218 Her twinning legs in timber meet.

†**Twinny.** *Obs. rare*[—1]. [f. TWIN B. 4; cf. *a twyn(n)y*, variant of ATWIN *advb. phr.*[1]]. In phr. *in twinny*, asunder, apart.

*c* **1380** WYCLIF *Wks.* (1880) 318 Many men when þey ben gederid preyen more plesingliche to god þen wen þei ben scaterid in twynny.

†**Twinse,** *v. Obs. rare*[—1]. (Meaning uncertain.)

*c* **1205** LAY. 4236 Þa kingges weoren deædde Heore duȝeðe to-dealde Twinseden cnihtes, here tir wes at-fallen.

**Twinship** (twi·nʃip). [f. TWIN *a.* or *sb.* + -SHIP.] The condition of being twin, or a twin; the relation of a twin or twins. *lit.* and *fig.*

**1674** N. FAIRFAX *Bulk & Selv.* 107 It [an atome or leasting] has neither East side nor West side;..top nor bottom,..nor any thing that speaks twinship to any thing else. **1796** BURNEY *Mem. Metastasio* I. 378 With all the tenderness of twinship. **1899** GRIFFITH JONES *Ascent through Christ* II. ii. 28 The two streams of mental and organic life coalesce.. and begin that marvellous twinship which ends only at death.

**Twin-sister.** (Also as two words.) [TWIN *a.* 3.] A sister born at the same birth, as one of twins. Also *fig.* (Cf. TWIN-BROTHER.)

**1707** NORRIS *Treat. Humility* v. 213 Humility..with its twin-sister meekness. *a* **1721** PRIOR *Colin's Mistakes* x, Twin Sisters still were Ignorance and Pride. **1798** WORDSW. *Peter Bell* Prol. xvi, A Boat twin-sister of the crescent-moon. **1884** W. G. HORDER in *Chr. World Pulpit* 12 Nov. 311/1 Music is twin-sister to poetry. **1885** MISS BRADDON *Wyllard's Weird* i, Twin sisters who had loved each other with more than common love.

Hence **Twin-sisterhood,** the relation of twin sisters.

**1824** MISS MITFORD *Village* Ser. I. (1863) 164 Never was the..tie of twin-sisterhood more closely knit than in these two charming young women.

**Twinter** (twi·ntəɹ), *a.* and *sb.* Chiefly *north.* and *Sc.* Forms: 5-6 twynter, (5 twyntour, 6 twintter, twyntter, tynter, twenter), 6- twinter; also 6 qwintter, 9 *Sc.* quinter. [Reduced f. OE. *twi-wintre, -winter* of two winters: see TWI- and WINTER, and cf. THRINTER. So WFris. *twinter-* two years old (of horses or cows; known to Kilian in *tweenter-, twinterdier*), and *twinter* (also *twainter*) a two-year-old horse or cow, NFris. *twenter* an ox of this age.]

**A.** *adj.* Of two winters; two years old: said of cattle and sheep (also of colts).

**1537** *N. C. Wills* (Surtees 1908) 103 To every oon..of my kynde servauntes..oon twynter calf. **1540** *Test. Ebor.* (Surtees) VI. 94, ij twintter bolokes..one twyntter heffer. **1582** *Shuttleworths' Acc.* (Chetham Soc.) 1 A twinter kowlt. **1620** *Ibid.* 245 A twinter steere. **1638** *Will E. Burton* in *Reliquary* VIII. 221 One twinter bay filly with a whyte foote. **1844** STEPHENS *Bk. Farm* II. 38 After a ewe has been shorn three times she is called a twinter ewe, that is, a two-winter ewe. **1876** *Whitby Gloss.*, *Twinter*, 'a twinter stot', an ox of two winters old.

**B.** *sb.* A two-year-old cow, ox, horse, or sheep.

**1404** *Durham Acc. Rolls* (Surtees) 399 Item xiiij twynterys. **1408** *Hist. MSS. Comm.*, *Var. Coll.* II. 16 Vnum twyntour. **1513** DOUGLAS *Æneis* V. ii. 105 Five twinteris britnit he,.. and tydy quyis. **1536** *Durham Acc. Rolls* 419, 4 Trynters, 7 Twynters, 9 Stirks. **1567** *Richmond. Wills* (Surtees) 204 One yonge colte beinge a twinter. **1570** *Wills & Inv. N. C.* (Surtees) I. 341, xxiij twenters, stotts and whies. **1674** BLOUNT *Glossogr.*, *Twinters*, Cattle of two Winters old, so called in Bedford-shire. *c* **1720** RAMSAY *Ram & Buck* 22 When sleet Made twinters and hog-wedders bleet. **1777** *Antiq.* in *Ann. Reg.* II. 149/1 Twinter, a calf two winters or two years old: Derbyshire. **1808** *Compl. Grazier* (ed. 3) 97 The name of the female neat cattle is for the first year, cow-calf, then a..twinter. **1868** *Jrnl. R. Agric. Soc.* Ser. II. IV. II. 428, I turned 20 yearly calves and 'twinters'—as two-year-old animals are locally termed—into a 6-acre field. *a* **1898** [see THRINTER].

**b.** *transf.* Applied to pasture for, or the right to pasture, a two-year-old sheep, in a common or jointly-held field.

**1846** *Award* cited in *High Crt. of Justice* (1892), *Chanc. Div.* (Coulston *v.* Harvey), Four gaits, two twinters, in Bolton Highfield. **1892** *Ibid.*, The Plaintiffs are entitled to 11 gaits 2 twinters and 2 claws or..22 A. 1 R. 35 P. And the Defendants to 2 gaits and 1 claw or..3 A. 2 R. 5 P.

**Twiny** (twəi·ni), *a. rare.* Also 9 twiney. [f. TWINE *sb.*[1] or *v.*[1] + -Y.] **a.** Of the nature of, or resembling, twine. **b.** Characterized by, or suggestive of, twining.

**1620** QUARLES *Jonah* (1638) 12 Arise O Sleeper,..Theres not a twiny thred 'twixt death and thee. **1771** J. FOOT *Penseroso* v. 203 Whilst swelling nets Their twiny bondage spread. *c* **1868** G. H. KINGSLEY *Sport & Trav.* iii. (1900) 56 Wait till you feel a twiney and twisty sensation which informs you of uneasiness at the other end [of the fishing-line]. *c* **1870** *Ibid.* v. 133 His subtle, twisty and twiny mind. **1902** *Westm. Gaz.* 20 Mar. 3/2 The fichu should be of Alençon lace in the cream or twiny tones.

†**Twire,** *sb.*[1] *Obs. slang.* Also 7 tweer. [f. TWIRE *v.*[1]] A glance, a leer.

**1676** ETHEREDGE *Man of Mode* III. iii, The affected smiles, the silly by-words, and Amorous Tweers, in passing. **1679** MRS. BEHN *Feigned Courtezans* I. ii, Such an Eye, so sparkling, with an amorous Twire. **1682** — *False Count* I. ii, Winks, and nods, and signes, and twires. **1719** D'URFEY *Pills* V. 74 You toss a twire, a grin.

†**Twire,** *sb.*[2] *Obs. rare*[—1]. (See quot.; but perhaps only a misprint for *twirl*.)

**1679** LOCKE *Obs. Silk* (1766) 71 They put the cocons in hot water, and so stirring them about with a kind of rod, the ends of the silk twires of the cocons stick to it.

**Twire** (twəiᵊɹ), *v.*[1] *arch.* and *dial.* Forms: 7 twyre, 7- tweer, twire. [Of obscure origin, but corresponding in form to MHG. *zwieren* (now Bavarian dial.) to blink, to peer. There is prob. no connexion with the cant word *tower, towre, toure*, given by Harman (1567) in his *Caveat* (1869) 84-6, and copied by Dekker and later writers.]

**1.** *intr.* To look narrowly or covertly; to peer; to peep. Also *fig.* of a light, etc.

*c* **1600** SHAKS. *Sonn.* xxviii, When sparkling stars twire not thou guil[d]'st th' euen. **1602** MARSTON *Ant. & Mel.* IV. Wks. 1856 I. 52, I saw a thing stir under a hedge, and I peep't, and I spyed a thing: and I peer'd, and I tweerd underneath. *a* **1625** FLETCHER *Women Pleased* IV. i, I saw the wench that twir'd and twinkled at thee The other day. **1637** B. JONSON *Sad Sheph.* II. ii, The common Parent of us all! Which Maids will twire at, 'tween their fingers. **1723** STEELE *Consc. Lovers* I. i, If I was rich, I could twire and loll as well as the best of them. **1874** SWINBURNE *Midsummer Holiday*, etc. (1889) 19 Star by star on the unsunned waters twiring down. **1893** *Wiltshire Gloss.* s.v., 'How he did twire an' twire at she, an' her wouldn't so much as gie 'un a look!'

†**2.** *intr.* Used in sense 'to wink'. *Obs. rare*[—1].

**1601** HOLLAND *Pliny* XI. xxxvii. I. 334 So hard a matter is it for a man to keepe his eies from twiring. And many men naturally cannot chuse but be evermore winking and twinckling with their eies.

Hence **Twi·ring** *vbl. sb.* and *ppl. a.*

**1604** MIDDLETON *Father Hubburd's T.* Wks. (Bullen) VIII. 99 The tweering constable of Finsbury with his bench of brown bill-men. **1612** DRAYTON *Poly-olb.* xiii. 169 The Sunne.. with a fervent eye lookes through the twyring glades. **1638** LISLE *Heliodorus* x. 172 The Wiseman lookt on King with twiring eyes. **1728** MRS. DELANY *Life & Corr.* (1861) I. 175 We had ogling and tweering [*printed* tweezing], and whispering and glancing. **1738** *The Briton Described* 13 And then for her Eyes, they are excellent at twiring. *a* **1832** MOTHERWELL *Facts fr. Fairyland* ii, By the winking light of the tweering star.

†**Twire,** *v.*[2] *Obs. rare*[—1]. (Perh. a misprint for TWIRL *v.*[1] 3.)

**1628** BURTON *Anat. Mel.* III. ii. III. i. (ed. 3) 490 No sooner doth a young man see his sweetheart coming, but he.. slickes his haire, twires his beard, &c.

**Twire,** obs. form of TUYERE.

†**Twirede,** *a. Obs.* [OE. *twirǣde*, f. *twi-*, TWI- + *rǣd*, REDE *sb.*[1]] Of two minds or counsels; undecided, irresolute; divided in mind, not unanimous.

*c* **888** K. ÆLFRED *Boeth.* xli. § 3 Hwæðer þu eft on ænȝum ȝeþeahte swa twioræde sie þæt þe helpe hwæðer hit ȝeweorðe, ðe hit no ne ȝeweorðe. *c* **1000** *Ags. Gosp.* Matt. xii. 25 Ælc rice þe byð twyræde on him sylfum byþ toworpen. *c* **1205** LAY. 19416 Bruttes hafden muchel mode & vnimete prute...And weoren alle twiræde. *c* **1250** *Gen. & Ex.* 3271 Egipcienes woren in twired wen Queðer he sulden folȝen or flen.

†**Twire-pipe.** *Obs. rare.* [In sense 2 f. *twire* TUYERE. Sense 1 may have the same origin.]

**1.** App. a contemptuous name for a musical pipe; in quots. applied to persons.

**1619** FLETCHER *Mons. Thomas* III. i, Ye are an Ass, a twirepipe, A Jeffery John bo peepe. *a* **1634** CHAPMAN (Webster), I have said..that you looked like Twire-pipe, the taborer.

**2.** A tuyere-pipe: see TUYERE b.

**1674** PETTY *Disc. Dupl. Proportion* 105 The Bellows.. rising in double Quickness admits double air..the whole passing through the same Twire-pipe in half the time.

†**Twirk,** *v. Obs. rare*[—1]. [App. from the same stem as *twirl*, with different suffix, but possibly a misprint.] *trans.* = TWIRL *v.*[1] 3.

**1599** BRETON *Praise of Vertuous Ladies* (Grosart) 57/2 If shee have her hand on the pette in her cheeke, he is twyrking of his mustachios.

**Twirl** (twɔ̄ɪl), *sb.* Also 6, 8 **twirle**, 7 **twerle**. [f. Twirl *v.*¹] The action or an act of twirling, or the condition of being twirled; a rapid whirling or spinning; a twist; a spin; a whirl; also *fig.*

**1598** Florio, *Giro*,..a twirle. **1700** T. Brown *Amusem. Ser. & Com., City Circle* 136 A Grave Old Gentleman..gave his Whiskers a Twirl. **1709–10** Steele *Tatler* No. 128 ¶ 4 The dextrous Twirl of your Mop. **1775** Adair *Amer. Ind.* 400 He commonly sends it [ball] the right course, by an artful sharp twirl. **1818** Moore *Fudge Fam. Paris* v. 2 Like a tee-totum, I'm all in a twirl. **1827** Southey *Devil's Walk* x, Satan gave thereat his tail A twirl of admiration. **1840** Dickens *Old C. Shop* viii, He performed..such spins and twirls as filled the company with astonishment. **1853** Kane *Grinnell Exp.* xiv. (1856) 106 A ballet-dancer in full twirl.

**b.** Anything that twirls or is twirled; † a reel, winch (*obs.*); each of the whorls of a shell; a curved line. Also *fig.*

*Steam twirl*, a revolving steam-heated cylinder for mixing materials in soap-making (*Cent. Dict., Supp.* 1909).

**1688** R. Holme *Armoury* III. xxii. (Roxb.) 277/2 An Instrument called a Twerle, or Line Reeles: It is to wind a long line of a fishing Rod vpon. **1696** *Phil. Trans.* XIX. 188 The inner Twirls of which Shell were preserved entire. **1716** M. Davies *Athen. Brit.* III. *Arianism* 12 Athanasius's Creed is a Twirle of Words. *a* **1728** Woodward *Nat. Hist. Fossils* II. (1729) 37 The Twirl in this is different from that of the others;..the Twirls turning from the Right-hand to the left. **1841** Carlyle *Misc., Baillie* (1857) IV. 230 Not a twirl in that cramp penmanship.

**Twirl** (twɔ̄ɪl), *v.*¹ Forms: 6 **twyrle**, 6–8 **twirle**, 7 **twurl**, 7–8 **twerle**, 7– **twirl**. [Of obscure origin: perh. merely imitative (or an alteration of *turl* Tirl *v.*³) after *whirl*. The initial *t-* and late appearance of the word are against direct connexion with Continental synonyms from the stem *þwer-*: cf. Thwerl *v.*]

**1.** *intr.* To rotate rapidly, to spin; to be whirled round or about; also to turn *round* quickly so as to face or point the other way; also *fig.* of the mind or head: to be in a whirl, be confused or giddy.

**1598** Florio, *Girare*,..to twirle about, to wander. *Ibid.*, *Girellare*, to twirle or gire about. **1611** Cotgr., *Pirouetter*, to whirle, twirle, turne swiftly about. **1621** Markham *Hunger's Prev.* 117 Vpon the least touch it will twerle and tourne as round as any Scopperill. **1639** S. Du Verger tr. *Camus' Admir. Events* 307 A Labyrinth where mens spirits twirle about and stray into acts so unreasonable, that they end in folly. **1712** Steele *Spect.* No. 466 ¶ 6 Such Impertinents as fly, hop, caper, tumble, twirl,..and..play a thousand Pranks. **1791** Cowper *Iliad* xxiii. 1047 His staff That twirling flies. **1792** Mme. D'Arblay *Diary* V. vii. 299 A grave man's voice behind me said, 'Is not that Miss Burney?' I twirled round and saw the Bishop of Dromore. **1830** Scott *Demonol.* viii. 235 Dost thou not twirl like a calf that hath the turn? **1860** Tyndall *Glac.* I. xx. 142 The [compass] needle..sometimes twirling swiftly round. **1879** G. Meredith *Egoist* III. xi. 240 My head twirls; I did unwisely to come out.

**b.** The verb-stem used adverbially.

**1806** Bloomfield *Wild Flowers* Poems (1845) 190 Twirl went his stick.

**2.** *trans.* To cause to rotate or spin; to turn (an object) round rapidly; to turn about in the hands; to spin between the finger and thumb, etc.; to twiddle idly or playfully.

*a* **1623** Fletcher *Love's Cure* III. iii, Her sighs, powerful as the violent North, Like a light feather twirl me round about. **1647** H. More *Poems* 196 'Bout which are hurld [the planets]..round on their own axes twurld. **1664** Power *Exp. Philos.* I. 55 Hairs..are..angular and corner'd, which you may even perceive by your fingers, by twirling a Horsehair in them. **1716** Gay *Trivia* II. 422 When..dexterous Damsels twirle the sprinkling Mop. **1797** Coleridge *Christabel* I. 48 There is not wind enough to twirl The one red leaf. **1812** H. & J. Smith *Rej. Addr.* ix. (1873) 85 Roll thy hoop, and twirl thy tops. **1832** G. R. Porter *Porcelain & Gl.* 184 The workman then dexterously twirls the punt.., the glass yields to the centrifugal impulse. **1871** Tyndall *Fragm. Sc.* (1879) II. v. 57 A boy twirls round his head a bullet at the end of a string.

**b.** *fig. To twirl* (a person) *round one's finger*: cf. Turn *v.* 9 c, Twiddle *v.*¹ 2 b.

**1748** Richardson *Clarissa* (1811) III. ix. 64 Who would not wish to outwit such girls, and to be able to twirl them round his finger?

**c.** To turn (one's fingers or thumbs) rapidly about one another; spec. *to twirl one's thumbs*, as an idle occupation when one has nothing to do. Cf. Twiddle *v.*¹ 2 c.

**1777** Mme. D'Arblay *Early Diary, Lett.* 27 Mar., Dr. Johnson..has a strange method of frequently twirling his fingers, and twisting his hands. **1816** *Remarks Eng. Mann.* 26 'What can I say?' 'Oh! any thing is better than sitting twirling your thumbs like a fool.' **1833** Ht. Martineau *Manch. Strike* vii. 77 Sitting down demurely..and twirling his thumbs. **1864** Miss Braddon *Henry Dunbar* iii. 23 Bad thoughts..come fastest when a fellow sits twirling his thumbs.

**d.** *transf.* To shake out or sprinkle by or as by twirling a mop.

**1762** Churchill *Ghost* IV. 49 Those, who Physic twirl, Full fraught with death, from ev'ry Curl. **1842** Motley *Corr.* (1889) I. iv. 117 The archbishop with a little mop or swab twirling water on all the dignitaries.

**3.** To twist spirally (threads, etc.); now *esp.* to twist (the moustache).

**1614** B. Jonson *Bart. Fair* II. iii, Neuer tuske, nor twirle your dibble. *a* **1619** Fletcher *Mad Lover* II. i, I'll take him And twirl his neck about. **1728** Morgan *Algiers* II. iv. 271 Sir, said he,..twirling his starched Mustachio, I am the Cavallero [etc.]. **1791** Cowper *Odyss.* VI. 379 Twirling her fleecy threads Tinged with sea-purple. **1882** Ouida *Maremma* I. 169 Joconda was silent, as she twirled her flax. **1894** Mrs. F. Elliot *Roman Gossip* iv. 121 He twirled his long moustache.

**4.** To move or cast with a rapid or violent turning motion; to whirl. Now *rare*.

**1646** Lilburne *Unhappy Game Scotch & Eng.* 10 Twerle up your Blew caps, and hurle them up at the Moone. **1648** Herrick *Hesper., N.-y. Gift to Sir S. Steward* 42 Carouse, Till Liber Pater twirles the house About your eares. **1695** Addison *Poems, King* 157 Misc. Wks. 1726 I. 13 Crags of broken Rocks are twirl'd on high. **1742** Richardson *Pamela* III. 392 The Knight following him with Outrage to the Top of a Pair of Stairs, he twirled him from Top to Bottom almost. **1848** Thackeray *Van. Fair* xl, She would ..twirl away his chair from the fire which he loved to look at.

**5.** *intr.* To twine, coil, curl. *rare*.

**1706**, *a* **1719** [see *twirled, twirling* below]. **1725** *Family Dict.* s. v. *Melon*, The Sun will soon draw the Heat of so fresh a Bed to that Degree, that..the two first Leaves.. of the Plant will twirl or coffer. **1840** Thackeray *Shabby-genteel Story* iv, His great Spanish cloak..of so prodigious a size that the tail of it, as it twirled over his shoulder, whisked away a lodging-card from the door of the house opposite. **1848** — *Van. Fair* lxiv, The monster's hideous tail..writhing and twirling.

Hence **Twirled** *ppl. a.*, **Twi·rling** *vbl. sb.* and *ppl. a.*

**1598** Florio, *Girata*,..a twirling of anything. **1611** Cotgr., *Giré*, veered, or turned..; twirled, whirled, or twyned about. *Ibid.*, *Pirouetteux*, whirling, twirling, trilling, turning swiftly about. **1623** Fletcher *Rule a Wife* II. iii, Leave twirling of your hat, and hold your head up, And speak to th' lady. **1626** Bacon *Sylva* § 845 The Twisting of Thred; And the Practice of Twirling about of Spindles. **1706** in *Hearne's Collect.* 19 Mar. (O.H.S.) I. 205 Fifty to one yᵉ twirl'd tail d Cur does win. *a* **1719** Addison *Ovid's Metam.* IV. 97 The wriggling snake is snatcht on high In eagle's claws,..Around the foe his twirling tail he flings. **1794** G. Adams *Nat. & Exp. Philos.* IV. xlvi. 291 [Electric] boats, with each of them a twirling fly..fixed to the top of the mast. **1822–9** Good *Study Med.* (ed. 3) V. 200 The sudden twirlings of the mouth..the jactitating struggle of the limbs. **1871** Tyndall *Fragm. Sc.* (1879) II. xiii. 307 The retention of the retinal impression transforms the little living rod into a twirling wheel. **1897** *Q. Rev.* July 230 Trying to unravel the twisted and twirled tangle of philosophies of life.

† **Twirl**, *v.*² *Obs. rare.* [Cf. prec. and Tirl *v.*² and *v.*³] *trans.* To lay *open* by rolling or turning back the covering. Also *intr.* for *refl.*

**1523** Fitzherb. *Husb.* § 55 Take bothe your handes, and twyrle vpon [*read* open] his [the sheep's] eye, and if he be ruddy, and haue reed stryndes, in the white of the eye, than he is sounde. *Ibid.* § 68 Her shap..wyll twyrle open, and close agayne.

**Twirl-** [Twirl *sb.* or *v.*¹ in comb.]: **twirl-blast**, **-wind**, a whirlwind; **twirl-mop** *a.*, that twirls a mop.

**1865** *Morn. Star* 22 July, This rock [Hoonister Crag, Rosthwaite] and its neighbourhood is famous for what is called hereabouts '*twirlblasts'—that is, in our southern dialect, 'whirlwinds'. **1765** E. Thompson *Meretriciad* 27 A venal trick..practis'd now by all the *twirl-mop maids. **1764** T. Brydges *Homer Travest.* (1797) II. 305 Have you not seen a sort of *twirlwind, Which country people call a whirlwind, Whip up a haycock from the ground?

**Twirler** (twɔ̄·ɪləɪ). [f. Twirl *v.*¹ + -er ¹.] One who or that which twirls.

In quot. 1827, a decoy for larks, consisting of a curved piece of wood set with small mirrors, mounted on a spindle and turned by a string.

**1808** *Sporting Mag.* XXXII. 134 The twirler is usually some gay youth..he whirls his cane in the air by means of a ribbon. **1827** J. H. H. in *Hone's Every-day Bk.* II. 93/1 The fascination of the twirler is so strong..After being fired at several times they [larks] return to the twirler. **1828** Miss Mitford *Village* Ser. III. 214 An household..that should shame all the twirlers of mops and brandishers of brooms in the county. *a* **1891** *Tribune Bk. of Sports* 81 (Cent.) Critics [in base-ball] are still looking for the pitcher par excellence...Their ideal twirler of the diminutive globe has not yet made his appearance.

**Twirlification** (twɔ̄·ɪlifikē·ʃən). *nonce-wd.* [f. Twirl: see -fication.] Twirling, gyrating.

**1834** M. Scott *Cruise Midge* (1859) 300 He again floundered past me with his partner..contriving in their complex twirlifications..to tread heavily on my toes.

**Twirligig** (twɔ̄·ɪligig). [f. Twirl *v.*¹ after *whirligig*.] A twirly pattern; a whirligig.

**1903** *19th Cent.* June 950 A lumpish, putty-coloured object ..embossed all over with serpentine flourishes and twirligigs.

**Twirly** (twɔ̄·ɪli), *a.* [f. Twirl *sb.* + -y.] Full of or characterized by twirls or curves.

**1887** *Story of a Kiss* I. iv. 56, I can never make out those twirly monograms. **1906** N. Munro in *Blackw. Mag.* July 18/1 A curious twirly wooden candlestick.

**Twiscar**, var. Tuskar, peat-cutting implement.

**Twisday, Twise**, obs. ff. Tuesday, Twice.

**Twisel, twissel** (twi·s'l, twi·z'l), *sb.* (*a.*) *Obs.* exc. *dial.* Forms: 1 **twisla**, **twisel-**; 4 **twisil**, 6 **twisel**, **twissell**, 9 **twissel**, (**twistle**, **twizzle**). [OE. *twisla* = OHG. *zwisila* (MHG. *zwisel*, G. *zwiesel*), f. *twi-* Twi-; cf. also ON. *kvísl*.]

**1.** A point or part at which anything divides into branches; a fork. Now *dial.*

**931** *Chart. Æðelstan* 21 June in Birch *Cart. Sax.* II. 360 Of þam mere on þan lace þær þa brocas twisliað; þanne of ðæm twislan on mær beorh. **1586** J. Hooker *Hist. Irel.* in *Holinshed* II. 43/1 The same were so soft, that with the weight of their bodies they sunke downe vp to the hard knees or twisels. **1847–78** Halliwell, *Twissel, Twistle*, that part of a tree where the branches divide from the stock. *West.* **1888** Elworthy *W. Somerset Word-bk.* 784 In the twizzle of that there pollard.

† **2.** A double twig or shoot. *Obs. rare.*

**1567** Turberv. *Poems, 'The Lover wisheth'* 34 As from a tree we sundrie times espie A twissell grow by Natures subtile might, And being two..For one are tane.

† **3.** *attrib.* or as *adj.* Double, twofold (in comb.).

*c* **1000** *Ælfric's Voc.* in Wr.-Wülcker 108/15 *Scinodens*, twiseltoðe. **1382** Wyclif *Prov.* viii. 13 The mouth of the twisil tunge I wlate. — *Ecclus.* v. 16 Be thou not clepid a twisil tunge, or a priue bacbiter. *Ibid.* vi. 1 Eche synnere enuyous and twisil tungid.

† **Twi·sel**, *v. Obs.* Forms: 1 **twislian**, 3 **twiselen**, 4 **twesel**, 5 **twysle**. [f. prec.; cf. MHG. *zwiselen* and ON. *kvísla*.] *intr.* To separate into two or more branches; to fork; to bifurcate. Hence † **Twi·sled** *ppl. a.*, † **Twi·sling** *vbl. sb.* and *ppl. a.*

**931** [see Twisel *sb.*]. **967** *Charter of Eadgar* in Kemble *Cod. Dipl.* III. 14 On ðone twisledan beam. *a* **1000** *Sax. Leechd.* III. 436 Æfter his forðsiþe Eadgar..þæs rices twislunge eft to annesse brohte. *c* **1000** in Wr.-Wülcker 148/25 *Scandula*, twisld corn. **1042** *Charter of Hardacnut* in Kemble *Cod. Dipl.* IV. 66 Ðær ða weʒes twisliʒað. *c* **1200** *Trin. Coll. Hom.* 117 Ðo openede þe holi gost him seluen to isende bi þan þe hem þuhte shapen alse tunge fele twiselende and on fires hewe. **1398** Trevisa *Barth. De P. R.* v. xxvi. (Bodl. MS.), Þe tweseled [*ed.* **1495** twyslyd] forkes ben nedeful.

**Twiser case**, obs. f. Tweezer-case.

† **Twish**, *int. Obs. rare.* [A natural utterance: cf. Tush *int.*] An exclamation of contempt or vexation.

**1577** Stanyhurst *Descr. Ireland* viii. in Holinshed *Chron.* (1587) II. 13/1 There is a cholerike or disdainfull interiection vsed in the Irish language called Boagh, which is as much in English as twish. **1583** — *Æneis* etc. (Arb.) 144 Twish, what woonder is yt, quod one of the coompanye, If [etc.].

† **Twisk**, obs. var. Tusk *sb.*²

**1611** Coryat *Crudities* 247 They wore double maskes upon their faces..with twiskes of downy or woolly stuffe covering their noses.

† **Twispeche**. *Obs.* [OE. *twispræc*, f. *twi-*, Twi- + *spræc* (later *spǣc*): see Speech *sb.*¹] Double or deceitful speech.

*a* **950** *Rituale Dunelm.* (Surtees) 25 Facon and eswico and aefisto and allo tuispreco. *c* **1200** *Trin. Coll. Hom.* 163 Ðe defles sed is hoker and scorn..cheast and twispeche.

**Twissel, Twissle**: see Twisel, Twistle.

**Twist** (twist), *sb.*¹ Forms: 4–6 **twyst**, **-e**, 4–7 **twiste**, (5 **twest**, **tweeste**, 5–6 **twys**, 6 **tweyste**, *Sc.* **tuist**), 4– **twist**. [Related to Twist *v.*, and presenting similar obscurities of history (except in senses directly derived from the verb). Sense 1 may be related to the OE. *-twist* which appears in *candel-twist* glossing L. *emunctoria*, and *mæst-twist* glossing L. *parastates*. Sense 2 corresponds to ON. *kvistr* (Norw. and Da. *kvist*, Sw. *qvist*), which may ultimately be from the same stem: Kilian also gives a Flemish *twist* 'rami abscissi, ramalia'. To sense 4 the only parallel appears to be Kilian's '*twist* i. *twijn*, filum duplex, retortum', the genuineness of which as a Flemish word is doubtful. (G. *twist*, cotton-twist, is from English.) In English there is no sense corresponding to MDu. and Du., MLG. and LG. *twist* (hence Da. and Sw. *tvist*), MHG. and G. *zwist* discord, dissension.]

**I.** A divided object or part.

† **1.** The flat part of a hinge, fastened on a door or gate, and turning on a hook or pintle fixed in the post: = Band *sb.*¹ 3. *Obs.*

**1350–1** in J. R. Magrath *Obituary Bk. Queen's Coll., Oxf.* 67 Recepta de dono Willelmi Muscham xvijˢ pro twystes portarum. **1388** Wyclif *Amos* viii. 3 And the herris [*gloss* ether twistis; Vulg. *cardines*] of the temple schulen greetli sowne in that dai. **1388–9** *Abingdon Rolls* (Camden) 54 In hokis, twystis, et clauis, xij d. **1404–5** *Ibid.* 69 In j hacche cum j twyste et opere ij s. **14..** *Beryn* 478 The Pardonere..went to have fond þe dor vp by þe haspe; & eke þe twist Held hym out a whils, & þe lok also. **1491–2** in Swayne *Sarum Churchw. Acc.* (1896) 40 Twistes and hokes necessary vnto the Wedyr Dorys. **1529** *Yatton Churchw. Acc.* (Som. Rec. Soc.) 145 Yᵉ levys of yᵉ wyndowes in yᵉ Church-howse, with hookys, twystys, and haspys. **1545** *Croscombe Churchw. Acc.* (Som. Rec. Soc.) 44 Paid for a tweyste and naylys and greffe, iiiᵈ. Paid for greffe thred and silke, iiiᵈ. *c* **1568** in Swayne *Sarum Churchw. Acc.* (1896) 114, iiij pere of twysse and ij pere of hookes. **1805** R. W. Dickson *Pract. Agric.* I. 71 Smith, for locks, hooks, and twists, latches, etc.

† **2.** A twig; a branch. *Obs.*

*c* **1374** Chaucer *Troylus* III. 1181 (1230) As a-bowte a tre with many a twyste [*v.rr.* twist, -e] Bytrent and wryþe the soote wode bynde. **1375** Barbour *Bruce* VII. 188 The kyng ..had drede of thai thre men...Tharfor he slepit as foul on twist. *c* **1386** Chaucer *Merch. T.* 1905 On his bak she stood And caughte hire by a twiste, and vp she gooth. **1423** Jas. I *Kingis Q.* xxxiii, On the small[e] grene twistis sat The lytill suete nyghtingale. *c* **1440** *Alph. Tales* 360/2 Þis man happend to be smyten in þe ee with a twyste, so þat he mot not se. **1513** Douglas *Æneis* III. i. 58 Ane vthir smale twist of a tree I chesit. **1583** Stubbes *Anat. Abus.* I. (1879) 76 So long as a sprigge, twist, or braunche, is yong, it is flexible and bowable. **1622** W. Whateley *God's Husb.* II. 2 The cutting off from the branches such vnprofitable and ouergrowing twists,..as doe no way benefit the branch.

**3.** The part of anything at which it divides or branches; *spec.* the junction of the thighs, the fork; now (exc. *arch.*) only that of sheep and cattle.

1398 TREVISA *Barth. De P. R.* v. xxxi. (Bodl. MS.), Þe boones of the rybbes..beth ybounde togedres in þe twiste of þe breest. *c* 1440 *Promp. Parv.* 504/2 Twest, or twyste, of þe eye (*H., P.* tweeste of the iye), *hirquus* [cf. 1677 COLES *Lat. Dict., Hirquus*, the corner of the eye]. 1572 J. JONES *Bathes Buckstone* 13 b, The one apply vnder the arme holes, and the other in the twyste. 1575 TURBERV. *Venerie* 36 Split one of his forefeete from the twiste of the cleas unto the ioynte of the foote. 1607 TOPSELL *Four-f. Beasts* (1658) 509 Bowes are requisite to remove them [squirrels] when they rest in the twists of trees. 1611 COTGR., *Fourcheure*..that part of the bodie from whence the thighes doe part; I thinke we call it the Twist. *a* 1668 DAVENANT *Siege* III. i, If thou dost grin I'll cleave thee from the Scalp, unto the Twist. 1719 DE FOE *Crusoe* (1840) I. ii. 25, I took him by surprise with my arm under his twist. 1799 A. YOUNG *Agric. Lincoln.* 359 The gambrels of the hind legs rather inclining inwards, and the twist fat. 1831 *Sutherland Farm Rep.* 82 in *Libr. Usef. Knowl., Husb.* III, The breast and twist much narrower than to all appearance was compatible with so broad a carcase. 1882 STEVENSON *New Arab. Nts.* (1901) 97/2 If I had my hand under your twist I would send you flying. 1899 *Jrnl. R. Agric. Soc.* Mar. 7 The breast, flank, and twist [of a bull] of great size.

†**b.** *transf.* See quot. *Obs.*

1706 PHILLIPS (ed. Kersey), *Twist*,..the Hollow on the inside of the Thigh;..among Carpenters it is taken for a piece of Timber otherwise call'd *the Girder*. 1823 CRABB *Technol. Dict., Twist*, another name for a girder.

**II.** The twisting of threads into a cord, and derived senses.

**4.** Thread or cord composed of two or more fibres or filaments of hemp, silk, wool, cotton, or the like, wound round one another; often with defining word, as *silk, woollen, cotton, gold* or *silver twist*.

1555 EDEN *Decades* 200 The other [cord] is grosser lyke the wycke or twyste of hempe. 1558 in Feuillerat *Revels Q. Eliz.* (1908) 93, iiij^or oz. di. silke twyste. 1591 SPENSER *M. Hubberd* 461 Ne to weare garments base of wollen twist, But with the finest silkes us to aray. 1601 J. WHEELER *Treat. Comm.* 110 White veluet ierkins cut, imbroidered with siluer twist. 1674 *Essex Papers* (Camden) I. 277 Rolling up Wooll into great Twist, & so passing it as Yarne. 1762 GOLDSM. *Cit. W.* liv, His coat was trimmed with tarnished twist. *c* 1850 *Arab. Nights* (Rtldg.) 306 A small silk purse..tied with a piece of twist.

**b.** *spec.* (*a*) in *Cotton-spinning*, warp yarn, which is more twisted in spinning, and stronger than weft; (*b*) fine silk thread used by tailors, hatters, etc. With *pl.*, a kind of this.

1805 *East Rep.* V. 175 The Battiers received orders from abroad for cotton twist. 1825 C. M. WESTMACOTT *Eng. Spy* I. 265 Buttons, twist, and small ware. 1851 L. D. B. GORDON *Art Jrnl. Illustr. Catal.* p. vi**/2 Twist is the term usually applied to the kind of yarn used for cotton warp; organzine to that for silk warp. 1890 'R. BOLDREWOOD' *Miner's Right* xxxi, A small piece of silk thread, known by tailors as 'twist'. 1891 *Daily News* 18 Nov. 2/7 Wefts are still more pressed for sale than twists.

**5.** A cord, thread, or the like, formed by twisting, spinning, or plaiting; in quot. 1872, a conical bag or wrapper made by twisting a piece of paper, a 'cornet' or 'screw'.

1598 SYLVESTER *Du Bartas* II. i. IV. *Handie-crafts* 293 On either horn a three-fold twist he ty'd Of Osiar twigs. 1603 B. JONSON *Jas. I's Entertainm.* Wks. (Rtldg.) 529/1 She..sits weaving certain small silver twists. 1607 SHAKS. *Cor.* v. vi. 96 Breaking his Oath and Resolution, like A twist of rotten Silke. 1662 GERBIER *Princ.* 5 Twists of Hair on both sides of their Cheeks. 1700 DRYDEN *Ovid's Met.* XII. 198 About his chin the twist He ty'd, and soon the strangl'd soul dismiss'd. 1740 CHEYNE *Regimen* 151 To suppose the Nerves to be..membranous Tubes, Twists or Ropes. 1791 COWPER *Odyss.* XVII. 238 His tatter'd wallet o'er his back.., suspended by a leathern twist. 1859 TENNYSON *Vivien* 70 A twist of gold was round her hair. 1872 *Routledge's Ev. Boy's Ann.* 127/2 A twist of newspaper, holding salt, was next placed on the table. 1906 ALICE WERNER *Natives Brit. Centr. Afr.* viii. 206 A few leaves, or a twist of grass, are put on the top to keep the water from spilling.

**b.** *Naut.* Each of the strands of which a rope consists. Also *to spin a twist* (*fig.*): see quot. 1867.

*c* 1635 CAPT. N. BOTELER *Dial. Sea Services* (1685) 192 The ends of the Strands or several Twists, are with a Fidd drawn into the ends of the other Ropes Strands, and this is called a Splice. 1769 FALCONER *Dict. Marine* (1789) Bb ij b, The twists or strands of a rope. 1867 SMYTH *Sailor's Wordbk., Spin a Twist* or *a Yarn*, to tell a long story; much prized in a dreary watch, if not tedious.

†**6.** *fig.* The continuation or course of life figured as a thread; cf. THREAD *sb.* 6 a. *Obs.*

1568 T. HOWELL *Arb. Amitie* (1879) 25 For thin is twist or fatall threed, on mortall wheele so spun. 1581 — *Deuises* (1879) 197 But when the twyste of this our tyme is wownde, No meanes by man may serve the same to stretch. 1596 SPENSER *F. Q.* IV. ii. 48 Cruell Atropos..cutting the twist in twaine. 1614 GORGES *Lucan* VI. 254 The Fatall sisters three,..their spinning twists did guide. 1638 FORD *Fancies* IV. i, 'Tis in my power to cut off The twist thy life is spun by.

**7.** In other figurative applications, e.g. a slight or weak support upon which something depends; a means of tracing one's way in a labyrinth; an intimate union or connexion; the composition or substance of something figured as being spun.

1580 LYLY *Euphues* (Arb.) 458 Vpon what a twist they hang that now are in honour. 1633 G. HERBERT *Temple, Pearl* iv, Through the labyrinths..thy silk twist let down from heav'n to me, Did both conduct and teach me. 1660 *Charac. Italy* 90 Nor doth her incolumity depend upon the slender twist of the life of one single person. 1675 BAXTER *Cath. Theol.* I. 54 Here is a wonderful inseparable twist; and in the main an Identity. *a* 1734 NORTH *Exam.* II. v. § 151 (1740) 410 We must necessarily have to do with him, because the Author has so taken him into his Twist, that we cannot baulk him.

**8.** A beverage consisting of a mixture of two liquors or ingredients, as tea and coffee, gin and brandy, etc.: see quots. *slang.*

*a* 1700 B. E. *Dict. Cant. Crew, Twist*, halt Tea, half Coffee. 1712 ADDISON *Spect.* No. 317 ⁋ 19 Coffee-house. Read the News. A Dish of Twist. 1725 *New Cant. Dict., Twist*,..Likewise Brandy and Eggs mixed. Hot-pot. 1823 JON BEE *Slang, Gin-twist*, hot water and gin, with sugar and lemon-juice, or orange ditto. 1826, 1849 [see GIN *sb.*[2] 2].

**9.** Tobacco made into a thick cord; a piece or 'length' of this. Cf. PIGTAIL 1 a.

1791 W. BARTRAM *Carolina* 499, I distributed my presents, giving him a very fine hankerchief and a twist of choice Tobacco. 1808 PIKE *Sources Mississ.* (1810) II. 121 The prize offered to the successful person was a jacket and a twist of tobacco. 1809 A. HENRY *Trav.* 315 Tobacco.. fetched one beaver-skin per foot of Spencer's twist. 1818 SCOTT *Hrt. Midl.* xl[i]v, Gang down to the Clachan and bring me up a pennyworth of twist. 1849 CUPPLES *Green Hand* iii, Cakes of cavendish, twists of negrohead, and coils of pigtail. 1886 HALL CAINE *Son of Hagar* III. i, Wot's to prevent me having a screw of twist on the strength of it? 1909 J. STARK *Priest Gordon of Aberdeen* ii. 22, I tried the daily use of small twist.

**10.** A small loaf made of one or more twisted rolls of dough; a small twisted roll of bread.

*a* 1845 HOOD *Love has not Eyes* iv, Though she's all so much awry, she can only eat a twist! 1852 DICKENS *Bleak Ho.* xix, Dainty new bread, crusty twists, cool fresh butter. 1893 EARL DUNMORE *Pamirs* I. 274 Three or four different sorts of bread, round balls, chupatties, twists [etc.].

**11.** Stringy india-rubber in the crude state made up in lumps like balls of cord.

1909 in *Cent. Dict. Supp.*

**III.** Senses denoting chiefly the action of the verb.

**12.** An act or the action of turning on or as on an axis; a turn; a twirl; the condition of being twisted or turned in this way; rotary motion, spin.

1576 GASCOIGNE *Grief of Joye* i. Wks. (Roxb.) II. 265 The strongest thryd y^t ever yet was sponne..Is nockthrowen yet even with y^e spindles twyst. 1762 STERNE *Tr. Shandy* V. v, Bending her head a little downwards, with a twist of her neck. 1799 A. YOUNG *Agric. Lincoln.* 151 It is gathered by hand, grasping the leaves of the plants, and taking them off with a twist. 1826 SAMOUELLE *Direct. Collect. Insects & Crust.* 63 The net should be of such a length, that, upon a slight twist, it may fall against one side of the hoop, and prevent the escape of the insect. 1840 THACKERAY *Shabby-genteel Story* ix, Mr. Fitch..gave a twist of the curling-tongs to his beard. 1849 H. MILLER *Footpr. Creat.* ix. (1874) 161 In order to accommodate it to the general twist, which rendered lateral what in other fishes is dorsal and abdominal. 1855 BROWNING *A Light Woman* x, [A pearl] 'Twas quenching a dozen blue-flies' thirst When I gave its stalk a twist. 1906 *Daily Chron.* 7 June 4/7 We have to allow for the twist of the earth,..mid-Europe time and Eastern Europe time ..are ahead of Greenwich.

**b.** *spec.* in *Arch.*: see quot. 1875.

1840 *Civil Eng. & Arch. Jrnl.* III. 232/2 A short portion of a course, or a single arch-stone, is very nearly contained between two planes slightly inclined to each other; and.. the loss of material arising from the *twist* of the stone must always be insignificant. 1875 KNIGHT *Dict. Mech., Twist* (3), *Archit.*, the wind of the bed-joint of each course of voussoirs in a skew arch.

**13. a.** In *Tennis, Cricket, Billiards*, etc.: Lateral spin imparted to a ball in striking or delivery, causing it to diverge on rebounding; 'screw'; a stroke by which such spin is given; the action or knack of giving this spin to a ball; also, a ball having such spin.

1699 E. S—CY *Country Gentl. Vade M.* 54 The Players [at Tennis]..talking of *Cuts* and *Twists*, and *Forces*. 1833 NYREN *Yng. Cricketer's Tutor* 68 The ball was delivered quite low, and with a twist. 1856 [see SCREW *sb.*[1] 11 b]. 1884 I. BLIGH in *Lillywhite's Cricket Ann.* 3 W. H. Cooper, as to whose powers of twist and singularity of method so much has been heard. 1889 S. GIBNEY in *Boys' Own Paper* 4 May 496/1 The way well pitched up balls to crump, And how the twists should smothered be.

**b.** *Physics.* Movement parallel to, combined with rotation about, an axis (as in the motion of a screw); also, the velocity of such movement (= *twist-velocity*). 1891 in *Cent. Dict.*

**14.** The amount or direction of twisting given to the strands of a rope (*rare*); also, the twisting given to yarn in spinning.

1712 ARBUTHNOT *John Bull* III. iii, Habbakuk brought him a smooth strong tough rope...Jack..found fault with the length, the thickness, and the twist. 1810 J. T. in *Risdon's Surv. Devon* p. xxv, The other yarn, of a softer twist, is called the abb or shoot. 1825 J. NICHOLSON *Operat. Mechanic* 383 When the spindles have given the requisite degree of twist to the yarn. 1831 G. R. PORTER *Silk Manuf.* 205 The action of steam..is found effectually and permanently to set the twist. 1839 URE *Dict. Arts* 983 The flat band, made of four ropes placed horizontally together, the ropes being laid alternately right and left...The ropes counteract one another in the twist. *c* 1905 in *Eng. Dial. Dict.* (W. Yks.), *Twist*,..the turns put into the end of thread by the rotation of the spindle.

**15.** The condition of being twisted spirally; the amount or degree of this; *spec.* the angle of torsion; also, a spirally twisted object or figure; a spiral line or pattern; *spec.* the rifling in the bore of a gun, etc. (Knight *Dict. Mech.* 1875).

*Damascus twist*: see DAMASCUS.

1711 ADDISON *Spect.* No. 120 ⁋ 3 There is not the least Turn in the Muscles or Twist in the Fibres of any one [animal], which does not render them more proper for that particular Animal's Way of Life than any other Cast or Texture of them would have been. 1774 GOLDSM. *Nat. Hist.* (1776) IV. 283 The tusks [of this elephant].. have a larger twist, or spiral curve, towards the smaller end. 1833 J. HOLLAND *Manuf. Metal* II. 100 The experience of the workmen [gun-making] enables them to produce any intricacy of twist by this drawing out, doubling and twisting. 1846 GREENER *Sc. Gunnery* 114 It is then twisted like a rope, or..wrung as wet clothes are, until it has from twelve to fourteen complete turns in the inch...Three of these rods are then placed together, with the inclinations of the twists running in opposite directions; they are then welded. *Ibid.* 368 The twist of the spirals..being one turn in four feet. 1858 — *Gunnery* 218 Drop a few drops of muriatic acid in a basin of water, and wash the barrel slightly, to brighten the twists. 1859 *Handbk. Turning* 113 Examine your work, and see whether the twists begin to appear...As the ivory twists are, of course, very delicate,.. employ the screw guides, as directed for the spiral turning. 1867 THOMSON & TAIT *Nat. Phil.* § 120 The whole twist of any length of a straight rod is the angle between the transverses of its ends. 1885 WATSON & BURBURY *Math. Th. Electr. & Magn.* I. 81 The suspending wire or fibre will be perfectly free from any twist or torsion.

**b.** *Dynamics.* Twisting strain or force; torque. 1891 in *Cent. Dict.*

**c.** *fig.* A means or opportunity of twisting; a hold. Cf. SCREW *sb.*[1] 2. *slang.*

1881 *Home Missionary* (N. Y.) Feb. 386 An artful scheme by which to get a twist on them for the extortion of money.

**16. a.** *Out of twist*, free from twisting or torsion.

1854 H. MILLER *Sch. & Schm.* x. (1858) 216 If their [the planets'] plane be, as a workman would say, out of twist, their lines will seem parallel. 1901 *J. Black's Illustr. Carp. & Build., Scaffolding* 34 As on the way the holes are bored will depend in a great measure whether the ladder is out of twist or not when finished, they should be made as true as possible.

**b.** A twisting or screwing of the body or features; a contortion or screw.

1865 DICKENS *Mut. Fr.* III. i, Another dry twist in place of a smile. 1896 *Pall Mall Mag.* Sept. 5 'Indeed!' said Mr. Paget, with an upward twist of his grizzled brows.

**c.** A strain or wrench (of a limb or joint).

1865 DICKENS *Mut. Fr.* I. vii, You have got a twist in that bone. 1868 ATKINSON *Cleveland Gloss., Twist*, a strain, or wrench; of a joint.

**17.** A hearty appetite. Cf. TWIST *v.* 13. *slang.*

1785 GROSE *Dict. Vulg. T.* s.v., A good twist, a good appetite. ? *a* 1830 in Norman *London Signs & Inscript.* iii. (1893) 63 Milo the Crotonian an ox slew with his fist, And ate it up at one meal, ye Gods what a glorious twist. 1834 W. H. AINSWORTH *Rookwood* IV. viii, What a devil of a twist he has got! 1861 HUGHES *Tom Brown at Oxf.* vi, You talking of my twist, indeed; you ate four chops and a whole chicken to-day, at dinner. 1890 'R. BOLDREWOOD' *Miner's Right* iv, 'Cyrus has such a tremendous appetite...' 'If I've got a good twist, I can do a day's work.'

**18.** An irregular bend; a crook, a kink; also, a confused intertwining, as of a yarn or thread; a tangle. Chiefly *fig.*

*A twist in one's tongue*, inability to articulate or pronounce clearly.

1776 FOOTE *Capuchin* III. Wks. 1799 II. 401, I am told I have a small twist in my tongue. 1806–7 J. BERESFORD *Miseries Hum. Life* (1826) III. v, Some plaguy twist in our horoscope. 1858 LONGF. *M. Standish* VIII. 75 She disentangled expertly Twist or knot in the yarn. 1897 *19th Cent.* Nov. 786 A twist in the language, an intricate turn, an idiomatic knot. 1903 *Westm. Gaz.* 23 Dec. 9/2 The twists into which some consciences have got tangled.

**19.** A turning aside, a deviation; also *fig.* a change of circumstances, vicissitude; in quot. 1884, the twisting flight of a snipe; also, a point or place at which a road alters its direction; a bend, turn (also *fig.*); often in phrase *twists and turns*, intricate windings, ins and outs.

1798 SOPHIA LEE *Canterb. T., Yng. Lady's T.* II. 6 Anxiously did she..form to every fantastic twist of fashion, Miss Arden's rich profusion of auburn hair. 1806–7 J. BERESFORD *Miseries Hum. Life* (1826) VI. Introd., A hot sun ..to stare in upon me all day..at every twist of the road. 1853 JERDAN *Autobiog.* IV. xvii. 330 After all his twists and turns of fortune. 1875 JOWETT *Plato* (ed. 2) III. 38 When men have learned to take a pleasure and pride in the twists and turns of the law. 1884 *St. James's Gaz.* 19 Dec. 6/2 Before the snipe got into his twist..the single-barrel seemed to drop the shot with certainty. 1884 TENNYSON *Becket* v. ii, He knows the twists and turnings of the place. 1897 G. ALLEN *Type-writer Girl* v, After various intricate twists and turns, ..I found myself at last by the side of a pond.

**20.** *fig.* **a.** An eccentric or perverted inclination or attitude; *esp.* a peculiar mental turn or bent; an intellectual or moral bias or obliquity; a craze, whim, crotchet.

1811 BYRON *Hints fr. Hor.* 734 *note*, If she don't take a poetical twist, and come forth as a shoe-making Sappho. 1813 SIR R. WILSON *Diary* in *Life* (1862) II. 204 He has a twist, or, as the Scotch say, a 'craze' on the subject of dress. 1840 DICKENS *Old C. Shop* xxxvi, If in a mind so beautiful any moral twist or bandiness could be found. 1842 L. HUNT *Men, Women, & B.* (1847) II. xii. 305 It took a twist of intrigue and worldliness. 1872 MORLEY *Voltaire* vi. (ed. 2) 311 The twist which polemical fury may give to the most acute intelligence. 1885 DUNCKLEY in *Manch. Exam.* 20 July 6/1 Attendance at Government night schools might easily give them a pauper twist for the rest of their lives.

**b.** A wresting, perversion, distortion.

1862 GOULBURN *Pers. Relig.* IV. vii. (1873) 304 What twists has the mind of man contrived to give it [the Gospel]. 1875 WHITNEY *Life, &c. of Lang.* v. 96 The most curious twist of meaning. 1876 DOUSE *Grimm's L.* § 34. 71 Minute phonetic twists in the several adopting dialects..might still wrench the sound on to widely divergent lines of debilitation.

**21.** *Anglo-Irish.* A spell or turn; a bout; a contest. Cf. TURN *sb.* 25. *rare.*

1846 J. KEEGAN *Leg. & Poems* (1907) 430 The great Queen's County bruiser..to take a twist with Davy Fetherstone.

**IV. 22.** *attrib.* and *Comb.*, as *twist-cop, hand, -loaf, manufacturer, service* (sense 13), *-spinning, tobacco*; **twist barrel**, a gun-barrel formed of a spirally twisted strip or strips of iron; hence **twist-barrelled** *a.*; **twist-bit**, = *twisted bit* (TWISTED 4); **twist-drill**: see quot.; **twist-frame**, a throstle for spinning cotton; **twist-gear**, a gear in which the teeth are helices (*Cent. Dict. Supp.* 1909); **twist-joint**, *Telegraphy*, a joint made by placing the ends of two wires side by side and coiling each round the other for a few turns (*Cent. Dict.* 1891); **twist knot**, a figure-of-eight knot, repeated or continued so as to form a kind of plait; **twist-lace** = BOBBIN-NET; †**twist line**: see TWINE *sb.*[1] 4 b; **twist-machine**: see quot.; also a machine for cutting spiral mouldings in wood-work (*Funk's Stand. Dict.* 1895); **twist-pinion** = *twist-wheel*; **twist-rail**, a banister-rail characterized by a twisted or curved end or part; **twist-shaft**, the shaft of the *twist-wheel*; **twist-stitch**, an embroidery stitch: see quot.; **twist-wheel**, in a spinning-machine, a wheel by which the number of turns put into the yarn is determined; **twist-yarn** = sense 4 b (*a*).

1833 J. HOLLAND *Manuf. Metal* II. 98 The *twist barrels ..are used for the most curious and expensive kinds of guns and pistols. 1881 GREENER *Gun* 81 The great step to the success of the double fowling-piece was the employment of twist barrels. 1858 — *Gunnery* 189 A *twist barrelled gun. 1901 *J. Black's Illustr. Carp. & Build., Scaffolding* 34 They must now be bored..with brace and *twist-bit. 1881 *Manch. Guard.* 12 Jan., Medium counts of *twist and weft cops. 1875 KNIGHT *Dict. Mech.*, **Twist-drill*, (Metal-working) a drill having a twisted body like that of an auger. 1888 HASLUCK *Model Engin. Handybk.* (1900) 66 A twist-drill will run through easily and will leave two holes. 1819 *Encycl. Brit.* Suppl. III. 396/2 The mule..contains a system of rollers like that belonging to the *twist frame. 1590 *Acc. Bk. W. Wray* in *Antiquary* XXXII. 371 Cre[mosin] and black *twiste fringe..twiste blacke fringe. 1886 *Daily News* 20 Oct. 6/2 The *twist hands or workmen who have charge of a machine earned their..seven pounds a week. 1871 *Routledge's Ev. Boy's Ann.* 246 The *twist knot is by no means so generally known. Dissected it is an ordinary 'three plait', though formed of one piece...If well done it forms a hard, tight, and compact long knot. 1840 *Civil Eng. & Arch. Jrnl.* III. 432/1 Improvements in machinery, for..making figured or ornamental bobbinnet or *twist-lace. 1856 KANE *Arct. Expl.* II. x. 100, I made my meat-ball like a *twist-loaf. 1875 KNIGHT *Dict. Mech.*, **Twist-machine*, one form of lace-making machine. 1800 *New Ann. Direct.* 235 *Twist Manufacturers. 1879 J. ROBERTSON in *Cassell's Techn. Educ.* IV. 397/2 The *twist-pinion requires to be changed when any material alteration is made in the count of the yarn. 1778 *Encycl. Brit.* (ed. 2) I. 618/1 Plate xxxviii. Shews the manner of squaring *twist-rails. 1901 *Munsey's Mag.* XXV. 657/1 Mahony was beaten at Newport..chiefly through the *twist service. 1884 W. S. B. MCLAREN *Spinning* (ed. 2) 139 The crown wheel..appears at first sight as if it were driven by the *twist shaft. 1825 J. NICHOLSON *Operat. Mechanic* 387 In water *twist-spinning, the operation of stretching is not introduced. 1882 CAULFEILD & SAWARD *Dict. Needlework* 180/1 *Cord Stitch*, a stitch used in Embroidery to cover straight threads thrown across spaces, and not run into the material; also known as *Twist Stitch...Throw a line of thread across a space and fasten it firmly. Return the thread to where it first started from by twisting it over and over the straight and tight line first made. 1894 H. NISBET *Bush Girl's Rom.* 63 He would be reduced once more to the old patched suit and station *twist tobacco. 1851 L. D. B. GORDON *Art Jrnl. Illustr. Catal.* p. vi**/2 The requisite quantity of twist..is regulated by the *twist-wheel. 1835 URE *Philos. Manuf.* 413 Spinning of *twist yarn is the sole business of the establishment. 1891 *Labour Commission Gloss.* s. v., Twist yarn is used for the warps which run lengthwise in a piece of cloth. ..Twist yarn is always made much stronger than weft, and is so called because more twists per inch are put into the yarn while being spun.

†**Twist**, ?*sb.*[2] *Obs. rare.* In 4 **twyst-**. [Perhaps identical with the second element of OE. *mæsttwist* (glossing L. *parastates*), which may be connected with TWIST *sb.*[1] 1–3.] Used with *line* and *rope* to designate some part of the tackle of a vessel.

1336 *Acc. Exch. K. R.* 20/20 (P.R.O.) De .xj. petris cordarum de Canabo..emptis..pro vno Twystrop inde faciendo. 1336–7 *Ibid.* 19/31 m. 5 In vj. petris corde de canabo..pro vno boltrope vno Twystrope et j. lychrop. 1356 in *Pipe Roll* 32 *Edw. III*, m. 34/2 (P.R.O.), xj. forloks, iij toppelynes, v. twystlyne [*sic*], vj tregetropes.

**Twist** (twist), *v.* Forms: 4–5 **twiste**, 4–6 **twyst**, 5 **twyste**, (4 **tuyst**), 6– **twist**. *Pa. t.* and *pple.* **twisted**; also 4–5 **twyst(e, twist(e**; (*pa. t.* 5 **tueste**, 7 *Sc.* **twust**; *pa. pple.* 6–7 **twist**). [Evidently (like TWINE *v.*[1]) a deriv. from the stem TWI-, denoting either division in two (Branch I) or combination of two (threads, etc.) into one (Branch II). With the former cf. Flem., Du., and LG. *twisten* to disagree, quarrel (hence Da. *tviste*, Sw. *tvista*), Icel. *tvistra* or *tvístra* to scatter (also *á tvist*, OIcel. *tvístróttr* scattered); with the latter cf. older Flem. (Kilian) *twisten* to twine (thread), Da. dial. *tviste, tweste.* Branch III would be a natural development of II, though actually recorded a century earlier.

The meaning of *twisteð* in *Trin. Coll. Hom.* 213 is obscure, and the passage appears to be in some way corrupt.]

**I.** To divide, separate.

†**1.** *intr.* To divide into branches; to branch. *Obs. rare.*

1340 *Ayenb.* 159 Yef þe onderstondingge is wrong, oþer yef huy tuysteþ..al þe inwyt ssel by þiestre...He tuysteþ ine tuo, huanne me wylneþ of one half to god, and of oþerhalf to þe wordle. 1398 TREVISA *Barth. De P. R.* v. xxi. (Bodl. MS.) lf. 12/1 The tunges of addres bene blacke..swifte in meuyng..þat meueþ þe tunge so swiftelich so þat on tunge semeþ iforked and twisted [*orig.* Qui tam velociter linguas agitat vt vna numero bifurcari videatur lingua].

**2.** *trans.* **a.** To prune, clip. *Obs.* or *dial.*

1483 *Cath. Angl.* 399/2 To Twyste, *defrondare.* 1535 COVERDALE *Isa.* v. 6, I will laye it waist, that it shall nether be twysted nor cut, but beare thornes and breares. — 2 *Esdras* xvi. 43 He that twysteth the vynyarde, as he that shal not gather the grapes. 1672 in W. Grainge *Nidderdale* (1863) 137 *note*, [The tenant also agrees] not to cut, fell, or twist the wood standing and growing thereon.

†**b.** *fig.* To detach, separate, take away. *Obs.*

*c* 1440 CAPGRAVE *St. Kath.* I. 103 He prechyd so ther þat [he] hem alle twyst [*v. r.* twyste] Fro all her maumentrye & fals be-leue. *Ibid.* II. 866, I haue ȝit no list þat ony man my maydynhod schuld twyst.

**II.** To combine, unite, and derived senses.

**3.** *trans.* To combine two or more yarns or fibres of (any suitable material) into a thread or cord by spinning; to form (a thread or cord) by spinning the yarns or strands. Also *absol.*

1471 *Mann. & Househ. Exp.* (Roxb.) 551 Alys Haweryng hat spowne and cardyd and twystyd tweyntey pownde of ȝerne. 1530 PALSGR. 764/2, I twyst threde, I twyne threde. This terme is northren; declared in 'I twyne'. 1595 SHAKS. *John* IV. iii. 128 The smallest thred That euer Spider twisted from her wombe Will serue to strangle thee. 1599 T. M[OUFET] *Silkwormes* 73 Man and maide Whilst winding, twisting, and in weauing, thay Now laugh, now chide. 1650 W. BROUGH *Sacr. Princ.* (1659) 458 Cords..if well twist and made will bind and hold any though never so strong. 1690 LUTTRELL *Brief Rel.* (1857) II. 3, 6000 *l.* worth of hay is already bought on the river Severn and ordered to be twisted and sent on board. 1725 DE FOE *Voy. round World* (1840) 347 Tow-lines..they supplied by twisting a strong tough kind of flag or rush. 1796 MORSE *Amer. Geog.* I. 557 Manufactory for spinning and twisting cotton. 1844 G. DODD *Textile Manuf.* vi. 184 Organzine, besides being wound, cleaned, and doubled, is twisted or thrown twice.

**b.** *fig.* or in fig. context.

1599 SHAKS. *Much Ado* I. i. 313 Was't not to this end, That thou beganst to twist so fine a story? 1643 HERLE *David's Song* 5 A double string,..twisted of two parts into a kind of discordant concord. 1663 BUTLER *Hud.* I. i. 157 He a rope of sand could twist As tough as learned Sorbonist. 1760–72 H. BROOKE *Fool of Qual.* (1809) III. 18 It twists the sacred and endearing cord of society. 1872 BAGEHOT *Physics & Pol.* (1876) 120 His life is twisted into a thousand curious habits. 1884 F. M. CRAWFORD *Rom. Singer* I. 17, I am trying hard to twist a rope of which I never held the other end.

**c.** *transf.* To plait, weave, twine, wreathe.

*a* 1592 T. WATSON *Poems* (Arb.) 15 Where Lawrell wreath's are twist for them alone, Whose gals are burst with often tasted sowre. 1693 *Patent Specif.* No. 313 A certaine Engine or Machine for the Makeing or Twisting of Whips. 1760–72 H. BROOKE *Fool of Qual.* (1809) III. 6 To twist the garland of your blessedness. 1878 M. A. BROWN *Nadeschda* 20 Of straw a girdle twisted up.

**4.** To join or unite by twining or interlacing; to twine *together*; to entwine (one thing) *with* or †*to* another; to intertwine, interweave.

1563 GOLDING *Cæsar* VII. (1565) 225 Fyue rowes of them ioyned and twysted one wythin another, so that whosoeuer ventured in, must nedes gore them selues vppon the sharpe pointes of the stakes. 1601 HOLLAND *Pliny* XVII. xxiii. I. 537 These meet one with another in the space betweene, and are interlaced, twisted, and tied together. 1634 SIR T. HERBERT *Trav.* 94 The people..thought to forbid..his desired entrance, by twisting one tree to another. 1687 A. LOVELL tr. *Thevenot's Trav.* I. 22 A Pillar made of three brazen Serpents twisted together. 1756–7 tr. *Keysler's Trav.* (1760) I. 234 The seat..is made of bark and ropes twisted together. 1825 SCOTT *Talism.* viii, A small silken bag made of network, twisted with silver. *Ibid.* xxvii, The sashes were twisted with silk and gold. 1827 FARADAY *Chem. Manip.* xxiv. (1842) 632 Twist together five or six folds of steel harpsichord wire.

**5.** *fig.* To unite, combine, connect, associate intimately, like strands in a cord.

1573–80 BARET *Alv.* T 460 To bind, or twist hard together, to mingle so together that one cannot tell what the thing meaneth. 1639 FULLER *Holy War* III. xxiv. (1840) 160 John de Bren..to twist his title with another string, married Maria Jole. 1646–8 G. DANIEL *Tomb Earl Strafford* ii, Our Monarch's Fate Was twist in his. 1652 BENLOWES *Theoph.* I. xcvi, Make arts thy tributaries, twist heart, tongue and pen. 1697 DRYDEN *Æneid* XI. 561 Pity your own, or pity our Estate; Nor twist our Fortunes with your sinking Fate. 1712 M. HENRY *Commun. w. God* i. Wks. 1853 I. 205/1 God has been pleased therein to twist interests with us. 1731 W. BOWMAN *Serm. Vers.* 24 The church then with the state was twisted.

**b.** *Twist in*, to initiate or swear in as a member or associate of the Luddites. *Twist out*: see quot. 1883; also *lit.*, to get out (a strand) from a cord by unravelling it.

1812 *Chron.* in *Ann. Reg.* 63/1 Offering five guineas bounty, and 15*s.* per week to all that would be twisted in. 1813 B. WALKER in *Examiner* 11 Jan. 21/2 The murder was well known amongst those twisted in. 1883 *Almondbury & Huddersfield Gloss.*, *Twisted out*, after the trials at York, an order in Council directed that..the Luddites.. should go before a magistrate, and be twisted out, as it was called; that is, they took the Oath of Allegiance. 1887 J. HUTCHISON *Lect. Philippians* iv. 35 The whole cordage.. has a red thread moving throughout it, which cannot be twisted out without undoing it all.

**c.** *fig.* To entangle or mix *up with* something; to get into a tangled or confused state; to confuse, confound.

1863 SUSAN WARNER *Old Helmet* 179 The question..was inextricably twisted up with the other question. 1908 RIDER HAGGARD *Ghost Kings* viii, They had twisted up the story ..into that [story] which they had narrated to her.

**6.** To wind or coil (a thread or the like) *on* or *round* something; to attach in this way; to encircle (an object) *with* or as with a thread, etc.; to entwine *in* something else.

1582 STANYHURST *Æneis* II. (Arb.) 66, I twisted a wallet On my broad shoulders. 16.. in Burton *Scot Abroad* I. iii. 150 He had long hair platt over his neck, whilk David Home..twust to his saddle-bow. 1710 W. KING *Heathen Gods & Heroes* x. (1722) 34 His Thighs were all twisted round with Folds of Vipers. 1820 W. IRVING *Sketch Bk.* I. 51 A few wild flowers were twisted in her fine hair. 1825 T. HOOK *Sayings* Ser. II. *Sutherl.* I. 21 Jane ran to a looking-glass and..twisted her limp ringlets round her long pale fingers into apologies for curls. *Ibid.*, *Passion & Princ.* xii. III. 268 Twisting silk on bits of cards cut star-wise. 1870 J. HAMILTON *Moses* v. 99 A sinful habit entwined and twisted round your souls. 1885 'MRS. ALEXANDER' *At Bay* x, Lambert twisted the comforter round his throat and face.

**7.** *intr.* and *refl.* To pass or move in a tortuous manner; to coil or twine *about* or *round*; to penetrate *into* something with a tortuous movement or action.

1635 QUARLES *Embl.* IV. xii. 43 O how these Armes..did twine, And strongly twist about his yeelding wast! 1644 EVELYN *Diary* 7 Mar., A fountaine of serpents twisting about a globe. *a* 1652 J. SMITH *Sel. Disc.* i. (1821) 7 Any filthy vice..perpetually twisting itself into the thread of our finest spun speculations. 1705 ADDISON *Italy* 391 (*Sienna*) Great Columns..finely engraven with Fruits and Foliage that run twisting about 'em from the very Top to the Bottom. 1774 GOLDSM. *Nat. Hist.* (1776) VII. 227 They [boas]..will dart down upon travellers, and twist themselves so closely round their bodies, as to dispatch them in a very few minutes. 1849 CUPPLES *Green Hand* xvi, Flowers, trailing and twisting in thick snaky coils close up the stems. 1850 HAWTHORNE *Scarlet L.* iii, A writhing horror twisted itself across his face. 1851 RUSKIN *Stones Ven.* I. App. viii. 364 The weeds..have twisted themselves into its crannies.

**III.** To wring, wrench.

†**8.** *trans.* To compress with a turning movement; to wring; also *fig.* to torment, harass. *Obs.* Cf. *tuaste* pa. t. (*c* 1325) in Ritson *Metr. Rom.* II. 272.

*c* 1374 CHAUCER *Troylus* IV. 226 (254) Þe furye and þe rage Whiche þat his herte twyste & faste þreste. *c* 1384 — *H. Fame* II. 267 For whan a pipe is blowen sharpe The aire ys twyst with violence And rent. *c* 1386 — *Wife's Prol.* 494 Ther was no wight saue god and he þat wiste In many wise how soore I hym twiste. — *Merch. T.* 761 She taketh hym by the hand and harde hym twiste.

**9.** To wring out of place or shape, or so as to change the shape; *esp.* to force (a limb, etc.) round so as to sprain it; to wrench. *To twist up*, to screw up into a rounded form. Also *refl.*

*c* 1530 *Hickscorner* B ij, *Imag.*..At tyburne..Some there taketh a fall that maketh theyr necke lame. *Frewyll.* Ye but can they go no more? *Imag.* Oh no man. The wrest is twyst so sore. 1655 FULLER *Ch. Hist.* IX. vii. § 36 The Doctor fairly twisted his wrists almost to the breaking thereof. *c* 1803 C. K. SHARPE *New Oxford Guide* ii, I twisted my ancle—foment it with grease. 1827 CARLYLE *Misc.*, *Richter* (1857) I. 2 This mirror is so twisted with convexities. 1844 W. H. MAXWELL *Wand. Highl.* II. xxi. 249 Twisting the neck of a skoray, or young kittiwake. 1857 HUGHES *Tom Brown* I. viii, [He] seized him [Tom] and twisted his arm. 1865 DICKENS *Mut. Fr.* I. vi, It seemed to twist itself into some likeness of boughs.

†**b.** *spec. To twist a horse*: see quot. *Obs.*

1727–41 CHAMBERS *Cycl.* s.v., To twist a horse, is violently to wring or twist his testicles twice about, which causes them to dry up, and deprives them of nourishment.

**c.** *pass.* To be hanged. *slang.*

1725 *New Cant. Dict.*, *Twisted*, executed, hanged. 1811 *Lexicon Balatr.* s. v. *Nose*, His pall nosed, and he was twisted for a crack,..was hanged for burglary.

**10.** To turn awry; to screw up or contract (the features, etc.); to contort, distort.

1789 W. BUCHAN *Dom. Med.* (1790) 433 In the fit..his extremities are bent or twisted various ways. 1818 SCOTT *Hrt. Midl.* xlvi, Sorely did he twist about his physiognomy, and much did he stumble in his speech, before he could express his idea. 1859 TENNYSON *Lancelot & Elaine* 1139 The dumb old servitor..Winking his eyes, and twisted all his face. 1867 AUG. J. E. WILSON *Vashti* xxx, A bitter smile twisted the muscles about Mrs. Gerome's mouth. 1898 'H. S. MERRIMAN' *Roden's Corner* viii, At times he twisted his lips, moistening them with his tongue.

**b.** *fig.* To wrest the form or meaning of; to pervert; to distort; to force a meaning from.

1821 SCOTT *Kenilw.* xiv, Twisting into all manner of uncouth and incomprehensible forms of speech the honest plain English phrase which God gave us to express our meaning withal. 1829 LYTTON *Disowned* xlviii, I tried to twist her words into a hundred meanings. 1853 KINGSLEY *Hypatia* viii, A mere logician, twisting Aristotle to mean what she knew..Aristotle never meant. 1871 PALGRAVE *Lyr. Poems* 120 A law no guile can twist to harm. 1883

*19th Cent.* May 730 Twisting my opinions into accordance with a party.

**11.** To force *down*, pull *off* or *out* with a turning strain; to wrench or wring *off*, etc. Also *fig.*

1784 COWPER *Task* IV. 62 A demagogue..with a dexterous jerk soon twists him down [from the summit of ambition]. 1804 C. B. BROWN tr. *Volney's View Soil U. S.* (Philad. ed.) 140 They [whirlwinds] twist off and lay level the largest trees. 1823 SCOTT *Quentin D.* v, Untwining his gold chain from his neck, Balafré twisted off, with his firm and strong-set teeth, about four inches from the one end of it. 1838 JAMES *Robber* vi, These foxes have almost twisted my thumbs off. 1890 GUNTER *Miss Nobody* xiii, A summons or writ or some other cursed legal thumb-screw to twist the dollars out of my pocket!

**12.** To form into a spiral; to bend, curve, or coil spirally; to screw *up*.

*a* 1744 POPE (J.), Either double it into a pyramidical, or twist it into a serpentine form. 1765 STERNE *Tr. Shandy* VIII. xi, By all that is hirsute and gashly! I cry, taking off my furred cap, and twisting it round my finger. 1818 SCOTT *Br. Lamm.* xxi, A cow chased by a whole nest of hornets, and her tail twisted over her rump like a corkscrew. *a* 1839 PRAED *Poems* (1864) I. 326 Twisting up his songs Into the sweetest candlepapers. 1843 HOLTZAPFFEL *Turning* I. 207 Some twist the iron before hammering to prevent it from becoming 'spilly'. 1858 GREENER *Gunnery* 195, I found that the inside was entirely composed of iron, over which the covering of Damascus had been twisted. 1861 BENTLEY *Man. Bot.* 512 Flowers usually symmetrical...Petals twisted in æstivation. 1875 BENNETT & DYER *Sachs' Bot.* 838 When the tendrils have fixed themselves by their extremities, they draw the stem towards the support by twisting themselves spirally. 1906 MARJ. BOWEN *Viper of Milan* x, He turned back into the corridor, twisting the ends of his scarlet robe between his fingers.

**b.** *To twist* (a person) *round one's finger*, to have completely under one's influence; so *to turn, twist, and wind* (one): cf. TURN *v.* 64.

1780 *Mirror* No. 95 ¶ 7 At the first glance I saw into him, and could now twist him round my finger. 1787 MME. D'ARBLAY *Diary* Aug., You turn, twist, and wind me just as you like. 1840 DICKENS *Barn. Rudge* vi, Women may twist me round their fingers at their pleasure. 1855 KINGSLEY *Westw. Ho!* xxix, The man has twisted the whole council round his finger.

**c.** *intr.* for *refl.* or *pass.*

1881 GREENER *Gun* 224 The rod is carefully watched while twisting, and should one part commence to twist more rapidly than another [etc.]. *a* 1886 in C. E. Pascoe *Lond. of To-day* xl. (ed. 3) 337 Seams are crooked and wrinkle, sleeves twist, the chest is tight,..&c. &c. The arrival of a new dress brings with it agonies.

**13.** *intr.* and *trans.* To eat heartily; also *to twist* (food) *down. slang.*

1694 MOTTEUX *Rabelais* v. v.17 Twist like Plough-jobbers, and Swill like Tinkers. *Ibid.* xxvii. 132 They us'd to twist store of Holy-bread, Cakes, Buns, Puffs, Lenten-Loaves, Jumbals and Biscuits. *a* 1700 B. E. *Dict. Cant. Crew*, *Twist*, to Eat. *To Twist lustily*, to Feed like a Farmer. 1785 GROSE *Dict. Vulg. T.* s.v. *Twist*, To twist it down apace, to eat heartily. 1817–18 COBBETT *Resid. U. S.* (1822) 165 She will twist down a half pound of beef with her 'potatoe', and has twisted down half a pound of buttered toast in the morning.

**IV.** To rotate, etc.

**14.** *trans.* To cause to rotate as on an axis; to turn (anything) round so as to alter its position or aspect. *To twist one's fingers*, to turn one's fingers about nervously.

1789 W. BUCHAN *Dom. Med.* (1790) 589 He must pull the head with considerable force, gently twisting it at the same time, if the face be turned to one side, till he perceives that the joint is replaced. 1796 MME. D'ARBLAY *Camilla* IV. 80 She twisted it..hastily round, to hide the hand-writing of the direction. 1827 SCOTT *Surg. Dau.* vi, I will twist your head round till your eyes look at the drummer's hand-writing on your back. 1864 LOWELL *Fireside Trav.* 264 Blocks of stone,..lowered, tipped, twisted, undermined, and generally capsized by the rains and frosts of centuries. 1885 'MRS. ALEXANDER' *Valerie's Fate* vi, Speak then, you stupid child, and don't stop short to twist your fingers.

**b.** *Cricket.* In bowling, to give a lateral spin to (the ball), so that it 'breaks' or turns aside on rebounding.

1833 NYREN *Yng. Cricketer's Tutor* 118 If either of your bowlers twist his balls, favour such twist as much as possible.

**15.** *intr.* To rotate, revolve; also, to turn so as to face another way.

1680 MOXON *Mech. Exerc.* x. 177 A strong Iron Screw.. with a square Shank near the Head, that..it may not twist about. 1850 TENNYSON *In Mem.* ci. 12 When the lesser wain Is twisting round the polar star. 1857 HUGHES *Tom Brown* II. viii, The ball comes skimming and twisting along about three feet from the ground. 1907 J. H. PATTERSON *Man-Eaters of Tsavo* xviii. 199 As we moved, the lion also twisted round and so always kept his head full on us.

**16.** *intr.* To turn aside and proceed in a new direction; *spec.* of a ball (at cricket, etc.): to turn aside or 'break' on rebounding; also, to proceed with frequent turns (often associated with *turn*); to follow a circuitous route; to wind, meander.

1833 NYREN *Yng. Cricketer's Tutor* 45 If the ball be struck to his right hand, he will surely find it twist to his left. 1851 LILLYWHITE *Guide Cricketers* 15 Try every manœuvre to make the ball twist and shoot after it touches the ground. 1852 DICKENS *Bleak Ho.* iv, We just twist up Chancery Lane. 1863 W. C. BALDWIN *Afr. Hunting* vii. 257 He turned, dodged, and twisted from side to side, with amazing quickness. 1879 S. C. BARTLETT *Egypt to Pal.* xiii. 289 The valley or ravine twisted this way and that. 1895 *Review of Rev.* Aug. 168 The stream twists down through the valley. 1906 MARJ. BOWEN *Viper of Milan* x, The steps were few in number, before they twisted abruptly out of sight.

**Twistable** (twi·stăb'l), *a.* [f. TWIST *v.* + -ABLE.] That may be twisted.

1853 LYNCH *Chr. Practicaln.* in *Lett. to Scattered* (1872) 364 Take the solemnity out of religion, and you do as if you should take the hardening element out of human bones. The bones would then become all soft and twistable. 1901 *N. & Q.* 9th Ser. VII. 468/2 Shades of meaning more or less twistable into that attributed to *-itis*.

**Twi·sted**, *ppl. a.* [f. as prec. + -ED [1].]

†**1.** Divided, branching. *Obs. rare*$^{-1}$.

1398 [see TWIST *v.* 1].

**2.** Consisting of two or more threads, strands, or the like twined together; (of a thread or strand) formed into a cord by being intertwined with another or others; made of spun or doubled thread, or by spinning; also *transf.* wreathed, plaited, interwoven.

*a* 1548 HALL *Chron., Hen. VI*, 135 An indissoluble knot, like the twisted tree, whiche cannot seuer. 1573–80 BARET *Alv.* T 456 Twined or twisted thred, *filum retortum*. 1590 SPENSER *F. Q.* II. xi. 22 In a canvas thin he was bedight, And girded with a belt of twisted brake. *a* 1603 *Council Order* in *Antiq. Rep.* (1807) I. 23 Twisted with two rows of twisted lace russet..the clothe itself set with the said twisted lace. 1609 BIBLE (Douay) *Exod.* xxxvi. 8 Ten curtines of twisted silke, and hyacinth, and purple, and scarlet twise died. 1718 BLACKMORE *Alfred* III. (1723) 92 Cables in Rings,.. Their twisted Lengths voluminous enfold. 1718 LADY M. W. MONTAGU *Let. to Mrs. Thistlethwayte* 25 Sept., We began to ascend Mount Cenis, being carried in little seats of twisted osiers. 1757 GRAY *Bard* 5 Helm, nor Hauberk's twisted mail. 1791 COWPER *Iliad* v. 135 Blood spouted through his twisted mail. 1794 SOUTHEY *Slave Trade* iv. 7 No tear escaped him, not one suffering groan Beneath the twisted thong. 1825 SCOTT *Talism.* iii, Mattresses, wrought of twisted flags, lay by the side of the cell. 1835 T. MITCHELL *Acharn. of Aristoph.* 400 *note*, A round twisted basket, in which any thing was carried. 1895 SCULLY *Kafir Stories* 24 A musical instrument..consisted of a stick about three feet long, bent into a bow by a string made of twisted sinews.

†**b.** *fig.* Intimately associated or connected; united; combined; also, consisting of two elements united. *Obs.*

1573–80 BARET *Alv.* T 460 Twisted together, hard to be loosed, intricate, doubtfull. 1642 GAUDEN *Three Serm.* 29 Hypocrisie is a double and twisted impiety. 1655 W. HAMMOND *Poems* (1906) 500 Our twisted lives must be cut both Together. 1665 GLANVILL *Scepsis Sci.* Addr. A iv, Their ..deep Sagacity, twisted Endeavours, ample Fortunes, and all other advantages.

**3.** Wrung out of shape; distorted; contorted; turned or bent awry; *spec.* in *Bot.* = CONTORTED 2; crooked, tortuous, winding; turned or wrung spirally, of coiled or screw-like form, spiral or helical; in *Geom.* applied to curves in space, as *twisted Cartesian, t. cubic*, etc. (see CURVATURE 1 b); also, involved, tangled, confused.

1725 W. HALFPENNY *Sound Building* 13 The two different Edges of a Twisted Schofeet. 1776 WITHERING *Brit. Plants* (1796) II. 319 Parnassia...Stem somewhat twisted. 1782 A. MONRO *Compar. Anat.* 167 The eight upper ribs were formerly classed into pairs,..to wit, the *crooked*, the *solid*, the *pectoral*, the *twisted*. 1828 STARK *Elem. Nat. Hist.* II. 135 *Siliquaria*, Lam.—*Serpula*, Lin. Shell tubular, irregularly twisted. 1830 CARLYLE *Richter Again* Ess. 1840 II. 297 Abounding..in the most twisted phraseology. 1831 SCOTT *Cast. Dang.* xvii, A clear fountain of living water bubbled forth from under the twisted roots of one of those trees. 1842 BISCHOFF *Woollen Manuf.* II. 355 They [horns] protrude nearly at right angles from the head, and then become twisted in a singular way. 1854 MURCHISON *Siluria* v. 93 Highly twisted micaceous schists. *a* 1861 T. WOOLNER *My Beautiful Lady, Her Gard.* iv, The mad gale had.. fiercely blown The stalks [of the lilies] in twisted heaps. 1876 HOOKER *Bot. Primer* 68 *Twisted*, when each overlaps by one margin the contiguous margin of that next to it. 1894 H. NISBET *Bush Girl's Rom.* 240 Worrogonga handed to her a small twisted note.

**4.** In special collocations: **twisted bit**, a bit of which the mouthpiece consists of a square bar spirally twisted; also in *Carpentry*: see quot.; **twisted drill** = *twist-drill* (TWIST *sb.*[1] 22); **twisted flower**, rendering of *Strophanthus*, name of a genus of tropical shrubs, natives of Asia and Africa, esp. applied to those species cultivated for the singularity of their flowers (*Cent. Dict.* 1891); **twisted horn** = TWISTY *sb.*; **twisted mouth**: see quot.; **twisted pillar**, a pillar having the appearance of being spirally twisted, or apparently consisting of two shafts intertwined; **twisted pine**, *Pinus contorta*, a small pine of the Pacific coast of North America, the twisted-branched pine; also *P. Teocote* of Mexico; **twisted stalk**, rendering of *Streptopus*, name of a genus of perennial herbaceous plants bearing bell-shaped flowers with curious bent stalks; **twisted stick** = *twisted horn*; **twisted suture**: see quot.; †**twisted tree**, ? a branch of willow or other tree formerly used in connexion with Easter celebrations.

1875 KNIGHT *Dict. Mech.*, **Twisted bit*.., a wood-boring tool adapted to be used in a brace. It is a..flat bar twisted into a spiral form and provided..with a cutter and a routing-table. 1884 F. J. BRITTEN *Watch & Clockm.* 95 For long holes of small diameter a *twisted drill is desirable. 1866 *Twisted horn [see TWISTY *sb.*]. 1875 KNIGHT *Dict. Mech.*, **Twisted mouth* (Manège), a bit whose mouthpiece has been twisted, to make it more severe than it otherwise would be. 1717 BERKELEY *Tour in Italy* Wks. 1871 IV. 550 The altars generally adorned with *twisted pillars. 1756–7 tr. *Keysler's Trav.* (1760) IV. 77 The great altar has sixteen twisted pillars of white and green marble. 1869 TOZER *Highl. Turkey* I. 238 Balustrades and windows with twisted pillars. 1866 *Treas. Bot.* s. v. *Pine*, *Twisted pine, *Pinus Teocote*. 1884 MILLER *Plant-n.*, Pine-tree, Twisted Mexican, *Pinus Teocote*. 1856 A. GRAY *Man. Bot.* (1860) 474 *Streptopus*, *Twisted-stalk. 1866 *Twisted stick [see TWISTY *sb.*]. 1767 GOOCH *Treat. Wounds* I. 154 The *twisted-suture ..is performed by introducing one, two or more, needles or pins through the whole substance of the lips of the wound, twisting a waxed thread neatly about them, in the form of a figure of 8. 1598 STOW *Surv.* 72 In the weeke before Easter had yee great shewes made for the fetching in of a *twisted Tree, or With, as they termed it, out of the woodes into the kinges house, and the like into euery mans house of honor or worship.

**5.** Comb., as *twisted-branched, -convolute, -locked.*

1830 LINDLEY *Nat. Syst. Bot.* 131 Æstivation for the most part twisted-convolute. 1862 *Eng. Wom. Dom. Mag.* IV. 218 Those frizzly-haired, lank-haired, twisted-locked, top-knotted foreigners. 1884 MILLER *Plant-n.*, *Pinus contorta*, twisted-branched pine.

Hence **Twi·stedly** *adv.*, in a twisted manner.

1910 *Westm. Gaz.* 2 Feb. 8/2 Every single strand of the tobacco smokes perpendicularly downwards instead of horizontally across, or twistedly diagonal. 1915 *Blackw. Mag.* May 590/1 A twistedly pathetic thing a battery team and limber is without a gun.

**Twister** (twi·stəɹ), *sb.* [f. TWIST *v.* + -ER [1].] One who or that which twists.

†**1.** One who prunes or clips trees. *Obs. rare*$^{-0}$.

1483 *Cath. Angl.* 399/2 A Twyster of trees, *defrondator*.

**2.** A girder. Cf. TWIST *sb.*[1] 3 b.

1875 KNIGHT *Dict. Mech.*, *Twister*..2, a girder.

**3.** One who (or that which) spins thread, cord, or the like; *spec.* one whose occupation is to twist together the ends of the yarns of the new warp to those of that already woven. Also *twister-in*.

1579 J. STUBBES *Gaping Gulf* B iv b, Which strong cord.. the Lorde..turned to the strangling of the twisters thereof. 1599 T. M[OUFET] *Silkewormes* 69 How many winders liue, How many twisters eke, and weauers thriue Vppon this trade? 1611 COTGR., *Retordeur*, a twister, twiner. 1723 *Lond. Gaz.* No. 6172/8 Samuel Brooke.., Twister. *Ibid.*, Nicholas Gudgeon.., Silver-Twister. 1799 *Hull Advertiser* 2 Mar. 4/4 The Man of the People..at a rope-maker's shop..besought..his interest..when the twister replied [etc.]. 1815 G. BEATTIE *John o' Arnha'* (1826) 36 Elspet, Mausie, fatal sisters, Of the thread of life the twisters. 1878 A. BARLOW *Hist. & Princ. Weaving* xxx. 311 The 'twister-in' has no difficulty in finding the proper threads to twist together. 1895 *Daily News* 3 July 7/5 The threatened lock-out..at Burnley has been averted by the settlement of the twisters' dispute.

**b.** A mechanical device for spinning yarns, etc.; *spec.* a throw-crook (*dial.*).

*a* 1703 WALLIS in J. Greenwood *Eng. Gram.* (1711) 283 He [a rope-maker], twerling his twister, makes a twist of the twine. 1875 KNIGHT *Dict. Mech.*, *Twister*, a reel used in twisting yarns or threads. 1890 *Gloucester. Gloss.*, *Twister*, an implement used for twisting straw ropes for thatching, resembling a brace and bit, except that the bit has a hooked end. 1903 *Dundee Advertiser* 25 July 9 This machine..does more work in a given time than any other type of twister.

**c.** A wheel, tourniquet, or other device by which torsional force is applied.

1833 LOUDON *Encycl. Archit.* § 2075 The Wringing-Machine..for small laundries. The articles to be wrung, when large, are taken out of the washing-tub, and, being passed over the pin,.. the two ends are put through the hole of the twister,..which is turned round by the spokes. 1892 *Columbus* (Ohio) *Dispatch* 24 May, One of the highwaymen..confessed his guilt after being tortured with 'twisters' and hot coals.

**4.** One who or that which turns about, turns from side to side, rotates, etc. †**a.** A twisting or twining shoot. *Obs. rare.*

1799 G. SMITH *Laboratory* I. 431 Fill a bag..of leaves and twisters of vine.

**b.** One who turns this way and that; *fig.* one who shuffles or prevaricates.

1834 BECKFORD *Italy*, etc. II. xvi. 359 The ambassador is.. no commonplace twister and turner in the paths of diplomacy. 1897 BLACKMORE in *Blackw. Mag.* July 61/2, I have handled a good many twisters and skippers in the way of savages.

**c.** *Cricket.* A delivery in which the ball twists or 'breaks'; a break; *transf.* in *Tennis* and other ball-games, a 'screw'.

1857 HUGHES *Tom Brown* II. vi, To come out..to Tom's wicket, and bowl slow twisters to him. 1862 CALVERLEY *Verses & Tr.* '*Hic vir, hic est*' viii, I have stood serene.. While the Buttress of the period Bowled me his peculiar twisters. 1884 MARSHALL *Tennis Cuts* 202 T was the Twister, that settled the rest.

**d.** *U.S.* In the Mississippi region: A whirling wind-storm; a cyclone, tornado.

1897 *Strand Mag.* Sept. 266/1 Kansas..is a favourite spot of the 'twisters' as the Westerns playfully term their windy enemy (the tornado). 1902 W. M. DAVIS *Elem. Phys. Geog.* ii. 67 Violent local storms..are often called cyclones, or prairie twisters, in the Mississippi valley, but the name tornado is to be preferred.

**e.** A handle operated by twisting or rotating it.

1902 F. T. BIDLAKE in *Cycl. Tour. Cl. Gaz.* Aug. 359/2 The..machine with the compound brake application, i. e., the combination of the lever and the twister.

**5.** One who curves, bends, or rolls something.

1879 *Cassell's Techn. Educ.* III. 158 The leaves are.. placed over charcoal fires...The twisters roll them over with their hands until twisted.

**6.** That which (or one who) wrings or causes

contortion; *esp. fig.* something that confounds, non-plusses, or 'doubles up', a 'staggerer' (*slang*).
1873 *Routledge's Yng. Gentl. Mag.* May 358/1 'Twister', broke in the petty officer; 'I tell you it's as true as gospel'. 1879 BLACK *Macleod of D.* xl, Well, you have had a twister; but you'll come through it. 1884 CLARK RUSSELL *Jack's Courtship* xvi, She had a letter from you this morning—a regular twister. 1893 *Daily Tel.* 1 May 5/1 This was evidently a twister for the beggar-boy.

**7.** A voracious feeder. *slang.* ? *Obs.*
1694 MOTTEUX *Rabelais* v. Prol. Avj b, What Swillers, what Twisters will there be!

**Twister** (twi·stəɹ), *v.* Now *dial.* [f. TWIST *v.* + -ER [5].]
†**1.** *trans.* and *intr.* To twist, spin thread. *Obs.*
*c* 1605 *Alleg. Worsted Weavers* (B. M. Add. MS. 12504, art. 64), Twistering one thridd of one coullour with another of another coullour. *Ibid.*, To twister a thridd of one colour with a thridd of another. 1687 R. FERRIER in *Camden Misc.* IX. VII. 30 Many..as they grow up, do work, some of whom twister, others net.
**2.** *intr.* To wind, meander. *dial.*
1872 [J. SPILLING] *Giles' Trip to Lond.* ii. 17 Straight on as ever yow can go in these twistering straats. 1895 *E. Anglian Gloss.*, *Twister*, to twist or turn.
Hence **Twi·stering** *ppl. a.*, winding, twisting; also † **Twi·sterer** *Obs.*, a twister or spinner.
1725 *Lond. Gaz.* No. 6380/13 Charles Scot,..Twisterer. 1872 Twistering [see 2 above].

**Twist-foot.** *rare*[−1]. [Translation of the generic name *Streptopus*.] = *Twisted stalk*, TWISTED 4.
1846–50 A. WOOD *Class-Bk. Bot.* 554 *Streptopus roseus*... Rose Twist-foot.

**Twistical** (twi·stikăl), *a. colloq.* [irreg. f. TWIST + -ICAL.] Somewhat twisted or crooked; *fig.* not straight or plain in character; morally or mentally tortuous.
1815 D. HUMPHREYS *Yankee in Eng.* 43 In his dealings with t'other sex, he is a leetle twistical. 1852 A. BALLOU *Spirit Manifest.* Pref. 9 They are..prejudiced, captious, twistical. 1890 *Harper's Mag.* Feb. 449/1 It lay on the route to Edinburgh, at a rather twistical sort of corner.

**Twistification** (twi:stifikēi·ʃən). *nonce-wd.* [f. as prec.: see -FICATION.] A twisting; a twisted object or part.
1835 BECKFORD *Recoll.* 137 To entertain any doubts of the supreme excellence of Don Emanuel's scollops and twistifications amounted to heresy. 1841 HAWTHORNE *Amer. Note-Bks.* (1883) 230 Dry jokes, the humor of which is so incorporated with the strange twistifications of his physiognomy, that [etc.].

**Twisting** (twi·stiŋ), *vbl. sb.* [f. TWIST *v.* + -ING [1].] The action of the verb TWIST.
†**1.** Pruning, clipping. (In quot. *attrib.*) *rare.*
1535 COVERDALE *Song Sol.* ii. 12 The floures are come vp in the felde, the twystinge tyme is come [*Vulg.* Tempus putationis advenit].
**2.** The spinning of thread, etc.; twining, wreathing, plaiting; also with *in* (in quot. 1812 *fig.* the swearing in of a Luddite), and *attrib.* In quot. *a* 1673 app. *concr.*
1552 HULOET, Twystyng wande, as wyker or osyer, *uimen, inis, uimineus, a, um,* of twystyng roddes. 1577 B. GOOGE *Heresbach's Husb.* 38 b, Flaxe and Hempe..serueth for webbes of Linnen, and twysting of Cordes. 1599 in *Archæologia* LXIV. 382 For mending the twisting wheele. 1649 MILTON *Eikon.* vi. Wks. 1851 III. 386 They..have to our Saviours crown of thorns no right at all. Thornes they may find anow of thir own gathering, and thir own twisting. 1668 WILKINS *Real Char.* 247 Making several vegetable or animal substances into Thred. Twisting,..Spinning. *a* 1673 T. HORTON *Serm.* xxii. (1679) 160/1 He can gather a Rod of these boughes, and make a scourge of these twistings. 1688 R. HOLME *Armoury* III. xxi. (Roxb.) 253/2 A Twisting wheele... This is an engine wherewith 2, 3 or more silk thrids are twisted, or turned all together into one entire double thrid. 1812 *Chron.* in *Ann. Reg.* 86/2 Thirty-eight were committed to Lancaster gaol, to take their trials for having administered the abominable and unlawful oath, known by the term of twisting-in. 1825 J. NICHOLSON *Operat. Mechanic* 421 The motions of both machines, excepting those of that set of twisting-spindles facing the opposite company, are then struck into geer. 1844 G. DODD *Textile Manuf.* vi. 188 There does not seem to be any definite distinction among silk-throwsters, between spinning, twisting, and throwing. 1878 A. BARLOW *Hist. & Princ. Weaving* xxx. 312 It is not to be wondered at that attempts should be made to perform twisting-in by mechanical means.
**3.** Wringing, screwing; spiral turning; contortion, distortion; *fig.* perversion or wresting of sense; *slang*, a scolding; a trouncing.
1725 W. HALFPENNY *Sound Building* 29 The Angles..in the Figure, do represent the Twisting of each Piece. 1738 SWIFT *Pol. Conversat.* Introd. 16 The Twistings and Movements, and different Postures of the Body. 1776 DA COSTA *Elem. Conchol.* vii. 148 The Vermiculi in general are of no determinate or fixed regular shape, from their windings and twistings. 1808 LADY SARAH LYTTELTON *Corr.* (1913) 14 A few pretty distortions of the features or graceful twistings of the body. 1818–20 E. THOMPSON tr. *Cullen's Nosol. Method.* (ed. 3) 224 Pain in the belly with a sense of twisting. 1827 FARADAY *Chem. Manip.* xix. (1842) 523 This should be done without any twisting or distortion of the glass. 1833 MARRYAT *P. Simple* xvi, I say, Bill, if them were we, what a precious twisting we should get to-morrow at six bells! 1890 *Daily News* 1 Dec. 6/2 Telling me that it [the letter] is being twisted this way and that, and asking me to put a stop to the twisting process.
**4.** Tortuous course; intricate winding; turning this way and that; *fig.* evasion, prevarication; also turning aside, or about; rotation.
1768 TUCKER *Lt. Nat.* (1834) I. 76 To follow..all the twistings and crossings, and entanglements in those intricate subjects that have hitherto perplexed the learned world. 1856 F. PERTHES *Mem.* II. vi. 94 What toil and trouble, what twisting and turning this undertaking has cost me. 1872 LIDDON *Elem. Relig.* iv. 154 A second regards sin as a twisting or perversion of the will from the right way. 1875 BENNETT & DYER *Sachs' Bot.* 188 A useful arrangement is..that all the parts..by a single twisting of the axis..assume those positions which are most favourable for the functions of the leaves... In the terminal buds of such shoots this twisting is no longer necessary. 1886 *Athenæum* 10 July 39/1 The twistings and eddyings of the political current.

**Twi·sting,** *ppl. a.* [f. as prec. + -ING [2].] That twists, in various senses of the verb; turning; wringing or wrenching; curving, winding, crooked; † interlacing (*obs.*); involved.
1683 MOXON *Mech. Exerc., Printing* xxiv. ꝑ 1 [To] hinder the Press from working into a twisting Position. 1712 J. JAMES tr. *Le Blond's Gardening* 156 Borders that are twisting and circular. 1761 YOUNG *Resignation* I. xxx, The twisting strings Of ardent hearts combin'd. 1835 R. WILLIS *Archit. Mid. Ages* vii. 74 The twisting form of the groin is disagreeable to the eye. 1872 H. W. BEECHER *Lect. Preaching* ix. 178 Some long sentences are good, but not twisting ones. 1882 *Daily Tel.* 4 May, The longitudinal or twisting strain, such..as a ship receives when she is struck at the same moment by a heavy sea on the starboard quarter and a heavy sea on the port bow. 1899 *Allbutt's Syst. Med.* VI. 676 They [pains] may be aching, burning, twisting or shooting in character. 1902 F. T. BIDLAKE in *Cycl. Tour. Cl. Gaz.* Aug. 360/1 Any further brake pressure put on by the lever will remain locked on by the twisting handle.
Hence **Twi·stingly** *adv.*, in a twisting manner.
1731 in BAILEY.

†**Twistkey.** *Obs.*[−1] [f. TWIST *v.*] A turnkey.
1617 EARL OF CORK *Diary* in *Lismore Papers* Ser. I. (1886) I. 178 John geffreys my twistekey died.

**Twistle** (twi·s'l), *sb. Sc.* Also **twissle.** [Cf. next.] A twist, a wrench (also *fig.*).
1785 BURNS *Twa Herds* iii, The Lord's cause ne'er gat sic a twistle, Sin' I hae min'. 1871 J. MILNE *Sel. Poems*, etc. 58 If he but aince come through thy twissle He'll rue sic gamin'. 1882 J. WALKER *Jaunt to Auld Reekie*, etc. 29 Screw the pegs wi cheepin twistle And strum the thairms. *Ibid.* 211 The deil gae a' their necks a twistle.

**Twi·stle,** *v. dial.* Forms: 8 *Sc.* **twisle,** 8–9 **twistle,** 9 **twissle** (*Sc.* **twussle**). [app. f. TWIST *v.* + -LE.] *trans.* To twist, twirl; to screw.
1788 PICKEN *Poems* Gloss., *Twisle*, to twist, fold. 1819 RENNIE *St. Patrick* II. 191 (Jam.) I'll twussle your thrapple in a jiffy. 1826– in various Eng. dial. glossaries (E.D.D.). 1886 COLE *S. W. Linc. Gloss.* 157 The wind seems to twistle the straw. 1890 *Anthony's Photogr. Bull.* III. 151 A tuft of clean cotton, formed into a ball and twistled on one side.

**Twistle,** variant of TWISEL.

**Twisty** (twi·sti), *a.* (*sb.*) [f. TWIST *sb.*[1] or *v.* + -Y.] Full of twists or turns; characterized by twisting or winding; also *fig.* dishonest, not straightforward. (Cf. *twistical.*)
1857 W. ARNOT *Let.* in *Life* vi. (1877) 330 It [a valley] was narrow and hilly and woody and beautiful and twisty. 1869 E. W. BENSON in *Life* (1900) I. ix. 309 Neither olive nor vine, only the poor twisty bramble. 1894 BLACKMORE *Perlycross* xxxviii, I just chucked 'un into a pool of watter, for to kape 'un out o' sight of twisty volk. 1905 *Daily Chron.* 21 July 4/7 A somewhat twisty redistribution of seats. 1912 D. CRAWFORD *Thinking Black* i. 7 This Africa for thousands of twisty miles ahead is..wholly innocent of roads.
**b.** *sb.* The fruit of the screw-tree, *Helicteres Isora*, of Southern India; see quot.
1866 *Treas. Bot.* 576/1 *H*[*elicteres*] *Isora* is a native of Southern India, where its singular twisted screw-like fruit, about two inches in length, is called 'twisted stick', 'twisted horn', or 'twisty', and..is supposed to be a sovereign remedy against colic or twistings of the bowels.
Hence **Twi·stiness,** the condition or quality of being twisty; **Twi·stiways, Twi·stiwise** *advbs.*, in a twisty manner. So **Twi·sty-wi·sty** *a. nonce-wd.*
1904 *Daily News* 16 July 4/2 As Miss Morison went upstream her progress was very tardy, a fact partly owing to the curious *twistiness of the river. 1903 *Speaker* 9 May 135/1 To drift *twistiways on the variant currents of men's thoughts. 1907 *Westm. Gaz.* 13 Sept. 2/1 Pace it [a 'magic' ring] three times round, '*twisty-wise', with face against the sun. 1892 KIPLING *Barrack-r. Ballads* 33 A single man gets bottled on them *twisty-wisty stairs.

**Twit** (twit), *sb.*[1] Also 6 **twyte.** [f. TWIT *v.*]
**1.** An act of twitting; a (light) censure or reproach; a taunt.
1528 in Strype *Eccl. Mem.* (1721) I. App. xvii. 38 Which bookes the sayd Frear dyd litle regard, and made a twyte of it. 1664 ETHEREDGE *Love in Tub* v. v, Upon Condition that there be no Twits of the Good Man departed. 1847 L. HUNT *Men, Women & B.* II. x. 224 An occasional twit at him for disappointing her.
**b.** *dial.* (See quot.)
*a* 1825 FORBY *Voc. E. Anglia*, *Twit*, a fit of hasty ill-humour; snappishness.
**2.** ? A person given to twitting; *dial.* a tale-bearer.
1719 D'URFEY *Pills* (1872) VI. 241 A silly, peevish Twit. 1896 *Warwick Gloss.* s. v., 'You are a twit'.

**Twit,** *sb.*[2] [Of obscure origin.] A fault or entanglement in a thread, which hinders the process of spinning or weaving.
1819 THOMSON *Poems* 27 (E.D.D.) Is 't a cursed wab o' yarn That winna work, for knots and twits? 1884 W. S. B. MᶜLAREN *Spinning* vii. (ed. 2) 131 Freedom from twits.

**Twit,** *sb.*[3]: see TWIT *int.*

**Twit** (twit), *v.* Forms: *α.* 6 **twyte, (twhyte),** 6–7 (9 *dial.*) **twite, (twight).** *β.* 6– **twit,** (7 **twitt, twytt**); 6 *pa. pple.* **twyte, twit.** [Orig. *twite* (with long *i*), aphetic form of ATWITE, q. v.]
**1.** *trans.* To blame, find fault with, censure, reproach, upbraid (a person), esp. in a light or annoying way; to cast an imputation upon; to taunt.
1530 PALSGR. 764/2, I twhyte one, I caste hym in the tethe or in the nose, *je luy reprouche*. This terme is also northren. *a* 1553 UDALL *Royster D.* II. iii. (Arb.) 36 No man for despite, By worde or by write His felowe to twite. 1573 G. HARVEY *Letter-bk.* (Camden) 127, I take him very..simpely wittid, That may the second tyme be iustly twittid. 1593 SHAKS. *2 Hen. VI*, III. i. 178 Hath he not twit our Soueraigne Lady here With ignominious words..? As if she had suborned some to sweare False allegations. 1633 T. ADAMS *Exp. 2 Peter* ii. 22 An Egyptian priest thus twitted Solon, You Grecians are ever Children. 1814 D'ISRAELI *Quarrels Auth.* (1867) 364 The Antiquarian Society were twitted as medal-scrapers. 1865 TROLLOPE *Belton Est.* viii, Anything would be better than being twitted in this way. How can I help it that I am not a man..?
**b.** Const. most usually *with*; also *about* (rare), *for*, *of* (now rare or obs.), *on*; † also with clause or infin. (*obs. rare*).
1563 HARDING *Answ. Welles Challenge* (1565) 6 The woont of some feastemakers, which of their neighbours twited with nyggardnes [etc.]. 1569 J. SANFORD tr. *Agrippa's Van. Artes* 116 b, And twite their husbandes with the courtly excesse. 1581 J. BELL *Haddon's Answ. Osor.* 374 Ill may the Snight the Woodcock twight for his long bill. 1586 A. DAY *Eng. Secretary* II. (1625) 80 To twit him, That he had like to haue knockt his hand against the gallowes. 1593 T. WATSON *Tears of Fancie* lviii, Yet still I twit my selfe of Surcuidrie. 1593 DRAYTON *Eclogues* ii. 14 Nor twit me so, my senses to have lost. 1612 BEAUM. & FL. *Cupid's Rev.* IV. iii, You do not twit me with my calling, neighbor? 1613 T. ADAMS *Heav. & Earth Reconciled* Wks. 1861 I. 469 Shall they twit us, that our *Our Father* hath taken from the church what their *Paternoster* bestowed on it? 1650 FULLER *Pisgah* II. ix. 186 Hannah though silent when twitted by Peninnah of barrenness, found her tongue when..taxed by Eli of drunkenness. 1664 H. MORE *Myst. Iniq.* vi. 19 Twitting them..for their Idolatry. 1743 FIELDING *Journey* I. xv, My friend..now twitting me with all his kindness,..discarded me for ever. 1791 BOSWELL *Johnson* Dec. an. 1775 (1831) III. 295 He was twitted by Mrs. Thrale for being very late. 1855 MACAULAY *Hist. Eng.* xix. IV. 308 Those who held this language were twitted with their inconsistency. 1870 *Lit. World* 16 Dec. 387 When twitted for his inconsistency. 1871 TYNDALL *Fragm. Sc.* (1879) II. xv. 381 The opponent of the undulatory theory might effectually twit the holder of it on his change of front. 1877 WHITTIER in Pickard *Life* (1894) II. 635 It is bad enough to be old, without being twitted of it. 1882 L'ESTRANGE *Friendships Miss Mitford* I. vii. 176 She was sometimes twitted about partialities for her cousin.
**c.** Also *to twit* (a person) *in the teeth.* *Obs.* or *arch.*
1579–80 NORTH *Plutarch* (1676) 386 In his youth he was fain to hire another mans house,..at a small rent, as afterwards he was twitted in the teeth withall. 1651 *Fuller's Abel Rediv., Bradford* (1867) I. 218 They twitted him in the teeth with heresy. 1729 GAY in *Swift's Lett.* (1766) II. 103 You have often twitted me in the teeth for hankering after the court. 1835 LYTTON *Rienzi* IV. i, They twit me in the teeth, because I cannot say who my father and mother were.
**2.** To condemn as a fault, blame, reprove, rebuke (an act, etc.); to cavil at, to disparage. Now *rare.*
1571 CAMPION *Hist. Irel.* II. viii. (1633) 105 Thus was Perkins bragge twighted. 1580 STANYHURST *Æneis*, etc. (Arb.) 152 Percase carpers wyl twight his iollitye youthful. 1592 GREENE *Upst. Courtier* To Rdrs. A iv, Though he speakes againste Veluet breeches..yet hee twits not the weede but the vice. 1673 HICKERINGILL *Greg. F. Greyb.* 214 Endeavouring to fool away twitting a good cause. 1675 tr. *Camden's Hist. Eliz.* I. 84 Others..twitted the Authority of the Queen's Majesty too much. 1876 J. WEISS *Wit, Hum. & Shaks.* iii. 87 The clown..remembers how the steward used to twit Olivia's contentment at his sallies.
†**b.** *Twit it*: to phrase it tauntingly; to utter a taunt or reproach. *Obs. rare.*
1570–6 LAMBARDE *Peramb. Kent* (1826) 276 This Archbishop..suffered the King to hold his stirup twise in one day in Normandie, but in *Prato proditorum*, as Mathew Parise very pretily twiteth it. 1673 HICKERINGILL *Greg. F. Greyb.* 24 To twit it home as wittily and effectually as he can.
**3.** *intr.* To tell tales; to blab. Now *dial.*
*a* 1643 [see TWITTING *vbl. sb.* 2]. 1854 MISS BAKER *Northampt. Gloss.* s. v., 'If he knows he'll twit'.

**Twit,** *int.* and *sb.*[3] Also 6 **twyt.**
†**1.** An imitation of the cry of an owl. Cf. TU-WHIT. *Obs. rare*[−1].
1591 LYLY *Endym.* III. iii, A goodly Owle..sitting vpon my shoulder, cryed twyt, twyt..I meruailed what the Owle said, til at the last, I perceiued twyt twyt, to it, to it.
**2.** An imitation of the shrill chirp of a small bird; hence as *sb.* a name for this. Cf. TWEET.
1820 CLARE *Rural Life* (ed. 3) 147 The flap of a leaf, and the twit of a bird. 1828 *Lights & Shades* II. 130 A fat chirping sparrow gave you a twit, twit, twit, that kept you awake.

**Twitch** (twitʃ), *sb.*[1] Also 6 **twycche, twytch-, twitche,** 6–8 **twich.** [f. TWITCH *v.*[1]]
**1.** An act of twitching; a sudden sharp pull or tug; a jerk; a pluck; a snatch.
1523 FITZHERB. *Husb.* § 15 'The oxe is neuer wo, tyll he to the harowe goo', And it is bycause it goeth by twytches. 1567 GOLDING *Ovid's Met.* IX. (1593) 211 Three times a twich Gaue Hercules, and could not wrinch my leaning breast him fro. 1607 HIERON *Wks.* I. 431 A single twine, which is snapt in sunder with a twitch. 1688 R. HOLME

*Armoury* III. xv. (Roxb.) 27/1 The bowes of the boat..would else be torne out with the twitches which the ship vnder saile would giue it. **1728–46** THOMSON *Spring* 412 Then fix, with gentle twitch, the barbed hook. **1821** CLARE *Vill. Minstr.* I. 154 A twitch at her sleeve!..a bramble had caught at her gown passing by. **1851** D. JERROLD *St. Giles* xvi. 169 He felt a twitch at his pocket, and..saw a child..carrying away a silk handkerchief.

**b.** *transf.* and *fig.* or in fig. context. *At a twitch*, in a moment, without delay.

**1528** *Impeachm. Wolsey* 174 in Furnivall *Ball. fr. MSS.* I. 357 They wold from þer bodyes þer hedis devyde, or hang them at A twycche. **1599** NASHE *Lenten Stuffe* (1871) 27 The city of Norwich, as in the *Præludium* hereof I had a twitch at. **1633** G. HERBERT *Temple, Church Porch* xxxvii, Think not thy fame at ev'ry twitch will break. **1649** MILTON *Eikon.* xxvii. Wks. 1851 III. 514 His Noose, which when he pleases to draw together with one twitch of his Negative, shall throttle a whole Nation.

**c.** *Twitch-up*, a pegged-down snare attached to an elastic sapling or the like, which springs up and strangles the game when sprung.

**1885** HORNADAY *2 Yrs. in Jungle* xxxvi. 428 A fine, large porcupine..caught by a hind foot in a twitch-up.

**2.** A sharp pain; a pinch, pang, twinge. Freq. of mental pain.

**1532** MORE *Confut. Tindale* Wks. 440/1 We sustayn.. euery man for himself the paynefull twitche of bodely death. **1573** TUSSER *Husb.* (1878) 118 Reward not thy sheepe (when ye take off his cote) with twitchis and patches. **1612** T. TAYLOR *Comm. Titus* ii. 11 (1619) 441 The smarting twitches of our consciences. **1688** WOOD *Life* 14 Nov. (O.H.S.) III. 282 A twich and paine in the instep. **1717** PRIOR *Alma* I. 458 Their Heart, descending to their Breeches, Must give their Stomach cruel twitches. **1796** MME. D'ARBLAY *Camilla* II. 421 [It] had caused his conscience to give him so many twitches, that it never let him rest a moment. **1821** LAMB *Elia* Ser. I. *Imperfect Sympathies*, My conscience..beginning to give some twitches. **1867** G. EASTON *Autobiog.* xiii. 178 Sensations very similar to a twitch of toothache.

**3.** †**a.** Forceps, tweezers. *Obs. rare*$^{-1}$. (Cf. QUITCH *sb.*[2])

**1596** BARROUGH *Meth. Physick* I. xxxvi. (ed. 3) 59 Take therfore a twich of siluer, & therewith lift up subtilly the vngle from the tunicle.

**b.** A noose or loop; *spec.* a noose which may be tightened by twisting the stick to the end of which it is attached, used to compress the lip or muzzle of a horse to restrain him during a painful operation.

(Quot. 1623 is doubtful: cf. TWITCH *v.*[1] 3 b.)

**1623** MIDDLETON *More Dissemblers* III. i. (1657) 34 Oh those dear Gipseys, they..eat sweet stoln Hens, pluckt over Pales or Hedges by a twitch. **1831** [YOUATT] *Horse* xviii. 321 Among the minor methods of restraint..are the twitch and the barnacles. **1894** ASTLEY *50 Years Life* II. 297 That horribly cruel invention, the twitch, is..twisted..tightly round the poor brute's tender upper lip. **1910** T. SHEPPARD in *Trans. E. Riding Antiq. Soc.* XVI. 41 Two holes have been pierced on each side of the projecting portion of the stern, evidently to receive a lashing or twitch which would pass to and from the sides, thus holding them firmly against the stern-board. **1910** *Times* 19 Mar. 4/2 Twitches were used for holding vicious or nervous horses for veterinary purposes or shoeing, or washing the legs.

**4.** *Mining.* A place in, or part of, a vein where it is compressed and narrowed.

**1653** MANLOVE *Lead-Mines* 265 (E.D.S.) Cauke, Sparr, Lid-Stones, Twitches, Daulings, and Pees. **1747** HOOSON *Miner's Dict.* s.v. *Brassil*, Some Veins that are Caukey are very subject to it; but more especially in Twitches, and hard Places. **1789** J. WILLIAMS *Min. Kingd.* I. 256, I saw coal..in the checks or twitches of those veins between the open bellies, not above one inch in thickness. **1821** W. FORSTER *Section Strata Newcastle-on-Tyne, etc.* (ed. 2) 236 Some..twitches carry a small rib of solid ore quite through.

**5.** A quick, involuntary, usually slight movement of a muscle, etc., esp. of nervous origin; a convulsive or spasmodic jerk or quiver.

**1718** QUINCY *Compl. Disp.* 173 Any Medicine which so far vellicates the ..Stomach and Bowels, as to draw them into convulsive Twitches. **1774** GOLDSM. *Nat. Hist.* (1776) II. 44 It is owing to these alterations that the mother so frequently feels those twitches, which are usually attended with pain. **1804** *Med. Jrnl.* XII. 112 Considerable pain in the head usually accompanied the convulsive twitches in the face. **1825** SCOTT *Talism.* xvii, Mark me the smallest twitch of the features, or wink of the eyelid. **1836** *Random Recoll. Ho. Lords* xiv. 315 A hasty scratch at the back of his head, accompanied with two or three twitches of his nose. **1897** MRS. E. L. VOYNICH *Gadfly* (1904) 47/1 That side of his face was affected with a nervous twitch.

**6.** A small lock of wool or flax twisted round the forefinger of the left hand in spinning.

*a* **1801** BLOOMFIELD *Rural T., Rich. & Kate* viii, She..laid aside her Lucks and Twitches.

**Twitch** (twitʃ), *sb.*[2] [Altered form of QUITCH *sb.*[1]] Couch-grass, *Triticum repens*; = COUCH *sb.*[2]

**1595** LODGE *Fig for Momus* III. 48 If thou espie within thy curious knot, Some tangling twitch, that doth thy flowers rot. **1620** MARKHAM *Farew. Husb.* (1625) 48 The sand that bringeth forth nothing but wyld Twitch, Bryars, Thorn-bush, and such like vndergrowth. **1733** W. ELLIS *Chiltern & Vale Farm.* 264 Lands which are over-run with Twitch or Couch-grass. **1816** G. SINCLAIR *Hort. Gram. Woburn.* (1825) 222 The *Trifolium medium* is inadmissible [in alternate husbandry] on account of its creeping roots constituting what in arable lands is termed *twitch.* **1821** CLARE *Vill. Minstr.* I. 202 The big clod..a hiding-place Breaking off the scorching sun Where the matted twitches run. **1827** — *Sheph. Cal.* 29 From teazing twitch, that in the spongy soil, Clings round the coulter. **1884** F. J. LLOYD *Science Agric.* 256 Of the weeds..none is more common or more troublesome than twitch, or couch grass.

**b.** *attrib.* and *Comb.*: **twitch-drag** (DRAG *sb.* 2 e), a drag or rake for clearing land of twitch; **twitch-fire**, a fire for burning twitch or other weeds; **twitch-grass**, (*a*) *Triticum repens*; (*b*) a species of fox-tail grass, *Alopecurus agrestis* (Britten and Holland, 1886); **twitch-rake** = *twitch-drag.*

**1799** A. YOUNG *Agric. Lincoln.* 69 A *twitch drag..for tearing out twitch. **1905** *Eng. Dial. Dict.*, **Twitch-fire.* **1908** [MISS FOWLER] *Betw. Trent & Ancholme* 81 The sweet-smelling twitch..fire. **1707** MORTIMER *Husb.* (1721) I. 312 *Twitch-grass is a very pernicious Weed to some Land. **1792** *Trans. Soc. Arts* X. 109, I sowed twitch-grass and rye-grass. **1805** R. W. DICKSON *Pract. Agric.* I. 8 The want of proper management..has suffered twitch-grass to become abundant. **1884** *St. James's Gaz.* 19 Sept. 6/1 In some wonderful way, twitch-grass sows itself on fields that were apparently clean. **1799** A. YOUNG *Agric. Lincoln.* 73 A *twitch rake, containing a double row of teeth. **1805** R. W. DICKSON *Pract. Agric.* I. 33 The Twitch-Rake.. necessary for the clearing of certain descriptions of land from these, as well as other kinds of weeds.

**Twitch** (twitʃ), *v.*[1] Forms: 4 **tuicche**, 5 **twych**, 5–6 **twycche**, 6 **twyche**, **twytche**, **twitche**, 6–9 **twich**, 5– **twitch**. *Pa. t.* and *pple.* 5 **twychyde**, 5– **twitched**, etc.; also 4 **twiȝt**, **-e**, *Sc.* **tuiȝt**, 4–5 **twyȝt**, **-e**, **twyght**, **-e**, **twyte**, **twite**, 4–7 **twight**. [ME. *twicchen* (found earliest in the comb. *to-twicchen*), = LG. *twikken*, MHG. and G. *zwicken* (OHG. **zwicjan*, pa. t. *kizwicta*), prob. representing an OE. **twiccan* related to *twiccian*, TWICK *v.*]

**1.** *trans.* To give a sudden abrupt pull at; to pluck; to jerk; to pluck (a person) *by* some part of the body or dress; also, to pluck (the strings of a musical instrument, etc.).

[*c* **1175**–*c* **1350**: see TO-TWITCH.] *c* **1450** *Mankind* 608 in *Macro Plays* 23, I was twychyde by þe neke; þe game was be-gunne; A grace was, þe halter brast asondur. **1587** GOLDING *De Mornay* xxii. (1592) 341 Notwithstanding that our Lawe in euery line..doe reproue vs for it, and after a sort twich vs euery howre by the Cote, to pull vs from it. **1658** BROMHALL *Treat. Specters* I. 44 This foul spirit often twitched and pulled them by the hair. **1704** SWIFT *T. Tub* xi, Providence either forgot or did not think it convenient to twitch me by the Elbow. **1715** S. CROXALL *Vision* 15 His fellow Bard..twitch'd the sounding Chords in solemn State. **1791** COWPER *Iliad* III. 458 She..twitch'd her fragrant robe. **1802** MAR. EDGEWORTH *Moral T.* (1816) I. xiii. 107 Their master twitched the rope, that was fastened round their necks. **1821** CLARE *Vill. Minstr.* I. 47 Such strength had they to twitch the thrumming string. **1849** J. FORBES *Physic. Holiday* ix. (1850) 90 The driver hardly twitched the reins or used the whip from first to last. **1889** GRETTON *Memory's Harkb.* 88 The rector went and twitched him by the sleeve.

**2.** *intr.* To pull or pluck sharply or forcibly; to give a sharp pull or jerk (*at* something); to tug. Also *fig.*

*c* **1305** *St. Lucy* 131 in *E. E. P.* (1862) 105 Hi gonne to drawe & tuicche And euere lai þis maide stille, hi ne miȝte hire enes icche. *c* **1386** CHAUCER *Friar's T.* 265 That was wel twight [*v. rr.* twyȝt, twite] myn owene lyard boy. *c* **1460** *Play Sacrament* 512 Now set on, felouse,..and pluke hys armes awey..; wat, y se he [? *read* y seye,] twycche, felovse, a ryght. **1575** TURBERV. *Falconrie* 210 When she sitteth always..twitching at her feathers with hir beake. **1824** W. IRVING *T. Trav.* I. 63 It seemed as if a legion of imps were twiching at him. **1829** LANDOR *Imag. Conv., Diog. & Plato* Wks. 1846 I. 455/1 Try to barter one with the other, amicably; and not to twitch and carp. **1871** B. TAYLOR *Faust* (1875) II. III. 222 The garment let not go. Already twitch The Demons at its skirts. **1913** EDITH WHARTON *Custom of Country* I. ii, Fidgeting, twitching at her draperies,..when people were noticing her.

**3.** *trans.* (With various advs. and preps.) To pull, draw, or take suddenly or with a jerk; to pull sharply or forcibly; to pluck, snatch. *To twitch up* (the strings of an instrument), to sound by plucking.

*c* **1320** *Sir Tristrem* 1952 Þe bord he fond of tviȝt. *c* **1374** CHAUCER *Troylus* IV. 1157 (1185) His swerde anon out of his shethe he twyghte. *c* **1380** *Sir Ferumb.* 1596 Hure swerdes out þay twyȝte. *a* **1450** *Le Morte Arth.* 1038 That purs..in hond he hente, A letter there-of than oute he twight. **1530** PALSGR. 764/2, I twytche, I pull a thynge sodaynely or hastely, *je happe*...He twitched it out of my handes or I was ware. **1549** COVERDALE, etc. *Erasm. Par. Jas.* v. 38 b, Those riches wherin now you most folishly put your confidence, being twitched awaye. **1575** TURBERV. *Falconrie* 141 Your hande being twitched away fearefully would make hir proceed the more eagerly. **1658** GURNALL *Chr. in Arm.* verse 14. III. xv. § 2. 302 Their fellows that were twitcht up by their gills from them even now with the anglers hook. **1674** BUNYAN *Light in Darkness* Wks. (ed. Offor) I. 412 He is mocked, spit upon, His beard is twitched from His cheeks. **1784** COWPER *Task* IV. 448 Twitched from the perch, He gives the princely bird..to his voracious bag. **1791** A. WILSON in *Poems & Lit. Prose* (1876) II. 77 Come twitch up the strings to great 'John Barleycorn'. **1833** MARRYAT *P. Simple* xxi, One of the strings..catching the lock of the musket carried by one of the sentries..and twitching it out of his hand. **1865** SWINBURNE *Atalanta* 2010 The King twitched his reins in and leapt down. **1876** *Trans. Clinical Soc.* IX. 5 In this eye I had afterwards to twitch away the partially detached piece.

*fig.* **1578** *Chr. Prayers* in *Priv. Prayers* (Parker Soc.) 557 Twitch our minds from time to time to the remembrance of so great happiness. **1653** J. OWEN *Dissert. Div. Just.* Wks. 1852 X. 600 He twitches the argument various ways.

**b.** To snatch by way of robbery or theft.

**1607** DEKKER & WILKINS *Jests*, etc. 39 He..gaue him a little Justle: and withall, twicht 3l. out of his pocket. **1655** tr. *Com. Hist. Francion* II. 33 To wander about the streets ..purposely to try if they could handsomely twich a Cloak. **1849** MRS. CARLYLE *Let. to Dr. Carlyle* Dec. in *New Lett. & Mem.* (1903) II. 10 Mercifully it was near home that he [a small dog] was twitched up [by a dog-stealer].

†**c.** *To twitch up*, to hang. *Obs.*

**1611** R. BRADLEY in *Coryat's Crudities* k ij, The Ducall Gallowes..Which twich him vp, when he offends their law. **1625** SANDERSON *Serm. Ps. cvi. 30* § 22 To twitch up a poor sheep-stealer.

**d.** *Lumbering.* See quots.

**1835–40** HALIBURTON *Clockm.* (1862) 262 He is a giant,.. and can twitch a mill-log as easy as a yoke of oxen can. **1848** BARTLETT *Dict. Amer.*, *To Twitch*, to draw timber along the ground by a chain. Used by lumbermen in Maine. **1905** *Terms Forestry & Logging* (*U. S. Dept. Agric.*, *Forestry* Bulletin lxi.), *Skid*, to draw logs from the stump to the skidway, landing, or mill...*Syn.* snake, twitch.

**4.** To pinch and pull at with or as with pincers or the like; to nip; to hurt or pain, as by doing this. Also *fig.*

*c* **1374** CHAUCER *Troylus* IV. 544 (572) Thus am I with desir and reson twyght. *c* **1412** HOCCLEVE *De Reg. Princ.* 5058 A wight..who is with greuous þoughtes twight. **1440** J. SHIRLEY *Dethe K. James* (1818) 22 A paire sharpe tangis, with the which he twitched and all to tare thare skynne and flessh. **1577–87** HOLINSHED *Chron.* (1807) III. 184 To twitch a quareller with such pinsars as wherewith afore he had nipt an other. *a* **1652** BROME *Eng. Moor* V. i, Had.. both been kil'd indeed, as you in jest, Where had been then your witty subtilty..? Ha! have I twight ye there? *a* **1680** CHARNOCK *Attrib. God* (1834) I. 19 Something in him twitching him upon the pursuit of uncomely actions. **1737** BRACKEN *Farriery Impr.* (1757) II. 174 Such Purges as vellicate and twitch the Nerves. **1760–72** H. BROOKE *Fool of Qual.* (1809) III. 144 His heart twitched him with a kind of compunction. **1851** D. JERROLD *St. Giles* iv. 31 [He] was twitched by a momentary surprise, but directly recovered himself. **1865** DICKENS *Mut. Fr.* I. xiii, I am tickled and twitched all over.

**5.** *intr. Mining.* Of a vein of ore: To contract; with *out*, to come to an end; = PINCH *v.* 14; also *trans.* of the containing rock: to converge upon and contract or close (a vein of ore); cf. PINCH *v.* 11.

**1709** T. ROBINSON *Nat. Hist. Westmld. & Cumbld.* xiv. 80 When the Vein opens wide in some place, and again closeth, or as the Miners speak, Twitcheth at both Ends, this is called a Belly of Ore, or Pipe-Ore. **1747** HOOSON *Miner's Dict.* V j, The Vein keeping a reasonable Compass, and cannot be said to be Twitched. **1789** J. WILLIAMS *Min. Kingd.* I. 255 The coal..grew thinner towards the ends of the belly or concavity of the vein, and it soon dwindled away to nothing, and twitched out entirely. **1836** R. FURNESS *Medicus-Magus* 17 Where wough or rider twitch'd a leading fast.

**6.** *trans.* To draw tight by means of a cord or the like; to tie, fasten, secure tightly or firmly. Also with the cord as object. Now *dial.*

**1615** G. SANDYS *Trav.* 63 They twitch the offender about the waist with a towell,..pricking him in the body, until they have drawn him within the compass of a span. **1634** T. JOHNSON tr. *Parey's Chirurg.* VII. xxii. (1678) 186 Ganglia ..must be tied with a string at the root, and every day twitched harder and harder. **1641** BEST *Farm. Bks.* (Surtees) 66 Twitch the other cooarde a little below the mouth of the newe hive. **1729** LAW *Serious C.* xix. (1732) 354 Her Stays which her Mother had ordered to be twitch'd so strait [etc.]. **1809** T. DONALDSON *Poems* 191 The Shoon indeed did leuk fu' weel,..Ye'd twitcht them weel thegither. **1877** *Holderness Gloss.* s.v., Twitch thi shavs (sheaves) tighther.

**b.** To castrate by means of a cord looped over the testicles and drawn tight; see also quot. 1841.

**1831** [YOUATT] *Horse* xii. 227 To the practice of some farmers, of twitching their colts at an early period, sometimes even so early as a month, we have stronger objection. **1841** HARTSHORNE *Salopia Antiq.* s.v. *Twitchel*, To twitch a horse, or apply to him a twitchel or twitch. **1877** in *N. W. Linc. Gloss.*

**7.** To draw *up* (a limb, etc.) sharply or with a jerk; to move (the skin, etc.) spasmodically or convulsively.

**1523** FITZHERB. *Husb.* § 108 The stryng halte..maketh him to twyche vp his legge sodeynly, and maketh hym to halte. **1616** SURFL. & MARKH. *Country Farme* 132 Ride him vpon new-plowed Lands, or in Wayes that are deepe and heauie, for that will make him twitch vp his legges, and strike them cleane and high. **1821** CLARE *Vill. Minstr.* I. 203 The cows..Twitching slow their fly-bit hides. **1863** GEO. ELIOT *Romola* xviii, A white rabbit..was twitching its nose with much content on a box full of bran. **1897** W. C. HAZLITT *Four Gen. Lit. Fam.* I. III. i. 239 As a young man [he] had a way of twitching his ears. **1899** *Allbutt's Syst. Med.* VII. 512 He rolled his eyes, clenched his hands, and twitched both arms and legs.

**b.** *intr.* Of a nerve, etc.: To twinge, 'shoot'.

*a* **1845** HOOD *True Story* ii, Why then they [teeth] only twitch'd the quicker.

**8.** *intr.* To proceed in a jerking or irregular way (*obs. rare*); now always in reference to involuntary bodily movements: to move in a jerky, spasmodic, or convulsive manner; to jerk, jump, start. Also *refl.* (const. *into*).

**1592** NASHE *Strange News* G iij, The Hexamiter verse ..goes twitching and hopping in our language like a man running vpon quagmiers vp the hill in one Syllable and downe the dale in another. **1832** HT. MARTINEAU *Weal & Woe* vii, His bony fingers sometimes twitching, sometimes drooping with an appearance of utter helplessness. **1839–40** W. IRVING *Wolfert's R.* (1855) 217, I tried to keep my countenance,..but it would not do. My muscles began to twitch. **1848** THACKERAY *Van. Fair* lviii, If the Major had twitched before, he started now. **1870** MORRIS *Earthly Par.* II. III. 513 His mouth twitched, though his eyes gazed steadily. **1871** B. TAYLOR *Faust* (1875) I. v. 87 In the last convulsion twitching. **1885** HOWELLS *Silas Lapham* (1891) I. 15 Some of the younger children had twitched themselves into wavering shadows [in a photograph]. **1899** *Allbutt's Syst. Med.* VII. 519 In 2 [cases] the eyes 'had been rolled about', and in 2 others they had twitched.

**b.** *intr.* To go with a sudden swift motion; to dart, shoot.

**1836** PARTINGTON *Brit. Cycl. Nat. Hist.* II. 139/2 It [the shag] floats with wonderful buoyancy in the air, twitches down to the water with the rapidity of lightning.

**9.** *Comb.*: **twitch-ballock**, an earwig; also, a large black beetle; **twitch-bell**, an earwig; **twitch-clock, -clog**, a cockroach. All *dial.*

**1658** ROWLAND *Moufet's Theat. Ins.* 1023 The Northern English by an obscene name call it [the earwig] *Twich-ballock. *a* **1800** PEGGE *Suppl. Grose, Twitch-ballock*, the large black beetle. *Lanc.* **1790** GROSE *Provinc. Gloss.* (ed. 2), **Twitchbell*, an earwig. *North.* **1825** in BROCKETT *N. C. Words.* **1863** in Robson *Bards of Tyne* 237 Nee spiders an twitchbells to 'larm ye. **1876** J. HARTLEY *Yorksher Puddin'* 187 Boxes full o' butterflies, an buzzards, an *twitchclocks.

Hence **Twitched**, **Twi·tching** *ppl. adjs.*

**1567** DRANT *Horace, Epist.* vi. D j, If that thy sydes, or Renes become With twitchinge stitche attainted. **1580** BABINGTON *Exp. Lord's Prayer* (1596) 274 His heart smote him,..and the woorde importeth a twiching smart. **1700** DRYDEN *Fables, Theod. & Hon.* 372 She..fear'd at ev'ry step a twitching sprite behind. **1821** CLARE *Vill. Minstr.* I. 5 The spinning-top whirl'd from the twitching string. **1881** MIVART *Cat* 137 The muscle by its contraction effects those twitching movements of which the cat's skin is capable. **1883** G. MEREDITH *Day Dau. Hades* vii, His twitched lips puffing to tell In music his tears and his need.

† **Twitch**, *v.*[2] *Obs. rare.* [Alteration of *quitch*, QUETCH *v.*, perhaps partly after prec.] *intr.* To move, stir.

**1543** BECON *Policy of War* Wks. 1564 I. 143 b, God wyll so watche the borders..of our Realmes that no Tyraunte shoulde..once be able to twytche agaynst vs. **1674** N. FAIRFAX *Bulk & Selv.* 127 Springs, some shaping or plastick, some bigning or growing, others barely stirring or twitching.

**Twitch** (twitʃ), *v.*[3] *dial.* [f. TWITCH *sb.*[2]] *intr.* To gather and destroy twitch or couch-grass; also *trans.* to clean (land) from twitch. Hence **Twi·tching** *vbl. sb.*

**1795** *Gentl. Mag.* Aug. 695/1 At Beighton, Derbyshire,..a respectable farmer was killed by lightning, as he was twitching in his land. **1799** A. YOUNG *Agric. Lincoln.* 398 Women..are employed in..picking up twitch to burn,..for twitching and weeding, they have, upon an average, 9*d.* per day. **1865** *Pall Mall G.* 13 May 2 They are employed in weeding, twitching, hoeing, and various other kinds of agricultural labour. **1886** *S.-W. Linc. Gloss.* s. v., I must twitch and do my land for wheat.

**Twitch**, obs. form of TOUCH.

**Twitchel**[1] (twi·tʃ'l). *dial.* Forms: 5 twe-, twychel(l, twachylle, 8–9 twitchel, -ell. [An alteration, or a variant with different suffix, of ME. *twychen*, late OE. *twichene*, OE. *twycene, twicen* a fork in a road, a forked way.

The form *twychen* survived in ME. times in Oxford in the names of special passages or lanes: see Wood *City of Oxford* (O.H.S.) I. viii. 187, 199, 223, etc., and Hurst *Oxford Topogr.* (O.H.S.) 186, 197. In Lanc. and Yorksh. the reduced form *twitch* is still in use. Cf. also TWITTEN.]

A narrow passage between walls or hedges. In quot. *c* 1460 *transf.*

**1435** *Nottingham Rec.* (1883) II. 357 Ye comon twechell yat lyges on ye northe syd ye Fleshusse. *Ibid.*, Twychel. **1484** *Ibid.* III. 229 Þe dore..þat gothe into the twychell betwix þe Shaumelles and þe Draperie. *c* **1460** *MS. Laud* 416 lf. 54 in *Rel. Ant.* II. 28 She..wyth her twachylle wille encrece and multeply. *a* **1800** PEGGE *Suppl. Grose, Twitchell*, a narrow passage, or alley, not a thoroughfare. Derb. **1848** A. B. EVANS *Leicester. Words, Phrases*, etc., *Twitchell*, a narrow passage or alley between houses. *a* **1889** *Notice* (Bedford) in *N. & Q.* 7th Ser. VII. 275/2 All persons passing by this twitchel are requested to go up or down directly.

**Twi·tchel**[2]. *dial.* [f. TWITCH *sb.*[1] or *v.*[1]] A noose; *spec.* = TWITCH *sb.*[1] 3 b. *dial.*

**1688** [implied in *twitchelling* below]. **1841** [see TWITCH *v.*[1] 6 b]. **1882** *Lanc. Gloss., Twitchel*, a short wooden lever with a loop of rope fastened to one end; the rope is put round the lower jaw of an unruly horse, and the stick is twisted round.

Hence **Twi·tchelled** (twi·chelt) *a.*, noosed, held in a noose; **Twi·tchelling**, the taking of fish with a noose.

**1688** CHETHAM *Angler's Vade-m.* Pref., The unlawful practice..of Damming, Groping, Spearing, Hanging, Twitchelling, [etc.]. **1855** E. WAUGH *Lanc. Life* (1857) 31 He wacken't an' stare't like a twichelt dog. **1865** B. BRIERLEY *Irkdale* II. 128 He geet how'd o' th' young womman, an' made her squeeal as leawd as a twitchelt gonner wi' th' squeeze he gan her.

**Twitcher** (twi·tʃəɹ). [f. TWITCH *v.*[1] + -ER[1].] One who or that which twitches.

**1.** An instrument for plucking or pinching something. † **a.** An instrument for clinching hog-rings; cf. *hog-ringer* (HOG *sb.*[1] 13). *Obs.* † **b.** = TWITCH *sb.*[1] 3 b. *Obs.* † **c.** Tweezers for extracting superfluous hairs. *Obs.* † **d.** Tweezers or nippers used in cookery for trimming or ornamenting pastry, etc. *Obs.*

**1573** TUSSER *Husb.* (1878) 38 Strong yoke for a hog, with a twicher and rings. **1688** R. HOLME *Armoury* III. 244/1 Yoke for Swine, Twitchers or Rings. *Ibid.* 302/2 Horse Twichers, or Bracks..to put on Horses Noses, when they will not stand quietly to be Shooed [etc.]. *Ibid.* 427/1 A Twitcher, or Twitchers; by them Hair superfluously growing in any part is pulled up by the Roots. *Ibid.* xxii. (Roxb.) 274/2 Instruments belonging to the Cook. The first is termed a Runner with Twichers. Some Cooks call these Iging [? edging] Irons.

**2.** One who or that which moves jerkily or spasmodically. *rare.*

**1793** MARY WOLLSTONECR. *Lett. to Imlay* viii. (1879) 19 Where shall I find a word to express the relationship which subsists between us? Shall I ask the little twitcher?

**3.** That which causes twitching; a severe blow; acute pain. *dial.*

**1828** *Craven Gloss., Twitcher*, a severe blow. **1877** *Sunday Mag.* 182 'The rheumatis' had, in his own phrase, 'caught him on the hop and given him a twitcher'.

**Twitching** (twi·tʃiŋ), *vbl. sb.*[1] [f. TWITCH *v.*[1] + -ING[1].] The action of the verb TWITCH; jerking, plucking; nipping; convulsive or spasmodic movement. Also *attrib.*

**1607** MARKHAM *Caval.* I. xviii. (1617) 75 Let them which haue hold vpon the halter, with twitchings and strainings torment him. **1626** BACON *Sylva* § 37 Almost all Purgers have a kind of Twitching and vellication besides the griping which commeth of winde. **1768** TUCKER *Lt. Nat.* I. xxxiii. (1834) I. 241 A man, who should find a troublesome twitching in his muscles, would do very wrong to destroy the tone of them. **1789** *Trans. Soc. Arts* VII. 189 Model of a machine for twitching of wool. **1799** *Med. Jrnl.* I. 480 Starting tremors, convulsive twitchings are frequent. **1831** CARLYLE in Froude *Life* (1882) II. 189 An occasional twitching up of the corners of the upper lip, and point of the nose. **1872** M. CREIGHTON *Hist. Ess.* ii. (1902) 101 His suffering was known only by..the twitching of his lips. **1881** *Trans. Obstet. Soc. Lond.* XXII. 20 The twitching attacks do not recur periodically and their duration is variable. **1899** *Allbutt's Syst. Med.* VIII. 589 The patient complains of..twitching of the extremities.

† **b.** *concr.* See quot. *Obs. rare.*

**1688** R. HOLME *Armoury* III. 300/1 *Twitchings*, the ends of Nails cut off, as of Horse-shooe Nails.

**Twitching**, *vbl. sb.*[2]: see TWITCH *v.*[3]

† **Twitchmill.** A nonce-rendering of G. *zwickmühle*, a certain advantage in the game of merels.

*c* **1640** H. BELL *Luther's Colloq. Mens.* (1652) 307 The Pope..maketh between the Emperor and French King a Twittchmill, without which two hee cannot subsist. *Ibid.*, Hee forsaketh not that Twittchmill with the Emperor and French King.

**Twitchy** (twi·tʃi), *a.*[1] [f. TWITCH *v.*[1] + -Y.]

**1.** Characterized by twitching; having a tendency to twitch; also, nervous, fidgety, irritable.

**1839** *Fraser's Mag.* XX. 671 Her lips were long, loose, and twitchy. **1861** DICKENS in *All Year Round* IV. 457 Faces peculiarly swollen, and twitchy about the nose. **1874** A. J. C. HARE *Story of my Life* (1900) IV. xvii. 245 An excellent person, but very nervous and twitchy. **1898** TALMAGE *Serm.* in *N. Y. Chr. Herald* 27 Apr. 368/3 Your nerves will become more twitchy and your dyspepsia more aggravated.

**2.** *Mining.* Cf. TWITCH *sb.*[1] 4, *v.*[1] 5.

**1747** HOOSON *Miner's Dict.* R ij b, Many good Veins that ..have been wrought to a vast Depth, yet it is found in the end to grow hard and Twitchey on the Soles.

**Twitchy** (twi·tʃi), *a.*[2] [f. TWITCH *sb.*[2] + -Y.] Full of or infested with twitch; made of twitch.

**1653** BLITHE *Eng. Improv. Impr.* xxviii. (ed. 3) 193 If upon a stony land, or twichy woody Land, it must be narrower. *Ibid.* 196 Lands..hard rooty, rushy, twichy, or any way unfeacible. **1829** *Glover's Hist. Derby* I. 195 He ploughs twitchy lands but once. *c* **1837** CLARE *To the Lark* iii. in *Life & Rem.* (1873) 137 How beautiful to see thee..Winnowing thy russet wings above thy twitchy nest.

**Twite** (twəit). [Imitative, from the note of the bird.] A species of linnet, *Linota flavirostris* or *L. montium*, found in hilly and moorland districts in the northern parts of Britain and in Scandinavia, and elsewhere as a winter visitant; also called Mountain Linnet or **Twite-finch.**

**1562** TURNER *Baths* Pref., Flockinge byrdes..linnettes, goldfinches, sparrowes and twyes [? twytes]. **1676** GREW *Musæum, Anat. Stomach & Guts* viii. 36 The Twite or Avicula Anadavadensis. **1773** BARRINGTON in *Phil. Trans.* LXIII. 282 *note*, The London bird-catchers also sell..the yellow hammer, twite and brambling as singing birds. **1815** STEPHENS in Shaw *Gen. Zool.* IX. 521 Twite Finch. **1876** SMILES *Sc. Natur.* xiii. (ed. 4) 260 The Twite..bred in suitable localities round the loch. **1894** R. B. SHARPE *Handbk. Birds Gt. Brit.* I. 43 The Twite is a moorland species...In winter it migrates south in large flocks, which frequent the neighbourhood of the coast, and enliven the marshes with their twittering song.

**Twite**, obs. or dial. form of TWIT *v.*

**Twithe**, obs. Sc. form of TOOTH.

**Twitten** (twi·t'n). *Sussex dial.* Also **twitting.** [Perh. related to LG. *twiete* alley, lane; but cf. also OE. *twicen* and TWITCHEL[1].] A narrow path or passage between two walls or hedges.

**1801** PENNANT *Journ. fr. Lond. to Isle of Wight* II. 77 Alleys, or, as they are called here [at Brighton] twittings, narrow passages, often not three feet wide. **1860** W. H. AINSWORTH *Ovingdean Grange* 334 Having tracked a series of 'twittens'..they issued forth into West-street. **1904** *Sat. Rev.* 2 Apr. 424/1 Along the bostals of the Downs and through the village twittens.

**Twitter** (twi·təɹ), *sb.*[1] [f. TWITTER *v.*[1]]

**1.** A condition of twittering or tremulous excitement (from eager desire, fear, etc.); a state of agitation; a flutter, a tremble. Now chiefly *dial.*

**1678** BUTLER *Hud.* III. I. 83 The ancient errant knights Won all their ladies' hearts in fights, And cut whole giants into fritters, To put them into amorous twitters. *a* **1734** NORTH *Exam.* I. iii. § 31 (1740) 141 The Attorney-General..was in a Twitter; for some of his Friends told him he would certainly be questioned for it in Parliament. **1802** G. COLMAN *Poor Gentleman* I. i, If I ben't all of a twitter to see my old John Harrowby again! **1825** J. NEAL *Bro. Jonathan* II. 151 A leap of the heart..and a sort of tingling twitter through all his blood. **1861** THACKERAY *Four Georges* iv. (1862) 198 In a twitter of indignation. **1869** TROLLOPE *He knew*, etc. xxxi, [She] was in a twitter, partly of expectation, and partly..of fear. **1869** LOUISA M. ALCOTT *Little Women* vi, Beth hurried on in a twitter of suspense.

**b.** A suppressed laugh, a titter; a fit of laughter. *dial.*

**1736** LEWIS *Isle of Tenet* Gloss. s. v. (E.D.S.), He is in a mighty twitter. **1847–78** HALLIWELL, *Twitter*,..(2) A fit of laughter. *Kent.*

**2.** An act or the action of twittering, as a bird; light tremulous chirping. Also *transf.* a sound resembling this.

**1842** BROWNING *Waring* I. vi. 35 As pours some pigeon.. her melodious cry Amid their [swallows'] barbarous twitter! **1849** W. S. MAYO *Kaloolah* v. (1850) 40 The hesitating twitter of the sleepy birds. **1871** BLACKIE *Four Phases* I. 43 A mere swallow-twitter of inarticulate jargon. **1902** SNAITH *Wayfarers* xvi, The ceaseless twitter of the rain on the road.

**Twi·tter**, *sb.*[2] [Dial. var. QUITTER *sb.*[1]]

**1.** *Farriery.* = QUITTER *sb.*[1] 2. Cf. TWITTER-BONE.

**1892** *Lincolnsh. N. & Q.* Apr. 45 *Twitter*, a tumour or gathering on a horse's foot, just above the hoof.

**2.** *Whaling.* The refuse of the case of the sperm-whale, consisting of a gummy and thready substance (*Cent. Dict.* 1891).

**Twi·tter**, *sb.*[3] *Sc.* and *north. dial.* [Cf. TWIT *sb.*[2] and TWITTER *v.*[2]] **a.** A thin part in a thread that is unequally spun. Also *transf.* **b.** A shred, a fragment. **c.** An entanglement; a complication.

**1721** KELLY *Sc. Prov.* 395 You are as small as the Twitter of a twin'd Rusky, a Taunt to a Maid, that would gladly be esteem'd neat, and small. **1825** JAMIESON s. v., Yarn is said to be twined to twitters, when twined too small...It is said of a lank delicate girl; 'She's a mere twitter'. **1847–78** HALLIWELL, *Twitters*, shreds; fragments. *North.* **1876** *Whitby Gloss., Twitters*, entangled threads; complications of all sorts.

**Twi·tter**, *sb.*[4] *rare.* [f. TWIT *v.* + -ER[1].] One who twits; *dial.* a tale-bearer.

**1854** MISS BAKER *Northampt. Gloss.* s.v., 'Don't tell him anything, he's a twitter.' **1882** in OGILVIE.

**Twitter** (twi·təɹ), *v.*[1] Forms: 4 twyter, twiter, 5– twitter. [Of imitative origin: cf. OHG. *zwizirôn, -erôn* (MHG. *zwitzern*, G. *zwitschern*), Du. *kwetteren*, and Sw. *qvittra*, Norw. dial. *kvittra, kvitra*, Da. *kvidre* (see QUITTER *v.*[2]), in sense 1.]

**1.** *intr.* Of a bird: To utter a succession of light tremulous notes; to chirp continuously with a tremulous effect.

*c* **1374** CHAUCER *Boeth.* III. met. ii. 54 (Camb. MS.) The Iangelynge bryd..enclosed in a streyht cage..twiterith desyrynge the wode with her swete voys. **1387** TREVISA *Higden* (Rolls) I. 237 Þe ny3tyngale in his note Twytereþ wel fawnyng Wiþ full swete song. **1697** DRYDEN *Virg. Georg.* IV. 434 Swallows twitter on the Chimney Tops. **1750** GRAY *Elegy* v, The swallow twittring from the straw-built shed. **1840** DICKENS *Barn. Rudge* i, Colonies of sparrows chirped and twittered in the eaves.

**b.** *transf.* Of a person: To sing after the above manner; also (esp. of a woman), to talk or chatter rapidly in a small or tremulous voice.

**1829** LADY GRANVILLE *Lett.* 22 Nov. (1894) II. 49 They.. are enchanted, twittering like hedge-sparrows. **1875** JOWETT *Plato* (ed. 2) III. 40 While a man is singing and twittering and pouring music like water through the funnel of his ears, the edge of his soul gradually wears away. **1879** K. S. MACQUOID *Berkshire Lady* 178 The old lady twittered and fluttered.

**2.** *trans.* Of a bird: To utter or express by twittering.

**1387** TREVISA *Higden* (Rolls) I. 237 Þe osul twytereþ mery songes. **1645** G. DANIEL *Poems* Wks. (Grosart) II. 70 The Squallid owle Twitters a midnight note. **1821** CLARE *Vill. Minstr.* II. 105 Linnets,..twittering their welcomes to the day's return. **1884** W. C. SMITH *Kildrostan* I. iii. 14 The swifts and swallows..Twitter their gossip in the evening light. **1891** FARRAR *Darkn. & Dawn* xxxvii, The very birds of the air seemed to flit away from him [Nero], twittering 'Matricide! matricide!'

**b.** *transf.* Of a person: cf. 1 b.

**1864** BROWNING *Youth & Art* iii, I..trilled and twittered, 'Kate Brown's on the boards ere long'. **1878** — *Poets Croisic* lxxi, These [lines], brisk as any finch, He twittered. **1900** SARAH GRAND *Babs* xvii, 'Really, Mrs. Kingconstance,' Miss Spice twittered excitedly, 'you are too kind!'

**3.** *intr.* To move tremulously, tremble, shake, quiver, shiver; *esp.* to tremble with excitement, eagerness, fear, etc.; to be in a flutter; hence, † to long eagerly, to hanker (*after*, or *to do* something). Now *dial.*

*a* **1616** BEAUM. & FL. *Scornf. Lady* IV. i, When it twitter'd to be at me. **1629** GAULE *Holy Madn.* 206 Hands clap, Fingers twitter. **1635** BROME *Sparagus Gard.* III. v, How the slave twitters. **1675** BUNYAN *Saved by Grace* Wks. (ed. Offor) I. 342 Doth not thy mouth water, doth not thy heart twitter at being saved? *a* **1688** — *Israel's Hope Encouraged* ibid. 620 Doth not all this discourse make thy heart twitter after the mercy that is with God? **1684** SOUTHERNE *Disappointm.* II. i, Her eyes and lips, see how they blubb and pout, and twitter and swell at you. **1821** CLARE *Vill. Minstr.* I. 46 Where the sunbeam twitter'd on the walls. *Ibid.* II. 92, I twitter'd like a leaf. **1861** THACKERAY *Four Georges* iv. (1876) 115 The bigness, boisterousness..appear to have.. set all the teacups twittering on the tray. **1878** STEVENSON *Inland Voy.* 114, I was..twittering with cold.

**b.** *trans.* To move (something) tremulously; to twiddle (the fingers). *rare*$^{-1}$.

**1855** THACKERAY *Newcomes* vii, Mademoiselle..was twittering her fingers.

**4.** *intr.* To laugh in a suppressed way, titter, giggle. *dial.*

**1687** MIÉGE *Gt. Fr. Dict.* II, To twitter, or snear at one, to laugh at him with some contempt, *se moquer de quêcun.* **1694** MOTTEUX *Rabelais* IV. lii. 204 The Maidens began to snicker,.. giggling and twittering among themselves. *a* **1700** B. E. *Dict. Cant. Crew, Twitter*, to Laugh much with little Noise. **1901** 'ZACK' *Dunstable Weir* 11 Folks would have twittered louder had they known whose fancy he was like to take.

**5.** *trans.* To bring *into* a specified condition by twittering. *rare*$^{-1}$.

**1861** T. L. PEACOCK *Gryll Gr.* xiv, The pianoforte is not much to my mind...Its incapability of sustaining a note has led..to those infinitesimal subdivisions of sound, in which all sentiment and expression are twittered and frittered into nothingness.

**Twi·tter,** *v.*$^2$ *Sc.* and *north. dial.* [Of obscure origin: cf. TWIT *sb.*$^2$ and TWITTER *sb.*$^3$] *trans.* To spin or twist unevenly, to make 'twitty'.

**1674** RAY *N. C. Words* 50 To Twitter Thread or Yarn, is to Spin it uneven. **1828** *Craven Gloss., Twitter*, to entangle, as thread which is too hard twisted. **1843** *Whistlebinkie* (1890) II. 165 Baith twittered and knotty's the thread o' our life.

**Twi·tter,** *v.*$^3$ Now *dial.* [f. TWIT *v.* + -ER$^5$.] *trans.* = TWIT *v.* 1; *dial.* to tease.

**1749** FIELDING *Tom Jones* VIII. vii, It doth not become such a one as you to twitter me. **1800** BROWNE *Poems* 155 (E.D.D.) She twitters me out of my life.

**Twittera·tion.** *nonce-wd.* [f. TWITTER *v.*$^1$ 3 + -ATION.] = TWITTER *sb.*$^1$ 1.

**1835–40** HALIBURTON *Clockm.* 373 (Cassell) When they struck up our blood-stirrin' national air, it made me feel all over in a twitteration. **1855** — *Nat. & Hum. Nat.* xiv. II. 50, I am so skeared, Sam, I feel all over of a twitteration.

**Twitter-bit.** (See quot.)

**1875** KNIGHT *Dict. Mech., Twitter-bit*, the bottom of the countersink which receives the head of the screw, uniting the halves of a pair of scissors.

**Twitter-bone.** *dial.* or *Obs.* [var. of *quitter-bone*, QUITTER *sb.*$^1$ 4.] A suppurating tumour on a horse's foot. Hence **Twitter-boned** *a.*, affected with a twitter-bone.

**1688** *Lond. Gaz.* No. 2395/4 A yellowish bay Horse,..a Twitterbone taken out of each hind Foot. **1759** STERNE *Tr. Shandy* I. x, His horse was either clapp'd, or..twitter-bon'd, or broken-winded. **1828** *Craven Gloss., Twitter-bone*, an excrescence on a horse's hoof.

**Twitterer** (twi·tərəɹ). [f. TWITTER *v.*$^1$ + -ER$^1$.] A bird that twitters; also *transf.* of a person (cf. TWITTER *v.*$^1$ 2 b).

**1834** R. MUDIE *Feathered Tribes Brit. Isles* (1841) I. 2 When the forest howls to its fury, driving the twitterers from the spray. **1890** O. CRAWFURD *Round Calendar in Portugal* 178 Several feeble-winged twitterers. **1895** J. G. WOOLLEY in *Voice* (N. Y.) 17 Oct. 2/1 A mere twitterer of lackadaisical platitudes.

**Twittering** (twi·təriŋ), *vbl. sb.* [f. TWITTER *v.*$^1$ + -ING$^1$.] The action of TWITTER *v.*$^1$

**1.** Light tremulous chirping of a bird or birds; a sound resembling or likened to this.

**1781** COWPER *Conversation* 448 Will the sweet warbler of the livelong night..Forget his harmony, with rapture heard, To learn the twittering of a meaner bird? **1824** LAMB *Elia* Ser. II. *Captain Jackson* (1833) 87 Chords responsive to the twitterings of that slender image of a voice. **1877** BARING-GOULD *Myst. Suffering* 87 The twanging of fiddles and twittering of flutes. **1877** BLACK *Green Past.* ii, The twittering of the young starlings in their nests.

**2.** Trembling; tremulous excitement; † eager desire or longing, hankering (*obs.*).

**1668** SEDLEY *Mulberry Gard.* v. i, Though you had a twittering to Althea, you will make ne'er the worse husband to Victoria. **1692** L'ESTRANGE *Fables* I. cccxxxii. 289 A Widow that had a Twittering toward a second Husband.

**Twi·ttering,** *ppl. a.* [f. as prec. + -ING$^2$.] That twitters.

**1.** Chirping lightly and tremulously, as a bird.

**1827** HOOD *Mids. Fairies* xxxi, We gather in loud choirs the twittering race. **1857** J. HAMILTON *Less. fr. Gt. Biog.* (1859) 172 New leaves are on the trees and twittering broods are in the nest.

**2.** Trembling, quivering; trembling with excitement or the like, in a flutter. Now *dial.*

**1681** W. ROBERTSON *Phraseol. Gen.* (1693) 1257, I am in a twittering case, *inter sacrum saxumque sto.* **1821** CLARE *Vill. Minstr.* II. 75 The sun now sinks behind the woodland green, And twittering spangles glow the leaves between. **1884** STEVENSON *Let. to Henley* Nov. (1899) I. 335 Hardly able to come downstairs for twittering knees.

Hence **Twi·tteringly** *adv.*

**1860** RUSSELL *Diary India* I. xvi. 255 A large zigzag fire of musketry goes twitteringly along the lines of the trenches.

† **Twitter-light.** *Obs. rare.* [?f. TWITTER *v.*$^1$ 3 + LIGHT *sb.* Cf. TWATTER-LIGHT.] Twilight.

**1607** MIDDLETON *Your Five Gallants* v. i, You can steale secretly hether..at twylight, twitterlights! *a* **1626** — *More Dissemblers* III. i, Come not till twitter light.

**Twi·tterly,** *a. rare*$^{-1}$. [f. TWITTER *sb.*$^1$ 1 or *v.*$^1$ 3 + -LY$^1$.] = next.

**1896** KIPLING *Seven Seas, Cholera Camp* (1897) 188 Our Colonel's white an' twitterly—'e gets no sleep nor food.

**Twittery** (twi·təri), *a.*$^1$ [f. TWITTER *sb.*$^1$ 1 or *v.*$^1$ + -Y.] Apt to twitter or tremble; feeble, shaky; also *fig.*

**1883** L. WINGFIELD *A. Rowe* II. iv. 92 Olivia was..twittery, nervous and sensitive. **1889** *Cornh. Mag.* July 69 A feeble, twittery tale of love. **1907** UNA L. SILBERRAD *Gd. Comrade* ii, The Captain was rather twittery at lunch.

**Twi·ttery,** *a.*$^2$ *Sc.* [f. TWITTER *sb.*$^3$ or *v.*$^2$] 'Slender; properly, spun very small' (Jam.).

**1819** *Edinb. Even. Cour.* 1 July (Jam.), Clothing.. far afore the twittery worn-wabs made now-a-days.

**Twitting** (twi·tiŋ), *vbl. sb.* [f. TWIT *v.* + -ING$^1$.] The action of the verb TWIT.

**1.** (Light) reproach or censure; taunting.

**1580** HOLLYBAND *Treas. Fr. Tong, Exprobation*, or *reproche*, a reproch, a twiting. **1586** A. DAY *Eng. Secretary* II. (1625) 48 Tush, pedegree, pedegree, here is nothing with you in hand but twitting with pedegree. **1611** COTGR., *Reproche*, an vpbraiding, twitting, or casting in the teeth. **1647** HEXHAM I, A twiting, *een verwijting.* **1891** E. W. GOSSE *Gossip in Library* xiv. 175 The only rough thing he ever did was the result of one such twitting.

**2.** Tale-telling, blabbing. Now *dial.*

*a* **1643** CARTWRIGHT *Ordinary* IV. iv, D' y' think I would undo me self by twitting?..I'm faithfull, And secret, though a Barber.

So **Twi·tting** *ppl. a.*, that twits; whence **Twi·ttingly** *adv.*, in the way of twitting, tauntingly.

**1675** tr. *Camden's Hist. Eliz.* I. 125 Having reckoned all his Civilities to the English Nation, he twittingly upbraided them therewith. **1838** B. CORNEY *Controversy* 20 The points whereon you may have been criticised rather twittingly.

**Twitting,** variant of TWITTEN.

† **Twi·ttle,** *v. Obs.* [app. altered from TITTLE *v.*$^1$; cf. TWITTLE-TWATTLE.] *trans.* To utter idly, chatter, babble: = TITTLE *v.*$^1$

**1577** STANYHURST *Descr. Irel.* Ep. to Sir H. Sidney, in Holinshed *Chron.* (1587) II. 6 His hystorie..twitled more tales out of schoole, and drowned weightyer matters in silence, then the Autor vpon better view..woulde haue permitted. *Ibid.* vi. 34/2 Such rumors noised, such tales bruted, such fables twitled, such vntrue reports twatled.

† **Twi·ttle-twa:t.** *Obs. rare*$^{-1}$. [app. shortened from next.] A tattler, babbler.

**1662** *Rump Songs* I. 52 Next come those idle Twittle-twats, Which calls me many God-knows-whats.

† **Twi·ttle-twa·ttle.** *Obs.* Also 6 **twitle twattle, twitell-twaytel.** [app. altered from TITTLE-TATTLE: see TWATTLE *sb.*$^1$] Idle talk, tittle-tattle. Also *attrib.*

**1556** OLDE *Antichrist* 7 b, Suche a kynde of religioun, as hath more twitle twattle toyes in it, then the Leuitical lawe. **1565** ABP. PARKER *Corr.* (Parker Soc.) 237 My lord of Leicester, they say, shall move..the Queen's Majesty,..and Mr. Cole is now at the Court.., which will overthrow all this attempt: and such twitell-twaytel there is much. *a* **1578** W. ROPER *Life Sir T. More* (1729) 89 She..not likinge suche talke, answered, twittle, twattle, twittle, twattle. **1668** R. L'ESTRANGE *Vis. Quev.* (1708) 244 The squalling of the Child, and the Twittle-Twattle-Gossipings of the Nurse and Midwife. **1719** D'URFEY *Pills* III. 250 Leave your twittle twattle.

† **Twit-twat.** *Obs. rare.* Also **twit twot.** [app. shortened from prec.]

† **1.** = prec. Also *attrib. Obs.*

**1677** YARRANTON *Eng. Improv.* 46 This way of ordering the young Women in Germany is one great cause that the German Women have so little of the twit twat. *Ibid.* 101 The strange News you hear at Coffee-houses..is generally idle Twit twot Discourse. *Ibid.* 170 Command Silence; Suffer not your Wives to use any Twit-twat.

**2.** A name for the house-sparrow.

**1891** in *Cent. Dict.*

**Twitty** (twi·ti), *a.*$^1$ *dial.* [f. TWIT *sb.*$^1$ + -Y.] See quots.

*a* **1825** FORBY *Voc. E. Anglia, Twitty, adj.* cross; snappish. **1893** ZINCKE *Wherstead* xxvi. (ed. 2) 251 (E. Anglian Dial.) 'Trunch' for short and thick; 'twitty' for snappish.

**Twi·tty,** *a.*$^2$ [f. TWIT *sb.*$^2$ + -Y.] Full of or containing 'twits': see TWIT *sb.*$^2$

**1884** W. S. B. MCLAREN *Spinning* (ed. 2) 119 Such a draft would..be too much for any wool and would make the sliver twitty. *Ibid.* 131 No yarn can spin well when it is twitty.

**Twitzer-case,** obs. f. TWEEZER-CASE.

† **Twive,** *v. Naut. Obs. rare.* Also **twyve.** [Of obscure origin.] *intr.* Of a ship at anchor: To swing up or down with the tide.

**1576** *Admir. Crt. Exam.* 22, 30 Aug.,The Salamon twyved to the Southwarde upp with the flud and when the water turned she twivid downe againe with the ebb. *Ibid.*, She twived upwards againe and therewith twyved uppon an anchor.

**'Twixt,** † **twixt** (twikst), *prep.* Forms: 4 **twix, tuyx,** 4, 6–7 *Sc.* **tuix,** 6–7 **twixt,** 7– **'twixt.** Aphetic form of ATWIXT, BETWIXT.

**13..** *Cursor M.* 3179 (Cott.) [Abraham] loked bi him tuyx þe thorns. *Ibid.* 22028 O fader and moder he sal be born.. Bituix a man and a womman..Noght tuix a biscop and a nun. **1570** *Satir. Poems Reform.* xx. 51 This I will say tuix sport and play. **1578** LYTE *Dodoens* II. xlviii. 206 The seede [of hyacinth] is drie in the thirde degree, yet temperate twixt heate and colde. **1611** SIR W. MURE *Misc. Poems* i. (*title*) Ane Conflict tuix Love and Ressoun. **1611** SHAKS. *Wint. T.* v. ii. 79 But, Oh the Noble Combat, that 'twixt Ioy and Sorrow, was fought in Paulina. **1634** SIR T. HERBERT *Trav.* 146 All the difference..twixt him and others. **1742** YOUNG *Nt. Th.* IX. 673 In thy nocturnal rove, one moment halt, 'Twixt stage and stage. **1885–94** R. BRIDGES *Eros & Psyche* May xxxi, He fondly kisst her.., And peace was 'twixt them.

† **b.** *Twixt and*, until (see BETWIXT A. 3), before. *Sc.* and *north. dial. Obs.*

**13..** *Cursor M.* 927 (Gött.) Þu sal bi þi bred ful dere, Tuix and þu again be gan. **1689** in *Acts Parlt. Scotl.* (1875) XII. 59/1 To compeir before the meetting twixt and þe 9th day of Apryle.

**c.** *Comb.*: **'twixt-brain** = *'tween-brain*: see 'TWEEN b.

**1878** BELL & LANKESTER tr. *Gegenbaur's Comp. Anat.* 503 These primitive cerebral vesicles give rise to new segments. ..The first is known as the Fore-brain or Prosencephalon; the next as the Twixt-brain or Thalamencephalon.

Also † **Twi·xten** (twyxten) *prep. Obs.* (Cf. BETWIXEN.)

*c* **1330** R. BRUNNE *Chron. Wace* (Rolls) 2282 [Lear] þoughte his doughtres gyue hosebandes, & twyxten hem parten his landes.

† **Twizeled,** *a. Obs. rare*$^{-1}$. [Perh. a survival of OE. *twisled* forked; but cf. TWIZZLE *v.*] (Meaning uncertain.)

**1685** *Lond. Gaz.* No. 2070/4 An Iron grey Gelding,..having upon each shoulder a twizeled Flower.

**Twizers,** obs. f. TWEEZERS.

**Twi·zzle,** *sb.* Chiefly *dial.* [Cf. next]

**1.** A twist or turn; a change of direction.

**1848** A. B. EVANS *Leicestersh. Words*, etc. s.v. *Twizzle*, There be so many turns and twizzles. **1876–** in dial. glossaries (Chesh., Shropsh., Warw., etc.).

**2.** In a spinning-machine, the eye of a flyer.

**1884** W. S. B. MCLAREN *Spinning* (ed. 2) 153 The flyer ..revolves 'the way the sun goes', the yarn is hooked into the flyer-eye, or twizzle, at its lower extremity.

**Twi·zzle,** *v. dial.* and *colloq.* [app. an imitative formation suggested by TWIST *v.*: cf. TWISTLE *v.*]

**1.** *intr.* To rotate rapidly, spin, twirl.

*a* **1825** FORBY *Voc. E. Anglia* s.v., He came twizzling down. **1886** P. ROBINSON *Valley Teet. Trees* 126 But those on the more exposed spots were fairly 'twizzling' like tops. **1898** KIPLING in *Morn. Post* 11 Nov. 5/2 From 6 to 10 p.m. one screw twizzled for the most part in the circumambient ether. **1908** W. W. JACOBS *Salthaven* ii, I suppose you never twizzle round on your chair.

**2.** *trans.* To twirl, twist; to turn round; to form by twisting.

**1854** BAKER *Northampt. Gloss.*, *Twizzle*, to twist, to twirl. Variously applied...Corn that is beat about by the wind in different directions, till it is twisted and entangled, is said to be *twizzled.* **1866** BROGDEN *Linc. Gloss.*, I have twizzled all the cotton. **1887** C. KEENE *Let.* in *Life* xii. (1892) 391 My friends directly after breakfast began twizzling up cigarettes. **1888** F. BARRETT *Recoiling Vengeance* vi, The girl he loved was being hugged and twizzled round by his rival. **1890** *N. & Q.* 7th Ser. IX. 138/1 If a couple of waxed-ends became twizzled [in the game of 'cob-nut']. **1905** *Longm. Mag.* June 134 'Shall us come and twizzle th' old churn?'

**Twizzle,** variant of TWISEL.

**Twke,** obs. Sc. pa. t. of TAKE *v.*

**Twm, twme, Twn,** obs. Sc. ff. TOOM, TON, TUN. **Twne,** obs. Sc. f. TIN, TUN.

**Two** (tū), *numeral a.*, *sb.* (*adv.*) Forms: see below; also TWAIN, TWAY. [OE. *twá* fem. and neut., *tú* neut., of the numeral of which the masc. *twégen* survives as TWAIN and TWAY. The forms in the cognate languages which more or less closely correspond to OE. *twá* and *tú* are OFris. *twâ* fem. and neut. (WFris. *twa*, EFris. *twô*, NFris. *tâw*, *tau*, *tô*, *tû*), MDu. and Du. *twee*, OS. *twâ*, *twô* fem., *twê* neut. (MLG. *twô*, *twu* fem., *twê* neut.; LG. *twê*, *twe*), OHG. *zwâ*, *zwô* fem., *zwei* neut. (MHG. *zwô*, *zwei*, G. *zwei*), ON. and Icel. *tveir* masc., *tvær* fem., *tvau* (*tvö*) neut. (Norw. dial. *tvei*, *tvæ*, *tvo*, *tvau*, etc.; Sw. *två*, Da. *to*), Goth. *twai* masc., *twōs* fem., *twa* neut. (For the forms corresponding to the OE. masc. *twégen* see TWAIN.) The word is common to all the Indo-European languages, as Skr. *dwau* masc., *dwē* fem. and neut., Gr. δύο, L. *duo*, OIr. *dá*, Lith. *du*, *dvi*, etc.

The genitive and dative forms (see A. 2 and A. 3) did not survive beyond the 13th century.

The pronunc. (*tū*), like that of *who* (hū) from OE. *hwá*, is due to labialization of the vowel by the *w* (cf. *womb*), which then disappeared before the related sound. The successive stages would thus be (twā, twǭ, twō, twū, tū).]

**A.** Illustration of Forms.

**1.** *nom.* and *acc.* **a.** 1, 4–5, *Sc.* 6 **tua**, 1–5, *dial.* -9, *Sc.* 5– **twa** (6 *Sc.* **thwa**), 8–9 *dial.* **twaa**; 7 *Sc.* **tuae**, 8– *Sc.* **twae**, 9 *north. dial.* **tweae, twea, tweea, twee.** (See also TWAY.)

The later Sc., and rare northern Eng., *twa* (twā, twǭ) in place of *twae*, *twea*, etc., is abnormal, but has parallels in *wha* WHO, and NA *adv.*$^2$ Examples are given under (*b*) below.

*Beowulf* 1194 Earmhreade twa. *a* **831** in *O. E. Texts* 444 An hriðer..& tua flicca. *Ibid.*, Fore Osuulfes sawle twa messan. *c* **893** K. ÆLFRED *Oros.* III. ii. § 1 Tua byriᵹ..on eorþan besuncon. *c* **1000** *Ags. Gosp.* Luke xvii. 35 Twa beoð ætgædere grindende. *c* **1000** ÆLFRIC *Gen.* xxv. 23 Twa þeoda..and twa folc. *Ibid.* xxvii. 9 Bring me twa þa betstan tyccenu. **1154** *O. E. Chron.* an. 1137 Ʒif twa men oþer III coman ridend to an tun. *c* **1230** *Hali Meid.* 35 Gulteð o twa half. *a* **1300** Tua [see B. I. 5 a]. **1340** HAMPOLE *Pr. Consc.* 987 Þe tother world..In twa partes divised may be. **1375** BARBOUR *Bruce* II. 234 Twa Erlis alsua with him war. *c* **1470** [see B. I. 2]. **1483** *Cath. Angl.* 398/2 Twa,..*duo.* **1513** DOUGLAS *Æneis* v. Prol. 17 Tua appetitis vneith accordis with vther. **1540** *Registr. Aberdon.* (Maitl. Cl.) I. 416 Mortificatioun..of thwa merkis ȝerelie. **1596** DALRYMPLE tr. *Leslie's Hist. Scot.* (S. T. S.) I. 3 The tua partes..ar called..from..the first tua sones. *c* **1620** HUME *Brit. Tongue* (1865) 8 Of this letter the latines themselfes had tuae other sounds. **1721** RAMSAY *Bessy Bell & Mary Gray* 27 Our fancies jee between you twae [*rime* Gray]. **1789** BURNS *Five Carlins* vii, But nae ane could their fancy please, O ne'er a ane but twae. **1802** ANDERSON *Cumbld. Ball., Nichol the Newsmonger* vii, I've twee, nit aw England can bang them. **1825** BROCKETT *N. C. Words*, Twea, twee, two. **1851** *Cumberld. Gloss.*, *Twea*, two. **1901** W. LAIDLAW *Poetry & Prose* 34 Twae windows. *Ibid.* 35 The twae were kind to ane an' a'.

(*b*) **1721** RAMSAY *Lucky Spence* xiii, I..whistl'd ben whiles ane, whiles twa. **1780** J. MAYNE *Siller Gun* I. xxvii, His Craft, the Hammermen, fu' braw, Led the Procession, twa and twa. **1815** SCOTT *Guy M.* xxii, I have six terriers at hame, forbye twa couple of slowhounds. **1828** *Craven Gloss.*, *Twaa*, two.

**β.** 3– two, 4–7 tuo, twoo, (5 thwo); *pl.* 7 twoes, 7–8 two's, 9 twos.

*c* **1200** *Trin. Coll. Hom.* 47 Two turtle briddes, ȝif hie was poure two duue briddes. ? *a* **1300** *Shires & Hundreds Eng.* in *O. E. Misc.* 145 Þis bis[co]pryche wes hwylen two bispriche. **13..** *Cursor M.* 16814 + 18 Vnto þe theues twoo [*rime* froo]. *c* **1330** R. BRUNNE *Chron.* (1810) 282 Tuo watres þer er togidir gon. *c* **1400** *Apol. Loll.* 38 Boþ thwo are dedly synne. *c* **1400** *Laud Troy-bk.* 18599 That the traytoures bothe two [*rime* so]. *c* **1420** *Chron. Vilod.* 3769 He hadde y-fedryde to-gedur his leygus two [*rime* þo]. **1447** BOKENHAM *Seyntys* (Roxb.) 75 For victory of tuo mo she must have. *a* **1548** Twoo [see B. I. 3 b]. **1560** DAUS tr. *Sleidane's Comm.* Pref. 4 It is set-forth..by mo than one or two. **1605** CAMDEN *Rem.* 191 Twoo Monkes. **1611** Twoes [see B. II. 2]. *c* **1620** A. HUME *Brit. Tongue* (1865) 16 At one consonant,..or at tuo consonantes. *c* **1659** *Roxb. Ball.* (1887) VI. 324 Here's a health to the Figure of Two [*rime* adieu]. **1697** [see B. I. 2 d]. **1845** BROWNING *Time's Revenges* 22, I am as sure that this he would do, As that Saint Paul's is striking two.

**γ.** 1 tuu, 1, 4 tu, 4–7 tow (5 thow, 6–7 towe). *Tu, tuu,* was only neuter in OE., in ME. *tow* was general in some dialects.

*c* **825** *Vesp. Psalter* lxi. 12 Tu [*L. duo*] ðas ic ȝeherde. *c* **887** *O. E. Chron.* an. 887 (Parker MS.) And tu [*Laud MS.* twa] folc-ȝefeoht ȝefuhton. *c* **890** tr. *Bæda's Hist.* III. xv. [xxi.] (1890) 222 Aan biscop sceolde beon ofer tuu folc. *a* **950** *Rituale Dunelm.* (Surtees) 106 Voeron..tvv in lichome anvm. *c* **950** *Lindisf. Gosp.* Matt. xxiv. 41 Tuu wif ȝegrundon on coernae. **13..** *Cursor M.* 16786 (Gött.) Þe stanes brast, þe temple clef in tu [*Trin.* in two]. **13..** *E. E. Allit. P.* B. 866, I haf a tresor in my telde of tow my fayre deȝter. **1422** tr. *Secreta Secret., Priv. Priv.* 164 The thow Sharpe eggis of youre Swerde. *c* **1440** *York Myst.* xix. 86 Tow townes betwene. **1510** in *10th Rep. Hist. MSS. Comm.* App. v. 394 Every couper shall gyve towe toune hopis for a penye. **1536** *Exhort. to North* 64 in Furnivall *Ball. fr. MSS.* I. 306 Bothe nowghty cromwell and the chancelleres towe [*rime* knowe]. **1597** *Vestry Bks.* (Surtees) 127 Paid..for mending of tow baudrigs to the bells, xv d. **1602** CAREW *Eng. Tongue* ℙ 19 Yf, like towe Turkeyes,..wee match it with our neighboures. **1666** WOOD *Life* 11 Dec. (O.H.S.) II. 95, I walked tow dayes before in the garden.

**δ.** 2–6 to, 4–6 too, 5–6 toe (6 tooe).

**1154** *O. E. Chron.* an. 1137 To munekes him namen and bebyried him. **1297** R. GLOUC. (Rolls) 11150 Wiþoute þe toun to mile. *c* **1330** R. BRUNNE *Chron. Wace* (Rolls) 330 Com of hym to noble sones. *c* **1400** Too [see B. I. 3 a]. *c* **1420** *Anturs of Arth.* xl. (Ireland MS.) Syxti maylis and moe, The squrd squappes in toe, His canel-bone allsoe. *c* **1440** *Promp. Parv.* 495/1 To, or tweyne (*K.* to, nowmere), *duo.* *c* **1460** J. METHAM *Wks.* (E.E.T.S.) 61/1625 Amoryus and Cleopes must dye ther with both to [*rime* so]. *a* **1500** *Brome Bk.* 17 Ȝe that haue sys, dewes, and too [*rime* goo]. *a* **1552** LELAND *Itin.* (1907) II. 141, I saw to antique heddes. **1552–3** *Inv. Ch. Goods, Staffs.* in *Ann. Lichfield* IV. 85 Tooe ornaments of dornex. **1558** in Feuillerat *Revels Q. Eliz.* (1908) 88 Syse, toe pannes—iiijd. **1567** DRANT *Horace, Epist.* II. ii. H iv, Too Orators..th' one was to the other..a faste ytrothed brother.

**2.** *genitive.* 1 tweȝa (twoeȝa), tweȝea, tweaȝea, tueȝa; tweȝra (twoeȝra, tuoeȝara), 2 tweiȝre, 2–3 tweire, 3 tweyre, twere.

*Beowulf* 2531 Uncer tweȝa. *c* **825** *Vesp. Hymns* vi. 2 In midle twoeȝa netna [*duorum animalium*] cuðas. *c* **890** tr. *Bæda's Hist.* I. xvi. [xxvii.] (1890) 70 Tweȝra ȝebroðra bearn oððe tweȝea ȝesweostra sunu & dohtor. *c* **897** K. ÆLFRED *Gregory's Past. C.* xiv. 86 Ðæt tweaȝea [*Hatton* tweȝea] bleo godweb. *c* **950** *Lindisf. Gosp.* John viii. 17 Tuoeȝara monna uittnesa. *c* **1000** *Ags. Gosp.* Matt. xviii. 16 On tweȝra oððe þreora ȝewittnesse [*Hatton* tweiȝre]. *c* **1200** *Trin. Coll. Hom.* 95 Tweire kinne. *a* **1250** *Owl & Night.* 991 Weþer is betere of twere [*v.r.* tweyre] twom.

**b.** *possessive genitive.* 6 twoos, twooes, 7 twoes, 7– two's.

**1510–20** Twoos [see B. I. 2]. **1587** Twooes [see B. I. 5 a]. **1619** HIERON *Wks.* I. 34 After a yeare or twoes nursing. **1676** RAY *Corr.* (1848) 126 A year or two's time. **1773** Two's [see B. I. 5 a].

**3.** *dative.* 1 twæm, tuæm, 1–3 twam, 3 twom.

*Beowulf* 1191 Be þæm ȝebroðrum twæm. *c* **890** tr. *Bæda's Hist.* I. x. [xiii.] (1890) 48 Betwih him twam. *c* **1000** *Ags. Gosp.* Matt. xxii. 40 On þysum twam [*Lindisf.* tuæm; *Rushw.* twæm] bebodum. *c* **1175** *Lamb. Hom.* 133 Of twam þingen. *a* **1250** Twom [see 2 above]. *c* **1275** *Woman of Samaria* 40 in *O. E. Misc.* 85 Bi-twene þis twam volke.

**B.** Signification.

The cardinal number next after one; one added to one: denoted by the symbols 2 or II.

**I.** *adj.*

**1.** In concord with a sb. expressed.

Frequent in proverbial expressions, as *to make two bites of a cherry* (BITE *sb.* 4, CHERRY *sb.* 1 b); *to have two strings to one's bow* (Bow *sb.*[1] 4 c); *of two evils* (or *ills*) *choose the less* (EVIL *sb.* 4, ILL *sb.* 5 b); *between two fires* (FIRE *sb.* 14); *two heads are better than one* (HEAD *sb.* 62); *as like as two peas* (PEA[1] 1 c); etc.

*Two men* (quot. 1533), the *duumviri*: see DUUMVIR.

*Beowulf* 1095 Ða hie ȝetruwedon on twa healfe fæste frioðuwære. *a* **900** *O. E. Martyrol.* 21 Sept. 172 Æfter Cristes upastignesse he ȝelærde twa [*v.r.* twua] mæȝða to godes ȝeleafan. *c* **1000** *Ags. Gosp.* Luke ii. 24 Twa turtlan, oððe tweȝen culfran briddas. *c* **1175** *Lamb. Hom.* 7 Þe castel þe wes aȝeines drih[t]nes twa leornikenehtes; he bitacnet þeos world. *a* **1225** *Ancr. R.* 10 Þer beoð two dolen to two manere of men. **13..** *Coer de L.* 504 Hys schelde in twoo peces off. *c* **1400** *Destr. Troy* 310 Tow pyllers he pight..Vppon Gades groundes. *c* **1485** *Digby Myst.* I. 240 To sle all the children..within to yeer of age. **1530** PALSGR. 594/1 Two wyttes be farre better than one. **1533** BELLENDEN *Livy* III. v. (S. T. S.) I. 256 The solempne preistis, namyt the two men, war commandit to serche þe werkis of Cibil. **1611** [TARLTON] *Jests* (1844) 21 Two tailors goe to a man. **1671** MILTON *P. R.* I. 159 To conquer Sin and Death the two grand foes. *c* **1765** GRAY *Satire* 16 As like as two beans. **1850** MCCOSH *Div. Govt.* III. ii. (1874) 335 The two inductive methods of acquiring knowledge..are observation and experiment. **1875** T. W. HIGGINSON *U. S. Hist.* vii. 49 No two explorers agreed about the actual shape of the coast.

**b.** With a superlative, either following (*the two best, eldest, first, last, next,* etc.; † formerly sometimes *two the first,* etc.), or in later use preceding (*the first two,* etc.): the latter is now somewhat more usual. Cf. FIRST *a.* 2 e, LAST *a.* 1 b. So with *former, latter.* (Also *absol.,* as in 2.)

*c* **1330** R. BRUNNE *Chron.* (1810) 52 Emme þe quene..of þe whilk was born Alfred & Edward, Hardknoute þe þrid, Þe tuo first of Eilred, of Knoute Hardknoute tid. *c* **1350** *Will. Palerne* 2162 Tvo þe bremest white beres þat euer burn on loked. *c* **1471** FORTESCUE *Wks.* (1869) 459 Than nedith it, that the Kyngs Lyvelood..be gretter than the Lyvelood of two the grettest Lords in Englond. **1556** OLDE *Antichrist* 70, I haue..expounded two the furst. **1560** DAUS tr. *Sleidane's Comm.* 44 b, Which two last were not agreed vpon. **1626** BACON *Sylva* § 249 [The echo] will..report you the whole three Words; And then the two latter Words..; and then the last Word alone. **1635** J. HAYWARD tr. *Biondi's Banish'd Virg.* Ep. Ded., The translation of the two first bookes of..Sir Phillip Sydney's Arcadia. **1669**– The last two [see LAST *a.* 1 b (*b*)]. **1688** DRYDEN *Lines on Milton,* To make a third, she joined the former two. **1692** BP. PATRICK *Answ. Touchstone* xiv. 100 The two first of them. *Ibid.,* The two next. **1704**– The first two [see FIRST *a.* 2 e (*c*)]. **1805** SOUTHEY *Let.* 15 Nov., in *Life* (1850) II. 353 The two best ships in the navy. **1829** JAS. MILL *Hum. Mind* (1869) II. 329 The association theory may account for the two last, but not for the former.

**c.** *Two parts*: two out of three equal parts (cf. PART *sb.* 5), two thirds (see 3 c). Chiefly *Sc.,* usually in form *the twa part* (sometimes as one word *twapart*). So *twa daill* (DEAL *sb.*[1] 1).

**1375** BARBOUR *Bruce* v. 47 Mair than twa part [*v. r.* partis] of his rout. *Ibid.* 369 In schort tym men mycht se ly þe twapart ded, or þan deand. *c* **1475** *Rauf Coilȝear* 123 He tyt the King be the nek, twa part in tene. **1535** STEWART *Cron. Scot.* (Rolls) II. 21 He loissit be Storme of the Se the Tua Part of his Schippis. **1565** *Reg. Privy Council Scot.* I. 334 To confisk thair gudis, the twa daill to the Quenis Majesteis behuif, and the thrid to the conservatour. *c* **1611** CHAPMAN *Iliad* x. 223 Two parts of night are past, the third is left. **1637–50** ROW *Hist. Kirk* (Wodrow Soc.) 36 Shall Papists peaceablie possess a twa-part of the patrimonie of the Kirk..., and shall Christ's Ministers..not have a third? **1678** SIR G. MACKENZIE *Crim. Laws Scot.* I. xxiii. § 7 (1699) 118 The two part thereof belongs to the King, and the third to the Sheriffs. **1808–25** JAMIESON, *Twa part, twaparte,* two thirds...This mode of expression is still quite common. ..*The twa part and third,* i. e., two thirds, and the remaining one.

**d.** *Two times* as advb. phr. (expressing repetition or multiplication) is now used only with a demonstrative or defining word; otherwise *twice* is substituted: see TWICE.

*a* **1450** *Knt. de la Tour* (1906) 43 The auicion come to hem bi two tymes. *c* **1489** CAXTON *Sonnes of Aymon* iii. 67 He was discomfyted two tymes. **1535** COVERDALE *Ecclus.* xlv. 14 Daylie perfourmed he his burntofferinges two tymes. **1574** HELLOWES *Gueuara's Fam. Ep.* (1577) 112 Two times I haue moued the Cardinal Tortosa in your busines. *Mod.* I have known it happen two separate times. I called upon him three times, but saw him only once; the other two times he was away.

**e.** As ordinal: = SECOND *a.* 1. Now only after the sb. (also *number two*); cf. II. 1 c.

**1586** W. WEBBE *Eng. Poetrie* (Arb.) 62 Make short either the two, foure, sixe, eight, tenne, twelue sillable. **1824** DE QUINCEY *Templars' Dial. Pol. Econ.* vi. § 2 in *Misc.* (1854) 251 Column two. **1911** *Act 1 & 2 Geo. V,* c. 14 § 1 The additional duty..imposed by the second paragraph of section two of that Act. *Mod.* Hymn number two.

**2.** *absol.* with ellipsis of sb. (which may usually be supplied from context; also often = 'two persons'), or after a pronoun or demonstrative, or as predicate. (For *both two* see BOTH A. 7.)

Also in proverbial expressions, as *two can play at that game*; *two's company, three's none* (COMPANY *sb.* 1 d).

*c* **882** *O. E. Chron.* an. 882 (Parker MS.) Ælfred..þara scipa tu [*Laud MS.* twa] ȝenam. *c* **890** tr. *Bæda's Hist.* I. xvi. [xxvii.] (1890) 70 Wer & wiif, heo tu beoð in anum lichoman. *c* **1175** *Lamb. Hom.* 31 He wule..eaten..et ane mele swa muchel swa et twam. *c* **1200** ORMIN 429 Swa ne didenn nohht ta twa. *a* **1225** *Ancr. R.* 202 Uor monie reisuns...Two ich chulle siggen. *Ibid.* 406, I þisse tweire monglunge. *a* **1300** *Cursor M.* 308 (Cott.) Þe hali gost comms of hem tua. *a* **1375** *Joseph Arim.* 184 Þe bark of þat on semede dimmore þen of þe oþer two. *c* **1425** *Cast. Persev.* 679 in *Macro Plays* 97 To may not to-gedyr stonde, but I, Bakbyter, be þe thyrde. *c* **1470** HENRY *Wallace* IV. 781 Twa him beheld, and said: 'We will go se'. **1510–20** *Compl. too late maryed* (1862) 3, I wyll..a wyfe to me take For to increase both our twoos lynage. **1535** COVERDALE *Eccl.* iv. 9 Two are better then one. **1556** *Chron. Gr. Friars* (Camden) 55 Too of the men that labord at yt. **1560** BIBLE (Genev.) *Amos* iii. 3 Can two walke together except thei be agreed? **1596** DALRYMPLE tr. *Leslie's Hist. Scot.* v. (S. T. S.) I. 298 Ilk of the tua slayis othir. *c* **1610** *Women Saints* 166 Committed to our twoes knowledge onelie. **1612** COLSON *Gen. Tresury* A j b, The generall parts..are only two, or of two sorts. *c* **1620** A. HUME *Brit. Tongue* (1865) 1 Nae tuae of the tuentie..wald agree. **1653** W. RAMESEY *Astrol. Restored* 335 Here is two to two,..we stand upon equal terms. **1768** PENNANT *Zool.* II. 363 The males, or Ruffs, assume such variety of colors..that it is scarce possible to see two alike. **1779** WARNER in Jesse *Selwyn & Contemp.* (1844) IV. 101 The Ministry carried it two to one. **1820** KEATS *Hyperion* I. 85 These two were postured motionless. **1847** HELPS *Friends in C.* I. vi. 94 What do you two..think about representative government? **18..** FLOR. MARRYAT (Dixon), Now, don't you call me any names, or you will find that two can play at that game. **1875** TENNYSON *Q. Mary* I. iv, The two were fellow-prisoners.

**b.** With ellipsis of *hours,* in stating the time of day; also *two o'clock.* Also with ellipsis of *years* (of age), as *a child of two.*

*c* **1485** in *Digby Myst.* (1882) 167 At the parvyse I wyll be.., be-twyn two and three. **1510** *Sel. Cases Star Chamb.* (Selden) II. 72 Abowt twoo of the Clok in the nyght. **1600** SHAKS. *A. Y. L.* IV. i. 183 By two a clock I will be with thee againe. **1795** MACNEILL *Will & Jean* xlvi, Now that nightly meetings Sat and drank frae sax till twa. **1799** WORDSW. *Lucy Gray* v, The minster-clock has just struck two. **1884** A. WAINWRIGHT in *Harper's Mag.* July 272/1 From two o'clock..until 'two-fifteen', the 'two-twenty' train gradually fills.

**c.** *In* († *on*) *two* (after vbs. expressing division or the like): into or in two parts or pieces. (See also A-TWO.)

*c* **890** *O. E. Chron.* an. 885 (Parker MS.) Her to dælde se fore sprecena here on tu [*v. r.* twa]. *c* **1000** *Ags. Gosp.* Mark xv. 38 Þæs temples wah-rift wæs tosliten on twa [*Lindisf. & Rushw.* in tuu]. *c* **1275** *Passion of our Lord* 448 in *O. E. Misc.* 50 Hi nolden hyne nouht delen a to ne a þreo. *a* **1300** *Cursor M.* 1957 (Cott.) O beist has clouen fote in tua [*v. rr.* to, two]. *c* **1400** *Laud Troy Bk.* 5942 Ther he smot on-two his polle. **1535** COVERDALE 1 *Sam.* ii. 31, I wyll breake thyne arme in two. **1623** GOUGE *Serm. Extent God's Provid.* § 15 The massy timber shivered in two. **1794–5** in B. Ward *Dawn Cath. Revival* (1909) II. 119 A Collier's vessel fell foul of ours, and broke the cable in two. **1805** MCINDOE *Poems* 107 This trout..Was faulded in twa like a speldin.

† (*b*) So as to be separate the one from the other; asunder, apart. *Obs.*

*c* **897** K. ÆLFRED *Gregory's Past. C.* vii. 49 Ðeah heo an tu tefleowe, ðeah wæs sio sæpryng sio soðe lufu. *c* **1000** ÆLFRIC *Hom.* I. 388 Ða..wearð him [*sc.* Paul and Barnabas] ȝeþuht þæt hi on-twa ferdon. *c* **1430** *Syr Tryam.* 60 Betwene the quene and the kyng Was grete sorowe..When they schulde parte in twoo.

**d.** *Two and two, two by two,* formerly also *by two and two*: in groups or sets of two; two at a time; by twos.

*c* **1000** ÆLFRIC *Hom.* II. 528 He sende hi twam and twam ætforan him. *c* **1290** *S. Eng. Leg.* I. 281/109 He saiȝ þe freres go þoruȝ þe londe, two and two. **13..** *Cursor M.* 1713 Ȝee sal..tak..Beist and fouxul..Þe meke be þam ai tua and tua, Þe wild do be þam-self al-sua. *c* **1400** MAUNDEV. (Roxb.) xix. 87 Before þe chariot gase..all þe maydens of þe cuntree, twa and twa togyder. *c* **1440** CAPGRAVE *St. Kath.* IV. 1264 The clerkis eke were sette be too and too. *a* **1533** LD. BERNERS *Huon* lxii. 216 Guyer held his brother Gerames by the hande, and so all the other .ii. and .ii. *c* **1575** J. HOOKER *Life Sir P. Carew* in *Archæologia* XXVIII. 144 Foremoste wente all the soylders..by tooe and tooe. **1604** E. G[RIMSTONE] *D'Acosta's Hist. Indies* VI. xxviii. 494 They daunced two and two. **1697** DRYDEN *Virg. Georg.* III. 270 Join'd with his School-Fellows by two and two [*rime* pursue]. **1709–10** ADDISON *Tatler* No. 120 ℙ 3 Coming out Two by Two, and marching up in Pairs. **1863** STANLEY *Serm. in East* App. I. 153 We started on foot, two and two, between two files of soldiers.

† **e.** *Rule of two* (Arith.): an inclusive name for the ordinary rules for finding a third number from two given numbers, viz. those of addition, subtraction, multiplication, and division. (Cf. *rule of three,* RULE *sb.* 8 b.) *Obs. rare.*

**1612** COLSON *Gen. Tresury* A j b, The..Rules of two, of three, of Reduction. *Ibid.* Bbb j/1 The Rule of Two is by two numbers knowne to finde out the third.., and is generally of two sorts, Rationall, and Proportionall. The Rule of Two Rationall..is of two sorts,..Addition..Substraction.

**3.** Forming compound numerals.

**a.** Added to multiples of ten, as *two-and-thirty,* now usually *thirty-two*; *a hundred and two.* So formerly (now rarely) with the ordinals, as *two-and-fiftieth* (now almost always *fifty-second*).

† *Two-and-thirty, a pip out* see PIP *sb.*[2] 1 b.

*Two-and-twentieth* (*Mus.*), a note 22 diatonic degrees (= 3 octaves) above or below a given note (both notes being reckoned); hence, an interval of 3 octaves; *spec.* an organ-stop formerly used, sounding 3 octaves above the normal pitch. (Now TWENTY-SECOND.)

*c* **893** K. ÆLFRED *Oros.* VI. ii. § 1 Þara twa & twentiȝra monna. *a* **900** *O. E. Martyrol.* 29 On þone twa & twentiȝðan dæȝ. *c* **961** ÆTHELWOLD *Rule St. Benet* xiii. (1885) 37 Se twa and feowertiȝeða sealm. *c* **1200** *Trin. Coll. Hom.* 47 On þe two and þrittuðe dai. **1297** R. GLOUC. (Rolls) 11861 To & tuenti kniȝtes. *c* **1380** *Antecrist* in Todd 3 *Treat. Wyclif* 121 In þe two and þritti boke. *c* **1400** *Destr. Troy*

2747 There were twenty and too. 1488–92 *Acc. Ld. High Treas. Scot.* I. 80 Sex score twa bedis and a knop. 1579 FULKE *Heskins' Parl.* 201 The two and twentieth Chapter. 1613 *Organ Specif. Worcester Cathedral*, In the chaire organ 1 flute of wood, 1 two and twentith of mettal. 1768 FOOTE *Devil on 2 Sticks* III. Wks. 1799 II. 276 The two-and-fiftieth part of a scruple. 1896 MRS. CAFFYN *Quaker Grandmother* 137 Two-and-thirty last March.

**b.** As multiplier before *dozen*, *score*, or before *hundred*, *thousand*, *million*, etc., or the ordinals of these.

Also in comb., as *two-hundred-mile-long* adj.; *two-hundred-pound* adj. (weighing, or costing, two hundred pounds).

*a* 900 *Cædmon's Exod.* 184 (Gr.) Hæfde him alesen leoda duȝeðe tireadiȝra twa þusendo. *c* 1000 *Ags. Gosp.* John vi. 7 On tweȝera hundred peneȝa wurþe. *c* 1205 LAY. 1556 Þa he hefde twa [*c* 1275 two] hundred mid sweorde to-hewen. *c* 1290 *S. Eng. Leg.* I. 91/145 In þe to hondrede ȝere. *a* 1548 HALL *Chron., Hen. VIII*, 147 b, Twoo hundred thousande Crounes. 1807 HERSCHEL in *Phil. Trans.* XCVII. 228 Its thickness at one end was 33, and at the other 31 two-hundredths of an inch. 1867 THIRLWALL *Lett.* (1881) II. 118 The two hundred mile long iceberg is still afloat. 1895 MRS. B. M. CROKER *Village Tales* (1896) 122 Tall and erect, ..carrying his two-score years with grace. 1897 *Outing* (U.S.) XXIX. 439/1 A two-hundred-pound buck.

**c.** As multiplier before an ordinal expressing an aliquot part (i. e. as numerator of a fraction), as *two-thirds*; also *attrib.* as *a two-thirds majority*.

[*c* 1643 LD. HERBERT *Autobiog.* (1824) 64 The other two third parts.] 1776 ADAM SMITH *W. N.* I. xi. III. (1869) I. 241 In the Saxon times the fleece was estimated at two-fifths of the value of the whole sheep. 1777 ROBERTSON *Hist. Amer.* (1783) III. 263 All laws..must be approved of by two-thirds of the members. 1888 RUTLEY *Rock-Forming Min.* 3 The wire is then bent to about two-thirds of a circle. 1910 H. W. STEED in *Encycl. Brit.* III. 38/2 The German parties ..stipulated that a two-thirds majority should be necessary for any alteration of the law.

**4.** In pregnant sense: = Two different, two distinct.

*To be in two minds*: see MIND *sb.*[1] 11 e.

1570 T. WILSON *Demosthenes* 42 *margin*, To say and to do are two things. 1603 SHAKS. *Meas. for M.* II. iv. 112 Ignomie in ransome, and free pardon Are of two houses. 1754 RICHARDSON *Grandison* (1811) I. xii. 71 A learned man and a linguist may very well be two persons. 1797 BURKE *Regic. Peace* iii. Wks. VIII. 273 But reason of state and common sense are two things. 1865 RUSKIN *Sesame* i. § 25 There need be no two opinions about these proceedings. 1895 G. S. STREET *Episodes* 134 Gerald in town and Gerald in the country were two people.

†**b.** *predicatively*: Discordant, disagreeing, at variance. (Cf. ONE 14, TWAIN B. 3 a.) *Obs.*

*c* 1645 HOWELL *Lett.* (1892) II. 547 The Author thereof and I are two in point of opinion. 1738 SWIFT *Pol. Conversat.* 105 When did you see your old Acquaintance, Mrs. Cloudy? You and She are Two, I hear.

**5. a.** *A ... or two*: an indefinite small number of (the things denoted by the sb.); one or two of...; a few... (For *one or two* see ONE B. I. 2 c.)

The whole phrase may take the possessive inflexion, as *a year or two's experience* = the experience of a year or two.

*a* 1300 *Cursor M.* 4342 (Cott.) Spek wit me a word or tua. 1543 *Sel. Cases Star Chamb.* (Selden) II. 267 A moneth or Towe before the said Faire. 1587 FLEMING *Contn. Holinshed* III. 1419/1 After a daie or twooes tariance. 1615–16 in J. C. Jeaffreson *Middlesex Co. Rec.* (1886) II. 113 To answere the causing of a tumult.., a poore man or two being much hurt. 1773 GOLDSM. *Stoops to Conq.* v. i, An hour or two's laughing with my daughter. 1861 M. PATTISON *Ess.* (1889) I. 45 The garden, where a vine or two and some of the finer sorts of fruit were trained.

**b.** *Two or three* (dial. *two-three*, Sc. *twa-three*): an indefinite (small or inconsiderable) number (of); a few.

1500–20 DUNBAR *Poems* lxxi. 4 Ȝeiris and dayis mo than two or thre. 1557 *Peebles Burgh Rec.* (1872) 240 The baillies, accumpanit with the thesaurare and tua thre honest men. 1669 *Extr. S. P. rel. Friends* IV. (1913) 296 Here is many theeues and two Three murtherers and aboue thirty quakers in the Castle. 1670 LADY MARY BERTIE in *12th Rep. Hist. MSS. Comm.* App. v. 21 The under pettycoatt very richly laced with two or three sorts of lace. 1785 BURNS *Death & Dr. Hornbk.* xxiv, In twa-three year. 1843 BORROW *Bible in Spain* xxviii. (Pelh. Libr.) 198 The walls being covered with books except in two or three places. 1893 STEVENSON *Catriona* xv. 166 She was daundering on the craigs wi' twa-three sodgers.

**c.** So rarely *two* simply.

1661 in *Extr. S. P. rel. Friends* II. (1911) 136 We humbly intreate two lynes from your hands.

**II.** *sb.*

**1.** The abstract number equal to one and one. Also in phrases, as *two and two make four*, used as a typically obvious or undeniable statement; *to put two and two together*, to consider two or several facts together and draw an inference; to reason about something and come to a conclusion (cf. PUT *v.* 52 e).

1697 COLLIER *Ess. Mor. Subj.* II. (1703) 85 The..notion.. is as clear as that two and two makes four. 1848 THACKERAY *Bk. Snobs* xvii, When will you acknowledge that two and two make four, and call a pikestaff a pikestaff? 1855 — *Newcomes* xlix, Putting two and two together..it was not difficult..to guess who the expected Marquis was. 1875 WHITNEY *Life Lang.* 279 Mathematics began with the apprehension that one and one are two. 1898 W. W. JACOBS *Sea Urchins, Disbursem. Sheet* (1906) 138 Twenty-eight twos equals fifty-six.

**b.** The figure (2) denoting this number.

1877 *Daily News* 21 Nov. 5/5 Two and two don't always make four, but sometimes 22. 1886 *Punch* 23 Feb. 84/2 '2222'. Four twos!

**c.** A person or thing denoted by this number, usually as being the second in a series. Also *number two*.

1890 [see NUMBER *sb.* 5]. 1890 *Eng. Illustr. Mag.* Apr. 499 Smith who rowed two in the last University race.

**2.** A group or set of two persons or things; a pair, couple. Usually in *pl.*

*a* 1585 POLWART *Flyting w. Montgomerie* 208 In anes and twaes. 1611 SHAKS. *Wint. T.* I. ii. 438 By twoes, and threes. 1625 in Rymer *Foedera* (1726) XVIII. 237/1 Eighte greate Rocke Rubies and twenty greate Pearles sett in twoes. *a* 1758 RAMSAY *Fables* xvii. 20 Pike out joys by twas and threes. 1865 KINGSLEY *Herew.* xxxiv, They would lodge by twos and threes..in the lonely farmhouse. 1902 VIOLET JACOB *Sheep-Stealers* ix, The people dispersed in twos and threes.

**b.** A card or domino, or the side of a die, marked with two pips or spots.

*a* 1500 *Brome Bk.* 17 Ȝe that haue sys, dewes, and too. 1680 COTTON *Compl. Gamester* (ed. 2) 12 You have..turn'd up two two's, or two treys. *Mod.* He took the trick with the two of trumps.

**c.** In military drill, A set of two men forming a unit in wheeling.

1796 *Instr. & Reg. Cavalry* (1813) 106 The two's must first wheel up, and then break into three's, and close up. 1833 *Regul. Instr. Cavalry* I. Plate 16 Twos from the Right at three horses length distance.

**d.** *Cricket.* A hit for which two runs are scored.

1881 *Daily News* 21 June 3/7 A capital innings, which included seven fours, a three, and four twos.

**e.** *slang* or *colloq.* Two pennyworth (of spirits).

1894 HENTY *Dorothy's Double* i, I don't mind if I do take a two of gin with you. 1896 *Daily News* 23 Sept. 3/5 He had had six twos of whiskey.

**f.** *Two-at-length*, a tandem.

1823 E. NARES *Heraldic Anomalies* (1824) I. 355 Driving their fours-in-hand, and twos-at-length.

**g.** *In two twos*: in a very short time; directly, immediately. *slang* or *colloq.*

1838 HALIBURTON *Clockm.* Ser. II. xiv. 211 The press can lash us up to a fury here in two twos any day. *Ibid.* xxi. 315 They'd soon set these matters right in two twos. 1882 STEVENSON *New Arab. Nts.* II. 112 The business was over in two twos.

†**III.** *adv.* = TWICE 2; followed by *so* and a word expressing quantity = twice as (much, etc.). *Obs.*

*c* 900 *O. E. Chron.* an. 897 Lang scipu..þa wæron fulneah tu swa lange swa þa oðru. 13.. *Coer de L.* 3128 The hethenes wer twoo so fele. *c* 1350 *Lybeaus Disc.* 1446 Now am y two so lyght. *c* 1420 *Sir Amadace* (Camden) l, He wold gif hom toe so muche..As any lord.

**IV.** Combinations (unlimited in number; the following are examples).

**1. a.** Adjectives formed of *two* with a sb. in sense 'of, pertaining to, consisting of, having, containing, measuring, etc. two of the things named', as *two-anna* (of the value of two annas), *-bond*, *-bout* (formed by two bouts of the plough), *-bushel*, *-cent*, *-chamber*, *-cylinder*, *-day*, *-deck*, *-figure*, *-floor*, *-fluid*, *-gallon*, *-groove*, *-guinea*, *-hour*, *-inch*, †*-kind*, *-light* (LIGHT *sb.* 10), *-man*, *-mast*, *-mile*, *-minute*, *-needle(s)*, *-ounce*, *-party*, *-phase* (PHASE 3; cf. THREE-*phase*), *-ply* (PLY *sb.* 1), *-pound*, *-quart*, *-rail*, *-room*, *-row*, *-shilling*, *-speed*, *-stall*, *-story*, *-stroke*, *-syllable*, *-wheel*. **b.** Parasynthetic adjectives formed on similar collocations, usually with -ED [2], in sense 'having or characterized by two of the things named', as *two-arched*, *-armed*, *-barred*, *-barrelled*, *-bedded*, *-bristled*, *-capsuled*, *-celled*, *-chambered*, *-coloured*, *-dimensioned*, *-flowered*, *-formed*, *-grained*, *-grooved*, *-handled*, *-horned*, *-humped*, *-lobed*, *-masted*, *-membered*, *-named*, *-necked*, *-nerved*, *-oared*, *-peaked*, *-petaled*, *-pronged*, *-ranked*, *-roomed*, *-rowed*, *-seeded*, *-shanked*, *-shaped*, *-spined*, *-spotted*, *-stalled*, *-storied*, *-stringed*, *-tined*, *-toed*, *-toothed*, *-topped*, *-valved*, *-wheeled*, *-winged*; also with other endings, as *two-dimensional*, *-handy* (see TWO-HANDED), *-monthly* (see 2). **c.** Parasynthetic sbs. in -ER [1], as *two-feeder*, *two-master* (a two-masted vessel), *-mover* (MOVER [1] 7), *-pounder*, *-sticker* (colloq. = two-master), *-wheeler*; see also **two-yearer** in 2, TWO-DECKER, TWO-HANDER. **d.** Adjectives formed of *two* in adverbial relation to an adj. or pple. (= in two, doubly), as *two-cleft*, *-ploughed*, *-soused*, *-twisted*: see also **two-high** in 2, TWO-FORKED, TWO-PARTED. **e.** Adjs. and sbs. formed from phrases, as *two-and-a-half-inch*, *two-days-old*, *two-feet-nine* adjs.; † *two-face-bearer* (cf. TWO-FACED), *two-pound-tenner*.

1899 *Westm. Gaz.* 9 Feb. 4/2 That hatch was of *two-and-a-half inch teak. 1882 F. M. CRAWFORD *Mr. Isaacs* xi, A *two-anna bit. 1897 W. C. HAZLITT *4 Generations* II. 183 The *two-arched bridge at Rugby. 1725 RAMSAY *Gentle Sheph.* v. iii. Prol., Sir William fills the *twa-arm'd chair. 1894 R. B. SHARPE *Handbk. Birds Gt. Brit.* I. 59 The *two-barred Crossbill. *Loxia bifasciata.* 1852 MUNDY *Our Antipodes* (1857) 114 *Two-barrelled guns. 1843 BORROW *Bible in Spain* vii. 42 A large *two-bedded room. 1900 *Daily News* 13 Oct. 6/4 The propeller is *two-bladed. 1674 RAY *Collect. Words, Mann. Wire Work* 133 A *two-bond wire as big as a great pack-thread. 1805 R. W. DICKSON *Pract. Agric.* I. 409 The *two-bout ridges, as they are called, may be the most advantageous. 1681 GREW *Musæum* I. VII. i. 156 The *Two-Bristled-Fly. 1796 W. H. MARSHALL *W. England* II. 61 The Corn Market well filled with long *two-bushel bags; chiefly of wheat. 1793 MARTYN *Lang. Bot.*, *Two-capsuled. *Ibid.*, *Bilocular* pericarp.. *two-celled, divided into two cells internally... Some seeds are also two-celled. 1902 ELIZ. L. BANKS *Newspaper Girl* xiv, Dinah got a letter through the American mail. She had fivepence to pay on it, because only a common *two-cent stamp had been stuck on it. 1898 *Daily News* 16 Feb. 7/6 The advantages or disadvantages of a bi-cameral system, ..a *two-Chamber system. 1851 RICHARDSON *Geol.* viii. (1855) 229 A *two-chambered heart. 1888 BRYCE *Amer. Commw.* II. II. xl. 86 Its two-chambered legislature. 1793 MARTYN *Lang. Bot.*, **Two-cleft*, or *Bifid...Utricularia* is an instance of the two-cleft perianth. 1648 HEXHAM II, *Twee-verwigh*, *Two-coloured, or Partie-coloured. 1827 GRIFFITH *Cuvier's Anim. Kingd.* V. 251 *Sciurus Bicolor* (Two-coloured Squirrel). 1885 W. PATER *Marius* II. xx, A two-sided or two-coloured thing. 1901 *Westm. Gaz.* 9 Dec. 8/2 Rigal, on his *two-cylinder, 12-h.p. tricycle. 1898 *Harper's Mag.* XCVI. 829 They..can only make *two-day..cruises. 1868 SWINBURNE *Blake* 9 The *two-days-old baby. 1797 *Encycl. Brit.* (ed. 3) XVII. 403/2 In all *two-deck ships it [the fire hearth] is placed under the forecastle. 1898 SIR W. CROOKES in *Daily News* 8 Sept. 6/3, I was like some *two-dimensional being who might stand at the singular point of a Riemann's surface, and thus find himself in ..inexplicable contact with a plane of existence not his own. 1885 W. K. CLIFFORD *Common Sense Exact Sc.* 223 *Two-dimensioned space. *c* 1515 *Cocke Lorell's B.* 11 Flaterers, and *two face berers. 1886 *Daily News* 18 Oct. 7/2 News Machine Wanted, fast *two-feeder. 1905 *Daily Chron.* 13 July 5/1 What is known as the *two-feet-nine seam. 1890 W. J. GORDON *Foundry* 223 The percentage of profit..may be a fraction with a *two-figure denominator. 1898 F. M. HUEFFER in *Contemp. Rev.* Aug. 182 A two-figure sketch by Burne-Jones. 1900 *Daily News* 11 July 7/5 A..*two-floor building. 1793 MARTYN *Lang. Bot.*, *Two-flowered peduncle. 1909 *Daily Chron.* 20 Mar. 3/5 Here you first find the two-flowered yellow violet..3,500 feet above the level of the sea. 1866 R. M. FERGUSON *Electr.* (1870) § 31 The *two-fluid theory of Dufay and Symmers, and the one-fluid theory of Franklin. 1876 PREECE & SIVEWRIGHT *Telegraphy* 244 Two-fluid batteries. 1743 FRANCIS tr. *Hor., Odes* II. xx. 2 A *two-form'd poet. 1693 T. POWER in *Dryden's Juvenal* XII. (1697) 307 A *two Gallon Draught. 1793 MARTYN *Lang. Bot.*, *Dicoccous* or **two-grained* capsule. ..Consisting of two cohering grains or cells, with one seed in each. 1846 GREENER *Sc. Gunnery* 357 A *two-grooved rifle. 1803 HATCHETT in *Phil. Trans.* XCIII. 137 A *two-guinea piece. 1818 COBBETT *Pol. Reg.* XXXIII. 368 A man, who, bred to the bar, had never had a two-guinea fee in his life. 1839 URE *Dict. Arts* 764 The fleshing knife; a large *two-handled implement [with] which the hide is scraped. 1877 J. D. CHAMBERS *Div. Worship* 258 A two-handled Chalice. 1561 DAUS tr. *Bullinger on Apoc.* (1573) 5 b, The old seuen-headed, and the new *twohorned beast. 1628 A. LEIGHTON *Zion's Plea agst. Prelacy* ix. (1842) 121 A two-horned idol, pushing both the Church and Commonwealth. 1781 PENNANT *Hist. Quad.* I. 136 Two-horned Rhinoceros. 1793 MARTYN *Lang. Bot.*, *Bicornes* (two-horned). Plants with anthers having two horns. 1848 MILL *Pol. Econ.* II. viii. § 3 (1876) 189 A cowhouse for two-horned cattle. 1900 *Westm. Gaz.* 15 Nov. 2/1 We..did not dismount except for a *two-hour halt till three p.m. 1834 *Nat. Philos.* III. *Phys. Geog.* 55/2 (Usef. Knowl. Soc.) The *two-humped or Bactrian camel. 1639 *Crabtree Lect.* 184, I will make you looke through a *two inch boord [*i. e.* pillory]. 1748 *Anson's Voy.* III. viii. 380 A strong net-work of two inch rope. 1859 F. A. GRIFFITHS *Artil. Man.* (1862) 309 A two-inch rope means a rope two inches in circumference. 1868 *Rep. U. S. Commissioner Agric.* (1869) 328 A fountain capable of filling ..a two-inch pipe. 1613 W. BROWNE *Brit. Past.* I. iv, The *two-kinde Bat. 1882 VINES *Sachs' Bot.* 466 Divisions take place in the epidermal cells by..which the wall becomes *two-layered. 1859 CORNWALLIS *Panorama New World* I. 221 The sunshine glancing through a *two-light window. 1793 MARTYN *Lang. Bot.*, *Two-lobed leaf. 1847 W. E. STEELE *Field Bot.* 167 *Neottia*, ..lip dependant, 2-lobed. 1895 *Outing* (U.S.) XXVI. 399/1 A *two-man balloon. 1911 *Q. Rev.* Jan. 215 The two-man Government..becomes one-man Government. 1775 DALRYMPLE in *Phil. Trans.* LXVIII. 400 A small *two-mast vessel. 1774 *Hull Dock Act* 33 *Two-masted vessels. 1899 QUILLER-COUCH *Ship of Stars* xxiv, That there *two-master's got a fool for skipper. 1905 *Westm. Gaz.* 29 Nov. 2/2 A *two-membered constituency. 1909 R. LAW *Tests of Life* i. 2 Two-membered sentences. 1875 W. S. HAYWARD *Love agst. World* 117 A *two-mile spin. 1895 *Outing* (U. S.) XXVII. 48/1 A *two-minute gait [*i. e.* at the rate of a mile in 2 minutes; cf. *two-forty* in 2]. 1905 *Westm. Gaz.* 23 Dec. 2/3 There were two-minute intervals between the start of each bob. 1891 *Athenæum* 31 Jan. 148/1 Thirty-six *two-movers. 1661 T. ROSS *Silius Italicus* I. 13 By the Banks of *two-nam'd Ister. 1854 J. SCOFFERN in *Orr's Circ. Sc., Chem.* 14 The mouths of a *two-necked bottle. 1890 BILLINGS *Med. Dict.*, **Two-needles operation*, tearing through a secondary cataract by two needles introduced from opposite sides. 1891 *Cent. Dict.*, Two-needle operation. 1833 HOOKER in Smith *Eng. Flora* V. I. 85 Leaves..*two-nerved at the base. 1899 DOYLE *Duet* Ded., The little *two-oared boats. 1838 DICKENS *O. Twist* xxiii, A *two-ounce tin tea-caddy. 1901 *Edin. Rev.* Oct. 506 It is..premature to suppose..that the *two-party system has..broken up. 1861 PALEY *Æschylus* (ed. 2) *Chœroph.* 1026 *note*, The *two-peaked hill of Parnassus. 1793 MARTYN *Lang. Bot.*, *Two-petalled corolla. 1909 *Cent. Dict. Suppl.*, *Two-phase circuit..Two-phase generator..Two-phase system. 1856 *Farmer's Mag.* Jan. 20 *Two-plowed furrows (that is, one plowed under another). 1847 WEBSTER, **Two-ply*..double; consisting of two thicknesses, as cloth. 1552 HULOET, *Two pounde weight, *dipondium.* 1887 *Roy. Proclam.* in *Standard* 18 May 3/2 Every Two Pound Piece should have the same obverse and reverse impression..as the Five Pound Piece. 1771 tr. *Pernety's Voy. Malouine Isl.* in *Ann. Reg.* (1771) II. 15/1 Round stones, of the size of a *two-pounder ball. 1836–9 DICKENS *Sk. Boz, Dancing Acad.*, Mr. Augustus Cooper had ordered a new coat..a *two-pound-tenner. **1825** T. HOOK *Sayings* Ser. II. *Man of Many Fr.* (Colburn) 104 *Two-pronged forks. **1727** *Fam. Dict.* s. v. *Fryars Balsam*, Put .. into a *Two-quart-Bottle. **1844** *Port Phillip Patriot* 25 July 3/6 A *two rail fence. **1793** MARTYN *Lang. Bot.* s. v. *Distichus*, A distich or *two-ranked stem or stalk. **1857** T. MOORE *Handbk. Brit. Ferns* (ed. 3) 38 Fructification forming two-ranked simple spikes. **1897** HUGHES *Medit. Malta* etc. *Fever* ii. 62 The staff-sergeant..occupied a *two-room quarter. **1897** *Daily News* 14 Apr. 5/1 A *two-roomed home. **1868** *Rep. U. S. Commissioner Agric.* (1869) 251 The Strength of *Two-Row Hedges when Pleached. **1793** MARTYN *Lang. Bot.*, Two-ranked or *Two-rowed. **1812** SIR J. SINCLAIR *Syst. Husb. Scot.* I. 247 Two-rowed barley. **1868** *Rep. U. S. Commissioner Agric.* (1869) 249 Two-rowed hedges. **1793** MARTYN *Lang. Bot.*, *Two-seeded fruit. **1621** G. SANDYS *Ovid's Met.* VIII. (1626) 156 *Two-shankt Compasses. **1756** P. BROWNE *Jamaica* 328 The larger Passion-flower with two-shanked leaves. **1613** HEYWOOD *Silver Age* III. Wks. 1874 III. 143 The *two-shap't Centaurs. **1717** ADDISON tr. *Ovid* II. *Coronis* 29 The two-shap'd Ericthonius. **1880** *Sat. Rev.* 2 Oct. 424/1 Our *two-shilling dinner. **1882** A. SOMERVILLE in G. Smith *Mod. Apostle* x. (1891) 240 Some two-shilling pieces. *a* **1625** FLETCHER *Bloody Bro.* IV. ii, Wholsom *two-sous'd petitoes. **1875** KNIGHT *Dict. Mech.*, **Two-speed Pulley*, a variable speed arrangement consisting of two fast pulleys, the shaft of one being tubular and sleeved upon that of the other. **1888** *Encycl. Brit.* XXIII. 560 Two-speed gears. **1785** PENNANT *Arct. Zool.* II. Suppl. 132 Stickleback. *Two-spined. **1803** SHAW *Gen. Zool.* IV. 476 Two-spined Sparus. *Ibid.* 608 Two-spined Stickleback. **1802** BINGLEY *Anim. Biog.* (1813) III. 130 The seven-spotted and *two-spotted lady-bug. **1859** W. COLLINS *Q. of Hearts* I. 242 A *two-stall stable. **1833** LOUDON *Encycl. Archit.* § 1829 A *two-stalled stable. **1884** *Leisure Hour* Aug. 505/2 Of modern racing schooners..the fastest *two-sticker ever designed. **1878** SMILES *Robt. Dick* ii. 9 A *two-storied.. house. **1880** J. DUNBAR *Pract. Papermaker* 9 A *two-storey building. **1776** BURNEY *Hist. Mus.* I. 206 This dichord, or *two-stringed instrument. **1855** BAIN *Senses & Int.* I. ii. § 21. (1864) 59 The *two-stroke movement of the lungs. **1900** *Engineering Mag.* XIX. 788/1 Two-Stroke Oil Engines. **1891** S. MOSTYN *Curatica* 47 Peace be to his *manes*—this, dear ladies, is a *two-syllable word. **1601** HOLLAND *Pliny* XVIII. vi. I. 557 If it be stonie, it would be digged with a mattocke or *two tined forkes. **1781** PENNANT *Hist. Quad.* II. 496 *Two-toed S[loth] with a round head. **1872** COUES *N. Amer. Birds* 49 The two-toed birds. **1802** R. HALL *Elem. Bot.* 192 *Two-toothed, *bidentatus*. **1828** STARK *Elem. Nat. Hist.* II. 57 Shell fusiform,..aperture two-toothed. **1616** CHAPMAN *Homer's Hymne to Apollo* 47 Their farr-stretcht valleys, and their *two-topt Hill. **1636** T. HEYWOOD in *Ann. Dubrensia* (1877) 69 Two-top't Pernassus. **1902** J. TORRANCE *Story Marātha Missions* vii. 62 The two-topped hill of Sitabaldi. **1649** MILTON *Eikon.* xxvii, To whip us with his *two-twisted Scorpions, both temporal and spiritual Tyranny. **1676** HOBBES *Iliad* 375 A high *two-valved door. **1771** *Phil. Trans.* LXI. 232 Two valved shells. **1889** *Science-Gossip* XXV. 219 Fruit,.. two-valved, dehiscing longitudinally. **1800** *Hull Advertiser* 19 July 2/4 A new *two-wheel cart barrow. **1663** BUTLER *Hud.* I. II. 328 A *two-wheel'd Chariot. **1733** TULL *Horse-Hoeing Husb.* xxi. 300 A common Two-Wheel'd-Plow. **1886** C. E. PASCOE *Lond. of To-day* xliii. (ed. 3) 376 Two-wheeled cabs. **1861** *Eng. Wom. Dom. Mag.* III. 44 What they call a 'gig' in those parts—a tall *two-wheeler. **1753** CHAMBERS *Cycl. Supp.*, *Ox-fly*,..a species of *two-winged fly.

**2.** Special Combinations: **two-bill**, = TWIBILL; †**two-blade(s** = TWAYBLADE; **two-blocks** *adv.* = *block and block* (BLOCK *sb.* 5 b), *chock-a-block* (CHOCK *adv.* c); **two-bottle** *a.*, applied to one who can drink two bottles of wine at a sitting; **two-clang**, *Acoustics* [CLANG *sb.* 3], a compound tone consisting of two simple tones; **two-coat** *a.*, requiring two coats, as work in plastering and painting; **two-cycle** *a.*, completing a series of operations in two cycles or strokes, as a gas-engine; **two-eared** *a.*, having two ears; two-handled; **two-ended** *a.*, having two ends (*spec.* with different properties, as a magnet); hence **two-endedness**; **two-eyed** *a.*, having two eyes; involving or adapted for the use of both eyes; **two-eyes** (*U.S. local*) = *twinberry* (see TWIN C.), from the two calyx-marks on the fruit (*Cent. Dict.* 1891); **two-field** *a.*, denoting a system of agriculture in which two fields are cropped and fallowed alternately; **two-finger**, one of a tribe in Surinam with deficient hands and feet (see quot.); **two-fisted** *a.* (*dial.* or *colloq.*), awkward with the hands, clumsy; **two-for-his-heels**, used jocularly for 'knave' (in allusion to the expression for the dealer's score on turning up a knave at cribbage: see HEEL *sb.*[1] 1 d); **two-forty**, *U.S. colloq.*, an expression for a high speed (properly, at the rate of a mile in 2 min. 40 sec., formerly a 'record' pace for trotting); **two-four** (usually $\frac{2}{4}$), *Mus.*, denoting a 'time' or rhythm with two crotchets in a bar; **two-furrow** *a.*, adapted for ploughing two furrows at once; **two-group**, a group of two, *e.g.* of two sound-units, as syllables forming an iamb or trochee; so **two-grouping**; **two-hearted** *a.*, double-hearted, deceitful; **two-heeled** *a.*, having two heels; in quot., two-edged (cf. HEEL *sb.*[1] 7 b); **two-high** *a.*, having two rolls one over another, as a rolling-mill (cf. *three-high* s. v. THREE B. III. 2); **two-horse** *a.*, drawn or worked by, or used with, two horses; **two-knot** *a.*, running two knots (see KNOT *sb.*[1] 3); **two-line, two-lined** *adjs.*, in *Printing*, extending through two lines, as a large capital letter; **two-lipped** (-lipt) *a.*, having two lips; *esp.* in *Bot.* of a corolla, calyx, etc.; bilabiate; **two-lofted** (*Sc.* **twa-**) *a.*, two-storied; **two-meal** *a.*, (*a*) of cheese: see quots. (cf. MEAL *sb.*[2] 3 a); (*b*) of or involving two meals a day; **two-monthly** *a.*, occurring every two months; see also quot. 1867; **two-oar**, a two-oared boat; **two-pair** *a.* (in full, *two-pair-of-stairs*), situated above two 'pairs' or flights of stairs, i. e. on the second floor; also *ellipt.* as *sb.* (*scil.* room); †**two-plait** (*two plette*), a double plait; **two-rhythm**, duple rhythm; †**two-sea'd** *a.*, situated between two seas (tr. L. *bimaris*); †**two-shafted** *a.*, of cloth, woven with two web-shafts (see SHAFT *sb.*[2] 9, and cf. THREE-*shafted*); **two-shear**, *a.* of a sheep, that has been shorn twice; *sb.* a two-shear sheep; also, the time or age of the second shearing; **Two-shoes**, nickname of the girl heroine of the History of Little Goody Two-Shoes; hence, a quasi-proper name for a child; **two-step**, a round dance characterized by sliding steps in duple rhythm; also, the music for such a dance; also *attrib.*; **two-teeth, -tooth,** *a.*, applied to sheep of from one to two years old: having two full-grown permanent teeth, double-toothed; also as *sb.*; **two-throw** *a.*, having two throws, as a crank (see THROW *sb.*[2] 2); **two-tongued** *a.*, having two tongues; *fig.* double-tongued, deceitful; **two-water** *a.*, *Naut.*, diluted with twice its bulk of water; **two-year** *a.* = TWO-YEAR-OLD; **two-yearer**, (*a*) a voyage lasting two years; (*b*) a pupil who has been at (Harrow) school two years; †**two-yearing** *a.*, of a beast, two years old; **two-yearling**, a beast of two years old; also *attrib.*

**1619** S. ATKINSON *Gold Mynes Scotl.* (Bann. Cl.) 1 To digg the next ground under that sodd..with a mattocke, picke, or *towbill. **1714** *Lond. Gaz.* No. 5258/4 Henry Bray..did give..Edward Hurly..a mortal Wound on the Head with a Two-Bill. **1807** VANCOUVER *Agric. Devon* (1813) 127 The grubbing of roots is generally performed with the two-bill, or double-bitted mattock. **1888** ELWORTHY *W. Somerset Word-bk.*, *Two-bill*, a double-ended mattock. Sometimes both ends are alike. **1605** TIMME *Quersit.* III. 177 Take of the rootes of angelica,..of bifolium or *two-blades. **1728** BRADLEY *Dict. Bot.*, *Ophris*, sive *Bifolium*,..Twyblade and Twablade. **1828** *Craven Gloss.*, *Twa-blade*, a plant with two leaves. *Ophrys ovata*. **1841** DANA *Seaman's Man.* 99 *Chock-a-block*. When the lower block of a tackle is run close up to the upper one, so that you can hoist no higher...Also called hoisting up **two-blocks*. **1855** THACKERAY *Newcomes* lix, This *two-bottle Mentor. **1874** L. STEPHEN *Hours in Library* (1876) II. 163 The two-bottle men who lingered till our day were..relics of the type which then gave the tone to society. **1894** CREIGHTON & TITCHENER tr. *Wundt's Hum. & Anim. Psychol.* v. § 2. 69 Similar simple periods are found to recur in the other harmonious *two-clangs [Ger. *Zweiklängen*]. **1833** LOUDON *Encycl. Archit.* § 936 All the ceilings..are to be finished with fine *two-coat plasterwork. **1847** SMEATON *Builder's Man.* 127 Lath, laid and set,..in plastering, signifying two-coat work. **1903** *Motor. Ann.* 273 He suggests the *two-cycle engine without valves as the most economical motor. **1520** *MS. Acc. St. John's Hosp., Canterb.*, A *ij erd basket. **1685** *Lond. Gaz.* No. 2068/4 One Tea Pot, one Silver Tankard wrought, one two Ear'd Pot. **1704** *Ibid.* No. 3984/4 A..Two-ear'd Cup. **1863** TYNDALL *Heat* xv. § 755. (1870) 522 The polarity of a magnet consists in its *two-endedness. **1864** *Reader* 19 Nov. 642/1 'A *Two-eyed Steak',..a Yarmouth bloater. **1876** STEWART & TAIT *Unseen Univ.* 21 Another class who regard a two-eyed man as a monster. **1892** GREENER *Breech-Loader* 92 The sportsman may..dispense with shooting correctors, two-eyed sights, *et id genus omne*. **1907** M. C. F. MORRIS *Nunburnholme* 250 The *two-field or three-field shift system. **1796** STEDMAN *Surinam* II. xxvi. 255 The Accorees, or *Two-fingers, live amongst the Seramaca negroes. **1859** GEO. ELIOT *A. Bede* vi, As poor a *two-fisted thing as ever I saw, you know you was. **1878** MRS. STOWE *Poganuc P.* vi, A stout, two-fisted farmer. **1837** DICKENS *Pickw.* xxvii, I am ashamed o' you, old *two-for-his-heels. **1889** FARMER *Americanisms*, *Two-forty*. To go at *two forty, or at two forty pace, is to proceed at a high rate of speed. The allusion is to the record pace at trotting matches, at one time a mile in two minutes forty seconds being considered very good. **1896** G. HUNTINGTON in *Chicago Advance* 26 Mar. 450/3 Now, get a two forty move on you, nags! **1848** RIMBAULT *First Bk. Piano.* 95 Where does the Accent fall in *Two-four Time? **1805** R. W. DICKSON *Pract. Agric.* I. 8 The double or *two-furrow plough. **1901** C. R. SQUIRE in *Amer. Jrnl. Psychol.* July–Oct. 535 The *two-group is psychologically simpler than the three-group. *Ibid.* 536 The natural tendency to a *two-grouping. **1654** A. GRAY *Serm.* (1755) 80 Many of us would be found *two-hearted men. *a* **1610** HEALEY *Theophrastus* (1636) 88 His *two-heel'd sword. **1875** KNIGHT *Dict. Mech.* s.v. *Rolling-mill Train*, *Two-high grooved rolls. **1798** R. DOUGLAS *Agric. Surv. Roxb.* 50 The plough is drawn by a strong stretcher, commonly called a *two-horse-tree. **1799** J. ROBERTSON *Agric. Perth* 525 Two-horse ploughs. **1812** SIR J. SINCLAIR *Syst. Husb. Scot.* I. 58 A two-horse cart. **1900** KROPOTKIN *Mem. Revolutionist* (1906) I. i. 4 Two-horse sledges. **1889** WESTGARTH *Austral. Progr.* 124 A *two-knot northerly current inshore. **1771** LUCKOMBE *Hist. Print.* 30 He used *two-line letters of a Gothic kind. **1892** A. OLDFIELD *Man. Typogr.* iv, Chapter Headings are usually set in a two-line titling. **1683** MOXON *Mech. Exerc.*, *Printing* xxii. ¶ 5 He begins his Chapter.. with a *Two-lin'd Letter. **1787** *Fam. Plants* I. 4 Nectary ..*two-lip'd. **1808** *Med. Jrnl.* XIX. 75 *G[enista] tinctoria*. ..Cal[yx] two-lipped. **1853** MISS PRATT *Wild Flowers* II. 18 They have..square stems, opposite leaves and two-lipped blossoms. **1818** SCOTT *Br. Lamm.* xxiv, Folk are far frae respecting me as they wad do if I lived in a *twa-lofted sclated house. **1784** TWAMLEY *Dairying* 57 What is generally known by the name of *Two-meal Cheese,..being made from one meal New Milk and one of old, or skimmed Milk. **1805** R. W. DICKSON *Pract. Agric.* II. 1011 Where two milkings are blended, or two-meal cheese made. **1901** *Daily Chron.* 3 Sept. 7/4 The generality of the two-meal system in hot countries. **1811** *Regul. & Ord. Army* 95 The Monthly Settlement in the Infantry and the *Two-Monthly Settlement in the Cavalry..have been duly made by the Captains. **1867** SMYTH *Sailor's Word-bk.*, *Two-monthly book*, a book kept by the captain's clerk, to be forwarded every two months, when possible. **1857** MRQ. DALHOUSIE in *Life* (1895) 208 Lots of eighteen-penny *two-oars. **1749** FIELDING *Tom Jones* XIV. iv, Nightingale should procure him either the ground-floor, or the *two pair of stairs. **1755** KIDGELL *Card* II. 179 The very two-pair-of-stairs Apartment. **1836** DICKENS *Sk. Boz, Our Parish* i, I rents a two-pair back, gentlemen. **1840** THACKERAY *Shabby-genteel Story* vii, There was a light in the garret, and another in the two-pair front. **1841** — *Gt. Hoggarty Diamond* ii, We occupied a very genteel two-pair. **1641** BEST *Farm. Bks.* (Surtees) 148 Bandes..made of the smallest haver-strawe,..first well twined, and after that twined togeather againe, after the manner of a *two plette. **1901** C. R. SQUIRE in *Amer. Jrnl. Psychol.* July–Oct. 536 Others explain this preference for the *two-rhythm as due to its accordance with the bodily rhythms, the expiration and inspiration of respiration, the diastole and systole of the heart [etc.]. **1621** G. SANDYS *Ovid's Met.* VI. (1626) 118 With all that *two-sead Isthmos Streights include. *c* **1440** *Promp. Parv.* 497/2 *Toschappyd clothe (*S.* tooschaptyd cloth), *bilix*. **1788** W. MARSHALL *Yorks.* II. 260 The wedders will fat at *two-sheer (that is, two to three years old) to thirty pounds a quarter. *c* **1830** *Glouc. Farm Rep.* 16 in *Libr. Usef. Knowl., Husb.* III, The two-shear, or four-teeth ewes. **1898** *Speaker* 5 Feb. 181 [The lamb] attained to the dignity of a two-shear. **1766** *Hist. Goody Two-Shoes* I. iii, The Pleasure she took in her two Shoes..by that Means [she] obtained the Name of Goody *Two-Shoes. **1870** EMERSON *Soc. & Solit., Dom. Life* Wks. (Bohn) III. 43 What a holiday is the first snow in which Twoshoes can be trusted abroad. **1900** in *Westm. Gaz.* 12 Apr. 2/3 The best dancer is the best man. She falls in love with him to the tune of a sighing waltz. She marries him to the tune of a *two-step. **1909** *Daily Chron.* 27 Jan. 7/4 The most popular steps are the two-step, waltz, schottische, three-step, and glide waltz. **1778** *Lett. & Pap. Agric. to Soc. at Bath* I. 42 The sheep most subject to it [the disease goggles] are *two teeth. *c* **1830** *Glouc. Farm Rep.* 16 in *Libr. Usef. Knowl., Husb.* III, The young or two-teeth ewes. **1875** KNIGHT *Dict. Mech.*, **Two-throw Crank*. **1393** LANGL. *P. Pl.* C. XXIII. 162 Here syre was a sysour þat neuere swor treuthe, On tomme *two-tounged. **1636** G. SANDYS *Paraphr. Ps.* xxvi. 35, I hate the two-tongu'd Hypocrite. **1815** MALCOLM *Sk. Persia* (1828) II. 156 'The fiery steed of the two-tongued pen' [a split reed] is allowed to run wild. **1776** *Carlisle Mag.* 13 July 22 It [the goggles] generally..attacks the younger sheep, more particularly the *two tooths. **1905** *Two-water..grog [see *three-water* s.v. THREE B. III. 2]. **1596–7** *Durham Wills* (Surtees) II. 268, iiij *two-yere cattell. **1894** DOYLE *Mem. S. Holmes* 81 I'm just off a *two-yearer in an eight-knot tramp. **1899** *Tit-Bits* 1 July 276/3 A 'three-yearer' may..be recognised by his stand-up collar and his tie-pin,..which an unfavored 'two-yearer' may look and long for. **1600** in W. F. Shaw *Mem. Eastry* (1876) 226 Item vij kine iij *towyearing beasts and four twelve monthings. **1577** B. GOOGE *Heresbach's Husb.* I. (1586) 43 b, My young breede, Yeerelinges, and *Twoyeerelinges. **1884** *W. Sussex Gaz.* 25 Sept., 10 good two-yearling wellbred Steers.

**Twoche**, obs. form of TOUCH.

**Two·-de:cker.** [f. TWO + DECK *sb.* + -ER[1]: see DECKER[2].]

**1.** A two-decked ship or boat; formerly *spec.* a line-of-battle ship carrying guns on two decks.

**1790** BEATSON *Nav. & Mil. Mem.* II. 140 We could perceive the ships to be French, the largest being a two-decker. **1833** MARRYAT *P. Simple* xiii, I was in the dock-yard, looking at a two-decker in the basin.

**2.** *transf.* and *fig.* Something consisting of two ranges or divisions, as a tram-car with seats on the roof and an additional roof over them; in quot. 1902, a play in two acts. Also *attrib.*

**1884** Two Decker Oven [see DECKER[2] 1]. **1902** *Westm. Gaz.* 20 Aug. 3/1 Unfortunately, it is a theory of managers that one poor three-act play is better than two good two-deckers. **1904** *Daily Chron.* 18 July 3/1 L.C.C. Two-deckers...on the ..tramways south of the Thames. **1905** *Outlook* 23 Dec. 903/2 The two-decker bed with its red and yellow curtains.

**Two-edged** (-edʒd, *poet.* -edʒėd), *a.* Having two edges; esp. of a sword, ax, etc., having two cutting edges, one on each side of the blade.

In quot. 1712–14 applied humorously to a pair of scissors. **1526** TINDALE *Heb.* iv. 12 The worde off god is..sharper then eny two edged swearde. **1546** *Lanc. Wills* (Chetham Soc.) II. 27 My greit twoo edged sword and my lesse tow edged sword. **1578** LYTE *Dodoens* IV. xxxi. 489 Turner calleth it..Axeworte, bycause Dioscorides saith the seede is lyke a two edged Axe. **1648** HEXHAM II, *Een twee-snijdigh swaert*, a two-edged sword. **1712–14** POPE *Rape Lock* III. 128 Clarissa drew..A two-edg'd weapon from her shining case. **1776** J. LEE *Introd. Bot.* Explan. Terms, *Anceps*, two-edged, flattened with two opposite sides sharp. **1850** W. IRVING *Mahomet* etc. xxxviii. II. 344 Alashtar..wielded a two-edged sword. **1875** BENNETT & DYER *Sachs' Bot.* 410 The ..apical cell..of *Isoëtes lacustris* is, according to Hofmeister, two-edged when the stem has two furrows.

**b.** *fig.* or in figurative allusion.

*a* **1625** FLETCHER *Hum. Lieutenant* III. iv, She has two-edged eyes; they kill o' both sides. **1661** BOYLE *Style of Script.* (1675) 126, I find all these Topicks..such two-edg'd Weapons, that they are as well applicable to the service of Falshood, as of Truth. **1878** BOSW. SMITH *Carthage* 82 Elephants were found to be a two-edged weapon which might be fatal to the hand which wielded it.

**Twoer** (tūˑəɹ). *colloq.* [f. TWO + -ER[1].] Something consisting of or counted as two; in quot. 1889, a hit at cricket for which two runs are or may be obtained.

**1889** *Boys' Own Paper* 23 Mar. 400/1 If he hits the ball far enough away for a twoer, he must run it. **1899** *N. & Q.* 9th Ser. III. 185/2 The value of the buttons..varied. There was the average unit, then 'twoers', as well as others of increased value.

**Two·-faced** (-fēist), *a.*

**1.** Having two faces: = DOUBLE-FACED 1.

**1659** T. PECKE *Parnassi Puerp.* 160 Janus..The Two-fac'd God. **1793** MARTYN *Lang. Bot.* s.v., Two-faced leaves. **1861** J. G. SHEPPARD *Fall of Rome* i. 13 January presents itself under the influence of the 'Two-faced Janus'.

**2.** *fig.* Deceitful, insincere: = DOUBLE-FACED 2.

*a* **1619** FLETCHER, etc. *Q. Corinth* III. ii, Who can trust The gentle looks and words of two-faced man? **1720** WELTON *Suffer. Son of God* II. xiv. 364 People, who, in Private.. approve of the principles of Religion, but act the Libertine in the Face of the World..These loose and Two-fac'd Christians. **1864** in J. H. Newman *Apol.* v. 429 Two-faced persons, who did not go simply and straightforwardly to work.

Hence **Two-facedness.**

**1882** in *Jamieson's Sc. Dict.* IV. 647. **1889** TALMAGE *Serm.* in *Voice* (N. Y.) 10 Oct., What subterfuge, what double-dealing, what two-facedness.

**Twofold** (tū·fōuld), *a.*, (*sb.*), *adv.* Forms: *α.* 2, 5– *Sc.*, **twafald,** 5 *Sc.* **twa faulde,** 9 *Sc.* **twafauld, (twa-fall).** *β.* 3 **twouold;** 4 **twofolde,** 6 **two folde, twofoulde,** 7 **twofolde;** 5–6 **two fold,** 7–9 **two-fold,** 7– **twofold.** [app. orig. a refashioning of TWIFOLD, after TWO; in later use perh. independently f. TWO + -FOLD.]

**A.** *adj.*

†**1.** Double (in *fig.* sense); double-minded, wavering. *Obs.*

*c* **1175** *Lamb. Hom.* 151 Anfald oðer twafald is ech mon... Þe twafalde Mon is unstaþelfest on alle his weies.

**2. a.** Consisting of two folds or layers.

*a* **1225** *Ancr. R.* 50 Þe cloð in ham beo twouold.

**b.** Folded or bent double. (Cf. B. 1.) *Sc.*

**1821** *Blackw. Mag.* Jan. 402/1 My auld auntie, wha's twafauld with the rheumatics.

**3.** Consisting of two combined; composed of two parts or elements; existing in two relations or manners; of two kinds; double, dual.

**a.** in abstract or general sense.

**1559** W. CUNNINGHAM *Cosmogr. Glasse* 17, I finde a twofoulde difference betwixt a sphere, and a circle. **1610** HOLLAND *Camden's Brit.* (1637) 102 A twofold victorie. **1691** NORRIS *Pract. Disc.* 321 The object of the Divine Will..is Twofold, either the object of his Will Decreeing, or..of his Will Commanding. **1774** GOLDSM. *Nat. Hist.* (1776) I. 399 The earth..seen with its twofold motion; producing, by the one, the change of seasons; and, by the other, the..vicissitudes of day and night. **1875** HELPS *Ess., Self-Discipl.* 19 Man, a creature of twofold nature, body and soul.

**b.** in concrete sense, of material objects.

**1605** SHAKS. *Macb.* IV. i. 121 Some..That two-fold Balles, and trebble Scepters carry. *a* **1721** PRIOR *2nd Hymn of Callimachus* 64 Ewes, that erst brought forth but single Lambs, Now drop'd their Two-fold Burdens. **1794** NELSON in Nicolas *Disp.* (1845) I. 379 Two three-fold blocks, and two two-fold blocks. **1888** *Lady* 25 Oct. 374/3 The two-fold [photograph] screens with..space for panel portraits.

**4.** Double in amount; twice as great.

**1812** CRABBE *Tales* xii. 176 More charming grew the Fair, And seem'd to watch him with a two-fold care. **1873** B. STEWART *Conserv. Force* iii. 49 The double system will now attract the single system with twofold force.

**5.** Of yarn: Consisting of two strands twisted into one.

**1880** *Daily News* 7 Dec. 2/8 Two-fold yarns are rather more in request. **1883** *Ibid.* 22 Oct. 7/1 Two-fold yarns.. command improved rates more readily than single wefts. **1894** *Ibid.* 20 Mar. 7/3 The trade in twofold yarns shows some improvement.

**b.** as *sb.* Also *attrib.*

**1884** W. S. B. MCLAREN *Spinning* (ed. 2) 239 Twisting two or more threads together that have already been each made into two-fold. **1888** *Daily News* 25 Sept. 2/5 Transactions in twofolds and singles are still somewhat restricted. **1895** *Ibid.* 3 Feb. 2/5 Twofold spinners are getting more work. **1910** *Encycl. Brit.* VII. 277/1 (*Cotton*), 40s mule, water twists and twofolds.

**B.** *adv.*

**1.** In two folds; so as to be folded or doubled. Chiefly *Sc.* of persons.

*c* **1394** *P. Pl. Crede* 516 Þe glose is so greit in gladding tales, þat turneþ vp two-folde vnteyned opon trewþe. *c* **1425** WYNTOUN *Cron.* VIII. xxxii. 5595 A stane..has hym ourtane, And twa faulde [*v. r.* twafald] downe can him bere. **1523** FITZHERB. *Husb.* § 62 Bynde a clothe two or thre folde vpon his foreheed. **1721** RAMSAY *Ode to Ph—* ix, Before auld age..lay ye twafald o'er a rung. *a* **1802** *Johnie of Breadislee* xviii. in Scott *Min.*, He's laid him twa-fald ower his steed. **1894** 'IAN MACLAREN' *Bonnie Brier Bush, Highl. Mystic* i, He wes bent twa fad; a' doot it's a titch o' rheumatism, or maybe lumbago.

**2.** To twice the amount, twice as much, doubly.

**1526** TINDALE *Matt.* xxiii. 15 Ye make hym two folde more the chylde off hell then ye youre selves are. **1637** GILLESPIE *Eng. Pop. Cerem.* II. i. 6 It twofolde more scandalizeth such a one.

Hence **Two·foldly** (also 2 **twafaldeliche**) *adv.*, in a twofold manner, doubly; **Two·foldness,** the quality of being twofold, doubleness, duality. So **Twofo·lded** *ppl. a.* [f. TWO + FOLDED], folded in two, folded double.

**1887** MORRIS *Odyss.* XII. 361 Wrapping it round *twofolded. *c* **1175** *Lamb. Hom.* 5 Nu ic eou habbe þet godspel iseid anfaldeliche, nu scule ȝe understonden *twafaldeliche þet hit bi-tacnet. **1648** HEXHAM II, *Tweevoudighlick,* Twofoldly or Doubly. **1827** COLERIDGE in *Lit. Rem.* (1839) IV. 310 The *twofoldness of the Christian Church. **1861** W. BARNES in *Macm. Mag.* June 128 That we should have two legs, or two hands,..this twofoldness of life-forms.

**Two-foot** (tū·fut), *a.*

**1.** †**a.** Having two feet, two-footed (*obs.*). **b.** Performed or executed with both feet (*rare*).

**1620** ROWLANDS *Night Raven* 3, I haunt not barnes, for either Mouse or Rat, As doth the searching two-foote flying Cat. **1902** *Munsey's Mag.* XXVI. 477/1 The two foot spin is one of the most sensational movements in figure skating.

**2.** Measuring two feet; two feet long, wide, or thick. *Two-foot rule*, a measuring rule two feet long. So **two-foot-wide** *a.*

**1664** BUTLER *Hud.* II. III. 13 A two-foot Trout. **1679** MOXON *Mech. Exerc.* vii. 129 If there be odd Inches, they measure them with the Two-foot Rule. **1855** J. PHILLIPS *Man. Geol.* 193 Two-foot coal. **1891** C. JAMES *Rom. Rigmarole* 127 Squeezed in between the two-foot-wide pavement and the centre of the roadway..was a row of canvas booths. **1903** *Heart of Heretic* xx. 152 We measure Him [God] by our little two-foot rule.

**Two-footed** (tū·fu:tėd), *a.* Having two feet; biped; two-legged; standing on two feet.

*c* **1374** CHAUCER *Boeth.* v. pr. iv. 128 (Camb. MS.) Man is a resonable two foted beest. **1495** *Trevisa's Barth. De P. R.* v. liv. (W. de W.) 171 The fete of fowles and of two foted beestes. **1601** HOLLAND *Pliny* I. 305 The Mice and Rats of Ægypt..walke like as if they were two-footed. **1607** [see BIPEDAL *a.* 2]. *a* **1661** HOLYDAY *Juvenal* ix. 170 He neglects me, and now seeks some other Two-footed sturdy asse. **1802** SHAW *Gen. Zool.* III. 311 Two-footed cylindric Lizard. **1839** CARLYLE *Chartism* iv. 125 There is not a horse willing to work but can get food..; a thing this two-footed worker has to seek for. **1864** TENNYSON *Aylmer's F.* 127 He [the dog] rose Twofooted at the limit of his chain.

**b.** *transf.* Performed by the two feet.

**1898** R. F. HORTON *Commandm. Jesus* i. 7 The third step in the two-footed progress.

**Two-forked** (tū·fǭɹkt), *a.* Having two divisions or branches like the prongs of a fork; bifurcate; dichotomous. Also *fig.*

**1579** FULKE *Heskins' Parl.* 107 This two forked reason. **1617** MORYSON *Itin.* I. 95 Towards the West-side of the City is a large market place twoforked. **1638** FEATLY *Strict. Lyndom.* II. 46 A dilemma or two-forked argument. *c* **1789** *Encycl. Brit.* (ed. 3) III. 440/2 *Caulis dichotomus*, a dichotomous or two-forked stem. **1793** MARTYN *Lang. Bot.* s.v., Two-forked, see *Dichotomous.* [Hence in Webster (1828), and in later Dicts.]

**Two·-hand,** *a.* Also 5 **two-handes.**

**1.** Requiring both hands to wield or manage: = next, 1.

*c* **1410** *Master of Game* (MS. Digby 182) xi, Makary had a gret twohande staffe. *a* **1440** *Sir Degrev.* 1643 Twohonde swerde. *c* **1500** *Melusine* xxii. 145 He held a two handes ax. **1630** *R. Johnson's Kingd. & Commw.* 312 Men of large stature..[who] serve onely with the Pike or two-hand-sword. **1807** HOGG *Gilmanscleuch* lvii, His twa-hand sword hang round his neck.

**2.** Done, or worked, by two persons: = next, 2. † *Two-hand battle*, a single combat, a duel (*obs.*).

*c* **1500** *Arnolde's Chron.* Index (1811) 2 That noo citezen doo twoo hand batayle. **1538** *MS. Acc. St. John's Hosp., Canterb.*, Payd for haftyng off the ij hand saw. **1614** *Ibid.*, Payd for the baryng of a too hand sawe xij d.

†**3.** Leading in two directions (right-hand and left-hand). *Obs. rare*$^{-1}$.

**1607** HIERON *Defence* I. 38 At some crosse or two hand way.

**Two·-ha·nded** (stress var.), *a.*

**1.** Wielded with both hands, as a sword, etc. (= prec. 1); involving the use of both hands.

**1432–50** tr. *Higden* (Rolls) VII. 243 Tailefer..toke a toohonded swerde, and..did slee oon of Ynglishe men. **1588** *Reg. Privy Council Scot.* IV. 277 With hagbute, bow, speir, or twa-handit swerd. **1637** MILTON *Lycidas* 130 That two-handed engine..Stands ready to smite. **1667** — *P. L.* VI. 251 With huge two-handed sway Brandisht aloft the horrid edge came down. **1814** SCOTT *Diary* 22 Aug., in *Lockhart*, The effigy of a warrior completely armed..with his hand on his two-handed broadsword. **1837** *Penny Cycl.* VIII. 283/1 This was probably the finger-alphabet from which our present two-handed one was derived. **1874** SWINBURNE *Bothwell* IV. ii, The sword Which was my grandsire's, whose two-handed stroke Did such-like service.

**2.** Wielded or worked by the hands of two persons, as a saw; engaged in or played by two persons, as a card-game, etc.: = prec. 2.

**1657** R. LIGON *Barbadoes* (1673) 41 Cutting it with two-handed Saws. **1680** COTTON *Compl. Gamester* x. 83 Some play at two handed, or three handed whist. **1827** J. WILSON *Noct. Ambr.* Wks. 1855 I. 274 I'm real happy..to think that we're to hae a twa-handed crack. **1853** SIR H. DOUGLAS *Milit. Bridges* vi. (ed. 3) 303 A plank..upon which..two men may stand to..work, conjointly, a heavy two-handed beetle. **1898** *To-Day* 5 Nov. 19/2 The Captain sat down to play two-handed poker with Chris.

**3.** *colloq.* Big, bulky, strapping. ? *Obs.*

**1687** T. BROWN *Saints in Uproar* Wks. 1730 I. 73 A huge two-handed lubber, St. Christopher I think they call him. **1692** tr. *C'tess D'Aunoy's Trav.* iii. (1706) 44 The Hair.. being..kept behind their Ears with a great Twohanded [mistranslating Fr. *doublé* 'lined'] Hat. *a* **1700** B. E. *Dict. Cant. Crew, Strapping-Lass*, a swinging two-handed Woman. **1749** FIELDING *Tom Jones* IX. iii, This Susan was as two-handed a wench (according to the phrase) as any in the country. **1830** LAMB *Let. to Wordsworth* 22 Jan., [Vulcan] the two-handed skinker.

**4.** Having two hands.

**1847** CARPENTER *Zool.* 132 *Bimana*, or two-handed Mammals. *Ibid.* 137 Man alone is two-handed.

**5.** Using both hands equally well, ambidextrous; dexterous, handy, efficient.

**1861** WHYTE MELVILLE *Good for Nothing* xxvii, A man soon learns to be two-handed in the bush.

Hence **Two-handedness.** So **Two-hander,** a two-handed sword; † **Two-handy** *a.* = sense 1.

**1891** *Home Missionary* (N. Y.) Jan. 389 A holy *two-handedness. **1888** *Archæologia* LI. 512 The sword..is an exceedingly handsome example of the *two-hander of the sixteenth century. **1648** HEXHAM II, *Een Slach-swaerdt*, a *two-handie Sword.

**Two-headed** (tū·he:dėd), *a.*

**1.** Having, or represented with, two heads.

*Two-headed snake* or *worm*, the amphisbæna (AMPHISBÆNA 2), formerly supposed to have two heads, one at each end of the body.

**1596** SPENSER *F. Q.* v. x. 10 His two-headed dogge that Orthrus hight. **1596** SHAKS. *Merch. V.* I. i. 50 By two-headed Ianus. **1708** SEWEL II, *Tweehoofdig*, two-headed. **1752** J. HILL *Hist. Anim.* 102 The Amphisbæna..has obtained, among the English, the name of the two-headed worm. **1796** MORSE *Amer. Geog.* I. 221 The two-headed snake. **1867** LATHAM *Black & White* 62 A two-headed iron bolt. **1899** T. NICOLL *Rec. Archæol. & Bible* vi. 193 The two-headed eagle of the Hittites..survives..as the symbol of imperial power in Austria and Russia to-day.

**2.** *fig.* Having or governed by two chiefs or rulers.

**1885** W. WILSON *Congress. Govt.* iv. 220 Doubts as to the .. advantage of a two-headed legislature. **1888** T. W. HIGGINSON *Women & Men* 93 If two business partners can work successfully on the two-headed plan, why [can] not two married persons do it?

**Two-leaf,** *a.* = next, a.

**1634** in *Archæologia* XXXV. 199 One two-leaf wyndowe. **1890** *Sale-Catal. Suffield House near Derby*, Deal table.. Two-leaf ditto.

**Two-leaved** (tū·līvd), *a.* Also 7 **-leaf(e)d.** Having or consisting of two leaves. **a.** Having two hinged or folding parts, as a door, table, etc. Also *fig.*

**1610** GUILLIM *Heraldry* II. i. (1660) 50 The two leaved silver gates. **1611** MIDDLETON & DEKKER *Roaring Girl* II. ii, The two-leav'd tongues of slander or of truth. **1611** COTGR., *Valve*, a foulding, or two-leafed doore, or window. **1626** tr. *Featly's Parallel.* A ij, A two leafed Tablet. *a* **1644** QUARLES *Sol. Recant.* ch. xii, Then shall the Castles two-leafd gates be barr'd. **1847** C. BRONTE *J. Eyre* xii, The great dining-room, whose two-leaved door stood open.

**b.** Having two foliage-leaves, or two petals or sepals; having leaves growing in pairs.

**1688** R. HOLME *Armoury* II. 115/2 Bifoile, or two leafed flower. **1793** MARTYN *Lang. Bot.*, Two-leaved calyx. **1894** J. MUIR *Mount. California* viii. 201 The Two-leaved Pine [*Pinus contorta*], more than any other, is subject to destruction by fire.

**c.** Of a book: Consisting of two leaves.

**1726** AYLIFFE *Parergon* 191 Her Register..was a two-leav'd Book of Record.

**Two-legged** (tū·legd, -le:gėd), *a.* Having two legs: usually as an epithet suggestive of a human being having the qualities of the animal named.

**1561** B. GOOGE *Palingenius' Zodiac Life* I. A vj b, What a sort ther be of twolegd Asses clothed In gold and silke and purple. **1575** *Gamm. Gurton* v. ii, Thy neighbours hens yu takest, and playes the two legged fox. **1693** DRYDEN *Juvenal* x. 388 Next to the Raven's Age, the Pylian King Was longest liv'd of any two-legg'd thing. **1719** DE FOE *Crusoe* (1840) I. xix. 348 A kind of two-legged wolves. **1815** SCOTT *Guy Mann.* xlviii, The mate of the two-legged Cerberus. **1858** CARLYLE *Fredk. Gt.* v. v. (1872) II. 97 Countries..infested with a new species of predatory two-legged animals: Prussian recruiters.

**Twolf,** obs. form of TWELVE.

**Twoling** (tū·liŋ). *rare*$^{-0}$. [f. TWO + -LING$^{1}$ 2.] A twin crystal (*Cent. Dict.*, 1891).

**Twoll, twolue,** obs. ff. TWELVE. **Twolthe,** obs. f. TWELFTH. **Twon, twone,** obs. pa. pples. of TWINE *v.*$^{1}$

**Twoness** (tū·nės). [f. TWO + -NESS.] The fact or condition of being two; duality, doubleness.

**1648** HEXHAM II, *Tweeheydt*, Twonesse, or Dualitie. **1829** JAS. MILL *Hum. Mind* (1869) II. 92 Abstract terms.. in place of which, the words oneness, twoness, threeness, might be substituted. **1892** SWEET *N. Eng. Gram.* 49 The singular expresses 'oneness'..The dual expresses 'twoness'. **1908** C. BIGG *Orig. Chr.* xxxii. (1909) 407 The original unity ..is now perceived to be a twoness.

†**Twoops.** *Obs.* (*colloq.* or *slang.*) Twopenny ale.

**1729** *Dulcinead* 5 Her Health he drinks when o'er his Cups, Which are brimful of Fitzy's Twoops.

**Two·-part,** *a.* Containing, consisting of, having, or involving two parts; composed in two parts, as a piece of music, or for two actors, as a play.

**1854** *Cherubini's Counterpoint* 20 It is prohibited in three-part-counterpoint, as in two-part-counterpoint, to make concealed fifths. **1894** S. FISKE *Holiday Stories* (1900) 207 Two-part comediettas.

So **Two-parted** *a.*, divided into two parts, bipartite.

**1793** MARTYN *Lang. Bot.*, *Two-parted leaf, perianth*,.. divided in two down to the base. **1830** LINDLEY *Nat. Syst. Bot.* 57 Calyx..tubular, with a two-parted limb.

**Twopence** (tɒ·pėns). Forms: see TWO and PENNY A. 2; also 6–7 **tuppens,** 7–9 **tuppence,** 8–9 *Sc.* **tippence.**

**1.** A sum of money equal to two pennies.

† *Penny of twopence* = sense 2: see PENNY 3.

1477 *Rolls of Parlt.* VI. 183/1 The Grotes, Pens of two Pens, and Pens, of this Reame. 1514 in *Eng. Gilds* (1870) 144 To the beddell of the seid Gilde Tuppens. 1641 *Sc. Acts Chas. I* (1817) V. 510/1 They might sell at tuppens a groatt & Sexpens.. They micht sell.. the deirest for a tippens. 1772–84 COOK *Voy.* (1790) I. 299 They were accosted by several Indians..and one of them undertook to carry them over..at two-pence per head. 1785 BURNS *Holy Fair* viii, A greedy glowr Black Bonnet throws, An' we maun draw our tippence. 1812 H. & J. SMITH *Rej. Addr., Theatre* 61 Boys who long linger at the gallery-door, With pence twice five—they want but twopence more. 1857 HUGHES *Tom Brown* I. ii, What can you expect for tuppence? 1872 RUSKIN *Fors Clav.* (1896) I. xix. 376 Work that will pay no dividend on their twopences.

**2.** An English silver coin of the value of two pennies: = HALF-GROAT (since 1662 coined only as Maundy money). **b.** A copper coin of this value issued in the reign of George III.

*c* 1450 *Mankind* 457 in *Macro Plays* 17 He louyth no grotis, nor pens or to-pens. 1597 SHAKS. 2 *Hen. IV*, IV. iii. 55 Like gilt two-pences. 1653 WALTON *Angler* xii. 231 A piece of reed..as big about as the compass of a two pence. 1684 E. CHAMBERLAYNE *St. Gt. Brit.* I. (ed. 15) 217 To scatter new-coyned two-pences in the..places where the King passes. 1712 *Mus. Thoresby.* (1713) 361 A very fair Canterbury Twopence [*temp.* Hen. VIII]. 1818 SCOTT *Br. Lamm.* xxxv, A when silver tippences to the poor folk. 1820 — *Let. to J. Ballantyne* 28 Mar., in *Lockhart*, I care not a bent twopence about their quarrels.

**3.** As type of a very small amount: now esp. in phr. (*not*) *to care twopence*.

1691 BAXTER *Repl. Beverley* 2 All our righteousness is not worth two-pence. *a* 1744 BRAMSTON *Art Politicks* 193 He cares not two-pence for the land-tax bill. 1752 FOOTE *Taste* I. (1781) 18 It does not signify Two Pence. 1894 G. W. APPLETON *Co-Respondent* I. 65 He asked me if you really cared twopence for Kate.

**b.** *fig.* Applied to a person of very little worth.

1866 SARTORIS *Week in French Country Ho.* (1902) 213 She was a wretched twopence of a woman.

**4. Twopence halfpenny**: a sum of money equal to two pennies and a halfpenny. Also *attrib.*

In attrib. use *twopenny-halfpenny* is more usual (see after next word), but in Sc. *twopence-halfpenny* is regular when the precise sum is intended, as in *a twopence-halfpenny stamp.*

16.. *Black Bk. Admiralty* (Rolls) I. 13 Each sea boy shall have twopence halfpenny per diem. 1849 THACKERAY *Pendennis* xl, Twopence-halfpenny for your thoughts. 1890 LE GALLIENNE *Meredith* 155 He does not weave two-pence-halfpenny mysteries.

**5.** *Herb twopence*: name given by Turner to the plant *Lysimachia Nummularia*, also called *twopenny grass* (see next, 3) or MONEYWORT, from its pairs of rounded leaves.

1548 TURNER *Names of Herbes* H ij, Centimorbia otherwise called Nummularia..may be called in englishe Herbe .ij. pence or two penigrasse because it hath two and two leaues standyng together of ech syde of the stalke lyke pence. 1597 GERARDE *Herbal* II. clxxxix. 505 Nummularia ..herbe Two pence, and Two pennie grasse. 1756 WATSON in *Phil. Trans.* XLIX. 815 The Nummularia, Moneywort, or Herb Twopence. 1861 MISS PRATT *Flower. Pl.* IV. 238 Creeping Loosestrife, Moneywort, or Herb-Twopence.

**6.** *attrib.* (= next, 1, 2) and *Comb.*

1762 STERNE *Tr. Shandy* V. xxxix, 'Tis not two-pence matter. 1827 SCOTT *Two Drovers* ii, Robin..proceeded to light his pipe, and call for a pint of twopenny. 'We have no twopence ale', answered..the landlord. 1889 STEVENSON *Let. to S. Colvin* 2 Dec., If we only had twopenceworth of wind.

**Twopenny** (tʊ·pĕni), *a.* and *sb.* Forms: see Two and PENNY; also 9 **tuppenny**; *Sc.* 8 **tippony, tippanny, 8–9 tippenny, tippeny,** 9 **tip'ny.**

**A.** *adj.* **1.** Of the value of, amounting to, or costing twopence.

*Twopenny faith*, the name by which Archbishop Hamilton's tract, *Ane Godlie Exhortatioun*, etc., published in 1559, was popularly known in Scotland.

1532 *Acc. Ld. High Treas. Scot.* VI. 156 Item, for vj scoir tuapenny breid..xx s. 1558–9 KNOX *Hist. Ref.* I. Wks. (1846) I. 291 The Bischoppis..sett furth somewhat in print, which of the People was called 'The Twa-penny Fayth'. 1589 NASHE *Anat. Absurditie* 17 The sum of their diuinitie consists in twopennie Catichismes. 1603 H. CROSSE *Vertues Commw.* (1878) 116 For a two-penny almes he may be throughly taught and made a perfect good scholler. 1625 MASSINGER *New Way* III. ii, Even starv'd for want of two-penny chops. 1705 *Lond. Gaz.* No. 4107/4 A Sable Tippet, with a black Two-peny Ribbon. 1825 JEFFERSON *Autobiog.* Wks. 1859 I. 106 A two-penny duty on tea. 1852 THACKERAY *Esmond* I. ii, His nephew slunk by..to his twopenny ordinary. 1873 RUSKIN *Fors Clav.* (1896) II. xxxviii. 295 People will eat twopenny herrings..when they wouldn't touch half-penny ones. 1907 *Westm. Gaz.* 11 Nov. 8/2 The same firm was authorised by George III to manufacture penny and twopenny pieces.

**b.** Involving an outlay of twopence; for the use of or admission to which there is a charge of twopence.

*Twopenny tube*, a popular name for the Central London Railway (see TUBE *sb.* 7 b), on which the fare was originally twopence for any distance.

1599 *Contract building Globe Theatre* in *Henslowe Papers* (1907) 6 The gentlemens roomes and Twoepennie roomes. 1601 B. JONSON *Poetaster* V. i, In taverns, two-penny rooms, tyring houses. 1765 *Chron.* in *Ann. Reg.* 70/1 Letting out two-penny lodgings. 1768 TUCKER *Lt. Nat.* (1834) I. 41 He..sits among his fellow topers at the two-penny club. 1814 J. BOSWELL in *Songs Justiciary Opera* (1816) 9 Mine's a tippeny eatin house. 1831 D. E. WILLIAMS *Life & Corr. Sir T. Lawrence* II. 23 Sources of petty gains—mere two-penny shows. 1900 [see TUBE *sb.* 7 b]. 1903 MCNEILL *Egregious English* 199 They saw Peter Robinson's and the tuppenny tube.

**c.** *Twopenny ale* (or *beer*), a quality of ale originally sold at twopence per quart; in Scotland, at twopence a Scotch pint (= 3 imperial pints).

1710 *Lond. Gaz.* No. 4668/1 Every Barrel of Twopenny Ale. 1798 W. HUTTON *Autobiog.* 6 My father treated us with a quart of twopenny beer. 1819 SCOTT *Leg. Montrose* iv, A huge barrel of twopenny ale.

**d.** *Twopenny post*: the London post (1801–1839) for conveyance of letters, etc. at an ordinary charge of twopence each. Also *attrib.*, as *twopenny postman*, etc.

1797–8 JANE AUSTEN *Sense & Sens.* xxvi, Marianne..requested the footman..to get that letter conveyed..to the two-penny post. 1838 DICKENS *O. Twist* xxix, To make an appointment by the twopenny post. 1887 T. A. TROLLOPE *What I remember* I. ii. 44 The twopenny post was considered an immense boon to Londoners.

1812 L. HUNT in *Examiner* 25 May 321/1 The two-penny postmen should ride about upon elephants. 1813 MOORE (*title*) Intercepted Letters; or, The Twopenny Post-Bag. 1830 *Parl. Papers* XIII. 46 The twopenny-post riders convey greater weights than the general-post riders.

**e.** Of iron: Costing twopence per pound.

1858 GREENER *Gunnery* 239 Making Double and Single Guns, with 'Twopenny' or 'Wedgebury Skelp Iron'.

**2.** *fig.* as a disparaging epithet: Of very little value; paltry, trumpery, trifling, worthless.

1560 JEWEL *Corr. Cole* I iv, To make the people thinke that we reade nothyng els but ij. penny doctoures, as ye cal them. 1643 S. MARSHALL *Lett.* 5 Even in a two-peny matter. 1739 CIBBER *Apol.* (1756) I. 243 Twopenny criticks must live as well as eighteenpenny authors. 1848 THACKERAY *Van. Fair* lxi, This woman, with her twopenny gentility.

†**3.** *Twopenny grass*, Herb twopence (see prec. 5).

1548, 1597 [see TWOPENCE 5]. 1578 LYTE *Dodoens* I. liv. 78 This herbe is now called..in English..two penny grasse.

†**4.** Applied to a ward in a prison. (The allusion is obscure.) *Obs. rare*$^{-1}$.

1605 CHAPMAN, etc. *Eastward Hoe* V. i. G iv b, I never knew ..Prisoners..more deuout. They will sit you vp all night singing of Psalmes,..onely, Securitie sings a note too high, sometimes, because hee lyes i' the Two-penny ward, farre off, and cannot take his tune.

**B.** *sb.* (ellipt. use of the adj.)

**1.** Short for *twopenny ale*: see 1 c above.

1711 RAMSAY *On Maggy Johnstoun* i, To braw tippony bid adieu. 1729 *Dulcinead* 5 *note*, The Old Swan in the Butcher-Row, noted for good Twopenny. 1762 BP. FORBES *Jrnl.* (1886) 181 To drink Tippanny and Whiskie. 1815 SCOTT *Guy M.* vi, The gossip over the good twopenny in every alehouse. 1858 M. PORTEOUS *Souter Johnny* 13 To appease their 'lowin' drouth' either with the Smith's 'tippeny' or the Landlord's 'strong drink'.

**2.** A twopenny piece (= TWOPENCE 2), or the sum of twopence.

1736 DRAKE *Eboracum* I. vi. 189 Pennyes or two pennyes, halfpennyes or farthings.

**3.** A jocular name for a child.

1844 MARY HOWITT *My Own Story* viii, 'Well, little Twopenny'..I..did not like to be called 'little Twopenny'.

So **Twopenny-halfpenny** (tʊ·pĕniˌhēⁱ·pĕni) *a.*, of the value of twopence-halfpenny; usually *fig.* as an epithet of disparagement (cf. A. 2 above).

1809 SOUTHEY in Robberds *Mem. W. Taylor* (1843) II. 268 Some little dirty twopenny-halfpenny piece of roguery. 1827 LYTTON *Pelham* II. xii, He..filched a twopenny-halfpenny gilt-chain out of..the pawnbroker's window. 1872 H. KINGSLEY *Hornby Mills* I. 30 They had lost a law-suit, a twopenny-halfpenny squabble about a trespass. *Mod.* A twopenny-halfpenny stamp.

**Two-pile** (tū·pəil), *a.* Applied to velvet in which the loops of the pile-warp are formed by two threads, producing a pile of double thickness: see PILE *sb.*[5] 2, and cf. THREE-PILE. Also **Two-piled** *a.* (in quot. *fig.*: cf. THREE-PILED 2).

1611 COTGR. s.v. *Poil*, *Velours à deux poils*, two-pile Veluet. 1678 DRYDEN *Limberham* I. i, Then she's a two-pil'd Punk, a Punk of two Descents.

**Two-sided** (tū·səi·dėd: stress var.), *a.* Having two sides, bilateral; *fig.* having two parts or aspects. Hence **Two-si·dedness.**

1863 TYNDALL *Heat* xv. § 755 (1870) 522 A kind of two-sidedness. 1869 — *Notes Lect. Light* iii. (1873) 116 The two-sidedness of that [polarized] light, in contrast to the all-sidedness of ordinary light. 1884 BOWER & SCOTT *De Bary's Phaner.* 409 To the second type belong..flat horizontal leaves...The chlorophyll-parenchyma..is severed into two different layers, each of which corresponds to one surface of the leaf. It may accordingly be termed the two-sided, the bifacial type. 1896 MRS. CAFFYN *Quaker Grandmother* 192 It's..in this case a two-sided custom.

**Twosome** (tū·sŏm), *sb.* and *a.* Chiefly *Sc.* (4–6 twasum, 9 twasome). [f. TWO + -SOME. Cf. WFris. *twaresom, -sum.*]

**A.** *sb.* Two persons together; two in company.

*c* 1375 *Sc. Leg. Saints* l. (*Katerine*) 691 Full Ioyfull þane þire twasum war. 1489 *Barbour's Bruce* x. 19 Twasum samyn mycht nocht rid. *a* 1578 LINDESAY (Pitscottie) *Chron. Scot.* (S.T.S.) I. 276 Thair was nane left onslaine bot himsellff his brother and twasum with thame. *a* 1802 *Auld Maitland* liii. in Scott *Minstr. Scott. Bord.* (1869) 157 The twa-some they hae slayne the ane. 1816 SCOTT *Bl. Dwarf* viii, The rest disperse by twasome and threesome. *c* 1870 *Jethart Worthies* (ed. 3) 58 The twosome kept the secret for a season or two. 1893 CROCKETT *Stickit Minister* x. 120 When the twasome had been haein' denner thegither.

**B.** *adj.* Performed by two together.

1825 JAMIESON, *Twasum* is still used to denote a dance, in which two persons are engaged; *a twasome dance*, i.e., a strathspey. 1830 GALT *Lawrie T.* VI. i, Whisking round and round the room to a two-some reel.

**Twound**, pa. t. and pple. of TWIND *v. Obs.*

**Two-way,** *a.*

Hexham (1648) renders Du. *twee-wegh* by 'a Two-way, or a double way'.

**1.** Having, or connected with, two ways, roads, or channels; situated where two ways meet.

*Two-way cock*, one with two outlets, which may act together or alternatively.

1571 GOLDING *Calvin on Ps.* xxv. 12 We stand as it were in a twowayleete, in every of our dooings, we hang in doubt, and are at our wittes end. 1618 BOLTON *Florus* I. ix. 36 Being situated in the middest betweene Latium and Tuscanie, as it were in a two-way-leet. 1844 STEPHENS *Bk. Farm* II. 209 The gauge-cock, of which there are usually two, but sometimes one, a two-way cock. 1903 *Daily Rec. & Mail* 15 Dec. 4 As a burglar may be driven out of the house by judicious handling of a two-way switch.

**2.** *Math.* Extending in two directions or dimensions, or having two modes of variation. (In quot. 1894 coinciding with sense 1.)

1891 *Cent. Dict.* s. v., A surface is a two-way spread. 1894 CAYLEY *Math. Papers* XIII. 507 The link may rotate in either direction..that is, $B$ may move from $B_1$ along $b$ in either of the two opposite senses, say $B_1$ is a 'two-way point'.

**Two·-year-old,** *a.* and *sb.*

**A.** *adj.* Of the age of two years. Chiefly of animals, *esp.* colts.

1601 in *T. Pont's Topogr. Acc. Cunningham* (Maitland Cl.) 180 Item, ane twa ȝeir auld bull. *c* 1686 *Depred. Clan Campbell* (1816) 31 [Three] tuo year old stots. 1805 R. W. DICKSON *Pract. Agric.* II. 1176 Young horses, as two-year old colts. 1835 JEKYLL *Corr.* (1894) 338 The two-year-old person on the throne of Spain. 1838 *Penny Cycl.* XII. 307/2 A three-year-old colt has his form and energies much more developed than a two-year-old one.

**B.** *sb.* An animal (*esp.* a colt) or child of two years of age. Also *attrib.*

1594–5 *Durham Wills* (Surtees) II. 254, iiij kyne and their calves, and fowre two-yere oldes. *a* 1600 in *T. Pont's Topogr. Acc. Cunningham* (Maitland Cl.) 178 Item, xiiij ȝoing beystis,..four twa ȝeir auldis and five ane ȝeir auld. *c* 1686 *Depred. Clan Campbell* (1816) 57 Nyne great coues, 2 tuo year olds. 1831 YOUATT *Horse* viii. 141 Is it possible to give this mouth to an early two-year-old? 1856 H. H. DIXON *Post & Paddock* iii. 56 Two-year-old racing lays the seeds of infirmity. *Ibid.* iii. 79 Very few two-year-olds were then trained. 1895 P. HEMINGWAY *Out of Egypt* I. iv. 46 The two-year-old [child] regarded him wonderingly.

**Twrn(e, Twrss**, obs. Sc. ff. TURN, TRUSS.

**Twussle**, Sc. var. TWISTLE.

†**Twy**, *v. Obs. rare.* (Meaning uncertain.)

A ME. survival of OE. *twīgan*, northern var. of *twēogan*, *twēon*, to doubt, hesitate, would suit the first passage, but not the second, unless a negative has been omitted. The sense of 'turn' would be appropriate in both passages.

*c* 1400 *Destr. Troy* 6360 The xij vnthwyuond, þat twyet not in fight Was..mightfull Henex. *Ibid.* 6378 With xxij vnthwyuond twyet to filde Dyomede, the derfe kyng.

**Twy**, obs. f. TWAY, two; var. TWIE *Obs.*, twice.

**Twy-**: see TWI-.

**Twyblade**, obs. f. TWAYBLADE. **Twych**, obs. Sc. f. TOUCH. **Twych, -e**, etc., obs. f. TWITCH. **Twychell**, obs. f. TWITCHEL[1]. **Twychen**: see note to TWITCHEL [1]. **Twye**, var. TWIE *Obs.*, twice.

†**Twy·eling.** *Obs. rare.* (Meaning uncertain.)

(Perh. an error for *wyeling*, var. of *wiȝeling*, *-ung*, OE. *wigelung* sorcery, witchcraft.)

*c* 1275 *Duty of Christians* i. in *O.E. Misc.* 141 Crist..yeue vs þat we moten fleo euer suneȝynge And þene feond and al his gleo and al his twyelinge.

**Twyer, -ere**, var. TUYERE.

**Twyes**, obs. form of TWICE.

†**Twyfyl.** *Obs. rare.* (Meaning uncertain.)

*c* 1460 *Towneley Myst.* xxx. 324 And nell with hir nyfyls of crisp and of sylke, Tent welle youre twyfyls, youre nek abowte as mylke.

**Twyght, twyȝt, -e**, obs. pa. t. and pple. of TWITCH *v.*[1] **Twyis, -iss**, obs. ff. TWICE. **Twyk**, obs. f. TWICK. **Twyle, twyll**, etc.: see TWILL, etc. **Twylt**, var. TWILT (obs. and dial. form of QUILT *sb.*[1], etc.). **Twyn**, obs. f. 'TWEEN, TWIN. **Twynch, -e, Twyncle**, obs. ff. TWINGE, TWINKLE. **Twyne, twynn(e**, obs. ff. TWIN.

†**Twynrys.** *Obs. rare*$^{-1}$. (Form and meaning doubtful.)

1513 DOUGLAS *Æneid* XII. vii. 55 (1553) Wyth his twynrys [*ed. Small* wynris] and grippand turkas sle, To thrist the hede and draw furth pressis he.

†**Twynt.** *Obs. rare.* Also twynte. [a. MDu. *twint* in similar use.] In negative expressions: a jot, a particle.

1399 LANGL. *Rich. Redeles* III. 81 Thus lafte þey þe leder þat hem wrong ladde, And tymed no twynte, but tolled her cornes. 14.. *Beryn* 433 So he þat payd for all in feer, [ne] hadde nat a twynt.

**Twynt(t)er**, obs. ff. TWINTER. **Twyrle**, obs. f. TWIRL. **Twys, twyse, twyss**, obs. ff. TWICE. **Twysday**, obs. f. TUESDAY. **Twysker, Twysle**, var. TUSKAR, TWISEL *v. Obs.* **Twyte**, var. THWITE, to cut; obs. f. TWIT; obs. pa. t. and pple. of TWITCH *v.*[1] **Twyter**, obs. f. TWITTER *v.*[1] **Twyvel**, obs. f. TWIBILL. **Twyys**, obs. f. TWICE.

† **Twyvete.** *Obs. rare.* Also twyfet. App. variant of TWIBIT (cf. *twyvel*, var. TWIBILL).

c 1500 *Debate Carpenter's Tools* 145 in Hazl. *E. P. P.* I. 84 3e, 3e, sayd the twyvete, Thryft I trow be fro your fette. *Ibid.* 157 Then be-spake the polyff, .. How, ser twyfet, me thinke 3ou grevyd.

**Ty**, obs. form of TIE.

**-ty**, *suffix*[1], denoting quality or condition, representing ME. *-tie, -tee, -te* (early ME. *-teð*), from OF. *-te* (mod.F. *-té*), earlier *-tet* (*-ted*) :—L. *-itātem*, nom. *-itās*. Such Latin types as *bonitātem, feritātem*, were in OF. normally reduced to two syllables (*bontet, fertet*) by elision of the *-i-* between the two stresses, so that *-tet*, later *-te*, became the regular form of the suffix. The final dental still appears in some early adoptions in ME., as *plenteð, plenteth* plenty (*c* 1250, in use till *c* 1600), and is characteristic of the Scottish forms *bountith, daintith*, and *poortith* (q. v.). The reduced form *-te*, however, is found in words recorded from shortly before or after 1200, such as *bonte* bounty, *cruelte* cruelty, *debonerte* debonairness, *deinte* dainty (sb.), *plente* plenty, *poverte* poverty, *purte* purity, and *vilte* vileness. Among others which appear somewhat later are *certeynte* certainty, *Cristente* Christenty, *freelte* frailty, *novelte* novelty, and *sotelte* subtlety. Varying forms of the stem are found in the words now or formerly represented by *beauty, fealty, lealty*, †*lewty, loyalty*, †*realty*, †*rialty*, and *royalty*. From the types *lealte, realte*, the ending *-alte* (mod.F. *-auté*) was in OF. extended to formations from different stems, and many words of this form (ultimately written with *-alty*) established themselves in English, as *admiralty, casualty, commonalty*, †*generalty, mayoralty*, †*principalty*, †*regalty, severalty, specialty, spiritualty, temporalty*. Most of these date from the 14th or early 15th century; *penalty* appears to be of later introduction (1512). An obsolete type of formation is exhibited by *curiouste, hid(e)ouste*, and *joyouste*. In OF. certain analogies led to the frequent substitution of *-ete* for *-te*, but this form of the suffix is only occasionally adopted in English, as in the obsolete *noblete, purete*, and *simplete*; the early *sauvete* is now represented by *safety*. Under Latin influence many words in OF. also appear with *-ite* (mod.F. *-ité*) in place of *-(e)te*; hence English forms in -ITY, which in many cases (as in F.) have supplanted those in *-ty*.

Although occurring in a large number of words the suffix has shown little productive power in English; *evelte, everlastingte*, and *overte* occur in the 14–15th cent., and *shrievalty, sheriffalty*, have had currency from the beginning of the 16th cent., but such formations are very rare.

Such words as *faculty, difficulty, honesty, modesty, puberty*, represent Latin formations in which the suffix *-tās* is directly added to a consonantal stem. The number of these in English, as in French, is very small.

The early form of the suffix (*-te*, or *-tee*) remained in use down to the 16th cent., but from the 15th was gradually supplanted by *-tie, -tye*, and the surviving *-ty*.

**-ty**, *suffix*[2], denoting 'ten', forming the second element of the decade numerals from 20 to 90 (in OE. to 120), as *twenty, thirty* (OE. *twentig, þritig*), etc. The OE. *-tig* (gen. sing. *-tiges*, gen. pl. *-tiga, -tigra*, dat. pl. *-tigum*) corresponds to OFris. *-tich, -tech* (pl. *-tiga, -tega*), MDu. *-tigh* (Du. *-tig*), OS. *-tig* (*-thig*), *-teg, -tich, -tech* (MLG. and LG. *-tig*), OHG. *-zug, -zuc, -zoch* (MHG. *-zec, -zic*, G. *-zig*), and is the same as ON. *tigr, tegr, tøgr, tugr* (pl. *tigir*, etc.) and Goth. *tigus* (pl. *tigjus*), which are not suffixed but remain independent words, as ON. *tveir tigir*, Goth. *twai tigjus*, twenty. For examples of the OE. forms and syntactical usage, see the various numerals.

† **Tyage** (tai·édʒ). *Obs. rare.* [f. TIE *v.* + -AGE.] The action of tying or mooring a vessel.

1504 *Sel. Cases Cct. Star Chamb.* (Selden) 212 Euery of the kynges liege people .. at their pleasure takyth there aucre holde & tyage in the seid streme & Reuer. *Ibid.* 223 He hath .. payd yerely for his Trow .. xxd. for his haling tyage and hoking att the seide brugge.

**Tyal, tyall**, variants of TIAL, *Obs.*

**Tyar**, obs. f. TEAR *sb.*[1], TIAR, TIRE *v.*[1]

**Tyara**, obs. f. TIARA. **Tyare**, obs. f. TIAR.

**Tyauve, tyave**, Sc. var. TAVE *v.*

**Tyburn** (tai·bɜ̄ɹn). Forms: 4 **Tybourne**, 4–7 **Tyborne**, 5–6 **Tiborne**, 5–7 **Tyburne**, 6 **Tibourne, -burne**, 6–7 **Tiburn**, 7 **Tiborn**, 8 **Tybourn**, 7– **Tyburn**. The place of public execution for Middlesex until 1783, situated at the junction of the present Oxford Street, Bayswater Road, and Edgeware Road. Hence in allusive use.

[*a* 1200 RALPH DE DICETO *Chron.* (Rolls) II. 143 (Hanging of Will. FitzOsbert in 1196) Per mediam civitatem trahitur ad furcas prope Tyburnam. Suspensus est.] 1377 LANGL. *P. Pl.* B. XII. 190 *Dominus pars hereditatis mee* is a meri verset, þat has take fro tybourne twenti stronge þeues. 1393 *Ibid.* C. VII. 368 Þe hangeman of tyborne. *c* 1450 *Brut* 443 To be drawe fro þe Toure of London thorugh þe Citee to Tiborne, & þere hangede & quartrede. *c* 1520 SKELTON *Magnyf.* 423 At the laste I brynge hym ryght To Tyburne, where they hange on hyght. 1580 CAMPION in *Hanmer's Answ.* (1581) 24 We haue a league, all the Iesuits in the worlde .. neuer to dispayre your recouerye whiles we haue a man left to enioy your tyburne or to be racked wyth your torments [etc.]. 1603 H. CROSSE *Vertues Commw.* (1878) 138 Many idle persons .. fall into offence of lawe, and are many times eaten vp by Tyborne. 1705 HICKERINGILL *Priest-cr.* II. iii. 30, I pity the Fate of Malefactors (as they go up Holborn towards Tybourn) though they deserve to be hang'd. 1783 *New Annual Reg.* II. 48 (Sept. 20) The malefactors .. convicted last week at the Old Bailey .. were executed at Tyburn.

*fig.* 1598 E. GILPIN *Skial.* (1878) 32 It is the scourge, the Tamberlaine of vice, The three square Tyborne of impieties.

*transf.* 1736 DRAKE *Eboracum* I. v. 171 August 23 [1649] were executed at Tyburn near York, Colonel John Morrice and Lieutenant Blackburn. 1904 DOM BEDE CAMM *Tyburn & Eng. Mart.* Introd. 12 The blessed Edmund Campion himself inaugurated this pilgrimage, just as the venerable Margaret Clitheroe began that to the York Tyburn.

**b.** *attrib.* and *Comb.*, as *Tyburn check, coach, collop, face, jig, piccadill, saint, stretch, string, tie, tiffany, tribe, wright*; **Tyburn blossom**: see quot. 1796; **Tyburn ticket**, a certificate formerly granted to one who secured the conviction of a felon, exempting the holder from all parochial duties in the parish where the offence was committed; **Tyburn tippet**: see TIPPET *sb.* 2; **Tyburn top**: see quot.; hence **Tyburn-topped** *a.*; **Tyburn tree**, the gallows.

1796 *Grose's Dict. Vulg. T.*, **Tyburn Blossom*, a young thief or pickpocket, who in time will ripen into fruit borne by the deadly never-green. 1827 LYTTON *Pelham* lxxxi, As pretty a Tyburn blossom as ever was brought up to ride a horse foaled by an acorn. *c* 1520 SKELTON *Magnyf.* 911 A *Tyborne checke Shall breke his necke. 1829 CARLYLE *Misc.* (1857) II. 27 At the tenth mile this *Tyburn-coach breaks down! *c* 1420 ? LYDG. *Assembly of Gods* 697 *Tyburne coloppys, and pursekytters. *c* 1515 *Cocke Lorells B.* 11 Tyburne collopes and peny pryckers. 1695 CONGREVE *Love for L.* II. vii, He has a damn'd *Tyburn-Face, without the Benefit o' the Clergy. 1698 FARQUHAR *Love & Bottle* II. ii, Which is best, Mr. Nimblewrist, an easy Minuet, or a *Tyburn Jigg? 1620 J. TAYLOR (Water P.) *Hempseed* Preamble 38 Till they put on a *Tyburne Pickadill. 1785 WOLCOTT (P. Pindar) *Odes to R. Acad.* v. 16 Your *Tyburn Saints will not your fame increase. 1573 TUSSER *Husb.* (1878) 214 To beg in age, Or else to fetch a *Tibourne stretch. 1882 J. WALKER *Jaunt to Auld Reekie* 4 He should dangle in a *Tyburn string. 1796 COLQUHOUN *Police of Metropolis* 203 For apprehending, and prosecuting to conviction, any person charged with horse-stealing, a *Tyburn ticket. 1813 *Examiner* 12 Apr. 232/1 Mr. Burton was also robbed, .. for which a man suffered death, on whose conviction the worthy old man received a Tyburn Ticket. 1816 *Rep. Committee on Police of Metropolis* 4 Is it not customary to give what is called 'a Tyburn Ticket' on some occasions? 1828 *Lights & Shades* II. 186 His brother was about to endure .. the '*Tyburn-tie'. 1612 ROWLANDS *Knave of Harts* 4 Neuer regarding Hang-mans feare, Till *Tyburne-tiffany he weare. 1549 *Tyburn tippet [see TIPPET *sb.* 2]. 1647 TRAPP *Comm.* 1 *Cor.* xiii. 3 And how many of our Popish Martyrs .. have worne the Tiburn-tippet, as Father Latimer phraseth it? 1830 MRS. BRAY *Fitz of F.* xxiv, Your glories aspire to a Tyburn tippet, and that will be the end of them. 1796 *Grose's Dict. Vulg. T.*, **Tyburn Top*, or *Foretop*, a wig with the foretop combed over the eyes in a knowing style. 1774 FOOTE *Cozeners* I. Wks. 1799 II. 153 See him on the turf, at Newmarket, in his *Tyburn-topp'd wig, tight boots, and round hat. 1727 GAY *Begg. Op.* III. xiii, I wonder we han't better Company, Upon *Tyburn Tree! 1851 BORROW *Lavengro* xxxix, Tyburn tree had long since been cut down. 1717 ROWE *Cruel Gift* Epil. 29 That *Tyburn-tribe of speech-making Non-jurors. 1589 [? LYLY] *Pappe w. Hatchet* B iij b, We neither feare Martin, .. nor of what occupation hee be, be a ship-wright, cart-wright, or *tiburn-wright.

**c.** *To preach at Tyburn cross*, to be hanged; in reference to the speeches permitted to those about to be executed.

1576 GASCOIGNE *Steele Gl.* (Arb.) 55 That Soldiours sterue, or preach at Tiborne crosse.

**Tyce**, variant of TICE *v.*

**Tychite** (tai·kəit). *Min.* [f. Gr. τύχη fortune, chance + -ITE[1], in reference to its accidental discovery.] A rare mineral consisting of carbonate and sulphate of magnesium and sodium, crystallizing in colourless octahedrons.

1909 in *Cent. Dict. Suppl.*

**Tycho-** (taiko), combining form repr. Gr. τύχη fortune, chance, used in a few recent scientific terms. **Ty:chopa·rthenoge·nesis**, exceptional or occasional parthenogenesis. **Tychopo·tamic** *a.* [Gr. ποταμός river], of occasional occurrence in or near rivers.

1900 B. D. JACKSON *Gloss. Bot. Terms, Tychopotamic.. Plankton*, the floating organisms of pools and river overflows (Zimmer). 1909 *Cent. Dict. Suppl.*, Tychoparthenogenesis.

**Tychonian** (taikōu·niăn), *a.* and *sb.* [f. mod.L. *Tychon-*, stem of *Tycho*, Latinized form of the Danish personal name *Tyge* + -IAN.] **a.** *adj.* = TYCHONIC. **b.** *sb.* A disciple or adherent of Tycho Brahe or of his system of astronomy. *rare.*

1647 BOYLE *Let.* 8 Apr., in Birch *Life* B.'s Wks. 1772 I. p. xxxix, The dissenting opinions of the Ptolemeans, the Tychonians [etc.]. 1710 J. HARRIS *Lex. Techn.* II, *Tychonian System* or *Hypothesis*, is so called from having been advanced to solve the Phænomena of Astronomy by the Noble Tycho Brahe. 1901 *Nature* 7 Nov. 7/1 In .. the Prague Town Hall an exhibition was held of several Tychonian relics.

**Tychonic** (taikǫ·nik), *a.* [f. as prec. + -IC.] Of or pertaining to the Danish astronomer Tycho Brahe (died 1601), or to his system of astronomy.

1670 FLAMSTEED in Rigaud *Corr. Sci. Men* (1841) II. 97, I had first notice of this star's varying from the Tychonic canon. 1678 CUDWORTH *Intell. Syst.* Pref. 3 The other (vulgarly so called) systems of the world .. the Ptolemaick, Tychonick, and Copernican. 1715 tr. *Gregory's Astron.* (1726) I. 187 The same Forces that are required in the Semi-Tychonic System, are required also in the Tychonic, since the same Motion of the Sun and Planets are supposed in both. 1870 R. A. PROCTOR in *Eng. Mech.* 4 Mar. 598/3 His ellipses were .. as available for the Tychonic system as for the Copernican.

**Tycht**, Sc. pa. pple. of TIGHT *v.*[1] *Obs.*

**Tyck, Tyckett, Tyckle**, obs. ff. TICK, etc.

‖**Tycoon** (taikū·n). Also **taikun.** [ad. Jap. *taikun* great lord or prince, f. Chinese *ta* great + *kiun* prince.] The title by which the shogun of Japan was described to foreigners.

1863 ALCOCK (*title*) The Capital of the Tycoon: A narrative of a three years' residence in Japan. *Ibid.* II. 491 The name by which this officer is commonly known is 'the Tycoon of Japan'. 1875 W. E. GRIFFIS in *N. Amer. Rev.* CXX. 287 There never was but one emperor in Japan, the Shogun was military usurper, and the bombastic title 'Tycoon' a diplomatic fraud. 1881 SIR R. ALCOCK in *Encycl. Brit.* XIII. 584/2 The title of *taikun* (often misspelt *tycoon*) was then for the first time used; it .. was employed for the occasion by the Tokugawa officials to convey the impression that their chief was in reality the lord paramount. 1887 L. OLIPHANT *Episodes* (1888) 186 Soldiers of the Tycoon, or Temporal Emperor [of Japan], as he was then [1861] called.

Hence **Tycoo·nate**, the office or dignity of a tycoon or the tycoons; **Tycoo·nism**, the system of temporal government by the tycoon.

1863 ALCOCK *Capital Tycoon* I. v. 135 The '*Tycoonat*', created by the strong arm and determined will of *Taikosama*. 1876 E. W. CLARK *Life Japan* 128 Shidz-u-o-ka .. became the St. Helena of Tycoonism.

**Tyd**, obs. f. TIDE *sb.* and *v.*, TITE *adv.*; var. TID *a. Obs.* **Tydance, -and(e, -annes, -ant**, obs. ff. TIDING, TIDINGS. **Tyddie**, obs. f. TIDY. **Tyde**, obs. f. TIDY; obs. pa. t. of TIE *v.* **Tydely**: see TIDELY *adv.* **Tyden**, obs. f. TIDE *v.*[1] **Tyder**, obs. f. THITHER.

† **Tydie.** *Obs. rare*—[1]. The name of some small bird; ? = TIDIFE.

1612 DRAYTON *Poly-olb.* xiii. 79 And of these chaunting fowls, the goldfinch not behind, That hath so many sorts descending from her kind. The tydie for her notes as delicate as they.

**Tydie**, obs. f. TIDY.

**Tydond, tydynde**, obs. ff. TIDING, TIDINGS.

**Tye, tie** (tai), *sb.*[1] *Obs.* exc. *dial.* and *local.* Forms: *a.* 1 téag, téʒ, téʒ, 5 tee; *β.* 1 tiʒ, 5 **tigh**, ty, 4– tye, 5–6, 9 tie. [OE. *téag, téah*, which agrees in forms with TIE *sb.* and TYE *sb.*[2], and is treated by Bosw.-Toller and Sweet as the same word. The sense-history is unknown; the connexion of the senses here included is also uncertain.]

† **1.** A small box or case for jewels and other valuables; a casket. *Obs.*

*a.* *c* 725 *Corpus Gloss.* (O.E.T.) 1300 *Mantega*, taeʒ. *Ibid.* 2010 *Tehis* [for *techis, thecis*], teʒum, fodrum. *c* 1000 ÆLFRIC *Saints' Lives* xxiii. 764 Þa feng se port-ʒerefa to þære teʒe and .. hi uninsæʒlode. 1027–34 *Laws of Cnut* II. c. 76 § 1 Hyre hordern and hyre cyste and hyre teʒe [*MS. B.* tæʒan]. 1477 *Inventory* in *Lanc. Wills* (1884) 4 A Tee w[th] other coofers.

*β.* *c* 1050 *Gloss* in Wr.-Wülcker 443/8 *Mantega*, tiʒ. 1390 GOWER *Conf.* II. 246 Tho tok sche forth a riche Tye Mad al of gold and of Perrie, Out of the which sche nam a Ring. *c* 1400 *Laud Troy Bk.* 5870 Thei robbed clene al that thei founde .. Off gold, siluer, & riche druri, That thei fond in coffres and ty. *Ibid.* 9983 3oure brochis brode & al 3oure byes That now ligges In 3oure tyes. *c* 1425 *Seven Sag.* (P.) 2951 Scho .. broght the rynge anoon That lay loken in hir tie [*rime* eie]. 1460 *Will of Spenser* (Somerset Ho.), Cum duabus cistis .. altera vocata spruce tigh. 1535 in Weaver *Wells Wills* (1890) 116 A croke, a tye, and v silver spones.

**2.** *Mining* (*Cornwall*). A deep trough or box used for collecting the dross and refuse in washing ore.

1531–2 *Act* 23 *Hen. VIII*, c. 8 § 1 Onelesse the saide diggar owner or wassher shall make .. sufficient hatches and tyes in the end of their buddels and cordes and therin putt .. all the sande stones gravell and robell digged about the inserching fynding and washing of the said Tynne there to be holly and suerlie kepte by the said hatches and ties oute and frome the said fresshe rivers. 1839 DE LA BECHE *Rep. Geol. Cornw.*, etc. xv. 578 The tye is a long, narrow, inclined furrow, through which passes a stream of water, three or four times larger than that used in buddling. 1839 URE *Dict. Arts* 1245 The latter is sometimes thrown away, and at others is subjected to the operation called the tie, viz., a washing upon the sloping bottom of a long trough.

**3.** A pit or trench from which turf or peat is dug. *local* (*Devonsh.*).

1836 A. E. BRAY *Descr. Tamar & Tavy* I. xx. 348 A turf tye, that is, a pit from which they dig turfs for fuel. 1873 *Q. Rev.* July 159 Dartmoor turf-cutters .. labouring in the solitary 'ties', as the turf-trenches are called.

**4.** The stuffed case forming a mattress or pillow:

= Tick *sb.*[2] Also *bed-tye*, *pillow-tye*. (Cf. Tay, tey.) Now *dial.*

1615 Crooke *Body of Man* 143 This Membrane..is rowled in plentifull fat, & so serueth the Kidneyes instead of a couering, of a tye, and of a soft pillow or bolster. 1847–78 [see Pillow *sb.* 6]. 1893 Baring-Gould *Cheap Jack Z.* I. vii. 110 We'll lift you on to a feather tye. 1898 Mrs. C. P. Penberthy *Warp & Woof Cornish Life* ii. 13 The bed-tie and pillows..was..in a pawn shop...There was the very tie, I knawed un in a minute.

**5.** *attrib.* and *Comb.* (in sense 2): **tye-lift** (see Lift *sb.*[2] 12); **tye-pit**, a pit for collecting the refuse in washing ore.

1602 Carew *Cornwall* 154 b, They have a tye-pit, not so much satisfying use, as relieving necessitie. 1778 W. Pryce *Min. Cornub.* 16 To take up the superficial streams, by.. grooves cut in the walls..of the Lode, to convey them either into the adit or tye lift of pumps. 1905 *Eng. Dial. Dict.* s.v. *Tye* (*Devon.*), 'Be careful now and don't go near the tie-pit.'

**Tye, tie** (təi), *sb.*[2] *local.* Forms: 1 téaȝ, 5– tye (also 7 tie). [OE. *téag*, by Bosw.-Toller and Sweet held to be the same word as Tie *sb.* and Tye *sb.*[1]; but the connexion of sense is unexplained. Bosw.-Toller also compares ON. *teigr* a strip of field or meadow-land, a close or paddock, which occurs freq. in names of meadows; but OE. *téag* and ON. *teigr* are not phonetically related.] An enclosed piece of land, enclosure, close; also, an extensive common pasture; a large common.

832 *Test. of Werhard* in Birch *Cart. Sax.* I. 559 Mansionem..et clausulam quod Angli dicunt *teage*, quæ pertinet ad prædictam mansionem. 853 *Charter of Ætheluulf* ibid. II. 61 Circumcincta est..a meritie Bromteaȝ. 1407 in *Essex Rev.* XIII. 204 [A freehold called] Tye-lond. 1488 *Maldon, Essex, Liber B.* lf. 39 (MS.) All that lane till they came dovne to Lymborn-broke on to the tye & comon ayenst Brodehedis. 1670 Blount *Law Dict.*, *Tigh* or *Teage*..a Close or Enclosure, a Croft...The word *Tigh* is still used in Kent in the same sense. *c* 1700 *Churchw. Acc. St. Dunstan's, Canterb.*, Woolvysty 3 acres of land lying within a cross. 1708 *Lond. Gaz.* No. 4453/4 Lost.., from the Tye in the Parish of Blackthorne.., a black Gelding. *a* 1825 Forby *Voc. E. Anglia*, *Tye*, an extensive common pasture. There are several tyes a few miles South of the central part of Suffolk; but in no other part of East Anglia. There are also some on the Northern border of Essex. 1884 *Daily News* 23 Sept. 6/6 In almost every parish was a 'heath', tie, common, or green, where the poor of the parish had certain rights. 1887 Parish & Shaw *Dict. Kentish Dial.*, *Tye, Tie*, an extensive common pasture. Such as Waldershare Tie.

**Tye, tie**, *v. Mining.* (*local.*) [f. Tye *sb.*[1] 2.] *trans.* To separate (the ore) from the dross or refuse by means of a 'tye'. Hence **Ty·ing** *vbl. sb.*

1757 in J. Lloyd *Old S. Wales Iron Works* (1906) 23 Pipes for carrying Air or Water underground through their lands, or Tying of Wase or Wases. 1839 De la Beche *Rep. Geol. Cornw.*, etc. xv. 578 Some kinds of ore..required other operations after roasting, generally either tying by itself, or tying and jigging. 1881 Raymond *Mining Gloss.*, *Strake* (*Corn.*), an inclined launder for separating or tying ground ore in water.

**Tye**, obs. form or var. of Tie.

‖ **Tyee, tyhee** (təi·ī). [Chinook jargon.]

**1.** A chief; a person of distinction. *slang. U.S.*

1909 in *Cent. Dict. Supp.* 1911 *Chambers' Jrnl.* July 439 Thither when a tyhee [*i.e.* a wealthy Chinaman] dies, wends a noisy procession.

**2.** The king-salmon or quinnat (*Oncorhynchus chouicha* or *quinnat*). Also *attrib.*

1902 Jordan & Evermann *Amer. Food & Game Fishes* 151 Chinook Salmon...Other names by which this fish is known are quinnat salmon,..tyee, tchaviche, and tschawytscha. 1903 *Blackw. Mag.* Mar. 373/1 The quinnat, chinook, or ty-hee (chief) commonly known as the Spring Salmon. 1909 *Morn. Leader* 6 Feb. 4/4 He caught four and Mr. Bonnell two 'Tyee' salmon;..only three other 'Tyees' were taken.

**Tyer**, obs. f. Tear *sb.*[1], Tire *sb.*[1] and *v.*[3], Tyre *sb.*[1]; var. Tier *sb.*[2], Tire *v.*[2], Tyre *sb.*[4] **Tyerce, Tyercell(e**, obs. ff. Tierce, Tercel. **Tyere**, obs. f. Tire *v.*[1] and [3]; var. Tyre *sb.*[1] *Obs.* **Tyers(e**, obs. ff. Tierce. **Tyesday**, Sc. f. Tuesday. **Tyf(e, tyff(e**, obs. ff. Tiff *v.*[1]

† **Tyft**, app. an obs. variant of Tuft *sb.* 3.

*c* 1450 *Godstow Reg.* 458, iij. acris of arable lond..with the mansion, tyftis of roddis, thorptis or croftis, and medis, at wyke. *Ibid.*, All the forsaid lond with the mansion, tyftis of twyggis, thorptis, medis,..and all other thyngis longyng to the said lond [cf. 139 toft of roddys; 679 tofte of Roddys].

**Tyg, tig** (tig). [Origin unknown.] A name said to have been formerly given in the Staffordshire potteries to a porringer; now applied by antiquaries and collectors to a drinking-cup with two or more handles, attributed to the 17th and 18th c.

1838 Bosworth *Anglo-Sax. Dict.* s.v. *Tigel*, To this day porringers are called tigs by the working potters. 1855 H. de la Beche & T. Reeks *Catal. Specimens Brit. Pottery*, etc., *Mus. Pract. Geol.* 116 Three handled tyg, a drinking cup of the time, so handled that three different persons, drinking out of it, and each using a separate handle, bring their mouths to different parts of the rim. 1865 Eliza Meteyard *Life J. Wedgwood* I. 76 The tyg or cup with two or more handles, was a favourite drinking vessel in the sixteenth and seventeenth centuries. 1880 C. H. Poole *Gloss. Stafford*, *Tyg*, a two-handled cup. 1892 Raine *Handbk. to York Museum* 169 Cruses and tygs of black and brown ware.

**Tyger**, obs. f. Tiger. **Tyȝe**, obs. f. Tie *v.*

**Tyȝl, Tyȝt**, obs. ff. Tile, Tite.

**Tyght(e**, obs. f. Theat, Tight; var. Tite *adv.*

**Tyhee**, obs. f. Tehee; var. Tyee.

**Tyik**, obs. Sc. f. Tick *sb.*[2], case for bed.

**Tying** (təi·iŋ), *vbl. sb.*[1] [f. Tie *v.* + -ing [1].]

**1.** The action of the verb Tie in various senses; fastening with a cord or string; connexion, binding, etc. Also *attrib.*

1480 *Wardr. Acc. Edw. IV* (1830) 123 For vj teyng haltres, price the pece xvj d. 1505 *Sel. Cases Crt. Star Chamb.* (Selden) 219 The kinges leege people..att ther pleasur take ther tying in the seide streme and on ther land adioyning. 1651 *Fuller's Abel Rediv.*, *Melancthon* (1867) I. 279 It was a tying void of sense and reason, to yield a subscription unto..things which..he did neither know nor understand. 1760–72 H. Brooke *Fool of Qual.* (1809) III. 89, I was still sore from the tyings and the bruises which I had received. 1809 *Med. Jrnl.* XXI. 424 When..ulceration takes place after the tying of an artery. 1833 Loudon *Encycl. Archit.* § 16 Cow-house, with a tying-post and trough for food. 1906 *Macm. Mag.* Apr. 447 A March brown [angling fly]..of the popular local tying.

**2.** *concr.* Something used for tying; something that ties, binds, or connects; a tie. ? *Obs.*

1548 Udall *Erasm. Par. Luke* i. 27 By and by..was the tying of his tounge looced. 1608 Topsell *Serpents* (1658) 652 A short stalk or tying, by which the Comb [in a wasps' nest]..is fastened..to the earth, or some tree. 1844 N. Paterson *Manse Gard.* 119 The paper may be kept in its place by pins, or a tying of twine.

**Tying**, *vbl. sb.*[2]: see Tye *v.*

**Ty·ing**, *ppl. a.* [f. Tie *v.* + -ing [2].] That ties: see the verb.

In some of the quots. this may be the vbl. sb. used *attrib.*

1552 Huloet, Tiynge bonde, *ligamentum*. 1688 R. Holme *Armoury* iii. 261/2 *Tying course*, [the bricks] as cover the top of the Arch. 1781 P. Beckford *Hunting* xx. 268 Old tyeing hounds..are..contrary to the true spirit of fox-hunting..continually bringing the pack back again. 1826 *Sporting Mag.* XVII. 233 Like unto the tying beagle which dwells upon the stale scent. 1827 Syd. Smith in *Edin. Rev.* XLV. 429 A tying-up..action. 1901 *J. Black's Illustr. Carp. & Build.*, *Home Handicr.* 61 Mortised through the tying rails.

**Tyir**, obs. Sc. f. Tire *v.*[1]

**Tyisce, tyist(e**, obs. Sc. ff. Tice *v.*

**Tyisday**, obs. Sc. f. Tuesday.

**Tyke** (təik). Chiefly *Sc.* and *north. dial.* Also 6 tyk, 6–9 tike. [a. ON. *tík* female dog, bitch (Norw. *tik*, also she-fox, vixen, Sw. dial. *tik*, older Da. *tig*); also MLG. *tike* bitch.]

**1.** A dog; usually in depreciation or contempt, a low-bred or coarse dog, a cur, a mongrel.

*c* 1400 *Melayne* 1325 Says Charls: 'þou false hethyn hownde, ..aythire of thies dayes Ilyke Hase þou stollen a waye lyke a tyke'. 1500–20 Dunbar *Of James Dog* 14 Poems (S.T.S.) 195 He barkis lyk ane midding tyk. 1570 Levins *Manip.* 122/25 A Tyke, dogge, *canis.* 1575 Churchyard *Chippes* (1817) 182 At great dogs the little tikes doe snarre. 1634 Heywood *Lanc. Witches* ii. Wks. 1874 IV. 199 Are Mr. Robinsons dogges turn'd tykes with a wanion? 1786 Burns *Twa Dogs* 29 He was a gash an' faithfu' tyke, As ever lap a sheugh or dike. 1815 Scott *Guy M.* lv, The mad randy gipsy, that had..been hounded like a stray tike from parish to parish. 1844 Stephens *Bk. Farm* II. 89 A drover of sheep should always be provided with a dog,..a knowing cautious tyke. 1861 J. Brown *Horæ Subs.* ii. 138 Toby was the most utterly shabby, vulgar, mean-looking cur I ever beheld—in one word, a tyke.

**2.** *transf.* Applied opprobriously to a man (rarely with similar force to a woman): A low-bred, lazy, mean, surly, or ill-mannered fellow; a boor. (Cf. Dog *sb.* 3 a, Hound *sb.*[1] 4 a.) Also said in playful reproof to a child.

? *a* 1400 *Morte Arth.* 3642 Hewe downe hertly ȝone heythene tykes! ? *a* 1500 *Chester Pl.* vii. 275 Lyther tyke, ..thy deedes are done. 1567 *Satir. Poems Reform.* xiv. 42 For me that Nobill of Renoun With ane Tyke, Tratour Hammiltoun, Was schot. 1599 Shaks. *Hen. V*, ii. i. 31 Base Tyke, cal'st thou mee Hoste? 1625 B. Jonson *Staple of N.* v. iv. 57 Yo'are a dissembling Tyke. 1681 Colvil *Whigs Supplic.* (1751) 87 Yet many utterly mislikes, That butcher Presbyterian tykes Should flee upon their throats and faces. 1806 Jamieson *Gude Wallace* in *Ball. & Songs* (1806) II. 174 Tyke, by the rude thou 'scapes nat sae. 1825 Brockett *N. C. Words*, *Tike* or *Tyke*, a person of bad character, a blunt or vulgar fellow. 1868 [see *tykishness* below]. 1894 *Daily News* 4 Oct. 7/2 Mr. R——..exclaimed, 'You dirty little tyke'.

**3.** A nickname for a Yorkshireman: in full *Yorkshire tyke*.

(Perhaps originally opprobrious; but now accepted and owned. It may have arisen from the fact that in Yorkshire *tyke* is in common use for *dog*.)

*a* 1700 B. E. *Dict. Cant. Crew*, *Yorkshire-Tike*, a Yorkshire manner of Man. *a* 1714 Prior *Wandering Pilgrim* vii, Could Yorkshire-Tyke but do the same, Then He like Them might thrive. 1761 *British Mag.* II. 464 I'se a poor Yorkshire tyke. 1820 Syd. Smith in *Life* x. (1884) 249 Give a tyke a bridle and he'll soon have a horse. 1856 [H. H. Dixon] *Post & Paddock* vi. 92 The tykes, who were very jealous of the honour of their jocks, did not relish their defeat. 1901 Harper *Great North Road* I. 268 By common consent, whatever its origin may have been, 'tyke', applied to a Yorkshireman, is taken in the complimentary sense.

**4.** *attrib.* and *Comb.*, as *tyke dog*, *-man*, *-sticker*.

*a* 1585 Polwart *Flyting w. Montgomerie* 787 Tyk stickar, poysond viccar, pot lickar! 1826 *Sporting Mag.* XVII. 283 A provincial touch..between Bob Luckman, a tyke-man, and John Bouck, a rat-trap. 1895 Crockett *Men of Moss-Hags* xxxiv, A great debate concerning this tyke dog.

Hence (*nonce-wds.*) **Ty·kedom**, the realm or community of tykes; humorously, Yorkshire (see 3); **Ty·kishness**, the character of a tyke.

1868 E. H. Yates *Wrecked in Port* iii, As the 'tyke' grew up she dropped all outward signs of tykeishness. 1905 *Westm. Gaz.* 18 Dec. 3/1 At Bradford or Sheffield or some other murky stronghold of Tykedom.

**Tyke**: see Tike [1]; obs. f. Tick *sb.*[1] and [2].

**Tykele, -ell**, obs. ff. Tickle.

‖ **Tykhana** (təikā·nä). *E. Ind.* [ad. Urdū (Pers.) *tahkhāna* nether house.] In India, an underground chamber to which to retire during the heat of the day.

1859 Lang *Wand. India* 196 These walls are those of the ty-khana—a vault beneath the dwelling from which the light is excluded. 1862 Beveridge *Hist. India* III. ix. iv. 629 Their families found good shelter in the tykhanas, or underground rooms. 1913 *Blackw. Mag.* May 687/2 Almost under our feet are the tykhanas.

**Tykkatt, Tykke, Tykle, -yl(l**, obs. ff. Ticket, Tick *sb.*[2], Tickle.

**Tyl**, obs. form of Till *prep.* and *conj.*

**Tyld, tylde**, var. Teld, Tild, *Obs.*

**Tyle**: see Tild, Tile, Till *v.*[1] and [3].

**Tyle**, in *tyle seed*: see Tilly *sb.*

**Tyle-berry.** The coral-plant, *Jatropha multifida*. 1866 *Treas. Bot.* 1185.

**Tyler**, obs. f. or var. Tiler.

**Tylerism** (təi·ləriz'm). [f. proper name *Tyler* (see defs.) + -ism.]

**1.** *U.S. Politics.* The practice or methods of President Tyler (see below).

1844 *Hallowell* (Maine) *Liberty Standard* 4 Apr., They would vote for Harrison..and have fallen under Tylerism.

**2.** The theological system of Dr. Bennet Tyler of Connecticut (1783–1858), which reaffirmed the doctrines of the older Calvinism as against Taylorism. 1891 in *Cent. Dict.*

So **Ty·lerize** *v.*, *intr.* to abandon the party to which one owes one's position or office, as President Tyler (1841–5) did; also *trans.* in causal sense.

1865 *Nation* (N. Y.) 24 Aug. 227 The Democratic party.. had two ways of returning..to office...They might either.. unseat the Administration, or else persuade the Executive to Tylerize. 1866 Pres. Johnson in *Morn. Star* 16 Mar. 5/3 It has been said..that here is a President who was elected by a party, and who on coming into power abandoned that party; that he has 'Tylerised' his Administration.

**Tylet**, var. Tillet [2] *Obs.*, lime-tree.

**Tylhexactine**: see Tylo-.

**Tylie**, obs. f. Till *v.*[1] **Tyll**, obs. f. Thill [1], Till; var. Tild *Obs.* **Tylle**, obs. f. Till, Twill *sb.*[1]

† **Tyllole.** *Obs. rare*[−1]. [a. OF. *tillole* (also *tignole*) in the same sense.] A device for bending a cross-bow.

1489 Caxton *Faytes of A.* ii. xxv. I v b, Tournes al newe for to bende crosbowes with all..othre tylloles for to bende crosbowes.

† **Tyllshite**, app. obs. for *twill-sheet*, Twill *sb.*[1] c.

1586 *Shuttleworths' Acc.* (Chetham Soc.) 34 Tyntie yardes of grete canves for to be a grete tyllshite, vij[s].

**Tylo-** (təilo), before a vowel or *h* tyl- (til), combining form repr. Gr. τύλος knob, or τύλη callus, cushion, used in a few terms of zoology. **Tylhexa·ctine** [see *hexactine* under Hexa-], a six-rayed sponge-spicule having a knob at the end of each ray. **Ty·loclad** [Gr. κλάδος shoot, branch], a sponge-spicule knobbed at one end and branched at the other. **Ty·lopod** [Gr. πούς, ποδ- foot], *a.* having pads on the digits instead of hoofs; belonging to the *Tylopoda*, a group of ruminants comprising the camels and llamas (synonymous with *Camelidæ*); *sb.* a member of the *Tylopoda*; so **Tylo·podous** *a.* **Ty·lostyle** [Gr. στῦλος pillar] (also in L. form **tylosty·lus**), a sponge-spicule of the form of a rod with a knob at one end (the other end being pointed); also *attrib.* or as *adj.*; so **Tylosty·lar, Tylosty·lote**, *adjs.*, pertaining to, or of the form of, a tylostyle.

1909 *Cent. Dict. Suppl.*, *Tylhexactine. 1888 Sollas in *Challenger Rep.* XXV. p. lv, **Tyloclad*. The esactine is tylote and the ecactine cladose. [1878 Bell *Gegenbaur's Comp. Anat.* 483 In the Tylopoda and Solidungula this end of the ulna has quite disappeared.] 1891 *Cent. Dict.*, *Tylopod, *Tylopodous. 1902 *Cassell's Encycl. Dict.*, *Suppl.*, *Tylostylar. 1886 R. von Lendenfeld in *Proc. Zool. Soc.* 21 Dec. 574 The supporting skeleton, composed of bundles of monaxonid not *tylostyle spicules, is strengthened by spongin. *Ibid.*, Spicules tetraxon, monaxon (tylostylus), or absent. 1887 Sollas in *Encycl. Brit.* XXII. 423/1 (*Sponges*) *Polymastidae.*—Skeleton consisting of styles radiately arranged and cortical tylostyles. 1886 R. von Lendenfeld in *Proc. Zool. Soc.* 21 Dec. 590 Spicules polyact, tetract, lithistid, *tylostylote, or stylote, never cemented with spongin.

**Tylose** (təi·lous). *Bot.* Also **thylose.** [a. F. *tylose* (Van Heurck), f. G. *thyllen* (1845), *tüllen* sb. pl., of doubtful origin.] An intrusive growth of the wall of a cell into the cavity of a vessel in woody tissue.

1872 Thiselton-Dyer in *Geol. Mag.* June 242 The most

curious feature about this wood is..the cellular mass (Tylose) with which the interior of the ducts is filled up. *Ibid.* 243 Many instances of Tylose are now known. **1884** BOWER & SCOTT *De Bary's Phaner.* 170 The formation of fresh thyloses may continue for a long time in a portion of a vessel.

‖ **Tylosis** (təilōu·sis). [mod.L., in sense 1 ad. Gr. τύλωσις formation of a callus (Galen), f. τύλος or τύλη: see TYLO- and -OSIS.]

**1.** *Path.* **a.** An inflammatory disease of the eyelids, characterized by thickening and hardening of their edges. **b.** An affection of the mucous membrane of the lips and mouth, characterized by whitish spots; leucoplacia. **c.** Callosity.

**1890** in BILLINGS *Med. Dict.* **1899** *Syd. Soc. Lex.*, *T[ylosis] palmæ*..callosity of the palm. *T. plantæ*.., a callosity occurring in the foot. **1899** *Allbutt's Syst. Med.* VIII. 689 Tylosis is usually painless.

¶**2.** *Bot.* = TYLOSE.

Perh. an erron. use arising from the pl. *tyloses* being taken as Latin.

**1876** J. H. BALFOUR in *Encycl. Brit.* IV. 87/1 These portions appear as cells filling the interior of the vessel, and are described under the name of *tylosis*. **1899** in *Syd. Soc. Lex.* **1900** B. D. JACKSON *Gloss. Bot. Terms, Tylose, Tylosis*.., a cell intruding into a duct.

**Tylostyle**, etc.: see TYLO-.

**Tylote** (təi·lout), *sb.* (*a.*) *Zool.* Also in L. form **tylotus** (təilōu·tǒs). [ad. Gr. τυλωτός knobbed, vbl. adj. f. τυλοῦν to make knobby, f. τύλος knob.] A sponge-spicule of the form of a cylindrical rod with a knob at each end; also *attrib.* or *adj.* Hence **Ty·lotate** *a.* [-ATE[2]], shaped like a tylote, knobbed; ‖ **Tyloto·xea** [OXEA], a spicule resembling a tylote but pointed at one end (whence **Tyloto·xeate** *a.*, shaped like a tylotoxea).

**1887** SOLLAS in *Encycl. Brit.* XXII. 416/2 (*Sponges*) The spicular rays often become cylindrical;..they are..frequently rounded off (*strongylate*), or thickened into knobs (*tylotate), or branched (*cladose*). *Ibid.* 417/2 The distal ends.. becoming slightly tylotate. *Ibid.* 417/1 The rhabdus..if knobbed at both ends [is known] as a **tylote*. **1888** — in *Challenger Rep.* XXV. p. lviii, *Tylostyle*. A style which is tylote at the origin. **1887** — in *Encycl. Brit.* XXII. 417/1 The tylote if pointed at one end is a **tylotoxea*. **1891** *Cent. Dict.* (citing SOLLAS) *Tylotoxeate. **1886** R. VON LENDENFELD in *Proc. Zool. Soc.* 21 Dec. 561 *Tylotus. A cylindrical rod with a knob at each end.

**Tylotic** (təilǫ·tik), *a. Path.* [f. TYLOSIS: see -OTIC.] Of, pertaining to, or affected with tylosis.

**1883** *Quain's Dict. Med.* 1645 The tylotic coating [of the tongue] presents a silvery or snow-white appearance. **1899** *Syd. Soc. Lex., Tylotic*, pertaining to, or affected with, a callosity.

**Tylsent**, early perverted form of TINSEL *sb.*[3]

† **Tylye**, obs. form of TAILYE.

**1666** *Caldwell Papers* (Maitl. Cl.) I. 135, I heirby bind me, my aires of tylye and provisione, to pay [etc.].

**Tylye**, obs. form of TILL *v.*[1]

† **Tylyester.** *Obs. rare.* Also **tylyystere.** [f. OE. *tili-an* (cf. TELING *vbl. sb.*) + *-estre* -STER.] An enchantress, sorceress.

**14..** *Voc.* in Wr.-Wülcker 582/4 *Facimia*, a forspeker or a tylyystere. *Ibid.* 582/22 *Fascennina, i. femina que novit incantare*, a tylyester.

† **Tymar**, var. TIMAR *Obs.*, a Turkish military fief.

*c* **1618** MORYSON *Itin.* IV. (1903) 17 For reuenues of Land, the Tymars giuen in farme only for life,..pay tythes and other duties to the Emperor.

**Tymbal**, var. TIMBAL. **Tymber, -ir, -re, -ur, -yr**, obs. ff. TIMBER, TIMBRE. **Tymble**, obs. f. THIMBLE. **Tymbrel, -ell(e, -ill**, obs. ff. TIMBREL.

† **Tymburnar.** *Obs. rare*⁻⁰. [Cf. TABORNER and TIMBRER.] A player on a timbrel.

**14..** *Nom.* in Wr.-Wülcker 693/13 *Hec timpanizatrix*, a tymburnar.

**Tyme**, obs. f. TEAM *sb.*, THYME, TIME; var. TEME *v. Obs.*

† **Tymer**, *v. Obs. rare*⁻⁰. [Of obscure origin.] *intr.* To work idly.

*c* **1440** *Promp. Parv.* 494/1 Tymeryn, *idem quod* tyffyn *supra.* [= TIFF *v.*[1] 3.]

**Tymer, Tymeral, Tymerous**, obs. ff. TIMBER *sb.*[1], TIMBREL *sb.*[2], TIMOROUS. **Tymir, -ire**, obs. ff. TIMBER. **Tymlie**, obs. Sc. f. TIMELY *adv.* **Tymmer, -ir, -yr**, obs. ff. TIMBER, TIMBRE.

† **Tymor, -our.** *Obs. rare*⁻¹. The name of some bird (if the reading is correct).

? *a* **1400** in Horstm. *Altengl. Leg.* (1881) 370/152 The pylycane & þe popyne-Jay The tymour & [*v.rr.* tymor and, tenure of] þe turtell trewe.

**Tymorous**, obs. f. TIMOROUS.

**Tymous**, obs. f. TIMEOUS.

**Tymp** (timp). Also 7 **timpe, timp.** [app. an abbreviation of TYMPAN. So F. *tympe, timpe*.]

**1.** The mouth of the hearth of a blast-furnace, through which the molten metal descends; formed by an arch of masonry (*tymp-arch*), or a block of stone or iron (*tymp-stone, tymp-plate*), or by two of these together.

**1645-50** BOATE *Irel. Nat. Hist.* (1860) 113 The [melted] Iron..descendeth to the lowest part of the furnace, called the Hearth; the which being filled..they unstop the Hearth and open the Mouth thereof (or the Timp as the Arts-men call it). **1686** PLOT *Staffordsh.* 162 Which four walls have the following names; that next the bellows, the tuarn or tuiron wall; that against it, the wind-wall or spirit-plate; that where the Metall comes out, the Timp or fire plate; that over against it, the back-wall. **1859** R. HUNT *Guide Mus. Pract. Geol.* (ed. 2) 195 A strong blast of air is..injected through *tuyeres*.., which are fixed in holes just above the level of the *tymp*, or block of sandstone which is adjusted at the base of the furnace.

**b.** *attrib.*, as *tymp arch, plate, stone, stopping.*

**1665** D. DUDLEY *Metallum Martis* (1855) 32 The Founder['s] terms,.. as the Timpe stones, the Wind-wall stones,..the Boshes. **1825** J. NICHOLSON *Operat. Mechanic* 331 Tymp-stone..Tymp-plate [*both mispr.* Lymp-]. **1839** URE *Dict. Arts* 691 [Iron blast furnace] Fig. 584 represents the hearth and boshes..*a* is the tymp stone, and *b* the tymp plate for confining the liquid metal in the hearth...The space under the tymp plate..is rammed full, for every cast, with strong loamy earth, or even fine clay; a process called the tymp stopping. **1876** ROUTLEDGE *Discov.* 29 The glassy looking slags..continually flowing over the tympstone. **1881** RAYMOND *Mining Gloss., Tymp*, a hollow iron casting, cooled interiorly by a current of water, and placed to protect the tymp-arch, or arch over the dam, in a blast furnace having a fore-hearth.

**2.** *Coal Mining.* A horizontal piece of timber for supporting the roof; also called *bar, cap*, or *lid*.

**1883** in GRESLEY *Gloss. Terms Coal Mining.*

**Tympan** (ti·mpăn). Also 1 **timpana**, 3-7 **timpane, timpan** (also 9 in sense 1 b), 4-8 **tympane**, (6 **tymphan, timphan**). [ad. L. *tympanum*, TYMPANUM, or a. OF. *tympan, timpan* (12th c. in Hatz.-Darm.; mod.F. *tympan*, = Pg. *tympano*, Sp. and It. *timpano*, in various senses). Cf. OHG. *timpana*, OIcel. *timpan*. In OE. and early ME. only in renderings of Biblical passages.]

**1.** A drum or similar instrument, as a timbrel or tambourine. *arch.*

*c* **825** *Vesp. Psalter* lxvii. 26 In midle iungra plæᵹiendra timpanan. *c* **897** K. ÆLFRED *Gregory's Past. C.* xlvi. 346 Lofiað God mid tympanan, ond on choro. *c* **1000** ÆLFRIC *Gen.* xxxi. 27 Mid lofsangum, & mid timpanum, & mid hearpum. *a* **1300** *E. E. Psalter* cxlix. 3 In timpan and sautre to him singe þai. *Ibid.* cl. 4 Loves him in crouth and timpane. **1303** R. BRUNNE *Handl. Synne* 7128 As þe bras, And as þe tympan, þat bete was. *c* **1400** *Lanfranc's Cirurg.* 283 Þese ben þe propre signes of tympanites: his wombe & þe regioun of his stomac schulen oonly be to-swolle, & alle his oþere lymes..wolen bicome smal, & if þou smitist him vpon his wombe, it wole soune as it were a tympan. **1413** *Pilgr. Sowle* (Caxton 1483) v. viii. 99 Dauyd ordeyned..instrumentes..organs and harpes, Symbals and sawtryes, Kroudes and tympans, Trompettes and tabours. **1503** *Acc. Ld. High Treas. Scot.* II. 392 Item..ane pair of tympanes to the King xxiiij s. **1606** G. W[OODCOCKE] *Hist. Ivstine* XLI. 128 They vse not to sound a trumpet, but a Timpane. *a* **1682** SIR T. BROWNE *Tracts* vi. (1684) 122 Bacchus gave the signal of Battel..not with Trumpets but with Tympans and Cymbals.

**b.** [Ir. *tiompan*.] An ancient Irish stringed instrument played with a bow.

**1432-50** tr. *Higden* (Rolls) I. 355 Men of Irlonde be experte specially in ij. kyndes of musike,..an harpe, and a tympan [L. *tympano*] stryngede and armede with cordes of brasse. **1862** O'CURRY *Anc. Irish* xxxvi. (1873) III. 362 The poem affords another proof that the Timpan was a stringed instrument; and..shows that it was..played on with a wand and hair, words that plainly enough describe a fiddle-bow. **1891** W. B. YEATS *C'tess Cathleen* Poems (1908) 10, I thought I heard far off tympans and harps.

† **2. a.** = TYMPANITES, TYMPANY 1. *Obs. rare.*

**1530** PALSGR. 281/2 Tympan a dysease in the bely, *enfleure.*

† **b.** *transf.* (See quot.) *Obs.*

**1555** EDEN *Decades* 142 The smaulest [pearls] differ from the byggest in a certayne swellynge or impostumation whiche the Spaniardes caule a tympane.

† **3.** = TYMPANUM 2. *Obs.*

**1549** COVERDALE, etc. *Erasm. Par. Jas.* 28 The worde of the Gospell..knocketh in vayne at the tympane of the ears; vnles it light depe in to the inwarde partes of the hearte. **1639** J. S. *Clidamas* 24 If what I speake may befit the tender tympane of a Ladyes eare. **1688** BURNET *Lett. Pres. St. Italy* 181 The violent noise..weakened the Tympan of his Ear. **1706** PHILLIPS (ed. Kersey), *Tympan*,..the Drum of the Ear.

**4.** An appliance in a printing-press, interposed between the platen or impression-cylinder and the sheet to be printed, in order to soften and equalize the pressure; in a hand press consisting of two frames (*outer* and *inner tympan*) with sheets of parchment or strong linen stretched upon them, and inclosing a packing either of blanket, rubber, or other soft substance, or sheets of paper, cardboard, cloth, or other harder material, according to the nature of the work to be printed.

**1580** HOLLYBAND *Treas. Fr. Tong, Le Chassis*, the tympane of a Printers presse. **1594** R. ASHLEY tr. *Loys le Roy* 22 Placing the leafe that is to be printed, on a double tympan or parchmin. **1683** MOXON *Mech. Exerc., Printing* x. ⁋ 10 The Tympan is a square Frame. **1728** CHAMBERS *Cycl.* s.v. *Printing*, On the Front of the Coffin are three Frames.., *viz.* the two Tympans and Frisket. **1824** J. JOHNSON *Typogr.* II. xv. 529 The tympans are covered with vellum, forrels, or parchment. **1869** W. B. in *Eng. Mech.* 24 Dec. 362/1 Make a tympan of thick cardboard. **1880** *Printing Times* 15 Mar. 63/1 Too much packing in a tympan is a great and common fault. **1885** C. G. W. LOCK *Workshop Receipts* Ser. IV. 404/1 A sheet of smooth card..should be laid over the picture before the leather tympan is closed down upon it.

**5.** *Arch.* = TYMPANUM 3.

**1704** J. HARRIS *Lex. Techn.* I, *Tympan of an Arch*, is a triangular Table placed in its Corners. *Ibid., Tympan*, is also attributed to the Pannels of Doors..and to the Dye or Square of Pedestals. **1767** DUCAREL *Anglo-Norman Antiq.* 88 Within the Tympan or panel of the pediment is a basso relievo. **1825** JAMIESON, *Timpan, tympany*, the middle part of the front of a house, raised above the level of the rest of the wall, resembling a gable...This is also called a *Tympany gavel*. **1893** E. H. BARKER *Wand. Southern Waters* 89 The composition, which fills the tympan of the scarcely-pointed arch, represents Christ surrounded by the twelve Apostles.

**6.** = TYMPANUM 4 b.

**1858** LARDNER *Hand-bk. Nat. Phil., Hydrost.* etc. 123 *The tympan.*—A form of wheel, which has received this name, is also used in France for irrigation.

**7.** A tense membrane or thin plate in any mechanical apparatus, e. g. in a phonograph.

**1883** GREER *Dict. Electr.* 170 This [carbon] lozenge is pressed gently by a tympan. **1900** *Daily News* 17 Nov. 6/3 The vibrating plate or tympan had not force enough to imprint the feeble sounds on the wax of the cylinder, and form a good record. *Ibid.*, This varying current in passing through the telephone..makes the iron plate or tympan vibrate and give out..a fairly correct imitation of the speaker's voice.

**8.** *attrib.* (in sense 4), as *tympan-cloth, -frame*; **tympan-sheet**, a sheet of paper, etc. laid on or fixed in the tympan, originally as a guide for placing the sheets to be printed.

**1683** MOXON *Mech. Exerc., Printing* xxiv. ⁋ 7 He takes a Sheet of Paper .. for a Tympan-sheet. *Ibid.* ⁋ 19 This Tympan-cloath is a Fine and even Linnen Cloath. **1771** LUCKOMBE *Hist. Print.* 345 The Tympan sheet..is only as a standing mark to lay all the other sheets exactly even upon. **1841** T. C. HANSARD *Print. & Type-founding* 109 They now choose their points, which are thin iron arms, having a short point projecting from the end, and made to screw on to the tympan-frame. **1911** WEBSTER s. v., In hand presses the tympan is double and consists of two sheets, usually of parchment, stretched on the tympan frame.

Hence † **Ty·mpaned** *a.* (*obs. nonce-wd.*), affected as with a 'tympan' (sense 2); inflated, puffed up; **Ty·mpaning** (tim-) *vbl. sb.* (*nonce-wd.*), the playing of a tympan (sense 1 b).

*a* **1640** DAY *Peregr. Schol.* (1881) 56 Philosophos..swolne and timpaned with presumption. **1862** O'CURRY *Anc. Irish* xxxvi. (1873) III. 363 The harper has exclusive harping... The Timpanist has exclusive timpaning (or Timpan playing).

**Tympanal** (ti·mpănăl), *a.* (*sb.*) *Anat.* and *Zool.* [f. TYMPAN-UM + -AL. So F. and Pg. *tympanal*.] = TYMPANIC 1.

**1822-9** GOOD *Study Med.* (ed. 3) IV. 273 An impeded motion of the air in the tympanal cavity. **1875** SIR W. TURNER in *Encycl. Brit.* I. 806/2 Alexander Achillini of Bologna.. the first who described the two tympanal bones, termed *malleus* and *incus*. **1887** *Amer. Naturalist* XXI. 579 The only organs [in insects] which might be interpreted as answering functionally to an ear are the so-called tympanal organs of Orthoptera.

**B.** *sb.* A tympanal or tympanic bone.

**1875** C. C. BLAKE *Zool.* 202 The upper jaw is represented by the vomer, the palatines, and the tympanals. **1883** *Science* I. 506/2 The tympanal is a horseshoe-like bone.

**Tympanectomy**: see TYMPANO-.

**Tympanic** (timpæ·nik), *a.* (*sb.*) [f. as prec. + -IC; cf. Gr. τυμπανικός suffering from tympanites. So F. *tympanique*, Pg. *tymp-*, Sp. *timpanico*.]

**1.** *Anat.* and *Zool.* Of, pertaining to, or connected with the tympanum, or drum of the ear (as *tympanic artery, bulla, cavity, membrane, muscle, nerve, ossicle*, etc.); of the nature of a tympanum.

*Tympanic bone*, in mammals, a bone of annular or tubular form supporting the tympanic membrane and surrounding the external auditory meatus (in the adult forming part of the temporal bone); in lower vertebrates, one of several bones variously supposed to be homologous with this, esp. the quadrate bone, which supports the lower jaw. *Tympanic pedicle*, the slender bone or series of bones by which the lower jaw is suspended in fishes. *Tympanic plate, ring*, the tympanic bone of mammals.

**1808** *Med. Jrnl.* XIX. 410 Other branches of the same nerve which supply the tympanic muscles. **1840** E. WILSON *Anat. Vade M.* (1842) 277 The Tympanic branch [of the glossopharyngeal nerve] is small. **1849** LYELL *2nd Visit U. S.* (1850) II. 75 The convoluted tympanic bones..characteristic of cetaceans. **1851** RICHARDSON *Geol.* viii. (1855) 308 The lower jaw is articulated to a tympanic bone as in reptiles. **1851** CARPENTER *Princ. Physiol.* § 825 The purpose of this Tympanic apparatus is..to receive the sonorous vibrations from the air, and to transmit them to the membranous wall of the labyrinth. **1860** TYNDALL *Glac.* 225 These aërial waves enter the external ear, meet..the so-called tympanic membrane. **1860** MAYNE *Expos. Lex., Tympanic Pedicle*, ..the large and long pedicle which supports the mandible in fishes,.. subdivided into sometimes two or three, and commonly into four pieces. **1876** *Nature* 20 July 253/2 Sawing out the temporal bone,..and exposing the tympanic bulla. **1893** NEWTON *Dict. Birds* 180 The quadrate bone.. in Mammals..is reduced and modified into the comparatively insignificant tympanic ring.

**b.** as *sb.* Short for *tympanic bone.*

**1851** RICHARDSON *Geol.* (1855) 287 The lower jaw..is articulated to the upper jaw by a distinct bone (the tympanic). **1881** MIVART *Cat* 65 Between the anterior end of the tympanic and the post-glenoid process is a narrow chink..which transmits the chorda tympani nerve.

**2.** Pertaining to or resembling a drum; in *Path.* tympanitic.

**1891** *Cent. Dict.* s. v., *Tympanic resonance*, tympanitic resonance.

**3.** *Arch.* Pertaining to a tympanum.

**1909** *Spectator* 6 Nov. Suppl. 713/1 The 'Doom' often

vividly depicted on the tympanic background, and the Saviour upon the cross in connexion with it.

† **Tympa·nical,** *a. Obs. rare.* [f. as prec. + -ICAL.] = TYMPANITIC.

1623 COCKERAM, *Tympanicall*, of or belonging to the tympanie. 1647 LILLY *Chr. Astrol.* xliv. 262 The Dropsie or Tympanicall humours.

**Tympanichord** (ti·mpăni-, timpæ·nikǭɹd). *Anat.* [f. TYMPANUM + Gr. χορδή CHORD *sb.*[1]] The *chorda tympani*, a branch of the facial nerve which traverses the mucous membrane of the tympanum. Hence **Tympanicho·rdal** *a.*, pertaining to the tympanichord.

1887 COUES (cited in *Cent. Dict.*).

**Tympanicity** (timpăni·sĭti). [f. TYMPANIC + -ITY.] The condition of being tympanic, or affected with tympanites.

1899 in *Syd. Soc. Lex.* 1903 *Lancet* 11 July 98/1 The area of gastric tympanicity was only slightly enlarged.

**Tympanie,** obs. form of TYMPANY.

**Tympaniform** (ti·mpăni-, timpæ·nifǭɹm), *a. Nat. Hist.* [ad. F. *tympaniforme* (Cuvier), f. TYMPANUM + *-forme*, -FORM.] Having the form of a drum, or (usually) of a drum-head; stretched like a drum-head: *spec.* applied to certain membranes in the bronchi of birds.

1854 BUSHNAN in *Circ. Sc.* (*c* 1865) I. 291/1 It is to this usually large portion of the wall of each bronchus that Cuvier gives the name, tympaniform membrane. 1893 NEWTON *Dict. Birds* 58 In almost all birds..the bronchi are strengthened by cartilaginous semirings; the ends of these ..are closed by the inner tympaniform membrane. *Ibid.* 940 *Syrinx trachealis*... Both inner and outer tympaniform membranes exist in the Bronchi. 1900 in B. D. JACKSON *Gloss. Bot. Terms.*

† **Tympa·nious,** *a. Obs. rare*⁻¹. [f. TYMPANY + -OUS.] Pertaining to or of the nature of a tympany.

1704 D'URFEY *Heir Adopted* cx, The dangerous secret of his life Shall never swell again a wife With a tympanious matter.

**Tympanism** (ti·mpăniz'm). *rare*⁻⁰. [cf. Gr. τυμπανισμός a beating of drums, ἀποτυμπανισμός a cudgelling: see TYMPANIZE and -ISM. So F. *tympanisme*, in sense 2.]

†**1.** (See quot., and cf. TYMPANIZE *v.* 3.) *Obs.*

1661 BLOUNT *Glossogr.* (ed. 2), *Tympanism*..a kind of torturing, used by the Jews, by beating one to death with Cudgels or Drum-sticks, *Heb.* 11. 35. 2 *Mac.* 6. 19.

**2.** *Path.* (See quot., and cf. TYMPANITES.)

1890 BILLINGS *Med. Dict.*, *Tympanism*, state of being distended with gas.

**Tympanist** (ti·mpănist). Also 9 tim-. [ad. F. *tympaniste*, It. *timpanista*, L. *tympanista*, Gr. τυμπανιστής, f. τυμπανίζειν TYMPANIZE, or f. *timpan* TYMPAN + -IST.] One who beats or plays upon a drum, a drummer. In quot. 1862, one who plays a tympan (TYMPAN 1 b).

1611 COTGR., *Tympaniste*, a Timpanist; a player on a Timpan, &c. 1656 BLOUNT *Glossogr.*, *Tympanist*, a Drumster or Taberer. 1862 in O'Curry *Anc. Irish* xxxi. (1873) III. 236 'Why is the *Timpan* called *Timpan Naimh* (or saint's Timpan), and yet no saint ever took a Timpan into his hands?' 'I do not know', said the timpanist. 1906 *Daily Chron.* 22 Sept. 1/3 Solo for Six Timpani and Orchestra...Timpanist—Mr. G. G. Cleather.

So † **Tympanister** [ad. L. *tympanistria*, a. Gr. τυμπανίστρια], a female player on a drum or tambourine.

1382 WYCLIF *Ps.* lxvii. 26 The princis camen befor ioyned with the singeris; in the myddel of the ȝunge wymmen tympanystris.

‖ **Tympanites** (timpănəi·tīz). *Path.* [Late L. *tympanītēs*, a. Gr. τυμπανίτης (Galen), f. τύμπανον drum: cf. ASCITES. So Pg. *tympanites*, F. *tympanite* (OF. *timpanides*), It. *timpanite*.] Distension of the abdomen by gas or air in the intestine, the peritoneal cavity, or the uterus.

1398 TREVISA *Barth. De P. R.* VII. lii. (Bodl. MS.) lf. 64 b/1 Þe ferþe [kind of dropsy] hatte Tympanytes..for if þe wombe is ysmete it sowneþ as a taboure oþer a tymber. *c* 1400 *Lanfranc's Cirurg.* 282 Þe .iij. [maner dropesie] is engendrid of greet wynd resolued of coold mater, & falliþ into þe holownes of þe wombe, & is clepid tympanites. *Ibid.* 283 [see TYMPAN 1]. 1651 BAXTER *Inf. Bapt.* 260 If a Physitian ask, How many Tympanites have you known cured? 1694 SALMON *Bate's Dispens.* (1713) 7/1 Water of black Cherries compound..is a most powerful Remedy in the Cure of a Tympanites. 1767 GOOCH *Treat. Wounds* I. 411 The Abdomen was..distended, as if the patient had been afflicted with an Ascites or Tympanites. 1872 T. G. THOMAS *Dis. Women* (ed. 3) 261 Abdominal enlargement from tympanites. 1899 [see TYPHOID *a.* 2 b].

**Tympanitic** (timpăni·tik), *a.* [ad. L. *tympanīticus*, f. *tympanītēs*: see prec. and -IC. So Pg. *tymp-*, Sp. and It. *timpanitico*.] Pertaining to, characteristic of, or affected with tympanites. *Tympanitic note, resonance*, or *sound*, a sound somewhat like that of a drum produced by percussion over the abdomen or other part when distended with gas or air.

1834 J. FORBES *Laennec's Dis. Chest* (ed. 4) 481 Some.. were of opinion that the..tympanitic resonance, on percussion, is of itself sufficient to point out pneumothorax. 1843 R. J. GRAVES *Syst. Clin. Med.* xiii. 142 His tongue was black and parched, his belly tympanitic. 1853 MARKHAM *Skoda's Auscult.*, etc. 255 The percussion-sound of the abdomen..being at one time distinctly tympanitic and clear, at another indistinct. 1860 TANNER *Pregnancy* ii. 67 Tympanitic distension of the intestines. 1899 *Allbutt's Syst. Med.* VII. 644 A tympanitic note on skull-percussion is suggestive that the abscess is situated in the cerebellum.

**b.** Giving a tympanitic sound.

1900 *Jrnl. Exp. Med.* 25 Oct. 140 The skin and subcutaneous tissues of the face, neck and chest were markedly swollen, and tympanitic on percussion.

So † **Tympani·tical** *a. Obs.* (in quot. 1772 *fig.*; cf. TYMPANY 2).

1656 BLOUNT *Glossogr.*, *Tympanitical*, that hath a Tympany or dropsy. 1772 NUGENT tr. *Hist. Friar Gerund* II. 202 Filling it with airy conceits, tympanitical thoughts,..and fantastical dissertations.

‖ **Tympanitis** (timpănəi·tis). *Path.* [In sense 1, an alteration of TYMPANITES; so Pg. *tymp-*, Sp. *timpanitis*, It. *timpanitide*. In sense 2, f. TYMPAN-UM + -ITIS.]

**1.** = TYMPANITES.

1797 M. BAILLIE *Morb. Anat.* (ed. 2) 205 When air is accumulated in very large quantity,..it forms a..disease called tympanitis... The belly is extremely swelled, with a very tense feeling. 1876 *Trans. Clinical Soc.* IX. 103 Bowels still unrelieved... The tympanitis has increased.

**2.** Inflammation of the lining membrane of the tympanum.

1857 DUNGLISON *Med. Lex.* 1890 BILLINGS *Med. Dict.*

† **Ty·mpanize,** *v. Obs.* Also 6–7 tim-. [ad. Gr. τυμπανίζειν to beat a drum, f. τύμπανον TYMPANUM; or late L. *tympanizāre* (in med.L. in sense 1 b below); cf. F. *tympaniser* (16th c.), to proclaim or decry loudly, Pg. *tympanisar* (med.).]

**1.** *trans.* To affect with a tympany (*lit.* or *fig.*); to distend (the abdomen, etc.) with gas; to inflate, puff up (with pride, etc.).

1593 NASHE *Christ's T.* (1613) 118 The therd sonne of Pride is Atheisme, which is when a man is so timpaniz'd with prosperity,..that he forgets he had a Maker. 1623 COCKERAM II, Swolne with watrish humors, *tympaniz'd*. 1647 C. HARVEY *Schola Cordis* XII. vi, My windy thoughts with pride are tympaniz'd. 1679 J. GOODMAN *Penit. Pard.* I. iv. (1713) 114 To have that element [water] forced down a man's throat till all the vessels of his body are stretched and tympanized.

**b.** *intr.* To be affected with a tympany; to swell (*lit.* and *fig.*).

1607 R. C[AREW] tr. *Estienne's World of Wonders* 157 Our Ladies..haue so many *prophylactica* to keepe their bellies from tympanizing. 1635 HEYWOOD *Hierarch.* VI. 352 Pride in their hearts doth swell and tympanise.

**2.** *intr.* To beat or play on a drum. *rare*⁻⁰.

1623 COCKERAM II, To beate a Drum, *tympanize*. 1656 BLOUNT *Glossogr.*, *Tympanize*, to play on a Drum, Taber or Tymbrel.

**3.** *trans.* To stretch on the rack.

A former interpretation of τυμπανίζειν in Heb. xi. 35 (prob. rather = to beat with a drum-stick: cf. TYMPANISM 1).

1647 TRAPP *Comm. Heb.* xi. 35 'Ετυμπανίσθησαν...They were tympanized, distended, stretched upon the rack as a sheeps-pelt is upon a drum-head. 1652 OLEY *Life G. Herbert* in *Rem.* A xj b, To be sawn asunder as Esay, stoned as Jeremy, made a Drum, or Tympanised, as other Saints of God were.

Hence † **Ty·mpanizing** *ppl. a.*

1607 WALKINGTON *Opt. Glass* i. 7 Swolne with timpanizing pride.

**Tympano-** (timpăno), before a vowel sometimes **tympan-**, combining form repr. Gr. τύμπανον or L. TYMPANUM, in recent terms of anatomy, etc. **Tympane·ctomy** [Gr. ἐκτομή excision], excision of the tympanic membrane. **Ty:mpano-ce·rvical** *a.* [CERVICAL], affecting the tympanum and the neck. **Ty:mpano-Eusta·chian** (-yustē·kiăn) *a.*, constituted by the tympanum and the Eustachian tube. **Ty:mpanohy·al** *a.*, pertaining to the tympanum and the hyoid arch; epithet of a small bone or cartilage at the base of the styloid process, which in early life becomes fused with the temporal bone; *sb.* = t. bone or cartilage. **Ty:mpanoma·lleal** *a.*, pertaining to the tympanic bone and the malleus; applied to a bone in the skull of batrachians and fishes. **Ty:mpanomandi·bular** *a.*, pertaining to the tympanum, or the tympanic bone, and the mandible or lower jaw-bone. **Ty:mpanoma·stoid** *a.*, pertaining to the tympanum and the mastoid cells. **Ty:mpano-occi·pital** *a.* and *sb.*, applied to a small bone or ossification connected with the ear and the exoccipital bone in birds, and held to be homologous with the tympanic bone in mammals (*Cent. Dict.* 1891). **Ty:mpano-perio·tic** *a.*, consisting of the tympanic bone and periotic bones united; *sb.*, a tympanoperiotic bone, as the ear-bone of a cetacean. **Tympano·phony** [Gr. φωνή voice], a sensation of ringing in the ears (cf. TYMPANUM 2). **Ty:mpanosquamo·sal** *a.*, pertaining to the tympanic and the squamosal bones. **Ty:mpanostape·dial** *a.*, 'pertaining to the tympanum and the stapes' (Dorland *Med. Dict.* 1900–13). **Ty:mpanote·mporal** *a.*, 'pertaining to the tympanum and the region over the temporal bone' (*ibid.*). **Tympano·tomy** [Gr. τομή cutting], incision through the tympanic membrane.

1900–13 DORLAND *Med. Dict.*, *Tympanectomy. *Ibid.* s.v. *Abscess*, **Tympanocervical a[bscess]*, an abscess arising in the tympanum and extending to the neck. 1890 BILLINGS *Med. Dict.*, **Tympano-Eustachian passage*, the tympanum and Eustachian tube considered together as a branchial cleft. 1872 MIVART *Elem. Anat.* 81 The styloid process.. is at birth separate from a little cylindrical piece of bone which afterwards forms its root, and which is called the *tympano-hyal. 1881 — *Cat* 78 At the end of the stylo-hyal is a cylindrical cartilage, the tympano-hyal. 1891 *Cent. Dict.*, *Tympanomalleal. 1900–13 in DORLAND *Med. Dict.* *a* 1909 STARKS *Synon. Fish Skeleton* 513 (Cent. D. Supp.). 1891 *Cent. Dict.*, *Tympanomandibular. *c* 1900 *Buck's Handbk. Med. Sci.* III. 697 (Cent. D. Supp.) *Tympanomastoid. 1870 ROLLESTON *Anim. Life* 8 A lamina of bone, which..serves..to keep the *tympano-periotic..in place. 1871 HUXLEY *Anat. Vert. Anim.* viii. 405 When the tympano-periotic bone and all the facial bones are removed. 1899 *Syd. Soc. Lex.*, **Tympanophony*, abnormal sounds in the ear, as echoes, &c. 1891 *Cent. Dict.*, *Tympanosquamosal. *c* 1900 *Buck's Handbk. Med. Sci.* III. 672 (Cent. D. Supp.) *Tympanotomy.

**Tympanoid** (ti·mpănoid), *a. Nat. Hist.* [ad. Gr. τυμπανοειδής, f. τύμπανον drum: see -OID.] Resembling a drum, or a drum-head.

1863 BERKELEY *Brit. Mosses* Gloss. 313 *Tympanoid*, resembling the head of a drum.

† **Ty·mpanous,** *a. Obs.* [f. TYMPAN-UM or TYMPAN-Y + -OUS.] Swollen as with a tympany; usually *fig.* inflated, puffed up; turgid, bombastic; hollow, empty, vain.

1624 MIDDLETON *Game at Chess* II. i, His proud tympanous master, swell'd with state-wind. 1635 HEYWOOD *Hierarch.* IV. 208 A Puny shall assume the name of Poet; And in a Tympanous and Thrasonicke stile [etc.]. 1648 SYMMONS *Vind. Chas. I* p. ii, Those new hopes being likely to prove tympanous. 1660 WATERHOUSE *Arms & Arm.* 26 That tympanous humour that swells up..light minds. 1669 COKAINE *Poems* 164 Her tympanous belly.

‖ **Tympanum** (ti·mpănǒm). Pl. **tympana.** [L. *tympanum* drum, wheel for raising weights, face of pediment, etc., a. Gr. τύμπανον drum, f. root of τύπτειν to strike, beat.]

**1.** A drum or similar instrument, as a tambourine or timbrel (esp. ancient); also, the stretched membrane of a drum, a drum-head.

1675 COVEL in *Early Voy. Levant* (Hakl. Soc.) 203, 6 Drumes, 4 trumpets, 2 kettle-drumes, and 4 tamburs (or tympanums) like sives cover'd with parchment at bottome. 1830 *Hobart Town Almanack* 92 The little tympanums which the Chinese hawk about the streets to amuse children. 1847 LEITCH tr. *C. O. Müller's Anc. Art* § 395 (1850) 520 She [Cybele] is recognised by the crown of flowers, the tympanum as a symbol of her enthusiastic worship, and the car yoked with lions. 1908 SIR H. JOHNSTON *Grenfell & Congo* I. xvi. 394 The slipping of his fingers down the cane set up a vibration of the tympanum of the drum.

**2.** *Anat.* The drum of the ear (med.L. *tympanum auris*, Albertus Magnus *c* 1255); the middle ear, consisting of a cavity in the temporal bone, filled with air, separated from the outer auditory canal by the tympanic membrane (*membrana tympani*) and from the inner ear by the membranes of the *fenestra ovalis* and *fenestra rotunda*, and containing the chain of small bones (auditory ossicles), or in lower vertebrates the single bone (*columella*), by which sound-vibrations are conveyed to the inner ear. Also often applied to the tympanic membrane simply.

In insects, a similar membrane with connected parts, in some cases supposed to constitute an organ of hearing (cf. quot. 1887 s.v. TYMPANAL *a.*).

1619 PURCHAS *Microcosmus* ix. 99 The passage auditorie being anfractuous, lest the *Tympanum* should by directer incursions be endangered. 1691 RAY *Creation* II. (1692) 38 At the end of this hole is a Membrane..stretched like the head of a Drum, and therefore by Anatomists called also *Tympanum*. 1709 STEELE *Tatler* No. 47 ¶ 3, I recited some Heroick Lines..which operated so strongly on the Tympanum of his Ear [etc.]. 1726 MONRO *Anat. Bones* (ed. 3) 97 The Cavity of the Ear, called *Tympanum*. 1840 G.V. ELLIS *Anat.* 282 The tympanum or middle ear is a circular space, situated in the base of the petrous portion of the temporal bone..; a chain of small bones crosses the cavity, to convey the undulations of sound to the labyrinth that is internal to it. 1856 TODD & BOWMAN *Phys. Anat.* II. 63 The tympanum..communicates..with the cavity of the throat through ..the Eustachian tube, whereby air has a free access into the tympanum. 1868 DUNCAN *Figuier's Insect W.* Introd. 6 The membrane..represents a trace of the tympanum which exists among the higher animals. 1871 ROSSETTI *Poems, Dante at Verona* xlvi, A Jester,..a ribald mouth to shout In Folly's horny tympanum Such things as make the wise man dumb. 1880 GÜNTHER *Fishes* 116 A tympanum, tympanic cavity [etc.] are..absent in..fishes.

**b.** *Ornith.* (*a*) Each of the two inflatable air-sacs at the sides of the neck in certain birds, as grouse. (*b*) Applied to the bony labyrinth at the base of the trachea in certain species of duck, having resonant membranes in its walls.

1873 COUES *Birds N. W.* (1874) 416 An illy-defined white area on each side of the neck, over the tympanum. 1896 NEWTON *Dict. Birds* 984 [In] the males of many..*Anseres*, some 6 or 8 of the lowest rings [of the trachea are] fused together..forming..the *bulba ossea* or labyrinth... This ..becomes very complicated in the group of 'Diving Ducks', forming in many cases a *tympanum*, whose bony walls are fenestrated and the spaces filled with a resonant membrane.

**3.** *Arch.* **a.** The die or cubical portion of a pedestal. **b.** The vertical recessed face of a pediment, often adorned with sculpture.

The sense 'panel of a door', given in the Glossary to Gwilt's *Encycl. Archit.*, and thence in mod. Dicts., is app. only Latin (Vitruvius).

**1658** tr. *Porta's Nat. Magic* XIX. v. 393 And in the upper surface of the Tympanum, bore the basis quite through with a little pipe, which enters into the hollow of the Tympanum. **1680** EVELYN *Diary* 18 Apr., The tympanum or gabal at the front [of Cashiobury] is a bass-relievo of Diana hunting. **1723** CHAMBERS tr. *Le Clerc's Treat. Archit.* I. 111 The Tympanum is either Triangular or Circular. **1841** W. SPALDING *Italy & It. Isl.* I. 161 The statues..which filled the tympana, or triangular spaces of the pediments at both ends of the temple. *a* **1878** SIR G. G. SCOTT *Lect. Archit.* (1879) I. 166 In the tympanum are sculptured scenes from Scripture history.

**4.** *Mech.* † **a.** The barrel of a capstan or similar apparatus for raising weights (? only Latin). *Obs.* **b.** A kind of wheel (originally drum-shaped) with curved radial partitions, used for raising water. **c.** A hollow wheel turned by two or more persons walking inside it, and communicating motion to a machine (*Cent. Dict.* 1891).

**1704** J. HARRIS *Lex. Techn.* I, *Tympanum*, in Mechanicks, is a Cylinder, but larger and shorter than the common Axis or Cylinder,..and..usually placed upon that Axis, and is much the same with the *Peritrochium*, which is a kind of Wheel..in whose Circumference are Staves or Levers to turn the Axis easily about, in order to raise the Weight required. **1875** KNIGHT *Dict. Mech.*, *Tympanum*, 1. An ancient form of wheel for elevating water...The Roman form of the *tympanum* is described by Vitruvius,..and was derived from Egypt...The *tympanum*, under the name of the *scoop-wheel*, is much used in the drainage of the fens in the East of England.

**5.** *Bot.* A membrane stretching across the mouth of the spore-case in some urn-mosses.

**1832** LINDLEY *Introd. Bot.* 201 Sometimes one membrane only remains,..stretching across the orifice of the theca, which is closed up by it; this is sometimes named the *tympanum*.

**Tympany** (ti·mpăni). Also 6 tympanye, 6–7 tym-, timpanie, timpany. [ad. med.L. *tympanias*, a. Gr. τυμπανίας, f. τύμπανον TYMPANUM.]

**1.** = TYMPANITES; also sometimes used vaguely for a morbid swelling or tumour of any kind. Common from 16th to 18th c. (with *a*, *the*, or without article); now *rare* or *arch.*

(*a*) **1528** PAYNEL *Salerne's Regim.* C iij b, A tympany..is ingendred..by coldenes of the stomake, and lyuer, not sufferyng mans drynke or meate to be conuerted in to good humours, but tourneth them in to ventosities. **1547** BOORDE *Brev. Health* cccxlv. 111 b, A tympany..doth make ones bely to swel lyke a taber. **1577–87** HOLINSHED *Chron.* III. 1131/1 Some..affirmed that she was deceiued by a timpanie..to thinke hirselfe with child. **1611** COTGR., *Mole*, a Timpanie, or Moone-calfe; a shapelesse lump of flesh, or hard swelling, in the wombe. **1635** N. R. *Camden's Hist. Eliz.* Introd., Q. Mary..left her life..of a sixe months Fever and a Tympany. **1706–7** FARQUHAR *Beaux' Strat.* I. i, She cured her of Three Tympanies, but the Fourth carried her off. **1754–64** SMELLIE *Midwif.* II. 82 She was grown very big; a circumstance she imputed to a dropsy or rather a tympany. **1860** EMERSON *Cond. Life, Culture* Wks. (Bohn) II. 363 Nature has no mercy,..makes a dropsy or a tympany of him.

(*b*) **1542** BOORDE *Dyetary* xxviii. (1870) 299 Yet the lyuer is drye, whether it be alchytes, Iposarca, Leucoflegmancia, or the tympany. **1612** WOODALL *Surg. Mate* Wks. (1653) 68 Cummin seed..is good against the chollick and tympany. **1661** LOVELL *Hist. Anim. & Min.* 178 It helps..the collick, tympany, and nephritick passion. **1747** WESLEY *Prim. Phy ic* (1762) 109 The Tympany or Windy Dropsy. **1844** BABINGTON tr. *Hecker's Epid. Middle Ages* 88 This practice of swathing was resorted to on account of the tympany which followed these spasmodic ravings.

(*c*) **1731** *Gentl. Mag.* I. Index, The Diseases and Casualties this year...Tympany, 3. **1796** E. DARWIN *Zoon.* (1802) III. 208 Tympany consists in an elastic tumor of the abdomen, which sounds on being struck. **1881** *Trans. Obstet. Soc.* XXII. 135 The movements of a coil of distended intestine as in some forms of tympany. **1901** W. OSLER *Princ. & Pract. Med.* i. 26 Obliteration of the liver flatness in the nipple line may be caused by excessive tympany.

† **b.** *transf.* or *allusively*, esp. in reference to pregnancy. *Obs.*

**1580** LYLY *Euphues* (Arb.) 238 My pursse now swelling with a timpany, I thought to serch al countries for a remedy. **1590** [TARLTON] *News Purgat.* (1844) 78 The maid fell sicke, and her disease was thought to be a timpany with two heeles. **1613** PURCHAS *Pilgrimage* IX. vii. 865 Sometimes the neighbour hils..tumble downe..in the plaine, thereby so amazing the fearefull Riuers, that they runne quite out of their Channels..or else stand still..and..fall into an vncouth tympanie, their bellies swelling into spacious..lakes. **1649** DAVENANT *Love & Hon.* IV. ii, Midwives believe that it foretells A hopefull timpany to come. **1663** DRYDEN *Wild Gallant* v. ii, A mere tympany..raised by a cushion. **1707** MRS. CENTLIVRE *Platonick Lady* II. i, If she has not twice slipt aside for a natural Tympany. **1711** ADDISON *Spect.* No. 127 ¶ 10 To Unhoop the Fair Sex, and cure this fashionable Tympany that is got among them.

**2.** *fig.* A swelling, as of pride, arrogance, self-conceit, etc., figured as a disease; a condition of being inflated or puffed up; an excess *of* something figured as a swelling; something big or pretentious, but empty or vain; inflated style, turgidity, bombast. Now *rare* or *Obs.*

**1581** J. BELL *Haddon's Answ. Osor.* 389 Why could your holy mother Church suffer so horrible a Tympany, and Imposthume within her owne bowels. **1602** WARNER *Alb. Eng.* Epit. (1612) 387 To this the Dukes Tympanie, the Commons..became Mid-wiues,..vntill..they had brought him a bed of a Kingdome. **1610** DONNE *Pseudo-martyr* 365 This Timpany, or false conception, by which spirituall power is blowne vp, and swelled with temporall. **1616** B. JONSON *Epigr.* xxviii, H' has tympanies of businesse, in his face. **1621** BURTON *Anat. Mel.* I. ii. III. xiv. (1651) 122 Puffed up with this Timpany of self conceit. **1639** FULLER *Holy War* v. xvii. 258 Some would cut off the flesh of the Churches necessary maintenance, under pretense to cure her of a tympanie of superfluities. **1676** E. BURY *Medit.* 214 Wealth many times swells men into a tympany, not easily cured. **1680** EARL ROSCOM. *Horace's Art Poetry* Poems (1780) 105 Others, that affect A lofty style, swell to a tympany. *a* **1703** BURKITT *On N. T.* Luke xiv. 11 He that before their eyes had cured a man of a bodily dropsy, attempts to cure [them] of the tympany of pride. **1723** DR. WHARTON *True Briton* No. 27 I. 233 What..was observ'd of Sejanus holds true of many later Tympanies of Grandeur. **1828** *Blackw. Mag.* XXIV. 906 Dr. Johnson..he charges..with a plethoric and tautologic tympany of sentence. **1829** SOUTHEY *Sir T. More* (1831) II. 288 He was afflicted with a tympany of mind produced by metaphysics. **1842** *Blackw. Mag.* LI. 15 It was the conceit..which turned out to be the sober truth; and our modesty..it was which turned out a windy tympany.

**3.** = TYMPAN 1, TYMPANUM 1. *rare. Obs.* or *arch.*

**1535** *Goodly Primer, Matins* Ps. cl. 4 Praise him with tympany and tabret. **1557** *Sarum Primer* B ij, Let them sing unto him with timpanie and harpe. **1875** BROWNING *Aristoph. Apol.*, *Herakles* 950 By the tympanies and the thyrsos hoist Of the Bromian revel-rout.

**4.** *Arch.* = TYMPAN 5, TYMPANUM 3 b. *Sc.*

**1825** [see TYMPAN 5].

**5.** *attrib.* and *Comb.*, as *tympany gavel* (GABLE *sb.*[1]), *window* (sense 4); *tympany-like* adj.

**1658** BROMHALL *Treat. Specters* I. 98 Out of a tympany-like ostentation. **1825** Tympany gavel [see TYMPAN 5]. **1849** *Glasgow Past & Present* (1884) I. 106 An old house with tympany windows.

Hence † **Tympanied** *ppl. a.* (*obs. nonce-wd.*), inflated as with a tympany, puffed up.

**1637** HEYWOOD *Dial.*, *Pelop. & Alope* Argt., Wks. 1874 VI. 297 More simple truth in their chaste loves, Than greater Ladies, tympany'de With much more honour, state, and pride.

**Tymper**, obs. f. TEMPER *sb.*

† **Tymyame**, var. *thymyame*, THYMIAMA *Obs.*

**1382** WYCLIF *Ezek.* xvi. 18 Myn oyle and my tymyame, [*gloss*] or encense.

**Tymyr, -yre**, obs. ff. TIMBER.

**Tymze**, obs. form of TEMSE, sieve.

**Tyn**, obs. f. TIN, TINE *v.*[2]; var. TINE *a. Obs.*

**Tynacle, -akle**, obs. ff. TUNICLE. **Tynage, -axe**, variants of TINAGE, *Obs.* a jar.

**Tyncke**, obs. f. TINK *v.*[1]

† **Tynclare**, obs. form of TINKLER[1].

**1560** *Abst. Protocols Town Cl. Glasgow* (1896) II. 79.

† **Tyncte.** *Obs.* app. = TAINT *sb.* 3.

**1456–7** *Paston Lett.* I. 406, I had lever paye xx. marke,..with myn enemyndz good love, than to yelde me to preson ayens here entent, and sewe forth the tyncte. And no trost ..that he wele bere owt the cost of the tyncte.

**Tynd(e**, var. TIND *v. Obs.* to kindle; obs. f. TINE *sb.*[1], *v.*[1]; obs. pa. pple. of TINE *v.*[2]

**Tyndallization** (ti·ndălǝizē^i·ʃǝn). [f. the name of John Tyndall, an English physicist (1820–1893); cf. PASTEURIZATION.] A method of sterilization in which time is allowed between repeated heatings for bacteria to develop; fractional or intermittent sterilization. So **Ty·ndallize** *v. trans.* to sterilize by this process (Webster, 1911).

*c* **1900** *Buck's Handbk. Med. Sci.* I. 686 (Cent. D. Supp.) Tyndallization. **1900–13** in DORLAND *Med. Dict.*

**Tynder**, obs. form of TINDER.

† **Tyndesawe.** *Obs. rare*^−1. [app. f. *saw* Sow *sb.*[3], with obscure first element.] A designation of a Lenten sowing.

*c* **1300** *Battle Abbey Custumals* (1889) 150 Ad semen Quadragesimale quod vocatur Tyndesawe.

† **Tyne**, app. an error for *cyue*, var. *cyuey*, *cyvey* (see CIVET *sb.*[3]) occurring in the same passages.

*c* **1430** *Two Cookery-bks.* 49 Take flowre, Almaunde milke, & Safroune, & make þer-of .iiij. tynez, & frye þi tynez in Oyle. *Ibid.* 50 Ley on þin cyvey a-bouyn þin Fyssche,..and caste a-bouyn Sugre of Alysaundre, & þer-vppe-on þine tyne.

**Tyne**, obs. f. THYINE, TIN, TIND, TINE.

† **Tynel, tynnell.** *Obs. rare.* [a. OF. *tinel* (= It. *tinello*) tub, vat, dim. of *tine* TINE *sb.*[3]] A vessel for holding liquids.

**1336–7** *Acc. Exch. K. R.* 19/31 m. 5 (P.R.O.) In ij. naugers emptis ad eandem..viij. d. Et in xxiiij tynels emptis de Rogero Hirdelere ad dictam nauem purificandam .ij. s. **1540** in V. Green *Hist. Worcester* (1796) II. App. 5 Inprimis, a holy water tynnell of selver and gylte.

**Tynie**, obs. f. TINY. **Tynke**, obs. f. TINK *v.*

**Tynnacle, -akel, -akil**, etc., obs. ff. TUNICLE.

**Tynne**, obs. f. TIN, TIND. **Tynsel, -il, -yll (-in, -yn)**, obs. ff. TINSEL *sb.*[3] **Tynt**, obs. f. TENT *sb.*[4], *v.*[1]; obs. pa. t. and pple. of TINE *v.*[2]

**Tyntare**, obs. f. *tine-tare*: see TINE *sb.*[4] b.

† **Tynte.** *Obs. rare.* [Of obscure origin: cf. ON. *tinta* fem., a small bottle, Norw. dial. *tint* a small vessel or measure; these are probably not native Scand. words.] (See quots.)

*c* **1440** *Promp. Parv.* 494/2 Tynte, mesure, *satum. Ibid.* 222/2 Half a buschel, or eytendele (..*H.*, *P.* or tynt), *satum.* **1552** HULOET, Tynte or halfe parte of a bushell, *semimodius.*

**Tynwald** (ti·nwǫ̆ld, tǝi·n-). Also 7 **Tynwold**, 7–8 **Tinewald**, 7, 9 **Tinwald.** [ad. early ON. **þingwall-*, stem of ON. *þingvǫllr* (gen. *-vallar*), f. *þing* THING *sb.*[2] + *vǫllr* field, level ground. The initial *t* for *th* is due to Manx phonetics. Of the same origin are the place-names *Tinwald* in Dumfriesshire, *Dingwall* in Ross-shire, and *Tingwall* in Shetland.] (Also *Tynwald Court.*) In the Isle of Man, an annual convention attended by the governor (representing the sovereign), a council acting as the upper house, and the House of Keys, at which the laws which have been enacted are proclaimed to the people. Also *attrib.*, as *Tynwald chapel, day, hill, mount.*

The MS. source of the earliest quots. dates from the beginning of the 17th century.

**1422** *Acts Sir John Stanley* (Manx Soc., vol. III) 71 This is..how you shalle be governed upon your Tynwald dayes. *Ibid.* 92 That the Tynwold be houldene two tymes in the yeare at the leaste. **1610** in *Mills' Statute Laws Isle of Man* (1821) 81 It is agreed..that after Midsomer Day next noe Tinwald shall be holden in this Isle upon the Lord's day. **1656** J. CHALONER *Descr. I. of Man* iv. in D. King *Vale Royall* IV. 16 The said Governour and Officers do usually call the 24 Keyes of the Island, especially once every year, *viz.* upon Midsummer day, at St. John's Chappel, to the Tinewald Court there, where upon a Hill near unto the said Chappel, all the Inhabitants of the Island, standing round about a fair Plain, they may hear the Laws and Ordinances agreed upon before in the Chappel aforesaid, published and declar'd unto them. *Ibid.* 17 If any Orders be agreed upon by the Officers, and 24 Keys, they are..at the next Tynwald, after, proclaimed for absolute Laws. **1701** in *Cowell's Interpr.* s. v. *Tinewald.* **1739** [see KEYS]. **1798** FELTHAM *Tour Isle of Man* xii. 144 The annual mode of promulgating the laws, is at the Tynwald hill. **1836** *Encycl. Brit.* (ed. 7) XIV. 211/2 [A law of the House of Keys] must be promulgated by the lieutenant-governor..on the top of an ancient tumulus called the Tynwald Mount. **1860** *All Year Round* No. 68. 420, I believe..though the language is still employed in some official formulæ of the Tynwald (or ancient court)..the ancient idiom of Mona is very near extinction. **1871** W. HARRISON (*title*) Records of the Tynwald and Saint John's Chapels in the Isle of Man. **1894** HALL CAINE *Little Man Isl.* 15 The open-air Parliament..meets once a year at St. John's, in the centre of the island, on the mount known as Tynwald Hill.

**Typ**, obs. form of TIP.

**Typacanthid, Typarchical**: see TYPO-.

**Typal** (tǝi·păl), *a.* [f. TYPE *sb.*[1] + -AL.]

**1.** Of the nature of, serving as, or answering to a type, pattern, or specimen; representative; typical.

**1853** BRIMLEY *Ess.*, *My Novel* 277 True typal varieties of English life. **1861** BERESF. HOPE *Eng. Cathedr. 19th C.* i. 18 The 'literate' may become the typal incumbent of England, and..the English clergyman—gentleman and scholar as well as Christian—become a thing of the past. **1882** DORLING in *Sunday Mag.* 196 A charming glimpse of a typal Welsh preacher.

**2.** Pertaining or relating to a type or symbol; symbolic; emblematic.

**1893** E. DINGLE (*title*) The typal use of the 22 letters of the Hebrew alphabet in the Psalms &c.

**3.** Of or pertaining to printing type; typographical.

**1882** J. PARKER *Apost. Life* I. 62 There are palpitations which cannot be reported, and tones which have no typal representation.

**Type** (tǝip), *sb.*[1] Also 6–7 tipe. [ad. F. *type* (16th c. in Littré) or L. *typus*, a. Gr. τύπος impression, figure, type, f. the root of τύπτειν to beat, strike.]

**1.** That by which something is symbolized or figured; anything having a symbolical signification; a symbol, emblem; *spec.* in *Theol.* a person, object, or event of Old Testament history, prefiguring some person or thing revealed in the new dispensation; correl. to *antitype*. *In* (*the*) *type*, in symbolic representation.

*c* **1470** HENRYSON *Mor. Fab.* (S. T. S.) 579 Suppose this be ane Fabill, And ouerheillit with typis figurall. **1590** 'HOBYNOLL' *To Learned Sheph.* v. in *Spenser's F. Q.* (Pref. Verses), That fare Ilands right, Which thou dost vayle in Type of Faery land, Elizas blessed field, that Albion hight. **1607** HIERON *Wks.* I. 104 The people of Israel were a tipe of Gods people: Canaan a tipe of heauen. **1654** JER. TAYLOR *Real Pres.* v. 103 He offered wine not water in the type..of his bloud. **1706** PRIOR *Ode to Queen* xxxiv, The British Rose, Type of sweet Rule, and gentle Majesty. **1781** FLETCHER *Lett.* Wks. 1795 VII. 236 [Marriage] the most perfect type of our Lords union with his church. **1829** *The Bengallee* 182 The Hookah's monstrous snake...That type of eastern Luxury's excess. **1851** KINGSLEY in *Life* (1878) I. 255 It is only in proportion as we appreciate and understand the types that we can understand the anti-types. **1863** MARY HOWITT *F. Bremer's Greece* II. xii. 29 A river is always the type of human life. **1875** MANNING *Mission H. Ghost* i. 15 Ceremonial actions, and washings, and purifications, which were the types and shadows of things to come.

**b.** An imperfect symbol or anticipation *of* something. *nonce-use.*

**1754** FOOTE *Knights* I. Wks. 1799 I. 62 The very abstract of penury! Sir John Cutler, with his transmigrated stockings, was but a type of him.

† **2.** A figure or picture of something; a representation; an image or imitation. *Obs. rare.*

**1559** W. CUNNINGHAM *Cosmogr. Glasse* 10 This Type do represent the world. *Ibid.* 156 Wherfore behold the tipe before placed. **1572** GASCOIGNE *Herbs, Voy. into Holland* 7, I must endite..A tipe of heauen, a liuely hew of hell. **1774** J. BRYANT *Mythol.* II. 445 Lunar amulets, or types of the Ark in the form of a crescent.

**b.** *Numism.* The figure on either side of a coin or medal.

**1785** HOLCROFT tr. *Mme. de Genlis' Tales Castle* (ed. 2) I. Notes 292 On the two sides..of a medal..are distinguished the type, and the inscription or legend. The type, or device, is the figure represented. **1853** HUMPHREYS *Coin-Coll. Man.* vi. 61 The crab, being perhaps at an early period made sacred to the river deity, became the principal type of the money of this city [Agrigentum]. **1904** W. M. RAMSAY *Lett. Seven Churches* xix. 262 Homer is one of the most frequent types on coins of the city.

**3.** A distinguishing mark or sign; a stamp. *rare.*

**1593** SHAKS. *3 Hen. VI*, I. iv. 121 Thy Father beares the type of King of Naples. **1613** — *Hen. VIII*, I. iii. 31 Tennis and tall Stockings, Short blistred Breeches, and those types of Trauell. **1692** PRIOR *Ode Imit. Horace* viii. 28 Heav'n as plainly pointed out the King, As when he at the Altar stood, In all his Types and Robes of Powr. **1862** BURTON *Bk. Hunter* (1863) 11 The types of a really hospitable country house were an anker of whisky always on the spigot, a caldron ever on the bubble with boiling water. *Ibid.* 44 All these things were the types of an intellectual vitality.

**4.** *Path.* The characteristic form of a fever; *esp.* the character of an intermittent fever as determined by its period. Cf. *type-fever* in 10. [So L. *typus.*] *Obs.* or merged in 5.

**1601** HOLLAND *Pliny* XXII. xiv. II. 122 The fever also, Of what type or kind it is. *Ibid.* XXVI. xi. 260 Some are wont to give of Cinque foile three leaves in a Tertian, and foure in a Quartane, and so rise to more according to the period or type of the rest. **1776** W. CULLEN *First Lines Pract. Physic* § 30 With respect to the form, or Type, of fevers. **1818–20** J. THOMPSON *Cullen's Nosol. Method.* (ed. 3) 187 [Fever] with intermission, varying (*a*) in type or period. **1858** COPLAND *Dict. Pract. Med.* I. 937 The type of masked ague is generally quotidian.

**5.** The general form, structure, or character distinguishing a particular kind, group, or class of beings or objects; hence *transf.* a pattern or model after which something is made.

**1843** MILL *Logic* IV. ii. § 3 (1856) II. 192 When we..see a creature resembling an animal, we compare it with our general conception of an animal; and if it agrees with that general conception, we include it in the class. The conception becomes the type of comparison. **1857** MAURICE *Ep. St. John* i. 3 The type upon which the whole was constructed. **1860** MOTLEY *Netherl.* (1868) I. i. 15 His face had lost all resemblance to the type of his heroic family. **1864** *Soc. Science Rev.* 3 Diseases are founded on types like animals, plants, systems of worlds [etc.]. **1874** BLACKIE *Self-Cult.* 4 The fundamental unity of type which the Divine reason has imposed on all things. **1874** PARKER *Goth. Archit.* I. i. 1 The original type of all Christian churches is universally acknowledged to have been the Roman Basilica. **1877** ROBERTS *Handbk. Med.* (ed. 3) I. 12 A few diseases exhibit well-marked types. **1880** *Mem. J. Legge* vi. 76 Every creature has a type, a peculiar character of its own.

**b.** *Ch. Hist.* [Gr. τύπος τῆς πίστεως type of the faith.] An edict of the Emperor Constans II, promulgated A. D. 648, prohibiting further discussion of the Monothelite controversy.

**1727–41** CHAMBERS *Cycl.*, *Type*, τυπος,..a name given to an edict of the Emperor Constans II...It had the name type, as being a kind of formulary of faith. **1854** MILMAN *Lat. Chr.* IV. vi. (1864) II. 322 The Ecthesis of Heraclius was replaced by the Type of Constans. The Type..aspired to silence by authority this interminable dispute. **1902** J. K. MANN *Hist. Popes* I. I. 381 Paul caused the Emperor Constans to issue the 'Type'...The 'Type' ordered the Ecthesis to be taken down, and forbade anyone in future to speak of either one or two wills or operations in Our Lord.

**6.** A kind, class, or order as distinguished by a particular character.

**1854** BREWSTER *More Worlds* iv. 73 On a planet more magnificent than ours, may there not be a type of reason of which the intellect of Newton is the lowest degree? **1855** MACAULAY *Hist. Eng.* xx. IV. 531 The Queen was sinking under small pox of the most malignant type. **1879** M. ARNOLD *Ess.*, *Porro unum est necess.* 152 The instruction in both is of the same type. **1888** BRYCE *Amer. Commw.* II. xlviii. 220 Three types of rural local government are discernible in America. **1897** D. W. FORREST *Christ of Hist. & Exp.* i. 31 It is a different type of moral character: another order of humanity. **1898** *Jrnl. Sch. Geog.* (U.S.) Oct. 306 The dominant weather type was clear, with light southerly winds and temperatures between 50° and 55°. This type was interrupted by two spells of cloudy weather, with northerly winds.

**7.** *transf.* A person or thing that exhibits the characteristic qualities of a class; a representative specimen; a typical example or instance.

**1842** PRICHARD *Nat. Hist. Man* (ed. 2) 333 The Tahitians are considered by Lesson as the type of the whole Polynesian race. *a* **1854** REED *Lect. Brit. Poets* v. (1857) 172 Shakspeare may be contemplated as the type of modern intellect and the representative of the European mind. **1865** DICKENS *Mut. Fr.* III. viii, It is a type of many. **1873** RUSKIN *Fors Clav.* xxxiv. (1896) II. 236 Sir Roger de Coverley is a character, as well as a type.

**b.** *spec.* A person or thing that exemplifies the ideal qualities or characteristics *of* a kind or order; a perfect example or specimen *of* something; a model, pattern, exemplar.

**1847** EMERSON *Repr. Men, Goethe* Wks. (Bohn) I. 392 He is the type of culture. *a* **1853** ROBERTSON *Lect., Wordsw.* 228 Arnold of Rugby is the type of English action; Wordsworth is the type of English thought. **1858** J. H. NEWMAN *Hist. Sk.* (1873) III. II. i. 221 Plato is the very type of soaring philosophy.

**8.** Technical uses from senses 5–7.

**a.** *Nat. Hist.*, etc. A certain general plan of structure characterizing a group of animals, plants, etc.; hence *transf.* a group or division of animals, etc., having a common form or structure.

**1850** MCCOSH *Div. Govt.* II. ii. (ed. 2) 162 In the organic kingdoms, there is an all-pervading system of types: there is a type for every particular species of plant and animal; a type for every leaf and every limb. **1850** TENNYSON *In Mem.* lv, So careful of the type she seems, So careless of the single life. **1867** DK. ARGYLL *Reign Law* iv. 215 The adaptability of the one Vertebrate Type to the..variety of Life to which it serves as..a home. **1872** OLIVER *Elem. Bot.* II. 122 You must try to refer to its type every flowering plant you meet with. **1877** HUXLEY *Anat. Inv. Anim.* i. 49 Such types or common plans as those of the *Arthropoda*, the *Annelida*, the *Mollusca* [etc.]. **1878** GURNEY *Crystallogr.* 30 By the type of symmetry of a crystal we mean the number and arrangement of its symmetral planes. **1892** WESTCOTT *Gospel of Life* 10 The product of any particular seed is fixed within the limits of a type.

**b.** *Nat. Hist.* A species or genus which most perfectly exhibits the essential characters of its family or group, and from which the family or group is (usually) named; an individual embodying all the distinctive characteristics of a species, etc.

**1840** WHEWELL *Philos. Induct. Sci.* VIII. ii. I. 476 A Type is an example of any class, for instance, a species of a genus, which is considered as eminently possessing the characters of the class. **1851** WOODWARD *Mollusca* I. 61 The type of each genus should be that species in which the characters of its group are best exhibited, and most evenly balanced. **1858** MAYNE *Expos. Lex.*, *Salicornieus*,..a tribe of the *Chenopodeæ* established by C. A. Meyer, having the *Salicornia* for their type.

**c.** *Chem.* A simple compound taken as representing the structure of more complex compounds.

**1852** WATTS tr. *Gmelin's Handbk. Chem.* VII. 15 Dumas' Theory of Substitution and of Types. **1857** MILLER *Elem. Chem.* (1862) III. 48 Water, hydrochloric, and hydrosulphuric acid are, therefore, the patterns or types upon which these several bodies are formed. **1868** WATTS *Dict. Chem.* V. 926 Bodies analogous in constitution, and exhibiting analogous reactions, are said to belong to the same type... In a wider sense, the formula HCl may be taken as the type of chlorides, bromides, iodides, fluorides, and cyanides.

**d.** *Math.* (See quots.)

**1891** *Cent. Dict.*, *Type* 12. In *math.*, a succession of symbols susceptible of + and − signs. **1911** WEBSTER, *Type*..6, the simplest of the forms equivalent with respect to a group.

**9.** A small rectangular block, usually of metal or wood, having on its upper end a raised letter, figure, or other character, for use in printing. *In types*, in type (see b). Also *fig.*

**1713** J. WATSON *Hist. Art Printing* 54 Christopher Plantin..printed..that fine Bible..whose Types were casten and made at Paris. **1727–41** CHAMBERS *Cycl.* s.v. *Printing*, The printing letters, characters, or types, as they are sometimes called. **1751** BERKELEY *Let. to Prior* 30 Mar., Wks. 1871 IV. 327 They are going to print..two editions..of Plato's works, in most magnificent types. **1799** *Monthly Rev.* XXX. 290 A method of printing maps and charts of any size by means of moveable types. **1829** MACAULAY *Westm. Reviewer's Def. Mill* (*ad fin.*), The preceding article was written, and was actually in types, when [etc.]. **1849** RUSKIN *Sev. Lamps* v. § 3 The types which once had the die of thought struck fresh upon them. **1880** VERN. LEE *Stud. Italy* III. ii. 102 Musical types had..been invented by an Italian.

**b.** *sing.* Types collectively; letter. *In type*, set up ready for printing.

**1778** V. KNOX *Ess.* xxxviii. 305 To trace the art in its gradual progress from the wooden and immoveable letter to the moveable and metal type. **1784** J. BELKNAP in *B. Papers* (1877) II. 179, I believe some brethren of the type are offended at it. **1837** SIR F. PALGRAVE *Merch. & Friar* Ded. (1844) 4 The work..had been kept in type for nearly a twelvemonth. **1852** DICKENS *Lett.* (1880) I. 291 This story goes straightway into type. **1869** TYNDALL *Notes Lect. Light* § 71 Compositors arrange their type in this backward fashion, the type being reversed by the process of printing. **1882** J. SOUTHWARD *Pract. Print.* (1884) 9 A bill of type is a table showing the number of each of the several sorts in a fount. **1904** R. J. FARRER *Garden Asia* 63 Not China, but Korea, was the inventor of movable type, and the true parent of printing.

**c.** *transf.* A printed character or characters, or an imitation of these.

**1784** COWPER *Task* v. 419 To read engraven on the mouldy walls [of the Bastille] In stagg'ring types, his predecessor's tale. **1831** BREWSTER *Optics* xxxviii. § 183. 320 To see small objects distinctly..such as..a small type. **1841** J. T. HEWLETT *Parish Clerk* I. 125 It was directed in the well-known type of Davy Diggs. **1872** RUSKIN *Fors Clav.* (1896) I. xvi. 321 Here it is in full type, for it is worth careful reading.

**10.** *attrib.* and *Comb.*, as *type-animal*, *-figure*, *-fossil*, *-man*, *-number*, *-phase*, *-phenomenon*, *-sample*, *-series*, *-set*, *-ship*, *-symptom*, *-theme*; in sense 9, as *type-arrangement*, *-body* (BODY *sb.* 13), *-case*, *-composition*, *-foundry*, *-mould*, *-punch*; objective, instrumental, etc., as *type-caster*, *-founder*; *type-casting*, *-composing*, *-creating*, *-distributing*, *-founding*, *-making*, sbs. and adjs.; *type-blackened*, *-cast*, adjs.; **type-bar**, (*a*) a line of type cast in a solid bar, as by the linotype; (*b*) in a typewriter, each of the bars carrying the letters or characters; **type-block**, a block having raised characters on its face, used to impress words or figures, as in gilding (Knight *Dict. Mech.* 1875); **type-blow**, the impact of the type on the paper in a typewriter; **type-carriage**, in a printing-machine, a frame carrying the form; **type-chart**, a chart or outline of a typical object or structure; **type-cutter**, one who engraves the dies or punches from which types are cast; a punch-cutter; so **type-cutting**; **type-cylinder**, the cylinder on which the types or plates are fastened in a rotary press; **type-desk**, a desk or table at which typewriting is done; **type-dressing**, the scraping, polishing, etc., of newly cast type: in quot. *attrib.*; † **type-fever**, an intermittent fever, an ague; **type-form**, (*a*) = FORM *sb.* 20; (*b*) a typical or representative form; **type-gauge**, (*a*) a gauge used by type-founders to test the size of type-bodies; (*b*) a type-measure (*Cassell's Encycl. Dict.*, 1888); **type-genus**, the genus which most perfectly exemplifies the essential characters of the family to which it belongs; *esp.* the genus from which the name of the family is taken; **type-high**, *a.* of the standard height of type (i. e. in Great Britain usually ·9175 in., in *U.S.* ·918 in.); *adv.* as high as, so as to correspond in height with, type; **type-holder**, an instrument for holding types, used for stamping or lettering books (*Cent. Dict.* 1891); **type-larval**, *a.* of or pertaining to a *type larva*, i. e. one which exhibits features characteristic of the group to which it belongs, which do not appear in the adult form; **type-letter**, each of the types or letters of a typewriter; **type-lever**, a lever by which a type or character is impressed, as in a linotype; **type-matter**, printed matter, letterpress; **type-measure**, **-measurer** (Knight *Dict. Mech.*), a rule showing the depth of the various kinds of type, used in calculating the number of lines or ems in composed type; **type-metal**, an alloy of lead and antimony, sometimes with tin or bismuth, of which printing types are cast; **type-music**, music printed from types; **type-page**, the page of type or letterpress as distinct from the paper-page on which it is printed; **type-paper**, paper suitable for typewriting; **type-printed** *a.*, printed from types; also, type-written; so **type-printing**; **type-rule** (*Funk's Stand. Dict.*, 1895); **type-scale** = *type-measure* (*Cent. Dict.* 1891); **type-script** [cf. *typoscript* TYPO-], *sb.* type-written matter or copy; *a.* typewritten; **type-setter**, a compositor; also, a composing-machine; so **type-setting**, *sb.* and *a.*, **type-set** *a.*; **type-slug** = *type-bar* a (*Funk's Stand. Dict.*, 1895); **type-species**, *Nat. Hist.* a species which most perfectly exemplifies its genus; *esp.* the species on which the genus is based; **type-specimen**, *Nat. Hist.* a specimen or individual on which the species is based, and from which the specific name is taken; also *fig.*; **type-sticker**, a compositor (*slang*); **type-system**, a system of teaching by types or representative specimens; **type-theory**, *Chem.* the theory of the derivation of compounds from types (sense 8 c) by substitution; **type-transliteration**, transliteration into modern type or letterpress; **type-value**, value as a type or standard of comparison; **type-wash**, a washing medium for type or plates (Webster, 1911); **type-wheel**, a wheel with raised characters on its periphery, as in the printing telegraph and in some typewriters; **type-work**, letterpress; also type-setting, composing. Also TYPEWRITER, etc.

**1850** *Jrnl. Asiatic Soc. Bengal* Jan. 35 This rare and beautiful creature [the giraffe], *type-animal of their land. *Ibid.* 36 The elephant is evidently with these people, the type-animal. **1877** W. BOYD *Descr. Model Newspaper*, A sheet .. regarding *type-arrangement, Excellent. **1886** *Science* 17 Sept. 252/2 As the *type-bar of a type-writer is connected with its key. **1891** in *Cent. Dict.* **1900** KIPLING in *Daily Express* 26 June 4/6 Allen wagged a *type-blackened forefinger across the table. **1901** *Phonetic Jrnl.* 15 June 371/1 In .. an electrical typewriter .. the *type-blow, or the hammer-blow, will be automatic. **1895** *Funk's Standard Dict.* s.v. *Point system*, Under this system the old names of *type-bodies, as *nonpareil* (now 6-point), *bourgeois* (now 9-point), etc., are in disuse. **1825** J. NICHOLSON *Operat. Mechanic* 307 By the farther motion of the *type carriage, the ink-table is caused to pass under four small elastic rollers. **1891** *Cent. Dict.*, *Type-case. **1909** H. HART in *Periodical* Feb. 294 A double-windowed room..was fitted up with compositors' frames and type-cases. **1876** *Nature* 18 May 43/2 This hammer..carries at its extremity a *type-cast letter. **1847** in *Inquiry Yorksh. Deaf & Dumb* (1870) 19 As a *type-caster..we consider him a good hand. **1875** KNIGHT *Dict. Mech.*, *Type-casting, .. Type casting and setting machine. **1897** *Daily News* 2 Feb. 2/1 The Wicks Rotary Type-Casting Machine can cast .. from 40,000 to 60,000 letters per hour. **1887** J. G. WOOD in *19th Cent.* Mar. 386 There are *type-charts of each organ. **1878** JEVONS *Prim. Pol. Econ.* 71 Some compositors still object to work in offices where *type-composing machines are introduced. **1881** *Instr. Census Clerks* (1886) 51 *Type cutter, founder. **1890** *Athenæum* 1 Mar. 281/3 He was a die-sinker and type-cutter. **1839** T. C. HANSARD *Print. & Type-founding* (1841) 156 An inking apparatus was applied to the *type-cylinder, and the paper was to be impressed by passing between the two. **1901** F. HARRISON in *19th Cent.* June 918 Every girl at a *type-desk or a telegraph office may live to reside in Fifth Avenue. **1875** KNIGHT *Dict.*

*Mech.* 2676/1 *Type-distributing machines have frequently been invented as companion machines to those for composing. *Ibid.*, **Type-dressing machine*.. passes the type set up in rows between a pair of knife-blades set in exact parallelism. **1819** Sir A. Boswell in *Poet. Wks. & Mem.* Introd. 33 Being infected with the *type-fever the fits have periodically returned. **1897** *Westm. Gaz.* 16 Mar. 2/1 Mr. Meredith..has himself drawn the great *type-figure of modern fiction..'The Egoist'. **1839** Ure *Dict. Arts* 1035 To adapt this method of inking to a flat *type-form machine. **1875** *Ibid.* III. 660 Mr. Applegarth..decided on abandoning the reciprocating motion of the type-form. **1900** F. H. Stoddard *Evol. Eng. Novel* 218 Mankind demands that it shall show conformity to a certain type-form. **1901** *Nature* 19 Dec. 168/1 The author divides the species into the type-form and four varieties. **1854** Murchison *Siluria* iii. 52 The *type-fossils..have not yet been detected. **1801** *Tilloch's Philos. Mag.* X. 270 A new art, that of the *type-founder. **1888** Burgon *Lives 12 Gd. Men* I. iii. 349 A heavy assortment of great and small pica, newly arrived from the type-founder. **1839** T. C. Hansard *Print. & Type-founding* (1841) 222 The invention of the art of *type-founding was a very early consequence of the discovery of the rude art of taking impressions from laboriously excised letters of wood and metal. **1875** W. Blades in *Bks. in Chains* (1892) Introd. 24 The first positive notice we have of type-founding in England is the fount of Saxon cut by John Day for Archbishop Parker and used in 1567. **1843** *Penny Cycl.* XXV. 454/1 The first and most important operation of a *type-foundry is the formation of the punches. **1840** Whewell *Philos. Induct. Sci.* viii. ii. I. 477 The type-species of every genus, the *type-genus of every family, is, then, one which possesses all the characters and properties of the genus in a marked and prominent manner. **1896** H. Woodward *Guide Fossil Reptiles Brit. Mus.* 65 Dr. Filhol records the type-genus from the Upper Eocene Phosphorites of France. **1896** T. L. De Vinne *Moxon's Mech. Exerc., Printing* 406 Brass Rule..cut in strips *type-high. **1890** W. J. Gordon *Foundry* 213 The copper electro is mounted type-high, and becomes the block from which the printing is made. **1884** Hyatt in *Proc. Boston Soc. Nat. Hist.* 5 Mar. 122 Their embryonic history has no stage which exhibits..a distinct *type-larval stage. **1876** *Nature* 18 May 43/2 Two keys struck at the same time must consequently cause two *type-letters to clash in their attempt to reach the same spot, the centre of the circle. **1908** *Daily Chron.* 26 Aug. 5/2 The typist has at his disposal all kinds of type on type wheels which are fixed at the end of *type levers. **1872** T. L. Cuyler *Heart Life* 25 He is the *type-man for thorough-going fidelity. **1906** Dk. Argyll *Autobiog. & Mem.* I. ii. 32 The type-man was Wolfe Tone, the unscrupulous Villain. **1892** *Advt.* in *Photogr. Ann.* II. p. clxiv, Phototype Prints are the best for reproducing Portraits [etc.]..*Type Matter requires a second printing. **1800** tr. *Lagrange's Chem.* I. 445 Antimony and lead form a most valuable mixture; it is that used for printing-types, and is called *Type-Metal. **1818** Todd, *To stereotype*, to make type-metal plates to print from at the letter-press. **1850** Ansted *Elem. Geol., Min.* etc. § 475 [Antimony] is used in the manufacture of type metal, of which it forms from one fourth to a twelfth part, the rest being lead, with a little tin, bismuth, and copper. **1882** J. Southward *Pract. Print.* (1884) 15 Type metal is of two kinds, ordinary and hard. **1843** *Penny Cycl.* XXV. 454/1 A *type-mould [illustrated]. **1882** J. Southward *Pract. Print.* (1884) 342 This system undoubtedly brings *type-music into disrepute. **1871** Kingsley *At Last* xiii, The nut ought to have..not one ovule, but three, the *type-number in palms. **1910** *Athenæum* 19 Mar. 348/1 The relation of *type-page to paper-page is.. still open, within certain limits, to individual taste. **1906** *Daily Chron.* 27 Jan. 6/4 They make the better-class papers known as 'banks', '*type' papers, 'drawing' papers, and high-class writing papers. **1911** *Edin. Rev.* July 103 Isolated .. caprices rather than *type-phases of animal literature. **1892** *Daily News* 26 Feb. 7/3, I searched Sampson before leaving..and found..two *type-printed statements relating to the charge. **1839** T. C. Hansard *Print. & Type-founding* (1841) 59 There does not appear to be any vestige of an art in any degree similar (such as block-printing) having been practised prior to the introduction of *type-printing. **1876** *Nature* 18 May 43/1 The sewing-machine or the more novel type-printing apparatus. **1888** *Arts & Crafts Catal.* 94 The current hand-writing may be elegant enough to be.. used as a model for the *type-punch engraver. **1894** *Daily News* 12 Sept. 7/1 *Type-samples of unmanufactured tobacco sent for trade purposes. **1893** A. Estoclet in *Nation* (N. Y.) 6 July 10/3 Writing..concerning a typewritten document.., I half apologetically used the word '*typescript'. **1906** N. W. Thomas *Kin. Org. & Group Marr. Austral.* Pref., He has read twice over my typescript MS, and my proofs. **1907** H. Wyndham *Flare of Footlights* xxix, Adrian recognized it as the typescript of his one-act play. **1887** J. G. Wood in *19th Cent.* Mar. 395, I would have a *type-series of the vertebrates, so that in going through the galleries the visitors would recognise the creatures they had seen grouped. **1903** *Westm. Gaz.* 17 Nov. 2/1 A *type set of the collections representing the massive rocks of the island. **1867** Brande & Cox *Dict. Sc.*, etc. s.v. *Telegraph*, The *type-set message. *Ibid.*, Ten *type-setters under Bonelli's system can compose at least 300 despatches per hour. **1888** *Cassell's Encycl. Dict.*, *Type-setter*, 2, a type-setting or composing machine. **1899** *Daily News* 24 June 4/4 When women first began as type-setters in Boston, the male type-setters struck. **1911** *T. P.'s Weekly* 29 Dec. 844/1 Young's Patent Composing Machine..was the name of the first practical type-setter, seventy years ago. **1867** Brande & Cox *Dict. Sc.* etc. s.v. *Telegraph*, Converting the telegraph stations..into so many *type-setting workshops. **1875** Knight *Dict. Mech.*, *Type-setting machine*, a composing-machine for type. **1886** *Science* 17 Sept. 254/1 Justification will be as easily accomplished as in ordinary type-setting. **1901** *Feilden's Mag.* IV. 421/1 The *type-ship, which has been tried on the measured mile. **1840** Whewell *Philos. Induct. Sci.* viii. ii. I. 476 All the species which have a greater affinity with this *type-species than with any others, form the genus. **1891** *Cent. Dict.*, *Type specimen. **1894** *Geol. Mag.* Oct. 435 J. Sowerby's type-specimens of *Ammonites Brocchii* are much more inflated than the present species. **1904** G. L. Kittredge *Eng. & Scot. Pop. Ball.* p. xxvi, 'The Hangman's Tree' is a survival of an archaic type-specimen. **1842** H. Greeley *Corr. R. W. Griswold* (1898) 104 Which you will keep out of the dirty hands of all *type-stickers. **1899** *Allbutt's Syst. Med.* VII. 591 All the *type symptoms of cerebellar abscess were present. **1901** *Nature* 26 Sept. 526/1 Prosecuting a more detailed study of individual forms, as with the now universal *type-system. **1901** *Daily Chron.* 14 June 3/4 In 'Rosmersholm' Ibsen has seized upon one of the great *type-themes of modern life. **1868** Watts *Dict. Chem.* V. 927 The law of substitution is the expression of facts, which the *type-theory was intended to explain. **1896** *Periodical* No. 1. 4 The unique MS...has been reproduced..in photo-facsimile and *type-transliteration. **1909** Marett *Threshold Relig.* Introd. (1914) 25 When..a set of useful contrasts is obtained by means of such bundles, each bundle..is said to have '*type-value'. **1849** Noad *Electricity* viii. (ed. 3) 381 The rotatory motion given to the *type wheel..until the required letter arrives opposite the paper. **1886** *Science* 17 Sept. 252/2 Fitted in vertical grooves in the periphery of the type-wheel are a number of steel types. **1910** H. C. G. Moule in *Fundamentals* II. vi. 107 The compositor 'justifies' a piece of *typework, when he corrects, brings into perfect order, as to spaces between words and letters, and so on, the types which he has set up.

Hence (*nonce-wds.*) **Ty·peful** *a.*, having the quality of a type; typical; symbolic; **Typefy** (təi·pĭfei), *v. trans.* to put into type, to print; **Ty·peless** *a.*, untyped, unprinted.

**1889** Lucia E. F. Kimball in *Chicago Advance* 16 May, How *typeful this lovely blossom of the rare, sweet souls who strive..to make the bare, ugly places brighter and better. **1856** Strang *Glasgow & Clubs* 25 The blatant blusterings of every charlatan..must be pencilled and *typefied, before the lapse of a few hours. **1845** Ford *Handbk. Spain* II. 708/1 Many authors..content to remain..in *typeless obscurity.

**Type**, *sb.*2: see Tipe *sb.*1

†**Type**, *sb.*3 Obs. var. of Tipe *sb.*2, trap.

**1799** *Hull Advertiser* 2 Feb. 3/3 [A] labourer..charged with entering the warren..and breaking open the lock of a type, and killing a rabbit therein.

**Type** (təip), *v.* [f. Type *sb.*1; cf. F. *typé* adj. (Littré), *typer* (ibid. *Suppl.*).]

**1.** *trans.* **a.** *Theol.* To prefigure or foreshadow as a type; to represent in prophetic similitude. Also *type forth*, *out*.

**1596** H. Clapham *Briefe Bible* I. 58 That specially typed out Our spotles Priest Iesus. **1606** J. Carpenter *Solomon's Solace* xxvii. 111 Wee see how he typeth the holy Messiah. **1633** Bp. Hall *Hard Texts, N. T.* 268 Which same thing is also typed forth unto us by Sinai and Jerusalem. **1690** C. Nesse *O. & N. Test.* I. 66 Adam..offer'd sacrifice which typed out Christ. **1827** Pollok *Course T.* v. 894 A time Typed by the Sabbath-day..When all had rest and peace.

**b.** To be the type or symbol of; to represent by a type or symbol; to symbolize: = Typify 1.

**1836** E. Howard *R. Reefer* xxxii, The old man's look.. was so wretched,..yet so fond—and was typed to my fancy so strongly by his little boat [etc.]. **1837** Campbell *Lines on Poland* 130 The Rainbow types Heaven's promise to my sight. **1839** Bailey *Festus* xi. (1848) 32/2 All nature typeth Thee and Thine. **1875** Tennyson *Q. Mary* III. iv, The cataract typed the headlong plunge and fall Of heresy to the pit.

**2.** To be an example or specimen of; to exemplify: = Typify 2. *rare.*

**1627** W. Sclater *Exp. 2 Thess.* (1629) 263 Pauls maine intention in typing or lineing out in his owne practise, what he prescribed to others. **1866** Blackie *Homer & Iliad* I. 25 The peculiar character..of Scottish piety, as it has been typed in Scotland now for more than three hundred years.

**b.** To be or furnish the pattern or model for.

**1836** Lytton *Athens* (1837) II. 55 On the Shield He bears his haughty ensign—typed by stars Gleaming athwart the sky.

**3.** To reproduce by means of type; to print. *rare.*

**1736** [see Typing *vbl. sb.*]. **1841** Miall in *Nonconf.* I. 13 A host of abstractions typed off with capital letters.

**4.** To write or copy by means of a type-writing machine; also *intr.* to practise typewriting; to typewrite.

**1888** *Scott. Leader* 28 Aug. 3 The operator..types at the rate of from fifty to sixty words a minute. **1888** *Pall Mall G.* 6 Oct. 15/1 Shorthand Evidence 'typed' from Dictation. **1897** G. Allen *Type-writer Girl* xvi, I went back to my machine and began typing mechanically. **1900** E. Wallace *Writ in Barracks* 114 'Tis the dainty hand that types it.

Hence **Ty·ping** *ppl. a.*

**1897** *Daily News* 21 Sept. 7/2 To transform..the secretaries into shorthand and typing clerks.

**-type** (təip), *suffix*, repr. F. *-type*, L. *-typus*, Gr. -τυπος, f. root of τύπτειν to beat, strike: cf. Type *sb.*1 The termination -τυπος was used in Greek to form adjs., in sense 'struck, driven, moulded', as ἀντίτυπος repelled, reflected (also in active sense 'repelling'), ἀρχέτυπος first-moulded, πρωτότυπος original, primitive (also used *absol.* as sbs.). These have been anglicized as sbs., *antitype*, *archetype*, *prototype*; and many technical words connected with printing and other modern processes of copying have been formed on the model of them, with the sense 'type, block, or plate for printing from', as in *electrotype*, *logotype*, *phonotype*, *stereotype*; 'impression or picture', also 'process of reproduction', as in *autotype*, *calotype*, *chrysotype*, *collotype*, *cyanotype*, *ferrotype*, *phototype*, *platinotype*, etc.; also in hybrid formations on Eng. words, as *colourtype*.

**Typed** (təipt, *poet.* təi·pĕd), *ppl. a.* [f. Type *v.* or *sb.*1 + -ed.]

**1.** Of or pertaining to a (specified) type; having a (certain) type or general character.

**1839** Bailey *Festus* xv. (1852) 170 Sun, planet, satellite, all typed spheres..it is mine To search and pass through. **1881** *Builder* XLI. 442 Medieval Church architecture..is characteristic and strongly typed.

**2.** In combination: That is printed in or with type of a specified kind.

**1831** J. Brown *Lett.* (1907) 7 A larger typed Testament which I think will suit your eyes.

**3.** That is printed or reproduced by means of a typewriter; typewritten.

**1890** *Daily News* 24 Feb. 5/6 'Typing' from copy,..dictation from 'typed matter'. **1895** A. W. Tuer in *Athenæum* 15 June 773/1 Some typed sample chapters.

†**Typed**, *a.* *Obs. rare.* [f. Type *sb.*3 + -ed 2.] Furnished with tipes or traps.

**1799** A. Young *Agric. Lincoln.* 385 A warren..carefully typed to catch all extra bucks.

**Typembryo** (təipe·mbriǫ). *Biol.* [f. Type *sb.*1 + Embryo.] The stage in the development of an embryo when the characteristic structure of its phylum or subkingdom begins to appear.

**1887** Hyatt in *Proc. Boston Nat. Hist. Soc.* 16 Nov. 398 Naming the embryo in these last stages the Typembryo. *Ibid.* 399 Typembryos serve to connect the earlier stages of the Neoembryos with the true larval stages which succeed the former.

**Typer** (təi·pəɹ). [f. Type *v.* + -er 1.] A type-writing machine: = Typewriter 1.

**1892** in *Boston* (Mass.) *Jrnl.* 27 May 4/7 For 'typewriter' (the machine) say 'typer'. **1915** *Morn. Post* 5 Feb. 2/1 It is.. typewritten, for..'we have bagged another German typer'.

**Typewrite** (təi·pɪrəit), *v.* [Back-formation from Typewriter.] *trans.* To print by means of a typewriter; to type; also *intr.* to use a typewriter, to practise typewriting.

**1887** in *Athenæum* 31 Dec. 878/1 Authors' MSS...typewritten at 1d. per folio. **1894** *Westm. Gaz.* 20 June 3/2 Eighteen machines,..the simplest of which type-writes a message by means of a single wire. **1897** G. Allen *Typewriter Girl* x, With my maimed fingers, it would be impossible for me to type-write for three days at least. **1898** *Westm. Gaz.* 5 Feb. 2/1 His..hero—a literary character—had fallen madly in love with the young lady who came to typewrite his novel.

So **Ty·pewriting** *vbl. sb.* and *ppl. a.*, **Ty·pewritten** *ppl. a.*

**1881** *X-Y-Z Guide* (N. Y.) Oct. 161 For sale..a type writing machine. **1885** *Pall Mall G.* 5 May 6/1 That new convenience of civilization a type writing office...Constant employment is now afforded to eight ladies in type-writing. **1888** *Ibid.* 6 Oct. 15/1 Typewritten documents cost no more than Law Engrossing. **1894** *Athenæum* 21 July 90/2 She forges type-written letters. **1897** G. Allen *Type-writer Girl* ii, Type-writing as an accomplishment is as diffused as the piano. **1912** *Times* 19 Dec. 13/2 A type-written copy of all the memoranda.

**Typewriter** (təi·pɪrəi:təɹ). [f. Type *sb.*1 + Writer.]

**1.** A writing-machine having types for the letters of the alphabet, figures, and punctuation-marks, so arranged on separate rods (or on the periphery of a wheel) that as each key of the machine is depressed the corresponding character is imprinted in line on a moving sheet.

**1875** Knight *Dict. Mech.* s. v., The Sholes type-writer..is about the size of the sewing-machine, and is worked with keys arranged in four banks or rows. **1881** *X-Y-Z Guide* (N. Y.) Oct. p. iv, Manufacturers of the best Type Writer in the market. **1897** G. Allen *Type-writer Girl* iii, My type-writer continued to go click, click, click. **1899** *Allbutt's Syst. Med.* VIII. 25 One typewriter..is worked by means of a handle which is grasped.

**2.** One who does typewriting, esp. as a regular occupation; = Typist 2.

**1884** *N. York Herald* 27 Oct. 7/2 Situation wanted—by lady, rapid stenographer and typewriter. **1887** *St. James's Gaz.* 22 Dec., Women..beat them [men] altogether as type-writers and 'dry-goods clerks'. **1895** *How to get Married* 86 The marriage of the type-writer and her employer is so frequent that it has passed into a joke.

**3.** *attrib.* and *Comb.*

**1889** *Pall Mall G.* 22 Oct. 2/1 The typewriter industry ..is a thing to itself. **1897** G. Allen *Type-writer Girl* xi, Ten thousand type-writer girls crowd London to-day. **1900** Doyle *Green Flag* 13 The typewriter-like clicking of the hopper. **1902** Eliz. L. Banks *Newspaper Girl* 4 My fingers ..flew over the typewriter keys. *Ibid.* 155, I took my type-writer brush out, as though to wash it in the kitchen sink.

**Typh** (təif). [Deduced from Typhus, Typhoid.] **Typh fever** (also simply **typh**): see quots.; **typh poison**, poison causing typh fever.

**1861** T. K. Chambers *Lect.* (1864) vi. 70 You saw a case of continued low fever (or as I shall call it for shortness Typh-fever) admitted four days ago. *Ibid.* 75, I have been led to believe that the exciting cause of typh-fever enters usually by the digestive canal. **1890** Billings *Med. Dict.*, *Typh fever*, a name proposed by Dr. Thomas King Chambers to include both typhus and enteric fevers. **1891** *Cent. Dict.*, Typh-poison. **1900–13** Dorland *Med. Dict.*, *Typh*, *typh-fever*, typhus and typhoid viewed together.

†**Typh**, obs. form of Tiphe.

**1600** Surflet *Country Farm* v. xvii. 688 Typh wheate is very like to our rye, and doth make a very blacke bread.

‖**Typha** (təi·fă). *Bot.* [mod.L., f. Gr. τύφη cat's-tail.] A genus of aquatic herbs (type of the N.O. *Typhaceæ*), containing the common cat's-tail or reed-mace (*T. latifolia*).

1548 TURNER *Names of Herbes* (E.D.S.) 79 Typha groweth in fennes and water sydes among the reedes...It is called in englishe cattes tayle, or a Reedmace. 1796 H. HUNTER tr. *St.-Pierre's Stud. Nat.* (1799) II. 143 The water-lentil of our marshes, as well as the typha of our rivers, has the middle of it's leaf swelled. 1838 MARY HOWITT *Birds & Fl., Lit. Streams* 23 Typha strong, and green bur-reed. 1861 BENTLEY *Man. Bot.* 688 The pollen of some species of *Typha* is edible.

**Typhaceous** (təifēⁱ·ʃəs), *a. Bot.* [f. mod.L. *Typhācē-æ*, f. *Typha*: see prec. and -ACEOUS.] Belonging to the Natural Order *Typhaceæ*.
1909 in *Cent. Dict. Suppl.*

**Typhe**, obs. form of TIPHE.

**Typhic** (ti·fik), *a. Path.* [f. TYPH-US + -IC; cf. F. *typhique*.] = TYPHOUS.
1860 MAYNE *Expos. Lex., Typhosepsis*, term for typhic or typhous putrefaction. 1890 BILLINGS *Med. Dict., Typhic*, typhoid.

**Typhine** (təi·fin). [f. TYPH-US + -INE 5.] The hypothetical infectious principle of typhus.
1864 FARR in *Rep. Regr. General* 34 Any zymotic matter such as varioline, scarlatinine, or typhine.

**Typhization** (təi-, tifizēⁱ·ʃən). *Path.* [f. TYPH-US + -IZE + -ATION.] Production of a morbid state by exposure to the infection of typhus.
1895 in *Funk's Stand. Dict.* 1900–13 in DORLAND *Med. Dict.*

‖ **Typhlitis** (tifləi·tis). *Path.* [mod.L., f. Gr. τυφλόν the cæcum or blind gut (neut. of τυφλός blind) + -ITIS.] Inflammation of the cæcum, cæcitis (often including that of the *appendix vermiformis*, now distinctively called *appendicitis*).
1857 in DUNGLISON *Med. Lex.* 1866 A. FLINT *Princ. Med.* (1880) 427 Inflammation of the caecum..constitutes an affection called *typhlitis, tuphlo-enteritis*, or *caecitis*. *Ibid.* 429 The term typhlitis is applied to inflammation of the vermiform appendix as well as to caecitis. 1891 *Pall Mall G.* 13 May 6/3 She died, after a short illness, of typhlitis.
Hence **Typhlitic** (tifli·tik) *a.*, pertaining to, of the nature of, or affected with typhlitis.
1891 in *Cent. Dict.*

**Typhlo-** (tiflo), before a vowel regularly **typhl-**, ad. Gr. τυφλο-, combining form of τυφλός blind: occurring in a few recent scientific and technical words, chiefly pathological and surgical terms relating to the cæcum (Gr. τυφλόν: see prec.). **Typhlatony** (-æ·tŏni), atony of the cæcum. **Typhle·ctomy** [Gr. ἐκτομή excision], excision of the cæcum. **Typhlenteri·tis**, more regular form of *typhlo-enteritis*. **Typhlodicliditis** (-diklidəi·tis) [Gr. δικλίς, δικλιδ- folding door], inflammation of the ileo-cæcal valve. **Typhlo-enteritis** (also **tuphlo-**) [Gr. ἔντερον intestine] = TYPHLITIS. **Ty·phlograph** (-graf) [-GRAPH: cf. F. *typhlographe* (Littré)], an apparatus for assisting the blind to write evenly. **Ty·phlolithi·asis** [LITHIASIS], formation of calculi or hard concretions in the cæcum. **Typhlo·logy** [-LOGY], the scientific knowledge relating to blindness. **Ty·phlopexy** [Gr. πῆξις fixation], the operation of fixing the cæcum to the wall of the abdomen. **Ty·phloste-no·sis** [Gr. στένωσις straitening, contraction], constriction of the cæcum. **Typhlo·tomy** [Gr. τομή cutting], incision into the cæcum.
1900–13 DORLAND *Med. Dict.*, **Typhlatony*, inefficiency of the motor activity of the cæcum. *Ibid.*, *Typhlectomy... *Typhlenteritis...*Typhlodicliditis. 1857 DUNGLISON *Med. Lex.*, *Tuphlo-enteritis. *Ibid.*, Typhlo-enteritis. 1866 [see TYPHLITIS]. 1896 *Westm. Gaz.* 2 May 2/3 Messrs. Jarrold send us a sample of what they..term 'The *Typhlograph'. It consists of a neat slope of hard wood with grooves on the surface, and it is designed to enable the blind to produce ordinary hand-writing in a straight line. 1898 *Internat. Cycl.* (N.Y.) II. 641 Mr. Gall's typhlograph is a much more perfect instrument. 1890 BILLINGS *Med. Dict.*, **Typhlolithiasis*. 1872 W. H. LEVY (*title*) Blindness and the Blind: or, a Treatise on the Science of *Typhlology. 1900–13 DORLAND *Med. Dict.*, Typhlopexia, *typhlopexy. 1890 BILLINGS *Med. Dict.*, *Typhlostenosis. 1903 *Lancet* 30 May 1511/1 Other operations may be required to relieve the patient, such as *typhlotomy, colotomy.

**Typhlope** (ti·floᵘp). *Zool. rare*$^{-0}$. [ad. mod.L. *Typhlop-, -ops*, ad. Gr. τυφλώψ, f. τυφλός blind + ὤψ eye, face.] A snake of the genus *Typhlops* or family *Typhlopidæ*; a blindworm.
1891 in *Cent. Dict.*

**Typhlophthalmic** (tiflǫfþæ·lmik), *a. Zool. rare*$^{-0}$. [f. mod.L. *Typhlophthalmi* (f. Gr. τυφλός blind + ὀφθαλμός eye) + -IC.] Belonging to the *Typhlophthalmi*, a superfamily of pleurodont lizards in Cope's classification.
1891 in *Cent. Dict.*

**Typhlosole** (ti·flosōul). *Zool.* Also **-solis**. [irreg. f. Gr. τυφλός blind + σωλήν channel, pipe.] A ridge or fold extending along the inner wall of the intestine and partly dividing the cavity of it, in various animals, as lampreys and certain ascidians, molluscs, and worms.
1859 *Todd's Cycl. Anat.* V. 297/2 In the Earth-worm, there is a singular apparatus, the typhlosole. 1877 HUXLEY *Anat. Inv. Anim.* x. 604 In many Ascidians, a strong fold of the endoderm of the intestine projects into its interior, as in Lamellibranchs and in the Earthworm, where such a fold constitutes the so-called typhlosole. 1881 DARWIN *Veg. Mould* 19 The intestine [of the earth-worm] presents a remarkable structure, the typhlosolis. 1888 ROLLESTON & JACKSON *Anim. Life* 435 The mid-gut..in the Lampreys contains a projecting fold or typhlosole.
Hence **Typhloso·lar** *a.*, pertaining to or of the nature of a typhlosole.
1887 BENHAM in *Q. Jrnl. Microsc. Sci.* Mar. 566 The dorsal trunk divides into two. A subneural vessel is present and a typhlosolar vessel.

**Typho-** (təifo), ad. Gr. τυφο-, combining form of τῦφος (see TYPHUS): used as combining form of TYPHUS or TYPHOID, in recent terms of pathology, etc. **Typho-adyna·mic** *a.* [ADYNAMIC], characterized by prostration as in typhus or typhoid fever. **Typhogenic** (-dʒe·nik) *a.* [see -GEN and -IC], producing typhus or typhoid fever. **Typholysin** (təifǫ·lisin), a lysin which destroys the bacilli of typhoid fever. **Typhomalarial** (-mălēᵊ·riăl) *a.*, applied to a fever exhibiting both typhoid and malarial symptoms, or to typhoid fever with malarial complications or of supposed malarial origin. **Ty:phopneumo·nia**, pneumonia complicated with typhoid fever, or exhibiting typhoid symptoms. **Typhoto·xin** [see TOXIN], a poisonous ptomaine obtained from cultures of the bacillus of typhoid fever.
1898 P. MANSON *Trop. Diseases* ii. 66 The fever may assume the *typho-adynamic type. 1900–13 DORLAND *Med. Dict.*, *Typhogenic. 1902 *Brit. Med. Jrnl.* 12 Apr. 920 *Typholysin, the lysin of cholera [etc.]. 1884 *Lisbon* (Dakota) *Star* 29 Aug., A severe attack of *typho-malarial fever. 1898 P. MANSON *Trop. Diseases* vi. 109 These cases are typho-malarial,..typhoid with a malarial complication. 1878 A. HAMILTON *Nerv. Dis.* 62 Typhoid, in some of its forms, or *typho-pneumonia, may resemble tubercular meningitis. 1890 BILLINGS *Med. Dict.*, *Typhotoxine, $C_7H_{17}NO_2$. 1901 W. OSLER *Princ. & Pract. Med.* i. (ed. 4) 8 Brieger isolated from cultures [of typhoid bacilli] a poison belonging to the group of ptomaines—typhotoxin.

†**Typho·dial**, *a. Obs. rare*$^{-1}$. [f. Gr. τυφώδης (f. τῦφος, TYPHUS + εἶδος form) + -IAL.] Resembling typhus: = TYPHOID *a.* 1.
1869 E. A. PARKES *Pract. Hygiene* (ed. 3) 72 Eight persons were affected with more or less typhodial symptoms.

**Typhœan** (təifī·ăn), *a.* [Properly *Typhoēan*, f. *Typhōeus*, Gr. Τυφωεύς, name of a giant of Greek mythology. (Cf. TYPHON [1].)] Belonging to or characteristic of Typhoeus.
1667 MILTON *P. L.* II. 539 Others with vast Typhœan rage..Rend up both Rocks and Hills, And ride the Air In whirlwind.

**Typhoid** (təi·foid), *a.* (*sb.*) *Path.* [f. TYPHUS + -OID; cf. Gr. τυφώδης, F. *typhoïde*, Pg. *typhoideo*, Sp., It. *tifoideo*.]
**1.** Resembling or characteristic of typhus; applied to a class of febrile diseases exhibiting symptoms similar to those of typhus, or to such symptoms themselves, esp. to a state of delirious stupor occurring in certain fevers.
1800 *Med. Jrnl.* III. 95 In its first stage, this fever did not appear to be contagious; but it was evidently so after the eleventh or fourteenth day, when the typhoid state was induced. 1813 J. THOMSON *Lect. Inflam.* 175 In low typhous fever, and in typhoid inflammatory affections. 1846 G. E. DAY tr. *Simon's Anim. Chem.* II. 245 The state of the urine in typhoid fevers. 1897 *Allbutt's Syst. Med.* II. 38 Acute general tuberculosis or acute typhoid tuberculosis as it is sometimes called. 1905 H. D. ROLLESTON *Dis. Liver* 316 A 'typhoid' or comatose condition ushers in death.
**2.** *Typhoid fever*: a specific eruptive fever (formerly supposed to be a variety of typhus), characterized by intestinal inflammation and ulceration: more distinctively, and now more usually, called *enteric fever*.
1845 BUDD *Dis. Liver* 70, I have never seen abscess of the liver noticed in conjunction with ulcerated intestine in typhoid fever. 1877 ROBERTS *Handbk. Med.* (ed. 3) I. 119 Typhoid fever originates from a specific poison, which is quite distinct from that causing typhus. 1890 *Lancet* 22 Nov. 1133/1 As to typhoid fever, the principal factor in its propagation was..drinking-water.
**b.** Of or pertaining to, characteristic of, or affected with typhoid fever.
1871 TYNDALL *Fragm. Sc.* (1879) I. v. 178 So surely does the typhoid virus increase and multiply into typhoid fever. 1890 BILLINGS *Med. Dict., Typhoid..tongue*, the black, dry tongue seen in enteric and typhus fevers. 1899 *Allbutt's Syst. Med.* VII. 483 The typhoid patient has some tympanites as a rule. *Ibid.* 600 A typhoid rash came out. 1904 *Brit. Med. Jrnl.* 10 Sept. 596 Infection with the typhoid bacillus.
**B.** *sb.* Short for *typhoid fever*: see 2 above.
*Pig typhoid*, a name for swine fever.
1861 TANNER *Pract. Med.* II. i. (ed. 4) 153 The fatal cases in typhus and typhoid are one in between five and six. 1887 *Times* 1 Feb. 9/6 Swine fever..being known in different parts of Great Britain by the names of pig typhoid, pig distemper. 1893 *Syd. Soc. Lex., Pig typhoid*, swine plague. 1898 *Daily News* 13 Dec. 3/4 Jenner's great contribution to medical knowledge was the differentiation of typhus and typhoid. 1902 R. BAGOT *Donna Diana* xxi, In typhoid there are often relapses.
**b.** A case of typhoid; a patient suffering from typhoid. *colloq.*
1890 *Pall Mall G.* 8 Sept. 2/3, I have heard of nurses who started out of their sleep and got out of bed under the impression they had still, as they put it, their 'two-hour typhoids to feed'. 1900 *Westm. Gaz.* 27 June 1/2 There were 316 patients, of whom half were typhoids.
**c.** *Comb.* as *typhoid-bacillus, -carrier, -infection*; *typhoid-contaminated, -like, -poisoned* adjs.
1897 *Allbutt's Syst. Med.* IV. 154 Pansini..obtained typhoid-like bacilli in three dysenteric abscesses. 1899 CAGNEY tr. *Jaksch's Clin. Diagn.* vi. (ed. 4) 246 The typhoid-bacillus..infests the discharges of this disease. 1902 *Daily Chron.* 18 Dec. 5/1 Typhoid-contaminated sewage. 1903 *Daily Mail* 10 Sept. 3/4 Typhoid-poisoned oysters. 1908 *Daily Chron.* 8 Sept. 4/4 Typhoid-infection on a large scale. *Ibid.*, 'Typhoid carriers', persons..long cured..of the active disease, yet act as culture-merchants of its germs.

**Typhoidal** (təifoi·dăl), *a.* [f. prec. + -AL.] Pertaining to or characteristic of typhoid fever; resembling or having the character of typhoid fever.
1882 *St. James's Gaz.* 15 Nov. 6 The milk-pail reeks with fever germs, The pump with seeds typhoidal. 1890 in *N. Y. Voice* 17 Apr., Miasmatic and typhoidal conditions. 1899 *Allbutt's Syst. Med.* VIII. 467 The fever..may be..ephemeral, remittent, .. continuous, typhoidal, according to the circumstances.

**Typholysin, Typhomalarial**: see TYPHO-.

‖ **Typhomania** (təifomēⁱ·niă). *Path.* [mod.L., ad. Gr. τυφωμανία (Hippocrates, Galen), f. τῦφος (see TYPHUS) + μανία madness, MANIA; by modern writers taken as f. TYPHUS (in the mod. sense) + MANIA.] Delirium accompanied with stupor, occurring in typhus and other fevers.
1693 tr. *Blancard's Phys. Dict.* (ed. 2), *Typhomania*, a Delirium with a Phrensy, and a Lethargy. 1783 W. CULLEN *First Lines Pract. Phys.* § 293 In the Nosology, I added the Typhomania to the character of Phrenitis. 1822–9 GOOD *Study Med.* (ed. 3) IV. 622 Imperfect lethargy,..the Typhomania of the Greek writers; the Coma Vigil of many later pathologists. 1857 DUNGLISON *Med. Lex., Typhomania*, the kind of delirium common in typhus. 1876 BRISTOWE *The. & Pract. Med.* (1878) 185 Occasionally the delirium [in typhus] is violent and maniacal,..but much more commonly it is of the low muttering kind, known by the name of 'typhomania'.

**Typhon** [1] (təi·fǫn). [a. L. *Tȳphōn*, a. Gr. Τυφῶν, name of a giant (see below); also, a tempestuous wind (see next); also applied to a comet or meteor.] The name of a giant or monster of ancient Greek mythology (according to Hesiod, the son of Typhoeus (see TYPHŒAN), and father of the Winds; later identified with Typhoeus), fabled to have been buried under Mount Etna, and represented as having a hundred heads and breathing out flames; also used as a name for the Egyptian evil divinity Set. Hence *allusively*.
1592 KYD *Sol. & Pers.* I. iii, *Bas.* What, wouldst thou haue me a Typhon, To beare vp Peleon or Ossa? *Pist.* Typhon me no Typhons. 1610 GUILLIM *Heraldry* I. i. (1660) 7 Ulysses bare a Dolphin and a Typhon breathing out flames of fire. 1611 SPEED *Hist. Gt. Brit.* IX. xx. § 14 This aery Typhon [Lambert Symnell], which grasped at the embracement of the two Kingdomes of England and Ireland. *a* 1649 DRUMM. OF HAWTH. *Poems* Wks. (1711) 40 Those brazen Typhons, which disgorge..metal, flame, and smoak. 1820 T. MITCHELL *Aristoph.* I. 202 He marches all elate 'Gainst that Typhon of the state, Storm and hurricane and tempest combining. *a* 1864 T. ARCHER in Macfarlane *Mem.* vii. (1867) 190 Boring away at Berosus and Sanchoniatho..at Demi-gods and Typhons.
*Comb.* 1598 SYLVESTER *Du Bartas* II. i. II. *Imposture* 637 Wo to the vain bravados Of Typhon-like invincible Armados. 1859 J. C. FAIRBAIRN *Hymns & Poems* 92 That brindled monster, typhon-born.

**Ty·phon** [2]. ? *Obs.* [ad. Gr. τυφῶν: see prec. In later use partly suggested by TYPHOON. Cf. F. *typhon*, Sp. *tifon*, It. *tifone*.] A whirlwind, cyclone, tornado; a violent storm of wind, a hurricane.
1555 EDEN *Decades* 21 These tempestes of the ayer (which the Grecians caule *Tiphones* that is whyrle wyndes) they caule, *Furacanes*. 1585 T. WASHINGTON tr. *Nicholay's Voy.* I. xi. 13 A wind called by the Gretians Typhon, of Plinie Vertex or Vortex. 1601 HOLLAND *Pliny* II. xlvii. I. 24 If the clift or breach bee not great, so that the wind be constrained to turn round, to rol and whirle in his discent,..it makes a whirlepuffe or ghust called Typhon. 1627 MAY *Lucan* VII. 177 Cloud breaking Typhons did arise. 1686 PLOT *Staffordsh.* 27 There happen'd a Typhon or Tornado-wind,..not above forty yards broad. 1699 Typhones [see TYPHOON β]. 1727–46 THOMSON *Summer* 984 The circling Typhon, whirl'd from point to point, Exhausting all the rage of all the sky. 1761 *Chron.* in *Ann. Reg.* 126/1 On the 4th of May, a most violent whirlwind of that kind commonly known by the name of Typhons, passed down Ashley river [S. Carolina]. 1820 T. S. HUGHES *Trav. Sicily* I. iv. 121 A violent sirocco blew from the S.E...As long as this Typhon prevails, the streets are generally deserted. 1826 HOOD *She is far fr. the Land* 21 All the sea-dangers,.. Tornadoes and typhons, And horrible syphons.
†**b.** Applied erroneously to a waterspout. (Cf. quot. 1625 s. v. TYPHOON *a.*) *Obs. rare*$^{-1}$.
1774 GOLDSM. *Nat. Hist.* I. xxi. 394, I am at a loss whether we ought to reckon these spouts called typhons; which are sometimes seen at land, of the same kind with those so often described by mariners, at sea.
†**c.** *spec.* = TYPHOON b. *Obs.*
1783 JUSTAMOND tr. *Raynal's Hist. Indies* III. 186 The storms they call typhons, which are peculiar to the seas of China.

**Typhonian** (təifōu·niăn), *a. Mythol.* [f. TYPHON [1] + -IAN; cf. Gr. Τυφώνιος, L. *Tȳphōneus*.] Pertaining to or connected with Typhon or Set.
1837 *Fraser's Mag.* XVI. 409 The greater bear appears under the typhonian figure of a pig standing on his hind-

legs. **1863** G. TREVOR *Anc. Egypt* ix. 200 Some of the paintings represent the spirits of the dead in Tartarus, armed with lances, fighting with the Typhonian animals, the hippopotamus, serpent, tortoise, and ass. **1877** S. LANE POOLE in *Encycl. Brit.* VII. 783/1 A gallery supported by Typhonian columns.

**Typhonic** (təifǫ·nik), *a.* [ad. Gr. Τυφωνικός, f. Τυφῶν: see TYPHON [1] and -IC.]

**1.** Having the character of a whirlwind or tornado; tempestuous. (In quots. in allusion to Gr. τυφωνικός in Acts xxvii. 14.)

[**1382** WYCLIF *Acts* xxvii. 14 The wynd Tiffonyk [**1388** Tifonyk: Vulg. *ventus typhonicus*], that is clepid north eest, or wynd of tempest.] **1865** *Pall Mall G.* 25 Aug. 11/1 Captain Spratt..was for some time in the Fair Havens, and..was caught by a real Euroclydon,..the gale having acquired a truly typhonic character by rushing down from the high land. **1895** W. M. RAMSAY *St. Paul the Trav.* xiv. § 4. 326 There struck down from the island a typhonic wind.

**2.** = TYPHONIAN.

**1874** BIRCH *1st & 2nd Egypt. Rooms Brit. Mus.* 19 Wooden head of a hippopotamus..sacred to Typhon, Thoueris and other Typhonic deities. **1894** *Western Daily News* 19 Sept., The history of Saturn is Typhonic or Satanic..; he is said to devour his children.

**Typhoon** (təifū·n). Forms: α. 6 touffon, 7 tuffon, -one, -in, tufon, -faon, tufan, 8 typhawn, 9 tuphan, toofan, touffan, tūfān. β. 7–9 tuffoon, 8–9 tiffoon. γ. 8 tay-fun, 9 ty-foong, tifoon, tyfoon, typhoon. [Two different Oriental words are included here: (1) the α-forms (like Pg. *tufão*, †*tufõe*) are a. Urdū (Persian and Arabic) طوفان *ṭūfān* a violent storm of wind and rain, a tempest, hurricane, tornado, commonly referred to Arab. طاف *ṭāfa*, to turn round (nouns of action طوف *ṭauf*, طوفان *ṭawafān*), but possibly an adoption of Gr. τυφῶν TYPHON [2]; (2) the β- and γ- forms represent Chinese *tai fung*, common dialect forms (as in Cantonese) of *ta* big, and *fêng* wind (hence also G. *teifun*). The spelling of the β-forms has apparently been influenced by that of the earlier-known Indian word, while that now current is due to association with TYPHON [2].]

**a.** A violent storm or tempest occurring in India († occas. with reference to other localities); **b.** A violent cyclonic storm or hurricane occurring in the China seas and adjacent regions, chiefly during the period from July to October.

α. **1588** T. HICKOCK tr. *Frederick's Voy.* 34 b, I went a boord of the Shippe of Bengala, at which time it was the yeere of Touffon. *Ibid.* 35 This Touffon or cruell storme endured three dayes and three nightes. **1614** PURCHAS *Pilgrimage* IV. xix. 448 The winde, which they call Tufan is so violent, that it driueth ships on the land, ouerthroweth men and houses. **1616** R. COCKS *Diary* (Hakl. Soc.) I. 163 Overcast wether, with a stiff gale wynd..towardes night proved a tuffon. **1625** PURCHAS *Pilgrims* I. I. vi. 20 Tempests, Huricanos, Tufons, Water-spouts. **1665** SIR T. HERBERT *Trav.* (1677) 11 It may also be remembred, that during this late tuffon, lightning was seen to fall and hang like fire. **1674** J. JOSSELYN *Two Voyages to N.-E.* 54 In the West-Indies in August and September the forcible North-wind, which though some call Tuffins or Hurricanes we must distinguish. **1793** W. HODGES *Trav. India* 132 The country people call them aundees, and typhawns. **1811** MRS. SHERWOOD in *Life* xxiii. (1847) 382 During a most tremendous touffan. **1826** HOCKLEY *Pandurang Hari* I. iv. 48, I..inquired how this *toofan* or storm had arisen. **1850** FANNY PARKS *Wand. Pilgr.* xliii. II. 53 The whirling clouds of the tūfān. **1885** LEWIN *Fly on Wheel* ii. 61 We ought to make ready for the coming 'tuphan' or tempest.

β. **1699** DAMPIER *Voy.* (1729) II. I. 35 The violent Storms called Tuffoons (Typhones). **1727** A. HAMILTON *New Acc. E. Ind.* II. xxxix. 89 September, they reacht the Coast of China, where meeting with a Tuffoon, or a North-east Storm, that often blows violently about that Season, they were forced to bear away. **1745** P. THOMAS *Voy. S. Seas* 274 Those dreadful Gusts of Wind called here [near Canton] by the Name of Tuffoons, of which the Chinese relate very amazing and incredible Effects. **1773** *Chron.* in *Ann. Reg.* 202/1 We had another tiffoon in August, when all the European ships at Wampoo drove with three anchors a-head. **1802** CAPT. ELMORE in *Naval Chron.* VIII. 381 In the event of a tuffoon coming on. **1831** TRELAWNY *Adv. Younger Son* I. 281, I should as soon have thought of anchoring on the sand-heads in a tiffoon.

γ. **1771** J. R. FORSTER tr. *Osbeck's Voy.* I. 169 Exceeding great storms (called Tay-fun by the Chinese). **1806** *Naval Chron.* XV. 465 A Danish..ship..encountered a Ty-foong. **1819** SHELLEY *Prometh. Unb.* II. iv. 170 My coursers..outstrip the Typhoon [*rime* moon]. **1832** LYELL *Princ. Geol.* II. 98 Captain W. H. Smyth informs me, that when cruizing ..amidst the Philippine Islands, he has..seen, after those dreadful hurricanes called typhoons, floating islands of wood, with trees growing upon them. **1848** S. W. WILLIAMS *Middle Kingd.* I. ii. 49 The increased temperature on the southern coast during..June and July operates..to produce violent storms along the seaboard, called tyfoons, from the Chinese *ta-fung*, or 'great wind'. **1900** *Jrnl. Sch. Geog.* (U.S.) June 224 The typhoon of the western Pacific Ocean is in many respects the counterpart of the West Indian hurricane.

*fig.* **1851** J. MILNE *Poems* 295 Thoughts have their Typhoons. **1898** *Allbutt's Syst. Med.* V. 807 Its [the heart's] workings..lie..in the track of emotional gales and typhoons.

**c.** *attrib.* and *Comb.*

**1880** MISS BIRD *Japan* II. 124 It was what they call a 'typhoon rain', without the typhoon. **1901** HALL & OSBORNE *Sunshine & Surf* ii. 17 Our track was well out of the typhoon district. **1907** *Manila Cablenews* 21 Aug. 8/5 The building is of concrete, earthquake- and typhoon-proof.

Hence **Typhoo·nish** *a.*, resembling or portending a typhoon.

**1880** CLARK RUSSELL *Sailor's Sweetheart* vi, That was a bright flash! Gad! That looked typhoonish! **1893** K. T. WEBBER in *Columbus* (Ohio) *Dispatch* 22 Nov., The weather ..had been very 'typhoonish'.

**Typhopneumonia, -toxin**: see TYPHO-.

**Typhous** (təi·fəs), *a. Path.* [f. TYPH-US + -OUS.] Pertaining to or having the character of typhus.

**1805** *Med. Jrnl.* XIV. 341 The district..has been..more free from typhous fever, than the more distant parts of the metropolis. **1822–9** GOOD *Study Med.* (ed. 3) II. 91 Prisoners confined in jails with typhous miasm around them. **1844** BABINGTON tr. *Hecker's Epidemics Mid. Ages* 237 Such opposite states are usual in all typhous fevers. **1857** DUNGLISON *Med. Lex.*, *Typhous Deposit*, a peculiar substance of new formation found in the areolar membrane..of the patches of Peyer in typhoid fever. **1897** *Allbutt's Syst. Med.* II. 364 The renal secretion..is..dark-coloured from typhous dissolution of the blood.

**Typhus** (təi·fŏs). [Late L. *tȳphus* in sense 1, and mod.L. (De Sauvages, 1759) in sense 2, ad. Gr. τῦφος smoke, vapour, conceit, vanity, stupor, f. τύφειν to smoke, smoulder. So (in sense 2) F. *typhus*, Sp. *tifus*, Pg. *typho*, Sp. and It. *tifo*.]

†**1.** Pride, haughtiness, conceit. *Obs.*

**1643** TUCKNEY *Balme of G.* 31 To bring down our loftinesse and pride,..to take down the Typhus of a *Britannia triumphans*, as some few yeares since we vainly boasted. [**1681** *Ess. Peace & Truth Ch.* 18 Proud and haughty Prelates (full of that *Typhus Secularis*—The old bane of the Church).]

**2.** *Path.* An acute infectious fever, characterized by great prostration and a petechial eruption; chiefly occurring in crowded tenements, etc.

**1785** D. CAMPBELL *Observ. Typhus* 7 We shall therefore, in speaking of this fever, either employ the technical term *Typhus*; or call it a low contagious fever. **1822–9** GOOD *Study Med.* (ed. 3) II. 239 The heavier, severer, or putrid typhus chiefly differs from the mild in the violence and rapidity of its march. **1866** A. FLINT *Princ. Med.* (1880) 967 The fever called typhus, known from the earliest antiquity, has received a great variety of names. The name typhus, introduced by Sauvages in 1759,..derived from τῦφος, denoting stupor,..relates to a feature..usually more or less prominent in this disease. **1875** B. W. RICHARDSON *Dis. Mod. Life* ii. 14 The black death is still represented in malignant typhus. **1897** *Allbutt's Syst. Med.* II. 354 Previous to the time of de Sauvages typhus was known as 'Pestilential' or 'Putrid Fever', or by some name suggested by the eruption or expressive of the locality in which it appeared, as 'Camp', 'Jail', 'Hospital' or 'Ship Fever'.

**b.** Also *typhus fever*.

**1789** G. BUCHANAN (*title*) Treatise on the Typhus Fever. **1818** SCOTT *Let. to Laidlaw* Mar., in *Lockhart*, Many of the better ranks are ill of the typhus fever. **1877** ROBERTS *Handbk. Med.* (ed. 3) I. 110 Typhus fever is generated by a specific poison, and is highly contagious.

**c.** *attrib.*, as *typhus case*, *contagion*, *epidemic*, *eruption*, *patient*.

**1799** J. FRANKS (*title*) On the Non-Existence of Typhus Contagion. **1843** R. J. GRAVES *Syst. Clin. Med.* iv. 41 The chief causes of typhus epidemics. **1876** BRISTOWE *The. & Pract. Med.* (1878) 189 It is important that typhus patients should be treated in large, airy, well-ventilated chambers. **1885–8** FAGGE & PYE-SMITH *Princ. Med.* (ed. 2) I. 146 He had headache and fever, and the typhus eruption followed in due course.

**Typic** (ti·pik), *a.* [a. F. *typique* (1582 in Hatz.-Darm.), ad. L. *typicus*, a. Gr. τυπικός typical, figurative, f. τύπος TYPE; see -IC. So Pg. *typico*, Sp. and It. *tipico*.]

**1.** = TYPICAL *a.* 1.

**1610** DONNE *Pseudo-martyr* 5 Those Typique times, and Sacrifices of the old law. **1692** J. SALTER *Triumphs Jesus* 7 Of various colour'd Plumes their wings are made The Rain-bows to 'em are but Typick shade. **1839** BAILEY *Festus* x. (1848) 110 This air-filled bowl is typic of the world. **1856** MRS. BROWNING *Aur. Leigh* IX. 134 Already swearing at my feet That I'm the typic She. **1886** SWINBURNE *Stud. Prose & Poetry* (1894) 181 With what passionate magnificence of rapture the poet would have sung the fall of the typic prison.

**2.** Of a fever: Conforming to a particular type (see TYPE *sb.*[1] 4); recurring at regular intervals; intermittent; periodic. ? *Obs.*

**1601** HOLLAND *Pliny* XXVIII. xvi. II. 335 As touching feavers,..if it bee any of these Typicke and Periodicall agues, which be intermittent and returne by fits. **1857** DUNGLISON *Med. Lex.*, *Typic, typical*,..characterized by periodicity, as a 'typical fever'; or one which observes a particular type.

**Typical** (ti·pikăl), *a.* [ad. med.L. *typicālis* figurative, symbolic (Thomas Aquinas, *c* 1150), f. L. *typicus* TYPIC: see -ICAL.]

**1.** Of the nature of, or serving as, a type or emblem; pertaining or relating to a type or types; symbolical, emblematic.

**1612** T. TAYLOR *Comm. Titus* i. 6 (1619) 99 Were they not all typicall representations of that spirituall holines, wherin even we ought to resemble them? **1616** BULLOKAR *Eng. Expos.*, *Typicall*, mysticall, or that which serueth as a shadow and figure of an other thing. **1631** GOUGE *God's Arrows* III. § 72. 319 Both the Psalmes are typicall, and prophesie of Christ, and his joyfull comming. *a* **1661** FULLER *Worthies*, *York* (1662) II. 230 He renewed the custome of expounding Scripture in a typicall way. **1711** HICKES *Two Treat. Chr. Priesth.* (1847) II. 188 The typical Melchisedec, the sacerdotal king of Salem. **1784** COWPER *Task* IV. 218 Ensanguin'd hearts, clubs typical of strife, And spades, the emblem of untimely graves. **1860** PUSEY *Min. Proph.* 601 In the daily sacrifice..the lamb..was typical of the precious blood-shedding of the Lamb without spot upon the Cross. **1865** R. W. DALE *Jew. Temp.* xiv. (1877) 159 The typical character of Old Testament ritualism, and of Old Testament history. **1898** C. BELL tr. *Huysman's Cathedral* xi. 223 Samuel, in many ways typical of Christ.

**2.** Having the qualities of a type or specimen; serving as a representative specimen of a class or kind.

**1860** TYNDALL *Glac.* II. App. 434 The facts which I have brought before you are typical facts. **1861** BENTLEY *Man. Bot.* 359 A perfectly normal and typical flower should possess a calyx, corolla, stamens, and carpels. **1874** PARKER *Goth. Archit.* I. v. 162 Exeter Cathedral is..the best typical example of the early part of this style. **1875** FORTNUM *Maiolica* ix. 81 Their style would be..typical of the Valencian pottery. **1881** FROUDE *Short Stud.* (1883) IV. II. vi. 249 Horace is a typical Roman of the intellectual sort.

**b.** *Nat. Hist.* That is the type of the genus, family, etc.

**1847** WEBSTER, *Typical*,..2. In *natural history*, pertaining to or constituting a type. **1861** *Rep. Smithsonian Instit.* 1860, 192 The typical genus, *Pleurotoma*.

**c.** *Path.* Of a fever: = TYPIC 2.

**1857** [see TYPIC 2]. **1875** tr. *von Ziemssen's Cycl. Med.* II. 599 Masked intermittents usually show themselves as typical neuralgia.

**3.** Of or pertaining to a type or representative specimen; distinctive, characteristic.

**1850** M<sup></sup>COSH *Div. Govt.* II. i. (1874) 123 The normal or typical number of toes is ten,..corresponding to the typical number of the digits. **1862** BURTON *Bk. Hunter* (1863) 290 Hitting off the deeper and typical characteristics of Scottish life. **1891** SWINBURNE *Stud. Prose & Poetry* (1894) 18 The typical English vices of egotism, hypocrisy, and envy.

**4.** Of or pertaining to printers' type; typographical. Now *rare* or *Obs.*

**1770** G. FAULKNER in *Abp. Boulter's Lett.* I. p. vii, I have ..corrected some typical errors that are in the London Edition. **1822** *Blackw. Mag.* XI. 7 Should you ever descend from your correctorship of typical errata. **1837** LOCKHART *Scott* xliv. (1839) VI. 87 Numerous typical errors which sprang of necessity from the author's inability to correct any proof-sheets.

Hence **Typica·lity** = TYPICALNESS.

**1863** H. JAMES *Substance & Shadow* 222 Such men..have spurned the empty typicality of the church. **1890** W. WHITMAN in *Pall Mall G.* 26 Aug. 7/2 If America is only for the rule and fashion and small typicality of other lands (the rule of the *état-major*) it is not the land I take it for. **1900** *Speaker* 22 Dec. 317/2 The propriety, justice and typicality of the picture.

**Typically** (ti·pikăli), *adv.* [f. TYPICAL + -LY [2].] In a typical manner.

**1.** By way of or by means of a type or types; figuratively; symbolically; emblematically.

**1605** WILLET *Hexapla Gen.* 455 It typically also setteth the practises of the scribes. **1617** COLLINS *Def. Bp. Ely* II. x. 506 How could the Priesthood of our Sauiour Christ be typically shaddowed and prefigured by two? **1692** BENTLEY *Boyle Lect.* ix. 334 The things they typically represented were come to pass. **1786** A. MACLEAN *Christ's Commission* I. 15 The nations of this world are neither typically nor spiritually related to God as His Church and Kingdom. **1836** J. GILBERT *Chr. Atonem.* Notes (1852) 335 What is true typically of the legal sacrifices, is true really of Christ's sacrifice. **1873** SYMONDS *Grk. Poets* iv. 193 We find the fundamental moral law of Nemesis as a part of the Divine government of the world expressed typically..in the Oresteia.

**2.** So as to constitute a type; in conformity with the type; representatively; characteristically.

**1868** CARPENTER in *Sci. Opinion* 6 Jan. (1869) 174/2 Numerous specimens of the typically triradiate. **1872** YEATS *Growth Comm.* 10 The Phoenicians were typically a nation of traders. **1910** SELIGMANN *Melanesians Brit. N. Guinea* Introd. 2 The character of its [the nose's] bridge varies, typically the nostrils are broad.

**Typicalness** (ti·pikălnės). [f. as prec. + -NESS.] The character or quality of being typical; *esp.* symbolic character.

**1633** AMES *Agst. Cerem.* I. 24 All Interpreters terme the types of the ould law ceremonies; for that spiritual disposition they have, and typicalnes which the Lord set upon them. **1649** ROBERTS *Clavis Bibl.* 560 His Typicalnesse herein remarkable; for Ionas was a singular type of Iesus Christ. **1865** *Lit. Churchman* 21 Oct. 443 Typicalness is a matter of the interior nature. **1903** A. B. DAVIDSON *O. Test. Proph.* xiv. 238 The Divine design is no part of their typicalness.

**Typification** (ti:pifikē^i^·ʃən). [Noun of action f. TYPIFY *v.*: see -FICATION.] The action of typifying; representation by a type or symbol; also, that which typifies, or serves as a type, symbol, or specimen of something; an exemplification.

**1811–31** BENTHAM *Lang.* Wks. 1843 VIII. 334 A distant and fanciful analogy which there is between the event typified and the real event made use of for typification. **1845** *Blackw. Mag.* LVII. 731 The four-paned rattling window of that clumsy typefication of slowness, misnamed a diligence. **1850** A. BAKER *Plea for Romanizers* 26 The typification, the earnest and the pledge by outward miracle, of the reality of the sacramental grace. **1893** E. L. WAKEMAN in *Columbus* (Ohio) *Dispatch* 19 Dec., A perfect typification of Norwegian childhood.

**Typify** (ti·pifəi), *v.* [f. L. *typus* TYPE *sb.*[1]: see -FY; cf. F. *typifié* (Littré).]

**1.** *trans.* To represent or express by a type or symbol; to serve as a type, figure, or emblem of; to symbolize; to prefigure.

**1634** WITHER *Emblemes* 5 Glorie by the wreath is typifide. **1646** SIR T. BROWNE *Pseud. Ep.* v. viii. 246 We cannot well conceive the wood a burthen for a boy, but such a one unto Isaac, as that which it typified was unto Christ. **1673** PENN *The Chr. a Quaker* xvi. 570 How can Christ be said to be typified out? **1730** WATERLAND *Script. Vind.* Pref. 8 That Fact expresses, prefigures, or typifies, another Fact of a higher and more important Nature. **1833** HT. MARTINEAU *Loom & Lugger* II. v. 103 A double death was to be typified by its fate. **1858** J. H. NEWMAN *Hist. Sk.* (1873) III. II. ii. 233 The Euxine! that strange mysterious sea, which typifies the abyss of outer darkness. **1864** BOWEN *Logic* viii. (1870) 248 A Syllogism, which is a union of three Judgments, is appropriately typified by a triangle, a union of three lines.

**2.** To serve as the typical specimen or characteristic example of (a class, family, etc.); to exhibit the essential characters of; to exemplify.

**1854** MURCHISON *Siluria* i. (1867) 7 Fossils which might typify such supposed older sediments. **1868** OWEN *Anat. Vertebr. Anim.* III. 374 The second deciduous molar..typifies the form of the upper sectorial, which is retained in the permanent dentition of several Viverrine and Musteline species.

Hence **Ty·pified** *ppl. a.*, **Ty·pifying** *vbl. sb.* and *ppl. a.* Also **Ty·pifier**, one who typifies (*rare*).

**1653** BAXTER *Worc. Petit. Def.* 13 The typifying use may cease. **1685** — *Paraphr. N. T.* Matt. v. 17 The Ceremonial part..was but a Typifying prediction of me. **1745** WARBURTON *Remarks Occas. Refl.* II. xviii. 95 A modern Typifier, who deals only in Similitudes and Correspondences. **1851** WARDLAW *Zech.* v. (1869) 98 As the typical Zerubbabel finished the typical temple, so surely shall the typified finish His.

**Typing** (tǝi·piŋ), *vbl. sb.* [f. TYPE *v.* + -ING [1].] The action of TYPE *v.* in various senses. Also *attrib.*

*a* **1638** MEDE *Wks.* (1672) 43 The Seven Arch-angels,..and the typing of them by the Seven Eyes and Horns of the Lamb. **1736** BYROM *Jrnl. & Lit. Rem.* (1856) II. I. 82 Dr. Mainwaring brought me a piece of Torlock's typing. **1876** MRS. WHITNEY *Sights & Ins.* vi, Somebody near, not going very deep, yet shivering faintly a typing in it. **1889** *Pall Mall G.* 21 Jan. 6/1 The application of the Tainter graphophone ..to typing purposes.

**Typism** (tǝi·piz'm). *rare*$^{-1}$. [f. TYPE *sb.*[1] + -ISM.] The character or quality of being typical or symbolic; symbolism.

**1850** J. BROWN *Disc. & Sayings our Lord* (1852) I. ii. 65 The economy, whose great characters were externality and typism, is about to close.

**Typist** (tǝi·pist). [f. TYPE *sb.*[1] + -IST.]

**1.** One who uses type; a printer, a compositor. In quot. *attrib.* *rare*$^{-1}$.

**1843** J. W. CROKER in *C. Papers* 5 Dec. (1884) III. 13 Some of them are probably typist errors.

**2.** One who does typewriting; = TYPEWRITER 2.

**1885** FREWEN in *Pall Mall G.* 5 May 6/2 The feelings with which a 'typist' contemplates the clumsy goose quill. *Ibid.* 9 May 2 If they are quick writers, the typists earn more than the sum mentioned. **1890** *Daily News* 24 Feb. 5/6 The Society of Typists announces a meeting at Exeter Hall on March 17 for the examination of 'type writer operators'. **1902** ELIZ. L. BANKS *Newspaper Girl* ii, I was a sort of private secretary and confidential typist to the proprietor of the *Daily Hustler*.

**Typo** (tǝi·po), *sb.* (*a.*) *slang.* [Short for *typographer* or *typographic.*] A typographer, a printer; *spec.* a compositor. **b.** *attrib.* or as *adj.* = TYPOGRAPHIC.

**1816** *Massachusetts Spy* 7 Aug. (Thornton), [Printers] will confer a favour on a brother typo [etc.]. **1858** *Printer* Dec. (Bartlett), A manuscript written in 1714–1716, by two ambitious typos. **1880** *Stationer* XXXV. 3 From the humble typo to the grand publisher in his chair. **1891** *Anthony's Photogr. Bull.* IV. 110 Good pressmen for color work, for litho. and typo. presses...What does a typo pressman know about lithographic inks, damping, [etc.]? **1893** LELAND *Mem.* I. 286 The typos, reporters, and subs [on a newspaper staff].

**Typo-** (tǝi·po, ti·po), before a vowel **typ-**, combining form repr. Gr. τύπος TYPE *sb.*[1], used chiefly in forming scientific and technical terms, and some nonce-words. **Typacanthid** (tǝip-, tipăkæ·nþid), *a.* [Gr. ἄκανθα spine], having the typical arrangement of spines, as a star-fish. **Typa·rchical** *a.* *nonce-wd.* [Gr. ἀρχή rule: cf. ARCHICAL], of or pertaining to the control of the printing-press. **Ty·pocrat** [after DEMOCRAT], one who rules by means of the press; so **Typocra·tic** *a.* (*nonce-wds.*). **Typo-etching**: see quot. **Ty·pogravure,** a method of printing pictures from half-tone blocks prepared by photo-engraving, and set up for printing with type-matter; also, a picture produced by this process. †**Typolite** (ti·pǒlǝit), *Geol.* (also *typolith*) [-LITE]: see quot. 1828. **Typolitho·graphy,** a process in which impressions from printers' type are reproduced by lithography (Webster, 1911); hence †**Typolitho·graphy** *v. trans.* to reproduce by this process; **Typolithogra·phic** *a.* pertaining to or produced by typolithography (Webster, 1911). **Typoma·nia** (*nonce-wd.*), (*a*) a craze for seeing one's writings or name in print; (*b*) a craze for typology or symbolism. **Typo·meter,** an instrument for measuring type-bodies. **Typonym** (tǝi·pǒnim), *Nat. Hist.* [after *eponym*, etc.], a name based on a type or specimen; hence **Typonymal** (-ǫ·nimăl), **Typonymic** (-ǒni·mik), *adjs.* **Ty·pophil** [-PHIL, -PHILE], one who has a fondness for or interest in typography. **Typoradio·graphy,** a method of making copies of a writing, etc. on sensitized sheets or films by radiography. **Typora·ma** [Gr. ὅραμα view, spectacle], a model or representation in facsimile. **Ty·poscribe,** a typist. **Ty·poscript,** typewriting, type-script. **Typo-te·legraph,** a telegraph instrument which automatically prints the messages it receives; so **Typo-tele·graphy.** **Typotheter** (-ǫ·þǐtǝɹ) [Gr. θετήρ, f. τιθέναι to set, place], a type-setting machine.

**1881** F. J. BELL in *Proc. Zool. Soc.* 3 May 502 When the spines retain the simpler disposition..seen in..most of the better known forms, we may speak of the arrangement as being *typacanthid. **1835** SOUTHEY *Doctor* cii. (1848) 233/2 Old Mr. Strahan the printer (the founder of his *typarchical dynasty). **1858** BAILEY *Age* 15 The *Typocrat now rules from coast to coast. **1854** E. MICHELSEN *England* 186 The English Constitution..is *typocratic, and written every day. **1888** J. SOUTHWARD in *Encycl. Brit.* XXIII. 704/1 In..*typo-etching, the drawing is made with ordinary lithographic ink on stone, or on paper and transferred to stone. It is then re-transferred to a plate of polished zinc by the ordinary lithographic process. **1885** *Academy* 20 June 445/2 A new process—'*typogravure'. **1890** WOODBURY *Encycl. Photogr.* 535 The Typogravure process is a method of obtaining half-tone pictures from copper relief plates. **1828** WEBSTER, **Typolite*, in natural history, a stone or fossil which has on it impressions or figures of plants and animals. *Cyc.* **1860** MAYNE *Expos. Lex.*, *Typolithus*,..a typolith. **1825** HONE *Every-day Bk.* I. 1038 A new musical work *typolithographied. **1882** O. W. HOLMES in *Atlantic Monthly* LI. 66 The slender intellectual endowments..which are so very frequently observed in association with *typomania. **1890** P. H. HUNTER *After Exile* II. iii. 57 The Jewish-Christian, misled by the prevailing typomania of his age. **1884** COUES in *Auk* Oct. 321 **Typonym*, a name based upon indication of a type species, or of a type specimen. **1889** *Pall Mall G.* 16 Feb. 1/2 Two publications which will receive and deserve the attention of all *typophils. **1899** *Sci. Amer.* 28 Jan. 51/1 Dr. Kolle now declares..that the process of *typo-radiography is..a self-evident and systematic method of procedure. *a* **1891** *First Year Silken Reign* 214 (Cent.) The *typorama, a plaster of Paris model of the Undercliff, Isle of Wight. **1893** N. H. DOLE in *Nation* (N.Y.) 13 July 27/2 For upwards of ten years..I have.. spoken and written of work thus composed as *typoscript. **1910** *Times* 26 Sept. 8/1, 40,000 articles..in the form of corrected typoscripts. **1888** *Encycl. Brit.* XXIII. 120/1 The automatic *typo-telegraph of Bonelli. **1903** *Electr. World & Engin.* 3 Oct. 377 (Cent. D. Supp.) *Typo-telegraphy. **1888** *Pall Mall G.* 10 Sept. 11/1 The *typotheter is a machine used for..setting type,..and requires no change in the type, material, or appliances now in use.

†**Typocosmy.** *Obs. rare.* [ad. mod.L. *typocosmia*, a. Gr. type *τυποκοσμία, f. τύπος type + κοσμεῖν to set in order.] A method or system, intended as an aid to learning, in which words or terms are grouped according to types or classes.

Blount's definition appears to be erroneous.

**1605** BACON *Adv. Learn.* II. xvii. § 14 Such was the trauaile of Raymundus Lullius, in making that Art, which beares his name; not vnlike to some Bookes of Typocosmy, which haue beene made since, beeing nothing but a Masse of words of all Arts. **1605** CAMDEN *Rem.* (1636) 112 To reduce surnames to a Methode, is matter for a Ramist, who should haply finde it to be a Typocosmie. **1656** BLOUNT *Glossogr.*, *Tipocosmy* or *Typocosmy* (*typocosmia*), a type or figure of the world.

**Typograph** (tǝi·p-, ti·pǒgrɑf). [a. F. *typographe* (1554 in Hatz.-Darm.), ad. med.L. *typographus*, f. Gr. τύπος (see TYPO-) + -γραφος (see -GRAPH). So Pg. *typographo*, Sp. and It. *tipografo.*]

**1.** A typographer or typographist.

**1737** OZELL *Rabelais* III. 281 A Fault of Mr Typograph's. **1833** MOORE *Mem.* (1854) VI. 329, I recollect having a little struggle with Simmons, my valuable Typograph, on this very point. **1880** (*title*) The Enemies of Books. By William Blades, Typograph.

**2.** A writing-machine for the blind in which pressure upon raised types causes the corresponding characters to be printed.

**1820** *Gentl. Mag.* May 446/1 A Duplex Typograph.. enables the blind to receive and communicate ideas by means of letters, upon a principle adapted to the sense of feeling. **1851** *Rep. Jurors, Exhibition of 1851* 311 Hughes..has exhibited a portable typograph or writing machine for the blind.

**3.** (See quot.)

**1886** *Science* 17 Sept. 252/1 There is now being perfected ..a machine intended to dispense with type and type-setters in certain kinds of printing. The 'standard typograph' is the name selected for it...The typograph is in reality a kind of type-writer, but, instead of printing upon paper, it produces indented or depressed characters upon a sheet of soft metal, from which an electrotype may be made.

**Typographer** (tǝip-, tipǫ·grăfǝɹ). [f. med.L. *typographus* (see prec.) + -ER [1].]

**1.** One who is skilled in typography; a printer.

**1643** SIR T. BROWNE *Relig. Med.* I. § 24 To maintain the trade and mystery of Typographers. **1683** MOXON *Mech. Exerc., Printing* i, By a Typographer, I do not mean a Printer...But by a Typographer, I mean such a one, who.. can either perform, or direct others to perform..all the Handy-works and Physical Operations relating to Typographie. **1715** M. DAVIES *Athen. Brit.* I. Pref. 9 The Vatican Typographers.., in Printing several Treatises. **1778** WARTON *Hist. Eng. Poetry* II. Addit. k j, A very antient edition..without date, place, or typographer. **1837** LOCKHART *Scott* II. i. 17 Whenever the poet hesitated about taking the hints of the zealous typographer.

†**2.** = TYPEWRITER 1. *Obs. rare.*

**1829** *Mechanics' Mag.* XII. 128 A curious machine..called a typographer. *Ibid.*, The time is near when a man..will instantly resort to his typographer, instead of his pen and ink.

**3.** A beetle, *Bostrychus* (or *Tomicus*) *typographicus*, which makes print-like markings in the bark of trees. Also called *typographic beetle.* Also *typographer* (*bark-*) *beetle.*

**1840** LOUDON tr. *Köllar's Treat. Insects* 357 The Typographer Bark-beetle. *Ibid.* 358 The larvæ..gnaw tortuous passages,..which, on account of their resemblance to letters, have obtained for the beetle the name of typographer. **1847** CARPENTER *Zool.* § 656 The Typographer beetle..devours, both in the larva and perfect states, the soft wood beneath the bark,..and thus causes the death of the tree.

**Typographic** (tǝip-, tipǒgræ·fik), *a.* [ad. med. L. *typographic-us* (1540 in *Corpus Reform.* (1843) XI. 818), f. *typographus* TYPOGRAPH: see -IC. So F. *typographique* (1710 in Hatz.-Darm.), Pg. *typographico*, Sp. and It. *tipografico.*] Of or pertaining to printing, typographical.

**1778** WARTON *Hist. Eng. Poetry* (1840) II. xxviii. 403 It was printed..in the infancy of the typographic art. **1794** MATTHIAS *Purs. Lit.* (1798) 337 My only objection is to the typographick pomp and expence of a book on such a subject. **1840** DE QUINCEY *Style* Wks. 1859 XI. 283 This typographic mystery..awoke and went back to sleep many times over from mere defect of materials. **1898** *Blackw. Mag.* Aug. 266/1 Typographic nudges and leers conveyed to the reader by capital letters, italics, dashes and asterisks.

**Typographical** (tǝip-, tipǒgræ·fikăl), *a.* [f. as prec. + -AL: see -ICAL.]

**1.** Of or pertaining to typography or printing; connected or dealing with printing.

**1593** J. UDALL *Key Holy Tongue* Printer's Note, The Typographical faultes, which perhaps haue scaped vs. **1611** in *Coryat's Crudities* Pref. Verses d vij, To Topographicall Typographicall Thomas. **1677** W. HUBBARD *Narrative* Pref., Faults..such as are meerly Typographical. **1757** BLACKSTONE *Let. to Dr. Randolph* 21 May 11 Mr. Mussendine's typographical character was entirely forgot in the university. **1790** V. KNOX *Winter Even.* (ed. 2) II. xxxiii. 229 That providential discovery, the typographical art. **1837** HALLAM *Hist. Lit.* I. iii. § 141 Some cities..had acquired a typographical reputation somewhat disproportioned to the local demand for books. **1847** L. HUNT *Men, Women, & B.* II. xi. 267 There were no stars, or other typographical symbols, indicating the passages omitted. **1874** ANDERSON *Missions Amer. Bd.* IV. xxxviii. 345 One of the most beautiful books, in its typographical execution, in the Arabic language.

**b.** Produced or expressed by typography or in print; printed.

**1803** SYD. SMITH *Wks.* (1859) I. 50/2 Not..a picture presenting us with an interesting epitome of the whole; but a typographical plan, detailing, with minute and fatiguing precision, every trifling circumstance, and every subordinate feature. **1806** in R. S. Fisher *Amer.* II. (1854) 323 That typographical thunder..has been muffled on this side of the Atlantic. **1868** *Pall Mall G.* 23 July 3 Typographical emphasis was given to the following advantages.

†**2.** (See quot.) *Obs. rare*$^{-0}$.

**1755** JOHNSON, *Typographical*, 1, emblematical; figurative. [Hence in later dicts.]

**Typogra·phically,** *adv.* [f. prec. + -LY [2].]

**1.** In a typographical way; in relation to or with respect to typography.

**1755** JOHNSON, *Typographically adv.*..2, after the manner of printers. **1802** WOODHOUSE in *Phil. Trans.* XCII. 88 Typographically considered, these expressions are more commodious than [etc.]. **1845** MISS MITFORD in L'Estrange *Life* (1870) III. xi. 197 Selling, for five shillings, books typographically worth about eightpence—poetically, good for nothing. **1893** J. L. SMITH in *World's Congr. Instr. Deaf* 254 An important requirement of the ideal institution newspaper is a high standard of excellence typographically.

†**2.** (See quot.) *Obs. rare*$^{-0}$.

**1755** JOHNSON, *Typographically*, 1, emblematically; figuratively. [Hence in later dicts.]

**Typographist** (tǝip-, tipǫ·grăfist). *rare.* [f. as TYPOGRAPH-ER + -IST.] One versed in the history or art of printing; a student of typography.

**1890** *Athenæum* 27 Sept. 412/1 [The origin of printing] seems still to excite strange passion in the minds of German and Dutch typographists...The grouping of [printing] types and the investigation of their evolution and relationship is the *ultima ratio* of the typographist.

So **Typo·graphize** *v.* (*nonce-wd.*), *trans.* to treat typographically, to describe in print.

**1811** BYRON *Bards & Rev.* liii. (ed. 5) *note*, He topographised and typographised King Priam's dominions.

**Typography** (tǝip-, tipǫ·grăfi). Also 7 tipo-. [a. F. *typographie* (1577 in Hatz.-Darm.), ad. mod. L. *typographia* (B. Veronensis, 1493), f. Gr. τύπος type + -γραφία writing: see TYPO- and -GRAPHY. So Pg. *typographia*, Sp. and It. *tipografia.*]

**1.** The art or practice of printing.

**1641** EVELYN *Diary* 28 Aug., The happy Monke whom they report to have been the first inventor of Typography. **1646** SIR T. BROWNE *Pseud. Ep.* I. viii. 34 Those diminutive, and pamphlet Treaties.., pieces maintaining rather Typography then verity. **1679** C. NESSE *Antichrist* 94 Typography or publick printing, a rare engine for communicating the knowledge of the truth. **1759** JOHNSON *Idler* No. 69. ⁋ 3 Caxton taught us typography about the year 1474. **1831** CARLYLE *Sart. Res.* I. vi, I consider those printed Paper Aprons, worn by the Parisian Cooks, as a new vent, though a slight one, for Typography. **1875** SCRIVENER *Lect. Text N. T.* 3 The first fruit of typography, the beautiful Latin Bible known as Cardinal Mazarin's.

† **b.** A printing establishment, a press. *Obs.*

**1660** in Blackstone *Let. to Dr. Randolph* 21 May 1757, 20 The overplus of the money..to be imployed in setting up and maintaining a learned typographie.

**2.** The action or process of printing; *esp.* the setting and arrangement of types and printing from them; typographical execution; hence, the arrangement and appearance of printed matter.

**1697** G. Keith *Sec. Narr. Proc. Turn.-Hall* 39 A Literal Fault in the Typography, as for *read* it was printed *real*. **1793** Boswell *Johnson* (ed. 2) Advert., The typography of both editions does honour to the press. **1817** Cobbett *Wks.* XXXII. 8 My name is placed in large characters,..here, merely in the typography of the thing, is a proof that [etc.]. **1853** Humphreys *Coin-Coll. Man.* xxvi. (1876) 405 Whose book is a fine monument of the typography of the period. **1900** *Jrnl. Sch. Geog.* (U.S.) Apr. 160 The typography is clear.

**b.** *transf.* Printed matter; letterpress. *rare.*

**1644** Milton *Areop.* (Arb.) 53 To catalogue all those Printers who are found frequently offending, and forbidd the importation of their whole suspected typography.

† **3.** (See quot.) *Obs. rare*$^{-0}$.

**1755** Johnson, *Typography*, 1, emblematical, figurative, or hieroglyphical representation.

**Typologic** (təip-, tipǫ·lǫ·dʒik), *a. rare.* [f. as next + -ic.] = next; in quot., relating to the study or subject of organic types (Type *sb.*[1] 8 a).

**1890** *Smithsonian Rep.* July 514 It is only very seldom.. that we can follow the typologic development.

**Typological** (təip-, tipǫ·lǫ·dʒikăl), *a.* [f. Typology + -ical.]

**1.** Of or pertaining to typology; relating to the study or interpretation of symbols.

**1845** P. Fairbairn *Typology Script.* (1857) I. i. 32 The typological System of the Cocceian School. **1868** J. A. Wylie *Road to Rome* iii. 30 The close of the typological dispensation. **1905** *Edin. Rev.* Oct. 333 No typological connexion was to be assumed between the subjects of the nave and the arch.

**2.** Pertaining to the art of printing, typographical.

**1882** *Trübner's Record* 127/2 Future writers on the Invention of Printing should..treat the question from a purely historical and typological point of view.

**3.** Pertaining to the study of numismatic types.

**1891** *Athenæum* 24 Oct. 554/1 From the evidence of recent finds and the author's typological studies it would further be shown that the whole chronological arrangement of the Syracusan coin-types..required radical revision.

**Typologist** (təipǫ·lǒdʒist). [f. next + -ist.] A student of typology.

**1841** W. L. Alexander *Connect. O. & N. Test.* viii. (1853) 314 If typologists had but kept fast hold of the principle, that nothing is typical which is not also symbolical [etc.]. **1898** J. H. Wilkinson in *Expositor* July 50 Justin..proceeded further to apply the ὕδωρ πιστόν to the wine of the Sacrament—no great liberty in a typologist.

**Typology** (təipǫ·lǒdʒi). [f. Gr. τύπος: see Typo- and -logy.]

**1.** The study of symbolic representation, *esp.* of the origin and meaning of Scripture types; also *transf.* symbolic significance, representation, or treatment; symbolism.

**1845** P. Fairbairn *Typology Script.* (1857) I. i. 1 The Typology of Scripture has been one of the most neglected departments of theological science. **1850** W. M. Hetherington in *Chr. Sabbath* (1852) X. 277 The true character of the Sabbath and the misapplication to it of the principle of typology. **1856** *Tait's Mag.* XXIII. 241 There is typology as well as a teleology in nature. **1862** Neale *Hymns East. Ch.* (1866) 82 S. Stephen the Sabaite is not deficient in richness of typology. **1867** H. Macmillan *Bible Teach.* vii. (1870) 139 He who understands the typology of plants, finds an eloquent tongue in every leaf. **1882** Farrar *Early Chr.* I. 105 Contrast the numerous errors and monstrously crude typology of the former [the Epistle of Barnabas] with the splendid spiritualism of the latter [the Epistle to the Hebrews].

**2.** The study of or a discourse on printing types or printing.

**1882** [implied in Typological *a.* 2].

**Typto, -ton,** etc.: see Tiptoe.

**Typtology** (tiptǫ·lǒdʒi). *rare*$^{-0}$. [irreg. f. Gr. τύπτειν to strike + -ology.] The theory or subject of spirit-rapping. So **Typtolo·gical** *a.*, pertaining to typtology; **Typto·logist**, a producer of, or believer in, spirit-rappings.

In recent Dicts.

**Tyr,** obs. f. Tire *sb.*[1] and *v.*[1]

† **Tyr,** *int. Obs. rare.* A call used to drive or direct sheep.

*c* **1460** *Towneley Myst.* xii. 113 *Secundus pastor.* I say, tyr! *Primus pastor.* I say, tyr, now agane!..*Secundus pastor.* Wold thou neuer so fane, Tup, I say, whyr!

**Tyran, -and,** etc., obs. ff. Tyrant.

† **Tyrandise.** *Obs.* Forms: 4–5 **tir-, tyraundise, -ys, -andise, -yse, tyrauntyse, tyrannyse.** [a. OF. *tirandise* (14th c. in Godef.), var. of *tirannise*, f. *tiran* Tyrant + *-ise* :—L. *-itia*: see -ise [2].]

**1.** The sway of a tyrant; absolute or despotic rule: = Tyranny 1. *rare.*

**1387** Trevisa *Higden* (Rolls) III. 269 Þat tyme þe firste Denys usede tiraundise [*v.r.* tyraundys] in Sicilia.

**2.** Oppressive or despotic government, action, or treatment: = Tyranny 3.

**1382** Wyclif *Wisd.* xvi. 4 It bihouede to them, hauntende tiraundise, deth to comen on with oute excusacioun. **1387** Trevisa *Higden* (Rolls) III. 283 Socrates was wel nygh alway in batayle, oþer in tyrauntise [**1480** Caxton, tyrannyse], oþer in fredom, hardiere þan bataille oþer tiraundise. **1390** Gower *Conf.* III. 382 He schal..Governe and lede in such a wise, So that ther be no tirandise. *c* **1450** *Cursor M.* 253 (Laud) To hem speke I alle-ther-most..That spendyþ her lyf in tyrandyse [*v.r.* truandis].

† **Ty·ranful,** *a. Obs. rare*$^{-1}$. [f. *tyran*, Tyrant + -ful.] Tyrannical, tyrannous.

**1533** Bellenden *Livy* iii. xii. (S.T.S.) I. 299 Traisting ay the mair distant and ferrare thay war fra the cumpany of þir ten tyranfull men, to be the ferrare fra every trubil approcheing.

**Tyranlie,** variant of Tyrantly.

**Tyranness** (təiᵊ·rănės). [f. L. *tyrann-us* Tyrant + -ess; cf. med.L. *tyrannissa* (1372 in Du Cange).] A female tyrant. Chiefly *fig.*

**1590** Spenser *F. Q.* i. v. 46 They were by law of that proud Tyrannesse [Dame Pride],..Condemned to that Dongeon mercilesse. **1607** Topsell *Four-f. Beasts* 462 Semiramis the Babilonian tyrannesse. **1614** Raleigh *Hist. World* ii. xxi. § 2 The house of David..was..rooted up, and the Crown of Juda in..possession of a cruel Tyrannesse. **1643** Milton *Divorce* i. xiii, Not to canonize Marriage either as a tyranness or a goddess over the enfranchised life and soul of man. **1706** Watts *Horæ Lyr.* ii. xvi. (1743) 171 Custom, that Tyranness of Fools. **1754** Richardson *Grandison* (1781) III. xi. 84 She was..indeed a tyranness, to all beneath her. **1814** Scott *Let. to J. B. S. Morritt* 11 Nov., in *Lockhart*, My Muse is a Tyranness, and not a Christian Queen. **1824** Heber *Narr. Journ. India* xix. (1828) II. 278 She [the Begum Sumroo] is, however, a sad tyranness. **1844** *Blackw. Mag.* LVI. 84 The lovely marble-souled tyranness has..turned back..a hundred, all worthily born.

† **Tyrannesse.** *Obs. rare.* [f. as prec. + -ess [2].] = Tyrandise 2.

**1432–50** tr. *Higden* (Rolls) III. 283 Socrates was alle moste contynually other in tyrannesse other in liberte moore cruelle and grevous then batayle.

† **Tyra·nnial,** *a. Obs.* [f. L. *tyrann-us* Tyrant + -ial.] = Tyrannic.

**1651** W. Jane Εἰκων Ακλαστος 216 Mahometts..Tyraniall vsurpation. **1788** Priestley *Lect. Hist.* v. xl. 291 The very names which have been used to express these tyrannial governments have grown..odious.

**Tyrannic** (ti-, təiræ·nik), *a.* Also 7 tir-. [ad. L. *tyrannicus*, a. Gr. τυραννικός, f. τύραννος Tyrant; cf. F. *tyrannique* (14th c. in Hatz.-Darm.), Pg. *tyrannico*, Sp. *tiranico*, It. *tirannico*.] = next.

**1491** Caxton *Vitas Patr.* (W. de W. 1495) ii. 272/2 We wyll dyscerne thabstynence dyuyne & holsome fro that whiche is tyrannyke & dyabolyke. *c* **1636** Denham *Passion of Dido* 115 Ah cruel Love!..Again she feels the smart Of a fresh wound from his tyrannic dart. **1695** Blackmore *Pr. Arth.* i. 52 The Pow'r of Hell and Sin's Tyrannick Yoke. **1704** Pope *Windsor For.* 74 The oppressor ruled tyrannick where he durst. **1768** H. Walpole *Hist. Doubts* 63 Henry was a tyrannic husband. **1793** Burke *Cond. Minority* Wks. VII. 267 Unprovoked rebellion and tyrannick usurpation. **1829** Hood *Dream of Eugene A.* xxvii, One stern tyrannic thought, that made All other thoughts its slave. **1868** M. E. G. Duff *Pol. Surv.* 85 The Anglo-Saxon, amongst weaker races, is apt to join the tyrannic School.

**Tyrannical** (ti-, təiræ·nikăl), *a.* Also 6–7 tir-. [f. as prec. + -al.]

**1.** Of, pertaining to, or befitting an absolute ruler or his government; arbitrary; despotic.

**1560** Daus tr. *Sleidane's Comm.* 410 Certain places of thempire wer brought into his tirannical power. **1601** R. Johnson *Kingd. & Commw.* (1603) 193 His gouernment is rather tyrannicall then kinglike: for he is absolute Lord of all the demeanes of the kingdome. **1603** Daniel *Def. Rhime* Wks. (1717) 14 Nor is this certain Limit observed in Sonnets, any tyrannical Bounding of the Conceit, but rather a reducing it in *girum*. **1638** Baker tr. *Balzac's Lett.* (vol. II) 3 So Tyrannicall an usurpation upon the liberty of mens spirits. **1706** Phillips (ed. Kersey), *Tyrannical*, or *Tyrannous*, belonging to Tyranny, imperious. **1838** Thirlwall *Greece* II. xii. 104 Miletus, after the overthrow of a tyrannical dynasty, was split into two factions.

**2. a.** Of the nature or character of a tyrant; acting or operating in an oppressive, cruel, or unjustly severe manner.

**1538** Starkey *England* i. iv. 115 We must schake of al such tyrannycal custumys and vnresonabyl bandys. *a* **1548** Hall *Chron., Hen. VI*, 167 A tyrannicall gouernor. **1606** Warner *Alb. Eng.* xiv. lxxxv. (1612) 351 A wretch so vitious, insolent, tyrannicall and prowd. **1618** D. Dyke *Two Treat., Sch. Afflict.* 328 Those tygerly and tyrannicall persecutours. **1685** Baxter *Paraphr. N. T.* 1 Cor. vii. 12 Such will be tyrannical and malicious Adversaries. **1791** Mrs. Radcliffe *Rom. Forest* v, If you must be tyrannical, Madam, indulge your humour in private. **1836** Marryat *Midsh. Easy* xii, Like all those who are seldom in command, the master was proportionally tyrannical and abusive. **1872** Morley *Voltaire* i. (1886) 12 A dark and tyrannical superstition.

**b.** Of, pertaining to, or befitting a tyrant; severely oppressive; despotically harsh or cruel.

**1579** E. K. *Gloss. Spenser's Sheph. Cal.* July 173 *In purple*, spoken of the Popes and Cardinalles, which vse such tyrannical colours and pompous paynting. **1592** tr. *Junius On Rev.* ix. 13 The first execution done upon the world by the tyrannical powers thereof. **1641** *More's Rich. III* Ded., The troublesome and tyrannicall government of usurping Richard the third. **1653** H. Cogan tr. *Pinto's Trav.* lxi. 248 They shall be chastised by the hand of the Most High God for the crimes of their tyrannicall lives. **1796** Morse *Amer. Geog.* II. 290 As to the king of Prussia, his conduct in Poland was the most tyrannical and oppressive that can be conceived. **1812** Scott *Let. to Southey* 4 June, in *Lockhart*, I am always prepared to expect the most tyrannical proceedings from professed demagogues. **1884** Pae *Eustace* 23 To his inferiors, his behaviour was most tyrannical.

**Tyra·nnically,** *adv.* [f. prec. + -ly [2].]

**1.** In a tyrannical manner; oppressively; despotically.

**1560** Daus tr. *Sleidane's Comm.* 216 Luther was in dede condemned..violently and tyrannically. **1653** H. Cogan tr. *Pinto's Trav.* lxi. 248 God hath made you Kings to use clemency towards men,..not to kill them tyrannically. **1699** Dampier *Voy.* II. i. iv. 78 These poor Prisoners..are tyranically insulted over by their rigid Creditors, till the debt is satisfied. **1756** C. Smart tr. *Horace, Sat.* ii. ii. (1826) II. 101 Such a man will not..be tyrannically cruel. **1839** James *Louis XIV*, III. 145 Colbert..pursuing not only eagerly, but somewhat tyrannically, his schemes. **1874** Spurgeon *Treas. Dav.* Ps. xcix. 4 His power never exerts itself tyrannically.

† **2.** As an intensive: Exceedingly; violently; vehemently. *Obs. colloq.*

**1602** Marston *Antonio's Rev.* v. iii, I am most tyrannically hungry. **1602** Shaks. *Ham.* ii. ii. 356 That crye out on the top of question; and are most tyrannically clap't for't. **1607** *Puritan* i. iv. 73, I warrant, my Kinsman's talking of me, for my left eare burnes most tyrannically.

So **Tyra·nnicalness,** tyrannical character. *rare.*

**1649** Roberts *Clavis Bibl.* 588 Which Chaldeans are described..By their..Tyrannicalnesse. **1727** in Bailey vol. II.

**Tyrannicidal** (ti-, təiræ:nisəi·dăl), *a.* [f. next + -al.] Pertaining or relating to tyrannicide; disposed or inclined to tyrannicide.

**1814** W. Taylor in *Monthly Rev.* LXXIII. 456 The seditious and tyrannicidal spirit. **1837** Hallam *Hist. Lit.* I. i. iv. § 46. 290 He has introduced a limitation of his tyrannicidal doctrine. **1853** Grote *Greece* ii. lxxxv. XI. 197 Such affection had to be overcome before he [Timoleon] accompanied his tyrannicidal friends to the acropolis. **1892** *Illustr. Lond. News* 8 Oct. 450/3 Dynamitical and tyrannicidal schemes.

**Tyrannicide** [1] (ti-, təiræ·nisəid). [a. F. *tyrannicide* (1583 in Hatz.-Darm.), ad. L. *tyrannicīda*, f. *tyrannus* Tyrant: see -cide 1. So It. *tirannicida*.] One who kills a tyrant.

**1657** W. Blois *Mod. Policies*, etc. (ed. 7) C vij, An honest Scot, who complains, that there are not some glorious rewards appointed for Tyrannicides. **1692** Washington tr. *Milton's Def. Pop.* v. M.'s Wks. (1847) 380/1 They..erect statues in their temples to the honour of tyrannicides. **1700** Toland *Harrington's Oceana* Pref. 9 Cremutius Cordus, who was condemn'd by that Monster Tiberius for speaking honorably of the immortal Tyrannicides Brutus and Cassius. **1809** *Edin. Rev.* Apr. 227 [Debry] proposed the formation of a corps of Tyrannicides. **1832** Carlyle *Misc., Boswell's Johnson* (1840) IV. 77 The English Nation had rebelled against a Tyrant; and, by the hands of religious tyrannicides, exacted stern vengeance of him. **1874** Symonds *Sk. Italy & Gr.* (1898) I. xv. 344 Memories of..Brutus, and other exalted tyrannicides, exalted his imagination. **1904** *Sat. Rev.* 30 July 144 The exact amount of blo-d-money received by each of the 'patriots', who posed as tyrannicides.

**Tyra·nnicide** [2]. [a. F. *tyrannicide* (16th c. in Hatz.-Darm.), ad. L. *tyrannicīdium*: see prec. and -cide 2. So Pg. *tyrannicidio*.] The killing or assassination of a tyrant.

**1650** Hobbes *De Corp. Pol.* 165 Tyrannicide, that is, the killing of a Tyrant, not onely Lawful, but also Laudable. **1751** Hume *Princ. Mor.* ii. iii. 29 Tyrannicide or the Assassination of Usurpers and oppressive Princes was highly prais'd in antient Times. **1790** Burke *Fr. Rev.* 93 It was in the most patient period of Roman servitude that themes of tyrannicide made the ordinary exercise of boys at school. **1809–10** Coleridge *Friend* i. xv. (1865) 212 It is difficult to conceive a case in which a good man would attempt tyrannicide. **1852** Miss Yonge *Cameos* (1877) II. xxiv. 263 Julian the Apostate is the first instance of tyrannicide that is adduced. **1873** Symonds *Grk. Poets* iii. 87 Theognis in one place actually advises tyrannicide.

† **Tyra·nnicly,** *adv. Obs. rare*$^{-1}$. In **6 -ykly.** [f. Tyrannic + -ly [2].] = Tyrannically.

**1539** Cromwell in Merriman *Life & Lett.* (1902) II. 188 The Duke of Holtz usurpatour of the kingdom of Denmerke by whose meanes his brother in lawe king christierne is kept tyrannykly in prison.

**Tyrannine** (ti·rănəin), *a. Ornith.* [f. mod.L. *Tyranninæ* (see def.), f. L. *tyrannus* Tyrant: see -ine [1].] Of or pertaining to the *Tyranninæ*, the typical subfamily of the tyrant-birds.

**1888** P. L. Sclater *Argentine Ornith.* I 148 The Bienteveo is in its habits the most interesting member of the Tyrannine family.

† **Tyra·nnious,** *a. Obs. rare.* [f. L. *tyrannus* Tyrant + -ious.] = Tyrannous. Hence † **Tyra·nniously** *adv. Obs.* = Tyrannously.

*c* **1561** T. Preston *Cambyses* D iv, The King is a tirant tirannious. **1584** Hudson *Du Bartas' Judith* iv. 224 Manasses then his wife would not controule Tyranniously. **1624** Bedell *Lett.* vii. 115 Doth hee tyranniously inforce his Colleagues to obedience also?

† **Ty·rannish,** *a. Obs. rare.* In 4 **tirannyssh.** [f. as prec. + -ish [1].] = Tyrannical.

**1390** Gower *Conf.* III. 246 The proude tirannyssh Romein Tarquinus. *Ibid.* 256 And thus this tirannysshe knyht Was soupled.

† **Tyrannism.** *Obs. rare*$^{-1}$. [f. as prec. + -ism.] The action or rule of a tyrant; absolute government; despotism.

**1591** Greene *Disc. Coosnage* (1859) 4 None could decipher Tyranisme better then Arestippus, not that his nature was cruell, but that he was nourtured with Dionisius.

† **Tyra·nnity.** *Sc. Obs. rare*$^{-1}$. [ad. OF.

*tirannitē*, or med.L. *tyrannitās* (Du Cange), f. *tyrannus*: see TYRANT and -ITY.] Tyranny.

1535 STEWART *Cron. Scot.* (Rolls) I. 91 Fra mansuetude and greit humanitie To tigirnes and greit tirannitie.

**Tyrannize** (ti·rănəiz), *v.* Also 6–7 tir-. [a. F. *tyranniser* (14th c. in Hatz.-Darm.), f. *tyran* TYRANT; cf. late L. *tyrannizāre* to act the tyrant, Gr. τυραννίζειν to side with a tyrant; also Pg. *tyrannizar*, Sp. *tiranizar*, It. *tirannizare*.]

**1. a.** *intr.* To be a despot or absolute ruler; to exercise absolute rule. Const. *over*.

1590 SPENSER *F. Q.* II. x. 57 Then gan Carausius tirannize anew, And gainst the Romanes bent their proper powre. 1628 HOBBES *Thucyd.* (1822) 9 Polycrates, who..tyrannized in Samos. 1737 WHISTON *Josephus, Antiq.* I. vi. § 2 Nimrod..stayed and tyrannized at Babylon. 1889 JACOBS *Æsop* 33 Here [at Athens] he 'tyrannised' in an easy-going way for ten years.

†**b.** *trans.* To have absolute sovereignty in or over; to rule over or dominate with absolute power. (Cf. 4.) Also *fig. Obs.*

1583 STOCKER *Civ. Warres Lowe C.* I. 6 The 12. articles.. inuented and practised by the Spanish Inquisition, to the end they might inuade, get, and tyrannize the Belgique prouinces. 1651 *Nicholas Papers* (Camden) 270 That whispering calumniator who hath of late tyrannized their eares. 1670 MILTON *Hist. Eng.* I. Wks. 1851 V. 5 Giants, who tyranniz'd the Ile, till Brutus came. 1795 WRAXALL *Hist. France* III. 175 His hopes of retaining the duchy of Brittany which he had tyrannized during a number of years.

**2.** *intr.* To reign tyrannically; to rule despotically or oppressively. Const. *over* († *on*, *upon*).

1494 FABYAN *Chron.* VI. cl. 138 Sigebertus was thus depryuyd..when he..had reygned or tyrannysyd two yeres. 1588 *Marprel. Epist.* (Arb.) 21 Oppressing and tyrannizing ouer her Maiesties subiects. *a* 1604 HANMER *Chron. Irel.* (1809) 136 Athelfrid the Saxon King of Northumbers, so tyrannized over the Britaines, that they were faine to take Ireland for their refuge. *a* 1641 BP. MOUNTAGU *Acts & Mon.* i. (1642) 20 The King of Egypt after Iosephs death..did tyrannize upon them with all extremity. 1741 PULTENEY in *Johnson's Debates* 16 Apr. (1787) I. 388 That power by which..the administration has tyrannized without controul. 1807 G. CHALMERS *Caledonia* I. II. vi. 309 The kings..had strengths, wherein they lived; and whence they tyrannized. 1814 SCOTT *Let. to J. S. B. Morritt* 30 Apr., in *Lockhart*, A glorious and stable peace with the country over which he tyrannized, and its lawful ruler.

**b.** *trans.* To spend (time) in tyrannizing. *rare*.

1649 MILTON *Eikon.* xxvii, Idlely raigning..he either tyranniz'd or trifl'd away those seventeen yeares of peace.

**3.** *intr.* To act tyrannically, play the tyrant; to exercise power or control oppressively or cruelly. Const. as in 2.

1529 FRITH *Antithesis* (1829) 314 Think you they would not let you know the cause and judgment, if they did justice & not tyrannize. 1590 MARLOWE *Edw. II*, I. ii, What! will they tyrannize upon the Church? 1621 BURTON *Anat. Mel.* I. ii. I. i. (1651) 38 A sacrilegious Frenchman..became frantick ..tyrannizing over his own flesh. 1639 FULLER *Holy War* III. xxvii. (1840) 167 They within the city, being themselves safe on shore, tyrannized on their poor brethren in shipwreck. 1690 C. NESSE *O. & N. Test.* I. 59 Popish prelates ..tyrannizing also over the bones of the dead. 1749 FIELDING *Tom Jones* I. vi, It is the nature of such persons ..to insult and tyrannise over little people. 1817 SHELLEY *Rev. Islam* Ded. iv, The selfish and the strong still tyrannize Without reproach or check. 1846 S. SHARPE *Hist. Egypt* xi. 364 The great were not allowed to tyrannize over the poor.

**b.** *fig.* of things.

1588 SHAKS. *Tit. A.* III. ii. 8 This poore right hand of mine, Is left to tirranize vppon my breast. 1615 W. LAWSON *Country Housew. Gard.* (1626) 39 A long, proud, and disorderly Cyon,..bearing no fruit, till it haue tyrannized ouer the whole tree. 1670 DRYDEN *1st Pt. Conq. Granada* v. i, Affairs of State..should not tyrannize on Love, but wait. 1805 FOSTER *Ess.* IV. vii. 217 The influences which tyrannise over human passions and opinions. 1833 J. H. NEWMAN *Arians* I. ii. (1876) 25 [The Arian heresy] made its way into the highest dignities of the Church..and tyrannized over the majority of her members who were orthodox believers. 1838–9 FR. A. KEMBLE *Resid. in Georgia* (1863) 19 The cold..tyrannizing over your region.

**4.** *trans.* To rule or govern tyrannically; to treat tyrannically, play the tyrant to or over. (Cf. 1 b.) Now *rare*.

*a* 1533 LD. BERNERS *Gold. Bk. M. Aurel.* (1546) H h ij, That one with tyranny shuld tyrannise dyuers other. 1594 DANIEL *Cleopatra* II. i, But that he must..tyrannize Th' afflicted Body of a woeful Woman. 1596 DANETT tr. *Comines* (1614) 183 Their subiects, whom they tyrannize and oppresse..without any compassion. 1649 MILTON *Eikon.* iv, Had ..rather sit still, and let his Country be tyrannized, than that the people..should..demand their rights. 1675 G. R. tr. *Le Grand's Man without Passion* 34 The Proud Mistresses of Beauty, that Tyrannize the Spirits of indiscreet men. 1761 MURPHY *Old Maid* II. i, Do not tyrannize me thus with alternate doubts and fears. 1783 JUSTAMOND tr. *Raynal's Hist. Indies* V. 268 They are tyrannized, mutilated, burnt, and put to death. 1896 *Daily News* 20 Feb. 6/1 A poor, weak ruler he was. The tyrant was tyrannised by the set about him.

**b.** *fig.* of things.

1588 W. BYRD *Psalmes*, etc. xxviii. 2 Pleasure..doth tirannize the ship. 1621 BURTON *Anat. Mel.* I. ii. IV. vi. (1628) 147 Poverty, which doth so tyrannize, crucifie, and generally depresse vs. 1741 MRS. MONTAGU *Lett.* (1813) I. 271 Happier are they who are governed by another's will than such as are tyrannized by their own. 1887 G. MEREDITH *Solon* iv, But shall the Present tyrannize us?

†**5.** To render tyrannical; to make oppressive. *Obs. rare*$^{-1}$.

1643 MILTON *Divorce* II. xx, The canon law.., whose boisterous edicts tyrannizing the blessed ordinance of marriage into the quality of a most unnatural..yoke [etc.].

Hence **Ty·rannized** *ppl. a.*, **Ty·rannizing** *vbl. sb.* and *ppl. a.*; whence **Ty·rannizingly** *adv.*

1589 *Hay any Work* 41 For their tyrannizing ouer him. 1611 SPEED *Hist. Gt. Brit.* VII. xviii. § 5. 290 His Christian heart pitying at such heathenish tyrannizings. 1642 MILTON *Apol. Smect.* Wks. 1851 III. 320 A slavish obedience without law; which is the known definition of a tyrant, and a tyranniz'd people. 1650 A. B. *Mutat. Polemo* 9 A self willed and wildly-Tyrannizing Monarch. *c* 1680 *Roxb. Ball.* (1887) VI. 290 Cupid, leave thy Tyrannizing! 1756 *World* No. 206 ⁋ 7 In..a few months, from being a restless, tyrannized, tormented wretch, I found myself a husband, a cuckold, and a happy man. *a* 1774 TUCKER *Lt. Nat.* (1834) II. 80 The crown, the church, and the barons, struggling which should have the tyrannizing over the people. 1790 HAN. MORE *Relig. Fash. World* (1791) 89 Those tyrannizing inclinations, which have so natural a tendency to enslave the human heart. 1832 H. MELVILE in *Preacher* III. 221/1 That infidelity which shall rule tyrannizingly over Christendom. 1881 *Athenæum* 27 Aug. 268/1 Intolerant of mean compliances and tyrannizing superiors. 1905 *Daily Chron.* 16 Feb. 5/2 The Church of the Concordat will be succeeded either by a free Church or by a tyrannised Church.

**Tyrannizer** (ti·rănəizəɹ). [f. prec. + -ER [1].] One who or that which tyrannizes; a tyrant.

1577 PATERICKE tr. *Gentillet* Pref. A iv b, Small potentates and tyrannizers. 1629 SIR W. MURE *True Crucifix* 2960 Maisters..May learne..To rule aright, not Tyrannizers proue. 1689 *Def. Liberty agst. Tyrants* 124 The Tyrannizer of Tyrants, Fear. 1882 P. HOOD *O. Cromwell* xvii. 226 When the will of the king became the tyrannizer of the country.

**Tyranno-** (ti-, təirǣ·no), before a vowel **tyrann-**, repr. Gr. τυραννο-, combining form of τύραννος TYRANT, occurs in a few nonce-formations, as **Tyrannoctonic** (-ǫktǫ·nik) *a.* [Gr. τυραννοκτόνος killer of a tyrant], tyrant-slaying; **Tyrannopho·bia** [-PHOBIA], dread of tyrants.

1651 HOBBES *Leviath.* II. xxix. 171 A certain *Tyrannophobia*, or feare of being strongly governed. 1789 PARR *Let. to Burney* Wks. 1828 VII. 411 What say you to this tyranno[c]tonic rigour which has overtaken Joseph and Gustavus?

**Tyrannoid** (ti·rănoid), *a. Ornith.* [f. L. *tyrannus* TYRANT + -OID.] Resembling or related to the tyrant-birds. 1891 in *Cent. Dict.*

**Tyrannous** (ti·rănəs), *a.* Also 6–7 tir-. [f. L. *tyrann-us* TYRANT + -OUS.]

**1.** Characterized by or inclined to tyranny; ruling or acting tyrannically; despotic.

1491 *Act 7 Hen. VII*, c. 18 Richard the iij[de]..of his cruell and tyrannous disposicion..caused [etc.]. 1531 TINDALE *Expos. 1 John* Prol. (1538) 3 b, When God visiteth vs with syckenes, pouerte, or what so euer aduersite it be, he doth it not of a tyrannous mynde to satisfye hys luste. 1577 tr. *Bullinger's Decades* (1592) 114 The tyrannous handes of any earthly Pharao. *c* 1600 SHAKS. *Sonn.* cxxxi, Thou art as tiranous..As those whose beauties proudly make them cruell. 1641 *Vind. Smectymnuus* 8 Those Bishops were Popish Tyrannous Bishops. 1760–72 H. BROOKE *Fool of Qual.* (1809) III. 34 Gave up the innocent many for a prey to the tyrannous few. 1876 GEO. ELIOT *Dan. Der.* III. xxv, To speak freely of a tyrannous patron behind his back.

**b.** *fig.* Exercising absolute dominion in some way; overpowering, irresistible; relentless; inexorable; severe.

1549 BIBLE *Ps.* xxv. 18 They beare a tyrannous hate agaynst me. 1592 SHAKS. *Rom. & Jul.* I. i. 176 Alas that loue so gentle in his view, Should be so tyrannous and rough in proofe. 1604 — *Oth.* III. iii. 447 Yeeld vp (O Loue) thy Crowne..To tyrannous Hate. 1644 MILTON *Educ.* Wks. (1847) 99/1 Flattery and court-shifts and tyrannous Aphorisms appear to them the highest points of wisdom. 1665 BOYLE *Occas. Refl.* IV. xvii, That Tyrannous thing, which we misname Civility. 1797–8 COLERIDGE *Anc. Mar.* I. xi, The Storm-blast..was tyrannous and strong. 1841–4 EMERSON *Ess.* Ser. II. i. (1876) 36 We have yet had no genius in America, with tyrannous eye, which knew the value of our incomparable materials. 1873 B. STEWART *Conserv. Force* v. 139 [Nature] is only tyrannous on the surface. 1876 GEO. ELIOT *Dan. Der.* IV. xxxii, To have spoken once is a tyrannous reason for speaking again. 1890 *Century Mag.* Feb. 574/1 The tyrannous moral Sense.

**2.** *transf.* Of the nature of or involving tyranny; oppressive, unjustly severe or cruel.

1556 OLDE *Antichrist* 51 b, The tyrannous power that they hade long wished for. 1585 T. WASHINGTON tr. *Nicholay's Voy.* IV. xxxi. 153 b, Princes should not vsurpe vpon tyrannous force. 1602 SHAKS. *Ham.* II. ii. 482 The parching streets That lend a tyrannous and damned light. 1637 EARL MONM. tr. *Malvezzi's Romulus & Tarquin* 146, I hold a good Principalitie as free, as a bad Common-wealth tyranous. 1709 STRYPE *Ann. Ref.* I. lvii. 583 That the election of ministers and bishops at this day was tyrannous. 1845 J. H. NEWMAN *Ess. Develop.* 167 As soon as the Empire relaxed its tyrannous oppression of the Church. 1870 J. R. SEELEY in *Macm. Mag.* Sept. 354/2 The Press.. would have an exceptional and almost tyrannous power.

**3.** Comb., as *tyrannous-minded*.

1590 HARINGTON *Apol. Poetrie* in *Orl. Fur.* ⁋ vj, For Tragedies.., that..of Richard the 3. would moue (I thinke) Phalaris the tyrannt, and terrifie all tyrannous minded men.

**Tyrannously** (ti·rănəsli), *adv.* [f. prec. + -LY [2]. Cf. OF. *tiranneusement*.] In a tyrannous manner; with tyrannical oppression or cruelty; despotically. Also *fig.*

1545 BRINKLOW *Compl.* xxii. (1874) 53 Let the kyngs grace consyder how tyrannosly..thei vsed part of his progenytors, kynges of Ingland. 1559 *Mirr. Mag., Rich. Plantagenet* iv, Waye how vsurpers tyrannously warke. 1596 SPENSER *F. Q.* v. ii. 13 They each at other tyrannously flew. 1612–16 *Liber Depositionum Archid. Colcestr.* lf. 70 b (MS.) Margaret Adams did vse her husband extreamly cruelly and tiranously. 1670 MILTON *Hist. Eng.* II. Wks. 1851 V. 46 Julius..tyrannously had made himself Emperor of the Roman Common-wealth. 1844 *Fraser's Mag.* XXX. 460/2 Monarchies more tyrannously monarchical. 1859 GEO. ELIOT *A. Bede* xxviii, His deed..was already governing him tyrannously. 1865 KINGSLEY *Herew.* Prelude, Right tyrannously..he lords it over her.

So **Ty·rannousness**, tyrannous character or quality.

1870 M. ARNOLD *St. Paul & Protestantism* 17 This proves well what the narrowness and tyrannousness of Puritanism dominant had really been. 1870 J. H. NEWMAN in *Life* (1912) II. xxix. 289, I cannot bear to think of the tyrannousness and cruelty of its advocates.

**Tyranny** (ti·răni), *sb.* Forms: 4–6 tir-, tyrannye, -ie, (5 thir-, thyrannye, tirandye, tyreny, terannye), 6 tiranni, tyranye (*Sc.* -y), tyrranie, 6–7 tiranny (tirr-), tyrannie, (7 tirany), 5– tyranny. [a. F. *tyrannie* (13th c. in Hatz.-Darm.), = Prov. *tirania*, Sp. *tirania*, It. *tirannia*, a. med.L. *tyrannia*, f. L. *tyrannus*, Gr. τύραννος TYRANT; cf. Gr. τυραννία (rare).]

**1.** The government of a tyrant or absolute ruler; the position or rule of a tyrant (in sense 1).

*c* 1374 CHAUCER *Anel. & Arc.* 66 And whan that old Creon [king of Thebes] gan espie How that the blode riall was brought edoun, He heled that Cite by his Thyrannye. 1579–80 NORTH *Plutarch* (1595) 94 They say that he aunswered his friendes, that principalitie and tirannie was indeede a goodly place. *Ibid.* 106 Solon liued long time after Pisistratus had vsurped the tyranny. 1614 RALEIGH *Hist. World* IV. vi. § 6 The Athenians..were fallen..vnder the tyranny of Lachares. 1671 MILTON *Samson* Pref., Of that honour Dionysius the elder was no less ambitious, then before of his attaining to the Tyranny. *a* 1727 NEWTON *Chronol. Amended* i. (1728) 124 Pisistratus began to affect the Tyranny of that city [Athens]. 1835 *Penny Cycl.* III. 15/1 Pisistratus and his son held the tyranny of Athens for thirty-six years. 1887 *Encycl. Brit.* XXII. 19/1 The tyranny of Dionysios fell, as usual, in the second generation.

**b.** In general sense: Absolute sovereignty.

1651 HOBBES *Leviath.* IV. xlvi, From Aristotle's civil philosophy, they have learned, to call all manner of commonwealths but the popular..tyranny. 1668 H. MORE *Div. Dial.* IV. vii. (1713) 300 Is it not absolute and unlimited Sovereignty,..which we from the Greeks call Tyranny? 1681 NEVILE *Plato Rediv.* 38 Aristotle..calls Tyranny the Corruption of Monarchy.

**c.** With *a* and *pl.* A state ruled by a tyrant or absolute prince; an absolute or despotic government.

1605 BACON *Adv. Learn.* I. viii. § 3 Honour in free Monarchies and Common wealths, had a sweetness more, than in Tyrannies. 1628 HOBBES *Thucyd.* (1822) 8 In most of the cities there were erected Tyrannies. 1672 TEMPLE *Ess. Govts.* Wks. 1731 I. 97 Some of the smaller States, but especially those of the Cities, fell often under Tyrannies, which spring naturally out of Popular Governments. 1712 SWIFT *Let. Eng. Tongue* ⁋ 5 The change of their [*i.e.* the Roman] government to a tyranny, which ruined the study of eloquence. 1838 ARNOLD *Hist. Rome* (1846) I. xxi. 454 All the ancient writers..call the Government of Dionysius a tyranny. 1881 JOWETT *Thucyd.* I. 10 The revenues of her [Hellas'] cities increased, and in most of them tyrannies were established; they had hitherto been ruled by hereditary kings, having fixed prerogatives.

**2.** The action or government of a tyrannical ruler; oppressive or unjustly severe government.

*c* 1385 CHAUCER *L. G. W.* Prol. 375 Tyrauntis of lumbardye That vsyn wilfulhed & tyrannye [*v.r.* tirandye]. 1390 GOWER *Conf.* III. 201 Of crualte the felonie Engendred is of tirannie. *c* 1430 LYDG. *Min. Poems* (Percy Soc.) 82 Roote of discorde is froward tyrannye. 1494 FABYAN *Chron.* I. vii. 12 Of this [Madan] is lytell or no memory made.., except y[t] some wryte of hym y[t] he vsed great Tyranny amonge his Brytons. 1495 *Trevisa's Barth. De P. R.* VI. xviii. (W. de W.) n iij/1 Ryghtful lordshyp ouersettith not his subgettes by tyranny, but he defendyth theym. 1555 EDEN *Decades* 258 The patriarch of Constantinople was oppressed by the Tiranni of the Turkes. 1586 T. B. *La Primaud. Fr. Acad.* I. (1594) 601 We may call that a tyrannie, when the prince accounteth all his will as a just law, and hath no care either of pietie, justice, or faith. 1594 SHAKS. *Rich. III*, v. iii. 168 The last was I that felt thy Tyranny. 1596 DALRYMPLE tr. *Leslie's Hist. Scot.* II. (S.T.S.) I. 137 The fyfte quha helde the gouernement..for his gret tirannie..he is slane. 1636 E. DACRES tr. *Machiavel's Disc. Livy* I. 172 That part of the nobility, that hath not a share in the Tyrannie, is alwayes enemy to the Tyrant. 1667 MILTON *P. L.* XII. 95 Tyrannie must be, Though to the Tyrant thereby no excuse. 1724 DE FOE *Mem. Cavalier* II. 167 Parliament Tyranny began to succeed Church Tyranny. 1792 *Anecd. W. Pitt* III. xl. 87 The House, in committing the City Magistrates to prison, without hearing their defence upon the point of privilege, had been guilty of a gross and palpable act of tyranny. 1835 THIRLWALL *Greece* I. x. 396 A monarchy, in which selfish aims predominate, becomes a tyranny. 1836 HOR. SMITH *Tin Trump.* (1876) 203 Sir Thos. More transported himself from the tyranny of Henry VIII into Utopia. 1863 FROUDE *Hist. Eng.* VII. i. 9 The accession of Mary had found the new opinions equally dishonoured by tyranny. 1883 — *Short Stud.* IV. iii. 263 In political catastrophes revolution is nearest when tyranny is at its worst.

**3.** Arbitrary or oppressive exercise of power; unjustly severe use of one's authority; despotic treatment or influence; harsh, severe, or unmerciful action; with *a* and *pl.*, an instance of this, a tyrannical act or proceeding.

*c* 1368 CHAUCER *Compl. Pite* 6 The cruelte and Tyrannye [*v. rr.* tirannye, thirannye] Of loue. 1390 GOWER *Conf.* III. 207 The tirannies whiche he wroght. *c* 1402 LYDG. *Compl.*

*Bl. Knt.* 665 Jelousye..That hath so longe..Werreyed Trouthe with his tirannye. *a* **1533** Ld. Berners *Gold. Bk. M. Aurel.* (1546) O j, He that hath muche, doeth tyranny to hym that hath but littell. **1560** Daus tr. *Sleidane's Comm.* 449 It is a starke tyranny that maried priestes should be put from the holy ministery. **1568** Jewel *Let. to Abp. Parker* 7 May, I am afraid of printers. Their tyranny is terrible. **1613** Purchas *Pilgrimage* (1614) 546 He delights to see men..torn with Elephants. Of these tyrannies he reckons many particulars which he saw. **1642** Fuller *Holy & Prof. St.* iv. x. 285 'Tis tyranny to trample on him that prostrates himself. **1664** H. More *Myst. Iniq.* xvii. 62 All the Frauds and Tyrannies of this Unchristian, though overmuch Anointed, Priesthood. **1709** Strype *Ann. Ref.* I. liii. 537 Among other his tyrannies,..the boy was gotten into Boner's house, and there whipped with rods in a most lamentable manner. **1747** Butler *Serm.* Wks. 1874 II. 302 The tyranny of our own lawless passions is the..most dangerous of all tyrannies. **1843** Prescott *Mexico* i. iii. (1864) 27 The worst kind of tyranny—that of a blind fanaticism. **1853** Kane *Grinnell Exp.* xl. (1856) 364, I commenced the anti-scorbutic tyranny at once. **1856** Kingsley *Lett.* (1878) I. 474 Lifting up your voice to expose the tyranny of 'Union' strikes. **1886** Sheldon tr. *Flaubert's Salammbô* 24 The tyrannies of discipline.

**b.** Violent or lawless action; violence, outrage, villany. *Obs.* or *arch.*

**1475** *Rolls of Parlt.* VI. 138/2 For fere of which Robberies and Tyrany, doon by the said Henry Bodrugan. **1547** *Reg. Privy Council Scot.* I. 75 The greit preparationis and tyrany divisit and ordanit be our saidis auld ynemeis. **1568** Grafton *Chron.* II. 250 When the Scottishe king had finished this hys tiranny vpon the Towne. **1570** *Sat. Poems Reform.* xx. 102 Be tyrannie, To sla our rycht Regent. **1603** Knolles *Hist. Turks* (1621) 142 Which crueltie he used, because they a little before had used the like tyrannie against his Turks.

Hence †**Ty·ranny** *v., intr.* = Tyrannize *v.* 3. *Obs. rare*—[1].

**1650** Gentilis *Considerations* 45 Our sense doth with ease tyranny over us.

**Tyrannykly,** var. Tyrannicly *adv. Obs.*

**Tyrant** (təi^ə·rănt), *sb.* Forms: *α.* 4 **tyraun**, 4–7 **tyran**, **-anne**, 5–7 **tyrane**, 6 **tiran**, **-aune**, 7 **tyrann**, *Sc.* 4 **terane**, 5–6 **tirrane**, 6 **tirane**, **tyrran(ne**; *β.* 3–5 (6 *Sc.*) **tir-**, **tyrand**, 4–5 **-ande**, **tir-**, **tyraund**, **terand** (also 6 *Sc.*), 5, 6 *Sc.* **tirr-**, **tyrrand**, (7 **tyrannd**); *γ.* 3 *pl.* **tyraunz**, 3–7 **tirant**, 4–5 **terant**, **-aunt**, 4–6 **tir-**, **tyraunt**, **-e**, (4 **tir-**, 5 **terawnte**, 6 *Sc.* **tirrant**), 6 **tyrante**, 5– **tyrant**. [a. OF. *tyrant* (12th c.), *tiran* (13th c.), F. *tyran* (14th c.) = Prov. *tiran*, Cat. *tira*, Sp. *tirano*, Pg. *tyranno*, It. *tiranno*, a. L. *tyrannus*, Gr. *τύραννος*.

The spelling with final *t* arose in OF. from association of the ending with that of present participles; cf. *suffragant* as variant of *suffragan*.]

**1.** One who seizes upon the sovereign power in a state without legal right; an absolute ruler; a usurper. (Chiefly in reference to ancient rulers, and in early use with suggestion of sense 3.)

*a* **1300** *Cursor M.* 21001 (Cott.) Vnder a tirand hight egeas Bonden on a rod he was. *c* **1330** R. Brunne *Chron.* (1810) 51 A bastard no kyngdom suld hald Bot if þat he it wan..Of tirant or of Sarazin. *c* **1374** Chaucer *Boeth.* iii. pr. v. 59 (Camb. MS.) A tyraunt þat was kyng of sysile. *c* **1470** Harding *Chron.* xxxi. ii, Eche Tyraunt was a Conqueroure. **1513** Douglas *Æneis* vi. ix. 197 Sum..Sald and betrasit thar natiue realm and land And tharin brocht a michty tirrand strang. **1542** Udall *Erasm. Apoph.* 39 The thirtie tyrannes had invaded & usurped the governance. **1593** Shaks. *3 Hen. VI*, iii. iii. 71 To proue him Tyrant, this reason may suffice, That Henry liueth still. **1622** Bacon *Hen. VII*, 1 Richard the third of that name, King in fact onely, but Tyrant both in Title and Regiment. **1653** Gataker *Vind. Annot. Jer.* 47 He..landed his forces, surprised Syracusa, and drave out the Tyranne. **1763** J. Brown *Poetry & Mus.* vii. 151 This Event happened..thro' the Authority of the thirty Tyrants. **1821** Byron *Juan* iii. lxxxvi, The tyrant of the Chersonese Was freedom's best and bravest friend; *That* tyrant was Miltiades! **1882** *Gd. Words* 181/1 In the fifth century before Christ, the tyrant Gelon extended its limits to embrace Acradina.

†**2.** A ruler, governor, prince. *Obs.*

*a* **1340** Hampole *Psalter* xxxii. 10 Princes, þat is,..tirauntis of þis warld. **1382** Wyclif *Dan.* i. 3 The sonys of Yrael, and of the kyngus bloode, and the children of tyrauntis. *c* **1430** Lydg. *Min. Poems* (Percy Soc.) 118 The hors..Withe his bellis and boosis brode of gold, Estate of tirauntis the poraile dothe expresse. *c* **1477** Caxton *Jason* 38 b, Dyomedes..brought with him xxx. of his tyrants. **1555** W. Watreman *Fardle Facions* i. vi. 90 The Troglodites..haue their heade ouer them, whome they call Tiraunte. **1609** Bible (Douay) *Dan.* iii. 2 The king sent to cal together the nobles, the magistrates, and judges, dukes, and tyrants, and rulers. **1737** Whiston *Josephus, Hist.* i. xii. § 2 Cassius..set tyrants over all Syria.

**3.** A king or ruler who exercises his power in an oppressive, unjust, or cruel manner; a despot.

**1297** R. Glouc. (Rolls) 7689 To hom þat wolde is wille do debonere he was & milde & to hom þat wiþsede strong tirant [*v.r.* tyraund]. *c* **1375** *Sc. Leg. Saints* ii. (*Paulus*) 647 Nero, þat tyran kene. *Ibid.* 796 Þe tyrand tuk on hand For to byrne þe gret cite Of rome. **1390** Gower *Conf.* III. 201 Evere yit it hath so stonde, That god a tirant overladde. **1422** tr. *Secreta Secret., Priv. Priv.* 181 Yf y [Cæsar] were a tyraunte, thow sholdyst Say no more so. *c* **1471** Fortescue *Wks.* (1869) 453 Whan a Kyng rulith his Realme onely to his own profytt, and not to the good of his Subgetts, he ys a Tyraunte. **1542** Udall *Erasm. Apoph.* 262 b, Sylla..afterwarde weaxed a cruell tyranne. **1587** Golding *De Mornay* xii. (1592) 172 Tyrannes..be but Gods scourges which he will cast into the fire when he hath done with them. **1601** Shaks. *Jul. C.* v. iv. 5 A Foe to Tyrants, and my Countries Friend. **1617** Bp. Hall *Quo Vadis* § 18 Their late Patron..was, after his death, in their Pulpits proclaimed *Tyran*, and worse. **1727** Gay *Fables* i. xlix. 5 Do not tyrants ..Think men were born for slaves to kings? **1831** Sir J. Sinclair *Corr.* II. 145 When Bonaparte put the Duke d'Enghien to death, all Paris felt so much horror..that the throne of the tyrant trembled under him. **1875** Stubbs *Const. Hist.* II. xvi. 350 The king had never been a tyrant. **1888** Bryce *Amer. Commw.* I. iv. 42 The weak points which had enabled George III to play the tyrant.

**4.** Any one who exercises power or authority oppressively, despotically, or cruelly; one who treats those under his control tyrannically.

*c* **1290** *Beket* 750 in *S. Eng. Leg.* I. 128 Ore louerd helpe nouþe seint thomas..A-mong so manie tyraunz for-to come þat weren alle is fon. *Ibid.* 753 In þe castel sat þe motinge of þis tyraunz ech-on. *a* **1340** Hampole *Psalter* ii. 9 Þou sall noght be tyraunt til þaim. **1387** Trevisa *Higden* (Rolls) VI. 209 Þe abbotes..for grete richesse beeþ proude, and bycomeþ tyrauntz. **1610** Shaks. *Temp.* ii. ii. 166 A plague vpon the Tyrant that I serue. **1750** Gray *Elegy* 58 Some village Hampden, that..The little Tyrant of his fields withstood. **1792** in *Gentl. Mag.* Dec. 1199/1 A man of republican levelling principles, who was the greatest of *tyrants* to his wife and family. **1817** Miss Mitford in L'Estrange *Life* (1870) II. i. 2 A sad tyrant, as my friends the Democrats sometimes are. **1848** Thackeray *Van. Fair* lxvii, It was William who defended him against a tyrant at the school where they were. **1908** R. Bagot *A. Cuthbert* iv, The marriage had not proved a happy one...He had been a domestic tyrant.

†**b.** By extension: Any one who acts in a cruel, violent, or wicked manner; a ruffian, desperado; a villain. Hence as a term of reproach. *Obs.*

*c* **1375** *Sc. Leg. Saints* i. (*Petrus*) 289 He folawit..Agan þat Terane [Simon Magus] for to stryfe. *Ibid.* xix. (*Cristofere*) 528 His tyranis furth can ryn, & did as he þaim bad in haste. **1377** Langl. *P. Pl.* B. i. 199 Attache þo tyrauntz [1393, tyrauns]..And fettereth fast falsenesse..And gurdeth of gyles hed. *c* **1430** *Chev. Assigne* 84 Tytlye tyrauntes tweyne..by þe byddynge of matabryne a-non þey her hente. *c* **1440** *York Myst.* xxxii. 227 Fals tiraunte [Judas], for þi tratoury þu art worþi to be hanged. **1457** Harding *Chron.* in *Eng. Hist. Rev.* Oct. (1912) 745 Your Iustyse of pese darr nought reply Suche tyrauntes that perteyne to any lorde. **1526** Tindale *1 Tim.* i. 13, I was a blasphemar, and a persecuter, and a tyraunt. **1561** S. Wythers tr. *Calvin's Treat. Relics* H vij b, The tirauntes that stoned him [Stephen]. *a* **1578** Lindesay (Pitscottie) *Chron. Scot.* (S.T.S.) I. xix. 86 He suburnit sum blody tyrantis to ly in ane quyit place..awaitand for the slaughter.

**c.** *fig.* Anything of which the action is likened to that of a tyrannical ruler.

**1508** Dunbar *Lament Makaris* 25 That strang vnmercifull tyrand [i.e. Death]. **1528** Paynel *Salerne's Regim.* O j, A pike (called the tyranne of fishes). **1579** Spenser *Sheph. Cal.* Oct. 98 Lordly loue is such a Tyranne fell. **1611** Shaks. *Cymb.* i. i. 84 O dissembling Curtesie! How fine this Tyrant Can tickle where she wounds? **1757** Gray *Bard* 130 Horrour, Tyrant of the throbbing breast. **1796** Eliza Hamilton *Lett. Hindoo Rajah* (1811) I. 11 When the tyrant pain had a little loosened the fetters of her power. **1847** Helps *Friends in C.* i. viii. 132 Public opinion, the greatest tyrant of these times.

**5.** *Ornith.* Any bird of the family *Tyrannidæ*; *esp.* any of several species of the genus *Tyrannus* (as *T. carolinensis*, the King-bird or bee-martin), noted for attacking and driving off any other bird approaching its nesting place. Also called *tyrant-bird*, *tyrant-flycatcher*.

**1730** Mortimer in *Phil. Trans.* XXXVI. 433 *Muscicapa coronâ rubrâ*, the Tyrant...He puts to Flight all Birds, both great and small, that come near his Station. **1731** M. Catesby *Nat. Hist. Carolina* I. 55 The Tyrant...The courage of this little Bird is singular. *a* **1841** Swainson in *Penny Cycl.* XXI. 415/2 The lesser tyrants (*Tyrannulæ*) are spread over the whole of America, where they represent the true flycatcher...The tyrants are bold and quarrelsome birds, particularly during the season of incubation. **1869** Gillmore tr. *Figuier's Rept. & Birds* (1870) 538 The Tyrants (*Tyrannus*) owe their name to their courageous, audacious, and quarrelsome character. **1895** Newton *Dict. Birds*, *Tyrant* or *Tyrant-bird*, Catesby applied it solely to ..the King-bird.., but apparently as much in reference to its bright crown..as to its tyrannical behaviour to other birds.

**6.** *attrib.* or as *adj.* That is a tyrant, tyrannical, tyrannous; also, characteristic of a tyrant.

**1297** R. Glouc. (Rolls) 8005 Milce nas þer mid him [King William] non..Ac as a tirant [*v.r.* terant] tormentor in speche & ek in dede. *c* **1375** *Sc. Leg. Saints* xvii. (*Martha*) 290 A tyrand man in vord & vark. **1390** Gower *Conf.* II. 316 That tirant raviner [Tereus], Whan that sche was in his pouer..Foryat he was a wedded man. *Ibid.* III. 148 Cirus the king tirant sche tok. **1456** Sir G. Haye *Law Arms* (S.T.S.) 32 Wikkit tyrane Emperouris and princis. **1572** *Reg. Privy Council Scot.* II. 140 Thair inordinat proceidingis, tirrant and tressonable attemptattis. **1585** T. Washington tr. *Nicholay's Voy.* iii. iii. 74 b, Sundry emperors tirants. **1600** Shaks. *A. Y. L.* i. ii. 300 Thus must I from the smoake into the smother, From tyrant Duke, vnto a tyrant Brother. **1624** Quarles *Job Militant* xv. 26 Hidden roots, wherewith they might appease Their Tyran'-stomakes. **1691** Swift *Athenian Soc.* x. Wks. 1755 IV. i. 236 The deluding muse..changes all to beauty, and the praise Of that proud tyrant sex of hers. **1730–46** Thomson *Autumn* 222 When tyrant custom had not shackled man. **1775** Abigail Adams *Fam. Lett.* (1876) 124 A reconciliation between our no longer parent state, but tyrant state, and these colonies. **1810** Crabbe *Borough* xxiv. 287 The tyrant-boy, whose sway All hearts acknowledge. **1835** Lytton *Rienzi* i. i, The excuse for these tyrant hypocrites to lift up their hands. **1839** Bailey *Festus* xxxi. (1852) 514 Those basest few who thought to win The tyrant monster's favour.

†**b.** as *adj.* in predicate. *Obs. rare.*

**1297** R. Glouc. (Rolls) 8615 So cruel ne so tirant ich wene no mon ne say. **1422** tr. *Secreta Secret., Priv. Priv.* 212 A man his..Tyraunt & Slow as a bere. *c* **1440** *Jacob's Well* 86 He is pruddere, þe more teraunt, þe more ouerledere, þe more cursyd lyvere, for his good. **1529** Rastell *Pastyme* (1811) 19 He was most tirant and cruell of all emperours.

**7.** *attrib.* and *Comb.*, as *tyrant-air*, *-craft*, *-killing*, *-kind*, *-murder*, *period*; *tyrant-hater*, *-killer*, *-queller*, *-slayer*, *-tamer*; *tyrant-hating*, *-quelling*, *-ridden*, *-scourging* adjs.; *tyrant-like* adj. and adv.; **tyrant-bird**: see sense 5; **tyrant-chat** (see quot.); **tyrant-fish**, a West Indian cutlass-fish, *Evoxymetopon tæniatus* (*Cent. Dict. Supp.*, 1909); **tyrant-flycatcher**, **tyrant-shrike**, species of *Tyrannus*, resembling, and formerly confused with, the *Muscicapidæ* and *Laniidæ*; **tyrant-wren**: see quot. for *tyrant-chat*.

**1746** Lockman *To 1st Promoter of Cambrick & Tea Bills* 29 [He] Lords it, with *tyrant-airs, o'er beast and man. **1888** *Cassell's Encycl. Dict.*, *Tyrant-bird. **1892** W. H. Hudson *Natur. La Plata* 35 Puma..following and harassing it [the jaguar] as a tyrant-bird harasses an eagle or hawk. **1885** *Stand. Nat. Hist.* IV. 468 We may now style various birds *tyrant-chats, tyrant-wrens, tyrant-flycatchers, etc., according to the more or less obvious resemblance they may have to the true (oscinine) chats, wrens, or flycatchers. **1812** Crabbe *Tales* xiv. 349 With *tyrant-craft, he then was still and calm. **1783** Latham *Synopsis Birds* III. 357 *Tyrant F[ycatcher]. Size of the Red-backed Shrike, or a trifle bigger... Inhabits Cayenne. **1839** Darwin *Voy. Nat.* xi. (1873) 237 Occasionally the plaintive note of a white-tufted tyrant-fly catcher..may be heard. **1879** E. P. Wright *Anim. Life* 243 The Tyrant Fly-catcher (*Tyrannus intrepidus*) is one of the migratory visitors of the United States, and often bears the name of 'King', as well as 'Tyrant'. **1819** Byron *Juan* Ded. x, He [Milton] closed the *tyrant-hater he begun. **1866** M. C. Tyler *Glimpses Eng.* (1898) 146 Two centuries of *tyrant-hating Russells. *a* **1586** Sidney *Arcadia* ii. (1622) 128 Killing many guiltlesse persons, either for affinitie to the tyrant, or enmitie to the *tyrant-killers. **1649** Canne *Gold. Rule* 36 Those monuments of tyrant-killers by antiquity were so honored. **1648** Milton *Tenure Kings* (1650) 20 Among the Jews this practice of *tyrant-killing was not unusual. **1726** Pope *Odyss.* xviii. 97 Echetus.. A tyrant, fiercest of the *tyrant-kind. **1532** Becon *Pomander of Prayer* (1578) 38 Forgeuing them, & praying for them whiche most *tyrauntlike handled thee. **1571** Golding *Calvin on Ps.* xlv. 7 Salomon reigneth not tyrantlike, as many Kynges do. **1629** H. Burton *Truth's Triumph* 21 The Prince of darkenesse, who tyrant-like ruleth in the children of disobedience. **1894** tr. *Pastor's Hist. Popes* IV. ii. v. 290 This crime was a *tyrant-murder of the ancient type. **1898** *Q. Rev.* July 106 Certain of the Mycenaean types..outlived the *Tyrant period. **1542** Udall *Erasm. Apoph.* i. 115 b, Harmodius & Aristogiton had been *tyrannequellers. **1819** Shelley *Prometh. Unb.* iv. i. 272 Golden spears With *tyrant-quelling myrtle overtwined. **1848** Mrs. Jameson *Sacr. & Leg. Art* (1850) 6 The *tyrant-ridden serf. **1591** Sylvester *Ivry* 385 Those King-correcting, *Tyrant-scourging Braves. **1809** Shaw *Gen. Zool.* VII. 304 *Tyrant Shrike..usually measuring about eight inches in length. **1826** Stephens *ibid.* XIII. ii. 133 Tyrant-Shrike..these inhabit the American continent: they..are said to defend their young against the attacks of Eagles. **1692** Washington tr. *Milton's Def. Pop.* ii. M.'s Wks. (1847) 354/1 The same emperour honoured the memory of Thraseas, and Helvidius [etc.], who all were *tyrant-slayers. **1910** P. Gardner in *Encycl. Brit.* XII. 480/1 The tyrant-slayers, Harmodius and Aristogiton. **1605** Sylvester *Du Bartas* ii. iii. iv. 704 Thy gracious God, the glorious *Tyrant-tamer. **1613** Heywood *Silver Age* iii. i, Nor will we cease till we haue purchas'd vs The name of Tyrant-tamer through the world.

Hence **Ty·rant** *v. intr.*, to play the tyrant, to tyrannize (also with *it*); whence **Ty·ranting** (†**tyranning**) *vbl. sb.*; **Ty·rantess**, a female tyrant, a tyranness.

**1596** Spenser *F. Q.* iv. vii. 1 Great God of love,..What glorie, or what guerdon hast thou found In feeble Ladies tyranning so sore? **1622** in Foster *Eng. Factories Ind.* (1908) II. 177 Hee persisted in his tyraninge. *a* **1661** Fuller *Worthies, Bucks.* (1662) i. 134 This encouraged the Irish Grandees (their *O's* and *Mac's*) to Rant and Tyrant it in their respective seignieuries. **1890** E. L. Arnold *Phra* iv, I was sorry for the tyrantess.

†**Ty·rantly,** *adv. Obs. rare.* Also **tyranlie.** [f. Tyrant + -ly [2].] Tyrannically.

*c* **1470** Harding *Chron.* xx. iv. (MS. Arch. Seld. B. 10) lf. 19 He..His commons alle with taxes did distreyne So tirantly he lefte þeim noght to spende. **1501** Douglas *Pal. Hon.* iii. xxxii, I saw..How tyranlie he Jowrie all oppresst. **1560** Becon *Flower Godly Prayers* Wks. II. 171 A multitude of enemies..haue all ready most tyrantelye spoyled me of my garmentes.

†**Ty·rantry.** *Obs.* Also 4 **tyrauntyre**, 4–5 **tir-**, **tyra(u)ntry**, **-ie**, **-ye**, **-e(e**, 5 **tyraunterie**, **terawntrye**; 4–5 **ter(r)andry**, 5 **tyrantry**, **-ie**; **tyranry**, **-ie.** [f. Tyrant + -ry. Cf. OF. *tiranerie.*] = Tyranny (in various senses).

**13..** *E. E. Allit. P.* (Morris) B. 187 Traysoun, & trichcherye, & tyrauntyre boþe. **1340** Hampole *Pr. Consc.* 1601 Now es luff turned tyll lychery, And ryghtwisnes tyll tyrauntry. **1382** Wyclif *Prol. Bible* iii. 4 The persecucioun and tirauntrie of Farao. *a* **1387** in *Archæologia* XVI. 83 His extorciones & his mayntenances and his tirranttrie of þat he hath take falsly ageyne þe Kynges lawes. *a* **1400–50** *Alexander* 4251 Þi [Alexander's] tent is all on terrandry & tourment of armys. **1435** Misyn *Fire of Love* i. xxxi. 68 Slike forsoth,..be power of þer tyrantry þe smale oppres. *c* **1449** Pecock *Repr.* iii. iv. (Rolls) 302 Into the avail of the vndirlingis; and not..by tyranrie into the avail oonli of the ouerers. *c* **1470** Henry *Wallace* ix. 206 In tyranny thus haiff we rongyn lang. **1483** *Cath. Angl.* 389/1 Tyrandry, *tirannides*. **1496** *Dives & Paup.* (W. de W.) i. lix. 100/2 Neyther they myght ne durste make suche solempnyte for tyrauntrye of the hethen people.

**Tyrantship** (təiᵊ·ræntʃip). *rare.* [f. TYRANT + -SHIP.] The condition or state of a tyrant, tyranny; also (with possessive), the personality of a tyrant.

*c* 1470 ASHBY *Active Policy Prince* 332 Rightwisnesse withoute pite is tiranship. *a* 1643 CARTWRIGHT *Siedge* II. iv, Saving your Tyrantship, you are a Fool. 1885 *Pall Mall G.* 19 Nov. 3/1 Tyrantship, not necessarily tyranny, was in those days a recognized profession.

† **Tyranture.** *Obs. rare*—⁰. = TYRANTRY.

*c* 1460 *Promp. Parv.* (E.E.T.S.) 476 Tyranture, *tirannis.*

**Tyraund, -aunt, -aundise,** etc.: see TYRANT, TYRANDISE.

† **Tyre, tire,** *sb.*[1] *Obs.* Forms: 5–6 **tire, tyre,** 6 **tyer(e.** [app. named from Tyre in Syria. Cf. OF. *tire, tyre,* silk cloth from Tyre.

'*Tire,* if not of Syrian growth, was probably a Calabrian or Sicilian wine, manufactured from the species of grape called [in Italian] *tirio'* (Furnivall in Note to quot. *c* 1460).]

A strong sweet wine imported in the 15th and 16th centuries. Also *attrib.*

1429 *Rolls of Parlt.* IV. 361/1 Tires and Romeneys at iiii marc'. *c* 1440 *Promp. Parv.* (E.E.T.S.) 483 Tyre wyne, or wyne tyre. *c* 1460 J. RUSSELL *Bk. Nurture* 119 The namys of swete wynes..Rompney of modon, Bastard, Tyre, Ozey. 1519 *Interl. Four Elem.* (Percy Soc.) 22 Ye shall have Spayneshe wyne and Gascoyn..Tyre, capryck, and malvesyne. 1526 *Pilgr. Perf.* (1531) 53 b, There groweth the myghty swete wynes, as malueseys, tyeres & muscadels. 1556 WITHALS *Dict.* (1566) H j/2 Tyre, *Vinum Tyrense, ex Tyro insula.* 1587 HARRISON *England* II. vi. in Holinshed *Chron.* I. 167/2 Whereof..Bastard, Tire, Oseie..are not least of all accompted of, bicause of their strength and valure.

† **Tyre,** *sb.*[2] *Obs.* [ad. med.L. *tirus* (Du Cange), *tyrus,* of uncertain origin. So OF. *tir, tyr, thire.*] The name of an alleged venomous snake of Syria and Arabia.

1471 RIPLEY *Comp. Alch.* III. ix. in Ashm. *Theatr. Chem. Brit.* (1652) 141 Thys Water ys lyke to the venemous Tyre, Wherewyth the myghty Tryacle ys wrought. 1608 TOPSELL *Serpents* (1658) 792 Of the Tyre. There be some which have confounded this Serpent with the Viper, and taken them both to be but one kinde, or at least the Tyre to be a kinde of Viper, because the Arabians call a Viper *Thiron. Ibid.,* This Tyre is called in Latine *Tyrus* and *Tyria,* and also among the Arabians..*Eosmari,* and *Alpfahex.*

† **Tyre,** *sb.*[3] *Obs. rare*—¹. [ad. med.L. *tyria, tiria,* ?fem. of *Tyrius* TYRIAN.] Name of a kind of leprosy: see quot.

1547 BOORDE *Brev. Health* cccxlix. (1557) 112 b, One of the kyndes of Leprousnes named Tiria. Tiria is the Latin worde. In Englyshe it is named the tyre or the propertie of an adder which is full of skales, so is this kynde of leprousnes full of skales and scabbes, corodyng the fleshe.

‖ **Tyre, tyer** (təiᵊɹ), *sb.*[4] *E. Ind.* Forms: 7 **tayer,** 7–8 **tair,** 7–9 **tire,** 8 **tayar,** 8–9 **tyer,** 9 **tyre.** [ad. Tamil *tayir.*] Name in India for curdled milk and cream beginning to sour.

1613 PURCHAS *Pilgrimage* v. xi. 428 Some held..that there were seuen Seas; one of salt-water, the second of fresh, the third of honey, the fourth of milke, the fift of Tair (which is creame beginning to sowre). 1699 DAMPIER *Voy.* II. I. 139 Tire is sold about the Streets there: 'tis thick sower milk. 1776 N. B. HALHED *Code Gentoo Laws* Pref. 41 Flesh, or Milk, or *Tyer* (Sour Cream) or *Ghee,* or bitter Oil. 1822 BABINGTON tr. *Beschi's Gooroo Paramartan* v. 80 A repast, in which there was no lack of ghee, or milk, or tyer. 1844 SOUTHEY *Life A. Bell* I. 192 He had been greatly displeased to see the bad milk and bad tire with which they were frequently supplied.

**Tyre** (təiᵊɹ), *sb.*[5] [A variant spelling of TIRE *sb.*[2], both being used indifferently in 15th and 16th c. In 17th c. *tire* became the settled spelling, and has so continued in U.S.; but in Gt. Britain *tyre* has been revived for the pneumatic tires of bicycles, carriages, and motor-cars, and is also sometimes used for iron or steel tires.]

**1.** The iron or steel rim of a wheel, *esp.* the steel rim of the driving wheel of a locomotive: = TIRE *sb.*[2] 2.

1796 W. FELTON *Carriages* Gloss., *Tyre,* the iron which rims the wheels. 1801 *Ibid.* II. 13 Extras to Wheels. Hooped tyre. Patent ditto. 1825 J. NICHOLSON *Operat. Mechanic* 647 The advantage of hooping cast iron wheels with malleable iron tyres or trods. 1838 BOURNE & BARTLEY *Patent Specif.* No. 7795, 6 Sept. 3 The felloe turned..to receive an ordinary outside hoop or tyre. 1862 SMILES *Engineers* III. 365 There are limits to the strength of iron, ..and there is a point at which both rails and tyres must break. 1865 *Athenæum* 30 Sept. 442/1 Prior to the invention of weldless tyres. 1889 G. FINDLAY *Eng. Railway* 130 A steel tyre, spun from a solid block of Bessemer steel, without a weld.

**2.** A rubber cushion around the wheel of a bicycle, motor-car, etc.: = TIRE *sb.*[2] 2 b.

1875 *Encycl. Brit.* III. 665/1 India-rubber tyres..were brought into requisition to relieve jolting. 1890 *Patent Specif.* No. 4206 Large rubber tyres..known commercially as (1) Pneumatic tyres, (2) Cushion tyres. 1891–1898 [see PNEUMATIC 1 b]. 1902 *Encycl. Brit.* XXVII. 325/1 In 1846 Mr. William Thompson had taken out a patent for a pneumatic tyre for carriages.

**3.** *attrib.* and *Comb.,* as *tyre-bar, -carrier, -cover, -fitter, -hoop, -inflator, -maker, -pump, -rim, -wheel.* (See also TIRE *sb.*[2] 3.)

1862 *Catal. Internat. Exhib., Brit.* II. No. 6264 Specimens of iron and steel, and Stocker's patent combined metal *tyre-bars. 1909 *Westm. Gaz.* 17 Nov. 5/2 The general fittings consist of two head-lights, wind-screen, clock, speedometer, two horns, and *tyre-carrier. 1903 *Motor. Ann.* 294 Brakes which act directly on the *tyre-cover cause it to deteriorate at an expensive rate. 1909 *Westm. Gaz.* 11 May 7/2 Carriage-builders, wheelwrights, carpenters, *tyre-fitters. 1865 *Athenæum* 30 Sept. 442/1 *Tyre-hoops for railway wheels. 1901 *Daily Chron.* 23 Sept. 8/5 Most of the *tyre inflators now made are provided with handles which telescope over the barrel. 1906 *Ibid.* 8 Sept. 3/7 Most *tyre pumps have a gauge on them to show the correct pressure. 1896 *Westm. Gaz.* 2 May 6/7 The Beeston Pneumatic Tyre Company..being unable to fulfil its orders for *tyre rims [etc.]. 1801 W. FELTON *Carriages* II. 38 A neat town Coach has..hooped *tyre wheels with moulded fellies.

Hence **Tyre** *v., trans.* to furnish with a tyre or tyres (= TIRE *v.*[4]); **Tyred** *ppl. a.,* furnished with a tyre or tyres: chiefly in compounds (= TIRED *ppl. a.*[2]); **Ty·reless** *a.,* having no tyres.

1909 MISS G. GUINNESS *Peru* xxi. 222 Sufficient rubber to *tyre 300,000 motor-cars. 1884 G. L. HILLER in *Longm. Mag.* III. 491 Using his *tyred but tireless steed [a bicycle]. 1886 Rubber-tyred [see RUBBER *sb.*[1] 13 c]. 1896 Pneumatic-tyred [see PNEUMATIC *a.* 5]. 1906 C. MANSFIELD *Girl & Gods* xv, The discordant hoot of the motor horn, the rumble of *tyreless vehicles.

† **Tyre,** Sc. aphetic f. *en-, intyre,* INTER *v.*

*a* 1500 *Wyntoun's Cron.* IX. 1096 (Cott. MS.) To Scoyne his men hym bare And honorably hym tyrit [*v. rr.* entyrit, enteryd] þar.

**Tyre,** obs. form of TIER *sb.*[1], TIRE.

**Tyrefull,** var. *tereful* obs., tedious: see TERE *a.*

**Tyrein** (təiᵊ·rɪ̄ˌin). *Chem. rare*—⁰. [f. Gr. τῦρός cheese, after *casein.*] A synonym of CASEIN.

1860 MAYNE *Expos. Lex., Tyreina,* the same as *Casein*: tyrein. 1890 in BILLINGS *Med. Dict.*

**Tyreling,** var. TIRELING *Obs.*

† **Tyr(e)ment,** Sc. aphetic f. INTERMENT.

1504 *Acc. Ld. High Treas. Scot.* II. 257 Quhen he passit to Sanct Androis to the Beschopes tyrement. 1513 DOUGLAS *Æneis* XI. ii. *heading,* ȝong Pallas corps is till Evander sent, With all honour accordyng hys tyrment. 1541 *Acc. Ld. High Treas. Scot.* VIII. 39 To cum to the quenis tyrement.

‖ **Tyremesis** (təire·mĭsis). *Path.* [mod.L., f. Gr. τῦρός cheese + ἔμεσις vomiting.] (See quot.)

1857 DUNGLISON *Med. Lex., Tyremesis,* vomiting of curdy matter, in infants especially.

**Tyreny,** obs. form of TYRANNY.

† **Tyret, tyrette,** obs. ff. TERRET.

1575 TURBERV. *Falconrie* Verses Commend. Hawking, To shape hir Jesse, hir Tyrets and hir line.

**Tyrian** (ti·riăn), *a.* and *sb.* [f. L. *Tyri-us* (f. *Tyrus* Tyre) + -AN.] **A.** *adj.* Of or belonging to, native of, or made in Tyre, an ancient Phœnician city on the Mediterranean, the centre of an extensive commerce.

In quot. 1634 alluding to the use of the pole-star (CYNOSURE 1) as a guide in navigation by the merchants of Tyre.

1513 DOUGLAS *Æneis* IV. iv. 67 The Tyrian menȝe skalis wydequhair. 1582 STANYHURST *Æneis* I. (Arb.) 28 Of Tyrian virgins too weare thus a quiuer is vsed. 1596 SHAKS. *Tam. Shr.* II. i. 351 My hangings all of tirian tapestry. 1634 MILTON *Comus* 342 Thou shalt be our star of Arcady, Or Tyrian Cynosure. 1746 FRANCIS tr. *Horace, Sat.* II. iv. 102 What! sweep with dirty broom a floor inlaid, Or on foul couches Tyrian carpets spread? 1893 M. G. EASTON *Illustr. Bible Dict.* (1894) 677/1 Tyrian merchants were the first who ventured to navigate the Mediterranean waters.

**b.** *spec.* In reference or allusion to the purple or crimson dye anciently made at Tyre from certain molluscs: see PURPLE B. 1 a.

1616 DRUMM. OF HAWTH. *Poems* I. D iij, Nor Temples spread with Flackes of Virgine Snow, Nor Snow of Cheekes with Tyrian Graine enroll'd. 1693 DRYDEN *Persius* ii. 117 Another finds the way to dye in Grain, And make Calabrian Wool receive the Tyrian Stain. 1700 — *Secular Masque* 56 The sprightly green has drunk the Tyrian dye [*i.e.* blood]. 1738 *Gentl. Mag.* VIII. 211/1 'Tis true, my form no Tyrian purples grace. 1877 G. F. MACLEAR *St. Mark* vii. (1879) 85 The dyes of the celebrated Tyrian purple. 1890 BILLINGS *Med. Dict., Tyrian blue,* aniline dye, of violet color; a nuclear stain for alcoholic preparations.

**B.** *sb.* A native or inhabitant of Tyre.

1513 DOUGLAS *Æneis* I. viii. 141 Betuix ane Troiane and ane Tiriane Na difference. *Ibid.* xi. 82 ȝow, my awin Tirianis. *c* 1614 SIR W. MURE *Dido & Æneas* I. 511 Even so the Tyrians, some a stately stage On arches rais'd for comedyes ereck. 1770 J. Z. HOLWELL *Orig. Princ. Anc. Bramins* viii. § 125 (1779) 165 The histories of the ancient Phenicians, Tyrians, and Carthaginians. 1893 M. G. EASTON *Illustr. Bible Dict.* (1894) 677/1 In the time of David, a friendly alliance was entered into between the Hebrews and the Tyrians.

**C.** *Comb.,* as *Tyrian-dyed, -hued* adjs.

1903 AGNES M. CLERKE *Probl. Astrophysics* 259 To put off its crocus-veil and shine Tyrian-hued. 1910 *Sat. Westm. Gaz.* 19 Feb. 6/1 The Tyrian-dyed curtain.

**Tyrite** (təiᵊ·rəit). *Min.* [f. Norw. *Tyr,* ON. *Týr,* the god of war (cf. TUESDAY) + -ITE[1].] A variety of, or mineral allied to, FERGUSONITE.

1855 FORBES in *Edin. New Philos. Jrnl.* I. 67 Tyrite..was found..by Mr. Dahl, at a place called Hampemijr, and was crystallized in prisms, having a quadratic section. 1857 — in *Philos. Mag.* Feb. 96 Tyrite and Fergusonite are closely allied, and may possibly be even identical. 1868 DANA *Min.* (ed. 5) 524 Tyrite..occurs in square pyramidal crystals like those of fergusonite. *Ibid.* 525 Tyrite is associated with euxenite at Hampemyr..and Helle.

† **Tyrl,** obs. f. THIRL *v.*[1], to perforate.

1519 HORMAN *Vulg.* 108 Boxen pypes be lyghtlyer tyrld through, or made holowe, than yuery pypis.

**Tyrleis,** obs. Sc. var. TRELLIS.

**Tyrment**: see TYREMENT.

**Tyro, Tyrocinium,** etc.: see TIRO, etc.

**Tyrogenous** (təirǫ·dʒĭnəs), *a. rare*—⁰. [f. Gr. τῦρός cheese + -GEN + -OUS.] 'Originating in cheese' (Dorland *Med. Dict.* 1900–13).

**Tyroglyphid** (təirǫ·glifid), *sb.* and *a. Zool.* [f. mod.L. *Tyroglyphid-æ,* pl., f. *Tyroglyphus,* name of the typical genus, f. Gr. τῦρός cheese + γλύφειν to carve.] **a.** *sb.* An acarid of the family *Tyroglyphidæ,* including the cheese-mites. **b.** *adj.* Belonging to this family.

1909 in *Cent. Dict. Supp.* 1914 *Brit. Mus. Return* 180.

**Tyroid** (təiᵊ·roid), *a. rare*—⁰. [f. Gr. τῦρός cheese: see -OID.] Resembling cheese; cheesy.

1900–13 in DORLAND *Med. Dict.*

**Tyrolean** (tirōᵘ·lĭăn), *a.* and *sb.* Also -ian. [f. *Tyrol* (see def.) + -EAN. Cf. F. *tyrolien.*] **a.** *adj.* Belonging to Tyrol (often called 'the Tyrol'), a province of Austria-Hungary. **b.** *sb.* A native or inhabitant of Tyrol. So **Tyroler** (ti·rǭləɹ) [G. *Tyroler, Tiroler*: see -ER] = *Tyrolean* b; **Tyrolese** (-ī·z) *a.* and *sb.* = *Tyrolean*; ‖ **Tyrolienne** (tiroliˌe·n) [F., fem. of *tyrolien* Tyrolean], a dance or song of the Tyrolese peasants, or in the style of this.

1809 *Repos. of Arts* II. 388/1 The attachment of the *Tyroleans..to their emperors was always firm. 1859 *Habits Gd. Soc.* vi. (new ed.) 232 Except for the occasional playing of Tyrolean minstrels, [the zither is] unknown in this country. 1906 *Temple Bar Mag.* Jan. 33 Green Tyrolean hats with feathers. 1909 *Cent. Dict. Supp.,* Tyrolian. 1891 *Cent. Dict.,* *Tyroler. 1899 *Daily News* 20 Dec. 6/6 They got guides familiar with the ground, and..outflanked the Tyrolers. 1809 *Repos. of Arts* II. 388 Portrait of the *Tyrolese Deputies. *Ibid.* 389 He stipulated that the privileges of the Tyrolese..should remain entire. 1844 A. P. DE LISLE in E. Purcell *Life* (1900) I. vii. 131 Columns of white Tyrolese marble. 1872 RUSKIN *Fors Clav.* (1896) I. xix. 373 The Tyrolese mountains. 1898 *Review of Rev.* Feb. 181/2 The Tyrolese..a sterling, sober-minded people. 1889 W. B. SQUIRE in Grove *Dict. Mus.* IV. 198 The best-known example of an artificial '*Tyrolienne' is the well-known 'Chœur Tyrolien' in Act iii of Rossini's 'Guillaume Tell'.

**Tyroleucin** (təiᵊrolˌiū·sin). *Chem.* Also -ine. [f. Gr. τῦρός cheese + LEUCIN.] A white crystalline substance ($C_7H_{11}NO_2$) produced by the decomposition of proteins.

1878 KINGZETT *Anim. Chem.* 366 Among the new products recently described by Schützenberger is a substance termed by him tyroleucin. 1881 WATTS *Dict. Chem.* VIII. 1682 Tyroleucine is a white crystalline deposit of chalky aspect, nearly tasteless.

**Tyroline** (ti·rǭləin). [? f. TYR-IAN *a.* + -OL + -INE [5].] A variety of aniline-violet.

1867 *Ure's Dict. Arts* (ed. 6) I. 170.

**Tyrolite** (ti·rǭləit). *Min.* [ad. G. *tirolit* (Haidinger, 1845), f. *Tyrol,* where found: see -ITE[1].] 'Hydrous arsenate of copper, found usually in reniform masses of pale green colour' (Chester).

1854 DANA *Min.* (1868) 570.

‖ **Tyroma** (təirōᵘ·mă). *Path.* [mod.L., ad. Gr. τύρωμα, f. τυροῦν to make into cheese, curdle, f. τῦρός cheese.] A morbid formation or tumour of a cheesy consistence. Hence **Tyro·matous** *a.,* of the nature of a tyroma.

1848 CRAIGIE *Elem. Anat.* I. xi. 222 *Tyroma glandularum.* Tyromatous deposition. *Ibid.,* I think that the term *Tyroma* (Τυρος, caseus) is most suited to express its nature. *Ibid.,* This tyromatous substance. 1880 W. AITKEN *Sc. & Pract. Med.* (ed. 7) II. 476 Strumous tumors, as tubercles of the brain, or tyroma.

† **Ty·roma:ncy.** *Obs.* Also tiro-. [ad. F. *tyromantie* (Rabelais), f. Gr. τῦρός cheese: see -MANCY.] Divination by means of cheese.

1652 GAULE *Magastrom.* xix. 166 *Tyromancy* [mispr. *Typomancy*], [divining] by the coagulation of cheese. 1656 BLOUNT *Glossogr., Tiromantie.* *a* 1693 *Urquhart's Rabelais* III. xxv, To have the truth..more fully..disclosed..by Tyromancy, whereof we make some Proof in a great Brehemont Cheese.

**Tyronic, -ism, -ist, -ize**: see TIRONIC.

**Tyrosin** (təiᵊ·rosin). *Chem.* Also -ine. [irreg. f. Gr. τῦρός cheese + -IN[1].] A white crystalline substance ($C_9H_{11}NO_3$) produced by the decomposition of proteins. Also *attrib.*

1857 MILLER *Elem. Chem.* III. 627 Tyrosine..was obtained by Liebig from the products of the fusion of well-dried cheese, fibrin, or albumen, with hydrate of potash. *Ibid.* 628 Tyrosine forms long fibrous crystals, which are very sparingly soluble in cold water. 1873 RALFE *Phys. Chem.* 72 Tyrosin...Associated with leucin it has been obtained from all the glandular organs and secretions of the body. *Ibid.,* On cooling, crystals of tyrosin will be deposited. 1897 *Allbutt's Syst. Med.* IV. 100 Tyrosin crystals were found in the urine.

Hence **Tyrosinase** (-ēⁱs) [after *diastase*], an oxidizing ferment which converts tyrosin into black pigments, as the inky secretion of the octopus.

1900 B. D. JACKSON *Gloss. Bot. Terms, Tyrosinase,* an oxidising enzyme which attacks the chromogen of certain Fungi. (Bertrand.)

‖ **Tyrosis** (təirōᵘ·sis). *Path.,* etc. [mod.L., ad. Gr. type *τύρωσις, f. τυροῦν: see TYROMA and -OSIS.] **a.** Curdling of milk, esp. in the stomach: = CASEATION a. **b.** = TYREMESIS. **c.** Cheesy degeneration: = CASEATION b.

1693 tr. *Blancard's Phys. Dict.* (ed. 2). 1857 DUNGLISON *Med. Lex.*, *Tyrosis*, Tyremesis. Also, the curdling of milk in the stomach. 1896 *Allbutt's Syst. Med.* I. 175 Caseation or Tyrosis is a mode of termination of necrosis.

‖ **Tyrotoxicon** (təiᵊrotǫ·ksikǫn). *Chem.* [mod. L., f. Gr. τῡρός cheese + τοξικόν poison.] A poisonous ptomaine (diazobenzene hydroxide, $C_6H_5N.N.OH$), produced by a microbe in stale cheese and milk; cheese-poison.

1886 *Sci. Amer.* 21 Aug. 112/3 About a year ago, Dr. Victor C. Vaughan, of the University of Michigan, succeeded in isolating from some samples of cheese..a highly poisonous ptomaine, which he named tyrotoxicon (cheese poison)...Further investigations have led to the discovery that tyrotoxicon may be developed in milk.

So **Tyroto·xin** [TOXIN] = *tyrotoxicon*; **Tyroto·xism**, cheese-poisoning.

1899 CAGNEY tr. *Jaksch's Clin. Diagn.* v. (ed. 4) 189 Vaughan obtained one of these bodies (tyrotoxin) from rotten cheese and bad milk. 1900–13 DORLAND *Med. Dict.*, *Tyrotoxism*, cheese-poisoning.

**Tyrran, -and, -anie,** etc. obs. ff. TYRANT, TYRANNY. **Tyrret,** obs. form of TERRET.

**Tyrrhene** (ti·rīn, tirī·n), *a.* and *sb.* Forms: 4–5 **Tyren,** 5 **Tyrene,** 6 **Tirrene,** 6–7 **Tyrrhen,** 6– **Tyrrhene.** [ad. L. *Tyrrhēnus* of or pertaining to the *Tyrrhēnī* (Gr. Τυρρηνοί) or Etruscans.] = next.

1387 TREVISA *Higden* (Rolls) II. 445 He passede..Hercules his pilers, and com in to þe see Tyren. 1432–50 tr. *Higden* (Rolls) VI. 369 From the occean of Briteyne unto the see Tyrene. 1513 DOUGLAS *Æneis* VII. xii. 54 In Itale strandis at the cost Tyrrhene. *Ibid.* VIII. viii. 164 Wyth brag of weyr and Tirrene trumpis sovn. 1634 MILTON *Comus* 49 Coasting the Tyrrhene shore. 1697 DRYDEN *Æneid* VIII. 729 The Trojan band, Who wait their leader to the Tyrrhene land. 1736 AINSWORTH *Lat. Dict.*, *Mezentius*,..a prince of the Tyrrhenes. 1882 'OUIDA' *Maremma* I. 147 One of the forgotten kings of the Tyrrhene people.

**Tyrrhenian** (tirī·niăn), *a.* and *sb.* [f. L. *Tyrrhēn-us* (see prec.) or *Tyrrhēnia* Etruria.] **a.** *adj.* Of or pertaining to the Tyrrheni or their country; Etruscan, Etrurian. **b.** *sb.* One of the Tyrrheni; an Etruscan.

*Tyrrhenian Sea*, the sea lying between the mainland of Italy and the islands of Corsica, Sardinia, and Sicily.

1660 STANLEY *Hist. Philos.* IX. *Pythagoras* i. (1687) 492/1 Suidas saith, That Pythagoras was..by birth a Tyrrhenian. 1711 J. CLARKE tr. *Grotius' Chr. Relig.* II. xii. 112 *note*, [See] Diodorus, Book v, concerning the Tyrrhenians. 1788 LEMPRIÈRE *Class. Dict.*, *Mezentius*, a king of the Tyrrhenians when Æneas came into Italy. 1797 *Encycl. Brit.* (ed. 3) XVI. 327 Æneas..steered his course for Italy across the Tyrrhenian sea. 1857 BIRCH *Anc. Pottery* (1858) II. 77 The amphora called Tyrrhenian differs only in its general proportion from the two preceding kinds.

**Tyrse.** *rare.* ? *Obs.* Also **thirsé.** [Properly *tirsé* (Forskål, 1775), *tyrsé* (G. Saint-Hilaire and Cuvier), ad. Arab. ترسة *tirsaʰ*, f. ترس *turs* shield.] The Egyptian soft-billed turtle, *Testudo triunguis.*

1807 HUNTER tr. *Sonnini's Trav. in Egypt* I. 301 The advantage with which this *thirsé* of the Egyptians and Nubians wages war with the crocodile. 1834 McMURTRIE *Cuvier's Anim. Kingd.* 171 *T. Ægyptiacus*...The Tyrse. 1839 *Encycl. Brit.* (ed. 7) XIX. 132/2 The Egyptian species or tyrse, the soft turtle of the Nile.

**Tyrtæan** (təɹtī·ăn), *a.* [f. proper name *Tyrtæus*, Gr. Τυρταῖος (see def.) + -AN.] Pertaining to or in the style of Tyrtæus, a Greek poet of the 7th century B.C., who composed martial songs for the Spartans; martial, warlike.

1879 SWINBURNE *Stud. Shaks.* (1880) 114 There was nothing of the dry Tyrtæan twang, the dull mechanic resonance. 1898 G. W. E RUSSELL *Collect. & Recollect.* 380 Twenty years ago..the music-halls rang with the 'Great MacDermott's' Tyrtæan strain:—We don't want to fight; but, by Jingo, if we do [etc.].

**Tyrtle, -tyll,** obs. forms of TURTLE *sb.*[1]

**Tysan, -ane, -ant,** obs. ff. PTISAN.

**Tysche, Tysday,** obs. Sc. ff. TISSUE, TUESDAY.

**Tyse,** var. TICE *v.*, to entice.

**Tysonian** (təisōu·niăn), *a.* *Anat.* [f. proper name *Tyson* (see def.) + -IAN.] Pertaining to or discovered by Edward Tyson, an English anatomist (1649–1708); applied to the sebaceous glands of the prepuce, also called *Tyson's glands.*

1891 in *Cent. Dict.* 1900–13 in DORLAND *Med. Dict.*

**Tysonite** (tai·sənəit). *Min.* [f. the name of S. T. *Tyson*, from whom it was received + -ITE [1].] A rare native fluoride of the cerium metals.

1880 ALLEN & COMSTOCK in *Amer. Jrnl. Sc. & Arts* XIX. 390 The formula $(Ce, La, Di)_2 Fl_6$ appears..to express the composition of the mineral...It should be regarded as a new species. We propose for it the name *Tysonite.*

**Tyss,** obs. Sc. f. TICE *v.*, to entice.

**Tyssew, tysshewe,** etc., obs. ff. TISSUE.

† **Tyssyke, tysyke,** obs. forms of PHTHISIC.

*c* 1450 *Nom.* in Wr.-Wülcker 708/5 *Hec tisis*, the tyssyke. *c* 1520 SKELTON *Magnyf.* 555 Can you a remedy for a tysyke?

**Tyst,** var. TICE *v.*, to entice. **Tyste, -tey, -tie, -ty,** dial. var. TEISTIE, Black Guillemot. **Tyster, -yre,** obs. Sc. ff. TESTER, canopy.

**Tyt,** obs. f. TIT, TITE. **Tytandis,** obs. f. TIDINGS. **Tyte, tytely,** obs. ff. TITE, TITELY.

† **Tytelet,** ? obs. f. TITLED *ppl. a.*

13.. *Gaw. & Gr. Knt.* 1515 F[or] to telle of þis teuelyng of þis trwe knyȝtez, Hit is þe tytelet token, & tyxt of her werkkez.

† **Tyte tust, tytetuste.** *Obs. rare*$^{-1}$. [app. related to *titty*, TUTTY *sb.*[2], in same sense; cf. TISTY-TOSTY, TUZZY-MUZZY.] A nosegay, posy.

*c* 1440 *Promp. Parv.* 494/2 Tyte tust, or tusmose of flowrys or othyr herbys [*S.* tytetuste or tussemose], *olfactorium.*

**Tythance, -and(es), -aundes,** obs. ff. TIDING(S. **Tythe,** var. TITHE. **Tythimal(l,** var. TITHYMAL *Obs.* **Tything,** obs. f. TIDING; var. TITHING. **Tythondys,** obs. f. TIDINGS. **Tytill, tytle,** obs. ff. TITLE, TITTLE. **Tytt(e,** obs. ff. TEAT, TITE.

† **Ty·tyfer.** *Obs.* Also 6 **tedyffre.** [Origin obscure: perh. akin to TIDIFE.] The name of some small bird.

*c* 1500 *Parl. Byrdes* 193 in Hazl. *E.P.P.* III. 177 The Tytyffer. I say, sayd the Tytyfer, we kentysshe men [*Lansdowne MS.*, Syth, quod the Tedyffre with the Norfolk men], We may not geue the Crow a penne.

**Tytyl, -yll,** obs. ff. TITLE, TITTLE. **Tytynge,** obs. f. TIDING. **Tytyuell, -villus:** see TITIVIL.

**Tyvys-, Tywes-, Tywysday,** obs. ff. TUESDAY. **Tywele,** variant of TWILLY *sb.*[1] *Obs.* **Tywell, tywlle,** obs. forms of TWILL *sb.*[1]

† **Tyxhyl,** obs. f. THIXEL (*dial.*).

*c* 1475 *Pict. Voc.* in Wr.-Wülcker 807/19 *Hec acia*, a tyxhyl.

**Tyxste:** see TEE *v.*[2] **Tyxt, tyxte,** obs. ff. TEXT. **Tyyn,** obs. f. THYINE.

**Tzar,** etc.: see CZAR, TSAR.

**Tzeiran,** var. DZEREN.

[1662 J. DAVIES tr. *Olearius' Voy. Ambass.* 226 A kind of Deer, which the Turks call *Tzeiran*, and the Persians, *Ahn.*] 1862 *Chambers' Encycl.* IV. 692/1 The bear of Tibet, the musk-deer, the tzeiran.., the Mongolian goat [etc.].

**Tzetse, tzetze,** var. TSETSE.

‖ **Tzigane** (tsigā·n), *sb.* and *a.* Also **tsigan(e, tzigan.** [a. F. *tzigane*, = Russian цыганъ, Ruthenian циганъ, Slovenian *Cigan*, Roumanian *Ţigan*, Lithuanian *Cigonas*, Bulgarian циганинъ, Croatian *Ciganin*; all from Magyar *cigány, czigány* (tsigā·ni). The spelling with *tz-* originated in German; a better Eng. spelling would be *tsigan*: cf. *Tsar.*]

**A.** *sb.* A Hungarian gipsy.

1887 *Pall Mall G.* 3 Mar. 5/2 The fiery Magyar, the melancholy Roumanian, the stolid Saxon, the merry, thieving Tzigane. 1898 *Tit-Bits* 7 May 114/1 The finest-looking people of Europe are the Tsiganes, or gipsies of Hungary. 1906 *Reader* 24 Nov. 124/1 The humblest peasant, even the nomad Tzigan, greasy, wild, and unkempt in appearance.

**B.** *adj.* That is a Tzigane; pertaining to or consisting of Tziganes.

1885 MABEL COLLINS *Prettiest Woman* vi, The Tzigane musicians were playing most exquisite music. 1888 E. GERARD *Land beyond Forest* II. xxvii. 13 Stripping a young Tzigane girl quite naked. 1912 *Daily News* 12 Apr. 6 The ..inevitable tzigane bands, valses, cake-walks.

Hence **Tziganologist** (tsigănǫ·lŏdʒist), **Tziga·nologue** (also **ts-**), one who studies or treats of the Tziganes.

1909 *Cent. Dict. Suppl.*, *Tsiganologist*, same as *Zinganologist.* 1911 *19th Cent.* Sept. 550 We owe our knowledge of it [Shelta] to Charles Godfrey Leland, a keen tsiganologue.

**Tzirid,** obs. f. JERID, wooden javelin.

# U.

**U** (yū), the 21st letter of the modern English, and the 20th of the ancient Roman alphabet, was in the latter identical in form and origin with V (q.v.), the same symbol being employed both as a vowel and a consonant. In Latin MSS. written in capitals the form V is retained; but in uncial MSS., of which the earliest specimens belong to the third or fourth century, the modified form ∪ appears, and is continued in the later half-uncial (from *c* 500) and minuscule MSS. (from the eighth century) as u. In Anglo-Saxon MSS. the latter form (u) was regularly employed as a minuscule to denote the vowel *u*, the corresponding form in capitals being either V or U. In early MSS. *u* and *uu* are also employed with the value of *w*, and very rarely *u* in place of *b* (later *f*) to denote intervocalic *v*; in late MSS. the substitution of *u* for *f* (= v) becomes fairly common, usually between vowels but sometimes also initially. In ME., after continental usage, the two symbols *u* and *v* were employed, but without clear distinction in value, each of them being used to denote either the vowel *u* or the consonant *v*. The practice with regard to the employment of the two forms varied considerably, but the general tendency was to write *v* initially and *u* in other positions, regardless of phonetic considerations, e.g. *vnder, vpon, vse* but *cure, full, huge*, and *vain, vice, vile* but *saue, euer, giuen*. For the sake of clearness, however, *v* was frequently preferred to *u*, especially in conjunction with *n* and *m*, as in *tvne, rovnd, mvse*. (In Scottish MSS. intervocalic *u* with the value of *v* is much rarer than in English, its place being largely taken by *f, ff, v* or *w*.) The early printers followed the common usage with regard to *u* and *v* in small letters; in capitals they employed only one symbol, viz. 𝔘 in black letter, and V in Roman. During the sixteenth century, however, continental printers began to distinguish between *u* and *v*, using the former as a vowel and the latter as a consonant. The distinction is found in Italian printing as early as 1524, but its general introduction dates from 1559–60, when it was employed in the *Grammatica* of Ramus; apparently the innovation was due to the printer rather than to the author. In English there were several attempts to introduce the distinction before 1600; after 1600 it rapidly became more common, and had come to be general by 1630. In capitals, however, V for some time continued to serve in the old double function, although U had been introduced in the work of Ramus. This was subsequently adopted and remained the usual form for the capital vowel until the close of the 17th century, after which it rapidly gave way to U, a form which is employed, though at first sparingly, from at least 1625. (In italic type the vowel was *V*, the consonant *V*.) From about 1700 the regular forms have been U u for the vowel, and V v for the consonant.

One result of the long-continued confusion of *u* and *v* was that in dictionaries, indexes, etc., words beginning with the vowel and with the consonant were combined in one list, *va-* being followed by *vb-* (i.e. *ub-*), *ve-* by *vf-*, etc. This practice was very commonly continued even after the two letters had been distinguished, and in English dictionaries remained as late as Todd's edition of Johnson (1818) and Richardson's dictionary (1837). When the two letters were separated, *v-* was sometimes placed before *u-*; a late example of this occurs in Jodrell's dictionary (1820). The modern arrangement, by which *u-* precedes *v-*, is found from at least the early part of the 18th cent., and has been usual in English dictionaries from that of Webster (1828) onwards.

In OE. the vowel-sounds denoted by *u* were those of Latin *u*, short and long, in the former case corresponding to that of mod.E. *pull, bush*, in the latter to that of *rude, brute*. In ME. the short *u* in native words partly retained its own sound, and was partly altered by lengthening or other phonetic changes; in some words the sound remained while the spelling was altered, as in *wolf* (OE. *wulf*), *woll* (OE. *wull*). The long *u* also retained its sound (unless when shortened before certain consonants), but was denoted by the new symbol *ou* derived from French spelling. Short and long *u* also freely occurred in words of French and Latin origin, but differed in quality from those of the native words, having the value of *ü, ǖ*; in the case of *ǖ* the difference continued to be marked, and the resultant sounds are now quite distinct. Under the influence of these forms southern ME. scribes substituted *u* for OE. *y, ý* (which had expressed the sounds *ü, ǖ*), writing *cun, cuðen*, etc., for OE. *cyn, cýðan*, which in midland and northern dialects became *kin, kithe*.

In mod.E. the short *u* of OE. (apart from changes due to lengthening, etc.) has normally become *v* (written *u* or *o*), as *dumb, sun, thus* = OE. *dumb, sunne, þus*, or *some, love* = OE. *sum, lufu*. This change apparently had not proceeded far enough to be clearly noticeable until the middle of the 17th century, and was probably not generally completed until the beginning of the 18th. Over all the north of England, however, and a large part of the midlands, the original sound of *u* remains in words of this class, and even in standard English it is preserved in a few instances after labial consonants, as in *bull, full, pull, bush, put*. Short *u* also has this sound in some common words not of native origin (mostly with labial initials), as *bushel, butcher, pudding, pulpit, push, sugar*. The OE. *ū* (ME. *ou*) has normally become the diphthong (au), written *ou* or *ow*, as in *thou, town* = OE. *þū, tūn*, but in a few instances has been shortened, as in *plum, thumb*. The ME. *ǖ* from French or Latin, on the other hand, has become the diphthong (iū, iūᵊ), written *u, ue*, or *u-e*, as in *huge, mute, future, cure*, with reduction to (*ū*, ūᵊ) after *s* (= ʃ, ʒ), *j*, and *r*, as in *sure, jury, brute, rule*, optionally after *l*, as in *lute, lure*, and more widely in American usage. This mode of spelling has also been extended to some native words which originally had a diphthong, and would normally be written with *ew*, as *hue, rue, true, truth* (compared with *new, grew, strew*). The same sounds (*iū, ū*) are also represented by *ui* in a few words, as *nuisance, bruise, fruit*.

In combination with other vowels *u* is employed in the groups *au* (ǭ), *eu* (iū), *ou* (with varying value, as in *foul, soul, four, young, route*), *ue* and *ui* (see above). It is silent after *g* in many words, as *guard, guide, plague*, and in final *-que*, as *masque, grotesque*. It has the value of *w* after *q* in other positions, and in various words after *g* and *s*, as *queen, quick, inquest*; *guano, iguana, anguish*; *suave, persuade*, etc.

The name of the letter down to the 16th century was *u*, pronounced like the long *u* of French or Latin origin, and consequently undergoing the same change to (iū) which took place in ordinary words. The completion of the change is indicated by the use of the letter (*u* or *v*) to represent the personal pronoun *you* in such passages as Shaks. *L.L.L.* v. i. 60 and Dekker and Webster *Westward Hoe* II. i. (Cf. I O U.) In Scotland the name (*ū*) was locally in use as late as the 19th century.

**I. 1.** Illustrations of the use of the letter or of its name.

α. *c* **1000** Ælfric *Gram.* ii. (Z.) 6, *h* and *k* ȝeendiað on *a* æfter rihte, *q* ȝeendað on *u*. *Ibid.* xxxi. (Z.) 197 *Mortuus sum* on twam uum, swaswa nan oðer. **1530** Palsgr. 7 *U*, in the frenche tong, where so ever he is a vowel by hymselfe, shall be sownded like as we sownde *ew*. **1588** Shaks. *L. L. L.* v. i. 60 *Peda.* I will repeat them: a e i. *Pag.* The Sheepe, the other two concludes it o u. **1668** O. Price *Eng. Orthogr.* 29 The u is two fold. 1. Short, as in but, must, burst. 2. Long, as in lute, muse, refuse. as if it were the compound of iw. **1727** Swift *Misc. in Verse* Wks. 1841 I. 783/1 And Q maintain'd 'twas but his due Still to keep company with U. **1768** Boswell *Corsica* Pref. p. xviii, Leaving out..u in the last syllable of words which used to end in our. **1843** *Penny Cycl.* XXV. 484/1 U is at one extremity of the series of vowel sounds, lying next to the vowel *o*. **1867** A. J. Ellis *E. E. Pronunc.* I. iii. 136 Many words now spelled with *u* were written with *ew* in the xvith century. **1888** Jacobi *Printers' Vocab.*, U is the nineteenth signature of the printer's alphabet.

β. **1526** *Pilgr. Perf.* (W. de W. 1531) 291 He reciteth an example of one Masseus a frere,..the whiche in suche ioye or iubile coude speke nothynge but .v. v. v. *c* **1532** Du Wes *Introd. Fr.* in Palsgr. 899 Ye shal pronounce..*v* after the Skottes, as in this worde *gud*. **1611** Cotgr. *Brief Direct.* 1 *V*, is sounded as if you would whistle it out, as in the word, a Lute. **1616** Bullokar, *Orthographie*, the art of writing words truely; as sonne of man, with an O: sunne that shineth, with the vowell v. **1710** Shaftesb. *Charac.* I. III. III. i. 288 The vowel *O* was form'd by an orbicular Disposition of the Mouth;..The Vowel *V* by a parallel Protrusion of the Lips.

**b.** = You *pron.* See I O U.

**1840** Sir N. C. Tindal in Manning and Granger *Reports* I. 48 There was no one but the plaintiff to whom the 'U' in the document [an I O U] could be applied.

**c.** *attrib.*, as *u-sound, -vowel*.

**1852** *Proc. Philol. Soc.* V. 198 The long vowel expressed by the diphthong *ou* is weakened, but not to the extinction of the *u* sound. **1886** *Encycl. Brit.* XXI. 272/1 Original root-syllables contained no simple *i-* and *u*-vowels, except as the second element of..diphthongs. **1888** *Ibid.* XXIII. 715/2 At the same time begins the corruption of *u* to the (so-called) *ŭ* sound in 'but,' 'shut', &c.; this is not a *u* sound at all.

**2.** Used with reference to the shape of the (capital) letter, esp. *attrib.* or *Comb.*, as *U-like, U-shaped* adjs., *U-shape*.

**1822–7** Good *Study Med.* (1829) I. 493 A minute semilunar bone, which, from its resemblance to the Greek letter *υ* or u-psilon, is called the hyoid or u-like bone. **1842** Parnell *Chem. Anal.* (1845) 457 The water in the bottle is withdrawn, air entering through the U-shaped tube at the same time. **1857** W. K. Loftus *Trav. & Res. Chaldæa & Susiana* xxi. 270 Three mud bricks were laid down in the form of the capital letter U. **1872** Coues *N. Amer. Birds* 234 Below, the spots fewer, brown, U-shaped. **1875** Bennett & Dyer tr. *Sachs's Bot.* 88 The mother-cells are so developed that from the young..epidermis-cell, a small piece is cut out on one side by a wall bent in a U-shape.

**b.** *attrib.*, in the sense 'shaped like the letter U', as *U bolt, -magnet, piece, plate, -rail, -tube*.

**1797** J. Curr *Coal Viewer* 63 The strength of the U plates must be the same as the spear plates. **1850** *Athenæum* 31 Aug. 922/2 By Arrangements of Coloured Liquids in a U Tube. **1868** *Rep. to Govt. U.S. Munitions War* 273 Iron rolled in the fashion of the ordinary U-rail for railroads. **1878** Abney *Photogr.* 289 A mirror..is suspended on two axes, x x, working a U-piece, s s. **1884** Knight *Dict. Mech.* Suppl. 911/1 *U bolt*, a clevis for the attachment of axles, rods, etc., in machinery and vehicles. **1888** *Scribner's Mag.* Aug. 177/2 Immediately below the bend of the U-magnet are the commutator segments.

**c.** Something shaped like the letter U.

**1897** *Allbutt's Syst. Med.* III. 814 The apex of the V or the bend of the U may become adherent to the mesentery.

**3.** Used to denote serial order.

Also employed as a symbol for purposes of calculation in quaternions, hydrodynamics, the theory of heat, etc.

**1900** *Dundee Advertiser* 14 Mar. 5 U Battery, which occupied a position to the north of the Boer centre, shelled the ridge thoroughly.

**II. 4.** Abbreviations: U = Uranium; U. C. = upcast shaft; U. K. = United Kingdom; U. P. = United Presbyterian; U.S., U.S.A. = United States (of America).

**1844** Fownes *Man. Chem.* 290 The equivalent of uranium is 60·. Its symbol is *U. **1883** Gresley *Gloss. Coal-M.* 266 *U.C., upcast shaft. **1892** *Daily News* 27 Oct. 7/4 The supplies at sea for *U.K. have decreased 32,000 quarters on the week...Supplies at sea for U.K. have further slightly decreased. **1865** *Slang Dict.* 265 *U.P., United Presbyterian. Scotch clerical Slang. **1878** *Chambers's Encycl.* IX. 647/1 Protracted negotiations for union between the U.P. and Free Churches have been without result. **1834** McCulloch *Dict. Commerce* (ed. 2) 843 American Tonnage. Entered into the *U.S...Departed from U.S. **1867** *Chambers's Encycl.* IX. 649/2 The U.S. are rich in mineral productions. **1901** *Daily Chron.* 12 Aug. 5/2 On Saturday we asked what language is U.S., which is announced as 'spoken' in the window of a City office.

**5.** *slang* or *colloq.* U.P., the spelling pronunciation of Up *adv.*, = over, finished, beyond remedy.

**1838** Dickens *O. Twist* xxiv, It's all U.P. there,..if she lasts a couple of hours, I shall be surprised. **1854** Miss Baker *Northampt. Gloss.* 370 'It's all U.P. with him;' i.e. all up either with his health, or circumstances. **1861** Whyte Melville *Good for Nothing* xxvii. II. 18 It's a long lane that has no turning, but I did think for five minutes afore I saw your fire that it was about U.P.

**U,** obs. var. Yew; var. *yu*, dial. f. Yule. **Ua-,** frequent ME. spelling for Va-. **Uald, Uas,** obs. Sc. ff. *would, was*. **U-batch,** var. *yu-batch*: see Yule. **Ubble, Ubbly(e,** obs. ff. Obley.

**Ub(b)ubboo,** variant of Hubbuboo.

**1702** Farquhar *Twin-Rivals* v. iii, Ububboo, a Witch, a Witch. **1851** Borrow *Lavengro* xi, Cut-throat kens, where thirty ruffians..would spring up with brandished sticks and an 'ubbubboo, like the blowing up of a powder-magazine'.

†**U·berant,** *a.* *Obs. rare.* [ad. L. *ūberant-, ūberans*, pres. pple. of *ūberāre*, f. *ūber* rich, plentiful.] Abundant, copious.

1622 G. FITZ-GEFFRY *Elisha* 14 Where the fountaine is vberant, needs must the streames bee fluent. 1624 *Gag for Pope* 56 Like vberant springs to send forth flowing streams of truth into the world. 1624 T. SCOTT *Belg. Souldier* 38 Whose vertue proued like an Vberant spring.

†**Uberate,** *v.*[1] *Obs.*—[0] Also hub-. [f. ppl. stem of L. *ūberāre*: cf. prec.] (See quots.)

1623 COCKERAM, *Huberate*, to make plentifull. 1656 BLOUNT *Glossogr.*, *Uberate*, to make plenteous and fruitfull.

†**Uberate,** *v.*[2] *Obs.*—[0] [f. L. *ūber* udder.] (See quot.)

1623 COCKERAM, *Vberate*, to give suck, to fatten with the brest. [Hence in Blount.]

**Uberous** (yū·bĕrəs), *a.* Now *rare.* [f. L. *ūber* rich, full, fruitful, abundant, etc. + -OUS, or ad. med.L. *ūberōsus*. Cf. mod.F. *ubéreux*.

Bailey (1727, vol. II) gives *uberose*, and (1721) *uberosity*.]

**1.** Supplying milk or nourishment in abundance. Said (*a*) of animals, etc., or (*b*) of the breasts.

In this sense prob. associated with L. *ūber* udder.

(*a*) 1624 QUARLES *Sion's Elegies* IV. vii, Milke, from the vberous Cow, Was ne're so pure in substance. 1632 — *Div. Fancies* I. xxxvii, How do our Pastures flourish, and refresh Our uberous Kine, so fair, so full of flesh! *a* 1635 NAUNTON *Fragm. Reg.* (Arb.) 51 My Lord..drew in too fast, like a childe sucking on an over-uberous Nurse. 1644 QUARLES *Sheph. Orac.* i, Our uberous ewes were evermore supplyed With twins, attending upon either side.

(*b*) 1634 SIR T. HERBERT *Trav.* 17 The women giue their Infants sucke as they hang at their backes, the vberous dugge stretched ouer her shoulder. 1635 QUARLES *Embl.* I. xii. 2 The ub'rous breasts, when fairly drawn, repast The thriving infant with their milkie flood. 1869 BROWNING *Ring & Bk.* IX. 53 Each feminine delight of florid lip,.. Marmoreal neck and bosom uberous.

**b.** Rich in fertilizing moisture. *rare*—[1].

*a* 1706 EVELYN *Sylva* II. viii. (1776) 426 This [water from ponds] approaches nearest to that of rain dropping from the uberous cloud, and is certainly the most natural and nursing.

†**2.** Of places: Richly productive; fertile. *Obs.*

*a* 1626 MIDDLETON *Mayor of Queenborough* II. iii, About the fruitful flanks of uberous Kent. 1634 SIR T. HERBERT *Trav.* 20 Cotton they [the Malagasy] haue store of, but most vberous in Fruits. 1651 HOWELL *Venice* 26 She [Padua] is situated in a most delightfull and uberous plain.

**3.** Abundant, copious, full.

1633 T. ADAMS *Exp. 2 Peter* iii. 18 If the young and tender grace of thankfulness do not fall into the hands of uberous and fruitful obedience, it will languish and pine away. 1747 *Gentl. Mag.* 242 Her uberous store, To these, parturient Earth unmidwif'd yields. 1839 *New Monthly Mag.* LVII. 408 Addressing himself to a lady of most uberous presence.

Hence **U·berousness,** plentifulness, fertileness.

1727 BAILEY (vol. II).

**Uberty** (yū·bəɹti). Now *rare.* Also 5 vberte, uberte(e; 7 ubertie. [a. OF. *uberté* (= It. *ubertà*, Pg. *uberdade*), or ad. L. *ūbertās*, f. *ūber*: cf. prec. and -TY.] Rich growth, fruitfulness, fertility; copiousness, abundance.

? *a* 1412 LYDG. *Two Merchants* 613 Greyne oppressith to moche vberte. *c* 1440 *Pallad. on Husb.* III. 104 A vine abundaunt ek thow take hem fro, And not hem take that ber a grape or too, But hem that kneleth doun for vberte. *Ibid.* VIII. 88 Of pasturyng they must haue vberte, Fro breris fer. 1491 CAXTON *Vitas Patr.* (W. de W. 1495) I. vii. 11 b/1 An ydolle, whyche somtyme was by prestes & other peple born in processyon for to obteyne uberte & habundaunce of rayne. 1603 FLORIO *Montaigne* I. xxx. (1632) 104 They yet enjoy that naturall ubertie and fruitfulnesse, which..doth in such plenteous abundance furnish them with all necessary things. 1623 COCKERAM, *Vbertie*, fertility, abundance. [Hence in Blount, Phillips, etc.] 1900 *Westm. Gaz.* 6 Apr. 7/3 So these happy volatile fellows talk on, with a uberty of optimism.

‖**U·bi.** *Obs.* [L. *ubi* where. So Sp. *ubi* place, room.]

**1.** Place, position; location. (In common use *c* 1640–1740.)

1614 T. ADAMS *Physicke fr. Heaven* in *Diuells Banket*, etc. 321 Euery spirituall Phisitian must keepe his right *vbi*. 1644 DIGBY *Nat. Bodies* i. (1645) 8 It is but assigning an Ubi to such a spirit and he is presently riveted to what place you please; and by multiplying the Ubies [etc.]. 1661 GLANVILL *Van. Dogm.* 101 Nor are we solicitous for the *Ubi* of Vertue, or any other Immaterial accident. 1704 NORRIS *Ideal World* II. iii. 223 Spirit cannot resist body, as being capable of coexisting in the same *ubi* with it. 1740 CHEYNE *Regimen* 215 That Bodies..must have an *Ubi*, a local permanent Situation at last, is certain.

**2.** Present place or location; whereabouts.

1778 H. WALPOLE *Let. to W. Mason* 15 May, The *ubi* of the Toulon squadron is not ascertained.

†**Ubia·tion.** *Obs.*—[1] [Cf. prec. and next.] The action of occupying a (new) place.

1624 F. WHITE *Repl. Fisher* 422 No substantiall thing is produced, but one substance succeedeth in the roome of another, by that which they stile vbiation.

**Ubication** (yūbikē[i]·ʃən). [ad. mod.L. **ubicātio* (cf. Sp. *ubicacion*, Pg. *ubicação*), f. **ubicāre* (Sp. *ubicarse* to be in a determinate place), f. L. *ubi* UBI.] The condition or fact of being in, or occupying, a certain place or position; location.

1644 DIGBY *Nat. Soule* v. § 9. 400 We conceiue these modifications of the thing, like substances; and..we call them by substantiue names, Whitenesse, Action, Vbication, Duration, &c. 1661 GLANVILL *Van. Dogm.* 101 Relations, Ubications, Duration, the vulgar Philosophy admits into the list of something. 1699 BURNET *39 Art.* xxviii. (1700) 324 They are accustomed to think that Ubication, or the being in a Place, is but an Accident to a Substance. 1837 WHEWELL *Hist. Induct. Sci.* II. VI. ii. § 5. 45 Arriaga, who wrote in 1639,..suggests that the board affects the upper weight, which it does not touch, by its ubication, or whereness. 1866 T. N. HARPER *Peace through Truth* Ser. I. 212 The *terminus ad quem* is already existing, and merely receives a new ubication. 1892 *Standard* 5 Aug., The constant identity of the ubication and direction of the lines [in Mars] proved their connection with the soil.

**Ubiety** (yubəi·ēti). [ad. mod.L. **ubietās*, f. L. *ubi* UBI.] Condition in respect of place or location; local relationship; whereness.

1674 N. FAIRFAX *Bulk & Selv.* 77 Being no wayes beclam'd with body as to ubiety or whereness. 1686 H. MORE *Real Pres.* 25 To make a body in this sense independent of Place or Ubiety, is as unconceivable as to make it independent of Time. 1733 WATTS *Scheme Ontol.* xii, Of time, and place, and ubiety. 1834 SOUTHEY *Doctor* cxcii. (1848) 509 O Soul of Sir John Cheke, thou wouldst have led me out of my way, if that had been possible,—if my ubiety did not so nearly resemble ubiquity. 1855 BAILEY *Mystic*, etc. 81 Vervain and magic haschisch, which endows Thought with ubiety. 1866 R. HOBSON *Chas. Waterton* iv. 92 Notwithstanding her uncertain tenure of ubiety,..she [the coot] patiently yielded to her lot.

**Ubiquarian** (yūbikwē[ə]·riăn), *sb.* and *a.* Also 8 ubiquerian. [f. L. *ubīque* wherever, anywhere, everywhere.]

**A.** *sb.* †**1.** *pl.* A society or club existing in the 18th cent. Also *attrib.* *Obs.*

1737 (*title*), A modest vindication of the illustrious order of Ubiquarians. *Ibid.* 23 The Ubiquarian Senate do not yet admit of this Difference. 1755 J. WITSELL in *Connoisseur* 27 Nov. 581 Laws, Rules, Regulations, or Orders, shall be formed for the Anti-Gallicans, Ubiquarians, Gregorians, or any private clubs and societies. 1761 *Ann. Reg., Charac.* II. 51/1 He was a respectable member of the Killers of Care, The Silenians,..Ubiquarians, &c.

**2.** A person who goes everywhere. *rare.*

1767 *Ann. Reg., Charac.* 62/2 The English being by their nature Ubiquarians, and seldom in one place long, must have painted canvas as quick as their ideas. 1812 *Sporting Mag.* XL. 281 That sporting ubiquarian, Colonel Thornton.

**B.** *adj.* **1.** Being or existing, present or found, everywhere; ubiquitous, ubiquitary.

1762 *Gentl. Mag.* Sept. 440/1 Happiness our friend shall be, Ubiquerian deity! 1784 COWPER *Tiroc.* 266 Have ye, ye sage intendants of the whole, An ubiquarian presence and controul. 1819 MACCULLOCH *West. Isl. Scot.* II. 321 Fingal ..the ubiquarian king and warrior is said to have occupied them. 1848 HAMPDEN *Bampt. Lect.* (ed. 3) 147 The Universal Governor, overshadowing all things with the ubiquarian tutelage of his Providence. 1891 C. DIXON *Idle Hours w. Nat.* 108 The ubiquarian House Sparrow has his home amongst the girders of the roof.

**2.** Met with or experienced everywhere.

1825 *Monthly Rev.* CVI. 490 It will facilitate, also, to men of note, who have occasion to travel, an ubiquarian reception.

†**Ubi·quious,** *a.* *Obs. rare.* [f. as prec. + -IOUS.] Ubiquitous.

1782 W. STEVENSON *Hymn to Deity* 31 Thro' stretch ubiquious, measureless expanse,..Abroad he moves in majesty of state. 1835 *Tait's Mag.* II. 93 The ubiquious Princess had arrived suddenly at Ostend.

**U·biquism.** *rare*—[1]. [Cf. next and -ISM. So Sp. *ubiquismo*.] = UBIQUITISM.

1891 *Athenæum* 28 March 403/3 In Switzerland he [Montaigne] questions Felix Plater..in regard to heretical doctrines such as Ubiquism.

**U·biquist.** *rare.* [a. F. *ubiquiste* (= Sp., Pg. *ubiquista*), f. L. *ubique* everywhere: see -IST.]

†**1.** (See quots.) *Obs.*

[1706 PHILLIPS (ed. Kersey), *Ubiquiste*, a Divinity-Doctor that belongs to no particular College in the University of Paris.] 1721 BAILEY, *Ubiquist* [from prec.]. 1728 CHAMBERS *Cycl.* s.v., In the University of Paris,..the Ubiquists are called simply Doctors in Theology.

**2.** = UBIQUITARIAN *sb.* 2.

1728 CHAMBERS *Cycl.* s.v., All the Ubiquists, however, are not agreed: Some of 'em, and among the rest the Swedes, hold that Jesus Christ, even during his Mortal Life, was every where. 1842 BRANDE *Dict. Sci.*, etc. *Ubiquists*, or *Ubiquitarians*, in Ecclesiastical History, a school of Lutheran divines; so called from their tenet that the body of Christ was present in the Eucharist in virtue of his divine omnipresence.

†**Ubiquit,** *v.* *Obs.*—[1] [Back-formation from UBIQUITOUS or -ITY.] *trans.* To make ubiquitous.

1676 MARVELL *Mr. Smirke* 33 This being done, then the Exposer ubiquits himself, peeping at the Key-holes, or picking the Locks of the Bed-chambers of all the Great Ministers.

†**Ubi·quitair,** *a.* *Obs.*—[1] [a. F. *ubiquitaire*.] = UBIQUITARY *a.* 2.

*c* 1645 HOWELL *Lett.* VI. xiii. (1650) I. 198 Of Him, whom Earth nor Air, Nor the vast mould Of Heaven can hould, Cause he's Vbiquitair.

†**Ubi·quitant.** *Obs.*—[1] [Cf. prec. and -ANT.] = UBIQUITARY *sb.* I.

1654 VILVAIN *Theol. Treat.* i. 9 They cannot be ubiquitants every wher or elswher at once.

**Ubiquitarian** (yubi·kwitē[ə]·riăn), *sb.* and *a.* [See UBIQUITARY and -IAN.]

**A.** *sb.* †**1.** = UBIQUITARY *sb.* I. *Obs.*

1644 *Thomasson Tracts* (Brit. Mus.) CLXIII. No. 12 A 4, He cannot heare..that Prince Rupert is approaching any-thing neare Yorke, yet they..prepare for him least that ubiquitarian steale on them unawares. 1663 R. HEAD *Hic et Ubique* 40 Why that Ubiquitarian, and his antick comrade Phantastick have lately borrowed monies of me. 1670 CLARKE *Nat. Hist. Nitre* 19 It [nitre] is an Ubiquitarian, though no place wil scarce hold it. *a* 1734 NORTH *Lives* (1826) III. 136 And I, that was no housekeeper, became an ubiquitarian till his lordship's death.

**2.** One of those Lutherans who maintained the doctrine that Christ's body was everywhere present at all times. Chiefly in *pl.*

1651 *Fuller's Abel Rediv., Sohnius* 384 Confuting the Ubiquitarians..so boldly, that he chose rather to hazard banishment then to connive at errors. 1660 HACKET *Serm. at Whitehall* 22 Mar. 20 The unrelenting Ubiquitarians among the rigid Lutherans. 1676 GLANVILL *Ess.* v. 25 The Ubiquitarians defend their Errors, by denying the judgement of Reason. 1704 NORRIS *Ideal World* II. xii. 511 Nay, perhaps, the Ubiquitarians may of the two have the better plea. 1798 HEY *Lect. Divinity* IV. IV. xxviii. § 10. 325 *note*, Luther is said to have given up this ubiquity as a proof of Christ's corporal presence in the Eucharist; but rigid Lutherans were still Ubiquitarians. 1874 J. H. BLUNT *Dict. Sects*, etc. (1886) 603 The Ubiquitarians are strong opponents of the Calvinistic and Zwinglian theories of the Holy Eucharist.

**B.** *adj.* **1.** Of or pertaining to, holding or maintaining, the doctrine of the Ubiquitarians.

1640 BP. HALL *Chr. Moder.* II. x. 79 The Calvinists brand Schlusselburgius for an Ubiquitarian hereticke. 1673 HICKMAN *Quinquart. Hist.* Ep. a b, The late Ubiquitarian Lutherans make a difference where they [Zwinglius and Luther] found none. *Ibid.* II. 366 Frederick the Prince was from his youth trained up and instructed in the Ubiquitarian Doctrine. 1882 FARRAR *Early Chr.* I. 350 *note*, The old Ubiquitarian controversy as to whether 'the right hand of God is everywhere'.

**2.** = UBIQUITARY *a.* 2. *rare.*

1641 LD. BROOKE *Disc. Nat. Episc.* II. ii. 71 No one man living could..Over-see it; except he could get the Pope to Transubstantiate him also, and so get a Ubiquitarian Body. 1828 *Examiner* 25/1 No ubiquitarian order should exist, with duties and interests paramount to those of national allegiance.

Hence **Ubiquita·rianism,** = UBIQUITISM.

1885 SCHAFF *Christ & Christianity* 75 The absolute ubiquitarianism of the Swabian school, and..the relative or hypothetical ubiquitarianism of the Saxon school.

†**Ubi·quitariness.** *Obs. rare.* [f. next + -NESS.] The quality of being ubiquitary.

1655 FULLER *Ch. Hist.* x. i. § 26 The Prelaticall party complained..of the ubiquitarinesse of some hands, the same being alwayes present at all Petitions. *a* 1661 — *Worthies, Lanc.* II. (1662) 119 He..was very obstreperous in arguing the case for Transubstantiation, and the Ubiquitariness of Christs body.

**Ubiquitary** (yubi·kwitări), *sb.* and *a.* [ad. mod.L. *ubiquitārius*, f. L. *ubīque* everywhere. Hence also F. *ubiquitaire*, Sp. and Pg. *ubiquitario*.]

**A.** *sb.* **1.** One who, or that which, is or can be everywhere at once. Now *rare.*

1587 HOLINSHED *Chron.* III. 579/2 There must needs be an errour..vnlesse we will grant the king and queene..to haue beene *Hic ibi simul*, which priuilege is granted to none but Ubiquitaries. 1599 B. JONSON *Cynthia's Rev.* II. iv, A Nymph..all motion, an ubiquitarie, Shee is euery where. 1615 P. SMALL in Farr *S. P. Jas. I* (1848) 332 Time is of the Ubiquitaries' race,—Time's here, Time's there, Time is in every place. 1638 BP. MOUNTAGUE *Art. Eng. Norwich* D., The Bishop is no Ubiquitary, that hee can discover every thing done. 1657 R. LIGON *Barbadoes* (1673) 63 Tables, cupbords, beds, stools, all are covered with them [*sc.* ants], so that they are a kind of Ubiquitaries. 1826 *Sporting Mag.* XVII. 262 Could it have been possible to have been an ubiquitary, I should have been with the Warwickshire, as well as with the Duke's hounds.

†**b.** *spec.* (See quot.) *Obs.*—[1]

1615 J. STEPHENS *Ess. & Charac.* xiv. 189 A Vbiquitarie Is a Iourney-man of all Trades, but no sauer because no setter vp.

†**c.** A clergyman having no settled benefice but taking duty anywhere. *Obs.*

1646 T. EDWARDS *Gangrena* I. 72 In a word, our Sectaries are become Pluralists, Nonresidents, and some of them Ubiquitaries, and are well paid for it. 1654 GAYTON *Pleas. Notes* III. viii. 117 The Priest being himself unbenefic'd, and an Ubiquetary, made bold..to pay the Non-Residentiaries ..for not stopping his mouth with a Living. 1663 BP. NICHOLSON *Expos. Catech.* Ep. Ded. A 3 These are not Ubiquitaries, and consequently are forced to be Non-residents.

†**2.** = UBIQUITARIAN *sb.* 2. *Obs.*

1585–7 T. ROGERS *39 Art.* (1625) 19 We altogether dissent ..from the Germaine Vbiquitaries..saying that Christ as man, is not onely in heauen, but in earth too at this instant. 1595 in Ellis *Orig. Lett.* Ser. III. IV. 116 A condemnacion of other reformed Churches, that did not agree with the Ubiquitaryes. 1614 BP. HALL *No Peace with Rome* § 181 Either Aquinas is false, or the papists vbiquitaries. 1654 JER. TAYLOR *Real Pres.* 156 To this the Answer is the same in effect which is given by the Roman Doctors, and by the Ubiquitaries, whom they call Hereticks. 1681 R. L'ESTRANGE *Apol. Protestants* IV. i. 98 There is no collecting from their Writings whether they were Consubstantiators or Ubiquitaries. 1709 STRYPE *Ann. Ref.* XXV. 252 Martyr in his lifetime dedicated to him his dialogue..against the Ubiquitaries.

**B.** *adj.* †**1.** = UBIQUITARIAN *a.* I. *Obs.*

1599 SANDYS *Europæ Spec.* (1632) 213 Besides the absurdity of their Ubiquitarie Chimera. *a* 1603 T. CARTWRIGHT *Confut. Rhem. N. T.* (1618) 721 The Iesuites deride the ubiquitarie Protestants, for that they could not finde how Christ should be present in all places by his Humanity, unlesse his Humanity were in every place where his Godhead is.

**2.** = UBIQUITOUS *a.* **a.** Of single persons, or the Deity. Now *rare* or *Obs.*

1609 *Ev. Woman in Hum.* IV. i. in Bullen *O. Pl.* IV, Nay looke up, beholde yon Christall pallace. There sits an ubiquitarie Judge. 1631 MASSINGER *Emperor East* I. ii, She can conjure, And I am her ubiquitary spirit. 1647 WARD *Simple Cobler* 57, I can as well admit an ubiquitary

King as another. 1673 DRYDEN *Marr. à la Mode* I. i, Besides the Court, she's the most eternal Visiter of the Town: And yet manages her time so well, that she seems ubiquitary. 1707 J. STEVENS tr. *Quevedo's Com. Wks.* (1709) 393 Then Jove said [to Olympus], Thou Vbiquitary God, shoot thy self into the World, and in a trice drag Fortune hither by the Ears. 1710 STEELE *Tatler* No. 244 ¶ 6, I remember at a full Table in the City, one of these ubiquitary Wits was entertaining the Company with a Soliloquy.

**b.** Of individual things, qualities, etc.

1625 JACKSON *Creed* V. xxvii. § 2 The fruition of His presence..cannot make saints or angels so capable of this ubiquitary knowledge as personal union with Him..might make Christ's body of ubiquitary local presence. 1640 HOWELL *Dodona's Gr.* 43 For wealth and an ubiquitary commerce none can exceed her. 1645 — *Twelve Treat.* (1661) 338 Their faculties have a kind of ubiquitary freedom, though the body be never so under restraint, as the Authors is. 1713 STEELE *Englishman* No. 22. 146 The ubiquitary Assistance of the Deity is celebrated by .. the Psalmist. 1738 *Phil. Trans.* XL. Suppl. 41 Whether God himself be not the immediate, acting, ubiquitary Cause of centripetal power. 1823 PALMERSTON *Opin. & Policy* (1852) 28 The surest though it may be the slow resource of Spain, is the desultory but ubiquitary resistance of her population.

**c.** Of a kind or class of persons or things.

1610 DONNE *Pseudo-martyr* § 35. 141 These vbiquitary Monks haue the aduantage of all others. 1642 FULLER *Holy & Prof. St.* III. xxiv. 220 It was in vain to erect any structure therein to restrain and keep his Ubiquitary beams. 1669 BAXTER *Power Mag. & Ch. Past.* I. (1671) 6 The Clergy are so numerous, subtile, ubicuitary and potent. 1709 MRS. MANLEY *Secret Mem.* (1720) II. 150 The God of Love finds little more Difficulty in Subduing the Grave than the Gay; the Desires he gives are alike Ubiquitary. 1853 G. JOHNSTON *Nat. Hist. E. Bord.* I. 121 A few, such as the Dandelion and the Daisy, may be said to be almost ubiquitary. *a* 1865 J. YOUNG *Life J. Welsh* v. i. (1866) 280 Scotsmen, in all ages roving and ubiquitary, were, at that time, settled in unprecedented numbers in..France. 1888 *Co-operative News* 4 Aug. 784 As I passed on I met two more of the ubiquitary fraternity.

**3.** Extending to all quarters; extremely wide or extensive. *rare.*

1652 URQUHART *Jewel* Wks. (1834) 194 [English] by its promiscuous and ubiquitary borrowing consisteth almost of all languages. *a* 1661 FULLER *Worthies, Barkshire* I. (1662) 92 It is impossible for any Author of a Voluminous Book consisting of several persons and circumstances..to have such Ubiquitary intelligence, as to apply the same infallibly to every particular. 1803 *Ann. Rev.* I. 257 The research displayed is ubiquitary, the materials are judiciously proportioned.

† **Ubi·quiter.** *Sc. Obs. rare.* [Cf. prec. and -ER [1].] = UBIQUITARIAN *sb.* 2.

1589 R. BRUCE *Serm. Sacram.* iii. (1590) M vj b, Will ȝe speare at the Vbiqviter, gif the true bodie of Christ be present? *a* 1599 ROLLOCK *Lect. Passion*, etc. xxxix. (1616) 381 If one goe to Germanie, he wil be an Vbiquiter, and in Rome a Papist, in Scotland a Christian.

**Ubiquitism** (yubi·kwitiz'm). [f. UBIQUIT-ARY + -ISM.] The doctrine of the omnipresence of Christ's body.

1617 COLLINS *Def. Bp. Ely* II. x. 413 Vnles you wil be so wood now, as to adde brutish Ubiquitisme to your barbarous Cyclopisme. 1630 DONNE *Serm., Easter-day* (1640) 253 *For he is risen*; And if this be a good reason, there is no Transubstantiation, no Ubiquitisme, for then Christ might have been there, though he were risen. 1728 CHAMBERS *Cycl.* s.v. *Ubiquists*, G. Hornius will only allow Brentius to be the first Propagator of Ubiquitism. 1857 PUSEY *Real Presence* i. (1869) 122 The 'Formula Concordiæ' admitted very little of the Ubiquitism of Breur; but it retained the original Ubiquitism of Luther.

† **Ubi·quitist.** *Obs.*[−1] [Cf. prec. and UBIQUIST 2.] = UBIQUITARIAN *sb.* 2.

1687 *Good Advice* 40 At this time there were Papists, Protestants, Evangelists, Præcisians, Ubiquitists, Familists or Enthusiasts and Anabaptists in England.

**Ubi·quitory,** *sb.* and *a.* *rare.* [-ORY.]

**A.** *sb.* = UBIQUITARY *sb.* 1.

1645 *Sacred Decretal* 4 Hee's such an Ubiquitory, wee know not how to deale with him.

**B.** *adj.* = UBIQUITARY *a.* 2 b.

1643 R. O. *Man's Mort.* v. 33 His humanitie not being vbiquitorie, that is, everie where at once, he must be in the creation, and in some certaine place of the creation. 1841 *Blackw. Mag.* L. 585 The arts have claimed..an ubiquitory citizenship everywhere.

**Ubiquitous** (yubi·kwitəs), *a.* [f. as UBIQUITARY + -OUS.] Present or appearing everywhere; omnipresent: **a.** Of single persons or things.

Of persons freq. with humorous exaggeration = 'turning up everywhere'.

1837 MISS SEDGWICK *Live & let Live* (1876) 60 Mrs. Broadson, who had an ubiquitous pair of ears. 1852 THACKERAY *Esmond* III. i, Here, as he lay nursing himself, ubiquitous Mr. Holt reappeared. 1860 PUSEY *Min. Proph.* 428 Heathendom was as a beleaguered city, mastered by an ubiquitous Presence, which they knew not how to meet. 1879 S. C. BARTLETT *Egypt to Pal.* i. 14 On crossing to the Continent, the marks of this ancient and ubiquitous force grew more continuous.

**b.** Of a kind or class of persons or things.

1840 E. NEWMAN *Brit. Ferns* (1844) 210 This fern appears to be ubiquitous in the moist woods and marshes. 1847 GROTE *Greece* II. xvii. III. 306 Informing himself, moreover, of passing events by means of ubiquitous spies and officials. 1878 BOSW. SMITH *Carthage* 4 Wherever a ship could penetrate,..there we find these ubiquitous, these irrepressible Phœnicians. 1887 *Pall Mall G.* 17 Dec. 2/2 The ubiquitous and unabashed British tourist.

Hence **Ubi·quitously** *adv.*, **Ubi·quitousness.**

1864 *Daily Tel.* 16 Aug., In spirit Mr. Dicey remains *ubiquitously impartial. 1882 *Standard* 25 Dec. 5/1 The modern spirit is ubiquitously triumphant. 1874 *Contemp. Rev.* XXV. 135, I have a spirit of which *ubiquitousness is an attribute. 1887 *Pall Mall G.* 8 Feb. 2/2 The coolness and courage he infused into his young troops by his ubiquitousness on the battlefield.

**Ubiquity** (yubi·kwiti). [ad. mod.L. *ubīquitas* (cf. F. *ubiquité* (17th c.), Sp. *ubicuidad*, Pg. *ubiquidade*), f. L. *ubīque* everywhere: see -ITY.]

**1.** *Theol.* The omnipresence of Christ or of his body, as maintained by the Ubiquitarians.

1579 FULKE *Heskins' Parl.* 173 If we found as good authoritie for the vbiquitie, or pluralitie of placing of his body as we finde for the feeding vs thereby into eternall life. 1597 HOOKER *Eccl. Pol.* v. lxvii. § 10 Out of which vbiquitie of his body they gather the presence thereof with that sanctified bread and wine. *a* 1617 BAYNE *On Eph.* (1618) 388 We see Vbiquity and all real Presence..ouerthrowne. 1624 BEDELL *Lett.* ii. 48 One side fetches arguments against vbiquitie from these places, and thereupon saith, the question is about these Articles. 1674 HICKMAN *Quinquart. Hist.* (ed. 2) 131 It seems, if men be never so violent for Ubiquity,..if they be but against Predestination, they shall pass for..Melancthonians. 1798 HEY *Lect. Div.* IV. IV. xxviii. § 10. 325 Luther..supported it [*sc.* consubstantiation], by what was called Ubiquity; by affirming, that the Son of God was every where, *ubique*. 1839 HALLAM *Hist. Lit.* II. ii. § 23 After the death of Melanchthon, a controversy, relating to the ubiquity, as it was called, of Christ's body, proceeded with much heat. 1882-3 SCHAFF *Encycl. Relig. Knowl.* III. 2414 Ubiquity is the doctrine ..of the omnipresence of the humanity, and more especially of the body, of Christ.

**2.** The capacity of being everywhere or in all places at the same time: **a.** In general use.

1597 HOOKER *Eccl. Pol.* v. liii. § 4 In the one there is attributed to God..death, whereof diuine nature is not capable; in the other vbiquitie vnto Man, which humane nature admitteth not. 1604 R. CAWDREY *Table Alph.*, *Vbiquitie*, presence of a person in all places. 1625 EARL CARLISLE in *Fortescue Papers* (Camden) 214, I could wishe..that you would borrow so muche of ubiquity as that your persone could be in the several places where your sufficiensy is so necessary. 1655 CLEVELAND *Gen. Poems*, etc. (1677) 142 Knowing that no place in the Nation is so remote, as not to share in the Ubiquity of your Care. 1713 CLARKE *Several Letters* (1716) 16 The Reason why you do not apprehend Ubiquity to be necessarily connected with Self-Existence. *a* 1721 PRIOR *On Coronation* i, Giving Poets to partake (Like those Deities they make) Of infinite Ubiquity. 1796 COLERIDGE *Destiny of Nations* 45 One all-conscious Spirit, which informs With absolute ubiquity of thought.. All his involved Monads. 1823 SCOTT *Quentin D.* xvi, The attention and activity which Quentin bestowed..had in it something that gave him the appearance of ubiquity. 1838 PRESCOTT *Ferd. & Is.* (1846) I. x. 427 Their vigilant adversary, who seemed now in their eyes to possess the powers of ubiquity. 1864 BOWEN *Logic* xiii. 422 It is admitted that this doctrine of the ubiquity of the mind to the body is incomprehensible.

**b.** As an attribute of God.

Variously taken as synonymous with, or as distinct from, *omnipresence*.

1607 J. DAVIES *Summa Totalis* E 2, For, so they must by his Immensitie, Which is the cause of his Vbiquity. 1664 H. MORE *Myst. Iniq.* ii. 36 It is an acknowledgement of one of the incommunicable Excellencies of God, viz. his Ubiquity. 1704 SWIFT *T. Tub* viii, This God, though endued with Ubiquity, was yet supposed to possess one peculiar Habitation. 1748 HARTLEY *Observ. Man* II. i. 34 By God's Omnipresence, or Ubiquity, we must be understood to mean that his Power and Knowlege extend to all Places. 1855 MILMAN *Lat. Chr.* VII. vi. (1864) IV. 167 The impartial ubiquity of God, the equable omnipresence of the Redeemer and the Holy Spirit throughout the whole universe. 1885 LYMAN ABBOTT in *Chr. World Pulpit* XXVIII. 179 Most Christians do not believe in the omnipresence of God; they only believe in His ubiquity.

**c.** *Law.* (See quots.)

1765 BLACKSTONE *Comm.* I. vii. 260 A consequence of this prerogative is the legal *ubiquity* of the king. His majesty, in the eye of the law, is always present in all his courts, though he cannot personally distribute justice...From this ubiquity it follows, that the king can never be nonsuit. 1841 in Peters *Rep. Supr. Crt. U.S.* XV. 6 The United States, in their sovereign capacity, have no particular place of domicile but possess, in contemplation of law, an ubiquity throughout the Union.

† **3.** Locality, region. *Obs.*[−1]

1633 B. JONSON *Love's Welcome* Wks. (1640) 275 A solemne Wight As you should meet In any street, In that Ubiquitie.

† **U·bity.** *Obs. rare.* [f. L. *ubi* UBI + -TY.] Place, locality.

1624 F. WHITE *Repl. Fisher* 451 An Angell being a finite creature, is at one instant difinitiuely in one vbitie onely. *Ibid.* 452 That which mooueth and passeth from one vbitie to another, is not in both the places at once.

**Uble, ubli, ubly,** obs. forms of OBLEY.

**U-block**; variant of *yu-block*: see YULE.

**U-boat.** [ad. G. *U-boot*, abbrev. of *Unterseeboot* 'under-sea-boat'.] A submarine.

In recent use (1913–).

† **Uch(e, vch(e,** obs. Sc. and north. ff. OUCH *sb.*

*c* 1375 [see OUCH *sb.* 1 β]. 1464 *Registr. Aberdon.* (Maitland) II. 163 Betuix þe tua vchis ij. litil garnatis; beneth þe secunde vche .ij. litil garnatis. 1488 *Acc. Ld. High Treas. Scot.* I. 81 In a litill paper within the said box, ane vche with a diamant. 1549 *Registr. Aberdon.* (Maitland) II. 196 In þe heid of þe samyn [monstrance] ane propir vch of gold. 1552 *N. Country Wills* (Surtees, 1908) 221 My best jewell which is an uche of golde after the fac[i]on of a bucle.

**Uch(e,** obs. forms of EACH *a.*

**Ud,** minced form of GOD. (Cf. AD, OD, UDS.)

1759 D. MALLET *Prol. to The Brothers* Wks. I. 41, I wish he would appear..Ud! I would give it him.

**'Ud,** abbrev. form of *would* WILL *v.*

**Udal** (yū·dăl). Forms: *α.* 6 **outhale, 6–7 outhell, owthell, 7 owthall; 6 uthall, -ail, 6–7 -ale, 7 -el.** *β.* **6–7 owdaill, 6– udal, 7 udail, udell, uddal, utal.** [Orkney and Shetland form of Norw. *odal, odel*, ON. *óðal* ODAL.]

**1.** *attrib.* **a.** *Udal land* or *lands*, land(s) in Orkney or Shetland held by the old native form of freehold tenure.

*α.* ?1502 in Peterkin *Rentals Orkney* (1820) I. 6 Tankarnes xij d terre uthall land. 1576 in *Reg. Mag. Sig. Scot.* (1890) 479/2 The said James outhale landis of Gartht, lyand within the parochin of Stronnes, Menland of Orknay. 1592 *Ibid.* (1892) 118/1 The haill skatt of the uthail land within the said yle baith butter and wadmell. 1609 *Ibid.* 129/1 Et omnium lie owthall-landis in dicto rentali content.

*β.* 1576 *Reg. Privy Council Scot.* II. 488 Being heretour of the udall land of the Yle of Gairsay in Orknay. 1633 *Reg. Mag. Sig. Scot.* 757/1, 1½ den. ex antiquo lie kingisland et ½ den. lie utalandis nuncupat. *Ibid.* 757/2, 24 den. kingisland et udailland in dicta villa. 1649 *Ibid.* 769/2 Towmale of uddalland vocat. Skegebuster. 1664 in Gifford *Descr. Zetland* (1886) 65 The lands called Udell-lands, lying within the said earldom. 1707 *Ibid.* 68 Sundry isles..udell-lands, and other lands. 1795 *Statist. Acc. Scot.* XV. 393 Some of the udal lands pay a small proportion of yearly rent to the King, and to the kirk. 1805 G. BARRY *Hist. Orkney Isl.* II. v. 219 These udal or allodial lands are directly opposed to fees or feus. 1884 *Scotsman* 26 July 3/1 Two Merks and One-Half Merk Udal Land.

† **b.** Placed after the sb. (sometimes in contrast to 'royal'). *Obs.*

1584 *Reg. Mag. Sig. Scot.* 264/1 Cum..scattis terrarum regalium et outhell de Southerbie..et owthell de Noltland. *Ibid.*, Cum scattis..terrarum regalium et owdaill de Sandweik. 1602 in A. Peterkin *Notes Orkney & Zetl.* (1822) App. 40 The richt and tytil of 6 mark land uthel, lyand in the town of Gruting. 1627 in Peterkin *Rentals Orkney* (1820) III. 45 Lynais is ane d. land outhell.

**c.** With other sbs., as *men, right, tenure*, etc.

*c* 1500 in A. Peterkin *Orkney & Zetl.* (1822) 88 The uthale men. 1587 in *Edinb. Antiq. Mag.* (1849) 60 He hes Reft and spulzeit diuerss of the uthallmen and heretors..of Orknay and Zetland of yair proper heritaige. 1669 in Peterkin *Orkney & Zetl.* (1822) 190 That their udal right may be sustained valid in all tyme coming. *a* 1688 J. WALLACE *Descr. Orkney* (1693) 94 *Udall-lands*, such as are possessed by the Udall-right, a possession the natives have successively without either Charter or Seasin. 1750 in Hibbert *Descr. Shetl. Isl.* (1822) 192 The udalmen were likewise called Rothmen or Roythmen; that is, self-holders. 1765-8 ERSKINE *Inst. Law Scot.* II. iii. § 18 The udal right of the stewartry of Orkney and Zetland is of the same nature. 1793 *Statist. Acc. Scot.* VII. 239 There are three kinds of tenure of lands in Scotland... Thirdly, the Udal, being a right compleat without writing. 1805 G. BARRY *Hist. Orkney Isl.* II. v. 219 The laws by which this udal property was inherited, sold, redeemed, or transmitted from one person to another. 1814 SCOTT *Diary* 4 August in *Lockhart*, The Udal proprietors have ceased to exist, yet proper feudal tenures seem ill understood. 1821 — *Pirate* xix, The wide Udal possessions of their father..were divided betwixt the brothers. 1909 J. GUNN *Orkney Bk.* 110 In Scotland land was held according to the feudal system, in Orkney according to the udal system.

**2.** The form of freehold tenure characteristic of Orkney and Shetland; land held in this way.

1588 *Reg. Mag. Sig. Scot.* 547/1 To be haldin..off our soverane lord..in fie, heretage, frie uthall and blensche for evir. 1750 in Hibbert *Descr. Shetl. Isl.* (1822) 192 Their udals, at this day, are not transmitted like other lands, but with the..compleat propriety and demesne of the subject.

**Udaller** (yū·dălər). Also 8 **udiller, udelar, 9 udeler, uddaler.** [f. prec. + -ER. Cf. ODALLER.] A tenant of land by udal right. Also *attrib.*

1669 in Peterkin *Orkney & Zetl.* (1822) 190 [An act] for the udallers of Orknay and Zetland. 1671 *Shetland Doct.* in *Proc. Soc. Antiq. Scot.* (1892) XXVI. 194 He..shall not suffer the same [lands] to be incrotched upon be the ffewaries, udallers and uythers. *Ibid.*, The ffewares, udallers, tennendes, occupiers of the landis [etc.]. 1733 GIFFORD *Descr. Zetland* (1886) 9 The head courts..where all the Udillers were obliged to convene. 1798 *Statist. Acc. Scot.* XX. 269 There are six udelars in Deerness. 1805 G. BARRY *Hist. Orkney Isl.* I. ii. 28 Men here called Udallers, who are little proprietors of land, that has never been held by the feudal tenure, nor subjected to either service or payment to any superior. 1821 SCOTT *Pirate* xvii, The stout-hearted and experienced general, for so the Udaller might be termed. 1884 *Gd. Words* Nov. 747/2 The last remains of the old udallers are to be found amongst the 'peerie (small) lairds' of Fladdabister.

**U·dally,** *adv.* [f. as prec. + -LY [2].] By udal right or tenure; under the udal system.

1909 J. GUNN *Orkney Bk.* 111 It must not be supposed that all the land in Orkney was held udally, or that all the inhabitants were udallers.

**Udder** (*v*·dəɹ). Forms: *α.* **1 udr-, 4 vddre, 5 vddyr (6 Sc. vdyr), 5–7 vdder (6 vtter, odder), 6– udder; 5–6 uther (9 Sc.), 6 other.** *β.* **5 iddyr, 6 ydder.** [OE. *úder* (once), = OS. *ūdar, ūder-*, MLG. (LG.) *ūder*, MDu. *ūder, uyder* (Du. *uier, uijer*, WFlem. *eur*; cf. WFris. *ūr* teat), OHG. *ūtar* (and *ūtiro*), MHG. *ūter* and *iuter* (G. *euter*):—OTeut. **ūđr-*, = Gr. *οὖθαρ*, Skr. *ūdhar, -as* (also *ūdhan*), L. *ūber*. By unexplained consonant change the corresponding ON. form is *júgr* EWER [3], YURE. It is doubtful whether an OTeut. variant, or an entirely different stem, is represented by OFris. *iader* (EFris. *jader, jæder*, NFris. *jidder*, etc., WFris. *jaer*), older Du. *jadder* (dial.

*jaar*), OS. *geder*, MLG. *geder*, *jeder* (LG. *jidder*, *jüdder*). In English the original long vowel has been regularly shortened before the consonant-group *-der*.]

**1.** The pendulous baggy organ, provided with two or more teats or nipples, by which the milk is secreted in certain female animals.

*a* **1000** *Kentish Gl.* 203 *Uberibus*, of udrum. **1398** TREVISA *Barth. De P. R.* XVIII. xviii. (Bodl. MS.), Þe Camel haþ foure tettes and tweyne vddres as þe cowe haþ. *a* **1425** tr. *Arderne's Treat. Fistula*, etc. 12 Wolle þat groweth atuix þe leggez of ane ewe about þe vdder. *c* **1440** *Promp. Parv.* 258/2 Iddyr, or vddyr of a beeste, *Uber*. **1515** BARCLAY *Egloges* iv. (1570) Ciij b/2 Your cowes others of milke replete and full. *Ibid.* Ciiij/1 Leane be my lambes,..And yet their dammes they dayly sucke so dry, That from the uthers no licoure can we wring. *c* **1518** SKELTON *Magnyf.* 1814, I saw a fox sucke on a kowes ydder; And with a lyme rodde I toke them bothe togyder. *c* **1534** in *Suss. Star Chamber Proc.* (1913) 21 The..Kyn were in suche payn for lake of myikyng that the mylke rane oute of there odderens and so lyke to be all perishte. **1577** B. GOOGE *Heresbach's Husb.* III. (1586) 139 b, The Lambe..must be sette on foote, and put to the dammes vdder. **1613** PURCHAS *Pilgrimage* IV. xi. 349 Next to the doore on the womens side..there is an Image with a Cowes Vdder for the women,..on the other side another with a Mares Vdder for the men. **1665** BOYLE *Occas. Refl.* IV. iii. 16, I..approach'd the place where the fair Milk-maid was solliciting the Udder of a fresh Cow. **1634** *Lond. Gaz.* No. 1910/4 A Red Cow of about 5 or 6 years old, with a White Udder. *c* **1720** W. GIBSON *Farrier's Guide* I. ii. (1738) 19 The Udder is another part peculiar to a Mare. **1773** JOHNSON in *Boswell* (1831) III. 47 Milk pressed from the swelling udder by the gentle hand of the beauteous milk-maid. **1799** *Med. Jrnl.* I. 314 A spurious cow-pox.. arising from pustules on the nipples or udder of the cow. **1847** W. C. L. MARTIN *Ox* 41/1 A twin heifer..which..was very handsome, with a well-formed udder, and was a good milker. **1867** BAKER *Nile Trib.* v. (1872) 75 The distended udders of thousands of camels were an assurance of plenty.

**b.** This part of an animal as an article of food.

**1474** in *Househ. Ord.* (1790) *32 The purveyors of beeves and muttons..hath to theire fees the oxe heads, muttons heades, the rumpes of every beefe, and the intrayles of every beaste excepte the oxe feete, and the uthers. **1598** *Epulario* Iiiij, Fifteene Egs, with a Cowes Udder wel sodden. **1660** PEPYS *Diary* 11 Oct., Mr. Creed and I to the Leg in King Street, where he and I, and my Will had a good udder to dinner. **1675** HANNAH WOOLLEY *Gentlew. Comp.* 158/1 Neats tongue and Udder roasted. **1721** *Queen's Closet* 99 To Roast a Cows Udder. **1842** A. COMBE *Physiol. Digestion* (ed. 4) 35 Four pounds of cow's udder and ten pounds of raw beef.

**2.** *poet.* (in *pl.*) A dug or teat. *rare.*

**1582** STANYHURST *Æneis* II. (Arb.) 55 Theyre whelps neere starued ar eager And expect vdders with dry iaws. **1600** SHAKS. *A. Y. L.* IV. iii. 115 Vnder which bushes shade A Lyonesse, with vdders all drawne drie, Lay cowching head on ground. **1887** BOWEN *Virg. Ecl.* III. 30 Twice each day she is milked; though still at her udders we leave Two young calves.

† **3.** The breast of a woman. *Obs.*⁻¹

*a* **1704** T. BROWN *Pleas Lett. to Gent.* Wks. 1709 III. II. 16 Their Udders swagging down to their Navils.

**4.** *attrib.* and *Comb.*, as *udder-cattle*, *-flank*, *part*; **udder-clap**, inflammation in the udder; **udder-ill** (see quot. 1847); **udder-lock** *sb.* (see quot. *a* 1808); *v. trans.*, to pull away the wool from the udders of (sheep).

*a* **1722** LISLE *Husb.* (1757) 214 The oak-buds killed five of the udder-cattle. *Ibid.* 345 It was the udder-flank, or throat, that they usually bit the sheep in. **1798** R. DOUGLAS *Agric. Roxb.* 156 *note*, All sheep are *udder-locked*, as it is here called, that being thought refreshing and salutary. **1806** A. HUNTER *Culina* (ed. 3) 256 Under the udder part of a leg of veal, there is a large piece of meat. *a* **1808** *Essays Highl. Soc.* III. 250 (Jam.) Udderlocks are the wool plucked from the udder. **1825** JAMIESON, *Udder-clap*, a sort of schirrous tumour affecting the udder of ewes, by an unexpected return of milk after being sometime *eild*. Teviotd. **1844** H. STEPHENS *Bk. Farm* II. 620 After recovery from lambing, the only complaint the ewe is subject to is inflammation in the udder, or *udder-clap*, or *garget*. **1847** W. C. L. MARTIN *Ox* 172/2 Loss of milk, or milk of a disgusting taste and odour, and consequently unfit for use, results from derangement of the digestive organs, and especially from morbid affections of the fourth stomach, and the animal is said to labour under 'udder-ill'.

Hence **U·dderful** *a.*, having a full udder; **U·dderless** *a.*, unsucked, motherless.

**1818** KEATS *Endym.* I. 210 All ye gentle girls who foster up Udderless lambs. **1879** MEREDITH *Egoist* Prelude, Listen..to an unleavened society: a low as of the udderful cow past milking hour!

**Udder, -ir,** dial. and obs. Sc. forms of OTHER.

**U·ddered,** *a.* [f. UDDER + -ED.]

† **1.** Suckled. *Obs.*⁻¹

**1582** STANYHURST *Æneis* IV. (Arb.) 108 Amydst rocks, Caucasus haggish Bred the, with a tigers soure milck vnseasoned, vdderd.

**2.** Having an udder or udders; provided with a teat or teats.

**1652** BENLOWES *Theoph.* XII. cxv, See where the udderd Cattle finde us food. **1714** GAY *Sheph. Week* II. 11 Marian, that soft could stroke the udder'd cow. **1725** POPE *Odyss.* IX. 282 Big-udder'd ewes, and goats of female kind. **1826** *Blackw. Mag.* XX. 782 A mother-matron, with a baboon visage, and uddered like a cow. **1870** MORRIS *Earthly Par.* III. 278 Deep-uddered kine Went lowing towards the pails at eventide. **1875** — *Æneid* VIII. 45 There lieth she All white along, and piglings white around her uddered sides.

**3.** Contained in the udder.

*a* **1814** A. BECKET *Genii* i. in *New Brit. Theatre* I. 518 Nor let the heifers of the vale In udder'd treasure ever fail.

† **U·ddery,** *a. Obs.*⁻¹ [f. UDDER + -Y.] Soft as the flesh of an udder.

**1398** TREVISA *Barth. De P. R.* V. xlviii. (Bodl. MS.), Constantine seiþ þat these stones þe substaunce of ham is ymade of vddry and cruddy flessch.

**Ude,** var. of *yode* went: see GO *v.* A 3.

**Udelar, -er,** obs. forms of UDALLER.

**Udell,** obs. form of UDAL.

**Udell,** variant of ALUDEL.

**1894** ROSCOE & SCHORLEMMER *Treat. Chem.* (new ed.) I. 201 Each cover is fitted with a leaden pipe, and this is connected with a series of glass or earthenware condensers, termed udells, fitting one into the other.

**Uder,** obs. Sc. form of OTHER.

† **Udfoot,** variant of *Ud's foot*: see UDS.

**1620** I. C. *Two Merry Milk-maids* I. iii. C 4, *Fer.* Vdfoot, what will the young Duke doe trow? *Ibid.*, *Jul.* Vdfoot, we shalbe whipt anon for this Abuse.

† **Udge,** var. JUDGE *v.* (attributed to Welsh speakers).

**1598** SHAKS. *Merry W.* I. i. 191 So got-udge me, that is a vertuous minde. **1603** DEKKER *Patient Grissill* 588 By Cods vdge me, is all true.

**Udged,** *a. Mining.* (See quot.)

**1883** GRESLEY *Gloss. Coal-M.* 266 *Udged*, loose, weak, liable to fall, sounding hollow, or unsound. A roof or a piece of side is said to *knock udged* when it produces a dead, hollow, unsafe sound, upon being knocked upon with a hammer, &c.

**Udiller,** obs. form of UDALLER. **Udimia,** obs. f. ŒDEMA. **Udir,** obs. Sc. f. OTHER.

**Udometer** (yudǫ·mĭtəɹ). [ad. F. *udomètre*, f. L. *ūdus* wet, damp: see -METER.] A rain-gauge.

**1825** *Reg. Arts & Sci.* III. 142 An improved Udometer, to shew the quantity of Rain fallen. **1873** *Routledge's Young Gentl. Mag.* Feb. 162/1 His thermometers,..hygrometers, and udometers.

Hence **Udome·tric** *a.* [F. *udométrique*.]

**1891** *Cent. Dict.*

† **Uds.** *Obs.* Also 7 ud's, udds, udz. [Minced form of *God's*, possessive of GOD *sb.*, or of *God s'* = God save. Cf. ADS and ODS.] A form of the name of God common in expletive oaths in the 17th century.

**1.** In possessive phrases (cf. GOD *sb.* 14), frequently written as one word, as *Ud's blood*, *bluff*, *bobblekens*, *-bows*, *-bud*, *-buddikins*, etc.

**1607** DEKKER & WEBSTER *Northw. Hoe* II. i, *Vds bloud ile laie him crosse vpon his coxcomb next daie. **1664** H. BOLD *Poems* 162 They swore Udz niggs, we swore *Udz bluffe. **1681** T. FLATMAN *Heraclitus Ridens* No. 42 (1713) II. 21 *Udds Bobblekens, quoth he, I were wet to the skin. **1684** D'URFEY *Sev. New Songs* 9 *Udsbows, cries my Country-man John, Was ever the like before seen? **1681** OTWAY *Soldier's Fort.* II. i, Ah! *udds-bud, they'd ..have stript for t'other Bottle. **1689** SHADWELL *Bury F.* II. 19 A very good jest! Udsbud, there's a pair of Gloves of the same mettle, to stop your pretty Mouth. **1740** tr. *De Mouhy's Fort. Country Maid* (1741) I. 59 *Udsbuddikins, were I in Colin's Place, I know what I would do. **1607** DEKKER & WEBSTER *Westw. Hoe* v. iii, *Vds Daggers? cannot sinne be set a shore once in a raigne vpon your Country quarters, but it must haue fidling? **1821** SCOTT *Kenilw.* iii, Uds daggers! I tell thee, man, mine own stock of assurance was too small to trade upon. **1607** DEKKER & WEBSTER *Westw. Hoe* IV. ii, *Vds death speake, or ile kil thee. **1702** VANBRUGH *False Friend* II. i, Keep a woman honest? Udsdeath! I'd as soon undertake to keep Portocarero honest! **1854** H. AINSWORTH *Flitch of Bacon* I. v. 43 'Udsdeath! I wish he hadn't arrested him here,' the landlord said. **1698** MOTTEUX *Quix.* (1733) I. 269 *Uds-diggers, quoth Sancho, I know her full well. *a* **1586** SIDNEY *Pansies Penshurst & Wilton* vi, Doth she call the faith of man In question? nay, *uds foot, she loves thee than. **1608** DAY *Hum. out of Br.* IV. iii, Vdsfoot, your iaylor, my lord. **1623** WEBSTER *Devil's Law-Case* IV. ii, Vd's foot, we are spoyled. **1630** DEKKER *2nd Pt. Honest Wh.* IV. i, Vds foot, Giue me some meate. **1676** D'URFEY *Madam Fickle* III. i, *Udshash! I'd like to have spoil'd all, I took him for a Morrice-Dancer. **1614** J. COOKE *Greene's Tu Quoque* E 1 b, *Vdslid, I'le not be out-brau'd. *Ibid.*, Vdslid, I am gleek't this time. *Ibid.* H 3 b, *Vds'life, this is excellent: now she talkes. **1706** VANBRUGH *Mistake* I. 92 Udslife! Sir! attack her with a fiddle! **1611** MIDDLETON & DEKKER *Roaring Girl* II. ii, *Vds light the tide's against me. **1618** N. FIELD *Amends for Ladies* I. (1639) B 2 b, Vd'slight whats the matter, wring him by the nose. **1632** MASSINGER & FIELD *Fatal Dowry* II. ii, Vd's-light, enjoy your wishes. **1680** DRYDEN *Limberham* IV. i, *Saint.* *Uds Niggers, but I will... *Wood.* Uds Niggers, I confess, is a very dreadful Oath. **1664** *Uds nigs [see *Uds bluff* above]. **1719** D'URFEY *Pills* IV. 96 Uds nigs, quoth I, what a Kirk beth' here. **1614** J. COOKE *Greene's Tu Quoque* B 2 b, *Vds pitty! unbutton man, thou'lt stifle her else. **1613** BEAUM. & FL. *Honest Man's Fort.* II. iv, *Udsprecious, we have lost a brother. **1821** SCOTT *Kenilw.* iv, Uds precious! madam, what make you here out of bounds? **1611** MIDDLETON & DEKKER *Roaring Girl* IV. ii. Kij, *Vds so Mol, where's that Trapdore? **1659** *Lady Alimony* II. i. B iij b, Uds so, will their dainty fingers tug in Alume work? **1695** CONGREVE *Love for L.* I. vi, Udso that's true, Mr. Valentine, I love Mirth, but Business must be done. **1697** VANBRUGH *Relapse* v. v, *Udsookers! they set my old blood a-fire! **1777** SHERIDAN *Trip Scarb.* v. ii, Udzookers! Now six words more, and I'll forgive them directly. **1611** MIDDLETON & DEKKER *Roaring Girl* IV. ii. I iij, *Vd' soule do but name that rascall. **1697** VANBRUGH *Relapse* III. v, *Udswoons! I'll give my wench a wedding-dinner. **1698** — *Æsop* II. 457 '*Udzwooks!' quoth he, 'With all your meat, I will maintain a dish of pease..Is much a better treat'. **1721** AMHERST *Terræ Fil.* No. 44 (1726) 236 Udzooks, I believe 'tis the hugest varsity alive.

**2.** In *Uds me*, *uds my life*: see GOD *sb.* 8 b.

**1635** [GLAPTHORNE] *Lady Mother* IV. i. in Bullen *O. Pl.* (1883) II. 169 Udsme, my lady! **1668** DRYDEN *Maiden Queen* v. i, Uds my life! here's the queen's music just going to us. **1702** FARQUHAR *Inconstant* II. ii, Uds my life—here's one.

**Uein, Ueir, Uell,** southern ME. varr. FAIN *adv.*, FAIR *a.*, FELL *v.* **Uell,** obs. Sc. f. WEAL *sb.* **Uerry,** southern ME. var. *ferre* FAR *v.*; obs. Sc. f. VERY *adv.* **Uewe,** obs. f. VIEW *sb.*

**Ufel,** obs. f. EVIL. **Ufemest,** var. OVEMEST *a. Obs.* **Ufenan, -en,** varr. OVENON, -AN *Obs.*

**Ufer** (yū·fəɹ). Also 9 upher. [Variant spelling of JUFFER. See also EUPHROE.] (See quot. 1842.)

**1754** T. GARDNER *Hist. Dunwich* 257 The Master found an Expedient to make a Stage with Ufers (he had on board), and Planks, to bear the Carriages. **1795** *Act 35 Geo. III*, c. 20 Sch. A, Ufers, imported from any Part of Europe, five Inches square and under eight Inches square, or if twenty-four Feet in Length or upwards. **1812** J. SMYTH *Pract. of Customs* (1821) 426 Ufers, being 5 inches square or upwards, are subject and liable to the Duties payable on Fir Timber. **1833** *Rep. Sel. Comm. on Munic. Corporations* 320 Water-bailiffs dues, payable to Corporation of Hull...Ufers, double ..—, single. **1842** GWILT *Archit.* 1049 *Uphers*, fir poles, from four to seven inches in diameter, and from twenty to forty feet in length.

**Ufere, Uferr-mar,** obs. ff. OVER *a.*, OVERMORE *adv.* **Uforbium,** obs. form of EUPHORBIUM.

**Ufreet,** variant of AFREET, EFREET.

**1847** L. HUNT *Jar Honey* i. (1848) 3 The vapour reached its height, and condensed,..and became an Ufreet (evil spirit), his head in the clouds, and his foot on the soil.

**Ug,** *sb. Obs.* exc. *dial.* [a. ON. *ugg-r*: cf. next. In mod. dial. use perh. from the vb.] Fear, dread.

*a* **1240** *Lofsong* in *O. E. Hom.* I. 209 For-ȝif me mine sunnen;..louerd, ich i-seo ham wiđ muchel ugge of þin eie.

**Ug** (ʋg), *v. Obs.* exc. *dial.* Forms: 3 *subj.* uggi, 4–6 ugge (vgge, 5 vggyn, -one), 5–6, 9 ugg (*Sc.* 5 owgg, 6 vgg, wegg), 5–6, 8–9 ug (5–6 vg, 6 *Sc.* wg); 5 ughe, uge. [a. ON. *ugga* to fear, dread, apprehend: cf. prec. and HUGGE *v.*]

**1.** *trans.* To inspire or affect with dread, loathing, or disgust.

*a* **1225** *Ancr. R.* 92 Ȝe schulen biholden sumetime touward te pine of helle, þet ou agrupie aȝean ham [*Titus MS.* þet ow uggi wið ham]. **1434** MISYN *Mending Life* 122 If my handis schyne as clennes,..ȝit sall þou toche me with fylth,..& my clothes sall vg me. *c* **1440** *Alph. Tales* 157 He spewid oute a grete froske...And when Nero lukid þervppon, hym vggid þerwith. *c* **1450** *St. Cuthbert* (Surtees) 7069 What he suld do he na wyste With þe sacrement..; him vgged to vse it and to ete. **1560** ROLLAND *Seven Sages* 124 My flesche it vggis quhen yt I tuitche his hyde. **1894** HESLOP *Northumbld. Gloss.* 754 He was ugged wi' eatin the stuff.

**2.** *intr.* To feel dread or apprehension, disgust or loathing. Usu. const. *at*, *of*, or *with*.

*a* **1340** HAMPOLE *Psalter* xxxiv. 7 Wha is þat vggis not with a way þat is bath myrke & sliþer. *c* **1340** — *Pr. Consc.* 6419 For þa paynes er swa fel and hard,..Þat ilk man may ugge, batheyhunge and alde, Þat heres þam be reherced and talde. *c* **1380** WYCLIF *Sel. Wks.* III. 117 Ne ugge þou not wiþ seknesse of þyn evyn Cristyn. *c* **1400** *Sc. Trojan War* II. 1097 Nought at the deth sche wggis there. **14..** *Tundale's Vis.* 317 Of hit was Tundale fulle yrke. When he hit sawe, he ugged sore. **1434** MISYN *Mending of Life* 122 My flesch makis me vg of my-self. *c* **1440** *Alph. Tales* 209 He vgged so with þe fend þat he cryed hugelie, & said he wold nott go with hym. *c* **1590** J. STEWART *Poems* (S.T.S.) II. 228 Glottonnie he vas so filthie fy, I vggit vith the discheis quhilk he buir. **1865** JANET HAMILTON *Poems* (1885) 100 It's no the wife that curls her nose At cogs o' sowens or cadger's brose, An' uggs at lang-kail.

† **b.** Const. *to* with inf. *Obs.*

*a* **1395** HYLTON *Scala Perf.* II. xv (W. de W. 1494), It is made..soo dredfull to her thynkynge that they uggen & lothen for to thinke vpon it. **1435** MISYN *Fire of Love* 43 Þa vg..to be borne to þer lust. *c* **1440** *Alph. Tales* 478 Becauce þou vggid to sla so mych innocent blude. *c* **1560** A. SCOTT *Poems* xxxiv. 119, I vg, for villanie, ȝour vycis to reherss. **1562** WINȜET *Vincent. Lirin.* xi. Wks. (S.T.S.) II. 31 Quhat materis I pray ȝow? I wg to tell.

**c.** *Sc.* (See quot.)

**1824** MACTAGGART *Gallovid. Encycl.*, *Ugg*, to vomit.

**3.** *trans.* To abhor, loathe, detest.

*a* **1340** HAMPOLE *Ps.* xli. 13 He þis felid of þe swetnes of heuen, and vggid þe perils of þe warld. *c* **1400** *Apol. Loll.* 109 Wylful begging of stalworþ men..of Salomon..is vggid, and many fold reprouid of holy doctoris. **1435** MISYN *Fire of Love* 64 A trew sawle..lufys meyknes; vaynglory it vggis, for myrth euer-lastyng onely desyrand. *a* **1568** '*My Mistres*' 26 in *Bannatyne Poems* (1881) VII. 1081, I hate and vgg hir greedie dispositioune. **1721** RAMSAY *To Earl Dalhousie* 47 What his kind frighted mother ugs, Is music to the soger's lugs. **1793** T. SCOTT *Poems* 367 Thus ane aye seekin' what another ugs. **1825** BROCKETT *N. C. Gloss.*, *Ug*, to feel abhorrence at.

Hence † **Ugged** *ppl. a.*, horrid, loathsome. *Obs.*⁻⁰ **U·gging** *ppl. a.*, causing loathing or disgust. *Sc.*

**1570** LEVINS *Manip.* 49/20 Vgged, *fædus*. **1832–53** A. MACLAGGAN in *Whistle-binkie* Ser. II. 118 I'm neither sae auld, auld, Nor am I sae gruesome or uggin.

**Uge,** ME. variant of HUGE *a.*

† **Ugertful,** *a. Sc. Obs.* Also ogert-. [f. OGART.] Proud; nice, squeamish.

**1755** FORBES *Jrnl. fr. London* 29 Ye ken well enough that I was never vera ogertfu'. *c* **1770** BEATTIE *To Alex. Ross* 63 Our fine newfangle sparks, I grant ye,..They're grown sae ugertfu' and vaunty. **1808** JAMIESON.

**U·gging,** *vbl. sb.* [f. UG *v.* + -ING [1].] Dread, fear, horror, loathing.

*c* 1250 *Gen. & Ex.* 950 Ðo cam on him vging [L. *horror*] and friȝt. *Ibid.* 2826 Vgging and dred me haueð numen. *a* 1340 HAMPOLE *Psalter, Song Moses* ii. 13 He fand him in land deserte: in stede of vggynge [L. *in loco horroris*], and in waste wildirnes. *Ibid.*, In þe wrechidnes of þis life, in þe qwilke is vggynge for drede of wa. 1650–1 R. BAILLIE *Lett. & Jrnls.* (1842) III. 126 The ugging of sundrie good people to see numbers of grievous bloodshedders ready to come in.

† **U·ggle**, *a. Obs.*—⁰ [f. the stem of UG *sb.* and *v.* Cf. OUGLE *a.*, and mod.Norw. *uggall* (Ross).] = UGLY *a.* 1.

1499 *Promp. Parv.* (Pynson), Vggyll, *horridus, horribilis.* [Pynson has also the verb *ugglyn* for *uggyn, uggone* (see UG *v.*) of the manuscripts.]

**Ugglesome** (*v*·g'lsəm), *a.* Now *rare.* Also 6–7 vgle-; 9 **ogglesome.** *β.* 6–7 **ouglesome.** [app. f. prec. + -SOME.] Fearful, horrible, gruesome.

*a.* 1561 T. HOBY tr. *Castiglione's Courtyer* III. (1577) Q viij, Some are compelled by their fathers to take olde men full of diseases vglesome and wayward. *Ibid.* IV. X iij b, A face darke, vglesome, vnpleasaunt, and to be shunned for yll. 1576 FOXE *A. & M.* (ed 3) 1904/2 When I beholde the amiable countenance of Christ..yᵉ vglesome [1563 vgsome] face of death doth not greatly trouble me. 1583 STUBBES *Anat. Abus.* I. (1877) 188 They shal be punished in fire and brimstone amongest the terrible Company of vgglesome Deuills. 1591—*Christal Glasse* C ij b, As though she saw some filthie vgglesome, and displeasant thing. 1617 J. MOORE *Mappe Mans Mort.* I. viii. 58 It shewed..our vglesome shape, most monstrous to beholde. 1855 *Chambers' Jrnl.* 7 July 13 This 'ugglesome beast' seldom troubles me, for his dwelling is in some secluded cleft of the stone. 1864 SALA in *Daily Tel.* 14 Nov., That weird and ogglesome beast the Wangdoodlum.

*β.* 1575 VAUTROLLIER *Luther on Ep. Gal.* 260 In the wilde wildernes, which being burnt vp with the heat of the Sunne, yeldeth an ouglesome habitation to the Monkes. 1608 DOD & CLEAVER *Expos. Prov.* xi–xii. 69 In the froward he seeth the work of the diuell, whereby they are deprauec and made most vile & ouglesome. 1622 S. WARD *Life of Faith in Death* (1627) 26 When I behold the ouglesome face of death, I am afrayd, but when I consider Christs amiable Countenance, I take heart againe. [Cf. quot. 1576 above.]

**Uggliness, Uggly**, obs. varr. UGLINESS, UGLY.

**Ugh** (uʰ, *v*ʰ), *int.* and *sb.* [Imitative.]

**1.** A representation of an inarticulate sound of the nature of a hollow cough; a sound or utterance of this nature.

1765 FOOTE *Commissary* I. (1782) 12 Ugh, ugh, ugh—[coughs]. 1822 SCOTT *Nigel* xxiii, The usurer..concluded his speech with a dry 'ugh, ugh'. 1859 THACKERAY *Virgin.* li, The next moment,..with an *ugh*, the Indian fell over my chest dead. 1887 L. OLIPHANT *Episodes* (1888) 70 My address was frequently interrupted by what Fenimore Cooper calls 'expressive ughs'.

**2.** An interjection expressive of disgust.

1837 HOWITT *Rur. Life* II. v. (1862) 140 The overhanging banks of the most transparent streams—ugh! they are now the very lurking-places of danger! 1855 BROWNING *Childe Roland* xxi, It may have been a water-rat I speared, But, ugh! it sounded like a baby's shriek. 1878 DALE *Lect. Preach.* viii. 242 Physic..all the year round;..ugh!—it is intolerable.

**Ugh(e**, obs. forms of YEW.

**Ughin**, var. of dial. *agin* AGAIN *prep.*

1767 S. PATERSON *Another Trav.* I. 368 Six to four ughin your lordship, and I say done first.

† **U·ghten.** *Obs.* Forms: 1 **uhtan**, 3 **uhhtenn**, 4 **vȝten, vghtene.** See also OUGHTEN. [Common Teutonic: OE. *ūhtan*, obl. form of **ūhte* wk. fem. = OS. *ūhta* (MLG. *uchten*, LG. *ucht*; MDu. *uchten, ochten*, Du. *ucht-, ochtend*), OHG. *ūhtā*, *uohtā* (MHG. *uohte, uhte*), Goth. *ūhtwō*, ON. and Icel. *ótta* (Norw. and Sw. *otta*) in the same sense: relationship to forms outside of Germanic is uncertain. In ME., as in MLG. and MDu., the oblique case in which the word commonly occurred was adopted in place of the original nominative.]

**1.** The part of the night immediately before daybreak; early morning.

*Beowulf* 126 Ða wæs on uhtan mid ærdæʒe Grendles guðcræft gumum undyrne. 971 *Blickling Hom.* 47 Syxtan siþe on niht ær he ræste, seofoþan siþe on uhtan. *c* 1000 *Saxon Leechd.* III. 20 Læt standan þreo niht; syle drincan ær uhton lytle ne scænc fulne. *c* 1200 ORMIN 2484 Godess enngell comm himm to Onn uhhtenn þær he sleppte. *a* 1300 *K. Horn* 1474 (Camb. MS.), Hi sloȝen & fuȝten, Þe niȝt & þe vȝten. 13.. *E. E. Allit. P.* B. 893 Ruddon of þe dayrawe ros vpon vȝten, When merk of þe mydnyȝt moȝt no more last. 13.. *St. Erkenwolde* 118 in Horstm. *Altengl. Leg.* (1881) 268 Ser Erkenwolde was vp in þe vghtene ere þene.

**2.** *attrib.* in *ughten-tide*; also **ughten-song**, = UHTSONG.

*c* 900 tr. *Bæda's Eccl. Hist.* IV. xii. 300 Neowe steorra..in uhttide [*Ca.* uhtantide] wæs ýpeornende. *c* 950 *Lindisf. Gosp.* Mk. xiii. 35 On uhte tid [*Rushw.* uhtu-tid] *vel* on honcroed. *c* 1200 ORMIN 5832 Hu Crist ras upp off dæþe Onn uhhtenntid te þridde daȝȝ. *Ibid.* 6360 Wiþþ daȝȝsang & wiþþ uhhtennsang, Wiþþ messess & wiþþ beness. 13.. [see next].

Hence **U·ghtening** (also *dial.* **oachenin**), in the same sense.

*a* 1300 *E. E. Psalter* lxxii. 14, I was swongen al þe dai, And in vghteninges [*Harl. MS.* uhtentide] mi þhraying ai. *Ibid.* c. 9 In vghteninge I slogh with hand Alle þe sinful of þe land. *c* 1900 *Eng. Dial. Dict.* (Caithness dial.), *Oachenin*, the early dawn.

**Uglesome**, variant of UGGLESOME *a.*

**Uglification** (*v*glifikēⁱ·ʃən). [f. next: see -FICATION.]

**1.** The action or process of making ugly.

1820 SHELLEY *Œd. Tyr.* I. 409 Where, for more glory, let the ceremony Take place of the uglification of the Queen. 1863 *N. & Q.* 3rd Ser. IV. 521 A more thorough uglification of our written or spoken language could hardly have been devised. 1890 *Longm. Mag.* Mar. 506 Their experiments in the science of comparative uglification.

**2.** That which renders ugly.

1893 *Westm. Gaz.* 8 Apr. 1/3 London..has no street architecture. It has no decorations, though it has many uglifications.

**Uglify** (*v*·glifəi), *v.* [f. UGLY *a.* + -FY.] *trans.* To make ugly or repulsive in appearance; to disfigure.

1576 NEWTON *Lemnie's Complex.* II. iii. 117 It defourmeth and vglyfyeth the skinne wyth dry, skuruye, skalie, mangie, and fylthye eruptions. 1650 B. *Discolliminium* 46 These derne, dreery, direfull dayes condunghill'd and uglified me into a darke dense lumpe. 1792 MME. D'ARBLAY *Diary* V. VII. 313 She is..completely a beauty...She uglifies everything near her. 1834 *Tait's Mag.* I. 613/1 When Mr. Luke marvelled at his daughter, disguised and uglified. 1857 HAWTHORNE *Eng. Note-bks.* (1870) II. 317, I remember little or nothing of this edifice, except that the Covenanters had uglified it with pews and a gallery, and whitewash. 1898 J. A. HOBSON *Ruskin* 304 The power exercised by irresponsible wealth..to uglify the outward aspects of life.

Hence **U·glifying** *ppl. a.*

1886 *New Princetown Rev.* I. 107 A protest against that uglifying process by which women are coaxed into resignation to old age and death.

**Uglily** (*v*·glili), *adv.* Also 4 **vgglili**, 6–7 **ouglily.** [f. UGLY *a.* + -LY ².] In an ugly manner, in senses of the adj.

*a* 1300 *Cursor M.* 29297 Þe man..þat kirkes brinnes or vgglili þar inwit sinnes,..he es cursd. *a* 1586 SIDNEY *Arcadia* III. (1912) 388 Fowler deaths had ouglily displayed their trayling guttes. 1615 G. SANDYS *Trav.* 134 Charon grim Ferri-man these streames doth guard, Vglily nastie. 1668 H. MORE *Div. Dial.* III. xv. (1713) 208 His Head uglily starting out from the midst of his Breast. 1685—*Paralip. Prophet.* Pref. p. xxiii, Two statuary Poppets.. must needs bear out Aaron's Breast-plate, very uglily and ill-favour'dly while they are there. 1755 JOHNSON, *Uglily*, filthily; with deformity; in such a manner as to raise dislike. 1834 SOUTHEY *Doctor* lxxxvii. (1848) 191 In those representations man indeed was not more uglily than fearfully made. 1869 D. W. FRESHFIELD *Central Caucasus & Bashan* ii. 19 The town is..uglily picturesque, if one may use such a phrase.

**Ugliness** (*v*·glinės). Forms: 4, 6– **ugli-** (4, 6–7 **vgli-**), 4, 7–8 **ugly-** (5 **vgly-**); 5 **vgg(e)ly-**, 7 **uggli-**; 6 **ougly-**, 6–7 **ougli-**, 9 *dial.* **oogli-**; also 4–5 **-nes**, 5–7 **-nesse.** [f. UGLY *a.* + -NESS.]

†**1.** Horror, dread, loathing. *Obs.*

*c* 1325 *Metr. Hom.* 21 For folc sal duin for din of se, And for baret that than sal be, Ouer al this werd bes rednes, Wandreth, and uglines. 1340 HAMPOLE *Pr. Consc.* 6832 'Þar nan ordre wonand es,' says he, 'Bot uglynes [L. *horror*] þat ever mare sal be'. *a* 1395 HYLTON *Scala Perf.* I. xxxvii. (W. de W. 1494), Some men he tempteth also and namely solitary men & wymmen by dredes and vglynes, and quakynges and shakynges. *a* 1400 *Relig. Pieces fr. Thornton MS.* 43 Whare we sulde hafe vgglynes als vn-till oure body, for to ete flesche, and drynke blude of man, oure Lorde Ihesu Criste turnede his flesche and his blude in liknes of brede and of wyne. *a* 1425 tr. *Arderne's Treat. Fistula*, etc. 8 Þof-al I suffre no-þing, vgglynes [L. *horror*] of suffryng holdeth me.

†**b.** A cause of horror or loathing. *Obs.*

1587 GOLDING *De Mornay* xvi. 294 What an ouglynesse then ought it to be vnto vs, when wee see how men..doe euery howre kill..and roote out one another?

**2.** The state of being ugly to look at; repulsiveness or marked inelegance of appearance: **a.** As an abstract quality.

Stronger in earlier than in later use.

*c* 1340 HAMPOLE *Pr. Consc.* 917 Aftir man,..vermyn es, And aftir vermyn stynkand uglynes. *c* 1440 *Promp. Parv.* 509/2 Vggelynesse, *horribilitas.* 1596 SPENSER *F. Q.* VI. vi. 10 But all her hinder parts did plaine expresse A monstrous Dragon, full of fearefull vglinesse. 1623 MIDDLETON *More Dissemblers* V. ii. 102 A thing whose face, through ugliness, frights children. 1642 MILTON *Apol. Smect.* Wks. 1851 III. 316 Which to dresse up and garnish with a devis'd bravery ..addes nothing but a deform'd uglinesse. 1703 ROWE *Fair Penit.* II. 22 You blast the Fair with Lies because they scorn you, Hate you like Age, like Ugliness and Impotence. 1756 BURKE *Subl. & B.* III. xxi, Though ugliness be the opposite to beauty it is not the opposite to proportion and fitness. 1798 S. & HT. LEE *Canterb. T.* II. 25 Her features had every disadvantage of ugliness, but that of being remarkable. 1820 KEATS *Lamia* I. 164 Of all these bereft, Nothing but pain and ugliness were left. 1844 KINGLAKE *Eothen* xvii, The awful haggardness that gave something of character to the faces of the men was sheer ugliness in the poor women. 1885–94 R. BRIDGES *Eros & Psyche* March v, She was as far From pictured beauty as is ugliness.

**b.** As a quality of particular things or persons.

*c* 1340 HAMPOLE *Pr. Consc.* 2364 Sen þe devel þus has tane his uglines Of þe filth of syn, þat swa filand es. *c* 1400 *Cursor M.* 27638 (Cott. Galba), When he wex proud..out of heuyn he fell to hell, And al his vglines he toke Of sin of pride. 1608 WILLET *Hexapla Exod.* 97 The Egyptians.. were..punished..with the number and vglines of them [frogs]. *a* 1618 SYLVESTER *Mem. Mortalitie* iii, Death's ouglinesse is but imagined; Under foule Vizard a faire Face shee wears. 1658 T. WALL *Charact. Enemies Ch.* 31 The ugliness of its [the leopard's] shape would more affright then the sweetness of its scent allure. 1756 MRS. CALDERWOOD in *Coltness Collect.* (Maitl. Cl.) 193 And what adds to the uglyness of the town is the dirty smoaky look it has. 1826 F. REYNOLDS *Life & Times* i. 19, I was perfectly startled at his ugliness. 1849 MACAULAY *Hist. Eng.* vi. II. 69 Charles, though he liked her conversation, laughed at her ugliness. 1861 M. PATTISON *Ess.* (1889) I. 45 High above, the Imperial double eagle figured in all its ugliness, like a scarecrow nailed to a barn door.

**c.** An instance of this quality; an ugly thing or feature.

1856 HAWTHORNE *Eng. Note-bks.* (1879) I. 313 All full of monstrosities and horrible uglinesses.

**3.** Moral repulsiveness or offensiveness; disgusting wickedness.

1601 BARLOW *Serm. Paules Crosse* B vij b, We, being commanded by authority,..did describe the nature and vglinesse of the rebellion. 1646 HAMMOND *Death-bed Repent.* 66 A consideration of the..detestable uglynesse of sinne. 1684 *Contempl. St. Man* I. ix. (1699) 95 The ugliness likewise of Human Nature shall be discovered. 1844 KINGLAKE *Eothen* v, A shock of this kind disclosing the *ugliness* of a cheat, is more..convincing than any mere proofs. 1858 HAWTHORNE *Fr. & It. Note-bks.* (1871) II. 3, I should like to know what it was..that made him insist upon having his actual likeness perpetrated, with all the ugliness of its animal and moral character. 1869 MᶜLAREN *Serm.* Ser. II. vii. 113 The Bible tells the shameful history in all its naked ugliness.

**4.** *dial.* Bad temper; disagreeableness.

1889 MABEL PEACOCK *Tales* 76, I knaw what he is, when he's full o' his ugliness.

† **U·glisome**, *a. Obs. rare.* Also 6 **oug(g)lisom(e.** [f. next + -SOME. Cf. UGGLESOME *a.*] Horrible, horrid; ugly.

1530 PALSGR. 328/1 Uglysome, *horryble, execrable.* 1583 STUBBES *Anat. Abus.* II. (1882) 51 Barbers are verie necessarie, for otherwise men should grow verie ougglisom and deformed.

**Ugly** (*v*·gli), *a., adv.*, and *sb.* Forms: *a.* 3 **uglike** (**iglie**), 4–5 **vg-, ugli**, 4– **ugly** (4–7 **vgly**, 5 **igly**, *Sc.* **wgly**, 5, 7 **vgely**), 6 **vg-, uglye**, 6–7 **vg-, uglie** (6 *Sc.* **wg-**); 4 **uggeli**, 5–6 **vggely(e, vggly(e**, 5–7 **vggly**; 4 **ogli**, 6 **oglie, oggly.** *β.* 5 **oughlye**, 7 **oughly**; 5–6 **owgly**, 6 **ouglye**, 6–7 **ougly**, **-lie**, 9 *dial.* **oogly.** *γ.* 4 **hoggyliche, hogely**, 6 **hogly**; 4–6 **hugly**, 5 **hughely**, 5–6 **houghly**, 6 **hougly.** [ad. ON. *ugglig-r* to be feared or dreaded, f. *ugga* UG *v.*: see -LY ¹.

The forms *iglie* in *Gen. & Ex.* 2918 and *igly* in the Harl. MS. of Chaucer *Clerk's T.* 673 are difficult to account for.]

**A.** *adj.* **1.** Having an appearance or aspect which causes dread or horror; frightful or horrible, esp. through deformity or squalor. (Now merged in sense 3.)

*a.* *c* 1250 *Gen. & Ex.* 2805 [Moses] it warp vt of hise hond, And wurð sone an uglike snake. *Ibid.* 2918 Moyseses migtful wand..wurð bi-foren pharaon An Iglie snake sone on-on. *a* 1300 *Cursor M.* 11606 Þar þai þam thoght to rest and slepe, Þar did þai mari for to light, Bot son þai sagh an vgli sight. *c* 1340 HAMPOLE *Pr. Consc.* 860 Nathyng es swa ugly, Als here es a mans dede body. *Ibid.* 6683 Swylk filthe and stynk es in þat ugly hole. 1423 JAS. I. *Kingis Q.* clxii, And vnderneth the quhele sawe I there Ane vgly pit, was depe as ony helle. *c* 1470 HENRY *Wallace* II. 247 Thai chargyt the geyler..to..bryng him wp out of that vgly sell. 1500–20 DUNBAR *Poems* xi. 20 Ȝit may thow be, within ane ȝeir, Ane vgsum, vglye tramort. *a* 1547 SURREY *Æneid* IV. 626 Agamemnons son:..That sitting found within the temples porche The vglie furies his slaughter to revenge. 1594 KYD *Cornelia* II. 13 Fayne would I die, but darksome vgly Death With-holds his darte, and in disdaine doth flye me. 1613 PURCHAS *Pilgrimage* VIII. vi. 639 The faces of their Priests are painted as vgly as they can deuise. 1643 A. ROSSE *Mel Helic.* 77 His snakie hairs doe shew how ugly he [*sc.* Cerberus] is in the sight of good men. 1667 MILTON *P. L.* XI. 464 O sight Of terrour, foul and ugly to behold, Horrid to think, how horrible to feel! 1680 OTWAY *Orphan* II. i, I struck The ugly brindled Monster to the heart. 1789 T. RUSSELL *Sonn.* xi, Uglier far than have been feign'd or fear'd, Ten thousand Phantoms to my sight appear'd.

*β.* 1426 LYDG. *De Guil. Pilgr.* 11036 Somwhyle, off dyrknesse And off the owgly ffoul thyknesse,..Thow shalt lese the syht off me. *c* 1430 LYDG. *Min. Poems* (Percy Soc.) 145 Yif he kaughte..Seyn that owgly careyn lamentable. 1550 CRAWLEY *Epigr.* 376 A greate mastyfe dogge and a foule ouglye beare. 1587 HOLINSHED *Chron.* III. 835/1 Suddenlie came out..eight wildmen,..with ouglie weapons & terrible visages. 1595 *Locrine* III. i. 7 Those ougly diuels of black Erebus, That might torment the damned traitors soule! 1601 HOLLAND *Pliny* XXVI. i. II. 240 These newcome diseases verely were..so foule and filthie, so loathsome and ougly, that a man would have chosen rather to die..than to bee so disfigured. 1633 P. FLETCHER *Purple Isl.* I. xl, Darknesse headlong fell, Frighted with suddain beams,..And plung'd her ougly head in deepest hell. 1640 GLAPTHORN *Ladies Privilege* III, But know the shape of Death Is not ougly to me.

*γ.* 13.. *Adultery* 85 in Herrig's *Archiv* LXXIX. 420 He ledd hym to an hogely hylle; þe erthe openyd & in þei ȝede. *c* 1375 *Sc. Leg. Saints* ii. (*Paul*) 1151 þan come a schadow full hugly, blak & blay, & stud hyme by. *c* 1470 HARDING *Chron.* CVII. vi. (1543) 107 b, Echeon their nose and ouer lippe ful right Cut of anone which was an hougly [*v.r.* hogly] sight. 1555 W. WATREMAN *Fardle Facions* I. iv. C ij, There be in it [Ethiopia] dyuers peoples of sondry phisonomy and shape, monstruous and of hugly shewe. 1565 STAPLETON tr. *Bede's Hist. Ch. Eng.* 95 These foure fyres encreasing by litle and litle so farr at the length extended, that ioyning altogether they grew to a great and houghly flame.

† **2.** Of events, times, etc.: Dreadful, terrible.

*a* 1300 *Cursor M.* 22519 Uggeli sal be þe fift dai, Mare þan ani tung can sai. *a* 1340 HAMPOLE *Psalter* ix. 37 Vgly is it to fall in þere hend, for þou bihaldis þe trauaile and þe sorow þat he has doen till haly men. 13.. *E. E. Allit. P.* B. 892 Bot þay wern wakned..Of on þe vglokest vnhap þat euer on erd suffred. *c* 1460 *Towneley Myst.* xvi. 142 Sich panys hard neuer man tell, For vgly and for fell. *a* 1586 SIDNEY *Ps.* (1823) VI. iii, Turn thee, sweete Lord, and from this ougly fall, My deere God, stay me. 1597 J. PAYNE

*Royal Exch.* 41 This wylie feynd geves not his onsett after his vglie and terrible maner.

**b.** Of sounds. (Passing into sense 6.)

*c* **1400** *Destr. Troy* 3701 With an ugli noise, noye for to here, Hit sundrit þere sailes & þere sad ropis. *c* **1400** MAUNDEV. (Roxb.) xxxi. 138 In þis vale er oft tymes herd.. voices vggly and hidous. *c* **1440** *York Myst.* xxxvii. 101 What! heris þou no3t þis vggely noyse. **1513** DOUGLAS *Æneid* III. iv. 31 The Harpyes..voce also wa wglie for to heir. **1550** LYNDESAY *Sq. Meldrum* 738 Than rais the reik with vglie crakkis. *a* **1585** MONTGOMERIE *Flyting* 503 The cry was sa ouglie, of elfes, aips, and owles. **1603** G. OWEN *Pembrokeshire* (1892) 249 At certaine tymes there is vgglye and terrible noyses and soundes hard to proceede from the same pitte. **1725** DE FOE *Voy. round World* (1840) 87 Great numbers came down to the shore, staring at us, and making confused ugly noises.

**3.** Offensive or repulsive to the eye; unpleasing in appearance; of disagreeable or unsightly aspect: **a.** Of persons.

*a.* *c* **1375** *Sc. Leg. Saints* ii. (*Paul*) 778 Þan sperit he [*sc.* Nero] rycht besyly, gyf þat he wes sa wgly Quhen he wes borne. *c* **1386** CHAUCER *Clerk's T.* 673 This vgly sergeant ..Hath hent hire sone þat ful was of beautee. *c* **1400** MAUNDEV. (Roxb.) xvii. 77 Þir wymmen er ri3t blak and vggly to behold. *c* **1480** HENRYSON *Test. Cres.* 372 He luikit on hir vglye Lipper face, The quhilk befor was quhite as Lillie flour. **1509** BARCLAY *Ship of Folys* (1570) 198 The uggly Maurians are also of this sect. *a* **1548** HALL *Chron., Hen. VIII*, 130 b, If the Frenche Quene, whiche was lame and ugly were dedde,..then waies might bee founde. **1580** H. GIFFORD *Gilloflowers, Dream* xv, An oggly creature, all in blacke. **1606** SHAKS. *Ant. & Cl.* II. v. 96 Had'st thou Narcissus in thy face to me, Thou would'st appeere most vgly. **1634** SIR T. HERBERT *Trav.* 49 They are the most vgly and impudent Whoores, in all Persia. *a* **1687** VILLIERS (Dk. Buckhm.) *Speeches* (1775) 237 Like ugly foolish children, whom, because of their deformity and want of wit, the parents are ashamed of. **1717** PRIOR *Alma* II. 350 Dames, who Native Beauty want, Still uglier look, the more They paint. **1742** BERKELEY *Lett.* Wks. 1871 IV. 286 You would be less zealous were the Queen old and ugly. **1794** S. WILLIAMS *Vermont* 195 They have all the same sallow complexion, deformed features, ugly appearance. **1815** SCOTT *Guy M.* liii, The fairy bride of Sir Gawaine..was more decrepit probably, and what is commonly called more ugly, than Meg Merrilies. **1858** HAWTHORNE *Fr. & It. Note-bks.* (1871) I. 98 A very ugly old man indeed—wrinkled, puckered, shrunken. **1879** FARRAR *St. Paul* (1883) 390 The ugly Greek who was the noblest of all Greeks.

*absol.* **1766** GOLDSM. *Vicar* xxxi, After having tried in vain [to find a wife], even amongst the pert and the ugly.

*β.* *c* **1400** *Rom. Rose* 3038 He was so hidous and so oughlye, I mene this that Trespasse hight. *c* **1407** LYDG. *Reson & Sens.* 1934 This lady, Dame hatrede, To-rent and owgly in her wede. **1548** UDALL *Erasm. Par. Mark* i. 16 Hence with this ougly and abhominable creature. **1598** R. HAYDOCKE tr. *Lomazzo* II. 133 Though a woman be faire, merry, and healthy and yet be dishonest, shee must needes seeme most ougly to an ingenuous and honest minde. **1610** SHAKS. *Temp.* IV. i. 192 And, as with age, his body ouglier growes, So his minde cankers.

*γ.* **1562** BULLEIN *Bulwarke, Sicke Men* 13 Keepe the mouth, teeth, and tongue cleane,..whych els shalbe corrupted, defiled, and so anoyed, that it shalbe..hugely and noysome to the beholders.

**b.** Of animals.

*c* **1375** *Sc. Leg. Saints* ii. (*Paul*) 780 Þat vgly padok þan gert he ta. **1444** *Pol. Poems* (Rolls) II. 218 The owgly bakke wyl gladly fleen be nyght Dirk cressetys and laumpys that been lyght. **1508** DUNBAR *Flyting* 185 Thow purehippit, vgly averill, With hurkland banis, holkand throw thy hyd. **1587** TURBERV. *Trag. T.* (1837) 31 Two monstrous mastyves eke he sawe that ran Close by her side, two ugly curres they were. **1614** SYLVESTER *Bethulia's Rescue* II. 175 Millions of millions of foule Frogs hee makes To cover Memphis with their ougly Frie. **1643** SIR T. BROWNE *Relig. Med.* I. § 16, I cannot tell by what Logick we call a Toad, a Beare, or an Elephant, ugly. **1699** DAMPIER *Voy.* II. II. ii. 59 The Monkies that are in these Parts are the ugliest I ever saw. **1774** GOLDSM. *Nat. Hist.* (1776) V. 355 In quadrupedes, the smallest animals are noxious, ugly and loathsome.

**c.** In miscellaneous uses.

*a.* **13..** *Seuyn Sages* (W.) 2782 With lang noses and mowthes wide, And vgly eres on ether syde. ? *a* **1400** *Morte Arth.* 1086 Erne had he fulle huge, and vgly to schewe, Wiþ eghne fulle horreble. *c* **1440** *York Myst.* xi. 265 Full vgly and full ill is it, þat was ful faire and fresshe before. **1561** T. NORTON *Calvin's Inst.* I. 52 Although we graunt that the Image of God was not altogether defaced and blotted out in him, yet was it so corrupted, that all that remaineth, is but vggly deformitie. **1577** in Hakluyt *Voy.* (1589) 626 For her ougly hewe and deformitie, we let her goe. **1604** E. G[RIMSTONE] *D'Acosta's Hist. Indies* v. xii. 360 They entred backward to their idol, and so went bending their bodies and head, after an vglie manner. **1680** C. NESSE *Church-Hist.* 122 An ugly image, half a fish and half a man. **1687** A. LOVELL tr. *Thevenot's Trav.* I. 26 The streets of Constantinople are very ugly, being for the most part narrow, crooked, up-hill and down-hill. **1763** J. BROWN *Poetry & Music* xiii. 227 *note*, May not the Voice and Figure of a distressed or joyous Object be so..ridiculous or ugly, as..to destroy the Sympathy of those who hear and see it? **1803** MAR. EDGEWORTH *Manufacturers* i, She made him pronounce an absurd eulogium on the ugliest thing in the room. **1865** TROLLOPE *Belton Est.* i. 5 The house itself was an ugly residence..built in the time of George II. **1875** J. P. HOPPS *Princ. Relig.* i. (1878) 6 Even poor savages who have never been taught any better, cling to an ugly idol,.. rather than be without a god at all.

*β.* **1547** BALDWIN *Mor. Philos.* (Palfr.) 124 Wherewith.. the figure of man is as it were by enchantment transformed into an ougly and loathsome image. **1581** A. HALL *Iliad* x. 181 This Dolon was of ougly shape. **1600** FAIRFAX *Tasso* VII. cxvi, Heau'ns glorious lampe wrapt in an ougly vaile Of shadowes darke. **1607** NORDEN *Surv. Dial.* 222 Without the aid and industrie of a skilfull husband, fairest grounds will become ougly.

**d.** In figurative contexts.

*c* **1440** *Jacob's Well* 246 Thynke of goddys presence, and be raysed to heuen be holy thou3t. Þanne se þe world foul & vggly, voyde of al goodnes. **1576** FLEMING *Panopl. Epist.* 339 An infinite number, whose malice is infected with many a foule and ougly disease. *a* **1586** SIDNEY *Arcadia* v. (1605) 445 While each conceite an ougly figure beares. **1601** YARINGTON *Two Lament. Trag.* II. i. in Bullen *O. Pl.* IV, Where shall we hide this trumpet of your shame, This timelesse ougly map of crueltie? **1615** J. CASTLE in *Crt. & Times Jas. I* (1848) I. 378 Those holy men ..had made him see this fearful error, and the ugly face of his sin. **1663** DAVENANT *2nd Pt. Siege of Rhodes* IV. i, Amazement is the uggli'st shape of fear. **1884** *Congregationalist* Jan. 14 The honest man must allow that there are ugly truths and lies with beautiful faces.

**4.** Morally offensive or repulsive; base, degraded, loathsome, vile. In later use also in weaker sense: Offending against propriety; highly objectionable.

*a.* *a* **1300** *Cursor M.* 1106 Þai thoght þat kynd him mond for-bede To haf don suilk an ogli dede. *Ibid.* 27612 Þai þat sua vgli athes suers, wonder es hou þis erth þam bers. *c* **1340** HAMPOLE *Prose Tr.* 33 A full forsakynge of..syne and of unclennes, with a gastely syghte of it how foule how vggly and how paynfull þat it es. *c* **1440** *Alph. Tales* 142 On a tyme þer was a scoler at Parissh, þat had done many vglie syn. **1583** BABINGTON *Commandm.* (1590) 54 Sight of vglie sinne lodging still in mee..will make mee praise His name. **1608** WILLET *Hexapla Exod.* 393 The most vile monstrous and vgly sinnes. **1650** BULWER *Anthropomet.* 199 Tokens that God was grievously offended with such ugly deeds. *a* **1658** CLEVELAND *Rustick Ramp.* (1687) 431 An abominable Ceremony, which had made their Impiety more ugly. **1732** BERKELEY *Alciphr.* III. § 11 Is it not..an ugly system in which you can suppose no law and prove no duty? **1816** J. WILSON *City of Plague* II. v. 110 But cutting throats in a churchyard Is something new, and 'tis an ugly practice. **1879** GEO. ELIOT *Theo. Such* 128, I cannot consider such courses any the less ugly because they are ascribed to temper. **1894** SIMPKINSON *Life & Times Laud* vi. 118 Gentlemen..who were sentenced to..do public penance in their own parish church for ugly acts of immorality.

*β.* **1584** CONSTABLE *Diana* III. ii, Like catife wretch by time and travell taught, His ougly ills in others good to hide. **1594** T. B. *La Primaud. Fr. Acad.* II. To Rdr., Surely of all Sathans delusions wrought by him in the hearts of vnbeleeuers, this monstrous error of atheisme is most ougly. **1602** WARNER *Alb. Eng.* XIII. lxxvii. (1612) 320 Wherein were acted ouglier things than to be found mong'st beasts. **1611** COTGR., *Landie deschiquetée*, an ouglie nickname for an ouerridden Hackney (or Harlot).

**5.** Offensive or unpleasant to the smell or taste; noisome, nasty.

*c* **1400** *Destr. Troy* 8732 How the korse might be keppit.. likyng to se; And not orible, ne vgly of odir to fele. **1668** CULPEPPER & COLE *Barthol. Anat.* I. xxviii. 70 Stinking things have filthy and ugly Vapors. **1693** EVELYN *De la Quint. Compl. Gard.* II. 148 Those kinds of rotten Dung are accompanied with an unpleasing smell that infects the Plants raised upon such Beds, and gives them an ugly Taste. **1707** MORTIMER *Husb.* (1721) II. 43 It yields an ugly stench in burning. **1712** W. ROGERS *Voy.* (1718) 149 The wind always blowing fresh over the land, brought an ugly noisome smell aboard from the Seals ashore. **1876** GEO. ELIOT *Dan. Der.* x, Archery has no ugly smell of brimstone.

**6.** Offensive to refined taste or good feelings; objectionable, disagreeable, unpleasant, not nice.

**1621** BURTON *Anat. Mel.* I. iv. III. i. 272 In the midst of these squalid, vgly, and such irksome dayes, they seek at last..to be eased of all by death. **1671** CLARENDON *Hist. Reb.* XI. § 243 When a Man might reasonably believe that less than a universal Defection of three Nations, could not have reduced a great King to so ugly a fate. **1697** tr. *C'tess D'Aunoy's Trav.* (1706) 126, I thought it very ugly, that an Old Woman such as that was which I saw there, should come and spurt Water out of her Mouth, in my Face. **1720** *Lett. Lond. Jrnl.* (1721) 48 It would be very pleasant, if it were not for the Abuse and ugly Language you meet with. **1722** DE FOE *Plague* (1754) 204 They call'd me..to an ugly and dangerous Office. **1754** W. GOODALL *Exam. Lett. Mary Q. Scots* I. i. 33 To affirm that it was to be found there, when it is not, has an extreme ugly aspect. **1806** SURR *Winter in Lond.* III. 128 The idea of having a daughter of sufficient age to be presented carries with it.. an ugly memento of the age of her mother. **1874** 'MAX ADELER' *Out of Hurly-burly* xiv. (Rtldg.) 176 With an ugly word upon his lips, he sprang from his seat. **1888** BURGON *Lives 12 Gd. Men* II. v. 18 The one person who comes out of that strife with an ugly stain upon his shield ..was the Prime Minister.

**b.** Causing disquiet or discomfort; of a very troublesome or awkward nature.

**1645** in *Verney Memoirs* (1904) I. 328 Sir Ralph replies at great length about 'this ugly business'. **1660** MARVELL *Corr.* Wks. (Grosart) II. 40 The last of December here was an ugly false report got abroad, that his Majesty was stabb'd. **1672** — *Reh. Transp.* I. 105 After things have been laid with all the depth of humane Policy, there happens lightly some ugly little contrary Accident. **1687** A. LOVELL tr. *Thevenot's Trav.* II. 11 Fearing that the Galleys..might serve him some ugly trick, he caused the Entry of it to be stopt up. **1711** SWIFT *Jrnl. to Stella* 4 Jan., I had an ugly giddy fit last night in my chamber. **1751** *Affect. Narr. of Wager* 17 For the more expeditiously retrieving this ugly Accident, the Commodore ordered several Carpenters on board her. **1792** BURKE *Let. to Sir H. Langrishe* Wks. 1842 I. 550 It is putting things into the position of an ugly alternative, into which I hope in God they never will be put. **1826** DISRAELI *Viv. Grey* II. xi, A horse which he was endeavouring to cure of some ugly tricks. **1852** THACKERAY *Esmond* I. xiii, My Lord Mohun (of whose exploits and fame some of the gentlemen of the University had brought down but ugly reports). **1890** *Spectator* 19 Apr., The Under-Secretary for Foreign Affairs..admitted some ugly facts.

**7. a.** Somewhat hazardous or perilous.

**1654** *Nicholas Papers* (Camden) II. 45, I know it is an ugly time to mention goeing into England. **1711** SWIFT *Jrnl. to Stella* 21 Jan., It is very ugly walking; a baker's boy broke his thigh yesterday. **1889** in *Eng. Dial. Dict.*

**b.** Suggestive of trouble or danger.

**1660** *Trial Regic.* 161, I was in the hall when that ugly Proclamation was proclaimed. **1719** DE FOE *Crusoe* II. (Globe) 352 They..let fall some dangerous ugly Words. **1780** COWPER *Lett.* Mar., A long preface such as mine is an ugly symptom and always forebodes great sterility in the following pages. **1801** S. & HT. LEE *Canterb. T.* IV. 376, I had an ugly presentiment of what was to be the subject of our conversation. **1853** KANE *Grinnell Exp.* xxix. (1856) 244 Poor Sir John Franklin! this night-drift is an ugly omen. **1888** E. MONEY *Dutch Maiden* 133 You think this looks ugly, but..a stern chase is a long chase.

**c.** Of the weather, sea, etc.: Unpleasantly or dangerously rough, stormy, or boisterous.

**1744** *Lond. Mag.* 143 But little Wind, and an ugly Swell. **1781** ARCHER in *Naval Chron.* (1804) XI. 289 Hold fast! that was an ugly sea... Another ugly sea: sent a Midshipman to bring news from the pumps. **1840** R. H. DANA *Bef. Mast* xxxv, It is blowing harder, and an ugly head sea is running. **1844** KINGLAKE *Eothen* xvii, With an ugly black sky above, and an angry sea beneath. **1847** ALB. SMITH *Chr. Tadpole* xxiii. (1879) 207 The flashes of lightning.. shewed that it was going to be an ugly night. **1900** J. H. HARRIS *Our Cove* ii. 14 You know the weather is going to be 'ugly', which means anything from tricky to downright bad.

**d.** In phr. *ugly customer*, a person who is likely to cause trouble, or be difficult to deal with.

**1811** *Sporting Mag.* XXXVIII. 56 He is a very ugly customer. **1819** *Metropolis* I. 241 Coachee, you've picked up an ugly customer there. **1844** DICKENS *Mart. Chuz.* xliii, In any such a cause you will find me, my young sir, an Ugly Customer! **1884** E. YATES *Recoll.* II. 207 The tone of the letter was exceedingly offensive and dictatorial, and it was evident that he was a very ugly customer.

**e.** *The ugly man*, the actual perpetrator of an act of garroting, as distinguished from his two accomplices. (Cf. NASTY *a.* 6.)

**1888** *Cassell's Encycl. Dict.*

**8.** Cross, angry, ill-tempered.

**1687** ALICE HATTON in *H. Corr.* (Camden) II. 65, I am sorry my ugly letter gave you any disturbance. **1848** DICKENS *Dombey* liv, He turned upon her with his ugliest look. **1855** HALIBURTON *Nat. & Hum. Nat.* I. ix. 286 Don't rile me, for I have an ugly pen, an ugly tongue, and an ugly temper. **1894** H. GARDENER *Unoff. Patriot* 163 I've had to buck up to some pretty ugly talk first and last.

**b.** In predicative use, esp. *to feel* or *look ugly*.

**1796** R. BAGE *Hermsprong* xxv, Lord Grondale looked ugly; the doctor did not know how to look. **1836** HALIBURTON *Clockmaker* Pref., I don't know as ever I felt so ugly afore since I was raised. *Ibid.* I. xii, Don't say that are any more.., for it makes me feel ugly. **1864** *Louie's Last Term* 122 You make me ten times worse every time I see you, you make me so ugly I don't know myself. **1896** *Daily News* 25 Feb. 3 It is amusing to see the clever promptitude with which they manage the brutes who look at all ugly.

**9.** *Comb.*, as *ugly-clouded, conditioned, faced, -headed, -tempered, visaged* adjs.; also *ugly-looking* adj.

(*a*) **1593** MARLOWE & CHAPMAN *Hero & Leander* IV. 331 So most vgly clowded was the light, That day was hid in day. **1602** CAREW *Cornwall* I. 34 b, The Seale..is..not vnlike a Pigge, vgly faced, and footed like a Moldwarp. **1634** MILTON *Comus* 695 What grim aspects are these, These oughly-headed Monsters? **1655** in *Verney Mem.* (1904) II. 25 The Example of very many..might somewhat excuse my signing that ugly conditioned Bond. **1849** CUPPLES *Green Hand* xi. (1856) 113 Ye're too tarnation ugly-faced for it, let alone colour. **1885** J. G. WALLER in *Archaeologia* XLIX. 205 On the opposite side is another ugly visaged figure. **1897** *Outing* XXIX. 590/2 A good-sized, well-fed, ugly-tempered creature, with a pair of magnificent tusks.

(*b*) **1771** SMOLLETT *Humph. Cl.* 31 May, A parcel of ugly-looking fellows came running into the water, and laid hold on our boat with great violence. **1820** BELZONI *Egypt & Nubia* III. 425 A sort of short ugly-looking fellow, turned up nose, long teeth out of his mouth, and uncommon thick lips. **1839** SIR C. NAPIER in Bruce *Life* iv. (1885) 132 A hundred fellows may get ugly-looking gashes.

**B.** *adv.* Horribly; terribly; uglily.

*c* **1375** *Sc. Leg. Saints* xxxiv. (*Pelagia*) 232 Þe feynde þarfor hye can cry, þat mony herde, ful vgly. *c* **1420** *Chron. Vilod.* 3988 An horribulle, foulle grome..hoggyliche lokede vpone herre wt horrible chere. *c* **1440** *Alph. Tales* 51 Yone yong man..stynkis mor vglie in þe sight of God..þan done all þe carion of þis werld. *c* **1440** *Promp. Parv.* 509/2 Vggely, or vggely wyse, *horribiliter*. **1678** BUNYAN *Pilgr.* (ed. 2) I. 187 But they desired him to let them go; with that he looked ugly upon them. **1876** [see PLUG-UGLY]. **1897** E. PHILLPOTTS *Lying Prophets* III. xi. 344 I'm punished ugly enough.

**C.** *sb.* **1.** An ugly person, animal, etc.

**1755** H. WALPOLE *Lett.* (1846) III. 100 There were all the beauties, and all the diamonds, and not a few of the uglies of London. **1790** MRS. WHEELER *Westmld. Dial.* (1821) 16 Monny a lump ea brass he hes teaan frae his poor barns an me, to carry to thor uglys. **1889** *Pall Mall G.* 27 June 6/1 Artists and actors,..peers and judges, beauties and uglies —they were all in the highest spirits. **1895** J. G. MILLAIS *Breath fr. Veldt* (1899) 161 There lay old Ugly *in extremis* with his..fine tusks directed towards us.

**2. a.** A kind of hood or shade attached to the front of a lady's bonnet or hat as a protection to the eyes. (In use *c* 1850.)

**1850** THACKERAY *Kickleburys on Rhine* (1851) 25 'Those hoods!' she said; 'we call those hoods Uglies!' **1856** H. MAYHEW *The Rhine* 107 The broad eaves project so far over that they remind you almost of a lady's 'ugly'. **1891** *Eng. Illustr. Mag.* Dec. 197 Most hideous folding shades of silk drawn on wires were affixed to the front of these bonnets, and deservedly called 'uglies'.

**b.** A knitted face-protector formerly worn in Canada. 1895 *Funk's Standard Dict.*

Hence **U·gly** *v. trans.*, to make ugly; to uglify.

1740 RICHARDSON *Pamela* (1824) I. 97 It is impossible I should love him; for his vices all ugly him over, as I may say. 1770 C. JENNER *Placid Man* v. iv, The idea of a ticket-porter stuck to every part of him, and uglied him all over.

**Uglyo·graphy.** [f. UGLY *a.* + -OGRAPHY. Used only by Southey.] Bad handwriting; uncouth spelling. Hence **Uglyo·graphize** *v. trans.*, to spell uncouthly.

1804 SOUTHEY *Lett.* (1856) I. 285, I do beseech you mend your uglyography. 1805 — *Madoc* (1807) II. Notes 200 Quetzalcohuatl, for such is the *uglyography* of his name. 1834 — *Doctor* ccxxiii. (1848) 604 How it would have been ..*uglyographised* by Elphinstone..I know not.

**Ugrian** (*ū*·grĭăn, yū·g-), *a.* and *sb.* [f. *Ugri*, the name given by early Russian writers to an Asiatic race dwelling east of the Ural Mountains.]

**A.** *adj.* Belonging to, of or pertaining to, a division of Ural-Altaic peoples, which includes the Finns and Magyars.

1841 PRICHARD *Phys. Hist. Mankind* III. 277 The fourth branch are the Ugorian races, the Ougres or Ugrian tribes. *Ibid.* 322 The proper Ostiaks of Ugrian origin. 1861 HULME tr. *Moquin-Tandon* I. v. 32 Tauraiinans...Divisions: 1, the Mongolian stock;..4, the Ugrian stock; 5, the Peninsular stock. 1889 S. BRYANT *Celtic Ireland* 5 The early Finnish or Ugrian type, that wandered westwards from the north-east.

**B.** *sb.* **1.** A member of the Ugrian stock.

1841 PRICHARD *Phys. Hist. Mankind* III. 274 In Asia various Tartar or Turkish tribes have encroached on the southern borders of the Tschudes and Ugrians. 1862 LATHAM *Elem. Compar. Philol.* 127 The Ugrians lead not only from Asia to Europe, but to America as well. 1889 S. BRYANT *Celtic Ireland* 5 Later immigrations..may have included.. mixtures of the Ugrian with the Celt.

**2.** The language of the Ugrians. Also *attrib.*

1862 LATHAM *Elem. Compar. Philol.* 150 The Votiak is the Ugrian of the Government of Viatka. 1877 *Encycl. Brit.* VII. 183/1 The following is the order of the groups, some of the more important languages..standing alone:—..Celtic, Lithuanic, Slavonic, Ugrian, Turkish.

**Ugric** (*ū*·grik, yū·g-), *a.* [f. as UGRI-AN + -IC. Cf. *Finno-Ugric* (1879) s.v. UGRO-.] = UGRIAN *a.*

1884 *Imp. Dict.*, *Ugric* a., same as Ugrian. 1886 M. A. MORRISON in *Jrnl. R. Asiatic Soc.* XVIII. II. 178 Finn. This group is almost altogether confined to Europe. Its four sub-branches are the Ugric, Finn proper, Volga-Finn, and Perm-Finn. *Ibid.*, The Magyar, one of the languages of the Ugric sub-branch.

† **Ugriness.** *Sc. Obs.*—[1] [Cf. UG *v.*] Horror.

*c* 1375 *Sc. Leg. Saints* vii. (*James Min.*) 716 In harte þai had sike wgrines, þat þai had no word for to say.

**Ugrio-**, variant of UGRO-.

1889 S. BRYANT *Celtic Ireland* 5 Later immigrations..may have included mixtures of a Ugrio-Iberian..stock.

**Ugro-** (*ū*·gro, yū·gro-), combining form of UGRIAN *a.*, used in a few terms, as *Ugro-Altaic*, *-Finnic*, *-Finnish*, *-Samoyede*, *-Slavonic*, *-Tartarian*.

1852 *Todd's Cycl. Anat.* IV. II. 1347 The Turanian, or Ugro-Tartarian [languages]..; spoken by the (Mongolian) people of High Asia and of certain parts of Northern Europe. 1879 *Encycl. Brit.* IX. 219/1 The term Finns..being, with its adjective Finnic or Finno-Ugric or Ugro-Finnic, the collective name of the westernmost branch of the great Uralo-Altaic family. 1883 MORFILL *Slavonic Lit.* ii. 31 In 681 the Slavonic settlers fell under the power of a tribe of Bulgarians, a Ugro-Finnish race. 1886 M. A. MORRISON in *Jrnl. R. Asiatic Soc.* XVIII. II. 177 Broadly speaking,.. the Ugro-Altaic languages are spoken over a region extending through more than 100 degrees of longitude. 1887 *Encycl. Brit.* XXII. 11/2 The Yeniseians were followed by the Ugro-Samoyedes. 1896 KEANE *Ethnology* ix. 201 [The] Bulgarians [are] Ugro-Slavonic.

**Ugsome** (*v*·gsŏm), *a.* Chiefly *north.* and *Sc.* Forms: 5 vg-, ugsom, 6 vgsoom; 5–6 vgsome (5 hwg-), 6 ougsome, 6– ugsome; *Sc.* 5–6 vg-, wgsum, 6–8 ugsum (6 -sume). [f. UG *v.* + -SOME.] Horrible, horrid, loathsome.

In older use common down to the latter part of the 16th cent. Literary currency in the 19th cent. is prob. due to the influence of Scott.

*c* 1400 *Destr. Troy* 877 He..was ware sone Of þe orible oxin, vgsome to se. *Ibid.* 12497 A thoner and a thicke rayne..With an ugsom noise. *c* 1425 WYNTOUN *Cron.* II. xi. 1011 Off þat incest fel murthir keyn, And ane vgsum manjory Off wlatsum corssis and vgly. *c* 1440 *Alph. Tales* 470 Þer he saw many vgsom turment and many dyvers kyndes of paynys. 1475 *Cath. Angl.* 191/2 Hwgsome, *abhominabilis*. 1509 FISHER 7 *Penit. Ps.* xxxviii. Wks. (1876) 49 Lyke as þe mornynge is a meane bytwene þe grete clerenes of þe sonne & þe vgsome derkenes of the nyght. 1549 LATIMER 7*th Serm. bef. Edw. VI* (Arb.) 186 Such an euyl fauoured face, such an vgsome countenaunce, such an horrible vysage. 1566 J. STUDLEY *Seneca's Medea* (1581) 134 O ougsome bugges, O gobblins grym of hell, I you intreat. 1583 MELBANCKE *Philotimus* C ij, And Morpheus [shall] present the with vgsome sights.

1724 RAMSAY *Vision* x, Infernal be thair hyre, Quha.. flang us Into this ugsum myre! 1790 A. WILSON 3*rd Epist. to W. Mitchell* Poet. Wks. (1846) 180 The carle..Aye puffin', or stuffin' Wi' ugsome chews his cheek. 1816 SCOTT *Antiq.* xxi, Like an auld dog that trails its useless ugsome carcass into some bush or bracken. 1832 LYTTON *Eugene A.* II. viii, 'Tis an ugsome bit of road,' said the corporal. 1875 BROWNING *Aristoph. Apol.* 1360 Attestation of the Muse That low-and-ugsome is not signed and sealed Incontrovertibly man's portion here

Hence **U·gsomely** *adv. rare.*

*c* 1440 *Alph. Tales* 181 Sodanlie as he lay, he began to cry vgsomlie. *a* 1578 LINDESAY (Pitscottie) *Chron. Scot.* (S.T.S.) I. 67 Thir same wordis war more wgsumlie crayit nor befoir. 1876 *Whitby Gloss.* 204 'It leuk'd at us varry ugsomely', savagely.

**Ugsomeness** (*v*·gsŏmnĕs). Also 5–6 vgsomnes (6 ug-), 5 hugsomenes, 6 *Sc.* vgsumnes. [f. prec. + -NESS.] † **a.** Loathing. *Obs.* **b.** The quality of being ugsome; loathsomeness; ugliness.

*c* 1440 *Alph. Tales* 117 He had lepre folk in so grete vgsomnes þat he myght not suffer to se þaim. 1483 *Cath. Angl.* 401/2 An Vgsomnes, *abhominacio*. 1509 FISHER 7 *Penit. Ps.* xxxviii. Wks. (1876) 81 Suche as be ouercomen by temptacyons are very blynde not perceyuynge þe vgsomnes of synne. 1549 LATIMER 7*th Serm. bef. Edw. VI* (Arb.) 185 The horrour and vgsomnes of death is sorer then death it selfe. *a* 1672 J. LIVINGSTONE in Tweedie *Sel. Biogr.* (Wodrow Soc.) I. 273 When sinlesse nature did sinlesly scunder at the infinite ugsomenes of the cup of wrath. 1834 WILSON in *Blackw. Mag.* XXXVI. 564 Some hideous witch-hag, to look on whose ugsomeness would be to die.

**Uh** (*v*[h]), *interj.* [Imitative: cf. UGH.] A representation of an inarticulate sound, such as that produced in coughing.

1605 B. JONSON *Volpone* I. iii, I feele mee going, (vh, vh, vh, vh.) I am sayling to my port, (vh, vh, vh, vh?) 1678 OTWAY *Friendship in F.* II. i, Uh gud murther, I had rather you had offer'd me a Toad. 1818 SCOTT *Br. Lamm.* xiii, Nae ill come ower them, I trust? Uh? 1818 — *Rob Roy* xxxi, Uh! uh! &c. &c. I am very happy to have this joyful opportunity.

‖ **Uhlan** (*ū*·lăn, yū·lăn). Also 8–9 ulan; 8 houlan, 9 hulan. [a. F. *uhlan, hulan, houlan*, G. *uhlan, ulan* (Da. and Sw. *ulan*, It. *ulano*), a. Polish *ułan, hułan* (Czech *ulan, hulan*, Serb. *ulan*, Russ. уланъ), ad. Turk. اوغلان *oghlān* (pop. *ōlān*), son, youth, servant.] A special type of cavalryman or lancer in various European armies (originally in Slavonic countries, esp. Poland; latterly spec. in the German Empire).

α. 1753 *Scots Mag.* Jan. 3/2 The surplus..consisted of Tartars and Ulans, whom he chose to keep in his pay. 1799 W. TOOKE *View Russian Emp.* I. 418 In their clothes they resembled the Poles, or rather the polish Ulans. 1802 JAMES *Milit. Dict.* s.v., The Ulans generally engage the enemy in small platoons or squads.

β. 1768 *Ann. Reg., Chron.* 126 They write from Warsaw, that an officer of Houlans..has been grievously insulted by a Russian officer. 1809 R. K. PORTER *Trav. Sk. Russia & Sweden* (1813) I. 171 One of the most superb regiments in the Russian service is that of the Hulans, commanded by the Archduke Constantine. 1837 CARLYLE *Fr. Rev.* III. I. i, Flying hulans and hussars have been seen on the Châlons road. 1851 GALLENGA *Italy* 131 Three squadrons of *hulans* and four companies of Croatians.

γ. 1771 *Gentl. Mag.* XLI. 478 The King [of Poland] was not escorted as usual by his guard of twelve Uhlans. 1809 *Lond. Chron.* 6 July 18/2 Three regiments of infantry, one of uhlans, and a battalion of the Bohemian Landwehr. 1889 BADEN-POWELL *Pigsticking* xi. 71 In that campaign, Hans Breitmann, serving as a uhlan, observed the number of sows that were about in the Ardennes.

*attrib.* 1812 *Examiner* 7 Dec. 781/1 Three Uhlan regiments of Guards. 1887 SIR W. W. HUNTER in Skrine *Life* xviii. (1901) 367 The horses go well, and my Uhlan groom is careful and intelligent.

*transf.* 1886 *Pall Mall G.* 6 March 5/2 Those uhlans of commerce who have lately been so urgently calling for the establishment of railway communication with China through Burmah.

Hence **U·hlaner.**

1886 W. J. TUCKER *E. Europe* 265 The cavalry officer, be he of the huszárs, the uhlaners, or of any other mounted body of men, represents in most cases blood and fortune.

**Uht-song** (*ū*χt-). *Eccl.* Now *Hist.* [OE. *úhtsang, -song*, f. *úhte* UGHTEN. Cf. OHG. *uhtisang*, ON. and Icel. *óttusǫngr* (MSw. *otto-, otta-, ottesang*, Sw. *ottesång*).] The ecclesiastical office celebrated just before daybreak; nocturns or matins.

*a* 900 *O. E. Martyrol.* 23 June 102 From uhtsanges tide heo a wunode..on hire ȝebede oð dæȝ. *c* 900 tr. *Bæda's Eccl. Hist.* IV. xxv. 348 Hu neah þære tide wære, þætte þa broðor arisan scolden..& heora uhtsong singan. *c* 960 *Rule St. Benet* ix. (Schröer) 33 On wintres timan is se uhtsang þus to beȝinnenne. *a* 1225 *Ancr. R.* 18 Þer efter anonriht vre Leafdi vhtsong siggeð oþisse wise. *Ibid.* 22 Biuoren Uhtsong & efter Prime.

1720 JOHNSON *Canons Ch. Engl., Elfric's Can.* xix, Let them sing..the Uht-song, the Prime-song, the Undern-song [etc]. 1844 LINGARD *Anglo-Sax. Ch.* (1858) I. vii. 272 *note*, The night-song..was frequently joined with the *uht-song*. 1853 ROCK *Ch. of Fathers* III. II. 11 The 'invitatory' at the beginning of uht-song or matins.

‖ **Uigur** (wī·gur), *sb.* and *a.* Also 8 Uigure, 9 Uighur, Ouigour. [ad. East Turkish اويغور *uighur*, f. *ui* to follow, fit, agree + *-gur* adj. suffix.]

**A.** *sb.* **1.** A member of the eastern branch of the Turkish race, which was prominent in Central Asia from the 8th to the 12th century.

1785 *Archaeol.* VII. 227 Perhaps it was the Uigures or Igureans, from whom the great founder of the Mongol monarchy first received letters and the art of writing. 1844 PRICHARD *Phys. Hist. Mankind* IV. 311 The celebrated Turkish race of the Ouigours. 1874 F. E. BURNETT tr. *Vambéry's Cent. Asia* 132 The Uigurs have played a very remarkable part in the history of the civilisation of Central Asia. 1888 *Encycl. Brit.* XXIII. 658/2 When we speak of Uigurs and Tatars, we mean tribes who style themselves Turks and really are such.

**2.** The language spoken by the Uigurs.

1843 *Penny Cycl.* XXV. 406/1 The Uighur was originally written with fourteen, and afterwards with sixteen letters, which..there is reason to believe..have been invented by the Uighurs themselves. 1862 LATHAM *Compar. Philol.* 102 Theoretically, the main differences between the Tshagatai and Uighur are considerable.

**B.** *adj.* Of or pertaining to, used by, the Uigurs.

1844 PRICHARD *Phys. Hist. Mankind* IV. 312 The Ouigour dialect..preserves the true characteristics and analogies of an oriental Tartarian idiom. *Ibid.* 313 He was the founder of the Ouigour empire. 1862 LATHAM *Compar. Philol.* 100 The Uighur Turks were the first of their stock to use an alphabet. *Ibid.* 102 A Uighur alphabet makes a Uighur work. 1870 HOWORTH in *Jrnl. Ethnol. Soc.* (N.S.) II. 87 The remains of the Ouigour literature.

Hence **Uigu·rean, Uigu·rian, Uigu·ric** *adjs.*

1773 *Archaeol.* II. 228 The Oigurian or Uigurean alphabet of 14 characters. 1844 PRICHARD *Phys. Hist. Mankind* IV. 316 As the Ouigourian and Mongolian alphabets have the same origin and form. 1874 F. E. BURNETT tr. *Vambéry's Cent. Asia* 131 The Uigurian race of the Turks. 1888 *Encycl. Brit.* XXIII. 662/1 But the oldest Turkish alphabet, the Uigurian, is a direct transformation of the Syriac. *Ibid.* XXIV. 2 The unassimilated Uiguric *kilur-im* answers to the Osmanli *kilur-um*.

**Uile**, obs. form of OIL *sb.*[1]

‖ **Uitlander** (oit-, *ū*·tlăndəɹ). [(Cape) Du., f. *uit* out + *land* land. Cf. G. *ausländer*.] = OUTLANDER b.

1892 [see OUTLANDER b]. 1893 *Natal Times* 30 Sept., The *uitlanders'* petitions for redress had been received with silence. 1901 *Contemp. Rev.* March 313 One of the most grievous blunders committed by the military authorities, has been in connection with the Uitlanders.

*attrib.* 1894 *Daily News* 31 May 2/6 The uitlander opinion, even in the Transvaal, was strongly alive to the advantages of the union. 1895 *Westm. Gaz.* 12 Dec. 7/1 He aims at the Presidency and counts on large uitlander support.

*transf.* 1902 *Fortn. Rev.* March 376 Disputes will not be avoided as the uitlanders [in Korea] become more numerous and powerful.

‖ **Ukase** (yūkē¹·s). Also 8 oukauze, ukause, 9 (o)ukaz. [ad. Russ. указъ *ukaz'*, f. указать *ukazat'* to show, direct, order, decree. Hence also F. *ukase, oukase*, Pg. *ukase*, Sp. *ucase*, G., Da., Sw. *ukas*.]

**1.** A decree or edict, having the force of law, issued by the Russian emperor or government.

α. 1729 CONSETT *Pres. State Russia* Pref. p. lxiv, A true Oukauze or Edict sign'd with her Imperial Majesty's own hand. 1797 W. TOOKE *Cath. II* (1798) III. 204 A gracious *ukause*..put an end to every process of more than ten years standing. 1833 R. PINKERTON *Russia* 62 The ukaz, which expelled them from the empire,..was dated March 13, 1820. 1877 D. M. WALLACE *Russia* i. 12 Fifteen years ago the domestic serfs were emancipated by Imperial Ukaz. 1894 *Times* 11 Dec. 8/3 In execution of the Imperial Oukaz to the Minister of Finance.

β. 1775 *Ann. Reg., Chron.* 120 The Empress of Russia issued an ukase, whereby various taxes are abolished. 1810 E. D. CLARKE *Trav. Russia* (1839) 28/1 A ukase had appeared, which forbade the importation of any kind of foreign literature. 1889 GUNTER *That Frenchman* xv. 193 The ukase of September has been issued—proclaiming, in time of peace, military law.

**2.** *transf.* Any proclamation or decree; an order or regulation of a final or arbitrary nature.

1818 LADY MORGAN *Fl. Macarthy* II. ii. (1819) 106 (Stanf.), He was even half inclined to send out an ukase to Jemmy Bryan, and his myrmidons, to hold themselves in readiness. 1859 KINGSLEY *Misc., Plays & Purit.* II. 136 That New England ukase of Cotton Mather's, which punished the woman who should kiss her infant on the Sabbath day. 1880 MRS. WHITNEY *Odd or Even?* xxx, Whatever the Autocrat of the Breakfast Table may have found true, or have recorded by his ukase, twenty years ago.

† **Ukrai·ner.** *Obs. rare.* [f. as next + -ER.] = UKRAINIAN *sb.* a.

*a* 1815 *Gentl. Mag.* LXXXV. II. 114 That by the Malorussians and Ukrainers is meant the same people, none are ignorant. 1815 *Ibid.* 602.

**Ukrainian** (yukrē¹·niăn), *a.* and *sb.* [f. *Ukraine*, an extensive district in the south of Russia, ad. Polish *Ukraina* or Russ. Украйна *Ukraïna*, specific use of *ukraïna* border, frontier, marches, f. *u-* at, beside + *kraĭ* edge, brink, etc.] **A.** *adj.* Of or pertaining to the Ukraine. **B.** *sb.* **a.** A native of the Ukraine; a Little-Russian or Ruthenian of that district. **b.** The Slavonic dialect spoken in the Ukraine; Malo-Russian, Ruthenian.

1816 *Gentl. Mag.* March 212 The so much vaunted liberty of the Ukrainian Kozaks. 1823 [ROBERTSON & BYERLEY] *Percy Anecd.* XIII. II. 79 Ukrainian Singers. *Ibid.*, The sweetness and unlimited combination and range of the voice of the Ukrainians. 1886 *Encycl. Brit.* XXI. 80/2 In western Russia, printing in Ukrainian is prohibited, and 'Russification' is being carried on among Ukrainians by the same means as those employed in Poland.

**Ulama, Ulan**, variants of ULEMA, UHLAN.

**-ular**, *suffix*, representing L. *-ulāris* (whence also F. *-ulaire*, Sp. and Pg. *-ular*, It. *-ulare, -olare*), formed by the addition of *-āris* -AR[1] to the diminutive suffix *-ul-*, and employed in adjs. derived from nouns ending in *-ulus, -ula, -ulum*, as *populāris, rēgulāris, sēculāris*, f. *populus, rēgula, sēculum*. A considerable number of these are recorded from classical or post-classical Latin, as *angulāris, annulāris, caniculāris, circulāris, fistulāris*, etc., and many of these have at various dates been adopted in English in the forms *angular, annular*.

etc. Many others are derived either from mediæval or modern Latin formations, or have been directly formed on Latin sbs., as *auricular, capsular, cellular, corpuscular, funicular, globular, jugular*, etc., the use of the suffix having steadily become more frequent (especially in scientific use) since the 17th century. When the primitive noun as well as the diminutive exists in English, and is in common use, the adj. in *-ular* is usually associated with it; thus *glandular* and *globular* commonly correspond to *gland, globe*, rather than to *glandule, globule*. This, however, has not given rise to much independent use of the suffix, which is normally confined to the above types.

**Ulcer** (*v*·lsəɹ), *sb.* Also 5-7 vlcer, 5-6 vlcere, 6 ulcere. [ad. L. *ulcer-, ulcus* neut. (related to Gr. ἕλκος), whence also It. *ulcera* fem., *ulcero* masc., Sp. and Pg. *ulcera* fem., F. *ulcère* masc. († and fem.), OF. *ulcere* (1314).]

1. *Path.* An erosive solution of continuity in any external or internal surface of the body, forming an open sore attended with a secretion of pus or other morbid matter.

*c* 1400 *Lanfranc's Cirurg.* 215 Þe cure of vlcers þat ben olde. *a* 1425 tr. *Arderne's Treat. Fistula*, etc. 35 Þe clensyng of þe vlcer of flessh mortified by þe forseid poudre. *Ibid.* 89 Sanguis veneris heleþ wele..depe woundez..and holow vlcerez. 1541 R. COPLAND *Galyen's Terap.* 2 F iv, Yf the lyppes of the vlcere appere harde and stony, they must be cutte. 1589 NASHE *Almond for Parrat* 10 The disease of disobedience proceeds from the swelling of pride, as madness from some vntollerable vlcer. 1615 H. CROOKE *Body of Man* 56 Why if a bone be caued or hollowed by an vlcer ..the flesh can neuer be generated ouer it? 1637 NABBES *Microcosm.* v, Conscience stain'd Is like a fretting ulcer. 1694 RAY in *Lett. Lit. Men* (Camden) 201 The ulcers upon my leg..are..broken out again. *c* 1720 W. GIBSON *Farrier's Guide* II. lv. (1738) 210 A small ulcer is more easily managed than one that is large. 1772 W. BUCHAN *Dom. Med.* l. 712 Ulcers may be the consequence of wounds, bruises, or imposthumes improperly treated. 1797 M. BAILLIE *Morb. Anat.* (1807) 154, I have reason to believe that ulcers of the stomach are often slow in their progress. 1846 BRITTAN tr. *Malgaigne's Oper. Surg.* 270 These foreign bodies introduced by the wound finished by transforming it into an ulcer. 1877 F. T. ROBERTS *Handbk. Med.* (ed. 3) I. 48 When inflammation destroys the tissues on a surface, an ulcer is formed.

*transf.* 1606 SHAKS. *Tr. & Cr.* I. i. 52 Thou..Powr'st in the open Vlcer of my heart, Her Eyes, her Haire [etc.].

b. Used in sing. as a generic term.

1623 LODGE *Poor Mans Talent* 13 For the Cancer, vlcer, and Noli me tangere. 1667 MILTON *P. L.* XI. 484 Intestin Stone and Ulcer, Colic pangs. 1749 HARTLEY *Observ. Man* I. 126 The subsequent Pain is to be referred to the Heads of Inflammation and Ulcer. 1820 GOOD *Nosology* 274 For so closely is ulcer connected with gangrene, that it cannot exist without it. *c* 1837 in A. Combe *Physiol. Digestion* (1842) ix. 250 Scurvy, typhoid fever, dysentery, and ulcer, which up to the period of the change had produced great havoc. 1884 BRYANT *Pract. Surg.* (ed. 4) I. 83 *marg.*, Local causes of ulcer. *Ibid.*, Constitutional causes of ulcer.

c. *attrib.* and *Comb.*

1611 COTGR., *Vlceratif*, .. vlcer-breeding. 1843 R. J. GRAVES *Syst. Clin. Med.* xxvi. 336 Enlargements of the tonsils, without any ulcer-like cavities, were not unfrequently observed. 1897 *Allbutt's Syst. Med.* II. 765 The mucous membrane overhanging the ulcer cavity is œdematous.

2. *fig.* Any corroding or corrupting influence; a morally diseased or unsound element; a plague-spot.

1592 tr. *Junius on Rev.* xvi. 2 It doeth signifie a spirituall ulcer. 1613-8 DANIEL *Coll. Hist. Eng.* Wks. (Grosart) IV. 211 Hee would not wrest any thing by an Imperiall power from the Kingdome (which might breed vlcers of dangerous nature). 1643 BAKER *Chron., Q. Eliz.* 105 This was the right way to finde, whether the ulcer of his minde were throughly cured or no. 1873-4 DIXON *Two Queens* XXI. iii. IV. 138 His enmity to some of the Reformers..was the ulcer of his fame.

b. Applied to persons. *rare.*

1602 MARSTON *Antonio's Rev.* I. iv, Yon putred ulcer of my roiall bloode. 1615 BRATHWAIT *Strappado* (1878) 34 This wicked vlcer that corrupts the state, Nere thinkes of death, till that it be too late.

**Ulcer** (*v*·lsəɹ), *v.* Now *rare.* [f. prec. In first quot. after F. *ulcérer.*] a. *absol.* To cause an ulcer or ulcers. b. *trans.* To ulcerate. Also *fig.*

1590 C'TESS PEMBROKE *Antonie* 284 And his [*sc.* Love's] sweet shafts, with whose shot none are kill'd, Which ulcer not. 1642 FULLER *Holy & Prof. St.* v. vi. 379 This by degrees abates the reverence of religion, and ulcers mens hearts with profaneness. 1694 *Acc. Sev. Late Voy.* Introd. p. xxii, The cold had prodigious effects on our men in Greenland,..as blistering, and ulcering their flesh. 1829 LYTTON *Disowned* xiv, Thought, feeling, the faculties and impulses of man, all ulcered into one great canker—Gain.

**U·lcerable**, *a.* *rare*—⁰. [Cf. prec. and -ABLE.] 'That may become ulcerated.'

1846 WORCESTER (citing *Quart. Rev.*).

†**U·lcerate**, *ppl. a.* *Obs.* [ad. L. *ulcerātus*, pa. pple. of *ulcerāre*: see next. So It. *ulcerato*, Sp. and Pg. *ulcerado*, F. *ulcéré.*] Ulcerated. Also *fig.*

*a* 1425 tr. *Arderne's Treat. Fistula*, etc. 2 Bothe his buttokis was so vlcerat and putrefied with in. 1541 R. COPLAND *Galyen's Terap.* 2 A iv, For the mystemperaunce of yᵉ fleshe vlcerate, or for the gatheryng of humours. 1609 [BP. W. BARLOW] *Answ. Nameless Cath.* 104 Vlcerate Apostemes must be launced. 1654 EARL MONM. tr. *Bentivoglio's Wars Flanders* 367 So the ulcerate part of Flanders makes the body of your whole Empire daily languish. 1720 W. GIBSON *Diet. Horses* i. (1726) 17 When the Cornet is large, it denotes an over-great Relaxation and Moisture in that Part, which is apt to turn ulcerate.

**Ulcerate** (*v*·lsəreɪt), *v.* [f. ppl. stem of L. *ulcerāre* (whence It. *ulcerare*, Sp. and Pg. *ulcerar*, F. *ulcérer*), f. *ulcer-, ulcus* ULCER *sb.*: see -ATE.]

1. *intr.* To form an ulcer; to break out into ulcers or purulent sores; to fester.

*a* 1425 tr. *Arderne's Treat. Fistula*, etc. 37 Þis sikenes lurkeþ wiþin þe lure in þe bigynnyng, but after processe of tyme it vlcerate, & fretyng þe lure goþe out. 1623 COCKERAM, *Vlcerate*, to blister, to breake out into sores. 1753 N. TORRIANO *Gangr. Sore Throat* 45 The Tonsils, says he, are often exposed to ulcerate. 1813 J. THOMSON *Lect. Inflam.* 387 A part never ulcerates till it has become inflamed. 1826 S. COOPER *First Lines Surg.* (ed. 5) 190 Inflaming the whole swelling, and causing it to ulcerate and slough. 1898 *Hutchinson's Arch. Surg.* IX. 313 The patches do not ulcerate or inflame.

*fig.* 1833 I. TAYLOR *Fanat.* ii. 49 When an affection, more sensitive than any other, is left to bleed and ulcerate in open air. 1850 BLACKIE *Æschylus* I. 154 More than a house may bear, whose wounds yet bleed, And ulcerate from the fangs of fate.

2. *trans.* To cause ulcers in or on.

*c* 1550 H. LLOYD *Treas. Health* 5 Sinapismus is an emplaster made of mustard to vlcerate the skynne & make the same red. 1604 R. CAWDREY *Table Alph.*, *Vlcerate*, to make full of sores, to blister. 1684 tr. *Bonet's Merc. Compit.* VII. 249 When signs of a Gangrene begin to appear..we must ulcerate the parts..with deep scarifications. 1753 *Phil. Trans.* XLVIII. 149 If either the stalks or leaves of this valuable plant are applied to the skin, they heat and ulcerate it. 1788 *Med. Commun.* II. 208 The discharge ..excoriates or ulcerates the membrane. 1843 YOUATT *Horse* (ed. 2) i. 14 The fetlock would be chafed and ulcerated, if the horse was ridden over ploughed grounds.

3. *fig.* To affect after the manner of an ulcer; to irritate; to wound or poison.

1647 N. BACON *Disc. Govt. Eng.* I. lxiv. 214 Wherein the King dealt with a tender hand, as if he feared to ulcerate any part, and especially the Clergy. 1768-74 TUCKER *Lt. Nat.* (1834) II. 656 By knowing the true place of the wound, we shall prevent its ulcerating the mind herself. 1792 BURKE *Let. to Sir H. Langrishe* Wks. VI. 362 The only reason which can be assigned for this disfranchisement, has a tendency more deeply to ulcerate their minds than the act of exclusion itself. 1849 MACAULAY *Hist. Eng.* vi. II. 46 A small knot of Roman Catholics whose hearts had been ulcerated by old injuries. *Ibid.* vii. II. 255 When her heart had been ulcerated by disasters and mortifications. 1879 FARRAR *St. Paul* viii, To brand consciences already ulcerated by a sense of guilt.

**U·lcerated,** *ppl. a.* [f. prec. + -ED.]

1. Converted into an ulcer; afflicted with ulcers; eroded with purulent sores.

1547 BOORDE *Brev. Health* § 377 Some be playne woundes .., some be festered, some be vlcerated and some hath fystures. 1580 HESTER tr. *Fioravanti's Disc. Chirurg.* 25 b, The cure of an Vlcerated legge. 1651 BAXTER *Inf. Bapt.* 274 It is only the ulcerated parts that honey doth bite and purge. 1695 J. EDWARDS *Perfect. Script.* 273 The falling out of his ulcerated bowels. 1721 R. KEITH tr. *T. à Kempis, Vall. Lillies* 56 The poor and ulcerated Lazarus, who after Death was joyfully received into Abraham's Bosom. 1787 *Med. Commun.* II. 384 The ulcerated sore-throat. 1797 M. BAILLIE *Morb. Anat.* (1807) 383 In advanced stages of the ulcerated uterus. 1799 *Med. Jrnl.* II. 89 The prevailing method of treating ulcerated legs. 1843 R. J. GRAVES *Syst. Clin. Med.* xxiii. 280 The lungs were extensively solidified, black, and ulcerated. 1872 COHEN *Dis. Throat* 89 Ulcerated sore throat is indicated by its name.

*transf.* 1842 LOUDON *Suburban Hort.* 649 Manure..causes the roots to branch and their rind to become ulcerated.

b. *fig.* (Cf. ULCERATE *v.* 3.)

1634 FORD *Perk. Warbeck* v. ii, Scorne weares onely Such fashion, as commends to gazers eyes Sad vlcerated Novelty. 1700 T. BROWN *Amusem. Ser. & Com.* ix. (1709) 99 They.. say that his conscience is Ulcerated. 1759 DILWORTH *Life of Pope* 28 Wrangling Dennis..with others of a like ulcerated understanding plied all the severity of censure they could, against it. 1875 JOWETT *Plato, Gorgias* (ed. 2) II. 399 The ulcerated and swollen condition of the State.

†2. Of matter: Rendered purulent. *Obs. rare.*

1580 HESTER tr. *Fioravanti's Disc. Chirurg.* 21 b, It is a grosse and vlcerated matter. 1660 R. COKE *Power & Subj.* 170 The wound is to be inquired into by good counsel; then the ulcerated matter, which does inwardly putrifie, is to be let out, that is, he purge himself through confession.

3. Of diseases: Characterized by the formation of ulcers in the affected part.

1706 PHILLIPS (ed. Kersey), s.v. *Cancer*, It is call'd an Occult, Latent, or Blind Cancer, but when bigger and open'd, it bears the Name of an Ulcerated Cancer. 1762 R. GUY *Pract. Obs. Cancers* 46 An ulcerated Cancer in the Breast. 1826 S. COOPER *First Lines Surg.* (ed. 5) 201 Another event, still more rare, is the actual cicatrization of an ulcerated cancer. 1878 HABERSHON *Dis. Abdomen* (ed. 3) 21 Ulcerated Stomatitis is especially seen in young children of 4 to 10 years of age.

**U·lcerating,** *ppl. a.* [f. as prec. + -ING ².]

1. Giving rise to ulcers. *rare*—⁰.

1611 COTGR., *Vlceratif*, vlceratiue, vlcerating, vlcer-breeding.

2. Developing into an ulcer or ulcers.

1843 R. J. GRAVES *Syst. Clin. Med.* xxix. 390 A few ulcerating points on the surface, were touched with nitrate of silver. 1890 *Retrospect Med.* CII. 384 An ulcerating malignant growth of the anterior vaginal wall.

**Ulceration** (*v*lsĕrē·ʃən). *Path.* Also 5 vlceracio(u)n, 6 -cyon, -tion. [ad. L. *ulcerātiōn-, ulcerātio*, noun of action f. *ulcerāre*: see ULCERATE *v.* Hence also F. *ulcération* (1314), Sp. *ulceracion*, Pg. *-ação*, It. *-azione.*]

1. The action, process, or state of forming ulcers or of becoming ulcerated.

*c* 1400 *Lanfranc's Cirurg.* 214 Þis wole not suffre þat þe matere schal make noon vlceracioun ne no fretyng. *a* 1425 tr. *Arderne's Treat. Fistula*, etc. 37 Signes, forsoþe, of his vlceracion bene þise. *c* 1530 *Judic. Urines* III. vii. 51 b *marg.*, Vlceracyon of the bladder. Vlceracyon of yᵉ reines. Vlceracyon of yᵉ liuer. 1541 R. COPLAND *Guydon's Form.* R iij b, Before the vlceracyon fyrste ought to be mynystred medycyns that be colde. 1611 COTGR., *Vlceration*, an ulceration; a making or growing vlcerous, a drawing to an vlcer. 1676 WISEMAN *Chirurg. Treat.* II. ii. 169 Where the Part hath been long affected with Vlceration, it..is very difficult to cicatrize. 1804 ABERNETHY *Surg. Obs.* 160 Some of these sores spread by ulceration, and some by sloughing. 1847 E. J. SEYMOUR *Severe Dis.* I. 16 Adhesion of the gall-bladder to the bowels and subsequent ulceration. 1876 BRISTOWE *Th. & Pract. Med.* (1878) 44 In ulceration the destruction of parts is molecular, or by small fragments, and progressive.

2. An ulcerous formation; an ulcer or group of ulcers.

1580 T. NEWTON *Approved Medicines* 57 b, Pryuet.. healeth vlcerations of the Mouthe that often happe in Children. 1599 A. M. tr. *Gabelhouer's Bk. Physicke* 178/2 A little bagge, as bigge that it may cover the vlceration. 1718 QUINCY *Compl. Disp.* 120 All Medicines of this Intention are suppos'd..to..fill up with new Flesh, all Ulcerations, and Foulnesses. 1725 *Fam. Dict.* s.v. *Lucatellus Balsam*, Such Coughs as give Suspicion of Tubercles and Ulcerations in the Lungs. 1804 ABERNETHY *Surg. Obs.* 124 He had an ulceration which spread over the palate. 1829 COOPER *Good's Study Med.* (ed. 3) III. 513 The disease generally commences on the alæ of the nose, with small tubercules, which gradually change into ulcerations.

**Ulcerative** (*v*·lsĕreɪtiv, -ătiv), *a.* [ad. med.L. *ulcerātīv-us*: see ULCERATE *v.* and -IVE. So F. *ulcératif, -ive* (1495), Sp., Pg., It. *ulcerativo.*]

1. Causing ulceration.

1575 J. BANISTER *Treat. Chyrurg.* 138 The properties of vlceratiue medicins, is to breake & blister the skinne, in what places they are laide. 1601 HOLLAND *Pliny* II. 158 The dregs of vinegre, must of necessitie be much more sharpe, biting, and ulcerative, than wine lees. 1813 J. THOMSON *Lect. Inflam.* 379 One, two, or three parts..were more susceptible of the ulcerative stimulus than the others.

2. Of the nature of ulceration.

1800 *Med. Jrnl.* IV. 489 Extensive erysipelas..followed in most [instances] by an immediate ulcerative process. 1835-6 *Todd's Cycl. Anat.* I. 444/2 The process of ulcerative absorption in any structure is scarcely understood. 1872 COHEN *Dis. Throat* 116 The ulcerative process may involve its cartilages as well as its mucous membrane. 1878 T. BRYANT *Pract. Surg.* I. 44 Opium is an admirable drug when the ulcerative action is present.

3. Accompanied or characterized by the formation of ulcers.

1813 J. THOMSON *Lect. Inflam.* 223 Mr. Hunter has divided inflammation..into adhesive, suppurative, and ulcerative. 1850 F. CHURCHILL *Dis. Children* II. vi. (1858) 471 Ulcerated sore mouth. Ulcerative stomatitis. 1879 *St. George's Hosp. Rep.* IX. 411 Ulcerative endocarditis of the heart-wall.

4. Due to, produced by, ulceration.

1876 BRISTOWE *Th. & Pract. Med.* (1878) 45 The chief removal of ulcerative detritus.

**U·lceratory**, *a.* [Cf. prec. and -ORY.] Ulcerative. (1891 *Cent. Dict.*)

**U·lcered,** *ppl. a.* [f. ULCER *sb.* or *v.* + -ED.]

1. = ULCERATED *ppl. a.* 1.

1575 J. BANISTER *Treat. Chyrurg.* 81 What meates are to be vsed as touching diet in vlcered bodies. 1576 G. BAKER tr. *Gesner's Jewell of Health* 58 b, This water..cureth the Bladder ulcered. 1610 HEALEY *St. Aug. Citie of God* I. xi. (1620) 19 One farre more sumptuous did the ministring Angell prepare for the poore vlcered begger in the sight of God. 1654 WHITLOCK *Zootomia* 386 Comparing his own sound Arme, with the Ulcer'd one of the Diseased. 1708 *Phil. Trans.* XXVI. 229 A Youth of Ten Years old, had his Gums much swelled and ulcered. 1807 SOUTHEY *Espriella's Lett.* II. 311 Colonel Despard..had been confined there..without fire, till his feet were ulcered with the frost. 1844 H. G. ROBINSON *Odes of Horace* I. xxv, When that lust, and hot desire,..Shall round your ulcer'd liver reign.

b. *fig.* = ULCERATED *ppl. a.* 1 b.

1602 MARSTON *Antonio's Rev.* v. i, Now gin the leprous cores of ulcered sins Wheale to a heade. 1616 R. C. *Times Whistle* (1871) 88 Lop of these vlcerd members of our land. 1699 R. L'ESTRANGE *Erasm. Colloq.* (1725) 162 Your Soul is yet fouler, than your Body, more putrid and ulcer'd, and yet more dangerously wounded. 1747 FRANCIS tr. *Horace, Epist.* I. xvi. 32 For Fools alone their ulcer'd Ills conceal.

†2. = ULCERATED *ppl. a.* 3. *Obs.*—¹

1622 R. BANISTER 413 *Diseases Eyes* O 10 b, Of vlcered Cancers, those onely are cut and seared, which are in the vppermost part of the body.

**Ulcerous** (*v*·lsĕrəs), *a.* [ad. L. *ulcerōs-us*, f. *ulcer-, ulcus* ULCER *sb.* Hence also It., Sp., Pg. *ulceroso*, F. *ulcéreux, -euse* (1554), Da. *ulcerøs.*]

1. Of the nature of an ulcer or ulcers; forming a purulent sore.

1577 B. GOOGE *Heresbach's Husb.* III. (1586) 144 The vlcerous places must be nointed with Vinegar. 1592 GREENE *Groat's W. Wit* (1617) 43 For my gluttony, I suffer hunger: ..for my adulterie, vlcerous sores. 1603 HOLLAND *Plutarch's Mor.* 97 Honie..being applied to a sore or ulcerous place, at the first doth smart and sting. 1607 SHAKS. *Timon* IV. iii. 39 Shee, whom the Spittle-house, and vlcerous sores, Would cast the gorge at. 1744 BERKELEY *Siris* § 21 In obstructions and ulcerous erosions of the inward parts. 1752 — *Th. Tar-water* Wks. 1871 III. 499 Good against ulcerous eruptions. 1789 A. DUNCAN *Mariner's Chron.* (1805) IV. 42 Their lips began to break out in watery and ulcerous blisters. 1834 J. FORBES *Laennec's Dis. Chest* (ed. 4) 279 The disease is curable..after the softening of the tubercles and the formation of an ulcerous excavation. **1897** *Allbutt's Syst. Med.* III. 886 In some instances the foreign bodies had escaped from the appendix through the ulcerous openings they had made in its walls.

*fig.* **1601** [? MARSTON] *Pasquil & Kath.* v. 20 Why, now the vlcerous swelling of my hate Is broken forth. **1602** MARSTON *Antonio's Rev.* IV. iii, The polluting filth Of ulcerous sinne.

**2.** Afflicted with an ulcer or ulcers; exhibiting ulceration.

**1599** B. JONSON *Ev. Man out of Hum., The Stage* 73 Euery seruile imitating spirit..striues to fling His vlc'rous body in the Thespian spring, And streight leaps forth a Poet. **1600** R. CAWDREY *Treasurie* 266 Scuruie, Scabbie, and vlcerous persons. **1605** SHAKS. *Macb.* IV. iii. 151 Strangely visited people All swolne and Vlcerous..he cures. **1662** HIBBERT *Body Divinity* I. 313 They observed..whether the bowels were of an unnatural colour, or ulcerous. **1899** *Allbutt's Syst. Med.* VI. 105 Cavities resulting from their destruction present irregular, anfractuous, ragged and ulcerous walls.

*absol.* **1889** H. M. STANLEY in *Stanley & Africa* xvii. (1890) 392 Assiduously dressing and trimming up the ulcerous ready for the march to Zanzibar.

**b.** *fig.* (Cf. ULCERATED *ppl. a.* 1 b.)

**1611** SPEED *Hist. Gt. Brit.* IX. xvi. § 20 A weauer (the Bailiffe of the Towne) was the vlcerous head, to which that corruption gathered. **1643** MILTON *Divorce* II. iii. Wks. 1851 IV. 65 Did God for this come down..to patch up an ulcerous and rott'n commonwealth with strict and stern injunctions? **1660** T. M. C. *Walker's Hist. Independ.* IV. 22 Belching forth the scandalous language of their ulcerous tongues to incense the People. **1879** H. GEORGE *Progr. & Pov.* x. v. (1881) 494 A just man would crush with his foot such an ulcerous ant-hill!

**3.** Developed in, proceeding from, ulcers.

**1660** O. SEDGWICK in Spurgeon *Treas. David* Ps. xix. 12 Methinks sin is..like evil and ulcerous humours. **1718** QUINCY *Compl. Disp.* 121 Ulcerous Exudations, which by their loose situations are easily carried along with the Medicine. **1844** G. S. FABER *Eight Dissert.* (1845) II. 311 By reason of some colouring ulcerous matter, the skin of the sufferer would pass through the different successive shades of dark red and lead colour and complete black.

**4.** Characteristic of, appropriate to, ulcers.

**1641** in Rushw. *Hist. Coll.* (1692) III. I. 218, I cannot but admire how this..Body of Judicature should swell up into such a vast and ulcerous dimension. *c* **1720** W. GIBSON *Farrier's Dispens.* III. xiv. (1721) 268/2 To dry up watry Corruptions, which create an ulcerous Disposition in the Legs. **1842** TENNYSON *St. Sim. Styl.* 13 Thrice ten years, Thrice multiplied by superhuman pangs,..In coughs,.. ulcerous throes and cramps. **1896** *Allbutt's Syst. Med.* I. 127 The development of ulcerous conditions when the process affects free surfaces.

**5.** = ULCERATED *ppl. a.* 3.

**1751** FOTHERGILL (*title*), Account of the Ulcerous Sore Throat. **1761** *Phil. Trans.* LII. 264 His disorder has been a malignant or ulcerous sore throat. **1859** SEMPLE *Diphtheria* 84 Severe and obstinate ulcerous inflammations of the skin and mucous tissue. **1889** DUNCAN *Clin. Lect. Dis. Women* (ed. 4) xxii. 189 A disease exactly resembling the acute ulcerous stomatitis of children.

Hence **U·lcerously** *adv.*; **U·lcerousness.**

**1727** BAILEY (vol. II), *Ulcerousness*, ulcerous State, Condition, or Quality. **1847** WEBSTER, *Ulcerously*.

**U·lcery,** *a. rare*[−1]. [f. ULCER *sb.*] Of the nature of an ulcer.

**1611** COTGR., *Mammelons*, be certaine little, red, hard, vlcerie, and teat-like swellings, which break out of the skin of the head.

**Ulche,** ME. variant of EACH *a.*

**U·lcuscle.** *rare*[−1]. [ad. L. *ulcusculum*, dim. of *ulcus* ULCER *sb.*] A small ulcer.

**1794** E. DARWIN *Zoon.* I. 400 The specific medicines.. act only by increasing the absorption of the matter in the ulcuscles of those diseases.

So **Ulcu·scule.** (Webster, 1847.)

**Ulde, -ere, -est,** ME. ff. ELD, -ER, -EST.

† **Uldron,** variant of *oldron* OLERON *Obs.*

**1550** *Admir. Crt. Exemplifications* 3, No. 167, Serten packes of canvas namyd uldrons of Methernek.

**Ule,** obs. var. OIL *sb.*[1]; obs. f. OWL *sb.*, YULE.

**-ule,** *suffix*, representing the Latin diminutive ending *-ulus, -ula, -ulum* (whence also F. *-ule*, Sp. and Pg. *-ulo, -ula*, It. *-ulo, -ula, -olo, -ola*), as in *globulus* globule, *glandula* glandule, *grānulum* granule. Among words now current with this ending a certain number correspond to actual Latin forms, as *capsule, cellule, ferule, macule, nodule, pustule, spherule, valvule*; others are of modern formation, as *anguillule*. Only a few of these were in use before the 17th century. Some examples, as *angule, circule, scrupule*, failed to establish themselves against the earlier forms of French origin in *-le*; others, as *formule*, have given way to the purely Latin form. In some cases both forms exist in scientific use, as *ligule* and *ligula, macule* and *macula, valvule* and *valvula*; in some the Latin form is commonly or exclusively employed, as *lingula, tabula*.

‖ **Ulema** (*ū·lĕmā*, *ū·lĕmă*, *u-*, *yulī·mă*). Also 7 **ulemi,** 9 **oulema, uhlema, oolama, ulama.** [a. Arab. (also Turk. and Pers.) علما *ʿulemā*, pl. of عالم *ʿālim* knowing, learned, f. *ʿalama* to know. Hence also Sp. *Ulema*, Pg. *Ulemas*, F. *Ulēma*.]

**1.** *pl.* or *collect.* Those who have had special training in the knowledge of Mohammedan religion and law, and are regarded by Moslems as the authorities on these matters; *spec.* the body of Mohammedan doctors under the headship of the Sheik-ul-islam, which exercises great political influence in the Turkish empire.

**1688** *Lond. Gaz.* No. 2313/2 The next day was a great Consultation held with the Ulemi or Interpreters of their Law. **1768** SIR J. PORTER *Observ. Turks* Pref. (1771) 30 They have the Ulema..composed of all the members of the church or law; a body of men..who stand as an intermediate order between the prince and people. **1803** *Edin. Rev.* II. 292 Russia, and imperial Rome, had its prætorian guards. Turkey has its *uhlema*. **1848** LAYARD *Nineveh* (1849) I. Introd. p. xxiv, The ulema having at length pronounced that these figures were the idols of the infidels, the Mohammedans..destroyed them. **1892** TENNYSON *Akbar's Dream* 45 But our Ulama..Are like wild brutes new-caged.

*attrib.* **1847** MRS. A. KERR tr. *Ranke's Hist. Servia* v. 89 The establishment of the influence of some great Ulema families which had become almost hereditary. **1888** *Encycl. Brit.* XXIII. 654/2 The juridical and spiritual precepts of the Koran and its '*ulemā* interpreters.

**2.** A Mohammedan doctor or divine.

*a* **1843** in Southey *Comm.-pl. Bk.* Ser. II. (1849) 350 A great part of the oulemas and of the people in office delayed not to partake of this luxury. **1848** W. H. KELLY tr. *L. Blanc's Hist. Ten Y.* I. 260 The divan was rescued from the mystic domination of the ulemas. **1882** *Macm. Mag.* XLVI. 474 The army was accompanied by a number of moullas and ulemas.

**-ulent,** *suffix*, ad. L. *-ulentus* employed to form adjs., usually with the force of 'abounding in', 'full of' (some thing or quality), as *fraudulentus* fraudulent, *opulentus* opulent, *truculentus* truculent, etc. (Variant forms of the suffix are *-olentus*, as in *vinolentus* vinolent, *violentus* violent, and *-ilentus* as in *gracilentus* slender, *pestilentus* pestilent.) A considerable number of the formations occurring in Latin have been adopted in English, and a few have been added either from mediæval or modern Latin, or by direct formation on Latin stems, as *cinerulent, flatulent, herbulent, nidorulent, torpulent*.

‖ **Ulex** (*yū·leks*). *Bot.* [mod.L. (Linnæus, 1737), a. L. *ulex* (Pliny) a shrub resembling rosemary.] A genus of thorny papilionaceous shrubs belonging to the order *Leguminosæ*; a plant belonging to this genus, esp. *Ulex Europæus* the common furze, gorse, or whin.

**1753** *Chambers' Cycl.* Suppl. s.v. **1755** *Dict. Arts & Sci.*, *Ulex*, in botany, a genus..of plants, with a papilionaceous flower; and an oblong turgid pod for its fruit. **1859** DARWIN *Orig. Spec.* xiii. (1860) 439 The embryonic leaves of the ulex or furze..are pinnate or divided like the ordinary leaves of the leguminosæ.

**Ulexine** (*yū·leksəin*). *Med.* [f. prec. + -INE.] An alkaloid prepared from the seeds of gorse.

**1887** *Brit. Med. Jrnl.* 21 May 1144/2 The value..of kavaine and ulexine as local anæsthetics. **1888** F. H. LESCHER *Recent Mat. Medica* (ed. 3) 88 Ulexine;..discovered by A. W. Gerrard. A powerful organic base, soluble in water, insoluble in ether.

**Ulexite** (*yū·leksəit*). *Chem.* [See quot. 1867.] (See quots. and BOROCALCITE.)

**1867** BRANDE & COX *Dict. Sci.*, etc. III. 892/2 *Ulexite*, a name given to native borate of lime (Hayesine), after Ulex, by whom it was analysed. **1875** *Ure's Dict. Arts* (ed. 7) III. 1050 *Ulexite*, a native borate of lime and soda, known also as Boronatrocalcite. It occurs at Iquique, in Peru; and in the Province of Tarapaca.

**Uley,** obs. Sc. variant of OIL *sb.*

**Ulican,** variant of ULLAGONE.

‖ **Ulicon** (*ū·likǫn*). Also **ulikon, eulachon, ulken;** and OOLAKAN, -CHAN, etc. [Native name in British Columbia.] A small fish of the north-western parts of North America, ascending the rivers in immense numbers to spawn; the candle-fish.

**1807** P. GASS *Jrnl.* 187 In the afternoon some of the natives came to visit us, and brought some of the small fish, which they call Ulken... At noon our fishermen returned with some ulken and sturgeon. **1880** *Libr. Univ. Knowl.* (N.Y.) I. 205 All the early navigators and explorers..have spoken of the immense numbers of salmon, cod, halibut, mullet, ulicon, etc. **1885** SIMMONDS *Animal Food Resources* ix. 318 The ulikon or oulachan (*Thaleichthys pacificus*, Gerard)..has long been an ichthyological curiosity...It is a small silvery fish, averaging about fourteen inches long, and in general appearance much resembling a smelt.

**Ulie,** obs. Sc. variant of OIL *sb.*

**Uli·ginal,** *a. Bot.* [f. L. *ūlīgin-* (see next) + -AL.] Growing in moist or wet ground.

**1863** J. G. BAKER *N. Yorksh. Stud. Bot.*, etc. 181 Aboriginal species characteristically paludal, uliginal, ericetal, and sylvestral.

**Uligino·se,** *a. rare.* [ad. L. *ūlīginōs-us* full of moisture, f. *ūlīgin-*, *ūlīgo* moisture, marshiness. Cf. It., Sp., Pg. *uliginoso*, F. *uligineux*.]

**1.** = ULIGINOUS *a.* 2 b. *rare*[−1].

*c* **1440** *Pallad. on Husb.* x. 29 This moone in lond vliginose or lene,..In thicked lond also, is to demene, When day and nyght yliche longe is holde.

**2.** *Bot.* = ULIGINAL *a.*

**1866** *Treas. Bot.*, *Uliginose*, growing in swampy places.

**Uliginous** (*yuli·dʒĭnəs*), *a.* [f. as prec., or directly f. L. *ūlīgin-* + -OUS. Cf. F. *uligineux* (of soil or plants).]

**1.** Of a watery, slimy, or oozy nature.

**1576** NEWTON *Lemnie's Complex.* II. iii. 109 b, For it is a certayne vliginous moystishnes and superfluous excrement, which ought rather to be sent out and purged. **1610** W. FOLKINGHAM *Art of Survey* I. x. 24 It reuiues the radicall and vliginous humour. *a* **1656** USSHER *Ann.* VI. (1658) 240 One Proxenus..found a spring of a fatty, and uliginous, or oily liquor. **1669** *Phil. Trans.* IV. 1132 The Birch and Alder feed more kindly on a thin uliginous moisture. *a* **1728** WOODWARD *Fossils* (1729) I. 118 The uliginous lacteous Matter,..in the Coral Fishings upon the Coast of Italy, was only a Collection of the Corallin Particles thus sustained in the Sea Water.

**2.** Of places: Soaked with water or moisture; water-logged, plashy, swampy.

**1610** W. FOLKINGHAM *Art of Survey* I. x. 33 Their vliginous and soaked Mosses doe recompence their meane ayre with vnctious Turffes. **1620** VENNER *Via Recta* i. 20 Contrary to this is that which is of a laxe and open substance, such as is commonly growen in low and vliginous places. **1664** EVELYN *Sylva* xv. 32 The water-galls, and uliginous parts of Forests that hardly bear any grass, do many times spontaneously produce it in abundance. **1699** — *Acetaria* (1729) 155 Those who live in marshes and uliginous Places like the Hundreds of Essex. **1867** SMYTH *Sailor's Word-bk.* 705 *Uliginous channels*, those connecting the branches of rivers, by cuts through the soil.

**b.** Similarly of soil.

**1650** CHARLETON tr. *Van Helmont's Paradoxes* 15 If..they are..buried in a muddy uliginous earth; when they begin to putrifie, they then operate upon..the Patient. **1802** R. HALL *Bot.* 192 *Uliginous Soil*,..spongy, filled with putrid water.

†**3.** Of air: Damp, moist. *Obs. rare.*

**1661** EVELYN *Fumifugium* Misc. Writ. (1805) I. 217 The impure and uliginous [air], as that which proceeds from stagnated places, is..the most vile and pestilent. **1697** R. PEIRCE *Bath Mem.* 85 He liv'd near the Fenns, to which Uliginous Air, was ascrib'd the beginning of his Illness.

† **Ulipy.** *Sc. Obs.* Also **vly-.** [Prob. ad. older Du. or Flem. **oliepij(e*, f. *olie* oil + *pij(e* PEE *sb.*[1] Cf. the equivalent WFlem. *oliebaai*.] ? An oilskin coat or jacket.

**1529** *Acc. Ld. High Treas. Scot.* V. 369 For ane coit of ulipy in all uncostis. *a* **1568** in *Bannatyne MS.* fol. 158 b, His clais is oft in wanting and sic is his gyis, He thrawis and he puttis fast at his vly pyis.

**Ulk,** ME. var. ILK *adjs.*; obs. Sc. f. WEEK.

**Ulken,** obs. var. ULICON. **Ulklie,** obs. Sc. f. WEEKLY. **'Ull,** dial. f. WILL *v.*

**Ullage** (*v·lėdʒ*), *sb.* Forms: 5 **oylage, vlage,** 6 *Sc.* **vlege,** 8- **ullage.** [ad. AF. *ulliage*, OF. *ouillage, eullage* (*heulliage*), *œillage* (also Anglo-L. *oliagium, oyll-, ull-, ulagium*), Pr. *ulhage, oulhage*, f. OF. *ouiller, eullier, oiller, œiller* (Anglo-L. *oillare*), Pr. *ulha, oulha*, to fill up (a barrel).

Forms with initial *a-* are also given by Godefroy, viz. *aouillage* and *aouillier, aoillier, aeullier*, etc. (1295-).]

**1.** The amount of wine or other liquor by which a cask or bottle falls short of being quite full (originally the quantity required to make good the loss by leakage or absorption).

[**1297** *Chanc. Misc.* (P.R.O.) Bd. 2 No. 15 (5), Tradidi etiam eidem vnam pipam pro oliagio predictorum doleorum. **1329** *Exchequer Rolls Scotl.* (1878) I. 224 De ij doliis et j pipa vini...Et in vllagio..j et dimidium. *a* **1377** *Rolls of Parlt.* II. 384 Item par Adam le Ken pur ulliage es Vins mesme l'an 1 ton' 1 pip'.]

**1444** *Compota Domest.* (Abbotsf. Cl. 1836) 26 In vlage et lecage per tempus predictum, [84] lagene [bere]. **1481-90** *Howard Househ. Bks.* (Roxb.) 288 Paid for iiij. galons wyne, iij. qrtes. for oylage for the ton wyne, iij. s. ij. d. **1565** *Burgh Rec. Edinb.* (1875) III. 211 The twn of wyne at this present..xvj crownis of the sone;..item, of fraucht xvj crownis sone; item, for vlege vj li. **1706** PHILLIPS (ed. Kersey), *Ullage* of a Cask, is what such a Vessel wants of being full. **1749** W. YEO *Ullaging & Inching* 3 As often as these Lines are used for determining the Ullages of Casks. **1755** *Dict. Arts & Sci.* s.v., The ullage of a vessel, whose axis is parallel to the horizon, may be found thus. **1833** LOUDON *Encycl. Archit.* § 1324 It is usually tunned into hogsheads of a hundred gallons each, leaving a few gallons ullage. **1835** MARRYAT *Olla Podr.* III. 297 (*Moonshine*), I held the bottle up to the candle to ascertain the ullage. **1885** W. ECOCKES in *Civilian* 3 Jan. 141/2 A work..comprising tables of ullages of casks, whose bung diameters range from 15 to 40 inches.

**b.** *On ullage*, (in a vessel) not completely full.

**1863** T. G. SHAW *Wine, Vine & Cellar* xi. 302 It is injurious to Rhenish wine to be left on ullage. **1880** *Act* 43 & 44 *Vic.* c. 24 § 43 The casks in which spirits are removed may be either full or..on ullage. **1883** *Times* 17 Nov. 10 The wines should not remain long on ullage.

**2. a.** (See quots.)

**1832** S. ROOSE *Ullaging* 5 By knowing the vacuity, and subtracting it from the whole content, leaves the Ullage or the quantity of liquor then in the cask. **1867** SMYTH *Sailor's Word-bk.* 705 *Ullage*, the remainder in a cask or package which has leaked or been partially used. **1883** *Encycl. Brit.* XVI. 28/2 The quantity of liquor contained in a cask partially filled and the capacity of the portion which is empty are termed respectively the wet and dry ullage.

**b.** *slang.* (See quots.)

**1874** *Slang Dict.* 332 *Ullages*, the wine of all sorts left in the bottoms of glasses at a public dinner. **1889** *Pall Mall G.* 21 Aug. 2/1 'Pray what is "ullage"?' 'The washings out of casks, sir,' replied my friend.

**3.** *transf.* **a.** Liquid that has oozed through a substance.

**1824** T. HOGG *Carnation* 50 Upon this stratum or bed of dung..the ullage occasioned from time to time by the rains will all be received.

**b.** The waste of metal in engraving.

**1860** *Cornh. Mag.* I. 272 In graving deep, tiny spirals of gold and silver curl away from the trenchant tool, and there is precious ullage in chasing and burnishing—spirals and ullage worth money in the market.

**c.** *Naut.* (See quots.)

**1901** *Daily Chron.* 23 May 5/1 The mass of her crew will all too probably be 'ullage'—to use the naval term for a preponderance of undesirables. **1904** KIPLING *Traffics & Discov.* 113 'You're a disgrace to the Service, and your boat's offal.' 'Awful?' I said. 'No—offal—tripes—swipes—ullage.'

**4.** *attrib.*, as *ullage bottle, cask, contents.*

**1743** BULKELEY & CUMMINS *Voy. S. Seas* 46 This Morning found the Store Tent robbed of Brandy; filled up all the ullage Casks. **1784** J. BOYDELL (*title*), The Ullage Cask Gauger; comprised in a series of Tables..whereby the Ullage Contents of any Cask..is at one view known. **1812** J. SMYTH *Pract. of Customs* (1821) 363 The ullage cask.. must be re-gauged, as must all casks entered for exportation. *Ibid.* 409 Landing Ullage Contents. **1864** *Daily Tel.* 4 June, There is scarcely a ship..in which the examining officer's attention is not called to ullage casks. **1889** *Pall Mall G.* 19 Jan. 7 It might have been made by putting two ullage bottles into one.

**U·llage,** *v.* [f. prec.]

**1.** *trans.* To calculate the amount of ullage in (a cask).

**1749** W. YEO (*title*), The Method of Ullaging and Inching all sorts of Casks and other Utensils used by Common Brewers, Victuallers, Distillers, &c. **1832** S. ROOSE *Ullaging* 11 To Ullage a Cask in the form of the frustum of a Cone.

**2. a.** To draw or tap to a slight extent. **b.** To fill up again (an ullaged cask, etc.).

**1881** *Standard* 3 Oct. 2/1 There..a cask of some rare vintage was 'ullaged,' with a biscuit and cheese accompaniment. **1888** *Wine, Sp. & Beer* 8 Mar. 186/1 To stir in some pure olive oil..and then flood the oil out by ullaging.

Hence **U·llaging** *vbl. sb.*

**1749** W. YEO *Ullaging & Inching* p. iii, That part of it [*sc.* gauging] which relates to the Ullaging of Casks. **1832** S. ROOSE *Ullaging* 5 The Ullaging of a Cask is to find how much liquor there is in it, when it is not full.

**U·llaged,** *ppl. a.* [f. prec. or the sb. + -ED. Cf. *unullaged* (1646).]

**1.** Of a cask or bottle: Short of contents.

**1549** in R. G. Marsden *Sel. Pleas Crt. Admir.* (Selden Soc.) II. 59 One hundreth and fyftie tonnes of wyne full and ullagid. **1867** SMYTH *Sailor's Word-bk.* 705 *Ullaged* is used for damaged, short of contents. **1908** ATTON & HOLLAND *King's Customs* 195 A demijohn or two in the captain's locker, and an ullaged anker in the forecastle.

**2.** Of wine: Affected in quality by the presence of ullage.

**1907** *Sat. Rev.* 29 June 815/1 Without..the clash of personalities the story is like a bottle of ullaged wine.

**3.** *transf.* Of inferior quality; refuse.

**1892** *Spectator* 9 Jan. 41/1 If you have to feed ten men on twopence, you must buy ullaged flour.

**U·llager.** [f. ULLAGE *v.*] One who ascertains the amount of ullage.

**1885** W. ECOCKES (*title*), The Ullager's Pocket Gem, comprising tables for finding the ullages of casks.

‖ **Ullagone,** *sb.* and *int.* *Anglo-Irish.* Also **ullagoane, ullaghone, ul(l)agon, hullagone, ullagawn, ulican.** [ad. Ir. Gael. *olagón, ologón, olagán*, of imitative origin.] A cry of lamentation, a wail; *spec.* a funeral lament. Also as *int.*

**1828** T. C. CROKER *Fairy Leg. & Tradit. S. Irel.* II. 191, I heard the dismallest ullagoane in the world, enough to break any one's heart. *Ibid.* 236 Oh ullagone, ullagone! this is a wide world. **1845** MRS. S. C. HALL *Whiteboy* v, A scream—loud and long—as of a woman in bitter trouble; it was, in fact, a 'keen', a regular 'ullagawn'. **1901** W. BARRY *Wizard's Knot* 219 (E.D.D.), It was a dirge, an ulagón, over Cathal, and his ruined walls.

Hence ‖ **Ullagone** *v. intr.*, to wail or lament loudly.

**1828** T. C. CROKER *Fairy Leg. & Tradit. S. Irel.* II. 76 Then the poor woman began to cry and ullagoane so finely that it would do any one good to hear her.

**Ulle,** obs. Sc. var. OIL *sb.*

**Ullmannite** (ʌ·lmănəit). *Min.* [From the name of Prof. J. C. *Ullmann* + -ITE [1]; in sense b named by J. Fröbel in 1850.] (See quots.)

† **a. 1839** *Penny Cycl.* XIV. 382/1 Phosphate of Manganese and Iron: Ullmannite...Occurs at Limoges in France.

**b. 1868** WATTS *Dict. Chem.* V. 936 *Ullmanite*, antimonial or antimonio-arsenical nickel-glance. **1875** *Ure's Dict. Arts* (ed. 7) III. 1050 *Ullmannite*, an antimonio-sulphide of nickel, occasionally containing arsenic. It occurs at Freusberg, in Nassau.

**Ully,** obs. Sc. variant of OIL *sb.*

**Ulma·ceous,** *a.* *Bot.* [f. mod.L. *Ulmace-æ*, an order of plants including the elm, f. L. *ulm-us* ULME.] (See quot.)

**1849** CRAIG, *Ulmaceous*, pertaining to the elm; belonging to the order Ulmaceæ.

**Ulmate** (ʌ·lmēt). *Chem.* [f. ULM-IC *a.*: see -ATE [4]. So F. *ulmate*, Pg. *ulmato.*] A salt produced by the action of ulmic acid.

**1836** BRANDE *Man. Chem.* 924 A brown liquid is obtained (ulmate of potassa), from which acids throw down ulmin. **1843** *Penny Cycl.* XXV. 491/1 When cold, the product, which contains ulmate of potash, is dissolved in water.

**Ulme.** *Obs.* or *dial.* [ad. L. *ulm-us* elm. Cf. G. *ulme*, Du. *olm.*] An elm-tree. (Cf. ULM-TREE.)

The forms *olm, holm, uim*, are recorded as surviving in northern English and southern Scottish dialects in the latter part of the 19th cent.

**1567** DRANT *Horace, Epist.* I. vii. D vj, Our cittizen is now a Corridon. He trimmes his ulmes. **1698** J. FRYER *Acc. E. India & P.* 295 A Catalogue of Plants growing at Spahaun...Sycamore. Ivy...Poplar. Ulmes. Willows.

**Ulmic** (ʌ·lmik), *a.* *Chem.* [f. L. *ulm-us* elm, after ULMIN. Cf. F. *ulmique*, Pg. *ulmico.*] *Ulmic acid*: **a.** = ULMIN 1.

A distinction between ulmic acid and ulmin or ulmine has been made by various chemists, but without agreement in the precise application of the terms.

**1831** T. THOMSON *Chem. Inorg. Bodies* II. 105 Ulmic acid appears to be a vegetable substance of very great importance..obtained from the exudation of the elm by dissolving the exudation in water and precipitating the ulmic acid. **1836** BRANDE *Man. Chem.* 923 As it [*sc.* ulmin] combines with bases, Boullay terms it *ulmic acid*... He represents ulmin, or ulmic acid, as a compound [etc.]. **1868** WATTS *Dict. Chem.* V. 936 The name 'ulmic acid', or 'ulmin', was given by Klaproth to a gummy substance contained in the black alkaline excrescences on the stems of unhealthy trees, especially of elms.

**b.** = ULMIN 2.

**1843** *Penny Cycl.* XXV. 491/1 Ulmic acid plays an important part in manures and soils, and what is called moss-water owes its peculiar properties to its presence. **1868** WATTS *Dict. Chem.* V. 936 The ammoniacal solution .. deposits brown or black gelatinous flocks of ulmic acid.

**Ulmin** (ʌ·lmin). *Chem.* Also **ulmine.** [f. L. *ulm-us* elm + -IN: named by Thomson. Cf. F. *ulmine*, Pg. *ulmina.*]

**1.** A substance which exudes spontaneously from the inner bark of the elm and some other trees; *spec.* the final stage of this as a distinct chemical principle.

*α.* **1813** T. THOMSON *Syst. Chem.* (1817) IV. 48 Ulmin.. was first noticed in 1804, by Klaproth, who found it in a spontaneous exudation from the elm. **1819** BRANDE *Chem.* 366 Ulmin is of a dark brown colour, with scarcely any taste or smell...The exudation from the elm is generally combined with carbonate of potassa, and is therefore readily soluble in water. **1842** *Penny Cycl.* XXII. 26/1 Simaruba is the bark of the root of the Simaruba amara...Its chief constituents are..ulmin, mucilage, and some salts.

*β.* **1838** TUPPER *Proverb. Philos.* Notes 219 With reference to the elm, I would remark, that no use has yet been discovered in the principle called 'ulmine'. **1853** ROYLE *Mat. Med.* (ed. 2) 632 It [the bark of Elm] contains Tannin..and a peculiar mucilaginous or gummy principle, called Ulmine.

**2.** A dark-brown or black product resulting from the decay of wood or vegetable matter, or artificially obtained by the action of powerful chemical agents on sugar and some other substances.

*α.* **1843** *Penny Cycl.* XXV. 491/1 Ulmin, or ulmic acid, may be artificially obtained..by the following process. **1857** MILLER *Elem. Chem., Org.* 54 If the solution [of sugar] be kept boiling for some hours,..a certain quantity of formic acid, and of a brown sparingly soluble substance termed *ulmin*, are produced. **1868** WATTS *Dict. Chem.* V. 936 Ulmin is also the name of a brown pigment, produced by the action of strong acids or alkalis on various organic bodies.

*β.* **1848** FOWNES *Chem.* (ed. 2) 371 *note*, This [substance] is generally called ulmic or humic acid, and its origin ascribed to the reaction of the alkali on the ulmine or humus of the soil. **1861** GESNER *Coal, Petrol.*, etc. (1865) 128 The decay of wood is produced by oxidation, and ulmine is the result.

**U·lmous,** *a.* *Chem.* [f. as prec. + -OUS.] Partaking of the character of ulmin.

**1868** WATTS *Dict. Chem.* V. 936 Ulmous or Humous Substances.

† **Ulm-tree.** *Obs. rare.* [f. L. *ulm-us* elm + TREE *sb.* Cf. ULME and MHG. *ulmboum*, Du. *olmboom.*] An elm-tree.

*c* **1000** ÆLFRIC *Gloss.* in Wr.-Wülcker 138 *Ulmus*, ulmtreow. **1382** WYCLIF *Isaiah* xli. 19, I shal sette in desert fyrr tree, and vlm tree, and box togidere.

‖ **Ulna** (ʌ·lnă). *Anat.* [L. *ulna* (hence also It., Pg. *ulna*), related to Gr. ὠλένη and OE. *eln* ELL [1] (cf. ELBOW *sb.*).]

**1.** The large inner bone of the fore-arm, extending from the elbow to the wrist.

**1541** R. COPLAND *Guydon's Quest. Chirurg.* G j b, The arme..is deuyded in thre great partyes. One is called vlna, the other lytel arme. *Ibid.* G i j, Howe many bones are in yᵉ fyrste parte of the great hande that is named vlna or adiutor? **1646** SIR T. BROWNE *Pseud. Ep.* IV. iv. 184 The other or lower division of the artery descendeth by the ulna. **1693** tr. *Blancard's Phys. Dict.* (ed. 2), *Ulna*,..the greater Bone, betwixt the Arm and the Wrist, which is jointed upward with the Shoulder. **1726** MONRO *Anat. Bones* (1741) 252 At the superior Extremity of the Ulna are two Processes. **1728** CHAMBERS *Cycl.* s.v., The Ulna lies on the inside of the Fore-Arm, reaching from the Elbow to the Wrist. **1803** *Med. Jrnl.* X. 558 The head of this bone was separated from the surrounding parts, as well as its union with the ulna. **1825** T. HOOK *Sayings* Ser. II. *Doubts and F.* i, Who conceived that some desperate injury had been done to her Ladyship's radius or ulna. **1881** *Med. Temp. Jrnl.* XLVI. 86 There was discharge from incisions both at the back and front of the hand and over the lower part of the ulna.

**2.** The corresponding bone of the foreleg in quadrupeds, and of the wing in birds.

**1831** YOUATT *Horse* xiii. 236 The long and front bone, called the *radius*, is nearly straight...The short and hinder bone is called the *ulna*. **1839** *Penny Cycl.* XIV. 69/1 In the ruminants generally the ulna is scarcely more than an appendage to the radius. **1879** E. P. WRIGHT *Anim. Life* 57 The fore-arm [in bats] consists of a rudimentary ulna, and a long, curved radius. **1884** COUES *N. Amer. Birds* 107 The enlarged proximal extremity of the ulna is called the olecranon, or 'head of the elbow'.

**3.** *Palæont.* and *Ichthyol.* (See quots.)

(*a*) **1839** G. ROBERTS *Dict. Geol.*, *Ulna*.., the bone or plate which, together with the radius, forms the first row, after the humerus, in the *front* paddles of an ichthyosaurus and plesiosaurus.

(*b*) *a* **1843** *Encycl. Metrop.* (1845) VII. 303/1 Between the lower edge of the spoke-bone and the upper edge of the ulna or cubit. **1854** OWEN *Orr's Circ. Sci., Org. Nat.* I. 175 Of the two flat bones connecting the fin with the coracoid, the upper one is the 'ulna'.

**U·lnad,** *adv.* [f. prec. + -AD.] Toward the ulnar aspect of the forearm.

**1803** BARCLAY *New Anat. Nomencl.* 166 Ulnad will signify towards the ulnar aspect. **1808** — *Muscular Motions* 384 When it is rolled radiad or ulnad, the power of the one will be necessarily increased proportionally as that of the other is diminished.

**Ulnage** (ʌ·lnėdʒ). *Obs.* exc. *Hist.* [ad. med.L. *ulnagium* (14th c.), f. L. *ulna* after OF. *aulnage* ALNAGE.]

**1.** = ALNAGE 1.

**1447** *Ord. Exchequer* 35. c. 62 (6) A v b, For euerye foreyn accompte of sheryffes and vlnage. **1454** *Rolls of Parlt.* V. 247 The Fermours of the Ulnage in the Counte of Somers[et] yerely. **1495** *Act* 11 *Hen. VII*, c. 62 § 1 The fermour of Ulnage in the Citie of Coventre.

**2.** = ALNAGE 2.

**1450** in *Archaeol.* (1770) I. 92 The issues and profits coming of the ulnage and subsidue of wollen clothes. **1450** *Rolls of Parlt.* V. 186/1 To be taken of the Subsidie and ulnage of Clothes. **1545** *Lanc. Wills* (Chetham Soc.) II. 61 My lease wyche I have of the ulnage and subsidie within the countie palatyne of Lancast[er].

**Ulnager** (ʌ·lnėdʒəɹ). *Hist.* [f. prec. + -ER [1].] = ALNAGER.

**1750** in *10th Rep. Hist. MSS. Comm.* (1885) App. I. 304 [Prosecuting his suit for the recovery of the patent office of] Ulnager [in Dublin]. **1832** *Rolls Parlt.* VII. 953/1 Office of Ulnager of Worsteds. **1867** BRANDE & COX *Dict. Sci.*, etc. III. 893/2 These officers were called *alnagers* or *ulnagers*, and the accounts rendered by them to the exchequer are still preserved.

**Ulnar** (ʌ·lnăɹ), *a.* and *sb.* *Anat.* [f. ULN-A + -AR. So F. *ulnaire*, Pg. *ulnar*, Sp. *ulnario.*]

**1.** Pertaining to the ulna, in various senses: **a.** In *ulnar artery, nerve, vein*, etc.

**1741** MONRO *Anat. Nerves* (ed. 3) 70 The ulnar Nerve is in the Palm of the Hand. **1800** *Phil. Trans.* XC. 103 The median proceeding along the arm, with the large blood-vessels, and giving off two branches of communication with the ulnar nerve. **1813** J. THOMSON *Lect. Inflam.* 267 As the brachial [artery] is sometimes observed to be divided..into radial and ulnar arteries. **1840** E. WILSON *Anat. Vade Mecum* vi. 318 The posterior ulnar vein. **1870** ROLLESTON *Anim. Life* 9 The ulnar sesamoid bone, or 'os pisiforme', is not reckoned as a carpal bone. **1885** *Buck's Handbk. Med. Sci.* I. 313/2 The ulnar nerve is placed to the inner side of the artery in the wrist.

**b.** With other sbs.

**1803** [see ULNAD *adv.*]. **1808** BARCLAY *Muscular Motions* p. xx, An aspect..towards the side on which the ulna is situated [is] *ulnar*. **1846** BRITTAN tr. *Malgaigne's Man. Oper. Surg.* 6 During the operation the ulnar border of the left hand should be pressed on the skin behind the right. **1854** OWEN in *Orr's Circ. Sci., Org. Nat.* I. 190 The ulnar portion of the bone developes a short .. olecranon. **1872** HUMPHRY *Myology* 185 Towards the ulnar side of the hand these tendons are usually absent.

**2.** *absol.* as *sb.* The ulnar nerve.

**1899** *Allbutt's Syst. Med.* VIII. 9 The physician then examines the nerve-trunks of both limbs simultaneously by means of gentle pressure on the ulnars behind the olecranons.

**Ulno-** (ʌ·lno), combining form (on Greek types) of ULNA, occurring in a few technical terms, as *ulnocarpal, -metacarpal, -radial.*

*a* **1843** *Encycl. Metrop.* (1845) VII. 327/2 In the Penguins, the Ulno-carpal bone..is largely developed.

**Ulode·ndroid,** *a.* *rare*[−1]. [f. mod.L. *Ulodendr-on* (see def.), f. Gr. οὖλος crisp, curly + δένδρον tree.] Of or connected with *Ulodendron*, a genus of extinct fossil plants.

**1900** *Nature* 15 Nov. 53/2 The nature of the large scars on the well-known Ulodendroid branches.

**Uloid** (yū·loid), *a.* and *sb.* *Path.* [f. Gr. οὐλή scar + -OID.] **a.** *adj.* Having the appearance of a scar or cicatrix. **b.** *sb.* A scar-like spot or mark on the skin.

**1901** DORLAND *Med. Dict.* (ed. 2).

**-ulose,** a compound adjectival suffix representing L. *-ulōsus*, formed by the addition of *-ōsus* (see -OSE) to stems in *-ul-us, -a, -um*, as *angulōsus* from *angulus*, *fābulōsus* from *fābula*, *perīculōsus* from *perīculum*. Such formations are rare in earlier Latin, but a considerable number are employed by post-Augustan writers, as Pliny, Columella, etc. Among the English examples which have their source in classical or post-classical forms are *angulose, calculose, fabulose, fistulose, glandulose, nebulose, pustulose, ramulose, sabulose, vermiculose.* On the analogy of these, various others have been introduced, as *flosculose, globulose, granulose, scrofulose, siliculose, tubulose, tumulose.* These forms are parallel to a certain number of those in -ULOUS, being as a rule either obsolete variants of these, or introduced later in order to convey the distinction commonly observed between the endings -OSE and -OUS.

**Ulotrichan** (yulǫ·trikăn). [Cf. next.] A person belonging to the crisp-haired division of mankind.

1888 *Cassell's Encycl. Dict.*

**Ulotrichous** (yulǫ·trikəs), *a.* Also oulo-. [f. mod.L. *Ulotrichi* (see def.), f. Gr. οὖλος crisp, curly + -τριχος -haired, f. τριχ-, θρίξ hair. Cf. F. *ulotrique*, Pg. *ulotrico*.] Of or belonging to the *Ulotrichi*, the division of mankind (in Bory de St. Vincent's classification) having crisp or woolly hair.

1857 MAYNE *Expos. Lex.* 847/2 Oulotrichous. 1884 *Imp. Dict.* 1909 A. C. HADDON *Races of Man* 3 These three varieties [of hair, *i.e.* straight, wavy, and woolly] are now termed leiotrichous, cymotrichous, and ulotrichous.

**-ulous,** a compound adjectival suffix representing the two Latin endings *-ulōsus* and *-ulus*. In the former case there are frequently variants in *-ulose*, which in modern use are as a rule more specific in meaning. To this class belong *angulous, calculous, fabulous, fistulous*, etc. (see -ULOSE); also *crapulous, meticulous, populous, scrupulous*, etc. The number of purely modern formations is not large. To the group which corresponds to Latin forms in *-ulus* belong *bibulous, credulous, emulous, garrulous, pendulous, sedulous, stridulous, tremulous*. In a very few instances both forms occur in Latin, as *querulus*, rarely *querulōsus*, querulous; *rīdiculus*, rarely *rīdiculōsus*, ridiculous.

†**Ulpic.** *Obs. rare.* In 5 vlpike. [ad. L. *ulpicum*.] A kind of leek.

*c* 1440 *Pallad. on Husb.* II. 224 Al the route Of rucul serue hit like this, cool also, Garlec, vlpike ek sowe hem now bo too. *Ibid.* IV. 166, XII. 71.

**Ulster** (ʋ·lstəɹ). [The name of the most northerly of the four provinces of Ireland.

The name occurs in ME. (14–15th cent.) as *Ulster* (also *Hulster*) and in the fuller form *Ulvester* (in Sc. also as *Ullister, Ulsister*, and *Ulcister*), = AF. (*a* 1225) *Ulvestre* (*Hulv-*), Anglo-L. (*c* 1200) *Ulvestera, -tira, -tria*, corresponding to ON. *Ulfastir*, a variant of the more usual *Ulaztir, Ulaðstir* (also *Ulaþscir*), the first element of which is the Irish *Ulaidh* (gen. *Uladh*), men of Ulster. The origin of the suffix, which also appears in Leinster and Munster (Ir. Gael. *Laighean, Mumha*), is not clear, but it may represent Ir. *tír* land.]

**1.** *pl.* Ulstermen (forming a regiment). *rare.*

1649 CROMWELL *Let.* 19 Dec. (Carlyle), Being informed that..Lieutenant-general Ferral with his Ulsters was to march out of Waterford,..I ordered Colonel Zanchy..to march..to the relief of our friends. *Ibid.*, The Ulsters.. made indeed for the time a good resistance.

**2.** The king-of-arms for Ireland.

1552 EDWARD VI *Jrnl.* in *Lit. Rem.* (Roxburghe Cl.) II. 395, [February] 2. Ther was a king of armes made for Irland, whose name was Ulster, and his province was al Irland. 1627 CHAS. I in *State Papers, Ireland* (1900) 223 You shall also see Ulster (who is the Chief Herald) countenanced in a herald's commission of visitation of various places in Ireland. 1712 *Lond. Gaz.* No. 4970/2 Coat of his Arms carried by Ulster King of Arms. 1857 *Lit. Rem. Edw. VI* (Roxb. Cl.) II. 395 *n.*, The arms given to the office of Ulster were, Argent, St. George's cross, and on a chief gules a lion between a harp and portcullis, all or. 1880 *Encycl. Brit.* XI. 688/1 In Ireland also there is but one king-at-arms, Ulster.

**3.** A long, loose overcoat of frieze or other rough cloth, frequently with a waist-belt.

The 'Ulster Overcoat' was introduced by J. G. M'Gee & Co. of Belfast in 1867; the abbreviated name has been in common use from 1879.

1878 H. S. LEIGH *Town Garland* 87 When the Ulster descends from its home on the hook, And the warmth-giving wrappers return from the wash. 1879 MISS BRADDON *Cloven Foot* xii. 110 Celia running home..with all her wedding finery smothered under a waterproof Ulster. 1888 RIDER HAGGARD *Col. Quaritch* III. xi. 169 He put on a pair of shooting-boots, an old coat, and an ulster.

*attrib.* 1878 *Era Almanack* 35 The ulster epidemic was raging even at this time. 1879 E. O'DONOVAN *Merv Oasis* xvi. (1883) 174 Over my shoulders was a drenched leopard skin, beneath which could be seen my travel-stained, much-worn ulster overcoat. 1880 *Cassell's Family Mag.* 122 The ulster muff is of a rectangular shape.

**4.** *attrib.* Used to designate the custom prevalent in Ulster by which a tenant has certain rights of occupancy, disposal, or compensation, in regard to land held by him; usually *Ulster tenant-right.*

1870 *Act* 33–34 *Victoria* c. 46 § 1 The usages prevalent in the province of Ulster, which are known as, and in this Act intended to be included under, the denomination of the Ulster tenant-right custom, are hereby declared to be legal. 1878 [see TENANT-RIGHT]. 1879 H. GEORGE *Progr. & Pov.* VI. i. (1881) 291 If what is known as the Ulster tenant right were extended to the whole of Great Britain, it would be but to carve out of the estate of the landlord, an estate for the tenant. 1882 M. ARNOLD *Irish Ess.*, etc. 28 It has been suggested..by the Ulster custom of compensating them [*sc.* tenants] for their improvements, and letting them sell the value which by their improvements they had added to the property.

**b.** *Ulsterman*, a native or inhabitant of Ulster.

In recent use also *Ulsterite*. Cf. ULTONIAN.

1845 CARLYLE *Cromwell* I. 497 'Lieutenant-General Ferral with his Ulsters;' *note*, Ulster-men. 1868 (*title*), Modern Ireland: its Vital Questions, Secret Societies, and Government: by an Ulsterman.

Hence (from sense 3) **U·lstered** *a.*, wearing an ulster. **Ulstere·tte,** a small or light ulster. **U·lstering,** material suitable for ulsters.

1880 MISS BROUGHTON *Second Thoughts* I. v. 62 A few *ulstered, comforted men, stamping up and down, waiting for the night mail. 1889 SKRINE *Mem. Thring* 201 The group of flannelled and ulstered players. 1887 J. ASHBY STERRY *Lazy Minstrel* (1892) 171 My smart *ulsterette, e'en a poet might sing, 'Tis white corduroy, with a rose-coloured lining! 1888 *Cambridge* (Mass.) *Tribune* 24 Nov., These 'Inverness' overcoats are close-fitting, and when worn without the cape have the appearance of an ulsterette. 1888 *Myra's Jrnl.* 1 Nov. 656/1 Patterns of Cloths, Homespuns, and *Ulsterings for ladies' and children's jackets and ulsters. 1890 *Textile News* 20 June (List Manufacturers), Fancy meltons, ulsterings, costumes, coatings, &c.

**Ult.,** abbrev. of ULTIMO.

1750 DUNCOMBE in *Lett. Eminent Persons* (1772) II. 170, I have read yours of the 30th ult. with great pleasure. 1767 J. GARDEN *Elegant Epist.* (1790) 730/1, I am..favoured with your's of the 25th ult. 1798 *York Courant* 1 Oct. 2/5 On Saturday the first ult a new peal of six bells..was opened. 1815 *Sporting Mag.* XLV. 354 On the 3d ult. they fell in with a fox.

†**Ultagh, -ogh.** *Anglo-Irish. Obs.* Also Ultock. [a. Ir. Gael. *Ultach*, f. *Ult-*, stem of OIr. *Ulaid* (d. pl. *Ultaib*, a. pl. *Ultu*) men of Ulster.] An Ulsterman.

1649 in *Contemp. Hist. Irel.* (Ir. Archæol. Soc.) II. 335 Those under the command of George Monro, part whereof were formerly his own, and part were of Owen ONeals Ultoghs. 1652–3 *Ibid.* III. 370 Created Earle of Tyrone, by the Ultaghes. 1690 J. MACKENZIE *Siege London-Derry* 48/1 Great numbers of Women and Boys (which the Ultoghs always carry along with them, when they expect spoil).

*attrib.* 1688 in Somers *Tracts* (1814) XI. 451 How often do we now hear the Ultock Irish boast of their merit.

**Ulterior** (ʋltīə·riəɹ), *a.* and *sb.* [a. L. *ulterior* further, more distant, comp. of **ulter* (cf. *ultrā, ultrō* advs.) that is beyond. Hence also It. *ulteriore*, Sp. and Pg. *ulterior*, F. *ultérieur* (16th c.).]

**A.** *adj.* **1.** Lying beyond that which is immediate or present; coming at a subsequent point or stage; further, future.

1646 SIR T. BROWNE *Pseud. Ep.* II. i. 49 If the prescription of time, and numerositie of assertors, were a sufficient demonstration, we might sit downe herein, as an unquestionable truth; nor should there need *vlterior* disquisition. 1661 BOYLE *Style of Script.* 211 The Ulterior Accomplishment of that Part of it [*sc.* Scripture], which once Promis'd God's People, that Kings should be its Nursing Fathers. 1816 A. KNOX *Rem.* (1834) I. 54 These changes were meant by Providence to subserve ulterior movements. 1827 JARMAN *Powell's Devises* II. 75 The principle which confers upon him the ulterior interest in the lands directed to be sold would seem to exclude him in the converse case. 1856 FROUDE *Hist. Eng.* (1858) I. iv. 336 The request was only preparatory to ulterior measures. 1884 *Manch. Exam.* 10 May 5/4 The attitude and disposition of those Powers, as bearing upon their ulterior action, necessarily enter into the question.

**b.** *spec.* Lying beyond what is openly stated, avowed, or evident; intentionally kept in the background or concealed.

1735 BOLINGBROKE *Study Hist.* viii. (1752) II. 98 By reserving still a right of making ulterior demands, they reduced the Carthaginians at last to the necessity of abandoning their city, or of continuing the war. 1825 T. HOOK *Sayings* Ser. II. *Man of Many Fr.* (Colburn) 86 Without any knowledge of her uncle's ulterior intentions on the subject. 1856 *N. Brit. Rev.* XXVI. 197 There is no reason for suspecting him of ulterior designs of a deeper and more treacherous dye. 1877 FROUDE *Short Stud.* (1883) IV. I. iii. 30 He was ..the most unlikely..to have adopted a course so marked without some ulterior purpose.

**2.** Lying on the further side of a point or boundary; more remote in position.

1721 BAILEY, *Ulterior*, on the farther Side. 1798 *Phil. Trans.* LXXXVIII. 167 This scale..containing three parallel lines engraven thereon, on the exterior and ulterior of which are three divisions. 1817 CHALMERS *Astron. Disc.* iii. (1852) 68 To shoot afar into those ulterior regions which are beyond the limits of our astronomy. 1864 BAILEY *Festus* (ed. 7) 120 The thunderous bars Of Heaven's ulterior orb.

**B.** *sb.* A further aim or end.

1843 CHALMERS in Hanna *Mem.* (1852) IV. xviii. 351 This will open..a bright and beautiful ulterior, to which every eye should be directed.

Hence **Ulterio·rity,** an ulterior thing or matter.

1814 PARR *Let. to S. Butler* 1 Apr., Wks. 1828 VII. 363, I shall say something about the ulteriorities, and you must sympathise and co-operate with me.

**Ulte·riorly,** *adv.* [f. ULTERIOR *a.* + -LY [2].] At (or to) a further stage or point; subsequently; afterwards.

1818 BENTHAM *Ch. Eng.*, *Catech. Exam.* 209 The future probable Bell-taught and ulteriorly teachable Parish Schoolboy. 1833 CARLYLE *Misc. Ess.*, *Diderot* (1888) 32 Nor do the generality, on either side, yet see whither ulteriorly it is tending. 1854 J. S. C. ABBOTT *Napoleon* (1855) II. xxxv. 663 Beneath its lofty dome, where the massive tomb of Napoleon was ulteriorly to be erected, a magnificent cenotaph was reared.

**Ultimacy** (ʋ·ltimăsi). [f. ULTIM-ATE *a.*: see -ACY.] The quality or state of being ultimate.

1842 SIR W. HAMILTON *Diss.* in *Reid's Wks.* II. 760 The simplicity, ultimacy, and incomprehensibility of our original apprehensions. *a* 1848 W. A. BUTLER *Hist. Anc. Philos.* (1856) I. 161 The ultimacy of the laws of motion has been lately made the subject of disquisition. 1893 FAIRBAIRN *Christ in Mod. Theol.* II. II. iii. 430 As to the ultimacy of the will Calvin is explicit.

**Ultimata,** pl. of ULTIMATUM *sb.*

**Ultimate** (ʋ·ltimĕt), *a.* and *sb.* [ad. late L. *ultimāt-us*, pa. pple. of *ultimāre* to be at the end, f. *ultimus* last, final: see ULTIME *a.*]

**A.** *adj.* **1.** Of ends, designs, etc.: Lying beyond all others; forming the final aim or object.

1654 JER. TAYLOR *Real Pres.* i. 10 The faithful and pious communicants receive the ultimate end of his presence, that is, spiritual blessings. 1664 POWER *Exp. Philos.* I. 67 In the obtainment of which he hath come to the ultimate design of his endeavours. 1675 BAXTER *Cath. Theol.* I. I. 61 God is this ultimate End of man,..to which all are means. *a* 1721 PRIOR *Dial. Dead* iii. Wks. 1907 II. 258 The beginning, Progress, and Ultimate end of Thought. 1758 JOHNSON *Idler* No. 1 ⁋ 3 To be idle is the ultimate purpose of the busy. 1782 PRIESTLEY *Corrupt. Chr.* I. Pref. p. xiii, If my proper and ultimate object be considered. 1847 G. HARRIS *Life Ld. Hardwicke* I. iv. 354 A far higher and nobler reward is their ultimate aim. *a* 1871 GROTE *Eth. Fragm.* iv. (1876) 72 They would..esteem different agents in proportion as they tended to assist these same ultimate purposes. 1892 H. LANE *Differ. Rheum. Dis.* (ed. 2) vi. 119 The ultimate goal of all our investigations and observations.

**2.** Coming at the end of a process, course of action, etc., or as the last in a succession or series; arrived at as a final result or in the last resort.

1660 R. COKE *Justice Vind.* 8, I am content with Aristotle's definition of the will,..That it is the ultimate resolution, end, or determination of counsel. 1671 MILTON *P. R.* III. 210 My harbour and my ultimate repose, The end I would attain, my final good. 1755 YOUNG *Centaur* ii. Wks. 1757 IV. 159 All agree, that several goods being proposed for our ultimate enjoyment, it is impossible in our nature not to chuse the best. 1785 PALEY *Mor. Philos.* VI. xii. (1818) II. 426 Containing that which in peace and war is equally unjustifiable—ultimate and gratuitous mischief. 1827 FARADAY *Chem. Manip.* ii. (1842) 30 The oscillations..will be found to be quick, and the beam will soon take its ultimate state of rest. 1841 MIALL in *Nonconf.* I. 2 Ultimate success will require union, patience, persevering energy. 1860 RUSKIN *Unto this Last* (1862) 8 No man ever knew, or can know, what will be the ultimate result to himself, or to others, of any given line of conduct. 1890 H. LANE *Differ. Rheum. Dis.* 5 Not to exhaust the subject, nor even to lead the way to the ultimate hope of eradicating the source and origin of the evil.

**b.** Of resolves, etc.: Final, determinate, absolute.

1687 MIÈGE *Gt. Fr. Dict.* II. s.v., This is the ultimate Resolution. 1779 J. MOORE *View Soc. France* (1789) I. i. 4, I have now formed an ultimate resolution against gaming. 1786 JEFFERSON *Writ.* (1859) I. 570 An ultimate opinion should not be formed till we see Mr. Randall. 1803 in Gurw. *Wellington's Desp.* (1837) II. 138 *note*, I consented to wait till then for their ultimate decision.

**c.** Putting an end to further continuance, development, or action; final, decisive.

1755 JOHNSON, *End*,..ultimate state; final doom. 1781 COWPER *Hope* 640 Nature opposes..This riving stroke, this ultimate divorce. 1803 MALTHUS *Popul.* (1817) I. 17 The ultimate check to population appears then to be a want of food. 1827 POLLOK *Course T.* VI. 365 Some disaster great and ultimate. 1838 PRESCOTT *Ferd. & Is.* Introd. ii. I. 79 To protect the subject from the oppressions of the crown and its officers, over all which cases it possessed original and ultimate jurisdiction. 1870 MOZLEY *Univ. Serm.* iii. (1877) 60 The natural philosopher is practically assured from the concurrence of data before him, of a result, before the ultimate test is got.

**d.** Forming a final stage, point, or limit; beyond which there is no advance or progress.

1794 G. ADAMS *Nat. & Exp. Philos.* I. v. 204, I informed them that the creatures [larvæ] before us were not in their ultimate state, but were the produce of the bee-fly. 1815 J. SMITH *Panorama Sci. & Art* II. 34 This salt..causes the hair to contract itself, until it has attained the ultimate limit of its contraction. 1869 RANKINE *Mach. & Millwork* 497 The ultimate shearing strength, or modulus of resistance to shearing. 1878 B. TAYLOR *Deukalion* III. v. 127 Why should I conceal The ultimate barrier where I needs must pause?

**3.** Beyond which no advance can be made by investigation or analysis; forming a limit or final stage in respect of nature or quality; fundamental or elemental.

1659 PEARSON *Creed* ii. 147 We must acknowledge that the actuall giving of salvation to us, is the ultimate and conclusive ground of the title *Saviour*. 1681 *Ess. Peace & Truth Ch.* 9 Man therefore is justly defined to be a Rational Religious Creature, therein consisting the formal ultimate difference from a Brute. 1739 HUME *Hum. Nat.* Introd. (1874) I. 308 Any hypothesis, that pretends to discover the ultimate original qualities of human nature. 1749 HARTLEY *Observ. Man* II. 32 Since God is the ultimate Author of all Motion, we must suppose him to be immaterial. 1792 N. CHIPMAN *Rep.* (1871) 53 The King was, in view of the law, the ultimate owner of all lands within his dominions. 1808 JEBB in *Knox & Jebb's Corr.* (1834) I. 453 There are ultimate truths, far above human ken. 1836 J. GILBERT *Chr. Atonem.* iv. (1852) 113 The ultimate law of moral agents must be the will of God. 1850 M'COSH *Div. Govt.* III. i. (1874) 295 In the inquiry into virtue and vice, we come back to ultimate principles, on which all morality rests. 1880 SAYCE *Introd. Sci. Lang.* (1890) I. 113 The sentence, in short, is..the ultimate starting-point of all our linguistic inquiries.

**b.** Of material things, *esp.* of the component particles of matter.

1808 BARCLAY *Muscular Motions* 273 These fibres, composed of the fibres that are called *ultimate*, are seldom seen extending from the one extremity of a muscle to the other. 1815 J. SMITH *Panorama Sci. & Art* II. 303 All that can be affirmed of the state in which the ultimate particles of matter exist, is only the result of conjecture. 1836–41 BRANDE *Chem.* (ed. 5) 1053 Although the ultimate principles of vegetable substances are few in number. 1857 MILLER *Elem. Chem., Org.* 11 To determine the relative proportion in which each of the ultimate elements exists. 1871 TYNDALL

*Fragm. Sci.* (1879) II. vi. 81 This formative power,..ready to..build the ultimate particles of matter into definite shapes.

*transf.* **1831** T. P. Jones *New Convers. Chem.* xxviii. 282 When we decompose them [*sc.* proximate principles], to ascertain how much they contain of each of the simple bodies, the operation is called *ultimate analysis.* **1857** Miller *Elem. Chem., Org.* 6 The determination of the proportions..furnishes an illustration of what is meant by *ultimate* organic analysis.

**c.** *Math. Ultimate ratio,* the final limiting ratio between two variable quantities which simultaneously approach definite fixed values or limits. (Correl. to *prime ratio*: see Prime *a.* 9 d.)

**1729** A. Motte tr. *Newton's Principia* I. 46 The ultimate ratio of the arc, chord, and tangent, any one to any other, is the ratio of equality. **1749** Hartley *Observ. Man* II. 32 According to the mathematical Doctrine of ultimate Ratios, not even an infinite Series..could remove it. **1818** Vince *Fluxions* (ed. 5) 16 The ingenious..Author of the *Analyst* ..went upon the term *ultimate* ratio, assuming equality where it was never intended. **1842** Brande *Dict. Sci.*, etc. 974/2 They are called prime ratios, or ultimate ratios, according as the ratios of the variables are considered as receding from, or approaching to, the ratios of the limits.

**4.** Not followed by another; last. *rare*$^{-1}$.

**1728** Morgan *Algiers* II. iv. 292 Returning home, he bad farewel to the fluid Element; this being his ultimate Expedition.

**5.** Forming a result or conclusion of a character different from the starting-point or present state; eventual, resultant.

**1777** Priestley *Disc. Philos. Necess.* Ded. p. ix, All seeming discord is real harmony, and all apparent evil, ultimate good. **1795** Burke *Th. Scarcity* Wks. 1842 II. 253 The quiet of the town is purchased by the ruin of the country, and the ultimate wretchedness of both. **1832** Ht. Martineau *Homes Abroad* ix. 127 One yields temporary benefit to a few at the expense of ultimate injury to the many. **1874** Green *Short Hist.* iv. § 1. 161 Neither trick nor conquest could shake the firm faith of the Celt in the ultimate victory of his race.

**6.** Final, last; occurring in, or falling on, the last syllable of a word.

**1837** G. Phillips *Syriac Gram.* 28 If the ultimate syllable be perfect without the terminating consonant. **1862** Marsh *Lect. Eng. Lang.* 380 The great frequency of ultimate and penultimate accentuation.

**7.** Most remote in space or position. *rare*$^{-1}$.

**1848** Johnston in *Proc. Berw. Nat. Club* II. 297 The ultimate [joint] armed with a long curved..claw.

**B.** *sb.* **1.** The final point or result; the end or conclusion; the last step.

**1681** Rycaut tr. *Gracian's Critick* 113 Ordinary Toyes, applauded by a Castilian, for but being his own, with praises as might befit the ultimate of all Perfection. **1718** J. Fox *Wanderer* 72, I..once hoped I might attain to the very Ultimate of what you propos'd by Sunday last. **1728** Eliza Heywood tr. *Mme. de Gomez's Belle A.* (1732) II. 2 Thelamont,..having now obtain'd the ultimate of his Desires, appear'd more bright and gay than ever. **1794** Hutton *Philos. Light*, etc. 211 A proper fulminating composition, which seems to be the ultimate to which we may proceed. **1820** Shelley *Ess. & Lett.* (1852) II. 225, I shall write to you the ultimates of my Commission in my next letter. **1852** Bailey *Festus* (ed. 5) 534 Ends and beginnings mingle at the last; All ultimates are foreordained. **1890** Booth *Darkest Eng.* II. vi. 230 They carried their principles of freedom and license to the logical ultimate.

**2.** The point at which investigation or analysis stops; a final or fundamental fact or principle.

**1709** Mrs. Manley *Secret Mem.* (1720) IV. 101 It was not her Fault that she became not Mistress of the great Secret, the Ultimate of Chymistry. **1774** J. Bryant *Mythol.* I. p. xii, The Deluge..was esteemed..the ultimate of Gentile history. *Ibid.* II. 267 The ancient Poet..spoke of him as the father of mankind. In short he was the ultimate, to which Grecian history referred. **1841** *Blackw. Mag.* XLIX. 152 Mind seems as it were to be getting loose upon space. It reposes upon no religious ultimates. **1862** H. Spencer *First Princ.* II. iii. § 50 (1875) 169 We come down then finally to Force, as the ultimate of ultimates. **1866** E. P. Whipple *Character & Characteristic Men* 268 If he calls his notion Law and makes law an ultimate, beyond which the human reason cannot go.

**Ultimate** (ʊ·ltimeᶦt), *v.*$^1$ [f. prec. or L. *ultimāt-*, ppl. stem of *ultimāre* (cf. It. *ultimare*, Sp. and Pg. *ultimar* to finish).]

**1.** *trans.* To carry to an end; to complete.

**1849** E. H. Sears *Regeneration* III. i. (1859) 131 Works are filled and vitalized by that angelic benevolence which is not complete until clothed and ultimated in action. **1866** Bessie R. Parkes *Vignettes* 399 My parents had seen my education ultimated in practical life. **1881** E. S. Holden *Sir W. Herschel* 53 His researches on the construction of the heavens would have been made; those were in his brain, and must have been ultimated.

*refl.* **1860** Emerson *Cond. Life* viii. 169 It is the soundness of the bones that ultimates itself in a peach-bloom complexion. **1880** Howells *Undisc. Country* iii. 50 A ferment of the kind he speaks of in the world of spirits would be more apt to ultimate itself here in the mind than in the stomach. **1885** L. Oliphant *Sympneumata* 14 The moral forces which ultimate themselves dynamically in the actions of men.

**2.** *intr.* To result finally; to end (*in* something).

*c* **1834** A. H. Stephens in Johnston & Browne *Life* (1878) 95 How the thing will ultimate I cannot tell. **1868** L. Oliphant *Let.* in *Life* (1891) viii. II. 41 We have no place here for those who like to meditate, unless the meditation ultimates in useful work. **1887** *Pop. Sci. Monthly* Aug. 564/2 Believing that they..must ultimate..in an increase of egoism.

**U·ltimate,** *v.*$^2$ *rare.* [Back-formation from Ultimatum *sb.*] *trans.* = Ultimatum *v.*

**1892** *Black & White* 30 Jan. 135/2 President Harrison has at last 'ultimated' Chili, as the Americans will probably soon be saying. **1898** *Pall Mall G.* 28 Sept. 2 At last the four Powers are going to ultimate the Sultan about the Turkish troops in Crete.

**Ultimately** (ʊ·ltimeᶦtli), *adv.* [f. Ultimate *a.* + -ly $^2$.]

**1.** In the last resort; when carried to the natural or logical conclusion; fundamentally.

**1660** R. Coke *Justice Vind.* Pref. 13 If I could not ultimately resolve the Dictates of my Reason as a Christian, into plain places of Scripture. **1690** Locke *Hum. Und.* II. i. § 2 In one word, From Experience: in that, all our Knowledge is founded; and from that it ultimately derives it self. ?**1743** in *10th Rep. Hist. MSS. Comm.* App. I. 279 To which nevertheless their Immunities must ultimately resort. **1775** Johnson *Tax. no Tyr.* 23 All government is ultimately and essentially absolute. **1776** Gibbon *Decl. & F.* vi. (1782) I. 185 The young emperor, on whose personal qualities the happiness or misery of the Roman world must ultimately depend. **1835** Newman *Par. Serm.* (1837) I. iv. 64 What will it ultimately profit a man to profess without understanding? **1866** Crump *Banking* v. 131 Credit given to the holder of a bill by the person ultimately liable is considered equivalent to payment. **1869** Mozley *Univ. Serm.* i. (1877) 18 Every kingdom ultimately depends on moral influence and not on physical force.

**2.** In the end; at the last: **a.** As the conclusion or final stage of a process, course of action, etc.

**1755** Johnson, *Finally*, 1. Ultimately; lastly; in conclusion. [Quoting Milton *Samson A.* 1296.] **1794** Matthias *Purs. Lit.* (1798) 306 All passions submit ultimately..to the inability of gratifying them. **1796** Mme. D'Arblay *Camilla* IX. iii, The heart-breaking event to which it had ultimately led. **1818** Mrs. Shelley *Frankenst.* iii, I doubted not that I should ultimately succeed. **1839** James *Louis XIV*, III. 235 It became daily apparent to all parties that war must ultimately be the result. **1860** Holland *Miss Gilbert* ii. 19 It was supposed by the gossips of the village that Dr. Gilbert would ultimately marry Aunt Catharine. **1878** Lecky *Eng. in 18th C.* I. iii. 452 It is of the nature of a constitution so formed as ours..ultimately to work well.

**b.** As a point in a series, or in time.

**1818** Cruise *Digest* (ed. 2) II. 430 A feoffment was made to the use of the feoffor for his life..and ultimately to the use of himself and his heirs for ever. **1827** Faraday *Chem. Manip.* ii. (1842) 37 It economises time to have the smaller weights arranged in order..and ultimately the large weights. **1880** Trollope *Duke's Children* I. iii. 35 Frank's mother.. would sometimes surmise..that the entire property must ultimately come to him. **1884** Thompson *Tumours of Bladder* 33 He..suffered much for a long time; ultimately there was some improvement.

**3.** In a final or conclusive manner; definitely.

**1785** Jefferson *Corr.* Wks. 1859 I. 342 These questions, however, cannot be decided, ultimately, at this day. **1793** — *Writ.* (1830) IV. 479 It had no right to dismember or alienate any portion of territory once ultimately consolidated with us. **1798** S. & Ht. Lee *Canterb. T.* II. 206 Yet nothing but a favourable judgment from the civilians in England could ultimately relieve [his] mind.

**U·ltimateness.** [f. as prec. + -ness.] The quality of being ultimate; finality.

**1884** *Century Mag.* XXVIII. 636 To have in it a certain completeness, ultimateness, and sacredness.

**Ultima Thule**: see Thule.

**Ultimation** (ʊltimeᶦ·ʃən). [f. L. *ultimāt-*, *ultimāre*: see Ultimate *v.*$^1$ Cf. It. *ultimazione.*] The action or process of bringing to an ultimate result; final issue or development.

**1791** H. Walpole *Let. to Miss Berry* 23 June, As this must take its passage..early to-morrow morning,..I shall perhaps not know the ultimation, but you probably will before you receive this. **1805** Eugenia di Acton *Nuns of Desert* I. 117 The ultimation of their meditated kindness, was only to bestow upon her an indisputable right to the title of a penitent. **1858** Sears *Athan.* III. ii. 258 The words *heaven* and *hell*, as they are used in popular speech, describe the complete ultimations of good and evil. **1883** L. Oliphant *Altiora Peto* II. 65 When a sufficient number have..attained a sufficient development for the ultimation of new results.

So **U·ltimatiza·tion.** *rare.*

**1885** L. Oliphant *Sympneumata* 117 Because of this abnormal ultimatisation of organisms in this subsurface world.

**U·ltimative,** *adj.* *rare*$^{-1}$. [f. as prec.] That tends to produce some final result.

**1885** L. Oliphant *Sympneumata* 239 The ultimative or operative region of earthly manhood.

**Ultimatum** (ʊltimeᶦ·tɒm), *sb.* Pl. **-ata** (-ēᶦ·tă). [ad. late L. *ultimātum*, neut. sing. of *ultimātus*, pa. pple. of *ultimāre*: see Ultimate *v.*$^1$ So in F., It., Pg., G., Du., etc.]

**1.** In diplomacy, the final terms presented by one power (or group of powers) to another, the rejection of which may lead to the severing of diplomatic relations, and eventually to a declaration of war.

*sing.* **1731** *Gentl. Mag.* Jan. 39/1 There are privately handed about here Copies of the *Ultimatum* (or last Proposals) of the Allies of Seville, as transmitted hither from Paris. **1759** Smollett *Hist. Eng.* VIII. (ed. 3) IX. 143 He delivered to the mediator an ultimatum, importing, That he adhered to the treaties of Westphalia and Nimeguen. **1784–5** *Ann. Reg., Hist. Europe* 107/1 A new statement of the emperor's claims and demands, described as his *ultimatum*, was presented to the Dutch ministers. **1832** tr. *Sismondi's Ital. Rep.* xiii. 287 Charles still insisted on disgraceful conditions, which his secretary read as his ultimatum. **1876** Bancroft *Hist. U.S.* VI. lviii. 482 Fitzherbert ..reflected that peace with the United States would be the best means of forcing France and Spain to declare their ultimatum.

*pl.* **1773** *Ann. Reg., Hist. Europe* 40/2 The delegates were also appointed..to receive the ultimata of the three powers. **1796** Hamilton *Wks.* (1886) VII. 121 In general, where more had been obtained by a treaty than the *ultimata* prescribed to the negotiator, it would be inexpedient to publish those *ultimata*. **1859** L. Oliphant *China & Japan* I. 98 Mr. Wade..proceeded..to Canton, and delivered the *ultimata* of the French and English plenipotentiaries. **1883** *Harper's Mag.* April 676/1 *note*, Different ultimata had been adopted with respect to the boundaries.

**b.** *transf.* A final condition or stipulation; one's last word on a matter.

**1733** Swift *Let. to Pope* 31 Mar., But, there must be some stipulations for my riding, with other necessary postulatums, and ultimatums. **1787** M. Cutler in *Life*, etc. (1888) I. 299 We therefore begged leave to state to the Board the terms on which we were ready to close the contract, and that those terms must be our *Ultimatum*. **1813** *Examiner* 11 Jan. 23/1 His Lordship would require, as the ultimatum, ..that a competent portion of the natives shall perform duty under British Officers. **1848** Dickens *Dombey* xl, I have stated my *ultimatum*, Madam. **1869** Trollope *He knew*, etc. xxxvii. (1878) 207 The official shrugged his shoulders and signified that his ultimatum had been pronounced.

**2.** The final point, extreme limit; an ultimate end or aim.

**1748** Richardson *Clarissa* (1768) III. 53 That single pressure..delighted me more than ever I was delighted with the *Ultimatum* with any other woman. **1793** R. Willett in *Archaeologia* XI. 196 The size of our ships seems now to have reached nearly its ultimatum. **1804** Jebb *Corr.* (1834) I. 153 And now I will tell you an ultimatum, which I would far prefer,..the librarianship of Armagh. **1804** Eugenia de Acton *Tale without Title* II. 26 Their ultimatum was obtained, and they were considered as persons of consequence.

**b.** Const. *of.*

**1770** *Monthly Rev.* 502 This surely is the *ultimatum* of astronomical precision. **1790** *Bystander* 308 The ultimatum of earthly enjoyment was to give him invitations to their houses. **1802** Mrs. E. Parsons *Myst. Visit* I. 132 To be married was still the ultimatum of her wishes. **1812** Shelley *Proposals* Pr. Wks. 1888 I. 280 The attainment of the good which I propose as the ultimatum of philanthropic exertion. **1856** Kane *Arct. Expl.* I. x. 114 At last we came to the Esquimaux ultimatum of simplicity,—raw meat and a fur bag. **1888** J. Ellis *New Chr.* ii. 51 If..all chemical and mechanical changes, or effects, are but the ultimatum of spiritual causes.

**c.** Final lot or destiny. *rare*$^{-1}$.

**1861** G. Moore *Lost Tribes* iv. 84 To trace the meaning of God's handwriting concerning the origin and ultimatum of our race.

† **3.** *slang.* The hinder parts; the buttocks. *Obs.*

**1823** C. Westmacott *Points of Misery* iii. 31 Old Brummagem and the fat lady being thrown head downwards, formed an excellent step-ladder with their *ultimatums* for the purpose. **1824** in *Spirit Pub. Jrnls.* (1825) 38 He..at the same time felt his spinal extremities and his ultimatum covered by a shower of slimy material of a very offensive odour. **1825** C. Westmacott *Eng. Spy* I. 165 As for the inexpressibles they hung round his *ultimatum* like petticoat trousers.

**4.** A primary element, beyond which analysis becomes impossible; something fundamental.

**1858** O. W. Holmes *Aut. Breakf.-t.* i. (1859) 10 No men can have satisfactory relations with each other until they have agreed on certain *ultimata* of belief not to be disturbed in ordinary conversation. **1867** H. Macmillan *Bible Teach.* i. 22 The truth is, that all our scientific investigations will never conduct us to the ultimatum—the commencement of matter. **1868** Bain *Ment. & Mor. Sci.*, *Ethics* II. 498 Sensible Perception,..whereby we perceive that the triangle before us is a geometrical ultimatum.

**5.** Furthest destination; most distant point (to be) reached.

**1862** Carlyle *Fredk. Gt.* XI. ii. III. 44 Almost to the coast of the Baltic; their ultimatum there a place called Köslin.

Hence **Ultima·tum** *v. trans.*, to present with an ultimatum. (Cf. Ultimate *v.*$^2$)

**1897** *Pall Mall G.* 23 Sept. 2 General Woodford never ultimatumed the fiery untamed Duke of Tetuan.

† **Ultime,** *a. Obs.* Also ultim. [ad. L. *ultimus*, superl. of **ulter*: cf. Ulterior. So It., Sp., Pg. *ultimo*, OF. *ultime*.] Ultimate, final.

**1626** Bacon *Nat. Hist.* § 99 Whereby the true and Ultime Operations of Heat are not attained. **1654** H. L'Estrange *Chas. I* (1655) 105 Nothing was wanting now to the perfecting of this League, but the ultime and compleating act, the solemn confirmation by Oath. **1659** — *Alliance Div. Off.* 295 The perficient and ultim act of marriage.

**Ultimity** (ʊlti·mĭti). Now *rare.* [f. as prec. + -ity. Cf. med.L. *ultimitas.*]

**1.** The final point or ultimate development of an action or thing; the last stage.

**1613** Bacon *Let. to Jas. I*, Wks. 1868 XI. x. 369 That those tragical arguments and (as the schoolmen call them) ultimities of persuasions which were used last Parliament should for ever be abolished. **1626** — *Sylva* § 838 The Degrees of Alteration, of one Body into another, from Crudity to Perfect Concoction; which is the ultimity of that Action, or Processe. *a* **1706** Evelyn *Hist. Relig.* (1850) I. 77 [The Almighty] knows all that does not actually exist, even the ultimities of what can or may be.

**2.** An ultimate principle or fact.

**1898** *Expositor* June 453 In everything appertaining to origins and causes, to ultimities and universalities.

† **Ultimo,** *sb. Obs.*$^{-1}$ [?a It., Sp., or Pg. *ultimo*: see Ultime *a.*] = Ultimum.

**1622** in Foster *Eng. Factories Ind.* (1908) II. 11 Which is as farr as the Nabobs perwanna importes, and is the ultimo of there and our owne expectacions.

‖ **Ultimo** (ʊ·ltimo), *a.* and *adv.* [L. *ultimō* (sc. *diē* or *mense*), abl. sing. masc. of *ultimus* last. So in G., Du., Sw., etc.]

†1. On the last day (of a specified month). *Obs.*
1582 ALLEN *Martyrd. Fr. E. Campion* (1908) 17 In the xxij yere of the raigne of our soveraine Lady the Queene, Maij vltimo. 1682 SCARLETT *Exchanges* 102 If it be dated *ultimo* February, then its not due till the *ultimo* March. *Ibid.*, If for the 30th of June he write *ultimo*, it will not be due till *ultimo* July.

2. Of last month. (Abbreviated ULT. and ULTO.)
1616 R. COCKS *Diary* (Hakl. Soc.) I. 125, I receved a letter from Mr. Wickham, dated..the 22th ultimo. 1683 W. HEDGES *Diary* (Hakl. Soc.) I. 63 Letters from Cassumbazar advised Thomas Bromly dyed ye 29 Ultimo. 1754 WASHINGTON *Let.* Writ. 1889 I. 70 The 25th ultimo,..I received ye news of your Honour's arrival. 1792 *Ibid.* (1891) XII. 242, I was very glad to receive your letter of the 31st ultimo. 1823 COL. HAWKER *Diary* (1893) I. 261 The morning of the 31st ultimo. 1841 HAWTHORNE in J. Hawthorne *N. Hawthorne & Wife* (1885) I. 227, I took up my abode here on the 12th ultimo.

**Ultimoge·niture.** [f. L. *ultim-us* last; after PRIMOGENITURE.] The mode of succession by which the right of inheritance pertains to the youngest of a family, as in borough-english.
1882 C. ELTON *Orig. Eng. Hist.* 185 'Ultimogeniture,' the awkward term proposed by the Real Property Commissioners of the last generation. 1883 GOMME in *Athenæum* 29 Dec. 865/3 The divergent lines of succession known as ultimogeniture and primogeniture.

† **U·ltimum.** *Obs.*⁻¹ [L., neut. sing. of *ultimus* last.] The final point or limit.
1649 G. DANIEL *Trinarch., Rich. II*, liv, Something has euer bin The Vltimum; and there is yet one step Beyond a Possibilitie to heap.

† **U·ltion.** *Obs. rare.* Also 6 *Sc.* vltioun. [ad. L. *ultiōn-, ultio*, noun of action f. the stem of *ulcisci* to avenge. So OF. *ultion, ulcion*, It. *ulzione*.] Vengeance, revenge, avengement.
c1550 ROLLAND *Crt. Venus* III. 582 Quhairfoir the greit vltioun First come on him and his pepill Ilkone. 1623 COCKERAM, *Vltion*, reuenge. 1657 TOMLINSON *Renou's Disp.* 132 A medicament..should leave in the mouth the ultion of the fault therein committed. 1682 SIR T. BROWNE *Chr. Mor.* III. § 12 To do good for evil [is] a soft and melting ultion, a method taught from Heaven to keep all smooth on Earth.

**Ulto.**, abbrev. of ULTIMO *adv.* 2.
1796 BP. G. HAY in *Ushaw Mag.* Dec. (1913) 284, I had left Edinr. on the 29 Ulto. 1847 *Theatr. Times* 7 Aug. 247 This house opened for a week's season on the 24th ulto.

**Ultonian** (*vltōu·niăn*), *a.* and *sb.* [f. med.L. *Ultonia* Ulster, f. OIr. *Ult-, Ulaid*: see ULTAGH.]
A. *adj.* Of or belonging to Ulster.
1766 O'CONOR *Dissert. Hist. Irel.* 50 The Ultonian Heberians followed the Example. *Ibid.* 158 The Establishment of the Ultonian Oeconomy by Kimbaoth. 1865 S. FERGUSON *Lays Western Gael, Tain-Quest* 23 In the ransom-races..to run 'Gainst the fleet Ultonian horses. 1880 *Encycl. Brit.* XIII. 245/2 The origin of the clan of Degaid is obscure; one story makes it Ultonian, and the other Erimonian.
B. *sb.* An inhabitant or native of Ulster.
1781 C. VALLANCEY *Lit. Irish in Heathen Times* 9 He..was banished by the Ultonians the year following. 1837 W. F. SKENE *Highlanders* I. viii. 210 The Ultonians, or inhabitants of the north of Ireland, were Cruithne. 1880 *Encycl. Brit.* XIII. 246/1 If the Scots failed to subdue the south thoroughly, they succeeded in crushing the Ultonians.

**Ultra** (*v·ltră*), *a.* and *sb.* [Independent use of ULTRA-, orig. as an abbreviation of F. *ultra-royaliste*, and app. mainly due to Lady Morgan. Cf. F. *ultra* sb. (in senses B. 1 and 2).]
A. *adj.* 1. Ultra-royalist.
1817 LADY MORGAN *France* II. (1818) I. 225 The gradual alteration in tone and manner of the *ultra* circles, during my residence at Paris, was extremely obvious. 1818 — *Autobiog.* (1859) 236 The ministry, it is thought, will be ultra. 1819 HELEN M. WILLIAMS *Lett. France* 195 No sooner did the tidings..reach Nismes, than the *Ultra*-party seized a pretext for new disturbances. 1828 LYTTON *Pelham* xv, Monsieur d'A—, a man of much conversational talent and some celebrity as an ultra writer.
2. Of persons or parties: Holding extreme views in politics or other matters of opinion.
1820 H. MATTHEWS *Diary of Invalid* (ed. 2) 492 Shifting its support as it may find danger from the encroachment of either of the ultra parties of the state. 1837 LOCKHART *Scott* (1839) IX. 119 The lofty impartiality with which Scott treats the personal character of Buonaparte was of course sure to make all ultra-politicians at home and abroad condemn his representation. 1864 J. H. NEWMAN *Apol.* 401 The said authority may be supported by a violent ultra-party.
3. Going beyond what is usual or ordinary; excessive, extreme, immoderate.
*attrib.* 1818 in *Lady Morgan's Autobiog.* (1859) 213 It will afford me equal pleasure if Lady Morgan should turn into ridicule, and excite to ultra rage, those who are envious of her. 1824 W. IRVING *T. Trav.* II. 147 A little wearied by this story, and by the ultra zeal of his countrymen. 1834 SIR W. HAMILTON *Discuss.* (1853) 502 Bishop Marsh,..whom no one assuredly will suspect of aught but ultra reverence to the Church of England.
*pred.* 1819 *Metropolis* III. 122 The term over-dressed does not mean over-clad, but applies to their being ultra in the caricature of fashion. 1864 LOWELL *Lincoln* Prose Wks. 1890 V. 187 All that he did was sure to be virulently attacked as ultra by one side. 1884 JEFFERIES *Life of Fields* 246 It is so great and ponderous, and ultra in size.
4. Expressive of extreme views.
1827 SCOTT *Let. to Lockhart* 26 Apr., I own I think Ultra-writing only disgusts people, unless it is in the way of a downright invective.
B. *sb.* 1. An ultra-royalist (in France).
1817 LADY MORGAN *France* II. (1818) I. 237 The royalists abuse the *ultras*; the *ultras* abuse the government; the constitutionalists laugh at both. 1821 MOORE *Mem.* (1853) III. 253 Went with Villamil to dine with General Fuller at Versailles; a party of ultras. 1831 in Gen. P. Thompson *Exerc.* (1842) I. 475, I remember a deputy, a good ultra too, once saying..that Charles X was losing the confidence and affection of his people. 1864 *Month* I. 357 She [Madame Récamier] equally welcomed ultras and liberals.
2. One who holds extreme opinions, particularly in religion or politics.
1826 SCOTT *Diary* 20 Jan., Making mutual concessions and balancing the constitution against the ultras of both parties. 1829 *Blackw. Mag.* XXV. 273 It must therefore stigmatize every man who..acts upon principle as an Ultra and a person of extreme opinions. 1860 FROUDE *Hist. Eng.* V. 391 To the last he was considered by the ultras as timid and intellectually weak. 1884 *American* IX. 69 The ultras of their own party denounce the Ministry as having betrayed their friends.
3. One who goes to the extreme of fashion.
1819 F. MACDONOGH *Hermit in Lond.* I. 55 Bad horsemen and pedestrian women, ultras in conceit and in dress. 1825 T. HOOK *Sayings* Ser. II. *Passion & Princ.* v, Even the parson dined at five, and he was the village *ultra* in points of fashion and etiquette. 1828 P. CUNNINGHAM *N. S. Wales* (ed. 3) II. 112 Cards are ceremoniously left, and rules of precedence..punctiliously insisted on by some of our *ultras*.

‖ **U·ltra**, *prep.* [L. *ultrā* beyond. Cf. F., Pg. *ultra*, It. *oltre*.]
1. In the phr. *ultra vires* (vəiᵊ·rīz), beyond the powers or legal authority (*of* a person, etc.; also used with ellipsis of *for*).
1793 [EARL DUNDONALD] *Descr. Estate Culross* 59 This has proved, and must always prove, *ultra vires* of any one individual. 1806 G. HUTCHESON *Treat. Justice of Peace*, etc. II. 564 *note*, This judgment has been appealed from, as *ultra vires*, as far as regards the directions for building the cruive dike. 1884 *Law Times* LXXVIII. 116/1 It was not *ultra vires* the directors to advance money on such security.
2. Lying beyond. (Cf. ULTRA- 1 c.)
1883 *Ch. Times* XXI. 939/2 As the human eye is sensible only of impressions of light ranging from red to violet, it follows that we cannot be conscious of any hue ultra either of these.

**Ultra-** (*v·ltră*), *prefix*, representing L. *ultrā* beyond, employed as a prefix in the post-classical *ultrāmundānus* ultramundane, and the later *ultrāmarīnus* ultramarine, and *ultrāmontānus* ultramontane. On these models are formed the types illustrated in senses 1 and 2. The further development represented by sense 3 apparently originated in French with the terms *ultra-révolutionnaire* and *ultra-royaliste*, and has become very prolific in English use, as well as in the Romanic languages and in German, Swedish, and Danish.
1. Signifying 'lying spatially beyond or on the other side of': a. With sbs., as *ultraequinoctials* (pl.), those who live beyond the equinox.
1551 ROBINSON tr. *More's Utopia* I. (1895) 112 For (as there Cronicles testifie) before our arriuall ther they neuer harde any thinge of vs, whome they call the ultraequinoctialles.
b. With adjs., as *ultra-Gangetic, -Martian, -median, -terrene, -terrestrial, -zodiacal*.
Also *ultra-galactic, -stellar, -tropical*. (In recent Dicts.).
1833 *Edin. Rev.* Oct. 197 The..hypothesis of Olbers respecting the formation of the four ultra-zodiacal planets. 1836 J. F. DAVIS *Chinese* I. iii. 81 The usual cautious and exclusive spirit of the ultra-gangetic nations. 1858 GLADSTONE *Homer* III. 288 Homer had conceived the existence of what we may call ultra-terrene parts, both westwards and eastwards. 1860 OLMSTEAD *Mech. Heavens* 271 The Asteroids, or Ultra-Zodiacal Planets. 1902 *Proc. Zool. Soc. Lond.* 115 On the hind wing the ultramedian blue band is replaced by a narrow line. 1905 *Athenæum* 11 Mar. 312/3 [A rotation] longer than that of any of the great ultra-Martian planets.
c. *Ultra-red, -violet*, applied to the rays lying beyond the two ends of the visible spectrum. (So F. *ultra-rouge, -violet*.) Also *absol.*
The ultra-red rays are also called *infra-red*.
1870 TYNDALL *Heat* (ed. 4) xiii. § 612. 439 The failure..proved the invisible rays to be exclusively ultra-red. 1875 tr. *Vogel's Chem. Light* vii. 60 We name the invisible tones of colour above violet ultra-violet, and those beyond red ultra-red. 1837 *Encycl. Brit.* XXII. 375/2 The remarkable series of ultra-violet lines..in the spectra of some stars. *Ibid.*, A number of lines in the ultra-violet.
2. With adjs., signifying 'going beyond, surpassing, or transcending the limits of' (the specified concept), as *ultra-human, -microscopic, -natural, -pecuniary*, etc.
Also *ultra-atomic, -gaseous, -material*. (In recent Dicts.)
1818 COLERIDGE in *Lit. Rem.* (1836) I. 185 All other super or *ultra-human beings. 1856 R. A. VAUGHAN *Mystics* (1860) I. 99 The intellectual refinements of an ultra-human spiritualism. 1883 JEFFERIES *Story of my Heart* 63 All things being ultra-human and without design. 1870 TYNDALL *Heat* (ed. 4) xv. § 754. 521 To make our precipitated particles grow from an infinitesimal and altogether *ultra-microscopic size. 1905 *Daily News* 18 May 8 An optical appliance for making visible ultramicroscopic particles in fluids. 1850 GROTE *Greece* II. lxvii. (1862) VI. 29 The *ultra-natural sublimity of the legendary characters disappears. 1802–12 BENTHAM *Ration. Judic. Evid.* (1827) V. 138 Suppose the punishment *ultra-pecuniary: suppose man's life at stake. 1850 GROTE *Greece* II. lxvii. (1862) VI. 70 The word Existence, as they understood it, did not mean phænomenal, but *ultra-phænomenal existence. 1865 — *Plato* I. ii. 97 The real, absolute, ontological, ultra-phenomenal, or Noumenal world. 1883 J. PARKER *Tyne Chylde* 152 Is it possible..to return to the meridian of absolute neutrality as regards *ultraphysical questions? 1894 B. KIDD *Soc. Evolution* vii. 184 That *ultra-rational system of ethics upon which our civilisation is founded. 1895 *Educational Rev.* Sept. 117 Science itself not unfrequently derives motive power from an *ultra-scientific source. 1851 MANSEL *Proleg. Log.* (1860) 18 It would not be difficult to shew that the *ultra-sensational philosophy is that which could most easily dispense with the necessity of introducing language at all. 1882 TYNDALL in *Longm. Mag.* I. 35 There is..boldness..in the attempt to make these *ultra-sensible actions generally intelligible. 1833 CARLYLE *Extr. Jrnl.* 28 Oct., in Froude *First Forty Y.* (1882) II. xvi. 372 The *ultra-sensual surrounds the sensual and gives it meaning.
b. In the sense of 'exceeding in respect of quantity or number', as *ultra-centenarianism* (of human life), *-dimidiate, -total*.
1847 HAMILTON *Let. to De Morgan* 43 If the one extreme coincide with the middle, to the extent of a half (dimidiate quantification); and the other, to the extent of aught more than a half, (ultradimidiate quantification). *Ibid.* 41 In regard to the ultratotal quantification of the middle term. 1864 BOWEN *Logic* viii. 251 This notation can represent equally total and ultratotal distribution. 1879 W. J. THOMS *Longevity* p. xxvi, A very large number of cases of alleged ultra-Centenarianism.
3. Signifying an excessive or extreme degree of the quality or condition expressed by the adjective forming the second element of the compound, as *ultra-affected, -Anglican, -Arctic, -believing*, etc.
First in *ultra-fashionable, -revolutionary*, but in very common, and steadily-increasing, use from about 1830. Only a few of the earlier or more important examples are given here. The distinction from sense 2 is not always quite clear.
1819 *Metropolis* I. 234 The *ultra-affected D-s-y gave us a drop in for a few minutes. 1834 SIR W. HAMILTON *Discuss.* (1853) 533 [Bishop Marsh] peculiarly affects an *ultra-Anglican orthodoxy. 1866 *Ch. Times* 27 Jan., The narrow and intolerant spirit of the ultra-Anglican School. 1856 KANE *Arct. Expl.* I. xx. 205 The ability of Europeans or Americans to inure themselves to an *ultra-Arctic climate. 1829 SOUTHEY *Sir T. More* I. 259 The unbelieving clergy are better than the *ultra-believing in this respect. 1836 J. GILBERT *Chr. Atonem.* vii. (1852) 190 The patrons of this theory are *ultra-benevolent towards the transgressors of law. 1816–30 BENTHAM *Offic. Apt. Maximized, Extr. Const. Code* (1830) 11 Repugnant to these same principles is all *ultra-concomitant remuneration. 1868 BOYD *Lessons Mid. Age* 106 Excellent men, *ultra-conservative in all things. 1870 DISRAELI *Lothair* I. viii. 69 Theodora is..*ultra-cosmopolitan and has invented a new religion. 1838 LOWELL *Lett.* (1894) I. 33, I am fast becoming *ultra-democratic. 1861 G. MUSGRAVE *By-Roads* 323 Owing to ultra-democratic feeling and low radicalism. 1841 F. E. PAGET *Tales Village* Ser. II. x. 197 There is more than one society, which..has already assumed (if I may coin such a word) *ultra-episcopal functions. 1831 *Eclectic Rev.* Apr. 307 A fearless and uncompromising asserter of..*ultra-evangelical doctrines. 1802 in *Spirit Pub. Jrnls.* VI. 91 No female, in the dress of the *ultra-fashionable, can be seen in the streets with the smallest regard to decency. 1841 THACKERAY *Ess., Lett., Sk.*, etc., *Men & Coats* Wks. 1900 XIII. 369 A person who sports an ultra-fashionable costume. 1859 *All Year Round* No. 33. 150 Its combination of the *ultra-feudal with the ultra-modern. 1842 DE QUINCEY *Mod. Greece* Wks. 1890 VII. 351 The Italian, in many features of Gallic insensibility, will be found *ultra-Gallican. 1843 MILL *Logic* I. iii. § 7 The *ultra-German and ontological character of his philosophy. 1848 MRS. JAMESON *Sacr. & Leg. Art* (1850) 107 What may be called the ultra German style. 1866 MRS. H. WOOD *St. Martin's Eve* xxii. (1874) 259 He was given to be *ultra honourable, and to maintain silence in such a case. 1824 SCOTT *Redgauntlet* ch. xvii, The most frank-hearted and *ultra-liberal lass that had ever lived. 1856 GEO. ELIOT *Ess.* (1884) 117 Börne..was a remarkable political writer of the ultra-Liberal party in Germany. 1881 *Times* 3 Jan. 9/4 One of the most notorious consequences of this *ultra-logical mode of conducting affairs is the instability of French Ministries. 1861 MAY *Const. Hist.* (1863) I. iii. 144 A joint address was agreed upon by both Houses,—*ultra-loyal, according to the fashion of the time. 1848 THACKERAY *Van. Fair* xxvi, Who does not know how *ultra-maternal grandmothers are? 1840 EARL ABERDEEN in Charteris *Life Jas. Robertson* v. (1863) 112 It will only be approved of by the old *ultra-moderate party. 1843 *Penny Cycl.* XXV. 296/2 The followers of the *ultra-modern school. 1830 *Fraser's Mag.* II. 598 His *ultramulish obstinacy in persisting. a1832 BENTHAM *Deontol.* xii. (1834) I. 171 They spread into divers circles, domestic,..national, *ultra-national, universal. 1877 GEIKIE *Christ* lvi. (1879) 676 He would embitter Himself with the ultra-national party. 1876 C. M. DAVIES *Unorth. Lond.* 60 He will see nothing but an *ultra-ornate service of the most decorous kind. 1830 PUSEY *Hist. Enq.* II. 327 It is not clear from this extract whether he is immediately speaking of *ultra-orthodox or fanatic opponents. 1844 *Civil Eng. & Arch. Jrnl.* Oct. 376/1 The *ultra-Pecksniffian taste displayed in the portico. 1842 BORROW *Bible in Spain* xxxviii, Several of the *ultra-popish bishops, then resident in Madrid, had denounced the Bible. 1841 A. P. DE LISLE in E. Purcell *Life* (1900) I. vi. 108 The *Ultra Protestant Parsons are quite beside themselves, they rave like maniacs. 1846 HOOK *Ch. Dict.* (ed. 5) 853 Some ultra-protestant sects..have irreverently used sitting as the posture of receiving the Lord's Supper. 1847 L. HUNT *Men, Women, & B.* (1876) 343 Lady Mary herself had an *ultra-prudent sympathy with her husband. 1820 SHELLEY *Œd. Tyr.* I. 200 Prating there of commerce, public faith, Economy,..And other topics, *ultra-radical. 1845 LD. CAMPBELL *Chancellors* xxxviii. (1857) II. 151 There were a few ultra-radical members still not satisfied. 1826 SOUTHEY *Vind. Eccl. Angl.* 198 Music and poetry were as much in request..in those days as they are now among the most *ultra-refined circles. 1890 'R. BOLDREWOOD' *Col. Reformer* (1891) 269 An ultra-refined aristocrat. 1831 CARLYLE in Froude *First Forty Years* (1882) II. viii. 177 They were all prophetical, Toryish, *ultra-religious. 1850 GROTE *Greece* II. lix. (1862) V. 248 His decorous private life and ultra-religious habits. 1793 HELEN M. WILLIAMS *Lett. France* (1795) II. 13 He had sufficient address to lead them to make some extravagant proposition, which he denominated *ultra-revolutionary, and for which he sent them to the scaffold. 1845 *Encycl. Metrop.* XIII. 370/2 Robespierre..

accordingly..took an early occasion to associate the ultra-revolutionary party with the foreign enemies of the republic. **1819** HELEN M. WILLIAMS *Lett. France* 61 A party, too well known by the denomination of *ultra-royalist. **1821** *Edin. Rev.* XXXVI. 139 This ultra-royalist spirit, diffused by the priests and emigrants. **1836** H. COLERIDGE *North. Worthies* (1852) I. 38 Their intolerant and ultra-royalist principles. **1823** BENTHAM *Mem. & Corr.* Wks. 1843 X. 536 Then came the servile poet and novelist, Sir Walter Scott: and then the *ultra-servile sack guzzler, Southey. **1832** COLERIDGE *Table-t.* 16 Aug., The discipline at Christ's Hospital in my time was *ultra-Spartan. **1853** MISS YONGE *Heir of Redclyffe* vii, Really it is so *ultra-splendid as to deserve notice! **1885** *Spectator* 18 July 945/2 He does not emulate the *ultra-strict veracity of the Quaker. **1829** MOORE *Mem.* (1854) VI. 41 Murray full of *ultra-Tory predictions about Peel; that he is a ruined man [etc.]. **1843** SYD. SMITH *Wks.* (1850) 683 Let me beg of my dear Ultras not to imagine..that they could form an Ultra-tory Administration. **1851** G. F. RICHARDSON *Geol.* (1855) 438 Groves and forests of the luxuriant vegetation of an *ultra-tropical climate were swept away by floods and inundations.

**b.** In some special terms, as *ultra-basic, -brachycephalic, -dolichocephalic, -elliptic.*

**1893** GEIKIE *Text-bk. Geol.* (ed. 3) VI. I. 681 Crystalline rocks, which range from amorphous masses..to basic or even what are called '*ultra-basic' compounds. **1898** *Nature* 3 Feb. 315/2 He..had arrived at certain very definite views concerning the constant association of the crystalline form of carbon with the ultrabasic rocks. **1886** J. G. GARSON in *Jrnl. Anthropol. Inst.* XVI. 14 The..third group on either side is called ultradolichocephalic and *ultrabrachycephalic respectively. **1900** DENIKER *Races of Man* ii. 58 *note*, Cephalic index of the skull:..from 90 and upwards, ultra-brachycephalic. **1877** CAYLEY *Math. Papers* X. 162 Göpel and Rosenhain each connect the theory with that of the *ultra-elliptic functions involving the radical $\sqrt{X}$ [etc.].

**c.** Similarly with advs.

**1871** MISS MULOCK *Fair France* i. 9 And what possible harm can it do a man to greet his neighbour civilly, even ultra-politely, rather than grumpily? **1883** MEREDITH *Poems & Lyrics* 139 All in honour still; Oh, all in honour, ultra-honourably!

**4.** With sbs. in the same sense: **a.** Denoting persons.

Many of these are adjs. used substantively.

**1817** MAR. EDGEWORTH *On Bores* Wks. 1833 XVIII. 318 Well-bred persons, abhorring the pedantry of the blues, are usually *anti-blues*, or **ultra-antis*. **1850** MARSDEN *Early Purit.* (1853) 338 Whitgift..was, in modern language, an *Ultra-Calvinist. **1868** G. DUFF *Pol. Surv.* 12 The struggles between *ultra-centralizers and ultra-federalists. **1836** GEN. P. THOMPSON *Let.* in *Exerc.* (1842) IV. 124 Among the names..are many, like Hermes, Nereus,..which modern *ultra-christians would have thought formidably heathenish. **1821** H. MORE in Roberts *Mem.* (1835) IV. 179 The *ultra-educationist would despise these limits. **1834** MAR. EDGEWORTH *Helen* xxxv. III. 66 One born and bred such an *ultra exclusive as Louisa Castlefort. **1829** T. HOOK *Bank to Barnes* 146 The forthcoming novel has long kept the *ultra fashionables on the tiptoe of expectation. **1868** *Ultra-federalist [see *ultra-centralizer*]. **1866** G. TALBOT in E. Purcell *Life A. P. de Lisle* (1900) I. xv. 408 The [architectural] designs excited the admiration even of the *Ultra-Goths present. **1818** BYRON *Juan* Ded. xvii, Is it not so, my Tory, *ultra-Julian? **1824** MISS MITFORD *Village* Ser. I. (1863) 208 He is an *ultra-liberal, quotes Cobbett, and goes rather too far. **1860** W. G. CLARK in *Vac. Tour* (1864) 6 The ultra-liberals are blind to facts and consequences. **1857** PUSEY *Real Presence* i. (1869) 112 The error of the Sacramentaries was opposed by the error of the *Ultra Lutherans. **1816** SOUTHEY *Ess.* (1832) I. 281 The *amateurs outrés* of horse-racing, or *ultra-men of the turf. **1852** S. R. MAITLAND *Eight Ess.* 158 'Just so,' replies the *ultra-papist; 'I believe you'. **1827** G. HIGGINS *Celtic Druids* 136 The *ultra pietists make a terrible outcry. **1818** BENTHAM *Ch. Eng., Catech. Exam.* 334 If the number of livings be greater than two,..he may be termed an *Ultra-Pluralist. **1818** *Q. Rev.* XVIII. 504 In the opinion of the *ultra-presbyterians. **1835** HOOK *Ch. Dict.* (1842) 501 The use of the ring in marriage used to be regarded as a remnant of Popery by *ultra-protestants. **1841** A. P. DE LISLE in E. Purcell *Life* (1900) I. xi. 208 That still more monstrous idea held by ultra-Protestants that the Catholick Church consists of all sects of nominal Christians. **1850** MARSDEN *Early Purit.* (1853) 49 The *ultra-puritans regarded them as semi-papists. **1834** GREVILLE *Mem.* (1874) III. 54 Lord Wharncliffe..says that the constituency of the great towns is composed of *ultra-Radicals. **1871** M. COLLINS *Marq. & Merch.* II. iii. 58 You're an ultra-Radical. **1858** FROUDE *Hist. Eng.* IV. 114 At home, the virulence of the *ultra-reactionaries..recommenced. **1867** LATHAM *Black & White* Pref. p. vi, They are the successful men, who have made money, and are not disposed to be *ultra-Republicans in future. **1845** *Encycl. Metrop.* XIII. 370/2 The progress of Hebert and the *ultra-revolutionists was still more distasteful to him [Danton] than to Robespierre. **1848** BLACKIE in *Class. Mus.* V. 72 Dante..said many things in his divine poem..offensive to the *ultra-Romanists. **1818** LADY MORGAN *Autobiog.* (1859) 276, I dread the machinations of the *ultra royalists and the Bourbon princes. **1845** LD. CAMPBELL *Chancellors* xcv. (1857) IV. 302 It was thought fit to balance them by some determined ultra-royalists. **1816** SOUTHEY *Ess.* (1832) I. 356 Such was the system of government established in France by the Perfect Emperor of the *Ultra-Whigs and Extra-Reformers.

**b.** Denoting actions, qualities, etc.

**1858** H. MARTINEAU *Hist. Peru* 169 The government was declared to have gone over to *ultra-abolitionism. **1845** FORD *Handbk. Spain* II. 656 Napier, in his *ultra advocacy of Soult, says [etc.]. **1831** *Edin. Rev.* LIV. 387 He parades an *ultra-Byronism. **1841** MIALL in *Nonconf.* I. 73 In connection with Laudism and *ultra-churchism. **1850** L. HUNT *Autobiog.* I. ii. 70, I found myself..cultivating a perplexed *ultra-conscientiousness with my mother. **1828** P. CUNNINGHAM *N. S. Wales* (ed. 3) II. 16 His *ultra-dandyism of speech, dress, and manner, made his presence a sort of *sine qua non* in every merry meeting. **1863** A. BLOMFIELD *Mem. Bp. Blomfield* I. iv. 106 Reports of his *ultra-discipline.. may have reached you. **1856** R. A. VAUGHAN *Mystics* (1860) I. 279 It is sickening to hear the unctuous talk with which now-a-days *ultra-liberalism will sometimes stretch out a hand to spiritual tyranny. **1857** PUSEY *Real Presence* i. (1869) 122 Amid the conflict of parties, the 'Formula Concordiæ' moderated the extremes of *Ultra-Lutheranism. **1847** L. HUNT *Men, Women, & B.* II. v. 70 The account is singular and interesting, as a specimen of the highest *ultra-manners of those times. **1877** C. GEIKIE *Christ* lvi. (1879) 676 With craft, the *ultra-orthodoxy of the Pharisaic party allied itself with the loyalist faction. **1818** BENTHAM *Ch. Eng.* 336 In these cases of *Ultra-Pluralism, whereabouts are the eyes of the Archbishop? **1842** PUSEY *Crisis Eng. Ch.* 30 Cases in which persons who were going over from *Ultra-Protestantism, have been thankful to be stayed, and found their rest in the true doctrines of our Church. **1858** SEARS *Athan.* III. ii. 267 It is only our ultra Protestantism that involves us in these difficulties and absurdities. **1825** HAZLITT *Spirit of Age* 147 They are a relief to the mind.. heated with *ultra-radicalism. **1847** W. C. L. MARTIN *Ox* 63/1 There is, perhaps, something of *ultra-refinement in this view of the matter. **1816–30** BENTHAM *Offic. Apt. Maximized, Extr. Const. Code* (1830) 12 Completely needless, and thence unjustifiable, is all such *ultra-remuneration. **1865** *Ch. Times* 28 Oct. 341 The Puritan outcry about the '*ultra-ritualism' at St. Michael's Church. **1815** *Ann. Reg., Gen. Hist.* 94 A preponderance of what is called *ultra-royalism, which opposes the moderation of the court. **1871** LOWELL *Pope* Prose Wks. 1890 IV. 18 The *ultra-spiritualism of the Puritans. **1829** MOORE *Mem.* (1854) VI. 44 Some of the Handelian part of the selections might be called the *ultra-Toryism of music.

**Ultra-crepida·rian,** *a.* and *sb.* [f. the Latin phrase *ultrā crepidam* 'beyond the sole' in allusion to the reply of Apelles to the cobbler.

The form in which the reply is given by Pliny (*Nat. Hist.* XXXV. x. § 36) is *ne supra crepidam judicaret.* Valerius Maximus (VIII. xii. 3) expresses it by *supra plantam ascendere vetuit.*]

**A.** *adj.* Going beyond one's proper province; giving opinions on matters beyond one's knowledge.

**1819** HAZLITT *Letter to W. Gifford* Wks. 1902 I. 368 You have been well called an Ultra-Crepidarian critic. **1822** — *Table-T.* II. vi. 143 The last sort I shall mention are verbal critics—mere word-catchers. [*Note*] The title of Ultra-Crepidarian critics has been given to a variety of this species. **1832** *Examiner* 662/1 He takes a fancy to teach that 'Ultra-crepidarian Critic' his own theory. **1872** F. HALL *Rec. Exemplif. False Philol.* 112 His assumption of judicial assessorship, as a critic of English, is, therefore, to borrow a word from Hazlitt, altogether ultra-crepidarian.

**B.** *sb.* One who ventures beyond his scope; an ignorant or presumptuous critic.

**1825** BEDDOES *Let.* in *Poems* (1851) p. xxxviii, The 'Fatal Dowry' has been cobbled, I see, by some purblind ultra-crepidarian. **1831** *Q. Rev.* XLIV. 77 Two of these ultra-crepidarians are included in Mr. Southey's present chapter of chronicles.

Hence **Ultracrepida·rianism.**

*a* **1876** M. COLLINS *Pen Sketches by Vanished Hand* (1879) I. 242 A brochure on *The Laws of Verse*, which is curious as exemplifying what a great wit called 'ultracrepidarianism'.

So † **Ultracre·pidast,** = B. above. *Obs. rare*⁻¹. **Ultra-cre·pidate** *v. intr.*, to venture beyond one's scope. **Ultracrepida·tion, -cre·pidizing,** the action or fact of criticizing ignorantly.

**1640** HENSHAW *Horæ Succ.* II. Ep. Ded. 1, I cannot but condemne those *ultra-crepitasts* [*sic*] that, with Festus, will teach Saint Paul divinity. **1800** COLERIDGE in *Sir H. Davy's Rem.* (1858) 78, I was a well-meaning *sutor* who had ultra-crepidated with more zeal than wisdom. *Ibid.* 83 All this is ultra crepidation. **1837** S. R. MAITLAND *6 Lett. Fox's A. & M.* p. ix, There is among the infinity of anonymous writing, compiling, concocting,..so much pretence (if I may make a word.., so much ultracrepidizing) that [etc.]. **1882** FARRAR in *Contemp. Rev.* Mar. 374 It is always dangerous, as Coleridge phrased it, to ultra-crepidate.

**Ultrafi·dian,** *a.* [f. the L. phrase *ultrā fidem* 'beyond faith'.] Going beyond mere faith; blindly credulous. Also **Ultrafi·dianism.**

**1825** COLERIDGE *Aids Refl.* viii, Sir Thomas Brown..could answer all the objections of the Devil and Reason 'with the old resolution he had learnt of Tertullian: Certum est quia impossibile est!'..Now this I call Ultra-fidianism. *a* **1849** H. COLERIDGE *Ess.* (1851) II. 96 The great moralist, who balanced an ultrafidian credulity in the supernatural with an extraordinary degree of scepticism in things natural and human. **1865** *Reader* 14 Jan. 43/2 It must be, however, a strangely incurious and ultrafidian mind that can consent to rest there..simply at another's bidding.

**Ultrage,** obs. form of OUTRAGE.

**Ultra·geous,** *a. rare.* [f. ULTRA *a.* or *sb.*, after *outrageous.*] Violently extreme.

**1823** G. CANNING *Let.* in *Q. Rev.* July (1897) 129 The French Government..suffered themselves to be driven on.. by the Ultrageous party of their followers. *Ibid.*, Another of an opposite sort may spring up, in an Ultrageous fashion.

**Ultraism** (*v*·ltrăˌiz'm). [f. ULTRA *a.* + -ISM. So Sw. *ultraism*, G. *ultraismus.* Cf. F. *ultracisme.*] The principles or tenets of one who holds extreme opinions on any question; the fact of holding such opinions.

**1821** H. MORE in Roberts *Mem.* (1835) IV. 178, I think there is ultraism on both sides of the question. **1842** G. S. FABER *Prov. Lett.* (1844) II. 116 The Ultraism of those, who..would fain establish a bundle of Unscripturalities as the catholic doctrine of the primitive Church. **1880** O. JOHNSON *W. L. Garrison* 32 How foolish to throw away all chances of doing any good by such ultraism!

**b.** An instance of this.

**1824** MEDWIN *Convers. Byron* II. 5 To the great horror of the former, she soon sported her Ultraisms. **1857** O. BROWNSON *Convert* Wks. 1882–7 V. 46 My alleged Ultraisms and tendency to run to extremes. **1865** J. H. NEWMAN in Ward *Life* (1912) xxiii. II. 102, I abominate the fierce tyranny which..calls to account everyone who ventures to keep clear of ultra-isms.

**Ultraist** (*v*·ltrăˌist). [f. as prec. + -IST. So Sw. *ultraist.*] One who holds extreme opinions; an extremist.

**1842** G. S. FABER *Prim. Doctr. Election* (ed. 2) I. i. 5 *note*, Those high-vaulting Ultraists, who professedly treat with contempt the harmonious voice of Aboriginal Antiquity. **1875** O. W. HOLMES *Old Vol. Life, Crime and Automatism* (1891) 357 Obviously these reformers are not fanatics; they are not ultraists or Utopians.

Hence **Ultrai·stic** *a.*, tending to extremes in opinion or practice.

**1840** G. S. FABER *Christ's Disc. Capernaum* Ded. p. xx, Our ultraistic friend, .. in his own insulated strength confident against the world in arms. **1877** SPARROW *Serm.* ix. 115 This unmeasured, exaggerated and ultraistic mode of drawing inferences.

**Ultramarine** (*v*ltrămărī·n), *a.* and *sb.* [ad. med.L. *ultrāmarīn-us*, f. L. *ultrā* beyond + *mare* sea: see ULTRA-. Cf. Sp. and Pg. *ultramarino*, It. *oltramarino*, OF. *ultremarin, oltre-* (obs. F. *outremarin*); also as sb. (sense B. 1) Sp. *ultramarino*, G., Sw., Da. *ultramarin*, Du. *-marijn*; Sp., Pg. *ultramar*, F. *outremer.*]

**A.** *adj.* **1.** Situated beyond the sea. Now *rare.*

**1652** FRENCH *Yorksh. Spa* vii. 65 In a moorish, boggie ground, ariseth a Spring of a Vitrioline tast.., resembling much those ultramarine Spaws. **1681** H. NEVILE *Plato Rediv.* 47 In the several Countries of Padua, Brescia, Vicenza, Verona,..as also in the Ultramarine Provinces. **1769** BURKE *Obs. Pres. St. Nat.* Wks. 1842 I. 80 He tells them that the loss of her ultramarine dominions lessens her expences. **1828** SIR W. NAPIER *Penins. War* I. ii. I. 15 The ultramarine dominions of the exiled family to be equally divided between the contracting parties. **1852** GROTE *Greece* II. lxxix. X. 419 The project of stretching across the Ægean for ultramarine dependencies.

**2.** (See defs.)

**1656** BLOUNT *Glossogr.*, *Ultramarine*, coming from beyond Sea. **1802** JAMES *Milit. Dict.*, *Ultramarine*, from beyond the sea—foreign.

**3.** *Ultramarine blue* (or *colour*): **a.** A pigment or colouring matter of various shades of blue, originally obtained from the mineral lapis lazuli and named with reference to the foreign origin of this. († Also with *green.*)

So Sp. and Pg. *azul ultramarino*, It. *azzurro oltremarino.*

**1686** AGLIONBY *Painting Illustr.* I. 23 In imploying of fine Colours, as fine lacks Ultra Marine Green, &c. **1698** FRYER *Acc. E. India & P.* 332 From this Stone [*sc.* Lapis Lazuli] is made that Colour they name Ultra-marine Blue. *a* **1775** J. HILL (Jod.), To it the painters are indebted for their beautiful ultramarine colour, which is by a calcination of lapis lazuli. **1816** P. CLEAVELAND *Min.* 258 Its chief use is to furnish the ultramarine blue, a pigment remarkable for the durability of its color. **1879** *Cassell's Techn. Educ.* IV. 222/1 If the body is to be blue, mix ultramarine blue with one half raw oil and turpentine.

**b.** A blue colour like that of this pigment.

**1781** [see next]. **1845** *Florist's Jrnl.* 229 It differs materially in the colour, the flowers of the present species being a bright ultra-marine blue. **1882** *Garden* 22 Apr. 283/3 The glowing ultramarine blue of the flowers is strikingly brilliant.

**4.** Of a special deep-blue colour. (Cf. prec.)

**1781** LATHAM *Gen. Synop. Birds* I. 413 Ultramarine R[oller]. ..The whole plumage of a rich glossy ultramarine blue. **1783** *Ibid.* III. 301 Ultramarine F[inch]. The plumage wholly of a fine deep blue. **1867** MISS BRADDON *Rupert Godwin* I. i. 5 The deep crimson of the brick-work, .. sharply defined against an ultramarine sky.

**B.** *sb.* **1.** = A. 3.

**1598** HAYDOCKE tr. *Lomazzo's Artes* III. v. 101 Of Blewes, ..the greater part of Azures, specially the vltramarine. *c* **1650** NORGATE *Miniatura* (1919) 49 The rest of the skie..is made with Ultramarine and White. **1677** GREW *Disc. Colours Plants* iii. § 28 The Flower of Lathyrus or Parseverlasting ..is changed from a Peach, to as pure a Blew, as the best Vltramarine. **1683** TRYON *Way to Health* 229 Take Indigo, Vltramarine, or any Blew, and mix it with White, and it makes a Skie to what degree you please. **1731** *Gentl. Mag.* I. 449 Capt. Goslin presented some blue Colour, with a Specimen which shew'd it to exceed the common Ultramarine. **1762–71** H. WALPOLE *Vertue's Anecd. Paint.* (1786) II. 234 It would be a very long time before the worth of 200*l.* in ultramarine could be employed in miniatures. **1816** P. CLEAVELAND *Min.* 258 The particles of the ultramarine, being thus rendered smooth and slippery, escape. **1859** R. HUNT *Guide Mus. Pract. Geol.* (ed. 2) 256 An artificial ultramarine is prepared by mixing clay, carbonate of soda, and sulphur. **1880** J. DUNBAR *Pract. Papermaker* 60 The above tests are..a safeguard to any paper-maker in buying ultramarines.

*attrib.* **1839** URE *Dict. Arts* 1262 The remainder of the mass..yields an inferior pigment, called ultramarine ashes. **1868** WATTS *Dict. Chem.* V. 937 A pale-blue powder called ultramarine ash. **1881** *Instr. Census Clerks* (1885) 58 Ultramarine Maker. Verditer Maker. **1888** *Encycl. Brit.* XXIII. 721/2 There are very few ultramarine works in other countries, and none, as far as we know, in Great Britain.

**b.** With distinguishing terms (see quots.).

**1728** CHAMBERS *Cycl.* s.v., There is another Kind, call'd Common or Dutch Ultramarine. **1867** *Chambers' Encycl.* IX. 625 The term *Yellow Ultramarine* is sometimes given commercially to chromate of baryta, a yellow insoluble powder used as a pigment. **1868** WATTS *Dict. Chem.* V. 937 The green ultramarine thus obtained is ground in a mill, and then roasted, with addition of sulphur, to convert it into blue ultramarine. **1879** *Cassell's Techn. Educ.* I. 221/2 The best imitation, or German ultramarine. *Ibid.* III. 20/1 The blue colour of artificial ultramarine. **1888** *Encycl. Brit.* XXIII. 722/1 Silica ultramarine is soda-ash ultramarine in whose preparation a quantity of finely divided silica..has been added. *Ibid.*, Since 1873 the Nuremberg works have been producing four varieties of magnificently violet ultramarine.

**2.** = A. 3 b.

1695 DRYDEN tr. *Dufresnoy's Art Paint.* § 354 Red Oker is one of the most heavy Colours...Ultramarine, or azure, is very light and a very sweet Colour. 1696 PATRICK *Comm. Exod.* xxv. (1697) 479 Maimonides expresses it the Colour of the Firmament; and Kimchi calls it ultramarine. 1860 TYNDALL *Glac.* I. iv. 34 The lake at some distance was of a deep ultramarine. 1868 W. S. O. tr. *Figuier's Ocean World* i. (1872) 13 The ocean, seen by reflection, presents a fine azure blue or ultramarine.

So † **Ultramari·nish** *a.*, = prec. A. 3. *Obs.*

1667 DENHAM *Direct. Paint.* I. iv, Use nothing but Ultra-Marinish Blue.

**Ultramontane** (vltrămǫ·ntēⁱn), *sb.* and *a.* Also 7 -an, -aine; 7 oltra-. [ad. med.L. *ultrā-montān-us*, f. L. *ultrā* beyond + *mont-*, *mons* mountain (sc. the Alps). So F. *ultramontain* (1323; also OF. *outremontain*, *-an*), Sp. and Pg. *ultramontano*, It. *oltramontano*; G. *ultramontan*, Du. *-montaan*. Cf. TRAMONTANE *a.* and *sb.*]

**A.** *sb.* **1.** *Eccl. Hist.* **a.** A representative of the Roman Catholic Church north of the Alps as opposed to the ecclesiastics in Italy. Now *rare.*

1592 BACON *Obs. Libel* in *Resuscitatio* (1657) 147 Those that know any Thing of the Respects of Conclaves, know, that he is not Papable: First, because he is an Vltramontane, of which sort, there hath been none, these Fifty years. 1620 BRENT tr. *Sarpi's Hist. Council of Trent* v. 463 The Cardinals saw no other meanes to oppose these attemp[t]s, but by sending a great number of Italian Prelats, who, being vnited together, will overcome all the Vltramontans. 1651 *Life Father Sarpi* 157 The Oltramontanes..did greedily reade and receive whatsoever came abroade. 1769 ROBERTSON *Chas. V*, III. 46 Perhaps the cardinals durst not venture to provoke the people of Rome..by placing another *ultra-montane* on the papal throne. 1855 MILMAN *Lat. Chr.* VI. 10 He [Pope Urban VI] openly avowed his design to make so large a nomination [of cardinals] that the Italians should resume their ascendancy over the Ultramontanes.

**b.** A strong adherent or supporter of the Papal authority; an ultramontanist. (Cf. B. 1 b.)

In this connexion the point of view is that of France or other countries north of the Alps.

1873 SPENCER *Stud. Sociol.* xii. (1874) 299 To the Ultramontane, holding that the temporal welfare no less than the eternal salvation of men depends on submission to the Church, it is incredible that Church-authority has but a transitory value. 1876 GLADSTONE in *Contemp. Rev.* June 4 The most violent Ultramontane, the most determined Agnostic, may alike make excellent Erastians. ? 1882 TENNYSON *In Mem. W. G. Ward* 4 My friend, the most unworldly of mankind, Most generous of all Ultramontanes, Ward.

**2.** An inhabitant or native of a country north of the Alps.

*c* 1618 MORYSON *Itin.* IV. (1903) 429 In Bologna..the Vltramontans and Citramontans are each governed by their owne Statutes. 1626 C. POTTER tr. *Sarpi's Hist. Quarrels* 331 The Venetians..resolued..to make ready all their Troupes, Italians and Albans, with some others of the Vltramontans. 1696 PHILLIPS (ed. 5) s.v., The Italians call all on this side the Alpes, Ultra-montanes, or People living beyond the Alpes. 1730 A. GORDON *Maffei's Amphith.* 195 The Original was bought by some Ultramontane or another, and so published we know not by whom. 1851 GALLENGA *Italy* II. iii. 74 Schiller was, of course, the best understood and appreciated of all the ultramontanes.

**3.** (See quot.)

1875 *Dublin Mag.* Sept. 317 A group of troubadours in the most northerly districts of Provence, who were called 'Ultramontanes' by the poets of the plains south of the Garonne and the Cevennes.

**B.** *adj.* **1. a.** Of or belonging to, connected with, derived from, the countries or peoples lying to the north of the Alps.

*c* 1618 MORYSON *Itin.* IV. (1903) 427 The Rector Vltramontane (that is of the nations beyond the Alps) must be chosen by the former yeares Rectour and by the newe Counselors. 1687 *Lond. Gaz.* No. 2209/2 An Officer in the service of the Duke of Savoy, has agreed with the Senate to raise 600 Ultramontaine Horse. 1829 SCOTT *Anne of G.* xxx, Your speech smacks of the northern, or Norman-French...But you are a minstrel, perhaps, from these ultramontane parts. 1832 tr. *Sismondi's Ital. Rep.* v. 128 Henry VII. departed from Pisa, commanding 2500 ultramontane and 1500 Italian cavalry. 1855 MILMAN *Lat. Chr.* VI. 12 The Ultramontane Cardinals would not tamely abandon a power which had given them..the spiritual supremacy of the world for seventy years. *Ibid.* 19 The Pope's courtiers of ultramontane birth or opinions.

**b.** Of, belonging to, or characteristic of, the Italian party in the Church of Rome; holding or implying extreme views in favour of the papal authority. (Cf. A. 1 b.)

1728 CHAMBERS *Cycl.* s.v. *Tramontan*, The French Lawyers give the same Title of..Ultramontane Doctors to the Italian Canonists..who go upon Rules and Maxims, too favourable to the Court of Rome. 1819 HELEN M. WILLIAMS *Lett. France* 100 Nations are tired of those ultra-montane mysteries. 1846 G. OLIVER *Monast. Dioec. Exon.* 424 *note*, A papal bull settled the question respecting the capacity of the mendicant orders to purchase in a manner eminently ultramontane. 1873-4 DIXON *Two Queens* XIII. v. III. 27 The ultra-montane school of canonists asserted, that a pope had power to publish such an act.

*transf.* 1899 T. G. SELBY *Unheeding God* xi. 201 Some of his [Darwin's] most fervent disciples no longer adopt that ultramontane attitude.

**2.** In general sense: Situated beyond, belonging to the other side of, the mountains.

1786 JEFFERSON *Writ.* (1859) I. 587 How may the ultramontane territory be disposed of so as to produce the greatest ..benefit to the inhabitants of the maritime States of the Union? 1809 A. HENRY *Trav.* 325 They were in possession of several ultramontane prisoners, two of whom we purchased.

**Ultramontanism** (vltrămǫ·ntăniz'm). [ad. F. *ultramontanisme* (18th c.), = Sp., Pg. *ultramontanismo*: see prec. and -ISM.] The principles and practice of the ultramontane party in the Church of Rome; the doctrine of absolute papal supremacy.

1827 *Westm. Rev.* Jan. 80 That what he calls ultramontanism may be maintained..to be an orthodox tenet of the Catholic church. 1854 LD. HOUGHTON in T. W. Reid *Life* (1891) I. xi. 498 Cullen's ultramontanism is doing good in denationalising the priesthood. 1878 DOWDEN *Stud. Lit.* 323 Ultramontanism in its strictest form was the creed of Lamennais.

**Ultramo·ntanist.** [Cf. prec. and -IST.]

**1.** An adherent of ultramontane principles and doctrines; a supporter of the absolute supremacy of the Pope.

1826 SOUTHEY *Vind. Eccl. Angl.* 3 The English Romanists will proudly acknowledge you for their advocate (whatever may be thought by the Ultra-Montanists), as one in whose hands their cause will lose nothing in strength. 1839 HALLAM *Hist. Lit.* III. ii. § 12 This opposition to the extreme line of the ultra-montanists might be well compatible with a tendency towards much that the reformers had denounced. 1885 W. W. ROBERTS *Pontif. Decrees* Introd. 12 How can the Ultramontanist meet the mistake that Rome made in condemning heliocentricism?

*attrib.* 1839 *Fraser's Mag.* XIX. 274 This paper..is an ultra-montanist paper. 1884 *Encycl. Brit.* XVII. 754/2 This bold proclamation of Ultramontanist doctrine.

**2.** = ULTRAMONTANE *sb.* 1 a. *rare*⁻¹.

1855 MILMAN *Lat. Chr.* VI. 13 As Ultramontanists it was their interest, their inclination, to espouse the Ultramontane cause.

**Ultramo·ntanizing,** *vbl. sb.* [Cf. prec. and -IZE.] The process of making ultramontane in character.

1893 *Dublin Rev.* Apr. 250 The Romanising or Ultramontanising of English worship, as it would be called in our days.

**Ultramundane** (vltrămv·ndēⁱn), *sb.* and *a.* [ad. late L. *ultrāmundānus*, f. *ultrā* beyond + *mundus* the world. Cf. F. *ultramondain*, Sp. *ultra-*, It. *oltramundano.*]

† **A.** *sb. pl.* Matters lying outside the physical world; metaphysics. *Obs.*⁻¹

1549 CHALONER *Erasm. on Folly* M ij, He had spent whole xxxvi yeeres togithers in studiyng the Phisicals and Vltramundans of Duns and Aristotle.

**B.** *adj.* Lying beyond or outside of the world; of or belonging to things beyond the limits of the solar system.

1656 BLOUNT *Glossogr.*, *Ultramundane*,..supercelestial, beyond or above the sky. Dr. Charl. 1665 BOYLE *Occas. Refl.*, *Occas. Medit.* 35 A Faculty..by whose help the restless mind..roves about in the ultra-mundane spaces, and considers how farr they reach. 1697 J. SERGEANT *Solid Philos.* 180 They will needs conceit there is some Ultramundane kind of Thing existent out of the world. 1807 *Edin. Rev.* X. 147 The particles by which this effect is brought about, are called by Le Sage..the ultramundane atoms. 1845 J. H. NEWMAN in Ward *Life* (1912) iii. I. 80 He dies a Pantheist denying that there is an Ultramundane God. 1876 P. G. TAIT *Rec. Adv. Phys. Sci.* (1885) 368 The very ingenious idea of the ultra-mundane corpuscles, the outcome of the lifework of Le Sage.

† **Ultra-, Ultrequidance,** variants of OUTRECUIDANCE *Obs.*

1541 *St. Papers Hen. VIII*, VIII. 545 He made..protestation, that the same..passed him..only uppon wilfulness and ultraquidance, which he confessed had been in him.

† **Ultrice.** *Obs.*⁻¹ [a. OF. *ultrice*, ad. L. *ultrīc-em*, *ultrix*, fem. of *ultor* avenger.] A female avenger.

1490 CAXTON *Eneydos* xxvii. 99 O cruelle vltryces, wycked vengeresses, Furyes infernalle & Iusticers of helle.

**Ultro-moti·vity.** *rare*⁻¹. [f. L. *ultrō* (see next) + MOTIVITY.] Capability of spontaneous movement.

1854 HICKOK *Sci. Mind* 278 Pure spontaneity has..merely a simple ultro-motivity to its object.

**Ultroneous** (vltrōu·niəs), *a.* [f. L. *ultrōne-us*, f. *ultrō* of one's own accord, voluntarily. Cf. Sp., Pg., It. *ultroneo.*] Made, offered, etc., of one's own accord; spontaneous, voluntary.

1637 GILLESPIE *Eng. Pop. Cerem.* II. ix. 43 This Argument of Scandall, the Pastor can make good against the Fornicator, out of his owne ultroneous and unrequired concession of the indifferency of Fornication. 1657 J. WATTS *Vind. Ch. Eng.* 144 A superiour may do..an ultroneous honour, if he will, to his inferior. 1817 J. FERGUSSON *Rep. Consist. Crt. Scotl.* 257 *note*, Testimony given by a witness not cited is liable to objection, as ultroneous. 1852 SIR W. HAMILTON *Discuss.* (1853) App. iii. 811 The exercise of the student in the University classes, should be partly exigible, partly ultroneous. 1894 BRETT in *19th Cent.* June 914 That worthy body of doctrinaires were responsible for the ultroneous rule of Palmerston.

**b.** *Sc. Law.* Of witnesses: (see quots.).

1824 G. TAIT *On Evidence* 379 Witnesses..if they come into Court..without being cited..are called ultroneous witnesses. 1838 W. BELL *Dict. Law Scot.* 371 Ultroneous witnesses, *i.e.* witnesses who offer their testimony without being regularly cited, were formerly inadmissable; but this objection seems now only to affect their credibility.

**Ultro·neously,** *adv.* [f. prec. + -LY ².] Of one's own accord; spontaneously, voluntarily.

1627 W. SCLATER *Exp. 2 Thess.* (1629) 75 Is it warrantable vltroneously to offer our selues to Martyrdome? 1657 REEVE *God's Plea* 28 He [God] doth love himselfe necessarily, but all other things ultroneously. 1847 SIR W. HAMILTON *Let. to De Morgan* 30 In the second, (what you omit to mention,) copies were through your friend Dr. — ultroneously proffered. 1883 *Saturday Review* 21 July 65 Mr. Gladstone and his colleagues wantonly, ultroneously,..have themselves interpreted and settled a..complicated point.

**Ultro·neousness.** *rare.* [f. as prec. + -NESS.] Voluntary action; spontaneity.

1623 W. SCLATER *Tythes* f 2 b, Law is not here opposed to no Law, or iniunction to vltroneousnesse of Tything. 1858-61 J. BROWN *Horae Subs.* (1863) 222 The law of personality, of ultroneousness, of free will, that which in a great measure makes us what we are.

† **Ululable,** *a.* *Obs.*⁻⁰ [ad. L. (post-classical) *ululābilis.*] 'Howling, yelling' (Bailey, 1721).

**Ululant** (v·liulănt, yū·l-), *a.* [a. L. *ululant-*, *ululans*, pres. pple. of *ululāre*: see next.]

**1.** Having the character of ululation.

1868 G. MACDONALD *R. Falconer* xxx, He burst out laughing, after a doubtful and ululant fashion. 1901 EDITH RICKERT in *Academy* 16 Mar. 236/2 An ululant tumult, that bounds and rebounds.

**2.** Ululating, howling.

1896 A. LANG *Walton's Angler* Introd. p. xli, They were better than Quakers, naked and ululant.

**Ululate** (v·liulēⁱt, yū·l-), *v.* [f. L. *ululāt-*, ppl. stem of *ululāre* (hence It. *ululare*, Sp., Pg., Pr. *ulular*, Fr. *ululer*), of imitative origin: cf. *ulula* screech-owl.] *intr.* To howl or wail; to lament loudly.

1623 COCKERAM, *Vlulate*, to howle like a dog or wolfe. 1638 SIR T. HERBERT *Trav.* (ed. 2) 124 Troopes of Jackalls ..all the while ululating and in offensive noises barking and eccohing out their sacriledge. 1826 *Lancet* 59 Poor Sir Peter ululates plaintively as an Irish Benshee over the fate of his College. 1832 GEN. P. THOMPSON *Exerc.* (1842) II. 321 Men must have been sadly beaten, when they ululate in this sort. 1893 'Q' (QUILLER COUCH) *Delect. Duchy* 171 The widow so often interrupted the service to ululate that the town clock had struck four when I hurried back.

Hence **U·lulating** *ppl. a.*

1894 N. BROOKS *Tales Maine Coast* 8 Nance Pegg knew the times and seasons of the ululating and melancholy loon.

**Ululation** (vliulēⁱ·ʃən, yū·l-). [ad. L. *ululātiōn-*, *ululātio*, noun of action f. *ululāre*: see prec. So obs. F. *ululation*, *-acion.*]

**1.** A howl or wail; a cry of lamentation.

1599 R. LINCHE *Fount. Anc. Fiction* O j b, Scilla,..with her vncouth and lowd barking and howling, make[s] the waters thereabout resound with an incredible report and eccho of such her strange vlulations. 1606 DEKKER *Newes fr. Hell* Wks. (Grosart) II. 130 What tongue is able to relate the grones and vlulations of a wretch so distressed? 1654 R. CODRINGTON tr. *Iustine* XII. 191 They did by instinct break forth into the sacred ululations of the God. 1689 R. COX *Hibernia Angl.* I. *Appar.* 1 2, They bury their Dead with great Ululations or *Allelews.* 1812 COLMAN *Poet. Vagaries*, *Lady of Wreck* xxxi, Again the horns were fill'd by all, And ululations shook the Hall. 1827-39 DE QUINCEY *Murder* Postscr., Wks. 1854 IV. 100 The ululation of vengeance which ascended instantaneously from the individual street. 1856 F. E. PAGET *Owlet of Owlst.* 169 Master Maximilian checked his ululations. 1881 *Blackw. Mag.* Sept. 341 The women..burst forth in a shrill scream, with a quaver or ululation resembling the note of the screech-owl.

**2.** The action of howling or wailing.

? 1799 COLERIDGE *Mahomet* 11 The people with mad shouts Thundering now, and now with saddest ululation Flew. 1848 LOWELL *Biglow P.* Ser. I. ix. Introd., The laborers..are heard to shout from behind the scenes in a singular tone resembling ululation. 1886 SWINBURNE *Misc.* 98 Who uttered in public or in private such high-pitched notes of ululation and imprecation.

† **U·lulative,** *a.* *Obs.*⁻¹ [See ULULATE *v.* and -ATIVE.] Wailing, lamenting.

1490 CAXTON *Eneydos* xxvii. 99 Lady & mastresse of alle artes & scyences magyques, ryght often called wyth voyces vlulatyue,..in tyme of nyght obscure.

**Ululatory** (vliulē·təri, yū·l-), *a.* [Cf. prec. and -ATORY.] = ULULANT *ppl. a.*

1831 *Fraser's Mag.* IV. 931 The matutinal ululatory summons of the dairy-maid. 1890 *Sat. Rev.* 13 Sept. 326/1 The overworked and ululatory brains ['that called out so loudly for rest'].

**Ululu·.** Also u-lu-lu. [Imitative. Cf. dial. *whillilew*, *whillaloo*, Ir. Gael. *uileliúgh.*] A wailing cry; a wail of lamentation.

1854 THOREAU *Walden*, *Sounds* (1884) 135 When other birds are still the screech owls take up the strain, like mourning women their ancient u-lu-lu. *a* 1873 MRS. SPOFFORD in *Casquet of Lit.* (1873) IV. 13/2, I raised such a ululu that presently mother took me in hand again severely.

‖ **Ulva** (v·lvă). *Bot.* [L. *ulva* sedge.] An alga forming the typical genus of the order *Ulvaceæ*; the laver or sea-lettuce.

1706 PHILLIPS (ed. Kersey), *Ulva*, Reet, or Weed of the Sea, Sea-grass; also Weeds growing in Pools, or standing Waters. 1753 *Chambers' Cycl.* Suppl. s.v., Bauhine makes the Ulva a purple sea-moss allied to the alga. 1850 MISS PRATT *Comm. Things of Sea-side* ii. 160 The Ulvæ, or Lavers, are flat green leaves, very transparent, and easily torn, and when laid on paper are scarcely thicker than gold-beater's skin. 1857 J. G. WOOD *Comm. Objects Seashore* 44, I found that the ulva had risen in the water, and was hanging in most elegant festoons from the surface. 1871 KINGSLEY *At Last* i, Here and there floated large fronds of a lettuce-like weed, seemingly an ulva.

**Ulva·ceous,** *a. Bot.* [f. mod.L. *Ulvaceæ*: see prec.] Resembling or belonging to the *Ulvaceæ*.

**1891** *Cent. Dict.*

**† Ulvo·se,** *a. Obs.*—⁰ [See Ulva and -ose.] 'Full of reeds or weeds' (Bailey, vol. II, 1727).

**Uly(e,** obs. Sc. variants of Oil *sb.*, Oily *a.*

**† Ulȝeat.** *Sc. Obs.*—¹ [var. *olyet* Oillet.] A stud for armour.

**1507** *Acc. Ld. High Treas. Scot.* III. 254 For l stuthes with ruffis callit ulȝeatis for the Kingis panses and mailȝeis, weyand v unce j quartar, iijli, xixs. ijd.

**Ulyie,** obs. Sc. form of Oil *sb.*[1]

**Ulyssean** (yuli·sīăn), *a.* [f. L. *Ulysses* (also *Ulixes*), ad. Gr. Ὀδυσσεύς Odysseus, king of Ithaca and hero of the Odyssey.] Of, belonging to, or connected with Ulysses; *spec.* characteristic of, or resembling, Ulysses in craft or deceit, or in extensive wanderings.

In quots. 1700, 1746 the metre shows the stressing to be *Ulysse'an*.

**1639** T. Bancroft *Epigr. & Epit.* B 3 b, This Vlyssean course of yours Vs of your worthier qualities assures. **1676** Bp. N. French *Vnkinde Desertor* xvi. Wks. 1846 II. 151 His subuerting our union with Vlyssean practizes. **1700** Dryden *Ovid's Met.* xiii. 100 That this is not a Fable forg'd by me, Like one of his, an Ulyssean Lie. **1746** Francis tr. *Horace, Epist.* i. vi. 95 Then let us..like th' abandon'd Ulyssean Crew, Our Ithaca forgot, forbidden Joys pursue. **a 1850** Marg. Fuller *Life Without & Within* (1862) 55 It is said..that the modern Greeks are Ulyssean in this respect, never telling straightforward truth, when deceit will answer the purpose. **1875** W. D. Geddes in *Contemp. Rev.* July 256 The pathos culminates in the Ulyssean part of the 'Iliad', the humour in the 'Odyssey' itself. **1889** *Scottish Leader* 13 April 6 Sir Samuel Baker..is one of the best living specimens of the Ulyssean Englishman.

**Ulzie,** obs. Sc. form of Oil *sb.*[1]

**Um, 'um,** var. of 'Em, Hem *pron.*

Common in 17th c. writers; now only *dial.*

**1606** Chapman *Gentlem. Usher* ii. i. 82 Come strew this roome afresh; spread here this carpet...Come sir Giles Goosecap, I must do all my selfe, lay me vm thus. **c 1610** Beaum. & Fl. *Philaster* i. i, But ever when he turned His tender eyes upon 'um, he would weep. **1664** Dryden & Howard *Ind. Queen* v. i, How can the Gods delight in humane blood? Think 'um not cruel; if you think 'um good. **1689** *Pol. Ballads* (1860) II. 12 May they all repent 'um And to Holland be sent home, On condition we lose all the money we lent 'um. **1859** J. Richardson *Song. Sol.* v. 3 I've weish't my feet; hoo s'all I soil um? **1887** Jefferies *Amaryllis* iii. 19 Th' pigeons have been at um, they be 'mazing fond of um, so be the larks.

**Um** ('m), *int.* [Imitative. Cf. Hum *int.*]

**1.** Used to indicate hesitating or inarticulate utterance on the part of a speaker.

**1672** Vanbrugh *Mistake* iv. i, Certain Immotions, which—um—cause, as one may suppose, a sort of convulsive—yes—Hurricanious—um—Like in short; a Woman, is like the Devil. **1748** Richardson *Clarissa* VI. 101 'Madam—I cannot excuse myself'—um, um, um, um, um, um—'I must own to you, Madam, that [etc.]'.

**2.** Used to indicate hesitation or doubt in replying to another.

**1777** Sheridan *Trip Scarb.* iii. ii, *Love* [*less*]. (Kissing her.) In matters of love, a woman's oath is no more to be minded than a man's. *Ber.* Um! **1818** Scott *Rob Roy* x, 'Was this selection of studies Rashleigh's choice, or your own, Miss Vernon?' I asked. 'Um!' said she, as if hesitating to answer my question. **1844** Alb. Smith *Adv. Mr. Ledbury* (1856) I. xiii. 99 Um! I don't see the..necessity. **1898** 'Merriman' *Roden's Corner* ii. 19 'Is it..the Victoria Cross?' she asked. 'Um—yes,' admitted White.

**† Um-,** *prefix*, a reduced form of Umb-, perh. directly ad. ON. *um-* (Icel. and Norw. *um-*, MSw. *um-*, *om-*, Sw. and Da. *om-*); a similar reduction has taken place in OFris. *um-* (Fris. *om-*, *âm-*), MDu. *um-*, *om-* (Du. *om-*), MLG. and MHG. (also G.) *um-*, and in the occasional OE. *ym-*, *em-* for *ymb-*, *emb-*. The more important words with this form of the prefix are Umbrace *v.*, Umbraid *v.*, Umgang *sb.*, etc.; the following rarer verbs are chiefly found in northern texts of the 14th century:—**umbehold**, to look about; **umcast** (see quot.); **umclap**, to surround, invest; **umclead**, to clothe about; **umclip**, to surround; **umclose**, to close in, invest; **umfold**, to enclose, surround, **umgripe**, to embrace, enfold; **umheed**, to look about; **umhill**, to cover; **umsee** (*refl.*), to take heed; **umseek**, to search for; **umshade**, **-shadow**, to shade about, to protect; **umshine**, to shine about; **umstand**, to stand round, to guard; **umtiff**, to deck out, adorn; **umwrithe**, to wind round, entwine.

The majority of these have corresponding forms in Umbe-, and a certain number also appear with Umb-. In the cognate languages the following parallel forms with similar significations occur:—umclead, MDu. *omcleeden* (p.p. *omghecleet*), Norw. *umklædd* p.p.; umfold, Da. *omfolde*, G. *umfalten* (MHG. *umbefalten*), Du. *omvouwen*; umgripe, MDu. *omme-*, *omgripen* (Du. *omgrijpen*), MLG. *ummegripen* (MHG. *umbegrîfen*), NFris. *âmgrip*, MSw. *umgripa*, older Da. *omgribe*; umsee, WFris. *omsjen*, NFris. *âmse*, MDu. *omme-*, *om-*, *umsien* (Du. *omzien*), MSw. *umsea*, older Da. *omse* (also OFris. *umbesia*, MDu. *ombesien*, OHG. *umbisehan*, *umbesehen*, OE. *ymbséon*); umseek, MDu. *omme-*, *omsoeken*, MSw. *omsökia*, older Da. *omsøge*; umshade, MLG. *ummescheden*, NFris. *âmskadi*; umshadow, MDu. *ommescaduwen* (Du. *omschaduwen*), MHG. *umbeschatewen*, *-schetewen*; umshine, MDu. *omme-*, Du. *omschijnen*, MHG. *umbeschînen*, MSw. *omskina*, OE. *ymbscínan*; umstand, MDu. *omme-*, *omstaen* (Du. *omstaan*), G. *umstehen*, older Da. *omstande*; umwrithe, Da. *omvride*, Sw. *omvrida*.

**a 1400-50** *Alexander* 731 (Ashm. MS.), *Vn-behalde þe wele on ilk halfe & haue a gud eȝe. **1887** *Jamieson's Sc. Dict.* Suppl. 250/1 'To **umcast* a splice,' to fasten it by a wrapping of cord. **a 1400-50** *Alexander* 2473 (Ashm. MS.), With þat þe kyng & his kniȝtis *vm-clappis þe cite. **a 1340** Hampole *Psalter* xliv. 15 Þe doghtirs of þe kynge..in hemmyngis of gold, *vmcled in sernesis. **a 1300** *E. E. Psalter* xlvii. 11 Vmgiues Syon, and *vmklippes it; Telles in his toures yhit. **c 1400** *Destr. Troy* 4255 [A place] *Vmclosit with a course of the colde ythes, With a serkle of the se þat soght þere aboute. *Ibid.* 9027 The Duke of Athens..& derf Menelaus..Vmcloset the kyng and his knightes als. **1515** *Scottish Field* 268 in *Chetham Misc.* (1856) II, He umclosed that castell, clene round aboute. **a 1400-50** *Alexander* 4717 Now gase he..& a fild entris, *Vmfaldin with a faire wod. **a 1300** *E. E. Psalter* lxxviii. 8 Ne mine of our alde wickenesses, for-þi; Tite *vmgripe vs þi merci. **a 1400-50** *Alexander* 731 (Dubl. MS.), *Vmhede þe wele on ilke halfe & haue a god Eȝe. **a 1340** Hampole *Psalter* xliii. 21 Þe shadow of ded *vmhild vs. *Ibid.* liv. 5 Dred and qwakynge com on me, and myrknes vmhild me. **a 1400-50** *Alexander* 3728 For-þi..*vmse þe be tyme, Quat tene & torfare may tide, & tent to þine ende. **a 1300** *Cursor M.* 15846 Quar-for haf yee taken me, And als a theif *vm-soght? **c 1460** *Towneley Myst.* x. 128 The holy gost shall light in the,..he shall *vmshade and fulfyll That thi madynhede shall neuer spyll. **a 1300** *E. E. Psalter* xc. 4 With his sculdres sal he *vmschadow þe al. **a 1340** Hampole *Psalter* cxxxix. 8 Þou vmshadoud abouen my heuyd in day of bataile. *Ibid.* xc. 4 He sall gif þe vmshadowynge. **a 1400** *New Test.* (Paues) Acts xxvi. 13 A lyghte þat *vmschone me and hem þat wore wiþ me. **a 1300** *E. E. Psalter* cxl. 3 Set, lauerd, to mi mouth yheming, And to mi lippes doer of *vmstanding [L. *ostium circumstantiæ*]. *Ibid.* cxliii. 14 Doghtres of þam samen-dight, *Vmtiffed als licknes of kirke bright. **a 1340** Hampole *Psalter* cxviii. 61 Cordis of synful has *vmwrithyn me.

**Umage,** obs. f. Homage. **'Uman,** Sc. f. Woman. **Umast,** variant Umest *a. Sc. Obs.*

**Umb,** variant of Umbe *prep. Obs.*

**† Umb-,** *prefix*, app. ad. ON. *umb-* (earlier form of *um-* Um-), corresponding to MLG. and MHG. *umb-*, OE. *ymb-*, *emb-* (see Umbe-). In ME. this form of the prefix is much rarer than the reduced Um- or the extended Umbe-, and occurs only in the following verbs:—**umbcast**, to surround; **umbclose**, to enclose; **umbfold**, to embrace; **umblay**, to wrap round; **umblook**, to look round; **umbset**, **-stead**, to surround; **umbthink**, to bethink (oneself *of* something).

The OE. *ymb-* was extensively employed in compound verbs, as *ymbclippan*, *-lócian*, *-settan*, *-snīðan*, *-standan*, *-þencan*, etc., and although not the phonetic antecedent of ME. *umb-* may have had some influence on its use.

**c 1400** *Destr. Troy* 10420 Achilles..meuyt to his Mirmydons in maner before, Þe kyng to *vmbcast, & close hym with-in. **c 1330** R. Brunne *Chron. Wace* (Rolls) 4080 Lud..*vmb-closed it [*sc.* London] wyþ a walle. **c 1400** *Destr. Troy* 8496 Sho braid with the barne to þe bare erthe, *Vmbfoldyt his fete, felle vnto swone. **a 1300** *Cursor M.* 22069 (Edinb.), And als it in ur leuedi liȝte, Þe hali gaste þurȝ godis miȝte, And *umblaide hir wiþ his leme To brede bate blisful barneteme. **c 1375** *Ibid.* 26406 (Fairf.), Þer-of saltow þe *vmbloke, of cases iiij, I finde in boke. **c 1400** *Destr. Troy* 10433 Þe Mirmydons to Menon myghtily þronge, *Vmbset hym on yche side, sesit hym onon. **c 1450** *Mirk's Festial* 64 Techyng his good chyldryn, forto haue yn mynde how hard he ys *vmbstad wyth deth on yche syde. **a 1300** *Cursor M.* 21667 (Edin.), Qua wil *umbþink him in his mode Mai finde fele takins of þe rode. **c 1375** *Ibid.* 19891 (Fairf.), Quiles saint peter him vmbþoȝt of þis siȝt quat hit takin muȝt.

**† Umbe,** *prep.* and *adv. Obs.* Forms: 1–2 ymbe (imbe), 1–5 umbe (3 ummbe), 3–4 umben; 5 umb. [Partly (1) OE. *ymbe* (with equivalent forms in the other Germanic languages; see below), whence southern ME. *üimbe* (see also Embe *prep.*); partly (2) an adoption of ON. *umb* (earlier form of *um*; cf. Um- and Umb-), whence the midland and northern forms. The form *ummbe* in the Ormulum is disyllabic (cf. *inne*, *onne*, *offe*, etc.), and so presumably are the ME. examples of the adv.

The Germanic forms corresponding to OE. *ymbe* (*embe*), *ymb*, are OFris. *umbe*, *umme*, *um*, *ombe*, *omme*, *om* (WFris. *om*), MDu. *omme*, *om* (Du. *om*), OS. *umbi*, *um* (MLG. *umbe*, *umb*, *umme*), OHG. *umbi* (*umpi*), *umbe* (MHG. *umbe*, *umme*, *umb*, *umm*, *um*; also *ümbe*, etc.; G. *um*), ON. *umb*, *um* (Icel. and Norw. *um*, Sw. and Da. *om*). The stem is represented in other Indo-European languages by Gr. ἀμφί (ἀμφίς), ἀμφι-, L. *ambi-*, Gaulish *ambi-*, Irish *imb-*, *im*(*m*-).]

**A.** *prep.* **1.** Around, about.

*Beowulf* 2883 Werȝendra to lyt þrong ymbe þeoden. *Ibid.* 3170 Þa ymbe hlæw riodan hildedeore. **971** *Blickling Hom.* 141 Ealle þa þe ymbe me standaþ. **c 1000** *Sax. Leechd.* I. 218 Wið bæt reng-wyrmas ymbe þone nafolan deriȝen. **a 1310** in Wright *Lyric P.* ix. 35 Hire gurdel of bete gold is al, Umben hire middel smal. **13..** *E. E. Allit. P.* B. 879 Þus þay þrobled & þrong & þrwe umbe his erez. **13..** *Gaw. & Gr. Knt.* 1830 Ho laȝt a lace lyȝtly, þat leke umbe hir sydez. **a 1400-50** *Alexander* 2209 (Dubl. MS.), Alexander als belyfe all vmbe þe cyte Mase iiij Mille to fonde. **c 1400** *Destr. Troy* 335 Vmbe the sercle of the Citie was sothely a playne. *Ibid.* 8745 A tabernacle triet & tristyly wroght;..Hit was atiryt vmb the top all with triet stones.

**2.** About, concerning, of.

*Beowulf* 2070 Ic sceal forð sprecan ȝen ymbe Grendel. **c 900** tr. *Baeda's Hist.* v. xii. (1890) 422 Se arwyrða bisscop ..feorr & wide Godes word ymbe Cristes ȝeleafan bodade & lærde. **c 1000** *Ags. Psalter* (Thorpe) xxxvii. 18 Forþæm ic andette Gode min unriht, and ic þence ymbe mine synna. **? a 1100** *O. E. Chron.* an. 1070, Þa þa hi þyder comon & umbe oþer þing ȝesprecon hæfdon umbe þæt hi sprecan woldon. **c 1175** *Lamb. Hom.* 95 He dude þet heo weren..bodiende umbe godes riche. *Ibid.* 147 Þreo roden beoð þa ich umbe speche. **c 1200** Ormin 304 Þatt tiss Elysabæþ, Þatt we nu mælenn ummbe, Wass þuss off Aaroness kinn.

**b.** Busied with, aiming at, seeking after.

**c 1000** Ælfric *Hom.* I. 12 Ac hi æfre beoð ymbe þæt an, hu hi maȝon Gode hyrsumian. **a 1200** *St. Marher.* 6 Helle hundes..haue al biset me, ah þu, hehe healent, beo umbe me to helpen. **a 1225** *Ancr. R.* 218 He..makeð hire ueire cheres, & is vmbe eueriches weis þet heo him luuie inwardliche in hire heorte. **c 1225** in *Rel. Ant.* II. 5 For-þi he is eaver umben to reare sum ladðe.

**3.** After (in time).

**c 1000** Ælfric *Gen.* xvii. 21 Min wedd soðlice ic sette to Isaace, þone þe Sarra þe acenð on þisre tide nu ymbe twelfmonð. **a 1122** *O. E. Chron.* Pref. (Laud MS.), And þa ȝelamp hit imbe ȝeara rina, þæt Scotta sum-dæl ȝewat of Ybernian on Brittene. **c 1205** *Lay.* 2632 Vmben ane stunde, þa scipen ȝaru weoren. *Ibid.* 6617 Hit wes vmbe fif winter, seoððe he heonne ferde. **a 1225** *Leg. Kath.* 518 Þes sondesmon, umbe long, þa he hefde al þet lond ourgan & þurhsoht, com [etc.].

**4.** *Umbe throwe*, = Umbewhile *adv.* 2.

**a 1310** in Wright *Lyric P.* iv. 25 We shule aryse ur fader byfore, thah fon us fallen umbe throwe.

**B.** *adv.* About, round.

*Beowulf* 2597 Nealles him on heape hand-ȝesteallan, æðelinga bearn, ymbe ȝestodon. **13..** *E. E. Allit. P.* C. 309 Þe grete flem of þy flod folded me vmbe. **a 1400-50** *Alexander* 2762 (Dubl. MS.), The ledes oute of Landace & all þe Landes vmbe. **c 1400** *Destr. Troy* 1455 Grete Troy was vp tild with mony toures vmbe. **c 1440** *Pallad. on Husb.* vii. 106 Do donge vppon and vmbe on euery side, And bynde hit to.

**† Umbe-,** *prefix* (also 3 ummbe-, 4–5 vmbe-, 5 vnbe-, unbe-, 6 *Sc.* wmbe-, ombe-; 4 vnbi-, 4–5 vmbi-, 5 vmby-, unby-, 6 *Sc.* onby-), partly (in southern ME. texts) representing OE. *ymbe-* (see prec.), but chiefly either an extended form of Umb- (cf. prec.) or a combination of Um- with Be-. Forms with the double prefix (*ommebe-* or *ombe-*) are very common in Middle Dutch, not infrequent in older Danish (*ombe-*), and occur occasionally in MLG.; it is possible that their prevalence in MDu. may have contributed to the extensive use of such forms in ME. Originally the *um-* was probably added to verbs which already had the prefix *be-* (as *beclip*, *belap*, etc.), and in most cases the two forms (with *be-* and *umbe-*) coexist with the same signification. In addition to those treated as main words (viz. Umbecast, -clip, -go, -lap, -lay, -set, -think) the following examples occur in ME. texts, chiefly of the 14th and 15th centuries:—**umbebraid**, to turn round; **umbecarve**, to circumcise; **umbeclap**, to embrace, to enclose; **umbeclead**, to clothe, wrap up; **umbeclose**, to enclose, enwrap; **umbedelve**, to dig round; **umbedraw**, to withdraw; **umbefold**, to surround, to embrace; **umbegang**, to go round, to surround; **umbegild**, to gild about; **umbegive**, to surround; **umbegrip**, to grasp; **umbegrow**, to grow round, overgrow; **umbelie**, to surround; **umbelook**, to look about; **umbelouk**, to include, comprehend; **umbepitch**, **umbereach**, to surround; **umberow**, to row about; **umberun**, to surround; **umbeshadow**, to shade about; **umbeshear**, to circumcise; **umbeshine**, to shine about; **umbesiege**, to besiege, environ; **umbespread**, to spread about; **umbestand**, to stand round, surround; **umbeswey**, to encircle; **umbethonre**, to encompass, surround; **umbetigh**, to encircle, surround; **umbeviron**, to environ; **umbewalt**, to surround; **umbeweave**, to enwrap; **umbewend**, to imbed, enclose; **umbewet**, to wet about.

Of these the following have parallels with the compound prefix (*um-be-*) in the cognate languages:—umbeclead, MDu. *ommebecleden* (p.p. *-cleet*); umbegrip, older Da. *ombegribe* (cf. MDu. *ombegrijp* sb.); umbelie, MLG. *ummebeliggen*; umbelook, NFris. *ombiluke*; umbelouk, MDu. *ommebeluken*, *ombeluken* (p.p. *-beloken*); umbeshine, MDu. *ombeschijnen*; umbestand, NFris. *ombistuun*, MDu. *omme-*, *ombestaen* (p.p.); umbetigh, NFris. *ombitiin*. Several of these, and many of the others, also correspond in sense to OE. formations with *ymb-* (less commonly *ymbe-*) or to equivalent forms in the other languages, e.g. umbecarve, OE. *ymbceorfan*; umbedelve, (OE. *ymbdelf* sb.), MDu. and Du. *omdelven*; umbegang, OE. *ymbgangan*, OFris. *ummegunga*, OHG. *umbigangan*, etc.: cf. the examples given under Um-.

**13..** *E. E. Allit. P.* B. 1622 When he com bifore þe kyng & clanly had halsed, Baltazar *vmbe-brayde hym & 'leue sir', he sayde. **a 1240** *Lofsong* in *O.E. Hom.* I. 207 Ich bide be..bi his blodi rune þat ron,..In *umbekeoruunge, in his blod swetunge. **? a 1400** *Morte Arth.* 1779 Thane syr Cador of Cornewayle *Umbeclappes the cors, and kyssez hyme ofte. **a 1400-50** *Alexander* 4171 Þan vmbyclappis þaim a cloude & couirs all ouire. **c 1400** *Anturs of Arth.* x. (Thornton MS.), Alle glowede als gledis the gaste whare scho glydis, *Vmbyclede in a clowde. **c 1400** *Ibid.* ix. (Ireland MS.), Alle bare was the body, and blak by the bone, *Vmbeclosut in a cloude, in clething evyl clad. **c 1440** *Pallad. on Husb.* iii. 533 Ek now is to repare

Rosayres olde & drynesse of to pare. Now *vmbedelue hem. *Ibid.* IV. 324 In heruest & in ver hem vmbidelue. **1456** Sir G. HAYE *Law Arms* (S.T.S.) 53 Thai war fayn..to *unbedraw thame agayn to thair pavilliones. **1513** DOUGLAS *Æneid* XII. Prol. 6 Mais onbydrew, for all his grundin glave. **13..** *Gaw. & Gr. Knt.* 181 Fayre fannand fax *vmbe-foldes his schulderes. **14..** *Siege Jerus.* (E.E.T.S.) 12/219 To seint Peter þe pope 30 platte to þe grounde, Vmbe-felde his fete, & to þe freke saide. *c* **1200** *Trin. Coll. Hom.* 191 Alse þe apostle seið..Ðurch onde com deað in to þe worelde al *umbegonge. *c* **1440** tr. *Palladius on Husb.* IV. 437 With seefroth other haue hem vmbiyonge [L. *circumdederunt*]. *a* **1400-50** *Alexander* 4899 ȝit was a mynstir on þe mounte of metall as þe nobill, *Vmbegildid with a garden of golden vynes. *a* **1400** in *Hampole's Psalter* (1884) p. xviii, For *vmbegyuen me hathe euels of þe whiche noumber is noght. ?*a* **1400** *Morte Arth.* 3758 Bot sir Gawayne..*Vmbegrippys a spere, and to a gome rynnys. *Ibid.* 3944 Sir Gawayne..Vmbegrippede the girse, and one grouffe fallene. **13..** *E. E. Allit. P.* B. 488 A bronch of olyue, Gracyously *vmbe-grouen al with grene leuez. *Ibid.* B. 836 Þe borȝ was al vp;..To *vmbe-lyȝe lothez hous þe ledez to take. *a* **1300** *Cursor M.* 8468 O prouerbes es þat toþer boke, Þat lers man him *vm-biloke Agains þis werld wikcedhede. *Ibid.* 23705 Yee cristen men, yow vmbilok,..O yur lijf þat yee her lede. *a* **1400** *Pistill of Susan* 291 Vmbiloke ȝou, lordes, such lawes ben leiþ. **1357** *Lay Folks Catech.* (T.) 259 This ten Comandementz that I haue nowe rekend Er *umbilouked in twa of the godspell. **13..** *E. E. Allit. P.* A. 1052 Þe hyȝe trone þer moȝt ȝe hede With alle þe apparaylmente *vmbepyȝte. **1513** DOUGLAS *Æneid* II. x. 155 The fader of goddis and king of men With thunderis blast me smate.. And with his fyry lewyne me *wmberauch. *Ibid.* VI. i. 134 Thocht..hard fortoun has wmberaucht The Troianis, and persewit vnfreindfully. *c* **1205** LAY. 114 Eneas þe duc, mid his drihtfolcke,..moni lond *umbe-rowen. *c* **1440** *Pallad. on Husb.* I. 324 Wyth orchard, or with gardyn, or with mede, Se that thyn hous with hem be *vmbironne. **14..** *With an O and an I* in *Anglia* XXVII. 286 Þe haly gast.. *Vmbeschadow þe sall wiþouten ony syn. *c* **1450** *Mirk's Festial* 106 Þe Holy Gost wythouten any werke of man, þat schall vmbeschadow þe wythout. *c* **1200** ORMIN 4132 Þatt cnif wass..Forr *tummbesherenn shapp þærwiþþ Off þeȝȝre cnapechilldre. *Ibid.* 4080 To wurrþenn ummbeshorenn, swa To clennsenn hemm off sinne. **13..** *E. E. Allit. P.* C. 455 Þe schyre sunne hit *vmbe-schon. **1422** YONGE tr. *Secreta Secret.* 182 The grete lordis of laynyster, seynge har Prynce i-putte to myschefe, and in euery Partie *vmbesegid wyth enemys. **1513** DOUGLAS *Æneid* X. ii. 85 The Troiane adulterar Ombesegyt the cite of Spartha. *c* **1400** *Laud Troy Bk.* 10563 Alle that feld was *vmbesprade Off dede knyȝtes. *c* **1300** *Havelok* 1875 Huwe rauen.. saw how þe laddes wode Hauelok his louerd *umbistode, And beten on him. **13..** *E. E. Allit. P.* B. 1380 Þe bourȝ [Babylon] was so brod & so bigge alce,..*Vmbe-sweyed on vch a syde with seuen grete wateres. *a* **1400-50** *Alexander* 3857 Þan come he streke on a staunke..*Umby-thonred with a thike wod thre mile a-boute. *Ibid.* 4806 Þai ware vmbe-thonrid in þat thede with slike a thike cloude, Þat þai miȝt fele it with þaire fiste. **13..** *Gaw. & Gr. Knt.* 770 A castel..Pyched on a prayere, a park al aboute, With a pyked palays, pyned ful þik, Þat *vmbe-teȝe mony tre mo þen two myle. **1375** BARBOUR *Bruce* XI. 640 (Edin. MS.), I will me speid To help hym, for he has ned; All *umbe-weround with hys fayis is he. **13..** *E. E. Allit. P.* B. 1181 Þe gentylest of Iudee in Ierusalem [he] biseged, *Vmbe-walt alle þe walles wyth wyȝes ful stronge. **13..** *Gaw. & Gr. Knt.* 581 Þe brawden bryne of bryȝt stel ryngez, *Vmbe-weued þat wyȝ, vpon wlonk stuffe. **1338** R. BRUNNE *Chron.* (1725) I. 117 A hede þat was of smyten,..þis squier.. sette it on a spere, in an orfreis vnbiweued. *c* **1440** *Pallad. on Husb.* XII. 221 The rootis wel in dongynge *vmbiwende. In faat lond moyst thei ioyfulliche ascende. *Ibid.* III. 675 The rootes ek ycutte & *vmbiwette With donge is good her spryngyng forto glade.

**b.** In the advs. **umbetrin, -turn**, round about.

*c* **1200** ORMIN 17563 Onn heffness whel all ummbetrin, Þurrh Godd tatt swillc itt wrohhte. **13..** *Gaw. & Gr. Knt.* 184 A much berd as a busk ouer his brest henges, Þat wyth his hiȝlich here, þat of his hed reches, Was euesed al vmbe-torne, a-bof his elbowes.

† **Umbecast**, *v. Obs.* Forms: 4 vmbecast (5 *p. t.* -caste), 4 (5 *p. t.*) vmbekest; 4 *p. t.* vmbikest, 5 vmbycast(e. [f. UMBE- + CAST *v.* (or UM- + BECAST *v.*). Cf. *umbcast* s.v. UMB-, and *umcast* s.v. UM-.]

**1.** *trans.* To surround, encircle.

*c* **1350** *Will. Palerne* 2319 Þei herd an huge route of horse þat hel al a-boute, & herd þat quarrere vmbe-cast & al þe cuntre wide. *Ibid.* 4693 Whan al þe cuntre was umbe-cast with clene men of armes. *c* **1400** *Laud Troy Bk.* 5505 The Gregeis vmbikest his cart With many a knyȝt hardi and smart. *c* **1410** *Master of Game* (MS. Digby 182) xxv, Þen ought þe lymmer..vmbycaste with his lymer þe whart þat þe deere is into.

**b.** To make the circuit of; to go round.

**13..** *E. E. Allit. P.* B. 478 When ho fyndez no folde her fote on to pyche, Ho vmbe-kestez þe coste & þe kyst sechez. *c* **1475** *Rauf Coilȝear* 410 He vmbekest the countrie outwith the toun. He saw na thing on steir, Nouther fer nor neir.

**2.** To enclose, confine.

*c* **1440** *York Myst.* xxxiii. 467, *i Mil.* All in cordis his coorse vmbycast. *ii Mil.* Late vs bynde hym in bandis all bare.

**3.** To consider, meditate (*that*, etc.).

**1375** BARBOUR *Bruce* V. 552 He vmbethocht him at the last, And in his hert can vmbecast, That the king had in custum ay [etc.]. *c* **1425** WYNTOUN *Cron.* VII. viii. 2029 (Wemyss MS.), All þarby Off þat thing thocht gret ferly, And vmbekest in þare entent.

**4.** *intr.* Of a hunting dog: = CAST *v.* 60.

**1470-85** MALORY *Arthur* XVIII. xxi. 764 Whan the hynde came to the welle..the dogges came after and vmbecaste aboute, for she had lost the veray parfyte feaute of the hynde.

**Umbeclap, -clead**: see UMBE-.



† **Umbeclip**, *v.*[1] *Obs.*[−1] In 3 ummbeclippenn. [f. UMBE- + CLIP *v.*[2]] *trans.* To circumcise.

*c* **1200** ORMIN 15009 Forr he let hise kinness menn Hiss shapp himm ummbeclippenn.

† **Umbeclip**, *v.*[2] *Obs.* In 4-5 vmbeclyppe, -clippe, 5 vmbiclyppe. [See UMBE- and BECLIP *v.*[1] OE. *ymbclyppan* occurs in the same sense.] *trans.* To surround, encircle.

**13..** *Gaw. & Gr. Knt.* 616 Þe cercle was more o prys. Þat vmbe-clypped hys croun. *a* **1395** HYLTON *Scala Perf.* (W. de W. 1494) II. xxxvii, Sothfastnes shall vmbiclyppe [ed. 1533 becleppe] the wyth a sheelde. *c* **1400** *Anturs of Arth.* x. (Douce MS.), Al glowed as a glede þe goste þere ho glides, Vmbeclipped him with a cloude, of cle[th]yng vnclere. *c* **1450** *Mirk's Festial* 64 The sykyngys of deth hauen vmbeclypped me.

**Umbeclose, -delve, -draw**, etc.: see UMBE-.

† **Umbego**, *v. Obs.* Also 4 vnbigo, 5 vmbego, vmbigo, vmbygo. [f. UMBE- + GO *v.* Cf. MDu. *ommebegaen*, and UMGO *v.*] *trans.* To go around, to encircle; to surround *with* something.

*c* **1300** *Havelok* 1842 Þe laddes were kaske and teyte, And vn-bi-yeden him ilkon, Sum smot with tre, and sum wit ston. **13..** *E. E. Allit. P.* A. 210 Her lere leke al hyr vmbe-gon. *c* **1400** *Laud Troy Bk.* 9468 Rofe and wal and euery a gable,..Courbel, beme, and euery a ston, With riche gold was vmbygon. **1430-40** in *MS. Bodl. 423* fol. 186 b, A weddynge cote...the whiche shuld be a maydens cote, vmbigoon with diuersitees of vertues. *c* **1440** *Pallad. on Husb.* II. 197 In herbis letuce vmbigoon wol growe.

**Umbegrip, -grow, -hold**: see UMBE-, UM-.

**Umbel** (*v*·mb'l). Also 6-9 umbell, 6-8 umble, 8 umbil. [ad. L. *umbella* sun-shade, parasol, dim. of *umbra* shadow. So Sp. *umbela*, Pg. and It. *umbella*, F. *ombelle*, †*umbelle* (16th c.), Sw. *umbell*. Cf. It. *ombrella*.]

**1.** *Bot.* A mass of inflorescence borne upon pedicels of nearly equal length springing from a common centre. Cf. UMBELLA 1.

**1597** GERARDE *Herbal* I. xvi. 19 His stalke is long, big and square,..and on his top a chaffie vmbell or tuft like vnto the true Cyperus. *Ibid.* II. ccccxiv. 904 The flowers stande at the tops of the stalkes in small spokie vmbles. **1634** T. JOHNSON *Parey's Chirurg. Wks.* XXVII. xii. 1103 Almost all hearbes that carry their flowres and seeds in an umbell, have seeds of a hot, subtle, and aiery substance. **1652** CULPEPPER *Eng. Physic.* 48 The middle part being hollow and low, and the outer stalks rising high, maketh the whole Umbel to shew like a Birds nest. **1682** *Nat. Hist. Coffee*, etc. 28 On the top of the Branches [of the elder]..there spring sweet and crisped umbels, swelling with white odoriferous Flowers. **1731** P. MILLER *Gard. Dict.* s.v. *Umbella*, That Umbel which consists of Pedicles only, is call'd a Simple Umbel; that which is compos'd both of Rays and Pedicles, is call'd a Compound Umbel. **1785** MARTYN *Lett. Bot.* v. (1794) 54 At first sight you would say, here is an umbellate plant. In looking at it, you would find a large or universal umbel, a small or partial umbel [etc.]. **1832** *Veg. Subst. Food* 192 The water-parsnip bears its flowers in umbels close upon the fruits of the stem. **1859** GEO. ELIOT *A. Bede* ii, The gently-curving stems of the feathered grass..and the white umbels of the hemlocks lining the bushy hedgerows. **1882** *Garden* 11 Feb. 93/1 Nearly the whole of the flowers composing the umbel were succeeded by capsules.

*attrib.* and *Comb.* **1683** J. REID *Scots Gard'ner* (1907) 98 The wild service,..when spread over with their umbelfashion'd bright red fruit. **1712** PETIVER in *Phil. Trans.* XXVII. 420 The Flowers pale,..in an umbel-like tuft. **1725** *Fam. Dict.* s.v. *Guaiacum*, The Flowers appear umbel-wise and are of a pale yellow. **1802** R. HALL *Elem. Bot.* 192 *Umbelliferous*,..umbel-bearing. **1829** LOUDON *Encycl. Pl.* (1836) 268 Umbel-flowered. **1858** R. HOGG *Veg. Kingd.* 370 Umbelliferæ.—Umbelflowers. **1861** S. THOMSON *Wild Fl.* II. (ed. 4) 121 The fruit of the composites, like that of the umbel-bearers, looks like a seed. **1870** HOOKER *Stud. Flora* 166 *Silaus pratensis*...Umbel-rays 1-2 in., few or many, incurved.

† **b.** An umbelliferous plant. *Obs. rare.*

**1702** FLOYER in *Phil. Trans.* XXIII. 1167, I refer the Umbells to the Grasses, because of their Sweetness and Joynted Stalks. **1713** PETIVER *Ibid.* XXVIII. 189 The Peculiarity of this Umbell, is to have its Root Leaves deeply cut.

**2.** *Zool.* An umbelliform arrangement of parts.

**1870** H. A. NICHOLSON *Man. Zool.* I. 311 *Umbellate*,.. forming an umbel; i.e. a number of nearly equal *radii* all proceeding from one point. **1891** *Cent. Dict.*, *Umbellularia*,..a genus of deep-sea alcyonarian polyps, having the polypites clustered in an umbel on top of the polypidom.

† **Umbelap**, *v. Obs.* Forms: 5 um-, vmbelappe (6 vn-); 4-5 vmbilappe, vmbylap(p. [See UMBE- and BELAP *v.*, and cf. UMLAP *v.*] *trans.* To encompass, surround.

*a* **1350** *St. Andrew* 243 in Horstm. *Altengl. Leg.* (1881) 7 Þar come a light in Doun fro þe heuyn..And vmbilappid his bodi about. ?*a* **1400** *Morte Arth.* 1819 The kynge of Lebe has laughte a stede þat hym lykede, And comes in lordely.., Umbelappez þe lumpe, and lattes in sondre. *c* **1400** MAUNDEV. (Roxb.) xxviii. 128 A thikke mirkness..vmbelapped þe emperour and all his oste. *c* **1440** *Alph. Tales* 423 When I dyed devuls vmbelappid me. *c* **1440** *Gesta Rom.* xcv. 426 (Add. MS.), Thou mayste aske, why this man disserued contricion, that wes vmbelapped with so many synnes. **1502** ATKYNSON tr. *De Imitatione* III. lxii. (1893) 254 If it touch the, yet let it nat throwe þe downe, ne longe vnbelappe the.

† **Umbelay**, *v. Obs.* Also 4 vmbelai, vmbilay; vmbe-, vmbi-, vmbyley. [See UMBE- and BELAY *v.* (and cf. *umblay* s.v. UMB-, and UMLAY *v.*). So MDu. *omme-*, *ombeleggen*.] *trans.* To beset, surround, encompass.

*a* **1300** *Cursor M.* 1336 Þis tre, þat i of for-wit said, A neddur hit hade al vmbilaid. **13..** *Ibid.* 22069 (Gött.), Als it in vr leuedi light,—þe hali-gast wid goddes might,—And vmbilaid hir wid his leme To brede þat blisful barnteme. *c* **1330** R. BRUNNE *Chron. Wace* (Rolls) 8278 Totenesse was vmbyleyd Wyþ schipes. **1338** — *Chron.* (1810) 297 Þat was his folie, so long in his bed gan ligge, Untille þe Waleis partie had vmbilaid þe brigge.

**Umbelic(k, -ique**, obs. forms of UMBILIC *sb.*

**Umbelical**, obs. form of UMBILICAL *a.*

**Umbelie**: see UMBE-.

‖ **Umbella** (*v*mbe·lă). [L.: see UMBEL.]

**1.** *Bot.* An umbel.

[**1693** tr. *Blancard's Phys. Dict.* (ed. 2), *Umbellæ*, the Tops of Plants that are like a Bird's Nest.] **1699** EVELYN *Acetaria* 25 Fennel..expels Wind, sharpens the Sight, and recreates the Brain; especially the tender *Umbella* and Seed-Pods. **1725** *Fam. Dict.* s.v. *Moly*, Bearing a great Umbella of starlike purple Flowers, that continue long before they decay. **1832** LINDLEY *Introd. Bot.* 111 Unless they applied the same term to the umbella, the spica, and all other forms of inflorescence. **1856** HENSLOW *Dict. Bot. Terms* 206 *Umbelliferus*, bearing umbels. Assuming the form as an umbella.

**2.** *Zool.* A more or less convex disk supporting the tentacula in Medusæ.

**1834** MCMURTRIE *Cuvier's Anim. Kingd.* 480 The tentacula, whether situated on the margin of the umbella or round the mouth, vary, not only according to the species, but to the age of the animal.

**Umbellal**, *a. Bot.* [Cf. prec. and -AL.] Consisting of plants with umbellate flowers.

**1836** LINDLEY *Nat. Syst. Bot.* (ed. 2) 21 A plant of the Umbellal alliance. **1846** — *Veg. Kingd.* 773 Umbellal Exogens, with didymous fruit, and a double epigynous disk.

**U·mbellar**, *a. Bot.* [f. as prec. + -AR.] 'Pertaining to an umbel; having the form of an umbel' (Webster, 1828-32).

**Umbellate** (*v*·mbelėt), *a.* [ad. mod.L. *umbellāt-us*, f. L. *umbella* parasol, UMBELLA: see -ATE[2]. So Sw. *umbellat*, F. *ombellé*.]

**1.** *Bot.* **a.** Of flowers: Forming, arranged in, an umbel or umbels.

**1760** J. LEE *Introd. Bot.* I. xix. (1765) 50 An *Umbellate* Flower is an aggregate one, consisting of many Florets placed on a Receptacle, on fastigiate Peduncles that are all produced from the same point. **1793** [see UMBELLED *a.*]. **1807** J. E. SMITH *Phys. Bot.* 239 Its ultimate terminations are sometimes obscurely umbellate, especially while in blossom. **1826** SAMOUELLE *Direct. Collect. Insects & Crust.* 28 Alighting on the blossoms of trees and shrubs, and particularly on flowers of the umbellate kind. **1872** OLIVER *Elem. Bot.* II. 184 Common Ivy...A climbing evergreen shrub, with..inconspicuous umbellate flowers.

**b.** Of plants: Having flowers in umbels.

**1785** MARTYN *Lett. Bot.* v. (1794) 53 This then is the proper character of the umbellate tribe. **1822-7** GOOD *Study Med.* (1829) I. 174 The umbellate order affords also a rich variety of carminatives.

**2.** *Zool.* Provided with, or forming, an umbel; umbelliferous; umbelliform.

**1870** [see UMBEL 2].

Hence **U·mbellately** *adv.*, in umbels.

**1887** GARNSEY & BALFOUR tr. *De Bary's Fungi* v. 153 A creeping endophytic mycelium and straight erect simple sporophores ending in umbellately arranged heads of basidia.

**U·mbellated**, *a. Bot.* [f. as prec. + -ED.] = UMBELLATE *a.* 1: **a.** Of flowers, etc.

**1676** GREW *Anat. Flowers* II. App. § 15 [Flowers] stand ..either without Stalks..or with Stalks, that is, Umbellated as Fenil, &c. **1756** P. BROWNE *Jamaica* 183 The flowers are disposed in umbellated groups. **1797** HOLCROFT tr. *Stolberg's Trav.* III. xc, A plant which bears an umbellated flower, or tuft.

**b.** Of plants.

**1731** P. MILLER *Gard. Dict.* s.v. *Jacobæa*, Shrubby African Ragwort, with hoary Leaves like the umbellated Wormwood. **1812** *New Bot. Garden* I. 97 Umbellated Butomus, or Flowering Rush. **1871** GARROD *Mat. Med.* (ed. 3) 413 Chimaphila, or umbellated winter green.

**U·mbelled**, *a. Bot.* [f. UMBEL + -ED[2].] = prec.

**1793** MARTYN *Lang. Bot.* s.v. *Umbella*, Flowers growing in this manner are called *Umbellati*, Umbellate or Umbelled flowers. **1812** *New. Bot. Garden* I. 7 The peduncles from the summit of the stem, umbelled, villose. **1830** LINDLEY *Nat. Syst. Bot.* 29 Inflorescence panicled or umbelled. **1869** RUSKIN *Q. of Air* § 77 In the celery and radish, you have the two great groups of umbelled and cruciferous plants.

**U·mbellet.** *Bot. rare.* [f. UMBEL + -LET.] = UMBELLULE.

**1793** MARTYN *Lang. Bot.*, *Umbellula*, an Umbellule or Umbellet. **1806** GALPINE *Brit. Bot.* 127 Umbels trifid, naked: umbellets 3-seeded. **1857** A. GRAY *First Less. Bot.* xi. 81 Here the whole is termed a *compound umbel*; and the smaller or partial umbels take the name in English of *umbellets*.

**Umbe·llicle.** *Bot. rare*[−0]. [f. UMBEL or UMBELLA.] An umbellule.

**1828-32** WEBSTER, *Umbellicle*, a little or partial umbel.

**Umbellifer** (*v*mbe·lifəɪ). *Bot.* [mod.L.: see UMBELLIFEROUS *a.*] A plant belonging to the natural order *Umbelliferæ*, having umbellate flowers.

**1718** OZELL tr. *Tournefort's Voy.* II. vi. 214 It is an Umbellifer, to speak like a Botanist, the Root whereof goes a foot and a half down. **1727** BAILEY (vol. II), *Umbellifer*, signifies a Plant that bears many Flowers, dispos'd somewhat like an Umbrella, growing upon many Foot-stalks proceeding from the same Center. **1846** LINDLEY *Veg. Kingd.* 773 If Botanists form their ideas of an Umbellifer from the ordinary appearance of such plants in Europe. **1861** S. THOMSON *Wild Fl.* II. (ed. 4) 120 The blossoms of umbellifers vary. **1872** OLIVER *Elem. Bot.* II. 183, So many species are dangerous, that Umbellifers generally are regarded as suspicious.

**Umbelliferone** (vmbeli·fĕroun). *Chem.* Also -on. [f. prec. + -ONE.] A colourless, tasteless, crystalline substance obtained from the bark of mezereon, and, by distillation, from various umbellifers.

**1868** WATTS *Dict. Chem.* V. 938 Umbelliferone forms colourless rhombic prisms, having a faint silky lustre. **1876** HARLEY *Royle's Mat. Med.* (ed. 6) 598 The resin yields oils of a green or purple tint, and about ½ per cent. of umbelliferone, $C_9H_6C_3$, which is isomeric with quinone.

**Umbelliferous** (vmbeli·fĕrəs), *a.* [f. mod.L. *umbellifer*, f. L. *umbella* UMBELLA + *-fer* bearing: see -FEROUS. Cf. It. *umbellifero* (*ombrellifero*), Sp. *umbelifero*, F. *ombellifère*, †*umbellifère* (1698).]

**1.** *Bot.* Bearing flowers arranged in umbels; of or belonging to the order of *Umbelliferæ*.

**1662** RAY *Rem.* (1760) 260, I observed, creeping upon the Ground, a small umbelliferous Plant. **1668** WILKINS *Real Char.* II. iv. § 4. 88 Umbelliferous herbs whose leaves are more broad and less finely cut. **1731** MILLER *Gard. Dict.* s.v. *Foeniculum*, Fennel..is an Umbelliferous Plant, whose Leaves are divided into Capillaceous Jags. **1776** WITHERING *Brit. Plants* Introd. p. xxxv, Carrot,..an example of the Umbelliferous or Rundle-bearing plants. **1785** MARTYN *Lett. Bot.* v. (1794) 55 The umbelliferous tribe is numerous. **1842** LOUDON *Suburban Hort.* 651 The parsnep..is an umbelliferous biennial. **1862** H. W. BELLEW *Pol. Mission Afghanistan* 471 A great variety of labiate and umbelliferous herbs. **1887** BENTLEY *Man. Bot.* (ed. 5) 576 The poisonous or non-poisonous properties of some other species of Umbelliferous plants.

**2.** Produced by or grown on umbelliferous plants.

**1753** *Chambers' Cycl.* Suppl., *Apium*,..a genus of plants. ..The flower is of the umbelliferous kind, and is rosaceous. **1847** in Royle *Mat. Med.* 420, I have examined another kind of Umbelliferous fruit in the collection of Dr. Royle. **1876** HARLEY *Royle's Mat. Med.* (ed. 6) 581 Cumin is carminative like the other umbelliferous fruits.

**3.** Umbelliform.

**1896** *Westm. Gaz.* 10 Sept. 3/2 That gored and umbelliferous skirt, that monster hat.

**U·mbelliflo·rous**, *a. Bot.* [Cf. prec.] Having an umbellate inflorescence.

**1895** *Funk's Stand. Dict.*

**Umbe·lliform**, *a. rare*—¹. [f. L. *umbella* (cf. above) + -(I)FORM. Cf. F. *ombelliforme*.] Having the form of an umbel.

**1891** *Cent. Dict.*, *Umbellate*,.. umbelliferous,.. umbelliform. **1898** H. C. PORTER tr. *Strasburger's Bot.* 544 The designation of the whole order as *Umbellifloræ* has reference to the umbelliform manner of branching displayed in the floral region.

**Umbellule** (vmbe·liŭl). *Bot.* [ad. mod.L. *umbellula*, f. UMBELLA: see -ULE. Cf. F. *ombellule*.] A partial or secondary umbel; an umbellet.

Also (in recent Dicts.) *umbellulate*, *-ated* adjs.

**1793** MARTYN *Lang. Bot.*, *Umbellula*, an Umbellule or Umbellet. **1796** WITHERING *Brit. Plants* (ed. 3) I. 204 Leafits acute, as long as the umbellule. **1812** *New Bot. Garden* I. 8 The flowers in umbels, umbellules..in pairs. **1843** *Penny Cycl.* XXV. 498/1 If the primary pedicels have other smaller pedicels, which form of themselves a smaller umbel,..the umbel is said to be compound, and the smaller umbels are called umbellules. **1861** BENTLEY *Man. Bot.* 190 Another [involucre] at the base of each of the partial umbels or umbellules.

**Umbelook, -louke, -pitch**: see UMBE-.

**Umber**, *sb.*¹ Now *dial.* Forms: 4–7 **vmbre, umbre,** 4–7 **vmber** (7 **vmbier**), 5– **umber**; 5 **owmbre, ovmbre, ovmbere**; *dial.* 7 **oumar,** 7–9 **oumer,** 9 **oumber, oomer,** etc. [a. OF. *umbre* (*ombre*) or ad. L. *umbra* shade, shadow. Cf. F. *ombre*, Pr. *umbra*, *ombra*, It. *ombra*, It. and Sp. *ombria*, Sp. and Pg. *umbria*.]

**1.** Shade, shadow.

*a* **1300** *Cursor M.* 8017 Qua mai rest him in þer vmber, Es nathing þat mai him cumber. *Ibid.* 8451 Vnder þe vmber o þat tre, þe kind o thinges lerd he. **13..** *E. E. Allit. P.* B. 524 Sesounez schal yow neuer sese of sede ne of heruest, Ne hete, ne no harde forst, vmbre ne droȝþe. **1382** WYCLIF *Ps.* cvi. 10 The sitteris in dercnessis, and in the vmbre of deth. *c* **1407** LYDG. *Reson & Sens.* 1242 Pallas.. Fleyng had about her hede Of Cynetys ful grete novmbre, Makyng in maner of an ovmbre. *c* **1440** *Pallad. on Husb.* XI. 329 Or flouris swete of vyne or other tre, In vmbre dried, may reserued be. **1470–85** MALORY *Arthur* VIII. i. 274 Thenne the gentylwoman leyd her vnder an vmbre of a grete tree. **1549** *Compl. Scot.* vi. 56 The mune is maid obscure..be rason that the vmbre and schaddou of the eird empeschis hyr to resaue lycht fra the soune. **1572** BOSSEWELL *Armorie* II. 25 Of whatsoever colour the fielde is of, the vmbre or shadowe of the token or signe borne in the fielde is traced of a contrarie color. **1673** *Yorkshire Dial.* 32 (E.D.S.), Put th' Whyes a-mel yon Stirks an' Steers, I' th' Oumar, an' sneck the lear-deers. **1677** NICOLSON *Cumbld. Gloss.* in *Trans. Roy. Soc. Lit.* (1870) IX. 317 *Oumer*, shade. [Hence in Ray, etc.] **1781–** in northern dial. glossaries (*Eng. Dial. Dict.* s.v. *Oumer*).

†**b.** The shadow of the pointer on a sundial or quadrant. *Obs.*

**1382** WYCLIF 2 *Kings* xx. 11 The prophete..brouȝt aȝeyn the vmbre by the lynys..in the orloge of Achaz. *a* **1400** in Halliwell *Rara Mathem.* (1841) 58 Byholde vpon what place of þe quadrant þe perpendicle falles, for ouþer it wille falle on þe vmbre toward or on þe vmbre froward.

†**c.** Reflection. (Cf. SHADOW *sb.* 5.) *Obs.*

*c* **1407** LYDG. *Reson & Sens.* 3846 Love him shal so dysfigure, To doon hys besy myght and peyn Hys ovne vmbre to restreyn.

†**2.** In various figurative uses. *Obs.*

*c* **1380** WYCLIF *Sel. Wks.* I. 355 Þe vertue of God makiþ umbre, whanne in a lowe place it lettiþ heete of synne. *c* **1425** *St. Mary of Oignies* II. x. 30 in *Anglia* VIII. 176 After þat she hadde sitten..vndir þe vmbre of hym þat she desyred. **1430–40** LYDG. *Bochas* I. xii. (1544) 23 In euery cost his renoun did shyne. The fame therof was clipsed wᵗ none vmbre. *c* **1450** — *Secrees* 402 Your studye ay stood, and your dilligence bryght as Apollo, with oute shadwe or Owmbre. **1481** CAXTON *Botoner's Tulle on Old Age* Pref., Whiche lytil volume I haue emprysed tenprynte vnder the vmbre and shadowe of the noble protection of our moost dradde soueraynı. **1573** in *Cath. Tractates* (S.T.S.) 26 In the synagoge, quhilk wes bot ane schaddou and vmbre of the trew kirk. **1581** *Ibid.* 137.

†**3.** *Under (the) umber of* (or *for*), under the cloak or colour of; on pretence of. *Obs.*

**1423** JAS. I *Kingis Q.* cxxxiv, Suich feynit treuth is all bot trechorye, Vnder the vmbre of hid ypocrisye. **1430** *Rolls of Parlt.* IV. 501/1 To considre..how under ye umbre of such Vidimus, all an hole Navy of Adversaries myght ..daily vetaill, stuffe and refreshe yair partie. **1475** *Bk. Noblesse* (Roxb.) 3 Tho roughe subtile wirkingis conspired and wroughte be the Frenshe partie undre the umbre and coloure of trewis. **1518** H. WATSON *Hist. Oliver of Castile* (Roxb.) P 4 How Arthur vnder the vmbre for to goo to Saynt James, departed for to fynde his felowe Olyuer.

†**4.** The visor of a helmet. Cf. UMBRERE. *Obs.*

**14..** *Guy Warw.* (C.) 8346 He opyned vmber that tyde, And keeled hym on euery syde. **1555** *Lydgate's Chron. Troy* III. xxii. Pj/2 His swerde so mightely gan race Through the vmber [*MSS.* vmbrere, vmbrel] into Troylus face, That he hym gaue a large mortall wounde. *Ibid.* Pi j/2 Cedeus wᵗ his swerde such a stroke him sette, That through yᵉ vmber out his eye he smette. **1603** STOW *Surv.* 385 The Esquier tooke his axe, and smote many blowes on the knight, and made him let fall his axe, and brake vp his vmber three times. **1616** J. LANE *Contn. Sqr.'s T.* XI. 261 The next that entred was a mightie knight..Whose bever and his vmbier closd vp weare.

**Umber** (v·mbəɹ), *sb.*² Forms: 5 **vmbre,** 6– **umber** (6–7 **vmber**), 7, 9 **humber,** 7–8 **omber;** 7 **omer,** 9 *dial.* **oumer.** [a. OF. *umbre*, *ombre* (also *humble*; mod.F. *umble*, *omble*; Sp. *umbla*, *ombla*, Pg. *umbla*), or ad. L. *umbra* UMBRA ².] = GRAYLING.

**1496** *Fysshynge w. Angle* (1883) 23 The grayllynge by a nother name callyd vmbre is a delycyous fysshe to mannys mouthe. *a* **1550** LELAND *Itin.* (1769) V. 68 In the Lake be Umbers, yn Walsche *Cangans*, and great Store of Pykes, wherof many cum into Wy River. **1615** MARKHAM *Pleas. Princes* iv. (1635) 23 The Humber haunts the clayie Rivers of hie Countries. *Ibid.* vi. 32 The Barbell, or Grayling, which some call the Vmber, are very crafty Fishes. **1662** R. VENABLES *Exper. Angler* v. 55 The Umber is generally taken with the same baits as the Trout. *a* **1672** WILLUGHBY *Hist. Pisc.* (1686) Tab. N. 8 *Thymus et Thymalus* Salv[ian], a Greyling or Omer. *Eboracensibus.* **1740** R. BROOKES *Art of Angling* I. ix. 33 The Grayling or Umber..is in proportion neither so broad nor so thick as a Trout. **1758** *Descr. Thames* 178 Next to the Trout I place the Graylin or Umber, which are thought by some to differ. **1817–22** *Encycl. Metrop.* (1845) XIV. 585/1 The Grayling, or Umber, spawns in May, and is in the best condition in November. **1853** J. JACKSON (*title*), The Practical Fly-Fisher, more particularly for Grayling or Umber.

**U·mber**, *sb.*³ Also 6–9 **umbre,** 6–7 **vmber.** [ad. F. *ombre* (also *terre d'ombre*) or It. *ombra* (also *terra di ombra*), either meaning 'shadow' (see UMBER *sb.*¹) or from L. *Umbra*, fem. of *Umber*, belonging to the province Umbria (cf. *Umbrica crēta*, Pliny). Hence also G. *umbra*, *umber-erde*, Da. and Sw. *umber*, *umbra*, Du. *omber*, but Sp. and Pg. *sombra* (= shadow) and *tierra* (Pg. *terra*) *de sombra*.]

**1.** A brown earth used as a pigment; also, the colour of this.

**1568** [see *umber-colour*, sense 3]. **1599** B. JONSON *Cynthia's Revels* v. ii, The gloves are right, sir; you shall bury them ..seven years, and they shall still retain their first scent, true Spanish. There's ambre in the umbre. **1600** SHAKS. *A. Y. L.* I. iii. 114 Ile put my selfe in poore and meane attire, And with a kinde of vmber smirch my face. **1612** PEACHAM *Gentl. Exerc.* 80 Vmber is a more sad colour. *c* **1650** in Norgate *Miniatura* (1919) 97 For the Black Cercle of the eye take Umber, Coale black, and a little whyte. **1753** *Chambers' Cycl.* Suppl. *App.*, *Umber.* This earth when burnt makes a good shade for gold. **1755** *Gentl. Mag.* XXV. 447/2 Sea sand, that in colour resembles unburnt umber, but is lighter and more yellow. **1815** J. SMITH *Panorama Sci. & Art* II. 744 Dark back-grounds may be composed of bistre, umber, or Cologne earth. **1842** LOUDON *Suburban Hort.* 167 Certain colours, having a greater affinity for water than for oil (such as blacks, umbers, and ochres), are liable to be affected by damp. **1899** *Pall Mall Mag.* Jan. 90 The scheme of colour is composed of the yellows, umbers, and reds which Rembrandt loved so intensely.

**b.** *Burnt umber*, a special preparation of the pigment rendering it redder in colour. Also *attrib.*

*c* **1650** NORGATE *Miniatura* (1919) 40 The deepning being made with Lake and burnt Umber, the heigthning of pure Gold. **1660** *Albert Durer Revived* 12 Shadow it with the water of Burnt Umber. **1787** W. WILLIAMS *Mechanic Oil Colours* 42 Burnt umber, a very quick drier. **1843** WINSOR & NEWTON *Hand-bk. Water Col.* 27 Burnt Umber, a quiet brown colour, affording clear and warm shadows. **1843** THACKERAY *Jerome Paturot* Wks. 1900 XIII. 388 The Jew-boy.., the burnt-umber Malay who sweeps crossings, save money. **1886** RUSKIN *Præterita* I. 396 To crumble burnt umber with a dry brush for foliage and foreground.

**2.** One or other of various moths.

**1832** J. RENNIE *Consp. Butterfl. & M.* 103 The Scarce Umbre (*L. prosapiaria*) appears in October or November. *Ibid.*, The Umbre (*C. defoliaria*) appears the end of October, in woods and copses. **1887** *Nicholson's Illustr. Dict. Gardening* IV. 122 *Hybernia defoliaria*, or the Mottled Umber.., and *H. aurantiaria*, or the Scarce Umber.

**3.** *attrib.* and *Comb.*, as *umber-colour*; *umber-black, -brown, -coloured, -rufous, -tinted* adjs.; †**umber-owe,** a kind of madder.

**1845** *Encycl. Metrop.* XXV. 882/2 A tufted *umber-black plant. **1832** T. BROWN *Bk. Butterflies & M.* (1834) I. 171 The pupa is of a burnt *umber-brown colour. **1859** B. CLEMENS *Tineina N. Amer.* (1872) 25 The head is umbre-brown. **1887** W. PHILLIPS *Brit. Discomycetes* 59 The hymenium is dark umber-brown, externally a little lighter. *c* **1568** in Swayne *Sarum Churchw. Acc.* (1896) 116 Yᵉ paynter for *vmber coller. **1816** W. SMITH *Strata Ident.* 3 The soil is of a mellow brown or umber colour. **1817** STEPHENS in *Shaw's Gen. Zool.* X. II. 335 The upper parts of the body *umber-coloured. **1832** T. BROWN *Bk. Butterflies & M.* (1834) I. 217 With..three umber-coloured spots towards the lower edge of the under wings. **1881** *Instr. Census Clerks* (1885) 85 *Umber Mine Agent. *Ibid.*, *Umber Miner. *a* **1661** FULLER *Worthies*, *Kent* II. (1662) 57 There are three kinds thereof. 1. Crop-Madder. 2. *Umber-owe. 3. Pipe or Fat-Madder. **1836** BERKELEY *Fungi* in *Smith's Eng. Flora* V. II. 17 Pileus dry squamulose *umber-rufous. **1895** *Daily News* 20 Dec. 5/2 Delicately arched nostrils, sensuously-moulded lips, and *umber-tinted hair.

**b.** Attrib. in the sense of 'umber-coloured'.

**1802** SHAW *Gen. Zool.* III. I. 226 Umbre Lizard. **1803** *Ibid.* IV. II. 384 Umbre Acanthurus. **1832** J. RENNIE *Consp. Butterfl. & M.* 103 The Umbre Link (*Hibernia connectaria*) appears in November and December. **1866** MISS MULOCK *Noble Life* x, The black woods—black, or with a faint umber shadow running through them. **1870** DISRAELI *Lothair* xxxviii, The golden and umber vapours fell into forms that..depicted the objects of his frequent meditation. **1881** ELEANOR A. ORMEROD *Injur. Insects* (1890) 337 The caterpillar of the Mottled Umber Moth is a 'looper'.

**Umber** *sb.*⁴, aphetic f. NUMBER *sb.*

The form *imber* (sb. and v.) is found in modern East Anglian dialect. (Cf. UMBER *v.*²)

*c* **1400** *Laud Troy Bk.* 4319 He sclow that tyme without-outen vmbre Mo Troyens than I can numbre. **1746** *Exmoor Vocab.* in *Gentl. Mag.* July 408 *Umber*, number.

**Umber**, variant of UMBRE (the bird).

**U·mber**, *v.*¹ Chiefly *dial.* In 5 **oumbre, owmbre,** 7 **vmbre,** 9 *dial.* **oumer, owmer, oomer,** etc. [ad. OF. *umbrer*, *ombrer* (mod.F. *ombrer* to shade in painting), ad. L. *umbrāre* (whence also It. *ombrare*), f. *umbra* UMBER *sb.*¹] *trans.* To shade, to protect.

*c* **1400** MAUNDEV. (Roxb.) xvii. 78 It will couer and oumbre all his body for þe sonne. *Ibid.* xxii. 100 It will couer all þe body and owmbre it fra þe sonne. **1611** COTGR., *Ombré*, vmbred, or shadowed; (a tearme in Blason). **1790** GROSE *Prov. Gloss.*, *Oumert*, shaded with trees or buildings. **1828** *Craven Gloss.* (ed. 2), *Oumer*, to shadow. *Ibid.*, That birk oumers 't gait. *a* **1867** in Harland & Wilkinson *Lanc. Folk-Lore* 60 T' leaves on t' trees, they owm'ered t' land, And fadin' was the summer light.

Hence **U·mbering** *ppl. a.*

**1872** DIXON *Milkin' Time* (E.D.D.), The branches of the owmering yew. **1880** A. B. TODD *August* Poet. Wks. (1906) 209 When winds grew hush'd, and umbering trees were still.

†**U·mber**, *v.*² *Obs.*—¹ In 5 **vmbre.** [Aphetic f. NUMBER *v.* Cf. UMBER *sb.*⁴] *trans.* To number.

*c* **1400** *Laud Troy Bk.* 370 He sclow champiouns without-outen nombre, So manye that no man myȝt hem vmbre.

**U·mber**, *v.*³ Also 7 **vmbre,** 7–8 **umbre.** [f. UMBER *sb.*³] *trans.* To stain or paint with umber; to make of a dark brown colour.

**1610** B. JONSON *Alch.* v. v, You..told her, you had tane the paines To dye your beard, and vmbre o'er your face. **1615** MARKHAM *Pleas. Princes* ii. (1635) 7 He which is a master in this Art will Vmber, and darken the Rod. **1623** MIDDLETON & ROWLEY *Sp. Gipsy* II. i, No red-ochre rascals umbered with soot and bacon as the English gipsies are. **1735** *Dict. Polygraph.* I. Q 5 After the faces have been umbred, shadow the hair. **1813** HOGG *Queen's Wake* I. *Young Kennedy* i, When the gusts of October had rifled the thorn, Had dappled the woodland, and umbered the plain.

**Umbereach**: see UMBE-.

**U·mbered**, *ppl. a.* Also 9 **umbred.** [f. UMBER *sb.*³ or *v.*³ + -ED.] Stained or painted with umber; made of a dark brown colour; embrowned, darkened.

In some quots. the sense 'shadowed, darkened by shade' (cf. UMBER *v.*¹) is possible.

**1599** SHAKS. *Hen. V*, IV. Prologue 9 Fire answers fire, and through their paly flames Each Battaile sees the others vmber'd face. **1624** HEYWOOD *Captives* II. ii. in Bullen *O. Pl.* IV, Fayre flesh and cleane they bothe appeare And not like gypsies umber'd. **1716** POPE *Iliad* VIII. 706 Full fifty guards each flaming pile attend, Whose umber'd arms, by fits, thick flashes send. **1805–6** CARY *Dante, Inf.* III. 110 Thus go they over through the umber'd wave. **1813** SCOTT *Trierm.* I. x, Amid whose yawning gulfs the sun Cast umber'd radiance red and dun. **1860** O. W. HOLMES *Elsie V.* xi. (1891) 154 The bistred or umbered beauties of mingled blood among whom he had been living. **1877** MALLOCK *New Republic* v. i. II. 232 A circular domed temple of umbred marble.

**Umberere**, variant of UMBRERE *Obs.*

†**Umberment.** *Obs.* [Cf. UMBER *sb.*⁴ and *v.*²] Number, multitude.

Modern Kentish dial. *umblement* 'number, complement', is prob. a survival of this.

1550-3 *Decaye Eng.* in *Supplic.* (1871) 96 Where tillage was wont to be, nowe is it stored wyth greate vmberment of shepe, & they that haue great vmberment of shepe, must nedes haue greate store of woll.

**Umberow**: see UMBE-.

† **Umberst**, *a. Obs.*⁻¹ [? superl. of **umberous* NUMBEROUS *a.* Cf. UMBER *sb.*⁴] ? Most numerous.

1599 *Warn. Faire Wom.* II. 198 Methought you.. went into a garden, and there was the vmberst sorte of flowers that euer I see.

† **Umberty.** *Obs. rare.* In 6 omberty, vmbertie. [App. an alteration of UBERTY, after UMBER *sb.*⁴] Abundance.

1575 LANEHAM *Lett.* (1871) 30 In Philosophy.. I think he be az naturally ouerseen: beside poetrie and Astronomie, and oother hid sciencez, as I may gesse by the omberty of hiz books. 1589 *Marprel. Epit.* E iij b, What bommination vmbertie of reasons here be,.. and yet euerye one false.

**Umberun**: see UMBE-.

**U·mbery**, *a.* [f. UMBER *sb.*³ + -Y.] Of the colour of umber; dark brown.

1834 H. MILLER *Scenes & Leg.* vi. (1857) 76 They admitted ..a sort of umbery twilight. 1862 THORNBURY *Turner* I. 55 Turner..sketching the river and boats with the conventional Indian ink and umbery sails. 1902 *Academy* 28 June 22/2 The flesh is not white, but umbery gold.

† **Umbeschew**, *v. Sc. Obs.* Also 5 umbechew, 6 vm-, wmschew, vmchev-, vmchow. [f. UMB- + ESCHEW *v.* The reason for the prefix is not clear.] *trans.* To avoid, shun. Hence † **Umschewing** *vbl. sb.*

*a.* 1456 SIR G. HAY *Gov. Princes* Wks. (S.T.S.) II. 120 Off sik thing men suld have counsale of medicineris as maladyes that men may nocht gudely umbechew. *a* 1500 in *Ratis Raving*, etc. 90 Thir ar the thewis.. Quilkis fullis oys comonly; Quhay lovis honor suld thaim vmbeschew. 1514 *Extr. Aberd. Rec.* (1844) I. 90 It is thoucht expedient,..to vmbeschew the said seknes, that thar be bot thre portis haldin oppin for cuming of strangearis.

*β.* 1530 *Extr. Aberd. Rec.* (1844) I. 448 To ewaid and vmchow trubill of thair innymeis. 1547 *Rec. Elgin* (1903) I. 91 The vmcheving of the apperand schayth and damagh of the haill commond veill.

† **Umbeset**, *v. Obs.* In later use *Sc.* Forms: *a.* 4- umbeset, 4-5 vmbesette, 5-6 -set(t, wmbeset, 6 -sett, 6 ombeset(t; 4 umbisett(e, 4 vmbi-, 5 vmbysett. *β.* 5 vnbesette, 6-7 -set, 6 unbeset, wnbesett. [See UMBE- and BESET *v.*, and cf. *umbset* s.v. UMB- and UMSET *v.* So MDu. *omme-*, *ombeset* p.p., MDa. *ombesat* p.p.] *trans.* To surround, encompass, beset.

*a. a* 1300 *Cursor M.* 7179 Þai vmbisett þat tun a-bute. *Ibid.* 19775 Petre..to þis licam com þat lai, Wit pouer widus vm-bi-sett. 1375 BARBOUR *Bruce* VI. 535 The kyng wes in gret iuperdy, That wes on athir syde vmbeset With fayis. *Ibid.* IX. 706 He till the hous went hastely, And vmbeset it all about. *c* 1400 *Apol. Loll.* 48 Þe auter is vmbeset wiþ stonis. *c* 1470 HENRY *Wallace* V. 168 At syndry furdis the gait thai vmbeset. 1513 DOUGLAS *Æneid* XI. xiv. 22 Quhou huge dolfnes, and schamful cowardice, Hes ombeset 3our myndis apon sik wys. *c* 1550 ROLLAND *Crt. Venus* I. 113 With Iacinth fine, and Topazion sa fair,..Was vmbeset his body ouir all quhair. 1587 *Reg. Privy Counc. Scot.* IV. 162 Thai..umbesettis thair hie wayes in thair ganging and cuming fra thair parroche kirk.

*β. c* 1440 *Gesta Rom.* lxv. 281 (Add. MS.), Whan the Steward was thus vnbesette with thise iij. bestes, he was right sory. *a* 1575 *Diurn. Occurr.* (Bann. Cl.) 168 Certane personis..quha was werry bent to haue vnbesett him in the waij betuix Edinburgh and Berwick. 1582-8 *Hist. James VI* (1804) 112 Thairfoir Lord Claud Hamiltoun unbeset the way with sum chosen men. 1624 in *Abbotsford Club Misc.* 144 Thomas Logie..meitting ane number of cattis..quhilk vnbesett him, the said Thomas saw 3our face vpoun ane of [the] cattis.

Hence † **Umbese·tting** *vbl. sb. Obs.*

1543 *Acc. Ld. High Treas. Scot.* VIII. 244 To underly the law for thair tressonable umbesetting of the gait. 1551 *Ibid.* X. 35 To have underlyne the lawis for unbesetting of the said Alexander Cummyng of Alteir gait. 1624 in *Abbotsford Club Misc.* 144 Anent the vnbesetting of the cattis.

**Umbeshadow, -shear, -shine, -siege, -spread, -stand**: see UMBE-.

† **Umbestound**, *adv. Obs.* Forms: 3 vmbe stunde, umbestunde, 4 vmbesto(u)nde, 5 *Sc.* vmbestount. [OE. *ymbe* (*embe*) *stunde*: see UMBE *prep.* and STOUND *sb.*¹] **a.** At times; sometimes. **b.** After a (short) time.

[993 *Battle of Maldon* 271 Æfre embe stunde he sealde sume wunde.] *c* 1205 LAY. 11969 Þa vmbe stunde ne sæ3e heo noht of londe. *a* 1225 *Ancr. R.* 344 Ich am of-dred leste I go driuinde oðerhwules to swuðe uorðward upe fole þouhtes, and fule umbestunde. *a* 1300 *Havelok* 2297 He is birkabeynes sone, Þe king þat was vmbe stonde wone For to yeme [us] and wel were. 13.. *E. E. Allit. P.* C. 122 O Folez in folk felez oþer whyle, & vnderstondes vmbestounde,.. Hope 3e þat he heres not þat eres alle made? 1375 BARBOUR *Bruce* VII. 398 The kyng..Wes in Carrik, quhar vmbestount He vald vend vith his men till hount.

So † **Umbestounds** *adv. Obs.*

13.. *E. E. Allit. P.* C. 7 Þen is better to abyde þe bur vmbe-stoundes, Þen ay þrow forth my þro, þa3 me þynk ylle.

**Umbeswey**: see UMBE-.

**Umbethi·nk, un-**, *v. Obs.* exc. *dial.* Forms: *a.* 3 ummbeþennkenn, 5 umbethenke; 4 vmbethynk(e, 4-6 vmbe-, umbethink (5-6 *Sc.* wmbe-); 4 vmby-, 4-5 vmbithynk(e. *β.* 4-7 vnbethink (4 vnbi-; 6 -thynk), 7, 8-9 *dial.*, unbethink (9 *dial.* on-). [See UMBE- and BETHINK *v.*¹ and cf. UMTHINK *v.*]

† **1.** *trans.* (with objective clause). To think about, to consider; to remember (*how*, *that*, etc.). *Obs.*

*c* 1200 ORMIN 2953 3iff þatt icc..mikell ummbeþennke, Whillc gate icc mu3he cwemenn Godd. *c* 1340 HAMPOLE *Psalter* lxxxvi. 13 Londe of forgettinge is in þas þat vnbethinks not þat þai salbe demed rightwisly. *c* 1380 WYCLIF in *MS. Bodl. 288* fol. 250/1 Makiþ knowen in þe folk þe fyndingis of him: vmbiþinkiþ for his name is hi3. 1483 *Cath. Angl.* 403/1 To Vmbethynke, *recogitare*. 1501 DOUGLAS *Pal. Hon.* I. lxx, I vmbethocht how Ioue and auld Saturne, Intill ane wolf thay did Lycaon turne.

**2.** *refl.* To bethink (oneself); to call to mind: **a.** With obj. clause or inf.

*a. a* 1300 *Cursor M.* 2999 For I me vm-bithoght Yee war men þat godd duted noght. *c* 1340 HAMPOLE *Prose Tr.* 10 Vmbethynke the þat thou halowe þi halydaye. 1375 BARBOUR *Bruce* V. 613 'A! schir, vmbethinkis 3ow,' said he, 'How neir to 3ou that I suld be'. *c* 1400 *Ywaine & Gaw.* 1583 Sir Ywaine umbithoght him than He had forgeten his leman. *c* 1425 WYNTOUN *Cron.* IV. ii. 130 He..wmbethoucht [*v.r.*(*c* 1520) vnbethocht] hym inkyrly Withe qwhat turmentis men mycht be Punyst for þar iniquite. *c* 1460 *Towneley Myst.* i. 123 Therfor, felow, hold thi peasse, and vmbithynke the what thou saysse.

*β. c* 1520 [see 2 *a*]. 1685 COTTON *Montaigne* (1711) I. xii. 60 The Lacedæmonian Foot.. unbethought themselves to disperse and retire. *Ibid.* II. xii. 365 Nicetas of Syracusa unbethought him to maintain, that it was the Earth that mov'd. 1703 A. DE LA PRYME *Short View Hist. Winterton* in *Archaeol.* XL. 234 William the Conqueror haveing the whole Nation at Command begun to unbethink himself, how he might gratify his Favourites. 1863 MRS. GASKELL *Sylvia's L.* vii, They'll prize what I leave 'em if I could only onbethink me what they would like.

**b.** Const. *of* or *on.* Also *intr.*

*a. c* 1375 *Cursor M.* 1325 (Fairf.), Of steppis he vmbe-þo3t him þan þat falowed for syn of man. 1375 BARBOUR *Bruce* III. 352 The king umbethocht him off a thing. 1422 tr. *Secreta Secret., Priv. Priv.* 150 Vmbethynke vs of the moste noble lordis as to worthely lorshuppe that afor this tymes weryn. 1456 SIR G. HAYE *Govt. Princes* (S.T.S.) 164 Will thou umbethink the wele of all that I have said. 1513 DOUGLAS *Æneid* I. x. 32 Quharfore I vmbethink me of ane trane, This quene first for to caucht in luvis lace. 1560 ROLLAND *Seven Sages* 87 He vmbethocht him self of ane consait.

*β.* ? *a* 1500 *Chester Pl.* xxiv. 430 How durst you euer doe amysse, when you vnbethoughte you of this? ? *a* 1600 *Sir Lionel* 35 in *Percy Folio, Ball. & Rom.* (1867) I. 76 He.. vnbethought him of a while [= wile], how he might that wilde bore beguile. 1630 W. FREAKE *Doctrines Jesuites* II. 59 The Iesuites vnbethought themselues further of this Stratagem. 1686 G. STUART *Joco-Ser. Disc.* 4 When I unbethink me of thae frights and fears This poor auld grey beard hangs dreeping with tears. *c* 1746 J. COLLIER (Tim Bobbin) *View Lanc. Dial.* Wks. (1862) 11 On then I unbethowt meh o me Sawt. 1788 W. H. MARSHALL *Rur. Econ. Yorks.* II. s.v., I unbethought myself on't. 1892 SARAH HEWETT *Peas. Sp. Devon* 139 Well, I'm baggered ef I ant ajist unbethowted o' 't.

**c.** Without const.

*a. a* 1300 *Cursor M.* 3622 A wyel sco hir vmbithogt. 1375 BARBOUR *Bruce* XVII. 40 Quhen the marschall the letteris saw, He vmbethoucht him than a thraw. *c* 1440 *Alph. Tales* 17 Sho satt still & vmbethoght hur, & knew his falssett well enogh. *Ibid.* 237 Als oft sithes as I se a tade, I vmbethynk me, & thankis God þat gaf me so fayr a form. *a* 1500 in *Ratis Raving*, etc. 13 Quhen I wmbethocht me, and turnyt my mynd in my self, thinkand of al my warldly werkis.

*β.* 1535 COVERDALE 2 *Sam.* xiv. 14 And God will not take awaye the lyfe, but vnbethynketh himselfe. 1603 *Philotus* lxxvi, Quhen I haue vnbethocht me thryse, I can na better way deuyse. *a* 1666 C. HOOLE *School-Colloquies* (1688) 190 Let me unbethink myself a little. *c* 1800 PEGGE *Anecd. Eng. Lang.* (1814) 250 Similar to this word *unbeknown* is an expression used in some parts of England, where people say, 'I un-bethought myself': i.e. I recollected. 1857 WAUGH *Lanc. Life* 207 He's the very mon for yo! Aw've just unbethought mo! 1879 MISS JACKSON *Shropsh. Wordbk.* 460, I should a done that wrung, if I 'adna jest unbethought me in time.

**3.** In *pa. pple.* After reflection.

1422 tr. *Secreta Secret., Priv. Priv.* 138 If hit happe a kynge to do any thynge vnawyssely, he owyth hit repel vnbethoght avysely, and wyth reyson know his defaute.

Hence **Umbethi·nking** *vbl. sb.*; **Umbethou·ght** *ppl. a.*

1422 tr. *Secreta Secret., Priv. Priv.* 155 The more ryche man be and manaunt, the more hym be-howyth that he be vmbethoght. *Ibid.* 157 Whoso wyse is and vmbethoght, he wille not begyle, ne begilid he nel not be. *c* 1440 *Alph. Tales* 293 To restrene hur wepyng sho lefte thynkyng of þe manhede of Criste & toke hur to vmbethynkyng of His godded. 1548 UDALL *Erasm. Par., Luke* xii. 115 To take folie and unbethinking to be of his counsayle.

**Umbethonre, -tigh, -trin, -turn, -viron, -wall, -weave, -wend, -wet**: see UMBE-.

† **Umbewhi·le**, *adv. Obs.* Also 3 umbe hwile, 4 vmbywhile (4 unbe-, 5 vnbi-). [OE. *ymb*(*e*) *hwile*: see UMBE *prep.* and WHILE *sb.* Cf. UMWHILE.]

**1.** After a time.

971 *Blickling Hom.* 217 Þa wæs ymb hwile, ða 3efelde he þæt se deada man his leomu ealle astyrede. *a* 1225 *Leg. Kath.* 12 Weox umbe hwile [*Royal MS.* umbe hwiles] wreððe ham bitweonen.

**2.** At times; sometimes.

*c* 1230 *Hali Meid.* 27 Nawt ane on ende; ah eauer umbehwile. *a* 1310 in Wright *Lyric P.* xv. 49 Sleuthe ant slep mi bedyner, that weneth me unbe-while. Umbe-while y am to whene, when y shal murthes meten. 1393 LANGL. *P. Pl.* C. VII. 396 (MS. Laud 656), [They] setyn til euesang range & songe vmbywhile.

**Umbfold**: see UMB-.

**Umbier**, variant of UMBER *sb.*¹

† **Umbil.** *Obs.*⁻⁰ [ad. L. *umbil-īcus*: see next. F. *nombril* is used in the same sense.] (See quot.)

1688 R. HOLME *Armoury* II. 85/1 The umbil is the navel, or daulk in any fruit, just against the stalk; it is also taken for the crown, top, or head of an apple, where the blossom is.

**Umbilic** (*v*mbi·lik), *sb.* Forms: *a.* 7 vmbilike, -icke, umbilick, umbelic(k, 7, 9 umbilic. *β.* 7 vmbilique, umbelique. [ad. L. *umbilīc-us* UMBILICUS, related to Gr. ὀμφαλός, and ultimately to NAVEL *sb.* Hence also F. *ombilic*, † *umbilic* (1556), It. *um-*, *ombilico*, *ombellico*, Sp. *ombligo*, Pg. *umbigo*. In sense 1 prob. stressed *umbili·c*.]

† **1.** The centre; the middle point or part. *Obs.*

*a.* 1607 BP. J. KING *Serm. 5 Nov.* 23 For the perpetration of it they went downe into the bowells of the earth, but for the inuention to the very vmbilicke, and centre of the earth. 1608 — *Serm. 24 Mar.* 19 The verie middle and vmbilicke of natures prefined time. 1638 SIR T. HERBERT *Trav.* (ed. 2) 113 Ormus is as it were the umbelick of the gulph. *Ibid.* 265 Hell is in the Umbelic or navell of the world.

*β.* 1612 PEACHAM *Gentl. Exerc.* III. 143 It was round, and equall from the vmbelique or middle point, to euery side. 1615 SIR E. HOBY *Curry-combe* vi. 248 Not only in Wales and Scotland, but euen in the vmbilique of the Saxons Dominion. 1638 SIR T. HERBERT *Trav.* (ed. 2) 214 In the umbelique or mid-part of this spatious Court is a quadrangular Tanck or Pond.

**2.** *Geom.* (See quots. 1875-6.)

1843 MACCULLAGH in *Proc. R. Irish Acad.* (1846) II. 458 The focal hyperbola of the ellipsoid and the focal ellipse of the hyperboloid of two sheets, are umbilicar focals, and pass through the umbilics of these surfaces. 1875 P. FROST *Solid Geom.* (ed. 2) I. 166 The point-circles in which the variable circle terminates are called *umbilics*. 1876 *Handbk. Sci. App. S. Kens.* 46 At special points, called umbilics, the greatest and least curvatures (and therefore all the curvatures) are equal to one another. The sphere has the peculiarity that every point on it is an umbilic.

† **Umbi·lic**, *a. Obs.* Also 6 vm-, 7 umbilique, 8 umbilick. [ad. L. *umbilīc-us* (see prec.), the ending being taken as adjectival.]

**1.** *Umbilic point*, a central point.

**a.** *Her.* 1586 FERNE *Blaz. Gentrie* 105 Counterchanging of them by the fesse or vmbilique point of the sheeld. *Ibid.* 184 This scutcheon..was of old named fessey target bycause that the fesse or vmbilique point of the coate armor is occupied with a targe or sheeld.

**b.** *Math.* 1700 MOXON *Math. Dict.*, *Umbilique Points*, or the 2 Focus or Centre-Points in an Elipsis.

**2.** (See quot.)

1681 tr. *Willis' Rem. Med. Wks.* Vocab., *Umbilic*, belonging to the navel, or of the likeness or shape of the navel.

**Umbilical** (*v*mbi·likăl), *a.* and *sb.* Also 6 vmbelycall, 8 umbelical, 7 vm-, umbilicall, 8 umbillical. [ad. med.L. *umbilicāl-is*, f. *umbilīc-us* UMBILIC *sb.* Cf. It. *umbilicale*, *ombelicale*, Sp. and Pg. *umbilical*, F. *ombilical* (1541), † *umbilical* (Cotgr.).]

**A.** *adj.* **1.** *Anat.* Of or pertaining to the umbilicus or navel.

1541 R. COPLAND *Guydon's Quest. Chirurg.* H ij, The party vmbelycall synual is fro ye nauyll downwarde. 1704 J. HARRIS *Lex. Techn.* I, *Umbilical Region*, is that part of the Abdomen lying round about the Navel. 1728 CHAMBERS *Cycl.* s.v. *Liver*, One [fissure] thro' which the Umbilical Ligament passes. 1808 BARCLAY *Muscular Motions* 348 A tendon, which..divides in the region called *umbilical* into two strata. 1846 BRITTAN tr. *Malgaigne's Man. Oper. Surg.* 434 The umbilical ring..is but slightly resistant and very dilatable for some time after birth. 1859 BULLOCK *Cazeaux' Midwif.* 128 The umbilical depression, which in the two first months seems deeper, disappears gradually as gestation progresses. 1881 MIVART *Cat* 185 On this account the ventral part of the groove is called the umbilical fissure.

**b.** In *umbilical artery*, *vein*, *vessel*.

1615 CROOKE *Body of Man* 710 The Infant..draweth the nourishment into the Liuer through the vmbilicall veine by a naturall instinct. 1656 BLOUNT *Glossogr.*, *Umbilical Arteries*, are two Arteries marching from the Navil, through *Peritonæum* to the sides of the Bladder. 1667 *Phil. Trans.* II. 512 The Embrio doth breath, but not feed, through the Umbilical vessels. 1725 *Fam. Dict.* s.v. *Liver*, These two Lobes [of the Liver] are separated by a Scissure or Cleft, through which the Umbelical Vein enters. 1774 GOLDSMITH *Nat. Hist.* (1862) I. ii. 158 The bloodvessels that go to the placenta..are plainly seen issuing from the navel (being therefore called the umbilical vessels). 1831 R. KNOX *Cloquet's Anat.* 715 The umbilical artery always furnishes three or four, which ramify in the walls of the bladder. 1841 T. R. JONES *Anim. Kingd.* 629 The arteries ..represent the umbilical arteries of the human fetus.

**c.** *Path.* and *Med.* Affecting, proceeding from, or applied to, the navel.

1797 *Encycl. Brit.* (ed. 3) XVIII. 155 In umbilical hernia the parts protruded pass out at the umbilicus, and are commonly the intestines, or omentum, or both. 1862 HABERSHON *Dis. Abdomen* (ed. 2) 570 Strumous Peritonitis. Fæcal Abscess. Umbilical Discharge. 1875 KNIGHT *Dict. Mech.* 2678/1 *Umbilical bandage*, .. a broad band of fabric which is buckled around the umbilical region of the body to serve as an abdominal supporter and for palliating umbilical hernia. *Ibid.*, An umbilical truss, designed for the same purpose.

**d.** Connected on the female side.

1888 *N. & Q.* 7th Ser. V. 493/2 The direct lineal ancestress in the female line, or what is sometimes termed umbilical or uterine ancestress.

**2.** *Umbilical cord*: **a.** The flexible string which attaches the fœtus to the placenta; the navel-string.

1753 *Chambers' Cycl.* Suppl. s.v. *Navel*, The umbilical cord or navel-string of the new-born infant. 1803 *Med. Jrnl.* IX. 74 He combats the opinion..that the death of the child necessarily follows from the neglect of tying the umbilical cord after delivery. 1847 W. C. L. MARTIN *Ox* 167/2 Some farmers after the birth of the calf attach a small weight to the umbilical cord, in order to facilitate the separation and expulsion of the placenta. 1888 *Buck's Handbk. Med. Sci.* VI. 22/2 The umbilical cord normally presents torsions.

*fig.* 1847 EMERSON *Repr. Men, Swedenborg* Wks. (Bohn) I. 334 With a force of many men, he could never break the umbilical cord which held him to nature. 1859 I. TAYLOR *Logic in Theol.* 217 That intercourse which..is linking England with India—that umbilical cord through which the circulation, to and fro, is going on.

**b.** *Bot.* The small peduncle which attaches a seed to the placenta. Similarly *umbilical bundle, vessel.*

1731 P. MILLER *Gard. Dict.* s.v. *Vegetation*, This fermented Liquor is convey'd by the Umbilical Vessel to the Trunk of the little Plant. 1819 LINDLEY tr. *Richard's Obs. Fruits & Seeds* 6 Every visible process of the trophosperm which bears a single seed is known by the name of umbilical chord. 1830 — *Nat. Syst. Bot.* 150 Seeds attached by umbilical cords to placentæ. 1875 BENNETT & DYER tr. *Sachs's Bot.* 252 From it [an umbilicus] a denser bundle of threads runs downwards to the peridium, the umbilical bundle.

**3.** *Conchol.* Provided or connected with, of the nature of, an umbilicus.

1755 *Gentl. Mag.* XXV. 128 The particular species of the *Nautilus*, as shells, are the papiraceous, the eared, and the umbilical. 1822 J. PARKINSON *Outl. Oryctol.* 147 In some instances the umbilical termination [of a shell] is filled, as if by an exudation of callus. 1894 *Geol. Mag.* Oct. 438 The Australian form is distinguished by the greater prominence of its short umbilical ribs.

**4.** *Geom.* Forming, or pertaining to, an umbilicus.

1728 CHAMBERS *Cycl.*, *Umbilical Points*, in Mathematicks, the same with *Foci*. 1841 J. R. YOUNG *Math. Dissert.* ii. 34 Dupin..clearly saw that Mouge had misinterpreted this symbol in his investigation of umbilical points. 1851 SYLVESTER in *Lond.* etc. *Phil. Mag.* Feb. 136 *note*, As the two surfaces jut one close into the other at this point, it would perhaps be not improper to designate the contact at such point as umbilical. 1863 FROST & WOLSTENHOLME *Solid Geom.* 144 The fixed point is called an umbilical focus, the intersection of the planes a directrix, and the constant ratio the umbilical modulus.

**5.** Occupying a central point or position.

1742 *De Foe's Tour Gt. Brit.* (ed. 3) II. 293 The Chapter-house is large, supported, as to its arched Roof, by one umbilical pillar. 1760 STERNE *Tr. Shandy* I. xxiii, His soul might as well, unless for mere ceremony, or the trifling advantage which the umbilical point gave her,..play the fool out o' doors as in her own house. 1774 J. BRYANT *Mythol.* I. 243 The Ætolians were stiled umbilical; and looked upon themselves as the central people in Greece.

**B.** *sb. pl.* The umbilical vessels.

1774 COOPER in *Phil. Trans.* LXV. 316 It is plain also, that the blood passed..through the hypogastrics and umbilicals to the placenta.

**†Umbilica·lity.** *Obs.* [f. prec. + -ITY.]

**1.** A close or intimate connexion.

1646 SIR T. BROWNE *Pseud. Ep.* v. v. 240 In his immortall and diviner part hee seemed to hold a nearer coherence, and an umbilicality even with God himselfe.

**2.** An umbilical cord.

1658 J. ROBINSON *Endoxa* vii. 44, I know, after two or three days incubation, that there is a Sanguine-like string; ..but that that should be the Umbilicality of the Chicken, is not by sight demonstrable.

**Umbi·lically,** *adv.* [f. as prec. + -LY [2].] By means of an umbilicus or umbilical cord; in the region of the navel.

1821 W. P. C. BARTON *Flora N. Amer.* I. 97 Seeds numerous, attached umbilically to a central receptacle.

**Umbilica·nimism.** *rare.* [f. L. *umbilīc-us* UMBILICUS + *anima* soul, after late Gr. ὀμφαλόψυχος.] The practice of looking steadfastly at the navel, followed by the Hesychasts, in expectation of an outward exhibition of the light supposed to dwell within the soul of man.

1874 J. H. BLUNT *Dict. Sects* 192/1 The Light theory and Umbilicanimism of the Hesychasts.

**Umbi·licar,** *a.* *Geom.* [f. UMBILIC-US + -AR. Cf. late L. *umbilicāris* (Tertullian).] Of or belonging to the umbilicus.

1843 MACCULLAGH in *Proc. R. Irish Acad.* (1846) II. 458 A focal which is not modular may be called *umbilicar*, because it intersects the surface in the umbilics. *Ibid.* 469 A focal point which is at once modular and umbilicar. 1870 CAYLEY *Math. Papers* VIII. 326 The contacts arise, as will appear, from the umbilici of the ellipsoid, and may be termed 'umbilicar centres', or 'omphaloi'.

**† Umbi·licary,** *a.* *Obs.*—[1] [f. obs. F. *umbilicar* (Rabelais), ad. late L. *umbilicāris*: see prec.] Lying in the region of the navel.

*a* 1693 *Urquhart's Rabelais* III. xxxiv. 290, I will..grope her Pulse, and see the Disposition of her Hypogaster, together with her Umbilicary Parts [F. *parties umbilicares*].

**Umbilicate** (*v*mbi·likĕt), *a.* [ad. L. *umbilīcāt-us*, f. *umbilīcus* UMBILICUS. Cf. It. *umbilicato, ombelicato*, F. *ombiliqué*.] Resembling a navel; having a depression like the navel.

1698 W. KING tr. *Sorbière's Journ. Lond.* 15 He has several other Curiosities; among the rest was a Roman Glass, whose very bottom was smoth and very little umbilicate. 1785 MARTYN *Lett. Bot.* xxxii. (1794) 499 Umbilicate [section], or hollowed like the navel, and sooty, or appearing black, or as if burnt. 1826 KIRBY & SP. *Entomol.* IV. 270 *Umbilicate*,..when a variole, tubercle granule, &c. has a depression in its centre. 1842 JOHNSTON in *Proc. Berw. Nat. Club* II. 30 There is no spire, nor is the apex umbilicate. 1897 W. E. STEELE *Field Bot.* 81 Cal[yx] with 30 furrows, conical, umbilicate at base.

**Umbi·licate,** *v.* [Cf. prec. and UMBILICATION.] *intr.* To become umbilicate.

*c* 1900 *Buck's Handbk. Med. Sci.* VII. 250 (Cent. Suppl.).

**Umbi·licated,** *a.* [f. as prec. + -ED.] Having a depression like the navel; umbilicate. (Chiefly in special applications: see quots.)

**a.** 1698 W. KING tr. *Sorbière's Journ. Lond.* 15 He show'd me, likewise, a great Rummer of two Quarts..: I found that the foot of the latter was more Vmbilicated than the former.

**b.** *Bot.* 1693 *Phil. Trans.* XVII. 928 The Fourth Section contains such Trees and Shrubs as have an Umbilicated Fruit. 1725 SLOANE *Jamaica* II. 76 To that follows many crown'd or umbilicated berries. 1756 P. BROWNE *Jamaica* 203 The larger Colts-foot, with umbilicated leaves. 1771 DUCHESS PORTLAND *Let.* in Mrs. Delany *Life & Corr.* Ser. II. (1862) I. 359, I fancy I left the umbilicated lichen at Ilam. 1845 *Florist's Jrnl.* (1846) VI. 196 The plant..is at first rotund, in age becoming more oblong, umbilicated at the top.

**c.** *Conch.* 1776 DA COSTA *Elem. Conchol.* x. 202 The umbilicated whitish thin Snail. 1822 J. PARKINSON *Outl. Oryctol.* 155 The columella umbilicated and slightly grooved at its base. 1851 S. P. WOODWARD *Mollusca* I. 100 The axis of the shell, around which the whorls are coiled, is sometimes open or hollow; in which case, the shell is said to be perforated, or umbilicated. 1880 *Linn. Soc. Jrnl.* XV. 95 Shell high, conical, tectiform, carinated, umbilicated, with a flattish depressedly conical base.

**d.** *Ent.* 1819 SAMOUELLE *Entomol. Compend.* 190 Black, shining, impressed-punctate, cicatriculose; the punctures umbilicated, the umbilici perforate. 1826 KIRBY & SPENCE *Entomol.* III. 509 In *Fulgora Diadema* they [stemmata] are also umbilicated, but the *umbilicus* is circular.

**e.** *Path.* and *Anat.* 1834 *Cycl. Pract. Med.* III 738/2 This central depression, or *umbilicated* form of vesicle (as it is sometimes called), is very characteristic of small-pox. 1877 COUES *Fur Anim.* i. 13 At each side of this fossa.. is found an umbilicated papilla. 1897 *Allbutt's Syst. Med.* II. 519 A pustular rash,..but without umbilicated pustules.

**Umbilication** (*v*mbilikēⁱ·ʃən). *Path.* [f. L. *umbilīc-us* UMBILICUS + -ATION.] A central depression on the upper part of a pock or other vesicle on the skin; also, the condition of being so depressed.

1873 F. T. ROBERTS *Handbk. Med.* 182 After a while the umbilication disappears, the pock becoming either rounded or pointed at the top. 1880 A. FLINT *Princ. Med.* 618 The umbilication, which can sometimes be felt on the cancerous nodules, may be of assistance in the diagnosis. 1899 *Allbutt's Syst. Med.* VIII. 876 As the tumour increases in size, one or more depressions, or umbilications, are observed on the surface.

**Umbili·ciform,** *a.* *rare.* [f. L. *umbilīc-us* + -(I)FORM.] Having the form of an umbilicus; navel-like.

1893 GADOW in Newton *Dict. Birds* 239 The umbiliciform pit,..which marks the point of junction with the rhachis and hyporhachis.

**Umbili·cular,** *a.* *rare*—[1]. [f. L. *umbilīc-us* (see next) + -ULAR.] Directed towards the navel.

1883 BOODLE in *Pop. Sci. Monthly* Feb. 513 The writers who have drawn attention off mere umbilicular contemplation.

‖ **Umbilicus** (*v*mbiləi·kŏs, *v*mbi·likŏs). Pl. **-ici** (-əi·səi, -isəi). [L. *umbilīcus*: see UMBILIC *sb.*]

**1.** *Anat.* The central depression in the abdomen, marking the point of attachment of the umbilical cord; the navel.

[1615 CROOKE *Body of Man* (1631) 81 They are called *Vasa Vmbilicalia*, because they passe through the Nauell which is called *Vmbilicus*. 1693 tr. *Blancard's Phys. Dict.* (ed. 2), *Umbilicus*, the Navel, or Boss in the middle of the Abdomen, to which the Navel-string in a Fœtus is joined. 1728 CHAMBERS *Cycl.* s.v. *Abdomen*, The middle part of the Umbilical [region], is called the *Umbilicus*, or Navel.] 1799 *Med. Jrnl.* I. 422 Immediately over the left rectus muscle, at its half intersection below the umbilicus. 1834 J. FORBES *Laennec's Dis. Chest.* (ed. 4) 345 This tumour increased and extended towards the umbilicus. 1876 BRISTOWE *Th. & Pract. Med.* (1878) 650 In which case the general symmetry of the belly is maintained, but the umbilicus is usually deeply sunk.

**b.** *Bot.* The part of a seed by which it is attached to the placenta.

1837 P. KEITH *Bot. Lex.* 89 They are then nourished by means of an *umbilicus*, which we cannot but regard as an external root. 1857 M. J. BERKELEY *Cryptog. Bot.* § 108. 135 *Acetabularia* bears a whorl of threads,..seated on a delicate peduncle, with a few free-branched threads springing from the umbilicus. 1866 *Treas. Bot.* 1190/1 *Umbilicus*, the hilum of a seed; the scar formed by its separation from the placenta.

**c.** *transf.* The central point.

1897–8 G. T. STOKES *Worthies Irish Ch.* i. 5 Killare in the county of Westmeath, formerly regarded as the umbilicus of Ireland.

**†2.** (See quot.) *Obs.*

1688 R. HOLME *Armoury* II. 363/1 An Umbilicus or Navel shell..is a kind of writhen cockle or shell fish wrinkled and turned in on the top like a Navel.

**3.** *Geom.* **†a.** A focus. *Obs.*

1704 J. HARRIS *Lex. Techn.* I, *Umbelicus* in an Ellipsis, &c. is that Focus about which the Motion of any Revolving Body is made, and which it respects as its Centre. So that either Focus may be called by this Name. 1728 CHAMBERS *Cycl.* s.v. *Moon*, These smaller [planets] must move in Ellipses having their Umbilici in the Centres of the larger.

**b.** A point in a surface through which all its lines of curvature pass.

1841 J. R. YOUNG *Math. Dissert.* ii. 36 The perplexities and mistakes in the theory of umbilici. 1863 P. FROST & WOLSTENHOLME *Solid Geom.* 418 To determine the conditions for an umbilicus. *Ibid.* 420 To determine the number of umbilici on a surface of the $n^{th}$ degree.

**4.** A small depression or hollow suggestive of a navel. (Chiefly in special applications.)

**a.** *Bot.* 1809 BROWN in *Trans. Linnean Soc.* (1811) X. 36 It is not accompanied by the usual position or even uniformity in the situation of the external umbilicus. 1812 *New. Bot. Garden* I. 42 The berries are round with a depressed umbilicus. 1845 *Florist's Jrnl.* (1846) VI. 196 In the umbilicus alone, whence the flowers appear, there are a few small brown rigid setæ rather than spines.

**b.** *Ent.* 1819, 1826 [see UMBILICATED *a.* d]. 1828 STARK *Elem. Nat. Hist.* II. 380 An indistinct style inclosed in an umbilicus at its extremity.

**c.** *Zool.* 1822 J. PARKINSON *Outl. Oryctol.* 147 The substance round which the turns are formed, is on the left side of the shell, and terminates at its base; sometimes in a point, and sometimes in a hollow, which is termed an umbilicus. 1851 WOODWARD *Mollusca* I. 84 The umbilicus is small or obsolete in the typical nautili. 1890 *Science-Gossip* XXVI. 242/2 A variety of *Helix hortensis*..having..traces of white between the bands,..and white continuous over the umbilicus.

**d.** *Ornith.* 1878 DUNMAN *Gloss. Biol. Terms* (1889) 152 *Umbilicus*,..the name given to two apertures (*superior* and *inferior*) in the calamus of a bird's feather.

**e.** *Path.* *a* 1883 FAGGE *Princ. & Pract. Med.* (1886) II. 612 The cavity is 'pocketed' and shows a central depression or *umbilicus*.

**Umbisett(e, Umbith**: see UMBESET, UMBOTH.

**Umblay**: see UMB-. **Umble**, var. HUMBLE *a.*, HUMMEL. **Umblement**, *dial.*: see UMBERMENT.

**Umbles** (*v*·mb'lz). Also 5 owmlys, 6 umblys, vmblis, 7–9 (in comb.) umble-. [var. of NUMBLES: see also HUMBLE *sb.*]

**1.** The edible inward parts of an animal, usually of a deer.

14.. *Voc.* in Wr.-Wülcker 616 *Tispatum*, umbles. 14.. *Nom.* Ibid. 678 *Hoc burburium*, owmlys. *a* 1500 *For to serve a Lord* in *Babees Bk.* (1868) 377 Brawne with mustard, umblys of a dere or of a sepe. 1523 SKELTON *Garl. Laurel* 1240 The vmblis of venyson..To fayre maistres Anne that shuld haue be sent. 1558 PHAER *Æneid* v. M 2 On umbles fat they feede, and broche, and broyle. 1587 HARRISON *England* II. xix. (1877) I. 305 The ordinarie fee, and parts of the deere giuen vnto the keeper by a custome, who..hath the skin, head, vmbles, chine, and shoulders. 1616 SURFL. & MARKH. *Country Farme* 585 Fine, daintie, and tender bodies, as..Umbles, Chickens, Calves feete, or any other good thing. 1662 J. DAVIES tr. *Mandelslo's Trav.* 208 They sell the flesh of them to the Chineses,..eating themselves onely the Umbles and Paunch. 1665 PEPYS *Diary* 13 Sept., He did give us the meanest dinner, (of beef, shoulder and umbles of venison). 1725 *Fam. Dict.*, *Black Puddings*;.. the best Method to make them..is, to boil the Umbles of a Hog tender. 1741 *Compl. Fam. Piece* I. ii. 175 Take the Umbles of a Deer, parboil them, clear off all the Fat from them. 1826 SCOTT *Woodst.* iii, Where..monarchs..amused themselves with broiling the umbles, or dowsets, of the deer, upon the glowing embers.

**b.** *transf.* and *fig.* (of persons).

1536 in W. H. Turner *Select. Rec. Oxford* (1880) 137, I trust shortly to wash my hands in yᵉ umbles of yᵉ..knaves. 1611 MIDDLETON & DEKKER *Roaring Girl* III. i, A good well-set fellow, if his spirit Be answerable to his umbles. 1826 SCOTT *Woodst* xviii, I'll give them leave to give mine umbles to the kites and ravens if they find me conferring my confidence where it is not safe.

**2.** *attrib.* in *umble-pie.* (Cf. HUMBLE PIE, and *numble-pie* s.v. NUMBLES β.)

1663 PEPYS *Diary* 8 July, Mrs. Turner..did bring us an umble pie hot out of her oven. 1683 *Accomplisht Lady's Delight*, 17 A dish of fruits. 18 An umble pye. 1728 E. SMITH *Compl. Housew.* A viij, First Course..Westphalia-Ham and Chickens..Venison Pasty..Umble-Pies. 1736 BAILEY *Household Dict.* s.v., [To make] An Umble Pye. Boil the umbles of a deer till they are very tender [etc.]. 1864 LOWELL *McClellan or Lincoln?* Prose Wks. 1890 V. 158 Disguise it as you will, flavor it as you will, call it what you will, umble-pie is umble-pie, and nothing else.

**† Umblete,** var. HUMBLETE (humility). *Obs.*

1377 LANGL. *P. Pl.* B. v. 629 (MS. Rawl. Poet. 38) fol. 24 Þere aren seven ȝiftes, þat seruen treuthe euere;..þat on hatte abstinence, and vmblete an other.

**† Umblico·metry.** *Obs.*—[1] (Meaning doubtful.) Perhaps intended for *umbilicometry*, as the passage deals with methods of judging character from physical peculiarities.

1653 R. SANDERS *Physiogn.* 145 These Greeks know also *Umblicometry*, and divers others; but as for Physiognomie they place it according to this Figure.

**Umblook**: see UMB-.

**Umbly**, obs. form of HUMBLY *adv.*

‖ **Umbo** (*v*·mbo). Pl. **umbones** (*v*mbōᵘ·nīz), **umbos.** [L. *umbo, umbōnis* shield-boss, knob, projection, etc. Cf. F. *ombon* (in sense 1).]

**1.** The boss of a shield, usually in or near the centre, and sometimes having a sharp point.

1721 SWIFT *Poems, George-nim-Dan-Dean's Answ. to Sheridan* 33 Like the umbo of the Romans Which fiercest foes could break by no means. 1753 *Chambers' Cycl.* Suppl., *Umbo*, in antiquity, the round protuberant part of a shield. 1851 D. WILSON *Preh. Ann.* II. iv. 268 Many of the shields of the same period were made chiefly of wood and leather, with the central umbo of bronze. 1899 R. MUNRO *Prehist. Scot.* vii. 240 Similar relics..were associated with the iron umbo of a shield.

**2.** A projection of a round or conical form; a knob.

1753 *Chambers' Cycl.* Suppl., *Umbunculus*..was afterwards used to express the inequalities on the surfaces of flints and agates, which frequently are roundish and obtuse and represent a kind of umbones. **1832** GELL *Pompeiana* I. vi. 116 The hot-water bath..consists in a vase or tazza of white marble...In the centre is a projection, or umbo, rising from the bottom.

**3. a.** *Conch.* The point at which a univalve shell, or each valve of a bivalve shell, is most protuberant.

*sing.* **1822** J. PARKINSON *Outl. Oryctol.* 228 *Terebratula semiglobosa*:..tumid, very smooth; umbo raised, margin entirely without plicæ. **1877** SIR C. W. THOMSON *Voy. Challenger* II. i. 5 The carina is a handsome plate, very uniformly arched, with the umbo placed at the apex.

*pl.* **1824** *Q. Jrnl. Sci.* XVII. 16 The umbones, which are unusually small, have scarcely any convexity. **1849** DANA *Geol.* (1850) App. i. 699 A byssiferous canal passing out of the umbos at the margin of the shell. **1870** ROLLESTON *Anim. Life* 54 The bivalve shell of the fresh-water mussel, ..with its ligament and its umbones.

**b.** *Ent.* (See quot.)

**1826** KIRBY & SP. *Entomol.* III. 368 *Umbones* (the Bosses), two moveable bosses surmounted by a spine, with which the Prothorax of the Coleopterous genus *Macropus* is armed.

**c.** *Bot.* The knob or prominence in the centre of the pileus of a fungus.

**1836** BERKELEY *Fungi* in *Smith's Eng. Flora* V. II. 28 *Agaricus rufus*... Pileus 3 inches broad, plano-convex, slightly or strongly umbonate with a depression round the umbo as the plant advances. **1871** M. C. COOKE *Handbk. Brit. Fungi* 186 Pileus 1–2 in. broad, purple brown,..umbonate, the umbo generally subumbilicate.

**d.** *Zool.* One of the perforated ambulacral plates of echinoderms.

**1877** *Encycl. Brit.* VII. 630/1 The ambulacra..have near their outer edge small shield-like spaces, *umbones*,..perforated by pairs of small orifices or pores for the protrusion of the feet.

**4.** *Path.* A central patch in an efflorescence or other affection of the skin.

**1822–7** GOOD *Study Med.* (1829) V. 559 Efflorescence in blushing patches;..often alternately fading and reviving; sometimes with a colourless umbo. *Ibid.* 625 Even the area partakes of the vesication and becomes an umbo.

**5.** *Anat.* (See first quot.)

**1877** BURNETT *Ear* 51 The lower end of the manubrium draws the *membrana tympani* inward very markedly, and forms that depressed spot in the centre called the umbo. **1902** HUGHES & KEITH *Man. Pract. Anat.* III. 281 The membrane is concave externally, the umbo forming the deepest point of the concavity.

**Umbo, Umbois**, variants of UMBOTH *Sc. Obs.*

**Umbonal** (*v*·mbonăl), *a.* [f. L. *umbōn-*, *umbo* UMBO + -AL.] Of, belonging to, situated near, the umbo; of the nature of an umbo.

**1854** S. P. WOODWARD *Mollusca* II. 316 Shell smooth, oblong;..umbonal rib extending across the interior of the valve. **1866** R. TATE *Brit. Mollusks* ii. 12 In the interior of the shell, the following..are to be distinguished: The umbonal cavity corresponding to the umbo [etc.]. **1888** ROLLESTON & JACKSON *Anim. Life* 124 A line..drawn to the ventral margin from the centre of the umbonal region.

**Umbonate** (*v*·mbonĕt), *a.* [f. as prec. + -ATE.]

**1.** Furnished with, rising up in, an umbo or boss. Chiefly *Bot.*

**1829** LOUDON *Encycl. Plants* (1836) 987 *Agaricus asper*. ..Cap somewhat umbonate rough with acute warts. **1857** BERKELEY *Cryptog. Bot.* § 532 In the other genus [Cryptangium].., the operculum is acuminate instead of umbonate. **1887** W. PHILLIPS *Brit. Discomycetes* 393 Spermogonia .. punctiform, black, acutely umbonate.

**2.** Formed into an umbo or knob.

**1891** *Cent. Dict.*

So **U·mbonated** *a. rare*[–1].

**1752** HILL *Hist. Anim.* 127 The fine, roundish, umbonated Cochlea. **1847** WEBSTER, *Umbonated*, in botany, having a boss or elevated point in the middle.

**Umbona·tion.** *rare*[–1]. [Cf. prec. and -ATION.] A formation of the nature of an umbo.

**1872** H. C. WOOD *Fresh-Water Algæ* (1874) 101 Tubercles, obtuse or sharp simple or forked spines, hair-like processes, umbonations, &c.

**U·mbone.** Now *rare* or *Obs.* [ad. L. *umbōn-*, stem of *umbo* UMBO.]

†**1.** *Bot.* A style or pistil. *Obs.*

**1633** *Gerarde's Herbal* I. xcii. 166 Each of these floures hath six leaues,..with so many white chiues or threds, and a little blewish umbone in the midst. **1708** KERSEY, *Umbone* or *Horn*, ..any pointed Style or Head in the middle of a Flower. **1725** *Fam. Dict.* s.v. *Virginia Climber*, The Leaves are of a whitish Colour,..but the strongest Part is the Umbone, which rises in the middle. **1728** CHAMBERS *Cycl.* s.v., There is also an Umbone call'd doubly-pointed, or by-parted, as in the Peony; and sometimes the Umbone has four sharp Points.

**2.** *Conch.* = UMBO 3 a.

**1867** MURCHISON *Siluria* (ed. 4) ix. 195 Beneath the beak or umbone a small area pierced by a round foramen.

**Umbones**, pl. of UMBO.

**Umbo·nial**, *a. rare*[–1]. [Cf. UMBONAL *a.*] Of or belonging to the umbo of a shell.

**1824** *Q. Jrnl. Sci.* XVII. 16 Four series of short oblique grooves, or of indented wrinkles, three of which are arranged in a direction with the umbonial slope.

So **Umbo·nic** *a.*

**1877** HUXLEY *Anat. Inv. Anim.* viii. 473 Sometimes the umbonic cone is prolonged and bent inwards.

**Umbo·nically**, *adv. rare*[–1]. [f. L. *umbōn-*, *umbo* UMBO: cf. prec. and -AL, -LY.] In the manner of an umbo or shield-boss.

**1654** GAYTON *Pleas. Notes* IV. viii. 218 The Trunke hose, and Codpiece umbonically prominent, and significant as a Digitus Mercurialis.

**Umbo·nulate**, *a. Bot.* [ad. mod.L. *umbonulāt-us*, f. L. *umbōn-* UMBO: see -ULE and -ATE.]

**1866** *Treas. Bot.* 1190/1 *Umbonulate*, terminated by a very small boss or nipple.

†**Umboth.** *Ork. and Shetl. Obs.* Also 6 umbuth, umbo, umbuss, -bois, 9 umbith. [a. ON. *umboð* (Norw. *umbod*, Sw. and Da. *ombud*) agency, office, f. *um-* UM- + *boð* command, etc.]

**1.** Agency, procuratory, part (in affairs).

**1509** *Earldom of Orkney* (S.H.S.) 84 Schir Nycol Haucru, ..persone of Orphare, in his said fadaris umbuth. **1510** in *Scottish Jrnl. Topog.* etc. II. 88 Sir Vilȝem Sinclar..sueand for Justice Rychert Sinclar, in ye umbuss of Jhone Adesone one ye tayne part, and Vilȝam flet in h[i]s awyne umbuss on ye tother part.

**2.** (See quots. *a* 1688 and 1733.) Also *umboth duty, tithe.*

**1577** *Reg. Privy Council Scot.* II. 648 To pay the Bischoppis dewitie callit the bischoppis umbois in Zeitland, quhilk he hes in tak and assedatioun. *a* **1688** J. WALLACE *Descr. Orkney* (1693) 94 *Umboth*, the great Tiend of either half of the Parish: so called because every other year it was changed with the Minister for his half: for the word *Umboth* signifieth time about. **1733** T. GIFFORD *Descr. Zetland Islands* (1886) 56 That rent called Umboth duty, that is the bishop's rents of Zetland, for which..the bishop has the equivalent rent in Orkney. *Ibid.* The Umboth tythes are for the most part a rental tythe. *a* **1800** *MS. Acc. Lands Unst* 2 (Jam.), In the Parish of Unst, the teind of which being umboth, or free parsonage teind, is..payable to Lord Dundas,..who has right to the Bishop's reserved teinds. **1809** EDMONDSTON *Zetl. Isl.* I. iv. 163 The corn teind is divided between the minister and the proprietor of the crown rents, and the share of the latter is denominated *umbith* or *umboth* duty. **1866** EDMONSTON *Shetland Gloss.* 135.

†**Umbothman.** *Obs.* Also 5 vmbythisman. [a. ON. *umboðsmann* (nom. *-maðr*; = Norw. *umbodsmann*, Sw. and Da. *ombudsman*), f. *umboð*: see prec.] An agent or procurator.

**1482–3** in *Rec. Earldom of Orkney* (S.H.S.) 194 Andro Quhitquiysson and Jonat Mawnus..witht consent of our vmbythisman..have sauld a half penny land lyand in Wasbuster. **1557** *Ibid.* 108 Thome .. maid Villiam Corgell yongest his procuratour and umbothman, and gave him his full power to defend his landis, housis, and heritage.

‖**Umbra**[1] (*v*·mbră). Pl. **umbræ** (*v*·mbrī). [L. *umbra* shade, shadow, UMBER *sb.*[1] Cf. It. *ombra*, *ombria*, F. *ombre*.]

**1.** The shade of a deceased person; a phantom or ghost. Also *fig.*

**1599** B. JONSON *Cynthia's Rev.* Induct., The *umbræ* or ghosts of some three or four playes, departed a dozen yeeres since. **1654** GAYTON *Pleas. Notes* III. iii. 78 Such kind of Tones as these the *Umbræ* use, when they call upon Charon for a Boat. **1654** tr. *Scudery's Curia Pol.* Pref., I have not troubled their famous umbra's, whom an innocent kind of Magick hath so often summoned from their Royal Tombs. **1878** BESANT & RICE *Celia's Arb.* xi, The faint and dimly-seen ghost of a possible repentance,..a spectral umbra pointing heavenward. **1883** *Sat. Rev.* 21 Apr. 486/1 Had Lord Beaconsfield ever indulged in such rashness, his *umbra* might point out..the disaster and the disgrace which have followed on their neglect of the warning.

**b.** (See quot.)

*a* **1652** J. SMITH *Sel. Disc.* v. 176 The spiritual vehicle of the soul,..a kind of umbra or aërial mantle in which the soul wraps herself.

**2.** A mere shadow of something. In quot. *fig.*

**1634** RAINBOW *Labour* (1635) 33 The pride of those..who are their owne umbra's, the servants and shadowes of their owne reflected shadowes.

**b.** An uninvited guest accompanying one who is invited.

**1696** S. SEWALL *Diary* 7 May, And let my dear Wife and all my children partake in this priviledge, and that not as Umbras, but on their own account. **1724** MOFFET *Hesperi-neso-gr.* (1755) 9 Most of the guests their umbra's brought And sauce that money never bought. *c* **1800** R. CUMBERLAND *John De Lancaster* (1809) II. 71 Mr. David Owen and his umbra in the bottle green were missing. **1834** LYTTON *Pompeii* I. iii, The sixth banqueter, who was the umbra of Clodius,..muttered also '*Ædepol*'.

**3.** Shade; shadow.

**1638** SIR T. HERBERT *Trav.* (ed. 2) 5 To all in the temperate Zone, in the Sunnes Meridian their shadowes cast North, having past the Zenith, the shade or umbra becomes contrary. **1856** RUSKIN *Mod. Paint.* IV. v. v. § 11 If any of these wayward umbræ are faithfully remembered and set down by the painter, they nearly always have an unaccountable look.

**4.** *Astr.* **a.** The shadow cast by the earth or moon as visible in an eclipse; now *spec.* that portion in which the shadow is complete, as contrasted with the *penumbra*.

**1679** MOXON *Math. Dict.*, *Umbra*, a shadow, a word oft used in the obscuration [*sic*] of Eclipses. **1812** WOODHOUSE *Astron.* xxxv. 344 The cones of the umbra and penumbra.. formed by lines drawn from the Sun and touching the Earth's surface. **1833** HERSCHEL *Astron.* vi. 225 Owing to the great size of the earth, the cone of its umbra always projects far beyond the moon. **1868** LOCKYER *Elem. Astron.* § 237 If the Sun were a point of light merely, the shadow would be all umbra.

**b.** In sun-spots: (see quots.).

The earlier *nucleus* and *umbra* correspond respectively to the modern *umbra* and *penumbra*.

**1788** *Encycl. Brit.* (ed. 3) II. 434/2 The increase of a spot is gradual, the breadth of the nucleus and umbra dilating at the same time. *Ibid.*, Small umbræ are often seen without nuclei. **1860** OLMSTED *Mech. Heavens* x. 103 A solar spot usually consists of two parts, the nucleus and the umbra...The umbra is a wide margin, of lighter shade, and is often of greater extent than the nucleus. **1868** LOCKYER *Guillemin's Heavens* (ed. 3) 32 The spots consist almost invariably of one or several dark portions called umbræ, which seem black when compared with the luminous parts of the disk. **1878** NEWCOMB *Pop. Astron.* III. ii. 245 The shaded penumbra seems to form the sides of the cavity, while the umbra is the invisible bottom.

**5.** *Algebra.* A symbol which requires to be paired with another in order to denote a quantity.

**1851** SYLVESTER in *Lond.* etc. *Phil. Mag.* Apr. 296 Each quantity is now represented by two letters; the letters themselves, taken separately, being symbols neither of quantity nor of operation, but mere umbræ or ideal elements of quantitative symbols. **1855** RANKINE *Misc. Sci. Papers* (1881) 139 The tasinomic coefficients for oblique axes may be regarded as compounded of umbræ.

‖**U·mbra**[2]. *rare.* [L. *umbra*, perh. the same word as prec.]

**1.** The grayling; = UMBER *sb.*[2]

**1610** HOLLAND *Camden's Brit.* 627 Both these rivers are full of salmons and trouts, but Wy of the twaine is the better, affording the best kind of them which they call Vmbras. **1708** KERSEY, *Umbra*,..the Vmber, a sort of Fish. **1769** PENNANT *Brit. Zool.* III. 262 It is a very swift swimmer and disappears like the transient passage of a shadow, from whence we believe is derived the name of Umbra.

**2.** A sciænoid fish of the genus *Umbrina*, esp. the Mediterranean species *U. cirrosa*.

**1753** *Chambers' Cycl.* Suppl. s.v. **1755** *Dict. Arts & Sci.*, *Sciæna*,..this genus comprehends the umbra and the umbrino. **1854** BADHAM *Halieut.* 43 A sandy bottom, though not absolutely bad for flat fish, suits the pelagians..best; such as, e.g. auratas, the dentex, and Punic and indigenous umbras.

**Umbra**, obs. form of OMRAH.

†**Umbrace**, *v. Obs. rare.* [Alteration of EMBRACE *v.*, by substitution of UM-.] *trans.* To surround; to obtain.

*c* **1350** *St. Agatha* 101 in Horstm. *Altengl. Leg.* (1881) 46 And with fire if þou [? me] vmbraste With dew of heuin it sal be waste. **13..** *Adultery* 46 *Ibid.* 369 With schryft of mouth & penans smerte They wene þer blys forto vnbrace [*v.rr.* vmbrace, vmbras].

**Umbra·cious**, *a. rare*[–1]. [Irreg. f. L. *umbra* UMBRA[1].] Shady, umbrageous.

**1839** STONEHOUSE *Axholme* 226 Planted with elms, sycamores, and chesnuts..., which have already become very umbracious.

**Umbra·ciousness.** *rare*[–1]. [Cf. prec.] The quality of giving shade.

**1661** MORGAN *Sph. Gentry* I. viii. 109 The umbraciousnesse of the Tree he compaires to the dark life of Man, through which the Sun is not able to pierce.

†**Umbracle.** *Obs.* Also 6 *Sc.* vmbrakill, -kle. [ad. L. *umbrācul-um* shady place, etc., dim. of *umbra* UMBRA[1]. Cf. obs. F. *ombracle*, It. *ombraculo*, *-colo*, F. (bot.) *umbracule*.] Shade or shadow; a shady place.

*c* **1500** KENNEDY *Passion of Christ* 14 Haill, beyme to skaill of ded þe dirk vmbrakill! *Ibid.* 1312, 1395. **1500–20** DUNBAR *Poems* lxxxv. 20 Quhilk king ws bring vnto his ryng, Fro dethis dirk vmbrakle. **1609** J. DAVIES (Heref.) *Holy Roode* Wks. (Grosart) I. 15/1 That Tree (that Soule-refreshing Vmbracle Together with our Sinne) His shoulders teares. **1653** R. MASON in Bulwer *Anthropomet.* Let. to Author, Here were the Alleys and umbracles of his ordinary recesses.

**Umbra·culate**, *a. Ent.* [ad. mod.L. *umbrāculāt-us*, f. L. *umbrācul-um*: see prec.] (See quot.)

**1826** KIRBY & SP. *Entomol.* xlvi. IV. 307 *Umbraculate*.., when there is upon the head an umbrella-shaped process.

**Umbraculi-**, the stem of L. *umbrācul-um* sunshade (see UMBRACLE), employed in the botanical adjs. **umbraculi·ferous**, **umbra·culiform** [F. (bot.) *umbraculiforme*]: (see quots.).

**1847** WEBSTER, *Umbraculiform*, having the form of an umbraculum or arbor. **1857** A. GRAY *First Less. Bot.* 235 *Umbraculiform*, umbrella-shaped, like a Mushroom, or the top of the style of Sarracenia. **1862** MAYNE *Med. Voc.* 422 *Umbraculiferus*,..*Bot.*, formed like a parasol: umbraculiferous.

**Umbrage** (*v*·mbrĕdʒ), *sb.* Also 7–9 ombrage. [a. OF. *umbrage*, *ombrage* (F. *ombrage*), = Pr. *umbratge*:—L. *umbrāticum*, *-icus*, f. *umbra* shadow.]

†**1.** Shade, shadow. *Obs.*

**1426** LYDG. *De Guil. Pilgr.* 22310 The party off my vysage Whiche is clowded with vmbrage, Off cleernesse scholde haue no reporte. **1513** DOUGLAS *Æneid* XIII. Prol. 40 All the bewtie of the fructuus feyld Was wyth the erthis vmbrage clene ourheild. **1544** BETHAM *Precepts War* I. cci. I vij b, The lyghte, and also..the false vmbrage whych the Moone doth shewe fourthe. **1616** DRUMM. OF HAWTH. *Poems* II. (S.T.S.) I. 65 Deare amber Lockes gaue Vmbrage to her Face. **1654** tr. *Scudery's Curia Pol.* 129 If we be worsted in our nocturnall and more secret attempts, the darknesse will give an umbrage, and obscure our shame. **1655** F. G. tr. *Mlle. De Scudery's Artamenes* IV. II. 83 The Sun setting that Evening without any cloudy umbrage, it might almost be said that the Sun-beams did guild the whole Countrey. **1687** NORRIS *Coll. Misc.*, *Ode to Darkness* v, The Blest above do thy sweet umbrage prize. When Cloy'd with light, they veil their eyes.

**b.** *transf.* and *fig.* (Very common in the 17th c.)

*a.* *c* **1642** *Observ. his Majesty's late Answ. & Expresses* 18 To look into termes a little more narrower, and dispell umbrages. **1663** *Aron-bimnucha* 30 Those Clouds and Umbrages that did eclipse and darken the glory of the Gospel. **1684** HOWE *Redeemer's Tears* Wks. 1862 II. 269 A mind led..to transmit through a dark umbrage some glimmerings only of that excellent majesty which his Sonship..entitled him to. **1711** SHAFTESB. *Charac.* (1737) III. 322 Great Mysterys,..so wrap'd in Clouds, or hid in Umbrages,..that they may seem to have been left as Trials of our Industry. **1727** A. Hamilton *New Acc. E. Ind.* I. xxiii. 279 [To] live.. under the Badge and Umbrage of Ignominy and Shame. *a* **1763** Shenstone *Progr. Taste* II. 102 And o'er her charms with caution shown, Be still a graceful umbrage thrown.

*β.* **1660** Milton *Free Commw.* 448 Kingship, though looking big, yet indeed most pusillanimous,..startl'd at every Ombrage. **1669** Temple *Lett.* (1701) II. 65 To suspect that it was Artificial, and only intended to give an Ombrage or false Light to the Court of Sueden.

**2.** *spec.* Shade or shadow cast by trees or the like.

*α.* **1540–1** Elyot *Image Gov.* xxi. (1544) 38 b, The sayd trees gaue a commodyous and plesant vmbrage. *Ibid.* xxii. 42 Which trees did cast ouer the walles a pleasant vmbrage or shadowe. **1664** Evelyn *Sylva* vi. 24 [Ash-trees are] not to be planted for Umbrage, or Ornament; especially neer the Garden. **1665** Sir T. Herbert *Trav.* (1677) 115 The boughs..so circle the bole or trunk that it resembles an arch'd circumference affording umbrage and refreshment to some hundred men. **1675** Evelyn *Terra* (1676) 94 All shade is not unpropitious, where the Soil and Climate are benign, as well as that which casts the umbrage. **1757** Dyer *Fleece* I. 399 Accustom'd to the barriers of the rick, Or some warm umbrage. **1849** C. Bronte *Shirley* xiii, Often..she would spend a sunny afternoon in lying stirless on the turf, at the foot of some tree of friendly umbrage. **1865** A. Raleigh in *Rec. Life* xi. (1881) 138 We had crept up slowly through the leafy woods, and all at once we emerged from the umbrage and stood upon the hill-top. **1888** R. Buchanan *City of Dream* VIII. 171 The steed sprang on across the golden glade and plunged into the umbrage suddenly.

*β.* **1604** R. Cawdrey *Table Alph.*, *Ombrage*, shade, harbor, or bower to rest vnder. **1866** J. B. Rose tr. *Ovid's Met.* I. 447 On sounding pinions Cupid sped his flight To the deep ombrage of Parnassus' height.

**b.** Const. *of*, or with possessives.

**1596** R. L[inche] *Diella* (1877) 22 Where vnder vmbrage of some aged Tree, With lute in hand I sit. **1667** Milton *P. L.* IX. 1087 In some glade Obscur'd, where highest Woods impenetrable To Starr or Sun-light, spread thir umbrage broad. **1677** Plot *Oxfordsh.* 159 Under the umbrage of which Tree.. no less than 324 horses, or 4374 men, may sufficiently be shelter'd. **1708** J. Philips *Cyder* I. 141 They run To Grots, and Caves, and the cool Umbrage seek Of woven Arborets. **1772** S. Whyte *Poems* (1795) 186 In the brown umbrage of the wood, If lonely you retire. **1793** *Minstrel* II. 109 The heat increasing, the deep umbrage of the forest invited her into its closest paths. **1830** J. G. Strutt *Sylva Brit.* 118 Branches..spreading their umbrage to the circumference of two hundred and seven feet. **1875** Miss Braddon *Strange World* i, Two figures are seated.. beneath the umbrage of an ancient thorn.

**c.** The foliage of trees, etc., affording shade.

**1657** Tomlinson *Renou's Disp.* Pref. b ij, Here you may view.. the pleasant Umbrages sporting with Zephyrus-Nectar-Blooms. **1659** Hammond *On Ps.* cxxviii. 3 Olive-plants..were usually planted (as in arbours) to shade the table, entertainments being made without doors, in gardens, under that umbrage. **1727–46** Thomson *Summer* 626 Beside the dewy border let me sit,..There in that hollow'd rock, grotesque and wild,..and over head By flowering umbrage shaded. **1767** Jago *Edge-hill* I. 357 Beneath their waving Umbrage Flora spreads Her spotted Couch. **1789** E. Darwin *Bot. Gard.* I. (1791) 207 Delighted Thames through Tropic umbrage glides, And flowers antarctic, bending o'er his tides. **1811** Shelley *St. Irvyne* xi, The tall ash and oak, in mingled umbrage, sighed far above their heads. **1833** Lytton *Godolphin* xv, Then abruptly they rose, overspread with thick and tangled umbrage, several feet above the level of the river. **1885** Buchanan *Annan Water* ix, In one corner was an arbour almost buried in umbrage.

*transf.* **1739** R. Bull tr. *Dedekindus' Grobianus* 222 Mustachio's, far beyond the vulgar Size; O'er all thy Mouth their hairy Umbrage spread. **1828** Wordsw. *Triad* 188 Her brow hath opened on me—see it there, Brightening the umbrage of her hair.

*fig.* **1822** De Quincey *Confess.* II. 81 The calamities of my noviciate in London.. shot up and flourished afresh, and grew into a noxious umbrage that has overshadowed and darkened my latter years. **1871** Tyndall *Fragm. Sci.* (1879) I. xviii. 462 The light of law was for a time obscured by the thick umbrage of novel facts.

**3.** A shadowy appearance or indication, a semblance, outline, or faint representation, a glimmering or trace, *of* something. Now *rare*. (Common in 17th c.)

*α.* **1604** Shaks. *Ham.* V. ii. 125 (Q. 2), His semblable is his mirrour, & who els would trace him, his vmbrage, nothing more. **1644** Bulwer *Chirol.* 143 The arme shadowes out the second Person in the Trinity...The fingers give an umbrage of the Holy Spirit. **1686** Plot *Staffordsh.* 417 There yet remains some umbrage of a Dean and Prebends here to this very day. **1756** in *Palatine Note-book* (1881) I. 118/2 His whole Life.. may be look'd upon as an Umbrage of Troubles and Perplexities among vexatious Neighbours. **1856** Faber *Creator & Creature* II. i. (1886) 110 Joys angelical..are all but a manifold umbrage of the one joy of God.

*β.* **1640** Howell *Dodona's Grove* 30 It will breed scruples and ombrages of doubts in her confederats. **1652** — *Giraffi's Rev. Naples* II. 57 The people had shrewd ombrages of fear that he came to no good purpose.

†**b.** Without const.: An appearance or semblance. *Obs.*

**1639** Fuller *Holy War* V. xxv. 272 Some of them [*sc.* essays] being umbrages and State-representations rather than realities. **1649** Jer. Taylor *Gt. Exemp.* II. viii. 78 A penitent is not taken with umbrages and appearances, nor quits a reall good for an imaginary. **1678** Marvell *Growth Popery* Wks. 1875 IV. 395 It looks and gives an umbrage as if what he was to do was by your leave. **1680** De Britaine *Hum. Prud.* ii. 5 But Wise-men cannot be content to be abused with Umbrages, nor is the World any longer to be entertained with Dark Lanthorns.

†**c.** In emphatic or intensive use, with *all*, *any*, *even*, *the least*, etc. *Obs.*

*α.* **1649** Fuller *Just Man's Funeral* 10 The very umbrage of Religion hath a sovereign virtue in it. **1668** Earl Orrery in *St. Lett.* (1743) II. 340 To avoid even the umbrages of suspicion. **1675** V. Alsop *Anti-Sozzo* 556 Our Author,.. without any umbrage of a pretence from the Text,.. has laid them in saltire. **1703** Bp. T. Wilson in Keble *Life* v. (1863) 192 That so all umbrage of arbitrary government may be removed. *a* **1734** North *Examen* II. v. § 139 (1740) 402 Let any one see in that extended Sum of the Evidence..if there be the least Umbrage of a Reflection upon this Accident. **1737** [S. Berington] *Mem. G. de Lucca* (1738) 35 To take off all Umbrage of Jealousy, I give you leave to sell him to some honourable Person for a Slave.

*β.* *c* **1645** Howell *Lett.* (1650) I. 75 They parted for that time without the least ombrage of discontent. **1650** — *Giraffi's Rev. Naples* I. 17 Hereupon the Vice-Roy went unto them to take off all ombrages of distrust. **1692** Beverley *Conciliatory Disc.* 19 Thus are the Secrets of all Hearts, judged according to the Apostles Gospel...Some Ombrage of which Heathens have.

†**d.** A figure or type. *Obs.*

**1657** W. Morice *Coena quasi Κοινὴ* xvi. 297 Sometime they think hereticks set forth under the umbrage of Tares.

†**4.** A feeling of suspicion or doubt. *Obs.*

*α.* **1624** Bacon *Consid. War with Spain* (1629) 8 I say iust feare,..not out of vmbrages, light iealousnesse, apprehensions a farre off, but out of cleare foresight of imminent danger. **1639** Fuller *Holy War* I. ix. (1840) 15 Though umbrages and light jealousies..be too narrow to build a fair quarrel on. **1656** Heylin *Extraneus Vapulans* 63 He took some time to consider of it,..for removing of all such umbrages and misapprehensions, as otherwise that interparlance might have occasioned.

*β.* **1604** Bacon *Apol.* 27 And therefore good my Lord carie it so, as you take away by all meanes all ombrages and distasts from the Queene. *c* **1645** Howell *Lett.* VI. i. (1650) 180 Ther were som ombrages, and not only so, but open and actuall differences.

†**b.** A suspicion, hint, inkling, or slight idea, *of* a matter. *Obs.*

**1654–66** Earl Orrery *Parthen.* (1676) 800 They neuer had the least umbrage of the Truth. **1697** Dampier *Voy.* (1729) I. 310 We..found no Canoas, or People, that might give us any umbrage of a City, or place of Trade near at hand. *a* **1734** North *Examen* I. iii. § 59 (1740) 160 Nor is it less remarkable that such Preparations of Fleets, Transports, Armies,..were to be dispatched..and no Neighbour Nation jealous, nor England (so near) haue any Intelligence or Umbrage of it.

†**c.** A reason or ground for suspicion, or for some opinion. *Obs.*

**1664** Jer. Taylor *Dissuas. Popery* I. x. 70 S. Peter did not carry himself so as to give the least overture or umbrage to make any one suspect he had any such preheminence. **1673** *Lady's Call.* II. ii. § 3 Therefore they must be nicely careful to give their husbands no color, no least umbrage for it [*sc.* jealousy]. **1704** *Lond. Gaz.* No. 4054/1 Every Man..did his Duty, without the least Umbrage for Censure or Reflection. **1737** L. Clarke *Hist. Bible* (1740) II. 288 But there is not the least umbrage for such a conjecture to be found in the scripture. **1760–72** tr. *Juan & Ulloa's Voy.* (1807) I. 6 All umbrage would be thus removed from persons who might not be sufficiently acquainted with the nature of their design.

†**5.** Shelter, protection, screen. *Obs.*

**1607** Day *Trav. Eng. Bro.* Ded. (1881) 3 Wee our selues should haue a safe harbor and vmbrage for our well willing yet weake labours. **1658** R. Franck *North. Mem.* Ded. (1694) p. iv, In this Dilemma I left the University to seek Umbrage in the City of London. **1698** J. Fryer *Acc. E. India & P.* 98 Humble Suiters for the Umbrage of any of Quality, to skreen them from this Violence. **1730** T. Gent *Hist. York* Pref. p. iii, So that it flies to the Umbrage of the courteous Reader, to be favourable in its Reception. **1740** S. Richardson in *Corr.* (1804) I. p. lxxvi, I therefore ..struck a bold stroke,..having the umbrage of the Editor's character to screen myself behind.

†**b.** In the phr. *under the umbrage of*. *Obs.*

The material sense in quot. 1741 is unusual.

**1677** W Hubbard *Narrative* Pref., The Historicall discourse ensuing might pass into publick view under the umbrage of your Protection. **1683** W. Rogers *Scourge for G. Whitehead* 10 Whitehead, now sinking in his Reputation, ..seems to shelter himself under the Umbrage of W. P. **1709** Mrs. Manley *Secret Mem.* (1720) III. 207 A Prince.. is still answerable for all the Evil he suffers others to commit under the sacred Umbrage of his Name. **1741** A. Hill in *Richardson's Corr.* (1804) I. 71 Little Harry Campbell.. had been listening all this while upon the floor, under the umbrage of a pair of out-strutting hoops. **1776** P. Oliver in *T. Hutchinson's Diary*, etc. (1886) II. 109, I entered the House of Lords under the umbrage of Lord Polworth.

†**6.** A pretext or pretence; a colour or false show. *Obs.*

**1634** Bp. Hall *Contempl. N. T.*, *Christ before Pilate*, It is al the care of hypocrites to seek umbrages, and pretences for their hatefull purposes. **1662** Hickeringill *Apol. Distressed Innoc.* Wks. 1716 I. 272 Veiling the Murder with the Umbrage of Devotion and Justice. *a* **1693** Ld. Delamer *Wks.* (1694) 107 Truth will appear from under all the false glosses and umbrages that men may draw over it. **1706** *Phil. Trans.* XXV. 2416 So convincing an Experiment as this, which..leaves no manner of umbrage for any other Hypothesis to take place in it.

†**b.** In the phr. *under the umbrage of*. *Obs.*

Slight differences of usage are represented in the different groups of quotations.

(*a*) **1674** *Case of Bankers & Creditors* Pref. 3 This grievance of ours hath been represented to his Majesty under the pretence and umbrages of Royal Prerogative. **1681** Hickeringill *Sin Man-Catching* Wks. 1716 I. 174 [Villains] that commit the greatest Rapacities..under the umbrage, pretence and colour of Law and Justice. **1696** C. Leslie *Snake in Grass* (1697) 90 Otherwise, they may commit Theft, Sacrilege, and all other Immoralities under this Umbrage. **1727** A. Hamilton *New Acc. E. Ind.* II. xlvii. 176 To make him accuse rich Men,..that he might seize their Estates under the Umbrage of Justice and Law. **1735** Bolingbroke *On Parties* (ed. 2) viii. 87 To form a Party, and maintain a Struggle for personal Power, under the Pretence and Umbrage of Principle.

(*b*) **1679** J. Smith *Narr. Popish Plot* 30 Under the Umbrage of Repairing a College, they were providing for the Ruine of a Kingdom.

(*c*) **1709** Sacheverell *Serm.* 5 Nov. 9 Should we cover such a False Apostle under the Sacred Umbrage of a True Church-Man? **1720** Gordon & Trenchard *Independ. Whig* (1728) 284 Under the Colour and Umbrage of Significant and decent Ceremonies, the most ridiculous and immodest Usages have been introduced. **1723** Dk. Wharton *True Briton* I. 234 Under the Umbrage of Adorers, [they] make themselves Masters.

†**7.** *To be*, or *to stand, in* (..) *umbrage*, to be in disfavour. *Obs.*

*a* **1635** Naunton *Fragm. Reg.* (Arb.) 31 On the fall of the Duke he stood some yeers in umbrage, and without imployment. **1647** Clarendon *Hist. Reb.* II. § 102 Being suspected at least a Favourer of the Papists,..by which he was in great umbrage with the People. *a* **1649** Drumm. of Hawth. *Hist. Jas. V*, Wks. (1711) 110 He knew Sir James stood in some umbrage with the King.

**8.** Displeasure, annoyance, offence, resentment: **a.** In the phr. *to give* (..) *umbrage* (*to* a person or persons).

**1620** Brent tr. *Sarpi's Hist. Council Trent* I. 28 He.. therefore besought them to take away all those words that might give him any Vmbrage. **1668** Dryden *Evening's Love* IV, It will not be convenient to give him any umbrage, by seeing me with another person. *a* **1700** Evelyn *Diary* 5 May 1686, Which dispensation..gave umbrage (as well it might) to every good Protestant. **1740** Somerville *Hobbinol* I. 242 Be thou, my Muse! No leaky Blab, nor painful Umbrage give To wealthy Squire. **1771** J. Fletcher *Checks* Wks. 1795 II. 8 How often do men sneakingly forsake their friends, for fear of giving umbrage to a superior party or interest. **1796** Washington *Let.* Writ. 1892 XIII. 263 Unless my pacific disposition was displeasing, nothing else could have given umbrage by the most rigid construction of the letter. **1842** H. Rogers *Ess.* (1874) I. i. 5 The sermon, when printed, gave great umbrage to the parliamentary party. **1869** Rawlinson *Anc. Hist.* 314 Both Antiochus and Seleucus..abstained from any proceedings that could give umbrage to their new subjects.

**b.** In the phr. *to take* (..) *umbrage* (*at*; also without const. or with clause).

(*a*) **1680** Fountainhall *Chronol. Notes* (1822) 5 The Bishop ..took umbrage at his freedom of speech in the pulpit anent the government. **1683** Temple *Mem.* Wks. 1720 I. 439 The Allies had taken great Umbrage at my Journey to the Hague. **1725** De Foe *Voy. round World* (1840) 300 If any opposition should be offered them in the country, or any umbrage taken at their design. **1759** Robertson *Hist. Scot.* VIII. Wks. 1813 II. 49 James himself, though he prudently concealed it, took great umbrage at her behaviour. **1796** Mme. D'Arblay *Camilla* x. xiv, However, as to his having called me a blockhead, it's not what I take umbrage at. **1827** Hallam *Const. Hist.* v. (1876) I. 284 We find no mention of any umbrage being taken at certain strains of prerogatives. **1862** Kingsley *A. Locke* Pref. p. v, Many of them..have taken umbrage at certain scenes of Cambridge life drawn in this book. **1883** Sir T. Martin *Ld. Lyndhurst* ix. 231 A less kindly-tempered man..would have taken umbrage at the tone of this letter.

(*b*) **1723** *Present State of Russia* I. 197 The subjects of the Can of Schirvan began to take Umbrage. **1748** Smollett *R. Random* xi, Fearing the captain and his lady would take umbrage, and leave his carriage. **1813** Scott *Rokeby* III. xxi, Our stout Knight..Took umbrage that a friend so near Refused to share his chase and cheer. **1841** D'Israeli *Amen. Lit.* (1867) 594 Many close at hand took umbrage lest they themselves were being supplanted.

**c.** In other constructions.

**1724** R. Wodrow *Corr.* (1843) III. 140 They all have your case very much at heart, and all the umbrage is over. **1768** H. Walpole *Hist. Doubts* 23 Whether the steps taken by the queen gave them new cause of umbrage. **1856** Lever *Martins of Cro' M.* xx, A very good-natured laugh from the others showed how little umbrage the frank avowal excited.

**Umbrage** (*v*·mbrėdʒ), *v.* Also 7 **ombrage.** [f. prec., or ad. F. *ombrager*, *-ier*, † *umbrager*, *-ier*, f. *ombrage*: see prec. Cf. also It. *ombreggiare*.]

**1.** *trans.* To shade or shadow; also *fig.*, to overshadow, put in the shade.

*α.* **1647** Hexham I, To Vmbrage or shadow, *beschaduwen*. **1658** Jas. Webb tr. *Calprenède's Cleopatra* VIII. 93 A man ..whose valour umbraged theirs, and whose words they had found so true to their confusion. **1738** [G. Smith] *Cur. Relat.* I. iv. 465 They were separated from one another with Rails, and umbraged with a Sort of Canopy. **1804** Anna Seward *Mem. Darwin* 123 Rude gives an idea of barrenness, and Matlock is luxuriantly umbraged. **1888** *Harper's Mag.* April 733/2 A ridge or hillock heavily umbraged with the rounded foliage of evergreen oaks.

*β.* **1648** Hexham II, *Omschaduwen*,..to Shaddowe About, or to Ombrage. **1652** F. Kirkman *Clerio & Lozia* 16 His Hat was ombraged with a plume of black Herons Feathers.

†**2.** To colour over, disguise. *Obs.*[−1]

**1675** R. Burthogge *Causa Dei* 312 If she mentioned others, it was by way of caution, only to secure her self, and Umbrage what she said that it might down the better.

†**b.** To give a pretext or ground for. *Obs.*[−1]

**1689** Hickeringill *Modest Inquiries* 35 Like that young Gallant, studying what he should see in her [*sc.* an old woman] to Vmbrage the fondness of his Embraces.

**3.** To offend, displease. *rare.*

*a* **1894** Stevenson *St. Ives* xxiv, May I help myself to wine without umbraging you.

Hence **U·mbraged**, **U·mbraging** *ppl. adjs.*

**1663** Sir G. Mackenzie *Religious Stoic* i. 12 Intimating thereby that umbrag'd silence was an excellent Shryn for sincere devotions. **1683** Pettus *Fleta Min.* I. Ded., They are divulged either by umbraging Sophistications, or concealed under the Name of Philosophical Secrets. **1890**

*Lippincott's Mag.* May 667 A park, a wood, an umbraged lane.

**Umbrageous** (ʌmbrēⁱ·dʒəs), *a.* Also 6–8 umbragious, 7, 9 ombrageous (7 -ious). [ad. F. *ombrageux* (OF. also *-eus*), f. *ombrage* (see UMBRAGE *sb.*); or directly f. UMBRAGE *sb.* + -OUS.]

**1. a.** Forming or affording shade; shady.

**1587** A. DAY *Daphnis & Chloe* (1890) 69 First ranne hee to the foot of a hie and umbragious rocke. **1614** GORGES *Lucan* II. 63 Where these vmbragious mountaines stand. **1675** EVELYN *Terra* (1676) 93 Lastly, by shade Ground is render'd barren, and by the dripping of umbragious trees. **1725** POPE *Odyss.* VI. 149 Where the grove with leaves umbrageous bends, With forceful strength a branch the Heroe rends. **1790** *Phil. Trans.* LXXX. 351 Their tops are so very thick and umbrageous as to prevent even a very heavy rain from reaching the ground underneath. **1826** SCOTT *Woodst.* x, The towers of Woodstock arose high above the umbrageous shroud which the forest spread around the..mansion. **1846** J. BAXTER *Libr. Pract. Agric.* (ed. 4) I. 99 A handsome umbrageous tree, with a smooth bark, and shining leaves. **1873** SYMONDS *Grk. Poets* x. 310 Oaks with their umbrageous foliage..belong to the forests of the North.

**b.** Abounding in shade; shaded by trees or the like; overshadowed.

**1612** DRAYTON *Poly-olb.* xxii. 1619 Those past times..When as that woody kind, in our umbrageous wild,..In this their world of waste, the sovereign empire sway'd. **1632** LITHGOW *Trav.* iii. 81 A secure place of repose in a vmbragious Caue. **1666** HARVEY *Morb. Angl.* 215 Walk daily in a pleasant, airy, and umbragious Garden. **1742** GRAY *Propertius* III. 3 Fast by th' umbrageous vale lull'd to repose, Where Aganippe warbles as it flows. **1774** R. CUMBERLAND in *Westm. Mag.* II. 148 No cooling Grottoes, no umbrageous Groves, To win the Graces, and allure the Loves. **1811** SHELLEY *St. Irvyne* xi, The umbrageous loveliness of the surrounding country. **1846** HAWTHORNE *Mosses* I. i. 13 It makes us shiver to think of these deep umbrageous recesses. **1891** FARRAR *Darkn. & Dawn* lvi, Everyone should wander at will about the green copses, and the umbrageous retreats.

**c.** Caused by thick foliage.

**1830** J. G. STRUTT *Sylva Brit.* 54 The religious Mahometans chose to pray under old trees,..piously believing that the holy men of former times had prayed and meditated under their umbrageous shade. *a* **1854** J. WILSON in *Casquet of Lit.* (1896) V. 178/2 Dew and dreams dropping through their umbrageous twilight at eve or morn.

**2.** Of persons: Suspicious; jealous; apt or disposed to take offence.

α. **1601** R. JOHNSON *Kingd. & Commw.* 169 The inhabitants, ..partly by their forme of gouernment, whereby they are made vile, base and vmbragious, haue little valour or manhood left them. **1652** J. WRIGHT tr. *Camus' Nat. Paradox* III. Argt. 48 The King made jealous of the Queen, shee no less umbragious of him, and both for Iphigenes. **1758** WARBURTON *Div. Legat.* Pref., Of which, doubtless, the Romans were very jealous,..though not so extravagantly umbragious as our Critic's hypothesis obliges him to suppose. **1768** HURD in Warburton *Lett.* (1809) 425 Both susceptible of high passions in love and friendship; but, of the two, the Italian more constant, and less umbrageous. **1846** GROTE *Greece* II. vi. II. 503 The rural costume..which the Helot commonly wore, and the change of which exposed him to suspicion, if not to punishment, from his umbrageous masters. **1874** SYMONDS *Sk. Italy & Greece* (1898) I. vi. 107 The people are idle, haughty, umbrageous, fiery, quarrelsome [etc.].

β. **1630** DONNE *Serm.* lv. (1640) 557 At the beginning some men were a little ombrageous, and startling at the name of the Fathers. **1803** [? SIR L. HANSON] *Hist. Acc. Orders Knighth.* II. 306 More punctilious with respect to forms and Ceremonies: and excessively ombrageous, with regard to the Non-observance of trivial points.

**b.** Of disposition or nature.

*c* **1639** WOTTON *Let. Sir. E. Bacon* in *Reliq.* (1672) 430 But lest you should mistake, as some others have been apt to do here, in the present constitution of the court (which is very ombragious). **1652** J. WRIGHT tr. *Camus' Nat. Paradox* XII. 321 Let your rigour execute mee..all that your umbragious or Cholerick humour can suggest. **1667** G. DIGBY *Elvira* I. i, What power meer appearances have had..to destroy, With an umbragious nature, all that Love Was ever able..To found and to establish.

†**3.** Obscure; dubious. *Obs.*

**1635** J. REYNOLDS *God's Revenge* III. xiii. 256 That there was none other present but himselfe when his Master De Merson was murthered, it is umbragious, and leaves a..sting of suspition in their heads. *a* **1649** DRUMM. OF HAWTH. *Hist. Jas. II*, Wks. (1711) 24 By umbragious Ways he nourished Discontentments in all Parts of the Country. **1651** H. L'ESTRANGE *Answ. Mrq. Worcester* 61 We blesse God for the light they had, though umbrageous and clouded, yet was it such as discovered the nakednesse and shame of the Church of Rome.

Hence **Umbra·geously** *adv.*; **Umbra·geousness.**

**1639** DRUMM. OF HAWTH. *Mag. Mirror* Wks. (1711) 175 He had Intention to bring Novations into our Religion; tending *umbrageously, and under a Mask, to the Introduction of Popery. **1834** AINSWORTH *Rookwood* I. i, One tree..outflings..its arms umbrageously. **1614** RALEIGH *Hist. World* I. iv. § 3. 69 The exceeding *umbragiousnesse of this tree he compareth to the darke and shadowed life of man. **1755** JOHNSON, *Shadiness*,..umbrageousness. **1823** *Examiner* 106/2 Trees..spreading sideways with Asiatic grace and umbrageousness. **1837** *Blackw. Mag.* XLI. 512 A face incapable of a blush, partly from the umbrageousness of the whiskers. **1871** *Daily News* 28 July, The familiar umbrageousness of Croydon.

†**Umbraid,** *sb. Obs.* Forms: 4 vmbreyd, 4–5 vmbreide, 5 vm-, vnbreid; 5 vmbrayd(e, vnbraide. [var. of UPBRAID *sb.*: cf. next.] Upbraiding, reproach.

*c* **1330** R. BRUNNE *Chron. Wace* (Rolls) 3485 Wiþ suche vm reides þey hem missayde. *Ibid.* 7999 When wraþe bygynneþ, þen comeþ vmbreyd. *a* **1400–50** *Alexander* 1800 (Dubl. MS.), Lett neuer it be broght on brade for vmbrayd of shame, Þhe dout for þe dityng of darius pistell. *a* **1425** *Cursor M.* 5673 (Trin.), Moises for þis vmbreide Was dredinge in his herte. *a* **1470** HARDING *Chron.* CLIV. iv, He..letters sent hym, defyals and vmbrayde, Of hys suraunce and othe that he had erred.

†**Umbraid,** *v. Obs.* Forms: 4 vmbreyde, -breide, 5 vmbreid; 4–5 vmbraide, 5–6 vmbrayde (6 um-), 5 vmbrayed, 6 vmbrayd, -braid, -brade; 5 vnbrayd(e, -braide. [Alteration of UPBRAID *v.*, under the influence of verbs in UM-.] *trans.* To upbraid, reproach.

*c* **1330** R. BRUNNE *Chron. Wace* (Rolls) 8004 3yf þou me vmbreyde, þe schame ys þyn. **1390** GOWER *Conf.* II. 296 If so be that he him umbreide Of oght that hath be speke or do. *a* **1400** *Sir Beues* (S.) 2417 Thow shalt neuer vmbraide me, When þou comest hoom to my contre. **1432–50** tr. *Higden* (Rolls) III. 81 Then the suster of that Oracius.. vmbraydede here brother for the sleenge of here howsebonde. *c* **1450** *Mirk's Festial* 132 Þes þat..be vsed to swere horrybull oþys by Godys sydys and his blod, and vmbrayden God of his passyon. *c* **1489** CAXTON *Sonnes of Aymon* xvi. 377 Many tyme he hath vnbrayd vs therof. **1530** PALSGR. 766/1 What though he have done a mysse, it was nat thy parte to umbrayde hym. **1557** EDGEWORTH *Serm.* Repert., Fastinge..in the rogation weke is vmbrayded and mocked of noughty lyuers. **1597** J. PAYNE *Royal Exch.* 24 Manie a good Christian have bene no less vmbraded and reproched.

Hence †**Umbrai·ding** *vbl. sb. Obs.*

**1597** J. PAYNE *Royal Exch.* 15 Men love better gentle admonitions then bytter vmbradings.

**Umbral** (ʌ·mbrăl), *a.* [f. UMBRA[1] + -AL.]

**1.** *Algebra.* Based on the use of umbræ in notation; consisting of umbræ.

**1851** SYLVESTER in *Lond.* etc. *Phil. Mag.* Apr. 297 My system of umbral or biliteral notation. **1852** — in *Cambr. & Dubl. Math. Jrnl.* VII. 78 *note*, The umbral method of denoting such a function. **1893** CAYLEY *Math. Papers* (1897) XIII. 306 It does not appear that there is any monomial umbral expression for the last-mentioned form.

**2.** *Astr.* Pertaining to the umbra of sun-spots or eclipses.

**1867–77** G. F. CHAMBERS *Astron.* 7 *note*, The umbral structure [of a sun-spot] is quite complete, and made up of sunken banks of filaments. **1879** NEWCOMB & HOLDEN *Astron.* 286 The observations consisted in measuring the relative amounts of umbral, penumbral, and photospheric radiation. **1885** AGNES M. CLERKE *Pop. Hist. Astron.* 201 Vapours which are dispersed over the unbroken solar surface are accumulated in the umbral cavity.

**3.** *Geol.* The special designation of a series of rocks occurring in Pennsylvania.

**1858** H. D. ROGERS *Geol. Pennsylv.* I. 144 The Umbral Series contains, in Pennsylvania, but one formation—the Umbral Red Shale...Its prevailing character, which is that of a dark-brownish red shale and red sandstone, it steadily maintains throughout its range.

Hence **U·mbrally** *adv.*

**1852** SYLVESTER in *Cambr. & Dubl. Math. Jrnl.* VII. 87 Express *H* umbrally under the form [etc.]. **1853** — in *Phil. Trans.* CXLIII. 429 The determinants thus umbrally represented.

†**Umbra·na, -a·no,** app. ad. It. *umbrina*: see UMBRINA.

**1607** BEAUM. & FL. *Woman-Hater* I. i, Is the Umbranoes head as we commanded, sent to the sad Gondarino, our General? *Ibid.* I. ii, For the Dukes own Table, the head of an Umbrana.

†**Umbrary.** *Obs.*[—1] [Cf. UMBRERE, and obs. F. *ombraire* umbrella (Cotgr.).] Visor.

*c* **1442** *Chron. London* (ed. Nicholas, 1827) 130 In brekynge of his gauntelette and reysyng of his umbrary [*MS. Cleop. C. iv.* umbray].

†**Umbrate,** *a. Obs.* [ad. L. *umbrāt-us*, pa. pple. of *umbrāre*: see next.]

**1.** Shady; umbrageous.

**1501** DOUGLAS *Pal. Hon.* I. Prol. 40 The vmbrate treis that Tytan about wappit War portrait..Be goldin bemis.

**2.** *Her.* = UMBRATED *a.*

**1572** BOSSEWELL *Armorie* II. 25 b, But yet in my iudgement, they myghte alwayes (with conuenient differences) haue borne the same whole, and not vmbrate.

†**Umbrate,** *v. Obs.* [f. ppl. stem of L. *umbrāre* (whence It. *ombrare*, F. *ombrer*), f. *umbra* UMBRA[1]. Cf. the earlier *adumbrate*, *obumbrate*.]

**1.** *trans.* To shadow. Also *fig.*

**1623** COCKERAM, *Vmbrate*, to shadow. *c* **1630** RISDON *Surv. Devon* § 42 (1810) 48 Instead of *lux fiat*, it may be verified that they are umbrated thereby.

**2.** To adumbrate, indicate.

**1675** J. SMITH *Chr. Relig. Appeal* II. viii. 84 The Gospel ..exhibits to us the Substance of the Law's Types; wherein the things pertaining to the Person, Office, and Kingdom, of the Messias, were umbrated.

**U·mbrated,** *a. Her.* Also 7 umbreted. [See prec. and -ED[1]. So F. *ombré*.] Indicated or drawn in a faint or shadowy manner.

**1486** [see UMBRATION 1]. **1562** LEGH *Armory* 79 He beareth Or, a Lion Saliaunte vmbrated. This is as muche to saye, as the shadowe of a Lion;..he is but traced with a pencell. vpon the fielde. So that the fyelde sheweth throwghe him. **1572** BOSSEWELL *Armorie* II. 25 This crosse so vmbrated is thus to be blazed. A. beareth Or, a crosse Moloyne Vmbre. **1610** GUILLIM *Heraldry* II. iii. 42 The portraicting out of any thing umbrated, is nothing else but a sleight and single draught or purfle traced out with a pensile, expressing to the view a vacant forme of a thing deprived of all substance. **1688** HOLME *Armoury* IV. viii. (Roxb.) 354/1 Morholt de Irland. A. Barry vmbreted ouer all a Lion rampant G. *c* **1828** BERRY *Encycl. Her.* I. Gloss. s.v., A sun umbrated does not show the face as it is usually represented.

**Umbratic** (ʌmbræ·tik), *a. rare.* [ad. L. *umbrātic-us* staying in the shade, f. *umbra* UMBRA[1]. So Sp. and Pg. *umbratico*, It. *ombratico*, F. *ombratique*, † *umbratique*.]

**1.** Shadowy, foreshadowing.

*a* **1677** BARROW *Serm.* (1683) II. xxvii. 386 By virtue wherof those..umbratick representations..did obtain their substance, validity and effect.

**2.** Confined to the shade or to retirement; retired, secluded.

**1839** DE QUINCEY in *Tait's Mag.* VI. 364 The torpid dreams of what the Romans called an umbratic experience.

†**Umbra·tical,** *a. Obs.* [f. as prec. + -AL.]

**1.** Remaining in retirement or seclusion.

**1636** B. JONSON *Discov.* Wks. (1641) 94 So I can see whole volumes dispatch'd by the umbraticall Doctors on all sides. **1656** COLLOP *Poesis Rediv.* 18 On the Umbraticall Doctors on the Romish party.

**2.** Serving as a shadow or imperfect representation of something.

**1633** AMES *Agst. Cerem.* II. 219 If all umbraticall rites be Iudaicall, and therefore unlawfull, then all religious significant Ceremonies are Iewish and unlawfull. **1633** BP. HALL *Hard Texts, N. T.* 333 Whose service was altogether umbraticall and typical, shadowing and representing heavenly things. **1683** *Case of Inf.-Baptism* 24 The purging and cleansing Virtue in their Blood..was also but a faint and umbratical resemblance of the more noble and efficacious cleansing Virtue of his Blood.

**3.** Serving as a disguise or cloak.

**1662** HIBBERT *Body Div.* II. 122 Ye have learned..not to be guided by the ostentation or umbratical shews of any plausible tongue.

Hence †**Umbra·tically** *adv. Obs.*

**1683** *Case of Inf.-Baptism* 25 It never did Umbratically initiate Believers, or Umbratically, and in shew and Similitude only, confirm the Covenant.

**Umbratile** (ʌ·mbrătəil, -il), *a.* and *sb.* [ad. L. *umbrātil-is* keeping in the shade, private, retired, etc., f. *umbra* UMBRA[1]. So It. *umbratile*, *ombratile*, Pg. *umbratil*, F. *ombratile*, † *umbratile*.]

**A.** *adj.* **1.** † **a.** Spent within doors. *Obs.*[—1]

**1592** BACON *Confer. Pleasure* (1870) 24 A health..that hath not ben softened by an vmbratill life still vnder the rooffe.

**b.** Carried on in retirement or seclusion; not public or practical.

**1640** BP. REYNOLDS *Passions* xxxix. 511 The same speech may be excellent in an umbratile Exercitation, which would be too pedanticall, and smelling of the Lampe in a matter of serious and weighty debate. **1840** *British Critic* XXVIII. 370 Christianity..was not once that umbratile thing, that feeble exotic, shut up in churches, parsonages and parlours. **1845** M. PATTISON *Ess.* (1889) 3 A time of peace and security tends to foster an umbratile and academic science.

**c.** Staying or living in the shade or withindoors; recluse, retiring.

**1850** *Tait's Mag.* XVII. 431/2 Umbratile spectators may inquire what ought to be done. **1888** DOUGHTY *Arabia Deserta* II. 29 The third brother..was an umbratile young man, and very fanatical. **1898** L. JOHNSON in *Post Liminium* (1911) 207 Octavius the 'umbratile', quiet man was content with a miniature immortality.

**2.** Of, belonging to, or resembling a shadow or shadows.

**1632** B. JONSON *Magn. Lady* III. iii, Shadows have their figure, motion, And their umbratil action, from the real Posture and motion of the body's act.

**b.** Of a shadowy nature; unsubstantial; unreal. Now *rare* or *Obs.* (Common in 17th c.)

**1647** H. MORE *Song of Soul* Notes 337 But this life that we live disjoyned from God is but a shadow, and umbratil imitation of that. *Ibid.* 433 A kind of an umbratil vitalitie that the soul imparts to the body in the enlivening of it. **1656** JEANES *Fuln. Christ* 131 Body is opposed unto shadowes; and so a bodily inhabitation unto an umbratile. **1678** CUDWORTH *Intell. Syst.* 854 As themselves are juniors,..so are their effects..but slight, ludicrous and umbratil. *a* **1706** EVELYN *Hist. Relig.* (1850) I. p. xxvii, All we have of precious and worthy our solicitude in this umbratile and transitory passage. **1806** KNOX *Corr.* (1834) I. 290 As far as thought could proceed, without feeling,..the umbratile, without the real apprehension,—few men could outdo him.

†**c.** Serving as a token or type. *Obs.*[—1]

**1663** J. SPENCER *Prodigies* (1665) 199 The honor of being received at least as the umbratile Sign and Coming of the Son of Man.

**3.** Giving shade; shady.

**1659** GAYTON *Art Longevity* 79 Under a Sycamore Which with umbratile leaves will let no Sun Hurt your Silk-gown. **1866** BLACKMORE *Cradock Nowell* lxiii. (1883) 439 His hat was umbratile, as of the Pilgrim Fathers.

†**4.** Of colour: Shaded, dark. *Obs.*[—1]

**1678** *Phil. Trans.* XII. 949 Appearing sometimes of a more flourishing colour tending to Carnation; and sometimes more umbratile.

**B.** *sb.* One who spends his time in the shade.

**1888** DOUGHTY *Arabia Deserta* I. 248 Many thus are umbratiles in the booths, and give themselves almost to a perpetual slumber.

†**Umbra·tilous,** *a. Obs.* [f. as prec. + -OUS.] Shadowy, unreal; faint.

**1637** IRONSIDE *Seven Quest. Sabbath* To Rdr. B iij b, Least thou shouldst perhaps think I affected a Sciomachy or Umbratilous skirmish. **1640** G. WATTS tr. *Bacon's Adv.*

*Learn.* III. iv. 165 The handling of Finall Causes in the Physiques..hath given men occasion to rest satisfied in such specious, and umbratilous Causes. 1669 W. SIMPSON *Hydrol. Chym.* 273 An humane embryo..without sexual discrimination, onely an umbratilous figuration of the microcosme.

† **Umbration.** *Obs. rare.* [ad. L. type **umbrātio*, f. *umbrāre*: see UMBRATE *v.* So It. *ombrazione*.]

**1.** *Her.* A faintly outlined figure; = ADUMBRATION 4.

1486 *Bk. St. Albans, Her.* c viij, Another sampull is sene of the vmbracion of a certayn cros, and thys cros is calde a cros floree vmbratid;..bot truly spekyng and propurli it is no cros, bott a shadow of such a cros.

**2.** A shadowy indication or faint representation (*of* something).

*a* 1706 EVELYN *Hist. Relig.* (1850) I. 192 Which, though resembling, are yet but faint shadows and umbrations of that sublime nature. *Ibid.* 241 Nor all this by transient and superficial knowledge, figures, and umbrations, but immediate and intuitive notices.

† **Umbratious,** *a. Obs.*⁻¹ [Irreg. f. UMBRACE *sb.*] Suspicious.

*a* 1639 WOTTON *Parall. Essex & Buckhm.* in *Reliq.* (1651) 11 He was to wrastle with a Queens declyning, or rather with her very setting Age,..which..is commonly even of it selfe the more umbratious and apprehensive.

**Umbrave, -brawe, -braye,** obs. ff. OMRAH.

**Umbre** (*v*·mbəɪ). Also umber. [ad. L. *umbra* or F. *ombre* shade, shadow, after mod.L. *umbretta*, F. *ombrette*, Brisson's name for the bird.] An African bird (*Scopus umbretta*) with deep-brown plumage; the hammerhead or African crow. (Cf. UMBRETTE.)

1773 PENNANT *Gen. Birds* 44 Umbre. Bill, strong, thick, strait, compressed, the upper mandible composed of several pieces. 1785 LATHAM *Gen. Synop. Birds* III. I. 30 Tufted Umbre...Size of a Crow...The bill is three inches and a half in length. 1819 STEPHENS *Shaw's Gen. Zool.* XI. II. 636 Crested Umbre, with the whole body fuscous. 1848 *Maunder's Treas. Nat. Hist.* 716/1 The Crested Umbre (*Scopus umbretta*)..is..of an umber colour, and the male is crested. 1890 *Sat. Rev.* 1 Feb. 139/2 The umbre..feeds upon fish and frogs, worms, snails, and insects.

**Umbre,** obs. variant of OMBRE, UMBER *sb.*

† **Umbrel** [1]. *Obs.* Also 6 -ell. [ad. OF. *ombrel* shade: cf. UMBRERE.] The visor of a helmet.

[1437 in Meyrick *Ant. Armour* (1824) II. 127 Arma in primis v galee cum v umbrellˢ et iiii ventells.] *c* 1470 *Lydgate's Chron. Troy.* III. 1636 (MS. Digby 230), With his swerde so myȝtely [Ulysses] gan race Thoruȝ þe vmbrel in to Troylus face. 1530 PALSGR. 285/1 Umbrell of an heed pece, *uisiere.*

† **Umbrel** [2]. *Obs.* [Anglicized f. UMBRELLA; in first quot. ad. F. *ombrelle.*]

**1.** = UMBRELLA 1.

1603 FLORIO *Montaigne* III. ix. 583 These Vmbrels or riding canapies, which since the ancient Romanes, the Italians vse, doe more weary the armes, then ease the head. 1617 MORYSON *Itin.* III. 21 In hot regions, to avoid the heat of the sun in some places (as in Italy) they carry Umbrels, or things like a little canopy over their heads. 1694 D'URFEY *Don Quixote* I. 9 Thou shouldst walk in the Streets with thy Train held up, and two Embroidered Laqueys holding an Umbrel over thee.

**2.** (See quot.)

1688 HOLME *Armoury* III. 271/1 Antiquity did ever set forth the Virgin Mary after this form with her Umbrel or Shady Hat.

**Umbre·ll,** dial. f. UMBRELLA 2.

1857 WAUGH *Lanc. Life* 31 Aw've no moor use for a book nor a duck has for a umbrell. 1883 *Harper's Mag.* May 845/1 Better take this umbrell, hadn't ye?

**Umbrella** (*v*mbre·lă). Also 7 umbrellia, umbrilla. *β.* 7–9 umbrello (7 vn-), 7 vmbrillo, 8 umbrellow. *γ.* 7–8 ombrella. [ad. It. *ombrella* and *ombrello*, f. *ombra*:—L. *umbra* shade, UMBRA [1]. Cf. F. *ombrelle*, Sp. *umbrela* (zool.).]

**1.** A light portable screen or shade, usually circular in form and supported on a central stick or staff, used in hot countries as a protection for the head or person against the sun.

*α.* 1611 CORYAT *Crudities* 111 Many of them doe carry other fine things..which they commonly call in the Italian tongue 'umbrellaes'...These are made of leather something answerable to the forme of a little caunopy and hooped in the inside with divers little wooden hoopes that extend the umbrella in a pretty large compasse. 1668 DAVENANT *Man's the Master* II. i, A very desperate man..coming near so bright a Sun as you are without a Parasol, Umbrellia, or a Bondgrace. 1695 MOTTEUX *St. Olon's Morocco* 148 An Umbrella was carry'd over me, which in some manner defended me from the Heat of the Sun's Rays. 1716 GAY *Trivia* I. 213 Let Persian dames th' umbrella's ribs display, To guard their beauties from the sunny ray. *a* 1739 JARVIS *Don Quix.* I. I. iv, They carried umbrellas, and were attended by four servants on horseback. 1797 HOLCROFT tr. *Stolberg's Trav.* (ed. 2) III. lxxxix. 479 The heat began so early in the day that, at six o'clock, we were obliged to use our umbrellas. 1832 G. DOWNES *Lett. Cont. Countries* I. 341 The costume is very picturesque in this part of Tuscany, always excepting the monstrous yellow umbrella, which is part and parcel of it. 1850 EMERSON *Cond. Life, Culture* Wks. (Bohn) II. 373 In the city of Palermo, the street was in a blaze with scarlet umbrellas. 1875 JOWETT *Plato* (ed. 2) III. 103 He sees the rich man under an umbrella puffing and panting.

*β.* 1610 W. STRACHEY in Purchas *Pilgrims* (1625) IV. 1739 So broad are the leaves [of palms] as an Italian *Vmbrello.* 1611 COTGR., *Ombrelle*, an Vmbrello; a (fashion of) round and broad fanne, wherwith the Indians (and from them our great ones) preserue themselues from the heat of a scorching Sunne. 1662 J. DAVIES tr. *Mandelslo's Trav.* II. 138 Of the leaves they make sayles;..they make of them likewise Umbrelloes, Fans, Tents, Mats and Hats. 1697 DAMPIER *Voy.* (1699) 407 The Chinese..when they walk abroad..carry a small Umbrello in their Hands, wherewith they fence their Head from the Sun or the Rain. 1697 *Lady's Trav. Spain* (1706) 249 He commanded them to bring Umbrellos to defend us from the Sun. 1753 HANWAY *Trav.* II. xlii. I. 286, I observed that the Persians are not cautious..of the sun in any degree equal to the Portugueze; for the last seldom travel without a cloak and umbrello. 1755 SMOLLETT *Quix.* I. I. iv. I. 21 Six merchants of Toledo..who travelled with umbrelloes.

*γ.* *c* 1620 MORYSON *Itin.* IV. v. i. (1903) 442 Then followes the Duke in his Robes,..a Scudiero carying his ombrella betweene him and the sunne. 1710 C. SHADWELL *Fair Quaker Deal* IV. 40 Your Baubles of China, your Indian Ombrella, your Hair-Ring, and your own Picture.

**b.** In some Oriental and African countries used as a symbol of rank or state.

*α.* 1682 *Lond. Gaz.* No. 1721/4 In the Evening he visited his Highness Prince Rupert, to whom he presented the two great Umbrella's. 1718 *Entertainer* No. 16. 109 To score out a Pattern of Umbrella's for the King of Bantam. 1727 A. HAMILTON *New Acc. E. Ind.* II. xxxvi. 45 King of the White Elephant, and of the twenty four Somereroes or Umbrellaes. 1745 P. THOMAS *Jrnl. Anson's Voy.* 201 Mandarines..accompanied with all the Officers of their Tribunal, who surround them with Umbrella's and other Marks of their Dignity. 1849 LAYARD *Nineveh* I. x. 337 He is attended by two eunuchs, one holding the umbrella, the other his quiver and mace. 1888 *Times* 30 Oct. 6/1 The Shereefian Umbrella does not pass necessarily from father to son.

*β.* 1653 H. COGAN tr. *Pinto's Trav.* xxxiv. 135 Then next to them marches twelve men on horsback, called *Peretandas*, each of them carrying an Umbrello of carnation Sattin. 1678 J. PHILLIPS *Tavernier's Trav.* II. II. viii. 123 Upon each side of the Throne are plac'd two Parasols, or Umbrellos, the handles whereof are about eight foot high. 1688 HOLME *Armory* IV. xi. (Roxb.) 431/2 Then 24 Vnbrello's richly adorned and them as carry them 2 and 2 together. 1719 J. T. PHILLIPS *Thirty-four Confer.* 331 Women..attended him with Umbrello's,..and all the other Court Employments within Doors were all done by Women. 1745 ELIZA HEYWOOD *Female Spect.* No. 18 (1748) III. 301 Twelve stout Indians carried a canopy of yellow and green silk, under which all the royal family walked:—the rest had umbrelloes, supported by their own particular slaves.

**2.** A portable protection against bad weather, made of silk or similar material fastened on slender ribs, which are attached radially to a stick and can be readily raised so as to form a circular arched canopy.

*α.* 1634 SIR T. HERBERT *Trav.* 149 A Shagg or Yopangee which riding serues [in Persia] as an Vmbrella against raine. 1716 GAY *Trivia* I. 211 Good houswives..underneath th' umbrella's oily shed, Safe thro' the wet on clinking pattens tread. 1765 H. WALPOLE *Let. to J. Chute* 3 Oct., Servants..walk about the streets in the rain with umbrellas to avoid putting on their hats. 1787 *Phil. Trans.* LXXVII. 291 If the weather be rainy, an insulated umbrella may be carried in one hand. 1833 COL. HAWKER *Diary* (1893) II. 52 It poured with rain, and my umbrella broke all to pieces. 1856 EMERSON *Eng. Traits, Manners* ¶ 6 An Englishman walks in a pouring rain, swinging his closed umbrella like a walking-stick. 1882 MISS BRADDON *Mt. Royal* I. i. 34 She always carried her stout little umbrella, winter or summer.

*β.* 1697 [see 1 *β*]. 1704 SWIFT *T. Tub* xi, A large Skin of Parchment..served him for a Night-cap when he went to Bed, and for an Umbrello in rainy Weather. 1709 W. KING *Art of Love* 99, I might have made you such a fellow, As should have carry'd my Umbrello, Or bore a flambeau by my chair. 1731 *Phil. Trans.* XXXVII. 32 An Umbrello, suspended by a Packthread tied to the Handle of it, became strongly Electrical. 1732 *Inventory Sir R. Sutton's Goods* 7 Four Umbrellows.

**3.** Used in comparisons or similes, esp. with reference to shape.

*α.* 1616 B. JONSON *Devil an Ass* IV. iv, I saw i' the Court of Spaine once, A Lady fall i' the Kings sight, along. And there shee lay, flat spred, as an Vmbrella. 1630 DRAYTON *Muses Elizium* (1892) 15 Doues..Which..shall..like Vmbrellas with their feathers Sheeld you in all sorts of weathers. *a* 1680 BUTLER *Rem.* (1759) II. 99 Hats..With broad Brims sometimes like Umbrellas, And sometimes narrow as Punchinello's. 1726 SHELVOCKE *Voy. round World* (1757) 66 On this bank, or shoal, we saw great numbers of Clubbers appearing, like the tops of umbrellas. 1726 J. HOBSON *Diary* 8 Oct., in *Yorks. Diaries* (Surtees) 258 Out of all..came pyramidicall streams of light,..forming such a figure as a ladies' umbrella. 1796 WITHERING *Brit. Plants* (ed. 3) III. 646 The florets diverging from the centre, spreading outwards and downwards like an umbrella.

*β.* 1710 STEELE *Tatler* No. 116 ¶ 1 An engine of several legs, that could contract or open itself like the top of an umbrello. 1740 L. WHYTE *Dissert. Fashions* 66 Erst have I seen a little fellow, With Hat as large as Vmbrellow; It was the Mode for young and old.

† **4.** *fig.* **a.** A means of shelter or protection.

*α.* 1609 DONNE *Lett.* (1651) 63 We have an earthly cave, our bodies, to go into by consideration, and cool our selves; and..we have within us a torch, a soul, lighter and warmer than any without: we are therefore our own umbrella's and our own suns. 1624 FLETCHER *Rule a Wife* III. i, Is your heart at rest, Now you have got a shadow, an umbrella To keep the scorching worlds opinion From your fair credit. 1648 J. RAYMOND *Il Merc. Ital.* Pref. 1 A weather beaten Traveller needs no such Umbrilla as a Patron to shroud under. *a* 1734 NORTH *Examen* I. ii. (1740) 89, I have been, perhaps, too long in exposing the Author for holding up an Umbrella to keep his Earl in a Shade.

*β.* 1652 H. L'ESTRANGE *Amer. no Jewes* To Rdr., No other dedicatory Umbrello do I seek..to defend this work from the scorch of censure. 1670 PHILIPOT *Antiq. Hierol. & Gent.* Ded., This Treatise implores your Patronage as an Umbrello to over-shadow it. 1690 *Secr. Hist. Chas. II & Jas. II*, 112 The popular gentlemen were only made use of as Umbrello's to shade the conspirators from the scorching heat of the people's discontent.

† **b.** A screen or disguise. *Obs.*

1623 T. SCOTT *Tongue-Combat* 80 Yorke, Patton, and Symple, with many others, who may haue Dispensations for their Oathes, and Vmbrilloes for their humours. 1653 JER. TAYLOR *Serm. for Year* I. vi. 77 We shall dishonour the sufferings of our blessed Saviour, if we make them to be a Umbrello to shelter our impious and ungodly living. 1658 OSBORNE *Mem. Jas. I*, 45 Those brainsick fooles as..made Religion an Umbrella to impiety.

**5.** Anything serving as a protection or shelter from the sun, rain, etc.

1654 WHITLOCK *Zootomia* 403 How do they lessen the stately wonders of the Eye, into Cottages (I may say Snaile-like Umbrellos) meer shades, and Dormitorys. 1674 C. F. *Wit at a Venture* 38 Shroud the Sun, and let each tree To her a kind umbrella be. 1701 WOLLEY *Jrnl. New York* (1860) 25 Nature kindly..shelters it with the umbrella's of all sorts of Trees from pernicious Lakes. 1718 OZELL tr. *Tournefort's Voy.* I. 66 To skreen themselues from the sun, they haue no other way but to make a sort of Umbrella of their Handkerchief. 1838 BARHAM *Ingol. Leg.* Ser. I, *Witches' Frolic* (1905) 99 The straggling yew, His leafy umbrella, was wet through and through; Rob was half dead with cold. 1907 *Westm. Gaz.* 9 Feb. 2/2 Here and there a stone-pine with its great umbrella of dark foliage cast a more impenetrable shade.

† **b.** A sun-blind. *Obs.*

1687 MIÉGE *Gt. Fr. Dict.* II. s.v., To have an Umbrello before his Window to keep off the Sun [Fr. *un Paillasson*]. 1706 PHILLIPS (ed. Kersey), *Umbrello*,..a Wooden Frame cover'd with Cloth or Stuff, to keep off the Sun from a Window. 1709 MRS. MANLEY *Secret Mem.* I. 33 The Weather violently Hot, the Umbrelloes were let down from behind the Windows, the Sashes open.

**6.** A structure resembling in shape an outspread umbrella, or serving for protection against something.

1680–4 DINGLEY *Hist. from Marble* (Camden Soc.) p. xxxix, The Umbrello in yᵉ Bath was erected and leaded by Mr. Coo. 1719 D'URFEY *Pills* II. 125 Tho' at Cales they scap'ed our Guns, By strong wall'd umbrello. 1742 B. LANGLEY *Anc. Archit. Restored* Plate xxxi, The work contains several designs for Umbrellos, by which term the author indicates a roofed structure with open sides to be placed at the termination of a walk in a garden. 1844 H. H. WILSON *Brit. India* III. 51 A spire surmounted by a Tee or umbrella of open iron-work. 1883 GRESLEY *Gloss. Coal-m.* 266 *Umbrella* [= *Bonnet*, the overhead cover of a cage or swinging bont]. 1904 *Daily Chron.* 26 Oct. 4/5 It requires a pretty good umbrella of a trench to protect men from this death-shower.

**b.** Anything which temporarily or permanently has the form of an umbrella.

*c* 1770 *Art of Angling* 48 in Ruddiman *Coll.* (1773) 277 But mine is not the glory to unfurl The net's umbrello, with Herculean whirl. 1846 J. BAXTER *Libr. Pract. Agric.* (ed. 4) I. 106 The feathery-like points of the down..uniting together form a kind of inverted umbrella. 1866 E. C. RYE *Brit. Beetles* 225 The larvæ in this family have an ingenious but unpleasant habit of forming their excrement into an umbrella, as in *Crioceris*. 1885 *Pall Mall G.* 11 Mar. 11/1 The araucaria forests..fringing the tops of the hills..with delicate, long stilted umbrellas.

**c.** A broad-brimmed hat.

*a* 1803 C. L. LEWES in *Mem.* (1805) I. 25 A large slouched beaver umbrella, that wanted only a crape hatband to sanctify it for a funeral.

**7. a.** *Bot.* A part of a plant resembling an outspread umbrella.

1658 SIR T. BROWNE *Gard. Cyrus* iii. 47 Elegant clusters of Dragons..with an *umbrella* or skreening Leaf about them. 1712 tr. *Pomet's Hist. Drugs* I. 6 The Flowers grow in Umbrellos on the Tops of the thick Branches. 1809 *Naval Chron.* XXII. 493 The cap of a mushroom, which M. P...names umbrella.

**b.** *Zool.* The gelatinous disk or bell-shaped structure of a jelly-fish.

1834 GRIFFITH tr. *Cuvier* XII. 482 *Medusa* have a disk more or less convex above, similar to the head of a mushroom, and to which the name of *umbrella* has been given. 1861 J. R. GREENE *Man. Anim. Kingd., Cœlent.* 38 In the umbrella of the *Lucernaridæ*, both vesicles and pigment-spots seem to become united into a single organ. 1881 E. R. LANKESTER in *Jrnl. Microsc. Sci.* Jan. 122 The manubrium of Limnocodium is a somewhat quadrangular tube, which depends during life below the margin of the umbrella.

**c.** *Conch.* A limpet-like gastropod of the genus *Umbrella*; also the part of the shell resembling an open umbrella.

1841 *Penny Cycl.* XXI. 217/2 Umbrella with a flattened shell; the disk of the lower surface not radiated. 1861 P. P. CARPENTER in *Rep. Smithsonian Instit. 1860*, 230 The shell..entirely covers the animal; which..can move its long neck freely under its large umbrella. *Ibid.* 234 The Umbrellas are very large creatures, wearing a flat limpet on the middle of the back.

† **8.** *White umbrella*, the elder-tree. *Obs.*⁻¹

1658 SIR T. BROWNE *Gard. Cyrus* iii. 47 The white umbrella or medicall bush of Elder, is an Epitome of this order.

**9.** *attrib.* and *Comb.*, as *umbrella-case, -cover, covering, frame, -silk, -stand, -stick, -trade*; *umbrella-bearer, -maker, -mender*; *umbrella-shaped, -topped* adjs.; *umbrella-wise* adv.

1852 BONOMI *Nineveh & Palaces* (1853) 176 The king..is accompanied by his charioteer and *umbrella-bearer. 1891 KINNS *Graven in Rock* xvi. 599 In the left hand of the umbrella-bearer is an object like a fan or fly-trap. 1850

THACKERAY *Pendennis* lvii, His despatch-boxes and *umbrella-cases, his guide-books, passports, maps, and other elaborate necessaries of the English traveller. **1888** *Encycl. Brit.* XXIII. 723/1 In 1848 William Sangster patented the use of alpaca as an *umbrella covering material. **1837** HEBERT *Engin. & Mech. Encycl.* II. 829 *Umbrella frames of the usual construction. **1793–4** *Matthews's Bristol Directory*, Ashbury, William, *Umbrella-maker, Hope Square, Hotwells. **1813** *Examiner* 31 May 350/2 She has given 'mirth' to nobody except it be the ducks and the umbrella-makers. **1884** *Harper's Mag.* Feb. 375/1 An umbrella-maker had established his open-air shop. **1848** DICKENS *Dombey* iii, The summer sun..came with the water-carts and the old clothes-men,..and the *umbrella-mender. **1796** WITHERING *Brit. Plants* (ed. 3) I. 387 Capsule cylindrical, sitting on a hollow nearly globular or *umbrella-shaped receptacle. **1837** P. KEITH *Bot. Lex.* 298 The pileus or cap is the conical or umbrella-shaped organ that surmounts the stipe of the Agarics. **1862** ANSTED *Channel Isl.* II. ix. (ed. 2) 239 The umbrella-shaped body of this animal. **1888** *Encycl. Brit.* XXIII. 723/1 *Umbrella silk is principally made at Lyons and Crefeld. **1862** *Catal. Internat. Exhib., Brit.* II. No. 6061, Fenders, fire-irons, hat and *umbrella stands. **1879** MEREDITH *Egoist* xxv, He stepped to the umbrella-stand. There was then a general question whether Clara had taken her umbrella. **1875** KNIGHT *Dict. Mech.* 2679/1 In preparing an ordinary *umbrella-stick, it passes through 19 separate processes or movements. **1850** R. G. CUMMING *Hunter's Life S. Afr.* (1902) 61/1 Some friendly grove of *umbrella-topped mimosas. **1835** *Penny Cycl.* IV. 446/1 The *umbrella trade arose from the demand for the brass furniture of these useful contrivances. **1725** *Fam. Dict.* s.v. *Elder-Tree*, Its Flowers grow somewhat like Roses at the Tops of the Branches 'Umbrella or Parasole-wise.

**b.** In names of plants or trees, denoting 'shaped like, resembling, an umbrella', as *umbrella acacia, bush, -fir, grass, leaf, palm, -pine, -plant, -wort.*

**1882** *Garden* 11 March 166/3 The *Umbrella Acacia.. forms a dense globular head, which is certainly very conspicuous. **1889** MAIDEN *Useful Pl.* 363 *Acacia Oswaldi*,.. often called *Umbrella Bush, as it is a capital shade-tree. **1884** MILLER *Plant-n.* 247/2 *Sciadopitys*, *Umbrella-, or Parasol-, Pine or Fir. *Ibid.* 58/1 *Umbrella Grass. *Fuirena squarrosa* and *Panicum decompositum*. **1898** MORRIS *Austral Eng.* 487/1 It is called Umbrella-grass, from the shape of the branches at the top of the stem representing the ribs of an open umbrella. **1866** *Treas. Bot.* 412/1 The only species, *Diphylleia cymosa*, a native of Japan, and of the southern United States, is there called the *Umbrella Leaf. **1798** NEMNICH *Allg. Polyglotten-Lex.* II. 928 *Umbrella palm. *Corypha umbraculifera*. **1884** MILLER *Plant-n.* 210/1 *Kentia Canterburyana*, Umbrella Palm. **1873** HEMSLEY *Handbk. Trees & Shrubs* 435 *Sciadopitys verticillata*, *Umbrella-Pine. A large evergreen tree from 50 to 150 feet high. **1893** G. ALLEN *Scallywag* I. 141 Among the rosemary bushes and the scanty umbrella-pines. **1874** *Treas. Bot.* Suppl. 1350/1 *Umbrella-plant, *Saxifraga peltata*. **1829** LOUDON *Encycl. Plants* (1836) 36 *Calymenia*. *Umbrella-Wort. **1852** JOHNSON *Cottage Gard. Dict.* 671/2 *Oxybaphus*, Umbrella-wort.

**c.** In names of birds, etc., as *umbrella-ant, -bird, chatterer, shell, snake.*

**1883** W. FARREN *White Ants* vi. 61 In some ant colonies more than two distinct forms of workers are found. I may instance the Saüba, or *Umbrella ant of Brazil. **1891** *Cent. Dict.*, *Umbrella-ant*, a parasol-ant or leaf-carrying ant. **1850** A. R. WALLACE in *Ann. & Mag. Nat. Hist.* (1851) Ser. II. VIII. 429 The *Umbrella Bird is about the size of a crow. **1863** BATES *Nat. Amazon* II. iv. 283 The rare and curious Umbrella bird (*Cephalopterus ornatus*);..decorated with a crest of long, curved, hairy feathers having long bare quills, which, when raised, spread themselves out in the form of a fringed sun-shade over the head. *Ibid.* II. vi. 387 Birds and monkeys, in this glorious forest, were very abundant,..the *Umbrella Chatterer and curl-crested Toucans amongst the most beautiful of the birds. **1861** P. P. CARPENTER in *Rep. Smithsonian Instit. 1860*, 234 Family *Umbrellidæ*. (Chinese *Umbrella Shells.) **1881** *Cassell's Nat. Hist.* V. 226 The 'Chinese Umbrella-shell' has a small depressed Limpet-like shell, marked by concentric lines of growth. **1904** *Westm. Gaz.* 23 April 2/3 The natives call it Mtaba, or the *umbrella snake.

**10.** Special Combs., as **umbrella gingham**, gingham employed for covering umbrellas; **umbrella hat**, a hat similar in size or shape to an umbrella; **umbrella man**, (*a*) one who mends or sells umbrellas; (*b*) a street-vendor who displays his wares in an inverted open umbrella; **umbrella print-seller**, = prec. (*b*); **umbrella roof**, an arched roof resembling an umbrella; **umbrella sail**, a sail constructed partly on the principle of an umbrella; **umbrella tent**, a tent made on the umbrella principle; **umbrella warping** *Naut.* (see quot.).

**1834** *Tait's Mag.* I. 72/2 *Umbrella ginghams have remained steady for some time. **1817** COLERIDGE *Biog. Lit.* (1907) II. 150 Dutch women with large *umbrella hats shooting out half a yard before them. **1851** MAYHEW *Lond. Labour* I. 303 I learned from one '*umbrella man' that, six or seven years previously, he used to sell more portraits of 'Mr. Edmund Kean, as Richard III.', than of anything else. **1889** *Belgravia* Sept. 333 The umbrella-man..stopped beside a stile and put down his bundle of umbrellas. **1851** MAYHEW *Lond. Labour* I. 303 Sometimes, too, an '*umbrella print-seller' will have a few 'pictures in frames', on a sort of stand alongside the umbrella. **1847** LEITCH tr. *C. O. Müller's Anc. Art* § 106 (1850) 74 The Odeion also, a smaller theatre with an *umbrella roof, received its form at Athens. **1900** *Pearson's Mag.* Aug. 143 The *umbrella sail can be set or furled in a minute; it does not close up as does an umbrella, but each side shuts up like a fan. **1895** *Army & Navy Co-op. Soc. Price List* 15 Sept. Index p. lxxv, *Umbrella Tents. *Ibid.* 449 The Umbrella Garden Tent with Sloping Walls. **1867** SMYTH *Sailor's Word-bk.* 705 **Umbrella-warping*, a contrivance similar to an umbrella, by which ships in a calm can be warped ahead.

**Umbre·llaed**, *ppl. a.* [f. prec. + -ED [1].]

**1.** Protected or covered as by an umbrella. Also *fig.*

*c* **1800** SOUTHEY *Inscriptions* xvi. *Under An Oak* (1854) 100 This ancient oak Will parasol thee if the sun ride high, Or, should the sudden shower be falling fast, Here mayst thou rest umbrella'd. **1858** H. W. BEECHER *Life Thoughts* 142 Many..believe that they must come to Him [*sc.* God] under the covert of some apology, or beneath some umbrellaed excuse. **1885** W. P. BREED *Aboard & Abroad* 127 The landscape lovingly umbrellaed by smiling clouds that took turns in the task of keeping the direct sunbeams from our faces.

**2.** *Ornith.* (See quot. and cf. UMBRELLA 9 c.)

*a* **1807** SHAW *Nat. Misc.* XXI. pl. 897 The Umbrella'd Ampelis...Black Ampelis, with the vertical crest and pendent breast-feathers glossed with violet. The Umbrella'd Chatterer. *Cephalopterus ornatus*.

**3.** Provided with an umbrella or umbrellas.

**1834** *Tait's Mag.* I. 42/1 Who in their senses might hope to escape the drench?..umbrellaed or umbrellaless they must have it. **1863** *Morn. Star* 21 May, When the umbrellaed multitude swarmed down the centre of the course, the effect was most extraordinary. **1887** M. B. EDWARDS *Next of Kin Wanted* I. x. 135 Groups of mackintoshed, umbrella'd, behooded travellers.

**Umbre·llaless**, *a.* [f. as prec. + -LESS.] Unprovided with an umbrella.

**1834** [see prec. 3]. **1864** MISS YONGE *Trial* II. 224 Pacing on, umbrellaless, was a figure which made her hurry to overtake him. **1898** *Daily Tel.* 14 Dec. 10/2 The umbrellaless man who in a shower of rain, sought to run between the drops.

**Umbre·lla-like**, *a.* [f. as prec. + -LIKE.] Resembling an umbrella.

**1796** WITHERING *Brit. Plants* (ed. 3) IV. 340 Pileus umbrella-like, gold coloured. **1857** DUFFERIN *Lett. High Lat.* xi. 290 A dark mantle of tempestuous clouds, that stretched down in umbrella-like points towards the horizon. **1895** CLIVE HOLLAND *Jap. Wife* ix, A wonderful umbrella-like hat of huge diameter.

**Umbre·lla-tree.** [f. as prec. + TREE *sb.*]

**1.** One of various American magnolias, especially *Magnolia tripetala*, having the leaves arranged umbrella-wise at the ends of the branches.

**1738** *Phil. Trans.* XL. 350 *Magnolia, amplissimo flore albo, fructu coccineo*. The Umbrella-tree. **1796** W. H. MARSHALL *Planting* II. 210 The wood of the Umbrella Tree..is more spongy than any of the other species of Magnolia. **1814** PURSH *Flora Amer. Septentr.* II. 381 *Magnolia tripetala* ..is generally known by the name of Umbrella-tree. **1832** *Planting* 94 (L.U.K.), Magnolia tripetala, umbrella-tree, is found in soils deep and fertile in the northern parts of New York. **1884** *Cassell's Fam. Mag.* Mar. 239/1 Here the umbrella-trees shaded the streets.

**2.** One of a variety of trees whose leaves or habit of growth resemble an umbrella.

*c* **1790** *Encycl. Brit.* (ed. 3) V. 482/1 *Corypha*, Mountain Palm, or Umbrella Tree. **1834** CAUNTER *Orient. Ann.* v. 53 The chatta, or umbrella-tree, begins here to be plentiful. **1866** *Treas. Bot.* 1190/1 Umbrella-tree,..*Thespesia populnea* and *Pandanus odoratissimus*. *Ibid.*, Guinea Umbrella-Tree, *Paritium guineense*. **1883** *Sunday Mag.* Aug. 511/2 We saw a good many specimens of the 'umbrella-tree', as it is called, a sort of acacia. **1889** MAIDEN *Useful Pl.* 387 *Brassaia actinophylla*,..Umbrella Tree, the large leaves being set, like umbrella-ribs, at the top of numerous stems.

† **Umbre·llian**, *a. Obs.*⁻¹ [f. as next + -IAN.] Serving the purpose of an umbrella.

**1721** RAMSAY *Tartana* 101 On each motion wait th' umbrellian Plaids, Repelling dust when winds disturb the air.

**Umbre·lliform**, *a. Zool.* [f. UMBRELL-A + -(I)FORM.] Having the shape of an umbrella.

**1857** GOSSE *Omphalos* xi. 304 The pulmonigrade umbrelliform stage.

**Umbrello(w**, obs. variants of UMBRELLA.

† **U·mbrere.** *Obs.* Also 5 **oumbrer, owmbrer(e, vmberere, 6–7 vmbriere, 7 umbrier.** [app. a. AF. **umbrere*, f. *umbre* shade, shadow; cf. obs. F. *ombriere* umbrella (Cotgr.).] The visor of a helmet.

*a* **1400** *Sir Perc.* 678 For to see hyme with syghte, He putt his umbrere on highte. ? *a* **1400** *Morte Arth.* 943 To þe creste of þe clyffe he clymbez one lofte; Keste upe hys vmbrere, and kenly he lukes. **1448–9** J. METHAM *Wks.* (1916) 37 At þe fyrst metyng Amoryus þis odyr gan smyght Vp-on hys vmbrere. **1470–85** MALORY *Arthur* VIII. xli. 338 Thenne sire Lamorak knelyd adoune, and vnlaced fyrst his vmberere, and thenne his owne. **1590** SPENSER *F. Q.* III. i. 42 But the braue Mayd would not disarmed bee, But onely vented vp her vmbriere. **1596** *Ibid.* IV. iv. 44 He..therewith smote him on his vmbriere. **1655** tr. *Sorel's Com. Hist. Francion* VII. 4 It was cloven in the middle, as if it were the Umbrier of some Troopers old Head-piece.

† **Umbretary**, misprint for VULNERARY *a.*

**1601** HOLLAND *Pliny* II. 111 Being applied as a cataplasme with oyle rosat and milke, it is a vmbretarie medicine.

**Umbreted**, obs. variant of UMBRATED *a.*

**Umbre·tte.** [ad. mod.L. *umbretta* or F. *ombrette.*] = UMBRE.

**1884** *Athenæum* 29 Nov. 698/3 Communications and papers were read..by Mr. F. E. Beddard, on the anatomy of the umbrette (*Scopus umbretta*). **1890** *Daily News* 9 Jan. 3/8 Occasionally the umbrette relaxes the severity of its demeanour and executes a fantastic dance with outspread wings.

**Umbrian** (*v*·mbriăn), *sb.* and *a.* [f. L. *Umbr-, Umber* (a. and sb.) or *Umbria* (see def.) + -(I)AN.]

**A.** *sb.* **1.** An inhabitant or native of Umbria, a province of central Italy; *esp.* a member of the Italic race anciently inhabiting this district.

**1601** HOLLAND *Pliny* I. 36 The Babylonians count for day all the time betweene two sunne risings...The Vmbrians from noone to noone. **1693** DRYDEN *Persius* III. 140 The Greaz'd Advocate, that Grinds the Poor, Fat Fees from the defended Umbrian draws. **1843** MACAULAY *Horatius* xxii, The terror of the Umbrian, The terror of the Gaul. **1867** *Chambers' Encycl.* IX. 630/1 The Umbrians were considered in ancient times to be the oldest people of Italy. **1890** *Contemp. Rev.* Aug. 266 The pile dwelling in the Lake of Fimòn, near Vicenza, ..must have been founded very soon after the Umbrians first reached Italy.

**2.** The language anciently spoken in Umbria.

**1858** G. ROBERTSON *Earliest Inhabitants Italy* 9 The differences between the Oscan and the Umbrian with its kindred dialects. **1864** F. W. NEWMAN *Iguvine Inscriptions* p. xiv, The vowel-declensions of Umbrian. **1882** C. S. HALSEY *Etym. Latin & Greek* I. i. 2 This [division] includes ..2. The Latin, akin to which were the Oscan and the Umbrian of central Italy.

**B.** *adj.* **1.** Of or belonging to ancient Umbria, its inhabitants or language.

**1601** HOLLAND *Pliny* II. Index s.v., Vmbrian earth or chalke, for what it is good. **1697** DRYDEN *Æneid* XII. 1088 The persecuted creature..Turns here and there, to escape his Umbrian foe. **1845** *Encycl. Metrop.* XXV. 1345/1 The Umbrian, Oscan, and Samnite characters, are, with a few trifling exceptions, nearly identical with the Etruscan. **1864** F. W. NEWMAN *Iguvine Inscriptions* p. iii, The Umbrian tendency to assimilate *n* even in the middle of words. **1890** *Contemp. Rev.* Aug. 264 We now come to the third Italian race, which may be called the Umbrian or Latin race.

**2.** Of or pertaining to mediæval or modern Umbria. *Umbrian School*, the Italian school of painting developed in Umbria in the 15th century.

**1841** W. SPALDING *Italy & It. Isl.* II. 252 The Umbrian painters appear to have at first studied both the older Florentines and the decaying school of Siena. **1845** MRS. JAMESON *Early Italian Painters* I. 204 In the sentiment of their works they resembled the Umbrian school, but the manner of execution is different. **1883** W. SHARP in E. A. Sharp *Life* (1910) 88 Watching the sunset over the far-stretching Umbrian country.

**Umbridawes**: see EMBER [2] 2.

**Umbri·ferous**, *a.* [f. L. *umbrifer* (f. *umbra* shade) + -OUS. Cf. It. *ombrifero.*] Affording or giving shade; umbrageous.

**1616** W. FORDE *Serm.* Ep. Ded., She had, to shadow her from the sunnes scorching beames, a beautifull and umbriferous tree. **1665** SIR T. HERBERT *Trav.* (1677) 382 Several other sorts of Trees there are...One I took special notice of was above five yards about and of a reasonable height, but umbriferous it was not. **1819** H. BUSK *Vestriad* I. 576 Nor cypress, plane, and cedar interlace Their arms umbrif'rous.

Hence **Umbri·ferously** *adv.*; **Umbri·ferousness.**

**1727** BAILEY (vol. II), *Umbriferousness*, Shadow-bringing Quality. **1884** *Imp. Dict.* (citing Tyndall), *Umbriferously*, so as to make or cast a shade.

† **Umbril** [1]. *Obs. rare.* [ad. It. *umbrella* UMBRELLA. Cf. UMBREL [2].] A sun-shade, parasol, umbrella.

**1610** R. TOFTE *Hon. Acad.* II. 10 Her amorous eye-browes, somewhat blacke, serving as an Umbril for her diamond-like-eyes. **1612** SHELTON *Quix.* I. I. viii. 54 Two monkes.. wore masks with Spectacles in them, to keepe away the dust from their faces, and each of them besides bore their Vmbrilles.

† **Umbril** [2]. *Obs. rare.* [ad. F. *nombril* navel.] A centre. Also *attrib.*

**1630** WESTCOTE *View Devonsh.* (1845) 135 The great conduit which stands in the umbril point of the city. *Ibid.* 139 The umbril of the city where standeth a great water conduit.

**Umbril** [3]. *Hist.* [var. UMBREL [1].] **a.** A part of a helmet projecting above the eyes. **b.** A visor.

**1824** MEYRICK *Ant. Armour* II. 221 The helmet of the king is the casquetel, having no covering for the face, but merely an umbril. **1864** WEBSTER, *Umbrere*,.. an umbril; a visor. **1892** H. PYLE *Men of Iron* xxxii. 306 The Constable advanced to his side, and formally raising the umbril of the helmet, looked him in the face.

‖ **Umbri·na.** *Zool.* [mod.L. (Cuvier), a. Sp. and It. *umbrina* (It. also *ombrina*, F. *ombrine*, † *umbrine*), f. *umbra* UMBER *sb.*[2]] A fish of the genus *Umbrina*, chiefly found in warm seas.

**1834** MCMURTRIE *Cuvier's Anim. Kingd.* 197 Some of the species, such as the King-fisher (an *Umbrina*), inhabit the American seas. **1840** tr. *Cuvier's Anim. Kingd.* 296 Some of them are silvery, and attain the size of an Umbrina. **1884** *Longman's Mag.* March 530 The Umbrinas of European seas are well known for the drumming sound they make.

† **Umbri·philous**, *a. Obs.*⁻¹ [f. L. *umbra* shade: see -PHIL and -OUS.] Shade-loving; growing in the shade.

**1592** R. D. *Hypnerotomachia* 32 Heleborous [*sic*] Niger, or Melampodi, Trayfles, and such other Vmbriphilous hearbes.

**Umbro-** (*v*·mbro) comb. form, on Gr. models, of L. *Umbr-, Umber* (see UMBRIAN), occurring in a few terms, as *Umbro-Etruscan, -Latin, -Oscan, -Roman, -Sabellian, Samnite.*

Also, with reference to the Umbrian school of painting, *Umbro-Florentine, -Siennese* (1866).

**1853** *Jrnl. Ethnol. Soc.* (1856) IV. 67 This inscription differs from those which are found in the Umbro-Etruscan or Rasenic districts. **1858** G. ROBERTSON *Earliest Inhabitants Italy* 46 The migration of the Umbro-Sabellian races. **1862** T. CLARK *Handbk. Compar. Grammar* 24 The Latin language has..some such relation to the Umbro-Samnite, as the Ionic has to the Doric. 1880 *Encycl. Brit* XIII. 496/1 The features common to Umbro-Roman and the Neapolitan dialects. 1890 *Contemp. Rev.* Aug. 265 This Umbro-Latin Aryan race must have entered Italy considerably more than two thousand years before the commencement of our era.

**Umbrose** (ʊmbrōᵘ·s), *a. rare.* [ad. L. *umbrōsus*, f. *umbra* shade. Cf. Sp. and Pg. *umbroso*, It. *ombroso*, OF. *ombros.*]

1. Shady; giving shade.

*a* 1425 tr. *Arderne's Treat. Fistula*, etc. 75 Hyng it in ane vmbrose place vnto þat þer be had nede þer-of. 1721 BAILEY, *Umbrose*, shady, casting a great Shade. 1871 MACDONALD *Wks. Fancy & Imag., Roadside Poems* III. 187 Still as a pool in its own place, Unsunned within an umbrose wood.

2. *Ornith.* Dusky.

1783 LATHAM *Gen. Synop. Birds* IV. 437 Umbrose W[arbler];..upper parts greyish brown: on the back obscurely marked with black.

† **Umbro·sity.** *Obs. rare.* [ad. L. *umbrōsitas*, f. *umbrōsus*: see prec. and -ITY. Cf. It. *ombrosità*, obs. F. *ombrosité*, *umbrosité*.] The state or condition of being shady.

1646 SIR T. BROWNE *Pseud. Ep.* II. i. 55 Oyled paper.. becommeth more transparent, and admits the visible rayes with lesse umbrosity. 1650 BULWER *Anthropomet.* v. (1653) 100 Kypler would not have this notion neglected, that the Haires of the Eye-lids do chiefly conduce to their umbrosity.

† **Umbro·sous,** *a. Obs.*—⁰ [f. L. *umbrōs-us.*] 'Full of shadow' (Cockeram, 1623).

**Umbrous** (ʊ·mbrəs), *a.* Also 5 **vmbreuse.** [ad. F. *ombreux*, † *umbreux*, or L. *umbrōs-us*: cf. UMBROSE *a.*]

1. Lying in the shade; shady, shadowed.

1480 CAXTON *Myrr.* III. i. 130 The Sonne..maketh the day to growe byfore hym, and on that other parte the erthe is vmbreuse & derke by hynde hym. 1480 — *Ovid's Met.* x. i, The Kynge and the quene comanded that Erudice shold be called forth, which was in the umbrous valeye. 1657 TOMLINSON *Renou's Disp.* 334 It grows..in margins of fields, that are not umbrous. 1821 T. G. WAINEWRIGHT *Ess. & Crit.* (1880) 227 A meadow..umbrous with orange and cedar trees.

† 2. *fig.* (See quot.) *Obs.*—¹

1483 CAXTON *Gold. Leg.* 108 b/1 He was umbrouse or shadewous, that is to saye he was colde and refrigerat fro all concupyscence of the flesshe.

**Umbset, -stead, -think**: see UMB-.

**Umbuss, Umbuth**: see UMBOTH.

† **Umbwhile,** *adv. Obs.* = UMBEWHILE *adv.* 2.

1393 LANGL. *P. Pl.* C. VII. 396 Bargeynes and beuereges by-gunne to aryse, And setyn so til euesong rang and songe vmbwhyle [*v.r.* vmbwyle, vmbewhile].

**Umbyll,** obs. f. HUMBLE *a.* **Umchew,** var. UMBESCHEW *v. Obs.* **Umclap, -clead, -clip, -close**: see UM-. **Umeer,** variant of AMEER. **Umellete,** obs. f. HUMILITY.

**U·mest,** *a. Sc.* Now *rare.* Also 5 **humest,** 6 **vmest, wmest,** 8–9 **umist,** 9 **eemest;** 5 **humost,** 5–6 **um-, vmast,** 9 **eemost, yimost.** [OE. *ufemest*: see OVEMEST *a.*]

† 1. Of clothes: Uppermost, outermost; *spec.* applied to the coverlet of a bed, claimed by the priest as a perquisite on the death of a parishioner.

*c* 1400 *Sc. Trojan War* II. 1932 Pallamydes..tuke of baith hois & schone, And syne his vmast clath. *c* 1470 HENRY *Wallace* IX. 707 Wallace gert tak in haist thar humest weid. 1535 LYNDESAY *Satyre* 3900 From this day furth, thay salbe cleane denudit Baith of cors-present, cow, and vmest claith. 1567 *Gude & Godlie B.* (S.T.S.) 196 Preistis, tak na kyis, The vmest claith ȝe sall quyte clame. *a* 1578 LINDESAY (Pitscottie) *Chron. Scot.* (S.T.S.) I. 349 Thow gaif againe to the parochinaris the kow and the wmest cloth.

2. Of things or places: Lying uppermost or highest.

*c* 1425 WYNTOUN *Cron.* VIII. xxvii. 4652 Endlange þe wode war wayis twa: Þe erl in þe vmast lay of þa. 1456 SIR G. HAY *Gov. Princes* Wks. (S.T.S.) II. 123 The ground of the stomak is..mare forcy of degestioun na the humast part of the stomak. 1513 DOUGLAS *Æneid* XII. vi. 172 Turnus.. evin betwix the helm can him arras And vmast roll or hem of his curas. 1537 *Reg. Privy Seal Scot.* II. 352/2 The umest hous and duelling place of the land callit the Abbay ȝet. 1566 in Ramsay *Bamff Charters* (1915) 103 Quhill it cum to the entres of the umest forkis of the burn. 1710 RUDDIMAN *Gloss. Douglas' Æneis, Umist*, S. upmost, uppermost. *c* 1800– in glossaries and texts (Kinc., Aberdeen, Moray, Caithness, etc.: *Eng. Dial. Dict.* s.v. *Eemost*).

3. Most important or prominent. ? *Obs.*

1513 DOUGLAS *Æneid* I. vi. 66 Lang war the iniuris, the dowtis lang to be tawld; Bot I the vmest of the mater sall hauld. *a* 1578 LINDESAY (Pitscottie) *Chron. Scot.* (S.T.S.) I. 284 The Earle of Angus become werie prude and insolent .., thinkand quho ewer had right to the autorietie he sould be vmest.

**Umff,** var. UMPH. **Umfold**: see UM-.

† **Umgang.** *Obs.* In 4–5 vm-, 6 *Sc.* wn-; 4 vmgong. [ME. *umgang* (see UM- and GANG *sb.*¹), = ON. *umgangr* (Norw. *um-*, MSw. *um-*, *omgang*, Sw. *omgång*, Da. *omgang*), WFris. *omgang*, NFris. *omgang, âmgung*, MDu. *omme-*, *omganc* (Du. *omgang*), MLG. *umb(e)-*, *ummegank*, OHG. *umbiganc* (MHG. *umbe-*, *umbganc*, G. *umgang*), OE. *ymb(e)gang.*]

1. The act of going round; the distance covered in this way; circuit, circumference.

*a* 1300 *E. E. Psalter* xvii. 13 And he set mirkenes his lurking lang, His telde to be in his vmgange, Mirke watres þat war of hewe. *a* 1300 *Cursor M.* 9192 In his [Josiah's] time was Fordon þe tune of ninive, þat was of vmgang thre iorne. *a* 1340 HAMPOLE *Psalter* xi. 9 Vs þou kepis, bot wickid men gas in vmgange. *c* 1400 MAUNDEV. (Roxb.) xxi. 97 It es a grete ile and a faire; and þe vmgang þeroff es nere a thowsand myle. 1456 SIR G. HAYE *Law Arms* (S.T.S.) 56 [Carthage] had sexty thousand pass about the vmgang [*printed* vin-] of the toune. 1505 *Charters Crosraguel Abbey* (1886) I. 63 Becaus the said hous, smedy, orchard, and yarde ar within the yettis and umgang and wallis of the said abbay.

2. A turn or spell of work. *rare*—¹.

1538 *Aberdeen Reg.* XVI. (Jam.), For the parting of the said maisteris fysche thre tymmez on ane wngang, quhar thai suld be twa tymmez partit on ane haill day.

So † **Umga·nging** *vbl. sb.*, going round. *Obs.*

*a* 1340 HAMPOLE *Psalter* cxii. 3 By þe vmgangynge of þe sone..he signyfyes þe warld.

† **Umgive,** *v. Obs.* [f. UM- + GIVE *v.* Cf. WFris. *omjown* (p.p.), NFris. *åmjiw*, Du. *omgeven* (p.p.), OHG. *umbigeban* (MHG. *umbe-*, *umbgeben*, G. *umgeben*), Sw. *omgifva*, Da. *omgive.*] *trans.* To enclose, surround, environ.

*a* 1300 *E. E. Psalter* iii. 6 Noght sal i drede a thousand Of folk, ar me vmgyuand. *Ibid.* vii. 7 Rise, lauerd, in bode þou sent to be, And kirke of folke sal vmgif þe. *a* 1340 HAMPOLE *Psalter* iii. 6 All vices, þe whilk vmgifs men to dissaif þaim. *Ibid.* xxxix. 16 For vmgifen me has illes of þe whilke noumbire is noght. *a* 1400 *New Test.* (Paues) Acts xxviii. 20 Forwhi for þo hope of Israel I am vmgyuen (or, bounden) with þis cheyne.

† **Umgo,** *v. Obs.* [f. UM- + GO *v.* Cf. WFris. *omgean*, MDu. *omme-*, *omgaen* (Du. *omgaan*), MSw. *um-*, *omga* (Sw. *omgås* refl.), Da. *omgaa*, OE. *ymbgān*, MLG. *umb-*, *umm(e)gān*, OHG. *umbi-*, *umbegān* (G. *umgehen*). See also UMBEGO *v.*] *trans.* To go around; to encompass.

*a* 1300 *E. E. Psalter* xxvi. 11, I vmyhode, and offred in telde hisse Offrand of berand steuen þat isse. *Ibid.* lviii. 7 Þai be torned at euen, and hunger thole þa Als hundes, and cite þai sal vmga. *a* 1340 HAMPOLE *Psalter* xxvi. 11, I vmȝed & i offird in his tabernakile þe hoste of heghynge of voice.

**Umgripe**: see UM-.

† **Umh, Um'h,** obs. varr. of UM or UMPH.

1614 J. COOKE *Greene's Tu Quoque* B 4, *Bub.* Vmh, vmh, vmh. 1616 S. S. *Honest Lawyer* IV. G 1, Vm'h, my doubts Wrappe me in further maze. 1668 DRYDEN *Evening's Love* IV, Umh! thou awaken'st a most villainous apprehension in me! 1702 FARQUHAR *Inconstant* II. i, Umh.—before that any young..Rakelly Fellow shou'd play such Tricks with me, I wou'd wear my Teeth to the stumps. 1740 CIBBER *Apol.* (1756) II. 31 With a slow hesitation..he reply'd—Umh! the best—umh!—I have tasted a great while.

**Umheed, -hill**: see UM-.

**Umiak, umyak,** varr. OOMIAK (Eskimo boat).

1769, 1819 [see OOMIAK]. 1863 A. YOUNG *Naut. Dict.* (ed. 2) 431 In Greenland, the umyak is the boat worked exclusively by the women, as the kayak is by the men. 1884 *Good Words* Feb. 96/1 We quitted the whale-boat.. and took a small umiak, on account of weight. 1900 *Scribner's Mag.* Sept. 294/2 Well-made models of kayaks and umiaks.

† **Umlap,** *v. Obs.* [f. UM- + LAP *v.*² Cf. UMBELAP *v.*] *trans.* To encompass, surround.

*a* 1300 *Cursor M.* 2778 Þaa foles feluns þat war fuus, All vmlapped loth huse. *c* 1340 HAMPOLE *Pr. Consc.* 6937 Þai salle umlapp þam alle oboute, And gnaw on ilka lym and souke. *c* 1375 *Sc. Leg. Saints* ii. (Paul) 537 Fra hewine schane don a mekil lycht, And vmlappyt hym son all. *c* 1400 tr. *Secreta Secret., Gov. Lordsh.* 109 Þe nombre of ten ys þe perfeccion of hem þat enbracen ffourhede, & vmlappys it yn nombres. *c* 1440 *Alph. Tales* 367 Sodanlie he was vmlappid with a grete flok of myce. *Ibid.* 521 Þe se-flude vmlappid bothe hym & þe cow & þe calfe.

‖ **Umlaut** (u·mlaut). *Philol.* [G., f. *um-* about + *laut* sound.] A change in the sound of a vowel produced by partial assimilation to an adjacent sound (usually that of a vowel or semivowel in the following syllable); = MUTATION 4 b.

[1844 T. H. KEY *Alphabet* 169 The Influence of Assimilation. *Footnote*, Sometimes called by Germans 'umlaut'.] 1852 *Trans. Philol. Soc.* 25 June V. 200 The cognate languages clearly exhibit the fact, that the umlaut in these words has been produced by the weak vowel of a lost suffix. 1873 EARLE *Philol. Eng. Tongue* (ed. 2) § 127 The Umlaut of the Indo-European languages is a phenomenon of a different order. Here the vowel of the after-member of the word influences that which has gone before.

*attrib.* 1873 EARLE *Philol. Eng. Tongue* (ed. 2) § 128 Nowhere is any structural signification attached now to an Umlaut form, except [etc.]. 1879 *Ibid.* (ed. 3) § 381 The modern s being imposed upon the old umlaut plural. 1879 *Encycl. Brit.* X. 519/2 In most [German] Midland manuscripts no special signs for the Umlaut vowels are used, except *e.*

Hence **U·mlauted** *a.*, modified by umlaut; containing a vowel or vowels modified in this way.

1852 *Trans. Philol. Soc.* 25 June V. 200 In particular the umlaut-ed plurals appear not to have yet found a fitting explanation in English grammars. 1879 EARLE *Philol. Eng. Tongue* (ed. 3) § 381 It should be observed that there is no natural connection between Umlauted forms and Plurality.

† **Umlay,** *v. Obs.* [f. UM- + LAY *v.*¹ Cf. MDu. *omme-*, *omleggen* (Du. *omleggen*), Da. *omlægge*; OS. *umbileggian* (MLG. *ummeleggen*), MHG. *umbe-*, *umblegen* (G. *umlegen*). See also UMBELAY *v.*] *trans.* To surround.

*a* 1300 *Cursor M.* 1010 Paradis is..euer vmlaid wit lem and light. *Ibid.* 22069 In vr leuedi light þe hali-gast.., And vmlaid hir wit his lem.

† **Umlouk,** *v. Obs.* Also -luke, -lok(e. [f. UM- + LOUK *v.*² Cf. MDu. *omme-*, *omluken* (Du. *omluiken*), and see *umbelouk* under UMBE-.] *trans.* To surround, enclose.

*a* 1300 *Cursor M.* 22705 The see þat vmlukes þe land, And watres all that rinnes in strand, Al sal turn again to noght. *a* 1300 *E. E. Psalter* lxxvii. 68 He vmlouked in swerd his folke to be. *a* 1340 HAMPOLE *Psalter* cxliv. 3 He is incomprehensibil, for na stede, na thoght, may vmlouke him. *a* 1400–50 *Alexander* 4672 With soft serkis of silke ȝoure sidis [ȝe] vm-loke.

**Umman,** dial. form of WOMAN.

**Umor, Umour,** obs. ff. HUMOUR.

**Umph** (ʼmh), *int.* Also 6 vmff. [Imitative: cf. HUMPH and UMH.] An inarticulate sound, expressive of hesitation, doubt, or dissatisfaction.

*a* 1568 in *Bannatyne MS.* (Hunter. Club) 461/21 Vmff, quod the Helandman, and swere be yon kirk [etc.].

1782 MISS BURNEY *Cecilia* IV. vi, He only looked at her, and said 'umph?' *Ibid.* VII. ix, I really believe the gentleman's deaf! he won't so much as say *umph* and *hay*, now. 1800 MRS. HERVEY *Mourtray Fam.* II. 119 'Umph!' thought Emma, 'is he abusing the Turk now by way of a blind?' 1822 SCOTT *Nigel* v, 'Umph!' repeated Master George,..'what does *umph* mean?' 1826 — *Woodst.* iii, Commands—umph—I think the damsel might have tarried. 1894 A. GORDON *Northward Ho* 87 An occasional 'Oich! Oich!' from John, and a sympathetic 'Umph! Umph!' from Eppie.

Hence **Umph** *v. intr.*, to ejaculate 'umph'.

1894 HALL CAINE *Manxman* I. x. 48 Cæsar *umpht* and grunted. 1900 *Daily News* 30 June 4/1 'Umph,' replied Mr. Rhodes, in his grim, gruff way, 'Umph!' and he went away umphing.

**Umpirage** (ʊ·mpəirėdʒ). Forms: α. 5 **owmpreght,** 7 **umpridge, umpiridge, umperage, umpeerage.** β. 6– **umpirage** (7 **umpireage**). [f. next + -AGE.] The act of umpiring; the office or power of an umpire; the decision of an umpire, arbitration.

α. *c* 1490 *Plumpton Corr.* (Camden) 84 Wher it is so, uncle, at the matter betwyxt my servant and John Forest is put to iiij men, and the owmpreght of you. 1609 *N. Riding Rec.* (1884) I. 173 The arbitrament..of Tho. Warcupp and Anth. Byarley, gent., with the umpridge of Mr. Parson Lascells. 1649 BP. HALL *Cases Consc.* 301 The Prophet Malachi ..hath so fully decided the cause, as if it had been expresly referred to his umperage. 1661 *Andronicus* III. i. D 4 b, Here's Cleobulus, We will refer it to his Umpeerage. 1679 W. PENN *Addr. Prot.* II. 180 The Scriptures are made more doubtful than they are by such as would fain preserve to themselves the Umpiridge and Judgship of their Meaning.

β. 1519 *Plumpton Corr.* (Camden) 223 *n.*, The parties to abide the umpirage of Thomas Lord Cardinal..if given before the feast of All Saints. 1633 BP. MORTON *Discharge Five Imput.* 144 S. Augustine his Vmpirage and full Determination of this whole question, concerning the exposition of Christ his speech. 1643 NETHERSOLE *Proj. for Peace* (1648) 21 The finall Umpirage of such..matters, as cannot be resolved without the admission of forein arbitrement. 1675 J. SMITH *Chr. Relig. App.* I. 18 Augustus..referring the choice of an Heir, where he had so bad choice, to the umpirage of the Divine Wisdom. *a* 1715 BURNET *Own Time* (1766) I. 48 They hoped the umpirage of the war would fall into their hands. 1768 BLACKSTONE *Comm.* III. i. 17 Enacting..that their submission of the suit to arbitration or umpirage shall be made a rule of any of the king's courts of record. 1805 *East's Reports* V. 189 The time for making the umpirage was further extended. 1846 SUMNER *Scholar, Jurist*, etc. 62 When, in our age, two nations.. appeal to war.., they voluntarily adopt this unchristian umpirage of right. 1890 *Law Times* LXXXVIII. 358/1 We do not think it would be fair to cast upon the County Court judges the responsibilities of umpirage.

**Umpire** (ʊ·mpəiᵊɹ), *sb.* Forms: α. 5 **owmpere, ovmper, ompar.** β. 5–6 **umpere** (6 **vn-**), 6 **vmppere,** 6–7 **umpeer(e.** γ. 5–7 **umper** (5 **unpar**). δ. 6–7 **umpyer, -pier** (6 **impier**). ε. 6– **umpire** (7 **umpyre**). [Later form of NOUMPERE, by transference of the *n-* to the indefinite article, as in *adder, apron.*]

1. One who decides between disputants or contending parties and whose decision is usually accepted as final; an arbitrator.

α. ? *c* 1400 LYDG. *Æsop's Fab.* vi. 43 Among these owmperis was werre none, ne stryf. *c* 1440 *Promp. Parv.* 360/1 Nowmpere, or owmpere, *arbiter, sequester.* 1483 *Cath. Angl.* 263/2 An Ovmper (A. Ompar), *impar.*

β. *c* 1430 *Wyclif's Prol. Rom.* (MS. Rawl. C. 257 fol. 90 b/2), Þe apostle putte him bitwene as a meene, distriynge alle her questiouns, as a good vmpere. 1450 *Paston Lett.* I. 120 Take ȝe one, and he another; and if they may not accorde, ȝe and I to be umpere, for we stande bothe in like cas. 1552–3 in E. B. Jupp *Carpenters' Co.* (1887) 376 John abbott Rjchard tylton George Kyng John revell..for days men and master Russell for vmppere. 1567 JEWEL *Def. Apol.* II. 312 He is no indifferente umpeere, that firste diuideth Offices equally bitweene twoo, and afterwarde alloteth bothe offices to One alone. 1576 A. HALL *Acc. Quarrell* (1815) 25 The just and consionable dome of so graue umpeers. 1601 R. JOHNSON *Kingd. & Commw.* (1603) 255 They constitute him their arbitraitour and chiefe Vmpeere. 1649 BALL *Power of Kings* 6 These things they may doe as Judges Allegate, or Umpeeres for the People. 1688 R. HOLME *Armoury* II. 394/2 Being desired to be Umpeer between Apollo and Pan,.. Midas passed his verdict against Apollo.

γ. 1464, 1556 [see 2]. 1580 LYLY *Euphues* (Arb.) 421 The Ladie Flauia..commaunded them both to silence, willing Euphues as vmper in these matters, briefly to speake his minde. 1606 BP. W. BARLOW *Serm.* E j b, The best course..will bee..to make him the vmper, whom they make our Accuser. **1611** GRIMESTON *Hist. France* 969 Cardinall Medicis..was, as it were, an Vmper of all difficulties in this good and holy reconciliation.

*δ.* **1551** ROBINSON tr. *More's Utopia* Ded. (1895) 3 Some as an vmpier or a judge with my sentence finallye to discusse. **1577** *F. de L'isle's Legendarie* A vij b, The controuersie was referred vnto the arbitrement of three vmpiers. **1581** J. BELL *Haddon's Answ. Osor.* 168 If this Aunswere..shall seeme but of small credite with you, I will bryng you Augustine for an umpyer betwixt us. **1609** HOLLAND *Amm. Marcell.* 23, I rest waiting upon you as umpiers to know what ye advise. **1641** PRYNNE *Antip.* 274 The Lords in Parliament tooke an Oath to be indifferent umpiers betweene the Bishop and Duke.

*ε.* **1599** *Broughton's Let.* vii. 25 He, whom you..made vmpire of that..controuersie. **1606** J. CARPENTER *Solomon's Solace* xxviii. 115 If a man sinne against God, who shall bee his Umpire, or Dayes-man? **1640** QUARLES *Enchirid.* (1641) 13 When the Frog and the Mouse could not take up the Quarrell, the Kite was umpyre. **1681** H. NEVILE *Plato Rediv.* 152 A great person was to be chosen every Parliament, who should be as it were an Umpire between the King and his People. **1717** J. KEILL *Anim. Œcon.* (1738) 54 How could I wish for a more impartial Judge, or how could I choose a more proper Umpire? **1751** SMOLLETT *R. Random* xvii, The constable..pleaded our cause so effectually, that she condescended to make him umpire. **1815** *Zeluca* III. 268, I must become umpire between you and Mrs. Wolsey. **1835** LYTTON *Rienzi* x. iii, We might call in an umpire—a foreigner who had no interest in either faction. **1875** JOWETT *Plato* (ed. 2) I. 152 To choose an umpire of discourse would be unseemly.

**b.** *transf.* Something which serves to decide or settle a matter.

**1583** W. M. in Foxe *A. & M.* (ed. 4) II. 2139 Let Gods word be vnpere, To try our true religion, From this euill fauoured geere. **1600** ROWLAND *Lett. Humours Blood* v. 73 Make Steele and Iron vmpiers to the Fray. **1647** N. BACON *Disc. Govt. Eng.* I. xvi. 48 As if the Law were the sole umpire between King and people. **1662** STILLINGFL. *Orig. Sacræ* III. i. § 9 It is a sign there is little of reason left, where sense is made the only Umpire of all kinds of Beings. **1696** DOGGET *Country-Wake* III. ii. 30 Your Conscience must be Umper in this Case. **1718** ROWE tr. *Lucan* I. 205 The Sword is now the Umpire to decide. **1784** COWPER *Tiroc.* 29 The judgment, umpire in the strife That grace and nature have to wage through life. **1805–6** CARY *Dante, Inf.* XXII. 140 In the boiling lake both fell. The heat Was umpire soon between them. **1878** BROWNING *La Saisiaz* 55 Take thou, soul, thy solitary stand, Umpire to the champions Fancy, Reason.

†**c.** Something which stands between others either by way of connexion or separation. *Obs.*

**1598** SYLVESTER *Du Bartas* II. i. *Eden* 392 For spirits.. 'Twixt God and man retein a middle kinde; And (Umpires) mortall th' immortall joine. **1610** HOLLAND *Camden's Brit.* I. 745 Those mountaines, which..interpose themselves as Umpiers and Bounders between diverse shires.

**2.** *Law.* A third person appointed or called upon to decide a matter submitted to arbitrators who cannot agree. Cf. REFEREE *sb.* 2.

**1464** *Cov. Leet Bk.* 329 If in the mean tyme the seid iiij arbitrours can not accorde that then the seid Mair to be unpar. *Ibid.*, That..as the a-fore named iiij arbitrours.. cowde not accorde, that then the seid mair to be vmper. **1552** HULOET, Impier or umpier, a iudge or mediatoure taken besydes arbitors to deme a matter debated, wher the arbitrors can not agree, *sequestor*. **1556** in W. H. Turner *Select. Rec. Oxford* (1880) 257 To abyde the arbytrament of..arbytrators, ..and that Mr. Pollard shalbe umper. **1706** PHILLIPS (ed. Kersey), *Umpire*, a third Person chosen to put a final End to a Controversy left to the Determination of two Arbitrators. **1768** BLACKSTONE *Comm.* III. 16 If they [*sc.* the arbitrators] do not agree, it is usual to add, that another person be called in as umpire (*imperator*), to whose sole judgment it is then referred. **1838** W. BELL *Dict. Law Scot.* 692 An oversman is an umpire appointed by a submission to decide where two arbiters have differed in opinion, or he is named by the arbiters themselves. **1843** *Penny Cycl.* XXV. 501/2 The word umpire..in its legal sense..means a person named in the Submission, or under its authority, by the arbitrators to decide the matters referred, which the arbitrators either cannot or will not decide.

**3.** In games or contests: One to whose decision all doubtful points are referred, and who sees that the rules of the game or sport are not broken. Cf. REFEREE *sb.* 3 b.

**1714** in Parkyns *Inn-Play* (ed. 2) 63 [Wrestling], And in case they can't Decide such Differences, then they shall be referr'd solely to the Decision of the said Sir Thomas Parkyns as Umpire. **1778** C. JONES *Hoyle's Games Impr.* 201 The Umpires are the sole Judges of fair and unfair Play, and have a Power to determine all Disputes. **1837** DICKENS *Pickw.* vii, The umpires were stationed behind the wickets. **1857** HUGHES *Tom Brown* II. viii, Their leading men and umpire inspected the ground, criticising it rather unmercifully. **1884** *Times* 15 Sept. 7/3 [Football], Mr. Walker officiated as referee, and Messrs. Davies and Bryan as umpires.

*attrib.* **1889** *Infantry Drill* 406 Umpire Regulations. *Ibid.* 407 Orders from the Umpire Staff are to be considered as emanating directly from the Umpire-in-Chief.

**U·mpire,** *v.* Also 7 vmpeere, vmper. [f. prec.]

†**1.** *trans.* To adjudge, appoint (a person to an office), in virtue of being umpire. *Obs.*$^{-1}$

**1592** BACON *Observ. Libel* in *Resuscitatio* (1657) 123 That no King of Spain, nor Bishop of Rome, shall umpire, or promote, any beneficiary, or feodatory, King, as they designed to do.

†**2.** To decide between (persons) as umpire; to act as umpire to. *Obs. rare.*

**1611** T. JAMES *Corrupt. Scripture* IV. 19 Who shall reconcile or vmpire them, decide doubts, determine questions, and take vp all controuersies? *a* **1657** R. LOVEDAY *Lett.* (1663) 19 He is now the great Cardinal that umpires almost all Christendom.

**3.** To settle or decide (a matter in dispute) as umpire or after the manner of an umpire.

**1611** SPEED *Hist. Gt. Brit.* IX. viii. 24 The Pope..therfore vndertooke to vmpeere the debates betwixt those two great Enemies. **1622** MABBE tr. *Aleman's Guzman d'Alf.* I. 101 The Clergy-men interposed themselues; they were to vmpire the businesse betweene vs. **1637** CARTWRIGHT *Royal Slave* IV. iv, I have Two or three servants within call here, they Shall umpire this your variance. **1675** R. BURTHOGGE *Causa Dei* 379 It was the Office of the Druids..to decide and umpire Controversies. **1710** R. WARD *Life H. More* 121, I have heard him pleasantly speaking, How he was fain to umpire the matter between his Mirth and his Sadder Tempers.

**b.** *transf.* Of things.

**1609** [BP. W. BARLOW] *Answ. Nameless Cath.* 322 The question also then in hand beeing to bee vmper'd onely by the holy Scripture. **1629** N. CARPENTER *Achitophel* II. (1640) 115 Queasi stomacks had rather appetite should umpire their desires, then judgement. **1674** T. FLATMAN *Desperate Lover* 2/8 A turfe of grass or Monument of Stone Umpires the petty competition.

**4.** *spec.* To supervise (games or contests) in the capacity of umpire.

**1861** *Times* 12 July, The regatta yesterday was exceedingly well managed, and the races umpired by gentlemen of the Universities. **1884** *Harper's Mag.* Oct. 726/1 It is not an unusual sight to see a game among the officers 'umpired' by some..non-commissioned officer. **1887** *Field* 13 Aug. 283/3 The various competitions were umpired from the bows of a launch.

**b.** To give (a player) *out*, as umpire.

**1894** *Daily News* 20 June 5/2 Conceivably, he 'umpired out' the other side whenever he had an opportunity.

**5.** *intr.* To act as umpire. Also const. *between, betwixt.*

**1613** PURCHAS *Pilgrimage* (1614) 328 We list not to vmpire betwixt Geographers. *a* **1638** MEDE *Wks.* (1672) 746 Even Cæsar at first umpired between her and her brother, in matters of difference between them. *a* **1688** CUDWORTH *Freewill* (1838) 42 In this contest there is no necessary understanding interposing and coming in to umpire between, that does unavoidably and irresistibly determine one way or other. **1716** M. DAVIES *Athen. Brit.* II. 243, I am sure nothing can be justly pleaded in Bar to their undoubted Prerogative..to Umpire in this Contest about Primitive Christianity. **1881** W. THOMSON *Bacon & Shakespeare* 29 None will be readier than he to umpire justly. **1901** *Weekly Register* 22 Nov. 649/2 The famous cricketer, who often used to umpire at boys' matches.

**b.** With *it.*

**1620** BRATHWAIT *Five Senses* in *Archaica* (1815) II. 51 Nobly interposing himself..to umpire it, that it may be more evenly carried, and more equally composed. **1627** W. SCLATER *Exp. 2 Thess.* (1629) 299 While Thomas..must vmpire it in Religion. **1695** J. SAGE *Article* Wks. 1844 I. 268 She umpired it between the Queen of Scotland and those who appeared for her son.

Hence † **U·mpirer**, an umpire. *Obs. rare.*

**1650** FULLER *Pisgah* I. x. 32 If the extent of their dominions be surveyed, and our eye in the Map made umpirer therein, the case is clear. **1675** J. SMITH *Chr. Relig. Appeal* IV. 97 The Umpirers of Difference among the Nations of the World.

**U·mpireship.** Also 6 umpeere-, 6–7 umpier-. [f. UMPIRE *sb.*] The office of umpire, or the discharge of this; umpirage.

**1565** HARDING *Confut. Apol.* I. ix. 31 We refuse not tharbitrement and vmpireship of the holy ghost. **1567** JEWEL *Def. Apol.* 65 Ye saie, ye refuse not the Umpeereship, and iudgemente of the Holy Ghoste. **1613** JACKSON *Creed* II. xxvii. § 4. 431 Tyrannicall claime of soueraigntie, and imperiall vmpiership over all other Churches. **1819** MOORE *Mem.* (1853) II. 264, I..was proceeding to talk to him about our joint umpireship on Byron's poem. **1869** *Daily News* 26 May, He withdrew from the umpireship of a dog show because he objected to the admission of mutilated dogs.

**U·mpiress.** Also 7 ump(e)resse, 8 umpress. [f. UMPIRE *sb.* + -ESS.] A female umpire.

**1602** MARSTON *Ant. & Mel.* v. Wks. 1856 I. 58 Give mee the golden harpe: faith with your favour, ile be umperesse. **1651** HOWELL *Venice* 4 She [Venice] hath allwayes bin more inclined to peace than war, and chosen rather to be a Spectatrix or Umpresse, than a Gamestresse. **1715** tr. *C'tess D'Aunoy's Wks.* 18, I became an Umpress among the Wits, and Judge of their Works. **1889** *Pall Mall G.* 4 Mar. 1/2 Umpires, or rather umpiresses, for the women folk of the village had been invited to give judgment.

**U·mpiring,** *vbl. sb.* [f. UMPIRE *v.* + -ING [1].] The action of acting as an umpire, esp. of deciding doubtful points in games.

**1884** *Pall Mall G.* 15 July 5/1 Construction of asphalte courts; treatises on umpiring, the same on handicapping. **1894** *Westm. Gaz.* 30 July 3/2 Most of these faults would be checked by good umpiring.

*attrib.* **1884** *Marshall's Tennis Cuts* 102 Our suggestion of a band on these occasions was scouted with scorn by the eminent in the umpiring line. **1896** KNOWLES & MORTON *Baseball* 56 The whole season was a very trying one for the gentlemen who occupied the umpiring positions.

**U·mpirism.** *rare*$^{-1}$. [f. UMPIRE *sb.*] Umpirage.

**1792** ANNA SEWARD *Lett.* (1811) III. 150 If the umpireism of dispassionate examination is to be rejected, and the ardours of zeal confided in implicitly.

†**Umple.** *Obs.* Also 5 umpull. [a. OF. *omple* 'étoffe unie' (15th c. in Godefroy).] A fine kind of linen stuff.

**1457** *Inv. Ornaments in Lady Chapel Cirencester Abbey Ch.*, A new Kerchon of umpull. **1463** *Rolls Parlt.* V. 505 Kerchiefs..of..Lawne, Nyfels, Umple. *a* **1500** *Assemb. Ladies* 471 Bicause the wallis shone so bright, With fyne umple they were al over-sprad, To that intent, folk shuld nat hurte hir sight. ? *a* **1500** *London Lickpenny* (MS. Harl. 542) x, One bad me come nere, and by fine cloth of lawne, paris thred, Coton, and vmple.

**Umpra,** obs. form of OMRAH.

**Umquhile, umwhile** (*ʊ·*mhwəil), *adv.* and *a.* Now only *arch.* Forms: *α.* 2 um-wile, 4–5, 7–9 umwhile (4 homwill), 4, 6 umwhyle. *β.* *north.* 4–5 umquile (umquil, 4 umquille), vmqwhyle; *Sc.* 5 umqwhile (9 umquwhile), 5– umquhile (5–6 wmquhile), 5–7 umquhyle (5 wmquhyle, vm-, wmqwhyle); 5 umquhil, 5–7 umquhill (wm-; 7 wmquill). [Representing OE. *ymb hwīle* (see UMBEWHILE *adv.*), with substitution of UM- for *ymb-*. In later use specifically Scottish, whence the usual spelling with *-quh-*.]

**A.** †**1.** *adv.* At times; sometimes. *Obs.*

*α.* **1154** *O. E. Chron.* (Laud MS.) an. 1137, Hi læiden gæildes on the tunes æure um wile & clepeden it tenserie. **1303** R. BRUNNE *Handl. Synne* 2780 Fallace ys, as who seye, 'gyle', As many one sweryn vmwhyle. *c* **1330** — *Chron. Wace* (Rolls) 1415 Vmwhile west, vmwhile est, þer schipes driuen in many tempest. *a* **1340** HAMPOLE *Psalter* cxli. 6, I fled noght fra tribulacioun in saule, thof i fled vmwhile in body. **1377** LANGL. *P. Pl.* B. v. 345 Þere was laughyng and louryng..And seten so til euensonge and songen vmwhile. *a* **1529** SKELTON *Agst. Garnesche* ii. 11 Ye countyr vmwhyle to capcyously, and ar ye be dysiryd.

*β.* *a* **1300** *Cursor M.* 4319 Sua þou mai þe driue to ded, To ded vmquil, and to langur. *Ibid.* 10323 Þof godd vmquil be funden still. **1375** BARBOUR *Bruce* III. 262 To stand agayne thar fayis micht, Wmquhile with strenth, & quhile with slycht. *c* **1400** MAUNDEV. (Roxb.) vi. 20 Ay when him list, he gase to visit þam, and vmqwhyle ledes þam aboute with him. *a* **1500** *Ratis Raving* I. 1448 And eild.. Wmquhill is twrnyt with inwy, And wmquhill led with lichory. **1535** STEWART *Cron. Scot.* (Rolls) III. 525 That all this warld hes bene full of variance; Vmquhill in plesure and prosperitie, Vmquhill in pane and greit penuritie. *a* **1568** in *Bannatyne MS.* (Hunterian Cl.) 633 Vmquhile I syche and vmquhile I sing...Vmquhill I lawche and quhill I weip and wring.

**2.** At one time; at some previous time; formerly. *Obs.* exc. *arch.*

*c* **1375** *Sc. Leg. Saints* iii. (*Andrew*) 863 Ane bischope vmquhile, I herd say..Sancte Andrew in affecione Had ay. *a* **1400–50** *Alexander* 23 Oute in þe erth of Egipt enhabet vmquile þe wysest wees of the werd. *Ibid.* 3079 (Dubl. MS.), Nowe am I kest vnder, þat had of the Orient all ouer homage vmwhile. **1456** SIR G. HAYE *Law Arms* (S. T. S.) 2 Chaumerlayn umquhyle to..king Charles of Fraunce. *c* **1470** HENRY *Wallace* II. 207 O der Wallace, wmquhill was stark and stur, Thow most o neide in presoune till endur. **1508** DUNBAR *Poems* vii. *heading*, Lord Barnard Stewart,..Conquereur of Naplis and vmquhile constable general of the same. *c* **1550** LYNDESAY *Tragedy* Prol. 40 I am Dauid, that cairfull Cardinall,..That vmquhyle had so gret preeminens. **1567** *Satir. Poems Reform.* iv. 1 I, Henrie Stewart, vmquhile of Scotland King. [**1890** SERVICE *Notandums* 88 Her white cheek, umquhile red.]

†**3.** At some later time; by-and-by. *Obs.*

**1375** BARBOUR *Bruce* III. 256 For nane wate, in how litill space That god wmquhile will send his grace. **1513** DOUGLAS *Æneid* II. x. 209 And I wmquhill quhilk sal be clepit thi spous, Quham to sall we be left in this waist hous?

**B.** *adj.* Former, late: **a.** Of persons; *esp.* = now deceased.

In the first quot. perhaps still adverbial.

**1431** *Munim. de Melros* (Bann. Cl.) 521 Patrike off Dunbarr,.. brothir vmquhile of a hee & mychti lorde Sir George of Dunbarr. **1477** *Exch. Rolls Scotl.* VIII. 403 *note*, Landis..the quhilkis umquhile Cuthbert Colvile had of ws of before. **1490–1** *Acc. Ld. High Treas. Scot.* I. 197 A compositioun maid with vmquhile the Master of Craufurd. **1535** STEWART *Cron. Scot.* (Rolls) III. 519 James Stewart, Sone and Air..to vmquhill King Robert Stewart. **1583** in *Montgomerie's Poems* (S.T.S. 1910) 300 The testament..pertening to vmquhile ane richt honorabill Ladie Margaret Fraser.., relict of vmquhile Iohne Montgummerie. **1633** *Sc. Acts, Chas. I* (1870) V. 26/1 The fruites of benefice givin by his Majestie his said vmquhyle dearest father. *a* **1670** SPALDING *Troub. Chas. I* (1829) 9 Lachlan M'Intosh, ..brother to the umquhile laird of M'Intosh, William M'Intosh,..son to umquhile Lachlan Angus-son. **1714** RAMSAY *Elegy J. Cowper* xiii, Of umquhile John to lie or bann, Shaws but ill will. **1784** in *Nairne Peerage Evidence* (1874) 72 The goods and gear which pertained and belonged to umq[le] miss Brabazone Nairne. **1814** SCOTT *Wav.* x, The estate which devolved on this unhappy woman by a settlement of her umwhile husband. **1816** — *Old Mort.* iii, His uncle, as well as his umquhile father, is a roundhead, I presume. **1874** HISLOP *Bk. Sc. Anecdote* 725/1 The 'leader of the psalmody', as umquhile 'precentors' are now termed. **1886** RUSKIN *Præterita* I. 408 Her father visited his umquwhile clientage at the coal-wharves.

**b.** Of things. *rare.*

**1548** *Compl. Scotl.* i. 21 Quhat sal be said of athenes, the vmquhile fontane of sapiens. **1842** F. TROLLOPE *Vis. to Italy* I. x. 161, I went to see Europe's umwhile wonder and delight. **1854** H. MILLER *Sch. & Schm.* (1858) 356 When I last passed along the Coal-hill, I saw my umquhile house existing as a bit of dingy wall.

**Umra,** var. OMRAH. **Umschew,** var. UMBESCHEW *v. Obs.* **Umsee, -seek**: see UM-.

†**Umset,** *v. Obs.* Also 6 vnsett. [f. UM- + SET *v.* Cf. MDu. *omme-, omsetten* (Du. *omzetten*), MSw. *omsätia*, Da. *omsætte*; OHG. *umbi-, umpisezzan* (MHG. *umbesezzen, -setzen*, G. *umsetzen*), OE. *ymbsettan.*] *trans.* To surround, invest.

*a* **1300** *Cursor M.* 195 How Iuus iesu oft vmsette And for his sermon thrali threte. *Ibid.* 15012 Wit harp and pipe, and horn and trump, þe strette þai him vmsette. *c* 1340 HAMPOLE *Pr. Consc.* 1250 For-why here we er on many wyse Alle umset with sere enmys. *a* 1352 MINOT in *Pol. Poems* (Rolls) I. 77 With him come mani a kumly knight And all umset the bare obout. *c* 1400 *Destr. Troy* 6964 Cassibilan kynd brether þen þe kyng segh,..Vmset hym full sone in a sop hole. *a* 1600 *Flodden Field* lxxi. in Child *Ball.* III. 358/1 Sir Rice..Came with a feirce menye; He bent his bowes on the bent to abyde, And cleane vnsett the gallow-tree.

**Umshade, -shadow, -shine**: see UM-.

† **Umsiege,** *v. Obs.* [f. UM- + SIEGE *v.* Cf. *umbesiege* under UMBE-.] *trans.* To besiege.

*a* 1325 *Prose Psalter* xxi. 16 Þe counseil of wicked vmseged me. *a* 1340 HAMPOLE *Psalter* xxi. 11 Fat bulles me has vmseged. *c* 1440 *Alph. Tales* 220 When Titus had vmsegid Jerusalem ij yere. *Ibid.* 226 What cetie at þai vmsegid, þai trustid to gett & wyn itt.

**Umstand**: see UM-.

† **Umstou·nd,** *adv. Obs.* Also 4 **vmbstont, vmstount, -stunt,** 5 **vmstonte;** 4 **vmstond.** [ad. ON. *um stund* for a time. Cf. UMBESTOUND *adv.*] Sometimes.

*a* 1300 *Cursor M.* 4451 Ioseph sagh þam ai vmstunt To comforth þam wel was he wont. *Ibid.* 14033 A man quilum was wont Penis for to lene vm-stunt [*Gött.* vmstount]. *Ibid.* 28330 Ben i haue vmstond quare barne Wit-vten cristening was for-farne. *a* 1340 HAMPOLE *Psalter* Prol. 4 Vmstunt he spekis of crist in his godhed, vmstunt in his manhed. *c* 1450 *St. Cuthbert* (Surtees) 3323 His brethir come to him vmstonte, To visit him, as þai were wonte.

**Umstri·d,** *adv. north. dial.* Also 9 **(h)umpstridden.** [Pa. pple. next.] Astride, strideways.

1674 RAY *N. C. Words*, *Umstrid*, astride, astridlands. [Hence in Bailey and Grose.] **1828**– in dial. glossaries (Yks., Lancs.).

† **Umstri·de,** *v. Obs. rare.* [f. UM- + STRIDE *v.*] *trans.* To bestride.

*a* 1352 MINOT in *Pol. Poems* (Rolls) I. 68 The King of Beme had cares colde, That was ful hardy and bolde A stede to umstride. *c* 1400 *Ywaine & Gaw.* 1302 When he was dight in seker wede, Than he umstrade a nobil stede.

† **Umstroke.** *Obs. rare.* [f. UM- + STROKE *sb.*[1]] Edge, circumference.

1650 FULLER *Pisgah* I. xiv. 46 Such Towns as stand (as one may say) on tiptoes, on the very umstroke, or on any part of the utmost line of any Map. *Ibid.* v. xx. 182 Places situate on the Um-stroke (such the location of Aleppo in our Map) are not in their exact position.

† **Umthink,** *v. Obs.* Also 4 **vmthinc(k,** 5 *Sc.* **wmthink;** 4–6 **vmthynk(e,** 6 **vnþ-.** [f. UM- + THINK *v.*[2] Cf. WFris. *omtinke*, MSw. *omtänkia*, older Da. *omtænke*, obs. Icel. *umþenkja*, MLG. *ummedenken*, OE. *ymbþencan.* See also UMBETHINK *v.*]

**1.** *intr.* To bethink, consider, reflect. Also const. *of*, or with inf.

*a* 1300 *Cursor M.* 717 Sathan..vmthoght o þat thing to stint þat godd til ending god had mint. *Ibid.* 23709 (Edinb.), Quasum graiþeli wil vmþink, Þis werd es fals and ful of swink. *a* 1340 HAMPOLE *Psalter* xxi. 28 Þe kirke of all þe warld sall vmthynke of God, for þai had forgetyn him: & swa vmthynkand, þai sall be turnyd till him.

**b.** In *pa. pple.* Having taken thought.

*c* 1340 HAMPOLE *Psalter, Cant. Mariæ* 9 He receyfyd israel his barne, vmthouȝt [L. *recordatus*] of his mercy.

**2.** *refl.* To bethink (oneself). Also const. *of*, or with obj. clause or inf.

*a* 1300 *Cursor M.* 529 If þow wil þe vm-think, Þow may þam find with litul suink. *Ibid.* 5722 He vmthoght him in his hert Of his hiht lang siþen es gan. *c* 1325 *Metr. Hom.* (1862) 79 He umthoght him what was best, How he might this ilk nonne fange. *c* 1340 HAMPOLE *Psalter* ix. 12 Sekand þe blode of þaim he has vmthoght him. *Ibid.* He has vmthoght him to glorifie his seruantes. *a* 1400 *New Test.* (Paues) Acts xi. 16 Forsoþe I vmboghte me of þo wordes of oure Lorde. *c* 1440 *Alph. Tales* 31 'Son, vmthynk þe if þou hafe dissayvid any man be þis stane.' And at þis wurde he vmthoght hym & said [etc.]. *Ibid.* 351 Þat evur when he lukid þer-vppon, he sulde vmthynk hym of his dead. 15.. *Chester Pl.* xxiv. 430 (MS. Bodley 175), How durst you euer doo amisse When you vnþought you of þis?

**Umtiff**: see UM-. **Umwhile**: see UMQUHILE.

**Umwrithe**: see UM-. **Umyak,** var. UMIAK.

**Un-,** *prefix*[1], expressing negation, representing OE. *un-*, = OFris. *un-, on-, oen-* (WFris. *ûn-, on-*, EFris. *ün-*, NFris. *ün-*), MDu. (and Du.) *on-*, OS. (MLG., LG.), OHG. (MLG., G.), and Goth. *un-*, ON. *ú-, ó-* (Icel. *ó-*, Sw. *o-*, Norw. and Da. *u-*), corresponding to OIr. *in-, an-*, L. *in-* (*im-, il-, ir-, i-*), Gr. ἀν-, ἀ-, Arm. *an-*, Skr. *an-, a-*, Indo-Eur. *n̥, an ablaut-variant of *ne* not: see NE *adv.* The prefix has been very extensively employed in English, as in the other Germanic languages, and is now the one which can be used with the greatest freedom in new formations.

**2.** In OE. the number of recorded forms in *un-* is very large, the prefix being freely applied with a purely negative force to several parts of speech, which may be classified as follows: (*a*) simple adjectives, as *unbeald, unbliðe, unbrád, unclǽne, uncúþ, undéop*, etc., derivative adjs., as *unbealoful, unblódiȝ, ungyltig, unmeahtig, unclǽnlic, uncúðlic, uncynlic*, etc., and composite forms, as *uncampróf, undéopþancol, unfæstrǽd*, etc.; (*b*) simple adverbs, as *unéaðe, unefne, unfæzere, unfeorr*, etc., and derivative forms, as *unclǽnlice, uncúðlice, unéaðelice, unfæstlice*, etc.; (*c*) past participles of strong and weak verbs, as *unbeden, unbegunnen, unboren, undrifen, ungeboden, ungecnáwen*, etc., *unbyrged, undǽled, ungedered, unclǽnsod, ungeendod, ungehálgod, unboht*, etc.; (*d*) present participles, as *unberende, unbirnende, uncwaciende, uncweðende, unfélende*, etc.; (*e*) simple nouns, as *unár, unbealu, uncyst, unfriþ, unlagu, unþanc*, etc., and derivative forms, as *unclǽnness, unfægerness, uncúfscipe, unwisdóm*, etc. A prominent feature of the OE. examples is the prevalence of long derivative or compound formations, usually based upon, or corresponding to, Latin formations with *in-, im-, il-*, as *unaberendlic* intolerable, *unaberendlice* intolerably, *unbegripendlic* incomprehensible, *unbescéawodlice* inconsiderately, *unforhæfedness* incontinence. The greater number of such forms were no doubt artificial, and had little or no currency in ordinary language. In a small number of nouns *un-* appears with a pejorative in place of a negative sense, as *unǽt* excessive eating, *uncoðu* an evil disease, *uncræft* an evil art, and similarly *undǽd, undóm, unlagu, unrǽd, unsiþ, untíma, unweder.* Altogether the number of *un-* words recorded in OE. is about 1250, of which barely an eighth part survived beyond the OE. period.

**3.** The disappearance of so many of the OE. formations left early ME. with a very limited supply of *un-* words, even when new (or apparently new) examples are added to those inherited from the older language. A fair proportion even of this reduced stock proved unable to survive for more than half a century, and had passed out of use by 1250. A few of these, especially such as obviously had some general currency, are entered in their alphabetical places, but the greater number are given here (together with a few of somewhat later date) as properly belonging to the older period and having no direct influence upon the later development of the prefix. Most of these are composed of purely native elements, but a few show the beginnings of Scandinavian and French influence, as *ungrith, unhaȝerliȝ, unskatheful; unbispused, uncoverlich.*

In ME. transcripts of OE. homilies a few additional words are found, as *unafillendlich, unasecgliche, uniredliche, unisewenlich, untodele(n)dlich, unȝearu.*

**unagi·n** *a.* [cf. AGIN *v.*], without beginning; **unane·mned** *ppl. a.* [OE. *ánemnan* to declare], unnamed, indescribable; **unaw·ned** *ppl. a.* [f. AWN *v.*[2]], unmanifested, undeclared; **unaȝe·ten** *ppl. a.* [f. ANGET *v.*], unperceived; **unba·leful** *a.* [OE. *unbealoful*], harmless; **unba·rmed** *ppl. a.* [f. BARM *v.*], unleavened; **unbibu·ried** *ppl. a.* [OE. *unbebyrigǽd*], unburied; **unbihe·ve** *sb.* [cf. next] = *unbihoof*; **unbihe·ve** *a.* [OE. *unbehéfe*], disadvantageous, unprofitable; **unbihoo·f, -ho·fthe** [BEHOOF, BIHOFTHE], disadvantage, detriment; **unbise·(h)iness** [f. pa. pple. of BESEE *v.*], inattention, carelessness; **unbiso·rȝeliche** *adv.* [OE. *unbesorh* not cared for], roughly; **unbispu·sed** *ppl. a.* [after OE. *unbeweddod*], unmarried; **unbiwe·ne** *a.* [cf. OE. *unwéne*], unexpected; **unbo·ned** *ppl. a.* [f. BOON *v.*], unentreated; **unbo·telich** *a.* [f. BOOT *sb.*[1]], irremediable; **unco·verlich** *a.* [f. COVER *v.*[2] 2], irrecoverable; **uncu·nne** [cf. OE. *uncynn* a.], improper conduct; **uncu·nneliche** *v.* [f. OE. *cynn* KIN[1]], to denaturalize; **uncu·nness** [f. OE. *cunnan* to know], ignorance; **uncu·ððe** [OE. *uncyððu*], a strange land; **undea·ðlich** *a.* [OE. *undéaþlic*], immortal; **undea·ðlichness** [OE. *undéaþlicnes*], immortality; **undeaþshi·ldiȝness** [f. OE. *déaþscyldig*], exemption from death; **unde·rf,** *a.* [f. DERF *a.*], irresolute, weak; **undrei·nt** *p.p.* [f. DRENCH *v.*], undrowned; **undri·nkled** *p.p.* [f. DRENKLE *v.*], = prec.; **une·ndliche** *adv.* [cf. ON. *úendiliga*], infinitely; **unfa·ken** *a.* [OE. *unfácne*], guileless, innocent; **unfew·** *a.* [ON. *úfár*], many; **unforgo·lden** *p.p.* [OE. *unforgolden*], unrequited; **unforgu·lt** *ppl. a.* [f. FORGUILT *v.*], not affected with guilt; **unfra·me** [cf. ON. *úframi* backwardness], disadvantage, loss; **unfre·me** [OE. *unfremu*], = prec.; **unfri·th** [OE. *unfriþ*, ON. *úfriðr*], dissension, strife; **unfu·lhtned** [cf. FULHTNE *v.*], unbaptized; **unfullma·king** [cf. *fullmake* v., and OE. *unfulfremming*], imperfection; **unȝeri·m** *a.* [OE. *ungerim* sb.], numberless; **unghe·re** *adv.* [OE. *ungéara*], soon, quickly; **ungre·te** [cf. OE. *grýto*], want of size, smallness; **ungri·th** [f. GRITH *sb.*], insecurity, hurt; **unha·ȝherliȝ** *adv.* [see HAGHER *a.*, and cf. ON. *úhagliga*], unskilfully, awkwardly; **unhe·rsumness** [OE. *unhiersumnes*], disobedience; **unhu·htlic** *a.* [f. OE. *hyhtlic* HIGHTLY *a.*], unpleasant; **unicu·nde** *a.* [OE. *ungecynde*], not native, foreign; **unifei·e** *a.* [OE. *ungeféȝe*], = next; **unifo·h, -ivo·h,** *a.* [OE. *ungefóg*], immense; *adv.* extremely; **uniho·ded** *ppl. a.* [OE. *ungehádod*], not ordained; **unili·mp** [OE. *ungelimp*], misfortune, mishap; **unilo·ȝe** *p.p.* [f. ME. *iloȝe*, p.p. of LIE *v.*[2]], without falsehood; **unima·ke** [OE. *ungemaca*], a non-equal, a superior; **unimea·ð** *adv.*, = *unmeðe* (see below); **unique·me** *a.* [OE. *ungecwéme*], unpleasant, inconvenient; **uniri·ht** [f. OE. *ȝeriht*], injustice, wrong; **uniri·med** *ppl. a.* [OE. *ungerimed*], unnumbered; **uniru·de** *a.* [OE. *ungerýde*], = UNRIDE *a.*; **unisa·ht** *ppl. a.* [see SAUGHT *v.*], unreconciled; **unise·le** *sb.* [cf. SELE *sb.*], unhappiness, misery; **unise·le** *a.* [f. ISELE *a.*], = next; **unise·li** *a.* [OE. *ungesǽlig*: cf. ISELI *a.*], unhappy, wretched; **unise·liche** *adv.* [OE. *ungesǽllice*], unhappily, wretchedly; **unise·lth** [OE. *ungesǽlþ*: cf. ISELTH], unhappiness, misfortune; **unisi·bbe** [cf. OE. *unsib* and *gesib* a.], dissension, strife; **uniso·me** *a.* [OE. *ungesóm*: cf. ISOM(E *a.*], at variance; **unisu·nde** [cf. ISUNDE], unsoundness, injury; **unitha·rf** [cf. THARF *sb.*], evil, mischief; **unive·le** *a.*, = UNFELE *a.*; **uniwea·ld** [OE. *ungeweald*: cf. IWALD *sb.*], lack of control; **uniwe·lde** *a.* [OE. *ungewielde*], unwieldy; **uniwi·dere** [OE. *ungewidere*], bad weather; **uniwi·ll** [cf. IWILL], unwillingness; **uniwi·ne,** = UNWINE (an enemy); **uniwra·st** *a.*, = UNWRAST *a.*; **uniwre·nch,** = UNWRENCH *sb.*; **unla·ȝeliche, -like** *adv.* [f. LAWLY *adv.*], unlawfully; **unle·f** *a.* [OE. *ungeléaf*], unbelieving; **unle·flich** *a.* [OE. *ungeléaflic*], incredible; **unle·pped** *ppl. a.* [f. *lep* LAP *v.*], uncovered; **unli·f** *a.*, unleavened; **unli·mp,** = *unilimp*; **unli·ȝel** *a.* [f. LIE *v.*[2]], truthful; **unlo·thness** [cf. LOATHNESS 1], harmlessness, innocence; **unlu·de** [f. LUDE[1]], an unpleasant noise; **unlu·ved** *ppl. a.* [OE. *unlýfed, -liefed*], unallowed, illicit; **unmea·ðeliche** *adv.* [OE. *unmǽðlice*], immoderately; **unme·ðe** *adv.*, = prec.; **unme·ðlich** *a.* [OE. *unmǽðlic*], immoderate, excessive; **unme·ðship** [cf. prec.], impatience; **unmi·ðe** [f. MITHE *v.*], open speech; **unmu·ndlunge** *adv.* [OE. *unmyndlinga*], unexpectedly; **unne·d, -ne·t** *p.p.* [OE. *ungenīedd*], unconstrained; **unneo·d** [f. NEED *sb.*], disadvantage, loss; **unneo·melich** *a.* [f. NIM *v.*], untakable; **unre·cheleas** *a.* [see 5 a], reckless, careless; **unro·less** *a.* [see 5 a], restless; **unseȝ·endlic** *a.* [cf. OE. *unásecgendlic*], unspeakable; **unseȝ·endlike** *adv.* [cf. OE. *unásecgendlice*], unspeakably; **unse·ȝenlic, -se·helich** *a.* [OE. *ungesegenlic*], invisible; **unse·ȝenlike** *adv.* [cf. OE. *ungesewenlice*], invisibly; **unsha·thiȝ** *a.* [OE. *unsceaþþig*], harmless, innocent; **unsha·thiȝness** [OE. *unsceaþþignes*], innocence; **unshri·vel** *a.* [f. SHRIVE *v.*], neglectful of confession; **unsi·bbe,** = *unisibbe*; **unsi·the** [OE. *unsiþ*], mishap, misfortune; **unska·theful** *a.* [cf. OE. *unsceaþful*], harmless; **unsme·the** *a.* [OE. *unsméðe*], unsmooth; **unsta·thelfest** *a.* [OE. *unstaðolfæst*], unsteadfast; **unstreo·ned** *p.p.* [f. STRENE *v.*], unbegot; **unta·lelich** *a.* [f. TALE *sb.*], indescribable; **untheo·de** [f. THEDE], strangers; **untho·lelich** *a.* [f. THOLE *v.*], unendurable; **unthrow·lich** *a.* [cf. OE. *unþrówigendlic*], incapable of suffering; **unthu·ldeliche** *adv.* [cf. OE. *unþyldlicnes*], with lack of endurance; **unti·ming** [f. TIMING *vbl. sb.* 1], mishap, ill fortune; **untobri·tned** *ppl. a.* [f. TO-BRITTEN *v.*], undivided; **untode·led** *ppl. a.* [OE. *untódǽled*], = prec.; **untode·linde** *ppl. a.* [cf. prec.], indivisible; **untrow·ness** [cf. OE. *untréow, -tréowþ*], unfaithfulness, breach of trust; **untu·deri** *a.* [cf. OE. *untydrende*], barren; **untu·htle** [see TUHTLE], a bad habit or custom; **untwe·med** *ppl. a.* [f. TWEME *v.*], undivided; **unvo·nded** *ppl. a.* [cf. OE. *ungefandod*], untried; **unwa·ker** *a.* [f. WAKER *a.*], unwatchful; **unwa·ldes** *adv.* [OE. *ungewealdes*], unintentionally; **unwea·wed** *ppl. a.*, ? uncovered; **unwe·nd** *p.p.* [f. WEND *v.*], unturned; **unweo·te** [OE. *unwita*], an ignorant person; **unweo·teness,** = *unwiteness*; **unwha·rfed** *p.p.* [f. WHARF *v.*], unturned, unaltered; **unwha·te** [f. WHATE *sb.*], misfortune; **unwi·lle** *a.* [cf. UNWILL *sb.*], unwilling; **unwi·sdomness** [f. UNWISDOM], folly; **unwi·teness** [cf. *unweote* above], ignorance; **unwi·tless** *a.* [see 5 a], senseless, insensible; **unwi·tship** [cf. WITSHIP], folly; **unzy·ginde** *ppl. a.* [cf. OE. *unásecgende*], indescribable.

*a* 1225 *Juliana* 3 (Bodl. MS.), An godd *unagin, euch godes ful. *c* 1175 *Lamb. Hom.* 43 Innan þan ilke sea weren *unaneomned deor. *c* 1200 ORMIN 2003 Forr þatt itt shollde *unnawwnedd ben & all unncuþ & dærne. *Ibid.* 7227, 7381. *c* 1205 LAY 25797 Ȝif þu hine ifindest..and þu al *un-aȝeten [*c* 1275 on-aȝete] aȝein miht iwende. *c* 1200 *Trin. Coll. Hom.* 49 Duue ne harmeð none fuȝele..and ðus kið þat hie is admod & *unbaleful. *c* 1200 ORMIN 1591 Forr þerrflinng bræd iss clene bræd, Forr þatt itt iss *unnberrmedd. *a* 1225 *Leg. Kath.* 2243 He het..bihefden ham..& leauen hare bodies *unbiburiet alle, fode to wilde deor. *c* 1200 *Trin. Coll. Hom.* 121 Ure drihten..seh þat alle hie turnden fro him hem seluen to *unbihefe. *Ibid.* 7 Do þat ure sowle & ure lichame be biheue, & forlaten al þat hem beð *unbiheue. *a* 1240 *Sawles Warde* in *O. E. Hom.* I. 265 Nes na lessere mi tale þen wes murhðes sondes ne unbihefre to ow. *c* 1205 LAY. 8576 Forð ferde þe king..to his muchelen *vnbihoue [*c* 1275 unbiofþe]. *a* 1225 *Ancr. R.* 344 [The sin] of keorfunge, oðer of hurtunge, þuruh *unbiseinesse [*v.r.* -sehenesse]. *c* 1175 *Lamb. Hom.* 43 Herefter iseh paul hwer .iii. deoflen ledden an meiden swiðe *unbisorȝeliche. *c* 1200 *Trin. Coll. Hom.* 13 Þat man þe spuse haueð,..& þo þe beð *unbispused. *c* 1250 *Gen. & Ex.* 3777 Alle he sunken ðe erðe wið-in,..Swilc endesið *vn-bi-wen hauen. *c* 1200 ORMIN 17081 Forrþi toc Crist forrþrihht anan Unnbedenn & *unnbonedd Allræresst towarrd Nicodem. *c* 1230 *Hali Meid.* 17 Flih alle thinges, & forhuh ȝeorne þat tus *unbotelich lure of mahe arisen. *Ibid.* 27 Wið swuch *uncouerlich lure as meidenhades menske is. *c* 1200 *Trin. Coll. Hom.* 11 After clepenge, & ascinge, & *uncunne, & warienge,..& fele swilche deueles craftes. *c* 1230 *Hali Meid.* 35 Þis is sunne, & ec *uncunnelicheð þe. *c* 1250 *Hymn* in *Trin. Coll. Hom.* App. 258 Vre neode wel þu wost, & ure *unkunnesse in þine hond is michte mest; louerd þu vs blesce. 1357 *Lay Folks Catech.* (L.) 390 For non schuld excuse hym of vnkunnys for to cun hem. *a* 1225 *Ancr. R.* 140 Uor heo is her in *uncuððe, iput in one prisune. *c* 1200 *Trin. Coll. Hom.* 133 Adam..was *undeaðlich forte he sinede. *a* 1225 *Leg. Kath.* 2292 Þet þing þet schal arisen..of deað to lif undeðlich. *c* 1200 *Trin. Coll. Hom.* 33 Ðe [deflen] bireueden him alle his riche weden þat waren unerned giue, & *undeðlicnesse, & loðlesnesse. *c* 1200 ORMIN 17571 Sawle iss ec wurrþlike shridd .. Wiþþ *unndæþshildiȝnesse. *a* 1225 *Leg. Kath.* 1174 Ah al þe weane..wente upon þe unstrencðe of þet *underue flesch, þet he neodeles nom. *c* 1175 *Lamb. Hom.* 141 Þe see..adreinte pharao and al his ferede mid him, swa þet nes þere nefre an bileued *un-dreint. *c* 1250 *Gen. & Ex.* 3280 Of hem alle bi-leaf non fot *Vn-drincled in ðat salte spot. *a* 1225 *Ancr. R.* 398 Ne schal neuer heorte þenchen swuch seluhðe, þet ich nulle ȝiuen more uor þine luue, vnimeteliche and *vnendliche more. *c* 1200 ORMIN 4149 Forr Crist iss strang & stedefasst & findiȝ & *unnfakenn. *Ibid.* 13327. *Ibid.* 159 Oþre *unnfæwe shulenn ec Full glade & bliþe wurrþenn. *Ibid.* 792 Oþre menn unnfæwe. *c* 1175 *Lamb. Hom.* 41 Ne scule ȝe neure god don *unforgolden. *a* 1200 *Moral Ode* 59 (Lamb. MS.), Ne scal nan ufel bon unbocht ne nan god unforȝolden [*v.rr.* -ȝolde, -gulde]. *a* 1225 *Leg. Kath.* 231 Þes heouenliche lauerd luueð treowe bileaue & nowðer blod ne ban of *unforgult ahte. *c* 1230 *Hali Meid.* 43 And te oðre þat halden ham vnforgult & cleane, beon ase sikere. *c* 1250 *Gen. & Ex.* 1566 Riȝt is his name hoten iacob, to min *un-frame. *Ibid.* 3037 Knowen sal ben, ðe to un-frame, In euerilc lond min miȝte name. *a* 1200 *Moral Ode* 226 (Lambeth MS.), Ich ..wille..Warni hom wið hore *unfrome [*v.r.* unfreme] ȝif ho me wulleð lusten. *c* 1200 *Trin. Coll. Hom.* 195 Ðe man noteð wel his ȝiepshipe þe birgeð him seluen wið his aȝene soule unfreme, & erneð after his soule freme. *c* 1205 LAY. 2557 Membriz hefde inomen þat grið, ah sone he makede *unfrið. *Ibid.* 19404 Octa heold muche vnfrið, & Lot faht him ofte wið. *c* 1200 ORMIN 16895 Þatt lede þatt primmseȝȝnedd iss & iss ȝet all *unnfullhtnedd. *a* 1300 *E. E. Psalter* cxxxviii. 15 Þine eghen segh *unfulmaking mine. *c* 1200 ORMIN 18993 Forr mikell follc & *unnȝerim Iss ȝet to daȝȝ onn erþe. *c* 1250 *Gen. & Ex.* 3047 O morgen, ..ðhunder, and hail, and leuenes fir, Cam wel *vnghere. *a* 1250 *Owl & Night.* 752 (Jesus Coll. MS.), Hwy atwitestu me myne vnstrengþe & myne *vngrete & myn vnlengþe? *c* 1200 ORMIN 16280 Forr hefiȝ & forr sware *unngriþþ Þatt hæþenn follc þær wrohhte. *Ibid.* 425 Forr swa we don *unnhaȝherrliȝ Whattse we don to gode. *Ibid.* 4277 Þatt dæþess wunde, Þatt Adam haffde ȝifenn uss Þurrh hiss *unnherrsummnesse. *Ibid.* 13425. *c* 1205 LAY. 5101 Nis hit noht *un-huhtlic incker moder inc hateð. *Ibid.* 18429 Swa we scullen of londe driuen *vnicunde [*c* 1275 onicunde]. *Ibid.* 5573 Ferde he hauede inoh muchel and *vnifeie. *Ibid.* 8674 Of þon folke he sloh muchel & *unifoh [*c* 1275 onifoh]. *Ibid.* 23518. *Ibid.* 17883 Þe leome þe toward France droh, he wes briht *vnifoh. *a* 1250 *Owl & Night.* 1178 (Jesus Coll. MS.), Ertu ihoded oþer þu cursest *vnihoded? *c* 1200 *Trin. Coll. Hom.* 177 Ðe water stremes on-heueden up here undes, þat is þat folc þe sore bimurneð, & swiðe bimeneð swich *unilimp. *a* 1250 *Prov. Ælfred* 148 in *O. E. Misc.* 110 Strong..hit is to swynke a-yeyn vnylimpe. *c* 1380 *Sir Ferumb.* 511 Ȝunder at my sadel boȝe hongeþ o botel, Ful of baume *oun-y-loȝe ys he euery del. *c* 1205 LAY. 17961 Biuoren þa steorre wes þæ drake elcches wurmes *vnimake [*c* 1275 onimake]. *Ibid.* 19125. *a* 1225 *Juliana* 5 (Bodl. MS.), Wið *unimeað muchel hird & wið heh duheðe. *a* 1250 *Prov. Ælfred* 444 in *O. E. Misc.* 128 Þanne deþ hit sone þat þe biþ *vnyqueme. *c* 1205 LAY. 10281 In his herede he makede grið, & lette awæi þat *vniriht. *Ibid.* 433 Þa lette he riden *vnirimed folc. *a* 1240 *Sawles Warde* in *O. E. Hom.* I. 253 [To] þolien & a-beoren hare *unirude duntes. *c* 1175 *Lamb. Hom.* 39 Þu scalt sahtnien þa þe beoð *unisahte mid alle þine mahte. *c* 1205 LAY. 21788 Þa Scottes weoren to-deled mid muclen *vniselen ȝeond þa monie munten. *Ibid.* 26446 Þe cniht was *unisele. *c* 1250 *Moral Ode* 101 in *E. E. P.* (1862) 28 Niere no man elles dieð ne sic, ne non vn-ysele [*v.r.* vnsele]. *c* 1175 *Lamb. Hom.* 31 He his *uniseli ȝif him is lað to donne þis. *c* 1205 LAY. 4014 Þe uniselie moder mid sexe hine to-snæde. *a* 1225 *Ancr. R.* 68 Sum uniseli.. haueð ischriuen hire al to wundre. *c* 1205 LAY. 7022 Seoððen wes his sune king þe *vniseliche [*c* 1275 onselliche] luuede. *a* 1200 *Moral Ode* 198 Þurh him deð com in þis middenerd and oðer *uniselðe [*v.r.* unisalðe, vnyselyhþe]. *c* 1205 LAY. 2545 Bi-tweonen heom aræs..sleȝht & muchel seorwa, al for heora uniselðe. *Ibid.* 9845 Betere weore sæhte þene swulc *vnisibbe [*c* 1275 onsibbe]. *a* 1250 *Owl & Night.* 1522 (Cott. MS.), For hit itit ofte & ilome, þat wif & were beoþ *unisome. *c* 1205 LAY. 18452 Heo droȝen heore þermes mid muchele *vnisunde. *c* 1200 *Trin. Coll. Hom.* 65 *Pes cucurrit ad malum*, fot ȝide to *uniðor[f]. *c* 1205 LAY. 21744 Þat is a seolcuð mere..mid fiscen & mid feoȝelen, mid *uniuele þingen. *c* 1200 *Trin. Coll. Hom.* 63 Þat we hauen agilt..oðer þurh nuteluste, oðer þurh *uniweald,..oðer recheluste. *c* 1205 LAY. 5901 Fifti hundred cnihtes, mid alle heore wepnen, þe weoren *vniwælde; Þa oðere weoren swifte, heore wepnen weoren lihte. *c* 1175 *Lamb. Hom.* 115 Þene bið his erd ihened,..ȝe on hungre, ȝe on cwalme, ȝe on *uniwidere. *Ibid.* 69 Halde we us from *uniwil, & habben feir lete & ec skil. *c* 1205 LAY. 14466 Ȝif þu wult þe awraken .. & don þine *vniwinen [*c* 1275 onwines] wa. *Ibid.* 29609 Heom sceomeden wel sære þat þat *vniwraste moncun heom iscend hafden. *c* 1250 *Death* 94 in *O. E. Misc.* 174 For þine fule sunnen & for þin *uniwrenche [*v.r.* vny-]. *c* 1175 *Lamb. Hom.* 115 Wa þere þeode..þer þa aldormen etað on erne marȝen *u[n]laȝeliche. *c* 1200 ORMIN 15867 All alls he draf..Ut off hiss Faderr temmple Þatt follc þatt he þærinne sahh Unnlaȝhelike himm ledenn. *c* 1200 *Trin. Coll. Hom.* 125 For þu art *unlef mine worde, þu shalt beo dumb forte þat child beo boren. *Ibid.*, And for þese þre þing [he] let hit *unleflich, & ne lefde hit noht, þat þe engel him seide. *a* 1225 *Leg. Kath.* 345 Þet alle ower leasunges beoð unlefliche. *a* 1225 *Unlepped [see *unweawed* below]. *c* 1250 *Gen. & Ex.* 3153 Heued and fet, and in-rew meten, lesen fro ðe bones and eten, Wið wriðel and *vn-lif bread. *c* 1200 *Trin. Coll. Hom.* 61 Oðer þurh roberie, oðer þurh unrihte dom,..oðer þurh oðer *unlimp. *Ibid.* 195. *a* 1225 *Ancr. R.* 274 Al þis unlimp is icumen þuruh þe ȝetewardes slepe. *c* 1200 *Trin. Coll. Hom.* 131 *Un-liȝel man selde liȝeð, & soð-saȝel man seið ofte soð. *c* 1175 *Lamb. Hom.* 97 Heo deð þere monnan heortan..þet heo beoð liðe þurh un-cladnesse [*read* *unlaðnesse]. *a* 1225 *Ancr. R.* 340 Edmodnesse, & abstinence, kulure unloðnesse, & oðer swuch uertuz. *a* 1275 *Prov. Ælfred* 689 in *O. E. Misc.* 138 He wole maken fule luden; he wole grennen, cocken, & chiden, & hewere [=ever] faren mid *vnluden. *c* 1200 *Trin. Coll. Hom.* 71 Ȝif hit was don on untime, oðer on *unluuede stede, oðer mid unluued lete, oðer on unluued wise. *a* 1200 *St. Marher.* 15 Lutle ich mei makien to muchelin *unmeaðeliche, ȝef me hut ant heleð hit. *a* 1225 *Juliana* 4 (Royal MS.), Wið *unmeð muchel hird & unduhti duheðe. *a* 1225 *Ancr. R.* 238 And so hit *unmeðluker is, wrinnen aȝean þe uestluker. *Ibid.* 122 Auh nu is muche wunder of ure muchele *unmeðschipe. Understondeð þis word. *c* 1250 *Gen. & Ex.* 3973 Quuað ðis asse ðus wið *vn-miðe, 'Qui betes ðu me ðis ðridde siðe?' *a* 1225 *Ancr. R.* 280 Mid þen ilke turn he mei hine *unmunlunge aworpen. *a* 1240 *Sawles Warde* in *O. E. Hom.* I. 249 Hire wune is to cumen bi stale ferliche & unmundlunge hwen me least weneð. *c* 1200 ORMIN 11457 To don summ hæfedd sinne, All hise þannkess, all *unnnedd. *a* 1225 *Ancr. R.* 340 Vor þe eorðe al unnet.. bringeð forð misliche flures. *c* 1205 LAY. 308 Þe fader heo bi-eode to his aȝre *unneode [*c* 1275 on-neode]. *Ibid.* 8741 To þes kinges unneoden. *a* 1225 *Leg. Kath.* 1180 Ne mahte me nowðer godd,..ne halden ne neomen ȝet, for godd is *unneomelich. *a* 1225 *Ancr. R.* 388 Heo underueng al ase on *unrecheleas þing. *c* 1230 *Hali Meid.* 35 Þat *unroles uuel, þat pine upo pine, þat wondrende ȝeomerunge. *c* 1200 ORMIN 2823 Þin seollþe iss all *unnseȝȝenndlic. *Ibid.* 11177 O Godess name, þatt iss an Unnseȝȝenndliȝ Þrimmnesse. *Ibid.* 1760 *Unnseȝȝenndlike mare inoh þann aniȝ wihht maȝȝ þennkenn. *Ibid.* 17296 Forr gast iss all *unnseȝhennlic Biforenn flæshlic eȝhe. *Ibid.* 19465. *a* 1225 *Leg. Kath.* 254 Alre þinge schuppent, þet is godd unsehelich. *Ibid.* 904. *c* 1200 ORMIN 17241 Þær iss þa þatt illke mann *Unnseȝhennlike wharrfedd Fra flæsh till gast. *Ibid.* 19720. *Ibid.* 2889, I þatt tatt he ne wollde nohht *Unnshaþiȝ wimmann wreȝhenn. *Ibid.* 15946 Þatt shep iss all unnshaþiȝ der. *Ibid.* 1171 Ȝiff þatt tu follȝhesst soþ meocleȝȝc & soþ *unnshaþiȝnesse. *Ibid.* 14473. 1340 *Ayenb.* 32 Huanne he is sleuuol,..*onssriuel, uoryetinde, slak, and fallinde. *a* 1250 *Owl & Night.* 1164 (Cott. MS.), Þu ne singst neuer one siþe Þat hit nis for sum *unsiþe. *c* 1200 ORMIN 1176 Forr shep iss all *unnskaþefull & stille der & liþe. *Ibid.* 7915. *Ibid.* 9209 Whærse iss all *unnsmeþe get Þurrh bannkess & þurrh græfess. *c* 1175 *Lamb. Hom.* 151 Þe twafalde Mon is *unstaþelfest on alle his weies. *a* 1225 *Ancr. R.* 208 Vnstaðeluest bileaue aȝean holi lore, nis hit of prude? *c* 1205 LAY. 18882 For ȝet he beoð *unstreoned þa sturieð al þa þeoden. *a* 1225 *Ancr. R.* 144 Þe *untaleliche pinen þet no tunge ne mei tellen. *Ibid.* 410 Þeo blisse..is untalelich to alle worldliche tungen. *a* 1240 *Sawles Warde* in *O. E. Hom.* I. 251 Hell is..ful of sorhe untalelich, for ne mei na muð..rikenin hit ne tellen. *a* 1225 *Ancr. R.* 312 *Unðeode ledden uorð þis child in his warde. *a* 1240 *Sawles Warde* in *O. E. Hom.* I. 251 Helle is..ful of stench *unþolelich. *a* 1225 *Leg. Kath.* 1155 Godd, þe is *unþrowlich, þrowede, oðer þolede pine oðer passiun, o þe deore rode. *Ibid.* 161 Heo..ifont ter swiðe feole..þeotinde *unþuldeliche wið reowfule reames. *c* 1250 *Gen. & Ex.* 1180 On dreme him cam tiding for-quat He ðrowede and ðolede *un-timing ðat. *c* 1200 ORMIN 11179 Faderr, & Sune, & Haliȝ Gast, An Godd all *unntobrittnedd. *Ibid.* 11518 An Godd all *unntodæledd. *Ibid.* 18512, I Godess herrte..All hal & unntodæledd. 1340 *Ayenb.* 266 Ich yzeȝ þe ilke onspekynde an *on-todelinde mageste of þe holy trinyte be-gynnynge ne ende ne heþ. *a* 1200 *Moral Ode* 265 Þer inne boð..þa þe *untrownesse duden þon þe ho sculden bon holde. *c* 1250 *Gen. & Ex.* 964 Siðen bi-fel ðat sarrai, for ȝhe was longe *untuderi, Ȝhe bitagte abre maiden agar. *c* 1205 LAY. 24655 Elche *untuhtle heo talden vnwurðe. *a* 1225 *Juliana* 54 (Royal MS.), Nawt þreo godes, ah is an euer ihwer *untwemet [*Bodl. MS.* untweamet]. *a* 1225 *Ancr. R.* 232 Hwat wot, he seið, Salomon, þe þet is *unuonded? *Ibid.* 272 Hwon Recabes sunen..ivindeð so *unwaker & so nesche ȝeteward. *c* 1175 *Lamb. Hom.* 23 Hit nis nan wunder þah mon sunegie oðer hwile *unwaldes. *a* 1225 *Ancr. R.* 424 No mon ne i-seo ham *unweawed [*v.r.* unlepped] ne open heaued. *c* 1200 *Trin. Coll. Hom.* 163 Ac seðen hie henen wenden, atlai þat lond *unwend, & bicam waste. *a* 1225 *Ancr. R.* 8 Ȝif eni *unweote acseð ou of hwat ordre ȝe beon. *a* 1225 *Leg. Kath.* 1054 Unweoten, þe weneð þet hit beo swa as hit on ehe bereð ham. *a* 1240 *Sawles Warde* in *O. E. Hom.* I. 255 Þurh *unweotenesse ne mei ha nawt sunegin *c* 1200 ORMIN 18794, I Godess herrte,..Þat aȝȝ iss all *unnwharrfedd. *Ibid.* 18822. *a* 1250 *Owl & Night.* 1148 (Cott. MS.), Al þat þu singst raþe oþer late Hit is euer of manne *unwate [*v.r.* vnhwate]. *Ibid.* 1267. *a* 1225 *Ancr. R.* 238 Þeo uihteð treouliche þet..wiðsiggeð þe graunt þerof mid *unwille heorte. *c* 1200 *Trin. Coll. Hom.* 39 Ðe unwreste herde sit on *unwisdomnesse, for he ne can is orf ȝemen. *a* 1225 *Ancr. R.* 278 Sunne & ignorance, þet is, unwisdom & *unwitenesse. *a* 1225 *Leg. Kath.* 245 He ȝelt þe wurðmunt to witlese [*R.* *unwitlese, *B.* unwitelese] þing. *a* 1240 *Wohunge* in *O. E. Hom.* I. 275 For sunne & *unwitschipe, ne hafdes tu nowðer. 1340 *Ayenb.* 268 Hy byeþ glede of god *onzyginde, hy byeþ glede of zuo moche of hare oȝene holynesse.

**4.** When the words included in the previous section are eliminated, the early ME. instances of the prefix resolve themselves into the following classes: (*a*) survivals of OE. forms, chiefly adjectives, as *unclene*, *uncouth*, *unfele*, *unfere*, *unhole*, *unmilde*, *unorne*, *unsely*, and nouns, as *unhele*, *unlaȝe*, *unmiȝt*, *unrede*, *unriȝt*, *unsele*, *unthank*, *unclenenes*, *unwisdom*, and a few past participles, as *unbegun*, *unborn*, *unboȝt*, *unheled*, *unwemmed*, *unwounded*; (*b*) new formations from native elements, as *unbuȝsom*, *uncomely*, *unhende*, *unsiker*, *untidy* adjs., *unhope*, *unstrength*, *unwinne* sbs., *unbeten*, *undone*, *unshriven*, *undemed*, *unsouȝt* pa. pples.; (*c*) adoptions of Scandinavian forms, or new formations on Scandinavian bases, as *unmeek*, *unnait*, *unsauȝt*, *unsleȝe* adjs.; *unhap*, *unsauȝt*, *unskill* sbs., *unbigged* pa. pple.; (*d*) new formations on French bases, as *ungracious*, *unsavoury*, *untrussed*.

Down to 1300 these additions were comparatively few, and barely compensated for the disuse of obsolescent forms. About that date a southern writer like Robert of Gloucester uses only a small number of *un-* words, and most of these belong to the traditional stock. On the other hand, the northern *Cursor Mundi* has a rich variety of both old and new forms, and indicates clearly the beginning of a fresh period of development. The features which are most notable in this are: (*a*) the increased proportion of past pples. in comparison with adjs. and nouns; (*b*) the reappearance of pres. pples. (as *undeiand*, *unfeland*, *unseand*), which are wanting in earlier ME. texts; (*c*) the increase in the French element, as *uncertain*, *undevote*, *undispensed*, *unfelun*, *unfruitand*, *unlele*, *unleute*, *unmesure*, *unpais*, *unponist*, *unpurvaid*, *unquit*, *unresun*, *unresunable*, *unvised*, *unwily*. With this revival of the past and pres. pples., and the introduction of *-able*, the way was opened for some of the commonest uses of *un-* in the later language. The tendency thus indicated is clearly marked before the middle of the 14th century; Dan Michel uses pres. pples., as *onconnynde*, *onspekynde*, *onwytynde*, while Hampole has *unconable*, *uncurable*, *unsufferable*, and even *unfillable*, *unstirrable*. Before 1400 the period of free employment of the prefix had fully begun, as shown by the number of new formations appearing in the works of Chaucer, Wyclif, Trevisa, and others.

**b.** As in OE., the usual force of *un-* in ME. is purely negative. The pejorative sense however survived in a few words, as *unrede*, *unsithe*, *unthew*, *unwether*, *unwine*, *unwrench*, and appears also in *unlede*, *unlude*, *unthede*, *unwiȝt*; in *unbeast* it is employed with a French base.

**c.** The usual form of the prefix in ME. is *un-*, but *on-* appears in some English texts (as the later version of Layamon, the *Ayenbite*, and the *Promp. Parv.*), and is common in older Scottish, esp. in the 16th century; this form is still current in midland and south-western dialects and in Scotland. In *Sir Ferumbras* (*c* 1380) the form *oun-* is employed, and a pronunciation corresponding to this (*un-*) is still heard in Aberdeenshire. In detached use (see 5 d) the form (ōn), sometimes written *ohn*, is also employed in the same locality.

**5.** Some peculiarities in the use of *un-*, arising in the ME. period but surviving beyond it, require special notice.

**a.** It is sometimes redundantly prefixed to adjs. ending in *-less*. Early instances are *unrecheleas* reckless, *unroless* restless, *unwitles* insensible (see 3 above), and *ungiltles* guiltless (*Sir Tristr.* 2144). The type, however, chiefly belongs to the later 16th and the 17th cent.; among the instances from that period are *unboundless*, *uncomfortless*, *undauntless*, *uneffectless*, *unfathomless*, *unhelpless*, *unmatchless*, *unmerciless*, *unnumberless*, *unrecomptless*, *unremorseless*, *unrespectless*, *unshameless*, *unshapeless*, *untimeless*; as late as 1786 *unquestionless* is found, and *unrestless* exists in modern dialect.

**b.** From the 14th century onwards there was considerable variation, when the base was of Latin origin, between the Latin *in-*, *im-*, etc., and the native *un-*. Early examples of forms with *un-*, which either then or a little later have variants with *in-*, *im-*, are *unability*, *uncorrigible*, *uncorrupt*, *uncurable*, *undign*, *undiscreet*, *unmeasurable*, *unmovable*, *unnumerable*, *unperfect*, *unperfection*, *unportable*, *unpossible*. Similar formations continued to multiply during the following centuries, so that a large proportion of the words beginning with *il-*, *im-*, *in-*, *ir-* had corresponding forms in *un-*, as *unadequate*, *unadvertence*, *unarticulate*, *unartificial*, *unattentive*, *unaudible*, *unauspicious*, *uncapable*, etc. The culminating period of the double forms lies in the 17th century; since that time the tendency has been to differentiate, and to discard one or other of the doublets, the forms with *in-*, etc., being very commonly preferred when the whole word has a distinctively Latin character, as *inadequate*, *inadvertence*, *inarticulate*, etc. Even with such forms there is no absolute rule, and doublets are still numerous, as *in-* or *un-advisable*, *in-* or *unalienable*, etc. (See IN-[2].)

By inadvertence, or simple errors in printing, *un-* or *vn-* sometimes appears in works of the 16–17th cent. for *im-*, *in-*, or *em-*, *en-*, as *vncoraged* encouraged, *unlarge* enlarge, *unployed* employed, *unpoysonynge* empoisoning, *unflam'd* inflamed, *unpostumed* imposthumed.

**c.** When two or more negative terms occurred in the same clause and were coupled by *and* or *or*, the prefix was sometimes employed only with the first. The following are examples of this practice, which is especially common in Scottish of the 16th century.

*c* **1380** WYCLIF *Wks.* (1880) 129 To kepe hym self vnblekkid or defoulid fro þis world. *c* **1460** J. RUSSELL *Bk. Nurture* 944 Lett neuer wollyn cloth.. passe a seuenyght to be vnbrosshen & shakyn. *a* **1500** in *Ratis Raving* 3 The synis that he has done wnconfessyt of or rapentyt. **1506** in *Charters, &c., Edinb.* (1871) 189 Throw selling of clayth.. vnsene or customit be yow. **1565** *Rec. Earld. Orkney* 274 Uncoackit, compellit, or seducit be ony way. **1603** KNOLLES *Hist. Turks* (1621) 83 The insolent souldiers .. nothing dedicated to the seruice of God, left vnpolluted and defaced. *Ibid.* 91 Which companies..came neere vnto the towne vnseene or discouered. **1707** MORTIMER *Husb.* 608 Eggs, unbroken or crack'd.

**d.** When *un-* is prefixed to present or past participles, these are rarely employed in a true participial function, but become adjectival in character. Examples of the present participle, however, occasionally occur with a following object, or with a prepositional construction; and in Scottish use, from at least the 15th century, *un-* in such cases has acquired the sense of 'without'. More rarely, in the older language, it has the same sense with passive participles. Both constructions are still retained in north-eastern Scottish dialect, with the prefix in the form *on* or *ohn*, frequently written separate from the participle. (The spelling *ohn* is due to, or has led to, a false association with G. *ohne* without.) Examples of these uses are :—

(*a*) **1456** SIR G. HAYE *Law Arms* (S.T.S.) 155 All that I may gett apon him, unslaand him. *Ibid.* 163 How may than a man do till othir sik dissait, ungrevand God? **1573** *Reg. Privy Council Scot.* II. 215 [To] gif to thame..gude entreatment..unrasand the present pryces in ony thing. *a* **1578** LINDESAY (Pitscottie) *Chron. Scot.* (S.T.S.) II. 122 Sa mony as the bot wald hauld on drowning thame sellffis. **1588** *Reg. Privy Council Scot.* IV. 279 Thay depairtit furth agane.., undoing ony violent deid. **1621** LADY M. WROTH *Urania* 103 Vnknowne, and vndiscouering your selfe to any, you come among vs. **1632** LITHGOW *Trav.* I. 7 The harmlesse innocent, vnexpecting euill, may suddenly bee surprised. **1786** BURNS *Ep. Young Friend* viii, Resolutely keep its laws, Uncaring consequences. **1796** MRS. M. ROBINSON *Angelina* I. 176, I could perceive him..leaning pensively on his hand, and for whole hours unvarying his attitude. **1816** BYRON *Ch. Har.* III. xlvii, As stands a lofty mind, Worn, but unstooping to the baser crowd. **1845** BAILEY *Festus* (ed. 2) 375 Earth..basks in her own free light Unfed, unaided, unrequiring aught. **1885** A. O. LEGGE *Unpop. King* II. 295 To mount a ladder..untouching the rounds with their feet.

(*b*) **1456** SIR G. HAYE *Law Arms* (S.T.S.) 185 Be quhat resoune than suld he consent..till his awin scathe.., unmaid sekir to be amendit? **1597** *Trials for Witchcraft* in *Spalding Club Misc.* (1841) I. 91 To ryss airlie befoir the sone, on betechit hir self to God, and on spokin. **1871** W. ALEXANDER *Johnny Gibb* xlii, I'm nae responsible to gae afore Sir Simon onhed my papers upo' me. **1879** G. MACDONALD *Sir Gibbie* xxii, Wad ye hae a fellow-cratur live to a' eternity ohn been ashamed o' sic a thing's that?

**6.** During the 15th, 16th, and 17th centuries the use of *un-* steadily increased, a large number of words being thus formed which have permanently established themselves in the language, besides many more which occur only incidentally or rarely. The freedom with which the prefix could be used in new formations appears clearly in the dictionaries of Florio and Cotgrave, who constantly employ it in rendering Italian and French negative terms in *in-*, etc. As the use of *un-* or *in-* (see 5 b) was still largely a matter of choice, and many of the older formations were still current, the vocabulary of the 17th century exhibits many types in common use which are now rare or obsolete, and in general is extremely rich in words beginning with *un-*. During the 18th century many of the older forms disappeared, and new formations became more limited in number and variety, but the sense of freedom in the use of the prefix when desired is clearly shown by a large number of the examples given by Ash in his dictionary in 1775. These were obviously manufactured for the purpose, and when added to the genuine words which he has included, make up a total of about 5,000 entries. In this way Ash frequently anticipates the actual introduction of new formations. In the 19th century the use of the prefix became still more common, it being freely applied to almost any adjectival or participial form, until its employment has become almost unrestricted, within certain limits indicated below. On this account it is impossible to make a complete enumeration even of forms which have actually been used, still less of those which may be created at any time.

**b.** The form of the prefix indicates that it was originally unstressed (although in OE. poetry it may have stress and carry the alliterative letter), and normally it still bears this relationship to the main part of the word. There is, however, considerable tendency to give stress to it in rare or casual formations, and whenever the negation or contrast which it implies is at all emphatic. In such cases the compound may either have two equal stresses, or the prefix may have the stronger stress; the latter degree of emphasis is usually indicated by underlining or italicizing, and the use of the hyphen; e.g. 'he is distinctly *un*-literary'.

**c.** The following sections illustrate the usual types of current formations, with illustrations drawn from unimportant modern examples, which might be indefinitely increased. All older examples in actual use, and all words important either in themselves or on account of their source, are given in their alphabetical place in the main series. As a large number of these are purely negative and self-explanatory, the place of a definition is supplied by a reference to the section of this article under which the precise type of formation is explained and illustrated.

The entries in Ash (see above) have been regarded as worthy of note only when they anticipate the appearance of a word in actual use. In these cases a reference to Ash is given within parentheses.

A purely artificial formation (suggested by Euphuistic diction) is *un-to-be-imitated* (Scott *Monast.* xx).

**7.** *Un-* is freely prefixed to adjectives of all kinds, except where a Latin form in *in-*, etc., has definitely established itself in common use. Both forms, however, may co-exist, and in some cases a new formation with *un-* has been introduced when that with *in-* has acquired a connotation which it is desirable to avoid. The form with *un-* is then purely negative, while the other may have almost a positive sense, e.g. *un-moral* in contrast with *immoral*. (When the form with *un-* has similarly acquired a positive implication, the simple negative or neutral sense is expressed by the use of NON- or NOT-.) There is also considerable restriction in the use of *un-* with short simple adjectives of native origin, the negative of these being naturally supplied by another simple word of an opposite signification. There is thus little or no tendency now to employ such forms as *unbroad*, *undeep*, *unwide*, *unbold*, *unglad*, *ungood*, *unstrong*, *unwhole*, *unfew*, etc., which freely occur in the older language. On the other hand, derivative forms in *-al*, *-ant*, *-ar*, *-ary*, *-ent*, *-ful*, *-ic*, *-ical*, *-ile*, *-ish*, *-ive*, *-ly*, *-ory*, *-ous*, *-y*, etc., are too numerous to be completely recorded. The general character of the less usual or permanent of these and other adjectival forms is illustrated by the following examples, which are restricted to such as are recorded before 1890, and could be indefinitely increased by the addition of later or less noteworthy material.

In dictionaries of various dates many formations are given of which no real instance has been found. Levins (1570) has *unhateful*, *unprecious*. Florio (1598 and 1611) renders equivalent Italian words in *in-* by such forms as *unavailful*, *unbrittle*, *uncontinuall*, *uncoy*, *unempty*, *unfrail*, *unnice*, *unoffensible*, *unopen*, *unplenteous*, *unshrill*, *unvalorous*. Ash (1775) gives *unalphabetical*, *unattendant*, *uncohesive*, *uncompatible*, *uncompressible*, *uncompulsive*, etc. (about 80 in all). Later dictionaries (Webster, Worcester, etc.), with or without indication of source, have the entries *unabundant*, *unbiographical*, *uncogent*, *uncollectible*, *undeceptive*, *undeliberative*, etc.

**1888** *Pall Mall G.* 6 Oct. 6/1 That *unacoustic chamber in the Town Hall. **1883** *Contemp. Rev.* June 815 The Scotch are .. the most *unæsthetical. **1842** DE MORGAN *Diff. & Int. Calculus* 3, I should not care if anyone thought this Treatise *unalgebraical. **1862** CARLYLE *Fredk. Gt.* XIII. i. (1872) V. 6 *Unanarchic, disciplined at all points. **1867** *Macm. Mag.* Feb. 355/1 These found it consistent with their *unarduous duties to hold livings at a distance. **1880** WARREN *Book-plates* viii. 95 The only *unarmorial bookplates. **1877** 'H. A. PAGE' *De Quincey* I. viii. 151 Certain solitary *unassimilative elements in Wordsworth's character. **1881** *Athenæum* 2 Apr. 461/3 The *un-Attic character of the diction of the tragic poets. **1841** BOSANQUET *Rights Poor Vind.* 298 The sweeping and cleansing of the Augean Church, from motives the..most wholly *unaugean. **1846** MRS. GORE *Eng. Char.* (1852) 132 Certain fools cavil at Lady Consol's box at the Opera as *un-bankerish and prodigal. **1804** COLERIDGE in *Mem. Coleorton* (1887) I. 56 The effect of my own **unbellerophontic* countenance. **1861** W. BARNES in *Macm. Mag.* June 128 Where..a man's..arms are so short or *unbendsome. **1883** *Q. Rev.* Jan. 188 His picturesque, naïve, and *unbitter narrative. **1833** *Fraser's Mag.* VIII. 433 She is a very nice, *unbluestockingish, well-dressed..young lady. **1833** MOORE *Mem.* (1854) VI. 343 Considering all the *un-Brahminical things he has done. **1825** JAMIESON, **Onbraw*,..Ugly, not handsome;..Unbecoming. **1846** MRS. GORE *Eng. Char.* (1852) 91 He should look well-fed and *uncareworn. **1826** J. GILCHRIST *Lecture* 43 Too theoretic..for plain, **uncollegian* understandings. **1883** SIR H. OAKELEY *Bible Psalter* Pref. p. v, That the extensive compass of many of them renders their melodies *uncongregational. *a* **1831** BENTHAM *Univ. Gram.* Wks. 1843 VIII. 357/2 Interjections may be termed the *unconstructural parts of speech. **1863** *Life in South* II. 196 The British Consul..was deeper than ever in the pressure of *unconsular business. **1866** *N. & Q.* 22 Sept. 221 A slim middle-aged man, in quaint *uncontemporary habiliments. **1851** H. D. WOLFF *Madrilenia* (1853) 51 That timid and *uncontemptuous smile so much their characteristic. **1835–6** *Todd's Cycl. Anat.* I. 253/2 An *uncontractile ligamentous capsule. **1887** D. C. MURRAY *Old Blazer's Hero* x, With an eminently *unconversational aspect. **1881** *Blackw. Mag.* Mar. 369 A ripe scholar of old-fashioned and *uncrotchety beliefs. **1817** H. T. COLEBROOKE *Algebra*, etc. 12 The first [digit] is a cube's place; and the two next *uncubic. **1800** COLERIDGE *Unpubl. Lett. to Estlin* (1884) 78 How I did think of your Sunday suppers, their light *uncumbrous simplicity. **1812** W. TENNANT *Anster F.* IV. lxxiv, No man *undeaf could stockishly refrain. **1813** *Examiner* 12 Apr. 228/2 Questions..of that innoxious and *undeceptious cast. **1802–12** BENTHAM *Ration. Judic. Evid.* (1827) II. 643 Evidence being subservient to justice no otherwise than in so far as it is *undeceptitious. **1881** *Athenæum* 16 July 86/3 An inappropriate, *undecorative stamp on the cover. **1862** T. W. HIGGINSON *Army Life* (1870) 34, I am equable and *undepressible. **1870** *Sat. Rev.* 5 Feb. 194/2 The *undestructive revolution which his theory .. was certain to bring about. **1879** S. C. BARTLETT *Egypt to Pal.* xvii. 367 Various indications,..some of which are too general, or too *undeterminal, to aid in solving the question. **1847** H. BUSHNELL *Chr. Nurt.* iii. (1861) 283 This unetherial and *undiffusive kind of bliss. **1844** B. JOWETT in *Life Dean Lake* (1901) 166 The old Bishop, like Lee, is very *undonnish. **1872** HOWELLS *Wedding Journ.* (1892) 101, I speak of the *undressful sex alone. **1845** MRS. CARLYLE in Froude *Lett. & Mem.* (1883) I. 338, 'I find your toast **unegoist*,' said he. **1858** WILKINSON in Rawlinson *Herodotus* II. cxi. II. 182 *note*, The story about the women is equally *un-Egyptian. **1878** J. PAYN *By Proxy* x, His system of morality..is singularly deficient and *unelemental. **1856** OLMSTED *Slave States* 120 In the words of a certain *un-eminent Southern divine. **1814** *Ann. Reg.*, *Chron.* 284 He had demanded the place of marshal of the admiralty, not an *unemolumentary place. *c* **1813** *Epitaph Gen. Fitzpatrick* (Jod.), Through life he walk'd *unemulous of Fame. **1885** STEVENSON *Prince Otto* III. iv, I had no merit but a love, slavish and *unerect. **1828** E. IRVING *Last Days* 102 The word in our text is 'not eucharistical or *uneucharistical'. **1818** BENTHAM *Ch. Eng.* Introd. 18 The one short and *unexcludible prayer excepted. **1827** MOORE *Hist. Irel.* I. i. 5 The yet *unexcursive Greeks. **1802–12** BENTHAM *Ration. Judic. Evid.* (1827) IV. 599 The limited and *unextensible quantity of time allowed. **1862** BAGEHOT *Lit. Stud.* (1879) I. 236 The whole tide of abstract discussion is quite *unfemale. **1873** MRS. H. WOOD *Master of Greylands* i, Enough to give an *unfinancial man the night-mare. **1816** COLERIDGE *Lay Serm.* (Bohn) 329 The *unfoodful trees in the shadowy world of Maro. **1889** SKRINE *Mem. Thring* 251 The subtle, tender, yielding, *unforceful growth of tree and herb. **1871** PALGRAVE *Lyr. Poems* 78 Sigh not, if the smiling band Their *unforethoughtful brightness keep. **1840** CARLYLE *Heroes* vi. (1904) 209 The King coming to them in the rugged **un*formulistic state shall be no King. **1870** *Standard* 14 Dec., Till there is not a battered and *unfoul place left. **1879** F. W. ROBINSON *Bridge of Glass* I. i, When the victim is reticent and *unfretful. **1881** A. KNOX *New Playgr.* xiii. 315 These *unfrisky matrons were certainly safe. **1875** BLAKE *Zool.* 26 Two principal toes, with two *unfunctional and rudimentary ones. **1856** GOSSE *Tenby* v. 49 To be easily procured by the most *ungeological virtuosi. **1810** S. GREEN *Reformist* I. 206 The **un*gothic, and more modern, ménage of their master's sons. **1866** HOWELLS *Venet. Life* v. 67 A certain gliding, *ungradual locomotion, altogether spectral. **1856** J. A. SYMONDS *Let.* in *Life* (1895) I. iii. 81, I pick up a good many words and phrases in an easy and *ungrammary way. **1856** KANE *Arct. Expl.* II. i. 23 A manner so *ungrandisonian that I leave a special description..to my note-book. **1844** TUPPER *Heart* ii. 15 Notwithstanding all these *unheroinals, no one..could look upon Maria without pleasure. **1864** GROSART *Lambs all Safe* (1865) 96 My answer here is again *unhesitant and direct. **1840** *C. O. Müller's Hist. Lit. Greece* vi. § 4. 68 Yet the fundamental ideas of the Cypria are so *un-Homeric. **1849** HERSCHEL *Ess.* (1857) 626 Some *unhygrometric, non-metallic substance. **1886** H. SWEET in *Academy* 6 Feb. 94 In spite of the *unimpartial and personal tone of his remarks. **1810** BENTHAM *Packing* (1821) 265 Its only cognoscible, determinate and *unimpostrous state. **1887** *Athenæum* 8 Jan. 57/2 A series of accurate, but singularly *unincisive lectures. **1839** [MRS. MAITLAND] *Lett. fr. Madras* (1843) 275 The tracts which come from England are altogether **un-Indian*, and unfit to translate. **1831** *Edin. Rev.* LIII. 390 Not allowed to slumber in the quiescence of an *uninfringible monopoly. **1883** MRS. OLIPHANT *Sheridan* v. 170 Genial, not *uninnocent amusement. **1879** *Expositor* IX. 116 Modern editors have..treated the poem as *unintensive. **1894** *Law Notes* XIII. 227/1 These remarks are uncalled for and very '*unjudgely'. **1762** H. Walpole *Let. to Lady Hervey* 1 Oct., You are one of those *un-Lacedæmonian mothers. **1855** Pusey *Doctr. Real Presence* i. (1869) 101 An *un-Lutheran tone of teaching. **1880** S. Lanier *Poems* (1884) 110 Bring large Lucretius, with *unmaniac mind. **1802–12** Bentham *Ration. Judic. Evid.* (1827) I. 159 That self-criminative consciousness..which distinguishes it from *unmendacious falsehood. **1852** *Meanderings Mem.* I. 15 A thing *unmental, mannerless and crude. **1849** E. W. Benson in *Life* (1899) I. iv. 80 The *unmilitant part of the Church. **1839** J. Sterling *Ess.*, etc. (1848) I. 310 Compare ..a missionary Swartz with an *un-missionary Lord Clive or Hyder Ali. **1847** Ld. Cockburn *Jrnl.* (1874) II. 172 A mendicant peer is very *unmonarchical. **1874** Hazlitt *Mary & C. Lamb* 15 The sentence seemed *un-motto-ish. *a* **1851** Moir *Poems* (1852) II. 130 Before her stood the household wheel *unmurmurous, and the thread Still in her fingers lay. **1861** [Mrs. Penny] *Romance Dull Life* xl. 295 An *unnervous nature, blessed with social effrontery. **1818** J. Brown *Psyche* 137 In honesty, the *unnew notion Of giving Psyche loco-motion, Is traceable to merry Prior. **1880** Freeman in *Contemp. Rev.* June 971 The present *unnormal state of Thessaly, and..the causes which made it unnormal. **1887** Saintsbury *Hist. Elizab. Lit.* (1894) 366 His stepmother appears to have been most *unnovercal. **1850** S. Dobell *Roman* vii, The *unoblivious sun hath paused not once; Our time is far spent. *a* **1861** Clough *Poems*, etc. (1869) I. 333 Have we anything that will..be as bright and *un-obsolete a hundred and fifty years hence? **1862** Mrs. H. Wood *Mrs. Hallib.* (1864) III. xxiv. 461 Honey Fair used to be an unsightly and *unodoriferous place. **1885** *Pall Mall G.* 30 June 5/2 The popular, terse, and *unornate style. **1826** G. S. Faber *Diffic. Romanism* (1853) p. lxii, An *unpaginal reference to a pamphlet which he had published. **1860** Poynting *Glimpses Heaven* Introd. p. xxi, The conception of God here presented is intensely *unpantheistic. **1844** J. T. Hewlett *Parsons & W.* xix, Added to all these *unpapaverous influences. **1854** Ferrier *Inst. Metaph.* 444 A clear, detached,..genuine, or *unparasitical Being. **1868** Dickens *Lett.* 23 Jan., A clever, *unparsonic, and straightforward man. **1876** Bernstein *Five Senses* 282 Noise is produced by irregular, *unperiodical movements of those bodies which convey sound. **1871** Earle *Philol. Eng. Tongue* 385 It would be *unphilological to let them be absorbed into any class of words whatever. **1875** Jowett *Plato* (ed. 2) I. p. xxi, Respecting the *un-Platonic character of the Laws. **1882** Morris in Mackail *Life* (1899) II. 74 The surroundings of life are so stern and *unplayful. **1868** H. Bushnell *Serm. Living Subj.* 17 She is a person too *unpositive..to be affirmatively capable of anything. **1871** *Sat. Rev.* 4 Feb. 137/1 Prim English matrons, and Yankee girls of a very *unprim type indeed. **1882** *Athenæum* 11 Nov. 631/3 A family hitherto remarkable for its *unproliferous nature. **1858** H. Bushnell *Nat. & Supernatural* iii. (1864) 66 The immense array of mythologic and formally *unrational religions. **1864** Grosart *Lambs all Safe* (1865) 83 Wishing to be as brief, and..*unrepetitive as possible. **1881** H. James *Portr. Lady* lv, Whose footfall, on the *unresonant turf,..she had not heard. **1858** H. Bushnell *New Life* (1860) 229 The respectable sin..shades into the *unrespectable. **1888** Bryce *Amer. Commw.* II. ii. xlii. 121 The criticisms of a very *unreticent press. *Ibid.* III. iv. lxxx. 55 Religion apart, they are an *unreverential people. I do not mean irreverent. **1864** Spencer *Illustr. Progr.* 437 Out amid the fields, a formal house..strikes us as *unrural. **1879** C. Geikie *Eng. Reform.* xxiv. 428 [The Prayer Book] was made more thoroughly *unsacramentarian than it has ever been since. **1886** *Athenæum* 23 Oct. 528/2 The *unsacrificial nature of Buddhist worship. **1835** *Chamb. Jrnl.* 25 July 205 Now how little chance is there of all these being effected *unsanguineously. **1842** G. S. Faber *Prov. Lett.* (1844) II. 119 The cheap penalty of his *unschismatical independence. **1883** *Athenæum* 27 Jan. 128/2 Some of his sculptures are very effective, but *unsculptural. **1837** Carlyle *Fr. Rev.* iii. iii. iii, Marat..is heard to articulate these most *unsenatorial ejaculations. **1886** H. Tennyson *Jack & Bean Stalk* 11 Oh! what a cramp'd-up, small, *unsesquipedalian object! **1865** *Cornh. Mag.* Mar. 299 His kindly, unpretentious, but not *unshrewd, talk. **1865** D. W. Thompson *Odds & Ends* iii. 26 In our ordinary *unsilentious services. **1880** A. Raleigh *Way to the City* 266 To be unworldly is to be unsordid, *unslippery, unselfish. **1887** E. Johnson *Antiqua Mater* 251 Your *unslothful love unto the glory of God. **1797** *Monthly Mag.* III. 516 The cause..of unwearied power, and of *unsluggish energy. **1821** *Ibid.* LI. 12 The Romans appear to have had a strange propensity to the harsh and *unsonorous letters j and s. **1871** Morris in Mackail *Life* (1899) I. 237 Things pushing up through the clean *unsooty soil. **1862** T. W. Higginson *Army Life* (1870) 9 Something so *un-Southern, the camp of a regiment of black slaves. **1808** Wilford *Sacr. Isles* in *Asiat. Res.* VIII. 247 The first impression, originating from no *unspecious reasons. **1674** N. Fairfax *Bulk & Selv.* 129 So the seeds..when sown become barren or *unsproutful. **1881** Dowden in *Academy* 8 Jan. 21 An *unstrenuous mood of lingering delight. *a* **1861** D. Gray *Poet. Wks.* (1874) 48 The *unsubvertive temple of the soul! **1865** Carlyle *Fredk. Gt.* xviii. v, Next evening..Prince of Prussia strikes his tents again; rolls-off in very *unsuccinct condition. **1830** Disraeli in Monypenny *Life* (1910) I. ix. 161 The dry, round, *unsugary fig is a great whetter. **1873** Miss Broughton *Nancy* III. 11 He shall see how patient I am! how *unsulky! **1878** H. G. Guinness *Approaching End of Age* (1881) 129 The Apocalypse..translated into *unsymbolic language. **1809** *Med. Jrnl.* XXI. 207 Judgment weaker; memory *untenacious. **1880** Goldw. Smith in *Atlantic Monthly* No. 268. 210 *Untheistic science can take cognizance of nothing but facts. **1858** E. W. L. Davies *Algiers* i. 5 The *untidal character of the sea. **1674** N. Fairfax *Bulk & Selv.* 40 'Tis hoped we may have leave to settle Gods whole Everlastingness, as *untimesom. **1815** Mar. Edgeworth *Patronage* xxviii, The language of fine feeling is absolutely untranslateable, *untransfusible. **1867** H. Bushnell *Mor. Uses Dark Th.* 202 This most *untropical institution we call home. **1811** Spencer *Poems* 65 Love's yet *untruant pinions. **1824** in *Spirit Pub. Jrnls.* (1825) 303 Milton,..in a very *un-uxorious spirit, calls a wife—'A thorn intestine,..A cleaving mischief'. **1858** G. H. Lewes *Sea-Side Stud.* 223 He is, with all his learning, quite as *unveridical as Giulia Grisi. **1859** Hamley in Shand *Life* (1895) I. vi. 127 At present I am a kind of clean and *unverminous lazzarone. **1866** Blackmore *Cradock Nowell* xxiv, To tell the plain, *unvinous truth. **1869** Ruskin *Q. of Air* (1874) 168 The swallow, in that noisy, but modestly upside-down Babel of hers under the eaves, with its *unvolcanic slime of mortar. **1668** Wilkins *Real Char.* iii. vii. 341 A person insolutive..is a Bankrupt; *Vnwalkative, is a Cripple. **1889** Stevenson *Master Ballantrae* ix, About the top of it ran considerable bulwarks, which made the ship *unweatherly. **1882** *Macm. Mag.* XLVI. 213/1 His method of describing its inhabitants is..*un-Wordsworthian.

**b.** The use of *un-* with adjs. in *-able*, beginning in the 14th cent. (see 4 above), soon became common, and gave rise to a large number of formations in the 16th and subsequent centuries. In the modern period the examples become too numerous for illustration; in addition to those entered as main words, those given below (all earlier than 1890) will serve as specimens of the freedom with which new formations are created. These are sometimes due to an antithesis of the form 'not only . . but', as 'not only unpainted but unpaintable'. The unusual types *uncome-at-able* (1694–), *unget-at-able* (1862–) are later in date than the corresponding positive terms; for illustrations of similar forms see (*b*).

Cotgrave (1611) has *unaboardable, unaccompanable, unaccostable, uncorruptable, undisplayable, unendable, unexceedable, unexpressable, unexterminable*, etc. Florio (1611) has *unaccommodable, uncolourable, uncompassionable, unsuccourable, untrafficable, unwadable*, and Hexham (1648) *unbesteadable, unbindable, unlabourable.* Ash (1775) introduces about twenty-five new forms, as *unadmittable, unappropriable, uncreditable, unexhalable, unexterminable.* An extreme instance is *un-in-one-breath-utterable* (B. Jonson *Ev. Man in Hum.* i. v.).

**1831** *Blackw. Mag.* XXX. 105 His picture swam in lustre *unbedimmable by the mist of years. **1834** *Tait's Mag.* I. 439/2 The mighty treasures laid up unbonded and *unbondable within the teeming womb of Nature. **1887** *Pall Mall G.* 15 Oct. 4/1 Land in London is almost *unbuyable. **1832** Chalmers *Pol. Econ.* vi. 206 Food, speaking generally, is far more bulky and *uncarriageable than workmanship. **1884** *Sat. Rev.* 29 Nov. 16 They [groups of boroughs] are almost *uncaucusable. **1866** Ruskin *Crown Wild Olive* (1873) 60 They are as the *uncharmable serpent. **1881** R. G. White *England* 363 A dismal, cheerless, *uncheerable dankness. **1817** W. Kitchener *Apicius Rediv.* (1822) 77 Till they are trapped to buy some *unchewable old poultry. **1884** *Punch* 30 Aug. 101/1 He is such an obstinately *uncoaxable man. **1861** Van Evrie *Negroes* 100 The negress..with her short, stiff, *uncombable fleece of seeming wool. **1802–12** Bentham *Ration. Judic. Evid.* (1827) III. 564 An uncompleted and perhaps *uncompletable sentence. *Ibid.* V. 290 A suit..carried on upon unpremeditatable, *unconcertable, cross-examined evidence. **1840** Alison *Hist. Eur.* (1859) VIII. 670 *Unconfrontable excitement among the people. **1873** *Contemp. Rev.* XXII. 835 The desperate determination to conserve the *unconservable. **1865** D. W. Thompson *Odds & Ends* iii. 5 We are *uncontentable hangerels. **1845** Stocqueler *Handbk. Brit. India* (1854) 114 The grounding of the adventurer in this description of *unconveyable knowledge. **1884** *Pop. Sci. Monthly* Apr. 774 These volatile oils, when heated, ..are *uncookable. **1875** Helps *Soc. Pressure* ii. 24 It is almost *undealable with. **1878** Abney *Photogr.* xxxiv. 274 The image becomes *undevelopable. **1811** Miss L. M. Hawkins *C'tess & Gertr.* 364 By the natural and *undiscardable stratagem of her nature. **1834** *Blackw. Mag.* XXXV. 419 Sheer, downright,..and *undislodgeable obstinacy. **1884** Goldw. Smith in *Contemp. Rev.* Apr. 527 The ruler is an *undomicilable alien. **1864** F. W. Robinson *Mattie* I. 141 The driest, hardest, and most *undrawable of cigars. **1884** E. Abbott *Flatland* 86 Remaining henceforth thy docile pupil, thy *unemancipable slave. **1876** M. Collins *From Midn. to Midn.* II. ii. 250, I have had.. the most labyrinthine and *unentangleable nightmares. **1879** H. W. Warren *Recr. Astron.* xii. 261 But nature sustained by *unexpendable forces must abide. **1831** J. Wilson *Unimore* i. 85 Th' *uneyeable sun flames up the heavens. **1668** Wilkins *Real Char.* iii. vii. 341 A person insolutive,.. Unwalkative,..Non-surrective,..*Unfattable. **1884** J. Payn *Lit. Recol.* 14 Vivian had reached the rather *unfloggable age of seventeen. *a* **1860** J. Younger *Autobiog.* (1881) 206 This became an *ungratifiable passion. **1835** T. B. Thorpe in Griswold *Prose Writers Amer.* (1851) 549/2 That bar [=bear] was an *unhuntable bar, and died when his time come. **1875** Poste *Gaius* (ed. 2) i. Introd. 14 That is involuntary (*unimputable) which is caused by external compulsion or by ignorance. **1880** R. G. White *Every-Day Eng.* 143 The peculiar indescribable and *unindicable French sound. **1843** Lane *Select. fr. Kuran* Introd. 13 A vast desert to all but Arabs *unindwellable. **1813** Lady Lyttelton *Corr.* (1912) vii. 174 Men and women always in two distant and *unjoinable squadrons at the end of the room. **1802–12** Bentham *Ration. Judic. Evid.* (1827) II. 176 The testimony of expatriate and *unjusticiable witnesses. **1847** Burton *Ld. Lovat* iii. 72 That *unlearnable self-estimate which insensibly exacts obedience. **1831** *Blackw. Mag.* XXX. 507 The Reformers owe us an *unliquidateable debt of gratitude. **1810** Bentham *Packing* (1821) 137 To persevere in defeating the express words as well as *unmisconceivable intention, of a law. **1831** — *Corr.* Wks. 1843 XI. 70 My advice to jurymen is plain and *unmisunderstandable. **1885** R. Bridges *Nero* i. iv. iii. 1933 Out of thy cold *unmotionable ashes. **1829** S. Martin in J. Duns *Mem.* iii. 36 He complains of being..*unmouldable..and difficult to impress. **1805** Saunders *Min. Waters* 493 A dry *unperspirable state of the skin. **1888** Lane-Poole *Stratford de Redcliffe* I. 365 Some described him as 'the most *unpumpable of men'. **1838** Tupper *Proverb. Philos.* (1852) 415 Life is a constant force, spirit an *unquietable impetus. **1870** Miss Broughton *Red as a Rose* (1878) 127 Most energetic, most *unrebuffable. **1883** *Harper's Mag.* Feb. 347/2 [There are] such a variety of..legends that they are quite *unrecountable. **1851** W. H. Goold in *Owen's Wks.* IX. 461 *note*, The *unreiterable sacraments, to which ordination..belongs. **1884** *Century Mag.* XXIX. 81 An *unrestrictable commercial access to the markets and workshops of Europe. **1884** *Church Bells* 21 June 682/2 The bells of this church have been *unringable for some time. **1862** *Jrnl. Roy. Dubl. Soc.* 347 Rough vascular tissue, which is probably *unrollable spiral fibres. **1861** Thoreau *Lett.* (1865) 205 Excuse these pencil marks, but my inkstand is *unscrewable. **1881** *Nature* XXIII. 585 To show the hypothesis to be *unstateable. **1883** *Pall Mall G.* Suppl. 2 June, Unsinkable boats,..*unstaveable life-boats. *a* **1843** Southey *Comm.-pl. Bk.* (1851) IV. 429 Toads..so tough as to be almost *unstoneable. **1886** Earl Lytton *Lett.* (1906) II. xxi. 307 Churchill's 'Tory Democracy' they find still more *unswallowable. **1850** H. Bushnell *God in Christ* 311 We must bring this astounding *untheorizable fact into theory. **1883** *Harper's Mag.* July 177/1 Students and amateurs..labouring with *untranscribable details. **1877** E. G. Squier *Peru* (1878) 348 Some of these [causeways] are now so ruined as to be *untransitable. **1833** *Blackw. Mag.* XXXIII. 125 The *untroubleable regions of the skies. **1834** *Tait's Mag.* I. 39/2 Those..vehicles, that once rolled in slow and *unupsettable solemnity along. **1879** *Cassell's Techn. Educ.* IV. 46/1 These slabs must be *unwarpable. **1886** *American* XII. 164 Railroad property..spread over an unmanageable and *unwatchable area. **1845** O. Brownson *Wks.* 188. V. 358 A firm, unwavering and *unwaverable conviction. **1845** Stocqueler *Handbk. Brit. India* (1854) 103 Thus they become..worn..into such *unwhetstonable bluntness.

(*b*) *c* **1850** 'Dow jr.' in Jerdan *Yankee Hum.* (1853) 89 Ovid, whose veracity is *uncomeoverable, and can't be disputed. **1844** J. T. Hewlett *Parsons & W.* xi, *Un-do-without-able, which I think is a much more applicable word than indispensable. **1888** G. Grossmith *Society Clown* iv, A..bottle of '*undryupable ink'. **1873** Miss Braddon *Str. & Pilgr.* i. ix, Miss Disney is really the most *un-get-on-able-with girl. **1840** J. T. Hewlett *P. Priggins* i, Weather hot — blow-flies *un-keep-off-able. **1840** De Quincey *Style* Wks. 1859 XI. 244 Alcibiades..was too unsteady and..'unrelyable;' or, perhaps, in more correct English, too '*unrelyuponable'. **1862** H. Marryat *Year in Sweden* I. 407 In the earlier period of Scandinavian history, serpents and dragons were looked upon as *untalkaboutable subjects. *a* **1864** Hawthorne *Dr. Grimshawe* xxii. (1891) 301 The record..of a foot stamped down there in guilt and agony, and oozing out with *unwipeupable blood.

**c.** The use of *un-* with adjectives in *-like* is found from at least the close of the 16th cent., when *ungentlemanlike* appears. Others occur in the following century, as *unbodylike, ungodlike, unwarlike.* The free use of such forms, however, is characteristic of the 19th cent., and especially of the latter part of it. The following are examples of casual formations earlier than 1890.

**1886** *Pall Mall G.* 1 Nov. 13 So contemptible, detestable, and *un-actor-like a proceeding. **1674** N. Fairfax *Bulk & Selv.* 88 Their *unbodylike way of being somewhere. **1845** Fitzball *Maritana* ii. i. 18 Your costume is somewhat *unbridegroom-like. **1847** L. Hunt *Men, Women, & B.* I. 74 The hand [of the monkey]..mortifies one: it looks so very *unbrute-like. **1854** Grace Greenwood *Haps & Mishaps* 14 He met my advances in a most gracious and *un-Bumble-like manner. **1841** J. T. Hewlett *Parish Clerk* II. 37 He..killed it afterwards in a most *unbutcherlike way. **1865** Visct. Milton & W. B. Cheadle *N.-W. Passage by Land* viii. (1867) 112 Feeling very dismal and *un-Christmaslike. **1850** Marg. Fuller *Wom. 19th C.* (1862) 190 Gazing up at the clouds in a most *uncitizen-like fashion. **1838** Jas. Grant *Sk. Lond.* 160 Whose manner ..is the most *undeliberative-like that the human mind could fancy. **1856** Lever *Martins of Cro' M.* 249 Suffering a 'sea change'..as *unearthlike as well may be imagined. **1807** in *Spirit Pub. Jrnls.* XI. 352 Your scandalous and *un-Englishmanlike behaviour. **1823** *Blackw. Mag.* XIV. 563 An excessive dread of being caught in the *unfreemanlike sin of blushing. **1826** Miss Mitford *Village* Ser. ii. (1863) 451 Her manners were quite as *ungipsy-like as her apparel. **1823** in *Spirit Pub. Jrnls.* 151 The professor thought this conduct extremely rude and *ungoldsmithlike. **1868** Lanier *Jacquerie* i. 24 The pack..took revenge as bloody as a man's, *Unhoundlike, sudden. **1884** *Century Mag.* XXVII. 678 The rows of unhomelike and even *unhouselike dwelling-places. **1851** Mayne Reid *Scalp Hunt.* xxi, This was said in well-accentuated and most *un-Indian-like English. **1822** Mrs. Shelley in *Mem.* (1859) 215 Pardon me that I still write in this incoherent and *unletterlike manner. **1841** Thackeray *Men & Coats* Wks. 1900 XIII. 610 An affair of brocade that has always struck me as absurd and *un-Macbethlike. **1860** Tristram *Gt. Sahara* vi. 93 The strange and most *unmoslem-like ceremony of sacrificing a goat. **1803** *Edin. Rev.* II. 427 And it would have been highly *unneighbour-like to have neglected them. **1879** Dowden *Southey* v. 117 Southey had a most *unprophet-like craving for the creature comforts of beef and bread. **1851** G. H. Kingsley *Sp. & Trav.* (1900) 452 In a most *unsalmon-like manner. **1846** Mrs Gore *Eng. Char.* (1852) 155 Thrusting his paraphernalia into a drawer, with a most *unsecretary-like blush. **1802** Mrs. E. Parsons *Myst. Visit* II. 257 The *unsex-like wickedness of Mrs. Hood. **1805** *Edin. Rev* V. 399 The ..*unsquire-like employment of writing, printing and publishing. **1878** A. H. Markham *Gt Frozen Sea* xvi. 229 Conducting itself in a very erratic and *unstarlike manner. **1880** *Cassell's Mag.* June 440 Another *unsummer-like fashion is asserting itself this year. **1885** Gladstone in Morley *Life* (1905) II. viii. x. 426 It is so *unsundaylike and unrestful. **1825** J. Wilson *Noct. Ambr.* Wks. 1855 I. 2 So bright wavering and *unsurelike was the haill living world. **1828** *Lancet* 19 Jan. 592/1 The unfeeling, *unsurgeon-like conduct of Mr. Heyderman. **1877** S. Cox *Salv. Mundi* Preface p. x, It is surely an undignified and *unteacherlike procedure. *a* **1849** Poe *Poems* (1859) 66 *Unthought-like thoughts that are the souls of thought. **1869** H. Bushnell *Wom. S.* i. 13 What could be more *un-university-like? **1855** Smedley *Occult*

*Sciences* 150 Its water..extinguished torches.., but it possessed also the most *unwaterlike power of relighting them. **1797** Mrs. M. Robinson *Walsingham* III. 41 The *unzephyrlike hand of the angry Lady Fusby forcibly held me.

**8.** The prefixing of *un-* to past participles, common in OE. and revived in ME., was subsequently extended until it became the commonest of all uses of the prefix. The following varieties may be distinguished in the usual formations:

**a.** Simple past pples. in *-ed*. These form an inexhaustible class, largely represented among the main words, and including many more similar to those in the following list.

A few casual forms are employed by Florio (1611), as *uncomparted, unnotted*, and various others by Hexham (1648), as *unbalsamed, unbedabbled, unblued, uncalumniated, unchested*, etc. Ash (1775) carries this type of formation to great lengths, and enters about 800 words which are either not recorded, or are of rare occurrence, in actual use, as *unabetted, unaccited, unacquitted, unadjudged, unallured, unamplified, unappraised*, etc.

As subdivisions of this type, forms in *-ated* and *-ized* may be specially noted on account of their frequency. These are also largely represented in Ash's dictionary, which contains about 150 unused or rare forms in *-ated*, as *unaccumulated, uncamphorated, uncircumstantiated*, etc., and a score or so in *-ized*, as *unapostrophized, unaromatized, uncantonized*, etc.

On the double meaning of forms like *undressed, unhoused, unsheathed*, etc., see Un-[2] 8.

(*a*) **1846** Worcester (citing Haslam), **Unbandaged.* **1884** *Pall Mall G.* 15 Jan. 6/2 Who seldom see even an *unbesmutted blade of grass. **1827** Pollok *Course T.* viii. 91 No king, no subject was; unscutcheoned all,..uncoroneted, *unbestarred. **1846** Worcester (citing Scott), **Unboasted.* **1883** *Athenæum* 11 Aug. 182/3 It is a question..what power of resistance a solid '*unburrowed' soil might have offered. **1846** Worcester (citing West. Rev.), **Uncountervailed.* **1893** G. Allen *Scallywag* I. 206 Quite *undiscomposed by this..most startling announcement. **1878** Abney *Photogr.* 117 The *unemulsified collodion for the wet process. **1883** *Encycl. Brit.* XVI. 653/2 Others..discharge their eggs *unenclosed in capsules freely into the sea-water. **1865** Earle *Sax. Chron.* Introd. p. iv, Their *unfagged memory was richly stored with the events of their own day. **1872** W. R. Greg *Enigmas of Life* vii. 260 Naked truth, *unfilmed eyes, will do all that the most righteous vengeance could desire. **1887** *Encycl. Brit.* XXII. 386 The 'jerk' or *unflated aspirate. **1887** *Pall Mall G.* 8 Aug. 12/1 They wanted the line between the *unflogged class..and the flogged masses to remain. **1873** H. A. Wise *Seven Decades Union* 282 As large a solid piece of it as was left *unfrasseled by the concussions. **1871** Noyes *Hymns Mod. Man* 39 Perfection *unfreckled by flaws. **1883** Gresley *Gloss. Coal-m.* 268 **Unholed*, boardgates or other headings which are not driven through or thirled into the adjoining roadway. **1870** E. Peacock *Ralf Skirl.* I. 106 Because some..kitchen-girl has left the cow *unhoppled. **1881** Romanes in *Nature* XXIV. 185 Sources of intermediate or *uninferred knowledge. **1844** A. Mallalieu *Buenos Ayres*, etc. 62 The untamed *unlassoed steed. **1883** *Pall Mall G.* 28 Dec. 5/1 Dr. Schliemann recognized ..in the objects of gold the *unlooted 'treasure of Priam'. **1844** *Ayrshire Wreath* 190 Egbert *unlured by vow or gift Gaid furth withouten fear. **1844** Friedländer tr. *F. Bremer's Neighbours* II. 201, I was half fearful after this of expressing my yet *unmooted fears in reference to himself. **1884** *Pall Mall G.* 29 Aug. 2/1 Not only did they receive their rations in full, but also their pay *unmulcted. **1875** Rolleston *Addr. Dept. Anthrop. Brit. Assoc.* 7 The possession of an *unoverwhelmed numerical representation. **1875** Whyte Melville *Katerfelto* xi, Excuse my freedom in an *unpatched pair of breeches. **1884** Bourke *Snake Dance Moquis* vii. 68 The stones were uncut or *unpecked. **1886** *Pall Mall G.* 9 Dec. 3/2 The unregenerate and, as yet, *unpermeated Tory. **1887** *Q. Rev.* Oct. 537 *Unprenticed and ingenuous new voters. **1882** *Garden* 14 Jan. 24/2 The chief danger with *unputtied glass is found when fierce wind-storms prevail. **1864** *Realm* 18 May 5 Formless clothes whose folds, *unretrenched by artifice, follow nature's laws. **1838** *Penny Cycl.* X. 378/1 The sides of their ditches being *unreveted. **1884** *Gentl. Mag.* Feb. 125 He fell at the head of his own *unrevolted regiment. **1879** Lanier *Poems, To B. Taylor* 23 Not [to] drudge *unriched. **1881** R. G. White *Eng.* 371 Sheridan..leaves this trait of speech *unridiculed. **1885** Warren & Cleverly *Wand. Beetle* 52 The Gunner saw no fun in leaving stunning things *unsketched. *c* **1890** *Fred Wilson's Fate* 80 His record out of office [was] not by any means *unsmudged. **1884** *Spectator* 4 Oct. 1326/1 She has left some wood *unstacked at home. **1876** Brickwood *Boat-Racing* 63 Rowing with *unstraightened arms, or slackened muscles. **1888** Doughty *Arabia Deserta* I. 31 The unwilling contribution of the few *unsubmitted Idumean villages. **1863** Dicey *Federal St.* I. 27 Wherever there is a free and *unsubventioned press, you may be sure [etc.]. **1830** Mackintosh *Progr. Eth. Philos.* Wks. 1846 I. 128 That Dr. Adam Smith's ethical speculations are not so *unsuggested as they are beautiful. **1880** McCarthy *Own Times* III. 208 So long as the Bill of 1832 remained *unsupplemented. **1788** T. Munro, etc. *Olla Podrida* 25 Of difficulties *unsurmounted. **1876** Stone in *Jrnl. R. Geog. Soc.* XLVI. 58 The bodies of the men are often *untattooed. **1868** Visct. Strangford *Select.* (1869) II. 104 They would not have let the triumph pass untold and *untelegraphed. **1883** *Athenæum* 8 Sept. 300/2 Untrodden districts—..*untoured, unspoiled. **1887** *Spectator* 20 Aug. 1111 What is the Channel, so long as it remains *untunnelled. **1843** Tizard *Brewing* 444 New or *unvatted porter. **1871** *Athenæum* 3 June 679 Let them be *unvaunted and unpublished. **1867** *Routledge's Ev. Boy's Ann.* Aug. 471 In the *unvivified condition it absolutely becomes a poison instead of a vivifier.

(*b*) **1884** *American* VIII. 236 The oddest theory..with which *unconjugated individuals ever comforted themselves. **1886** C. Scott *Sheep-Farming* 208 Cotton cake, *undecorticated. **1886** B. Harte *Snow-bound* 18 The remaining and *undenominated passenger turned to Hale. **1884** *Spectator* No. 2914. 587/1 Mr. Besant's bowdlerised presentment cannot but tempt to the perusal of the *undepurated loot. **1882** *Pall Mall G.* 8 Apr. 3 The universal *undigitated stocking need not fear its rival. **1846** Worcester (citing Fleming), **Undisintegrated.* **1887** *Pall Mall G.* 5 Nov. 7/1 With *unexpropriated landlords..some sort of arrangement will be come to. **1881** *Standard* 7 Apr. 7/4 There are numerous dead and wounded still *unextricated from the ruins. **1885** *Athenæum* 12 Dec. 772/3 The medium..is *ungranulated ether. **1889** Geddes & Thomson *Evol. Sex* 78 The liberation of *unindividuated sex elements. **1881** *Nation* (N.Y.) XXXII. 426 A manuscript *unmanipulated by them would be of priceless value. **1881** Le Conte *Light* 172 Now a rectangular cross-image, if *unrotated, would project as the crosses in the corners. **1887** Cook *Sievers' O. E. Gram.* 168 The middle vowel has again forced an entrance from the *unsyncopated forms.

(*c*) **1886** *Pall Mall G.* 1 Oct. 4/1 A father of limited means and *uncapitalized income. **1885** Seth *Scott. Philos.* iv. 136 To this *uncategorised perception..Kant allows a wide range. **1852** *Meanderings of Mem.* I. 76 Hope, *uncelestialized by heathen hand. **1860** W. C. Lake in *Life* (1901) 199 Liddell, whom I found quite different and *undonicised (by the side of Whewell at least). **1855** Milman *Lat. Chr.* xiv. vi. (1864) IX. 218 Toulouse owns only her own *unidealised unromanticised Counts. **1885** *Athenæum* 20 June 788/1 The author's liberal use of *unitalicized.. French words. *a* **1861** Cunningham *Hist. Theol.* (1864) II. xxiv. 325 The sounder or *unsocinianized Arminians. **1830** Lamb *Let.* 24 May, I..know no more of stave and crochet Than did the *Un-Spaniardised Peruvians. **1864** *Sat. Rev.* 3 Dec., A mere *unspurgeonized profane grocer. **1885** *Pall Mall G.* 23 Jan. 5/1 *Unsubventionized English steamers. **1858** *Brownson's Q. Rev.* Apr. 198 Salvation lies in the supernatural order, and is not secured in the *unsupernaturalized by the simple negative merit of not sinning. **1844** Draper in *Philos. Mag.* July 2 The *untithonized chlorine shows no disposition to unite with its hydrogen. **1844** Noad *Electricity* (ed. 2) 267 If even the smallest quantity of liquid remains in the capsule, *unvaporized.

**b.** Past pples. with other endings, from strong or weak verbs. These form a much smaller class, but include a considerable number in common use, as *unbegun, unblown, unborn, unbought*, etc. A few are found with *-ate* for *-ated*, as *unevaporate, -exaggerate*, but these and others not permanently established in the language are of rare occurrence.

Examples in Ash are *unbeset, uncast, uninterwoven, unshotten, unshown, unslung*, etc.

**c.** Participial formations with *un-* frequently have a suffixed adverb or preposition (usually with a hyphen when the formation is used attributively). An early example of this is *unborne-away* (Caxton, 1483); others make their appearance in the 16th and 17th centuries, as *uncalled-for, uncared-for, unheard-of, unlooked-for, unthought-of*, etc. A number of these have become permanent and are in general use; the following are examples of more casual formations.

**1884** H. Spencer in *Contemp. Mag.* 613 Exceptional communities unaggressive and from special causes *unaggressed upon. **1858** Froude *Hist. Eng.* IV. 496 Unvouched for, *unalluded to by any contemporary authority as yet discovered. **1887** *Daily News* 3 Nov. 2/5 You have..allowed your conduct to remain unexplained and *unapologised for. **1855** Browning *Bp. Blougram's Apol.* 894 Not simply unbutted at, *unbickered with. **1847** Medwin *Shelley* I. 105 This startling and *unborne-out proposition. **1873** Waterford in Hare *Two Noble Lives* (1893) III. 325 [For my dance] I expect so many very young and pretty girls—the *un-come-out Durhams and Tankervilles. **1860** E. Venables *Isle of Wight* 332 Many a lovely nook..*unencroached upon as yet by gentility. **1836** R. M. M'Cheyne in *Mem.* (1872) 296 It had left some footpath *unglared across. **1832** Tennyson *Sonn., Alexander* 12 High things were spoken there, *unhanded down. **1863** Grosart *Small Sins* (ed. 2) 79, I do not say that his prayer will go unheard, much less *unhearkened to. **1839** Burgon *Life & Times Gresham* I. ii. 57 His administration..was very nearly *uninterfered with. **1830** J. G. Strutt *Sylva Brit.* 11 The extent to which the oak will throw its broad arms..when *unintruded upon. **1648** Hexham II, *Een Onbeslapen dochter*, a maide *Vnlien with, or a Virgine. **1828** *Craven Gloss.*, **Unmelled-on*, not meddled with. **1849** Mill *Ess.* (1859) II. 335 Justice..demand[s] that these unmerited attacks should not remain *unprotested against. **1871** Macduff *Mem. Patmos* vii. 90 As they sob their tale of *unresponded-to anguish. **1849** M. Arnold *Fragm. 'Antigone'* i, [He] makes his own welfare his *unswerv'd-from law. *a* **1674** Clarendon *Hist. Reb.* xvi. § 17 After he had lived some years in Paris *untaken notice of, indeed unknown.

**d.** A type of formation which is not very frequent is that in which the participle is preceded by a noun, usually with instrumental sense, as in the following examples.

**1595** *Polimanteia* (1881) 36 For not..aged censoring Cato might challenge greater priuiledge of trueth, then your free toongd and *vn-aw-bound skill. **1765** [E. Thompson] *Meretriciad* 26 She never vended goods *unduty paid. **1829** Bentham *Justice & Cod. Petit.* 104 Because by the judges, *unfee-fed as they would be, nothing would be to be got by it. **1895** L. A. Tollemache *B. Jowett* 135 The barren laurels of an *un-heaven-rewarded martyrdom. **1659** Fuller *App. Inj. Innoc.* II. 68 That single and signal instance of that *Unparliament-impowred Convocation. **1598** Barret *Theor. Warres* 5 The *vnsouldier-learned, to the vnlettered souldier may be paralleld as the Phisition Theorike to the grosse practitioner. **1605** Sylvester *Du Bartas* II. iii. iv. *Captains* 1022 Where, Learned men, *unsoule-clog'd (as it were) With servile gyves of Kings imperious Fear, Fly even to Heav'n. **1879** Rutley *Study Rocks* xiv. 300 Consisting partly of angular and comparatively *unwater-worn..materials.

**9.** Adjectival forms in *-ed*, from substantives, of the type *unbearded, unbodied, unfeathered*, etc. These are anticipated in OE. by such rare formations as *ungefeþered, ungewintred, unwǣded*, but otherwise belong to the 16th and subsequent centuries. The usual sense is 'not provided or furnished with', but sometimes 'not affected by', 'not treated with', etc.; in the latter case the use is not clearly distinguishable from the purely participial.

Ash gives such instances as *unaproned, unbrooched, unbuskined, unchevroned, uncliented, uncodded*, etc.

**1881** J. M. Brown *Student Life* 13 The *unancestored genius. **1873** *Daily News* 22 Aug., The barbarous exposure of them, *unblanketed in piquet line. **1846** Worcester (citing *Ed. Rev.*), **Unbuoyed*.., not buoyed. **1892** Stevenson *Across the Plains* 13 A butler perhaps rides as high over the *unbutlered. **1882** *Encycl. Brit.* XIV. 862/2 The *uncathedralled paganisms of American scenery and life. **1864** Sala in *Daily Tel.* 25 Feb., I wonder whether the *unchattelled farmer will keep his oath. **1885** *Jrnl. Science* July 389 The sewage of an *unclosetted town. **1877** Blackmore *Cripps* (1887) 240 His simple, unpractised, and *uncored heart. **1886** *Pall Mall G.* 3 Aug. 6/2 A supplementary *uncostumed choir..supported the singing. **1873** 'Susan Coolidge' *What Katy did at Sch.* xi. 183 As she looked up at the *uncottoned space at the top of the window. **1860** *All Year Round* No. 47. 493 With paint washed off and *undiamonded hair. **1887** D. A. Low *Machine Drawing* Pref. p. iii, An *undimensioned scale drawing. **1883** *19th Cent.* May 858 *Unfountained from above, the higher moral virtues would decay for lack of a meaning. **1864** Eliz. Murray *Ella Norman* II. 270 That on the left was a treeless, *ungrassed elevation. **1887** Rider Haggard *Jess* xiv, You must either knock under..or trek on into the *unhostelled wilderness. **1860** *All Year Round* No. 41. 344 A draught of pure *unincensed air from the open window. **1878** B. Taylor *Deukalion* II. v. 90 Druid oaks *Univied, stretch their stubborn arms abroad. **1880** Miss Bird *Japan* I. p. xxii, An *unmatted floor. **1821** *Examiner* 5 Aug. 482/1 The unbeneficed and *unparked. **1844** Poe *Mesmeric Rev.* Wks. 1864 I. 113 Until we arrive at a matter *unparticled—without particles. **1888** Rutley *Rock-Forming Min.* 142 A band of unstriated or *unpegged crystal. **1874** J. Addis *Eliz. Echoes* (1879) 110 Defiant Chestnuts prick the air, *Unpennon'd battle-spears arraying. **1861** *Times* 25 Feb. 8/5 The banks of our river *unquayed. **1863** *Not an Angel* II. 260 The *unrailwayed inhabitants of that neighbourhood. **1836** F. Mahony *Rel. Father Prout* (1859) 394 As for your critic,..We *unrancoured hope to see him. *a* **1871** De Morgan *Budget Parad.* (1872) 75 The following, of which I have an *unreferenced note. **1887** Meredith *Poet. Wks.* (1912) 332 Idly the flax wheel spun *unridered. **1877** Blackmore *Erema* xi, The riders struck the savage, *unrowelled spur into them. **1822** Wilkins *Body & Soul* I. 123 The picturesque appearance of the *unsabled mourners. **1852** *Meanderings of Mem.* I. 5 Worn As weary nakedness, *unshooned, unshorn. **1854** Hooker *Himal. Jrnls.* I. xi. 252 The ridge was *unsnowed a little way down the east flank. **1880** 'Mark Twain' *Tramp Abroad* I. 144 The only 'distinguished dead' who went down to the grave *unsonnetted. **1831** Scott *Jrnl.* 26 Nov., I got home about mid-night; but remain unpoetised and *unspeeched. **1648** Hexham II, *Ongespitst*, Vnpointed, or *Vnspired. **1866** in *Cassell's Techn. Educ.* (1879) IV. 108/2 The fold-yards are also kept *unspouted. **1823** E. Moor *Suffolk Words* 23 Where words occur, not readily understood by the *Unsuffolked reader, he is to take them as Suffolcisms. **1872** G. B. Cheever *Lect. Pilgr. Progr.* xiv. 345 What we know of the..state of *untabernacled souls is but little. **1890** 'R. Boldrewood' *Col. Reformer* (1891) 244 The serene *untempested heavens of the isles of the blest. **1860** O. W. Holmes *Elsie V.* xiv, There are states of mind..which remain not only unworded, but *unthoughted. **1867** H. Conybeare in *Fortn. Rev.* Nov. 514 There is a breadth of effect in the..*untraceried windows. **1888** Yeats *Wand. Oisin* Poems (1908) 259 His vast foot that lay Half in the *unvesselled sea. **1866** Crichton *Rambles Orcades* 34 Over country 'unrailway-ed' and '* unvilla-ed'.

**b.** Instances in which the noun is preceded by a qualifying word are not numerous, and such formations are usually individual or casual.

[**1650** Trapp *Comm. Lev.* xxi. 18 Lest his Ministerie bee sleighted for..unheavenlie mindedness.] **1870** *Routledge's Ev. Boy's Ann.* May, Suppl. 3/1 Plain white unwatermarked paper. **1872** Ruskin *Fors Clav.* xix. 6 My notion of.. charity is, by no means..the giving to unable-bodied paupers.

**10.** The use of *un-* with present participles, revived about 1300 (see 4 above), subsequently became common, and has given rise to a large number of permanent words, such as *unbecoming, unbending, unchanging, undoubting*, etc. (On the participial use of such forms see 5 d.) Examples of casual formations are given below.

Others occurring in Ash's dictionary are *unbeguiling, unbiasing, unblinding, unbuilding, unenticing, unflowing*, etc.

**1883** R. Bridges *Prometh.* 79 Hope..to cheer with visions fair Their *unamending pains. **1844** Wardlaw *Prov.* xxxix. (1869) II. 44 Doctrines of this easy *unannoying description. **1873** Ruskin *Fors Clav.* xxx. 2 He showed his wisdom in pleasant and *unappalling ways. **1845** R. W. Hamilton *Pop. Educ.* iii. (ed. 2) 40 Agriculture,..in the ordinary processes of its labour,..has been simple and *unarousing. **1876** Mrs. Whitney *Sights & Ins.* II. xxxviii. 673 There had been two wonderful tides, that which carried them forth, all uncertain, *unbelonging, separate. **1870** G. T. Dodds in Bonar *Life* ii. (1884) 70 Our study will be comparatively useless and *unbenefiting. **1885** *Pall Mall G.* 6 Feb. 6/1 A safe and *unblundering guide through the mazes. **1862** Furnivall *Handlyng Synne* Pref. p. ix, Ready to turn to account, though in an *unboring way, every opportunity. **1873** C. E. Norton *Lett.* (1913) I. viii. 471 Carlyle seemed a little weary, perhaps weakened by the mild *unbracing weather. **1837** Whittock *Bk. Trades* (1842) 358 None of these ends can be accomplished..unless this be done in a neat '*unbungling' manner. **1886**

*Academy* 14 Aug. 109/1 The Gaelic tribes of Ireland—that 'heap of *uncementing sand'. **1884** *Harper's Mag.* Apr. 659/2 Da Porta's..*uncommenting way of telling the story. **1857** Ld. Granville in *Life* (1905) I. x. 260, I encourage the correspondence by commonplace *uncommitting acknowledgements. **1784** R. Bage *Barham Downs* I. 101 *Unconcatenating blockhead! **1885** Ruskin *Præterita* I. x. 307 Most [forces] act irregularly, or else at *uncorresponding periods. **1858** Faber *Spir. Confer.* 136 Of all saving things, fear..is..the most *undeluding. **1823** D. McNicoll *Wks.* (1837) 118 *Undemurring confidence. **1856** Ruskin *Mod. Paint.* IV. v. 20 To burn *undisdaining upon the reeds of the river. **1865** Grosart *Mem. H. Palmer* 38 His was the omnipotence of the light,.. silent *undisplaying might. **1805** *Med. Jrnl.* XIV. 495 A simple *unembarrassing method of stopping the screw from being relaxed. **1883** *Athenæum* 15 Dec. 774/3 The stories are as *unfascinating as they can be made. **1887** J. Hutchison *Lect. Phil.* xvii. 187 The *unfaultfinding complacency with which he contemplated one of his later works. **1865** Mrs. Carlyle *Lett.* (1883) III. 263 She is so kind and *unfussing. *c* **1860** Faber *Hymn, Sacr. Heart* iii, In that *ungrowing vision nothing deepens, nothing brightens. **1876** Meredith *Beauch. Career* II. iv. 64 The *unlettering elusive moon. **1887** Morris *Odyss.* xii. 325 But *unlulling blew the south-wind. **1881** R. G. White *Eng.* 74 This *unmarring modesty of outward show. **1867** J. Thomson *Vane's Story*, etc. (1881) 113 Their eyes.. flashed.. like swift swords That leapt *unparrying to each other's heart. **1873** Miss Broughton *Nancy* II. 216, I pass and re-pass the cold River Gods of the *unplaying fountain. **1862** Mrs. Crosland *Mrs. Blake* II. 131 Men..profess..a certain horror of an '*unpraying' woman. **1822–7** Good *Study Med.* (1829) III. 18 In a pure and healthy, or *unpredisposing atmosphere. **1866** J. G. Murphy *Comm., Exodus* xxi. 14 The milder sentence of the *unpremeditating manslayer. **1866** S. B. James *Duty & Doctr.* (1871) 290 Eternity hastens on, and so many are unprepared, are *unpreparing, to meet it. **1864** *Realm* 24 Feb. 2 *Unpresaging of the complaints which will ere long issue from the offices. **1867** H. Bushnell *Mor. Uses Dark Things* 195 Tropical consciences, which are out-door, self-indulgent, *unpronouncing consciences. **1862** R. H. Patterson *Ess. Hist. & Art* 403 Secluded in position and *unproselytising in spirit. **1885** *Athenæum* 24 Oct. 533 His life was an *unprotesting protest against convention. **1821** Cobbett *Rur. Rides* (1885) I. 38 It is no very *unprovoking reflection. *c* **1800** Macneill *To Eliza* 43 Plaguing her plain, *unpuffing spouse, About his former oaths and vows. **1882** H. S. Holland *Logic & Life* (1885) 24 These impulses cannot be altogether blind and *unpurposing. **1881** Ruskin *Bible Amiens* iv. § 10 On the *unquaking and fruitful earth. *a* **1859** De Quincey *Posth. Wks.* (1891) I. 220 To explain the true character of note-writing—how compressed and *unrambling and direct it ought to be. **1878** S. Cox *Salv. Mundi* vii. (ed. 3) 145 Doomed to an endless and *unredeeming torment. **1880** S Lanier *Sunrise* Poems (1884) 8 The wave-serrate sea-rim sinks unjarring, *unreeling. **1874** L. Tollemache in *Fortn. Rev.* Feb. 229 We are..led to describe the poet..as an *unreforming optimist. **1869** Mrs. H. Wood *Roland Yorke* III. 173 To submit to it in *unrefuting tameness. **1854** Faber *Growth in Holiness* xiii. 223 Go walk by the shore of that *unresounding sea. **1858** J. Robertson *Poems* 78 As light is mixed in the *unretreating air. **1864** A. de Vere in *Reader* 30 Apr. 545/1 We part..With *unreverting faces, not ingrate. **1868** Pusey *Serm. Pharisaism* 11 Monuments..scarce held in being by our *unsacrificing gifts. **1845** *Florist's Jrnl.* (1846) VI. 177 An upright *unscrambling habit, and very blunt leaflets. **1888** Meredith *Poems* (1898) II. 143, I saw, *unsighting: her heart I saw. **1880** A. Raleigh *Way to City* (1881) 282 His goodness is a full and *unslacking stream. **1674** N. Fairfax *Bulk & Selv.* 47 All tastless, nothing relishing; all *unsmelling, nothing scented. **1873** Pater *Stud. Hist. Renaiss.* 74 This last passion would be the most *unsoftening .of all. **1848** Buckley *Iliad* 193 Both heard an *unsoothing reply. **1883** R. Bridges *Prometh.* 395 To sow thy seed Year after year in this *unsprouting soil. **1815** Chalmers *Let.* in *Life* (1851) II. 25 The more *unstaggering your faith is..the more is God well pleased with it. **1834** De Quincey *Autob. Sk.* Wks. 1853 I. 211 We were detained a few days in those *unsteaming times by foul winds. **1863** W. Lancaster *Præterita* 43, I lean on this *unstumbling oracle, And nourish hope. **1844** G. S. Faber *Eight Dissert.* (1845) II. 127 An *unsystematising perusal of the prophecy itself. **1885** *Irish Monthly* Nov. 598 The white monotony of *unthawing snow. **1858** H. Bushnell *Serm. New Life* 100 More ambitious and more *untransforming to the people. **1865** *Pall Mall G.* 29 Sept. 10/1 Novel sensations wherewith to enliven the *untravelling reader. **1888** A. S. Wilson *Lyric Hopeless Love* 162 Nor vow..nor sacred rite The *ununiting can unite. **1880** W. Watson *Prince's Quest*, etc. (1892) 94 So forward piloted.., she held her way *Unveering. **1878** Jessie Fothergill *First Violin* vi. iv, To finger, or blow into, or beat the dumb, *unvibrating things. **1878** B. Taylor *Deukalion* i. iv. 34 Gray sedges wave *Unwhispering ever, o'er the slimy flats. **1887** Morris *Odyss.* x. 282 Whither away..dost thou wander,..*Unwotting of the country?

**11.** In OE. adverbial formations in *-lice* formed a large portion of the words in *un-*. Very few of these survived in ME., but additions were gradually made which maintained the existence of the type (ending in *-liche* in southern dialects and *-ly* in the northern). Subsequently the use of *un-* with *-ly* again became common, independent of the form of the central element, which may be an adjective, present or past pple., etc. There are however two ways in which such formations may arise. Either the suffix *-ly* is added to a form already beginning with *un-*, or *un-* is prefixed to an adverb already formed with *-ly*. In most cases the difference in sense is slight or immaterial, but at times the distinction becomes important. If *unprofessionally* is formed from *unprofessional* it means 'at variance with, contrary to, professional rules or etiquette', if from *professionally* it means 'not in a professional manner or capacity'.

The following are miscellaneous examples of recent formations.

A few others occur in early dictionaries, as *unaccessively, unbewailably, unfalsely, unrecoverably.*

**1887** H. S. Holland *Creed & Char.* 126 So He pityingly, *unangrily pronounced. **1842** *Murray's Hand-bk. N. Italy* 21/2 The Cardinal..had most *uncardinally directed the painter [etc.]. **1869** W. G. Ward *Ess.* (1884) II. 243 These *uncatholicly educated Catholics who are the Church's most dangerous enemies. **1824** J. Gilchrist *Etym. Interpr.* 150 Many verbs..are employed both causatively and *uncausatively. **1816** Bentham *Chrestom.* Wks. 1843 VIII. 38 The short time necessary..would not be *unchrestomathically employed. **1871** Tyndall *Fragm. Sci.* (1879) II. viii. 130 If you wish to speak to me, plainly, honestly, and *undisputatiously. **1830** W. Taylor *Hist. Surv. Germ. Poetry* II. 369 The very words, which twice before They said by heart so *unerroneously. **1887** *Pall Mall G.* 18 Oct. 1/1 That her eyes are set not *ungreedily upon Morocco is notorious to every one. **1838** *Tait's Mag.* V. 279 She told her weeping tale..so mildly, and so *unhatingly towards the prisoners. **1783** *Satanical Remembrancer* 16 Our Irish Native *Van Sighè*, vulgarly and *unhibernically called *Banshee.* **1842** Pusey *Crisis Eng. Ch.* 9 It may be, that we may all together learn humility, and none..think *unhumbly of them. **1885** Stevenson in *Contemp. Rev.* Apr. 555 The groups which..break up the verse for utterance, fall *uniambically. **1884** W. M. Baker in *Harper's Mag.* Mar. 561/2 No woman could have done more, and so naturally and *unintrusively. **1884** A. C. Bickley *Geo. Fox* vii. 96 Lambert defended himself not altogether *unjesuitically. **1737** *Gentl. Mag.* VII. 13/2 *Unliterally and ungrammatically. **1833–40** J. H. Newman *Ch. of Fathers* 264 Olybrius, our virgin's father, who .. was *unmaturely carried off. **1873** B. Gregory *Holy Catholic Ch.* xv. 162 What boots it that the chain of bishops has become..inextricably entangled and *unmendably snapped? **1838** R. Bagot *Let.* in Liddon *Life Pusey* (1893) II. xxi. 57 Feeling sure that you will not think that I ever..acted *unopenly towards you. **1887** J. A. Wylie *Hist. Scott. Nation* II. xxii. 279 Heads so *unorthodoxically shorn. **1862** S. Lucas *Secularia* 327 He received an ostensible letter of recall, and with it a private letter apprising him that '*unostensibly his proceedings were approved of'. **1824** *Westm. Rev.* Jan. 143 Who had unprofessionally and *unpecuniarily burthened his memory with the dull details. **1875** Howells *Foregone Concl.* xv. 259 Some..harmless thing that she had *unpurposely bruised. **1889** Saltus *Truth about T. Varick* 165 The .. most *unrebuffably good-natured scoundrel that he had ever encountered. **1882** W. R. Greg *Misc. Ess.* ii. 31 As briefly and *unrhetorically as possible. **1859** Boyd *Recreat. Country Parson* (1862) 36 The massive foolscap..over which the pen so pleasantly and *unscratchingly glides. **1834** *New Monthly Mag.* XLII. 53 *Unsilenceably resounded in his ears the mandate. *a* **1864** Hawthorne *Amer. Note-bks.* (1883) 352 Last night was the most uncomfortably and *unsleepably sultry that we have experienced. **1855** Lynch *Rivulet* lxxvii. ii, *Unvauntingly, yet with defiance, One man the world may meet. **1852** Smedley *L. Arundel* xliii. 331 His ..tail, which was crumpled up *un-wag-ably in the corner.

**b.** *Un-* is seldom prefixed to simple adverbs. Even in OE. such formations are rare, though a few do occur, as *uneaðe, unefne, unfægere, unfeorr, unseldan, unsófte.* ME. retained most of these, but the number has at no time been greatly added to, and the later tendency is to discard such forms altogether.

**12.** The OE. use of *un-* with substantives (see 2 e above) survived very fully in ME., not only by the retention of old forms but by the introduction of many new, which continue to multiply in the later periods of the language. From the beginning the nouns have been almost entirely restricted to those of an abstract nature, so that forms with suffixes are numerous. In OE. and ME. the commonest of these is *-ness* (occasionally *-dom* and *-ship*); subsequently *-ation, -ity*, and *-ment* are frequent, as in the following selection of miscellaneous examples.

Florio (1611) has a certain number of casual formations, as *unacknowledgement, unartness, unbrittleness, undwellingness, uneloquence, unfrailness*, etc. Ash gives *unadequateness, uncommensurability, -ableness, unfrugalness, unliableness, unorganicalness*, and various others.

**1883** A. Stewart *Nether Lochaber* l. 316 The *unabidingness..of all sublunary things. **1887** *Athenæum* 6 Aug. 177/2 Some decidedly clever..observations upon the *unactuality of old art. **1853** Miss E. S. Sheppard *Ch. Auchester* II. 211 Here I suddenly arrested myself, for my *unaddress stared me in the face. **1884** *N. & Q.* 6 Sept. 189 The Church only crossed the Jordan, and that on dry land and in the purest *unalarm. *a* **1866** J. Grote *Exam. Utilit. Philos.* (1870) 324 The *unassociativeness of different races of man. **1864** Lowell *Fireside Trav.* 263 The picturesque vivacity and ever-renewing *unassuetude of the whole scene. **1884** *Athenæum* 23 Aug. 238 The onesidedness and *unbalancement of our best efforts. **1868** Ruskin *Time & Tide* (1872) 31, I must get back to the evil light, and *uncalm, of the places I was taking you through. **1844** Kinglake *Eothen* (1845) 324 *Unchangefulness in the midst of change. **1862** F. Hall *Hindu Philos. Syst.* 143 Atheism, injury to others, *uncompassion, falsehood, and so forth. **1873** Mrs. Whitney *Other Girls* xxx, *Unconsent to the divine impulse comes of incongruity. **1862** Spencer *First Princ.* (1870) 281 That increase of internal motion involves a progressing *unconsolidation. **1868** W. R. Greg *Lit. & Soc. Judgm.* 390 A match for bureaucratic immovability and (to coin a word) *unconvinceability. **1882** *Ch. Times* XX. 938 All that the State can aim at is *un-crime, whereas the work of the Church is to inculcate virtue. **1865** W. Kay *Crisis Hupfeldiana* 23 The *à priori* criticism, the *uncriticism, which is..chiefly intent on proving 'two main conclusions'. **1858** Sir C. Napier in *Times* 24 Nov. 9/5 This country must not be left in a state of *undefence. **1893** Goldw. Smith in *Contemp. Rev.* Dec. 800 There is also *undesign,.. there is waste, there is failure. **1853** Herschel *Fam. Lect. Sci.* vi. § 42 (1873) 258 The three primary colours, .. each in its highest degree of purity and *undilution. **1886** *Pall Mall G.* 12 July 10/1 Full of calmness, and courage, and quiet *undismay. **1866** Carlyle *Remin.* (1881) II. 21 My feeling with him was that of *unembarrassment. **1882** *Century Mag.* XXIV. 44, I had no power to return to my original *unembodiment. **1868** Dilke *Greater Brit.* I. i. vi. 70 A fog of *unenterprise hung over the land. **1877** M. Collins *Sweet & Twenty* I. xi, The *unfragrance of money adheres to him. **1889** *Pall Mall G.* 25 Mar. 2/3 The palpable *unfrankness of the addendum. **1886** *Encycl. Brit.* XX. 610/1 A more curious instance of *ungreediness for pelf than earlier cases which we have cited. **1852** De Morgan in Graves *Life Sir W. R. Hamilton* (1889) III. 418 A unanimous *uninfallibility would be just as drowsy a dormitory as an infallible Church. **1796** W. H. Marshall *W. England* II. 16 The roads, their *unlevelness apart, are among the best in the kingdom. **1843** *Civil Eng. & Arch. Jrnl.* VI. 40/1 A property almost peculiar to wrought iron, namely its all but *unmeltableness. **1847** H. Bushnell *Chr. Nurt.* iii. (1861) 65 The ostrich is nature's type of all *unmotherhood. **1879** G. Macdonald *Sir Gibbie* xii, The earthly hitherto—the final obstacle of *unobstancy. **1862** Mrs. H. Wood *Mrs. Hallib.* II. xv. 225 Cyril was looking on... His *unoccupation caught the Quaker's eye. **1884** *Harper's Mag.* June 73/2 The most..commendable feature of the charity is its privacy and *unostentation. **1877** Blackmore *Cripps* II. ii. 23 Every single fall or rise of nature's work..led her into various veins of inductive *unphilosophy. **1866** *Pall Mall G.* 12 May 12 Gaze down into the future upon the hateful Land of *Unpromise. **1802–12** Bentham *Ration. Judic. Evid.* (1827) II. 140 The publicity or *unpublicity of the process. **1883** E. Clodd in *Knowl.* 15 June 352/2 The *unrelation between religion and formulated theology. **1873** Mrs. Whitney *Other Girls* xxviii, The old story of worry, discontent, *unreliance, disruption. **1868** *Edin. Rev.* Apr. 435 Making due allowance..for a considerable amount of *unrepresentation on the part of our manufacturers. **1853** Faber *All for Jesus* 163 Anything like *unrespectability has been so completely avoided. **1825** Hogg *Queen Hynde* 164 To veil *unsanctitude within. **1865** W. G. Palgrave *Arabia* II. 230 An event followed by much confusion, shouting, and awkward *unseamanship. *c* **1843** Carlyle *Hist. Sk. Jas. I & Chas. I* (1898) 269 The English noses in their shapes and *unshapes. **1872** H. Bushnell *Serm. Living Subj.* 335 What kind of *unsociety we suffer when we have about us only persons very unequal. **1881** G. S. Hall *German Cult.* 230 The very possibility of *unspaciality or punctuality. **1878** J. W. Reynolds *Supernat. in Nat.* (1883) 109 Making stuff pass from a no sort of *unstickingness into some sort of holding-togetherness. **1872** Howells *Wedding Journ.* (1892) 296 The young girls .. had the true touch of provincial *unstylishness. **1802–12** Bentham *Ration. Judic. Evid.* (1827) I. 293 Suggestedness and *unsuggestedness. **1846** G. S. Faber *Lett. Tractar. Secess.* 271 To flounder in all the comfortless *untenacity of an ever-shifting quicksand. **1886** W. J. Amherst *Hist. Cath. Emanc.* I. 271 Ireland's **un*unanimity—if I may coin an expression—is England's opportunity. **1864** Ruskin in *Daily Tel.* 28 Oct., Intrinsic value or goodness in some things, and..intrinsic *unvalue or badness in other things.

**b.** The prefixing of *un-* to nouns used attributively is rare and usually not intended seriously.

**1673** Penn *The Chr. a Quaker* i. Wks. (1726) 523 The Unchange-Gospel-Rule to Believers. **1771** Lady Mary Coke *Jrnl.* 13 Aug., The reason of the discontent of the unquality Ladys is that they were laugh'd at by the great Ladys. **1823** Byron *Age of Bronze* xiv, Alas, the country! how shall tongue or pen Bewail her now *uncountry* gentlemen? **1852** S. R. Maitland *Eight Ess.* 236 It was a whim of the artist to sketch his subject in that occasional, uncompany costume. **1880** *Spectator* 3 Jan. 9/2 Single women, widows, and unbusiness men, are those on whom the blow chiefly fell.

Other examples are *uncurrency-style* (1852), *undining-room* (1845), *unhousehold-name* (1894), *unsociety-people* (1898).

**13.** In OE. there are a few instances of *un-* with verbal substantives in *-ung*, as *unbletsung, -brosnung, unmeltung*, etc. None of these survive in ME., and new forms in *-ing* are rare; *untiming* occurs *c* 1250, *uncunning c* 1300, *unknowing, unpunishing c* 1340. In the later language the usage also remains rare, and in nearly all verbal sbs. the prefix *un-* is Un-[2]; a few exceptions are recorded here.

**1538** Elyot, *Insolentia*,.. vnhaunting of a place. **1598** Florio, *Insepoltura*, the vnburying of one. *Ibid.*, *Ingenerabilita*, vnbegetting, ingenerabilitie. **1611** Florio, *Inconniuenza*, an vnmoouing or not twinkling of the eies. **1853** R. S. Surtees *Sponge's Sp. Tour* iii, His sellings and his returning, his lettings and his unlettings. **1886** Linskill *Haven under Hill* lxii, The great beauty which had been to Ermengarde Salvain as a hurt and an unblessing. **1887** *Daily Tel.* 20 Dec. (Cassell's), Why was this unowning of the plays necessary?

**14.** In OE. the use of *un-* with verbs is limited to formations from negative adjectives, as *unclǽnsian, unrótsian, untrumian* from *unclǽne, unrót, untrum.* (More commonly *ge-* is prefixed, as in *geunclǽnsian, geunrétan*, etc.) This type barely survived in ME., but *un-* began to be sparingly prefixed to ordinary verbs, as *untrowen* (*a* 1200) to disbelieve, *untrusten* (*a* 1225) to distrust, *unbetide* not to happen, *unbe* not to be, and similar formations are fairly common in the 16–17th c., as *unbecome, unbefit, unbelieve, unbeseem,* *uncomprehend*, *unconcern*, etc. Many of these are obviously suggested by the participial adjectives (*unbecoming*, etc.), which are quite regular in formation (see 10 above). The type is now rare, but occasional examples occur.

*a* **1175** *Twelfth Cent. Hom.* 118 Swa mucele swiðor him biteriæð & unswetiæþ alle þas eorðlice þing. *c* **1205** LAY. 11547 Vnhæle & ælde hæueð þene king vnbalded [*c* **1275** onbalded]. *Ibid.* 15037 Þa þat folc was icumen, þa was þe king swiðe untrumed [*c* **1275** ontromed]. *a* **1300** *Maximian* 65 (MS. Digby 86), Forþi min herte keldeþ And mi bodi ounbeldeþ.

**1843** E. JONES *Poems, Sens. & Event* 71 But the world unrecognized his visions of goodness. **1884** LORD R. CHURCHILL in *Pall Mall G.* 11 Aug. 10/1 This measure.. which, instead of improving the representation of the people, would only fatally unrepresent the people. **1902** *St. James's Gaz.* 31 Dec. 12/2 On the ground that the state of trade absolutely unwarrants it.

**15.** By confusion of thought, *un-* is sometimes used redundantly, especially in the 16th and 17th centuries, where a positive term is really intended. For examples see *undated* (1637), *undifference* (1654), *undifferency* (1583).

**Un-**, *prefix* [2], expressing reversal or deprivation, representing OE. *un-*, *on-*, = OFris. *und-*, *unt-*, *un-*, *ond-*, *ont-*, *on-*, MDu. and Du. *ont-*, OS. *ant-*, OHG. *ant-*, *int-* (MHG. and G. *ent-*), Goth. *ana-*, originally identical with AND- *prefix*.

**2.** From OE. more than a score of reversive verbs formed with *un-* (or its variant *on-*) are recorded, as *unbindan*, *uncnyttan*, *undón*, *unfealdan*, *ungyrdan*, *unhelian*, *unlúcan*, etc. Some of these were in common use; others occur rarely or in single instances. About half of the number (including all those mentioned above) survived in ME., and various new formations appear in texts from the first half of the 13th century, as *unbenden*, *undytten*, *unfast(n)en*, *unhaspen*, *unhillen*, *unlimen*, *unmensken*, *unsteken*; even at that date the prefix is used with verbs which are not of native origin. Similar formations from later ME. are *unbuckle*, *uncatch*, *unclench*, *uncover*, *unfetter*, *unkevel*, *unsew*, *unshut*, *unwrap*, *unyoke*. The following are examples of obsolete ME. forms :— **unha·dien** [OE. *unhádian*], to deprive of ecclesiastical orders; **unme·nsken** [f. MENSK *v.*], to dishonour; **unro·ne** [f. RONE *v.*], to make desolate; hence *unro·ningness*; **unteo·n** [f. *teon* TEE *v.*[1] 6 b], to fall apart.

*c* **1205** LAY. 13169 Buten he him plihte þæt he wolden vorð rihtes *vnhadien [*v. r.* onhodi] Costanz. *Ibid.* 13174 Þar he vnhadede his broðer. *a* **1200** *St. Marher.* 14 Heanlunges makeð ham wið heouenlich hirð ant *unmenskeð hamseolf bimong eorðlich men. *a* **1300** *E. E. Psalter* lxxviii. 7 For þai ete Jacob ilka lim, And *vnroned þe stede of him. *Ibid.* lxxii. 19 Hou ere þai made in vnronyngnesse! *a* **1310** in Wright *Lyric P.* 101 The fleyhs shal rotie from the bon, The senewes *untuen everuchon.

**b.** In the 16th century new formations with *un-* become very numerous and varied, and in the 17th the prefix is used with much greater freedom than is now possible. The lexicographers Florio and Cotgrave constantly employ it in rendering Italian words in *dis-* and *s-* and French words in *de-*, *des-*. By this time the prefix had developed several variations of sense which are still current, and are illustrated by modern examples in the following sections.

**3.** In OE. most of the forms with *un-* have for their second part a simple verb, either strong (as *unbindan*, *unfealdan*, *unlúcan*, etc.) or weak (as *uncnyttan*, *undón*, *ungierwan*, *ungyrdan*, etc.). In either case the prefix denotes a simple reversal of the action of the verb. Many of the new formations in ME. are of the same type, as *unbend*, *unclench*, *uncover*, *unfasten*, *unhasp*, *unhide*, *unshut*, etc., and additions to this class continue to be freely made at all subsequent periods. In addition to the numerous examples entered as main words, many others have been casually employed, similar to those here illustrated.

Florio and Cotgrave make extensive use of this type, e. g. *unastony*, *unbrand*, *uncancel*, *unclumse*, *unclutter*, *uncompass*, *uncurd*, *unfester*, *unflow*, etc. Ash gives *unbaste*, *unmoble*, *unsolder*, *unsort*, etc.

**1865** *Sat. Rev.* 9 Sept. 330/2 A boisterous English captain ..annexed them for a few weeks, and then had to *unannex them. **1838** [MRS. MAITLAND] *Lett. fr. Madras* (1843) 223 You had betrayed his intention...You tried to **un-betray* it afterwards,..but in vain. **1862** DE MORGAN in Graves *Life Sir W. R. Hamilton* (1889) III. 576 My belief is, that if you call *h* and *k* differentials, the community..will *uncall them. ?**1774** *Monody Death Goldsmith* 13 G.'s Wks. (1816) p. li, Thus some magician..*Uncears the pond'rous tombs. **1886** *Pall Mall G.* 22 Dec. 2/2 When he has changed his mind no power on earth can induce him to *unchange it. **1888** J. C. AMBROSE in *Union Signal* (Chicago) 19 Apr., The first hard work..on butter is to *unchurn it. **1891** M. COLE *Cy Ross* 12 Pull up for the night, *uncinch the packs. **1859** SEMPLE *Diphtheria* 316 Is this leading circumstance.. sufficient to make us *unclassify this disease? **1851** W. R. GREG *Creed of Christendom* xvi. 268 That everything done is done irrevocably—that even the Omnipotence of God cannot *uncommit a deed. **1860** TROLLOPE *Framley P.* xvii, Do no such thing, or you may too probably have to *uncongratulate me again. **1775** ASH, **Uncrook*.., to reduce from crookedness. **1868** E. YATES *Rocks Ahead* III. vii, I could hardly uncrook your fingers. **1898** B. GREGORY *Side Lights* 205 He..cannot possibly afford to *undecree his own infallibility. **1885** S. TROMHOLT *Aurora Borealis* II. 20 She looked as if she had never *undonned her funny garb since I saw her last. **1825** COLERIDGE *Aids Refl.* (1848) I. 288 To break this sensual charm, to *unfascinate these bedazzled brethren. **1818** COBBETT *Pol. Reg.* XXXIII. 527 To unthink their present thoughts and *unfeel their present feelings! **1862** [W. COOPER] *Yacht Sailor* xi. 142 The only perfect self-acting fid I ever saw..'fids' and '*unfids' itself. **1873** MISS BROUGHTON *Nancy* II. 241, I have my flax hair..curled, plaited, frizzed, and again *unfrizzed. **1891** ZANGWILL *Bachelor's Club* 35 His brow began to *unfurrow itself. **1883** *Century Mag.* Oct. 946/2 We could see them all busy *ungriping their lee boat. **1896** E. BERDOE *Browning & Chr. Faith* 180 It is not in him to *unhate his hates. **1889** *Blackw. Mag.* Oct. 456 It was unprecedented that..a weak hysterical subject should, after being *unhypnotised, remain so long in prostrate exhaustion. **1844** NOAD *Electricity* (ed. 2) 69 *Uninsulating the ball, insulating it, and then observing what change it had acquired. **1888** JACOBI *Printers' Vocab.*, **Uninterleave*, to withdraw the sheets which have been placed between printed work to prevent set-off. **1839** J. STERLING *Ess. & T.* (1848) I. 327 Self is thus..dis-individualized, *unisolated, rather universalized and idealized. **1775** ASH, **Unjamb*, .. to free from a pressure between two bodies. **1900** *Daily News* 7 Mar. 8/7 The gun..jammed less than any other machine gun, and could be easily unjammed. **1888** LEES & CLUTTERBUCK *B. C.* xxviii. (1892) 314 Presently..the monster had *unkilled himself..and swam happily away. **1611** FLORIO, *Dismentire*, to *vnlie. **1882** *Ch. Times* 10 Feb. 83 It is hardly necessary to 'unlie' the insinuation, as the French would say. **1845** *P. Parley's Ann.* VI. 361 How long it took to *unmat their hair. **1887** *Pall Mall G.* 19 Oct. 2/1 To *unmesmerize all those Christians whom the devil has mesmerized. **1809** *Ann. Reg., Chron.* 339/2 For heaven's sake, do not be *unmodelling my accounts again. **1817** PETTIGREW *Mem. Lettsom* II. 230 Let any person..*unprejudice his mind. **1844** WHEWELL in *Life* (1881) 308 Having puzzled and *unpuzzled myself. **1889** SAINTSBURY *Ess. Eng. Lit.* (1891) 31 You could play on Crabbe that odd trick..and *unrhyme him. **1812** J. H. VAUX *Flash Dict.*, **Unslour*, to unlock, unfasten, or unbutton. **1860** NARES *Seamanship* 112 *Unsnatch and shift the mast rope. **1887** in Prothero *Life of Bradshaw* (1888) 78 Some one '*unsported' him with a dinner-knife. **1833** *Fraser's Mag.* VIII. 309 It *unsquatted the incubus which so long oppressed me. **1856** J. STRANG *Glasgow & Clubs* 395 To *unswing a golden fleece was a common trick. **1869** ABBOT *Shaks. Gram.* Pref., So far from training we are *untraining our understanding. **1896** *Globe* 19 Dec. 1/4 It would have been as easy to take the stripes as to *unwhip those boys.

**4.** A small number of OE. verbs in *un-* imply removal or deprivation; these end in *-ian*, as *unhádian* to deprive of orders, *unhlidian* to remove the lid from, *uninseglian* to unseal, *unscógian* to unshoe. In ME. the type remains rare, but occurs in *unclead*, *unclothe*, *unhair*. At a later date it becomes more frequent, and is common in modern use.

Florio is especially lavish in new formations which have not obtained subsequent currency, as *unblossom*, *unbrain*, *unbridge*, *uncheek*, *uncheese*, *uncorn*, *uncorner*, *unflank*, *unfringe*, *ungarland*, etc.

**1882** R. G. INGERSOLL, etc. *Chr. Relig.* 44 Cradles would be robbed, and women's breasts *unbabed. **1798** FERRIAR *Illustr. Sterne* i. 8 In like manner, *unbolster Falstaff and his wit will affect us less. **1836** T. HOOK *G. Gurney* II. 260, I found the task of '*unbooting' one of much greater difficulty than I had anticipated. **1886** *Pall Mall G.* 2 Dec. 6 A native *unbraceleting or ungartering himself. **1611** COTGR., *Desbrodequiner*, to *vnbuskin; to plucke, or draw, off buskins. **1831** *Soc. Life Eng. & France* 198 Some subsequent attempts to unbuskin tragedy. **1611** COTGR., *Escremé*, *vncreamed. **1886** *Pall Mall G.* 28 Sept. 11/2 Adulterated or uncreamed..milk. **1826** BEDDOES *Let. to B. Procter* Poems (1851) 170 To rob him,—to *uncypress him in the light—To unmask all his secrets. **1874** S. LANIER *Poems, Corn* 190 Discrowned, *undaughtered, and alone. **1846** LANDOR *Imag. Conv.* Wks. I. 144/2 The chalice of poison,..by which their own hands were..*undirked, and paralysed. **1855** BAILEY *Mystic*, etc. 127 He, to his fate divine, *uneyes himself in vain. **1878** J. W. REYNOLDS *Supernat. in Nat.* (1880) 4 To *unfaith men takes from them everything which can preserve from evil and lead to good. **1859** SALA *Gas-light & D.* v. 62 He would..run down the doomed legislator.., and..*unfrank him on the spot. **1829** GEN. P. THOMPSON *Exerc.* (1842) I. 84 That the man..who goes to bed a freeholder, does not wake *unfreeholded on the morrow. **1791** LADY HAMILTON in Gamlin *Romney* (1894) 223 The little picture with the black hat. I wish you would *unfrill it. **1897** F. THOMPSON *Sel. Poems* 125 She..Her hand *ungauntlets in mild amity. **1861** *Temple Bar Mag.* III. 197 A hand of light *Unjewelleth the robe of night. **1821** *Sporting Mag.* IX. 51 Both were *unmettled by fast work. **1804** LARWOOD *No Gun Boats* 10 Let England *unpoignard her Dwarf Assassins. **1852** R. REDGRAVE in *Life* iv. (1891) 83 Here we were disrobed and *unsashed. **1888** 'B. CANE' *Haunted Tower* 307 He had *unspiled the water-cask. **1865** WILBERFORCE in *Life* (1882) III. 189 If he did not *unsurplice his choir and degrade his service to their Dissenting level. **1839** HOOD *Lines to Friend at Cobham* iii, Of hen and cock you'll have a stock, And death will oft *unthrob 'em. **1808** E. S. BARRETT *Miss-led General* 69 We must either embowel them, or they will *untripe us. **1889** TALMAGE *Serm.* 28 Apr., God is not dead. The chariots are *unwheeled.

**b.** A modification of this sense is that of freeing or releasing from something. This appears in ME. in *unfetter*, *unkevel*, *unyoke*, although in origin these may be simply reversive. In the later period the type has also become common, and is very largely represented from the close of the 16th century.

Florio and Cotgrave afford numerous examples, as *unbarb*, *unbit*, *unbunch*, *unchaff*, *uncrupper*, *ungravel*, *unhunger*, etc.

**1899** T. S. MOORE *Vinedresser* 74 His sword fell noisy to the ground While he *unbrooched his cloak. **1888** F. H. STODDARD in *Andover Rev.* Oct., [Matthew] Arnold has *un-Coleridged criticism. **1839** in Marindin *Lett. Ld. Blachford* (1896) 57, I can't fancy any more magnificent practice for a fidgety person who wanted to be *unfidgeted. **1839** BAILEY *Festus* 118 When heaven's light Pours itself on the page, .. *unglooming all its mighty meanings. **1868** EARL CLARENDON in *Life & Lett.* (1913) II. xxiii. 355, I wish he were *unhandcuffed from the party with which he can have no sympathy. **1881** *Cheq. Career* 335 *Unhobble the spare horses. **1888** JACOBI *Printers' Vocab.*, **Unlead*, to take out the leads from leaded matter. **1814** SCOTT *Wav.* lvi, *Unplaid yourself on the first opportunity. **1840** R. H. HORNE *Gregory VII*, IV. v. 74 It is his change That hath *unscarfed mine eyes. **1800** *Naval Chron.* IV. 523 The labourers .. *unshored the St. Joseph .. in the great dock. **1878** A. H. MARKHAM *Gt. Frozen Sea* xviii. 257 'Woolwich' was also '*unsnowed'. **1832** *Regul. & Instr. Cavalry* II. 43 The men..strap and *unswivel their carbines. *a* **1722** LISLE *Husb.* (1757) 387 If it is impracticable to accomplish both, the oats should be left *unthistled rather than the barley. **1897** MARY KINGSLEY *W. Africa* 280 To devote the rest of his evening..to *unthorning himself. **1845** T. W. COIT *Puritanism* 237 *Untrammeling human opinion and human will. **1815** T. SHUFFLETON *Amat. Wks.* 116 *Unzone the veil! produce the prize Which long has charm'd my roving eyes!

**5.** The use of *un-* to denote the removal or extraction (forcibly or otherwise) of a person or thing from a place or receptacle occurs in the 14th cent. in *unhouse*, and later in *unbody*, *unearth*, but does not become prominent till the beginning of the 17th, when Florio and Cotgrave afford many examples. In a few instances the sense passes into that of releasing or setting free from confinement, as in *uncage*, or of revealing to others, as in *unbosom*.

Among the instances occurring in Florio and Cotgrave are *unaerie*, *unbench*, *unborough*, *unbrake*, *unbranch*, *unchamber*, *unchest*, *unfurnace*, etc.

**1865** E. BURRITT *Walk to Land's End* 375 Then he *unbasketed our dinner. **1897** *Outing* XXIX. 491/1 The request that a number of soldiers be sent back to *unbog the wagon. **1822** W. TENNANT *Thane of Fife* VI. xxiii, He ..had *uncav'd his jars to heave their spirits up. **1883** H. DRUMMOND *Nat. Law in Spir. W.* i. (1884) 30 To do that, and rest in the contemplation, it has first to *uncentury itself. **1859** SALA *Tw. round Clock* (1861) 228, I fear the awful committee that..can *unclub a man for a few idle words inadvertently spoken. **1870** T. W. HIGGINSON *Army Life* 195 She shouted with delight at being suddenly *uncribbed and thrust into her little scarlet cloak. **1851** G. W. CURTIS *Nile Notes* XXV. 112 The cavalcade was magically *undonkeyed, the savages..tumbled off, while their beasts were yet in full motion. **1888** *Public Opinion* 29 June 811 Hearing that a mammoth had been unearthed, or rather *uniced, near the mouth of the Lena. **1883** *Daily News* 18 Sept. 3/3 Until the furniture and other articles..stored hastily .. have been *unstored and examined. **1846** LANDOR *Imag. Conv.* Wks. II. 45/1 All her wars for six hundred years have not done this; and the first trumpet will *untrance her. **1884** *Law Rep.* 12 Chanc. Div. 631 No offence was committed until the pigs were *untrucked, and the appellants had..no part in untrucking them.

**b.** In some formations belonging to this type *un-* is prefixed to a word either denoting the thing removed or the action of removal; in the latter case the sense of the prefix passes into that of *out*. Examples of these uses are :—

**1598** FLORIO, *Sbacciellare*,..to vngraine, or take out of the cods. **1611** COTGR., *Escerner*, to vnkernell; to take or cut a thing cleane out of the round place wherein it was. **1877** TALMAGE *Serm.* 316 He it is who undirks the lightning from the storm cloud.

**6.** In OE. the fact or process of depriving a person or thing of a certain quality or property was not expressed by the reversive *un-*, but by verbal formations based on adjectives already having the negative prefix (see UN-[1] 14), *Unable*, appearing towards the end of the 14th cent., may still belong to this type, but from the middle of the 16th century forms become frequent in which the prefix is clearly the reversive *un-*, employed both with adjs. and sbs. Both types are largely represented in Florio, and to a less extent in Cotgrave. **a.** When the formation has an adjectival base, the adjective may be used in its simple form, or with the suffix *-en*.

Examples from Florio and Cotgr. of the simple adj. form are *unbald*, *unbig*, *uncorrect*, *undizzy*, *ungiddy*, *unhoar*, etc.; and of forms in *-en*, *unfatten*, *ungreaten*, *unmoisten*, *unsharpen unthicken*, *unweaken*.

**1888** RUSKIN in *Pall Mall G.* 27 Oct. 5/2 Rosalind is extremely glad to get her face *unbrowned again. **1893** *Columbus* (Ohio) *Dispatch* 19 Sept., They found..the shops ill-regulated and the Frenchmen *un-Frenched. **1827** HARE *Guesses* (1859) 488 You may abuse and misuse: you cannot *ungood. **1747** E. POSTON *Pratler* I. 223 Thy Brother.. almost had the Name undone, And almost did *ungrand it. **1825** SOUTHEY *Let. to Mrs. S.* 7 July, Freshmen are called *greens*, and a ceremony was (and perhaps is) used in *ungreening them. **1827** O'CONNELL *Let.* in *Daily News* 17 Dec. (1888) 3/6, I will *un-Orange Ireland. **1887** BROWNING *Parleyings, F. Furini* i, Straight your bag *Unplumped itself. **1826** Scott 19 Mar. in *Croker Papers*, If you *unscotch us you will find us damned mischievous Englishmen.

**b.** Substantives are similarly employed without ending.

Florio has a number of examples, as *unbride, uncitizen, uncoward, undoctor, undwarf*, etc. Casual formations are frequently employed by Fuller, as *uncardinal, unchaplain, uncity, unmartyr*, etc.

**1867** Sir J. Y. Simpson in Duns *Mem.* xiv. (1873) 482 Often I wish I could *unbaronet myself. **1839** J. D. Coleridge in *Life Ld. Coleridge* (1904) I. 71 Herman Merivale *unbeared himself for five minutes. **1800** Mackintosh in *R. Hall's Wks.* (1832) VI. 129 They ought not to *uncitizen Tom Paine. **1797** Mrs. A. M. Bennett *Beggar Girl* (1813) V. 94 Recollections, unsupported by proofs, could neither *uncountess her nor rob her of the adoration her beauty excited. **1857** Heavysege *Saul* (1869) 145 It me *unfiends to see and listen to him. **1860** Reade *8th Commandm.* 24 It would be 'nefas' to *ungenius our geniuses. **1889** Talmage *Serm.* in *Voice* (N. Y.) 31 Oct., Every day there are Samsons *ungianted. **1870** C. W. Collins *Anc. Classics for Eng. Readers, Virg.* 182 An occasional burst of tears on Æneas's part would not have *unheroed him in our estimation one whit. **1839** J. Rogers *Antipopopr.* i. § 7. 87 They unavoidably fancy all other kirks to be no real or right kirks at all, *unkirking them. **1860** Milman in *Archaeol.* XXXVIII. 22 The remedy applicable to the condition of the Marches of Mercia and Wales was..to reduce and, so far, **unmarch* them. **1865** J. Grote *Explor. Philos.* I. 229 This..is described first as seeing nature in masquerade, and then as *unmasquerading her. **1877** E. FitzGerald *Lett.* (1889) I. 408 Thence I lately took down Mr. Lowell's (I have proposed to **unmister* him too), Lowell's Essays. **1870** C. Reade *Put yourself in his Place* I. v. 68 The hair, not in ropes—yet not so as to cord the mass, and *unsatin it quite. **1890** *Chamb. Jrnl.* 21 June 387/2 To break her spirit, and *unshrew her into somebody's very humble servant. **1674** N. Fairfax *Bulk & Selv.* 75 Our Watch would without more ado be utterly *unwatcht.

**c.** From sbs. (rarely from adjs.) there are numerous formations in **-(*i*)*fy***, and from both sbs. and adjs. in ***-ize***. Other endings, as *-ate*, are less usual.

(*a*) **1857** Dufferin *Lett. High Lat.* viii. 201 The idea of fog and ice in the month of June seemed so completely to *uncockneyfy us. **1834** Southey *Doctor* vi. (1848) 107 Unipsefying and *unegofying the *Ipsissimus Ego.* **1837** Darwin in *Life* (1887) I. 282, I think my silicified wood has *unflintified Mr. Brown's heart. **1882** Sala *Amer. Revis.* (1883) 241 A city on a scale of vastness which Sesostris, could he '*unmummify' himself, might admire. **1866** Ruskin *Eth. Dust* 36 What will you gain by *unpersonifying it? **1858** Faber *Foot of Cross* (1872) 231 Why should she stay her devotion, or *unsimplify her worship?

(*b*) **1883** *American* VII. 117 Foreign interests and alien population tend to *un-Americanize the place. **1895** *Spectator* 23 Nov. 731 The author scarcely deserves to be *unanonymised. **1860** Reade *8th Commandm.* 335 A noble international measure that..would have done much to *unbohemianize writers. **1891** W. S. Lilly *Shibboleths* 186 A certain number of the clergy..wished to *unclericalize themselves. **1876** *N. Amer. Rev.* Oct. 255 Its consequence was to *undemocratize the Democratic party. **1871** Proctor *Light Science* 338 To pluralize some of the objects,..to *undualize others. **1870** *Standard* 24 Nov., If the *unequalising process is to be carried any further. **1882** *St. James' Gaz.* 29 Mar. 3/1 We are invited to view..the Fenians *unfenianized. **1830** Pusey *Hist. Enq.* II. 392 The great body, which their excellent predecessors had endeavoured to *unformularize. **1898** Bodley *France* I. I. i. 67 German intermarriages have *un-gallicised the Swedish dynasty. **1852** Bristed *Five Yrs. Eng. Univ.* (ed. 2) 343 Unmanning and *un-gentlemanizing themselves to any extent. **1898** Bodley *France* I. I. iv. 222 As for the Alsacians, France took little pains to *un-germanize them. **1853** *Blackw. Mag.* LXXIV. 101 A hero, with out-staring eyes,..is sadly *unheroised. *a* **1876** Ht. Martineau *Autobiog.* (1877) II. 287 Let us *unindividualize ourselves. **1875** Shalders tr. *Godet's Comm. Luke* I. 386 Jesus desired..to reclaim the people, and prevent their being still more *unjudaized. **1862** De Morgan in Graves *Life Sir W. R. Hamilton* (1889) III. 571 He had..to back out of infinitesimals, in order to *unleibnitize his system. **1874** H. Bushnell *Forgiveness & Law* iv. 222 To *unlocalize, universalize, and make victorious the great salvation. **1838** G. S. Faber *Inquiry* 48 The paradoxical vineyard of *unmanicheanised Manicheism. **1884** Stoughton *Relig. in Eng.* I. 337 How could it, without *unmethodising Methodism? **1833** R. H. Froude *Rem.* (1838) I. 332 To..un-Protestantise, *un-Miltonise them. **1885** Masson *Carlyle* ii. 71 Mystics he could make nothing of except by *unmysticising them. **1833** *Blackw. Mag.* XXXIV. 540 Such a taste is there to vulgarize, to *unpoetize nature. **1852** Smedley *L. Arundel* xxix. 218 It will take me longer to *unpuppyise myself than I was aware of. **1889** *Times* 23 Feb. 7/1 His great anxiety was to *unradicalize himself. **1842** *Blackw. Mag.* LI. 163 The effect produced,..was, if the expression may be allowed, to *unrevelationize revelation. **1852** C. Wordsworth *Occas. Serm.* IV. 14 England romanized Ireland: and England ought to *unromanize it. **1885** *Cornh. Mag.* Mar. 271 Some of the chaunting was rather fine, but the orchestral accompaniment was decidedly *unsolemnising. **1899** R. Wallace *Geo. Buchanan* iv. 70 Had he been all his detractors call him, that would not have *unstoicized him. **1854** Faber *Growth in Holiness* x. (1872) 163 Human respect *unsupernaturalizes actions which are good in substance. **1852** Lewis *Meth. Observ. & Reas. in Pol.* I. 96 There are numerous influences at work to *untechnicalize it. **1873** J. Skinner *Let.* in *Life* xvi. (1884) 318 Those mad attempts to *untheologize (if I may coin a word) the language of theology.

**7.** With rare exceptions, the OE. verbs in *un-* are transitive, and this has always remained the prevailing use. In ME., however, intransitive uses of some common words are found, as *unbend, unclose, unlouk*, and in casual formations as *unbody*. In the later language the usage increases to some extent (as in *unfold*, etc.), but is chiefly confined to words having some currency.

Florio employs *unday, undebt, undroop, unsicken, unswell*. The following are rare modern instances.

**1816** Colman *Br. Grins, Champernoune* ii, His courtiers swore..They'd broil a pope to keep a place, So all unpapalized apace. **1831** Trelawny *Adv. Younger Son* II. 113 Look at him, he is unturbaning! **1862** Helps *Org. Daily Life* 108 The organization grinds on,..and it is very difficult to make the thing ungrind.

**8.** Verbal substantives, participial adjectives, and agent-nouns are naturally formed from verbs in *un-* as from simple verbs. These forms begin to appear in the 14th century, and become common in the later language.

Many of the past pples. and ppl. adjs., as *unbent, unbound, undressed, unfastened*, etc., coincide with formations in which the prefix is Un-[1], and the distinction in meaning is not always sufficiently clear to admit of an absolute separation between the forms. Either prefix is normally unstressed in all participial formations used predicatively, but commonly receives the main stress when employed attributively, as *an u·nbent bow, an u·nbound book*.

**9.** The redundant use of *un-* is rare, but occurs in OE. ***unliesan***, and ME. ***unloose***, which has succeeded in maintaining itself. Later instances are *unbare, unsolve, unstrip* (16–17th cent.), and the modern dialect forms *unempt(y), unrid, unthaw* (also locally *uneave*).

For occasional misuses of *un-* see *unloaden, unranked*.

**Un,** *sb.* An instance of the negative prefix Un-[1].

**1650** B. *Discolliminium* 7 It was a thousand pities those two *Un's* were put in.

**Un, 'un** [1], later dial. f. Hin(e *pers. pron.* 'him'.

**1633** B. Jonson *Tale Tub* I. iv, *Pup.* He is high Constable, And who should reade above un, or avore 'hun? **1749** Fielding *Tom Jones* vi. ii, Allworthy is a queer dog, and money has no effect o' un. **1785** [see Hin(e]. **1821** Scott *Kenilw.* xi, 'And what if I did see un, Master Crane?' replied Jack Hostler. **1825-** in dial. glossaries, etc. (*Eng. Dial. Dict.* s.v. *En*).

**Un, 'un** [2], dial. f. One *pron.* (senses 22 and 24).

**1821** Scott *Kenilw.* xii, Here's a gentleman..has given Sir Hugh a draught that is worth twenty of yon un. **1859** Geo. Eliot *A. Bede* xx, 'It [a rose] smells very sweet,' he said; 'those striped uns have no smell'.

**Un,** obs. form of On *prep.*, dial. f. And *conj.*

**Una** (yū·nă). [From the name of the first boat of the kind brought from America to England in 1853.] A catboat. Also *attrib.*

**1878** D. Kemp *Man. Yacht Sailing* xvi. 171 In less than a year there was a whole fleet of Unas at Cowes. *Ibid.* 174 The Cowes Una boat of the present time. **1880** G. C. Davies *Pract. Boat Sailing* 42 The mast is more inboard than the real Unas. **1889** E. F. Knight *Sailing* 36 The Cat or Una rig is generally preferred by the Americans.

**Unaba·ndoned,** *ppl. a.* (Un-[1] 8.) **1745** Young *Refl. Public Sit. Kingd.* 107 Which honest counsels never fail to fix In favour of an unabandon'd land.

**†Unaba·sed,** *ppl. a.*[1] *Obs.* Forms: 5 **unabaiste,** *Sc.* **-abasit, -yt,** 6 *Sc.* **onabasit, unabaset.** [Northern and Sc. var. Unabashed *a.*] Undaunted.

*?a* **1400** *Morte Arth.* 1378 Sir Boys vn-abaiste alle he buskes hyme a-gaynes. *c* **1470** Henry *Wallace* II. 48 He vnabasyt, and nocht gretlie agast, Vpon the hed ane with the steing hitt he. **1513** Douglas *Æneid* VI. iv. 54 Eneas vnabasit..Followis his gyde. *Ibid.* XI. xvi. 12 Opis..onabasit did behald the ficht. **1596** Dalrymple tr. *Leslie's Hist. Scot.* II. 437 At the altar he stude vnabaset without al feir.

**Unaba·sed,** *ppl. a.*[2] (Un-[1] 8.) **1659** Gauden *Tears Ch.* III. iv. 274 They easily preserved the doctrine of Christian Religion uncorrupted,..the reverence of Religion unabased.

**†Unaba·sedly,** *adv. Sc. Obs.* Forms: 4–5 **un-, onabasytly,** 5 **wn-, unabasitly** (6 **-lie**), **wnabayssitly,** 6 **unabaisitly** (**-lie**). [f. Unabased *ppl. a.*[1] + -ly [2].] Dauntlessly, boldly.

**1375** Barbour *Bruce* VI. 20 Var he nocht outrageous hardy, He had nocht swa vnabasitly Sa smertly seyn his avantage. *c* **1425** Wyntoun *Cron.* v. xi. 3032 He Wnabasitly maid entre..Wndere erd to þe dragoune. **1501** Douglas *Pal. Hon.* III. xxviii, Vnabasitlie this campioun saw I gang In a deip cisterne, and thair a lyoun sleuch. **1573** *Satir. Poems Reform.* xxxix. 359 He..stoutlie tuik on hand Richt vnabasitlie all that gait to gang.

**Unaba·shable,** *a.* (Un-[1] 7 b.) **1848** Landor *Exam. Shaks.* Wks. II. 290 It must be an unabashable man that ever shook his sides in their company. **1872** Lever *Ld. Kilgobbin* xiv, He is the most unabashable villain in Europe.

**Unabashed** (vnăbæ·ʃt), *ppl. a.* [Un-[1] 8.] Not abashed; bold, undaunted; not disconcerted or put out.

**1571** Golding *Calvin on Ps.* xxvii. 1 If wee dare not with unabashed minde set him ageinste all oure enemies. **1592** Warner *Alb. Eng.* VIII. xl. 177 Shee vnabashed, mounting now the Skaffold, theare attends The fatall Stroke. **1728** Pope *Dunc.* II. 147 Earless on high, stood unabash'd De Foe. **1772** Priestley *Inst. Relig.* (1782) II. 104, I..shall show an unabashed..countenance. **1851** Mrs. Browning *Casa Guidi Wind.* II. 749 Fix thy brave blue English eyes on mine..With unabashed and unabated gaze. **1891** Farrar *Darkn. & Dawn* xxxii, Detected in their theft, the priests were still unabashed.

Hence **Unaba·shedly** *adv.*

**1890** Talmage in *Voice* (N. Y.) 13 Feb., We go easily and unabashedly into sin.

**Unaba·table,** *a.* (Un-[1] 7 b.) **1837** Carlyle *Fr. Rev.* I. III. iv, The wise man..sees..all the symptoms he has ever met with in history,—*un*abateable by soothing Edicts.

**Unaba·ted,** *ppl. a.* (Un-[1] 8.)

*?a* **1611** Beaum. & Fl. *Four Plays in One* Wks. 1912 X. 296 Behold a princess..playing here the slave, To keep her husbands greatness unabated. **1676** Hobbes *Iliad* XIX. 295, I think yet Another time for Feast had better been;..whilst yet unabated is my Spleen. **1781** Gibbon *Decl. & F.* xxxi. (1787) III. 194 The king of the Goths..still advanced with unabated vigour. **1796** Mme. D'Arblay *Camilla* III. 393 Mrs. Arlbery felt provoked to find his power thus unabated. **1840** R. H. Dana *Bef. Mast* xxv, For three days and three nights the gale continued with unabated fury. **1857** Buckle *Civiliz.* I. vii. 456 For nearly fifty years the movement has continued with unabated speed.

Hence **Unaba·tedly** *adv.*

**1828** Carlyle *Misc.* (1857) I. 132 They chaunting unabatedly her extreme deficiency in personal charms. **1898** *Westm. Gaz.* 27 July 5/1 The war would be carried on unabatedly until something more tangible in the way of terms was proposed.

**Unaba·ting,** *ppl. a.* (Un-[1] 10.)

**1768–74** Tucker *Lt. Nat.* (1834) II. 103 That unabating activity, that serenity..which are characteristics of a perfect disciple. **1779** Hervey *Nav. Hist.* II. 165 The fleet remained ignorant of what had happened, and the fight was continued with unabating warmth. **1831** D. E. Williams *Life & Corr. Sir T. Lawrence* II. 264 The whole of which time he appeared in unabating spirits, and with not the slightest appearance of weakness. **1894** *Daily News* 5 Sept. 5/6 His unabating zeal for the Irish cause.

Hence **Unaba·tingly** *adv.*

**1793** *Minstrel* I. 174 The storm continued unabatingly.

**Unabbre·viated,** *ppl. a.* (Un-[1] 8.) [1775 Ash.] **1805** Tooke *Purley* II. viii. 498 Without taking..into our language the same unabbreviated verb. **1886** *Athenæum* 27 Nov. 714/1 Many of the 'points' in the narrative have been selected for printing without their context, but unabbreviated. **Unabho·rred,** *ppl. a.* (Un-[1] 8.) **1608** Sylvester tr. *Mathieu, Mem. Mortality* I. lxxx, Th' art loth to leave the Courts Delights, Devices Where None lives long vnbrav'd, or vnabhorred. **Unabi·ding,** *ppl. a.* (Un-[1] 10.) *c* **1430** *Life St. Kath.* (1884) 49 To see what medes and rewardes þay be þat crist ȝeueth to hyse seruauntys for þese vnabydyng thynges. **1849** Froude *Nemesis of Faith* 226 Markham's new faith fabric had been reared upon the clouds of sudden violent feeling, and no air castle was ever of more unabiding growth. **Unabi·dingly** *adv.* (Un-[1] 11), **Unabi·dingness** (Un-[1] 12). **1847** Webster.

**†Unabi·lity.** *Obs.* Also 5-6 **unabilite,** 6 **-itie, -itye;** 6–7 **unhabilitie,** 6 **-habylytee,** *Sc.* **wnhabilietie.** [Un-[1] 12, after OF. *inhabilité* (14th c.) or med.L. *inhabilitas* Inability.] The quality of being unable; inability. Freq. const. *for, of, to*, etc.

*c* **1400** *Apol. Loll.* 28 Þer ontrowþ, and vndisposicoun, and vnabilite to reseyue. **1509** Fisher *Serm.* Wks. (1876) 268, I knowe well myne vnworthynes & vnhabylytees to this so grete a mater. **1565** Stapleton *Fortr. Faith* 122 b, S. Basill excuseth him selfe of vnabilite to extoll sufficiently the vocation of couent Monkes. **1617** R. Wilkinson *Barwick Bridge* 31 The highest stile of praise is to professe our unability of expressing. **1644** Quarles *Barnabas & B.* (1651) 223 Thy unability for the work prophesies the impossibility of the reward. **1711** in *10th Rep. Hist. MSS. Comm.* App. V. 152 They alleadge for their justification an unability in stopping the foe. **1769** in *Cath. Rec. Soc. Publ.* (1914) XIV. 149 Not admitting any Solace but when constrain'd by an absolute Unability.

**Una·bject,** *a.* (Un-[1] 7.) **1850** Leigh Hunt *Autobiog.* xxv. III. 269 Such humble, yet un-abject, and truly religious souls, as cannot accept unintelligible and unworthy ties of conscience. **Unabju·red,** *ppl. a.* (Un-[1] 8.) **1549** Latimer *7th Serm. bef. Edw. VI* (Arb.) 189, I wyl aduyse you fyrst..to abiure al your fryendes, all your frindeshipe, leaue not one vnabiured.

**Unable** (vnē[i]·b'l), *a.* Forms: *α.* 4–7 **unhable,** (6 *Sc.* **wnhable, unhabil**). *β.* 4– **unable,** 5 **unabille, -abyll(e, -abull,** 5–6 **unabil(l;** 5 **onable,** 6 **-abil.** [Un-[1] 7 + Able *a.*, after OF. *inhabile* or L. *inhabilis* Inhabile *a.* Cf. MDu. *onabel.*]

**1.** Not able, not having ability or power, *to* do or perform (undergo or experience) something specified. (Chiefly of persons.)

*α.* *c* **1380** Wyclif *Wks.* (1880) 422 Al þes þat han chirchis aproprid faylen of þ is trewe seruyss herfore, & þus þei ben vnhable to preye, but preyen aȝen þer oune hed. **1552** Latimer *Serm. Gosp.* vi. 190 The person of the Church is ignoraunt and unhable to teach the word of God. **1590** Spenser *F. Q.* I. iv. 23 Vnfit he was for any worldly thing And eke vnhable once to stirre or go. **1596** *Ibid.* VI. i. 16 Me first he tooke, vnhable to withstond.

*β.* **1382** Wyclif *Isaiah* xl. 20 The stronge tree, and the vnable to roten ches the wise craftes man. *c* **1420** Lydg. *Ballad Commend. Our Lady* 15 Alas! unworthy I am and unable To love suche con. *c* **1470** Henry *Wallace* VII. 119 My witt vnabill is To runsik sic, for dreid I say off myss. **1526** *Pilgr. Perf.* (W. de W. 1531) 98 Thou shalte make thy selfe vnable to ryse and growe in goostlynesse. **1598** Yong *Diana* 57 To tell you now the life, that I led in his absence, ..my toong is far vnable. **1651** Hobbes *Leviath.* II. xxx. 181 Many men..become unable to maintain themselves by their labour. **1700** Prior *Carm. Sec.* xxiii, Lost in trackless Fields of shining Day, Unable to discern the Way. **1774** Goldsm. *Nat. Hist.* (1776) III. 402 As they are unable to escape by flight, the hunters..easily overpower them. **1836** Thirlwall *Greece* III. xvii. 3 The Persian governor, unable to hold out, and disdaining to surrender, set fire to the town. **1891** Farrar *Darkn. & Dawn* xx, Panting with wrath, he was unable even to return the greeting of Nero.

**b.** Const. *for* or *to* (with sbs.).

(*a*) **1456** Sir G. Haye *Law Arms* (S.T.S.) 109 Gif he be ane unworthy persone, and unhable tharto,..he degradis him. *a* **1470** H. Parker *Dives & Pauper* (W. de W. 1496) v. xviii. 220/1 Though his woodnes passe yet he is yrreguler & unable to goddes aulter. **1513** *Life Henry V* (1911) 83 The Kinge his father, who at that time was lymited, was vnable to the charge of the realme.

(*b*) **1568** GRAFTON *Chron.* II. 382 He was maymed with the stroke of an horse in his youth, and so made unhable for the governaunce of the Realme. **1598** GRENEWEY *Tacitus, Ann.* I. i. (1622) 2 Agrippa they accounted..yoong, and raw in state matters; vnable for so great a charge. **1668** WILKINS *Real Char.* II. i. § 4. 41 Either by restoring what is due, or by being rendred unable for it. **1841** CHAMBERS *Pop. Rhymes Scotl.* (1870) 76 She could not spin at all, and found herself quite unable for it.

† **c.** Used attributively with *to* following the noun. *Obs. rare.*

**1560** PILKINGTON *Expos. Aggeus* (1562) 59 An unable priest to teach, is good to nothinge in that kynde of lyfe or ministerye. *a* **1586** SIDNEY *Arcadia* I. xii. (1912) 80 Those troblesome effects..be not the faults of love, but of him that loves; as an unable vessel to beare such a licour. *c* **1640** J. SMYTH *Lives Berkeleys* (1883) II. 141, I stand an unable man to determine of either opinion.

**d.** Not knowing, ignorant. *rare*—¹.

*a* **1721** EUSDEN in *Addison's Cato* A.'s Misc. Wks. 1721 I. 267 Silent we stand, unable where to praise.

**2.** Of persons: Lacking ability in some implied respect; incompetent, inefficient.

**1395** PURVEY *Remonstr.* (1851) 112 It is gouernid by symonient bisshopis and vnable curatis. **1407** WILLIAM OF THORPE in Foxe *A. & M.* (1570) I. 648/2 These vnable priestes haue bene, and yet are, and shalbe, chiefe cause of pestilence of men. *a* **1513** FABYAN *Chron.* (1811) 548 Weale I wote, and knowlege, and deme myselfe to be and haue ben vnsuffycyent and vnable and also vnprofytable. **1544** BETHAM *Precepts War* I. cxcviii. I vj b, To sende forth thyne vnable souldyours..to be as a bayte..to thyne enemyes. **1612** BRINSLEY *Lud. Lit.* p iv, This indeuor..thus vndertaken by me the vnablest of many thousands. **1668** R. STEELE *Husbandman's Calling* v. (1672) 139 What if I leave a shiftless wife, and unable children behind me? **1710** SHAFTESB. *Charac., Adv. Author* (1737) I. 224 The greatest actions lose their force, and perish in the custody of unable and mean writers. *a* **1774** GOLDSM. *Hist. Greece* II. 167 No hopes of succour from such unable protectors. **1856** EMERSON *Eng. Traits, Manners* P 8, I hesitated to read and threw out for its impertinence many a disparaging phrase ..about poor, thin, unable mortals. **1877** OWEN *Wellesley's Desp.* p. xxvii, What would become of the system in *un*able hands?

**b.** Of faculties, actions, etc.: Characterized by want of ability; inefficient, ineffectual.

**1387–8** T. USK *Test. Love* III. i. (Skeat) l. 171 If any thing be insufficient or els mislyking, wyte that the leudnesse of myne unable conning. *c* **1400** MAUNDEV. (1839) xxxi. 315, I ..have ben..at many a faire Dede of Armes (alle be it that I dide none my self, for myn unable insuffisance). **1584** CONSTABLE *Diana* VII. vi, A dombe restraint Breakes forth in teares from mine unable mind. **1633** COWLEY *Constantia & Philetus* To Rdr. ii, As shee my vnabler quill did guide, Her briny teares did on the paper fall. *a* **1699** J. BEAUMONT *Psyche* XXI. lxxv, I..see thee more By this unable and denying Sight, Than they [etc.]. **1795** BURKE *Abridgm. Eng. Hist.* Wks. 1842 II. 523 Vortigern..opposed a mixture of timid war and unable negociation.

† **3. a.** Of persons: Incapable of, not qualified for, some position. *Obs.*

*c* **1380** WYCLIF *Wks.* (1880) 465 þat pope þat fayliþ heere oþer for kunnyng or for wille is vnhable to take to pope & lede his floc. **1390** GOWER *Conf.* III. 202 His nase of and his lippes bothe He kutte, for he wolde him lothe Unto the poeple and make unable. **1426** LYDG. *De Guil Pilgr.* 5108 But I sawh ther in presence, Somme pressen to the table That wer vnworthy & vnhable.

† **b.** Of things: Unfit or unsuitable for some purpose. *Obs.*

**1390** GOWER *Conf.* III. 104 Which of the poeple be forlete As lond desert that is unable, For it mai noght ben habitable. *c* **1440** *Pallad. on Husb.* I. 222 Diuide hit thus: that fatte & bering, able, Let plowe hit vp, & leef the lene, vnable, Couert in woode. **1444** *Maldon* (Essex) *Rec.* Liber 'A.' fol. 32 b, Item, that no bocher sle, ne selle, none vnhable flessh.

† **4. a.** Not able to be (done); impossible. *Obs.*

*c* **1400** *Destr. Troy* Prol. 46 How goddes foght in the filde, folke as þai were, And other errours vnable þat after were knowen, That poyetis of prise have preuyt vntrew. **1548** GESTE *Pr. Masse* 78 The wyche, as it is an attempte too unreasonable and unable, so passynge wycked, presumptuouse and detestable. **1567** *Reg. Privy Council Scot.* I. 512 How unabill it salbe to the nobilitie..alwayis to abyde and continew at Court.

† **b.** Awkward; unlucky. *Obs.*—¹

**1572** *Satir. Poems Reform.* xxxi. 94 Sen Fortoun, with a Reill, Hes wrocht thame ane vnabill charr.

**5.** Lacking in physical ability or strength; incapable of much bodily exertion; weak, feeble. In later use *Sc.*

**1577** B. GOOGE *Heresbach's Husb.* III. (1586) 144 b, Hee waxeth feeble, and vnable, before he bee sixe yeeres olde. **1591** SHAKS. I *Hen. VI*, IV. v. 4 When saplesse Age, and weake vnable limbes Should bring thy Father to his drooping Chaire. **1621** BURTON *Anat. Mel.* III. iii. I. ii, I haue an old grimme sire to my husband as bald as a gourde, as little and as vnable as a child. **1685** BAXTER *Paraphr. N. T.* Matt. xxv. 46 This doth not extend to condemn Infants or poor unable persons for not doing what they could not. **1764** GOLDSM. *Hist Eng. in Lett.* (1772) I. 168 Though unable by disease, yet they recompensed the defect by valour. **1818** SCOTT *Br. Lamm.* xv, Those unarmed and unable Mephibosheths, that are sure to be a burden to every one that takes them up. **1858–61** J. BROWN *Horæ Subs.* (1863) 163 No one could have suffered from..the misery of an unable body. **1896** CROCKETT *Grey Man* iv, He..was ever thereafter unable of his legs.

*transf.* **1601** YARINGTON *Two Lament. Trag.* i. ii. in Bullen *O. Pl.* IV, We do assure us of your love And care to guide his weake unhable youth In pathes of knowledge. **1607** HEYWOOD *Wom. Killed w. Kindn.* (1617) C 2 b, Sir I accept it, and remaine indebted Euen to the best of my vnable power.

† **Una·ble,** *v. Obs.* Also 5 unabyl, 6 -abill; 5–6 unhable. [UN-² 6 a, or f. UNABLE *a.*]

**1.** *trans.* To render unable, to unfit or incapacitate, *to* do something. Sometimes *spec.* in *Law*: To make legally incapable.

*c* **1380** WYCLIF *Sel. Wks.* I. 147 Myche more shulde worldely lordship unable men now to take þis Goost. *c* **1400** *Destr. Troy* 9423 He woundit hym wickedly in his wale face, And vnablit after with angur to fight. *a* **1470** HARDING *Chron.* CLVII. iii, This Edmond thelder soonne of Kyng Henry, Broke backed and bowbacked bore, Was vnabled to haue the monarche. **1567–9** JEWEL *Def. Apol.* (1611) 195 Then doth it [the vow] not of necessitie and fine force vnable a man to contract Matrimonie. **1613** SHERLEY *Trav. Persia* 32 The eldest son of the King remained at the Court of his father, administring all that, which his fathers defect of light vnabled him to doe. **1640** HABINGTON *Edw. IV*, 67 They..had been unabled to pay their usuall tribute to the King. *a* **1774** GOLDSM. *Hist. Greece* I. 207 Until both were utterly unabled to withstand the smallest efforts of foreign invasion.

*refl. c* **1380** WYCLIF *Wks.* (1880) 191 þei vnablen hem self to do þe office of prestis. *c* **1380** — *Serm.* Sel. Wks. II. 36 þre ordris in Cristis tyme unabliden hem to be of þis rewme.

**b.** Const. *to* (or *of*) an action, office, etc.

*a* **1395** HYLTON *Scala Perf.* II. xv. (W. de W. 1494), How louers of this worlde unable hem in dyuers maners to the refourmyng of her owne soule. *a* **1470** H. PARKER *Dives & Pauper* (W. de W. 1496) I. xxxviii. 79/1 He sholde be pryued of his benefyce yf that he hadde ony. Yf he had no benefyce he sholde be unabled and dysposed therto. **1560** KNOX *Bk. Common Order* (1901) 20 The crimes and vices that might unable them of the Ministry.

**2.** Without const.: To unfit or incapacitate, to deprive of ability or power, in some respect; to disable physically.

*c* **1380** WYCLIF *Sel. Wks.* I. 105 Siþ he..wiþdrawiþ never his grace, but ʒif man unable him selfe. *Ibid.* 219 As distempour of þe eir shal sle men and unable þe erþe. *c* **1450** in Aungier *Syon* (1840) 281 Whom euerychone and eche trespasyng in the premysses, we unable for euermore in the selfdede doyng. **1503** *Rolls of Parlt.* VI. 547/1 To the use, profitte or behove of any persone or persones by this Acte not attaynted nor unabled. **1582** STANYHURST *Æneis* III. (Arb.) 80, I through pangs vncoth vnhabled, With stutting stamering at leingth thus fumbled an aunswer. *a* **1641** BP. MOUNTAGU *Acts & Mon.* (1642) 285 That old Leacher, worne out and unabled, though he dyed his haire black that he might seeme to be young. **1654** GAYTON *Pleas. Notes* III. v. 100 That is to say, with three hard words, un-mule, un-leg, and un-able, Alanso Lopez. **1775** JOHNSON *Let.* in *Boswell* (1831) III. 255 Poor Lucy Porter has her hand in a bag, so unabled by the gout that she cannot dress herself.

**b.** To annul or cancel. *rare*—¹.

**1611** SPEED *Hist. Gt. Brit.* IX. xxi. § 134 Hee prepared himselfe to make his Wil, wherein howsoeuer titles had been vnhabled in Parliaments, he ordained his three children to succeede each after others.

Hence † **Una·bling** *vbl. sb. Obs.*

**1475** *Rolls of Parlt.* VI. 147/2 As if the said Acte of atteyndre or unablyng never had been made. **1503** *Ibid.* 548.

† **Una·bled,** *ppl. a. Obs. rare.* [UN-¹ 8.]

**1.** Unqualified.

**1497–8** in *Archæol. Jrnl.* XLIII. 168 It[e]m for a fyne lost by Will[ia]m Birchwold for settyng to werke a child vnabled & vnbound [= unapprenticed], x^d. **1653** GAUDEN *Hierasp.* 226 Compleating those sad effects, which disorderly, unordeined, unsent, and unabled Teachers..have already begun.

**2.** Not endowed with strength or vigour.

**1597** MIDDLETON *Wisd. Solomon* ii. 11 Wee are the cedars, they the mushromes bee, Vnabled shrubs, vnto an abled tree.

† **Una·bleness.** *Obs.* [f. UNABLE *a.*] The condition of being unable; inability, incapacity; disability. (Very common *c* 1500–1660.)

*c* **1380** WYCLIF *Wks.* (1880) 245 Siche men as desiren benefices schulden not haue hem, but men þat fleen hem for drede of vnabilnesse of hemself & grete charge, as dide moyses. *c* **1425** *Found. St. Bartholomew's* (E.E.T.S.) 4 Promysynge that he wolde be ware of alle passid vnhabilnesse, and yeue affectualy his diligence and laboure to that he hathe promysyd. **1501** in *Lett. Rich. III & Hen. VII* (Rolls) II. 100 The..commissary hath full power to dispense with that irregularity and to take away all infamy and unableness. **1560** PILKINGTON *Expos. Aggeus* (1562) 172 He biddeth us when we feele oure weakness & unablenes to fulfil his law, to come unto hym. **1638** JUNIUS *Paint. Ancients* 37 There is in us a certaine unablenesse of imitating such things as doe not very well agree with our naturall disposition. **1648** BOYLE *Seraph. Love* xiii. (1700) 71 To convince the World of their unableness to emerge and recover out of that deep Abyss, wherein the load of Sin..had precipitated Fall'n Man. **1727** BAILEY (vol. II) s.v. *Inability*.

† **Una·blety.** *Obs.* In 4–5 vnablete, -abilte. [f. UNABLE *a.* + -TY, prob. after OF. *inhabileté.*] = UNABILITY.

*c* **1380** WYCLIF *Wks.* (1880) 67 God wole not and may not brynge vnable men in-to benefices of þe chirche for his riȝtwysnesse & vnablete of hem self. *c* **1400** tr. *Secreta Secret., Gov. Lordsh.* 67 He may falle yn-to syknes, ffebylnes, and ynto oþer vnabiltez. **1425** *Rolls of Parlt.* IV. 267/2 Ye grete unabilte and unsuffisante, that the same Wauter felte in hymself, to touche thing yat was so chier.

**Una·bly,** *adv.* Now *rare* or *Obs.* [UN-¹ 11.] In an unable or incapable manner.

*a* **1400–50** *Alexander* 2308 Quat, & has þou ossed to Alexander þis ayndain wirdes, And me þus ill? vn-ably þine abet þou weris. *c* **1658** in *Lovelace's Poems* (1904) 212 Thy but unably-comprehending clay, To what could not be circumscrib'd gave way. **1710** SHAFTESB. *Charac.* (1711) I. 346 Facts unably related, tho with the greatest Sincerity and good Faith, may prove the worst sort of Deceit.

**Unabo·lishable,** *a.* (UN-¹ 7 b.) **1643** MILTON *Divorce* Wks. 1851 IV. 57 That Law [has been] proved to be morall, and unabolishable. **1645** — *Tetrach.* Ibid. IV. 215 By that unabolishable equity which it convaies to us. **1682** H. MORE *Annot. Glanvill's Lux O.* 257 There may be many other ..habitudes of Terms..every jot as unabolishable as this.

**Unabo·lished,** *ppl. a.* (UN-¹ 8.)

**1577** HOLINSHED *Chron.* I. 4/1 They [*sc.* Bards], of all the other sectes before specified, were suffred only to continue vnabolished in all ages. **1594** HOOKER *Eccl. Pol.* IV. xiv. § 1 The number of needlesse lawes vnabolisht, doth weaken the force of them that are necessarie. **1667** *Phil. Trans.* II. 579 With art and care those channels may be preserved un-abolisht. **1837** CARLYLE *Fr. Rev.* II. VI. i, Your unabolished Staff of the Guard..is in these very moments privily deliberating at the General's.

**Unabra·ded,** *ppl. a.* (UN-¹ 8.) **1827** FARADAY *Chem. Manip.* iii. (1842) 72 The learner should practise first on a piece of waste glass tube, commencing both from an unabraded surface and from a cross line. **1886** *Athenæum* 18 Dec. 830/1 In an area of about forty feet square were found nearly six hundred unabraded worked flints.

**Unabri·dg(e)able,** *a.* (UN-¹ 7 b.) **1802–12** BENTHAM *Ration. Judic. Evid.* (1827) IV. 154 The establishment of long and unabridgable intervals between these times.

**Unabri·dged,** *ppl. a.* [UN-¹ 8.] Not abridged, reduced, or shortened. In mod. use spec. of literary works.

**1599** SANDYS *Europæ Spec.* (1632) 111 In those places where their power remaineth yet unabridged. **1772** MASON *Eng. Gard.* I. 20 To the lawn [to] restore Its ample space, and bid it feast the sight With verdure pure, unbroken, unabridg'd. **1840** AINSWORTH *Tower of Lond.* (1864) 234 By which means your authority would be unabridged. **1864** PUSEY *Lect. Dan.* i. (1876) 49 Daniel and Ezra use unabridged, and so, older forms. **1894** A. E. WAITE *Paracelsus' Writ.* Title-p., Paracelsus the Great, now for the first time translated faithfully and unabridged into English.

**b.** *absol.* A copy of the 'unabridged edition' of Webster's Dictionary.

**1860** O. W. HOLMES *Prof. Breakf.-T.* ii. 36 You small boy there, hurry up that 'Webster's Unabridged'! **1894** H. GARDENER *Unoff. Patriot* 302 I'm not sure that I've spelled some of these words right, but my unabridged is not handy.

**Una·brogated,** *ppl. a.* Also 6 *Sc.* vnabrogat. (UN-¹ 8 and 8 b.)

**1535** STEWART *Cron. Scot.* (Rolls) I. 101 To caus thair lawis keip the strenth..that tha had maid vnabrogat at lenth. **1577** tr. *Bullinger's Decades* (1592) 410 The law, so far as it is the rule howe to liue well and happely,..doth remaine vnabrogated. **1818** G. S. FABER *Horæ Mosaicæ* II. 29 These priests must obviously have been priests according to the still unabrogated patriarchal dispensation. **1849** RUSKIN *Seven Lamps* i. § 6. 14 Let us not now lose sight of this broad and unabrogated principle.

**Unabru·pt,** *a.* (UN-¹ 7.) **1865** METEYARD *Life Wedgwood* I. 168 The highest effects are obtained from subdued tones, and unabrupt contrasts of colour, light and shade.

† **Unabsoi·led,** *ppl. a. Obs.*—¹ [UN-¹ 8: cf. ASSOIL *v.* 6.] Unsettled.

**1521** WOLSEY in *St. Papers Hen. VIII* (1830) I. 67 Soo that doubte remaynethe yet unabsoiled, as it did byfore my writyng.

† **Una·bsolute,** *a. Obs.* (UN-¹ 7.) **1697** COLLIER *Ess. Mor. Subj.* I. (1709) 174 Where Goodness is mutable, and Reason unabsolute, there must be Rigour to..check the Abuse of Liberty. **Unabso·lvable,** *a.* (UN-¹ 7 b.) **1635** J. HAYWARD tr. *Biondi's Banish'd Virg.* 17 The Gods are not so firmely bound by the unabsolveable oathes they vow by the infernall Lake.

**Unabso·lved,** *ppl. a.* [UN-¹ 8. Cf. G. *unabsolviert.*]

**1.** Not absolved. Also const. *of.*

**1611** FLORIO, *Innassolto*, vnabsolued. **1681** BAXTER *Acc. Sherlocke* iv. 186 Who shall Absolve the Patriarchs, Primates,..&c.? Must they be Unabsolved till a General Council do it? **1765** STERNE *Tr. Shandy* VII. xxiv, If we are ravished and die unabsolved of them. **1819** SCOTT *Ivanhoe* xliii, Slay him not,..unshriven and unabsolved. **1844** LADY G. FULLERTON *Ellen Middleton* III. xxi. 68 [I] always let him draw near to the altar alone; for, unforgiven, unabsolved, unreconciled, I dared not approach it.

† **2.** Unsettled, undecided. *Obs.*

An alteration of UNABSOILED *ppl. a.*

**1721** STRYPE *Eccl. Mem.* I. 33 So that doubt remaineth not [*sic*] unabsolved.

**Unabso·rbable,** *a.* (UN-¹ 7 b.) **1846** WORCESTER (citing Davy). **1899** *Westm. Gaz.* 6 Dec. 10/1 The carbon in the 'fog mixture' being of an unabsorbable nature.

**Unabso·rbed,** *ppl. a.* (UN-¹ 8.)

**1766** *Phil. Trans.* LVII. 99, I think we may fairly conclude that this unabsorbed part was intirely common air. **1791** *Ibid.* LXXXI. 370 Being then taken out, and the unabsorbed water hastily wiped from their surface, they were again weighed. **1863** TYNDALL *Heat* ix. (1870) 305 Where the waves pursue their way unabsorbed no motion of heat is imparted. **1885** *Pall Mall G.* 28 July 5/2 Within ten years the list of unabsorbed country banks will probably be a short one.

**Una·bstract,** *a.* (UN-¹ 7.) **1840** HERSCHELL *Ess.* (1857) 73 A theory..rude and unabstract in the form of its statement. **Unabsu·rd,** *a.* (UN-¹ 7.) **1742** YOUNG *Nt. Th.* VII. 514 What less than infinite, makes un-absurd Passions, which all on earth but more inflames? *c* **1815** JANE AUSTEN *Persuas.* viii, Doing it with so much sympathy and natural graces as showed the kindest considerations for all that was real and unabsurd in the parent's feelings.

† **Unabui·lyeit,** *ppl. a. Sc. Obs.*—¹ [UN-¹ 8.] Unarrayed.

*c* **1530** W. STEWART *To the King* 8 (Bann. MS.), Of alkin clething nakit and denud, Bair, vnabulyeit [*Maitl. MS.* onabilȝeit], as scho borne was.

**Unabu·sed,** *ppl. a.* (UN-¹ 8.) **1661** GLANVILL *Van. Dogm.* 100 More sober heads have a set of misconceits, which are as absurd to an unpassionated reason, as those to our unabused senses. **1678** CUDWORTH *Intell. Syst.* 69 The Opinion, that such Spirits were Incorporeal and Immaterial, could never enter into the minds of men by Nature, Unabused by Doctrine. **1864** PUSEY *Lect. Daniel* i. (1876) 19 Human greatness is, when unabused, a majestic sight.

**Unabu·sing,** *ppl. a.* (UN-[1] 10.) *a* **1628** F. GREVIL *Let. Hon. Lady* (1633) C iv, To giue all, and take nothing, proceeds of an uncaused goodnesse, and so necessarily of an vnabusing.

**Unacade·mic,** *a.* (UN-[1] 7. Cf. G. *unacademisch.*) **1844** H. ROGERS *Ess.* (1874) I. ii. 45 Having absented himself from certain 'exercises', and otherwise been guilty of sundry unacademic irregularities. **1897** FLANDRAU *Harvard Episodes* 78 Probably the most..unacademic person that ever answered to an official name.

**Unacade·mical,** *a.* (UN-[1] 7.) **1840** MOZLEY *Lett.* (1885) 98 Therefore his conduct is so much the more unacademical.

**Unacce·lerated,** *ppl. a.* (UN-[1] 8.) *a* **1774** GOLDSM. *Surv. Exp. Philos.* (1776) I. 135 The product will be the space described by the unaccelerated motion continued after the fall. **1893** *Brit. Jrnl. Photogr.* XL. 751 A simple unaccelerated drop-shutter.

**Unacce·nted,** *ppl. a.* [UN-[1] 8.] Not accented or stressed; unemphasized.

Hence (in recent use) *unaccentedness.*

**1598** FLORIO, *Disaccentato*, vnaccented, without an accent or due sound. **1728** CHAMBERS *Cycl.* s.v. *Accent*, Every Bar or Measure is divided into accented and unaccented Parts. **1768** *Phil. Trans.* LVIII. 256 As neither the Samnites nor the Etruscans had in their alphabet O, they used the simple unaccented V for that element. **1808** L. MURRAY *Eng. Gram.* I. 332 Unaccented syllables are generally short. **1873** H. C. BANISTER *Music* 12 In all measures, certain beats are accented, and the others unaccented. **1893** *Nation* (N.Y.) 12 Jan. 33/3 His outline drawings..are round and unaccented, and show little sense of structure.

**Unacce·ntuated,** *ppl. a.* (UN-[1] 8. Cf. G. *unaccentuirt*, Sw. *oaccentuerad.*) **1716** M. DAVIES *Athen. Brit.* II. 373 Of the same 12th Century were Folmar, Abaillard, Arnaldus Brixiensis [etc.],..all whose unaccentuated and recanted Arianism perish'd together. **1887** COOK *Sievers' O. E. Gram.* 114 This change occurs most frequently in an unaccentuated syllable.

**Unacce·pt,** *v. rare*[–1]. [UN-[2] 3.] *trans.* To cancel the acceptance of (a bill).

**1665** MARIUS *Adv. Conc. Bills Exchange* 24 The Acceptor would (if he could) unaccept the Bill, or make voyde his Acceptance thereof.

**Unacceptabi·lity.** (UN-[1] 12.) [**1775** ASH.] **1852** LD. COCKBURN *Jeffrey* I. 387 The people maintained..that popular unacceptability was of itself a ground on which the courts were entitled to reject. **1863** H. SPENCER *Ess.* III. 325 We shall find that its unacceptability becomes still more conspicuous when the analysis is pursued to the end.

**Unacceptable,** *a.* [UN-[1] 7 b and 5 b. For pronunciation see note to ACCEPTABLE *a.*] Not acceptable.

**1483** *Cath. Angl.* 2/2 Vn Acceptabylle, *ingratus,..non acceptabilis.* **1540** WYATT in Flügel *Neuengl. Lesebuch* I. 349, I can not ellis se what shold move this rigour..onles I peraventure be vnacceptable vnto hym. **1594** HOOKER *Eccl. Pol.* II. iv. § 5 To the author and God of our nature, how shal any operation proceeding in naturall sort, be in that respect vnacceptable? **1634** CANNE *Necess. Separ.* 27 A vaine worship: and therefore vnacceptable altogether to the Lord. **1697** BENTLEY *Phal.* (1699) 83 It will not be unacceptable to the Reader, to see some of it here corrected. **1710** PRIDEAUX *Orig. Tithes* v. 241 The new Laws of King Henry being very unacceptable to the English. **1753** WARBURTON in Harris *Hardwicke* (1847) II. 481 No favours from such a hand could be unacceptable. **1855** MACAULAY *Hist. Eng.* xxi. IV. 551 He still called himself a Whig, and was not unacceptable to many of the Whigs. **1880** MEREDITH *Tragic Com.* (1881) 165 An honourable son-in-law could not be unacceptable to him.

Hence **Unacceptableness; Unacceptably** *adv.*

**1648** HEXHAM II, *On-aengenaemheydt*, *Un-acceptableness. **1660** INGELO *Bentiv. & Ur.* I. (1682) 72 To correct the unacceptableness of his story. **1697** COLLIER *Ess. Mor. Subj.* I. (1709) 2, I hope this Alteration does not arise from any natural Antipathy I have to Sense; but from the unacceptableness of the Subject I am upon. **1873** MRS. WHITNEY *Other Girls* xxi, A tone timid with an apprehension of some possible unacceptableness. **1648** HEXHAM II, *On-aengenaemlick*, *Vn-acceptably. **1828**- in various Dicts.

**Unacce·ptance.** [UN-[1] 12.] Lack of acceptance.

**1865** M. ARNOLD *Ess. Crit.* iv. (1875) 148 Saint Theresa endured twenty years of unacceptance and of repulse in her prayers. **1898** SAINTSBURY *Short. Hist. Eng. Lit.* XI. iii. (1900) 772 Mr. Ruskin's ideas, when their first stage of unacceptance and their second of acceptance were over, came to be cavilled at.

**Unacce·ptant,** *a.* (UN-[1] 7.) **1865** RUSKIN *Eth. Dust* v. (1883) 85 Whatever dead substance, unacceptant of this energy, comes in their way, is..rejected.

**Unacce·pted,** *ppl. a.* [UN-[1] 8.] Not accepted; rejected.

**1612** T. TAYLOR *Comm. Titus* i. 8 Such cups of cold water shall not be vnaccepted nor unrewarded of him. **1718** PRIOR *Solomon* II. 212 Restless I follow'd this obdurate Maid..., Offer'd again the unaccepted Wreath. **1809** R. LANGFORD *Introd. Trade* 35 Unaccepted bills must be protested..on the very day when they become due. **1857** MISS WINKWORTH tr. *Tauler's Serm.* xviii. 322 Therefore, His gifts, which He offers without ceasing to every man, remain unaccepted. **1899** MISS B. HARRADEN *Fowler* 234 Davy always kept up the rôle of being an unaccepted sweetheart.

**† Unacce·ssible,** *a. Obs.* Also 6–7 -able. [UN-[1] 5 b.] = INACCESSIBLE *a.*

**α. 1596** RALEIGH *Discov. Guiana* 97 Whosoeuer shall first possesse it, it shall bee founde vnaccessable for anie Enemie. **1611** COTGR., *Vn lieu condemné*, an vncouth, or vnaccessable place. **1645** SLINGSBY *Diary* (1836) 167 By yᵉ wayes we took thro' yᵉ almost unaccessable mountains of Wales.

**β. 1600** E. BLOUNT tr. *Conestaggio* 263 Hauing viewed the Iland fortified on all parts where he might descend, and by nature vnaccessible. *a* **1641** BP. MOUNTAGU *Acts & Mon.* (1642) 536 The place was..unaccessible; none did or could come there but the High Priest, once every yeere. **1704** RAY *Creation* (ed. 4) I. 200 Things..too remote and unaccessible for us to penetrate or discover. **1768–74** TUCKER *Lt. Nat.* (1834) I. 527 The Creator dwells in unaccessible light, whereto we cannot draw near.

Hence **† Unacce·ssibleness; † Unacce·ssibly** *adv. Obs.*

**1615** G. SANDYS *Trav.* 183 Mountains; whereof some are cut (or naturally so) in degrees like allies, which would be else vnaccessably fruitlesse. *a* **1676** HALE *Prim. Orig. Man.* II. iv. (1677) 155 We cannot attain to any clear sensible discovery of them..by reason of their remoteness, distance, and unaccessibleness.

**Unacce·ssional,** *a.* (UN-[1] 7 and 5 b.) **1655** EARL ORRERY *Parthen.* I. II. 95 The Princess..has all the guifts of Nature in so unaccessionall a Degree, that nothing can excel the perfectnesse of her body but that of her Minde.

**Unacce·ssory,** *a.* (UN-[1] 7.) **1660** INGELO *Bentiv. & Ur.* II. (1682) 155 Altogether unaccessory to their Calamities. **1753** W. MELMOTH tr. *Cicero's Lett.* II. 145 Nor were you entirely unaccessory to my error.

**Unaccide·nted,** *a.*, (UN-[1] 9.) *c* **1740** J. BROWN in R. Mackenzie *Life* (1918) iii. 23 Reason told me that at least our unaccidented tongue could not much change names from what they were in the Greek.

**Unaccli·mated,** *ppl. a.* (UN-[1] 8.) **1846** WORCESTER (citing Patterson). **1852** T. ROSS tr. *Humboldt's Trav.* I. xi. 379 Their death often alarmed the unacclimated Europeans. **1883** *Cent. Mag.* July 425/2 The fatality of the epidemics was principally among the unacclimated.

**Unacclima·tion.** (UN-[1] 12.) **1866** A. FLINT *Princ. Med.* (1880) 1023 Unacclimation is a condition pertaining to individual susceptibility.

**Unaccli·matized,** *ppl. a.* (UN-[1] 8. Cf. G. *unacclimatisirt.*) **1863** *Waitz' Introd. Anthropol.* I. 125 Negroes of the third and fourth generation, who, after being acclimatized in North America had returned to Africa,..became subject to the same climatic diseases as other unacclimatized individuals. **1891** KIPLING *City Dreadf. Nt.* 80 The air..brings about, to the unacclimatised, a singing in the ears.

**† Unacco·mmodate,** *ppl. a. Obs.* [UN-[1] 8 b and 5 b.] Unsuited; unaccommodated.

*a* **1676** HALE *Prim. Orig. Man.* III. vi. (1677) 282 Yet in the first state of Humane Production all these Suppositions must be laid aside, as unaccommodate to that state. **1736** T. PRINCE *New Eng. Chronol.* II. i. 103 Infected with the Scurvy & other Diseases, which their long Voyage and unaccommodate [**1621** inacomodate] Condition brought upon them.

**Unacco·mmodated,** *ppl. a.* [UN-[1] 8.] Not accommodated; not possessed *of*, unprovided *with*.

**1605** SHAKS. *Lear* III. iv. 109 Vnaccommodated man, is no more but such a poore, bare, forked Animall as thou art. **1627** DONNE *Serm.* 41 Not angry so as that he left Moses unsatisfied or unaccommodated for the maine businesse. **1680** MOXON *Mech. Exerc.* 226 Being at that time..unaccommodated of a Lathe of my own, I intended to put them out to be Turned. **1726** WELSTED *Dissemb. Wanton* I. i, The resource of stale virgins, and unaccommodated prudes. **1818** LADY MORGAN *Autobiog.* (1859) 7, I hear that travelling in Italy is beyond everything desolate and unaccommodated. **1842** F. E. PAGET *Milf. Malv.* 161 So soon as he perceived a body of strangers unaccommodated with seats of any kind, he immediately opened his pew door, and beckoned them in.

**Unacco·mmodating,** *ppl. a.* (UN-[1] 10.) **1790** BEATSON *Nav. & Mil. Mem.* I. 94 His manners and temper were unaccommodating. **1854** DICKENS *Hard T.* I. i, His very neckcloth, trained to take him by the throat with an unaccommodating grasp,..helped the emphasis. **1897** HINDE *Fall Congo Arabs* 106 We had taken prisoner the unaccommodating chief.

**Unacco·mpanied,** *ppl. a.* [UN-[1] 8.]

**1.** Not accompanied or attended. Also const. *by*, or *with*.

**1545** RAYNALDE *Byrth Mankynde* 21 b, God..neuer createth no speciall pleasure vnaccompanyed with some sorowe. *a* **1600** HOOKER *Eccl. Pol.* VII. xxiv. § 18 The travels and crosses wherewith prelacy is never unaccompanied. **1605** SHAKS. *Macb.* I. iv. 40 Our eldest, Malcolme, whom we name hereafter, The Prince of Cumberland: which Honor must Not vnaccompanied, inuest him onely. **1709** *Tatler* No. 120 ⁋ 3 As I was single and unaccompanied, I was not permitted to enter the temple. **1763** J. BROWN *Poetry & Music* v. 47 The Melody of Instruments, unaccompany'd by Dance or Song. **1800** *Asiat. Ann. Reg., Misc. Tr.* 84/2 Persic odes, unaccompanied with translations. **1827** POLLOK *Course T.* x. 351 Thou goest..Not unaccompanied; all these, my saints, Go with Thee. **1891** FARRAR *Darkn. & Dawn* liii, Unaccompanied by Philetus, the actor went to the meeting.

**2.** Lacking instrumental accompaniment.

**1818** BUSBY *Gram. Mus.* 475 In Unaccompanied Recitative, the modulation has little or no dependence. **1876** STAINER & BARRETT *Dict. Mus. Terms* s.v. *Anthem*, Those choirs in which an unaccompanied service is sometimes performed.

**Unacco·mplishable,** *a.* (UN-[1] 7 b.)

**1675** *Art Contentm.* I. § 12. 179 It must be exceedingly bitter, to be thus condemned to endless unaccomplishable desires. **1812** CARY *Dante, Parad.* XXVI. 126 Or ever Nimrod's race Their unaccomplishable work began. **1868** RUSKIN *Sesame* (1871) 161 At these visions of theirs we have mocked, and held them for idle and vain, unreal and unaccomplishable.

**Unacco·mplished,** *ppl. a.* [UN-[1] 8.]

**1.** Not accomplished or achieved; uncompleted.

**1525** LD. BERNERS *Froiss.* II. cxiv. 329 Your wysshes and enterprises are more lyke to be vnacomplysshed than atchyued. **1590** SWINBURNE *Testaments* 133 The same is neither accompted for accomplished,..neither yet for vnaccomplished or deficient. **1667** MILTON *P. L.* III. 455 All th' unaccomplisht works of Natures hand, Abortive, monstrous, or unkindly mixt. **1736** THOMSON *Liberty* IV. 161 Yet dark beneath The suffering feature sullen vengeance lowrs Shame, indignation, unaccomplish'd rage. **1821** SHELLEY *Hellas* Prol. 51 Assemble, sons of God, To speed or to prevent or to suspend..The unaccomplished destiny. **1850** TENNYSON *In Mem.* xci, The hope of unaccomplish'd years Be large and lucid round thy brow.

**2.** Of persons: Not socially or intellectually accomplished.

*a* **1729** CONGREVE tr. *Ovid's Art Love* III, Still unaccomplish'd may the maid be thought, Who gracefully to dance was never taught. **1796** MME. D'ARBLAY *Camilla* II. 357 How many are there, amongst the untaught and unaccomplished, who would think [etc.]. **1826** MISS MITFORD *Our Village* Ser. II. (1863) 274 Unaccomplished they were of course, but they could never have been thought ignorant. **1874** MISS MULOCK *My Mother & I*, xiv, Not that she is ill-educated, or unaccomplished.

**Unacco·mplishment.** (UN-[1] 12.) **1643** MILTON *Divorce* Introd., Wks. 1851 IV. 4 Custom being but a meer face,..rests not in her unaccomplishment, untill by secret inclination she accorporat her self with error. *Ibid.* 24 Where the mind and person pleases aptly, there some unaccomplishment of the bodies delight may be better born with.

**† Unacco·mptably,** *adv. Obs.* (UN-[1] 11.) *a* **1677** BARROW *Serm.* Wks. 1686 III. 260 The which are alledged, not with intent to imply that God ever acteth unaccomptably, or without highest reason.

**† Unaccompted,** *ppl. a. Obs.* (UN-[1] 8.) *a* **1483** *Liber Niger* in *Househ. Ord.* (1790) 65 In case the accomptes passe, for lack of appearance of one of them [*sc.* the steward or treasurer], three dayes unaccompted.

**† Unacco·mptible,** *a. Obs.* (UN-[1] 7.) **1678** B. R. *Let. Pop. Friends* 4 What Protestant Scammony is strong enough to make a..Catholick Disgorge Infallibility, or the Popes unaccomptible Power?

**† Unacco·mptibly,** *adv. Obs.* (UN-[1] 11.) **1678** CUDWORTH *Intell. Syst.* I. iii. Contents § 10. 102 These Materialists..assigned no cause of Motion, but introduced it into the world unaccomptibly.

**Unacco·rdable,** *a.* (UN-[1] 7 b.)

**1456** SIR G. HAYE *Law Arms* (S.T.S.) 30 Thai ar..unacordable with wysare than thame self. **1611** FLORIO, *Inaccordabile*, vnaccordable, not to bee agreed vpon.

**† Unacco·rdance.** *Obs.*[–1] [UN-[1] 12 and 5 b.] Disagreement.

*c* **1449** PECOCK *Repr.* 263 These preiers, whiche mowen be seid as mad to the cros, mowen be saued fro inconuenience and vnaccordaunce.

**Unacco·rdant,** *a.* (UN-[1] 7 and 5 b.)

*a* **1470** HARDING *Chron.* CV. xiii, Athelbold..His stepdame wed, menne saied it was not faire,..Again the lawe and christen conscience, Vnaccordant with his magnificence. **1798** *Geraldina* II. 268 The present disposition of my spirits is not unaccordant to the sentiments of affection. **1879** FARRAR *St. Paul* I. 384 The rhythmic conclusion is not unaccordant with the style of his most elevated moods.

**Unacco·rded,** *ppl. a.* [UN-[1] 8.] Not agreed upon; not granted or bestowed.

**1645** BP. HALL *Peace-Maker* v. 43 The Divines..professed their agreement in all the maine and important points; leaving those parcels unaccorded, which are meet to be sent, and confined to the Schooles. **1883** R. BRIDGES *Prometheus* 1215 O Right's toil unrewarded! O Love's prize unaccorded.

**† Unacco·rding,** *ppl. a. Obs.* [UN-[1] 10.] Inaccordant.

**1398** TREVISA *Barth. De P. R.* IX. xv. (Bodl MS.), Þe Caniculer daies bygynneþ,..alle hoote passions encreseth, and þat tyme is moste disconuenient and vnacording to medicyne. *c* **1400** tr. *Secreta Secret., Gov. Lordsh.* 60 By þe wyndes comes corrupcions of þe eyr and norschight dedly venyms, and many oþer vnacordand þinges comes þerof. *a* **1470** HARDING *Chron.* XXX. iv, Drunken he was echedaye expresse, Vnaccordynge to a prince of worthynesse. **1530** R. WHYTFORD *Werke for Househ.* H 3 Ferre vnacordynge ben they for housbandes and ware housholders. **1756** PITT in Walpole *George II* (1822) II. 34 From such an unaccording assemblage of separate..powers with no system, a nullity results.

Hence **† Unacco·rdingly** *adv. Obs.*

*c* **1449** PECOCK *Repr.* 207 Ellis it wolde folewe that ther yn thei diden vnaccordingli and vnsemeli. **1519** HORMAN *Vulg.* 77 Many be occupyed vncomly, and vnaccordynglye about childrens matters. **1533** tr. *Erasmus' Com. Crede* 63 Yf ony man dyd tourne a temple made of stone..into a showemakers shope wolde not all men crye out that it were shamefully and vnaccordyngly don?

**Unaccountabi·lity.** (UN-[1] 12. See next.)

**1704** SWIFT *Let. to Tisdall* 20 Apr., There is more unaccountability in your letter's little finger than in mine's whole body. **1794** ANNA SEWARD *Lett.* (1811) IV. 31 With all his good taste in literature and ladies, he has some unaccountabilities—I was going to have said eccentricities. **1851** SIR F. PALGRAVE *Norm. & Eng.* I. 68 Moreover, many anomalies and unaccountabilities accompanied the growth. **1871** TYLOR *Prim. Cult.* I. 17 The notions of arbitrary impulses, causeless freaks, chance and nonsense and indefinite unaccountability.

**Unaccou·ntable,** *a.* and *sb.* [UN-[1] 7 b, 5 b.]

**A.** *adj.* **1.** That cannot be accounted for or explained; inexplicable. Also *absol.*

**1643** MILTON *Divorce* II. xxi. Wks. 1851 IV. 120 The unaccountable and secret reasons of disaffection between man and wife. **1689** [see UNACCOUNTED 2]. **1709** ADDISON *Tatler* No. 123 ⁋ 7 Those unaccountable Antipathies which some Persons are born with. **1776** DALRYMPLE *Ann. Scot.* I. 9 To this hardy atchievement, an unaccountable inactivity succeeded. **1834** LYTTON *Pompeii* I. v. 25 A sudden and unaccountable gloom came over each as they thus gazed. **1871** TYLOR *Prim. Cult.* I. 4 Where events look unaccountable,..to wait and watch in hope that the key to the problem may some day be found. **1895** MRS. WILSON *5 Years India* 281 The Hindu accounts for the unaccountable by calling it divine.

**b.** Of persons: Difficult to account for or make out; of a strange or puzzling disposition.

**1711** ADDISON *Spect.* No. 1 ⁋ 4, I..left the University, with the Character of an odd unaccountable Fellow, that had a great deal of Learning, if I would but show it. **1748** RICHARDSON *Clarissa* (1811) III. 329 Indeed, Mr. Lovelace, you are a very unaccountable man. **1774** FOOTE *Cozeners* II. Wks. 1799 II. 161 The family above..are a strange unaccountable tribe: Pray, who the deuce are they? **1801** Mar. Edgeworth *Moral T., Angelina* i, A self-willed, unaccountable romantic girl. **1873** 'Ouida' *Pascarel* II. 240 We Italians are an unaccountable people.

**2.** Not liable to be called to account; irresponsible: **a.** Of power, etc.

**1649** Milton *Eikon.* xi. Wks. 1851 III. 420 Hee met at first with Doctrines of unaccountable Prerogative; in them hee rested, because they pleas'd him. **1695** J. Sage *Cyprianic Age* 67 The Acknowledgment of his Supream and Unaccountable Power within his own District. **1724** R. Fiddes *Morality* Pref. p. lxxxiii, If man had an unaccountable power..a single tyrant..might lawfully destroy all the rest. **1736** *Gentl. Mag.* VI. 303/2 They have never since made any Demand for the Deficiencies; not that We are to suppose that it is supply'd by the Revenue's being unaccountable. **1861** Ld. Brougham *Brit. Const.* viii. 105 Each estate should have powers independent of all the others, and in the exercise of which it is unaccountable and supreme.

**b.** Of persons, etc.

**1677** *Spottiswood's Hist. Ch. Scot.* App. 31 The King is an absolute and unaccountable Monarch. **1683** *Brit. Spec.* 173 Governed by one Supreme, Absolute, Independent, Undeposable, and Unaccountable Head. **1713** Berkeley *Guard.* No. 3 ¶ 1 The Pleasures for which their Doctrines leave them [*sc.* abandoned young men] unaccountable. **1827** Pollok *Course T.* II. 38 All else was..unaccountable, by instinct led. But man He made of angel-form erect.

†**3.** Incalculable; uncountable. *Obs.*

**169.** Temple *Pop. Discontents* ii. ¶ 6 It is unaccountable what Treasures it would save this Nation, by preventing so many Wars..abroad. **1722** Wollaston *Relig. Nat.* v. § 14 To shew him..still more and more of these fixt lights, and to beget in him an apprehension of their unaccountable numbers.

**B.** *sb.* **1.** An unaccountable person.

**1748** Richardson *Clarissa* (1811) V. 314, I never heard of or saw such a dear unaccountable. **1825** Brockett *N. C. Gloss.* s.v. **1854** Miss Baker *Northampt. Gloss.* s.v., He's quite an unaccountable.

**2.** An unaccountable thing or event. *rare.*

**1789** M. Cutler in *Life*, etc. (1888) I. 448 It was an event, however, I could not fail of recording in my book of unaccountables. **1799** Mrs. J. West *Tale of Times* II. 250 It ..must be set down in the catalogue of my unaccountables.

**Unaccou·ntableness.** (Un-[1] 12.)

**1676** W. Allen *Address Nonconf.* 156 The unsafeness or unaccountableness of the way in which you conduct the people. **1696** C. Leslie *Snake in Grass* (1697) 254 What is an Universal Liberty, but Independancy and Unaccountableness in Practice and Conversation? **1713** Berkeley *Guard.* No. 70 The Unaccountableness of some Step of Providence or Point of Doctrine to his narrow Faculties. **1748** Richardson *Clarissa* (1811) V. 106 Jealousy of itself, to female minds, accounts for a thousand unaccountablenesses. **1814** Jane Austen *Mansf. Park* xxxii, As her unaccountableness was confirmed, his displeasure increased. **1874** Pusey *Lent. Serm.* 6 God has placed no limit to the wonderfulness, the unaccountableness of His mercies.

**Unaccou·ntably,** *adv.* [Un-[1] 11.]

†**1.** Without being liable to be called to account; irresponsibly. *Obs.*

**1679** Oates *Narr. Popish Plot* Ded. a 2 b, More to trust and rely upon Your Two Houses of Parliament..than to any..Ministers whatsoever, unaccountably, who may pretend to more Loyalty.

**2.** Inexplicably.

**1694** F. Bragge *Disc. Parables* xiii. 427 So unaccountably stupid and thoughtless are men for the generality. **1733** Cheyne *Eng. Malady* II. ix. § 7 (1734) 214 Which Symptoms, as they will come on unaccountably,..will go off as unaccountably. **1794** Mrs. Radcliffe *Myst. Udolpho* lv, He had felt suddenly and unaccountably reassured of her innocence. **1847** Meeson & Welsby *Rep.* XVI. 645 *note*, The season had proved unaccountably injurious to meat. **1885** *Manch. Exam.* 13 Jan. 5/4 The indifference of the clergy themselves to a defect which their flocks have so unaccountably condoned.

**Unaccou·nted,** *ppl. a.* [Un-[1] 8, 8 c.]

**1. a.** Not taken account *of. rare*—[1].

**1587** Golding *De Mornay* xxi. 328 A people being conquered, caried away,..vnaccounted of,..as the Iewes were.

**b.** Not accounted *for.*

**1799** J. Robertson *Agric. Perth* 392 Allowing the average of this increase to the fourteen unaccounted for. **1834** *Tait's Mag.* I. 697/1 Sir Robert Walpole..had left a million and a half of the public money unaccounted for. **1884** *Manch. Exam.* 22 Nov. 4/7 The voting papers were scrutinised with the exception of 547 remaining unaccounted for.

**2.** Of which no account is given.

**1689** *Apol. Fail. Walker's Acc.* 19 Those unaccounted (but not unaccountable) baffles giv'n to the reliefs sent to Derry. **1812** *Examiner* 5 Oct. 633/1 Which suffers an Irish Defaulter of unaccounted millions, to remain unaudited. **1827** Hallam *Const. Hist.* II. 56 *note*, They reported unaccounted balances of 1,509,161*l.*, besides much that was questionable in the payments.

**Unaccou·tred,** *ppl. a.* (Un-[1] 8.) **1749** Mrs. R. Goadby *Carew* ii. (1750) 24 He exchanged his Habit..for only an old Blanket... Being thus accoutred, or rather unaccoutred, he was now no other than poor Mad Tom. **Unaccre·ditated,** *ppl. a.* (Un-[1] 8.) **1806** R. Cumberland *Mem.* (1807) II. 53 He was driven to allude to these unaccreditated propositions.

**Unaccre·dited,** *ppl. a.* (Un-[1] 8.)

**1828–32** Webster s. v., The consul remained unaccredited. **1850** Kingsley *A. Locke* x, They're the unknown great—the unaccredited heroes, as Master Thomas Carlyle would say. **1882** Farrar *Early Chr.* I. 83 It is singular how very little is narrated of the rest [of the apostles], and how entirely that little depends upon loose and unaccredited tradition.

†**Una·ccuracy.** *Obs.*—[1] [Un-[1] 12 and 5 b.] = Inaccuracy.

**1702** S. Parker tr. *Cicero's De Finibus* II. 73 We'll not fall out with him for the Confusedness of his Method, because he professes and vindicates Unaccuracy and Negligence.

†**Una·ccurate,** *a. Obs.* [Un-[1] 7 and 5 b. Cf. G. *unaccurat.*] = Inaccurate *a.*

**1660** Boyle *New Exp. Phys. Mech.* xxxvi. 288 Some learned men have attempted it by wayes so unaccurate that they seeme to have much mistaken it. *a* **1680** Glanvill *Sadducismus* I. (1682) 1 The unaccurate product of a little leisure. **1723** Waterland *2nd Vind. Christ's Div.* 188 The latter has indeed, in an unaccurate Work, or perhaps corrupted, mentioned the Distinction.

†**Una·ccurately,** *adv. Obs.* [Un-[1] 11 and 5 b.] = Inaccurately *adv.*

**1674** Boyle *Excell. Theol.* 159 A Mathematician, when he probably conjectures at the compass of the Terrestrial Globe,..divides,..unaccurately, its Surface, first, into proportions of Sea and Land. **1710** *Managers' Pro & Con* M j b, The Parliament expressed themselves unaccurately. **1719** Waterland *Vind. Christ's Div.* 186 If ποιητὴς signified more than δημιουργὸς, Origen spoke very unaccurately.

†**Una·ccurateness.** *Obs.* [Un-[1] 12 and 5 b.] Inaccuracy.

?**1648** Boyle *Seraphic Love* To Rdr. (1660) A 3 b, They will passe by such unaccuratenesses as are wont to be incident to Composures of this Later Nature. **1665** Hooke *Microgr.* 247 The great unaccurateness of artificial works. **1705** Hearne *Collect.* 29 Aug. (O.H.S.) I. 38 The unaccurateness of divers particulars.

**Unaccu·rsed, unaccu·rst,** *ppl. a.* (Un-[1] 8.)

*a* **1674** T. Traherne *Poems Felicity* (1910) 16 All that in Visibles is Good, Or Pure, or Fair, or Unaccurst. **1727** Thomson *Britannia* 113 Pure is thy reign; when, unaccurs'd by blood, Nought, save the sweetness of indulgent showers, Trickling distils into the vernant glebe. **1828** Campbell *Emigrants for N. S. Wales* 70 With laws from Gothic bondage burst, And creeds by chartered priesthoods unaccurst.

**Unaccu·sable,** *a.* (Un-[1] 7 b. Cf. late L. *inaccūsābilis*, F. *inaccusable.*)

**1582** *Reg. Privy Council Scot.* III. 538 The saidis nobill men ..salbe untroublid and unaccusabill for that caus in tyme cuming. **1589** *Ibid.* IV. 406 To be free and unaccusable for thair ressett and furnissing grantit to the saidis Erllis. **1651** Stanley *Poems*, etc. 256 Persons exact and unaccusable in every part. **1853** Ruskin *Stones Ven.* II. vi. 160 They thus receive the results of the labour of inferior minds; and out of fragments full of imperfection,..indulgently raise up a stately and unaccusable whole. **1886** — *Præterita* (1899) I. iv. 117 As much trigonometry as made my mountain work..unaccusable.

Hence **Unaccu·sably** *adv.*

**1859** Ruskin *Arrows of Chace* (1880) I. 199 Every man.. unaccusably accomplished..for his place and function. **1870** — *Lect. Art* vi. 161 The slightest attempts to copy them will show you that the terminal lines are..unaccusably true.

**Unaccu·sed,** *ppl. a.* (Un-[1] 8.)

**1508** *Reg. Privy Seal Scotl.* I. 250/1 We..respittis thame to be..unaccusit, unpersewit, unfolowit in the law or by the law. **1520** *Caxton's Chron. Eng.* IV. 36 b/2 Also that no man vnaccused in a cryme shold be put frome his dygnyte or degree tyll he were conuycted. **1580** Lupton *Sivquila* 93 Many should be unaccused, that now are falsely accused. **1624** Heywood *Gunaik.* IV. 178 This was three times prooved, and he still came off unaccused. **1784** Cowper *Task* v. 398 There dwell the most forlorn of human kind; Immur'd though unaccus'd, condemn'd untried. **1796** Mme. D'Arblay *Camilla* III. 31 He felt..some consolation to find that Edgar..was untainted by deceit, unaccused of any evil. **1897** *Daily News* 15 Mar. 5/4 Ismail Pacha has also amused himself during the past week in making many arrests in the town of unaccused persons.

**Unaccu·sing,** *ppl. a.* (Un-[1] 10.) **1827** Pollok *Course T.* VII. 569 To censure, unaccusing minds.. Opposing. **Unaccu·stom,** *v.* (Un-[2] 3). **1580** Hollyband *Treas. Fr. Tong, Desaccoustumer*, to vnaccustome, to disuse. **1591** Percivall *Sp. Dict., Desabituar*, to vnaccustome. *Ibid., Desabituacion*, vnaccustoming.

†**Unaccu·stomable,** *adv. Obs.* [Un-[1] 7 b.] Unusual. Hence †**Unaccu·stomably** *adv. Obs.*

**1584** Lodge *Hist. Forbonius & Prisc.* (Shaks. Soc.) 94 Let it not seeme straunge unto thee, to beholde thine aged father's unaccustomable accesse, since he is now perplexed with unacquainted feares. **1651** Biggs *New Disp.* ¶ 230 The veins being now unnaturally and unaccustomably emptied.

†**Unaccu·stomarily,** *adv. Obs.* [Un-[1] 11.] Unusually, abnormally.

**1634** T. Johnson *Parey's Chirurg.* XVIII. vii. Wks. (1678) 417 These..are now suddenly and unaccustomarily supprest. **1655** Culpepper, etc. *Riverius* XIII. iii. 364 If the Belly be unaccustomarily bound, or loose.

**Unaccu·stomed,** *ppl. a.* [Un-[1] 8.]

**1.** Not customary; unfamiliar, unusual, strange.

**1526** *Pilgr. Perf.* (Pynson) 92 By the reason of their glorious presence and excellent lyght, unaccustomed to the sayd persons. **1560** Daus tr. *Sleidane's Comm.* 452 Such unaccustomed vices, and not everywhere used. **1621** in Foster *Eng. Factories Ind.* (1906) I. 260 Such unaccustomed raynes ..hath drowned the greatest parte of new indicoe in the countryes. **1656** Earl Monm. tr. *Boccalini's Advts. fr. Parnass.* I. xii. (1674) 15 [He] was met with unaccustomed demonstrations of honour. **1742** Gray *Propertius* II. i. 27 Nor I with unaccustomed vigour trace Back to its source divine the Julian race. **1840** Dickens *Old C. Shop* xvii, At sight of the strange room and its unaccustomed objects she started up in alarm. **1871** Morley *Crit. Misc.* Ser. I. 283 Firmer souls were not only exhilarated, but intoxicated by the potent and unaccustomed air.

†**b.** Const. *to* with inf. *Obs.*—[1]

**1607** Topsell *Four-f. Beasts* 64 They were wont also to sacrifice a bul to Neptune...But vnto Iupiter it was vnaccustomed to be offered.

**2.** Not accustomed or habituated. Const. *to.*

**1611** Bible *Jer.* xxxi. 18, I was chastised, as a bullocke vnaccustomed to the yoke. *a* **1680** Glanvill *Serm.* i. (1681) 90 The first steps are roughest to those feet that have been unaccustomed to it. **1728** Eliza Heywood tr. *Mme. de Gomez's Belle A.* (1732) II. 82 Your Heart, unaccustom'd to feel any very tender Impressions, felt some Concern for those you have inspir'd me with. **1797** S. & Ht. Lee *Canterb. T.* (1799) I. 352 Lothaire was unaccustomed to fear. **1846** Mrs. A. Marsh *Father Darcy* II. ii. 67 The abhorrence of bloodshed is common to all who are unaccustomed to it. **1891** Farrar *Darkn. & Dawn* lvii, Familiar with crime, he was unaccustomed to be charged with it.

**b.** Used (attrib. or absol.) without const.

**1653** W. Ramesey *Astrol. Restored* 170 Phlebotomy is not any wise dangerous to those that are accustomed therewith, but it may prove dangerous to the unaccustomed. **1794** Mrs. Radcliffe *Myst. Udolpho* xxxv, Circumstances that united to elevate the unaccustomed mind of Blanche to enthusiasm. **1859** Mansel *Lett., Lect.*, etc. (1873) 192 Quaint as the nomenclature may sound to unaccustomed ears. **1875** Whyte Melville *Katerfelto* xix, An unaccustomed horse would have stuck fast up to its girths before it had gone fifty yards.

†**3.** = Uncustomed *ppl. a. Obs.*

**1701** *Lond. Gaz.* No. 3737/4 Liable to be..seized in like manner as Prohibited and Unaccustomed Goods. **1715** *Ibid.* No. 5298/3 Prosecutions..concerning unaccustomed and Prohibited Goods.

Hence **Unaccu·stomedness.**

Also *unaccustomedly* (Torriano, 1659).

**1611** Cotgr., *Desaccoustumance*, a disuse, vnwontednesse, vnaccustomednesse. **1659** *Gentl. Calling* 435 The main cause of that disgust men have to this spiritual entercourse, is their unaccustomedness to it. **1866** *Lond. Rev.* 8 Dec. 623 It is permissible when it leads the worshipper to God, and does not, by its unaccustomedness, splendour, or intricacy, interpose itself as a veil between God and him. **1881** Mrs. Oliphant in *Macm. Mag.* Apr. 493/1 He was seated, not in any familiar corner, but with the forlornest unaccustomedness, in the middle of it.

**Unachie·vable,** *a.* (Un-[1] 7 b.)

**1657** Farindon *Serm.* 484 If..it should be unatchievable, not to be attained to by some. **1845** Carlyle *Cromwell* (1871) IV. 238 Projects unachievable, even the preface of them. **1899** *Westm. Gaz.* 15 Feb. 2/1 A reader of less nimble wits who has not caught the trick of suppressing the verbs and leaping to a meaning unachievable by syntax.

**Unachie·ved,** *ppl. a.* (Un-[1] 8.) **1603** Holland *Plutarch's Mor.* 794 The combat remained unatchived and unperfect, neither had it a certaine and doubtlesse conclusion. **1831** Scott *Ct. Rob.* x, So it is, the spell remains unachieved.

**Una·ching,** *ppl. a.* (Un-[1] 10.)

**1607** Shaks. *Cor.* II. ii. 155 To brag vnto them, thus I did, and thus Shew them th' vnaking Skarres, which I should hide. **1721** Cibber *Love in Riddle* I. i, The winter of unaching Age. **1757** Dyer *Fleece* I. 642 Pleasing weariness Soon our unaching heads to sleep inclines. **1822–7** Good *Study Med.* (1829) I. 532 Compressible Polypus..unaching, chiefly pale-red. **1828** Landor *Imag. Conv.* III. 312 Days of happiness like this I could recall and look back upon with unaching brow.

†**Una·chteled,** *ppl. a. Obs.*—[1] [Un-[1] 8 + *achtel, aghtle* Ettle *v.*] Unestimated.

*c* **1250** *Gen. & Ex.* 796 God gaf him ðor siluer and gold,.. Vn-achteled welðe he ðor bi-gat.

**Unaci·dulated,** *ppl. a.* (Un-[1] 8.) [**1775** Ash.] **1860** Grove *Corr. Phys. Forces*, etc. (1874) 416 With distilled water unacidulated I could observe no effect of electrolysis.

**Unacknow·ledged,** *ppl. a.* (Un-[1] 8.)

**1583** Golding *Calvin on Deut.* iii. 17/1 See (I say) how God is vnacknowledged of vs in his benefites. **1647** Clarendon *Hist. Reb.* I. § 160 The fear..of what was to come..from an unknown, at least an unacknowledg'd Successor, to the Crown. **1687** Rycaut *Hist. Turks* II. 228 The Ambassadour remained aboard unsaluted and unacknowledged by the publick Ministers of the City. **1751** Earl Orrery *Remarks Swift* (1752) 76 From the same causes, Stella remained an unacknowledged wife. **1796** Mme. D'Arblay *Camilla* x. xiii, A reciprocal confidence that left..not an action unrelated, not even a thought unacknowledged. **1835** T. Mitchell *Acharn. of Aristoph.* 230 *note*, The consequent dread that prevailed lest any of those gifts should appear to pass unacknowledged. **1871** Tylor *Prim. Cult.* I. 2 Nor ..in investigating the lower functions even of man, are these leading ideas unacknowledged.

**Unacknow·ledging,** *ppl. a.* (Un-[1] 10.)

**1611** Cotgr., *Mescognoissant*, vnacknowledging, ignorant, vngratefull. **1656** Earl Monm. tr. *Boccalini's Advts. fr. Parnass.* I. xxxiii. 38 He..desired, that as an unacknowledging and ungrateful man, he might receive condign punishment. **1697** Collier *Ess. Mor. Subj.* II. (1709) 35 Who could have imagined People so strangely stupid and unacknowledging? **1752** Mrs. Lennox *Fem. Quixote* III. viii. 208 Your Condition shall be never the worse for Miss Glanville's unacknowledging Temper...You are almost as unacknowledging as your Sister.

**Unacquai·nt,** *a.* Chiefly *Sc.* [Un-[1] 7.] = Unacquainted *ppl. a.* (Usu. const. *with.*)

**1587** T. Hughes *Misfort. Arthur* Induct., Good ladies, unacquaint with cunning reach. **1587** W. Fowler *Wks.* (S.T.S.) I. 26 The habit proude, vnsene, vnvsd, all new and vnacquent, I thair beheld. **1611** Sir W. Mure *Misc. Poems* ii. 47 Scho, spying me ȝit wnacquaint in loue, Hir new got dairts throught my puir hert did roue. **1628** — *Doomesday* 643 Satietie, which vnacquent With loathing, doth arise. *a* **1699** Kirkton *Hist. Ch. Scotl.* (1817) 280 Maxwell,..because he was unacquaint in the town,..came running into Nicol Moffat, stabler, his house in Horse-Wynd. **1716** Wodrow *Corr.* (1843) II. 216 Your Reverend colleague, to whom, though unacquaint, I give my dearest respects. *a* **1758** Ramsay *Some of the Contents* v, Thair forbeirs were unacquaint with feir. **1822** Galt *Provost* xxvi, We were unacquaint with the character of the man. **1840** Lowell *Irene* 23 And, though herself not unacquaint with care, Hath in her heart wide room for all that be.

†**Unacquai·nt,** *v. Obs. rare.* [Un-[2] 6 a.] *trans.* To deprive of acquaintance.

**1557** N. T. (Genev.) Epist. *iiii, What thing can ther be then that might vnacquaynte vs and dryue vs backe from this Gospel? 1697 J. Sergeant *Solid. Philos.* 360 Nor can the contrary be sustaind any other way, but by unacquainting us with our selves and our own kind.

**Unacquai·ntance.** (Un-1 12 and 5 b.)

1598 Florio, *Inesperientia*, inexperience, vnskilfulnes, vnacquaintance. 1627 Bp. Hall *Gt. Impostor* 507 Of this vnacquaintance, secondly, arises a dangerous mesprison of a mans selfe. 1659 T. Pecke *Parnassi Puerp.* 49 Therefore how many, and how Qualifi'd; By unacquaintance, could not be descry'd. 1786 A. Gib *Sacr. Contempl.* 381 There will be no unacquaintance among the individuals of the redeemed in heaven. 1882 Ld. Acton in *Life & Lett. Bp. Creighton* (1904) I. 229, I shall be very glad if I may consider the stage of unacquaintance as gone by.

b. Freq. const. *with*.

1646 R. Baillie *Anabaptism* (1647) 49 Through unacquaintance with the minde of the most. 1676 Glanvill *Ess.* vi. 28, I scorn the ordinary Tales of Prodigies, which proceed from superstitious Fears, and unacquaintance with Nature. 1716–20 *Lett. fr. Mist's Jrnl.* (1722) I. 300 Our as yet utter Unacquaintance with the real Folly and Vanity there is in every thing. 1777 Robertson *Hist. Amer.* vii. (1778) II. 319 The Peruvians, from their unacquaintance with the use of arches,..could not construct bridges either of stone or timber. 1814 Scott *Wav.* xxxi, Your..unacquaintance with the manners of the Highlands. 1895 Hunter *Old Missionary* iv. 106 Their unacquaintance with English made it difficult for them to master the..new Penal..Codes.

**Unacquai·nted,** *ppl. a.* [Un-1 8.]

†1. Of persons: Not personally known (to one). *Obs.* (Cf. 4.)

1529 More *Suppl. Souls* Wks. 288/1 Your humble & vnacquaynted, and half forgotten supplyantes. 1586 J. Hooker *Hist. Irel.* in *Holinshed* II. 155/2 He was more like a father than a freend, and more like a freend than an vnacquainted countriman. 1607 Dekker & Webster *Northw. Hoe* i. i, Being a Londoner though altogether vnacquainted, I haue requested his company at supper.

†2. Of things: Unknown, unfamiliar, strange, unusual. *Obs.* (Common *c* 1560–1640.)

1551 T. Wilson *Logike* Ep. to King A iv, I haue..enterprised to ioyne an acquaintaunce betwiene Logique, and my countrymen, from the whiche they haue bene hetherto barred, by tongues vnacquaynted. 1565 Jewel *Reply Harding* (1611) 53 Certainly this phrase was so farre vnacquainted and vnknowen in that World, that the very Originals of these Decrees haue it not. 1577 tr. *Bullinger's Decades* (1592) 467 The name of merites is an vnacquainted terme, not vsed in the scriptures. 1632 Lithgow *Trav.* x. 458, I was confident to dye a fearefull and vnacquainted death. 1672 Marvell *Reh. Transp.* i. 126 Although the other punishments are more severe, yet this being more new and unacquainted, I cannot pass it by.

†b. Const. *to*. *Obs. rare.*

1572 Buchanan *Detection Marie Q. of Scottes* H ij b, The kinde of disease, strange, vnknawin to the pepill, vnacquainted to phisitiones. 1598 Yong *Diana* 452 Marcelius, Diana, and Ismenia, were lodged in two chambers in the Palace,..lodgings vnacquainted to simple Shepherds.

3. Of persons (rarely of things): Having no acquaintance *with* (= knowledge of) something.

(*a*) 1563 Golding *Cæsar* iii. (1565) 70 b, Conueying thyther by water wold be very combersome, bycause the Romanes were vnacquainted wyth those countryes. 1647 Clarendon *Hist. Reb.* i. § 143 Sir Dudley Carleton..was unacquainted with the Government, Laws, and Customs of his own Country. 1736 Butler *Anal.* i. ii. Wks. 1874 I. 36 There may be some impossibilities in the nature of things, which we are unacquainted with. 1771 *Junius Lett.* lviii. (1788) 312, I profess to be unacquainted with his private character. 1815 Scott *Guy M.* liv, Hazlewood, unacquainted with their plan of assault, was a moment later. 1860 Tyndall *Glac.* ii. ix. 269 To those unacquainted with the fact of their motion,..the assertion that a glacier moves must appear..startling and incredible.

(*b*) 1605 Verstegan *Dec. Intell.* i. (1628) 1 The Irish language..is..vtterly vnacquainted with the names of England and of Englishmen. 1615 Sandys *Trav.* iv. 254 A bay..vnacquainted with tempests. 1646 P. Bulkeley *Gospel Covt.* iv. 303 Faith being..yet unacquainted with the Lords dealing with his people. 1860 Adler *Prov. Poet.* 351 This poetry was unacquainted with the dramatic form.

†b. Const. *in*, *of*, or *to*. *Obs.*

*a* 1586 Sidney *Arcadia* (1622) 360 So that poor Apollo was faine to leade a very miserable life, vnacquainted to worke, and never vsed to begge. 1704 Swift *T. Tub* Ded., Being very unacquainted in the style and form of dedications. 1787 Charlotte Smith *Romance Real Life* I. 290 A species of torture, but of the nature of which we are happily unacquainted in this country. 1805 tr. *Lafontaine's Hermann & E.* IV. 181 She is unacquainted of this circumstance, and she must remain in ignorance of it.

c. Without const.: Inexperienced; ignorant. Also with *that* and clause.

In quot. 1791 = in ignorance.

1581 Allen *Apol.* 121 Death and dungeons be not so terrible things to Christes souldiars, as they seeme to the vnacquainted. 1581 Studley *Medea* A v, Not any guilt thou shalt with unacquainted hand assay. 1632 Lithgow *Trav.* x. 426, I thinke it best to show the vnacquainted Reader, a reasonable satisfaction for [etc.]. 1663 Boyle *Usef. Exp. Nat. Philos.* i. i. 3 The surprizing spectacle of so many and various Objects, as presented themselves to her unacquainted Sight. 1791 J. Learmont *Poems* 15 Tho' unacquaintit she has wooet Wi' ane that is his fae. 1796 Mme. D'Arblay *Camilla* iv. v, Is she unacquainted that a little knowledge of books and languages is what alone I have been taught?

4. Of persons: Not having acquaintance, not being on terms of personal knowledge, *with* another. Also without const.: Not mutually acquainted.

1633 Massinger *Guardian* v. iv, You know the proscribed Severino,—he not unacquainted, but familiar, with The most of you. 1657 Reeve *God's Plea* 263 The Omniscient God is not unacquainted with them that are most dear to him, his Elect. 1766 Goldsm. *Vicar* xxviii, Sir,..you are unacquainted with the man that oppresses us. 1818 Scott *Br. Lamm.* xx, Were my mother to see you..I am sure she would approve; but you are unacquainted personally. 1892 H. Lane *Differ. Rheum. Dis.* (ed. 2) Pref., The exceeding kindness..with which friends, as well as critics, with whom I was personally unacquainted, received my first literary venture.

**Unacquai·ntedness.** [Un-1 12.] The state or fact of not being acquainted: a. Const. *with*.

1617 Hieron *Wks.* (1620) II. 380 Doe not cherish thy selfe in thy vnacquaintednesse with this broken heart. 1682 Flavel *Fear* 115 We may be excused for our fears, by reason of our own unacquaintedness with sufferings. 1764 T. Hutchinson *Hist. Mass.* i. (1765) 5 From unacquaintedness with the geography of the country. 1825–9 Mrs. Sherwood *Lady of Manor* II. xiv. 257, I have no doubt that I uttered many shocking avowals of my entire unacquaintedness with these things. 1851 I. Taylor *Wesley* 250 With our .. unacquaintedness with the manners and habits of the lower classes.

b. With *in*, *of*, or without const.

1667 *Inconveniences of Toleration* 6 It is nothing but unacquaintedness which makes them lyable to be so scared with all those terrible and groundless Stories. 1669 Earl Orrery *Parthen.* iii. v. 44 By their unacquaintedness in using of an Oar [they were] unable to Row. 1729 'Philalethes' *Enq. Price Coals* 35 What proceeded from an Unacquaintedness in some Part of this Affair. 1748 Richardson *Clarissa* (1811) II. xxxvii. 272 To what might not my youth, my sex, and unacquaintedness of the ways of that great, wicked town expose me?

**Unacqui·rable,** *a.* (Un-1 7 b.) 1640 Bp. Reynolds *Passions* xiii. 121 Sinners, conceiving happinesse as unacquirable by them, do grow to the Hating of it. 1882 G. Macdonald *Weighed & Wanting* II. vi. 53 An unacquirable gift, not necessarily associated with anything noble. **Unacqui·rableness.** (Un-1 12.) 1768–74 Tucker *Lt. Nat.* (1834) I. 217 As to the unacquirableness of virtue, this somewhat resembles Whitfield's day of grace, which being not yet come or being once past, no man can attain to righteousness.

**Unacqui·red,** *ppl. a.* [Un-1 8.]

1. Not acquired; unattained.

1653 Jer. Taylor *Serm. for Year* I. xii. 154 The work of God is left imperfect, and our persons ungracious, and our ends unacquired. 1656 W. Montague *Accompl. Wom.* Ep. Ded., So that this cannot enform your understanding in any new unacquired grace or vertue.

2. Not obtained from without; innate.

1793 Holcroft tr. *Lavater's Physiog.* xxix. 136 Can we call this feeling, internal unacquired sensation? 1870 Lowell *Among my Bks.* Ser. i. 164 We recognize his truth to Nature by an innate and unacquired sympathy.

†**Unacquit,** *ppl. a.* *Obs.*—1 [Un-1 7.] Unrequited.

1390 Gower *Conf.* I. 271 For it was nevere knowe yit That charite goth unaquit.

**Unacqui·tted,** *ppl. a.* (Un-1 8.) 1770 Hailes *Anc. Sc. Poems* 327 *Unquyt*, unacquitted, unpaid.

†**Unacquitting,** *vbl. sb.* [Un-1 13.] Failure in acquitting or clearing.

1648 W. Browne *Polexander* ii. iv. ¶¶¶¶j, He..besought his pardon for the long unacquitting himselfe of what he owed him.

†**Unact,** *v.* *Obs. rare.* [Un-2 3.] *trans.* To reverse in act; to undo.

1594 W. Percy *Cœlia* (1877) 5 My doome is past, nor can be now vnactit. 1628 Feltham *Resolves* ii. lxxxix. 257 The Act remaines adultery still;..nor can a Man vnact it againe.

**Una·ctable,** *a.* [Un-1 7 b.] That cannot be acted (on the stage); unsuitable for dramatic representation. Hence (in recent use) **Unactabi·lity.**

1810 Byron *Let. to Hodgson* 3 Oct., Before the fire was out, he writes..to inquire whether this farce was not converted into fuel, with about two thousand other unactable manuscripts. 1830 Miss Mitford in L'Estrange *Life* (1870) II. xiii. 298 Goldoni is the most insipid writer I ever read; Alfieri is a very fine one but unactable. 1871 *Public Opinion* 16 Dec. 778 Mr. Browning has written brief unactable dramas.

**Una·cted,** *a.* [Un-1 8.]

1. Not acted or carried out in action; unperformed.

1593 Shaks. *Lucr.* 527 The fault vnknowne, is as a thought vnacted. 1613 Sherley *Trav. Persia* 52 To leaue no meanes vnacted which might both assure them more, and him selfe with them. *a* 1688 Jordan *Muses Melody*, *To his disdainful Mistress* 17 Must I For some offence unacted, or unknown, Be tortur'd thus? 1706 [? Prior] *Ep. after Battle of Ramillies* 290 My sons lament, in distant dungeons thrown, Unacted crimes, and follies not their own. 1789 W. Blake *Marr. Heaven & Hell, Proverbs*, Sooner murder an infant in its cradle than nurse unacted desires. 1825 Scott *Talism.* xvii, I would buy with every jewel I have, that our fatal jest had remained unacted.

b. Const. *on*, *upon*.

1794 G. Adams *Nat. & Exp. Philos.* III. xxiv. 21 A mass of [units] lying together, unacted upon by a mechanical material agency. 1825 T. Hook *Sayings* Ser. ii. *Passion & Princ.* iv, I wish you to peruse it alone, and unacted upon by any extraneous influence. 1857 Miller *Elem. Chem.*, *Org.* 67 The second portion remains unacted on in the liquid.

2. Not acted upon; unformed. *rare*—1.

1700 W. Shippen in Rowe *Amb. Step-Moth.* iii. ii, When Matter yet unacted lay.

3. Not performed on the stage. Also *absol.* as *sb.*, those whose plays are not acted. In recent use.

**Una·cting,** *ppl. a.* (Un-1 10.) 1736 Hervey *Mem.* I. 82 The state of his mind..seemed still to be an entire apathy, unacting and unmoved. 1745 *Phil. Trans.* XLIV. 156 It is the white unacting Globules that do thus.

†**Una·ction.** *Obs.*—1 [Un-1 12, 5 b.] Inaction.

1698 tr. *Fénelon's Maxims of Saints* 98 'Tis better to remain in an absolute Unaction.

†**Una·ctive,** *a.* *Obs.* [Un-1 7 and 5 b.]

1. Habitually or naturally inactive; indisposed or unable to act; hence, sluggish, slothful: a. Of persons (or animals).

1591 G. Fletcher *Russe Commw.* (Hakl. Soc.) 146 For the most part, they are unweldy and unactive withall. 1657 Austen *Fruit Trees* ii. 177 It is an intolerable shame to some professors especially, to see them so lukewarme and unactive in the waies of God. 1696 Stanhope *Chr. Pattern* (1711) 126 When advancement to Heaven..is offered, they are slothful and unactive. 1726 Gibson *Dieting Horses* 14 Flanders Horses..are thereby render'd the more heavy and unactive. 1741 *Compl. Fam.-Piece* ii. ii. 346 Chub..are a strong unactive Fish.

*absol.* 1708 *Diss. Drunkenness* 12 It charms the Unactive, the Desperate and Crafty of either Sex.

b. Of material things.

1638 Quarles *Hieroglyph.* ii. (1669) 27 Nor hath unactive matter pow'r to soil Her pure and active form, as Jars corrupt their Oyl. 1694 Salmon *Bate's Dispens.* (1713) 528/2 The Points of the Acid of the Tartar..are too unactive, gross or blunt to insinuate themselves into the Pores of this Salt. 1704 Norris *Ideal World* ii. iii. 253 What a dead unactive thing matter is. 1729 Butler *Serm. Hum. Nat.* i. Wks. 1874 II. 387 The mere material body.., without the mind being a dead unactive thing.

c. Of mind or disposition.

1647 Clarendon *Hist. Reb.* v. § 340 The drowsy and unactive Genius of the Kingdom. *Ibid.* vi. § 182 The faculties and understandings of the lay councillors [grew] more dull, lazy, and unactive. 1704 J. Trapp *Abra-Mulé* ii. i. 544 Melancholy Blood retards the Springs Of his unactive Soul. 1724 R. Fiddes *Morality* Pref. p. xxxviii, Disquisitions of this kind are an argument of an unactive wit. 1746 *Brit. Mag.* 98 The Ignorance, or unactive inexperimenting Spirit of our Manufacturers.

d. Of immaterial things.

1649 Jer. Taylor *Gt. Exemp.* Ep. Ded. 1 The calentures of men breathe out in problemes and unactive discourses. 1686 W. de Britaine *Hum. Prudence* xvi. 74 He..may escape many dangers by his wary Conduct, but will fail of as many Successes by his unactive Fearfulness. *c* 1705 Bp. Berkeley in Fraser *Life* (1871) 445 Uneasiness, &c. are ideas, therefore unactive, therefore can do nothing. 1761 Hume *Hist. Eng.* III. xlviii. 45 His unactive virtue, the more it was extolled, the greater disregard was it exposed to.

2. Not active at a particular time; remaining quiescent or idle.

1599 Daniel *Musoph.* (1602) c iij b, That these more curious times, they might diuorce From the opinion..Of our disable and vnactiue force. 1643 Wither *Campo Musæ* 2 When I shall be dead, And lie unactive in a loanly roome. 1670 Cotton *Espernon* i. iii. 107 Neither was he in his retirement..either unactive in himself, or in a Scene improper for his Majesties Service. 1715 Pope *Iliad* iv. 425 Can'st thou, remote, the mingling Hosts descry, With Hands unactive, and a careless Eye? 1756 Johnson *Misc. Lives, K. of Prussia* Wks. 1787 IV. 557 All the vegetative powers are kept unactive by a long continuance of drought. 1757 Burke *Abridgm. Eng. Hist.* Wks. 1842 II. 516 The legates in Britain..remained unactive [till it could be determined for what master they were to conquer.

3. Marked or characterized by inaction.

1621 G. Sandys *Ovid's Met.* ii. (1626) 41 To Enuie's caue her course shee bent,..Repleat with sadnesse, and vnactiue cold. 1652 Evelyn *St. France* Misc. Writ. (1805) 81 The Gentry..are universally given to solitary and unactive lives in the country. 1711 Addison *Spect.* No. 93 ¶4 For the Employment of our dead unactive Hours. 1736 Butler *Anal.* v. 89 Nothing which we at present see, would lead us to the Thought of a solitary unactive State hereafter. 1777 Johnson *Let. to Mrs. Thrale* 27 Aug., I am here in unactive obscurity.

†**Una·ctive,** *v.* *Obs.* [Un-2 6 a.] *trans.* To unfit for action.

1639 Fuller *Holy War* 52 Though bookishnesse may unactive, yet learning doth accomplish a Prince. 1655 — *Ch. Hist.* viii. ii. 19 A man so buried in the speculations of School-Divinity, that it unactiv'd him to be practical in persecution.

†**Una·ctively,** *adv.* *Obs.* [Un-1 11 and 5 b.] = Inactively *adv.*

1611 Speed *Hist. Gt. Brit.* vii. viii. 236 That his time was so peaceably and vnactiuely spent, that it ministred not matter whereof to indite. 1661 Feltham *Resolves* ii. xlix. 281 He..that is illiterate, and unactively lives hamletted in some untravail'd village. 1693 Locke *Educ.* § 125 Mark how he spends his Time, whether he unactively loiters it away.

†**Una·ctiveness.** *Obs.* [Un-1 12.] = next.

1647 Jenkyn *Serm. bef. Peeres 27 Jan.* Pref., Cast off the spirit of sleep in respect of unactivenesse. 1683 Temple *Mem.* Wks. 1720 I. 406 To make amends for the Unactiveness of this Campaign in Flanders, the Confederates by Concert on all sides fell upon an Enterprize of great *Eclat*.

†**Unacti·vity.** *Obs.* [Un-1 12 and 5 b.] = Inactivity.

1654 Fuller *Two Serm.* 5 By their easinesse and unactivitie [they] betray themselves to that condition. *a* 1676 Hale *Prim. Orig. Man.* (1677) 98 To suppose them in an eternal rest and unactivity,..were to suppose them eternally kept in a useless, needless, imperfect state. 1740 Cheyne *Regimen* iv. 174 The human Soul..now confin'd to Darkness, Silence, and Unactivity.

**Una·ctual,** *a.* (Un-1 7.) 1871 Fraser *Berkeley* x. 377 Our now unactual past or future sense experience.

**Una·ctuated,** *ppl. a.* (Un-1 8.)

1661 Glanvill *Van. Dogm.* xvi. 153 The Peripatetick matter is a pure unactuated Power: and this conceited Vacuum a meer Receptibility. 1774 *Trinket* 50 The sprightly friend, unactuated by any softer passion. 1802 tr. *Ducray-Duminil's Victor* I. 171 What reliance was to be placed upon the faith of a banditti, unactuated by any sentiment of honour or delicacy? **1827** SCOTT *Let.* in *Lockhart* (1839) IX. 148 Unactuated by any feeling excepting the wish to do justice to all parties.

**Unacu·te,** *a.* (UN-[1] 7.) **1775** J. HARRIS *Philosoph. Arrangem.* (1841) 349 Acute sentiments often escape the comprehension of unacute hearers. **Unacu·ted,** *ppl. a.* (UN-[1] 8.) **1804** MITFORD *Inquiry* 268 Though..Latin..can have a long penultimate following an acuted antepenultimate,..yet..long vowels unacuted are numerous. **Unadaptabi·lity.** (UN-[1] 12 and 5 b.) **1829** BENTHAM *Justice & Cod. Petit.* Suppl. 11 So they be—either by unadaptability, or by their narrowness—..obstructive of all..change. **Unada·ptable,** *a.* (UN-[1] 7 b and 5 b.) **1882** A. GRAY in *Eclectic Mag.* XXXV. 738 Natural Selection continually took away the unadaptable, to give room and opportunity to the better-adapted. **1886** *Athenæum* 17 Apr. 530/2 'Tom Jones' is, in fact, unadaptable [as a play]. **Unada·pted,** *ppl. a.* (UN-[1] 8.) [**1775** ASH.] **1805** J. FOSTER *Ess.* II. ii. (1806) I. 148 They may form a strong character, in spite of the counteraction of an unadapted constitution. **1879** H. SPENCER *Data of Ethics* xiii. § 84. 223 The material aids to happiness which each received would be more or less unadapted to his requirements. **Unada·ptedness.** (UN-[1] 12.) **1846** WORCESTER (citing Foster). **1871** in Napheys *Prev. & Cure Dis.* II. iv. 557 The choicest articles of food are injurious to some persons by an obscure and inexplicable unadaptedness. **Unada·ptive,** *a.* (UN-[1] 7 and 5 b.) **1841** MYERS *Cath. Th.* III. § 27. 99 The words which Jesus..spoke in answer to the instincts of the unadaptive Baptist. **Una·dded,** *pa. pple.* (UN-[1] 8.) **1610** HEALEY *St. Aug. Citie of God* IX. xi. (1620) 332 Romulus..instituted the *Lemuralia* to be kept the third day of May, at such time as February was vnadded to the yeare.

**Unaddi·cted,** *ppl. a.* (UN-[1] 8.)
**1583** GOLDING *Calvin on Deut.* xciv. 1203 It behoued them to forget both father and mother, and to be vnaddicted to their fleshly affections. *a* **1670** HACKET *Abp. Williams* I. (1692) 9 To be unaddicted to belly-pampering, sleep, and carnal wantonness. **1670** G. H. *Hist. Cardinals* II. I. 119 A Pope..unaddicted to the advancement of his private Family. **1844** KINGLAKE *Eothen* xvii, Marlen..is..unaddicted to the practice of magical arts. **1859** SALA *Tw. round Clock* (1861) 317 The serious world is not at all unaddicted to good living.

†**Unaddi·tionable,** *a.* *Obs.*—[1] [UN-[1] 7 b.] Not worth counting in or adding.
**1716** M. DAVIES *Athen. Brit.* II. To Rdr. p. xiii, Some few Despicable Unadditionable Units or Unitarians.

†**Unaddi·tioned,** *a.* *Obs.*—[1] [UN-[1] 8.] Not provided with a title.
*a* **1661** FULLER *Worthies, Hereford* II. (1662) 46 He was a Knight, howsoever it cometh to passe he is here unadditioned.

†**Una·ddle,** *a.* *Obs.*—[1] [UN-[1] 7.] Not addled.
**1611** *Panegyr. Verses* in Coryat *Crudities* d vij, In Odcombe parish yet famous with his cradle, A chicke he hatcht was of an egge vnaddle.

**Unaddre·ssed,** *ppl. a.* (UN-[1] 8. Cf G. *unaddressirt.*) [**1775** ASH.] **1885** *Athenæum* 5 Dec. 732/3 A letter from Mrs. Byron..perhaps to Mr. Becker is unaddressed, and not dated further than 'Thursday 13th'.

**Unade·pt,** *sb.* and *a.* [UN-[1] 12, 7, and 5 b.] **a.** *sb.* One who is not an adept. **b.** *adj.* Not adept or proficient. Also *absol.*
**1742** YOUNG *Nt. Th.* IX. 649 I'll point out to thee Its various lessons; some that may surprise An un-adept in mysteries of Night. **1817** KEATINGE *Trav.* I. 42 The unadept in the valuable science of botany. **1818** MRS. SHELLEY *Frankenst.* ii, Thus for a time I was occupied by exploded systems, mingling, like an unadept, a thousand contradictory theories. **1830** BENTHAM *Offic. Apt. Maximized, Public Account Keeping* 10 To an unadept mind, what other idea than this is it in the nature of this appellation to suggest?

†**Una·dequate,** *a.* *Obs.* [UN-[1] 5 b.] = INADEQUATE *a.*
**1644** MILTON *Bucer on Div.* Wks. 1851 IV. 303 Be not bound about..by the scanty and unadequat and inconsistent Principles of such as condemn others for adhering to Traditions. **1651** BIGGS *New Disp.* ⁋ 35 The preposterous ignorance of the Constitution of man in generall..hath ..been a meanes to usher in that incongruous form of unadæquat remedies. **1709** HEARNE *Collect.* (O. H. S.) II. 234 Those who are unadequate Judges.

**Unadhe·rence.** *rare*—[1]. [UN-[1] 12. Cf. next.] Non-adherence.
**1728–31** *Lett. fr. Fog's Jrnl.* (1732) I. 17 In such a Government, Unadherence to the Rights and Privileges..of the Court, manifest a glorious Fortitude of Mind.

**Unadhe·rent,** *a.* (UN-[1] 7 and 5 b.) **1836–9** *Todd's Cycl. Anat.* II. 598/1 The inner surface [of the pericardium], like that of all the other serous membranes, is unadherent, smooth, and shining. **Unadhe·sive,** *a.* (UN-[1] 7 and 5 b.) **1815** KIRBY & SP. *Entomol.* xiii. (1816) I. 419 The unadhesive radii and exterior threads remain unsoiled. **1840** MARRYAT *Olla Podr.* III. 246 Her imperishable beauty and unadhesive cleanliness of person. **Una·djectived,** *ppl. a.* (UN-[1] 9.) **1805** TOOKE *Purley* II. vii. II. 469 As the Noun Adjective always signifies all that the unadjectived Noun signifies,..so must the Verb Adjective signify all that the unadjectived Verb signifies, and no more. **1815** RICHARDSON *Eng. Philol.* 28 We have also borrowed..adjectived signs from other languages, without always borrowing the unadjectived signs of the same ideas. **Unadjou·rned,** *ppl. a.* (UN-[1] 8.) **1648** HEXHAM II, *Ongedaeght*, Vncited, or Vn-adjourned. **1865** DICKENS *Mut. Fr.* IV. xi, Mrs. Sprodgkin was left still unadjourned in the hall. **Unadju·st,** *v.* (UN-[2] 3.) **1785** *Phil. Trans.* LXXV. 475 *note*, I have myself repeatedly adjusted the wires eight or ten times running, allowing another person to read off and unadjust each time. **Unadju·sted,** *ppl. a.* (UN-[1] 8.) **1775** JOHNSON *Tax. no Tyr.* 17 In countries where life was yet unadjusted and policy unformed. **1812** *Ann. Reg., Gen. Hist.* 2 Important differences between this country and the United States of America remained unadjusted. **1899** *Allbutt's Syst. Med.* VIII. 274 That his conduct is unadjusted to his circumstances is manifest.

**Unadmi·nistered,** *ppl. a.* [UN-[1] 8.] Not administered (esp. in law).
**1590** SWINBURNE *Testaments* 171 He maie commit the administration of the goods of the deceased vnadministred by thee. **1684** *Secr. Serv. Money Chas. & Jas.* (Camden) 97 Of the goods and chattels of John Eaton unadministred. *a* **1814** *Forgery* II. v. in *New Brit. Theatre* I. 455 Inquiry would perhaps but probe the wound, Leaving the cure still unadminister'd. **1884** *Law Times Rep.* 12 Apr. 205/2 The latter died on the 12th Dec. 1879, leaving the estate of the testatrix partly unadministered.

**Una·dmirable,** *a.* (UN-[1] 7 b.) **1853** RUSKIN *Stones Ven.* III. ii. § 3. 34 That the antagonistic Renaissance is, in the main, unworthy and unadmirable,..it was my principal purpose to show. **1866** CARLYLE *Remin.* I. 218 Very sumptuous, very cockneyish, strange and unadmirable to me.

**Unadmi·red,** *ppl. a.* (UN-[1] 8.)
**1707** MRS. BEHN in *Muses Mercury* Oct. 237 Then all your Glories unadmir'd will lie. **1781** V. KNOX *Lib. Educ.* xxi. 186 The story was entertaining, but the diction and the sentiment passed unadmired. **1827** POLLOK *Course T.* IX. 480 Nor 'mong the fairest unadmired..Distinguished stood the bard. **1865** TREVELYAN *Cawnpore* 6 The furniture ..is scattered about in most unadmired disorder.

**Unadmi·ring,** *ppl. a.* (UN-[1] 10 and 5 d.)
**1858** CARLYLE *Fredk. Gt.* II. xii. (1872) I. 119 Unadmiring posterity has confirmed the nickname. **1881** *Times* 20 Aug. 9/2 Before an impatient and unadmiring audience.

**b.** Used with ppl. construction.
**1876** MISS BROUGHTON *Joan* xxi, Joan looks away again, utterly unadmiring herself.

Hence **Unadmi·ringly** *adv.*
**1862** 'SHIRLEY' *Nugæ Crit.* iii. 150 One, whose massive brow and chiselled eyelids you..have noted not unadmiringly.

**Unadmi·tted,** *ppl. a.* [UN-[1] 8.]
**1.** Not allowed to enter.
**1616** in *Harl. Misc.* (Malh.) III. 327 It was not lawful for a Christian to enter unadmitted. **1801** SOUTHEY *Thalaba* IX. xxvi, On the sympathizing wax, The unadmitted flames play powerlessly.
**2.** Unacknowledged, unconfessed.
**1895** *Thinker* VIII. 440 Science has almost out-dogmatized the dogmatists, by teaching a practical though unadmitted atheism.

**Unadmo·nished,** *ppl. a.* (UN-[1] 8.)
*a* **1591** H. SMITH *Serm. Punishm. Jonah* i. Wks. 1867 II. 224 Let us take heed that a wicked one be not found amongst us unadmonished. **1645** MILTON *Tetrach.* Introd., Wks. 1851 IV. 136 Who..hath not forborn to scandalize him, unconferr'd with, unadmonisht, undealt with by any Pastorly or brotherly convincement. **1667** — *P. L.* V. 245. **1751** WARBURTON in *Pope's Works* IV. 138 *note*, He would not bear to see a friend..live in the miserable abuse of one of Nature's best gifts unadmonished of his folly. **1781** COWPER in *Priv. Corresp.* (1824) I. 106. I am sure you would not suffer me unadmonished to add myself to the multitude of insipid rhimers. **1862** T. A. TROLLOPE *Marietta* i, The pony, unadmonished save by a word, started off at a brisk trot.

**Unado·ptable,** *a.* (UN-[1] 7 b.) **1843** CARLYLE *Past & P.* II. xvii, The good [prayers] were found adoptable by men; ..the bad, found inappropriate, unadoptable, were gradually forgotten.

**Unado·pted,** *ppl. a.* (UN-[1] 8.)
**1659** MILTON *Civ. Power* Wks. 1851 V. 328 Hence it planely appeers, that if we be not free we are not sons, but still servants unadopted. **1765** LANGHORNE *Observ. Collins' Ode to Evening*, Blank verse.., though it has been generally received in the latter [kind of poetry], it is yet unadopted in the former. **1902** *Westm. Gaz.* 27 Oct. 4/2 Put aside, too, and unadopted by the Jewish writers are the statements of the extreme critical..school.

**Unado·red,** *ppl. a.* (UN-[1] 8.)
**1621** G. SANDYS *Ovid's Met.* VIII. (1626) 157 Nor vnreueng'd, said she, Though vn-adored, shall they vant we be. **1667** MILTON *P. L.* I. 738 Nor was his name unheard or unador'd In ancient Greece. **1742** YOUNG *Nt. Th.* IV. 383 By Thee, Oh most adorable! most unador'd! **1816** WORDSW. *Ode General Thanksgiving* 32 Thou..for thy bounty wert not unadored.

**Unado·ring,** *ppl. a.* (UN-[1] 10.) **1748** RICHARDSON *Clarissa* (1811) IV. 137 The complaisant gallant is so often preferred to the cold, the unadoring husband. **1845** MOZLEY *Ess.* (1878) II. 119 In proportion to the extent to which such a view obtains, worship must become necessarily unimpassionate and unadoring.

**Unado·rned,** *ppl. a.* (UN-[1] 8.)
**1634** MILTON *Comus* 23 All the Sea-girt Iles That like to rich and various gemms inlay The unadorned bosom of the Deep. **1667** — *P. L.* IV. 305 Shee as a vail down to the slender waste Her unadorned golden tresses wore. **1730** THOMSON *Autumn* 213 For loveliness Needs not the foreign aid of ornament, But is when unadorn'd adorn'd the most. **1777** SHERIDAN *Sch. Scand.*, *Portrait* 231 She, adorning fashion, unadorned by dress. **1813** BYRON *Br. Abydos* II. ix, That dagger..No longer glitter'd at his waist, Where pistols unadorn'd were braced. **1865** W. G. PALGRAVE *Arabia* I. 80 It is a very simple and unadorned construction. **1871** DARWIN *Desc. Man* II. xiii. (1890) 391 Eight or nine specimens..retained their unadorned winter plumage ..throughout the year.

**b.** In transf. or fig. applications.
**1647** CLARENDON *Hist. Reb.* I. § 142 A man..unadorned with parts of vigour and quickness. **1692** ATTERBURY *Serm.*, *Ps. l. 14* (1726) I. 31 Majestick Plainness and Simplicity of Thought..Unadorn'd by Words, Unenliven'd by Figures. **1744** AKENSIDE *Pleas. Imag.* I. 550 Where Virtue..doth forsake The unadorned condition of her birth. **1796** MME. D'ARBLAY *Camilla* VII. viii, The artlessness of unadorned truth. **1837** HALLAM *Hist. Lit.* I. iv. § 22 The speeches in this tragedy are sometimes too long, the style unadorned.

Hence **Unado·rnedly** *adv.*, **Unado·rnedness.**
**1727** BAILEY (vol. II), *Plainness*,..Unadornedness. **1820** *Monthly Rev.* XCI. 278 The merit of having recorded faithfully, and unadornedly, the observations made by him. **1847** H. MILLER *First Impr. Eng.* vii. (1857) 105 It was placed there, in its naked unadornedness.

**Unadroi·t,** *a.* (UN-[1] 7.) **1841** S. WARREN *Ten Thousand a Year* iii. I. 101 Various faint but unadroit hints and feelers of his had been thrown away. **Unadroi·tly,** *adv.* (UN-[1] 11.) **1839** THACKERAY *Major Gahagan* iv, The ..scimitar, fiercely but unadroitly drawn.

**Unadu·lterate,** *ppl. a.* [UN-[1] 8 b and 5 b.] Not adulterated or corrupted. Also *absol.*
**1664** H. MORE *Myst. Iniq.* 206 It cannot be judged pure and unadulterate Christianity. **1697** TUTCHIN *Search Honesty* iii, The Unadulterate Priesthood never knew The Glory, Strength, nor Lewdness of the New. **1716** GAY *Journ. to Exeter* 99 On unadulterate wine we here regale. **1798** CHARLOTTE SMITH *Yng. Philos.* IV. 71 You would have ..a beautiful piece of unadulterate clay, which you might mould as you would. **1841** I. TAYLOR *Spir. Chr.* 79 This doctrine when unadulterate..animates orthodoxy. **1879** MEREDITH *Egoist* xxxvii, The unadulterate is to be had only by faith in it or by waiting for it.

So **Unadu·lterately** *adv.*
**1638** W. GILBERTE in *Ussher's Lett.* (1686) 494 By Inductions, fresh and unadulteratly drawn from those Observations [of the Heavens].

**Unadu·lterated,** *ppl. a.* (UN-[1] 8.)
*a* **1719** ADDISON *Evid. Chr. Relig.* v. (1733) 41, I have only discovered one of those channels by which the history of our Saviour might be conveyed pure and unadulterated, through those several ages. **1765** BLACKSTONE *Comm.* I. 64 That these customs..continued down..to the present time, unchanged and unadulterated. **1823** J. BADCOCK *Dom. Amusem.* 30 Flour which is pure and unadulterated. **1881** WESTCOTT & HORT *Grk. N. T.* Introd. § 38 An unadulterated transcript of the original text.

Hence **Unadu·lteratedly** *adv.*
**1891** KIPLING *City Dreadf. Nt.*, *Railway Folk* i, Jamalpur is unadulteratedly 'Railway'.

**Unadu·lterously,** *adv.* (UN-[1] 11.) **1643** MILTON *Divorce* 10 Many beasts in voluntary and chosen couples live together as unadulterously, and are as truly maried in that respect.

**Unadva·nced,** *ppl. a.* Also 4–5 -avanced, 5 -avaunced. [UN-[1] 8.] Not advanced or promoted; not pushed forward.
**1390** GOWER *Conf.* II. 205 If it is along on me Of that ye unavanced be,..The sothe schal be proved nou. **1411–2** HOCCLEVE *De Reg. Princ.* 5274 So manny a worthi clerk famouse, In Oxinford, and in Cambrigge also, Stonde vnavanced. **1491** *Act 7 Hen. VII*, c. 12 *Preamble*, His Highnes..entendith to provyde..his children unavaunced to be preferred. **1603** KNOLLES *Hist. Turks* (1621) 832 In the meane time..matters stood stil altogether vnaduanced. **1741** T. ROBINSON *Gavelkind* App. Qq iv b, The youngest Son..was the Child, if any, left unadvanced at the Death of his Father. **1856** OLMSTED *Slave States* 367 Young men..unadvanced beyond the lowest knowledge of the elements of primary school learning. **1892** *Pall Mall G.* 26 Sept. 3/3 Both advanced and unadvanced members of unincorporated societies.

**Unadva·ncing,** *ppl. a.* (UN-[1] 10.) **1819** *Metropolis* III. 209 Her habit, her unadvancing air of modest timidity, ..all conspired to render her irresistible. **1850** L. HUNT *Autobiog.* III. xxv. 267 Let the imagination of him who thinks otherwise sit for ever with his unadvancing legs in the ditches of his ancestors.

†**Unadva·ntageable,** *a.* *Obs.*—[1] [UN-[1] 7 b.] Not advantageous or profitable.
**1603** CHETTLE *Engl. Mourn.-Garm.* B 4 b, So potent, that the Deputie had many dangerous and vnadvantageable skirmishes against him.

**Unadva·ntaged,** *ppl. a.* (UN-[1] 8.)
*a* **1661** FULLER *Worthies, Stafford.* (1840) 145, I have not met with a more noble family, measuring on the level of flat and unadvantaged antiquity. **1755** AMORY *Mem.* (1769) I. 149 Divine faith shines forth in breasts unadvantaged with human requirements.

**Unadve·ntured,** *ppl. a.* (UN-[1] 8.) **1548** HALL *Chron.* 261 For whose defence,..if necessitie require, my persone shall not be vnadventured. **Unadve·nturing,** *ppl. a.* (UN-[1] 10.) **1824** GODWIN *Hist. Commw.* I. 4 Men of a more cautious and unadventuring character.

**Unadve·nturous,** *a.* [UN-[1] 7 and 5 b.]
Hence, in recent use, *unadventurously*, *-ness.*
**1671** MILTON *P. R.* III. 243 The wisest, unexperienc't, will be ever..Irresolute, unhardy, unadventrous. **1861** CRAIK *Hist. Eng. Lit.* I. 35 His attempts are of the slightest character, and unadventurous as they are, nobody can undertake to say..whether they are well or ill done. **1890** 'R. BOLDREWOOD' *Col. Reformer* (1891) 312 The shorthorns and unadventurous beeves of more..succulent pastures.

†**Unadve·rtance.** *Obs.*—[1] [ad. OF. *inadvertance.*] Inadvertence.
**1483** CAXTON *Cato* F vj, To the ende that thou be not ouertaken by unaduertaunce or unwyttyngly.

†**Unadve·rtedly,** *adv.* *Obs.*—[1] [UN-[1] 11.] Without being noticed.
**1660** tr. *Amyraldus' Treat. conc. Relig.* III. iii. 343 As Sugar blended with his poisonous doctrines to make them be swallow'd more pleasingly and unadvertedly.

†**Unadve·rtency.** *Obs.* [UN-[1] 12 and 5 b.] = INADVERTENCY.
**1653** R. BAILLIE *Dissuas. Vind.* (1655) 62 In this unadvertency M. Marshall..has the good luck to be set at my side. **1656** EARL MONM. tr. *Boccalini's Advts. fr. Parnass.* 385 It was neither unadvertency, nor bestiality which made me do that to my Master Apuleius.

**Una·dvertised,** *ppl. a.* [UN-[1] 8 and 8 c.]
†**1.** Not advertised or warned; uninformed (*of* something). *Obs.*
**1450** *Paston Lett.* I. 176 My Lord York, unadvertised of the trouth, sent a lettre to my Lord Oxford. **1535** STEWART *Cron. Scot.* (Rolls) III. 362 All this..wes done In that intent to turne agane richt sone, Quhen that his fais sould vnaduerteist be. *a* **1548** HALL *Chron.*, *Hen. VI*, 174 The kyng was not ignorant of this assemble, nor yet vnaduertised of the dukes intent. **1627** *Lisander & Cal.* VIII. 157 Thus Lisander, unadvertized, could not come to the court

within the time hee was expected. 1652 LOVEDAY tr. *Calprenede's Cassandra* III. 212 That it was impossible for Roxina to be long unadvertis'd of his love.

2. Not announced or made known.

1864 *Daily Telegraph* 6 Aug., Strange storms, unadvertised by Admiral Fitzroy,..go eddying round us. 1874 A. WHITNEY *We Girls* xi. 229 The little unadvertised resources of New York.

**Una·dvertising,** *ppl. a.* (UN-[1] 10.) 1548 *Reg. Cupar Abbey* II. 55 Give ony of thame..permittis ony vtheris to ..tak away ony of the samyn [wood] vnaduertissand or stoppand at thair powar. 1834 *Tait's Mag.* 735/2 Lazarus with the dogs (the unadvertising dogs) licking his sores!

**Unadvi·sable,** *a.* [UN-[1] 7 b and 5 b.]

1. Of persons: That cannot or will not be advised; not open to advice.

1673 O. WALKER *Educ.* 77 Of angry persons some are.. sullen, intractable, unadvisable (a disposition mixed up of pride and melancholy). 1692 WOOD *Life* (O.H.S.) IV. 27, I hope his lordship will admit me to his favour, and not think I am unadviseable. 1762 WESLEY *Jrnl.* 3 July, There were none of them headstrong or unadvisable, none that were wiser than their teachers. 1802 H. MARTIN *Helen of Glenross* III. 216 Till now I have ever considered you, though too unadvisable, to be a man possessed of a considerable share of talents and understanding. 1865 CARLYLE *Fredk. Gt.* XIX. viii. (1873) VIII. 265, I am Astolpho warning Roger..not to trust himself to the Enchantress Alcina; but Roger was unadvisable.

2. Of things: Inexpedient, imprudent.

1758 LOWTH *Life Wm. of Wykeham* v. 155 Extreme rigour would have been unadviseable in the beginning of a new reign. 1837 CARLYLE *Fr. Rev.* I. v. i, Nay were resistance unadvisable, even dangerous, yet surely pause is very natural. 1897 *Allbutt's Syst. Med.* IV. 619 Alcohol in the form of diluted brandy or whisky is unadvisable.

Hence **Unadvi·sably** *adv.*

1702 *Lond. Gaz.* No. 3822/2 A Soldier..firing unadvisably upon a Centinel. 1877 RUSKIN *Fors Clav.* lxxxi. 257 It was unadvisably allowed by me to remain in small print.

**Unadvi·sableness.** [f. prec. + -NESS.] The quality of being unadvisable: a. Of persons.

1771 WESLEY *Wks.* (1872) V. 476 As he grows in pride, so he must grow in unadvisableness and in stubbornness also.

b. Of things.

In recent use (1891–) also *unadvisability* (for earlier *inadvisability*).

1833 GEN. P. THOMPSON *Exerc.* II. 374 In proof of the unadviseableness of permitting the extension of manufacturing industry. 1841 CRAIK in *Pict. Hist. Eng.* IX. vii. IV. 853/1 The impossibility or unadvisableness of carrying it [the Licensing Act] rigorously into execution. 1877 M. ARNOLD *Last Ess. on Church* 217 The unadvisableness of using the occasion of burial for passing sentence of condemnation..against the particular person dead.

**Unadvi·sed,** *a.* and *adv.* Forms: *a.* 4 onauysed, 5 -yd, onavised; 4–5 unauysed (4, 6 -id), 5–7 unauised (5 -yd); 4–5 unavised (5 -ede, -id), 4–6 unavysed (4 -id, 5 -et). *β.* 5–6 unaduysed, 6–7 unaduised (6 *Sc.* -it), -uized, 6– unadvised. [UN-[1] 8. Cf. MDu. *ongeavijst.*]

1. Of acts, words, etc.: Done or spoken without due consideration; rash, inconsiderate.

*a.* 13.. *E. E. Allit. P.* A. 292 Þre wordez has þou spoken at ene, Vn-avysed, for soþe, wern alle þre. *c* 1380 WYCLIF *Wks.* (1880) 389 So herode schulde have broke his oþe,..and sore a-repentid hym for his vnavysid swerynge. *a* 1450 *Knt. de la Tour* (1868) 126 Ofte tymes by vnauised speche of right is made the wronge. 1537 CROMWELL in Merriman *Life & Lett.* (1902) II. 86 They haue him in the lesse estimatyon for his vayn tytle and vnauised procedinges to the same. *β.* 1526 *Pilgr. Perf.* (W. de W. 1531) 158 For..suche cogitacions vnaduysed, eyther be lytell synne or none. 1579 NORTHBROOKE *Dicing* (1843) 168 By dauncing commeth filthie talke and communications, vnaduised promises. 1612 WOODALL *Surg. Mate* Wks. (1653) 334 Fearfull dangers ensue often by unadvised bleeding..in contagious times. 1677 W. HUBBARD *Narrative* 83 Provoked by the rash, unadvised, cruel act of some of the English. 1753 RICHARDSON *Grandison* (1781) III. xxix. 338 Lady Sforza..hinted, that the last interview between the young lady and me was an unadvised permission. 1769 BLACKSTONE *Comm.* IV. 123 Contempts against the king's title..are the denial of his right to the crown in common and unadvised discourse. 1833 I. TAYLOR *Fanat.* Pref. p. iv, An unskilful or unadvised treatment. 1876 BANCROFT *Hist. U.S.* I. vi. 155 Complaining..of his unadvised and dangerous dealings with the Indians.

2. Of persons: Imprudent, indiscreet, thoughtless. Also *transf.* of things.

*a.* 1382 WYCLIF *Prov.* xiii. 3 Who forsothe is vnauysid to speken, shal felen euelis. 1390 GOWER *Conf.* II. 43 Thou miht so per cas Ben ydel, as somtime was A kinges dowhter unavised. 1412–20 LYDG. *Chron. Troy* IV. 4617 Hem list no þing to be so rekkeles, Nor vn-avysed what hem ouȝt to do. *a* 1475 G. ASHBY *Dicta Philos.* 385 Unauised men, foles bene repute. 1530 PALSGR. 328/1 Unavysed, *maladuisé.* *β.* 1535 COVERDALE *Prov.* xxi. 5 He yt is vnaduysed, commeth vnto pouerte. 1566 PAINTER *Pal. Pleas.* II. 175 Here they may see the damage and hurt that unadvised youth incurreth. 1640 BP. HALL *Episc.* III. 223 Some bold unwarranted suggestion from an unadvised adversary. 1656 EARL MONM. tr. *Boccalini's Advts. fr. Parnass.* I. i. (1674) 3 Flies..which some unadvised men endeavouring to chase away..with a Dagger, have..cut their own Noses. 1726 LEONI *Alberti's Archit.* II. 99 Faults which the negligent and unadvised easily fall into. 1819 LAMB *St. Crispin to Mr. Gifford* I All unadvised, and in an evil hour,..you daft The lowly labours of the Gentle Craft. 1831 SCOTT *Ct. Rob.* xv, The thoughtless insult which the Count had been unadvised enough to put upon the Emperor the preceding day.

*transf.* 1600 S. NICHOLSON *Acolastus* (1876) 10 O vnaduised, Treason-working eyes, You are the cause my ife in passion dyes. 1621 QUARLES *Argalus & P.* I. Wks. (Grosart) III. 250/2 Her unadvised sickle shall not thrust Into her hopefull Harvest, ere needs must.

b. Similarly of conduct, disposition, etc.

1390 GOWER *Conf.* III. 274 Ther is yit more forto sein Of love which is unavised. *c* 1412 HOCCLEVE *De Reg. Princ.* 3104 A Prince mot..his angir refreyne, & ire, Lest þat vnavisid commocioun..sette his hert on fire. 1440 J. SHIRLEY *Dethe K. James* (1818) 25 O ye..mercilesse Scottisshe folke, ..full replet of unavisid folie. 1553 *Act* 1 *Mary* Sess. II. c. 1. § 2 Taking his foundation partly vpon his owne vnaduised judgment of the Scripture. 1590 SPENSER *F. Q.* I. iv. 34 His ruffin raiment..Which he had spilt..Through vnaduized rashnesse woxen wood. 1610 HOLLAND *Camden's Brit.* (1637) 454 Preserving..the Realme from that confusion which it after fell into by King John's unadvised carriage. 1638 QUARLES *Hieroglyph.* I. iii. 6 His knowledge climbs..and sometimes slips Through unadvised hast. 1726 LEONI *Alberti's Archit.* I. 21 b, Nero's unadvised fondness for building.

† c. Quasi-*adv.* Without consideration or reflection; unwarily, heedlessly. *Obs.*

*a.* 1420–2 LYDG. *Thebes* III. 4651 Wherfor ech man be war Vnavysed a werre to bygynne. *c* 1440 *Gesta Rom.* lxv. 289 (Add. MS.), He, as he rode vnavised, fille into one, and myght not come out, for the pitte was depe. 1483 *Vulgaria abs Terentio* 6 b, It forseth nott whedyr a woman do all thynges auysed or vnauysed.

*β.* 1535 COVERDALE *Prov.* xiii. 3 Who so speaketh vnaduysed, fyndeth harme. 1606 G. WOODCOCK *Lives Emperors* in *Hist. Ivstine* K k 5 The matter being vnaduised done, hee lost many of his men. 1627 MAY *Lucan* I. 543 The madd people all With hasty steppes so vnaduised runne, As if no way at all were left to shunne Their imminent, and feard distruction.

d. Not having consulted *with* another; not having been consulted *with.*

1579 FENTON *Guicciard.* (1618) 4 So Ludouyke Sforce,.. unadvised with others, had given counsell that the Embassadors..should all enter Rome in one day. 1649 MILTON *Eikon.* xii. Wks. 1851 III. 431 What should move the King ..to hold such frequent and close meetings with a Committy of Irish Papists..while the Parlament of England sate unadvis'd with. 1836 BROWNING & FOSTER *Life Strafford* (1892) 160 The Catholics..unadvised with each other, and utterly unprepared.

3. Not advised or warned. *rare*[−1].

*c* 1374 CHAUCER *Troylus* I. 378 Thus argumented he yn his gynnynge, Ful vnauysed of his wo comynge.

† 4. Not announced or foreshadowed. *Obs.*

*c* 1386 CHAUCER *Pars. T.* ¶ 449 Whan they sourden by freletee vnauysed and sodeynly withdrawen ayeyn. *a* 1395 HYLTON *Scala Perf.* II. xliii. (1507) Z viij b, The ghostly presence of Ihesu..bryngeth to his mynde..the wordes..of holy wrytte vnsoughte and vnauysed one after a nother.

† b. As *adv.* Without warning; unexpectedly.

1390 GOWER *Conf.* I. 133 The Camelion, Which..moste newe His colour, and thus unavised Fulofte time he stant desguised. *c* 1450 tr. *De Imitatione* I. xxiii. 31 Many men dien sodenly & unavised. 1483 CAXTON *Gold. Leg.* 377/2 To thende that sodaynly he shold falle up on this kyng unaduysed.

5. Not supplied with advice.

1851 TENNYSON *Q. Mary* II. ii, We..set no foot theretoward unadvised Of all our Privy Council. 1864 in Ld. Fitzmaurice *Life Granville* (1905) I. 469 How fearful it is to be suspected—uncheered—unguided and unadvised! 1876 J. C. BROWN *Reboisement in France* IV. v. § 10. 294 From the forbidding nature of the precipice, few would be bold enough to make the essay unadvised.

**Unadvi·sedly,** *adv.* Forms: as prec. + -lie, -ly(e (also 4 unauyssedly, 6 *Sc.* onavisitly). [f. prec. + -LY [2].]

1. Without consideration or reflection; imprudently, injudiciously; thoughtlessly, rashly, inadvisedly.

*a.* *c* 1340 HAMPOLE *Prose Tr.* 11 Þat þay say to þam na wordes of myssawe..ne of displesance vnauyssedly. *a* 1513 FABYAN *Chron.* VII. (1811) 666 Robert Byfelde, one of the shyreffs, vnauysidly knelyd downe nygh vnto the sayd mayer, wherof the mayer after reasonyd hym and layd it to his charge. 1513 DOUGLAS *Æneid* x. vii. 151 Quhill Alesus onavisitly Cled with hys scheyld Imaonus, hym by,..Hys breist stud nakyt.

*β.* 1474 CAXTON *Chesse* III. iv. G 4 b, It cometh of nature often tymes to women to geue counceyl shortly and unaduysedly to thynges that ben in doubte or perilous. 1581 MULCASTER *Positions* xxxvi. (1887) 138 By appointment, either vnaduisedly made, or aduisedly marred. 1620 VENNER *Via Recta* viii. 189 If it be immoderately, vntimely, and vnaduisedly vsed, it is no lesse hurtfull then Intemperance. 1657 TRAPP *Comm. Job* xlii. 4 He would speak no more so rashly, and unadvisedly as he had done, to God's dishonour. 1709 *Tatler* No. 147 ¶ 8, I shall decide nothing unadvisedly in Matters of this Nature. 1765 BLACKSTONE *Comm.* I. 187 Charles the first..having unadvisedly passed an act to continue the parliament then in being. 1808 SCOTT *Let. to Gifford* Oct. in *Lockhart,* If a weak brother will unadvisedly put forth his hand to support even the ark of the constitution, I would expose his arguments. 1866 GEO. ELIOT *F. Holt* v, There are ranks and degrees—and those who can serve in the higher must not unadvisedly change what seems to be a providential appointment.

† 2. Without warning; unexpectedly. *Obs.*

*c* 1535 in Strype *Eccl. Mem.* (1721) I. App. xlv. 125 Antichrist shal sodenly and unadvisedly come, and..destroy al mankind through his error. 1577 HANMER *Anc. Eccl. Hist.* (1663) 175 Petrus, who..suddenly and unadvisedly by the commandment of Maximinus was beheaded. 1699 N. MARSH in *Lett. Lit. Men* (Camden) 296 The pretended Mathematician has quite mistaken his measures, and, soaring too high, hath unadvisedly dropt into the pit.

**Unadvi·sedness.** [f. as prec. + -NESS.] The quality of being unadvised; want of consideration or reflection; imprudence, rashness; an instance of this.

*c* 1449 PECOCK *Repr.* 357 It is to be bileeued that Girald was bigilid (as manie othere writers bi liȝtnes and unavisidnes han be). 1542 UDALL *Erasm. Apoph.* 256 b, There was nothyng more unconvenable for a perfecte good Capitaine, then over muche hastyng & unavisednesse. 1583 GOLDING *Calvin on Deut.* cxlii. 875 How many faults do we commit through vnaduisednesse, when we thinke not on them? 1611 SPEED *Hist. Gt. Brit.* IX. xxiv. (1632) 1229 By his owne vnaduisednesse..hee clouded his honour. 1681 KETTLEWELL *Chr. Obedience* (1715) 564 All his unwill'd ignorances, and innocent unadvisednesses, upon his prayers for pardon shall be abated. 1780 BENTHAM *Princ. Legisl.* IX. § 16 In the case of *un*-advisedness with respect to any of the circumstances. *Ibid.* § 17 Un-advisedness coupled with heedlessness, and mis-advisedness coupled with rashness. 1853 JAS. HAMILTON *Life Bp. J. Hall* 167 The circumstance which implicated him was, at the worst, an act of unadvisedness.

† **Unadvi·sely,** *adv. Obs.* Also 4 vnauisely, 4–5 -auysely, 5 -awyssely. [f. UN-[1] 11 + *avisé* ADVISY *a.* + -LY [2]. Cf. UNAVISY *a.*] = UNADVISEDLY *adv.*

*c* 1380 WYCLIF *Wks.* (1880) 383 Þis symony & heresi so vnauysely brouȝte in-to þe chirche. 1422 tr. *Secreta Secret., Priv. Priv.* 138 If hit happe a kynge to do any thynge vnawyssely. *a* 1455 *Lett. Marg. Anjou & Bp. Beckington* (Camden) 99 Summe of your officers..unadvisely toke fro day to day the horses of our said tenants.

† **Unadvi·sement.** *Obs. rare.* In 6 vnaduyse-, *Sc.* vnadwysment. [UN-[1] 12.] Want of consideration or judgement.

1526 *Pilgr. Perf.* (W. de W. 1531) 90 b, Inconstancy or vnstablenes, heddynes or vnaduysement, inordinate loue that man or woman hath to them selfe. *a* 1600 MONTGOMERIE *Devot. Poems* v. 2 Since vnadwysment wraks or thou be war, To call for grace betyms at God begin.

† **Unadvi·sing,** *ppl. a. Obs.*[−1] [UN-[1] 10.] Imprudent.

1721 SOUTHERNE *Spartan Dame* II. i, The repented rashness of my youth, Whose unadvising folly gave me to Your sister's bed, now surfeited, and loath'd.

**Una·erated,** *ppl. a.* (UN-[1] 8.) 1796 KIRWAN *Elem. Min.* (ed. 2) I. 170 Here [it] is remarkable..that magnesia and calx should be unaerated. 1835–6 *Todd's Cycl. Anat.* I. 143/2 In this instance..the aerated and unaerated blood require to be..prevented from commingling. 1887 MOLONEY *Forestry W. Afr.* 152 The cloth is dipped into the extract unaerated, then freely exposed to the air.

**Unæsthe·tic,** *a.* (UN-[1] 7. Cf. INÆSTHETIC *a.*, and G. *unæstetisch.*)

1832 [S. AUSTIN] tr. *Tour Germ. Prince* III. xii. 332 This morning I went to church, with a full intention of being pious; but it did not succeed. Everything was too cold, dry, and unæsthetic. 1846 MILMAN *Ess., Newman* (1870) 352 Our unpoetic and unæsthetic (may we venture the word?) spirituality.

**Unafea·rd, -ed,** *a.* Now *arch* or *dial.* Also 6 vnaffear'd, *Sc.* onaffeired. [UN-[1] 8.] Unafraid.

15.. *Christ's Kirk* in *Bannatyne MS.* (Hunt. Club) 287 Than followit feymen rycht on-affeird. 1595 DANIEL *Civ. Wars* III. lxxviii, The king..plies his hands vndaunted, vnaffear'd, And with good hart, and life for life he stird. 1812 TENNANT *Anster F.* VI. xli, I was not unafeared. 1868 MORRIS *Earthly Par.* (1870) I. I. 400 The weasel peered From out the wheat stalks on her unafear'd. 1898 N. MUNRO *J. Splendid* viii, Down at the shore, unafeared of man, would be solitary hinds.

**Una·ffable,** *a.* (UN-[1] 7.)

1603 DANIEL *To Sir T. Egerton* xvii, When surly Law, sterne and vnaffable, Cares onely but itselfe to satisfie. 1633 T. ADAMS *Exp. 2 Peter* ii. 19 Nabal's servant was wearie of so unaffable, uncharitable, unreasonable a Master. 1736 NEAL *Hist. Purit.* III. 542 He [Charles I] was unaffable and difficult of address. 1770 ARMSTRONG *Imitations of Shaks.* 119 Of walking statues, ghosts unaffable. 1834 DE QUINCEY *Autobiog. Sk.* Wks. 1854 II. 189 Southey disliked in Wordsworth the air of dogmatism, and the unaffable haughtiness of his manner.

**Unaffe·cted,** *ppl. a.* [UN-[1] 8. Cf. G. *unaffectirt.*]

I. 1. Not adopted or assumed: a. Of qualities, feelings, etc.: Not simulated or pretended; real, genuine, sincere.

1592 DANIEL *Compl. Rosamund* lxxviii. A happy Country mayde, Whose vnaffected innocencie thinks No guilefull fraude. 1622 PEACHAM *Compl. Gent.* x. (1634) 90 Hee.. cannot with Virgill containe himselfe within that sweet, humble, and unaffected moderation. *a* 1656 BP. HALL *Serm. on Eccl. iii. 4* Wks. 1808 V. 571 Not in a hypocritical way of ostentation,..but in a wise, sober, seemly, unaffected deportment. 1710 STEELE *Tatler* No. 198 ¶ 2 There appeared in the Face of Cælia a Chearfulness, the constant Companion of unaffected Virtue. 1796 MME. D'ARBLAY *Camilla* III. 184 Sir Sedley received them with the most unaffected pleasure. 1825 SCOTT *Talism.* xvii, A hurried glance of undisguised and unaffected terror. 1884 *Manch. Exam.* 22 May 5/2 A war which the great majority of the nation regard with unaffected dislike.

b. Of style or discourse: Free from affected words or phrases; simple, natural.

1598 HAKLUYT *Voy.* Pref. ¶ 8 The harsh and vnaffected stile of his substantiall verses and the olde dialect of his wordes. 1619 T. MORE in A. Newman *Pleas. Vis.* A iij b, Like to thy modest selfe, thy happy veine Is vnaffected. 1659 RUSHW. *Hist. Coll.* I. Pref., I have esteemed the most unaffected and familiar Stile the best. 1711 STEELE *Spect.* No. 2 ¶ 3 Sir Andrew having a natural unaffected Eloquence. *a* 1721 SHEFFIELD (Dk. Buckhm.) *Wks.* (1723) I. 180 Here sweet Eloquence does always smile, In such a choice, yet unaffected Style, As must both Knowledge and Delight impart. 1818 SCOTT *Let.* in *Lockhart* (1837) IV. iv. 137 The letters you have published are, I think, his very best—lively, entertaining, and unaffected.

**c.** Of conduct, bearing, etc.: Free from affectation or artificiality.

1712 STEELE *Spect.* No. 284 ⁋ 1 An unaffected Behaviour is without question a very great Charm. 1791 MRS. RADCLIFFE *Rom. Forest* v, His Manners were unaffected and graceful rather than dignified. 1848 THACKERAY *Van. Fair* li, She said the wickedest things with the most simple unaffected air. 1876 MISS BRADDON *J. Haggard's Dau.* I. 67 Oswald was impressed by the simple pathos, the unaffected power, of the speaker.

†**2.** Not desired or aimed at. *Obs. rare.*

1611 SPEED *Hist. Gt. Brit.* VII. xliv. § 3. 358 A cloud appearing of bloud and fire, immediately after his vnaffected Coronation.

**3.** Of persons: Not affected, unartificial or unpretentious, in manners.

1677 MIEGE *Fr. Dict.* II, Unaffected, *qui n'est pas affecté.* a 1721 SHEFFIELD (Dk. Buckhm.) *Wks.* (1723) II. 266 Montagu, methinks, represents Adam in his innocence..; naked, but not ashamed, because unblemished and unaffected. 1729 T. COOKE *Tales*, etc. 88 Hence, says the Bird of Venus, Boaster fly;..Me Men, and Gods, with Admiration view, Plain, unaffected, with my glossy Hue. 1818 LADY MORGAN *Autobiog.* (1859) 21 He seems eminently intellectual, unaffected, and kind. 1889 LANG *Prince Prigio* ii. 13 What nice, unaffected princes they are!

**b.** Sincere, honest (in some respect).

1796 MME. D'ARBLAY *Camilla* V. 221 An unaffected admirer of all she had heard of [her] good qualities.

**II. 4.** Not affected or influenced in mind or feeling; untouched, unmoved. Also const. *by*, † *to*, † *with*.

c 1586 C'TESS PEMBROKE *Ps.* LVIII. ii, The aspick..On whom the charmer all in vaine applies His skillful'st spells.., self-deaf, and unaffected lies. c 1616 FLETCHER *Thierry & Theod.* II. i, A poor, cold, unspirited, unmanner'd, Unhonest, unaffected, undone, fool. 1729 LAW *Serious C.* iv. 67 The mock ceremony, instead of blessing our victuals, does but accustom us to trifle with devotion, and give us a habit of being unaffected with our prayers. 1741 RICHARDSON *Pamela* I. 177 How unaffected People were to the Distresses of others. 1803 *Censor* 1 Sept. 100 There is something..so moving in the narrative, that I think it is impossible any reader, however stoical, can remain unaffected. c 1820 MRS. SHERWOOD *Orange Grove* 17 The old man was quite unaffected, and looked quite stupid.

†**b.** Not inclined to a side or party. *Obs.*⁻¹

1619 SIR E. HERBERT in *Eng. & Germ.* (Camden Soc.) 85, I hope his Majestie will find this state so unaffected and neutrall, that..their irresolution will keep them indifferent.

**5.** Not attacked by disease or illness.

1797 M. BAILLIE *Morb. Anat.* (1807) 408 Scirrhous tumours occasionally arise in the vagina itself..when the uterus is unaffected. 1873 T. H. GREEN *Introd. Pathol.* (ed. 2) 281 In this stage [of nephritis] the tubes and their epithelium are unaffected.

**6.** Not acted upon or altered *by* some agent or influence.

1830 MACKINTOSH *Eth. Philos.* Wks. 1846 I. 24 That happiness consisted in virtuous pleasure, chiefly dependent on the state of mind, but not unaffected by outward agents, was the doctrine of both. 1875 JOWETT *Plato* (ed. 2) III. 615 Free from old age and unaffected by disease.

**b.** Similarly without const.

1833–4 J. PHILLIPS *Geol.* in *Encycl. Metrop.* (1845) VI. 656 A tremour which might shiver elastic flint,..but leave the chalk unaffected. 1890 *Retrospect Med.* CII. 182 Out of six cases treated..two were cured (?), three slightly relieved, and one unaffected.

**Unaffe·ctedly,** *adv.* [f. prec.] In an unaffected manner; without affectation.

1677 MIEGE *Fr. Dict.* II, Unaffectedly, *sans affectation.* 1693 CONGREVE *Old Batchelor* v. i, Yet, she was unaffectedly concern'd, he says; and often blush'd with Anger and Surprize. 1782 V. KNOX *Ess.* xxiii. (1819) I. 131 The purpose of history is truth, and truth requires no more than to be fairly, openly, and unaffectedly exhibited. 1794 R. J. SULIVAN *View Nat.* I. Pref. 7 He has unaffectedly to solicit the indulgence of the reader. 1808 L. MURRAY *Eng. Gram.* I. 232 A girl unaffectedly modest. *Ibid.* 270 He spoke unaffectedly and forcibly. 1896 T. F. TOUT *Edw. I*, iv. 68 Edward was deeply and unaffectedly religious.

**Unaffe·ctedness.** [f. as prec.] The quality of being unaffected.

†**1.** Impassiveness, indifference. *Obs.*

1670 *Devout Commun.* (1688) 203 Charge not upon me..my unpreparedness, unaffectedness. 1681 KETTLEWELL *Chr. Obedience* (1715) 528 The coldness and unaffectedness, the unsettledness and distractions, which they find in themselves when they are at prayers. 1694 — *Comp. Penitent* 55, I am grieved..for all my neglects of thy service, and for my insincerity and unaffectedness in performing it.

**2.** Freedom from affectation; naturalness.

1685 H. MORE *Paralip. Prophet.* vi. 38 Which Letter, as I said, is written with..unaffectedness and punctualness withal. 1752 *Narr. Journ. through Eng.* (1869) 32 She seemed to have all that delicacy and unaffectedness requisite to persons of the first rank. 1783 BLAIR *Lect.* xix. I. 398 The simplicity or unaffectedness of his manner, is the crowning ornament. 1861 THACKERAY *Four Georges* iv. (1862) 192 Not ill liked by the nation, which pardons youthful irregularities readily enough for the sake of pluck, unaffectedness and good-humour. 1882 J. A. ALLEN *Love Story Col. & Mrs. Hutchinson* 39 What dignity of bearing! yet withal What simple, winning unaffectedness!

†**Unaffe·ctible,** *a. Obs.*⁻¹ [UN-¹ 7.] That cannot be affected.

1678 CUDWORTH *Intell. Syst.* I. iv. § 36. 561 To what purpose any Devotional Addresses should be made by us to such an Unaffectible, Inflexible,..and Adamantine Being.

**Unaffe·cting,** *ppl. a.* [UN-¹ 10.]

†**1.** Free from affectation. *Obs.*

1602 *Ld. Cromwell* III. iii. 13 A most learned, yet vnaffecting spirit. 1713 STEELE *Spect.* No. 423 ⁋ 2 He carries on an unaffecting Exactness in his Dress and Manner. 1814 WORDSW. *Excurs.* VI. 578 Though a vulgar face..And unaffecting manners might at once Be recognised by all.

**2.** Not affecting or touching; having no effect upon the feelings.

1647 N. WARD *Simple Cobler* 87 Affected termes are unaffecting things to solid hearers. 1719 WATERLAND *Vind. Christ's Div.* 277 Abstract Reasons of Esteem, Honour, and Regard are unaffecting, without a mixture of something relative to Us. 1763 J. BROWN *Poetry & Music* xiii. 233 The Ode must be written in the Style of Passion; not with the Parade of unaffecting Imagery, or tedious Allegory. 1812 CRABBE *Tales* viii. 354 In her tall mirror then she shows a face, Still coldly fair with unaffecting grace. 1823 J. WILSON *Trials Marg. Lyndsay* i. 3 The narrative of whose fortunes may perhaps not be unaffecting to those who [etc.].

**Unaffe·ctionate,** *a.* [UN-¹ 7 and 5 b.]

†**1.** Unbiassed; impartial. *Obs.*⁻¹

1588 A. KING tr. *Canisius' Catech.* G vij b, I think it sall be acceptable to the vnaffectionat redar, giff..I sall pen ye occasion [etc.].

†**2.** Not endowed with feeling. *Obs.*⁻¹

1645 MILTON *Tetrach.* Wks. 1851 IV. 236 A helplesse, unaffectionate, and sullen masse whose very company represents the visible and exactest figure of lonelines it selfe.

†**3.** Not well affected. *Obs.*⁻¹

1787 JEFFERSON *Writ.* (1859) II. 108 His devotion to the principles of pure despotism, renders him unaffectionate to our governments.

**4.** Not affectionate; devoid of affection.

1815 MRS. PILKINGTON *Celebrity* III. 13 Sir Ferdinand,..returning to her hand the unaffectionate production, said [etc.]. 1830 H. N. COLERIDGE *Grk. Poets* (1834) 304 His demeanour towards his mother..is generally unaffectionate. 1875 RUSKIN *Fors Clav.* liv. 167 Not..that I grew up selfish or unaffectionate.

Hence **Unaffe·ctionately** *adv.*

1847 H. BUSHNELL *Chr. Nurt.* II. i. (1861) 241 If the child is..simply laid aside unaffectionately, in no warmth of motherly gentleness.

**Unaffe·ctioned,** *ppl. a.* (UN-¹ 8.) 1788 D. GILSON *Serm.* xv. 434 When..the sayings of Jesus are lost upon unaffectioned spirits. †**Unaffe·ctive,** *a. Obs.*⁻¹ (UN-¹ 7.) 1689 *Myst. Iniq.* 22 A superficial and unaffective Glance.

**Unaffi·anced,** *ppl. a.* (UN-¹ 8.)

1750 CARTE *Hist. Eng.* II. 612 The duke of Bourgogne, or the count of Hainault,..had no daughters unmarried or unaffianced. 1829 B. W. PROCTER in *Gem* 284 Did they not say this girl Was unaffianced? Ay, unwoo'd, unsought. 1898 TALMAGE in *Chr. Herald* (N. Y.) 19 Jan. 44/1 That at least that number of women shall be unaffianced for life.

**Unaffie·d,** *ppl. a.* [UN-¹ 8.] = prec.

1527 in Grose *Antiq. Rep.* (1809) IV. 670 The saide Andrewe then to be vnmaryed, vnaffied and vncontracted. c 1625 in *Verney Mem.* (1904) I. 72 That the ward unmarried, unaffyed, and uncontracted should..be sent to Lady Denham. 1857 EMERSON *Poems, Woodnotes* II. 231 Not unrelated, unaffied, But to each thought and thing allied.

†**Unaffi·led,** *ppl. a. Obs.*⁻¹ [UN-¹ 8.] Unpolished, rude.

1390 GOWER *Conf.* I. 119 No strengthe of love bowe mihte His herte, which is unaffiled.

**Unaffi·liated,** *ppl. a.* (UN-¹ 8.) 1849–50 ALISON *Hist. Eur.* II. vii. § 23. 134 No precautions [were] adopted..against the admission of unaffiliated members. 1859 *Sat. Rev.* 17 Dec. 728/2 Not to trust upright and able servants unaffiliated to the Society of Loyola. **Unaffi·rmed,** *ppl. a.* (UN-¹ 8.) 1620 DONNE *26 Serm.* (1660) 48 That Council [of Trent] will not say, that..we leave any truth unaffirmed, which the Primitive Church affirm'd to be necessary to salvation. **Unaffi·xed,** *ppl. a.* (UN-¹ 8.) 1602 WILLIS *Stenographie* D ij b, Vnaffixed Particles, as: furlong, despise.

**Unaffli·cted,** *ppl. a.* (UN-¹ 8.)

1599 DANIEL *Musophilus* 13 The whiles my vnafflicted minde doth feede On no vnholy thoughts for benefit. 1647 BP. HALL *Satan's Fiery Darts* II. iv. 163 Tell mee if thou canst, which of those Saints that are now shining bright in their heaven, hath got thither un-afflicted? 1665 BP. N. FRENCH *Hist. Wks.* (1846) I. 135 If such an one may not pass his days unafflicted. 1742 YOUNG *Nt. Th.* v. 333 Truth, radiant goddess!..shews the real estimate of things; Which no man, unafflicted, ever saw. 1872 RUSKIN *Fors Clav.* xvi. 13 [Wine] mellowed by pure chalk rock and unafflicted sunshine.

**Unaffli·cting,** *a.* (UN-¹ 10.) a 1711 KEN *Hymns Evang.* Poet. Wks. 1721 I. 174 And on the Stone an angel they behold, His Face like unafflicting Lightning bright. — *Christophel* Ibid. I. 420 As Moses..once saw God's trayling Beams with unafflicting Aw. **Unaffli·ctingly,** *adv.* (UN-¹ 11.) a 1711 KEN *Hymns Evang.* Poet. Wks. 1721 I. 94 Forth from the bosom of the fontal Sire Came the Eternal Word to wear our Clay And Godhead unafflictingly display. **Unaffo·rdable,** *a.* (UN-¹ 7 b.) 1825 BENTHAM *Offic. Apt. Maximized, Indic.* (1830) 77 The space and research necessary for such distinctions [is] altogether unaffordable. **Unaffra·nchized,** *ppl. a.* (UN-¹ 8.) 1611 COTGR. s.v. *Morte-main*, Illegitimated bastards, vnnaturalized strangers, and vnaffranchized villaines.

**Unaffri·ghted,** *ppl. a.* (UN-¹ 8.)

1586 MARLOWE *1st Pt. Tamburl.* IV. i, As Crocodiles that vnaffrighted rest While thundring Cannons rattle on their Skins. c 1620 FLETCHER & MASS. *Little Fr. Lawyer* I. i, He that through all these dreadfull passages Pursued and overtook them, unaffrighted, Deserves reward. 1641 T. HAYNE *M. Luther* 21 Multitius..with sharp wordes and threates so daunted the man, till now a clamorous, unaffrighted, bold face, terrible to all. 1718 *Entertainer* No. 13. 84 Henderson.., whom they traduced as timorous.., they found..unaffrighted with Threats, Reproaches, and Dangers. 1742 RICHARDSON *Pamela* III. 211, I was not guilty of any Freedoms, that her Modesty, unaffrighted, could reproach itself with having suffered. 1852 M. ARNOLD *Self-Depend.* v, Unaffrighted by the silence round them, Undistracted by the sights they see. 1886 A. WEIR *Hist. Basis Mod. Europe* (1889) 554 A generation grew up..which was unaffrighted by visions of fanaticism.

Hence **Unaffri·ghtedly** *adv.*

1891 H. HERMAN *His Angel* 121 When they could unaffrightedly bask in the sunshine of their mutual happiness.

**Unaffro·nted,** *ppl. a.* [UN-¹ 8.]

**1.** Not affronted or insulted.

1753 RICHARDSON *Grandison* (1781) III. xxx. 355 You went away unhurt and unaffronted. 1820 KEATS *Lamia* I. 101 And by my power is her beauty veil'd To keep it unaffronted, unassail'd By the love-glances of unlovely eyes.

**2.** Not confronted or faced.

1840 BROWNING *Sordello* I. 547 Rife With grandeurs, unaffronted to the last, Equal to being all! 1856 F. E. PAGET *Owlet of Owlst.* 57 But unaffronted, (we invent a very expressive word for the occasion,) he is impregnable.

†**Unaffro·ntive,** *a. Obs.*⁻¹ [UN-¹ 7.] Unresisting.

1720 WELTON *Suffer. Son of God* II. xxxi. 801 Such an unaffrontive Patience, and Resigned Disposition, is ever acceptable to God.

**Unafrai·d,** *a.* [UN-¹ 7.] Not afraid; undaunted, undismayed. Also const. *of.*

1423 JAS. I. *Kingis Q.* xxxv, Therewith vnaffraid,..From beugh to beugh thay hippit and thai plaid. 1535 STEWART *Cron. Scot.* (Rolls) I. 247 King Caratac, with curage vnaffrayit, Upoun ane plane the battell hes arrayit. 1584 HUDSON *Du Bartas' Judith* IV. (1608) 64 This while, the worthie widdow with her maid Past towards th' enmies camp not vnafraide. 1635 QUARLES *Embl.* IV. xiv. (1818) 251 Hath thy all-glorious Deity ne'er a shade..Where I might sit refreshed and unafraid? 1672 DRYDEN *Def. Epilogue* Ess. (ed. Ker) I. 169 By *unfeared* he [B. Jonson *Catiline* IV. i. 32] means *unafraid*: words of quite a contrary signification. 1725 RAMSAY *Gentl. Sheph.* III. i, He,..unafraid of fate, Contented spends his time. 1748 THOMSON *Cast. Indol.* II. xxviii, Where free, and unafraid, Amid the flowering brakes each coyer creature stray'd. 1856 MRS. BROWNING *Aur. Leigh* III. 169 Serene and unafraid of solitude I worked the short days out. 1895 CLIVE HOLLAND *Jap. Wife* iii, I never felt so unafraid of Lou..in all my life.

†**Unagainsay·ably,** *adv. Obs. rare.* [UN-¹ 11.] Undeniably.

c 1449 PECOCK *Repr.* I. xx. 130 This firste parte of this present book and The iust apprising of Holi Scripture..schewen vndoutabli and vnaȝenseiabily, that [etc.]. *Ibid.* III. xvi. 380. c 1456 — *Bk. of Faith* (1909) 222 If this be trewe, as it is unaȝenseiabili trewe.

†**Unagainsta·ndably,** *adv. Obs.*⁻¹ [UN-¹ 11.] Irresistibly.

c 1449 PECOCK *Repr.* v. ix. 533 If a manys riȝt iȝe sclaundre him (that is to seie, violentli and ferseli and as it were vnaȝenstondeabli bringith him into synne).

†**Una·ged,** *a. Obs.*⁻¹ [UN-¹ 9.] Not of age.

1486 *Bk. St. Albans, Her.* A vi b, Whan an unaged prynce is made Knyght or be crowned King.

**Una·geing,** *ppl. a.* (UN-¹ 10.) 1860 PUSEY *Min. Proph.* 414 He who admitteth faith and love to dwell in his heart hath as a requital, un-aging life. 1887 MORRIS *Odyss.* VII. 257 She..meant to make me be A deathless man for ever, and unageing all my days. **Una·ggravated,** *ppl. a.* (UN-¹ 8.) 1746 WESLEY *Princ. Methodist* 12 This is the real unaggravated charge. 1777 POTTER *Æschylus, Agamemnon* 284, I tremble now Hearing th' unaggravated truth. 1816 J. SCOTT *Vis. Paris* (ed. 5) 130 It is a sign that the virtue of a nation is spurious and debased, not that its vice is scanty and unaggravated. **Una·ggregated,** *ppl. a.* (UN-¹ 8.) 1871 FRASER *Berkeley* x. 390 Things I say, not mere unaggregated phenomena. **Unaggre·ssive,** *a.* (UN-¹ 7 and 5 b.) 1862 *Edin. Rev.* CXVI. 223 In the unaggressive position which England assumes these interests are identical. 1867 LEWES *Hist. Philos.* II. 207 There was something in the noble calmness and unagressive fearlessness of his attitude which acted like a mental tonic. **Unaggre·ssively,** *adv.* (UN-¹ 11.) 1899 MISS B. HARRADEN *Fowler* 8 Carrying everything before them, but carrying it gallantly and unaggressively. **Unaggre·ssiveness.** (UN-¹ 12.) 1870 *Pall Mall G.* 16 Dec. 3 It would be absurd to give credit for national unaggressiveness to a country parcelled out among a lot of squabbling princelings.

†**Unagha·st,** *a. Sc. Obs.* [UN-¹ 7.] Not aghast; unafraid.

a 1510 DOUGLAS *K. Hart* I. 184 Sone thai can thame dres, Full glaid thai glyde as gromes vnagaist. 1535 STEWART *Cron. Scot.* (Rolls) III. 249 To quhome agane richt sone in to that place He ansuer maid, rycht scharplie vnagast. a 1600 MONTGOMERIE *Misc. Poems* xiv. 32, I pas the tym but pain, And vnagast.

**Una·gitated,** *ppl. a.* [UN-¹ 8.]

**1.** Not physically moved or disturbed.

1638 SIR T. HERBERT *Trav.* (ed. 2) 128 Commonly the clouds here at Larr are undigested..and unagitated by the wind. 1747 *Gentl. Mag.* 523 The air stable, and the water unagitated.

**2.** Not mentally disturbed; not stirred or excited by emotion or unrest.

1772 *Test Filial Duty* II. 88 Unagitated by alternate hope and fear, the heart is quiet. 1844 *Mem. Babylonian Princess* II. 257 The steady and unagitated tread of some seaman. 1857 RUSKIN *Pol. Econ. Art* i. 34 What we mainly want, therefore, is a means of sufficient and unagitated employment.

Hence **Una·gitatedly** *adv.*

1894 MRS. DYER *Man's Keeping* (1899) 64 There was a perceptible pause before he spoke again, during which Urquhart unagitatedly waited.

†**Una·glet,** *v.* (UN-² 4.) 1530 PALSGR. 766/1, I unaglet a poynte, or lace, *je defferre*...I pray you, unaglet this poynt.

**Unagree·able,** *a.* Now *rare.* [UN-¹ 7 b.]

**1.** Not agreeable or pleasing; not to one's liking or taste; disagreeable, uncongenial. Also const. *to*, *unto.*

c 1374 CHAUCER *Boeth.* I. met. i. (1868) 4 But now..myn

vnpitouse lijf draweþ a-long vnagreable dwellynges in me. **1491** CAXTON *Vitas Patr.* (W. de W. 1495) I. clxiv. 173/1 In all maner of her dedes she was unagreable to god. **1547** SIR W. PAGET in Strype *Eccl. Mem.* (1721) II. vii. 57 Then shall it be well don..to send an express man, not unagreeable to any of both the parts. **1671** CLARENDON *Hist. Reb.* IX. § 1 We are now entering upon a time, the representation..whereof must be the most unpleasant..to the reader..and as unagreeable and difficult to the writer. **1683** J. L. in J. Pordage *Mystic Div.* To Rdr. 5 His Soul, which then groaned to be set loose from so unagreeable a Bodie. **1725** *Fam. Dict.* s.v. *Box*, The Excellency of its Wood makes amends for its unagreeable Smell. **1808** JANE AUSTEN *Lett.* (1884) I. 361 Mr. M. was not unagreeable, though nothing seemed to go right with him. **1866** *Lond. Rev.* 5 May 499/2 There is another class of persons who..are what one might call (if there were such a word in the English language) 'unagreeable' people.

†**2.** Unconformable or unsuitable *to*, inconsistent or incongruous *with*. *Obs.*

**1550** BALE *Apol.* 57 Here, how inconstaunt, unagreable, and contraryouse he is also to hymselfe. **1566** PAINTER *Pal. Pleas.* (1569) 86 b, Thinkinge it better..to haue a wife unagreable to his estate, then to suffer him to die for her sake. **1580** E. KNIGHT *Trial Truth* 12 The millers hackney vnagreeable with the true rules and accident of armes. **1624** HEYWOOD *Gunaik.* III. 151 Least any abject thing or unworthie may be objected against us unagreable with our blood and qualitie. **1667** MILTON *P. L.* X. 256 Let us try Adventrous work, yet to thy power and mine Not unagreeable. **1684** H. MORE *Answer* 42 Also it is unagreeable with the making the Christian Emperours the seventh Head. **1702** H. DODWELL *Apol.* § 14 in S. Parker *Cicero's De Finibus* b 4 b, This was thought to be the case of the *Biothanatoi*..which made it unagreeable to the Principles of Philosophy for any to imitate it.

Hence **Unagree·ableness.**

**1658** *Whole Duty Man* xii. § 8 That unagreeableness that was betwixt their practice, and their law. **1667** *Decay Chr. Piety* xvi. ₽ 2 A doctrine, whose unagreeableness to the gospel-œconomy rendred it suspicious.

**Unagree·ably,** *adv.* [UN-1 11.]

†**1.** Inconsistently. *Obs.*—1

**1546** BALE *Eng. Votaries* I. (1550) 4 b, Which thynge hath bene hytherto in all Englysh Chronicles, doubtfullie, vnagreablye, yea and vntruly treated.

**2.** Unpleasantly, disagreeably.

[**1775** ASH.] **1850** L. HUNT *Autobiog.* I. vii. 291 They.. were not unagreeably sprinkled with quotation.

**Unagree·d,** *ppl. a.* [UN-1 8.]

**1.** Not agreed or in accord (*with*).

**1525** LD. BERNERS *Froiss.* II. clxxxiv. 556 Thoughe the lordes departed euery daye vnagreed, yet they departed asonder right amiably. **1557–75** *Diurn. Occurr.* (Bann. Cl.) 188 Thaj depairtit agane unaggreit with the said regent. **1667** *Decay Chr. Piety* xi. § 8 If he find them unagreed upon the way, one disputing for this, and another for that,..he would sure retract his confidence.

†**2.** With *of*: Not agreed upon. *Obs.*—1

**1661** BOYLE *Style of Script.* (1675) 172 Which [part] is not onely less considerable, but is changeable and unagreed of.

**Unagree·ing,** *ppl. a.* (UN-1 10.) **1611** COTGR., *Incongrue*, incongruous, vnagreeing; absurd. **1654** COKAINE *Dianea* I. 9 The knight..conceived it unagreeing to his generous spirit to be cruell to a Carkass. **Unai·dable,** *a.* (UN-1 7b and 5b.) **1664** (SHAKS.) *All's Well* II. i. 122 (3rd Fol.) That labouring art can never ransome nature From her unaydible [1623 inaydible] estate. [**1755** JOHNSON.] **1866** CARLYLE *Remin.* (1881) II. 265 What a look,..unaidable, and like to break one's heart. **1871** — in *Lett. Mrs. Carlyle* (1883) III. 179 Such a deluge of..indescribable, unaidable pain, as I had never seen or dreamt of.

†**Unai·dant,** *a.* *Obs.*—1 [UN-1 7.] Not helpful.

**1667** WATERHOUSE *Fire Lond.* 170 Incontributive to the publique Charge, as well as unaydant to their own Expences.

**Unai·ded,** *ppl. a.* [UN-1 8.] Not aided; unassisted: **a.** In predicative use; also const. *by*.

**1667** MILTON *P. L.* VI. 141 Who,..with solitarie hand Reaching beyond all limit, at one blow Unaided could have finisht thee. **1791** COWPER *Iliad* XVI. 652 Thy allies, who, for thy sake,..Perish, unaided and unmiss'd by thee. **1796** MME. D'ARBLAY *Camilla* V. 376, I cannot support it unaided. **1860** TYNDALL *Glac.* I. i. 5 Mere reasoning, unaided by experiment, was incompetent to answer. **1888** BARRIE *When a Man's Single* (1900) 71/1 Angus is longing to pull us up the river unaided.

**b.** Attrib.; in later use esp. of the eye.

**1676** GLANVILL *Ess.* iii. 24 The distance of the Heavens is so vast, that our unaided Senses can give us but extreamly imperfect Informations of that Upper World. **1712** BLACKMORE *Creation* II. 77 Counting those the unaided eye Can see, or by invented tubes descry. **1773** *Observ. State Poor* 63 The terrors of unaided poverty would happily operate to the advantage of those, who..prodigally waste those earnings. **1827** SCOTT *Chron. Canongate* Introd., I had therefore the task of avowing myself..as the sole and unaided author of these Novels of Waverley. **1855** BAIN *Senses & Int.* III. iii. § 2 The multiplication of unaided eyes could never equal the vision of one person with a telescope.

Hence **Unai·dedly** *adv.*

**1859** G. WILSON *Mem. E. Forbes* ii. (1861) 42 Forbes.. had..unaidedly discovered the true scope of his intellect.

**Unai·ding,** *ppl. a.* (UN-1 10.) **1716** POPE *Iliad* VIII. 581 From fields forbidden we submiss refrain, With arms unaiding see our Argives slain. **Unai·ling,** *ppl. a.* (UN-1 10.) **1846** WORCESTER (citing Chatham), *Unailing*, a., free from disease; healthy.

†**Unai·mable,** *a.* *Obs.*—1 In 4 uneymable. [UN-1 7 b.] Unreckonable.

**1382** WYCLIF *Job* xxxvi. 26 Lo! God gret, ouercomende oure kunnyng; the noumbre of the ȝeris of hym uneymable [L. *inestimabilis*].

**Unai·med,** *ppl. a.* [UN-1 8.] **a.** Not aimed or pointed at a mark. **b.** With *at*: Not taken as a mark.

**1648** HEXHAM II, *Ongewickt*, Vn-aimed, Vnleveled. **1669** COKAINE *Poems, Let. to Earl Huntingdon* 86 So you (my Lord) for sweet conditions known, Parallels to your high birth, stand alone, Unaim'd and unarriv'd at. **1805** WORDSW. *Prelude* IV. 315 With din of instruments and shuffling feet,.. And unaimed prattle flying up and down. **1835** BROWNING *Paracelsus* V. 629 The tumult of unproved desire, the unaimed, Uncertain yearnings, aspirations blind. **1888** *Daily News* 6 Sept. 6/5 Swept by artillery fire and unaimed rifle fire at long ranges.

**Unai·ming,** *ppl. a.* (UN-1 10.) **1691** DRYDEN *K. Arthur* I. i, Your Charming Daughter, who like Love, Born Blind, Un-aiming hits, with surest Archery, And Innocently kills. *a* **1735** GRANVILLE *Poems* (1790) 86 The noisy Culverin, o'ercharg'd, lets fly, And burst unaiming in the rended sky.

**Unai·rable,** *a.* *Obs.*—1 [UN-1 7 b. Cf. AIRABLE *a.*] †Not capable of forming good music.

*a* **1619** CAMPION *Counterpoint* Wks. (1909) 217 If this be the right Base,..what a strange vnaireable change must the key then make from *F.* with the first third sharp to *G.* with *B.* flat.

**Unai·red,** *ppl. a.* [UN-1 8.]

†**1.** Untravelled. *Obs.*—1 (Cf. AIRED *ppl. a.* 2.)

?*a* **1616** BEAUM. & FL. *Q. Corinth* II. iv, Be not so improvident To forget your travelling pace, 'tis a main posture, And to all unayr'd Gentlemen will betray you.

**2.** Not exposed to the air or to heat so as to remove stagnant air or damp. (Cf. AIR *v.* 1, 2.)

**1682** OTWAY *Venice Preserved* III. ii, What feminine Tale hast thou been listening to, Of unayr'd shirts; Catharrs and Tooth Ach got By thin-sol'd shoos. **1740** MRS. DELANY in *Life & Corr.* (1861) II. 122 We are, I think, too much invalids to go into an unaired house. **1763** *Brit. Mag.* IV. 405 The ladies were under terrible apprehensions about damp sheets and unaired beds. **1826** SCOTT *Woodst.* iii, The state-rooms are unaired, and in indifferent order. **1865** TROLLOPE *Belton Est.* ix. 95 She had been wrong to go into such a place as the cold, unaired Court House.

**Unait,** variant of UNNAIT *a.* *Obs.*

†**Unaker.** *Obs.* (See quots.)

**1744** in *Dict. Nat. Biogr.* (1889) XX. 300/1 The material [for making china-ware] is an earth, the produce of the Cherokee nation in America, called by the natives *unaker*. **1885** *Encycl. Brit.* XIX. 641/1 The clay, which was called 'unaker,' was brought from America, and was probably an impure kind of kaolin.

**Unaki·n,** *a.* (UN-1 7.) **1864** F. W. ROBINSON *Mattie, a Stray* III. 175 Twice had the answer been deferred, for reasons unakin to each other. **1878** MISS FOTHERGILL *First Violin* VI. i, In former days there had been in his face something not unakin to this stormy, free night.

**Unal** (yū·năl), *a.* [f. L. *ūn-us* one + -AL.] Single; that is one only; based on unity.

**1883** MOMERIE *Personality* Introd. (ed. 2) 12 It [metaphysics] seeks a unal basis for the phenomena of nature and of human nature. **1892** 'UNITAS' *Unalism* Pref., The neglected Unal principle has its source in the Divine Oneness.

**Unala·rm,** *v.* (UN-2 3.) **1722** DE FOE *Plague* (1754) 21 The Distemper intermitted often at first; so they were as it were, alarm'd, and unalarm'd again.

**Unala·rmed,** *ppl. a.* (UN-1 8.)

**1756** MRS. DELANY in *Life & Corr.* (1861) III. 419, I am still unalarmed about the invasion, but don't find people are so apprehensive as at first. **1769** G. WHITE *Selborne* xxvi, A tame snake, which was..as sweet as any animal while in good humour and unalarmed. **1820** W. JAY *Prayers* 89 Unalarmed by fears, undistressed by pain. **1897** ANNE PAGE *Afternoon Ride* 61 A large iguana, waddling with serious mien and unalarmed leisure towards the drift.

**Unala·rming,** *a.* (UN-1 10.)

**1760–72** H. BROOKE *Fool of Qual.* (1792) III. 9 The seasonable precaution of breaking the matter to our father by unalarming degrees. **1803** *Ann. Rev.* I. 364 A disposition to make..slight unalarming reforms. **1868** MISS BRADDON *Dead Sea Fr.* III. iv. 61 Her illness was of a very slight and unalarming character.

†**Una·lchemy,** *v.* *Obs.*—1 [UN-2 3.] *trans.* To decompose chemically.

**1661** FELTHAM *Resolves* II. viii. 194 Like the only true Philosophers stone, he can unalchimy the Allay of life.

**Una·lcoholized,** *ppl. a.* (UN-1 8.) [**1775** ASH.] **1881** *Daily News* 21 June 6/8 During those two years..they were experimenting in the production of Unalcoholized Sherry. **1884** *Ch. Bells* 2 Feb. 214/1 *Vino Sacro*, the pure unalcoholised Sacramental wine. **Unale·rt,** *a.* (UN-1 7.) **1811** SOUTHEY *Inscript.*, *Affair Arroyo Molinos* 17 He..deem'd the British soldiers all too slow, To seize occasion, unalert in war. **1892** 'M. FIELD' *Sight & Song* 92 The offender callous, unalert.

**Una·lienable,** *a.* [UN-1 7 b and 5 b.] = INALIENABLE *a.*

**1611** COTGR., *Inalienable*, vnalienable; which cannot be sold, or passed away. **1641** EARL MONM. tr. *Biondi's Civil Warres* V. 125 Those countries..which for safety and reputation ought to be unalienable from the Crowne of England. **1688** *Answ. Talon's Plea* 27 This Monsieur Talon maintains to be an unalienable right of the Crown of France. **1743** J. MORRIS *Serm.* vii. 197 God..gives all men their being, and has an unalienable claim to their obedience. **1771** GOLDSM. *Hist. Eng.* II. 307 Giving these petty tyrants a power of selling their estates, which before his time were unalienable. **1841** STEPHEN *Comm. Laws Eng.* (1874) II. 13 Personal chattels cannot in any instance be rendered unalienable beyond the period prescribed. **1855** MACAULAY *Hist. Eng.* xvii. IV. 115 That all men were endowed by the Creator with an unalienable right to liberty.

**Una·lienably,** *adv.* [UN-1 11 and 5 b.] = INALIENABLY *adv.*

**1702** *Toleration* 3 It is..evident..that no Man may arrogate what is unalienably appropriated unto God. **1765** WILKES *Corr.* (1805) II. 193, I hope my friends..think of me..for my life unalienably attentive to my country. **1809** E. CHRISTIAN in *Blackstone's Comm.* I. 329 The parliament had the wisdom..to vest unalienably in commissioners the sum of 1,000,000 *l.* annually. **1881** EMMA WORBOISE *Sissie* xxv, The pittance that remained was hers—hers unalienably.

**Una·lienated,** *ppl. a.* [UN-1 8.]

**1.** Not estranged in feeling.

**1798** S. & HT. LEE *Canterb. T.* II. 513 Even if his heart should stand the test, and remain wholly uncorrupted, and unalienated. **1859** FARRAR *J. Home* 414 An effort was made by his few remaining and unalienated friends to provide for him the means of emigration.

**2.** Not alienated or transferred in respect of ownership.

**1851** SIR F. PALGRAVE *Norm. & Eng.* I. 5 His resources.. arose only from the very few royal domains as yet unalienated from the crown. **1887** MOLONEY *Forestry W. Africa* 6 The absence of compiled information of extent of lands sold and unalienated.

†**Una·liened,** *ppl. a.* [UN-1 8.] Unalienated.

**1596** BACON *Use Com. Law* (1635) 28 Some action must bee brought against the heire whilest the land or other inheritance resteth in him unaliened away. **1674** STAVELEY *Rom. Horseleech* 131 Her example was not followed by any of the Nobility, or others, who had incorporated any of the Abby Lands into their estates, but the Queen restored only what remained in the Crown un-aliened from the same.

**Unali·ke,** *adv.* [UN-1 11 b.] Differently.

**1616** GATAKER *Lots* 337 Which stickes if they light and lye both alike on the flat side, they account it a good signe; if unalike, an evill signe.

**Unalime·ntary,** *a.* (UN-1 7.) **1822** GOOD *Study Med.* I. 182 Unalimentary substances swallowed through bravado or by mistake, as knives, metallic money, or pieces of glass.

**U·nalism.** [f. UNAL *a.* + -ISM.] (See quot.)

**1892** 'UNITAS' *Unalism* i. 2 Unalism..has nothing whatever to do with Unitarianism. It means a system of thought and action which is in accordance with the Unal Rule.

**Unalist** (yū·nălist). [f. UNAL *a.* + -IST; cf. *pluralist.*] **a.** A holder of only one benefice. **b.** A believer in unalism.

**1743** R. NEWTON *Pluralities Indefensible* 198, I do deny, that, in the general, Pluralists have Greater Merit than Unalists. **1892** 'UNITAS' *Unalism* i. 2 Christian nations and Churches generally..are Double Deists, or Ditheists, instead of being Unalists, as they ought to be.

**Unali·ve,** *a.* [UN-1 7.] Not fully susceptible or awake *to* something.

**1828** L. HUNT *Byron & Contemp.* (ed. 2) I. 377 Dry, mechanical theorists, unalive to sentiment and fancy. **1855** BAGEHOT *Lit. Stud.* (1879) I. 16 An experienced and erudite Frenchman, not unalive to artistic effect. **1893** G. ALLEN *Scallywag* III. 9 He was not unalive to the advantages of keeping up his dormant connection.

**Unallay·able,** *a.* (UN-1 7 b.) **1801** SOUTHEY *Thalaba* VII. xvi, Belike he shall exchange..its cups of joy For the unallayable bitterness of Zaccoum's fruit accurst.

**Unallay·ed,** *ppl. a.* [UN-1 8.] Not allayed or mixed; unmixed, unqualified.

**1519** HORMAN *Vulg.* 165 b, He drynketh wyne vnalayed. **1648** BOYLE *Seraph. Love* i. (1700) 2 Unallay'd satisfactions are joys too Heavenly to fall to many men's shares on Earth. **1682** NORRIS *Hierocles* 90 Yet by the conjunction of good, he..at last enjoys pure and unallai'd pleasure with his vertue. **1796** CHARLOTTE SMITH *Marchmont* I. 46 Althea received this news with unallayed transport. **1817** COLERIDGE *Biogr. Lit.* xx. II. 114, I can bring to my recollection three persons..who had read the poems..with more and more unallayed pleasure. **1887** BOWEN *Æneid* V. 608 Deep her mighty designs, and her ancient wrath unallayed.

**b.** Const. *with* or *by*.

*a* **1676** HALE *Prim. Orig. Man.* IV. viii. (1677) 375 By this means their enjoyments are sincere, unallayed with fears or suspitions. **1751** SMOLLETT *Per. Pic.* civ, The most elevated transports of joy, unallayed with the least mixture of grief. **1762** FALCONER *Shipwr.* II. 379 Where perils unallay'd by hope appear. **1791** ANNA SEWARD *Lett.* (1811) III. 199 A source of lasting happiness..unallayed by private or public calamity.

**Unalle·ged,** *ppl. a.* (UN-1 8.) **1587** GOLDING *De Mornay* xiv. (1592) 224 If I haue left any thing vnalledged which might make to this purpose,..he which feeleth himself conuicted in himself, needeth no more diligent proofe than hath been made already. **Unallego·rical,** *a.* (UN-1 7. Cf. G. *unallegorisch.*) **1776** MICKLE tr. *Camoens' Lusiad* Introd. 138 *note*, The unallegorical opposition or concert of Christian and Pagan ideas. **Unalle·viable,** *a.* (UN-1 7 b.) **1816** SOUTHEY *Ess.* (1832) I. 241 It was vehement grief,.. unalleviated..and..unalleviable. **1887** H. DRUMMOND in G. A. Smith *Life* (1899) xi. 274 The thing that crushes is to look on silently at the unalleviable pain of those we love.

**Unalle·viated,** *ppl. a.* (UN-1 8.)

**1750** SECKER *Serm. 11 Mar.* (1771) 194 All Mischief of all Kinds befall us,..through the whole Course of Life, unalleviated by a Prospect of Recompense after Death. **1816** [see prec.]. **1866** J. C. COLQUHOUN *Wilberforce* 408 It is no wonder that he felt, and showed in his looks, the unalleviated strain. **1882** FARRAR *Early Chr.* I. 107 The world was settling into the sadness of unalleviated despair.

**Unalli·able,** *a.* (UN-1 7 b.)

**1740** CHEYNE *Regimen* 37 They are not incompatible and unallyable,..but they are contrary. **1792** BURKE *Corr.* (1844) III. 394 They had long shown themselves wholly adverse to, and unalliable with, the party. **1792** — *Let. to Langrishe* Wks. VI. 355 We look upon you..as perpetual and unalliable aliens.

**Unallie·d,** *ppl. a.* [UN-1 8.]

**1.** Not allied or related.

**1663** BOYLE *Usef. Exp. Nat. Philos.* II. v. 290 The greater their experience,..the greater indisposition it would give them to credit so unallied a truth. **1697** COLLIER *Ess. Mor. Subj.* II. (1703) 85 Extension and cogitation are unallied in their ideas. **1852** M. ARNOLD *Empedocles* II. 359 Still Thought and Mind Will hurry us..Over the unallied unopening Earth. **1862** SPENCER *First Princ.* II. xiv. § 113 (1875) 323 Year by year are established certain connexions among orders of phenomena that appear unallied.

**b.** Const. *to*.

1697 COLLIER *Ess. Mor. Subj.* I. (1709) 143 'Tis a Principle ..absolutely unallied to Reason and Good-nature. 1789 COWPER *Annus Mem.* 59 The eyes that never saw thee, shine With joy not unallied to thine. 1818 SCOTT *Br. Lamm.* xviii, She seemed to be an angel..unallied to the coarser mortals among whom she deigned to dwell for a season. 1864 CARLYLE *Fredk. Gt.* XVI. iii. IV. 280 He..regards with sublime pity, not unallied to contempt, all other diplomatic beings.

**2.** Having no ally or allies.

*a* 1797 H. WALPOLE *Geo. II* (1847) II. iv. 127 Unallied we could make no diversion to France. 1898 *Westm. Gaz.* 15 Apr. 5/3 Spain..enters upon the conflict unallied.

**Unallo·tted,** *ppl. a.* (UN-[1] 8.) [1775 ASH.] 1869 *Sat. Rev.* 9 Jan. 44/2 This shows how wise it is to have a spare hour or two unallotted in the scheme of days. 1883 *Law Rep.* 24 Chanc. Div. 375 As there were so many shares remaining unallotted, it shews that there were no other persons ready to take them.

**Unallow·able,** *a.* [UN-[1] 7 b.] Not allowable; inadmissible, impermissible.

1560 DAUS *Sleidane's Comm.* ij b, He neyther bringeth Scripture for hym, nor any thinge out of the auncient Doctours, but certein dreames of his owne, receiued of scoolemen by an vnallowable euill custome. 1577 tr. *Bullinger's Decades* (1592) 134 If we shall goe about to performe those ..vnallowable othes, then shal we..incurre the heauie wrath of the reuenging Lorde. 1645 MILTON *Tetrach.* To Parlt. A 2 b, It can be no immoderate, or unallowable course of seeking so..needfull reparations. *a* 1678 H. SCOUGAL *Disc. Imp. Subj.* (1735) 268 An unallowable patience in hearing his master dishonoured. 1726 BUTLER *Serm.* Pref., It is very unallowable for a work of imagination or entertainment not to be of easy comprehension. 1799 *Monthly Rev.* XXVIII. 526 The inferences deduced from them would still be unallowable. 1842 DE MORGAN *Diff. & Int. Calc.* 384 An infinite number of unallowable points. 1867 MACFARREN *Harmony* ii. 40 Whatever is unallowable for all the notes is, of course, forbidden for each particular one.

**Unallow·ed,** *ppl. a.* (UN-[1] 8 and 8 c.)

1632 SHERWOOD, Unalowed, *desavoüé*. 1686 HORNECK *Crucif. Jesus* xiv. 322 No unallowed of miscarriages, I mean miscarriages against the settled bent and resolutions of our souls, can be said to null this covenant. 1785 *Liberal Amer.* II. 257, I saw two virtuous hearts struggling with an unallowed passion. 1842 PUSEY *Crisis Eng. Ch.* 26 There must be risk that persons will seek unity in unallowed ways of their own. 1874 — *Lent. Serm.* 84 To use unallowed what is another's is to steal.

**Unalloy·ed,** *ppl. a.* (UN-[1] 8.)

*fig.* *a* 1672 STERRY *Freed. Will* (1675) 9 Being it self in its absoluteness,..unalloyed by any differences of mixtures. 1737 WEST *Let.* in *Gray's Poems* (1775) 27 Four-and-twenty hours of pure unalloy'd health together. 1796 MME. D'ARBLAY *Camilla* V. 183 A pity..unalloyed with any blame. 1860 MOTLEY *Netherl.* vi. (1868) I. 358 There is hardly a character in history upon which the imagination can dwell with more unalloyed delight. 1869 TOZER *Highl. Turkey* I. 131 The purest religious influences, unalloyed by superstition.

*lit.* 1760–72 H. BROOKE *Fool of Qual.* (1792) V. 216 A coffin of unalloyed and beaten silver. 1812 SIR H. DAVY *Chem. Philos.* 385 Iron..is capable of acquiring magnetism, though in its unalloyed state it retains it only a very short time.

**Unallu·rable,** *a.* (UN-[1] 7 b.) 1812 *Monthly Rev.* LXVII. 296 Uniformity in religious opinion was the unallurable phœnix, for which reformation professed to spread her nets. **Unallu·ring,** *ppl. a.* (UN-[1] 10.) [1775 ASH.] 1805 M. A. SHEE *Rhymes on Art* (1806) 106 *note*, Our national mode of worship;..there is a coldness about it, an unalluring formality. *c* 1855 LYTTON in *Life* (1883) I. iii. 26 Those Muses which had seemed so unalluring to her childhood took a softer aspect. 1863 — *Caxtoniana* II. 201 They maintained the continuance after death of an unsatisfactory, unalluring state of being. **Una·lmsed,** *a.* (UN-[1] 9.) 1827 POLLOK *Course T.* III. 279 He ..with a look Which hell might be ashamed of, drove the poor Away unalmsed.

**Una·lphabeted,** *a.* [UN-[1] 9.] Not acquainted with the alphabet. Also *fig.*

1799 COLERIDGE *Lett.* (1895) 305 The inhabitants..are bigots, unalphabeted in the first feelings of liberality. 1832 — *Ibid.* 764 An almost unalphabeted but very sensible woman.

**Unalphabe·tic,** *a.* (UN-[1] 7.) 1883 BURTON & CAMERON *Gold Coast* I. v. 127 In fact, the Guanches of Tenerife were unalphabetic. **Una·ltarlike,** *a.* (UN-[1] 7 c.) 1640 SIR E. DERING *Carmelite* (1641) 34 You may guesse how un-altarlike these Tables were. **Unalterabi·lity.** (UN-[1] 12 and 5 b.) 1847 SMEATON *Builders' Man.* 143 It is used for housepainting, less..in regard to its unalterability, than to its solubility. 1885 *Law Times* LXXVIII. 315/2 Not that there was any sanctity or unalterability inherent in the memorandum.

**Una·lterable,** *a.* [UN-[1] 7 b and 5 b.] That cannot be altered or changed: **a.** In general use.

1611 FLORIO, *Inpermutabile*, vnalterable. 1656 BRAMHALL *Replication* 5 The essences of things are unalterable. 1694 F. BRAGGE *Disc. Parables* xii. 397 Whatever alteration is made in the state..of the soul..shall be from henceforth for ever unalterable. 1729 POPE *Let. to Swift* 9 Oct., The doctor is unalterable, both in friendship and quadrille. 1794 HUTTON *Philos. Light*, etc. 286 Space, which is unalterable, and in which bodies are conceived to move. 1815 J. SMITH *Panorama Sci. & Art* II. 451 Alone, it [*sc.* silex] is unalterable by the strongest heat. 1864 BOWEN *Logic* xii. 400 What is called physical necessity is nothing but a conviction that the relation of an Efficient Cause to its effect is unalterable.

**b.** Of resolves, decisions, laws, etc.

1631 GOUGE *God's Arrows* I. § 67. 112 Vow with an unalterable resolution to performe what you vow. 1699 BURNET *39 Art.* xxxiv. 370 No rule made in such matters is to be held unalterable, but may be changed upon occasion. 1779 *Mirror* No. 67, Her resolution was taken; and she repeatedly assured me, that her motives made it unalterable. 1781 COWPER *Conversat.* 467 'Tis an unalterable fix'd decree, That none could frame or ratify but she. 1815 J. CORMACK *Abol. Fem. Infanticide Guzerat* x. 195 Not less unalterable did the Jahrejahs of Guzerat pronounce the horrid practice of infanticide. 1890 'R. BOLDREWOOD' *Col. Reformer* (1891) 199, I do not see why it should be an unalterable law.

**c.** Of feelings. (Common in 18th cent.)

1716 POPE *Let. to Lady Montagu* 18 Aug., With all unalterable esteem and sincerity. 1776 MICKLE tr. *Camoens' Lusiad* Dissert. 160/1 Perceiving the unalterable hatred which the League bore to his religion. 1841 BREWSTER *Mart. Sci.* II. iii. (1856) 133 Tycho received..an assurance of his Majesty's unalterable attachment.

**Una·lterableness.** [f. prec.: see UN-[1] 12.] The quality of being unalterable.

1620 BP. HALL *Hon. Marr. Clergy* I. xxii. 123 When he finds an vnalterablenesse in the determination of these degrees. 1649 F. ROBERTS *Clavis Bibl.* 372 The unalterablenesse of Gods work. 1699 BURNET *39 Art.* xxxiv. 372 The Second Branch of this Article is against the Unalterableness of Laws made in matters indifferent. *a* 1728 WOODWARD *Fossils* I. 186 The Unalterableness of the Corpuscles. 1817 HAZLITT *Char. Shaks.* (1838) 287 The unalterableness of his resolutions. 1850 L. HUNT *Autobiog.* III. xxv. 283 A bull declaring the unalterableness of every papal dogma. 1866 GEO. ELIOT *F. Holt* xxxiv. III. 6 Our minds get tricks and attitudes as our bodies do—and age stiffens them into unalterableness.

**Una·lterably,** *adv.* (UN-[1] 11.)

1643 LIGHTFOOT *Glean. Ex.* (1648) 22 That must be of a Lambe or kid unalterably. 1697 COLLIER *Ess. Mor. Subj.* I. (1703) 90 It is the part of true magnanimity to adhere unalterably to a wise choice. 1725 BOLINGBROKE *Let. to Swift* 24 July, To pass an act, which fixing my fortune unalterably to this country, fixes my person here also. 1796 MME. D'ARBLAY *Camilla* I. 9 His temper was unalterably sweet. 1830 HERSCHEL *Study Nat. Phil.* I. iii. 39 These primary qualities originally and unalterably impressed on matter. 1894 H. GARDENER *Unoff. Patriot* 56 Upon that point his mind was clearly and unalterably made up.

†**Una·lterate,** *ppl. a. Sc. Obs.*[−1] [UN-[1] 8 b.] Unaltered.

153. BELLENDEN *Benner of Pietie* 35 (Bann. MS.), Thy word eterne but end is permanent, Vnalterat but mvtabilitie.

**Unaltera·tion.** (UN-[1] 12.) *a* 1676 HALES *Prim. Orig. Man.* I. iii. (1677) 86 The supposition..of any corruptible or alterable Being, in a state of incorruption or unalteration.

**Una·ltered,** *ppl. a.* [UN-[1] 8.] Unchanged.

1551 RECORDE *Pathw. Knowl.* I. v, Then do I set one foote of the compas vnaltered in D, and stretch the other in the circular line. 1597 HOOKER *Eccl. Pol.* V. liv. § 5 Neyther are..the state and qualitie of our substance so vnaltered, but that there are in it many glorious effects proceeding from so neere copulation with deitie. 1615 CHAPMAN *Odyss.* V. 148 Affirming that th' unaltered Destinies..have decreed he shall not die. 1653 W. RAMESEY *Astrol. Restored* 226 The Government or Rule then setled shall continue firm and unaltered 57 years. 1763 SIR W. JONES *Caissa* Poems, etc. (1777) 131 In one unalter'd line they tempt the fight. 1796 MME. D'ARBLAY *Camilla* IV. 302, I should have assured you of my unaltered regard. 1855 MACAULAY *Hist. Eng.* xix. IV. 315 The valuation made in 1692 has remained unaltered down to our own time. 1882 MINCHIN *Unipl. Kinemat.* 27 The distance between them being altered or unaltered.

**Una·ltering,** *ppl. a.* (UN-[1] 10.) 1813 SHELLEY *Q. Mab* VII. 6 Tempered disdain in his unaltering eye, Mixed with a quiet smile, shone calmly forth. 1877 'H. A. PAGE' *De Quincey* II. xix. 166 Unaltering friendship for him remains as his record in this particular. **Una·lumed,** *ppl. a.* (UN-[1] 9.) 1811 *Self-Instructor* 536 A scabrous matter, such as unallumed cloth is. **Unama·lgamable,** *a.* (UN-[1] 7 b.) 1828 SOUTHEY *Lett.* (1856) IV. 86 Coarse materials predominate in the unamalgamable composition. 1865 C. J. VAUGHAN *Plain Words* vi. (1866) 106 That remote and unamalgamable thing we have always fancied to be religion. **Unama·lgamated,** *ppl. a.* (UN-[1] 8. Cf. G. *unamalgamirt.*) 1825 *Monthly Rev.* CVI. 19 His three unamalgamated provinces. 1844 NOAD *Electricity* (ed. 2) 184 Gas from the unamalgamated part of the copper. 1855 I. TAYLOR *Restor. Belief* (1856) 42 The mass combines the two unamalgamated and adverse elements. **Unama·lgamating,** *ppl. a.* (UN-[1] 10.) 1820 T. L. PEACOCK *Misc.* Wks. 1875 III. 335 A heterogeneous congeries of unamalgamating manners. 1865 W. G. PALGRAVE *Arabia* II. 271 An influence hardly to be understood by our own unamalgamating Anglo-Saxon. **Unama·ssed,** *ppl. a.* (UN-[1] 8.) 1700 S. PARKER *Six Philos. Ess.* 4 Why might it not be as well a drift or shower of Atoms yet unamass'd, disorderly dancing one amongst another, and at various distances?

**Unama·zed,** *ppl. a.* (UN-[1] 8.)

1598 FLORIO, *Interrito*, without feare, vnamazed. 1624 QUARLES *Job* xvii. 50 Who comprehends the Lightning, or the Thunder? Who sees, who heares them, vnamaz'd with wonder? 1667 MILTON *P. L.* IX. 552 Into the Heart of Eve his words made way, Though at the voice much marveling; at length Not unamaz'd, she thus in answer spake. 1899 *Westm. Gaz.* 28 Sept. 3/3 It is possible to be unamazed at the modesty of the man who Englished it.

**Unambigu·ity.** (UN-[1] 12.) 1842 G. S. FABER *Prov. Lett.* (1844) II. 203 Its unambiguity is the more fully established, because the language is not that of a single individual.

**Unambi·guous,** *a.* (UN-[1] 7.)

1751 CHESTERF. *Lett.* xlv. (1774) II. 189 Every paragraph should be so clear, and unambiguous, that the dullest fellow in the world may not be able to mistake it. 1785 REID *Intell. Powers* II. viii. 273 Malebranche is perfectly clear and unambiguous in this matter. 1804 *Phil. Trans.* XCIV. 219 The concise and unambiguous expression of the conditions of a problem in algebraic language. 1883 in *Law Times Rep.* (1884) 26 Apr. 273/2 If..that had been intended, the Legislature would have so enacted in express and unambiguous terms.

Hence **Unambi·guously** *adv.*

1790 G. WALKER *Serm.* II. xxiii. 164 The promises of the Gospel..do clearly and unambiguously confirm the hope. 1802 *Phil. Trans.* XCII. 111 The law of the series is truly and unambiguously represented. 1866 J. MARTINEAU *Ess.* I. 162 All the physical indications point unambiguously the same way.

**Unambi·tion.** [UN-[1] 12.] Lack of ambition.

1781 EARL MALMESBURY *Diaries & Corr.* I. 487 The idea of the moderation and unambition of the French Ministry is..solidly established. 1850 F. W. NEWMAN *Phases of Faith* 31 Now indeed they are weak: now they profess unworldliness and unambition.

**Unambi·tious,** *a.* [UN-[1] 7 and 5 b.] Not ambitious or aspiring; devoid of ambition: **a.** Of thoughts, occupations, productions, etc.

16.. *Nobody & Someb.* in Simpson *Sch. Shaks.* (1878) I. 332 My unambitious thoughts have bin long tird With this great charge. 1656 COWLEY *Praise Pindar* iv, Whilst, alas, my tim'erous Muse Unambitious tracks pursues. 1713 *Guard.* No. 167 ¶ 3 Train them up in the humble unambitious Pursuits of Knowledge. 1768 BOSWELL *Corsica* Dedication p. v, Predicting greatness to those who afterwards pass their days in unambitious indolence. 1814 WORDSW. *Excurs.* V. 111 The calm delights Of unambitious piety he chose. 1862 LATHAM *Channel Isl.* III. xviii. (ed. 2) 430 The bottom of this unambitious window..is but four feet from the ground. 1887 *Spectator* 25 Mar. 421/2 He can produce an unambitious though not unsatisfying tiny cabinet picture.

**b.** Of persons, the mind, etc.

1621 G. SANDYS *Ovid's Met.* I. (1626) 3 Then, vnambitious Mortals knew no more, But their owne Countrie's Nature-bounded shore. 1728 YOUNG *Love Fame* II. 291 Is thy ambition sweating for a rhyme; Thou unambitious fool, at this late time? 1784 COWPER *Task* IV. 798 An unambitious mind, content In the low vale of life. 1816 BYRON *Ch. Har.* III. lxiv, Stainless victories, Won by the unambitious heart and hand Of a proud, brotherly, and civic band. 1893 LIDDON *Life Pusey* I. App. 455 That unenterprising and unambitious but useful class of the English gentry.

Hence **Unambi·tiously** *adv.*, **-ness.**

1746 HERVEY *Medit.* (1818) 120 While others, free from all aspiring views, creep unambitiously on the ground, and look like the commonalty of the kind. *a* 1755 CONYBEARE (Mason), Others through unambitiousness of temper are gradually sinking. 1791 COLERIDGE *Math. Problem* iii. 10 Unambitiously join'd in equality's band. 1814 WORDSW. *Excurs.* VII. 473 That monumental stone..unambitiously relates How long..The sad privation was by him endured. 1847 LYTTON *Lucretia* 19 He felt a lively satisfaction at the thought of leaving his friend honourably, if unambitiously, provided for.

**Unambro·sial,** *a.* (UN-[1] 7.) 1839 J. STERLING *Ess.*, etc. (1848) I. 316 Jove, whose shake of his un-ambrosial wig once ruled the world. **Una·mbush,** *v.* (UN-[2] 3.) 1650 FULLER *Pisgah* II. xii. 254 Such ambushes are now adays unambushed, by the general suspicion all have of them. **Uname·nability.** (UN-[1] 12.) 1865 *Cornh. Mag.* May 591 One set of features characteristic of pestilence is the suddenness of its onset; its unamenability to the resources of the healing art.

**Uname·nable,** *a.* (UN-[1] 7 b.)

1771 E. LONG *Trial of Dog 'Porter'* in Hone *Every-day Bk.* II. 209 Laws to which he was unamenable. 1802–12 BENTHAM *Ration. Judic. Evid.* (1827) II. 599 Superior and unamenable power. 1868 VISCT. STRANGFORD *Select.* (1869) II. 251 Tibet, Afghanistan, and all Indian frontier countries are classed in the same category as unamenable to civilised laws. 1877 SIR H. TAYLOR *Autobiog.* (1885) I. 139 The good easy Chancellor of the Exchequer was overruled by the stout and unamenable Secretary.

**Uname·ndable,** *a.* (UN-[1] 7 b.)

*c* 1450 HOLLAND *Howlat* 928 'My first making,' quoth scho, 'was vnamendable'. *c* 1550 CHEKE *Let.* in *Athenæum* 28 Aug. (1909) 237/2 If you think yourself unamendable. 1561 DAUS tr. *Bullinger on Apoc.* (1573) 112 His vnamendable wickednes and continuall blasphemy. 1583 GOLDING *Calvin on Deut.* i. 6 Let vs aduise our selues to make our profit therof and let vs not be vnamendable. 1646 BAILLIE *Lett. & Jrnls.* (1841) II. 378 The Independents miserable unamendable designe to keep all things from any conclusion. 1653 tr. *Carmeni's Nissena* 10 Struck with admiration to behold those..unamendable beauties. 1729 POPE *Let. to Swift* 9 Oct., [Gay] is the same man. So is every one here that you know: mankind is unamendable. 1817 BENTHAM *Parl. Reform* Introd. 174 A pure and ever unamendable despotism. 1853 WHEWELL *Grotius* II. 277 When a man who is unamendable is removed from life, that he may not commit more or greater crimes.

**Uname·nded,** *ppl. a.* (UN-[1] 8.)

1382 WYCLIF *2 Chron.* Prol., Bot to the blame of wrijters it is to wijten, while of the vnamendid thei wrijten vnamendide thingis. 1525 LD. BERNERS *Froiss.* II. CCXXXV. [ccxxxi.] 729 This can nat longe endure vnamended. 1549 COVERDALE, etc. *Erasm. Par. 2 Cor.* 63 So wryte I..also to all such, as are offenders, yf I fynde them vnamended. 1583 GOLDING *Calvin on Deut.* iii. 681 Forasmuch as God hath called you and you continue vnamended. 1648 HEXHAM II, *Ongebetert*, Vnbettered, or Vn-amended. 1726 THEOBALD (*title*), Shakespeare restored: or, a Specimen of the Many Errors, as well Committed, as Unamended, by Mr. Pope in his Late Edition of this Poet. 1779 JOHNSON *L. P.*, *Pope* Wks. IV. 105 He never passed a fault unamended by indifference. 1853 LD. J. RUSSELL in Walpole *Life* (1889) II. 187 We surely cannot again present to him the same note unamended. 1884 *Law Times* 24 May 59/2 The present clause of the Bill, if unamended, would change that law: hence his proposal.

**Uname·rced,** *ppl. a.* (UN-[1] 8.) [1775 ASH.] 1872 BROWNING *Fifine* xxxiii, Such tribute body pays to time; but, unamerced, The soul..boasts old treasure multiplied.

**Un-Ame·rican,** *a.* [UN-[1] 7.] Not in consonance with American characteristics.

Similarly, in recent use, *un-Americanism*, *un-American-looking*.

1818 M. BIRKBECK *Notes Amer.* 28 Ninety marble capitals have been imported at vast cost from Italy,..and shew how *un*-American is the whole plan. **1894** *Daily News* 30 Apr. 5/3 However it came about, it is un-American and should be repudiated by the people. **1902** Eliz. Banks *Newspaper Girl* 55 She refused on the ground that it was both unbecoming and un-American.

**Unamiabi·lity.** [Un-[1] 12.] Unamiableness. **1829** Beddoes *Let.* in *Poems* (1851) p. lxxxvi, The ruling unamiability of the principal characters. **1866** Seeley *Ecce Homo* 154 There is an extreme degree of unamiability which quenches this love in us. **1880** 'Ouida' *Moths* II. iii. 55 It would be impossible to suspect the Princess of unamiability.

**Una·miable,** *a.* [Un-[1] 7 b and 5 b.] Not amiable, in senses of that adj.: **a.** Of things (chiefly abstract) or acts.

*c* **1480** Henryson *Fables, Trial of Fox* xx, My mycht is.. Angrie, austerne, and als vnamiable To all that standis fray to myne estait. **1565** Cooper *Thesaurus, Inamabilis*,.. vnamiable: without grace or pleasantnesse woorthie fauour. **1603** Holland *Plutarch's Mor.* 1140 If love be away,..the act thereof remaineth altogether not expetible, dishonourable, without grace and unamiable. **1708** J. Philips *Cyder* I. 563 Nor are the Hills unamiable, whose Tops To Heav'n aspire. **1796** Mme. D'Arblay *Camilla* V. 83 Extremes, nearly as pernicious, though not so unamiable as the vices. **1849** Macaulay *Hist. Eng.* iv. I. 500 Three poor labouring men, deeply imbued with this unamiable divinity, were arrested. **1884** *St. James's Gaz.* 9 Sept. 6/1 The Greenore steamer..surmounted the unamiable waves of the Channel.

**b.** Of persons.

**1711** Addison *Spect.* No. 261 ⁋ 4 True Love has ten thousand Griefs..that render a Man unamiable in the Eyes of the Person whose Affection he sollicits. **1778** Miss Burney *Evelina* xl, The distaste I already felt for these unamiable sisters. **1832** Lytton *Eugene A.* i. 4 What in the world makes a man of just pride appear so unamiable as the sense of dependence? **1884** *Spectator* 4 Oct. 1325/1 There is no more unamiable character in the whole of history than Frederick William I.

**c.** Of conduct, disposition, etc.

**1774** Mrs. Delany in *Life & Corr.* (1862) II. 65 His conduct had been unamiable and careless. **1779** *Mirror* No. 33, A tolerable person, and I think not an unamiable temper. **1818** Scott *Hrt. Midl.* xlv, This unamiable..disposition of mind broke forth in sundry unfounded criticisms. **1849** Macaulay *Hist. Eng.* iv. I. 450 His countenance and his voice must always have been unamiable. **1890** Baker *Wild Beasts* I. 306 The difficulty was increased by the cheetah making unamiable faces as the man approached.

Hence **Una·miableness, Una·miably** *adv.*

**1611** Florio, *Inamabilità*, *vnamiablenesse, vnlouingnesse. **1668** Wilkins *Real Char.* iii. vii. § 6. 341 Passive, to be done, *Unamiableness.* *a* **1797** H. Walpole *Mem. Geo. II* (1847) III. vi. 162 The unamiableness of the characters he blamed imprinted those dislikes. **1840** L. Hunt *Leg. Florence* i. i, He does her the honour of making her..Grateful return for his unamiableness, Love without bounds, in short, for his self-love. **1874** Ruskin *Val D'Arno* cxxxi. (1886) 63 Pacific Florence, in her pride of victory, was beginning to show unamiableness of temper. **1849** Macaulay *Hist. Eng.* ix. II. 423 Their national antipathies were, indeed, in that age, unreasonably and *unamiably strong.

**Una·micable,** *a.* (Un-[1] 7 b and 5 b.) **1732** Berkeley *Serm. to S. P. G.* Wks. 1871 III. 245 That narrowness of spirit which formerly kept them at such an unamicable distance from us. **Una·morous,** *a.* (Un-[1] 7.) **1668** Wilkins *Real Char.* 341 Adjective,..Active, to do, *Unamourous.* **1877** Sir H. Taylor *Autobiog.* (1885) I. 52 My admiration was wholly unamorous, but it was very ardent.

**†Unamo·ved,** *ppl. a. Sc. Obs.*—[1] [Un-[1] 8.] Unmoved.

**1513** Douglas *Æneid* ix. iii. 113 The hie curage and forcy hardyment Baid onamovit in Turnus stout entent.

**Unamu·sable,** *a.* (Un-[1] 7 b.)

**1812** *Monthly Rev.* LXVII. 143 With the revenues of a nation at his fingers-ends, he was still unamusable. **1841** *Tait's Mag.* VIII. 620 An unamusable and capricious fashionable audience. **1865** Miss Braddon *Sir Jasper* v, Ambitious Madame de Maintenon found it a hard thing to amuse the unamusable.

**Unamu·sed,** *ppl. a.* (Un-[1] 8.)

**1742** Young *Nt. Th.* ii. 246 O ye Lorenzos of our age! who deem One moment unamus'd a misery Not made for feeble man! **1795** V. Knox *Chr. Philos.* lv. 405 They fly to various scenes of public resort, in the midst of amusements, unamused. **1809** Syd. Smith in Lady Holland *Mem.* (1855) II. 55 Instead of being unamused by trifles, I am..amused by them a great deal too much. **1890** 'R. Boldrewood' *Col. Reformer* (1891) 264 He played..well enough..to enliven their somewhat unamused evenings.

**Unamu·sing,** *ppl. a.* (Un-[1] 10.)

**1799** *Mirror* No. 10, To a stranger it would have been not unamusing. **1812** *Q. Rev.* VII. 384 It cannot be unamusing to speculate on what Warburton would have achieved. **1893** Swinburne *Stud. Prose & Poetry* (1894) 74 'Wit at Several Weapons,' a violent farce, outrageous but not unamusing.

Hence **Unamu·singly** *adv.*

**1889** Swinburne *Study B. Jonson* i. 76 It is neither coarse nor tedious, and takes up but very little space; and that not unamusingly.

**Unamu·sive,** *a.* (Un-[1] 7.) **1755** Shenstone *Lett.* lxxxiii. Wks. 1777 III. 254, I have passed a very dull and unamusive winter. **Unanacreo·ntic,** *a.* (Un-[1] 7.) **1809** Malkin *Gil Blas* viii. ix. ⁋ 13, An ode of Anacreon, translated into most un-anacreontic Spanish verse.

**†Unana·lied,** *ppl. a. Sc. Obs.*—[1] [Un-[1] 8.] Unalienated.

**1508** *Reg. Privy Seal Scotl.* I. 253/1 For keping of his heretage..unsparpalit and unanalyt in favouris of his sone.

**Unanalo·gical,** *a.* (Un-[1] 7.) **1755** Johnson, *Shine*, n.s.,.. is a word, though not unanalogical, yet ungraceful, and little used. **Unana·logous,** *a.* (Un-[1] 7.) **1782** Eliz. Blower *Geo. Bateman* III. 83 For reasons totally unanalogous to real humanity. **1816** Bentham *Chrestom.* Wks. 1843 VIII. 181 An objection not unanalogous to that which is above applied to the word power. **1837** Lytton *Athens* II. 326 A conflict between the negroes and the planters in modern times, may not be unanalogous to that of the helots and the Spartans.

**Una·naly·sable,** *a.* (Un-[1] 7 b.)

**1829** Jas. Mill *Hum. Mind* (1869) II. 146 We have an indivisible, unanalysable, mode of consciousness, distinct from all modes of passive sensation. **1882** Seeley *Nat. Relig.* 47 Witness the instinctive, as we say, and unanalysable skill sometimes possessed by savages.

**Una·nalysed,** *ppl. a.* (Un-[1] 8.)

**1668** Boyle *Phys.-Chym. Ess., Salt-Petre* § 5 Some large Crystals of refin'd and unanalyz'd Nitre..appear'd to have each of them six flat sides. **1754** Warburton *Bolingbroke's Philos.* ii. 164 There he would stop: and leave the other side of the eternal reason, unanalyzed. **1794** Hutton *Philos. Light*, etc. 326 To attempt to philosophise with those vulgar notions, or unanalysed ideas, leads only to the confusion of our knowledge. **1820** Hazlitt *Table-T.* Ser. ii. ii. (1869) 37 This sort of unmeaning, unanalysed reputation. **1865** Mrs. Whitney *Gayworthys* II. 116 There was a joy of claim and confidence, unanalysed, between them in that instant. **1871** R. H. Hutton *Ess.* (1876) I. 9 Moral freedom..may be superseded..by the single unanalysed predominance of another's wish.

**Unanaly·tic,** *a.* (Un-[1] 7.) **1884** Browning *Ferishtah, Cherries* 93 My father took The..gold, Nor cared to count what sparkled here and there, Sagely unanalytic. **Unanaly·tical,** *a.* (Un-[1] 7.) **1840** Mill *Diss. & Disc.* (1859) I. 450 It would be difficult to find,..in the works of analytical minds, anything more entirely unanalytical. **1884** J. Tait *Mind in Matter* iv. 128 In unanalytical ages, the knowledge of God was moral rather than intellectual. **Unana·tomizable,** *a.* (Un-[1] 7 b.) **1861** T. L. Peacock *Gryll Gr.* xiii, What can be more pitiable than the right-hand man..with the dish twisted round.., digging..for a joint which he cannot find, and wishing the unanatomisable *volaille* behind a Russian screen with the footmen? **Una·ncestried,** *a.* (Un-[1] 9 b.) **1864** Lowell *Study Wind.* (1870) 163 As God made Adam, out of the very earth, unancestried, unprivileged, unknown.

**Una·nchor,** *v.* [Un-[2] 4 b. Cf. Du. *ontankeren.*] *trans.* To loose from anchor.

**1648** Hexham ii, *Ontanckert*, un-anckred, or, the Ancker wound up. **1649** G. Daniel *Trinarch.* To Rdr. 193 Whose Cable Pietie vn-Anchored, Yet fixt her vessell steddie, in the Bed Of many waters meeting. **1847** De Quincey *Span. Mil. Nun* Wks. 1854 III. 10 Now, then, through three-fourths of an hour Kate will have free elbow-room for unanchoring her boat.

*refl.* and *absol.* **1878** Dallinger in *Proc. Roy. Soc. Lond.* XXVII. 337 [It attaches] itself to one of the springing forms, which at once unanchors itself, and both together swim freely and vigorously about. [**1878** *Pop. Sci. Monthly* Aug. 511/2 It soon comes in contact with a colony of the organism in the perfectly flagellate condition, attaches itself to one of them, which soon unanchors, and both swim away.]

**Una·nchored,** *ppl. a.* (Un-[1] 8.)

**1651** Davenant *Gondibert* ii. vii. xxxix, She dreams Herself into possession of desires, And trusts unanchored hope in fleeting streams. **1652** Benlowes *Theoph.* iv. xxxv, All Hope's unanchor'd but in that. **1725** Pope *Odyss.* ix. 158 A port there is, inclos'd on either side, Where ships may rest, unanchor'd and unty'd. **1876** Mrs. Whitney *Sights & Ins.* II. xxxvii. 663, I had lived such a wandering, unanchored life. **1880** L. Wallace *Ben-Hur* 457 Over all the clouds floated like sailed ships unanchored.

**Una·nchylosed,** *ppl. a.* (Un-[1] 8.) **1839–47** Owen in *Todd's Cycl. Anat.* III. 269/2 In the skull of the mature Wombat..the ex-occipitals were still unanchylosed. **1854** — in *Orr's Circ. Sc., Org. Nat.* I. 217 Their pleurapophyses are unanchylosed.

**Unane·led,** *ppl. a.* Forms: 7 vnnaneld, 8 unanell'd, 9 -el'd, -eled; 8 unanneald, 8–9 -ealed, 9 -eal'd, unaneal'd, -ealed. [Un-[1] 8.] Not having received extreme unction. Also *fig.*

**1602** Shaks. *Ham.* i. v. 77 Cut off euen in the Blossomes of my Sinne, Vnhouzzled, disappointed, vnnaneld. ? **1740** W. Thompson *Hymn to May* xxix, O may the man that shall his image scorn,..Die unanell'd and dead, by dogs and kites be torn. **1759** Sterne *Tr. Shandy* ii. x, Obadiah had led him in as he was, unwiped, unappointed, unannealed. **1816** Byron *Siege Cor.* xxvii, Unanel'd he pass'd away,..To the last a Renegade. *a* **1851** Moir *De Quincey's Rev.* ii. viii, How awful it is for the soul of man Unanneal'd to pass away! **1897** Abp. Benson *Cyprian* 98 The divine acceptance of the unaneled penitent.

**Un-a·ngel,** *v.* (Un-[2] 6 b) **1641** 'Smectymnuus' *Vind. Answ.* § 13. 140 Rather then you will not prove the Angell of Thyatira to be an individuall Bishop, you will *un-Angell* him. **Unange·lic,** *a.* (Un-[1] 7.) **1890** S. J. Duncan *Soc. Depart.* 236 We,..to persuade ourselves that we had not really died and gone to heaven, took a most unangelic tiffin. **1893** W. H. Hudson *Idle Days in Patagonia* 230 We are hardly in a position just yet to dispense with the unangelic qualities, even in this exceedingly complex state. **Unange·lical,** *a.* (Un-[1] 7.) *a* **1711** Ken *Edmund* Poet. Wks. 1721 II. 96 Angel he seems, but yet methinks his speech Strives something unangelical to teach. **Una·ngered,** *ppl. a.* (Un-[1] 8.) **1813** T. Busby *Lucretius* II. vi. 465 Strike with consuming flame the Good, the Wise, And bring destruction from un-angered skies. **1909** *Westm. Gaz.* 31 July 13/1 Unhorrified, unangered, suave and grand [he] Looked on the Cid. **Una·nglican,** *a.* (Un-[1] 7.) **1842** G. S. Faber *Prov. Lett.* (1844) II. 15 Episcopal admonitions and censures..directed against their own unscriptural and unanglican speculations. **Una·ngry,** *a.* (Un-[1] 7.) **1876** Morris *Sigurd* ii. 159 Look down with unangry eyes on us to-day alive. **Una·ngular,** *a.* (Un-[1] 7.) **1756** Burke *Subl. & B.* iii. xxiv, His state of mind, on feeling soft, smooth, variegated, unangular bodies. **Unanimadve·rted,** *ppl. a.* (Un-[1] 8 c.) **1816** Keatinge *Trav.* I. 125 The state of..refinement of a people is to be judged of by what they applaud on a theatre, where the emotion may be gratified unanimadverted on. **Una·nimalized,** *ppl. a.* (Un-[1] 8.) *a* **1778** C. Darwin *Acc. Retrograde Motions* (1780) 47 A great quantity of pale unanimalized urine is discharged.

**†Una·nimate,** *a. Obs.*—[1] [f. L. *ūnanim-is, -us* + -ate [2].] Of one mind.

**1633** Cowley *Pyramus & Thisbe* 32 Age had cracked the wall which did them part, This the vnanimate couple soone did spye.

**Unanimate** (yunæ·nime[i]t), *v.* [f. as prec. + -ate [3].] *trans.* To make of one mind; to cause to be unanimous.

**1702** C. Mather *Magn. Chr.* iv. vi. 190/1 Even such was the Friendship, that Vnanimated our Oakes and our Shepard. **1886** *Sat. Rev.* 20 Nov. 683 It has become.. necessary for the great Liberal party..to unite and unanimate itself still further by a League of its own.

**†Una·nimate,** *ppl. a. Obs.* [Un-[1] 8 b and 5 b.] = Unanimated *ppl. a.* 1.

**1614** Tomkis *Albumazar* ii. v. (1615) E ij, I'le rather change fiue, then apparrell one: For men haue liuing soules, cloathes are vnanimate. **1652** Earl Monm. tr. *Bentivoglio's Hist. Relat.* 13 The..Mariners, who are the animated Instruments of Navigation,..yield not in number to the other unanimate necessaries.

**Una·nimated,** *ppl. a.* [Un-[1] 8. Cf. prec.]

**1.** Not animated or endowed with life.

**1697** Dryden *Æneis* Ded., Ess. (ed. Ker) II. 231 Part of them kindled into life, and part a lump of unformed unanimated mud. **1799** Corry *Sat. Lond.* (1803) 60 How infinitely superior are those animated originals of feminine perfection,..when compared with the unanimated beauties of even the Venus de Medici. **1834** W. Godwin *Lives Necromancers* 144 The ghost of the dead man stood erect before her, trembling at the view of his own unanimated limbs.

**2.** Dull, inanimate; not enlivened.

**1734** *Prompter* 19 Nov. 2/1 The empty, unanimated Briskness of a Fop, a Fool, or a Courtier. **1779** Johnson *L. P., Thomson* Wks. IV. 172 Of a dull countenance, and a gross, unanimated, uninviting appearance. **1815** Scott *Paul's Lett.* (1839) 193 The total absence of cattle from the fields, gives a dull and unanimated air to a French landscape. **1816** — *Old Mort.* xviii, A square face, and a set of stupid and unanimated features.

**3.** Not inspired or actuated *by* something.

**1856** R. A. Vaughan *Mystics* (1860) I. iii. iii. 70 The understanding had been over-tasked—set to work unanimated and unaided by the conscience and the heart.

**† Una·nimately,** *adv. Obs. rare.* [f. Unanimate *a.*] = Unanimously *adv.*

**1599** Nashe *Lenten Stuffe* 49 To the water foules vnanimately they recourse, and besought Ducke, and Drake, ..of their oary assistance. **1610** Marcelline *Triumphs Jas. I*, 49 So that all vnanimately or with one consent, were in duty compelled to respect him.

**Una·nimating,** *ppl. a.* (Un-[1] 10.) [**1775** Ash.] **1785** Reid *Intell. Powers* iv. iv. 388 Whose imagination..grovels in a field of mean, unanimating, and uninteresting objects. **1790** Burke *Fr. Rev.* Wks. V. 131 The still unanimating repose of publick prosperity.

**† Unanime,** *a. Obs.* Also unanim. [ad. L. *ūnanim-is, -us*, f. *ūn-us* one + *animus* mind. So F., Sp., Pg., It. *unanime.*] = Unanimous *a.*

Common 1610–1650, esp. with *consent.*

**1610** Donne *Pseudo-martyr* 213 For your first title..you haue the intire and vnanime consent and concurrence of the whole Christian Church. **1635** Pagitt *Christianogr.* App. 20 First, they make a generall Confession, which they follow the Priest in: and assent in an Unanim Amen. **1656** A. Wright *Five Serm.* 157 The frame and context of the place hath drawn that unanime Exposition from all.

Hence **†Una·nimely** *adv. Obs.*

**1625** Donne *Serm.* 3 Apr. 15 Those Fundamentall things, which are unanimely professed by both. **1626** — *Serm., John xiv. 2* (1640) 740 Where all the Fathers are unanimely and diametrally against them.

**Unanimity** (yūnăni·mĭti). Also 5 -te, 6 -tee, 6–7 -tie. [ad. OF. *unanimite* (14th c.; F. *unanimité*, = It. *unanimità*, Sp. *-idad*, Pg. *-idade*), ad. L. *ūnanimitās* (rare), f. *ūnanimis, -us*: see prec.] The state of being unanimous or of one mind; agreement in opinion.

**1436** *Libel Eng. Policy* in *Pol. Poems* (Rolls) II. 201 Set many wittes wythoutene variaunce To one accorde and unanimite. **1579** Fulke *Heskins' Parl.* 478 Our Lords sacrifices doe declare the Christian vnanimitie, which is knitted vnto him with an insuperable vnitie. **1581** Lambarde *Eiren.* i. ii. (1588) 8 To reduce the people to an vniuersall unanimitie (or agreement of minds). **1603** B. Jonson *K. Jas.'s Entertainm.* Wks. (1616) 847 Her selfe personating the vnanimity, or consent of soule, in all inhabitants of the city to his seruice. **1680** C. Nesse *Church-Hist.* 425 Christian Princes..might have by their unanimity and united armies given a stop to..this severe scourge. **1762** in *10th Rep. Hist. MSS. Comm.* App. I. 345 May it produce Peace abroad, and cheerful unanimity at home. **1781** Johnson *Let. to Mrs. Thrale* 14 Nov., I..love them because they love each other. Of this consanguineous unanimity I have had never much experience. **1822** Byron *Juan* vii. li, A general council, in which unanimity, That stranger to most councils, here prevail'd. **1859** Mill *Liberty* ii. (1865) 28/1 Persons..who form an exception to the apparent unanimity of the world on any subject. **1897** Gladstone *E. Crisis* 16 Parliament, upon that question, would speak with unanimity.

**b.** Const. *of.*

**1712** Steele *Spect.* No. 280 ⁋ 2 A certain Unanimity of Taste and Judgment. **1815** *Ann. Reg., Gen. Hist.* 65 The acceptance of the new act by nearly a unanimity of votes. **1839** James *Louis XIV*, II. 201 This unanimity of object seems to me to have given ultimate predominance to the royal party. **1869** Farrar *Fam. Speech* iii. (1873) 106 Animated by a sublime unanimity of purpose.

**Unanimous** (yunæ·niməs), *a.* [f. L. *ūnanim-is, -us*: see Unanime *a.*]

**1.** Of persons: Of one mind or opinion; agreed.

1624 DONNE *Serm.* Wks. 1839 IV. 585 Be the fathers as clear, and as unanimous as they will in it. 1637 R. HUMFREY tr. *St. Ambrose* I. 70 Let not thine unanimous friend nor thy brother know what thou dost. 1697 ADDISON *Ess. Georgics* ¶ 1 All are Unanimous in giving him the Precedence to Hesiod in his Georgics. 1744 HARRIS *Three Treat.* Wks. (1841) 43 You cannot forget (for we were both unanimous) the contempt in which we held those superficial censurers. 1783 W. THOMSON *Watson's Philip III*, VI. 475 The council was unanimous that he ought immediately to be recalled. 1849 MACAULAY *Hist. Eng.* vi. II. 146 The English Roman Catholics .. were almost unanimous in favour of the Act of Settlement. 1873 HAMERTON *Intell. Life* x. v. 388 Physicians are unanimous in their preference of early to late work.

**2.** Of beliefs, statements, actions, etc.: Exhibiting general agreement or consent.

1675 tr. *Camden's Hist. Eliz.* III. 402 The universall and unanimous Belief of all men carried it for certain Truth, that a most invincible Armada was rigged and prepared in Spain against England. 1691 WOOD *Ath. Oxon* II. 685 Dr. Atkins was nominated by the unanimous Votes of the said Presbytery. *a* 1727 NEWTON *Chronol. Amended* vi. (1728) 352 By the unanimous consent of all Chronologers. 1772 BURKE *Corr.* (1844) I. 363 Without their own vigorous and unanimous efforts in their own cause, our endeavours will be of no service. 1856 FROUDE *Hist. Eng.* (1858) II. vii. 22 The nation seemed to unite in an unanimous declaration of freedom. 1875 JOWETT *Plato* (ed. 2) V. 3 The genuineness of the Laws is sufficiently proved..by the unanimous voice of later antiquity.

**Una·nimously,** *adv.* [f. prec. + -LY [2].] In a unanimous manner.

†**1.** In unanimity or harmony. *Obs.*

*a* 1619 FOTHERBY *Atheom.* I. v. § 2 (1622) 31 'Religion [is] the foundation of euery Citie,' both gathering men, and holding them vnanimously together. 1633 BP. HALL *Hard Texts, Ps.* cxxii. 3 Jerusalem is stately built,..And is strongly, and unanimously compacted together. 1648 STANLEY *Aurora* 44 Pausanias and Aurora living and loving so unanimously that every day seemed the first of their marriage.

**2.** With unanimity; with agreement in aim, opinion, or action.

1611 SPEED *Hist. Gt. Brit.* IX. viii. § 5. 485/1 Him they had all..vnanimiously [*sic*] Elected. 1631 *Star Chamb. Cases* (Camden) 64 It was unanimously declared by the whole Court that his Majestie proceeded herein legally and rightfully for the benefit of his crowne and people. 1737 WATERLAND *Eucharist* 2 It is of great Moment..to observe what they unanimously agreed in. 1794 R. J. SULIVAN *View Nat.* xliv. II. 272 The collecting of the Sacred Writings is unanimously ascribed by both Jews and Christians to Ezra. 1826 F. REYNOLDS *Life & Times* II. 165 Being unanimously elected, I immediately assumed.. the uniform of the club. 1855 MACAULAY *Hist. Eng.* xi. III. 40 An address was unanimously voted requesting the King to take effectual steps for the suppression of the rebellion. 1884 A. R. PENNINGTON *Wiclif* ix. 289 They had unanimously resolved that they [*sc.* books] should be committed to the flames.

†**3.** In combination; conjointly. *Obs.*

1655 MRQ. WORCESTER *Cent. Inv.* § 16 A Sea-castle or Fortification..to divide it self into three Ships...And even whilest it is a Fort or Castle they shall be unanimously steered. *Ibid.* § 98.

**Una·nimousness.** [f. as prec. + -NESS.] The quality or fact of being unanimous.

[1775 ASH.] 1828–32 WEBSTER s.v., The unanimousness of a vote.

†**Una·nimy,** *v. Obs.*[−1] [f. L. *ūnanim-is*: see UNANIME *a.*] *trans.* To combine harmoniously.

1602 WARNER *Alb. Eng.* XI. lxvii. 285 With Marriage, that preferreth vs, and stayes vs in content, Vnanimieth weale or woe, as either vs is sent.

**Unannea·led,** *a.* [UN-[1] 8.] Untempered.

1745 *Phil. Trans.* XLIII. 505 Some Experiments lately made..upon the Fragility of unannealed glass Vessels. 1753 *Chambers' Cycl.* Suppl. s.v., Unannealed Bottles, or Bologna Bottles. *a* 1853 PEREIRA *Polarized Light* (1854) 149 The dissected unannealed glasses, sold in the opticians' shops. 1869 SIR E. REED *Shipbuild.* xvi. 312 We find that the drilled unannealed plates gave an average of 41·075 tons per square inch.

*fig.* 1855 BREWSTER *Newton* II. xvii. 134 The stability of a mind unannealed by the world.

**Unannealed,** variant of UNANELED *ppl. a.*

**Unanne·xed,** *ppl. a.* (UN-[1] 8.) [1775 ASH.] 1867 BURTON *Hist. Scot.* I. i. 44 The unannexed districts of the British Isles. 1884 *Pall Mall G.* 11 Oct. 1/1 The internationalization of all the unannexed lands of the world. **Unanni·hilable,** *a.* (UN-[1] 7 b.) 1678 CUDWORTH *Intell. Syst.* I. iv. § 36. 559 They were not only Eternal Emanations ..but also necessary, and therefore are they both also absolutely undestroyable and unannihilable. **Unanni·hilate,** *ppl. a.* (UN-[1] 8 b.) 1804 BLAKE *Milton* Poet. Wks. (1913) 372 Lest the Last Judgement come and find me unannihilate. **Unanni·hilated,** *ppl. a.* (UN-[1] 8.) [1775 ASH.] 1797 *Monthly Rev.* XXIII. 569 A portion even of the interest of the unannihilated debt is now discharged in specie. **Una·nnotated,** *ppl. a.* (UN-[1] 8.) 1859 G. WILSON *Mem. E. Forbes* v. (1861) 153 It is partly a Commonplace Book for unannotated extracts, partly a record of original observations. 1884 *Athenæum* 8 Mar. 310/3 An unannotated edition of the 'Poetical Works of Keats'. **Unannou·nced,** *ppl. a.* (UN-[1] 8.) [1775 ASH.] 1825 SCOTT *Talism.* xviii, Behind him glided as a spectre, unannounced, yet unopposed, the savage form of the hermit of Engaddi. 1891 HARDY *Tess* liii, Her letter made him ask himself if it would be wise to confront her unannounced in the presence of her parents.

**Unannoy·ed,** *ppl. a.* (UN-[1] 8.)

*a* 1470 HARDING *Chron.* CIV. vii, To the sea they went agayne vnanoyed. 1791 COWPER *Iliad* XIV. 487 The double guard preserv'd him unannoy'd. 1865 W. G. PALGRAVE *Arabia* II. 224 Next morning we took a small boat, and unannoyed this time by the custom-house officers..we crossed over to Moharrek.

**Unannu·lled,** *ppl. a.* (UN-[1] 8.)

1579 *Reg. Privy Council Scot.* III. 239 In respect of the said marriage standing unannullit. 1832 SOUTHEY *Hist. Penins. War* III. 63 For sanctioned it was by being allowed to appear in the Regency's Gazette unannulled and uncensured.

**Unanoi·nted,** *ppl. a.* (UN-[1] 8.)

1649 LOVELACE *Lucasta* Poems (1904) 82 Sweeter and sweeter whisleth He To un-anointed Axel-tree. 1726 BAILEY (ed. 3), *Unannealed*, unanointed, *i.e.* without extreme Unction. 1846 R. FORD *Gatherings fr. Spain* (1906) 304 In order to ensure success, no step in the official ladder must be left unanointed. 1885 *Harper's Mag.* Dec. 90/1 The wind..waltzing about with screaming and creaking an unanointed weather-cock.

**Una·nswerabi·lity.** (UN-[1] 12.) *a* 1849 POE *Marginalia* cii, The beauty of these *exposés* must lie in the precision and unanswerability with which they are given.

**Una·nswerable,** *a.* [UN-[1] 7 b.]

†**1.** Wanting in correspondence or agreement; discrepant, dissimilar. *Obs.*

1611 FLORIO, *Inrispondéuole*, vnanswerable. 1665 SIR T. HERBERT *Trav.* (1677) 86 His good will was much, but the success unanswerable. 1674 N. FAIRFAX *Bulk & Selv.* 133 Another man..may make over the beginnings of manliness.., with a liveliness no ways unanswerable.

†**b.** Const. *to.* Also quasi-*adv.* *Obs.*

(*a*) 1614 W. B. *Philosopher's Banquet* (ed. 2) 244 A man of so large a stature and bodie,..a woman so small and vnanswereable therevnto. 1616 J. HAYWARD *Sanct. Troub. Soul* I. xv. (1620) 325, I yeeld thee praises (O Lord) although base and bare, and farre vnanswerable to thy deserts. 1660 *Seas. Exhort.* 13 Our barrenness and unanswerable walking to the Gospel of Christ.

(*b*) 1657 AUSTEN *Fruit Trees* II. 93 When the enemies of God see professours..behave themselves unanswerable to their profession, these things reflect even upon God. 1670 *Devout Commun.* (1688) 175, I have walked..unanswerable to those multiplied obligations laid upon me.

**2.** That cannot be answered; not admitting of an answer.

1613 PURCHAS *Pilgrimage* IX. xv. 747 A Bishop in America hath written a large and vnanswerable Treatise of the..vnchristian Antichristian proceedings in the new World. 1690 C. NESSE *O. & N. Test.* I. 29 The unanswerable argument of [*i. e.* for] his knowledge and wisdom. 1709 BERKELEY *Th. Vision* § 1 A new and unanswerable proof of the Existence and immediate Operation of God. 1796 MME. D'ARBLAY *Camilla* VIII. x. IV. 379 Edgar sighed, but acknowledged this question to be unanswerable. 1814 BYRON *Corsair* II. xv, Oh! too convincing—dangerously dear—In woman's eye the unanswerable tear! 1852 MRS. STOWE *Uncle Tom's C.* xxviii, A solving of all moral problems by an unanswerable wisdom! 1894 MRS. DYAN *Man's Keeping* (1899) 271 She never plied him with embarrassing, unanswerable questions.

**3.** Unable to answer; irresponsible.

1884 *Manch. Exam.* 21 July 4 He committed the offence ..whilst suffering from a fit, and unanswerable for his acts.

**Una·nswerableness.** [UN-[1] 12.]

†**1.** The character of not answering or being responsive. Also const. *to.* *Obs.*

1625 BP. HALL *Serm. Thanksgiving* (1626) 21 How can we but hate this vnkind, and vnjust, vnanswerablenesse. *a* 1656 — *Rem. Wks.* (1660) 26 Being conscious..of my unanswerableness to so great expectation. 1677 GILPIN *Demonol.* (1867) 315 The greatness of the disappointment under special service, the unworthy neglect and unanswerableness to special favours, are extraordinary provocations.

**2.** The condition of not admitting of an answer.

1627 PERROT *Tithes* Ep. Ded. A ij b, That great opinion that most men have of the unanswerablenes of Mr. Seldens History of Tithes. *a* 1631 DONNE *Serm., Ps. lxxxix. 47* (1640) 267 We shall first, for our generall humiliation, consider the unanswerablenesse of this question, There is no man that lives, and shall not see death. 1817 SHELLEY *Rev. Islam* Preface *note*, A commentary illustrative of the unanswerableness of 'Political Justice'. 1879 MINTO *Defoe* 33 He proved with provoking unanswerableness that all honest Dissenters were noways concerned in the Bill.

**Una·nswerably,** *adv.* [UN-[1] 11.]

**1.** In a manner not capable of being answered or refuted; irrefutably.

1584 FENNER *Def. Ministers* (1587) 107 But vnto this we haue answered unanswerably. 1624 GATAKER *Transubst.* 68 So plainely and unanswerably doe they teach the literall understanding of our Saviours words. 1679 MARG. MASON *Tickler Tickled* 6 This was certainly and unanswerably a knowledge sufficient of the persons. 1710 STEELE *Tatler* No. 195 ¶ 6, I have unanswerably proved, that Jointures and Settlements are the Bane of Happiness. 1782 MME. D'ARBLAY *Let.* May, All you say about the annuity and the money appears to me unanswerably right. 1802 SYD. SMITH *Wks.* (1859) I. 14/2 Errors that have been so frequently, and so unanswerably exposed. 1884 LD. COLERIDGE in *Law Times Rep.* 2 Aug. 694/2 The judgment..interprets the statute quite rightly and unanswerably.

**2.** Unconformably, unsuitably.

1656 BAXTER *Reformed Pastor* (1862) 209 [To] deliver the message of God so..unanswerably to its dignity, and the need of men's souls.

**Una·nswered,** *ppl. a.* (UN-[1] 8.)

1390 GOWER *Conf.* I. 250 Bot for nothing that evere he can He mihte as thanne noght ben herd, So that his cleym is unansuerd. 1464 *Cov. Leet Bk.* 323 That hit were doughtfull sich suggestion to remayn vnanswered. 1532 MORE *Confut. Tindale* III. 281 Tyndale wolde haue sayed I hadde dissymyled, and lefte vnanswered his chyefe reason of all. 1585 T. WASHINGTON tr. *Nicholay's Voy.* I. xix. 22 [They began] to shoote at the castle with great furie, which was not leaft vnanswered. 1611 SHAKS. *Wint. T.* v. i. 229 Your Petition Is yet vn-answer'd. 1653 W. RAMESEY *Astrol. Restored* 37 The Art remains still unshaken, and it [= a book] unanswered. 1738 WESLEY *Ps.* VI. iv, Weary of my unanswered Groans, Yet still with never-ceasing Moans I languish for Relief. 1796 MME. D'ARBLAY *Camilla* II. xi, His unanswered observations contributed but little to enliven the walk. 1843 MRS. CARLYLE *Lett.* (1883) I. 276 She has left my last letter unanswered. 1901 *Spectator* 20 July 92/2 The arguments so ably re-stated..are not only unanswered but unanswerable.

**Una·nswering,** *ppl. a.* (UN-[1] 10.) 1624 SANDERSON *Serm.* I. 226 Many of the creatures being now rebellious and noysom unto man, and unanswering his commands and expectations. 1861 SIR T. MARTIN *Catullus, To Calvus* 4 When..friendship weeps, and clasps the unanswering urn. **Unantagoni·stic,** *a.* (UN-[1] 7.) 1858 STOPFORD BROOKE in Jacks *Life & Lett.* (1917) I. 110 They are on the whole such lifeless, unantagonistic creatures. **Unanta·gonized,** *ppl. a.* (UN-[1] 8.) 1862 SPENCER *First Princ.* (1870) 246 An unantagonized force in one direction. 1899 *Allbutt's Syst. Med.* VII. 376 The occurrence of rigidity..is due to the 'unantagonised' or 'unrestrained' influence exerted by the cerebellum.

**Unanti·cipated,** *ppl. a.* (UN-[1] 8.)

*a* 1779 WARBURTON *Div. Legat.* v. App., Wks. 1788 III. 183 This possibly might have recurred to his Lordship, while he was boasting of his new and unanticipated objection. 1827 FARADAY *Chem. Manip.* xxiii. 565 Those who have suddenly had occasion to collect gas from natural or unanticipated sources. 1891 MEREDITH *One of our Conq.* xxv, They left hurriedly; I think it was unanticipated by Nesta.

**Unanti·cipatingly,** *adv.* (UN-[1] 11.) 1891 MEREDITH *One of our Conq.* xxvii, She had come unanticipatingly, without design, except perhaps to get a superior being to..restrain a gambler's hand. **Unanti·cipative,** *a.* (UN-[1] 7.) 1847 H. MILLER *First Impr. Eng.* xvii. (1857) 309 They perished ignorant of the past, and unanticipative of the future. 1891 V. C. COTES *2 Girls on Barge* 6 He stood with unanticipative resignation, this old carpenter. **Una·ntiquated,** *ppl. a.* (UN-[1] 8.) 1859 RUSKIN in *R. & Rossetti* (1899) 230, I plead with you for entire clearness of modern and unantiquated expression.

**Una·nxious,** *a.* (UN-[1] 7.)

1742 YOUNG *Nt. Th.* I. 414 When young, indeed, In full content, we sometimes nobly rest, Unanxious for ourselves. *a* 1774 TUCKER *Lt. Nat.* (1834) II. 642 To keep the mind ..unanxious for success in her eagerest pursuits. 1844 THACKERAY *B. Lyndon* vi, I am not unanxious to experience on myself the effect of the war passion. 1870 W. R. GREG *Polit. Problems* 161 The career of these classes, instead of being easier and more unanxious than it was,..has become ..a ceaseless struggle.

Hence **Una·nxiously** *adv.*

1762 *J. Philips' Poems, Life* 10 This gentleman..sat as unanxiously easy as he did, even in a much humbler fortune. 1861 WISEMAN *Lenten Past.* in *Times* 12 Feb. 5/6 We can safely and unanxiously commit to..our devoted clergy the task [etc.]. 1885 FINLAYSON *Biol. Relig.* 52 He ought to do all these things unanxiously.

**Unapo·cryphal,** *a.* (UN-[1] 7.) 1644 MILTON *Areop.* (Arb.) 43 Yet God in that unapocryphall vision, said..Rise Peter, kill and eat.

**Unapologe·tic,** *a.* (UN-[1] 7. Cf. G. *unapologetisch.*)

1834 LYTTON *Pompeii* II. iv, With that sort of quiet and unapologetic air, which seemed to consider the right as a thing of course. 1868 W. R. GREG *Lit. & Soc. Judgm.* 203 The unapologetic and as it were physiological coolness of his analysis. 1892 SWINBURNE *Stud. Prose & Poetry* (1894) 236 The humorous little word of unapologetic apology.

**Unapo·statized,** *ppl. a.* (UN-[1] 8.) 1684 H. MORE *Answer* 77 The Vision .. prefigures the purity and unapostatized state of the primitive Church. *Ibid.* 367 Characterizing the true Church and unapostatized Evangelical Christians. **Unapo·statizedness.** (UN-[1] 12.) 1684 H. MORE *Answer* 411 The Purity and Unapostatizedness of the Primitive Church.

**Unaposto·lic,** *a.* (UN-[1] 7. Cf. G. *unapostolisch.*)

1675 [BP. CROFT] *Naked Truth* 25, I know full well this unapostolick way of Preaching was used by some of the Ancient Fathers. 1850 F. W. NEWMAN *Phases of Faith* 14 My repugnance to Infant Baptism was really intense, and my conviction that it is unapostolic as strong then as now. 1876 RUSKIN *Fors Clav.* lxv. 160, I can't think whom the unapostolic William was named after.

**Unaposto·lical,** *a.* (UN-[1] 7.) 1837 SYD. SMITH *Let. to Singleton* Wks. 1859 II. 158/2 An opulence which my clever friend the Examiner would pronounce to be unapostolical. **Unaposto·lically,** *adv.* (UN-[1] 11.) 1868 J. A. WYLIE *Road to Rome* xi. 142 They died, and were succeeded by others unapostolically ordained. 1884 W. S. LILLY *Anc. Relig. & Mod. Th.* 64 [Evangelicalism] had ended unapostolically in the preaching of foolishness.

†**Unappai·r,** *v. Obs.*[−1] [UN-[1] 15.] *intr.* To become impaired, to fade.

1426 LYDG. *De Guil. Pilgr.* 19210 Lyche a ffloure that dothe vnapayre Whanne it is plukkyd and leyde lowe.

†**Unappai·rable,** *a. Obs.*[−1] [UN-[1] 7 b.] Incapable of being impaired; unfading.

1574 tr. *Marlorat's Apocalips* 300 It signifieth y[t] the blissed sort are crowned with an vnappairable & flaming crowne of euerlasting life.

†**Unappai·red,** *ppl. a. Obs.* [UN-[1] 8.] Unimpaired.

1561 T. NORTON *Calvin's Inst.* IV. 161 Y[t] euery man may kepe his own safe & vnappeired. 1571 GOLDING *Calvin on Ps.* ii. 4 His power..contineweth sauf and unappayred, whatsoever men doo practise against it. 1587 — *De Mornay* xiv. 199 Ye shall see a man forgoe all his sences..and yet haue both life and reason vnappayred.

**Unappa·lled,** *ppl. a.* (UN-[1] 8.)

1578 BANISTER *Hist. Man* VII. 89 Others, with senses vnappalled,..haue plowed a path directly over the mountaine. 1586 T. B. *La Primaud. Fr. Acad.* (1589) 282 Sustaining also with a great and unappalled hart, most cruel torments. 1611 SPEED *Hist. Gt. Brit.* IX. vii. § 68 Applying vnto him certaine verses of Lucan, in commendation of his vnapalled constancy. 1671 MILTON *P. R.* IV. 425 Some bent at thee thir fiery darts, while thou Sat'st unappall'd in calm and sinless peace 1713 Young *Last Day* III. 168 The sons of light scarce unappal'd look down. *a* 1774 Tucker *Lt. Nat.* (1834) II. 229 Unhurt by toils and labours, unappalled by dangers. 1821 Scott *Pirate* xxxvii, The unappalled, dignified, and commanding manner of Minna Troil over-awed him. 1851 Longf. *Gold. Leg.* I. *Castle of Vautsberg*, Unappalled By fear of death, or priestly word.

**† Unappa·rel,** *v. Obs.* [Un-² 4.] *trans.* To disrobe, undress. Also *fig.*

1577 Hanmer *Anc. Eccl. Hist.* (1663) 65 The fiery pile being prepared, he unapparelled himself. 1586 J. Mush *Life Margt. Clitherow* (1849) 194 She requested them that the women might unapparel her. 1602 Middleton *Blurt Master Constable* II. ii. D ij, Ladies vnapparell your deare beauties. 1614 Donne *Obsequies Ld. Harrington* 12 That I can studie thee, And, by these meditations refin'd, Can unapparell and enlarge my minde.

**Unappa·relled,** *ppl. a.* (Un-¹ 8.)

1622 Bacon *Holy War* (1629) 103 In Peru, though they were unapparelled People, according to the Clime [etc.]. 1624 Quarles *Job* Sect. xv. M j b, If e're (alone) my lips did taste my bread,.. Or bent my hand to doe the Orphane wrong, Or saw him naked, vnapparell'd long. 1656 Heylin *Surv. France* 118 Most immodestly unapparelled. 1872 Calverley *Fly Leaves* (1903) 93 All unapparell'd, barefoot all, She ran to that old ruin'd wall.

**Unappa·rent,** *a.* (Un-¹ 7.)

1554 Knox *Faythfull Admon.* F 8 b, To..obeye that whych God commaundeth is neuer so harde, so vnapparent or contrarie to their affeccions. 1614 Latham *Falconry* (1633) 102 For the liuer or the disease thereof, is so secret and vnapparant, that..it is neuer mistrusted nor thought of. 1645 Milton *Tetrach.* Wks. 1851 IV. 193 Bitter actions of despight too suttle and too unapparent for Law to deal with. 1667 — *P. L.* VII. 103 He heares..the rising Birth Of Nature from the unapparent Deep. 1725 Pope *Odyss.* II. 152 On foreign shores Ulysses treads, Or glides a ghost with unapparent shades. 1755 Young *Centaur* i. Wks. 1757 IV. 129 A fire elemental is diffused through all nature, though .. unapparent in most parts of our globe. 1816 Shelley *Dæmon* I. 42 The dark blue orbs that burn below With unapparent fire. 1890 Hosmer *Anglo-Sax. Freedom* 129 Nowhere, probably, was the popular moot utterly unapparent.

*absol.* 1821 Shelley *Adonais* xlv, The inheritors of unfulfilled renown Rose from their thrones, built beyond mortal thought, Far in the Unapparent.

Hence **Unappa·rently** *adv.*

1599 Sandys *Europæ Spec.* (1632) 94 To avoid the contagion of the disease or seducement by the dangerously and unapparently diseased.

**† Unappa·ssionate,** *a.* (Un-¹ 7), **-ately** *adv.* (Un-¹ 11.)

1598 Yong *Diana* 53 If Paris had iudged like a prudent and vnappassionate iudge. *Ibid.* 148 But thinking of the matter vnappassionately, it was now better for me.

**Unappea·lable,** *a.* [Un-¹ 7 b.] That cannot be appealed against (or *from*).

1635 J. Hayward tr. *Biondi's Banish'd Virg.* 30 An unappealable sentence of death. 1642 *Vind. King* 15 The sole unappealable Judge of all things. 1678 Cudworth *Intell. Syst.* I. v. 898 There being no ultimate judgment unappealable from, there could never be any final determination of controversies. 1747 Carte *Hist. Eng.* I. 259 The Bishops..maintaining their just and unappealable authority. 1786 Seward *Lett.* (1811) I. 229 A man of ability, with an air of unappealable decision, perpetually pronouncing in modern poets that to be obscure, which is clear as day-light. 1860 Ld. Lytton *Lucile* II. iv. § I. 11 Muse or Spirit, that inspirest..the deep drama of man !.. First and last unappealable arbitress, thou ! 1874 Gladstone *Rome*, etc., *Vatican Decrees* 38 The judgments of this Pope..are unappealable and irreversible.

Hence **Unappea·lableness, -ably** *adv.*

1651 Durham *Maran-atha* (1652) 23 The un-appealablenesse from this judgement. 1840 De Quincey *Mod. Superstit.* Wks. 1854 III. 314 The *victa causa*..stood, as regarded heavenly verdicts, unappealably condemned.

**Unappea·ling,** *ppl. a.* (Un-¹ 10.) 1846 Worcester (citing South). 1856 Ruskin *Mod. Paint.* IV. v. xviii. § 9 Without some correlative understanding in the spectator, Titian's work..must be utterly dead and unappealing to him. 1865 C. Stanford *Symb. Christ* vii. (1878) 190 Hidden meanings sparkle out from lines in his Bible that before seemed blank and unappealing.

**† Unappea·ring,** *ppl. a. Obs.* [Un-¹ 10.] Unapparent.

1554 Knox *Faythf. Admon.* H 7 b, God hath a thousand meanes (very unapperyng to mannes iudgement) wherby he wyll delyuer..his afflicted churche. 1638 Mayne *Lucian* (1664) 388, I plainly see the Images of all things, you unappearing; my self elsewhere. 1640 Fuller *Joseph's Coat* I. (1867) 108 Their knowledge..[being] increased insensibly and by unappearing degrees.

**Unappea·sable,** *a.* [Un-¹ 7 b.] That cannot be appeased or placated; implacable, insatiable: **a.** Of feelings, activities, etc.

1561 T. Norton *Calvin's Inst.* II. vii. (1634) 158 They presse us, I say, and doe pursue us with an unappeasable rigour. 1571 Golding *Calvin on Ps.* xxxiv. 1 He..burned against him with unappeasable hatred. 1581 J. Bell *Haddon's Answ. Osor.* 407 Such unappeasable contention and brawlyng about the mainteynaunce of Purgatory. 1602 Warner *Alb. Eng.* Epit. 360 They pursued such vnapeasable and tyrannous warre that [etc.]. 1671 Milton *Samson* 963 Thy anger, unappeasable, still rages, Eternal tempest never to be calm'd. 1779 Johnson *L. P.*, *Addison* ¶ 37 The author..wandered..behind the scenes with restless and unappeasable solicitude. 1822 Lamb *Elia* I. *Artif. Comedy*, The eternal tormenting unappeasable vigilance.. of present fashionable tragedy. 1845 Hamilton *Pop. Educ.* ix. (ed. 2) 256 The ambition of the Papal See is unappeasable. 1870 Lowell *Among my Bks.* Ser. I. (1873) 292 The unappeasable apprehension of a German for his biographer.

**b.** Of persons (or other agents).

1577 tr. *Bullinger's Decades* (1592) 574 There is no faith in a hard, stubborne, and vnappeasable man. 1578 *Chr. Prayers* in *Priv. Prayers* (1851) 543 Set thyself in our defence against this our unappeasable adversary. 1611 Speed *Hist. Gt. Brit.* IX. xx. 31 The turbulent, and vnappeaceable Dutchesse of Burgundy. 1632 Lithgow *Trav.* I. 26 [They are] so vnappeasable in anger, that they cowardly murther their enemies. *a* 1711 Ken *Hymns Festiv.* Poet. Wks. 1721 I. 234 With envious Rage I saw them swell, All unappeasable as Hell. 1839 Dickens *Nickleby* xliii, A real live furious and most unappeasable Saracen. 1872 M. Collins *Two Plunges for Pearl* I. ix. 183 One makes it a vast machine, moving blindly in an unalterable groove, driven by an unappeasable fate.

Hence **Unappea·sableness, -ably** *adv.*

1611 Florio, *Implacabilita*, vnappeasablenesse. [Also in Bailey and Ash.] 1647 Hexham I, Vnappeasably, *onversoeneliicken*. 1837 Lytton *Athens* II. 310 Those twin rocks ..between which the sea..roars unappeasably through its mists of foam. 1865 Carlyle *Fredk. Gt.* XXI. v. (1872) X. 63 He grieves unappeasably to have lost Friedrich. 1871 Lowell *Stud. Wind.* (1886) 129 He is pertinaciously and unappeasably dull.

**Unappea·sed,** *ppl. a.* (Un-¹ 8.)

1588 Shaks. *Tit. A.* I. i. 100 Giue vs the proudest prisoner of the Gothes, That we may..sacrifice his flesh :..That so the shadowes be not vnappeas'd. 1597 Hooker *Eccl. Pol.* v. xlviii. § 9 Gods heauie indignation and wrath towards mankinde as yet vnappeased. *a* 1637 B. Jonson *Horace's Art Poet.* 172 If againe Honour'd Achilles' chance by thee be seiz'd, Keepe him still active, angry, un-appeas'd. 1718 Pope *Iliad* XIV. 567 Not unappeased he enters Pluto's gate, Who leaves a brother to revenge his fate. 1828 Lytton *Pelham* III. xiii, He was too lost in his still unappeased rage to heed me. 1864 R. F. Burton *Mission to Gelele* I. 9 The unappeased elements gathered strength for a fresh outburst.

**† Unappe·llable,** *a. Obs.*—¹ [Un-¹ 7 b: cf. Appellate *ppl. a.*] = Unappealable *a.*

1661 Feltham *Resolves* (ed. 8) II. lxxxiii. 370 Who shall be Judg, whether..I shall take upon me to be supreme and unappellable?

**Unappen·daged,** *a.* (Un-¹ 9.) 1827 Pollok *Course T.* VIII. 107 It was a congregation vast of men: Of unappendaged and unvarnished men.

**† Unapperceived,** *ppl. a. Obs. rare.* [Un-¹ 8.] Unperceived.

1390 Gower *Conf.* II. 337 Wher that Diane hirselve stod, Sche thoghte come unaperceived. *Ibid.* 367 His pourpos aboute he broghte, And wente awey unaparceived.

**Unappertai·ning,** *ppl. a.* (Un-¹ 10.) 1645 Symonds *Diary* (Camden) 274 Tire others easier eares with these Unapperteyning storyes. 1800 W. Taylor n Robberds *Mem.* (1843) I. 344, I steadily disadvise spoiling your new edition of Chatterton by tacking to it any unappertaining stuff of mine. **Una·ppetizing,** *ppl. a.* (Un-¹ 10.) 1884 *Graphic* 18 Oct. 399/2 The food is too often frequently coarsely-prepared, pretentious and unappetising. 1890 *Times* 15 Mar. 11/2 Within the unappetizing husk which surrounds the question there is a kernel of interest.

**Unapplau·ded,** *ppl. a.* (Un-¹ 8.)

1739 R. Bull tr. *Dedekindus' Grobianus* 153 You'll something find to act, as well as they, Nor unapplauded be for what you say. *a* 1774 Goldsm. tr. *Scarron's Com. Romance* (1775) I. 9 His merit did not pass unobserved or unapplauded. 1855 [J. R. Leifchild] *Cornwall* 293, I should envy the man that faith of assurance which could support him in such an extremity..unwitnessed, unapplauded. 1863 Kinglake *Crimea* II. 112 The patient unapplauded toil by which he prepared the end.

**Unapplau·sive,** *a.* (Un-¹ 7.) 1837 Carlyle *Fr. Rev.* II. v. x, At which Festival the Public again assists, *unapplausive*. 1872 Geo. Eliot *Middlem.* xx, The cold, shadowy, unapplausive audience of his life.

**† Unappli·able,** *a. Obs.* [Un-¹ 7 b.] Inapplicable.

1588 J. Harvey *Disc. Probl.* 96 Shall you not find the said esteemed number of that yeere vnapliable to any such purposes, or intents? 1644 Milton *Areop.* (Arb.) 44 Best books to a naughty mind are not unappliable to occasions of evill. *a* 1661 Fuller *Worthies, Cambridge*. I. (1662) 150 All unappliable in any peculiar manner to the people of this County. 1675 R. Burthogge *Causa Dei* 116 Who seeth not how unapplyable to either Proposition in the mention'd Argument this Answer is?

**Unappli·anced,** *a.* (Un-¹ 9.) 1844 Talfourd *Athenian Captive* IV. ii, The sun-like face Of unappllanced virtue.

**† Una·pplicable,** *a. Obs.* [Un-¹ 7 b.] = Inapplicable *a.*

1647 Clarendon *Hist. Reb.* v. § 11 His Majesty..saw all those..either totally aliened from his service,..or, like men in a trance, unapplicable to it. 1690 Locke *Hum. Und.* IV. xii. § 7 The Ideas that demonstratively shew the equality or inequality of unapplicable Quantities. 1741 C. Middleton *Cicero* I. vi. 406 A consecration, legally performed, made the thing consecrated unapplicable ever after to any private use. 1765 Blackstone *Comm.* I. 12 The Roman pandects will furnish us with a piece of history not unapplicable to our present purpose.

**Unapplie·d,** *ppl. a.* [Un-¹ 8.] Not applied, in various senses.

1540 Hyrde tr. *Vives' Instr. Chr. Wom.* I. i. 1 Quintilian in his boke, where he doth instruct and teache an oratour, wylleth his begynnyng and entrance to be taken from the cradel, and no tyme to be slacked vnaplied towarde thende and purpose of the faccultee entended. 1605 Bacon *Adv. Learn.* II. xxi. § 5 Because they were men dedicated to a private, free, unapplied course of life. 1681 Flavel *Meth. Grace* i. 2 Never was any wound healed by a prepared, but unapplied plaister. 1751 Warburton *Pope's Wks.* IV. 28 *note*, While a character is unapplied, all the various parts of it will be considered together. 1785 J. Phillips *Treat. Inland Nav.* 39 The money would lie useless and unapplied a great part of the time. 1832 Babbage *Econ. Manuf.* xxxv. (ed. 3) 388 We may remark that the sea itself offers a perennial source of power hitherto almost unapplied. 1889 S. Walpole *Ld. J. Russell* I. 272 The remedies which Lord John had desired to provide were still unapplied.

**Unappoi·nt,** *v.* [Un-² 3.] *trans.* To cancel.

1682 Mrs. Behn *City Heiress* IV. i, 'Twas an appointment only, hum, which I shall now make bold to unappoint, render null, void, and of none effect.

**Unappoi·ntable,** *a.* (Un-¹ 7 b.)

1664 H. More *Myst. Iniq.* 95 This Infallible Judge being not appointed by God, and being unappointable by man. 1836 Carlyle *Corr. w. Emerson* (1883) I. 103, I suppose there is no more unpromotable, unappointable man now living in England than I.

**Unappoi·nted,** *ppl. a.* [Un-¹ 8.]

**1.** Not appointed, in various senses.

1560 Pilkington *Expos. Aggeus* I iij, Nay how shall they come together, except place and time be appoynted? How shal they know when and whither to resort, vnappoynted? *a* 1586 Sidney *Arcadia* III. v. (1912) 377 Else the very griefe & feare would prove her unappointed executioners. 1782 V. Knox *Ess.* vi. (1819) I. 34 The operations of this engine of oppression, in the hands of an interested plebeian, unappointed, unauthorised. 1800 *Law Rep.* 29 Ch. Div. 521 So much thereof as should remain unappointed or undisposed of.

**2.** Not fitted out with requisites; unequipped.

1579 Gosson *Sch. Abuse* (Arb.) 64 Finding them selues vnappointed for the fielde, [they] keepe a farre off. 1759 [see Unaneled *ppl. a.*]. 1837 Carlyle *Fr. Rev.* II. v. xi, Troops badly commanded, shall we say? Or troops intrinsically bad? Unappointed, undisciplined, mutinous.

**Unappo·rtioned,** *ppl. a.* (Un-¹ 8.) [1775 Ash.] 1792 A. Hamilton *Wks.* (1886) VII. 53 This second process leaves a residue of eight out of the 120 members unapportioned. **Una·ppositely,** *adv.* (Un-¹ 11.) 1680 H. More *Apocal. Apoc.* Epil. 292 To the fourth and last [argument] he answers not unappositely.

**Unappre·ciable,** *a.* [Un-¹ 7 b and 5 b.] Inappreciable.

1822 *Blackw. Mag.* XII. 53 After reading the above unappreciable epistle..we forthwith sweetened our fragrant lymph with two supernumerary lumps. 1849 F. W. Newman *Soul* iv. § 2 Where that holy spirit of Intercession lives, the whole man must be wonderfully perfect, nor would this be an unappreciable fact. 1864 *Times* 24 Dec., It was never worth while for the sake of a sum which would be unappreciable as a national debt to create an unpopular..system of national taxation.

**Unappre·ciated,** *ppl. a.* [Un-¹ 8.] **a.** Not duly appreciated or valued. **b.** Not properly estimated.

1828–32 Webster. 1835 *Court Mag.* VI. 132 Though her powers in parts of passion, energy and pathos, are not unappreciated. 1868 Miss Braddon *Run to Earth* III. i. 5 She loves him, although she knows that her affection is unreturned, unappreciated. 1893 Liddon, etc. *Life Pusey* I. xi. 271 The yet unappreciated power of Romanism.

**Unappre·ciating,** *ppl. a.* (Un-¹ 10.) 1833 S. Austin *Charac. Goethe* I. 304 The unworthy and unappreciating mention of such names as Wordsworth, Southey, and Coleridge. 1871 Tylor *Prim. Cult.* I. 20 The unappreciating hatred and ridicule that is lavished by narrow hostile zeal on Brahmanism, Buddhism, Zoroastrism. **Unapprecia·tion.** (Un-¹ 12 and 5 b.) 1886 *Pall Mall G.* 29 Jan. 8/2 A singular unappreciation of the condition of things. **Unappre·ciative,** *a.* (Un-¹ 7 and 5 b.) 1857 C. E. Norton *Lett.* (1913) I. iv. 172 The reviews are cold and unappreciative. 1868 Visct. Strangford *Selection* (1869) I. 202 It is full time to enter into a special examination of his Eastern policy, contrasting it, when necessary, with his own curiously unappreciative exposition of the same.

**Unapprehe·nded,** *ppl. a.* [Un-¹ 8.]

**1.** Not apprehended by the mind.

1597 Hooker *Eccl. Pol.* v. ii. § 1 They of whom God is altogether vnapprehended, are but few in number. 1668 Clarendon *Vind.* Tracts (1727) 48 Bringing heinous crimes to light..by means unapprehended by the guilty. 1896 A. Morrison *Child of the Jago* xxi. 205 He had a shapeless, unapprehended notion that Canary was the sole creature alive that could understand and feel with him.

**2.** Not arrested.

1611 Cotgr., *Descalengé*, vnarrested, vnapprehended. 1764 Burn *Poor Laws* 207 The clause..whereby a rogue and vagabond..was to be sent to the place where he last passed unapprehended.

**Unapprehe·nding,** *ppl. a.* [Un-¹ 10.] Lacking in apprehension.

1794 Godwin *Caleb Williams* 112 How much had he to struggle with in this respect in the unapprehending obstinacy of some of his Macedonians? 1891 Hardy *Tess* xxxv, You are an unapprehending peasant woman.

**† Unapprehe·nsible,** *a. Obs.* [Un-¹ 7, 5 b.]

**1.** That cannot be apprehended.

1613 Sir W. Alexander in Sidney *Arcadia* (1622) 333 O how the soule, apt for all impressions transcending reason, can comprehend unapprehensible things! *a* 1715 South *Serm.* (1744) VII. 94 Which assertions..leave it unapprehensible what place can reasonably be left for addressing exhortations to the will. *a* 1761 Law *Behmen's Myst. Magnum* xx. (1772) 85 It stood hidden in God, and was unapprehensible.

**2.** Incapable of apprehending.

1613 Heywood *Bras. Age* II. ii, How harshly doth your wisedome sound in th'eares Of these Barbarians, dull, vnapprehensible.

**Unapprehe·nsive,** *a.* [Un-¹ 7 and 5 b.]

**1.** Not apprehensive or quick to understand; stupid, unintelligent.

1624 Donne *Devot.* Med. xiv. (ed. 2) 321 When they [*sc.* honours and pleasures] come in an vnapprehensive Age, they come..as a Pardon, when the head is off. 1670 Milton *Hist. Eng.* III. Wks. 1851 V. 130 Unapprehensive, yet impudent; suttle Prowlers, Pastors in Name, but indeed Wolves. 1770 Gray in *Corr. w. Nicholls* (1843) 104 Pray let the next you send me be halt and blind, dull, unapprehensive, and wrong headed. 1786 *Francis the Philanthropist* I. 66 The wine was sour, the sheets wet,.. and the servants unapprehensive and impertinent. 1825 Scott *Betrothed* v, Frame not thyself more unapprehensive than nature hath formed thee. 1840 J. H. Newman *Par. Serm.* (1842) V. iii. 41 They look at them as infants gaze at the objects which meet their eyes, in a vague unapprehensive way.

**2.** Not anticipative or fearful *of* danger, etc.

**1666** W. Boghurst *Loimographia* (1894) 28 The patient being unapprehensive of his danger. **1672** Wilkins *Nat. Relig.* 267 That stupor and benummedness of spirit, whereby men are made unapprehensive of their afflictions. **1728** Eliza Heywood tr. *Mme. de Gomez's Belle A.* (1732) II. 227 Unapprehensive of the Destiny which attended him. **1805** Wordsw. *Prelude* II. 455 And for this cause to thee I speak, unapprehensive of contempt. **1854** J. S. C. Abbott *Napoleon* (1885) I. xxvi. 409 For there were thousands of travelers on the Continent, unapprehensive of danger.

**b.** With clause, or without const.

*a* **1705** J. Howe *Living Temple* I. ii. § 8, I am not unapprehensive that I might..have proceeded in another method. **1742** Blair *Grave* 477 In gamesome Mood To frolick on Eternity's dread Brink, Unapprehensive. **1753** Richardson *Grandison* (1781) I. xxxix. 283 My heart is a little lighter: Yet not unapprehensive. **1829** Scott *Anne of G.* ix, In the hour of unaffected and unapprehensive ease and simplicity. **1853** Kane *Grinnell Exp.* xxxvii. (1856) 340 *note*, The animals were entirely unapprehensive.

**Unapprehe·nsively,** *adv.* [Un-1 11 b.] † Undiscoverably, imperceptibly.

*a* **1659** Osborne *Observ. Turks* Wks. (1673) 317 Till a reverence..be real, or unapprehensively feigned, it is folly to expect performance of Oaths in the Members.

**Unapprehe·nsiveness.** [Un-1 12.] Lack of apprehension.

**1661** Baxter *Mor. Prognost.* (1680) I. § 4 If..a Natural Unapprehensiveness Blocks up the Way, even Time and Labour will never..bring any, to any great Eminency of Understanding. **1671** Woodhead *St. Teresa* II. xix. 127 By reason of the Unapprehensiveness which God puts into us. **1748** Richardson *Clarissa* (1811) III. ii. 6 Unthinking creatures have some comfort in the shortness of their views; in their unapprehensiveness. *c* **1833** Mrs. Sherwood *Life* xxxi. (1854) 567 That unaccountable unapprehensiveness which so often foreruns any severe affliction.

**Unappre·nticed,** *ppl. a.* (Un-1 8.) [1775 Ash.] **1809** *Crit. Rev.* XVI. 500 How many await, unapprenticed, for the interference of some overseer in their behalf?

**Unappri·sed,** *ppl. a.* [Un-1 8.] Not apprised or informed: **a.** Const. *of.*

**1728** R. Morris *Ess. Anc. Archit.* p. xxii, Those who are unappriz'd of the minuter Proportions. **1798** S. & Ht. Lee *Canterb. T.* II. 58 But he, unapprised of the anxious expectation he excited, loitered by the way. **1835** I. Taylor *Spir. Despot.* iv. 144 The author must not be supposed.. unapprised of the vast controversy of which it has been the subject. **1852** Mundy *Antipodes* (1857) 211 Aware that Darlington had been a Probation Station, and unapprised of its abandonment.

**b.** With dependent clause, or without const.

**1742** Young *Nt. Th.* v. 539 Some mischievously weep, not unappris'd, Tears, sometimes, aid the conquest of an eye. **1746** Wesley *Princ. Methodist* 49, I suppose, you are not unapprized, That during this Period..they were continually relieved by the Prayers of the Faithful. **1783** Pott *Chirurg. Wks.* II. 65, I also am not unapprized what influence a successful operation has had. **1816** P. Hervé *Beauties of Paris* I. 238 Truly mortifying is it to the unapprized visitor to one of the first theatres in Europe, to find [etc.] **1847** Grote *Greece* II. xxxii. (1862) IV. 268 They doubtless were not unapprised that the Spartans had actually equipped an army for the support of Crœsus.

**Unapproachabi·lity.** (Un-1 12 and 5 b.) **1846** Mrs. Gore *Eng. Char.* Introd., My Lord Duke, no longer arrayed in his star, garter, and unapproachability, can be trafficked with. **1902** S. E. White *Blazed Trail* xxx, The lumber-jack demands in his boss a certain fundamental unapproachability.

**Unapproa·chable,** *a.* (and *sb.*). [Un-1 7 b and 5 b.]

**1.** Of things or places: That cannot be approached; inaccessible.

**1581** A. Gilby *Test. 12 Patriarchs* 28 We went to a strong walled, and vnapproachable Citie..whiche threatened to kill vs. **1583** Golding *Calvin on Deut.* xxii. 130 To the ende that wee shoulde learne to be humble and to know that hee dwelleth in vnapproachable light. **1625** K. Long tr. *Barclay's Argenis* III. vii. 175 The Hill is unapproachable toward the Sea-side. **1685** Boyle *High Veneration* § 6. 5 God..is said to inhabite an unapproachable Light, which humane Speculations cannot penetrate. **1742** Young *Nt. Th.* IX. 850 He resides above them all, In glory's unapproachable recess. **1816** Scott *Old Mort.* xliii, All alone, and in a place of almost unapproachable seclusion. **1891** Farrar *Darkn. & Dawn* l, There were districts in which the heat was so intense that they were unapproachable.

*fig.* **1686** tr. *Chardin's Trav. Persia* 51 Which sort of Policy, having neither Art nor Principles, was as it were unapproachable.

**2.** That cannot be approached in confidence or intimacy.

**1848** Dickens *Dombey* liii, Mr. Dombey is unapproachable by any one, and his state of mind is haughty, rash, unreasonable, and ungovernable, now. **1855** — *Mut. Fr.* III. viii, All such things she would hear discussed, as we..in our unapproachable magnificence never hear them. **1904** Mrs. M. Creighton *Life Bp. Creighton* vi. I. 158 The fisherfolk ..had..the most imagination, and the hinds were the most unapproachable.

**3.** Beyond the reach of rivalry; matchless.

**1831** Carlyle *Sart. Res.* III. xi, The epithet *schneidermässig* (tailor-like) betokens an otherwise unapproachable degree of pusillanimity. **1856** Froude *Hist. Eng.* (1858) I. i. 68 Out of the illuminations arose those paintings which remain unapproached and unapproachable in their excellence. **1871** E. F. Burr *Ad Fidem* xiv. 280 A sermon of unapproachable eloquence, and pathos.

**4.** *absol.* as *sb.* One who, or that which, cannot be approached or equalled.

**1800** Coleridge *Piccolom.* III. i, We shall view The Unapproachable glide out in splendour. **1821** Shelley *Sonn. Byron* 6 A worm whose life may share A portion of the unapproachable. **1886** *Academy* 22 May 357/3 One or two [translations] from Heine come as near to the unapproachable as can fairly be expected.

Hence **Unapproa·chableness, -ably** *adv.*

**1727** Bailey (vol. II), *Inaccessibleness*, *unapproachableness. **1825** *Eng. Life* II. 82 He became resolutely silent and did not attempt to overcome his unapproachableness. **1874** Lisle Carr *J. Gwynne* I. iii. 94 The unapproachableness of the disdainful governess. **1846** Worcester, **Unapproachably*, so as not to be approached. Dr. Allen. **1863** Ld. Lytton *Ring Amasis* I. 36 The habitual consciousness of an unapproachably high social position. **1890** 'R. Boldrewood' *Miner's Right* (1899) 177/2 The illustrious Jake Challerson, unapproachably apparelled, redolent of fabulous wealth.

**Unapproa·ched,** *ppl. a.* [Un-1 8.] Not approached; not reached by advance (in space or attainment).

**1667** Milton *P. L.* III. 4 Since God is light, And never but in unapproached light Dwelt from Eternitie. **1725** Pope *Odyss.* XIX. 53 Celestials, mantl'd in excess of light, Can visit unapproach'd by mortal sight. **1817** Wordsw. *Lament Mary Q. Scots* 19 Me, unapproached by any friend, Save those who to my sorrows lend Tears due unto their own. **1856** [see Unapproachable *a.* 3]. **1864** *Realm* 22 June 8 To form..a national style such as is yet unapproached by native composers.

*absol.* *c* **1854** Faber *Hymn*, '*Harsh Judgements*' x, Thou art the Unapproached, whose height Enables Thee to stoop.

**Unappro·priate,** *ppl. a.* [Un-1 8 b, 5 b.]

**1.** Not appropriated or assigned.

**1767** Warburton *Serm.* Wks. 1788 V. 513 Goods, which God, at first, created un-appropriate; and Nature threw in common to all her children. **1832** C. M. Goodridge *Voy. South Seas* Title-p., A Statistical View of Van Diemen's Land, Giving its..Roads and Public Works, Unappropriate Land [etc.].

**2.** = Inappropriate *a.*

**1818** Bentham *Ch. Eng., Catech. Exam.* 153 With the exception of the Scriptural, and surely not unappropriate, part of the subject. **1822** T. Taylor *Apuleius* 234 He assigned unappropriate causes. **1898** *Daily News* 12 May 7/5 He would not say that the treatment..would be unappropriate for pelvic inflammation.

Hence **Unappro·priateness.**

**1838** [Mrs. Maitland] *Lett. fr. Madras* (1843) 208 They had contrived with great ingenuity every possible unappropriateness that could be devised.

**Unappro·priated,** *ppl. a.* [Un-1 8.]

**1.** Not allocated or assigned to a special person, thing, or purpose.

**1756** J. Warton *Ess. Pope* I. iii. 147 Ovid could not restrain the luxuriancy of his genius..from wandering with an endless variety of flowery and unappropriated similitudes. **1791** Boswell *Johnson* II. 365 He has not owned to whom he was obliged; so that the acknowledgement is unappropriated to his Grace. **1806** Surr *Winter in Lond.* I. 21 There remained thirty thousand pounds unappropriated, and the whole was at her own disposal. **1872** Howells *Wedding Journ.* (1892) 310 She had found..certain odd corners in her trunks still unappropriated.

**2.** Not taken in possession by any one.

**1776** Burney *Hist. Mus.* I. 1 The land of conjecture, however, is so extensive and unappropriated, that every new cultivator has a right to break up fresh ground. **1796** Mathias *Purs. Lit.* II. (1797) 24 This character..shall ever remain unappropriated by me. **1814** Jane Austen *Mansf. Park* viii, The envied seat, the post of honour, was unappropriated. **1884** *Law Times Rep.* 19 Apr. 230/2 A common supply of unappropriated water in deep water-bearing strata.

**Unappro·priating,** *vbl. sb.* (Un-2 3.) **1641** Milton *Reform.* II. 85 The unappropriating, and unmonopolizing the rewards of learning and industry, from the greasie clutch of ignorance, and high feeding. **Unappro·vable,** *a.* (Un-1 7 b.) **1647** Trapp *Comm., 2 Cor.* xiii. 6 We are no reprobates, counterfeits, or unapprovable, opposed to approved. **1685** H. More *Reflect. Baxter* 1 Seven unapprovable Particulars noted in the said Advertisement.

**Unappro·ved,** *ppl. a.* [Un-1 8.]

**†1.** Not proved to be skilled. *Obs.*[-1]

**1421** *Rolls of Parlt.* IV. 158/1 Many unconnyng an[d] unapproved in the forsayd science practiseth.

**†2.** Not demonstrated; unproved. *Obs.*

**1597** Shaks. *Lover's Compl.* 53 O false blood thou register of lies, What vnapproued witnes doost thou beare! **1597** Hooker *Eccl. Pol.* v. lxii. § 16 The nullity of baptism in regard of the like defect is only a few men's new, ungrounded, and as yet unapproved imagination. **1598** Florio *Dict.* Ep. Ded., Rashnes in assuming so much for it that yet is vnapprooued.

**3.** Not approved or sanctioned.

**1667** Milton *P. L.* v. 118 Evil into the mind of God or Man May come and go, so unapprov'd, and leave No spot or blame behind. **1812** Crabbe *Tales* ix. 77 A Doctor Campbell..Declared his passion, and proclaim'd his worth; Not unapproved. **1827** Pollok *Course T.* VIII. 193 Unprofitable seemed, and unapproved That day, the sullen, self-vindictive life Of the recluse. **1902** *Westm. Gaz.* 20 May 3 He recognised forces unapproved by the Royal College of Surgeons.

**Unappro·ven,** *ppl. a.* *Sc.* [Un-1 8 b.] = prec. 1.

**1619** A. Simson in *Sel. Biog.* (Wodrow Soc.) I. 105 Our unapproven hand may loss them and tyne our travells.

**Unappro·ving,** *ppl. a.* (Un-1 10.) **1787** Hawkins *Life Johnson* 225 He looked upon the restraints on a life of pleasure with an unapproving eye. [Also in recent use, with adv. *unapprovingly*.]

**Una·pt,** *a.* [Un-1 7 and 5 b.]

**†1.** Of persons or things: Unfitted or unfit *to* do something. *Obs.*

*c* **1374** Chaucer *Troylus* I. 971 Was neuere man ne woman yet bygete, That was vnapt to suffren loues hete Celestial. **1504** Atkynson tr. *De Imitatione* II. viii. 186 Whan grace deperteth fro the soule it is faynt & frayle, vnapte to do or to suffre that vertue commaundith. **1597** Hooker *Eccl. Pol.* v. lxi. § 1 *note*, Those which were baptized in their beds were thereby made vnapt to haue any place amongst the clergie. **1610** J. Dove *Advt. Seminaries* 52, I might happily have persuaded them,..had they not been as a plot of ground unapt to receive good seed. **1654** Gayton *Pleas. Notes* IV. v. 199, I had some guests that were very unapt to sleep anywhere but in their own houses. **1682** Norris *Hierocles* 19 Those which constantly contemplate God, and are unapt to converse on earth. **1726** De Foe *Hist. Devil* (1840) 106 The wood unapt to burn by the moisture which fell, scarce received the fire I brought to kindle it. **1736** Butler *Anal.* II. vi. 225 In Proportion to Defects in the Understanding, Men are unapt to see lower Degrees of Evidence.

**2.** Unfit or unsuited *for* some use or purpose: **a.** Of persons.

*a* **1513** Fabyan *Chron.* VII. 408 A great nombre of olde men and women, and children, vnapt for ye warre. **1595** Daniel *Civ. Wars* IV. xxix, The Earle being..Vnapt for issue, it must needes descend on those of his being next of Clarence race. *a* **1648** Ld. Herbert *Hen. VIII* (1683) 33 Courtiers have those [arts] by which they govern their Princes, when through any indisposition they grow unapt for affairs. **1654** H. L'Estrange *Chas. I* (1655) 1 He was exceeding feeble in his lower parts,..whereby he was unapt for exercises of activity. **1791** Cowper *Odyss.* XXI. 159, I shall prove of little force Hereafter, and for manly feats unapt. **1850** Ht. Martineau *Hist. Eng.* II. 224 Unapt for combination..as his colleagues were, his..indifference went to increase the evil.

**b.** Of things.

**1579** Fulke *Heskins' Parl.* 20 A minde vnapte for the contemplation of this doctrine. **1608** Willet *Hexapla Exod.* 836 Such beasts..being vncleane, and vnapt for food. **1633** Bp. Hall *Occas. Medit.* 108 Is there any thing more heavy, and unapt for motion then Iron, or steele? **1736** Butler *Anal.* I. vi. 116 Whoever will consider, how unapt for Speculation, rude and uncultivated Minds are. **1765** Sterne *Tr. Shandy* VII. xxx, I..have a brain so entirely unapt for every thing of that kind. **1826** Kirby & Sp. *Introd. Entomol.* III. xxxiv. 429 In the Lamellicorn beetles..they [*sc.* mandibles] are soft, membranous, and unapt for mastication. **1873** M. Arnold *Lit. & Dogma* (1876) 9 There are heads unapt for this sort of work.

**†3.** Unsuited or unadapted *to* some end. *Obs.*

**1539** N. T. (Cranmer) *Tit.* i. 16 They are..vnapte vnto euery good worcke. **1579** Gosson *Sch. Abuse* (Arb.) 72 We must neither be laboured too muche..nor loyter too long, for making ourselues vnapt to any thing. **1620** Venner *Via Recta* viii. 179 Men after a full meale are..very vnapt vnto any labour.., either of minde or body. **1647** Jer. Taylor *Lib. Proph.* ii. 47 That..every clause in the Creed should be clear, and..inopportune and vnapt to variety of interpretation.

**4.** Without const. Unfitted, unsuited, unadapted: **†a.** Of persons. *Obs.*

*a* **1513** Fabyan *Chron.* VII. (1811) 422 An vnredy and dispurueyed hoost for the warre, as..spyrytuell men of the churche, with husbonde men and other vnapte people. **1577** tr. *Bullinger's Decades* (1592) 269 He must be no litherbacke, vnapt, or slothfull fellow. *a* **1621** Bacon *Disc. Saville* in *Resuscitatio* (1657) 230 The contrary Advantage (in Natures very dull, and unapt) of working Alacrity, by framing an Exercise with some Delight, or affection. *a* **1656** Hales *Gold. Rem.* (1688) 277 The longer we defer, the more unapt still we grow. *a* **1680** Butler *Rem.* (1759) I. 402 Such Men are commonly the most unapt in Things, that require Judgment and Reason.

**b.** Of things.

**1588** Lambarde *Eiren.* IV. Epil., I may neyther altogether condemne it as unapt, nor reiect it as unserviceable. **1598** Greene *Jas. IV*, II. ii, When the mould is barraine and vnapt, They toyle, they plow, and make the fallow fatte. **1638** Penkethman *Artach.* K 4 The whole Earth..is growne more unapt and backwards in bearing. **1650** Jer. Taylor *Holy Living* ii. § 6. 132 There are many worse [diseases] then to dye with an atrophy or Consumption, or unapt and courser nourishment. **1818** Cruise *Digest* (ed. 2) IV. 261 Such a union was very unapt and improper. **1842** H. Rogers *Introd. Burke's Wks.* I. 56 Thus disorders become incurable ..by the unapt and violent nature of the remedies.

**5.** Of language, etc.: Unsuitable, inappropriate.

**1553** Wilson *Art Rhet.* 88 *marg.*, Vnapte vsyng of apt wordes. **1588** E. Yorke in *Antiq. Rep.* (1807) I. 261 Of which worde of Calibre, came first this unapt terme wee use to call a Harquebuze a Calliver. **1634** W. Tirwhyt tr. *Balzac's Lett.* A 2 Those, who with unapt complements imagine they have composed a good letter. **1783** Colman *Prose Sev. Occas., Ep. Pisos* (1787) III. 13 Chaunting no odes between the acts, that seem unapt, or foreign to the general theme. **1796** Mrs. M. Robinson *Angelina* I. 228 Seldom she speaks: if question'd, she returns The answer incoherent and unapt. **1821** Scott *Pirate* xxv, No unapt representation of the sea in the Vision of Mirza. **1866** Geo. Eliot *F. Holt* xvi, Your comparison is not unapt, sir.

**6.** Of things: Not readily tending or likely *to* do something.

**1587** Turberv. *Trag. T.* (1837) 64 But commonly when men in fancie burne, Then womens hartes are most unapt to turne. **1597** Hooker *Eccl. Pol.* v. iii. § 1 Feare..is of all affections (anger excepted) the vnaptest to admit any conference with reason. *a* **1628** F. Grevil *Cælica* liv, Rage, feare, griefe, Powers as unapt to take, as give reliefe. **1665** Hooke *Microgr.* 13 The parts of the body of some are so loose from one another, and so unapt to cohere,..that [etc.]. **1819** Scott *Ivanhoe* xl, A mind which was unapt to apprehend danger. **1856** Bryant *Yellow Violet* v, Unapt the passing view to meet, When loftier flowers are flaunting nigh.

**b.** Of persons: Not apt or prone, not readily disposed, *to* do something.

**1640** Wilkins *New Planet* II. 32 Men being naturally unapt to beleeve any thing that seemes contrary to their senses. **1665** Hooke *Microgr.* 242, I am not unapt to think, that the Vale may have Vegetables analogous to our Grass, Shrubs, and Trees. **1785** T. Balguy *Disc.* 5 Unaccustomed to suffer harm, we are unapt to suspect it. **1828** Scott *F. M. Perth* viii, You may have thought me unapt to be moved by light complaints. **1874** Micklethwaite *Mod. Par. Churches* 241 Men of little creative power, but not unapt to take up ideas suggested to them.

**c.** Without const.: Unready, backward.

**1849** Mill *Ess.* (1859) II. 401 Lord Brougham has condescended to bestow upon these unapt scholars his view of some of the essential requisites of a popular Constitution.

†**Una·pt,** *v.* *Obs.* [f. prec., or Un-² 6 a + Apt *a.*] *trans.* To render unapt.

**1593** Nashe *Christ's T.* (1613) 156 Our full platters..vnapt vs to any exercise of Christianitie. **1628** R. Hobart *Edw. II*, cccxvii, Let not..false surmises Unapt their meanes, and crosse their owne devises. **1641** *Exam. Abstr. Answ. agst. Votes Bps. in Parl.* 77 It puts them out of their Calling, unapts them for the proper worke of it.

† **Una·ptitude.** *Obs.*⁻¹ [Un-¹ 12 and 5 b.] Inaptitude. (Const. *of* = for.)

**1545** Raynald *Byrth Mankynde* 144 Most communely the vnaptitude of conception (in women hauynge ther helth) springeth of the superfluyte of cold & moyst humours.

**Una·ptly,** *adv.* [Un-¹ 11 and 5 b.] Inaptly.

**1548** Udall, etc. *Erasm. Par. Luke* Pref., Why than should the ghospell seme to be vnaptely sent vnto those which are handlers and louers of the ghospell? **1579** W. Wilkinson *Confut. Fam. Love* 20 Yet are these places by him very vnskilfully cited and vnaptly to the purpose. *c* **1643** Ld. Herbert *Autobiog.* (1824) 56 It may be not unaptly called the paying our debts with another Man's money. **1659** *Gentl. Calling* 57 In this respect therefore I may not unaptly apply that Exhortation which the Apostle makes in another. **1748** Smollett *R. Random* xxxiii, This composition was, by the sailors, not unaptly stiled *Necessity*. **1798** S. & Ht. Lee *Canterb. T.* II. 101 Dennis, my silver-headed foster-father, may not unaptly personate my real one. **1852** Mrs. Stowe *Uncle Tom's C.* xi, Mr. Wilson's mind was one of those that may not unaptly be represented by a bale of cotton. **1866** Felton *Anc. & Mod. Gr.* I. 168 A soft, yet spicy vivacity, in which it has been not unaptly compared to the Castillian.

**Una·ptness.** [Un-¹ 12 and 5 b.] Inaptitude.

**1557** *Act* 4 & 5 *Phil. & Mary* c. 3 § 1 The same Disability and Unaptness notwithstanding, the same unable and unmeet Persons..have been also released. **1595** Daniel *Civ. Wars* iv. xviii, And languishing luxuriousnes had spred Feeble vnaptnes ouer all the land. **1605** Verstegan *Dec. Intell.* ix. 291 The trees grow but low..by reason of the vnaptnesse of the soyle. **1652** W. Hartley *Inf. Bapt.* 12 The prohibition hath peculiar relation to the unaptness of the sacrificers. **1676** *Phil. Trans.* II. 739 That seminal root..hindred by the unaptness of the place. **1710** Norris *Chr. Prud.* ii. 98 He often fails as to his Means, as well as to his End, I don't mean as to their unaptness.

**b.** Const. *for*, *to* (with sb. or inf.).

**1548** Elyot, *Prosedanium*, a disease which happeneth to ..beastes, whiche is vnaptenesse to generacion through to muche labour. **1600** W. Watson *Decacordon* (1602) 165 M. Blackwels simplicitie and vnaptnesse to gouerne. **1654** *Nicholas Papers* (Camden) II. 55 The naturall unaptness hee has for that exercise. **1670** Clarendon *Contempl. Ps.* Tracts (1727) 729 An unaptness to be confident of what they see and feel. *a* **1688** W. Clagett 17 *Serm.* (1699) 216 There will be laziness and slothfulness, and unaptness for instruction. **1860** Rawlinson *Herodotus* ix. lxx. IV. 442 *note*, A general unaptness for the mechanical arts?

**Unaraced**: see Unraced *ppl. a.* *Obs.*

**Una·rbitrariness.** (Un-¹ 12.) **1825** Coleridge in *Lit. Rem.* (1836) II. 359 The coincidences would bring the truth, the unarbitrariness, of the preceding exposition as near to demonstration as can rationally be required. **Una·rbitrary,** *a.* (Un-¹ 7.) **1793** Holcroft tr. *Lavater's Physiog.* iv. 35 If unarbitrary Nature patched up countenances like arbitrary Art. **Una·rbitrated,** *ppl. a.* (Un-¹ 8.) **1821** Shelley *Let. to T. L. Peacock* 10 Aug., All these [animals] ..walk about the house, which every now and then resounds with their unarbitrated quarrels.

**Unarch** (vnā·ɹtʃ), *v.* [Un-² 3.] *trans.* and *intr.* To uncurve; to straighten.

**1598** Florio, *Disarcare*, to vnbend, to vnarche. **1885** Jefferies *Open Air* (1890) 234 His flexible back bends and undulates, arches and unarches, rises and falls as a wave rises and rolls on.

**Unarchdea·con,** *v.* (Un-² 6 b.) **1555** Philpot *Exam.* 100 In dede M[aster] D[octor] ye haue among you vnarchediaconed me as nowe.

**Una·rched,** *a.* [Un-¹ 9.]

**1.** Not covered over with an arch.

**1658** Osborne *Adv. Son* (1896) 132 [A] tomb also hinders the variety of such contingent Resurrections as unarched Bodies enjoy.

**2.** Not provided with arches.

**1832** Froude in *Rem.* (1838) I. 299 The awkwardness of mixing up arched and unarched architecture is thus entirely avoided.

**Unarchite·ctural,** *a.* [Un-¹ 7.]

**1.** Not in accordance with the principles of architecture.

**1849** Ruskin *Sev. Lamps* ii. § 18. 47 It is lawful to paint either pictures or patterns...But it is not less true, that such practices are essentially unarchitectural. **1862** E. Falkener *Ephesus* i. iv. 49 The old style of building, which, from its irregularity and unarchitectural character, resembled that still used in Eastern climates. **1873** Mrs. Whitney *Other Girls* xxxi, An odd rambling wing,..slanting off at a wholly unarchitectural angle from the main house.

**2.** Not skilled in architecture.

**1884** *Pall Mall G.* 18 July 11/1 It is difficult from the mere text of this report for the unarchitectural reader to get a clear notion of what is proposed.

**Una·rguable,** *a.* (Un-¹ 7 b and 5 b.) **1881** *Times* 11 May 6/5 The President said that point was wholly unarguable. **1885** *Law Times* LXXIX. 244/1 The case for the first mortgagee would have been absolutely unarguable.

**Una·rgued,** *ppl. a.* (Un-¹ 8.)

**1616** B. Jonson *Epigr.* i. cx, He wrote with the same spirit that he fought; Not that his work lived in the hands of foes, Unargued then. **1628** Bp. Hall *Old Relig.* Ep. Ded. ¶ vj, No corner of truth hath lyen vnsearcht, no plea vnargued. **1667** Milton *P. L.* iv. 636 To whom thus Eve..: My Author and Disposer, what thou bidst Unargu'd I obey; so God ordains. **1777** Howard *Prisons Eng.* (1780) 152 The orders given by the commissary of the marines encharged with the care of prisoners are to be strictly complied with unargued and undisputed.

**Unargume·ntative,** *a.* (Un-¹ 7.)

**1722** *Lett. fr. Mist's Jrnl.* I. Pref. p. ii, The most.. impudent and unargumentative weekly Paper the Town was ever infested with. **1837** G. S. Faber *Prim. Doctr. Justif.* v. 235 The doctrine would not have been a whit the worse, had the..unargumentative curses been omitted. **1870** J. H. Newman *Gram. Assent* i. v. 119 The inward voice of that solemn Monitor, personal, peremptory, unargumentative.

Hence **Unargume·ntatively** *adv.*

**1840** G. S. Faber *Prim. Doctr. Regen.* 66 Just as if the writers unargumentatively thought, that no one..could ever doubt its propriety.

**Unari·sen,** *ppl. a.* (Un-¹ 8 b.) **1865** Swinburne *Hesperia* 74 Now that the white skies thrill with a moon unarisen. **1894** *Woman's Signal* 5 Apr. 224/2 A working principle.. as yet unarisen in the public mind. **Unaristocra·tic,** *a.* (Un-¹ 7.) **1841** in Monypenny *Disraeli* (1912) II. 123 We do not know the latest appointments; but up to the latest, except Gladstone, there is not one single untitled or unaristocratic individual. **1863** *Sat. Rev.* 7 Feb. 183/2 Stung at times into unaristocratic ebullitions of rather helpless spleen. **Unarithme·tic,** *a.* *Obs.*⁻¹ (Un-¹ 7.) **1789** H. Walpole *Let. to Mrs. H. More* 4 Nov., My head is as unmechanic as it is un-arithmetic, un-geometric, un-metaphysic, un-commercial. **Unarithme·tical,** *a.* (Un-¹ 7.) **1671** Crowne *Juliana* 1, Five times ten hundred crowns! most monstrous, prodigious, gigantique, pedantique, unarithmetical sum. **1858** Miss Mulock *Th. about Wom.* vi. 156 Unarithmetical ladies, who have always reckoned their accounts by sixpences. **Una·rk,** *v.* (Un-² 5.) **1611** J. Davies *Sco. Folly* cclxxxv, Till thou be left vpon Th' Armenian mount of safety, ioy and rest; Where when thou art thou maist thyselfe vn-arke.

**Una·rm,** *v.* Also 4–5 onarm (4 oun-), 4–7 unarme (5 *Sc.* wnarm). [Un-² 4.]

**1.** *trans.* To relieve (a person) of armour; to assist in putting off armour.

13.. *Sir Beues* (A.) 1081 King Ermin..clepede is douȝter & saide: 'Iosian, þe faire maide, Vn-arme Beues, he wer at mete. *c* **1386** Chaucer *Sqr.'s T.* 173 This knyght is to his chambre lad anoon, And is vnarmed, and vn to mete yset. **1470–85** Malory *Arthur* vii. xviii. 241 The mayden Lynet..vnarmed hym and serched his woundes. *c* **1489** Caxton *Sonnes of Aymon* xv. 357 He made hym to be vnarmed, and made his wounde to be wrapped. **1568** Grafton *Chron.* II. 252 Assoone as the King was vnarmed, he..went vp to the Castell to salute the Countesse of Sarisbury. **1573** in Feuillerat *Revels Q. Eliz.* (1908) 202 [To] Roger Tyndall..for his seruauntes Attendaunces to arme & vnarme the children in the play. **1606** Shaks. *Tr. & Cr.* iii. i. 163 Sweet Hellen, I must woe you, To helpe vnarme our Hector...You shall..disarme great Hector. **1720** Mrs. Manley *Power of Love* (1741) 337 [He] commanded the Conqueror should be unarm'd and set before his Face, to receive the Reward due to his Valour.

*absol.* **1606** Shaks. *Ant. & Cl.* iv. xiv. 35 Vnarme Eros, the long dayes taske is done, And we must sleepe.

**b.** *refl.* To free or strip (oneself) of armour. (Also with *head* as obj.)

13.. *Guy Warw.* (A.) 5506 Otus to his pauiloun he ȝede, & vnarmed him of his wede. *c* **1400** *Laud Troy Bk.* 10241 Vn-Arme the at my prayere. *c* **1430** *Pilgr. Lyf Manhode* i. cxxxiv. (1869) 70 Allas, whi woldest thou euere vnarme thee? *c* **1477** Caxton *Jason* 7 b, The Iousters vnarmed them, And put hem in fayr araye. *a* **1533** Ld. Berners *Huon* lix. 206 They vnarmyd them, and went to dyner. **1581** A. Hall *Iliad* iv. 66 He soft vnarmes him, and his scarfe, and Curet off doth take. **1609** Heywood *Brit. Troy* xiii. lxxxv, King Priam by Antenors mouth desires To unarme him streight and to the Courte returne. **1624** — *Gunaik.* v. 246 When with the slaughter of his enemies tyred He doff'd his cushes, and unarm'd his head. **1719** D'Urfey *Pills* I. 175 The Great Mars of the Battle unarms him and plays. **1823** Scott *Quentin D.* xxxvi, Go, tell no man to unarm himself; and let them shoot, in case of necessity.

*absol.* *c* **1450** *Merlin* xxvii. 555 Elizer was besy to serue sir Gawein..and helped him to vn-arme. **1606** Shaks. *Tr. & Cr.* i. i. 1 Call here my Varlet, I vnarme againe. *Ibid.* v. iii. 3 Vnarme, vnarme, and doe not fight to day. *a* **1625** Fletcher *Hum. Lieut.* iii. vi, Will ye unarm, and yield your selves his prisoners?

† **2.** To deprive of arms or armour; to disarm.

**1560** Daus tr. *Sleidane's Comm.* 101 To send their ayde agaynst the Turke..were to unarme them selves and to cut their owne senewes. **1569** J. Sanford tr. *Agrippa's Van. Artes* 125 b, To kill them, to take them, to unarme them, to spoile them. *a* **1618** Raleigh *Maxims St.* in *Rem.* (1661) 43 To unarm his people of weapons, money, and all means, whereby they may resist his power. **1635** Pagitt *Christianogr.* i. ii. (1636) 48 The Turke usually in his Conquests unarmeth the Christians. **1654** Earl Monm. tr. *Bentivoglio's Wars Flanders* 106 A Brigade of the Spanish foot forthwith entered the Town, and unarmed every one therein.

† **b.** *transf.* and *fig.* *Obs.*

**1568** Grafton *Chron.* II. 757 If deuision and dissencion of their friendes had not vnarmed them, and left them destitute. **1646** Sir T. Browne *Pseud. Ep.* 385 Galen.. would not leave unto the world too subtile a Theory of Poisons; unarming thereby the malice of venemous spirits. *a* **1668** Davenant *Epithal.* Wks. (1673) 312 So an excessive purity of Love Unarmes you to invite offence.

† **3.** To empty or strip of arms. *Obs.*

**1560** Daus tr. *Sleidane's Comm.* 405 By unarmyng the armaries, and openyng the waye to confiscation. **1636** G. Sandys *Paraphr., Ps.* xlvi, He breaks their Bowes, unarmes their Quivers, The bloody Speare in pieces shivers. **1665** Manley *Grotius' Low C. Wars* 209 The Queen..Commands by her Letter, the Lord Admirall Howard..that he should unarm and discharge the best of her Ships.

† **4.** To disarm, render harmless. *Obs.*⁻¹

**1700** Dryden *Ovid's Met.* viii. *Meleager* 120 No blood he drew; Dian unarm'd the Javelin as it flew.

**Una·rmed,** *ppl. a.* Also 3 uniarmed, 5 *Sc.* unermyt, onarmed. [Un-¹ 8.]

**1.** Not armed; having no armour or weapons.

**1297** R. Glouc. (Rolls) 11274 Vn iarmed out he wende to þe barons wel stille. *c* **1330** *Arth. & Merl.* 6947 (Kölbing), Vnarmed were þe paiens alle, Our folk hem gun to talle. **1387** Trevisa *Higden* (Rolls) I. 353 Þey fiȝteþ vnarmed, naked in body. **1412–20** Lydg. *Chron. Troy* iii. 1719 Cruelly þei had his hede of smet, For he vnarmyd al at meschef stood. **1456** Sir G. Haye *Law Arms* (S.T.S.) 113 A man that is outhir unarmyt, or evill armyt may nocht hald felde in bataill place. *a* **1533** Ld. Berners *Huon* lxvii. 230 All his company were vnarmed, & all the other .xl. were clene armed. **1579** W. Wilkinson *Confut. Fam. Love* Ep. Ded. *iij, Neither are able many of them being vnarmed to withstand the enemy. **1632** W. Lithgow *Trav.* iii. 89, I neuer could see a Greeke come forth of his house vnarmed. **1671** Milton *P. R.* iv. 626 He all unarm'd Shall chase thee with the terror of his voice. **1748** *Anson's Voy.* ii. vi. 200 He came down unarmed to a centinel of ours. **1794** S. Williams *Vermont* 170 An unarmed defenceless stranger. **1839** Thirlwall *Greece* VI. 223 The Thracians were keeping very negligent guard, and, in imagined security, were mostly unarmed. **1882** De Windt *Equator* 69 The remainder of the tribe were unarmed, as it is made a strict rule in Sarawak that..all arms..shall be left behind.

*absol.* **1590** Barwick *Disc. Weapons* 10 b, The musket.. will kill the armed of proofe at ten skore yardes,..and the vnarmed at thirty skore.

*transf.* **1634** Milton *Comus* 582 Th' unarmed weakness of one Virgin Alone, and helpless! **1827** Pollok *Course T.* ix. 965 Sin's dark tactics, such as boyish man, Unarmed by strength divine, could ill withstand.

**2.** Of animals, etc.: Not fitted for attack; not furnished with horns, teeth, or the like.

**1398** Trevisa *Barth. De P. R.* xviii. lxxx. (Bodl. MS.), The schepe..is a nesche beeste and bereþ wolle & is vnarmed & plesinge in herte. **1649** Lovelace *Lucasta* Poems (1904) 95 A Falcon..Unarm'd of Wings and Scaly Oare. **1804** Shaw *Gen. Zool.* V. i. 14 Unarmed Silure, *Silurus Inermis*. **1834** McMurtrie *Cuvier's Anim. Kingd.* 495 *Furcularia*...The body is unarmed. **1855** *Orr's Circ. Sci., Inorg. Nat.* 108 Reptiles..whose two tusks, in an otherwise unarmed jaw, strikingly distinguish them from any of their contemporaries. **1869** Tanner *Clin. Med.* (ed. 2) 309 The unarmed or beef tape-worm,..as its name implies, is unfurnished with hooks around its head.

**3.** Of plants: Destitute of prickles, spines, or thorns.

**1676** Grew *Anat. Flowers* ii. App. § 11 The Top is Thorny, as in Furz; or Vnarmed. Vnarmed, either produced, that is, poynted, or at least, Roundish. **1793** Martyn *Lang. Bot.*, *Inerme folium*, an unarmed leaf. **1845** Steele *Field Bot.* 218 Bracts of invol. linear-lanceolate, almost unarmed. **1855** Miss Pratt *Flower. Pl.* II. 298 Unarmed Hornwort. Fruit without either spines or tubercles. **1870** Hooker *Stud. Flora* 107 *Prunus communis*,.. Sub-sp. *domestica*;..branches straight unarmed.

**4.** Of things: Not provided with anything that assists or strengthens.

**1693** Dryden *Juvenal* x. 319 The same foulness does to Age belong, The self same Palsie,..And Gums unarm'd to mumble Meat in vain. *a* **1721** Prior *Journ. to Copt-Hall* 12, I mount, and great as Hudibrass, With unarm'd kick urge on my horse. **1860** Tyndall *Glac.* i. xxvii. 200 Pattens ..sank less deeply than the unarmed feet. **1860** Emerson *Cond. Life* v. 156 In Siberia, a late traveller found men who could see the satellites of Jupiter with their unarmed eye.

† **5.** Of a magnet: Not provided with an armature. *Obs.*

**1662** J. Bargrave *Pope Alex. VII* (1867) 120 Two large loadstones, one armed with steel...The other..is unarmed. **1730** *Phil. Trans.* XXXVI. 325, I placed the Pole of the upper Armour about 4 or 5 Inches from the Top of the unarmed Bar. **1777** *Ibid.* LXVII. 135 A fine, smooth, unarmed load-stone.

Hence **Una·rmedness.**

**1684** H. More *Answer* 208 This Lamblike condition of it is chiefly represented in this present Vision, its seeming harmlesness and unarmedness.

**Una·rmoured,** *a.* [Un-¹ 9.]

**1.** Of vessels: Not armour-clad.

**1869** Sir E. Reed *Our Iron-Clad Ships* iv. 73 When we pass from unarmoured to armoured ships, the contrast is still more striking. **1879** *Cassell's Techn. Educ.* IV. 61/1 In the unarmoured iron ships recently built for the navy tie-plates have been entirely dispensed with.

**2.** Of persons: Not protected by armour.

**1873** Morris *Love is Enough* 18 Barehanded, unarmoured, he handled the spear-shaft. **1892** Tennyson *Foresters* iv, And walkest [thou] here Unarmour'd? all these walks are Robin Hood's And sometimes perilous.

**Unarou·sed,** *ppl. a.* (Un-¹ 8.) **1855** Singleton *Virgil* II. 207 Burns Unaroused and moveless hitherto Ausonia. **Unarrai·gnable,** *a.* (Un-¹ 7 b.) **1886** Swinburne *Misc.* 52 Work unarraignable alike by fair means or foul. **Unarrai·gned,** *ppl. a.* (Un-¹ 8.) **1595** Daniel *Civ. Wars* iii. xxii, Neuer shall this poore breath of mine consent That he..Should here be iudgd vnheard, and vnaraignd. **1858** Merivale *Hist. Rom. Emp.* lii. (1865) VI. 286 He did not venture to command his execution, unarraigned and unconvicted. **Unarra·nged,** *ppl. a.* (Un-¹ 8.) [1775 Ash.] **1791** Boswell *Johnson* an. 1737, The *disjecta membra* scattered throughout, and as yet unarranged. **1840** Carlyle *Heroes* v. (1904) 160 How many powerful forces are seen working in a wasteful, chaotic, altogether unarranged manner. **1897** Pullen Burry *Blotted Out* 51 Death is an unsurveyed land, an unarranged science.

†**Unarray·**, *v. Obs.* [UN-² 4.] *trans.* To deprive of array; *esp.* to undress, disrobe.

14.. *Chaucer's Sqr.'s T.* 173 (Camb. MS.), This knyght ..is on-arayed [*other MSS.* vnarmed] & to mete i-set. *a* 1483 *Liber Niger* in S. Pegge *Cur. Misc.* (1782) 79 Two [Esquires of the Body] to be attendant on the King's person to array and unarray him. 1483 *Cath. Angl.* 12/1 To vn Aray, *exornare, & cetera; vbi* to dysaray. 1590 STOCKWOOD *Eng. Accidence* 65 This verbe *exuo*, of araying, or rather indeed of vnaraying, hath two accusative cases. 1601 LAMBARDE *Dict. Angl. Topogr.* (1730) 69 She forthwith unarrayed her selfe, untrussed her Heare.

**Unarray·ed**, *ppl. a.* [UN-¹ 8.]

1. Not arrayed or put in order.

*c* 1340 HAMPOLE *Prose Tr.* 28 If þou..latis þame spill for defaute of kepynge—unarayede, unkepide,..thou pleses Hym noghte. 1390 GOWER *Conf.* III. 175, I sih also The noble peple of Irahel Dispers as schep upon an hell, Withoute a kepere unarraied. *c* 1400 *Brut* 13 Whan Humbar saw hem come, he was sore adrad, forasmyche as his men wist it not, & also þey were vnarrayed. 1727 BAILEY (vol. II), *Unarrayed*, not ranged in Order of Battle.

2. Not dressed; unclothed; unarmed.

*c* 1380 *Sir Ferumb.* 821 Duke Roland þan was sore amayed, So wern þe doþþepers,..for þay wern oun-araid. *c* 1440 *York Myst.* xxiv. 6 We will bere witnesse..How we hir raysed all vnarayed,..Wher sche was with hir leman laide. *a* 1450 *Knt. de la Tour* (1906) 153 There shall now be sheued you of the good ladyes that were vnaraied, duellynge in Rome. 1611 COTGR., *Desabillé*, vncloathed, vndressed, vnarrayed. 1665 DRYDEN *Ind. Emp.* I. i, As if this Infant World, yet unarray'd, Naked and bare, in Nature's Lap were laid. 1685 — *Thren. August.* 54 Half unarray'd he ran to his Relief, So hasty and so artless was his Grief. 1839 BAILEY *Festus* 187 Thou art as the cloudless moon, Undimmed and unarrayed; No robe hast thou.

**Unarre·stable**, *a.* (UN-¹ 7 b), **-ably**, *adv.* (UN-¹ 11). 1855 PRINCE ALBERT *Sp. in B'ham* 22 Nov., The former is an unarrestable movement towards the fountain of truth. 1884 E. ABBOTT *Flatland* 75, I could feel him slowly and unarrestably slipping from my contact.

**Unarre·sted**, *ppl. a.* [UN-¹ 8. Cf. MDu. *ongearresteert.*]

1. Not arrested or apprehended.

*c* 1400 *Beryn* 2188, I woll..assay, yf I may, in eny maner wise, Ascapen vnarestid more in suche maner wise. 1498, 1531 [see UNATTACHED *ppl. a.* 1]. 1533 MORE *Apol.* 259 b, By thys pacyfyers good deuyse, heretykes maye go unarrested. 1611 COTGR., *Descalengé*, vnarrested, vnapprehended. 1891 E. KINGLAKE *Australian at Home* 77 The wife of a certain unarrested absconder was observed to have command of plenty of money.

2. Not stopped or checked.

1733 TULL *Horse-Hoeing Husb.* xiv. 199 The under Stratum must be the richer for receiving what the upper Stratum lets pass Unarrested. 1859 TENNENT *Ceylon* II. VII. v. 197 The temples of Kandy..are dilapidated edifices, apparently perishing from unarrested decay. 1869 G. LAWSON *Dis. Eye* (1874) 79 If the disease be unarrested by treatment, the whole pupillary margin becomes sealed to the lens capsule.

**Unarri·ved**, *ppl. a.* [UN-¹ 8.]

1. Not yet arrived (at a place, or in time).

1626 in Foster *Eng. Factories India* (1909) III. 155 The shipps expected and unarrived. 1742 YOUNG *Nt. Th.* IX. 294 These, as two monarchs, on their borders meet, (Monarchs of all elaps'd, or unarriv'd!)

b. That has not yet attained success.

1902 *Academy* 25 Jan. 76/2 Liverpool offers great possibilities to the unarrived novelist.

2. Not yet arrived *at*; unattained.

1669 [see UNAIMED *ppl. a.*].

**Una·rrogant**, *a.* (UN-¹ 7.) 1831 D. E. WILLIAMS *Sir T. Lawrence* I. 12 He had an unarrogant self-possession which few men enjoy. **Una·rrogating**, *ppl. a.* (UN-¹ 10.) 1742 MELMOTH *Fitzosborne Lett.* (1763) 349 Whoever pursues his speculations with this humble unarrogating temper of mind [etc.]. 1854 E. SARGENT *Peculiar* I. 152 The quiet unarrogating air of one whose nobility is a part of his nature.

† **Una·rted**, *a. Obs.* [UN-¹ 9.]

1. Ignorant of the arts; unskilled.

1603 FLORIO *Montaigne* I. li. 166 They are..rude, simple, and unarted in the combate of talking. 1606 WARNER *Alb. Engl.* XIV. To Rdr., Shunne Eares vnarted, rude, precise. 1699 CIBBER *Xerxes* II, I am unarted, Sir, in any grace of speech To stir the soul! My words are plain and honest.

2. Unartificial; plain.

1628 FELTHAM *Resolves* II. xcix. 291 Wise Innocence, friends like, and good Vnarted-meat, kind neighbourhood.

**Una·rtful**, *a.* [UN-¹ 7.]

1. Not artificial or contrived; artless.

1669 DRYDEN & DAVENANT *Tempest* III. (1670) 32 I'm sure unartful truth lies open In her mind, as Crystal streams their sandy bottom shew. 1693 CONGREVE in *Dryden's Juvenal* XI. (1697) 291 A chearful Sweetness in his Looks he has, And Innocence unartful in his Face. 1713 *Guard.* No. 127 *Crt. Venus* 70 Unartful Tears, and hectick Looks, that show With silent Eloquence the Lover's Woe. 1763 FALCONER *Fond Lover* 14 Since all her thoughts by sense refined, Unartful truth express. 1820 W. TOOKE tr. *Lucian* I. 147 Much less can it be affirmed, that it [*sc.* spunging] is an unartful art. 1899 VERRAL in A. C. Brown *Life E. W. Benson* (1900) I. 219 The same delightful and unartful arts were displayed.

b. Free from artifice or cunning.

1703 ROWE *Fair Penit.* II. ii. 596 This Son, if Fame mistakes not, is more hot, More open, and unartful.

2. Displaying no technical skill; inartistic.

1675 COCKER *Morals* 49 Rashness draws crooked and unartful Lines. 1703 SAVAGE *Lett. Antients* ix. 52 Beneath this humble Roof he stood, and this plain unartful Floor supported him. 1712 BLACKMORE *Creation* III. 179 So full of faults is all the unartful frame. 1759 GOLDSM. *Bee* No. 5. 90 To have almost every personage on the scene almost of the same character..was unartful in the poet to the last degree. 1883 *Pall Mall G.* 24 Nov. 4/2 Prose which borrows in a manner pleasant enough in result, and by no means unartful, the more obvious and seductive attractions of verse.

b. Of persons: Unskilful, maladroit. *rare.*

1683 MRS. BEHN *Yng. King* II. iii, I am a man, whose martial disposition Renders unartful in my language. 1709 MRS. MANLEY *Secret Mem.* (1720) IV. 88 A swift and sure Contempt succeeds upon what-ever the unartful Husband shall happen to do after.

Hence **Una·rtfully** *adv.*

1724 SWIFT *Drapier's Lett.* iii. Wks. 1841 II. 17/2 The report, which, although it be not unartfully drawn,..yet there was no great skill required to detect the many mistakes..in it. 1726 — *Gulliver* IV. ii, Matts of straw, not unartfully made. 1793 *Minstrel* III. 137, I discovered a door, not unartfully concealed by some rude chizeling in the rock. 1840 THACKERAY *Pict. Rhapsody* 116 This plan has been not unartfully contrived.

**Unarti·culate**, *a.* [UN-¹ 7 and 5 b.]

†1. = INARTICULATE *a.* 2. *Obs.*

1603 J. DAVIES (Heref.) *Microcosmos* Wks. (Grosart) I. 12/2 No Beast..But in his voice (though vnarticulate) Salutes these times. 1611 COTGR., *Sphinge*, the..Sphinx..; his vnarticulate voice like that of a hastie speaker.

2. = INARTICULATE *a.* 1.

1855 PUSEY *Doctr. Real Presence* Note 440 The one..is upright, articulate,..but the other..is round, unarticulate, inanimate.

**Unarti·culated**, *ppl. a.* [UN-¹ 8. Cf. G. *unarticulirt*, Sw. *oarticulerad.*]

1. Not articulated or distinct.

*a* 1700 KEN *Hymnarium* Poet. Wks. 1721 II. 25 God from the Moment we draw breath,..Our words, when unarticulated, hears. 1823 LAMB *Let. Old Gentl.* Misc. Wks. (1871) 451 That unarticulated language, which was before the written tongue. 1840 WILLIS *Loiterings* II. 139 The touching attitudes and utter abandonment of all around to their unarticulated devotions.

2. Not jointed; not fitted together.

1861 HULME tr. *Moquin-Tandon* II. VII. xiii. 399 The egg encloses a short unarticulated embryo. *a* 1894 C. H. PEARSON in Stebbing *Life* (1900) 77 A cupboard full of unarticulated human bones.

**Unartifi·cial**, *a.* [UN-¹ 7 and 5 b.]

1. Not displaying special art or skill; unskilful, inartistic, clumsy. Now *rare* or *Obs.*

1591 HARINGTON *Orl. Fur.* Pref., If I shold confesse..that my verse is vnartificiall, the stile rude, the phrase barbarous. 1597 MORLEY *Introd. Mus.* 80 It is an vnartificiall kinde of descanting in the middle of a lesson, to let the plainsong sing alone. 1602 CAMPION *Art Eng. Poesie* Ded., The vulgar and vnarteficiall custome of riming. 1702 S. PARKER tr. *Cicero's De Finibus* III. 154 The Common-Places and suggestions of your Advocates for Pleasure are, at best, but very Shallow and Unartificial. 1790 BURKE *Fr. Rev.* 275 They have levelled and crushed together all the orders which they found, even under the coarse unartificial arrangement of the monarchy. 1825 BENTHAM *Ration. Reward* 204 Art and science, on the one hand, and unartificial practice and unscientific knowledge, on the other.

2. Not artificial; simple, natural.

1603 FLORIO *Montaigne* III. xii. 628 It representeth in an vn-artificiall boldnesse, and infantine securitie, the pure impression and first ignorance of nature. 1656 EARL MONM. tr. *Boccalini's Advts. fr. Parnass.* I. lxxvii. (1674) 100 Men who live in sincerity..., with an undisguised and unartificial goodness. 1799 *Monthly Rev.* XXX. 345 Example arising from a natural unartificial developement of incidents.

**Unartifi·cially**, *adv.* [f. prec.] † Inartistically, unskilfully.

1591 HARINGTON *Orl. Fur.* Pref., And yet for Ariostos tales that many thinke vnartificially brought in, Homer his selfe hath the like. 1598 HAKLUYT *Voy.* I. 484 The barrel is rudely and vnartificially made. 1622 PEACHAM *Compl. Gent.* x. (1634) 89 Hee goeth unartificially to worke even in the very beginning. 1670 MILTON *Hist. Eng.* III. Wks. 1851 V. 102 The material being only Turf, and by the rude multitude unartificially built up.., avail'd them little. 1706 STEVENS *Span. Dict.* I, *Inhabilmente*, unhandily, unartificially, unskilfully, ignorantly.

**Unarti·stic**, *a.* (UN-¹ 7 and 5 b.) 1854 GRACE GREENWOOD *Haps & Mishaps* 68 It certainly strikes the unartistic as a most unsuitable alliance. 1865 *Athenæum* No. 1955. 520/3 A vague unartistic tale. **Una·rtistlike**, *a.* and *adv.* (UN-¹ 7 c and 11 b.) 1654 GAYTON *Pleas. Notes* III. iii. 81 It was very improper, and unartist-like done in Sancho, to permit him to sleep. 1757 GROSE *Voy. E. Indies* 173 Their naval, like their other architecture, has always something clumsy, unfinished, and unartist-like in it. 1837 LYTTON *Athens* II. 115 The elaborate description of this work [a bridge] given by Herodotus proves it to have been no clumsy or unartistlike performance.

† **U·nary.** *Obs.*⁻¹ [f. L. *ūn-us* one.] A unit.

1576 FLEMING tr. *Caius' Dogs* (1880) 36 This countrey was cleerely discharged of rauenyng wolfes, & none at all left, no, not to the least number, or the beginnyng of a number, which is an Vnari.

**Unasce·ndable**, *a.* (UN-¹ 7 b.) 1615 G. SANDYS *Trav.* 171 He..confined the Royall progeny within high and vnascendable mountaines. 1628 FELTHAM *Resolves* II. [I.] xxix. 90 A Hill almost vn-ascendable. 1801 SOUTHEY *Thalaba* XII. xvi, The depth was unascendable. **Unasce·nded**, *ppl. a.* (UN-¹ 8.) 1821 SHELLEY *Adonais* xlvi, It was for thee yon kingless sphere has long Swung blind in unascended majesty. 1861 F. W. JACOMB in *Peaks, Passes & Glaciers* Ser. II. I. 315 Removing a mountain from the unascended list. **Unasce·ndible**, *a.* (UN-¹ 7.) 1801 SOUTHEY *Thalaba* VII. iv, The heights precipitous, Impending crags, rocks unascendible. **Unascertai·nable**, *a.* (UN-¹ 7 b.) 1802-12 BENTHAM *Ration. Judic. Evid.* (1827) V. 237 It is only..to an amount altogether precarious and unascertainable, that it does away the mischief. 1876 A. S. MURRAY *Mythol.* 14 By keeping constantly before the mind a sense of the unascertainable and infinite powers of nature.

**Unascertai·ned**, *ppl. a.* [UN-¹ 8.] † **a.** Not certified or apprised. *Obs.* **b.** Not ascertained or known.

1628 in Foster *Eng. Factories India* (1909) III. 193 What is become of Beale, whether living or dead, we are yett unascertained. 1751 HARRIS *Hermes* II. i. (1765) 217 The Article (A) leaves the Individual itself unascertained, whereas the Article (The) ascertains the Individual also. 1784 COOK *Third Voy.* VI. iv. III. 269 The only part of the Russian empire that now remains unascertained. 1815 J. SMITH *Panorama Sci. & Art* II. 319 The standard temperatures desired, remained unascertained till the time of Newton. 1879 *St. George's Hosp. Rep.* IX. 127 An unascertained quantity of oxalic acid and white precipitate.

† **Unascri·ed**, *ppl. a. Obs.*⁻¹ [UN-¹ 8.] Undescried, unobserved.

*a* 1548 HALL *Chron., Hen. VIII*, 32 So that alwaies it was forsene that..the Frenchemen shoulde not come on them sodainly vnaskryed.

**Unasha·med**, *ppl. a.* (UN-¹ 8.)

Hence, in recent use, *unashamedly* adv., *-ness.*

1600 FAIRFAX *Tasso* V. lxxi, This foolish crew of louers, vnashamed,..Ran forward still, in this disordred sort. 1619 H. HUTTON *Follie's Anat.* (Percy Soc.) 24 See this incarnate monster of her sex Play the virago, unashamde, perplext. 1827 POLLOK *Course T.* VIII. 782 Lust of wealth and power Inordinate, and lewdness unashamed. 1855 BROWNING *Two in Campagna* vii, Let us, O my dove, Let us be unashamed of soul. 1887 LOWELL *Democracy*, etc. 100 Coleridge's words have the unashamed nakedness of Scripture.

**Una·sinous**, *a.* [f. L. *ūn-us* one + *asinus* ass, after *unanimous*.] Agreeing in stupidity.

1656 HOBBES *Six Lessons* vi. ad fin., Go your wayes you uncivil Ecclesiasticks,..De-doctors of Morality, unasinous collegues [etc.].

**Una·sk**, *v.* (UN-² 3.) 1843 GEO. ELIOT in Cross *Life* (1885) I. 120, I cannot desire that you should unask violin and Flute, unless a postponement would be..as agreeable to you and them. **Una·skable**, *a.* (UN-¹ 7 b.) 1854 FERRIER *Inst. Metaph.* IX. xxxv. 498 The truths which it has reached renders that question absurd. It is unanswerable, because it is unaskable.

**Una·sked**, *ppl. a.* Also 6, 9 *dial.*, unaxed. [UN-¹ 8, 8 c.]

1. Without being asked; not requested or intreated; uninvited.

*a* 1225 *Ancr. R.* 338 Þe hwule þet tu const siggen out [in shrift], seie al unasked. 1456 SIR G. HAYE *Law Arms* (S. T. S.) 139 Gyf a knycht..had gevyn a coursour to the Provost of Paris unaskit. 1582 STANYHURST *Æneis* II. (Arb.) 55 In gentil manner thus he soone discoursed, vnasked. 1628 J. TAYLOR (Water P.) *Penniless Pilgr.* Wks. (1630) 123/1 Master Taylor, at the Sarazen's head, Vnask'd (vnpaid for) me both lodg'd and fed. 1697 DRYDEN *Virg. Past.* III. 100 Fair Amyntas comes unasked to me, And offers love. 1710 PRIOR *Examiner, To Earl Godolphin* 10 Unask'd you offer, and unseen you give. 1746 FRANCIS tr. *Hor., Sat.* I. iii. 3 Sing they can never at a friend's request, Yet chant it forth, unask'd, from morn till night. 1810 CRABBE *Borough* xviii. 56 He shows the shipping;.. He makes (unask'd) their ports and business known. 1879 MEREDITH *Egoist* xxiv, She went to the music-rack and gave the song unasked.

† b. Left uninvited. *Sc. Obs.*

*c* 1730 BURT *Lett. N. Scot.* (1754) II. 204, I have several times been unasked to eat.

2. Not asked for; not made the subject of a request.

1456 SIR G. HAYE *Law Arms* (S. T. S.) 96 Quhat thingis ..has sauf condyt be privilege unaskit at the princis. 1529 S. FISH *Supplic. Beggars* (1871) 8 There was giuen theim ynough vnaxed. 1592 SHAKS. *Ven. & Ad.* 102 Yet hath he ..begg'd for that which thou unask'd shalt have. 1618 J. TAYLOR (Water P.) *Penniless Pilgr.* Wks. (1630) 123/2, I thought it no good manners to refuse, But thank'd him for his kinde vnasked gift. 1658 OSBORNE *Jas. I*, 53 The Scots, by whom nothing was unasked, and to whom nothing was denied. 1712 ADDISON *Spect.* No. 357 ¶ 10 Adam..expostulates with his Creator for having given him an unasked Existence. 1751 WARBURTON *Pope's Wks.* IX. 247 *note*, To the issue of that unasked and unsought compliment these words allude. 1819 SCOTT *Leg. Montrose* x, He delivered his unasked opinion as follows. 1870 MORRIS *Earthly Par.* II. III. 426 Indeed I thought That news of ill unasked would soon be brought.

b. Similarly with *for.*

1714 MANDEVILLE *Fab. Bees* (1733) II. 117 The unask'd-for bounty and downright generosity of his benefactor. 1861 LADY LYTTELTON *Let.* 15 Dec., The Queen..sent me an account on the 10th (unasked for..) through Lady Augusta Bruce. 1876 T. HARDY *Ethelberta* xxxvi, An unasked-for concession to their cause.

**Una·sking**, *ppl. a.* (UN-¹ 10.)

1722 WOLLASTON *Relig. Nat.* V. 116 That he..should have many things granted him, which are not given to the careless, obdurate, unasking part of mankind. 1799 in *Spirit Pub. Jrnls.* III. 271 Laid under contribution to the unasking necessities of the pupil of Mercury. 1876 LANIER *Clover* 97 This cool, unasking Ox Comes browsing o'er my hills and vales of Time.

b. In ppl. use: Without asking for. (UN-¹ 5 d.)

1754 SHEBBEARE *Matrimony* (1766) I. 225 Unasking more, he implored only the Continuation of Health to himself and Family.

† **Unaspe·cted**, *ppl. a. Obs.*⁻¹ [UN-¹ 8: cf. ASPECT *v.* I.] Unsuspected, unexpected.

1578 FLORIO *1st Fruites* 86 The forreyne knyfe dothe disbarke it [*sc.* a tree], the bee of unaspected causes dooth consume it.

† **Unaspe·ctive**, *a. Obs.*⁻¹ [UN-¹ 7 + ASPECT *v.*] Unregardful.

1661 FELTHAM *Resolves* II. lxxiv. 348 In which the Holy Ghost is not wholly unaspective to the custome that was used among men.

† **Unaspie·d**, *ppl. a. Obs.* = UNESPIED *ppl. a.* *c* **1400** *Destr. Troy* 1428 Of a sparke unaspied, spred vnder askys, May feston vp fyre to mony freike sorow. **1508** DUNBAR *Tua Mariit Wemen* 427 That I may spy, vnaspyit, a space me beside.

**Una·spirated**, *ppl. a.* (UN-[1] 8. Cf. G. *unaspirirt.*) [**1775** ASH.] **1793** PARR *Combe's Horace* Wks. 1828 III. 33 Lambin gives ὄρνυμι for the Æolic verb unaspirated. **1887** *Pall Mall G.* 26 Aug. 3/1 Mr. and Mrs. Williamson's unaspirated piety might have been spared with advantage.

**Unaspi·ring**, *ppl. a.* (UN-[1] 10.) *a* **1729** J. ROGERS *Serm.* (1736) 173 An easy unaspiring Temper which rests satisfy'd with its present Share of the Bounties of Providence. **1806** R. MANT *Poems, To Bp. Durham* I. 2 She loves..To cheer with unaspiring lay The dear domestic shade. **1852** LD. COCKBURN *Jeffrey* I. 103 The unaspiring life, I believe, has the least positive wretchedness.

Hence **Unaspi·ringness.**

**1681** *Whole Duty Nations* 64 The Humility, Modesty, and unaspiringness of Christianity. **1861** MILL *Repr. Govt.* iii. 64 Inactivity, unaspiringness, absence of desire, are a more fatal hindrance to improvement than any misdirection of energy.

**Una·ss**, *v.* (UN-[2] 5.) **1654** GAYTON *Pleas. Notes* IV. iii. 184 Gines Passamont..With Sancho's Asse unto a Fare was packing; The quick-eyed Bore had spied him, and unass'd him.

**Unassai·lable**, *a.* [UN-[1] 7 b.]

**1.** Not assailable; not open to assault or attack. Also *fig.*

**1596** SPENSER *F. Q.* V. ix. 5 Thereto both his owne wylie wit (she sayd), And eke the fastnesse of his dwelling place, Both vnassaylable, gaue him great ayde. **1601** SHAKS. *Jul. C.* III. i. 69, I do know but One That vnassayleable holds on his Ranke, Vnshak'd of Motion. **1825** J. NEAL *Bro. Jonathan* III. 121 He was always the same,..alike unassailable—inscrutable. **1841** ELPHINSTONE *Hist. Ind.* I. 543 The chief had occupied an unassailable position, but was drawn out by a pretended flight. **1871** MACDUFF *Mem. Patmos* xii. 167 They have a..heritage of tribulation: but their spiritual safety is unassailable.

**2.** Not open to adverse criticism.

**1830** MACKINTOSH *Progr. Eth. Philos.* Wks. 1846 I. 120 In both cases he occupies the unassailable ground of an appeal to consciousness. **1884** *Manch. Exam.* 17 Sept. 4/6 The President's address..does not actually lead us to any unassailable conclusions.

Hence **Unassai·lableness**; **-ably** *adv.*

Also, in recent use, *unassailability*.

**1870** *Pall Mall G.* 20 Oct. 3 America possesses over us the advantages of distance and unassailableness. **1876** BANCROFT *Hist. U. S.* VI. xxxvii. 184 The two oceans, between which the republic has unassailably intrenched itself.

**Unassai·led**, *ppl. a.* (UN-[1] 8.) *a* **1586** SIDNEY *Arcadia* III. vii. (1912) 385 The quietnesse of his unassailed senses. **1593** SHAKS. *2 Hen. VI*, VI. ii. 18 It greeues my soule to leaue thee vnassail'd. **1634** MILTON *Comus* 220 The Supreme good..Would send a glistring Guardian if need were To keep my life and honour unassail'd. **1735** THOMSON *Liberty* III. 456 Unarm'd he stray'd, unguarded, unassail'd. **1819** SCOTT *Ivanhoe* xliv, If unassailed, we depart assailing no one. **1887** MOLONEY *Forestry W. Africa* 194 Nevertheless the trade in jute holds its own unassailed.

**Unassa·ssinated**, *ppl. a.* (UN-[1] 8.) **1842** POE *Marie Roget* Wks. 1865 I. 227 If starting from the living Marie, we find her, yet find her unassassinated.

**Unassau·ltable**, *a.* (UN-[1] 7 b.) **1571** GOLDING *Calvin on Ps.* xlviii. 11 A Citie very wel fortified and unassaultable. **1582** BENTLEY *Mon. Matrones* 334 When I bethinke me what a tower of strength..and unassaultable habitation thou hast euer beene. **1611** SPEED *Hist. Gt. Brit.* IX. xxiii. 114 A breach made in the wall, not farre from the Water-gate, but yet vnassaultable, the English within so maintained the defence. **1653** A. WILSON *Jas. I*, 216 It is a great disadvantage for living Bodies to fight against dead Walls, being so high, and unassaultable. *a* **1711** KEN *Christophil* Poet. Wks. 1721 I. 516 O Realm of undisturb'd repose, Thrones unassaultable by Woes!

**Unassau·lted**, *ppl. a.* (UN-[1] 8.) **1611** SPEED *Hist. Gt. Brit.* v. vi. § 17. 37 The German Saxons..neuer left their attempts vnassaulted till they set the glorious diademe thereof vpon their owne heads. **1655** MOUFET & BENNET *Health's Improv.* (1746) 207 He..left no fair Woman unassaulted. *a* **1711** KEN *Psyche* Poet. Wks. 1721 IV. 209 That I secure may grow, When unassaulted by my Foe. **1758** JOHNSON *Idler* No. 20 ¶ 11 The commanders ..durst not leave the place unassaulted.

**Unassay·ed**, *ppl. a.* (UN-[1] 8.) *c* **1374** CHAUCER *Boeth.* II. pr. iv. (1868) 42 Alwey to euery man þere is..somwhat þat vnassaied he ne wot not, or ellys he dredeþ þat he haþ assaied. *c* **1403** LYDG. *Temple Glas* 1249 For vn-assaied men may no troupe preue. **1513** DOUGLAS *Æneid* VIII. iv. 58 Na maner of wickitnes nor dissait Mycht be, that he ne durst nocht tak on hand, Ne onassait leif. **1560** DAUS tr. *Sleidane's Comm.* 195 b, Who leaveth no waye unassayed to accomplyshe his ambition. **1617** MORYSON *Itin.* I. 275 These good fellowes leave nothing unassaied, in the wished discovery of these fraudes. **1649** MILTON *Eikon.* xi. Wks. 1851 III. 427 To be rid of these mortifying Propositions he leaves no tyrannical evasion unassaid. **1708** PHILIPS *Cyder* I. 362 They sedulously think To meliorate thy Stock; no Way, or Rule Be unassay'd. **1784** COWPER *Task* III. 451 To raise the prickly and green-coated gourd, ..is an art..at this moment unassay'd in song. **1912** LADY BURGHCLERE *Life Dk. Ormonde* I. x. 317 He could not afford to leave unassayed any issue that promised escape.

**Unasse·nting**, *ppl. a.* (UN-[1] 10.) **1836** SIR H. TAYLOR *Statesman* xiii. 88 Otherwise the hand, if an unassenting one, will carry an advantage over the head. **1883** MISS BETHAM-EDWARDS *Disarmed* xx, Arthura smiled, a sad, unassenting smile. **Unasse·rted**, *ppl. a.* (UN-[1] 8.) [**1775** ASH.] **1856** LEVER *Martins of Cro' M.* lxv, He is now back here once more; come to insist upon his long unasserted rights. **Unasse·rtive**, *a.* (UN-[1] 7.) **1861** DICKENS *Gt. Expect.* lvii, He would sit and talk to me..in the old unassertive protecting way. **1882** *Ch. Q. Rev.* Apr. 140 Unanxious and unassertive, where certainty fails it.

† **Unasse·rved**, *ppl. a. Obs. rare.* [UN-[1] 8.] **a.** Unserved. **b.** Undeserved.

*c* **1400** *Beryn* 56 'Graunt mercy, gentil Sir!' quod she, 'þat yee been vnaservid'. *c* **1400** *R. Gloucester's Chron.* 1256 (MS. Digby 205), I haue holde him on his londe and my mede þer of is That he me wolde dryue awey and unasserued j wis.

**Unassi·duous**, *a.* (UN-[1] 7.) **1776** BENTHAM *On Govt.* Wks. 1843 I. 295 All these leading points,..with as many points of detail subservient to each as a meditation not unassiduous has suggested.

**Unassi·gnable**, *a.* (UN-[1] 7 b.)

Hence, in recent use, *unassignability*.

**1674** N. FAIRFAX *Bulk & Selv.* 62, I see this roomthiness in the whole, must as well have unassignable parts or such as cannot be laid out. **1780** T. TWINING in R. Twining *Recreat. & Stud.* (1882) 76 In gracing, he does the most beautiful, most unassignable..things I ever heard. **1780** BENTHAM *Princ. Legisl.* xii. § 15 Such party may be either an assignable individual..or else a multitude of unassignable individuals. **1883** SIR E. E. KAY in *Weekly Notes* 15 Dec. 212/1 A vested reversionary interest subject to a life interest in leasehold property..[is] not an unassignable possibility.

**Unassi·gned**, *ppl. a.* (UN-[1] 8.) **1495** *Cov. Leet Bk.* 565 Yf..eny persone vnassigned take vppon hym to ruyde contrarie to þis ordenaunce, they to lese at euery defalt x s. **1812** WOODHOUSE *Astron.* xvii. 181 Effects with unassigned causes. **1870** SWINBURNE *Ess. & Stud.* (1875) 341 Many sketches by hands unknown...Also unassigned, is a vigorous drawing of a monk's head.

**Unassi·milable**, *a.* (UN-[1] 7 b and 5 b.) **1873** E. H. CLARKE *Sex in Educ.* 23 Our girls revel in those unassimilable abominations. **1882** *Athenæum* 4 Mar. 286/1 America is being invaded by Socialist Germans..and unassimilable Chinese. **Unassi·milatable**, *a.* (UN-[1] 7 b.) **1858** J. H. BENNET *Nutrition* iv. 89 The kidneys..[remove] from the circulating fluid effete unassimilatable nutritive elements.

**Unassi·milated**, *ppl. a.* (UN-[1] 8. Cf. G. *unassimilirt.*) **1748** HARTLEY *Observ. Man* I. iii. § 6. 393 It circulates with the Fluids in an unassimilated State. **1811** ABERNETHY *Surg. Wks.* (1827) II. 201 Much unassimilated matter being conveyed into the blood with the chyle. **1866** WHIPPLE *Char. & Charac. Men* 11 Unassimilated knowledge—knowledge that does not form part of the mind, but is attached to it.

**Unassi·milating**, *ppl. a.* (UN-[1] 10.) **1796** MME. D'ARBLAY *Camilla* I. i, [Fortune's] most rapid vicissitudes, her most unassimilating eccentricities, are..distanced by the wilder wonders of the Heart of man. **Unassi·stant**, *a.* (UN-[1] 7.) **1796** *Plain Sense* (ed. 2) III. 203 To suffer..her most strenuous protector, thus to depart unassistant to her wants,..pressed..heavily on her mind.

**Unassi·sted**, *ppl. a.* (UN-[1] 8.)

Hence, in recent use, *unassistedly* adv.

**1614** GORGES *Lucan* v. 179 Cæsar..As vnassisted now he stands: And almost left to his owne sword. **1705** CLARKE *Disc. Attributes* II. xiii, Many of them not discoverable by bare Reason unassisted with Revelation. **1751** EARL ORRERY *Remarks Swift* (1752) 120 The pure instincts of brutes, unassisted by any knowledge of letters. **1820** SCOTT *Monast.* ii, In case of assault, the proprietor would have to rely upon his own unassisted strength. **1849** RUSKIN *Sev. Lamps* ii. § 7. 33 The pillars would be, if unassisted, too slight for the weight.

**b.** *spec.* Of the eye or sight: Unaided, naked.

**1661** BOYLE *Certain Physiol. Ess.* (1669) 196 Notwithstanding the unassisted Eye can discern no such matter. **1707** *Curios. in Husb. & Gard.* 27 A naked and unassisted Eye. **1781** COWPER *Retirem.* 56 Contrivance intricate, express'd with ease, Where unassisted sight no beauty sees. **1794** G. ADAMS *Nat. & Exp. Philos.* I. i. 28 Microscopical observations that discover animals, thousands of which could scarce form a particle perceptible to the unassisted sense. **1865** MRS. L. L. CLARKE *Common Seaweeds* ii. 42 How could we with the unassisted eye see aught that is lovely in those dark purple or olive-brown tufts?

**Unassi·sting**, *ppl. a.* (UN-[1] 10.) **1694** DRYDEN *Love Triumph.* IV. i, They stretch their unassisting Hands in vain, But none will plunge into the raging Main, To save the sinking Passenger from Death. **1716** POPE *Iliad* v. 395 Nor Sthenelus, with unassisting hands, Remain'd unheedful of his lord's commands.

**Unassi·zed**, *ppl. a.* [UN-[1] 8.] † Not brought up to the proper assize; under weight.

**1616** *Southampton Court Leet Rec.* (1907) III. 512 We have ..from eache of them..taken some smale quantities of there howsholde vnassized bread.

**Unasso·ciable**, *a.* (UN-[1] 7 b.) **1816** J. GILCHRIST *Philos. Etym.* 215 Not to mention the unassociable, repellent natures of their tastes and styles. **1829** JAS. MILL *Hum. Mind* (1869) I. 98 There is therefore a further condition required to render two ideas unassociable. **Unasso·ciably**, *adv.* (UN-[1] 11.) **1892** PATER *Marius* II. 72 The immemorial waterfall, plunging down so unassociably among those human habitations.

† **Unasso·ciate**, *ppl. a. Obs.* [UN-[1] 8 b.] = next. (Const. *of* = with.)

**1545** RAYNALD *Byrth Mankynde* 17 Nether is there any notable vaine vnassotiat of an artyre. *Ibid.* 33 None of this vaynes run to the matrice or otherwhere, vnassosiat of an Artyre.

**Unasso·ciated**, *ppl. a.* (UN-[1] 8.) **1709** SHAFTESB. *Charac.* (1711) II. 313 Even on the supposal, that there was ever such a Condition or State of Men, when as yet they were unassociated, unacquainted. **1790** HAMILTON *Wks.* (1886) VII. 48 The accommodation..of unassociated persons and families who may emigrate thither. **1839** DE LA BECHE *Rep. Geol. Cornwall*, etc. x. 286 The manganese ores of North Devon are, however, unassociated with trappean rocks. **1897** *Westm. Gaz.* 17 Mar. 2/2 In this case the unassociated schools were better off than the associated.

**Unassoi·led**, *a.* [UN-[1] 8.]

**1.** Not assoiled; not absolved from sin.

*c* **1440** *Alph. Tales* 16 He was wrothe þat þis monke died vnasoylid. *a* **1513** FABYAN *Chron.* VII. 335 This Frederyke dyed vnassoylyd. **1844** MRS. BROWNING *Lost Bower* xxxiv, Unassoiled by Ave Marys Which the passing pilgrim prays. **1888** LOWELL *Heartsease & Rue* 71 The unclean bird Hooting to unassoiled shapes as they pass.

† **2.** Not settled; undecided. *Obs. rare.*

**1387** TREVISA *Higden* (Rolls) VII. 451 Þe pope..now..leveþ þe stryf al unassoilled [L. *indeterminatum*]. *a* **1513** FABYAN *Chron.* VII. ccxxviii. 257 The pope gaue suche a defuse sentence in this mater yᵗ he lefte yᵉ stryfe vndetermyned & vnassoyled.

**Unasso·rted**, *ppl. a.* (UN-[1] 8. Cf. G. *unassortirt.*) [**1775** ASH.] **1865** GLADSTONE *Farew. Addr. Edin. Univ.* 24 They were no longer a chaotic assemblage of unassorted or even conflicting units. **1877** RAYMOND *Statist. Mines & Mining* 253 Assays, unassorted, from $200 to $300.

**Unassua·geable**, *a.* (UN-[1] 7 b.) **1611** FLORIO, *Inplacabile*, vnasswageable. **1802–12** BENTHAM *Ration. Judic. Evid.* Wks. 1843 VII. 436 No mischief is so unassuageable as that which employs for its instrument a mass of corrupted language. **1817** SHELLEY *Address* Pr. Wks. 1888 I. 374 A calamity..such as the English nation ought to mourn with an unassuageable grief. **1884** G. MACDONALD *Unspoken Serm.* Ser. II. 39 The unassuageable rest of repulsion with which he regards such conditions.

**Unassua·ged**, *ppl. a.* (UN-[1] 8.) **1654** R. BAKER tr. *Balzac's Lett.* (vol. II) I. 119 There is no..pain unasswaged by his words before it be expelled by his wit. **1784** COWPER *Task* VI. 463 The pangs Of hunger unassuag'd. **1799** CAMPBELL *Pleas. Hope* II. 434 That spark .. shall beam on Joy's interminable years, Unveiled by darkness, unassuaged by tears. **1815** WORDSW. *Artigal & Elidure* 35 Till she, in jealous fury unassuaged, Had slain his paramour. **1892** *Pall Mall G.* 11 Oct. 2/3 The unassuaged agony of the animal.

**Unassu·med**, *ppl. a.* (UN-[1] 8.) [**1775** ASH.] **1818** HAZLITT *Table T.* xviii, The true, unassumed equality of greatness.

**Unassu·ming**, *ppl. a.* [UN-[1] 10.] Free from assumption; unpretentious: **a.** Of persons.

**1726** THOMSON *Winter* 772 See now the cause, Why unassuming worth in secret liv'd, And dy'd, neglected. **1780** *Mirror* No. 90, In his manners simple and unassuming. **1839** DICKENS *Nickleby* xviii, A very unassuming young woman. **1862** CALVERLEY *Verses & Transl.* (ed. 2) 49 Once, an unassuming Freshman Through these wilds I wandered on.

**b.** Of character or manners.

**1796** MME. D'ARBLAY *Camilla* IV. 401 His character [was] unassuming. **1797** S. & HT. LEE *Canterb. T.* (1799) I. 369 The unassuming and simple dignity of Lothaire. **1805** SOUTHEY in *Ann. Rev.* III. 570 A gentleman of unassuming talents. **1875** JOWETT *Plato* (ed. 2) II. 392 He walks about on the sea shore in an unassuming way.

**c.** Of things.

**1805** WORDSW. *Prelude* XIII. 46 The unassuming things that hold A silent station in this beauteous world. **1838** LYTTON *Alice* I. v, The expensive, yet unassuming *robe de soie*. **1896** MRS. CAFFYN *Quaker Grandmother* 146 Stopping to hit at the blackened unassuming remains of a dock.

Hence **Unassu·mingness.**

Also, in recent use, *unassumingly* adv.

**1768** *Woman of Honor* I. 48 An unassumingness, which was the result of most perfect modesty. **1799** SOUTHEY in Robberds *Mem. W. Taylor* (1843) I. 303 Davy is a surprising young man, and one who, by his unassumingness,..soon conciliates our affections. **1830** JAMES *Darnley* xxi, A sort of unassumingness, which seemed to hold his own high qualities as light, silenced much envy. **1876** MRS. WHITNEY *Sights & Insights* xii. 124 That unassumingness which is conscious of nothing to assume.

† **Unassu·re**, *a. Obs.*[−1] [Cf. UNASSURED and SURE *a.*] Unreliable.

**1531** in Ellis *Orig. Lett.* Ser. III. II. 216, I..wyll prove myselff, though the powrest,..yet not the vnassurest or vntrustiest of your freends.

† **Unassu·re**, *v. Obs.*[−1] [UN-[2] 3.] *trans.* To cancel the assurance of.

**1643** CARYL *Sacr. Covt.* 20 When at any time ye can..be resolved that these are insufficient grounds of making a Covenant,..ye may goe, and un-assure the Covenant which ye make this day.

**Unassu·red**, *ppl. a.* [UN-[1] 8.]

**1.** Not assured or safe; insecure.

*c* **1430** LYDG. *Min. Poems* (Percy Soc.) 76 Riche with wysshis, pore of possessioune; Stable unassured, assured eke unstable. **1596** SPENSER *Hymn of Love* 263 The doubts, the daungers, the delayes,..The fayned friends, the unassured foes. **1611** COTGR., *Desassurer*, to disassure;..to make vnsetled, vnassured. **1647** N. BACON *Disc. Govt. Eng.* I. xlv. 117 In the middest of his strong and conquering army he held himselfe unassured. **1896** *Daily News* 29 Oct. 6/5 The confusion..superinduced by unassured peace.

**2.** Not certain or sure (*of* something).

*a* **1529** SKELTON *Replyc.* 93 Your selfe thus ye discured As clerkes vnassured, With ignorance obscured. **1577** tr. *Bullinger's Decades* (1592) 504 The sentence definitive is suspended or else it is otherwise ghessed at by humane and vnassured suspition. **1646** SIR T. BROWNE *Pseud. Ep.* 194 To invent or assign a cause, when we remain unsatisfied or unassured of the effect. **1651** HOBBES *Leviath.* II. xxvii. 156 When men are by any accident unassured they have slept, [dreams] seem to be reall Visions. **1736** THOMSON *Liberty* V. 718 As thick to view these varied Wonders rose, Shook all my soul with transport, unassur'd, The Vision broke. **1776** M. MORGANN *Ess. Dram. Char. Falstaff* (1777) 12 Their ill-gotten..gold feels loose in their unassured grasp.

**3.** Not self-possessed or confident; not sure of oneself or of one's safety.

**1627** *Lisander & Cal.* v. 81 A troubled countenance and an unassured voice. **1697** COLLIER *Ess. Mor. Subj.* II. (1709) 153 He that is Embarrassed in his Liberty, is apt to be unassur'd in his Actions. **1713** *Guard.* No. 32 ¶ 8 He moved towards her with an easie but unassured air. **1760–72** H. BROOKE *Fool of Qual.* (1809) IV. 73 [They] stood yet awhile, pale, astonished, and unassured. **1821–2** WORDSW. *Eccl. Sonn.* III. xxxvii. 8 Had we, like them, endured Sore stress of apprehension,..From month to month trembling and unassured. 1825 SCOTT *Betrothed* xxvii, Lady Eveline approached his bedside with unassured steps, fearing she knew not what.

**4.** Not insured against loss or damage.

1828–32 WEBSTER s.v.

Hence **Unassu·redly** *adv.*, **Unassu·redness.**

1648 HEXHAM II, *Ongewisselick*, Vncertainly, or Vnassuredly. 1660 INGELO *Bentiv. & Ur.* I. (1682) 130 Incredulous Philosophers, of whose vitious lives I cannot but think their unassuredness in this matter to have been a great cause.

**Unasto·nished,** *ppl. a.* (UN-¹ 8.)

1533 BELLENDEN *Livy* v. xxi. (S.T.S.) II. 220 Fabius..past sturdelie throw all þe statiouns and watche of Inemyis vnastonist be ony of þare wourdis or terrouris. c 1605 ROWLEY *Birth Merl.* IV. i, Mother speak freely and unastonished; That which you dared to act, dread not to name. 1621 SANDYS *Ovid's Met.* VIII. 267 She..vnlocks a posterne doore: Then past the foe (bold by her merit made), Vnto the King not vn-astonisht, said. 1828 CARLYLE *Misc.*(1857) I. 224 Cool, unastonished, holding his equal rank from Nature herself. 1891 CONST. MACEWEN *3 Women in 1 Boat* 117 Xenia rose slowly, indifferently, and quite unastonished from her lounge.

†**Unastrai·ned,** *ppl. a. Obs.*—¹ In 5 *Sc.* vnastrenȝet. [UN-¹ 8.] Unconstrained.

c 1375 *Sc. Leg. Saints* iii. (*Andrew*) 341 He tholit þar one for to hynge, vnastrenȝet, bot of fre will.

**Unastrono·mical,** *a.* (UN-¹ 7.) a 1849 POE *Eureka* Wks. 1865 II. 127 The difficulty, if not impossibility, of presenting..to the unastronomical, a picture at all comprehensible. 1887 RUSKIN *Præterita* II. 391 This—unastronomical readers will please to note—being one of the leaden influences on me of the planet Saturn.

**Unat,** variant of UNNAIT *a. Obs.*

**Unathle·tic,** *a.* (UN-¹ 7.) 1759 H. WALPOLE *Let. to Mann* 13 Sept., With your unathletic constitution I think you will have a greater weight of glory to represent than you can bear. 1888 *Daily News* 25 Aug. 5/2 The absence of nerves in the unathletic Chinaman.

**Unato·nable,** *a.* Also -eable. [UN-¹ 7 b.]

†**1.** Unaccordable. *Obs.*—¹

1645 MILTON *Tetrach.* Wks. 1851 IV. 267 He who sees not this argument how plainly it serves to divorce any untunable, or unattonable matrimony, sees little.

**2.** Irreconcilable.

1683 HOWE *Union among Prot.* Wks. 1724 II. 243 If such men were capable of being reason'd with..I would ask them, 'What, are you altogether unatoneable? Will nothing divert you from this pursuit?' 1830 W. TAYLOR *Hist. Surv. Germ. Poetry* I. 213 How the waves rush, the thunders roar, and the voice of winds tells of this unatonable vengeance. 1853 RUSKIN *Stones Ven.* II. viii. § 45. 322 The great unatoneable division between the disciple and the adversary.

**3.** That cannot be atoned for or expiated.

1689 *Apol. Fail. Walker's Acc.* 19 The unattoneable Guilt of retarding the Conveyance of those Arms and Ammunition. 1881 W. COLLINS *Black Robe* I. x, I have committed the one unatonable and unpardonable sin.

**Unato·ned,** *ppl. a.* [UN-¹ 8, 8 c.]

**1.** Not atoned for or expiated. Also with *for.*

(*a*) 1727 THOMSON *Britannia* 60 And his guilty stores, Won by the ravage of a butcher'd world, Yet unatton'd, sunk in the swallowing deep. 1771 MRS. GRIFFITH *Hist. Lady Barton* III. 220 There is a hope beyond the grave, and nought but vice, unatoned by penitence and piety, need ever urge despair! 1811 SCOTT *Don Roderick* II. xlix, Nor unatoned, where freedom's foes prevail, Remain'd their savage waste. 1837 LYTTON *Athens* II. 7 Time past on, the injury was unatoned, the remembrance remained.

(*b*) 1753 RICHARDSON *Grandison* (1781) V. x. 50, I acquainted her with his former fault, unatoned for as it was. 1856 LEVER *Martins of Cro' M.* 279 The great fact remained unatoned for—his family, his own connexions, 'had done nothing for him'. 1876 BANCROFT *Hist. U.S.* III. i. 316 They cherished a deep sense of the wrongs unatoned for and unavenged.

†**2.** Unreconciled. *Obs.*—¹

1730 T. BOSTON *View Covt. Grace* (1734) 167 That Spirit they could not have from an unattoned God.

**Unato·ning,** *ppl. a.* (UN-¹ 10.) 1838 LYTTON *Alice* XI. iv, What hand could dare to send a criminal..so black with crime, unatoning, unrepentant, and unprepared, before the judgment seat of the All-Just?

**Unatta·ch,** *v.* [UN-² 4 b.] *trans.* To free from attachment.

1671 F. PHILIPPS *Reg. Necess.* 246 When it is and hath been not unusual for the Judges..to free or unattach goods attached in the City of Lond.

**Unatta·chable,** *a.* (UN-¹ 7 b.) 1843 in *Life A. Fonblanque* (1874) 257 There is no temple, and the unattached and unattachable gates are mere lumber.

**Unatta·ched,** *ppl. a.* Also 5–6 *Sc.* -attechit. [UN-¹ 8.]

†**1.** Not arrested or seized. *Obs.*

1498 *Reg. Privy Seal Scotl.* I. 34/2 All his men..to be une-sumond, une-attechit, une-arrestit, in his or thairis persoun or gudis. 1531 *Ibid.* II. 134/2 The saidis personis ..to be unattechit, unarrestit,..and untrublit. 1639 R. JUNIUS *Sin Stigm.* 368 He that is pursued, will cry, Stop Theife, that by this meanes he may escape unattached.

**2.** Not attached or united (*to* something).

In the first set of quots. used with reference to physical attachment or connexion.

(*a*) 1822 J. PARKINSON *Outl. Oryctol.* 96 Mr. Mantell.. ascertained it to have been an unattached animal, and without a column. 1861 H. MACMILLAN *Footn. fr. Page Nat.* 46 It [the bog-moss] has no roots whatever, but floats unattached in an upright position in the water. 1878 ABNEY *Photogr.* 100 Bromide of silver with unattached atoms of metallic silver, is formed.

(*b*) a 1821 V. KNOX *Spir. Despotism* § 34 True patriotism and true philosophy, unattached to names of particular men, or even to parties. 1844 DISRAELI *Coningsby* VIII. vi, Her eye soon glanced over the page, unattached by its contents. 1885 'MRS. ALEXANDER' *At Bay* iii, 'Pray do not trouble yourself,' returned Deering hastily, 'I can exist for half an hour in an unattached condition'.

**3.** Of persons: Not attached to, or definitely associated with, a particular body, institution, sphere of work, etc.: **a.** Of military officers: Not attached to a particular regiment or company.

1796 *List Officers Army* 13 Thomas Nesbitt,..Capt. of Foot, unattached. 1806 *Ibid.* 17 Late Unattached Officers. 1826 *Gentl. Mag.* I. 638 Promotions..J. Haverfield, from unattached full pay. 1835 MARRYAT *Olla Podr.* vii, He was put on full pay unattached. 1852 BURN *Naval & Milit. Dict.* s.v. *Disponibilité*, To place on the unattached list. 1859 J. LANG *Wand. India* 363 As a General of Division, he had been unattached, and had never done a single day's duty. 1876 VOYLE & STEVENSON *Milit. Dict.* 445/1 *Unattached list*, in the British army, officers not attached to regiments.

**b.** Of clergy: Not attached to a particular diocese or church.

1865 PUSEY *Truth Eng. Ch.* 285 *note*, Lord Westbury has ..declared him in fact an unattached Bishop. 1902 R. BAGOT *Donna Diana* v. 43 One of the unattached priests to be met with by hundreds in the streets of Rome.

**c.** Of students: Not attached to any college; non-collegiate. Also *transf.* and as *sb.*

1870–1 *Ann. Rep. Deleg. Stud. not attached* 16 A Grocers' Company's Exhibitioner and Unattached Student in the University of Oxford. *Ibid.* 4 The amount of intellectual life and industry developed by the Unattached system. 1897 ESCOTT *Soc. Transform. Vict. Age* xiv. 184 The Davis scholarship in Chinese was for the fifth time won a few years ago by an unattached.

**d.** In miscellaneous uses.

1888 'R. BOLDREWOOD' *Robbery under Arms* xl, We must get you in the police force..or make you an inspector, unattached. 1893 JOYCE *Short Hist. Irel.* 70 The oldest.. passed out of the organization altogether, and became an ordinary unattached member of the tribe. 1899 *Daily News* 26 June 8/4 Reporters attached to no particular journal have dashed up with news.., though the importance of the unattached men has waned.

**4.** Not engaged or married. Also *absol.*

1874 LISLE CARR *J. Gwynne* II. vii. 184 You lovers have such a provoking way of showing your immense superiority to us unattached creatures. 1897 *Westm. Gaz.* 9 Dec. 10/1 We are absolutely out of single young ladies just now, and ..they specially invited some charming 'unattached' from Johannesburg.

**b.** Not belonging to any family, owner, etc.

1888 *Pall Mall G.* 11 Oct. 11/2 That would bring to decent places the unattached children. 1898 *Tit-Bits* 26 Feb. 420/2, 40000 cats,..of which half are 'unattached', and live largely on refuse.

**c.** Not assigned to any special group.

1899 *Allbutt's Syst. Med.* VIII. 855 The Microsporon Audouini is as yet 'unattached'.

**Unatta·ckable,** *a.* [UN-¹ 7 b.]

**1.** Not liable or open to assault.

1805 LD. GRENVILLE in Dk. Buckingham *Mem. Geo. III*, (1855) III. 457, I am confident that Toulon is absolutely unattackable with such a force as you speak of. 1862 CARLYLE *Fredk. Gt.* XIII. xii. (1872) V. 122 Height which he judged unattackable, and on the side of which he pitches his camp accordingly.

**2.** Not susceptible to the effects of detrimental or dissolvent agencies.

1881 *Nature* XXIV. 249/1 The oxides formed on the surface may preserve it by their very presence, furnishing a sort of unattackable varnish. 1882 *U.S. Rep. Prec. Met.* 649 To make some of the particles of gold wholly unattackable by mercury.

Hence **Unatta·ckably** *adv.*

1865 CARLYLE *Fredk. Gt.* XVIII. xiii. (1872) VIII. 56 So unattackably strong was this position at Klein Kamin.

**Unatta·cked,** *ppl. a.* (UN-¹ 8.)

1663 COWLEY *Cutter Coleman-St.* Pref. ad fin., There are others..who think it a sign of weakness or stupidity to let anything pass by them unattaqued. 1693 *Mem. Ct. Teckely* II. 145 It having not been imagin'd that the Turks would leave behind them Comorra and Raab unattack'd. 1772 BURKE *Sp. Acts Uniformity* Wks. 1812 V. 325 However, as none of them wholly abandon that post, it will not be safe to leave it behind me unattacked. 1828 LYTTON *Pelham* III. iii, I am undisturbed and unattacked in the enjoyments best suited to my taste. 1878 ABNEY *Photogr.* 28 Treat all these residues with nitric acid, and they will all be found to remain unattacked by it.

**Unattainabi·lity.** (UN-¹ 12 and next.) 1850 CARLYLE *Latter Day Pamphlets, Jesuitism* 29 Moral evil is unattainability of Pig's-wash; moral good, attainability of ditto.

**Unattai·nable,** *a.* and *sb.* [UN-¹ 7 b and 12.]

**A.** *adj.* That cannot be attained or reached.

1662 BP. HOPKINS *Serm., Funeral* (1685) 52 Those thirty or forty years, which were judged by thee in thy childhood an unattainable age. 1690 LOCKE *Hum. Und.* II. xxi. § 40 The will..cannot, at any time, be moved towards what is judged, at that time, unattainable. 1736 POPE *Let. to Swift* 25 Mar., A View of the useful and therefore attainable, and of the un-useful and therefore un-attainable, Arts. 1771 *Junius' Lett.* lxiii. (1788) 334 This, though a wicked purpose, is neither absurd nor unattainable. 1809 *Edin. Rev.* XIV. 283 The great body of the people never yet engaged eagerly in the pursuit of an unattainable object. 1860 RUSKIN *Unto this Last* (1862) 80 Though absolute justice be unattainable, as much justice as we need for all practical use is attainable.

**B.** *sb.* **1.** An unattainable thing. *rare.*

1661 GLANVILL *Van. Dogm.* 112 *Temperamentum ad pondus*, may well be reckon'd among the three Philosophical unattainables. 1786 COWPER *Let. to Lady Hesketh* 10 Apr., Range and jack [in a kitchen] are not unattainables; they may be easily supplied.

**2.** With *the*: That which is not attainable.

1857 MAURICE *Ep. St. John* xx. 340 In one sense I can admit that man is always striving after the unattainable. 1882 MISS BRADDON *Mt. Royal* I. iii. 101 All women sigh for the unattainable.

Hence **Unattai·nableness; -ably** *adv.*

1690 LOCKE *Hum. Und.* II. xx. § 11 Despair is the thought of the unattainableness of any Good. 1863 HAWTHORNE *Our Old Home* (1879) 371 A strange repulsion and unattainableness in the very spell that made her beautiful. 1894 HALL CAINE *Manxman* III. xxv, She would be with him always;..the more reproachfully and unattainably, because she would be the wife of another man.

**Unattai·ned,** *a.* and *sb.* [UN-¹ 8.]

†**1.** Untouched, unaffected. *Obs.*—¹

1613 SIR A. SHERLEY *Trav. Persia* 136 Any of those bring extrinsicke danger, or intrinsicke errours, from both which you must liue free and vnattained.

**2.** Not attained or reached.

1671 CLARENDON *Dial.* Tracts (1727) 326 The art of Logick..is rarely unattained there by any who spend their time there with any application. 1774 GOLDSMITH *Nat. Hist.* (1776) II. 92 When the mind reflects with regret upon some good unattained or lost. 1794 MRS. RADCLIFFE *Myst. Udolpho* xxvi, Unless the crime..was instigated merely by resentment, .. its object must be unattained till the niece was also dead. 1868 MORRIS *Earthly Par.* (1870) I. II. 585 Days once bright, With foolish hopes of unattained delight.

**b.** *sb.* With *the*: That which is not attained.

1854 LONGF. *Epimetheus* xii, Thou makest each mystery clearer, And the unattained seems nearer. 1870 WHITTIER *My Triumph* vii, I better know than all How little I have gained, How vast the unattained.

**Unattai·ning,** *a.* (UN-¹ 10.) 1831 CARLYLE *Sart. Res.* II. iv, No mortal's endeavour or attainment will..content the as yet unendeavouring, unattaining young gentleman.

**Unattai·nt,** *a.* [UN-¹ 7: cf. next.]

**1.** = UNATTAINTED *ppl. a.* 2.

1649 G. DANIEL *Trinarch., Rich. II*, cclxxv, These, by a Publicke Act, stand vnattaint. *Ibid., Hen. IV*, xxii, The rest who fell Confederates with them, are vn-attaint.

**2.** = UNATTAINTED *ppl. a.* 1.

1850 S. DOBELL *Roman* ii, Unattaint, Perchance the Arethusan blood of Rome Hath coursed the conduits of a tyrant's veins. 1856 E. FITZGERALD *Salaman* (1909) 59 From Darkness came to Light a Child, Of Carnal Composition unattaint.

**Unattai·nted,** *ppl. a.* [UN-¹ 8.]

**1.** Unstained, unspotted; free from blemish.

1592 SHAKS. *Rom. & Jul.* I. ii. 90 With vnattainted eye, Compare her face with some that I shall show. 1600 W. WATSON *Decacordon* (1602) 274 [The catholics] liue in sorrow, heauiness, and suspition had of their vnattainted loyalties in generall, for some priuate offences in speciall. 1641 MILTON *Reformation* II. Wks. 1851 III. 54 To..ingage the unattainted Honour of English Knighthood..for so unworthy a purpose. 1716 SWIFT *Misc. Poems, To Earl of Oxford* 8 Virtue repuls't, yet knows not to repine; But shall with unattainted Honour shine. 1845 HIRST *Com. Mammoth*, etc. 44 That bears on high in knightly fight An unattainted crest.

**2.** Not attainted in law.

1794 W. HUTCHINSON *Hist. Cumbld.* I. 378 Whereupon it was adjudged that the title remained unattainted. 1821 BYRON *Two Foscari* I. i, Wouldst thou have His state descend to his children, as it must, If he die unattainted?

**Unatte·mpered,** *ppl. a.* (UN-¹ 8.) [1775 ASH.] 1884 WYLIE *Hist. Protestantism* VIII. i. I. 411/1 Nor have their souls remained unattempered by the grandeurs amid which they daily move. **Unatte·mptable,** *a.* (UN-¹ 7 b.) 1656 CROMWELL *Let.* 28 April (Carlyle), Whether Cadiz itself be unattemptable. 1865 CARLYLE *Fredk. Gt.* XX. v. (1872) IX. 94 Hopes there were of getting back Dresden itself; but that, on closer view, proved unattemptable.

**Unatte·mpted,** *ppl. a.* [UN-¹ 8.]

**1.** Not attempted or tried.

a 1548 HALL *Chron., Hen. VI*, 105 b, Thei..assauted the walles, and left no thyng vnattempted, whiche might bee to theim, any aduantage. a 1586 SIDNEY *Arcadia* II. xv. (1912) 250 Leaving no meanes unattempted of destroying his son. 1655 *Nicholas Papers* (Camden) II. 191 Yet no meanes shall bee vnattempted to discharge my duty. 1667 MILTON *P. L.* I. 16 Things unattempted yet in Prose or Rhime. 1734 *Col. Rec. Pennsylv.* III. 561 That we might leave no means unattempted for the Relief of these..Men. 1744 AKENSIDE *Pleas. Imag.* I. 696 To adorn This unattempted theme. 1816 BENTHAM *Chrestom.* 239 The imperfection, so long as the work has any use, will not afford any sufficient reason for leaving it unattempted. 1846 MRS. A. MARSH *Father Darcy* II. xiii. 230 Whatever the work left unattempted at home [etc.].

**2.** Upon, or against, which no attempt has been made.

1595 SHAKS. *John* II. i. 591 My hand, as vnattempted yet, Like a poore begger, raileth on the rich. 1687 SHADWELL *Juvenal* 372 While flourishing Troy Yet unattempted, did full peace enjoy. a 1704 T. BROWN *Walks round London, Westm.-Abby* (1709) 48 The Thief stole the Head and left the Trunk unattempted.

**Unatte·mpting,** *ppl. a.* [UN-¹ 5 d and 10.]

†**a.** Not attempting. *Sc. Obs.* **b.** Unenterprising.

1585 *Reg. Privy Council Scot.* III. 759 That thay contene thameselfis, in peceable and quiet maner at this tyme, unattempting ony..revenge aganis ony Englishman. 1730 WATERLAND *Script. Vind.* Pref. 23 Many have been too forward and enterprizing in that way..; and many also have been too cautious and unattempting.

**Unatte·ndance.** [UN-¹ 12.] †Inattention.

c 1449 PECOCK *Repr.* IV. ix. 470 Al tho lay persoonys..y biseche for to attende into these thingis,..whos vnattendaunce hath causid ful myche yuel.

**Unatte·nded,** *ppl. a.* [UN-¹ 8.]

**1.** Not attended or waited upon; unaccompanied.

1603 DRAYTON *Bar. Wars* v. xxiv, Car'd for of none, nor look'd on, vnattended, Sadly returning, with a heauie

Heart. **1667** MILTON *P. L.* VIII. 60 Forth she went; Nor unattended, for on her as Queen A pomp of winning Graces waited still. **1708** POPE *Lett.* (1735) I. 66 What a Number have here drop'd off, and left the poor surviving seven unattended! *a* **1795** PHILIDOR *Studies of Chess* (1817) 36 The unattended king should advance to intercept the pawn. **1846** MRS. GORE *Eng. Char.* (1852) 60 It suited him to ride thither unattended. **1895** SWETTENHAM *Malay Sk.* 119 The Shabandar, unarmed and unattended, accompanied him.

**b.** Of horses, etc.: With no one in attendance.

**1796** COLERIDGE *Destiny of Nations* 197 In the first entrance of the level road An unattended team! **1897** *Daily News* 5 Oct. 6/3 When vehicles were left unattended the wheels should be chained.

**2.** Not attended or accompanied *by* or *with* some thing, circumstance, etc.

(*a*) **1687** DRYDEN *Hind & P.* III. 607 Night came, but unattended with repose. **1768–74** TUCKER *Lt. Nat.* (1834) II. 678 Every benefit..procured for any individual,..if unattended with bad consequences, is a profit made to the whole. **1787** W. TICKELL *Acc. New Chym. Med.* (title-page), Its specific virtue in..all coughs unattended with inflammation. **1837** LYTTON *Athens* II. 4 It seldom happens that their renown in life was unattended with reverses equally signal. **1885** *Manch. Exam.* 6 Jan. 5/2 The collision was unattended with grave consequences.

(*b*) **1726** POPE *Odyss.* XIX. 601 Unattended by sincere repose, The night assists my ever-wakeful woes. **1749** FIELDING *Tom Jones* VIII. xi, I could have gladly embraced Death, ..if it had offered itself to my Choice unattended by Shame. **1847** W. C. L. MARTIN *Ox* 11/1 Nor is the chase unattended by danger, for a wounded bison often turns on his assailant. **1884** *Manch. Exam.* 12 Sept. 5/3 The accident to the Fenella..was fortunately unattended by worse consequences.

**3.** Not attended *to*. (Also without prep.)

**1729** BOYER *Dict. Royal* II, Unattended to, (disregarded) ..*negligé*. **1791** COWPER *Retired Cat* 66 The sun descended, And puss remain'd still unattended. **1803** *Edwin* III. ix. 150 No circumstance, however trivial, should be unattended to, from whence aid to our purpose may be derived. **1874** RUSKIN *Fors Clav.* IV. xxxvii. 4, I don't suppose any man with a tongue in his head and zeal to use it was ever left so entirely unattended to.

**Unatte·nding,** *ppl. a.* [UN-[1] 10.] Inattentive.

**1634** MILTON *Comus* 272 Nay gentle Shepherd ill is lost that praise That is addrest to unattending Ears.

**Unatte·ntion.** *Obs.*[−1] (UN-[1] 12 and 5 b.) **1691** NORRIS *Pract. Disc.* 290 Our Unattention is the Shield that repels thy Darts.

† **Unatte·ntive,** *a. Obs.* [UN-[1] 5 b.] = INATTENTIVE *a.*

**1591** HARINGTON *Orl. Fur.* Pref., A loose vnattentiue reader will hardly carrie away any part of the storie. **1665** BOYLE *Occas. Refl.* IV. Advt., A Reader that is not Unattentive, may easily collect.. That they were written several years ago. **1710** STEELE *Tatler* No. 167 ⁋ 3 Young Men, who are too unattentive to receive Lectures. **1768–74** TUCKER *Lt. Nat.* (1834) II. 547 There is a virtue in keeping one's self unconcerned at abuse or slander, unattentive to noise and impertinence.

Hence † **Unatte·ntively** *adv.*, **-ness.** *Obs.*

**1611** COTGR., *Sourdement*, deafely; also vnattentiuely. *a* **1649** DRUMM. OF HAWTH. *Hist. Jas. III*, Wks. (1711) 44 By the ambition and unattentiveness of his friends, his worth was made the scaffold of his ruine. **1682** NORRIS *Heirocles* 133 Their unattentiveness to the Instructions of others.

**Unatte·nuated,** *ppl. a.* (UN-[1] 8.) **1727** *Vin. Britan.* 42 The gross and unattenuated Parts of the Liquor. **1826** *Art of Brewing* (ed. 2) 31 Keeping a quantity of this fermentable matter unattenuated. *c* **1900** *Buck's Handbk. Med. Sci.* VI. 833 (Cent. Suppl.), Rabbits inoculated with unattenuated rabies virus.

**Unatte·sted,** *ppl. a.* (UN-[1] 8.)

**1665** J. SPENCER *Vulg. Proph.* 83 All these unattested Prophets generally fail in all their Prophecies. *a* **1677** BARROW *On the Creed* (1697) 27 Thus..God has not left himself unattested, doing good. **1818** CRUISE *Digest* (ed. 2) VI. 84 A charge by an unattested codicil will not be good. **1853** GROTE *Greece* II. lxxxviii. XI. 454 *note*, This is the best opinion which I can form on matters lamentably unattested and uncertain. **1858** LD. ST. LEONARDS *Handy-bk. Prop. Law* xviii. 143 If there are any interlineations in your will unattested, it will be presumed that they were made after the execution of your will.

**Unatti·re,** *v.* (UN-[2] 7.) **1791** MME. D'ARBLAY *Diary* (1842) V. 209 We both left Mrs. Schwellenberg to unattire.

**Unatti·red,** *ppl. a.* [UN-[1] 8.] Unclothed.

*c* **1400** *Laud Troy Bk.* 8300 Sithen I se the, I haue desired to se the, Ector, vn-atired. **1624** BOLTON *Nero* 247 Coignes represent that lady in this vnattired dresse, and posture. **1781** COWPER *Table T.* 722 Unattir'd in that becoming vest Religion weaves for her, and half undress'd. **1813** *J. N. Brewer's Beauties Eng. & Wales* XII. II. 449 Mrs. Lucy Waters, with an unattired infant.

**Unattra·ctable,** *a.* (UN-[1] 7 b.) **1802** *Phil. Trans.* XCII. 188, I separated the particles attractable by a magnet; and digested the unattractable portion with nitric acid.

**Unattra·cted,** *ppl. a.* (UN-[1] 8.) **1727** THOMSON *To Mem. Newton* 55 The tide revertive, unattracted, leaves A yellow waste of idle sands behind. **1909** *Pall Mall G.* 12 Apr. 6/2 Those who are unattracted by the South Pole. **Unattra·cting,** *ppl. a.* (UN-[1] 10.) **1776** S. J. PRATT *Pupil of Pleas.* (1777) I. 219 A woman whom even the depredations of four lingering months, passed in the languors of sickness, have not rendered unattracting.

**Unattra·ctive,** *a.* (UN-[1] 7.) Also *Comb.*

[**1775** ASH.] **1813** SHELLEY *Q. Mab* v. 29 Compelled, by its deformity, to screen.. Its unattractive lineaments. **1880** MCCARTHY *Own Times* IV. 56 It was evident..that the proposed measure was only..a compromise of the most unattractive kind. **1897** *Outing* (U.S.) XXX. 242/1 A very unattractive-looking dog that put us into precipitate flight.

Hence **Unattra·ctively** *adv.*, **-ness.**

**1836** JAS. GRANT *Random Recoll. Ho. Lords* xvi. 379 The unattractiveness of his manner. **1862** [ELIZ. JOHNSTON] *Gifts & Graces* xvi. 159 The..condition of lady-like unattractiveness so indispensable in a governess. **1863** A. GILCHRIST *Life Blake* (1880) I. 426 They are very small and very unattractively engraved.

**Unattri·butable,** *a.* (UN-[1] 7 b.) **1812** [LEIGH HUNT] in *Examiner* 11 May 289/2 Whatever may be the..cause of the misfortune, and however unattributable to the people.

**Unattu·ned,** *ppl. a.* (UN-[1] 8.) [**1775** ASH.] **1792** *Elvina* II. 23 Spirits..so unattuned as mine. **1806** SURR *Winter in Lond.* III. 185 Wild and unattuned to the social duties. **1887** SWINBURNE *Stud. Prose & Poetry* (1894) 135 A poor creature whose ear was yet unattuned to the cadence of 'chants democratic'.

‖ **Unau** (yū·nǭ). *Zool.* [Brazilian of the Island of Maranhão.] The South American two-toed sloth, *Cholopus didactylus.*

Adopted by Buffon from C. d'Abbeville *Mission des Pères Capucins*, etc. (1614) 252. Of the two kinds there mentioned by the names of *Unaü* and *Unaü ouassou* the former is Buffon's *Ai*, the latter his *Unau.*

**1774** GOLDSM. *Nat. Hist.* IV. xxii. 343 Of the sloth there are two different kinds,..the one, which in its native country is called the unan [*sic*], having only two claws upon each foot. **1834** MCMURTRIE *Cuvier's Anim. Kingd.* 93 Only one species [of *Bradypus*] is known, the Unau.., less uniform in its organisation than the Aï. **1872** HUMPHRY *Myology* 21 A recess and dimple in the astragalus of Unau and of Aï.

† **Unau·dible,** *a. Obs.* [UN-[1] 7 and 5 b.] = INAUDIBLE *a.*

**1611** FLORIO, *Inaudibile*, vnaudible, not to be heard. **1650** R. STAPYLTON *Strada's Low C. Wars* VII. 68 The man read it in French, and Low Dutch, but with such a hoarse vnaudible Voyce, that very few understood him. **1667** *Decay Chr. Piety* ii. ⁋ 18 Shall the superaddition of our Religion damp ours into a whisper, a soft unaudible sound. **1784** R. BAGE *Barham Downs* II. 106 Only heaven has blessed him with the gift of unaudible sighing.

**Unau·dienced,** *ppl. a.* (UN-[1] 8.) **1748** RICHARDSON *Clarissa* (1811) V. 183 To send back to town, un-audienced, unseen, a man of his business and importance! **Unau·dited,** *ppl. a.* (UN-[1] 8.) **1812** *Examiner* 5 Oct. 633/1 Which suffers an Irish Defaulter of unaccounted millions, to remain unaudited..after his dismissal. **1869** J. MARTINEAU *Ess.* II. 57 Honorable men do not wish their accounts to pass unaudited. **Unaugme·ntable,** *a.* (UN-[1] 7 b.) **1868** W. R. GREG *Lit. & Soc. Judgm.* 372 If, indeed, there were only a certain fixed and unaugmentable quantity of work to be done.

**Unaugme·nted,** *ppl. a.* [UN-[1] 8.] Not augmented or increased; in later use *spec.* of Greek verbs (see AUGMENT *sb.* 2).

**1555** EDEN *Decades* (Arb.) 296 The residue of the nyght that receaueth no light by the sayde..twilightes, is accomplysshed by the lyght of the moone, so that the nyghtes are seldome vnaugmented. **1648** HEXHAM II, *Ongegrooted*, vnaugmented. **1776** RICHARDSON *Arabic Grammar* 28 Chiefly from the simple or unaugmented three-letter words and their feminines. **1848** VEITCH *Irreg. Grk. Verbs* (1856) s.v. Ἀναλίσκω, Thuc. and the Trag. seem to have preferred the unaugmented, Plato and the Orators the augmented forms.

† **Unau·gurate,** *a. Obs.*[−1] [UN-[1] 8 b: cf. AUGURATE *v.*] Unconsecrated by augury.

**1600** HOLLAND *Livy, Topogr. Rome* vii. 1365 In it the Senat sate in counsell, because they might not assemble in any place unaugurate or unhallowed.

† **Unauspi·cious,** *a. Obs.* [UN-[1] 7 and 5 b.] = INAUSPICIOUS *a.*

**1601** SHAKS. *Twel. N.* v. i. 116 To whose ingrate, and vnauspicious Altars My soule the faithfull'st offrings haue breath'd out. **1656** EARL MONM. tr. *Boccalini's Advts. fr. Parnass.* II. l. (1674) 200 Some unauspitious Aspects of the Heavens. **1708** ROWE *Royal Convert* IV, Seo. Haste, and break off your unauspicious Rites: The instant Dangers summon you away. **1768** *Woman of Honor* II. 232 To consummate so unauspicious a sacrifice as that must be.

Hence † **Unauspi·ciously** *adv. Obs.*

*a* **1797** H. WALPOLE *Mem. Geo. II* (1847) III. x. 276 A Minister so unauspiciously seconded by fortune.

**Unauste·re,** *a.* (UN-[1] 7.) **1740** in Richardson *Pamela* (1741) I. p. xix, A gradual moral Sunshine of un-austere and compassionate Virtue shall break upon the World.

**Unauthe·ntic,** *a.* (UN-[1] 7 and 5 b.)

**1631** BRATHWAIT *Whimzies, Zealous Brother* 119 He vents such unauthenticke stuffe, as it proves pregnantly from what spirit it comes. **1660** GAUDEN *God's Gt. Demonstr.* 51 Thy humane traditions, and unauthentick because uncatholick observations, instead of Christ's institutions. **1778** WARTON *Dissert.* in *Hist. Eng. Poetry* (1781) p. xx, Shakespeare is thought to have formed his play [*Anthony and Cleopatra*] on this story from North's translation of Amyot's unauthentic French Plutarch. **1831–3** E. BURTON *Eccl. Hist.* xxii. (1845) 474 The evidence is equally unauthentic, which speaks of Zoticus, an Armenian Bishop, being put to death at this same period. **1851** I. TAYLOR *Wesley* (1852) 132 But the Methodists took orders in another manner, less direct and explicit indeed, but yet..not unauthentic or unimportant.

**Unauthe·ntical,** *a.* (UN-[1] 7.) **1549** COVERDALE, etc. *Rev.* xxii. 40 Nor it is not lawfull to confirme and mainteyne any maner of doctrine, concerninge our faithe and relygion by the auctoritie of any suche vnauenticall bookes. **Unauthe·ntically,** *adv.* (UN-[1] 11.) **1600** W. WATSON *Decacordon* IX. x. (1602) 332 A maxime in the lawes, either vnauthentically defined, or remaining litigious.

**Unauthe·nticated,** *ppl. a.* (UN-[1] 8.)

**1787** WHITAKER *Mary Q. Scots Vind.* I. 62 They thus condemn the Queen..upon letters unauthenticated by the producers. **1823** LINGARD *Hist. Eng.* VI. 316 The contradictory and unauthenticated statements of her friends and enemies. **1882** FARRAR *Early Chr.* II. 533 No Apostolic Church would have paid attention to an unauthenticated epistle.

**Unauthenti·city.** (UN-[1] 12.)

**1776** MICKLE *Camoens' Lusiad* Introduction 130 Though Voltaire still retains this sentence, its unauthenticity has been detected by several critics. **1862** LATHAM *Channel Isl.* II. xiii. (ed. 2) 325 The general unauthenticity of all the earliest monastic grants and charters. **1890** GLADSTONE *Impregnable Rock* v. 187 The question is not so much what particulars can be convicted of unauthenticity.

**Unauthe·nticness.** (UN-[1] 12.) **1657** J. SERGEANT *Schism Dispach't* 533 The perfect weaknes of his corroboratory proof, and utter unauthenticknes of the Welsh Pueriles.

**Unau·thorish,** *a.* (UN-[1] 7.) **1798** COLERIDGE *Let.* in *Biogr. Epist.* (1911) I. 161 May God love you and me, who am, with most unauthorish feelings, your true friend.

**Unautho·ritative,** *a.* (UN-[1] 7 and 5 b.)

**1644** HUNTON *Vind. Treat. Monarchy* v. 39 Is that.. Authoritative; or merely Consiliarie and unauthoritative? **1780** BENTHAM *Princ. Legisl.* xix. § 22 A Book of expository Jurisprudence is either authoritative or unauthoritative. **1851** H. W. TORRENS *Jrnl. Asiat. Soc. Bengal* 14 The vague and unauthoritative character of this learned writer's deductions. **1884** DOWELL *Taxation* IV. iii. I. 67 An abstract, imperfect and unauthoritative, of the Regent's Act of confirmation.

Hence **Unautho·ritatively** *adv.*; **-ness.**

**1644** HUNTON *Vind. Treat. Monarchy* iv. 27 It brings an illegality and unauthoritativenesse on acts exceeding. *a* **1827** in Bentham *Ration. Judic. Evid.* V. 595 *note*, To speak of the unauthoritatively..described act as evidence of the authoritatively..expressed one.

**Unautho·ritied,** *ppl. a.* [UN-[1] 8.] Unauthorized.

**1641** MILTON *Animadv.* Wks. 1851 III. 185 Nor to do thus are we unautoritied either from the morall precept of Salomon..nor from the example of Christ.

**Unau·thorize,** *v.* Also 6 -ysh. [UN-[2] 3.] *trans.* † To reject or annul the authority of.

**1554** BALE *Declar. Bonner's Art.* xix. 68 He hathe vnauthoryshed his owne naturall king Edwarde the syxte, notynge hym an vsurper. **1611** COTGR., *Exauthorer*, to exauthorize, or vnauthorize; to dispossesse of, or degrade from, authoritie.

**Unau·thorized,** *ppl. a.* (UN-[1] 8.)

**1596** WARNER *Alb. Eng.* XII. lxxii. (1612) 300 To armor vnauthorised should subiects neuer ronne. **1597** HOOKER *Eccl. Pol.* v. lxii. § 16 The exercise of vnauthorized iurisdiction. *a* **1637** B. JONSON *Underw., Vis. Muses M. Drayton* 46 A wild and an unauthoris'd wickedness! **1684** T. GODDARD *Plato's Demon* 14 Any private person, who unauthoriz'd by our lawful Government, shall publish any arguments or discourse [etc.]. ? **1760–1** GRAY *Metrum* Wks. 1884 I. 325 [To] insert words and syllables, unauthorized by the oldest manuscripts. **1858** FROUDE *Hist. Eng.* IV. 290 Henry so far listened..as to forbid the sale of unauthorized editions. **1885** J. MARTINEAU *Types Eth. Th.* II. II. iii. i. § 1 He was threatened with penalties still unrepealed for unauthorised theological teaching.

Hence **Unau·thorizedly** *adv.*

**1854** GROSART *Spenser's Wks.* III. 29/2 The spelling and grammatical forms, etc., of the later date are made to supplant..the earlier—unauthorisedly.

**Unavai·l,** *v.* [UN-[1] 14, after *unavailing*.] *trans.* and *intr.* To be of no avail (to); to fail.

**1866** J. B. ROSE tr. *Ovid's Met.* 23 Aye, all my knowledge unavails its lord. *Ibid.* 186 And lest medicaments should unavail [Medea] Chanted another magic silent spell.

**Unavai·lable,** *a.* [UN-[1] 7 b and 5 b.]

**1.** Unavailing; inefficacious; ineffectual.

**1549** COVERDALE, etc. *Erasm. Par. Jas.* 31 b, Of like sorte doubtles shall the profession of faith, whiche consisteth only in worde and worketh nothynge in dede, bee vnauayleable, but lyeth slugging like as it were deade. *a* **1600** HOOKER *Eccl. Pol.* VII. xi. § 2 Their proofs are unavailable to shew, that Scripture affordeth no evidence for the inequality of Pastors. **1616** J. HAYWARD *Sanct. Troub. Soul* I. v. (1620) 86 Where shall I hide?..To go forward it will be intolerable,.. to turne aside vnauailable. **1673** DRYDEN *Marr. à la Mode* IV. i, Your pity, madam, is generous, but 'tis unavailable. **1746** HERVEY *Medit.* 81 What can they do in this Day of Visitation?..To fly, will be impossible; to justify themselves, impracticable; and now, to make any Supplications, unavailable. **1777** POTTER *Æschylus, Prom. Chained* 12 To complain, or not complain, alike Is unavailable. **1808** *Mem. Female Philos.* II. 91 They displayed..the greatest valour and patriotism, but they were, alas, wholly unavailable in opposition to a superior force. **1850** MERIVALE *Rom. Emp.* xiii. (1865) II. 120 He unburdened his feelings to Atticus in unavailable lamentations.

**2.** Not available; incapable of being used.

**1855** *Orr's Circ. Sci., Inorg. Nat.* 202 Storage in reservoirs ..if the river supply is for any reason unavailable. **1888** BRYCE *Amer. Commw.* III. lxx. II. 558 In the event of the man they chiefly favour proving 'unavailable'.

**Unavai·lableness.** (UN-[1] 12.)

Also, in recent use, *unavailability*.

**1548** GESTE *Pr. Masse* E j b, Whych dyde [= deed] as it is a grounded proufe of falshode so of y[e] vnauaileablenes of y[e] masse. **1599** SANDYS *Europæ Spec.* (1605) L 3 b, Doubting else the vnavaileablenesse of those former inconveniences. **1611** W. SCLATER *Key* (1629) 130 Vncertaintie,.. vnprofitablenesse, and vnauaileablenesse eyther to decline wrath, or procure saluation. **1638** — *Serm. Experimentall* 63 The unavaileablenesse of all outward benefits, to stead us in the day of Gods wrath. **1829** E. BATHER *Serm.* II. 564 The utter unavailableness of man's presumed merits. **1870** RUSKIN *Lect. Art* v. 123 The impossibility of using it [oil-colour] with safety..and its unavailableness for note-book sketches and memoranda.

**Unavai·lably,** *adv.* (UN-[1] 11.) **1860** RUSKIN *Mod. Paint.* V. VI. viii. § 5, I know that nearly all in such matters must be said or shown, unavailably.

**Unavai·ling,** *ppl. a.* (UN-[1] 10.)

**1670** DRYDEN *Conq. Granada* III. i, I..would your unavailing Valour call, From aiding those whom Heav'n has doom'd to fall. **1728** ELIZA HEYWOOD tr. *Mme. de Gomez's Belle A.* (1732) II. 286 In hope that..I might bring him to a just Sense of his Folly, and cure a Passion so unavailing. **1788** GIBBON *Decl. & F.* l. V. 216 Their mummies were embalmed..to preserve the ancient mansion of the soul, during a period of three thousand years. But the attempt is partial and unavailing. 1843 BETHUNE *Sc. Fireside Stor.* 117 The heavy sea which was then running, rendered their efforts unavailing. 1891 FARRAR *Darkn. & Dawn* lv, The inventiveness of cruelty which Tigellinus and Nero studied.. amid the faint, unavailing remonstrances of Poppæa.

Hence **Unavai·lingly** *adv.*

1810 LEE *Odes Pindar* vii. 83 Approaching age serene I view, Nor unavailingly deplore The time, when I shall be no more. 1885 *Law Rep.* 10 P.D. 99 Every effort was unavailingly made to avoid the collision.

**†Unava·luable,** *a. Obs.*—[1] [UN-[1] 7 b + obs. F. *avaluer* (Cotgr. *avalluer*) to value.] Inestimable.

1638 KNYVETT in Ellis *Orig. Lett.* Ser. I. IV. 211 For not only the estate went to wrack, but neglected my education and breeding, a loss to me unvalleuable.

**Unava(u)nced,** obs. ff. UNADVANCED.

**Unave·ngeable,** *a.* (UN-[1] 7 b.) 1814 WORDSW. *Excurs.* III. 375 Wrongs unredressed, or insults unavenged And unavengeable.

**Unave·nged,** *ppl. a.* Also 6 vnad-. (UN-[1] 8.)

1481 CAXTON *Reynard* ii. (Arb.) 6 That shal I neuer hyde ne suffre it vnauengyd. 1548 UDALL, etc. *Erasm. Par. Rev.* xxii. 40 God wyll not suffer any suche thing to be vnpunysshed nor vnaduenged. 1670 MILTON *Hist. Eng.* IV. 169 They were by him and his Heathen Neighbours cruelly butchered; yet not unaveng'd. 1790 [see UNAVOWED *ppl. a.*]. 1816 SCOTT *Old Mort.* xxvii, The sword of liberty ..is in my hand, and I will neither fall meanly nor unavenged. 1859 TENNYSON *Marriage of Geraint* 1544 Tyrants in their day of power, With life-long injuries burning unavenged. 1876 [see UNATONED *ppl. a.* 1].

**Unave·nging,** *ppl. a.* (UN-[1] 10.) 1827 CAMPBELL *Lines St. Greece* vi, To see her unavenging ships Ride fast by Greece's funeral pile. **Una·venued,** *a.* (UN-[1] 9.) 1827 POLLOK *Course T.* IX. 1173 The gulf Of an unavenued,..Interminable, dark Futurity. **Unave·rred,** *ppl. a.* (UN-[1] 8.) [1775 ASH.] 1850 MRS. BROWNING *Sonn. fr. Portug.* xxxi, With souls that tremble through Their happy eyelids from an unaverred Yet prodigal inward joy. **Unave·rtable,** *a.* (UN-[1] 7 b and 5 b.) 1829 SOUTHEY in *For. Rev. & Cont. Misc.* III. 3 The Moorish historian considers it as an unavertable fatality. 1882 *U.S. Rep. Prec. Met.* 540 The theory of an unavertable decline of the Australian gold fields. **Unave·rted,** *ppl. a.* (UN-[1] 8.) 1753 RICHARDSON *Grandison* (1781) VI. xiii. 264 He stole gently my handkerchief from my half-hid face; with it he dried my unaverted cheek. 1820 SHELLEY *Œd. Tyr.* I. 374 Let not man or beast Behold their face with unaverted eyes! 1836 J. H. NEWMAN in *Lyra Apost.* (1849) 3 Upon Death's unaverted day As I speed upward. **Una·vian,** *a.* (UN-[1] 7.) 1890 W. H. HUDSON *Natur. La Plata* ii. (1892) 27 Its [the rhea's] figure and carriage have a quaint majestic grace, somewhat unavian in character.

**Unavised, -ly,** obs. varr. UNADVISED, -LY.

**†Unavisy,** *a. Obs. rare.* [f. UN-[1] 7 + *avisy* ADVISY *a.*] Not well-advised.

*c* 1420 *Prose Life Alex.* 13 Þe vnavesy lightenesse of ȝonge men. *c* 1425 *St. Mary Oignies* in *Anglia* VIII. 138 Soo þat hee, vnavisy man,..leeryd with schame by experiens what hee schulde doo.

‖ **Una voce** (yū·neɪ vōu·sɪ). [L. *ūnā* abl. sing. fem. of *ūnus* one + *vōce*, abl. sing. of *vox* voice.] With one voice; unanimously.

1567 HARMAN *Caveat* vi. 14 And, *vna voce* all sayde that no such man dwelte in their streate. 1619 BACON *Lett. & Rem.* (1734) 100 Unto which..all the Lords and the rest *unâ voce* assented. *a* 1708 T. WARD *Eng. Reform.* I. (1710) 113 The Congregation hearing this, Cry'd, *Vnâ voce*, So it is. 1758 J. S. *Le Dran's Observ. Surg.* (1771) 194 We concluded, *una Voce*, to leave all Things in the same Condition. 1834 DICKENS *Sk. Boz, Mrs. J. Porter*, 'It's sure to do.' 'Sure! sure!' cried all the performers *unâ voce.*

**Unavoi·dable,** *a.* [UN-[1] 7 b and 5 b.]

1. Not avoidable; that cannot be avoided or escaped; inevitable.

1577 tr. *Bullinger's Decades* (1592) 511 If..meere and vnauoidable violence is offered to a godlie man. 1600 E. BLOUNT tr. *Conestaggio* 241 Beeing an vnauoydable passage for the ships that come from the Indies. *a* 1688 CUDWORTH *Immut. Mor.* (1731) 11 The necessary and unavoidable Consequences of this Opinion. 1718 LADY M. W. MONTAGU *Let. to C'tess Mar* 10 Mar., Surprise at her beauty and manner.. is unavoidable at the first sight. 1782 MISS BURNEY *Cecilia* v. xiii, The change of habitation that now seemed unavoidable. 1826 F. REYNOLDS *Life & Times* II. 406 Within, and without, the walls of his theatre, he has a host of unavoidable enemies. 1885 'MRS. ALEXANDER' *At Bay* i, You may be sure the delay was unavoidable or I should not have kept you waiting.

2. *Law.* Not liable to be voided.

1628 COKE *On Litt.* 2 b, But if the man of non sane memory recouer his memory, and agree vnto it, it is vnauoydable.

Hence **Unavoi·dableness.**

Also, in recent use, *unavoidability.*

1599 SANDYS *Europæ Spec.* (1632) 115 The unavoidablenesse of those former inconveniences. 1653 GATAKER *Vind. Annot. Jer.* 103 The unavoidablenes of the Evils by these signs portended. *a* 1688 W. CLAGETT *17 Serm.* (1699) 206 The unavoidableness of heresies in the church. 1894 *Current Hist.* (Buffalo, N.Y.) IV. 900 Francis Joseph, convinced of the unavoidableness of the proposed reforms, supported his ministers steadfastly.

**Unavoi·dably,** *adv.* (UN-[1] 11 and 5 b.)

1608 H. CLAPHAM *Errour Left Hand* 86 Then it vnauoidably followeth, that [etc.]. 1695 LD. PRESTON *Boeth.* II. 66 They whom they have left must unavoidably submit to Poverty. 1744 BERKELEY *Siris* § 256 Natural evils will sometimes unavoidably ensue. 1798 COXE *Walpole* I. 727 The time unavoidably to be taken up in drawing orders at the exchequer. 1827 JARMAN *Powell's Devises* II. 177 Different minds will almost unavoidably form different opinions. 1861 MILL *Repr. Govt.* (1865) 4/1 There have been states of society in which even a monarchy..unavoidably broke up into petty principalities.

**Unavoi·ded,** *ppl. a.* [UN-[1] 8.]

1. Not avoided or escaped.

1565 GOLDING *Ovid's Met.* II. 24 b, Phebus..by and by with deadly stripe of unauoyded blow strake through the breast. 1596 DRAYTON *Legends* iv. 670 O powerfull Doome of unavoyded Fate. 1616 B. JONSON *Epigr.* I. xciv, Yet, Satires, since the most of mankind bee Their vn-auoided subiect, fewest see. 1642 H. MORE *Song Soul* IV. xix, The silent Preachers thoughts..will..Find each man out, and in a moment hit With unavoyded force. 1842 IS. WILLIAMS *Baptistery* I. ix. (1874) 109 Every night He sends his image, wraps us in his cove Of unavoided sleep.

† 2. a. Unavoidable; inevitable. *Obs.*

1591 SHAKS. 1 *Hen. VI*, IV. v. 8 A terrible and vnauoyded danger. 1594 — *Rich. III*, IV. iv. 218 All vnauoyded is the doome of Destiny.

† b. Unexceptionable; irrefutable. *Obs.*—[1]

1617 MIDDLETON *Fair Quarrel* v. i, Mine accusation shall haue firme euidence. I will produce an unauoided witnes.

**Unavou·chable,** *a.* (UN-[1] 7.) 1650 FULLER *Pisgah* III. xii. 403 What ever politick palliations may be pleaded for the contrary, such sacrilidge was unavouchable in it self. *Ibid.* v. iii. 149 An opinion..unavouchable by any strong arguments. **Unavou·ched,** *ppl. a.* (UN-[1] 8.) 1628 GAULE *Pract. The.* (1629) 182 They lash out the largest pennyworths, whose Ware is either vnknowne, or vnauouched. **Unavow·able,** *a.* (UN-[1] 7 b.) [1775 ASH.] 1802 BENTHAM *Panopt. Corr.* Wks. 1843 XI. 140 Any such clandestine and dishonourable, and unavowable and unavowed assurance. 1892 *Times* 26 Apr. 9/3 Gladstonian adhesion to crazy and unavowable schemes.

**Unavow·ed,** *ppl. a.* (UN-[1] 8.)

[1775 ASH.] 1790 BURKE *Fr. Rev.* 124 If the French king ..has in his own person..really deserved these unavowed, but unavenged, murderous attempts. 1850 L. HUNT *Autobiog.* xii. II. 94 Coleridge..lamented that an endeavour unavowed had been made to catch his tone. 1876 GLADSTONE in *Contemp. Rev.* June 5 Votaries who are scattered and isolated; or whose creed is unavowed.

Hence **Unavow·edly** *adv.*

1861 MAINE *Anc. Law* ii. (1866) 31 The moment the judgment has been rendered and reported, we slide unconsciously or unavowedly into..a new train of thought.

**†Unawait,** error for *in* (or *on*) *await*: see AWAIT *sb.* 1 b.

1452 *Paston Lett.* I. 238 Item, iij. of the seid felechep lay unawayte upon Emond Brome,..and toke hym presoner.

**Unawa·kable,** *a.* (UN-[1] 7 b.) 1691 E. TAYLOR *Behmen's Theos. Philos.* 348 In the Eternal Nature lyeth the Turba, though unawakable.

**Unawa·ked,** *ppl. a.* [UN-[1] 8.] = next.

1647 HEXHAM I, Vnawaked, *ongeweckt.* 1721 YOUNG *Revenge* IV. i, How soft the breast, on which I laid my peace For years to slumber, unawak'd by care! 1742 — *Nt. Th.* II. 618 Strange! the theme..shou'd sleep unsung! And yet it sleeps, by genius unawak'd.

**Unawa·kened,** *ppl. a.* (UN-[1] 8.)

1705 ATTERBURY *Serm. Luke xvi. 31* (1726) II. 57 Every day the Impression loses somewhat of its Force,..till at length it comes..to operate..faintly upon careless unawaken'd Minds. 1762 WESLEY *Jrnl.* 29 July (1827) III. 103 A harmless, unawakened..woman came to one of the meetings for prayer. 1819 SHELLEY *Ode West Wind* 68 Be through my lips to unawakened earth The trumpet of a prophecy! 1860 W. L. COLLINS *Luck of Ladysmede* (1862) I. 275 The eyes..in whose soft depths a mighty unawakened love had seemed always sleeping. 1899 *Educ. Rev.* Dec. 472 The dull and unawakened have their rights.

Hence **Unawa·kenedness.**

1879 MEREDITH *Egoist* x, Chewing the cud in the happy pastures of unawakenedness.

**Unawa·kening,** *ppl. a.* (UN-[1] 10.) 1846 WORCESTER (citing Foster). 1866 M. ARNOLD *Thyrsis* xvii, There thine earth-forgetting eyelids keep The morningless and unawakening sleep. **Unawa·king,** *ppl. a.* (UN-[1] 10.) 1863 [H. W. WHEELWRIGHT] *Spring Lapl.* 131, I should.. gradually pass off into an unawaking slumber. **Unawa·rded,** *ppl. a.* (UN-[1] 8.) [1775 ASH.] 1897 *Outing* XXX. 346/1 The cup offered..to the member who should ride upon the road the greatest number of days..is unawarded after a whole year having elapsed.

**Unaware** (vnăwēə·ɪ), *adv.* and *a.* [UN-[1] 11 b and 7: cf. UNIWARE and UNWARE.]

A. *adv.* 1. = UNAWARES *adv.* 1 a.

1592 SHAKS. *Ven. & Ad.* 823 As one that unaware Hath dropp'd a precious jewel in the flood. 1667 MILTON *P. L.* II. 156 Will he, so wise, let loose at once his ire, Belike through impotence, or unaware. 1700 DRYDEN *Pal. & Arc.* II. 18 To his Keeper this [beverage] he brought, Who swallow'd unaware the sleepy Draught. *a* 1800 COWPER *Odyss.* (ed. 2) XIX. 634 She pours her echoing voice,..Deploring Itylus, whom she destroy'd (Her son by royal Zethus) unaware. 1862 MRS. BROWNING *False Step* ii, Thou only hast stepped unaware,—Malice, not one can impute.

2. = UNAWARES *adv.* 2.

1667 MILTON *P. L.* III. 547 Some high-climbing Hill, Which to his eye discovers unaware The goodly prospect. 1700 DRYDEN *Pal. & Arc.* I. 258 A Glance of some new Goddess gave the Wound, Whom, like Acteon, unaware I found. 1818 KEATS *Endym.* IV. 879 Long have I sought for rest, and, unaware, Behold I find it! 1885-94 R. BRIDGES *Eros & Psyche* Apr. xxviii, A Zephyr..gathering round her unware Fill'd with his breath her vesture and her veil.

3. In phr. *at unaware*: cf. UNAWARES *adv.* 4.

1598 R. BERNARD tr. *Terence, Heautont.* IV. i, Thou doest all things at unaware and unadvisedly. 1644 T. CASE *Serm., Quarrel of the Covenant* 6 Floods of wrath and vengeance might break in upon them at unaware. 1700 DRYDEN *Pal. & Arc.* I. 492 A Serpent shoots his Sting at unaware. 1855 BROWNING *An Epistle* 296 So we met In this old sleepy town at unaware, The man and I. 1866 CHR. ROSETTI *Prince's Progr.*, etc. 20 At unaware They met eye to eye.

B. *adj.* 1. Not aware; not cognizant; ignorant. Const. *of*, or with clause.

1704 SWIFT *T. Tub* i, I am not unaware how the Productions of the Grub-street Brotherhood have..fallen under many Prejudices. 1809-10 COLERIDGE *Friend* (1865) 121 Of this important fact Rousseau was by no means unaware. 1866 G. MACDONALD *Ann. Q. Neighb.* iii. (1878) 34 He spoke in the most matter-of-fact tone, unaware of anything poetic in what he said.

2. Reckless; lacking caution; unwary.

1817 SHELLEY *Rev. Islam* VI. xv, I lost all sense or care, And like the rest I grew desperate and unaware.

Hence † **Unawa·red** *a.*; **Unawa·redly** *adv.*; **Unawa·reness.**

1652 SPARKE *Prim. Devot.* (1663) 114 A barbarous surprise of unawared sufferers, affording them neither opportunity of defence or preparation. 1847 L. HUNT *Men, Women & B.* I. ix. 145 He stood holding the door open,..in the blandest tones of unawareness saying—'Ah, dear me—I'm very—I beg pardon'. 1895 W. SHARP in *Life* xv. (1910) 244 It is unawaredly that she whispers to me.

**Unawares** (vnăwēə·ɪz), *adv.* Also 6 unawarres, 7 unawars. [f. as prec. + -S. Cf. UNIWARES, UNWARES *advs.*]

1. a. Without being aware; unconsciously; inadvertently; unintentionally. Cf. UNAWARE *adv.* 1.

1535 COVERDALE *Josh.* xx. 5 They shall not delyuer the deedslayer in to his handes, for so moch as he hath slayne his neghboure vnawarres. 1585 T. WASHINGTON tr. *Nicholay's Voy.* II. vi. 35 b, If any drinke of it vnawares. 1641 J. JACKSON *True Evang. T.* I. 70 Lactantius was slipt unawares into this opinion, and S. Ierome doth..animadvert him for it. 1699 R. L'ESTRANGE *Erasm. Colloq.* (1725) 276 Money might lie upon the Ground, and they tread upon it unawares. 1726 BERKELEY *Let.* Wks. 1871 IV. 139, I have unawares run into this long account. 1787 BENTHAM *Def. Usury* xiii. 184 So great a master having fallen unawares into an error. 1832 HT. MARTINEAU *Weal & Woe* ix. 133, I might have spoken unawares, with authority. 1865 KINGSLEY *Heroes* II. ii, I will tell you, lest you rush upon your ruin unawares.

b. Without being noticed; unobserved.

1667 DRYDEN & DAVENANT *Tempest* III. ii, I fear'd the pleasing form of this young man Might unawares possess your tender breast. 1690 LOCKE *Hum. Und.* III. i. § 5 By which we may give some kind of guess,..how Nature, even in the naming of Things, unawares suggested to Men the Originals and Principles of all their Knowledg. 1718 PRIOR *Solomon* Pref. ₱ 8 Age steals upon Us unawares. 1796 MME. D'ARBLAY *Camilla* V. 531 [In] confidence unlimited ..hours might have passed, unnumbered and unawares.

2. Without intimation or warning (given or received); unexpectedly, suddenly.

1535 COVERDALE *Ps.* xxxiv. 8 Let a sodane destruccion come vpon him vnawarres. 1584 R. SCOT *Discov. Witchcr.* II. ii. (1886) 16 Witches must be examined as suddenlie, and as unawares as is possible. 1657 TRAPP *Comm. Job* i. 19 No guest cometh unawares to him who keeps a constant table. 1667 MILTON *P. L.* II. 932 He..meets A vast vacuitie: all unawares Fluttring his pennons vain plumb down he drops. 1712 STEELE *Spect.* No. 504 ₱ 1 Commend me also to those who..do not give up their Pretensions to Mirth. These can slap you on the Back unawares. 1796 MME. D'ARBLAY *Camilla* II. 353 He had just surprised her in tears, by coming upon her unawares. 1812 BYRON *Ch. Har.* II. lxxi, He that unawares had there ygazed With gaping wonderment had stared aghast. 1869 FREEMAN *Norm. Conq.* vii. (1877) II. 63 The King, accompanied by the three great Earls, came unawares upon the Lady.

b. In the phr. *to take* (or *catch*) .. *unawares.*

1593 SHAKS. 3 *Hen. VI*, IV. viii. 63 Away betimes, before his forces ioyne, And take the great-growne Traytor vnawares. 1791 BURNS *Tam O'Shanter* 86 Glowring round wi' prudent cares, Lest bogles catch him unawares. 1849 LYTTON *Caxtons* I. iii, He seemed incapable of acting for himself; he,..if taken unawares, was pretty sure to be the dupe. 1865 KINGSLEY *Herew.* ii, The famous soubriquet of 'Wake'; the Watcher, whom no man ever took unawares.

3. In quasi-adj. use: † a. Ignorant, not aware, *of* something. *Obs.*—[1] (Cf. UNAWARE *a.* 1.)

1548 COVERDALE, etc. *Erasm. Par. Acts* 36 b, But thou, in persecucion of my disciples,..doest persecute me also, vnawares thereof. 1567 MAPLET *Gr. Forest* 86 b, He, as they are vnawares of him, sodainely snatcheth vp with his Pawes certaine of them.

b. Unknown, unperceived, unrealized. Const. *to* or † *of* (oneself or another).

1548 UDALL, etc. *Erasm. Par. John* 94 b, Neyther is it vnawares to me that ye shall not fully vnderstande these thynges whiche I nowe speake. 1584 *Leycesters Commonw.* (1641) 36 They sent on day (unawares to her) for Doctor Bayly, and desired him to perswade her to take some little potion at his hands. 1635 J. HAYWARD tr. *Biondi's Banish'd Virg.* 140, I submissively kneeling down, and kissing his [hand] unawares of him. 1643 E. SYMMONS *Loyal Subjects Belief* 75 It is not wisdome for any man..to trust himself in a suspicious path, lest unawares to himselfe and them, he be on the sudden *in mediis malis.* 1748 RICHARDSON *Clarissa* (1811) VI. 70 Unawares to myself, I had moved onward. 1857 KINGSLEY *Two Y. Ago* I. 144 She found..that she watched, almost unawares to herself, for his passing. 1874 S. WILBERFORCE *Ess.* II. 15 The very features of men..assume, unawares to themselves, something of unnatural severity.

4. In phr. *at unawares*: a. = sense 2.

1564 HAWARD *Eutropius* III. 31 Anniball assaultinge Eneus Fulvius at unawares beinge then in Italye slue him. 1593 SHAKS. 3 *Hen. VI*, IV. iv. 9 He is taken prisoner, Either betrayd by falshood of his Guard, Or by his Foe surpriz'd at vnawares. 1622 R. HAWKINS *Voy. S. Sea* (1847) 90 We used all our best endevours to take them at unawares, yet comming within fortie paces, we were discovered. *a* 1667 COWLEY *Ess. in Verse & Pr., Avarice*, He..Must run the danger..of the rapid stream it self which may At unawares bear him perhaps away. 1737 WHISTON *Josephus, Antiq.* II. x. § 2 Serpents..some of which..fly in the air, and so come upon men at unawares. *a* 1774 GOLDSM. *Hist. Greece* II. 225 Darius fearing he should be attacked at unawares,.. obliged his soldiers to continue the whole night under arms.

1822 SCOTT *Halidon Hill* I. ii. 167 You might slay him At unawares before he saw your blade drawn. 1868 NETTLESHIP *Ess. Browning* i. 40 It is like coming to the edge of a precipice at unawares.

b. = sense 1 a and 1 b.

1596 DANETT tr. *Comines* (1614) 129 The King feared especially..least some word should escape him at vnawares. 1613 PURCHAS *Pilgrimage* (1614) 570 A Roman, at vnawares hauing killed a Cat, could not..be detained from their butcherly furie. 1679 C. NESSE *Antichrist* 213 It stole into the world..unsensibly and at unawares. 1853 MISS YONGE *Heir of Redclyffe* xv, All this was told at unawares, drawn forth by different questions and remarks, till Guy inquired how much 'it would take to give them a start?' 1870 CHR. ROSSETTI *Poems* (1904) 65 When friend shall no more envy friend Nor vex his friend at unawares.

† **Unawa·rnist,** *ppl. a. Sc. Obs.* [UN-1 8: cf. UNWARNIST.] Unannounced. So †**Unawa·rnistly** *adv.*, without warning. *Obs.*

1533 BELLENDEN *Livy* II. x. (S.T.S.) I. 165 Brokin of þare purpois be vnawarnist cummyng of romane legiouns. *Ibid.* IV. xii. II. 89 This l. posthvmeus..Invadit þe Inemyis vnawarnistlie.

**Unaw·ed,** *ppl. a.* [UN-1 8.] Not awed or awestruck. Also const. *by.*

1693 DRYDEN *Ovid's Met.* I. 116 Unforc'd by Punishment, un-aw'd by fear, His words were simple, and his Soul sincere. 1728 POPE *Dunciad* III. 223 Persist, by all divine in Man unaw'd. 1768–74 TUCKER *Lt. Nat.* (1834) I. 669, I have proceeded all along with an unawed freedom, doing my utmost to cast all prejudices aside. 1807 BYRON *Episode of Nisus* 95 With anxious tremors, yet unawed by fear, The faithful pair before the throne appear. 1867 H. MACMILLAN *Bible Teach.* 73 The pine..standing lonely and unawed..in the midst of fearful horizons of snow-mountain and glacier.

**Unaw·ful,** *a.* [UN-1 7.]

†1. Not inspired or tinged with awe. *Obs.*

1627 WREN *Serm. bef. King* 17 Feb. 33 All negligent and perfunctorie performance of our Religion, all slight and unawful Expressions in it, as in Gods presence, are the foulest Scorn and Abasement that may be. 1656 JEANES *Fuln. Christ* 70 Men come with as unprepared, unreverent, unawfull, and undevout thoughts and affections to a sermon, as to a play.

2. Not inspiring or causing awe.

1799 H. T. COLEBROOKE in *Life* (1873) 422 In the valleys the gloomy confined view is not unawful. 1826 MILMAN *Anne Boleyn* iii. 50, I go..where wild men howl around Their blood stain'd altars—to uplift th' unknown, Unawful Crucifix.

† **Unaw·ned,** *ppl. a. Obs.* (See UN-1 3.)

**Unaw·ned,** *a.* [UN-1 9.] Awnless.

1821 W. P. C. BARTON *Flora N. Amer.* I. 105 Anthers linear, unawned.

**Una·zotized,** *ppl. a.* [UN-1 8.] Not deprived of oxygen.

1828 *Lancet* 29 Mar. 940/1 Unazotised food increased the symptoms. 1861 BENTLEY *Man. Bot.* 726 The various azotized and unazotized compounds which are concerned in the development of new tissues.

**Un-ba·ckboarded,** *a.* (UN-1 9.) 1858 MRS. GORE *Heckington* xvi, God be praised! there is still one good, natural, honest, un-backboarded girl left in the world.

**Unba·cked,** *a.* [UN-1 8.]

1. Of horses: Unmounted; untrained.

1592 SHAKS. *Ven. & Ad.* 320 The vnbackt breeder full of fears, Iealous of catching, swiftly doth forsake him. 1613 W. BROWNE *Brit. Past.* I. v. 98 A stubborne Nagge of Galloway; Or vnback'd Iennet, or a Flanders Mare. 1656 STANLEY *Hist. Philos.* IV. (1687) 136/2 Being demanded how the Learned differ from the unlearned, he answered, as Horses unback'd from such as are well manag'd. 1753 HOGARTH *Anal. Beauty* xvii. 223 A fine Arabian war-horse, unbacked, and at liberty, and in a wanton trot. 1787 *Generous Attachment* II. 66 My Louisa's long unbacked mare..frisked like a fawn across the neighbouring meadow.

2. Not backed or supported; not endorsed.

1609 DANIEL *Civ. Wars* III. lxxix, He..will not avouch thy fact, But let the weight of thine owne infamie Fall on thee, vnsupported, and vnbackt. 1642 H. MORE *Song of Soul* To Rdr., Nor is reason unback'd with better principles mathematically satisfiable in matters of this kind. 1658 EARL MONM. tr. *Paruta's Wars Cyprus* 34 Most..were new men, and unexperienced, especially being unback'd by Horse. 1846 MRS. GORE *Eng. Char.* (1852) 115 A sucking politician unbacked by parliamentary interest. 1854 H. MILLER *Sch. & Schm.* (1858) 548 They were in danger of being put down, unbacked by the popular support which in such a cause they deserved. 1892 *Daily News* 25 May 2/3 An arrangement which gives only an unbacked promise of half interest.

b. Not backed by betting.

1883 *Times* 22 Oct. 10/2 This year he took part in the race for the Great Yarmouth Handicap,..but he was unbacked and unplaced.

3. Not furnished with a back or backing.

1861 *Daily Tel.* 19 Aug., The target fired at was an unbacked slab of wrought iron. 1895 *Funk's Stand. Dict.*, *Unbacked*, having no back, as a stool.

† **Unbad,** obs. variant of UNBID *ppl. a.*

1642 H. MORE *Song of Soul* II. ii, Men ybrought Into some spacious room, who when they've had A turn or two, go out, although unbad.

**Unba·dged,** *ppl. a.* (UN-1 8.) 1875 BROWNING *Aristoph. Apol.* 195 No unbadged buffoon is licensed here To shame us all. **Unba·ffleable,** *a.* (UN-1 7.) 1827 *Examiner* 642 Extraordinary penetration and unbaffleable acuteness.

**Unba·ffled,** *ppl. a.* (UN-1 8.)

1795 SOUTHEY *Joan of Arc* I. 251 'Maiden, thou hast done Thy mission here,' the unbaffled fiend replied. 1829 LYTTON *Disowned* ii, The first glow and life of youth,..unbaffled in a single hope. 1855 BROWNING *Old Pict. Florence* xxxvi, That morning the scaffold Is broken away, and the long-pent fire..unbaffled Springs from its sleep.

**Unba·g,** *v.* [UN-2 5.] *trans.* To take or let out of a bag.

1611 FLORIO, *Dissaccare*, to emptie out of a sacke, to vnbag. 1854 DE QUINCEY *War* Wks. 1862 IV. 279 To carry the knaves like foxes in a bag to the English border and there unbag them. 1860 GEO. ELIOT *Mill on Floss* III. iii, Mrs. Tulliver, with a confused impression that it was a great occasion, like a funeral, unbagged the bell-rope tassels, and unpinned the curtains. 1884 *Pall Mall G.* 5 Mar. 3/2 A crowd of spectators assembled to see the fox unbagged.

**Unbai·lable,** *a.* [UN-1 7 b.] a. Not entitled to be released on bail. b. Not admitting of bail.

1627 in Birch *Crt. & Times Chas. I* (1848) I. 295 If the cause be unexpressed, he shall be unbailable. *a* 1718 PENN *Life* Wks. 1726 I. 228 We are..then thrown into a noisom Gaol, and there we must lie unbailable. 1861 W. S. PERRY *Hist. Ch. Eng.* I. iv. 185 The unbailable imprisonment which lighted upon those who declined it. 1884 *Imp. Dict.* s. v., The offence is unbailable.

**Unbai·n,** *a.* Now only *dial.* Also 4–5 vnbayn(e, -bein, 5 -beyne, 9 *dial.* unbane. [f. UN-1 7 + BAIN *a.*, or ad. ON. *úbeinn* not straight, crooked (Norw. *ubein* crooked, awkward).]

†1. Not ready or willing; disobedient. *Obs.*

*a* 1300 *Cursor M.* 17735 He sal find mani bern vnbain, For mani sal him sai again. *c* 1400 *Rule St. Benet* (Verse) 1639 If ony be so vnbayne In word or werk to groch ogayn, ..With penance sal scho be chastid. *c* 1460 *Towneley Myst.* xxiv. 356 Thou shall forthynk it, in fayth; Fy, what thou art fre! vnbychid, vnbayn! ? *a* 1500 *Chester Pl.* II. 338 Thus shalt thou lyve,..for thou hast bene to me vnbeyne.

†b. Unfriendly, disagreeable. *Obs.*

*a* 1300 *Prov. Hending* in *Anglia* IV. 186 Drawe þine honde sone aȝein, ȝef man doth þe ouht unbein, Þar þine herte is ilende.

†2. Slow, inactive. *Obs.*—1

*a* 1470 HARDING *Chron.* LXIII. xii, So was he kyng of Brytain then again, And sone then after, he fell in age vnbain.

3. *dial.* Inconvenient, awkward.

1828 *Craven Gloss.*, *Unbane*, inconvenient, distant. 1863 MRS. TOOGOOD *Spec. Yorksh. Dial.* (MS.), I ought to have a fork; the spade is very unbane for the work. 1899 *Leeds Merc. Suppl.* 5 Aug. (E.D.D.), T' doors is as unbane as can be.

**Unbai·t,** *v.* (UN-2 4.) 1598 FLORIO, *Disinuescare*, to vnsnare, to vnbaite. 1844 *P. Parley's Ann.* V. 231 As to cheese, I'll unbait all the mousetraps for you; but you shall not eat dry bread.

**Unbai·ted,** *ppl. a.* [UN-1 8.]

1. Not baited or worried by dogs.

15.. J. BALNAVIS '*O Gallandis all*' 86 (Bann. MS.), Ouer oft to hound in vnkowth ground, Thow ma tak vp vnbaittit. 1672 in Picton *L'pool Munic. Rec.* (1883) I. 341 a bull unbaited.

2. Not furnished with bait.

1880 CARNEGIE *Pract. Trapping* 61 A sure way of catching this destructive little animal..is to cut a groove in some of the posts or gate posts, in which set an unbaited steel trap. 1905 *Macm. Mag.* Dec. 90 Two rods dangled an unbaited hook and a bedraggled fly in the water.

**Unbai·zed** *a.* (UN-1 9.) 1853 C. BRONTE *Villette* xxviii, It slid down the polished slope of the varnished and unbaized desk.

**Unba·ked** (vnbē·kt), *ppl. a.* Also 6 unbackte. [UN-1 8. Cf. Sw. *obakad*, Da. *ubagt.*]

1. Of tiles, brick, etc.: Not baked in a kiln; not exposed to heat.

1563 HYLL *Art Garden.* (1574) 32 Ye water, in which the vnbaked Tile hath bene soked, poured vpon their holes, doth destroy them. 1579 LANGHAM *Gard. Health* (1633) 191 The stones burned in an vnbaked pot..and the ashes burnt wil serue for Spodium. 1598 FLORIO, *Mattoni crudi*, vnbaked brickes, white bricks. 1787 *Phil. Trans.* LXXVII. 291 This handle consists of turned unbaked mahogany. 1853 J. LANG *Wetherbys* 171 Badly-built walls, which had been made of unbaked bricks to save expense! 1869 TOZER *Highl. Turkey* I. 375 Miserable hovels of unbaked brick.

2. Of bread, etc.: Not prepared by baking.

1577 tr. *Bullinger's Decades* (1592) 370 There was offered ..cleane meale vnbaked. 1578 LYTE *Dodoens* II. cxvi. 310 Maynardus..putteth it into the midle of an vnbackte loafe, so letting it bake vntil the bread be wel backte. 1611 FLORIO, *Incotto*, vnsodden, vnbaked, vnrosted, vnboyled. 1727 BAILEY (vol. II), *Dough*,..the Mass of Bread unbaked. 1769 COOK *Voy. round World* I. xvii. (1773) 202 A quart of the pounded bread-fruit, which is as substantial as the thickest unbaked custard.

3. *fig.* Left in an unfinished or immature state.

1601 SHAKS. *All's Well* IV. v. 3 All the vnbak'd and dowy youth of a nation. *a* 1625 FLETCHER *Elder Brother* II. ii, A little unbak'd Poetry, such as the Dablers of our time contrive. 1635 PAGITT *Christianogr.* II. vi. (1636) 40 Their Masse was then unmoulded, Transubstantiation unbaked.

† **Unba·ken,** *ppl. a. Obs.*—1 [UN-1 8 b. Cf. MDu. *ongebacken* (Du. *-bakken*), OHG. *ungipachan* (MHG. *ungebachen*, G. *-backen*).] = prec. 1.

1549 *Compl. Scot.* vi. 46 Ane of the tabilis vas of baikyn stane, and the tothir tabil of onbaykyn stane.

**Unba·lance,** *sb.* (UN-1 12.) 1887 *Alienist & Neurol.* Oct. 524 The paralyzing influence..arising from congenital deficiency and unbalance. 1895 *Strand Mag.* Oct. 383/1 His mind was still in a terrible state of unbalance.

**Unba·lance,** *v.* [UN-2 3.]

†1. *trans.* = UNBALLAST *v.* 1. *Obs.*—1 (Cf. BALANCE *v.* 17.)

1586 B. YOUNG *Guazzo's Civ. Conv.* IV. 193 b, He..without anie more wordes unballanced [It. *votò*] the ship.

2. To throw (a person or thing) off the balance.

1856 RUSKIN *Mod. Paint.* III. IV. xii. § 10 His ways are stedfast; it is not this or that new sight which will at once unbalance him. 1892 *Pall Mall G.* 21 Jan. 3/2 Alcohol.. disturbs and unbalances the nervous system.

Hence **Unba·lancing** *vbl. sb.*

1889 *Pop. Sci. Monthly* July 368 A further unbalancing of the relations between the railroad companies and the public.

**Unba·lanceably,** *adv.* (UN-1 11.) 1661 FELTHAM *Resolves*, etc. 392 Albeit his loss without Gods mercy was unballanceably irrecoverable.

**Unba·lanced,** *ppl. a.* [UN-1 8.]

1. Not balanced or equably poised: a. Of the mind, judgement, etc., or persons in respect of these.

1650 BP. HALL *Cases Consc.* (ed. 2) 388 Wherein yet I cannot much blame an unballanced judgement, whiles I find the Septuagint contrary to themselves. 1737 POPE *Hor. Epist.* I. vi. 25 Thus good or bad, to one extreme betray Th' unbalanc'd Mind, and snatch the Man away. 1882 J. PARKER *Apost. Life* I. 62 We know what he has been up to this time, ardent, impulsive, unbalanced, enthusiastic, cowardly. 1886 A. WEIR *Hist. Basis Mod. Europe* (1889) 111 Interference with the old order was so far-reaching, that the minds of all were quite unbalanced.

b. Of material things.

1732 POPE *Ess. Man* I. 251 Let Earth unbalanc'd from her orbit fly. 1784 COWPER *Task* v. 40 No needless care, Lest storms should overset the leaning pile Deciduous, or its own unbalanc'd weight. 1835 *Court Mag.* VI. 192/1, I was several times unbalanced, and on the very point of being hurled backward into the gulf. 1901 *Feilden's Mag.* IV. 442/2 A running test of 16 hrs. with an average unbalanced load of 3,000 lbs.

c. *fig.* or *transf.* in various senses.

1712 BLACKMORE *Creation* III. 487 Then would unbalanc'd heat licentious reign. 1818 BYRON *Ch. Har.* IV. cxxxii, Thou, who never yet of human wrong Left the unbalanced scale. 1855 BAIN *Senses & Int.* II. ii. § 9 The variegated aspects of the fields and gardens..have more beauty than the unbalanced verdure of the leaf. 1879 R. K. DOUGLAS *Confucianism* iii. 91 He hated those who possess valour unbalanced by the observance of propriety. 1899 *Allbutt's Syst. Med.* VIII. 333 Deviation takes place in the opposite direction through the unbalanced action of the healthy muscles on the unparalysed side.

2. Of an account: (see BALANCE *v.* 14).

1828–32 WEBSTER, *Unbalanced*,..not brought to an equality of debt and credit. 1902 *Daily Chron.* 25 Nov. 6/2 Complicated, confused, and unbalanced accounts.

**Unba·le,** *v.* [UN-2 5.] *trans.* To undo (goods) from a bale or bales. Hence **Unba·led** *ppl. a.*

1752 *Phil. Trans.* XLVII. 516 There should be found very honest men..who will take the trouble of seeing all the good unbaled, and every particular parcel exposed to the air. 1879 T. H. S. ESCOTT *England* I. 221 The unbaled cotton..passes through a series of machines.

**Unba·lked,** *ppl. a.* (UN-1 8.) 1888 TALMAGE in *Voice* (N.Y.) 10 May, That passion of jealousy, livid, hungry, unbalked, rages on.

**Unba·ll,** *v.* [UN-2 5: cf. UNBALE *v.*] *trans.* To unpack.

*a* 1694 SIR A. BALFOUR *Lett.* (1700) 96 You must..then cause unball them at the Custom-house, and set your Mark upon them.

† **Unba·llassed,** *ppl. a. Obs.* Also 7 vnballac't, -aced. [UN-1 8.] = UNBALLASTED.

1606 BP. HALL *Heaven upon Earth* § 25. 185 A light, vnballaced vessell, that rises and falls with euery wave. 1621 G. SANDYS *Ovid's Met.* II. (1626) 25 As vnballac't ships are rockt and tost With tumbling Waues. 1694 ADDISON *Ovid's Met.* II. Wks. 1721 I. 157 As at sea th' unballass'd vessel rides Cast to and fro.

† **Unba·llast,** *ppl. a. Obs.* [var. of prec. Cf. Du. *ongeballast.*] = UNBALLASTED.

1622 T. SCOTT *Belg. Pismire* Pref., I have..saved much I might have lost, had I ventured any thing in so light, weake, and vnbalast a bottom. 1655 GURNALL *Chr. in Arm.* I. 275 The opinion of others, whose breath of applause possibly was a means to over-set thy unballast spirit. 1659 W. CHAMBERLAYNE *Pharonnida* II. 103 The vexed prince,.. to entertain Them now with strength unballast, calls in haste His late neglected Council.

**Unba·llast,** *v.* [UN-2 4. Cf. Du. *ontballasten.*]

1. *Naut.* To clear (a ship) of ballast. Also **Unba·llasting** *vbl. sb.*

*a* 1684 LEIGHTON *Com. Pet.* v. 6 (1849) II. 460 It is necessary time and pains that is given to the unballasting of a ship. 1769 FALCONER *Dict. Marine* (1780), *To unbalast*, to discharge the ballast of a ship. [Hence in later dicts.] *Ibid.* (French Terms), [The] *Maître de quai*..is besides to appoint the proper places for ballasting and unballasting vessels.

2. *fig.* To render unsteady.

1836 *Blackw. Mag.* XXXIX. 466 This pleasure..more completely unballasts the mind than any other.

**Unba·llasted,** *ppl. a.* [UN-1 8.]

1. Of vessels: Not ballasted or rendered steady by ballast.

1657 F. COCKIN *Div. Blossomes* 22 And such a heart, like an unballast'd Ship, Is turned o'r with e'ry breath of wind. 1678 CUDWORTH *Intell. Syst.* I. iv. § 31. 472 These have cut off the most excellent Fulcrum of the Soul,..by means whereof, like unballasted ships, they are tossed up and down perpetually. 1829 I. TAYLOR *Enthus.* ii. 41 Yesterday the unballasted vessel was seen hanging out all the gaiety of its colours. 1897 *Outing* (U.S.) XXX. 334/1 No better demonstration of the superiority of the light-draught and unballasted sailboat over the deep, heavy one has been given.

b. *fig.* Not steadied or kept in order by serious or solid qualities.

1644 MILTON *Educ.* 2 To be tost and turmoild with their unballasted wits in fathomles and unquiet deeps of controversie. 1670 C. GATAKER in *Gataker's Antid. Errour* Ep. Ded. A iij, The shame and misery will light heavie at last upon these unballasted mindes. 1697 COLLIER *Ess. Mor. Subj.* I. (1703) 182 An unexperienced unballasted

Divine must be an improper missionary. 1701 — *M. Aurel., Life* p. xxiv, Lucius Verus had none of these good Qualities; his Inclinations were eager, unballasted, and lewd. 1796 CHARLOTTE SMITH *Marchmont* III. 144 The unballasted head of Linda .. was quite overset. 1809 SOUTHEY *Lett.* (1856) II. 151 Both these men are such unballasted politicians, that the public mind could not be worse guided. 1870 LOWELL *Study Wind.* 179 Percival.. offers an example..of the poetic temperament unballasted with those less obvious qualities, which make the poetic faculty.

**2.** Of a railway line: Not filled in with ballast. 1887 M. ROBERTS *Western Avernus* 204, I could not step in between, for the line was unballasted. 1891 *Cycling* 21 Feb. 75 Riding over the 'sleepers' on an unballasted railroad would be preferable.

**Unba·ndage,** *v.* [UN-² 4.] *trans.* To remove the bandage from. Also *absol.*

1840 MARRYAT *Poor Jack* xliii, The hospital mates unbandaged Spicer's leg. 1857 R. TOMES *Amer. in Japan* viii. 181 Dr. Parker prevailed upon a girl of thirteen, who was a patient in the hospital, to unbandage in the presence of her mother. 1899 *Westm. Gaz.* 8 Sept. 3/2 Mr. L. (the oculist..) unbandaged the weak eye for a few moments.

**Unba·nded,** *ppl. a.* [UN-¹ 8.] Not furnished with a band or bands. Also *fig.*

1570 *Wills & Inv. N. Co.* (Surtees, 1835) 329 It[e]m I do gyue and bequiethe vnto my doughtor margreatt dychbourne a brass pan vnbanded. 1600 SHAKS. *A.Y.L.* III. ii. 397 Your hose should be vngarter'd, your bonnet vnbanded, your sleeue vnbutton'd. 1608 *Merry Devil Edmonton* V. i. 85 Did not this good knight..Confesse with you,..To deale with him about th' unbanded marriage Betwixt him and that faire young Millisent?

† **Unba·ndoned,** *ppl. a. Sc. Obs.*⁻¹ [UN-¹ 8.] Not kept under control; loose.

1375 BARBOUR *Bruce* x. 382 (Camb. MS.), Richt as thai ky and oxin weir, That war vnbawndonit left therout.

**Unba·nished,** *ppl. a.* (UN-¹ 8.)

1533 BELLENDEN *Livy* v. xv. (S.T.S.) II. 197 Quhen Camyllus..was on þis wise exilit, quhilk remanand still..vnbanist, Rome micht never hive bene tane. 1597 WARNER *Alb. Eng.* v. xxvii. 137 Make-shifts, and Bawdes did thriue, Nor was an ancient English Peere vnbanisht or aliue. 1648 HEXHAM II, *Ongebannen*, Vnbanished, or Vn-exiled. 1821 BENTHAM *Lib. Press* 17 Under whom it has hitherto been my good hap to live unhanged, unsabred, unimprisoned, unbanished, and unruined.

**Unba·nk,** *v.*¹ [UN-² 4.]

**1.** *trans.* To free from a bank or barrier. In quot. *fig.*

1842 SIR H. TAYLOR *Edwin the Fair* I. v. 36 Unbank the hours To that soft overflow which bids the heart Yield increase of delight.

**2.** To clear (a fire) from banked-up matter.

1890 *Sci. Amer.* 17 May 315/3 The first duty of an engineer..is to ascertain how many gauges of water there are in his boilers. Never unbank or replenish the fires until this is done.

**Unba·nk,** *v.*² (UN-² 4: cf. BANK *sb.*³ 7.)

1834 CALHOUN *Wks.* (1874) II. 363 We must..use a bank to unbank the banks, to the extent that may be necessary.

**Unba·nkable,** *a.* (UN-¹ 7 b.) 1864 *Weekly Times* (N.Y.) 9 Apr., The loss the treasury may sustain from unbankable notes. 1890 GILDERSLEEVE *Ess. & Stud.* 55 A poor exchange for the treasure of German idealism, unbankable as it is. **Unba·nked,** *ppl. a.* (UN-¹ 8.) [1775 ASH.] 1893 *Cycling* 82 [The cycle-tracks] were unbanked, and in some cases the corners were very sharp. **Unba·nnered,** *ppl. a.* (UN-¹ 8.) 1827 POLLOK *Course T.* VII. 421 Innumerable armies rose, unbannered all.

**Unbapti·ze,** *v.* [UN-² 3.] *trans.* To divest (a person) of the effect of baptism. Also *absol.*

1611 FLORIO, *Sbattezzare*, to vnchristen, to vnbaptize. 1641 MILTON *Ch. Govt.* II. ii. 55 Ye have bin bold,..baptizing the Christian infant with a solemne sprinkle, and unbaptizing for your own part with a profane and impious forefinger. 1709 J. JOHNSON *Clergym. Vade M.* II. p. lxxi, The Priest can baptize, but he can't un-baptize. *a* 1714 M. HENRY *Treat. Baptism* Wks. 1853 I. 549/1 To unchurch, unchristianize, unbaptize, all those who are not in every thing of our length, is..destructive to the catholic church. 1841 A. R. C. DALLAS *Past. Superintend.* 147 Therefore, a person who acts thus would become a heathen if he could unbaptize himself. 1858 *Edin. Rev.* July 220 In the Roman Catholic Church..a man can no more be unmarried than he can be unbaptized.

**Unbapti·zed,** *ppl. a.* (UN-¹ 8.)

*c* 1375 *Sc. Leg. Saints* xxxiii. (*George*) 789 Quhat..sal be of me gyf I de in sic degre vnbaptyst ȝet? 14.. *With an O and an I* in *Anglia* XXVII. 288 He þat will lende Vnbaptist, he bese feffed wiþ þe fende. 14.. *Siege Jerus.* (E.E.T.S.) 155 ȝit vnbaptized wer boþe Barnabe & Poule. 1534 MORE *Treat. Passion* Wks. 1287/2 As for infantes dyeng vnbaptised .., many men wil peraduenture thynk otherwyse. 1586 WARNER *Alb. Eng.* IV. xxi. (1592) 90 He putteth all to Sword and Seas that vnbaptized wair. 1651 BAXTER *Inf. Bapt.* 71 It is true that many unbaptized are in the Kingdom of Christ. 1689 SHERLOCK *Death* iii. § 7 They are in the state of unbaptized Jews. 1708 J. PHILIPS *Cyder* II. 652 Th' unbaptiz'd Turk Dreads War from utmost Thule. 1796 COLERIDGE *To a Friend* 11 And with those recreant unbaptized heels Thou'rt flying from thy bounden ministeries. 1826 SCOTT *Woodst.* ii, Unbaptized dog, speak civil of the Martyr in my presence. 1867 PEARSON *Hist. Eng.* I. 153 He bethought himself of asking what fate his unbaptized ancestors were undergoing.

**Unbapti·zing,** *ppl. a.* (UN-¹ 10.) 1846 WORCESTER (citing Coleridge), *Unbaptizing, a.*, not baptizing.

**Unbar,** *v.* [UN-² 3 and 7.] **a.** *trans.* To remove the bar from (a door or gate, etc.); to unfasten, undo. Also *absol.*

13.. *Gaw. & Gr. Knt.* 2070 The brygge was brayde doun, & þe brode gatez Vnbarred, & born open. 1433 LYDG. *St. Edmund* III. 1201 A-nother [thief] besy..To vnpyke lokys, a-nother to vnbarre. *c* 1450 *Mirk's Festial* 42 Thomas ȝede to þe dyr, and vnbarret þe dyrre. *c* 1530 LD. BERNERS *Arth. Lyt. Bryt.* (1814) 81 He vnbarred helmes, and claue asounder sheldes. 1590 SPENSER *F. Q.* II. xi. 17 He behight Those gates to be vnbar'd, and forth he went. 1603 KNOLLES *Hist. Turks* (1621) 995 The Turkes..vncouered and vnbarred their artillerie against the assailants. *c* 1620 FLETCHER & MASSINGER *Trag. Barnavelt* v. iii, Who Unbard the Havens that the floating Merchant Might clap his lynnen wings up to the windes. 1700 DRYDEN *Ovid's Met., Ajax* XIII. 573 Sure I may..Enter the Town, I then unbarr'd the Gates, When I remov'd their tutelary Fates. 1752 JOHNSON *Rambler* No. 190 ₱ 7 The servant immediately confessed that he unbarred the door. 1815 SCOTT *Guy M.* xlv, The house-door was next unbarred, unlocked, and unchained. 1859 DICKENS *Haunted House* iv, With soothing words the sister bade her wait, Until she brought the key to unbar the gate.

**b.** In fig. context.

1601 WEEVER *Mirr. Mart.* C iij b, Looke when the sun.. doth rise, Soone as the morne vnbarres her christall gate. 1611 SHAKS. *Cymb.* V. iv. 8 Th' sure Physitian, Death, who is the key T' vnbarre these Lockes. 1667 MILTON *P.L.* VI. 4 Till Morn..with rosie hand Unbarr'd the gates of Light. 1725 POPE *Odyss.* IV. 412 The morn..Unbarr'd the portal of the roseate East. 1746 HERVEY *Medit.* (1818) 87 The returning hours have unbarred the gates of light. 1855 BREWSTER *Newton* II. xvii. 133 That intellectual strength which had unbarred the strongholds of the universe. 1867 RUSKIN *Time & Tide* iv. § 17 You practical English!—will you ever unbar the shutters of your brains? 1878 SEELEY *Stein* III. 565 There is nothing he likes better than unbarring restrictions, throwing open closed doors.

**c.** *intr.* To undergo unbarring.

1748 RICHARDSON *Clarissa* (1811) IV. 396, I heard her lady's door, with hasty violence unbar, unbolt, unlock, and open.

Hence **Unba·rring** *vbl. sb.* and *ppl. a.*

1611 FLORIO, *Sbaraglio*, rout, vnbarring, scattring. 1829 SCOTT *Anne of G.* xix, They heard the noise of the unbolting and unbarring of the gates of the inn. 1834 MARRYAT *P. Simple* xix, The unbarring of the prison doors. 1857 DICKENS *Dorrit* I. xvi, The possibility of her father's release from prison by the unbarring hand of death.

**Unba·rbarize,** *v.* [UN-² 6 c.] *trans.* To render less barbarous; to civilize. Hence (or f. UN-¹ 8) **Unba·rbarized** *ppl. a.*, civilized.

1648 J. BEAUMONT *Psyche* VIII. ccxxv, Mothers Who in their arms their tender Burdens brought, A sight which might all Beasts unbarbarize. 1719 OZELL tr. *Misson's Mem.* 150 Of these original Irish, most of the Persons of Quality understand English, and lead a Life totally unbarbarized. 1752 CHESTERF. *Lett.* cclxxviii (1792) III. 275 The courts of Manheim and Bonn I take to be a little more unbarbarised than some others. 1812 SOUTHEY *Let. to Landor* 16 April, Peru may be unbarbarized—made worse than it was under the Incas by the victory of the Indians. 1893 G. TYRRELL in M. D. Petre *Life* (1912) II. ii. 57 If Newman were studied and assimilated it would tend to unbarbarise us.

† **Unba·rbed,** *ppl. a.*¹ *Obs.* [UN-¹ 8. See BARB *v.* 1 and 2.]

**1.** O cloth: Not barbed or clipped.

1535 *Act 27 Hen. VIII*, c. 13 § 1 No wollen cloth..shuld be conveyed ouer the See vnrowed, unbarbed and unshorne. 1541–2 *Act* 33 *Hen. VIII*, c. 19 Any coloured Clothe above the value of thre poundes, unrowed, unbarbed or unshorne. 1643 *Docq. Lett. Pat. at Oxf.* (1837) 363 To transporte all wollen clothes vnrowed, vnbarbd, vnshorne, and not fully drest.

**2.** *poet.* Unmown, uncut.

1612 DRAYTON *Poly-olb.* xiii. 112 When with his hounds The laboring Hunter tufts the thicke unbarbed grounds Where harbor'd is the Hart. 1652 BENLOWES *Theoph.* XII. lvii, The Virgin-meads, whose gaies Unbarb'd perk up to prank the curled stream.

**Unba·rbed,** *ppl. a.*² [UN-¹ 8 + BARBED *ppl. a.*²] Unarmed; not caparisoned; unbarded.

1565 COOPER *Thesaurus*, *Equus patens vulneri*, a horse vnbarbed, and in daunger to be wounded. 1607 SHAKS. *Cor.* III. ii. 99 Must I goe shew them my vnbarb'd Sconce?

**Unba·rbed,** *ppl. a.*³ [UN-¹ 8 + BARBED *ppl. a.*¹] Not furnished with a barb or barbs. Also *fig.*

1844 J. TOMLIN *Mission. Jrnls.* 84 The point sharp as the finest needle, but unbarbed. 1880 DAWSON *Fossil Men* v. (1882) 135 In the north barbed bone spears were used, and also little unbarbed bones with two elastic pieces of wood at the sides.

**b.** Const. *by.* (Cf. BARB *v.* 4.)

1863 MISS BRADDON *Aurora Floyd* i, The busy tongues.. were not unbarbed by malice.

**Unba·rbered,** *ppl. a.* (UN-¹ 8.) 1845 THACKERAY *Journ. fr. Cornhill to Cairo* ix, We'd a hundred Jews to larboard, Unwashed, uncombed, unbarbered. 1891 *Century Mag.* Dec. 236 Their long black locks unbarbered.

**Unba·rded,** *ppl. a.* [UN-¹ 8.] = UNBARRED *ppl. a.*²

1598 BARRET *Theor. Warres* v. ii. 142 Well mounted vpon a strong horse vnbarded. 1846 H. W. TORRENS *Rem. Milit. Hist.* 95 The real Grecian cavalry..used un-barded horses.

† **Unba·re,** *a. Obs.*⁻¹ [UN-² 9.] = UNBARED *ppl. a.*

1624 HEYWOOD *Gunaik.* VIII. 391 The people stare To see my garments torne, and brests unbare.

**Unba·re,** *v.* Now *rare.* [UN-² 9.] *trans.* To lay bare, to expose to view. (Cf. BARE *v.*)

1530 PALSGR. 766/1, I unbare a thyng, *je desnue. Ibid.*, Sythe I se the vysage, it is ynough, I wyll unbare nothing else. 1598 TOFTE *Alba* (1880) 108 Because thou seest myselfe with Love I cloathe, Another shall despoyle me and vnbare. 1615 SYLVESTER *Job Triumphant* II. 204 Destruction's Sword shall hunt him every hower, Consume his Sinews, and un-bare his Skin. 1630 LORD *Banians* Ep. Ded. A 2 b, Not unbaring the roote of their guilt and criminalitie. 1650 H. MORE *Observ.* in *Enthus. Tri.*, etc. (1656) 108 He has not done that which is impossible to doe, unbare to us the very substance of the Form. 1858 FARRAR *Eric* II. ii, The least boys seemed the greatest proficients in unbaring, without a blush, its hideous ugliness.

Hence **Unba·red** *ppl. a*, **Unba·ring** *vbl. sb.*

1585 Q. ELIZ. in Motley *Netherl.* (1868) I. vi. 340 This is no small succour, and no little unbaring of this realm of mine. *a* 1665 J. GOODWIN *Filled w. the Spirit* (1867) 203 When there is an unbared arm of God, then the work is said to be done from heaven. 1879 FARRAR *St. Paul* (1883) 418 The unbared palpitations of his inmost being.

**Unba·rgained,** *ppl. a.* (UN-¹ 8.) 1839 *Times* 1 Apr., An unbought, unbargained support to the Conservative government. 1874 H. SIDGWICK *Meth. Ethics* IV. iii. 409 Sometimes such unbargained requital is even legally obligatory.

**Unba·rk,** *v.*¹ [UN-² 4 + BARK *sb.*¹] *trans.* To deprive or strip of bark. (Cf. BARK *v.*² 3.)

*c* 1557 ABP. PARKER *Ps.* lxxviii. 224 He dyd unbarke of vyne the trees. 1589 FLEMING *Virg. Georg.* II. 30 Smooth canes and poles of byrch Peeld or vnbarkt. 1626 BACON *Sylva* § 654 A Branch of a Tree being Un-barked some space at the Bottome. 1654 GAYTON *Pleas. Notes* IV. 209 Spoyling the stick and unbarking that body, which is vitiated.. by the approach of outward air. 1677 PLOT *Oxfordsh.* 165 The Tree being within as hollow as a Drum, and its outmost surface, where unbark'd, dead and dry beside. 1719 LONDON & WISE *Compl. Gard.* 103 In speaking of good and bad Roots, it may be thought, that the meaning of these is only such as are broken, or unbarked.

**Unba·rk,** *v.*² Now *dial.* or *Obs.* [UN-² 5 + BARK *sb.*²] To disembark.

1555 EDEN *Decades* (Arb.) 194 The gouernour had vnbarked .xvi. horses which were also at the battayle. 1560 DAUS tr. *Sleidane's Comm.* 83 The Emperoure unbarked hym selfe in spayne & arryved at Genes. 1599 HAKLUYT *Voy.* II. I. 214 Where they..doe vnbarke themselues and vnlade their goods. *c* 1850 in *Eng. Dial. Dict.* (Devonshire dial.).

**Unba·rked,** *ppl. a.* [UN-¹ 8 + BARK *v.*²]

† **1.** Not treated with bark; untanned. *Obs.*⁻¹ So Sw. *obarkad*, Da. *ubarket.*

1569 *Richmond. Wills* (Surtees) 218, ij barked horse skyns, and one vnbarked.

**2.** Not stripped of bark.

1839 MARRYAT *Diary Amer.* Ser. I. I. 237 The other had an unbarked hickory stick. 1890 'R. BOLDREWOOD' *Col. Reformer* (1891) 185 The unbarked pine-posts of the rude verandah.

**Unba·rking,** *ppl. a.* (UN-¹ 10.) 1833 MRS. BROWNING *Prometh. Bound* Poems 1850 I. 177 The griffins, those unbarking dogs of Zeus.

**Unbarmed**: see UN-¹ 4.

**Unba·rrable,** *a.* (See UN-¹ 7 b and next.) 1818 CRUISE *Digest* (ed. 2) V. 525 An entail..had lasted three hundred and sixty years... Its having been so long unbarred, gives a presumption, that the owners knew it was unbarrable.

**Unba·rred,** *ppl. a.* [UN-¹ 8.]

**1.** Of harbours: Not obstructed by a bar.

*a* 1550 LELAND *Itin.* III. (1907) 192 Ther cam to this place ons, the haven beyng onbarrid and syns chokid with tynne workes, good talle shippes. 1796 MORSE *Amer. Geog.* II. 177 These are..the principal unbarred havens.

**2.** Not secured or blocked with a bar or bars.

1603 HOLLAND *Plutarch's Mor.* 165 Making no resistance to his appetites and demaunds, but letting all ly unfortified, unbard, and unlockt. 1708 J. PHILIPS *Cyder* I. 656 Weymouth,..whose hospitable Gate, Unbarr'd to All, invites a numerous Train Of daily Guests. 1811 LD. DUDLEY *Lett. to 'Ivy'* (1905) 147 The doors are all left unbarred, and yet I never heard of anything being stolen. 1871 *Daily News* 18 Sept., Gallopers explored the railway line right and left to find sound bridges or unbarred level crossings.

**3.** *Law.* Not excluded or blocked. (BAR *v.* 5 b.)

1818 [see UNBARRABLE *a.*]. 1877 BLACKMORE *Erema* li, As to the property,..the greater part would descend to me under unbarred settlement.

**4.** Not marked with a bar or minus sign.

1878 GURNEY *Crystallogr.* 16 All of these numbers are unbarred.

**5.** Of music: Not divided into bars.

1879 *Grove's Dict. Mus.* I. 137/2 In this kind of unbarred music the relative value of the notes must be..preserved. 1901 *Westm. Gaz.* 5 Feb. 1/3 Old madrigals from the separate and unbarred part books for the Musical Antiquarian Society.

**Unba·rrel,** *v.* (UN-² 5.) 1611 FLORIO, *Sbarillare*, to vnbarrell. [1775 ASH.] 1889 J. L. HILL in *Minutes Congreg. Council* 295 How can we, upon the spot, unbarrel the salt? **Unba·rrelable,** *a.* (UN-¹ 7.) 1838 EMERSON *Addr., Lit. Ethics*, Truth is..so..unbarrelable a commodity, that it is as bad to catch as light. **Unba·rrelled,** *ppl. a.* (UN-¹ 8.) 1482 in *Charters, etc. Edinb.* (1871) 168 Salmound and sic lyke fish vnbaralit. **Unba·rrenness.** (UN-¹ 12.) 1656 JEANES *Fuln. Christ* 161 From all which he concludeth the perpetuity, indeficiency, and unbarrenness of the Church.

**Unba·rricade,** *v.* [UN-² 4.] *trans.* To free from a barricade or barrier.

1623 WEBSTER *Duchess Malfi* V. v, You shall not unbarracade the doore To let in rescew. 1768 STERNE *Sent. Journ., Passport*, The Bastile is not an evil to be despised—but.. unbarricade the door—..the evil vanishes.

**Unbarrica·doed,** *ppl. a.* (UN-¹ 8.) [1775 ASH.] 1795 BURKE *Let. to W. Elliott* Wks. VII. 351 What he could find in the glutted markets, the unbarricadoed streets.

† **Unba·rrowed,** *ppl. a. Obs.* [UN-¹ 8: cf. BAROWE *v.* and UNBERRIED.] Unthreshed.

1569 *Richmond. Wills* (Surtees) 218 Haver barrowid and unbarrowed bye estimacion xv quertars..; I. stroke queat unbarrowed.

**Unba·se,** *a.* (UN-¹ 7.) 1601–3 DANIEL *Cert. Epist.* 42 Wks. (Grosart) I. 218 How should we know thy soule had beene secur'd In honest counsels and in way vnbase! **Unba·sed,** *a.* (UN-¹ 8.) 1860 PUSEY *Min. Proph.* 82 From that unsolid, unbased, inflated greatness it vanisheth in air. 1884 H. SPENCER in *Contemp. Rev.* July 25 The theory commonly accepted is ill-based or unbased.

† **Unba·shed**, *ppl. a. Obs.*—1 [UN-1 8.] = UNABASHED *ppl. a.*

**1536** *Stories & Proph. Script.* H viij, Geue vs a bolde and an onbashed harte to resiste all temptacions.

**Unba·shful**, *a.* (UN-1 7.)

**1563** MAN *Musculus' Commonpl.* 13 b, The benefite of clere conscience, and the unbashfull [L. *intrepidæ*] familiaritie with God. **1600** SHAKS. *A. Y. L.* II. iii. 50 In my youth I ..did not with vnbashfull forehead woe The meanes of weaknesse and debilitie. **1611** FLORIO, *Inuerecondo*, vnbashfull, impudent. **1834** WORDSW. *Even. Voluntaries* vi. 17 Meek eve shuts up the whole usurping host (Unbashful dwarfs each glittering at his post). **1858** MASSON *Milton* I. 280 Throughout all Milton's works there may be discerned a vein of noble egotism, of unbashful self-assertion. **1887** SWINBURNE *Stud. Prose & Poetry* (1894) 140 The laurels of Gotham, with which the critical sages..have bedecked his unbashful brows.

Hence **Unba·shfully** *adv.*, **Unba·shfulness.**

**1795** *Monthly Rev.* XVIII. 129 Probably Mr. Pye cared not unbashfully to contest the authority of Aristotle. **1611** FLORIO, *Inuerecondia*, vnbashfulnes, impudency.

**Unba·stardized**, *ppl. a.* (UN-1 8.) **1769** H. WALPOLE *Let. to Mr. Cole* 12 Aug., Abp. Wareham's tomb at Canterbury being .. the last example of unbastardized Gothic. **1794** W. ROBERTS *Looker-on* No. 90 III. 448 A line of honest yeomanry, untainted by spurious grandeur, ..unbastardized by kings and nobles. **Unbastilled**, *a.* (UN-1 9.) **1817** BENTHAM *Parl. Reform* (1818) 77 So long, in a word, as it shall be my lot to remain alive, unkilled, and unbastiled.

**Unba·ted**, *ppl. a.* [UN-1 8.]

**1.** = UNABATED *ppl. a.*

**1596** SHAKS. *Merch. V.* II. vi. 11 Where is the horse that doth vntread againe His tedious measures with the vnbated fire, That he did pace them first? **1611** B. JONSON *Cataline* III. iv, My guards Are you, great Powers, and the unbated strengths Of a firm conscience. **1670** COTTON *Espernon* I. II. 80 His brave, and unbated Courage. **1680** OTWAY *Orphan* IV. vi, I still love him with unbated Passion. **1810** SCOTT *Lady of L.* I. vii, Alone, but with unbated zeal, That horseman plied the scourge and steel. **1892** 'M. FIELD' *Sight & Song* 95 Yet round the place whence flows Thy blood Thy conscious palm with fervour of unbated will doth cling.

† **2.** Not bated or blunted. *Obs.*

**1602** SHAKS. *Ham.* IV vii. 139 You may choose A Sword vnbaited, and in a passe of practice, Requit him for your Father. **1815** W. H. IRELAND *Scribbleomania* v, At ye I point the lance unbated by the poison of envy. [**1826** SCOTT *Woodst.* xxxii, I would have struck him through..with an unbated weapon, as Will says.]

**Unba·thed**, *ppl. a.* (UN-1 8.)

**1570** FOXE *A. & M.* (ed. 2) I. 57 He leaped out of the bathe vnbathed, because he feared the bathe shoulde haue fallen. *a* **1625** FLETCHER, etc. *Love's Pilgr.* III. ii, Let her but shew me A ruin'd cheek like mine, that holds his colour;..An unbathed body. **1697** DRYDEN *Æneis* VII. 1103 Her flying feet unbathed on billows hung. **1700** — *Cymon & Iph.* 599 The Blade return'd unbath'd, and to the Handle bent. **1791** COWPER *Odyss.* XIX. 409 For how, my honour'd inmate! shalt thou learn..if unbathed, unoil'd, Ill-clad, thou sojourn here? **1803** VISCT. STRANGFORD *Poems of Camoens, Sonn.* xx (1810) 106 Not unbath'd by Memory's warmest tear! **1888** *Pall Mall G.* 12 Sept. 2/2 During the three days that we spent under his roof I remained unbathed.

**Unba·ting**, *ppl. a.* (UN-1 10.) **1744** AKENSIDE *Pleas. Imag.* III. 373 The virgin's radiant eye, Superior to disease, ..Shines with unbating lustre. **Unba·tterable**, *a.* (UN-1 7 b.) **1576** FLEMING *Panopl. Epist.* 266 Not taking strong towers, huge castles, and unbatterable walls for their fortifications.

**Unba·ttered**, *ppl. a.* (UN-1 8.)

**1603** KNOLLES *Hist. Turks* (1621) 324 If these wals stood still firme, and vnbattered. **1605** SHAKS. *Macb.* v. vii. 19 Else my Sword with an vnbattered edge I sheath againe vndeeded. **1607** DEKKER *Knt.'s Conjur.* iv. F ij, Captains, some in guilt armour (vnbattred), some in buffe Ierkens. **1837** CARLYLE *Fr. Rev.* III. I. vii, Brunswick may *re*cross the dell,..not unbattered by the way.

**Unbawndonit**: see UNBANDONED *ppl. a.*

**Unbay**, error for *im-*, EMBAY *v.*1 I.

**1625** J. GLANVILLE *Voy. to Cadiz* (1883) 111 It was dangerous, in tyme of Winter, to unbay our selves soe deepelie as wee must doe by touching att Bayon.

† **Unbay**, *v. Obs.*—1 [UN-2 4 b + BAY *sb.*5] *trans.* To free from barrier or restraint.

**1687** NORRIS *Coll. Misc.* 326, I ought now to let loose the reins of my affections, to unbay the current of my Passion.

† **Unba·zled**, *ppl. a. Sc. Obs.* [UN-2 4: cf. Sc. dial. (Roxb.) *bizzel* 'a hoop or ring round the end of any tube' (Jam.).] ? Having the ring(s) started or loose.

**1719** in W. R. Mackintosh *Glimpses of Kirkwall* (1887) 81 The guns belonging to the Brugh have been long unwrought for whereby they or some of them may be unbazled.

**Unbe·**, *v.*1 *rare.* [UN-1 14.] *intr.* To lack being; to be non-existent.

**1434** MISYN *Mending Life* 122 As qwo say: syn in vs may vnrene [= not reign], bot it may not vnbe. *a* **1795** *Bonnie James Campbell* iv. in Child *Ballads* IV. (1890) 143/2 My house is unbigged, my barn's unbeen. **1885** R. F. BURTON *Arab. Nts.* IV. 248 This ecstasy would see my being unbe. **1898** T. HARDY *Wessex Poems* 182 But for the charge that blessed things I'd liefer have unbe.

**Unbe·**, *v.*2 [UN-2 4.] *trans.* To deprive of being; to make non-existent.

**1624** *Trag. Nero* III. iii. in Bullen *O. Pl.* (1882) I. 51 How oft, with danger of the field beset Or with home mutineys, would he unbee Himselfe. **1646** S. BOLTON *Arraignm. Err.* 13 God..could as easily destroy them, as subdue them, unbee them as conquer them. **1759** R. SHIRRA in *Rem.* (1850) 118 He would not only dethrone, but un-be God, un-God him.

**Unbea·coned**, *ppl. a.* (UN-1 8.) **1828** CAMPBELL *Departure of Emigrants* 72 Where shipless seas now wash unbeaconed crags. **1850** *Illustr. London News* 25 May 372/1 Her starboard bow suddenly struck upon the dangerous and unbeaconed rocks in question. **Unbea·med**, *ppl. a.* (UN-2 8.) *a* **1843** SOUTHEY *Comm.-Pl. Bk.* (1851) IV. 198 The barber...Without his wig he is Jove without his thunder. Venus uncestused, Phœbus unbeamed.

**Unbea·r**, *v.* [UN-2 4 b.] *trans.* To free (a horse) from the bearing-rein.

**1853** DICKENS *Bleak Ho.* lvi, Unbear him half a moment to freshen him up.

**Unbea·rable**, *a.* [UN-1 7 b.] Unendurable, intolerable.

*c* **1449** PECOCK *Repr.* v. v. 507 This man hath a bodili sijknes..bi which he schal lyue in huge vnberable peine or be deed. **1601** SIR W. BROWN in A. Collins *Lett. & Mem. State* (1746) II. 228 The hurt Men..make such a noysom Smell in the Towne, that is allmost vnberable. **1690** C. NESSE *O. & N. Test.* I. 175 The first covenant..hath impossible as well as unbearable conditions. **1791-3** in *Spirit Public Jrnls.* (1799) I. 159 The consumption of provisions in such an army as this, may be objected to as unbearable. **1812** J. HENRY *Camp. agst. Quebec* 212 He was almost unbearable to many men. **1875** C. L. KENNEY *Mem. M. W. Balfe* 60 This state of mind was heightened to an almost unbearable strain of suspense.

Hence **Unbea·rableness, Unbea·rably** *adv.*

**1730** BAILEY (fol.), *Insupportableness*, *unbearableness. **1867** MISS BROUGHTON *Cometh up like a Flower* vi, This bearableness or unbearableness of the various burdens laid on the shoulders of poor humanity. **1873** *Daily News* 26 Aug., An ordinary mortal would have found the beach in the middle of the day hot to unbearableness. **1809** MALKIN *Gil Blas* VII. i. ¶ 11 You are become so *unbearably hateful to her. **1862** C. H. AÏDÉ *Carr of Carlyon* II. 255 Since her dog's death she had been more unbearably silly..than ever.

**Unbea·rd**, *v.* (UN-2 4.) **1598** FLORIO, *Sbarbare*,..to vnbeard, to cut off ones beard. **1786** tr. *Dulaure's Pogonologia* 127 One of their lay brethren..unbearded all of them whilst they were asleep.

**Unbea·rded**, *a.* [UN-1 9. Cf. NFris. *ünbiarded*, Du. *ongebaard* (Kilian *onghebaerdt*), G. (botan.) *ungebartet*.]

**1.** Of persons: Not having a beard.

**1560** BECON *Jewel of Joy* Pref., What a swarme of popyshe shauelyngs brought he forth, .. some bearded, some vnbearded. **1567** DRANT *Horace, Ep.* A v, Unbearded youth, at last rid from the Tutors barring charge. **1586** J. DAVIS in Hakluyt *Voy.* (1600) III. 104 The people are of good stature ..; the most part vnbearded,..and close toothed. *a* **1637** B. JONSON *Horace, Art Poet.* 230 Th' unbearded youth, his guardian once being gone, Loves dogs and horses. *a* **1653** G. DANIEL *Idyll.* iii. 162 Truth shall find A Narrow Roome to tread in, and the few Vn-bearded Criticks, Cloth her out a new. **1855** SINGLETON *Virgil* II. 186 O'er it stand amazed The inexperienced and unbearded groups. **1891** KINNS *Graven in Rock* xvi. 599 Behind the king stands an unbearded officer.

**2.** Of plants, etc.: Not furnished with bristles or hairy tufts; awnless.

**1688** DRYDEN *Brit. Rediv.* 260 As when a sudden Storm of Hail and Rain Beats to the ground the yet unbearded Grain. **1882** *Garden* 28 Jan. 66/3 The throat of the flower is unbearded.

**Unbea·ring**, *ppl. a.* [UN-1 10. Cf. OHG. *unberenti, -perendi*, Goth. *unbairands*.] Unfertile, unproductive, barren.

*c* **825** *Vesp. Psalter* cxii. 9 Se eardian doeð unbeorende [L. *sterilem*] in huse modur bearna. *c* **950** *Lindisf. Gosp.* John xv. 2 *marg.*, þæt unberende treo he ȝenimes. *c* **1000** ÆLFRIC *Deut.* vii. 13 Ne bið mid eow nan þing unberendes ne on mannum ne on nytenum. *c* **1200** *Trin. Coll. Hom.* 125 Þe holi man .. was of michel elde, & his woreldes make was..unberinde. **1685** DRYDEN *Horace, Ep.* ii. 21 [He] Does .. with his pruneing hook disjoyn Unbearing Branches from their Head. **1853** J. G. MURPHY *Comm., Gen.* xi. 6 Unwittingly provide a store for the unbearing period of the year. **1874** C. R. SMITH *Rural Life Shaks.* 4 Fruit-trees must be continually lacerated to decrease the growth of unbearing wood.

† **Unbea·st**, *sb. north.* and *Sc. Obs.* Also 4–5 vnbest(e, 6 wn-, vnbeast, 6 vn-, 9 unbeist, 8 *Sc.* onbeast. [UN-1 12. Cf. MDu. and Du. *ondier*, MHG. and G. *untier*, Da. and Norw. *udyr*, Sw. *odjur*.] A wild beast; a monster; a ravenous or vile animal. Also *transf.*

*a* **1300** *Cursor M.* 19859 Quen petre þais vnbestes sagh, O þaim þan thoght him mikel agh. *c* **1375** *Sc. Leg. Saints* xvi. (*Magdalene*) 502 Pytuisly þe prince can pray, þat þai hyr kest nocht in þe se, met til vnbestis to be. *c* **1400** *Destr. Troy.* 7766 He auntrid on this Vnbest angardly fast. *a* **1585** MONTGOMERIE *Flyting* 258 (Tullibardine MS.), Bot this bargane, vnbeist, deir sall þou by it. **1629** Z. BOYD *Last Battell* i. 47 Fye upon barnes, a nest for myce and rattons. Would yee desire to liue for to enioye the leauinges of vnbeastes? **1768** ROSS *Helenore* I. 8 Has the onbeast your lambie taen awa'? *Ibid.* I. 18. **1808** JAMIESON s.v. *Onbeast, Unbeist*,..a noxious member of human society; Ang[us].

**Unbea·st**, *v.* (UN-2 6 b.) **1611** FLORIO, *Disbestiare*, to vnbeast, to vnrude. **1621** G. SANDYS *Ovid's Met.* II. (1626) 35 Let him vnbeast the beast..and her wanton shape restore.

† **Unbeat**, obs. variant of UNBEATEN *ppl. a.*

**1533** BELLENDEN *Livy* II. v. (S.T.S.) I. 145 Nocht was left þareof vnbet doun bot ane small parte. **1635** BRATHWAIT *Arc. Princ.* Ded., You shall here meet with an Author walking in an unbeat path.

**Unbea·table**, *a.* (UN-1 7.) **1897** *Outing* (U.S.) XXIX. 483/2 The dogs..were, however, very pretty and almost unbeatable on the show-bench.

**Unbea·ten**, *ppl. a.* [UN-1 8 b.]

**1.** Not beaten or struck.

*a* **1275** *Prov. Ælfred* 448 in *O. E. Misc.* 129 Betere is child vnboren þenne vnbeten. *a* **1635** CORBET *Iter Bor.* Poems (1647) 12 His Mare went truer then his Chronicle; And even for Conscience sake unspurr'd, unbeaten, Brought us sixe miles, and turn'd taile to New-Eaton.

**b.** Not pounded; not broken up or softened by pounding.

**1607** TOPSELL *Four-f. Beasts* 515 Yoong mice being beaten into small bits or peeces...The same being vnbeaten and roasted. **1655** MOUFET & BENNET *Health's Improvement* 169 Stockfish whilst it is unbeaten is called Buckhorne, because it is so tough; when it is beaten upon the stock, it is termed stockfish. **1903** *Westm. Gaz.* 3 June 5/3 The daily labour required is the picking of 2 lb. of unbeaten or 4 lb. of beaten oakum.

**2.** Not beaten or trodden down. Also *fig.*

**1617** MORYSON *Itin.* I. 294 The unbeaten waies make them [miles] seeme longer. **1634** W. WOOD *New Engl. Prosp.* I. ii, To hit home through the unbeaten Woods, was strange. **1690** T. BURNET *Theory Earth* II. 142 Natural reason can determine neither of these, sees no tract to follow in these unbeaten paths. **1716** SWIFT *Horace* III. ii. 12 Some new unbeaten passage to the sky. **1796** MORSE *Amer. Geog.* I. Pref. p. iii, He does not pretend that this design is completed;..he has trodden, comparatively, an unbeaten path. **1807** T. THOMSON *Chem.* (ed. 3) II. 144 One of the first excursions made by that illustrious philosopher into the then unbeaten tracts of pneumatic chemistry. **1880** MISS BIRD (*title*), Unbeaten Tracks in Japan.

**3.** Not conquered or defeated.

**1757** *Pol. Ballads* (1860) II. 338 What joy it must be to a nation like Britain, To see such a Fleet return safe and unbeaten! **1884** ST. L. HERBERT in *Fortn. Rev.* Feb. 243 The Basutos, unbeaten, are thrown back upon the Imperial Government.

**4.** Not scoured for game.

**1882** *N. Y. Tribune* 12 July, With these companions the sportsman is taken over unbeaten ground.

**Unbeau·teous**, *a.* (UN-1 7.) *a* **1660** HAMMOND *Serm. Luke xviii. 11* Wks. 1684 IV. 610 The sanctifying spirit that beautifies the soul, is an humbling spirit also, to make it unbeauteous in its own eyes. **1839** LADY LYTTON *Cheveley* i, They .. turned away from every inn within that most dirty and unbeauteous town. **1876** MARY M. GRANT *Sun-Maid* i, The long tracts through which the railroad passes..are very dreary and unbeauteous. **Unbeau·teousness.** (UN-1 12.) **1886** MISS BRADDON *One Thing Needful* x, She had felt keenly the sting of her own unbeauteousness.

**Unbeau·tified**, *ppl. a.* (UN-1 8.)

**1625** QUARLES *Sion's Sonn.* xii. 4 Thy Necke (vnbeautifyde with borrow'd grace) Is whiter then the Lillies of thy face. **1680** C. NESSE *Church-Hist.* 137 Nature had spent all her strength in beautifying their bodies,..but she had left their souls altogether unbeautified. **1871** SMILES *Charac.* xi. 314 Fine features unbeautified by sentiment or good-nature.

**Unbeau·tiful**, *a.* (UN-1 7.)

**1495** *Trevisa's Barth. De P. R.* XIX. viii. (W. de W.) hh vij b/2 Euery mannes face is moste made bewtefull or vnbewtefull with colour. **1580** LUPTON *Sivquila* 60 Both fayre and foule, beautiful and unbeautiful, go so al alike, that none can know the fair from the foule. **1647** CLARENDON *Contempl. Ps.* Tracts (1727) 503 If we..by..adorning it [*sc.* guilt] with specious Excuses..render it less unbeautiful and unpleasant to our View. *a* **1680** CHARNOCK *Attrib. God* (1834) II. 223 To..deny him this, is to frame him as an unbeautiful monster, a deformed power. **1692** SOUTH *Serm.* (1727) III. xi. 434, I cannot persuade myself, that God ever designed his Church for a rude, naked, unbeautiful Lump. **1828** TENNYSON *Lover's Tale* I. 342 Nothing in nature is unbeautiful. **1870** SWINBURNE *Ess. & Stud.* (1875) 379 No good art is unbeautiful; but much able and effective work may be, and is.

*absol.* **1887** HISSEY *Holiday on Road* 299 Once the unbeautiful puts her foot in anywhere, there..she remains.

Hence **Unbeau·tifully** *adv.* (1847 Webster), **Unbeau·tifulness** (1727 Bailey).

**Unbeau·tify**, *v.* [UN-2 6 c.] *trans.* To render unbeautiful.

**1570** LEVINS *Manip.* 98 To vnbeautifie, *dedecorare.* **1611** FLORIO, *Disabellire*, .. to vnbeautyfie. *a* **1680** CHARNOCK *Attrib. God* (1834) I. 753 Sin unbeautifies man, and ravisheth his excellency. **1729** W. REEVE *Serm.* 20 They depreciate and unbeautify the whole work of Redemption. **1798** LAMB *The Witch* in Lucas *Lamb & Lloyds* (1898) 94 Heaven's music, which is order, seems unstrung, And this brave world ..unbeautify'd, Disorder'd, marr'd. **1876** W. ALEXANDER *Witness Ps. to Christ* (1877) 181 It is characteristic that the same hand should have unbeautified the Psalms for a shallow generation.

† **Unbeau·ty**, *v. Obs. rare.* [UN-2 4.] = prec.

**1495** *Trevisa's Barth. De P. R.* XVII. lxxv. (W. de W.) U iv b/2 The floure.. defoyleth nother vnbewtieth the rodde: but makyth it .. perfyte & fayr. **1611** FLORIO, *Disbellettare*, to vnpaint, or vnbeautie.

**Unbea·vered**, *a.*1 (UN-1 9 or UN-2 4 + BEAVER1.) **1720** GAY *The Espousal* 81 Brethren unbeaver'd then shall bow their head. **Unbea·vered**, *a.*2 (UN-1 9 or UN-2 4 + BEAVER2.) *a* **1851** MOIR *Sir Eliduc* xvi, From the echoing streets of Exeter March'd a thousand men and more, With banners, and unbeaver'd all. **Unbeclo·gged**, *ppl. a.* (UN-1 8.) **1674** N. FAIRFAX *Bulk & Selv.* 40 'Tis hoped we may have leave to settle Gods whole Everlastingness, as untimesom, and altogether unbeclogg'd with onwardness. **Unbeclou·ded**, *ppl. a.* (UN-1 8.) **1709** WATTS *Hymn, 'There is a land'* v, Oh! could we..see the Canaan that we love With unbeclouded eyes! **1857** SUSANNA WINKWORTH tr. *Life Tauler* 251 The beams of the eternal and divine sun..shining with unbeclouded force. **1884** J. PARKER *Apost. Life* III. 68 On another day, unbeclouded and infinite in light, thou wilt show the answer to the riddle.

**Unbeco·me**, *v.*1 [UN-2 4.] *trans.* To deprive (*of* something).

**1624** HEYWOOD *Captives* I. i, Shall I, bycause hee perisht in the sea,..Despoyle my shipps, and unbecom the deepes Of theire fayre Sayles and tackles?

**Unbeco·me**, *v.*2 [UN-1 14: cf. UNBECOMING *ppl. a.*] *trans.* To fail to become or suit; to be unbecoming to.

1628 ABP. WILLIAMS *Serm.* 8 It doth not vnbecome fortunate men to swell a little. 1653 SHIRLEY *Court Secret* II. i, It will not unbecome your royal justice To let me know his crime. 1679 PENN *Addr. Prot.* II. vi. (1692) 221 They draw to Strife,..Hatred and Persecutions, which unbecome the Man of God. 1716 M. DAVIES *Athen. Brit.* III. Ded. A j b, I thought it did not unbecome me..to pay and raise such Tribute of Loyalty and Gratitude as lay in my Power. 1893 YEATS *Celtic Twilight* p. x, I..shall be well content if it do not unbecome me.

† **Unbecoˑmed,** *ppl. a. Obs.*—1 [UN-1 8 c: the sense of *become* is unusual.] Unadorned *with* something.

1646 J. GREGORY *Notes & Obs.* 113 The Earth was without Forme and voide, i. e...unbecomed with that glorious furniture which now it hath.

† **Unbecoˑmely,** *a. Obs.* Forms: 3 unbicomelich, -cumeliche, 4 onebycomeleche. [UN-1 11.] Unbecoming; unsuitable.

c 1200 *Trin. Coll. Hom.* 97 Hwu come þu [h]ider in mid unbicumeliche weden? a 1300 *K. Horn* 1145 He makede him vn-bicomelich, Hes [= as] he nas neuremore ilich. c 1315 SHOREHAM *Poems* VII. 589 One-by-comeleche þyng hyt were, ȝef eny loȝ þer leþy were.

Unbecoˑming, *vbl. sb.* (UN-2 8.) 1883 MAUDSLEY *Body & Will* III. vii. 317 Are we to look forward to a continued becoming or to an ultimate unbecoming of things? Will evolution on earth go on for ever?

**Unbecoˑming,** *ppl. a.* [UN-1 10 and 5 d.] Not becoming or befitting; unsuitable; improper.

a. Without const.

1598 FLORIO, *Inconueneuole*,..vnbeseeming, vnbecomming. 1605 SHAKS. *Macb.* III. i. 14 If he had beene forgotten, It had bene as a gap in our great Feast, And all-thing vnbecomming. 1659 W. CHAMBERLAYNE *Pharonnida* III. 187 Some this bold Act of her's Term un-becoming Passion. 1688 in Ellis *Orig. Lett.* Ser. II. IV. 155 One of his own officers..had provoked Mr. Howard to give him some unbecoming language. 1727 SWIFT *To Young Lady* Wks. 1755 II. II. 49 Those of our sex, who presume to take unbecoming liberty before you. 1775 SHERIDAN *St. Patrick's Day* I. ii, It is very unbecoming in you to want to have the last word with your Mamma. 1816 J. WILSON *City of Plague* II. i. 209 With frantic outcry and with violent steps Most unbecoming mid the hush of death. 1855 MACAULAY *Hist. Eng.* xxi. IV. 541 They pointed out ..with a grave irony which is not unbecoming, the absurdities..of the statute. 1885 SIR J. HANNEN in *Law Rep.* 15 Q.B.D. 143 It would be highly unbecoming if the justices were present when the medical man made his examination.

b. Governing a sb. (Cf. BECOME *v.* 8 b.)

1658 *Whole Duty Man* x. § 23 This savageness..is so unbecoming the nature of a man, that [etc.]. 1670 COTTON *Espernon* I. I. 12 An assiduity and diligence unbecoming his Spirit, and Blood. 1749 FIELDING *Tom Jones* v. viii, Behaviour, so unbecoming a Christian. a 1774 GOLDSM. *Hist. Greece* I. 21 They..had a power of arresting..their kings, if they acted unbecoming their station. 1830 SCOTT *Pirate* vii. *note*, The woman's dwelling and appearance were not unbecoming her pretensions. 1842 TENNYSON *Ulysses* 53 Some work of noble note may yet be done, Not unbecoming men that strove with Gods. 1882 *Daily News* 22 Aug. 6/4 Temper unbecoming of all places the Judgment seat.

c. Const. *of.*

1741 CHESTERF. *Lett.* May, What was not unbecoming of a child would be disgraceful to a youth. c 1800 R. CUMBERLAND *John De Lancaster* (1809) II. 254 You must not do what is unbecoming of your situation. 1803 *Censor* 1 Nov. 124 He never offered any thing unbecoming of a man who has serious intentions of wedding a woman. 1862 J. F. STEPHEN *Def. Rowl. Williams* 180 It would be unbecoming, I think, of the character of any man [etc.].

**Unbecoˑmingly,** *adv.* (UN-1 11.)

1653 H. MORE *Conject. Cabbal.* (1713) 203 He has unbecomingly and indiscreetly ventured out of his own Sphere. 1742 RICHARDSON *Pamela* IV. 231 A Gentleman would not attempt to penetrate unbecomingly, thro' the Disguises that a Lady thinks proper to assume. 1749 CHESTERF. *Lett.* 7 Feb. (1774) I. 393 What Cicero, very absurdly and unbecomingly for a Philosopher, says with regard to Plato. 1843 BETHUNE *Sc. Fireside Stor.* 99 For one so near her grave,..I must confess I have acted unbecomingly. 1876 T. HARDY *Ethelberta* xlviii, Why did you come so mysteriously, and, I must say, unbecomingly?

**Unbecoˑmingness.** (UN-1 12.)

1652 J. HALL *Height of Eloquence* p. ix, All these extream unbecomingnesses have defaced Eloquence. 1693 LOCKE *Educ.* § 75 If Words are sometimes to be used, they ought to be grave, kind and sober, representing the ill, or unbecomingness of the Fault. 1810 BENTHAM *Packing* (1821) 98 Flippancy...Deviation from decency...Unbecomingness. 1872 GEO. ELIOT *Middlem.* xxxiv, She felt the unbecomingness of saying anything that might convey a notion of it to others.

**Unbeˑd,** *v.* [UN-2 5.] *trans.* To remove from a bed; to disembed. Also *refl.*

1611 FLORIO, *Dislettare*, to vnbed, to vncouch. 1653 WALTON *Angler* v. 129 That learned man has made me to believe that Eeles unbed themselves, and stir at the noise of the thunder. 1821 CLARE *Vill. Minstr.* II. 122 The plough unbeds the worms. 1883 R. BRIDGES *Prometheus* 102 In the ruined dwellings and old tombs He dug, unbedding from the wormed ooze Vessels and tools.

**Unbeˑdded,** *ppl. a.* [UN-1 8.]

1. *Geol.* Not arranged in beds.

1842 SEDGWICK in *Hudson's Guide Lakes* (1843) 198 Great masses of granite and other kinds of crystalline unbedded rock. 1890 *Q. Jrnl. Geol. Soc.* Aug. 393 There are two crags,..of which one is slate, striking directly at the other which is unbedded grit.

2. Not put to bed. (In quot. *spec.*)

1877 SIR H. TAYLOR *Edwin the Fair* III. viii. Wks. II. 121 We deem'd it best that this unbedded bride Should visit Chester, there to live recluse.

**Unbedewˑed,** *ppl. a.* (UN-1 8.) [1775 ASH.] 1860 PUSEY *Min. Proph.* 14 The soul of the sinner..is unbedewed by God's grace, unwatered by the Fountain of living waters. **Unbediˑmmed,** *ppl. a.* (UN-1 8.) [1775 ASH.] 1840 WORDSW. *Misc. Sonn.* III. xxxii, 'Tis a fruitless task to paint for me, Who..By the habitual light of memory see Eyes unbedimmed. 1857 SUSANNA WINKWORTH tr. *Life Tauler* 333 There reigns perpetual light, clear and unbedimmed. **Unbediˑnned,** *ppl. a.* (UN-1 8.) 1816 L. HUNT *Rimini* I. 131 A princely music unbedinned with drums.

† **Unbeeˑned,** *ppl. a. Obs.*—1 [UN-2 8: cf. UNBE *v.*2] Deprived of existence.

1642 H. MORE *Song of Soul* II. I. I. xv, The hidden might And root of motion unliv'd, unbeen'd they leave In their vain thoughts.

**Unbefiˑt,** *v.* [UN-1 14.] *trans.* To be unfitting or unbecoming for.

1621 QUARLES *Hadassa* Med. 10 Wks. (Grosart) II. 57/2 Kings by their Royall priuiledge may doe, What vnbefits a mind to search into. 1624 — *Job* xvi. 104 It vnbefits our wills, to stint his pleasure.

**Unbefiˑtting,** *ppl. a.* [UN-1 10 and 5 d.] Not befitting or suitable: a. Without const.

1588 SHAKS. *L.L.L.* v. ii. 770 Loue is full of vnbefitting straines. 1659 MILTON *Civ. Power* 48 Then was the state of rigor, childhood, bondage and works, to all which force was not unbefitting. 1836 J. GILBERT *Chr. Atonem.* ix. (1852) 275 To imagine that,..were of all extravagances the most wild and unbefitting. 1864 PUSEY *Lect. Daniel* viii. 472 It would be unbefitting to speak of the Creator as the 'throne' of the creature. 1891 MEREDITH *One of our Conq.* xxx, Mrs. Blathenoy resented her unbefitting queenly style.

b. Governing a sb. (Cf. BEFIT *v.* 1.)

a 1643 J. SHUTE *Judgem. & Mercy* ix. (1645) 198 Moses.. loved not to..provoke him [Pharaoh] and use him unbefitting a Magistrate. 1667 MILTON *P. L.* IV. 759 Farr be it, that I should..think thee unbefitting holiest place. 1815 L. HUNT *Feast Poets* 70 The stanza..has always an air of direct imitation, which is unbefitting the dignity of an original seriousness. 1880 MISS BRADDON *Just as I am* vii, She never wore a garment unbefitting her years. 1890 'R. BOLDREWOOD' *Col. Reformer* (1891) 115 A species of rest..not unbefitting the day.

Hence **Unbefiˑttingly** *adv.*, **Unbefiˑttingness.**

1871 MACDUFF *Mem. Patmos* iv. 49 The form which these seven letters or addresses assume is unique; or, as it has not unbefittingly been called, 'artistic'. 1865 PUSEY *Truth Eng. Ch.* 194 The longing for the vision of God, from which the unbefittingness, yet cleaving to her, still excludes her.

Unbefooˑl, *v.* (UN-2 3.) a 1684 LEIGHTON *Serm. Ps. cvii. 43* Wks. (1859) 512/2 The strange woman..calls the fools to befool them:..but wisdom calls them, to unbefool them. a 1716 SOUTH *Serm.* (1744) VII. viii. 175 He that recovers a fool must first unbefool him to that degree, as to perswade him of his folly. **Unbefrieˑnd,** *v.* (UN-1 14.) 1884 *American* XXIX. 104 And will not unbefriend the enterprising any more than the timid.

**Unbefrieˑnded,** *ppl. a.* (UN-1 8.)

1628 WITHER *Brit. Rememb.* VIII. 1212 All those reeds on which thou hast depended, Will faile thy trust, and leave thee unbefriended. a 1661 FULLER *Worthies, Berkshire* I. (1662) 94 God and himself raised him to the eminency he attained unto, unbefriended with any extraction. 1767 *Woman of Fashion* I. 134, I am..convinced of your Readiness to afford an Asylum to hopeless and unbefriended Innocence. 1800 CAMPBELL *Scene in Bavaria* viii. Forsaken scene, how like to thee The fate of unbefriended Worth! 1842 MIALL in *Nonconf.* II. 1 Alone and unbefriended,..it set out on its course. 1877 'H. A. PAGE' *De Quincey* I. iv. 72 Whilst he had every hardship to face that is most painful in unbefriended poverty.

*absol.* 1717 KILLINGBECK *Serm.* xiii. 287 The Patronage of the Poor and Unbefriended.

**Unbegeˑt,** *v.* [UN-2 3.] *trans.* To annul or undo the begetting of.

a 1625 FLETCHER *Hum. Lieut.* IV. ii, I'le raise 'em to a Regiment, and then command 'em, When they turn disobedient, unbeget 'em. 1676 DRYDEN *Aurengzebe* I. i, He .., Repining that he must preserve his Crown, Wishes.. he could unbeget Those Rebel-Sons, who dare t' usurp his Seat. a 1721 SHEFFIELD (Dk. Buckhm.) *Wks.* (1753) II. 200 There would be yet a greater pleasure in unbegetting such a Son, if possible. c 1825 BEDDOES *Poems, Torrismond* I. iv, Unwrap me of my years, And hunt me..Into my mother's womb! there unbeget me!

† Unbegete (also -ȝet), obs. var. UNBEGOTTEN.

a 1300 *XV Signa* 31 in *E. E. P.* (1862) 8 We wold louerd þat we ner in world icome forto bene and vnbeȝet of ure fader wer. c 1450 *Cov. Myst.* (Shaks. Soc.) 274 Bettyr it hadde hym for to a be Bothe unborn and unbegete.

Unbeˑggared, *ppl. a.* (UN-2 8.) 1538 LATIMER *Let. to Cromwell* 6 Oct., Rem. (Parker Soc.) 403 Popishness changed into holiness, beggars unbeggared to avoid beggary.

**Unbeˑgged,** *ppl. a.* [UN-1 8.] a. Not begged or entreated. b. Not obtained by begging.

1579 *Sc. Acts Jas. VI* (1814) III. 141/1 To see quhat they may be maid content..to accept daylie to leif on vnbeggit. 1634 MASSINGER *Very Woman* Epil., If you are pleased, unbegged you will bestow A gentle censure. 1648 HEXHAM II, *Ongebedelt broodt*, Vnbegged bread. 1683 E. HOOKER *Pref. Pordage's Mystic Div.* 91 His (unexspected, undeserved, tho' I trust not undesired and unbegged) Mercie. c 1828 PRAED *Poems, Parting* ix, When between us lay Long tracks of sand and sea, The carrier pigeon went his way Unbegged, unbought, by me.

**Unbegiˑlt,** *ppl. a.* (UN-1 8 b.) 1850 S. DOBELL *Roman* viii. Poet. Wks. 1875 I. 151 That uncrown'd presence, unbegilt, unfeather'd, Naked and full of God. 1850 SIR H. TAYLOR *Virgin Widow* v. v. 178 Sire, the sense Of loyal service done is, unbegilt, Worth..the ransom of a King.

**Unbegiˑnning,** *ppl. a.* [UN-1 10.] Having no beginning.

1591 SYLVESTER *Du Bartas* I. i. 343 [The world is] nought but all, in't selfe including All: An un-beginning, midlesse, endlesse Ball. 1756 LAW *Lett. Important Subj.* 118 The unbeginning, never-ending, never-changing trinity of love. a 1761 — *Behmen's Myst. Magnum* iv. (1772) 18 Threefold in its eternal unbeginning Birth. 1842 MRS. BROWNING *Grk. Chr. Poets* IV. ad fin., That unbeginning light of Thine. 1887 E. JOHNSON *Antiq. Mater* 217 The doctrine of the unbeginning and unknowable God.

Hence **Unbegiˑnningly** *adv.*, **-ness.**

1674 N. FAIRFAX *Bulk & Selv.* 165 You can no wayes halve them, and say, This half is unbeginningly, and that unendingly. 1862 F. HALL *Hindu Philos. Syst.* 35 By the unbeginningness of transmigration.

**Unbegiˑrt,** *ppl. a.* (UN-1 8 b.) 1603 DEEBLE in J. Davies (Heref.) *Microcosmos* P p, That curious Hand Which could the Pen most perfectly commaund Had not a Finger unbegirt with Gold.

† **Unbegoˑt,** *ppl. a. Obs.* [UN-1 8 b.] = next.

1593 SHAKS. *Rich. II*, III. iii. 88 They shall strike Your Children yet vnborne, and vnbegot. 1604 *Primer Blessed Virgin, Hymns* 20 Vnto the father unbegot, And to his sole begotten sonne. 1667 MILTON *P. L.* x. 988 In thy power It lies, yet ere Conception to prevent The Race unblest, to being yet unbegot.

**Unbegoˑtten,** *ppl. a.* [UN-1 8 b.] Ungenerated.

1532 SIR T. MORE *Confut. Tindale* IV. Wks. 580/2 Wherein the sonnes will that is yet vnbegotten, can nothyng make nor marre. 1561 T. NORTON *Calvin's Inst.* I. 40 By the Scriptures we teach..that the essence as well of the Sonn as of the Holy ghost is vnbegotten. 1587 GOLDING *De Mornay* (1592) 133 The world euerlasting and unbegotten. 1613–31 *Primer our Lady* (1669) 367 Glorie to th' unbegotten Father, And to the sole begotten Son. 1678 CUDWORTH *Intell. Syst.* I. iv. § 36. 587 The First Divine Hypostasis is altogether Unbegotten from any other. 1884 ADDIS & ARNOLD *Cath. Dict.* (1897) 895/2 The Father is unbegotten, the Son begotten.

Hence **Unbegoˑttenly** *adv.*, **Unbegoˑttenness.**

1631 I. R. *Pair Spectacles* ix. 340 Consubstantiality of the sonne, Diuinity of the Holy Ghost, and euen vnbegottenesse of the Father. 1736 CHANDLER *Hist. Persec.* 49 The son co-exists with God unbegottenly.

† **Unbegraˑve,** *ppl. a. Obs.* [UN-1 8 b + BEGRAVE *v.* 1. Cf. MDu. and Du. *onbegraven*, MHG. and G. *unbegraben*, Da. *ubegraven*, etc.] Unburied.

1513 DOUGLAS *Æneid* XI. i. 54 Lat ws to erd haue The corpsis of our fallowis onbegraue.

**Unbeguiˑle,** *v.* [UN-2 3.] *trans.* To undeceive.

1601 DANIEL *Let. fr. Octavia* li, Break from these snares —thy judgment unbeguile. 1654 H. L'ESTRANGE *Chas. I* (1655) 182 The Archbishop..resolved to speak out, and unbeguile them both. a 1711 KEN *Preparat.* Poet. Wks. 1721 IV. 58 Our God in that great King design'd To unbeguile each Worldly mind.

**Unbeguiˑled,** *ppl. a.* (UN-1 8.)

a 1533 LD. BERNERS *Gold. Bk. M. Aurel.* xlii. (1535) 76 b, And to the entent thou lyue vnbegiled I will tell the a secrete. a 1729 CONGREVE *Homer's Hymn to Venus* 14 Blue-ey'd Minerva free preserves her heart, A virgin unbeguil'd by Cupid's art. 1820 SHELLEY *Hymn Merc.* xxvi, The Goddess, his fair mother, unbeguiled, Knew all that he had done being abroad. 1833 TENNYSON *Lady Clara Vere De V.* 5 At me you smiled, but unbeguiled I saw the snare.

**Unbeguiˑleful,** *a.* (UN-1 7.) 1604 R. CAWDREY *Table Alph.* (1613), *Infallible*, undeceiueable, vnbeguilefull. **Unbeguiˑlefulness.** (UN-1 12.) c 1456 PECOCK *Bk. of Faith* (1909) 156 He knewe bi experience the treuthe and the sadnes and the unbigilefulnes of hise felowis.

**Unbeguˑn,** *ppl. a.* Forms: 1 unbegunnen, 3 unnbigunnenn, 4 unbegunne (7 vn-), 6 vnbegon(ne, vnbegun, 7- unbegun. [UN-1 8 b. Cf. Du. *onbegonnen*, OHG. *unbegunnen.*]

1. That had no beginning; ever existent.

c 1000 ÆLFRIC *Saints' Lives* I. 16 An ælmihtiȝ god æfre unbegunnen and unȝeændod. c 1200 ORMIN 18574 Forr eȝȝþerr iss wiþþutenn ord, & æfre all unnbigunnenn. 1390 GOWER *Conf.* III. 275 The myhti god, which unbegunne Stant of himself. 1610 J. HEALEY *St. Aug. Citie of God* XII. xvii. 458 Hee needed none of these creatures,..hauing continued.. blessed without them, from all vn-begunne eternity. a 1680 CHARNOCK *Attrib. God* (1834) I. 375 We were nothing from an unbegun eternity. 1872 LIDDON *Elem. Relig.* ii. 79 That unbegun, unending, self-existent Life; that boundless Intelligence,..what is He, our God, to us?

2. Not yet begun; not commenced.

1562 W. WIGHTMAN Ep. Ded., in Phaer *Æneid* (ed. 2) 1 He..promised to vse all hys possible diligence for the finishing of the other three bookes then vtterly vnbegonne. a 1568 ASCHAM *Scholem.* II. (Arb.) 159 The other part of the head beyng hidden, the bodie and the rest of the members vnbegon. 1597 HOOKER *Eccl. Pol.* v. lvi. § 5 A worke vnbegun is in the Artificer which afterward bringeth it into effect. 1706 WATTS *Horæ Lyr.* III. 266 Nations unborn, and ages unbegun. 1738 *Gentl. Mag.* VIII. 485/2 Therefore, tho' more than half my days are done, My days of life are un-begun. 1812 *Monthly Mag.* XXXIV. 14 We prevent what is unbegun, we hinder what is unfinished. 1868 MRS. WHITNEY *P. Strong* xvi, The smoothness of that which is unbegun.

**Unbeheaˑded,** *ppl. a.* (UN-1 8.) a 1578 LINDESAY (Pitscottie) *Chron. Scot.* (S.T.S.) II. 49 *marg.*, The erle of angus eschaippit onbeheiddit be meanis of the lard of blanerne.

**Unbeheˑld,** *ppl. a.* (UN-1 8 b.)

1667 MILTON *P. L.* IV. 674 These then, though unbeheld in deep of night, Shine not in vain. 1796 ANNA SEWARD *Lett.* (1811) IV. 172 In my best days, however I might admire and revere unbeheld excellence,..yet [etc.]. 1819 SHELLEY *Cenci* II. i. 192 Constellations quenched in murkiest cloud, In which I walk secure and unbeheld Towards my purpose. 1867 G. MACDONALD *Poems* 3 The good, the heavenly land, Though unbeheld, quite near them lay.

**Unbehoˑldable,** *a.* (UN-1 7 b.) 1855 PUSEY *Doct. Real Presence* Note 2. 173 Afterwards his face is changed by brightness unbeholdable. 1862 R. H. PATTERSON *Ess. Hist. & Art* 392 The mystery of whose unbeholdable splendours not unaptly symbolised the presence of Him.

**Unbeho·lden,** *ppl. a.* [Un-[1] 8 b.]

**1.** Not under an obligation (*to* a person); independent. *rare.*

**1674** N. Fairfax *Bulk & Selv.* 18 Both unmade by God, and unbeholden to, or independent on God. *c* **1848** J. Keegan *Leg. & Poems* (1907) 489 Dandy Delaney and his family grew rich all at once. People..wondered how the mischief he grew so 'unbeholden' in a moment.

**2.** Unbeheld, unseen.

**1820** Shelley *Skylark* 48 Like a glow-worm golden.. Scattering unbeholden Its aëreal hue. **1867** Jean Ingelow *Poems, Tired* v, And were it good to go, And unbeholden in the vessel's wake Look on the man thou lovedst, and forgive. **1876** Swinburne *Erechtheus* 813 At a shrine unbeloved of a God unbeholden a gift shall be given for the land.

Hence **Unbeho·ldenness.** *rare*[—1].

**1674** N. Fairfax *Bulk & Selv.* 63 They who hold this wild emptiness, hold also..its independency on, or unbeholdenness to, God himself.

†**Unbeho·lding,** *ppl. a. Obs.* [Un-[1] 10.] = Unbeholden 1.

**1615** G. Sandys *Trav.* 182 Where we saw..a fountaine not vnbeholding to Art. **1654–66** Earl Orrery *Parthen.* (1676) 164 Perhaps I have not been unbeholding to her.

†**Unbeho·vable,** *a. Obs. rare.* Also 5 vnbehuvable. [Un-[1] 7 b.] Unsuitable; unprofitable.

*c* **1440** *Alph. Tales* 63 Þan Joseph thoght þat & sho hatid euer-ilk a man, sho sulde not be vnbehuvable vnto hym. **1550** Cheke in *Harington's Nugæ Ant.* (1804) I. 42 Heareby all sortes of students..be..enabled to attaine to a greater and perfecter trade of learning, not unbehovable for the commonwelthe.

†**Unbeho·veful,** *a. Obs.* [Un-[1] 7.] Not profitable or useful; unnecessary.

**1429** *Rolls of Parlt.* V. 417/2 [Fortresses and places] suche as shall be thoght..unbehovefull. *c* **1520** Barclay *Jugurtha* 4 b, Neuertheles so to do it is vnbehouefull & vnexpedyent. **1619** W. Sclater *Exp. 1 Thess.* (1630) 554 Things lawfull in themselues may be vnseemely for our state and calling; vnbehouefull also to benefit of others. **1624** Bp. Mountagu *New Gagg* 205 We hold it needlesse,..as unbehoovefull, and to no purpose. **1648** Hexham ii, *Onbehoeflick*, Vnbehovefull.

†**Unbeho·vely,** *a. Obs. rare.* [Un-[1] 7.] = prec.

**1390** Gower *Conf.* III. 123 Scorpio..of his kinde is moiste and cold And unbehovely manyfold. *Ibid.* 372, I am unbehovely Your Court fro this day forth to serve. **14..** *Voc.* in Wr.-Wülcker 588 *Illicitus*, vnbehouely *vel* unlefful.

**Unbeho·ving.** (Un-[1] 12.) **1844** Mrs. Browning *Woman's Shortcoming* v, Unless you can dream that his faith is fast, Through behoving and unbehoving.

†**Unbe·ing,** *vbl. sb. Obs.* [Un-[1] 13.] Absence or lack of being; non-existence.

**1435** Misyn *Fire of Love* 84 To deed hastand & to vnbeingis to mevingis of fleschly affeccions. **1587** Golding *De Mornay* ii. (1592) 22 A tending to the vtter vnbeing or not being of the whole. *Ibid.* 23 Which matter they termed the verie vnbeing, that is to saye, in verie troth no being at all.

†**Unbe·ing,** *ppl. a. Obs.* [Un-[1] 10.] Non-existent.

**1607** J. Davies (Heref.) *Summa Totalis* Wks. (Grosart) I. 23/1 Those Things haue euer an vnbeing Beeing Which in his Vnderstanding onely Bee. *a* **1631** Donne *Ess. Divinity* (1651) 130 All [those] now eminent and in actions, and all yet undiscovered, and unbeing. **1682** Sir T. Browne *Chr. Mor.* 119 He must answer, who asked it; who understands entities of preordination, and beings yet unbeing.

**Unbeke·nd, -kent,** *ppl. a. Sc.* and *north.* [Un-[1] 8, 8 b. Cf. WFris. *on-*, *ûnbikend*, Du. and Flem. *onbekend*, †*onbekendt*, G. *unbekannt*, Sw. *obekant*, Da. *ubekendt*.] Unknown.

**1513** Douglas *Æneid* viii. ii. 15 And thou, O haly fader Tiberyne,..Ressaue Eneas to ȝou onbekend [*v.r.* vn-]. *Ibid.* ix. vii. 61 Quham the dissaitfull onbekend [*v.r.* vm-] dern way.. Betrasit had. **1808** Jamieson, *Unbekent.* **1894** Heslop *Northumbld. Gloss.* 754.

**Unbeknow·n,** *ppl. a.* Also *dial.* onbeknown, unbeknawn, etc. [Un-[1] 8 b.]

**1.** In absolute or adverbial const. in the phrase *unbeknown to*, without the knowledge of.

**1636** T. Goodwin *Return of Prayers* iv. 75 To sympathize with another in praying for such a thing unbeknowne one to another. **1836–7** Dickens *Sk. Boz, Seven Dials*, If my 'usband had treated her with a drain..unbeknown to me, I'd tear her precious eyes out. **1837** — *Pickw.* xxxiv, 'I was there,' resumed Mrs. Cluppins, 'unbeknown to Mrs. Bardell'. **1885** *Law Times* 28 Feb. 321/2 The chalk had been opened..unbeknown to the tenant.

*ellipt.* **1866** Reade *G. Gaunt* xvi, I shall send you some stock from the castle, and you can cook his vegetables in good strong gravy, unbeknown. **1896** Housman *Shropshire Lad* xxi, My love rose up so early And stole out unbeknown.

**2.** Unknown; lying outside of one's knowledge or acquaintance. Also *absol.*

**1824** *Monthly Mag.* LVII. 408 They agreed to be both at the tourney, But unbeknown and clad in common armure. **1861** Clough *Poems*, etc. (1869) I. 262 Gentlemen unbeknown to ladies give their arms to ladies aforesaid, to conduct them into dinner. **1888** *Pall Mall G.* 7 May 2/2 He..is loath to prophesy as to what is possible or is not possible in that 'land of the unbeknown'.

**Unbeknow·nst,** *a.* or *adv. colloq.* and *dial.* Also unbeknowns, etc. [f. prec. The analogy on which the *-s* or *-st* has been added is not clear: cf. the earlier Unknownst.] = Unbeknown 2.

**1854** Huxley in L. Huxley *Life & Lett.* (1910) I. 111, I hate doing anything of the kind 'unbeknownst' to people. **1854** *Poultry Chron.* I. 331/1 It was found that she was sitting on a nest of eggs,—unbeknownst. **1887** Kipling *Plain Tales fr. Hills* (1888) 147 Perhaps they were afraid that their wives had come from Homo unbeknownst.

**Unbelaw·yered,** *a.* (Un-[1] 9.) **1830** *Westm. Rev.* Oct. 445 Not to speak of unsold justice, unbelawyered justice.

**Unbe·lched,** *ppl. a.* (Un-[1] 8.) **1854** S. Dobell *Balder* xxiv. 169 Like an embowelled earthquake yet unbelched.

**Unbeld,** obs. variant of Unbold *a.*

**Unbeleue,** obs. f. Unbelief, -lieve *v.*[1]

**Unbelie·d,** *ppl. a.* (Un-[1] 8.) [**1775** Ash.] **1834** Wordsw. '*Soft as a Cloud*' 24 If yet To-morrow, unbelied, may say, I come to open out [etc.].

**Unbelie·f.** Forms: *a.* 2 unbelefe, 4 vnbylefe; 3 unbileue, -leaue, 4 vnbi-, vnbyleue, 4, 6 unbeleue (4 -leeue, 6 -leve). *β.* 6 vnbelefe, 6–7 -leefe, -liefe, 6– unbelief (6–7 -liefe). [Un-[1] 12.] Absence or lack of belief; disbelief, incredulity.

**a.** In matters of religion.

*a.* *c* **1160** *Hatton Gosp.* Mark xvi. 14 Heom atewede se hælend & here unbelefen & heora heorten ȝe-tremede. *c* **1200** *Trin. Coll. Hom.* 81 He..blamede here un-bileue & here unwreste liflode. *a* **1225** *Leg. Kath.* 259 Wið neauer an ne kecched he creftiluker cang men, ne leadeð to unbileaue. **1382** Wyclif *Matt.* xiii. 58 He dide nat there manye vertues, for the vnbyleue of hem. *a* **1400** *New Test.* (Paues) Heb. iii. 12 Loke ȝe, wheþer þer be in any of ȝou an efel herte of vnbylefe. **1526** Tindale *Rom.* xi. 20 Be cause of vnbeleve they are broken of. **1567** *Gude & Godlie B.* (S.T.S.) 13 Saif vs..from dispair, From unbeleue, and Lollardis lair.

*β.* **1531** Tindale *Exp. 1 John* ii. (1538) 39 The doctrine of them..that say, vnbelefe to be the mother of al vyce. **1597** Hooker *Eccl. Pol.* v. xxii. § 4 Their vnbeleefe in that case we may not impute vnto any weakness..in the meanes. **1634** Milton *Comus* 519 Such there be, but unbelief is blind. **1680** Flavel *Meth. Grace* xxxii, Positive Unbelief, is the Sin of Men and Women under the Gospel. **1705** Atterbury *Serm.* (1726) II. 51 For the Mind doth, by every degree of affected Unbelief, contract more and more of a general Indisposition towards Believing. **1809–10** Coleridge *Friend* (1865) 57 As much as I love my fellow-men, so much and no more will I be intolerant of their heresies and unbelief. **1858** J. Martineau *Stud. Chr.* 27 The second of these books would be condemned for heresy, and the first for unbelief. **1897** Liddon, etc. *Life Pusey* IV. iii. 73 Those forms of German unbelief with which..he had become painfully familiar at Göttingen.

**b.** In general use.

**1649** J. Taylor (Water P.) *Western Voy.* 15 It is a hazard of the losse of a traveller's liberty by either their unbeliefe or misprision. *a* **1800** Cowper *Odyssey* (ed. 2) xiv. 177 Since, hopeless of thy lord's return, Thou art thus resolute in unbelief. **1855** *Poultry Chron.* II. 566/1 The tables were turned on me by the man, who had I suppose observed my previous gesture of unbelief. **1900** *Longm. Mag.* Mar. 465, I had received the news with contemptuous unbelief.

**c.** Personified.

**1744** Akenside *Pleas. Imag.* iii. 122 Where watchful Unbelief Darts through the thin pretence her squinting eye. **1781** Cowper *Truth* 445 Thus often unbelief, grown sick of life, Flies to the tempting pool. or felon knife.

†**Unbelie·fful,** *a. Obs.* Forms: *a.* 4–5 unbileveful, vnbileueful. *β.* 4–5 vnbeleffful, vnbileefful(l, vnbyleeful. [Un-[1] 7, or f. prec. + -ful.]

**1.** Unbelieving; wanting in belief. Also *absol.*

*a.* *c* **1380** Wyclif *Sel. Wks.* II. 149 He þat is unbileveful to þe sone, shal not se þe blis of hevene. **1388** — *Deut.* i. 26 ȝe weren vnbileueful to the word of oure Lord God.

*β.* *c* **1380** Wyclif *Wks.* (1880) 45 Who euere of freris bi inspiracioun of god wilen goon among sarasyns & oþere vnbelefful. **1382** — *Acts* xxvi. 19, I was not vnbileefful to heuenly visioun. *c* **1430–40** *R. Gloucester's Chron.* (Rolls) 4920+20 To byleue [= remain] þere Among mys bylyuede [MS. *e* vnbelefful] men.

**2.** Incredible. *rare*[—1].

**1388** Wyclif *Judg.* xx. 5 Thei bitraueliden my wijf with vnbileueful woodnesse of letcherie.

Hence †**Unbelie·ffulness.** *Obs.*[—1]

**1382** Wyclif *Mark* ix. 23 Lord, I bileue; help thou myn vnbileeufulnesse.

**Unbelievabi·lity.** (Un-[1] 12: see next.) Also, in recent use, *unbelievableness.*

**1851** Carlyle *Sterling* i. xv, Boiling mud-oceans of Hypocrisy and Unbelievability.

**Unbelie·vable,** *a.* Also 6 vnbeleu(e)able, 6–7 vnbeleeu(e)able; 7 unbeleavable; 6 unbelieuable. [Un-[1] 7 b.] That cannot be believed; incredible.

**1548** Geste *Pr. Masse* A viij b, Which graunt [= admission] as it is erronyouse and vnbeleueable so vngodly and exchuable. **1549** Coverdale, etc. *Erasm. Par. Acts* vii. 36 Though it semed to be a thynge vnbeleuable that was promysed,..Abraham beleued. **1580** *Apol. Prince of Orange* liv, Some..will thinke it vnbeleeueable,that euer there could be founde, such great inconstancie in them. **1624** Heywood *Gunaik.* vii. 346 Hugotio..began to recite many unbeleavable things concerning his appetite in his youth. **1633** J. Done tr. *Aristeas' Hist. Septuagint* 63 This is a thing yet more admirable, and almost vnbeleeuable. **1797** Mrs. Radcliffe *Italian* xxii, However unbelievable it may seem, you may depend upon it, it is all true. **1833** Carlyle *Misc. Ess., Diderot* (1888) V. 52 He believes that pleasure is pleasant: that a lie is unbelievable. **1895** Saintsbury *Corrected Impressions* xv. 144 Almost unbelievable faults of taste.

Hence **Unbelie·vably** *adv.*

**1839** Bailey *Festus* 359 Made pure, and unbelievably uplift Above their present state. **1893** *Chamb. Jrnl.* 19 Aug. 514/1 It seemed almost unbelievably sweet.

**Unbelie·ve,** *v.*[1] Also 6 vnbeleue, 7 -leeue. [Un-[1] 14.] To disbelieve: **a.** *trans.*

**1547** Baldwin *Mor. Philos.* (1550) G v b, Aristotle..beeyng asked what vauntage a man might get by lying, he answered: to be vnbeleued whan he telleth truth. **1615** Daniel *Hymen's Triumph* ii. ii, A counterfeited shew Of passion, which you may..Make him as easily to vnbeleeue, As what he neuer saw. **1646** Sir T. Browne *Pseud. Ep.* i. viii. (1686) 24 Such as amass all relations, must erre in some, and may without offence be unbelieved in many. **1672** Eachard *Lett.* 70, I must desire you to unbelieve all that you have said. **1711** *Medley* No. 42 He seems to think he may..make us unbelieve what we have seen. **1813** J. Adams *Wks.* (1856) X. 57 What does Priestley mean by an unbeliever, when he applies it to you? How much did he unbelieve himself? **1872** Lever *Ld. Kilgobbin* lxxix, Fellows who are realistic, ..who have little to speculate on and less to unbelieve.

**b.** *intr.* or *absol.*

**1687** *Reason. Toleration* 2 Let neither Her nor Him that unbelieves depart, if pleased to stay. *a* **1718** Penn *Tracts* Wks. 1726 I. 451 Where Men believe, not because it is True, but because they are required to do so, there they will unbelieve. **1855** Browning *Bp. Blougram's Apol.* 263 And so you live to sleep as I to wake, To unbelieve as I to still believe?

**Unbelie·ve,** *v.*[2] [Un-[2] 4.] *trans.* To give up belief in; to discard or abandon (belief).

**1605** Daniel *Queen's Arcadia* v. iv. (1606) Kiij, How were I cleer'd of griefe, Had I the power to vnbeleeue beliefe. **1795** Paine *Age of Reason* ii. 8 To believe therefore the Bible to be true, we must unbelieve all our belief in the moral justice of God. **1837** Ht. Martineau *Soc. Amer.* II. 38 *note*, You know nothing of those people. They will believe everything, and unbelieve nothing.

**Unbelie·ved,** *ppl. a.* Forms: 3 unbilefde, -bileued; 4 vnbylefed, 5 vnbeleued, etc.; 7– unbelieved. [Un-[1] 8.]

†**1.** Unbelieving. *Obs.*

*c* **1200** *Trin. Coll. Hom.* 81 Þe grimliche wordes þe ure helende..gaf to andswere þe unbilefde iudeuisshe men. *a* **1225** *Ancr. R.* 260 Unbileued he is þet luueð to muchel & ȝisceð worldes weole & wunne. *a* **1400** *New Test.* (Paues) Titus i. 16 Þei beþ abhomynabel, & vnbylefed, & reprefabel to eferich good werk. *c* **1450** *Mirk's Festial* i. 139 Phylyp was send..forto prech Godis worde to þe vnbeleued pepull.

† **2.** Unbelievable, incredible. *Obs.*

*c* **1425** in *Anglia* X. 342 Turmentede with vnbylevede sorowe. **1581** Sidney *Apol. Poetrie* (Arb.) 19 Nay, to so vnbeleeued a poynt hee proceeded, as that no earthly thing bred such wonder to a Prince, as to be a good horseman. **1611** Beaum. & Fl. *King & No King* ii. ii, I made his valour stoop, and brought that name soar'd to so unbeliev'd a height, to fall beneath mine.

**3.** Not believed; disbelieved.

**1603** Shaks. *Meas. for M.* v. i. 119 Heauen shield your Grace from woe As I thus wrong'd, hence vnbeleeued goe. *a* **1619** Fotherby *Atheom.* Pref. (1622) B ij b, But yet specially, in the first point, of beleeuing that there is a God, that is of all the rest the most vnbeleeued. **1655** J. Jane in *Nicholas Papers* (Camden) II. 223 It cannot be long vnbeleeved, being soe farr advanced especially in the French leauge. **1819** Wordsw. *Haunted Tree* 27 Nor is it unbelieved, By ruder fancy, that a troubled ghost Haunts the old trunk. **1844** Kinglake *Eothen* viii, The unbelieved Cassandra was right after all. **1877** Ruskin *Fors Clav.* lxxxi. 250 All which teachings have..passed from deed and truth into mere monotony of unbelieved phrase.

**Unbelie·ver.** [Un-[1] 12.] One who does not believe; *spec.* one who does not accept a particular religious belief, an infidel.

**1526** Tindale 2 *Cor.* vi. 14 Beare nott the yooke wyth the vnbelevers. **1597** Hooker *Eccl. Pol.* v. lxxx. § 2 The name of Pagans, which properly signifieth country people, came to be used in common speech for the same that infidels and vnbeleeuers were. **1618** J. Taylor (Water P.) *Pennyles Pilgr.* F ij, This sounds like a lie to an vnbeleeuer; but I..knowe that I speake within the compasse of truth. **1653** W. Ramesey *Astrol. Restored* 32 In the dark corners of the Gentiles, who were then unbelievers. **1709** Addison *Tatler* No. 111 ℙ4 To become conspicuous, [he] declares that he is an Unbeliever. **1777** Priestley *Matt. & Spir.* I. Pref. (1782) p. viii, The cry against me as an unbeliever..was..general and loud. **1825** Scott *Talism.* iii, The miseries imposed by the unbelievers upon the Latin Christians in the Holy Land. **1837** W. A. Butler *Serm. Doctr. & Pract.* Ser. ii. xx. (1856) 202 The unbeliever may chafe at the mysteries of faith.

**Unbelie·ving,** *vbl. sb.* [Un-[1] 13.] The action of not believing; disbelief; an instance of this.

*a* **1400** *New Test.* (Paues) Heb. iii. 19 Þei ne myȝte not entren in-to his reste for hure vnbylefynge. **1611** Cotgr., *Incredulité*,..vnbeleeuing, lacke of beliefe. **1627** R. Ashley *Almansor* 60 God permitteth vnbeleeuing in this world. **1883** J. M. Wilson *Theory Inspiration* ii. 30 It is as wrong to count a man a fool for believing as for unbelieving.

**Unbelie·ving,** *ppl. a.* [Un-[1] 10.] Not giving or having belief (esp. in religious matters); incredulous; infidel.

*a* **1400** *New Test.* (Paues) Heb. iii. 18 To whom swor he þat þei schulden noȝt entren in-to his reste, bote to þilke þat weren vnbylefynge? **1526** Tindale 1 *Cor.* vii. 14 For the vnbelevynge husbande is sanctifyed by the wyfe: and the vnbelevynge wyfe ys sanctifyed by the husbande. **1567** Jewel *Def. Apol.* ii. vi. Div. 3. 141 As often as he shutteth vp the Gate of the Kingdome of Heauen against vnbeleeuing, and stubborne persons. **1613–6** W. Browne *Brit. Past.* ii. iv, Which vnbeleeuing man, that is not mov'd To credit aught, if not by reason prov'd,..Held as most fabulous. *a* **1656** Hales *Gold. Rem.* i. (1673) 95 'Tis true indeed, in spight of unbeleiving miscreants, it hath pleased God..to save those that are his. **1725** Pope *Odyss.* xiv. 431 And why, oh swain of unbelieving mind!..Doubt you my oath? **1728** Eliza Heywood tr. *Mme. de Gomez' Belle A.* (1732) II. 270 There is nothing I would not endeavour to suffer, or perform, to keep you mine, indifferent and unbelieving as you are. **1825** Scott *Talism.* iii, A barefooted friar would have been a better associate than the gay but unbelieving Paynim. **1864** Pusey *Lect. Daniel* (1876) 110 It is no uncommon resource of unbelieving criticism. **1875** Jowett *Plato* (ed. 2) III. 41 The age of miracles has ceased, and the world is an unbelieving world.

*absol.* **1526** Tindale *Rev.* xxi. 8 The fearfull and vnbelevynge, and the abhominable, and murdres. **1594** Drayton *Sonn.* Minor Poems (1907) 7 See myracles, ye vnbeleeuing; see A dumbe-born Muse made to expresse the mind.

Hence **Unbelie·vingly** *adv.*; **-belie·vingness.** 1685 BAXTER *Paraphr. N. T.* 1 Pet. ii. 7 Even they that *unbelievingly reject..the Gospel, and disobey it. *a* 1708 BEVERIDGE *Thes. Theol.* (1711) I. 340 He is angry with them [*sc.* the wicked]..For all Actions; are done 1) From wrong Principle. 2)..Inobedientially. 3. Unbelievingly. 1350 LYNCH *Theoph. Trinal* vii. 134 Many true things we unbelievingly say. 1561 T. NORTON *Calvin's Inst.* I. 34 It is therfore no maruell if Christ alleged his miracles to confound the *unbeleuingnesse of the Jewes. 1581 J. BELL *Haddon's Answ. Osor.* 231 The fault hereof is their own unbeleevingnes, not the will of God.

**Unbelo·ved,** *ppl. a.* (UN-[1] 8.) 1597 WARNER *Alb. Eng.* IX. xlvi. 217 Eccho, an amiable Nymph, long amorous of him, But louing, vnbeloued. 1647 CLARENDON *Hist. Reb.* II. § 101 If it had not concerned a person notoriously unbeloved, and so the more unpitied. 1697 DRYDEN *Æneid* I. 536 Whoe'er you are—not unbeloved by Heaven..—Have courage. 1706 WATTS *Horæ Lyr.* I. 118 Wild and wand'ring all alone, Unbeloved and unknown. 1815 SHELLEY *Summer Evening* 5 Silence and Twilight, unbeloved of men. 1890 BAKER *Wild Beasts* I. 230 A tiger or some unbeloved animal was before them.

*absol.* 1820 LAMB (*title*), The Unbeloved.

†**Unbe·lt,** *ppl. a. Obs.* [UN-[1] 8 b.] Unbelted. 1662 HIBBERT *Body Divinity* I. 130 Truely here (as one saith well) if ever *unbelt unblest*; he is a loose man that wants this girdle of sincerity.

**Unbe·lt,** *v.* [UN-[2] 4 and 5.]

**1.** *trans.* To ungird. 1483 *Cath. Angl.* 27/2 To vn Belte, *discingere, incingere.*

**2.** To detach or remove (a sword, etc.) by unfastening the belt. 1814 SCOTT *Lord of Isles* III. xxiii, But why waste time in idle words? Sit to your cheer—unbelt your swords. 1825 — *Talism.* xxvii, As if thy knight, who hath not yet buckled on his armour, were unbelting it in triumph. 1879 J. D. LONG *Æneid* IX. 389 From off His shoulder he unbelts the golden sword.

**Unbe·lted,** *a.* (UN-[1] 9.) 1814 BYRON *Lara* I. xii, They ..snatch'd in startled haste unbelted brands. 1870 BRYANT *Iliad* XVI. II. 135 Sarpedon as he saw his friends The unbelted Lycians. 1880 L. WALLACE *Ben-Hur* 32 He wears ..a loose gown, sleeveless, unbelted, and dropping from the neck to the knee. **Unbemoa·ned,** *ppl. a.* (UN-[1] 8.) 1623 tr. *Favine's Theat. Hon.* v. i. 41 By his vnbemoaned death, Henry his Brother..came to enioy the Crowne of England. *a* 1711 KEN *Hymns Evang.* Poet. Wks. 1721 I. 375 When he..Had no known Sin left unbemoan'd, And with fresh Tears had God aton'd. 1827 POLLOK *Course T.* II. 773 God..lets them ever try..To walk alone, unguided, unbemoaned, Where Evil dwells.

**Unbe·nd,** *v.* [UN-[2] 3 and 7.]

**I.** *trans.* **1.** To release or relax (a bow) from tension; to unstring. *c* 1250 *Gen. & Ex.* 483 Lamech wið wreðe is knape nam, Vn-bente is boȝe, and bet, and sloȝ. *c* 1290 *St. John* 331 in *S. Eng. Leg.* I. 412 Þare-aftur sone he nam is bouwe, and unbende it ase he couþe. *c* 1375 *Sc. Leg. Saints* v. (*John*) 481 Þar-for he his bow vnbent. Þane sad sancte Iohne: 'tel þi entent, quhy þu vnbent þi bow sa sone'. 1390 GOWER *Conf.* I. 108 Thanne was I furthest ate laste, And as a foll my bowe unbende. 1413 *26 Pol. Poems* 53 Pray we god his bowe of wraþþe vnbende. *c* 1440 *Alph. Tales* 274 Þe apostell askid hym whi it was vnbendid. 1503-4 *Act 19 Hen. VII*, c. 4 Yf..servauntes..shote with their Crosebowe otherwyse than..to unbend the same. 1530 PALSGR. 766/1 Unbende your bowes, syrs, nowe you come in to the towne. 1614 PURCHAS *Pilgrimage* VI. v. (ed. 2) 590 Others 3. times vnbent their bows, & thrice again bent them whiles their horses ran. 1627 DRAYTON *Agincourt* 61 Their bloody swords they quietly had sheath'd, And their strong bowes already were unbent. 1825 SCOTT *Talism.* xii, Unbend thy arblast, and come into the moonlight.

†**b.** To uncock (a fire-arm). *Obs.*[—1] 1632 LITHGOW *Trav.* VIII. 351 Holding vp my hand, and imploring for our liues.., they vnbend their fire-locks, and.. did me homage.

†**2.** To slacken or weaken. *Obs.* 1605 SHAKS. *Macb.* II. ii. 45 You doe vnbend your Noble strength, to thinke So braine-sickly of things. 1611 — *Cymb.* III. iv. 111 Why hast thou gone so farre To be vn-bent? 1831 JAMES *Phil. Augustus* vi, My curse upon time! for he..saps our castles, and unbends our sinews.

**3.** *fig.* To relax, to give relaxation to (one's mind, etc.); to free from serious occupations. 1594 SOUTHWELL *M. Magd. Funeral Teares* (1823) 139 Unlesse thou wilt unbend her thoughts, that her eyes may fully see thee. 1604 MARSTON *Malcontent* III. ii. E j b, Thou that..Vnbendst the feebled vaines of sweatie labour. 1656 COWLEY *Pindar. Odes, To Dr. Scarborough* vi, Unbend sometimes thy restless care. 1725 POPE *Odyss.* I. 335 Social mirth unbent his serious soul. 1753 HANWAY *Trav.* VII. xcviii. (1762) I. 459 In this palace..the king most unbends his mind. 1839 HALLAM *Hist. Lit.* III. vi. § 5 The extemporaneous comedy had always been the amusement.. of all who wished to unbend their minds. 1856 *N. Brit. Rev.* XXVI. 217 The mind of the reader is unbent, he puts aside for a time his own cares.

*refl.* 1672 WYCHERLEY *Love in Wood* v. ii, Men in office too, that adjourn their cares and businesses, to come and unbend themselves at night here. 1711 ADDISON *Spect.* No. 93 ¶ 10 The Mind never unbends itself so agreeably as in the Conversation of a well chosen Friend. 1791 BOSWELL *Johnson* Ded., Dr. Clarke..was unbending himself with a few friends in the most playful and frolicksome manner. 1891 L. FALCONER *Mlle. Ixe* ii. 38 A very different person from the Mademoiselle Ixe who unbent herself with Evelyn.

**4.** *Naut.* To unfasten, untie, undo (a cable, line, or sail). 1627 CAPT. SMITH *Seaman's Gram.* vii. 30 [To] vnbend the Cable, is..to take it away, which we vsually doe when we are at Sea. 1720 DE FOE *Capt. Singleton* (1906) 220 We immediately unbent all our sails,..and set up seven or eight tents with them. 1745 P. THOMAS *Jrnl. Anson's Voy.* 27 We split the Foresail and unbent it, and bent another. 1793 SMEATON *Edystone L.* § 158 We found it equally difficult to get the bridle chain unbent from the swivel. 1840 R. H. DANA *Bef. Mast* xxvi, We unbent the mainsail, and formed an awning with it. 1875 *Board of Trade Instr. Saving Life by Rocket*, Unbend the Rocket Line from the Warp. 1882 NARES *Seamanship* (ed. 6) 124 What ropes are bent and unbent from the sail?

**5.** To allow or cause (the brow) to relax from a serious, severe, or frowning aspect. 1718 PRIOR *Henry & Emma* 6 Wilt thou awhile unbend thy serious Brow? *Ibid.* 138 A softer Look unbends his op'ning Brow. 1811 LAMB *Hogarth* Wks. 1909 I. 110 The ..joke which has unbent his care-worn hard-working visage. 1816 BYRON *Parisina* xx, But never..smile his brow unbended.

**6.** To straighten from a bent or curved position; to unfold. Also *refl.* 1663 BP. PATRICK *Parab. Pilgr.* xxx, They are the Souls whose Prayers God hears, who employ their hands as soon as they have unbent their knees. 1817 KIRBY & SPENCE *Entomol.* xxiii. II. 315 These [spines] are of great use in pushing them off when the legs are unbended. 1834-6 P. BARLOW in *Encycl. Metrop.* (1845) VIII. 99/2 A spring, which, in order that it may exert any force or give motion to a Machine, must first unbend itself. 1886 *N. Zealand Herald* 8 Nov. 6/5 Three nets were unbent and a number of opening games played.

*absol.* 1816 KIRBY & SP. *Entomol.* xxiii. (1817) II. 315 They bend their legs like the grasshoppers, and then unbending kick them out with violence.

**II.** *intr.* or *absol.* †**7.** To abandon an effort or attempt. *Obs. rare.* *a* 1400-50 *Alexander* 1744 (Dubl. MS.) For-þi is better vnbende & of þi brathe leue. *Ibid.* 1974 For-þi it wer better vnbenden or þou bale suffre.

**8. a.** To free oneself from constraint or ceremony; to act in an unconstrained or genial manner; to relax one's seriousness or severity. 1746 FRANCIS tr. *Horace, Epist.* I. xviii. 106 Yet oft at home you can unbend, And even to trifling Sports descend. 1784 COWPER *Tiroc.* 608 Ev'n in his pastimes he requires a friend, To warn, and teach him safely to unbend. 1831 D. E. WILLIAMS *Life & Corr. Sir T. Lawrence* II. 351 *note*, He seemed to unbend, and give way to his humour. 1869 FREEMAN *Norm. Conq.* vii. (1877) II. 28 In private company though he never forgot his rank, he could unbend.

**b.** Of the features: To lose severity; to relax. 1818 SCOTT *Rob Roy* xviii, His hard features gradually unbent. 1897 A. DOBSON *Poems, Tale of Polypheme* xviii, Soon the Child Filled the lone shore with louder merriment, And e'en the Cyclops' heavy brow unbent.

**c.** To relax in purpose. 1877 C. GEIKIE *Christ* xxxv. (1879) 413 His soul never unbent from its grand enthusiasm.

**9.** To alter from a bend or curve; to become straight or less curved. 1815 J. SMITH *Panorama Sci. & Art* II. 35 The spring, by unbending at the same time, loses a part of its power. 1861 GEO. ELIOT *Silas M.* xii, But the complete torpor came at last: the fingers lost their tension, the arms unbent. 1867 AUGUSTA WILSON *Vashti* xxx, The brow wore its heavy cloud, and the arch of the lip had not unbent.

**Unbe·ndable,** *a.* (UN-[1] 7 b.) [1775 ASH.] 1884 G. MACDONALD tr. *Lett. fr. Hell* (1885) 62 In such things her will was unbendable. 1889 BADEN-POWELL *Pigsticking* 94 The neck connecting the socket to the blade should be strong and unbendable.

**Unbe·nded,** *ppl. a.*[1] [f. UNBEND *v.*] Relaxed. 1693 *Humours Town* A 6 b, If it does but Contribute to your Diversion, at your more unbended Hours. 1745 ELIZA HEYWOOD *Female Spect.* No. 10 (1748) II. 192 The constantly chearful and entertaining companion of his more unbended moments. 1751 SMOLLETT *Per. Pick.* ii, His features were a little unbended. 1751 JOHNSON *Rambler* No. 89 ¶ 12 A wise and good man is never so amiable as in his unbended and familiar intervals.

**Unbe·nded,** *ppl. a.*[2] [UN-[1] 8.] Not bent. 1648 HEXHAM II, *Onbesweken*, Vnbowed, or Vnbended. 1726 POPE *Odyss.* XXI. 62 She..To the proud Suitors bears in pensive state Th' unbended bow, and arrows wing'd with Fate.

**Unbe·nder.** *rare*[—1]. [f. UNBEND *v.*] That which unbends or relaxes. 1637 QUARLES *Elegie* i, Away, those Ioyes:..The late vnbenders of my thoughtfull minde.

**Unbe·nding,** *vbl. sb.* [f. UNBEND *v.*] The action of the verb, esp. in senses 3 and 8. 1552 HULOET, Vnbendinge, *remissio.* 1611 COTGR., *Destenture*, an vnbending, vnstretching, slackening, loossing. 1648 HEXHAM, *Ontspanninge*, a Loosening, an Vnbending, or an Vnspanning. 1693 DRYDEN *Juvenal's Sat.* Ded. (1697) p. xxix, Recreation, for the unbending of our Minds. 1709 MRS. MANLEY *Secret Mem.* (1720) IV. 105 He found his Understanding return with double Force after such Unbendings. 1756 *Monitor* No. 53 II. 12 The rest of the evening was spent in table talk, and the easy unbendings of these little nocturnal assemblies. 1840 DICKENS *Old C. Shop* xxxvi, With such unbendings did Richard..relieve the tedium of his confinement. 1859 G. A. SALA *Tw. round Clock* 218 He was of a disposition, save in casual moments of unbending, quite surprising for its saturnine taciturnity.

**b.** *attrib.* (or *ppl. a.*). 1701 ROWE *Amb. Step-Moth.* Ded., I hope it may indifferently Entertain your Lordship at an unbending hour. 1740 CIBBER *Apol.* I. Ded. (1756) p. viii, Where like the fam'd orator of old, when publick cares permit, you pass so many rational unbending hours.

**Unbe·nding,** *ppl. a.* [UN-[1] 10.]

**1.** Not giving way or departing from a position or principle; unyielding, inflexible, steady: **a.** Of feelings, dispositions, etc. *a* 1688 CUDWORTH *Immut. Mor.* (1731) 270 Truth is the most Unbending and Uncompliable..Thing in the World. 1800 MRS. HERVEY *Mourtray Fam.* IV. 115 Recollect, that Mr. Silbourne is rather of an unbending temper. 1848 LYTTON *Harold* VIII. iv, His unbending hate of all that was Norman. 1861 MAY *Const. Hist.* (1863) I. i. 82 A kind but most unbending answer was returned to Mr. Pitt.

**b.** Of persons. 1796 MATHIAS *Purs. Lit.* (1798) 128 Firm, constant, and unbending, he has the principles of a man, who knows and feels what is demanded of him by his country. 1831 SCOTT *Ct. Rob.* xxxiii, The veteran and unbending conspirator, Harpax, thus strengthened..the failing spirits of Stephanos. 1871 C. GIBBON *Lack of Gold* viii, Annie knew how doggedly unbending her father was.

**2.** Not bending or curving; rigid; *esp.* of persons, remaining erect, not stooping. 1709 POPE *Ess. Crit.* 373 Swift Camilla..Flies o'er th' unbending corn. 1726-45 THOMSON *Winter* 1064 Ye noble few! who here unbending stand Beneath life's pressure, yet bear up a while. 1802 PALEY *Nat. Theol.* xvi, The short unbending neck of the elephant is compensated by the length and flexibility of his proboscis. 1884 F. M. CRAWFORD *Rom. Singer* I. 25 The tall old foreigner stood erect and unbending.

Hence **Unbe·ndingly** *adv.*, **Unbe·ndingness.** 1847 WEBSTER, *Unbendingly. 1894 C. N. ROBINSON *Brit. Fleet* 439 The usage of the time was unbendingly severe. 1824 LANDOR *Imag. Conv.* I. 96 *note*, *Unbendingness, in the moral as in the vegetable world, is an indication as frequently of unsoundness as of strength. 1855 I. TAYLOR *Restor. Belief* (1856) 59 The spread of Christianity,..[considering] its unbendingness, and the furious hostility it encountered,..is proof of its reality. 1891 MEREDITH *One of our Conq.* xxxviii, She met them with the slender unbendingness that was her own.

†**Unbene,** *a. Obs.*[—1] [UN-[1] 7: see BEIN *a.*] Ungenial, wild and rugged. 13.. *Gaw. & Gr. Knt.* 710 Þe knyȝt tok gates straunge, In mony a bonk vnbene.

**Unbe·neficed,** *ppl. a.* (UN-[1] 8.) 1623 MARSTON *Duchess of Malfi* III. ii, No question but many an unbenefic'd scholar Shall pray for you for this deed. 1697 COLLIER *Ess. Mor. Subj.* I. (1709) 50 There would be a strange Improvement in the unbeneficed Clergy, if they had a better Salary. 1749 FIELDING *Tom Jones* XIV. viii, The brother..married the daughter of an unbeneficed clergyman. 1828 *Q. Rev.* XXXVII. 39 Some hoary, unbeneficed Oxonian unburthening his heart in a garret. 1884 *Gentl. Mag.* Feb. 106 Me the unbeneficed and insignificant, with my wretched pittance of £80 per annum.

**Unbene·ficent,** *a.* (UN-[1] 7.) 1822 'P. BEAUCHAMP' (Geo. Grote) *Anal. Infl. Nat. Relig.* (1875) 21 If..he is depicted as unbeneficent—as having personal affections seldom coincident with human happiness. 1864 *Sat. Rev.* XVIII. 398/2 Mr. Sturm..had a face..fit to belong to some wood-god (not unbeneficent) of heathen fable.

**Unbenefi·cial,** *a.* (UN-[1] 7.) 1626 BP. H. KING *Serm. Deliverance* 63 Salubrity of Aire is His Gift; shift of Places, smells to prepossesse the Senses, but for Him had been vnbeneficiall. 1687 NORRIS *Coll. Misc.* (1699) 125 That it becomes unbeneficial to him [*sc.* God]..is purely by accident. 1718 *Entertainer* No. 24. 162 If duly apply'd, it may be, not unbeneficial. 1828 P. CUNNINGHAM *N. S. Wales* (ed. 3) II. 70 It would admit an exchange among ourselves beneficially, instead of an unbeneficial exchange with distant parts. 1839 PALMERSTON in G. H. Francis *Opin. & Pol.* (1852) 418 We shall be doing that which will not be unbeneficial or unacceptable to some of those persons.

**Unbe·nefitable,** *a. rare.* (UN-[1] 7 b.) 1688 NORRIS *Love* I. v. 59 This is plain in God, who..is the most self-sufficient and unbenefitable..Being.

**Unbe·nefited,** *ppl. a.* (UN-[1] 8.) 1735 POPE *Let. to Swift* Wks. 1751 IX. 195 A friend and benefactor even to your un-friended and un-benefited Nation. 1753 RICHARDSON *Grandison* (1781) V. xxvii. 166 Religion..will not, I hope, leave me unbenefited by its all-chearing influence. *a* 1821 V. KNOX *Liberal Educ.* App. Wks. 1824 IV. 263 Men who have acquired their excellence ..uninstructed by the tuition, unbenefited by the foundations, and undignified by the graduation of Oxford and Cambridge. 1879 *St. George's Hosp. Rep.* IX. 57 Unbenefited by treatment.

**Unbene·volence.** *rare.* (UN-[1] 12.) 1688 COLLIER *Several Disc.* (1725) 352 To imagine God has ordered this World for the Advantage of..Pride, of Sordidness, and Unbenevolence,..seems inconsistent with his Attributes. 1720 — *Further Def. Restor. Prayer-bk.* 79 I'm sorry to see such Marks of Unbenevolence.

**Unbene·volent,** *a.* (UN-[1] 7.) 1697 COLLIER *Ess. Mor. Subj.* I. (1703) 106 To be fond of anything,..because the generality of mankind wants it,..arises from an unbenevolent and ungenerous temper. 1701 — *M. Anton.* (1726) 205 If not, they [the gods] must either be mistaken in their measures, or unbenevolent in their design. 1775 S. J. PRATT *Liberal Opin.* xiv. (1783) I. 83 To prevent an action, which I thought, on all hands, unlawful and unbenevolent. *a* 1832 BENTHAM *Deontol.* i. (1834) II. 65 The meekness of a man whose meekness is pernicious to others, and useless to himself, is unbenevolent, and the contrary of virtuous. 1853 G. J. CAYLEY *Las Alforjas* II. 291 Another interstice of apathy, followed by a frown of unbenevolent impatience.

**Unbeni·ght,** *v.* [UN-[2] 4 b.] *trans.* To free from night or obscurity. 1621 QUARLES *Argalus & P.* I, Wks. (Grosart) III. 252/2 When sad Athleia's dreame had unbenighted Her slumbering eyes, her busie thoughts were frighted. 1638 — *Hieroglyph.* i. 20 Ibid. 187/1 Thou great Originall of Light, Whose errour-chacing beams do unbenight The very soul of darknesse. 1674 N. FAIRFAX *Bulk & Selv.* 40 Having thus far unbenighted our selvs, and clear'd our way.

**Unbeni·ghted,** *ppl. a.* (UN-[1] 8.) 1667 MILTON *P. L.* x. 682 To them Day Had unbenighted shon.

**Unbeni·gn,** *a.* (UN-[1] 7.) 1651 CROMWELL *Let. to Greenwood* 4 Feb. (Carlyle), I should wrong it..if, either by pretended modesty or in any unbenign way, I should dispute the acceptance of it. 1667

MILTON *P. L.* x. 661 When to joyne In Synod unbenigne. **1698** *Christ Exalted* cix. 88, I proceed to convince..my Dear Kratiste of his unbenign Temper. **1809-14** WORDSW. *Excurs.* IV. 1014 As if the act removed..all traces from the good Man's heart Of unbenign aversion.

Hence **Unbeni·gnly** *adv.*

*a* **1892** TENNYSON *Hendecasyllabics* 21 As some..half coquette-like Maiden, not to be greeted unbenignly.

**Unbeni·gnant,** *a.* (UN-¹ 7.) **1856** HAWTHORNE *Eng. Note-bks.* (1879) II. 76 A thoughtful..and not unbenignant face. **1860** GEO. ELIOT in Cross *Life* (1885) II. 202 A really grand woman of fifty, with firm mouth and knitted brow, yet not unbenignant. **Unbeni·gnity.** (UN-¹ 12.) **1867** H. BUSHNELL *Mor. Uses Dark Th.* 188 We have, in our winter, a whole season of the year that bears a look of unbenignity.

**Unbe·nt,** *ppl. a.* [UN-¹ 8 b; also (in sense 1) f. UNBEND *v.*]

**1.** Not bowed or curved; also, freed from bending, straightened.

**1483** *Cath. Angl.* 28/1 Vn Bent, *laxus, relaxus.* **1611** COTGR., *Desbandé*, disbanded; vnbent; vnbound. **1813** BYRON *Giaour* 27 His queen, the garden queen, his Rose, Unbent by winds, unchill'd by snows. **1860** GOSSE *Rom. Nat. Hist.* 61 These venerable giants of the forest, that have stood unbent beneath the weight of a thousand years.

**b.** Of a bow: Not bent; released from a bent state.

**1513** DOUGLAS *Æneid* XI. xvii. 18 [They] on thar wery schuldris wyth greit schame Thar byg bowys onbent has tursit hame. **1601** DONNE *Progr. Soul* 390 Like an unbent bow, carelesly His sinewy Proboscis did remisly lie. **1663** BP. PATRICK *Parab. Pilgr.* xxii, Do not think you shall be in danger to lose the Victory over them, if you suffer your Bow sometimes to be unbent. **1728** ELIZA HEYWOOD tr. *Mme. de Gomez's Belle A.* (1732) II. 41 She had a Quiver at her Back, and an unbent Bow in her Hand. **1830-4** WHITTIER *Mogg Megone* 386, I only meant To draw up again the bow unbent.

**2.** Not wrinkled or knit.

**1593** SHAKS. *Lucr.* 1509 An humble gate, calme looks, eyes wayling still, A brow vnbent that seem'd to welcome wo.

**3.** *fig.* Not subdued or made subservient.

**1697** DRYDEN *Æneis* VI. 143 Thou, secure of soul, unbent with woes. *a* **1718** PRIOR *Solomon* II. 554 She looks with Majesty, and moves with State: Unbent her Soul, and in Misfortune great, She scorns the World. **1825** SCOTT *Betrothed* xxix, The high-spirited entreaties of Eveline, unbent by adversity and want, gradually lost effect on the defenders of the castle. **1845** [see UNBETTERED *ppl. a.*].

**Unbenu·mb,** *v.* [UN-² 3.] *trans.* To free from numbness. Hence **Unbenu·mbing** *vbl. sb.*

**1598** SYLVESTER *Du Bartas* II. i. IV. *Handy-cr.* 237 The fire Dries his dank Cloathes,..And un-benums his sinnews and his flesh. **1603** FLORIO *Montaigne* III. iii. 492 Most wittes haue neede of extravagant stuffe, to vn-benumme and exercise themselues. **1611** COTGR., *Desdormissement*,..a quickening, or vnbenumming. **1624** QUARLES *Job* xvi. 25 The vertue of his breath, can vnbenumme The frozen lips, and strike the speaker dumme. **1706** STEVENS I, *Desentorpecer*, to unbenum.

**Unbenu·mbed,** *ppl. a.* (UN-¹ 8.) **1861** GEO. ELIOT *Silas M.* xii, She knew this well; and yet, in the moments of wretched unbenumbed consciousness [etc.]. **Unbepi·ssed,** *ppl. a.* (UN-¹ 8.) *a* **1550** *Image Hypocr.* III. 172 in *Skelton's Wks.* (1843) II. 435/1 He is sutch a scolde, That no play may hym holde For anger vnbepyst. **Unbepra·nked,** *ppl. a.* (UN-¹ 8.) **1594** CAREW *Tasso* (1881) 31 And of her wooers vnbeprancт and sole, Both from the land, and from the lookes she stole.

**Unbequea·thed,** *ppl. a.* Also 5 unbequethyn, -queithen, 6 -queith. [UN-¹ 8 and 8 b.] Not bequeathed.

α. **1483** in *Somerset Med. Wills* (1901) 243 My money and plate that remayneth unbequethyn to be kept by my seid executours. **1494** [see UNBESET]. **1521** in *Test. Ebor.* (Surtees) VI. 4 The residew of..my goodes unbequeith I freely gif unto Jenett my wif. **1553** *Wills & Inv. N. C.* (Surtees, 1835) 141 The Resydew off all my goods vnbequeith I gyue to my brother.

β. *c* **1525** *Lanc. Wills* (Chetham Soc.) I. 3, I will and beqweth..all the residew of my goodes unbeqwethed unto the mariage of my son. **1544** *Knaresb. Wills* (Surtees) I. 42, I gyffe all my goodes unbequythed to the usse of Richard my sonne. *a* **1613** OVERBURY *Characters* (1615) Hj b, He croakes like a raven against the death of rich men, and so gets a Legacy vnbequeath'd. **1618** in *Buccleuch MSS.* (Hist. MSS. Comm.) I. 253 He hath..given him the residue of his goods unbequeathed. **1655** FULLER *Hist. Cambr.* (1840) 214 She left..five thousand pounds, besides her goods unbequeathed, for the erection of a College. **1829** S. H. CASSAN *Lives Bps. Bath & Wells* 224 The residue, unbequeathed, was applied to the Vicars' Close at Wells. **1846** GROTE *Greece* II. vi. (1862) II. 475 Conflicting claims at law for the hand of an unbequeathed orphan heiress.

*fig.* **1622** MAY *Heir* II. D j, Her Ladies heart doe yet stand free And vnbequeath'd to any.

† **Unbeque·st(ed,** *ppl. a. Obs.* [UN-¹ 8, 8 b.] = prec.

**1506** *Test. Ebor.* (Surtees) IV. 255 All my oder goods unbequest I gyf them to Kateryn my wife. **1527** *Lanc. Wills* (Chetham Soc.) I. 18, I will that all my goodis moveable and unmoveable unbequest be sold. **1540** *Test. Ebor.* (Surtees) VI. 108 Residue of my goodes unbequested I put unto the full disposicion of my sones. **1564** *Richmond. Wills* (Surtees) 175 All my goods unbequested I give and bequeth to Cecile Swale my wiff.

† **Unbequo·then,** obs. var. of UNBEQUEATHED.

**1482** MARG. PASTON in *P. Lett.* III. 288 The residewe of the stuffe of myn houshold unbiquothen.

**Unberea·ved,** *ppl. a.* (UN-¹ 8.) **1889** *Sat. Rev.* 23 Mar. 359/2 That iron philosopher..had, in his unbereaved moments, a keen eye for the main chance. **Unberea·ven,** *ppl. a.* (UN-¹ 8 b.) **1849** MRS. BROWNING *Child's Grave* xxiv, Arms, empty of her child, she lifts, With spirit unbereaven.

**Unbere·ft,** *ppl. a.* (UN-¹ 8 b.)

**1621** G. SANDYS *Æneis* I. 411 Lost Phrygia I with twenty ships forsooke;..seauen, unbereft By seas, and cruell stormes, alone are left. **1648** HEXHAM II, *Onberooft*, Vnbereft, or Vnspoiled. **1820** WORDSW. *River Duddon, Faery Chasm* 3 A sky-blue stone, within this sunless cleft, Is of the very footmarks unbereft Which tiny Elves impressed. **1839** WHITTIER *Relic* 24 Flower of a perished garland left, Of life and beauty unbereft!

† **Unberi·sped,** *ppl. a. Obs.*⁻¹ [ad. Du. and Flem. *onberispt*, f. *berispen* BERISP *v.*] Uncensured, unreproved.

**1481** CAXTON *Reynard* xvi. (Arb.) 36 Tho commanded the kynge openly that eche of them shold be stylle, and suffre the foxe to saye vnberisped what that he wolde.

**Unberou·ged,** *ppl. a.* (UN-¹ 8.) **1778** *The Auction* 3 Half-dress'd and unberoug'd, she hastes away.

**Unbe·rried,** *ppl. a.* [UN-¹ 8: see BERRY *v.*¹, and cf. UNBARROWED *ppl. a.* So Norw. dial. *ubard, obart.*] Unthreshed.

**1570** *Wills & Inv. N. C.* (Surtees, 1835) 341 In vnberied whete xiiij thraves;..in pease vnberied iij quarters. **1582-3** *Durham Wills* II. 77 In corne berryed and vnberyed.

**Unbe·rthed,** *ppl. a.* [UN-¹ 8: see BERTH *v.*²] Unboarded.

**1589** in *N. & Q.* 9th Ser. X. 373/2 The church stool which is appointed for women to sit in, is very insufficient, being unbirthed and kept very fowle. **1640** *Ibid.* VII. 505/2 That many of the pews..are old, ruinous, unbirthed.

**Unbesee·m,** *v.* [UN-¹ 14.]

**1.** *trans.* To be unseemly or unbecoming for (a person); to suit (one) badly.

*a* **1657** R. LOVEDAY *Lett.* (1663) 30, I..write his Letters, and [do] whatever else that unbeseems not his command or my obedience. **1678** GALE *Crt. Gentiles* IV. III. Pref. A ij, Passionate emotions, personal reflexions, or whatever may unbeseem one that lies under essential obligation [etc.]. **1846** H. G. ROBINSON *Odes of Horace* II. xii, Whom it ne'er unbeseem'd to bear foot in the dance.

**2.** To fail in, fall short of.

**1812** BYRON *Ch. Har., To Ianthe* ii. Ah! may'st thou ever be what now thou art, Nor unbeseem the promise of thy spring. **1870** CREASY *Hist. Eng.* II. 336 But he soon unbeseemed that promise.

**Unbesee·ming,** *a.* [UN-¹ 10 and 5 d.]

**1.** With object: Not beseeming or befitting (a person, etc.); unbecoming or inappropriate to. (Very common in 17th c.)

**1583** GOLDING *Calvin on Deut.* lxv. 394 Nowe it were vnbeseeming his power that hee coulde not execute the thing that he had determined with himselfe. **1586** T. B. *La Primaud. Fr. Acad.* I. 191 They judged the verie remembrance thereof to be unwoorthie & unbeseeming men of honor. **1631** GOUGE *God's Arrows* I. § 27 You shall find them all to be very toyes, much unbeseeming Gods excellent Majesty. **1651** WITTIE tr. *Primrose's Pop. Err.* I. ii. 40 But some thinke it a thing unbeseeming the dignitie of a physician, to prepare his Medicines. **1676** HALE *Contempl.* I. 493 An unnecessary breaking of the rest of this day, and unbeseeming the solemnity of it. **1721** in *Cath. Rec. Soc. Publ.* VIII. 301 As being a thing Unbeseeming a Religious house. *a* **1721** SHEFFIELD (Dk. of Buckhm.) *Wks.* (1753) II. 153 The truth of it is, a criminal there had put me into a passion, a little unbeseeming a Judge. **1880** SWINBURNE *Study Shaks.* (1895) 60 An office..no more unbeseeming the pupil hand of the future master, than [etc.].

† **b.** In quasi-adverbial use. *Obs.*

**1645** TOMBES *Anthropol.* 9 Ye doe unbeseeming your priviledge. **1655** GURNALL *Chr. in Arm.* II. xviii. § 2. 190 He dare not think or speak unbeseeming the glory or goodnesse of God.

**2.** Unbecoming; offending against propriety or good taste. (Very common in 17th c.)

**1594** HOOKER *Eccl. Pol.* I. viii. § 9 All those things which men by the light of their naturall vnderstanding euidently know..to be vnseeming or vnbeseeming. **1621** BURTON *Anat. Mel.* I. ii. III. xiii, They..break many times into violent passions, oaths, imprecations and unbeseeming speeches. **1664** PEPYS *Diary* 23 Sept., Minnes took occasion, in the most childish and unbeseeming manner, to reproach us all. **1671** H. M. tr. *Erasm. Colloq.* 433 What is more unbeseeming, than that an ignoble merchant should have store of money. **1716** M. DAVIES *Athen. Brit.* I. 296 Larding their unbeseeming and inconsistent Prophecies, with..incongruous Latin. **1825** LAMB *Elia* II. *The Wedding*, The unbeseeming artifices, by which some wives push on the matrimonial projects of their daughters. *a* **1843** SOUTHEY *Doctor* ccxxii, Nor has it any unbeseeming levity, like this which is among Browne's poems. **1860** GEO. ELIOT in Cross *Life* (1885) II. 244 The Almighty above is as unbeseeming as painted Almighties usually are.

Hence **Unbesee·mingly** *adv.*, **-see·mingness.**

**1617** COLLINS *Def. Bp. Ely* II. x. 497 They dare not for horrour say that our Sauiour did vnwisely, or any way *vnbeseemingly. **1660** STANLEY *Hist. Philos.* IX. (1687) 521/2 They, under the pretence of his Doctrine, do many strange things, inveigling the young men unbeseemingly. *a* **1677** BARROW *Serm. Phil. iv. 11* Wks. 1686 III. 63 All reason dictateth ..that in being discontented we behave our selves very unbeseemingly and unworthily. **1623** BP. HALL *Contempl.*, *O. T* XVIII. iv, Against the disguise she had pleaded the 'unbeseemingnesse for her person and state. **1674** N. FAIRFAX *Bulk & Selv.* 191 That would be an unbeseemingness. **1723** DK. WHARTON *True Briton* No. 48 II. 422 He is to learn from the Unbeseemingness and Intemperances of others Passions, the better how to govern his own.

**Unbesee·mly,** *a. rare.* [UN-¹ 11.] Unseemly.

**1648** HEXHAM II, *Onbehoorlick*, Vnbeseemly. **1801** ELIZ. HELME *St. Mag.'s Cave* xi. (1819) I. 121 It is unbeseemly for youth to press thus before age to the grave.

† **Unbesee·n,** *a. Obs.*⁻¹ [UN-¹ 8 b.] Unprovided, destitute, devoid.

**1390** GOWER *Conf.* III. 280 Love, which is unbesein Of alle reson. as men sein.

† **Unbesee·nness.** *Obs.*⁻¹ [Cf. prec.] Heedlessness; want of care.

*a* **1225** *Ancr. R.* 344 Of alle kudde & kuðe sunnen, ase.. of keorfunge, oðer of hurtunge, þuruh unbiseinesse [*MS. T.* unbisehenesse].

**Unbeset,** var. UMBESET *v. Obs.*

† **Unbese·t,** *ppl. a. Obs.* [UN-¹ 8 b + BESET *v.* 8.] Not bestowed or apportioned.

**1494** *Will Maude Parterich* 23 Feb. (Somerset Ho.), As long as my goodis vnbyset and vnbequeithen will strecche to.

**Unbesie·ged,** *ppl. a.* (UN-¹ 8.) **1610** HEALEY *St. Aug. Citie of God* 148 But Sulmo..being unbesieged..was.. appointed for a direct spoile. **1644** PRYNNE & WALKER *Fiennes' Trial* 89 Unlesse they leave the Castles unbesieged.

**Unbeso·t,** *v. rare.* [UN-² 3.] *trans.* To free from dulness or stupidity.

**1603** FLORIO *Montaigne* III. v. 532 He that could recouer or vn-besot man, from so..verball a superstition, should not much prejudice the world. **1611** COTGR., *Dessoter*, to vnbesot; to quicken, refine, or cleere a dull vnderstanding.

**Unbeso·tted,** *ppl. a.* (UN-¹ 8.) **1875** RUSKIN *Fors Clav.* liii. 126 The meaning of the parable, heard with ears unbesotted, is this.

**Unbesou·ght,** *ppl. a.* (UN-¹ 8 b.)

**1667** MILTON *P. L.* X. 1058 Least Cold Or Heat should injure us, his timely care Hath unbesaught provided. **1739** 'R. BULL' tr. *Dedekindus Grobianus* 173 In case they come, which sure no Mortal ought, Unlook'd for, unexpected, unbesought, Receive 'em not. **1827** POLLOK *Course T.* VII. 20 Thus the bard, Not unbesought, again resumed his song. **1874** HOLLAND *Mistr. Manse* iv. 30 Poor precious gift, that goes for nought From willing heart and ready hand, And wins no favor unbesought.

† **Unbesou·nd,** *ppl. a. Obs.*⁻¹ [UN-¹ 8 b.] Not sounded.

*c* **1532** DU WES *Introd. Fr.* in *Palsgr.* 898 What letters shall be lefte unbesounde.

† **Unbespea·k,** *v. Obs.* [UN-² 3.] *trans.* To countermand; to cancel an order or request for.

**1661** PEPYS *Diary* 30 Oct., Pretending that the corps stinks, they will bury it to-night privately, and so will unbespeak all their guests. **1693** — *Let.* in *Academy* 9 Aug. (1890) 109/3 You will force me elce to..unbespeake yᵉ continuance of a Kindenesse I cannot repay. **1740** GARRICK *Lying Valet* I, I can immediately run back and unbespeak what I have order'd. **1743** MRS. DELANY in *Life & Corr.* (1861) II. 207 He says he has not strength to perform the journey. The lodgings are unbespoke, the coach forbid.

**Unbespo·ken,** *ppl. a.* Also 8 unbespoke. [UN-¹ 8 b.] Not bespoken; not ordered, engaged, or arranged for.

**1681** DRYDEN *Abs. & Achit.* I. 242 Swift, unbespoken Pomps, thy steps proclaim. **1796** *Campaigns 1793-4* I. I. ix. 85 Oh, spare me a Muse (if there's one unbespoke). **1843** GEO. ELIOT in Cross *Life* (1885) I. 124 We need not be idle in imparting all that is pure and lovely to children whose minds are unbespoken. **1860** EMERSON *Cond. Life* vi. (1861) 118 The horses come up with the family carriage unbespoken to the door.

**Unbespri·nkled,** *ppl. a.* (UN-¹ 8.) **1653** URQUHART *Rabelais* II. xxii. 153 These villainous dogs..left none of her attire unbesprinkled with their staling.

**Unbestow·ed,** *ppl. a.* (UN-¹ 8.)

**1534** MORE *Comf. agst. Trib.* III. xiii. Pvj, He woulde not haue lefte them vnbestowed, if he had foreknowen the chaunce. **1581** MULCASTER *Positions* xxxvi. (1887) 137 Is not that most dangerous..as the vnbestowed scoller by profession is? **1622** BACON *Hen. VII*, 216 Hee had now but one Sonne, and one Daughter vnbestowed. **1794** WORDSW. *Guilt & Sorrow* lix, Comfort by prouder mansions unbestowed Their wearied frames, she hoped, would soon regale.

† **Unbe·t,** *ppl. a. Obs.* [UN-¹ 8 b + BEET *v.* Cf. OE. *ungebētt*, ON. *úbǿttr.*] Unamended.

*c* **1200** *Trin. Coll. Hom.* 173 He bit here unbette sennes ..cumen biforen hem. *a* **1300** *Cursor M.* 26649 A sin or tua Vnbette þai drau ai toward maa. *Ibid.* 28371 My suernes me has don for-gette And many sinnes left vn-bett.

**Unbe·t,** *v. rare*⁻¹. [UN-² 3.] *trans.* To free from a bet.

**1668** DRYDEN *Even. Love* V. i, I'll be unbetted again if you please, Sir, and leave you all the Honour of it.

† **Unbetea·ming,** *ppl. a. Obs.*⁻¹ [UN-¹ 10 + BETEEM *v.*] Unconsenting.

**1642** D. ROGERS *Naaman* 274 Cease thine enmity, thine hard thoughts, thine unbeteaming heart.

**Unbetea·red,** *ppl. a.* (UN-¹ 8.) **1635** J. HAYWARD tr. *Biondi's Banish'd Virg.* 30 With unbeteared eyes to see him at parting. *Ibid.* 217 There was not an unbeteared eye among all the spectators.

**Unbethink,** variant of UMBETHINK *v.*

**Unbethou·ght,** *ppl. a.* [UN-¹ 8 b. Cf. MDu. *onbedocht, -dacht* (Du. *-dacht*), G. *unbedacht* thoughtless.]

**1.** Unpremeditated; also as *adv.*, without premeditation, unintentionally, unexpectedly. Now *dial.*

**1558** PHAER *Æneid* II. D 4 b, As one that unbethought hath hapt some snake among the briers To tread. **1823** E. MOOR *Suffolk Words* 458 *Unbethowt*, unpremeditated, unintentionally. ''Twas wholly unbethowt o' me.' **1854** MISS BAKER *Northampt. Gloss.* 368.

**2.** Unthought of, unrealized.

**1855** BAILEY *Mystic*, etc. 135 When, i' th' end, Unnumbered times, duration unbethought, Have passed.

† **Unbeti·de,** *v. Obs. rare.* [UN-¹ 14.] *intr.* To fail to happen.

*c* **1374** CHAUCER *Boeth.* V. pr. iv. (1868) 161 þilke þinges þat þe prescience woot byforn ne mowen nat vnbitide, þat is to seyn þat þei moten bitide. *Ibid.* pr. vi. 175 þat þilke þinge þat god seeþ to bytide it ne may nat vnbytide.

**Unbeto·ken,** *v.* (UN-¹ 14.) **1844** LD. HOUGHTON *Mem. Many Scenes* 151 Like a glorious maiden dreaming music in the drowsy heat, Lies the City, unbetokening where its myriad pulses beat.

**Unbetray·ed,** *ppl. a.* (UN-[1] 8.)
1595 DANIEL *Civ. Wars* III. xli. 52 For many being priuy to the fact How hard it is to keepe it vnbetray'd? 1805 WORDSW. *Sonn. fr. Michael Angelo* i. 2 Yes! hope may with my strong desire keep pace, And I be undeluded, unbetrayed. 1821 SHELLEY *Epipsych., Fragm.* 42 Start not—the thing you are is unbetrayed.

**Unbetray·ing,** *ppl. a.* (UN-[1] 10.) 1788 ANNA SEWARD *Lett.* (1811) II. 8 It is either genuine, or assumed with guarded and unbetraying art. 1893 K. GRAHAM *Pagan Papers* 64 Only we three, the wide world over, she and I, and the unbetraying gate. **Unbetro·thed,** *ppl. a.* (UN-[1] 8.) 1577 tr. *Bullinger's Decades* II. x. (1592) 231 Some ..are of opinion that they are not culpable of adultery, if they haue the company of an vnbetrothed maiden. 1660 R. COKE *Power & Subj.* 153 If a man corrupt a virgin unbetrothed, .. let him be fined. 1904 HOWITT *Native Tribes S.E. Australia* v. 178 Some other woman .. who has an unbetrothed daughter.

**Unbe·tterable,** *a.* [UN-[1] 7 b.] Incapable of being improved.
1806 *Ann. Rev.* IV. 82 The country is not only bad but unbetterable. 1874 RUSKIN *Fors Clav.* xl. IV. 76 A lovely, classic, unbetterable sentence of Marmontel's, perfect in wisdom and modesty.

**Unbe·ttered,** *ppl. a.* [UN-[1] 8. Cf. Du. *ongebeterd*, MHG. *ungebezzert* (G. *-bessert*), MSw. *obätrad*.] Not made better; unimproved.
1628 WITHER *Brit. Rememb.* IV. 941 All they that goe Unbetter'd from such objects, worse doe grow. 1648 SPARKE *Pref. to J. Shute's Sarah & Hagar* b j, He..so tempered the wine and oil together, that none (but through his own default) might go away unbettered. 1813 SHELLEY *Q. Mab* IV. 81 From kings, and priests, and statesmen, war arose, Whose safety is man's deep unbettered woe. 1845 BAILEY *Festus* (ed. 2) 310 Even these.. Unbent, unbettered will again rush forth In all the might of madness and despair.

† **Unbe·tty,** *v. Cant.* [UN-[2] 3.] (See quot.)
1812 J. H. VAUX *Flash Dict.* s.v. *Betty*, To *unbetty*, or *betty* a lock, is to open or relock it, by means of the betty [= a picklock].

**Unbe·velled,** *ppl. a.* (UN-[1] 8.)
1592 KYD *Sp. Trag.* III. xi. 23 A sonne, The more he growes .., The more vnsquard, unbeuelled he appeares. 1621 QUARLES *Div. Poems, Esther* Med. 19 The Law of God..doth iustly paize The ballances of his [*sc.* man's] vnbeuelled wayes. 1851 RUSKIN *Stones Ven.* I. xvi. § 5 The bevelled wall cannot conveniently carry an unbevelled arch. 1875 *Carpentry & Join.* 47 A chisel is inclined to draw into the work on the plain or unbevelled side.

**Unbewai·led,** *ppl. a.* (UN-[1] 8.)
1586 W. WARNER *Alb. Eng.* IV. xxi. (1592) 88 He wandred vnbewailed long, as man whom men exempt From house, and helpe. 1606 SHAKS. *Ant. & Cl.* III. vi. 85 But let determin'd things to destinie Hold vnbewayl'd their way. 1661 HICKERINGILL *Jamaica* 99 Not unbewail'd was his Catastrophe. 1676 HOBBES *Iliad* 338 Why should this come now into my head, When unbewail'd Patroclus lieth still? 1837–8 SOUTHEY *Poems, To Hymen* iii, Tho' doomed perchance to die Alone and unbewailed.

**Unbewai·ling,** *ppl. a.* (UN-[1] 10.) 1820 SHELLEY *Prometh. Unb.* II. iv. 16 The radiant looks of unbewailing flowers. *Ibid.* II. v. 71.

† **Unbewa·re,** *adv. Obs.* [Alteration of UNWARE *adv.*, after BEWARE *v.*] = UNAWARE *adv.*
1489 CAXTON *Faytes of A.* I. x. 28 To com by thees wayes vpon theyre enemyes vnbeware. *c* 1489 — *Blanchardyn* xxx. 113 A grete sorowe toke hym at his herte of that he was so taken vnbeware. 1565 GOLDING *Ovid's Met.* I. (1593) 7 He meant..To steale upon me in the night and kill me unbeware.

† **Unbewa·res,** *adv. Obs.* [Cf. prec.] = UNAWARES *adv.*
1483 *Vulgaria abs Terentio* 23 b, He com vnbywarse. 1508 FISHER 7 *Penit. Ps.* cii. Wks. (1876) 192 Leest peraventure sodeynly vnbewares it fall in decaye. 1550 BALE *Apol.* 25 Fulfyll not that thou hast vowed vnbewares. *a* 1557 ABP. PARKER *Ps.* F ij, And thus I offend unbewares, thoughe afterwards I perceiue it.

**Unbewi·lder,** *v.* (UN-[2] 3.) 1668 H. MORE *Div. Dial.* v. xvii. (1713) 464 For it can be no unbecoming office to unbewilder some over-serious Souls, that may be too much captivated with such kind of Writers. **Unbewi·ldered,** *ppl. a.* (UN-[1] 8.) [1775 ASH.] 1805 WORDSW. *Prelude* VI. 41 What keen research, Unbiassed, unbewildered, and unawed. 1855 MILMAN *Lat. Chr.* XIV. iii. VI. 461 Yet he himself seems to walk unbewildered in his own labyrinth.

**Unbewi·tch,** *v.* [UN-[2] 3.] *trans.* To deliver from witchcraft; to disenchant.
1584 R. SCOT *Discov. Witchcr.* XII. xviii. (1886) 219 There be masses of purpose for this matter, to unbewitch the bewitched. 1646 GAULE *Cases Consc.* 4 Their bewitched body or goods has served to unbewitch them. 1679 OATES *Serm. at St. Michaels* Pref. A 4 b, That God..would unbewitch this Roman Catholick Synagogue, who believe none to be Christians but themselves. 1751 LAVINGTON *Enthus. Meth. & Papists* III. (1754) 194 Barbara Dorea..confessed that she had unbewitched several whom she herself had bewitched.

**Unbewi·tched,** *ppl. a.* (UN-[1] 8.) 1648 BP. HALL *Select Th.* § 12 A Christian can hold his eyes and yet behold beauty, unbewitched. 1827 POLLOK *Course T.* IX. 242 By fashion's revelry uncharmed, By honour unbewitched—he left the chase Of vanity. **Unbewi·tching,** *ppl. a.* (UN-[1] 10.) 1859 G. MEREDITH *R. Feverel* xxi, A similar unbewitching fear. **Unbewray·ed,** *ppl. a.* (UN-[1] 10.) 1605 DANIEL *Philotas* III. i, And that the keeping of it [i. e. an offence] vnbewraid, Was that I held the rumor vaine to be. **Unbewri·tten,** *ppl. a.* (UN-[1] 8.) 1820 in Mrs. Wyndham *Corr. Lady Lyttleton* (1912) 228 This perfectly fresh and unbewritten sort of subject.

**Unbi·as,** *v.* [UN-[2] 3.] *trans.* To free from bias.
1708 SWIFT *Sent. Ch. Eng. Man* Wks. 1755 II. I. 54 The truest service a private man may hope to do his country is, by unbiassing his mind as much as possible.

**Unbi·assable,** *a.* (UN-[1] 7 b.) 1714 G. LOCKHART *Mem. Affairs Scot.* (ed. 3) 214 His being esteem'd by People of all Parties, on Account of his eminently unbyassable Honesty and Integrity.

**Unbiassed** (ʊnbəi·ăst), *a.* Forms: 7–8 unbyassed, 7– unbiassed, 8– unbiased; 7–8 unbyass'd (7 -byas'd), unbiass'd (7, 9 -bias'd), 8 unbyast. [UN-[1] 8.]

1. Of bowls, etc.: Having no bias.
1607 G. WILKINS *Miseries Enforced Marr.* IV, These men ..headlong run, like an unbias'd bowl. 1825 J. NICHOLSON *Operat. Mechanic* 173 The piston, therefore, being in an unbiassed state, as regards the pressure, will again be raised to its original situation by the counterpoise weights.

2. *fig.* Not unduly or improperly influenced or inclined; unprejudiced, impartial: **a.** Of persons.
1647 CLARENDON *Hist. Reb.* II. § 77 They were as sure, that so many so unbiass'd men, would never be elected again. 1686 W. HOPKINS tr. *Ratramnus* Dissert. v. (1688) 100 Which are the Sentiments of Ratramnus, as will evidently appear to any unbyass'd Reader. 1710 *Tatler* No. 235 ⁋ 2 My Lady..is wholly unbiassed in dispensing her Favours among them. 1775 WESLEY *Calm Address* 12, I am unbiassed: I have nothing to hope or fear from either side. 1823 KEBLE *Serm.* iii. (1848) 72 A considerate unbiassed man, acting steadily by this rule. 1861 BROUGHAM *Brit. Const.* xvii. 265 Its [the House of Lords'] veto upon all the measures that pass the Commons,..its more calm deliberation on all questions, unbiassed by mob clamour.
*absol.* *c* 1721 MRQ. TULLIBARDINE in *10th Rep. Hist. MSS. Comm.* App. I. 126 The unbiass'd are strangely disjoynted through the busie artifice of those who find their account in unexpressable confusion.

**b.** Of the judgement, mind, feeling, standards of action, etc.
1654 WHITLOCK *Zootomia* 209 In humane Learning I appeale to every Mans own impartiall Breast, whether he can boast an unbiassed Judgement? 1673 DRYDEN *Amboyna* Ded. A iij, You have serv'd him with unbyass'd Honor, and with unshaken resolution. 1724 SWIFT *Drapier's Lett.* Wks. 1755 V. II. 104 The minds of a jury, which ought to be wholly free and unbyassed. 1776 GIBBON *Decl. & F.* x. I. 252 He submitted the choice of the censor to the unbiassed voice of the senate. 1808 HELEN ST. VICTOR *Ruins of Rigonda* II. 6 A heart, unbiassed to any particular individual. 1846 MRS. GORE *Eng. Char.* I. 117 The Linkman sees with unbiassed eyes, and declaims with unblushing enunciation. 1873 C. M. DAVIES *Unorthod. Lond.* (1876) 104 And probably in no section of religious development is this unbiassed judgement more essentially necessary.

**c.** Of particular actions, opinions, etc.
1668 TEMPLE *Let. to Bridgman* Wks. 1720 II. 63 The general Opinion conceived here, of your Lordship's..unbiass'd Pursuit of the true Interest of the Kingdom. 1690 LOCKE *Hum. Und.* I. iv. § 25 Without any other design, than an unbiass'd enquiry after Truth. 1742 RICHARDSON *Pamela* III. 248 He will judge us according to the unforced and unbyassed Use we make of that Light. 1791 BURKE *Corr.* (1844) III. 193 All..which a man without authority can give,—his unbiassed opinion, his honest advice, and his best reasons. 1812 SIR H. DAVY *Chem. Philos.* 25 Every field of enquiry was open for the free and unbiassed exercise of the powers of genius. 1843 BETHUNE *Sc. Fireside Stor.* 72 Upon these concurring circumstances—supported as they were by the unbiassed testimony of Dr. G——, he was set at liberty. 1862 H. SPENCER *First Princ.* I. i. § 6 (1875) 20 An unbiassed consideration of its general aspects.

3. As *adv.* = next. *rare*[—1].
1796 MME. D'ARBLAY *Camilla* VII. iv, If impartially and unbiassed, the Major is refused.

Hence **Unbi·assedly** *adv.*, **Unbi·assedness.**
1676 *Doctrine of Devils* 159 As is plain, if any man do but *unbyassedly consider the several places, where the word is used, as I have intimated afore. 1699 LOCKE in Fox Bourne *Life* (1876) II. xv. 472 With a free mind that unbiassedly pursues truth it cannot be other wise. 1718 HICKES & NELSON *J. Kettlewell* III. ciii. 443 Who..shall Faithfully and Unbyasedly Persue the Blessed Work of Christian Union. 1886 *Cyclist* 25 Aug. 1165/1 The same printer very unbiassedly turned out both bills. 1660 *Bp. Hall's Remains* Pref. b ij b, He claims the liberty of reserving his own Judgement, and more especially to pag. 387. where in the close of the Tract his *unbyassedness is clearly professed. 1692 LOCKE *Toleration* Wks. 1714 III. 462 'Tis Want of Attention and Unbyassedness in you, that puts your Religion past doubt with you.

**Unbi·blical,** *a.* (UN-[1] 7. Cf. Du. *onbijbelsch*, G. *unbiblisch*, Sw. *obiblisk*.)
1828 PUSEY *Hist. Enq.* I. 92 Even unbiblical terminology, except what was admitted by the universal church, was excluded. 1875 E. WHITE *Life in Christ* v. xxviii, The custom..of representing Faith and Reason as opposites, is unbiblical and pernicious.

**Unbi·bulous,** *a.* (UN-[1] 7.) 1864 J. ORMSBY *Autumn Rambles N. Africa* 44 Bushes of an unbibulous kind of brushwood that seemed to have taken a pledge of total abstinence early in life.

† **Unbi·ched,** *a. Obs.*[—1] App. = BICCHED *a.*
*c* 1460 *Towneley Myst.* xxiv. 356 Thou shall forthynk it, in faythe; Fy, what thou art fre! vnbychid, vnbayn!

**Unbi·ckered,** *ppl. a.* (UN-[1] 8 c.) 1855 BROWNING *Bp. Blougram* 894 You are not I—Who needs must make earth mine and feed my fill Not simply unbutted at, unbickered with, But [etc.].

**Unbi·d,** *ppl. a.* Also 5 vnbedde. [UN-[1] 8 b.]

1. = UNBIDDEN *ppl. a.*
14.. *Gosp. Nicodemus* (A.) 174 Þis messagere to ihesu knelid;..Þes baners sone gan helde And bowed to ihesu vnbedde. 1593 SHAKS. 3 *Hen. VI*, v. i. 18 Oh vnbid spight, is sportfull Edward come? 1623 J. TAYLOR (Water P.) *Discov. by Sea* A vij, The waues amaine (vnbid) oft boorded vs. 1661 PEPYS *Diary* 3 Feb., So to Mr. Fox's, unbidd; where I had a good dinner and special company. 1700 DRYDEN *Iliad* I. 784 He said no more but crown'd a Bowl, unbid: The laughing Nectar overlook'd the Lid. 1715 POPE *Iliad* II. 485 And Menelaus came, unbid, the last. 1725 — *Odyss.* VII. 269 As yet, unbid they never grac'd our feast. 1827 POLLOK *Course T.* VIII. 16 The ministers Of God's unsparing vengeance waited, still Unbid. 1876 [see UNBODEN *ppl. a.* 1].

† 2. Unprayed for. *Obs.*
1590 SPENSER *F. Q.* I. ix. 54 He chose an halter from among the rest, And with it hung himselfe, vnbid vnblest.

**Unbi·d,** *v.* [UN-[2] 3.] *absol.* To cancel a command or invitation.
1597 J. KING *On Jonas* (1618) 450 A man may impute it to unconstancy, to bid, and vnbid. 1598 FLORIO, *Disinuitare*, to vnuie at any game, to vnbid, to disinuite.

**Unbi·ddable,** *a.* (UN-[1] 7 b.) 1825 JAMIESON. 1831 COBBETT *Eng. Spelling-Bk.* 91 He was not in general what is called an unbidable child. 1899 CROCKETT *Black Douglas* xxi, A great ram-stam, unbiddable, unhallowed deevil he is.

**Unbi·dden,** *ppl. a.* Forms: 1, 4–5 unbeden (3 *Orm.* unnbedenn); 4 vnbiden, 5 -bidyn, -byden; 4, 6–7 vn-, 6– unbidden. [UN-[1] 8 b. Cf. NFris. *ünbeden*, MDu. and Du. *ongebeden*, MHG. and G. *ungebeten*, ON. *úbeðinn*, Icel. *óbeðinn* (Norw. *ubeden*).] Not asked or invited; not commanded or directed.
*pred.* *c* 1010 ÆLFRIC *Past. Ep.* xlix. in Thorpe *Anc. Laws* (1840) II. 386 Sume preostas..unbedene gaderiað hi to ðam lice. *c* 1200 ORMIN 17081 Forrþi toc Crist forrþrihht anan Unnbedenn & unnbonedd .. To mælenn & to spellenn. *a* 1300 *Cursor M.* 14912 He wil him all vnbiden [*v.r.* vnbidden] bede. *c* 1380 WYCLIF *Serm.* Sel. Wks. II. 120 And siþ alle þes failen to men, how shulden þei fiȝte unbeden of God? *c* 1400 *Destr. Troy* 9943 Breisaid the burd, vnbidyn of hir fader, Full duly to Dyamede dressit to wend. 1427 *Wills & Inv. N. C.* (Surtees) I. 74 Þai þat come thidir þat tyme vnbyden be fewe. 1583 in Strype *Ann. Ref.* (1709) III. xvi. 183 The painful pastors and ministers of the Word ..are condemned,..Some for leaving the Holidays unbidden. 1608 DOD & CLEAVER *Expos. Prov.* xi–xii. 122 That we goe not unsent, nor come unbidden. 1685 BAXTER *Paraphr. N. T.* Matt. xiv. 28 Yet none must tempt God, nor go unbidden into danger. 1726 POPE *Odyss.* XVII. 365 Adown his cheek a tear unbidden stole. 1796 MME. D'ARBLAY *Camilla* x. x, Thou art come, uncalled, unbidden, thy task unfulfilled, thy peace unearned. 1842 MANNING *Serm.* ii. (1848) I. 30 Thoughts..thrust themselves unbidden now into the abode where they were wont to be welcomed before. 1859 TENNYSON *Merlin & V.* 426 And beasts themselves would worship; camels knelt Unbidden. 1873 BLACK *Pr. Thule* iv. 47 Tears had sprung to her eyes unbidden.
*attrib.* *a* 1425 *Cursor M.* 14243 (Trin.), Þere were fele hem to rewe And also mony vnbeden iewe Þider coom. 1548 UDALL, etc. *Erasm. Par. Luke* vii. 74 She did not onely ieoperde as an vnbidden geaste boldely to entre into the house of a Pharisee, but [etc.]. 1573 G. HARVEY *Letter-bk.* (Camden) 42 He lookith like..an unbidden geste that knowes not where to sitt him downe. 1620 BRINSLEY *Virgil* 58/3, I do not sing vnbidden (vncommanded) things. 1697 DRYDEN *Virg. Georg.* I. 227 Burrs and Brambles, an unbidden Crew Of graceless guests, th' unhappy Field subdue. 1718 POPE *Iliad* XIV. 396 Glad earth..from her bosom pours Unbidden herbs, and voluntary flowers. 1805 SCOTT *Last Minstrel* IV. xxv, Gush'd to her eye the unbidden tear. 1850 F. W. NEWMAN *Phases Faith* 163 Judaism also unlearnt polygamy, and made an unbidden improvement upon Moses.

**Unbide,** variant of ONBIDE.

**Unbi·gged,** *ppl. a.* Also *Sc.* 5–6 vnbiggit. [UN-[1] 8. Cf. ON. and Icel. *ú-*, *óbygðr* (Norw. *ubygd*, older Da. *ubygget*, *ubygt*, Sw. *obyggd*).] **a.** Uninhabited. **b.** Unbuilt. **c.** Not built upon.
*c* 1200 ORMIN 3199 He..flæh himm inntill wesste land þær itt wass all unbiggedd. 1496 *Acc. Ld. High Treas. Scot.* I. 270 For tymmir and diuers odir expens maid apone the bigging of the harnes mill, quhilk ȝit is vnbiggit. 1555 *Sc. Acts, Mary* (1814) II. 490/1 Gif the awnaris lattis the ground to be vnbiggit. 1597 SKENE *De Verb. Sign.* s.v. *Annuell*, Quhen the ground and propertie of onie land bigged or vnbigged, is disponed and annalied. *a* 1795 *Bonnie James Campbell* iv. in Child *Ballads* IV. (1890) 143/2 My house is unbigged,.. My corn's unshorn.

**Unbi·goted,** *a.* (UN-[1] 9.) 1711 ADDISON *Spect.* No. 213 ⁋ 15 Erasmus, who was an unbigotted Roman Catholick. 1784 R. BAGE *Barham Downs* II. 311 Sir George has free notions; the Professor is an unbigotted Catholic. 1841 F. E. PAGET *Tales of Village* (1852) 317 He is..so unbigotted, has such a liberal mind,..that it was quite impossible not to admire him. 1894 BLACKMORE *Perlycross* xliv, A Protestant not quite unbigoted.

† **Unbiheve,** *sb.* and *a.*: see UN-[1] 3.

**Unbi·lified,** *ppl. a.* (UN-[1] 8.) 1823 LOCKHART *Reg. Dalton* II. vii, A firm, sound, unseasoned, and unbilified stomach.

**Unbi·lled,** *ppl. a.* [UN-[1] 8.] Not enrolled.
1587 HARRISON *England* II. xvi. (1877) I. 280 A third part of this like multitude [of soldiers] was left vnbilled and vncalled.

**Unbi·lleting,** *vbl. sb.* (UN-[1] 13.) 1654 H. L'ESTRANGE *Chas. I* (1655) 78 Personal liberty being thus setled, next they fall upon..the unbilleting of Souldiers and nulling of Martiall Law in times of peace.

**Unbi·nd,** *v.* Forms: (see UN-[2] and BIND *v.*). [OE. *unbindan* (f. UN-[2] 3 + BIND *v.*), *onbindan*, = Du. *ontbinden*, G. *entbinden*.]

1. *trans.* To free from a band, bond, or tie; to make loose or free by undoing a band, etc. Also *absol.*
*c* 950 *Lindisf. Gosp.* Matt. xxi. 2 Ȝe infindes asal ȝebunden & fola mið hia, unbindas & to-lædas me. *Ibid.* Luke xiii. 15 An eȝhuelc iuer on symbel-doeȝ ne unbindeð *vel* woxo his *vel* assald of bósih. *c* 1175 *Lamb. Hom.* 5 Ure drihten sende his .ii. apostles..þet heo unbunden þat assa. *c* 1250 *Gen. & Ex.* 2223 Quan men ðo seckes ðor un-bond, And in

ðe coren ðo aȝtes fond. **1382** WYCLIF *Luke* xix. 31 And if ony man schal axe, whi ȝe vnbynden [*sc.* the ass], thus ȝe schulen seye to him. **1426** LYDG. *De Guil. Pilgr.* 3038 Pereyl off deth..ys a cause evydent That thow mayst wel.. The swerd ydrawe,..And the keyes vnbynde also. *c* **1450** LOVELICH *Grail* xlix. 213 Thanne let this Sarrazin Iosephe vnbynde his hondis that bownden weren behinde. **1484** CAXTON *Fables of Alfonce* ix, Whanne the nyght was come, the labourer vnbonde his oxen. **1596** SHAKS. *Tam. Shr.* II. i. 4 For these other goods, Vnbinde my hands, Ile pull them off my selfe. **1669** STURMY *Mariner's Mag.* I. ii. 17 Get the Sail into the Ship, and unbind all things clear of it. **1683** J. REID *Scots Gard'ner* (1907) 71 Set the graff on the west-side...Unbind when you find their bands harme them. **1707** MORTIMER *Husb.* (1721) II. 262 When you unbind them you may discern which are good and have taken, and which not. **1791** MRS. RADCLIFFE *Rom. Forest* ix, The ruffians unbound me from my horse. **1821** SCOTT *Kenilw.* xxxix, He unbound his horse from the tree.

*fig.* *c* **1000** ÆLFRIC *Hom.* I. 352 Þæs fæder tungan his nama unband. *c* **1400** *Rom. Rose* 2226 To vilayne speche in no degre Late never thi lippe vnbounden be. **1859** TENNYSON *Guinevere* 164 O maiden,..Sing, and unbind my heart that I may weep.

**b.** *transf.* To loosen, open up or out, set free, detach, etc.

**1577** GRANGE *Golden Aphrod.*, etc. S j b, So doth the morne (me thinkes) vnclose and eke vnbinde, Each thing whiche in the night, are closed in their kynde. **1633** FLETCHER *Purple Isl.* I. xxxvi, Vain men, too fondly wise, who plough the seas,..The earths vast limits dayly more unbinde! **1697** DRYDEN *Virg. Georg.* I. 64 While Earth unbinds Her frozen Bosom to the Western Winds. **1735** A. HILL *Zara* v. 60 His absence shall unbind his sister's tongue. **1743** FRANCIS tr. *Hor., Odes* I. xxii. 18 Place me where never Summer Breeze Unbinds the Glebe, or warms the Trees. **1781** COWPER *Tiroc.* 439 The most disint'rested and virtuous minds, In early years connected, time unbinds. **1817** SHELLEY *Rev. Islam* VII. xl, Like wind Which..can wake the still cloud, and unbind The strength of tempest.

**c.** To take the bandage off (a limb or wound).

**1639** T. DE GRAY *Expert Farrier* 30 Binde upon it a linnen cloth,..then..unbinde the foot. **1699** DAMPIER *Voy.* II. II. 91 The next Morning the Cloath being rubb'd off, I unbound it, and found the Worm broken off, and the Hole quite healed up. **1821** BYRON *Sardanap.* III. i, I will unbind your wound and tend it.

**2.** *fig.* **a.** In renderings of Matt. xvi. 19, etc. Cf. LOOSE *v.* 1 c.

*c* **950** *Lindisf. Gosp.* Matt. xvi. 19 Suæ huæt ðu unbindes ofer eorðu bið unbunden in heofnum. *c* **1000** ÆLFRIC *Hom.* I. 542 Swa hwæt swa hi unbindað ofer eorðan, þæt bið unbunden on heofonum. *c* **1200** *Trin. Coll. Hom.* 65 Al þat prest bindeð soðliche buð ibunden & al þat he unbindeð beð unbunden. **1382** WYCLIF *Matt.* xviii. 18 What euere thingis ȝee shulen vnbynde vpon erthe, tho shulen be vnbounden and in heuenes. *c* **1400** LOVE *Bonavent. Mirr.* (1908) 123 What that ȝe vnbynde in erthe schal be vnbounden in heuene.

*absol.* **1820** WORDSW. *Processions* 67 That licentious craving in the mind To act the God among external things, To bind, on apt suggestion, or unbind. **1822** — *Eccl. Sonn.* I. xxxix, Through earth and heaven to bind and to unbind!

†**b.** To free from sin or its consequences; to absolve. *Obs.*

*c* **950** *Lindisf. Gosp.* Luke, Contents lxxvi, Ðone aldormon unband [L. *absoluit*] seðe cuom hal ȝedoe þætte losade. *c* **1000** ÆLFRIC *Hom.* I. 234 Forði sceolon ða lareowas ða unbindan fram heora synnum þa ðe Crist ȝeliffæst þurh onbryrdnysse. *a* **1200** *Vices & Virtues* 53 Hwa se..is mid heued-senne ibunden, þe naure ne mai ben unbunden bute ðurh priestes muðe oðer ðurh biscopes. *c* **1275** *Passion Our Lord* 630 in *O. E. Misc.* 55 Þeo þat ye aleseþ here of heore sunnes bende, Hi schulle beon vnbunden euer buten ende. **1303** R. BRUNNE *Handl. Synne* 1014 Certys we ouȝt þan with ful mynde To preye god vs of synne vnbynde. *c* **1400** *Rom. Rose* 6416, I am unbounde;..For he that myght hath in his honde, Of alle my synnes me unbonde. *a* **1450** *Knt. de la Tour* (1906) 53 The deuell holdithe hem bounde in his seruice till thei be vnbounde by confession.

*absol.* *a* **1300** *Cursor M.* 28742 Sin crist is buxum to vnbind, Qui sal man preist ouer hard find. **1340** *Ayenb.* 172 He ssel zeche zuych ane confessour, þet conne bynde and onbynde. **1396–7** in *Eng. Hist. Rev.* (1907) XXII. 301 Þei seyn þat..þei mown cursyn and blissin, byndin and unbyndin at here owne wil. *c* **1440** *Jacob's Well* 63 Here it semyth þat acursyng byndyth, & absolucyoun vnbyndyth.

†**c.** To set free, deliver, cure (from sickness or trouble). *Obs.*

*c* **950** *Lindisf. Gosp.* Luke xiii. 16 Ðios..dohter abrahames ..ne were..reht to unbindanne *vel* to undoanne of bend ðissum dæȝe symbles? *c* **1000** *Saxon Leechd.* I. 98 Ȝyf hwa on þære untrumnysse sy þæt he sy cis, þonne meaht ðu hine unbindan. *c* **1385** CHAUCER *L. G. W.* 1339 *Dido*, O cloth, whil Jubiter hyt leste, Take now my soule, vnbynd me of thys vnreste. *c* **1430** *Hymns Virgin* (1867) 97 How myȝt god me of care vnbinde Siþen god loueþ trouþe so verrili? *c* **1440** *Jacob's Well* 63 ȝysterday, whan þe absolucyoun was red ouyr my graue, I was vnboundyn of my peyne.

†**d.** To make free, to release, from some legal restraint or obligation. Also *absol.* *Obs.*

**1297** R. GLOUC. (Rolls) 3370 In oþer halue he founde Ioye in is herte, uor þe contasse of spoushod was vnbunde. *Ibid.* 649 Þo was he al clene louerd, to binde & unbinde. **1340** *Ayenb.* 97 Laȝe is yzed þeruore þet hy hare-zelue ne byn ake þe oþre byndeþ and þis onbynt. **1382** WYCLIF *Rom.* vii. 6 Now forsothe we ben vnbounden fro the lawe of deeth. *c* **1386** CHAUCER *Merch. Prol.* 14 Were I vnbounden al so moot I thee I wolde neuere eft comen in the snare [of marriage]. *a* **1470** H. PARKER *Dives & Pauper* (W. de W. 1496) IV. vi. 166/2 By his relygyon he is unbounden from this commaundement. **1491** CAXTON *Vitas Patr.* (W. de W. 1495) V. xiv. 344/2, I praye the that it please the to doo to me that grace..to unbynde me of the sentence of excomynycacyon in whiche I am bounden. **1581** MARBECK *Bk. of Notes* 978 New things, that is, the sweete tidings of yᵉ Gospell to vnbinde us.

†**e.** *absol.* To give up an enterprise. *Obs. rare.*

*a* **1400–50** *Alexander* 1744 (Ashm. MS.), Forthi is bettir vnbynd & of þe brathe leue. *Ibid.* 1974 For-þi ware bettir vnbynde or þou bale suffire.

**3. a.** To set (a person) free from bonds; to restore to personal liberty in this way. Also in fig. context.

*c* **950** *Rit. Eccl. Dunelm.* (Surtees) 7 From synna bendum unbundeno..vsig..ȝihald. *c* **1000** ÆLFRIC *Hom.* I. 466 Æfter his behate ic ðe unbinde, þæt þu fare to westene. *a* **1023** WULFSTAN *Hom.* (1883) 83 Æfter þusend ȝearum bið Satanas unbunden. *c* **1200** ORMIN 3682 Forr þatt he wollde unnbindenn uss Off hellepiness bandess. *c* **1300** *Havelok* 601 [They] Vnkeueleden him, and swiþe unbounden. *c* **1350** *Will. Palerne* 1227 Þan þei him vnbond bliue & brouȝt him his stede. **1382** WYCLIF *Acts* xxii. 30 Forsoth in the day suynge he..vnbound him. *a* **1425** *Cursor M.* 14912 (Trin.) Þat wiþ þe fend dwellynge ware He wolde hem vnbynde in dede. **1483** CAXTON *Gold. Leg.* 180/1 Thenne came an aungel that unbonde them. *a* **1533** LD. BERNERS *Huon* l. 168, I requyre the vnbynd me & brynge me out of this dolouros payne. **1588** SHAKS. *Tit. A.* III. i. 24 Vnbinde my sonnes, reuerse the doome of death. **1635** *Life Long Meg of Westm.* (1871) 27 Help to unbind me, for I am undone, and almost killed. **1799** *Hull Advertiser* 3 Aug. 4/1 A.. girl..tied up by both arms to a tree...I implored that she might be immediately unbound. **1817** SHELLEY *Rev. Islam* III. xiii. 2 They bore me to a cavern in the hill Beneath that column, and unbound me there. **1839** WHITTIER *World's Convention* 228 Methinks I see my country rise:..Her captives from their chains unbound. **1851** — *Pris. Naples* 13 Whom man hath bound let Thy right hand unbind.

*fig.* **1390** GOWER *Conf.* III. 369 Sche which mai the hertes bynde In loves cause and ek unbinde. **1400–10** CLANVOWE *Cuckow & Night.* ii, The god of love..can binden and unbinden eke What he wol have bounden or unbounde.

†**b.** To deliver (a woman). *Obs.*[−1]

*c* **1325** *Lai le Freine* 85 Sone therafter bifel a cas, That hirself with child was. When God wild sche was unbounde, And deliuerd.

†**c.** To clear of phlegm. *Obs.*[−0]

**1552** HULOET, Vnbynde the breaste, *expectoro.*

**4.** To unfasten, untie, undo (a bond, cord, etc.).

*c* **950** *Lindisf. Gosp.* Luke iii. 16 Ðæs ne am ic wyrðe to unbindanne ðuongas sceoea his. *c* **1200** ORMIN 10412 Þa shollde an oþerr cumenn forþ..& shollde unnbindenn þin shoþwang. *c* **1205** LAY. 5926 Heo unbunde þa locun, drowen ut þa baiȝes. **1382** WYCLIF *Acts* xvi. 26 And a-noon alle the doris ben openyd, and the bondis of alle ben vnbounden. **1426** LYDG. *De Guil. Pilgr.* 22028 For the osyers nygh echon Were broke ffyrste.., Wherffore the hoopys were vnbounde. **1596** SPENSER *F. Q.* VI. xi. 8 But she resolu'd no remedy to fynde,..Till Fortune would her captiue bonds vnbynde. **1697** DRYDEN *Æneis* VII. 563 Unbind your fillets, loose your flowing hair. **1757** W. WILKIE *Epigon.* VI. 170 They..the helmet loos'd, the buckled mail unbound. **1791** COWPER *Odyss.* V. 419 Unbind the zone, Which thou shalt cast far distant from the shore Into the deep. **1812** BYRON *Ch. Har.* III. civ, 'Twas the ground Where early Love his Psyche's zone unbound. **1820** SHELLEY *Vis. Sea* 56 The sharks and the dogfish their grave-clothes unbound.

**b.** In fig. context.

*c* **950** *Lindisf. Gosp.* Mark vii. 35 Sona untyndo woeron earo his & un-bunden wæs ȝebend tungæs his. *a* **1200** *Moral Ode* 188 in *O.E. Hom.* I. 171 Vre bendes he vnbond & bohte us mid his blode. **1388** WYCLIF *Isaiah* lviii. 6 Vnbynde thou the byndingis togidere of vnpitee. *a* **1500** *Ratis Raving* I. 1067 Gyf thai twa frendis can nocht find That scho may syk a band [*sc.* as that of marriage] wnbynd, I pray thee, reul the as thai red. **1559** *Mirr. Mag., Dk. Clarence* xi, Loves strongest bandes vnkindnes doth vnbinde. **1728** POPE *Dunc.* I. 24 Whether thou..magnify Mankind, Or thy griev'd Country's copper chains unbind. **1744** BERKELEY *Siris* § 302 Theology and philosophy gently unbind the ligaments that chain the soul down to the earth. **1810** SCOTT *Lady of L.* v. xxviii, Those cords of love I should unbind, Which knit my country and my kind. **1843** WHITTIER *Knight of St. John* 70 Then let the Paynim work his will, And death unbind my chain.

**c.** *fig.* To dissolve, undo, destroy.

*c* **1200** ORMIN 15590 Ure Laferrd..seȝȝde: Unnbindeþþ all þiss temmple, & icc Itt i þre daȝhess reȝȝse. *c* **1374** CHAUCER *Troylus* IV. 675 Al þe world ne koude here loue vnbynde, Ne Troylus out of here herte caste. *c* **1386** — *Pars. T.* ⁋ 511 Thanne cometh discord that vnbyndeth alle manere of freendshipe. *c* **1430** *Pilgr. Lyf Manhode* IV. l. (1869) 200 Þis byndinge, quod she, is cleped silence; Benedicite, þis is þilke þat oonliche vnbynt it. **1490** CAXTON *How to Die* (1491) 19 Thou vnbindest the synne of all the worlde. **1529** MORE *Suppl. Soulys* 28 b, By thys place ye se..that cryste at hys resurreccyon dyd lose and vnbynd paynys in hell. **1643** BAKER *Chron., Hen. VIII*, 19 Both Kings had given authority..to the Cardinall to affirme and confirme, to bind or unbind, whatsoever should be in difference betweene them. **1697** DRYDEN *Æneis* IV. 704 Her charms unbind The chains of love, or fix them on the mind. *Ibid.* XII. 304 No force, no fortune, shall my vows unbind, Or shake the steadfast tenor of my mind.

†**5. a.** *absol.* To aid the natural flux of the bowels. **b.** *trans.* To detach, clear away. *Obs.*

**1398** TREVISA *Barth. De P. R.* VII. lxix. (Bodl. MS.) fol. 73 b/2 With laxatyue medicens we laxeþ & vnbindeþ as with scamony. **1541** *Bk. Properties Herbs* E ij, Thys herbe.. wyll vnbinde wormes in a mannes stomake.

**6.** *intr.* †**a.** To dissolve. *Obs.*[−1]

*c* **1450** *M. E. Med. Bk.* (Heinrich) 220 Tak gomme of chyrytrees, or of plumtrees,..& put hyt in old wyn forto onbynde.

**b.** To become loosened.

**1827** KEBLE *Chr. Year* St. Peter xvi, Touch'd he upstarts—his chains unbind.

Hence **Unbi·nder**, one who unbinds.

**1837** LYTTON *Athens* II. 17 Bacchus,..the God of the Vineyard and the 'Unbinder of galling cares'.

**Unbi·nding**, *vbl. sb.* [f. prec. + -ING [1].] The action of the verb in various senses.

**1382** WYCLIF *Prol. Bible* ii. 3 In the tyme of Antecrist, and of vnbyndyng of Sathanas. **1382** — *1 Cor.* vii. 27 Thou art boundyn to a wyf, nyle thou seke vnbyndyng. *c* **1400** tr. *Secreta Secret., Gov. Lordsh.* 101 But it nedys be doon with consideracion..yn byndynge, & vnbyndynge. **1598** FLORIO, *Stralciamenti*, vntanglings, vnbindings, vntyings. **1641** MILTON *Animadv.* 52 There comes another strange Gardener that..challenges as his right the binding or unbinding of every flower. **1875** POSTE *Gaius* III. (ed. 2) 443 Nothing more natural than the likeness of the means of binding and of unbinding.

**Unbi·nding**, *ppl. a.*[1] [UN-[1] 10.] Not binding; *esp.* having no binding force, invalid.

**1652** *Persuasive to Compliance* 14 Rules..unbinding to the Parliament. **1803** in *Spirit Publ. Jrnls.* VII. 189 Assurances of the most satisfactory and yet unbinding nature. **1846** M'GEE *Gallery Irish Writers* 121 He published a treatise against the proceedings of the nuncio as uncanonical and unbinding. **1853** KANE *Grinnell Exp.* xxx. (1856) 263 It is drawn on like the shirt, and, except at the neck, is perfectly loose and unbinding.

**Unbi·nding**, *ppl. a.*[2] [f. UNBIND *v.*] Loosening, dissolving.

**1791** COWPER *Yardley Oak* 78a (MS.), All-binding frost and all unbinding thaw.

**Unbir·dlimed**, *ppl. a.* (UN-[1] 8 and UN-[2] 8.) **1800** COLERIDGE in Campbell *Life* (1894) vi. 112 If God grant me health, I shall have my wings wholly unbirdlimed.

**Unbi·rdly**, *a.* [UN-[1] 7.] Unlike a bird; not maintaining the character of a bird.

*a* **1667** COWLEY *Verses & Ess., Ode upon Liberty* iii, None so degenerous and unbirdly prove,..None but a few unhappy Houshold Foul. [**1834** K. H. DIGBY *Mores Cath.* v. vi. 185 If we would not degenerate below our species, and even unbirdly prove, we should rise to salute the dawn.]

**Unbi·rsed**, *ppl. a.* *north.* and *Sc.* [UN-[1] 8.] Unbruised.

**1435** MISYN *Fire of Love* II. vi. 82 Goddis holy lufar in cristis name onbyrsyd & als [it] wer without stryfe gladynde. **15..** *Christ's Kirk* xv. (Bann. MS.), He come hame with vnbirsd banis, Quhair fechtaris wer mischevit.

**Unbi·rthday.** (UN-[1] 12 b.) **1871** 'L. CARROLL' *Through Looking-Glass* vi, 'What *is* an un-birthday present?' 'A present given when it isn't your birthday, of course.'

**Unbi·shop**, *v.* [UN-[2] 6 b and 4.]

**1.** *trans.* To deprive of the office of bishop.

**1598** FLORIO, *Smetriare*, to vnmytre, to vnbishop, to degrade from a mytre. **1628** in *Cosin's Corr.* (Surtees) I. 153 You in the north, I in the south, are the object of toungs and penns, and I must be unbishop't a-geyne. **1657** TRAPP *Comm. Job* xxxi. 30 The one died ere he came home, and the other was unbishoped. **1691** GRASCOMBE *Reply Vind. Disc. Unreasonableness New Separation* 11/2 It was in their power to take away our Orders, and Unpriest and Unbishop us.

*refl.* **1641** MILTON *Reform.* I. Wks. 1851 III. 11 When he steps up into the Chayre of Pontificall Pride,..then he degrades, then he un-Bishops himselfe. **1680** *Spirit of Popery* 15 By which he did really unbishop himself.

**2.** To deprive (a place) of a bishop. *rare*[−1].

*a* **1661** FULLER *Worthies, Glouc.* I. (1662) 368 Some questioned its Charter, and would have had it Un-Citied, because Un-Bishoped in our Civil Wars.

Hence **Unbi·shop(p)ing** *vbl. sb.*

**1636** PRYNNE (*title*), The Vnbishoping of Timothy and Titvs. **1641** *Lords Spiritual* 7 That this un-bishoping intends onely the losse of his Barony and place in Parliament. **1711–2** M. HENRY *Life P. Henry* vii. Wks. 1853 II. 691/2 Much was said, *pro* and *con*, touching..the bishoping and unbishoping of Timothy and Titus [etc.].

**Unbi·shop(p)ed**, *ppl. a.*[1] Also 5 *Sc.* wnbyschoppyt. [UN-[1] 8.]

**1.** Not blessed or confirmed by a bishop.

*a* **970** *Canons Edgar* c. 15 And we læraδ..þæt ænig man to lange unbiscopod ne wurðe. *a* **1023** WULFSTAN *Hom.* (1883) 120 We lærað, þæt man æniȝne ne læte unbiscpod [*v.r.* unbiscopod] to lange. *a* **1225** *Ancr. R.* 208 Al so as..longe beon unbishoped, & falsliche igon to schrifte. *c* **1470** HENRY *Wallace* VII. 549 Wnbyschoppyt ȝeit, for suth I trow ye be; Your selff sall fyrst his blyssyng tak for me. [**1844** LINGARD *Anglo-Sax. Ch.* (1858) I. vii. 298 *note*, That no man remain unbishoped too long.]

**2.** Not consecrated as a bishop.

**1601** F. GODWIN *Bps. of Eng.* 373 Much against his will he died vnbishopped twelue daies after his nomination.

**Unbi·shop(p)ed**, *ppl. a.*[2] [UN-[2] 8, or f. UNBISHOP *v.*] Deprived of the status of a bishop.

**1563** FOXE *A. & M.* 1353/1 Shaxton byshop of Salisburye resigned also with him his bishoprick. And so these two remained a great space vnbishopped. **1607** HARINGTON *Nugæ Ant.* (1804) II. 32 Once I thought to have sayd somwhat of Bonner, because I may remember him living in the late Queens tyme unbishopped. **1666** SOUTH *Dolben Consecr. Serm.* 2, I must professe that I cannot look upon Titus as so far Vnbishopt yet but that he still exhibits to us all the Essentials of that Jurisdiction.

**Unbi·shoply**, *a.* (UN-[1] 7.) **1865** RUSKIN *Sesame* i. § 22 The most unbishoply character a man can have is therefore to be Blind. **1876** FREEMAN *Norm. Conq.* V. xxv. 576 After the days of the unbishoply Ulf had passed away.

**Unbi·t**, *ppl. a.* (UN-[1] 8 b.) **1742** YOUNG *Nt. Th.* IV. 108 Some avocation deeming it——to die; Unbit by rage canine of dying rich.

**Unbi·t**, *v.* [UN-[2] 4 b.] *trans.* To free (a horse) from the bit. Also *absol.*

**1565–6** BLUNDEVIL *Horsemanship* IV. lxx. (1580) 29 b, Then vnbitte him, and if it bee in Winter, offer him a hande full of Wheaten strawe. **1639** T. DE GRAY *Expert Farrier* 116 Let him stand upon his trench foure or five houres,..then unbit him, and give him sweet hay. **1662** J. DAVIES tr. *Olearius' Voy. Ambass.* 228 We were told the Herb of it is..venemous,..upon which accompt it was, that we durst not unbit that day. 1775 S. J. PRATT *Liberal Opin.* cxi. (1783) IV. 51 Jack Bookwit..unbitted his horse.

**Unbi·tt,** *v.* [UN-[2] 3.] *trans.* To uncoil or unfasten (a cable) from the bitts. Also *absol.*

1769 FALCONER *Dict. Marine* (1780), *Unbitting*, the operation of removing the turns of a cable from off the bits. *Ibid.*, *Débitter le cable*, to unbit the cable. *a* 1860 H. STUART *Seaman's Catech.* 54 It is used for stoppering the cable, when bitting or unbitting. 1883 *Man. Seamanship for Boys* 189 A..Blake's stopper..is used for stoppering the cable to bitt or unbitt it.

Hence **Unbi·tted** *ppl. a.*[1]

1864 *Daily Tel.* 25 Feb., In what particular the public money is running through Admiralty hawse-pipes like an unbitted cable.

**Unbi·tted,** *ppl. a.*[2] [UN-[1] 8.] Not furnished with a bit; unbridled, unrestrained. Also *fig.*

*a* 1586 SIDNEY *Astr. & Stella* Sonn. xxxviii, This night while..vnbitted thought Doth fall to stray. 1604 SHAKS. *Oth.* I. iii. 335 We haue Reason to coole our raging Motions, our carnall Stings, or vnbitted Lusts. 1628 FELTHAM *Resolves* II. xciii. 270 A limitlesse tongue is a strange vnbitted Beast, to worry one with. 1826 MRS. SHELLEY *Last Man* II. 248 Like a troop of unbitted steeds. 1882 STEVENSON *Mem. & Portr.* xii. (1887) 211 The same fatal conflicts of unbitted nature with too rigid custom.

**Unbi·tten,** *ppl. a.* (UN-[1] 8 b.) 1796 W. H. MARSHALL *Rur. Econ. W. England* II. 204 Instance of unbitten aftergrass. **Unbla·cked,** *ppl. a.* (UN-[1] 8.) 1836 *Hood's Comic Ann.* 80 So like Othello, with his face unblack'd. 1887 T. HARDY *Woodlanders* II. viii. 143 He..had sometimes been..seen on Sundays with unblacked boots. **Unbla·ckened,** *ppl. a.* (UN-[1] 8.) 1864 *Lond. Rev.* 28 May 563 A fair spring day, with the young green of the trees still unscorched by sun and unblackened by smoke. 1867 M. ARNOLD *Epil. to Lessing's Laocoon*, The grass had still the green of May, And still the unblacken'd elms were gay.

**Unbla·de,** *v.* [UN-[2] 6 b.] *trans.* To divest of the character of a blade or ruffian.

1633 SHIRLEY *Gamester* v. i, I shall take it as a favour too If, for the same price that you made him valiant, You will unblade him.

**Unbla·meable, unbla·mable,** *a.* [UN-[1] 7 b.] Blameless, irreproachable.

1531 TINDALE *Exp. 1 John* (1537) 100 A man of maruaylous integrete and vnblameable. 1579 W. WILKINSON *Confut. Fam. Love* Ep. Ded. *iij b, [They] would fayne in lyfe seeme innocent and vnblameable. 1612 T. TAYLOR *Comm. Titus* i. 6 (1619) 93 *margin*, The most commendable conformitie is to ioyne to vncorrupt doctrine an vnblameable life. 1693 *Apol. Clergy Scot.* 15, I know not a more unblamable Company of men upon Earth than the Episcopal Clergy of Scotland. 1738 WARBURTON *Div. Legat.* I. v. I. 72 His Followers, whom their very Enemies acknowledged to be unblameable in their actions. 1781 COWPER *Hope* 622 If, unblameable in word and thought, A *man* arise. 1840 CARLYLE *Heroes* iv. 230 That Scotland would forgive him [Knox] for having been worth to it any million 'unblamable' Scotchmen that need no forgiveness!

Hence **Unbla·m(e)ableness.**

1638 BP. REYNOLDS *Serm. 12 July* 42 Piety and unblameablenesse of living. *a* 1661 FULLER *Worthies, Lanc.* II. (1662) 107 Elizabeths unblameableness, .. the Canaanitish Womans faith, Mary Magdalens charity. 1698 KILLINGBECK *Serm.* (1717) 23 The Integrity of his Heart, and the Unblamableness of his Life.

**Unbla·meably, unbla·mably,** *adv.* [UN-[1] 11.] Blamelessly, irreproachably.

1539 BIBLE (Great) *1 Thess.* ii. 10 Ye are witnesses..how holyly and iustly and vnblameably we behaued oure selues. 1612 T. TAYLOR *Comm. Titus* ii. 7 It is possible for a man by grace to liue vnblameably. 1650 JER. TAYLOR *Holy Living* I. iii. 33 It is a great..ingagement to do unblameably, when we act before that Judge, who is infallible in his sentence. 1712 ADDISON *Spect.* No. 343 ¶ 4 From that time forth I lived so very unblameably, that I was made President of a College of Brachmans. 1883 F. D. HUNTINGTON in J. G. Butler *Bible-Work* (1887) II. 266 Even in these self-seeking earthly streets the Christian is to walk unselfishly and unblamably.

**Unbla·med,** *ppl. a.* [UN-[1] 8. Cf. MDu. *ongeblaemt.*] Not found fault with; uncensured.

14.. *Love-Longing* in *Rel. Ant.* I. 71 Wo worth hope unblamyd! 1570 LEVINS *Manip.* 50 Vnblamed, *inculpatus.* 1596 SPENSER *F. Q.* VI. ii. 43 Ioying together in vnblam'd delight. 1603 B. JONSON *Sejanus* II. iv, They that durst to strike At so exampless, and unblamed a life. 1651 STANLEY *Poems, Moschus* 42 Before unblam'd Europa's feet he stood. 1700 DRYDEN *Flower & Leaf* 513 And all her Train with leavy Chaplets crown'd Were for unblam'd Virginity renown'd. 1725 POPE *Odyss.* I. 207 Unblam'd abundance crown'd the royal board. 1767 SIR W. JONES *Seven Fountains* Poems (1777) 38 Say, gentle damsel, may I ask unblam'd, How this gay isle, and splendid seats are nam'd? 1840 CARLYLE *Heroes* vi. 359 Now he was, there as he stood recognised unblamed, the virtual King of England. 1876 GEO. ELIOT *Dan. Der.* lxii, The bright, unblamed young fellow.

† **Unbla·meful,** *a. Obs.*[—1] [UN-[1] 7.] Blameless. So † **Unbla·mefully** *adv.*

*c* 1400 *Apol. Loll.* 17 Þe kirk may not do it iustli, ne vnblamfully. 1570 LEVINS *Manip.* 186 Vnblameful, *inculpabilis.*

**Unbla·nched,** *ppl. a.* [UN-[1] 8.] Not bleached.

*a* 1420 *Liber Cocorum* (1862) 11 Take almondes unblanchyd, wasshe hom and grynd. 1598 *Epulario* D j, Take a pound and a half of Almonds vnblanched. 1658 A. FOX *Würtz' Surg., Children's Bk.* 342 Course unblanched linnen. 1725 *Fam. Dict.* s.v. *Sallet*, With unblanch'd Endive, Succory and Purslane. 1842 LOUDON *Suburban Hort.* 677 The points of the unblanched leaves are used to flavour soups.

† **Unbla·nked,** *ppl. a. Obs.*[—1] [UN-[1] 8 + BLANK *v.* 2.] Not disconcerted or silenced.

1570 FOXE *A. & M.* (ed. 2) I. 753/1 Yet was ther none of al those that interrupted him which scaped vnblanckt, but he brought them all to confusion.

**Unbla·sted,** *ppl. a.* (UN-[1] 8.)

1589 WARNER *Alb. Eng.* v. xxiii. (1592) 102 We here a blisfull Vintage gayne, That .. euermore vnblasted may remaine. 1612 PEACHAM *Minerva Brit.* 209 Th' vnblasted bay, to conquests due. 1742 YOUNG *Nt. Th.* III. 79 Those Few our noxious Fate unblasted leaves In this inclement Clime of human Life. 1819 BYRON *Proph. Dante* I. 16 Midst whom..Beatrice..led the mortal guest, Unblasted by the glory, though he trod From star to star.

**Unbla·zoned,** *ppl. a.* (UN-[1] 8.) [1775 ASH.] 1830 W. COBBETT *Rur. Rides* (1853) 578 The memory of the virtuous Catharine is unblazoned. 1859 TENNYSON *Elaine* 378 When Lavaine Returning brought the yet-unblazon'd shield.

**Unblea·ched,** *ppl. a.* [UN-[1] 8. Cf. MDu. and Du. *ongebleekt*, G. *ungebleicht*, Sw. *oblekt*, Da. *ubleget, -blegt.*] Not bleached. Also *ellipt.*

1531-2 *Durham Househ. Bk.* (Surtees) 68 Et in 15½ ulnis unbleched emptis. 1570 *Wills & Inv. N. C.* (Surtees, 1835) 337 Thre peces of vnbleched lynne xxx[s]. 1648 HEXHAM II, *Ongebleyckt lijnwaedt*, Vnbleached linen. 1756 F. HOME *Exper. Bleaching* 182 Into this mixture the same quantity of the same unbleached cloth was put. 1842 MRS. CARLYLE *Lett.* (1883) I. 175 Mr. Byng..was dressed from head to foot in unbleached linen. 1880 *Plain Hints Needlework* 79 In the North, .. unbleached diaper can be procured.

*transf.* and *fig.* 1815 JANE AUSTEN *Emma* lv, The stain of illegitimacy, unbleached by nobility or wealth, would have been a stain indeed. 1865 *Slang Dict.* 264 *Unbleached American*, the new Yankee term for coloured natives of the United States.

**Unblea·ching,** *ppl. a.* (UN-[1] 10.) 1812 BYRON *Ch. Har.* I. lxxxviii, Let their bleach'd bones, and blood's unbleaching stain, Long mark the battle-field with hideous awe.

† **Unble·cked,** *ppl. a. Obs.* [UN-[1] 8.] Unstained.

*c* 1380 WYCLIF *Wks.* (1880) 129 Þis is clene religion..to kepe hym self vnblekkid or defoulid fro þis world. *Ibid.* 211 Ypocritis of feyned religion..kepe not hem self vnbleckid fro þis world. 1535 STEWART *Cron. Scot.* (Rolls) III. 130 Syne efter that this ladie he did wed.., Quhilk..Martha.. In all hir tyme wnblekkit wes with blame.

**Unble·d,** *ppl. a.* (UN-[1] 8 b.) 1835 SANGRADO (*title*), The Great Unbled. An Allegorical Tale. **Unblee·ding,** *ppl. a.* (UN-[1] 10.) *a* 1619 DANIEL *To Sir T. Egerton* v. in *Panegyrike*, etc. (1623) 50 Making as deepe, although unbleeding wounds. 1812 BYRON *Ch. Har.* I. xci, To..mix unbleeding with the boasted slain.

**Unble·mishable,** *a.* (UN-[1] 7 b.)

1607 DEKKER *Knt.'s Conjur.* (1842) 69 It went away chaste and vnblemishable. 1625 *Modell Wit* 67 Her inhærent vnblemishable vertue and honor. 1651 W. JANE *Image Unbroken* 229 A sobrietie vnblemishable by a Traytours malice. 1720 WELTON *Suffer. Son of God* II. xiv. 369 So Pure and Unblemishable was His conversation, that He defied His Enemies to convince Him of any sin. 1875 MYERS *Poems* 98 Her sweet unblemishable soul.

**Unble·mished,** *ppl. a.* Forms: (see BLEMISH *v.*). [UN-[1] 8.]

**1.** Free from moral blemish or stain: **a.** Of persons. Also *absol.*

13.. *E. E. Allit. P.* A. 782 Vnblemyst I am wyth-outen blot. 1626 QUARLES *Feast for Worms* 1594 His Spouse is chaste, vnblemisht with a spot. 1646 CRASHAW *Sospetto d'Herode* xxiv, The unblemisht Lambe, blessed for ever, Should take the marke of sin, and paine of sence. 1711 POPE *Temp. Fame* 523 Unblemish'd let me live, or die unknown! 1784 COWPER *Task* III. 83 'Twas..an wholesome rigour in the main, And taught th' unblemish'd to preserve with care That purity, whose loss was loss of all. 1800 *Misc. Tr.* in *Asiat. Ann. Reg.* 58/2 Fines are enacted for abandoning an unblemished girl, and forgiving a blemished damsel. 1870 BRYANT *Iliad* VI. I. 194 Priam's sons in law And their unblemished consorts.

**b.** Of honour, name, character, etc.

1432 *Paston Lett.* I. 35 The said Erle..desired, and ever shal, to kepe his trouthe and worship unblemysshed. *a* 1475 ASHBY *Dicta Philos.* 1155 Thus ye shul..come to grete glory and noble fame Thurgh your goode liffe & vnblemyshed name. 1634 MILTON *Comus* 215 O welcom pure-ey'd Faith, ..And thou unblemish't form of Chastity. 1670 PETTUS *Fodinæ Reg.* 45 They must be Men of upright and unblemisht Lives and Conversations. 1738 WARBURTON *Div. Legat.* II. iv. I. 139 He should be of an unblemished and virtuous Character. 1779 *Mirror* No. 33, I am now in affluent circumstances, and I have reason to think that I am so with an unblemished character. 1823 SCOTT *Quentin D.* xviii, For the unblemished faith and unfaded honour of Scotland. 1855 MACAULAY *Hist. Eng.* xix. IV. 387 All the authority which belongs to unblemished integrity.

**2.** Not substantially or materially blemished or impaired.

*c* 1450 *St. Cuthbert* (Surtees) 6802 Þe text of wangels fell in þe water... Þe text was foun vnblemyst þare. *c* 1460 FORTESCUE *Abs. & Lim. Mon.* vii. (1885) 125 For be this meane þe kynges estate shall alwey be kept vnblemyshed. *a* 1500 in *Arnolde's Chron.* (1811) 19 So that all the forsayd citezens of London..haue alle the frauncheses of the wareyn and forest vnblemysshyd. 1596 SPENSER *F. Q.* v. xi. 62 What foule disgrace is this,..To blot your beautie that vnblemisht is? 1598 HAKLUYT *Voy.* I. 618 The religious houses only being spared, and left vnblemished. 1625 QUARLES *Sion's Sonn.* xvii. 3 His eyes are..Vnblemisht, vndistayned with a spot. 1883 SCHAFF *Encycl. Relig. Knowl.* 2365 The tenth one [of cattle, etc.] being set apart, no matter whether it were bad or good, blemished or unblemished.

Hence **Unble·mishedness.**

1656 JEANES *Fuln. Christ* 239 The unblemishednesse required in all the Priests, that ministered in the sanctuary. 1680 H. MORE *Apocal. Apoc.* 58 After a due search into their Pedigree, and the unblemishedness of their body. 1681-6 J. SCOTT *Chr. Life* (1747) III. 148 The Necessity of a moral Cleanness and Unblemishedness.

**Unble·mishing,** *ppl. a.* (UN-[1] 10.) 1661 FELTHAM *Serm. Luke xiv. 20* in *Resolves*, etc. (ed. 8) 392 If at most they leave a Mote behind, it is but dead, and with the next fair wind unblemishing blowes away.

**Unble·nched,** *ppl. a.* [UN-[1] 8.]

**1.** Not blenched or turned aside; undismayed, unflinching.

1634 MILTON *Comus* 430 Yea there, where very desolation dwels,..She may pass on with unblench't majesty. 1839 HALLAM *Hist. Lit.* (1855) IV. 101 His eye roams unblenched in the light, before which that of Pascal had been veiled in awe. 1863 IS. WILLIAMS *Baptistery* II. xxiv. (1874) 90 He who seem'd an unblench'd eye to bear. 1876 BANCROFT *Hist. U.S.* IV. xxiv. 494 Wesley's mental constitution was not robust enough to gaze on the future with unblenched calm.

**2.** Unstained, untarnished.

Perh. vaguely associated with BLENCH *v.*[2]

1813 COLERIDGE *Night-Scene* 66, I swore to her, that were she red with guilt, I would exchange my unblenched state with hers. 1815 — *Zapolya, Prelude* I. 286 Let the Queen Dowager, with unblench'd honours, Resume her state.

**Unble·nching,** *ppl. a.* (UN-[1] 10.) [1828 WEBSTER.] 1837 R. NICOLL *Poems* (1842) 132 The Poor and Honest Man can stand, With an unblenching brow, Before Earth's highest. 1843 PRESCOTT *Mexico* v. iii. (1864) 293 He looked with an unblenching eye on his past reverses. 1898 WATTS-DUNTON *Aylwin* II. iv, So different from the unblenching child who loved to stand hatless! **Unble·nchingly,** *adv.* (UN-[1] 11.) 1864 E. SARGENT *Peculiar* I. 27 Mrs. Charlton..looked him unblenchingly in the face. 1885 *Athenæum* 3 Jan. 8/3 He takes his death as the English hero should take death, unblenchingly. **Unble·ndable,** *a.* (UN-[1] 7 b.) 1716 M. DAVIES *Athen. Brit.* III. 67 The Romists value themselves to an unblendable Obstinacy, upon such pretended Superiority of Parts and Performances.

**Unble·nded,** *ppl. a.* (UN-[1] 8.)

*c* 1340 HAMPOLE *Prose Tr.* 8 Thay hafe othyr vertus vnblendide with þe fylthe of syne and vnclene luste. 1611 FLORIO, *Immescolato*, vnmingled, vnblended. 1624 QUARLES *Job* vi. 31 The Hiue No hony yeelds, vnblended with the Wax. 1661 GLANVILL *Van. Dogm.* vii. 65 It dwels no where in unblended proportions on this side the Empyreum. 1795 ANNA SEWARD *Lett.* (1811) IV. 108 Her lilies and roses are exchanged for the unblended flush of sun-burnt health. 1820 SHELLEY *Arethusa* iii, Behind her descended Her billows, unblended With the brackish Dorian stream. 1887 MORRIS *Odyss.* IX. 204 The drink of the Gods, unblended sweet wine, for me did he pour Into twelve fulfilled pitchers.

**Unble·nt,** *ppl. a.* (UN-[1] 8 b.) 1835 *Court Mag.* VI. 229/1 Nothing could exceed the distortion of those naturally large and unblent lineaments. 1882 *Good Literature* 8 Apr., Born of the old Puritan stock, unblent with other strains.

**Unble·ss,** *v.* [UN-[2] 3.] *trans.* To deprive of a blessing or of happiness.

1600 SHAKS. *Sonn.* iii. 4 That face should forme an other, Whose fresh repaire if now thou not renewest, Thou doo'st beguile the world, vnblesse some mother. 1631 QUARLES *Samson* Wks. (Grosart) II. 149/1 Too great excesse Makes Ioy a Madnesse, and does quite unblesse So sweet a gift. 1641 M. FRANK *Serm., Annunc.* (1672) 319 Because they bless her too much, these unbless her quite.

**Unble·ssed, unble·st,** *ppl. a.* Forms: (see BLESS *v.*). [UN-[1] 8.]

**1.** Not formally blessed or consecrated.

*c* 1310 in Horstm. *Altengl. Leg.* (1881) 231 Þer ich finde a wiif þat liȝter is of barn,..ȝif it be vnblisced, y croke it fot or arm. 1340 *Ayenb.* 41 Huanne me stelþ..be kueade skele out of holy stede yblissede þinges oþer onblissede, huet þet hit by. *c* 1530 MORE *Answ. Frith* Wks. 842/2 Whether the blessed sacrament be consecrate or vnconsecrate, .. [he] biddeth care not but take it for all that vnblessed as it is. 1546 *Wyclif's Wycket* A viij, Ye gyve vs after the breade wyne and water, and sometymes clene water vnblessed rather coniured.

**b.** Deprived of, excluded from, left without, a blessing or benediction.

1590 SPENSER *F. Q.* I. ix. 54 He chose an halter from among the rest, And with it hung himselfe, vnbid vnblest. 1633 BP. HALL *Contempl., N. T.* IV. xii, 'Ungirt, unblessed,' was the old word; as not ready till they were girded. 1687 DRYDEN *Hind & P.* III. 637 He breath'd his last, exposed to open air, And there his corps, unbless'd, is hanging still. 1757 GRAY *Bard* 102 Stay, oh stay! nor thus forlorn Leave me unbless'd, unpitied, here to mourn. 1783 CRABBE *Village* I. 346 The crowd retire distress'd, To think a poor man's bones should lie unbless'd. 1818 BYRON *Ch. Har.* IV. lxviii, Pass not unblest the Genius of the place! 1847 H. BUSHNELL *Chr. Nurt.* II. ii, This always unblessed, tedious look of sanctimony.

**2.** Not blessed in fortune or lot; unfortunate, wretched, miserable.

1340-70 *Alex. & Dind.* 1124 ȝe ben vn-blessed of lif, for.. Þat ȝe holden so her holsome dedes Gret wante is of wo & wikkede paine. *c* 1375 *Cursor M.* 13108 (Fairf.), Þat man salle vn-blessed be þe quilk trawes noȝt in me. *c* 1400 *Laud Troy Bk.* 5883 That day the Troyens were glad... But Ector was that day vnblessed, Off grace certes that day he myssed. *c* 1450 *Myrr. our Ladye* 220 O moste blyssed of women, socoure vs vnblyssed synners. 1592 WARNER *Alb. Eng.* VII. xxxvii. 166 What might remaine but death for me that liued so vnblest? 1604 SHAKS. *Oth.* v. i. 34 Minion, your deere lyes dead, And your vnblest Fate highes. 1649 MILTON *Eikon.* ix. 79 That unblest expedition to the Jle of Rhee. 1675 HOBBES *Odyssey* (1677) 25 Unblest Ulysses, who at Ilium Together with you fought. *a* 1721 PRIOR *Fortune-Teller* 27 What matters, if unblest in love, How long or short my life will prove? 1798 *Monthly Mag.* IV. 48 Unchang'd, eternal be your misery. I rule you, and am only more unblest. 1848 BAILEY *Festus* (ed. 3) 169 Which is more unblest Whose love is shunned or sought let time attest! 1865 DICKENS *Mut. Fr.* III. i, Gaslights flared in the shops with a haggard and unblest air.

*absol.* 1814 WORDSW. *Excurs.* II. 596 That poor Man taken hence to-day..must be deemed, I fear, Of the unblest.

**3.** Unhallowed, unholy; wicked, evil, malignant.

1388 WYCLIF *Ecclus.* xxvii. 24 To schewe opynli the pryuytees of a frend, is dispeir of a soule vnblessid. 1426 AUDELAY *Poems* (Percy Soc.) 15 We were put in paradise to have wele withoutyn woo Hent we had unblest brokyn the commaundmentis of our Kyng. *c* 1450 *Mirk's Festial* 219

Then sayde Laurens: 'Vnblessyd, þes tormentys I haue ȝore desyred'. *c* **1520** SKELTON *Magnyf.* 134 If Lyberte sholde lepe and renne where he lyst, It were no vertue, it were a thynge vnblyst. **1591** SPENSER *M. Hubberd* 915 For none but such as this bold Ape vnblest Can euer thriue in that vnluckie quest. **1610** BP. CARLETON *Jurisd.* 71 This vnblessed deuise of forgerie, being attempted in a number of decretall Epistles. **1667** MILTON *P. L.* I. 238 Such resting found the sole Of unblest feet. **1697** DRYDEN *Virg. Georg.* I. 229 Oats unblest, and Darnel domineers, And shoots its head above the shining Ears. **1761** GRAY *Odin* 35 Who is he, with voice unblest, That calls me from the bed of rest? **1793** HOLCROFT *Lavater's Physiog.* i. 11 Wilt thou teach man the unblessed art of judging his brother by the ambiguous expressions of his countenance? **1800** COLERIDGE *Christabel* II. 529, I had vowed with music loud To clear yon wood from thing unblest. **1837** CARLYLE *Fr. Rev.* II. v. v, Why were not [they]..in their beds, that unblessed Varennes Night! **1840** — *Heroes* v. 304 The world..can either have it as blessed continuous summer-sunshine, or as unblessed black thunder and tornado.

**4.** Not favoured or made happy *by* or *with* something.

**1743** FRANCIS tr. *Hor., Odes* I. xx. 15 My meagre Cup's unblest With the rich Formian, or Falernian Vine. **1795** CAMPBELL *Elegy* 13 The cloudy heavens unblest by summer's smile. **1844** H. G. ROBINSON *Odes of Horace* I. xxxi, Nor let me an old age prolong, Unhonour'd or unblest by song. **1848** W. H. KELLY tr. *L. Blanc's Hist. Ten Y.* II. 269 Lyons was plunged into a silence, unblessed with repose.

Hence **Unble·ssedness.**

**1549** COVERDALE, etc. *Erasm. Par. Rev.* xix. 32 An euerlasting supper of al bitternes & vnblessednes wherof they maye eate and be partakers altogether. **1836** T. HOOK *G. Gurney* I. 141 Without having changed her state of single-unblessedness. **1881** BRUCE *Chief End Rev.* vi. 302 The grace of God is represented as finding men in a state of serious moral corruption and consequent unblessedness.

**Unble·ssing,** *ppl. a.* (UN-[1] 10.) **1760–72** H. BROOKE *Fool of Qual.* (1809) IV. 11 All the..fond relations..must ever have remained, unblessing and as dead. **1842** GEO. ELIOT in Cross *Life* (1885) I. 116, I..have thought..my life the shallowest, muddiest, most unblessing stream.

† **Unble·stful,** *a. Obs.*[—1] [UN-[1] 7.] = UNBLESSED *ppl. a.* 2.

**1608** SYLVESTER *Du Bartas* III. II. iv. *Schisme* 417 Th' unsavory breath of Serpents crawling o're The Lybians pestfull and un-blest-full shore.

**Unbli·ghted,** *ppl. a.* (UN-[1] 8.)

**1784** COWPER *Task* IV. 334 In such a world; so thorny, and where none Finds happiness unblighted. **1792** CHARLOTTE SMITH *Desmond* II. 217 That world which has, at your age, and with your unblighted prospects, so many charms. **1827** LYTTON *Falkland* 233 She went to that last home with a blest and unblighted name. **1861** H. MACMILLAN *Footnotes Page Nat.* 34 Though subjected to the scorching rays of the summer's sun, they [*sc.* mosses] continue green and unblighted.

Hence **Unbli·ghtedly** *adv.*

[**1847** WEBSTER.] **1871** B. TAYLOR *Faust* v. vi. 373 Roses ..Branching unblightedly, Budding delightedly.

**Unbli·nd,** *a.* (UN-[1] 7.) **1818** KEATS *Visit Burns's Country* 48 That he may..keep his vision clear from speck, his inward sight unblind.

**Unbli·nd,** *v.* [UN-[2] 3. Cf. Du. *ontblinden.*]

**1.** *trans.* To free from blindness.

In some instances implying sense 2.

**1598** MARLOWE & CHAPMAN *Hero & Leander* III. 365 We know not how to vow, till loue vnblinde vs. **1605** SYLVESTER *Miracle of Peace* xxiv, Unblinde thy blinde soule, ope thine inward sight. **1681** RYCAUT tr. *Gracian's Critick* 202 How well is my innocency..rewarded, wherewith I desire to unblind the World.

**2.** = UNBLINDFOLD *v.*

**1590** R. W[ILSON] *Three Lords & Ladies Lond.* I. I iij b, Wel one day he wil pay for all. Vnblind Simplicity. **1608** ARMIN *Nest Ninn.* (1842) 20 They all shout aloud and cry rarely well done, and one unblindes him, while another puts the glove on the speare. **1632** BROME *Crt. Beggar* III. i, Here set him downe: unbind him and unblind him. **1655** tr. *Sorel's Com. Hist. Francion* IX. 16 Having unblinded him, they demanded of him, who did put him there?

**Unbli·nded,** *ppl. a.* [UN-[1] 8.]

**1.** Not blinded or deprived of sight.

**1611** FLORIO, *Inorbato*,..vnblinded. **1833** TENNYSON *Pal. Art* 42 Who shall gaze upon My palace with unblinded eyes?

**2.** *fig.* Not deluded or deceived.

**1755** *Man* No. 20. 8 A man unblinded by prejudice, is not far from being a Christian. **1797** COLERIDGE *Let. to Cottle* 8 June, I speak with heartfelt sincerity and, I think, unblinded judgment. **1802–12** BENTHAM *Ration. Judic. Evid.* (1827) I. 287 A judgment unblinded by prejudice. **1871** RUSKIN *Fors Clav.* vii. 24 Learn..how to obey good Men, who are living, breathing unblinded law.

**Unbli·nded,** *a.* [UN-[1] 9.] Not furnished with, or covered by, a window-blind.

**1862** MRS. NORTON *Lady of La Garaye* IV. 113 The cold fine star That glitters through the unblinded window-pane. **1876** T. HARDY *Ethelberta* xlv, An unblinded window revealed inside it a room bright and warm.

**Unbli·ndfold,** *v.* Also 5 vnblyndfelle, 6 vnblindefilde. [UN-[2] 4.] *trans.* To unbandage (the eyes); to free (a person or animal) from a bandage over the eyes. Also *fig.*

*c* **1430** *Pilgr. Lyf Manhode* IV. xix. (1869) 186 Þat þei vnblyndfelle so here eyen þat þei mown biholde to þe heuene. **1580** HOLLYBAND *Treas. Fr. Tong, Dessiller*, to vnwrappe his eies,..to vnblindefilde. **1596** SPENSER *F. Q.* VI. vii. 33 He bad his eyes to be vnblindfold both, That he might see his men. **1607** MARKHAM *Cavel.* VIII. (1617) 28 You may blindfolde the horse and.. after vnblindfolde him. **1643** PRYNNE *Sov. Power Parl.* II. 79 Which I hope will fully un-blindfold the hood-winkt world.

**Unbli·nkingly,** *adv.* (UN-[1] 11.)

Also, in recent use, *unblinking* adj.

**1867** AUGUSTA WILSON *Vashti* v, Her large, brilliant eyes followed the sinking sun as steadily—as unblinkingly—as an eagle's. **1888** *Daily News* 7 Dec. 3/2 Until now he had looked none in the face. Now, however, he did it unblinkingly.

**Unbli·ss.** [UN-[1] 12. So OE. *unbliss.*] Lack of bliss; unhappiness.

*a* **1628** F. GREVIL *Poems, Inquisition upon Fame and Hon.* II. xix, So as between perfection, and unblisse, Man, out of man, will make himself a frame.

**Unbli·ssful,** *a.* [UN-[1] 7.] Unhappy; destitute of bliss.

**1340–70** *Alex. & Dind.* 543 To ȝoure souorain of sinne [ye] sacrifice maken Wiþ þat vnblisful blod þat þei bled hauen. **1382** WYCLIF *Prov.* xix. 26 Who tormentith the fader, and fleeth the modir, shenful shal be, and vnblisful [L. *infelix*]. **1833** TENNYSON *Dream Fair Wom.* xxi, From within me a clear under-tone Thrill'd thro' mine ears in that unblissful clime. **1868** MORRIS *Earthly Par.* (1870) I. I. 149 Ah! soothly, well remembered Was that unblissful wretched home.

† **Unbli·the,** *a. Obs.* Forms: (see UN-[1] and BLITHE *a.*). [OE. *unblīðe* (f. *un-* UN-[1] 7 + *blīðe* BLITHE *a.*), = MDu. *onblide* (Kilian *-blijde*), OHG. *unblīdi*, *-plīdi* (MHG. *unblīde*), ON. and Icel. *ú-*, *óblíðr* (Sw. *oblid*, Da. *ublid*).]

**1.** Unhappy; sad, sorrowful; not delighted.

*Beowulf* 131 Mære þeoden..unbliðe sæt, þolode ðryðswyð, þegnsorge dreah. *c* **897** K. ÆLFRED *Gregory's Past. C.* xxvii. 187 Moniȝe beoð ðeah bliðe & eac unbliðe..for ðæs blodes styringe. *c* **1000** ÆLFRIC *Saints' Lives* xxxiii. 348 Þa se abbod þis gehyrde þa wearð he swyðe unbliðe. *a* **1250** *Owl & Night.* 1585 Þe lauerd into þare þeode Fareþ ut.., An[d] is þat gode wif unbliþe For hire lauerdes houdsiþe. *a* **1300** *Cursor M.* 14867 Þai went þam ham, all þat sith, Bath wrath, waful, and vn-blith. **13..** *Gaw. & Gr. Knt.* 746 With mony bryddez vnblyþe vpon bare twyges, Þat pitosly þer piped for pyne of þe colde. *c* **1400** *Destr. Troy* 8029 For Bresaide the bright vnblithe was his chere. **1535** STEWART *Cron. Scot.* (Rolls) II. 272 So Columba tuik on him greit cuir And bissines, suppois he wes wnblyth.

**2.** Of things: Unpleasant, disagreeable.

In OE. also of persons = showing displeasure.

*c* **1320** *Sir Tristr.* 240 As god wil, it schal be, Vnbliþe. **13..** *E. E. Allit. P.* B. 1017 Þer faure citees wern set, nov is a see called,..Blo, blubrande, & blak, vnblyþe to neȝe. *a* **1400–50** *Alexander* 48 Þan was him bodword vnblyth broȝt to þe sale.

Hence † **Unbli·thely** *adv. Obs.*

**1415** *Pol. Poems* (Rolls) II. 127 Many of hem her hertblode Unblythly bledden upon that bent.

**Unblo·ck,** *v.* [UN-[2] 3.]

**1.** *trans.* To free from an obstruction; to open up, to clear. Also *fig.*

**1611** COTGR., *Desblouquer*, to vnblocke, or open the (blocktvp) passages of. **1656** BAXTER *Reformed Pastor* 193 Our credit may do much to remove prejudice, and to unblock the entrance into mens minds.

**2.** *Cards.* To give free scope to (a partner's suit) by playing an unnecessarily high card. Also *absol.*

**1885** 'CAVENDISH' *Whist Developments* Pref. p. x, The cases where the leader's partner, when he does not head the trick, should play to unblock by retaining his lowest card (playing a higher one). **1899** MELROSE *Solo Whist* 12 This principle is known in whist as 'unblocking' partner's suit.

Hence **Unblo·cking** *vbl. sb.*

**1885** 'CAVENDISH' *Whist Developments* Pref. p. x, Hitherto it has been left to the ingenuity of individuals..to decide when and how the unblocking should be done.

**Unblo·cked,** *ppl. a.* (UN-[1] 8 c.) **1662** GURNALL *Chr. in Arm.* III. 83 This River is unblockt up which makes glad the City of God.

**Unbloo·ded,** *ppl. a.* [UN-[1] 8.]

**1.** = next 1.

[**1775** ASH.] **1784** COWPER *Task* v. 215 The shrew'd Contriver who first..forced the blunt and yet unblooded [**1800** unbloodied] steel To a keen edge. **1818** MILMAN *Samor* 78 To Hela's realm, Unblooded, woundless, must the maid descend. **1831** SCOTT *Ct. Rob.* vii, As a man who dies in peace, and with unblooded hand.

**2.** Of an animal: 'Not marked or distinguished with improved blood'.

**1860** WORCESTER (citing J. N. Brown).

**Unbloo·died,** *ppl. a.* [UN-[1] 8.]

**1.** Not smeared or stained with blood.

**1593** SHAKS. *2 Hen. VI*, III. ii. 193 Who finds the Partridge in the Puttocks Nest, But may imagine how the Bird was dead, Although the Kyte soare with vnbloudied Beake? **1791** HUDDESFORD *Salmag., Monody Death of Dick* 138 Within the tender velvet of his paw Tho' yet unbloodied lurks each virgin claw. **1825** SCOTT *Betrothed* xv, The spirit of the murdered person,..if favourable,..appears with a smiling aspect, and crosses them with her unbloodied hand. **1881** SWINBURNE *Mary Stuart* I. i. 29, I am sick with shame to hear men's jangling tongues Outnoise their swords unbloodied.

† **2.** = UNBLOODY *a.* 2 b. *Obs.*[—1]

**1644** SIR E. DERING *Prop. Sacr.* 39 Your Sacrifice is ἀναίμακτος, *unbloudyed.*

**Unbloo·dily,** *adv.* Also 6 vnbloudely, 7 unbloudily. [UN-[1] 11.] In a bloodless manner; without shedding of blood. (Chiefly *Theol.*)

**1548** GESTE *Pr. Masse* C vi b, Ye ones offering of christ neuer to be reuyued eyther.. bloudely or vnbloudely to purge our synnes withal. **1565** HARDING *Answ. M. Ivelles Chalenge* 145 The lambe of God being layed and sacrificed of priestes vnbloudely. **1624** GATAKER *Transubst.* 46 He saith, that Christs blood is offered in the Eucharist, unbloodily, or not as blood. **1670** C. GATAKER *Harmony Truth* 67 To beleive that the blood of Christ is really shed in the Sacrament unbloodily. **1749** WESLEY *Wks.* (1872) X. 120 In the sacrifice of the mass, the same Christ is contained, and unbloodily offered.

**Unbloo·dy,** *a.* [UN-[1] 7. So OE. *unblōdig* (once), = Du. *onbloedig*, G. *unblutig*, ON. *úblóðigr*, Da. *ublodig*, Sw. *oblodig.*]

**1.** Not attended with (much or any) bloodshed.

**1544** BETHAM *Precepts War* I. cxciv. I v, Nothynge is more profytable,..then by vnbloudye battayle to wynne the mastrye. **1553** BRENDE *Q. Curtius* IV. 47 b, There were slaine of the Percians and Arabies ten thousand, and the victorye was not vnblodye vnto the Macedones. **1607** TOPSELL *Four-f. Beasts* 88 The Spartanes..esteemed more of an vnbloudy then a bloudy victory. **1654** R. CODRINGTON tr. *Iustine* v. 82 They fell not in a sluggish or an unbloody war, but fought to the last man. **1670** MILTON *Hist. Eng.* II. Wks. 1851 V. 64 Petilius Cerealis..had to doe with the populous Brigantes in many Battails, and som of those, not unbloodie. **1870** BRYANT *Iliad* XVII. II. 177 The strife was not unbloody, though of Greeks There perished fewer.

**2.** Not involving the shedding of blood; not characterized by bloodshed.

**1548** [see b]. **1577** HANMER *Anc. Eccl. Hist.* (1663) 201 The unbloody and spiritual Sacrifices of prayers. **1590** SWINBURNE *Testaments* 67 Verie likelie it is to bee vrged with more violent arguments .. then by the vnbloodie blowes of bare words. **1606** SYLVESTER *Du Bartas* II. iv. *Magnif.* 868 Here, many a Mars un-bloudy Combats fights. **1649** MILTON *Eikon.* ix. Wks. 1851 III. 402 Those many.. corporal inflictions wherwith his raign also before this Warr was not unbloodie. **1702** ECHARD *Eccl. Hist.* (1710) 26 Prohibiting the use of wine, and using only inanimate and unbloody sacrifices. *a* **1797** H. WALPOLE *Mem. Geo. II* (1822) I. 324 By the character of the age that disposition is systematized into little mischiefs and unbloody treacheries. **1858** FROUDE *Hist. Eng.* III. 154/2 *note*, The cause of the unbloody termination of the crisis was more creditable to the rebel leaders. **1899** CAPT. A. T. MAHAN *Lessons of War with Spain*, etc. (1900) iii. 106 Blockade..is but one form of the unbloody pressure brought to bear upon an enemy by interruption of his commerce.

**b.** *Theol.* Used with reference to the eucharist, esp. in the phrase *unbloody sacrifice.*

**1548** GESTE *Pr. Masse* C vi b, Theyr auouching .. our synnes clerely to be clensed wyth theyr vnsufferable & vnbloudye sacryfyce of christ. **1559** BP. SCOTT in Strype *Ann. Ref.* (1709) I. App. x. 30 Manyfestly affirmynge Christe to be offered daylye after an unbloody manner. **1581** J. BELL *Haddon's Answ. Osor.* 432 That unbloudy Sacrifice of the body and bloud of Christ, which is dayly exequuted by so many handes of sacrificing shavelinges. **1620** BP. HALL *Hon. Marr. Clergy* Conclusion, I leave my refuter..to the acting of his vnbloudie executions of the Sonne of God. **1651** C. CARTWRIGHT *Cert. Relig.* I. 71 S. Clem. Apost. calleth it a reasonable, unbloudy, and Mysticall Sacrament. **1712** P. METCALFE *Life St. Winefride* (1917) 23 Saint Beuno was preparing to offer the Unbloody Sacrifice of our Redemption. **1753** CHALLONER *Cath. Chr. Instr.* 81 In the Sacrifice of the Altar he [Christ] only dies mystically, and therefore this is an unbloody Sacrifice. **1833** J. WATERWORTH tr. *Veron's Rule Cath. Faith* 127 In this divine sacrifice..the same Christ is present and offered in an unbloody manner, who..offered himself in a bloody manner. **1860** PUSEY *Min. Proph.* 595 To Malachi alone it was reserved to prophesy of the unbloody Sacrifice.

**3.** Not covered or smeared with blood. *Unbloody grave*, that of one who has not died by bloodshed.

*a* **1590** *1st Pt. Contention* E 3, Although the kyte soare with unbloodie beake. *a* **1699** J. BEAUMONT *Psyche* XVI. xciv, Prayers and Persuasions her Engins be, Prepared pure unbloody Bays to gain. **1733** [see UNBRIBED]. **1819** SCOTT *Leg. Montrose* xiv, You might yet lay your head on an unbloody pillow to-night. **1829** — *Anne of G.* xx, As thou desirest to sleep in an unbloody grave, let me warn thee, that the secrets of this night shall remain with thee.

† **4.** Having no blood; bloodless. *Obs.*[—1]

**1615** CROOKE *Body of Man* 258 All these kinds of generation are maimed and imperfect, and therfore the creatures so procreated, are called..vnbloodye and insectile creatures.

**5.** Not bloodthirsty; averse to bloodshed.

*c* **1665** MRS. HUTCHINSON *Mem. Col. Hutchinson* (1846) 339 His unbloody nature desiring to spare the rest of the delinquents. **1824** LANDOR *Imag. Conv.* I. 324 Such is the characteristic expression of this brave unbloody people.

Hence **Unbloo·diness.**

**1851** W. ANDERSON *The Mass* iv. 48 The unbloodiness of the Mass.

**Unbloo·med,** *ppl. a.* (UN-[1] 8.) **1501** DOUGLAS *Pal. Hon.* I. iii, Muscane treis.., Combust, barrant, vnblomit and vnleifit. **1528** LYNDESAY *Dreme* 76 Because vnblomit was baith bank and braye. **1892** *Daily News* 20 Dec. 3/8 Unbloomed pieces of Odontoglossum. **Unblo·ssomed,** *ppl. a.* (UN-[1] 8, UN-[1] 9.) **1611** FLORIO, *Sfioreggiato*, vnblossomed, disflowred. **1861** W. BILLINGTON *Sheen & Shade* 23 Like dainty fruit on the unblossomed boughs. **Unblo·ssoming,** *ppl. a.* (UN-[1] 10.) **1699** EVELYN *Kal. Hort.* (ed. 9) May 60 You may now give a third Pruning to Peach-trees, taking away and pinching off unblossoming Branches.

**Unblo·tted,** *ppl. a.* (UN-[1] 8.)

*a* **1548** HALL *Chron., Hen. VI*, 172 Few or none of this company were unblotted, or undestroied by this dolorous drink of dissimulacion. **1612** BRINSLEY *Lud. Lit.* 39 That the schollars..keep their copies and books fair, vnblotted and vnscrauled. **1615** SYLVESTER *Job Triumph.* I. 69 A man..Of Life unblotted, and unspotted Fame. **1809** [see UNBLURRED]. **1841** D'ISRAELI *Amen. Lit.* (1867) 475 He seems to have been satisfied with his first unblotted thoughts. **1862** T. A. TROLLOPE *Marietta* vii, You would by such an alliance blot the hitherto unblotted scutcheon, which [etc.].

† **Unblow·ed,** *ppl. a. Obs.*[—1] [UN-[1] 8.] = UNBLOWN *ppl. a.*[2]

**1623** (SHAKS.) *Rich. III*, IV. iv. 10 Ah my poore Princes! ah my tender Babes: My vnblowed [*Quartos* vnblowne] Flowres, new appearing sweets.

**Unblow·n,** *ppl. a.*1 [Un-1 8 b, 8 c + Blown *ppl. a.*1]

1. Not driven, tossed, or fanned by the wind.

1638 G. Sandys *Paraphr. Job* xx. 27 Thick darknesse shall infold, a fire unblowne Devoure his Race. 1648 B. Duppa *Soules Solil.* 17 He..might the next year at his return find the same Letters un-blowne away. 1835 Campbell *Fragm. Oratorio Bk. Job* 29 By the fire of his conscience he perisheth In an unblown flame. 1878 B. Taylor *Deukalion* iii. v. 125 Groping first on fields of unblown mist.

2. With *-out*: Not extinguished.

1642 H. More *Song of Soul* i. ii. cxviii, When others eyes plainly can nothing see, Then thy prodigious lamps by night unwet And unblown-out, can read right readily.

3. Not sounded.

1815 Byron *Hebrew Mel., Destr. Sennacherib* v, The tents were all silent, the banners alone, The lances unlifted, the trumpet unblown.

**Unblow·n,** *ppl. a.*2 [Un-1 8 b + Blown *ppl. a.*2] Of flowers: Unopened; still in the bud.

1587 Golding *De Mornay* xiii. 213 The little flowers, which wee see vnblowen in the morning and withered at night. 1775 T. Percival *Ess.* (1776) III. 203 A purple flower, unblown, was suspended in the vessel with the lilas. *a* 1822 [see Unborn *ppl. a.* 1 b]. 1845 Ballard & Garrod *Mat. Med.* 226 *Rosa Gallica*. The dried petals of the shops are the unblown flower-buds. 1850 *Jrnl. Asiatic Soc. Bengal* XIX. 18 *note*, The formation shaped like the unblown water-lily.

*fig.* 1594 Shaks. *Rich. III* (1597) iv. iv. 10 Ah my young princes, ah my tender babes! My vnblowne flowers. *a* 1625 Fletcher *Hum. Lieut.* ii. iv, How yet unripe we were, unblown, unharden'd. *a* 1625—*Love's Pilgrimage* iii. ii, I hold my beauty..As right and rich as hers,..My youth as much unblown. 1784 Cowper *Tiroc.* 446 Boys are at best but pretty buds unblown. 1821 Shelley *Epipsych.* 265 As hair grown gray O'er a young brow, they hid its unblown prime With ruins of unseasonable time. 1893 B. Carman *Lyrics, Why* i, A name unknown, Whose fame unblown Sleeps in the hills.

**Unblu·nder,** *v.* (Un-2 4 b.) 1665 J. Sergeant *Sure Footing* 214 In the mean time let him consider what Logick tells us, that The Conclusion is in the Premises, which reflexion will much unblunder his Thoughts.

**Unblu·nted,** *ppl. a.* (Un-1 8.)

1656 Cowley *Davideis* iii. 12 A Sword whose weight without a blow might slay, Able unblunted to cut Hosts away. 1775 S. J. Pratt *Liberal Opin.* lvi. (1783) II. 168 My feelings were, as yet, unblunted by habitual trespasses. 1779 *Mirror* No. 67, While the warm feelings of benevolence remain unblunted by those artificial manners. 1818 Byron *Juan* xvi. cix, Anacreon only had the soul to tie an Unwithering myrtle round the unblunted dart Of Eros. 1867 Mrs. Whitney *L. Goldthwaite* viii. (1873) 127 The full white light of such unblunted day. *a* 1894 Stevenson *South Seas* ii. ii, [I] woke again with an unblunted sense of my surroundings.

**Unblu·rred,** *ppl. a.* (Un-1 8.) 1809 W. Blake *Descr. Catal.* 51 Mr. B. left it [a picture] unblotted and unblurred. 1880 Baring-Gould *Mehalah* iii. (1884) 43 The sky was absolutely unblurred, and thick besprint with stars.

**Unblu·sh,** *v.* [Un-2 7.] *fig.* To cease to be ashamed.

1620 tr. *St. Augustine's Confessions* viii. ii. 350 Esteeming himselfe guilty..if he should be ashamed,..he did vnblush, and shew a bold face against errour.

† **Unblu·shed,** *ppl. a.*1 *Obs.*-1 [Prob. ad. Du. or Flem. *ongebluscht*: see Blesche *v.*] Unslaked.

*c* 1550 *Vertuous Scholehous* B ij b, Nowe arte thou lyke vnto vnblusshed lymestone, whiche, whan colde water is poured vpon it,..smoketh and burneth vnnaturally.

**Unblu·shed,** *ppl. a.*2 (Un-1 8.)

1854 S. Dobell *Balder* i. 4 Who to me Is as your airy fragrance and mere hues To your unblushed substantial.

**Unblu·shing,** *vbl. sb.* [Un-1 13 or Un-2 8.] The fact of not blushing or of recovering from a blush.

1596 Warner *Alb. Eng.* xi. lxvi. (1597) 280 Her blusshing, and vnblushing, made that Stafford doubted whether It pleased, or displeased.

**Unblu·shing,** *ppl. a.* [Un-1 10.]

1. Not blushing or reddening.

1595 Daniel *Civ. Wars* ii. lvi, People vntrue To God and man,..And with vnblushing faces formost thrust. *a* 1711 Ken *Hymnotheo* ix, That [Beauty] modest, pure, this full of Stain, Unblushing, vain. *a* 1757 T. Edwards *Sonn.* xiv. 3 That bold bad man..pretending still With hard unblushing front the public good. 1773 Goldsm. *Stoops to Conq.* Epil., Th' unblushing Barmaid at a country inn. 1815 W. H. Ireland *Scribbleomania* 124 Bold and unblushing comes Theodore Hooke, For ever enroll'd in rank plagiary's book. 1865 Ellen C. Clayton *Cruel Fort.* I. 207 The very next day, perhaps, she would utter a falsehood with the most unblushing face.

2. Immodest, shameless, unabashed.

1736 Thomson *Liberty* v. 180 The buzz Of masquerade unblushing. 1776 Mickle *Camoens' Lusiad* Introd. 128 This last unblushing falsity, that Gama prays to Christ. 1849 Macaulay *Hist. Eng.* ix. II. 415 He tried to show.. that strenuous and unblushing servility, even when least successful, was a sure title to his favour. 1875 Jowett *Plato* (ed. 2) V. 14 In several passages the Athenian praises himself in the most unblushing manner.

Hence **Unblu·shingly** *adv.*, **Unblu·shingness.**

1782 V. Knox *Ess.* viii. I. 38 They..end with bankruptcy as naturally, as unreluctantly, and as *unblushingly, as if it had been the object of their pursuit. 1812 'Lucius' in *Examiner* 5 Oct. 633/1 Though undenied, and even unblushingly acknowledged. 1894 Sir E. Sullivan *Woman* 26 They so unblushingly affect virtues that they have not got. 1891 Meredith *One of our Conq.* xxxviii, The appalling theme..was taken for a proof of the girl's *unblushingness.

**Unboa·rded,** *ppl. a.* (Un-1 8.) 1825 J. Nicholson *Operat. Mechanic* 451 It is at last brought to a part that is left unboarded and it falls through into troughs placed to receive it. 1892 G. Hake *Mem. 80 Y.* lxvi. 281 The floor is, in one place, ostentatiously unboarded, to show the foundation to be rock.

**Unboa·stful,** *a.* (Un-1 7.)

1727-46 Thomson *Summer* 684 Oft in humble station dwells Unboastful worth, above fastidious pomp. 1747 Collins *Ode Simplicity* ii, O chaste, unboastful Nymph, to thee I call! 1868 Milman *St. Paul's* xix. 494 Unlike most great men, the more he is revealed to posterity, [Wellington] shows more substantial, unboastful, unquestionable greatness. 1890 Ld. Coleridge in J. E. Butler *Recoll. G. Butler* (1893) 483 An athlete quite unboastful, a sportsman silent about his exploits.

**Unboa·sting,** *ppl. a.* (Un-1 10.) 1802 Mrs. J. West *Infidel Father* III. 346 The same manly virtue..and unboasting goodness. 1854 Cdl. Wiseman *Fabiola* (1855) 174 So frank, so generous, so brave, yet so unboasting.

**Unboa·ted,** *ppl. a.* [Un-2 8.] Disembarked; landed from a boat.

1688 R. Holme *Armoury* iii. xv. (Roxb.) 26/2 The Oare by beating the water forceth the boate forward to the place desired: the hooks holds it close to the shoare till all be vnboated.

**Unbo·den,** *ppl. a.* *Obs.* exc. *dial.* [Un-1 8 b. Cf. OE. *unzeboden*, = MDu. and Du. *ongeboden*, MHG. and G. *ungeboten*, ON. and Icel. *ú-*, *óboðinn* (Norw. *uboden*, Da. *ubuden*, Sw. *objuden*).]

1. Uninvited; unbidden.

*a* 1300 *Cursor M.* 14243 Þar was fele boden, als i tru, And mani als-sua vnboden Iuu þider com. 1876 Robinson *Whitby Gloss.* 204 *Unbid*,..or *Unbodden*, uninvited.

†2. *Sc.* Not provided with arms. *Obs.*-1

1456 *Sc. Acts, Jas. II* (1814) II. 45/2 And at na pure man, na vnbodyn, be chargyt to cum to ony raidis in Inglande.

**Unbo·died,** *a.* and *ppl. a.* [Un-1 9 and Un-2 8.]

1. Of souls or spirits: Having no body; not invested with a body; also, removed from the body, disembodied.

The two senses are not clearly distinguishable.

*attrib.* 1532 More *Confut. Tindale* Wks. 387/1 By his power mai the bodily water as wel be a working instrument upon ye vnbodied & vnbodily soule. 1589 Warner *Alb. Eng.* vi. xxxii. (1592) 143 He wonne his Subiects loue,..But, as must ours, so lastly his vn-bodied Soule departs. 1643 Digby *Observ. Sir T. Browne's Relig. Med.* 10 A Separated and unbodyed Soule. 1696 Stanhope *Chr. Pattern* (1711) 177 To indulge those longings and pleasures, which refined and unbodied spirits feel. 1711 Pope *Temple Fame* 101 These..call'd th' unbody'd shades To midnight banquets in the glimm'ring glades. 1721 Tickell *Epist. Death of Addison* 48 In what new region to the just assign'd, What new employments please the unbodied mind? 1791 Cowper *Iliad* ix. 510 No force arrests Or may constrain th' unbodied spirit back. 1810 Crabbe *Borough* xxii. 327 There were they, hard by me in the tide, The three unbodied forms. 1827 Keble *Chr. Year* 2 Lent v, Then may th' unbodied soul in safety fleet Through the dark curtains of the world above.

*pred.* 1513 Douglas *Æneid* iii. v. 42 Oft wald sche cleip and call, and oneith stint, Apone the saulis that wnbodeit war, Besyde Hectouris void tomb standand thair. 1665 J. Spencer *Vulg. Proph.* 71 The Souls of men become half unbodyed, while they hang upon the lips of these extraordinary persons. 1678 *Lively Oracles* iii. § 23 (1684) 270 We must be unbodied our selves before we can perfectly conceive what he is. 1726 Pope *Odyssey* xxiv. 19 The spectres..rest at last, where souls unbodied dwell. *c* 1750 Collins *Ode Superst. Highl.* 60 When, o'er the wat'ry strath, or quaggy moss, They see the gliding ghosts unbodied troop. 1818 Byron *Ch. Har.* iv. ix, My spirit shall resume it—if we may Unbodied choose a sanctuary.

2. Of abstract or immaterial things: Not having a corporeal form.

1606 Shaks. *Tr. & Cr.* i. iii. 16 That vnbodied figure of the thought That gaue't surmised shape. 1678 Cudworth *Intell. Syst.* i. iii. § 37. 157 As Knowledge and Understanding only, which is Art naked, abstract and unbodied. *c* 1800 H. K. White *On Survey Heavens* v, Say, foolish one—can that unbodied fame.. Give a new zest to bliss? 1820 Shelley *Skylark* 15 Thou dost float and run; Like an unbodied joy whose race is just begun. *a* 1851 Moir *Poems, Night-Hawk* xiii, Most lonely voice! most wild unbodied scream!

3. Of substances or material things: Not having a definite form.

1630 Davenant *Just Italian* Wks. (1673) 457 Wilt thou not bleed? not yet? I skirmish with unbodied air. 1651 French *Distill.* v. 163 Salts unbodied are farre more acid then when they have assumed a body. 1652 — *Yorksh. Spa* vii. 67 Those spirits,..becoming to be unbodied (for before they were incorporated with the water),..penetrate even the glass it self. 1845 Bailey *Festus* (ed. 2) 215 Command of mind alone, and of the world Unbodied and all-lovely.

**Unbo·dily,** *a.* Now *rare*. [Un-1 7.] Incorporeal.

1398 Trevisa *Barth. De P. R.* iii. iii. (Tollem. MS.), A soule is an unbodili..substance. 1435 Misyn *Fire of Love* 76 Þe lufar..byrnand into vnbodily halsynge. *c* 1491 *Chast. Goddes Chyld.* 47 Whanne the insighte of the sowle..is cleerly fastnyd in unbodely substaunce. 1532 More *Confut. Tindale* Wks. 387/1 That ye bodely water can not worke vpon the vnbodyly soule. 1587 Golding *De Mornay* xiv. (1592) 203 Herevpon inseweth another controuersie, whether this substance bee a bodily or an vnbodily substance. 1610 Healey *St. Aug. Citie of God* xi. xxi. 424 His intention runnes not from thought to thought, all thinges hee knowes are in his vnbodily presence. 1686 Parr *Life of Ussher* App. 14 The real presence of a Body, and yet unbodily; I suppose those that speak thus, understand as little as I do. 1876 Emerson *Lett. & Soc. Aims, Immort.* Wks. (Bohn) III. 288 Thinking the soul as unbodily among bodies,..the wise man casts off all grief.

Hence **Unbo·diliness.**

1611 Florio, *Incorporeita*, vnbodilinesse.

**Unbo·ding,** *ppl. a.* [Un-1 10 and 5 d.]

1. *Sc.* 'Unpropitious, unpromising' (Jam., 1825).

2. Not anticipating.

1842 Tennyson *Will Waterproof* vi, I grow in worth, and wit, and sense, Unboding critic-pen.

**Unbo·dkined,** *a.* (Un-1 9.) 1844 Mrs. Browning *Duchess May* lxii, Calm she stood; unbodkined through, fell her dark hair to her shoe.

**Unbo·dy,** *v.* [Un-2 7 and 3.]

†1. *intr.* To leave or quit the body. *Obs.*

*c* 1374 Chaucer *Troylus* v. 1550 The fate wold his soule sholde vnbodye, And shapen hadde a mene it out to dryue. 1387-8 T. Usk *Test. Love* i. i. (Skeat) l. 88 These diseses mowen wel, by duresse of sorowe, make my lyfe to unbodye, and so for to dye.

2. *trans.* To remove from the body; to disembody.

*a* 1548 Hall *Chron., Hen. VI*, 83 Death..vnbodiyng the solle of this godly prince,..appalled the hertes..of the Englishe nacion. 1577 Holinshed *Chron.* I. *Hist. Scot.* 138/1 Herevpon followed a feuer..that after xiiij. monethes space vnbodied his ghost. 1602 Warner *Alb. Eng.* Epit. (1612) 394 Prince Edward,..also formerly vnbodied by that Tyrant Gloucester. 1650 T. Vaughan *Anthroposophia* 53, I am unbodi'd by thy Books, and Thee, And in thy Papers finde my Extasie. 1753 A. Murphy *Gray's-Inn Jrnl.* No. 60 II. 46 As soon as the Spirit shall be unbodied, it will instantly smile at our wisest Employments in this World. 1787 *Generous Attachment* I. 174 Would to heaven it was in my power to unbody myself, and like a celestial being, to come to you on a sun beam!

*fig.* 1678 Cudworth *Intell. Syst.* i. ii. 51 Plato and Aristotle ..took..the Theology and Doctrine of Incorporeals, but Unbodied, and Devested of its most Proper and convenient Vehicle, the Atomical Physiology.

†b. *Chem.* To render amorphous. *Obs.*-1

1651 French *Distill.* v. 163 We must..consider which way we may unbody Nitre (because it is scarse possible to get it before it hath received its body).

**Unbodylike** *a.*: see Un-1 7 c.

**Unbo·ggy,** *a.* (Un-1 7.) 1887 Ruskin *Præterita* II. 358 One of the best bits of unboggy ground by the Tummel.

**Unboi·led,** *ppl. a.* (Un-1 8.)

1611 Florio, *Incotto*, vnsodden, vnbaked, vnrosted, vnboyled. 1622 Malynes *Anc. Law-Merch.* 233 Strong wort new runne, or vnboyled wort also luke warme. 1698 *Phil. Trans.* XX. 439 When as the same Water un-boyl'd rose ⅞. 1756 F. Home *Exper. Bleaching* 273 Six grains of the effete lime required 26 drops..to saturate it; 6 gr. of the unboiled, 41 drops. 1794 G. Adams *Nat. & Exp. Philos.* II. xx. 378 Where this transparent blue colour of the unboiled lobster is thinner. 1847 W. C. L. Martin *Ox* 149/1 This disease generally occurs in stalled cattle fed upon unboiled potatoes. 1875 Huxley & Martin *Elem. Biol.* (1877) 29 In a day or two abundant Bacteria will be found in the unboiled flask.

**Unboi·sterous,** *a.* (Un-1 7.) 1768-74 Tucker *Lt. Nat.* (1834) II. 404 Christians of all denominations..will find themselves actuated by the same spirit of a steady, unboisterous zeal.

**Unbokel,** variant of Unbuckle *v.*

**Unbo·ld,** *a.* ? *Obs.* Forms: α. 1 unbeald, 3 onbald, 1, 3-6 un-, vnbald (4 -baald, -balde), 6, 9 *Sc.* unbauld; 4-5 un-, vnbolde, 4, 6 onbolde, 6-7 vnbould. β. 4-5 un-, vnbelde. [Un-1 7. Cf. OHG. *unbald*.] Lacking in boldness; deficient in self-confidence or energy; timid, bashful; backward, slow.

α. *c* 897 K. Ælfred *Gregory's Past. C.* xl. 289 He for his monnðwærnesse aslawað, & wierð to unbeald. *a* 900 Cynewulf *Juliana* 427 Wende ic, þæt þu þy wærra weorþan sceolde..& þy unbealdra. *c* 1205 Lay. 16306 Þer fore maȝen Bruttes beon muchele þe vnbaldur [*c* 1275 onbaldere]. *Ibid.* 28159 Þa weoren Bruttisce men swiðe vnbalde uorþæn. *a* 1310 in Wright *Lyric P.* xxxvi. 100 When we shule suen thy wounde blede, to speke thenne we bueth unbolde. 13.. *Minor Poems of Vernon MS.* xxxvii. 172 As a lord schalt þou be cald, Þer oþure schul stonde behynde vnbald. *c* 1460 *Lament. Virg.* in *Chester Pl.* (Shaks. Soc.) II. 206/2 But whan he lyste they were on slepe, For to wakyn they were unbolde. *c* 1480 Henryson *Thre Deid Pollis* 8 (Bann. MS.), Off thy self, man, thow may be richt vnbald. 1530 Palsgr. 632, I make unbolde or shamfull. *Ibid.*, Twenty honest women can nat make her onbolde agayne. 1611 Florio, *Inaudace*, vndaring, cowardly, fearefull, vnbould. 1825 Jamieson, *Unbauld*, humble, self-abased, *Clydes[dale]*.

β. 13.. *Sir Beues* (A.) 47 Man, whan he falleþ in to elde, Feble a wexeþ and vnbelde Þourȝ riȝt resoun. 13.. *Metr. Hom.* (Vernon MS.) in Herrig's *Archiv.* LVII. 277 Whon þis Monk com to feir elde To wrechen ouht he was vnbelde. *a* 1470 Harding *Chron.* ccix. iii, The which the duke of Burgoyn wold haue weld, Because to hym they were so vnbelde, Theim to haue slayn.

**Unbo·ldened,** *ppl. a.* (Un-1 8.) 1591 Daniel *To C'tess Pembroke* Wks. (Grosart) I. 33 My vnboldned Muse is forced to appeare so rawly in publique. **Unbo·ldness.** (Un-1 12.) *c* 1520 Barclay *Jugurth* 81 b, For a great part therof is wasted and spent..by the vnbol[d]nesse and cowardyse of their captayns. 1611 Florio, *Sbaldanza*, vnboldnesse, vnhardinesse.

† **Unbo·lne,** *v.* *Obs. rare*. [Un-2 7.] *intr.* Of a swelling: To go down; to subside.

*a* 1425 tr. *Arderne's Treat. Fistula*, etc. 93 It makeþ þe place for to vnbolne, and it remeueþ þe rede colour.

**Unbo·lt,** *v.* [Un-2 7 and 3.]

1. *intr.* Of a door: To have the bolt withdrawn.

1470-85 Malory *Arthur* xi. i. 571 And when he came to the chamber..the dores of yron vnlocked and vnbolted. 1680 Otway *Orphan* iii. *Stage Direct.*, The door unbolts. 1711 Mrs. Centlivre *Marplot* i, Ha! the door unbolts; which way shall I get rid of this puppy? 1748 [see Unbar *v.* c].

**2.** *trans.* To draw back the bolt of, to unfasten (a door, etc.).

1598 FLORIO, *Discadenacciare*, to vnboult a doore, to vnbar. 1606 SHAKS. *Tr. & Cr.* IV. ii. 3 Ile call mine Vnckle down; He shall vnbolt the Gates. 1650 ALSOP *Serm.* in A. B. Grosart *Small Sins* (1863) 75 *note*, They bring little boys along with them,..who..unbolt the doors, and let in the whole company of thieves. 1760–72 H. BROOKE *Fool of Qual.* (1809) IV. 124 He..unbolted a door that opened into a garden. 1767 *Phil. Trans.* LVIII. 7, I tried the experiment of unbolting my windows. 1819 SCOTT *Ivanhoe* xx, The hermit speedily unbolted his portal. 1835 DICKENS *Pickwick* xxvii, Putting his arm over the half-door of the bar, coolly unbolting it, and leisurely walking in. 1887 BOWEN *Æneid* II. 266 [They] unbolt Troy's gates, to the hosts of the fleet Entrance give.

**b.** In fig. contexts.

1601 DENT *Pathw. Heaven* 258 To betray vs into the hands of Satan: ye to vnbolt the doore, and let him in to cut our throats. 1648 BP. HALL *Breathings Devout Soul* (1851) 194 To enable me with strength to turn the key, and to unbolt this unwieldy bar of my soul. 1828 T. BROWN *Serm.* 116 We cannot unbolt or break open the gate of the temple of Knowledge.

†**c.** *absol.* To unfold, explain. *Obs.*

1607 SHAKS. *Timon* I. i. 51 *Painter.* How shall I vnderstand you? *Poet.* I will vnboult to you.

**3.** To withdraw, draw back (a bolt).

1655 MRQ. WORCESTER *Cent. Inv.* § 69 To bolt and unbolt ..an hundred Bolts through fifty Staples, two in each.

**4.** To detach by the removal of bolts.

1793 *Trans. Soc. Enc. Arts*, etc. (ed. 2) V. 207 By unbolting and taking off the side pipe.

Hence **Unbo·lting** *vbl. sb.*

[1775 ASH.] 1829 SCOTT *Anne of G.* xix, The noise of the unbolting and unbarring of the gates.

**Unbo·lted,** *ppl. a.*[1] [UN-[1] 8 and UN-[2] 8.]

**1.** Not fastened with a bolt; released by withdrawal of a bolt.

*c* 1580 *Bugbears* I. ii. 132 A window which I left unbolted. 1711 MRS. CENTLIVRE *Marplot* 1, Let me see, is my trap-door unbolted? 1779 JOHNSON *L. P., Milton* (1868) 45 To sleep with doors unbolted. 1874 SWINBURNE *Bothwell* II. xviii, The strait garden-plot.. Whereto the door that opens from beneath Shall stand unbolted. 1891 C. ROBERTS *Adrift Amer.* 57 Most are content to hunt for an unbolted end door.

**2.** Not fastened together with a bolt or bolts.

1793 SMEATON *Edystone L.* § 262 The bolt and shackle.. might get its forelock broken or beat out, and then..it could not be long before the shackle became unbolted.

**Unbo·lted,** *ppl. a.*[2] Also 6 vnbulted, 6–7 unboulted. [UN-[1] 8.] Not bolted or sifted.

1598 FLORIO, *Semolato*, a kind of course vnboulted bread, full of branne. 1611 COTGR., *Pain de fenestre*,..bread made of vnboulted corne. 1616 SURFL. & MARKH. *Country Farme* V. xx. 577 It is made of meale vnboulted, the branne and the meale being all knodden together. 1857 R. TOMES *Amer. in Japan* ix. 200 The flour, however, remains unbolted, but makes a good and sweet bread. 1871 NAPHEYS *Prev. & Cure Dis.* II. i. 406 Take a tablespoonful of unbolted flour.

*fig.* 1570 FOXE *A. & M.* (ed. 2) III. 2033/2 Leauyng the very truth of the matter vnbulted out by the word of God. 1605 SHAKS. *Lear* II. ii. 70, I will tread this vnboulted villaine into morter, and daube the wall of a Iakes with him.

†**Unbo·mbast,** *v. Obs.*—[1] [UN-[2] 3.] *trans.* To take the stuffing out of.

1596 NASHE *Saffron-Walden* Wks. (Grosart) III. 49, I came to vnrip and vnbumbast this Gargantuan bag-pudding, and found nothing in it but dogs-tripes..and sheepes gutts.

**Unbonairty**: see UNDEBONAIRTY *Obs.*

**Unbo·nded,** *ppl. a.* (UN-[1] 8.) 1878 ABNEY *Photogr.* 102 The unbonded atom of silver in the subsalt. 1880 F. G. LEE *Ch. under Q. Eliz.* I. p. xlii, Without it the others are unbonded together.

**Unbo·ne,** *v.* (UN-[2] 4.)

1570 LEVINS *Manip.* 168 To Vnbone, *exossare*. 1598 FLORIO, *Disossare*, to vnbone, to pull out the bones. 1611 COTGR., *Desossé*, vnboned; whose bones are taken out. 1642 MILTON *Apol. Smect.* Wks. 1851 III. 267 So many of the young Divines..have bin seene so oft upon the Stage writhing and unboning their Clergie limmes.

**Unbo·ned,** *ppl. a.* [UN-[1] 8.]

**1.** Not furnished with a bone; boneless.

*a* 1650 MAY *Satir. Puppy* (1657) 32 Her Chastitie being starv'd..and her Fort vanquisht by an unboned Member (the Tongue).

**2.** Not manured with bones.

1849 JOHNSTON *Exp. Agric.* 57 On the old boned field, the crop was four times as bulky as on the unboned field.

**3.** Of meat: Not having the bone(s) removed.

**Unbo·nnet,** *v.* [UN-[2] 7 and 4.]

**1.** *intr.* To remove the bonnet.

1810 SCOTT *Lady of L.* V. xvii, With that he..Unbonneted, and by the wave Sate down his brow and hands to lave. 1850 MRS. GASKELL *Let.* in *Life of C. Bronte* (1857) II. vii. 171, I went up to unbonnet, &c.; came down to tea.

**b.** *esp.* To do this as a mark of respect; to uncover. Also *refl.*

1821 SCOTT *Kenilw.* vii, They hurried to bespeak favour by hastily unbonneting. 1829 — *Anne of G.* xxxii, Do nothing but rise, unbonnet yourself, and be silent. 1879 DIXON *Windsor* I. ii. 14 His pride disdained to unbonnet in the presence of a King of Scots.

**2.** *trans.* To remove the bonnet from.

1828 MISS MITFORD *Village* II. 62 She sat down on her dear sofa, and was forthwith unclogged..and unbonneted. 1868 F. E. PAGET *Lucretia* 183 When people attempt to exert a power which they do not possess,—be they judges unbonneting quakers, or bishops exasperated at 'ribbons'. 1896 *Daily News* 4 Apr. 2/3 Even a foreigner may only disregard the pious custom..at the imminent risk of being rudely 'unbonneted' by any devout Russian whom he may happen to encounter.

Hence **Unbo·nneting** *vbl. sb.*

*c* 1844 MRS. BROWNING *Lett. R. H. Horne* xliii. (1877) II. 24, I excuse the unbonneting. You are Orion, and I can estimate you.

**Unbo·nneted,** *ppl. a.* [UN-[1] 8.]

**1.** Not wearing a bonnet; having the head uncovered, *spec.* as a mark of respect. Also *fig.*

1604 SHAKS. *Oth.* I. ii. 23 My demerites May speake (vnbonneted) to as proud a Fortune As this that I haue reach'd. 1605 — *Lear* III. i. 14 (Qo. 1), This night..vnbonneted he runnes, And bids what will take all. 1818 LAMB *Sonn.* x, Wet and chilly on thy deck I stood Unbonneted and gazed upon the flood. 1823 SCOTT *Quentin D.* xxvi, 'No,' replied the gray-headed seneschal, who attended upon him unbonneted. 1863 THORNBURY *True as Steel* I. 208 Standing unbonneted before his good master.

**2.** Of the head: Not covered by a bonnet.

1820 SCOTT *Monast.* xi, Halbert, his head unbonneted,.. sped up..the little valley of Glendearg. 1876 MARIA M. GRANT *Sun-Maid* ix, A broad parasol shielded her unbonneted head.

**Unbo·nny,** *a. dial.* (UN-[1] 7.) 1830 J. WILSON *Noctes Ambr.* (1856) III. 71 *North.* She sat and smiled to see her long dishevelled tresses reflected in the Fairy's Pool. *Shepherd.* That's no unbonny. 1894 CROCKETT *Lilac Sunbonnet* 34 'Deed I'm nane sae unbonny yet.

**Unboo·ked,** *ppl. a.* [UN-[1] 8. Cf. Du. *ongeboekt*, G. *ungebucht*.] **a.** Not entered, registered, or recorded in a book. **b.** Not booklearned.

Also, in recent use, 'not pre-engaged by booking'.

1586 HOOKER *Hist. Irel.* in *Holinshed* II. 140/1 If any of them were found vnbooked and not registered, that he should be used as a fellon where so euer he was taken. 1859 MASSON *Brit. Novelists* iv. 220 There are rich fields of yet unbooked English life both in northern and in southern England. 1870 LOWELL *Study Wind.* 139 From the unbooked freshness of the Scottish peasant to the most far-sought phrase of literary curiosity.

**Unboo·kish,** *a.* [UN-[1] 7.]

**1.** Not bookish or studious; unlearned.

1604 SHAKS. *Oth.* IV. i. 102 His vnbookish Ielousie must construe Poore Cassio's smiles, gestures, and light behauiours Quite in the wrong. 1644 MILTON *Areop.* (Arb.) 36 It is to be wonder'd how museless and unbookish they were. 1792 G. WAKEFIELD *Mem.* (1804) II. 135 Alexander, like the unbookish bigots who are molesting me, would take offence at the speculations of his preceptor. 1863 *N. & Q.* 3rd Ser. III. 349 We would submit the following explanation of the unbookish housekeeper's little bill. 1882 *Century Mag.* XXIII. 951 Even the most unbookish reader will kindle into a momentary sympathy.

**2.** Free from bookishness.

1887 *Spect.* 19 Mar. 382 Luther, the most unbookish of men.

**Unboo·klearned,** *ppl. a.* (UN-[1] 8 d.)

1633 D. R[OGERS] *Treatise of Sacr.* ii. 67 Meane folkes who..being unbook-learned cannot comprehend such depths as these. *a* 1661 FULLER *Worthies, Northampton* (1662) II. 291 The History of the Bible..hath done as much good to un-book-learn'd people, as any of that kind.

**Unboo·t,** *v.* [UN-[2] 4 and 7.]

**1.** *trans.* To take the boots off (a person).

1598 FLORIO, *Distiuallare*, to vnboote, to pull off boots. 1611 COTGR., *Dehousé*,..vnbooted, or whose boots are pulled off. 1865 J. M. LUDLOW *Epics Mid. Ages* II. 219 Has he no servant nor squire to unboot him? 1893 *Voice* (N. Y.) 21 Sept., 'I will never unboot the son of a slave,' was the lady's gracious response, referring to a marriage ceremony of the time.

**2.** *absol.* To take off one's own boots.

1812 BYRON *Waltz* To Publ., I unbooted, and went to a ball. 1873 LELAND *Egypt. Sketch-Bk.* 97 They were very particular at the door in making us unboot and put on canoes of the native pattern.

**Unboo·ted,** *ppl. a.* (UN-[1] 8 or UN-[2] 8.) 1727 BAILEY (vol. II). 1881 *Cheq. Career* 39 Their comely unbooted feet in the stirrup-irons.

†**Unbo·re,** *ppl. a. Obs.* [UN-[1] 8 b.] = UNBORN *ppl. a.*

*a* 1250 *Prov. Alfred* 449 in *O. E. Misc.* 128 Betere is child vnbore þane vnbuhsum. *c* 1290 *S. Eng. Leg.* I. 19/2 Miracle ore louerd dude for him þe ȝuyt he was un-bore. 1390 GOWER *Conf.* I. 149 Sche wissheth forto ben unbore. *c* 1400 *Beryn* 1210 It wer better he were vnbore, For he doith nat ellis, save atte hazard pley. 1605 SYLVESTER *Du Bartas* II. iii. II. *Fathers* 133 But (O!) more millions of Babes yet un-bore, Then there be sands upon the Libyan shore.

**Unbo·red,** *ppl. a.* Also 7 unboared. (UN-[1] 8. Cf. Du. *ongeboord*, G. *ungebohrt*.)

1598 FLORIO, *Disforato*, without holes, vnbored. 1626 B. JONSON *Staple of N.* II. iv, We ha the dullest, Most unboar'd Eares for verse amongst our females. 1799 G. SMITH *Laboratory* I. 16 It is best to give the turner an unbored rocket. 1829 *Nat. Philos.* I. *Heat* ii. 4 (U.K.), He took an unbored cannon, with the large projecting piece..which is usually cast with cannon to ensure solidity. 1861 *Rep. Smithsonian Instit.* 1860 215 A flat, spiral shell exactly like an unbored *Haliotis*. 1868 G. STEPHENS *Runic Mon.* II. 576 The unbored and therefore current Roman Coins.

**Unbo·rn,** *ppl. a.* [OE. *unboren* (UN-[1] 8 b), = OFris. *un-*, *oen-*, *onbern* (WFris. *on-*, *ûnberne*), MDu. and Du. *ongeboren*, OHG. *ungi-*, *ungaporan* (MHG. *ungeborn*, G. *-boren*), ON. and Icel. *ú-*, *óborinn* (MSw. *oborin*, *-burin*, Norw. *uboren*, Da. *ubaaren*).]

**1.** Not yet born; still to be born. (Freq. with preceding *yet*.) Also in fig. context.

*c* 897 K. ÆLFRED *Gregory's Past. C.* xlviii. 367 Mid ðy ðe hie ofsniðen mid ðy seaxe hefiȝlices ȝedwolan ða unborenan bearn, ðe..beoð mid wordum ȝeeacnode on ȝeleaffullra mode. *c* 1000 ÆLFRIC *Lives Saints* xxiii. 429 Ure hælend se þe unborenum cildum lif sylð on heora modra innoðe. *c* 1200 ORMIN 17327 Forr þatt Nicodem wass ȝet Unnborenn i þatt time Off Haliȝ Gast. *c* 1375 *Cursor M.* 12232 (Fair.), I wende my make ware vnborne [*Cott.* noght born]. *c* 1386 CHAUCER *Melib.* ¶ 2231 Ther is ful many a child vnborn of his mooder that shal sterue yong by cause of that ilke werre. *c* 1465 *Chevy Chase* 9 The chylde may rue that ys vn-born, it wos the mor pitte. 1535 COVERDALE *Eccl.* iv. 2 Wherfore I iudged..him that is yet vnborne to be better at ease then they both. 1560 DAUS tr. *Sleidane's Comm.* 118 b, Young chyldren, as well borne as unborne. 1624 ELIZ. JOCELIN (*title*), The Mothers Legacie, To her vnborne Childe. 1695 PRIOR *Ode after Queen's Death* iii, Ages to come, and Men unborn Shall bless her Name. 1717 POPE *Iliad* x. 61 Yet such his acts, as Greeks unborn shall tell. 1779 WARNER in Jesse *Selwyn & Contemp.* (1844) IV. 294 They had just discovered, by what means I know no more than the child unborn, that [etc.]. 1818 CRUISE *Digest* (ed. 2) VI. 190 The devise would have been void, being to an unborn person for life. 1840 THIRLWALL *Greece* VII. lvi. 169 The throne was to be shared between an idiot and an infant yet unborn. 1887 *Spectator* 22 Oct. 1406 The total abolition of settlements upon unborn lives.

**b.** *transf.* or *fig.* Of time, etc.

1596 SHAKS. 1 *Hen. IV*, V. i. 21 A Portent Of broached Mischeefe, to the vnborne Times. 1667 MILTON *P. L.* VII. 220 Nor staid [He], but..in Paternal Glorie rode Farr into Chaos, and the World unborn. 1712 *Spect.* No. 316 ¶ 5 The present Time alone is ours, the future is yet unborn. 1757 GRAY *Bard* 108 Ye unborn Ages, crowd not on my soul! 1776 GIBBON *Decl. & F.* i. (1782) I. 26 Venice was yet unborn; but the territories of that state..were inhabited by the Venetians. 1822 SHELLEY *Unfinished Drama* 203 A nook of unblown violets And lilies-of-the-valley yet unborn. — *To Jane, Invit.* 7 The brightest hour of unborn Spring. 1884 *Chr. Treasury* Feb. 92/2 It is not a function of human intellect to read the secrets of unborn ages.

**2.** Not born; deprived of birth. Also *fig.*

*a* 1275 *Prov. Ælfred* 447 in *O. E. Misc.* 129 For betere is child vnboren þenne vnbeten. *a* 1300 *Cursor M.* 15372 To mare blis it had him ben Vnborn if þat he ware. *c* 1386 CHAUCER *Shipman's T.* 1372 Yet were me leuere that I were vnborn Than me were doon a sclaundre or vileynye. 14.. *Lat. & Eng. Prov.* (MS. Douce 52) fol. 27 Better is a chylde vnborne þen vnlerned. *c* 1450 *Mirk's Festial* 87 Yf God had don vengeans, anon the world had ben endyd mony a day agoo, and so mony had be vnborne, þat now ben holy sayntys yn Heuen. 1546 J. HEYWOOD *Prov.* (1867) 20 Better vnborne than vntought, I haue heard saie. 1595 DANIEL *Civ. Wars* II. xcvii, This mighty burthen wherewithall they goe Dies vndeliuered, perishes vnborne. 1618 BP. HALL *Contempl. N.T.* I. i, Many a father repents him of his fruitfulnesse, and hath such sons as he wishes unborne. *c* 1645 HEYWOOD & ROWLEY *Fortune by Land & Sea* III, These mischiefs make me wish my self unborn. *a* 1661 [see UNBRED *ppl. a.* 2].

*transf.* 1390 GOWER *Conf.* II. 109 Withdrawgh the Banere of thin Armes, And let thi lyhtes ben unborn.

**3.** Existing without having been born.

1821 SHELLEY *Hellas* 769 Look on that which cannot change—the One, The unborn and the undying.

**Unbo·rne,** *ppl. a.* [UN-[1] 8 b.] Not borne or carried *away* or *out*.

1483 CAXTON *Gold. Leg.* 89/1 On a tyme whan the Jewe was oute theuys cam and robbed alle his goodes and lefte unborn away only thymage. 1847 MEDWIN *Shelley* I. 105 This startling and unborne-out proposition.

**Unbo·rrowed,** *ppl. a.* [UN-[1] 8. Cf. obs. Da. *uborget*.] Not borrowed or taken on loan; esp. *fig.*, not adopted from another, native, inherent, original. (Common from *c* 1700.)

1638 G. DANIEL *Eclog* i. 256 Oh doe not thinke but She may be as faire In nature's bounties, with vnborrwed haire. 1697 DRYDEN *Virg. Past.* IV. 52 The luxurious father of the fold, With native purple and unborrowed gold, Beneath his pompous fleece shall proudly sweat. 1704 *Moderat. Displ.* ix, Bathillo, in his own unborrow'd Strains, Young Sacharissa's Angel Form profanes. 1742 RICHARDSON *Pamela* III. 325 For your Arguments are always new and unborrow'd. 1793 W. ROBERTS *Looker-on* No. 43 (1794) II. 144 His taste was unborrowed, as well as the principles on which he supported it. 1828 LD. GRENVILLE *Sinking Fund* 55 Every portion of unborrowed wealth which this fund has ever received. 1871 FRASER *Life Berkeley* ix. 351 His unborrowed, evidently self-elaborated thought.

**Unbo·rrowing,** *ppl. a.* (UN-[1] 10.) 1776 MICKLE tr. *Camoens' Lusiad* Introd. 134 In this unborrowing sameness, he artfully interweaves the history of Portugal.

**Unbo·som,** *v.* [UN-[2] 5. Cf. Du. *ontboezemen*.]

**1.** *trans.* To bring out from the breast or heart; to give vent to; *esp.* to disclose, reveal.

1588 SHAKS. *L. L. L.* V. ii. 141 Their seuerall counsels they vnbosome shall. 1645 QUARLES *Sol. Recant.* V. 31 Here may thy Griefs unbosome all their grones. *a* 1652 J. SMITH *Sel. Disc.* ix. (1821) 412 But God..is pleased to unbosom his secrets, and most clearly to manifest the way into the holiest of all. 1715 DE FOE *Fam. Instruct.* I. i. (1841) II. 9, I have longed a great while to unbosom my sorrows to somebody. 1749 FIELDING *Tom Jones* XVI. viii, He then unbosomed the violence of his passion to Lady Bellaston. 1844 THIRLWALL *Greece* VIII. 149 It was difficult to find a friend to whom he could safely unbosom his views or wishes. 1854 J. S. C. ABBOTT *Napoleon* (1855) II. xxv. 468 He was freely unbosoming his perplexities and his anguish to General Coletta.

**b.** *refl.* To disclose or reveal one's thoughts, secrets, etc.

1628 T. BALL *Life Preston* (1885) 171 To him he, therefore, now unbossomed himselfe. 1673 *True Worship God* 44 When men unbosome themselves to their Ministers. 1712 STEELE *Spect.* No. 528 ¶ 1, [I] have now taken Pen, Ink, and Paper, and am resolv'd to unbosom my self to you. 1749 FIELDING *Tom Jones* XIV. ix, Mr. Nightingale, taking the old gentleman with him up stairs,..unbosomed himself as follows. 1803 *Censor* 1 Oct. 110 Having been lately in great distress of mind,..I was led..to unbosom myself to several friends. 1848 THACKERAY *Van. Fair* vi, The fat fellow could not be brought to unbosom himself of his great secret-

**c.** *absol.* = prec.

**1733** P. SHAW tr. *Bacon's De Sap. Vet.* B.'s Phil. Wks. I. 593 Princes usually treat such Persons familiarly; and.. think they may with safety unbosom to them. **1772** FOOTE *Nabob* I. Wks. 1799 II. 295 Similarity of sentiments..may have induced him to unbosom to you. **1804** H. K. WHITE *Lett. to B. Maddock* Sept., I am long before I can unbosom to a friend. **1879** MEREDITH *Egoist* xxix, She was really the last person to whom he could unbosom.

**2.** To lay open or disclose to the eye.

**1610** G. FLETCHER *Christ's Vict. & Tri.* II. xi, Rose-buds bright, Unbosoming their brests against the light. **1728–46** THOMSON *Spring* 526 Along these blushing borders, bright with dew,..Fair-handed Spring unbosoms every grace. **1845** BAILEY *Festus* (ed. 2) 258 The world in vain unbosometh her beauty, We have no list to live.

**3.** To empty or exhaust (the bosom). *rare*⁻¹.

**1610** G. FLETCHER *Christ's Vict. & Tri.* I. xiii, Greefes companie..That lankes the cheekes, and pales the freshest sight, Unbosoming the cheerefull brest of all delight.

Hence **Unbo·somer.**

**1850** THACKERAY *Pendennis* xxiv, That great unbosomer of secrets, a cigar. **1895** PURCELL *Life Cdl. Manning* I. xxii. 475 Not as a teacher, but as an unbosomer of his own burdens.

**Unbota·nical,** *a.* (UN-[1] 7.) [1775 ASH.] **1883** G. ALLEN in *Longm. Mag.* July 306 The two plants really differ sufficiently to attract the attention of an unbotanical eye.

**Unbo·ttle,** *v.* [UN-[2] 5.] *trans.* To extract from, or let out of, a bottle. Also *fig.*

**1821** *Q. Rev.* XXIV. 497 As good an insight..as Don Cleophas, by the help of the unbottled Asmodeus, obtained into the intrigues of Madrid. **1862** CARLYLE *Fredk. Gt.* XII. iii. (1872) IV. 149 The general population ..turned out, with emotion again like to unbottle itself. **1895** *Advance* (Chicago) 18 Apr. 1038/2 Without warning he [a blue-jay] unbottled his shrillest whistle.

**Unbo·ttom,** *v.* [UN-[2] 4 and 7.]

**1.** *trans.* To divest of a bottom or foundation; †*fig.*, to deprive of support or stay; to unsettle or make unstable.

**1598** FLORIO, *Diffondare*, to vnbottom. **1642** D. ROGERS *Naaman* 156, I am willing to be informed,..yea, to unbottome my selfe of my old rotten mixtures. **1655** GURNALL *Chr. in Arm.* I. 252 This one consideration might be of excellent use to unbottom a sinner, and abase him so as never to have high thought of himself. **1693** G. FIRMIN *Rev. Davis's Vind.* i. 6 Commonly when we speak of unbottoming a Man from himself, we mean [from] his own goodness.

**2.** *intr.* To make oneself bare-breeched.

**1651** CLEVELAND *Poems, News fr. Newcastle* 45 Then you'll unbottom, though December blow, And sweat i' th' midst of Isicles and Snow.

**Unbo·ttomed,** *ppl. a.*[1] [UN-[1] 8.]

**1.** Having no bottom; bottomless. Also *fig.*

**1615** SYLVESTER *Tobacco Battered* 192 Tobacco's smoakie Mists Which..No small addition of Adustion fit Bring to the smoak of the Unbottom'd Pit. **1630** J. TAYLOR (Water P.) *World's Eighth Wonder* Wks. II. 67/1 The nine and forty wenches, water filling, In tubs vnbottom'd, which was euer spilling. **1667** MILTON *P. L.* II. 405 Who shall tempt with wandring feet The dark unbottom'd infinite Abyss? **1704** *Moderat. Displ.* x, From Faction's dark unbottom'd Cell I come. **1778** *Conciliation* 7 Mir'd and flound'ring in th' unbottom'd Pit. **1802** LEYDEN *Mermaid* 44 If, from the unbottom'd deep,..The sea-snake heave his snowy mane.

**b.** *fig.* Unfathomable.

**1760–72** H. BROOKE *Fool of Qual.* (1809) I. 150, I will no longer..make my ignorance a sounding-line for his [God's] unbottomed wisdom.

**2.** Having no proper foundation; unsupported; not founded *on* or *in* something.

**1640** GAUDEN *Love of Truth* (1641) 21 For errour is so feeble and unbottomed, that it must have some butresses and seeming basis of truth to support it. **1650** ASHMOLE *Chym. Collect.* Prol. 3 Others there are, who out of Ignorance or Mistake, have delivered blinde and unbottomed Fictions. **1675** H. MORE in R. Ward *Life* (1710) 272 The Question,..whether there be no Love unbottomed on Self-love? **1742** YOUNG *Nt. Th.* VIII. 801 Can joy, unbottom'd in reflection, stand? And, in a tempest, can reflection live?

**Unbo·ttomed,** *ppl. a.*[2] [UN-[2] 8.] Deprived of a bottom or foundation; unsettled.

**1674** PENN *Christian Quaker* I. xxv. 126 Thus is this Man Unravel'd, Unreligion'd, Unbottom'd as to his former State. *a* **1684** LEIGHTON *Comm. 1 Pet.* iii. (1849) 263 You are your own deceivers in it,..and are not careful to have your souls really unbottomed from themselves, and built upon Christ.

**Unbought** (vnbǭ·t), *ppl. a.* Forms: (see BUY *v.*). [UN-[1] 8 b.]

**1.** Not bought; unpurchased.

*c* **950** *Lindisf. Gosp.* Matt. x. 8 Unboht *vel* unceaped (L. *gratis*) ȝie onfengon, unboht sellas. *a* **1300** *Prov. Hendyng* in *Rel. Ant.* I. 114 Of un-boht hude men kerveth brod thong. *a* **1300** *Cursor M.* 5410 In all egypti lefte he na land Vn-boght in-til þe king hand. **1535** STEWART *Cron. Scot.* (Rolls) II. 451 Thus tha strave about ane wnbocht gait. *a* **1593** MARLOWE *Ovid's Elegies* I. x. 43 Thankes worthely are due for things vnbought. *c* **1600** CHALKHILL *Thealma & Cl.* (1683) 24 On unbought Delicates their Hunger fed. **1637** COWLEY *Sylva, A Vote* xi, In this true delight, These unbought sports, and happy state, I would not feare, nor wish my fate. *c* **1720** PRIOR *Pontius & Pontia* 23 Some hair I have, I'm sure, unbought, Pray bring your brother-wits to see't. **1790** BURKE *Fr. Rev.* 113 The unbought grace of life ..is gone! **1845** *Kitto's Cycl. Bibl. Lit.* (1847) I. 604/1 Wandering shepherds..depending solely upon the unbought gifts of nature. **1895** CORNISH *Wild England* 310 The unbought beauty of the county is still its main and most potent charm.

†**2.** Unpunished. *Obs.*⁻¹

*a* **1200** *Moral Ode* 59 (Lamb. MS.), Ne scal nan ufel bon unbocht, ne nan god unforȝolden.

**Unbou·nd,** *ppl. a.*[1] Forms: (see BIND *v.*). [UN-[1] 8 b. Cf. MDu. and Du. *ongebonden*, MHG. and G. *ungebunden*, NFris. *ünbünjen*, ON. and Icel. *ú-*, *óbundinn* (Da. *ubunden*, Sw. *obunden*).]

**1.** Not bound or tied up; unfastened. Also with *up*.

*a.* *a* **900** *Laws of Ælfred* c. 35 Ȝif he hine to preoste bescire unbundenne, mid xxx scill. ȝebete. *a* **1000** *Ags. Riddles* xxiii. [xxiv.] 15 Nelle ic unbunden ænigum hyran, nymðe searosælod. *c* **1375** *Sc. Leg. Saints* xlvii. (*Euphemia*) 49 Vnbundine [he] gert hir cum þare Ymang þame þat bundyn var sar. **1523** FITZHERB. *Husb.* § 28 So the barley lyeth vnbounden .iii. or .iiii. dayes.., and than to bynde it.

*β.* *c* **1440** *Alph. Tales* 357 With þe ta syde of hur heade vnbun vpp sho ran to feght agayn þaim of Babilon. **1570** LEVINS *Manip.* 221 Vnbound, *liber*. **1600** FAIRFAX *Tasso* XVI. xviii, Her lockes vnbound, wau'd in the wanton winde. **1667** MILTON *P. L.* III. 603 Though..they binde Volatil Hermes, and call up unbound In various shapes old Proteus from the Sea. **1757** W. WILKIE *Epigon.* II. 47 Now, tam'd by age, his coursers stood unbound. **1808** SCOTT *Marm.* IV. iv, Some damsel flying fast, With hair unbound, and looks aghast. **1892** GUNTER *Miss Dividends* (1893) 248 The moonlight shining through the car window gets into her unbound hair.

**b.** *fig.* Unconfined, unconstrained; not bound by any engagement, vow, etc.

**1390** GOWER *Conf.* II. 393 It helpeth more..than forto crave Of othre men and make him bounde, Wher elles he mai stonde unbounde. *c* **1470** *Gol. & Gaw.* 1040 Bot ilk berne has bene vnbundin with blame. **1532** MORE *Confut. Tindale* Wks. 684/1 God..hauing his power absolute, fre, and vnbounden vnto any maner of hys ordinary course. **1603** J. DAVIES (Heref.) *Microcosmos* Wks. (Grosart) I. 66/1 To court bright beauty match'd, as t'were vnbound. **1790** COWPER *Mother's Pict.* 87, I should ill requite thee to constrain Thy unbound spirit into bonds again. **1859** TENNYSON *Elaine* 1377 Yet thee She fail'd to bind, tho' being, as I think, Unbound as yet.

**c.** Not bound as apprentice. *rare*.

**1497–8** in *Archæol. Jrnl.* XLIII. 168 A fyne lost by R. Bancrofte for..settyng to werk a child vnbound & vnablid.

**2.** Not secured with a band or border of some strong material.

**1531** *Rec. St. Mary at Hill* 38, viij kettelles bound and vnbond. **1547** in Feuillerat *Revels Edw. VI* (1914) 17 One Black chest bounde with Irone & ij other Chestes vnbounde.

**3.** Of books: Not provided with a binding or cover. Also with *up*.

**1541** *Acts Privy Council* 25 Apr., Anthony Marler.. might sell the bibles of the Gret volume unbounde for x. s sterl[ing]. **1549** (Mar.) *Bk. Com. Prayer* Colophon, That no maner of person do sell this present booke unbounde, aboue the price of ii. Shyllynges the piece. **1690** LOCKE *Hum. Und.* III. x. § 27 A Book-seller, who had in his Ware-house Volumes that lay there unbound, and without Titles. **1720** HEARNE *Collect.* (O.H.S.) VII. 161 The Textus..will be sent unbound, as desired. **1831** CARLYLE *Sart. Res.* I. xi, One other leaf of that mighty volume..left to fly abroad, unprinted, unpublished, unbound up. **1896** T. L. DE VINNE *Moxon's Mech. Exerc., Printing* 401 The complete book on printing, unbound, then cost 14s. 4d.

*fig.* **1592** SHAKS. *Rom. & Jul.* I. iii. 87 This precious Booke of Loue, this vnbound Louer, To Beautifie him, onely lacks a Couer.

**4.** Of substances: In a loose or free state.

**1697** DRYDEN *Virg. Georg.* I. 98 While the Turf lies open, and unbound, Succeeding Suns may bake the Mellow Ground. **1902** *Brit. Med. Jrnl.* 14 June 146 Their methods ..would only extract and precipitate the unbound purin.

**Unbou·nd,** *ppl. a.*[2] *rare*⁻¹. [UN-[1] 8 + BOUND *ppl. a.*[1]] Unprovided, destitute.

*a* **1300** *Cursor M.* 24034, I stakerd sua i moght not stand, Bot als þai me up-held wit hand Vn-bun was i o bote.

†**Unbou·nd,** *ppl. a.*[3] *Obs.* [UN-[1] + BOUND *v.*] Unbounded; boundless.

**1593** Q. ELIZ. *Boeth.* II. pr. vii. 53 The lasting of any longest tyme, if it be matcht with vnbounde eternitie, not small but none shall seeme. *a* **1619** FOTHERBY *Atheom.* II. ii. § 1 (1622) 198 The vnlimited and vnbound extension of the Appetites of Man. *c* **1658** *Elegy on Cleveland* 16 C.'s Wks. (1687) 284 Such was the Fate of my weak Streams, that ran To drown themselves in th'unbound Ocean. *c* **1725** RAMSAY *Some of Contents* ii, Dunbar does with unbound ingyne, In satyre, joke, and in the serious schyne.

**Unbou·nd,** *v. rare.* [UN-[2] 3.] *trans.* To deprive of bounds or limits.

**1598** SYLVESTER *Du Bartas* III. ii. *Colonies* 178 The thirst of Vengeance, and that puffing breath Of elvish Honour.. Un-bound all Countries. **1612** DRAYTON *Poly-olb.* v. 104 Gowr, whose promontory (plac'd to check the ocean's pow'r) Kept in Severne yet herself, till being growne too great Shee with extended armes unbounds her ancient seat.

**Unbound,** pa. pple. of UNBIND *v.*

**Unbou·ndable,** *a.* (UN-[1] 7 b.) **1622** R. HARRIS *Gods Goodnes* 17 Mercy in the first sense, is Negatiuely endlesse, that is, vncapable of end, because vnboundable for being. **1837** EMERSON *Misc.* (1855) 91 Who shall set a barrier on any one side to this unbounded, unboundable empire?

**Unbou·ndably,** *adv.* (UN-[1] 11.) **1607** DEKKER *Westw. Hoe* Wks. 1873 II. 289, I am so infinitly, so vnboundably beholding to you.

**Unbou·nded,** *ppl. a.* [UN-[1] 8.]

**1.** Not bounded or limited in extent. Also *fig.*, of the Deity.

**1598** FLORIO, *Interminato*, vnbounded, boundles, vnlimited. **1667** MILTON *P. L.* x. 471 With what paine [I have] Voyag'd th' unreal, vast, unbounded deep Of horrible confusion. *a* **1711** KEN *Hymns Festiv.* Poet. Wks. 1721 I. 270 God's Presence is himself; for none Unbounded is but God alone. **1730** THOMSON *Autumn* 902 Mean-time, light-shadowing all, a sober calm Fleeces unbounded ether. **1808** SCOTT *Marm.* IV. Introd. 160 The wild unbounded hills we ranged. **1821** BYRON *Heav. & Earth* I. iii, Earth shall be ocean! And no breath, Save of the winds, be on the unbounded wave! **1870–2** LIDDON *Elem. Relig.* iv. § 1 The Unbounded, All-powerful Being is alone the good.

**b.** Unlimited in amount.

**1646** CRASHAW *Steps to Temple, Miracle of Multiplyed Loaves* 3 See here an easie Feast,..A subtle Harvest of unbounded bread. **1695** PRIOR *Ode Queen's Death* xxiii, As Waters from her Sluces, flow'd Unbounded Sorrow from her Eyes. **1709** HEARNE in *R. Glouc. Chron.* (1724) II. 603 Ador'd and flatter'd upon account of their Dignity and unbounded Wealth. **1763** WILKES *Corr.* (1805) I. 89 Testimonies of an unbounded confidence in your veracity and good faith. **1849** MACAULAY *Hist. Eng.* vii. II. 257 The writers generally expressed unbounded reverence and affection for William. **1867** DICKENS *Lett.* (1880) II. 272 The enthusiasm has been unbounded. **1897** MARY KINGSLEY *W. Africa* 474 Owing entirely to..her own unbounded courage and energy.

**2.** Not restrained or kept within limits; unchecked, uncontrolled.

Not always clearly distinguishable from prec. sense.

**1608** CHAPMAN *Byron's Consp.* II. i. 47 In such air breathe his unbounded spirits, Which therefore well will fit such conjurations. **1647** N. WARD *Simple Cobler* 49 They are a good People, that undoe not their Prince, by any one of their unbounded Liberties. **1736** BUTLER *Anal.* I. v. Wks. 1874 I. 108 Prosperity itself..begets extravagant and unbounded thoughts. **1794** R. J. SULIVAN *View Nat.* I. iii. 14 Their unbounded claims..to temporal..dominion. **1823** SCOTT *Quentin D.* i, A tone of romantic and chivalrous gallantry (which, however, was often disgraced by unbounded license). **1830** HERSCHEL *Study Nat. Phil.* 7 Cherishing as a vital principle an unbounded spirit of enquiry. **1854** BANCROFT *Hist. U. S.* I. ii. 34 Leaving his wife to govern the island, he and his company, full of unbounded expectations, embarked for Florida.

**3.** Of persons (and animals): Unchecked or uncontrolled in action.

**1612** *Two Noble K.* I. ii. 70 A most unbounded Tyrant. **1656** COWLEY *Davideis* IV. 241 Let his power loose, and you shall quickly see How mild a thing unbounded Man will be. **1681** DRYDEN *Abs. & Achit.* I. 762 Then they are left Defenceless, to the Sword Of each unbounded, Arbitrary Lord. **1725** DE FOE *Voy. round World* (1840) 312 The fellows were so rude, so ungovernable and so unbounded in their hunting after gold. **1728** SAVAGE *Bastard* 19 Nature's unbounded son, he stands alone, His heart unbiass'd, and his mind his own. **1818** SCOTT *Hrt. Midl.* xxxvi, Numberless flocks and herds, which seemed to wander unrestrained and unbounded through the rich pastures.

**b.** Profusely generous or liberal.

*a* **1704** T. BROWN *Praise Drunken.* Wks. 1730 I. 35 Their darling humour, avarice, is lost, and their hearts become unbounded, and free as the God by whom they are possess'd. **1825** SCOTT *Talism.* xxiii, It is well known that the high esteem of the European knowledge and courage made the Soldan unbounded in his gifts to those who..had been induced to take the turban.

**Unbou·ndedly,** *adv.* [f. prec.] Without limitation; beyond all bounds.

**1611** COTGR., *Librement*, freely, frankly, vnboundedly. **1619** HIERON *Wks.* II. 431 Nor to bee so vnboundedly subiect vnto kings, as not to regard what is owing from us vnto God. **1674** *Govt. Tongue* ix. § 1. 150 So unboundedly mischievous is that petulant member, that heaven and earth are not wide enough for its range. **1781** H. DOWNMAN tr. *Voltaire's Dram. Wks.* I. 248 My heart relies upon thy faith, Unboundedly relies. **1845** BAILEY *Festus* (ed. 2) 227, I was born To gratify myself unboundedly, So that I wronged none else. **1881** MRS. H. HUNT *Child. Jerus.* 122 She was unboundedly fond of babies.

**Unbou·ndedness.** [f. as prec.] Unlimitedness, boundlessness.

**1640** BP. REYNOLDS *Passions* xviii. 192 This unboundednesse of Desires we are to take heed of. **1678** CUDWORTH *Intell. Syst.* 389 The unlimitedness and unboundedness of its power, declareth it to be infinite. **1715** CHEYNE *Philos. Princ. Nat. Relig.* II. ii. 58 Infinitude [imports] the unboundedness of these Degrees of Affections, or Properties. **1839** BAILEY *Festus* 240 When thus to one poor spirit He gives His hand, He seems to impart His own unboundedness Of bliss. **1860** PUSEY *Min. Proph.* 321 With increased knowledge of Him, come higher perceptions of the unboundedness of God's love to us.

**Unbounden,** obs. var. UNBOUND *ppl. a.*, and obs. pa. pple. of UNBIND *v.*

†**Unbou·ndless,** *a. Obs.*⁻¹ [UN-[1] 5 a.] Unbounded, boundless.

**1624** in Capt. J. Smith *Virginia* III. ii. 45 Thus God vnboundlesse by his power, Made them thus kind.

**Unbou·nteous,** *a.* (UN-[1] 7.) **1645** MILTON *Tetrach.* Wks. 1851 IV. 156 Nay such an unbounteous giver we should make him, as in the fables Jupiter was to Ixion.

**Unbou·ntifulness.** (UN-[1] 12.) **1660** INGELO *Bentiv. & Ur.* I. (1682) 144 Want..is not from God's unbountifulness, but men's folly and wickedness. **1730** BAILEY (fol.), *Illiberality*,..unbountifulness.

†**Unbow·,** *v. Obs.* [UN-[2] 3.] *trans.* To unbend, to straighten.

**1538** ELYOT, *Decircino*,..to vnbowe, or to bringe out of compasse, or roundenesse. **1621** QUARLES *Hadassa* ii. Wks. (Grosart) II. 57/2 Her lowly bended body she vnbow'd. **1653** H. MORE *Antid. Ath.* II. i. § 6 As in little pieces of Wood naturally bow'd like a Man's Elbow, the Carver doth not unbow it but..shapes it into the Compleat Figure of a Man's Arm.

*fig.* **1639** FULLER *Holy War* III. vi. (1840) 124 Because looking back would unbow his resolution.

†**Unbow·able,** *a. Obs.* [UN-[1] 7 b.] Unbendable, inflexible.

**1537** BIBLE (Matthew) *Ps.* ii. 9 *note*, A rodde of yron for a sure and unbowable domynyon. **1583** STUBBES *Anat. Abus.* I. (1879) 76 So long as a sprigge, twist, or braunche, is yong, it is flexible and bowable.., but if we tarie till it be a great tree, it is inflexible and unbowable. **1611** COTGR., *Imployable*, inflexible, vnbowable.

**Unbow·dlerized,** *ppl. a.* (Un-1 8.) **1894** Wilkins & Vivian *Green Bay Tree* II. 50 A private and unbowdlerized version of 'Helen of Troy'. **1896** Mrs. Caffyn *Quaker Grandmother* 54 An entirely un-bowdlerised library.

**Unbow·ed,** *ppl. a.* [Un-1 8.] Not bowed or bent. Freq. *fig.*

*c* **1374** Chaucer *Boeth.* iv. met. vii. (1868) 148 þe laste of his labours was þat he sustenede þe heuene vpon his nekke vnbowed. **1593** Shaks. 2 *Hen. VI*, iii. i. 16 He..passeth by with stiffe vnbowed Knee. **1610** — *Temp.* i. ii. 116 Confederates..To giue him Annuall tribute..and bend The Dukedom yet vnbow'd..To most ignoble stooping. **1648** Hexham ii, *Ongekromt*, Vncrooked, or Vnbowed. **1816** Byron *Ch. Har.* iii. xxxix, He stood unbow'd beneath the ills upon him piled. **1865** W. G. Palgrave *Arabia* I. 205 His tall stature, absolutely unbowed by years. **1879** M. Pattison *Milton* 131 In Andrew Marvel Milton found one congenial spirit, incorruptible amid poverty, unbowed by defeat.

**Unbow·ed,** *a.* [Un-1 + Bow *sb.*1] Of pigs: Not furnished with a bow-shaped piece of wood to impede their movements.

**1624** in H. Maclean *Watermillock Reg.* (1908) 157 That none..shall keep their swine unbowed..sub poena for every swine so unbowed iiij d. **1794** W. Hutchinson *Hist. Cumbld.* I. 163 *note*, The tenants are subject to pains..for swine going unbowed in the time of harvest.

† **Unbow·el,** *v. Obs.* [Un-2 4.]

**1.** *trans.* To disembowel (a person or animal); to eviscerate, exenterate.

**1552** Huloet, Vnbowell, *exentero.* **1591** R. W[ilmot] *Tancred & Gism.* Argt., Afterward .. he commanded the Earle to be attached, imprisoned, strangled, vnbowelled. **1606** S. Gardiner *Bk. Angling* 123 The hand of this cunning worke-man vnbowelleth him. **1651** Howell *Venice* 84 After the Duke is dead, he is unbowell'd, his body embalm'd. *a* **1691** Boyle *Hist. Air* (1692) 182 This prepared, they first unbowelled the corps.

*fig.* **1592** Nashe *Four Lett. Confut.* Wks. (Grosart) II. 198 Before I vnbowell the leane Carcase of thy book any further. **1654** Cokaine *Dianea* iv. 336 All Vices are Vices; but Cruelty holds the preheminence. It spoiles, unbowels, unsoules the World. **1713** C'tess Winchelsea *Misc. Poems* 389 Wou'd you then have me live, when thus unbowell'd, Without the Charms of my Aristor's presence?

**b.** *refl.* (*a*) To exhaust oneself; to expend one's strength or means; (*b*) to unbosom oneself.

(*a*) **1647** A. Ross *Mystag. Poet.* i. (1675) 30 Covetous men are like spiders, they unbowel, that is they consume and spend themselves with care and toyl to catch a fly. **1650** Howell *Giraffi's Rev. Naples* i. 27 With such cries..they did unbowell themselves to provide furniture for the War. (*b*) **1650** H. Brooke *Conserv. Health* 205 Thus..did this famous Deviner unbowel himself and thereby..made some amends for his former impostures. **1655** Sanderson *Serm.* (1681) ii. Pref., Since I had thus adventured to unbowel my self.

**2.** *fig.* To empty of contents; to open up; to make hollow. Also in fig. context.

**1597** J. King *On Jonas* (1618) 78 They ransack all the corners of the shippe, vnbowell her inmost cells, throwe out commodities. **1610** *Histrio-m.* iii. 62 Then stooping suiters ..May groaning come, unbowelling the bagges Of their rich burthens in your wide-mouth'd deskes. **1646** Gataker *Mistake Removed* To Rdr. 2 Partly to unbowel and lay open some part of that unsound stuff that lies closely couched in this covert vault. *a* **1785** Glover *Athenaid* xxvii, A native arch .. Expands before an excavation deep, Unbowelling the hill.

**b.** To open up or disclose by investigation or exposition. (Common in 17th c.)

**1606** J. King *Serm.* Sept. 15 The whole book of God must be vnbowelled, and all the wit of man ransackt, to finde out a stile honorable enough for their new erected presbytery. **1659** E. Hopton *Encomium* in T. Barker *Art of Angling* (ed. 2), Thou hast unbowell'd Dame Natures part In a *Vade mecum*. **1693** Norris *Pract. Disc.* (1698) IV. 178 When this Great Thought comes to be open'd and unbowell'd, to be unravell'd and laid bare.

**c.** To display or reveal.

**1650** Baxter *Saints' R.* i. vii. 91 When we shall feed at Josephs own house,..when he shall fully unbowel his love unto us, and take us to dwell in Goshen by him.

Hence † **Unbow·elling** *vbl. sb. Obs.*

*a* **1639** Spottiswoode *Hist. Ch. Scot.* (1655) vi. xiii. 306 Whether they perceived any sign of poyson at his unbowelling. *a* **1653** Binning *Serm.* (1845) 340 The not unbowelling of our hidden affections. **1694** Westmacott *Script. Herb.* 41 The embalmer..then salted, without any Incision or unbowelling, the whole body with Sal Nitri.

† **Unbow·elled,** *ppl. a. Obs.* [f. prec.] Disembowelled. Also *fig.*

**1592** Kyd *Sp. Trag.* i. ii. 61 There legs and armes lye bleeding on the grasse, Mingled with weapons, and vnboweld steedes. **1637** N. Whiting *Albino & Bellama* 32 Th' hollow belly of th' un-boweld earth. **1655** Vaughan *Silex Scint.* i. (1858) 27 Unbowel'd nature, shew'd thee her recruits And change of suits.

**Unbow·elled,** *a.* [Un-1 9.] Having no bowels; *fig.* unaffectionate, pitiless.

**1592** R. D. *Hypnerotomachia* 17, I issued foorth of the unbowelled monster. **1656** Earl Monm. tr. *Boccalini's Advts. fr. Parnass.*, etc. 241 The unbowel'd love which they bear unto them, is more prejudicial to them, then is their enemies implacable hatred. *Ibid.*, *Pol. Touchstone* 403 That unbowel'd beyond-sea Renegado. **1815** Milman *Fazio* (1821) 81 As deaf and hollow as the unbowell'd winds.

**Unbow·ing,** *ppl. a.* [Un-1 10.] Unbending, unyielding. Hence **Unbow·ingness.**

*a* **1300** *Cursor M.* 27243 Wandring in quere, Vn-boandnes a-bote þe autere. *Ibid.* 27796 O suernes cums..Hardnes of hert and vnboand [*v.rr.* vnbowand, vnboghande]. **1382** Wyclif *Heb.* x. 23 We..holde the confessioun of oure hope vnbowynge, or that may not be foldyn.

**Unbow·some,** *a. Obs.* exc. *dial.* [Un-1 7. Cf. NFris. *ünbügsom*, MDu. *onboochsam*, Du. *onbuigzaam*, G. *unbeugsam.*]

**1.** = Unbuxom *a.* 1.

*c* **1290** *S. Eng. Leg.* I. 266/185 Ake þat ich onbouȝsum ne beo i-seie..I-chulle bidde for þe, mi leoue fader. **1340** *Ayenb.* 21 Þou hest y-by onboȝsam to þine uader and to þine moder. *c* **1340** Hampole *Pr. Consc.* 8596 Grysely devels salle gang and com On þe synfulle þat tylle God war unbowsom. **1818** Hogg *Brownie of B.* i, Ye hae a dour, stiff, unbowsom kind o' nature in ye.

**2.** *dial.* Unbending, stiff.

**1818** Hogg *Wool-gatherer* Tales (1866) 80/2 It makes.. but an unbowsome overleather. **1894** Heslop *Northumbld. Gloss.* 755 He's..ungainly an' unbowsome.

Hence **Unbow·someness.**

**1340** *Ayenb.* 33 Þe uerste [point] is onboȝsamnesse, huanne þe man nele do þet me him zayþ ine penonce. *c* **1400** *Cursor M.* 27616 (Cott. Galba), Of pride cumes als vnbowsumnes. *c* **1450** *St. Cuthbert* (Surtees) 3377 Þai wer glad and somwhat shamed,..Þaim shamed of þair vnbowsomnes.

**Unbo·x,** *v.* [Un-2 5.] *trans.* To take out of a box.

**1611** Cotgr., *Desböeter*, to vnbox, or take out of a box. **1817** Keats *Let.* Wks. 1889 III. 51, I went and unbox'd a Shakespeare. **1864** P. M. Irving *Life W. Irving* IV. 31 He brought home also a picture...After tea he took mallet and chisel, and proceeded to unbox it. **1883** *Standard* 10 Aug. 2/1 Minehead reached, horses were quickly unboxed.

**Unboy·,** *v.* [Un-2 7 and 6 b.] **a.** *intr.* To grow out of boyhood. **b.** *trans.* To divest of boyishness; to make a man of.

**1611** Florio, *Sgarzonare*, to become from a boy to a man, to vnboy, to vnlackie. **1647** Clarendon *Hist. Reb.* viii. § 179 He began to say..that it was now time to unboy him, by putting him into some action and acquaintance with business.

**Unboy·ish,** *a.* (Un-1 7.) **1864** Miss Yonge *Trial* I. 277 The steady low voice, and unboyish language. **1881** Mary C. Hay *Missing*, etc. II. 43 It might have grown into an idle and unboyish habit.

**Unbra·ce,** *v.* [Un-2 3.]

**1.** *refl.* or *trans.* To free (oneself or another) from bands or braces forming part of clothing or armour. Also *absol.*

*c* **1400** *Laud Troy Bk.* 7007 Ector affter euere chases, At eche a lepe his stede vnbrasis. **1420–2** Lydgate *Thebes* 4284 He alighte doun, And brotherly, with a pitous face, To saue his lyf gan hym to vnbrace. **1598** Florio, *Sbracciarsi*, to vnbrace ones selfe. **1633** Rowley *Match at Midn.* iv, *Widow.* You will not be so uncivil to unbrace you here?.. *Alex.* I will off with my doublet to my very shirt. **1637** Heywood *Pleas. Dial.* xviii. 147 *Par.* Have them all stript naked.. *Merc.* Vnbrace your selues, put off, and nothing hide.

**b.** *fig.* To lay open; to disclose, reveal.

**1607** Tourneur *Rev. Trag.* iv, Now y'are both present, I will unbrace such a close private villain Unto your vengeful swords.

**2.** *trans.* To undo, to loosen or untie, to relax (a band, grasp, etc.).

*c* **1475** *Rauf Coilȝear* 629 The ȝaip ȝeman to the ȝet is gane; Enbraissit [*read* vn-] the bandis beliue. *c* **1475** *Lament. Mary Magd.* xxxi, Than gan I there min armes to vnbrace Up lifting my handes ful mourningly. **1590** Spenser *F. Q.* ii. iv. 9 The knight..Knit all his forces, and gan soone vnbrace His grasping hold. **1598** Yong *Diana* 189 A faire and daintie hand he did vnbrace. **1718** Pope *Iliad* xiv. 245 The queen of love..from her fragrant breast the zone unbraced. **1762–9** Falconer *Shipwr.* ii. 521 Arion..The cordage of the leeward guns unbraced.

**b.** To loosen, detach, or set free by the undoing or removal of braces or bonds.

**1593** Nashe *Christ's T.* Wks. (Grosart) IV. 71 The resplendent eye-out-brauing buildings of your Temple, (like a Drum) shal be vngirt & vnbraced. **1627** Drayton *Agincourt* ccix, Now with mayne blowes their Armours are vnbras'd. **1654** Whitelocke *Jrnl. Swed. Emb.* (1772) II. 365 The gunner was so amazed with the daunger, that he forgott to unbrace the gunnes, and shott away the maine sheate. **1714** '*Nestor Ironside*' *Orig. Canto Spenser* xli, So gan they soon her Armoury unbrace. **1813** Scott *Trierm.* ii. xxiv, Gay shields were cleft, and crests defaced, And steel coats riven, and helms unbraced. **1828** Landor *Imag. Conv.* III. 133 Unbrace his armour—loose the helmet first.

**c.** To relax the tension of (a drum).

**1593** [see 2 b]. **1636** Massinger *Bashf. Lover* iv. i, Had you been Employed to mediate your father's cause, My drum had been unbraced, my trumpet hung up. **1691** Dryden *K. Arthur* iii. i, Furl up our Colours, and Unbrace our Drums.

† **3.** To carve (a mallard or duck). *Obs.*

The two earlier instances are repeated in many later copies of the list of 'proper terms'.

*c* **1470** *Hors, Shepe, & G.* (Roxb.) 33 A malard unbrased; a cony unlaced. **1508** W. de Worde *Bk. Keruynge* in *Babees Bk.* (1868) 265 Vnbrace that malarde. **1687** J. Shirley *Rich Closet of Rarities* 52 In unbracing a Mallard, Observe that you raise up the pinion and leg, not taking them off. **1688** R. Holme *Armoury* iii. 78 Unbrace that Duck or Mallard. **1771** Mrs. Haywood *New Present for Maid* 269 To unbrace a Duck. *Ibid.* 270 To unbrace a Mallard. **1804** Farley *Lond. Art Cookery* (ed. 10) 293 To unbrace a mallard or duck, first raise the pinions and legs.

**4.** *fig.* † **a.** To allow or make (the heart) to relax in feeling; to free (oneself) from restraint.

*c* **1485** Skelton *Death Edw. IV*, 93 O ye curtes commyns, your hertis vnbrace Benyngly now to pray for me also. ? *a* **1500** *Chester Pl.*, *Ador. Sheph.* 448 Nowe pray we to hym with good intent, And sing I will, and me unbrace. ? **1511** Sir T. Phelyppis in *Early XVI Cent. Lyrics* lxvii. 24 The rose I suppose thyn hart vnbrace.

**b.** To render lax or slack; *esp.* to deprive of firmness or strength in this way; to enfeeble, weaken.

**1711** Addison *Spect.* No. 249 ¶ 5 Laughter, while it lasts, slackens and unbraces the Mind, weakens the Faculties. **1715** Pope *Iliad* iv. 365 But wasting years, that wither human race, Exhaust thy spirits, and thy arms unbrace. **1758** Johnson *Idler* No. 9 ¶ 2 What rules has he proposed totally to unbrace the slackened nerve? **1799** *Phil. Trans.* XC. 2 The muscles of the malleus having been deemed sufficient for bracing and unbracing it. **1865** Lowell *Wks.* (1890) V. 293 The war..which invigorated bolder men, unbraced him. **1884** *Fortn. Rev.* Jan. 37 Everything has been done that could be done..to unbrace the sinew of national resistance.

**c.** *absol.* To become lax; to lose firmness.

**1693** Dryden *Juvenal* vi. 210 Let her Eyes lessen, and her Skin unbrace. **1699** Garth *Dispens.* 37 At thy Approach the Springs of Nature start, The Nerves unbrace. *a* **1718** Parnell *Gift of Poetry* 455 When spirits stop their course, when nerves unbrace, And outward action and perception cease.

**Unbra·ced,** *ppl. a.* [Un-1 8 or Un-2 8.]

**1.** With dress or part of dress unfastened or loosened.

*c* **1510** Barclay *Mirr. Gd. Manners* (1570) E v, Their false heare inuolued, in nettes intricate, Their brestes vnbraced, their smerking paynted chin. *a* **1529** Skelton *E. Rummyng* 134 Some wenches come vnlased, Some huswyues come vnbrased. **1601** Holland *Pliny* II. 308 Women,.. with their haire hanging loose about their eares, vngirt, vnlaced, and vnbraced. **1602** Shaks. *Ham.* ii. i. 78 Lord Hamlet with his doublet all vnbrac'd, No hat vpon his head. **1622** Fletcher *Sea-Voy.* ii. i, Methought a sweet young man..Stole slylie to my Cabin all unbrac'd. **1821** Scott *Kenilw.* xiv, He found Lord Sussex dressed, but unbraced and lying on his couch. **1875** Whyte Melville *Katerfelto* xiii. 120 Presently steals in a slipshod drawer, unbraced, uncombed, unwashed.

**2.** Of a drum: Not made tight or tense; released from tension.

**1625** B. Jonson *Staple of N.* Induct., He doth sit like an vnbrac'd Drum with one of his heads beaten out. **1669** Dryden *Tyrannic Love* i. i, Like the hoarse murmurs of a trumpet's sound, And drums unbraced. **1703** Prior *Advice to Painter* 43 Near this, erected on a Drum unbrac'd, Let Heaven's and James's Enemy be plac'd. **1713** Mrs. Centlivre *Wonder* ii. i, Poor Gentleman, he is as melancholy as an unbraced drum.

**3.** Loosened, relaxed. Also *fig.*

**1621** Quarles *Argalus & P.* (1678) 55 The little winged god with arm unbrac'd, And Bow unbent. **1760** *Cautions & Adv. Officers of Army* 98 Little Good can be expected from him whose..unbraced Nerves..denote him fitter for his Grave..than for his Duty. **1776** Paine *Com. Sense* (1791) 73 The property of no man is secure in the present unbraced system of things.

**4.** Not braced or strengthened (*by* something).

**1809–10** Coleridge *Friend* (1865) 216 Their sensibilities unbraced by the co-operation of fixed principles. **1883** H. Drummond *Nat. Law in Spir. W.* (1884) 354 His character untouched, his will unbraced.

**Unbra·celeted,** *a.* (Un-1 9.) **1855** Patmore *Angel in Ho.* ii. iii. 2 With arm and wrist All warmth and light, unbraceleted. † **Unbra·ck,** *v. Obs.* (Un-2 5: cf. Brack *sb.*5) **1611** Florio, *Scassare vn pezzo*, to vnstocke, to vnbracke or dismount a piece. **Unbra·gging,** *ppl. a.* (Un-1 10.) **1570** Levins *Manip.* 137 Vnbragging, *inglorius.* **Unbrai·d,** *v.* (Un-2 3.) **1828–32** Webster, *Unbraid*, to separate the strands of a braid. **1880** J. Cook *Monday Lect.* Ser. i. 6, I shall unbraid the reasoning and show its strands

**Unbrai·ded,** *ppl. a.* [Un-1 8.]

† **1.** Untarnished, undamaged. *Obs.*—1

**1611** Shaks. *Wint. T.* iv. iv. 204 Thou talkest of an admirable conceited fellow, has he any vnbraided Wares?

**2.** Not braided or plaited.

**1821** Scott *Kenilw.* vii, Her unbraided hair escaping from under her midnight coif. **1879** H. W. Warren *Recr. Astron.* ii. 30 Just above the color vibrations of the unbraided sunbeam.

**Unbrai·led,** *ppl. a.* [Un-1 8.] Not confined by a brail or thong.

**1618** Latham *Falconry* (1633) 97 Beware you giue no traines vnbrayld of both wings, vntill the Hawke be well blouded.

† **Unbrai·ned,** *ppl. a. Obs.*—1 [Un-1 8.] Not deprived of brains.

*c* **1614** Fletcher *Wit at Sev. Weapons* iv. i, Hast thou ever hope To come i' the same roome where lovers are; And scape unbrain'd with one of their velvet slippers?

**Unbra·n,** *v.* [Un-2 4.] *trans.* To divest of bran. Hence **Unbra·nning** *vbl. sb.*

**1863** Wynter *Subtle Brains* 383 The invaluable process of unbranning wheat. **1884** Knight *Dict. Mech.* Suppl. 911/1 *Unbranning machine*, a machine for removing the bran or cuticle of the wheat grain.

**Unbra·nched,** *a.* [Un-1 9.]

**1.** Of trees or plants, their stems, etc.: Not furnished with branches.

**1665** Rea *Flora* 96 The Lily Asphodells flower in the end of May;..the unbranched kind is the first and the branched the last. **1731** Miller *Gard. Dict.* s.v. *Palma*, The Palm-Tree..hath a single unbranch'd Stalk. **1753** *Chambers' Cycl.* Suppl. s.v. *Filix*, The unbranched, dentated fern. **1855** Miss Pratt *Flower. Pl.* (1861) V. 314 Unbranched Upright Bur-reed. **1897** Mary Kingsley *W. Africa* 464 A great hard wood forest tree, which has a tall unbranched stem, terminating in a crown of branches.

**2.** Not divided into branches; having no ramifications. Chiefly *Bot.* and *Zool.*

**1796** Withering *Brit. Plants* (ed. 3) III. 755 Leaves generally unbranched. **1847** W. E. Steele *Field Bot.* 171 Leaves with unbranched mostly parallel ribs. **1857** T. Moore

*Handbk. Brit. Ferns* (ed. 3) 58 The veins, which are alternate, mostly unbranched, and extending to the margin. **1875** HUXLEY & MARTIN *Elem. Biol.* (1877) 37 A bud-like process is thrown out, which, usually, grows only into a very short unbranched hypha.

**Unbra·nched,** *ppl. a.* [UN-¹ 8.] Not deprived of branches.

**1572** MASCALL *Plant. & Graff.* (1592) 37 The other sorts of Trees may well passe vnbranched, if they haue not too great or large branches.

**Unbra·nching,** *ppl. a.* (UN-¹ 10.) **1774** GOLDSM. *Nat. Hist.* III. iii. 80 The other has black unbranching hollow horns that never fall. **1826** KIRBY & SP. *Entomol.* III. xxviii. 12 He has made the first deviation from the beaten track of an unbroken and unbranching series.

**Unbra·nded,** *ppl. a.* (UN-¹ 8.)

**1641** MILTON *Animadv.* Wks. 1851 III. 230 Lest his conversation unprohibited, or unbranded, might breath a pestilentiall murrein into the other sheepe. **1886** *Daily News* 4 June 6/3 Butter:..price of unbranded, 78*s*, 71*s*, 66*s*. **1890** 'R. BOLDREWOOD' *Col. Reformer* (1891) 232 Cows, unbranded calves, and pen-branded bullocks. **1892** *Academy* 23 Jan. 81/3 What is false and heartless is not allowed to pass unbranded under its screen of art.

**Unbra·ndied,** *a.* (UN-¹ 9.) **1862** T. A. TROLLOPE *Marietta* I. x. 195 Unbrandied juice of the grape.

† **Unbra·ngled,** *ppl. a. Sc. Obs. rare.* [UN-¹ 8.] Not shaken or made uncertain.

**1671** R. MACWARD *True Nonconf.* 368 The more serious Presbyterians..remain stedfast and unbrangled with these delusions. *c* **1730** T. BOSTON *Life* ix. (1908) 182 God's calling me to the place remained clear, plain, and unbrangled.

**Unbranning**: see UNBRAN *v.*

† **Unbra·nslable,** *a. Obs.*⁻¹ [UN-¹ 7 b: cf. BRANLE *v.*] Unshakable.

**1633** LD. WARRISTON *Diary* (S.H.S.) I. 170 On the quhilk tuo my saule doeth bottom itself as one ane unbranslable rok.

† **Unbras·hed,** *ppl. a. Obs.*⁻¹ [UN-¹ 8.] Unattacked, unassailed.

**1596** DALRYMPLE tr. *Leslie's Hist. Scot.* (S.T.S.) I. 104 Quhen the armie is in sicht, the space of thrie dayes thay byd nocht vnbrachte with vs.

**Unbra·ve,** *a.* (UN-¹ 7.) *a* **1681** T. RAYMOND *Autobiog.* (Camden) 35 Soe I had in this brave place [the Hague] a very unbrave life. **Unbra·ved,** *ppl. a.* (UN-¹ 8.) **1608** SYLVESTER tr. *Mathieu, Mem. Mortality* I. lxxx, Th' art loth to leave the Courts Delights, Devices, Where None lives long vnbrav'd, or vnabhorred. **Unbra·ze,** *v.* (UN-² 4.) [**1775** ASH, *Unbraze*.., to unsolder brass.] **1898** *Cycling* 19 A useful bar is made by unbrazing the central lap-joint. **Unbrea·chable,** *a.* (UN-¹ 7 b.) **1866** M. ARNOLD *Thyrsis* 156 Unbreachable the fort Of the long-batter'd world uplifts its wall. **Unbrea·ched,** *ppl. a.* (UN-¹ 8.) **1876** SWINBURNE *Erechtheus* 1451 Unbreached of warring waters Athens like a sea rock stands.

**Unbrea·kable,** *a.* (UN-¹ 7 b.)

*c* **1480** HENRYSON *Orpheus & Eurydice* 405 Hard is þi law, þi bandis vnbrekable. **1611** COTGR., *Irrefragable*,..vnbreakable. **1845** BAILEY *Festus* (ed. 2) 130 He made earth,..Lined it with fire, and round its heart-fire bowed Rock-ribs unbreakable. **1890** *Spectator* 20 Sept. 374/2 This Moloch that devours young girls' lives is an idol that appears unbreakable.

**Unbrea·kfasted,** *a.* (UN-¹ 9.) **1646** J. HALL *Poems* 43 Three such as you Unbreakfasted might sterve Seraglio. **1826** DISRAELI *V. Grey* v. ii, I see you smile at my supposing a horseman unbreakfasted. **1847** L. HUNT *Men, Women & B.* I. ix. 159 This personage..persisted in giving poor unbreakfasted Jack in charge. **1865** TREVELYAN *Cawnpore* 115 Half-clad, unbreakfasted,..our countrymen huddled..into the precincts of the fatal earthwork. **Unbrea·king,** *ppl. a.* (UN-¹ 10.) **1869** MORRIS *Earthly Par.* II. III. 183 And ever as the shadows fell, More formless grew the unbreaking swell Far out to sea. **1876** GEO. ELIOT *Dan. Der.* xl, Part of my Jewish heritage is an unbreaking patience.

**Unbrea·st,** *v.* [UN-² 5.] *trans.* To take or force out from the breast; to unbosom. Chiefly *fig.*

**1559** *Mirr. Mag.* (1563) C vii, My fault wherein because mine vncle tolde..I found the meanes his bowels to vnbrest. **1603** FLORIO *Montaigne* I. xvii. 28 Feare then vnbreasts all wit, That in my minde did sit. **1631** P. FLETCHER *Pisc. Eclogs* IV. xxiv, Could'st thou unmask their pomp, unbreast their heart, How would'st thou laugh at this rich beggerie! **1633** — *Purple Isl.* XII. lxiii, Out from his mouth a two-edg'd sword he darts;..And with his keenest point unbreasts the naked hearts.

Hence **Unbrea·sted** *ppl. a.*

**1610** G. FLETCHER *Christ's Tri.* II. xl, To whose open eye The hearts of wicked men unbrested lie.

**Unbrea·thable,** *a.* (UN-¹ 7 b.) **1846** WORCESTER (citing F. Butler). **1862** *Cornh. Mag.* VI. 485 No one pretends that the worst air in a closed railway carriage is unbreathable. *c* **1882** CHR. ROSSETTI *Resurgam* Poems (1891) 378 He stumbles on the darkened mountain-head, Left breathless in the unbreathable thin air.

**Unbrea·the,** *v.* [UN-² 7.] *intr.* To cease to breathe; to expire, die.

**1589** WARNER *Alb. Eng.* VI. xxxiii. 144 Now is the time and place (sweete Frends) and we the Persons be That must giue England breath, or els vnbreath for her must we.

**Unbrea·thed,** (*ppl.*) *a.* [UN-¹ 8, 8 c, 9. For pronunc. see BREATHED *ppl. a.*]

† **1.** Unexercised; unpractised. *Obs.*

**1590** COKAINE *Treat. Hunting* C 4 Who so hunteth vnbreathed hounds at the Bucke first in hot weather. **1590** SHAKS. *Mid. N.* v. i. 73 Hard handed men,..Which neuer labour'd in their mindes till now; And now haue toyled their vnbreathed memories With this same play. **1620** QUARLES *Jonah* 99 A Muse vnbreath'd, vnlikely to obtaine An easie honour, by so stout a Traine. **1644** MILTON *Areop.* (Arb.) 45, I cannot praise a fugitive and cloister'd vertue, unexercis'd and unbreath'd.

**2. a.** Not having recovered breath.

**1692** PRIOR *Ode Imit. Hor.* v, Yon' Hero, crown'd with blooming Victory,..And yet unbreath'd from Battles gain'd.

**b.** Not out of breath or exhausted.

**1901** KIPLING *Kim* 369 Kim's messenger dropped from the steep pasture as unbreathed as when she had set out.

**3.** Not breathed (*upon*); not respired.

**1817** MOORE *Lalla Rookh, Veiled Prophet* II. 186 When from those lips, unbreath'd upon for years, I shall again kiss off the soul-felt tears. **1831** WORDSW. *Yarrow Revisited* VI. 9 Rocks, rivers, and smooth lakes more clear than glass Untouched, unbreathed upon. **1884** *Imp. Dict.* s.v., Air unbreathed.

**4.** Not uttered or whispered.

*a* **1827** J. HISLOP *Cameronian's Dream* 30 The vengeance that darkened their brow was unbreathed.

**Unbrea·thing,** *ppl. a.* [UN-¹ 10.]

**1.** Not breathing or respiring; *esp.* holding the breath; breathless.

**1709** *Rowe's Shaksp., Rich. III*, III. vii. 25 Like dumb statues or unbreathing stones. **1736** A. HILL *Zara* v. i, Th' unbreathing World is hush'd, as if it heard, And listen'd to, your Sorrows. **1789** E. DARWIN *Bot. Gard.* II. (1791) 53 Silent with upturned eyes unbreathing crowds Pursue the floating wonder to the clouds. **1814** WORDSW. *Excurs.* IV. 1281 Hushed As the unbreathing air, when not a leaf Stirs in the mighty woods. **1824** GALT *Rothelan* III. 237 The audience sat in silent admiration and unbreathing astonishment. *a* **1867** WILLIS *Lazarus & Mary* 68 A fearful and unbreathing hush, Stiller than night's last hour.

**2.** Not taking breath; continuous.

**1893** *Scribner's Mag.* June 821/1 It is neither recital, analysis, nor exposition; but soaring, sweeping, unbreathing rhapsody.

**Unbre·d,** *ppl. a.* [UN-¹ 8 b.]

† **1.** Unborn. *Obs.*⁻¹

*c* **1600** SHAKS. *Sonn.* civ, For feare of which, heare this thou age vnbred, Ere you were borne was beauties summer dead.

**2.** Not properly bred or brought up; not imbued with good manners; unmannerly, ill-bred.

**1622** in Foster *Eng. Factories Ind.* (1908) II. 146 Borish unbred upstartts, whoe abound in all pryde and insolenceey. *a* **1661** FULLER *Worthies* I. (1662) 34 Seeing much of Truth is contained in our English Proverb, It is as good to be unborn as unbred. **1700** CONGREVE *Way of World* III. xvii, My nephew's a little unbred, you'll pardon him, madam. **1712** STEELE *Spect.* No. 492 ⁋ 2 A little Country Girl..that makes her use of being young and unbred. **1760–2** GOLDSM. *Cit. W.* xxxix, Would he not be reckoned more fantastically savage than even his unbred footman?

**b.** Not trained *in*, not brought up *to*, some occupation.

*a* **1683** OLDHAM *Wks.* (1686) 68 Dull Northern Brains, in these deep Arts unbred, Know nought but to cut Throats. **1697** DRYDEN *Æneis* VII. 1096 A warrior dame; Unbred to spinning, in the loom unskilled. **1878** *N. Amer. Rev.* CXXVI. 304 With no education,..often unbred to any handicraft.

† **Unbre·de,** *v. Obs.*⁻¹ (Meaning obscure.)

**13..** *Satire* in *Pol. Songs* (Camden) 156 Heore boc ase unbredes. Heo wendeth bokes un-brad.

**Unbree·ch,** *v.* [UN-² 4. Cf. Du. *ontbroeken.*]

**1.** *trans.* To remove the breech or breeching from (a cannon, etc.).

*a* **1548** HALL *Chron., Hen. VIII*, 259 b, The portes [were] left open,..and the greate ordinaunce vnbreched, so that when the ship should turne, the water entered, and sodainly she sanke. **1598** FLORIO, *Scalcagnare*,..to vnbreech, to vnheele, to vnstock, or dismount any kinde of great ordinance or artillerie. *c* **1620** FLETCHER & MASS. *Double Marriage* II. i, *Gun.* Let the worst come, I can unbreech a Cannon, and without much help Turn her into the Keel. **1625** MARKHAM *Souldiers Accid.* 8 He shall..shew them how to scoure their Pieces, and..how to vnbreetch them.

**2.** To strip (a person) of breeches.

**1598** FLORIO, *Scalcidre*, to vnhose, to unshoe,..to vnbreech. **1835** *Court Mag.* VI. 20, I was afraid of feeling for my snuff-box, lest I should unbreech half Naples. **1846** LANDOR *Imag. Conv.* Wks. I. 29 Kings have been stripped bare, and emperors unbreeched, by the popes. *a* **1896** MORRIS *Sundering Flood* (1897) 123 If I catch thee not and unbreech thee and whip thee as a grammar master his scholar, then [etc.]

Hence **Unbree·ching** *vbl. sb.*

**1598** FLORIO, *Scalciatura*, an..vnhosing, vnbreeching.

**Unbree·ched,** *a.* [UN-¹ 9.] Not dressed in breeches.

**1611** SHAKS. *Wint. T.* I. ii. 158 Me thoughts I did requoyle Twentie three yeeres, and saw my selfe vn-breech'd, In my greene Veluet Coat. **1800** WORDSW. *Two Thieves* 13 The One, yet unbreeched, is not three birthdays old. *c* **1837** HAWTHORNE *Twice-told T.* (1851) I. vi. 112 All at once, the devil of their fathers entered into the unbreeched fanatics. **1879** DOWDEN *Southey* i. 5 Southey, an unbreeched boy of three years, was borne away one morning..to be handed over to the tender mercies of a school-mistress.

**Unbrent,** obs. f. UNBURNT.

**Unbresed,** obs. f. UNBRUISED.

**Unbrew·ed,** *ppl. a.* (UN-¹ 8.) **1725** *Fam. Dict.* s.v. *Straw*, In case you have not sweet Wine, take some thick or unbrew'd Wine of the Colour of Bulls Blood. **1742** YOUNG *Nt. Th.* VII. 288 They graze the turf untill'd; they drink the stream Unbrew'd, and ever full.

† **Unbrew·ing.** *Obs.*⁻¹ A fanciful name for a 'company' (of carvers).

**1486** *Bk. St. Albans* f vij, A vnbrewyng of kerueris.

**Unbri·bable,** *a.* (UN-¹ 7 b.)

**1661** FELTHAM *Resolves* (ed. 8) II. lxxxiii. 68 Though it be cry'd up for impartial and unbribeable, yet I do not see but in many 'tis erroneous, mutable, and uncertain. **1678** CUDWORTH *Intell. Syst.* I. iv. § 16. 291 God is..the Head or Leader of all Good, Unbribable. **1849** THOREAU *Week Concord Riv.* Wedn. 304 The impartial and unbribable beneficence of Nature. **1862** THORNBURY *Turner* II. 169 My object is..to draw his real likeness with the unbribable fidelity of a photograph. **1893** SALTUS *Madam Sapphira* 166 Beyond that we won't go. The unbribable Comstock won't let us.

**Unbri·bed,** *ppl. a.* [UN-¹ 8.]

**1.** Not bribed; not corrupted by bribery.

**1607** TOURNEUR *Rev. Trag.* I. ii, The justice Of that unbribed euerlasting law. **1646** G. DANIEL *Poems* Wks. (Grossart) I. 56 She commands Who ballanceth the world with unbrib'd hands. **1668** DRYDEN *Dram. Poesy* Ess. (ed. Ker) I. 44 That praise or censure is certainly the most sincere, which unbribed posterity shall give us. **1733** POPE *Ess. Man* III. 158 Unbrib'd, unbloody, stood the blameless priest. **1796** MME. D'ARBLAY *Camilla* V. 230 [He was] unbribed by the high praise of his son. **1802–12** BENTHAM *Ration. Judic. Evid.* (1827) II. 424 Two hundred unbribed witnesses agree in deposing that..he was seen by them at Prague. **1845** ELIZA COOK *Old Man's Marvel* xix, It [the heart] stands unbribed by an Eastern mine—For a ducat of dross 'tis bought and sold.

*fig.* **1608** BEAUM. & FL. *Four Pl. in One* Wks. 1912 X. 340 Have I not here enough to thank Heaven for?..The water that I touch, unbrib'd with odours To make me sweet to others.

**2.** Not obtained or brought about by bribery.

**1667** R. WILD *Poems* (1870) 75 Unbribed loyalty! his highest reach Was to be Master Calamy, and preach. **1735** THOMSON *Liberty* I. 79 The commonweal inspiring every tongue With fervent eloquence, unbrib'd, and bold. **1781** COWPER *Hope* 580 Paul's love of Christ, and steadiness unbrib'd. **1802–12** BENTHAM *Ration. Judic. Evid.* (1827) V. 93 Perjury, if unbribed, will be without a motive.

† **Unbri·che,** *a. Obs.* In 4 vnbryche. [OE. *unbryce*: see BRICHE *a.*] Useless, unserviceable.

**1303** R. BRUNNE *Handl. Synne* 6786 God..deyneþ nat to nemne hys name,..But calleþ hym yn þe gospel, ryche, As vnkynde and vnbryche.

**Unbri·ck,** *v.* [UN-² 4.] *trans.* To remove bricks from; to open up, set free, by the removal of bricks.

**1598** FLORIO, *Smattonare*, to vnpaue, to vnbrick, to pull downe bricks. **1873** WHITNEY *Other Girls* xx, Couldn't the fire-place be unbricked? **1900** *Academy* 4 Aug. 90/2 A climber had stuck there [in a narrow chimney] and died before he could be unbricked.

*fig.* **1894** B. PAIN *Kindn. Celestial* 179 Three days after the engagement he had unbricked 'a bright and sunny temperament' in my father.

**Unbri·cked,** *ppl. a.* (UN-¹ 8.) **1814** *Monthly Mag.* July 594 No more than 130 yards of the tunnel..were unbricked on the 31st of May. **1894** *Daily News* 6 Sept. 1/3 He desired to be buried in an unbricked grave. **Unbri·dgeable,** *a.* (UN-¹ 7 b.) **1799** SOUTHEY in *Sir H. Davy's Rem.* (1858) 37 One channel,..unbridgeable from its depth, unpassable from its whirlpools. **1879** LEWES *Study Psychol.* 50 An unbridgeable gulf, which no dexterity of speculation can pass. **1881** *Standard* 30 Aug. 3/4 Between them there was an all but unbridgeable abyss. **Unbri·dged,** *ppl. a.* (UN-¹ 8.) **1800** WORDSW. *Brothers* 254 Every water-course And unbridged stream.. Was swoln into a noisy rivulet. **1852** MRS. STOWE *Uncle Tom's C.* xiv. 121 The gulf of separation was unbridged by even a friendly word or signal. **1884** *Spectator* 4 Oct. 1322/1 The traveller who left England with the intention of proceeding overland to Ceylon, with the exception of the three unbridged channels.

**Unbri·dle,** *v.* [UN-² 4 b. Cf. Du. *ontbreidelen.*]

**1.** *trans.* To remove the bridle from (a horse). Also *absol.*

? *a* **1400** *Morte Arth.* 2509 Thare vnbrydilles theis bolde, and baytes þeire horses. *c* **1435** *Torr. Portugal* 1552 Down light this gentille knyght..And vnbrydelid his stede. *c* **1450** *Mirk's Festial* 56 He fell wod, and so vnbrydylt his hors þat bare hym into a maner of þe lordes. **1530** PALSGR. 766/2 Unbrideil my horse and gyve hym otes. **1607** MARKHAM *Cavel.* III. (1617) 31 Then you shal come vnto him and vnbridle him. **1643** TRAPP *Comm. Gen.* xxiii. 2 They would neither unbridle their horses, nor untie their armor. **1809** MALKIN *Gil Blas* VI. ii. ⁋ 1 We unbridled our horses, and turned them out to grass. **1890** L. C. D'OYLE *Notches* 134 He led the horses by their bridles down to the gate of the enclosure; here he unbridled them and let them go.

**b.** *transf.* and *fig.* To free from restraint.

*a* **1440** *Found. St. Bartholomew's* (E. E. T. S.) 57 The tonge was vnbridilid to blasfemy and rybawdy. **1567** *Trial Treas.* (Percy Soc.) 23, I doubte not but I shal be unbridled by Luste. **1576** GASCOIGNE *Philomene* li, Forth he floong the raines, Unbridling blinde desire. **1604** T. WRIGHT *Passions* I. iii. 14 Selfe-love..inticeth the citizens..to prosecute pleasures, unbridle their senses. **1648** J. BEAUMONT *Psyche* VIII. cclvii, Loe, There unbridle thy Extremitie, And give thee leave in free carreer to goe.

**c.** *absol.* (in fig. use). To stop or halt.

**1653** URQUHART *Rabelais* I. xxii, Then did he sleep without unbrideling until eight a clock.

**2.** *Surg.* To free (a wound) from a bridle. (See BRIDLE *sb.* 5 b.)

**1758** J. S. *Le Dran's Observ. Surg.* (1771) 333, I had not sufficiently unbridled it, nor penetrated deep enough into the Body of the Muscles.

**Unbri·dled,** *ppl. a.* [UN-¹ 8. Cf. MDu. *ongebreidelt.*]

**1.** *fig.* Not restrained or held in check; absolutely uncontrolled or ungoverned: **a.** Of conduct, feeling, utterance, etc.

*c* **1374** CHAUCER *Troylus* III. 429 He..in hym self wiþ manhod gan restreyne, Eche rakel dede and eche vnbrydled chere. *c* **1412** HOCCLEVE *De Reg. Princ.* 2433 Vnbridlid wordes ofte man by-weepiþ. **1412–20** LYDG. *Chron. Troy* I. 2019 No cher vnbridlid þat tyme hir asterte. *c* **1530** *Remedy of Love* Prol., Seeing the manifolde inconuenience Falling by vnbrideled prosperitie. **1561** T. NORTON *Calvin's Inst.* I. 4 We reade of none that euer did breake forth into more presumptuous and vnbridled despising of God, than Caius Caligula. **1590** SWINBURNE *Testaments* 200 By this meane to restraine the vnbrideled lusts of some. **1626** T. H[AWKINS] *Caussin's Holy Crt.* 120 After the concupiscences of the belly, commeth vnbridled irreuerence. **1642** MILTON *Apol.*

*Smect.* Wks. 1851 III. 273, I go on to shew you the unbridl'd impudence of this loose rayler. **1711** STEELE *Spect.* No. 38 ¶ 5 When we give the Passion for Praise an unbridled Liberty. **1751** EARL ORRERY *Remarks Swift* (1752) 99 A wild unbridled indulgence of his own humour and disposition. **1821** SCOTT *Kenilw.* xxxi, His flights are too unbridled for any place but Parnassus. **1855** PALEY *Æschylus* Pref. (1861) p. xxiii, To keep in check the otherwise unbridled passions of a fickle multitude. **1888** BRYCE *Amer. Commw.* I. iii. 25 *note*, An alarming example of what the unbridled rule of the multitude may come to.

**b.** Of persons, the mind, tongue, etc.

*a* **1547** SURREY *Paraphr. Ps. lv.* 13 Rayne those vnbrydled tungs; breake that coniured league. *a* **1548** HALL *Chron., Hen. V*, 56 b, When he had once tamed and framed to his purpose this young unbrideled gentleman. **1581** A. HALL *Iliad* IV. 69 After our vnbrideled youth coms sage and wrinckled yeares. **1606** SHAKS. *Tr. & Cr.* III. ii. 130 My thoughts were like vnbrideled children grow[n] Too head-strong for their mother. **1644** MILTON *Areop.* (Arb.) 37 Nævius was quickly cast into prison for his unbridl'd pen. **1676** HOBBES *Iliad* I. 322 That they may be To Gods and Men, and to th' unbridled man My witnesses. **1840** ALISON *Hist. Eur.* VIII. liii. § 39. 433 The usual..intemperance of the unbridled populace of great towns. **1876** BANCROFT *Hist. U.S.* I. xviii. 517 They were exposed, without defence, to the fury of an unbridled soldiery.

**c.** Of natural forces.

?**1814** WORDSW. *Brownie's Cell* 64 Towers rent, winds combating with woods, Lands deluged by unbridled floods.

**2.** Not furnished with a bridle.

**1553** EDEN *Treat. New Ind.* (Arb.) 16 They are all vnbrideled, hauinge neither withe nor coller aboute theyr neckes. **1600** HAKLUYT *Voy.* III. 315 They fel on running like vnbridled horses, through the middest of the thickest woods. **1656** EARL MONM. tr. *Boccalini, Pol. Touchstone* (1674) 253 That unbridled Horse which the State bears for her Ensign. **1694** MOTTEUX *Rabelais* IV. xlviii. 188 An unbridled Mule, with green Trappings. **1798** *Hull Advertiser* 8 Sept. 1/4 Our picquets were attacked; this caused some bustle, as our horses were all unbridled. **1841** SPALDING *Italy & It. Isl.* II. 27 Pride, clothed in a lion's skin, rushes forward on an unbridled horse. **1872** HEAD *Sel. Grk. Coins Brit. Mus.* 16 The unbridled horse may be a symbol of Liberty.

Hence **Unbri·dledly** *adv.*; **Unbri·dledness.**

**1561** T. NORTON *Calvin's Inst.* I. 37 Yet the boldnesse of Sophisters could not be restrained by them from babling *vnbrideledly. **1591** SYLVESTER *Du Bartas* I. iii. 211 Yet true it is, that humane things (seem) slide Unbridledly with so uncertain tide [etc.]. **1571** GOLDING *Calvin on Ps.* v. 5 With howe muche more *unbrydlednesse his enemies ronne royet. *a* **1639** W. WHATELEY *Prototypes* II. xxvi. (1640) 65 The unbridlednesse of your evill natures. *a* **1684** LEIGHTON *Comm. 1 Pet.* v. (1819) II. 322 The presumption and unbridledness of youth require the pressing and binding on of this rule.

**Unbrie·fed,** *ppl. a.* (UN-[1] 8.) **1889** *Pall Mall G.* 18 Dec. 6/2 The Great Unbriefed—or *un*learned counsel as they are sometimes called.

**Unbri·ght,** *a.* (UN-[1] 7; cf. OE. *unbeorhte* adv.)

**1523** [COVERDALE] *Old God* (1534) B j, Beynge through dust & longe beynge unoccupied, unbright and defiled with ruste. **1570** LEVINS *Manip.* 119 Vnbright, *illucidus*.

**Unbri·ghtened,** *ppl. a.* (UN-[1] 8.) **1827** COLERIDGE *Work without Hope* 11 With lips unbrightened, wreathless brow, I stroll. **1873** MORLEY *Rousseau* II. 29 Saint Preux's egoism is unbrightened by a single ray of tender abnegation.

**Unbri·ned,** *ppl. a.* (UN-[1] 8.) **1733** TULL *Horse-Hoeing Husb.* xii. 144 The Oldest Farmer believ'd Brining to be but a Fancy, and sow'd his Seed Unbrined.

**Un-Bri·tish,** *a.* (UN-[1] 7.)

**1746** YOUNG *Thoughts on Late Reb.* 191 By thoughts inglorious, and un-British deeds, Their cancell'd will is impiously profaned. **1754** H. WALPOLE *Mem. Geo. II* (1822) I. 328 As un-British an age as ever was. **1755** YOUNG *Centaur* vi, May they cease from this hour to sing or dance ..our British, unbritish youth, manhood, and age, out of their senses! **1894** *Daily News* 12 Nov. 6/4 This extraordinary and most un-British freedom from prejudice.

**Unbrizzed,** Sc. form of UNBRUISED.

**Unbroa·ched,** *ppl. a.* (UN-[1] 8.)

**1689** *Gazophyl. Angl., To Blink beer*,..to keep it unbroached, till it grow sharp. **1742** YOUNG *Nt. Th.* III. 319 His luxuries have left him..No maiden relishes, unbroacht delights. *Ibid.* VIII. 671 His full draught of pleasure, from a cask Unbroach'd by just authority. **1824** MISS FERRIER *Inher.* iii, Which she was reading unconsciously for the third time with unbroached delight. **1871** HAWTHORNE *Sept. Felton* (1879) 176 Septimius..left the box unbroached.

†**Unbroa·ded,** *ppl. a.* *Obs.*[-1] [UN-[1] 8: see BROWD *v.*] Unbraided.

**1590** C'TESS PEMBROKE *Antonie* 302 The Comets flaming through the scat'red clouds With fiery beames, most like vnbroaded haires.

†**Unbroi·d,** *v.* *Obs.*[-1] [UN-[2] 3.] *trans.* To unbraid, disentangle, make plain.

**1586** STANYHURST *Descr. Irel.* Ep. Ded. in *Holinshed*, That I maie the sooner unbroid the pelfish trash that is wrapt within this treatise.

†**Unbroi·ded, -en,** *ppl. a.* *Obs.* [UN-[1] 8, 8 b.] Unbraided, loose, dishevelled.

*c* **1374** CHAUCER *Troylus* IV. 817 The myghty tresses of here sonnyssh herys Vnbroyden hangen al aboute here eris. **1582** STANYHURST *Æneis* II. (Arb.) 56 Lo ye; the wood virgin, with locks vnbroyded is haled Cassandra.

**Unbroi·led,** *ppl. a.* (UN-[1] 8.) **1623** FLETCHER & ROWLEY *Maid in Mill* IV. ii, Do not look to find..so much flesh unbroil'd of all that mountain, As a worm might sup on.

**Unbro·ke,** *ppl. a.* [var. of next.]

**1.** = UNBROKEN *ppl. a.* 1.

*a* **1325** *MS. Rawl. B.* 520 fol. 31 b, Þulke þat we graunteden to holde..in þe forme hol bi-forseide ant vnbroke. *c* **1460** *Oseney Reg.* 14 Ordeynyng þat all maner possessions.. to þem, and to þere successours sure and vnbroke abyde. *Ibid.* 161 Þat sure and vnbroke hit abide. **1593** SHAKS. *Rich. II*, IV. i. 215 God keepe all Vowes vnbroke are made to thee. *a* **1637** B. JONSON *Underw., to Browne*, See, that thou By off'ring not more sureties, than inow, Hold thyne owne worth unbroke.

**2.** = UNBROKEN *ppl. a.* 2. Also *fig.*

**1632** LITHGOW *Trav.* V. 182 These Iarres are all..interlarded with pitch to preserue the earthen vessells vnbroke a sunder. **1725** POPE *Odyss.* VIII. 149 How broad his shoulders spread! By age unbroke! **1762** WILKES *Corr.* (1805) III. 43, I.. return it with the seal unbroke, as the clearest demonstration that I never have read the contents of it. **1805** SCOTT *Last Minstrel* IV. xxi, Unbroke by age, erect his seat. **1845** LONGF. *Arrow* iii, Long, long afterward, in an oak I found the arrow, still unbroke.

**3.** = UNBROKEN *ppl. a.* 4.

*a* **1716** ADDISON tr. *Horace* III. iii, Wild from the desart and unbroke: In vain they foam'd. **1743** FRANCIS tr. *Hor., Odes* II. v. 1 See, thy Heifer's yet unbroke To the Labours of the Yoke. **1810** SOUTHEY *Kehama* VIII. ii, His neck unbroke to mortal yoke, Like Nature free the Steed must be. **1842** BORROW *Bible in Spain* xix, He was a black Andalusian stallion,..unbroke, savage, and furious. **1865** TOM TAYLOR *Ballads & Songs of Brittany* 172 An unbroke filly.

**4.** = UNBROKEN *ppl. a.* 5.

**1793** WORDSW. *Evening Walk* 429 The scene is waken'd, yet its peace unbroke, By silver'd wreaths of quiet charcoal smoke. **1808** SCOTT *Marm.* III. vi, All gaz'd at length in silence drear, Unbroke, save when..Some yeoman..whisper'd forth his mind. **1816** BYRON *Siege Cor.* xi, That deep silence was unbroke, Save where the watch his signal spoke.

**Unbro·ken,** *ppl. a.* [UN-[1] 8 b. Cf. MDu. and Du. *ongebroken*, MHG. and G. *ungebrochen*.]

**1.** Of compacts, etc.: Not broken or infringed; unviolated, inviolate.

*a* **1300** *Cursor M.* 611 Bot for to hald it wel vnbroken, þe forbot þat was be-twix þam spoken. **1580** HOLLYBAND, *Inviolé*, inuiolated, sound, vnbroken. **1667** MILTON *P. L.* II. 691 That Traitor Angel,..Who first broke peace in Heav'n and Faith, till then Unbrok'n. **1743** FRANCIS tr. *Hor., Odes* I. xvii. 20 To sing frail Circe's guilty Fire, And chaste Penelope's unbroken Vow.

**2.** Of material things: Not broken or fractured; intact, whole.

**1495** *Trevisa's Barth. De P. R.* XIX. cxxx. 939 Men in olde tyme callyd a thynge y[t] was hoole and vnbroken, *Solidum et Totum*. **1585** T. WASHINGTON tr. *Nicholay's Voy.* I. xviii. 21 [There are] many towers and goodly buildings ruined.., amongst which, one which was vnbroken. **1613** TOURNEUR *Pr. Henry* 97, I wonder how Or he or anye other souldier now Can hold his sword unbroken. **1697** DRYDEN *Virg. Georg.* IV. 426 His bowels, bruised within, Betray no wound on his unbroken skin. **1707** MORTIMER *Husb.* (1721) II. 357 Put into the Hogshead ten new-laid Eggs, unbroken or cracked. **1790** J. BRUCE *Source Nile* II. 460 The seal [was] examined, and declared to be the patriarch's, and unbroken. **1864** MRS. CARLYLE *Lett.* (1883) III. 218 There is hardly a kitchen utensil left unbroken. **1889** J. C. JEAFFRESON *Q. of Naples & Nelson* I. iii. 93 Escaping..with unbroken bones. *fig.* *a* **1650** CRASHAW *Carmen, Answ. for Hope* 16 Nor will the virgin joyes we wed Come lesse unbroken to our bed. **1753** RICHARDSON *Grandison* (1781) II. xxxvi. 341 My fortune, which is unbroken, is the same sum that he gave my Brothers.

**3.** Not crushed, humbled, or subdued; not impaired or weakened.

**1513** DOUGLAS *Æneid* XII. i. 4 Turnus..saw thar curage faill,..Quhilk war tofor onbrokin and stowt of hart. **1549** COVERDALE, etc. *Erasm. Par. 1 John* ii. 47 A mynde that is vnbroken and vnconquered agaynst al wanton enticementes. **1609** B. JONSON *Masque of Queenes* Wks. (1660) 960 A Heroine of a most inuincible and vnbroken fortitude. **1612** *Two Noble K.* V. iv. 101 If thy heart, Thy worthie, manly heart, be yet unbroken. **1697** DRYDEN *Æneis* X. 1102 But, glancing thence, the yet unbroken force Took a new bent obliquely. **1796** MME. D'ARBLAY *Camilla* V. 288 Her, as yet, unbroken powers of encountering adversity. **1817** LADY MORGAN *France* II. (1818) I. 261 Courage unsubdued, spirits unbroken, indignation unrestrained. **1856** KANE *Arct. Expl.* I. xviii. 219 The journey was an arduous one to be undertaken, even by unbroken men. **1907** *Verney Mem.* II 239 Her..cheerful spirits, unbroken by poverty and dependence.

**4.** Of horses, etc.: Not tamed or rendered tractable; untrained.

**1538** ELYOT, *Indomitus*, wylde, vnbroken. **1542** UDALL *Erasm. Apoph.* 230 To ride the vnbroken horse Bucephalus. **1593** NASHE *Christ's T.* Wks. (Grosart) IV. 170 We are the vnbroken-Colt..which hee [*sc.* Our Lord] commaunded (with the Asse) to be brought vnto hym. **1705** STANHOPE *Paraphr.* I. 30 A Colt unbroken on which never Man had sat. **1806–7** J. BERESFORD *Miseries Hum. Life* (1826) II. xxvii, Driving an unbroken horse. **1864** BOYD *Ess., Commonpl. Philos.* vii. 203 No man likes to think that he is being managed as Mr. Rarey might manage an unbroken colt. **1908** *Animal Managem.* 252 Traders carrying unbroken horses through the tropics.

*transf.* **1743** FRANCIS tr. *Hor., Epodes* vii. 7 Britons yet unbroken to our War, In Chains should follow our triumphal Car. **1747** RICHARDSON *Clarissa* (1811) I. xvii. 119 You are young and unbroken.

**5.** Not interrupted or disturbed; continuous, uniform.

**1561** T. NORTON *Calvin's Inst.* I. 5 b, There ought to haue ben one continual vnbroken course of obedience in their whole lyfe. *a* **1578** LINDESAY (Pitscottie) *Chron. Scot.* (S.T.S.) I. 23 Sick amitie and freindscheip..that all men supponit the samyn for to indure for ever and euer onbrokin. **1722** WOLLASTON *Relig. Nat.* iii. 60 Truth is the offspring of silence, unbroken meditations, and thoughts often revised and corrected. **1736** BUTLER *Anal.* II. vii. 260 An unbroken Genealogy of Mankind for many Ages. **1783** BURKE *Rep. Aff. India* Wks. 1842 II. 11 It required an unbroken attention, ..to form a true judgment. **1825** WATERTON *Wand. S. Amer.* I. (1903) 2 An unbroken range of forest covers each bank of the river. **1852** ROBERTSON *Serm.* Ser. III. xii. (1882) 151 One unbroken series of cruelty and crime. **1887** BOWEN *Æneid* I. 495 While yet silent he stands in a long and unbroken gaze.

**b.** Const. *by*.

**1743** FRANCIS tr. *Hor., Odes* I. xiii. 19 In equal rapture, and sincere delights, Unbroken by complaints or strife. **1796** MME. D'ARBLAY *Camilla* III. 137 Miss Dennel grew..weary with the length of the way, unbroken by any company. **1809** CAMPBELL *Gert. Wyom.* I. x, Many a halcyon day he lived to see Unbroken but by one misfortune dire. **1882** DE WINDT *Equator* 66 The landscape being unbroken by hill or habitation of any kind.

**6.** Of ground: Not broken by ploughing or digging. Also with *up*.

**1579–80** NORTH *Plutarch* (1595) 26 They did take off the plougheshare, and drew the ploughe, with leauing a certain space of earthe vnbroken up. **1638** JUNIUS *Paint. Ancients* 245 An unbroken and untilled ground doth now and then bring forth goodly hearbs. **1646** EARL MONM. tr. *Biondi's Civil Wars* IX. 206 The ground is for the most part unbroken up. **1697** DRYDEN *Virg. Georg.* I. 75 E'er we stir the yet unbroken Ground. **1746** FRANCIS tr. *Horace, Epist.* I. xiv. 36 You complain, that with unceasing Toil, You break, alas! the long unbroken Soil. **1855** DELAMER *Kitchen Garden* (1861) 142 If you are making a new garden on unbroken ground.

**7.** Not broken in ranks; not thrown into disorder.

**1721** DE FOE *Mem. Cavalier* (1840) 129 The imperialists, eager in the pursuit, left him unbroken. **1781** GIBBON *Decl. & F.* xxx. III. 153 He..withdrew from the field of battle, with the greatest part of his cavalry entire and unbroken. **1855** MACAULAY *Hist. Eng.* xvii. IV. 93 The obscurity enabled Sarsfield, with a few squadrons which still remained unbroken, to cover the retreat. **1898** *Westm. Gaz.* 24 Sept. 2/1 As cavalry are not ordinarily required to charge large masses of unbroken infantry.

**8.** *Bot.* Not variegated. (Cf. BREAK *v.* 32 c.)

**1829** LOUDON *Encycl. Plants* (1836) 267 Instead of saving the seed..from the finest variegated tulips, they prefer unbroken flowers or breeders.

Hence **Unbro·kenly** *adv.*, **Unbro·kenness.**

**1850** LYNCH *Theoph. Trinal* xii. 232 The years *unbrokenly march on. **1866** LIDDON *Bampt. Lect.* vi. (1875) 322 Like a ray of light from the parent fire with which it is unbrokenly joined. **1849** ROCK *Ch. of Fathers* I. iii. 246 The unbroken wholeness of this Altar-stone was a symbol of the *unbrokenness of the Church. **1889** ABP. BENSON in A. C. Benson *Life* (1900) II. 284 The whole crowded congregation sing in most perfect unbrokenness.

**Unbroo·kable,** *a.* (UN-[1] 7 b.) **1633** T. ADAMS *Exp. 2 Peter* ii. 8 How unbrookable is dulness in any work to a man of spirit! **1835** HOGG *Tales & Sk.* (1837) V. 357 A feeling of horror that was quite unbrookable.

**Unbro·sten,** *ppl. a.* [UN-[1] 8 b. Cf. OHG. and MHG. *ungebrosten*, Du. *ongeborsten*.] Unburst.

**13..** *E. E. Allit. P.* B. 365 Was no brymme þat abod vnbrosten bylyue. **1876** *Whitby Gloss.* 204/2 *Unbrussen*.

**Unbro·ther,** *v.* [UN-[2] 6 b.] *trans.* To deprive of brotherhood.

**1634** BP. HALL *Contempl. N. T.* IV. xxxiii. 520 It is not in the power of the sins of our infirmities to unbrother us. **1657** M. LAWRENCE *Use & Pract. Faith* 211 Yet he beareth with them; he will not presently cast them off, and unbrother them. **1752** YOUNG *Brothers* III. i, Unson'd! unbrother'd! nay, unhumaniz'd! Far from affection, as thou'rt near in blood! **1804** *Ann. Rev.* II. 197/2 Brother Broomhall turned metaphysician...As they could not confute *Mr.* Broomhall (for of course he was immediately unbrothered) they excommunicated him.

**Unbro·thered,** *ppl. a.* [UN-[1] 8.] Not provided with a brother. Also *fig.*

**1798** *Monthly Mag.* VI. 454 He from Thrugelmer descends, Aurgelmer's unbrother'd son. **1853** MISS E. S. SHEPPARD *Ch. Auchester* III. 194 The perfect form, the distinct conception of this unbrothered work.

**Unbro·therlike,** *a.* [UN-[1] 7 c.] = UNBROTHERLY *a.*

**1594** WEST *2nd Pt. Symbol. Chancerie* § 118 To thintent onely and thereby of set purpose, malice, and unbrotherlyke dealing to defraude..your said Orator. **1667** *Decay Chr. Piety* xvii. ¶ 3, I mean Victor's unbrotherlike heat towards the Eastern churches in the controversie about Easter. **1877** TENNYSON *Harold* V. i, O brother, most unbrotherlike to me, Thou gavest thy voice against me in my life.

**Unbro·therliness.** (f. next. See UN-[1] 12.)

**1647** N. WARD *Simple Cobler* 32 Nor would I declaime of the uncomlinesse, unbrotherlinesse, unseasonablenesse and unreasonablenesse of these direfull digladiations. **1885** C. J. LYALL *Anc. Arab. Poetry* 112 Ye took your stand far away from unbrotherliness.

**Unbro·therly,** *a.* [UN-[1] 7. Cf. Du. *onbroederlijk*, G. *unbrüderlich*.] Not brotherly or characteristic of a brother.

**1586** FERNE *Blaz. Gentrie* 113 The treacherous and vnbrotherly attempts of..the Kinges brother. **1605** WILLET *Hexapla Gen.* 470 Dishonouring their holy profession with vnbrotherlie strife. **1680** MATHER *Irenicum* 3 Forbearing and avoiding unbrotherly and provoking terms and words. **1741** RICHARDSON *Pamela* IV. 36 How did all their Hearts burn with sordid and unbrotherly Envy against their Father's favourite Son? **1796** *Monthly Mag.* I. 200 The people no longer view them with..mistrust, or unbrotherly emotions. **1829** SCOTT *Anne of G.* v, Here is the scroll, coldly worded, but far less unkindly than his unbrotherly message. **1891** F. W. NEWMAN *J. H. Newman* 21, I shall be told that these revelations are unbrotherly.

†**Unbro·therly,** *adv.* *Obs.* [UN-[1] 11. Cf. ON. *úbróðurliga*.] In a manner or spirit unbefitting a brother.

**1574** WHITGIFT *Def. Aunsw.* i. 74 As the name was first by the Papistes maliciously inuented, so is it of you verie vnbrotherly confirmed. **1605** CAMDEN *Rem.* 202 Brotherly to pardon his manifolde offences, that he had vnbrotherly committed against him. *a* **1635** SIBBES *Confer. Christ & Mary* (1656) 31 They had dealt most unbrotherly with him.

**Unbrou·ght,** *ppl. a.* [UN-[1] 8 b, 8 c.] Not brought (*forth, in*, or *into*).

**1525** TINDALE *N. T.* Prol. A serpent yet yonge, or yett unbrought forthe. **1595** DANIEL *Civ. Wars* III. xxii, Iudges incompetent To iudge their king unlawfully detaind, And vnbrought forth to plead his guiltles cause. **1600** FAIRFAX *Tasso* x. xviii, If in thy skilfull hart this lore be writ To tell th' euent of things to end vnbrought. **1817** KEATINGE *Trav.* II. 138 Not a foot of vertical superficies should remain unbrought into account.

**Unbrui·sed,** *ppl. a.* [UN-[1] 8.]

**1.** Not injured by bruising or crushing.

*c* **1440** *Pallad. on Husb.* III. 353 So sawe hit that the bark vnbresed be. **1526** *Pilgr. Perf.* (W. de W. 1531) 83 A floure, whan it is fresshe,..vnbrused & hole, is moche delectable & swete. **1579** SPENSER *Sheph. Cal.* Oct. 42 Doubted Knights, whose..helmes vnbruzed wexen dayly browne. **1606** SHAKS. *Tr. & Cr.* Prol. 14 On Dardan Plaines The fresh and yet vnbruised Greekes do pitch Their braue Pauillions. *a* **1652** BROME *City Wit* v. i, Unbruised bones, and smooth foreheads to face both. **1801** SURR *Splendid Misery* I. 172 Foul imps of ignominy will squat their loathsome forms on my unbruised bones. **1816** SCOTT *Antiq.* viii, The callant had come off wi' unbrizzed banes. **1900** F. T. BULLEN *Men Merch. Service* xxxii, One man..beat me until there was not a square inch of my small body unbruised.

*fig.* **1455** *Rolls of Parlt.* V. 280/2 Alwey kepyng oure trouthe to his said Highnesse unspotted and unbrused.

**2.** Not crushed small; unpounded.

**1607** TOPSELL *Four-f. Beasts* 327 It should seeme that none of his meate should fall thereinto vnbruised. **1802** PALEY *Nat. Theol.* ix. § 6. 1 The rough action of the unbruised spiculæ. **1844** H. STEPHENS *Bk. Farm* II. 191 The horses fed on unbruised raw and on boiled grain, gave results..very nearly alike.

**Unbru·shed,** *ppl. a.* (UN-[1] 8.) **1640** FULLER *Joseph's Coat* vi. (1867) 167 Men of a rugged, unbrushed nature, such as were never licked, hewn, or polished. **1888** BARRIE *When a Man's Single* iii, The coat had hung unbrushed on a nail for many years. †**Unbru·shen,** *ppl. a. Obs.* (UN-[1] 8 b.) *c* **1460** J. RUSSELL *Bk. Nurture* 944 Lett neuer wollyn cloth ne furre passe a seuenyght to be vnbrosshen & shakyn. **Unbru·talize,** *v.* (UN-[2] 6 a *c.*) **1852** MILL *Lett.* (1910) I. v. 165 All reading..which must tend to ..give them some of the meaning of self-devotion and heroism, in short, to unbrutalise them. **1862** H. KINGSLEY *Ravenshoe* lii, I am afraid of their getting too much unbrutalized for another struggle like ours. **Unbru·te,** *v.* (UN-[2] 6 b.) **1670** PENN *Lib. Consc.* Wks. 1782 III. 21 That it does not unbrute us, but unman us. **1687** A. LOVELL tr. *Bergerac's Com. Hist.* 49 Not being able to unbrute my self so soon. **Unbru·tify,** *v.* (UN-[2] 6 c.) **1812** TENNANT *Anster F.* III. xiv, The very waving of her arm Had pow'r a brutish lout to unbrutify and charm. **Unbru·tized,** *ppl. a.* (UN-[1] 8.) *a* **1711** KEN *Hymnotheo* Poet. Wks. 1721 III. 336, I certain am I must the Godhead fear, Since all Men unbrutis'd some God revere.

†**Unbu·bble,** *v. Obs.*—[1] [UN-[2] 3.] *trans.* To explode, dispel.

*a* **1640** JACKSON *Wks.* (1844) VII. 416 So may every novice in arts unbubble all that some great..schoolmen have been twenty or thirty years in contriving.

**Unbu·cked,** *ppl. a.* (UN-[1] 8 + BUCK *v.*[2]) **1638** MAYNE *Lucian* (1664) 337 'Tis not in a Lyons skinne, as I have heard, said Dinomachus, but in a Virgin Hindes skinne unbuckt.

**Unbu·ckle,** *v.* [UN-[2] 4 b.]

**1.** *trans.* To unfasten the buckle of (a shoe, belt, etc.); to undo or set free in this way.

*c* **1386** CHAUCER *Sqr.'s T.* 555 Ne neuere..Ne koude man..Countrefete the Sophymes of his Art Ne were worthy vnbokelen his galoche. **1393** LANGL. *P. Pl.* C. xx. 68 He vnbokelede hus boteles, and bobe he a-tamede. *c* **1430** *Pilgr. Lyf Manhode* I. cxxxviii. (1869) 72 Thanne the bocle j vnboclede. **1470–85** MALORY *Arthur* x. lx. 516 Soo the varlet wente to vnbockel his helme. **1548** UDALL, etc. *Erasm. Par. Luke* iii. 32 b, I..am vnworthy to vnbuccle the latchet of his shoes. **1577** *Test. 12 Patriarchs* (1604) 90 The young man unbuckled Joseph's shoes at the gate. **1606** SHAKS. *Ant. & Cl.* IV. iv. 12 He that vnbuckles this, till we do please To daft for our Repose, shall heare a storme. **1755** YOUNG *Centaur* v. Wks. 1757 IV. 223 This is a militant state; nor must man unbuckle his armour, till he puts on his shroud. **1820** SCOTT *Monast.* vi, He is like a miser, who will not unbuckle his purse to bestow a farthing. **1860** FROUDE *Hist. Eng.* V. 389 Dropping his cloak he unbuckled his sword. **1886** C. E. PASCOE *London of To-day* i. (ed. 3) 23 The Major..fell to unbuckling the straps of his trunk.

**b.** In fig. context. (Cf. MAIL *sb.*[3] 1 c.)

*c* **1386** CHAUCER *Miller's Prologue* 7 This gooth aright vnbokeled is the Male; Lat se now who shal telle another tale. *a* **1400** *Partonope* 7308 Of þi woo vnbocle þi male, And tell me all the verey troube. *a* **1600** DELONEY *Gentle Craft* II. viii. Wks. (1912) 186 Neuer be afraid man to vnbuckle Your Budget of close counsell to me. **1805** *Ann. Rev.* III. 164 We much doubt whether any one, not educated in the catholic schools, could have detected where the collar may best be unbuckled.

**c.** *fig.* To free or separate *from*; to open up, display; to detach, break off.

*a* **1548** HALL *Chron., Hen. VI*, 177 b, This noble realme.. shall neuer be vnbuckeled from her quotidian feuer. **1638** BRATHWAIT *Barnabees Jrnl.* (1818) 191 Some comfort unbuckle, my sweet honeysuckle. **1736** [CHETWOOD] *Voy. Vaughan* (1760) I. 264 The congregation immediately unbuckled their Devotions, and were crouding out as fast as they cou'd.

**2.** *absol.* To undo the buckle or buckles of a belt, garment, etc.

**1611** BEAUM. & FL. *King & No King* III, Why do you wear a Sword then? Come unbuckle...Unbuckle I say, and give it me. **1611** SHAKS. *Wint. T.* IV. iv. 659 Vnbuckle, vnbuckle. Fortunate Mistresse..you must retire your selfe Into some Couert. **1649** DAVENANT *Love & Hon.* I. i. 160 Unbuckle, Calladine, the day is hott. **1836** DICKENS *Sk. Boz, Gt. Winglebury Duel*, Up started the ostlers..unstrapping, and unchaining, and unbuckling.

**b.** *transf.* To become slack.

**1648** J. BEAUMONT *Psyche* XIII. clxxxii, His Joints unbuckled; and his Eyes did start; His hair stood staring up.

**c.** *fig.* To unbend, become less stiff.

**1886** STEVENSON *Kidnapped* viii, Even the captain..would sometimes unbuckle a bit, and tell me of the fine countries he had visited.

Hence **Unbu·ckling** *vbl. sb.*

**1598** FLORIO, *Sfibbiatura*, an vnbuckling, an vnlacing. *a* **1859** DE QUINCEY *Posth. Wks.* (1891) I. 272 Through the unbuckling of human nature under higher inspirations.

**Unbu·ckled,** *ppl. a.* [UN-[2] 8 and UN-[1] 8.] **a.** Having the buckle undone. **b.** Having the buckle not fastened.

In quot. *c* 1723 misused for 'not unbuckled' (in sense 2).

*c* **1489** CAXTON *Sonnes of Aymon* i. 42 There sholde ye haue seen..many..helmes vnbocled and sore beten. **1667** MILTON *P. L.* XI. 245 His starrie Helme unbuckl'd shew'd him prime In Manhood. *c* **1723** RAMSAY *The Nuptials* 145 That zone ..lang unbuckled grows a hatefu' thing. **1809** *Med. Jrnl.* XXI. 389 The girths being unbuckled, the whole of the back may be exposed and dressed. **1825** SCOTT *Talism.* ii, The long and ponderous Gothic war-sword which was flung unbuckled on the same sod. **1875** BEDFORD *Sailor's Pocket Bk.* vii. 220 Whilst in the boats they are to keep them unbuckled.

**Unbu·ckramed,** *a.* (UN-[1] 9.) **1813** COLMAN *Broad Grins, Vagaries Vind.* li, Thence I appeal, for judgment on my pen, To moral but unbuckram'd gentlemen. **Unbu·d,** *v.* (UN-[2] 4.) **1669** WORLIDGE *Syst. Agric.* (1681) 220 In a little time they have almost totally unbudded the Plumtrees, Currant-trees, &c. of a whole Town. **Unbu·dded,** *ppl. a.* (UN-[1] 8.) **1820** KEATS *Lamia* II. 54 Like the hid scent in an unbudded rose. **Unbu·dget,** *v.* (UN-[2] 3.) **1611** FLORIO, *Sbolgettare*, to vnbudget. **1843** [JAMES] *Commissioner* 62 Mr. Longmore was infinitely relieved by unbudgetting his griefs. **1886** *Gd. Words* 332 He had made the most extraordinary unbudgettings about his pet bees, guinea-pigs [etc.]. **Unbu·ffeted,** *ppl. a.* (UN-[1] 8.) [**1775** ASH.] **1855** LYNCH *Rivulet* LXXXVIII. vi, While unconfused by riot, Unbuffeted by storm.

**Unbui·ld,** *v.* [UN-[2] 3.] *trans.* To pull down, destroy, demolish (a building or structure).

**1607** SHAKS. *Cor.* III. i. 198 To vnbuild the Citie, and to lay all flat. **1642** T. GOODWIN *Zerub.*, etc. 25 Thou didst unbuild Hierusalem and my Temple. **1684** T. BURNET *Theory Earth* I. 91 God builds and unbuilds worlds: and who shall build up that arch that was broke down at the deluge? **1751** LABELYE *Westm. Bridge* 81 Whilst the Arches were unbuilding and taking down. **1820** SHELLEY *Cloud* 84, I arise and unbuild it again. **1829** CARLYLE *Misc.* (1857) II. 49 The Ephesian Temple..could be unbuilt by one madman, in a single hour. **1878** BROWNING *Poets Croisic* 13 Priestesses Unbuilt and then rebuilt it every May.

**b.** In fig. uses. Also *absol.*

**1640** HABINGTON *Edw. IV*, 75 The Almightie..permitted perjurie now to unbuild the greatnesse of Lancaster. **1667** MILTON *P. L.* VIII. 81 When they come to model Heav'n,.. how they will weild The mightie frame, how build, unbuild. *Ibid.* XII. 526 What will they then..but unbuild His living Temples, built by Faith to stand? **1856** R. A. VAUGHAN *Mystics* (1860) I. v. i. 112 First of all exercising the extraordinary will to the utmost to unbuild his body. **1875** WHITNEY *Life Lang.* iv. 74 The component elements of speech are first unified, then unbuilt and destroyed.

Hence **Unbui·lding** *vbl. sb.*

**1879** TRENCH *Poems* 155 Build it this time..A holy house, ..And we, though in the unbuilding there be pain, Will still affirm,—'tis well.

**Unbui·lded,** *ppl. a.* [UN-[1] 8.]

**1.** = UNBUILT *ppl. a.*

**1519** in *Somerset. & Dorset. N. & Q.* (1893) III. 244 Every half yere that the said sidehouse shall be unbuylded or unreedefyed. **1535** COVERDALE *Isaiah* vi. 11 Till the londe be also desolate, and lye vnbuylded. **1560** PILKINGTON *Expos. Aggeus* (1562) 163 Chuse you whether ye will let my house lye unbuylded stil,..or ye will repare it diligently.

*fig.* **1594** HOOKER *Eccl. Pol.* II. vii. § 5 When bare and vnbuilded conclusions are put into their mindes..they fall into anguish and perplexitie.

**2.** Not employed in building.

**1867** HOWELLS *Ital. Journ.* iii. 21 Mixing their weary brick and mortar with the earth's unbuilded dust.

**Unbui·lt,** *ppl. a.* [UN-[1] 8 b, 8 c: cf. prec.]

**1.** Not (yet) built or erected.

**1455–6** *Cal. Anc. Rec. Dublin* (1889) 290 Yf yt be unbylyt aftyr the fyrst yere..than the Mayre..shold require hym to repeyre hit. **1582** STANYHURST *Æneis* III. (Arb.) 74 Theare picht he his kingdoom, for then Troy cittye was vnbuylt, And castels stood not. **1612** DRAYTON *Poly-olb.* iv. 375 Tuisco, Gomer's son, from unbuilt Babel brought His people to that place. **1697** COLLIER *Ess. Mor. Subj.* II. (ed. 2) 5 The Rhodian Colossus had been lost;..the Egyptian Pyramids unbuilt. **1861** BERESF. HOPE *Eng. Cathedr. 19th C.* iv. 112 As I have given some unbuilt designs of modern architects.

**b.** Made without building.

**1882** J. PARKER *Apost. Life* I. 48 Elijah hid himself in an unbuilt chamber in the rock.

**2.** Of land: Not occupied with buildings; not built on or *upon*.

**1631** WEEVER *Anc. Funeral Mon.* 607 All which he pulled downe,..leauing the ground vnbuilt for a Cemitery or Churchyard. **1819** in Picton *L'pool Munic. Rec.* (1886) II. 378 Such part of their unbuilt land as will be sufficient for a Public Market. **1855** [J. R. LEIFCHILD] *Cornwall* 66 Scarcely in any other district so open and unbuilt on, would you find the agriculturist so completely subdued. **1893** A. CAWSTON *Street Improv. London* 124 In the as yet unbuilt parts grounds are to be reserved.

**Unbu·lk,** *v.* (UN-[2] 3.)

Probably an error for UNBUCKLE *v.* 1 b.

**1536** *Pilgr. T.* 272 in Thynne *Animadv.* (1875) 84 'But her,' he sayd, 'cowd I tell a tall', 'now I pray the,' quod I, 'vnbulke thy malle, and tell forthe'.

**Unbu·lky,** *a.* (UN-[1] 7.) **1678** CUDWORTH *Intell. Syst.* 780 Incorporeal..activities,..though they act upon bulk and extension, yet are themselves unbulkie, and devoid of quantity and dimensions. **1848** MILL *Pol. Econ.* III. xix. § 2 (1876) 369 This..must be occasioned by..the unbulky character of these commodities. **Unbu·mptious,** *a.* (UN-[1] 7.) **1865** TENNYSON in Ld. Tennyson *Mem.* (1897) I.. 28 Me, who am physically the most unbumptious of men and authors. **Unbu·nched,** *ppl. a.* (UN-[1] 8.) **1615** *Marr. & Wiving* xi. in *Harl. Misc.* (1809) II. 173 This destiny shall preserve him, to wear his brow..as unbunched as the front of a bachelor.

**Unbu·ndle,** *v.* [UN-[2] 3.] *trans.* To unpack, take out of a bundle. Also *fig.*

**1606** S. GARDINER *Bk. Angling* 111 Who so is a wise merchant will not vnbundle his seuerall wares to such. **1611** FLORIO, *Disfagottare*, to vnfaggot, to vnbundle. *a* **1739** JARVIS *Quix.* (1749) II. III. vi. 220 Unbundle your griefs, madam, and let us into the particulars.

**Unbu·ng,** *v.* [UN-[2] 3.] *trans.* To take the bung out of (a barrel). Hence **Unbu·nging** *vbl. sb.*

**1611** COTGR., *Detapper*, to vnbung, to open the bung-hole of. *a* **1693** *Urquhart's Rabelais* III. Prol. 6 There did he..unbung it,..unstopple it. **1694** MOTTEUX *Rabelais* IV. li. 199 This Stuff has unbung'd the Orifice of my Mustard-Barrel. **1742** *Lond. & Country Brew.* II. (1743) 143 When Servants have the Bunging and Unbunging of such Casks of Malt-Liquors.

**Unbu·nged,** *ppl. a.* (UN-[1] 8 or UN-[2] 8.) **1731** MILLER *Gard. Dict.* s.v. *Wine*, Let it [the vessel] stand unbung'd 'till cool. **1817** W. SELWYN *Law Nisi Prius* (ed. 4) II. 1261 The act of the warehouseman in leaving them unbunged after filling them up. **1897** *Daily News* 23 July 3/1 Unbunged barrels were left at the mercy of the rising water, the contents being spoilt. **Unbuoy·ant,** *a.* (UN-[1] 7.) **1866** J. B. ROSE tr. *Ovid's Met.* I Unfirm the earth, unbuoyant was the wave.

**Unbu·rden, unbu·rthen,** *v.* [UN-[2] 4 b. Cf. G. *entbürden*.]

**1.** *trans.* To unload; to free from a load or burden. Chiefly *fig.*, to relieve (a person, the mind, etc.) by the removal or disclosure of something. Freq. const. *of*.

α. **1538** ELYOT Addit., *Exonero, -rare*, to discharge or vnburdeyn. **1568** *Gismond of Salerne* I. ii. 34, I may perhappes devise some way to be unburdened of my life. **1622** S. WARD *Life of Faith in Death* (1627) 105 The inner man ages not, ..but rather lifts vp the head,..and expects to be unburdened. **1634** SIR T. HAWKINS *Pol. Observ.* 11 Tiberius by him unburdened from the greater toyles of Empire,..would not so soone..precipitate him. **1797** MRS RADCLIFFE *Italian* xii, I would fain sing to unburden it of some of its joy. **1846** MRS. A. MARSH *Father Darcy* II. xi. 204 She felt that irresistible necessity to unburden her heart. **1858** SEARS *Athan.* II. iii. 194 They unburden their minds to each other.

β. *a* **1595** SOUTHWELL *Hundred Medit.* (1873) 231 Thou.. commandest us to love to unburthen us of the heavy weight and griefs that we suffer. **1597** A. M. tr. *Guillemeau's Fr. Chirurg.* 22 b/2 Ther ensueth an effluxion of bloode, because that parte may be therof released and vnburthened. **1641** CHAS. I *Commons Remonstr.* Wks. 1662 II. 68 We desire to unburthen the Consciences of men of needless and superstitious Ceremonies. **1671** H. M. tr. *Erasm. Colloq.* 406 If I had not unburthened my Boat, I had been cast away together with my Boat, passengers, and fraught. **1777** SHERIDAN *Sch. Scand.* IV. iii, There is a subject, my dear Friend, on which I wish to unburthen my Mind to you. **1796** MORSE *Amer. Geog.* II. 17 The glutton..unburthens his stomach by squeezing himself between two close-standing trees. **1820** SHELLEY *Liberty* xix, As summer clouds dissolve, unburthened of their rain. **1875** WHYTE MELVILLE *Katerfelto* iv. 31 He unburthened his mind while watching Waif's stealthy movements.

**b.** *refl.*

**1589** GREENE *Menaphon* (Arb.) 67 Fame..vnburdened hir selfe of hir secrets in the presence of yong Pleusidippus. **1600** HAKLUYT *Voy.* III. 81 It is not possible that so great course of floods..can be digested here without vnburdening themselues into some open Sea beyond this place. **1634** SIR T. HERBERT *Trav.* 54 A violent storme of raine vnburthened it selfe. **1674** tr. *Scheffer's Lapland* xxxiv. 146 Several less rivers unburdening themselves at last into the Bothnick sea. **1859** J. LANG *Wand. India* 400 A trooper in the dragoons..thus unburthened himself. **1862** TROLLOPE *Orley F.* xxxi, She thought to herself that she would..then unburthen herself of the whole story.

**2.** To cast off, get rid of, discharge, after the manner of a burden; to disclose, reveal.

*a* **1593** MARLOWE & NASHE *Dido* v. i, The Sunne from Egypt shall rich odors bring, Wherewith his burning beames ..Shall here vnburden their exhaled sweetes. **1596** SHAKS. *Merch. V.* I. i. 133 From your loue I haue a warrantie To vnburthen all my plots and purposes. **1830** LYTTON *P. Clifford* iv, All that rage which it was necessary for her comfort that she should unburthen somewhere. **1876** E. MELLOR *Priesth.* viii. 372 There is, at times, a great relief in unburdening to a friend the sins and sorrows of one's life.

Hence **Unbu·rdening** *vbl. sb.*; **Unbu·rdenment.**

**1550** THOMAS *Ital. Dict.*, *Scaricamento*, a dischardge or vnburdenyng. **1848** MRS. GASKELL *Mary Barton* ii, The unburdening of her fears and thoughts to her friend. **1892** MRS. H. WARD *David Grieve* II. vii, A moment of unburdenment, of intimacy. **1902** *Fortn. Rev.* June 1048 The unburdening of sins is generally a more irksome task.

**Unbu·rdened,** *ppl. a.* (UN-[1] 8 and UN-[2] 8.)

**1548** *Act 2 & 3 Edw. VI*, c. 21 § 1 Beinge free and unburdened from the care and coste of fyndinge Wyef and Children. **1605** SHAKS. *Lear* I. i. 42 Conferring them on yonger strengths, while we Vnburthen'd crawle toward death. **1724** SWIFT *Poems, On Dreams* 8 When in bed we rest our weary limbs, The mind unburden'd sports in various whims. **1775** BURKE *Sp. Concil. Amer.* Wks. III. 116 The obedient colonies in this scheme are heavily taxed; the refractory remain unburthened. **1875** C. L. KENNEY *Mem. M. W. Balfe* 148 His exchequer would be unburdened with superfluous expenses. **1883** STEVENSON *Silverado Sq.* 122 Even for a man unburthened, the ascent was toilsome and precarious.

**Unbu·rdensome,** *a.* (UN-[1] 7.) **1792** G. WAKEFIELD *Mem.* (1804) I. 363 Judiciall processes, speedy, decisive, and unburdensome. **1817** COLERIDGE *Biog. Lit.* xi. (1882) 111 The establishment presents a patronage at once..effective and unburthensome. **Unbu·rdensomeness.** (f. prec.;

see UN-[1] 12.) **1795** BENTHAM *Supply without Burthen* 27 Thus stands the resource in point of unburthensomeness.

**Unbu·rgessed,** *a.* (UN-[2] 8.) **1671** E. CHAMBERLAYNE *Pres. St. Eng.* II. 136 The petty decayed Burroughs [petitioned] that they might not be obliged to send Burgesses to Parlament, whereby it came to pass that divers were unburgessed.

**Unbu·riable,** *a.* (UN-[1] 7 b.) **1853** G. J. CAYLEY *Las Alforjas* I. 203 It would be an inconvenience to have an unpleasant, unburiable moral corpse of an unjustly supposed immoral ancester always lying at their door. **1872** TENNYSON *Gareth & Lynette* 79 A yet-warm corpse, and yet unburiable.

**Unbu·rial.** [UN-[2] 8.] Disinterment.

**1872** RUSKIN *Fors Clav.* xv. 15 The persons thus reverenced in their burial, or unburial, being all, by profession, soldiers.

**Unbu·ried,** *ppl. a.* Forms: (see BURY *v.*). [UN-[1] 8.] Not buried; not interred.

*a* **900** *O. E. Martyrol.* 22 Jan. 28 Se casere þa bebead þæt hine man forlete unbyrgedne. *a* **1225** *Ancr. R.* 352 Þe dead nis [*v.r.* ne wis] nout of, þauh he ligge unburied & rotie buuen eorðe. **1297** R. GLOUC. (Rolls) 4486 Men bysyde of þe lond he let burye is fon, Vor he ne kepte uor reuþe þat þer were vnbured non. *c* **1386** CHAUCER *Frankl. T.* 713 His loue rather for to dyen chees Than for to suffre his body vnburyed be. *c* **1430** *Life St. Kath.* (1884) 59 He bad þat.. her hedes [should be] smyten of and her bodyes left vnburyed. **1460** CAPGRAVE *Chron.* (Rolls) 75, xxx. dayes lay his body onburied, til Seynt Petir..bad him bery it. **1513** DOUGLAS *Æneid* XI. vii. 191 So that we..Be nocht down strowit in the feildis ded, In cumpaneis vnberyit or bewalit. **1560** DAUS tr. *Sleidane's Comm.* 286 b, Wherof the one departed xi yeares past,..and remayned unburied hitherto. **1600** HAKLUYT *Voy.* III. 806 Euery Fort had in it one cast peece, which peeces were buryed in the ground, the cariages were standing in their place vnburied. **1697** DRYDEN *Æneis* XI. 4 The pious chief, whom double cares attend For his unbury'd soldiers and his friend. *a* **1745** SWIFT *Hen. II,* Wks. 1768 IV. 317 When he..found that..he must draw upon himself the scandal of keeping a father unburied. **1836** THIRLWALL *Greece* III. xxvi. 449 The sight of the unburied dead struck their surviving friends with pious grief. **1891** FARRAR *Darkn. & Dawn* lxv, The stench of an unburied corpse which lay by the roadside.

**Unburle·squed,** *ppl. a.* (UN-[1] 8.) **1827** POLLOK *Course T.* VII. 586 Unfaded work of Deity, And unburlesqued by mortal's puny skill. **1876** MEREDITH *Beauch. Career* i, Politics..(enough, when unburlesqued, to blow the down off the gossamer-stump of fiction..) must be treated of.

**†Unbu·rly,** *a.* and *adv. Obs.* In 5 unborely, vnburely. [UN-[1] 7 and 11.] Uncomely; not elegant(ly).

*a* **1400** *Sir Perc.* 525 Thofe he unborely were dyghte. *c* **1475** *Rauf Coilȝear* 522 Thocht thair brandis be blak and vnburely. *Ibid.* 807 His blonk was vnburely, braid and ouir hie.

**Unbu·rn,** *v.* [UN-[2] 3.] *trans.* To restore from the effects of burning.

**1815** J. SMITH *Panorama Sci. & Art* II. 485 To deprive them of oxygen is virtually to unburn them. **1869** *Q. Rev.* CXXVI. 263 The duty of the plant, on the other hand, is to unburn carbonic acid, to sunder the molecules of that compound back again to their elements of carbon and oxygen.

Hence **Unbu·rning** *vbl. sb.*

**1866** ODLING *Anim. Chem.* 72 The heat absorbed in the unburning, so to speak, of the hydrogen.

**Unbu·rnable,** *a.* (UN-[1] 7 b.) **1881** *Harper's Weekly* XXV. 455 There is scarcely a town that does not contain his unburnable chests [= safes].

**Unbu·rning,** *ppl. a.* (UN-[1] 10; cf. OE. *unbyrnende.*) **1644** DIGBY *Nat. Bodies* vii. (1658) 61 The unburning fire (which we call light) streaming from the flame of a candle. **1822** T. TAYLOR *Apuleius* 263 The purity of the vivific and unburning fire of the heavens. **1867** MORRIS *Jason* II. 666 Some happy summer isle Whereon the kind unburning sun doth smile For ever.

**Unbu·rnished,** *ppl. a.* (UN-[1] 8.)

**1691** *Lond. Gaz.* No. 2654/4, 7 Silver Tankards, one unburnished weighing about 32 Ounces. **1795** SOUTHEY *Joan of Arc* VII. 40 Their bucklers lay Unburnish'd and defiled. **1842** TENNYSON *Ulysses* 23 How dull it is to pause, to make an end, To rust unburnish'd, not to shine in use! **1894** *Daily News* 11 Nov. 5/2 An olive branch in old unburnished gold is..thrown across the oak branches.

**Unbu·rnt, unbu·rned,** *ppl. a.* Forms: (see BURN *v.*). [UN-[1] 8 and 8 b. Cf. MDu. *onghebernt, -brant,* Du. *ongebrand,* G. *ungebrannt,* ON. and Icel. *úbrendr, óbrendr* (Sw. *obrand,* Da. *ubrændt*).]

**1.** Not burnt or consumed by fire.

*α. c* **1290** *S. Eng. Leg.* I. 29/97 His bones þat weren bi-left vn-barnd amidde þe se to caste. *c* **1440** *Alph. Tales* 162 Þat was fon vnbyrnyd emang þe hate colis. **1563** FOXE *A. & M.* 1224/1, I will geue vi fagottes to burne the with all or thou shuldest be vnburned. **1607** SHAKS. *Cor.* V. i. 27 He said, 'twas folly, For one poore graine or two, to leaue vnburnt, And still to nose th' offence. **1623** BINGHAM *Xenophon* 57 They came..to the vnburnt villages, setting afire the villages, where they last quartered. **1676** GREW *Exper. Luctation* iii. § 11 Egg-shells..being burnt, are far stronger Medicines, than when unburnt. **1715** DESAGULIERS *Fires Impr.* 133 Put what Wood is left unburn'd over them. **1849** THOMS tr. *Worsaae's Primeval Antiq. Denmark* 94 The ancient cromlechs or giants' chambers, with unburnt bodies and objects of stone. **1884** *Health Exhib. Catal.* 71/2 Stoves..constructed specially to bring all the air into the room..pure and warm but unburnt.

*β. c* **1384** CHAUCER *H. Fame* I. 173 Anchises..Bare the goddesse of the londe Thilke that vnbrende were. **1412–20** LYDG. *Chron. Troy* IV. 6527 Þei ne lefte with-inne þe cite No þing vnbrent. *c* **1450** *Mirk's Festial* 163 So [he] sauet his bokes vnbrent þrogh þe grace and þe mercy of God. **1509** BARCLAY *Shyp of Folys* (1570) 171 Because the lightning or thunder violent..suffreth thee and thy house to be vnbrent. **1568** GRAFTON *Chron.* II. 346 They..made a road into Scotland,..and left nothing vnbrent to Edenbourgh.

*γ. c* **1375** *Sc. Leg. Saints* xxvii. (*Machor*) 188 Þe barne stil can ly, Ay kepand it sa godis grace þat in þe fyr vnbrynt it was. *c* **1480** HENRYSON *Annunciation* 40 The low of luf haldand þe hete Vnbrynt full blithlie birnis. **1555** *Sc. Acts, Mary* (1814) II. 490/1 Gif samekill restis vnbrint of the haill tenement. **1571–2** *Reg. Privy Council Scot.* II. 121 For sauftie of the houssis..being within the same unbrint and dimolissit.

*fig. a* **1584** MONTGOMERIE *Cherrie & Slae* (1597) 243 Bot now na bluid in me remaines, Vnbrunt and bruilȝeit throw my vaines, Be luiffis bellowes blawin.

**2.** Not subjected to the action of fire for a specific purpose. Esp. of bricks, clay, lime, etc.

**1626** BACON *Sylva* § 898 We see also, that burnt wine is more hard and astringent, than wine unburnt. *c* **1650** NORGATE *Miniatura* (1919) 15 Cologne Earth unburnt..is a very good colour for deepe shadowes. **1815** ELPHINSTONE *Acc. Caubul* (1842) I. 305 The commonest house by far is built of unburned brick. **1877** RAYMOND *Statist. Mines & Mining* 382 When the pile is finished the outside crust of unburned pyrites is taken off and put onto the next pile.

**Unbu·rrow,** *v.* [UN-[2] 7 and 5.] **a.** *intr.* To come out of a burrow. Also *fig.* **b.** *trans.* To bring or force out of a burrow.

**1744** in *10th Rep. Hist. MSS. Comm.* App. I. 280 If Ma[rsha]l Saxe will not unburrow I have advised our sending strong partys of horse [etc.]. **1827** J. MONTGOMERY *Pelican Isl.* III. 158 Hence the young brood, that never knew a parent, Unburrowed and by instinct sought the sea. **1860** DICKENS *Uncomm. Trav.* x, He feigns that he can bring down sparrows, and unburrow rats.

**Unbu·rse,** *v. Obs.*[−0] (UN-[2] 5.) **1570** LEVINS *Manip.* 191 To Dispurse, *expendere.* To Disburse, *idem...* To Vnburse and Vnpurse, *idem.*

**Unbu·rst,** *ppl. a.* (UN-[1] 8 b; cf. UNBROSTEN.)

**1782** F. DOUGLAS *E. Coast Scot.* 44 In one of them, called the Murray-gate,..several bombs, unburst, were lately found, deep sunk in the earth. **1855** T. R. JONES *Anim. Kingd.* (ed. 2) 333 Another membrane, which in the unburst egg is external to this and lines the interior of the shell.

**Unbu·rstable,** *a.* (UN-[1] 7.) **1890** *Times* 25 Oct. 5/1 The power that will make guns unburstable and armour impenetrable.

**Unburthen, -ed, -some,** varr. UNBURDEN, etc.

**Unbu·ry,** *v.* [UN-[2] 3.] *trans.* To disinter; to take out of the ground again.

**14..** *Voc.* in Wr.-Wülcker 581 *Exhumo,* to vnberye. **1481** CAXTON *Godfrey* cvi. 162 Whan the peple afoote knewe this, they ranne, And there vnburyed them, And toke them out of theyr sepultures and graues. **1530** PALSGR. 766/2 It shulde seme that he hath done some great offence, that they unbury hym nowe. **1567** JEWEL *Def. Apol.* 100 The same Pope Steuin vnburied his Predecessour Pope Formosus, and defaced, and mangled his naked carkesse. **1605** WILLET *Hexapla Gen.* 250 The Sichemites..would rather haue vnburied them. **1647** TRAPP *Comm. Rev.* xi. 9 They unburied and burned the bones of Hermannus Ferrariensis after they had sainted him. **1848** GALLENGA *Italy* I. 61 As long as there remain..inscriptions to decipher, or ruins to unbury. **1876** LOWELL *Among my Bks.* Ser. II. 132 The medicine by which vampires were cured was to unbury them, drive a stake through them [etc.].

**b.** *fig.* or in fig. context.

**1620** SHELTON *Quix.* II. xlix. 321 Because they come not in a fit time to haue audience: straight they back-bite..him, gnaw his bones, and vnbury his ancestors. *a* **1739** JARVIS *Quix.* (1749) II. III. v. 217 Speaking ill of us, unburying our bones, and burying our reputations. **1839** LYTTON *Richelieu* I. i, Your breast holds both my secrets; Never Unbury either! **1862** H. AÏDÉ *Carr of Carrlyon* I. 309 The secret is ours. No one has a right to demand us to unbury our past. **1887** BROWNING *Parleyings, Fust & Friends,* Unbury that brow! Look up, that thy judge may read clear in thine eyes!

Hence **Unbu·rying** *vbl. sb.*

**1899** S. BUTLER *Shaks. Sonn.* 117 To suppose that he sanctioned the unburying, is to deny the commonest instinct of humanity.

**Unbu·sied,** *ppl. a.* (UN-[1] 8. Cf. Du. *ongebezigd.*)

**1570** T. WILSON tr. *Demosth. Orat.* vii. 101 Why wouldest thou not rather follow a quiet and vnbusied life? **1628** J. DOUGHTY *Serm. Church-schismes* 13 Rather then rest vnbusied, they will doe some vnnecessary mischiefe. **1658** ROWLAND tr. *Moufet's Theat. Ins.* 920 Yet..they are not unbusied neither; but they build houses for the Kings.

**Unbu·siness.** (UN-[1] 12 b.) **1901** *Westm. Gaz.* 19 Mar. 4/2 The unbusiness methods which mark the administration of the War Office.

**Unbu·siness-like,** *a.* (UN-[1] 7 c.) **1824** SCOTT *Redgauntlet* ch. ii, His own very unbusiness-like mistake of shuffling the Provost's letter..among some papers belonging to Peter Peebles's affairs. **1862** HELPS *Organiz. Daily Life* 21 Great efforts will be made in a scattered, uncomprehensive, and unbusiness-like way.

**Unbu·sk,** *v.* [UN-[2] 4 and 7.] *trans.* and *intr.* To undress.

**1596** NASHE *Saffron Walden* Wks. (Grosart) III. 178, I would we might know her, and see her vnbuskt and naked once. **1673** R. HEAD *Canting Acad.* 29 We had got Money enough to new cloath our selves, which we did, having first unbusk'd.

**Unbu·sked,** *ppl. a.* (UN-[1] 8.) **1798** MACNEILL *Poems, Sc. Muse* xxxiv, 'Tween pastoral Tweed and wand'ring Ayr, Whar unbusked nature blooms sae fair.

**Unbustling,** *ppl. a.* (UN-[1] 10.) **1826** SHERER *Notes & Refl. Ramble in Germany* 223 She..then resumed her occupation with a plain unbustling air.

**Unbu·sy,** *a.* (UN-[1] 7.) **1731** A. HILL *Adv. Poets* Ep. p. xiv, I am so devoted a Lover of a private, and unbusy Life. **1747** RICHARDSON *Clarissa* (1811) I. xviii. 132 [She] continued looking into a drawer among laces and linen in a way neither busy, nor unbusy. **1827** COLERIDGE *Work without Hope* 5 All Nature seems at work,..And I, the while, the sole unbusy thing. **1852** *Meanderings of Mem.* I. 196 If bigotted, or most unbusy herd, O'er stocked with time and talent, were preferred.

**Unbu·sy,** *v.* (UN-[2] 6 a.) *a* **1657** R. LOVEDAY *Lett.* (1663) 120 Error has humbled my Reason, and unbusied my reaches at futurity to a quiet resignation to the great Disposer.

**Unbu·tchered,** *ppl. a.* (UN-[1] 8.) **1835** LYTTON *Rienzi* IX. iv, To live unbutchered by the Barons, and untaxed by their governors.

**Unbu·tted,** *ppl. a.* (UN-[1] 8 c.) **1855** [see UNBICKERED].

**Unbu·ttered,** *ppl. a.* [UN-[1] 8. Cf. Du. *ongeboterd.*] Not spread (or cooked) with butter.

**1584** COGAN *Haven Health* 29 The greene beanes they vse to butter, & the other they eate with salt vnbuttered. **1655** MOUFET & BENNET *Health's Improv.* 40 If it be too lean and dry..it is far worse, and nourisheth the body no more then a piece of unbuttered stockfish. **1869** MRS. WHITNEY *Hitherto* I. vii. 145 The going in to eat beans or porridge and unbuttered bread.

**Unbu·tton,** *v.* [UN-[2] 3.]

**1.** *trans.* To unfasten (buttons); to undo the buttons of (a garment).

*c* **1325** *Gloss. W. de Bibbesw.* in Wright *Voc.* 149 Unbotone [*glossing* Tachet]. *c* **1530** REDFORDE *Play Wit & Sci.* (Shaks. Soc.) 29 Unbuttun thy cote, foole; canst thow do nothyng? **1653** H. COGAN tr. *Pinto's Trav.* xxix. 113 Hereupon she unbottoned one of the sleeves of a red Satin Gown she had on. **1688** R. HOLME *Armoury* IV. xi. (Roxb.) 447/1 The oyntment being thus prepared, the Kings buttons are to be vnbottoned. **1727** SWIFT *Circumcision E. Curll* Wks. 1755 III. I. 166 Six Jews..laid hands upon him, and unbuttoning his breeches threw him upon the table. **1829** LYTTON *Disowned* 28 The stranger slowly unbuttoned his gaiters. **1891** C. ROBERTS *Adrift Amer.* 118 Unbuttoning my coat I pulled my six-shooter round handy over my right hip.

*fig.* **1593** G. HARVEY *Pierce's Super.* Wks. (Grosart) II. 124 Vnbutton thy vanity, and Vnlase thy folly. **1652** J. WRIGHT tr. *Camus' Nat. Paradox* v. 107 Wee shall never have done contesting..unless I quite unbutton my breast to you. **1830** GALT *Lawrie T.* II. vii. (1849) 64 Unbuttoning my bosom and showing him all the profitable secrets I had learnt in business. **1892** STEVENSON *Across the Plains* 25, I..unbuttoned my wrath under the similitude of ironical submission.

**b.** With personal object. Also *refl.*

**1596** SHAKS. *1 Hen. IV,* I. ii. 3 Thou art so fat-witted with drinking of olde Sacke, and vnbuttoning thee after Supper. **1619** R. JONES *Serm. Resurr.* (1659) 64 Help them, good Women! unbutton the Souldiers, ye need not fear their Halberts. **1650** GREAVES *Seraglio* 5 He puts off his uppermost Coat,..then turns up his sleeves, and unbuttoneth himself. **1696** VANBRUGH *Relapse* II. i, Call a surgeon there.—Unbutton him quickly. **1784** COWPER *Tiroc.* 304 The little ones, unbutton'd, glowing hot, Playing our games.

*absol.* **1725** *Fam. Dict.* s.v. *Swoon,* The most common way of relieving the Patient, is to throw Water in his Face; to make him lie on his Back, to unbutton or unlace.

**c.** *absol.* To undo one's own buttons; also (quot. 1605), to become unbuttoned.

**1605** SHAKS. *Lear* III. iv. 112 Off, off you Lendings: Come, vnbutton heere. **1664** [J. SCUDAMORE] *Homer à la Mode* 54 Till th' were so cramd with beef and mutton, That every one was faine t' unbutton. *a* **1697** AUBREY *Lives* (1898) I. 110 A man that is buttond or laced too hard, must unbutton before he can be at his ease. **1760–72** H. BROOKE *Fool of Qual.* (1809) III. 142 Gluttony stuffs till it pants, and unbuttons and stuffs again. **1817–8** COBBETT *Resid. U.S.* (1822) 201 You are here disgusted with none of those eaters by reputation that are found..in England: fellows that unbutton at it.

**2.** *transf.* To open up or unfold (a bud).

**1663** BP. PATRICK *Parab. Pilgr.* xxxvii, It swells into small knobs or buttons..Suppose you should unbutton it as soon as it swells,..would you not endanger the spoiling of its beauties?

Hence **Unbu·ttoning** *vbl. sb.*

**1591** PERCIVALL, *Desabotonadura,* vnbuttoning. **1892** *Photogr. Ann.* II. p. xxxi, With the unbuttoning of a strap ..three legs unfold and give us a most rigid Tripod.

**Unbu·ttoned,** *ppl. a.* [UN-[1] 8.]

**1.** Not furnished with a button or buttons.

**1583** *Rates of Custome Ho.* F iv, Caps vnbuttoned English the dosen xvi s. viij d. **1902** *Daily Chron.* 8 Dec. 3/6 Woe to the man who has to encounter an enemy like M. Merignac with a duelling sword or an unbuttoned foil.

**2.** Not fastened with buttons; having the buttons unfastened.

In some instances possibly f. UNBUTTON *v.*

**1592** GREENE *Courtier* D iv b, A thredbare blacke coate vnbuttond before vpon the brest. **1600** SHAKS. *A. Y. L.* III. ii. 398 Your hose should be vngarter'd, your bonnet vnbanded, your sleeue vnbutton'd. **1645** MILTON *Colast.* Wks. 1851 IV. 368 This is not for an unbutton'd fellow to discuss in the Garret, at his tressle. **1711** ADDISON *Spect.* No. 129 ¶ 9 His new silk Waistcoat, which was unbutton'd in several Places to let us see that he had a clean Shirt on. **1790** J. C. SMYTH in *Med. Commun.* II 477, I..found him.. sitting in a great chair with the collar of his shirt unbuttoned. **1832** LYTTON *Eugene A.* I. ii, The one short, dry, fragile, and betraying a love of ease in his unbuttoned vest. **1854** A. FONBLANQUE in *Life & Labours* vi. (1874) 513 If he had seen the same officer with an unbuttoned jacket, or any other disorder in his dress.

*fig.* **1898** *Westm. Gaz.* 27 Oct. 4/1 An example of the master in an unwontedly unbuttoned mood.

**Unbu·ttressed,** *ppl. a.* (UN-[1] 8.) **1849** FREEMAN *Archit.* 280 The analogy which its vast, unbroken, unbuttressed height bears to the campaniles of that country. **1893** *Archaeol.* LIII. 550 On account of its unbuttressed length.

**†Unbu·xom,** *a. Obs.* Forms: (see BUXOM *a.*). [UN-[1] 7. Cf. UNBOWSOME *a.*]

**1.** Not submissive or compliant; intractable, disobedient. Freq. const. *to.*

*a* **1250** *Prov. Ælfred* 450 in *O. E. Misc.* 128 Betere is child vnbore, þane vnbuhsum. *a* **1300** *Cursor M.* 28089 To crist ic haue vn-buxum bene. *c* **1330** R. BRUNNE *Chron. Wace* (Rolls) 15378 Monk ne clerk wolde þey non spare, For þey byforn unbuxom ware. **1380** *Lay Folks Catech.* 713 (Lamb. MS.), Rebel men..ben vnbuxum to cryst and his chyrche. *c* **1440** *Jacob's Well* 112 Þis vyce makyth a mannys herte hard & vnbuxom to god. *a* **1470** H. PARKER *Dives &*

*Pauper* (1496) IV. viii. 171/1 Childern unbuxum to fader & moder sholde be stoned to deth. **1559** AYLMER *Harborowe* Q 4 God punished that sinne with another by sending them vnbuxome hartes.

*absol.* **1389** in *Eng. Gilds* (1870) 5 ȝif eny be rebelle..þe forsaide bretherhede shul be helpyng aȝeins þe rebelle and vnboxhum.

**2.** Unready to bend; stiff.

*c* **1412** HOCCLEVE *De Reg. Princ.* 985 My bak unbuxum hath swich thyng forsworne, At instance of writing,..That stowpyng hath hym spilt with his labour.

Hence **†Unbu·xomly** *adv. Obs.*

**1390** GOWER *Conf.* I. 88 Evere unbuxomly thei pleigne Upon fortune. *Ibid.* III. 212 The more unbuxomliche he cride. *a* **1400** *MS. Harl.* 2260 fol. 3, I usedde wronge with my body, And serves the unbuxumly.

**†Unbu·xomhead.** *Obs.*—[1] [f. prec.] **a.** Disobedience. **b.** Stiffness of body.

*c* **1250** *Gen. & Ex.* 345 Vn-buxumhed he hauen hem don, Vn-buxumhed is hem cumen on; Vn-welde woren..Here owen limes hem wið-in.

**†Unbu·xomness.** *Obs.* [f. as prec.] Disobedience; obstinacy.

*a* **1300** *Cursor M.* 27616 O pride bicums vnbuxumnes, Strif, and strutt, and frawardnes. *c* **1315** SHOREHAM VII. 806 God wyste wel þat man schold erry, And þorȝ on-boxamnesse uerry Fram alle healþe. **1390** GOWER *Conf.* I. 89 And in this wise I me confesse Of that ye clepe unbuxomnesse. **1426** AUDELAY *Poems* (Percy Soc.) 18 Aȝayns my gret goodnes Thai chewyn me unbuxumnes. *c* **1450** *Mirk's Festial* 22 When angeles seon þat hor Lorde was wroth wyth man for vnbuxamnes. *c* **1530** *Songs, Carols*, etc. (E.E.T.S.) 55 Marcy, God, & forgevenes For pride & for vnbuxvmnes!

**Unc**, var. UNK *pron.* **Unca**, var. UNCO *Sc.*

**Unca·bined**, *a.* (UN-[1] 9.) **1891** HARDY *Tess* ii, There was an uncribbed, uncabined aspect in his eyes and attire.

**Unca·bled**, *a.* (UN-[1] 9.) **1791** COWPER *Odyss.* XIII. 117 Within it, ships (The port once gain'd) uncabled ride secure. **1872** J. S. JEANS *Western Worthies* 93 The uncabled oceans that separate the families of the earth.

**Unca'd**, Sc. f. UNCALLED.

**Unca·denced**, *ppl. a.* (UN-[1] 8.) *c* **1838** MRS. BROWNING *Pet-Name* i, I have a name, a little name, Uncadenced for the ear.

**Uncage**, *v.* [UN-[2] 5.] *trans.* To let or take out of a cage. Also *fig.*

**1620** SHELTON *Quix.* II. xxxviii. 250 But pray vncage your griefes, and tell them us. **1659** TORRIANO, *Sgabbiare*, to uncage, to let loose. **1660** KATH. PHILIPS *Poems* (1664) 77 Thou wert all Soul, and through thy Eyes it shin'd: Asham'd and angry to be so confin'd, It long'd to be uncag'd. **1837** W. A. BUTLER *Serm.* Ser. II. xxii. (1856) 326 The aged saint, ..turning round, bade them uncage the lions. **1855** J. R. LEIFCHILD] *Cornwall* 167 Let Imagination have her flight, uncage her, and sit down on the top of this smooth bank.

Hence **Unca·ged** *ppl. a.*[1]

**1647** FANSHAWE *Poems, Virgil's Æneas* 296 This said, cut off her hayre, Heat left her, and th' uncaged Soule flew through the Ayre.

**Unca·ged**, *ppl. a.*[2] [UN-[1] 8.] Not shut up or confined in a cage.

*a* **1734** POPE *Epigr. Dennis* 7 Uncag'd then let the harmless monster rage. **1775** ASH, *Uncaged*,..not put into a cage. **1890** 'R. BOLDREWOOD' *Col. Reformer* (1891) 260 The capture of an uncaged bird. **1893** in J. H. Barrows *World's Parlt. Relig.* II. 820 The [Jewish] spirit..shows in this free land the elasticity of the uncaged eagle.

**Uncairdly**, var. UNCAREDLY *adv. Obs.*

**Uncalca·reous**, *a.* (UN-[1] 7.) **1793** SMEATON *Edystone L.* § 193 It may be accounted a pure limestone..as containing no uncalcareous matter. **Uncalcified**, *ppl. a.* (UN-[1] 8.) **1854** OWEN in *Orr's Circ. Sci., Org. Nat.* I. 295 Certain tracts of that soft and vascular substance were left uncalcified. **1880** HUXLEY *Crayfish* iv. 155 An uncalcified plate, bent into the form of a half cylinder.

**Unca·lcined**, *ppl. a.* (UN-[1] 8.)

**1601** HOLLAND *Pliny* II. 588 The same are much used also crude and uncalcined..for the king's evill. **1676** GREW *Exper. Luctation* iii. § 17 Millepedes likewise calcined, makes a stronger Effervescence, than when uncalcined. **1796** KIRWAN *Elem. Min.* (ed. 2) I. 395 Limestones are frequently ejected from volcanos uncalcined. **1839** URE *Dict. Arts* 322 A small quantity of uncalcined matt must be introduced. **1861** SIR W. FAIRBAIRN *Iron* 76 The use of raw coal and uncalcined ore.

**Unca·lculable**, *a.* (UN-[1] 7 b and 5 b.) **1848** MILL *Pol. Economy* II. vii. § 4. 337 The habit of foreign service, by opening to the children a career indefinite and uncalculable, sometimes calls forth a superabundant population. **Unca·lculableness.** (UN-[1] 12 and 5 b.) **1831** J. FOSTER *Lett.* in Ryland *Life* (1846) II. 192 There are few things more remarkable than the total uncalculableness, if I may make such a word, of the ultimate local destinations of a young family.

**Unca·lculated**, *ppl. a.* (UN-[1] 8.)

**1828** *Life Planter Jamaica* 153 In addition to these uncalculated incidents, the wet weather retarded the forwarding of the work. **1856** KANE *Arct. Expl.* I. xxxii. 443 This uncalculated accession of numbers makes our little room too crowded. **1883** SIR N. LINDLEY in *Law Rep.* 25 Chan. Div. 355 If the Plaintiff were to sue the Defendant again for that uncalculated interest, his action would be considered frivolous.

**Unca·lculating**, *ppl. a.* (UN-[1] 10.)

*a* **1832** BENTHAM *Deontol.* ii. (1834) II. 84 That sacrifice is mere asceticism;..it is miscalculating or uncalculating blindness. **1861** GEO. ELIOT *Silas M.* iii, Trying to turn his gloom into uncalculating anger. **1873** W. CORY *Lett. & Jrnls.* (1897) 331 These uncalculating disinterested lovers of truth.

Hence **Unca·lculatingly** *adv.*

**1852** HAWTHORNE *Blithedale Rom.* ix, She seemed ready to fling it away..uncalculatingly. *a* **1853** ROBERTSON *Lect.* ii. (1858) 192 It consecrated certain acts as right, uncalculatingly, and independently of consequences.

**Unca·lendared**, *ppl. a.* [UN-[2] 8 and UN-[1] 8.] **a.** Removed from a calendar or roll. **b.** Not entered in a calendar.

**1654** GAYTON *Pleas. Notes* III. vii. 113 He..is Uncalendred for ever, and his name expung'd the Ephemerides of King Arthurs Knights. **1850** BLACKIE *Æschylus* II. 39 The flower-strewn Spring, and the fruit-laden Summer, Uncalendered, unregistered, returned. **1898** *Westm. Gaz.* 7 Dec. 5/1 With certain other uncalendared manuscripts placed at his disposal by Lord Salisbury.

**Unca·lled**, *ppl. a.* Also 8– *Sc.* unca'd. [UN-[1] 8, 8 c. Cf. MSw. and Sw. *okallad*, Da. *ukaldet*.]

**1.** Not called or summoned; not invited.

*a* **1400-50** *Alexander* 832 And I to consaile vn-callid I can noȝt þar-on. *c* **1440** *Alph. Tales* 243 Þis Hillarius come to þis cowncell vncallid. *a* **1500** in *Ratis Raving*, etc. 9 Be curtas ay in company: To consell cum þow nocht wncald. **1533** MORE *Debell. Salem* Wks. 973/1 The ordinary shal know who can tell more, and will also if they be called and sworen, and wyll not vncalled and vnsworen, tel no tale at all. **1587** HARRISON *England* II. xvi. (1877) 280 Yet were they not so narrowlie taken, but that a third part of this like multitude was left vnbilled and vncalled. **1667** MILTON *P. L.* IX. 523 Hee boulder now, uncall'd before her stood. **1697** DRYDEN *Virgil* Postscr., For who would give physic to the great, when he is uncalled? **1796** MME. D'ARBLAY *Camilla* X. iii, [He] would, uncalled, have given his whole attention. **1810** SHELLEY *Spectral Horseman* 20 The shade of a murdered man, Who has rushed uncalled to the throne of his God. **1856** MRS. BROWNING *Aur. Leigh* IV. 84 He came uncalled wherever grief had come. **1861** MRS. H. WOOD *East Lynne* III. xix, Uncalled, unprepared,..you hurried that unfortunate man into eternity.

**b.** *transf.* Of things.

*a* **1586** SIDNEY *Astr. & Stella* Sonn. lxi, Oft with true sighes, oft with vncalled teares,..I Stella's eyes assaid. **1751** JOHNSON *Rambler* No. 175 ¶ 2 The knowledge of crimes intrudes uncalled and undesired. *c* **1790** COWPER *Comm. Milton's P. L.* II. 220 Rhyme is apt to come uncalled, and to writers of blank verse is often extremely troublesome. *a* **1839** PRAED *Poems* (1865) II. 15 Sudden tears uncalled spring up. **1885** 'MRS. ALEXANDER' *Valerie's Fate* vi, Bestowing frequent sudden uncalled hugs and kisses on her friend.

**2.** *spec.* Not called or summoned by some power or influence to a special function or state.

**1561** T. NORTON *Calvin's Inst.* IV. xviii. § 9. 144 b, They must confesse yt the honour is not of God, into which they haue with wicked rashnes broken in vncalled. **1619** HIERON Wks. I. 11 All preaching, all exercises of religion ayme at one of these two, either to conuert those that are vncalled, or to builde vp those which are conuerted. **1662** H. HIBBERT *Body Divinity* II. 155 We pray thee then, O Heavenly Father, to call the uncalled Jew and Gentile. **1690** C. NESSE *O. & N. Test.* I. 142 Such as continue in an uncall'd condition yield up themselves to Satan. *c* **1700** PRIOR *Sat. Poets* 128 Something beyond the uncall'd drudging Tribe, Beyond what Bayes can write, or I describe.

**b.** Not invited to a pastorate.

**1854** H. MILLER *Sch. & Schm.* vii. (1860) 74/1 Better be a poor mason, better be anything honest, however humble,—than an un-called Minister.

**3.** With *for*: Not called for; not asked for or requested; unnecessary, intrusive.

Hence, in recent use, *uncalled-for-ness.*

*pred.* *a* **1610** HEALEY *Theophrastus* (1636) 90 When the people consult,..hee steppeth forth uncalled for. **1623** MASSINGER *Dk. Milan* I. iii, *Enter Francisco. Sforza.* Why, uncalled for? **1824** MISS L. M. HAWKINS *Annaline* II. 168 The thought comes uncalled for into my mind. **1846** J. BAXTER *Libr. Pract. Agric.* (ed. 4) I. p. xv, The course he had adopted was uncalled for. **1867** TROLLOPE *Chron. Barset* II. lxvii. 242 No one could now press uncalled-for into his study.

*attrib.* **1635-56** COWLEY *Davideis* III. ad fin., Uncall'd for sighs oft from her bosome flew. **1817** BENNET in *Parl. Deb.* 340 He would oppose..this arbitrary, impolitic, and uncalled-for measure. **1843** R. J. GRAVES *Syst. Clin. Med.* xxix. 393 The uncalled for administration of mercury. **1874** BURNAND *My Time* vi. 50 A satisfactory issue of an uncalled-for interference.

**4.** Of capital: Not called up.

**1882** *Pall Mall G.* 26 July 6/1 The whole of the remaining uncalled capital would have to be called up in order to pay the creditors.

**Unca·llow**, *sb. local.* [f. next.] = CALLOW *sb.* 3.

**1787** W. H. MARSHALL *Norfolk* (1795) I. 151 The depth of uncallow is generally very unequal. *Ibid.* II. Gloss., *Uncallow*, the earth which covers a jam of marl. **1841** *Civil Eng. & Arch. Jrnl.* IV. 341/2 To the above must be added the expenses for removing the uncallow. **1871** J. PHILLIPS *Geol. Oxf. & Vall. Thames* 471 Thick bed of 'Uncallow', consisting of gravel, brickearth, loam, and sand, in horizontal, curved, and aggregated masses.

**Unca·llow**, *v. local.* [UN-[2] 4 + CALLOW *sb.* 3.] *trans.* To clear (clay, marl, etc.) of the surface soil; to remove (soil) for this purpose. Also *intr.* Hence **Unca·llowing** *vbl. sb.*

**1729** *Act 2 Geo. II*, 313 They are hereby obliged and required to uncallow and take off all the Soil, Mould, or other Compost, lying upon the said Earth. **1787** W. H. MARSHALL *Norfolk* (1795) I. 396 *note*, One individual gives 4d...and 6d...a load for casting; besides the uncallowing, which he pays for extra by the day. **1824** *Mechanics' Mag.* No. 33. 77 This is done by removing the vegetable mould from the surface, which is called uncallowing. **1842** *Civil Eng. & Arch. Jrnl.* V. 85/2 The uncallowing and resoiling together ..must be taken at the lowest price of 3d. and 3½d.

**Unca·lm**, *sb.*: see UN-[1] 12.

**Unca·lm**, *v.* [UN-[2] 6 a.] *trans.* To deprive of calm; to agitate, disturb.

**1655** VAUGHAN *Silex Scint.*, *Storm* ii, Thus the enlarg'd, enraged air Uncalms these [waters] to a flood. **1665** DRYDEN *Ind. Emp.* II. iv, What strange disquiet has uncalmed your breast?

**Unca·lm**, *a.* (UN-[1] 7.) **1817** MOORE *Lalla Rookh*, *Veiled Prophet* I. 378 The momentary meteors sent Across th' uncalm, but beauteous firmament. **Unca·mbered**, *ppl. a.* (UN-[1] 8.) **1881** COLQUHOUN *Let.* in *Times* 11 Apr. 10/5 If the boats were laid on a straight or uncambered keel.

**Unca·mp**, *v.* (UN-[2] 5.)

**1670** MILTON *Hist. Brit.* Wks. 1851 V. 37 Freeing themselvs from the fear of like invasions heerafter,..if they could but now uncamp thir Enemies.

**Unca·ncellable**, *a.* (UN-[1] 7 b.)

**1606** *True & Perfect Relat.* H h 3 It is cleare that..onely by the character of regall unction uncancellable he was so far priviledged. **1646** EARL MONM. tr. *Biondi's Civil Wars* VIII. 136 To cancell the uncancellable memory of his cruelty. **1716** M. DAVIES *Athen. Brit.* II. 151 He would..have laid uncancellable obligations at home and abroad.

**Unca·ncelled**, *ppl. a.* (UN-[1] 8.)

**1557** RECORDE *Whetst.* O j b, The whole nomber aboue that is vncancelled. **1594** CONSTABLE *Diana* VII. iv, When posteritie in time to come, shall finde th' uncanceld tenor of her vow. **1622** MALYNES *Anc. Law-Merch.* 226 The new bond being made, the old is void, and yet may be vncancelled. **1675** DRYDEN *Aurengz.* IV. (1676) 64, I onely mourn my yet uncancell'd score. **1772** *Phil. Trans.* LXII. 334 The first uncancelled number that appears in the series, after 3, is 5. **1836** KEBLE in *Lyra Apost.* (1849) 220 O trust his seal Baptismal, yet uncancelled on thy brow. **1875** JEVONS *Money* xviii. 218 Equal in amount to the aggregate of the uncancelled notes.

**Unca·ndid**, *a.* [UN-[1] 7.] Not candid or open; disingenuous: **a.** Of opinions, utterances, etc.

**1681** KETTLEWELL *Meas. Chr. Obed.* v. iii. 633 Peevish, or uncourteous, or uncandid..behaviour. **1694** — *Compan. Penitent* 59, All the..evil and uncandid surmises..which I stand guilty of towards any. **1759** FRANKLIN *Ess.* Wks. 1840 III. 305 How grossly uncandid and clumsily crafty this rhapsody was, appears at the first glance. **1771** *Encycl. Brit.* I. 651/2 The experiment is incomplete, and the conclusion drawn from it uncandid and precipitate. **1825** COLERIDGE *Aids Refl.* (1848) I. 84 That Leighton attached a definite sense to the words above quoted, it would be uncandid to doubt. **1884** CHURCH *Bacon* i. 26 Bacon's reply ..is not more one-sided and uncandid than the pamphlet which it answers.

**b.** Of persons.

**1771** SMOLLETT *Humph. Cl.* 8 June, Will you be so uncandid as to exclaim against Italy for the practice of common assassination? **1784** COWPER *Task* III. 275 The proud, uncandid, insincere, Or negligent, inquirer. **1849** MACAULAY *Hist. Eng.* i. I. 27 The temper, not of judges, but of angry and uncandid advocates.

Hence **Unca·ndidly** *adv.*; **Unca·ndidness.**

**1681** KETTLEWELL *Measures Chr. Obed.* v. iii. 633 Has any man..committed any action of..Uncandidness, Unmercifulness, Unpeaceableness, or the like? **1754** MISS TALBOT *Lett.* (1809) II. 160 The uncandidness of disliking and throwing aside such a book, on casually dipping into the midst of it. **1800** *Asiat. Ann. Reg., Proc. E. Ind. Ho.* 132/1 It had been most uncandidly, because untruly argued. **1852** READE *Peg Woff.* x. 195 She offered to come to him. He answered uncandidly.

**Unca·ndied**, *ppl. a.* (UN-[2] 8. Cf. DISCANDY *v.*) **1612** *Two Noble K.* I. i. 115 O my petition was Set downe in yce, which by hot greefe uncandied Melts into drops.

**Unca·ndour.** [UN-[1] 12.] Lack of candour.

**1879** HOWELLS *L. Aroostook* (1884) II. 178 A generous uncandour like this. **1892** WHITNEY *Max Müller* 79 What I had more right to object to was the uncandour and misrepresentation.

**Unca·nkered**, *ppl. a.* (UN-[1] 8.) **1768-74** TUCKER *Lt. Nat.* (1834) II. 111 Provided he employ healthy stocks of the genuine kind, uncankered with prejudice or peculiarity..the fruits will be the same.

**Unca·nnily**, *adv.* [f. UNCANNY *a.*]

**1.** *dial.* (See quot.)

**1825** BROCKETT *N. C. Gloss.*, *Uncannily*, unthinkingly, thoughtlessly.

**2.** In an uncomfortably strange manner; weirdly.

**1873** MURDOCH *Doric Lyre* 98 Slates an' tiles an' chimla cans Uncannily were fa'in'. **1888** R. BUCHANAN *Heir of Linne* xxv, He talks so uncannily. **1895** *Atlantic Monthly* Aug. 225 A gigantic eye which uncannily turns around.

**Unca·nniness.** [f. next.] The quality or state of being uncanny; unpleasant strangeness.

**1860** GEO. ELIOT *Mill on Fl.* VI. iii, Now I see how it is you..have learned so much since you left school; which always seemed to me witchcraft before—part of your general uncanniness. **1880** *Contemp. Rev.* Sept. 382 They gain a terrible reality from the uncanniness of their surroundings. **1893** LELAND *Mem.* I. 39 There was a quaint uncanniness, as of something unknown, in my nature.

**Unca·nny**, *a.* Orig. *Sc.* and *north.* Also 6–7 uncannie, 7 unkannie, 8 **unkanny.** [UN-[1] 7.]

**†1.** Mischievous, malicious. *Obs.*—[1]

**1596** DALRYMPLE tr. *Leslie's Hist. Scotl.* II. 58 Sum now, vncannie sawers, sew sum causes of contentioun betuene the Chanceller and the Gouernour.

**2.** Careless, incautious.

**1638** R. BAILLIE *Lett. & Jrnls.* (1841) I. 100, I [was].. made hopefull he would not suffer it to be spoiled by the imprudencie of mony uncannie hands which are about it. **1825** BROCKETT *N. C. Gloss.*, *Uncanny*, giddy, careless, imprudent.

**†3.** Unreliable, not to be trusted. *Obs.*

**1639** R. BAILLIE *Lett. & Jrnls.* (1841) I. 211 It was thought meet..to make all, without dinn, march forward, leist his unkannie trewes-men should light on to call [= drive] them up in their rear. **17..** PENNECUIK *Coll.* (1787) 36 You're an hawk of an unkanny nest.

**4.** Of persons: Not quite safe to trust to, or have dealings with, as being associated with supernatural arts or powers.

**1773** R. FERGUSSON *Poems* (1789) II. 8 For this some ca'd him an uncanny wight; The clash gaed round, 'he had the second sight'. **1815** SCOTT *Guy M.* liii. I wish she binna uncanny! her words dinna seem to come in God's name, or like other folk's. **1868** NETTLESHIP *Ess. Browning* II. 68 These gipsies were a queer uncanny folk. **1884** J. GILMOUR *Mongols* 241 The Mongols..were inclined to think him uncanny.

**b.** Partaking of a supernatural character; mysterious, weird, uncomfortably strange or unfamiliar. (Common from *c* 1850.)

**1843** LYTTON *Last Bar.* I. vii, If men, gentlemen born, will read uncanny books,..why they must resolve to reap what they sow. **1856** EMERSON *Eng. Traits, Stonehenge*, We walked in and out, and took again and again a fresh look at the uncanny stones. **1882** MISS BRADDON *Mt. Royal* II. x. 229 A slate quarry under the cliff—a scene of uncanny grandeur.

**c.** In comb. *uncanny-looking* adj.

**1861** MISS E. A. BEAUFORT *Egypt. Sepul. & Syr. Shr.* II. xx. 184 Between the hill of Ophel and the strange, uncanny-looking village of Siloam. **1886** CORBETT *Fall of Asgard* I. 38 Frightened at her uncanny-looking companion's strange talk.

**5.** Unpleasantly severe or hard.

**1773** R. FERGUSSON *Poems* (1789) II. 69 Whinstanes..May thole the prancing feet o' naigs, Nor ever fear uncanny hotches Frae clumsy carts or hackney-coaches. **1814** SCOTT *Wav.* lxvi, I rode whip and spur to fetch the Chevalier..; and an uncanny coup I gat for my pains.

**6.** Dangerous, unsafe.

**1785** *Poems Buchan Dial.* 7 Thus wi' uncanny pranks he fights. **1837** LOCKHART *Scott* IV. vii. 217 He said it was *uncanny*, and would certainly have felt it very uncomfortable, not to welcome the new year in the midst of his family and a few old friends. *a* **1882** W. DICKINSON *Lit. Rem.* (1888) 193 (E.D.D.), Times was raderly uncanny than, An' laal better now.

**Uncano·nic,** *a.* [UN-[1] 7.] = next.

*a* **1711** KEN *Dedicat.* Poet. Wks. 1721 I. 2 Forc'd from my Flock by uncanonick Heat, In singing Hymns, thus solace my Retreat. **1868** BROWNING *Ring & Bk.* x. 70 This act was uncanonic and a fault.

**Uncano·nical,** *a.* [UN-[1] 7.]

**1.** Not in accordance with ecclesiastical canons.

**1632** *Star Chamb. Cases* (Camden) 172 He sought for this place in an uncanonicall order. **1676** MARVELL *Gen. Councils* Wks. (Grosart) IV. 104 And God forbid too that any measure of wealth should render a clergyman uncanonical. **1693** LUTTRELL *Brief Rel.* (1857) III. 17 Yesterday lord bishop of Llandaff exhibited articles..against Dr. Jones..for uncanonicall practices and misdemeanours committed by him. **1709** BINGHAM *Orig. Eccl.* II. 172 Among his other Irregularities he [*sc.* Novatian] was ordained at an uncanonical Hour. **1760** STERNE *Tr. Shandy* IV. xxvi, A single word and no more [was] uttered..—a word I am ashamed to write—yet must be written—must be read—illegal—uncanonical. **1845** LD. CAMPBELL *Chancellors* ix. (1857) I. 130 Uncanonical and forced elections..were made to vacant ecclesiastical dignities. **1872** FREEMAN *Hist. Ess.* (ed. 2) Pref., The marriage of his widow was uncanonical.

**b.** Of dress, pastimes, etc.: Unclerical; unbecoming to 'the cloth'.

**1747** CARTE *Hist. Eng.* I. 676 Wearing long hair, and a dress in any respect uncanonical. **1809** MALKIN *Gil Blas* VII. vi. ₱1 In the archbishop's palace..all such profane shews were condemned as uncanonical. **1819** SCOTT *Ivanhoe* xvii, Are you not afraid he may pay you a visit during some of your uncanonical pastimes? **1829** — *Anne of G.* xv, Begirt, not with a suitable sash such as clergymen wear, but with a most uncanonical buff-belt. **1867** FELTON *Anc. & Mod. Gr.* II. iii. 299 He [St. George] exhibited a most uncanonical greed for money.

**2.** Not belonging to the canon of Scripture.

**1835** *Penny Cycl.* IV. 369/1 Lists of Biblical books were promulgated by the orthodox Greek church in order to prevent the use of Apocryphal or uncanonical books. **1884** CHURTON (*title*), The Uncanonical and Apocryphal Scriptures, being the additions to the Old Testament Canon.

Hence **Uncano·nicalness.**

**1655** FULLER *Ch. Hist.* III. 38 This made him connive at Jeffery Plantaginet his holding the Bishoprick of Lincoln, though uncanonicalness on uncanonicalness met in his person. **1684** BP. LLOYD *Ch. Govt. Brit.* vi. 130 Here was another Uncanonicalness,..that he intruded into a See, into which another had been Elected.

**Uncano·nically,** *adv.* [f. prec.] Not canonically or in a canonical manner.

**1713** E. CALAMY *Life Baxter* (ed. 2) I. 508 He admits that the deposed Bishop was unjustly depriv'd and the New one Uncanonically promoted. **1774** J. COLLYER *Hist. Eng.* II. 150 He had been uncanonically elected. **1842** WRIGHT *Biog. Brit.* 174 He had been consecrated uncanonically by British bishops. **1865** KINGSLEY *Herew.* i, Now, why were the two ecclesiastics so uncanonically kind to this wicked youth?

**Unca·nonize,** *v.* [UN-[2] 6 c.]

**1.** *trans.* To remove from the canon or calendar of saints.

**1607** R. C[AREW] tr. *Estienne's World Wond.* 348 A Monke ..who was almost as soone vncanonized as canonized. **1651** JANE *Image Unbr.* 32 The Authors Pageantry playing with a picture is not the way to uncannonize a saint. **1751** LAVINGTON *Enthus. Meth. & Papists* III. (1754) 214 He [Boniface VIII] uncanonized St. Herman of France, and ordered his Bones to be dug up and burned.

**2.** To reject from the canon of Scripture, or of authoritative writings.

*a* **1706** EVELYN *Hist. Relig.* (1850) I. 409 And it is enough to read the two last verses of the second of Maccabees quite to uncanonize them. **1812** JEFFERSON *Writ.* (1830) IV. 179 The exclusion from the courts of the malign influence of all authorities after the *Georgium sidus* became ascendant, would uncanonize Blackstone.

**Unca·nonized,** *ppl. a.* [UN-[1] 8.]

**1.** Not admitted into the canon of Scripture.

**1548** GESTE *Pr. Masse* 129 The last consayl..regestered ye bible bokes without any mencion made of the Machabees at al, which argueth that then the bokes of Machabees were uncanonised. **1860** WESTCOTT in *Smith's Dict. Bible* I. 251/1 The uncanonical books were described simply as 'those without', or 'those uncanonized'.

**2.** Not formally recognized (as a saint).

*a* **1643** A. TOWNSHEND *Poems* (1912) 34 If he tooke the style before, And name uncanonized wore,..This Saint [etc.]. **1718** ATTERBURY *Serm. Acts xxvi. 26* (1734) III. 17 The Members of it boast very much of mighty Signs and Wonders wrought by some Canonized, and some Uncanonized Saints; their Legends, their Sermons are full of them. **1771** MRS. GRIFFITH *Hist. Lady Barton* III. 220, I passed six days with this uncanonized saint. **1862** MISS BRADDON *Lady Audley* xiv, The uncanonized saint and benefactress to the poor.

**Unca·nopied,** *ppl. a.* (UN-[1] 8.) **1613** W. BROWNE *Brit. Past.* I. iv. 74 Gladly I tooke the place the sheepe had giuen, Uncanopy'd of any thing but heauen.

**Unca·nvassed,** *ppl. a.* [UN-[1] 8.] Not canvassed, in various senses of the verb.

[**1775** ASH.] *a* **1797** H. WALPOLE *Mem. Geo. II* (1847) II. i. 3 His brother..rose..to a distinguished situation entirely unsought, uncanvassed. **1822** T. MITCHELL *Com. Aristoph.* II. 246 Where the loud-voiced herald cries, 'Who's uncanvass'd?—let him rise!' **1884** *Law Times* 13 Dec. 120 There is not a large town in England except London in which such transactions would be allowed to pass uncanvassed.

**Unca·p,** *v.* [UN-[2] 4.]

**1.** *trans.* To remove the cap from (the head or a person). Also *absol.*

**1566** PAINTER *Pal. Pleas.* li. 219 All they that weare hornes, be pardoned to weare their capps...For they be so sweete and pleasaunt, as they vncappe no man. **1598** FLORIO, *Sberettare*, to vncap, to put off hat or cap. **1836** L. HUNT *Poems, Bodryddan* 98 The gard'ner..Uncapp'd his bent old silver hair. **1875** H. JAMES *Transatlantic Sk.* 247, I felt really like uncapping, with a kind of reverence.

**2.** To divest (a thing) of a cap or covering.

**1688** R. HOLME *Armoury* III. xix. (Roxb.) 170/2 The Words of command for the pistolls. 1. Vncape your pistolls. 2. Draw forth your pistoll. **1711** *Milit. & Sea Dict.* (ed. 4), Uncap your Cartridges, Is to take off the Top of the Paper, which is folded down at the End, that so the Powder may fall loose to the Touch-hole. **1750** W. ELLIS *Mod. Husbandm.* VI. I. v. 28 Farmers are emboldened to let their wheat stand ..in the field without uncapping. **1859** JEPHSON & REEVE *Brittany* 88 Mr. Taylor was watching eagerly for a sign from me to uncap the lenses. **1859** F. A. GRIFFITHS *Artill. Man.* (1862) 112 No. 3 loads, assists to ram home, elevates, uncaps fuze when in bore.

†**Uncapabi·lity.** *Obs.*[−1] [Cf. next.] = INCAPABILITY.

*c* **1642** TWYNE in Wood *Life* (O. H. S.) I. 84 The Vice-chancellour's supposed uncapabilitie.

†**Unca·pable,** *a. Obs.* [UN-[1] 7 b and 5 b.]

**1.** = INCAPABLE *a.* 1.

**1587** W. FOWLER *Wks.* (S.T.S.) I. 98 My daisled eyes, vncapable of suche a splendant light. **1634** ABP. WILLIAMS in *Laud's Wks.* (1857) VI. 405, I do endeavour, by my life and conversation, to make myself a vessel not altogether uncapable of that sacred oil. **1637** C. DOW *Answ. to H. Burton* 40 Men were uncapable of these doctrines. **1713** STEELE *Englishm.* No. 55. 356, I know some..uncapable of the deep Secrets which lie in their Bosoms.

**2.** = INCAPABLE *a.* 2.

**1586** T. B. *La Primaud. Fr. Acad.* I. 191 The brutish part of the soule, depending of the feeding beast, and uncapeable of reason. **1597** HOOKER *Eccl. Pol.* v. xlix. § 3 Such as should be vncapable of so great a blessing. **1626** PRYNNE *Perpet. Regen. Man's Est.* 55 These promises which I haue mentioned must needes be absolute.., because that most of them are vncapable of any condition. *a* **1677** HALE *Prim. Orig. Man.* I. v. 113 All which will produce multitudes uncapable of Infinitude, as much as the several individuals of Mankind. **1683** KENNET *Erasm. on Folly* (1709) 30 He would be..uncapable of any ease or satisfaction. **1737** WATERLAND *Eucharist* 111 Being utterly uncapable of any certain Proof, the Argument built thereupon, must of consequence fall to the Ground.

**3.** = INCAPABLE *a.* 3.

**1611** TOURNEUR *Ath. Trag.* II. i, I am uncapable of comfort. **1651** HOBBES *Leviath.* I. xvi. 81 There are few things, that are uncapable of being represented by Fiction. **1717** J. KEILL *Anim. Œcon.* (1738) 263 Things that lessen Perspiration, by being uncapable of Reduction. **1758** REID tr. *Macquer's Chym.* I. 6 The Earth, which we look upon as uncapable of vitrification.

**4.** = INCAPABLE *a.* 4 and 4 b.

**1596** SHAKS. *Merch. V.* IV. i. 5 Thou art come to answere A stonie aduersary, an inhumane wretch, Vncapable of pitty. **1619** NAUNTON in *Fortescue Papers* (Camden) 105 It would make him uncapable to do the service he pretends he can from Rome and other partes. **1642** *Complaint Ho. Comm.* 19 We shal be made uncapable of taking fruit by it. **1716** M. DAVIES *Athen. Brit.* II. 426 He is as uncapable to calculate Eclipses as he is unfit..to Judge of the three first Christian Centuries. **1745** P. THOMAS *Jrnl. Anson's Voy.* 154 Left us..to help ourselves, of which we were utterly uncapable. **1775** ADAIR *Amer. Ind.* 176 Which might..render them uncapable of receiving the supposed divine inspiration. **1805–6** CARY *Dante, Inf.* XXXIII. 91 Them..their tender years, thou modern Thebes, did make Uncapable of guilt.

**5.** = INCAPABLE *a.* 5. Also *absol.*

**1627** HAKEWILL *Apol.* Preface c v, Nature hath not made vs more vncapable then our Auncestours. **1632** LITHGOW *Trav.* x. 437 Preachers..who make conscience of their calling, and liue as Lanthorns to vncapable ignorants. **1653** R. SANDERS *Physiogn.* A 3 b, The eyes of the uncapable and ignorant debase, rather than illustrate and adorn them. **1712** W. ROGERS *Voy.* (1718) 309 Who have put the care of the said ship under an uncapable command. **1719** in W. S. Perry *Hist. Coll. Amer. Col. Ch.* (1871) I. 221 Of which we are very uncapable Judges.

**6.** = INCAPABLE *a.* 6.

**1589** *Act 31 Eliz.* c. 6 § 2 Everie person, by whom..anye Monye..shalbe given or agreed to be payde,..shalbe uncapeable of that Place or Roome for that tyme or turne. **1602** *Hist. Eng.* in *Harl. Misc.* (1809) II. 439 A notorious offender, exempt from the ordinary protection of the laws, uncapable of any preferment. **1678** SIR G. MACKENZIE *Crim. Laws Scot.* I. xvii. § 10 (1699) 93 For though the Law make them uncapable to succeed as Heirs, yet it does not make them uncapable to receive a Disposition. **1706** DE FOE *Jure Div.* VIII. 189 The League deposed Henry the IIId, and declar'd him a Tyrant, a Murtherer, and uncapable to Reign. **1726** SWIFT *Gulliver* I. vi, The disbelief of a divine Providence renders a man uncapable of holding any public station.

Hence †**Unca·pableness.** *Obs.*

**1611** COTGR., *Incapacité*,.. incapacitie, vncapablenesse. **1612** T. TAYLOR *Comm. Titus* iii. 6. 662 Oh let vs bewaile our owne vncapablenesse in the sence of our wants. **1657** J. WATTS *Vind. Ch. Eng.* 106 By reason of your uncapableness of them, by your ignorance. **1727** BAILEY (vol. II), *Illacerableness*, wholeness, or uncapableness of being torn.

**Uncapa·cious,** *a.* (UN-[1] 7 and 5 b.)

**1635** HEYWOOD *Hierarchy* II. 77 It is not fit..to enquire for that, which should we finde, Our limited and uncapacious minde Could not conceiue. *c* **1638** FELTHAM *Let. to Johnson* in *Resolves*, etc. (1661) 87 The poor and uncapacious Vulgar think him to be such as they see. **1854** JAMES *Ticonderoga* III. 81 The narrow-minded man, the man of an uncapacious soul. *a* **1859** DE QUINCEY *Posth. Wks.* (1891) I. 279 It is remarkable how mean, vulgar, and uncapacious has been the range of intellect in many first-rate Grecians.

†**Uncapa·citate,** *v. Obs.* [UN-[2] 3.] *trans.* = INCAPACITATE *v.*

**1668** H. MORE *Div. Dial.* iv. II. 17 Tell me the difference that uncapacitates the one from being the members of the Kingdom of God more then the other. **1693** *Mem. Ct. Teckely* I. 45 Separating from Count Strasoldo..instead of entring Bosnia with him after the defeat of the Basha: Which uncapacitated Scrasoldo [*sic*] to do anything.

†**Uncapa·city.** *Obs.* (UN-[1] 12 and 5 b.) **1681** BAXTER *Answ. Dodwell* ii. 16 One who hath no Authority through uncapacity, or usurpation. **Uncapa·risoned,** *ppl. a.* (UN-[1] 8.) [**1775** ASH.] **1865** MRS. WHITNEY *Gayworthys* xv, The uncaparisoned steed.

† **Unca·pe,** *v. Obs.*[−1] (Of obscure meaning.) The interpretations 'to unbag' or 'to uncouple' are not supported by any evidence.

**1598** SHAKS. *Merry W.* III. iii. 173 Ile warrant wee'le vnkennell the Fox. Let me stop this way first: so, now vncape.

**Unca·pped,** *ppl. a.* (UN-[1] 8.)

**1548–63** BECON *New Catech.* (1564) I. 330 b, A sorte of Popettes standing in euerye corner of the Church, some holdinge in theyr handes a Swoorde,..some capped, some vncapped. **1670** G. H. *Hist. Cardinals* II. III. 186 The Nuntio [was] uncapt for some time, and not one word to be heard of his promotion. **1850** L. HUNT *Autobiog.* xx. (1860) 347 The large wrinkled features of the old women, with their uncapped gray hair, strike you at first as singularly plain. **1902** FAIRBAIRN in *Expositor* Sept. 171 The great mountains raised.. their uncapped heads crowned with perennial snow.

**Unca·pper.** [f. UNCAP *v.* 2.] A tool for removing an exploded cap from a gun.

**1895** *Funk's Stand. Dict.*

**Unca·pping,** *vbl. sb.* [f. UNCAP *v.*] The action of removing a cap or cover. Also *attrib.*

**1681** HICKERINGILL *Dial. Def. Fullwood's Leges Angl.* 6, I now find thy knack at capping of verses and uncapping of names. **1886** *Pall Mall G.* 23 Sept. 6/2, I claim that we are before them in the matter of uncapping machines [for honey-combs].

**Uncapsi·zable,** *a.* (UN-[1] 7 b.) **1883** *Fisheries Exhib. Catal.* 48 Life Boat Buoy, uncapsizable, carries provisions and water; also signal lights. **1883** *Harper's Mag.* Aug. 442/2 The rule..produced a boat that was..uncapsizable. **Unca·ptained,** *ppl. a.* (UN-[1] 8.) **1895** MEREDITH *Amazing Marr.* xlvi, An uncaptained vessel in the winds on high seas. **Unca·ptious,** *a.* (UN-[1] 7.) **1661** FELTHAM *Resolves* II. xliii. (ed. 8) 267 Among uncaptious and candid Natures, plainness and freedom are the preserves of amity. **1860** *Times* 26 Oct. 5/1 Supporters of a fair and uncaptious interpretation of Government rights.

**Unca·ptivate,** *v.* [UN-[2] 3.] *trans.* To free from captivity.

**1611** COTGR., *Decaptiver*, to vncaptiuate; free from captiuite, set at libertie. **1681** RYCAUT tr. *Gracian's Critick* 134 To consult about a remedy which might uncaptivate his beloved Friend.

**Unca·ptivated,** *ppl. a.* (UN-[1] 8.)

**1678** CUDWORTH *Intell. Syst.* Pref. 12 Those of the most accomplished intellectuals and uncaptivated minds. **1700** *Paper to W. Penn* 21 And this may be a Conviction to any of them that are but uncaptivated to observe what they find usual, and will confess it.

**Unca·ptived,** *ppl. a.* [UN-[1] 8: cf. prec.] Not made captive.

**1601** DANIEL *Cleopatra* I. Wks. F v b, For come what will, this stands, I must die free, And die my selfe vncaptiu'd and vnwonne. **1629** H. BURTON *Truth's Triumph* 23 Innocent as Adam,..his will most free, vntainted, vncaptiued. **1669** *Address to Hopef. Yng. Gentry Eng.* 110 The first and wisest of men had not larger notices of the creation, than the uncaptiv'd spirit instantly enters upon.

**Unca·ptured,** *ppl. a.* (UN-[1] 8.) **1885** *Pall Mall G.* 15 May 3/2 As long as Riel is uncaptured the Canadian Government is not out of the wood. **Unca·rded,** *ppl. a.* (UN-[1] 8. Cf. Sw. *okardad.*) [**1775** ASH.] *a* **1833** in Carlyle *Misc.* (1840) IV. 375 Uncombed, uncarded, like a mass of tarry wool.

**Unca·rdinal,** *v.* (UN-[2] 6 b.)

**1642** FULLER *Holy & Prof. St.* v. vii. 383 Borgia's active spirit disliked the profession,..wherefore he quickly got a dispensation to uncardinall himself. **1654** GAYTON *Pleas. Notes* IV. ix. 230 Ungovern'd, Uncardinall'd, Unlorded, Outed of all his hopes, but not Unworded. **1746** YOUNG *Th. Late Rebellion* 87 On what then smote his heart, uncardinal'd, And sunk beneath the level of a man?

**Unca·red-for,** *a.* [UN-[1] 8 c.] Not cared for or looked after; untended, neglected.

*pred.* 1597 HOOKER *Eccl. Pol.* v. i. § 4 Their Kings..left their owne and their peoples ghostly condition vncared for. 1775 ASH, *Uncared*.., not regarded;..' It was uncared for'. 1818 SCOTT *Br. Lamm.* xxi, Circumstances which, in families of rank, are left uncared for, because it is supposed impossible they can be neglected. 1850 TENNYSON *In Mem.* ci, The brook shall.., Uncared for, gird the windy grove. 1894 *Persian Pict.* 40 Somewhat desolate and uncared-for in appearance.

*attrib.* 1621 G. SANDYS *Ovid's Met.* II. (1626) 37 He fetcht a grone,..And now vncar'd-for odours powr'd vpon her. 1856 *N. Brit. Rev.* XXVI. 109 A slatternly wife and eight or ten uncared-for children. 1887 MOLONEY *Forestry W. Africa* 171, I have seen species of this plant in an uncultivated and uncared-for state in the interior districts of the Gold Coast.

† **Unca·redly,** *adv. Sc. Obs.* [UN-1 11.] Without taking care; recklessly.

1590 BUREL *Pilg.* II. in Watson *Scots Poems* (1709) II. 45 Dispairdly, vncairdly, I hasert ouer the hill.

**Unca·reful,** *a.* [UN-1 7.]

**1.** Not exercising care; careless, not cautious or watchful.

*c* 1533 LATIMER in Foxe *A. & M.* (1563) 1317/1 We be secure & vncarefull, as though false Prophetes coulde not haue meddled with vs. 1592 BRETON *C'tess Pembrooke's Loue* Wks. (Grosart) I. 25/1 Vnhappy hart, that euer thee offended,..Vncarefull eare, that euer tale attended! 1604 T. WRIGHT *Passions* II. ii. 58 An vncarefull Magistrate neglecteth the good of the common-weale. 1647 BP. REYNOLDS *Passions* iii. 15 An eagernesse to take in, makes uncareful to retain. 1861 FLOR. NIGHTINGALE *Nursing* (ed. 2) 83 Careful nursing has done in a few weeks what uncareful medical observation has declared it impossible to do in less than two years. 1867 HOWELLS *Ital. Journ.* xi. (1883) I. 165, I had noticed (in an uncareful fashion enough, no doubt) the great changes which had taken place in Italy.

**2.** Not taking any care or consideration *of* or *for* (a thing or person).

1559–60 *MS. Cott. Caligula* B ix, Our eyes are opened, we espy how uncareful they have been of our weile at all tymes. 1572 H. MIDDELMORE in Ellis *Orig. Lett.* Ser. II. III. 7 So ame I not uncarefull of hir in any thinge that I maye knowe to be for hir preservation and good. 1662 J. CHANDLER *Van Helmont's Oriat.* 263 Such [Gods] as are uncareful of us, and despisers of small matters, and therefore also ignorant of us. 1664 CHAS. II *Sp. Both Ho. Parlt* 6 That Bill..passed in a Time very uncareful for the Dignity of the Crown, or the Security of the People. 1882 MRS. OLIPHANT *Lit. Hist. Eng.* I. 90 A delusion..which..he suddenly adopts and sanctions, uncareful of the misery which it might produce. 1897 *Ch. Times* 6 Aug. 135/2 The exclusiveness of official Anglicanism, un-careful of the masses, and caring only for the big purses.

**3.** Free from care; not anxious or troubled.

1643 QUARLES *Emblems* IV. xiii. 40 There shall thy soul possesse uncarefull treasure. 1646 — *Judgem. & Mercy* Wks. (Grosart) I. 97/1 How hast thou liv'd O my uncarefull soule to see these prophesies fulfill'd? 1858 HAWTHORNE *Fr. & It. Note-bks.* II. 291 This journey from Rome has been one of the brightest and most uncareful interludes of my life. 1874 RUSKIN *Val D'Arno* (1886) 117 The uncareful happiness of men clothed without labour, and fed without fear.

Hence **Unca·refully** *adv.*, **Unca·refulness.**

1567 PAYNELL *Treas. Amadis of Gaule* 255 [We] shall soone breake them, being thus open, and it may be through uncarefulnesse and negligence chauncing unto them. 1654–66 EARL ORRERY *Parthen.* (1676) 548 He began so uncarefully to thrust at my Prince.

**Uncare·ssed,** *ppl. a.* (UN-1 8.) 1814 WORDSW. *Excurs.* IV. 577 He, whose hours Are by domestic pleasure uncaressed And unenlivened. 1825 LYTTON in *Life & Lett.* (1883) II. 23 Contempt for all encaged starlings, who have not the privilege of being as free and uncaressed as myself. **Unca·ricatured,** *ppl. a.* (UN-1 8.) 1880 RUSKIN in *19th Cent.* June 948 That book is an earnest and uncaricatured record of states of criminal life.

**Unca·ring,** *ppl. a.* (UN-1 10 and 5 d.)

1786 BURNS *Ep. Young Friend* viii, Debar a' side-pretences, And resolutely keep its laws, Uncaring consequences. 1826 MISS MITFORD *Village* Ser. II. (1863) 275 She was so overflowing with health and spirits, so fearless and uncaring. 1844 KINGLAKE *Eothen* xxvii, A few Persian carpets,—thrown about near the divan,—give to the room an appearance of uncaring luxury. 1896 KIPLING *Seven Seas, Hymn bef. Action* ii, Deaf ear and soul uncaring, We seek Thy mercy now!

Hence **Unca·ringly** *adv.*

1868 H. BUSHNELL *Serm. Living Subj.* 208 Put into language unspoken, it says, 'Plunge thyself uncaringly into evil'.

† **Unca·rnate,** *a. Obs.*–1 [UN-1 7, after INCARNATE.] Not incarnate.

1646 SIR T. BROWNE *Pseud. Ep.* VII. xvi. 372 Nor need we be afraid to ascribe that unto the incarnate Son, which sometimes is attributed unto the uncarnate Father.

† **Unca·rnating,** *vbl. sb. Obs.* [UN-2 8: cf. prec.] The action of rendering unincarnate.

1659 GAUDEN *Tears Ch.* II. xvi. 198 They set forth their pageantries of new-drest Divinity to be..spirituall manifestations,..unheard-of emanations,..the uncarnating of a Christian [etc.].

**Uncarni·vorous,** *a.* (UN-1 7.) 1822 T. L. PEACOCK *Maid Marian* xv, The fast-day dinner of an uncarnivorous friar.

**Unca·rpeted,** *a.* (UN-1 9.)

[1775 ASH.] 1816 J. SCOTT *Vis. Paris* (ed. 5) 117 A small room or two, uncarpeted and bare, must be hired. 1860 MARIA L. CHARLESWORTH *Eng. Yeomen* xxx. (1861) 392 You scarcely heard a footfall, though the parlour boards were uncarpeted. 1894 DOYLE *S. Holmes* 63 Little rooms, uncarpeted and uncurtained.

**Unca·rried,** *ppl. a.* (UN-1 8.)

1584–5 *Act 27 Eliz.* c. 19 § 3 In default therof, [to] pay.. for euerie such load [of gravel, etc.] due and uncarried, Two Shillings and Sixe Pence. [1775 ASH.] 1890 *Pall Mall G.* 1 Sept. 5/1 Operations are..much hampered by the standing and uncarried crops.

**Unca·rt,** *v.* [UN-2 5.] *trans.* To take out of a cart; to unload from a cart.

1641 J. TAYLOR (Water P.) *Last Voy.* A 7 b, I being vncarted (with my boate) at a place called Stonehouse. 1857 GEO. ELIOT *Scenes Cler. Life, A. Barton* ii, He carted and uncarted the manure with a sort of flunkey grace. 1865 M. COLLINS *Who is the Heir?* xxxi, A noble deer was uncarted, and went straight away without a pause. 1890 BAKER *Wild Beasts* I. 300 We now uncarted a fresh cheetah.

**Unca·rtable,** *a.* [UN-1 7 b.] † On which carting is impossible.

1658 FRANCK *Northern Mem.* (1694) 195 What have we here? Cawses [= causeways] uncartable, and Pavements unpracticable, pointed with rocky stumpy Stones.

**Unca·rved,** *ppl. a.* [UN-1 8.]

**1.** Not carved or cut up for eating.

*a* 1592 GREENE *Jas. IV*, I. ii, I cannot abide..a fat capon vncaru'd.

**2.** Not carved or cut artistically or ornamentally.

1611 FLORIO, *Inscolpito*, vncarued, vngrauen. 1613–39 I. JONES in Leoni *Palladio's Archit.* (1742) II. 45 This Architrave is..uncarv'd. 1830 *Q. Rev.* XLIII. 21 It was a rude uncarved wooden log about six feet long. 1831 W. ELLIS *Polynesian Res.* (ed. 2) I. xiv. 354 A straight log of hard casuarina wood,..uncarved, but decorated with feathers.

**Uncase,** *v.* [UN-2 4 and 5.]

**1.** *trans.* † **a.** To skin or flay (an animal or person). *Obs.*

1575 TURBERV. *Faulconrie* 12 As well the browne Eagles as the blacke are skynned and uncased as the Vultures be. 1591 SPENSER *M. Hubberd* 1380 The Foxe, first Author of that treacherie, He did vncase, and then away let flie. 1638 *Guillim's Heraldry* III. xiv. 176 You shall say a Foxe is Vncased. 1658–9 MORRICE in *Burton's Diary* (1828) IV. 191 Cambyses once uncased a corrupt judge, and made a cushion of his skin for his son to sit on. 1677 W. HUBBARD *Narrative* Postscr. 10 As men use to do with a slaughtered Beast before they uncase him.

*absol.* 1712 STEELE *Spect.* No. 473 ¶ 1 It can be proved upon him, that he cuts up, disjoints, and uncases with incomparable Dexterity.

**b.** To strip (a person); to undress.

1570–6 LAMBARDE *Peramb. Kent* (1826) 147 He was openly uncased, boxed about the eares, and sent to the next Iustice. 1599 NASHE *Lenten Stuffe* Wks. (Grosart) V. 261 He tare him from his throne, and vncased him of his habiliments. 1600 HOLLAND *Livy* XXIX. ix. 715 Whiles there was some time spent in turning them out of their apparrell and uncasing them. 1635 [GLAPTHORNE] *Lady Mother* I. i. in Bullen *O. Pl.* (1883) II. 107 If you uncase him, you will find his sattin dublett naught but fore sleaves and breast. 1699 FARQUHAR *Constant Couple* v. ii, I'll ha' you into the dungeon, and uncase you. 1823 MRS. SHERWOOD *Henry Milner* III. xxi, He..uncased him from a huge great coat.

*refl.* 1588 GREENE *Pandosto* (1843) 42 Dorastus..went to the grove where hee had his rich apparel, and there uncasing himself as secretly as might be [etc.]. 1596 SHAKS. *Tam. Shr.* I. i. 212 Tranio at once Vncase thee: take my Coulord hat and cloake. *a* 1634 CHAPMAN *Alphonsus* III. i. 227, I.. straight untruss'd my points, uncas'd myself. 1704 NORRIS *Ideal World* II. vii. 338 It seems impossible that bodies should thus intirely and simultaneously strip and uncase themselves of these their outer coats or membranes.

**c.** *absol.* To put off a garment or garments.

1588 SHAKS. *L. L. L.* v. ii. 707 Do you not see Pompey is vncasing for the combat? 1622 FLETCHER *Prophetess* IV. vi, I know that glory Is like Alcides's Shirt..: when we would uncase, It brings along with it both flesh and sinews. 1691 J. WILSON *Belphegor* III. v, The Sham won't pass on me—Come, come—uncase. 1733 FIELDING *Don Quix. in Eng.* II. vi, Sancho, uncase this instant, and handle that squire as he deserves. 1781 C. JOHNSTON *Hist. J. Juniper* I. 192 As soon as they arrived at the Jew's Kennel in Houndsditch, our hero directly uncased. 1837 BARHAM *Ingol. Leg.* Ser. I. *Leech of Folkestone*, Quick, Master Marsh! uncase, or you perish!

**2.** *fig.* To uncover, lay bare, expose to view or observation.

1587 HOLINSHED *Chron.* I. 77/1 He vncased the crooked conditions which he had couertlie concealed. *a* 1591 R. GREENHAM *Wks.* (1599) 56 Nakedly to vncase thy sins before God, is a hard thing to flesh and blood. 1627 HAKEWILL *Apol.* (1630) 520 His hypocrisie shall be uncased and laid open to the view of the world. 1642 FULLER *Holy & Prof. St.* v. viii. 390 Thus God at last shall uncase the closest dissembler to the sight of men. 1677 GILPIN *Demonol.* (1867) 23 Those secret thinkings;..the very inside and outside of them are uncased, cut up and anatomised by his eye. 1710 PALMER *Proverbs* 167 A hypocrite shou'd be uncas'd and shewn to the world.

**b.** To strip or deprive *of* something.

1583 MELBANCKE *Philotimus* T ij b, Thy prickemedaintie Cornelius shallbee vncased of his vaine vizarde, and disburdened..of his hypocriticall apparitions. 1613 DAY *Dyall* xii. (1614) 326 What? to uncase themselves of al they had, and to give it to the Poore?

**c.** To take out of the body.

1629 QUARLES *Argalus & P.* I. Wks. (Grosart) III. 252/2 Death could ne'r uncase Thy soule. 1631 — *Samson* Ibid. II. 160/1 Betwixt them both, his fury did uncase A thousand soules.

**3.** To free from a casing or covering.

1643 A. ROSSE *Mel Helic.* 41 O Lord, when thou dost call on me, Uncase my eyes, that I may see.

**4.** To draw or take out of a case or cover.

1589 GREENE *Tully's Love* Wks. (Grosart) VII. 126 As the foes of Perseus when hee vncased the head of Medusa. 1600–9 ROWLANDS *Knaue of Clubbes* (Hunterian Cl.) 8 A swaggering rogue breakes open dore, And's Rapier did vncase. 1688 R. HOLME *Armoury* III. xix. (Roxb.) 153/1 Take forth your Granade. Shut your pouch. Vncase your fuse. 1742 *Lond. & Country Brew.* I. (ed. 4) 19 Here they save the Charge of emptying or uncasing it out of the Bin. 1791 COWPER *Iliad* IV. 122 So Pallas spake, to whom infatuate he Listening, uncased at once his polish'd bow. 1802 JAMES *Milit. Dict.*, *To uncase*, in a military sense to display, to exhibit—As to uncase the colours. 1826 P. POUNDEN *France & Italy* 66 A crystal coffin in a small repository..being uncased to our view. 1893 *Daily News* 14 Dec. 2/2 The gun was here uncased by an officer and handed to the witness.

† **5.** To cast, throw off. *Obs.*–1

1582 STANYHURST *Æneis* II. (Arb.) 58 The owtpeaking from weeds of poysoned adder,..His slough vncasing.

Hence **Unca·sed** *ppl. a.*[1]

1598 E. GUILPIN *Skial.* (1878) 42 Who for deluding vs, to plague their sinne, Are turnd to counterfaits, which their vncasde skin Quickly discouers. 1611 COTGR., *Salcoque*, an vncased Prawne. 1658 J. ROBINSON *Endoxa* i. 19 What an uncased or discovered Hypocrite is, I could never apprehend. 1760 *Impostors Detected* IV. viii. II. 232 D. Nunez was not a little surprised at seeing me at that time of night, and so uncased. 1791 COWPER *Odyss.* XI. 741 With uncas'd bow and arrow on the string. 1809 MALKIN *Gil Blas* I. ix. ¶ 4 Leaving the carriage and the uncased carcases by the road-side. 1818 SCOTT *Rob Roy* xxxi, He arose a forked, uncased, bald-pated, beggarly-looking scarecrow.

**Unca·sed,** *ppl. a.*[2] [UN-1 8.] Not cased.

1840 CLOUGH *Early Poems* 1 Come back again, my olden heart!—With incrustations of the years Uncased as yet.

**Unca·semated,** *a.* (UN-1 9.) 1611 COTGR., *Veues mortes*, close, or vncasemated windowes. **Unca·shed,** *ppl. a.* (UN-1 8.) 1896 *Harper's Mag.* XCIII. 35/1 It happened.. that I had two or three uncashed checks in my pocket.

**Unca·sing,** *vbl. sb.* [f. UNCASE *v.*] The action of taking out of a case, etc.

1589 NASHE *Almond for Parrat* 12, I am a shreud fellow at the vncasing of a fox. 1613 PURCHAS *Pilgrimage* (1614) 356 Goropius bestowes much paines in the vncasing of them. 1642 MILTON *Animadv.* Pref., In the serious uncasing of a grand imposture. 1693 EVELYN *Misc. Wks.* (1825) 719 Un-casing, for the taking them out of the case or vessel. *a* 1701 SEDLEY *Tyrant K. of Crete* II. iv, Sir, commit the uncasing Him to me!

**Unca·sk,** *v.* [UN-2 5.] *trans.* To take or bring out of a cask; *fig.* to open up.

1594 NASHE *Unfort. Trav.* Wks. (Grosart) V. 69 Oratorie vncaske the bard hutch of thy complements, and with the triumphantest troupe in thy treasurie doe trewage vnto him. 1630 J. TAYLOR (Water P.) *Eighth Wond. World* Wks. II. 60/1 If thou in kindnesse wilt accept this taske, Hereafter I will better things vn-caske.

**Unca·sque,** *v.* (UN-2 5.)

1818 MILMAN *Samor* 158 Through files of warriors, who uncasque their brows To fill their curious gaze, she hurries on. 1880 BARING-GOULD *Mehalah* xxi. II. 101 There she was wont to uncasque, and ruffle out her white cap.

† **Unca·ssable,** *a.*, **Unca·ssed,** *ppl. a. Obs.* (UN-1 7 b, 8. See CASS *v.*)

1599 Q. ELIZ. in Moryson *Itin.* (1617) II. 56 You may keep the Captaines uncassed, but not give any warrant to them to supply their Companies with any more Irish. 1609 SKENE *Reg. Maj.* 12 In that case he affirmes the brieve to be valide, and vncassable.

**Unca·ssock,** *v.* (UN-2 5.)

1645 *Sacred Decretal* 2 He hath so uncassock'd our misterious divinity.

**Unca·st,** *ppl. a.* Also *Sc.* 5 vncastyne, 6 -castin. [UN-1 8. Cf. Sw. *okastad.*]

**1.** Not cast or thrown.

*c* 1375 *Sc. Leg. Saints* vii. (*James*) 246 Þat stane one stane in-to þat towne suld nocht be lefit vncastyne done. 1533 BELLENDEN *Livy* II. xx. (S. T. S.) I. 209 Þe dartis war left vncastin on athir side. *a* 1547 SURREY *Æneid* II. (1557) C j, But sone an other sort stept in theyr stede, No stone vnthrown, nor yet no dart vncast. 1662 R. VENABLES *Exper. Angler* x. 100 The flie were better uncast, because it frights the fish.

**2.** Not founded or moulded by casting.

1617 *Bk. Rates Marchandise* N j b, Leade.. vncast the Fodder..xx.l...cast, the Fodder..xx.l.

**3.** Not reckoned (*up*) or calculated.

1598 SYLVESTER *Du Bartas* II. *Ded. Sonn.* ii, Our small Art's-stock .. is even beggered with th' uncast Expense. 1745 *De Foe's Eng. Tradesm.* xxxii. (1841) II. 58 Other accounts are left open and uncast up.

**4.** Not disfigured by a squint.

1629 GAULE *Holy Madn.* 328 He sees well, and his eyes were uncast.

**Unca·st,** *v.* (UN-2 3.) 1874 LD. COLERIDGE in *Life* (1904) II. 244 The die is cast: it cannot be uncast now.

† **Unca·stigate,** *ppl. a. Obs.*–1 [UN-1 8 b.] = next.

1539 TAVERNER *Bible* Ded., But now though many faultes perchaunce be yet left behind vncastigat,..I trust your maiestie..wyll pardon me.

**Unca·stigated,** *ppl. a.* (UN-1 8.)

1657 TOMLINSON *Renou's Disp.* 582 Trochisks of Alhandal were safer then Coloquintida uncastigated. 1812 L. HUNT in *Examiner* 14 Sept. 589/1 Any uncastigated edition of such a writer. 1896 *Daily News* 7 Dec. 4/7 The editor alone walks the earth uncastigated.

**Unca·stle,** *v.* (UN-2 5.)

1611 FLORIO, *Discastellare*, to vncastle. 1655 FULLER *Ch. Hist.* III. xii. 27 He uncastled Roger of Salisbury, Alexander of Lincoln, and Nigellus of Ely. *a* 1661 — *Worthies, Lond.* (1662) II. 197 The first of these [houses] is so uncastelled, the Glory of the second so obscured, that very few know..where these houses were fixed. 1775 ASH, *Uncastle*.., to drive out of a castle.

**Unca·strated,** *ppl. a.* [UN-1 8.]

**1.** Not castrated; ungelded; entire.

1725 *Fam. Dict.*, *Ram*, the uncastrated Male of the Sheep-Kind. 1764 C. CHURCHILL *The Times* 29 Where is the Mother, ..Who not permits, e'en for the sake of pray'r, A Priest, uncastrated, to enter there?

**2.** Not mutilated or expurgated.

1737 OLDYS *Librarian* 159 *note*, About the middle of the late King's Reign, an uncastrated Copy did arise. 1817 D'ISRAELI *Cur. Lit.* III. 196 *note*, It is a quarto tract,.. inserted in the uncastrated edition of Milton's prose works in 1738. 1822–56 DE QUINCEY *Confess.* (1862) 145 An uncastrated Decamerone or other dazzling κειμήλιον. 1886 *Athenæum* 16 Jan. 103/2 The genuine Giunta uncastrated edition [fetched] 81 *l.*

**Unca·sual,** *a.* (UN-[1] 7.) *a* 1618 SYLVESTER *Panaretus* 781 Besides th' off-cutting of All Passages,.. Is even to conquer by uncasuall course. †**Unca·suistly,** *adv. Obs.* (UN-[1] 11.) 1649 *Bounds Publ. Obed.* 3 With an acknowledgement of their authority and right, which is very uncasuistly and unconscientiously inserted here.

**Unca·talogued,** *ppl. a.* (UN-[1] 8.)

1837 J. H. NEWMAN *Proph. Office Ch.* 249 Unsorted and uncatalogued treasures. 1858 O. W. HOLMES *Aut. Breakf.-t.* iv. 81 Then we will go together into the solemn archives of Oblivion's Uncatalogued Library! 1870 J. H. NEWMAN *Gram. Assent* II. viii. 297 The combination of many uncatalogued experiences floating in my memory.

**Unca·tchable,** *a.* (UN-[1] 7 b.) 1824 MISS MITFORD *Village* Ser. I. (1863) 152 She was a sad romp;..as uncertain as a butterfly, as uncatchable as a swallow! 1892 *Star* 13 May 1/7 Some Indian gentlemen with uncatchable names were much admired.

**U·ncate,** *a. Bot.* [ad. L. *uncāt-us*, f. *unc-us* hook.] = UNCINATE *a.*

1866 *Treas. Bot.* 1191/1 *Uncate*,..hooked; curved suddenly back at the point.

**Uncatechized** (ʋnkæ·tĭkəizd), *ppl. a.* [UN-[1] 8.] Not formally instructed or examined in religion. Also *absol.*

1619 W. SCLATER *Exp.* 1 *Thess.* (1630) 28 The manner of ascending to assurance of Election,..wherein..these men are yet uncatechized. 1667 *Decay Chr. Piety* iii. § 6. 218 But would God the uncatechiz'd were the only persons we had to complain of in this matter. 1685 J. SCOTT *Chr. Life* II. 137 The hair-brain'd and uncatechised youths of the Town. 1832 MACGILLIVRAY *Trav. Humboldt* xvii. 237 They found six houses inhabited by uncatechised Guahiboes. 1842 PUSEY in Liddon *Life* (1893) I. xi. 258 It will be thrust on minds unprepared, and on an uncatechised Church.

Hence **Unca·techizedness.**

1659 GAUDEN *Tears Ch.* IV. xxiii. 619 What means the Uncatechisedness, the Sottishness, Profaneness, Impudence and Irreligion which are so much spreading and prevailing?

**Uncathedralled,** *a.*: see UN-[1] 9.

**Uncatholic** (ʋnkæ·þŏlik), *a.* and *sb.* [UN-[1] 7 and 12.]

**A.** *adj.* Not catholic or universal, in an ecclesiastical sense; also *spec.*, not Roman-Catholic.

1601 [? W. WATSON] *Imp. Consid. Sec. Priests* (1675) 61 This intolerable and very uncatholick course thus held by divers, to the great offence of many good Catholicks. 1660 GAUDEN *God's Gt. Demonstr.* 51 Thy humane traditions, and unauthentick because uncatholick observations, instead of Christ's institutions. 1678 T. JONES *Heart & its Sov.* 522 Our Romanists..are so restrain'd, and Vncatholick, and Jewish-like, in the bounds of their Church, which they so confine to Rome. 1685 J. SCOTT *Chr. Life* II. vii. § 9 Now that Church which requires sinful or uncatholick Terms of Communion, doth hereby exclude..all Parts of the Catholick Church from its Communion. 1711 G. HICKES *Two Treat. Chr. Priesth.* (1847) I. 271 A new uncatholic mission of their own creating. 1845 J. H. NEWMAN *Ess. Developm.* 328 Such a doctrine is in no sense uncatholic. 1896 GORE *R. C. Claims* App. I. 210 We in the Church of England..are yet unfettered by any uncatholic dogma.

*transf.* 1624 MIDDLETON *Game at Chess* II. i, I'll tell thee what a most uncatholic jest He put upon me once.

**B.** *sb.* One who is not a Catholic.

1865 PUSEY *Truth Eng. Ch.* 133 The Bishop of Trèves doubted for a time on account of the un-Catholics, but decided that the decree would be advantageous.

**Uncatho·licalness.** (See prec. and UN-[1] 12.) Also, in recent use, *uncatholicity*.

1695 J. SAGE *Fundamental Charter* (1697) 247 The impoliticalness the uncatholicalness of most, if not all, of these Propositions.

**Uncatho·licize,** *v.* (UN-[2] 6 c.)

1806 G. S. FABER *Disc. Prophecies* (1814) II. 279 As I have no inclination to uncatholicise myself. 1842 PUSEY *Crisis Eng. Ch.* 126 Our Church has been in part un-Catholicized by those who helped in a degree to unsecularize her.

Hence **Uncatho·licized** *ppl. a.*, **Uncatho·licizing** *vbl. sb.*

1822 C. BUTLER *Remin.* xv. 211 The uncatholicizing of the calendar. 1824 BENTHAM *Bk. Fallacies* Wks. 1843 II. 468/2 All the doctors..of the as yet uncatholicized university of Mexico. 1863 O'DWYER *Pius IX*, xxxi. 188 In reformed and uncatholicised England.

**Uncatholicly,** *adv.*: see UN-[1] 11.

**Unca·ttle,** *v.* (UN-[2] 4.)

1643 *Merc. Brit.* No. 27. 213 Colonell Cromwell hath uncatteled them about Oxford, and..both drove away the Cattell & the Rebells into Oxford at the same time.

**Uncau·ght,** *ppl. a.* (UN-[1] 8 b.)

1340–70 *Alex. & Dind.* 38 þei þou fonde wiþ þi folk to fiȝhte wiþ us alle, We schulle us kepe on-cauȝt oure cauus wiþ-inne. ? *a* 1500 *Chester Pl.* XVIII. 117 He scapeth not vncought. 1605 SHAKS. *Lear* II. i. 59 Let him fly farre: Not in this Land shall he remaine vncaught. 1619 HIERON *Wks.* I. 639 The state of men by nature, who bee as fishes ranging after their owne disposition, vncaught. 1711 GAY *Rural Sports* 145 His bosom glows with treasures yet uncaught. 1820 C. R. MATURIN *Melmoth* (1892) III. xxviii. 147 Whenever you have seen the tear, which your hand might have wiped away, fall uncaught. 1894 BARING-GOULD *Kitty Alone* II. 95, I live in fear of him as long as he is uncaught.

**Uncau·lk,** *v.* (UN-[2] 3.) 1608 SYLVESTER *Du Bartas* II. iv. *Schisme* 949 The billows, beating round about the ship, Unchauk [*sic*] her keel, and all her seams unrip.

**Uncau·lked,** *ppl. a.* (UN-[1] 8.) 1748 SMOLLETT *R. Random* xxiv. 164 Another observing my wounds, which remained exposed to the air, told me, my seams were uncaulked. 1841 LEVER *C. O'Malley* xxxi. 166 Where the uncaulked deck but filters every rain on your head.

†**Uncau·ponated,** *ppl. a. Obs.* [UN-[1] 8.] Not sold, or tampered with, by hucksters.

*a* 1752 SMART *Hop Garden* I. 176 When great Eliza reign'd.., when our brave sires Drank valour from uncauponated beer.

**Uncau·sed,** *ppl. a.* (UN-[1] 8.)

Common from *c* 1730; hence (in recent use) *uncausedness*.

*a* 1628 F. GREVIL *Let. to Honorable Lady* (1633) C iv, To giue all, and take nothing, proceeds of an uncaused goodnesse, and so necessarily of an vnabusing. 1722 WOLLASTON *Relig. Nat.* v. 65 Where there is a subordination of causes and effects, there must necessarily be a cause in nature prior to the rest, uncaused. 1768–74 TUCKER *Lt. Nat.* (1834) I. 366 We know that He is almighty, self-existent, uncaused. 1796 BP. WATSON *Apol. Bible* 367 What think you of an uncaused cause of every thing? 1849 H. SPENCER in *Academy* 25 June (1904) 690/1 An uncaused deity is just as inconceivable as an uncaused universe. 1871 TYLOR *Prim. Cult.* I. 4 He has simply thrown out..the whole fabric of motiveless will and uncaused spontaneity.

†**Uncau·telous,** *a. Obs.* [UN-[1] 7 and 5 b.] Incautious, unwary.

1628 PRYNNE *Brief Survay* 2 They may the more insensibly Insinuate..themselues into the Hearts, and Intralls, of vncautelous, and ouer-credulous Christians. *a* 1656 HALES *Gold. Rem.* I. (1673) 284, I would you would advise him to beware of such uncautelous speeches. 1697 EVELYN *Numism.* ix. 316 Those of Savoy, Swisserland, and many parts of Germany, which abound in Foxes, etc., are the dullest, simplest, and most uncautelous of all their Neighbours.

Hence †**Uncau·telousness.** *Obs.*

*a* 1656 HALES *Gold. Rem.* I. (1673) 256 He hath laid it down in such terms, that nothing but negligence and uncautelousness can hazard it.

†**Uncau·tioned,** *ppl. a. Obs.* = next.

1671 R. MACWARD *True Nonconf.* 383 Your blunt and uncautioned general, viz. that private persons may punish crimes in case of the supinness of the Magistrat.

†**Uncau·tious,** *a. Obs.* [UN-[1] 7 and 5 b.] Incautious. Also *absol.*

1644 DIGBY *Nat. Bodies* xii. § 6. 105 A man that was vncautious and sucked strongly that had his foreteeth beaten out by the blow of the bullett ascending. 1677 GILPIN *Demonol.* (1867) 31 There is no small cunning and working of Satan in them, insomuch that the uncautious and injudicious are deceived. 1710 PALMER *Proverbs* Pref. p. xiv, An uncautious wanton writer can possibly give the vice he has too lusciously describ'd. 1741 RICHARDSON *Pamela* I. 205 O what has this uncautious man said?

Hence †**Uncau·tiously** *adv.*, †**Uncau·tiousness.**

1680 H. DODWELL *Two Lett.* (1691) 154 Arguments..endangered by the very uncautiousness of the expression. 1721 WATERLAND *Case Arian-Subscr. Consid.* iv. 41 (Plea xiv. § 4), It is very uncautiously and unaccurately said, that King Charles I. patronized the Subscribing the same Articles either in contradictory, or different Senses. 1759 GOLDSM. *Bee* No. 7. 128 Uncautiously suffering this jealousy to corrode in her breast.

†**Unce.** *Obs.*[−1] [ad. L. *uncus*.] A claw.

1609 HEYWOOD *Brit. Troy* VII. lxxvi, The Riuer-waking-Serpent to make sleepe, Whose horride crest, blew scales, and vnces blacke, Threat euery one a death.

**Unce,** obs. f. OUNCE *sb.*[1] and *sb.*[2]

†**Uncea·sable,** *a. Obs.* [UN-[1] 7 b.] Incessant.

1604 DEKKER *Magnif. Entertainm. K. Jas.* Wks. 1873 I. 268 Zealous prayers, and unceasable wishes for his more speedy and longed-for arrivall. 1611 COTGR., *Incessible*, vnceasable, vnendable, vndeterminable.

**Uncea·sed,** *ppl. a.* (UN-[1] 8.)

1598 SYLVESTER *Du Bartas* II. ii. *Colonies* 244 Not that I send Sem, at one flight unceast, From Babylon unto the farthest East.

**Uncea·sing,** *ppl. a.* Also 4–5 vnce(e)s(s)ynge, 5 vncecynge. [UN-[1] 10.] Never ceasing, incessant, continuous. (Common from *c* 1750.)

1382 WYCLIF 2 *Pet.* ii. 14 Hauynge iȝen ful of auoutrie, and vncesynge trespasse, deceyuynge vnstedefast soules. 1410 *Prymer* in Maskell *Mon. Rit.* III. 16 To the cherubyn and seraphym crien with uncecynge vois. 1743 FRANCIS tr. *Hor., Odes* III. xxix. 9 Nor [do thou] with unceasing Joy survey Fair Æsula's declining Fields. 1774 GOLDSM. *Nat. Hist.* (1776) VIII. 157 Still millions more [of gnats] succeed, and produce unceasing torment. 1803 MALTHUS *Popul.* I. vi. 75 The efforts of the German nations to colonize or plunder were unceasing. 1842 MANNING *Serm.* i. (1848) I. 6 Carrying on unceasing, universal warfare against Heaven. 1873 LELAND *Egypt. Sketch-Bk.* 196 They are still singing, those unceasing children of Egypt, that quaint old refrain.

Hence **Uncea·singness.**

1727 BAILEY (vol. II), *Incessantness*, Continualness, Unceasingness. (Also in recent use.)

**Uncea·singly,** *adv.* Also 4 vncesendly, -cessandly, -seshandle; 5 vncessyngly, -sessyngly, unsessyngly. [f. prec. + -LY [2].] Without ceasing; incessantly.

*c* 1340 HAMPOLE *Prose Tr.* 3 Wharefore, what may do faile vn-to hym þat couaytes vn-cessandly for to lufe þe name of Ihesu? 1382 WYCLIF *Isaiah* Prol., For the present bacbityng by which me enemys vncesendely to-tern, he to me ȝelde meede in tyme to come. *c* 1425 *Found. St. Barth.* II. xxviii, All the benefetys..that hath be don yn the portys of the see ..unsessyngly. 1435 MISYN *Fire of Love* 101 þat þai godis giftis knawand in al þer hart hym þa suld glorify & lufe vncessyngly. 1779 *Mirror* No. 37, To wear high feathers, and to wave them more unceasingly than any other ladies. 1809 PINKNEY *Trav. France* 147 They are temperate, unceasingly gay, and sufficiently clad. 1880 'OUIDA' *Moths* I. vii. 161 She was harassed by the sense of being unceasingly criticised.

**Uncei·led,** *ppl. a.* (UN-[1] 8.)

[1775 ASH.] 1819 CRABBE *T. of Hall* xii. 708 The roof, unceil'd in patches, gave the snow Entrance within. 1865 KINGSLEY *Herew.* iii, A low lean-to roof; the slates and rafters unceiled. 1891 T. HARDY *Tess* xxxviii, The room below being unceiled she could hear most of what went on there.

**Uncei·linged,** *a.* (UN-[1] 9.) 1849 LEVER *Con Cregan* v, In a large unceilinged room..sat Betty in a straw chair.

**Uncele,** var. UNSEEL *v. Obs.*

**Unce·lebrated,** *ppl. a.* [UN-[1] 8.]

**1.** Not observed with festivities or in some formal manner; not specially honoured or extolled.

1660 MILTON *Free Commw.* Wks. 1851 V. 425 Nor was.. our Victory..unprais'd or uncelebrated in a written Monument. 1667 — *P. L.* VII. 253 Thus was the first Day Eev'n and Morn: Nor past uncelebrated, nor unsung By the Celestial Quires. 1736 POPE *Let. to Swift* 30 Dec., I have seen a royal birth-day uncelebrated but by one vile Ode, and one hired bonfire. 1781 MRS. GRANT *Lett. fr. Mount.* (1813) II. xiv. 75 The freedom, ease, and gaiety, which..has not passed uncelebrated or unsung. *a* 1843 SOUTHEY *Comm.-pl. Bk.* Ser. II. (1849) 138 Christmas *un*celebrated there.

**2.** Not famed or renowned.

1740 CIBBER *Apol.* (1756) II. 4 There came over from Dublin Theatre two uncelebrated actors to pick up a few pence among us. 1782 V. KNOX *Ess.* lxvi. I. 288 Such is that uncelebrated virtue, common and moral honesty. 1840 WILLIS *Loiterings Trav.* III. 38 This out-of-door's world, unvisited and uncelebrated.

**Uncele·stial,** *a.* (UN-[1] 7.)

1661 FELTHAM *Resolves* (ed. 8) II. lvi. 301 It..gives the lips a trembling; the eyes an uncelestial and declining look. 1742 YOUNG *Nt. Th.* IX. 713 'Tis nature's structure, broke by stubborn will, Breeds all that un-celestial discord there. 1860 TROLLOPE *Framley P.* xxiii, Any uncelestial envy or malice. 1897 BLACKMORE *Dariel* 193 And the last of these was Dariel, looking as if she had never dreamed of anything uncelestial.

**Unce·llar,** *v.* (UN-[2] 5.)

1611 FLORIO, *Discantinare*, to vncellar. 1879 J. TODHUNTER *Alcestis* 78 Set the banqueting-hall in order;..uncellar my choicest wines.

**Unce·llared,** *ppl. a.* (UN-[1] 8.)

1564 *Reg. Privy Council Scot.* I. 299 That it remane within schip onsellarit to that effect for the space of four dayis.

**Unceme·nt,** *v.* (UN-[2] 3.)

*a* 1634 CHAPMAN & SHIRLEY *Chabot* IV. i. 56 They have frighted My fancy into my dreams with their close whispers How to uncement your affections.

**Unceme·nted,** *ppl. a.* (UN-[1] 8.)

1717 BERKELEY *Jrnl. Tour Italy* 28 May, Wks. 1871 IV. 552 Parched pasture, amidst wall of huge uncemented stones grown rough with age. 1841 W. SPALDING *Italy & It. Isl.* I. 312 Some huge fragments of uncemented blocks. 1851 RUSKIN *Stones Ven.* I. vi. § 2 With all the joints, perhaps uncemented, or imperfectly filled up with cement, open to the sky.

**b.** *transf.* and *fig.*

1783 BEATTIE *Theory Lang.* II. iv. 480 This uncemented composition has of late become fashionable among the French and their imitators. 1792 CHARLOTTE SMITH *Desmond* II. 53 That, uncemented by blood, the noble and simply majestic temple of liberty will arise. 1856 MERIVALE *Rom. Emp.* xxxix. (1865) IV. 379 The state itself has seemed..to become a mere collection of uncemented atoms. 1864 PUSEY *Lect. Daniel* (1876) 412 Subdued, but warlike nations, uncemented into one with the conquering empire.

**Unce·nsored,** *ppl. a.* (UN-[1] 8.) 1890 *Blackw. Mag.* Oct. 442 No foreign journalist may send uncensored telegrams to his editor.

**Uncenso·rious,** *a.* (UN-[1] 7.)

*a* 1711 KEN *Edmund* Poet. Wks. 1721 II. 272 Her Speech was uncensorious and restrain'd. 1823 DE QUINCEY *Lett. to Yng. Man* Wks. 1860 XIV. 19 Leibnitz was always uncensorious, and yet patient of censure. 1881 L. A. TOLLEMACHE in *Jrnl. Educ.* Oct. 225 Straightway the dove was expelled for his uncensorious mildness.

**Unce·nsurable,** *a.* (UN-[1] 7 b.)

1643 PRYNNE *Sov. Power Parl.* III. 121 Our Opposites must grant all Bishops, Priests, Ministers,..as irresistible, uncensurable, undeprivable. 1678 CUDWORTH *Intell. Syst.* I. v. 897 These sovereign legislative powers may be said to be..un-judicable or un-censurable by any humane court. 1810 BENTHAM *Packing* (1821) 58 An interest, than which ..nothing should be more innocent and uncensurable. *a* 1817 T. DWIGHT *Trav. New Eng.*, etc. (1821) II. 112, I have been informed..that he was uncensurable in his life.

**Unce·nsured,** *ppl. a.* (UN-[1] 8.)

1574 *Life 70th Abp. Canterb.* To Rdr. E 2 b, A masse of there intolerable superstitions deeds and sayinges vncensured. 1606 SYLVESTER *Du Bartas* II. iv. *Tropheis* 1055 But David's foule defect Was yet un-seen, un-censur'd, unsuspect. 1645 MILTON *Tetrach.* Introd., It was preacht before ye..that there was a wicked Book abroad, and ye were taxt of sin that it was yet uncensur'd. 1693 DRYDEN *Persius* I. 219 Rather than so, uncensur'd let 'em be. 1728 R. MORRIS *Ess. Anc. Archit.* 65 From these considerations I pass not uncensur'd. 1767 WILKES *Corr.* (1805) III. 101 All these papers have passed uncensured..by the two houses of parliament. 1849 MACAULAY *Hist. Eng.* vi. II. 11 This breach of the law for a time passed uncensured. 1879 FARRAR *St. Paul* (1883) 754 Children of God, uncensured in the midst of a crooked and distorted generation.

**Unce·ntral,** *a.* (UN-[1] 7.) 1782 PAINE *Let. Abbé Raynel* (1791) 54 The greater part of the Abbe's writings..appear to me uncentral and burthened with variety.

**Unce·ntre,** *v.* [UN-[2] 5.] *trans.* To remove from or as from a centre. Also *refl.*

1625 T. ADAMS *Serm.* Wks. (1629) 944 Let the heart be vncentred from Christ, it is dead. 1642 H. MORE *Song of Soul* III. 3 For then we fell,..Uncentring our selves from our great stay. 1693 NORRIS *Pract. Disc.* III. 195 To find herself loosen'd and uncenter'd from the Creature, and not lodg'd upon God. 1788 WESLEY *Wks.* (1872) VI. 447 Whatever uncentres the mind from God does properly dissipate us.

Hence **Unce·ntring** *vbl. sb.*

**1669** *Address to hopef. yng. Gentry Eng.* Ep. Ded. A 2 b, His vanity to promise the uncentring of that vast body and unweildy.

**Unce·ntred,** *ppl. a.* (UN-[1] 8.) **1652** BENLOWES *Theoph.* VII. xi, Jehovah's zone to this uncentred ball Ecliptick and meridionall. **1829** LYTTON *Disowned* xxxviii, Hers is the real and uncentred poetry of being, which pervades and surrounds her as with an air. **Unce·reclothed,** *a.* (UN-[1] 9.) **1862** GRATTAN *Beaten Paths* I. 142 The unsepulchred, uncoffined, and uncereclothed tailor. **Unce·remented,** *ppl. a.* (UN-[1] 8.) **1880** T. HODGKIN *Italy & her Invaders* III. vii, The bodies were unwashed, uncemented.

**Unceremo·nious,** *a.* [UN-[1] 7.]

**1.** Of conduct, actions, etc.: Characterized by lack of ceremony or formality.

**1598** CHAPMAN *Contn. Marlowe's Hero & Leander* III. 156 She vanisht, leauing pierst Leanders hart With sence of his vnceremonious part. **1727** BLACKWALL *Sacr. Class.* (ed. 2) I. 206 In the more plain and unceremonious times it [woman] was a title apply'd to ladies of the greatest quality and merit. **1779** J. MOORE *View Soc. France* II. lxxxv. 332 The unceremonious and easy manner, in which this great prince lives with his subjects. **1825** SCOTT *Talism.* viii, Expressing strongly the displeasure he felt at this unceremonious rebuke. **1891** FARRAR *Darkn. & Dawn* xxxix, Now the people laughed at the unceremonious way in which he shook one of them.

**2.** Of persons, etc.: Acting without ceremony.

**1831** SCOTT *Ct. Rob.* xiii, If it happens that they actually need gold, they are sufficiently unceremonious in taking it. **1832** LYTTON *Eugene A.* I. v, Forgive me if I seem unceremonious—adieu.

Hence **Unceremo·niously** *adv.*, **-mo·niousness.**

**1755** JOHNSON, *Familiarly*, *unceremoniously; with freedom like that of long acquaintance. **1796** MME. D'ARBLAY *Camilla* VI. xv, Resentful of the liberty he had so unceremoniously taken. **1825** SCOTT *Betrothed* xvii, The message of the Archbishop, so unceremoniously delivered. **1878** CHURCH *Bacon* ix. (1884) 215 Setting down unceremoniously ..the real rules which he had felt to be true. **1815** JANE AUSTEN *Emma* xii, All the *unceremoniousness of perfect amity. **1866** GEO. ELIOT *F. Holt* v, 'Well, they're right enough there,' said Felix, with his usual unceremoniousness.

**† Unce·rt,** *a. Sc. Obs. rare.* [ad. L. *incert-us*: cf. UN-[1] 5 b.] Uncertain.

**1543** *Sc. Acts, Mary* (1814) II. 440/2 Tharfor þe said decret of forfaltour is vncert, Inept, and generale, & following and promulgate vpoune ane vnecert, Inept & generale libell.

**Unce·rtain,** *a.* Forms: (see UN-[1] and CERTAIN *a.*). [UN-[1] 7; cf. F. *incertain* INCERTAIN *a.*, and L. *incertus*.]

**1. a.** Not determinate or fixed in point of time or occurrence; that may happen earlier or later.

*a* **1300** *Cursor M.* 23733 Es nathing certainur þan dede, Ne vncertainner þan es þe tide. *c* **1340** HAMPOLE *Pr. Consc.* 1952 What es mare uncertayn thyng, Þan es þe tyme of the dede commyng. **1388** WYCLIF *Wisd.* x. 7 Trees hauynge fruytis in vncerteyn tyme. *c* **1480** HENRYSON *Thre Deid Pollis* 12 (Bann. MS.), The hour of deth and place Is vncertane. **1526** *Pilgr. Perf.* (W. de W. 1531) 240 Vncertayne is thy deth, remember thyne ende. **1549** *Compl. Scot.* 36 The terme of cristis cumming is schort, ande the day oncertane. **1560** DAUS tr. *Sleidane's Comm.* 462 b, To be differred to a tyme uncerten. *a* **1627** SIR J. BEAUMONT *Miserable St. Man* 39 Which fixe our minds on that vncertaine day When these shall faile, most certaine to decay. **1811** *Regul. & Ord. Army* 135 The Captain and Subaltern of the Day of each Regiment are to visit the Hospital at different and uncertain Hours.

**b.** Not determinate or fixed in amount, number, or extent.

**1303** R. BRUNNE *Handl. Synne* 6688 Betwyxe oure ioye, and ȝoure peyne, ys endles tyme, and vncerteyne. **1382** WYCLIF *Job* xv. 20 The noumbre of ȝeris of his tiraundise is vncertein. *c* **1460** FORTESCUE *Abs. & Lim. Mon.* ix. (1885) 127 Sithyn the said extraordinarie charges bith so vncertayne þat thai be not estymable. **1725** *Fam. Dict.* s.v. *Yard-land*, This uncertain quantity in 28 of Edward IV. is call'd a Verge of Land. **1774** GOLDSM. *Nat. Hist.* I. 339 The activity of the winds, their continual change, and uncertain duration. **1775** JOHNSON *Tax. no Tyr.* 14 A duty of very uncertain extent. **1816** SHELLEY *Hymn Intell. Beauty* IV. 2 Love, Hope, and Self-esteem, like clouds depart And come, for some uncertain moments lent. **1839** STONEHOUSE *Axholme* 25 The warp along the shores of the Trent forms a bed of uncertain thickness.

**c.** Having no regular shape. *rare*—[1].

**1742** LEONI *Palladio's Archit.* I. 81 It was pav'd with uncertain Stones, that is, such as had unequal sides and angles.

**2.** Not certain or determined in respect of occurrence; dependent on chance or accident.

**1303** R. BRUNNE *Handl. Synne* 5995 Here mercy ys ful on-certeyn But þey ȝelde hem here gode aȝeyn. **1484** *Coventry Leet Bk.* 518 Because they shuld not come in þe market ..Howe-so-euer þe price of whete went higher or lower, which was thought vncerteyn. **1589** PUTTENHAM *Eng. Poesie* I. xix. 32 The things future, being also euents very vncertaine, and such as can not possibly be knowne because they be not yet. **1634** MILTON *Comus* 360 Peace brother, be not over-exquisite To cast the fashion of uncertain evils. **1818** CRUISE *Digest* (ed. 2) II. 269 Such remainder is contingent, because it is uncertain which of them will survive. **1853** ABP. THOMSON *Laws Th.* (ed. 3) § 124. 332 Uncertain events are those wherein no cause or law appears, to determine the occurrence of one rather than of another. **1880** *Science-Gossip* XXV. 116/1 There are small ledges here and there formed..by the uncertain deposit of material, or by the uncertain slip of shingle.

**b.** Devoid of, lacking in, certainty or settled character; liable to change or accident.

**1477** *Rolls of Parlt.* VI. 168/1 The lyf of every creature is uncertayn. **1503–4** *Act 19 Hen. VII*, c. 25 *Preamble*, Lyfe [is] as uncertayne to suche as survyve as was to them now departed. **1526** TINDALE *1 Tim.* vi. 17 Charge them..that they be not excedynge wyse, and that they trust not in the vncertayne riches, but in the livynge god. **1607** SHAKS. *Timon* V. i. 205 Their Aches, losses, Their pangs of Loue, with other incident throwes That Natures fragile Vessell doth sustaine In lifes vncertaine voyage. **1655** STANLEY *Hist. Philos.* III. (1687) 86/2 He ought not voluntarily to thrust himself into destruction..; that he should leave his Children in an uncertain mean estate. **1690** LOCKE *Hum. Und.* I. iii. § 13 Truth and Certainty..are not at all secured by them: But Men are in the same uncertain, floating estate with, as without them. **1743** FRANCIS tr. *Hor., Odes* III. xxix. 39 For the World's uncertain Fate Alarm'd. **1828** LYTTON *Pelham* III. x, My mother was much better, but still in a very uncertain and dangerous state of health. **1850** MCCOSH *Div. Govt.* II. ii. (1874) 163 There is nothing so uncertain as bodily health and human destiny. **1891** FARRAR *Darkn. & Dawn* xlv, His philosophic teacher.. persuaded him that a firm death was preferable to troubled and uncertain life.

**3.** About which one cannot be certain or assured; subject to doubt.

**1338** R. BRUNNE *Chron.* (1810) 324 Who may now in Rome haf any sikernesse, þat þer is hiest dome, & ȝit vncerteyn es? *c* **1374** CHAUCER *Boeth.* v. pr. iii. (1868) 154 Þan ne sholde þer ben no stedfast prescience of þinge to comen but raþer an vncerteyn oppinioun. **1382** WYCLIF *1 Cor.* ix. 26 Therfore I renne so, not as into an uncerteyn thing; thus I fiȝte, not as betynge the eyr. *c* **1400** *Destr. Troy* 9206 Hit semith me vnsertain, all serchyng of wayes. **1484** CAXTON *Fables of Auian* xvi, Men ought not to lete goo..what they be sure of, hopynge to haue afterwards that..whiche is vncertayne. **1555** EDEN *Decades* (Arb.) 126 Petrus Arias..hath offered hym selfe to aduenture his lyfe..vnder vncerteyne hope of gayne. **1596** SHAKS. *1 Hen. IV*, II. iii. 12 The purpose you vndertake is dangerous, the Friends you haue named vncertaine. **1634** SIR T. HERBERT *Trav.* 2 Vncertaine stories, which not only perplexe the hearers, but beget incredulitie, oftentimes amongst the credulous. **1669** STURMY *Mariner's Mag.* V. xii. 70 It is very difficult, and a thing uncertain also to arrive herein unto Exactness. **1718** PRIOR *Solomon* I. 740 Forc'd by reflective Reason I confess, That human Science is uncertain Guess. **1794** S. WILLIAMS *Vermont* (1809) I. vii. 221 If the facts had been true, the conclusions which have been drawn from them would have been wholly uncertain. **1798** WORDSW. *Tintern Abbey* 19 With some uncertain notice, as might seem Of vagrant dwellers in the houseless woods. **1827** FARADAY *Chem. Manip.* xxi. 548 New, important, and uncertain or unexpected results, are to be repeated once or twice.

*absol.* **1484** CAXTON *Fables of Auian* xvi, Men ought not to leue that thynge whiche is sure & certayne, for hope to haue the vncertayn. **1548** HALL *Chron. Hen. VI*, 129 It was not the poynt of a wiseman, to leave and let passe, the certain for the uncertain.

**b.** Of ways, etc.: Not clearly leading to a certain goal or destination.

*c* **1380** WYCLIF *Sel. Wks.* III. 363 Certis þat man were a fool þat wolde take þis uncerteine weie, and leeve þe certeyn witt and feyþ. **1565** COOPER *Thesaurus*, *Iter ambiguum*, vncertayne way. **1594** SHAKS. *Rich. III*, IV. ii. 64 Murther her Brothers, and then marry her, Vncertaine way of gaine. **1640** DENHAM *Cooper's H.* (1655) 295 He..more Repents his courage, then his feare before; Finds that uncertaine waies unsafest are. **1653** J. TAYLOR (Water P.) *title*, The certain Travailes of an uncertain Journey. **1784** COWPER *Task* III. 3 One who, long in thickets and in brakes Entangled, winds now this way and now that His devious course uncertain, seeking home. **1805** WORDSW. *Prelude* VI. 696 Doubting not that..by no uncertain path..Led, as before, we should behold the scene. **1818** KEATS *Endym.* II. 48 For many days, Has he been wandering in uncertain ways: Through wilderness.

**c.** That cannot be relied on to produce a particular result.

**1382** WYCLIF *Wisd.* ix. 14 The thoȝtis forsothe of deadli men [ben] dredful, and vncerteyn oure purueauncis. **1596** SPENSER *F. Q.* VI. iv. 25 So vp and downe he wandred many a mile, With wearie trauell and vncertaine toile. **1759** R. BROWN *Compl. Farmer* II. 119 Hops are a very uncertain crop. **1765** *Museum Rust.* IV. 314 He admits the spring-sowing to be uncertain. **1781** GIBBON *Decl. & F.* xxx. III. 175 These expensive and uncertain treaties. **1833** *Penny Cycl.* I. 186 In this arid region..maize, barley, and caffre corn, afford the husbandman a miserable and uncertain crop.

**4.** Not known with certainty; not established or proved beyond doubt; doubtful, dubious.

*a* **1325** *Prose Psalter* l. 7 Þe vncerteyn þynges and pryue of þy wisdom þou made to me apert. **1338** R. BRUNNE *Chron.* (1810) 334 Roberte's men þei slowe, þe numbre vncerteyn. **1387** TREVISA *Higden* (Rolls) II. 63 Hit is vncerteyn who bulde first þis citee. **1538** STARKEY *England* (1878) 61 Fortune, or els what other name soeuer you wyl gyue to the blynd and vncertayne causys wych be not in mannys powar. **1561** T. NORTON *Calvin's Inst.* 22 Euen the wisest of them..in theyr prayers do cal vpon vncertayne gods. *a* **1578** LINDESAY (Pitscottie) *Chron. Scot.* (S. T. S.) I. 68 The Earle of Saillisberrie quho was slaine be the schot of ane goun, wncertane hou or be quhat way. **1610** HOLLAND *Camden's Brit.* (1637) 288 Uncertaine it is, whether he made these buildings, or the buildings made him. **1639** LD. BALMERINO in 10*th Rep. Hist. MSS. Comm.* App. I. 48 Occurrents heere are vncertain. **1732** BERKELEY *Alciphr.* VI. § 5 What was uncertain in the primitive times cannot be undoubted in the subsequent. **1807** ROBINSON *Archæol. Græca* III. xiv. 260 It is uncertain who was the inventor of divination by sacrifices...By some it is ascribed to the Hetrurians. **1875** JOWETT *Plato* (ed. 2) IV. 121 The relation [of the Parmenides] to the other writings of Plato is..uncertain.

**b.** Without clear signification; ambiguous.

**1382** WYCLIF *1 Cor.* xiv. 8 If the trumpe ȝyue vncerteyn vois [1388 soune], who schal make him silf redy to bateil? **1611** BIBLE *1 Cor.* xiv. 8 If the trumpet giue an vncertaine sound. **1663** BP. PATRICK *Parab. Pilgr.* xvi, Metaphorical or borrowed words, which..make an uncertain sound, and leave the mind in confusion. **1818** CRUISE *Digest* (ed. 2) IV. 298 *marg.*, Where a Deed is uncertain, it is void. **1905** G. THORNE *Lost Cause* x, When the most influential part of the Press began to speak with no uncertain voice.

**c.** Not clearly identified, located, or determined.

**1617** MORYSON *Itin.* I. 192 Which King Phillip Augustus began to build in..1257, the foundations being before laid by an uncertaine founder. **1631** WEEVER *Anc. Funeral Mon.* 518 The vncertaine buriall of Vortimer..was in some part of this Citie. **1638** *Guillim's Heraldry* (ed. 3) I. vi. 41 According to that saying of an uncertaine Author. **1817** BYRON *Beppo* xxii, The years Which certain people call a 'certain age', Which yet the most uncertain age appears. **1821** SCOTT *Kenilw.* xxv, A large and massive Keep, which formed the citadel of the Castle, was of uncertain though great antiquity. **1900** A. S. MURRAY *Catal. Sculpt. Parthen. in Brit. Mus.* 77 No. 30 is a maiden holding an uncertain object, perhaps a footstool, on her left arm.

**d.** Not clearly defined or outlined.

**1638** JUNIUS *Paint. Ancients* 89 The uncertaine shapes of clouds most commonly are likened unto anything our wandering minde conceiveth. **1833** TENNYSON *Palace of Art* 238 But in dark corners of her palace stood Uncertain shapes. **1853** KANE *Grinnell Exp.* xlvii. (1856) 444 Every thing, in short, grew blurred and uncertain.

**5.** Not certain to remain in one state or condition; unsteady, variable, fitful.

**1591** SHAKS. *Two Gent.* I. iii. 85 How this spring of loue resembleth The vncertaine glory of an Aprill day. *c* **1600** — *Sonn.* cxlvii, My loue is as a feauer,..Feeding on that which doth preserue the ill, Th' vncertaine sicklie appetite to please. **1694** J. SMITH *Horolog. Disquisit.* 87 To make the more certain Guess at what Weather will after ensue, especially if the Glass be at Changeable and Uncertain. **1738** GRAY *Tasso* 48 As when athwart the dusky woods by night The uncertain crescent gleams a sickly light. **1743** FRANCIS tr. *Hor., Odes* I. xiii. 6 On my cheek th' uncertain color dies. **1753** MISS COLLIER *Art Torment.* I. i, When the weather is quite uncertain. **1794** MRS. RADCLIFFE *Myst. Udolpho* xxix, The moon gave a faint and uncertain light, for heavy vapours surrounded it. **1805** SCOTT *Last Minstrel* Introd. 85 Amid the strings his fingers stray'd, And an uncertain warbling made. **1828** SIR J. E. SMITH *Eng. Flora* II. 109 It may be observed that our uncertain summer is established by the time the Elder is in full flower. **1866** HOWELLS *Venetian Life* ii, I could see by that uncertain glimmer how fair was all, but not how sad and old.

**b.** Of persons: Variable, fickle, changeable, capricious.

?*a* **1611** BEAUM. & FL. *Four Plays, Tri. Death* ii, Uncertain as the Sea, Sir, Proud and deceitful as his sins Great Master. *a* **1625** FLETCHER *Double Marr.* I. i, Thou art constant; I an uncertain fool, a most blind fool. **1664** J. WILSON *A. Commenius* V. viii, The uncertain people, Constant to nothing but inconstancy. *a* **1721** PRIOR *Ess. Opinion* ?13 If You trace this Man thro life..You will find him always uncertain. **1808** SCOTT *Marm.* VI. xxx, O, Woman! in our hours of ease, Uncertain, coy, and hard to please.

**6.** Of persons: Not fully confident or assured *of* something.

*c* **1400** *Destr. Troy* 2050 Now Priam..[was] Uncertain of his Sister for seyng hir euer. **1548** UDALL, etc. *Erasm. Par. Mark* xiii. 83 b, These seruauntes, because they be vncertayne of theyr Lordes returnyng home, do styl endeuoyre them selues to do theyr office & duety. **1596** SHAKS. *1 Hen. IV*, I. i. 61 He..in the very heate And pride of their contention, did take horse, Vncertaine of the issue any way. **1631** WEEVER *Anc. Funeral Mon.* 579 He..being infected with the plague,..was landed about Portsmouth, and being vncertaine of any house, died vnder a hedge. **1670** MILTON *Hist. Eng.* III. 110 Thir [*sc.* the Saxons'] multitude wander'd yet uncertain of habitation. **1718** PRIOR *Solomon* III. 290 What is a King?..To blind Events, and fickle Chance a Slave: Seeking to settle what for ever flies; Sure of the Toil, uncertain of the Prize.

**b.** Const. *how, what, whether*, etc.: Having no clear knowledge; in a state of doubt.

**1526** *Pilgr. Perf.* (W. de W. 1531) 7 Whan he is vncerteyn whether he shall be iudged for euermore to ioye or to payne. **1560** DAUS tr. *Sleidane's Comm.* 444 b, And the people be lefte in this doutfull state of thinges, to be uncertaine howe paciently all menne woulde take it. **1597** HOOKER *Eccl. Pol.* V. lxii. § 18 St. Augustine was not himselfe vncertaine what to thinke. **1697** DRYDEN *Æneis* III. 9 Uncertain yet to find What place the gods for our repose assigned. **1794** MRS. RADCLIFFE *Myst. Udolpho* xxxiv, As she advanced, terrified and uncertain what to do. **1796** MME. D'ARBLAY *Camilla* VI. xiii, Camilla was still more agitated; for though uncertain if she were right or wrong in the appeal she meant to make [etc.]. **1851** THACKERAY *Eng. Hum.* vi. 302 He is always looking in my face, watching his effect, uncertain whether I think him an impostor or not. **1865** MRS. CARLYLE *Lett.* (1883) III. 253, I am uncertain how long he will be away.

**c.** Undecided; not directed to a definite end.

**1382** WYCLIF *1 Sam.* xxiii. 13 Dauid..and his men..hidir and thider weren vagaunt vncerteyn [L. *incerti*]. **1607** SHAKS. *Cor.* V. vi. 17 The People will remaine vncertaine, whil'st 'Twixt you there's difference. **1697** DRYDEN *Æneis* VII. 692 Ascanius young, and eager of his Game, Soon bent his Bow, uncertain in his Aim. **1808** SCOTT *Marm.* III. xx, The King Lord Gifford's castle sought, Deep labouring with uncertain thought. **1821** — *Kenilw.* xxv, That anxious and uncertain gaze, which indicated a doubt whether her brain was settled. **1855** *Poultry Chron.* III. 428/1 In their droning flight they move very irregularly, darting hither and thither, with an uncertain aim.

**† 7.** *Into uncertain*, at random. *Obs.*

**1382** WYCLIF *1 Kings* xxii. 34 A maner man bente a boowe, into vncerteyn [L. *in incertum*]. — *2 Chron.* xviii. 33 Oon of the puple in to vncerteyn kast an arowe.

**8.** Quasi-*adv.* In an uncertain manner.

*a* **1718** PRIOR *Cloe Hunting* 4 She lost her Way, And thro' the Woods uncertain chanc'd to stray. **1784** COWPER *Task* I. 358 The constant flail, That seems to swing uncertain, and yet falls Full on the destin'd ear.

**† Unce·rtain,** *v. Obs. rare.* [f. prec.] *trans.* To render uncertain.

**1614** RALEIGH *Hist. World* I. i. § 11. 14 It being manifest, that the diuersity of seasons, the Winters, and Sommers, more hot and cold, are not so vncertained by the Sunne and Moone alone. *a* **1619** FOTHERBY *Atheom.* I. xiii. § 4 (1622) 145 It might greatly vncertaine the mindes of the people about it.

† **Unce·rtained**, *ppl. a.* *Obs.*⁻¹ [Un-1 8.] = Uncertain *a.* 6 b.

1470 *Reb. Linc.* (Camden) 16 The tewsday, in the mornyng, the King, uncerteined how they wolde demean theym upon the saide summons.., addressed hymself to the felde.

**Unce·rtainly**, *adv.* [Un-1 11.]

**1.** In an uncertain or variable manner; at random, by chance or accident.

1387 Trevisa *Higden* (Rolls) III. 217 þese trowed þat al þing was vncertenliche i-made. 1530 Palsgr. 160 They use these sixe..uncertainly, somtyme of the masculyne gendre and somtyme of the feminyne. 1590 Sir J. Smyth *Disc. Weapons* 12 With the swelling of the salt water..they shall shoote verie vncertainlie. 1678 Cudworth *Intell. Syst.* Pref., That Motion of Sensless Atoms Declining Uncertainly from the Perpendicular. 1737 Whiston *Josephus, Antiq.* v. vii. § 7 The affairs of the Hebrews were managed uncertainly, and tended to disorder, and to the contempt of God.

**b.** At an indefinite time. *rare*⁻¹.

1683 E. Hooker *Pref. Pordage's Mystic Div.* 25 When the inexorabl Messenger, whose Name is the First Death, shal com (as certenly, and yet, as uncertenly hee wil).

**2.** Without definite result, course, or aim.

1555 Eden *Decades* (Arb.) 129 Whyle the matter was thus vncerteynly debated. 1567 Jewel *Def. Apol.* 152 Therefore the Prieste iudginge that, yᵗ he cannot know, muste needes wander vncertainely, and be a very doubtful Iudge. 1603 Holland *Plutarch's Mor.* 484 It were better for them to settle in any one certaine place whatsoever, than still to wander uncertainely upon the seas. 1662 Playford *Skill Mus.* iii. (1674) 38 Doing that safely and resolutely which others attempt timorously and uncertainly. 1696 Whiston *Th. Earth* iii. (1722) 278 [They] floated in the Waters among one another uncertainly. 1883 *Century Mag.* XXVI. 44 The poor beast ran uncertainly in all directions.

**3.** Without clear or definite knowledge or statement; doubtfully, undecidedly.

1613 *William I* in *Harl. Misc.* (Malh.) III. 144 The slaughter of the English is uncertainly reported. 1664 Pepys *Diary* 11 Nov., Some in Germany do derive themselves from the patrician families of Rome, but that uncertainly. 1742 *Jura Ecclesiastica* II. 351 To that two great Objections were made, that this Custom is unreasonable in itself and uncertainly set forth. 1795 *Phil. Trans.* LXXXV. 154, I have perceived this phænomenon only eleven times with perfect certainty, and only a few other times uncertainly. 1860 Pusey *Min. Proph.* 104 Joel foretold, not as uncertainly, not as anticipation, or hope, or longing, but absolutely and distinctly, that [etc.]. 1878 Lady Brassey *Voy. Sunbeam* xv. 255 A group of low islets whose position is very uncertainly indicated in the charts.

**Unce·rtainness.** *rare*⁻¹. [f. as prec.] = next.

1601 W. Cornwallis *Ess.* ii. xxx. R iv b, All which..carry man from his destinated mediocritie, & so leaues him to the pleasure of irresolution and vncertainenesse. 1677 Miege ii. s.v., Uncertainness what to do.

**Unce·rtainty.** [Un-1 12 and 5 b.]

**1.** The quality of being uncertain in respect of duration, continuance, occurrence, etc.; liability to chance or accident.

For the phrase *the glorious uncertainty of the law* see Glorious *a.* 5 b.

1382 Wyclif 1 *Tim.* vi. 17 Nethir for to hope in vncerteynte of richessis, but in quyk God. 1495 *Act 11 Hen. VII*, c. 36 *Preamble*, Greate uncertente and troble myght herafter growe bytwyne the seid Duches and the seid nowe Duke. 1526 *Pilgr. Perf.* (W. de W. 1531) 230 Bothe for the vncertaynty of the same [life], and also for the paynfulnes.. therof. a 1548 Hall *Chron., Hen. IV*, 20 Whose study was euer to procure malice, and to set al thynges in broile and vncertentie. a 1586 Sidney *Arcadia* ii. xxvi. (1912) 318 The uncertainty of his estate made you take armes. 1617 Moryson *Itin.* i. 278 By reason of the aforesaid uncertaintie in receiving money by billes of exchange. 1677 Yarranton *Eng. Improv.* 19 Such hazards at Sea as attend Merchants, with the badness and uncertainty of Personal Security. 1755 Earl of Corke in J. Duncombe *Lett.* (1773) III. 29 The uncertainty of the weather was still more surprising than the cold: we have had all kinds of seasons in a day. 1794 R. J. Sulivan *View Nature* I. 164 There is, besides this, great uncertainty of colour, according as the heat varies. 1810 Scott *Lady of L.* iii. ii, Neither broken nor at rest; In bright uncertainty they lie. 1860 Tyndall *Glac.* i. xi. 75 The uncertainty of the footing between the blocks of ice.

**b.** With *a* and pl. Something of which the occurrence, result, etc., is uncertain.

1619 in Foster *Eng. Factories India* (1906) I. 174, I send him not uppon uncertayntyes but uppon sure grounds. 1653 J. Hall *Paradoxes* 37 We love to toyl for uncertainties, and in this are worse then children. 1691 *Andros Tracts* II. 251 Most of the Persons in our Government understand little or nothing of Trade, and so they leave it always at uncertainties. 1712 Lady M. W. Montagu *Let. to Mr. W. Montagu* 9 Dec., I would not advise you to neglect a certainty for an uncertainty. 1757 Pitt in *10th Rep. Hist. MSS. Comm.* App. I. 214 Exposed to the most alarming Uncertainties. 1782 Miss Burney *Cecilia* iii. ix, Mr. Arnott was wretched from a thousand uncertainties. 1846 Mrs. A. Marsh *Father Darcy* II. viii. 141 Every thing seems so certain, so inevitable, a consequence of the enterprise—yet my mind is harassed by uncertainties. 1864 Bowen *Logic* xiii. 443 The probability..of two independent uncertainties happening conjointly.

**c.** An uncertain gain or emolument.

1650 Greaves *Seraglio* 168 He hath then but a thousand aspars a day, as the Cadeeleschers have..; howbeit their uncertainties amount alwayes to a far greater matter.

**2.** The state of not being definitely known or perfectly clear; doubtfulness or vagueness.

c 1380 Wyclif *Sel. Wks.* II. 133 Þat sum men graunten and sum men denyen, for uncerteynte of þe dede. 1395 Purvey *Remonstr.* (1851) 47 The multitude and vncertaynte of siche lawis. 1565 Cooper *Thesaurus, Incertum*,..doubtfulnesse: vncertaintie. 1599 Hakluyt *Voy.* II. Pref. *4 b, Besides the foresaid vncertaintie, into what dangers and difficulties they plunged themselues..I tremble to recount. a 1633 Austin *Medit.* (1635) 95 This is the briefe of the uncertainty of the History. 1696 Whiston *The. Earth* iii. (1722) 285, I might..leave the following Conjectures to the same State of Uncertainty they have hitherto been in. 1765 *Museum Rust.* IV. 291 The uncertainty in which of the stages the delineation of the plant has been taken. 1802 T. Thomson *Chem.* ii. v. II. 189 He acknowledged..that there were two sources of uncertainty, which rendered his conclusions not altogether to be depended upon. 1869 Froude *Short Stud.* Ser. ii. *Educ.* (1871) 322 So far as our special occupations go, there is no uncertainty. 1902 J. Gairdner *Eng. Ch. 16th Cent.* viii. 141 The name of the celebrant was kept a profound secret, and to this day it is a matter of uncertainty.

**b.** *Law.* In phr. *bad*, or *void, for uncertainty.*

1818 Cruise *Digest* (ed. 2) IV. 298 Where the words of a deed are so uncertain that the intention of the parties cannot be discovered, the deed will be void. Thus a gift..to one of the children of J. S., he having four children, is void for uncertainty. 1890 Sir A. Charles in *Law Times Rep.* LXIII. 767/1 There is some variation in the mode in which the custom is stated, but not enough to make it bad for uncertainty.

**c.** Something not definitely known or knowable; a doubtful point.

1387 Trevisa *Higden* (Rolls) II. 377 It is vncerteynte whiche Mercurius þis was. 1577 tr. *Bullinger's Decades* (1592) 24 What..is more euident than that which..no man doeth referre to darkenesse and vncertainties. 1590 Shaks. *Com. Err.* ii. ii. 187 Vntill I know this sure vncertaintie, Ile entertaine the free'd [*sic*] fallacie. 1653 W. Ramesey *Astrol. Restored* 38 To what end..is it for a man to busie his head about such uncertainties. 1878 Stanley *Addr. & Serm. U.S.* iii. (1883) 141 Many a one..has been perplexed by the uncertainties and contentions of history. 1889 *Renan's Bk. Job* p. xxxix, There is but one remedy for such uncertainties.

**3.** The state or character of being uncertain in mind; a state of doubt; want of assurance or confidence; hesitation, irresolution.

1548 Elyot, *Suspensio*, a hangyng vp; also doubte or vncertayntee of the mynde. 1598 R. Bernard tr. *Terence, Phormio* iv. iii, Let me vnderstande..if they will giue me her, that I may let this alone, least I stay in an vncertaintie. 1607 Shaks. *Cor.* iii. iii. 124, I banish you, And heere remaine with your vncertaintie. Let euery feeble Rumor shake your hearts. 1635 D. Dickson *Expl. Hebr.* x. 242 Doeth not this Exhortation importe the Elects vnsetlednesse, and vncertayntie of perseverance? 1746 Wesley *Princ. Methodist* 43 When I have been in great distress of soul, or in utter uncertainty how to act in an important case. 1794 Mrs. Radcliffe *Myst. Udolpho* i, She was compelled to rest in uncertainty. 1851 Hawthorne *Ho. Sev. Gables* ix, Pacing the room..with the uncertainty that characterized all his movements. 1879 Lubbock *Addr. Pol. & Educ.* iii. 57 Uncertainty as to the educational value of Science.

*pl.* 1846 Mrs. A. Marsh *Father Darcy* II. viii. 139, I marvel at..these hesitations and uncertainties in a man of your resolution. 1851 Carlyle *Sterling* ii. iii, I suppose, he was full of uncertainties.

† **b.** In phr. *at uncertainty, upon uncertainties.*

1668 Howe *Bless. Righteous* (1825) 267 Though he be upon great uncertainties as to his enjoyment of them. 1690 Locke *2nd Let. Toleration* Wks. 1714 II. 272 Whereby we are as much still at Uncertainty, as we were before, who those are who..are to be punished.

**Uncerti·ficated**, *ppl. a.* (Un-1 8.)

Frequent in recent use, esp. of teachers.

1836–7 Dickens *Sk. Boz, Scenes* xiii, A disappointed eighth-rate actor, a retired smuggler, or an uncertificated bankrupt. 1868 M. Pattison *Academ. Org.* iv. 88 Study not merely private and uncertificated, but evidenced by a regular appearance in the public schools for disputation.

**Unce·rtified**, *ppl. a.* [Un-1 8.]

**1.** Not made certain; not assured.

1535 Stewart *Cron. Scot.* (Rolls) II. 170 Vncertifieit tha war into sic thing Into that cace quhome that tha wald mak king. 1801 Southey *Thalaba* vi. xviii, The astonish'd Thalaba..closed his eyes, And open'd them again; And yet uncertified, He prest them close.

**2.** Not attested as certain; not guaranteed by certification.

1681 *Calr. Treas. Bks.* 7 That he do not issue out process upon any uncertified bond. 1760–1 Smollett *Launcelot Greaves* xx, The mercy of the legislature in favor of insolvent debtors, is never extended to uncertified bankrupts taken in execution. 1846 Grote *Greece* i. xix. II. 47 Any chronological system which may be applied to it, must be essentially uncertified and illusory. 1876 Meredith *Beauch. Career* xxxiv, She touched the double chords within us which are..a divine discord if an uncertified harmony.

**Unce·rtitude.** [Un-1 12.] = Incertitude.

1541 Cranmer in *St. Papers Hen. VIII*, I. 717 Wheropon myght growe most uncertitude of Your Graces succession, with..unquietnes..to this Realme. 1870 J. H. Newman *Gram. Assent* ii. vi. 194 That uncertitude on the subject is just the explanation..of the strange violence of language.

† **Unce·ssable**, *a.* *Obs.*⁻¹ = Incessable *a.*

1596 Z. J. tr. *Lavardin's Hist. Scanderbeg* 212 Mahomet was noted aboue the rest to vse an vncessable kind of diligence.

† **Unce·ssant**, *a.* *Obs.* Also 6 vnceassa(u)nt, -cessaunt. [Un-1 7 and 5 b.] = Incessant *a.* (Very common c 1550–1690.)

*α.* 1548 Udall *Erasm. Par. Luke* xxiv. 178 b, Hauyng within hymself a perpetuall vnceassaunt power to dooe whatsoeuer his wille is. 1592 Kyd *Murther I. Brewen* Wks. (1901) 293 Bloud is an vnceassant crier in the eares of the Lord.

*β.* 1555 Eden *Decades* (Arb.) 161 The vncessaunt mouynge and impulsion of the heauens. 1583 Babington *Commandm.* (1590) 190 Parents, that take such intollerable and vncessant paines to leaue much vnto their children. a 1641 Bp. Mountagu *Acts & Mon.* (1642) 429 Wicked mens soules they thrust and imprison in a darksome roome below, where torments uncessant doe attend them. a 1661 Holyday *Juvenal* (1673) 263 They..bid their sons with uncessant industry imploy their time. 1692 Ray *Creation* ii. 47 The Heart..by its uncessant Motion distributing the Blood.

† **Unce·ssantly**, *adv.* *Obs.* Also 5 vncessantle, 6 vncessaunt(e)ly(e, 6–7 uncessantlie; 6 vnceassantly. [Cf. prec.] = Incessantly *adv.* (Very common c 1550–1690.)

c 1460 *Towneley Myst.* iii. 147 It shall begyn full sone to rayn vncessantle. 1548 Udall *Erasm. Par. Luke* xix. 147 b, But the Iewes..kepyng sylence of the glorie of Christ .., the stones vnceassauntely crye it out. 1576 Fleming *Panopl. Epist.* 282 Such a one searcheth the very heart and entrayles of the ground, for gold and siluer, unceassantly. 1600 Holland *Livy* xxxii. xv. 817 The assault and batterie continuing uncessantly both night & day, overcame at length the..valour of the Macedonians. 1651 H. More *2nd Lash* in *Enthus. Tri.*, etc. (1656) 213 Putting the body ..into a perpetuall motion, so that the parts fridge one against another uncessantly. 1691 Norris *Pract. Disc.* 329 They..must needs..be carried out uncessantly and intirely toward the Supream Good.

† **Unce·ssantness.** *Obs.* [Cf. prec.] = Incessantness.

1627 H. Scudder *Chr. Daily Walk* xvi. § 6 (1637) 639 Those [evil thoughts] which come onely from Satan, may usually bee knowne..by their suddennesse and uncessantnesse. 1677 Gilpin *Demonol.* iii. 19 If they urge the uncessantness of the Devil's Attempts, Christ and others have felt the like.

**Unce·stused**, *a.* (Un-2 8.) a 1843 Southey *Comm.-Pl. Bk.* (1851) IV. 198 Without his wig he is Jove without his thunder. Venus uncestused, Phœbus unbeamed.

**Unch**, obs. form of Inch *sb.*1

† **Unch**, reduced form of Nuncheon.

*Nunch* is common in English dialect use.

1668 R. B. *Adagia Scot.* 7 An unch is a feast (of Bread and Cheese).

**Uncha·fed**, *ppl. a.* (Un-1 8.) [1775 Ash.] 1865 *Pall Mall G.* 19 June 4/2 One is glad..to be dismissed in peace, unchafed and unwearied.

† **Unchaghe.** *Obs.*⁻¹ [a. Ir. *óinseach*.] A foolish or wanton woman.

1534 *St. Papers Hen. VIII*, II. 215 That no Yryshe.. bardes, unchaghes, nor messangers, come to desire any goodes of any man dwellinge within the Inglyshrie.

**Unchai·n**, *v.* [Un-2 4 b.]

**1.** *trans.* To set free, release, from a chain or chains; to remove the chain(s) from.

1582 N. Lichefield tr. *Castanheda's Conq. E. Ind.* i. lxxiii. 150 Being in a readinesse to uncheine his Mastes, he was presently informed that the king of Calicut was reforming a new his Castles. 1591 Shaks. 1 *Hen. VI*, v. iii. 31 Vnchaine your spirits now with spelling Charmes, And try if they can gaine your liberty. 1664 Dryden & Howard *Ind. Queen* iii. i, They may By force unchain, and crown him in a day. 1679 Alsop *Melius Inq.* i. ii. 108 When the Righteous God saw it necessary to unchain the Devil, and let him loose upon the English Protestants. 1704 Prior *Prol. Her Majesty's Birth-day* 37 So was his Fame compleat, and Andromede unchain'd. 1831–7 Praed *Bridal of Belmont* 113 The young Count clambered down the rock, Unfurled the sail, unchained the oar. 1868 Dickens *Uncomm. Trav.* xxviii, He used his utmost influence to get the man unchained from the bedstead.

*absol.* 1836 Dickens *Sk. Boz, Gt. Winglebury Duel*, Up started the ostlers..unstrapping, and unchaining, and unbuckling, and dragging willing horses out.

**b.** *transf.* and *fig.* To set free; to liberate.

1793 H. Walpole in Miss Berry *Jrnls. & Corr.* (1865) I. 425, I unchain my impatience, which has behaved like an angel. 1796 Coleridge *Destiny of Nations* 111 Yet the wizard her..Forces to unchain the foodful progeny Of the Ocean stream. 1811 H. G. Knight *Phrosyne* 40 Stern Winter..Unleafs the forest, and unchains the wind. 1855 [J. D. Burn] *Autobiog. Beggar Boy* (1859) 13 You may form some little opinion of my position when my father unchained his lawless desires. 1890 'R. Boldrewood' *Col. Reformer* (1891) 175 The storm..swept over..as if a fresh blast had been unchained among the far south ice-fields.

**2.** To free from obstruction by the removal of a chain. Also *fig.*

1613–6 W. Browne *Brit. Past.* ii. iii, Gaze on mine eyes, whose life-infusing beames Haue powre to melt the Icy Northern streames, And so inflame the Gods of those bound Seas They should vnchaine their virgin passages. 1663 Davenant *Siege of Rhodes* i. 31 Away! unchain the Streets, unearth the Ports!..And bravely sally out from all the Forts!

Hence **Unchai·ning** *vbl. sb.*

[1775 Ash.] a 1835 Mrs. Hemans *Carolan's Prophecy* 13 Many stood waiting around, in silent earnestness, Th' unchaining of his soul. 1871 W. B. Jerrold *At Home in Paris* ii. vii. II. 147 It was a wicked, reckless unchaining of the hates long nursed, of the two foremost military nations of the world.

**Unchai·nable**, *a.* (Un-1 7 b.) c 1836 Mangan *Poems* (1903) 9 Though he were even a pleasant salmon in the unchainable sea. 1899 F. T. Bullen *Way Navy* 12 Like sentient monsters mad with unchainable energy.

**Unchai·ned**, *ppl. a.* (Un-1 8.)

1660 Ingelo *Bentiv. & Ur.* ii. (1682) 184 The unchain'd Barges separated themselves from one another. 1704 Prior *Let. to M. Boileau Despreaux* 174 The Eagle,..Unchain'd and Free, directs her upward Flight. a 1721 — *Female Phaeton* vi, Dearest Mamma, for once let me, Unchain'd, my Fortune try. 1742 Young *Nt. Th.* ix. 614 Come, my Prometheus, from thy pointed rock Of false ambition if unchain'd, we'll mount. 1816 Byron *Siege Cor.* viii, Given to none, Had young Francesca's hand remain'd Still by the church's bonds unchain'd. 1865 Esquiros *Cornwall* 156 One must have lived there to know what is the violence of the unchained winds.

**Unchai·r**, *v.* (Un-2 5.)

1645 Tombes *Anthropol.* 10 What is this lesse then to unchaire Christ?

**Uncha·lked**, *ppl. a.* [1775 Ash.] 1786 *Phil. Trans.*

LXXVII. 30 No other book would do the same, though the sides were scraped unchalked.

**Uncha·llengeable**, *a.* (Un-[1] 7 b.)
1611 Speed *Hist. Gt. Brit.* ix. xx. 731/1 Our vulgar Bookes extant can hardly passe with a Iury of ordinary Criticks and Censors for vnchallengeable euidence. 1824 Scott *St. Ronan's* xxxiii, His title and his paternal fortune, which he thought..might be rendered unchallengeable. 1847 Ld. Lindsay *Sk. Hist. Chr. Art* I. 61 The Byzantines.. maintained a pre-eminence, unchallenged and unchallengeable, in the three sister arts. 1880 Muirhead *Gaius* ii. § 119 *note*, A man, whose position as heir under the civil law was unchallenged and unchallengeable.
Hence **Uncha·llengeably** *adv.*
1827 Scott *Napoleon* c. VIII. 330 Annual expositions of national receipt and expenditure..which were, to outward appearance, unchallengeably accurate. 1866 F. G. Stephens *Eng. Children* (1867) 32 This is unchallengeably true.

**Uncha·llenged**, *ppl. a.* (Un-[1] 8.)
*a* 1639 Spottiswoode *Hist. Ch. Scot.* (1655) ii. 97 He was.. much hated by the clergy... Notthelesse he went unchallenged and was not brought in question. 1805 Scott *Last Minstr.* v. xii, Unchallenged thus, the warder's post, The court, unchallenged, thus he cross'd. 1847, 1880 [see Unchallengeable *a.*]. 1898 'Merriman' *Roden's Corner* xvii. 176 'Yes,' continued the unchallenged speaker, in .. the typical voice of the tavern-talker.

**Uncha·mbered**, *ppl. a.* (Un-[1] 8.)
1650 Fuller *Pisgah* 373 The east end where the Porch stood, was clear, and unchambered. 1870 E. T. Stevens *Flint Chips* 392 *note*, Skulls from unchambered long barrows in South Wilts. 1895 *Chambers's Encycl.* VII. 409 This shell [of the nautilus] is unchambered, and peculiar to the females.

**Uncha·mpioned**, *ppl. a.* (Un-[1] 8.) 1819 Scott *Ivanhoe* xxxix, Championed or unchampioned, thou diest by the stake and faggot. 1872 *Spectator* 5 Oct. 1261 Will he, isolated and unchampioned, have the courage solemnly to bring his matters of complaint before a committee of squires.

**Uncha·nce.** *north.* and *Sc.* [Un-[1] 12. Cf. Wanchance.] Mischance, misfortune.
*a* 1400–50 *Alexander* 822* (Dublin MS.), [He] Comand kenely hys knyghtez to kepe to hys blonkez, Þat no vnchaunce þaim achefe. 1535 Stewart *Cron. Scot.* (Rolls) III. 405 Quhen this wnchance wes to king Richart kend. 1823 Galt *Gilhaize* lxxvi, Those grevious unchances which darkened the latter days of so many of the pious.

**Uncha·ncellor**, *v.* (Un-[2] 6 b.)
1676 Row *Contn. Blair's Autobiog.* xii. (1848) 512 The King took from Hyde the great seals (so he was unchancellered).

**Uncha·ncy**, *a.* Chiefly *Sc.* [Un-[1] 7. Cf. Wanchancy *a.*]
**1.** Ill-omened, ill-fated, unfortunate.
1533 Bellenden *Livy* ii. iv. (S.T.S) I. 142 Sen his hous was vnchancy, & his son dede. 1536 — *Cron. Scot.* (1821) II. 468 The lordis thocht that Johne was ane unchancy name to be ane king. 1589 Warner *Alb. Eng.* vi. xxxii. 141 Lastly slaine By Edward, whilst he did vphold vnchancie Henries Raigne. 1768 Ross *Helenore* ii. 98, I.. monie a weary foot synsyne hae gane, Born i' the yerd wi' that unchancy coat. 1863 *N. & Q.* 3rd Ser. IV. 264 Another of this difficult lady's unchancy wooers was a Scottish laird. 1893 Stevenson *Catriona* xiii, The devil any other sight or sound in that unchancy place.
**b.** Inconvenient, ill-timed.
1860 Trollope *Framley P.* xxix, Why had his Grace come at so unchancy a moment?
**2.** Dangerous; not safe to meddle with.
1786 Burns *To J. Kennedy* i, Down the gate, in faith, they're worse, And mair unchancy. 1818 Scott *Rob Roy* xxiii, We gang-there-out Hieland bodies are an unchancy generation when you speak to us o' bondage. 1833 M. Scott *Tom Cringle* xii, A stalwart unchancy customer, who will not be gainsaid or contradicted. 1874 Wood *Nat. Hist.* 281 The Brown Owl,..when roused to anger or urged by despair, is a remarkably unchancy antagonist.

**Unchangeabi·lity.** [f. next.] = Unchangeableness.
*c* 1400 *Pilgr. Sowle* (Caxton, 1483) ii. lii. 54 He myght not be refourmyd by cause of his vnchangeabylyte. 1813 T. Busby *Lucretius* I. i. Comm. p. xviii, Objections like these only serve to throw difficulties in the way of our faith in the unchangeability of the Divine Being. 1865 Livingstone *Zambesi* xxiv. 509 The African traditions which seem possessed of the same unchangeability as the arts to which they relate.

**Uncha·ngeable**, *a.* [Un-[1] 7 b and 5 b.] That cannot change or be changed; not liable to change; immutable, invariable.
Also, in recent use, 'not exchangeable'.
*a* 1340 Hampole *Psalter* iv. 9 It is tendant in til lastandnes and vnchaungeabile ioy. *c* 1340 — *Pr. Consc.* 8232 How God invysible es, And unchaungeable, and endles. 1382 Wyclif *Job* xv. 15 Among his seintus noon is vnchaungable. *c* 1430 *Life St. Kath.* xiii. (1884) 28 For god is vnbodyly inuisible and vnchaungeable. 1434 Misyn *Mending Life* 106 Qwhat is turnyng fro god bot turnynge fro guyde vnchawngabyll to guyde chawngabyll. 1526 *Pilgr. Perf.* (W. de W. 1531) 271 b, Seynge in spiryt the immutable or vnchaungeable trewth of god. 1587 Golding *De Mornay* iv. (1592) 44 By this terme Vnchangeable we deny him to be lyke the immortall soules, which admit passions. *a* 1610 Healey *Cebes* (1636) 152 Shee giueth the true knowledge of profitable things a gift of unchangeable goodnesse and security. 1676 Hale *Contempl.* i. 191 An eternal state of unchangeable and perfect happiness shall succeed. 1732 Berkeley *Alciphr.* vi. § 31 Although the light of truth be unchangeable. 1774 Goldsm. *Nat. Hist.* I. xx. 341 They..talk of a friend or a mistress as fixed and unchangeable as the winds. 1817 J. Scott *Paris Revisit.* (ed. 4) 71 The latter method will inevitably produce..a more unchangeable fidelity. 1855 Macaulay *Hist. Eng.* xiv. III. 450 The thousands of clergymen, who had so loudly boasted of the unchangeable loyalty of their order. 1867 H. Macmillan *Bible Teach.* xvi. 322 About the average age of forty, when the character becomes unchangeable.

*absol.* 1875 Jowett *Plato* (ed. 2) III. 535 For the unchangeable is never older or younger.

**Uncha·ngeableness.** [f. prec. + -ness.] Immutability.
1548 Elyot *Immutabilitas*,..vnchaungeablenesse, constancie. 1587 Golding *De Mornay* xvii. (1592) 279 Surely the vnchangeableness of Spirits was created to depend vppon their linking in with their maker. 1607 Hieron *Wks.* I. 156 The stablenesse and vnchangeablenesse of that worke of saluation which is wrought by Christ Jesus. *a* 1653 Gouge *Comm. Heb.* xii. (1655) 271 The Apostle giveth us to understand .. the unchangeablenesse of the Gospel. 1736 Chandler *Hist. Persec.* 51 He expressly asserts the immutability and unchangeableness of the Son. 1777 Priestley *Matt. & Spir.* (1782) I. xvi. 190 The eternity and unchangeableness of the first cause stands upon the very same grounds. 1827 Faraday *Chem. Manip.* ii. 28 This is fully compensated by the unchangeableness in weight. 1871 Jowett *Plato* I. 427 The realm of purity, and eternity, and immortality, and unchangeableness.

**Uncha·ngeably**, *adv.* [f. as prec. + -ly.] Immutably.
*a* 1340 Hampole *Psalter* lxxxviii. 35 Antyme, þat is, vnchaungabilly i sware in my haligh. 1608 Willet *Hexapla Exod.* 790 God yet himselfe being vnchangeablie present. 1682 Norris *Hierocles* 17 Shining with him in a happy life, but not uniformly and unchangeably. 1743 J. Morris *Serm.* ii. 37 Him, who is so perfectly wise, so unchangeably happy. 1781 Cowper *Table-t.* 443 A dire effect, by one of nature's laws Unchangeably connected with its cause. 1829 Southey *All for Love* i. xxi, Therein to be for life and death Unchangeably array'd. 1875 J. P. Hopps *Princ. Relig.* viii. 26 There is such a thing as the eternally right and the unchangeably good.

**Uncha·nged**, *ppl. a.* [Un-[1] 8.] Unaltered.
1387 Trevisa *Higden* (Rolls) II. 431 [To] chaunge þe liknesse wiþ oute and leue þe kynde vnchaunged wiþ ynne. *c* 1420 Lydg. *Ballad Commend. our Lady* 95 Thu louyst hem unchaungid þat serue the. 1532 More *Confut. Tindale* 135 He shold rather haue kepte styll the worde *presbyteros* vnchaunged, bycause that worde is yt yᵗ sygnyfyeth authoryte wyth the grekes. *a* 1586 Sidney *Arcadia* i. v. (1912) 34 Malice sooner ceased, then her unchanged patience. 1633 P. Fletcher *Purple Isl.* x. xli, The faces change prov'd th' hearts unchanged grace. 1667 Milton *P. L.* vii. 24 More safe I Sing with mortal voice, unchang'd To hoarce or mute. 1718 Prior *Solomon* i. 64 Whilst the distinguish'd Yew is ever seen, Unchang'd his Branch, and permanent his Green. 1794 Mrs. Radcliffe *Myst. Udolpho* xxxiv, Tell him my heart is unchanged. 1827 Scott *Highl. Widow* v, Noon found him in the same unchanged posture. 1894 Sir E. Sullivan *Woman* 23 Throughout Asia and Africa the relative position of women, legal and social, is unchanged.
Hence **Uncha·ngedness.**
1880 Mrs. Craik *Poems, Immutable* 31 Yet still Our change yearns after Thine unchangedness.

**Uncha·nging**, *ppl. a.* (Un-[1] 10.)
1593 Shaks. *3 Hen. VI*, i. iv. 116 But that thy Face is Vizard-like, vnchanging,..I would assay..to make thee blush. *a* 1625 Fletcher *Fair Maid Inn* iii. i, The husband Of my remembrance and unchanging vowes. 1709 Pope *Ess. Crit.* 315 But true expression, like th' unchanging Sun, Clears and improves whate'er it shines upon. 1757 W. Wilkie *Epigon.* vii. 198 If fame's unchanging voice to all the earth, With truth, proclaims you author of my birth. 1792 Burns *The Posie* ii The hyacinth's for constancy wi' its unchanging blue. 1812 Sir H. Davy *Chem. Philos.* 91 The summits [of the Andes] are covered with unchanging snows. 1856 Kane *Arct. Expl.* I. xxv. 326 The horizon showed an unchanging circle of ice. 1875 Jowett *Plato* (ed. 2) I. 456 The soul.. being in communion with the unchanging is unchanging.
Hence **Uncha·ngingness.**
1878 A. L. Walker *Lady's Holm* II. viii. 163 No place.. has the same look of unchangingness.

**Uncha·ngingly**, *adv.* (Un-[1] 11.)
1435 Misyn *Fire of Love* 14 So þe generacion of þe sone with þe euerlastynge of þe godhede vnchaungyngly bydis. 1817 Moore *Lalla Rookh, Nourmahal* 130 There's a beauty, for ever unchangingly bright. 1827 — *Epicur.* xvii. (ed. 4) 271 God..proceeds..unchangingly to the great, final object of his providence. 1883 Whitelaw *Sophocles, Œd. Col.* 613 And the same spirit never of friend and friend, Or state with state, abides unchangingly.

**Uncha·nnelled**, (*ppl.*) *a.* (Un-[1] 8 and 9.)
1600 S. Nicholson *Acolastus* (1876) 65 Then brake th' vnchannel'd issue of mine eyes, My teares gaue vent vnto my tired soule. 1712 Blackmore *Creation* vii. 622 She next essay'd the embryo's rise to trace From an unfashion'd, rude, unchannell'd mass. [1775 Ash.] 1872 *Daily News* 12 Oct., The lanes and byways unchannelled.

**Uncha·nted**, *ppl. a.* (Un-[1] 8.) [1775 Ash.] 1820 Shelley *Prometh. Unb.* i. 513 Leave Hell's secrets half unchanted To the maniac dreamer. 1840 Mangan *Poems* (1903) 14 The Chief whom nothing daunted..fell in distant Spain, unchronicled, unchanted!

**Uncha·peroned**, *ppl. a.* (Un-[1] 8.)
1858 Miss Mulock *Th. ab. Women* 33 Anxious mothers, who would not for worlds be guilty of the indecorum of sending their daughters unchaperoned to the theatre or a ball. 1886 Miss Braddon *One Thing Needful* vii, She was willing..to allow her daughter to stroll across the fields unchaperoned.

**Uncha·plain**, *v.* (Un-[2] 6 b.)
*a* 1661 Fuller *Worthies, Dorset* i. (1662) 280 Dr. Hackwel, for opposing the Spanish Match, was un-Chaplain'd and banished the Court.

**Uncha·pleted**, *ppl. a.* (Un-[1] 8.) 1864 Swinburne *Atalanta* (1865) 114 With unchapleted hair, With unfilleted cheek. 1870 Morris *Earthly Par.* III. iv. 51 Her golden head,..uncoifed, unchapleted.

**Uncha·racter**, *v.* (Un-[2] 6 b.)
1570 Foxe *A. & M.* (ed. 2) 193/1 Making of a priest a non priest, or a layman: vncharacteryng his owne order.

**Uncha·ractered**, *ppl. a.* [Un-[1] 8.]
**1.** Having no distinctive sign.
1633 C. Butler *Eng. Gram.* To Rdr., If first wee reforme our Alphabet, by adding those uncharactered letters which are wanting, and giving fit names to those that want them.
**2.** Of persons: Destitute of moral character.
1841 Gen. P. Thompson *Exerc.* (1842) VI. 37 The profligate and the uncharactered of both sexes.

**Uncharacteri·stic**, *a.* (Un-[1] 7.)
1753 Richardson *Grandison* (1781) IV. xviii. 141 Wisdom itself..is sometimes thought to sit ungracefully, when it is uncharacteristick, not to the man, but to the times. 1807 Opie in *Lect. Paint.* iv. (1848) 329 Important events disgraced by mean and uncharacteristic agents. 1853 Ruskin *Stones Ven.* II. v. § 26. 139 This cross, though graceful and rich,..is uncharacteristic in one respect. 1893 F. Adams *New Egypt* 41 Everything that is characteristic of the Egyptian is uncharacteristic of the Arabian.

**Uncharacteri·stically**, *adv.* (Un-[1] 11.)
1753 Richardson *Grandison* (1781) V. xxxi. 208 They won't let me write on,..or I should not have concluded so uncharacteristically. 1804 *Something Odd* II. 76 A quantity of fair hair floated gracefully (uncharacteristically I might also add) upon the shoulders. 1856 Ruskin *Mod. Paint.* III. iv. xiii. § 26 His ideas respecting all landscape being not uncharacteristically summed, finally, by Pallas herself. 1898 *Century Mag.* LV. 772 It ends, uncharacteristically enough, in rich simplicity.

**Uncha·racterized**, *ppl. a.* (Un-[1] 8.) 1701 Beverley *Apoc. Quest.* 13 Seeing the Time between the Weeks and the 1260 Days, would be otherways uncharacteriz'd, and the Space unknown. 1862 E. Falkener *Ephesus*, etc. ii. iv. 268 Vitruvius's definition of *hypæthros* is said to be uncharacterized by his usual precision.

**Uncha·rge**, *v.* Now *rare.* [Un-[2] 3.]
**1.** *trans.* To free from a charge or burden.
1303 R. Brunne *Handl. Synne* 11942 But yn euery tyme þat þou shryuest þe, Of pyne shalt þou vncharged be. 1377 Langl. *P. Pl.* B. xv. 338 For charite with-oute chalengynge vnchargeth þe soule. *c* 1430 *Pilgr. Lyf Manhode* ii. xlvii. (1869) 94 So miche we dide, she and j, þat þe contracte was ouerthrowe from me, and j vncharged.
*absol.* 1340 *Ayenb.* 97 Þe oþere [law] chargeþ: and þis onchargeþ.
**b.** To acquit of guilt.
1602 Shaks. *Ham.* iv. vii. 68 Euen his Mother shall vncharge the practice, And call it accident.
**2.** To unload; to discharge (a vessel).
13.. *Coer de L.* 2584 The drowmound..was drownyd in the flood, Ar halff unchargyd wer that good. 13.. *Propr. Sanct.* (Vernon MS.) in Herrig's *Archiv* LXXXI. 312/171 A beest þat charged is In plaas Mai not passe þorwh narwh paas Til he vncharged be þat tide. 1388 Wyclif *Acts* xxi. 3 We ..seiliden in to Sirie, and camen to Tire. For there the schip schulde be vnchargid. *c* 1425 *Eng. Conq. Ireland* 10 Thay vncharged hare shippes, & made ham loges on lond. *c* 1475 *Cath. Angl.* 59/1 To vn-charge; *vbi* to discharge.
*transf.* 1387 Trevisa *Higden* (Rolls) VII. 201 After mete þey wente into þe feeld by cause for to uncharge þaire stomakes.
**3.** To remove the charge from (a gun).
1687 Miége *Gt. Fr. Dict.* i, *Decharger un Canon, en ôter la charge*, to uncharge a Gun.

**Uncha·rgeable**, *a.* (Un-[1] 7 b.)
1649 Jer. Taylor *Gt. Exemp.* ii. x. 136 Offer was made of private and unchargeable arbitrators. 1659 *Gentl. Calling* ix. § 8 Will any man renounce a rich unchargeable reversion, when he is not only wooed, but bribed..not to disclaim it?

† **Uncha·rgeant**, *a.* *Obs.*[−1] (Un-[1] 7.)
*c* 1380 Wyclif *Sel. Wks.* III. 412 Siþ Crist ches to be unchargeaunte to þo puple, ne gif non occasioun of avarise to oþer, þei shulden fle þis doynge.

**Uncha·rged**, *ppl. a.* [Un-[1] 8.]
**1.** † **a.** Not called upon; unsummoned. *Obs.*
1456 Sir G. Haye *Law Arms* (S. T. S.) 91 Gyf a man gais to the weris unchargit, sall he tak wagis? 1539 *Reg. Privy Seal Scot.* II. 472/2 The said Johnne to be..unchargit to find souerte to the law.
**b.** Not burdened (*with* something).
*c* 1475 *Golagros & Gaw.* 435 Sen hail our doughty elderis has bene endurand, Thriuandly in this thede, vnchargit as thril. 1746 Eliza Heywood *Female Spect.* No. 24 (1748) IV. 317 When the Almighty, offended with our presumption, gives his fiat to our wishes, they seldom come uncharged with ills. 1896 *Westm. Gaz.* 23 Sept. 5/1 The national desire to be at any rate uncharged with responsibility.
**c.** Not formally accused.
1900 *Westm. Gaz.* 3 Apr. 3/2 His two native evangelists, who were arrested with him, are reported to be still in prison, untried and uncharged.
**2.** Unassailed, unattacked.
1607 Shaks. *Timon* v. iv. 56 Then there's my Gloue Desend and open your vncharged Ports.
**3.** *Her.* Not furnished with a charge.
1610 Guillim *Heraldry* ii. v. 49 The Bend containeth in breadth the fifth part of the Field, as it is vncharged. 1845 *Antiq. & Archit. Year Bk.* 312 Beneath each figure appears a shield, but uncharged.
**4. a.** Not loaded with powder and shot.
1719 De Foe *Crusoe* i. (Globe) 307 Snapping an uncharg'd Pistol, close to the Powder, [I] set it on fire. 1745 Mrs. Eliz. Montagu *Corr.* (1906) I. 203 The first was my servant, valiantly armed with two uncharged pistols. *a* 1829 *Parcy Reed* xv. in Child *Ball.* III. 26/2 You have left me in a fair field standin, And in my hand an uncharged gun.
**b.** Not charged with electricity.
1815 J. Smith *Panorama Sci. & Art* II. 263 A coating was then put on the uncharged glass. 1873 Maxwell *Electr. & Magn.* I. 53 When they are gone, other uncharged particles [of air] take their place.
**c.** Not furnished with a load.
1796 T. Twining *Trav. India*, etc. (1893) 157 The jolting of the uncharged machine became almost insupportable.
**5.** Not subjected to a financial charge.
1894 *Daily Tel.* 5 Dec. 5/7 A Four and a Half per Cent. Gold Loan, secured on the uncharged revenues of the Treaty ports.

**Uncha·riot**, *v.* (Un-[2] 5.)

*c* 1715 POPE *Lett* (1735) I. 140 The poor distressed Roman Catholics, now unhors'd and uncharioted. 1877 TALMAGE *Serm.* 9, The Lord has unhorsed us, uncharioted us.

**Uncha·ritable**, *a.* Also *Sc* 5 uncheritable. [UN-[1] 7 b and 5 b.] Not charitable; lacking in charity: **a.** Of persons, etc.

1456 SIR G. HAYE *Law of Armes* (S.T.S.) 237 And rycht sa..gif thare war ane uncheritable prelate, quhilk war..a counsailour to mak were. 1548 UDALL, etc. *Erasm. Par. Mark* xi. 71 b, With his frownyng browes, with his stately loke, with his contencious or vncharitable mouthe. 1592 G. HARVEY *Four Lett.* iii. Wks. (Grosart) I. 195 His conclusion, That the worlde was vncharitable, and he ordained to be miserable. 1646 CRASHAW *Steps to Temple, Charity* 58 What can the poore hope from us, when we bee Uncharitable ev'n to Charitie? 1673 *Lady's Call.* I. i. § 29 In this uncharitable age, things are apt to be denominated not from the greater but worser part. 1743 J. MORRIS *Serm.* ii. 49 If he remains uncharitable he is utterly unfit for heaven. 1828 LYTTON *Pelham* III. iv, Why be so uncharitable to this poor and persecuted principle? 1880 'OUIDA' *Moths* III. 82 People are so horridly uncharitable.

*absol.* 1837 W. IRVING *Adv. Capt. Bonneville* II. 191 The uncharitable were apt to surmise that he had, in the interim, been well used up in a buffalo hunt.

**b.** Of actions, feelings, etc.

*a* 1631 DONNE *Serm., Ps. li.* 7 (1640) 640 An uncharitable condemning of other men. 1683 D. A. *Art Converse* 22 With most uncharitable exaggerations of their least, or fancied misdemeanours. 1764 BURN *Poor Laws* 137 It were an uncharitable action to relieve them in a course of idleness. 1814 WORDSW. *Excurs.* VII. 775 Her uncharitable acts, I trust, And harsh unkindnesses are all forgiven. 1833 H. COLERIDGE *Lives Northerns* 11 Marvell..never again uttered so uncharitable a surmise as that with regard to Morus.

**Uncha·ritableness.** [f. prec. + -NESS.] The quality or character of being uncharitable.

1548-9 (Mar.) *Bk. Com. Prayer, Litany*, From enuy, hatred, and malice, and all uncharitablenes, Good lorde, deliuer us. 1581 SIDNEY *Apol. Poetrie* (Arb.) 35 The morrall common places of vncharitablenes, and humblenes. 1641 SMECTYMNUUS *Answ.* § 18 (1653) 74 It is no unusuall thing with the Prelats..to charge such as protest..with uncharitablenes and Schisme. 1653 JER. TAYLOR *Serm. for Year, Winter* ii. 17 The uncharitablenesse of men towards his poor. 1719 WATERLAND *Christ's Div. Vind.* 418 There's no uncharitableness in believing, that He gives us at least his own true meaning. 1836 HOR. SMITH *Tin Trump.* (1876) 193 Those outpourings of envy or uncharitableness which inevitably harden the heart. 1867 AUGUSTA WILSON *Vashti* xxi, I never before heard you utter sentiments that trenched so closely upon harsh uncharitableness.

**Uncha·ritably**, *adv.* [UN-[1] 11 b.] In an uncharitable manner; without charity.

*c* 1386 CHAUCER *Pars. T.* ¶ 626 If he repreue hym vncharitably of synne..thanne apperteneth that to the reioysynge of the deuel. 1529 *Act 21 Hen. VIII*, c. 4 § 1 The resydue of the same Executours uncharytably..have refused to intermedle..with the execucion of the said wyll. *a* 1548 HALL *Chron., Hen. IV*, 7 He uncharitably commaunded that no man..should once entreate him for the retourne of Henry nowe duke of Lancastre. 1624 GATAKER *Transubst.* 147 He very uncharitably passeth them by. 1656 COWLEY *Pindar. Odes, Life* iii, We..wish uncharitably for them, To be as long a Dying as Methusalem. 1728 ELIZA HEYWOOD tr. *Mme. de Gomez's Belle A.* (1732) II. 288, I know not..which of my Actions should make you judge so uncharitably of me. 1831 JAMES *Phil. Augustus* II. iv, You speak but uncharitably of the reverend canon of St. Berthe's. 1860 TRENCH *Serm. in Westm. Abb.* xi. 122 We pray that we may not speak uncharitably; but oh! let us pray that we may not think uncharitably.

**Uncha·rity.** (UN-[1] 12 and 5 b.)

*a* 1548 HALL *Chron., Edw. IV*, 200 The mother of this pernicious commocion was uncharitie, or very impietie. 1598 E. GUILPIN *Skial.* A v, It is a strange seeld seene vncharitie, To make fooles of themselues to hinder thee. 1643 SIR T. BROWNE *Relig. Med.* I. § 56 Thus we,..with as much uncharity as ignorance, doe erre..in points, not onely of our own, but on[e] anothers salvation. 1691 NORRIS *Pract. Disc.* 53, I might without any danger of Censoriousness or Uncharity, write Mystery upon the Triple crown. 1722 WODROW *Corr.* (1843) II. 655 Forgive the seeming uncharity in the supposition; I shall be glad it be groundless. 1837 JEFFREY in Ld. Cockburn *Life* (1852) II. 293 But I will have no uncharity. They too should have been richer. 1874 FARRAR *Christ* (ed. 2) II. xliv. 118 The frenzy which filled them when He set at naught their Sabbatarian uncharities.

**Uncha·rm**, *v.* [UN-[2] 3.]

**1.** *trans.* To deprive of magical powers; to nullify the efficacy or virtue of (a charm).

1575 VAUTROLLIER *Luther on Ep. Gal.* (1577) 95 We labour both by preaching and wryting vnto you, to vncharme that sorcerie wherewith the false apostles haue bewitched you. 1612 J. DAVIES (Heref.) *Muse's Sacr.* Wks. (Grosart) II. 53/1 Vncharme the Charmes then, of these grieuous ioyes, that still allure my sense of them to taste. 1624 HEYWOOD *Gunaik.* VIII. 402 Amasis King of Egypt was by the like exorcisme bound..till those ligatorie spells were after uncharmed. 1860 J. WOLFF *Trav. & Adv.* I. 362 The Russians convinced them that they could uncharm a talisman.

**2.** To free from a spell or from enchantment; to deliver from the influence of a charm. Also *absol.*

1621 LADY M. WROTH *Urania* 554 He ran to take her vp, and try how to vncharme her, but he was instantly throwne out of the Caue in a trance. 1638 GODOLPHIN in G. Sandys *Paraphr. Divine Poems* Pref. Verses **j b, That Harp, whose Charms uncharm'd the brest Of troubled Saul. 1688 E. RAVENSCROFT *London Cuckolds* 71, I will go home to my Wife, and uncharm her Mouth, and set her Tongue at Liberty. 1779 MME. D'ARBLAY *Diary* 16 June, She charms and uncharms in a moment; she is a bane and an antidote at the same time. 1883 MEREDITH *Lett.* (1912) II. 341 Where to go this year I do not know; perhaps nowhere. My last year's experience uncharmed me.

**b.** To deprive or rob of charm or fascination.

1835 WILLIS *Pencillings* II. xli. 28 But one look at the terms that might describe it, written on paper, uncharms even the remembrance.

**Uncha·rmed**, *ppl. a.* [UN-[2] 8.] Not subject to a spell or charm; not invested with charm; not delighted or pleased.

1592 SHAKS. *Rom. & Jul.* I. i. 217 From loues weake childish Bow, she liues vncharm'd. 1757 H. WALPOLE *Let. to Mann* 20 Nov., Still uncharmed, he said it was too little! 1818 COLERIDGE *Let. to Mrs. Gillman* (1895) 691 We come to a wood, full of birds and not uncharmed by nightingales. 1857 TENNYSON *Merlin & Vivien* 549 That full heart of yours.. may now assure you mine; So live uncharm'd.

**Uncha·rming**, *ppl. a.* (UN-[1] 10.)

1687 DRYDEN *Hind & P.* III. 209 Conscience would not let him rest: I mean, not till..old, uncharming Catherine was remov'd. 1892 *Pall Mall G.* 15 Nov. 3/1 He earned no little distinction by keeping outside that uncharming circle.

**Uncha·rnel**, *v.* [UN-[2] 5.] *trans.* To take out of a charnel. Hence **Uncha·rnelled** *ppl. a.*

*c* 1805 H. K. WHITE *Poems* (1825) 366 They tell..of uncharnell'd spectres, seen to glide Along the lone wood's unfrequented path. 1817 BYRON *Manfred* II. iv. 82 *Nemesis.* Whom wouldst thou Uncharnel? *Man.* One without a tomb—call up Astarte. 1831 TRELAWNY *Adv. Younger Son* III. 232 More like corpses uncharnelled, than living men.

**Uncha·rred**, *ppl. a.* Also 8 -chared. (UN-[1] 8.)

[1775 ASH, *Uncharred.*] 1799 J. ROBERTSON *Agric. Perth* 30 It is also calculated for drying malt, to which the acid, the oily particles and phlegm of unchared coals would be detrimental. 1898 *Daily News* 23 Nov. 6/6 Charred wood was more active than uncharred.

**Uncha·rted**, *ppl. a.* [UN-[1] 8.] Of which there is not a map or chart. (Common in recent use.)

[1847 WEBSTER.] 1895 *Pop. Sci. Monthly* July 404 To establish the latitude and longitude of uncharted places. 1897 *Edin. Rev.* Oct. 322 In tracking the Siberian coast through the month of August, many uncharted islands were discovered.

† **Uncha·rteral**, *a. Obs*[−1]. [UN-[1] 7.] Not in accordance with a charter.

*a* 1718 PENN *Tracts* Wks. 1726 I. 687 The most ignominious Death of our Country..was hardly satisfaction enough to the Kingdom, for their Uncharterall Proceeding.

**Uncha·rtered**, *ppl. a.* [UN-[1] 8.]

**1.** *fig.* Not authorized as by the terms of a charter; irregular, lawless.

1805 WORDSW. *Ode to Duty* 37 Me this unchartered freedom tires. 1863 COWDEN CLARKE *Shaks. Char.* ix. 215 The unchartered wind that 'bloweth where it listeth'. 1885 *Athenæum* 25 July 105/1 Faust..has mistaken unchartered freedom and limitless desires for the true human ideal.

**2.** Not furnished with a charter; not formally privileged or constituted.

1818 HALLAM *Mid. Ages* (1872) III. 112 The representation of unchartered, or at least unincorporated boroughs. 1822 J. FLINT *Lett. Amer.* 283 At the time when this happened, the people had just become jealous of unchartered banks. 1901 *Harper's Mag.* CII. 700/1 The Squatters—or unchartered settlers—roamed, at first, rent free.

**Uncha·ry**, *a.* (UN-[1] 7.)

1601 SHAKS. *Twel. N.* III. iv. 222, I haue said too much vnto a hart of stone, And laid mine honour too vnchary on't. 1818 KEATS *Endym.* II. 532 The unchariest muse To embracements warm as theirs makes coy excuse. 1856 MRS. BROWNING *Aur. Leigh* II. 622 To make a good man, which my brother was, Unchary of the duties of his house.

**Unchas·ed**, *ppl. a.* (UN-[1] 8.)

*a* 1533 LD. BERNERS *Gold. Bk. M. Aurel.* (1535) 101 b, They leaue no cattayle vnslayne, no gardeyne vnrobbed, no wyld beest vnchased. 1533 BELLENDEN *Livy* I. xxi. (S. T. S.) I. 118 The vnchangeabil seit of god terminus (quhilk alanerlie.. sal abide vnchasit away fra his mansioun). 1648 HEXHAM II, *Ongejaeght*, Vnhunted, or Vnchased.

**Uncha·ste**, *a.* [UN-[1] 7.] Not chaste; lacking chastity; impure, lascivious: **a.** Of persons, etc.

1382 WYCLIF *Rev.* xxii. 15 Forsothe with oute forth, houndes, and venym doers,..and vnchaast men, and manquellers. 1387 TREVISA *Higden* (Rolls) II. 173 Sardanapallus.. was ful vnchast, and..þey þat beeþ swiþe vnchaste beeþ i-cleped Sardanapally. *c* 1422 HOCCLEVE *Min. Poems* 216 This tale ..is of a womman þat was vnchaast. 1526 *Pilgr. Perf.* (W. de W. 1531) 95 He is so incontynent & vnchaste yt his mynde is blynde. 1564 tr. *Martyr's Comm. Judges* xxi. 287 b, Sempronia a certayne lasciuious & vnchast woman. 1626 BACON *New Atl.* (1650) 23 Their usuall saying is, That whosoever is unchaste cannot reverence himselfe. 1671 MILTON *Samson* 321 To seek in marriage that fallacious Bride, Unclean, unchaste. 1780 COWPER *The Doves* 29 If, fickle and unchaste,..Thou couldst become unkind at last, And scorn thy present lot. 1856 MRS. BROWNING *Aur. Leigh* VII. 71 These unchaste girls are always impudent.

*absol.* 1390 GOWER *Conf.* III. 269 And thus thunchaste was chastised. 1712 STEELE *Spect.* No. 286 ¶ 1 The Unchaste are provoked to see their Vice exposed. 1888 *Hooker's Wks.* III. 789/2 The unchaste, excluded from absolution by Tertullian.

**b.** Of life, habits, etc.

1541 *Act* 33 *Hen. VIII*, c. 21 § 8 Withoute plaine declaracion before of her unchaste lief. 1546 BALE (*title*), The Actes of Englysh votaryes, comprehendynge their vnchast practyses and examples by all ages. 1605 SHAKS. *Lear* I. i. 231 It is ..No vnchaste action or dishonoured step That hath depriu'd me of your Grace and fauour. 1663 BP. PATRICK *Parab. Pilgr.* xxiii. (1687) 237 What a loss they are at sometimes.. to satisfie an unchaste desire? 1711 SHAFTESB. *Charac.* II. 109 Even the unchastest Love borrows largely from this Source. 1849 ROBERTSON *Serm.* Ser. I. ix. (1855) 145 You read of the victims of unchaste life hurried on the dark whirlwind for ever.

**Uncha·stely**, *adv.* [f. prec. + -LY.[2]] In an unchaste manner; impurely.

*c* 1340 HAMPOLE *Prose Tr.* 6 A ȝonge mane,..vn-chastely and delycyousely lyfande and full of many synnys. 1340-70 *Alisaunder* 36 Hue loued so lecherie & lustes of synne, Þat her chylder hue chese unchastly to haue. 1548 UDALL, etc. *Erasm. Par. John* iv. 23 One that had naughtely & vnchastely misused her body with diuerse. *a* 1586 SIDNEY *Arcadia* II. xv. (1912) 245 She (unchastly attempting his wonted fancies) found..a bitter refusall. 1634 HABINGTON *Castara* I. (Arb.) 36 Who while he ey'd, Vnchastely, such a beauty,..Turn'd marble. 1690 C. NESSE *O. & N. Test.* I. 316 Dinah,..whom..he had unjustly as well as unchastly possessed.

**Uncha·stened**, *ppl. a.* (UN-[1] 8.)

1641 MILTON *Ch. Govt.* II. Concl. 62 A sort of formal outside men..whose unchast'nd and unwrought minds [were] never yet..subdu'd under the true lore of religion. 1760-72 H. BROOKE *Fool of Qual.* (1809) III. 136 He..has left his own household unchastened and unguided. 1819 KEATS *Otho* I. ii, I blush to think of my unchasten'd tongue. 1846 RUSKIN *Mod. Paint.* II. III. x. § 6 In language coarse, in thought undisciplined, in all unchastened. 1875 MAINE *Hist. Inst.* i. 6 A school [of thought] almost infamous for the unchastened license of its speculations on history and philology.

**Uncha·steness.** [f. UNCHASTE *a.* + -NESS.] The quality or state of being unchaste; impurity.

1530 PALSGR. 285/1 Unchastnesse, *impudicité.* 1548 CRANMER *Catech.* 66 Wher yought doth both heare and see vnchastnes, there the infection of vncleannes spreadeth abrode. 1610 HEALEY *St. Aug. Citie of God* I. xviii. (1620) 27 It were no vnchastenesse in her to suffer the rape vnwillingly. 1653 BAXTER *Worcester Petit. Def.* 38 Would you permit any rogues that will, to have access to your wives, and solicit them to Unchasteness? 1828 E. IRVING *Last Days* 239 If I were to come to speak of unchasteness.

† **Uncha·stied**, *ppl. a. Obs.*[−1] [UN-[1] 8 + CHASTY *v.*] Unchastised.

*c* 1340 HAMPOLE *Pr. Consc.* 5544 Yhit sons and doghters þat unchastyd war Sal accuse þair fadirs and modirs þar.

**Unchasti·sable**, *a.* Also 6 *Sc.* vnchestiable. (UN-[1] 7 b.)

1382 WYCLIF *Ezek.* ii. 4 The sones ben of hard face, and of herte vnchaastisable,..to whom I sende thee. *c* 1430 LYDG. *Min. Poems* (Percy Soc.) 57 A chield to thryve that is unchastisable,..It may wele ryme, but it accordith nought. [*c* 1580 *Maitland Folio MS.* (S T.S.) lv. 36 A chyld to thryff quhilk is vnchestiable.] 1645 MILTON *Tetrach.* Wks. 1851 IV. 194 The hard hearts of others unchastisable in those judicial Courts, were so remitted there, as bound over to the higher Session of Conscience.

**Unchasti·sed**, *ppl. a.* (UN-[1] 8.)

*c* 1380 WYCLIF *Wks.* (1880) 272 A bischop þat consentiþ to oþer mennus synnes schulde raþere be clepid an vnchastised hound þan a bischop. 1388 — *Ecclus.* xxx. 8 An hors vntemyd, ether vnchastisid, schal ascape hard, and a sone vnchastisid schal ascape heedi. *a* 1533 LD. BERNERS *Gold Bk. M. Aurel.* xlviii. (1535) 94, I neuer lefte ylnesse vnchastysed, nor goodnesse without rewarde. *a* 1547 SURREY *Paraphr. Eccles.* iv. 2 Wks. (1815) 73 When I bethought me well, under the restless Sun By folk of power what cruel works unchastised were done. 1688 SHADWELL *Sqr. Alsatia* III, Do you think you shall dishonour this family and debauch my sister, unchastiz'd? 1711 in 10th *Rep. Hist. MSS. Comm.* App. V. 123 The rebells..must not goe unchastized. 1779 COWPER *Olney Hymns* xxxvii. Oh! hadst thou left me unchastiz'd, Thy precept I had still despis'd. *a* 1814 *Intrigues of a Day* III. i, in *New Brit. Theatre* I. 116, I think it my duty, as a member of society, not to let it pass unchastised.

**Uncha·stity.** [UN-[1] 12 and 5 b.] Lack of chastity; sexual impurity; lasciviousness.

1382 WYCLIF *Rom.* xiii. 13 Not in couchis and vnchastitees, not in stryf and in enuye. *a* 1400 *Pauline Ep.* (Powell) 2 Cor. xii. 21 Penaunce of þeyre vnclennesse..and vnchastite | at þey han done. 1483 *Cath. Angl.* 60/1 Vn Chastite, *incontinencia.* 1550 BALE *Apol.* 141 b, They haue in confessions, made kinges wiues and daughters to make vowes of vnchastyte vnto them. 1599 NASHE *Lenten Stuffe* 42 That she might liue chaste vestall Priest to Venus the queene of vnchastitie. 1639 HABINGTON *Castara* II. (Arb.) 80 Against them who lay unchastity to the sex of Women. 1685 BAXTER *Paraphr. N. T.* 1 Tim. v. 1-2 Carefully shunning all that savoureth of Immodesty or Unchastity. *a* 1763 W. KING *Polit. & Lit. Anecd.* (1819) 49 It might perhaps be too severe a censure to charge a woman with unchastity, who had only transgressed with one man. 1846 WRIGHT *Ess. Mid. Ages* I. ii. 56 [In] the thirteenth century..unchastity was certainly not regarded as one of the greatest of sins. 1871 B. TAYLOR *Faust* (1875) I. 297 Church-penance for unchastity was formerly common in England.

**Unchaw·**, *v.* (UN-[2] 3.)

1611 COTGR., *Desmacher*, to vnchaw. 1616 J. LANE *Contn. Sqr.'s T.* 95 *note*, Th'intestine motive wheareof tind his blood, and soone causd to vnchawe his late chawd cud.

**Unchaw·ed**, *ppl. a.* [UN-[1] 8.] = UNCHEWED.

1566 BLUNDEVIL *Horsemanship* IV. xl. (1580) 18 b, To let his meate fall out of his mouth, or at the least to keepe it in his mouth vnchawed. 1600 J. LANE *Tom Tel-troth* 609 Bits vnchaw'de in her bulke, as in a forge, Kindle the coales whereof foule lust is bred. 1693 DRYDEN *Persius* v. 8 Why wou'dst thou these mighty Morselschuse, Of Words unchaw'd, and fit to choak the Muse?

So **Unchaw·n** *ppl. a.* (UN-[1] 8 b.)

1648 HEXHAM II, *Ongeknauwt*, vnchawne.

**Unchea·t**, *v.* (UN-[2] 3.)

1650 H. MORE *Observ.* in *Enthus. Tri.*, etc. (1656) L 2 b, Nor could his lofty soul so low descend But to uncheat the World; a noble end. 1681 CROWNE *Hen. VI*, I, They are fools, and know not men, nor what they love; Uncheat 'em; but however save the King.

**Unchea·ted**, *ppl. a.* (UN-[1] 8.)

1746-7 W. COLLINS *The Manners* 19 Youth of the quick uncheated sight, Thy walks, Observance, more invite! 1820 T. MITCHELL *Com. Aristoph.* I. 101 Uncheated he his stalls may spread, nor lose his time and labour.

† **Unche·ck**, *v. Obs.*[−1] [UN-[1] 14.] *trans.* To fail to check.

1607 SHAKS. *Timon* IV. iii. 447 The Lawes, your curbe and whip, in their rough power Ha's vncheck'd Theft.

**Unche·ckable,** *a.* (Un-¹ 7 b.) *a* 1734 North *Lives* (1826) II. 217 His lordship used him in his most private and uncheckable trusts. 1836 T. Hook *G. Gurney* (1850) III. 389 Wells,..whose volubility when once 'off' was uncheckable,.. would not let me pause here. 1881 *Echo* 11 Apr. 3/6 Flying before the uncheckable onslaughts of the interviewers.

**Unche·cked,** *ppl. a.* [Un-¹ 8.] Not checked or repressed; unrestrained. Also const. *by*.

1469 in *Househ. Ord.* (1790) 92 Clerkes at wages certein, unchekked, to have a yeoman and groome's parte. 1533 More *Apol.* xlvii. Wks. 921/1 Yet he they suffred boldely to talke vnchecked. 1577 G. Whetstone in Gascoigne *Steele Gl.*, etc. (Arb.) 18 Trueth is the garde, that keepeth men vnchect. 1667 Milton *P. L.* viii. 189 Apte the Mind or Fancie is to roave Uncheckt. 1683 Burnet tr. *More's Utopia* (1753) 114 If they were not strictly restrained from all unchecked Appetites. 1732 Pope *Ess. Man* ii. 40 Man's superior part Uncheck'd may rise, and climb from art to art. 1783 Burke *Rep. Aff. India* Wks. XI. 100 The effects of commercial servitude during its unchecked existence. 1813 Shelley *Q. Mab* ix. 84 The growing longings of its dawning love, Unchecked by dull and selfish chastity. 1844 H. H. Wilson *Brit. India* II. 170 The mountaineers..were committing unchecked ravages in retaliation for invaded rights. 1891 Farrar *Darkn. & Dawn* lvi, Mankind was to see.. unchecked power smitten with fatal impotence.

† **b.** Of a report: Uncontradicted. *Obs.*

1596 Shaks. *Merch. V.* iii. i. 2 It liues there vncheckt, that Anthonio hath a ship..wrackt on the narrow Seas. 1619 Visct. Doncaster *Let.* in *Eng. & Germ.* (Camden) 208 There is there an unchecqued report these three or foure dayes that the Count of Mansfelt [etc.].

**Unchee·red,** *ppl. a.* (Un-¹ 8.)

[1775 Ash.] 1817 Wordsw. *Ode to Lycoris* 24 Yet cool the space within, and not uncheered..By stealthy influx of the timid day. 1849 M. Arnold *Resignation* 235 Who treads at ease life's uncheer'd ways. 1864 Trevelyan *Compet. Wallah* (1866) 301 He must go through the dreary remainder of life uncheered by friendship.

**Unchee·rful,** *a.* [Un-¹ 7.]

**1.** Not enlivening or gladdening; cheerless.

*c* 1449 Pecock *Repr.* ii. xvi. 244 Forto cleue to a thing as to his Soureyn Lord..and ȝit for to haue noon homelynes with the same thing were an vncheerful thing. 1586 Bright *Melanch.* xvii. 103 The body thus possessed with the vnchearefull darknes of melancholie. 1593 Shaks. *Lucr.* 1024 In vaine I raile at oportunitie, At time, at Tarqvin, and vnchearfull night. 1648 Milton *Ps.* lxxxviii. 11 My life at death's uncherful dore Unto the grave draws nigh. 1656 Cowley *Davideis* iv. 536 'Twas the last Morning whose uncheardful Rise, Sad Jabes was to view with both their Eyes. 1798 Jane Austen *Northang. Abb.* xxi, The furniture..was handsome and comfortable, and the air of the room altogether far from uncheerful. 1853 Ruskin *Stones Ven.* II. iv. § 10. 63 The Cathedral square..laid out in rigid divisions of smooth grass and gravel walk, yet not uncheerful. 1856 Hawthorne *Eng. Note-bks.* (1879) I. 256 It is an uncheerful old hotel.

**2.** Not exhibiting, or partaking of, cheerfulness.

*c* 1550 *Dice Play* (Percy Soc.) 6 Stalking up and down.. with such heavy and uncheerful countenance, as if he had some hammers working in his head. 1596 Spenser *F. Q.* v. vii. 18 But by the change of her vncheareful looke, They might perceiue she was not well in plight. 1712 Addison *Spect.* No. 483 ¶ 1 People of gloomy uncheerful Imaginations. 1753 Richardson *Grandison* (1781) I. v. 24, I cannot bear an uncheerful brow in a servant. 1882 C. E. Norton *Lett.* (1913) II. x. 131 'Ah, Charles,' he answered, with a not uncheerful smile, 'there are no good days now'. 1892 G. Hake *Mem. 80 Yrs.* lxviii. 293 A quiet, not uncheerful, but almost complaining way.

**b.** Not cheerfully performed.

*a* 1684 Leighton *Comm. 1 Pet.* iii. 1 (1849) II. 4 Now, if it be such obedience as ought to arise from a special kind of love, then the wife would remember this, that it must not be constrained, uncheerful obedience. 1858 Faber *Spir. Confer.* 115 There is no vigour in uncheerful penance.

**3.** Of persons: Lacking in cheerfulness; melancholy, gloomy. Also *transf.*

1612 Bp. Hall *Contempl., O. T.* iv. iv, Wheresoeuer meere Nature is, she is..niggardly in her grants, and vncheerfull. 1621 Burton *Anat. Mel.* i. iii. i. i. 231 They be commonly leane, hirsute, vncheareful in countenance. 1680-1 Penn in *Wks. I. Pennington* I. p. viii, When he did Speak, he was Serious, yet sweet and not uncheerful. 1740 Cibber *Apol.* (1756) I. 17 Let them call me any fool but an unchearful one. 1860 Bushnell *New Life* i. 7 There ought never to be a discouraged or uncheerful being in the world. 1862 Lytton *Str. Story* xlviii, She said that Lilian was quiet, not uncheerful.

Hence **Unchee·rfully** *adv.*

*a* 1628 Preston *New Covt.* (1634) 104 Who comes not more uncheerfully before God, because of it? 1753 Richardson *Grandison* (1781) VII. xvii. 98 We had hopes..she would be brought to give her hand, not uncheerfully, to the Count of Belvedere. 1890 'R. Boldrewood' *Col. Reformer* (1891) 299 Save for the inevitable death-scene of the morrow, the evening would have passed not uncheerfully.

**Unchee·rfulness.** [f. prec. + -ness.] The quality or state of being uncheerful.

1617 Hieron *Wks.* II. 342 It is a checke to our common lumpishnesse and vncheerefulnesse. 1647 Clarendon *Hist. Reb.* vii. § 231 Those indispositions..grew into a perfect habit of unchearfulness. 1712 Addison *Spect.* No. 494 ¶ 2 There are many Persons, who, by a natural Unchearfulness of Heart,..love to indulge this uncomfortable way of Life. 1733 W. Crawford *Infidelity* (1836) 211 Lumpish uncheerfulness may not be taken for gospel sorrow.

**Unchee·ring,** *ppl. a.* (Un-¹ 10.) 1796 *Monthly Mag.* II. 451 The kiss of thy mistress shall be cold and uncheering. 1856 Froude *Hist. Eng.* I. 79 It is not uncheering to look back upon a time when the nation was in a normal condition of militancy against social injustice. 1871 B. Taylor *Faust* (1875) II. ii. i. 87 The incomprehensible disappearing Of that great man to him is most uncheering.

† **Unchee·rly,** *a. Obs.*⁻¹ (Un-¹ 7.)

1627 J. Carter *Plain Expos.* 109 A very narrow way or lane (which we know is often mirie, and many wayes vncheerly to travellers.)

**Unchee·ry,** *a.* (Un-¹ 7.)

1760 Sterne *Serm.* (1766) I. ii. 31 The sad accidents of life, and the uncheary hours which perpetually overtake us. *Ibid.* IV. vii. 16 In some uncheary corner it nourishes its discontent. 1847 Mary Howitt *Ballads* 58 The chill light from the window fades; The fire it burneth all uncheery. 1871 B. Taylor *Faust* (1875) II. iii. 224 Bat-like to squeak and twitter In whispers uncheery and ghostly.

† **Unche·que,** *a. Obs.*⁻¹ [Un-¹ 7: see Check *v.* 9.] Without check or stoppage.

1671 F. Philipps *Reg. Necess.* 367 That such of them as have none Offices..to the value of two pence by the day, shall have the wages of six pence by the day uncheque.

**Unche·quered,** *ppl. a.* (Un-¹ 8.)

1796 Mme. D'Arblay *Camilla* vii. ii, Ah! what in this lower sphere can be unchequered? 1825 Jefferson *Autobiog.* Wks. 1859 I. 51, I had lived the last ten years in unchequered happiness. 1840 Arnold *Hist. Rome* II. 243 Nor was even this latter period of the contest unchequered by some changes of fortune. 1877 R. H. Horne in F. Collins *M. Collins' Lett. & Friendships* I. 37 My pleasant and unchequered memory of Mortimer Collins.

**Unche·rished,** *ppl. a.* (Un-¹ 8.)

13.. *E. E. Allit. P.* B. 1125 And if hit cheue þe chaunce vncheryst ho worþe. [1775 Ash.] 1817 Kirby & Sp. *Entomol.* xix. II. 136 An infant..fed with unwholesome food, or uncherished by genial warmth. 1859 Cornwallis *Panorama New World* I. 186 The obscure light shed by the yet uncherished fires.

**Unche·rishing,** *ppl. a.* (Un-¹ 10.) 1876 Geo. Eliot *Dan Der.* xxxiii, When the uncherishing years have thrust it far onward in the ever-new procession of youth and age.

**Unchestiable**: see Unchastisable *a.*

**Unchew·ed,** *ppl. a.* [Un-¹ 8. Cf. Unchawed *ppl. a.*, and MDu. *ongecouwet, -kauwet*, Du. *ongekaauwd*, G. *ungekaut*.] Not chewed.

1646 Quarles *Sheph. Orac.* ix, Say, do you eat and grind it,..Or like an unchew'd Pill, but swallow't down? 1697 Dryden *Æneis* x. 1025 His mouth runs o're With unchew'd morsels. 1742 Young *Nt. Th.* v. 973 All,..wide-expanding their voracious jaws, Morsel on morsel swallow down unchew'd. 1766 *Compl. Farmer* s.v. *Cubbitting* O 2/2, Horses addicted to this vice are but of small value; they drop a great part of their food unchewed. 1884 Browning *Ferishtah, Two Camels*, No sprig Of toothsome chervil must I leave unchewed!

*fig.* 1643-5 Milton *Divorce* Introd., If she presume to bring forth ought, that sorts not with their unchew'd notions and suppositions. 1681 Dryden *Abs. & Achit.* i. 113 Not weigh'd or winnow'd by the Multitude, But swallow'd in the Mass, unchewed and crude.

**Unchi·d,** *ppl. a.* [Un-¹ 8 b.] = next.

[1846 Worcester.] 1860 *Macm. Mag.* Aug. 292 There, unchid, her tears may flow. 1893 *Westm. Gaz.* 22 Sept. 3/2 Meditating..on his own sins, and leaving the world to sin unchid.

**Unchi·dden,** *ppl. a.* (Un-¹ 8 b.)

1472 *Paston Lett.* III. 50 We go not to bed unchedyn lyghtly, all that we do is ille doon. 1614 T. A. in Latham *Falconry* A iv, Pleasure it selfe hath still vnchidden stood. 1753 Glover *Boadicea* iii. i, While massacre, unchidden, cloys his famine, And quaffs the blood of nations. 1826 Miss Mitford *Village* Ser. ii. (1863) 295 It was no time for scolding; so the whole chain of delinquents..escaped unchidden. 1870 Morris *Earthly Par.* II. iii. 366 Still stronger grew that thought, Unheeded, and unchidden.

**Unchi·ld,** *v.* [Un-² 4 and 6 b.]

**1.** To deprive of children; to make childless.

1605 Earl Stirling *Alexandr. Trag.* iv. ii, First orphan'd, widdow'd, and vnchilded last, A daughter, wife, and mother all accurst. 1607 Shaks. *Cor.* v. vi. 153 Though in this City hee Hath widdowed and vnchilded many a one. 1791 Cowper *Iliad* xxii. 48 He hath unchilded me of many a son.

**2.** To deprive of the status of a child or of the qualities peculiar to childhood.

1615 Bp. Hall *Contempl., O. T.* x. iii, Whosoever now dispose of themselves without their parents, they do wilfully unchild themselves. 1864 Browning *Mr. Sludge* Wks. 1888 VII. 230 In brief, she may unchild the child I am.

**Unchi·lded,** *ppl. a.* [f. prec. or Un-¹ 8.] Destitute or deprived of children; childless.

1610 Healey *St. Aug. Citie of God* xv. xv. (1620) 521 Nor is it credible that their fathers liued all this while either immature or vnmarried or vnchilded. 1866 J. Conington *Æneid* 58 With death in view, the unchilded sire Checked not the utterance of his ire. 1882 Swinburne *Tristr. of Lyonesse*, etc. 155 So bitter burned within the unchilded wife A virgin lust for vengeance.

**Unchi·ldish,** *a.* (Un-¹ 7.)

1586 W. Webbe *Eng. Poetrie* (Arb.) 45 Some..haue especially made choyse of such vnchildish stuffe, to reade vnto young Schollers.

**Unchi·ldlike,** *a.* (Un-¹ 7 c.)

[1775 Ash, *Unchildlike*.., unlike a child, unbecoming a child.] 1840 Dickens *Barn. Rudge* xxv, Something infinitely worse, so ghastly and unchild-like in its cunning. 1879 Miss Bird *Rocky Mts.* 53 The family consists of a grown-up son..and three hard, unchildlike younger children.

† **Unchi·ldly,** *a. Obs.*⁻¹ [Un-¹ 7.] Unfilial, undutiful.

1597 Beard *Theatre God's Judgem.* (1612) 222 He first remoued his lodging..to a base vnder roome, and after shewed him many other vnkind and vnchildlie parts.

**Unchi·lled,** *ppl. a.* (Un-¹ 8.)

1794 Mrs. Radcliffe *Myst. Udolpho* i, Yet, amidst the changing visions of life, his principles remained unshaken, his benevolence unchilled. 1813 Byron *Giaour* 27 His Queen, the garden queen, his Rose, Unbent by winds, unchill'd by snows. 1856 Kane *Arct. Expl.* I. xxxi. 434 Even an Arctic temperature leaves the mind unchilled. 1890 'R. Boldrewood' *Col. Reformer* (1891) 130 The prompt and unchilled service atones fully for want of artistic merit.

**Unchi·nked,** *ppl. a.* (Un-¹ 8.) 1879 Miss Bird *Rocky Mts.* 45 The very wall was in holes, the logs were unchinked. 1883 *Harper's Mag.* Sept. 625 Her eyes wandered over.. the unchinked, dirty cabin.

**Unchi·pped,** *ppl. a.* (Un-¹ 8.)

1647 Herrick *Noble Numb., Thanksgiving to God* 22 A little Byn, Which keeps my little loafe of Bread Unchipt, unflead. 1854 *Poultry Chron.* I. 296/2 Nine healthy living chicks and five unchipped eggs. 1865 Lubbock *Preh. Times* 251 One of these peculiar forms has one side left unchipped.

**Unchiro·tonize**: see Chirotonize *v.*

**Unchi·selled,** *ppl. a.* (Un-¹ 8.)

1772 J. Ives *H. Swinden's Gt. Yarmouth* Pref. 1 The unchizelled stone, or rudest hieroglyphic, accompanied the songs of the Bards, to perpetuate a whole nation. 1830 *Westm. Rev.* Jan. 46 Unchiselled stones, according to Pausanias, were the first images of the gods of the Greeks. 1854 Grace Greenwood *Haps & Mishaps* 3 The pure and graceful Greek column makes no solid or defiant show of strength, like the unchiselled stone or the jagged rock.

**Unchi·valric,** *a.* [Un-¹ 7.] = next.

1851 *Westm. Rev.* April 12 With much self-gratulation on our own unchivalric aspect. 1868 W. R. Greg *Lit. & Soc. Judgm.* 217 A coarseness and a cruelty, as well as an unchivalric and ungenerous roughness.

**Unchi·valrous,** *a.* (Un-¹ 7.)

1846 Worcester (citing Scott). 1853 C. Bronte *Villette* xxxvii, Such a bad pupil, monsieur! so thankless, cold-hearted, unchivalrous, unforgiving. 1880 Swinburne *Stud. Shaks.* 274 A garb of transforming verse under a guise at once weak and wordy, coarse and unchivalrous.

Hence **Unchi·valrously** *adv.*

[1847 Webster.] 1889 *Sat. Rev.* 26 Jan. 103 He somewhat unchivalrously refused her request..for a safe-conduct.

**Unchi·valry.** (Un-¹ 12.)

1858 Kingsley *Misc., Winter-Gard.* I. 148 That world-famous ancestor of his, whose deeds of unchivalry were the delight..of knight and kaiser..in the Middle Age. 1865 — *Herew.* xxvi, All the chivalry, and the unchivalry, of the Baltic shores.

**Uncho·ke,** *v.* (Un-² 3.)

1588 Lucar tr. *Tartaglia's Colloq. Shooting* 36 If the Artillery should be choked with nayles or otherwise, whether it be possible to devise a waie to unchoke quickly the same Artillery. 1888 *Times* (weekly ed.) 3 Feb. 3/3 She tried to unchoke it and took three parts of a pailful out.

**Uncho·ked,** *ppl. a.* (Un-¹ 8.) 1833 Poe *Tales, MS. in Bottle* (1902) 54 We found the pumps unchoked. 1860 H. Gouger *Two Yrs. Imprisonment* xxiii. 255, I..again luxuriated in a well-cleansed exterior, and pores unchoked with grime. **Uncho·leric,** *a.* (Un-¹ 7.) 1831 Carlyle *Sart. Res.* ii. iv, On some points, as his *Excellenz* was not uncholeric, I found it more pleasant to keep silence. **Unchoo·sable,** *a.* (Un-¹ 7 b.) 1858 Carlyle *Fredk. Gt.* iv. iii. I. 407 A man..unchoosable at hustings or in caucus.

**Unchoo·sing,** *ppl. a.* (Un-¹ 10.)

*a* 1586 Sidney *Arcadia* i. (1598) 94 Like a Lambe, whose damme away is fet, (Stolne from her young by theeues vnchoosing-haste). 1660 Jer. Taylor *Ductor* iv. i. rule i. § 17 They are natural, or unavoidable, or the productions of fancy, or some other unchusing faculty.

**Uncho·pped,** *ppl. a.* (Un-¹ 8.) 1648 Hexham ii, *Ongehackelt*, Vnhackt, or Vnchopt. 1891 C. Roberts *Adrift Amer.* 101 A large stack of unchopped firewood. **Uncho·ral,** *a.* (Un-¹ 7.) 1865 Miss Yonge *Clever Woman of Fam.* iii, Cathedral music had been too natural to him for the endurance of an unchoral service. **Uncho·rded,** *ppl. a.* (Un-¹ 8.) 1859 Ld. Lytton *Wanderer* (ed. 2) 189 From the unchorded harp and vacant shell New notes reveal.

**Uncho·sen,** *ppl. a.* (Un-¹ 8 b.)

1529 More *Dyaloge* iv. Wks. 273/2 And that euery man is either chosen or vnchosen... And yf we bee of the vnchosen sorte, no good dede can auail vs. *c* 1592 Marlowe *Jew of Malta* ii, In spite of these swine-eating Christians, (Vnchosen Nation, neuer circumciz'd). 1644 Milton *Areop.* (Arb.) 54 To be made the perpetuall reader of unchosen books and pamphlets. 1655 Jer. Taylor *Unum Necess.* vi. i. § 29 To be born, was a thing wholly involuntary and unchosen. 1712 Blackmore *Creation* v. 397 Can actions be denominated wise,..The means unchosen, and unknown the end? 1814 Wordsw. *Excurs.* vii. 309 [To] Beguile A solitude, unchosen, unprofessed. 1871 Carlyle in *Mrs. Carlyle's Lett.* (1883) II. 249 [She] never did complain once of her unchosen sufferings..under the writing of that sad book.

*absol.* 1849 Froude *Nemesis of Faith* 127 The sucking children of the unchosen were not saved in Noah's flood.

**Unchri·som,** *a. rare*⁻¹. [Un-¹ 7.] Unchristened.

1831 Lamb *Elia* ii. *Shade of Elliston*, The schoolmen admitted a receptacle apart for Patriarchs and un-chrisom Babes.

† **Unchri·sted,** *ppl. a. Obs.* [Un-² 6 b.] Deprived of the attributes or nature of Christ.

1646 Evance *Noble Ord.* 42 God blasphemed, Christ unchristed. 1654 T. Warren *Unbeleevers* 145 Let some frenzy take them and bereave them of their reason..and they are un-Christed again. 1677 W. Hughes *Man of Sin* ii. iii. 45 Is She not..God Un-godded, and Christ Unchristed; in saying, That at death there is none other Hope but She?

† **Unchri·sten,** *a. Obs.* [OE. *uncristen* (see Un-¹ 7 and Christen *a.*), = ON. *úkristinn* (Da. *ukristen*, Sw. *okristen*), OHG. *unchristâni* (MHG. *unkristen*).] = Unchristian *a.* Also *absol.*

*c* 1000 tr. *Baeda's Eccl. Hist.* iv. xvi. (MSS. O and Ca.) Ðeah ðe hi þa ȝyta uncristene wæron. 1362 Langl. *P. Pl.* A. i. 91 Clerkes þat knowen hit scholde techen hit aboute, For Cristene and vn-cristen him cleymeþ vchone. *c* 1400 *Rowland & Otuel* 218 For-thi hathe he sent the worde by mee, Þat þou schall vn-cristen bee. 1456 Sir G. Haye *Law Arms* (S.T.S.) 86 And a cristyn man war in a bataill..agayn the uncristyn. *Ibid.* 298 Paganis that we call unCristyn men. 1509 Barclay *Shyp of Folys* (1570) 201 All the land about, Trembling for feare of the unchristen route, Of cursed Turkes and other infidels. 1553 *Respublica* i. i. 71 My veray trewe vnchristen Name ys Avarice.

Hence † **Unchri·stenness.** *Obs.*—[1]
*c* 1548 in Strype *Cranmer* II. viii. (1694) 176 Making the same..a Den or Sink of all Unchristiness.

**Unchri·sten,** *v.* [Un-[2] 3.]

**1.** *trans.* To reverse the christening of; to deprive of the name given at christening.

**1598** Florio, *Sbattezzare*, to vnchristen, to forget ones proper name. **1831** *Q. Rev.* XLV. 416 The church of St. Geneviève was once more unchristened, and ana-paganized by its absurd name of the Pantheon. **1868** H. Bushnell *Serm. Living Subj.* 167 These desolating doubts.. are present as powers of the air to unchristen the new born thoughts of religion as fast as they arrive. **1893** in J. H. Barrows *World's Parlt. Relig.* II. 1152 Before you can strip the discovery [of America] of its religious character, you must unchristen the admiral's flagship.

† **2.** = Unchristianize *v.* *Obs.*

**1643–5** Milton *Divorce* II. xxii, To constrain him furder were to unchristen him, to unman him. **1653** Baxter *Chr. Concord* 50 They would unchristen all the Reformed Christians in all these Nations. **1670** — *Cure Ch. Div.* 296 Therefore on one side let us take heed how we unchurch and unchristen any with whom we do not corporally join. **1718** Cibber *Non-juror* Prol., There safe, he lets his thundring Censures fly, Unchristens, damns us, gives our Laws the Lie.

Hence **Unchri·stening** *ppl. a.*

**1659** Baxter *Key Cath.* II. iii. 429 It would be a damning unchristening sin to deny the Headship of the Pope or General Council, if they were indeed the Head of the Church.

**Unchri·stened,** *ppl. a.* [Un-[1] 8. Cf. MSw. *okristnadher*, and Unkirsened *ppl. a.*]

**1.** Not made Christian; not converted to Christianity, unbaptized.

*c* **1330** R. Brunne *Chron. Wace* (Rolls) 11974 Me þynkeþ hit were but tynt, þe stounde, To write þe names of so fele hounde þat were vncristned in þys mounde. *c* **1350** *Lybeaus Disc.* 1358 What wendest thou, fendes fere? Uncrystenede that were Tyll y saw the wyth syght. *c* **1400** *Apol. Loll.* 2 Corneli centurio, ȝet vncristund, is clensid wiþ þe Hooli Goost. *c* **1440** *Alph. Tales* 219 þai & all þer howsold become crestend, þat war haythen befor and vncristend. **1470–85** Malory *Arthur* IX. xxvii. 381 Nay said syre Persydes, hit is syr Palomydes, that is yet vncrystened. *a* **1548** Hall *Chron., Hen. VII*, 23 b, The Moores or Mawritane nacion, beyng infideles and vnchristened people. **1570–6** Lambarde *Peramb. Kent* (1826) 211 A Pagan (or unchristened) King of Northumberland, had married a Christian woman. **1649** Jer. Taylor *Gt. Exemp.* III. xvii. 74 The Holy-land is now in the dominion of unchristened Saracens. **1659** Baxter *Key Cath.* II. iii. 429 Else most of the Christians of the world at this day are Apostates and unchristened. **1825** Scott *Talism.* xxv, Edith Plantagenet scorns the homage of an unchristened Pagan. **1868** J. H. Newman *Verses Var. Occas.* 114 Why should we fear, the Son now lacks His place Where roams unchristened man? **1881** *Athenæum* 24 Sept. 393/2 A survival of the feasts of our unchristened forefathers.

*transf.* **1805** Scott *Last Minstrel* III. ix, Those iron clasps.. Would not yield to unchristen'd hand. **1899** R. Bridges *Poet. Wks.* (1912) 348 Thy soft unchristen'd smile, That shadows neither love nor guile.

**b.** *spec.* Of children. Also *transf.*

**1725** Ramsay *Gentle Sheph.* II. ii, At midnight hours o'er the kirkyard she raves, And howks unchristen'd weans out of their graves. **1777** Brand *Pop. Antiq.* 74 *note*, Children dying unbaptized;.. It is thought here very unlucky to go over their Graves. It is vulgarly called going over 'unchristened Ground'. **1791** Burns *Tam o' Shanter* 132 Twa span-lang, wee, unchristen'd bairns. **1855** Macaulay *Hist. Eng.* xiv. III. 462 Annihilation is the fate of the greater part of mankind, of heathens, of Mahometans, of unchristened babes.

**2.** Unnamed.

**1832** Miss Mitford *Village* Ser. v. (1863) 456, I do not mean, in this catalogue, to include the large proportion of bright, shallow trouting-streams, for the most part unchristened and unregistered. **1853** E. K. Kane *Grinnell Exp.* xxiv. (1856) 194 A large cape and several smaller headlands were seen,.. all on the western side. They remain unchristened.

† **Unchri·stenlike,** *a.* *Obs.*—[1] [Un-[1] 7 c.] = Unchristianlike *a.*

**1570** Dee *Math. Pref.* A ij, Their particular deuises, fables, ..and vnchristenlike slaunders.

† **Unchri·stenly,** *adv.* *Obs.* [Un-[1] 11.] = Unchristianly *adv.*

**1535** Shaxton in Strype *Eccl. Mem.* (1721) I. App. lxi. 152 Take al in good part... Construe nothing unchristenly: & become again my good Lord. *a* **1568** Coverdale *Bk. Death* (1579) vii. 28 It is better to liue ill, then to dye well. Whiche wordes are very vnchristenly spoken.

**Unchri·stian,** *a.* and *sb.* [Un-[1] 7 and 12. Cf. Unchristen *a.*]

**1.** Of persons: Not Christian; not professing, or converted to, Christianity; devoid of Christian principles or feeling.

**1555** Latimer in Foxe *A. & M.* (1563) 1373/1 That iurisdiction whiche the vnchristian Princes before by tyranny did resiste. **1594** Hooker *Eccl. Pol.* II. v. § 7 Whereupon grew a question, whether a Christian Souldier might herein doe as the vnchristian did. **1606** *Arraignem. & Execution Late Traitors* (1872) 5 They wanted nothing, that.. was thought fit, and, indeed, too good for so unchristian offenders. **1755** Magens *Insurances* II. 250 Any Turkish, Moorish, Barbarian or other unchristian Pirates. **1852** Mrs. Stowe *Uncle Tom's C.* xiv, 'Well, I hate those old slaveholders!' said the boy, who felt as unchristian as became any modern reformer. **1864** Miss Yonge in *Mag. for Young* May 152 The allowing an untaught un-Christian population to grow up among them.

**b.** Imposed by non-Christians.

**1816** Byron *Siege Corinth* ix, Ere that faithless truce was broke Which freed her from the unchristian yoke

**c.** *sb.* One who is not a Christian.

**1827** Carlyle *Germ. Rom.* III. 285 This morning the little Unchristian, my godson, was precisely the person least attended to.

**2.** Of actions, etc.: At variance with Christian principles; devoid of Christian spirit; unbefitting or unbecoming a Christian.

**1581** Aldersey in Hakluyt *Voy.* (1599) II. 152 We are not indeede all good Christians, for there are in the ship some that hold very vnchristian opinions. **1585–7** T. Rogers *39 Art.* iv. (1633) 18 Vtterly false then, and vnchristian is the opinion of those men. **1605** *London Prodigal* III. ii. 185 That were vnchristian, and an vnhumane part. **1651** Hobbes *Leviath.* III. xlii. 279 Disciples that obstinately continue in an unchristian life. **1679** Sharp *Serm. St. Margaret's 11 Apr.* 18, I mean the Unnatural, Un-Christian Feuds and Divisions that are amongst us. **1729** Berkeley *Skel. Serm.* Wks. 1871 IV. 639 Their own unchristian life and neglect of instruction. **1755** Young *Centaur* i. Wks. 1757 IV. 115 He was for making religion familiar and inoffensive. And so he did; and unchristian too. **1812** Henry *Camp. agst. Quebec* 131 The unchristian wish, that he might be hanged. **1849** Macaulay *Hist. Eng.* viii. II. 389 He..had repeatedly assailed them with unjust and unchristian asperity. **1876** Bancroft *Hist. U.S.* I. v. 131 Some years later, John de Wycliffe asserted strongly the unchristian character of slavery.

**b.** Improper; unnatural; objectionable.

**1630** *R. Johnson's Kingd. & Commw.* 475 The most Unchristian abuse is, that in every great towne he hath a Caback (or Tap-house) to sell Aqua-vite. **1633** Fletcher & Shirley *Night Walker* III, My Aunt has turn'd me out a doors, she has, At this unchristian hour. **1831** Trelawny *Adv. Younger Son* III. 89 This was the unchristianest, beastliest liquor I ever tasted.

† **Unchri·stian,** *v.* *Obs.* [Un-[2] 6 a. Cf. Du. *ontchristenen* (Sewel).] = Unchristianize *v.*

**1633** Prynne *Histrio-m.* 172 Is this a light..effeminacie, for men..thus..to vnman, vnchristian, vncreate themselues? **1658** Baxter *Saving Faith* § 8. 60 If I deny this, I must unchurch and unchristian almost all.. of the Churches and Christians in the world. **1661** Beveridge *Priv. Th.* II. (1730) 46 By this means, he renouncing his Baptism, blasphemes Christ, unchristians himself. **1712** Bp. Talbot *Charge* 16 How many Thousands does this Doctrine unchristian of those that were born..from..1648, to..1660?

**Unchri·stianed,** *ppl. a.* (Un-[1] 8.)

**1579** W. Wilkinson *Confut. Fam. Love* 53 b, Hee trembled and was affrayde..which was an vnchristianed Heathen man.

**Unchristia·nity.** [Un-[1] 12.] Lack of Christianity.

**1652** Heylyn *Cosmogr.* 297 The customs have not more unchristianity in them, than this of those Scotish Christians. **1859** *Habits of Gd. Society* 46 It is not mere vulgarity, it is positive unchristianity, hopeless injustice. **1885** Abp. Benson in A. C. Benson *Life* (1899) II. i. 60 Is Unchristianity and Antichristianity to invade us yet more?

**Unchri·stianize,** *v.* [Un-[2] 6 c.] *trans.* To deprive of the character or status of being Christian; to render unchristian.

*a* **1714** M. Henry *Treat. Baptism* v. Wks. 1853 I. 549/1 To unchurch, unchristianize, unbaptize, all those who are not in every thing of our length. **1746** *Brit. Mag.* 95 Debasing and unchristianizing the more polite and younger Part of the Nation. **1839** *Morn. Herald* 1 July, To enslave the people and un-Christianise the country. **1850** Newman *Diffic. Anglic.* I. i. (1891) I. 24 Why, half the country is unbaptized... Shall the country unchristianize itself? *a* **1878** Sir G. Scott *Lect. Archit.* I. 13 Surely this does not unchristianise the already Christian architecture of the soldiers of the Cross.

Hence **Unchri·stianized** *ppl. a.*[1], **-izing** *vbl. sb.*

**1636** H. Burton *Apology of Appeale* 20 The basenesse of Degenerate English Spirits, become so unchristianized, as [etc.]. **1853** Bright *Sp., Admiss. Jews to Parlt.* (1868) 524 Whence this notion or feeling of unchristianising springs.

**Unchri·stianized,** *ppl. a.*[2] (Un-[1] 8.)

**1778** Apthorpe *Preval. Chr.* 43 These nations, as yet unchristianized, found no power in Italy more respectable than that of the bishops of Rome. **1849** Kingsley *Misc., N. Devon* (1860) II. 300 There before me great countries untilled, uncivilized, unchristianized. **1859** W. Anderson *Disc.* (1860) 88 That must be a lifeless heart which lies cold and inanimate within the bosom of every unchristianized man.

**Unchri·stianlike,** *a.* (Un-[1] 7 c.)

**1610** in *Harl. Misc.* (Malh.) III. 111 This vnchristian-like conspiracie. **1646** E. F[isher] *Marrow Mod. Divin.* (ed. 2) 3 Neither let us have such unchristianlike expressions amongst us. **1709** Steele *Tatler* No. 38 ⁋ 1 That Unchristian-like and Bloody Custom of Duelling. **1754** *Connoisseur* No. 13. 77 That unchristian-like instrument the Jews-Harp. **1824** Miss L. M. Hawkins *Annaline* I. 188 Do not think that any observations I make are allied to so unchristianlike a spirit. **1866** *Routledge's Ev. Boy's Ann.* 197 It is one of the most ungentlemanly and blackguardly things.., not to say unchristianlike and despicable.

**Unchri·stianlike,** *adv.* (Un-[1] 11 b.)

**1700–1** R. Gough *Hist. Myddle* (1875) 184 Hee grievously complained that his nephew had soe unchristian-like used his owne father. **1784** P. Wright *New Bk. Martyrs* 796/1, I thank God I have not led my life as unchristian-like as many have done.

† **Unchri·stianly,** *a.* *Obs.* (Un-[1] 7.)

**1643–5** Milton *Divorce* II. xx, A most unnatural and unchristianly yoke. **1645** — *Colast.* Wks. 1851 IV. 364 Whom to leave thus without remedy..I say is most unchristianly.

**Unchri·stianly,** *adv.* (Un-[1] 11.)

**1547** J. Harrison *Exhort. Scottes* 209 The feldes lie ful of their bodies, whose deathes thei moste cruelly and vnchristianly haue procured. **1599** Hakluyt *Voy.* II. 309 As they behaued themselues most vnchristianly toward their brethren, so and much more vngodly..did they towards God. **1654** Gataker *Disc. Apol.* 71 A wicked and wretched censure, most uncharitable and unchristianlie passed upon persons of well-known piety. **1694** F. Bragge *Disc. Parables* II. 50 Why must communicating with such ministers..be unchristianly abstained from? **1743** Wesley *Jrnl.* (1749) 69, I look upon myself to be under no kind of obligation..to observe any thing contained in that scandalous paper, so unchristianly imposed upon me. **1879** Meredith *Egoist* xxxi, She feared he might be speaking unchristianly.

**Unchri·stianness.** [f. Unchristian *a.*] The character of being unchristian.

**1648–9** *Eikon Bas.* xxiv. 207 The Unchristianness of those denials. **1667** *Decay Chr. Piety* xx. ⁋ 1 We have now seen the unhappy riddle of the unchristianness of Christians unfolded.

**Unchri·stlike,** *a.* (Un-[1] 7 c.)

**1869** W. P. Mackay *Grace & Truth* (1875) 153 Un-Christlike divisions in the Church of the living God. **1884** *Oxf. & Cambr. Undergrad. Jrnl.* 14 Feb. 232/1 The most un-Christ-like outcome of a so-called science.

Hence **Unchri·stlikeness.**

**1882** 'Edna Lyall' *Donovan* xxxiv, The un-Christlikeness of Christians.

**Unchri·stly,** *a.* (Un-[1] 7.)

**1880** *World of Cant* x. 73 Both your objects and your means are unchristly. **1901** *Pop. Sci. Monthly* LVIII. 435/1 Ages have..fought over..this subject until history points with scarlet finger to unchristly deeds and impotent creeds, all in His name.

Hence **Unchri·stliness.**

**1905** Mrs. J. E. Butler *Autobiog.* (1909) 307 The manifest unchristliness of the teaching of many of the churches.

**Unchro·nicled,** *ppl. a.* (Un-[1] 8.)

**1598** *Mucedorus* Epilogue 19 Studie to act deedes yet vnchronicled. **1833** L. Ritchie *Wand. by Loire* 194 Events of the most stupendous magnitude passed unchronicled. **1840** [see Unchanted *ppl. a.*]. **1885** J. E. Taylor *Brit. Fossils* ii. 49 The heroes..of many an unchronicled feud and deed of daring.

**Unchronolo·gical,** *a.* [Un-[1] 7.]

**1.** Not chronological; not arranged in order of time; not in accordance with chronology.

**1763** Burn *Eccl. Law* II. 320 This is unchronological and absurd. **1801** R. Patton *Asiat. Mon.* 149 The history is called, 'A modern unchronological Account of Bengal'. **1841** L. Hunt *Seer* II. (1864) 18 But the truth of the painting makes amends, as in the unchronological pictures of old masters. **1882** Farrar *Early Chr.* II. 348 *note*, The assertion ..is an unchronological guess.

**2.** Of persons: Not skilled in, not observing, chronology.

**1817** Byron *Let. to Murray* 26 Apr., What is necessary but a bust and..a date? the last for the unchronological, of whom I am one. **1827** G. S. Faber *Sacr. Calend. Prophecy* (1844) I. 29 All the matters, which unchronological prophets describe as taking place at the epoch of the Restoration of Judah.

Hence **Unchronolo·gically** *adv.*

**1879** Farrar *St. Paul* (1883) 7 Mentioned only so cursorily, ..so unchronologically, that scarcely one of them can be dwelt upon.

**Unchu·rch,** *v.* [Un-[2] 4, 5, and 6 b.]

**1.** *trans.* To remove or exclude (individuals) from membership of a church; to shut out from church privileges; to excommunicate.

*a* **1620** J. Dyke *Sel. Serm.* (1640) 372 Hee will cast men out of the Temple, will unchurch them,..because men doe not buy in the Temple. **1655** Fuller *Ch. Hist.* IX. i. § 52 These holy men..were loath to unchurch any, and drive them off from an Ecclesiastical communion for such petty differences. **1677** W. Hughes *Man of Sin* II. xii. 217 Gregory 3d...lets fly against the Emperour Leo also, to Unchurch and Uncrown him together. *a* **1703** Burkitt *On N. T., 2 Cor.* i. 24 Our apostle doth not unchurch them.., but endeavours to reform their disorders. **1711** *Medley* No. 21. 243 All Candidates,.. if they vote with Dissenters, are (however Orthodox themselves) *ipso facto* unchurch'd. **1876** Fairbairn in *Contemp. Rev.* June 127 He did not mean to be unchurched, was thoroughly happy and at home in the Christian religion.

*absol.* *a* **1658** Durham *Comm. Revelation* ii. 6–7 (1660) 91 They might Excommunicate and un-Church for spiritual offences.

*refl.* **1813** Bp. J. Milner in Husenbeth *Life* (1862) 225 By his obstinacy in adhering to his schismatical errors, [he] does in fact unchurch himself.

**2.** To exclude (a number or class of persons) from participation in the Church (or some branch of it); to divest (a community) of the character of a church; to deprive of the possession of a church.

**1633** Sanderson *Serm.* (1681) II. 43 These our brethren..of the separation are so violent and peremptory in unchurching all the world but themselves. **1657** J. Watts *Vind. Ch. Eng.* 8 If they be able to unchurch England, they may unchurch also all the World. **1709** J. Johnson *Clergym. Vade M.* II. p. xcvi, We are told..that by this judgment and practice we unchurch all foreign protestants. **1752** Carte *Hist. Eng.* III. 578 Unchurching all bodies of Christians who did not adopt this discipline of his predecessor Calvin's invention. **1773** J. Allen *Serm. at S. Mary's, Oxf.* 12 A contempt of morality would be a reason sufficient for unchurching any Communion. **1833** *Tracts for Times* No. 4. 5 Do you then unchurch all the Presbyterians, all Christians who have no Bishops? **1856** Emerson *Eng. Traits, Relig.* Wks. (Bohn) II. 101 Of course, money will..steadily work to..unchurch the people to whom it was bequeathed. **1892** *Guardian* 28 Sept. 1447/1 It 'unchurches' whole communities of sincere Christians.

*refl.* **1679** C. Nesse *Antid. agst. Popery* 102 The Jews..did apostatize, .. unchurching and uncovenanting themselves. *c* **1700** Howe in H. Rogers *Life* x. (1863) 306 This Church.. has not, by adding some much disputed things,..thereby unchurched itself.

**b.** With *church* as object. (Cf. *unkirk* Un-[2] 6 b.)

**1636** Prynne *Unbish. Tim.* (1661) 80 They..Un-church most Protestant Churches in foreign parts, and Un-minister their Ministers. **1680** C. Nesse *Church Hist.* 404 He wrote those seven Epistles to the seven Churches which were not un-churched. **1711** G. Hickes *Two Treat. Chr. Priesth.* (1847) I. 270 Invidious clamour..for unchurching the reformed churches. **1830** Cassan *Lives Bps. Bath & Wells* II. 36 His Lordship's argument thus practically unchurches the

Church. **1889** GORE *R. C. Claims* x. 162 But undiscipline does not unchurch a church.

**Unchu·rched,** *ppl. a.* [UN-[1] 8 and UN-[2] 8: cf. prec.] **a.** Excluded from, deprived of, (the status of) a church. **b.** Not provided or connected with a church. **c.** (See quot. 1727.)

**1681** BAXTER *Answ. Dodwell* iii. 21 The Protestant Churches are in the same unchurched damnable case that have Bishops. **1727** BAILEY (vol. II), *Unchurched*, dissolved from being a Church, excommunicated; also not churched, as a Woman that has lain in. **1870** M. D. CONWAY *Earthw. Pilgr.* xxvi. 311 The great interests of our time gather about the unchurched world. **1889** J. H. WARD *Church in Modern Society* 224 There is more activity to-day in the churches, but there are also more unchurched people than ever before.

**Unchu·rching,** *vbl. sb.* [f. UNCHURCH *v.*] The action of the verb, in various senses.

**1655** BAXTER *Quaker's Catech.* Pref., The decrying of the Ministry, the unchurching of our Churches. *a* **1658** DURHAM *Comm. Revelation* ii. 6–7 (1660) 99 Un-Churching and Excommunication in such cases, is an Ordinance of Jesus Christ. *a* **1715** BURNET *Own Time* (1897) I. 247 King James..thought it went too far towards the unchurching of all those who had not bishops among them. **1852** H. NEWLAND *Lect. Tractar.* 61, I wish I had time to say a few words on..the unchurching of our neighbours.

**Unchu·rching,** *ppl. a.* [f. as prec.] That unchurches.

**1681** BAXTER *Search Schism.* ii. 26 Bishop Gunning and Mr. Dodwell hence draw dismal degrading and unchurching Consequences. **1721** A. CAMPBELL *Doctr. Mid. State* Pref., Those Men, who..valued themselves chiefly..upon their own Unchurching Principles. **1846** G. B. CHEEVER *Lect. Pilgr. Progr.* vi. 79 He..was completely free from the unchurching spirit of his age.

**Unchu·rchlike,** *a.* (UN-[1] 7 c.)

**1642** MILTON *Apol. Smect.* Wks. 1851 III. 290 Shall not all the mischiefe which other men do, be layd to his charge, if they doe it by that unchurchlike power which he defends. **1711** *Medley* No. 21. 243 The Name Church-men..not only ..wipes off all former Blemishes how unchurch-like soever, but [etc.]. **1845** G. A. POOLE *Churches* i. 3 We have trim, parsimonious, unchurchlike preaching-houses, under the name of churches. **1881** *Lond. & Provinc. Music Trades Rev.* 15 Feb. 7/3 This anthem is..crude, amateurish, and unchurchlike.

**Unchu·rchly,** *a.* (UN-[1] 7: cf. G. *unkirchlich.*)

**1858** in *Lit. Churchman* 15 May 184/1 A sentence which, according to their own explanation, arose from the unchurchly tone of the lectures themselves. **1883** P. BROOKS *Serm. in Eng. Ch.* 280 Churchmen..bringing to the Church unchurchly hearts.

**Unchut,** obs. variant of UNCOUTH *a.*

**Unci,** pl. of UNCUS.

‖ **Uncia** (*v*·nʃiă). Pl. **unciæ** (*v*·nʃiˌī). [L. *uncia* a twelfth part (spec. of a pound or foot): see INCH *sb.*[1] and OUNCE *sb.*[1]]

†**1.** *Math.* (See quot. 1704.) *Obs.*

**1695** *Phil. Trans.* XIX. 60 That admirable Invention of Mr. Newton, whereby he determines the *Unciæ* or Numbers prefixt to the Members composing Powers. **1704** J. HARRIS *Lex. Techn.* I, *Unciæ*, in Algebra, signify those Numbers which are prefixed before the Letters of the Members of any Power produced from a Binomial, Residual, or Multinomial Root. **1763** W. EMERSON *Meth. Increments* 106 Where the numeral coefficients are the unciæ of the several powers of a binomial.

**2.** A Roman copper coin, equal in value to the twelfth part of the 'as'.

**1834** *Penny Cycl.* II. 431/2 The *Uncia*,..or piece of one ounce, is marked by a single globule. **1853** HUMPHREYS *Coin-coll. Man.* I. 260 The uncia here engraved is of the same period as that of the 'as' of nine-and-a-half ounces.

**Uncial** (*v*·nʃăl), *a.* and *sb.* [ad. L. *unciāl-is* pertaining to a twelfth part, f. *uncia* UNCIA. In sense 2 after L. *unciales litteræ* (Jerome). Hence also It. *onciale*, Sp. *uncial*, Pg. *oncial*, F. *oncial* (*uncial*), G., Sw. *uncial.*]

**A.** *adj.* **1. a.** Pertaining to, connected with, etc., an inch or an ounce.

**1650** J. WYBARD *Tactometria* 305 The solid measure of one ounce-troy will be (in unciall or inch-measure) 1·8947 inch; and of one ounce-avoirdupois, 1·72556 inch. **1656** BLOUNT *Glossogr.* [copying Cooper], *Uncial*, of or belonging to an ounce or inch. **1824** SCOTT *Redgauntlet* Concl., I am sorry I have not room (the frank being only uncial) for his farther observations.

**b.** Based on a duodecimal division; divided into twelve equal parts.

**1842** *Smith's Dict. Grk. & Rom. Antiq.* s.v. *Uncia*, The uncial system was adopted by the Greeks of Sicily. **1853** HUMPHREYS *Coin-coll. Man.* II. 375 *note*, It seems probable that both the name of the weight, and the uncial coinage, may have been derived from Sicily. **1884** *Encycl. Brit.* XVII. 652/2 The denarius was struck at 80 to the pound, and the as became uncial.

**2.** Of letters or writing: Having the large rounded forms (not joined to each other) characteristic of early Greek and Latin manuscripts; also (in looser use), of large size, capital.

The term is also applied to letters having the form of the uncial, irrespective of size. When used in its strict sense, *uncial* is distinguished from *capital*, which denotes the more original, unrounded forms of the letters.

Jerome's *unciales litteræ* (Prol. Job) is commonly explained as meaning 'letters of an inch long'; his use of the word is accompanied by the phrase *ut vulgo aiunt*, and the literal sense was perhaps not seriously intended. The emendations *initiales* 'initial' and *uncinales* 'hooked, bent', have been suggested.

**1712** HENLEY tr. *Montfaucon's Trav. Italy* ii. 19 The Book is writ in the Oblong uncial Character. *a* **1734** NORTH *Lives* (1826) I. 20 It is not well to write, as the fashion now is, uncial or semiuncial letters. **1784** ASTLE *Orig. & Progr. Writ.* 82 Uncial writing began to be adopted about the middle of the fifth century. **1844** S. R. MAITLAND *Dark Ages* 207 A copy of the Gospels,..written in uncial characters. **1869** J. J. RAVEN *Ch. Bells Cambr.* (1881) 12 Bells inscribed in the uncial mediæval lettering, commonly called Longobardic. **1881** T. WALROND in *Macm. Mag.* XLIV. 151 All those that have been mentioned are written in the great uncial or capital character.

*Comb.* **1885** *Encycl. Brit.* XVIII. 150/2 The minuscule character is maintained intact, without intrusion of larger or uncial-formed letters.

**b.** Written, cut, etc., in uncial characters.

**1849** CURZON *Monast. Levant* xi. 134 The one [inscription] on the other side was either Coptic or uncial Greek. **1863** *Smith's Dict. Bible* III. 1201 *note*, An uncial MS., brought by Tischendorf from St. Catherine's Monastery. **1885** H. SWEET *Oldest Eng. Texts* 422 The latest uncial charter..is dated 736, and..it is Mercian.

**c.** Characterized by the use of large letters.

**1876** GEO. ELIOT *Dan. Der.* II. xiv, The address was in a lady's handwriting (of the delicate kind which used to be esteemed feminine before the present uncial period).

**B.** *sb.* **1.** An uncial or capital letter.

**1775** ASH, *Uncial*.., a letter of a larger size formerly used in inscriptions. **1784** ASTLE *Orig. & Progr. Writ.* 66 All writing may be divided into capitals, uncials, and small letters. **1860** I. TAYLOR *Ess.* iii. 203 His [Franklin's] name, until his later years, drew after it no cumbrous length of academic Uncials. **1875** SCRIVENER *Lect. Text N. Test.* 19 These uncials attract the eye for their minuteness.

**b.** An uncial style of writing.

So F. *onciale* fem., *oncial* masc.

**1883** I. TAYLOR *Alphabet* viii. § 6 II. 204 In the 7th century the Irish uncial..came into competition with the Roman uncial. **1885** *Encycl. Brit.* XVIII. 148/1 In this class of writing there is again the same dearth of dated MSS. as in the round uncial.

**2.** A manuscript written in uncial characters.

**1881** WESTCOTT & HORT *Grk. N. Test.* Introd. § 98 The Greek MSS. of the New Testament are divided into two classes,—Uncials and Cursives. **1883** SCHAFF *Hist. Chr. Church, Apost. Chr.* lxxxi. II. 642 *note*, It is omitted in several uncials and ancient versions.

**U·ncialize,** *v.* [f. prec.] *trans.* To convert into uncial characters; to write in uncials. Hence **U·ncialized** *ppl. a.*

**1883** I. TAYLOR *Alphabet* viii. § 6 II. 204 The Irish uncial, which was the old Roman cursive uncialized. *Ibid.*, The Glagolitic might prove to be merely an uncialized form of the Greek cursive.

**U·ncially,** *adv.* [f. UNCIAL *a.*]

†**1.** In uncial measurement. *Obs.*

**1650** J. WYBARD *Tactometria* 306 And so the solid measure of one pound-troy of water, wil be, Uncially, 22·7368; and of one pound-avoirdupois, wil be Uncially 27·609.

**2.** In uncial letters.

**1885** H. SWEET *Oldest Eng. Texts* 422 As there is an entire absence of Northumbrian charters and of uncially written West-Saxon ones.

†**U·nciary,** *a.* *Obs.*[—1] [ad. L. *unciāri-us*, f. *uncia* UNCIA. Hence also F. *onciaire.*] Amounting to a twelfth part. (Wrongly explained in quot.)

**1586** T. B. *La Primaud. Fr. Acad.* I. 497 There was a lawe amongst the ancient Grecians and Romanes, which forbad all usurie surmounting one pennie for a hundred by the yeere, and they called it vnciarie vsurie.

**Unci·catrized,** *ppl. a.* (UN-[1] 8.)

[**1775** ASH.] **1841** T. R. JONES *Anim. Kingd.* 301 The wound remains uncicatrised until the next moult. **1854** DE QUINCEY *Autobiog. Sk.* Wks. II. 271 Nothing was new, nothing was raw and uncicatrized.

**Unciform** (*v*·nsifǫ̈m), *a.* and *sb.* *Anat.* [ad. mod.L. *unciform-is*, f. L. *unc-us* hook. So F. and Sp. *unciforme.*] **A.** *adj.* Hook-shaped; esp. *unciform bone, process.*

(*a*) **1733–4** G. DOUGLAS tr. *Winslow's Anat. Expos.* (1756) 84 In the fourth Bone..we are to consider the..hooked or Unciform Apophysis. **1831** R. KNOX *Cloquet's Anat.* 105 The inferior turbinated bone..which..seems suspended by its unciform process. **1855** HOLDEN *Hum. Osteol.* 74 The unciform process..is connected..with the inferior spongy bone and the superior maxillary bone.

(*b*) **1840** E. WILSON *Anat. Vade M.* 198 The *Flexor ossis metacarpi*..arises from the unciform bone and annular ligament. **1861** HULME tr. *Moquin-Tandon* I. ii. 4 The carpus has 8 bones arranged in two rows...In the second..is the trapezium, the trapezoid, the os magnum, and the unciform bone. **1884** COUES *N. Amer. Birds* 107 A carpal bone, supposed to be *unciform*, later fusing with metacarpus.

**B.** *sb.* The unciform bone of the wrist.

Also used in the L. form *unciforme* (sc. *os*).

**1840** G. V. ELLIS *Anat.* 439 One is placed on each side of the os magnum, uniting this bone to the trapezoides on the one hand, and to the unciform on the other.

**Unci·liated,** *ppl. a.* (UN-[1] 8.)

**1851** G. F. RICHARDSON *Geol.* viii. 217 The Anthozoa have unciliated tentacula, no intestinal appendage to the stomach [etc.]. **1860** *Encycl. Brit.* (ed. 8) XXI. 1008/2 The majority of the species produce only unciliated gelatinous grains.

**Uncinate** (*v*·nsinĕt), *a.* and *sb.* [ad. L. *uncīnāt-us*, f. *uncīn-us* hook. Hence also It. *uncinato.*]

**A.** *adj.* Hooked; furnished with hooks; unciform, uncinated: **a.** *Bot.*

**1760** J. LEE *Introd. Bot.* I. xiv. (1765) 36 *Uncinate*, hooked. **1830** LINDLEY *Nat. Syst. Bot.* 58 Flowers in terminal and lateral racemes, covered with uncinate hairs. **1870** HOOKER *Stud. Flora* 375 Grasswrack;..embryo large, ovoid, with a small uncinate subulate plumule.

**b.** *Anat.* and *Zool.*

**1826** KIRBY & SP. *Entomol.* xlvi. IV. 322 Antennæ. Uncinate (*Uncinatæ*), when their apex is incurved so as to form a kind of hook. **1852** DANA *Crust.* I. 191 The moveable finger being very strongly uncinate. **1884** COUES *N. Amer. Birds* 142 These 'sacral ribs' are furthermore distinguished by being devoid of the epipleural or uncinate processes.

**B.** *sb.* An uncinate process.

**1891** *Cent. Dict.* **1903** *Proc. Zool. Soc. Lond.* 17 Mar. 274 The third pair [of ribs] always bear uncinates. *Ibid.*, The uncinates are broad and strong.

**U·ncinated,** *ppl. a.* [f. as prec. + -ED.] = UNCINATE *a.*

**1752** J. HILL *Hist. Anim.* 579 The Capra, with erect, uncinated horns. The Rupicapra, or Chamoise. **1772** *Phil. Trans.* LXIII. 150 The whole skin tough, covered with five rows of uncinated scales. **1826** KIRBY & SP. *Entomol.* III. xxxv. 630 The uncinated, forked,..and insulated nervures of Coleopterous insects. **1851** S. P. WOODWARD *Mollusca* I. (1856) 72 The uncinated calamaries are solitary animals, frequenting the open sea.

**Unci·nch,** *v.* (UN-[2] 3 or 4 b.) **1891** M. COLE *Cy Ross* 12 Pull up for the night, uncinch the packs. **1900** VACHELL *J. Charity* xx. 272 He and Quijas had dismounted and had uncinched their horses. **Unci·nct,** *ppl. a.* (UN-[1] 8 b.) **1880** BROWNING *Pan & Luna* 28 She teemed Herself with whiteness,—virginal, uncinct By any halo. **Unci·nctured,** *ppl. a.* (UN-[1] 8.) **1775** H. DOWNMAN *Infancy* II. (1803) 97 Cloath'd be thy child;..but in airy garb, Loose, and uncinctured. **1791** COWPER *Iliad* XVI. 510 When he saw Such havoc made of his uncinctured friends.

‖ **Uncinus** (*v*nsəi·nɒ̆s). *Zool.* Pl. **uncini** (-nəi). [L. *uncīnus*, f. *uncus* hook.] A hook-shaped part or process; esp. one of the hook-like teeth of molluscs.

**1851** S. P. WOODWARD *Mollusca* I. 113 Lingual dentition like murex erinaceus; teeth transverse, 3 crested; uncini small, simple. **1859** J. R. GREENE *Man. Anim. Kingd.* I. *Protozoa* 67 The 'setæ' or ciliary bristles of *Oxytricha*, ..the 'uncini' (hooks) and 'styles' of *Euplotes*. **1878** BELL tr. *Gegenbaur's Comp. Anat.* 360 The outermost uncini of the transverse rows may..also be articulated.

†**Unci·pher,** *v.* *Obs.* [UN-[2] 6 b.] *trans.* To decipher. (Common in 17th c.)

**1598** FLORIO *Disciferare*, to vncifer, to decifer. **1640** HOWELL *Dodona's Gr.* 170 The bookes of Kings are written in darke Characters which few can uncypher. **1644–5** in *Charles I's Wks.* (1662) 322 If You believe that I should be capable to shew them to any, onely to Lord Jer. to uncypher them. **1668** TEMPLE *Let. Ld. Arlington* Wks. 1720 II. 96 Your Lordship will have found that all I could uncipher in your last was already performed here. **1710** STEELE *Tatler* No. 195 ⁋2, I wanted the true Key to uncipher your Mysteries. **1737** in *10th Rep. Hist. MSS. Comm.* App. I. 474 Send me his answer if you can Uncypher or guess the Meaning of ye Spanish Phisick Latin.

**Unci·rcular,** *a.* (UN-[1] 7.) **1775** R. CHANDLER *Trav. Asia M.* (1825) I. 4 The other portion [of the sun] put on several uncircular forms. **Unci·rculated,** *ppl. a.* (UN-[1] 8.) [**1775** ASH.] **1880** *Plain Hints Needlework* 39 We live in crowded rooms with gas-consumed and uncirculated air.

†**Uncircumcided,** obs. var. UNCIRCUMCISED.

**1382** WYCLIF *Josh.* v. 6 The puple that is bore in deseert bi fourti yeer..were uncircumcidid to the tyme that thei weren wastid. **1382** — *Jer.* vi. 10 Lo! vncircumcidid the eres of hem. **1535** COVERDALE *Gen.* xxxiv. 14 That can we not do, to geue oure sister to an vncircumcided man.

†**Uncircumcis,** *ppl. a.* *Obs.*[—1] [Cf. CIRCUMCIS *pa. pple.*] = next.

*c* **1250** *Gen. & Ex.* 2841 Moyses and hise wif sephoram And hise childre wið him nam; And ðat on was vncircumcis.

**Unci·rcumcised,** *ppl. a.* [UN-[1] 8 and 5 b.]

**1.** Not having undergone circumcision. Also *absol.*

**1387** TREVISA *Higden* (Rolls) IV. 115 By ensample of hem meny of þe Iewes..lefte hem uncircumsised, and cleped hem self Antiochenes. *c* **1400** *Apol. Loll.* 35 Ilk alien kynd & vncircumsisid in hert, and vncircumsisid in flesch, schal not go in to my sanctuari. **1526** TINDALE *Rom.* ii. 26 Yf the vncircumcised kepe the right thynges contayned in the lawe, shall not his vncircumcision be counted for circumcision? **1565** ALLEN *Def. Purg.* xvii. 285 b, Iudas or any other in the lawe, offered for his friend, or any man elles being vncircumcised. **1608** BP. HALL *Epistles* v. iv, As a seale of the righteousnes of that faith, which he had when he was vncircumcised. **1668** DRYDEN *Evening's Love* III, We of the Uncircumcised, in a civil way, as Lovers, have somewhat the advantage of your Musullman. **1685** BAXTER *Paraphr. N. T.* Gal. v. 6 For in our State of Christianity..a Man shall not be accepted and justified as circumcised, or as uncircumcised. **1825** SCOTT *Talism.* ix, I will not reason with one uncircumcised upon the virtue of the medicines. **1850** F. W. NEWMAN *Phases Faith* 180 In the conversion of Cornelius was the justification of Peter for admitting uncircumcised Gentiles.

*transf.* **1535** COVERDALE *Lev.* xix. 23 All maner trees wherof men eate..: thre yeares shal ye holde them for vncircumcysed. [Also in later versions.]

**2.** *fig.* Not spiritually chastened or purified; irreligious; heathen. Also *absol.*

*a* **1400** *New Test.* (Paues) Acts vii. 51 Harde-frownted ande vncircumsised hertes ande eares. *c* **1400** *Apol. Loll.* 34 Alien sonis vncircumsicid in hert. **1526** TINDALE *Acts* vii. 51 Ye stiffenecked and of vncircumcised hertes and eares: ye have allwayes resisted agaynste the holy goost. **1591** SYLVESTER *Du Bartas* I. ii. 1185 Uncircumcised! O hard hearts! At least Let's think that God those Waters doth digest In that steep place. **1642** MILTON *Apol. Smect.* Wks. 1851 III. 310 In the Hebrew text, which is so necessary to be understood, except it be some few of them, their lips are utterly uncircumcis'd. **1685** BAXTER *Paraphr. N. T.* Acts vii. 51 Ye are an unruly obstinate people, whose hearts are unreformed and uncircumcised. **1800** WEEMS *Washington* xi. (1877) 149 The pirates of Morocco laying their uncircumcised hands on our rich commerce in the Mediterranean. **1825** SCOTT *Betrothed* vii, Such an uncircumcised Philistine as thou or thy master.

Hence **Uncircumci·sedness.**
1583 GOLDING *Calvin on Deut.* lxxii. 442 This people..who therefore were oftentimes vpbrayded with the vncircumcisednes of their heartes. *a* 1639 WHATELEY *Prototypes* I. xvi. (1640) 158 We make use of the outward seale, thereby to be made to see and feel our uncircumcisedness of heart.

**Uncircumci·sion.** (UN-[1] 12 and 5 b.)
1526 TINDALE *Rom.* ii. 25 But if thou breake the lawe thy circumcision is made vncircumcision. 1561 T. NORTON *Calvin's Inst.* II. 145 Now there is no respect of Greke or Jewe, circumcision or vncircumcision. 1643–5 MILTON *Divorce* II. vi, How vain then,..to exact a circumcision of flesh from an infant,..and to dispence an uncircumcision in the soul of a grown man. 1685 BAXTER *Paraphr. N. T.* Gal. vi. 16 Placing acceptable Religion in this, and not in Circumcision or Uncircumcision. 1816 SCOTT *Old Mort.* xxvii, Even while thou..wert fighting in the ranks of uncircumcision. 1879 FARRAR *St. Paul* I. 163 The idle fancies that circumcision alone was enough to save them from God's wrath, and that uncircumcision was worse than crime.

**Uncircumlo·cutory,** *a.* (UN-[1] 7.) 1808 BENTHAM *Sc. Reform* 104 Those instruments of distinct conception, as well as unambiguous and uncircumlocutory reference.

**Uncircumscri·bable,** *a.* (UN-[1] 7 b.)
1608 tr. *Gregory's Dial.* (1874) 216 He is uncircumscribable and invisible. 1698 NORRIS *Treat. Sev. Subj.* 395, I do not see how they can make it, or he can call it Uncircumscribable. *a* 1706 EVELYN *Hist. Relig.* (1850) I. 99 Now, that which was first has no parts or dimensions, and is therefore..uncircumscribable, and immense. 1848 BAILEY *Festus* (ed. 3) 202 In so far as worded it is not The entire truth uncircumscribable.

**Unci·rcumscribed,** *ppl. a.* (UN-[1] 8.)
1610 HEALEY *St. Aug. Citie of God* x. xiii. 379 Hee desired to behold that cleare vncircumscribed nature [of God]. 1642 CHAS. I *Mess. both Houses* 28 Apr. 3 So arbitrary and uncircumscribed a Power. *a* 1672 STERRY *Freedom Will* (1675) 12 The uncircumscribed Amplitude and Majesty of God. 1713 *Guard.* No. 164 ¶ 3 The Pow'r of Pluto stretches all around, Uncircumscrib'd by Nature's utmost Bound. 1798 *Monthly Mag.* V. 280 They boast the proud recommendation of moral beauty, in the most extensive and uncircumscribed acceptation of the term. 1820 SHELLEY *Prometh. Unb.* III. iv. 194 The loathsome mask has fallen, the man remains Sceptreless, free, uncircumscribed. 1881 MRS. C. PRAED *Policy & P.* I. 264 Imagination presented an uncircumscribed field of action.
*absol.* 1635 A. STAFFORD *Fem. Glory* (1869) 184 Thou Circumscription (if I may so say) of the Uncircumscribed!

Hence **Unci·rcumscribedness.**
1679 J. GOODMAN *Penitent Pardoned* I. ii. (1713) 27 The uncircumscribedness of the divine Goodness.

† **Unci·rcumscript,** *ppl. a.* [UN-[1] 8 b.] = prec.
*c* 1374 CHAUCER *Troylus* V. 1865 Thow..That regnest ay yn thre, and two, and oon, Vncircumscript [*v.r.* -scrit] and al mayst circumscryue. 1649 G. DANIEL *Trinarch., Hen. V*, xxix, The vnresisted Emanations Of a true Maiestie..baffle Questions To their Activity vncircumscript.

**Uncircumscri·ptible,** *a.* (UN-[1] 7 and 5 b.)
1577 tr. *Bullinger's Decades* IV. iii. 606 His eternall..power and vnspeakable maiestie are altogether vncircumscriptible.

**Uncircumscri·ption.** (UN-[1] 12 and 5 b.)
1852 BP. FORBES *Nicene Cr.* 145 Immensity, and uncircumscription, and supralocal existence, are the qualities of the true God.

**Unci·rcumspect,** *a.* [UN-[1] 7 and 5 b.]
**1.** Of persons: Not circumspect or cautious; imprudent, unwary.
1502 ATKYNSON tr. *De Imitatione* I. xxiii. 173 O thou vncircumspecte soule, of howe great perell & fere myghtest thou delyuer thy selfe of nowe. 1540 ELYOT *Image Gov.* 143 If there had been a senate uncircumspect,..or an Emperour a tyranne. 1632 J. HAYWOOD tr. *Biondi's Eromena* 119 Yet was I not therein uncircumspect, for some of them I tooke.., others would I not take. 1669 CLARENDON *Ess.* Tracts (1727) 157 Such like trivial imaginations, which make us so unwary in all our actions, so uncircumspect throughout the course of our lives. 1886 A. WEIR *Hist. Basis Mod. Europe* (1889) 38 The evident connection between the causes of his failure and his uncircumspect philanthropic temperament.
**2.** Of actions, etc.: Not marked by circumspection; incautious.
1563 FOXE *A. & M.* 605/2 Dalaber goes on, '..by this your vncircumspecte comminge vnto me, and speaking so before this yonge man, ye haue disclosed your selfe and vtterlye vndone me'. 1625 K. LONG tr. *Barclay's Argenis* IV. xi. 275 Of her owne will, with a rash and uncircumspect hastinesse, she looked upon the shoulder of the child. 1682 BUNYAN *Holy War* (1905) 220 Yet I cannot but (a little) chide you for your late uncircumspect action.

**Uncircumspe·ction.** (UN-[1] 12 and 5 b.)
1598 GRENEWEY *Tacitus, Ann.* IV. viii. (1622) 101 The witlesse vncircumspection of such as thinke..they can also extinguish the memory of future times. 1810 G. LAWSON *Serm.* ix. 314 Your spiritual ardour is greatly abated through your uncircumspection.

**Unci·rcumspectly,** *adv.* (UN-[1] 11 and 5 b.)
1535 JOYE *Apol. Tindale* (Arb.) 30 Sithe he cannot iustifye his writing so vncircumspectly put forth. 1560 DAUS tr. *Sleidane's Comm.* 300 In case you wyll obstinatly perseuer in the opinion, whiche very vncircumspectly you haue ones embraced. 1611 SPEED *Hist. Gt. Brit.* VI. vi. § 18. 63 They intercepted the scattered troopes of the Romanes that vncircumspectly wasted and spoiled the Country. 1669 EARL ORRERY *Parthen.* (1676) 746 He sounded his inclinations.. so uncircumspectly, that he discover'd his own.

**Unci·rcumstanced,** *ppl. a.* [UN-[1] 8.] Not justified or supported by circumstances.
1678 RYMER *Trag. last Age* 113 Both the Kings behaviour and hers, uncircumstanc'd as we have them, are every way so harsh..that [etc.]. 1766 *Museum Rust.* VI. 12 He should have considered, that no sensible man can pay any regard to so uncircumstanced an account as he gives.

**Uncircumsta·ntial,** *a.* (UN-[1] 7.)
1646 SIR T. BROWNE *Pseud. Ep.* VII. i. 340 The like particulars although they seem uncircumstantiall are oft set downe in holy Scripture. 1752 *Phil. Trans.* XLVIII. 18 Cleomedes, who perhaps saw the same treatise of Hipparchus, is as uncircumstantial as Theon. 1823 BENTHAM *Not Paul* 332 Note here two things—the narrator one of the party; the narrative so loose and uncircumstantial.

**Uncisor'd,** obs. f. UNSCISSORED *ppl. a.*

**Unci·te,** *v.* (UN-[2] 3.) 1721 AMHERST *Terræ Fil.* No. 24 (1726) 126 Whom he order'd to cite the two proctors of the university into the court; as soon as the proctor had done this, the vice-chancellor order'd him to uncite them.

**Unci·ted,** *ppl. a.* [UN-[1] 8.]
**1.** Not called or summoned.
1584 R. SCOT *Discov. Witchcr.* II. iii. (1886) 18 A witnesse uncited, and offering himselfe in this case is to be heard. 1622 in Rushw. *Hist. Coll.* (1659) I. 72 So principal a Person ..who uncited, unheard, and without all knowledge of the Cause hath been condemned. 1665 BOYLE *Occas. Refl.* V. v. 161 There being nothing more easie,..than for Multitudes to pass uncited before Man's Tribunal, to receive their Condemnation at God's.
**2.** Not quoted or mentioned.
1581 J. BELL *Haddon's Answ. Osor.* 116 Here withall is also coupled that saying of Christ with like uncited place. 'They that' [etc.]. 1891 MEREDITH *One of our Conq.* xxxiv, She had her charges to bring against them for injustice: uncited, unstirred charges.

**Unci·tied,** *a.* (UN-[1] 9.)
1802 LANDOR *Crysaor* 80, I am Jove, Thou Neptune: happier in uncitied realms. 1844 LD. HOUGHTON *Mem. Many Scenes, Valentia* 202 For thou..Wilt..bid him dwell at peace with thee In thy uncitied modesty.

**Unci·ty,** *v.* [UN-[2] 6 b.] *trans.* **a.** To deprive of the privileges of a city. **b.** To destroy as a city.
*a* 1661 FULLER *Worthies, Glouc.* I. (1662) 368 Seeing some questioned its Charter, and would have had it Un-Citied, because Un-Bishoped in our Civil Wars. 1850 BLACKIE *Æschylus* I. 211 The ancient city of famous Priam thou Didst sheer uncity.

**Unci·vic,** *a.* (UN-[1] 7.) 1791 MACKINTOSH *Vind. Gallicæ* Wks. 1846 III. 28 The spirit of resistance to uncivic commands broke forth at once in every part of the empire. 1828 *Lights & Shades* I. 129 So uncivic and anti-commercial an offence. 1892 J. W. HEADLAM in *Classical Rev.* 297/2 Anyone who incurred suspicion of uncivic conduct, either political or moral, would be summoned before the Council.

**Unci·vil,** *a.* [UN-[1] 7 and 5 b.]
**1.** Not civilized; barbarous; unrefined: †**a.** Of persons. *Obs.*
1553 BRENDE *Q. Curtius* IV. 35 The Bactrians be the most hardiest people amongst these nations, uncivill men. 1590 SPENSER *F. Q.* II. vii. 3 He sitting found in secret shade, An vncouth, saluage, and vnciuile wight. 1630 *R. Johnson's Kingd. & Commw.* 336 Among all men that professe Christ, there is not a more uncivill creature than the Calabrian. 1644 [H. PARKER] *Jus Populi* 42 No creature is now so uncivill or untame as Man.
**b.** Of actions, places, times, etc.
1553 BRENDE *Q. Curtius* v. 86 This nacion for al their vncyuill and rude maner, could not escape to be subdued with the same force of fortune y[t] others were. 1596 SPENSER *State Irel.* Wks. (Globe) 633/1, I thought this manner of lewd crying and howling not impertinent to be noted as uncivill and Scythian-like. 1650 BULWER *Anthropomet.* 113 They of Goa also eat their pottage with their hands, mocking at the use of spoons as if they were uncivil. 1663 DAVENANT *Siege of Rhodes* II. i, Their gladness is but an uncivil Noise. 1790 BURKE *Fr. Rev.* Wks. V. 88 Men cannot enjoy the rights of an uncivil and of a civil state together. 1890 *Charity Organis. Rev.* Jan. 5 So is their project of feeding a barbarous and uncivil method in civic administration.
† **2. a.** Undeveloped, rude, primitive. *Obs.*
1572 TWYNE *Dionysius' Surv. World* E vij b, These inhabite a very wilde, and vnciuile countrey, the mould beeing very sandy, and not meete for anye tillage. 1632 LITHGOW *Trav.* x. 433 Bad and unciuill Husbandry in Ireland.
† **b.** Irresponsive to culture. *Obs.*
1675 EVELYN *Terra* (1676) 69 That Soil may be so strangely alter'd..as to render the harsh and most uncivil Clay obsequious to the Husbandman. 1733 TULL *Horse-hoeing Husb.* 50 *note*, I take harsh uncivil Clay to be the least Profitable of any to keep in Tillage.
**3.** Not civil or courteous, impolite; rough, rude, lacking in manners: **a.** Of actions, etc.
1591 SHAKS. *Two Gentl.* V. iv. 60 Ruffian: let goe that rude vnciuill touch, Thou friend of an ill fashion. 1596 *Edward III*, II. ii. 60 Now we thinke it an vnciuill thing, To trouble heauen with such harsh resounds. 1613 W. BROWNE *Brit. Past.* I. iv. 439 [They] Bad me begone; and then (in terms uncivil) Did call me counterfait, witch, hag, whore, divell. 1653 W. RAMESEY *Astrol. Restored* 25 The which rugged, preposterous and uncivil answer, caused me presently to believe him to be whom I found him at the last. 1685 BAXTER *Paraphr. N. T.* Acts xv. 12 The proud Magisterial Talkers..stop and silence him by rude uncivil interruption, on pretence that he is too long. 1796 MME. D'ARBLAY *Camilla* VII. xi, I'm not going to offer any thing uncivil. 1824 SCOTT *St. Ronan's* xiii, Having found himself aggrieved by the uncivil behaviour of..Francis Tyrrel. 1878 BROWNING *Poets Croisic* xciv, You've learnt your lesson ..By this uncivil answer of La Roque.
*Comb.* 1600 NASHE *Summers Last Will* iv, Presumptuous Ver, vnciuill-nurturde boy, Think'st I will be derided thus of thee?
**b.** Of persons.
1611 COTGR., *Mauduict*,..ill brought vp, vnciuile, rude. 1619 BEAUM. & FL. *Knight of Malta* V. i, Hard-hearted, and uncivil Oriana. 1663 BP. PATRICK *Parab. Pilgr.* xxxv, He was forced to be more uncivil to her than otherwise he should have been. 1712 ARBUTHNOT *John Bull* I. viii, He was a very uncivil fellow to use such coarse language before People of Condition. 1758 JOHNSON *Idler* No. 16 ¶ 7 His riches neither made him uncivil nor negligent. 1845 JAMES *Arrah Neil* III. ii, We do not intend to be uncivil to you. 1882 MISS BRADDON *Mt. Royal* II. v. 87 He was not absolutely uncivil to his cousin.
**4.** Not decent or seemly; indecorous.
1586 T. B. *La Primaud. Fr. Acad.* I. 172 No effeminate or loose maners, no clownish or vncivill fashions are seene in him. 1611 SPEED *Theat. Gt. Brit.* xxvii. (1614) 53/1 Her faire haire..so covered her nakednes, that no part of her body was uncivil to sight. 1682 BUNYAN *Holy War* (1905) 377 His two servants..catcht them together in uncivil manner more than once. 1687 DRYDEN *Hind & P.* III. 1010 That he should..vex th' Etherial Pow'rs With midnight Mattins at uncivil Hours.
**5.** Not in accordance with civic unity; contrary to civil well-being.
1597 BEARD *Theatre God's Judgem.* (1612) 277 So that great trouble and vnciuill warres were growne vp..in euerie corner of the realme. 1620 J. TAYLOR (Water P.) *Jack a Lent* B ij b, They run starke mad, assembling in routs and throngs numberlesse of vngouerned numbers, with vnciuill ciuill commotions. 1642–4 VICARS *God in Mount* (1844) 29 Our home-bred and inbred distractions and uncivill-civill warres. 1647 N. WARD *Simple Cobler* 2 Civill Commotions make roome for uncivill practises. 1871 R. ELLIS tr. *Catullus* lxvii. 13 Comes to the light some mischief, a deed uncivil arising.
† **6.** Not civilian. *Obs.*[—1]
1590 SWINBURNE *Testaments* 67 To be decided and ruled by the dead stroke of vnciuill and martial cannons, rather then by anie rule of the ciuill or cannon lawe.

† **Unci·vil,** *v. Obs.*[—1] [UN-[2] 6 a.] *trans.* To render uncivil.
1615 DANIEL *Hymen's Triumph* IV. iii, I trust your lonenesse hath not so Vnciuil'd you, to force a messenger To doe against good manners, and his will.

**Unci·vilish,** *a.* (UN-[1] 7.)
1828 LANDOR *Imag. Conv.* III. 280 It is uncivilish to speak to a lady, with a leg of a turkey in limbo, between the gullet and grinder.

**Uncivi·lity.** Now *rare.* [UN-[1] 12 and 5 b.] Absence or lack of civilization or of civility.
1598 FLORIO, *Immodestia*, immodestie, intemperancie, vnciuilitie. 1612 PEACHAM *Gentl. Exerc.* II. ii. 121 His crabbed lookes signifie the sauage vnciuility of the people in those parts. 1648 GAGE *West Ind.* xiii. 73 Their uncivility and barbarous properties tell us that they are most like the Tartars of any. 1697 T. BROWN *Dispens.* II. Wks. 1709 III. III. 67 If thee woul't have no Excuse made for thy Uncivility, I have done. 1830 CUNNINGHAM *Brit. Paint.* II. 78 The uncivility of his opponents.

**Unci·vilizable,** *a.* (UN-[1] 7 b.)
1879 M. PATTISON *Milton* 99 Though the savage Irish are barbarians, uncivilised and uncivilisable. 1880 MISS BIRD *Japan* II. 74 They are uncivilisable and altogether irreclaimable savages.

**Unci·viliza·tion.** (UN-[1] 12 and 5 b.)
[1828–32 WEBSTER.] 1884 *Blackw. Mag.* Mar. 307 They, in their uncivilisation, would have regarded me with contempt.

**Unci·vilize,** *v.* [UN-[2] 6 c.] *trans.* To deprive of civil, civilized, or civic character; to decivilize. Also *absol.*
1603 J. DAVIES (Heref.) *Microcosmos* Wks. (Grosart) I. 18/1 When the civill Sword's vncivilliz'd In mightiest Empires. 1633 ROWLEY *Match at Midn.* IV. H 2 b, I will uncivillize that injured civilitie which you so scurvily slander. 1690 T. BURNET *Theory Earth* II. 16 That is commonly the vanity of great empires, to uncivilize in a manner all the rest of the world. 1811 *Henry & Isabella* II. 207 If the principle of force is to be sanctioned, the tendency of it is to uncivilize. *Ibid.* 212 Nor do I mean to deny that ..it would not have the same effect of uncivilizing.

**Unci·vilized,** *ppl. a.* [UN-[1] 8 and 5 b.] Not civilized; barbarous.
1607 TOPSELL *Four-f. Beasts* 334 Vulgar, illiterate, and vnciuilized men, do participate in their conditions, the labors and enuye of brute beasts. 1647 COWLEY *Mistr., Welcome* iii, What joy couldst take, or what repose In Countrys so unciviliz'd as those? 1711 ADDISON *Spect.* No. 119 ¶ 5 Several of our Men of the Town..make use of the most coarse uncivilized Words in our Language. 1777 COOK *Voy. Pacific* I. viii. (1784) I. 159 They shew as much ingenuity, both in invention and execution, as any uncivilized nations under similar circumstances. 1825 T. HOOK *Sayings* Ser. II. *Man of Many Friends* I. 283 The young gentlemen..with difficulty suppressed a most uncivilized laugh. 1869 DOWDEN *Stud. Lit.* (1890) 161 The first thing we are tempted to say of him..is that he was emphatically an uncivilized man.

Hence **Unci·vilizedness.**
1879 M. ARNOLD *Mixed Ess., Equality* 86 We owe..our uncivilisedness to inequality.

**Unci·villy,** *adv.* [UN-[1] 11.] In an uncivil manner; not in accordance with civility; roughly, rudely; † barbarously.
1577 tr. *Bullinger's Decades* II. v. (1592) 150 Al vertue..is vtterly ouerthrowen,..virgins defiled, matrones vnciuilly dealt withall. 1581 PETTIE tr. *Guazzo's Civ. Conv.* I. (1586) 22, I must first aske if you know anie citizen which liueth unciuillie. 1600 HOLLAND *Livy* 897 He was loth to converse there uncivilly, at so unseasonable a time. 1646 SIR T. BROWNE *Pseud. Ep.* (ed. 2) I. i. 3 When he brake forth as desperately as before he had done uncivilly. 1676 SHADWELL *Libertine* III, Ha! 'tis uncivilly done to leave a man in a strange country. 1798 SOUTHEY *Lett.* (1856) I. 51 Some English soldiers storm the ale-house, and are proceeding to behave somewhat uncivilly to Joan and her sister. 1825 SCOTT *Betrothed* xvii, Turning sternly on the huntsman, as one who has been hastily and uncivilly roused from a reverie. 1888 FREEMAN *Four Oxford Lect.* ii. 99 Those Breton followers of Ralph of Wader whom Lanfranc so uncivilly called 'filth'.

**Uncizar'd,** obs. f. UNSCISSORED *ppl. a.*

† **Uncked,** *a. Obs.*[—1] [f. L. *unc-us* hook.] Hooked, uncate.
1621 QUARLES *Esther* Sect. vii, Enuie did ope her snakedeuouring Iawes, Foamd frothy blood, and bent her vnked [ed. 1717: uncked] Pawes.

† **Unckle,** obs. var. INKLE *sb.*

*c* 1545 in *Fabric Rolls York Minster* (Surtees) 136 For ij peeces of buckerham, 12*s*. For ij do. of white unckle.., 7*d*.

**Unckle,** obs. f. UNCLE.

**Uncla·d,** *ppl. a.* [UN-¹ 8 b. Cf. MDu. *ongecleet* (Du. *ongekleed*), MHG. *ungekleidet, -kleit*, ON. and Icel. *ú-, óklæddr* (Norw. *uklædd*, MSw. and Sw. *oklädd*, Da. *uklædt*).] Not clad or clothed; undressed; naked.

*c* 1420 *Avow. Arth.* liv, Qwenne ho se him vnclad, Then the lady wex drede. 1500 *Ortus Vocab.* (W. de W.) S viij b, *Inuestitus*, vncladde. 1531 ELYOT *Gov.* II. xii, He was a shamed to approche nigh to it, beinge in so simple astate and unklad. 1647 HEXHAM I, Vnclothed or unclad, *ontkleedt*. 1761 GLOVER *Medea* I. i, Creon knows, thy altar Unclad with garlands still proclaims thy firmness Against his daughter's marriage. 1768 MURPHY *Desert Isl.* II, That I may sit, With unclad sides, upon some blasted heath. 1827 POLLOK *Course T.* IX. 1095 Decrepit, withered wretch, unhoused, unclad. 1855 MILMAN *Lat. Chr.* XIV. ix. VI. 601 Men, women, rose unclad from their tombs.

**Unclad,** pa. t. and pple. of UNCLEAD *v.*

**Unclai·med,** *ppl. a.* (UN-¹ 8.)

1600 SHAKS. *A. Y. L.* II. vii. 87 If he be free, Why then my taxing like a wild-goose flies Vnclaim'd of any man. 1738 JOHNSON *London* 173 Has Heav'n reserv'd, in pity to the poor,..No peaceful desert yet unclaim'd by Spain? 1783 CRABBE *Village* II. 26 Yet still, ye humbler friends, enjoy your hour, This is your portion, yet unclaim'd of power. 1826 SOUTHEY *Vind. Eccl. Angl.* 306 The quiet, unassuming, unclaimed influence of the one may appear to you less than it ought to be. 1867 SMYTH *Sailor's Word-bk.* 705 *Unclaimed*, as Derelict. Vessels found at sea..are good prizes, if not claimed within 366 days.

**Unclainte,** obs. pa. t. of UNCLENCH *v.*

**Uncla·morous,** *a.* (UN-¹ 7.) 1849 LYTTON *K. Arthur* V. xxvii, The Prophet mark'd the deep unclamorous vow Of the pent passion.

**Uncla·mp,** *v.* (UN-² 3.)

1809 *Phil. Trans.* XCIX. 120 Unclamp the apparatus. 1849 HERSCHEL *Astron.* 106 Now unclamp the level, and.. turn round the circle on the axis. 1860 H. STUART *Seaman's Catech.* 46 The outside men will..unclamp the booms.

† **Unclap,** *v. Obs.* [UN-² 3.] *trans.* To open up.

1621 T. WILLIAMSON tr. *Goulart's Wise Vieillard* A 4 b, My fingers did euen itch to set pen to paper, and to vnclappe so good a Worke.

**Uncla·rified,** *ppl. a.* (UN-¹ 8.)

1591 PERCIVALL *Sp. Dict.*, *Agraz*, a sower grape, honie vnmade, oile vnclarified, Veriuice. 1599 A. M. tr. *Gabelhouer's Bk. Physicke* 45/2 Then take vnclarifyede rosin. 1620 VENNER *Via Recta* vi. 104 It is..hurtfull to such as abound with winde, especially the crude and vnclarified honie. 1725 *Fam. Dict.* s.v. *Whey*, Its best they should take it unclarify'd. [1755 JOHNSON (quoting Bacon), and in later Dicts.]

**Uncla·shing,** *ppl. a.* (UN-¹ 10.) 1642 W. PRICE *Serm.* 24 Like the æviternall unclashing sway of the Orbs in the Heavens. 1825 R. WILSON *Sk. Hist. Hawick* 297 In this momentous matter [*sc.* religion] human interests are so *unclashing*,..that [etc.]. 1854 CDL. WISEMAN *Fabiola* (1855) 312 Glorious Church of Christ! great in the unclashing combination of thy unity!

**Uncla·sp,** *v.* [UN-² 3 and 7.]

**1.** *trans.* To unfasten the clasp(s) of.

1530 PALSGR. 766/2, I pray you, unclaspe my boke, for I am nat stronge ynough. 1592 *Soliman & Pers.* II. i. 85, I must vnclaspe me, or my heart will breake. 1611 COTGR., *Desagrafer*, to vnclaspe, vngraple, vnhaspe. *a* 1699 J. BEAUMONT *Psyche* XVI. xvii, Disrobe me of my Beauty..; Unclasp my Joints; unlace my nerves. 1798 EDGEWORTH *Pract. Educ.* (1811) I. 110 A little boy..trying to clasp and unclasp a lady's bracelet. 1805 SCOTT *Last Minstrel* V. xxiv, His beaver did he not unclasp. 1859 TENNYSON *Elaine* 975 Then, when she heard his horse upon the stones, Unclasping flung the casement back. 1891 FARRAR *Darkn. & Dawn* xiv, He unclasped the armlet from his wrist.

**b.** In fig. context.

1592 DANIEL *Delia* i, Heere I vnclaspe the booke of my charg'd soule. 1607 DEKKER *Hist. Sir T. Wyatt* Wks. 1873 III. 100 When the blacke booke of my crime's vnclaspt. 1633 DRUMM. OF HAWTH. *Entertainm. Chas. I*, ii. 31 Heavens volume to unclaspe, wast pages spread, Mysterious golden cyphers cleere to reade. 1833-4 *Encycl. Metrop.* (1845) VI. 688/2 It will be prudent before thus entangling ourselves in fetters which it may be difficult to unclasp, to wait for a full investigation of the subject.

† **c.** *fig.* To open up, display. *Obs.*

1599 SHAKS. *Much Ado* I. i. 325, I will..tell faire Hero I am Claudio, And in her bosome Ile unclaspe my heart. 1611 — *Wint. T.* III. ii. 168 He..to my Kingly Guest Vnclasp'd my practise. 1637 N. WHITING *Albino & Bellama* 5 All had their speakers which unclasp'd their graces.

**2.** To loosen the grasp or hold of; to open or force open (the clasped hand).

1627 MAY *Lucan* IV. G v, His fresh limmes vnclaspe the others hands. 1681 FLAVEL *Right Man's Ref.* 251 Neither of them..can unclasp the arms of divine love. 1810 SCOTT *Lady of L.* II. xxxiv, Sullen and slowly they unclasp, As struck with shame, their desperate grasp. 1831 JAMES *Phil. Augustus* iv, Unclasping his arms from the slight, beautiful form round which they were thrown. 1898 'MERRIMAN' *Roden's Corner* i, Von Holzen..softly unclasped the dead man's hand, taking from it the crumpled notes.

**b.** *intr.* To relax a grip or grasp.

1608 SHAKS. *Per.* II. iii. 107 Vnclaspe, vnclaspe. Thankes Gentlemen to all. 1751 SMOLLETT *Per. Pic.* xxix, The cudgel flew from his unclasping hand. 1850 LYNCH *Theoph. Trinal* vi. 110 The jaws of their grave shall unclasp. 1851 LONGF. *Gold. Leg.* ii. *Village Church*, I feel my feeble hands unclasp, And sink discouraged into night!

**3.** *trans.* To release from a clasp or grip.

1885 'MRS. ALEXANDER' *At Bay* ix, He remained silent for a minute, his hands clasping and unclasping the arms of his chair.

Hence **Uncla·sping** *vbl. sb.*

1592 *Soliman & Pers.* II. i. 87 But inward cares are most pent in with greefe; Vnclasping, therefore, yeeldes me no releefe. 1599 B. JONSON *Ev. Man out of Hum.* II. ii, A whole volume of humour, and worthy the vnclasping.

**Uncla·sped,** *ppl. a.* [f. UNCLASP *v.* 1 or UN-¹ 8 + CLASPED *ppl. a.*] Having the clasp undone or not fastened. Also *fig.*

1609 J. DAVIES *Holy Roode* G, None other Booke but thy vnclasped Side (Wherein's contain'd all Skils Angelical). 1628 GAULE *Pract. The.* (1629) 24 In him Law and Gospell conspire together; the Law as a closed Gospell; the Gospell as an vnclasped Law. 1825 SCOTT *Talism.* viii, The hood which he wore,..now unclasped and thrown back for heat. 1856 J. RICHARDSON *Recoll.* I. iii. 69 He was an incessant talker... When once unclasped, it was with difficulty he could again be closed. 1880 L. WALLACE *Ben-Hur* 474 Iras began, toying the while with one of her unclasped bracelets.

**Uncla·sping,** *ppl. a.*¹ (UN-¹ 10.) 1640 O. SEDGWICK *Christs Counsell* 174 The impotency..of an unholding and unclasping memory. **Uncla·sping,** *ppl. a.*² (See UNCLASP *v.* 2 b, quot. 1751.)

**Uncla·ss,** *v.* (UN-² 6 b.)

1873 MORLEY *Rousseau* I. 108 *note*, 'A bourgeois unclassed by an alliance with a tavern servant';..but surely Rousseau had unclassed himself long before.

**Uncla·ssable,** *a.* (UN-¹ 7 b.) 1848 RICKMAN *Styles Archit. Eng.* 234 Roslyn chapel..is certainly unclassable as a whole, being unlike any other building in Great Britain of its age. 1870 H. SPENCER *Psychology* (ed. 2) I. II. i. 148 Mind remains unclassable and therefore unknowable. **Uncla·ssed,** *ppl. a.* (UN-¹ 8.) 1820 SHELLEY *Prometh. Unb.* III. iv. 195 The man remains..Equal, unclassed, tribeless, and nationless. 1865 TYLOR *Early Hist. Man.* viii. 203 He would have to leave a large fraction of the whole in an unclassed heap.

**Uncla·ssic,** *a.* (UN-¹ 7.)

1728 POPE *Dunc.* III. 258 Angel of Dulness, sent to scatter round His magic charms o'er all unclassic ground. 1894 *Outing* (U.S.) XXIV. 46/2 It is now known as the unclassic and plebeian Bay de Vache.

**Uncla·ssical,** *a.* (UN-¹ 7.)

1725 BLACKWALL *Sacr. Class.* (1727) I. 76 That it [*sc.* the repetition] is not unclassical but pure, I shall shew by parallel forms of expression in the noblest classics. 1767 S. PATERSON *Another Trav.* I. 350 They are either too classical (You are unclassical) or too illiterate. *c* 1828 ARNOLD in Stanley *Life & Corr.* (1844) I. 50 If the sermons are read, I do not care one farthing if the readers think me the most unclassical writer in the English language. 1871 BLACKIE *Four Phases* i. 11 The Athenian philosopher made a jest of his unclassical nose.

Hence **Uncla·ssically** *adv.*

[1775 ASH.] 1860 J. WHITESIDE *Italy* xvii. 168 As we reach the unclassically-named town of Poggibonsi.

**Uncla·ssifiable,** *a.* (UN-¹ 7 b.) *a* 1849 POE *E. B. Browning* Wks. 1865 III. 401 Setting aside..certain rare commentators..—creatures neither precisely men, women, nor Mary Wollstonecraft's—..as unclassifiable. 1875 [see next].

**Uncla·ssified,** *ppl. a.* (UN-¹ 8.)

1865 TYLOR *Early Hist. Man.* i. 12 Our accounts of the culture of the lower races, being mostly unclassified. 1875 WHITNEY *Life Lang.* v. 82 Neglecting the unclassified and perhaps in part unclassifiable residue. 1884 J. TAIT *Mind in Matter* 132 Like the flora and the fauna in nature, miracles are unclassified in the Bible.

**Unclay·,** *v.* (UN-² 4 b.)

1655 JER. TAYLOR *Guide Devot.* 144 Oh, end the Strife, And part us, that in Peace I may Unclay My wearied Spirit. [1706 STEVENS I, *Desembarrar*, to unclay, to undaub.] 1796 C. MARSHALL *Gardening* xx. (1813) 407 Graffs that have clearly taken, unclay and unbind.

**Unclay·ed,** *ppl. a.* (UN-¹ 8.) 1883 *Daily News* 26 Sept. 3/4, 600 bags unclayed Manilla [sugar].

**Uncle** (ʌ·ŋk'l), *sb.* Forms: α. 3-7 **vncle** (5 **wncle**), 4- **uncle** (5-6 **oncle**). β. 4, 6-8 **unkle** (vn-), 6-7 **unckle** (vn-, 7 wn-). γ. 4 **unkel**, 5 **vnkel**, 6 **unkell** (vn-), 5-6 **vn-**, **unkil**(1, **-kyll** (5 **hunckyl**, **oncyll**, **ownkyll**, 6 **onkill**); 5 **vn-**, **uncull**, 6 **unckall**. See also NUNCLE. [a. AF. *uncle*, OF. *uncle*, *oncle* (mod.F. *oncle*, whence G., Da., Sw. *onkel*), = Pr. *oncle*, *avoncle*, Roum. *unchiu*:—L. *avunculus* mother's brother.]

**1.** A brother of one's father or mother; also, an aunt's husband (= uncle-in-law).

α. *c* 1290 *S. Eng. Leg.* I. 20/27 To his vncle he gan go, þe Erchebischop of caunterburi. 1297 R. GLOUC. (Rolls) 1937 Þre vnclen is moder adde. *c* 1380 *Sir Ferumb.* 169 Þe duk ..drow ys swerd anon, & wolde ys vncle þar-wiþ herte. 1387 TREVISA *Higden* (Rolls) III. 389 Alisaundre exiled dwelled awhile wiþ his uncle in Epirus. 1412-20 LYDG. *Chron. Troy* I. 3751 Iason..gan his vncle in ful lowe maner First to þanke. 1475 *Bk. Noblesse* (Roxb.) 15 Henry the vᵗᵉ..made Thomas Beauford then erle Dorset hys oncle capteyn of yt. *c* 1500 *Melusine* xix. 97 For neuer I shall ete tyl that ye be hanged with your vncle. *c* 1520 BARCLAY *Jugurth* vi. (1557) 6 b, Se that ye worshipe and loue this Jugurth your worthy vncle. 1581 G. PETTIE tr. *Guazzo's Civ. Conv.* III. (1586) 120 b, In families there are the Uncle and the Nephew, the Father in law and the Sonne in law [etc.]. 1653 W. RAMESEY *Astrol. Restored* 109 [This] signifieth..also the Uncle or Ant of the Querent by the fathers side. 1725 RAMSAY *Gentle Sheph.* V. iii, At last he spak and won, And hopes to be our honest uncle's son. 1756-7 tr. *Keysler's Trav.* (1760) IV. 214 Offering him the immediate payment of a debt due to his uncle. 1818 CRUISE *Digest* (ed. 2) III. 353 If the son, in this case, die without issue, and his uncle enter into the land. 1866 GEO. ELIOT *Felix Holt* i, Your uncle thought I ought to have you to myself in the first hour or two.

β. *c* 1380 WYCLIF *Sel. Wks.* III. 475 How may oure hyȝe prestis..be grettur worldly lordis þen..kyngus unklis ande kyngus sonys? 1565 COOPER *Thesaurus*, *Auunculus*, the vnkle on the mothers side. 1584 *Knaresb. Wills* (Surtees) I. 145 Ric. Roundell ther unckle. 1610 HOLLAND *Camden's Brit.* (1637) 696 King Edward the Fifth his Unkle by the mothers side. *a* 1699 LADY HALKETT *Autobiog.* (Camden) 32 Pretending his wife was dead,..and that her uncle Sir Ralph S. had assured them both of itt. *a* 1727 NEWTON *Chronol. Amended* ii. (1728) 239 Orus, with his mother Isis,..and unkle Typhon. 1779 JOHNSON *L. P.*, *Pope* Wks. IV. 15 She was obliged to converse only with those from whom her unkle had nothing to fear.

γ. 1387 TREVISA *Higden* (Rolls) IV. 235 Herodias, þat was afterwarde Phelip his wif, þat was Aristobolus his eme and unkel. 1415 SIR T. GREY in *43 Deputy Keeper Public Records* 585 Þe Erle of Somerset zowr uncull. 1451 *Paston Lett.* I. 202 On of myn unkyll men..told it myn unkill. 1472 *Ibid.* III. 41 Item, as for myn ownkyll William, I have spook with hym. 1539 *Cal. Anc. Rec. Dublin* (1889) 407 For as mych as my sayd unkyll ys well willyng. 1540 CROMWELL in Merriman *Life & Lett.* (1902) II. 255 A true copie of your unckall ys testament and last will. 1570 LEVINS *Manip.* 126 An Vnkil, *auunculus*.

**b.** *Uncle-in-law*, the husband of one's aunt.

1561 *Child-Marriages* 3 All the premisses this deponent knowis to be true, bie cause he is Vncle-in-lawe to the said Homfrey. 1667 DUCHESS OF NEWCASTLE *Life Duke of N.* (1886) I. 2 These two brothers were partly bred with Gilbert, Earl of Shrewsbury, their uncle-in-law. 1779 *Mirror* No. 53 P 8 Among the rest was my uncle-in-law's partner

**c.** In allusive use.

In the first two quots. directly from French usage.

1578 H. WOTTON *Courtlie Controv.* 275 Wheras other men accustome to visite their vncle when they determine to take truce for a time with their amorous trauailes. 1611 COTGR. s.v. *Oncle*, He is my neerest friend that fills my bellie; or he is my kindest vncle who doth feed me. 1678 RAY *Prov.* 227 She is one of mine Aunts that made mine Uncle go a begging. 1785 GROSE *Dict. Vulgar T.* s.v., He is gone to visit his uncle, saying of one who leaves his wife soon after marriage.

**d.** *Welsh uncle* (see later quots.).

1747 T. CARTE *Hist. England* I. 210 Aeddon, who was welsh-uncle to Rydderch, made his escape to the Isle of Man. 1820 SOUTHEY *Wesley* II. 108 He was placed under the care of the husband of his father's first cousin; which remote relationship comes under the comprehensive term of a Welsh Uncle. 1868 FREEMAN *Norm. Conq.* II. App. 645 A 'Welsh uncle', that is the first cousin of a parent.

**e.** *Dutch uncle* (see quots.).

1838 J. C. NEAL *Charcoal Sk.* 201 If you keep a cutting didoes, I must talk to you both like a Dutch uncle. 1853 *N. & Q.* 1st Ser. VII. 65/2 In some parts of America, when a person has determined to give another a regular lecture, he will often be heard to say, 'I will talk to him like a Dutch uncle'; that is, he shall not escape this time. 1869 *East Anglian* III. 350 There were the squires on the bench, but I took heart, and talked to 'em like a Dutch uncle. 1873 HELPS *Anim. & Mast.* v. 131 Milverton..began reasoning with the boys; talking to them like a Dutch uncle.. about their cruelty.

**2.** Used in addressing or designating one's uncle.

*c* 1374 CHAUCER *Troylus* II. 210 Nay blame haf I, my vncle, quod she þenne. 1547 EDWARD VI in Ellis *Orig. Lett.* Ser. I. II. 148 Derest Vncle,..we have at good length vnderstanded..the good success [etc.]. ? *c* 1570 *Bugbears* V. vii. 97 O good vncle Donatus, ther is cawse I shold love you. 1598 SHAKS. *Merry W.* III. iv. 49 Pray you Vncle, tel Mist. Anne the iest how my Father stole two Geese out of a Pen, good Vnckle. 1640 BROME *Antipodes* III. v, *Beg.* Sir excuse me... *Gal.* Yet good unkle. 1656 STANLEY *Hist. Philos.* Ded., The gratitude of, Dear Uncle, Your most affectionate Nephew. 1700 N. ROUS in *Jrnl. Friends' Hist. Soc.* (1912) IX. 184 With mine and Wifes..kind respects to Unckle and Aunt Abrams,..I rest [etc.]. 1793 MRS. INCHBOLD *Midn. Hour* II, Do not be alarmed, uncle; force is seldom used but to her that is willing. 1828 SCOTT *F. M. Perth* xxiii, Uncle, you are a good huntsman. 1850 TENNYSON *In Mem.* lxxxiv, When..boys of thine Had babbled 'Uncle' on my knee.

**b.** *local* and *U.S.* Used as a form of address to non-relatives, esp. to elderly men.

1793 *Gentl. Mag.* Dec. 1083/2 It is common in Cornwall to call all elderly persons Aunt or Uncle, prefixed to their names. 1835 J. H. INGRAHAM *South West* II. 241 Nor are planters indifferent to the comfort of their gray-headed slaves... They always address them in a mild and pleasant manner as 'Uncle' or 'Aunty'. 1853 LOWELL *Wks.* (1890) I. 16 Formerly, every New England town had its representative uncle. 1855 KINGSLEY *Westw. Ho!* xx, 'Put this coat on your back, uncle,' says some one. 1859 BARTLETT *Dict. Amer.* (ed. 2) 492 *Uncle*, used in the Middle and Southern States in accosting an elderly colored man.

*transf.* 1847 EMERSON *Repr. Men, Plato* ad fin., Plain old uncle as he [Socrates] was,..the rumour ran, that [etc.].

**c.** *Uncle Sam*, the government (or people) of the United States of America.

The history of the expression has been traced by A. Matthews in *Proc. Amer. Antiq. Soc.* XIX. 21-65; see also R. H. Thornton *Amer. Glossary* 916. The suggestion that it arose as a facetious interpretation of the letters U.S. is as old as the first recorded instances, and later statements connecting it with different government officials of the name of Samuel appear to be unfounded.

1813 *Troy Post* 7 Sept. (Matthews), Loss upon loss, and no ill luck stir[r]ing but what lights upon Uncle Sam's shoulders. 1839 N. HAWTHORNE in Longfellow *Life* (1891) I. 334 Uncle Sam is rather despotic as to the disposal of my time. 1850 — *Scarlet L.* Introd. (1852) 3 The thirteen stripes turned vertically,..thus indicating that a civil..post of Uncle Sam's government is here established. 1884 *Harper's Mag.* June 48/1 To cheat Uncle Sam in revenue matters is regarded as a ..venial sin.

**d.** *Uncle George*, King George III.

1829 MARRYAT *F. Mildmay* iii, We make *uncle George* suffer for the stores.

**3.** *slang.* A pawnbroker.

Usually preceded by a possessive pronoun.

1756 TOLDERVY *Hist. 2 Orphans* IV. 113 The next week carried the new cloaths, which they bought at Bath, to their uncles (if Humphry's expression may be used). **1796** GROSE *The Olio* 230 A shirt and hose I'd at my uncle's lodg'd. **1807** E. S. BARRETT *Rising Sun* II. 131 The bed-furniture was carefully preserved by my uncle, and when.. I had gained a bed, and money enough to redeem the furniture, I put them up. **1855** THACKERAY *Newcomes* xii, 'Dine in your frock,..if your dress-coat is in the country.' 'It is at present at an uncle's.' **1869** M. COLLINS *Ivory Gate* II. i. 19 You may want to take it to your uncle, you know, now that your secretaryship is about to be abolished.

4. *appositive* and *Comb.*, as *uncle devil, father, -guardian, -marquis*; *uncle-given* adj.

**1602** SHAKS. *Ham.* II. ii. 393 My Vnckle Father, and Aunt Mother are deceiu'd. **1638** FORD *Fancies* II. ii, Our great uncle-marquis, Disabled from his cradle. **1789** M. MADAN tr. *Persius* II. 292 *note*, The relish or savour of morose uncle-guardians. **1828** *Lights & Shades* I. 27 At the very first uncle-given dinner. **1897** MARY KINGSLEY *W. Africa* 93 Any leg or arm I saw that uncle devil pulling out to place within reach of the crocodiles.

Hence **U·nclehood**. *rare*$^{-1}$.

**1846** B. BARTON *Select.* (1849) 100 Those five uncles of mine..grew not up to mature uncle-hood.

**U·ncle**, *v.* [f. prec.]

1. *trans.* To address (one) as uncle.

**1593** SHAKS. *Rich. II*, II. iii. 85 Grace me no Grace, nor Vncle me, I am no Traytors Vnckle. **1872** B. TAYLOR in *Life & Lett.* (1884) II. 592, I am 'uncled' from morning till night. **1884** J. T. TROWBRIDGE *Farnell's Folly* I. xix. 196 Uncle! uncle!' chattered old Carolus,..'don't uncle me!'

†2. To cheat or swindle (*of* something). *Obs.*

Perhaps originally implying a pretence of being uncle to the person victimized; but the association with COZEN *v.* and *sb.*, which appears in the quots., makes it also possible that *uncle* is merely a punning variation of *cousin*.

*a* **1592** GREENE *Selimus* (1594) H ij, This is some cousoning conicatching crosbiter, that would faine perswade me he knowes me, and so vnder a tence of familiaritie and acquaintance, vncle me of victuals. **1606** *Sir G. Goosecappe* V. i, And Neece tho you have cosind me in this, Ile uncle you yet in an other thing. **1608** DEKKER *Belman of London* Wks. (Grosart) III. 127 If the Cozen be such an Asse to goe into a tauerne, then he is sure to be vnckled.

†b. To deprive (an uncle) *of* life. *Obs.*$^{-1}$

**1602** CHETTLE *Hoffman* I. (1631) C 3, Vncle, ile vncle thee of thy proud life.

**-uncle**, *suffix*, representing OF. *-uncle* (*-oncle*) and ultimately L. *-unculus, -uncula*, in a few words, in most of which it retains its diminutive force. The earliest of these is *carbuncle* from the 13–14th cent.; †*portiuncle* appears in the 15th, *caruncle, furuncle, homuncle* in the 17th, *peduncle* in the 18th, and *oratiuncle* in the 19th. New formations without Latin originals are rare, and the suffix has little independent existence though occasionally employed as in the following examples.

**1825** BENTHAM *Offic. Apt. Maximized, Indic.* (1830) 71 Not a *reformatiuncle* of his (as Hartley would have called it) did Romilly ever bring forward, that he had not first brought to me. **1875** [see PSEUDONYMUNCLE].

**Unclea·d**, *v.* *Obs.* or *arch.* Also 4 vncleth(e; *pa. t.* 4 vnclede, 5 -cledde, 5–6 -cled; 4–5, 7, 9 unclad; *p.p.* 7 vncled, -clad. [UN-$^2$ 4. Cf. MDu. *ontcleden* (*-cleiden*), Du. *ontkleeden*, G. *entkleiden*.]

1. *trans.* To unclothe, undress. Also *refl.*

*a* **1300** *Cursor M.* 16339 Pilate..Of his clothes vn-clethes him. *c* **1375** *Sc. Leg. Saints* xxx. (*Theodera*) 781 Þe abbot ..vncled hyr, as custum was, þe ded body for to wesche. *c* **1400** *Rule St. Benet* (Prose) 145 Þe Priores sal hafe hir befor þe auter & vncleth hir of hir seculer clething. **1483** CAXTON *Gold. Leg.* 85 b/1 He dyspoylled and unclad hym and gaf hys clothys unto the bochyers. *c* **1520** M. NISBET *Matt.* xxvii. 31 Thai vncled him of the mantil. **1842** TENNYSON *Godiva* 48 Godiva..Unclad herself in haste.

2. *fig.* To divest oneself of; to put off.

**1659** W. CHAMBERLAYNE *Pharonnida* I. 44 Argalia thus unclad Amazements dark disguise. *Ibid.* IV. 81 We there unclad All our deform'd misfortunes.

**Unclea·n**, *a.* Forms: (see CLEAN *a.*). [OE. *unclǽne*: see UN-$^1$ 7 and CLEAN *a.*]

1. Morally impure or defiled; unchaste: a. Of persons.

*a* **900** CYNEWULF *Crist* 1017 Woruldmonna seo unclæne ȝecynd. *a* **1100** *Voc.* in Wr.-Wülcker 308 *Incestus*, unclæne. *c* **1325** *Spec. Gy Warw.* 834 For ȝit wole he noht sinne fle: Iwis, vnclene he shal be. **1340–70** *Alex. & Dind.* 636 Þanne schulle ȝe for ȝour sinne soffre paine, For ȝe unclene bi cleped & cleuen in ȝour sinne. *c* **1440** *Promp. Parv.* 364/2 Onclene, *immundus, inpurus.* **1490** in *Somerset Med. Wills* (1901) 292 After her deceese, other else that she mary, other leve unclene of her body ayenst the lawes of God. **1526** TINDALE *Eph.* v. 5 No whormonger, other vnclene person, or coveteous person. **1596** DALRYMPLE tr. *Leslie's Hist. Scot.* (S.T.S.) I. 240 Quhen he gathiret his vile, vnhonest, maist impure, and vncleine secte. **1667** MILTON *P. L.* IX. 1098 That this new commer, Shame, There sit not, and reproach us as unclean. **1680** *Charac. Town-miss* (Hindley, III) 8 She becomes a Loathsome thing, too unclean to enter into Heaven. **1738** WESLEY *Ps.* v. ii, In Souls unholy and unclean Thou never canst delight. **1755** — *Jrnl.* (1761) III. 5 The fierce, unclean, brutish, blasphemous Antinomians.

*absol.* **1382** WYCLIF *Eccl.* ix. 2 Alle thingus euenli comen ..to the goode and to the euele, to the clene and to the vnclene. **1535** COVERDALE *Ibid.*, It goeth..with the good & cleane as with the vncleane. **1569** J. SANFORD tr. *Agrippa's Van. Artes* lviii. 83 b, Sinners with the faithfull,..the vncleane with yᵉ cleane.

b. Of thoughts, conduct, etc.

*a* **900** CYNEWULF *Crist* 1316 Þær we nu maȝon..ȝeseon on ussum sawlum..unclæne inȝeþoncas. **971** *Blickl. Hom.* 25 Moniȝe men syndon þe..beoþ besmitene mid þem unclænan firen-luste. **1297** R. GLOUC. (Rolls) 7208 Vor prustes mid vnclene honden & mid lechors mod Al isoyled sacrieþ godes fless & is blod. *a* **1300** *Cursor M.* 28509, I haf þam wit delt..Wit handling vnhende, kissyng vnclene. **13..** *E. E. Allit. P.* B. 710 Now haf þay skyfted my skyl & scorned natwre, & henttez þem in heþyng an vsage vn-clene. *c* **1400** *Prymer* 49 From vnclene þouȝtis, lord, deliuere us! *c* **1480** HENRYSON *Test. Cres.* 285 Thus hir leuing vnclene and Lecherous Scho wald returne on me and my Mother. **1526** *Pilgr. Perf.* (W. de W. 1531) 84 b, With elacyon of mynde, or other vycyous and vnclene thoughtes. **1567** *Gude & Godlie B.* (S.T.S.) I Then sal thay..cause them to put away baudrie & vnclene sangis. **1605** BACON *Adv. Learn.* I. i. § 3 It is mere imposture..to offer to the author of truth the unclean sacrifice of a lie. **1651** [see 2]. **1707** WATTS *Hymn, 'Vain are the Hopes'* i, Their Hearts by Nature [are] all unclean. **1728** POPE *Dunciad* II. 99 Her servants..List'ning delighted to the jest unclean Of link-boys vile. **1781** COWPER *Tiroc.* 735 If thy table be indeed unclean, Foul with excess, and with discourse obscene. **1889** R. BUCHANAN in *Contemp. Rev.* Dec. 925 Unclean sexual pathology..now threatens the Drama.

2. *Unclean spirit*, a wicked spirit; a demon. Also *transf.*

*c* **950** *Lindisf. Gosp.* Mark i. 26 Se gast unclænæ..of-eode from him. *c* **1000** ÆLFRIC *Gloss.* in Wr.-Wülcker 144 *Spiracula*, unclænra gasta wunungstow. *c* **1200** ORMIN 4635 Forr deofell iss unnclene gast, & lufeþþ unnclænnesse. **1382** WYCLIF *Mark* i. 23 In the synagoge of hem was a man in an vnclene spirit. *a* **1400** *New Test.* (Paues) Acts v. 16 Hem þat wore traueiled wiþ vnclene spirittes. [**1534** TINDALE *Luke* iv. 33 A man which had a sprete of an vncleane devell.] **1548** UDALL, etc. *Erasm. Par. Matt.* xii. 56 b, Whan the vnclene spirite is gone out of a man. **1651** HOBBES *Leviath.* I. viii. 38 The spirit of man, when it produceth unclean actions, is ordinarily called an unclean spirit. **1727** DE FOE *Syst. Magic.* I. ii. (1840) 53 A cage of devils, and as the text calls them, unclean spirits. **1861** PALEY *Æschylus* (ed. 2) *Supplices* 637 *note*, Hence μιάστωρ became a general term for an unclean spirit, or evil genius. **1870** DICKENS *E. Drood* i, He has to withdraw himself to a lean arm-chair.. until he has got the better of this unclean spirit of imitation.

3. Of animals: Regarded as defiled or impure, and *esp.* as unfit to be eaten on that account. Hence also of food.

*c* **900** tr. *Baeda's Hist.* I. xxvii. (1890) 80 Mid þy seo æ moniȝ þing bewereð to etanne swa swa unclæne. *a* **1000** *Colloq. Ælfric* in Wr.-Wülcker 93 Hwæt ȝif hit unclæne beoþ fixas? Ic utwyrpe þa unclænan ut, & ȝenime me clæne to mete. *a* **1300** *Cursor M.* 1960, I warn yow als-sua all be-deine Ete o na best o kind vn-clene. **1382** WYCLIF *Lev.* xi. 8 Ne towche ȝe the careyns, for thei ben vnclene to ȝow. *c* **1400** *Destr. Troy* 11185 Let hir bones with baret abide in this aire, As a caren vncleane, for hir curst dedis. **1535** COVERDALE *Hosea* ix. 3 But Ephraim..eateth vncleane thinges amonge the Assirians. **1597** HOOKER *Eccl. Pol.* v. lxviii. § 1 They are Dogges, swine, vncleane beasts. **1604** E. G[RIMSTONE] *D'Acosta's Hist. Indies* VII. ii. 497 They hunted..vncleane beasts, as snakes, lizards, locusts and wormes. **1671** MILTON *P. R.* II. 328 Nor mention I Meats by the Law unclean, or offer'd first To Idols. **1796** H. HUNTER tr. *St.-Pierre's Stud. Nat.* (1799) I. 347 Why are those animals pronounced unclean? **1841** LANE *Arab. Nts.* I. 18 The distinctions of clean and unclean meats. **1854** BADHAM *Halieut.* 61 The remarkable Divine interdict obliging the Jews to abstain from certain fish as unclean. **1864** PUSEY *Lect. Daniel* (1876) 322 Eating of unclean food.

b. In general use: Ceremonially impure.

*c* **1200** ORMIN 1712 He wass unnclene þohh þatt daȝȝ anan till efenn. *c* **1250** *Gen. & Ex.* 1867 Aȝte unclene ne wulde he beren, for he dredde him it sulde him deren. *a* **1300** *Cursor M.* 19932 Nu wit sight i haf it sene þat o man-kind es nan vnclene. **1382** WYCLIF *Lev.* xii. 2 She shal be vnclene seuen dayes. *c* **1450** *Mirk's Festial* 57 A woman þat was delyuerde of a man-chyld sculd be holden vnclene by þe lawe vii dayes aftyr hur burth. **1535** COVERDALE *Lev.* xi. 38 Whan there is water poured vpon the sede, and afterwarde eny soch deed carcase falleth theron, then shall it be vncleane vnto you. **1630** J. TAYLOR (Water P.) *Jack a Lent* Wks. 119/1, I hold it a conscience to abstaine from flesh-eating in Lent: not that I thinke it to bee vncleane to the cleane. **1643** CARYL *Expos. Job* I. 1326 The uncleanness of the giver renders his gift unclean. **1836** J. H. NEWMAN *Par. Serm.* (ed. 2) II. xxi. 335 The Gentiles were no longer common or unclean. **1855** PUSEY *Doctr. Real Presence* Note S. 429 But if he who is merely unclean..has so fearful a judgment, how much more will he, who is in sin,..draw upon himself a more dreadful punishment!

*transf.* **1880** MISS BRADDON *Just as I am* xxvii, Avonmore is one of the genteelest towns in England. There is positively nothing common or unclean in it.

4. Not physically clean; dirty, filthy, foul. Of the tongue: Coated with fur.

*a* **1250** *Owl & Night.* 91 Þu art lodlich & vnclene Bi þine neste ich hit mene. **1297** R. GLOUC. (Rolls) 8969 Is þis wel ido þat þou þes vnclene limes handlest & kust so? **1390** GOWER *Conf.* I. 179 For who so wole his handes lime, Thei mosten be the more unclene. *a* **1400** *Octavian* 885 Clement broght forthe the schylde and spere, That were uncomely for to were, Alle sutty, blakk, and unclene. **1440** J. SHIRLEY *Dethe K. James* (1818) 17 The Kyng..cryed..that they shuld cume with shettes, and drawe hym up owt of that uncleyne place of the privay. **1552** HULOET, Vncleane,.. Loke in filthy and fowle. **1600** SHAKS. *A. Y. L.* III. iii. 36 To cast away honestie vppon a foule slut, were to put good meate into an vncleane dish. **1609** DEKKER *Gull's Horn-bk.* iii. 14 To carry away all noisome filth that is swept out of vncleane corners. **1683** BURNET tr. *More's Utopia* 92 Nor do they suffer any thing that is foul or unclean to be brought within their Towns. **1800** *Med. Jrnl.* IV. 423 As soon as they see an unclean tongue, an emetic is pronounced unquestionably necessary. **1864** HAZLITT in *E. P. P.* III. 131 The moist and unclean thumbs of a wide circle of readers. **1898** *Westm. Gaz.* 12 May 5/2 A common way of introducing it to the system is by the use of an unclean instrument.

*absol.* **1382** WYCLIF *Eccl.* xxxiv. 4 Of the vnclene what shal ben clensid?

†b. Of air or smells: Foul, impure. *Obs.*

*c* **1400** *Destr. Troy* 1639 The clowdes hom clede in vnclene ayre. *c* **1440** *Pallad. on Husb.* I. 35 Al this is preef of holsum aier and clene, And ther as is contrair is aier vnclene. *Ibid.* IV. 971 From bathes aliene, vnclene odure,..auyse Thee wel to been.

c. Of land: Foul with weeds, etc. *rare*$^{-1}$.

*c* **1440** *Pallad. on Husb.* II. 74 The lond vnclene al doluen up mot be, Of rootis, fern, & weed, to mak hit fre.

d. Of fish: In an unhealthy or unwholesome condition.

**1861** *Act* 24–5 *Vict.* c. 109 § 14 No Person shall..wilfully take any unclean or unseasonable Salmon. **1883** *Standard* 13 Jan. 3/6 Summoned for being in the possession of five unclean salmon.

**Unclea·nable**, *a.* (UN-$^1$ 7 b.) **1724** SWIFT *Blunders & Misfort. Quilca* Wks. 1841 II. 78/2 The empty bottles all uncleanable. **Unclea·ned**, *ppl. a.* (UN-$^1$ 8.) **1859** R. F. BURTON *Centr. Afr.* in *Jrnl. Geog. Soc.* XXIX. 437 The Americans exported the gum uncleaned, because the operation is better performed at Salem. **1902** *Munsey's Mag.* XXVI. 492/1 Should father find the tables and counter and windows uncleaned, my back would suffer.

**Unclea·nliness.** [f. next + -NESS. Cf. MDu. *onclein-, oncleenlijcheit.*]

1. Lack of moral cleanness; moral impurity.

**1509** BARCLAY *Shyp of Folys* (1570) 238 The newe disguises hath..come to Englande, and eche vnclenlynes Doth leade vs wretches. **1540** HYRDE tr. *Vives' Instr. Chr. Wom.* Pref. A iv b, I wolde not fall in to any vnclenlynes, which were the grettest shame that can be, for hym that shuld be a maister of chastitie. **1603** SHAKS. *Meas. for M.* II. i. 82 My wife.. might haue bin accus'd in fornication, adultery, and all vncleanlinesse there.

2. Want of physical cleanliness.

**1542** UDALL *Erasm. Apoph.* 142 b, Beeyng chidden, for yᵗ he was a gooer into places full of..vnclenelynesse. **1598** FLORIO, *Immonditia*, vnclenlines, filthines. **1722** *Lond. Gaz.* No. 6057/1 The Poverty and Uncleanliness of the Parents. **1802** MRS. SHERWOOD *Susan Gray* 18 However poor you may be, there can be no necessity for uncleanliness. **1859** R. F. BURTON *Centr. Afr.* in *Jrnl. Geog. Soc.* XXIX. 417 The village..is not only healthier,..despite its uncleanliness, but is also more comfortable. **1899** *Allbutt's Syst. Med.* VIII. 747 Personal uncleanliness is a powerful general cause [of Acnitis].

**Unclea·nly**, *a.* [OE. *unclǽnlic*: see UN-$^1$ 7 and CLEANLY *a.* Cf. MDu. *oncleinlijc, oncleenlijc* foul, dirty.]

1. Morally or spiritually impure.

*c* **950** *Rit. Eccl. Dunelm.* (Surtees) 110 *Contactus inlicitorum fugat*, cunnvnga þa vnclænlico ȝifliæ. **1340** *Ayenb.* 42 Ich clepie onclenlich: huanne þe seruises byeþ y-do uor onclenliche cause. **1526** TINDALE 2 *Pet.* ii. 7 Lot vexed with the unclenly conversacion off the wicked. **1548** UDALL, etc. *Erasm. Par. Acts* xii. 45 b, And princes on the other parte flatter the people, exhibitinge vnto them shewes to gase vpon, and vncleanly playes. **1598** TOFTE *Alba* Div. Poems (1880) 131 Soyled with beastly Thoughts vncleanly gore. **1604** SHAKS. *Oth.* III. iii. 139 Who ha's that breast so pure, Wherein vncleanly Apprehensions Keepe Leetes, and Law-dayes. **1710** ADDISON *Tatler* No. 224 ¶ 8, I cannot excuse my fellow-Labourers for admitting into their Papers several uncleanly Advertisements. **1788** V. KNOX *Winter Even.* li. (1790) II. 368 He pursues his subject so far, as frequently to lead his reader to uncleanly scenes. **1871** FARRAR *Witn. Hist.* iv. 138 Yet there was a needless and uncleanly abjectness in several of his precepts.

2. Lacking in physical cleanness; dirty, foul, filthy.

**1398** TREVISA *Barth. De P. R.* XVII. xi. (1495) 609 Men that must nedes passe by stynkyng places other vnclenly rotyn places. **1502** ARNOLDE *Chron.* 108 Item that many of the priestis and clerkis often were foule and unclenly surplesis. **1548** ELYOT, *Incultus*, vncleanly apparaylyng, contrary to *Cultus*; negligence in apparaylyng. **1595** SHAKS. *John* IV. iii. 112 Th' vncleanly sauours of a Slaughter-house. **1604** JAS. I. *Counterbl. to Tobacco* (Arb.) 100 The vncleanly and adust constitution of their bodies. **1670** CLARENDON *Ess.* Tracts (1727) 173 This uncomely and uncleanly wardrobe. **1756** C. LUCAS *Ess. Waters* III. 261 Who is there so uncleanly..as to wash his feet in the water used by another? **1805** *Med. Jrnl.* XIV. 340 The crouded and uncleanly parts of the town. **1849** ROCK *Ch. of Fathers* I. ii. 188 Long hair on a clergyman, besides being uncleanly, is quite against the canons of the Church. **1896** KIPLING *Seven Seas, The King* iii, By sleight of sword we may not win, But scuffle 'mid uncleanly smoke Of arquebus and culverin.

**Unclea·nly**, *adv.* [OE. *unclǽnlice*: see UN-$^1$ 11 and CLEANLY *adv.*] In an unclean manner; foully, filthily.

*c* **1000** ÆLFRIC *Hom.* I. 432 We wilniað mid urum hlaforde clænlice sweltan, swiðor ðonne unclænlice mid eow lybban. **1583** BABINGTON *Commandm.* (1590) 178 Wee walke and talke idlely, vainly, vncleanly, and vngodlily. **1584** COGAN *Haven Health* 262 Much people in small roume, liuing vncleanly and sluttishly. **1611** COTGR., *Impurement*, impurely, foulely, filthily, vncleanely. **1621** BURTON *Anat. Mel.* I. ii. II. v. (1651) 83 The inhabitants are slovens, and the streets uncleanly kept. **1727** BAILEY (vol. II), *Uncleanly*, filthily.

**Unclea·nness.** [OE. *unclǽnnes*, f. *unclǽne* UNCLEAN *a.* Cf. CLEANNESS.]

1. The quality or state of being morally or spiritually unclean; moral impurity; an instance of this.

*c* **897** K. ÆLFRED *Gregory's Past. C.* xiii. 75 Se reccere sceal bion simle clæne on his ȝeðohte, ðætte nan unclænnes hine ne besmite. *c* **1000** *Ags. Gosp.* Matt. xxiii. 25 Ȝe synt innan fulle reaflaces and unclænnysse. *a* **1100** in Napier *O. E. Glosses* I. 4225 *Lasciviæ obscenitatis*, wrænre unclænnysse. *c* **1200** ORMIN 2168 Swa summ þatt laþe maȝȝdenn iss þat sekeþþ unnclænnesse. **1297** R. GLOUC. (Rolls) 8949 Vor me ne miȝte hire neuere ise vnclannesse [*v.r.* vnclennysse] do ene. **1340** *Ayenb.* 203 Uoule wordes þet wendeþ to ribaudye and to onclennesse. **1382** WYCLIF 2 *Pet.* ii. 20 Men forsakinge the defoulinges, or vnclennesses, of the world. **1411–2** HOCCLEVE *De Reg. Princ.* 3724 Natheles eschued he þe taast

Of vnclennesse, and kepte his body chaast. *c* 1450 CAPGRAVE *Life St. Aug.* xxiv. 33 Sche defouled neuer hir lippis with no vnclennesse. 1526 *Pilgr. Perf.* (W. de W. 1531) 90 b, Scurrilite or spekynge of fylthy wordes, vnclennes, moche speche or many wordes. 1577 HOLINSHED *Chron.* II. 340/2 Diuers of those .. myghte haply fall into moste horrible vncleannesse. 1611 BIBLE *Ezek.* xxxvi. 29, I wil also saue you from all your vncleannesses. 1643 MILTON *Divorce* 16 Let him not put her away for the meer surmise of Judaicall uncleannes. 1714 BERKELEY *Serm.* Wks. 1871 IV. 606 Their Sacred Rites were polluted with acts of uncleanness and debauchery. 1748 SMOLLETT *R. Random* vii, There being no scandal equal to that of uncleanness. 1865 C. J. VAUGHAN *Plain Words* iv. (1866) 70 Still is the living fountain open for all sin and all uncleanness.

**2.** Physical impurity; filthiness, foulness; squalor.

*c* 950 *Rit. Eccl. Dunelm.* (Surtees) 121 Svæ hvæd in hvsvm .. þas yð eft astrægde beværle vnclænnisse [L. *careat immunditia*]. *a* 1100 in Napier *O. E. Glosses* I. 4455 *Olidos squalores*, fule unclænnessa. 1390 GOWER *Conf.* III. 100 The Splen doth him to lawhe and pleie, Whan al unclennesse is aweie. 1487 *Rolls of Parlt.* VI. 391/1 To great hurt and disease of the Kyngs Leige People .. goyng .. in the said Stretis and Suburbes, and also grete unclenness of the same. 1534 *Act 26 Hen. VIII*, c. 8 Vacant groundes .. replenisshed with muche vncleanes & filth to the great annusance of the said inhabitantes. 1598 GRENEWEY *Tacitus, Ann.* XII. xi. (1622) 172 The horse-men .. were put to flight .. by reason of the difficulties and vncleannesse of the place. 1663 COWLEY *Ess. in Verse & Pr.* viii, Yet the very sight of Uncleanness is loathsome to the Cleanly.

**Unclea·nsable**, *a.* *rare*⁻⁰. (UN-¹ 7 b.)

1483 *Cath. Angl.* 66/1 Vn Clenceabylle, *inexpiabilis, inpurgabilis*.

**Unclea·nse**, *v.* [UN-² 3; cf. OE. *unclǣnsian*.] *trans.* To make (or declare) unclean.

1585 T. WASHINGTON tr. *Nicholay's Voy.* IV. ii. 115 No drop of the bloud should fall into the water, least the same shuld therby be polluted and vncleansed. 1872 J. G. MURPHY *Comm., Lev.* xiv. 7 As the priest uncleanses, that is, pronounces unclean, the leper.

**Unclea·nsed**, *ppl. a.* [UN-¹ 8.] Not cleansed or made clean.

*c* 897 K. ÆLFRED *Gregory's Past C.* vii. 51 Ðylæs ænig unclænsod dorste on swa micelne haliȝdom fon ðære clænan ðeȝnenga ðæs sacerdhades. *c* 1200 ORMIN 10617 Þatt all follc wass unnclennsedd Off þatt missdede þatt wass don Þurrh Adam & þurrh Eve. 1439 *Rolls Parlt.* V. 32/1 Eny such Espiceries ungarbeled and unclensyd. 1467 in *Eng. Gilds* (1870) 385 That no blode putte be vnclensyd ouer a day and a night. 1549 COVERDALE, etc. *Erasm. Par. 1 Cor.* xi. 32 b, He without reuerence, and with an vnclensed conscience presumed to come vnto so great a misterie. 1555 EDEN *Decades* (Arb.) 268 It is sould vnclensed or vnpurged. 1632 SHERWOOD, Uncleansed, *non nettoyé*. 1821 SCOTT *Kenilw.* xxxi, We forgive your audacity, and your uncleansed boots withal. 1886 *Encycl. Brit.* XXI. 712/1 The imperfectly cleansed sewage and the wholly uncleansed surplus.

Hence **Unclea·nsedness.**

1622 W. WHATELY *God's Husb.* II. 122 You would not suffer your selfe-loue to hinder you from taking notice of your vncleansednesse.

**Unclea·r**, *a.* [UN-¹ 7. Cf. WFris. *ûn-, onklear* (at variance), MDu. *onclaer* (*oncleer*), Du. *onklaar*, MLG. *unklâr*, G. *unklar*, ON. *úklárr* (Norw. *uklaar*, Da. *uklar*, Sw. *oklar*).]

**1.** Not clear or distinct; not easy to understand; obscure, dark.

13.. *E. E. Allit. P.* C. 307, I calde & þou knew myn vncler steuen. *?a* 1500 *Chester Pl.* XVI. 279 But my might in this manere Will I not proue, .. my cause unclear Were then, in good fay. *a* 1513 FABYAN *Chron.* 2 Ryght mysty storyes, doughtfull and vnclere. 1611 TOURNEUR *Ath. Trag.* IV. iii, The time, the place, All circumstances argue that unclear. 1678 SIR G. MACKENZIE *Crim. Laws Scot.* II. xxix. § ii. (1699) 277 It were very hard upon testimonies, that have so unclear a *causa scientiæ*.., to take a way a mans life. 1798 *Monthly Mag.* VI. 99 The mythological allusions in the 10th, 11th and 12th verses are unclear. 1828 PUSEY *Hist. Eng.* I. p. xiv, To fix the stamp of misconception upon every thing else which is unclear in the work. 1884 LD. COLERIDGE in *Law Times Rep.* L. 297/2 That these otherwise clear and plain words are made doubtful and unclear by the 3rd clause of this section.

**b.** Not clear in understanding, perception, or statement; confused.

*c* 1430 LYDG. *Min. Poems* (Percy Soc.) 27 A philosophre .. Had a frend that somwhat was aged, In suche tymes as wyttes wex uncler. 1734 LD. HERVEY *Mem. Geo. II* (1848) I. 324 From having a most unclear head .. he was absolutely useless to his brother. 1828 PUSEY *Hist. Eng.* I. 142 The unsystematic and unclear mind of his disciple. 1885 *Century Mag.* XXXI. 276 So unclear in their statements that we can make nothing of them.

**c.** Of persons: Uncertain, doubtful (about something).

1671 [R. MACWARD] *True Nonconf.* 172 If you be still unclear, answere this demand with your self in sobriety. 1715 WODROW *Corr.* (1843) II. 94 The whole brethren present seemed very unclear as to the abjuration. 1886 SIR J. PAGET *Lett.* 7 Aug. in *Mem.* vi. 362, I am unclear as to their [*sc.* certain patients'] names.

**2.** Not clear of, not free from, fault or blame.

*a* 1400 *Pistill of Susan* 306 Nou schal þi concience be knowen, þat euer was vnclere. 1426 AUDELAY *Poems* 13 Thai are the lanternys of lyf .. Bot thai be caȝt with covetyse with conscions unclere. 1607 TOURNEUR *Rev. Trag.* II. D iv b, I haue great sins; I must haue daies .. To lift 'em out, and not to die vncleere.

**3.** Not clear or bright; dark, thick.

*c* 1400 *Anturs of Arth.* x, Al glowed as a glede þe goste þere ho glides, Vmbeclipped him with a cloude, of cle[th]yng vnclere. 1527 ANDREW *Brunswyke's Distyll. Waters* B ij, Lyquor or sape, which ye wyl puryfye from all trowblious and unclere substaunces. 1535 COVERDALE *Esther* xi. 8 Ye same daye was full of darcknes & very vncleare, full of trouble & anguysh. 1594 CAREW *Tasso* (1881) 80 Sometimes the Sun shines through white cloud vncleere.

*fig.* *c* 1440 CAPGRAVE *Life St. Kath.* v. 1207 Fro al onclennesse Of lust and filthe, and fro that loue on-clere Whiche þei calle letcherie. 1639 G. DANIEL *Ecclus.* xvii. 80 Those Horrid Crimes of Mortalls Shall appeare Vgly and Monstrous, vile, deform'd, vncleare.

**Unclea·red**, *ppl. a.* [UN-¹ 8.]

**1.** Not cleared off or settled; undischarged.

1637 RUTHERFORD *Lett.* (1664) 132 When he & I fall in reckoning, we are both behinde, .. & so marches lie still unrid & counts uncleared betwixt us. 172. RAMSAY *Evergreen* Gloss., *Unquit*, uncleared or unpaid.

**2.** Not cleared or freed from something which encumbers; *esp.* not cleared of trees.

1772 COOK *Voy.* I. v. (1773) 60 There was neither gnat nor musquito, .. which perhaps is more than can be said of any other uncleared country. 1805 R. W. DICKSON *Pract. Agric.* I. 391 The water .. is conveyed in a rut perpetually descending along the whole line of the uncleared moss. 1822 J. FLINT *Lett. Amer.* 239 In the uncleared woods, which are not suitable pastures for sheep. 1829 TYTLER *Hist. Scot.* (1864) I. 234 Savage animals abounded as much in Scotland as in the other uncleared and wooded regions of northern Europe. 1880 J. C. CRAWFORD *N. Zealand & Australia* 27 The whole distance traversed .. was through dense and uncleared forest.

**3.** Not freed from the imputation of guilt.

1724 SAVAGE *Sir T. Overbury* IV. i. 35 To fly, wou'd be, to leave my Fame unclear'd. 1903 *Westm. Gaz.* 26 Jan. 8/2 Were the Crown to .. release the prisoner, he would for ever remain an 'uncleared' man.

**4.** Not cleared *up*; not removed or explained.

1802-12 BENTHAM *Ration. Judic. Evid.* (1827) II. 405 A repugnancy, which, for want of cross-examination, remains uncleared up. 1861 [F. W. ROBINSON] *Under the Spell* III. 237 That would necessitate another long night of suspense, with doubts 'uncleared'.

**5.** Not freed from impurities; not made clear or transparent.

1837 M. DONOVAN *Dom. Econ.* II. 343 It appears to me that uncleared coffee has a less agreeable taste than the same quality if transparent.

**Unclea·rly**, *adv.* (UN-¹ 11.)

1844 DARWIN in *Life & Lett.* (1887) II. 29 If I had seen how hypothetical [is] the little, which I have unclearly written, I would not [etc.]. 1875 WHITNEY *Life Lang.* xv. 317 The germs of all the most important modern doctrines, .. but unclearly apprehended.

**Unclea·rness.** [f. UNCLEAR *a.*] Lack of clearness; obscurity.

*a* 1658 DURHAM *Comm. Rev.* xvii. (1660) 665 From this unclearnesse it ariseth, that it is hotly disputed. *a* 1718 PENN *Tracts* Wks. 1726 I. 748 The Voluminousness of the Books is no small Token of the Unclearness of the Writers. 1811-31 BENTHAM *Logic* Wks. 1843 VIII. 242/2 Where unclearness (why not unclearness as well as uncleanness) has place in a discourse. 1842 PUSEY *Crisis Eng. Ch.* 51 It is no disrespect to speak of the unclearness or narrowness of a system. 1881 W. R. SMITH *Old Test. in Jew. Ch.* v. 29 This unclearness of view rests upon an error.

**Unclea·vable**, *a.* (UN-¹ 7 b.) 1839 URE *Dict. Arts*, etc. 744 Opal, or uncleavable quartz. 1855 *Orr's Circ. Sci., Geol.*, etc. 514 Uncleavable Staphyline Malachite.

**Unclea·ve**, *v.* [UN-² 7.] *intr.* To become unfastened or detached. So **Unclea·ving** *vbl. sb.*

1596 THOMAS *Dict.* (1606), *Deglutinatio*, an vncleauing or vngluing. 1648 GAGE *West Ind.* xii. 45 Which did glew so strong, that it scarce ever uncleaved again.

**Unclea·ved**, *ppl. a.* (UN-¹ 8.) 1882 GEIKIE *Text-bk. Geol.* IV. vi. 522 Fragments of cleaved rocks in an uncleaved conglomerate.

**Uncle·ft**, *ppl. a.* (UN-¹ 8 b. Cf. Du. *ongekliefd*.)

1611 COTGR., *Bois de brin*, round, or vncleft-small-wood. 1647 HEXHAM I, Vncleft, *ongedeylt*. [Also in later Dicts.]

† **Uncle·ment**, *a.* *Obs.* [UN-¹ 7 and 5 b.] = INCLEMENT *a.*

1598 FLORIO, *Incleménte*, .. mercilesse, sterne, fell, vnclement. 1611 COTGR., *Inclement*, vnclement; rigorous, austere. 1751 YOUNG *Nt. Th.* III. 80 Those few [buds which] our noxious fate unblasted leaves, In this unclement [1742 inclement] clime of human life.

**Uncle·nch**, *v.* [UN-² 3. Cf. UNCLINCH *v.*]

**1.** *trans.* To undo the clenching of (bars, etc.).

1340-70 *Alisaunder* 1172 Hee unclosed þe caue, unclainte þe barres. 1775 ASH, *Unclench*, .. to raise the point of a bended nail. 1825 [see UNCLENCHING *vbl. sb.*].

**2.** To relax or open (the clenched hand, a grip or clutch, etc.).

[1775 ASH.] 1816 *Monthly Mag.* XLI. 143 Nor dares unclench the hand of her relief. 1868 BROWNING *Ring & Bk.* x. 600 Revenge .. would pluck pang forth, but unclench No gripe in the act, let fall no money-piece. 1888 'J. S. WINTER' *Bootle's Childr.* vii, So he stood there clenching and unclenching his hands, .. the very picture of misery.

*fig.* 1839 BAILEY *Festus, L'Envoi* 361 God was with him; and bade old Time, to the youth, Unclench his heart.

**b.** To cause to relax; to force open.

1793 *Minstrel* III. 70, I flew on the wretch who held him, unclenched his grasping hand from the throat of my darling. 1841 DICKENS *Barn. Rudge* lxxi, 'We have time for no more of this,' cried the man, unclenching her hands, and throwing her roughly off. 1888 G. E. POST in *Centen. Conf. Missions* I. 323 A grasp of iron which the crusaders could not unclench.

**c.** *refl.* and *absol.* Of the hand: To relax from a clenched state.

[1755 JOHNSON.] 1900 *Daily News* 11 Oct. 3/1 The nervous hand, clenching and unclenching as his passions swayed him. 1901 MRS. E. L. VOYNICH *Jack Raymond* 87 He let his hand fall by his side, and unclench itself slowly.

**3.** *trans.* To loosen from a grasp or hold.

1860 FARRAR *Orig. Lang.* (1865) 2 Her lessons .. have been unclenched by sheer labour from the granite hand of nature. 1871 R. ELLIS *Catullus* xxv. 9 Unglue the nails adroit to steal, unclench the spoil.

Hence **Uncle·nching** *vbl. sb.*

[1775 ASH.] 1825 SCOTT *Betrothed* Concl., Hasten thy unclenching and undoing of rivets.

**Uncle·rgiable**, *a.* (UN-¹ 7 b.) 1802-12 BENTHAM *Ration. Judic. Evid.* (1827) III. 556 In the penal branch, in cases of felony unclergyable and clergyable. 1819 MACDONALD in *Rep. fr. Comm., Crim. Laws* VIII. 49 The Black Act is full of unclergyable felonies.

**Uncle·rgy**, *v.* *rare*⁻¹. (UN-² 6 b.)

1695 HICKERINGILL *Lay-Clergy* Wks. 1716 I. 348 Till Holy Church was pleased to Depose, Disrobe, and unclergy the Traytor or Murderer.

**Uncle·rical**, *a.* [UN-¹ 7.] Not appropriate to, or characteristic of, the clergy or a clergyman.

1762 FOOTE *Orator* I. Wks. 1799 I. 201 Many individuals .. are obliged to have recourse to very unclerical professions for the support of themselves and families. 1788 V. KNOX *Winter Even.* (1790) II. xiii. 88, I have no doubt but that it is one reason why many clergymen are seen to take delight in unclerical occupations. 1848 THACKERAY *Van. Fair* xxxiv, I am a martyr to duty and to your odious unclerical habit of hunting. 1865 MRS. WHITNEY *Gayworthys* ii, A very unclerical gesture of—to say the least—impatience.

Hence **Uncle·rically** *adv.*

1883 *Harper's Mag.* June 5/2 The .. canons unclerically .. fell upon him.

**Uncle·rklike**, *a.* (UN-¹ 7 c.)

1647 JER. TAYLOR *Lib. Proph.* vi. 118 Such an emendation as is a plain contradiction to the sense, and that so un-clerklike.

**Uncle·rkly**, *a.* (UN-¹ 7.) 1875 BLACKMORE *Alice Lorraine* II. i. 4 This unclerkly clerk had a good supper. 1895 *Athenæum* 4 May 567/2 The manuscript .. was a very unclerkly one. **Uncle·rkly**, *adv.* (UN-¹ 11.) 1531 S. VAUGHAN in Ellis *Orig. Lett.* Ser. III. II. 208 You wrot that the answer whiche he made to the Chancellour was unclerkly done.

**U·ncleship.** [f. UNCLE *sb.* + -SHIP.] The state or condition of being an uncle; the relationship of an uncle.

1742 RICHARDSON *Pamela* IV. 410 Must you, my Lord, .. add to my Plagues, if I have any? Is this your Uncleship? 1826 LAMB *Elia* II. *Wedding*, I feel a sort of cousinhood, or uncleship, for the season. 1827 SOUTHEY *Lett.* (1856) IV. 51 And how, Mr. Bedford, do you feel yourself under the honours of uncleship? 1881 *Athenæum* 24 Dec. 844/1 She was a niece of that unlucky General .. whose uncleship bribed Southey into omitting a sentence in his 'Peninsular War'.

**Uncle·ver**, *a.* (UN-¹ 7.)

Also, in recent use, *uncleverly*, *uncleverness*.

[1775 ASH.] 1870 *Daily News* 23 Dec., Those garments .. which her lazy or unclever fingers do not care to preserve tidy. 1890 SARA J. DUNCAN *Social Depart.* 112 We felt most clumsy and bungling and unclever.

**Unclew·**, **unclue·**, *v.* [UN-² 3.]

**1.** *trans.* To unwind, undo; *fig.* to ruin.

1607 SHAKS. *Timon* I. i. 167 If I should pay you for't as 'tis extold, It would vnclew me quite. *c* 1645 HOWELL *Lett.* IV. Ded., They [*sc.* letters] can the Cabinets of Kings unscrue, And hardest intricacies of State unclue. 1654 E. JOHNSON *Wonder-wrkg. Provid.* 221 With watry tears unclued we will be, From creature-comforts. 1855 SINGLETON *Virgil* II. 72 Dædalus himself The cheats and windings of the dome unclewed.

*refl.* 1622 MABBE tr. *Aleman's Guzman d'Alf.* I. (To Vulgar), Who is he, that can be so happy, as to vnclue himselfe from this Labyrinth?

**2.** To let down the clews or lower ends of (a sail).

1855 SINGLETON *Virgil* I. 384 Take your seats upon the banks; Unclew the sails with speed. 1899 *Atlantic Monthly* Aug. 197 The sailboat .. lay alongside the wooden pier, with ballast stowed amidships and her mutton-ham unclewed.

**U·nclify**, *v.* [f. UNCLE *sb.*] *trans.* To make an uncle of.

1799 LAMB *Let. to Southey* 21 Jan., Did Lord Falkland die before Worcester fight? In that case I must make bold to unclify some other nobleman.

**Uncli·mbable**, *a.* (UN-¹ 7 b.)

In frequent use from *c* 1880.

1533 BELLENDEN *Livy* v. xv. (S. T. S.) II. 199 At þe fute of þe montanis, quhilkis stude sa hie aganis him þat þai apperit vnclymabil. 1827 *Lincoln & Lincolnshire Cabinet* 9 The almost unclim[b]able street which, as before stated, runs directly up the hill. 1892 RIDER HAGGARD *Nada the Lily* 211 It was of no great height, and yet unclimbable, for .. the sides of it were sheer.

**Uncli·mbed**, *ppl. a.* (UN-¹ 8.)

[1775 ASH.] 1800 *Monthly Mag.* X. 426 When on mountains unclimb'd encamps tremendous a nigh storm. 1856 MASSON *Ess., Shaks. & Goethe* 24 Like a universal ivy, which has left no wall uncovered, no pinnacle unclimbed.

**Uncli·nch**, *v.* [UN-² 3.] *trans.* = UNCLENCH *v.* Hence **Uncli·nching** *vbl. sb.*

1598 FLORIO, *Sbrancare*, .. to rid or free from any pawes or clawes, to vnclinch. 1688 R. L'ESTRANGE *Brief Hist. Times* III. 158 When the Word was once pass'd, and the Charge Rivetted to Somerset-House, there was No Recalling, No Unclinching of it. 1699 GARTH *Dispens.* v. 66 The Hero thus his Enterprise recalls, His Fist unclinches, and the Weapon falls. 1720 *Humourist* 25 The Miser, when Love has once warm'd his Heart, unclinches both his Fists, and throws away his Money in Handfuls. 1752 YOUNG *Brothers* IV. i, Unclinch thy talons from thy prey. 1887 RIDER HAGGARD *Jess* ii, Clinching and unclinching his great hand.

**Uncli·nched**, *ppl. a.* (UN-¹ 8.) 1877 MORLEY *Crit. Misc.* Ser. II. 287 We may think the reasoning .. halt of foot; we may discern arguments unclinched.

**Uncli·ng**, *v.* [UN-² 7 and 3.]

**1.** *intr.* To loosen hold.

1645 MILTON *Tetrach.* 11 A canonicall infection liver-grown to their sides; which perhaps will never uncling, without the strong abstersive of som heroick magistrat. 1710 J. NORRIS *Chr. Prud.* viii. 358 When even this cleaving Folly..shall uncling and drop from us.

**2.** *trans.* To unclasp; to loosen from clinging.

*a* 1711 KEN *Preparatives* Poet. Wks. 1721 IV. 34, I have got the Wing, You without Fear your Fingers may uncling. 1750 G. HUGHES *Barbados* 305 It is found to be a difficult task for a very able man to uncling one of them from the rocks.

**Unclip,** *v. rare*⁻¹. [UN-² 3.] *trans.* To unclasp.

1598 MARSTON *Sco. Villanie* I. (1599) 171 Daphne, vnclip thine armes from my sad brow.

**Uncli·pped, -cli·pt,** *ppl. a.* [UN-¹ 8. Cf. Da. *uklippet*, Sw. *oklippt*.] Not clipped or cut: **a.** Of hair, wings, etc., or with reference to these.

1388 WYCLIF 2 *Sam.* xix. 24 Myphibosech..cam doun.. with berd vnclippid, in to the comyng of the kyng. 1483 *Cath. Angl.* 67 (Vn) Clippyd, *intonsus.* 1573 TUSSER *Husb.* (1878) 118 Let lambes go vnclipped, till June be halfe worne. 1586 FERNE *Blaz. Gentrie* 20 Hath your Eagle her wings vnclipped? 1658 *Melrose Regality Rec.* (S. H. S.) I. 193 He ought therefore to deliver the ewes with their lambs, unclipped. 1878 BROWNING *Poets Croisic* 101 Grant A fledgeling novice that with wing unclipt She soar her little circuit.

**b.** Of money.

1691 LOCKE *Consid. Money* Wks. 1714 II. 45 Clip'd and unclip'd money will always buy an equal quantity of any thing else. 1696 DE LA PRYME *Diary* (Surtees) 98, I have seen unclip'd half crowns that has weigh'd down fifteen shillings clipt. 1823 BYRON *Juan* XII. xii, Ingots, bags of dollars, coins (Not of old victors,..But) of fine unclipt gold.

†**Uncli·psed,** *ppl. a. Obs.*⁻¹ [UN-¹ 8.] Not eclipsed.

*c* 1485 *Digby Myst.* (1882) III. 1349 O, þe on-clypsyd sonne, tempyll of salamon!

**Uncli·t,** *v.* [UN-² 3: cf. CLITCH *v.*] *trans.* To unfasten.

1587 M. GROVE *Pelops & Hipp.* (1878) 91 My lady cals it follie plaine, With toong such hardned knot to knit, As all the teeth with helpe of braine, Shall ne be able to vnclit.

**Uncloa·k,** *v.* [UN-² 4.]

**1.** *trans.* To divest of, free from, a cloak. Chiefly *refl.* Also *absol.*

1598 FLORIO, *Smantellare*, to vnmantle, to vncloke. 1775 ASH, *Uncloak*.., to take off a cloak, to free from the incumberance of a cloak. 1816 SCOTT *Old Mort.* iii, The young plebian,..as he took his stand, half-uncloaked his rustic countenance. 1826 — *Woodst.* xxx, A bustle occurred in receiving the General, assisting him to uncloak himself. 1845 FORD *Handbk. Spain* I. 146 All men give the wall to her, many uncloak themselves. *Ibid.* 201 Spaniards always uncloak when..the host or the king passes by.

**2.** *fig.* To expose, lay bare, reveal.

1659 *Gentl. Calling* (1696) 124 Will none have so much Charity, so much Zeal for publick Concern, as to uncloak this Impostor? *a* 1847 ELIZA COOK *Poems, He that is without Sin* ii, The herd, Whose dark and evil works are all uncloaked. 1877 MRS. OLIPHANT *Makers Flor.* xii. 302 The price of uncloaking the false pretensions of the..priest.

Hence **Uncloa·king** *vbl. sb.* Also *attrib.*

[1775 ASH.] 1845 FORD *Handbk. Spain* xviii. 249 Uncloaking in Spain is..a mark of respect, and is equivalent to our taking off the hat. 1877 MRS. FORRESTER *Mignon* II. 56 Kitty is awaiting her friend..in the uncloaking room.

**Uncloa·ked,** *ppl. a.* [UN-¹ 8.] Not provided with, or covered by, a cloak. Also *fig.* and *absol.*

1540 MORYSINE *Vives' Introd. Wysd.* K iij, It is better, that all thinges be open, playne, uncloked, and symple. 1839 LEVER *Lorreq.* v. 34 It being now settled to my satisfaction, that Mr. Beamish and the great uncloaked were 'convertible terms'. 1862 J. SPENCE *Amer.* 164 It must stand out unshielded, uncloaked, in the light of open day.

**Unclo·g,** *v.*¹ [UN-² 4 b.] *trans.* To free from a clog, hindrance, or encumbrance.

1607 SHAKS. *Cor.* IV. ii. 47 Could I meete 'em But once a day, it would vnclogge my heart of what lyes heauy too't. 1678 G. G. in H. Scougal *Wks.* (1735) 304 Such ardent sighs, and groanings,..as perhaps unclog'd his spirit, and made his soul take its flight, so soon. 1766 MRS. S. PENNINGTON *Lett.* III. 172 Soft magic welcome, welcome angel dream, Unclog me quick, and let me far expand. 1834 HT. MARTINEAU *Moral* III. 119 Which must..unclog the system of manufactures and commerce. 1886 LESTER *Under Fig Trees* 161 You can't be stooping down for ever to unclog your machine.

**Unclo·g,** *v.*² [UN-² 4.] *trans.* To divest of clogs or pattens.

1828 [see UNBONNET *v.*²].

**Unclo·gged,** *ppl. a.* [UN-¹ 8.] Not clogged or hampered.

1563 FOXE *A. & M.* 1046/2 That we may liue and kepe our consciences vnclogged. 1654 WHITLOCK *Zootomia* 345 Ranging Licentiousnesse, which such Satyrists call Liberty, and unclogged Freedome. *a* 1721 SHEFFIELD (Dk. Buckhm.) *Wks.* (1753) I. 312 Our minds unclogg'd with farther care, Except to overcome or die. 1742 RICHARDSON *Pamela* III. 356 The Wheels of Nature being unclogg'd, new-oiled, as it were, and set right. 1839 DE LA BECHE *Rep. Geol. Cornwall*, etc. iv. 101 Thus leaving the subject unclogged by this kind of entanglement.

**Uncloi·ster,** *v.* [UN-² 5.] *trans.* To turn out of, remove from, a cloister; to set free, liberate.

1611 FLORIO, *Dischiostrare*, to vncloister. 1687 NORRIS *Paraphr. 3rd Chap. Job* vi, Why did I not uncloister'd from the Womb Take my next lodging in a Tomb? 1795 tr. *Mercier's Fragm. Pol. & Hist.* II. 424 These..burnt the archives, and uncloistered the monks and nuns. 1856 *N. Brit. Rev.* XXVI. 276 The monks and friars were uncloistered.

Hence **Uncloi·stered** *ppl. a.*¹

1627 P. FLETCHER *Locusts* IV. x, Can that uncloist'red Frier with those light armes..Wake all the sleeping world? 1853 CDL. WISEMAN *Ess.* iii. 97 He was brother to the patron and was..an uncloistered friar.

**Uncloi·stered,** *ppl. a.*² [UN-¹ 8.] Not shut up in a cloister; not organized as a cloister.

1652 BENLOWES *Theoph.* XII. xxxiii, Uncloystred, we this course beyond Courts splendor love. 1859 SALA *Tw. round Clock* (1861) 115 These *preux chevalières* of womanhood, these uncloistered nuns. 1902 MRS. TOUT in *Owens Coll. Hist. Ess.* 51 This order arose in an uncloistered institute for the Christian education of young girls.

*transf.* 1874 RUSKIN *Val D'Arno* ii. § 35 If you..return to the uncloistered sunlight of the piazza.

**Unclo·sable,** *a.* (UN-¹ 7 b.)

1820 L. HUNT *Indicator* No. 14, Another..shall find his eyes as uncloseable as a statue's. 1866 NEALE *Sequences & Hymns* 139 Who are these that next the unclosable portals.. Gather in one.

**Unclo·se,** *a.* Now *rare.* [UN-¹ 7.] **a.** Not closed; open. **b.** Unreserved. **c.** Not intimate; distant.

*c* 1400 *Destr. Troy* 4688 The Grekes..Comyn to the castell, (vnclose were the yatis). 1605 SYLVESTER *Du Bartas* II. iii. *Captains* 1075 Known Designs are dangerous to act: And th' vnclose Chief did never noble fact. 1651 *Buchanan's Detection Mary Q. Scots* 59 A house..not [only]..unclose, but [even] open to pass through. 1659 A. HAY *Diary* (S.H.S.) 227 Notwithstanding my unclose walking, yet the Lord had been very kind to me.

**Unclo·se,** *v.* [UN-² 3 and 7.]

**1.** *trans.* To make open; to cause to open.

13.. *E. E. Allit. P.* B. 1438 He with keyes vn-closes kystes ful mony. *c* 1430 LYDG. *Min. Poems* (Percy Soc.) 23 Aurora, ageyne the morowe gray, Causith the daysy hir croune to unclose. 1530 PALSGR. 766/2 These letters shall nat be unclosed for me, I wot nat from whence they come. 1555 EDEN *Decades* (Arb.) 101 They vnclose and shake theyr handes. *c* 1586 C'TESS PEMBROKE *Ps.* (1823) LXXVIII. x, He unclos'd the garners of the skies. 1700 DRYDEN *Cymon & Iph.* 177 At length awaking, Iphigene the fair..Unclos'd her eyes. 1761 GRAY *Descent Odin* 49 Unwilling I my lips unclose. 1794 MRS. RADCLIFFE *Myst. Udolpho* viii, She unclosed the casement to listen to the strains of the music. 1827 SCOTT *Surg. Dau.* ix, Surely the demons of Ambition and Avarice will unclose the talons which they have fixed upon this man. 1852 MRS. STOWE *Uncle Tom's C.* ix, The woman slowly unclosed her large dark eyes, and looked vacantly at her.

*absol.* 1426 LYDG. *De Guil. Pilgr.* 20333 Yiff they hadde commyssioun..Bothe to shette and ek vnclose.

**b.** *fig.* To disclose, make known, reveal.

13.. *E. E. Allit. P.* B. 26 Me mynez on one amonge oþer, as maþew recordez, Þat þus of clannesse vn-closez a ful cler speche. 1426 LYDG. *De Guil. Pilgr.* 2760 How sore aforn that they yt close, ye muste hem make yt to vnclose By trewe reuelacyon. 1446 — *Two Nightingale P.* ii. 51 The briddes song I shal to the vnclose. 1877 MRS. OLIPHANT *Makers Flor.* viii. 212 He..uncloses the treasures of that celestial wisdom which speaks to men.

†**c.** To detach, unharness. *Obs.*⁻¹

1615 CHAPMAN *Odyss.* IV. 32 Inform your pleasure, if we shall unclose Their horse from coach.

**2.** *intr.* To become open.

*c* 1385 CHAUCER *L. G. W.* Prol. 65 Hire [the daisy's] chere is pleynly sprad in the brightnesse Of the sonne for ther yt wol vnclose. *c* 1400 *Destr. Troy* 807 In hor mouthe caste [it], And þai clappe shall full clene, & neuer vnclose aftur. *c* 1440 *Pallad. on Husb.* VI. 218 Take roses that bigynneth forto vnclose. 1725 POPE *Odyss.* XVIII. 235 Wak'd at their steps, her flowing eyes unclose. *a* 1785 GLOVER *Athenaid* XXVII, Now they reach The further mouth unclosing in a dale Abrupt. 1808 HELEN ST. VICTOR *Ruins of Rigonda* II. 94 She perceived her curtains unclose, and the form of her mother leaning over her. 1880 'OUIDA' *Moths* I. 54 She heard the door underneath unclose.

†**3.** *trans.* To hatch. *Obs.* (Cf. DISCLOSE *v.* 3 b.)

1486 *Bk. St. Albans, Hawking* a ij, And when they [*sc.* hawks] bene unclosed and begynneth to feder any thyng of lengthe anoon be kynde they will draw somwatt out of the nest. 1581 MARBECK *Bk. of Notes* 325 Of Eagles it maie be taken, that their young ones doe sucke bloud anone after they be unclosed.

Hence **Unclo·sing** *vbl. sb.*

1705 STEVENS II. s.v., An Unclosing of that which was shut, *abertura.* 1840 POE *W. Wilson* Wks. 1864 I. 428 The violent, although partial unclosing of the door. 1874 *Contemp. Rev.* Oct. 690 The unclosing of the potential parts of a plant in its development from a germ.

**Unclo·sed,** *ppl. a.* [UN-¹ 8.]

**1.** Not enclosed or shut in; unenclosed.

*c* 1400 *Rom. Rose* 3921, I wole with siker walle Close bothe roses and roser. I have to longe..Left hem unclosid wilfully. 1426 LYDG. *De Guil. Pilgr.* 3208 Thogh thow sest hem bothe the two Ber swerd And keyes in ther hond Naked & vnclosyd. 1523 LD. BERNERS *Froiss.* I. ccccxxx. 306 And a thre leages in yᵉ way there stode the towne of Mardyke, a great vyllage on the see syde vnclosed. 1543 *Act* 35 *Hen. VIII*, c. 17 § 2 Every Month that the same Coppice.. shall..be unclosed, not fenced, saved or preserved.

**2.** Not closed; open.

*c* 1450 *Merlin* xxix. 597 Than thei..be-helde towarde the see where thei saugh the cristin a litill vn-closed. *c* 1470 *Gol. & Gaw.* 60 The berne bovnit to the burgh with ane blith cheir, Fand the yettis vnclosit, and thrang in full thra. 1563 SHUTE *Archit.* C iij, The other side is lefte vnclosed. 1790 COLERIDGE *Inside the Coach* 2 'Tis hard on Bagshot Heath to try Unclosed to keep the weary eye. 1827 SCOTT *Highl. Widow* iv, Night by night..she removed from her unclosed door to throw herself on her restless pallet. 1888 HON. MORTEN *Sk. Hospital Life* 35 If a man ..has the smallest unclosed wound on his body.

**b.** *transf.* Of an account. (See CLOSE *v.* 8.)

1723 STEELE *Consc. Lovers* IV. i. 63, I don't love to leave any part of the Account unclos'd.

**3.** Not joined so as to enclose a space. (Cf. CLOSE *v.* 11.)

1551 RECORDE *Pathw. Knowl.* I. Defin., To speake properlie, a figure is euer made by platte formes, and not of bare lines unclosed.

**Unclo·sing,** *ppl. a.*¹ [UN-¹ 10.] Not coming close; keeping apart.

1643 MILTON *Divorce* 6 Where the minde and person pleases aptly, there some unaccomplishment of the bodies delight may be better born with, then when the minde hangs off in an unclosing disproportion.

**Unclo·sing,** *ppl. a.*² [f. UNCLOSE *v.*] That uncloses(s); opening.

1792 J. BARLOW *Conspir. Kings* 159 The hour is come, the world's unclosing eyes Discern with rapture where its wisdom lies. 1831 T. L. PEACOCK *Crotchet Castle* iv, The Captain anxiously watched the unclosing door for the form of his beloved. 1894 AUG. WEBSTER *Mother & Daughter* (1895) 28 The flower's unclosing growth.

**Unclo·the,** *v.* [UN-² 4; cf. UNCLEAD *v.*]

**1.** *trans.* To divest (a person) of clothing; to undress; to strip.

*c* 1300 *Havelok* 659 Grim dede maken a ful fayr bed; Vncloþede him, and dede him þer-inne. 1382 WYCLIF *Matt.* xxvii. 28 And thei vnclothinge hym, diden aboute hym a rede mantel. 1485 in *Rutland Papers* (Camden) 16 Wher as the King shalbe vnraied and vnclothed by his Chamberlayn. 1556 *Aurelio & Isab.* (1608) P iv, They unclothede him of his garmentes. 1632 LITHGOW *Trav.* x. 476, I was..vnclothed to my skin. 1790 BURNS *Let.* in Cromek *Reliques* (1808) 101 Unclothing the naturalist [in a picture], and giving him a rather more resolute look.

*transf.* *c* 1440 *Pallad. on Husb.* IV. 449 In the wynter seson, Couert of stre their coldes most appeson. When somer comth, vnclothe hem.

**b.** *refl.* († Also with double object.)

1382 WYCLIF *Ezek.* xliv. 19 Thei shuln vnclothe hem her clothingus. *c* 1489 CAXTON *Sonnes of Aymon* xxii. 491 He wente to his chambre, & vnclothed hymselfe from his goode raymentes. 1530 PALSGR. 766/2 Unclothe you at ones, for you shall be trymmed starke naked. 1585 T. WASHINGTON tr. *Nicholay's Voy.* II. xxi. 58 Seats..vppon the whiche they vncloth themselues. 1604 E. G[RIMSTONE] *D'Acosta's Hist. Indies* v. xxiv. 397 The ceremonies, dancing and sacrifice ended, they went to vnclothe themselves.

*transf.* 1661 MORGAN *Sph. Gentry* I. vi. 87 The Sheep doth uncloth it self to apparel man.

**c.** In various figurative uses.

1526 *Pilgr. Perf.* (W. de W. 1531) 82 To vnclothe our olde man and make hym all naked, that he may be renewed in god. 1586 T. B. *La Primaud. Fr. Acad.* I. 440 Let us learne to uncloath our harts of all envie and hatred. 1622 S. WARD *Life of Faith in Death* 104 Though they doe not Cynically reuile the body as a Clog, a prison,..yet are they willing, yea and sigh to be vncloathed. 1632 J. HAYWARD tr. *Biondi's Eromena* 23 You'l uncloath your owne shame, and thereby procure your selfe many losses and disgraces. 1671 FLAVEL *Fount. Life* v. 13 The Seleusians affirmed that He unclothed himself of His Humanity. 1849 STOVEL *Canne's Necess.* 55 The sombre but joyous magnanimity of Frith unclothed an element in human nature which human expedients can never overcome. 1870 NEWMAN *Gram. Assent* II. x, Why am I..unclothing my mind of that large outfit of existing thoughts,..desires, and hopes, which make me what I am?

**2.** To strip of leaves or vegetation.

In the first quot. perhaps *intr.*, 'to shed the leaves'.

*a* 1547 SURREY in *Tottel's Misc.* (Arb.) 16 When Boreas gan his raigne, And euery tree vnclothed fast, as nature taught them plaine. 1613 DENNIS *Secr. Angling* I. v, When.. blustring Boreas with his chilling cold, Vnclothed hath the Trees of Sommers greene. 1707 MORTIMER *Husb.* Ss 3 b, Nov[ember]..generally proves dry, and the Earth and Trees are wholly uncloathed.

**3.** To remove a cloth or cloths from.

In early quots. perh. strictly *uncloth.*

1607 MARKHAM *Cavel.* III. (1617) 21 First let your Groom vncloath him, then..dresse him in such sort as belongs to his place and office. 1623 — *Eng. Housew.* v. 217 Couer it ouer with some thicke wollen clothes,..the warmth whereof will make it Come presently: which once perceiued, then forthwith vncloth it. 1825 J. NICHOLSON *Operat. Mechanic* 39 Many wind-mills are provided with flying-balls, which, by very ingenious mechanism, clothe and unclothe the sails just in proportion to the strength of the wind. 1893 *N. & Q.* 8th Ser. III. 75/2 When the force of the wind increased, the miller was obliged to bring each of the sails in succession to the ground, in order to 'unclothe' it.

Hence **Unclo·thing** *vbl. sb.*

1643 CARYL *Expos. Job* I. 104 Death is called an uncloathing,..because it pulleth all outward things off from a man. 1650 BAXTER *Saints' R.* v. § 2. 54 If unclothing be the thing thou fearest; why, it is, that thou mayst have better clothing put on.

**Unclo·thed,** *ppl. a.* [UN-¹ 8.]

**1.** Not covered with clothes; bare, naked.

1440 J. SHIRLEY *Dethe K. James* (1818) 15 The Kyng.. stondyng in his night gowne, all unclothid save his shirt, his cape [etc.]. 1495 *Trevisa's Barth. De P. R.* XVIII. ix. 762 A serpent dredyth a nakyd man & dare not touche hym though he lepe on hym whan he is vnclothed. 1601 LD. MOUNTJOY *Let.* in Moryson *Itin.* II. (1617) 204 Then will the souldier be vnclothed, which rather then he will indure, he will runne away. 1616 SURFL. & MARKH. *Country Farme* I. xxviii. 128 Vpon his necke, and other outward parts which are vnclothed. 1816 BYRON *Siege Cor.* xxvi, Their leader's nervous arm is bare,..Unclothed to the shoulder it waves them on. 1862 SHARPE *Egypt. Antiq. Brit. Mus.* 13 The unclothed parts of their bodies are painted red. 1874 LISLE CARR *J. Gwynne* I. vii. 237 Prone to cravings after a savage ideal of untaught, unclothed freedom.

*transf.* 1581 HOWELL *Devises* (1906) 32, I sawe the naked Fields vnclothde on euery side. 1855 *Orr's Circ. Sci., Inorg. Nat.* 85 The unclothed jaws—covered with hard enamel instead of skin—are lined with a double row of teeth.

**2.** Not covered with a cloth or cloths.

1856 KANE *Arct. Expl.* II. ix. 93 [The table] still stands in its simple dignity, an unclothed platform of boards. 1891 E. KINGLAKE *Australian at Home* 94 A plainly furnished room with an unclothed deal table.

Hence **Unclo·thedly** *adv.*

*a* 1648 *Ess. on Death* in *Bacon's Remaines* (1648) 8 Forgetting how unclothedly they came hither, or with what naked ornaments they were arrayed. 1683 E. HOOKER *Pref. Pordage's Mystic Div.* 67 Where, unclothedly, uncoveredly, nakedly, uncompoundedly,..Hee stood.

**Unclo·tted,** *ppl. a.* (UN-[1] 8.) 1770 HEWSON *Blood* in *Phil. Trans.* LX. 380, I had the curiosity to compare..the clotted part with the unclotted.

**Unclou·d,** *v.* [UN-[2] 4 b.]

**1.** *trans.* To clear or free from clouds.

1598 FLORIO, *Disnebbiare*, to vncloude, to cleere vp. *c* 1610 BEAUM. & FL. *Philaster* IV. i, 'Tis the King Will have it so, whose breath can still the winds, Uncloud the Sun. 1652 BENLOWES *Theoph.* v. lxxiii, This Monarch Star, Making his progresse through the Signes, unclouds the air.

**2.** *transf.* and *fig.* To free from obscurity or gloom; to clear, make clear.

1594 *Constable's Diana* Printer to Rdr., Obscur'd wonders ..visited me.., and I in regard of Aeneas honour, have vnclouded them vnto the worlde. 1607 EARL STIRLING *J. Cæsar* IV. i, When friend-ship one of them pretends, The other likewise doth un-cloud the face. *a* 1711 KEN *Hymnotheo* Poet. Wks. 1721 III. 375 Down from high Heav'n rush'd a strong gracious Wind, Dispelling Mists, unclouding ev'ry Mind. 1789 T. TWINING *Aristotle's Treat. Poetry* (1812) I. 305 It is in the true spirit of a modern drinking song; recommending it to the servant to uncloud his brow. 1891 C. E. NORTON *Dante's Purgat.* xxviii. 179 The psalm..affords light which may uncloud your understanding.

*refl.* *a* 1672 P. S[TERRY] *Appear. God to Man* Wks. (1710) 328 Things seen in their Unseen and Divine Forms, unclouding themselves, shining out upon the Soul.

**3.** *absol.* To become clear.

1874 KINGSLEY *Lett.*, etc. (1877) II. 431, I am hopeful that as she gets weaker the brain will uncloud. 1879 G. MACDONALD *P. Faber* I. xv. 176 Every now and then she cast up a glance, and there were black suns unclouding over a white sea.

Hence **Unclou·ding** *vbl. sb.*

1704 NORRIS *Ideal World* II. iii. 162 It is for the unclouding of both, to observe a definitive strickness in the use of our words.

**Unclou·ded,** *ppl. a.* [UN-[1] 8.]

**1.** Not obscured or darkened by clouds.

1595 G. W. *On Spenser's Sonn.* 3 But when they see his glorious raies vnclowded, With steddy steps they keepe the perfect way. 1639 HABINGTON *Castara* II. (Arb.) 91 Th' unclouded Sun had never showne them day Till that bright minute. 1655 VAUGHAN *Silex Scint.* II. *Ascension-day* 46 All the Planets did unclouded pass. 1765 WILKES *Corr.* (1805) II. 160 A fine blue the arch of heaven is here,—pure, serene, and unclouded. 1796 H. HUNTER *St.-Pierre's Stud. Nat.* (1799) II. 36 The unclouded azure in the Heavens. 1858 LARDNER *Handbk. Nat. Phil.* 377 A clear unclouded sky in the absence of the sun radiates but little heat towards the earth. 1887 BOWEN *Æneid* III. 518 He beholds that the heavens are one unclouded expanse.

**2.** *transf.* and *fig.* Not darkened or obscured.

1641 MILTON *Ch. Govt.* II. ii, That more then angelick brightnes, the unclouded serenity of Christian Religion. *c* 1645 HOWELL *Lett.* (1650) I. 355 A clear unclouded countenance. *a* 1711 KEN *Sion* Poet. Wks. 1721 IV. 398 And where the Mind falls short, Love taking Flight, Obtains of God a more unclouded Sight. 1796 MME. D'ARBLAY *Camilla* V. 189 A brighter, though not unclouded scene, was exhibited at Cleves. 1821 SCOTT *Kenilw.* vi, The graceful ease and unclouded front of an accomplished courtier. 1847 C. BRONTE *J. Eyre* xxxviii, No fear of death will darken St. John's last hour: his mind will be unclouded. 1890 'R. BOLDREWOOD' *Miner's Right* (1899) 160/2 My conscience was unclouded.

Hence **Unclou·dedly** *adv.*; **Unclou·dedness**.

1648 BOYLE *Seraph. Love* iii. (1700) 14 The Love..that makes nothing more conducive to it than the greatest uncloudedness of the Eye. 1804 EUGENIA DE ACTON *Tale without Title* I. 62 Why then, fond foolish heart, so sad! Think not to pass uncloudedly thy days.

**Unclou·dy,** *a.* (UN-[1] 7.)

1675 GASCOIGNE in Rigaud *Corr. Sci. Men* (1841) I. 223 A clearer and more uncloudy sky than ordinarily England doth allow. 1711 GAY *Rural Sports* I. 108 Now..twinkling orbs bestrow th' uncloudy skies.

**Unclou·red,** *ppl. a.* *Sc.* [UN-[1] 8.] Not injured with blows or hard knocks.

1719 RAMSAY *Ep. to Hamilton* 4 Aug. vii, Be thy Crown ay unclowr'd in Quarrel.

**Unclo·ven,** *ppl. a.* (UN-[1] 8 b. Cf. MDu. *ongecloven*, MSw. *oclyffvin*, Sw. *oklufven*.)

1620 FLETCHER *Chances* II. i, My skull's uncloven yet, let me but kill. 1725 *Fam. Dict.* s.v. *Animal*, There are those that are cloven-footed; as black Cattle; or uncloven, as Horses. 1842 BORROW *Bible in Spain* v, They will not partake of the beast of the uncloven foot. 1893 SWINBURNE *Stud. Prose & Poetry* (1894) 290 A sea uncloven by the share or by the prow of an adventurer in verse.

**Uncloy·,** *v.* [UN-[2] 3.] *trans.* (See quots., and cf. CLOY *v.*[1] 1 and 4. In this sense *Obs.*)

1611 COTGR., *Descloüer*, to vnnayle, or vncloy; to loose, pull off, draw out, a nayle. 1627 CAPT. SMITH *Seaman's Gram.* xiv. 68 To uncloy her [*sc.* a gun], is to put..oile.. about the naile to make it glib, and by a traine giue fire to her by her mouth, and so blow it out.

**Uncloy·ed,** *ppl. a.* [UN-[1] 8.]

†**1.** Unhurt, uninjured. *Obs.*

1562 PHAER *Æneid* x. Dd ij b, Yet..let me Ascanius keepe vncloyed: Let me my nephew small withdraw from Mars.

**2.** Not cloyed or surfeited.

1627 SANDERSON *Serm.* I. 268 Depending upon the ministry thereof with unsatisfied ears and unwearied attention, and feeding thereon with uncloyed appetites. *a* 1703 POMFRET *Ode Gen. Conflagration* xiii, Where undisturb'd uncloyed they will possess Divine substantial happiness. 1797 GODWIN *Enquirer* I. xv. 139 The man of genius..feeds with an uncloyed appetite. 1827 KEBLE *Chr. Y., 4th Sun. Advent* viii, These eyes..In fearless love and hope uncloy'd For ever on that ocean bright Empower'd to gaze. 1866 LIDDON *Bampt. Lect.* v. (1875) 230 All His infinite powers and faculties turn ever inward with uncloyed delight.

**Uncloy·ing,** *ppl. a.* (UN-[1] 10.)

1768–74 TUCKER *Lt. Nat.* (1834) II. 263 Thou endest not but in endless, uncloying fruition. 1819 SHELLEY *Cyclops* 364 The Cyclops vermilion, With slaughter uncloying, Now feasts on the dead. 1856 GRINDON *Life* xx. (1875) 253 The pure and uncloying charms of virtue and nature.

**Unclu·bbable,** *a.* (UN-[1] 7 b.)

Hence, in recent use, *unclubbability*.

?1764 JOHNSON in Mme. D'Arblay *Diary* (1842) I. 66 Sir John was a most unclubable man! 1859 SALA *Tw. round Clock* (1861) 215 Moreover, they are a people who drink *standing*,..a most unclubable characteristic. 1867 E. YATES *Forlorn Hope* x, Kilsyth is not popular at Barnes's, being decidedly an unclubbable man.

**Unclue,** var. UNCLEW *v.*

**Unclu·ng,** *ppl. a.* (UN-[1] 8 b. Cf. CLUNG *ppl. a.* 2.)

1587 GOLDING *De Mornay* xv. 233 Or els the earth yet yoong ..the seede thereof vncloong Reteined still in fruitfull wombe.

**Unclu·tch,** *v.* (UN-[2] 3.)

1667 *Decay Chr. Piety* iv. ¶ 3, If the terrors of the Lord could not have force enough..to unclutch his griping hand, or disseize him of his prey. 1816 SCOTT *Bl. Dwarf* viii, It unclutched the burden, and let it drop..upon the ground. 1864 E. SARGENT *Peculiar* III. 56, I should not feel much compunction in compelling such a man to unclutch his riches.

**Unco** (*v·ŋkǒ*), *a.*, *adv.*, and *sb.* *Sc.* and *north. dial.* Also 5 vnkow, 6 vncow, 7, 9 uncow, 8–9 unko, 9 unco', unca. [Shortening of UNCOUTH *a.*]

**A.** *adj.* **1.** Unknown, strange; unusual.

*c* 1410 *Chaucer's Troylus* III. 1797 (Campsall MS.), And ouer al þis so wel koude he deuyse Of sentement and in so vnkow wyse, Al his aray, þat [etc.]. 1500–20 DUNBAR *Poems* xxxi. 13 He that..schuttis syne at ane vncow schell,..He wirkis sorrow to him sell. 1596 DALRYMPLE tr. *Leslie's Hist. Scot.* (S.T.S.) II. 132 At this tyme an vncow and sair seiknes ..invadet hail Scotland. 1683 LAW *Mem.* (1818) 246 Taken with an uncow disease, like unto convulsion fits. 1725 RAMSAY *Gentl. Sheph.* III. ii, They're here that ken, and here that disna ken The wimpled meaning of your unko tale. 1785 BURNS *Halloween* xxviii, Wi' merry sangs, an' friendly cracks,..And unco tales, an' funnie jokes. 1816 SCOTT *Antiq.* xxxii, It was an unco thing to bid a mother leave her ain house wi' the tear in her ee. 1871 W. ALEXANDER *Johnny Gibb* xliv. 306 Buyin' a twa three rigs o' grun' an' sittin' doon wi' a' thing unco aboot's.

**b.** Weird, uncanny.

1828 MOIR *Mansie Wauch* x, It was an unco thought, and garred all my flesh creep. 1893 STEVENSON *Catriona* xv, It was an unco place by night, unco by day.

**2.** Remarkable, notable, great, large.

1724 *Ramsay's Tea-t. Misc.* (1733) I. 25, I had amaist forgot My mistress and my song to boot, And that's an unco faut I wate. 1786 BURNS *The Calf* 4 There's yoursel just now, God knows, an unco Calf! 1815 SCOTT *Guy M.* xi, [The boy's disappearance] made an unca noise ower a' this country. 1820 — *Monast.* xxxiii, It would be an unco task to mend the yetts. 1869 A. MACDONALD *Love, Law & Theol.* viii. 133 She thinks an unco heep o' Mr. Ochtertyre.

**B.** *adv.* Extremely, remarkably, very.

1724 *Ramsay's Tea-t. Misc.* (1733) I. 26, I hate to live; but O I'm wae And unko sweer to die. 1786 BURNS *Twa Dogs* 116 Whyles twalpennie-worth o' nappy Can mak the bodies unco happy. 1816 SCOTT *Antiq.* xi, Though you're near enough, yet Miss Grizel has an unco close grip. 1869 C. GIBBON *R. Gray* iv, Ye're getting unco fine in your ways.

**b.** *The unco guid*, those who are professedly strict in matters of morals and religion.

1786 BURNS (*title*), Address to the Unco Guid, or the Rigidly Righteous. 1859 *Habits of Gd. Society* iv. 160 Indifference and consequent inattention to dress,..extolled by the 'unco gude' as a virtue. 1887 *Daily Tel.* 12 Mar. 5/2 The absurdities initiated by the 'unco' guid' in their futile attempts to promote public morality by legislation.

**C.** *sb.* **1.** A strange or unusual thing or tale; a novelty or piece of news. Usu. *pl.*

1785 BURNS *Cotter's Sat. Nt.* v, Each tells the uncos that he sees or hears. 1822 GALT *Steam-Boat* xvii. 359, I..was thankful for being returned in safety among my friends, after seeing such uncos. 1886 B. BRIERLEY *Cast upon World* xi. (E.D.D.), Jone knew all the 'uncos' that were afloat.

**2.** A stranger.

1800 ADAIR in Currie *Burns' Wks.* I. 172 She gave as her first toast after dinner, *Awa, Uncos*, or, away with the strangers. 1821 GALT *Ann. Parish* xx, We had advised her, by course of post, of our coming, and intendment to lodge with her, as uncos and strangers.

**Uncoa·ch,** *v.* (UN-[2] 5.)

1615 CHAPMAN *Odyss.* VI. 124 These (here arriv'd) the Mules vncoacht, and draue Vp to the gulphie riuers shore. 1630 DAVENANT *Cruel Brother* III, Watch my Lords comming from the Duke, and bring Me word, before he is vncoach'd.

**Unco,a·cted,** *ppl. a.* [UN-[1] 8 and 5 b.]

**1.** Not compelled or constrained.

1545 *St. Papers Hen. VIII*, V. 485 Donald Maclane of Kengerloch, wncoakit or incompulsit. 1567 TURBERV. *Epit.*, etc. 4 b, With free and vncoacted minde. 1577 tr. *Bullinger's Decades* III. ix. 470 Such an vncoacted affection, voluntarie loue, and free goodwill as children..beare to their parents.

**2.** Not forced together.

1642 H. MORE *Song of Soul* To Rdr., All homogeneall, simple, single,..unknotted, uncoacted.

**Unco,a·gulable,** *a.* (UN-[1] 7 b and 5 b.) 1669 W. SIMPSON *Hydrol. Chym.* 103 This wild uncoagulable spirit we call wind. 1809 *Phil. Trans.* XCIX. 333 It appeared that..it might be dissolved in alcohol, and thereby become uncoagulable. 1836–9 *Todd's Cycl. Anat.* II. 152/1 The animal matters thus mixed with the blood..constitute the..uncoagulable animal matter of the blood.

**Unco,a·gulated,** *ppl. a.* (UN-[1] 8.)

1770 *Phil. Trans.* LX. 408 A part of the blood..was found uncoagulated thirteen hours after death. 1845 TODD & BOWMAN *Phys. Anat.* I. 39 Not a particle of caseine..will remain uncoagulated. 1873 ROLFE *Phys. Chem.* 153 Place in it 5 ounces of fresh uncoagulated blood.

**Unco,a·gulating,** *ppl. a.* (UN-[1] 10.)

1822–7 GOOD *Study Med.* (1829) IV. 402 The blood itself was black, uncoagulating, and of an oily appearance.

†**Un-coalcarrying,** *ppl. a.* *Obs.*[—1] (See UN-[1] 10 and COAL *sb.*[1] 12.)

1611 CHAPMAN *May Day* III, Now sir he (being of an vncole-carrying spirit) fals foule on him, cals him gull openly.

**Uncoa·t,** *v.* (UN-[2] 4.)

1571 GOLDING *Calvin on Ps.* l. 1 To bee uncoted out of that their masking garment of holynesse, whereof they vaunted themselves.

**Uncoa·ted,** *ppl. a.* [UN-[1] 8.]

**1.** Not covered with a coating of some substance.

1663 BOYLE *Usef. Exp. Nat. Philos.* II. App. 351 Put it into a strong glasse retort uncoated. 1798 *Phil. Trans.* LXXXVIII. 577 When the flints appeared perfectly uncoated, and in their usual state, I decanted the liquor. 1800 *Ibid.* XC. 339 A piece of the polished or uncoated red coral was now taken. 1878 ABNEY *Photogr.* 26 If the plate be exposed..with the uncoated side next the image.

**2.** Not wearing a coat.

1853 G. JOHNSTON *Nat. Hist. E. Bord.* I. 106 You must add life to the landscape:..the uncoated ploughman [etc.].

**Unco·ck,** *v.*[1] [UN-[2] 3.]

†**1.** *trans.* To take (the match) out of the cock of the old matchlock gun. Also *absol.*, and with *piece* as obj. *Obs.*

1598 BARRET *Theor. Warres* 33 Let him vncocke his match, clap his musket vpon his shoulder, and so retire. 1639 *Verney Papers* (Camden) 240 Charles Price..bedd them uncock theyr peeces. 1650 R. ELTON *Military Art* (1659) 192 Uncock, and return your Match.

**2.** To lower the cock or hammer of (a fire-arm) in order to prevent accidental discharge.

[1775 ASH.] 1804 tr. *La Martelier's Three Gil Blas* I. 30 One of my pistols, which..I had forgot to uncock, went off. 1818 SCOTT *Br. Lamm.* xxxiii, Ravenswood..uncocked and returned his pistol to his belt. 1824 W. IRVING *T. Trav.* (1849) 422 The pistol was uncocked; the burden was resumed.

**Unco·ck,** *v.*[2] (UN-[2] 3. Cf. COCK *v.*[4])

1844 J. T. HEWLETT *Parsons & W.* v, To uncock and toss about Farmer Read's hay.

**Unco·cked,** *ppl. a.*[1] [UN-[1] 8.] Of a hat: Not cocked or turned up.

1721 RAMSAY *Morning Interview* 13 The sons of Bacchus stagger home to rest, With tatter'd wigs, foul shoes, and uncock'd hats. 1751 JOHNSON *Rambler* No. 109 ¶ 6 With ..my hair unpowdered, and my hat uncocked. 1785 GROSE *Dict. Vulgar T.*, *Zouch*, or *Slouch*, a slouched hat; a hat with its brims let down, or uncocked.

**Unco·cked,** *ppl. a.*[2] [UN-[1] 8.] Of crops: Not put up in cocks.

1641 BEST *Farm. Bks.* (Surtees) 58 If theire come any great raines, then they [pease] are better uncocked then cocked.

**Unco·cted,** *ppl. a.* [UN-[1] 8 and 5 b.] Not properly prepared or digested by heat, etc.; crude.

1598 SYLVESTER *Du Bartas* II. i. III. *Furies* 481 An impotence for Generation's-deed, And lust-lesse Issue of th' uncocted seed. 1601 HOLLAND *Pliny* II. 476 [Vermilion] uncocted and crude is..brought to Rome in the masse as it lay within the veine. 1622 DONNE *Serm.* xvi. 157 In a devotion perchance indigested, uncocted, and retaining yet some crudities.

† **Uncod,** obs. var. UNCOUTH *a.* or UNKED *a.*

1399 *Pol. Poems* (Rolls) I. 364 Her eldest bryd his taken her fro, into an uncod place.

**Unco·dified,** *ppl. a.* (UN-[1] 8.) 1867 *Nation* 12 Sept. 205 The uncodified regulations required by public opinion. †**Un-co·dpieced,** *a.* *Obs.*[—1] (UN-[1] 9.) 1580 G. HARVEY *Let. to Spenser* S.'s Wks. (1912) 625/2 Largebelled Kodpeasd Dublet, vnkodpeased halfe hose. **Unco·erced,** *ppl. a.* (UN-[1] 8.) 1791–2 BENTHAM *Anarchical Fallacies* Wks. 1843 II. 505 The liberty which the law ought to..leave uncoerced, unremoved. 1802–12 — *Ration. Judic. Evid.* (1827) V. 657 Gain or loss..from the uncoerced conduct of individuals. 1864 SIR F. PALGRAVE *Norm. & Eng.* III. 363 The first community which had made a formal and uncoerced submission of their own free will.

**Unco·ffer,** *v.* [UN-[2] 5.] *trans.* To take out of a coffer.

*c* 1412 HOCCLEVE *De Reg. Princ.* 4245 Þe bagged gold by þe marchaunt hym lent He hath vncofred. *a* 1470 HARDING *Chron.* CXXII. i, Then went he furth to Duram wher he offred, And to the Churche he gaue great good vncoffred.

**Unco·ffered,** *ppl. a.* (UN-[1] 8.) 1870 BARING-GOULD *In Exitu Israel* I. viii. 118 There remained still one of Gabrielle's dresses uncoffered.

**Unco·ffined,** *ppl. a.*[1] [UN-[1] 8.] Not enclosed in a coffin.

1648 HEXHAM II, *Ongekist*, Vnchested, or Vncoffined. *a* 1680 GLANVILL *Sadducismus* II. (1681) 218 An uncoffined body being laid in a ground exposed to wet [etc.]. 1742 BLAIR *Grave* 152 A Dungeon-Slave, that's bury'd In the High-way, unshrouded and uncoffin'd. 1855 [J. R. LEIFCHILD] *Cornwall* 30 A small ancient dungeon, wherein were found the uncoffined bones of a large man. 1884 *Athenæum* 16 Aug. 203/3 This is the last instance we remember of a body being buried uncoffined when laid in consecrated ground with the rites of the Church.

**Unco·ffined,** *ppl. a.*[2] [UN-[2] 8.] Taken out of a coffin.

1836 F. MAHONY *Rel. Father Prout* 164 A newly uncoffined mummy (warranted of the era of Sesostris).

**Unco·ft,** *ppl. a.* *Sc.* [UN-[1] 8 b. Cf. MDu. and Du. *ungekocht*.] Unbought.

1536 BELLENDEN *Descr. Alb.* iv. in *Cron. Scot.* (1541) B ij b, Thay mycht..haif all necessaris within thaym self vncoft. 15.. J. BALNAVIS '*O Gallandis all*' 15 (Maitland MS.), With stufe oncoft, set vpone loft, Aneuch is ewin a feist. 1721 KELLY *Sc. Prov.* 388 You strive about uncoft Gait [*i.e.* goats]. 1737 RAMSAY *Sc. Prov.* xliii. 116 Ye cangle about uncoft kids.

**Unco·gged**, *ppl. a.*[1] [UN-[1] 8 + COG *v.*[1]] Not blocked or stopped.
1637 GILLESPIE *Eng. Pop. Cerem.* Ep. A ij b, Those who are wealthy and well at ease, and mounted aloft upon the uncogged wheeles of prosperous fortune.

**Unco·gged**, *ppl. a.*[2] [UN-[1] 8 + COG *v.*[3]] Of dice: Not cogged or loaded.
1870 LOWELL *Among my Bks.* Ser. I. (1873) 230 Honest dice, uncogged by those three hoary sharpers, Prerogative, Patricianism, and Priestcraft.

†**Unco·gible**, *a. Obs.*[—1] [UN-[1] 7 + L. *cōgĕre* to compel.] Incapable of being constrained.
1646 S. BOLTON *Arraignm. Err.* 314 Those acts of conscience which are internall, are free and uncogible; they fall not under mans cognizance.

† **Unco·gitable**, *a. Obs.* (UN-[1] 7 b and 5 b.)
1529 MORE *Suppl. Souls* 43 But [they] haue in them selfe a farre more excellent syght,..by meanys vncogitable to man. 1534 — *Comf. agst. Trib.* III. xxvi. (1553) Uvj, Ye Ioys of heauen are..to mannes hearte vncogitable.

**Unco·gnisant**, *a.* (UN-[1] 7.) 1860 GOSSE *Rom. Nat. Hist.* 153 There exists a world of animated beings..of which our senses are altogether uncognisant.

**Uncogni·zable**, *a.* (UN-[1] 7 b and 5 b.)
1720 WELTON *Suffer. Son of God* I. iii. 39 Constrain'd to continue in that Covert, and Uncognisable State,..many Years. 1827 *Perils & Captivity* in *Constable's Misc.* 326 Until he came to the spot where their corpses laid, already putrid and uncognizable. 1849 HERSCHEL *Outl. Astron.* 590 This displacement, however, is..uncognizable by any phænomenon, so long as the solar motion remains invariable.

**Uncogni·zed**, *ppl. a.* (UN-[1] 8.) 1877 BLACKIE *Wise Men* 216 So all in all, believe me, Lies hidden, uncognised.

**Uncognoscibi·lity.** (UN-[1] 12 and 5 b.)
1802–12 BENTHAM *Ration. Judic. Evid.* (1827) IV. 152 Making more and more rubbish, with the help of factitious and groundless diversification, thence uncognoscibility, uncertainty, and so forth. 1865 MILL *Exam. Hamilton* 56 Our author has merely proved the uncognoscibility of a being which is nothing but infinite.

**Uncogno·scible**, *a.* (UN-[1] 7 and 5 b.)
1810 BENTHAM *Packing* (1821) 23 Rendering the subject.. as incomprehensible, or..as uncognoscible as possible. 1840 POLSON *Law & Lawyers* (1858) 197 Perhaps abstractedly speaking law phrases are not one whit more barbarous and uncognoscible than those of any other science.

† **Uncohe·rent**, *a. Obs.* (UN-[1] 7 and 5 b.)
1588 FRAUNCE *Lawiers Log.* Ded., Neyther himselfe can well understand his unjoynted discourse, nor the hearers conceave his uncoherent jangling. 1611 FLORIO, *Incoherente*, vncoherent.

**Uncoi·f**, *v.* (UN-[2] 3.)
1598 FLORIO, *Dischiomare*, to vnhaire, to vncoiffe, to disheuell, to touze ones haire. 1611 COTGR., *Descoeffer*, to vncoife; to disarray,..vncouer, the head. c 1714 POPE, etc. *Mem. M. Scriblerus* vi. Wks. 1797 VI. 109 Yonder are two Apple-women scolding, and just ready to uncoif one another. 1876 F. K. ROBINSON *Whitby Gloss.* 205.

**Uncoi·fed**, *ppl. a.* (UN-[1] 8 and UN-[2] 8.)
1611 COTGR., *Descoeffé*, vncoifed. 1727 BAILEY (vol. II). 1742 YOUNG *Nt. Th.* VIII. 601 Lorenzo! thou, her majesty's renown'd, Tho' uncoift, counsel, learned in the world! 1870 [see UNCHAPLETED].

**Uncoi·l**, *v.* [UN-[2] 3.]
**1.** *trans.* To unwind; to take out of a coiled state.
1713 DERHAM *Phys.-Theol.* x. (1727) 406 *note*, Between which [great fibres], may be seen the Spiral Air-Vessels (like Threads of Cobweb) a little uncoiled. 1811 *2nd Rep. Records Irel.* 26 The Parliament Rolls..often extend many perches in length; actually requiring a machine to uncoil and wind them up. 1839 DARWIN *Voy. Nat.* i. 19 Where the stream uncoils into long streaks the froth collected in the eddies. 1860 TYNDALL *Glac.* I. xi. 73 We..paused while our guide uncoiled a rope and tied us all together.
*refl.* 1824 DIBDIN *Libr. Comp.* 742 His muse..is capable of uncoiling and rousing herself, as it were, for attacks of tremendous severity. 1859 TENNYSON *Vivien* 738 The snake of gold slid from her hair, the braid Slipt and uncoil'd itself.
**2.** *absol.* To become uncoiled.
1854 OWEN in *Orr's Circ. Sci., Org. Nat.* I. 195 The constrictor slowly uncoils. 1870 HOOKER *Stud. Flora* 472 Elaters, which are coiled round the spore when moist, and uncoil when dry.
Hence **Uncoi·led** *ppl. a.*; **Uncoi·ling** *vbl. sb.*
1839 URE *Dict. Arts*, etc. 1284 The coiling and uncoiling of the cord. 1844 W. UPTON *Physioglyphics* 176 The English capital represents it uncoiled, but still quiescent. 1856 EMERSON *Eng. Traits, Result*, Who would see the uncoiling of that tremendous spring.

† **Uncoi·n**, var. of (or error for) UNCOINED *ppl. a.*
1640 SHIRLEY *Arcadia* II. i, Be there a myne Of Coyne or vncoyne mettall, it is mine.

**Uncoi·n**, *v.* (UN-[2] 3.)
1833 HT. MARTINEAU *Berkeley* I. ii. 33 Every week uncoins what was coined the week before. 1875 JEVONS *Money* viii. 81 These are the people who frequently uncoin money, either by melting it, or by exporting it.

**Uncoi·ned**, *ppl. a.* (UN-[1] 8.)
1423 *Rolls of Parlt.* IV. 256/2 Silver is bought and soold unkoyned atte pris of xxxii *s.* the pound of troie. c 1550 R. BIESTON *Bayte Fortune* A vj, That tyme was I vncoyned, therfore man chaunge thy mynde To blame me of all euylles. 1555 EDEN *Decades W. Ind.* (Arb.) 290 The Ruthenians vse money vncoyned. 1625 T. GODWIN *Moses & Aaron* (1641) 269 Though at last they used coined money, yet at first they weighed their money, uncoined. 1696 *Lond. Gaz.* No. 3238/3 A free Exportation of Gold and Silver, both coined and uncoined. 1715 LEONI *Palladio's Archit.* (1742) II. 80 The first Money in Rome, was of Brass, and uncoined. 1790 in *Nairne Peerage Evidence* (1874) 99 Gold & silver coined & uncoined. 1862 *Lond. Rev.* 23 Aug. 175 All the mentions of money in the Bible before the Babylonian captivity may be explained as of uncoined money. 1886 *Pall Mall G.* 12 June 9/2 The scarcity of the supply both of the coined and uncoined metal.

*fig.* 1599 SHAKS. *Hen. V*, v. ii. 164 While thou liu'st, deare Kate, take a fellow of plaine and vncoyned Constancie.

**Unco·ked**, *ppl. a.* (UN-[1] 8.) 1868 JOYNSON *Metals* 24 Uncoked coal—that is,..coal in its ordinary condition.

**U·nco-like**, *a.* and *adv. Sc.* [f. UNCO *a.*] **a.** *adv.* In a strange manner. **b.** *adj.* Strange; abnormal.
1636 RUTHERFORD *Lett.* (1836) I. 126 He looked fremed and unco-like upon me when I came first here. 1842 D. VEDDER *Poems* 139 Rax doon the nuts, ye uncolike loon. 1891 H. JOHNSTON *Kilmallie* I. iii, It's an unco-like suspicion, I'm sure.

**Unco·llar**, *v.* (UN-[2] 4 b.)
1611 COTGR., *Escollelé*, vncollered; whose coller is taken off, or pulled away. 1613 PURCHAS *Pilgr.* (1614) 702 Then they are vncollared, freed, and dignified with the Title of Soldiours. 1755 *Mem. Capt. P. Drake* II. i. 2, I..unbridled and [un]collared my Horse, and put the Hay before him.

**Uncolla·ted**, *ppl. a.* (UN-[1] 8.)
[1775 ASH.] 1787 WHITAKER *Mary Q. Scots Vind.* I. 62 They thus condemn the Queen..upon letters unauthenticated by the producers, uncollated by themselves. 1885 *Athenæum* 2 May 566/3 The text of various MSS. of the Septuagint unknown or uncollated in Montfaucon's time.

**Uncolle·cted**, *ppl. a.* (UN-[1] 8.)
**a.** Of persons, the mind, etc.: (see COLLECT *v.* 3).
1611 BEAUM. & FL. *Maid's Trag.* IV. ii, What a wild beast is uncollected man! 1613–6 BROWNE *Brit. Past.* I. i, Fearing lest those often idle fits Might clean expel her uncollected wits. 1639 BP. REYNOLDS *Lord's Supper* xviii, Sudden, uncomposed, & uncollected thoughts. 1718 PRIOR *Solomon* II. 291 Asham'd, confus'd I..to my Soul yet uncollected said: Into Thy self, fond Solomon, return. 1833 MARRYAT *P. Simple* lxiii, My mind was so uncollected..that I could not feel assured of it for a minute.
**b.** Of things: (see COLLECT *v.* I, I b).
1730 THOMSON *Autumn* 731 As when of old.., Light, uncollected, thro' the Chaos urg'd Its infant way. 1828–32 WEBSTER s.v., Uncollected taxes; debts uncollected. 1847 L. HUNT Title-p., Men, Women, and Books. A Selection.. from his uncollected Prose Writings.

**Uncolle·giate**, *v.* (UN-[2] 6 c.) 1851 HANNA *Chalmers* III. 446 The uncollegiating of the five parishes which enjoyed a double ministry. 1867 BLACK *Hist. Brechin* (ed. 2) xi. 278 There is a talk of uncollegiating the parish church. **Uncollo·quial**, *a.* (UN-[1] 7.) 1840 *London & Westminster Rev.* XXXIII. 113 It is impossible that the impression made upon the audience of the native storytellers can be of the same uncolloquial and semi-scriptural sort..as that which [etc.]. **Uncolo·nial**, *a.* (UN-[1] 7.) 1861 DICKENS *Gt. Expect.* xlv. III. 92 A certain person not altogether of uncolonial pursuits. **Unco·lonize**, *v.* (UN-[2] 6 c.) 1824 MEDWIN *Convers. Byron* I. 96 When once she obtained a footing inside my door,..I had great difficulty in uncolonizing her.

**Unco·lourably**, *adv.* (UN-[1] 11.)
1541 WYATT *Decl.* in *Poems* (1913) II. 265 Syncearely and vncolourably from tyme to tyme to declare the trouthe.

**Unco·loured**, *ppl. a.* [UN-[1] 8.]
**1.** Not having a colour or colours.
1538 ELYOT, *Abaphus*, vndied or vncoloured. 1541 R. COPLAND *Galyen's Terap.* 2 C iij, The partye of the vlcere that is stony and harde and vncoloured ought to be cut. 1667 MILTON *P. L.* v. 189 Whether to deck with Clouds the uncolourd skie, Or wet the thirstie Earth with falling showers. a 1684 LEIGHTON *Com.* 1 *Pet.* (1693) 184 When you look..through pure uncolour'd glass, you receive the clear light. 1784 COWPER *Task* VI. 178 All this uniform, uncolour'd scene, Shall..flush into variety again. 1843 PRICHARD *Nat. Hist. Man* 89 When the light..shone through the transparent texture uncoloured. 1876 O. C. STONE in *Jrnl. R. Geog. Soc.* XLVI. 42 The substitution of a yellow-stained belt for a plain uncoloured one.
**2.** *fig.* **a.** Not invested with any specious or deceptive appearance or quality; open, undisguised; not influenced or affected *by* something.
1585 ABP. SANDYS *Serm.* 21 Without trecherie and deceit, ..in naked simplicitie, in trueth vncoloured. 1775 BURKE *Corr.* (1844) II. 65 The insolent and uncoloured act of injustice which has been done to my brother. 1827 CARLYLE *Misc.* (1840) I. 30 Such, seen through no uncoloured medium, ..are some features of..Richter and his works. 1868 FARRAR *Seekers* I. ii. (1875) 32 They have been even entirely uncoloured by his teaching.
**b.** Plain, simple.
?1845 DE QUINCEY *Ess.*, *J. Foster* Wks. (1858) 292 The uncoloured style of his general diction.
Hence **Unco·louredly** *adv.*; **Unco·louredness.**
1561 T. NORTON *Calvin's Inst.* III. 216 They saw themselues to be openly and uncoloredly scorned of the Pope and his Bulbearers. 1660 H. MORE *Myst. Godl.* I. x. 30 *marg.*, The invisibility and uncolouredness of the Air is called Hades or Hell.

**Unco·lted**, *a.* [UN-[2] 8.] Deprived of a horse.
1596 SHAKS. 1 *Hen. IV*, II. ii. 41 *Falstaff.* What a plague meane ye to colt me thus? *Prince.* Thou ly'st, thou art not colted, thou art vncolted.

**Unco·mbated**, *ppl. a.* (UN-[1] 8.)
1649 LOVELACE *Poems* 102 Captive they in Triumph lead each eare and eye, Claiming uncombated the Victorie. 1796 MME. D'ARBLAY *Camilla* III. 65 The uncombated sway of an unavailing, however well-placed attachment.

**Unco·mbed**, *ppl. a.* Also 6 vncomde, vncomed, 7 vnkombt; *Sc.* and *north.* 7 unkamed, 9 unkaimed. [UN-[1] 8. Cf. UNKEMPT *ppl. a.* and Sw. *okammad*, Du. *ongekamd.*]
**1.** Not combed; not dressed or smoothed with a comb: **a.** Of hair (or of persons in this respect).
1561 T. NORTON *Calvin's Inst.* IV. xii. § 17. 79 Accused men..with long hanging beard, with vncombed heare. 1591 SPENSER *Daphnaida* 43 His carelesse locks, vncombed and vnshorne, Hong long adowne. 1606 DANIEL *Queen's Arcadia* 2509 Worthier people too, of subtler spirits, Then these vnfashion'd and vncomb'd rude swaines. 1648 CRASHAW *Steps to Temple, Sospetto* ix, Their lockes are beds of uncomb'd snakes. 1745 MRS. MONTAGU *Corr.* (1906) I. 203 The doctor's man, whose uncombed hair so resembled the mane of the horse he rode. 1809–11 COMBE *Syntax* XXIII. 98 My uncomb'd wig,—my suit of black. 1849–50 ALISON *Hist. Eur.* XII. lxxix. § 43. 37 The rustic air and uncombed locks of these Scandinavian warriors. 1883 *Sword & Trowel* July 355 All these ragged, unwashed, uncombed children.
**b.** Of wool.
1642 *Bk. Rates Merchandizes* H 2 b, Irish wooll uncomb'd the hundred weight,..£2. 16s. 1844 H. STEPHENS *Bk. Farm* III. 894 Combed and uncombed wool of different varieties.
**2.** *fig.* Rude, inelegant. (Cf. INCOMPT *a.*)
1633 P. FLETCHER *Purple Isl.* III. iii, How may I hope to quit your strong desires, In verse uncomb'd such wonders comprehending?

**Uncombi·nable**, *a.* (UN-[1] 7 b.) 1791 WALKER *Pronouncing Dict.* s.v. *Chamber*, *mb* being uncombinable consonants, we cannot end the first syllable with *a.* 1871 BROWNING *Pr. Hohenstiel-Schw.* Wks. 1896 II. 307 Health, strength, beauty,..uncombinable with flesh and blood.

**Uncombi·ne**, *v.* [UN-[2] 3.] *trans.* To disunite.
1595 DANIEL *Civ. Wars* III. vi, When out-breaking vengeance vncombines The ill-ioyn'd plots so fairly ouercast. 1847 DICKENS *Haunted Man* i, Some of these phantoms trembling at heart like things that knew his power to uncombine them.

**Uncombi·ned**, *ppl. a.* (UN-[1] 8.)
1611 FLORIO, *Incombinato*, vncombined. 1803 WELLESLEY in Owen *Desp.* (1877) 222 Uncombined with the power of Scindiah, Holkar will not probably venture to resist the Peishwa. 1858 H. BUSHNELL *Nat. & Supernat.* ix. (1864) 251 Nature, unapplied or uncombined by our wills, could do no such thing.
**b.** *spec.* in chemical or technical use.
1785 *Phil. Trans.* LXXV. 293 There was never any sensible quantity of uncombined fixed air mixed with the inflammable air. 1825 J. NICHOLSON *Operat. Mechanic* 708 The specific gravity of the alloy is greater than that of the two metals in an uncombined state. 1876 TAIT *Rec. Adv. Phys. Sci.* vii. (ed. 2) 161 There may be..enormous masses of as yet uncombined iron and uncombined sulphur.

**Uncombi·ning**, *ppl. a.* (UN-[1] 10.)
1643 MILTON *Divorce* 18 To sowe the furrow of mans nativity with seed of two incoherent and uncombining dispositions. 1651 JER. TAYLOR *Serm. for Year* II. ii. 22 His purposes untwist, as easily as the rude conjuncture of uncombining cables, in the violence of a Northern tempest.
Hence **Uncombi·ningness.**
1850 *Tait's Mag.* XVII. 735/1 The very same characteristics of inertia, unintellectuality, and uncombiningness.

†**Uncombu·st**, *ppl. a. Obs.* (UN-[1] 8 b.) a 1568 in *Bannatyne MS.* (Hunter. Club) 110/43 Thow, Moyses busk remanyng vncombust. 1673 HICKERINGILL *Greg. F. Greyb.* 34 Jove being uncombust and free. **Uncombu·stible**, *a.* (UN-[1] 7.) 1576 G. BAKER tr. *Gesner's Jewell of Health* 191 An oyle of Naphta, that is of Brimstone uncombustible or never burned.

† **Uncome**, *sb. Obs.* [Of obscure formation: see ONCOME *sb.* and ANCOME.]
**1.** = ONCOME *sb.* 1.
1538 ELYOT, *Aduentitius morbus*, syckenes that cometh without our defaute, and of some menne is called an vncome.
**2.** = ANCOME, INCOME *sb.*[2]
1542–3 *Act* 34 & 35 *Hen. VIII*, c. 8 § 1 Vncomes of handes ..& such other like diseases. 1562 BULLEIN *Bulwarke, Dial. Sorenes & Chir.* 10 b, Apostumacions that sprynge of blood, or choller, be diuersly termed by sundrie names as botches,..uncomes. 1597 GERARDE *Herbal* 362 An impostume in the ioints of the fingers (called among the vulgare sort a fellon or vncome). 1601 HOLLAND *Pliny* II. 188 The seed [of the tamarisk]..is singular good for any uncom or fellon. 1697 *View Penal Laws* 208 It is lawful for persons skilful in the Nature of Herbs..to Practise and Minister to any outward Sore, Uncom, Wound.

**Unco·me**, *ppl. a.* Now *north. dial.* Also *Sc.* 6 uncum, vncuming, 7 oncum. [UN-[2] 8 b. Cf. ON. and Icel. *ú-*, *ókominn* (Norw. *ukomen*, MSw. *okomin*).] Not (yet) arrived.
1512 *Acc. Ld. High Treas. Scot.* IV. 295 The Kingis schippis boght and as ȝit uncum to Scotland. 1535 STEWART *Cron. Scot.* (Rolls) III. 441 The lordis..Quhilk in England vncuming hame war than. 1649 I. BASIRE *Corr.* (1831) 98 A bill of 50 *l* which should have come in August last, is yet uncome. 1659 *Knaresb. Wills* (Surtees) II. 240 Yeares of a lease..which are yet uncome and unexpired. a 1670 SPALDING *Troub. Chas. I* (1851) II. 343 He mist sum of Strathbogie men oncum thair. 1828 *Craven Gloss.*, *Uncome*, not come. 1877 *Holderness Gloss.* 151 He's uncome yit.

**Uncome-a·t-able**, *a.* (Freq. unhyphened.) Also 7 uncomatible, 8–9 -able. [UN-[1] 7 b.] Unattainable; inaccessible.
Characterized by Johnson as 'a low, corrupt word'.
α. 1694 CONGREVE *Double-Dealer* II. v, My Honour is infallible and uncomatible. 1706 E. WARD *Wooden World Diss.* (1708) 69 It's an uncomatable Mark, that's certain. 1726 *Adv. Capt. R. Boyle* (1768) 231 The Juice of the Grape is very uncomatable there. 1822 SCOTT *Nigel* xxxii, To whom, I doubt, he awes an uncomatable sum.
β. 1709 STEELE *Tatler* No. 12 ⁋ 18 He has a perfect Art in being unintelligible in Discourse, and uncomeatable in Business. 1732 *Hist. Litteraria* III. 549 Some have asserted ..that Truth was absolutely uncomeatable. 1818 MISS MITFORD in L'Estrange *Life* (1870) II. 35 He is un-come-at-able. One never knows where to catch him. 1847 *Illustr. Lond. News* 4 Sept. 158, I have never seen so uncomeatable a place. 1890 D. C. MURRAY *John Vale's Guardian* xv, The hidden uncomeatable parts of his purchase.
Hence **Uncome-a·t-ableness.**
1727 BAILEY (vol. II).

† **Unco·melily**, *adv. Obs.* (UN-[1] 11.)
c 1420 *Anturs of Arth.* 106 (Thornton MS.), Bare was hir body, and..Alle by-claggede in claye, vn-comlyly clede. 1561 T. NORTON *Calvin's Inst.* IV. v. § 17. 31 The dignitie

of the Church is by that magnificence not vncomlily vpholden. **1658** GURNALL *Chr. in Arm.* II. (1669) 50/1 He walks not haltingly and uncomelily.

**Unco·meliness.** [f. next.]

1. The quality of being uncomely; want of comeliness († or seemliness); an uncomely feature.

**1542** BECON *Potation for Lent* G iij, To make clene yᵉ face of our hart, from all fylthinesse of synnes & from the vncomelynes of trespasse. **1589** PUTTENHAM *Eng. Poesie* III. xxiv. (Arb.) 297 In euery vncomlinesse there must be a certaine absurditie and disproportion to nature. **1624** HEYWOOD *Gunaik.* II. 64 They raysed a kind of uncomelinesse and deformitie in the faces of such as playd upon them. **1670** MILTON *Hist. Brit.* II. 60 Her own Subjects, who detested ..the uncomeliness of thir Subjection to the Monarchie of a Woeman. **1711** STEELE *Spect.* No. 52 ⁋ 3 The native and unaffected Uncomeliness of her Person. **1795** BURKE *Abridgm. Eng. Hist.* Wks. 1842 II. 509 He has joined to these powers of living existence uncomeliness, want of strength, want of distinction. **1865** M. ARNOLD *Ess. Crit.* iv. (1875) 164 That brick-and-mortar image of English Protestantism, representing it in all its prose, all its uncomeliness.

†2. Unruliness. *Obs.*⁻¹

**1607** MARKHAM *Cavel.* v. 22 If you finde his [a horse's] vncomelinesse onelye proceedes from ticklishnesse.

**Unco·mely,** *a.* [UN-¹ 7.]

1. Not pleasing or agreeable to the moral sense or to notions of propriety; unbecoming, improper, unseemly.

*c* **1230** *Hali Meid.* 25 As tah ha nefden wit in ham ne tweire schead as mon haueð, ba of god & of uuel, of cumelich & of uncumelich [*v.r.* vnkumelich]. **1362** LANGL. *P. Pl.* A. x. 180 Hit is an vn-Comely Couple.. To ȝeuen a ȝong wenche to an old feble Mon. *a* **1400** *Sir Degrev.* 1638 The body syttys opon the hors, Hyt was uncomely to the cors. **1538** STARKEY *England* 52 He..began to persuade the rest..to forsake that rudnes & vncomly lyfe. **1583** BABINGTON *Commandm.* (1590) 271 Whereunto for an other inticement to vncleannes, wee may referre all vndecent and vncomely pictures. **1622** in *Harl. Misc.* (Malh.) III. 459 All such reasons are uncomely and unchristian to be objected. **1653** A. WILSON *Jas. I*, 39 If any man speaks any thing uncomely there, the Chancellour ..interrupts him. *a* **1683** OWEN *Two Discourses Holy Spirit* II. iv. (1693) 169 Uncomely Artifices of intreiguing Secular Courts. **1759** ROBERTSON *Hist. Scot.* App. x, To avoid broad and uncomely speech.

2. Not pleasing or agreeable to the senses; not comely or fair to look upon. Also *absol.*

*a* **1400** *Octavian* 884 Clement broght forthe schylde and spere, That were uncomely for to were, Alle sutty, blakk, and unclene. **1513** MORE *Hist. Rich. III*, Wks. 36/2 In hys later dayes with ouer liberall diet, sommewhat corpulente and boorelye, and nathelesse not vncomelye. **1531** ELYOT *Gov.* I. xi, We se, that therof..the childrens personages do waxe uncomely and lasse growe in stature. **1607** MARKHAM *Cavel.* IV. (1617) 36 To make horses amble without either marring their mouthes, vnsetling their heads, or breeding any other vncomely disorders. **1611** BIBLE 1 *Cor.* xii. 23 Our vncomely parts haue more abundant comlinesse. **1710** STEELE *Spect.* No. 17 ⁋ 1 Since our Persons are not of our own Making, when they are such as appear Defective or Uncomely, it is, methinks, an honest and laudable Fortitude to dare to be Ugly. **1824** BYRON *Def. Transf.* I. i, Your aspect is Dusky, but not uncomely. **1847** BRONTE *J. Eyre* xvi, Mrs. Poole's square, flat figure, and uncomely, dry, even coarse face. **1865** WHITTIER *Margaret Smith's Jrnl.* 12 Nov. 1678, Charity ..maketh the weak strong and the uncomely beautiful.

†**Unco·mely,** *adv. Obs.* [UN-¹ 11.] In an uncomely manner; unsuitably, unbecomingly.

*c* **1375** *Cursor M.* 891 (Fairf.), Worme þou sal be vncumly diȝt, mare þan any oþer wiȝt. *c* **1420** *Anturs of Arth.* 106 (Douce MS.), Bare was þe body, and..Al bi-clagged in clay, vncomly cladde. *c* **1510** BARCLAY *Mirr. Gd. Manners* (1570) A ij, A man with hoare heres vncomely doth incline To misframed fables or gesture feminine. **1542** UDALL *Erasm. Apoph.* 300 Will noman chastice this feloe here uncomely demeanyng hymself? **1605** BACON *Adv. Learn.* I. iii. § 9 The great Ladie..would needs haue him carie her little Dogge, which he doing officiously, and yet vncomely, the Page scoffed. **1619** FLETCHER & MASS. *False One* III. i, 'Tis most uncomely spoken.

**Unco·mfort,** *sb.* (UN-¹ 12.)

**1805** MISS BERRY *Jrnls. & Corr.* (1865) II. 297 No uncomforts of situation, no sufferings, shall ever tempt me to any step [etc.]. **1853** G. J. CAYLEY *Las Alforjas* I. 154 Getting tired of..the uncomfort of our rude, straw-stuffed pads.

**Unco·mfort,** *v. rare*⁻¹. (UN-² 3.)

**1637** WHITING *Albino & Bell.* 22 The gods..have ravel'd thy content, Sorrowes uncomfort will thy virgine yeares.

**Unco·mfortable,** *a.* [UN-¹ 7 b and 5 b.]

1. Not comforting; causing or involving discomfort or uneasiness; disquieting.

**1592** SHAKS. *Rom. & Jul.* IV. v. 60 Vncomfortable time, why cam'st thou now To murther, murther our solemnitie? **1615** G. SANDYS *Trav.* 92 The lightning ministring uncomfortable light, intermixed with thunder and tempests. **1653** W. RAMESEY *Astrol. Restored* To Rdr. 8 But pass we these five troublesome, uncomfortable years also. **1680** W. ALLEN *Peace & Unity* Pref. p. iii, To put an end to our dishonourable and uncomfortable contentions. **1711** ADDISON *Spect.* No. 159 ⁋ 8 The Genius..bid me quit so uncomfortable a Prospect. **1785** BURNEY in *Parr's Wks.* (1828) VII. 397, I lament..the uncomfortable account which you give of your health. **1843** PRESCOTT *Mexico* III. i. (1850) I. 347 They were too sanguine to allow such uncomfortable surmises long to dwell in their minds. **1873** TRISTRAM *Moab* i. 16 The Jehalin look..most uncomfortable ruffians to meet in an unfriendly way.

†2. Incapable of being comforted; inconsolable.

**1592** R. D. *Hypnerotomachia* 22 b, The uncomfortable and still mourning Cyparissus. **1611** COTGR., *Inconsolable*, inconsolable, vncomfortable, not to be comforted. **1667** MARVELL *Corr.* Wks. (Grosart) II. 402 On a private loss,..to be impatient, to be uncomfortable, would be to dispute with God.

3. Feeling discomfort; ill at ease; uneasy.

**1796** MME. D'ARBLAY *Camilla* IV. 427 [She was] impelled by this notion, yet wavering, dissatisfied and uncomfortable. **1825** J. NEAL *Bro. Jonathan* I. 3 The whole family were afraid of him;..felt uncomfortable, if he looked into their eyes. **1841** HELPS *Ess., Aids Contentm.* (1842) 16 They are most uncomfortable if their little projects do not turn out according to their fancy. **1887** *Spectator* 20 Aug. 1115 One of them wanting the window open and the other wanting it shut, one of them must be uncomfortable.

**Unco·mfortableness.** [f. prec.]

†1. Inconsolableness. *Obs.*⁻¹

*a* **1639** W. WHATELEY *Prototypes* I. xxi. (1640) 267 Isaac outlived Josephs selling into Egypt, and was afflicted in Jacobs uncomfortablenesse under that crosse. **1727** BAILEY (vol. II), *Inconsolableness*, a State of uncomfortableness, or that will not admit of Comfort.

2. The quality or state of causing or involving discomfort.

**1677** MIÉGE, Uncomfortableness, *l'état triste, ou fâcheux de quelque chose.* **1727** BAILEY (vol. II), *Uncomfortableness*, Uneasiness, Unpleasingness. **1743** BULKELEY & CUMMINS *Voy. S. Seas* 82 Add to our Uneasiness, the Uncomfortableness of the Climate. **1795** FRANCES DILLON in *Jerningham Lett.* (1896) I. 83 The Uncomfortableness of y[ou]r long absence. **1853** KANE *Grinnell Exp.* xxix. (1856) 240 Our abiding-place below has a smoky atmosphere of lamplit uncomfortableness. **1856** HAWTHORNE *Eng. Note-bks.* (1879) I. 379 The vile uncomfortableness of a military life.

3. The fact of feeling uncomfortable.

**1828** LYTTON *Pelham* II. xxv, There is such a certain uncomfortableness always occasioned to the mind by stillness and mystery united, that [etc.]. **1847** MRS. SHERWOOD *Fairchild Family* III. ii. 24 Ready to cry from fatigue, sleep, and uncomfortableness. **1872** HUXLEY *Physiol.* viii. 188 Such are the sensations of uncomfortableness.

**Unco·mfortably,** *adv.* [f. as prec.] In an uncomfortable manner; with discomfort or uneasiness, disagreeably; † inconsolably.

*c* **1425** *St. Mary of Oignies* II. iii. 13 in *Anglia* VIII. 158 Þe holy man..made dule vncomfortably for defoylynge of chirches. *a* **1548** HALL *Chron., Hen. V*, 60 b, This miserable people vncomfortably forsaken & vnnaturally dispised of their owne nacion. **1594** DRAYTON *Matilda* xxxvi, Thus in my closet being left alone, Vpon the floore vncomfortably lying. **1612** T. TAYLOR *Comm. Titus* iii. 6 Water is so necessarie a creature, as nothing can be more dangerously or vncomfortably wanting to the life of man. **1643–5** MILTON *Divorce* II. viii, Rather then to live uncomfortably and unhappily both to himself and to his wife,..he might dismisse her. **1719** DE FOE *Crusoe* I. (Globe) 112, I wander'd about very uncomfortably. **1796** MRS. M. ROBINSON *Angelina* I. 104, I felt most uncomfortably, and would have given anything I possess to have been out of the carriage. **1856** KANE *Arct. Expl.* II. ix. 96 Long and uncomfortably have I pondered over these opposing calls. **1879** *Cassell's Techn. Educ.* IV. 236/1 The native article becomes uncomfortably sticky in the heat of tropical climates.

**Unco·mforted,** *ppl. a.* (UN-¹ 8.)

**1583** BABINGTON *Commandm.* (1590) 344 It is very barbarous crueltie to leaue them vtterly vncomforted, with any portion of that which was taken about them. *a* **1586** SIDNEY *Arcadia* I. xvii. (1912) 110 So (uncomforted therein) [he] sent him away. *a* **1625** BEAUM. & FL. *Laws of Candy* III. i, Let me yet by these Awake your love to my uncomforted Brother. **1797** COLERIDGE *Dungeon* 12 And this is their best cure! uncomforted And friendless solitude. **1832** TENNYSON *Œnone* 256 Lest their shrill happy laughter come to me Walking the cold and starless road of Death Uncomforted. **1835** TRENCH *Justin Martyr* 130 Our great Father, when he sat Uncomforted on Ararat.

**Unco·mforting,** *ppl. a.* (UN-¹ 10.) **1798** *Monthly Mag.* IV. 47, I wander And look upon the busy Danaids Alike uncomforting, uncomforted. †**Unco·mfortless,** *a. Obs.* (UN-¹ 5 a.) **1598** YONG *Diana* 235 Wofull man vncomfortlesse, and sad. †**Unco·ming,** *vbl. sb. Obs.*⁻¹ (UN-¹ 13.) **1593** T. MATHEWS in Tytler *Hist. Scotl.* (1864) IV. 199 Mr. Lock, whom these two days he hath looked for, and mervaileth not a little at his uncoming.

†**Uncomma·nd,** *v. Obs.*⁻¹ [UN-² 3.] *trans.* To countermand, to abrogate.

*c* **1430** *Pilgr. Lyf Manhode* II. xxi. (1869) 83 Wolt thou hold the gospel at fable and lesinge? thou seist it vncomanded that that god hath ordeyned.

**Uncomma·nded,** *ppl. a.* [UN-² 8.]

1. Not ordered to be done or observed.

**14..** *Chaucer's Parl. Foules* 518 (Camb. MS.), For office vncommaundet full ofte anoyth. **1538** BALE *Thre Lawes* 1682 In vayne offer yow that vncommaunded seruyce. **1594** HOOKER *Eccl. Pol.* IV. vii. § 5 Except the one doe auoid whatsoeuer Rites and Ceremonies vncommanded of God the other doth embrace. **1643** *Let. from Grave Gentleman* 3 The People, engaged..under Pretence of an uncommanded protestation. **1692** SOUTH *Serm.* (1697) I. 39 Those affected, uncommanded, absurd Austerities,..exercised by some of the Romish Profession. **1723** ATTERBURY *Serm.* (1726) I. x. 352 They were, I say, Uncommanded Instances of Virtue. **1794** MRS. PIOZZI *Synon.* II. 323 Such uncommanded seclusion is evil for society.

2. Not ordered to do something.

**1534** MORE *Comf. agst. Trib.* III. Wks. 1224/1 That they maye..commaunde and controlle other menne, and liue vncommaunded them selfe. *a* **1586** SIDNEY *Arcadia* v. (1598) 449 Pardon me most honoured Iudge, saith he, that vncommaunded I begin my speech vnto you. **1646** EARL MONM. tr. *Biondi's Civil Warres* VI. 54 Lewis after this commanded his men to retire; and Edwards men forthwith withdrew uncommanded. *a* **1667** COWLEY *On Death W. Hervey* i, My eyes with Tears did uncommanded flow. *a* **1716** BLACKALL *Wks.* (1723) I. 133 If any private Soldier quits his Station, and runs himself uncommanded upon a dangerous Adventure, he deserves Reproof.

3. Not dominated or overlooked (*by* something).

**1693** *Mem. Ct. Teckely* III. 56 Being seated upon an inaccessible Rock uncommanded,..a few Men might be able to defend it against a great Army. **1821** BYRON *Sardanap.* V. i, The river's broad and swoln, and uncommanded..by these besiegers. **1829** SCOTT *Anne of G.* xv, It was in a corner,.. uncommanded by any of the angles of the fortification.

Hence **Uncomma·ndedness.**

**1646** HAMMOND *Tracts* Pref., Perswading themselves and others..that the uncommandednesse of any thing induces that excesse.

**Uncomma·nder-like,** *a.* (UN-¹ 7 c.)

**1644** MILTON *Divorce* II. xi. 53 What more un-Judge-like, more un-Magistrate-like, and..more un-commander-like?

**Uncomme·ndable,** *a.* (UN-¹ 7 b and 5 b.)

**1509** BARCLAY *Shyp of Folys* (1570) 228 It is thing lawfull and not vncommendable. **1548** UDALL *Erasm. Par. Luke* Pref. C j b, It is vncommendable thorough vain arrogancie to take vpon vs that we haue not. **1603** BRETON *Dial. Pith & Pleas.* Wks. (Grosart) II. 9/2 The most dishonourable, and vncommendable of all creatures in the world. **1697** JOS. WOODWARD *Relig. Soc.* i. (1701) 15, I know no worldly, sinister, or uncommendable design proposed or prosecuted thereby. **1758** WALPOLE *Catal. Roy. Authors* (1759) II. 172 This is the only uncommendable performance of our Author's life.

Hence **Uncomme·ndably** *adv.*

**1589** PUTTENHAM *Eng. Poesie* II. xii[i]. (Arb.) 126 As he that translated certaine bookes of Virgils Eneydos in such measures and not vncommendably. **1882** *Academy* 16 Dec. 433/3 He dipped a little into scholarship, too, and not uncommendably.

**Uncomme·nded,** *ppl. a.* (UN-¹ 8.) **1570** LEVINS *Manip.* 50 Vncommended, *illaudatus.* **1645** WALLER '*Goe lovely Rose*' ii, Hadst thou sprung In deserts where no men abide, Thou must have uncommended dy'd. †**Uncomme·nsurate,** *a. Obs.* (UN-¹ 7 and 5 b.) **1676** GLANVILL *Ess.* i. 18 Our Senses are short, imperfect, and uncommensurate to the vastness and profundity of things. **1702** S. PARKER tr. *Cicero's De Finibus* IV. 237 Upon what Account therefore is Man so singular as to..take up with a *Summum Bonum* uncommensurate to the whole of his Person? **Uncomme·nted,** *ppl. a.* (UN-¹ 8.) **1751** J. BROWN *Shaftesb. Charac.* 318 The only method..is to search for them in the uncommented pages of the Gospel. **1877** BROWNING *La Saisiaz* 359 T'aversed heart must tell its story uncommented on. **Uncomme·rciable,** *a.* (UN-¹ 7 b.) **1787** JEFFERSON *Writ.* (1859) II. 189 By prohibiting all his Majesty's subjects from dealing in tobacco, one third of the exports of the United States are rendered uncommerciable here.

**Uncomme·rcial,** *a.* (UN-¹ 7.)

**1768** PENNANT *Brit. Zool.* I. 23 The uncommercial genius of the people. **1796** H. HUNTER tr. *St.-Pierre's Stud. Nat.* (1799) III. 116 There reigned at that time so much honesty and simplicity in this un-commercial island, that [etc.]. **1860** DICKENS (*title*), The Uncommercial Traveller. **1892** E. REEVES *Homeward Bound* 271 Cordova..is the quiet, uncommercial centre of an excellent wheat and olive country.

**Uncommi·ngled,** *ppl. a.* (UN-¹ 8.) **1861** S. WILBERFORCE *Ess.* (1874) I. 181 Both natures being uncommingled, though both eternally united in the person of the Son. **Unco·mminuted,** *ppl. a.* (UN-¹ 8.) **1757** *Phil. Trans.* L. 156 This part will be retained, after long trituration,..uncomminuted by the pestle. **Uncommi·serated,** *ppl. a.* (UN-¹ 8.) **1611** SPEED *Hist. Gt. Brit.* IX. xvi. § 45. 831/2 Thus Sommerset, and the English, are compelled to quit Normandy, not onely inglorious, but also in England it selfe vncommiserated. **Uncommi·serating,** *ppl. a.* (UN-¹ 10.) **1679** *Establ. Test* 41 Oh Injustice and uncommiserating Cruelty!

**Uncommi·ssioned,** *ppl. a.* [UN-¹ 8.]

1. Not commissioned or authorized.

**1659** FULLER *App. Inj. Innoc.* (1840) 618 Commissioned plunder begun with the war, but uncommissioned plunder was before it. *a* **1711** KEN *Anodynes* Poet. Wks. 1721 III. 460 Whose Voice I labour to suppress; While she my State bemoans, In uncommission'd Sighs and Groans. **1738** WARBURTON *Div. Legat.* I. 168 A little Priest's bringing the Mysteries into Etruria, on his own head; uncommissioned by his Superiors. **1802–12** BENTHAM *Ration. Judic. Evid.* (1827) I. 533 Uncommissioned inspecting judges. **1842** PUSEY *Crisis Eng. Ch.* 107 The one holds Ordination to be derived from the Apostles; the other, that Presbyters, uncommissioned, may confer it.

2. Of ships: = NON-COMMISSIONED *a.* 2.

**1863** *Lond. Rev.* 10 Jan. 7 The order of Earl Russell to detain her at Nassau must have been made under the impression that she would have reached that port uncommissioned.

**Uncommi·tted,** *ppl. a.* [UN-¹ 8.]

1. Not entrusted or delegated.

*c* **1381** CHAUCER *Parl. Foules* 518 Whoso hyt doth full fowle hymsylf accloyeth For offyce vncommyttyd oft anoyeth.

2. Not committed or perpetrated; (left) undone.

**1598** BARRET *Theor. Warres* 11 Gracelesse fellowes which do leaue no kinde of rauening crueltie vncommitted. **1607** HIERON *Wks.* I. 183 He would haue giuen a world, if he had beene able, that the fact of betraying Christ had beene vncommitted. **1643** HAMMOND *Lent Serm. at Oxford* Wks. 1683 IV. 511 Because he hath..no strength to maintain, no injury to provoke the uncommitted sin. **1814** BYRON *Corsair* II. xi. 22 She scarce had left an uncommitted crime. **1891** MEREDITH *One of our Conq.* xxxiv, To have the forgiveness for her uncommitted sin dashed in her face.

3. Not referred to a committee.

**1807** JEFFERSON *Writ.* (1830) IV. 95 We propose..to leave the question of war, non-intercourse, or other measures, uncommitted, to the legislature.

4. Not pledged to any particular course.

**1814** CHALMERS *Let.* in Hanna *Life* (1849) I. 444, I trust you will concede to me the right of bringing a free and uncommitted mind to this matter. **1826** DISRAELI *Viv. Grey* III. i, A young man, uncommitted in political principles. **1884** *Manch. Exam.* 28 Oct. 5/3 Up to the present..the deputation..prefer to regard themselves as uncommitted.

**Uncommi·xed,** *ppl. a.* (UN-¹ 8 and 5 b.)

*c* **1611** CHAPMAN *Iliad* x. 369 The Thracian quarter lies Utmost of all and uncommix'd with Trojan regiments. **1660** J. H[ARDING] *Basil. Valent. Chariot Antim.* 3 The Chaff being separated from the uncommix'd and undefiled Corn. **1814** SOUTHEY *Roderick* xv. 250 A feeling uncommixed with sense of guilt Or shame..thrill'd through the King.

†**Uncommo·ded,** *ppl. a. Obs.* (UN-¹ 8 and 5 b.)

**1683** MOXON *Mech. Exerc., Printing* ii. ⁋ 1 A Window..on the North-side the Room, that the Press-men..may be the less uncommoded with the heat of the Sun.

† **Uncommo·dious,** *a. Obs.* (UN-1 7 and 5 b.) **1539** ELYOT *Cast. Helthe* (1541) 54 b, If any grefe hapneth of the heade, vomite is than uncommodious. **1597** BEARD *Theatre God's Judgem.* (1612) 463 How hurtfull and vncommodious the desire..was vnto them. **1643–5** MILTON *Divorce* II. xxi, To forbid dislike..were indeed an uncommodious rudenesse, not a just power. **1680** MOXON *Mech. Exerc.* x. 184 To tire it [the leg] quickly with bringing it down again, after it is raised to so uncommodious a position.

So † **Uncommo·diously** *adv. Obs.*
**1545** ELYOT, *Incommode*,..vncommodiously, ylle fauouredly. **1647** HEXHAM I, Vncommodiously, *ongerievelick*.

**Unco·mmon,** *a.* (and *adv.*). [UN-1 7.]

**1.** Not possessed in common. *rare*—1.
**1548** UDALL, etc., *Erasm. Par. John* xiv. 85 b, Betwene vs two is no vnlykenes, or any thyng vncommon as touchyng the hier, and our diuine nature.

**2.** Not commonly (to be) met with; not of ordinary occurrence; unusual, rare.
**1611** COTGR., *Incommune*, vncommon; or, not common. **1665** BOYLE *Occas. Refl.* VI. vi. 209 'Tis so uncommon a thing to see Tulips last till Roses come to be blown. **1676** GLANVILL *Ess.* vi. 28 To give us some general notice of those uncommon Events which they foresee. **1712** ADDISON *Spect.* No. 421 ¶ 2 Whatever is New or Uncommon is apt to delight the Imagination. **1732** BERKELEY *Alciphr.* v. § 20 Nor is it an uncommon thing to behold ignorance and zeal united in men. **1770** *Junius Lett.* xli. (1788) 227 Yours is not an uncommon character. **1818** BYRON *Juan* I. i, I want a hero: an uncommon want, When every year and month sends forth a new one. **1884** THOMPSON *Tumours of Bladder* 1 There is little doubt that these growths are by no means uncommon.
*absol.* **1806** SURR *Winter in Lond.* II. 58 He was compelled to admit, that the uncommon is nevertheless the possible.

**3.** Unusual in amount, extent, or degree; remarkably great; above the ordinary.
**1700** PRIOR *Carm. Sec.* xxiii, She, from the noble Precipices thrown, Comes rushing with uncommon Ruin down. **1736** BERKELEY *Disc.* Wks. III. 427 Such bad notions have..been propagated with uncommon industry in these kingdoms. **1774** J. BRYANT *Mythol.* II. 100 Semiramis, a woman of uncommon endowments, and great personal charms. **1825** COBBETT *Rur. Rides* 450 He seems to have taken uncommon pains in the execution of this work. **1864** FROUDE *Short Stud.* (1867) I. 2 He was a man of uncommon power.

**4.** Of an unusual type or character; exceptional in kind or quality. Also *absol.*
**1705** ADDISON *Italy* Pref., His masterly and uncommon Observations on the Religion and Governments of Italy. **1758** S. HAYWARD *Serm.* xvii. 550 We could not but value so uncommon a friend. **1819** SHELLEY *Peter Bell 3rd* IV. xvi, The Devil was no uncommon creature. **1882** W. SHARP *Rossetti* iii. 105 The spiritual is ever foreign to the material, the *un*common to the common.

**5.** *Mus.* (See quot.)
*c* **1833** *Encycl. Metrop.* (1845) V. 778 *Uncommon chord*, the chord of the sixth, not so called because unusual or improper, but in contradistinction to the common chord.

**6.** As *adv.* = UNCOMMONLY *adv.* 2. *colloq.* or *dial.*
**1784** *New Spectator* No. 15. 1 To hear another of austere gravity, burst into an uncommon loud fit of laughter at a trifling incident. **1818** LADY MORGAN *Autobiog.* (1859) 190 He was uncommon afraid of the custom-house officers. **1851** KINGSLEY *Yeast* ix, He consorts with them poachers, sir, uncommon. I hope he ben't one himself. **1891** 'J. S. WINTER' *Lumley* i, They're an uncommon thirsty lot to-night.

**Unco·mmonable,** *a.* (UN-1 7 b.) **1768** BLACKSTONE *Comm.* III. 237 In case..the uncommonable cattle of a commoner be found upon the land.

**Unco·mmonly,** *adv.* [Cf. UNCOMMON *a.* and UN-1 11.]

**1.** *Not uncommonly*, not rarely; pretty frequently.
**1747** J. SMITH *Mem. Wool* Pref. a j *note*, A Person more than ordinarily concerned, and not uncommonly employed. **1883** STUBBS *Med. & Mod. Hist.* xv. (1886) 343 We are not uncommonly told that Henry VII. had not in his own person the shadow of hereditary right.

**2.** In an uncommon or unusual degree; unusually, remarkably.
**1751** EARL ORRERY *Remarks Swift* (1752) 10 Otherwise it was thought impossible, that he could be so uncommonly munificent to a young man, no ways related to him. **1794** MRS. RADCLIFFE *Myst. Udolpho* liv, There was something in his countenance uncommonly interesting. **1840** R. H. DANA *Bef. Mast* xxiv, He wrote an uncommonly handsome hand. **1885** *Truth* 28 May 847/2 The high-priced nobodies who..do so uncommonly little.

**Unco·mmonness.** [f. UNCOMMON *a.*] The quality or state of being uncommon; unusualness.
**1705** ADDISON *Italy* 225 Our admiration of 'em does not so much arise out of their Greatness as Uncommonness. **1730** GAY *Let. to Swift* 6 Dec., For the uncommonness of the thing, I fansy, your curiosity will prevail over your fear. **1830** CARLYLE *Misc.* (1840) II. 365 Some features of originality, as well as of uncommonness. **1882** *Pall Mall G.* 8 April, This ..presents the common with due uncommonness and suggestiveness.

**Unco·mmonplace,** *a.* (UN-1 7.)
**1873** HELPS *Anim. & Mast.* i. (1875) 23 Everything seems clever and uncommonplace in a language of which you know but little. **1887** LD. GRANVILLE in Fitzmaurice *Life* (1905) II. 497 The charm of your..uncommonplace character.

**Uncommu·nicable,** *a.* [UN-1 7 b and 5 b.]

**1.** That cannot or may not be communicated; incommunicable.
**1382** WYCLIF *Wisd.* xiv. 21 The vncomunycable name to stones and trees thei putten. **1555** EDEN *Decades* (Arb.) 297 The diuine prouidence hath made nothynge vncommunicable. **1587** GOLDING *De Mornay* vi. (1592) 70 Men were forbidden to vtter the vncommunicable name of God. **1612** SELDEN *Illustr. Drayton's Poly-olb.* xiii. 269 A perfect and uncommunicable power royall. **1650** COWLEY *Let.* 9 July, Wks. (Grosart) II. 348/2 Their hopes of an uncommunicable Victory. **1742** WARBURTON in *Pope's Wks.* (1788) VI. 135 His having no Delight in any thing uncommunicated or uncommunicable. **1780** BURKE *Sp. at Bristol* Wks. 1808 III. 369 The peculiar, reserved, uncommunicable rights of England. **1833** LD. HOUGHTON *Mem. Many Scenes, To Landor* (1844) 144 The power of uncommunicable Art.

† **2.** Uncommunicative. *Obs.*—1
**1628** FELTHAM *Resolves* II. vii. 16 Neither [master nor servant] can haue comfort, where both are vncommunicable.

Hence **Uncommu·nicably** *adv.*
**1817** SHELLEY *To Constantia Singing* 12 A breathless awe, ..Wild, sweet, but uncommunicably strange.

† **Uncommu·nicant.** *Obs.*—1 [UN-1 12.] = NON-COMMUNICANT. **1600** *Vestry Bks.* (Surtees) 278 Our certificate concerninge the recusantes and uncommunicantes. † **Uncommu·nicate,** *a. Obs.*—1 [UN-1 7 and 5 b.] = next. **1664** H. MORE *Antid. Idolatry* ii. 34 If it be not, we give an uncommunicate Excellency to the Creature, and rob God of his Right and Honour.

**Uncommu·nicated,** *ppl. a.* (UN-1 8 and 5 b.)
**1597** HOOKER *Eccl. Pol.* v. liii. § 1 Whatsoeuer is naturall to Deitie, the same remaineth in Christ vncommunicated vnto his Manhood. **1647** CLARENDON *Contempl. Ps.* Tracts (1727) 438 Whose uncommunicated prerogative it is, to discern clearly the thoughts and inclinations of all hearts. **1720** WATERLAND *Eight Serm.* 224 Supreme Power, whether communicated or uncommunicated, is supreme Power. **1826** SOUTHEY *Vind. Eccl. Angl.* 278 Disposed to uphold the[ir] ascendancy..by uncommunicated knowledge, and unrelenting severity.

**Uncommu·nicating,** *ppl. a.* (UN-1 10, 5 b.)
**1650** JER. TAYLOR *Funeral Serm. C'tess Carbery* 5 There are exterminating Angels that fly wrapt up in the curtains of immateriality and an uncommunicating nature. **1765** BLACKSTONE *Comm.* I. 95 From a diversity of practice in two large and uncommunicating jurisdictions. **1801** SOUTHEY *Thalaba* IV. xxv, In uncommunicating misery Silent they stood. **1821** LAMB *Elia* I. *Quakers' Meeting*, The uncommunicating muteness of fishes.

**Uncommu·nicative,** *a.* (UN-1 7 and 5 b.)
**1691** NORRIS *Pract. Disc.* 297 To be selfish and straitlaced, niggardly and covetous, reserved and uncommunicative. **1730** SWIFT *Dean's Reasons* 43 Whose uncommunicative heart Will scarce one precious word impart. **1756** COWPER *Wks.* (1837) XV. 285 Our nation has, indeed, been generally supposed to be of a sullen and uncommunicative disposition. **1807** G. CHALMERS *Caledonia* I. Pref. p. vii, The scholars of Scotland remained inert, and uncommunicative of what they did not know. **1865** W. G. PALGRAVE *Arabia* II. 296 We made sail..in company with some islanders, silent uncommunicative men.

Hence **Uncommu·nicativeness.**
**1748** RICHARDSON *Clarissa* (1811) IV. 291, I might justify my secrecy and uncommunicativeness by her own. **1829** DISRAELI in Monypenny *Life* (1910) I. 122 Though generally accused of uncommunicativeness, I like a gentle chat with a friend. **1851** GALLENGA *Italy* i. 22 The Italians had given him blame for a dark simulation—which proceeded from sheer timidity and uncommunicativeness.

**Uncommu·ted,** *ppl. a.* (UN-1 8.)
**1870** W. R. GREG *Polit. Problems* 151 He believes (correctly) that his fair share, uncommuted and unadvanced, would be 23*s.* in good years. **1872** GEO. ELIOT *Middlem.* v, Such a lady gave a neighbourliness to both rank and religion, and mitigated the business of uncommuted tithe.

**Uncompa·ct,** *a.* (UN-1 7 and 5 b.)
**1705** ADDISON *Italy* 237 How could a Liquid, that lay hardening by degrees, settle in such a furrow'd uncompact Surface?

**Uncompa·cted,** *ppl. a.* (UN-1 8 and 5 b.)
**1661** FELTHAM *Resolves* (ed. 8) II. xxiii. 230 He catches at that which is not yet in his reach; which seems to unfold but an uncompacted mind. **1781** JOHNSON *L.P., Lyttelton*, Lord Lyttelton..had a slender uncompacted frame, and a meagre face. **1793** W. ROBERTS *Looker-on* No. 36 (1794) II. 31 Democracies were all either loose and uncompacted, or violent and distorted. **1863** DANA *Man. Geol.* 49 Whether solid or uncompacted earth.

† **Uncompanable,** *a. Obs.* Also 6 vncompaignable. [UN-1 7 b.] Uncompanionable.
**1555** WATREMAN *Fardle Facions* II. iv. 143 Thei ware sterne men, and vncompaignable. **1611** COTGR., *Insociable*, vnsociable, vncompanable.

† **Uncompane,** *v. Obs.*—1 [UN-1 14 or UN-2 7.] *intr.* To avoid or shun society. **1589** WARNER *Alb. Eng.* VI. xxix. 128 She vncompaned, To flie He bids her solitarie moodes.

**Unco·mpanied,** *ppl. a.* [UN-1 8.] Unaccompanied.
*a* **1547** SURREY *Æneid* IV. (1557) F ij b, And still her thought, that she was left alone Vncompanied great viages to wende. **1570** LEVINS *Manip.* 50 Vncompanied, *incomitatus*. **1600** FAIRFAX *Tasso* I. xlviii, Yet thence she fled, uncompaned, unsought. **1791** COWPER *Odyss.* v. 38 Our fixt resolve, that brave Ulysses thence Depart, uncompanied by God or man. **1814** SOUTHEY *Roderick* III. 161 The daughters of the land.. to the Mosque Holding uncompanied their jealous way.

**Uncompa·nionable,** *a.* [UN-1 7 b.]

**1.** Of persons: Not companionable; unsociable.
**1748** RICHARDSON *Clarissa* VII. 149 Uncompanionable poor creatures. **1796–7** JANE AUSTEN *Pride & Prej.* xxvii, With such a mother and such uncompanionable sisters, home could not be faultless. **1819** SHELLEY *Cyclops* 425 Do you desire, or not, to fly This uncompanionable man? **1873** HELPS *Anim. & Mast.* viii. 177 But any thing more uncompanionable than the society of London cannot well be imagined.

**2.** Of things: Not fitted to go together.
**1855** [J. D. BURN] *Autobiog. Beggar Boy* (1859) 121 Philosophy and hungry bellies are as uncompanionable as they were at the siege of Jerusalem!

**Uncompa·nioned,** *ppl. a.* [UN-1 8.]

**1.** Unmatched, unequalled.
**1608** MACHIN *Dumbe Knight* I. i, Dost thou not thinke She is..Vnparalleld, and vncompanioned?

**2.** Not provided with a companion; not accompanied by any other (person or thing).
**1809** CAMPBELL *Gert. Wyom.* I. xii, All uncompanioned else her heart had gone. *a* **1851** MOIR *Poems, Tombless Man* iii, With uncompanion'd step, measured and slow,.. Up a long vista'd avenue I wound. **1863** LD. LYTTON *Ring Amasis* I. II. I. v. 264 Now, completely uncompanioned, he had withdrawn himself from his retinue.

**b.** Characterized by the absence or want of a companion or companionship.
**1822** J. WILSON *Lights & Shadows Sc. Life* 229 In his hours of uncompanioned darkness. **1860** LD. LYTTON *Lucile* II. iii. § 5. 18 A sense Of his own uncompanion'd, remote, and intense Isolation. **1885** M. ARNOLD *Poor Matthias*, Fare for ever well, nor fear..to stray Down the uncompanion'd way!

**Unco·mparable,** *a.* [UN-1 7 b and 5 b.]

† **1.** = INCOMPARABLE *a. Obs.*
**1382** WYCLIF *Judith* x. 4 That she aperede to the eȝen of alle men with fairnesse vncomparable. **1483** CAXTON *Cato* e iv b, I consydere and suppose that god is so ouer souerayn and uncomparable and unlyke. **1548** GESTE *Pr. Masse* A v b, What an vnspeakable and vncomparable vyce is thee Pryuee Masse. **1586** F. GREVILLE in Sidney *Poems* (1873) I. p. xix, Sir Philip's uncomparable judgement. **1634** P. SMITH in Fuller *Abel Rediv.* (1867) II. 316 Had that father been born and lived in Italy or France, his wit, though uncomparable, had been much more refined.

**2.** Incapable of being compared (to anything else).
**1826** SOUTHEY *Vind. Eccl. Angl.* 177 An unexpressible, uncomparable, unimaginable stench.

Hence **Unco·mparably** *adv.*
**1548** GESTE *Pr. Masse* E v b, By reason wherof thee priest sacryfyce as it most hyghly empayrethe christes honoure & maiestie so vncomperablely offendeth god.

**Uncompa·ratively,** *adv.* [UN-1 11.] †Absolutely, positively. **1702** S. PARKER tr. *Cicero's De Finibus* III. 174 Whatever touches not upon the Confines of Vertue or Vice is in its own Nature Uncomparatively Indifferent. **Uncompa·red,** *ppl. a.* (UN-1 8.) **1755** YOUNG *Centaur* ii. Wks. 1757 IV. 146 Come you..to make these young criminals appear more innocent, than they could appear uncompared with superior indiscretion?

**Unco·mpassable,** *a.* (UN-1 7 b.)
*c* **1530** tr. *Erasmus' Serm. Ch. Jesus* (1901) 7 He abydeth in hymselfe vncompassable and vnmeasurable. **1611** FLORIO s.v. *Incircondéuole*. **1644** DIGBY *Nat. Soul* Concl. 456 So extreme must the rauenous inclemency..be of such an vncompassable desire gnawing eternally vpon the soule.

**Unco·mpassed,** *a.* [UN-1 9.] Not provided with a compass.
**1827** POLLOK *Course T.* II. 242 Choosing, thus unshipped, Uncompassed, unprovisioned, and bestormed, To swim a sea of breadth immeasurable. *a* **1844** CAMPBELL *Napoleon & Brit. Sailor* 35 A wherry..Untarr'd, uncompass'd, and unkeel'd, No sail, no rudder.

**Unco·mpassed,** *ppl. a.* [UN-1 8.] Not bounded or circumscribed; unlimited.
**1577** tr. *Bullinger's Decades* Preface, The Churche in this time is like lande that hath lyen..vnmanured, vncompassed, vntilled. **1602** J. DAVIES (Heref.) *Mirum in Modum* i. Wks. (Grosart) I. 5/1 Center of true Rest, Compass'd with glory, and vncompass'd blisse. **1642** H. MORE *Song of Soul* II. III. iv. 27 Why not dispred The world withouten bounds, endlesse uncompassed? **1665** CODRINGTON *Life Earl Essex* 11 When the ambition and the excesse of the Bishops did swell them up to such an uncompassed greatnesse.

**Uncompa·ssionate,** *a.* [UN-1 7 and 5 b.] Wanting in compassion; unfeeling.
**1591** SHAKS. *Two Gent.* III. i. 231 Neither bended knees,.. nor siluer-shedding teares Could penetrate her vncompassionate Sire. *a* **1663** SANDERSON *Serm., Ad Magist.* (1681) 80 To wrestle with the unjust and bitter upbraidings of unreasonable and uncompassionate men. **1671** MILTON *Samson* 818 If thou in strength all mortals dost exceed, In uncompassionate anger do not so. **1792** G. WAKEFIELD *Mem.* (1804) II. 392 Nor can a single syllable in support of such uncompassionate persuasions be produced from the Christian Scriptures. **1871** ALABASTER *Wheel of Law* 61 This is uncompassionate and wicked. **1877** WALLACE *Russia* iii. 39 The personification of uncompassionate, inflexible law.
*absol.* **1688** COLLIER *Several Disc.* (1725) 351 The Designing, the Parsimonious and Uncompassionate.

Hence **Uncompa·ssionately** *adv.*; **-ness.**
**1608** HIERON *Wks.* I. 743 The vncompassionatenesse which I finde among the men of this yron age. **1612** SHELTON *Quix.* I. III. x. 225 Catching hold of one anothers beards, and be-fisting themselues..vncompassionately. **1862** F. HALL *Hindu Philos. Syst.* 124 Cruelty is uncompassionateness.

**Uncompa·ssionated,** *ppl. a.* (UN-1 8.) **1867** 'OUIDA' *Idalia* xxix, Those..uncompassionated millions who are the prey alike of despot and of demagogue. **1882** FARRAR *Early Christianity* I. 159 Once not a people, but now a people of God; once uncompassionated, but compassionated now. **Uncompa·ssionating,** *ppl. a.* (UN-1 10.) *a* **1711** KEN *Edmund* Poet. Wks. 1721 II. 279 They..with an uncompassionating Eye Into their panting Breasts began to pry. **Uncompa·ssioned,** *ppl. a.* (UN-1 8.) **1827** POLLOK *Course T.* III. 597 A cold..Forsaken thing, that wandered on, forlorn, Undestined, uncompassioned, unupheld. **Uncompee·red,** *ppl. a.* (UN-1 8.) **1602** WARNER *Alb. Eng.* XII. lxxviii. (1612) 321 For Good must God be vncompeer'd. **Uncompe·llable, -ible,** *a.* (UN-1 7, 7 b.) **1613** DRUMM. OF HAWTH. *Cypress Grove* Wks. (S.T.S.) II. 91 Thy Will is vncompellable [**1711** uncompellible], resisting Force, daunting Necessitie, despising Danger. **1661** FELTHAM *On Luke* xiv. 20 in *Resolves* (ed. 8) 386 A noble Courtesie..conquers the uncompellable mind, and disinterests Man of himself.

**Uncompe·lled,** *ppl. a.* (UN-1 8.)
**1470–1** *Rolls of Parlt.* VI. 233/1 The other pety Capytaynes affermed to be trewe at their Dethes, uncompelled, unstured or undesired soo to doo. **1548** PATTEN *Exped. Scotl.* O j b, Thear wear but fewe of Lordes..and gentlemen in the feld, but..did thearin right willyngly & vncompeld their partes. **1549** COVERDALE, etc. *Erasm. Par.* 1 *Tim.* 4 b, They..runne vncompelled, and doe more than al the whole law requireth. **1621** G. SANDYS *Ovid's Met.* I. 3 The Golden Age was first; which vncompeld, And without rule, in Faith and Truth exceld. **1648** BOYLE *Seraph. Love* xxv. (1700) 152 The

amorous Needle, once joyn'd unto the Load-stone, would never uncompell'd forsake the inchanting Mineral. **1725** Pope *Odyss.* ii. 420 But..swear To keep my voyage from the royal ear, Nor uncompelled the dang'rous truth betray. **1816** Byron *Childe Harold* iii. xii, Still uncompell'd, He would not yield dominion of his mind. **1856** Mrs. Browning *Aur. Leigh* iv. 544 Of course the people came in uncompelled.

**Uncompe·nsable**, *a.* (Un-1 7 b and 5 b.) **1734** Watts *Reliq. Jur.* 121 The Destruction of such a rare Piece of Workmanship would have been an uncompensable Loss.

**Unco·mpensated**, *ppl. a.* [Un-1 8.]

1. Not compensated by any gain or good.

**1774** Burke *Sp. Amer. Tax.* 23 To join together the restraints of an universal..monopoly, with an universal..taxation, is an unnatural union; perfect uncompensated slavery. **1787** *Ann. Reg., Hist. Eur.* 81/1 Mr. Fox inferred that the revenue of this country would suffer a very serious and uncompensated loss. **1802–12** Bentham *Ration. Judic. Evid.* (1827) III. 484 The vexation and expense incident to the production of it, is uncompensated. **1898** *Educat. Rev.* Oct. 277 Their story is one of almost universal and uncompensated disappointment.

2. Not balanced or made up for.

**1789** *Phil. Trans.* LXXIX. 283 The uncompensated electricity which is as essential to the charge as that which is in equilibrio. **1835** Mrs. Somerville *Connex. Phys. Sci.* iii. (ed. 2) 22 An uncompensated portion of the direct motion.

3. Unrecompensed.

**1830** Cobbett *Rur. Rides* 163 That gentleman remains uncompensated for his sufferings. **1882** *Amer. Missionary* (N. Y.) Apr. 100 The House of Refuge,..to whose interest he gave untiring and uncompensated time and attention.

†**Unco·mpetence.** *Obs.*—1 [Un-1 12 and 5 b.] Want of fittingness. **1541** R. Copland *Galyen's Terap.* 2 E j b, In Ametrie, that is to saye, in vncompetence and immoderacyon. †**Unco·mpetent**, *a. Obs.* [Un-1 7 and 5 b.] Incompetent. **1563** Foxe *A. & M.* 721 Him that is conuented before an vncompetente and suspecte iudge. **1659** *Gentl. Calling* (1696) 45 All, whose value and wishes of a Mahometan Paradise render them not uncompetent to estimate these purer and refined pleasures. †**Uncompetible**, *a. Obs.*—1 (Un-1 7 and 5 b.) *a* **1628** Ld. Brooke *Alaham* ii. ii, He first despiseth thee, Then triumphs in thy once forsaken loue; Proclaimes deceipt to be thy state of mind, Vncompetible, vnpossible to finde. **Uncompe·titive**, *a.* (Un-1 7.) **1885** Ruskin in *Pall Mall G.* 2 Mar. 4/2 An English officer,..totally inexperienced in war,..uncompetitive in any manner of examination. **1886** Hissey *On Box Seat* 242 The shops are uncompetitive of course, and..provokingly uninteresting. **Uncompla·cent**, *a.* (Un-1 7.) **1805** Foster *Ess.* (1806) I. 189 This new desire must have been a very uncomplacent associate for them. **Uncomplai·ned**, *ppl. a.* (Un-1 8.) **1648** Hexham ii, *Onbeklaeght*, Vncomplained. **1691** T. H[ale] *Acc. New Invent.* f 7 Instances of Complaints.., and observation of a greater number of Ships resting uncomplained of.

**Uncomplai·ning**, *ppl. a.* (Un-1 10.)

**1744** Thomson *Spring* 390 The bleeding Breast Of the weak, helpless, uncomplaining Wretch. **1816** Shelley *Sunset* 48 Whether the dead..are the uncomplaining things they seem. **1848** Dickens *Dombey* iii, The child..was so gentle, so quiet, and uncomplaining. **1873** Symonds *Grk. Poets* 295 The uncomplaining submission of Iphigeneia and Polyxena.

Hence **Uncomplai·ningly** *adv.*; **-ness.**

[**1847** Webster.] **1861** Whyte Melville *Good for Nothing* I. 68 Ada bore with it all, sadly, but uncomplainingly. **1876** Smiles *Sc. Natur.* xiii. (ed. 4) 252 Edward's perseverance, self-denial, and uncomplainingness.

**Unco·mplaisance.** (Un-1 12.) **1707** Norris *Treat. Humility* vii. 311 Pride is hated..as an uncomplaisance, as something that opposes and hinders, and stands in the way.

**Unco·mplaisant**, *a.* (Un-1 8.)

**1693** Locke *Educ.* § 143 A natural Roughness, which makes a Man uncomplaisant to others. **1704** Cibber *Careless Husb.* iv. 73 This is very Uncomplaisant to Engross so Agreeable a Part of the Company to yourself. *a* **1734** North *Lives* I. 93 His lordship, of one that was not morose and uncomplaisant, was the most sober that [etc.]. **1802** *Phil. Trans.* XCI. 154 This metal is so uncomplaisant as to retain the white colour.

Hence **Unco·mplaisantly** *adv.*

**1766** Blackstone *Comm.* II. xiv. 213 Thus sons shall be admitted before daughters; or, as our male lawgivers have somewhat uncomplaisantly expressed it, the worthiest of blood shall be preferred.

**Unco·mplemental**, *a.* (Un-1 7. Cf. Complemental *a.* 6.) **1673** Cave *Prim. Chr.* ii. iii. 61 The severe and uncomplemental man..bluntly entertained her with this discourse.

†**Uncomple·te**, *a. Obs.* (Un-1 7 and 5 b.)

**1398** Trevisa *Barth. De P. R.* xix. lxxix. (1495) ll v b/2 Wynde egges..ben lesse in quantite for they ben vncomplete. *c* **1430** *Art of Nombryng* 19 The last ternary other uncomplete nombre. **1611** Cotgr., *Imperfaict*, imperfect, vncompleat. **1725** Pope *Odyss.* I. p. xii, These various incidents..are only the uncompleat and unfinish'd parts of one and the same Action and Fable.

**Uncomple·ted**, *ppl. a.* (Un-1 8 and 5 b.)

**1513** Douglas *Æneid* vii. Prol. 148, I..wolx ennoyit.., Thair restit vncompleitit so gret ane part. **1661** Feltham *On Luke* xiv. 20 in *Resolves*, etc. (ed. 8) 393 Marriage is Creations perfectness, barren Virginity is but uncompleted Man. **1681** Burnet *Hist. Ref.* II. 363 The other more pressing things that were still uncompleted. *a* **1771** Gray *Dante* 44 In low and uncompleated Sounds I heard 'em wail for Bread. **1858** Longf. *M. Standish* ix. 67 Each with his plan for the day, and the work that was left uncompleted. **1875** J. P. Hopps *Princ. Relig.* xiv. 46 The salvation that is left uncompleted here will be continued in the brighter world beyond.

†**Uncomple·tely**, *adv. Obs.*—1 (Un-1 11 and 5 b.) *c* **1380** Wyclif *Sel. Wks.* II. 197 And þes blasfemes out of bileve, þat seien þat Crist spekiþ here falsely or uncompletly. **Unco·mplex**, *a.* (Un-1 7 and 5 b.) **1702** S. Parker tr. *Cicero's De Finibus* v. 292 The Six Uncomplex Acceptations of *Summum Bonum* I have now laid before you. **1854** Mill *Lett.* (1910) II. 368 Small things, or at least things uncomplex and composed of few parts.

**Uncompli·able**, *a.* (Un-1 7 b and 5 b.)

**1626** in *Cosin's Corr.* (Surtees) I. 95 The disposition of some men..who will not be won, but are uncompliable and intractable. **1687** H. More *Answ. Psychop.* (1689) 127 How uncompliable this Difference is with History.

Hence **Uncompliabi·lity, -ableness.**

**1687** H. More *Contn. Remark. Stor.* (1689) 427 His displeasure against her uncompliableness. **1880** Burton *Reign Anne* I. ii. 62 Their uncompliability was neutral, not active.

**Uncompli·ant**, *a.* (Un-1 7 and 5 b.)

**1659** Gauden *Tears Ch.* iii. xv. 305 By which you and they must needs be so well informed, as to be justly opposite and uncompliant to those Errours. **1678** Cudworth *Intell. Syst.* i. v. 672 When..the stubborn necessity of matter proves uncompliant. **1768–74** Tucker *Lt. Nat.* (1834) II. 581 They generate a stiffness and preciseness.., rendering men troublesome and uncompliant. **1828** D'Israeli *Chas. I*, I. viii. 259 The King, in despair, dissolved this uncompliant Parliament. **1860** W. L. Collins *Luck of Ladysmede* (1862) I. 320 A miserable wife, as some said,—an uncompliant mistress, according to others.

**Unco·mplicated**, *ppl. a.* (Un-1 8.)

[**1775** Ash.] **1792** Burke *Let. Sir H. Langrishe* Wks. VI. 369 You may leave that deliberation of a parliamentary reform..uncomplicated and unembarrassed with the other question. **1879** Spencer *Data of Ethics* viii. § 51. 139 Observing, in their uncomplicated forms, what are the negative conditions to harmonious social life. **1881** *Macm. Mag.* XLIII. 359/2 The worship..in its primitive form, and uncomplicated with elements of later mythic growth.

b. *spec.* in *Path.*

**1835–6** *Todd's Cycl. Anat.* I. 456/1 In a simple and uncomplicated case [of necrosis] recovery is nearly certain. **1871** A. Meadows *Man. Midwifery* (ed. 2) 418 Thus what was originally simple uncomplicated local inflammation may become a specific contagious disease.

**Uncomplime·ntary**, *a.* (Un-1 7.) **1846** Worcester (citing *Qu. Rev.*). **1861** Mill *Repr. Govt.* (1865) 88/1 If he forms an uncomplimentary opinion of their part in the affair. **1878** *Masque Poets* 228 With Robert Lorne's Florinda's name was coupled In terms uncomplimentary to both.

**Uncomply·ing**, *ppl. a.* (Un-1 10 and 5 b.)

**1643** Milton *Divorce* 11 When he shall find himselfe bound fast to an uncomplying discord of nature. *a* **1661** Fuller *Worthies, Carmarthen.* iv. (1662) 27 A man not unlearned, but somewhat indiscreet, or rather uncomplying, which procured him much trouble. **1724** Swift *Verses Whitshed's Motto on Coach* 14 To shew my Fury Against an uncomplying Jury. **1777** Robertson *Hist. Amer.* vi. (1778) II. 234 He was endowed only with integrity and courage; the former harsh and uncomplying. **1834** De Quincey in *Tait's Mag.* I. 21/2 His sturdy and uncomplying morality. **1862** S. Lucas *Secularia* 197 Others of the company..incurred the Protector's displeasure by too uncomplying principles.

**Uncompo·sable**, *a.* (Un-1 7 b.)

**1640** Ld. Digby *Sp. Triennial Parl.* 14 All the rest of the world at the same time in Tempest, in Combustions, in uncomposable Warres. *a* **1734** North *Exam.* i. ii. § 63 A Difference..at length flamed so high as to be uncomposeable.

**Uncompo·sed**, *ppl. a.* [Un-1 8 and 5 b.]

1. Not composed or made up; not composite.

**1570** Billingsley *Euclid* vii. def. xii. 186 Numbers vncomposed, haue no part to measure them, but onely vnitie. **1644** Digby *Nat. Soul* i. § 3. 358 We can not diuide the actions of mans mind, further then into apprehensions; and therefore we called them simple and vncomposed.

2. Not put together in proper form.

**1598** Florio, *Discomposto*, vncomposed, shapelesse, formelesse. *c* **1610** *Women Saints* 189, I haue sett downe her life in playne and vncomposed wordes. **1753** Hogarth *Anal. Beauty* ii. 17 Variety uncomposed, and without design, is confusion and deformity. **1838** Carlyle *Misc.* (1857) IV. 140 Scott's Biography if uncomposed, lies..here, in the elementary state, and can at any time be composed, if necessary.

3. Not reduced to an orderly or tranquil state; disordered, excited.

**1601** B. Jonson *Ev. Man in Hum.* (Qo.) v. i. 526 It is a vertue that persues Any saue rude and vncomposed spirites. **1639** Bp. Reynolds *Lord's Supper* xviii, Sudden, uncomposed, & uncollected thoughts. **1691** Hartcliffe *Virtues* 205 The Scum of an empty Mind, the very froth of an unsetled and uncomposed Spirit.

b. Unregulated; disorderly.

**1631** Brathwait *Whimzies, Traveller* 93 Not an irregular haire about him, nor an unset looke to attend him, nor an uncomposed cringe to accoutre him. **1649** *Alcoran* 411 The uncomposed gestures of the drunkard.

4. Not brought into a state of concord.

**1650** R. Stapylton *Strada's Low C. Wars* v. 133 In his Letters to the Governess, the Emperour promised her his endeavours, if any thing was yet uncomposed. **1651** C. Cartwright *Cert. Relig.* i. 87 Whilst the Catholicks have no jars undecided, no differences uncomposed.

†**Uncompou·nd**, *a. Obs.* (Un-1 7 and 5 b.)

**1539** Elyot *Cast. Helthe* (1541) 1 b, The Elementes be those originall thinges unmyxt and uncompounde, of whose..myxture all other thynges be compacte. **1557** Recorde *Whetst.* A iij b, 2. is accompted truely an euen number, originall, and vncompounde.

**Uncompou·ndable**, *a.* (Un-1 7 b.) **1691** E. Taylor *Behmen's Theos. Philos.* 66 Tin and silver..coming of different Properties are uncompoundable.

**Uncompou·nded**, *ppl. a.* [Un-1 8 and 5 b.]

1. Not compounded; not made up of various elements; unmixed: a. Of the Deity or his essence.

**1587** Golding *De Mornay* iv. 45 By these conclusions we come to another, which is, that God is not compounded. [*marg.*] God is single and vncompounded. **1602** Warner *Alb. Eng.* xiii. lxxix. 326 Sufficeth vs to know he is..Vnpassiue, vnmateriall, vncompounded. *a* **1619** Fotherby *Atheom.* ii. x. § 3 (1622) 304 His vncompounded simplicitie, is the true matter of his Vnitie. *a* **1676** Hales *Prim. Orig. Man.* i. i. (1677) 11 Though he is but one, and one most simple uncompounded Being. **1720** Waterland *Eight Serm.* 200 The proof of the Father's being..one simple, uncompounded, undivided, intelligent Agent. *a* **1751** Bolingbroke *Philos.* Wks. 1754 V. 77 Various manifestations of the infinite wisdom of one simple uncompounded being. **1867** Bp. Forbes *Explan. 39 Art.* i. 10 If God is absolutely, He is simple and uncompounded.

b. Of material things, their nature or qualities.

**1615** H. Crooke *Body of Man* i. xx. 32 Aristotle calleth them..Simple and vncompounded Parts, because they are not compounded of other parts. **1665** Hooke *Microgr.* 1 We must endevour to follow Nature in the more plain and easie ways she treads in the most simple and uncompounded bodies. **1742** H. Baker *Microsc.* i. Introd. 12 In the School of Nature we must begin with..the smallest and most uncompounded Parts. **1794** Hutton *Philos. Light*, etc. 212 The antiphlogistic theory maintains, that sulphur and metals are simple substances, or to us uncompounded bodies. **1808** J. Webster *Nat. Philos.* 171 The divisions of the uncompounded colours on the spectrum. **1875** E. White *Life in Christ* i. viii. (1878) 72 That the soul of man is an uncompounded substance, or indivisible essence, has never been proved.

*fig.* *a* **1633** W. Austin *Medit.* (1635) 103 Alwaies, in secret, Men are most direct, plaine, and uncompounded: when (often) in publike they play the Hypocrites. **1703** Mrs. Centlivre *Stolen Heiress* iv, It was her single uncompounded self, her self without addition that I lov'd.

c. Of ideas, abstractions, etc.

**1650** Earl Monm. tr. *Senault's Man bec. Guilty* 115 Christian Eloquence is uncompounded. **1690** Locke *Hum. Und.* ii. ii. § 1 Those simple Ideas; which being each in itself uncompounded, contains in it nothing but one uniform Appearance. **1713** Berkeley *Hylas & Phil.* i. Wks. 1871 I. 267 Fire affects you only with one simple, or uncompounded idea. **1785** Reid *Intell. Powers* 234 To consider them as one uncompounded operation. **1822–7** Good *Study Med.* (1829) IV. 16 The sensorial power in its simplest and uncompounded state. **1862** Marsh *Lect. Eng. Lang.* iii. 62 It is, however, rarely the case that a simple uncompounded word so well repays the labour of investigation.

d. Const. *with.*

*a* **1633** W. Austin *Medit.* (1635) 33 They were simple men, uncompounded with the world. **1803** W. Blackburne in *Med. Jrnl.* X. 463 Accumulated human effluvia..uncompounded with limose or paludous gas.

†2. = Uncomposed *ppl. a.* 3. *Obs.*

**1659** Rushworth *Hist. Coll.* I. 2 To keep his Majesty from declaring himself opposite to Spain in the business of Cleves and Juliers, which still remained uncompounded.

Hence **Uncompou·ndedly** *adv.*; **-ness.**

**1628** T. Spencer *Logick* 163 It is a simple Axiome: because one thing barely, and *vncompoundedly, is referred to another. **1683** [see Unclothedly *adv.*]. **1653** Blithe *Eng. Improver Impr.* xxi. 136 The description of it [*sc.* marl] is not so much in Colour..as in the Purity and *uncompoundedness of it. **1835** *Blackw. Mag.* XXXVIII. 751 There is a oneness, a wholeness, an uncompoundedness of character in these elect instruments.

**Uncompou·nding**, *ppl. a.* (Un-1 10.) **1782** J. Brown *Comp. View Nat. & Rev. Relig.* iv. i. 298 It is an uncompounding union, both the united natures retaining their distinct essential properties. **1821** *Tales Landlord, Fair Witch of Glas Llyn* II. 191 His wanton cruelty was accepted as the pledge of uncompounding sincerity. **Uncomprehe·nd**, *v.* (Un-1 14.) **1602–3** Daniel *Musophilus* 656 If this grosse spirit..Neglect, distaste, vncomprehend, disdaine.

**Uncomprehe·nded**, *ppl. a.* (Un-1 8 and 5 b.)

**1598** Florio, *Incompreso*, vncomprehended, incomprehensible. **1829** Lytton *Devereux* iii. vii, What wonder that ye should have gleaned from the uncomprehended earth an answer to the enigmas of Fate! **1866** Geo. Eliot *F. Holt* xi, A large experience in the effect of uncomprehended words.

**Uncomprehe·nding**, *ppl. a.* (Un-1 10, 5 b.)

**1838** Mrs. Browning *Song agst. Singing* iv, Thou..Wouldst..Upturn thy bright uncomprehending eyes And bid me play instead. **1871** Farrar *Witn. Hist* ii. 64 The light which..shone quietly in the uncomprehending darkness.

Hence **Uncomprehe·ndingly** *adv.*

**1858** Miss Mulock *Th. ab. Wom.* 260 Tell her this, and the chances are she will stare at you uncomprehendingly.

†**Uncomprehe·nsible**, *a. Obs.* [Un-1 7 and 5 b.] = Incomprehensible *a.*

**1388** Wyclif *Jer.* xxxii. 19 Greet in councel, and vncomprehensible in thouȝt. *c* **1532** Du Wes *Introd. Fr.* in *Palsgr.* 1057 [The soul] is vncomprehensyble. **1567–9** Jewel *Def. Apol.* 239 It is vntoucheable, and vncomprehensible vnto our senses. **1587** Golding *De Mornay* xxiv. (1592) 370 The matters of God which are vncomprehensible to man. **1740** Cheyne *Regimen* 185 An uncomprehensible and inexplicable Mystery.

**Uncomprehe·nsion.** (Un-1 12 and 5 b.) **1862** Mrs. Oliphant *Last of Mortimers* II. 27 The child looked up..with an amazed uncomprehension of any order issued to her.

**Uncomprehe·nsive**, *a.* [Un-1 7 and 5 b.]

†1. That cannot be comprehended. *Obs.*

**1606** Shaks. *Tr. & Cr.* iii. iii. 198 The prouidence that's in a watchfull State..Findes bottome in th' vncomprehensiue deepes.

2. Lacking in comprehension.

**1667** South *Serm.* (1697) II. 46 Some narrow-spirited, Uncomprehensive Zealots, who know not the world.

3. Not sufficiently comprehensive or inclusive.

**1862** Helps *Org. Daily Life* 21 Great efforts will be made in a scattered, uncomprehensive, and unbusiness-like way.

**Uncompre·ssed**, *ppl. a.* (Un-1 8.)

**1666** Boyle *Orig. Forms & Qual.* (1667) 17 The Learned Horstius..ascribes the Indolence of the Part, whil'st uncompress'd, to some slimy Juice. **1713** Derham *Phys.-Theol.* 5 *note*, I shall leave the ingenious Reader to judge what the cause was of both the Birds living longer in compressed, than uncompressed Air. **1808** J. Webster *Nat. Philos.* 77 It produces considerable pain in the part which is uncompressed. **1863** Tyndall *Heat* ii. 24 The uncompressed lead they said had a greater capacity for heat than the compressed substance.

**Uncompri·zed**, *ppl. a.* (Un-1 8.)

**1598** Drayton *Heroical Ep.* xii. 31 Whose vncomprised wisedomes did fore-see, That you in marriage should be linck'd to mee. **1610** HEALEY *St. Aug. Citie of God* 213 It is no way credible that he would leave the kingdomes of men.. uncomprized in..his eternall providence. **1652** BENLOWES *Theoph.* v. lxxiii, Thou all-comprizing, uncompriz'd!

**Unco·mpromised,** *ppl. a.* (UN-[1] 8.) [1775 ASH.] **1882** MISS BRADDON *Mt.-Royal* I. iv. 105 He might..ride off at the last uncompromised.

**Unco·mpromising,** *ppl. a.* [UN-[1] 10.] Not willing or seeking to compromise; unyielding, unbending; stiff, stubborn: **a.** Of persons.

**1828** LYTTON *Pelham* II. i, We must pursue the same course —stern and uncompromising. **1849** MACAULAY *Hist. Eng.* v. I. 541 The most honest, fearless, and uncompromising republican of his time. **1863** 'OUIDA' *Held in Bondage* vi, Among uncompromising patriots as among poor foreigners.

**b.** Of feelings, attitudes of mind, etc.

**1830** *Forrester* III. 89 [He was] aroused..to a full sense of the danger he had incurred by his uncompromising hostility. **1885** 'MRS. ALEXANDER' *At Bay* vii, Whose uncompromising sincerity might convince the hardest skeptic of its reality.

**c.** *fig.* Of things.

**1875** LADY BARKER *Year's Housekeeping S. Africa* i. (1877) 7 The 'Devil's Peak' is uncompromising enough for any one's taste. **1889** HISSEY *Tour in Phaeton* 363 A square house 'with no nonsense about it',..an uncompromising square house.

Hence **Unco·mpromisingly** *adv.*; **-ness.**

**1837** PUSEY *Let.* in Liddon *Life* (1894) I. 388 However *uncompromisingly they maintain the maxim. **1888** MISS BRADDON *Fatal Three* I. iv, The dressmaker sent home three new frocks, all uncompromisingly ugly. **1865** PUSEY *Eiren.* 284 The *uncompromisingness of the Church of England in maintaining Catholic truth. **1894** *Fortn. Rev.* May 690 Even her uncompromisingness is preferable to the ostentatious abandonment of principles.

†**Uncompt,** *a. Obs.* [UN-[1] 7 and 5 b.]

**1.** Of persons: Not neat in dress or appearance.

*a* **1641** BP. MOUNTAGU *Acts & Mon.* (1642) 247 The cited to appeare in Court, came in humble manner,..attired in black, uncompt, undrest. **1647** N. BACON *Disc. Govt. Eng.* I. xli. 104 Nor was this the originall trick of the rude and uncompt Germans, or Barbarous Britons, but of the wise Greeks.

**2.** Of style: Incompt, inelegant, unpolished.

**1633** PRYNNE *Histriomastix* 925 Whenever I fell to read the Prophets after I had beene reading Tully and Plautus, ..their uncompt stile became irkesome to me.

**Uncompu·lsory,** *a.* (UN-[1] 7.) **1567** in Tytler *Hist. Scot.* (1864) III. 271, I asked him what freewill there might be, or uncompulsory consent, for a prisoner. **Uncompu·table,** *a.* (UN-[1] 7 b and 5 b.) **1678** CUDWORTH *Intell. Syst.* I. iv. § 14. 241 Proclus contends..that the world had lasted such a length of time, as was in a manner inestimable to us, or uncomputable by us. **Uncompu·ted,** *ppl. a.* (UN-[1] 8.) [1775 ASH.] **1885** *Leeds Mercury* 31 Jan. 7/2 The millions of dollars..required to provide these Civil War pensions seem to have been uncomputed.

†**Unco·nable,** *a. Obs.* [UN-[1] 7 b.] Improper, unbefitting.

*a* **1340** HAMPOLE *Psalter* lxxii. 9 Þair bostus speche, sua vncunable was, þat it passed in[to] þe earth. *Ibid., Cant. Marie* 1 Þat soul worshippys god, þe whilk..vnkonnabil beryng heghis not. *c* **1440** *Jacob's Well* 294 Vnconable ioye of ony wordly vanyte.

Hence †**Unco·nableness; -ablety; -ably** *adv.*

*a* **1340** HAMPOLE *Psalter* xxxviii. 1 Þe haly man..thynkis ..to be still, þat he say nathynge vnconabilly. *Ibid.* lxxii. 14 If god war nought wytand al things, or punyscht not synne, þere vnconabiltes folouid. *Ibid.* cv. 31 Moyses wes for þe mykil vnconabilnes of þe folk lettid in thoght.

**Unconand,** obs. f. UNCUNNING.

†**Unconca·tenable,** *a. Obs.* (UN-[1] 7 b. Cf. CONCATENATE *v.*)

**1654** GAYTON *Pleas. Notes* III. viii. 117 His Auditory smiling at..what an irreconcileable piece of Scripture they had proposed, and unconcatenable to his usuall subject.

**Unconcea·lable,** *a.* (UN-[1] 7 b.)

Also, in recent use, *unconcealably* adv.

**1809–14** WORDSW. *Excurs.* VI. 158 Through his frame it crept With slow mutation unconcealable. **1860** EMERSON *Cond. Life, Behaviour* Wks. (Bohn) II. 380 The power of manners is incessant,—an element as unconcealable as fire. **1879** H. GEORGE *Progr. & Pov.* VIII. iii. (1881) 375 The immovable and unconcealable character of the land itself.

**Unconcea·led,** *ppl. a.* (UN-[1] 8.)

[1775 ASH.] **1839** DE LA BECHE *Rep. Geol. Cornwall*, etc. iii. 71 The whole is unconcealed by more modern deposits. **1860** TRISTRAM *Gt. Sahara* iv. 62 The nests which are.. unprotected and unconcealed among the mud and grass.

**Unconcea·ling,** *ppl. a.* (UN-[1] 10.) **1804** *Ann. Rev.* II. 289 To what dire resources the alarmists at length had to recur, is thus related by this unconcealing writer. *a* **1822** SHELLEY *Matilda* 30 This [water], whose unconcealing dew, Dark, dark, yet clear, moved under the obscure Eternal shades. **Unconce·ded,** *ppl. a.* (UN-[1] 8.) **1674** BOYLE *Excell. Theol.* II. v. 229, I should have forborn to make use of divers of the arguments I have employed, as fetched from unconceded topicks. **Unconcei·ted,** *a.* (UN-[1] 9.) [1775 ASH.] **1838** LD. COLERIDGE in E. H. Coleridge *Life* (1904) I. 50, I pray God I may be humble and unconceited like you. **Unconcei·tedly,** *adv.* (UN-[1] 11.) **1812** *Examiner* 24 Aug. 541/1 You..(very unconceitedly to be sure) boast that you do not condescend to read it.

**Unconcei·vable,** *a.* [UN-[1] 7 b and 5 b.] Inconceivable. (Common in 17–18th c.)

**1611** COTGR., *Incomprehensible*, incomprehensible, vnconceiueable. **1612** T. TAYLOR *Comm., Titus* ii. 14 Christ.. willingly suffered such torments as are vnconceiuable. **1647** TRAPP *Comm. Rev.* ii. 17 The feast of a good conscience, which is unconceivable and full of glory. **1705** STANHOPE *Paraphr.* II. 203 Many and great Pleasures, yet hidden from our Eyes, unutterable, unconceivable. **1768** *Woman of Honor* II. 133 The effect this had..would be unconceivable but for one just reflexion. **1838** [see UNCONCEIVED *ppl. a.* 1]. **1867** PUSEY *Eleven Addresses* xi. (1908) 143 The souls of those, who are departed hence in the grace of God, are in unconceivable bliss.

Hence **Unconcei·vableness.**

**1611** COTGR., *Incomprehensibilité*, incomprehensiblenesse, vnconceiuablenesse. **1655** H. MORE *App. Antid. Ath.* (1712) 185 The unconceivableness of that line that is produced by the Motion of a Globe on a Plane. **1704** NORRIS *Ideal World* II. vii. 337 The unconceivablenesse of supposing that a body..should always send forth from itself species on all sides. **1854** HALLAM *Hist. Lit.* (ed. 4) III. iii. § 119 *marg.*, Unconceivableness of infinity.

**Unconcei·vably,** *adv.* [f. prec.] = INCONCEIVABLY *adv.*

**1630** BP. HALL *Serm., Hypocrite* Wks. 1837 V. 381 How then? what is their case? Surely inexplicably, unconceivably fearful. **1683** E. HOOKER *Pref. Pordage's Mystic Div.* 67 Imperceptibl subtilities of unconceivably profound Contemplators. *a* **1711** KEN *Hymnotheo* Poet. Wks. 1721 III. 45 Yet curs'd Abaddon's Diabolick Crew, Death's Terrors unconceivably outdo. **1861** PAGE *Past & Pr. Life of Globe* 239 The divine idea of moral perfection..[is] unconceivably unattainable by created existences.

**Unconcei·ved,** *ppl. a.* [UN-[1] 8.]

**1. a.** Not conceived or thought of; unimagined.

**1434** MISYN *Mending of Life* 126 God truly is infinit.., of all wroght kyndes vnconsauyd. **1591** SYLVESTER *Du Bartas* I. iii. 949 Renowned Load-stone, which on Iron acts, ..Attracts it strangely..With unknow'n cords, with unconceived hooks. **1598** BP. HALL *Sat.* Postscr., Sith..that is almost unseene which is unconceived. **1648** J. BEAUMONT *Psyche* XIV. lxii, Judas who neer this place did frying lie With unconceived anguish gnash'd his teeth. **1710** BERKELEY *Princ. Hum. Knowl.* § 23 It is necessary that you conceive them existing unconceived or unthought of. **1742** YOUNG *Nt. Th.* I. 111 They live! they greatly live a life on earth Unkindl'd, unconceiv'd. **1838** POE *A. G. Pym* Wks. 1864 IV. 89 Events..of the most unconceived and unconceivable character. **1871** MORLEY *Vauvenargues* in *Crit. Misc.* Ser. I. (1878) 9 The Encyclopædia was yet unconceived.

†**b.** Uncomprehended; not understood. *Obs.*[—1]

**1619** PURCHAS *Microcosmus* lxix. 689 In the meane while, sometimes without dores, on Horse-backe, they heare their vn-conceiued Liturgie.

**2.** Not brought into being; not properly formed or developed.

**1599** MARSTON *Sco. Villanie* III. ix. G viij b, Whilst I..abuse chast virgin time, Deflowring her with unconceiued time. **1848** BAILEY *Festus* (ed. 3) 205 All the forms Of plant, fish, brute, bird, insect, and the lives Insensible and unconceived.

**Unconcei·ving,** *ppl. a.* [UN-[1] 10.] Not apprehending or understanding; dull-witted.

**1593** NASHE *Strange Newes* Wks. (Grosart) II. 253 Art thou so innocent & vnconceiuing that thou shouldst ere hope to dash mee quite out of request? **1614** R. TAILOR *Hog hath lost Pearl* III. E j b, Why should I teach them, and go beate my braines, To instruct vnapt, and vnconceauing dolts? **1740** CIBBER *Apol.* (1756) I. 124 A broad laughing voice,..round shoulders, an unconceiving eye.

**Unconce·rn,** *sb.* [UN-[1] 12.] Lack of concern, anxiety, or solicitude; indifference, equanimity.

**1711** STEELE *Spect.* No. 75 ¶ 5 He..is in a fair way of doing all things with a graceful Unconcern, and Gentleman-like Ease. **1769** E. BANCROFT *Guiana* 326 Their unconcern for futurity..is by no means singular. **1849** EASTWICK *Dry Leaves* 93 Their faces were pale with terror, and they vainly attempted to simulate unconcern. **1865** W. G. PALGRAVE *Arabia* I. 116 We put on an appearance of great ignorance and unconcern.

†**Unconce·rn,** *v.*[1] *Obs.* [UN-[1] 14.] *refl.* Not to concern or interest (oneself) *in* a thing.

**1670** PENN *Tracts* Wks. 1726 I. 488, I might here over-look his abusive reflections upon me..by unconcerning my self in the Matter. **1682** GREW *Anat. Plants* 220, I also know, that Your Lordship unconcerneth Your self..in what I even now spake.

**Unconce·rn,** *v.*[2] *rare.* [UN-[2] 3.] *trans.* To free from concern or anxiety.

**1653** SHIRLEY *Court Secret* II. iv, I was taking pains to unconcern the jealousie Of Antonio, and find him my own Rivall.

**Unconce·rned,** *ppl. a.* [UN-[1] 8.]

**1.** Devoid of concern or interest; uninterested, indifferent, unmoved.

? *c* **1635** WALLER *Misc., On Lady Isabella* 2 Such moving sounds from such a careless touch! So unconcern'd her self, and we so much! **1659** *Gentl. Calling* (1696) 2, I have been no unconcerned..Spectator of the Depression the Gentry have fallen under. **1725** POPE *Odyss.* XXIII. 169 Canst thou, oh cruel! unconcern'd survey Thy lost Ulysses, on this signal day? **1796** MME. D'ARBLAY *Camilla* III. 81 See but how he smiles..in defiance of all his efforts to look unconcerned! **1822** SCOTT *Peveril* xxxiii, Had Peveril come thither as an unconcerned visitor, his heart would have sunk within him.

**b.** Const. *about, at, in.*

**1659** PEARSON *Creed* vii. 614 If there were no other judge beside our own soules, we should be..wholly unconcern'd in our own condemnations. **1697** COLLIER *Ess. Mor. Subj.* I. (1709) 155 To suppose that he has made the Nature of Man such, that..he should be unconcerned about the Happiness of his Neighbour. **1749** FIELDING *Tom Jones* IV. xiii, He was not unconcerned at the accident. **1822** LAMB *Elia* I. *Artificial Comedy*, A passing pageant, where we should sit as unconcerned at the issues,..as at a battle of the frogs and mice.

**c.** Of feeling, conduct, etc.

**1658** PHILLIPS, *Indifference*, a carelesse, general, and unconcerned affection. **1702** ECHARD *Eccl. Hist.* (1710) 617 The holy man gave him an unconcern'd answer. **1820** HAZLITT *Lect. Dram. Lit.* 14 The same strength and depth and richness,..poured out in unconcerned profusion from the lap of nature. **1853** R. S. SURTEES *Sponge's Sp. Tour* xxxvii, He saw Soapey Sponge's preparations for departure with an unconcerned air.

**2.** Not affected by concern or anxiety; free from solicitude; undisturbed.

**1660** COWLEY *Ode his Majesty's Restoration* xv, Methoughts I saw the three Judæan Youths..In the Chaldæan Furnace walk; How chearfully and unconcern'd they talk! **1685** DRYDEN *Thren. August.* i, We liv'd as unconcern'd and happily As the first Age in Natures golden Scene. **1747** HERVEY *Medit., Contempl. Night* (1840) 226 To be utterly unconcerned, where it is the truest wisdom to take the alarm. **1800** MRS. HERVEY *Mourtray Fam.* II. 226 If I had been cool and unconcerned..; but I was in a fright. **1897** MARY KINGSLEY *W. Africa* 351, I attempted to look as unconcerned as possible.

**3.** Indifferent or uninterested between two parties; disinterested, impartial.

**1664** ATKYNS *Orig. Printing* Ded. C ij b, I have so far prevailed upon your Royal Goodness, as to make an unconcern'd Councel what is best to be done. **1697** DRYDEN *Æneis* X. 166 Each to his proper fortune stand or fall; Equal and unconcerned I look on all. *a* **1718** PRIOR *Poems, Democritus & Heraclitus* 5 Between You both I unconcern'd stand by. **1748** SMOLLETT *R. Random* xxx, I begged to be examined by some unconcerned person on board.

**4.** Not concerned or involved, having no part or share, *in* something.

**1647** CLARENDON *Hist. Reb.* II. § 7 They believed there was no part of their Civil Government, uninvaded by them, and no Persons of what Quality soever unconcerned and..unhurt in them. **1683** *Apol. Prot. France* i. 9 The two Successors of Henry the Fourth look'd not upon themselves as unconcern'd in this Edict. **1764** HARMER *Observ.* iv. § 14. 163 The robb of grapes..is, I should think, unconcerned in this enquiry.

**b.** Not concerned or occupied *with* something.

**1667** MILTON *P. L.* XI. 174 The Morn, All unconcern'd with our unrest, begins Her rosie progress smiling. **1732** BERKELEY *Alciphr.* IV. § 16 They were indolent gods, unconcerned with human affairs.

**c.** Without const. Also *ellipt.*, not affected by drink; sober. (Cf. CONCERNED *ppl. a.* 2.)

**1668** HOWE *Bless. Righteous* 5 Not..as an unconcern'd circumstance, that hath nothing to do with the businesse spoken of. **1699** BENTLEY *Phal.* Pref. p. lxxvi, It's a very difficult thing, for a person unconcern'd and out of the reach of Harm, to be a fair Arbitrator there. **1748** RICHARDSON *Clarissa* VII. 373 Mowbray and Tourville grew very noisy. ..As to myself, the little part I had taken in their gaiety kept me unconcerned.

**Unconce·rnedly,** *adv.* [f. prec. + -LY [2].] In an unconcerned manner; without anxiety or concern; with indifference.

**1636** *Destr. Troy* I Not the most cruel of Our conquering Foes So unconcern'dly can relate our woes, As not to lend a tear. **1679** EVERARD *Popish Plot* 12, I unconcernedly expected a speedy enlargement. *a* **1721** SHEFFIELD (Dk. Buckhm.) *Wks.* (1723) II. 81 To discourse about the serving of the Tide..as coolly, and unconcernedly, as if it had been only a common journey. **1768–74** TUCKER *Lt. Nat.* (1834) I. 603 We shall never do it..unconcernedly, but as an unavoidable means for attaining some greater good. **1828** LYTTON *Pelham* III. i, Thrusting the miniature in my bosom, and turning unconcernedly away. **1872** BLACK *Adv. Phaeton* xv. 208 We were unconcernedly having luncheon.

**Unconce·rnedness.** [f. as prec. + -NESS.] The quality or state of being unconcerned; freedom from anxiety; indifference.

**1647** CLARENDON *Hist. Reb.* I. § 46 So little dejected with it, that he answered the Articles with great steddyness, and unconcernedness. **1675** WYCHERLEY *Country Wife* V. i, To shew my unconcernedness, I'll come to your wedding. **1738** GRAY *Let.* Poems (1775) 36 My resolution and unconcernedness in the midst of evils. **1768–74** TUCKER *Lt. Nat.* (1834) II. 65 To attain a perfect unconcernedness at every-thing past,..is more plausible in theory, than feasible in practice. **1800** MRS. HERVEY *Mourtray Fam.* I. 9 He possessed great equanimity of temper, and a quiet unconcernedness of mind. **1860** PUSEY *Min. Proph.* 290 This union of inherent strength and unconcernedness about foreign aid is an adequate test of days anterior to Ahaz.

**Unconce·rning,** *ppl. a.* [UN-[1] 10 and 5 d.] Not concerning or affecting one; unconnected with one's affairs or interests; having no importance or relevance.

**1612** DONNE *Progr. Soule, 2nd Anniv.* 285 To know but Catechismes and Alphabets Of unconcerning things, matters of fact. **1651** FULLER *Abel Rediv., Jerome* (1867) I. 29 They vexed him with trivial objections about unconcerning matters. **1742** MELMOTH *Fitzosborne Lett.* (1763) 438 With other topics of the same unconcerning kind. *a* **1779** WARBURTON *Unpubl. Papers* (1841) 568 It will teach him to distinguish real from imaginary knowledge,..useful from unconcerning. **1821** COLERIDGE *Lett., Convers.*, etc. II. 22 Lonely in an unconcerning crowd of human figures. **1833** LAMB *Elia* II. *Barrenness Imag. Faculty in Modern Art*, As if unconscious of Bacchus, or but idly casting her eyes as upon some unconcerning pageant,..Ariadne is still pacing the..shore.

†**b.** Const. *to*, or with direct object. *Obs.*

**1647** L. HAWARD *Charges Crown Rev.* Ded., Having medled with the publishing of such a Subject so unconcerning my own quality. **1654** WHITLOCK *Zootomia* 87 They will satisfie the Patients thirst with cooling Juleps, be they never so improper for the Malignity Nature hath to struggle with, or unconcerning her assistance to resist. **1667** *Decay Chr. Piety* V. ¶ 10. 228 Those things that are either impossible in their nature, or unconcerning to us, cannot beget it.

**Unconce·rnment.** [UN-[1] 12.] The fact of not concerning oneself; unconcern.

**1660** STANLEY *Hist. Philos.* IX. (1687) 507/1 This happened from two Causes, as well by reason of the unconcernment of the Cities..as by reason of the Death of the most excellent persons. **1676** GLANVILL *Ess.* I. 31 If there be any repose attainable by the Methods of Reason, there is nothing so like to afford it, as unconcernment in doubtful Opinions. **1716–7** BENTLEY *Serm.* xi. 383 The Seat of Selfishness and of Unconcernment for all about him. **1832** W. STEPHENSON *Gates-*

*head Local Poems* 69 No matter where these daring souls have been, They always are in unconcernment seen. **1892** *Nation* (N.Y.) 12 May 364 They show the scholar among his books, handling his thoughts with a certain unconcernment.

† **Unconce·rnness.** *Obs.*—1 = prec.

**1700** BLACKMORE *Job* xix. 80 Job in Affliction you refuse to know, And a shy Stranger's unconcernness show.

**Unconce·rted,** *ppl. a.* (UN-1 8.)

**1594** CAREW *Huarte's Exam. Wits* (1616) 215 The Stoicks held opinion, that..there was another [cause] vnwise and vnconcerted, whose workes prooued without order. **1711** SHAFTESB. *Charac.* III. 325 A Company where alternate Discourse is carry'd on, in un-concerted Measure, and unpremeditated Language. **1793** *Monthly Rev.* X. 376 In so much that the unconcerted composition of the gospels..is with some difficulty to be proved.

**Unconce·ssible,** *a.* (UN-1 7.)

**1643** HUNTON *Treat. Mon.* II. vii. 69 It is strange to see, how in this Epidemicall division of the Kingdome, the Abettors of both parts claime this unconcessible Judgement.

† **Unconci·liable,** *a.* *Obs.*—1 (UN-1 7 b, 5 b.)

**1610** J. MELVILL *Diary* (Wodrow Soc.) 554 Peace betwixt the unconciliabill natiounes of Scottis and English.

**Unconci·liated,** *ppl. a.* (UN-1 8.) **1828–32** WEBSTER. **1868** *Once a Week* 18 Jan. 66/2 But the company was unconciliated. **Unconci·liating,** *ppl. a.* (UN-1 10.) **1807** COXE *House of Austria* I. v. 72 He offended the natives by his stern and unconciliating manners. **1855** MACAULAY *Hist. Eng.* xv. III. 578 His clemency was peculiar to himself. ..It was cold, unconciliating, inflexible.

**Unconci·liatory,** *a.* (UN-1 7.)

**1789** JEFFERSON *Writ.* (1859) II. 572 Ternant will see that his predecessor is recalled for unconciliatory conduct. **1861** TROLLOPE *Tales All Countries* I. 4 She was..unconciliatory when any change even for a day was proposed to her. **1873** SYMONDS *Grk. Poets* iii. 90 We may gather..that his friend Cyrnus was of a rash and haughty and unconciliatory temper.

**Unconclu·dable,** *a.* (UN-1 7 b.) **1642** J. BALL *Answ. to Can.* I. 131 To reason from the effect of things (you say) is unsound and unconcludable. **1653** H. MORE *Conject. Cabbal.* A 4, Nor does it at all follow, because a truth is delivered by way of Tradition, that it is unconcludable by Reason.

**Unconclu·ded,** *ppl. a.* (UN-1 8.)

**1564** PALFREYMAN *Baldwin's Mor. Philos.* 146 So many matters laid aside and left vnconcluded. *a* **1633** AUSTIN *Medit.* (1635) 73 But this (as well as the rest) stands unconcluded, since (peradventure) God would not have it certainely knowne. **1822** RANKEN *Hist. France* IX. x. ii. 241 The court pronounced the business unconcluded. **1837** LYTTON *Athens* I. 103 Yet he wrote in an age when the struggle was still unconcluded. **1886** A. WEIR *Hist. Basis Mod. Europe* (1889) 165 When the peace of Amiens was yet unconcluded.

† **Unconclu·dency.** *Obs.*—1 (UN-1 12 and 5 b.)

**1654** HAMMOND *Answ. Animadv. Ignat.* iv. § 1. 91 Produced by me as an argument to convince the unconcludency of Blondel's collection.

† **Unconclu·dent,** *a.* *Obs.* (UN-1 7 and 5 b.)

**1634** JACKSON *Creed* VII. xv. § 3 It was then an allegation unconcludent and impertinent..to say [etc.]. **1647** HAMMOND *Power of Keys* iv. 80 The arguments..being utterly unconcludent against us. *a* **1676** HALE *Prim. Orig. Man.* I. vi. (1677) 116 All our Argumentations touching them are inevident and unconcludent.

**Unconclu·dible,** *a.* (UN-1 7.) **1647** H. MORE *Song of Soul* Notes 352 Endeavouring..to comprehend and conclude that which is so unconcludible and incomprehensible.

† **Unconclu·ding,** *ppl. a.* *Obs.* [UN-1 10 and 5 b.] Inconclusive.

*a* **1643** LD. FALKLAND, etc. *Infallibility* (1646) 200 You are to wise to claime by *Tu es Petrus* or any other so unconcluding an argument. **1662** H. MORE *Philos. Writ.* Pref. Gen. p. iii, The Author's Excuse for his omitting.. to confute the unconcluding Reasons some use for the proof of a God. **1713** E. CALAMY *Life R. Baxter* xiii. 356 He shews his arguments both *ad Rem* and *ad Hominem* to be unconcluding.

Hence † **Unconclu·dingness.** *Obs.*

**1647** JER. TAYLOR *Lib. Proph.* vi. 110 The uncertainty of the truth of its decrees, by reason of the unconcludingnesse of the Arguments brought to attest it. **1661** BOYLE *Scept. Chym.* IV. (1680) 440 The unconcludingness of the Analytical Experiments vulgarly Relyed on.

† **Unconclu·sive,** *a.* *Obs.* (UN-1 7 and 5 b.)

**1640** HAMMOND *Poor Man's Tithing* Wks. 1684 IV. 554 Had the Promises been of any other sort,..the Apostles illation..had been utterly unconclusive, if not impertinent. **1672** H. DODWELL *Two Lett.* Pref. C iij, There being no more politick way for betraying the Truth..than to offer to defend it by unconclusive arguments.

Hence † **Unconclu·sively** *adv.*, **-ness.** *Obs.*

**1660** COKE *Justice Vind.* 13 When a man talks unconclusively, they say he talks not sense. **1723** MATHER *Vind. Bible* 209 The appearing unconclusiveness of the reasoning used in Scripture.

† **Unconco·ct,** *a.* [UN-1 7 and 5 b.] = next.

**1591** SYLVESTER *Du Bartas* I. ii. 132 Too-much Moist, which (unconcoct within) The Liver spreads betwixt the flesh and skin. **1625** HART *Anat. Ur.* II. i. 53 A great agitation and stirring of crude and vnconcoct humours.

**Unconco·cted,** *ppl. a.* [UN-1 8 and 5 b.]

**1.** Not digested in the stomach.

**1611** FLORIO, *Indigesto*, vndigested, vnconcocted. **1615** CROOKE *Body of Man* 110 The stomacke ..receyueth the meate when it is harder and vnconcocted. **1651** WITTIE tr. *Primrose's Pop. Err.* III. 150 The meat..being unconcocted doth encrease the disease, and the symptomes thereof. **1774** GOLDSM. *Nat. Hist.* V. 244 The red-beaked toucan..feeds chiefly upon pepper,..gorging itself in such a manner that it voids it crude and unconcocted. **1802** LAMB *John Woodvil* IV. i. 2 A weight of wine lies heavy on my head, The unconcocted follies of last night.

**2.** Not brought to a proper state or condition; crude, immature.

**1649** E. REYNOLDS *Hosea* iii. 12 Those fruites..are sowre, unsavoury, and unconcocted. **1693** SIR T. P. BLOUNT *Nat. Hist.* 250 Erastus affirms..that in Germany there hath been Unripe and Unconcocted Silver found in Mines. **1726** LEONI *Alberti's Archit.* I. 34 When it [*sc.* lime] is used too soon.., there will be some small unconcocted Stones in it. **1770** LANGHORNE *Plutarch* (1879) II. 792/1 The fruits were so crude and unconcocted, that they pined away and decayed.

**3.** *fig.* Not properly worked up or elaborated.

*c* **1628** DONNE *Serm.* (1640) 599 Ever more there will be some things raw and unconcocted in every church. **1658** OSBORN *Adv. Son* Wks. (1673) 89 Such unconcocted Rebellions turn seldom to the hurt of any, but the Parties that promote them. **1745** WESLEY *Wks.* (1872) XII. 68 Such frothy, unconcocted trifles, such undigested crudities, as a man of learning.. would have been ashamed to set his name to. **1846** LANDOR *Imag. Conv.* Wks. I. 201/2 The smoky, verminous, unconcocted doctrine of passive obedience.

† **Unconco·ction.** *Obs.*—1 (UN-1 12 and 5 b.)

**1662** J. CHANDLER *Van Helmont's Oriat.* 199 Because the one only ignorance of ferments hath caused digestions, and the remedies of unconcoction to be unknown.

**Unconcu·rrent,** *a.* (UN-1 7 and 5 b.) **1613–8** DANIEL *Coll. Hist. Eng.* (1626) 49 A league, consisting of seuerall Nations, emulous and vnconcurrent in their courses.

**Unconcu·rring,** *ppl. a.* (UN-1 10 and 5 b.)

**1639** FULLER *Holy War* v. xiii. 251 The confluence of Princes otherwise unconcurring in their severall courses. **1728** SAVAGE *Bastard* 36 While your backward Will retrench'd Desire, And unconcurring Spirits lent no Fire.

**Uncondemnable,** *a.* (UN-1 7 b.)

**1643** PRYNNE *Sov. Power Parl.* III. 121 Therefore our Opposites must grant all Bishops, Priests, Ministers,..as irresistible, uncensurable, undeprivable, uncondemnable, for any crimes whatsoever, as they say kings are.

**Uncondemned,** *ppl. a.* (UN-1 8.)

**1526** TINDALE *Acts* xxii. 25 Ys it laufull for you to scourge a Romain vncondempned? *c* **1545** BRINKLOW *Compl.* xii. (1874) 27 To put a man to death vncondemnyd is to commyt murder. **1600** [see UNCONFUTED]. **1680** BAXTER *Answ. Stillingfl.* xxxvii. 62 How few were there un-Cursed, and un-Condemned in the Roman World? **1842** MANNING *Serm.* xvi. (1848) I. 236 Set side by side..your rules and your acts; and who shall go uncondemned? **1861** STANLEY *East. Ch.* p. l, See..what evils are left uncondemned.

**Uncondensable,** *a.* (UN-1 7 b and 5 b.) **1846** WORCESTER (citing Turner). **1857** MILLER *Elem. Chem., Org.* ix. 555 A large amount of volatile matter is expelled, partly in the form of uncondensable gases.

**Uncondensed,** *ppl. a.* [UN-1 8.]

**1.** Not condensed or compressed.

*a* **1711** KEN *Hymnotheo* Poet. Wks. 1721 III. 212 By Manna uncondens'd, and Heav'nly Dew. **1859** GREGORY *Egypt* I. 330 The clouds, the centre of which furrowed by uncondensed lightnings, reflected a silvery light.

**2.** *spec.* (See CONDENSED *ppl. a.* 2.)

**1810** HENRY *Chem.* (ed. 6) I. 43 The gas passes, uncondensed, through the second right-angled tube. **1838** GRANVILLE *Spas Germ.* 255 The steam, at such a temperature, must differ little from that of uncondensed distilled water. **1862** MILLER *Elem. Chem., Org.* (ed. 2) ix. 638 The remaining portion of the distillate, consisting of uncondensed gases.

† **Uncondesce·ndable,** *a.* *Obs.*—1 [UN-1 7 b.] Incapable of coming down.

**1683** E. HOOKER *Pref. Pordage's Mystic Div.* 67 These Sublimities in Religion,..uncondescendabl to the meerly Rational, or uncompliabl with the Rules of Syllogism.

**Uncondesce·nding,** *ppl. a.* (UN-1 10.) **1660** GAUDEN *God's Gt. Demonstr.* 16 Who will carry himself..with an uncondescending height, and divine stiffness against those that are not humble in his sight. **Uncondesce·nsion.** (UN-1 12.) **1681** J. KETTLEWELL *Meas. Chr. Obed.* II. iv. 165 The Law..against uncourteousness, against stiffness or uncondescension. *Ibid.* II. vi. 197 Stateliness or difficulty of access and uncondescension. † **Uncondesce·nsive,** *a.* *Obs.*—1 (UN-1 7.) **1681** J. KETTLEWELL *Meas. Chr. Obed.* v. iii. 633 Has any man..been surprized into rash words and censures, ..or uncandid, or uncondescensive behaviour?

† **Uncondi·ted,** *ppl. a.* *Obs.*—1 [UN-1 8.] Unseasoned, unflavoured.

*a* **1667** JER. TAYLOR *Suppl. Serm. for Year* (1678) 86 While he estimates the secrets of Religion by such Measures, they must needs seem as insipid as..the uncondited Mushroom.

† **Uncondi·tionable,** *a.* *Obs.*—1 = next.

**1642** *View Print. Bk. int. Observat.* 7 The King hath in nothing appertaining to His Crown, an unconditionable Property.

**Uncondi·tional,** *a.* [UN-1 7 and 5 b.] Not limited by or subject to conditions or stipulations; absolute, unlimited, complete.

**1666** DRYDEN *Ann. Mirab.* cclxix, O pass not, Lord, an absolute Decree, Or bind thy Sentence unconditional. **1726** AYLIFFE *Parergon* 19 Our Saviour left a Power in his Church to absolve men from their Sins; but this was not an absolute or unconditional Power. **1776** ADAM SMITH *W. N.* II. ii. I. 399 The obligation of an immediate and unconditional payment of such bank notes as soon as presented. **1839** JAMES *Louis XIV*, I. 404 The chamber of accounts leaned towards unconditional obedience, and prepared to quit Paris. **1844–8** H. H. WILSON *Brit. India* II. 351 He pretended that he had come to offer an unconditional surrender of the fortress. **1885** 'MRS. ALEXANDER' *At Bay* viii, There must be nothing about possibility..Give me an unconditional promise, or I shall not leave you!

Hence **Uncondi·tionalness.**

**1843** MILL *Logic* I. 372 If there be any meaning which confessedly belongs to the term necessity, it is unconditionalness. **1884** *Expositor* Feb. 151 The unconditionalness of God's election.

**Unconditiona·lity.** [f. prec. Cf. INCONDITIONALITY.] The quality of being unconditional.

*a* **1714** M. HENRY *Treat. Baptism* ii. Wks. 1853 I. 509/1 Those who speak so much of free grace, and the unconditionality of the gospel covenant. **1811–31** BENTHAM *Univ. Gram.* Wks. 1843 VIII. 355/2 The verb at large, considered independently of..conditionality and unconditionality. **1870** J. H. NEWMAN *Gram. Assent* iv. 38 The reality of the thesis is almost a condition of its unconditionality.

**Uncondi·tionally,** *adv.* [UN-1 11.] Without conditions.

*a* **1660** HAMMOND *Serm. 2 Cor. vii. 1* Wks. 1684 IV. 503 We are the special Favorites to whom those Promises are unconditionally consign'd. **1743** WESLEY *Jrnl.* 23 Aug., That God before the foundation of the world, did unconditionally elect certain persons to do certain works. **1791** BOSWELL *Johnson* July 1762, Thus, then,..there was nothing inconsistent..in Johnson's accepting of a pension so unconditionally and so honourably offered to him. **1837** HT. MARTINEAU *Soc. Amer.* III. 287 That faith which would lead them..to appropriate all truth, fearlessly and unconditionally. **1882** FARRAR *Early Chr.* II. 469 Yet Christ prayed unconditionally for his murderers.

**Uncondi·tionate,** *a.* [UN-1 7 and 5 b.] Not subject to or limited by conditions.

**1642** *Answ. to Printed Bk.* 11 So unconditionate and high a propriety in all the Subjects lives. **1668** H. MORE *Div. Dial.* I. xx. 84 The Divine Decrees, when they finde not men fitting Tools, make them so, where Prophecies are peremptory or unconditionate.

So **Uncondi·tionated** *ppl. a.*

**1836** F. MAHONY *Reliques Father Prout, Painter, Barry* (1859) 503 He claimed..unconditionated pedigree, ascending ..to the ancient masters of the world.

**Uncondi·tionately,** *adv.* [UN-1 11.] Unconditionally.

**1670** CUDWORTH *Serm. 1 Cor. xv. 57*, 234 The Divine Spirit of Grace doth not work absolutely, unconditionately, and irresistibly in the Souls of men. **1695** KENNETT *Par. Antiq.* ix. 607 All Ecclesiastical dues are to be voluntarily and unconditionately paid. **1820** MILNER *Suppl. Mem. Eng. Cath.* 28 In those times..no orthodox Catholic could unconditionately swear that [etc.].

**Uncondi·tioned,** *ppl. a.* [UN-1 8.]

**1.** Not subject to, or dependent upon, conditions or stipulations.

*a* **1631** DONNE *Serm.* xxxix. (1640) 391 Thou must stay out that time,..and by no practice, no not so much as by a deliberate wish, or unconditioned prayer, seeke to be delivered of it. **1692** BEVERLEY *Disc. Dr. Crisp* 10 Therein it must needs be, as unconditioned, as Election is. **1712** BERKELEY *Pass. Obed.* Wks. 1871 III. 139, I speak of non-resistance as an absolute, unconditioned, unlimited duty. **1776** GIBBON *Decl. & F.* xi. I. 301 With the choice only of submitting to his unconditioned mercy, or waiting the utmost severity of his resentment. **1852** BAILEY *Festus* (ed. 5) 491 Who thus pour forth Unmeasured, unconditioned, your divine Riches of works and words. **1864** R. A. ARNOLD *Cotton Famine* 477 They had grown used to 'th' relief', and regarded it as their unconditioned right.

**2.** Not dependent upon, or determined by, an antecedent condition.

**1829** SIR W. HAMILTON in *Edin. Rev.* L. 204 We are.. inspired with a belief in the existence of something unconditioned beyond the sphere of all comprehensible reality. **1846** LEWES *Hist. Philos.* IV. 205 An entirely unconditioned Thought. **1862** H. SPENCER *First Princ.* I. iii. § 15 (1875) 50 If Space and Time are the conditions under which we think, then when we think of Space and Time themselves, our thoughts must be unconditioned.

**3.** *absol.* That which is not subject to the conditions of finite existence and cognition.

**1829** SIR W. HAMILTON in *Edin. Rev.* L. 198 The first of these ideas..is variously expressed, under the terms unity, identity, substance, absolute cause, the infinite, pure thought, &c.; we would briefly call it the *unconditioned*. **1836**—*Metaph.* xxxviii. (1859) II. 373 The Conditioned is that which is alone conceivable or cogitable; the Unconditioned, that which is inconceivable or incogitable. **1877** E. CAIRD *Philos. Kant* iii. 45 The form of time, in which we always find condition beyond condition, cause beyond cause, and never reach the unconditioned, the *causa sui*.

Hence **Uncondi·tionedness.**

**1860** J. YOUNG *Prov. Reason* 47 Only through and on account of this undefinedness (unconditionedness) is Being Non-Being. **1903** *Edin. Rev.* July 71 Nor is the test of this unconditionedness arbitrary.

**Uncondo·led,** *ppl. a.* (UN-1 8.) *a* **1711** KEN *Hymns Evang.* Poet. Wks. 1721 I. 102 Bless'd are the Merciful,.. Who uncondol'd pass no one's Sorrow by.

**Uncondu·cing,** *ppl. a.* (UN-1 10.)

**1660** JER. TAYLOR *Duct. Dubit.* I. iv. Wks. IX. 209 The affairs of the world..are..unconducing to the affairs of the spirit. **1675** E. PHILLIPS *Theat. Poet.* Pref. 4 b, I judged it a Work in some sort not unconducing to a public benefit.

**Uncondu·cive,** *a.* (UN-1 7 and 5 b.)

**1661** BOYLE *Style Script.* (1675) 79 Those volumes, which ..must contain nothing unconducive to those designs. **1776** S. JENYNS *Internal Evid. Chr. Relig.* 33 A religion..totally unconducive to any worldly purpose. **1802–12** BENTHAM *Ration. Judic. Evid.* (1827) IV. 435 A short experiment will be found not unconducive to his purpose.

**Uncondu·cted,** *ppl. a.* (UN-1 8.) *a* **1677** BARROW *Serm. Jer. li. 15* Wks. 1686 II. 96 An undisciplined and unconducted troop of atoms rambling up and down confusedly.

**U·nconess.** *Sc.* [f. UNCO *a.*] Strangeness.

**1637** RUTHERFORD *Lett.* (1836) I. 330 Our Lord loveth not niceness and dryness and unconess in friends. **1652** WARISTON *Diary* (S.H.S.) II. 164 My awen mynd found an uncounesse and deadnesse of my sprite in exercises.

**Unconfe·cted,** *ppl. a.* (UN-1 8.) **1650** BULWER *Anthropomet.* 119 If it carry the unconfected meat, it works nothing upon the meat. **Unconfe·derated,** *ppl. a.* (UN-1 8.) [**1775** ASH.] **1802–12** BENTHAM *Ration. Judic. Evid.* (1827) V. 118 If..it be necessary for the acquirer to have recourse to an ordinary and unconfederated dealer. **Unconfe·rred,** *ppl. a.* (UN-1 8). **1645** MILTON *Tetrach.* Introd., Who..hath not forborn to scandalize him, unconferr'd with, unadmonisht, undealt with by any Pastorly or brotherly convincement.

**Unconfe·ss,** *v.* (UN-2 3.) **1749** LAVINGTON *Enthus. Meth. & Papists* II. Pref. (1754) p. xxvi, Whether..I have not in some measure unconfessed my confessions.

**Unconfe·ssed,** *ppl. a.* Also 6 *Sc.* wnconfessyt, 7–8 unconfest. [Un-[1] 8.]

**1.** Not confessed or avowed; unacknowledged. † Also const. *of*.

*a* **1500** in *Ratis Raving*, etc. 3 He bryngis to his mynd.. the synis that he has done, wnconfessyt of or rapentyt. **1509** Fisher *Wks.* (1876) 86, I shall..thynke on my synne that no thynge of it be vncontryte & vnconfessed. **1526** *Pilgr. Perf.* (W. de W. 1531) 227 b, Leuyng no mortall synne vnconfessed. **1648** Hexham II, *Ongebiecht*, Vnconfessed. **1863** Julia Kavanagh *Q. Mab* II. 306 It was love mutual—unconfessed, but ardent and impassioned. **1871** R. H. Hutton *Ess.* I. 4 All unconscious and unconfessed acts of surrender to the divine influence.

**b.** Of persons: Not self-avowed.

**1742** Young *Nt. Th.* v. 817 Like princes unconfest in foreign courts, Who travel under cover. **1898** A. MacKennal in *Life* xix. (1905) 314, I think that unconfessed Christians.. must have brought the gospel into Britain.

**2.** Not having confessed; unshriven.

**1607** J. Carpenter *Plaine Mans Plough* 205 For want of Confession, thou shalt be damned, as unconfest. **1638** *Penit. Conf.* xii. (1657) 331 He came into the Forest to hunt, and there was wounded with an arrow; and forthwith died impenitent and unconfessed. **1808** Scott *Marm.* I. Introd. 267 A sinful man, and unconfess'd, He took the Sangreal's holy quest. **1810** — *Lady of L.* III. v, Alice..lock'd her secret in her breast, And died in travail, unconfess'd. **1889** 'Mark Twain' *Yankee at Crt. K. Arthur* xvii, It were peril to my own soul to let him die unconfessed and unabsolved.

**Unconfe·ssing,** *ppl. a.* (Un-[1] 10.)

**1641** Milton *Animadv.* 57 Because hee may not as a Judge sit out the wrangling noyse of litigious Courts to shreeve the purses of unconfessing and unmortify'd sinners.

**Unco·nfidence.** (Un-[1] 12 and 5 b.)

*a* **1670** Hacket *Abp. Williams* I. (1692) 124 In all his employments for this [the Spanish] match,..he never raised his style higher when he wrote than with Ifs and suppositive unconfidence.

**Unco·nfident,** *a.* (Un-[1] 7 and 5 b.)

Also, in recent use, *unconfidently* adv.

*a* **1652** A. Wilson *Jas. I* (1653) 51 The Jesuits unconfident of him (inclining more to the hot zeal of Spain) one of their Instruments stab'd him into the mouth with a knife, without much hurt. **1869** *Athenæum* 13 Feb. 242/1, I mean, us unconfident lovers. **1871** Ruskin *Fors Clav.* ix. 8 [He] turned to me with an anxious, yet not unconfident expression.

**Unconfide·ntial,** *a.* (Un-[1] 7.)

**1772** Burke *Corr.* (1844) I. 384 As I have stated this matter so much at large,..it is not necessary to say more by this unconfidential conveyance. **1834** Lytton *Pompeii* I. vi, Why is it to me thou art thus unconfidential? **1839** *John Bull* 15 Apr., Showing however unconfidential they may be, that they are at any rate confident men. **1847** Mrs. Gore *Castles in Air* I. xi. 227 The unconfidential terms on which we lived.

**Unconfi·ding,** *ppl. a.* (Un-[1] 10.) **1820** Mrs. Opie *Tales of Heart* IV. 344 Rash unconfiding boy! **1870** J. Bruce *Life Gideon* xx. 368 Gideon's for long unconfiding and undutiful because unbelieving demeanour.

**Unconfi·nable,** *a.* (Un-[1] 7 b and 5 b.)

**1598** Shaks. *Merry W.* II. ii. 21 You stand vpon your honor: why, (thou vnconfinable basenesse), it is as much as I can doe to keepe the termes of my honor precise. **1669** Earl Orrery *Parthen.* (1676) 771 Your pity is so great and unconfinable. **1794** G. Adams *Nat. & Exp. Philos.* (1806) I. 523 [Light and caloric] being of too subtile a nature to be confined in any vessel that we possess, have..been termed unconfinable bodies. **1815** J. Smith *Panorama Sci. & Art* II. 291 Light and caloric, those unconfinable powers which so many of these manipulations elicit or require. **1820** W. Irving *Sketch Bk.* (1821) I. 152 It is the divine attribute of the imagination, that it is irrepressible, unconfinable.

Hence **Unconfi·nably** *adv.*

*a* **1657** R. Loveday *Lett.* (1663) 161 But I outrun the Constable: Dear Brother, Unconfinably yours to serve you, R. L.

**Unconfi·ne,** *v.* [Un-[2] 4 b.] *trans.* To release from restraint; to give free course to.

**1651** Stanley *Poems* 16 Yet there's a way to unconfine thy heart. *a* **1711** Ken *Hymnotheo* Poet. Wks. III. 35 Curs'd Infidelity to reinstil, Unfix the Mind, and unconfine the Will. **1820** Keats *Isabella* xxi, Each unconfines His bitter thoughts to other.

**Unconfi·ned,** *ppl. a.*[1] [Un-[1] 8.]

**1.** Not restrained or restricted in respect of freedom of action. Also const. *to*.

**1607** Beaum. & Fl. *Woman Hater* III. i, Were we not made our selves, free, unconfin'd Commanders of our own affections? **1624** Massinger *Renegado* I. ii, It is his pleasure.., provided (For so far I am unconfined) that I Affect and like your person. **1694** *Gracian's Courtier's Orac.* 49 Never to be too forward nor passionate, is the sign of a free and unconfined heart. **1709** Pope *Ess. Crit.* 639 Blest with a taste exact, yet unconfin'd. **1711** Steele *Spect.* No. 2 ¶ 1 His being unconfined to Modes and Forms. **1784** Cowper *Task* III. 713 Pure is the nymph, though lib'ral of her smiles, And chaste, though unconfin'd, whom I extol. **1808** Scott *Marm.* IV. Introd. 163 Oft our talk its topic chang'd, And..Rang'd, unconfin'd, from grave to gay. **1820** J. P. Neale *Views Seats Eng.*, etc. III. *Porkington* 2 To the east the eye roams unconfined over the rich and highly ornamented plains of Shropshire.

**b.** Unlimited, unbounded.

**1626** Massinger *Roman Actor* I. ii, As his rule is infinite, his pleasures Are unconfined. **1662** Bp. Hopkins *Serm.* (1685) 26 We begin to grow more unconfined in our knowledge, as well as our being. *a* **1672** Sterry *Freed. Will* (1675) 109 As an heavenly Marriage eternally established in its own unconfined Unity. *a* **1721** Prior *Ess. Opinion* Wks. 1907 II. 202 However our Vanities or desires are unconfined. **1738** Glover *Leonidas* XII. 82 Now devastation, unconfin'd, involves The Malian fields. **1818** Cruise *Digest* (ed. 2) IV. 279 The former was subject to some restraint..; the latter consisting in general and unconfined dominion.

**2.** Not kept in confinement; not shut up or enclosed; not secured or kept in place.

**1649** Lovelace *To Althea* i, When Love with unconfined wings Hovers within my Gates. *a* **1711** Ken *Psyche* Poet. Wks. IV. 299 The Soul in Vision seem'd from Flesh unloos'd To fly abroad, and spatiate unconfin'd. **1739** 'R. Bull' tr. *Dedekindus' Grobianus* 5 Thy Hairs, uncut and unconfin'd, With loose Disorder wanton in the Wind. **1762** R. Guy *Pract. Obs. Cancers* 30 The Matter having a free and unconfined Discharge. **1808** Scott *Marm.* III. Introd. 22 Then, wild as cloud, or stream, or gale, Flow on, flow unconfin'd, my Tale! **1832** Ht. Martineau *Ella of Gar.* i. 9 Her hair [was] unconfined by any cap. **1892** Greener *Breech Loader* 163 Unconfined wood powder..may be ignited without obtaining a third of the available explosive force.

Hence **Unconfi·nedly** *adv.*; **Unconfi·nedness.**

**1654–66** Earl Orrery *Parthen.* (1676) 598 Sorrow, to which they so justly and unconfinedly abandon'd themselves. **1673** A. Walker *Lees Lachrymans* 3 The healthful Vigour, the agile Unconfinedness,..of his Youth. **1687** Dryden *Hind & P.* II. 617 Prove any Church, oppos'd to this our head, So one, so pure, so unconfin'dly spread. **1899** *Macm. Mag.* LXXIX. 455/2 The sense of the desert was upon me, the embracing, soothing spirit of unconfinedness.

**Unconfi·ned,** *ppl. a.*[2] [Un-[2] 8.] Released from confinement.

**1833** Tennyson *Two Voices* 371 And men,..From cells of madness unconfined, Oft lose whole years of darker mind.

**Unconfi·ning,** *ppl. a.* (Un-[1] 8.) **1846** Worcester (citing Chesterfield). **Unconfi·rm,** *v.* (Un-[2] 3.) **1550** Bale *Eng. Votaries* II. 66 Anselme intreated for hys dysgraded abbottes and vnconfirmed prelates, whyche was graunted forthwith, and they restored to their dygnytees. **1598** Florio, *Disconfermare*, to vnconfirme, to disestablish. **1843** Carlyle *Past & Pr.* II. ix, Long ages of..entirely confirmed Valethood—which will have to *un*confirm itself again.

**Unconfi·rmed,** *ppl. a.* [Un-[1] 8 and 5 b.]

**1.** Not having received the rite of confirmation.

**1565** Calfhill *Answ. Martiall* 99, I besech you, how many be suffered to dye, vnconfirmed.

**2.** Not strengthened or fortified; not yet made firm or sure.

*c* **1592** Marlowe *Jew of Malta* III. iii, Then were my thoughts so fraile And vnconfirm'd, And I was chain'd to follies of the world. **1609** Daniel *Civ. Wars* IV. xxxvi, In th' unconfirmed troupes, much fear did breed. **1706** Rowe *Ulysses* IV, A boy! ..feeble in Infancy, Essaying the first Rudiments of Manhood, With Strength unpractis'd yet, and unconfirm'd. **1750** *Phil. Trans.* XLVI. 399 As I observed the Callus to be unconfirmed, I re-applied the Bandage. **1795** Southey *Joan of Arc* I. 98 Thoughts of politic craftiness arose Within him, and his faith, yet unconfirm'd, Determin'd to prompt action.

† **b.** Uninstructed, ignorant. *Obs.*

**1588** Shaks. *L. L. L.* IV. ii. 19 After his..vntrained, or rather vnlettered, or ratherest vnconfirmed fashion. **1599** — *Much Ado* III. iii. 120 *Con.* I wonder at it. *Bor.* That shewes thou art vnconfirm'd.

**c.** Not supported or established by further evidence; uncorroborated.

**1671** Milton *P. R.* I. 29 Nor was long His witness unconfirm'd. **1781** V. Knox *Liberal Education* Concl. 359 Their [*sc.* French] recent histories are destitute of dignity, both of diction and sentiment, and unconfirmed by authorities. **1897** *Westm. Gaz.* 26 Aug. 2/1 The report that 300 of these brave fellows have been cut to pieces is unconfirmed.

**3.** Not formally confirmed or sanctioned.

**1656** Bramhall *Replic.* ii. 105 Therefore we give the same priviledges to a Councell unconfirmed..and to a Councell confirmed by the Pope.

† **Unconfo·rm,** *a. Obs.* [Un-[1] 7 and 5 b.]

**1.** = Inconform *a.*

**1653** Gauden *Hierasp.* 74 How unscriptural, how unconform to the examples of all ancient Churches,..do they seem to many judicious and gracious Christians? **1667** Milton *P. L.* V. 259 From hence..he sees, Not unconform to other shining Globes, Earth and the Gard'n of God.

**2.** = Non-conform *a.*

**1653** R. Baillie *Dissuas. Vind.* (1655) 74 Not only the Separatists but the unconform ministers. **1676** John Row *Contin. Blair's Autobiog.* viii. (1848) 113 The preaching of the Word by honest unconform and anti-prelatic men.

**Unconformabi·lity.** [Un-[1] 12. Cf. next.] The state or quality of being unconformable. Chiefly *Geol.*

**1833** Lyell *Princ. Geol.* III. 30 The frequent unconformability in the stratification of the inferior and overlying formation. **1865** Livingstone *Zambesi* ii. 54 A picture of dislocation or unconformability which would gladden a geological lecturer's heart. **1873** Earle *Philol. Eng. Tongue* (ed. 2) § 6 One important cause of unconformability is the introduction of foreign words.

**Unconfo·rmable,** *a.* [Un-[1] 7 b and 5 b.]

**1.** Not conformable or correspondent *to* something. Also without const.

**1594** Hooker *Eccl. Pol.* III. vii. § 4 Vnto those generall rules.. we doe not defend that we may hold any thing vnconformable. **1598–9** E. Forde *Parismus* II. (1672) 73 So far is this Picture unconformable to the perfect description of her cælestial perfections, as far as is black from white. *a* **1688** Cudworth *Immut. Mor.* (1731) 157 This must not be granted, that the Modes of Conception in the Understanding..are disagreeable to the Reality of the Things conceived by them; and so being unconformable, are therefore False. **1711** Steele *Spect.* No. 145 ¶ 7 We retain still a Quilted one [*sc.* petticoat] underneath, which makes us not altogether unconformable to the Fashion. **1726** Leoni *Alberti's Archit.* I. 11 The..Parts may not be unconformable to the Rules of Art. **1802–12** Bentham *Ration. Judic. Evid.* (1827) I. 156 In so far as it is the will..of the witness, that his testimony..be in any respect unconformable to the real state of the case. **1883** M. Pattison *Mem.* (1885) 299 He wanted to get me out as an unconformable element.

**b.** Of persons: Unwilling to conform. (Cf. next.)

**1647** Clarendon *Hist. Reb.* I. § 173 That People..would not appear unconformable to his Majesty's wish in any particular. **1728** Morgan *Algiers* I. iv. 76 His libidinous and unconformable Proselytes.

**2.** *spec.* in *Eng. Hist.* Not conforming to the usages of the Church of England, in later use esp. as prescribed by the Act of Uniformity of 1662. Also const. *to*. (Cf. Non-conformable *a.*)

**1611** A. Stafford *Niobe* 175 These men, whose puritie hath made them vnconformable to the present Discipline of the Church. **1647** Clarendon *Hist. Reb.* IV. § 10 The recommending some seditious, Unconformable Ministers, to be Lecturers in Churches about London. **1672** Baxter *Bagshaw's Scand.* iii. 32 Could you wish..that the.. Protestant Religion were kept up by none but the unconformable Ministers in private? **1732** Neal *Hist. Purit.* I. 307 Many ministers of his diocese being returned unconformable, were suspended. **1736** Chandler *Hist. Persec.* 358 A warrant from the Council..to stop all ministers unconformable to the discipline and ceremonies of the Church. **1861** W. S. Perry *Hist. Ch. Eng.* I. xvi. 591 Unconformable clergy could be reduced..into a sullen outward compliance.

**3.** *Geol.* Not having the same direction or plane of stratification. Also const. *to*.

**1813** Bakewell *Introd. Geol.* (1815) 76 Granite is sometimes met with not under the slate rocks, but resting upon them in an unconformable position. **1830** Lyell *Princ. Geol.* I. 201 The travertin is unconformable to the lacustrine beds. **1882** Geikie *Text bk. Geol.* IV. x. 601 Wherever one series of rocks is found to rest upon a highly denuded surface of an older series, the junction is unconformable.

Hence **Unconfo·rmableness.**

**1711** *Phil. Trans.* XXVII. 329 The unconformableness that the Figure of the compounded Globe had to a perfect Sphere.

**Unconfo·rmably,** *adv.* [Un-[1] 11.] *Geol.* In an unconformable manner or position.

**1839** Murchison *Silur. Syst.* I. xxxiv. 451 In the former district, it has just been shown to lie unconformably upon the coal measures and more ancient strata. **1875** Dawson *Dawn of Life* ii. 9 The crumpled..strata..are seen to underlie unconformably.

**Unconfo·rmed,** *ppl. a.* [Un-[1] 8.]

† **1.** Not conforming; nonconformist. *Obs.*

*a* **1631** Donne *Lett.* (1651) 36 That more single [duellism], and almost self-homicide, between the unconformed Ministers, and Bishops. **1676** Row *Contn. Blair's Autobiog.* xii. (1848) 454 All the unconformed ministers were summoned..to come to their meeting.

**2.** *Geol.* (Cf. Unconformable *a.* 3.)

**1833–4** J. Phillips *Geol.* in *Encycl. Metrop.* (1845) VI. 656/2 A little appearance of the chalk is observable North of the coal of Elberfeld, to which it is unconformed. **1876** Page *Adv. Text-bk. Geol.* 325 Where any beds of the oolitic system are really unconformed to others of the same system below them.

Hence **Unconfo·rmedly** *adv.*

**1833–4** J. Phillips *Geol.* in *Encycl. Metrop.* (1845) VI. 590/1 The Northern and Southern portion of this great tract.. agree in being..covered unconformedly by the magnesian limestone.

**Unconfo·rming,** *ppl. a.* [Un-[1] 10.] Failing or refusing to conform; *spec.* = Nonconforming.

**1641** *Vind. Smect.* xiii. 131 There is one practice of our Bishops he is something more laborious to justifie: That is, their casting out unconforming brethren. **1656** Sanderson *Serm.* (1689) 13 Unconforming Ministers have no cause to complain. **1680** *Dial. Pope & Phanatick* 7 We post within the Establish'd Church as many Unconforming Ministers as we can. **1753** Chesterf. in *World* No. 29. 256 To be plagued ..by the unconforming obstinacy, the low vulgar excesses,.. of my son. **1821** Wordsw. *Eccl. Sonn., Clerical Integrity* 2 Nor shall the eternal roll of praise reject Those Unconforming; whom one rigorous day Drives from their Cures. **1825** *Monthly Rev.* CVI. 513 Calvinistic laymen are seldom tolerant, their women less unconforming.

† **Unconfo·rmist.** *Obs.* [Un-[1] 12 and 5 b.] = Nonconformist.

**1640** R. Baillie *Canterb. Self-convict.* 117 Since by severe punishment the number of the unconformists have decayed, ..their cause can not bee from God. **1653** — *Dissuas. Vind.* (1655) 15 This no meer unconformists had ever done. **1688** C'tess of Clare in *Buccleuch MSS.* (Hist. MSS. Comm.) I. 348 Mr. Gilbert, an unconformist minister.

† **Unconfo·rmitable,** *a. Obs.*[−1] [Un-[1] 7 b: cf. next.] = Unconformable *a.* 2.

**1647** Clarendon *Hist. Reb.* III. § 15 (1888) I. 232 *note*, Many preachers, whom he named and who he knew were of precious memory with the unconformitable party.

† **Unconfo·rmitant.** *Obs. rare.* [Un-[1] 12.] = Nonconformitant.

**1605** Hieron *Short Dial.* 43 The vnconformitant and the not subscriber for just reasons perswading his conscience. **1629** W. Sclater *Exp. 2 Thess.* 82 What one Separatist, or but vnconfor[mi]tant, hath the contrary course wonne?

**Unconfo·rmity.** [Un-[1] 12 and 5 b.]

**1.** Lack of conformity (*to* something).

*a* **1600** Hooker *Eccl. Pol.* VII. xxiii. § 11 So odiously to be upbraided with unconformity unto the pattern of our Lord and Saviour's estate. *a* **1716** South *Serm.* (1717) III. 435 The Moral Goodness or Evil of men's Actions, which consist in their Conformity, or Unconformity to Right Reason. **1728** R. Morris *Ess. Anc. Archit.* 69 In a direct Unconformity to the Rules. **1781** M. Madan *Thelyphthora* III. Pref. p. vii, He..has been at the pains to shew its unconformity to the Divine system, in the former parts of this work.

† **2.** = Nonconformity. *Obs.*

**1635** Bp. of Peterborough in *Buccleuch MSS.* (Hist. MSS. Comm.) I. 275 No man's learning and piety shall excuse, with me, his unconformity. **1657** J. Sergeant *Schism Dispach't* 580 To wit, distractions, dissentions, Unconformity, with a perpetually-fleeting Changeablenes of their tenet. *a* **1677** Manton *Serm. John xvii. 11* Wks. 1872 X. 330 Every modest dissent and unconformity is branded with the name of schism.

**3.** *Geol.* The fact of being unconformable or unconformed; difference of plane.

1829 J. PHILLIPS *Geol. Yorks.* I. 125 Proving the great unconformity of strata beneath the Yorkshire wolds. 1880 HAUGHTON *Phys. Geogr.* iii. 81 The general unconformity of the Permian and Triassic rocks.

**b.** With *a* and pl. An instance of this.

1863 J. G. MURPHY *Com., Gen.* i. 12–13 The stratifications of the earth's crust with all their slips, elevations, depressions, unconformities. 1895 J. W. POWELL in *Nat. Geog. Monogr.* I. i. 18 Ore deposits are often found in unconformities.

**Unconfou·nd,** *v.* [UN-² 3.] *trans.* To free from confusion.

1648 MILTON *Tenure Kings* (1649) 40 His people..now.. against thir own disciplin,..absolve him, unconfound him, though unconverted, unrepentant.

**Unconfou·nded,** *ppl. a.* (UN-¹ 8.)

1577 tr. *Bullinger's Decades* 677 The selfe same sonne is.. true God and man..abideing in two vnconfounded natures. 1612 W. SCLATER *Ministers Portion* 36 Alienation of possessions..was flatly forbidden..that Christs linage and descent might bee kept vnconfounded. 1676 BOYLE in *Phil. Trans.* XI. 783 As if some odd subtile matter..interposed, to keep them unconfounded. 1758 WARBURTON *Div. Legat.* IV. § 6 II. 414 The only place where they could remain, for so long a time, safe and unconfounded with the natives. 1836 I. TAYLOR *Phys. The. Another Life* (1858) 113 Then does the mind hold each of these sets of signs..unconfounded and distinct. 1856 G. WILSON *Gateways Knowl.* (1859) 50 Music forms the universal language which..the confusion of Babel left unconfounded.

Hence **Unconfou·ndedly** *adv.*

1664 H. MORE *Myst. Iniq.* Apol. 525 Son, Lord, onely-begotten, acknowledged to be unconfoundedly, immutably, indivisibly and inseparably in two natures.

**Unconfro·nted,** *ppl. a.* (UN-¹ 8.)

*a* 1656 USSHER *Ann.* vi. (1658) 555 To provide, that they should die free women and unconfronted. 1802–12 BENTHAM *Ration. Judic. Evid.* (1827) II. 141 If these several modes ..were to be left altogether unconfronted and uncompared. 1891 *Pall Mall G.* 9 Nov. 6/2 Are these by no means ineffectual tactics to go on unconfronted, unchecked?

**Unconfu·sed,** *ppl. a.* (UN-¹ 8 and 5 b.)

1609 J. DAVIES *Holy Roode* G 3 b, Ye vnconfused orders Angellick In order come to take this Blood effuz'd. 1635 JACKSON *Creed* VIII. vi. § 3 The diversity of these two natures might still remaine unconfused without diversity of persons. *a* 1676 HALES *Prim. Orig. Man.* I. ii. (1677) 56 In that it is more distinct and unconfused than the sensitive Memory. 1768–74 TUCKER *Lt. Nat.* (1834) I. 304 When we see qualities affecting our senses, we may have an unconfused idea of something exerting them. 1853 RUSKIN *Stones Ven.* II. vi. § 97. 222 A few of the most common forms are represented, unconfused by exterior mouldings. 1882 *Edin. Rev.* Oct. 344 He keeps his eyes open and his senses unconfused by prejudice or sentiment.

Hence **Unconfu·sedly** *adv.*

1655 MRQ. WORCESTER *Cent. Inv.* § 42 To write..by these three Senses as perfectly, distinctly and unconfusedly, yea as readily as by the sight. 1690 LOCKE *Hum. Und.* IV. vii. § 4 He knows them distinctly and unconfusedly one from another. 1709 BERKELEY *Th. Vision* § 50 To treat accurately and unconfusedly of vision.

**Unconfu·table,** *a.* (UN-¹ 7 b and 5 b.)

1643 CHAS. I *Treaty at Oxford* Wks. 1662 II. 285 So just and unconfutable a Censure. 1684 CUDWORTH *Let.* in Birch *Life R. Boyle* (1744) 257 Your pieces of natural history are unconfutable. *a* 1849 H. COLERIDGE *Ess.* (1851) I. 259 Though ..little beholden to the privileged orders, Mr. Green was a sound unconfutable Tory.

**Unconfu·ted,** *ppl. a.* (UN-¹ 8.)

1600 NASHE *Summer's Last Will* D 2, If Enuy vnconfuted may accuse, Then Innocence must vncondemned dye. 1645 MILTON *Tetrach.*, To Parlt. A 4, That what he writes though unconfuted, must therefore be mistrusted. 1720 WATERLAND *Eight Serm.* Pref. p. xxviii, It is in vain to think of any Expedients in this affair, while our Doctrine stands unconfuted. 1760 LAW *Spir. Prayer* II. 60 Till then, the Appeal must, and therefore will for ever, stand unconfuted.

**Uncongea·l,** *v.* [UN-² 3 and 7.] *trans.* and *intr.* To unfreeze; to thaw.

1593 NASHE *Christ's T.* Wks. (Grosart) IV. 246 The infected ayre will vncongeale, and the wombes of the contagious Clowdes will be clensed. 1664 POWER *Exp. Philos.* I. 35 When I came again about two or three hours after to uncongeal the Liquor, by keeping the glass in my warm hand. 1833 TENNYSON *Two Voices* 407 Like soften'd airs that blowing steal, When meres begin to uncongeal.

**Uncongea·lable,** *a.* (UN-¹ 7 b and 5 b.)

1611 COTGR., *Incongelable*, vncongealable, not to bee congealed. 1794 R. J. SULIVAN *View Nat.* I. 191 Air..being uncongealable, or incapable of being fixed by any known method. 1799 SOUTHEY *Nondescripts, Cool Reflect.* 22 A road whose white intensity Would now make platina uncongealable Like quicksilver.

**Uncongea·led,** *ppl. a.* (UN-¹ 8.)

1646 SIR T. BROWNE *Pseud. Ep.* II. i. 51 The aqueous parts will freeze, but the spirit retyre and be found uncongealed in the center. *a* 1700 EVELYN *Diary* 3 Feb. 1645, A quantity of uncongealed water. 1816 BYRON *Parisina* xx, Those tears ..in its depth endure, Unseen, unwept, but uncongeal'd. 1883 *Standard* 31 Aug. 3/6 Congealed or uncongealed milk.

**Unconge·nial,** *a.* [UN-¹ 7 and 5 b.]

**1.** Not congenial or kindred; unsympathetic.

[1775 ASH.] 1813 SCOTT *Rokeby* II. iv, And small the intercourse, I ween, Such uncongenial souls between. 1846 TRENCH *Mirac.* xxix. (1862) 402 The disturbing influences of that uncongenial circle. 1884 BLACK *Jud. Shakes.* xiii, Refusing to harbor such uncongenial guests.

**2.** Unsuited to the nature of the thing mentioned or under consideration.

1788 V. KNOX *Winter Even.* xxx. (1790) II. 202 In England, a cold northern country, where I imagine its growth is impeded by an uncongenial climate. 1830 LYELL *Princ. Geol.* III. vii. (1835) III. 86 Insects..can readily spread themselves wherever their progress is not opposed by uncongenial climates. 1846 J. BAXTER *Libr. Pract. Agric.* (ed. 4) I. 67 The stratum beneath,..if uncongenial to the growth of the tree, will assuredly cause it to canker. 1873 SYMONDS *Grk. Poets* v. 136 Into the Æolian style Anacreon introduced a new and uncongenial element.

**3.** Not suited or agreeable to one's temperament; not to one's taste.

1805 *Ann. Rev.* III. 58 This is best resisted by uncongenial employment during youth. 1860 MRS. CARLYLE *Lett.* (1883) III. 20 The reading of that book will be an even more uncongenial job. 1905 'GUY THORNE' *Lost Cause* iii, He felt that he was in a thoroughly uncongenial atmosphere.

**b.** Const. *to, with.* † Also as *adv.*, in disagreement, at variance *with.*

1799 SICKELMORE *Agnes & Leonora* II. 190 They trusted.. that their father..would..relinquish his intention of marrying his daughter uncongenial with her wishes. 1812 SHELLEY in Dowden *Life* (1887) I. 221 Oxonian society was insipid to me, uncongenial with my habits of thinking. 1839 HALLAM *Hist. Lit.* III. ii. § 25 This..important book..must have been very uncongenial to the ruling party. 1871 JOWETT *Plato* I. 66 The good is congenial, and the evil uncongenial to every one.

**Uncongenia·lity.** [Cf. prec. and UN-¹ 12.] The quality or state of being uncongenial.

1805 FOSTER *Ess.* IV. ii. 129 This feeling of uncongeniality. 1848 DICKENS *Dombey* xxx, Dombey found no uncongeniality in an air of scant and gloomy state that pervaded the room. 1873 MORLEY *Rousseau* II. 298 The vicious excess..in his character..was irritated into further activity by the uncongeniality of the surrounding medium.

† **Uncongru·ity.** *Obs.* (UN-¹ 12 and 5 b.)

*c* 1449 PECOCK *Repr.* II. xviii. 255 And thei ordeyneden.. certein figuris..forto excuse tho spechis fro vncongruyte of gramer. 1587 GOLDING *De Mornay* xi. (1592) 155 There starts me vp a whole world of Grammarians, which inforce their wittes..to finde some elegancie in thine vncongruities.

† **Unco·ngruous,** *a. Obs.* (UN-¹ 7 and 5 b.)

1709 in Hardiman *O'Flaherty's Iar Connaught* (1845) 441 Hanmer,..to rectify that as uncongruous, must invent that they were consecrated by the Archbishops of Canterbury.

**Unconje·cturable,** *a.* (UN-¹ 7 b.)

1806 J. WILSON *Let.* in *Mem.* iv. (1879) 78, I have long been conjecturing the reason of your unconjecturable silence. 1829 BENTHAM *Justice & Cod. Petit.* 88 Not to speak of an unconjecturable variety of other circumstances. 1863 LYTTON *Caxtoniana* I. 308 Thus Faith..loses itself no more among the phantom shadows of the Unknown and Unconjecturable.

So **Unconjecturabi·lity.**

1802–12 BENTHAM *Rationale* (1827) IV. 37 From this unconjecturability, two..advantages accrue to the partnership.

**Unconje·ctured,** *ppl. a.* (UN-¹ 8.)

*a* 1647 BOYLE in Birch *Life* (1744) 27 The true cause.. remained long unconjectured, until the effects betrayed it. 1850 TENNYSON *In Mem.* xciii, Therefore from thy sightless range With gods in unconjectured bliss,..Descend, and touch, and enter. 1862 LYTTON *Str. Story* I. 165, I imagined that.. the discovery might lead to some sublime and unconjectured secrets of science.

**Unco·njugal,** *a.* (UN-¹ 7.)

1644 MILTON *Divorce* I. i, What hinders that more then the unfitnes and defectivenes of an unconjugal mind. 1671 — *Samson* 979 My name..may stand defam'd, With malediction mention'd, and the blot Of falshood most unconjugal traduc't. 1809 MALKIN *Gil Blas* IV. iv. ¶ 18 An unconjugal and litigious defence of her insulted virtue. 1877 BLACKMORE *Cripps* xxi, Unconjugal, perhaps, is what I mean; unuxorial, or what it may be.

**Unconju·nctive,** *a.* (UN-¹ 7.) 1644 MILTON *Divorce* II. xvi, Parted from each other, as two persons unconiunctive and unmariable together. **Unco·njured,** *ppl. a.* [UN-¹ 8.] † Unconsecrated. 1546 *Wyckliffe's Wycket* (1828) p. xii, Then makest thou to worshyppe a false god in the chalyce, whych is unconjured when ye worshyp the breade. **Unconne·ct,** *v.* [UN-² 3.] *trans.* To disconnect. 1796 LAMB *Lett.* (1904) I. 36, I can unconnect myself with him, and shall manage all my father's moneys in future myself.

**Unconne·cted,** *ppl. a.* [UN-¹ 8 and 5 b.]

**1.** Not connected or associated *with* something.

1736 BUTLER *Anal.* I. i. 13 There would be no apprehension that any other power or event unconnected with this of death would destroy these faculties. 1796 MORSE *Amer. Geog.* I. 471 The colony of New Haven, though unconnected with the colony of Connecticut. 1842 SEDGWICK in *Hudson's Guide Lakes* (1843) 191 We find..great masses of alluvial drift, entirely unconnected with any erosion of the existing rivers. 1885 *Law Times* 10 Jan. 183/1 A surveyor..who is entirely unconnected with the neighbourhood.

*ellipt.* 1813 SHELLEY *Q. Mab* IV. 74 This is no unconnected misery, Nor stands uncaused, and irretrievable.

**b.** Not physically joined *with* something.

1829 T. CASTLE *Introd. Bot.* 150 The flowers have upwards of twenty-five stamens, all unconnected with the calyx.

**2.** Characterized by want of connexion.

1762 GIBBON *Misc. Wks.* (1814) V. 250 His epistles,..translated in a very bad style, and unconnected method. 1824 L. MURRAY *Eng. Gram.* (ed. 5) I. 193 As the fashionable mode of unconnected composition is less improving to the mind of the reader. 1886 WILLIS & CLARK *Cambridge* III. 249 His buildings are disposed in an unconnected manner about a quadrangular court.

**3.** Not joined together in order or sequence; disunited, isolated.

1777 RICHARDSON *Pers. Dict.* 1925 Incongruous, unconnected speech. 1791 BOSWELL *Johnson* (1831) I. 180 Addison's note was a fiction, in which unconnected fragments of his lucubrations were purposely jumbled together. 1809–10 COLERIDGE *Friend* (1865) 9 These short and unconnected sentences are easily and instantly understood. 1889 GRETTON *Memory's Harkb.* 55, I simply record unconnected anecdotes and disjointed facts.

**4.** Not having personal connexions; not related by family ties, common aims, etc.

1802 MAR. EDGEWORTH *Moral T.*, *A Summons*, An individual in society who has friends..and a home, is in a more desirable situation than an unconnected being. 1822 BYRON *Werner* IV. i. 516, I could only guess at one, And he to me a stranger, unconnected. 1846 MRS. GORE *Eng. Char.* I. 40 But without this..what would become of the vapid, unmeaning, unconnected Lady P——?

**Unconne·ctedly,** *adv.* [f. prec.] In an unconnected manner; disconnectedly.

1778 TOOKE *Let. to Dunning* ad fin., He thought the best way to make his zany talk unconnectedly and nonsensically, was [etc.]. 1799 V. KNOX *Lord's Supper* xvii. Wks. 1824 VII. 423 This petition therefore comes in very abruptly and unconnectedly. 1817 J. SCOTT *Paris Revisit.* (ed. 4) 389 Enabling them to regard it unconnectedly with circumstances of humiliation. 1841 MARRYAT *Poacher* xxxix, They..would talk unconnectedly, running from one subject to another. 1877 RAYMOND *Statist. Mines & Mining* 192 Twenty-six mining districts are distributed irregularly over the county, occupying unconnectedly the various mountain-ranges.

**Unconne·ctedness.** [f. as prec.] The quality or state of being unconnected.

1772 MACKENZIE *Man World* I. xxix, She relapsed into her former unconnectedness. 1780 M. MADAN *Thelyphthora* (1781) I. 146 The marriage destroys their unconnectedness, distinctness, and independency on each other. 1837 LANDOR *Pentameron, 4th Day's Interv.* Wks. 1853 II. 339/2 The loose and shallow foundation of so vast a structure; its unconnectedness. 1877 'H. A. PAGE' *De Quincey* II. xix. 168 Hence the unconnectedness, the obtrusive digressions and rangings from date to date.

**Unconne·ction.** (UN-¹ 12 and 5 b.)

*a* 1756 CHANDLER *Life of David* (1766) I. 113 There is a force and elegance in the very unconnection of the expressions. 1794 *Monthly Rev.* XIV. 320 English ode-writers.. seem..to have considered eccentricity and unconnection as the very characteristics of their task. *a* 1834 COLERIDGE *Notes & Lect.* (1849) I. 14 That unconnection by contradictions of the inward being, to which all folly is owing. 1876 MRS. WHITNEY *Sights & Ins.* xiii, [These ideas] rushed through my thought in a connected unconnection.

**Unco·nned,** *ppl. a.* (UN-¹ 8.) 1742 SHENSTONE *Schoolmistr.* ii, They..oft-times on vagaries idly bent, For unkempt hair, or task unconn'd, are sorely shent.

† **Unconne·xed,** *ppl. a. Obs.*⁻¹ (UN-¹ 8.)

1716 M. DAVIES *Athen. Brit.* II. 304 In the unconnex'd heaping of Texts in that and most of his Sermons.

**Unconning,** obs. f. UNCUNNING *sb.* and *a.*

**Unconni·ving,** *ppl. a.* (UN-¹ 10.) 1671 MILTON *P. R.* I. 363 To that hideous place not so confin'd By rigour unconniving.

**Unco·nquerable,** *a.* [UN-¹ 7 b and 5 b.]

**1.** Of persons, places, etc.: That cannot be overcome by conquest or force of arms; not yielding to superior force; invincible.

1598 FLORIO, *Inuincibile*, inuincible, vnconquerable. 1608 J. KING *Serm. 24 Mar.* 10 Whose priuiledge and right vnquestionable, is, *per me reges regnant*, and his might vnconquerable. 1632 LITHGOW *Trav.* I. 40 There is neither out-going nor in-comming, without a Pylot, which maketh the Citty vnconquerable. 1649 MILTON *Eikon.* ix. 76 So farr was any man.. from esteeming him unconquerable. 1760 PITT in Ellis *Orig. Lett.* Ser. II. IV. 421 To give stability and happiness to the fortunes of this unconquerable Monarch. 1798 PENNANT *Hindoostan* II. 196 The most unconquerable fort in the world. 1855 SINGLETON *Virgil* II. 360 The buckler, which the Lord of Fire himself Vouchsafed, unconquerable. 1878 BOSW. SMITH *Carthage* 315 They forgot now that..Hannibal was still in Italy, still unconquered, and, as far as they knew, unconquerable.

**b.** Of the mind, feelings, etc., with similar implication.

(*a*) 1667 MILTON *P. L.* I. 106 All is not lost; the unconquerable Will, And study of revenge, immortal hate. 1702 ROWE *Tamerl.* III. i, But to subdue th' unconquerable Mind,..Impossible! 1754 GRAY *Progr. Poesy* 65 Th' unconquerable Mind, and Freedom's holy flame. 1802 WORDSW. *Poems Independence & Liberty* I. viii. 14 Man's unconquerable mind. 1875 HENLEY *Life & Death* iv, *Bk. Verses* (1888) 56, I thank whatever gods may be For my unconquerable soul.

(*b*) 1776 GIBBON *Decl. & F.* xii. I. 339 Their unconquerable love of freedom, rising against despotism, provoked them into hasty rebellions. 1797 MRS. RADCLIFFE *Italian* xvi, He fought with unconquerable audacity and fierceness. 1825 SCOTT *Talism.* ii, Animated by a zeal as fiery as their own, and possessed of as unconquerable courage, address, and success in arms. 1881 JOWETT *Thucyd.* I. 154 The unconquerable quality which is inherent in our minds.

**2.** Incapable of being overcome, mastered, brought under control, etc.

1642 FULLER *Holy & Prof. St.* II. viii. 78 Nothing was unconquerable to his pains, who had a golden wit in an iron body. 1654 COKAINE *Dianea* I. 53 That there was nothing more unconquerable than love. 1695 LD. PRESTON *Boeth.* IV. 166 By this almost unconquerable Bent and Help of Nature. 1771 BEATTIE *Minstrel* I. i, Check'd by the scoff of pride, by envy's frown, And poverty's unconquerable bar. 1781 GIBBON *Decl. & F.* xviii. II. 118 Yet he mentions with admiration the unconquerable fertility of the soil. 1828 D'ISRAELI *Chas. I*, I. i. 7 Something of pity and terror must blend with the story of a noble mind wrestling with unconquerable Fate. 1846 TRENCH *Mirac.* Introd. (1862) 72 His argument is..unconquerable so long as it is permitted to rest upon the earth out of which it sprung. *a* 1881 A. BARRATT *Phys. Metempiric* (1883) 17 As this assumption..is perhaps not wholly unconquerable, it will be wise not to lay too much stress on it.

**b.** Of feelings. (Cf. INVINCIBLE *a.* 1 b.)

1727 DE FOE *Hist. Appar.* x. I. 73 An unconquerable aversion to any restraint. 1767 WILKES *Corr.* (1805) III. 217 The same fixed and unconquerable hatred to the enemies of freedom. 1798 S. & HT. LEE *Canterb. T.* II. 492 Actuated by an unconquerable curiosity. 1828 TYTLER *Hist. Scot.* (1864) I. 49 His unconquerable thirst of vengeance against the English influenced their choice. 1863 GEO. ELIOT *Romola* III. vi, Romola..shrank with unconquerable disgust from the shrill excitability of those illuminated women.

**Unco·nquerableness.** [f. prec. + -NESS.] The quality or state of being unconquerable.

1647 SPRIGG *Anglia Rediv.* To Englishmen, We would least of all be thought..to fixe unconquerablenesse..upon this Army. 1652 HEYLIN *Cosmogr.* II. 254 When all the Persians soothed the King in the unconquerableness of his forces; Artabanus told him [etc.]. 1866 RUSKIN *Eth. Dust* 182 Some real notion of the extent and the unconquerableness of our ignorance. 1901 'LINESMAN' *Words by Eyewitness* (1902) 75 The greatest of the three failures which..nerved her retreating soldiers to a pitch of absolute unconquerableness.

**Unco·nquerably,** *adv.* [f. as prec. + -LY[2].] In an unconquerable manner or degree; invincibly.

1654 COKAINE *Dianea* 220 Which..obtained more hearts which gave up their Liberties to it, than it met with eyes that unconquerably could behold it. 1725 POPE *Odyss.* XI. 356 Wild, furious herds, unconquerably strong! 1797 FRERE in *Anti-Jacobin* 25 Dec. (1852) 26 True to herself unconquerably bold. 1826 MISS MITFORD *Village* Ser. II. (1863) 342 But it would not do: she was unconquerably stupid. 1849 MACAULAY *Hist. Eng.* vi. II. 103 His temper acrimonious, turbulent, and unconquerably stubborn.

**Unco·nquered,** *ppl. a.* [UN-[1] 8.] Not conquered or vanquished: **a.** Of persons, places, etc.

1549 UDALL, etc. *Erasm. Par. 1 John* ii. 47 A mynde that is vnbroken and vnconquered agaynst al wanton enticementes, agaynst all iniuries, sheweth a man to be a Christian. 1591 SHAKS. *1 Hen. VI*, IV. ii. 32 Loe, there thou standst a breathing valiant man Of an inuincible vnconquer'd spirit. 1618 J. TAYLOR (Water P.) *Penniless Pilgr.* Wks. (1630) 129/2, I haue seene many Straights and Fortresses.., but they must all giue place to this vnconquered Castle, both for strength and scituation. 1684 BURNET tr. *More's Utop.* 1 Henry the 8th, the unconquered King of England. 1715 POPE *Iliad* I. 378 That imperious, that unconquer'd soul, No laws can limit, no respect control. 1765 BLACKSTONE *Comm.* I. 93 Wales had continued independent of England, unconquered and uncultivated. 1813 BYRON *Corsair* III. i, The mountain shadows kiss Thy glorious gulf, unconquer'd Salamis! 1867 'OUIDA' *C. Castlemaine's Gage* 3 So she would put them all aside..and go on her own way, proud, peerless,..conquering and unconquered.

**b.** Of things, in various applications.

1651 WITTIE *Primrose's Pop. Err.* I. viii. 30 Wood annointed with Alome remaines unconquered of the fire. *a* 1718 PRIOR *Henry & Emma* 22 While my Notes to future Times proclaim Unconquer'd Love. 1750 tr. *Leonardus' Mirr. Stones* 63 The diamond..had its name from the Greek interpretation, which is, an unconquered virtue. 1813 SHELLEY *Q. Mab* III. 97 The unconquered powers Of precedent and custom interpose Between a king and virtue. 1860 TYNDALL *Glac.* I. xi. 78 The chief difficulties remained unconquered. 1887 *Spectator* 5 Nov. 1497 Saint Elias,..the still unconquered peak of Alaska.

† **Unco·nquest,** *ppl. a.* [UN-[1] 8 b.] = prec.

1584 HUDSON *Du Bartas' Judith* v. 30 But now..his minde doth frame To conquer this most chast vnconquest Dame. *a* 1600 MONTGOMERIE *Sonn.* viii. 5 The hundreth saxt, by lyne, vnconqueist king.

**Unco·nscienced,** *a.* (UN-[1] 9.) 1833 TENNYSON in *Mem.* (1897) I. 130 That luxurious, eye-glass-wearing, unconscienced fellow. 1888 *Andover Rev.* Oct. 363 The riot of unconscienced power.

† **Unco·nsciencely,** *adv. Obs.* [UN-[1] 11.] = UNCONSCIENTIOUSLY *adv.*

1450 *Rolls of Parlt.* V. 206/1 The seid late predecessours have made divers Relesses, Obligacions, and other Suertees unconciensly. 1485 *Rolls of Parlt.* VI. 322/1 The said Morgan..unconsciencely causyd theym to fynde by their Verdyt, that [etc.].

**Unconscie·ntious,** *a.* [UN-[1] 7.] Not conscientious; not scrupulous or careful: **a.** Of actions, etc.

[1775 ASH.] 1791 BOSWELL *Johnson* (1831) III. 183 Johnson was shocked at this unconscientious conduct. 1803 MACKINTOSH *Def. Peltier* Wks. 1846 III. 246 An immoderate and unconscientious exercise of power. 1818 SCOTT *Rob Roy* xvii, This base and unconscientious scheme of plundering his benefactor. 1884 *Law Times* 11 Oct. 382 The Act supposes that the real owner is actuated by unconscientious motives.

**b.** Of persons.

1827 SCOTT *Napoleon* v, This unconscientious tribunal found the prisoner guilty. 1827 — *Surg. Dau.* xii, An able and active, but unconscientious man. 1884 H. SPENCER in *Pop. Sci. Monthly* XXIV. 732 Representatives are unconscientious enough to vote for bills [etc.].

Hence **Unconscie·ntiousness.**

1860 FROUDE *Hist. Eng.* V. 256 The Earl of Warwick himself was untroubled with religious convictions of any kind, and might take either side with equal unconscientiousness. 1879 SPENCER *Data Ethics* xii. 210 Not in large ways only..does each suffer from the general unconscientiousness.

**Unconscie·ntiously,** *adv.* [f. prec. + -LY.[2]] In an unconscientious manner; unscrupulously.

1649 [see UNCASUISTLY *adv.*]. 1780 *Ann. Reg., Chron.* 208/2 The attorney had acted very unconscientiously. 1855 PUSEY *Doctr. Real Presence* Note S. 428 In that, unconscientiously and unprofitably,..he approacheth thanklessly to such a mystery, he bringeth on him the judgment of slothfulness. 1898 G. W. STEEVENS *Egypt* xix. 219 The Chicago colonel unconscientiously copies them.

**Unco·nscionable,** *a.* (*sb.*, *adv.*). [UN-[1] 7 b, 5 b.]

**1.** Of persons: Having no conscience; not controlled by conscience; unscrupulous; unreasonably grasping, extortionate, harsh, etc.

1570 ABP. PARKER *Corr.* (Parker Soc.) 374 Christ's holy religion,..as it may be choked with overmuch in unconscionable men's hands, so it will fall to ground amongst beggars. 1583 STUBBES *Anat. Abus.* II. (1882) 51 Least these cunning barbers might seeme vnconscionable in asking much for their paines. 1611 SPEED *Hist. Gt. Brit.* IX. iii. § 20 None were rich but Treasurers and Collectors, none in fauour but vnconscionable Lawyers. 1667 WATERHOUSE *Fire Lond.* 31 Occupancy is judged by men unconscionable, the best title. 1681 DRYDEN *Abs. & Achit.* To Rdr., You cannot be so Unconscionable, as to charge me for not Subscribing of my Name. 1708 MRS. CENTLIVRE *Busy Body* II, Can you be so unconscionable, Madam, to let me say all these fine things to you without one single Compliment in return? 1765 STERNE *Tr. Shandy* VII. xvii, How can that unconscionable coachman talk so much bawdy to that lean horse? 1824 W. IRVING *T. Trav.* I. 242 Sometimes the unconscionable editors will clip our paragraphs. 1865 DICKENS *Mut. Fr.* I. viii, I am not so unconscionable as to think it likely. 1885 'MRS. ALEXANDER' *Valerie's Fate* i, What an unconscionable old slave-holder!..Why do you submit to such an imposition?

*absol.* 1623 HALL *Contempl., O. T.* XIX. ii, The unconscionable will know no other law, but their profit, their pleasure.

**b.** With depreciatory terms, as an intensive.

1597 BEARD *Theatre God's Judgem.* (1612) 457 Barnabe, Vicount of Milan,..was an vnconscionable oppressor of his subjects and tenants. 1609 W. M. *Man in Moone* (1849) 27 He is an insatiable cormorant,..a mercilesse mony-monger, ..and unconscionable extortioner. 1655 FULLER *Ch. Hist.* I. v. § 30 Unconscionable Liars, though they most hurt themselves, do the least harm others. 1687 M. CLIFFORD *Notes Dryden* ii. 7 You are therefore a strange unconscionable Thief. 1732 FIELDING *Miser* v. xviii, I am an unconscionable beggar. 1755 SMOLLETT *Quix.* (1803) IV. 93 Your excellency may perceive what a shameless and unconscionable rogue he is.

**c.** As *sb.* An arrant rogue.

1825 KNAPP & BALDWIN *Newgate Cal.* III. 496/1 One of the trading unconscionables.

**2.** Of actions, etc.: Showing no regard for conscience; not in accordance with what is right or reasonable.

1565 CALFHILL *Answ. Martial* 79 Was not thys a goodly councell then? The cause so vnlawfull?..The order so vnconscionable? Brag, as ye please, of your Nice councell. 1586 J. HOOKER *Hist. Irel.* in *Holinshed* II. 106/2 Which he rather of pleasure vttered, than of anie vnconscionable meaning purposed to haue doone. 1628 WITHER *Brit. Rememb.* VI. 1251 Ev'n in our Court of Conscience, some things are Unconscionable. 1653 PRYNNE *Gospel-plea* 14 It must needs be most unjust, unreasonable, unconscionable, and against the common rules of war. 1656 H. PHILLIPS *Purch. Patt.* (1676) 145 The errour..is so much the more unconscionable, because it gives the buyer so much less than his due. 1738 A. HILL *Let. to Pope* 29 Aug., When I remember'd you had read it four times, I found not enough of the Poet, within me, to presume the unconscionable fifth. 1796 MME. D'ARBLAY *Camilla* III. 425 So difficult was even this, in an affair so dark and unconscionable. 1828 KEIGHTLEY *Fairy Mythol.* (1850) 95 They plundered their pantries in a most unconscionable manner. 1890 *Spectator* 19 July, St. Kevin's behaviour on a famous occasion was not quite so unconscionable as that attributed to him by Moore.

**b.** Unreasonably excessive.

*a* 1586 SIDNEY *Arcadia* I. xv. (1912) 99 She tooke the advauntage one daye uppon Phalantus unconscionable prayinges of her. 1598 B. JONSON *Ev. Man in Hum.* I. ii, Draw your bill of charges, as unconscionable as any Guildhall verdict will giue it you. 1601 F. GODWIN *Bps. of Eng.* 295 That wrongfull and vnconscionable raunsome. 1654 WHITELOCKE *Jrnl. Swed. Emb.* (1772) II. 264 Such is their unconscionable exaction uppon strangers. 1671 MILTON *Samson* 1245 His Giantship is gone somewhat crestfall'n, Stalking with less unconsci'nable strides, And lower looks. 1760 STERNE *Tr. Shandy* III. xxxiii, What an unconscionable jointure, my dear, do we pay out of this small estate of ours! 1785 MARTYN *Lett. Bot.* x. (1794) 108 This letter not being of so unconscionable a length as the former. 1818 SCOTT *Hrt. Midl.* xii, We are out unconscionable sums just for barkened hides and leather. 1849 MACAULAY *Hist. Eng.* iv. I. 439 He had been, he said, a most unconscionable time dying. 1871 'HOLME LEE' *Miss Barrington* II. xiii. 203 He had stayed an unconscionable time—had made her quite a visitation.

**c.** As an intensive: Egregious, arrant.

1593 *Tell-Troth's N. Y. Gift* (1876) 14 To blabb such vnconscionable vntrothes. 1603 H. CROSSE *Vertues Commw.* (1878) 43 Tearing out the bowelles of his brethren, with vsurie, extortion, and vnconscionable brokerie. 1650 FULLER *Pisgah* v. i. 143 It seems not onely an ungentile harshness, but an unconscionable injustice. *a* 1734 NORTH *Exam.* III. ix. § 14 (1740) 657 A due Reward of unconscionable Cheating. 1782–3 W. F. MARTYN *Geog. Mag.* I. 308 Which sum he consented to abate in favour of those who were called upon to make up the amount of this unconscionable imposition.

**3.** As *adv.* = UNCONSCIONABLY *adv.* 2.

1596 NASHE *Saffron Walden* F ij, Tis an vnconscionable vast gorbellied Volume. 1807–8 W. IRVING *Salmag.* (1824) 272 One of Christopher's unconscionable long stories. 1847 ROBB *Squatter Life* (Bartlett), 'That's an unconscionable slick gal of your'n,' says I.

**Unco·nscionableness.** [f. prec.] The quality or state of being unconscionable; unscrupulousness, unreasonableness.

1607 HIERON *Defence* I. 179 Observe further, his unconscionablenes and whether..he hath not sold himselfe to speake he careth not what. 1657 G. STARKEY *Helmont's Vind.* 173 A cover-slut of idleness, ignorance, and unconscionableness. 1670 BAXTER *Cure Ch. Div.* 380 Are not the most conscientious, necessary helpers of the Ministry, by their example, to cure the unconscionableness of the rest?

**Unco·nscionably,** *adv.* [f. as prec.]

**1.** In an unconscionable manner; without regard for conscience; unreasonably.

1583 GOLDING *Calvin on Deut.* ii. 65 If a poore man deale vnconscionably when he hath not wherewith to liue,..yet shall he bee condemned. 1589 *Acts Privy Council* (1898) XVII. 19 He was verie unconscionablie dealte and proceeded withall by his credytours. 1631 T. POWELL *Tom All Trades* (1876) 161 To a good old Vsurer, or one that had got his great estate together vnconscionably. 1646 P. BULKELEY *Gospel Covt.* IV. 298 Such as live loosely, carnally, unconscionably, doe but deceive themselves. 1705 HICKERINGILL *Priest-cr.* II. v. 56 The..Avarice and Ambition of some Highflyers, have..most Unchristian like and Unconsionably..endeavoured to monopolize by Law all Places of Honour, Profit, Trust.

**2.** To an unconscionable extent or degree; inordinately.

1583 STUBBES *Anat. Abus.* II. (1882) 37 For whereas the others inhanse the price of their hides excessiuely, these felowes racke it very vnconcionably. 1602 in Moryson *Itin.* II. (1617) 265 Her Subiects.., by the excessiue rates in the sale of all commodities, haue beene vnconscionably ouercharged. *a* 1661 FULLER *Worthies, Cheshire* I. (1662) 171 Some have Flesh, Salt,..but so unconscionably dear, that Common people have little comfort therein. 1672 MARVELL *Reh. Transp.* I. 270 The Fanaticks..made them pay for it most unconscionably and through the nose. 1771 MME. D'ARBLAY *Early Diary* Aug., His visit was unconscionably long, and..I had the whole weight of it. 1787 BECKFORD *Italy*, etc. (1834) II. 54, I felt no inclination to prolong a walk which already had been prolonged unconscionably. 1863 *N. & Q.* 3rd Ser. IV. 214 Having trespassed unconscionably on your valuable space, I will now conclude at once. 1884 A. BIRRELL *Obiter Dicta* Ser. I. 183 The age has remained transitional so unconscionably long.

**Unco·nscious,** *a.* [UN-[1] 7 and 5 b.]

**1.** Not conscious or knowing within oneself; unaware, regardless, heedless.

1712 BLACKMORE *Creation* VI. 646 Unconscious we these motions never heed, Whether they err, or by just laws proceed. 1848 DICKENS *Dombey* xiii, As he stood..surveying his (of course unconscious) clerk, from head to foot. 1889 *Anthony's Photogr. Bull.* II. 202, I mean the unconscious model, i.e., one taken unawares with a detective camera.

**b.** Const. *of*, *that*, etc.

1712 BLACKMORE *Creation* VII. 632 Through every dark recess [they] pursue their flight, Unconscious of the road. 1789 BURNS *Kirk's Alarm* vii, Are ye huirdin' the penny, Unconscious what evils await? 1820 SCORESBY *Acc. Arctic Reg.* II. 172 Never having been disturbed, these animals were unconscious of danger. 1841 CARLYLE *Heroes* i. (1904) 33 Silent, with closed lips, as I fancy them, unconscious that they were specially brave. 1863 KINGLAKE *Crimea* I. 158 All this time he was unconscious of exercising any ascendancy.

**2.** Not characterized by, or endowed with, the faculty or presence of consciousness.

1712 BLACKMORE *Creation* III. 266 Unconscious causes only still impart Their utmost skill, their utmost power exert. 1744 AKENSIDE *Pleas. Imag.* I. 527 For what are all The forms which brute, unconscious matter wears, Greatness of bulk, or symmetry of parts? 1802 PALEY *Nat. Theol.* iv. § 1. 55 Can any distinction be assigned..between the producing watch, and the producing plant? both passive, unconscious substances. 1890 W. JAMES *Princ. Psych.* I. 199 Sleep, fainting, coma, epilepsy, and other 'unconscious' conditions.

*absol.* 1843 CARLYLE *Past & Pr.* II. xv, The Unconscious is the alone Complete. 1876 *Westm. Review* XLIX. 512 Those who are acquainted with the 'pessimist' conclusions of the 'philosophy of the Unconscious'. 1884 COUPLAND (*title*), Philosophy of the Unconscious, by Eduard von Hartmann.

**b.** Temporarily devoid of consciousness.

1860 O. W. HOLMES *Elsie Venner* xxvi. (1861) 302 A man is stunned by a blow with a stick on the head. He becomes unconscious. 1890 *Retrospect Med.* CII. 118 The patient had a temperature of 105·8° for thirty-six hours, and was unconscious for twenty-four hours.

**3.** Not realized or known as existing in oneself.

1800 COLERIDGE *Christabel* II. xxvii, Still picturing that look askance With forced unconscious sympathy Full before her father's view. 1870 L'ESTRANGE *Miss Mitford* I. vi. 166 And is not the sunny felicity of childhood in itself unconscious virtue? 1890 'R. BOLDREWOOD' *Col. Reformer* (1891) 150 [She] rode..extremely well, and with an unconscious grace.

*absol.* 1817 COLERIDGE *Biogr. Lit., Poesy or Art*, In every work of art there is a reconcilement of the external with the internal; the conscious is so impressed on the unconscious as to appear in it.

**4.** Not attended by, or present to, consciousness; performed, employed, etc., without conscious action.

*Unconscious cerebration*: see CEREBRATION.

1820 LAMB *Elia* I. *Oxford in Vacation*, He has long taken up his unconscious abode, amid an incongruous assembly of attorneys, attorneys' clerks [etc.]. 1836 C. WORDSWORTH *Athens* xxiii. (1855) 156 It may be considered as an unconscious emblem of the consecration of earthly history and glory and majesty to the Cross. 1866 J. MARTINEAU *Ess.* I. 133 It is wrong to punish an unconscious act. 1878 S. BUTLER *Life & Habit* ii. 26 In like manner, the most perfect humour and irony is generally quite unconscious.

**Unco·nsciously,** *adv.* [f. prec.] In an unconscious manner; without conscious action or effort.

1779 JOHNSON *L. P., Milton* Wks. II. 119, I cannot but remark a kind of respect, perhaps unconsciously, paid to this great man by his biographers. 1813 SHELLEY *Q. Mab* III. 234 Man, like these passive things, Thy will unconsciously fulfilleth. 1856 FROUDE *Hist. Eng.* (1858) I. v. 422 The populace of England were unconsciously on the rapid road to protestantism. 1887 W. P. FRITH *Autobiog.* I. xx. 243 Pretty groups of ladies were to be found..unconsciously forming themselves into very paintable compositions.

**Unco·nsciousness.** [f. as prec.]

**1.** The state or fact of being mentally unconscious or unaware *of* something.

1779–81 JOHNSON *L. P., Addison* Wks. III. 51 The work did not suffer much by his unconsciousness of its commencement. 1794 PALEY *Evid.* I. ix. § 1 We perceive also in Clement a total unconsciousness of doubt whether these were the real words of Christ. 1837 HT. MARTINEAU *Soc. Amer.* II. 336 In a society where things like these are said and done ..there is a prevalent unconsciousness of the existing wrong. 1870 J. H. NEWMAN *Gram. Assent* II. vi. 181 Our unconsciousness of those innumerable acts of assent, which we are incessantly making.

**b.** Without const.

1828 LYTTON *Pelham* III. xx, It was Dawson who shut the door, through utter unconsciousness. 1882 FARRAR *Early Chr.* I. 264 Josephus..falsifies and colours...Philo on the other hand wrote with far greater unconsciousness.

**2.** The fact of being devoid of consciousness.

1759 JOHNSON *Rasselas* xlvii, All the notices of sense and

investigations of science concur to prove the unconsciousness of matter.

**3.** The state of being unconscious; loss of consciousness; insensibility.

1849 Froude *Nemesis of Faith* 223 When he came he found her in a state of almost unconsciousness. 1863 Morris *Earthly Par.* (1870) II. III. 135 The peace of dull unconsciousness His wild torn heart at last did bless. 1890 *Retrospect Med.* CII. 160 A longer or shorter period of continued unconsciousness, without convulsion.

**Unco·nsecrate,** *v.* [Un-[2] 3.] *trans.* To render unconsecrated; to desecrate or profane.

1598 Florio, *Disconsecrare*, to degrade, to profane, to vnconsecrate. *a* 1660 Hammond *Serm., 2 Cor. vii. 1* (1664) 86 Heaven must be unconsecrated by such violence. 1667 South *Serm., Ps. lxxxvii. 2* (1715) I. 258 The Sins of Israel had even unconsecrated and prophaned that Sacred Edifice. 1711 *Brit. Apollo* III. No. 143. 3/1 To Unconsecrate his Dust. 1768–74 Tucker *Lt. Nat.* (1834) II. 450, I should apprehend it might by natural effect prove an unconsecrating the place with respect to myself.

**Unco·nsecrate,** *ppl. a.* [Un-[1] 8 b.] = next.

1529 More *Dyaloge* I. xiv. Wks. 134/2 Diuers times she was houseled..with an host vnconsecrate. *Ibid.* II. 193/1 If we worshippe an host in the masse which percase the neglygence or malice of some lewde priest hath left vnconsecrat. 1607 G. Wilkins *Miseries Enforced Marr.* K iij b, Here wil I seale the children that are born, From wombes vnconsecrate. 1673 [R. Leigh] *Transp. Reh.* 13 Except only this unconsecrate Lay-Clergy. 1850 J. Martineau *Misc.* (1852) 330 The heroes of modern fiction and biography are unconsecrate according to the measure of theology.

**Unco·nsecrated,** *ppl. a.* (Un-[1] 8.)

1579 Fulke *Heskins' Parl.* 99 It was better then yᵉ vnconsecrated bread and wine. 1641 Milton *Ch. Govt.* II. iii. 54 They fear religion..and think..that any uncleannesse is more sutable to their unconsecrated estate. 1684 Bunyan *Pilgr.* II. 159 One questioned if it was lawful to go upon unconsecrated Ground. 1790 Pennant *London* 116 A chapel was erected, well-pewed, well-warmed, dedicated, unendowed, unconsecrated. 1816 Byron *Parisina* xix, No tomb, no memory had they; Theirs was unconsecrated clay. 1848 Thackeray *Van. Fair* xxxv, There the young officer was laid by his friend, in the unconsecrated corner of the garden.

**Unconsenta·neous,** *a.* (Un-[1] 7.) 1818 T. L. Peacock *Nightmare Abbey* iv, The results are unconsentaneous, and their respective necessitated volitions clash.

**Unconse·nted,** *ppl. a.* (Un-[1] 8 and 8 c.)

1631 Fuller *David's Punishm.* xvi. in *Joseph's Coat*, etc. (1867) 233 Sins unconsented to no souls impair. 1643 Milton *Divorce* Pref., Not that licence and levity and unconsented breach of faith should herein be countenanc't. 1668 Clarendon *Vind.* Tracts (1727) 79 He read all the articles..which remained undetermined and unconsented to. 1800 *Monthly Mag.* VIII. 601 From Scandinavia have poured the only barbarians who ever achieved an unconsented conquest of the British isles.

**Unconse·nting,** *ppl. a.* (Un-[1] 10.)

*a* 1693 T. Yalden *Rape of Theutilla* 42 Vanquish'd by that repose from which he flies, Now slumbers close his unconsenting eyes. 1713 Rowe *Jane Shore* v. i, Tho' the King by Force possest her Person, Her unconsenting Heart dwelt still with you. 1725 Pope *Odyss.* xv. 221 Let not Pisistratus in vain be prest, Nor unconsenting hear his friend's request. *a* 1859 De Quincey *Posth. Wks.* (1891) I. 192 Blood, lawless blood—a horrid Moloch..revelling in a thousand unconsenting women. 1889 *Anthony's Photogr. Bull.* II. 20 The right to photograph unconsenting strangers.

**Unconseque·ntial,** *a.* [Un-[1] 7 and 5 b.]

**1.** Not properly or necessarily following or ensuing; inconsequential.

1769 Blackstone *Comm.* IV. 37 A, though accessory to the burning, is not accessory to the robbery, for that is a thing of a distinct and unconsequential nature. 1779–81 Johnson *L. P., Waller* Wks. II. 261 Some applications may be thought too remote and unconsequential: as in the verses on the *Lady dancing*. *a* 1849 Poe *F. S. Osgood* Wks. 1865 III. 90 The 'situations' of Elfrida are improbable or ultra-romantic, and its incidents unconsequential. 1885 *Athenæum* 19 Dec. 804/3 Her punishment is..too unconsequential to be accepted as a natural transcript from every-day life.

**2.** Of no consequence; insignificant.

1782 I. Reed *Baker's Biog. Dram.* I. 187/2 Notwithstanding an unconsequential figure and uncommon timidity, he says, he succeeded beyond his most sanguine expectations. 1789 Mrs. Piozzi *Journ. France* I. 146 [It] is..crowded with small unconsequential figures.

†**Unco·nsequently,** *adv. Obs.* (Un-[1] 11 and 5 b.) 1565 Cooper *Thesaurus, Insequenter*,..vnconsequently: not to the purpose. 1647 Hexham I, Vnconsequently, *niet ten proposte*. **Unconse·rvative,** *a.* (Un-[1] 7.) 1877 D. M. Wallace *Russia* I. i. 11 Even in unconservative Russia customs outlive the conditions that created them.

†**Unconsi·derable,** *a. Obs.* [Un-[1] 7 b.] = Inconsiderable *a.*

1643 Prynne *Sov. Power Parl.* II. 43 Better then either the King himselfe, his Cabinet-Counsell, or any unconsiderable Privadoes, Courtiers, Favorites. 1654–66 Earl Orrery *Parthen.* (1676) 501 My Crime..merited a higher punishment than these unconsiderable wounds. 1668 Cressy *Ch. Hist. Brit.* Errata, Unconsiderable ones [*sc.* errors] which have hapned by mistake of single Letters resembling one the other.

†**Unconsi·derance.** *Obs.*[−1] (Un-[1] 12 and 5 b.) 1546 Bale *1st Exam. Anne Askewe* Concl. 44 b, If I should holde my peace,..my conscyence wolde both accuse me and condempne me of vnconsyderaunce of my lorde God.

†**Unconsi·derate,** *a. Obs.* (Un-[1] 7 and 5 b.)

1594 Daniel *Cleopatra* I. i vij, Thus much beguiled haue Poore vnconsiderat wights These momentary pleasures, fugitiue delights. 1612 Cotta (*title*), A Short Discouerie of the Vnobserued Dangers of seuerall sorts of ignorant and vnconsiderate Practisers of Physicke in England.

Hence †**Unconsi·derately** *adv.*; **-ness.** *Obs.*

1570 T. Norton tr. *Nowel's Catech.* III. 56 They that come rashly and vnconsiderately to prayer. 1611 Florio, *Inconsideranza*, vnconsideratenesse. 1621 G. Sandys *Ovid's Met.* III. (1626) 56 [He] Admireth all;..And vnconsiderately himselfe desir'd.

†**Unconsidera·tion.** *Obs.* (Un-[1] 12 and 5 b).

*c* 1449 Pecock *Repr.* I. xvi. 89 The vnconsideracion of this..hath be a greet cause of the wickidli enfectid scole of heresie among the lay peple in Ynglond. *Ibid.* IV. ix. 474.

**Unconsi·dered,** *ppl. a.* [Un-[1] 8 and 5 b.]

**1.** Not considered or thought of; not taken into consideration.

1587 Golding *De Mornay* xii. (1592) 167 Those that haue the distributing of goods and honors, are blamed for leauing them vnconsidered. 1611 Shaks. *Wint. T.* IV. iii. 26 A snapper-vp of vnconsidered trifles. 1613 — *Hen. VIII*, I. ii. 17 That you would..Not vnconsidered leaue your Honour, ..is the poynt Of my Petition. 1619 Donne *Serm.* 139 This is the unexpected and unconsidered strangenesse of that day. 1729 Young *Merchant* Contents, The unconsidered benefits of liberty. 1826 Miss Mitford *Village* Ser. II. (1863) 454 The gift of some unconsidered trifles. 1856 Froude *Hist. Eng.* I. 152 There was a third party in the country, unconsidered as yet, who [etc.]. 1873 Proctor *Expanse Heav.* viii. 86 A different opinion has long been entertained, owing to the details of the matter being left unconsidered.

**2.** Unaccompanied by, not done with, consideration or intention.

1876 T. Hardy *Ethelberta* xxv, She got up in an unconsidered and unusual impulse to seek relief. 1877 Mrs. Oliphant *Makers Flor.* iii. 82 The cruel levity of these probably unconsidered jests.

†**Unconsi·derer.** *Obs.*[−1] (Un-[1] 12)

*c* 1456 Pecock *Bk. of Faith* (1909) 122 Which favour, peraventure, sum hasty unconsidere(r)s schulen not aspie.

**Unconsi·dering,** *ppl. a.* (Un-[1] 10 and 5 b.)

1660 *Rope for Pol* To Rdr., 'Tis incredible what influence they had upon numbers of unconsidering persons. 1682 T. Flatman *Heraclitus Ridens* No. 79 (1713) II. 237 They take up with the unconsidering People who admire their Wealth. 1700 Blackmore *Paraphr., Moses' Song* 246 O that these unconsidering tribes were wise! 1710 Swift *Jrnl. to Stella* 13 Oct., I'll never do it again, though all mankind should persuade me, unconsidering puppies!

*absol.* 1691 Locke *Tolerat.* III. viii. 172 Some of the ignorant and unconsidering that are in the National Church.

**Unconsi·gned,** *ppl. a.* (Un-[1] 8.)

1647 Jer. Taylor *Lib. Proph.* xviii. 227 This mercy which appertaines to Infants is so secret and undeclar'd and unconsign'd. 1891 M. Cole *Cy Ross* 142 The ship sped on, bearing its unconsigned merchandise of sin to a haven of safety.

†**Unconsi·stent,** *a. Obs.* (Un-[1] 7 and 5 b.)

1638 Chillingw. *Relig. Prot.* I. ii. § 65. 76 Nor lyable to any such exception, as is unconsistent with due Intention in giving the Sacrament of Orders.

**Unconso·ciable,** *a.* [Un-[1] 7 b: cf. Consociate *v.*] Incapable of being united.

1697 J. Sergeant *Solid Philos.* 90 To clap these most unconsociable Things, Light and Darkness, into one Dusky Compound.

**Unconso·lable,** *a.* (Un-[1] 7 b and 5 b.)

*a* 1618 Raleigh *Son's Advice* Rem. (1664) 115 Oh how unconsolable were your case, your friends being fled. 1654–66 Earl Orrery *Parthen.* (1676) 598 This relation..had a resembling operation on the unconsolable Emilia. 1731 Fielding *Mod. Husb.* v. ix, What an unconsolable creature would you be if [etc.].

Hence **Unconso·lably** *adv.*

1895 W. Platt *Women*, etc. 61 She went off and wept unconsolably.

**Unconso·latory,** *a.* (Un-[1] 7.) 1760 Sterne *Lett.* (1775) I. 91 The consolation you give me..is very unconsolatory. 1803 Mary Charlton *Wife & Mistress* III. 73 Laura, wearied by this unconsolatory nonsense, shook her head.

**Unconso·led,** *ppl. a.* (Un-[1] 8.)

1814 Wordsw. *Excurs.* IV. 310 Therefore, not unconsoled, I wait. 1860 Ellicott *Life Our Lord* viii. 384 Standing weeping by the tomb, unconsoled and inconsolable. 1879 B. Taylor *Stud. Germ. Lit.* 82 Tristan is wandering alone and unconsoled.

**Unconso·lidated,** *ppl. a.* (Un-[1] 8.)

[1775 Ash.] 1802 Playfair *Illustr. Hutton. Th.* 49 The opposite sides of the rock..have the interval between them filled with soft and unconsolidated earth. 1851 Carpenter *Man. Phys.* (ed. 2) 263 Having the fibrous element of the shell..unconsolidated by the intervening deposit of chalky particles. 1874 Stubbs *Const. Hist.* I. iii. 41 They are not only unconquered, but unconsolidated.

**Unconso·ling,** *ppl. a.* (Un-[1] 10.) 1846 Worcester (citing Buckminster). **Unco·nsonancy.** (Un-[1] 12.) 1665 J. Sergeant *Sure Footing* 216 Not to note the unconsonancy of this carriage, I shall yeild him the honour [etc.].

**Unco·nsonant,** *a.* [Un-[1] 7.] = Inconsonant *a.* **a.** Const. *to* or *with*.

1535 Stewart *Cron. Scot.* (Rolls) III. 33 Vnconsonand is to the veritie To do to ws so greit inormitie. *a* 1600 Hooker *Serm. on Pride* IV. § 1 If..it be a thing most unequal and unconsonant unto justice. 1657 Tomlinson *Renou's Disp.* Pref., Which is not altogether unconsonant to reason. *a* 1676 Hale *Prim. Orig. Man.* III. ii. (1677) 260 As his Supposition of these *Semina*, thus casually produc'd, seems unconsonant both to the Reason and Course of Nature. 1805 Foster *Ess.* IV. v. 183 A certain order of opinions unconsonant, or at least not identical, with the principles of that religion. 1843 in J. Hawthorne *N. Hawthorne & Wife* (1885) I. vi. 273 It was a magnificent comedy to watch him,..so unconsonant to what was about him.

**b.** Without const.

1597 Hooker *Eccl. Pol.* v. li. § 3 It seemeth a thing vnconsonant that the world should honor any other as the Sauiour but him whom it honoreth as the creator of the world. 1658 Manton *Exp. Jude 4* Wks. 1871 V. 167 To observe..whether we embrace it upon undue grounds, or match it with unconsonant practices. 1665 J. Sergeant *Sure Footing* 241 If he does, he must hold it was Eternal; If not, how unconsonant is his parallel?

Hence **Unco·nsonantly** *adv.*

1863 Cowden Clarke *Shaks. Char.* v. 128 He is gradually led on to act unconsonantly with his real nature.

**Unconspi·cuous,** *a.* (Un-[1] 7 and 5 b.)

1802–12 Bentham *Ration. Judic. Evid.* (1827) V. 659 Latent and unconspicuous the single force of a pecuniary interest is capable of rising. 1816 — *Chrestom.* 187 These properties are..recondite and unconspicuous. 1861 Mill *Utilit.* ii. 22 A part however small and unconspicuous, in the endeavour. 1874 Micklethwaite *Mod. Par. Churches* 216 Placing ventilators in some unconspicuous positions in the walls.

**Unconspi·ringness.** (Un-[1] 12.) 1661 Boyle *Style of Script.* 76 A Harmony whose Dissonances serve but to manifest the Sincerity and Unconspiringnesse of the Writers.

†**Unconstabi·lity.** [Un-[1] 12. Cf. late L. *inconstābilītio*.] Want of stability; changeableness.

1611 Speed *Hist. Gt. Brit.* VI. xlviii. § 2. 166 Gregory Nazianzen charging him with..vnconstability, sayth; That by..his vnsteady and halting pace [etc.].

†**Unco·nstance.** *Obs.* (Un-[1] 12 and 5 b.)

*c* 1449 Pecock *Repr.* II. vii. 177 Forto remove..al vnstable vnconstaunce and variaunce and vnperseueraunce. 1603 Holland *Plutarch's Mor.* 1034 So great unconstance and repugnance of words, as to affirme one and the same nature to be created and uncreated.

†**Unco·nstancy.** *Obs.* [Un-[1] 12 and 5 b.]

**1.** = Inconstancy 1.

1548 Elyot, *Instabilitas*, vnconstancie, instabilitee. 1583 Golding *Calvin on Deut.* i. 2 Because he saw the lightnes and unconstancy of the people. 1605 Bacon *Adv. Learn.* I. v. § 2 We see..the leuitie and vnconstancie of mens iudgements. 1652 J. Wright tr. *Camus' Nat. Paradox* II. 45 The thoughts of them..who are not Reeds of the Desart in unconstancy, but Pillars of the Temple of Stability. 1699 Burnet *39 Art.* xxviii. 335 The scandalous Unconstancy of the Councils of those Ages.

**2.** = Inconstancy 2.

1587 Golding *De Mornay* xi. (1592) 162 The vnmoouable decree of his euerlasting Prouidence, which..directeth all the vnconstancies of this world to one certeine end. 1627 in Rushw. *Hist. Coll.* (1659) I. 485 The Frame of other States are subject, some to Unconstancy, some to Faction..and to many Distempers. 1650 Baxter *Saints' R.* I. vii. (1662) 95 But there is none of this unconstancy, nor mixtures in Heaven.

†**Unco·nstant,** *a. Obs.* [Un-[1] 7 and 5 b.]

**1.** = Inconstant *a.* 1.

*c* 1480 Henryson *Test. Cres.* 570 Traisting in vther als greit vnfaithfulnes, Als vnconstant, and als vntrew of fay. 1483 Caxton *Cato* c vj, And by the contrarye the man unconstaunt ..falleth in to many vyces and synnes. 1564 Palfreyman *Baldwin's Mor. Philos.* 45 All men are ignorant, and as fraile and vnconstant as ye shadow of smoke. 1581 Pettie tr. *Guazzo's Civ. Conv.* I. (1586) 26 b, To some, stout hardinesse, and deuout holinesse, haue been alwaies proper and naturall, who neuerthelesse are worldlings and vnconstant. 1602 Fulbecke *Pandects* 89 For the Ægyptians as others report of them, are men vnconstant, raging, proude,..desirous of nouelties. 1647 N. Bacon *Disc. Govt. Eng.* I. lxvi. 229 They found the King either wilfull or unconstant. 1693 *Mem. Ct. Teckely* IV. 25 The Will of the Soveraign, which is as unconstant as his Passions. 1712 Arbuthnot *John Bull* I. v, Bull ..was..of a very unconstant temper.

*Comb.* 1653 R. Sanders *Physiogn.* 194 A mutable, wavering, unconstant-minded person.

**b.** *spec.* Unfaithful in love or wedlock.

1561 *Chaucer's Wks.* 340 A balade whiche Chaucer made agaynst women vnconstaunt. 1593 Marlowe *Edw. II*, v. i, My vnconstant Queene, Who spots my nuptiall bed with infamie. 1611 Beaum. & Fl. *King & No King* IV, She lives to tell thee thou art more unconstant, Than all ill women ever were together. 1676 D'Urfey *Mme. Fickle* IV. i, I am grown jealous of my Mistress, several Reports declare she is unconstant. 1757 W. Wilkie *Epigon.* VII. 196 To reclaim The hero's love,..If e'er, devoted to a stranger's charms, He stray'd, unconstant, to her widow'd arms.

**c.** Of actions, conduct, etc.

1549 *Compl. Scot.* xii. 100 Thai culd nocht meruel aneucht of his onconstant ansuer. 1563 B. Googe *Eglogs* vii. (Arb.) 59 Men do smarte not through your words but your vnconstant deeds. 1609 Daniel *Civ. Wars* VIII. lxxxvii, Without which, nor his Greatnes, nor his Wits, Could ward him from the Kings vnconstant fits. 1621 Quarles *Hadassa* Introd., Bleare-eyd mortals,..with vnconstant frailty,..vary From what is good, to what is cleane contrary. 1694 Kettlewell *Comp. Penitent* 66 My good Thoughts are unconstant and Changeable.

**2.** = Inconstant *a.* 2.

1574 Hyll *Conject. Weather* ii, The winter shall be windie and unstable, the Spring windy, and unconstant of weather. 1592 tr. *Junius on Rev.* xvii. 15 As unconstant and variable as are the waters. *a* 1619 Fotherby *Atheom.* II. viii. § 2 (1622) 284 Error is alwayes vnconstant, and neuer true vnto it selfe. 1645 Quarles *Sol. Recant.* III. 21 Vnconstant earth! what can thy treasure show, That is not, like thy self, unconstant too? 1691 T. H[ale] *Acc. New Invent.* 79 An unconstant and unequal decay. 1703 R. Neve *City & C. Purchaser* 3 Being kept in an unconstant Temper, it decays in a little time. 1721 Ramsay *Keitha* 93 The powers..dinna like to gie o'er meikle trust To this unconstant earth, with what's divine.

**b.** = Inconstant *a.* 2 b.

1610 Fletcher *Faithf. Sheph.* II. i, Ne'r did my unconstant eye yet greet That beauty.

†**Unco·nstantly,** *adv. Obs.* [f. prec.] = Inconstantly *adv.*

*a* 1542 Wyatt *Sonnet, 'Alas the greefe'* iii, in *Anglia* XVIII. 275 O cruell causer of vndeserued chaunge, by greatt desire vnconstantly to raunge. 1586 T. B. *La Primaud. Fr. Acad.* I. 121 Philosophie is..not a plaie or prittle prattle, unconstantlie uttered to obtaine honor onelie. 1607 Middleton *Fam. Love* I. ii, As chaff, which when our nourishing grains Are winnow'd from them, unconstantly they fly. 1650 Hobbes *Hum. Nat.* v, Consider..how unconstantly names have been settled, and how subject they are to equivocation. 1714 Fortescue-Aland *Pref. Fortescue's Abs. & Lim. Mon.* 7 The others have only Names and Words, and such as sometimes are unconstantly used.

† **Unco·nstantness.** [f. as prec.] Inconstancy.
**1551** BIBLE 2 *Cor.* i. *note*, Yea, yea, Nay, nay ;..in this place they are taken for vnconstauntenes of mynde, as to say both yea, and naye to one thynge. **1581** T. HOWELL *Deuises* (1879) 175 Which change full oft hath falne through her vnconstantnesse. **1600** SIR W. CORNWALLIS *Ess.* i. B j b, So much haue I hated this giddy vnconstantnesse.

† **Unco·nstanty,** variant of UNCONSTANCY.
**1563** *Wills & Inv. N. C.* (Surtees) 213 I..knowing the constantie of Death & ye vnconstantie of ye houre & time.

**Unco·nstellated,** *ppl. a.* (UN-¹ 8.) **1782–3** W. F. MARTYN *Geog. Mag.* I. Introd. 13 Observations on the unconstellated bodies. **1866** J. B. ROSE tr. *Ovid's Met.* 230 The great brother twins, not yet on high, Unconstellated yet. **Unco·nstituted,** *ppl. a.* (UN-¹ 8.) **1660** WATERHOUSE *Arms* 186 Whatever is new, unconstituted, and of a spurious birth.

**Unconstitu·tional,** *a.* [UN-¹ 7.]
**1.** Not in harmony with, or authorized by, the political constitution ; at variance with the recognized principles of the state.
**1765** BLACKSTONE *Comm.* I. 245 Whenever the unconstitutional oppressions, even of the Sovereign power,..threaten desolation to a State. **1770** *Junius Lett.* xxxix. (1778) 220 The unconstitutional employment of the military. **1849** MACAULAY *Hist. Eng.* vii. II. 210 That the Declaration of Indulgence was unconstitutional is a point on which both the great English parties have always been entirely agreed. **1893** *Times* 29 Apr., Lord S. described such a step as in the highest degree unconstitutional.
**2.** Not inherent in, or in accordance with, a person's constitution.
**1794** GODWIN *Caleb Williams* 198 The keeper once more made his appearance..with his former unconstitutional and ambiguous humanity.
Hence **Unconstitu·tionally** *adv.*
**1791** *Gentl. Mag.* Jan. 32, I am concerned..to see you unconstitutionally adopting a French word when there is no occasion. **1845** LD. CAMPBELL *Chancellors* (1857) IV. lxxxix. 215 The bill had been unconstitutionally got rid of. **1889** SIR S. WALPOLE *Life Ld. J. Russell* xxiv. II. 202 It was..asserted..that the Prince was interfering unconstitutionally both in foreign and domestic affairs.

**Unconstitutiona·lity.** [f. prec.] The quality of being unconstitutional.
**1795** WASHINGTON *Let.* Writ. 1892 XIII. 73 The unconstitutionality of the measure. **1850** GROTE *Greece* II. lxii. VIII. 48 Indictment on the score of informality, illegality, or unconstitutionality. **1890** HOSMER *Anglo-Sax. Freedom* 215 A popular explanation of the unconstitutionality of government acts.

**Unconstrai·nable,** *a.* (UN-¹ 7 b.)
**1659** MILTON *Civil Power* Wks. 1851 V. 319 Both our beleef and practise..flow from faculties of the inward man, free and unconstrainable of themselves by nature.

**Unconstrai·ned,** *ppl. a.* [UN-¹ 8.]
**1.** Not constrained or forced ; not acting under constraint or compulsion.
*c* **1386** CHAUCER *Doctor's T.* 61 And of hir owene vertu vnconstreyned She hath ful ofte tyme syk hire feyned. **1513** DOUGLAS *Æneid* VII. v. 25 Vnconstrenyt, nocht be law bound thairtill, Bot be our inclinatioun and fre will Just and equale. **1548** UDALL, etc. *Erasm. Par. John* xix. 108 b, The luste to reuenge was so greate, that vnconstrayned they adiudged themselues to perpetuall bondage. *a* **1614** DONNE Βιαθανατος (1664) 201 He dyed, as the same man sayes, with the same zeale as Christ, unconstrained. **1665** GLANVILL *Def. Van. Dogm.* 27 A free and unconstrained will. *a* **1704** T. BROWN *Sat. agst. Woman* Wks. 1730 I. 56 Unconstrain'd by want of choice they lie Wallowing in all the filth of boundless luxury. **1827** POLLOK *Course T.* II. 145 Making His soul an offering for sin,..By doing, suffering, dying, unconstrained. **1831** SCOTT *Ct. Rob.* xxviii, Let me find my way to the grave, unnoticed, unconstrained.
† **b.** Without exertion. *Obs.*—¹
**1539** ELYOT *Cast. Helthe* (1541) 55 b, If he whiche oftentymes unconstrayned hath had great sieges [=evacuations], be sodeynly stopped.
**2.** Not done, made, given, etc., under constraint or compulsion ; free, spontaneous.
**1535** *Act 27 Hen. VIII*, c. 25 The voluntary and vnconstreined almes & charitie of the parishens. *a* **1600** HOOKER *Two Serm. Jude* i § 12 What meaneth this Apostasie and vnconstrained departure? Why doe His seruants so willingly forsake him? **1632** LITHGOW *Trav.* I. 7 Thy voluntary wandring, and vnconstrayned exyle. **1656** BRAMHALL *Replic.* iii. 116 These Acts were unconstrained. *a* **1704** T. BROWN *Let. Dissent. Preacher* Wks. 1711 IV. 191 Thanks must be Voluntary; not only unconstrain'd, but unsolicited. **1770** GIBBON *Misc. Wks.* (1814) IV. 504 The unconstrained workings of nature.
**3.** Free from constraint or embarrassment ; natural.
**1704** *Moderat. Displ.* iv, So Free, so Unconstrain'd in his Address. **1707** SIR W. HOPE *New Method Fencing* vii. 205 In a Good Guard, the whole Body should be easy, and as much unconstrain'd as possible. **1759** STERNE *Tr. Shandy* II. xvii, He looked frank,—unconstrained,—something assured,—but not bordering upon assurance. **1818** SCOTT *Rob Roy* ix, Dismissing from his countenance some part of the hypocritical affectation of humility..and saying, with a more frank and unconstrained air [etc.].
**4.** Not subject to restraint ; unrestrained.
**1796** MME. D'ARBLAY *Camilla* IV. 278 The unconstrained freedom with which he was empowered to have more books upon the table. **1891** FARRAR *Darkn. & Dawn* xlvii, The intercourse which the prisoner could hold with any who came to visit him was unconstrained.
Hence **Unconstrai·nedness.**
**1656** EARL ORRERY *Parthen.* III. IV. 12 He acquitted himselfe with so much grace and unconstrainednesse in the dance.

**Unconstrai·nedly,** *adv.* [f. prec.] In an unconstrained manner ; without constraint.
**1561** T. NORTON *Calvin's Inst.* I. 16 b, Vnconstrainedly publishing..that the principall auncester of the familie..was an abhominable doer. **1594** HOOKER *Eccl. Pol.* IV. vii. § 6 To thinke..that..wee did vnconstrainedly those things, for which conscience was pretended. **1686** PLOT *Staffordsh.* 14 Some of the Witches..unconstrainedly confest, that the Devil appeared to them like a short black Man. **1854** FABER *Hymn*, '*The Eternal Years*' xiv, Keep unconstrain'dly in this thought, Thy loves..and tears. **1875** GLADSTONE *Glean.* (1879) VI. 107 So long..as it naturally and unconstrainedly bears some sense not entailing such a consequence.

**Unconstrai·ning,** *ppl. a.* (UN-¹ 10.)
**1644** MILTON *Areop.* (Arb.) 51 Those unwritt'n, or at least unconstraining laws of vertuous education. **1691** NORRIS *Pract. Disc.* 80 When the Allurements to Vice were strong, and the ingagements to Duty but weak and unconstraining.

**Unconstrai·nt.** (UN-¹ 12.)
**1711** H. FELTON *Classicks* (1718) 56 Dryden..wanted that Easiness,..that Air of Freedom and Unconstraint,..which is more sensibly to be perceived, than described. **1851** D. COLERIDGE *H. Coleridge's Ess.*, etc. II. 268 The characteristic unconstraint and naïveté of the style carries with it an air of genuineness. **1865** MRS. WHITNEY *Gayworthys* xxviii, It was so hard for him with..his habits of unconstraint, to remember the traditional sanctities of the place.

**Unconstru·able,** *a.* (UN-¹ 7 b and 5 b.) **1856** DOVE *Logic Chr. Faith* IV. i. § 1 Nothing and infinity are equally unconstruable to human thought. **1896** *Law Times* CII. 125/1 He pourtrays the Legislature passing unconstruable statutes. **Unconstru·ctive,** *a.* (UN-¹ 7.) **1859** R. F. BURTON *Centr. Afr.* in *Jrnl. Geog. Soc.* XXIX. 45 The unconstructive African..loves his hut, and has a superstitious horror of stone walls. **Unconstru·ed,** *ppl. a.* (UN-¹ 8.) **1755** YOUNG *Centaur* ii, Does this yet unconstrued, undecyphered creature consider himself as an immortal being? **Unconsu·ltable,** *a.* (UN-¹ 7 b and 5 b.) **1843** E. FORBES *Let.* in Wilson & Geikie *Mem.* xi. (1861) 330 The Zoological Society's collection is boxed up and unconsultable in an old warehouse. **1887** H. G. HEWLETT in *Academy* 26 Mar. 220/1 The preparation of trustworthy calendars and indexes to records previously unconsultable.

**Unconsu·lted,** *ppl. a.* [UN-¹ 8 and 5 b.]
† **1.** Uncounselled, unadvised. *Obs.*—¹
**1567** *Reg. Privy Council Scot.* I. 515 Quhat is abill to be objectit that evir hir Majestie tuke on hand unconsultit be the nobill men, hir Counsall.
**2.** Not consulted (*with*) or referred to.
**1619** SIR J. SEMPIL *Sacrilege Handled* Ded., God was vnconsulted ;..his Church spoyled ; the Commons oppressed. **1642** MILTON *Apol. Smect.* 7 A suspicion that in setting forth this pamphlet the Remonstrant was not unconsulted with. **1829** CASSAN *Lives Bps. of Bath & Wells* 268 He left no history or chronicle of this nation unconsulted. **1847** DE QUINCEY *Milton* Wks. 1857 VII. 318 The reasons assigned to Labienus for passing the oracle of the Libyan Jupiter unconsulted. **1884** *St. James' Gaz.* 4 Apr. 5/2 Our feelings having been entirely unconsulted in the matter.

**Unconsu·lting,** *ppl. a.* [UN-¹ 10 and 5 d.]
**1.** Taking no counsel ; inconsiderate, rash.
*a* **1586** SIDNEY *Arcadia* II. xxii. (1912) 290 It was the faire Zelmane,..whom unconsulting affection..had made borrowe so much of her naturall modestie, as [etc.].
**2.** With object : Without consulting (something).
**1848** LYTTON *Harold* XI. vii, The oath that would bestow on a stranger the fates of a nation, against its knowledge, and unconsulting its laws.

**Unconsu·mable,** *a.* [UN-¹ 7 b and 5 b.]
**1.** That cannot be consumed ; inexhaustible.
**1571** GOLDING *Calvin on Ps.* xviii. 17 From whence the rivers have so unconsumable store and abundance of waters. **1586** T. B. *La Primaud. Fr. Acad.* I. 418 The wealth which proceedeth from liberalitie is unconsumeable. **1615** G. SANDYS *Trav.* 127 [Arms and legs] from the Mummes (whereof there are an vnconsumeable number).
**2.** Incapable of being destroyed by fire.
**1670** BROOKS *Wks.* (1867) VI. 207 How will an unconsumable soul and body be able to endure the scorching flames of hell for ever? **1859** SALA *Tw. round Clock* (1861) 381 It was ..suggested that he was unconsumable, made of asbestos. **1870** MEREDITH *Odes Fr. Hist.* (1898) 57 Ever invoking fire from heaven, the fire Has grasped her, unconsumable.

**Unconsu·med,** *ppl. a.* (UN-¹ 8 and 5 b.)
**1549** *Compl. Scot.* vi. 46 Of this sort the art of astronomie suld ay remane onconsumit. **1627** MAY *Lucan* VIII. P vij, The bones halfe-burnt, not yett dissolu'd hee takes, Stil full of nerues, and vnconsumed marrow. **1697** CONGREVE *Mourn. Bride* II. v, The poor remains..Yet fresh and unconsum'd by time and worms. **1724** RAMSAY *Health* 86 Long unconsum'd the oak can bear the beams. **1818** CRUISE *Digest* (ed. 2) V. 91 Every such fine..should be of the same force and effect, as if it had still remained upon record unconsumed or not lost. **1857** MILLER *Elem. Chem., Org.* 329 A charred mass remains, consisting of carbonate of potash and unconsumed carbon.

**Unconsu·ming,** *ppl. a.* (UN-¹ 10.)
**1628** FELTHAM *Resolves* II. xxv. 80 Though pleasure merries the Sences for a while : yet horror after vultures the vnconsuming heart. [**1718** *Entertainer* No. 15. 97 No sooner shall the enjoyment be over, when Horrour will..act the Promethean Vulture upon the unconsuming Conscience.] **1836** KEBLE in *Lyra Apost.* (1849) 204 God of the unconsuming fire, On Horeb seen of old. **1851** TRENCH *Sonnet* Poems (1865) 92 It straightway kindled then, and was afire, And with the unconsuming radiance blended.

**Unconsu·mmate,** *ppl. a.* [UN-¹ 8 b and 5 b. Cf. next.] Not consummated ; uncompleted.
**1609** BIBLE (Douay) *Deut.* xxiv. *comm.*, Nothing..can loose the band of Mariage..unconsummate, but death, or solemne vow in an approved rule of religion. *a* **1643** W. CARTWRIGHT *Siege* III. i, I cannot then retire me from the sin, Though I do leave the action unconsummate. **1702** S. PARKER tr. *Cicero's De Finibus* III. 196 Whatever Action bears the Name of a Compleat Good one is a Duty perform'd, as there is also Duty Unconsummate. **1868** BROWNING *Ring & Bk.* IX. 421 The unconsummate blow, Adroitly baulked by her.

**Unco·nsummated,** *ppl. a.* (UN-¹ 8.) **1813** T. BUSBY *Lucretius* I. III. 1138 Joys unconsummated round thee play. **1852** IS. WILLIAMS *Apocalypse* 119 The unnumbered company [intimates] the gathering in as yet unconsummated.

**Unconta·gious,** *a.* (UN-¹ 7.) **1822** GOOD *Study Med.* II. 71 The production of uncontagious intermittent fever.

**Uncontai·nable,** *a.* (UN-¹ 7 b.)
**1618** T. ADAMS *Generat. Serpents* Wks. (1629) 890 His vncontainable poyson would soone burst him. **1681** RYCAUT tr. *Gracian's Critick* 40 Pythagoras calls it a Tuned-Harp, whose measure and harmony wraps up our Contemplations and Thoughts with uncontainable Ravishments. **1883** *Harper's Mag.* Jan. 284/2 Jim had an awkward expression of uncontainable happiness.

**Uncontai·ned,** *ppl. a.* (UN-¹ 8.) *c* **1611** CHAPMAN *Iliad* I. 93 This still will empty in our hearts His deathful quiver, uncontain'd till to her loved sire The black-eyed damsel be resign'd. **1836** EMERSON *Nature* 13 I am the lover of uncontained and immortal beauty. **Unconta·minable,** *a.* (UN-¹ 7 b and 5 b.) **1657** EARL MONM. tr. *Paruta's Pol. Disc.* 52 So well disposed towards the good of their Country, and so uncontaminable by any other affection.

**Unconta·minate,** *ppl. a.* (UN-¹ 8 b and 5 b.)
**1675** COCKER *Morals* 24 A Conscience uncontaminate. **1784** COWPER *Task* VI. 789 The pure and uncontam'nate blood. **1842** R. I. WILBERFORCE *Rutilius & Lucius* 164 The corrupted traditions..flowed from a source which originally was clear and uncontaminate. **1876** LOWELL *Among my Bks.* Ser. II. 249 Abstinence, exercise, and uncontaminate air.

**Unconta·minated,** *ppl. a.* (UN-¹ 8 and 5 b.)
**1611** COTGR., *Incontaminé*, vncontaminated, vnpolluted. **1774** GOLDSM. *Nat. Hist.* II. xvi. 375 Nature has providently stopped the fruitfulness of these ill-formed productions, in order to preserve the form of every animal uncontaminated. **1832** MISS MITFORD *Village* Ser. v. 7 Our village, though in the centre of the insurgents, continued uncontaminated. **1879** FROUDE *Cæsar* ii. 19 Whose minds were still uncontaminated, in whom the ancient habits of life still survived.

**Unconte·mned,** *ppl. a.* (UN-¹ 8.)
**1613** SHAKS. *Hen. VIII*, III. ii. 10 Which of the Peeres Haue vncontemn'd gone by him? **1634** HABINGTON *Castara* II. *Wife*, Shee is so true a friend, her Husband may to her communicate even his ambitions, and if successe Crowne not expectation, remaine neverthelesse uncontemned.
Hence **Unconte·mnedly** *adv.*
**1628** FELTHAM *Resolves* II. 296, I beg no more, then may keepe mee vncontemnedly, and vnpittiedly-honest.

**Uncontemplated,** *ppl. a.* (UN-¹ 8.)
**1709** SHAFTESB. *Charac.* (1711) II. 424 Never can the Form be of real force where it is uncontemplated,..unexamin'd. **1837** LYTTON *Athens* II. 268 So do the most important results arise from causes uncontemplated by the providence of statesmen. **1860** DICKENS *Uncomm. Trav.* x, He may be seen..haling the blind man away on expeditions wholly uncontemplated by..the man.

**Uncontempora·neous,** *a.* (UN-¹ 7.) **1859** G. WILSON *Mem. E. Forbes* i. (1861) 26 The uncontemporaneous events which are recorded in the same page of an almanac. **1870** LOWELL *Among my Bks.* Ser. I. 6 Unless, like Goethe, he is of a singularly uncontemporaneous nature. **Unconte·nded,** *ppl. a.* (UN-¹ 8.) **1697** DRYDEN *Æneis* V. 510 Permit me, Chief, permit without Delay, To lead this uncontended Gift away. **Unconte·nding,** *ppl. a.* (UN-¹ 10.) **1748** RICHARDSON *Clarissa* (1811) III. 248 Thou knowest my generosity to my uncontending Rosebud. **1881** RUSKIN *Lett. to Faunthorpe* (1895) I. 43 The recognition of uncontending and natural worth.

**Unconte·nt,** *sb.* [UN-¹ 12.] Absence of content ; dissatisfaction.
**1873** MISS BROUGHTON *Nancy* II. 131 Over all the landscape there is a look of plaintive uncontent.

**Unconte·nt,** *a.* [UN-¹ 7.] = next.
**1502** ARNOLDE *Chron.* (1811) 125 And so wolde leue dyuers persones that I am in dett to vncontent. **1591** *Troub. Raigne K. John* (1611) A 2, Yet Iohn your Lord, contented vncontent, Will (as he may) sustaine the heauy yoke Of pressing cares. **1885** L. OLIPHANT *Sympneumata* 167 The records of the intellect..cannot evince a perfect understanding..of this vast subject, so long as..its moral whole is uncontent.

**Unconte·nted,** *ppl. a.* [UN-¹ 8. Cf. DISCONTENTED.] Not contented ; unsatisfied.
**1568** T. HOWELL *Newe Sonets* (1879) 124 Mewsing how I best might ease mine vncontented minde. **1586** T. B. *La Primaud. Fr. Acad.* I. 31 Perturbations..which fill the soule with endlesse trouble and disquietnes, causing man to live alwaies uncontented. **1605** DANIEL *Philotas* Ded. A iv, When your iudgment shal ariue so far, As t' ouerlooke th' intricate designes Of vncontented man. **1675** *Art Contentm.* I. xii, The torture which every repining uncontented spirit provides for its self. **1718** G. SEWELL *Proclam. Cupid* 4 Thus uncontented with a private Wrong, He spreads his Baseness with a busie Tongue. **1861** MILL *Repr. Govt.* (1865) 24/1 Nothing is more certain, than that improvement in human affairs is wholly the work of the uncontented characters.
Hence **Unconte·ntedness.**
*a* **1660** HAMMOND *Fundamentals* xi. Wks. 1674 I. 298 Contentedness is most eminently one of these specialties,..as it is opposed to ambition, covetousness, injustice, uncontentedness.

**Unconte·nting,** *ppl. a.* (UN-¹ 10.) **1698** NORRIS *Pract. Disc.* IV. 357 His Future Expectations shall prove every whit as vain and uncontenting as his past Fruitions. **Unconte·ntingness.** (UN-¹ 12.) **1648** BOYLE *Seraph. Love* viii. (1700) 51 The decreed uncontentingness of all other goods.

**Unconte·ntious,** *a.* (UN-¹ 7.)
Also, in recent use, *uncontentiousness.*
**1828** PUSEY *Hist. Eng.* I. 66 Either pupils of Calixtus, or of the same uncontentious disposition. **1868** E. EDWARDS *Ralegh* I. iv. 63 [He] proposed that all difficulty..should be referred to lawyers for uncontentious decision. **1884** *Manch. Exam.* 25 June 6/1 A comparatively uncontentious measure.

**Unconte·stable,** *a.* (UN-¹ 7 b and 5 b.)
**1681** *Whole Duty Nations* 13 Religion..being a most uncontestable duty and obligation in those lesser Kingdoms, Families. **1714** SWIFT *Pres. St. Aff.* Wks. 1755 II. I. 217, I must therefore lay it down as an uncontestable truth. **1725** *Fam. Dict.* s.v. *Vegetation*, As to what is said concerning the heat of the Sun, it is uncontestable. **1826** *Westm. Rev.* Oct. 483 The arrangement, which Mr. Humphreys, and with uncontestable reason, proposes. **1831** LD. PALMERSTON in *Westm. Rev.* July (1855) 60 *note*, The will of a sovereign whose rights are uncontestable.

Hence **Unconte·stably** *adv.*

1709 (*title*), An Exact Narrative of the many Surprizing Matters of Fact uncontestably wrought by an Evil Spirit. 1740–1 *Johnson's Parliamentary Debates* (1787) I. 201 That where this maxim is not..adhered to, rights and liberties are empty sounds, is uncontestably evident.

**Unconte·sted,** *ppl. a.* (Un-[1] 8 and 5 b.)

1678 Oldham *On Wks. B. Jonson* x, Poems (1684) 81 Thou thy own Works didst strictly try By known and uncontested Rules of Poetry. 1692 Norris *Curs. Reflect.* 14, I affirm that there are..as uncontested Propositions in Morality as in any other Science. 1750 Johnson *Rambler* No. 45 ¶ 2 You seem..to have allowed as an uncontested principle, that marriage is generally unhappy. 1800 *Misc. Tr.* in *Asiat. Ann. Reg.* 248/1 The Goosaigns maintained an uncontested authority, till the arrival of about 12 or 14,000 Seik horsemen. 1855 Macaulay *Hist. Eng.* xvii. IV. 47 A government of which the title was uncontested. 1874 Disraeli in Froude *Carlyle's Life in Lond.* xxxiii. (1884) II. 429, I see only two living names which..stand out in uncontested superiority.

Hence **Unconte·stedly** *adv.*

1699 T. Baker *Refl. Learn.* ii. 10 As for the Greek [tongue], which is uncontestedly Learned, most know, how copious it is. 1719 J. T. Phillips tr. *Thirty-four Confer.* 298 These sorts of Beads had been for some thousand Years uncontestedly an efficacious Medecine for Souls.

† **Unco·ntinent,** *a.* *Obs.* [Un-[1] 7 b.] = Incontinent *a.* Also † **Unco·ntinently** *adv.*

1382 Wyclif 2 *Tim.* iii. 2 Men schulen be..fals blameris, vncontynent, vnmylde. *a* 1420 *Wycliffite Bible* (1850) III. 12 *marg.*, He that is vncontynent, ether a lecchour, renneth in to the snare of synne. 1565 Cooper *Thesaurus, Incontinens*,..vncontinent. *Ibid.*, *Incontinenter*,..vncontinently. 1598 Florio, *Incontinente*, vncontinent, vncleane of life.

† **Uncontinent,** var. Incontinent *adv.*

1506 in *Charters*, etc. *Edinb.* (1871) 189 We charge you straitlie and commandis vncontinent [etc.].

**Unco·ntinented,** *a.* (Un-[1] 9.) 1847 Emerson *Poems, Monadnoc*, The bullet of the earth Whereon ye sail, Tumbling steep In the uncontinented deep. **Unconti·nued,** *ppl. a.* (Un-[1] 8.) 1576 Abp. Sandys *Serm.* (1585) 171 Their seruice was vnrewarded, because it was vncontinued. **Unconti·nuous,** *a.* (Un-[1] 7 and 5 b.) 1846 Mozley *Ess.* (1878) II. 154 A succession of momentary, uncontinuous, fragmentary impulses, ideas, and feelings. 1863 Cowden Clarke *Shaks. Char.* x. 257 He is light-minded, being inconsequent and uncontinuous, which is very French. **Unconto·rted,** *ppl. a.* (Un-[1] 8.) 1834 Foster in Ryland *Life & Corr.* (1846) II. 248 If..the diction be perspicuous, natural, and uncontorted.

**Uncontra·ct,** *v.* [Un-[2] 3.] To relax, unbend.

1628 Feltham *Resolves* ii. lvi. 162 The best way is, to vncontract the brow, and let the worlds mad spleene fret.

**Uncontra·cted,** *ppl. a.* [Un-[1] 7 b and 5 b.]

† **1.** Not affianced or betrothed. *Obs.*

1527 [see Unaffied]. 1564–5 *Reg. Privy Council Scot.* I. 325 He sould..keip the said Jane..as fre woman uncontractit or mariit..for the space of ane yeir. *c* 1625 [see Unaffied].

**2.** Not brought into smaller compass.

1758 Johnson *Idler* No. 9 ¶ 2 To give the smooth feature and the uncontracted muscle. 1864 Pusey *Lect. Daniel* i. 49 In the Biblical Chaldee the older uncontracted forms prevail. 1877 Raymond *Mines & M.* 116 This serpentine belt..extending its course southeasterly with uncontracted dimensions.

**Uncontradi·ctable,** *a.* (Un-[1] 7 b and 5 b.)

1707 *Curios. in Husb. & Gard.* 134 We know by uncontradictable Experiments, that Nitre..attracts..Humidity. 1825 Bentham *Offic. Apt. Maximized, Indicat.* (1830) 70 That confidence-commanding and uncontradictable hand.

Hence **Uncontradi·ctably** *adv.*

1862 T. A. Trollope *Marietta* I. iv. 64 The means by which one moral nature speaks..uncontradictably to another.

**Uncontradi·cted,** *ppl. a.* (Un-[1] 8.)

1606 Warner *Alb. Eng.* xv. xcvi. 383 And new Rome,.. Vncontradicted, for that Plot from Hell the Palme doth win. 1651 Hobbes *Leviath.* i. xvi. 83 The excesse of Negatives, standing uncontradicted, are the onely voyce the Representative hath. 1748 Hartley *Observ. Man* ii. ii. § 21. 92 The People..let it pass uncontradicted. 1815 J. Smith *Panorama Sci. & Art* II. 71 The inference drawn by the Florentines, remained uncontradicted by any experiment, till about 1762. 1885 *Law Rep.* 14 Q. B. Div. 248 There was uncontradicted evidence given at the trial that [etc.].

Hence **Uncontradi·ctedly** *adv.*

1652 Gaule *Magastrom.* 129 So they may (more easily and uncontradictedly) resist the truth.

**Uncontradi·ctory,** *a.* (Un-[1] 7.)

In quot. = uncontradictable.

1698 Norris *Pract. Disc.* (1707) IV. 231 He need not deny it because it is an uncontradictory Truth.

**Uncontrite,** *a.* (Un-[1] 7.)

*c* 1440 *Jacob's Well* 167 Sche wolde no3t leve here synne & dyed vncontrite. 1509 [see Unconfessed 1]. 1646 Hammond *Pract. Catech.* i. iii. (ed. 2) 28 [The priest] by absolving an uncontrite sinner, cannot sure make him contrite. 1861 Lytton & Fane *Tannhäuser* 96 Even though unabsolved, not uncontrite.

**Uncontri·ved,** *ppl. a.* (Un-[1] 8.)

1612 W. Parkes *Curtaine-Dr.* (1876) 49 If he shall practise vncontriued conclusions vpon our liues. 1646 Sir T. Browne *Pseud. Ep.* i. xi. 44 Thus hath he deluded many Nations.. from casuall and uncontrived contingences divining events succeeding. 1790 Paley *Horæ Paul.* iv. § 8 A species of confirmation..evidently uncontrived.

**Uncontri·ving,** *ppl. a.* (Un-[1] 10.) 1774 Goldsm. *Nat. Hist.* I. xxii. 401 To the savage uncontriving man the earth is an abode of desolation. **Uncontro·l.** (Un-[1] 12.) 1861 Mrs. H. Wood *East Lynne* i. xvi, She burst forth in passionate uncontrol.

**Uncontro·llable,** *a.* [Un-[1] 7 b and 5 b.]

† **1.** Incontrovertible, indisputable, irrefutable.

1577 tr. *Bullinger's Decades* iii. ix. 460 That diuine saying of Sainct Peter remaineth for euer vncomptroleable. 1602 Warner *Alb. Eng.* Epit. (1606) 362 It is to be noted, as warranted out of vncontrowlable authours, that [etc.] 1646 Sir T. Browne *Pseud. Ep.* vi. i. 273 His labours are rationall, and uncontroulable upon the grounds assumed. 1673 Cave *Prim. Chr.* iii. iii. 304 He makes it an uncontrollable Argument of the Truth. 1701 Swift *Contests Nobles & Comm.* i, The error of those, who think it an uncontrollable maxim, that power is always safer lodged in many hands than in one. 1738 — *Pol. Conversat.* Introd. 74.

**2.** Not subject to control from a higher authority; absolute.

1593 G. Harvey *Pierce's Super.* Wks. (Grosart) II. 180 Armed with that supreme & Vncontrowlable authoritie, which they affect in causes Ecclesiasticall. 1630 *R. Johnson's Kingd. & Commw.* 526 His sentence in matters of Law and Religion is uncontrollable. 1672 Marvell *Reh. Transp.* i. 140 He had vested them with an..unlimited power, and uncontroulable in the Government of Religion. 1711 Steele *Spect.* No. 167 ¶ 3, I have grasped imaginary Scepters, and delivered uncontroulable Edicts. 1752 Hume *Ess. & Treat.* (1777) I. 39 Authority..can never..become quite entire and uncontroulable. 1809 Mar. Edgeworth *Manœuvring* xv, She had an uncontroulable right to marry as she thought proper. 1836 J. Gilbert *Chr. Atonem.* ii. 49 The power of the Creator over all his creatures is entirely uncontrollable.

**b.** In quasi-adverbial use.

*a* 1704 T. Brown *Praise Drunkenness* Wks. 1730 I. 35 Consider whether 'tis not the Drunkard, that..acts so uncontroulable as the Gods themselves.

**3.** That cannot be controlled or restrained.

1648 R. Josselin *Diary* (1908) 54 The wofull uncontroulable encrease of all manner of wickedness. 1665 Sir T. Herbert *Trav.* (1677) 262 Cardarigas..fancies to himself that they were brought thither by some uncontroulable destiny to be destroyed. 1748 Richardson *Clarissa* (1811) I. i. 2 His natural imperiousness and fierce and uncontroulable temper. 1823 Scott *Quentin D.* ix, His horse, seizing the bit with his teeth, went forth at an uncontrollable gallop. 1846 McCulloch *Acc. Brit. Empire* (1854) II. 629 Poverty and misery produced by accidental and uncontrollable causes. 1879 H. C. Wood *Therap.* 570 Hydrophobia is a perfectly uncontrollable disease.

*absol.* 1754 Richardson *Corr.* (1804) IV. 89 Dr. Young is another uncontrollable, therefore unaccountable. 1819 Shelley *Ode West Wind* 47 The impulse of thy strength, only less free Than thou. O uncontrollable!

**Uncontro·llableness.** [f. prec.] The state or quality of being uncontrollable.

Also, in recent use, *uncontrollability.*

1634 Bp. Hall *Contempl., N.T.* iv. vii, Vices,..when they grow inveterate, have a strong plea for their abode and uncontroulableness. 1673 Cave *Prim. Chr.* iii. ii. 243 The Uncontrolableness of the Miracles performed in his Name. 1748 Richardson *Clarissa* (1811) II. xxx. 192 My charge upon him of unpoliteness and uncontroulableness. 1833 Carlyle *Misc. Ess., Diderot* (1888) 62 With vehemence enough, with even a female uncontrollableness. 1862 Mill *Syst. Logic* (ed. 5) II. 416 [It] cannot fail..to create a feeling of uncontrollableness in the former also.

**Uncontro·llably,** *adv.* [f. as prec. Cf. Incontrollably *adv.*]

† **1. a.** As if uncontrovertible. *Obs.*

1629 Prynne *Ch. Eng.* 52 Being alwayes..unanimously, professedly and uncontrollablie entertained. 1646 Sir T. Browne *Pseud. Ep.* vi. viii. 312 Hereof uncontroulably and under generall consent many opinions are passant, which notwithstanding..do admit of doubt.

† **b.** Incontrovertibly, indisputably. *Obs.*

1676 Hale *Contempl.* i. 222 Abundantly and uncontrollably convincing the reality of our Saviour's death and true Resurrection. 1678 Jones *Heart & Right Sov.* 134 Our Brittish Churches appear to be uncontrollably of apostolical descent.

**2.** Without submission to control or restraint; absolutely; unrestrainedly.

1637 *Declar. Pfaltzgrave's Faith* 34 In which Commandement God hath forbidden two things vncontroleably. 1672 [H. Stubbe] *Rosemary & Bayes* 22, I conceive it is uncontroulably settled by law. 1768 Tucker *Lt. Nat.* III. 311 Though it be certain God may uncontrolably and lawfully deal with his creatures as he pleases. 1809 Mar. Edgeworth *Manœuvring* xv, He became uncontrouladly impatient to declare his own attachment. 1873 Symonds *Grk. Poets* i. 26 Pericles governed the most uncontrollably free of nations by Reason.

**Uncontro·lled,** *ppl. a.* [Un-[1] 8 and 5 b.]

**1.** Not subjected to control; unrestrained, ungoverned, unchecked: **a.** In predicative use.

1513 More *Hist. Rich. III*, Wks. 56 To rule..ye realm at their pleasure, & therbi to pil and spoil whom thei list vncontroled. 1595 Spenser *Col. Clout* 662 Happie I him hold, That may that blessed presence still enioy, Of fortune and of enuy vncomptrold. 1614 Gorges *Lucan* iv. 147 The coasts on both sides shall behold Valour vn-vanquisht vncontrold. 1655 *Nicholas Papers* (Camden) II. 311 To suffer so greate a prodigy of baseness to goe vncontrolld, were an injury to humane society. *a* 1718 Prior *Cloe Jealous* x, Fall uncontroll'd my Tears, and free. 1755 Young *Centaur* i, Thus the sluices are set open for all sensuality..to pour in uncontrouled. 1844 H. H. Wilson *Brit. India* III. 541 The whole of India would fall under the dominion of one Governor, unassisted and uncontrolled. 1890 'R. Boldrewood' *Col. Reformer* (1891) 332 Possessing no very near relatives, she was uncontrolled as to her..mode of life.

**b.** In attributive use.

*c* 1586 C'tess Pembroke *Ps.* (1823) lxxv. ii, Then [will I] denounce my uncontrolled pleasure. *a* 1592 Greene *Selimus* 961 Or have the uncontrolled Christians Unsheath'd their swords to make more war on us? 1614 Markham *Cheap Husb.* i. i. 2 He withstandeth all effects of sicknesse, with vncontroled constancy. 1660 *Gentl. Calling* 46 The Affections ..will have as free and uncontrolled a sway in men, as they have in meer animals. 1742 Richardson *Pamela* IV. 56 An Example to all who know him and his uncontrouled Temper. 1777 Robertson *Hist. Amer.* ii. (1778) I. 156 They flattered themselves that now they should enjoy an uncontrouled liberty. 1824 Dibdin *Libr. Comp.* 745 *note*, The spleen.. broke out with uncontrolled bitterness in..the Third Canto. 1875 Jowett *Plato* (ed. 2) III. 112 The uncontrolled licence and freedom of the democrat.

† **2.** Not checked by comparison with facts; untested as to accuracy. *Obs.*

1529 More *Suppl. Souls* Wks. 297/2 Sith he knoweth hys tale false: it is wisdome to leue the time vnknowen, that hys lye may bee vncontrolled. 1584 in *Cath. Rec. Soc. Publ.* V. 81 To make this slaunder more probable, Or at the lest to be the longer uncontrowled.

† **3.** Not called in question; not gainsaid or disproved; undisputed. *Obs.*

1534 More *Comf. agst. Trib.* iii. Wks. 1223/2 If he perceyued that they sayde but the trouthe, he woulde lette it passe by, vncontrolled. 1591 *Troub. Raigne K. John* ii. (1611) 86 Faire Lewis of Fraunce..Hath title of an vncontrouled strength To England. 1672–5 Comber *Comp. Temple* (1702) 44 The main part of them is genuine, as the uncontrouled Tradition of the Eastern Church assures us. 1724 Swift *Drapier's Lett.* 14 Dec., I ever thought it the most uncontrouled and universally agreed maxim. 1731 — *Let. to Ventoso* 28 Apr., It is an uncontrolled truth.

Hence **Uncontro·lledly** *adv.*

1579 Knewstub *Confut.* To Rdr., The sinnes of our Countrey ..are done so openly and so vncontrolledly in the sight of the Lord. 1667 Flavel *Saint Indeed* (1754) 17 To let thy heart habitually and uncontrouledly wander from God. 1768–74 Tucker *Lt. Nat.* (1834) II. 559 Men commonly place it in a license to do uncontrolledly whatever their desires..shall prompt them to. 1855 Doran *Queens of Eng.* I. ix. 400 Uncontrolledly exercising the power she had attained.

† **Uncontrove·rsable,** *a.* *Obs.* (Un-[1] 7 b.) 1617 Hales *Gold. Rem.* i. (1673) 18 The litteral, plain, and uncontroversable meaning of Scripture. † **Unco·ntroversed,** *ppl. a.* *Obs.* (Un-[1] 8.) 1634 Jackson *Creed* vii. iii. § 3 The deduction of Mathematicall conclusions from the uncontrovers'd Maximes of the same Art.

**Uncontrove·rsial,** *a.* (Un-[1] 7.)

1861 J. G. Sheppard *Fall Rome* vii. 359 Races of uncontroversial warriors, such as were the Vandals and the Goths. 1870 J. H. Newman *Gram. Assent* i. v. 144 Foreign, strange, and hard to the pious but uncontroversial mind.

So **Uncontrove·rsially** *adv.*

1847 Pusey *Paradise Chr. Soul* v. Advert. p. viii, No one can look uncontroversially at such occasional addresses.

† **Uncontrove·rsory,** *a.* *Obs.* [Un-[1] 7.] = prec.

1641 Bp. Hall *Def. Humble Remonstr.* ii. 10 The Devotion of it yeeldeth no cause of offence to a very Popes eare, as onely ayming at an uncontroversory Piety.

† **Uncontrove·rtably,** *adv.* *Obs.* [Un-[1] 11.] = Uncontrovertibly.

*a* 1658 Durham *Comm. Rev.* xvii. (1660) 660 These things being..uncontrovertably applicable to Rome.

**Uncontrove·rted,** *ppl. a.* (Un-[1] 8.)

1654 Wariston *Diary* (S.H.S.) II. 250 They..wer angrye to heare of the acts of uncontraverted assemblies. *a* 1674 Clarendon *Surv. Leviath.* (1676) 63 His speculation is contradicted by constant and uncontroverted practice. 1712 Addison *Spect.* No. 529 ¶ 6 A standing and uncontroverted Principle. 1771 *Junius Lett.* xlviii. (1788) 264 The resolutions..stand upon your Journals, uncontroverted and unrepealed. 1800 *Med. Jrnl.* III. 527 It is uncontroverted that the original author intended to destroy contagious matter.

Hence **Uncontrove·rtedly** *adv.*

1644 Bp. Maxwell *Prerog. Chr. Kings* ii. 31 By Thrones, Dominions, Principalities and Powers, uncontrovertedly Angels are meant. 1705 Clarke *Disc. Nat. Relig.* xiv. (1738) 445 Most of the Books were uncontrovertedly written by the Apostles themselves.

**Uncontrove·rtible,** *a.* (Un-[1] 7 and 5 b.)

1664 H. More *Myst. Iniq.* 350, I mean the latter end of his real and uncontrovertible reign,..not that imaginary one. 1693 *Humours Town* 62 A good Assurance dubs any one an uncontrovertible Critick. 1742 *Johnson's Parliamentary Debates* II. 251 Even the positions..which are laid down as uncontrovertible, are generally false. 1794 R. J. Sulivan *View Nat.* xliv. II. 253 This is a position, uncontrovertible in some points, but in others..much to be doubted. 1818 Bentham *Ch. Eng.* Introd. 13 May not then this position be stated as uncontrovertible? 1894 H. Gardener *Unoff. Patriot* 24 The watchwords and uncontrovertible basis of belief for the succeeding generation.

Hence **Uncontrove·rtibly** *adv.*

1755 Johnson, *Incontestably*,..indisputably; uncontrovertibly. 1770 — *False Alarm* (ed. 2) 24 It is uncontrovertibly certain, that [etc.]. 1818 Bentham *Ch. Eng.* p. xli, Shew me ..that proposition in Euclid which is more uncontrovertibly demonstrated than is this one.

† **Unconfu·nded,** *ppl. a.* *Obs.*—[1] (Un-[1] 8 and 5 b.) 1599 A. M. tr. *Gabelhouer's Bk. Physicke* 125/1 Take Horsedung, as much as an Egge,..& half a drag. of vncountunded Safferne. † **Unconvale·sced,** *ppl. a.* *Obs.*—[1] (Un-[1] 8.) 1590–1 *Reg. Privy Council Scot.* IV. 578 He wes lyand bedfast,..unconvalesitt of the said woundis. **Unco·nvenable,** *a.* *Obs.*—[1] (Un-[1] 7.) 1542 Udall *Erasm. Apoph.* 256 b, Yt there was nothyng more unconvenable for a perfecte good Capitaine, then over muche hastyng. **Unconve·ned,** *ppl. a.* (Un-[1] 8.) [1775 Ash.] 1855 Grote *Greece* ii. lxii, [The conspirators'] design was to appropriate the powers of government..; leaving this body of Five-thousand not merely unconvened, but non-existent.

† **Unconve·nience.** *Obs.* (Un-[1] 12 and 5 b.)

1535 in *Lett. Suppress. Monast.* (Camden) 56 We shall not be drevyn be necessyte nether to begge, nor to fall to no other unconveniyence. 1635 Feltham *Resolves* ii. iii. 325 If I must have one, give me an unconvenience, not a mischiefe.

**Unconve·nient,** *a.* and *sb.* *Obs.* exc. *dial.* [Un-[1] 7, 5 b, and 12.]

**A.** *adj.* = Inconvenient *a.* (in various senses).

1450–80 tr. *Secreta Secret.* 8 The name of skarste is vnconvenient to a kyng. 1523 Fitzherb. *Husb.* § 154 It shoulde seme vnconuenient for a temporall man to take vpon hym to shewe or teache any suche spirytuall matters. 1551 Robinson tr. *More's Utopia* ii. (1895) 278 It were an vnconuenient thinge, that the blessed shoulde not be at libertye to goo whether they wold. 1590 *Disc. Span. Invasion* in *Harl. Misc.* (1809) II. 158 It seemed unconvenient that he should in every thing be inferior to the Englishmen. 1683 Moxon

*Mech. Exerc., Printing* p. iii, A Low Case is unconvenient for a Compositer to work at. 1880- in dial. glossaries.

†**B.** *sb.* = INCONVENIENT *sb.* 3. *Obs.*

?*c* 1536 in Ellis *Orig. Lett.* Ser. III. III. 43 It was thoght.. the matter..wolde have growen to forther vnconueniaunts.

Hence **Unconve·niently** *adv.*

1538 ELYOT, *Indecore*, vnhonestly, vnconueniently. 1548 UDALL, etc. *Erasm. Par. John* xix. 108 b, That it myght appeare howe vnconueniently the cryme of any cruell auctoritie..was layd agaynst hym. 1561-6 *Child-Marriages* 112 She..had sene the said Custance Wade and Robert Rile..unconvenientlie together in the..chambre.

**Unconve·ntional,** *a.* [UN-[1] 7.] Not limited or bound down by convention; free and easy.

Also, in recent use, *unconventionally* adv.

1839 G. DARLEY *Beaumont & Fletcher's Wks.* I. Introd. p. xxxii, The unsettled and unconventional state of our language at that period. 1861 [H. S. CUNNINGHAM] *Wheat & Tares* 387 His views as to grammar were entirely unconventional. 1884 E. DREW *Elocutionist* Nov. 3/1 The book ..is entirely unconventional.

Hence **Unconve·ntionalism.**

1868 *Round Table* No. 202. 374 The freedom and unconventionalism in such writing. 1883 *Nonconf. & Indep.* 28 Dec. 1167 The work needs freshness and unconventionalism.

**Unconve:ntiona·lity.** (UN-[1] 12. Cf. prec.)

1854 H. SPENCER *Ess.* I. 153 Such of his unconventionalities as can be attributed only to eccentricity, he has no qualms about. 1866 G. MACDONALD *Ann. Q. Neighb.* xxii. (1878) 396 The fact of his unconventionality and justice in leaving his property to my sister.

**Unconve·ntioned,** *a.* (UN-[1] 9.) 1876 WHITTIER *June on Merrimac* 77 What cares the unconventioned wood For pass-words of the town?

**Unconve·rsable,** *a.* Also -ible. [UN-[1] 7 b, 7, and 5 b.] Unfit or unsuitable for social converse.

α. 1593 NASHE *Strange Newes* Ep. Ded., I loue and admire thy pleasant wittie humor, which no care or crosse can make vnconuersable. 1681 J. SCOTT *Chr. Life* I. iii. § 3 In what a miserable state shall we be, when every Member of our Society shall be of the same unconversable Temper with our selves. 1697 COLLIER *Ess. Mor. Subj.* I. (1703) 79 What a rugged, tempestuous, unconversable mortal was Achilles. 1728 SWIFT *Let. to Carteret* 18 Jan., If I had not been confined to my chamber by the continuance of my unconversable disorder [*i.e.* deafness]. 1803 LAMB *Let. to Manning* in *Final Mem.* vii. 69 Among nasty, unconversable, horse-belching, Tartar-people.

β. 1674 *Govt. Tongue* 158 Nothing rendering a man so unconversible [as pride]. 1687 *Lond. Gaz.* No. 2302/2 The Ignorance or unconversible Humor of the Turks. 1736 H. WALPOLE *Lett.* (1861) I. 9 Great mathematicians have been of great use, but the generality of them are quite unconversible.

Hence **Unconve·rsableness.**

1684 H. MORE *Answer* 315 Contemptuousness, Malapertness against their Betters,..Unconversableness. 1702 S. PARKER tr. *Cicero's De Finibus* I. 45 The many Dangers and Frights that go along with Unconversableness and Solitude.

**Unco·nversant,** *a.* (UN-[1] 7 and 5 b.)

*a* 1674 CLARENDON *Surv. Leviath.* (1676) 57 If Mr. Hobbes were not strangely unconversant with the transactions of those times. 1708 T. MADOX *Exchequer* Pref. p. xvi, Persons who are haply unconversant in disquisitions of this kind. 1813 T. BUSBY *Lucretius* I. III. Comm. p. xxxiii, A being, unconversant with its own existence. 1853 *Topographer & Geneal.* II. 6 Though this may sound marvellous to those unconversant with the subject.

**Unconversible**: see UNCONVERSABLE. **Unconve·rsing,** *ppl. a.* (UN-[1] 10.) 1643-5 MILTON *Divorce* I. iii, How preposterous [it is] in the Canon Law..to have had no care about the unconversing inability of minde. **Unconve·rsion.** (UN-[1] 12, 5 b.) 1846 WORCESTER (citing *Ch. Ob.*). 1861 F. W. ROBINSON *No Church* I. viii. 169 He might never wake again, but die..in his brutal ignorance and unconversion.

**Unconve·rt,** *v.* [UN-[2] 3.]

**1.** *trans.* To transform.

1654 GAYTON *Pleas. Notes* IV. xvii. 258 Who with head full addle, Would unconvert his Pannell from a saddle.

**2.** To undo the conversion of.

1825 R. P. WARD *Tremaine* II. xv. 146 As he indeed wished to convert Monsieur Dupuis, so the valet..thought it but a fair return of kindness to endeavour to unconvert her. 1887 *Advance* (Chicago) 1 Dec. 760 We are not suffering so much from disturbing methods of converting people, as we are from the influences which un-convert them.

**Unconve·rted,** *ppl. a.* [UN-[1] 8 and 5 b.]

**1.** That has not been brought over to a religious faith or profession; not changed from one faith or opinion to another.

1648 [see UNCONFOUND *v.*]. 1685 BAXTER *Paraphr. N. T.* Matt. xxv. 7 Self-love, and fear, will make them cry for Mercy, with some kind of Repentance, though they be unconverted. 1745 WESLEY *Answ. Ch.* 35 Our Lord commanded those very Men who were then unconverted,..to do this in Remembrance of Him. 1825 SCOTT *Talism.* viii, There is no doubt that the primitive Christians used the services of the unconverted heathen. 1865 B. NORTH *Ourselves* 7 These are solemn statements, and surely they should make every unconverted man who hears them, Think.

*transf. a* 1864 FERRIER *Grk. Philos.* (1866) I. xii. 340 The ignorant and unconverted soul supposes that its knowledge of sensible objects is due to the impressions which it receives.

*absol.* 1657 BAXTER *Treat. Conversion* (title-p.), The lamentable State of the Unconverted. 1672 ALLEINE *Alarm* iv. 88 Some of the Unconverted carry their marks in their foreheads, more openly. *a* 1805 PALEY *Serm. Several Subjects* vii, It has been usual to divide all mankind into two classes, the converted and the unconverted. 1828 CARLYLE *Misc.* (1857) I. 239 They are in the camp of the Unconverted.

**2.** 'Not turned or changed from one form to another' (Webster, 1828-32).

**3.** *Law.* (See CONVERT *v.* 15.)

1884 V. R. SMITH in *Law Times Rep.* LI. 83/2 The premises ..were taken improperly, and are therefore unconverted.

**Unconve·rtible,** *a.* [UN-[1] 7 and 5 b.] Incapable of conversion (in various senses); inconvertible.

1695 CONGREVE *Love for L.* IV. xii, Ill stars, and unconvertible ignorance attend him! 1805 *Ann. Rev.* III. 622 The Mohammedans have been found unconvertible for this plain reason. 1864 BOWEN *Logic* v. 139 Unconvertible are A and B.

Hence **Unconvertibi·lity.**

1804 SOUTHEY *Lett.* (1856) I. 285 That the common opinion of the unconvertibility of this people is ill-founded.

**Unconvey·ed,** *ppl. a.* (UN-[1] 8 and 8 c.)

14.. *Chaucer's Parl. Foules* 518 (MS. St. John's, Oxf.) For office vnconveyid offt tym Anoyithe. 1696 STANHOPE *Chr. Pattern* (1711) 218 No property or claim any longer remaining unconveyed over.

†**Unconvi·ct,** *ppl. a. Obs.* [UN-[1] 8 b.] = next.

*a* 1618 SYLVESTER *Job* IV. 12 Against Job began his wrath to flame,..And..his Foe-friends, for so strict Condemning Job, untry'd and unconvict.

**Unconvi·cted,** *ppl. a.* (UN-[1] 8.)

1675 OTWAY *Alcibiades* IV. iii, The basest wretch not unconvicted dies. 1760 STERNE *Tr. Shandy* IV. *Slawkenb.'s Tale*, Am I to be the sport of Fortune and Slander—destined to be driven forth unconvicted—unheard—untouched? 1828 P. CUNNINGHAM *N. S. Wales* (ed. 3) II. 135, I see no reason whatever for excluding a man who has been once convicted, from any office the unconvicted now enjoy here. 1858 MERIVALE *Rom. Emp.* lii. (1865) VI. 286 He did not venture to command his execution, unarraigned and unconvicted. 1894 H. NISBET *Bush Girl's Rom.* 20 To personate the dead but unconvicted criminal.

**Unconvi·nce,** *v.* (UN-[2] 3.) 1815 *Zeluca* II. 42 Mrs. Delvayne said she would..unconvince herself if possible. **Unconvinceabi·lity.** 1868 [see UN-[1] 12]. **Unconvi·nceable,** *a.* (UN-[1] 7 b.) 1875 RUSKIN *Fors Clav.* lii. 100 [The bees] knocking themselves..again and again, unconvinceable of their fallacy. 1887 RIDER HAGGARD *Jess* xiv, Sturdy, determined, unconvinceable Englishmen.

**Unconvi·nced,** *ppl. a.* [UN-[1] 8.]

†**1.** Undisproved, unrefuted. *Obs.*[-1]

1643-5 MILTON *Divorce* II. xv, He lets go that sophistry unconvinc't, for that had bin to teach them else.

**2.** Not convinced or persuaded.

1675 J. OWEN *Indwelling Sin* xiii. (1732) 175 God is pleased to leave no Generation unconvinced of this Truth. 1681 FLAVEL *Meth. Grace* iv. 73 Never was there one tear of true repentance seen to drop from the eye of an unconvinced sinner. 1797 MRS. RADCLIFFE *Italian* ii, Vivaldi quitted her unconvinced by her arguments, and unmoved in his designs. 1819 LADY MORGAN *Autobiog.* (1859) 313 The man retired, satisfied at not losing his place, but unconvinced of his error. 1897 MARY KINGSLEY *W. Africa* 426 The official is unconvinced and goes up the ladder to see other officers about it.

Hence **Unconvi·ncedly** *adv.*; **-convi·ncedness.**

1642 D. ROGERS *Naaman* 847 Another let is unconvincedness of heart. 1850 F. W. NEWMAN *Phases* iv. 120 The soul ..has to learn from, and unconvincedly submit to, some external authority.

**Unconvincibi·lity.** (UN-[1] 12 and 5 b.) 1883 *Blackw. Mag.* Apr. 534/1 The obdurate unconvincibility of a fool. **Unconvi·ncible,** *a.* (UN-[1] 7 and 5 b.) 1787 tr. *Klopstock's Messiah* III. 102 Of an unconvincible mind. [In recent use.]

**Unconvi·ncing,** *ppl. a.* (UN-[1] 10.)

1653 MILTON *Hirelings* Wks. 1851 V. 357 To heap such unconvincing Citations as these in Religion,..argues not much Learning nor Judgment. 1885 W. S. GILBERT *Mikado* II. 41 A bald and unconvincing narrative.

Hence **Unconvi·ncingly** *adv.*

1891 F. W. NEWMAN *Cdl. Newman* 18 He quoted Scripture unconvincingly.

**Unco·nvoluted,** *ppl. a.* (UN-[1] 8.) *c* 1842 *Todd's Cycl. Anat.* III. 291/2 In the Phalangers.., the surface of the cerebral hemispheres is..unconvoluted. **Unconvu·lsed,** *ppl. a.* (UN-[1] 8.) 1794 G. ADAMS *Nat. & Exp. Philos.* I. ii. 59 The liquor will flow out steadily and unconvulsed.

**Uncoo·ked,** *ppl. a.* [UN-[1] 8. Cf. Du. *ongekookt*, G. *ungekocht*, Sw. *okokt*, Da. *ukogt*.]

**1.** Not cooked for eating.

[1775 ASH.] 1846 SOYER *Cookery* 381 Half a pound of lean uncooked ham. 1856 KANE *Arct. Expl.* II. i. 21 Fire would ruin the..vitality which belongs to its uncooked juices. 1870 N. F. HELE *Aldeburgh* vii. 78 They would eat freely of birds and uncooked liver.

**2.** *fig.* Not altered to suit a purpose.

1860 GEN. P. THOMPSON *Audi Alt.* III. clxxx. 223 The earliest reports..(which are always most to be depended on, as being un-cooked). 1865 BUCKSTONE in *Morn. Star* 13 Apr., We always present an uncooked balance-sheet.

**Uncooled,** *ppl. a.* Also 6 *Sc.* onculyt. (UN-[1] 8.)

1513 DOUGLAS *Æneid* XI. v. 65 And ȝit all warm, onculyt, sone thai have Bedelvyn thame, and in the erd begrave. 1648 HEXHAM II, *Ongekoelt*, vncooled. 1894 F. A. STEEL *Potter's Thumb* iii, Insipid as uncooled water on a summer's day.

**Uncoo·pered,** *ppl. a.* (UN-[1] 8.) 1757 W. THOMPSON *R. N. Adv.* 36 Your Memorialist..Prevented many hundred of Casks fresh packed, from being many Weeks uncoopered. **Unco-o·rdinated,** *ppl. a.* (UN-[1] 8.) 1892 *Spectator* 30 Apr. 612/2 There is plenty of imagination in the story, but it is uncoördinated.

**Unco·pe,** *v.* (UN-[2] 3: see COPE *sb.*[1] 9.)

1703 R. NEVE *City & C. Purchaser* 19 To remove the Earth over the Stones, or uncope it, as Workmen call it. *Ibid.* 256 The Stone..lay almost level with the Ground, and requir'd but very little uncopeing.

**Unco·ped,** *ppl. a.* (UN-[1] 8 c.)

1594 NASHE *Unfort. Trav.* Wks. (Grosart) V. 58 Those that beholding him at the stake yet vncoapte with, wisht him a sutable death to his vgly shape.

**Unco·piable,** *a.* (UN-[1] 7 b.)

1846 WORCESTER (citing Ware). 1856 RUSKIN *Mod. Paint.* III. IV. ix. § 17 His [*sc.* Turner's] finish is so delicate as to be nearly uncopiable. 1870 LOWELL *Among my Bks.* Ser. I. (1873) 226 This country-tradesman's son..could set high-bred wits..uncopiable lessons in drawing gentlemen.

**Unco·pied,** *ppl. a.* (UN-[1] 8.)

1737 W. KNOWLER in *Camden Misc.* IX. (1895) p. ix, There is four or five times the number of Letters uncopied for one transcribed. 1859 LADY MORGAN *Autobiog.* p. vii, The autograph letters, from which uncopied they have been printed.

†**Uncoqued,** *ppl. a. Obs.* [UN-[1] 8.] Uncooked.

1617 AINSWORTH *Annot. Exod.* xvi. 31 As it was gathered, and uncoqued, [it] was like honey wafers.

**Uncoque·ttish,** *a.* (UN-[1] 7.)

Also, in recent use, *uncoquettishness.*

1798 JANE AUSTEN *Northang. Abb.* vii, So pure and uncoquettish were her feelings. 1876 *Daily News* 8 Nov. 5/6 With a not uncoquettish shrug of the shoulders.

**Unco·rd,** *v.* [UN-[2] 4 b.] *trans.* To unstring (a bow); to free or disengage from a cord or cords.

*c* 1430 *Pilgr. Lyf Manhode* IV. lviii. (1869) 204 þe corde [with] which þe bowe was corded, and þat j haue vncorded. 1611 COTGR. s.v. *Desencordé*. 1622 MABBE tr. *Aleman's Guzman d'Alf.* II. 73 His servants punctually performed that, which his Master had commanded him; vn-cording..the very selfe-same Trunke. ?1712 *Dangerous Present* 4 If the Box had been uncorded, and the Cords drawn leisurely. 1754 G. K. in *Connoisseur* No. 33. 198 Pinning baskets, and cording trunks; as again..in unpinning, uncording, locking up foul linnen. 1842 BORROW *Bible in Spain* viii, The fellow..began to pull the trunks off the sumpter mule and commenced uncording them.

**Unco·rdial,** *a.* Also 5 *Sc.* -uall. [UN-[1] 7.]

†**1.** *Sc.* Uncongenial. *Obs.*[-1]

*c* 1470 HENRY *Wallace* IX. 430 Still in to pes he couth nocht lang endur; Wncorduall it was till his natur.

**2.** Not cordial; lacking in heartiness.

1643 PRYNNE *Sov. Power Parl.* III. 150 In which to be..cold, uncordiall, or timerous.., demerits a perpetuall brand of infamy. 1797 JANE AUSTEN *Sense & Sens.* xxxiv, A little proud-looking woman of uncordial address. 1824 SCOTT *St. Ronan's* xxv, We were bundled off to Scotland, coupled up like two pointers in a dog-cart, and..with much the same uncordial feeling towards each other. 1871 MEREDITH *H. Richmond* xxxvii, I took upon myself to be..always courteous, deliberate in my replies, and not uncordial.

Hence **Unco·rdially** *adv.*

1811 *Ora & Juliet* 50 She begged his forgiveness, which he granted, though somewhat uncordially.

†**Unco·re,** *ppl. a. Obs.*[-1] [UN-[1] 8 b.] Unchosen; not employed.

13.. *St. Gregory* (Vernon MS.) 530 Be stille, dame, and hold þi pes, let suche wordus ben vnkore.

**Unco·re,** *v.* (UN-[2] 3.)

1611 FLORIO, *Dis-callire*, to suple, to vnharden, to vncore. 1615 CHAPMAN *Odyss.* XVII. 194 Your son..knows clearly nothing more, Hear me yet speak, that can the truth uncore.

‖**Uncore prist.** *Obs.* [AF. *uncore* (F. *encore*) still + *prist* (F. *prêt*) ready.] (See quot. 1607.)

1607 COWELL *Interpr.*, *Vncore prist*, is a plee for the Defendant, being sewed for a debt due at a day past, to saue the forfeiture of his bond; saying, that he tendered the dept at the time and place, and that there was none to receiue it, and that he is now also readie to pay the same. *a* 1613 OVERBURY *Characters, Meere Common Lawyer* (1615) E 4 His loue letters..are stuft with Discontinuances, Remitters, and *Vncore prists*. 1685 J. KEBLE *Rep. K. B.* II. 178 He pleaded a tender by the Stranger and did not say *uncore prist*, for which cause the Plaintiff demurred. 1768 BLACKSTONE *Comm.* III. 303.

**Unco·rk,** *v.* [UN-[2] 3.]

**1.** *trans.* To draw the cork of (a bottle, etc.).

1727 POPE, etc. *Art of Sinking* 113 Uncork the bottle. 1784 *Phil. Trans.* LXXIV. 375 The funnel was taken out,.. and uncorked over a weighed cup. 1848 THACKERAY *Van. Fair* vi, He made the salad; and uncorked the Champagne. 1894 H. NISBET *Bush Girl's Rom.* 222 Timothy..brought out a fresh bottle of brandy. This he uncorked cautiously.

**b.** *transf.* and *fig.*

1749 FIELDING *Tom Jones* XVII. iv, The froth bursting forth from his lips the moment they were uncorked. 1892 ZANGWILL *Childr. Ghetto* I. x, In the ferment of freethought he had uncorked his soul, and it had run over with much froth. 1894 A. ROBERTSON *Nuggets*, etc. 17 Their courage had been uncorked.., and they felt as limp as a wet rag.

**2.** To draw out, withdraw (a cork, etc.).

1740 CHEYNE *Regimen* p. xlix, To uncork the Plugs, and concreted Recrements, that stop the Mouths of the perspiratory Glands.

Hence **Unco·rker**; **Unco·rking** *vbl. sb.*

1855 OWEN in R. Owen *Life* (1894) ii. 8 The uncorker uncorks the bottle. 1881 MISS BRADDON *Asphodel* I. 250 She sat..sipping her lemonade, half of which had been lost in the process of uncorking.

**Unco·rked,** *ppl. a.* [UN-[1] 8 and UN-[2] 8.] Not fitted or stopped with a cork; also, having the cork removed.

1791 O'KEEFFE *Wild Oats* I. i, You found the tenth bottle uncorked. 1835 *Wilson's Tales Borders* I. 305/1 Dead as uncorked small beer that has stood an hour in the sun. 1854 P. B. ST. JOHN *Amy Moss* 206 The whiskey bottle stood before him uncorked. 1878 ABNEY *Photogr.* 148 The water ..should stand in an uncorked bottle for twenty-four hours.

†**Unco·rn.** [UN-[1] 4 b.] Evil grain; 'wild oats'.

1513 DOUGLAS *Æneid* IV. Prol. 13 Quhar schame is lost, thair..Ripis ȝour perellus fruitis and oncorn. 1710 RUDDIMAN *Gloss. Douglas' Æneis* s.v., In some places of Scotland they say, that one hath sown his uncorn.

**Unco·ronated,** *a.* (UN-[1] 8. Cf. next.) 1802 H. MARTIN *Helen of Glenross* III. 162 If an uncoronated cloathing was put on any one of these ducal steeds, he would kick it to pieces. **Unco·roneted,** *a.* (UN-[1] 8.) 1817 BENTHAM *Parl. Reform* Introd. 19 Great Landholding, and as yet uncoroneted Commoners, styled Country Gentlemen. 1852 ROBERTSON *Lect.* (1858) 159 That daring warrior..who has been laid aside uncoroneted and almost unhonoured.

**Unco·rporal,** *a.* ? *Obs.* (UN-[1] 7 and 5 b.)

1565 GOLDING *Ovid's Met.* Epist. (1567) b j b, God the father ..made first of all Both heauen and earth vncorporall. 1570 T. NORTON tr. *Nowel's Catech.* 25 b, God..made..the vncorporall spirites whom we call Angels. 1590 SWINBURN

*Testaments* 218 All the goods, & cattels,..whether they bee moueable or immoueable, corporal or vncorporall.

**Unco·rpulent,** *a.* (Un-[1] 7.) **1827** Pollok *Course T.* viii. 70 The man Of tithes,..ungowned, unbeneficed, Uncorpulent.

**Uncorre·ct,** *ppl. a.* and *a.* [Un-[1] 8 b, 7, 5 b.]

†**1.** = Uncorrected *ppl. a. Obs.*

**1502** Atkynson tr. *De Imitatione* i. xvi. (1893) 165 We wolde that other that offendeth shulde be straitly correcte & our selfe more coulpable vncorrecte. **1553** *Respublica* Prol. 51 That yls whiche long tyme have reigned vncorrecte shall nowe foreuer bee redressed with effecte.

**2.** = Incorrect *a.*

**1568** Charteris *Pref. Lyndesay's Wks.* A j b, Quhat difference is betuix..correct and vncorrect Imprenting, salbe cleirlie sene. **1669** Dryden *Wild Gallant* Pref. A 2 b, You have..receiv'd with Applause, as bad, and as uncorrect Playes from other Men. **1702** *Eng. Theophrast.* 23 The Ancients, tho' generally uneven and uncorrect, have yet here and there some fine touches. **1752** Salmon *Universal Trav.* i. viii. 20 Before the Missionaries taught them, their tables of eclipses were very uncorrect.

**Uncorre·ctable,** *a.* (Un-[1] 7 b.)

Also, in recent use, *uncorrectible.*

**1560** Whitehorne *Arte Warre* 6 b, Parte of theim are wonte to bee enemies of warre, parte vncorrectable.

**Uncorre·cted,** *ppl. a.* [Un-[1] 8 and 5 b.]

**1.** Not freed from error or inexactness; not revised or emended.

**1387** Trevisa *Higden* (Rolls) III. 73 He putte Ianeuer and Feuerrer to þe bygynnynge of þe ȝere, and so þe ȝere lefte among þe Romayns vncorrected anon to Iulius Cesar his tyme. **1548** Elyot, *Incorrectus*,..vncorrected. **1598** Florio, *Scorretto*, vncorrected, vnpolished, rude, rough. **1699** Bentley *Phalaris* 251 Whole Lines were omitted by the Stone-Cutter, and pass'd uncorrected. **1711** G. Hickes *Two Treat. Chr. Priesth.* (ed. 3) I. 170 If these holy Men's Notion..be..a Mistake, it..stood uncorrected for almost sixteen hundred Years. **1798** Southey *Lett.* (1856) I. 55 They are, I know, hastily written and uncorrected. **1819** Shelley *Let.* Pr. Wks. 1888 II. 299 You are to write me uncorrected letters, just as the words come. **1837** Goring & Pritchard *Microgr.* 77 Perfectly direct day-light also gives apparent achromatism with any common uncorrected lenses.

**2.** Not chastised or punished.

**1475** *Bk. Noblesse* (Roxb.) 56 So many wrecchid synnes as among us dailie uncorrectid hathe reigned. **1513** More *Hist. Rich. III*, Wks. 40/1 Robbers and riuers walking at libertie vncorrected. **1548** Elyot, *Incastigatus*,..not chastised: vncorrected. **1647** Hexham i, Vncorrected, *ongestraft.* **1670** Baxter *Cure Ch. Div.* 338 Parents must not be so patient with sin as to leave their children uncorrected.

**3.** Not improved by training or discipline; not guided into the proper course.

**1599** Shaks. *Hen. V*, v. ii. 50 The freckled Cowslip, Burnet and greene Clouer, Wanting the Sythe, withall vncorrected, ranke; Conceiues by idlenesse. **1718** *Freethinker* No. 23 ⁋ 6 Amongst the many Abuses, of which we stand uncorrected. **1750** Carte *Hist. Eng.* II. 790 A fine youth, but..having too much of his mother's spirit, uncorrected as yet by reflection and experience. **1865** Froude *Short Stud.* (1867) I. 161 Submissiveness, humility, obedience produce if uncorrected in politics a nation of slaves.

**4.** Not counteracted or neutralized.

**1694** Salmon *Bate's Dispens.* (1713) 373/2 If any of the kinds of Flowers be used uncorrected, it is much better to use their Infusion in Wine. **1825** Scott *Betrothed* xxi, During slumber, when Imagination, uncorrected by the organs of sense, weaves her own fantastic web. **1899** *Allbutt's Syst. Med.* VI. 829 Such consequences may be produced in uncorrected hypermetropia.

†**Uncorre·ctly,** *adv. Obs.* (Un-[1] 11, 5 b.)

**1706** Stevens *Span. Dict.* i, *Incorrectamente*, uncorrectly. **1716** M. Davies *Athen. Brit.* iii. *Diss. Physick* 32 It had been printed long before uncorrectly, at Norimberg 1532.

†**Uncorre·ctness.** *Obs.* (Un-[1] 12, 5 b.)

**1669** Dryden *Wild Gallant* Pref., I doubt not but you will see in it the uncorrectness of a young writer. **1711** Shaftesb. *Charac.* III. 274 Their Remis[s]ness, Uncorrectness, Insipidness, and downright Ignorance of all literate Art.

**Unco·rrelated,** *ppl. a.* (Un-[1] 8.) **1881** *Med. Rev.* II. 43 Occurring at haphazard, or as uncorrelated coincidences.

**Uncorrespo·ndency.** (Un-[1] 12, 5 b: cf. next.)

**1659** Gauden *Tears Ch.* iv. xi. 459 This uncorrespondency, to which I am upon those grounds compelled.

**Uncorrespo·ndent,** *a.* (Un-[1] 7 and 5 b.)

*a* **1631** Sir W. Cornwallis *Ess.* ii. lii. (1632) 334 Wee must offer the eyes of men nothing vncorrespondent to the peculiar grace of our callings. **1659** Gauden *Tears Ch.* iii. xxviii. 363 Vicious extremes..are contrary to each other, and yet uncorrespondent with that vertue from which they are divided. **1784** J. Potter *Virtuous Villagers* I. 43 Nothing can be more preposterous or uncorrespondent. **1844** Elliott *Horæ Apoc.* (1862) IV. 14 Very much as in a famous, and probably not uncorrespondent, prophecy of Ezekiel.

**Uncorrespo·nding,** *ppl. a.* (Un-[1] 10 and 5 b.)

**1826** Lamb *Elia* ii. *Pop. Fallacies* xiii, His insufferable procerity of stature, and uncorresponding dwarfishness of observation. **1886** [see Un-[1] 10].

†**Unco·rrigible,** *a. Obs.* (Un-[1] 7 and 5 b.)

*a* **1420** *Wycliffite Bible* (1850) III. 39 *marg.*, Stryue thou not..with vncorrigible men bi word of blamyng. *c* **1440** *Gesta Rom.* xxxvii. 151 We vncorrigible wrecchis conne not sece of oure synnynge. **1539** Elyot *Cast. Helthe* 69 Either for vncorrigible vices, or infortunate chances. **1583** Golding *Calvin on Deut.* xiii. 77 To blinde the reprobates and such as are vncorrigible. **1655** Gurnall *Chr. in Arm.* i. (1669) 62/1 We wrestle against Providence, when uncorrigible under the..dispensations of God towards us. **1692** South *Serm.* (1697) I. 489 Such is the peculiar Insolence of this sort of Men, such the uncorrigible Vileness of all slavish Spirits.

**Uncorro·borated,** *ppl. a.* (Un-[1] 8.) [**1775** Ash.] **1911** Craik *Clarendon* I. 100 He found a 'copy' of a paper which supported his father's uncorroborated evidence. **Uncorro·ded,** *ppl. a.* (Un-[1] 8.) **1685** Boyle *Salubr. Air* 65 It will leave all the rest uncorroded, and fall onely upon the Gold.

**Unco·rrugated,** *ppl. a.* (Un-[1] 8.) **1863** Cowden Clarke *Shaks. Char.* ix. 228 How the velvets would have escaped with uncorrugated pile! †**Uncorru·mped,** *ppl. a. Obs.* [Un-[1] 8.] Uncorrupted. *a* **1400–50** *Alexander* 4334 For þe aire within oure habitacle is ai vn-corumpid.

**Uncorru·pt,** *a.* [Un-[1] 7 and 5 b.]

**1.** = Incorrupt *a.* 1.

**1382** Wyclif 1 *Cor.* ix. 25 Thei [strive]..that thei take a coruptible crowne, we forsothe vncorupt. *a* **1425** tr. *Arderne's Treat. Fistula*, etc. 43 It is certayne þat bones shul noȝt be corrupte wiþin a fourtniȝt if þai war vncorrupte afore þat tyme. *c* **1450** Capgrave *Life St. Gilbert* 75 Ther was bred kept sextene ȝere aftir his deth, on-corupte, on-mouled. *a* **1513** Fabyan *Chron.* v. cxxvii. 108 Thou shalt fynde our thre bodyes hoole & vncorrupte. **1555** Eden *Decades* (Arb.) 264 If it [*sc.* ruby] coomme owt of the fyer vncorrupte, it becommeth of the coloure of a burnynge cole. **1600** Surflet *Countrie Farme* iii. xliii. 509 The leaues of the Bay tree doe preserue, keepe vncorrupt and make faster the fish that is fried. **1692** Ray *Disc.* ii. iv. (1693) 127 The real Shells themselves..remaining still entire and uncorrupt. **1733** Tull *Horse-Hoeing Husb.* viii. 82 The Seeds..are so hardy, as to lie sound and uncorrupt for many Years..in the Earth. **1794** R. J. Sulivan *View Nat.* I. 254 So that several substances may be preserved in it uncorrupt for a considerable time.

**2.** = Incorrupt *a.* 2.

*c* **1440** *Alph. Tales* 344 Sho sent hur one þat was a maydyn and vncorrupte. **1535** Coverdale *Wisd.* vi. 19 The kepinge of yᵉ lawes is perfeccion & an vn corrupte life. **1561** T. Norton *Calvin's Inst.* iii. 269 Honest in dede and of vncorrupt maners. **1597** Hooker *Eccl. Pol.* v. lvi. § 8 That which in him made our nature vncorrupt. **1638** Junius *Paint. Ancients* 6 Such Artificers..carry in their mind an uncorrupt image of perfect beautie. **1670** Cotton *Espernon* ii. vii. 304, I have..preserv'd my Hands clean, my Conscience uncorrupt. **1725** Berkeley *Proposal*, etc., Wks. 1871 III. 215 The pure uncorrupt doctrine of the gospel. **1784** Cowper *Task* ii. 400, I would express him simple, grave, sincere; In doctrine uncorrupt. *c* **1814** Southey *Ode War Amer.* vi, Thy martyrs purchased at the stake Faith uncorrupt for thine inheritance. **1871** Meredith *H. Richmond* liv, History, like the air we breathe, must be in motion to keep us uncorrupt.

**b.** Of language, texts, etc.

**1596** Dalrymple tr. *Leslie's Hist. Scot.* (S.T.S.) I. 95 Mair than 2 thowsand ȝeirs thay haue keipet the toung hail vncorrupte. **1600** E. Blount tr. *Conestaggio* 1 An enimie to the vncorrupt writing of Historiographers. **1693** J. Edwards *Author. O. & N. Test.* 53 These Masoretick Doctors have kept it [*sc.* the Hebrew text] undepraved and uncorrupt. **1845** Kitto *Cycl. Bibl. Lit.* I. 377/1 That..their writings..should be preserved entire and uncorrupt.

**3.** = Incorrupt *a.* 3.

**1651** Hobbes *Leviath.* i. x. 42 A learned and uncorrupt Judge. **1656** Earl Monm. tr. *Boccalini's Advts. fr. Parnass.* i. v. (1674) 9 The eternal glory of the uncorrupt Venetian Justice. **1724** Swift *Drapier's Lett.* Wks. 1755 V. ii. 114 The greatest, the wisest, and the most uncorrupt minister I ever conversed with. **1774** J. Reade in *Buccleuch MSS.* (Hist. MSS. Comm.) I. 416 A respectable, unshaken, uncorrupt majority. **1841** Borrow *Zincali* I. xii. i. 192 Pure and uncorrupt justice has never existed in Spain.

**Uncorru·pted,** *ppl. a.* [Un-[1] 8 and 5 b.]

**1.** Of organic matter: Not corrupted or decomposed.

*c* **1400** *Destr. Troy* 8724 The body..may not long vpon loft ly vncorruppit. **1555** Eden *Decades* (Arb.) 131 Only one remayned vncorrupted, the other being putrified by reason of the longe vyage. **1610** Holland *Camden's Brit.* (1637) 541 His hand remained heere uncorrupted many hundred yeeres after. **1615** G. Sandys *Trav.* 134 The iuyce of Cedars..preserued them vncorrupted. **1707** Mortimer *Husb.* (1721) I. 286 It keepeth all things uncorrupted which are put into it. **1734** tr. *Rollin's Anc. Hist.* xvi. i. (1827) VI. 344 The body continued uncorrupted all that time. **1870** Bryant *Iliad* xix. II. 230 The body shall remain Even more than uncorrupted.

**2.** Of persons: Not rendered morally unsound; not debased or depraved; not influenced by bribes.

**1565** Cooper *Thesaurus*, *Integri testes*, witnesses vncorrupted. **1570** T. Norton tr. *Nowel's Catech.* 41 b, Their life, which..shalbe examined by the vncorrupted and seuere iudge according to the truth. **1599** *Life Sir T. More* in Wordsw. *Eccl. Biog.* (1853) II. 185 John More his father a civill man,..just, and uncorrupted. **1620** Middleton & Rowley *World Tost at Tennis* 826 Thou, uncorrupted Lawyer, Virtue's great miracle. **1732** Pope *Epit. on Gay* 6 Above Temptation, in a low Estate, And uncorrupted, ev'n among the Great. **1754** Wilkes *Corr.* (1805) I. 26 Gentlemen, I come here uncorrupting, and I promise you I shall ever be uncorrupted. **1849–50** Alison *Hist. Eur.* VIII. li. § 8. 231 Calamities..draw forth the energy of the uncorrupted portion of mankind. **1875** Jowett *Plato* (ed. 2) I. 367 Not the corrupted youth only,..but their uncorrupted elder relatives.

**b.** Of personal attributes, actions, etc.

**1571** Golding *Calvin on Ps.* lxvi. 245 He expresseth trew and uncorrupted woorshippinge. *a* **1586** Sidney *Arcadia* iii. (1912) 401 Glad to receyve an uncorrupted libertie. **1615** G. Sandys *Trav.* 8 The nuptiall sheetes..are..preserued..as a testimonie of their vncorrupted virginities. **1697** Dryden *Æneis* viii. 548 Thus frugally they earn their children's bread, And uncorrupted keep their nuptial bed. **1713** Berkeley *Guardian* No. 49 ⁋ 5 It is this alone that makes them desirable to an uncorrupted taste. **1797** S. & Ht. Lee *Canterb. T.* (1799) I. 303 The lad, whose good-nature was yet uncorrupted by the world, greeted her with cordiality. **1847** Helps *Friends in C.* i. i. 7 To do that, he must have an uncorrupted judgment.

**3.** Unadulterated.

**1539** Elyot *Cast. Helthe* (1541) 57 So true a poticary, that hath always drowges uncorrupted. **1683** *Roxb. Ball.* (1885) V. 564 Springs and Streams that still run pure, Nature's uncorrupted Goods.

Hence **Uncorru·ptedly** *adv.*; **-ru·ptedness.**

**1570** T. Norton tr. *Nowel's Catech.* 2 b, How godlynesse, holynesse, and Religion, are to be purely and vncorruptedly yelded to God. **1611** Florio, *Incorrottibilita*, vncorruptednesse. **1644** Milton *Areop.* (Arb.) 48 The grace of infallibility, and uncorruptednesse. **1783** Blair *Lect. Rhet.* xxviii. II. 97 The purity and uncorruptedness of their morals. **1882** Mayne Reid in *N.Y. Tribune* 19 July, Even when the contest is conducted..uncorruptedly.

**Uncorru·ptible,** *a.* [Un-[1] 7 and 5 b.]

**1.** = Incorruptible *a.* 1.

**1382** Wyclif *John* Prol., Bigynnynge the work of an vncoruptible word, other Goddis sone. **1382** — *Rom.* i. 23 The glorie of God vncorruptible. **1535** Coverdale 1 *Peter* v. 4 Ye shal receaue the vncorruptible crowne of glory. **1594** Carew *Huarte's Exam. Wits* (1616) 49 One of the greatest arguments..that the reasonable soule is vncorruptible. **1611** Bible *Rom.* i. 23 The glory of the vncorruptible God.

**2.** = Incorruptible *a.* 2.

**1843** tr. *Custine's Empire of Czar* II. 316 It was to the advice of these uncorruptible men that he owed much of his glory. **1897** Olive Schreiner *Trooper P. Halket* Ded., An uncorruptible justice and a broad humanity.

Hence **Uncorruptibi·lity; -ru·ptibleness.**

**1382** Wyclif 1 *Pet.* iii. 4 The ilke that is the hid man of herte, in vncoruptibilite of quyete..and mylde spirit. **1579** Fulke *Heskins' Parl.* 186 This corruptible nature..could not..be brought to vncorruptiblenesse and life. **1645** Pagitt *Heresiogr.* (1661) 150 They that teach this, do thereby deny the uncorruptiblenesse of that divine seed.

**Uncorru·pting,** *ppl. a.* (Un-[1] 10.)

*a* **1711** Ken *Hymns Festiv.* Poet. Wks. 1721 I. 223 For uncorrupting Myrrh, an Heart sincere I'll bring. **1754** [see Uncorrupted *ppl. a.* 2].

**Uncorru·ption.** [Un-[1] 12 and 5 b.] Absence of corruption; uncorrupt character or condition.

**1382** Wyclif *Rom.* ii. 7 Glorie, and honour, and vncorripcioun, to hem sekynge euerelasting lyf. *a* **1420** *Wycliffite Bible* Wisd. vi. 19 *marg.*, That is, of goostly vncorrupcioun, bi eschewing of synne. **1526** Tindale *Titus* ii. 7 Shew vncorrupcion, honestie, and the wholsome worde which cannot be rebuked. **1542** Udall *Erasm. Apoph.* 74 b, Onely in the children remained the aunciente integritee & uncorrupcion. **1802–12** Bentham *Ration. Judic. Evid.* (1827) IV. 56 That perfect purity and uncorruption which has so long been regarded as a characteristic..of an English judge. **1824** — *Bk. Fallacies* iv. vii. 284.

**Uncorru·ptive,** *a.* (Un-[1] 7 and 5 b.)

**1737** R. Glover *Leonidas* vii. 412 Those other climes of uncorruptive joy, Which Heav'n in dark futurity conceals.

**Uncorru·ptly,** *adv.* [Un-[1] 11 and 5 b.] In an uncorrupt manner; genuinely; correctly.

**1553** Brende *Q. Curtius* vii. 57, I shall declare vncorruptly the sayinges which the eldest of those embassadours dyd speake. **1565** Cooper *Thesaurus* s.v. *Integre*, To bestow his time vncorruptely and honestly. **1647** Hexham i, Vncorruptly, *onverderflick.* *a* **1700** Evelyn *Diary* 8 Feb. 1678, The Conte de Castel Mellor..had behaved himselfe..uncorruptly in all his ministrie. **1736** Butler *Anal.* i. vi. 164 Whether the revelation itself be uncorruptly handed down.

**Uncorru·ptness.** [Un-[1] 12 and 5 b.] The quality of being uncorrupt; incorruptness.

**1583** Golding *Calvin on Deut.* xlviii. 287 Wee must..worshippe him with such vncorruptnesse, as all ydoles bee vtterly cast downe. **1611** Bible *Titus* ii. 7 In doctrine shewing vncorruptnesse, gravity, sinceritie. **1671** E. Chamberlayne *Pres. St. Eng.* i. (ed. 5) 194 These are the Principal Judges,..persons for Knowledge, Courage, Uncorruptness, &c., equal..to any other in former Kings Raigns. *c* **1728** Earl of Ailesbury *Mem.* (1890) 705 He makes amends by the high stock he hath of zeal, industry and uncorruptness. [**1860** S. Wilberforce *Addr. Cand. Ordination* 124 Gravity, sincerity, uncorruptness and habitual soundness of speech.]

†**Unco·rsayed,** *ppl. a. Obs.*—[1] (Un-[1] 8. Sense doubtful.) *a* **1400–50** *Alexander* 3775 Sone as þai wist of his will þai wiȝtly him sente Ten vncorsayd coltis.

† **Unco·rse,** *v. Obs.* Also 5 vncorce. [Un-[2] 5.] *trans.* To remove from the body.

*c* **1470** Harding *Chron.* xcv. x, This Audry..In Ely bode ..To tyme hir soule were lesed and vncorced. *Ibid.* cv. xv, Before his soule was passed and vncorced.

**Unco·rseted,** *ppl. a.* (Un-[1] 8.) **1856** P. H. Gosse *Tenby* ii, The busy bathing-women—uncouth, uncorsetted figures.

†**Unco·rven,** *ppl. a.* [Un-[1] 8 b. Cf. MDu. *ongecorven*, Du. *ongekorven.*] Unpruned.

*c* **1380** Chaucer *Former Age* 14 Vn-koruen [*v.r.* Vncaruyn] and vn-grobbed lay the vyne.

†**Unco·st**[1]. *Obs.*—[1] [Un-[1] 4 b + Cost *sb.*[1]] Bad disposition, evil nature.

*c* **1220** *Bestiary* 192 in *O. E. Misc.* 7 Oc walke..mildelike among men; no mod ðu ne cune,..ne mannes vncost.

†**Uncost**[2]. *Obs.* [ad. MDu. (also mod.Du.) *onkosten* pl., f. *on-* Un-[1] 4 b + *kost* Cost *sb.*[2] So G. *unkosten.*] Additional or incidental expenses. (Cf. Oncost.)

*c* **1480** *Howard Househ. Bks.* (Roxb.) 285 Paid for the aparayll of a chymeny...Item, for uncostes of the same to brynge it to the water syde, .xd. **1488** *Acta Dom. Audit.* (1839) 117/1 Þe Custemez, fraucht & vncostis maid be the said george of þe said malt. **1511–2** *Acc. Ld. High Treas. Scot.* IV. 334 For fraucht of sex kistis of sukkoure,..and for the uncostis of thame fra the Feir to Leith. **1581** *Burgh Rec. Edinb.* (1882) IV. 217 The pryce he gaif thairfor with all vncostes maid thairon to be payit to him.

**Unco·st**[3]. [Un-[1] 12.] Lack of cost.

**1868** Pusey *Serm. Pharisaism* 9 Such acts..cost us individually little,..and may give evidence of their valuelessness by their uncost.

**Unco·stly,** *a.* [Un-[1] 7. Cf. MDu. *oncostelijc*, *-lic*, Du. *onkostelijk*, MLG. *unkostlik.*] Inexpensive.

**1638** Junius *Paint. Ancients* 52 Making a very fine and uncostly shew. **1651** Jer. Taylor *Serm. for Year* i. xv. 186 A mans spirit is naturally carelesse of baser and uncostly materials. **1798** *Poetry Anti-Jacobin* No. 15. 76 Uncostly cabbage springs from cabbage seed. **1837** Lockhart *Scott* (1839) VII. 384 A volume every second month in this new and uncostly form. **1893** J. W. Barry *Stud. Corsica* 204 The simple, primitive, and uncostly type that one sees at Pompeii.

Hence **Unco·stliness.**
1861 Mill *Utilit.* ii. 11 The greater permanency, safety, uncostliness,..of the former [pleasures].

**Uncou·ch,** *v.* [Un-$^2$ 5 and 7.]
**1.** *trans.* To raise up from a couch.
c1430 *Pilgr. Lyf Manhode* II. xxxv. (1869) 154 It is a god that..wole that men cowchen him ofte and vncowche him. 1611 Florio, *Dislettare,* to vnbed, to vncouch.
**2.** To drive (an animal) out of its lair. Also *fig.*
a1562 G. Cavendish *Wolsey* (1893) 89 The kyng..commaunded the hunts to oncouche the boore. 1609 T. Jackson *Londons New-Yeeres Gift* 14 b, They are resembled vnto Foxes, whom we are now to vncouch. *Ibid.* 20 b, In the next place, we are to vncouch the Foxes Ecclesiasticall.
**b.** *intr.* Of an animal: To come out of its lair.
1860 Ld. Lytton *Lucile* II. iv. § II. 4 As a young fawn uncouches..from the fern where some hunter approaches.
Hence **Uncou·ched** *ppl. a.*, **Uncou·ching** *vbl. sb.*
1609 T. Jackson (*title*), Londons New-Yeeres Gift, or the Vncovching of the Foxe. *Ibid.* Ded. A ij b, My selfe [shall] remaine the safer from the teeth of vncouched Foxes, if [etc.].

**Uncou·nsellable,** *a.* [Un-$^1$ 7 b, 5 b.]
**1.** Of persons: Not open to counsel.
Very common in the 17th century.
a1578 Lindesay (Pitscottie) *Chron. Scot.* (S.T.S.) I. 266 Takand no thocht as ane man wncons[al]able. 1646 J. Whitaker *Uzziah* 28 Pride..makes the soul unconsellable. 1680 C. Nesse *Ch. Hist.* 60 Those sturdy rebels were uncounsellable. 1825 Jamieson, *Unbiddable,* unadvisable, uncounselable.
†**2.** Of things: Inadvisable. *Obs.*
a1674 Clarendon *Hist. Reb.* (J.), It would have been uncounsellable to have march'd to any distance, and have left such an enemy at their backs.

**Uncou·nselled,** *ppl. a.* (Un-$^1$ 8.)
c1400 *Rom. Rose* 6868 Wher so they clad or naked be Vnconceiled goth ther noon fro me. a1500 *Voc.* in *MS. Harl.* 2257 fol. 69 b, *Inconsultus,* vnconsiled. 1648 Hexham II, *Onberaden,* Vncouncelled. 1786 *Francis the Philanthropist* III. 110 Parentless, uncounselled, and unguided, I yielded to his solicitations. 1796 Burke *Let. Noble Lord* Wks. VIII. 17 When it appeared, nothing to subdue it was left uncounselled, nor unexecuted, as far as I could prevail. 1818 Scott *Br. Lamm.* xxix, Alone and uncounselled, I involved myself in these perils. 1887 Bowen *Æneid* III. 452 Pilgrims depart uncounselled, and bear no love to the shrine.

**Uncou·ntable,** *a.* [Un-$^1$ 7 b.]
**1.** = Unaccountable *a.* 2 b. *Obs.*$^{-1}$
a1400-50 *Bk. Curtasye* 544 in *Babees Bk.*, The Controllour shalle wryte to hym,..Vncountabulle he is, as y 3ou say.
**2.** Too numerous to be counted; innumerable.
1582 Stanyhurst *Æneis,* etc. (Arb.) 142 But toe what eend labor I..Thee stars too number, poincts playnely vncountabil opning. 1586 W. Webbe *Eng. Poetrie* (Arb.) 36 The vncountable rabble of ryming Ballet makers. 1614 Raleigh *Hist. World* I. i. § 11. 15 So were not those vncountable glorious bodies set in the firmament, to no other end, than to adorne it. 1829 Marryat *F. Mildmay* xix, Nests in numbers uncountable. 1876 Mrs. Whitney *Sights & Ins.* xxi, Millions of little uncountable, inseparable threads.
**b.** Of the pulse, etc.: Too rapid to be counted.
1823 Gr. Kennedy *Father Clement* x. (1824) 203 Ernest gave his hand, and Dormer pressed it on his temples. The full throb seemed uncountable. 1897 *Allbutt's Syst. Med.* III. 623 The tongue soon becomes dry, the pulse is uncountable.
**3.** Inestimable, immense.
1858 Carlyle *Fredk. Gt.* III. viii. I. 263 Which has been of uncountable advantage to Brandenburg. 1860 *Cornh. Mag.* 134 To give uncountable happiness and delight to the world.
Hence **Uncou·ntably** *adv.*
1599 Nashe *Lenten Stuffe* 27 Her Maiesties tributes and customes..augmenteth and enlargeth vncountably.

**Uncou·nted,** *ppl. a.* (Un-$^1$ 8.)
a1500 in *Makculloch & Gray MSS.* (S.T.S.) 55 Kingis & knichtis in company Vncountit curiously vp I kest. 1597 Shaks. 2 *Hen. IV,* Induct. 18 The blunt Monster, with vncounted heads, The still discordant, wauering Multitude. 1611 Cotgr. s.v. *Brebis,* The wolfe eats counted, as well as uncounted, sheepe. 1677 Sir T. Herbert *Trav.* (ed. 3) 375 Above threescore millions of Men, Women being uncounted. 1782 Johnson *Ode Death Levet* viii, The busy day—the peaceful night, Unfelt, uncounted, glided by. 1802-12 Bentham *Ration. Judic. Evid.* (1827) V. 700 A mass of uncounted money. 1837 Carlyle *Misc.* (1840) V. 17 How they lay, for uncounted ages and æons,..Silently imbedded in the rock. 1868 Morris *Earthly Par.* (1870) I. II. 511 Upon the floor uncounted medals lay.

**Uncou·ntenanced,** *ppl. a.* (Un-$^1$ 8.)
1776 Mickle *Camoens' Lusiad* Introd. 129 Fanshaw's Lusiad, where..there are puns, conceits, and low quaint expressions, uncountenanced by the original. 1820 T. Mitchell *Aristoph.* I. 159 Desertion, uncountenanced as yet by the example of the unprincipled Alcibiades, was held in strong and merited abhorrence.

**Uncountera·cted,** *ppl. a.* (Un-$^1$ 8.)
1809-10 Coleridge *Friend* (1818) III. 256 Some general law by the untempered and uncounteracted action of which both would be prevented. a1864 Ferrier *Grk. Philos.* (1866) I. x. 217 All the..difficulties..would continue uncounteracted.

**Uncounterba·lanced,** *ppl. a.* (Un-$^1$ 8.)
1780 Bentham *Princ. Legisl.* xii. § 23 In proportion to that part of the primary [mischief] which remains unexcluded or uncounterbalanced. 1862 Lytton *Str. Story* II. 226 Power infinitely greater, and, when uncounterbalanced, infinitely more dangerous than that which superstition exaggerates in magic.

**Uncou·nterfeit,** *a.* (Un-$^1$ 7.)
a1542 Wyatt in *Anglia* (1896) XIX. 186 And as it is it doeth appeare Vncontrefaict mistrust to barr. c1585 [R. Browne] *Answ. Cartwright* 24 They are true and vncounterfaite sacraments. a1626 Bp. Andrewes *Serm.* (1629) 64 If it be true, and vncounterfeit, a first degree it is, and not lightly to be accompted of. 1669 Cokaine *Poems* 150 Her breath was sweet as Venus bower of bliss, Her joyes uncounterfeit; and not remiss. 1834 De Quincey *Autob. Sk.* Wks. 1853 I. 98 These proportions are best measured from the fathoming ground of a real uncounterfeit sympathy.

**Uncou·nterfeit,** *v.* (Un-$^2$ 3.)
1580 T. Lupton *Sivqila* 10 *Sivqila.* Alas, they counterfaite themselues, vntyll they get in. *Omen.* And when they vncounterfeite themselues againe, why are they not thrust out?

**Uncou·nterfeited,** *ppl. a.* (Un-$^1$ 8.)
1571 Golding *Calvin on Ps.* Ep. Ded. 2 If your vertues be uncounterfayted. 1613 Sir W. Alexander in Sidney *Arcadia* (1622) 343 Hee went with an vncounterfeited reuerence. 1625 K. Long tr. *Barclay's Argenis* v. xiv. 383 All that were present honoured this reall and uncounterfeited vertue.

**Uncounterma·ndable,** *a.* (Un-$^1$ 7 b.) 1846 Worcester (citing M. Hale). **Uncou·ntrified,** *ppl. a.* (Un-$^1$ 8.) 1839 Hood *Rur. Felicity* 86 So one isn't so very uncountrified in the very heart of the town.

**Uncountry**: see Un-$^1$ 12 b.

**Uncou·ple,** *v.* [Un-$^2$ 4 b. Cf. MDu. *ontcoppelen, -copplen,* Du. *ontkoppelen.*]
**1.** *trans.* To release (dogs) from being fastened together in couples; to set free for the chase.
13.. *Guy Warw.* (A.) 2512 A gret bore þai founden, y-wis, & hij uncopled her houndis. 1390 Gower *Conf.* I. 119 The houndes weren in a throwe Uncoupled and the hornes blowe. c1410 *Master of Game* (MS. Digby 182) xiii, þe firste bolde houndes hunteth alle manere of beestes þat his maister will vncouple hym to. a1450 *Knt. de la Tour* (1868) 43 The houndes were uncoupeled on hem, and chaced and bote hem spitously bi the eeres and thies. 1555 *Instit. Gentl.* H vj b, Likewise huntyng in his kinde, as to fleshe a dogge, to vncupple houndes, to followe them [etc.]. 1576 Turberv. *Venerie* 102 They shall place their houndes in some faire place.., forbidding the varlet that he uncouple them not without their knowledge. 1600 Surflet *Countrie Farme* VII. xxv. 847 He must not vncouple any of his dogs; but onely marke the way that the Hart runneth. 1821 Scott *Kenilw.* xii, Ere we had uncoupled the hounds, he..turns bridle..and leaves us to hunt at leisure by ourselves. 1842 Mrs. Gore, etc. *Fascination* xi, Order the hounds to be uncoupled, and I will beat the underwood with three or four of the surest.
**b.** *absol.* (Also in fig. use.)
c1386 Chaucer *Monk's T.* 512 He maked hym so konnyng and so sowple That longe tyme it was er tirannye Or any vice dorste on hym vncowple. c1410 *Master of Game* (MS. Digby 182) xxxv, Þe herte houndes..þat before haue be ladde by somme forster or parker þedur as þei shull vncouple. 1596 *Edward III,* I. ii. 91 What, are the stealing Foxes fled and gone, Before we could vncupple at their heeles? 1599 Shaks. *Mids. N.* IV. i. 112 My Loue shall heare the musicke of my hounds. Vncouple in the Westerne valley.
**2.** To unfasten, disconnect, detach.
a1533 Ld. Berners *Gold. Bk. M. Aurel.* (1546) N nj b, How far is our vnderstandyng vncoupled for thy thoughtes. 1548 Udall, etc. *Erasm. Par. John* xiv. 87 b, That shall so couple you and vs together, that neyther lyfe nor death can vncouple vs. 1581 Mulcaster *Positions* xxxv. (1887) 124 Being so neare companions in linke, and not to be vncoupled in learning. 1685 Dryden *Lucretius* III. 10 When our mortal frame shall be disjoyn'd, The lifeless Lump uncoupled from the mind, From sense of grief and pain we shall be free. 1786 Jefferson *Writ.* (1859) II. 23 Congress have desired those States to uncouple the grants, so that each may come into force separately. 1858 O. W. Holmes *Aut. Breakf.-t.* viii, Will nobody block those wheels, uncouple that pinion, cut the string that holds those weights? 1884 *Harper's Mag.* July 273/1 The locomotive is uncoupled from the cars.
Hence **Uncou·pled** *ppl. a.*$^1$, **Uncou·pler.**
1687 Dryden *Pal. & Arc.* II. 236 Th' appointed Place In which th' uncoupl'd Hounds began the Chace. 1705 Stevens II, An Uncoupler, *desuñidor.* 1728 Chambers *Cycl., Decouple,* in Heraldry, the same as *Uncoupled,* i.e. parted or sever'd. 1803 Scott *Cadyow Castle* x, Steeds snort; uncoupled stag-hounds bay.

**Uncou·pled,** *ppl. a.*$^2$ [Un-$^1$ 8. Cf. MDu. *ongecoppelt,* Du. *ongekoppeld.*] Not coupled or joined; left detached or separate.
1377 Langl. *P. Pl.* B. Prol. 162 Vncoupled þei wenden Boþe in wareine & in waste where hem leue lyketh. *Ibid.* 206 Coupled & vncoupled. c1430 Lydg. *Min. Poems* (Percy Soc.) 32 Thouhe she be yong, yet wol she wele abide, Uncoupled to a fresshe man of iunesse. 1589 Puttenham *Eng. Poesie* II. x. (Arb.) 102 There is a band to be giuen euery verse in a staffe, so as none fall out alone or vncoupled. 1625 Milton *On Death of Fair Infant* 13 Th' infamous blot, Of long-uncoupled bed, and childless eld. 1659 Chamberlayne *Pharonnida* (T.), Vows, whose harsh events must be Uncoupled cold virginity. 1818 Colebrooke *Obligations* 55 Exorbitancy of price too, uncoupled with fraud. 1869 Colburn in *Eng. Mech.* 19 Mar. 579/2 There was not..an engine..having..uncoupled driving-wheels.

**Uncou·pling,** *vbl. sb.* [f. Uncouple *v.*] The action of the verb.
c1369 Chaucer *Dethe Blaunche* 377 With a grete horne [he] blewe thre mote At the vncoupylynge of hys houndys. c1410 *Master of Game* (MS. Digby 182) xxxv, He shulde blowe iii. longe moot to þe vncoupelynge. 1470-85 Malory *Arthur* x. lii. 500 To the vncoupelynge, to the sekynge, to the rechate [etc.]. 1611 Cotgr., *Descouple,* the vncoupling of houndes, or loosing them after their game.

**Uncoura·geous,** *a.* (Un-$^1$ 7.) 1878 Dowden *Stud. Lit.* 123 Wordsworth's..uncourageous elder years.

**Uncou·rsed,** *a.* [Un-$^1$ 9.] Of masonry: Not laid or set in courses.
1825 J. Nicholson *Operat. Mechanic* 537 In uncoursed rubble the stones are placed promiscuously in the wall. 1886 Willis & Clark *Cambridge* I. 17 Its wall..is of rough uncoursed rubble work.

**Uncou·rted,** *ppl. a.* (Un-$^1$ 8.)
1595 Daniel *Civ. Wars* II. lii, Uncourted, unrespected, unobeyed. 1640 Habington *Castara* III. (Arb.) 117 While I my life of fame beguile And under my owne vine uncourted sit. 1714 Mandeville *Fab. Bees* (1733) II. 224 No female of twelve would be refractory, if applied to; or remain long uncourted, if there were men. 1796 Mme. D'Arblay *Camilla* V. 295 Devotion paid straight forward, and uncourted.

**Uncou·rteous,** *a.* [Un-$^1$ 7.] Wanting in courtesy; discourteous: **a.** Of persons.
α. 1303 R. Brunne *Handl. Synne* 6798 Þys ryche man, as þe gospel seys, Was but to o man vncurteys. a1352 Minot in *Pol. Poems* (Rolls) I. 79 Unkind he was and uncurtayse. a1400-50 *Bk. Curtasye* 128 in *Babees Bk.*, Dip not þi thombe þy drynke into, þou art uncurtayse yf þou hit do. 1470-85 Malory *Arthur* IV. xxiii. 151 Yf syre Pelleas had ben as vncurteis to yow as ye haue ben to hym ye hadde bene a dede knyghte. 1533 More *Apol.* ix. Wks. 865/2 Were not a manne..worthye to bee compted vncourteyse, that woulde [etc.]. 1548 Elyot, *Inclemens,*..vngentil: vncurteis.
β. 13.. *E. E. Allit. P.* A. 303, I halde þat iueler lyttel to prayse,..& much to blame & vn-cortoyse. 1530 Palsgr. 328 Uncourtoyse, *ingrat.* 1552 Huloet, Vncurtoyse, *illiberalis.*
γ. 1426 Audelay *Poems* (Percy Soc.) 14 He is unkynd and uncurtes. 1456 Sir G. Haye *Law Arms* (S.T.S.) 222 Quhasa did the contrair he war ungentill, uncurtas, and unconnand. ?a1500 *Chester Pl.* II. 105 God forbyde that we were So uncurtise to you heare. 1542 Udall *Erasm. Apoph.* 264 b, Hymselfe remained prisoner emong the most uncourtise Silicians. 1575 Laneham *Let.* 41 Yoor only prezens shallbe matter sufficient of abandoning this vncurtess knight.
δ. 1535 Coverdale *Bar.* iv. 15 An vncurteous people, and of a straunge language. 1551 Recorde *Pathw. Knowl.* Pref., If I were as vncurteous as you vnkind, I shuld vtterly refuse to do them any good. 1652 J. Taylor (Water P.) *Short Relat. Long Journ.* (Spenser Soc.) 23 Then most uncurteous Mistris, quoth I, I doubt I must bee necessitated to take up my lodging in the Field. 1801 *Lusignan* II. 49 Strangers, you seem not uncourteous. 1858 Trollope *Dr. Thorne* xxxiii, She was more than ordinarily anxious not to appear uncourteous or unkind to him.
**b.** Of actions, speech, etc.
c1490 *Plumpton Corr.* (Camden) 71, I besech you speake to my master, that no uncurtes dealing be had with none of his servants. a1548 Hall *Chron., Hen. IV,* 19 He beyng netteled with these uncurteous ye unvertuous prickes & thornes, serched out the authours. 1594 Hooker *Eccl. Pol.* IV. xiii. § 10 They ease us of that vncourteous burden. 1601 Shaks. *Twel. N.* v. i. 369 Vpon some stubborne and vncourteous parts We had conceiu'd against him. 1828 Scott *F. M. Perth* xxiv, It would be, therefore, uncourteous to leave my readers under any doubt concerning the agency. 1875 W. S. Hayward *Love agst. World* 11, 'I know what I am doing,' was the uncourteous reply.

**Uncou·rteously,** *adv.* [f. prec. + -ly$^2$. Cf. ON. *úkurteisliga* and Incourteously.] In an uncourteous manner; discourteously, uncivilly.
α. 1338 R. Brunne *Chron.* (1810) 143 Loke how kyng Philip said vncurteisly, Daþet haf his lip, & his nose þerby. 1393 Langl. *P. Pl.* C. xiv. 172 Ich took kepe How vn-corteisliche þe cok hus kynde forth strenede. 1477 Earl Rivers *Dictes* (1877) 56 b, If he demaunde ony thing he shal axe it vncurtaisly. 1565 Cooper *Thesaurus* s.v. *Inclementer,* To speake vncourteisly or churlishly to his father.
β. c1485 *Digby Myst.* (1882) IV. 655 He & I com both of your kyn, And that ye kithe vn-curteslye. 1523 Ld. Berners *Froiss.* I. cccxxxii. 131 b/1 They be men of warr, suche as can nat lyue, but by pyllage & robbery: and haue vncurtesly ouer ryden oure countrees. 1548 Cranmer *Catech.* 49 b, Beware good children y$^t$ you dispise not your parentes, or vncurtesely entreat them.
γ. 1535 Coverdale 1 *Esdras* vi. 33 To deale vncurteously with the house of the Lorde at Ierusalem. 1575 Vautrollier *Luther on Ep. Gal.* 25 Paul might have handled the Galatians more uncurteously. 1632 Sherwood, Vncourteously, *incivilement.* 1849 Eastwick *Dry Leaves* 118 They were.. at last dismissed uncourteously with a refusal. 1856 Kane *Arct. Expl.* II. ix. 94 A cordial meal it is. I am sorry to hurry over it so uncourteously.

**Uncou·rteousness.** [f. as prec. + -ness.] The quality of being uncourteous; discourtesy.
1530 Palsgr. 285/1 Uncourtesnesse, *ingratitude.* 1531 Tindale *Exp. 1 John* (1537) 99 Al blameth his vncourteousnesse. 1597 J. King *On Jonas* (1618) 598 The time inuiting mee thereunto,..and the vncurteousnes of these our times, requiring no less. 1681 [see Uncondescension]. 1843 *Florist's Jrnl.* (1846) IV. 95 He accuses us of 'uncourteousness' and 'partiality'.

†**Uncou·rtesy.** *Obs.* [Un-$^1$ 12. Cf. ON. *úkurteisi.*] Discourtesy, incivility.
c1380 *Sir Ferumb.* 2058 'Mahoun,' quaþ sche, '3yue þe schame for þyn oncortesye!' c1400 *Rom. Rose* 3587, I wole in no wise..Denye that ye haue asked heere; It were to gret uncurtesie. c1449 Pecock *Repr.* II. iii. 151 Thou art to be excusid of vncurtesie bi thi greet folie and madnes. 1523 Ld. Berners *Froiss.* I. cvii. 129 Certaynly cosyn, ye haue done me great vncourtesy, to fight with our ennemyes without me. 1569 Newton *Cicero's Olde Age* 4 Unbrideled insolencie, and blunt uncurtesie. 1605 *1st Pt. Jeronimo* II. iii. 97 Your wife condemns you of a vncurtesie.

**Uncou·rtierlike,** *a.* (Un-$^1$ 7 c.)
1786 Mme. D'Arblay *Diary* (1842) III. 103 Here we had new court scenery, in which I acted but an uncourtier-like part. 1812 R. H. in *Examiner* 23 Nov. 747/2 Excuse my ..uncourtier like language. 1857 Ld. Granville in Ld. Fitzmaurice *Life* (1905) I. ix. 224 He talked of the advantages and disadvantages of being Prince of Wales in a very uncourtierlike manner.

**Uncou·rting,** *ppl. a.* (Un-$^1$ 10 and 5 d.)
1744 Eliza Heywood *Female Spect.* No. 3 (1748) I. 133 Uncourting, unindebted to favour, a native greatness shines through his whole deportment. 1887 C. C. R. *Minora Carmina* 303 She came.., Uncourting gaze of curious men.

**Uncou·rtlike,** *a.* (Un-$^1$ 7 c.)
1659 Fuller *App. Inj. Innoc.* III. 21 The roughnesse of his uncourt-like nature, sweetned many men when they least looked for it. 1733 Ld. Chesterf. in *Lett. C'tess Suffolk* (1824) II. 63 Your letter..I must look upon as a most uncommon and uncourtlike piece of friendship. 1865 Stopford Brooke in *Life & Lett.* (1917) I. x. 179 He is—they say on account of this uncourtlike manner—a great favourite with the Queen.

**Uncou·rtliness.** [f. next.] Lack of courtliness; uncourtly behaviour.
1668 H. More *Div. Dial.* v. xxi. (1713) 474 A great piece

of roughness, rudeness and uncourtliness. **1710** ADDISON *Whig Exam.* No. 5 ⁋ 11 Notwithstanding the uncourtliness of their phrases the sense was very honest. **1748** RICHARDSON *Clarissa* (1811) I. v. 34 Our sex perhaps expect to hear a little—uncourtliness shall I call it? from the husband.

**Uncou·rtly,** *a.* [UN-[1] 7.]

**1.** Not adapted or suited to the Court; *esp.* not sufficiently polished or refined: **a.** Of persons, their attributes, etc.

**1598** CHAPMAN *Contn. Marlowe's Hero & Leander* III. 251 This euent vncourtly Hero thought Her inward guilt would in her lookes haue wrought. **1632** MASSINGER & FIELD *Fatal Dowry* III. i, You will find it safer Rather to be uncourtly than immodest. *a* **1662** HEYLIN *Laud* (1668) 57 A man of independent Fortune..but otherwise of an uncourtly disposition. **1759** STERNE *Tr. Shandy* II. ix, A little squat, uncourtly figure. **1838** EMERSON *Misc. Papers, Milton* Wks. (Bohn) III. 294 Lord Bacon..shrinks and falters before the absolute and uncourtly Puritan. **1876** BANCROFT *Hist. U.S.* IV. xxiv. 491 The retired and uncourtly scholar.

**b.** Of things or actions.

**1640** HABINGTON *Q. of Arragon* I. i. B ij b, His Garbe was so uncourtly. **1727** POPE *Let. to Gay* 16 Oct., I can only add a plain, uncourtly Speech. **1775** ADAIR *Amer. Ind.* 341 The uncourtly leave he took of our gallant, and faithful old friends. **1827** POLLOK *Course T.* IX. 653 No longer hid by coarse uncourtly garb.

**2.** Not subservient to, not seeking to please, the Court.

**1712** SWIFT *Cond. Allies* Wks. 1751 II. 127 The present Lord Treasurer,..not entering into those refinements of paying the public money upon private considerations, hath been so uncourtly as to stop it. **1821** W. H. LYTTELTON in *Corr. Lady Lyttelton* ix. (1912) 237 The Archbishop's sermon [at the Coronation]..., on the whole uncourtly enough to..displease the courtiers. **1855** MACAULAY *Hist. Eng.* xx. IV. 476 Two eminent orators, who had, during some years, been on the uncourtly side of every question.

**U·ncous,** *a. rare.* [f. L. *unc-us* hook, or *unc-us* adj., hooked.] Hooked, curved.

**1658** SIR T. BROWNE *Gard. Cyrus* iii. 124 The calicular shafts [of the teasel] and uncous disposure of their extremities. *a* **1682** — *Pseud. Ep.* (1686) v. i. 191 The uncous and pointed extremity of their Bill.

**Uncouth** (ʋnkū·þ), *a.* and *sb.* Forms: *α.* 1 uncuþ, 1–3 uncuð (3 vn-), 2 unkuþ, 3 -kuð, 4 un-, vncuth (-cut), 5 vnchut; 3 vnecouþ, 3–4 onecouþ, 4 vnkouþ; 4–7 vn-, 4– uncouth (5–6 *Sc.* wn-, 6 on-), 4–6 vnkouth (5 -koud, 6 *Sc.* wn-, onkouth), 6 *Sc.* oncoutht, 6–8 uncooth, 7 uncough; 4 oncouþe, 4–5 vn-, unkouþe, 4–6 vn-, uncouthe (4 -kouthe, 5 *Sc.* wncou(y)the, 6 vncovthe); 3–5 vncowþe, -the (5 -k(u)owtbe), 4 vnkowth (6 on-), 5 oncowth, 6 oncowght. *β.* 2 uncoð-, 3 vncoþ-, vnekoþ-, 4 vnchoþe, 5 -koth, 5–6 -cothe, 6–7 vn-, uncoth. (See also UNQUOD, -QUOTH, and UNCO.) [OE. *uncūþ* (f. UN-[1] + *cūþ* COUTH *a.*), = MDu. *oncont* (Du. *onkond*), OHG. *unkund*, *-chunt* (MHG. *unkunt*), ON. *úkunnr* (obs. Da. *ukund*), Goth. *unkunþs*. In many examples from the 17th and 18th centuries the exact sense is difficult to determine.]

**A.** *adj.* †**1.** Of facts or matters of knowledge: Unknown; also, not certainly known, uncertain. *Obs.*

*c* **897** K. ÆLFRED *Gregory's Past. C.* Pref. ad fin., Uncuð [hit is] hu longe ðær swæ gelærede biscepas sien. *c* **900** tr. *Baeda's Hist.* II. xiii. (1890) 134 To wi metenesse þære tide, þe us uncuð is. **971** *Blickl. Hom.* 51 Us is swiþe uncuþ hwæt ure yrfeweardas..don willon æfter urum life. *c* **1000** ÆLFRIC *On Old Test.* (Gr.) 4 God..sealde heora ælcum synderlice spræce, þæt heora ælcum wæs uncuð, hwæt oðer sæde. *a* **1200** *Vices & Virtues* 23 Ic bliðeliche ðine rad wile blesten,..3if ðu me ðin uncuðe name woldest kyðen. **1303** R. BRUNNE *Handl. Synne* 4296 Ful fewe bedys are yn hys mouþe, He vsyþ none; þey are vncouthe. **1423** JAS. I *Kingis Q.* lxiii. Quhen sall 3our merci rew vpon 3our man, Quhois seruice is 3it vncouth vnto 3ow? **1447** BOKENHAM *Seyntys* Introd. (Roxb.) 4 Wych story is no thyng unkuowthe At mownt Flask. **1533** BELLENDEN *Livy* I. viii. (S.T.S.) I. 48 This ordour of preisthede was..nocht vncouth to þe pepill of albane. *a* **1577** GASCOIGNE *Dan Barth.* Wks. (1587) 101 With stopping sobs..he sought To utter that which was to one uncouth. **1616** BOYS *Wks.* (1622) 871 Now the whole superficies of the earth as well vncouth as discouered, is but a little point. **1650** R. GELL *Serm.* 8 Aug. 2 A kind of attestation not uncouth among the Poets.

**2.** With which one is not acquainted or familiar; unfamiliar, unaccustomed, strange: **a.** Of ways, paths, etc. (frequently passing into sense 5).

*α.* *Beowulf* 1410 Ofereode þa æþelinga bearn..enge anpaðas, uncuð gelad. *a* **1000** *Boeth. Metr.* xiii. 58 Merecondel scyfð on ofdæle, uncuðne weg nihtes geneðeð. **1387–8** T. USK *Test. Love* II. xi. (Skeat) l. 45 Folisshe ignoraunce misledeth wandring wrecches by uncouth wayes that shulden be forleten. *c* **1450** *Merlin* xx. 314 Ride euer be nyght and by the moste vn-cowth weyes that ye may. **1582** STANYHURST *Æneis* II. (Arb.) 67, I wandred through streets and passages vncooth. **1611** FLORIO, *Inuio sentiere*, an vngone, vntroden or vncouth path or way. **1667** MILTON *P. L.* x. 475 But I toild out my uncouth passage, forc't to ride Th' untractable Abysse. **1691** SWIFT *Athenian Soc.* Wks. 1755 IV. I. 231 To grope her uncouth way After a mighty light that leads her wand'ring eye. **1704** — *T. Tub* xi, They would make choice of the..most uncouth rounds..that they might be sure to avoid one another.

*β.* **1579** FENTON *Guicciard.* XIV. 829 Fraunces Sforce taking a straunge and vncothe waye, was receyued at Sesto by Prospero. **1583** GREENE *Alcida* Wks. (Grosart) IX. 55 Wandring awhile by many vncoth paths, at last wee came into a faire place. **1600** J. LANE *Tom Tel-troth* 69 Nature.. Is now inforc'd in vncoth walkes to stray.

**b.** Of lands or places.

*α.* *c* **960** *Rule St. Benet* lxi. 109 Se utancumena munuc, þe of uncuðum eardum cymð. *c* **1175** *Lamb. Hom.* 157 Wume nu ..þet ic scal wunien in unkuþe londe. *c* **1200** *Trin. Coll. Hom.* 53 Hu muge we singen godes loft song in uncuðe londe? *c* **1290** *S. Eng. Leg.* I. 325 Þus feor in one-couþe londe Mit deol and soruwe ich habbe i-leoued. **13..** *Guy Warw.* (A.) 1192 Time it is þat ich fond To winne priis in vncouþe lond. *c* **1400** *Destr. Troy* 12510 The sea..Depertid the pepull, pyne to be-hold, In costes vnkowthe. *a* **1450** *Le Morte Arth.* 851 She it yaff to the scottisshe knight, For he was of an vnkouth stede. *a* **1470** HARDING *Chron.* CCXLI. vii, Who hath power to make you resistence In any wise, in any vncouth lande? **1534** MORE *Comf. agst. Trib.* III. Wks. 1237/2 When they shall..cary vs farre from home into a straunge vncouth lande. **1632** RUTHERFORD *Lett.* (1862) I. xxvi. 97 The silly stranger in an uncouth country must take with a smoky inn. **1671** MILTON *Samson* 333 Brethren and men of Dan, for such ye seem, Though in this uncouth place. **1722** DE FOE *Plague* (1840) 97 [They] wandered into fields and woods, and into secret uncouth places. **1824** SCOTT *Redgauntlet* let. xi, Ye see, birkie, it is nae chancy thing to tak a stranger traveller for a guide, when you are in an uncouth land.

*β.* **1297** R. GLOUC. (Rolls) 6445 Þat he hom to deþe bro3te So ver in vnekoþe lond, þat no mon of hom ne io3te. *c* **1400** *Destr. Troy* 531 A sure knyghte..ayres into vnkoth lond auntres to seche.

**c.** Of persons.

For the early legal use see HOGHENHINE. For the phrase *uncouth, unkissed*, see UNKISSED.

*c* **893** K. ÆLFRED *Oros.* VI. xxxi. 286 Þa com him ongean an uncuð mon, & ofstong Iulianus. *c* **1000** *Ags. Gosp.* John x. 5 Ne fyliað hig uncuþum,..forþam þe hig ne gecneowon uncuþra stefne. *c* **1000** ÆLFRIC *Saints' Lives* xxiii. 613 Þæt þær gelæht wære binnan þære byrig an uncuð geong man. *a* **1175** *Cott. Hom.* 231 Scewie we þes uncoðe mæn ur 3efo. *c* **1205** LAY. 7107 Seoððen her com vncuð folc faren in þessere þeode. *a* **1225** *Ancr. R.* 54 A meiden..eode vt uor to biholden uncuðe wummen. *a* **1300** *Cursor M.* 5495 Þar ras an vncut king þat had to ioseph na knauing. **1362** LANGL. *P. Pl.* A. VIII. 141 Vnkouþe knihtes schul come þi kingdam to clayme. *c* **1400** *Ywaine & Gaw.* 501 Unkowth men wele may he shende, That to his felows es so unhende. **1446** LYDG. *Nightingale Poems* ii. 44 From the god of love To me was sent an vnkouth messangier. **1470–85** MALORY *Arthur* III. vi. 105 Vncouth men ye shold debate with al & no broder with broder. **1596** WARNER *Alb. Eng.* XI. lxii. (1612) 272 They, seeing vncouth Men and Ships, weare wondringly agaste.

**d.** Of peoples or nations.

*c* **1000** ÆLFRIC *Deut.* xxviii. 36 Drihten sent uncuðe þeode ofer eow, þa þe ge ne cunnon. *a* **1300** *Cursor M.* 1171 In vncuth lede sal end mi wa. *Ibid.* 4177 Þan sagh þai cumand be þe stret Marchands of an vncuth thede. *c* **1400** *St. Alexius* (Trin.) 258 Tydynges none hy ne bro3te Of his sone, þat him so3te In vncouþe þede. *c* **1450** LYDG. *Secrees* 219 In Rethoryk he hadde experyence Of euery strange, unkouth nacyoun.

† **e.** *Sc.* Pertaining to other nations; foreign. *Obs.*

**1533** BELLENDEN *Livy* II. xv. (S.T.S.) I. 187 How beit þe ciete was in quiet þis 3ere but ony vncouth or domestic weris. *Ibid.* v. xxiv. II. 232 Nocht standing oure neir þe sey to resaif dammaige be perell of oncouth flotis.

**3.** Of an unknown or unfamiliar character; unusual, uncommon, strange; marvellous. Now *rare.*

Very common *c* 1590–1700. In later use passing into 6.

*Beowulf* 876 Secg..welhwylc gecwæð, þæt he fram Sigemunde secgan hyrde ellendædum uncuþes fela. *c* **900** tr. *Baeda's Hist.* II. xii. (1890) 128 Þa geseah he..sumne mon wið his gongan..uncuðes gegyrlan. *c* **1000** *Sax. Leechd.* I. 194 Gif men þæt heafod berste, oððe uncuð swyle ongesitte. *a* **1122** *O. E. Chron.* an. 1106, Hig ma on þison timon uncuðra steorra gesawon. *c* **1200** ORMIN 228 Þe33 wisstenn þatt himm wass þatt da33 Summ unncuþ sihhþe shæwedd. *a* **1300** *Cursor M.* 22494 Efter þe tua fules þe þrid, An uncuth dai þan es it kidd. **1340–70** *Alisaunder* 683 Queme yee me might, Of this unkouth case too karp þe soothe. *c* **1384** CHAUCER *H. Fame* I. 1279 Ther saugh I Colle tregetour Vpon a table of Sygamour Pley an vncouthe thynge to telle. *c* **1386** — *Sqr.'s T.* 284 Who couþe telle you þe forme of daunces So vncouthe. *c* **1430** LYDG. *Min. Poems* (Percy Soc.) 25 The tragides divers and unkouth Of morall Senec. **1430–40** — *Bochas* IX. xxxiii. 34 b, His vncouth story breuely to compyle. **1448–9** METHAM *Amoryus & Cl.* 1278 The venym owte off hys tayle in-to hys mowth He drawyth anone..; Thow yt gretly be meruulus and oncowth. *a* **1513** FABYAN *Chron.* v. lxxxiii. 61 The Kynge had maryed a woman of vncowght beleue. **1548** UDALL, etc. *Erasm. Par. Matt.* xxi. 101 Moued with this uncouthe syght. **1582** STANYHURST *Æneis* III. (Arb.) 80, I through pangs vncoth vnhabled,..thus fumbled an aunswer. **1603** B. JONSON *Sejanus* III. iii, It is no uncouth thing To see fresh buildings from old ruines spring. **1648** *Hunting of Fox* 24 Saint Bridgit her selfe, the mother of so many uncouth Revelations. **1693** N. MATHER in Owen *Holy Spirit* Pref., Novel and uncouth Terms foreign to the Things of God. **1710** BERKELEY *Princ. Hum. Knowl.* I. § 1 We are insensibly drawn into uncouth paradoxes. **1748** HARTLEY *Observ. Man* I. iii. 350 The Speculations may seem uncouth to those who are not conversant in Mathematical Inquiries. **1801** tr. *Gabrielli's Myst. Husb.* III. 173 When James's uncouth story was absolutely confirmed. **1847** G. HARRIS *Ld. Hardwicke* II. viii. 237 To gaze on the uncouth, unaccustomed spectacle presented by the Highlanders. **1864** BOWEN *Logic* v. 136 It would certainly be accounted a forced and uncouth assertion.

† **b.** Alien or foreign *to* something. *Obs. rare.*

*c* **1374** CHAUCER *Boeth.* II. pr. ii. (1868) 34 Syn þat stedfastnesse is vnkouþ to my maneres. **1697** J. SERGEANT *Solid Philos.* 273 Any other and higher Points, especially such as are Uncouth to..Natural Reason.

† **c.** Unrecognizable. *Obs.*—[1]

**1390** GOWER *Conf.* II. 318 So what with blod and what with teres..He made hire faire face uncouth.

† **4.** Of a strange and unpleasant or distasteful character. *Obs.*

*c* **1380** WYCLIF *Sel. Wks.* III. 242 Þis unkouþe discencioun þat is bitwixe þes popes. **1430–40** LYDG. *Bochas* II. xxviii. (1554) 64 Atwene them, there was an uncouth strife. **1586** DAY *Eng. Secretorie* I. (1625) 46 The sight became so vncouth, as all men shamed, each one feared, and none durst abide it. **1641** BROME *Joviall Crew* I. (1652) B iv, I hop'd thou hadst abjur'd that uncough practice. **1696** WHISTON *The. Earth* (1722) 7 An uncouth and incredible system. **1719** DE FOE *Crusoe* II. (Globe) 382 The Sight, you may be sure, was something uncouth to our Spaniards. **1785** BURKE *Nabob Arcot* Wks. IV. 320 To some the subject is strange and uncouth; to several harsh and distasteful. **1797** GODWIN *Enquirer* I. vi. 43 They will not accept an uncouth and disgustful lesson.

† **b.** Of smells, sounds, etc. *Obs.*

**1600** HOLLAND *Livy* XXI. lv. 425 The Elephants..frighted the horses especially, & not onely with the straunge sight, but also with as uncouth a sent and savor. **1658** ROWLAND tr. *Moufet's Theat. Ins.* 909 Poysoned Honey..hath a strange and uncouth smell. **1665** SIR T. HERBERT *Trav.* (1677) 29 Toddy..tasts like Rhenish; at first draught it is uncouth, but every draught tasts better than other. **1720** DE FOE *Capt. Singleton* xv. (1840) 257 A strange noise more uncouth than any they had ever heard.

† **c.** Unseemly, indecorous. *Obs.*

**1589** GREENE *Menaphon* (Arb.) 40 Samela meruailed at such an vncouth banquet. **1600** FAIRFAX *Tasso* I. xviii. 4 Nor sweld his brest with vncouth pride therefore, That heau'n on him aboue this charge had laide. **1659** BROME *Eng. Moor* I. iii, Which uncouth Policie to sorrow leads Thousands a thousand wayes.

**5.** Of places: Not commonly known or frequented; solitary, desolate, wild, rugged, rough.

*α.* *a* **1542** WYATT in *Anglia* (1897) XX. 432 So close the Cave was and unkouth Yᵗ none but God was record off his payne. **1600** SHAKS. *A. Y. L.* II. vi. 6 If this vncouth Forrest yeeld any thing sauage, I wil either be food for it, or bring it for foode to thee. **1633** T. STAFFORD *Pac. Hib.* I. xviii. (1821) 191 Lurking in desart, uncouth, and unknowen places. **1653** H. COGAN *Diod. Sic.* 256 Wandring alone through desert and uncouth places, he died with sorrow. **1728** MORGAN *Algiers* I. iii. 72, I have met with the Ruins of several stately Buildings..in uncooth Mountains. **1748** *Anson's Voy.* I. vii. 73 This uncouth and rugged coast. **1814** SCOTT *Wav.* lxiii, He soon pursued a very uncouth path. **1830** J. G. STRUTT *Sylva Brit.* 119 The Prior of St. Mary's at York was chosen Abbot by the Monks; with whom they withdrew into this uncouth desert.

*β.* **1582** STANYHURST *Æneis* IV. (Arb.) 99 When they toe thee mountayns and too layrs vncoth aproched. **1595** *Locrine* III. vi. 7 Where may I finde some hollow vncoth rocke, Where I may..ban my fill?

**b.** Of life, surroundings, etc.: Unattractive, unpleasant, uncomfortable. *Obs.* or *arch.*

**1611** CORYAT *Crudities* 409 Duke Iohn..liued a most vncouth and solitary life in the desert forrests. *a* **1627** MIDDLETON *Witch* II. i, 'Tis so uncouth Living i' th' country, now I'm us'd to th' city. **1670** CLARENDON *Hist. Reb.* XII. § 130 [He] order'd his other small Troops to contain themselves in those uncouth Quarters, in which they were. **1685** in *Verney Mem.* (1907) II. 404 This place is very uncouth to me now you are gone out of it! **1888** STEVENSON *Black Arrow* III. iv, The pair were left to their uncouth reflections for the night.

† **c.** Strange; uneasy; at a loss. *Obs.*—[1]

**1660** PEPYS *Diary* 26 May, All the great company being gone, I found myself very uncouth all this day for want thereof.

**6.** Of an unfamiliar or strange appearance or form; *spec.*, having an odd, uncomely, awkward, or clumsy shape or bearing.

**1513** DOUGLAS *Æneid* XI. xv. 12 In brovne sangwane weill dycht Abuf hys onkouth armour blomand brycht. **1600** FAIRFAX *Tasso* II. 38 In vncouth armes yclad and strange disguise. **1613** PURCHAS *Pilgrimage* 685 An vncouth Idoll, great and hollow, fastened in the wall with lime. **1653** H. MORE *Antid. Ath.* II. ii. § 14 The Frost and Wind will draw upon Doors and glass-Windows pretty uncouth streaks like feathers and other fooleries. **1713** POPE *Windsor For.* 403 Then ships of uncouth form shall stem the tide. **1770** COOK *Voy. round World* II. ix. (1773) III. 453 The dress of a New Zealander is certainly..the most uncouth that can be imagined. **1838** LYTTON *Leila* I. v, A profusion of strange and uncouth instruments and machines. **1845** FORD *Handbk. Spain* I. 53 The ponies of Gallicia, although ugly and uncouth, are admirably suited to the wild hilly country. **1879** H. PHILLIPS *Notes Coins* 12 A heavy and uncouth gold British coin of remote antiquity.

**b.** Of persons: Awkward and uncultured in appearance or manners. Also *transf.*

**1732** SIR C. WOGAN *Let. to Swift* 27 Feb., The very name of Irish carries so uncouth an idea along with it. **1740** SOMERVILLE *Hobbinolia* I. 165 The jocund Troop..incessant shake Their uncouth brawny Limbs. **1798** S. & HT. LEE *Canterb. T.* II. 64, I have never seen this redoubtable, troublesome, uncouth cousin of mine. **1825** MACAULAY *Ess., Milton* (1851) I. 24 People saw nothing of the godly but their uncouth visages. **1828** LYTTON *Pelham* iii, A raw, uncouth sort of young man, with a green coat and lank hair. **1868** FARRAR *Seekers* I. vi. (1875) 75 He dragged out an uncouth panic-stricken mortal.

*Comb.* **1809** W. IRVING *Knickerb.* (1861) 57 Several uncouth-looking beings seated on rocks. **1869** TOZER *Highl. Turkey* I. 292 The shepherds were an uncouth-looking set.

**c.** Of language, style, etc.

**1694** PENN *Rise & Progr. Quakers* v, Though that side of his understanding which lay next to the world, and especially the expression of it, might sound uncouth and unfashionable to nice ears. **1699** GARTH *Dispens.* IV. 50 Harsh words, tho' pertinent, uncouth appear. **1717** LADY MONTAGU *Let. to Pope* 1 Apr., An expression in an ancient author..may be extremely fine with them, when at the same time it looks low or uncouth to us. **1762** FALCONER *Shipwr.* I. 82 Tho' terms uncouth shou'd strike th' offended ear, For sake of truth the uncouth measures bear. **1773** MRS. CHAPONE *Improv. Mind* (1774) II. 128 Buried in obsolete words and uncouth constructions. *a* **1834** COLERIDGE *Shaks. Notes* (1875) 145 The scholastic and uncouth words homogeneity, proportionateness. **1870** LOWELL *Among my Bks.* 162 Where it does not make Shakespeare write bad sense, uncouth metre, or false grammar.

*absol.* **1737** POPE *Hor., Ep.* II. ii. 174 Prune the luxuriant, the uncouth refine, But show no mercy to an empty line.

**d.** Of manners, actions, etc.
**1740** JOHNSON *Life Drake* Wks. IV. 426 Nor were their other customs less wild or uncouth. **1763** J. BROWN *Poetry & Music* iii. 27 Their Gestures are uncouth and horrid. **1837** W. IRVING *Capt. Bonneville* I. 274 It was a day of uncouth gambols, and frolics, and rude feasting. **1850** ADLER *Prov. Poet.* ii. 29 The uncouth heroism of the barbarous times. **1868** NETTLESHIP *Ess. Browning* ii. 62 This uncouth mind, so cramped..by the exigencies..of rhythm and rhyme.

†**7.** Unknowing, ignorant. Also *absol. Obs. rare.*
*c* **1220** *Bestiary* 112 in *O. E. Misc.* 4 His muð is ȝet wel unkuð wi ) pater noster and crede. *Ibid.* 512 Ðer-fore oðre fisses to him draȝen;..of his swike he arn uncuð. *c* **1340** HAMPOLE *Prose Tr.* 25 For he taght the vn-couthe and vn-kunnynge by his prechynge. **1624** in *Abbotsford Club Misc.* 4 *margin*, The pannell denyet not, but scho said scho was vncouth, and wist not quhat to say.

**B. 1.** *absol.* An unknown person; a stranger.
*a* **1225** *Ancr. R.* 348 Ich halsie ou..alse unkuðe & pile-grimes, þet ȝe wi holden ou from vlesliche lustes. *a* **1300** *Cursor M.* 6835 To pilgrime and to vncuth þou ber þe wit þi dedis cuth. **1340** *Ayenb.* 37 Þe priue þyeues byeþ þo þet ne steleþ naȝt of oncouþe ac of prives. **14..** *Sir Beues* (C.) 2134 'What þow?' sche seyde, 'þou onkowth?'

**2.** *sb. pl.* Things not commonly known; news.
*a* **1529** SKELTON *Col. Clout* 1054 The people..wyl talke of such vncouthes. **1684** G. MERITON *Yorks. Dial.* 42 What uncuths hes ta brought Come tell me seaun? *c* **1746** J. COLLIER (Tim Bobbin) *View Lanc. Dial.* Wks. (1775) 33 I'd ash him ..whot Uncoth's he heard sturrink. **1828** *Craven Gloss.*

†**3.** *spec.* (See quot.) *Obs.*[−1]
**1589** PUTTENHAM *Eng. Poesie* III. xxii. (Arb.) 262 Ye haue another vicious speech which the Greekes call *Acyron*, we call him the vncouthe, and is when we vse an obscure and darke word.

**Uncou·thie,** *a. Sc.* [UN-[1] 7.] Dreary; uncomfortable; unfriendly.
**1768** ROSS *Helenore* II. 68 Tyn heart, tyn a'; we'll even tak sic bield, As thir uncouthy heather hills can yield. **1835** D. WEBSTER *Orig. Sc. Rhymes* 25 (E. D. D.), Think ye the auld uncouthie byke Wad wish them parted?

**Uncou·thly,** *a.* [f. UNCOUTH *a.*] Awkward.
**1821** CLARE *Vill. Minstr.* I. 19 A more uncouthly lout was hardly seen Beneath the shroud of ignorance than he.

**Uncou·thly,** *adv.* [f. as prec. + -LY [2].] In a strange, unfamiliar, or uncouth manner.
*c* **900** *Laws K. Ælfred* c. 47 (Liebermann), Þam elðeodeȝan & utancumenan ne læt ðu no uncuðlice wið hine. *c* **1200** ORMIN 14341 Þatt he spacc till hiss moderr þær Þuss unn-cuþliȝ wiþþ worde. *a* **1300** *Cursor M.* 4818 Cuth þai wit him na kything tak, And vncuthli to þam he spak. ?*a* **1366** CHAUCER *Rom. Rose* 584 She hadde no thought..but if it were oonly To graythe hir wel and vncouthly. **1423** JAS. I *Kingis Q.* ix, Is none estate nor age Ensured, more the prince nor than the page: So vncouthly hir werdes sche deuidith. *c* **1440** *Promp. Parv.* 511/1 Vncowthly, *extranee.* **1535** STEWART *Cron. Scot.* (Rolls) II. 396 Out throw the horne ilkone that tyme tha spak Richt vncouthlie, and with sic awfull sound. **1703** ROWE *Fair Penit.* v. i. H iij, What Charnel has been rifl'd for these Bones? Fye! this is Pageantry; they look uncouthly. **1777** SHERIDAN *Sch. Scand.*, *Portrait* 50 She,..Not stiff with prudence, nor uncouthly wild. **1784** COWPER *Task* IV. 276 The shadow..Dancing uncouthly to the quiv'ring flame. **1834** J. FOSTER *Ess. Evils Pop. Ignorance* 246 These are still further and most uncouthly confounded by the admixture of the ancient heathen notion of fate. **1881** FOWLER *Bacon* 160 What are, somewhat uncouthly, called the Idealists, the Materialists, and the Dualists.

**Uncou·thness.** [f. as prec.] The quality or condition of being uncouth, in various senses.
**1435** MISYN *Fire of Love* 2 For vncuthnes of slike helefull habundance oft-tymes haue I gropyd my breste. **1442** *Rec. Coldingham Priory* (Surtees) I. 138 The unkouthness at is lyke to ryss be[tween] S[r] Alex[r] Howme & S[r] David Howme. **1600** *Gowrie's Conspir.* in *Select. fr. Harl. Misc.* (1793) 192 His hienes beeing stricken in great admiration..of the vn-couthnes of the tale. **1628** *World Encomp. by Sir F. Drake* 13 Notwithstanding the vncouthnes of the way. **1654–66** EARL ORRERY *Parthen.* (1676) 267 My Prince, by the uncouthness of the ground, advanced slowly with his Battalion. **1672** MARVELL *Reh. Transp.* I. 220 A peculiar uncouthness and obscurity of stile. **1712** STEELE *Spect.* No. 514 ⁋ 4 Some in the Habit of Laplanders,..notwithstanding the Uncouthness of their Dress, had lately obtained a Place upon the Mountain. **1778** [W. H. MARSHALL] *Minutes Agric., Digest* 47 The uncouthness of the Yoke and Goad. **1815** JANE AUSTEN *Emma* iv, The uncouthness of a voice, which I heard to be wholly unmodulated. **1871** FREEMAN *Norm. Conq.* IV. xviii. 154 The building whose combined uncouthness of outline and perfection of detail makes it unique among English churches.

**Uncou·thsome,** *a. rare.* [UN-[1] 7.] Unfavourable, unpleasant.
**1684** tr. *Bucaniers Amer.* I. i. 3 This uncouthsom weather being spent, we had again the use of very favourable gales. **1824** J. TELFER *Border Ball.* 65 The witches..grinded with their mucke-rake teeth, Uncouthsome to the view.

†**Unco·venable,** *a. Obs.* [UN-[1] 7 b.]
**1.** Inappropriate, unsuitable, unfitting.
In the first quot. rendering L. *importuna.*
*c* **1374** CHAUCER *Boeth.* IV. pr. vi. (1868) 141 Perauenture þe nature of som man is so ouerþrowyng to yuel and so vn-couenable [etc.]. **1382** WYCLIF 1 *Tim.* iv. 7 Forsothe schonye thou vncouenable fablis and veyn. *a* **1425** tr. *Arderne's Treat. Fistula*, etc. 47 Oon aposteme come to a man..þat was hard to breke for vncouenable emplastres putte þer-to first. *c* **1450** tr. *De Imitatione* I. xxi. 26 Yeue not þiself to uncouenable gladnes. **1477** EARL RIVERS *Dictes* 41 Do not vncouenable werkis, take compaynie with wyse men and studie in their bookis.

**2.** Unseasonable.
*c* **1380** WYCLIF *Sel. Wks.* II. 121 We mai lerne, over þis, to fede not uncovenable axingis. **1382** — 1 *Kings* iii. 20 Risynge with silence of the vnkouenable niȝt, she took my sone fro myn syde.

Hence †**Unco·venably** *adv. Obs.*
**1382** WYCLIF *Ecclus.* xxxii. 6 Vncouenabli wile thou not ben enhauncid in thi wisdam. **1387** TREVISA *Higden* (Rolls) VI. 473 Sche was þerfore i-blamed of seint Ethelwold, and sche answerede noþer uncovenabeliche noþer ful curteisliche.

**Unco·venant,** *v.* (UN-[2] 3.)
**1643** W. GREENHILL *Axe at Root* 8 Now the Lord did un-covenant them, un-church them, un-power them. **1679** C. NESSE *Antid. agst. Popery* 102 The Jews..did apostatize, ..unchurching and uncovenanting themselves. **1881** *Edin. Rev.* Apr. 483 There it was that, so to speak, Carlyle un-covenanted himself.

**Unco·venanted,** *ppl. a.* [UN-[1] 8.]
**1.** Not promised or secured by a (*spec.* a Divine) covenant.
**1648** HEXHAM II, *Onbevoorwaerdet*, Vncovenanted. **1689** SHERLOCK *Death* iii. § 7 (1731) 207 They must be saved by uncovenanted Grace and Mercy. *a* **1711** KEN *Hymnarium* Poet. Wks. 1721 II. 133 Since we the Grace that we obtain, By Supereffluence uncovenanted gain. *a* **1806** BP. HORSLEY *Serm.* (1816) III. xxxviii. 165, I will cast me on his free un-covenanted mercy. **1887** S. COX *Expositions* Ser. III. xiii. 177 On the testimony of the Bible itself..his uncovenanted mercies are just as sure as his covenanted mercies.

**b.** Lying outside of any Divine covenant.
**1858** J. MARTINEAU *Stud. Chr.* 114 Many a parable did Jesus utter, proclaiming his Father's intended mercy to the uncovenanted nations. **1860** BP. S. WILBERFORCE *Addr. Ordination* 41 Men who lay in the uncovenanted darkness of a fallen nature.

**2.** Not sanctioned by, not in accordance with, a covenant or agreement.
**1727** E. LAWRENCE *Duty of Steward* 55, I have known Instances of Gentlemen's Estates sinking very much by irregular and uncovenanted practices.

**3.** Not bound by a covenant; *spec.* in the Indian Civil Service (cf. COVENANTED *ppl a.* 4).
**1790** BURKE *Fr. Rev.* 88 The first fundamental right of uncovenanted man, that is, to judge for himself, and to assert his own cause. **1845** STOCQUELER *Handbk. Brit. India* (1854) 105 The uncovenanted servants, the East Indians, and the natives themselves. **1884** *Truth* 13 Mar. 386/2 A member of the uncovenanted service of India.

**b.** Not having subscribed the Covenant.
**1818** SCOTT *Hrt. Midl.* xviii, The present government, which, however mild and paternal, was still uncovenanted. **1855** MACAULAY *Hist. Eng.* III. 706 These men continued ..to disclaim all allegiance to an uncovenanted Sovereign. **1889** LOWELL *Latest Lit. Ess.*, *Walton* (1891) 74 Some foraging party from Leslie's army which would not have spared his uncovenanted chickens.

**Unco·venanter.** (UN-[1] 12.)
**1640–1** *Kirkcudbr. War-Comm. Min. Bk.* (1855) 131 Johne Cutlar..declares no..uncovenanters within his bounds.

**Unco·ver,** *v.* Also 4–5 vnkeuer(e, 5 oncowyr, 5–6 vncouere, etc. [UN-[2] 3, 5, 7.]
**1.** *fig.* To disclose, lay bare, make known.
*a* **1300** *Cursor M.* 27425 And sua his rede ask he þat naman scrift vn-couer[d] be. **1628** FELTHAM *Resolves* II. xvii. 52 In our demaunds, we vncouer our owne desires. **1649** MILTON *Eikon.* xxviii. 238 Neither was it to cover thir perjury as he accuses, but to uncover his perjury to the Oath of his Coronation. **1674** JEAKE *Arith.* (1696) 405, I now come to review them in their common nature..and uncover their Comparative Elements. **1891** HARDY *Tess* xlix, The terrible evening over the hearth, when her simple soul uncovered itself to his.

**2.** To lay open or bare by the removal of some covering thing or matter.
*a* **1375** *Joseph Arim.* 559 Eualac..vn-keuered his scheld & on þe cros biholdes. *c* **1400** *Brut* I. 125 þis Hardiknoght ..lete vncouere his broþer Harolde, and smote of his Heuede..at Westmynstr. **14..** *Three Kings Cologne* 28 (Camb. MS.), Whan hit [the snow] is vncouered oute of þe chaf, anoone hit dissolueþ and wasteþ awey. *c* **1430** *Pilgr. Lyf Manhode* I. xxxv. (1869) 22 It is bettere the keyes..ben hid than vnhyd, For al bi times may men come to vnkeuere both that oon and that oother. **1553** BRENDE *Q. Curtius* IV. 56 The teares yet distilling downe his chekes [he] vn-couered his face. **1597** A. M. tr. *Guillemeau's Fr. Chirurg.* 9/2 Which we can not certaynlye espye, without makinge denudatione of the Cranium, and to our sight vncover it. **1603** [see UNBAR *v.* a]. **1779** *Mirror* No. 64, That mental feast with which I was to be regaled when the table should be uncovered. **1796** MME. D'ARBLAY *Camilla* V. 276 Weeping always, and never..uncovering her face. **1839** YEOWELL *Anc. Brit. Ch.* xii. (1847) 133 Human bones, which from time to time have been uncovered by the winds, and lie bleaching on the sand. **1892** *Photogr. Ann.* II. 414 It really does uncover the inches set forth below, whereas many other patterns only uncover about two-thirds.

**b.** To make bare or naked by removal of clothing; to expose unclothed or unveiled.
**1530** PALSGR. 767/1 Uncover this man, take awaye the clothes. **1560** BIBLE (Genev.) *Isaiah* xlvii. 2 Vncouer y[e] legge, & passe through the floods. **1609** — (Douay) *Ibid.*, Discouer the shoulder, vncouer the thighes. **1769** COOK *Voy. round World* I. xix. (1773) 242 When an Indian is about to worship at the Morai, or brings his offering to the altar, he always uncovers his body to the waste. **1815** J. SMITH *Panorama Sci. & Art* II. 200 On uncovering the foot, at that part was found a blue mark. **1875** JOWETT *Plato* (ed. 2) I. 167 Uncover your chest and back to me that I may have a better view.
*refl.* **1535** COVERDALE 2 *Sam.* vi. 20 The kynge..hath vn-couered himselfe before the maydens of his seruauntes. **1734** in Sale *Koran* 291 *note*, It being reckoned..indecent, for a woman..to uncover her self before one who is an infidel.
*absol.* **1713** ADDISON *Guard.* No. 109 ⁋ 3 We were forced to uncover after them, being unwilling to give out so soon.

**c.** To drive (a fox) out of cover.
**1812** *Sporting Mag.* XXXIX. 185 Proceeding to Minting Wood, they uncovered a fox. **1824** MACTAGGART *Gallovid. Encycl.* 414 The hounds could not uncover him, so the ron was set in flames about his lugs.

**3.** To remove a cover or covering from, to take the cover or top off (something).
*c* **1400** *Beryn* 3935 The Cup was vncoverid, þe swerd was out i-brayid. *c* **1410** *Sir Cleges* 364 Sir Cleges oncowyrd the panyere, And schewed..the cheryse. **1507** *Coventry Leet Bk.* 609 That on Joh. a Woode, mercer, let on-couere the Redde diche, which renneth throwgh his gardeyn. **1534** TINDALE *Mark* ii. 4 They vncovered the rofe of the housse where he was. **1586** J. HOOKER *Hist. Irel.* in *Holinshed* II. 114/1 The churches for the most part were all destroied & vncouered. **1699** DAMPIER *Voy.* II. 47 A long Pole or Bambo..with a Cutting-hook at the end of it, purposely for uncovering the houses. **1737** CHALLONER *Cath. Chr. Instr.* (1753) 220 Our Altars we also uncovered and stript of all their Ornaments.

**4.** To remove the hat from (the head), as a mark of reverence, respect, or courtesy.
**1530** PALSGR. 767/1 Why do you thus, I pray you, be nat uncovered for me. **1535** COVERDALE *Lev.* x. 6 Ye shall not vncouer youre heades, ner rente youre clothes. **1608** *Yorkshire Trag.* iii. 60, I that neuer could abide to vncouer my head ith Church. **1699** DAMPIER *Voy.* II. 129 None of the Eastern people use the Complement of uncovering their Heads when they meet, as we do.

**b.** *absol.*
**1627** MAY *Lucan* IX. S 3 b, Thus hauing spoke Straight hee vncouers, and presents the head. **1841** MACAULAY *Ess.*, *W. Hastings* (1851) 595 The House of Commons which uncovered and stood up to receive him. **1889** F. E. GRETTON *Memory's Harkb.* 37 He stopped short, reverentially uncovered, and stood bare-headed till the line of mourners had passed.

**5.** *Mil.* **a.** To expose, leave open, by the moving or manœuvring of men. **b.** To leave unprotected by withdrawal of troops.
**1796** *Instr. & Reg. Cavalry* (1813) 122 As soon as the rear division is uncovered, it receives the word, *March!* **1802** JAMES *Milit. Dict.* s. v., The different leading companies or divisions, &c. successively uncover those in their rear. **1832** *Prop. Reg. Instr. Cavalry* III. 72 The Troop..advances till its right uncovers the left of the Base Troop. **1899** *Daily News* 27 Mar. 7/4 The old battle lines surrounding the city are maintained, and the city cannot be safely uncovered.

**Unco·verable,** *a.* (UN-[1] 7 b.) **1837** CARLYLE *Fr. Rev.* III. II. v, To stretch out the old Formula.., so that it may cover the new, contradictory, entirely *un*coverable Thing?

**Unco·vered,** *ppl. a.* [UN-[1] 8.]
**1.** Not roofed or closed in overhead; not sheltered by a roof.
*c* **1400** *Destr. Troy* 11667 The walles were wroght to þe wale rofe, All clanly by course vncouert aboue. **1563** GOLDING *Cæsar* VII. (1565) 192 Bycause they saw the penthouses of our turrettes burned downe, and that oure men could not with ease go vncouered to saue them. **1587** *Southampton Court Leet Rec.* (1906) II. 255 The wollon hawle is vncovered and decayed which wee desier maye be amended. **1600** J. PORY tr. *Leo's Africa* III. 125 The middle part of the house is alwaies open or uncouered. **1697** DRYDEN *Æneis* II. 700 Uncovered but by heaven, there stood in view An altar.

**2.** Not covered by clothing; bare, naked.
*c* **1400** T. CHESTRE *Launfal* 291 For hete her clothes down sche dede, Almest to her gerdyl stede, Than lay sche uncovert. **1535** COVERDALE *Gen.* ix. 21 Noe..was dronken, and laye vncouered in his tente. **1560** BIBLE (Genev.) *Isaiah* xx. 4 Bothe yong men and olde men,..with their buttockes vncouered. **1605** SHAKS. *Lear* III. iv. 106 Thou wert better in a Graue, then to answere with thy vncouer'd body, this extremitie of the Skies. **1827** FARADAY *Chem. Manip.* ii. (1842) 54 It is requisite that the bottle should not be handled by uncovered hands. **1851** LONGF. *Gold. Leg.* V. *At Foot of Alps*, A band of pilgrims, moving slowly On their long journey, with uncovered feet.

**b.** Not wearing a hat; bareheaded.
**1570** in W. H. Turner *Select. Rec. Oxford* (1880) 331 Every man..spekeyng within the same Counsell howse, shall stand upp bare headed or uncovered. **1593** SHAKS. 2 *Hen. VI*, IV. i. 128 Rather let my head..dance vpon a bloody pole, Then stand vncouer'd to the Vulgar Groome. **1611** BIBLE 1 *Cor.* xi. 13 Is it comely that a woman pray vnto God vncouered? *a* **1656** BP. HALL *Rem. Wks.* (1660) 242 The French Divines preach with their hats on, ours uncovered. **1710** ADDISON *Tatler* No. 253 ⁋ 3 The Censor, who continued hitherto uncovered, put on his hat with great dignity. **1831** SCOTT *Ct. Rob.* ix, Sitting stationary..when so many noble knights.. stand uncovered around. **1884** *Manch. Exam.* 26 Nov. 5/1 The members of the House of Commons stand uncovered, the peers sit and wear their hats.

**c.** Of women: Unveiled.
**1585** T. WASHINGTON tr. *Nicholay's Voy.* I. viii. 8 b, The wiues of the Turkes..are not seene goe vncouered.

**3.** Having no covering; left open or exposed; not covered by or *with* (also † *of*) something.
**1530** PALSGR. 840/1 Oncovered, *a descouuert.* **1563** HYLL *Art Garden.* (1593) 12 They wil also that those furrowes so lie all the winter open and vncouered. **1638** MAYNE *Lucian* (1664) 24 Let's finde out some eminent place, uncovered with Snow, where we may the firmelier chain him. **1650** EARL MONM. tr. *Senault's Man bec. Guilty* 368 Whilst any mountains were yet uncovered with water, the remainders of man-kind were fixed there. **1692** RAY *Disc.* II. (1693) 65 He sent forth Birds, that he might try whether they could espy any Land uncovered of Water. **1793** COWPER *A Tale* 17 The heaths uncover'd, and the moors, Except with snow. **1807** WORDSW. *White Doe* VI. 144 One of the Norton Tenantry Espied the uncovered Corse. **1819** SCOTT *Ivanhoe* iii, The board was uncovered by a cloth. **1827** FARADAY *Chem. Manip.* iv. (1842) 93 The sand being cleared off..leaves the metal uncovered. **1875** W. S. HAYWARD *Love agst. World* i, The polished oak flooring, uncovered by carpet.

**b.** Not furnished with the usual covering.
**1565** in Hay Fleming *Reform. Scotl.* (1910) 610 Item, in the lauche chalmer, four stullis oncoverit. **1907** E. GLYN *3 Weeks* xiv, The bed unmade and piled with uncovered hotel pillows.

†**4.** Not having a cover laid for meals. *Obs.*
**1494** in *Househ. Ord.* (1790) 116 For all manner of estates that are to bee uncovered.

**5.** Not protected or screened by another or others. (See COVER *v.*[1] 8 and 12.)

*a* **1795** PHILIDOR *Studies of Chess* (1817) 98 It would be scarcely possible to prevent the uncovered king..from doubling on the same line. **1832** *Prop. Reg. Instr. Cavalry* II. 17 If the numbers are uneven, the last man but one.. must remain uncovered.

**6.** Not covered by insurance.

**1892** *Pall Mall G.* 22 Aug. 2/1 The building only was insured, and all the furnishings were uncovered.

Hence **Unco·veredly** *adv.*

**1683** E. HOOKER *Pref. Pordage's Mystic Div.* 67 Where, unclothedly, uncoveredly, nakedly,..Hee stood.

**Unco·vering,** *vbl. sb.* [f. UNCOVER *v.*] The action of the verb, in various senses.

**1495** *Trevisa's Barth. De P. R.* v. xxvii. 137 [In acute fevers] vncouerynge and puttynge out of bare armes is token of deth. **1598** FLORIO, *Scomiglio*, an vncouering, an vnhilling. **1611** COTGR., *Descouvrement*, a discouering, vncouering, detecting, disclosing. **1647** T. MOORE (*title*), An Uncovering of Mysterious Deceits. **1817** J. SCOTT *Paris Revisit.* (ed. 4) 70 The uncovering of the established and fruitful face of things. **1855** MACAULAY *Hist. Eng.* xiv. III. 414 That the sitting and rising, the covering and the uncovering, should have been regulated by exactly the same etiquette. **1895** *Athenæum* 5 Oct. 460/2 To carry out a complete uncovering of the immense accumulations of rubbish.

† **Unco·vert,** *a.* [UN-[1] 7.] = DISCOVERT *a.*

**1485** *Rolls of Parlt.* VI. 285 To vest and be in her sole.., as she were sole and uncovert. **1487** *Act 4 Hen. VII*, c. 24 Five yeais next after that they..be..uncovert, and of whole Mind.

**Unco·veted,** *ppl. a.* (UN-[1] 8.)

**1760–72** H. BROOKE *Fool of Quality* xiv. (1792) III. 45 Uncoveted wealth came pouring in upon me. **1833** MRS. BROWNING *Prometh. Bound* 163, I..keep An uncoveted watch o'er the world and the deep. **1882** 'F. ANSTEY' *Vice Versâ* v. 92 He had contrived..to evade the uncoveted wooden spoon by just two places.

**Unco·vetingly,** *adv.* (UN-[1] 11.) **1862** R. H. PATTERSON *Ess. Hist. & Art* 47 To beg for the rose, yet look uncovetingly on the dandelion.

**Unco·vetous,** *a.* (UN-[1] 7.)

*a* **1500** *Ratis Raving* I. 624 Scho is louand in kind lawtee, Vncouatice, of gyftys free. **1648** HEXHAM II, *Onbegeerigh*, Vncovetous. **1871** RUSKIN *Fors Clav.* v. 22 An uncalculating and uncovetous wisdom. *Ibid.* x. 7 The healthy delight of uncovetous admiration.

**Uncow,** obs. f. UNCO.

**Uncow·ed,** *ppl. a.* (UN-[1] 8.) **1891** MISS DOWIE *Girl in Karp.* 127 The children sharp, clever, and uncowed.

**Uncow·l,** *v.* (UN-[2] 4.)

**1611** COTGR., *Descapuchonner*, to vnhood, vncowle, vncouer. **1812** COLERIDGE *Remorse* I. ii. 260, I pray you, think us friends—uncowl your face. **1829** I. TAYLOR *Enthus.* ix. 242 Let him uncowl his ears, and cover his naked feet. **1840** BROWNING *Sordello* VI. 348 One blood-drop to the bowl Which brimful tempts the sluggish asp uncowl At last.

**Uncow·led,** *ppl. a.* (UN-[1] 8.)

**1728** POPE *Dunc.* III. 114 Behold yon' Isle, by Palmers, Pilgrims trod, Men bearded, bald, cowl'd, uncowl'd, shod, unshod. **1868** GEO. ELIOT *Sp. Gypsy* III. 301 To work the will of a more tyrannous friend Than any uncowled father.

**Uncra·cked,** *ppl. a.* (UN-[1] 8.)

**1581** BP. AYLMER in Nicolas *Mem. Sir C. Hatton* (1847) 240 If you will have..your credit kept uncracked for commending me. **1623** MIDDLETON & ROWLEY *Sp. Gipsy* IV. i, The uncrack'd diamond of my faith shall hold. **1648** SANDERSON *Serm.* (1681) II. 226 The ice..is of that firmness, that it will bear a loaden cart uncrackt. **1763** CHURCHILL *Ghost* IV. 1397 Good men..With names uncrack'd, and credit sound. **1826** LAMB *Lett* (1886) II. 228 Heaven send him his jars un-crack'd. **1891** KIPLING *Light that Failed* (1900) 244 The person who demanded muffins and an uncracked teapot.

**Uncra·ftily,** *adv.* [UN-[1] 11.] † Unskilfully.

**1519** HORMAN *Vulg.* 42 b, Woundis..yf they be touchyd vncraftelye out of season,..waxe angry and rauncleth. **1538** ELYOT, *Infabre*, vnkunningly, vncraftily.

**Uncra·ftiness.** [UN-[1] 12.] † Unskilfulness.

*c* **1520** BARCLAY *Jugurth* 88 They dispyse my..vnnoble lynage, and I dyspyse the vncraftynesse and slouthe of them.

**Uncra·fty,** *a.* [UN-[1] 7. Cf. (with the sense of 'weak, feeble') OS. *unkrahtag*, MDu. *oncrachtich, -crechtich, -creftich* (older Du. *onkrachtig*), MLG. *unkrechtich*, OHG. *unchreftic* (MHG. *unkreftig*, G. *unkräftig*), MDa. *ukraftig*.]

† **1.** Not dexterous or ingenious; unskilful. *Obs.*

**1483** *Cath. Angl.* 80/1 Vn Crafty, *inartificiosus*. *c* **1520** BARCLAY *Jugurth* 47 Whiche armye was vncraftie, sluggishe and feble. **1533** BELLENDEN *Livy* I. iii. (S.T.S.) I. 23 Þe rude and vncrafty pepill of þat regioun.

**2.** Not crafty or cunning; guileless.

**1647** HEXHAM I, Vncraftie, *sonder schalckheyt*. **1660** JER. TAYLOR *Ductor* Pref. (1676) p. vii, By the new methods, a Simple and Uncrafty Man cannot be wise unto salvation.

**Uncra·mp,** *v.* (UN-[2] 3.)

**1851** SIR F. PALGRAVE *Norm. & Eng.* I. 353 Uncramping or shattering the pedestals supporting the idols. **1860** MISS YONGE *Stokesley Secr.* viii, Susie extended each hand to its broadest stretch to uncramp them.

**Uncra·mped,** *ppl. a.* (UN-[1] 8.)

**1797** *Monthly Rev.* XXIV. 194 Providing him with the means of pursuing his inquiries uncramped and at leisure. **1860** PUSEY *Min. Proph.* 519 An unconfined, uncramped population, spreading itself freely, without restraint of walls. **1899** RODWAY *Guiana Wilds* 109 Their broad backs were quite unaffected by burning sun or pouring rain, and their limbs uncramped by sitting on the bottom of the canoe.

Hence **Uncra·mpedness.**

**1882** *Academy* 18 Nov. 358 The free handling and absolute uncrampedness of the landscape.

**Uncra·nnied,** *ppl. a.* (UN-[1] 8.)

? *a* **1625** WEBSTER *Appius & Virg.* I. iii, Trust my bosom To be the closet of your private griefs: Believe me, I am uncrannied. *a* **1627** DRAYTON *Sheph. Sirena* 70 There is nothing to that friend, To whose close vncrannied brest, We our secret thoughts may send. **1649** G. DANIEL *Trinarch., Hen. V*, cxxix, Where Loyaltie vncranied, doth keepe out The Subtle Flame, the Fæces, cannot doe't.

**Uncrava·tted,** *ppl. a.* (UN-[1] 8.) **1847** HELPS *Friends in C.* I. ii. 31 A great, unhatted, uncravated, bearded man.

**Uncra·vingly,** *adv.* (UN-[1] 11.) **1849** M. ARNOLD *Resignation* 161 Beautiful eyes meet his; and he Bears to admire uncravingly.

**Uncra·zed,** *ppl. a.* (UN-[1] 8.)

**1608** HEYWOOD *Lucrece* IV. iv, So I keep unstain'd The uncraz'd honour I have yet maintain'd. **1613–8** DANIEL *Coll. Hist. Eng.* (1626) 119 Who in that broken time, onely held vncrased..the part of an euen Counsellour and Officer.

**Uncre,a·table,** *a.* (UN-[1] 7 b.)

**1846** WORCESTER (citing Tillock). **1883** H. DRUMMOND *Nat. Law in Spir. W.* 297 Matter is uncreatable and indestructible.

Hence **Uncre,atabi·lity; Uncre,a·tableness.**

**1878** NEWCOMB *Pop. Astron.* IV. iii. 502 The uncreatableness and indestructibility of matter. **1883** *Glasgow Weekly Her.* 6 Oct. 8/2 The incontrovertibility of matter and energy ..and their consequent indestructibility and uncreatability.

**Uncre,a·te,** *ppl. a.* [UN-[1] 8 b and 5 b.] = UNCREATED *ppl. a.*

**1548–9** *Bk. Com. Prayer, Quicunque vult*, The father uncreate, the sonne uncreate, and the holy gost uncreate. **1608** L. MACHIN *Dumbe Knight* III. i, A creature vncreate in paradise, And one thats onely of a womans making. **1807** OPIE in *Lect. Paint.* i. (1848) 240 All that poets yet have feigned..of uncreate or unembodied being. **1842** MANNING *Serm.* (1848) I. i. 3 We talk of powers, and qualities,..and the like; but..they do not exist apart from beings, create or uncreate. **1870** MYERS *Poems* 120 Then in scorn My lips are silent; uncreate, unborn, Evanishes the visionary lay.

*absol.* **1851** KINGSLEY *Yeast* xvii, You can only see the Uncreate in the Create—the Infinite in the Finite.

**Uncre,a·te,** *v.* [UN-[2] 3.] *trans.* To undo the creation of; to unmake. Also *refl.*

**1633** PRYNNE *Histrio-m.* 172 Is this a light, a despicable effeminacie, for men..thus purposely..to vnman, vnchristian, vncreate themselves? **1640** HABINGTON *Edw. IV*, 37 It was as easie for him to uncreate as to create a King. **1690** C. NESSE *O. & N. Test.* I. 2 When we are once created in Christ, we can, indeed, do something to uncreate our selves. **1760–72** H. BROOKE *Fool of Qual.* (1809) III. 107 Could I have had my wish, creation would again have been uncreated. **1847** BUSHNELL *Chr. Nurt.* viii. (1861) 209 One religion was creating and the other uncreating manhood. **1894** *Fallen Angels* xxi. 112 God himself could not preserve the unfilial from suffering, save by uncreating them.

*absol.* *a* **1634** CHAPMAN & SHIRLEY *Chabot* v. i. 89 With one breath they uncreate. **1651** STANLEY *Poems* 74 Thus thy diviner Muse a power 'bove Fate May boast, that can both make and uncreate. **1744** YOUNG *Nt. Th.* VII. 1221 But tho' you can deform, you can't destroy; To curse, not uncreate, is all your pow'r.

**Uncre,a·ted,** *ppl. a.* [UN-[1] 8 and 5 b.]

**1.** Not brought into existence by a special act of creation; of a self-existent or eternal nature.

**1548–9** *Bk Com. Prayer, Quicunque vult*, As also there be not..three uncreated: but one uncreated. **1587** GOLDING *De Mornay* ix. (1592) 118 If it were created after the example of a thing vncreated, can it come to passe that it should be euerlasting? *a* **1633** W. AUSTIN *Medit.* (1635) 246 Certaine Hereticks held them [*sc.* angels] to be uncreated, and Coëternall with God. **1667** MILTON *P. L.* II. 150 To perish..in the wide womb of uncreated night. **1704** CLARKE *Attributes* iii (1738) 22 Original Being, Uncreated, Independent, and of it self Eternal. **1777** PRIESTLEY *Matt. & Spir.* (1782) I. xix. 225 Uncreated light could not be seen by mortal eyes. **1801** SOUTHEY *Thalaba* IV. ix, Of these Angels' fate Thus in the uncreated book is written. **1860** PUSEY *Min. Proph.* 481 Love, joy, peace..are created in man. Only in God they exist, undivided, uncreated.

*absol.* **1678** CUDWORTH *Intell. Syst.* Pref., The Pagan Polytheism and Idolatry consisted not in worshipping Many Creators, or Uncreateds, but [etc.]. **1805** WORDSW. *Prelude* II. 413 Every form of creature..looked Towards the Uncreated with a countenance Of adoration. **1877** SPARROW *Serm.* vi. 78 What we are as creatures we never can know, as we ought, but by studying the uncreated.

**2.** Not created; not brought into being.

**1607** BEAUM. & FL. *Woman-Hater* II. i, Nor will I Wish my self uncreated for this evil. **1667** MILTON *P. L.* VI. 268 How hast thou..into Nature brought Miserie, uncreated till the crime Of thy Rebellion? **1890** *Spectator* 18 Oct., In the case of an uncreated book, of course the argument is infinitely stronger.

**Uncre,a·tedness.** [f. prec.] The quality or state of being uncreated.

**1648** HEXHAM II, *Ongeschapenheydt*, Vncreatednesse, or Vnshapennesse. **1678** CUDWORTH *Intell. Syst.* I. iv. § 6. 197 Some Modern Sects..do also assert the Vncreatedness of the Matter. *a* **1740** WATERLAND *Wks.* (1823) II. 326 Making a distinction between derived uncreatedness, and underived uncreatedness. **1857** SUSANNA WINKWORTH tr. *Life Tauler* 288 God..is equal to the soul as touching freedom, and unequal as touching uncreatedness, for the soul is created. **1877** W. BRIGHT in *Dict. Chr. Biog.* I. 181/2 When Arius..expressly denied..the uncreatedness of the Son of God.

**Uncre,a·ting,** *ppl. a.* [f. UNCREATE *v.*] Destroying; reducing to nonentity.

**1742** POPE *Dunc.* IV. 654 Light dies before thy uncreating word. **1820** SHELLEY *Naples* 138 The Anarchs of the North lead forth their legions Like Chaos o'er creation, uncreating.

**Uncre,a·tion.** [UN-[2] 8: cf. prec.] The action of uncreating.

**1884** *Edin. Rev.* Oct. 334 The famous lines on the uncreation of the world by 'Chaos old'. **1885** G. MACDONALD *Book of Strife* 16 Dec., A thing..Which uncreation can alone release.

**Uncre,a·tive,** *a.* (UN-[1] 7 and 5 b.) **1855** MILMAN *Lat. Chr.* XIV. viii. VI. 566 The East..settled down in unprogressive, uncreative acquiescence, and went on copying that type. **Uncre,a·tiveness.** (UN-[1] 12.) **1855** LEWES *Goethe* I. III. viii. 291 The contempt of Prometheus for the idleness, the uncreativeness of the Gods. **Uncrea·tural,** *a.* (UN-[1] 7.) **1649** J. ELLISTONE tr. *Behmen's Epistles* 30 We our selves are the property of the foure Elements, and they are in Us creaturall; and without us they are uncreaturall.

**Uncrea·turely,** *a.* [UN-[1] 7.] Not belonging, natural, or proper to creatures.

**1668** HOWE *Bless. Righteous* (1825) 89 That diabolical uncreaturely pride that is long since banished heaven. **1707** NORRIS *Treat. Humility* vii. 295 Hatred of God..is strictly an uncreaturely sin. **1877** SPARROW *Serm.* 334 The proud, selfish, ungrateful, rebellious, impious, uncreaturely temper.

† **Uncre·dible,** *a.* *Obs.* [UN-[1] 7 and 5 b.]

**1.** = INCREDIBLE *a.* 1. (Common *c* 1550–1650.)

*c* **1440** *Wycliffite Bible* Judg. xx. 5 (MS. Bodl. 277), Þei han traueilid my wijf wiþ vncredible wodnesse of leccherie. **1482** *Monk of Evesham* xlix. (Arb.) 98 An oncredyble and inestymable conforte of ioye and plesure. **1560** DAUS tr. *Sleidane's Comm.* 424 b, It is vncredible, with what rebukes and railinges yͤ people receiued hym. **1605** BACON *Adv. Learn.* I. iv. § 10 Rarities and reports, that seeme vncredible. **1653** HOLCROFT *Procopius, Vandal Wars* II. 47 A thing seeming difficult, and uncredible to such as have not seen our former actions. **1680** MORDEN *Geog. Rect., Turkey* 356 Taken by..Mustapha..with an uncredible Slaughter.

**2.** Incredulous. *rare.*

**1553** *Douglas's Æneid* IV. 87 Quhy dois he refuse my wourdis and prayers To lat entyr in hys dul vncredyble [*Small* vntretable] eris?

Hence † **Uncredibi·lity;** † **Uncre·dibly** *adv.*

**1486** *Bk. St. Albans* f vj b, An vncredibilitie of Cocoldis. **1565** STAPLETON tr. *Bede's Hist. Ch. Eng.* Pref. 9 We see as much vncredibilite..in the one as in the other. **1565** COOPER *Thesaurus, Incredibiliter*,..vncredibly: meruaylously.

† **Uncre·dit,** *v.* *Obs.* [UN-[1] 14 and UN-[2] 3.] *trans.* To distrust; to discredit.

**1615** DANIEL *Hymens Triumph* II. ii, Such meanes can wit deuise To make mens mindes vncredit their owne eies. **1628** FELTHAM *Resolves* II. xxi. 70 Affirmations are apter to winne beliefe, then Negatiues to vncredit them. **1655** FULLER *Ch. Hist.* XI. ii. § 82. 156 Then was it Kilvert his designe to uncredit the Testimony of Pregion, by charging him with several accusations.

**Uncre·ditable,** *a.* [UN-[1] 7 b and 5 b.] Discreditable; disreputable.

**1643** HAMMOND *Serm.* Wks. 1684 IV. 511 He..that abstains only from uncreditable or unfashionable, from branded or disused sins. **1688** COLLIER *Several Disc.* (1725) 2 The Design..being to make all Injustice and Encroachment an uncreditable, as well as an unprofitable Practice. **1710** PALMER *Proverbs* 342 A brawl, in which both parties use a hundred impertinent and uncreditable expressions. **1782** PALEY *Serm.* 21 Sept., The vocation in time comes to be thought mean and uncreditable. **1818** BENTHAM *Ch. Eng., Catech. Exam.* 427 No need has he of any such uncreditable and hazardous practice. **1866** *Illustr. Lond. News* 1 Dec. 526 The credit which Mr..has received ..is very uncreditable to the English nation.

Hence **Uncre·ditableness.**

**1667** *Causes Decay Chr. Piety* xix. 419 To all other disswasives we may add this of the Uncreditableness.

**Uncre·dited,** *ppl. a.* (UN-[1] 8 and 5 b.)

**1586** WARNER *Alb. Eng.* II. ix. (1592) 36 It cannot weepe, nor wring the handes, but say that she did so: And saieth so vncredited. **1607** CHAPMAN *Rev. Bussy D'Ambois* Plays 1873 II. 140 God (said she) Would haue me vtter things vncredited. **1670** CLARENDON *Contempl. Ps.* Tracts (1727) 532 Who..does render..their virulent suggestions against our reputations ineffectual and uncredited. **1777** *Ann. Reg., Antiq.* 134/2 This opinion remained..uncredited by all skilful medallists. **1828** *Lights & Shades* II. 133 Being at the same time..unmannered, uncredited, unwitted.

**Uncree·ping,** *ppl. a.* (UN-[1] 10.) **1727** *Fam. Dict.* s.v. *Dog's Cawl*, The uncreeping *Apocynon* shoots forth great Twigs of an ill Scent.

**Uncre·sted,** *ppl. a.*[1] [UN-[1] 8.] Not adorned or furnished with a crest.

**1655** MOUFET & BENNET *Health's Improv.* 103 Some of each sort are high crested like a lapwing, others uncrested. **1757** DYER *Fleece* IV. 436 Soldier, and statesman, and uncrested chief. **1888** GUNTER *Mr. Potter* ix. 117 Plain letter paper and uncrested envelope.

**Uncre·sted,** *ppl. a.*[2] [UN-[2] 8.] Deprived of a crest.

**1611** COTGR., *Ecreté*, topped, vncrested; whose top or crest is taken off. **1834** DE QUINCEY *Autob. Sk.* Wks. 1853 I. 181 *note*, Supposing the city to be uncrested, as it were; its upper tiers to be what the sailors call unshipped.

**Uncri·bbed,** *ppl. a.*: see UNCABINED *a.*

**Uncrie·d,** *ppl. a.* [UN-[1] 8 c.] *Uncried up*, not extolled or praised.

**1630** B. JONSON *New Inn* IV. ii, *Huf.* So you will name no Spaniard, I will pledge you. *Tip.* I rather choose to thirst, ..Then leaue that creame of nations vncry'd vp.

**Uncri·minal,** *a.* (UN-[1] 7.) **1864** CARLYLE *Fredk. Gt.* XVI. xi. IV. 432 With other the like uncriminal fancies. **1881** *Daily News* 25 Jan. 3/1 The uncriminal but powerful organization of the Land League. **Uncri·minally,** *adv.* (UN-[1] 11.) *a* **1864** HAWTHORNE *S. Felton* (1883) 258 A human life, taken (however uncriminally) by his own hands.

**Uncri·ppled,** *ppl. a.* (UN-[1] 8.)

*a* **1800** COWPER *Odyss.* (ed. 2) xx. 437, I have eyes and ears, Two feet uncrippled. **1812** CARY *Dante, Purgat.* xxv. 2 It was an hour, when he who climbs, had need To walk uncrippled. **1894** *Daily News* 11 June 8/2 Love of beauty and of uncrippled happiness.

**Uncri·sp,** *v.* (UN-[2] 3.) **1598** FLORIO, *Discrespare*, to vncurle, to vnfrizle, to vncrispe, to vnwrinkle. **Uncri·sped,** *ppl. a.* (UN-[2] 8.) **1827** HOOD *Hero & Leander* lxiii, His uncrispt locks uncurling in the brine.

**Uncri·tical,** *a.* [UN-[1] 7. Cf. Du. *onkritisch*, G. *unkritisch*, Da. *ukritisk*.]

**1.** Not critical; lacking in judgement; not addicted to criticism.

**1659** GAUDEN *Tears Church* I. i. 24 We are not so rude understanders, or uncritical speakers. **1767** STERNE *Tr. Shandy* x. xxiv, A most uncritical fever which attacked me at the beginning of this chapter. **1826** MISS MITFORD *Village* Ser. II. (1863) 361 She discovered none of the imputed sublimity; her uncritical eye could only scan the tremendous number of pages. **1854** MAURICE *Mor. & Met. Philos.* (ed. 2) 20 It has been the ungrateful fashion of some modern historians to speak of him as an uncritical retailer of anecdotes. **1890** 'R. BOLDREWOOD' *Col. Reformer* xx, He played..well enough to satisfy the uncritical audience. *absol.* **1874** SPENCER *Study Sociol.* v. 81 Statements..readily accepted by the uncritical who believe all they see in print.

**2.** Showing lack of criticism or critical exactness; not in accordance with critical methods.

**1846** J. KENRICK *Ess. Primæval Hist.* Pref. p. xii, An arbitrary and uncritical preference of the Septuagint to the Hebrew. **1855** J. PHILLIPS *Man. Geology* 420 A perverse and uncritical application of the Mosaic narrative. **1874** MAHAFFY *Soc. Life Greece* vii. 215 It is uncritical to judge an age by its greatest men.

Hence **Uncri·tically** *adv.*

**1807** G. CHALMERS *Caledonia* I. 402 Huntington, however, copies it, uncritically. **1858** SPENCER in *Westm. Rev.* July 195 We see that the notion, of late years idly repeated and uncritically received,..involves us in sundry absurdities. **1895** *Blackw. Mag.* Nov. 634/1 You took with you a temperament uncritically alert to fresh impressions.

**Uncri·ticizable,** *a.* (UN-[1] 7 b.) **1858** HAWTHORNE *Fr. & It. Note bks.* (1872) II. 137 Pictures..cold, proper, and uncriticizable. **Uncri·ticized,** *ppl. a.* (UN-[1] 8.) **1846** WORCESTER (citing Scott). **1884** *Pall Mall G.* 9 Dec. 3/1 The most intolerable government in the world—an absolute and uncriticized bureaucracy. **Uncri·ticizingly,** *adv.* (UN-[1] 11.) **1850** F. W. NEWMAN *Phases* vi. 212 The claims ..implied..the duty of all to sit at his feet uncriticizingly.

**Uncroo·ked,** *ppl. a.* (UN-[1] 8.)

**1611** FLORIO, *Inobliquo*, vncrooked, straight. **1618** FLETCHER *Loyal Subj.* III. ii, Now you have moulded us.. To easie and obedient ways, uncrooked, Where the fair mind can never lose nor loiter. **1776** S. J. PRATT *Pupil of Pleas.* (1777) I. 184 Plain, clear, clean, uncrooked honesty.

**Uncro·pped,** *ppl. a.* [UN-[1] 8.]

**1.** Of flowers, etc.: Not cut or plucked; not eaten by cattle. Also *fig.*

**1601** SHAKS. *All's Well* v. iii. 328 If thou beest yet a fresh vncropped flower, Choose thou thy husband, and Ile pay thy dower. **1610** FLETCHER *Faithf. Sheph.* I. i, If I keep My Virgin Flower uncropt, pure, chaste, and fair. **1667** MILTON *P. L.* IV. 731 Where thy abundance wants Partakers, and uncropt falls to the ground. **1825** J. NEAL *Bro. Jonathan* III. 396 A bright circle of uncropped herbage was about the root. **1835** E. JESSE *Glean. Nat. Hist.* Ser. III. 228 Nature has given them a distaste for several flowers which are..left uncropped.

**2.** Not cropped or cut; left uncut.

**1802** COLEMAN *Br. Grins, Knt. & Friar* (1819) 101 Uncropp'd his ears, undock'd his flowing tail. **1895** *Westm. Gaz.* 7 June 3 Nineteen black-and-tans with uncropped ears. *Ibid.*, The first prize..was won by..an uncropped dog.

**3.** Of land: Not used for cropping.

**1857** MILLER *Elem. Chem., Org.* xiii. § 1. 733 Allowing the land to lie uncropped for a year.

**Uncro·ss,** *v.* [UN-[2] 3.] *trans.* To take out of, change back from, a crossed position.

**1599** G. SILVER *Paradoxes Def.* 4 He shal haue great disaduantage, both in making of a strong crosse, and also in vncrossing againe. **1611** COTGR., *Descroiser*, to vncrosse; to open,..lay, or set straight a thing which stands acrosse. **1760** STERNE *Tr. Shandy* IV. *Slawkenb. Tale*, Having uncrossed his arms with the same solemnity with which he crossed them. **1815** SCOTT *Guy M.* iii, The Dominie groaned deeply, uncrossed his legs. **1871** 'M. LEGRAND' *Cambr. Freshm.* ix. 169 Mr. Samuel uncrossed the knives, and let the salt lie, in a reckless manner.

**Uncro·ssable,** *a.* (UN-[1] 7 b.) **1882** R. H. PATTERSON *New Gold. Age* I. 112 The hardly known region beyond the almost uncrossable mountain wall.

**Uncro·ssed,** *ppl. a.* [UN-[1] 8.]

**1.** Not wearing or invested with a cross.

**1560** BECON *Jewel of Joy* Pref., What a swarme of popyshe shauelyngs brought he forth,..some crossed, some vncrossed. **1858** BAILEY *Age* 78 Unstarred, uncrossed, uneagled, pure of mind.

†**2.** Not obliterated or cancelled. (See CROSS *v.* 4.)

**1611** SHAKS. *Cymb.* III. iii. 26 Such gaine the Cap of him, that makes him fine, Yet keepes his Booke vncros'd. **1640** *Wand. Jew telling Fortunes* C 2, These rich clothes cost me nothing, the Mercers uncrost booke shall sweare for me. **1690** NORRIS *Beatitudes* Ep. Ded., I am got too far in your Accounts..; some part of them I must ever leave uncrossed as a standing Hold upon me.

**3.** *fig.* Not thwarted or opposed.

*a* **1634** CHAPMAN *Rev. for Honour* III. i. 118 With as secure an ease 'T shall be accomplish'd as the blest desires Of uncross'd lovers. **1833** WORDSW. *Sonn.*, '*Desire we past*' 8 Conquering Reason, if self-glorified, Can nowhere move uncrossed by some new wall Or gulf of mystery. **1899** *Allbutt's Syst. Med.* VI. 516 An uncrossed influence arising somewhere above the lower end of the fourth ventricle. *absol.* **1846** LANDOR *Imag. Conv.* I. 249/2 The studious ..the unhardened in politics, the uncrossed in literature.

**4.** Of a cheque: (see CROSS *v.* 7 c).

**1884** *Law Times* 29 Nov. 79/2 Three..were crossed generally 'and Co.', and three were uncrossed.

**Uncross-exa·minable,** *a.* (UN-[1] 7 b), **-exa·mined,** *ppl. a.* (UN-[1] 8.) **1802–12** BENTHAM *Ration. Judic. Evid.* (1827) V. 285 Unsanctioned and uncross-examinable evidences. *Ibid.* III. 563 The evidence unsanctioned, and the author uncross-examined. *a* **1873** MILL *Ess. Relig.* (1874) 236 The uncross-examined testimony of extremely ignorant people.

**Uncro·ssly,** *adv.* [UN-[1] 11.] Not adversely.

**1615** *Marr. & Wiving* in *Harl. Misc.* (Malh.) III. 253 That the joy their forward youth hath sought, Uncrossly matched, may come more near their thought.

**Uncrow·ded,** *ppl. a.* (UN-[1] 8.)

**1701** ADDISON *Let. Italy* 76, Wks. 1721 I. 49 An amphitheater's amazing height..That on its publick shows Unpeopled Rome, And held Uncrowded nations in its womb. **1732** J. WHALEY *Poems* 162 There roll your River's wide extended Waves, That on its Side uncrouded Fleets receives. **1791** COWPER *Yardley Oak* 55 The numerous flock That graz'd it stood beneath that ample cope Uncrowded. *a* **1817** T. DWIGHT *Trav. New Eng.*, etc. (1821) II. 412 The situation is..at a sufficient distance from the Green Mountains to furnish a fine, uncrowded view of them. **1899** A. WRIGHT *Depopulation* 124 Strong for what? For the crowded millions, or for their uncrowded masters only?

**Uncrow·n,** *v.* [UN-[2] 4. Cf. Du. *ontkroonen* (Sewel), G. *entkrönen.*]

**1.** *trans.* To take the crown from (a ruler); to deprive of royalty.

*a* **1300** *Cursor M.* 9084 'Tas of,' he said, 'mi kinges croun þat i na langer agh to bere...I will þat yee vncroun me'. **1593** SHAKS. 3 *Hen. VI*, III. iii. 232 He hath done me wrong, And therefore Ile vn-Crowne him, er't be long. **1605** SYLVESTER *Du Bartas* II. iii. II. 85 The voyce which made all things, Which sceptereth Shepheards, and un-crowneth Kings. **1645** E. CALAMY *Indictm. Eng.* 18 They seeke his life, and would uncrowne Him and his Posteritie. **1705** HICKERINGILL *Priest-cr.* (1721) I. 39 The insulting Priest.. let him know, that he that Crown'd him could Uncrown him. **1747** W. HORSLEY *Fool* (1748) II. 222 Where an Inquisitor-General..is uncrowning the Monarchy. **1855** MACAULAY *Hist. Eng.* xi. III. 7 They had meant to obtain from him some guarantee..., but not to uncrown and banish him. *fig.* **1638** FORD *Lady's Trial* II. iv, Prepare a welcome to uncrown the greatness Of his prevailing fates. *refl.* **1846** *Literary Gaz.* Oct. 842 Francis II uncrowned himself, declaring that the holy Roman empire was at an end.

**2.** To remove a crown from (the head); to divest *of* (a crown).

**1598** FLORIO, *Disghirlandare*, to vngarlande, to vncrowne. *a* **1658** LOVELACE *Poems* (1864) 167 Of the wet pearls uncrown thy hair. **1697** DRYDEN *Æneis* XII. 449 The Italians strip the dead Of his rich armour, and uncrown his head.

**b.** *fig.* To uncover; to display.

**1849** M. ARNOLD *Shakespeare* 4 The loftiest hill That to the stars uncrowns his majesty.

Hence **Uncrow·ning** *vbl. sb.*

**1611** SPEED *Hist. Gt. Brit.* IX. viii. § 45. 499/1 That the mindes of the vulgar should not bee vnpossessed with like expectation of Iohns vn-crowning. **1862** R. H. PATTERSON *Ess. Hist. & Art* 357 The uncrowning of the Seven-Hilled Queen by the barbarians of the North.

**Uncrow·ned,** *ppl. a.* [UN-[1] 8. Cf. MDu. *ongecroont*, Du. *ongekroond*, G. *ungekrönt.*]

†**1.** Untonsured. *Obs.*[—1]

**1393** LANGL. *P. Pl.* C. VI. 62 Hit by-comeþ for clerkus crist for to seruen, And knaues vncrouned to cart and to worche.

**2.** Not invested with a crown.

**1634** BP. HALL *Contempl. N. T.*, *Faithful Canaanite*, Never did such grace goe away uncrowned. **1810** CRABBE *Borough* xi. 58 Unlike the nobler beast, the Bear is bound, And with the Crown so near him, scowls uncrown'd. **1889** R. BRIDGES *Sonn.* lxvii, And Autumn with a sad smile fled uncrown'd From fruitless orchards and unripen'd grain.

**3.** Not consummated or perfected.

**1742** BLAIR *Grave* 731 The glad Soul Has not a Wish uncrown'd.

**Uncru·cified,** *ppl. a.* (UN-[1] 8.) **1528** TINDALE *Obed. Chr. Man* 87 b, Yf Christe had not rebuked the Phareses.. he mighte haue be vncrucified vnto this daye.

†**Uncru·d,** *v. Obs.* [UN-[2] 3.] = UNCURD *v.*

**1398** TREVISA *Barth. De P. R.* XIX. li. (Bodl. MS.), It is tempred wiþ a litel hony and salte and þan it cruddeþ neuer but vncruddeþ [**1495** vncurdyth] ȝif it bigynneþ to crudde in þe stomake. **1598** FLORIO, *Squagliare*, to..vncrud milk.

**Uncru·dded,** *ppl. a.* [UN-[1] 8.] = UNCURDLED.

**1594** SPENSER *Epithal.* 175 Her brest like to a bowle of creame vncrudded.

**Uncru·de,** *a.* (UN-[1] 7.)

**1574** NEWTON *Health Mag.* 31 b, Hippocrates commaundeth vs to minister Phisicke to those thinges that be concoct and to mooue the vncrude. **1675** EVELYN *Terra* 161 Mingle the residue with the grosser Compost..frequently moistned with uncrude water.

**Uncru·el,** *a.* (UN-[1] 7.)

**1611** FLORIO, *Incrudele*, vncruell, milde. **1720** MRS. MANLEY *Power of Love* (1741) 272 If this Gentleman..had pressed her to make Him happy,..the uncruel fair One would not have been so hard-hearted to deny him. **1863** COWDEN CLARKE *Shaks. Char.* xiv. 363 Such a destiny would have been a sorry climax to thy uncruel misdemeanours.

**Uncru·mbled,** *ppl. a.* (UN-[1] 8.) [**1775** ASH.] **1878** B. TAYLOR *Deukalion* I. iii. 30 There the sun Sheds..hoary splendor on uncrumbled stone.

**Uncru·mple,** *v.* [UN-[2] 3.]

**1.** *trans.* To restore from a crumpled state.

**1611** COTGR., *Deffroncer*, to vnfrounce, vnwrinckle, vncrumple. *Ibid.*, *Desplissure*, an vnfoulding, vnplaiting, vnwrinkling, vncrumpling. **1863** LYTTON *Caxtoniana* I. vii. 92 No hand save his own could uncrumple the rose-leaf that chafed him. **1887** BROWNING *Parleyings, G. de Lairesse* v, Crisp buds a struggling bee Uncrumples.

**2.** *intr.* To become free from crumples.

**1866** M. ARNOLD *Thyrsis* 84 Next year he will return,.. With whitening hedges, and uncrumpling fern.

**Uncru·mpled,** *ppl. a.* (UN-[1] 8.)

**1854** CDL. WISEMAN *Fabiola* (1855) 39 The same scarf streams out, like a pennant, unruffled and uncrumpled by the breeze. **1873** BROWNING *Red Cott. Nt.-cap* 37 The varech limit-line, Burnt cinder-black with brown uncrumpled swathe Of berried softness.

**Uncru·shable,** *a.* (UN-[1] 7 b.)

**1873** MISS BRADDON *Str. & Pilgr.* I. xiii, 'I have more sense of the fitness of things,' replied the uncrushable youngest. **1894** *Westm. Gaz.* 22 Feb. 3/3 Its good wearing and uncrushable habit recommend it still more.

**Uncru·shed,** *ppl. a.* (UN-[1] 8.)

**1626** JACKSON *Creed* VIII. xxxi. § 6 The adoration of this serpent, whilst it stood uncrusht, was..the most preposterous idolatry. **1759** STERNE *Tr. Shandy* II. xix, Provided all goes right after, and his cerebellum escapes uncrushed. **1856** MRS. BROWNING *Aur. Leigh* I. 457 Her head uncrushed by that round weight of hat. **1875** HUXLEY & MARTIN *Elem. Biol.* (1877) 8 Note the..solid and uncrushed transparent sacs; the soft crushed stained protoplasm.

**Uncru·sted,** *ppl. a.* (UN-[1] 8.) [**1775** ASH.] **1880** *Contemp. Rev.* Feb. 210 An incandescent, uncrusted molten ball.

†**Uncry·,** *v.* [UN-[2] 3.] *trans.* To countermand.

**1594** CAREW *Tasso* (1881) 66 Who in his name their ouerhardinesse Vncries, and straight to turne doth straight impose.

**Uncry·stalled,** *ppl. a.* (UN-[1] 8.) **1796** KIRWAN *Elem. Min.* (ed. 2) I. 446 The adherence of some uncrystalled substance. **Uncry·stalline,** *a.* (UN-[1] 7.) **1833–4** J. PHILLIPS *Geol.* in *Encycl. Metrop.* (1845) VI. 702/1 The exterior of most uncrystalline rocks..seems to be slowly eaten away. **1875** RUSKIN *Fors Clav.* lx. 329, Such uncrystalline termination must now happen to all my work.

**Uncrystalli·zable,** *a.* (UN-[1] 7 b.)

**1791** W. HAMILTON *Berthollet's Dyeing* I. I. i. xii. 37 The uncrystallizable residue of the alum. **1812** SIR H. DAVY *Chem. Philos.* 496 This body is strongly acid and uncrystallizable. **1839** URE *Dict. Arts* 398 The small quantity of uncrystallizable sugar present in them. **1887** A. M. BROWN *Anim. Alkaloids* 142 Azotized uncrystallizable substances.

Hence **Uncrystallizabi·lity.**

**1841** BRANDE *Chem.* (ed. 5) 1077 The uncrystallizability of molasses is partly referable to a similar cause.

**Uncry·stallized,** *ppl. a.* (UN-[1] 8.)

**1759** STERNE *Tr. Shandy* I. xxiii, A dark covering of uncrystalized flesh and blood. **1794** R. J. SULIVAN *View Nat.* I. 467 The spherical..masses called geodes, are also crystaline, though they are, as it were, externally uncrystalized. **1830** HERSCHEL *Study Nat. Phil.* 242 The division of bodies into crystallized and uncrystallized, or imperfectly crystallized. **1874** GARROD & BAXTER *Mat. Med.* 277 Amorphous quinine, which bears the same relation to the crystallized alkaloid as uncrystallized syrup does to ordinary sugar.

†**Unct,** *v.* Chiefly *Sc. Obs.* Also 5–6 vnt-, 5 vynte. [f. L. *unct-*, ppl. stem of *ungĕre*, *unguĕre* to smear, etc.] *trans.* To anoint.

**14..** *Voc.* in Wr.-Wülcker 577/44 *Delibutus*, bebawdyd or vntyd. *c* **1425** WYNTOUN *Cron.* VIII. xxii. 2930 All kingis of Scotland Suld be sa vnctit befor regnand. *c* **1500** KENNEDY *Passion of Christ* 358 Thai laithly lippis vntit with fals tressoun. **1549** *Compl. Scot.* iv. 30 Osias vas bot aucht ȝeir of aige quhen he vas vnctit kyng. **1596** H. CLAPHAM *Briefe Bible* I. 75 [David] having raigned..33 yeares in Ierusalem, where he was the third time vncted.

Hence †**U·ncting** *vbl. sb. Obs.*

**1551** HAMILTON *Catechism* 131 Quhen the uncting is compleit, yair followis ane Catechisme.

†**U·ncteous,** obs. var. UNCTIOUS *a.*

**1601** HOLLAND *Pliny* II. 510 The same also in the bruising will..be uncteous or fattie. **1603** — *Plutarch's Mor.* 659 That sea water is uncteous, Aristotle..beareth witnesse.

**Unction** (ʋ·ŋkʃən). Forms: 4–5 vnccioun, 5–6 vnccion (5 -ione, 6 -yon); 5 unxioun; 5–6 uncion (5 ovncion); 5 unctioun, 6–7 vnction (6 vun-), 6– unction. [ad. L. *unctiōn-*, *unctio*, noun of action f. *unct-*, *ung(u)ĕre*: see UNCT *v.* So F. *onction* (12th c.), It. *unzione*, Sp. *uncion*, Pg. *unção.*]

**1.** The action of anointing with oil as a religious rite or symbol; occas. *ellipt.* = b.

**1387** TREVISA *Higden* (Rolls) I. 113 Seynt Austyn..clepeþ it [*sc.* Mount Olivet] þe hulle of crisma and of vnccioun. *c* **1400** MAUNDEV. (Roxb.) iii. 10 Þai make bot ane vnccioun, when þai christen childer. *c* **1430** LYDG. *Min. Poems* (Percy Soc.) 253 The hooly unctioun, shrift, hosyl, repentaunce. ? *a* **1500** *Chester Pl.* VIII. 289 Then both vnctions, sacrafices, and rites Ceremoniall Of the old Testament..shall vtterly cease. **1560** DAUS tr. *Sleidane's Comm.* 24 Then [he] treateth also of the other foure [sacraments], confirmation, order, matrimonye and Unction. **1697** J. POTTER *Antiq. Greece* II. ii. (1715) 196 The Act of Consecration chiefly consisted in the Unction, which was a ceremony derived from the most primitive Antiquity. **1745** BUTLER *Lives Saints* (1821) XI. 169 The ancient councils order them [*sc.* altars] to be consecrated by the unction of chrism, and the blessing of priests. **1768–74** TUCKER *Lt. Nat.* (1834) II. 414 The primitive fathers..practised exorcisms, unctions, signatures of the cross, and lustrations by holy water. **1856** R. A. VAUGHAN *Mystics* (1860) I. 94 The three sacraments,—Baptism, the Eucharist, and Unction. **1879** R. T. SMITH *Basil Gt.* x. 121 We bless both the water of baptism and the oil of unction. *personif.* *c* **1425** LYDG. *Assembly of Gods* 1444 Then came to the fylde the mynystre fynall, Called Holy Vnccion, with a crysmatory.

**b.** *Extreme unction*: see EXTREME *a.* 3.

**1513** *Life Hen. V* (1911) 182 After he had receaued the Sacraments of the Alter, and of extreame vunction. **1558** BP. WATSON *Sev. Sacram.* xxx. 193 To remoue these twoo euils, God hath ordeyned this Sacrament of extreme Unction to bee ministred. **1579** [see EXTREME *a.* 3]. **1602** J. COLVILLE *Parænese* u j, Dispysing the Sacrament of the altar, Celibat and extrem Vnction as many do nou a dayis. **1663** DRYDEN *Rival Ladies* v. ii, 'Tis like giving the extream Unction In the beginning of a Sickness. **1734** in *Cath. Rec. Soc. Publ.* (1914) XIV. 122 Her last Sickness.. only left time for yͤ Extrem unction. **1783** W. THOMSON *Watson's Philip III* (1839) 373 The blessed sacrament was administered to him about midnight. He received the extreme unction at two o'clock in the morning. **1871** MISS MULOCK *Fair France* vii. 218 He told us a woman lay dying, and the priest was administering extreme unction.

**2.** The action of anointing as a symbol of investing with a certain office, esp. that of kingship.

*c* **1400** *Three Kings Cologne* (1886) 32 Þe Iwes..seyden þat longe tyme aftir þe Natiuite of crist her vnccioun cesyd noȝt, but þey had many kyngis aftir. *a* **1500** *Cov. Corpus*

*Christi Pl.* ii. 204 Of that kyng that I ma haue a syght,.. At whose cumyng the tru ovncion of Juda schall seyse. **1626** D'Ewes in Ellis *Orig. Lett.* Ser. i. III. 218 The Archbishop performed the unction, which I doubted hee should not. **1690** Boyle *Chr. Virtuoso* ii. 30 The Heavenly Coronation has a Virtue like that of the Unction of Saul. **1757** Burke *Abridgm. Eng. Hist.* Wks. X. 430 He proceeded..to London to be crowned, and to sanctify by the solemnity of the unction the choice of the people. **1761** Hume *Hist. Eng.* I. ii. 43 Leo III gave Alfred the royal unction. **1845** Sarah Austin *Ranke's Hist. Ref.* I. 19 Otho could receive the unction without scruple. **1869** Freeman *Norm. Conq.* (1875) III. xi. 41 The hands of Stigand might not administer an unction which was held to confer somewhat of sacramental grace.

**3.** *fig.* A spiritual influence acting upon a person. Chiefly in renderings and echoes of 1 John ii. 20 and of the hymn *Veni, Creator spiritus* 8.

**1382** Wyclif 1 *John* ii. 20 But ȝe han vnccioun of the Holy Goost, and han knowe alle thinges. **1526** *Pilgr. Perf.* (W. de W. 1531) 154 They can not leaue & forsake the delectable wyne of contemplacyon & swete vnccyon of oyle of the holy goost. **1549** (Mar.) *Bk. Com. Prayer, Order. Priests*, Thou art the very comforter..and Unction spirituall. **1597** Hooker *Eccl. Pol.* v. lv. § 6 There is no other way how it should grow but either by the grace of vnion with deitie, or by the grace of vnction receiued from deitie. **1627** Cosin '*Veni Creator*,' Thou the anointing Spirit art;.. Thy blessed vnction from aboue Is comfort, life, and fire of loue. **1663** Bp. Patrick *Parab. Pilgr.* xxxvi, When he felt those distillations on his head, he could think of nothing else but the Vnction from above. **1693** Dryden '*Creator Spirit*' ii, Come, and thy Sacred Unction bring To Sanctifie us, while we sing! **1763** J. Payne tr. *Imit. Christ* iii. xix. 214 Give me, instead of all worldly comfort, the Divine Unction of Thy Holy Spirit. **1858** Neale *Bernard de M.* (1865) 26 The mention of thy glory Is unction to the breast. **1869** Freeman *Norm. Conq.* III. xi. 46 So now the oil poured on the head of God's servant might be a true sign of the inner unction of the heart.

**b.** Deep spiritual feeling, or the manifestation of this in language and utterance; a manner suggestive of religious earnestness or appreciation of spiritual things.

In later use freq. in depreciative sense, implying that the feeling or manner is superficial or assumed, or is tinged with obvious self-complacency.

**1692** Burnet *Past. Care* Pref. p. xxxiv, I began my Studies in Divinity with reading these, and I never yet grew weary of them; they..carry so much of unction and life in them, that [etc.]. **1817** Lady Morgan *France* (1818) I. 85 The peasantry..were seen..chaunting the office with as much faith and unction as if they had been paid. **1830** Coleridge *Table-t.* 1 June, There is a great decay of devotional unction in the numerous books of prayers put out now-a-days. **1870** Lowell *Among my Bks.* 235 That clerical unction which in a vulgar nature so easily degenerates into greasiness.

**c.** *transf.* A manner of utterance or address showing real appreciation or enjoyment of the subject or situation.

**1815** Scott *Guy M.* xvi, I have heard you too often describe the scene with comic unction. **1849** C. Bronte *Shirley* vi, He delivered the haughty speech of Caius Marcius to the starving citizens with unction. **1886** *Pall Mall G.* 7 Dec. 4/2 Is an actor subject to dismissal..because he does not 'throw enough unction' into his part?

**4.** The action of anointing or rubbing with an ointment or oil as a lubricating or preserving substance.

**1580** Hester tr. *Fioravanti's Disc. Chirurg.* 21 The first thing is to euacuate the stomacke, the second to sweate, the thirde vnccion. **1605** B. Jonson *Volpone* ii. i, Applying onely a warme napkin to the place, after the vnction and fricace. **1632** Lithgow *Trav.* (1906) 235 We saw..the place of Unction, which is a foure squared stone;..on which (say they) the dead body of our Saviour lay, and was embalmed. **1726** Pope *Odyss.* xix. 590 The bath renew'd, she ends the pleasing toil With plenteous unction of ambrosial oil. **1740** Johnson *Life Drake* Wks. IV. 425 In hot countries,..the natives only use unction to preserve them from the other extreme of weather. **1887** D. Maguire *Art Massage* iii. (ed. 4) 39 Unction does not, properly speaking, form part of the manipulations classified amongst frictions.

**5.** Any soft composition used for anointing or lubricating; an unguent or ointment.

**1580** Hester tr. *Fioravanti's Disc. Chirurg.* 26 b, Glisters, Vomittes, Purgations, and Vnctions;..the vnctions dissolue the winde. **1602** Shaks. *Ham.* iv. vii. 142, I bought an Vnction of a Mountebanke. **1631** Mabbe *Celestina* vi. 78 Clothing them [*sc.* their faces] with diuers colourings, glissenings, paintings, vnctions, oyntments. **1760** R. James *Canine Madness* 132 He must..get a considerable quantity of the unction rubbed into the arm-pits. **1860** Froude *Hist. Eng.* VI. 101 The next day, Arras having sent the necessary unction, the ceremony was performed at the Abbey. **1884** F. J. Britten *Watch & Clockm.* 202 The unction or paste obtained by rubbing two blue stones together.

*fig.* **1657** Trapp *Comm. Esther* ii. 12 Let women learn and labour to smell of Christ, who is the royal Unction.

**b.** *fig.* A soothing influence or reflection.

**1602** Shaks. *Ham.* iii. iv. 145 Lay not a flattering Vnction to your soule, That not your trespasse, but my madnesse speakes. **1836** Hor. Smith *Tin Trump.* I. 7 The stings of conscience would be intolerable, could we not lay some flattering unction to our souls. **1877** Farrar *Days of Youth* 108 Think not to lay to your diseased conscience the flattering unction that your sin was the result of circumstance.

**U·nctional,** *a.* [f. prec. 3 b.] Full of spiritual unction; deeply religious.

**1849** Tweedie *Life J. Macdonald* iv. 398 The discourse.. is rich, unctional, and full. **1864** *Mem. G. Paterson* 31 There was..no glib use of a sweet unctional phraseology.

**U·nctionless,** *a.* [f. as prec.] Devoid of spiritual unction.

**1842** *Blackw. Mag.* LI. 163 Tillotson and Burnet..show it in all the unctionless elegance..of its philosophic good sense.

**† U·nctious,** *a.* *Obs.* Also 5–6 vnctius, vnctyous, 6–7 vnctious. [f. L. *unct-um* ointment: see -ious.] = Unctuous *a.* 1. (Common *c* 1600–1725).

**1477** Norton *Ord. Alch.* v. (MS. Ashm. 1445) fol. 67 Þe same degrees..Vnctius sapor engender euer shall. **1542** Boorde *Dyetary* xiii. (1870) 265 Euery thyng that is vnctious..doth swymme aboue in the brynkes of the stomacke. **1594** Carew *Huarte's Exam. Wits* vi. 84 That [moisture] which springs from the aire maketh them to prooue vnctious and ful of oyle and fat. **1639** T. de Gray *Expert Farrier* 274, I will never use any other oyle or vnctious matter in any medicine. **1697** Tryon *Way to Health* vi. (ed. 3) 100 Whereby it is made more Spirituous than other Waters, and of a fat unctious Quality. **1764** Harmer *Observ.* 408 Lamps that are supplied with more than ordinary quantities of oyl, or other unctious substances.

*fig.* **1645** Quarles *Sol. Recant.* vi. 66 Or is she gone to oyle the wings of Time With unctious pleasures in some foraine Clime? **1646** — *Judgem. & Mercy* Wks. (Grosart) I. 69 Steepe thy stupid senses in unctious, in delightful sports.

Hence **† U·nctiousness.** *Obs.*

**1560** Whitehorne *Ord. Souldiours* 27 So that nothinge else be burnte but..certaine grosse vnctiousnes of the saltepeter. *a* **1661** Fuller *Worthies, Warwick.* iii. (1662) 115 It burneth..clear and bright, as if the Sappe thereof had a fire-feeding Unctiousness therein.

**Unctment,** obs. Sc. f. Ointment.

**† Unctuo·se,** *a.* *Obs. rare.* [ad. med.L. *unctuōsus.*] = Unctuous *a.*

*c* **1400** *Lanfranc's Cirurg.* 137 Also y seye þat oyle of roses ..is noȝt vnctuose, but is dreyȝe. **1471** Ripley *Comp. Alch.* i. vi. (MS. Ashm. 1445), And we make calxes vnctuose both white & red.

**Unctuosity** (ʌŋktiuˌǫ·sĭti). Forms: 4–5 vnctuosite, 6 -yte, 6–7 -itie, 7 -ity; 6 vnctuositee, 7 unctuositie, -ocity, 7– unctuosity. [a. OF. *unctuosite* (F. *onctuosité*), or ad. med.L. *unctuōsitas*, f. *unctuōs-us* Unctuous: see -ity. Cf. It. *untuosità*, *untosità*, Sp. *untuosidad*, Pg. *unctuosidade.*]

**1.** Unctuousness; oiliness, greasiness.

**1398** Trevisa *Barth. De P. R.* xix. xxxiii. (Bodl. MS.), For vnctuosite leide to þe tunge openeþ swiþe & dissolueþ, & sotel substaunce entreþ ful swiþe. *c* **1400** tr. *Secreta Secret., Gov. Lordsh.* 98 Swetnesse, bitternesse, saltnesse, & vnctuosite. **1539** Elyot *Cast. Helthe* (1541) 37 Whay,..by the vnctuositee of the butter,..is both moist and norishing. **1562** Boorde *Dyetary* xiii. E j, The vnctuosyte of it doth..augmente the heate of the lyuer. **1601** Holland *Pliny* II. 558 A certaine unctuositie or fattinesse it carrieth with it. **1644** Digby *Nat. Bodies* xix. § 8. 173 They haue a high degree of aqueous humidity ioyned with their vnctuosity. **1712** tr. *Pomet's Hist. Drugs* I. 102 The more nitrous and fossile the Salts are, the more Unctuosity they have. **1756** C. Lucas *Ess. Waters* II. 58 The gentlemen who talk of..unctuosity in sea water. **1805** Saunders *Min. Waters* 487 Inhabitants of hot climates, protected by the greater unctuosity of their skin,..are enabled to lead an almost amphibious life. **1873** *Beeton's Dict. Comm., Musk* ..comes to us dry, with a kind of unctuosity.

**2.** *fig.* Unctuous religiosity or complacency.

**1884** Tennyson *Becket* iii. iii, From whence there puffed out such an incense of unctuosity into the nostrils of our Gods of Church and State. **1885** *Spectator* 22 Aug. 1114/1 The author's style,..its well-known grace, and its at least equally well-known unctuosity.

**Unctuous** (ʌ·ŋktiuəs), *a.* Also 4–7 vnctuous, 6 ounctuous; 5, 7 vnctuos. [ad. med.L. *unctuōs-us*, f. L. *unct-um* ointment, f. *unct-*, ppl. stem of *ung(u)ĕre* to anoint. Cf. OF. *unctueus* (F. *onctueux*), It. and Sp. *untuoso*, Pg. *unctuoso.*]

**1.** Of the nature or quality of an unguent or ointment; oily, greasy.

**1387** Trevisa *Higden* (Rolls) I. 113 Þe fruit of olyue is ful of liȝt, likynge, and vnctuous. **1528** Paynell *Salerne's Regim.* b ij b, The vnctuous fleme whiche is engendred by mynglynge, of vnctuous bloud and fleme. **1555** Eden *Decades* (Arb.) 293 Gummes..and other vnctuous frutes and trees growing in hotte regions. **1604** F. Hering *Mod. Defence* 22 Sallet oile, butter, or any other vnctuous things. *a* **1691** Boyle *Hist. Air* (1692) 202 As if all the unctuous parts that were wanting in the dried portion of the cheese had retired thither. **1733** *Phil. Trans.* XXXVIII. 64 When this Operation succeeds rightly, there comes forth, First, a thick unctuous Oil. **1818** *Art Preserv. Feet* 105 The unctuous matter which exudes from excretory vessels. **1875** C. C. Blake *Zool.* 152 The poison itself is an unctuous gelatinous fluid.

**b.** Of meat: Greasy, fat, rich. Now *arch.*

**1495** *Trevisa's Barth. De P. R.* xix. xlv. 883 Vnctuous meete fletyth aboue for the lyghtnesse therof. **1539** Elyot *Cast. Helthe* (1541) 18 b, Meates..fatte and vnctuous, nourisheth, and maketh soluble. **1555** Eden *Decades* (Arb.) 147 When their fingers are imbrued with any ounctuous meates. **1610** B. Jonson *Alch.* ii. ii, The swelling vnctuous paps Of a fat pregnant sow. **1650** Bulwer *Anthrop.* 241 They feed upon unctuous and sweet meats. **1821** Lamb *Elia* i. *Grace before Meat*, Those unctuous morsels of deer's flesh.

*transf.* **1675** Grew *Disc. Tastes Plants* i. § 13 Contrary to an Unctuous Taste, are Astringent and Pungent. **1879** *Cassell's Techn. Educ.* IV. 162/2 The exquisite and unctuous taste which this excellent mollusk gives.

**c.** Characterized by the presence of oil or fat.

**1641** Milton *Reform.* ii. Wks. 1851 III. 66 Warming their Palace Kitchins, and from thence their unctuous and epicurean paunches, with the almes of the blind. **1768** [see 1 d]. **1791** Cowper *Iliad* ii. 664 Pallas rear'd him: her own unctuous fane She made his habitation. **1837** Dickens *Pickw.* iv, There was something in the sound of the last word, which roused the unctuous boy. **1856** Emerson *Eng. Traits, Charac.* Wks. (Bohn) II. 62 English day-labourers..are of an unctuous texture.

**d.** *Unctuous sucker*: (see quot.).

**1768** Pennant *Brit. Zool.* (1776) III. 135 Unctuous Sucker. This fish takes the name of sea snail from the soft and unctuous texture of its body, resembling that of the land snail.

**2.** Of ground or soil: Of a soft adhesive nature; fat, rich.

**1555** Eden *Decades* (Arb.) 227 As fat and vnctuous groundes ..yelde a fast and firme moysture. **1675** Evelyn *Terra* (1676) 30 Good and excellent Earth should be..not too unctuous nor too lean. **1693** — *De la Quint. Compl. Gard.* I. 18 Some [soils] are Unctuous and Sticking together. **1707** Mortimer *Husb.* 68 A soft unctuous Chalk, which is the best for Lands. **1777** Robertson *Hist. Amer.* (1778) I. 474 Their hunger is so great as compels them to eat..a kind of unctuous earth. **1813** Bakewell *Introd. Geol.* (1815) 297 When the matrix, or the substance which principally fills veins, is a soft unctuous clay. **1839** Murchison *Silurian System* 435 A layer of unctuous shale or fuller's earth. **1867** D. G. Mitchell *Rural Studies* 293 There are farms I know, unctuous with an accumulated fertility.

**3.** Of vapours, etc.: Partaking of the nature of oil or grease.

**1606** N. B[axter] *Sydney's Ourania* D 3 b, For Shepheards fayne..That from Bodyes buried in Summer season, An vnctuos vapour, hot and dry, doth rise. **1610** B. Jonson *Alch.* ii. iii, A humide exhalation, which we call *Materia liquida*, or the vnctuous water. **1635–56** Cowley *Davideis* iii. Note xl, Lambent fire is, A thin unctuous exhalation made out of the Spirits of Animals. **1712** Blackmore *Creation* iv. 173 Evening trains of unctuous vapours. **1774** Goldsm. *Nat. Hist.* I. 390 Falling stars, which are thought to be no more than unctuous vapours, raised from the earth to small heights. **1812** Sir H. Davy *Chem. Philos.* Introd. 19 Unctuous or inflammable gas. **1820** Shelley *Sensit. Pl.* iii. 74 Unctuous meteors from spray to spray..flitted in broad noonday Unseen. **1840** Dickens *Old C. Shop* xviii, And an unctuous steam came floating out.

**4.** Having an oily or greasy feel or appearance. Also of feel, touch, etc.

**1668** Wilkins *Real Char.* 82 Being of an unctuous touch, and used for Sallets. **1804** Abernethy *Surg. Obs.* 44 But it is not at all unctuous to the touch. **1828** J. E. Smith *Eng. Flora* II. 9 Pubescence mealy, friable, and unctuous. **1863** Hawthorne *Our Old Home* (1879) 96 Excellently carved in oak, now black with time and unctuous with kitchen-smoke. **1876** Duhring *Dis. Skin* 17 To the touch the skin has a soft, smooth, somewhat unctuous feel.

**5.** Characterized by spiritual unction (in later use *esp.* of an assumed or superficial nature); complacently agreeable or self-satisfied: **a.** Of persons.

**1742** Cheyne in *Byrom's Rem.* (1857) 331, I think him..more plain,..luminous, and unctuous, than any I ever met with. **1854** *Poultry Chron.* I. 292/2 Bland, unctuous, and rosy as they appear, they are nevertheless excessively fastidious. **1882** J. Ashton *Soc. Life Reign Q. Anne* II. 138 A Quaker could not be drawn without being caricatured into an unctuous rogue. **1896** 'Ian Maclaren' *Kate Carnegie* 171 A certain class of smug, self-contented, unctuous men.

**b.** Of speech, conduct, etc.

**1822** Lamb *Elia* i. *Chimney-Sweepers*, It was a pleasure to see the sable younkers lick in the unctuous meat, with *his* more unctuous sayings. **1848** Dickens *Dombey* iv, Laying an unctuous emphasis upon the words. **1871** Morley *Carlyle* in *Crit. Misc.* Ser. i. 217 In the corrupt and unctuous forms of a mechanical religious profession.

**U·nctuously,** *adv.* [f. prec. + -ly [2].] In an unctuous manner; with unction.

**1864** Webster. **1872** Goldw. Smith in *Fortn. Rev.* Mar. 246 The [religious] faith in the name of which the aristocracy had unctuously stolen the property of the nation. **1888** Miss Braddon *Fatal Three* i. v, 'I think hers is about the best case,' answered the Doctor unctuously.

**U·nctuousness.** Also 4 vnctuosnes. [f. as prec. + -ness.] The quality or state of being unctuous.

**1398** Trevisa *Barth. De P. R.* xix. xxxiii. (Bodl. MS.), Somme vnctuous þinges greueþ þe breste wᵗ drynes þᵗ is þerin, as it fareþ in oile of nottes, for suche haue not pure vnctuosnes. **1644** Digby *Nat. Bodies* xxix. (1658) 316 Softnesse, unctuousnesse, and viscousnesse, encreaseth blacknesse. **1682** T. Gibson *Anat.* (1697) 25 Whilst Nature takes care that it..besmear both the Stomach and Intestines with its Unctuousness. **1705** Addison *Italy* (1733) 140 Its Unctuousness will make it heavy. **1758** Reid tr. *Macquer's Chym.* I. 23 We shall afterwards see that, bating this unctuousness, it has none of the properties of oils. **1891** W. A. Jamieson *Dis. Skin* (ed. 3) i. 11 The office of the coil glands is to impart unctuousness to the skin.

*fig.* **1866** *Pall Mall G.* 3 Jan., The coarse, self-exhibiting unctuousness with which his book overflows.

**† Uncture.** *Obs.* [a. OF. *uncture* (*ungture*, *ointure*), or ad. L. *unctūra*, f. *unct-*, *ung(u)ĕre*. So Sp. and Pg. *untura.*] Ointment.

*c* **1400** *Lanfranc's Cirurg.* 41 For þys vncture ratefieþ & efenyþ þo placys by whom akþe goþ to þe brayn. *Ibid.* 103 Þenne y dede efte sonys þe same medycine & þe same vncture. *c* **1440** *Pallad. on Husb.* vi. 128 For sheep yshorn make vncture of lupynys.

**Uncu·ckold,** *v.* (Un-[2] 3.) **1789** J. Moore *Zeluco* xxi, I never yet heard of any method by which a man can be uncuckolded. **Uncu·ckolded,** *ppl. a.* (Un-[1] 8.) **1606** Shaks. *Ant. & Cl.* i. ii. 76 It is a deadly sorrow, to beholde a foule Knaue vncuckolded. **Uncu·dgelled,** *ppl. a.* (Un-[1] 8.) **1682** Shadwell *Medal* 1 The fool uncudgell'd, for one Libel swells.

**U·ncular,** *a.* *rare*[−1]. [f. Uncle *sb.*, after *avuncular.*] Belonging to an uncle.

**1847** De Quincey *Span. Nun* vi. Misc. (1854) 12 The grave Don..clasped the hopeful young gentleman..to his *uncular* and rather angular breast.

**Uncu·lled,** *ppl. a.* (Un-[1] 8.)

**1667** Milton *P. L.* xi. 436 A sweatie Reaper from his Tillage brought First Fruits,..Uncull'd, as came to hand. **1820** Wordsw. *River Duddon* vii. 12 There are whose calmer mind it would content To be an unculled floweret of the glen. **1826** Galt *Last of Lairds* i. 7 She was neither particular in her attire, nor methodical in her work, and her words were unculled.

† **Uncu·lpable,** *a. Obs.* [Un-1 7 b, 5 b.] Not culpable or blameworthy; free from fault or blame.
1382 Wyclif *Num.* xxxii. 22 Thanne ȝe shulen be vnculpable anentis God, and anentis Irael. 1532 More *Confut. Tindale* Wks. 355/1 For then is the fayth of the church in that point infallyble, or at ye lest vnculpable. 1594 Hooker *Eccl. Pol.* iii. vii. § 2 Which the Iewes obseruing as yet vnwritten,..are notwithstanding in that respect vnculpable. 1613 Jackson *Creed* ii. vii. § 11 We vpon inuincible or vnculpable ignorance, did not apprehend it for such. 1659 Stanley *Hist. Philos.* xiii. (1687) 912 It behoves us..not to suffer wickedness to escape unculpable. 1748 Richardson *Clarissa* VII. 55 You shall set over me, instead of my poor obliging, but really unculpable Hannah, your Betty Barnes.

† **Uncu·lt,** *a. Obs.* [Un-1 7, 5 b.] Uncultured.
1675 J. Smith *Chr. Relig. App.* ii. i. 4 The Gallick Druides (that most uncult Tribe of Divines).

† **Uncu·lted,** *ppl. a.* [Un-1 8.] Uncultivated.
1548 *Act* 2 & 3 *Edw. VI*, c. 13 § 16 The saide Countrey of Wales was throughe civile dissencion uncultcd. 1685 R. Burton *Eng. Emp. Amer.* vii. 107 Whatever wast or uncultcd Country is the Discovery of any Prince, it is the Right of that Prince.

**Uncu·ltivable,** *a.* (Un-1 7 b.)
1663 Heath *Flagellum* (1672) 12 Which like Weeds, sprung out of his rank and uncultivable nature. 1849 *Florist* 185 This interesting class of plants..a few years ago were thought uncultivable by common people. 1869 Ruskin *Q. of Air* § 79 The sedges are essentially the clothing of waste, and more or less poor or uncultivable soils.
Hence **Uncultivabi·lity.**
1880 A. Gray *Struct. Bot.* iii. § 1. 38 This occurs in species of Gerardia and other plants of the same family, the uncultivability of which is thereby explained.
**Uncu·ltivatable,** *a.* (Un-1 7 b.) 1870 *Putnam's Mag.* Sept. 290/1 The land..is..perfectly uncultivatable.

**Uncu·ltivate,** *ppl. a.* [Un-1 8 b, 5 b.] = next.
1659 H. More *Immort. Soul* iii. x. 428 The greatest part of the Universe..would lye as it were uncultivate, like a desart of sand. 1694 Addison *Acc. Eng. Poets* 19 An age that yet uncultivate and rude, Where-e'er the poet's fancy led, pursu'd..the unfrequented floods. 1732 J. Whaley *Poems* 286 A pleasing Wildness..., That seems uncultivate and rude to lie. 1785 Anna Seward *Lett.* (1811) I. 36 Uncultivate minds are always in extremes respecting those high abilities whose elevation they cannot clearly discern.

**Uncu·ltivated,** *ppl. a.* [Un-1 8 and 5 b.]
**1.** *fig.* Of persons, their faculties, etc.: Not improved by education or training; uncultured.
1646 Sir T. Browne *Pseud. Ep.* i. iii. 8 Whereof their uncultivated understandings scarce holding any theory, they are but bad discerners of verity. 1746 Hervey *Medit.* (1818) 145 Such are the usual products of savage nature! such, the furniture of the uncultivated soul! 1796 Mme. D'Arblay *Camilla* III. 146 Mr. Dennel was a man as unfavoured by nature as he was uncultivated by art. 1864 Mrs. Carlyle *Lett.* (1883) III. 224 He was a coarse, uncultivated man. 1898 J. Arch *Story of Life* 247 Their uncultivated minds were like dark lanterns with a rushlight inside.
**b.** Of nations, times, etc.: Not improved by culture; uncivilized.
1725 Berkeley *Proposal* Wks. 1871 III. 227 They shew as much natural sense as other uncultivated nations. 1779 *Mirror* No. 13, The rude and uncultivated age in which the poet is supposed to have lived. 1817 Jas. Mill *Brit. India* Pref. p. xiii, Tacitus..was certainly not acquainted with the language of our uncultivated ancestors.
**2.** Of land: Not cultivated or laboured; untilled.
1683 Burnet tr. *More's Utopia* 90 A part of their Soil, of which they make no use, but let it lie idle and uncultivated. 1697 Dryden *Æneis* i. 425 It looked a wild uncultivated shore. 1719 Swift *Hist. Engl.* Wks. 1841 I. 555/1 The fields lay uncultivated, all the arts of civil life were banished. 1781 Gibbon *Decl. & F.* xviii. II. 95 A more numerous band..were easily admitted to share a superfluous waste of uncultivated land. 1849 Macaulay *Hist. Eng.* iii. I. 313 How many square miles, which were formerly uncultivated or ill cultivated, have..been fenced and carefully tilled. 1869 Tozer *Highl. Turkey* I. 340 The open country extends in a sea of green vegetation, which gives way..to uncultivated land.
*fig.* 1693 *Ladies Petit.* in *Harl. Misc.* (1809) IV. 329 Will you not provide that so many longing young ladies shall not lie unploughed, unharrowed, and uncultivated? 1738 Wollaston *Relig. Nat.* (ed. 6) § 3. 55, I believe many more [things] will in time be cleard, which..are yet in their dark and uncultivated estate. 1828 B. White in Liddon *Life Pusey* (1893) I. 166 The growth of some weeds which were breaking out in the long uncultivated ground of my mind.
**b.** Of plants: Not produced or improved by cultivation; growing without tillage or care.
1697 Dryden *Virg. Georg.* ii. 601 Trees of Nature, and each common Bush, Uncultivated thrive. 1809 W. Irving *Knickerb.* i. v, The roots and uncultivated fruits of the earth. 1871 Garrod *Mat. Med.* (ed. 3) 286 The uncultivated plant is stated to be preferable to the cultivated.
**3.** Not attended to or practised; not properly trained or developed.
1684-5 Boyle *Min. Waters* 110 A First essay upon so difficult and uncultivated a Subject as I have ventur'd to treat of. 1712 Steele *Spect.* No. 334 ¶ 3 The Art [of dancing]..lies altogether uncultivated. 1751 Earl Orrery *Remarks Swift* (1752) 50 Swift indeed has left no weapon of sarcasm untried, no branch of satyr uncultivated. 1796 Mme. D'Arblay *Camilla* IV. 93 The superior force of goodness, even where most simple and uncultivated. 1837 Hallam *Hist. Lit.* i. iv. § 11 He became..a comic writer ..in the same vein of uncultivated genius.
Hence **Uncu·ltivatedness.**
1764 Harmer *Observ.* Pref., There is a sameness in human nature every where, under the like degree of uncultivatedness.

**Uncultiva·tion.** [Un-1 12 and 5 b.] Lack of cultivation; want of culture.
1796 J. Moser *Hermit of Caucasus* I. 52 The disorder and uncultivation that reigned in it. 1829 Carlyle *Misc.* (1857) II. 112 It is the sign of uncultivation to wonder. 1840 Mill *Diss. & Disc.* (1859) I. 94 The question often is, which is least prejudicial.., uncultivation or malcultivation?

† **Uncu·ltived,** *ppl. a. Obs.* [Un-1 8.] = Uncultivated *ppl. a.* 2.
1605 Verstegan *Dec. Intell.* ix. 292 Leyland, [so named] of the lying *legh* or empty thereof, to wit, vncultyued. 1614 Raleigh *Hist. World* ii. xvii. 484 Hee had now both horse and chariots good store to cary his prouisions through those vncultived places.

**Uncu·lturable,** *a.* [Un-1 7 b and 5 b.] Incapable of receiving culture or cultivation.
1860 I. Taylor *Spir. Hebrew Poetry* (1873) 118 The endeavour to find your way to the mind and heart of untutored and of unculturable and sanguinary savages. 1881 *Athenæum* 10 Sept. 329/2 The existence of large areas of forest, mountain, and unculturable waste in each province.

**Uncu·lture.** [Un-1 12, 5 b.] Lack of culture.
c 1624 Bp. Hall *Serm.* Wks. 1837 V. 205 Idleness, ill-husbandry, in mistiming, neglect of meet helps, unculture, ill choice of seeds. 1812 Shelley *Let. to E. Hitchener* 6 June, Might not your father,..led on by the unculture of his mind, form conclusions of the utmost asperity? 1896 *Daily News* 10 Mar. 6/4 The humiliation of western culture before Russian unculture and Turkish fanaticism.

**Uncu·ltured,** *ppl. a.* [Un-1 8.]
**1.** Of soil or plants: Not cultivated or subjected to cultivation.
1555 Eden *Decades* (Arb.) 299 By reason of so many marisshes,..it is yet rude vncultured, and lyttle knowen. 1607 J. Carpenter *Plaine Mans Plough* 197 Brambles and tares, such as naturally spring of evill and uncultured fields. 1633 Bp. Hall *Hard Texts* 85 Some obscure valley that lies..utterly uncultured. 1762-9 Falconer *Shipwr.* iii. 247 A sanguine train, With midnight ravage, scour the uncultured plain. 1804 Charlotte Smith *Conversations*, etc. I. 150 Blushing, the uncultured Rose Hangs high her beauteous blossoms there. 1872 Stopford Brooke in L. P. Jacks *Life & Lett.* (1917) I. xiii. 267 The uncultured breast of Blackford and the Pentlands.
**2.** *fig.* Not developed or improved by education; not characterized by culture; unrefined.
1777 T. Swift *Gamblers* i. 56 At school half brute, the self-same passions roll, And stamp for life his low, uncultur'd soul. 1796 Mme. D'Arblay *Camilla* II. 369 Those who unite native hardness with uncultured minds and manners. 1840 Carlyle *Heroes* ii. (1904) 67 The man [Mahomet] was an uncultured semi-barbarous Son of Nature. 1878 Bosw. Smith *Carthage* 277 He was a rough soldier, uncultured as Marius and hardly less cruel.

**Uncu·mber,** *v.* [Un-2 3.] *trans.* To free from encumbrance; to disencumber. Also *refl.*
c 1440 *Pallad. on Husb.* vi. 51 Haue up this stones; storne [*sic*] vnto the wallis, They may thy feeld vnkomber & defende. 1529 More *Dyaloge* ii. x. 60 b/2 For a pek of otys she wyll not fayle to vncumber theym of theyr husbondys. 1571 Golding *Calvin on Ps.* xviii. 37 When he was browght to utter despayre, he was uncombered agein by the help of God. 1620 Shelton *Quix.* ii. lviii. 385 When Don Quixote saw himselfe in open field, free and vn-cumbred from Altisidora's wooing. 1876 *Whitby Gloss.* 205.

**Uncu·mbered,** *ppl. a.* [Un-1 8. Cf. MSw. *okumbradh*.] Not encumbered.
1551 Recorde *Pathw. Knowl.* To Rdr., For neither is.. mi laiser so quiet and vncombered, that I maie perform iustlie so learned a laboure. 1600 Hakluyt *Voy.* III. 64 But a seruant,..a good footman, and vncombred with any furniture.. ouertooke one of them. 1699 Dryden *To J. Driden* 18 Lord of your self, uncumber'd with a Wife. 1738 Pope *Epil. Sat.* i. 31, I have..Seen him, uncumber'd with the Venal tribe, Smile without Art. 1748 Thomson *Cast. Indol.* ii. xxii, Unless..mighty patrons the coy sisters call Up to the sun-shine of uncumber'd ease. 1823 J. Badcock *Dom. Amusem.* 210 He is..uncumbered with the concealment sometimes practised, of bushes or sprigs hung about his person. 1870 Bryant *Iliad* viii. I. 261 The Trojans,..In a clear space uncumbered by the slain, Held council.

† **Uncu·nning,** *sb. Obs.* Forms: (see Cunning *sb.*). [Un-1 12.] Lack of knowledge; ignorance. Common in 14-15th c.
c 1290 *Beket* 1028 in *S. Eng. Leg.* I. 136 For euere ich dradde for oncunninge mi soule forto spille. 1338 R. Brunne *Chron.* (1810) 256, I wite þis no man, Bot myn vnconyng, þis folie my self bigan. c 1380 Wyclif *Sel. Wks.* II. 394 Þerfore trewe men in Crist shulden be wel paied of þis uncunnyng. c 1412 Hoccleve *De Reg. Princ.* 325 Myn vnkonyng of þat me schal excuse, Of whiche matere knowleche haue I non. c 1449 Pecock *Repr.* ii. iv. 156 At whiche men mowe lawȝe and take bourde for her symplenes or her vnkunnyng as of folis. a 1470 H. Parker *Dives & Pauper* (W. de W. 1496) i. lvii. 99/1 They wolde excuse them by uncunnynge yf they dyde amys.

**Uncu·nning,** *a.* Now *arch.* Forms: (see Cunning *a.*). [Un-1 10. Cf. OHG. *unchunnênti*, Goth. *unkunnands*.]
**1.** Of persons: Ignorant, unlearned, unskilful.
α. 1340 *Ayenb.* 59 Hi..ziggeþ þet hi byeþ..zuo zenuol and zuo onconnynde. c 1340 Hampole *Pr. Consc.* 152 Bot som men has wytte to understand, And yhit þai er ful unkunand. c 1400 *Rowland & O.* 293 Unconnande Sarazene,..in þis place þi wykkednes es ȝare. 1456 Sir G. Haye *Law Arms* (S.T.S.) 222 Quhasa did the contrair he war ungentill, uncurtas, and unconnand.
β. c 1374 Chaucer *Boeth.* i. pr. i. (1868) 7 Any vnkonnyng and vnprofitable man. c 1420 *Chron. Vilod.* 4 þys werke, þat y, so vnconnynge, Presumpswysly haue vndertake. c 1450 *Mirk's Festial* 213 Lest any vnconyng man take on for anoþir, I will tell you þes woymen. 1483 Caxton *Gold. Leg.* 287/1 The bisshop repreuyd hym sore as unconnyng and an ydeote. 1549 Chaloner *Erasm. on Folly* F iv, The rasher, the uncunnynger, and lesse circumspect,..the more yet is he regarded. a 1577 Sir T. Smith *Commw. Eng.* iii. viii. (1584) 112 Some vncunning Lawyers that would make a newe barbarous Latine worde to betoken lande giuen *in fidem*. 1601 Munday & Chettle *Death Earl Huntington* v. ii, Thus is Matildaes story showne in act, And rough heawen out by an vncunning hand. [1791 Wolcot (P. Pindar) *Ode to my Ass* ix, But I'm a modest, not unconnyinge elf. 1792 — *Odes Kien Long* v. ii, This to my simple and unconnying mind Seems œconomical.] 1826-7 K. Digby *Broadst. Hon.* ii, *Tancredus* (1828) 280 A theme which requires a far less earthly and uncunning tongue than mine.
**b.** *absol.* (chiefly as pl.).
1338 R. Brunne *Chron.* (1810) 244 Wardeyns gode he sette, ..Justise þat þe lawe gette to vnkonand þei kende. 1477 Earl Rivers *Dictes* (1877) 36 b, A wyseman ought not to exalte him self byfore the vnconning. 1495 *Festivall* 186 b, The fyrst is teche the vnconnynge that he sauour rightfully. 1511-2 *Act* 3 *Hen. VIII*, c. xi, Many of the Kynges liege people..cannot descerne the uncunnyng from the cunnyng.
**c.** Const. *in*, *of*, or with inf.
a 1340 Hampole *Psalter* cxviii. 92 He is vnkunand in gastly batayle. 1357 *Lay Folks Catech.* (Lamb. MS.) 1146 To teche men þat be vncunnynge of goddys lawe. 1377 Langl. *P. Pl.* B. xii. 185 Person or parisch prest,..Vnconnynge to lere lewed men. c 1440 *Gesta Rom.* xliii. 170 (Harl. MS.), They coude fynde noon, but that they wer corrupte,..or vncunnynge in the mystery. a 1450 *Knt. de la Tour* (1868) 159 That is gret pite, as in youthe to be vncunnynge and vnknowynge of hym selff. [1888 Doughty *Arabia Deserta* I. 278 But ye be also uncunning in many things, which the Aarab ken.]
**2.** Of actions, etc.: Arising from, indicative of, ignorance or unskilfulness.
1387 Trevisa *Higden* (Rolls) VII. 245 William put þat knyȝt out of þat chivalrie, for he hadde i-doo an unkonnynge dede. c 1449 Pecock *Repr.* i. x. 51 The wanton and vnkunnyng bering of hem whiche wolen not allowe eny gouernaunce to be the lawe..of God. 1549 Coverdale, etc. *Erasm. Par. Titus* iii. 31 b, Folyshe and vnconnyng questions, and entangled genealogies. a 1652 Brome *City Wit* i. i. Wks. 1873 I. 284 If my uncunning Disposition be my only vice.
So † **Uncu·nninghead, -ship.** *Obs.*
a 1300 *Cursor M.* 26306, I wat not quar-on it es lang, Queþer on mi plight or on þin,..Or min vnconanscipe [*v.r.* unkunnandeshepe], mai fall. 1340 *Ayenb.* 33 Efterward comþ slacnesse;..hit comþ of onconnyndehede, and of fole hete. *Ibid.* 40 Be hare kueadnesse, oþer uor onconynghede.

**Uncu·nningly,** *adv.* [f. prec.] In an uncunning manner; ignorantly, unskilfully.
a 1340 Hampole *Psalter* lxxiv. 2 For many fals breþere vnconandly demes, crist says.., i sall deme rightwisnes. 1397 *Rolls of Parlt.* III. 379/1, I dede evyll and unkunnyngelych. 1408 tr. *Vegetius' De re milit.* (MS. Digby 233) fol. 185/2 Long tyme of pees haþ maad vs to chese vnkonnyngliche oure knyȝtes. c 1440 *Pallad. on Husb.* iv. 87 Vnconnyngly they do right as they are. 1519 Horman *Vulg.* 218 b, This mater was vncunnyngly or indiscretly handled. 1550 Bale *Eng. Votaries* ii. 88 b, And whan she had vnconnyngly perfourmed that acte, they toke vp the peces. 1632 Sherwood, Vncunningly, *lourdement*.

**Uncu·nningness.** [f. as prec.] Ignorance; unskilfulness.
a 1325 *Prose Psalter* lxxxi. 5 Hii ne wyst nouȝt ne vnderstode nowit, and hii ne gon in vnconandnes [*v.r.* vncunnyngnes]. 1375 *Cursor M.* 27571 (Fair.), Oft be-tidis þat man I-wis be-comis proude for vn-kunningnes. 1408 tr. *Vegetius' De re milit.* (MS. Digby 233) fol. 186/2 Vnkonnyngnesse of swymmynge. 1422 Yonge tr. *Secreta Secret.* 235 Ful smale leggis tokenyth vnconyngnesse. c 1475 *Partenay* 12 By lachesse, Or..by vnconnyngnesse. 1513 Douglas *Æneid* viii. Prol. 87 Clerkis for oncunnandnes mysknawis ilk wycht.

† **Uncunyed,** *ppl. a. Sc. Obs.* [Un-1 8.] Uncoined. 1513 Douglas *Æneid* x. ix. 53 Ane huge wecht of fynast gold tharby, Oncunȝeit ȝit. a 1572 Knox *Hist. Ref.* Wks. 1846 I. 373 Silver, gold, and mettall, alsweill cunȝeit as uncunȝeit.
**Uncu·p,** *v.* (Un-2 5.) 1857 Heavysege *Saul* (1869) 222 This victory's new-risen splendour Hath gathered and uncupped itself, as if An ocean were condensed there to a drop.
**Uncu·pidate,** *a.* [Un-1 8 b.] Divested of the form of Cupid. 1631 P. Fletcher *Sicelides* iii. iv, Now must I be vncupidate, & shortly appeare here Cosmafied. **Uncu·pped,** *ppl. a.* (Un-2 8.) 1861 Morris *Jason* x. 328 On their heads fell down The uncupped acorn, and the long leaves brown.

† **Uncu·rable,** *a. Obs.* [Un-1 7 b and 5 b. Cf. MDu. *oncurable*.]
**1.** = Incurable *a.* 1. (Common c 1400-1650.)
**a.** Of wounds, diseases, etc.
1382 Wyclif *Deut.* xxxii. 33 Venym of eddres vncurable. 1388 — *Isaiah* xiv. 6 The ȝerde of lordis, that beet puplis..with vncurable wounde. a 1425 tr. *Arderne's Treat. Fistula*, etc. 4, I afferme noȝt that I miȝt hele al ffistulae in ano, ffor som ben vncurable. c 1450 Lydg. *Secrees* 1425 The tyme dyuerse ..sodeynly men schent, be seknessys which be unkurable. 1526 *Pilgr. Perf.* (W. de W. 1531) 82 Lepry, fransy, & suche other, whiche be in maner vncurable. 1562 Turner *Baths* Pref., Many sore and otherwyse uncurable syknesses. 1593 Shaks. 2 *Hen. VI*, iii. i. 286 Send Succours (Lords) and stop the Rage betime, Before the Wound doe grow vncurable. 1622 Gataker *Spirituall Watch* 86 Decay of nature, old age, and some vncureable diseases. 1650 Trapp *Comm. Exod.* xv. 26 To an Almightie Physician no diseas is uncurable.
*fig.* 1652 Heylyn *Cosmogr.* iv. 22 Of all Surfeits this of Forraign supplies is most uncurable.
**b.** Of persons. Also *fig.*
a 1425 tr. *Arderne's Treat. Fistula*, etc. 1 Sir Adam..made for to aske counsel at all the lechez and cirurgienz that he myȝt fynde...And all forsoke hym for vncurable. c 1440 *Gesta Rom.* xxxvii. 152 (Add. MS.), Yit he dothe many synnes ayenst god, and so he is vncurable. 1560 Daus tr. *Sleidane's Comm.* 36 b, As al those Romish be utterly uncurable. 1609 Bible (Douay) *Deut.* xxviii. 35 Be thou uncurable from the sole of thy foote unto the toppe of thy head. 1657 Sparrow *Bk. Com. Prayer* 138 Malice or revenge which makes us unpardonable and uncurable. 1775 Ash.
**2.** *transf.* and *fig.* = Incurable *a.* 2.
a 1340 Hampole *Psalter* cxxxix. 3 Thai hafe..malice vncurabil in þaire hert. c 1545 H. Rhodes *Bk. Nurture* B iij, An olde man & a yonge woman, to satysfye is vncurable. 1626 in Foster *Eng. Factories India* (1909) III. 136 Her

leake prooved uncureable. **1650** BAXTER *Saints' R.* III. iii. (1662) 325 An eternal, absolute, tormenting, uncurable despair. *a* **1676** HALE *Prim. Orig. Man.* I. iv. (1677) 103 The absurdities and incongruities..are infinite and uncurable.

Hence † **Uncu·rableness**; † **Uncu·rably** *adv.*

*a* **1425** tr. *Arderne's Treat. Fistula*, etc. 38 Whiche..makeþ euermore pronosticacion..als wele of deþ as of vncurablenes. **1548** UDALL *Erasm. Par. Luke* v. 59 b, Wheras theim selfes wer euen for this verai poynte vncurably wicked enemies of God. **1643** MILTON *Divorce* vii. *heading*, A matrimony found to be uncurably unfit. **1651** BIGGS *New Disp.* ¶ 61 The uncurableness of diseases.

**Uncu·rb**, *v.* [UN-[2] 4 b.] *trans.* To free (a horse) from a curb. Also *fig.*

**1580** HOLLYBAND *Treas. Fr. Tong*, *Desgourmer vn cheval*, to vncurbe a horse. **1684** T. GODDARD *Plato's Demon* 160, It is like uncurbing, or laying the Reins upon the Necks of headstrong Horses. **1729** YOUNG *Merchant* v. ix, Who curbs the tide, Uncurbs, extends, throws wide Britannia's reign.

**Uncu·rbable**, *a.* (UN-[1] 7 b.)

**1606** SHAKS. *Ant. & Cl.* II. ii. 67 So much vncurbable, her Garboiles (Cæsar) Made out of her impatience.

**Uncu·rbed**, *ppl. a.* [UN-[1] 8.]

**1.** Not curbed; unchecked, unrestrained.

**1599** SHAKS. *Hen. V*, I. ii. 243 Therefore with franke and with vncurbed plainnesse, Tell vs the Dolphins minde. **1621** QUARLES *Div. Poems*, *Esther* Med. 19 True 'tis, the Law of God's the rule and squire, Whereby to limit Man's vncurb'd desire. **1660** H. MORE *Myst. Godl.* v. xvii. 207 Their death conducing so much to the uncurbed fruition of all worldly and carnal enjoyments. **1734** tr. *Rollin's Anc. Hist.* (1827) I. 120 So licentious and uncurbed a liberty. **1821** KEATS *Sonn.*, *On Peace* 13 Give thy kings law—leave not uncurbed the great. **1879** DIXON *Windsor* I. vii. 67 Uncurbed by scruple, she gave orders to employ material force.

**2.** Free from a curb.

**1680** C. NESSE *Church-Hist.* 143 Absaloms mule..runs from under him with the reins uncurbed. **1801** SOUTHEY *Thalaba* VI. iv, But when he saw the mouth Uncurb'd, the unbridled neck, Then his heart leapt. **1825** LONGF. *Burial of Minnisink* 38 Leading the war-horse of their chief,..Uncurbed, unreined, and riderless.

Hence **Uncu·rbedly** *adv.*

**1685** H. MORE *Illustr.* 150 The King of Pride, or Antichrist, reigneth uncurbedly for a time.

**Uncu·rd**, *v.* (UN-[2] 3.) **1495** [see UNCRUD *v.*] **1598** FLORIO, *Disquagliare*, to vncurd as milk is. **1611** COTGR., *Se Descailler*, to resolue, vncurd, fall asunder.

**Uncu·rdled**, *ppl. a.* (UN-[1] 8.)

[**1775** ASH.] **1823** BYRON *Juan* IX. xliii, White stockings drawn uncurdled as new milk O'er limbs whose symmetry set off the silk. **1894** H. NISBET *Bush Girl's Rom.* 11 His coming disciples were still in long clothes,..being satisfied then with their milk uncurdled.

**Uncu·rdling**, *vbl. sb.* (UN-[2] 8.) **1673** *Phil. Trans.* VIII. 6169 The Secretion of the Serum from the blood is ingeniously cleared up by the curdling and un-curdling of Milk.

† **Uncu·re**, *v. Obs.* [UN-[2] 3 + CURE *v.*[2]] *trans.* To uncover; to disclose.

*c* **1440** *Promp. Parv.* 364/2 Oncuryn, or on-hyllyn, *detego*, *discooperio*. *c* **1450** LYDG. & BURGH *Secrees* 2347 Swyfft massageerys..To whoom thou mayst thy wyl also vncure. *c* **1485** *Digby Myst.* (1882) III. 769 He hath oncuryd þe therknesse of þe clowdy nyth.

**Uncu·red**, *ppl. a.* [UN-[1] 8.]

**1.** Not healed or restored to health; not remedied.

**a.** Of wounds, diseases, etc.

**1548** ELYOT, *Incuratus*,..vncured, vnhealed. **1597** A. M. tr. *Guillemeau's Fr. Chirurg.* 30 b/1 The perforation of the artery tarrieth vncured and open. **1676** HOBBES *Iliad* 119 Let them imbark at least in haste, and bear Along with them their wounds uncured home. **1819** SCOTT *Ivanhoe* xliii, Thy wounds are uncured—Meet not that proud man. **1879** *St. George's Hosp. Rep.* IX. 742 The mother had milk-fever and abscess of breast. This last remained uncured.

*fig.* **1598–9** B. JONSON *Case is Altered* v. iv, I am ashamed That my extreame affection to my sonne Should giue my honour so vncur'd a maine. **1642** FULLER *Holy & Prof. St.* II. xxiv. 152 Thus..the Wounds to the Commonwealth (in the breach of the Laws) are left uncured. *a* **1683** OWEN *Two Disc. Holy Spirit* (1693) 74 The uncured Darkness of their Minds. **1793** COWPER *Stanza for Year* 33 That want, uncur'd.., Speaks him a criminal, assur'd Of everlasting death. **1884** SIR C. S. C. BOWEN in *Law Rep.* 12 Q.B.D. 170 The blot in the proceedings of the respondent still remains uncured.

**b.** Of persons. Also *fig.*

**1601** SIR W. BROWN in Collins *Lett. & Mem. State* (1746) II. 228 The hurt Men that lye in the Streets, vncured, for Want of Surgins, make..a noysom Smell. **1674** R. GODFREY *Inj. & Ab. Physic* 150 Many times..they go uncured through deficiency in Medicine. **1757** BURKE *Abridgm. Eng. Hist.* III. iv. Wks. 1812 X. 432 Uncured by his misfortunes of a loose generosity,..he..mortgaged every branch of his revenue. **1825** SCOTT *Talism.* xiv, We physicians are sworn not to send away a patient uncured. **1899** *Allbutt's Syst. Med.* VII. 683 It does not appear that there is any material difference in the percentage of cured and uncured cases.

**2.** Not dressed or prepared for keeping.

**1622** in Foster *Eng. Factories Ind.* (1908) II. 103, [4000 pieces of cloth,] most partt uncurd, but ours are all cured. **1770** *Phil. Trans.* LX. 304 The certain consequence..will be, that maggots will be generated in such uncured parts [of stuffed birds]. **1828** SPEARMAN *Brit. Gunner* (ed. 2) 77 Cartridges, uncured. **1883** DAY *Indian Fish* 3 (Fish. Exhib. Publ.), Inland places having no special facilities for carriage do not receive uncured sea fish in a wholesome condition.

† **3.** Of land: Not cleared for cultivation. *Obs.*

**1719** DE FOE *Crusoe* I. 37, I purchased as much Land that was uncur'd, as my Money would reach.

**Uncu·rious**, *a.* [UN-[1] 7 and 5 b.]

**1.** Of persons: = INCURIOUS *a.* 2.

**1570** LEVINS *Manip.* 226 Uncuriouse, *incurius, ignauus*. **1621** QUARLES *Div. Poems*, *Esther* To Rdr., It is enough for an vncurious questioner to know it was indited by the Spirit of God. **1641** — *Enchyridion* IV. lxxxviii, If thou art not worth more than the world can make thee, thy Redeemer had a bad pennyworth, or thou an uncurious Redeemer. **1712** STEELE *Spect.* No. 340, That I have not been so uncurious a Spectator, as not to have seen Prince Eugene. **1716–7** in *Collect. Hist. Aberdeen & Banff* (Spalding Club) I. 39 A most elegant and powerfull preacher,..uncurious of politeness, save in the pulpit.

† **2.** = INCURIOUS *a.* 5. *Obs.*

**1598** SYLVESTER *Du Bartas* II. i. IV. *Handycrafts* Argt., The praise of Peace, the miserable states Of Eden's Exiles: their un-curious Cates: Their simple habit, silly habitation.

† **3.** = INCURIOUS *a.* 6. *Obs.*

**1601–3** DANIEL *Ep. Sir T. Egerton* 54 The state of truth..dwells free in the open plaine, Vncurious, Gentle, easie of accesse.

**4.** = INCURIOUS *a.* 7.

**1684–5** BOYLE *Min. Waters* 69 This Glass was judged capable of holding Water enough for not uncurious Tryals. **1712** STEELE *Spect.* No. 546 ¶ 1 He added very many Particulars not uncurious concerning the Manner of taking an Audience. **1768** *Woman of Honor* I. 96, I was by chance witness to a not uncurious scene. **1846** THACKERAY *Crit. Rev.* Wks. 1886 XXIII. 97 A not uncurious specimen of the biography of a literary man. *a* **1860** H. H. WILSON *Ess. & Lect.* (1862) I. 136 It is not an uncurious feature..that the veneration paid to their Gosáins is paid solely to their descent.

**Uncu·riously**, *adv.* [UN-[1] 11; cf. prec.]

† **1.** In a plain or unelaborate manner. *Obs.*

**1490** CAXTON *Eneydos* ii. 15 Ensiewed creusa his wyf, vncuryously aourned, Nothyng appertenaunt to thestate Royall. **1611** COTGR., *Incurieusement*, vncuriously, plainely, after a homely manner. **1716–20** *Lett. fr. Mist's Jrnl.* (1722) I. 284 Handling the Subject uncuriously and unpolitely.

**2.** Without curiosity. Cf. INCURIOUSLY *adv.*

**1667** G. DIGBY *Elvira* I. 15, I should have thought you strangely chang'd in humour Should you have gone away so uncuriously. **1862** 'SHIRLEY' (J. Skelton) *Nugæ Crit.* xi. 483, I began, not uncuriously, to peruse these latest products of the English imagination.

**Uncu·rl**, *v.* [UN-[2] 7 and 3.]

**1.** *intr.* To come out of curl; to unfold from a curved or spiral form.

**1583** SHAKS. *Tit. A.* II. iii. 34 My fleece of Woolly haire, that now vncurles, Euen as an Adder when she doth vnrowle. **1601** B. JONSON *Poetaster* Introd. 8 Cling to my necke, and wrists, my louing wormes, And cast you round, in soft and amorous foulds, Till I doe bid, vncurle. **1697** DRYDEN *Virg. Georg.* IV. 693 The Furies harken, and their Snakes uncurl. **1827** HOOD *Hero & Leander* lxiii, His uncrispt locks uncurling in the brine. **1873** 'OUIDA' *Pascarel* II. 162 The green corn uncurling underneath the blossoming vines.

**2.** *trans.* To take out of curl; to untwist.

**1598** FLORIO, *Discrespare*, to vncurle, to vnfrizle, to vncrispe. **1687** DRYDEN *Hind & P.* III. 270 He sheathes his paws, uncurls his angry mane. **1697** — *Æneis* v. 167 The raging billows..Uncurl their ridgy backs, and at his foot appear. **1816** SCOTT *Bl. Dwarf* xvi, On the other side sate Isabella,..her long hair uncurled by the evening damps. **1848** THACKERAY *Van. Fair* i, A black servant, who reposed on the box beside the fat coachman, uncurled his bandy legs. **1887** M. ARNOLD *Kaiser Dead* x, I see the tail,..In moments of disgrace uncurl'd, Then at a pardoning word refurl'd.

*refl.* **1606** DEKKER *Seuen Deadly Sinnes* 32 The vgliest Serpent hath not vncurld himselfe. **1884** *Nonconf. & Indep.* 5 June 545/1 The bracken has not yet uncurled itself.

**Uncu·rled**, *ppl. a.* [UN-[1] 8, or f. prec.]

**1.** Of hair: Not formed into, or growing in, curls or ringlets; out of curl.

**1596** SPENSER *F. Q.* IV. vii. 40 His faire lockes..He let to grow and griesly to concrew, Vncomb'd, vncurl'd, and carelesly vnshed. **1611** L. BARRY *Ram Alley* II. i, Thy head, Which is with greasy hair orespred, And being vncurld and black as cole [etc.]. **1693** CONGREVE in *Dryden's Juvenal* XI. (1697) 291 Two home-bred Youths..With honest Faces, tho' with uncurl'd Hair. **1712–4** POPE *Rape Lock* v. 26 Curl'd or uncurl'd, since Locks will turn to gray. **1796** MORSE *Amer. Geog.* I. 72 Their black hair, long and uncurled. **1828** SCOTT *Tapestr. Chamb.* ¶ 25 His hair..was dishevelled, uncurled, void of powder, and dank with dew. **1848** LYTTON *Harold* I. i, His forehead shaded with short thick hair, uncurled, but black..as the wings of a raven.

**b.** Not adorned with curls or ringlets.

**1799** in *Spirit Pub. Jrnls.* III. 322 Leave me uncurl'd, undinner'd, here to mourn.

**2.** Not disposed in coils or spiral convolutions; also, relaxed from a spiral form.

**1597** MIDDLETON *Wisd. Solomon* iii. 1 The adder is not always seen uncurl'd. **1708** POPE *Ode St. Cecilia's Day* iv, The Furies sink upon their iron beds, And snakes uncurl'd hang list'ning round their heads. **1820** KEATS *Hyperion* II. 46 A serpent's plashy neck; its barbed tongue Squeez'd from the gorge, and all its uncurl'd length Dead. **1841** T. R. JONES *Anim. Kingd.* 259 When not in use, the proboscis is coiled up..; but when uncurled, its structure is readily examined.

**Uncu·rling**, *ppl. a.* (UN-[1] 10.)

**1728** THOMSON *Spring* 185 Th' uncurling Floods, diffus'd In glassy Breadth, seem, thro' delusive Lapse Forgetful of their Course. **1800** *Monthly Mag.* VIII. 726 When on the tea's uncurling leaves it lies, With golden hues the porcelain vases flow. **1854** WHYTE MELVILLE *Gen. Bounce* (1855) 119 None..would have thought the long golden brown hair spoiled by hanging down in those rich, uncurling clusters. **1883** DIXON *Mano* I. ii. 5 A heavy fall Of dark uncurling hair flowed either side.

**Uncu·rrent**, *a.* [UN-[1] 7.]

**1.** Of money: Not current; not in circulation.

**1601** SHAKS. *Twel. N.* III. iii. 16, I can no other answer make, but thankes, And thankes: and euer oft good turnes, Are shuffel'd off with such vncurrant pay. **1639** S. DU VERGER tr. *Camus' Admir. Events* a 3 It is a strange thing, that reasonable spirits can be payd with such counterfeit and uncurrant coyne. **1655** tr. *Sorel's Com. Hist. Francion* II. 39 My neighbours..cryed me down more than uncurrent Money. **1855** W. IRVING *Washington* lxii. II. 497 Paper money issued by Congress which was uncurrent among the Canadians. **1883** *Encycl. Brit.* XVI. 484 After a certain amount of wear a gold coin..loses weight and becomes legally uncurrent.

*fig.* **1618** FLETCHER *Loyal Subj.* II. v, Thou crackt uncurrant Lord. **1646** G. DANIEL *Poems* Wks. (Grosart) I. 201 Such for vncurrant Knights or new-coyn'd Squire Might suite. **1827** POLLOK *Course T.* VIII. 597 Honour..Bearing the signature of Time alone, Uncurrent in Eternity, and base!

**2.** Not commonly accepted or recognized.

**1611** SHAKS. *Wint. T.* III. ii. 50 Since he came, With what encounter so vncurrant, I Haue strayn'd t'appeare thus. **1639** LD. DIGBY, etc. *Lett. conc. Relig.* (1651) 77 Conceits of their own, and other uncurrent doctrines. **1665** BOYLE *Occas. Refl.* II. xiii. 233 'Tis hard..to be sure, that his present Repentance is not of the same ignoble and uncurrent kind.

**3.** Of a warrant: Having no legal force; invalid.

**1647** CLARENDON *Hist. Reb.* v. § 156 The Messenger would scarce have return'd to have reported how uncurrent such Warrants were like to be in York.

Hence **Uncu·rrentness.**

**1641** SIR T. ROE *Sp.* in *Harl. Misc.* (Malh.) IV. 457 Another cause of scarcity of coin, may be the over-strict rule of the uncurrentness of any good coin.

**Uncu·rried**, *ppl. a.* (UN-[1] 8.)

*c* **1616** FLETCHER *Thierry & Theod.* v. i, Out upon you, you uncurried colts. **1734** *Prompter* 29 Nov. 2/2 Stray'd, ..a lean, ragged, uncurried creature, call'd Common Sense. **1888** DOUGHTY *Arabia Deserta* I. vii. 198 We saw the Prince's gift-mare standing,..weak, and uncurried.

**Uncu·rse**, *v.* (UN-[2] 3.)

**1593** SHAKS. *Rich. II*, III. ii. 137 Againe vncurse their Soules; their peace is made With Heads, and not with Hands. *c* **1831** H. COLERIDGE *Ess.* (1851) I. 180 Old Prynne and Jeremy Collier, if their hearts were in the right place,..would have uncursed the stage.

**Uncu·rsed, uncu·rst**, *ppl. a.* (UN-[1] 8.)

*a* **1628** F. GREVIL *Cælica* cii, All things vncurst, nothing yet done amisse, And so in him no base of his defection. **1680** BAXTER *Answ. Stillingfl.* xxxvii. 62 How few were there un-Cursed, and un-Condemned in the Roman World? **1759** YOUNG *Conject. Orig. Composition* 60 What we mean by Blank verse, is verse unfallen, uncurst. **1827** POLLOK *Course T.* VII. 497 That morn When first they met in Paradise, unfallen, Uncursed. **1843** LD. COCKBURN *Jrnl.* (1874) II. 5, I see no ground for expecting that..we can even be uncursed by these heartrending visitations.

**Uncu·rsing**, *ppl. a.* (UN-[1] 10.) **1806** WOLCOT (P. Pindar) *Tristia* Wks. 1812 V. 317 How thou..with uncursing breath Couldst see Saint Paul..Stoned,..a second time, to death.

**Uncurtai·led**, *ppl. a.* (UN-[1] 8.)

**1741** RICHARDSON *Pamela* II. 21 Will you,..on your Honour, let me see them uncurtail'd, and not offer to make them away? **1820** T. MITCHELL *Aristoph.* I. 25 To our share Fell some fine oxen—whole, sirs,—uncurtail'd. **1856** FROUDE *Hist. Eng.* (1858) I. iv. 288 Making use of their yet uncurtailed powers of persecution. **1861** W. S. PERRY *Hist. Ch. Eng.* I. iv. 171 The ancient canon law was still in force, uncurtailed by the Reformation.

**Uncu·rtain**, *v.* [UN-[2] 4.] *trans.* To remove a curtain or veil from; to disclose or reveal. Also *refl.*

**1628** FELTHAM *Resolves* II. l. 147 The honest man will rather be a graue to his neighbours failes, then any way vncurtaine them. **1659** W. CHAMBERLAYNE *Pharonnida* III. 186 She in these words uncurtains mystick Fate. **1817** MOORE *Lalla Rookh*, *Veiled Prophet* 766 Now thou seest my soul's angelic hue, 'Tis time these features were uncurtain'd too. **1858** CARLYLE *Fredk. Gt.* IX. x. II. 499 Watching the great Wartheatre uncurtain itself in this manner, from Dantzig down to Naples. **1887** BOWEN *Æneid* IV. 120 When Phœbus at earliest morn..with radiant light uncurtains the land.

*absol.* **1897** 'O. RHOSCOMYL' *White Rose Arno* 242 The tender smile of Night's white queen uncurtained to the world.

**Uncu·rtained**, *a.* (UN-[1] 8.)

[**1775** ASH.] **1804** J. GRAHAME *Sabbath* 49 The toil Of ministering around th' uncurtain'd couch Of pain and poverty. **1842** DICKENS *Amer. Notes* (1850) 49/2 A blazing fire shone through the uncurtained windows. **1865** MISS BRADDON *Eleanor's Vict.* ii, Broad uncurtained open windows.

‖ **Uncus** (*v*·ŋkǒs). *Zool.*, etc. Pl. **unci** (*v*·nsəi). [L. *uncus* hook.] A hook or hook-like process.

**1826** KIRBY & SP. *Entomol.* III. 390 *Unci* (the *Unci*), two pair of robust organs..with which the anus of *Locusta*.. is furnished. **1888** ROLLESTON & JACKSON *Anim. Life* 158 A stout decurved pointed process terminating in two hooks, the *uncus* of Gosse or *tegumen* of White. **1899** *Allbutt's Syst. Med.* VII. 324 Smell was impaired on the side of the lesion, by a tumour which caused erosion of the uncus.

**Uncu·shioned**, *ppl. a.* (UN-[1] 8.) [**1775** ASH.] **1873** MRS. WHITNEY *Other Girls* xxvii, There were window-seats in the two windows, uncushioned. **Uncu·sped**, *a.* (UN-[1] 9.) **1859** RUSKIN *Perspective* 116 A square niche of good Veronese Gothic, with an uncusped arch.

† **Uncu·stom**, *sb. Sc. Obs.* [UN-[1] 4 b.] An improper or illegal tax.

**1569** *Reg. Privy Council Scot.* Ser. I. I. 672 He hes send his officiaris to tak up uncustomes sic as ane cott hen..from every cottar.

† **Uncu·stom**, *v.* [UN-[2] 3.] To disaccustom.

**1530** PALSGR. 767/1, I uncustume, I leave of a thyng that I was wonte to use, *je desacoustume*. *Ibid.*, I coulde shoote with any man that came, but nowe I am uncustomed. **1570** LEVINS *Manip.* 162 To Vncustome, *desuefacere*.

**Uncu·stomable**, *a.* [UN-[1] 7 b.]

† **1.** Not according to custom; unusual. *Obs.*

**1387** TREVISA *Higden* (Rolls) VIII. 241 Þe pope greved þe chirches of Engelond wiþ taxes..undewe and uncustemable. **1570** LEVINS *Manip.* 4 Vncustomable, *inconsuetus*.

**2.** Of goods: Not liable to pay custom.

**1727** BAILEY (vol. II).

**Uncu·stomary**, *a.* [UN-[1] 7.] Not according to custom; unusual, unwonted.

**1650** H. BROOKE *Conserv. Health* 115 Meats also that are uncustomary..must very sparely be fed upon. **1744** T. BIRCH *Life R. Boyle* 296 In such private meetings it was not uncustomary for any one of the hearers, who was unsatisfied about any matter then uttered, to give in his objections. **1798** PENNANT *Hindoostan* I. 173 A female reign in these parts is not uncustomary. **1802–12** BENTHAM *Ration. Judic. Evid.* (1827) I. 11 If the lamb were to be cut up into uncustomary joints. **1871** ALABASTER *Wheel of Law* 208 Such is not uncustomary among the higher classes.

**†Uncu·stomate,** *ppl. a. Sc. Obs.* [UN-¹ 8 b.] Not having paid duty.

**1510** *Reg. Privy Seal Scotl.* I. 326/2 With power to eschaete all custumable gudis passand furth of the realme uncustumate. **1565** *Reg. Privy Council Scot.* I. 332 Certane malivolus personis.. fraudulentlie transportis thair gudis and marchandices, sumtymes uncustumat.

**Uncu·stomed,** *ppl. a.* [UN-¹ 8.]

**1.** Of merchandise: On which no custom or duty has been paid. †Also, not charged with or liable to duty.

**1393** *Rec. Elgin* (New Spald. Cl. 1903) I. 19 Al ye wol, ye clathe and al vthir thyngis yᵗ gais be schipe owte of wre hafine of Spee vncustomyt. **1427** *Rolls of Parlt.* IV. 318/1 To passe oute of this Royaume be way of Marchandise, uncustumed. **1487** *Naval Acc. Hen. VII* (1896) 32, vij hausers forfetted..in bringyng the same on land uncustumed. *a* **1548** HALL *Chron., Hen. VIII*, 65 A great numbre of rascal & pedlers..brought ouer hattes and cappes, and diuerse merchaundise vncustomed. **1594** J. DICKENSON *Arisbas* (1878) 48 Hee had aboord certayne vnlawfull and vncustomed wares. **1631** HEYWOOD *Fair Maid of West* v, An Englishman Hath forfeited his ship for goods uncustom'd. **1669** STURMY *Mariner's Mag., Penalties & Forfeit.* 7 Liberty to go on board and take out Prohibited and Uncustomed Goods. **1718–9** *Act 5 Geo. I*, c. 11 (*title*), An Act against clandestine running of uncustomed Goods. **1733** *Gentl. Mag.* May 266/2 The Watchmen..seized 1100 Weight of uncustom'd Tea. *c* **1820** HOGG *Tales & Sk.* (1836) I. 304 Uncustomed wine and spirits. **1887** *Times* 10 Sept. 4/4 Dealing with uncustomed goods—i.e., tobacco—with intent to defraud Her Majesty's Customs.

**2.** Unaccustomed *to* something. *Obs.* or *arch.*

*c* **1520** BARCLAY *Jugurth* (1557) 41 b, Other vncustomed to suche busynesse of batayle..fered the losse of their libertie. **1607** C. LEVER *A Crucifix* cxv, To adulation they vncustomd are. **1791** COWPER *Odyss.* VIII. 553 Glad he beheld The steaming vase, uncustom'd to its use E'er since his voyage from the isle of fair Calypso. **1877** BLACKIE *Wise Men* 179 They show like moles uncustomed to the light.

**3.** Not customary; unusual. *Obs* or *arch.*

**1552** HULOET, Vncustomed or out of vse, *disuetus*. **1565** STAPLETON tr. *Bede's Hist. Ch. Eng.* 79 An Abbat..to whom ..the bishops them selues ought after a straunge and vncustomed order to be subiect. **1581** MARBECK *Bk. of Notes* 730 A Miracle is a worke, hard and vncustomed by the power of God. **1603** FLORIO *Montaigne* I. xxv. 85 My father purposed to make mee learne it [*sc.* Greek] by arte; But by new and vncustomed meanes. **1872** BLACKIE *Lays Highl.* 35, I feel the keen, uncustomed temper of the thin, clear air.

**Uncu·t,** *ppl. a.* Also 5 unkyt. [UN-¹ 8 b, 8 c.]

**1.** Not cut, gashed, or wounded with a sharp-edged instrument; not having received a cut.

**1426** AUDELAY *Poems* (Percy Soc.) 12 Who mai kepe hym unkyt fro a kene knyfe, ȝif he boldly that blad touche in his tene. **1615** *Work for Cutlers* 4 Ile make a Capon of you before I haue done with you, you shall nere come home vncut Ile warrant you. **1623** MASSINGER & FIELD *Bondman* IV. ii, *Gracculo.* [We'll] not leave One house unfired. *Cimbrio.* Or throat uncut of those We have in our power. **1834** M. SCOTT *Cruise Midge* (1863) 236 An open book, the leaves kept down..by a most enticing uncut pine apple. **1840** ELIZA COOK *To Favourite Pony* v, Thy knees uncut, my bones unshatter'd.

**b.** Without being operated on.

*a* **1548** HALL *Chron., Edw. V*, 1 b, Shee could not be delivered of hym uncut.

**2.** That has not been subjected to cutting; not severed by cutting; not mown, lopped, etc.

**1548** UDALL, etc. *Erasm. Par. John* xix. 110 Therfore the souldiers thought good that it should be kept whole unkut. **1583** GREENE *Mamillia* Wks. (Grosart) II. 49 The grasse looketh better being vncut, then that which withereth with the sieth. *a* **1593** MARLOWE *Ovid's Elegies* III. i. 1 An old wood, stands vncut of long yeares space. **1639** HORN & ROB. *Gate Lang. Unl.* lxi. § 641 Heathenish Priests in their Temples & uncut groves, dedicated presents. **1745** *Transl. & Paraphr. Sc. Ch.* XXIV. i, Say, grows the Rush without the Mire?.. Green and Uncut, it quickly fades. **1841** ELPHINSTONE *Hist. Ind.* I. 27 Clad in bark,.. with his hair and nails uncut. **1846** J. BAXTER *Libr. Pract. Agric.* (ed. 4) II. 323 Keep these branches uncut till you arrive at the season of grafting. **1835** *Times* (weekly ed.) 25 Sept. 13/4 A few of the fields being still uncut.

**b.** With *down* or *up*.

**1546** J. HEYWOOD *Prov.* (1867) 27 He that hangth him selfe a sondaie Shall hang still vncut downe a mondaie for mee. **1607** BEAUM. & FL. *Woman Hater* I. ii, Great, cumbersom, un-cut-up pies..to make a shew with.

**3.** Not fashioned or shaped by cutting.

*Uncut diamond, velvet*, etc.: cf. CUT *ppl. a.*

**1596** *Acc. Bk. W. Wray* in *Antiquary* XXXII. 281, j li. cut and uncut fringe, iiij *s.* **1605** DRAYTON *Poems* 69 b, Which being now but in so meane a bed, Is like an vncut diamond in lead. *a* **1700** EVELYN *Diary* 22 Oct. 1644, With a terrace at each side having rustic uncut balustrades. **1771** MME. D'ARBLAY *Early Diary* (1889) I. 121 She fixed upon a suite of dark blue, uncut velvet. **1875** KNIGHT *Dict. Mech.* 695/2 Until 1476..the diamond was worn uncut. **1902** MARSHALL *Metal Tools* 41 Most flat files are provided with one plain, uncut edge.

**4.** Of books: Not having the leaves cut open.

**1828** MACAULAY *Misc. Writ.* (1860) I. 273 The new novel lies uncut. **1850** MRS. CARLYLE *Lett.* (1883) II. 125 The new 'Copperfield'..to this hour remains uncut. **1893** LIDDON, etc. *Life Pusey* I. xii. 276 The copy of the published sermon which was sent him 'from the author' is still uncut.

**b.** Not having the margins cut down.

**1809** DIBDIN *Bibliomania* 60 Uncut Copies,..books of which the edges have never been sheared by the binder's tools. *Ibid.* 61 An uncut first Shakspeare, as well as an uncut first Homer. **1863** HOTTEN *Hand-bk. Topogr.* 95/1 Fine uncut copy (sells at £4 5s.) 35s. **1888** JACOBI *Printers' Vocab.*, *Uncut edges*, books not cut down, but not necessarily 'unopened'.

**c.** *transf.* Given to collecting 'uncut' books.

**1862** BURTON *Bk. Hunter* (1882) 19 He was not a black letter man or a tall copyist or an uncut man.

**5.** Not curtailed or shortened.

**1896** *Westm. Gaz.* 7 Dec. 3/2 The uncut 'first night' is apt to cause great injustice to the performers.

**†Uncu·t,** *v. Obs.* [UN-² 9.] *trans.* To sever by cutting.

**1611** SPEED *Hist. Gt. Brit.* IX. xvi. 13 Behold how God began to vncut the knot of those bands with which the English held France bound. **1622** *Prosopopoeia* in *Phœnix Brit.* (1732) I. 314 You see it is of a greater Consequence than to uncut a Gordian Knot.

**†Uncu·ted,** *a. Obs.*⁻¹ [UN-¹ 9 + *cute* CUIT.] Not converted into cuit or sweet wine.

**1615** G. SANDYS *Trav.* 224 Wines that seldome come vnto vs vncuted, but excellent where not.

**Unceweme,** var. UNQUEME *a. Obs.*

**Uncy·nical,** *a.* (UN-¹ 7.) **1824** BYRON *Juan* XVI. xliii. *note*, A table-cloth, or some other expensive and uncynical piece of furniture. **Uncy·nically,** *adv.* (UN-¹ 11.) **1895** MEREDITH *Amazing Marr.* xxxviii, Must we be proxy if we are profoundly, uncynically sincere? **Uncy·pressed,** *a.* (UN-¹ 9.) **1799** in *Spirit Pub. Jrnls.* III. 105 Slow to th' uncypress'd church-yard he was borne.

**†Und.** *Obs. rare.* Also 2 unde, 6 vnd. [a. OF. *unde*, or ad. L. *unda* wave.] A wave; *Her.*, a wave-like marking. (Cf. UNDEE *a.*)

*c* **1200** *Trin. Coll. Hom.* 177 Ðe water stremes on-heueden up here undes [L. *fluctus*]. **1490** CAXTON *Eneydos* ii. 15 By troblous reuolucyons of the vndes or wawes [they] were broughte into the Ile of Anchandron. **1592** WYRLEY *Armorie* 12 John Basset of new place..left the Labell, and charged the blacke vnds with manie besants dispersed all ouer them. [**1694** MOTTEUX *Rabelais* 249 Lute, Unds and Sands did long our March oppose.]

**†Undade, -adie,** *a. Obs.* [Cf. prec.] *Her.* = UNDATED *a.*, UNDEE *a.*

**1562** LEIGH *Armorie* 137 He beareth Or, and Tenne, parted per Saltier Vndade, which is as much to say as watried with a flood. **1572** BOSSEWELL *Armorie* III. 9 b, These bendes sinister vndadie or waterie, maye foreshowe some..enterprise done by force, violence, or rage of the waters.

**†Unda·ftiness.** *Obs.*⁻¹ [UN-¹ 12.] Untidiness.

**1555** WATREMAN *Fardle Facions* II. iv. I vj b, As for checkes or reuilinges, was to them muske and Honie, and slouenly vndaftinesse, a greate comelinesse.

**†Undai·nteous,** *a. Obs.*⁻¹ [UN-¹ 7.] Not dainty through rarity.

*c* **1449** PECOCK *Repr.* II. viii. 184 Tho ymagis..schulde be vndeinteose for the grete plente of hem;..plente is no deinte.

**Unda·m,** *v.* [UN-² 3.]

**1.** *trans.* To release from a dam. Also *fig.*

**1697** DRYDEN *Virg. Georg.* I. 160 The wary Ploughman, on the Mountain's Brow, Undams his watry Stores. **1885** *Pall Mall G.* 27 Oct. 5/1 A stream of impertinent chatter such as the most voluble sciolist would hesitate to undam.

**2.** To deprive of a protective dam.

*a* **1713** A. PITCAIRNE in *N. & Q.* Ser. v. VIII. 498/1 Amphibious wretches, Sudden be your fall! May man undam you, And God damn you all! (Cf. UNDAMN *v.*)

**Unda·mageable,** *a.* (UN-¹ 7 b.) **1648** HEXHAM II, *Ondeerlick*, vndammageable. **1884** *Stubbs' Mercantile Circular* 30 Jan. 94/1 Iron wire declared to be undamageable.

**Unda·maged,** *ppl. a.* (UN-¹ 8.)

**1648** HEXHAM II, *Onbeschadight*, Vndammaged, or Vnharmed. **1708** J. PHILIPS *Cyder* I. 305 Thou'lt find that Plants will frequent Changes try, Undamag'd, and their marriageable Arms Conjoin with others. **1859** GEO. ELIOT *A. Bede* xxvii, So long as there was hope of gathering in their own corn undamaged. **1897** MARY KINGSLEY *W. Africa* 604 The only point I congratulate myself on is having got my men up so high, and back again, undamaged.

**Unda·masked,** *a.* (UN-¹ 9.) **1838** ELIZA COOK *Old Water-Mill* vi, Our seats were undamasked, our partners were rough. **Unda·mmed,** *ppl. a.* (UN-¹ 8.) *a* **1849** POE *Monos & Una* Wks. 1865 II. 278 Holy, august and blissful days, when blue rivers ran undammed, between hills unhewn. **1896** *Fortn. Rev.* LIX. 632 The undammed stream of sarcasm, invective and calumny.

**Unda·mn,** *v.* (UN-² 3. Also a punning variant of UNDAM *v.* 2.)

**1719** T. GORDON *Cordial for Low Spirits* (1763) 90 The most gross sinners are now innocent, being undamned by the priest. **1741** *Pol. Ballads* (1860) II. 267 Let France damn the Germans, and undamn the Dutch. **1809** in *Spirit Pub. Jrnls.* XIII. 206 Turned-in to my cot; muttered a short prayer; d—nd the French; *und*—d the Dutch.

**Unda·mned,** *ppl. a.* (UN-¹ 8.)

**1382** WYCLIF *Acts* xxii. 25 If it is leeful to ȝou, for to scourge a man Romayn, and vndampned? *a* **1400** *New Test.* (Paues) Acts xvi. 37 Þei hauen beten vs vnrightly ande vndampned. *c* **1450** *Mirk's Festial* 89 Þen schall non scape vndampned. **1631** DEKKER *Match me in London* III, A Broaker that's vndamn'd for halfe a dram For halfe a scruple. **1852** JAMES *Pequinillo* III. 125 'I hope my blood will remain und—d,' replied Doctor Pequinillo. **1862** T. A. TROLLOPE *Marietta* II. xi. 191 Thus the work dragged on—undamned—to the end of the first act.

**†Unda·mnified,** *ppl. a. Obs.* [UN-¹ 8.] Undamaged, unimpaired.

**1576** FLEMING *Panopl. Epist.* 199 Returne I pray thee, returne, in hope to be saued harmelesse and undamnified. **1658** EARL MONM. tr. *Paruta's Wars Cyprus* 140 He..past through the midst of our Fleet with some 30 gallies, undamnified. **1686** *Lond. Gaz.* No. 2197/3 There remains not one Beam undamnified. **1709** T. ROBINSON *Vind. Mosaick Syst.* 31 To keep undamnify'd his..beloved Hypothesis.

**Unda·mped,** *ppl. a.* [UN-¹ 8.]

**1.** Of persons, their spirits, etc.: Not discouraged or checked; undepressed.

**1742** YOUNG *Nt. Th.* II. 693 Undampt by doubt, undarken'd by despair, Philander, thus, augustly rears his head. **1792** S. ROGERS *Pleas. Mem.* I. 301 Undamped by time, the generous Instinct grows. **1834** WORDSW. *Lines Album C'tess Lonsdale* 62 They, who mark thy course,..See cheerfulness undamped by stealing Time. **1863** *N. & Q.* 3rd Ser. III. 506 With ardour undamped, and obstinacy undrowned.

**b.** *spec.* (See quots. and DAMP *v.* 1 c.)

**1883** A. J. HIPKINS in Grove *Dict. Mus.* III. 636 In the edition of 1797 he remarks that the undamped register of the Fortepiano is the most agreeable. **1906** *Westm. Gaz.* 28 Nov. 5/2 He obtained a million or more vibrations per second, and..produced continuous or undamped waves.

**2.** Not damped or made wet.

**1898** *Westm. Gaz.* 10 Sept. 8/2 Having a surface undamped by rain.

**Unda·ncing,** *ppl. a.* (UN-¹ 10.) **1633** PRYNNE *Histrio-m.* 249 If this be true, how many happy Husbands are there now, when there are so few undancing wives?

**Unda·ngered,** *ppl. a.* (UN-¹ 8.)

*c* **1400** *Beryn* 2410 For, had ye dwellid within yeur shippis, ..Then had yee been vndaungerid, & quyt of al hir wrong. **1816** J. SCOTT *Visit Paris* (ed. 5) 245 Undangered and inevitable duration can be promised to nothing in this world.

**Unda·ngerous,** *a.* (UN-¹ 7.)

**1727** THOMSON *Britannia* 205 Then cherish this, this unexpensive power, Undangerous to the public. **1818** BENTHAM *Ch. Eng.*, *Catech. Exam.* 113 To which these modern effusions..are but inadequate, and not altogether undangerous, substitutes. **1831** GEN. P. THOMPSON *Exerc.* (1842) I. 423 The charge..was not more futile,..and it may be added undangerous, than that advanced against the Radicals.

Hence **Unda·ngerousness.**

**1817** BENTHAM *Parl. Reform* Introd. p. i, The necessity,—and..the undangerousness,—of a Parliamentary Reform.

**Unda·red,** *ppl. a.* (UN-¹ 8.) **1587** HUGHES *Misfort. Arth.* I. ii, O wrong content with no reuenge; seeke out Vndared plagues. **1611** FLORIO, *Inauso*, vndaring, vndared.

**Unda·ring,** *ppl. a.* (UN-¹ 10.)

Also *undaringness* (Florio s.v. *Inaudacia*).

**1611** FLORIO, *Inaudace*, vndaring, cowardly. **1650** LLUELLYN *Elegie* in *J. Gregory's Posthuma*, Graie Customs, which our dead dismettled Sloth Gave up, to surfet the undaring Moth. **1815** J. CORMACK *Abol. Fem. Infanticide Guzerat* xii. 219 We might be excused..for cherishing hopes of a very undaring nature. **1877** LANIER *Poems, Florida Sunday* 57 Mine thy dole Of shut undaring wings.

**Unda·rk,** *a.* (UN-¹ 7.) **1876** MORRIS *Sigurd* I. 4 On Mid-Summer Even ere the undark night began. **Unda·rk,** *v.* (UN-² 6 a.) **1644** QUARLES *Sheph. Oracles* v, How each spark Contends for greater brightnes, to undark The shades of night. **Unda·rken,** *v.* (UN-² 3.) **1598** FLORIO, *Stenebrare*, to..cleare vp, to vndarken. **1866** W. STOKES in Meyer *Voy. Bran* (1895) I. 222 Chief lights irradiating and undarkening the City.

**Unda·rkened,** *ppl. a.* (UN-¹ 8.)

**1742** [see UNDAMPED 1]. **1818** SHELLEY *Marenghi* 20 Reconciling factions..swear to keep each spirit Undarkened by their country's last eclipse. **1847** J. MARTINEAU *Chr. Life* 130 A heaven undarkened by a doubt. **1889** RUSKIN *Præterita* III. 181 Fireflies..shone fitfully in the still undarkened air.

**Unda·rned,** *ppl. a.* (UN-¹ 8.)

**1797** BRYDGES *Hom. Trav.* I. 337 His dear Nelly, who had scarce An undarn'd smicket. **1880** LEE *Church under Q. Eliz.* I. 317 His lawn-sleeves perfectly clean and undarned. **1894** ELIZ. BANKS *Camp. Curiosity* 29 Basket upon basket of gentlemen's undarned socks.

**Unda·shed,** *ppl. a.* [UN-¹ 8.]

**1.** Not discouraged or dismayed; undaunted.

**1601** DANIEL *Civ. Wars* VI. lxxviii, Yet standes he stiffe, vndasht, vnterrifi'd. **1616** R. WELDON in B. Holyday *Persius* A vij, I think't a taske too great for humane sleights, Vngraueld or vndasht to passe those streights. **1896** C. ALLEN *Papier Mâché* 12 'But who plays on them now?' asked Paul, undashed by this dismal possibility of a future.

**2.** Not mingled *with*, or affected *by*, something.

**1803** *Edwin* III. vii. 125 And may the tide of friendship gently glide undashed with sorrow. **1868** MILMAN *St. Paul's* xi. 267 Whose creed was therefore in a continual state of change, not undashed with doubt. **1885** *Athenæum* 2 May 565/1 The same quaint humour not undashed by pathos.

**3.** Not provided with a dash or dashes.

**1879** *Encycl. Brit.* X. 401/2 Replacing the dashed letters by those undashed ones which denote the same points.

**Unda·table,** *a.* (UN-¹ 7 b.) **1882** *Schaff's Encycl. Relig. Knowl.* 74 A momentous but undatable event.

**U·ndated,** *a.* Now *rare* or *Obs.* [f. med.L. *undātus*, f. L. *unda* wave.]

**1.** *Her.* = UNDEE *a.*, WAVY *a.*

**1486** *Bk. St. Albans, Her.* 94 Palyt armys oftyme ar founde vndatyt, that is to say watteri. *Ibid.*, They be called barrit vndatit for they be made of ij colouris metyng togedre by the maner of a floyng watre. **1572** BOSSEWELL *Armorie* II. 31 b, These pales may be borne vndated, whiche is as moche as to saye, as watered with a floode.

**2.** *Ornith.* Having wavy markings.

Also *Bot.*, waved (Webster, 1828, citing Lee).

**1783** LATHAM *Gen. Synop. Birds* IV. 391 Undated L[ark]. *Ibid.* 477 Undated W[arbler].

**Unda·ted,** *ppl. a.* [UN-¹ 8. Cf. G. *undatirt*, Du. *ongedateerd*, Sw. *odaterad*.]

**1.** Not furnished or marked with a date; left without indication of date.

**1570** FOXE *Acts & Mon.* (ed. 2) 383/1 The certein tyme.. I cannot searche out, neyther may it be [in] his epistles vndated, easly found out. **1658** SIR T. BROWNE *Hydriot.* 24 The undated ruines of winds, flouds or earthquakes. **1710** H. BEDFORD *Vind. Ch. Eng.* 177 The Latin Edition..is without Numbers, as well as his undated English one. **1824** MISS MITFORD *Village* Ser. I. 159 The precious epistle was undated. **1856** FROUDE *Hist. Eng.* I. 383 This letter is undated, but it was written..some time in the year 1532. 1886 Willis & Clark *Cambridge* II. 104 The Statement is undated. *Ibid.* 578 The list..is unfortunately undated.

**2.** Having no fixed date or limit; unending.

In quot. 1637 misused for 'dated'.

1624 Quarles *Sion's Elegies* II. xxii, Yet my vndated Euills, no time will minish, Though Yeers, and Months, though Daies and Howers, finish. 1637 D. Digges *Elegy* in *Jonsonus Virbius* (1638) 23 They did receive new life from you; Which shall not be undated, since thy breath Is able to immortall, after death.

**3.** Marked by no striking events.

1878 W. C. Smith *Hilda* 184 A wild, black night of tempest, such as men remember long In the dull undated life of a sleepy country town.

† **Unda·tion.** *Obs. rare.* [ad. L. type *undātio, f. L. *undāre* to rise in waves. Cf. OF. *undation, -acion.*] A waving; an undulation.

1656 Blount *Glossogr.*, *Undation*, a flowing or rising of waves. 1668 Culpepper & Cole *Barthol. Anat.* II. vi. 101 A certain Undation or waving towards one side according to the carriage of the right Ventricle.

**Undau·b,** *v.* (Un-2 3.) 1611 Cotgr., *Desenduire*, to vndawbe; to bare; to pull the dawbing off. 1620 Brinsley *Virgil* 129 If..you will emptie (Vndaube or vncouer) their stately seate [*sc.* the honeycombs]. **Undau·bed,** *ppl. a.* (Un-1 8.) 1648 Hexham II, *Ongemortert*, Vnplaistered, or Vndawbed. 1885 *Harper's Mag.* Dec. 136 Within the rude stable of unhewn logs, all undaubed. **Undau·ghterly,** *a.* (Un-1 7.) 1748 Richardson *Clarissa* VII. 149 Any-thing undaughterly, unsisterly, or unlike a kinswoman. 1886 *Academy* 6 Mar. 162 It was at least ungenerous and undaughterly for Capri to expose all the seamy side of his nature to her friend.

**Undau·ntable,** *a.* [Un-1 7 b.] That cannot be daunted; indomitable. (Freq. in 17th c.)

1587 Harmar tr. *Beza* 381 The vndauntable insolencie of Pharao. 1593 G. Harvey *Pierce's Super.* Wks. (Grosart) II. 112 He will welcome me with a fierce reioynder:..and so forth *in infinitum*, with an vndauntable courage. 1611 Speed *Hist. Gt. Brit.* IX. xxiv. § 222 Their enemies no lesse fierce and vndauntable, then fortunate. 1631 Weever *Anc. Funeral Mon.* 589 Of an haughtie and vndauntable spirit. *a*1670 Hacket *Life Abp. Williams* I. (1693) 181 That heroick and undauntable Boldness. 1848 Dickens *Dombey* liv, She was resolute, he saw; undauntable.

**Undau·nted,** *ppl. a.* [Un-1 8.]

†**1.** Of horses: Not broken in; untamed. *Obs.*

1422 Yonge tr. *Secreta Secret.* 168 Hit happid, that Traiane his Sonne rode an hors vndauntid. *c*1560 A. Scott *Poems* (S.T.S.) xxx. 11 Thay rin lyk wyld vndantit hors, But brydillis, to and fro.

†**b.** *transf.* Unbridled, unrestrained. *Obs.*

Chiefly used by Sc. writers of the 16th cent.

1513 Douglas *Æneid* VI. iv. 82 The felloun Hungir with hir vndantit rage. 1535 Stewart *Cron. Scot.* (Rolls) I. 103 This king he wox rycht vile;..Drokkit and dull throw vndantit delyte. *c*1550 Rolland *Crt. Venus* I. 341 Weill I knaw thy vndantid barnage Will haif ane May. 1683 D. A. *Art Converse* 21 Nothing [is] more destructive than an undaunted passion.

†**c.** *Sc.* Undisciplined; disorderly. *Obs.*

1533 Bellenden *Livy* III. v. (S.T.S.) I. 261 Ane cumpanye of ȝoung vndantit men. 1549 *Compl. Scot.* xv. 128 Rustical and inciuile, ondantit, ignorant, dullit slauis.

†**2.** Unsubdued, unconquered. *Obs. rare.*

1513 Douglas *Æneid* IV. i. 84 Heir the vndantit folk of Numyda duell. *a*1547 Surrey *Æneid* IV. 52 Eke the vndaunted Numides compasse thee.

**3.** Of persons: Not daunted or discouraged; undismayed; intrepid.

1587 Turberv. *Trag. T.* (1837) 126 The tone Rossilion calde, a bold undaunted knight. 1594 *Selimus* D ij, They are strong vndanted enemies. 1635–56 Cowley *Davideis* III. 125 Th' undaunted Prince, though thus well guarded here, Yet his stout Soul durst for his Parents fear. 1671 Clarendon *Dial.* Tracts (1727) 290 They are undaunted when it may be we look pale. 1697 Dryden *Virg. Georg.* IV. 113 To War they follow their undaunted King. 1708 J. Philips *Cyder* I. (1728) 31 Where shall we find Men more undaunted, ..More prodigal of Life? 1781 Cowper *Table-t.* 366 Undaunted still, though wearied and perplex'd. 1828 D'Israeli *Chas. I*, I. xii. 325 The courtly patriot was disconcerted; the undaunted Duke was facing his accuser. 1891 Farrar *Darkn. & Dawn* vii, If he had been a Regulus or a Fabricius he could not have been more undaunted.

*transf.* 1820 Wordsw. *River Duddon* IV. 9 Starts from a dizzy steep the undaunted Rill.

**b.** Of courage, spirit, etc.

1591 Sylvester *Du Bartas* I. ii. 806 Th' vndaunted strength of the Diuine right-hand. 1631 Gouge *God's Arrows* III. Ep. Ded. p. iv/1 Joshua, a Generall of an undaunted spirit. 1663 Bp. Patrick *Parab. Pilgr.* xviii, I have known many Pilgrims of great courage and undaunted Resolution. 1727 Gay *Fables* I. x. 1 The man who with undaunted toils Sails unknown seas. 1759 Robertson *Hist. Scot.* III. Wks. 1813 I. 167 The spirit of Knox, however, still remained undaunted and erect. 1855 Macaulay *Hist. Eng.* xvii. IV. 54 With undaunted courage, with considerable talents.., he was emphatically a bad man. 1868 Milman *St. Paul's* 306 Norfolk's..undaunted mendacity..was unknown to Nowell.

**Undau·ntedly,** *adv.* [f. prec.] In an undaunted manner; without fear; boldly.

1598 Florio, *Strenuamente*, valiantly, stoutly,..vndauntedly, courageouslie. 1610 Healey *St. Aug. Citie of God* 326 Our martyrs..bore all tortures undauntedly. 1653 Gataker *Vind. Annot. Jer.* 51 The Roman Souldiery..undauntedly and cheerfully addressed themselves to encounter with the enemy. 1694 Kettlewell *Comp. Persecuted* 145 Give me Courage..to behave myself undauntedly. *a*1720 Sewel *Hist. Quakers* (1795) I. 3 He had preached the gospel undauntedly. 1742 Fielding *J. Andrews* IV. xiv, She walked undauntedly to Slipslop's room. 1852 Miss Yonge *Cameos* I. xxx. 259 The princes undauntedly strove to collect their shattered forces. 1894 Baring-Gould *Deserts S. France* II. 270 He stood upright, proudly and undauntedly facing the soldiers.

**Undau·ntedness.** [f. as prec.] The quality or state of being undaunted. (Freq. in 17th c.)

1598 Florio, *Strenuita*, valiancie,..courage, vndantednes. 1626 Gouge *Serm. Dignity Chivalry* § 6 Stoutnesse and courage of mind, Vndauntednesse in danger, Discretion mixed with passion. *a*1656 Ussher *Ann.* (1658) 300 Antigonus..stood amazed at this bold attempt of his, and undauntednesse of his high courage. 1709 S. Clarke *Serm. Vict. near Mons* 16 'Tis by his blessing..that generals are inspir'd with wisdom, and troops with undauntedness and bravery. 1879 S. Brooke *Milton* 12 He moved so that men said he had courage and undauntedness.

**Undau·nting,** *ppl. a.* [Un-1 10.] Not quailing.

1786 Burns *Ep. to Young Friend* 84 May Prudence, Fortitude and Truth, Erect your brow undaunting!

† **Undau·ntless,** *a. Obs.*$^{-1}$ (Un-1 15.) 1654 Earl Monm. tr. *Bentivoglio's Wars Flanders* 106 Death will come the more welcome, when sought..with undauntless valour.

† **Undau·ntoned,** *ppl. a. Sc. Obs.* [Un-1 8.] Not tamed or broken in; unsubdued.

1609 Skene *Reg. Maj.* 5 That..he may breake downe the proudnes of the vnreulie and vndantoned people. *a*1653 Binning *Serm.* (1743) 564 To tame and danton that undantoned wild beast. 1678 *Geneal. Campbells* in *Highland Papers* (S.H.S.) II. 77 He was a wild undauntoned person.

**Undaw·ned,** *ppl. a.* (Un-1 8.) 1854 J. S. C. Abbott *Napoleon* (1855) I. xxx. 472 The gloom of the yet undawned morning. *a*1860 D. Gray *Luggie*, etc. (1862) 9 The light Quickens in the undawned east. **Undaw·ning,** *ppl. a.* (Un-1 10.) 1784 Cowper *Task* IV. 130 Thou hold'st the sun A pris'ner in the yet undawning east.

**Unda·zed,** *ppl. a.* (Un-1 8.)

1757 W. Thompson *Hymn to May* xvi. 13 He who undaz'd can wander o'er her face, May gain upon the solar-blaze at noon. 1868 Adah I. Menken *Infelicia* 101 The Eagle's gray eyes..Undazed by the sun. 1871 B. Taylor *Faust* (1875) II. III. 198 Her glance Gods only bear undazed.

**Unda·zzle,** *v.* (Un-2 3 and 7.)

1611 Florio, *Sbarbagliare*,..to vndazle. 1833 Tennyson *Dream Fair Wom.* xlv, Slowly my sense undazzled.

**Unda·zzled,** *ppl. a.* (Un-1 8.)

1644 Milton *Areop.* (Arb.) 72 Kindling her undazl'd eyes at the full midday beam. 1665 Boyle *Occas. Refl.* IV. iii. 16 Ev'n upon such bright Eyes..I could gaze undazel'd enough to approve my self a right Eagle. 1743 Francis tr. *Hor., Odes* II. ii. 28 To him..Who can a treasur'd Mass of Gold With firm, undazzled Eye behold. 1799 Campbell *Pleas. Hope* II. 270 As the spirit eyes, with eagle gaze, The noon of Heaven undazzled by the blaze. 1834 A. F. Tytler *Univ. Hist.* (1850) II. 278 Undazzled by the splendor of so high an object of ambition. 1875 Jowett *Plato* (ed. 2) III. 137 There too he may remain undazzled by wealth or the allurements of evil.

**Unda·zzling,** *ppl. a.* (Un-1 10.)

1601–3 Daniel *Ep. Ld. H. Howard* 80 They carry things assuredlie Vndazling of theire owne or others sight. 1814 in *Orr's Circ. Sci., Pract. Chem.* (1856) 498 [The light was] soft and undazzling as moonlight. 1846 Keble *Lyra Innoc.* (ed. 3) 347 To His Sight Heaven's secrets are undazzling light. 1855 W. Irving *Washington* xviii. I. 151 The sterling, enduring, but undazzling qualities of Washington.

**Unde, Undé,** varr. Undee *a.*

**Undea·d,** *a.* [Un-1 7. Cf. ON. *údauðr.*] Not dead; alive.

*a*1400–50 *Alexander* 158 And many was þe bald berne at banned þar quile, þat euer he dured þat day vndede opon erthe. *c*1475 *Rauf Coilȝear* 855 Ane of vs sall neuer hine Vndeid in this place. 1548 Udall, etc. *Erasm. Par. John* vi. 41 b, Where as all men did eat therof, they neuerthelès dyed, nether did any one of so great a number remain vndead. 1592 Warner *Alb. Eng.* VII. xxxiv. 149 The same..That thought he liued not because his Neeces weare vndead.

**Undea·dened,** *ppl. a.* (Un-1 8.)

1813 T. Busby *Lucretius* I. III. 119 While o'er the soul undeadened transports steal. 1856 R. A. Vaughan *Mystics* x. i. II. 172 That heaven, where..glorious powers shall be gloriously developed, undeadened by any lethargy. 1895 *Outing* XXVI. 70/1 The noises, which wide-open windows admitted undeadened.

† **Undea·dliness.** [f. next.] Immortality.

*c*1000 Ælfric *Hom.* II. 484 Ure æhta sind ece on heofenum, þær ðær undeadlicnys ricsað. *a*1225 *Leg. Kath.* 1119 He ne losede na lif, onont þet he godd wes, ne undedlichnesse onont his drihtnesse. *c*1380 *Lay Folks' Catech.* (L.) 1115 He wyle cloþe oure sowlys..with þe stole of vndedlynesse and blysse of heuyn. *c*1420 *Prose Life Alexander* 73 'Gyffe vs,' quoþ þay, 'vndedlynesse, so þat we mow noȝte dye'. 1481 Botoner *Tulle on Old Age* (Caxton) H v, It nedith not also that I speke euir of the undedlynesse of the soules, but I hode..that the soules of men be undedly.

**Undea·dly,** *a.* [Un-1 7. OE. had both *undéadlic* and *undéaþlic* (see Un-1 3), corresponding to OHG. *untôdlîh* (MHG. *untötlich*, G. *untödtlich*), ON. *údauðligr* (Sw. *odödlig*, Da. *udødelig*).]

†**1.** Not subject to death; immortal. *Obs.*

*c*950 *Rit. Eccl. Dunelm.* (Surtees) 169 Haliȝ God,..strong, haliȝ, & vndeadlic. *c*1000 Ælfric *Hom.* I. 150 He..wunað ..undeadlic, se þe ær his ðrowunge wæs deadlic. *c*1000 — *Saints' Lives* iv. 385 Þær bið æfre ece fyr and undeadlic wyrm. *a*1200 *St. Marher.* 10 Keiser of kinges, drihtin undedlich. *a*1225 *Leg. Kath.* 390 Hwen þu forcweðest, for þi Crist, ure undedliche godes. *c*1230 *Hali Meid.* 39 Eadi is te were ..hwas streon is undeadlich. *a*1340 Hampole *Psalter* xxiii. 4 He..feland his saule vndedly, enterly gaf him til godis luf. 1382 Wyclif *1 Tim.* i. 17 To the kyng of worldis, vndeedly and invisyble God aloone, honour and glorie. *c*1425 *St. Christina* iii. in *Anglia* VIII. 120/45 To suffre peynes of an vndeedly soule by a deedly body. *c*1449 Pecock *Repr.* II. xvi. 243 Tho spiritis were vnmade and vndeedli withoute bigynnyng or eending in tyme. ?1554 Coverdale *Hope of Faithful* xxiv. 169 Vndeadlye or immortall is it called, because it neuer ceaseth to lyue. 1612 T. James *Corrupt. Scripture* III. 8 For rightfulnes is euerlasting and vndeadlie.

**2.** Not causing death; not mortal.

*c*1611 Chapman *Iliad* XI. 390 Ulysses knowing well The wound undeadly..Thus spake to Socus.

**Undea·f,** *v.* (Un-2 6 a) 1593 Shaks. *Rich. II*, II. i. 16 Though Richard my liues counsell would not heare My deaths sad tale, may yet vndeafe his eare.

**Undea·lt,** *ppl. a.* [Un-1 8 b. Cf. OFris. *unideld, ondeld*, MDu. *ongedeelt* (Du. *-deeld*), OHG. *unchideilit* (G. *ungeteilt*), ON. *údeildr* (Da. *udelt*, Sw. *odelad*) undivided, unshared.]

**1.** Undivided. (OE. *undǽled.*)

*a*1300 *Cursor M.* 9761 An-fald godd vndelt es he.

**2.** Not dealt *with.*

1645 Milton *Tetrach.* Introd., Unadmonisht, undealt with by any Pastorly or brotherly convincement. 1648 Hexham II, *Ongehandelt*, Vnhandled, or Vndealt withall. 1870 Proctor *Other Worlds* xiii. 319 *note*, Certain difficulties suggest themselves which must not be left undealt with.

**Undea·n,** *v.* (Un-2 6 b.) 1857 Trollope *Barchester T.* xlvi, Thorne gave him a look which undeaned him completely.

**Undea·r,** *a.* [OE. *undéore* (see Un-1 7 and Dear *a.*1), = MDu. *ondiere, -dure, -duyr* (older Du. *ondier*), OHG. *undiuri, -tiuri* (MHG. *untiure*), ON. *údýrr* (Icel. *ódýr*).]

†**1.** Of little value or estimation; worthless, cheap. *Obs.*

*c*897 K. Ælfred *Gregory's Past. C.* lvii. 439 He nemde ða undiorestan wyrta ðe on wyrttunum weaxe. *c*1000 Ælfric *Gloss.* in Wr.-Wülcker 130 *Vile ualet*, undeor hit is. *a*1225 *Ancr. R.* 408 Vndeore he makeð God, & to unwurð mid alle, þet for eni worldliche luue his luue trukie. *a*1300 *Cursor M.* 16034 Parfai, pilate, wel þou aght to hald him ful vn-dere.

**2.** Not dear; not regarded with affection.

1748 Richardson *Clarissa* (1811) IV. 168 So hasty, dearest Madam—And so slow, undearest Sir, I could have said. 1790 Mme. D'Arblay *Diary* V. IV. 182 Adieu, my dear friends! Adieu—undear December! 1881 Mrs. A. R. Ellis *Sylvestra* II. 76 One art Sylvestra gained, not undear to her, ..the getting-up of 'small linen'.

**Undea·thlich,** *a.*, etc.: see Un-1 3.

**Undeba·rred,** *ppl. a.* (Un-1 8.)

1595 Daniel *Civ. Wars* V. v, For warelesse insolence whilst vndebard Of bounding awe, runnes on to such excesse. 1852 M. Arnold *Summer Night* 59 Awhile he [*sc.* Man] holds some false sway, undebarr'd By thwarting signs.

**Undeba·sed,** *ppl. a.* (Un-1 8.)

1753 Glover *Boadicea* I. ad fin., We can shew..Firm hearts, and manners undebased by fraud. 1768–74 Tucker *Lt. Nat.* (1834) II. 24 So..gold is pure when undebased by any alloy. 1825 Southey *Tale Paraguay* IV. v, A peaceful lot ..By Avarice undebased, exempt from care. 1846 *P. Parley's Ann.* VII. 191 The lama seems to be the only animal that is undebased by being subjected to man.

**Undeba·table,** *a.* (Un-1 7 b.)

Also, in recent use, *undebatably* adv.

1869 F. W. Newman *Misc.* 200 Seas, Deserts or great Mountain ranges have always been the chief arbiters in this undebateable question. 1898 *Mission. Herald* (Boston) Mar. 104/2 The pastors settled it by saying it was undebatable.

**Undeba·ted,** *ppl. a* (Un-1 8.)

1620 Donne *Serm.* Wks. 1839 IV. 551 It must not be a rash, a sudden, an undebated Resolution. 1648 Milton *Observ. Art. Peace* Wks. 1851 IV. 563 Men whose serious consideration thereof hath left no certain precept, or example undebated. 1897 *Daily News* 15 Mar. 5/1 The undebated clauses of the Home Rule Bill.

**Undebau·ched,** *ppl. a.* (Un-1 8.)

*a*1656 Bp. Hall *Rem. Wks.* (1660) 255 He sends us for the determination of decency, to the judgment of our right reason, undebauched nature, and approved custome. 1693 Dryden *Juvenal* VI. 17 For when the World was bucksom, fresh, and young, Her Sons were undebauch'd, and therefore strong. 1710 *Tatler* No. 191 ¶ 2 There are some that preserve their Relish undebauched with common Impressions. 1784 Cowper *Task* III. 744 Were England now What England was; plain, hospitable, kind, And undebauch'd.

**Undebi·litated,** *ppl. a.* (Un-1 8.) [1775 Ash.] 1879 Spencer *Data of Ethics* vi. 89 Those who are undebilitated by voluntary or enforced submission to actions injurious to the organism. **Undebi·litating,** *ppl. a.* (Un-1 10.) 1811 Abernethy *Surg. Obs.* II. 208 Unirritating and undebilitating doses..were given. † **Undebonai·rty.** *Obs.*$^{-1}$ [Un-1 12.] Ungraciousness. 13.. *Prose Psalter* lxxii. 6 Hij ben couerd wyþ her wickednes and vndebonerte [*v.r.* vnbonerte].

† **Unde·bted,** *ppl. a. Obs.*$^{-1}$ [Un-1 8.] Not due as a debt or obligation.

*a*1564 Becon *Art. Chr. Relig.* iv, The goodnesse of God,.. which by the vndebted death of the same hys sonne, had chosen them into the inherytaunce of euerlasting life.

**Undecagon** (vndekăgǫn). *Geom.* [Irreg. f. L. *undec-im* eleven, after *decagon* (cf. Hendecagon). So Sp. and Pg. *undecágono*, F. *ondécagone.*] A plane figure having eleven sides and angles.

1728 Chambers *Cycl.*, *Undecagon*, is a regular Polygon of eleven Sides. 1798 Hutton *Course Math.* (1806) I. 271. 1879 *Cassell's Techn. Educ.* I. 251.

**Undecay·able,** *a.* (Un-1 7 b.)

1534 More *Treat. Passion* Introd., Wks. 1270/2 The infinite perfection of their..vndecayable glory. 1586 Day *Eng. Secretorie* I. (1595) 145 Feruent and assured loue grounded vpon the vndecaiable staie and prop of your vertues. *c*1610 *Women Saints* 78 Let vs liue..that..we may receyue in heauen vnmeasurable and vndecayable ioyes. 1872 Hawthorne *S. Felton* (1883) 318 Safe against disease, and undecayable by age.

**Undecay·ed,** *ppl. a.* Also 6 *Sc.* **ondekeyt.** [Un-1 8.]

**1.** Not decayed or impaired; not reduced in quality or condition.

1513 Douglas *Æneid* x. xiv. 71 Hys stalwart hart And curage ondekeyt was gude in neyd. 1697 Dryden *Æneis* x. 860 How fierce in fight, with courage undecay'd; Judge if such warriors want immortal aid. 1815 Byron *Hebrew Mel.*, '*When coldness wraps*' ii, Eternal, boundless, undecay'd, A thought unseen, but seeing all. 1869 Dk. Argyle *Primeval*

*Man* IV. 158 Accidents which did not happen to civilized nations so long as their civilization was yet undecayed.

**2.** That has not begun to crumble or fall in pieces; not physically wasted.

1632 W. LITHGOW *Trav.* III. 86 The Temple..is a worke.. as yet vndecayed. *a* 1682 SIR T. BROWNE *Tracts* (1683) 39 Coffins of this Wood, which he found yet fresh and undecayed. 1799 KIRWAN *Geol. Ess.* 198 We find the quantity of iron much the same as in undecayed basalts. 1826 KIRBY & SP. *Entomol.* IV. xlviii. 469 The one in a putrescent and the other in an undecayed state. 1864 J. RAINE *Hexham* (Surtees) I. Pref. p. lv, In the grave were..a chasuble, a tunic, and a napkin uninjured and undecayed.

Hence **Undecay·edness.**

1650 TRAPP *Comm. Num.* xi. 7 This might be some cause of Moses his undecayedness.

**Undecay·ing,** *ppl. a.* (UN-[1] 10.)

1599 DANIEL *Musoph.* Wks. (1602) A vj, These Lines are ..the arteries, And vndecaying life-strings of those harts That stil shall pant. 1641 MILTON *Prel. Episc.* 11 The intire, the spotlesse, and undecaying robe of Truth. 1725 POPE *Odyss.* IX. 239 Unmingled wine, Mellifluous, undecaying, and divine! 1810 SOUTHEY *Kehama* x. vii, Every amaranthine flower Its deathless blossom interweaves With bright and undecaying leaves. 1868 W. CORY *Lett. & Jrnls.* (1897) 128, I don't care for Henri Deux and the undecaying Diane.

**Undecea·sed,** *ppl. a.* (UN-[1] 8.)

*a* 1585 MONTGOMERIE *Cherry & Slae* (1597) 272 Like to ane fische fast in the nette, In dead-thraw vndeceist. 1589 WARNER *Alb. Eng.* VI. xxix. 127 For often Vprores did ensue for him, as vndeceast. *c* 1611 CHAPMAN *Iliad* XIII. 679 Of whom, some were not to be found unhurt, or undeceas'd.

**Undecei·tful,** *a.* (UN-[1] 7.) Also **-fully** *adv.*

1571 GOLDING *Calvin on Ps.* xviii. 31 God helpeth his seruants vndeceytfully. 1682 GREW *Anat. Roots* iv. § 14 Undeceitful and accurate Observation of both their Number, and Size, must be made by the Microscope. 1744 AKENSIDE *Pleas. Imag.* I. 383 Where is..the seal of undeceitful good, To save your search from folly?

**Undecei·vable,** *a.* [UN-[1] 7 b.]

†**1.** Incapable of deceiving; undeceptive; certain, sure. *Obs.*

1534 MORE *Comf. agst. Trib.* II. xvi. (1553) I vj, Shall you not lacke to enquyer, by what sure & vndeceiuable tokens, a man maye descerne yᵉ true reuelacions from yᵉ false illusions? 1581 J. BELL *Haddon's Answ. Osor.* 453 b, Where be those irreproveable Testimonyes, and undeceiveable examples, whereupon you crake so lustely? 1650 BAXTER *Saints' R.* II. iv. (1662) 220 The way that this Testimony hath come down to us is a certain and undeceivable way. 1669 STURMY *Mariner's Mag.* v. viii. 26 These Rules are undeceivable with Authority.

**2.** Incapable of being deceived.

1608 BP. HALL *Epist.* I. i, Shame not to haue the weake eyes of the world see that, which once your vndeceiuable Iudge shall see. 1687 BOYLE *Martyrd. Theodora* ii. 20 They look on Sufferers for truth with His undeceiveable Eyes. 1827 POLLOK *Course T.* VIII. 290 His votaries, who left the earth Secure of bliss, around him, undeceived, Stood, undeceivable till then. 1860 RUSKIN *Mod. Paint.* V. VI. ix. § 14 An undeceivable common sense, and an obstinate rectitude.

Hence **Undecei·vableness; Undecei·vably** *adv.*

1560 BECON *New Catech.* Wks. 1564 I. 314 b, Tokens or markes, whereby we may truely and vndeceaueably knowe the true Catholyke and Apostolyke church. 1685 H. MORE *Paralip. Prophet.* Pref. p. xii, To acknowledge the Autority and Undeceivedness..though not Undeceivableness or Infallibility of the ancient Catholick Church.

**Undecei·ve,** *v.* [UN-[2] 3.]

**1.** *trans.* To free (a person) from deception or mistake; to deliver from an erroneous idea.

1598 FLORIO, *Disingannare*, to vndeceiue, to cleare, to free or resolue from any doubt. 1651 BAXTER *Let. to Ch. at Bewdley* 9 If this much will not undeceive the misled, let them for me be deceived still. 1687 T. BROWN *Saints in Uproar* Wks. 1730 I. 83, I am resolved to undeceive mankind. 1712 tr. *Pomet's Hist. Drugs* I. 215, I think my self oblig'd to undeceive the Publick. 1769 *Junius Lett.* xxxv. (1788) 182 Nothing less than your own misfortunes can undeceive you. 1839 ALISON *Hist. Eur.* liv. VII. 305 No sooner was he undeceived in this particular, than he despatched the most pressing orders. 1875 W. S. HAYWARD *Love agst. World* 45, I will very soon undeceive his lordship. *refl.* 1687 MIÉGE II, To undeceive himself, *se desabuser*. 1708 J. HUGHES tr. *Fontenelle's Dial.* I. v. 21 Undeceive yourself, I beseech you. 1829 LYTTON *Devereux* II. vii, It is hard to undeceive ourselves. 1890 'R. BOLDREWOOD' *Miner's Right* ii, My heart had only now undeceived itself.

**b.** Const. *of* (an error, etc.).

1653 W. RAMESEY *Astrol. Restored* To Rdr. 1 To undeceive my Country men of such Calumnies as are cast upon this..study. 1710 J. CLARKE tr. *Rohault's Nat. Philos.* (1729) I. Pref., A Man who had undeceived the World of an ancient Errour. 1823 SOUTHEY *Hist. Penins. War* I. 427 He was undeceived of both errors in the Peninsula.

**2.** To instruct by removal of error.

1649 MILTON *Eikon.* i. 13 Thus much be said in general to his Prayers;..anough to undeceive us what esteem we are to set upon the rest.

**Undecei·ved,** *ppl. a.* [UN-[1] 8.] Not deceived or imposed upon.

*c* 1400 *Apol. Loll.* 15 To haue þe more clere and vndeceyuid knowyng of þis mater. 1529 MORE *Dyaloge* II. Wks. 186/2 It may well..happen, that the good men wel beleuing & vndeceiued, be those that beleue the worship of ymages & praying to saintes to be ydolatry. 1747 LD. LYTTELTON *Monody* xii, A prudence undeceiving, undeceiv'd, That nor too little, nor too much believ'd. 1799 WORDSW. *Ruth* 148 Deliberately, and undeceived, Those wild men's vices he received. 1827 [see UNDECEIVABLE *a.* 2].

*absol.* 1832 WORDSW. *Rural Illusions* 29 The World's illusive shows For the undeceived..Are melancholy things.

Hence **Undecei·vedness.**

1685 [see UNDECEIVABLENESS].

**Undecei·ver.** [f. UNDECEIVE *v.*] One who or that which undeceives.

1643 (*title*), The Vn-Deceiver. 1668 R. L'ESTRANGE *Vis. Quev.* (1708) 114 Some call me the Plain-Dealer; others, the Undeceiver General. 1825 LYTTON *Falkland* 20 My manhood has been the undeceiver of my youth.

**Undecei·ving,** *vbl. sb.* [f. as prec.] The action of the verb.

1648 [P. HEYLYN] (*title*), The Undeceiving of the People in point of Tithes. 1652 T. NICOLS *Lapidary* Title-p., Cautions for the undeceiving of all those that deal with Pretious Stones. *a* 1708 BEVERIDGE *Thes. Theol.* (1711) III. 331 Godliness is profitable for the soul..in its will, by undeceiving of it. 1886 HALL CAINE *Son of Hagar* I. ii, The undeceiving came at length, and then the Laird Fisher was old and poor.

**Undecei·ving,** *ppl. a.* (UN-[1] 10.)

*a* 1586 SIDNEY *Arcadia* III. x. (1912) 403 In paying the tribute of undeceyving skill. 1607 HIERON *Wks.* I. 319 Who would not esteeme such vndeceiuing engagements of Gods vnchanging loue? 1704 NORRIS *Ideal World* II. iii. 170 The undeceiving answers of Truth itself,..whose instructions are faithful and unerring. 1747 [see UNDECEIVED].

**Unde·cency.** Now *Obs.* or *rare.* [UN-[1] 12 and 5 b: cf. UNDECENT *a.*] = INDECENCY 1.

1589 PUTTENHAM *Eng. Poesie* III. xxiii. (Arb.) 271 Diuers points, in which the wise and learned men of times past haue noted much decency or vndecencie. 1656 *Clarke Papers* (Camden) III. 75 Upon a motion against blackpatches used by women on their faces, all undecency in apparrell was also moved again. 1692 SOUTH *Serm.* (1697) I. 482 From this springs the Notion of Decency or Undecency; that which becomes or mis-becomes.

**b.** = INDECENCY 1 b.

1624 GATAKER *Transubst.* 189 It should be subject to many undecencies, as corruption, putrefaction, mice-eating. 1660 JER. TAYLOR *Worthy Commun.* Introd. 5 A disproportionate instrument is an undecency, and makes the effect impossible. *a* 1716 SOUTH *Serm.* (1744) VII. 30 Every vacuity is (as it were) the hunger of the creation, both an undecency, and a torment.

**Undece·nnary,** *a. rare.* [f. L. *undec-im* eleven, after *decennary.*] Given, occurring, or observed every eleventh year, or once in every eleven years.

*a* 1847 E. STILES (Webster), It appears from an undecennary account laid before Parliament.

So **Undece·nnial** *a.* (1864 WEBSTER.)

**Unde·cent,** *a. Obs.* exc. *dial.* Also 5 vndesent, 7, 9 *dial.*, ondecent. [UN-[1] 7 and 5 b.]

**1.** Unfitting, unbecoming, improper; = INDECENT *a.* 1. Now *arch.*

1546 *Supplic. Poore Commons* (1871) 72 That it were farre vndesent to musell the oxe that trauaylleth all the daye. 1576 FLEMING *Panopl. Epist.* 177, I thincke it undecent, that I writing of mine owne matters, should, in yours, shewe mee selfe negligent. 1608 D. T[UVILL] *Ess. Pol. & Mor.* 51 b, As beeing a thing altogether vndecent, that one of her composition should any way intermeddle with Armes. 1658 T. WALL *Charact. Enemies Ch.* Ded. 1 To entitle a Book to the name of a Brother, is neither unusual or undecent. 1703 R. NEVE *City & C. Purch.* 86 It would be undecent to see a great Fabrick, consist of little Apartments. *a* 1721 SHEFFIELD (Dk. Buckhm.) *Wks.* (1723) II. 208 'Tis surely not undecent to mention one's self when 'tis rather with censure than approbation. 1823 LAMB *To Southey* Wks. 1908 I. 290, I have endeavoured there to rescue a voluntary duty..from the charge of an undecent formality.

**b.** Const. *for* (a person).

1559 MORWYNG *Evonym.* 196 All the use of Cosmetical.. thinges oughte to be taken for unhonest and undecent for a man that is..godly minded. 1581 PETTIE *Guazzo's Civ. Conv.* III. (1586) 159 It is an undecent thinge for a woman to resemble a man. 1604 T. WRIGHT *Passions* IV. ii. § I. 127 Such passions are..vndecent for graue persons. 1660 N. INGELO *Bentiv. & Ur.* II. (1682) 113 [No more] than it is undecent for a man to stand upon two Feet. 1685 SOUTH *Serm.* (1727) V. i. 28 It is very undecent for a Master to jest or play with his Scholars.

†**2.** Uncomely, unhandsome, unbecomingly mean; = INDECENT *a.* 2. *Obs.*

1622 WITHER *Philarete* (1633) F 5 b, 'Twixt the Eyes, no hollow place, Wrinkle nor undecent space, Disproportions her in ought. 1637-8 in Willis & Clark *Cambridge* (1886) I. 118 Fairer accesse to their Chappell, wᶜʰ is now most undecent. 1670 DRYDEN *2nd Pt. Conq. Granada* I, *Ozym.* I cast it from me, like a Garment torn, Ragged, and too undecent to be worn.

**3.** Offensive to propriety or moral feeling; = INDECENT *a.* 3. Now *dial.*

1563 *Homilies* II. *Excess of Apparel* P 10 Thou..makest of thy vndecent apparell of thy body, the deuilles nette. 1573-80 G. HARVEY *Letter-bk.* Wks. (Grosart) I. 135 What Stoick or Eremite will bar them of any merriments and iestes that are not ether merely undecent or simple unhonest? 1654 GATAKER *Disc. Apol.* 77 Away with all undecent, unwashed and defiled langage. 1693 *Dryden's Juvenal* XIV. (1697) 342 Much more is it their Duty to their Children, that nothing appear corrupt or undecent in their Family. 1711 E. WARD *Quix.* 111 He spy'd her stretch'd out in an undecent Manner on the Ground. 1717 *Entertainer* No. 8. 48 Shocking Sentences and Undecent Dialogues. 1810 S. GREEN *Reformist* I. 86 Aren't you ashamed, you undecent fellow, to be appearing on the staircase in that there manner? 1861 J. BARR *Poems* 108 (E.D.D.), 'Twas a shamefu' undecent remark.

†**Unde·cently,** *adv. Obs.* [Cf. UN-[1] 11 and 5 b, and prec.]

**1.** Unbecomingly, unsuitably, improperly; = INDECENTLY *adv.*

1563 *Homilies* II. *Sacrament* I. P 2 Lest..this comfortable medicine of the soule vndecently receaued, tende to our greater harme. 1577 tr. *Bullinger's Decades* (1592) 637 Hee ought to be free, least the image of God should seeme to bee bond vndecently. 1628 T. SPENCER *Logick* 171 We may not thinke, that he hath omitted it: for that is to charge him vndecently:..and against reason. 1671 GREW *Anat. Plants* iii. App. § 4 The Branches whereof.. must needs by their own weight, and that of their Fruit, undecently fall. 1716 M. DAVIES *Athen. Brit.* II. 96 He made early Applications to King Henry's Queen Dowager, who comply'd with him a little undecently.

**2.** Unhandsomely, inelegantly.

1587 *Presentmt.* in *Essex Rev.* XV. 43 The church is undecently and unsemely and filthily kept. 1644 LAUD *Hist. Troub. & Trials* (1695) xxxii. 310, I say so too, or else my Chappel must lye more undecently than is fit to express. 1664 J. WEBB *Stone-Heng* (1725) 38 They are most undecently high, saith Scamozzi. 1673 *Lady's Call.* I. v. § 32 Shall she take no care how sordidly, how undecently she appear when the King of Kings gives audience?

**3.** With impropriety or indecency.

1589 PUTTENHAM *Eng. Poesie* III. xxiii. (Arb.) 275 It was not vndecently spoken.., for it was the cleanliest excuse he could make. 1603 FLORIO *Montaigne* III. v. 522, I know a hundred Cuckolds, which are so, honestlie and little vndecently. 1655 STANLEY *Hist. Philos.* III. (1687) 92/2 Another time she offered to go to a publick show attired undecently. 1689 BURNET *Trav.* iii. (1750) 140 The great Libertinage that is so undecently practised by most Sorts of People at Venice.

**Undece·ption.** [UN-[2] 8.] The action of undeceiving or the fact of being undeceived.

1694 *Gracian's Courtier's Orac.* 191 At present undeception is politick, it goes commonly betwixt two lights. 1820 C. R. MATURIN *Melmoth* xxix. IV. 309 Oh Margaret—that undeception plants a dagger in the heart. 1870 R. BLACK tr. *Guizot's France* I. xiii. 301 Length of life brings, in the soul of the ambitious, days of hearty undeception.

**Undeceptious, -titious**: see UN-[1] 7.

**Undece·ptive,** *a.* (UN-[1] 7.) 1846 WORCESTER (citing Foster). 1883 D. C. MURRAY *Hearts* i. (1885) 2 With an undeceptive pretence of gaiety.

**Undeci·dable,** *a.* [UN-[1] 7 b.] Incapable of being decided.

1640 BP. HALL *Episc.* III. v. 244 Things so utterly undetermined, that they are indeed altogether undecidable. 1683 MOXON *Mech. Exerc., Printing* 1 An undecidable Controversie about the original Contriver..remains on foot. 1737 L. CLARKE *Hist. Bible* (1740) II. 224 The question being undecidable among themselves, they appeal to Jerusalem. 1845 CARLYLE *Cromwell* (1872) V. 16 As this matter of the Kingship is to me even now, very 'dark' and undecidable!

**Undeci·de,** *v.* (UN-[2] 3 and 7.)

1601 DANIEL *Civ. Wars* VI. xc, To vndiscide The late concluded Act they held for vaine. 1853 MRS. GASKELL *Ruth* xxi, She was weary of hearing all the..deciding, and undeciding, and re-deciding, before it was possible for her to go.

**Undeci·ded,** *ppl. a.* and *sb.* [UN-[1] 8.]

**A.** *adj.* **1.** Not decided; unsettled; uncertain.

1540 in *Charters, etc. Edinb.* (1871) 212 The pley beand.. as yet ondecidit, na innovatioun suld be maid. 1588 LAMBARDE *Eiren.* III. i. 330, I find it both doubted and undecided. 1603 FLORIO *Montaigne* I. xxvi. 89 Glory..forbids vs to leaue any thing vnresolued or vndecided. 1651 HOBBES *Leviath.* I. xv. 78 For else the question is undecided, and left to force. 1697 DRYDEN *Virg. Georg.* IV. 132 A Cast of scatter'd Dust will..undecided leave the Fortune of the Day. 1731 *Hist. Litteraria* III. 762 Finding, that notwithstanding the great pains he had taken, many Controversies remained still undecided. 1782 MISS BURNEY *Cecilia* II. vi, If any thing is yet undecided, it will not, perhaps, be amiss that I should be consulted. 1825 J. NICHOLSON *Operat. Mechanic* 671 It appears to us that this point still remains in a very undecided state. 1853 RUSKIN *Stones Ven.* (1874) II. vi. § 91. 217 This is not an unimportant distinction, nor an undecided one.

**b.** Lacking in decision or definiteness.

1828 LYTTON *Pelham* III. vii, To engage a certain rather than a doubtful and undecided support. 1864 TREVELYAN *Compet. Wallah* (1866) 292 To have..an undecided opinion on the question of Eternal Punishment.

**c.** *Coursing.* Not decided between the competing dogs; indecisive.

1839 in Youatt *Dog* (1845) 261 In running a match the judge may declare the course to be undecided. 1856 'STONEHENGE' *Brit. Sports* 206, etc.

**2.** Irresolute, hesitating.

1779 *Mirror* No. 66, He knows..that the undecided mind, without choice or active sense of propriety, is equally accessible to the next [feelings] that occur. 1791 COWPER *Iliad* I. 242 So doubted he, and undecided yet Stood drawing forth his faulchion huge. 1860 TYNDALL *Glac.* I. xi. 71 The man.. stood beside the chasm manifestly undecided as to whether he should take the step. 1875 JOWETT *Plato* (ed. 2) III. 173 When action above all things is required he is undecided.

**B.** *sb. Coursing.* An indecisive course.

1876 *Coursing Calendar* 5 Miss Steel and No More ran a short undecided. *Ibid.* 222 We did not make the anticipated headway, only getting thirty courses, including the two undecideds.

Hence **Undeci·dedly** *adv.*

[1847 WEBSTER.] 1856 OLMSTED *Slave States* 19 They seem to move very awkwardly, slowly, and undecidedly. 1885 SIR J. F. STEPHEN in *Law Q. Rev.* Jan. 8 Their language hovers undecidedly between two meanings.

**Undeci·ding,** *ppl. a.* (UN-[1] 10.) 1802 WOLCOT (P. Pindar) *Gt. Cry & Little Wool* IX. ii, A certain Law Lord of our days, A great *un*-deciding decider. 1846 WORCESTER (citing Burke).

**Undeci·duous,** *a.* (UN-[1] 7 and 5 b.)

1851 MRS. BROWNING *Casa Guidi Wind.* II. 380 From bole to bole Of immemorial, undeciduous trees. 1893 W. H. HUDSON *Patagonia* 136 The grey undeciduous foliage of the tree and shrub vegetation.

**Unde·cimal,** *a.* [f. L. *undecim* eleven.] Characterized in some way by the number eleven.

1804 SHAW *Gen. Zool.* V. I. 24 Undecimal Silure... Silure with single dorsal fin of eleven rays. 1845 *Encycl. Metrop.* XXV. 1397/1 The numeration [of the New Zealanders] is undecimal by successive multiples of eleven.

**Unde·ciman,** *a.* [f. as prec.] Connected with eleven o'clock. Also **Undecima·rian** *a.*

**1883** *Ch. Times* 27 Apr. 293 The service began at ten instead of eleven. After this revolt from the true *Undeciman Faith [etc.]. **1874** MICKLETHWAITE *Mod. Par. Churches* 308 But, says *undecimarian respectability, we should go to church to say our prayers and be preached to.

**Undecimarti·culate,** *a. Zool.* [f. L. *undecim* eleven + *articul-us* joint.] Having eleven sections.

**1856** W. CLARK *Van der Hoeven's Zool.* I. 340 Antennæ undecimarticulate, perfoliate.

‖ **Undeci·mvir.** *Gr. Antiq.* Also **undecem-**. [f. L. *undecim* eleven + *vir* man, after Gr. οἱ ἕνδεκα.] *pl.* The body of eleven magistrates in ancient Athens. Hence **Undeci·mvirate.**

**1728** CHAMBERS *Cycl.* s.v., The Functions of the *Undecimviri* at Athens, were much the same as those of the *Prevots de Marechaussee* in France. **1775** ASH, *Undecemvirate*.., the office or dignity of the undecemviri.

**Undeci·pher,** *v.* [UN-[2] 9.] *trans.* **a.** To decipher. **b.** To make undecipherable.

**1654** GAYTON *Pleas. Notes* I. ii. 6 It were very good policy in times of warre, suites, or jealousie, to learne to undecipher mouths, lookes, and gates. **1764** D. E. BAKER *Compan. to Play-house* II. s.v. *Denham*, All his Letters..were constantly decypher'd [= ciphered] and undecyphered by Mr. Cowley. **1856** E. FITZGERALD *Salámán* Prelim., Oh distracted Lover! writing What the Sword-wind of the Desert Undeciphers so that no one After you shall understand.

**Undeci·pherable,** *a.* [UN-[1] 7 b and 5 b.] That cannot be deciphered or made out; indecipherable: **a.** Of writings, inscriptions, etc.

**1758** H. WALPOLE *Lett. to Mann* 23 Feb. (1846) III. 346 Your copyist or his original have made undecypherable mistakes. *a* **1827** MISS BENGER in *Literary Souvenir* 39 This paper..being in many parts almost undecypherable. **1862** STANLEY *Serm. in East* (1863) 136 In another fifty years it is probable that many of them will be almost undecypherable. **1877** 'H. A. PAGE' *De Quincey* II. xviii. 128 The rest of this letter is so mutilated as to be undecipherable.

**b.** *transf.*

**1757** CHESTERF. *Let.* in *Misc. Wks.* (1777) II. 435 Public matters have been long, and are still, too undecypherable for me to understand, consequently to relate. **1822–56** DE QUINCEY *Confess.* (1862) 272 Its cause, its nature, and its undecipherable issue. **1850** GROTE *Greece* VIII. 574 In settling the undecipherable portions of the problem. **1876** T. HARDY *Ethelberta* This deep undecipherable habit sometimes suggested..Ethelberta's busy brain to her sisters.

Hence **Undecipherabi·lity**; **-ably** *adv.*

**1847** WEBSTER, *Undecipherably*. **1881** RUSKIN *Morn. Florence* 35 The whole landscape is quite undecipherably changed and spoiled. **1890** *Standard* 17 Jan. 5/3 Owing to the undecipherability of many of the signatures.

**Undeci·phered,** *ppl. a.* [UN-[1] 8.] Not deciphered or made out.

*a* **1668** DAVENANT *Philos. Disquisition* Wks. (1673) 326 She steals to Natures Closet, and from thence, Brings nought but undecypher'd Characters. **1755** YOUNG *Centaur* ii. Wks. 1757 IV. 153 Does this yet unconstrued, undecyphered creature consider himself as an immortal being? **1827** HOOD *Hero & Leander* lvii, As one, who pores on undecypher'd books, Strains vain surmise. **1897** P. WARUNG *Tales Old Régime* 231 The fear that..any written message from their friend..might remain undeciphered.

† **Undeci·sed,** *ppl. a.* [UN-[1] 8.] Undecided.

**1528** in *Lett. Suppress. Monast.* (Camden) 3 For the tryall of certen laundes and rightus which lately did depende..in contraversie, and yet doith depende undecised.

† **Undeci·sion.** *Obs.* (UN-[1] 12 and 5 b.)

**1611** COTGR., *Indecision*, an vndecision; a doubtfull, vndetermined, or vncleered state of things. **1795** *Jemima* I. 56 This state of torturing undecision shall terminate.

**Undeci·sive,** *a.* [UN-[1] 7 and 5 b.]

**1.** = INDECISIVE *a.* 1.

**1661** GLANVILL *Van. Dogm.* 132 The two Nations differing about the antiquity of their Language, made appeal to an undecisive experiment. **1769** *Junius' Lett.* xxxv. (1788) 178 Undecisive qualifying measures will disgrace your government still more than open violence. **1796** KIRWAN *Elem. Min.* (ed. 2) I. 24 The analyses..present different results, and consequently are undecisive. **1807** G. CHALMERS *Caledonia* I. 291 At Air-Gialla..an undecisive conflict was fought. **1855** SINGLETON *Virgil* I. 278 When a bull..from his neck Hath shaken out the undecisive axe.

**2.** = INDECISIVE *a.* 2.

**1780** *Mirror* No. 104, My poor friend, naturally of an undecisive temper,..had accustomed himself to deliberate on every trifle. **1802** WOLCOT (P. Pindar) *Pitt & Statue* Wks. 1812 IV. 510 So very undecisive in decision, Leaving for future Chancery-traps provision.

Hence **Undeci·sively** *adv.*; **Undeci·siveness.**

**1771** MACPHERSON *Introd. Hist. Gt. Brit.* 174 Their lawgiver and prophets..speak very obscurely, as well as undecisively, upon the subject. **1778** *Ann. Reg., Hist.* 30/2 The undecisiveness of the campaign had..occasioned a prodigious desertion on both sides.

**Unde·ck,** *v.* (UN-[2] 3.)

**1593** SHAKS. *Rich. II*, IV. i. 250, I haue giuen here my Soules consent T' vndeck the pompous Body of a King. **1598** FLORIO, *Disornare*, to disadorne, to vndeck.

**Unde·cked,** *ppl. a.* [UN-[1] 8.]

**1.** Not decked, adorned, or embellished.

**1570** LEVINS *Manip.* 50 Vndecked, *incultus*. **1596** *Edward III*, I. ii. 150 The ground, vndect with natures tapestrie, Seemes barrayne. **1621** G. SANDYS *Ovid's Met.* xi. (1626) 225 A Fane, vndeckt with gold or marble stone Adioynes. **1667** MILTON *P. L.* v. 380 Eve Undeckt, save with her self.., Stood to entertain her guest from Heav'n. **1740** DYER *Ruins Rome* 247 Those piles undeck'd, capacious, vast. **1811** WILLAN in *Archaeol.* XVII. 162 *Undight*, undressed, or undecked.

**2.** Not furnished with a deck or decks.

**1769** FALCONER *Dict. Marine* (1780) s.v. *Couloirs*, The sides of undecked vessels. **1824** SMYTH *Mem. Sicily*, etc. iv. 123 The undecked boats of the Rhegians. **1841** EMERSON *Ess., Self-reliance* Wks. (Bohn) I. 37 Columbus found the New World in an undecked boat. **1894** C. N. ROBINSON *Brit. Fleet* 202 Large, undecked row-boats.

**Undecla·rable,** *a.* (UN-[1] 7 b and 5 b.)

*c* **1449** PECOCK *Repr.* II. xvi. 245 Of the spirit and of the ymage to gidere in an vndeclarable maner schulde be maad a sensible God. **1675** PENN *Summons to Christendom* Wks. 1782 III. 319 Oh the peace, the joy, the pleasure and the undeclarable comfort!

**Undecla·red,** *ppl. a.* (UN-[1] 8.)

**1526** *Pilgr. Perf.* (W. de W. 1531) 172 b, Here we may perceyue that we touched in the first peticyon, & lefte vndeclared. *a* **1548** HALL *Chron., Hen. VI*, 185 The breaches whereof, he neither forgat, nor omitted vndeclared. **1599** *Life Sir T. More* III. in Wordsw. *Eccl. Biog.* (1818) II. 180 Seeing to declare the causes is so dangerous, then to leave them undeclared is no obstinacie. **1647** JER. TAYLOR *Lib. Proph.* xviii. 227 This mercy which appertaines to Infants is so secret and undeclared and unconsign'd. *a* **1665** J. GOODWIN *Filled w. the Spirit* (1867) 487 If we consider God..as undeclared unto the world in that covenant and word. **1751** SMOLLETT *Per. Pic.* lxviii, Pickle's intention..was still dubious and undeclared. **1840** THACKERAY *Shabby-genteel Story* v, He was allowed to remain in the house, an undeclared but very assiduous lover. **1884** *American* IX. 182 A war nearly unprovoked and entirely undeclared.

**Undecli·nable,** *a.* [UN-[1] 7 b and 5 b.]

**1.** *Gram.* = INDECLINABLE *a.* 3.

**1530** PALSGR. 77 Any other of the partes that be undeclynable. **1775** ASH, *Undeclinable*.., not admitting a change of termination.

**2.** Unswerving; = INDECLINABLE *a.* 1.

**1610** HEALEY *St. Aug. Citie of God* XXII. XXX. 919 An vndeclinable and sted-fast delight of not sinning.

**3.** Unavoidable; = INDECLINABLE *a.* 2.

**1652** CHARLETON *Darkn. Atheism Dispelled* 242 The malignant impressions of the Stars, epidemick contagions, or other undeclinable Accidents. *a* **1670** HACKET *Abp. Williams* I. (1693) 107, I have shewn how blameless the Lord Keeper was, and that the Offence on his Part was undeclinable. *a* **1711** KEN *Hymnotheo* Poet. Wks. 1721 III. 90 At ev'ry Sense..Shall Horrors undeclinable rush in.

**4.** That cannot be refused.

**1641** SIR E. DERING *Carmelite* 20, I offer you a fair tryall, and Iudges undeclinable.

Hence **Undecli·nably** *adv.*, †unswervingly.

**1662** STILLINGFL. *Orig. Sacræ* III. iii. § 15 Speaking of those souls which are undeclinably good.

† **Undecli·ne,** *v.* [UN-[1] 14.] = DESCEND *v.* 7 b.

**1651** CLEVELAND *Poems* 5 Were the note I sing Above heavens *Ela*, should I undecline, And with a deep-mouth'd Gammut sound agen.., I could not reach her worth.

**Undecli·ned,** *ppl. a.* [UN-[1] 8.]

**1.** *Gram.* Having no cases marked by variations in the termination.

In the following quot. the meaning is not clear:—**1509** FISHER 7 *Penit. Ps.* xxxviii. ee vij, This verbe morior after saynt Augustyne is vndeclyned.

**1530** PALSGR. 77 Partes that be undeclyned. *nous* and *vous* remayne undeclyned. **1565** COOPER *Thesaurus* (*) 4 This varietie of construction is not onely to be considered in the diuersity of cases, but also of other partes vndeclined. **1612** BRINSLEY *Lud. Lit.* vi. (1627) 56 The other foure last are undeclined; that is, such as cannot be so turned, and have but onely one ending. *a* **1721** PRIOR *Dial. Dead, Chas. & Clenard* P 2 Adverb, Conjonction, Preposition, Interjection undeclined. **1733** J. BRAMSTON *Man of Taste* 6 Good Parts are better than Eight Parts of Speech: Since these declin'd those undeclin'd they call, I thank my Stars, that I declin'd 'em all.

† **2.** Not turned aside. *Obs.*—[1]

**1638** G. SANDYS *Paraphr. Job* 31 For in his tract my wary feet have stept; His undeclined wayes precisely kept.

**Undecli·ning,** *ppl. a.* (UN-[1] 10.) **1820** SHELLEY *Prometh. Unb.* I. 281 [I] thus devote to sleepless agony, This undeclining head.

† **Undeco·ct,** *a. Obs.* [UN-[1] 7] Undigested.

**1542** BOORDE *Dyetary* xi. (1870) 261 Hote breade is vnholsome.., haustyng vndecoct humours.

**Undeco·cted,** *ppl. a.* [UN-[1] 8.] †Uncooked.

**1542** BOORDE *Dyetary* xiii. (1870) 267 Rawe crayme undecocted, eaten with strawberyes or hurtes.

**Undecompo·sable,** *a.* [UN-[1] 7 b and 5 b.] = INDECOMPOSABLE *a.* Also const. *by*.

**1807** SOUTHEY *Espriella's Lett.* III. 363 Nothing will vegetate upon it, and it is undecomposable by the weather. **1865** MILL *Exam. Hamilton* 13 Many of our intellectual ideas are regarded by him as ultimate and undecomposable facts. **1870** JEVONS *Elem. Logic* ii. 15 A simple undecomposable substance called by chemists an element.

**Undecompo·sed,** *ppl. a.* [UN-[1] 8.] Not decomposed: **a.** Of chemical or mineral substances.

**1758** REID tr. *Macquer's Chym.* I. 248 If the Fixed Alkali be desired perfectly free from any mixture of undecomposed Nitre. **1789** *Phil. Trans.* LXXIX. 307 The volatile alkali ..will frequently pass over in great quantities undecomposed. **1849** D. CAMPBELL *Inorg. Chem.* 49 Sometimes there is a very small quantity of undecomposed matter remaining undissolved. **1880** J. LOMAS *Man. Alkali Trade* 277 Large quantities of undecomposed manganese.

**b.** Of substances liable to organic decay.

*a* **1835** MCCULLOCH *Attributes* (1837) III. xlii. 120 The fallen wood in particular is useless to future vegetation while it is undecomposed. **1855** *Orr's Circ. Sci., Inorg. Nat.* 64 The flesh having been preserved in a sufficiently undecomposed state to serve as food for wild animals.

**Undecompo·sible,** *a.* [UN-[1] 7 and 5 b.] = UNDECOMPOSABLE *a.* Also **Undecomposibi·lity.**

**1866** ODLING *Anim. Chem.* 126 Its undecomposibility save by oxidation. *Ibid.* 129 Without this additional oxygen it has hitherto proved undecomposible. **1879** *Cassell's Techn. Educ.* I. 211 The other colours of the spectrum are due to simple or undecomposible rays.

**Undecompou·nded,** *ppl. a.* (UN-[1] 8.)

**1795** *Phil. Trans.* LXXXV. 340 Wrought iron is to be considered as a simple or undecompounded body. **1804** *Edin. Rev.* IV. 126 A number of substances which are still undecompounded. **1843** *Civil Eng. & Arch. Jrnl.* VI. 420/1 The earths being classed as undecompounded bodies.

**Unde·corated,** *ppl. a.* (UN-[1] 8.)

*a* **1763** SHENSTONE *Ess., Gardening* Wks. 1777 II. 113 A sufficient quantity of undecorated space is necessary to exhibit such decorations to advantage. **1844** MARY HOWITT *My Own Story* ix. 84 His horn, undecorated with ribands. **1874** LUBBOCK *Mod. Savages* 107 If in the very low races the women are often wholly undecorated [etc.]. **1897** J. R. TANNER in *Eng. Hist. Rev.* XII. 31 The Commons found the undecorated facts alarming enough.

**Unde·corative,** *a.* (UN-[1] 7.) **1881** [see UN-[1] 7]. **1886** RUSKIN *Præterita* II. v. 162 The undecorative structural arrangement, Swiss to the very heart..of it. **Undecrea·sing,** *ppl. a.* (UN-[1] 10.) **1587** GOLDING *De Mornay* vi. 72 To be short, he calleth him ye myndly speech,..vncorruptible, vnincreasing, vndecreasing,..and firstbeknowne after God. **Undecree·,** *v.* (UN-[2] 3.) **1667** WATERHOUSE *Fire Lond.* 182 Be that Judgment, O Lord, undecreed by thee. **1691** DRYDEN *K. Arthur* III. ii, As if eternal doom Could be reversed, and undecreed for me. **1898** [see UN-[2] 3]. **Undecri·ed,** *ppl. a.* (UN-[1] 8.) [**1775** ASH.] **1868** H. BUSHNELL *Serm. Living Subj.* 292 They fall into their places, unenvied, undecried.

**Unde·dicated,** *ppl. a.* (UN-[1] 8.)

**1661** BOYLE *Style of Script.* Ep. Ded. 2 That I should let this Book come forth Undedicated. **1675** HAN. WOOLLEY *Gentlewom. Comp.* 100 You would not let one minute pass undedicated to some good employment. **1794** W. TINDAL *Hist. Evesham* 31 It is difficult to conceive..that it should have remained long undedicated after being built. **1881** *Times* 20 Dec. 4/1 With the intention of walking over the defendant's undedicated land.

**Undee, undé(e,** *a. Her.* Also 6–7 (9) **unde.** [a. OF. *unde, -ee* (F. *ondé, -ée*), f. L. *unda* (F. *onde*) wave, UND.] Having the form of waves; wavy. (Cf. UNDY *a.*, OUNDY *a.*, UNDATED *a.*, UNDADE *a.*)

**1513** in Glover *Hist. Derby* (1829) I. App. 61, 3 barrs upon his nek, sabul unde or wave. **1572** BOSSEWELL *Armorie* 26 Crosses,..vairee, vndee, nebulee, cordee [etc.]. *Ibid.* II. 28 G. beareth Or and Gules, parted per Pale, vndee. It is termed Vndee, because two colors are caried one into an other, by the maner of water troubled with ye wind. **1611** GUILLIM *Heraldry* II. v. 50 This is termed a Bend Vnde. **1688** R. HOLME *Armoury* I. 19/1 Wavee, or Wavey, or Waved, or Unde, or Surged. *c* **1828** BERRY *Encycl. Her.* I. Gloss., *Unde, Undée*..is applied to charges, the edges of which curve and recurve, like the waves of water. **1863** BOUTELL *Her. Hist. & Pop.* xxi. 287 Barry undée of six, arg. and az. **1868** CUSSANS *Her.* (1893) 47 The lines by which a shield is divided..may assume any of the..forms:..Undé, or Wavy. Nebulé [etc.].

† **Undee·ded,** *a. Obs.*—[1] (UN-[1] 9.)

**1605** SHAKS. *Macb.* v. vii. 20 Either thou Macbeth, Or else my Sword with an vnbattered edge I sheath againe vndeeded.

**Undee·med,** *ppl. a.* [UN-[1] 8.]

† **1.** Not judged or condemned; uncensured. *Obs.*

*c* **1200** ORMIN 16725 Whase lefeþþ upponn himm, þatt mann iss all unndemedd. *Ibid.* 17045 Ec off þatt, tatt illc an mann Iss all þwerrt ut unndemedd. *c* **1460** *Towneley Myst.* xxi. 230 Sir, the law will not he gang on nokyn wyse Vndemyd. **1500–20** DUNBAR *Poems* xviii. 50 Do weill, and sett not by demying, For no man sall vndemit be.

**2.** Unsuspected, unimagined.

**1845** BAILEY *Festus* (ed. 2) 152 The words of gods, And fragments of the undeemed tongues of Heaven. **1856** VAUGHAN *Mystics* vi. vi. I. 394 The consciousness that all possessed is but a drop of the illimitable undeemed Perfection yet beyond.

**Undee·mous,** *a. Sc.* and † *north.* Forms: 4 **vndemes**, 6 **vndemus, -ous**, 9 **undeemous, -deemis, ondeemas**, etc. [ad. ON. *údǽmis*, gen. of *údǽmi* (Norw. *udøme*, MSw. *odöme*) an unexampled or monstrous thing or deed, f. *ú-* UN-[1] + *dǽmi* example, instance, related to DEEM *v.*, DOOM *sb.* The ending has partly been taken as -OUS.] Unexampled, unparalleled, extraordinary, remarkable.

*a* **1300** *Cursor M.* 23235 (Gött.), The fiȝft [pain] es vndemes of dint [*Cott.* vnclemes dint; *Edinb.* vndemenes of dint], þat þa wreches þar sal hint. **1536** BELLENDEN *Cron. Scot.* I. vii. (1541) 6 b/2 Suppone we be vincust (quhilk may nocht succeid but vndemus murdir of ȝow) than sall ye be ane facyll pray to ȝour ennymes. *Ibid.* vi. xvi. 76 b/2 Thay ruschit.. on the said Romanis; and maid sic vndemus slauchter on thaym, that [etc.]. **1596** DALRYMPLE tr. *Leslie's Hist. Scot.* I. 349 Edward..gathiris..ane armie vndemous. **1808** JAMIESON s.v., *Undeemis..money*, a countless sum. **1871** W. ALEXANDER *Johnny Gibb* x, An ondeemas thing o' siller.

Hence **Undee·mously** *adv. Sc.*

**1846** W. CROSS *Disruption* xiv, It's groun just undeemously since we cam' to Embro'.

**Undeep,** *sb.* [f. next.] A shoal, shallow place.

**1513** DOUGLAS *Æneid* v. iv. 114 First Sergest behind sone left hes he, Wreland on skelleis and wndepis of the see. **1847** G. LEE tr. *Hist. Ceylon* 6 Some of their vessels were driven into the undeeps near the place..called Chilaw.

**Undee·p,** *a.* [OE. *undéop* (see UN-[1] 7 and DEEP *a.*), = WFris. *ûn-, ondjip*, Du. and Flem. *ondiep*, G. *untief*.] Not deep; shallow.

*c* **897** K. ÆLFRED *Gregory's Past. C.* lxv. 469 Nis ðæt rædlic ðing, ȝif swa hlutor wæter hlud and undiop toflowð æfter feldum. *Ibid.* lxiii. 459 On ðæt undiope mod. **1154** *O. E. Chron.* (Laud MS.) an. 1137, Sume hi diden in crucethus, ðæt is in an cæste þat was scort & nareu & undep. **1597** A. M. tr. *Guillemeau's Fr. Chirurg.* 4/2 Smalle and vndiepe woundes. **1675** *Phil. Trans.* VI. 3074 These Galleys are of great use both in Rivers and Un-deep Seas.

**Undefa·ceable,** *a.* (UN-[1] 7 b.)

**1587** in T. NORTON *Calvin's Inst.* Table XX x 6, Of the undelible character or undefaceable marke of the oyle wherewith popish Priestes are annointed at their creation. **1611** COTGR., *Ineffaçable*, vneffaceable, vndefaceable.

**Undefa·ced,** *ppl. a.* [UN-[1] 8.]

**1.** Not defaced or disfigured; not destroyed.

*c* 1400 *Destr. Troy* 8730 He fraynet..How the korse might be keppit..Fresshe, vndefacede, & in fyne hew. 1537 *Lett. Suppr. Monast.* (Camden) 164 The churche and house remenythe as yet undefacede. 1566 *Eng. Ch. Furniture* (Peacock, 1866) 115 John hyxon haythe ij candelstickes & sensors vndefased. 1582 *Wills & Inv. N. C.* (Surtees, 1860) 100 The chamber, as yt now standeth, vndefaced. 1631 WEEVER *Anc. Funeral Mon.* To Rdr., Such memorials..as were remaining yet vndefaced. 1676 HOBBES *Iliad* 374 Yet is his body uncorrupt,..And..doth whole remain And undefac'd, the bloud all washt away. 1772 [SHRUBSOLE & DENNE] *Hist. Rochester* 63 The monuments of the dead..escaped undefaced. 1839 DARWIN *Voy. Nat.* xxiii. 604 The primeval forests undefaced by the hand of man. 1863 WHYTE MELVILLE *Gladiators* III. 165 Never again would she lie in the moonlight, beautiful and gracious and undefaced.

**2.** Not obliterated or blotted out; uneffaced.

1565 *MS. Cott. Cal. B. 10.* fol. 270 Which charters remain still undefaced. *a* 1619 FOTHERBY *Atheom.* I. iii. § 3 (1622) 19 There is a sense of God still vndefac't. 1633 T. NASHE *Quaternio* (1636) 224 Both he and shee are branded with infamie, and the stigmaticall characters remaine as yet vndefaced in them. 1709 *Brit. Apollo* II. No. 15. 1/2 Undefac'd Impressions of our Maker's Image. 1818 SCOTT *Br. Lamm.* xxi, The softer substances, when they receive an impression, retain it undefaced. 1873 W. CORY *Lett. & Jrnls.* (1897) 333 The undefaced cross and bull on the door-post.

**Undefa·lcated,** *ppl. a.* [UN-[1] 8.] Not curtailed or reduced; undiminished.

*a* 1745 SWIFT *Wks.* 1841 II. 223/2 A real undefalcated income of 600 *l.* a-year. 1802–12 BENTHAM *Ration. Judic. Evid.* (1827) V. 187 A perfect and undefalcated interest in the establishment of the will.

† **Undefa·me,** irreg. var. of next. *Obs.*

1560 ROLLAND *Seven Sages* 10 Lord, I am auld, and neuer [*sic*] vndefame On ȝour counsall, and hes bene mony ȝeir.

**Undefa·med,** *ppl. a.* (UN-[1] 8.)

*a* 1450 *Knt. de la Tour* (1868) 36 Ther she might abide atte home with her worshippe saued, vndefamed of her good name. 1530–1 *Act 22 Hen. VIII*, c. 14 Whiche appertayne to the libertie of the kynges subiectes undefamed. 1578 *Reg. Privy Council Scot.* III. 60 He is ane trew man, knawin honest and undefamit sen he was borne. 1623 tr. *Favine's Theat. Hon.* III. vi. 374 That the Order may remaine pure and vndefamed, according as it ought to doe. 1648 HEXHAM II, *Onbefaemt*, Vndefamed.

†**Undefa·tigable,** *a. Obs.* (UN-[1] 7 b and 5 b.)

1630 tr. *Camden's Hist. Eliz.* IV. 89 Meane while, the Lord Deputy with vndefatigable paynes prosecuteth Mac-Hugh. 1662 GURNALL *Chr. in Arm.* III. xx. § 1 Men, furnished by the blessing of God on their undefatigable labours and studies.

† **Undefau·lting,** *ppl. a.* [UN-[1] 10.] Unfailing.

*a* 1440 *Found. St. Bartholomew's* (E.E.T.S.) 45 He preyid the vndefawtynd mercy of criyst.

†**Undefea·sed,** *ppl. a. Sc. Obs.* [UN-[1] 8.] Undischarged.

1492 *Acta Dom. Conc.* (1839) 273/1 Þat þe said James sall content & pay to þe said Johne þe somme of v li contenit in þe said sentence arbitrale & vndefesit tharintill.

† **Undefea·sible,** *a. Obs.* Also -able. [UN-[1] 7, 7 b.] = INDEFEASIBLE *a.* (Freq. in 17th c.)

1461 *Rolls of Parlt.* V. 465/2 By auncient maters of..notable recorde undefaisible. 1548 UDALL *Erasm. Par. Luke* xxii. 165 And the said victorie consisteth in the vndefeasable scriptures of ye olde and newe testament. 1650 ELDERFIELD *Tythes* 38 Foundation of dominion cannot but have settled me a sufficient title and undefeasible. 1695 TRYON *Dreams* vii. 117 This great and undefeazable Law of the Creator.

**Undefea·t,** *v.* (UN-[2] 3.) 1746 GRAY *Let. to Walpole* 3 Feb., Our defeat to be sure is a rueful affair..; but the Duke is gone it seems..to undefeat us again. **Undefea·table,** *a.* (UN-[1] 7 b and 5 b.) *a* 1640 JACKSON *Creed* x. iv. § 2 Either by the power of their almighty Creator, or by the undefeatable contrivance of his wisdom. [Also in recent use.]

**Undefea·ted,** *ppl. a.* (UN-[1] 8.)

[1775 ASH.] 1818 SHELLEY *Rosalind* 701 Faith, the Python, undefeated, Even to its blood-stained steps dragged on Her foul and wounded train. 1875 WHYTE-MELVILLE *Katerfelto* ii, Game-cocks, of which he owned a choice and undefeated breed. [Common in recent use.]

Hence **Undefea·tedly** *adv.*

1897 QUILLER-COUCH in Stevenson *St. Ives* xxxiii, He was pale, but undefeatedly voluble.

**Unde·fecated,** *ppl. a.* (UN-[1] 8.) 1817 GODWIN *Mandeville* II. vi. 115 Mine was pure, simple, undefecated rage, that did not dream of controling itself. **Undefe·ctive,** *a.* (UN-[1] 7, 5 b.) 1599 SANDYS *Europæ Spec.* (1632) 45 The most heavenly order reaching from the heighth of al power to the very lowest of all subjection, with admirable harmony and undefectiue corespondence. **Undefe·ctiveness.** (UN-[1] 12.) 1702 S. PARKER tr. *Cicero's De Finibus* v. 318 As certainly as our Nature is desirous of Consummation and Undefectiveness.

† **Undefe·nced,** *ppl. a. Obs.* [UN-[1] 8.]

**1.** = UNDEFENDED *ppl. a.* 2.

1451 CAPGRAVE *Life St. Gilbert* 94 So was our old man eke disposed þat he wold not leue þe lyues old on-defensed. 1544 BETHAM *Precepts Warr* II. li. L ij b, Let hym beware that he leaue not his campe vndefenced and vnmanned. 1586 DAY *Eng. Secretorie* II. (1595) 100 The nature of the Dolphin is not to suffer the yong ones of her kind to straggle vndefenced. 1609 BIBLE (Douay) *Gen.* xlii. 12 You came to consider the undefensed partes of this land. 1652 HEYLYN *Cosmogr.* 4 God sends man into the world..naked, and weak, and undefenced against all violences and dangers.

**2.** Unfenced.

1607 J. NORDEN *Surv. Dial.* v. 239 It is common..where men sow their corne, in undefenced grounds, there they make a dead hay..to keepe the cattle from the corne.

**Undefe·nded,** *ppl. a.* [UN-[1] 8.]

†**1.** Not forbidden. *Obs.*

1399 GOWER *Praise of Peace* 223 We..soeffrin every lond To slen ech other as thing undefendid. 1598 FLORIO, *Indiffeso*, vndefended, not forbidden.

**2.** Not defended or guarded; unprotected.

1564 DORMAN *Proofe Cert. Articles Relig.* 28 b, Why haue they left him so long vndefended, who did no other thing then whereof them selues wer the authors. 1660 JER. TAYLOR *Ductor* I. iv. rule 2 § 22 If a sober man shall stand alone unarm'd, undefended, or unprovided, and shall tell that he will make the Sun stand still. 1687 DRYDEN *Hind & P.* III. 626 The rest were strugling still with death, and lay The Crows and Ravens rights, an undefended prey. 1795 BURKE *Let. to W. Elliot* Wks. VII. 363 Property, left undefended by principles, became a repository of spoils to tempt cupidity. 1810 CRABBE *Borough* I. 136 There stands a cottage with an open door, Its garden undefended blooms before. 1869 TOZER *Highl. Turkey* I. 200 [A] bridge..with a single lofty arch undefended by a parapet.

**3.** *Law.* **a.** Not defended; not assisted by legal defence.

1607 COWELL *Interpr.*, *Informatus non sum*, is a formall aunswer or of course made by an atturney,..by the which he is deemed to leaue his client vndefended. 1832 MISS MITFORD *Village* v. (1863) 323 The judge..hearing that he was a voluntary witness for the undefended prisoner, proceeded to question him. 1900 *Daily News* 4 May 5/5 The accused is undefended.

**b.** Against which no defence is raised.

1898 *Daily News* 26 July 8/7 The undefended petition of Major..for a divorce. 1899 *Ibid.* 4 May 8/4 Action was brought against him..and was undefended.

**Undefe·nding,** *ppl. a.* (UN-[1] 10.)

1651 JER. TAYLOR *Serm. for Year* I. xx. 253 Birds, sheep, and bevers, who..have not the foresight to avoid a snare, but by their fear and undefending follies are driven thither. 1888 O. CRAWFURD *Sylvia Arden* 320 Having to slay an undefending man in cold blood.

† **Undefe·nsable,** *a. Obs.* Also 7 -ceable. [UN-[1] 7 b.] **a.** = next 2. **b.** Unpreventable.

*c* 1412 HOCCLEVE *De Reg. Princ.* 2619 Wearmes bere A-geyn the armed men, hem for to dere, And naght a-geyn children vndefensable. *c* 1440 *Jacob's Well* 194 A knyȝt wyth-outen armoure, or armoure wyth-outen a knyȝt, is vndefensable. 1622 CALLIS *Stat. Sewers* (1647) 114 Things which happen extraordinarily by the Sea or great waters..are counted inevitable and undefenceable.

**Undefe·nsible,** *a.* [UN-[1] 7 and 5 b.]

**1.** = INDEFENSIBLE *a.* 2.

1529 MORE *Dyaloge* IV. Wks. 256/2 Luther hath bee fayne for the defence of his vndefencible errours, to..forsake al ye maner of profe & trial. 1830 *Westm. Rev.* July 85 Perhaps it is to a little undefensible latitude this way..that he owes a portion of the affected contempt of Pope, Swift, and Co.

**2.** Incapable of defence. Also *absol.*

1616 SURFL. & MARKH. *Country Farme* v. v. 531 To take away the stones were to impouerish the ground, and make it bare and vndefensible both against the wind, heat, and cold. 1661 J. DAVIES *Civ. Warres* 87 He..enters the unarmed and undefencible Town without resistance. 1661 FELTHAM *Resolves* (ed. 8) II. i. 174 How below the gallantry of man is it, to tyrannize upon the undefensible and senselesse?

† **Undefe·nsive,** *a. Obs.* (UN-[1] 7 and 5 b.)

1587 A. DAY *Daphnis & Chloe* (1890) 16 Loue..had..prepared a secrete ambush wherewith to frame some notable breache into the vndefensiue imaginations of these..louers.

**Undefere·ntially,** *adv.* (UN-[1] 11.) 1876 RUSKIN *Fors Clav.* lxix. 291, I looked at him, in one sense, not undeferentially. **Undefi·cient,** *a.* (UN-[1] 7, 5 b.) 1854 PATMORE *Angel in Ho.*, *Betrothal* 71 And therefore in herself she stands Adorn'd with undeficient grace.

† **Undefie·d,** *ppl. a.*[1] *Obs.* [UN-[1] 8.] Undigested; unconcocted.

1398 TREVISA *Barth. De P.R.* IV. ix. (Tollem. MS.), Aristotel sayeþ þat flemme is an undefied superfluite of mete. *Ibid.* v. xxxix. (Bodl. MS.), If þe blood is vndefied þe body þat is ifed þerewith swelleþ and strecchiþ. *c* 1440 *Promp. Parv.* 364/2 On-defyyd, *indigestus*. *c* 1450–80 tr. *Secreta Secret.* 25 That mete dwellith vndefied in þe bottom of the stomak.

**Undefie·d,** *ppl. a.*[2] (UN-[1] 8.)

1590 SPENSER *F. Q.* II. viii. 31 Miscreant, thou broken hast The law of armes, to strike foe vndefide. 1670 DRYDEN *1st Pt. Conq. Granada* I, Tarifa..Chang'd his blunt Cane for a Steel-pointed Dart, And..basely threw it at him, undefy'd.

**Undefi·lable,** *a.* (UN-[1] 7 b.) 1855 CDL. WISEMAN *Fabiola* xvi. 99 Simple as light is His nature, one and the same every where, indivisible, undefilable.

**Undefi·led,** *ppl. a.* [UN-[1] 8.]

**1.** Not rendered morally foul or impure; unpolluted, untainted.

13..*E. E. Allit. P.* A. 725 He com þyder ryȝt as a chylde, Harmlez, trwe & vnde-fylde. *c* 1440 CAPGRAVE *Life St. Kath.* v. 576 He offred hym-selue on-to the fadyr of blis An oste ful clene, ondefiled with synne. 1504 C'TESS RICHMOND tr. *De Imitatione* IV. ii. (1893) 263 Lorde, kepe my herte and my body vndefyled. 1561 T. NORTON *Calvin's Inst.* I. 13 The law of the Lord (sayth he) is vndefiled, conuerting soules. 1628 SIR W. MURE *Spir. Hymne* 16 That I may spreade thy praise, thy might, With heart pure, vndefyl'de. 1662 STILLINGFL. *Orig. Sacræ* III. iii. § 7 He had a pure and undefiled soul. 1784 COWPER *Task* III. 260 Immortal Hale!..fam'd For sanctity of manners undefil'd. *a* 1839 PRAED *Legend of Drachenfels* Poems 1864 I. 150 Thou, in whose all-searching sight No human thing is undefiled. 1851 FROUDE *Short Stud.* (1867) I. 379 To..keep themselves if possible undefiled by so much as one corrupt thought.

*absol.* 1611 BIBLE *Ps.* cxix. 1 Blessed are the vndefiled in the way. 1837 MONSELL *Hymn*, '*God of that glorious gift*' v, Make him and keep him Thine own child, Meek follower of the Undefiled!

**b.** Sexually pure or unpolluted; chaste.

*c* 1450 *Cov. Myst.* (Shaks. Soc.) 141 A mayd undefyled I hope he xal me preve. *c* 1470 *Pol., Rel., & L. Poems* (1903) 4 Thove vergyne knight of whom we synge, Vn-Deffiled sithe thy begynnyng. 1531 ELYOT *Gov.* III. xviii, But whan he knewe that they were of noble lignage, he sent them undefiled to their parentes and kynnes folke. 1539 CRANMER *Heb.* xiii. 4 Wedlocke is to be had in honoure among all men, and the bed vndefyled. 1611 BIBLE *Wisd.* xiv. 24 They kept neither liues nor mariages any longer vndefiled. 1667 MILTON *P. L.* IV. 761 Perpetual Fountain of Domestic sweets, Whose Bed is undefil'd and chast pronounc't. 1710 STEELE *Tatler* No. 210 ¶ 6, I have lived a pure and undefiled Virgin these Twenty seven Years. 1793 COWPER *A Tale* 6 Husband..and wife may boast Their union undefil'd. 1816 BYRON *Siege Corinth* xxvii, She is safe..In heaven;..Far from thee, and undefiled.

† **2.** Undefaced, unimpaired. *Obs. rare.*

1432–50 tr. *Higden* (Rolls) I. 185 That mownte..in whom letters wryten [in dust] were founde vndefilede [L. *illibatæ*] at the end of the yere. *c* 1460 *Oseney Reg.* 14 And what-soeuer thyng..may be i-purchased, to þem or to þere successours..vnbroke and undefylyd [L. *illibata*] abyde.

**3.** Not rendered foul or dirty. Also *fig.*

1590 SPENSER *F. Q.* IV. ii. 32 Dan Chaucer, well of English vndefyled. 1660 J. H[ARDING] *Basil. Valent. Chariot Antim.* 3 The Chaff being separated from the uncommix'd and undefiled Corn. 1718 LADY M. W. MONTAGU *Verses written in the Chiosk at Pera* 34 The streams still murmur, undefil'd with rain. 1821 WORDSW. *Mem. Tour Continent* XXXIII. 35 A sea-green river,..With current swift and undefiled. 1826 SCOTT *Woodst.* ii, Perhaps it is a punishment on me, who thought the loyalty of my house was like undefiled ermine.

**4.** Not violated or desecrated.

1586 J. MUSH *Life Margt. Clitherow* in Morris *Troub. Cath. Forefathers* Ser. III. (1877) 363 Insomuch as now not one Religious house standeth, not one altar unrased and undefiled. 1715 ROWE *Lady Jane Grey* II, Mercyful, great Defender! Preserve thy holy Altars undefil'd. 1818 BYRON *Ch. Har.* IV. cliv, In this eternal ark of worship undefiled. 1865 MISS YONGE *Clever Woman of Family* I. ix. 225 He did think he had one lawn in the world undefiled by those horrible [croquet] hoops!

Hence **Undefi·ledly** *adv.*; **Undefi·ledness.**

1548 UDALL, etc. *Erasm. Par. Matt.* v. 24 But I wyll haue Matrimonye obserued more holyly and *vndefyledly amonge them that professe the new lawe. 1583 GOLDING *Calvin on Deut.* xxxiv. 200 Wee cannot serue him vndefyledly, except wee bee separated from the defylings that are contrarie to him. 1868 NETTLESHIP *Ess. Browning* 215 Here only could he be led to yearn undefiledly..after truths. 1571 GOLDING *Calvin on Ps.* li. 8 God requireth *undefylednesse in the inward partes. ? 1657 FARINDON *Serm.* xiii. (1672) I. 274 The colours and Beauty of it [*sc.* religion]; first, in its Purity..; secondly, its Vndefiledness, having no pollution.

**Undefi·nable,** *a.* and *sb.* (UN-[1] 7 b, 5 b.)

1694 LOCKE *Hum. Und.* (ed. 2) III. iv. § 4 *marg.*, Names of simple Ideas undefinable. 1750 CHESTERF. *Lett.* (1774) 49 That is the occasion in which manners, dexterity, address, and the undefineable *je ne sçais quoi*, triumph. 1780 BURKE *Œcon. Reform* Wks. III. 306 Other persons meriting as little as they do, might be put upon it to an undefinable amount. 1827 DISRAELI *V. Grey* v. xv, When he was experiencing emotions, which, though undefinable, he felt to be new. 1884 CHURCH *Bacon* viii. 201 The undefinable but very real character of greatness.

*sb.* 1809 MALKIN *Gil Blas* X. xii. ¶ 23, I had no mind to meddle any more with the dish of undefinables.

Hence **Undefi·nableness; Undefi·nably** *adv.*

? 1705 BERKELEY in Fraser *Life* (1871) 437 There may be another cause of the undefinableness of certain ideas,..viz. the want of names. 1886 W. J. TUCKER *E. Europe* 127 Every village one passes through has..something undefinably characteristic about it.

**Undefi·ned,** *ppl. a.* [UN-[1] 8.] Not defined or clearly marked; indefinite.

1611 FLORIO, *Indefinito*, vndefined. 1658 PHILLIPS, *Indefinite*, not limited, undefined, undetermined. 1716 ADDISON *Freeholder* No. 31 ¶ 5 The Terms which the Author makes use of are loose, general, and undefined. 1797 GODWIN *Enquirer* I. xii. 105 A sort of floating and undefined reverie. 1844 KINGLAKE *Eothen* viii, The prestige created by the rumours of her high and undefined rank. 1875 JOWETT *Plato* (ed. 2) IV. 156 Theology..is full of undefined terms which have distracted the human mind for ages.

Hence **Undefi·nedly** *adv.*; **Undefi·nedness.**

1827 MONTGOMERY *Pelican Isl.* IX. 190 His soul explored immensity, In search of something undefinedly great. *a* 1832 BENTHAM *Language* Wks. 1843 VIII. 304/1 Clearness, as opposed to: 1. Obscurity, 2. Ambiguity, 3. Undefinedness. 1860 J. YOUNG *Prov. Reason* 47 Only through and on account of this undefinedness,..is Being non-Being.

† **Unde·finite,** *a.* [UN-[1] 7.] = INDEFINITE *a.*

1589 NASHE *Anat. Absurd.* Epistle, The vndefinite desire to be suppliant vnto you in some subiect of witte. 1603 FLORIO *Montaigne* I. ix. 17 The opposite of truth hath many shapes, and an undefinite field.

**Undefle·cted,** *ppl. a.* (UN-[1] 8.)

1852 BAILEY *Festus* (ed. 5) 475 The sun-sire and the deathworld too, And undeflected spirit, pure from Heaven. 1882 GEIKIE *Text-bk. Geol.* IV. vii. i. § 3. 554 The dykes may be traced undeflected across some of the largest faults.

† **Undeflore,** *a. Obs.* [UN-[1] 7.] = INDEFLORE *a.*

*a* 1568 BELLENDEN *Benner of Pietie* 138 (Bann. MS.), The secund wes ane richt excellent thing, Quhen moderfull wes the Virgin, vndefloir.

**Undeflow·ered,** *ppl. a.* (UN-[1] 8.)

(*a*) *a* 1533 LD. BERNERS *Gold. Bk. M. Aurel.* ii. (1535) 101 b, They leaue no cattayle vnslayne, no gardeyne vnrobbed, no wyld beest vnchased, nor no mayde vndefloured. 1602 DEKKER *Satirom.* Wks. 1873 I. 225 A charme, that shall lay downe the spirit of lust, and keep thee undeflowerd. 1641 EARL MONM. tr. *Biondi's Civil Wars* II. 83 No maidenhood was undeflowred, nor marriage bed unviolated.

(*b*) 1641 MILTON *Reform.* II. Wks. 1851 III. 65 Much more may a King injoy his rights, and Prerogatives undeflowr'd, untouch'd. 1678 CUDWORTH *Intell. Syst.* I. v. 728 The Atomick Philosophy [has been] restored, as it was in its first genuine and virgin state, undeflowred as yet by Atheists. 1746 YOUNG *Nt. Th.* IX. 1210 Minds elevate..alone obtain Full relish of existence un-deflower'd. *a* 1861 D. GRAY *Poet. Wks.* (1874) 23 He feels As one newborn to being undeflowered.

† **Undefoi·led,** *ppl. a. Obs. rare.* (UN-[1] 8. Cf. *defoil* DEFOUL *v.*)

*a* 1325 *Prose Psalter* (1891) 193 Þe which bot ȝif ichon kepe hole & nouȝt de-fouled [*v.r.* vndefoylid],..he shal peris wyþ-outen ende. [1859 J. T. STATON *Song Sol.* vi. 9 Ma dove, ma undefoilt, is but one.]

† **Undefoi·ling,** *vbl. sb. Obs.* (UN-¹ 13; cf. prec.) *c* 1425 *St. Mary of Oignies* II. iii. 26 in *Anglia* VIII. 158 Vndefoylynge of þe forseyde holy virgyns.

**Undefo·rmed,** *ppl. a.* (UN-¹ 8.) 1672–3 GREW *Anat. Roots* I. v. § 8 To be chosen, while the Plant is yet growing; at which time, it may be often found dry, yet undeformed. *c* 1714 POPE *Let.* Wks. 1751 VII. 127 The sight of so many gallant fellows, with all the pomp and glare of war, yet undeform'd by battles,..may possibly invite your curiosity. 1812 BRACKENRIDGE *Views Louisiana* (1814) 34 Those clean smooth meadows,..covered with a short sweet grass.., undeformed by a single weed! 1886 E. WARD *Dress Problem* v. 84 Strong, healthy lungs and an undeformed pelvis.

† **Undefou·led,** *ppl. a. Obs.* (UN-¹ 8.) Common from *c* 1380 to 1450. 13.. *Propr. Sanct.* (Vernon MS.) 95 in Herrig's *Archiv* LXXXI. 86 He him kneuh for Innocent And vndefoulet. *c* 1374 CHAUCER *Boeth.* II. pr. iv. (1868) 40 Yif þat þilke þing ..be kept to þe..vnwemmed and vndefouled. *c* 1410 HOCCLEVE *Mother of God* 1 Modir of god and virgyne vndeffouled! *a* 1450 *Knt. de la Tour* (1868) 157 She that hathe atte al tymes putte her payne in trauaile to kepe her body vndefouled and in clennesse. 1483 CAXTON *Gold. Leg.* 392/1 That I may haue the prepucye vndefouled.

† **Undefou·lingness.** (UN-¹ 12.) *c* 1400 *Wycliffite Bible* 1 Pet. iii. 4 The hid man of herte, in vncoruptibilite [*MS. New Coll.* 67 vndefoulingnesse] of quyete..and mylde spirit.

**Undefray·ed,** *ppl. a.* (UN-¹ 8.) 1611 COTGR., *Insolu*, vnpayed, vndischarged, vndefrayed. 1727 BAILEY (vol. II). 1817 *Monthly Rev.* LXXXIV. 520 The expences of alterations at Osmanstadt were still undefrayed. 1842 MADDEN *United Irishmen* I. x. 325 No expenses of these gentlemen were left undefrayed.

**Undege·neracy.** (UN-¹ 12.) 1793 HOLCROFT tr. *Lavater's Physiog.* xxxv. 180 Much has been said of the openness, undegeneracy, simplicity and ingenuousness of a childish and youthful countenance.

**Undege·nerate,** *a.* (UN-¹ 7.) 1743 BLAIR *Grave* 470 Fantastic schemes, which the long livers In the world's hale and undegenerate days Could scarce have leisure for. 1822 CAMPBELL '*Men of England*' i, Men whose undegenerate spirit Has been proved on land and flood. 1854 H. MILLER *Sch. & Schm.* xiii. (1860) 135/1 While the as yet undegenerate plant had merely borne atop a few florets. 1870 RUSKIN *Lect. Art* i. 27 We are still undegenerate in race. 1897 *Allbutt's Syst. Med.* VII. 229 The quick normal response of the undegenerate muscle-fibres to the negative closure.

**Undege·nerated,** *ppl. a.* (UN-¹ 8.) 1794 MRS. PIOZZI *Synon.* I. 354, I believe large oxen..do no more work..than beasts of the common undegenerated size. 1897 *Trans. Amer. Pediatric Soc.* IX. 168 A constant and potent factor in..maintaining the type undegenerated.

**Undege·nerating,** *ppl. a.* (UN-¹ 10.) 1606 in Nichols *Progr. Jas. I* (1828) II. 51 We of hereditary and fee-simple blood, and undegenerating valour. 1693 EVELYN tr. *De la Quint. Compl. Gardener, Melons* 1 The most Undegenerating sort of Melons are..of a middling Size. 1753 WEST *Odes Pindar, Nemean Odes* xi, Him, whose undegenerating Breast Swells with a Tide of Spartan Blood.

†**Undegra·de,** obs. Sc. var. of next. *c* 1560 A. SCOTT *Poems* (S.T.S.) xiv. 13 In lykwayis dois hir bewty vndegraid Transcend all vþiris, wyfe, wedow, or maid.

**Undegra·ded,** *ppl. a.* (UN-¹ 8.) [1775 ASH.] 1821 V. KNOX *Rem. Grammar Schools* 24 The intention of a founder in preserving grammar studies undegraded ought to be held sacred. 1825 SCOTT *Talism.* xv, It is King Richard's pleasure that you die undegraded. 1853 RUSKIN *Stones Ven.* II. vi. 179 It can shrink into a turret,..or spring into a spire, with undegraded grace.

**Unde·ified,** *ppl. a.* [f. next.] Reduced from the position of a deity. 1643–5 MILTON *Divorce* I. vi, That originall and firie vertue giv'n him by Fate, all on a sudden goes out and leaves him undeifi'd and despoil'd of all his force. 1858 FROUDE *Hist. Eng.* III. xv. 287 The undeified images passed by a swift transition to the flames.

**Unde·ify,** *v.* [UN-² 6 c.] *trans.* To deprive of the status, character, or qualities of a deity. 1637 R. ASHLEY tr. *Malvezzi's David Persecuted* 119 All sinners in regard of themselves doe undeifie him. 1664 H. MORE *Myst. Iniq.* vi. 121 It is plainly to un-deify him, if I may so speak, and to declare him to be no God at all. 1711 ADDISON *Spect.* No. 73 ¶ 11 An Idol may be Undeified by many accidental Causes. 1789 J. WHITE *Earl Strongbow* I. 93 Modern Nobles who employ their pens in writing down religion, and undeifying their Redeemer. 1845 R. WARDLAW in *Ess. Chr. Union* vi. 307 The acknowledgement of Him undeified all else besides. 1871 MACDUFF *Patmos* 161 Let us not dethrone and undeify the great Maker and Sustainer. *refl.* 1675 J. SMITH *Chr. Relig. App.* I. 15 They must undeifie themselves, and become no Gods of other Cities, before they are allowed to be Gods in that. 1700 ASGILL *Argument* 36 God cannot lie without undeifying himself. 1709 *Brit. Apollo* II. No. 44. 2/1 To act contrary to his own.. Eternal Essence, and Consequently to Un-Deify himself. *absol.* 1718 WODROW *Corr.* (1843) II. 353 This would infer a superior excellency in the First, and undeify.

Hence **Unde·ifying** *vbl. sb.* and *ppl. a.* 1637 R. ASHLEY tr. *Malvezzi's David Persecuted* 4 It is an undeifying of God. *a* 1680 CHARNOCK *Attrib. God* (1834) I. 201 When we come before him with undeifying thoughts of him. 1864 PUSEY *Lect. Daniel* 271 *note*, The whole boasted theory then..was at stake, and, with it, the whole undeifying of prophecy.

**Undei·stical,** *a.* (UN-¹ 7.) 1755 YOUNG *Centaur* 218, I, therefore, drop this dispute, not only as Unchristian, but Undeistical too.

**Undeje·cted,** *ppl. a.* (UN-¹ 8.) 1613 WITHER *Abuses Stript* Ep. Ded. A v, In despight of outward Destinies haue a care to keepe an vndeiected heart still free for Vertue. 1645 QUARLES *Sol. Recant.* vii. 19 Wisdome affords more strength, more fortifies The undejected courage of the wise. 1729 CONGREVE *Epist. to Ld. Cobham* 6 Not so robust in Body, as in Mind, And always undejected, tho' declin'd. 1782 V. KNOX *Ess.* iv. I. 19 We shall indeed often fall; but let us rise again undejected. 1862 LYTTON *Str. Story* ii, My children would have entered on manhood..undejected by the charity of strangers.

**Undela·ted,** *ppl. a.* (UN-¹ 8.) 1597 in *Maitland Cl. Misc.* (1840) I. 129 That na eldar..suffir ane singill woman..to dwell hir allane in ane hous undelaited to the sessioune of the kirk. **Undelay·able,** *a.* (UN-¹ 7 b.) 1628 FELTHAM *Resolves* II. xxii. 72 With what vndelayable heate, does the lime-twig'd Louer court a deseruing Beautie? 1887 LOWELL *Democr.*, etc. 6 The undelayable year has rolled round.

**Undelay·ed,** *ppl. a.*¹ [UN-¹ 8 + DELAY *v.*¹] Not delayed or deferred; unretarded; immediate. 1439 in *Fenland N. & Q.* July (1905) 221 Hasty and undelaied provision of gret and notable puissance. 1472 *Paston Lett.* III. 64 The Kynge hathe specially doon for me in thy case,..that iff thys fayle..I shalle have ondelayed justyce. 1540 *Act 32 Hen. VIII*, c. 48 More redy & vndelaied paimentes herafter shalbe had and made to all officers. 1591 in Picton *L'pool Munic. Rec.* (1883) I. 82 The first buier of the same shall..geve undelaied notice..hereof to Mr. Maior. 1611 SPEED *Hist. Gt. Brit.* IX. xxiv. § 190 The demand of the Queene was, to haue..a present and vndelayed truce. 1667 in *10th Rep. Hist. MSS. Comm.* App. V. 40 It may please your Grace to require the said Christopher..to make your petitioner undelayed satisfaction. *a* 1711 KEN *Serm.* Wks. (1838) 204, I earnestly exhort you to a serious and undelayed repentance. 1818 SCOTT *Rob Roy* x, He wished to get back to his own country, undelayed and unembarrassed by any..judicial inquiries.

**b.** quasi-*adv.* Without delay. 1470 HARDING *Chron.* CXIX. iv, Vpon the holy euangelis sworne vndelayed, The kyng graunted hym his grace. 1653 MILTON *Ps.* vii. 59 His ill trade Of violence will undelay'd Fall on his crown with ruine steep.

Hence **Undelay·edly** *adv.* 1534 HEN. VIII in Froude *Hist. Eng.* (1858) II. 231 We.. command you that you do make, undelayedly, and with all speed and diligence,..advertisement to us. 1603 FLORIO *Montaigne* II. v. 213 All the assemblie, and even his accuser himselfe did vndelayedly follow him towards the temple.

† **Undelay·ed,** *ppl. a.*² *Obs.* [UN-¹ 8 + DELAY *v.*²] Undiluted; not weakened by dilution. 1600 SURFLET *Countrie Farme* VI. xxii. 780 The learned.. haue alwaies reiected and disallowed pure and vndelaied wine. 1601 HOLLAND *Pliny* II. 174 The same being vsed with pure vndelaied wine, is singular for the prick of scorpions.

**Undelay·ing,** *ppl. a.* (UN-¹ 10.) 1791 COWPER *Iliad* XXIII. 163 Undelaying each Complied, and in bright arms stood soon array'd. 1820 SHELLEY *Prometh. Unb.* III. iii. 157 Trampling the..glassy lakes With feet unwet, unwearied, undelaying. 1882 MYERS *Renewal of Youth* 76 Yon unhurrying undelaying star.

**Undele·ctable,** *a.* (UN-¹ 7 b and 5 b.) 1610 HEALEY *St. Aug. Citie of God* IX. xv. 352 The diuels immortality is miserable: But Christs mortality hath nothing vndelectable. 1760 STERNE *Tr. Shandy* IV. xxvii, The genial warmth..was not undelectable for the first twenty or five-and-twenty seconds.

**Unde·legated,** *ppl. a.* (UN-¹ 8.) 1790 BURKE *Fr. Rev.* Wks. V. 398 It is one instance, among many indeed, of your assumption of undelegated power. 1815 *Monthly Rev.* LXXVII. 468 [He] would never have usurped an undelegated authority.

**Undeli·berate,** *a.* (UN-¹ 7 and 5 b.) 15.. [see UNDELIVERED *ppl. a.*²]. 1593 NASHE *Christ's T.* 91 b, Let not worldlings iudge thee inconstant, or vndeliberate in thy choyse. 1753 RICHARDSON *Grandison* (1781) V. xxxviii. 237 It was not a request made on undeliberate motives. 1874 LOWELL *Agassiz* III. i, With no pedant blindness to the worth Of undeliberate mirth. 1876 RUSKIN *Fors Clav.* lxviii. 271 The difference between deliberate and undeliberate heartlessness..is for God to judge.

Hence **Undeli·berateness.** 1817 COLERIDGE *Biog. Lit.* (1907) II. 41 With due allowances for the undeliberateness, and less connected train, of thinking natural and proper to conversation.

**Undeli·berated,** *ppl. a.* (UN-¹ 8 and 5 b.) *a* 1674 CLARENDON *Hist. Reb.* VIII. § 87 The strange manner of the Prince's coming, and undeliberated throwing himself and all the King's hopes into that suddain and unnecessary Engagement. 1874 PUSEY *Lent. Serm.* 352 Our undeliberated close-cleaving weaknesses.

**Undeli·berating,** *ppl. a.* (UN-¹ 10.) *a* 1763 SHENSTONE *Economy* II. 78 It much avails to seize the present hour, And, undeliberating, call around Thy hungry creditors. 1768 STERNE *Sent. Journ.* (1782) II. 10 She did it of herself with..undeliberating simplicity.

† **Unde·lible,** *a.* [UN-¹ 7.] = INDELIBLE *a.* 1534 MORE *Treat. Passion* Wks. 1316/2 The caracter and spirituall token, by baptisme imprinted in the soule, is vndelible and neuer canne be putte out. 1587 [see UNDEFACEABLE *a.*]. 1679 JENISON *Popish Plot* 13 Which I knew would undergo an undeleble blot. 1747 CARTE *Hist. Eng.* I. 213 That army composed of their followers, was branded with an undelible mark of reproach.

**Undeli·cious,** *a.* [UN-¹ 7.] †**a.** Not dainty or delicate. *Obs.* **b.** Not pleasant or agreeable. *a* 1618 SYLVESTER tr. *Mathieu's Mem. Mortalitie* II. xcvii, Little sufficeth Life in th' un-delicious. 1829 I. TAYLOR *Enthus.* ix. 246 The spiritual Monk..there passed his hours, not uncheered, not undelicious, in prayer and meditation.

**Undeli·ght.** [UN-¹ 12.] Lack of delight. 1821 SHELLEY *Ginevra* 20 The weary glare..Vexing the sense with gorgeous undelight. 1835 TRENCH *Poems* 176 If at seasons this world's undelight oppressed him.

**Undeli·ghted,** *ppl. a.* (UN-¹ 8.) 1667 MILTON *P. L.* IV. 286 From this Assyrian Garden, where the Fiend Saw undelighted all delight. 1713 *Guardian* No. 68 ¶ 2 If she has no Relish for rural Views, but is undelighted with Streams, Fields and Groves. *a* 1763 SHENSTONE *Ess.* Wks. 1765 II. 228, I love painting and statuary so well, as to be not undelighted with moderate performances. 1805 WORDSW. *Prelude* III. 217 Could I behold.., with undelighted heart, So many happy youths? 1852 M. ARNOLD *Empedocles* II. 296 Uncaring and undelighted.

**Undeli·ghtful,** *a.* (UN-¹ 7.) Frequently used with preceding negative. 1585 BULLOKAR *Æsops Fablz* 155 Go-away henc' with a mischef, with that thy vn-deliht-ful howsband. 1599 DANIEL *Let. Octavia* xli, Wretched Mankind, wherfore hath nature made The lawfull vndelightfull? 1616 BRETON *Good & Bad* Wks. (Grosart) II. 5/2 Hee is..an vndelightfull friend, and a tormentor of himselfe. 1662 J. DAVIES tr. *Olearius' Voy. Ambass.* 274 The Dancing of the Women..was not undelightfull. 1682 SIR T. BROWNE *Chr. Mor.* III. § 22 In such an Age Delights will be undelightful and Pleasures grow stale unto him. 1742 RICHARDSON *Pamela* IV. 221, I am now..quitting this undelightful Town, as it has been, and is, to me. 1775 S. J. PRATT *Liberal Opin.* xcviii. (1783) III. 215, I never felt such feverish, yet not undelightful attacks before. *c* 1819 SHELLEY *Ess. & Lett.* (1887) 305 Tacitus, or Livius,.. are..undelightful and uninstructive in translation. 1876 MRS. OLIPHANT *Curate in Charge* viii, The odour of this very undelightful feature in the scene.

Hence **Undeli·ghtfully** *adv.*; **-fulness.** 1653 *Cloria & Narcissus* I. (1665) 79 They soon retired, with the undelightfulness of the prospect, into their own Lodgings. 1783 JOHNSON *Let. to Mrs. Thrale* 13 Aug., Ovid says that the sun is undelightfully uniform. 1893 SWINBURNE *Stud. Prose & Poetry* (1894) 32 In this..his real..kinship to his beloved Dr. Johnson..was not undelightfully manifest.

**Undeli·ghting,** *ppl. a.* [UN-¹ 10.] **1.** Taking no delight or pleasure (*in* something). 1570 FOXE *A. & M.* (ed. 2) 37/1 The vndelityng wil of man to God and hys word. 1798 *Monthly Mag.* VI. 556 Undelighting in so artificial a deception, he would have fallen off in the courage to persevere.

**2.** Affording no delight or pleasure. 1768–74 TUCKER *Lt. Nat.* (1834) II. 546 What keeps them in slavery under an undelighting habit, but because it would cost them pains to break it?

**Undeli·ghtsome,** *a.* (UN-¹ 7.) *c* 1586 C'TESS PEMBROKE *Ps.* CXXXIX. iv, O whither might I take my way?..To dead mens undelightsome stay? There is thy walk. **Undeli·neable,** *a.* (UN-¹ 7 b.) 1767 MRS. S. PENNINGTON *Lett.* I. 122 The utter impossibility of expressing what they feel to be equally true and undelineable.

**Undeli·verable,** *a.* (UN-¹ 7 b.) In recent use esp. of postal matter, as in quot. 1862. 1843 CARLYLE *Past & Pr.* II. xvii, Fix thyself in Dandyhood, undeliverable: it is thy doom. 1862 TROLLOPE *N. Amer.* II. 388 The task of returning to their writers undelivered and undeliverable letters.

† **Undeli·verance.** [UN-¹ 12.] Non-delivery. *a* 1578 LINDESAY (Pitscottie) *Chron. Scot.* (S.T.S.) II. 313 The erle of argyle vas put to the horne for ondelyuerance of certaine jowallis.

**Undeli·vered,** *ppl. a.*¹ [UN-¹ 8 + DELIVER *v.*¹] **1.** Not handed over or transferred to another's possession; not delivered or distributed. 1472–3 *Rolls of Parlt.* VI. 5/2 [The money] there to be kept, undelyvered by eny mean unto You, Soverayn Lord. 1561–2 *Reg. Privy Council Scot.* I. 203 To keip the samyn in his handis and keping undeliverit to George Dowglas. *a* 1600 HOOKER *Eccl. Pol.* VII. xxiv. § 17 To withdraw any mite of that..bequeathed, though as yet undelivered into the sacred treasure of God. 1640–1 *Kirkcudbr. War-Comm. Min. Bk.* (1855) 79 We resolve to keip the commissione undelyverit till we heir from you. 1767 in *Nairne Peerage Evidence* (1874) 169 These presents shall be habit and repute a valid & delivered evident albeit found..undelivered the time of my death. 1775 SHERIDAN *Duenna* I. iii, I must slip out to seal it up, as undelivered. 1842 TYTLER *Hist. Scot.* (1864) IV. 29 If he found the fortress..undelivered, he was to remonstrate loudly against its being surrendered. 1887 *Daily News* 6 Oct. 2/8 Discovery of undelivered letters.

**2.** Not set free or released. Also const. *from.* *a* 1513 FABYAN *Chron.* VII. 382 The prynce..remayned longe after vndelyuered wᵗ many other prysoners. 1653 MILTON *Hirelings* Wks. 1851 V. 339 To deliver us the only People of all Protestants left still undeliver'd from the Oppressions of a simonious decimating Clergy. 1721 STRYPE *Eccl. Mem.* III. xliii. 355 He..did as much as possible he might to see them undelivered. 1837 WORDSW. *White Doe* Introd., The soul..from mortal bonds Yet undelivered.

† **3.** Not dispatched or disposed of. *Obs.*—¹ 1535 STEWART *Cron. Scot.* (Rolls) II. 240 The Saxone herald thair remaning maid, ȝit vndeliuerit on his ansuer baid.

**4.** Of a child: Not brought forth or born. 1595 DANIEL *Civ. Wars* II. xcvii, This mighty burthen wherewithall they goe Dies vndeliuered, perishes vnborne.

**5.** Of a woman: Not disburdened of offspring. 1799 *Med. Jrnl.* II. 434 It is not improbable that..the poor woman..survived as long as she would have done, if she had been permitted to perish undelivered. 1871 A. MEADOWS *Man. Midwifery* (ed. 2) 242 Rather than see the mother die undelivered, I used the perforator and extracted.

**6.** Not made or attempted. 1895 *Review of Rev.* Aug. 148 An attack, which now, alas, must remain for ever undelivered.

† **Undeli·vered,** *ppl. a.*² *Obs.*—¹ [UN-¹ 8 + DELIVER *v.*²] Unconsidered; unwise. *c* 1425 WYNTOUN *Cron.* V. xi. 3172 Off þare counsall and assent, And vndeliuerit [15.. *Lansdowne MS.* vndeliberait] avisment, Thare estait þai renunsit haill.

**Undeli·very.** [UN-¹ 12.] Non-delivery. 1679 in W. M. Morison *Dict. Decis.* (1807) 16178 The defences, for Lothian, which resolved into two, the incompleteness, and undelivery [etc.].

**Undelu·dable,** *a.* (UN-¹ 7 b.) 1839 J. STERLING *Ess.*, etc. (1848) I. 365 Those who hold themselves undeludable.

**Undelu·de,** *v.* [UN-² 3.] *trans.* To free from delusion or deception; to undeceive. 1654 EARL ORRERY *Parthen.* (1676) 77 All things had contributed to undelude you. *a* 1711 KEN *Hymnotheo* Poet.

Wks. 1721 III. 325 She..Would not consult her Adam first, lest she Should by his Counsel undeluded be.

**Undelu·ded,** *ppl. a.* (UN-[1] 8.)

**1746** YOUNG *Nt. Th.* IX. 1022 There..she [the soul] can rove at large;..And, undeluded, grasp at something great. **1756** *Demi-Rep* 22 Ye undeluded shun the flow'ry shore, Nor split, where thousands have been wreck'd before! **1816** BYRON *A Sketch* 20 That high Soul..panted for the truth it could not hear, With longing breast and undeluded ear.

**Unde·luged,** *ppl. a.* (UN-[1] 8.) **1791** COWPER *Odyssey* XXIV. 621 Peace, O ye men of Ithaca! while yet The field remains undeluged with your blood. **1819** CAMPBELL *Rainbow* 21 When o'er the green, undeluged earth, Heaven's covenant thou didst shine. **Undelu·sive,** *a.* (UN-[1] 7.) **1817** BENTHAM *Parl. Reform* Introd. 104 Sound, dispassionate, and undelusive information. **1829** WORDSW. *Humanity* 14 Inviting..ears and eyes To watch for undelusive auguries.

**Unde·lve,** *v.* [UN-[2] 9.] *trans.* To dig up.

**1340** *Ayenb.* 61 Þet is þe felliste best þet me clepeþ hyane, þet ondelfþ þe bodies of dyade men and hise eteþ.

**Unde·lved,** *ppl. a.* (UN-[1] 8.)

**1602** *Kyd's Sp. Trag.* III. xii. A 84 All the undelued mynes cannot buy An ounce of iustice. **1623** LISLE *Ælfric on O. & N. Test.* Ded. xviii, This three-cornered Ile,..Unfens'd, undelv'd, ungardined, unset. **1794** SOUTHEY *Botany Bay Ecl.* i, Welcome, ye wild plains Unbroken by the plough, undelved by hand Of patient rustic.

**Undema·gnetizable,** *a.* (UN-[1] 7 b.) **1876** *S. Kensington Mus. Catal.* No. 1703, Pair of Undemagnetisable Coils, designed in 1866. **1882** *Crystal Palace Internat. Electric Exhib. Catal.* 17 Brittan's Undemagnetizable Needle.

**Undema·nded,** *ppl. a.* (UN-[1] 8.)

**1513** DOUGLAS *Æneid* VI. viii. 46 Vndemandit, with freyndly wordis and soundis Enee hym grat, sayand [etc.]. *a* **1652** BROME *Mad Couple* III. i, Will you never..receive that onely fit for you to understand, which I deliver to you undemanded? **1748** THOMSON *Cast. Indol.* I. xxxiv, Some hand unseen these silently display'd, Even undemanded by a sign or sound. **1796** MME. D'ARBLAY *Camilla* V. 409 To present herself.. undemanded and unforgiven at Etherington, she thought impossible. **1860** FORSTER *Gr. Remonstr.* 28 With new conditions of restraint and constitutional safeguards before undemanded, assistance is rendered again.

**† Undeme·rited,** *ppl. a. Obs.* [UN-[1] 8.] Unmerited; undeserved.

**1629** PRYNNE *God no Impostor* 13 Pulling downe many vndemerited blessings, vpon Reprobates and Castawayes. **1644** — *Check to Britannicus* 4 His undemerited free Pardon.

**† Unde·mnified,** *ppl. a. Obs. rare.* [UN-[1] 8: cf. INDEMNIFY *v.*[2]] Uninjured, unhurt.

**1576** NEWTON *Lemnie's Complex.* 15 b, Hee therefore that woulde preserue his spirites vndemnifyed..must endeuour.. to keepe his body in right good plight. **1608** WILLET *Hexapla Exod.* 487 How much should he remaine vndemnified,.. which goeth to the bosome of his mother the Church?

**Undemocra·tic,** *a.* (UN-[1] 7.)

**1839** T. MITCHELL *Frogs of Aristoph.* Introd. p. cv, Æschylus, young, ardent, and at that time not undemocratic in his politics. **1856** OLMSTED *Slave States* 183 Through a similar undemocratic, uneconomical and unjust..exercise of power. **1895** *Thinker* VIII. 252 All assumptions of sacerdotal superiority and sanctity are undemocratic.

Hence **Undemocra·tically** *adv.*

**1865** E. BURRITT *Walk to Land's End* 363 How we glory in the humble origin, as it is most undemocratically called, of our great men!

**Undemo·lishable,** *a.* (UN-[1] 7 b.) **1837** CARLYLE *Fr. Rev.* II. v. xii, Will jingle and fanfaronade demolish the Veto; or will the Veto..remain undemolishable by these?

**Undemo·lished,** *ppl. a.* (UN-[1] 8.)

**1571–2** *Reg. Privy Council Scot.* Ser. I. II. 121 For sauftie of the houssis..being within the same unbrint and [un]dimolissit. **1610** J. HEALEY *St. Aug. Citie of God* 82 This Nasica would haue Carthage stand stil vndemolished. **1634** SIR T. HERBERT *Trav.* 117 A stately Palace, which remayned vndemolisht for many ages. **1708** J. PHILIPS *Cyder* I. 182 Then also, tho' to foreign Yoke submiss, She undemolish'd stood, and even 'till now Perhaps had stood. **1837** CARLYLE *Fr. Rev.* II. III. v, Vincennes stands undemolished, reparable.

**Undemonstrable,** *a.* (UN-[1] 7 b and 5 b.)

**1594** HOOKER *Eccl. Pol.* III. ix. § 2 Out of the precepts of the lawe of nature as out of certaine common & vndemonstrable principles. **1865** *Reader* 14 Oct. 420/2 The theological or undemonstrable part of the question.

**Undemonstrated,** *ppl. a.* (UN-[1] 8.)

**1648** HEXHAM II, *Onbetoont*, Vnshowne, or Vndemonstrated. **1657** HOBBES *Absurd Geom.* Wks. 1845 VII. 378 Your first forty-one propositions are undemonstrated. **1794** *Monthly Rev.* XIV. 285 We seek in vain for the facts that should disprove..this undemonstrated but very possible circumstance. **1833** HAMPDEN *Bampt. Lect.* 433 He professes also not to rest the proof of his point on mere undemonstrated faith, but on exact argument. **1870** J. H. NEWMAN *Gram. Assent* II. viii. 334 We are bound to give heed to the undemonstrated sayings and opinions of the experienced and aged.

**Undemo·nstrative,** *a.* [UN-[1] 7.]

**1.** Not given to, or characterized by, outward expression (of the feelings, etc.).

**1846** *Edin. Rev.* Jan. 48 That type of an undemonstrative Englishwoman, Cordelia. **1847** C. BRONTË *Jane Eyre* xxix, 'You *shall*,' repeated Mary, in the tone of undemonstrative sincerity which seemed natural to her. **1880** MRS. ROLLINS *New Eng. Bygones* (1883) 87 Repulsive spectacles..on the surface of its pure, calm, undemonstrative life.

**2.** *Gram.* (Cf. DEMONSTRATIVE *a.* 3.)

**1871** EARLE *Philol. Eng. Tongue* 457 Two or three very undemonstrative conjunctions, such as *if, but, for, that,* &c.

Hence **Undemo·nstratively** *adv.*; **-iveness.**

**1858** MISS MULOCK *Th. ab. Wom.* 167 Its total absence of sentimentality, its undemonstrativeness, depth, and power. **1864** W. HANNA *Earlier Years our Lord's Life* vi. 133 Living so naturally, unostentatiously, undemonstratively.

**Undemu·re,** *a.* (UN-[1] 7.) **1538** BALE *Thre Lawes* II. A viij b, The beastes oft vndemure, Whych were left to mannys cure, Wyll hym sumtyme deuoure. **Unde·n,** *v.* (UN-[2] 5.) **1598** FLORIO, *Scopare*,..to rouze, to vndenne, to vnkenell. **1613** HEYWOOD *Braz. Age* II. ii, Some plant the toiles, others brauely mount To unden this sauadge.

**Undeni·able,** *a.* [UN-[1] 7 b and 5 b.]

**1.** That cannot be denied or refuted; incontrovertible, indisputable.

**1547** COVERDALE *Old Faith* E viij b, Now is it certayne and vndenyable, that he which speaketh, & he to whom ought is spoken, are not one, but two personnes. **1594** HOOKER *Eccl. Pol.* II. vii. § 9 If there be either vndeniable appearance that so it doth [avouch], or reason such as cannot deceiue. **1631** GOUGE *God's Arrows* I. Ded. p. vii, This ancient, undeniable aphorisme. **1651** BAXTER *Inf. Bapt.* 229, I will name some undeniable Arguments. **1727** DE FOE *Hist. Appar.* ii. (1840) 19 These apparitions of angels..are undeniable on other occasions. **1794** R. J. SULIVAN *View Nat.* I. 455 The fact is undeniable. **1809–10** COLERIDGE *Friend* (1865) 118 The system commences with an undeniable truth, and an important deduction therefrom equally undeniable. **1880** SWINBURNE *Stud. Shaks.* 301 What he did say was undeniable by any but those who trusted only to their ear.

b. Of witnesses: Irrefragable.

**1619** MRQ. BUCKHM. in *Fortescue Papers* (Camden) 78 You were accused of nothing that was not proved by oath of divers witnesses alltogither undeniable. **1663** BP. PATRICK *Parab. Pilgr.* xxviii, Together with the testimony of many undeniable Witnesses. **1855** MILMAN *Lat. Chr.* IX. v. IV. 111 *note*, The historians, all ecclesiastics, are undeniable witnesses. **1883** *Contemp. Rev.* June 774 Karema is there as an undeniable witness of the success of these efforts.

**2.** Incapable of being refused; admitting or accepting no denial.

**1549** OLDE *Erasm. Par. Peter* Dedication, I toke it in hande for none other ende, but only to doe at my hartie frendes vndenyable request. **1649** JER. TAYLOR *Gt. Exemp.* II. xii. 42 The multitude found him out, imprisoning him in their circuits and undeniable attendances. *Ibid.* III. xiv. 42 The seeming denial made her importunity more bold and undenyable. **1839** LADY LYTTON *Cheveley* (ed. 2) III. vi. 150 Thoughts, those..undeniable visitors, *will* intrude.

**3.** Not open to objection; unexceptional, excellent.

**1793** SMEATON *Edystone L.* Contents p. ix, Moorstone being undeniable. **1799** H. MITCHELL *Scotticisms* 87 His public character is undeniable. **1808** *Times* 2 Mar. 4/1 Nursery Maid..; can have an undeniable character from the Lady she last served. **1861** WHYTE-MELVILLE *Market Harb.* viii, Her foot and ankle were undeniable, and her hands white and well-shaped. **1884** *Graphic* 9 Aug. 134/1 Italian fruits ..are open to much criticism, but the grapes and green figs are undeniable.

*absol.* **1861** WHYTE MELVILLE *Market Harb.* xx, A dry biscuit and a magnum of the undeniable make their appearance.

Hence **Undeni·ableness.**

**1654** WHITLOCK *Zootomia* 254 What Author so ever denyeth the undeniablenesse of any of our received Tenets. **1677** GILPIN *Demonol.* (1867) 463 The plainness and undeniableness of this inference. **1889** *19th Cent.* Sept. 404 The undeniableness of the facts he adduces.

**Undeni·ably,** *adv.* [f. prec.]

**1.** In an undeniable manner; so that denial (of the fact) is impossible; incontrovertibly.

**1646** SIR T. BROWNE *Pseud. Ep.* VI. viii. 314 It is undeniably rejected by the Modernes, and must be warily received by any. **1679** BEDLOE *Popish Plot* Ep. A 2 b, By this Letter ..the Witnesses evidence..is undeniably confirmed. **1758** MRS. DELANY *Life & Corr.* (1861) III. 483 My present situation is undeniably an anxious one. **1825** MCCULLOCH *Pol. Econ.* II. ii. 135 It is undeniably certain we shall have to export ten or twenty millions worth..to pay them. **1848** DICKENS *Dombey* i, The son was an undeniably fine infant. **1881** JOWETT *Thucyd.* I. 47 The event proved undeniably that the fate of Hellas depended on her navy.

**2.** Without heeding any denial, refusal, or protest.

**1705** tr. *Bosman's Guinea* 74 Some Negroes are so unreasonable that they will undeniably take back all their pure Gold.

**Undeni·ed,** *ppl. a.* Also 7 -denayed. (UN-[1] 8.)

**1621** QUARLES *Div. Poems, Esther* ii, Perhaps (Asuerus) Vashti might haue stayed Vnsent for, and thy selfe been vndenayed. **1660** *Trial Regic.* 11, I think it is an undenied consequence, He must needs be Superiour over them. **1760** LAW *Spir. Prayer* I. 63 If self is undenied, if thou livest to thine own will,..thou art dead whilst thou livest. **1887** *Pall Mall G.* 1 July 1/1 This is undenied and undeniable.

Hence **Undeni·edly** *adv.*

**1837** G. S. FABER *Prim. Doctr. Justif.* 226 For there, undeniedly and undeniably in the case of the regenerated and converted, the Apostle says: The Flesh [etc.].

**Unde·nizened,** *ppl. a.* (UN-[1] 8.) **1635** HEYWOOD *Hierarchie* IV. 208 Words at which th' Ignorant laugh, but the Learn'd smile, Because Adulterate and Vndenizen'd. **Unde·nizing,** *vbl. sb.* (UN-[2] 3, 8.) **1716** M. DAVIES *Athen. Brit.* II. To Rdr. p. v, To give the Athenian Law..a new Vigour and Sanction, under the Forfeiture and Penalty of Undenizing and Expulsion.

**Undeno·mina·tional,** *a.* [UN-[1] 7.] Not belonging to any particular religious denomination.

Freq. in recent use in connexion with religious education in elementary schools.

**1871** *Athenæum* 15 Apr. 465 It has ruled that the new Board schools are to be strictly undenominational. **1885** *Manch. Exam.* 20 Mar. 8/5 The..advantage of an undenominational system of education.

Hence **Undenomina·tionalism, -alist, -alize** *v.*, **-ally** *adv.*

**1883** *Christian* 1 Nov. 12/2 His strong protest against *undenominationalism..does not appear to us well-timed. **1884** *Pall Mall G.* 14 Aug. 4/2 The most animated debate of the whole Conference was that between Churchmen and *undenominationalists. **1895** *Forum* (N.Y.) June 435 Our own scattered colleges, now '*undenominationalized', if not secularized, can be gathered into groups and unified. **1906** *Westm. Gaz.* 8 Feb. 2 How this is to be done *undenominationally I do not know.

**Undeno·ted,** *ppl. a.* (UN-[1] 8.) **1859** CORNWALLIS *New World* I. 52 Many a lifeless tenant of an undenoted grave. **1882** STEVENSON *Mem. & Portraits* iii. (1887) 41 Among the thousand undenoted countenances of the city street. **Undenou·nced,** *ppl. a.* (UN-[1] 8.) [**1775** ASH.] **1837** CARLYLE *Fr. Rev.* III. II. vi, Let him withdraw again; not undenounced. **1896** LD. ROSEBERY in *Daily News* 10 Oct. 2/5 There is a much more drastic instrument in existence undenounced, unrepealed. **Undenu·ded,** *ppl. a.* (UN-[1] 8.) **1872** W. S. SYMONDS *Rec. Rocks* xi. 406 An outlier of undenuded rocks.

**† Undepa·rtable,** *a. Obs.* [UN-[1] 7 b and 5 b.] Inseparable; indivisible.

*c* **1374** CHAUCER *Boeth.* IV. pr. iii. (1868) 120 No wise man ne may doute of þe vndepartable peyne of shrewes. **1382** WYCLIF *Luke* 1st Prol., Bi the entringe of the generacioun of vndepartable God. *c* **1450** tr. *De Imitatione* III. xxvii. 97 Ioyne me to þe wiþ an undepartable bonde of loue. **1483** *Cath. Angl.* 96 Vn Departiabylle, *indiuisibilis, indiuiduus.*

Hence **Undepa·rtableness; Undepa·rtably** *adv.*

*c* **1449** PECOCK *Repr.* I. iii. 15 Tweyne pointis of matrimonie, which ben vndepartabilnes and fleischli vce of bodies into childe bigeting. *c* **1456** — *Bk. of Faith* (1909) 245 Oon man to have bi the lawe oon wyf undepartabili. *a* **1470** H. PARKER *Dives & Pauper* (W. de W. 1496) VI. viii. 244/2 There wolde no man knytte hym undepartably to ony woman.

**Undepa·rted,** *ppl. a.* [UN-[1] 8 and 5 b.] † Not parted or separated; undivided.

**1430–40** LYDG. *Bochas* I. viii. (1544) 13 b, And, undeparted, [I] yeue to you mine herte. **1453** *Rolls of Parlt.* V. 231/2 Kept hole, undepartid, undevided and unsevered. *a* **1470** HARDING *Chron.* CCVI. iv, Twenty strokes with euery wepen smyten, Vndeparted without any mote. **1610** HEALEY *St. Aug. Citie of God* 475 Thus is hee..not yet in death, because the soule is vndeparted.

**Undepa·rting,** *vbl. sb.* [UN-[1] 13.] † Absence of separation. *c* **1400** tr. *Secreta Secret., Gov. Lordsh.* 90 In þe whilk we sall determyn of singuleryte, and vndepartyng of some planetis vegetablez.

**Undepa·rting,** *ppl. a.* (UN-[1] 10.)

**1581** *Reg. Privy Council Scot.* III. 436 He hes..kepit the said burgh, undeparting as yit thairfra. **1587** *Ibid.* IV. 195 The Senatouris to remane undepairting oute of the burgh. **1842** WORDSW. *Poems of Fancy* XXIX. 23 Each stood companionless and eyed This undeparting Flower in crimson dyed.

**Undepe·ndable,** *a.* [UN-[1] 7 b.] Not to be depended upon; unreliable, untrustworthy.

**1860** *Sat. Rev.* 10 Mar. 303/2 The praises of the official world are, from obvious reasons, quite undependable. **1865** W. G. PALGRAVE *Arabia* I. 193 The fickle and undependable Bedouins. **1894** 'J. S. WINTER' *Red-Coat* 63 Just a fickle, changeable thing,..an undependable nothing.

**Undepe·nding,** *ppl. a.* [UN-[1] 10 and 5 b.]

**1.** Not depending *from* or *on* something.

**1649** MILTON *Eikon.* x. Wks. 1851 III. 414 If the power of the Sword were any where separate and undepending from the power of Law. **1659** — *Hirelings* Ibid. V. 387 While they are thus upheld undepending on the Church, on which alone they anciently depended.

**2.** Not dependent; independent.

**1649** MILTON *Observ. Peace Ormond* Wks. 1851 IV. 569 [To] claim an absolute and undepending Jurisdiction. **1712** [P. METCALFE] *Life St. Winefride* 19 That with an undepending Freedom, they might be more absolute Masters of short time. **1724** SWIFT *Drapier's Lett.* Wks. 1755 V. II. 60 But the landed undepending men..will never receive it.

**† Undephle·gmated,** *ppl. a. Obs.* (UN-[1] 8.)

**1664** BOYLE *Exp. Colours* III. xl. 309 Common and undephlegmated Aqua-fortis. **1758** *Elaboratory laid Open* 161 The undephlegmated spirit may be used.

So **† Undephle·gmed** *ppl. a. Obs.*

**1673** *Phil. Trans.* VIII. 6002 Not when 'tis undephlegmed, but when highly rectified.

**Undeplo·red,** *ppl. a.* (UN-[1] 8.)

Chiefly in renderings of Greek and Latin originals.

*c* **1611** CHAPMAN *Iliad* XXII. 330 Dead, vndeplor'd, Vnsepulcherd, he lies at fleete, vnthought on. **1621** G. SANDYS *Ovid's Met.* XI. (1626) 232 Arise, weepe, put on black: nor vndeplor'd For pitie send me to the Stygian Ford. **1654** OWEN *Doctr. Saints' Persev.* 17 With these Garlands..doth he surround the Head of the Sacrifice,..that so it may fall an undeplored Victim. **1791** COWPER *Odyss.* XI. 60 But we had left his corse In Circe's palace, tombless, undeplored. **1818** BYRON *Ch. Har.* IV. xliii, Then might'st thou,..less desired, Be homely and be peaceful, undeplored For thy destructive charms. **1855** SINGLETON *Virgil* II. 442 We, despicable souls, A rout unsepulchred and undeplored.

**Undepo·sable,** *a.* (UN-[1] 7 b and 5 b.) **1669** E. CHAMBERLAYNE *Pres. St. Eng.* 83 England is an Hereditary Paternal Monarchy, governed by one Supreme, Independent, and Undeposable Head. **1855** [see next]. **Undepo·sed,** *ppl. a.* (UN-[1] 8.) **1624** BEDELL *Lett.* i. 43 They are Martyrs that are executed for plotting to blow him vp with Gun-powder, though vndeposed. **1855** MILMAN *Lat. Chr.* VII. iii. (1864) IV. 115 The actual, undeposed, undeposable King. **Undepo·sited,** *ppl. a.* (UN-[1] 8.) **1646** HAMMOND *Tracts* 37 The hypocrisy of him which keeps any one close undeposited sin upon his soul.

**Undepra·ved,** *ppl. a.* [UN-[1] 8.]

**1.** Not morally depraved or corrupted; not lowered in character or tone.

**1646–7** J. HALL *Poems* 95 There did he loose his snowy Innocence, His undepraved will. **1660** STANLEY *Hist. Philos.* XIII. (1687) 909/2 Thus doth every undepraved animal, its own nature judging incorruptly and entirely. **1697** COLLIER *Ess. Mor. Subj.* I. (1703) 152 If we hearken to the undepraved suggestions of our minds. **1782** V. KNOX *Ess.* (1819) II. lxxi. 67 Who possess all the faculties of perception, in a state undepraved by artificial refinement. **1784** COWPER *Task* I. 124 The palate, undeprav'd By culinary arts. **1826** *Q. Rev.* XXXIII. 283 Men whose sense of right and wrong is undepraved.

**2.** Not vitiated textually.

**1686** W. HOPKINS tr. *Ratramnus* Dissert. ii. (1688) 33 Whether it [a book] be come pure and undepraved to our hands, I shall enquire in the next chapter. **1693** J. EDWARDS *Author. O. & N. Test.* 53 These Masoretick Doctors..have kept it [*sc.* the Hebrew text] undepraved and uncorrupt.

Hence **Undepra·vedness.**

1723 MATHER *Vind. Bible* 337 The sense of the place pleads for the undepravedness of the Hebrew in this verse.

**Undepre·ciated,** *ppl. a.* (UN-[1] 8.)
1818 COLEBROOKE *Obligations* 30 Movables..of small account and such as could not be preserved undepreciated. 1845 MCCULLOCH *Taxation* II. xii. 369 Loans and engagements..[to] be made good in an undepreciated currency.

**Undepre·ssed, -pre·st,** *ppl. a.* [UN-[1] 8.]
**1.** Not depressed in spirit; not dejected.
1697 D. F. *Char. Dr. S. Annesley* 6 When Griefs come threatning on, or Comfort flows, He was undepress'd by these, unrais'd by those. 1782 D. E. BAKER *Biog. Dram.* I. 222 He maintained his wit and good humour undepressed by misfortunes. 1813 BYRON *Corsair* II. viii, 'Tis he indeed—disarm'd but undeprest. 1880 MCCARTHY *Own Times* III. 225 Undepressed by early poverty, unspoiled by later and almost unequalled success.
**2.** Not pressed down or bent; not hollowed or sunken.
1807 WORDSW. *White Doe* III. 146 A stature undepressed in size, Unbent, which rather seemed to rise. 1819 SCOTT *Ivanhoe* xxxv, His gait, undepressed by age and toil, was erect. 1879 *St. George's Hosp. Rep.* IX. 314 The depressed bone was much driven in, and the margins of the surrounding undepressed portions formed..irregular edges.

**Undepri·vable,** *a.* (UN-[1] 7 b, 5 b.) 1643 [see UNCONDEMNABLE *a.*]. 1860 READE *8th Commandm.* 15 He could not give me any undeprivable possession of his work.

**Undepri·ved,** *ppl. a.* (UN-[1] 8.)
1564 HAWARD *Eutropius* To Rdr. 7 Worthy to be..undepryved of theyr wel deserved prayse. 1655 FULLER *Ch. Hist.* VIII. i. § 20 Only two Protestant Bishops..found the favour to be last undone, as remaining un-deprived at the beginning of the Parliament. 1700 DRYDEN *Fables, Gd. Parson* 126 Much to himself he thought; but little spoke: And, Undepriv'd, his Benefice forsook. 1709 STRYPE *Ann. Ref.* I. xii. 154 Papers wherein..are shewn, who were dead, who deprived, and who were yet alive and undeprived.

**Under,** *sb. rare.* [f. UNDER *adv.* and UNDER- *prefix* [1].]
**1. a.** A state of lowness or inferiority. In phr. *to be at a great under.* Now *dial.*
1600 HOLLAND *Livy* XXII. lxi. 471 They were unwilling..that Anniball (who as the voyce went, was at a very great under for money) should be inriched thereby. 1869 *Lonsdale Gloss.* 89/2 *To be at a girt under,* to be in a state of thraldom, subdued.
**b.** *dial.* An undervalue.
1828 CARR *Craven Gloss.* s.v.
**2.** *pl.* Underclothes, underwear.
1731 FIELDING *Letter-writers* Wks. 1775 II. 158 He'll make us pope [= pawn] our unders for the reckoning: we'll not go with him. 1905 'E. NESBIT' *Amulet* vii, Let's..get into flannels. We can't go in our unders.

**Under,** obs. var. UNDERN *sb.*

**U·nder,** *a.* [f. UNDER- *prefix* [1], detached from compounds on the analogy of OVER *a.*
There is no clear distinction between the prefix and the adj. when immediately preceding a noun, beyond the writing of the latter as a separate word.]
**1.** Having a lower or underlying place or position; lying beneath or at a lower level: **a.** Of places, their contents or inhabitants.
*a* 1300 *Cursor M.* 541 Þe ouer fir gis man his sight, Þat ouer air of hering might; Þis vnder wynd him gis his aand. 1597 BEARD *Theatre God's Judgem.* (1612) 222 He first remoued his lodging..to a base vnder roome. *c* 1611 CHAPMAN *Iliad* XIX. 2 The Morne arose, and..Gaue light to all, As well to gods, as men of th' vnder globe. 1632 LITHGOW *Trav.* II. 49 The Sunne had imparted his brightnesse to our vnder neighbours. 1874 SWINBURNE *Bothwell* IV. i, For look where yonder..Comes up to usward from the under field One with a flag of message. 1897 *Daily News* 15 Oct. 5/2 He took to the water, disappeared, leaving it on the low under bank of the stream.
**b.** Of things (esp. one of a pair).
1648 [see SUB- 10]. 1669 STURMY *Mariner's Mag.* VII. iii. 7 The Wyre at the under end at D. 1704 *Dict. Rust.* (1726) s.v. *Cart,* The under pieces which keep the bottom of the Cart together. 1723 CHAMBERS tr. *Le Clerc's Treat. Archit.* I. 89 The upper Order must always be less Massive than the under. 1774 GOLDSM. *Nat. Hist.* II. v. 91 Those [adults] whose upper and under row of teeth are equally prominent. 1839 URE *Dict. Arts* 765 The upper stopcock is closed, and the under is opened to run off the liquor. 1859 TENNYSON *Geraint & Enid* 675 At this he turn'd all red.., Now gnaw'd his under, now his upper lip.
**2. a.** Lying under (so as to be covered).
1547 in Feuillerat *Revels Edw. VI* (1914) 12 Twoo vnder ffrockes without sleves. 1611 BIBLE 2 *Esdras* xii. 19 The eight small vnder feathers sticking to her wings. 1611 FLORIO, *Sottocoperta,* an vnder couerlet. 1746 *Exmoor Scolding* (E.D.S.) 30 That wan tha liv'st up to tha Cot, tha wart the Old Rager Hill's Under Bed-blonket. 1819 S. BUTLER in *Life & Lett.* (1896) I. 164 One under and one good upper blanket. 1872 [see UNDER-GARMENT].
**b.** Facing downwards.
1731 P. MILLER *Gard. Dict.* s.v. *Leaves,* The upper and under Surfaces of the two Leaves. 1738 [see UNDERSIDE β]. 1839 URE *Dict. Arts* 999 The under face of the licker-up is made rough like a rasp. 1892 *Photogr. Ann.* II. 267 This lever is sunk into the under surface of D.
**c.** Of sound: Low, subdued.
1806 WOLCOT (P. Pindar) *Tristia* Wks. 1812 V. 319 Tones in the Minor Key, so sweet, so under. 1834 WORDSW. *Lines in Album of C'tess Lonsdale* 33 Those self-solacing, those under, notes Trilled by the redbreast.
**3.** Inferior, subordinate; of lower rank or position.
1580 *Brief Disc. why Cath. refuse to goe to Ch.* 41 b, For that they haue not receaued the vnder Orders, which they should haue done before Preisthoode. 1611 COTGR., *Soubzacazement,* a dead Fief, rent secke, mesne, or vnder rent. 1693 *Humours Town* 86 The under classes of them, Attorneys, Sollicitors, and Pettifoggers. 1727 POPE, etc. *Art of Sinking* 120 For the under characters, gather them from Homer and Virgil, and change the names as occasion serves. 1823 EGAN *Grose's Dict. Vulgar T., Under dubber,* a turnkey. 1890 R. C. LEHMANN *H. Fludyer* 33 The poor dear servants..going in batches to the pantomime—at least, the under ones.
**4.** Below the proper standard, amount, etc.; defective, insufficient.
1673 *Essex Papers* (Camden) 103 Getting a long Lease of it at an under rent from ye Citty. 1710 PALMER *Proverbs* 294 Men..rarely fail of over-measure in the return of an injury, and under in the acknowledgment of a kindness. 1737 BRACKEN *Farriery Impr.* (1757) II. 258 'Tis best to begin rather with an under than over Dose. 1817 KEATINGE *Trav.* I. 9 Flat tracts of hungry pasture ground in under proportion to the tillage.

**Under** (ʊ·ndəɹ), *prep.* Forms: 1– under (3 *Orm.* unnderr), 3–7 vnder (5–7 wnder), 4–5 vndere, undere (undre), vndire, 4–6 vn-, wn-, undir, 4–5 vn-, undur, 4–5 vndyr (5 hun-, 6 wn-); 4 vnþer, 5 vnther, vnþur; 4–6, 7 *Sc.,* onder (4 honder), 5 ondre, ondyr, 5–6 ondir; 5 onþer, onther; *Sc.* 8 oner, 9 oonder, oon'er, unner. [Common Teutonic: OE. *under,* = OFris. *under, onder* (WFris. *ûnder, onder,* NFris. *onner, önner*), OLFr. *under, undir* (MDu. and Du. *onder*), OS. *undar* (MLG. *under,* LG. *under, unner*), OHG. *untar, untir, undar, undir* (MHG. and G. *unter*), ON. and Icel. *undir* (Norw., Sw., Da. *under*), Goth. *undar.* The stem is regarded as identical with that of Skr. *ádharas* lower, inferior (*adhamás* lowest, *adhás* below, down), and L. *infrā.*]
**I.** In senses denoting position beneath or below something, so as to have it above or overhead, or to be covered by it.
**1.** With reference to: **a.** The heavens or heavenly bodies. (See also HEAVEN *sb.* 1, SUN *sb.* 1 e, COPE *sb.*[1] 7, CANOPY *sb.* 2 b.)
*Beowulf* 8 He..weox under wolcnum. *Ibid.* 51 Hæleð under heofenum. *a* 900 CYNEWULF *Elene* 13 (Gr.), Æðelinges weox rice under roderum. *c* 1000 ÆLFRIC *Gen.* i. 7 Þa wæteru þe wæron under þære fæstnisse. *c* 1175 *Lamb. Hom.* 151 Ure drihten him solf..seide þet under houene ne [wes] nan his ilike. *c* 1205– [see SUN *sb.* 1 e]. 1340–70 *Alex. & Dind.* 219 We weren tauht..Þat non haþel vndur heuene so holi is founde. *a* 1400–50 *Alexander* 247 Þare enhabetis in þat erd ..Þe wisest wees in þis werd þe welken vndire. *c* 1400 *Destr. Troy* 3873 Was neuer kyng vnder cloude his knightes more louet. 1458 AGNES PASTON in *P. Lett.* I. 423 The blyssyng of all seyntes undir heven. *a* 1542 WYATT in *Tottel's Misc.* (Arb.) 64 Thinke not alone vnder the sunne Vnquit to cause thy louers plaine. 1555 [see FIRMAMENT 1]. 1609 BIBLE (Douay) *Deut.* xxix. 20 Our Lord abolish his name vnder heauen. 1644 MILTON *Educ.* 7 They are by a sudden.. watch word, to be call'd out to their military motions, under skie or covert, according to the season. 1712 BERKELEY *Pass. Obed.* Wks. 1871 III. 108 In every kingdom or society of men under heaven. 1766 GOLDSM. *Vicar* xiv, The greatest rascal under the canopy of heaven. 1821 WORDSW. *Three Cottage Girls* 56 Gay vision under sullen skies! 1885 *Manch. Exam.* 29 June 5/3 They rush off immediately..and bathe under a hot and broiling sun.
†**b.** The Deity as dwelling in heaven. *Obs.*
*c* 1205 LAY. 27976 Neoðeles heo auered weoren..þat nusten heo under criste nenne ræd godne. *c* 1320 *Cast. Love* 225 Þat vche þing vnder heuene-driht So muche les of strengþe and miht. *c* 1400 *Destr. Troy* 11776 There is no greuaunce so grete vndur god one, As the glemyng of gold.
**c.** Special parts of the heavens, esp. as indicating terrestrial locality.
*c* 1391 CHAUCER *Astrol.* I. § 21 Whan the planetes ben vnder thilke signes, þei causen vs..effectes lik to the operaciouns of bestes. *c* 1400 [see PLANET *sb.*[1] 1 b]. 1432–50 [see POLE *sb.*[2] 1]. *c* 1450 HOLLAND *Howlat* 31 Under the Cirkill solar thir sauorus seidis War nurist be dame Natur. 1559 W. CUNNINGHAM *Cosmogr. Glasse* 82 There be some that suppose..Paradise to be situated vnder th' Equinoctiall. 1590 SPENSER *F. Q.* III. iii. 6 The learned Merlin well could tell, Vnder what coast of heauen the man did dwell. 1611 R. JOHNSON *Kingd. & Commw.* 437 Authours affirme, that vnder the very pole lyeth a black and high rocke. 1634 HERBERT *Trav.* 186 This day we were under nine degrees fifteene minutes North. 1679 MOXON *Math. Dict.* 162 Under the Sun Beams. 1728 CHAMBERS *Cycl.* s.v. *Current,* Under the Equator, where the Motion of the Earth is the greatest. 1783 JUSTAMOND tr. *Raynal's Hist. Indies* (ed. 3) I. 3 A man living under the equator or under the pole.
**d.** The stars as having influence on persons.
1583 STUBBES *Anat. Abus.* II. I 4, Whether all the host of Pharao were borne vnder one and the same starre and planet. 1590 SPENSER *F. Q.* II. ii. 2 Ah lucklesse babe, borne vnder cruell starre. 1601 [see STAR *sb.* 3]. *a* 1715 BURNET *Own Time* (1724) I. 525 Great applications were made to the Duke for saving his life: But he was not born under a pardoning planet. 1823 SCOTT *Quentin D.* xii, This..youth has his destiny under the same constellation with mine. 1837 [see PLANET *sb.*[1] 1 b].
**2.** With reference to the surface of the earth or water. (Cf. UNDERGROUND *adv.*)
In early use without *the* before the noun.
*Beowulf* 1656 Ic þæt unsofte ealdre ȝediȝde, wiȝȝe under wætere. *Ibid.* 2415 Goldmaðmas heold eald under eorðan. *a* 900 CYNEWULF *Elene* 218 (Gr.), Hwær se wuldres beam haliȝ under hrusan hyded wære. *a* 1300 *Cursor M.* 1079 Þe bodi moght he nan-gat hide, For vnder erth most it not rest. *c* 1330 R. BRUNNE *Chron. Wace* (Rolls) 2068 He dide hure kepe Vnder erthe in a seler depe. 1398 TREVISA *Barth. De P. R.* VI. ii. (Bodl. MS.), He is iputte aside and iberied vndur þe erthe. *c* 1400 *Gamelyn* 68 A-none as he was dede and vnder gras grave. 1477 EARL RIVERS (Caxton) *Dictes* 22 But nowe they may not be perceyued for they ar hidde vnther the erthe. *c* 1511 *1st Eng. Bk. Amer.* Introd. (Arb.) 28/1 There dwellyng is vnder the erthe. 1530 PALSGR. 328/1 Under the grounde, *soubzterraine.* 1555 EDEN *Decades* (Arb.) 142 They had certeyne dyuers or fysshers exercised..in swymmynge vnder the water. 1601 HOLLAND *Pliny* II. 408 Anon it is swallowed up within a hole under the ground. 1721 [see TURF *sb.*[1] 2]. 1790 [see EARTH *sb.*[1] 2]. 1818 CRUISE *Digest* (ed. 2) V. 21 In cases of copyholds, a lord may have a right under the soil of the copyholder. 1880 R. M. BALLANTYNE (*title*), Under the Waves; or, Diving in Deep Waters.
**3.** With words denoting natural or artificial structures or means of shelter; freq. = beneath the cover or shelter of.
See also GLASS *sb.*[1] 3 b, HATCH *sb.*[1] 3, 4, ROOF *sb.* 1 b. For examples with abstract terms see COVER *sb.*[1] 3 c, COVERT *sb.* 2 c, SHADE *sb.* 8, UMBRAGE *sb.* 2 b.
*a* 900 CYNEWULF *Elene* 653 (Gr.), Ȝe þa byrȝenna under stanhleoðum..on ȝewritu setton. 971 *Blickl. Hom.* 209 Under þæm stane wæs niccra eardung & wearȝa. *c* 1000 ÆLFRIC *Gen.* xxi. 15 Heo þa alede þone sunu under sumum treowe. *a* 1310 in Wright *Lyric P.* xiii. 44 Wormes woweth under cloude [= clod]. 1338 R. BRUNNE *Chron.* (1810) 14 Sibriht, þat I of told,..Þat a suynhird slouh vnder a busk of thorn. 1340–70 *Alex. & Dind.* 435 We ne han none hous bote holus in þe holou cauus Vndur hillus ful hie. *c* 1374 CHAUCER *Anel. & Arc.* 19 Thow..Syngest with voice memorial in þe shade Vndir the laurier. *c* 1400 MAUNDEV. (Roxb.) iii. 9 Vnder þe stages er stables. 1422 YONG tr. *Secreta Secret.* 192 Lik as a man ne restith not well vndir a dropping hous. *c* 1470 *Gol. & Gaw.* 356 Thus with trety ye cast yon trew vndre tyld. 1508 DUNBAR *Tua Mariit Wemen* 11, I hard, vnder ane holyn..Ane hie speiche at my hand. 1571 CAMPION *Hist. Irel.* II. ix. (1633) 115 You are served under a Canopy. 1585 T. WASHINGTON tr. *Nicholay's Voy.* II. vi. 36 [He] giueth vnto the inhabitants..these trees ..vpon condition that euery one..shall trim them & keep the ground cleane that is vnder them. 1662 *Extr. St. Papers Friends* Ser. II. (1911) 148 These Anabaptist..meete ..privately vnder hedges at vnseasonable houres in the night. 1693 *Humours Town* 43 If they had kept under their own Vine in the Country. 1711 STEELE *Spect.* 82 ¶ 1 Passing under Ludgate the other Day, I heard a Voice bawling for Charity. 1761 MRS. F. SHERIDAN *Sidney Bidulph* I. 319 Whatever your designs may be, it will be less to my dishonour if you prosecute them from under your husband's roof. 1843 *Fraser's Mag.* XXVIII. 649 Under this canopy was the coffin. 1891 FARRAR *Darkn. & Dawn* lxiv, They reached the green level under the trees.
*fig.* 1711 *Spect.* No. 67 ¶ 5, I love to shelter my self under the Examples of Great Men.
**b.** *Sc.* With reference to the cover or shelter of darkness. *Under night,* during the night, by night.
*Under cloud of night*: see CLOUD *sb.* 9.
1434 *Extr. Aberd. Reg.* (1844) I. 391 That na fischar of sawmound..house nane bot thai be tane vndir nycht, and on the morn brocht to the markete. 1508 KENNEDIE *Flyting w. Dunbar* 428 And ondir nycht quhyle stall thou staggis & stirkis. 1567 *Reg. Privy Council Scot.* I. 592 The said Oliver..come to the said Androis dwelling hous..under silence of nycht. 1725 RAMSAY *Gentle Sheph.* II. iii, He brought east the howdy under night. 1730 T. BOSTON *Mem.* xi. (1899) 371 Under night we lost the way again. 1824 MACTAGGART *Gallovid. Encycl.* 450 To sing undernight for 'bawbees' in the large towns on their way. 1844 H. STEPHENS *Bk. Farm* I. 129 Some mares..are known to drop their foals under night in the stable.
**4.** In general use.
In some phrases with development of figurative senses: see FOOT *sb.* 33, NOSE *sb.* 7 b, ROSE *sb.* 7, WING *sb.* *Under metal*: see METAL *sb.* 7. In quot. 1553 the reference is app. to relative position on the map.
*c* 825 *Vesp. Ps.* ix. 28 Under tungan his [bioð] ȝewin & sar. *c* 950 *Lindisf. Gosp.* Mark iv. 21 Hueðer cuom leht-fæt..þætte under mitta..ȝesetted bið *vel* under bed. *a* 1000 *Kent. Gloss.* in Wr.-Wülcker 82 *Sub ascella sua,* under his oxne. *a* 1250 *Owl & Night.* 86 Þe were icundere to one frogge Þat sit at Mulne vnder cogge. *c* 1320 *Sir Tristr.* 1947 A siue he fond tite And bond vnder his fete. *c* 1386 CHAUCER *Knt.'s T.* 1727 And in that selue moment Palamon Is vnder Venus Estward in the place. *a* 1400 *Octouian* 1851, I fond my chyld lye yn oo place, Onther a lyoun..With whelpys tweyne. *c* 1430 *Art of Nombryng* (E.E.T.S.) 15 Therfor vnder the last in an od place sette me most fynde a digit. 1508 KENNEDIE *Flyting w. Dunbar* 364 Thou wald be fayn to gnaw,..Wnder my burd, smoch banis behynd doggis bakkis. 1523 FITZHERB. *Husb.* § 27 If it be a newe house, they thacke it vnder theyr fote. 1553 EDEN *Treat. New Ind.* (Arb.) 8 The situation of the cytie of Saba in Ethiopia vnder Egipt. 1669 STURMY *Mariner's Mag.* v. xii. 72 If the said Work be under the Platform, Substract the Difference found by your Quadrant. 1683 MOXON *Mech. Exerc., Printing* xi. ¶ 23 The Stoking-hole lying far under the Caldron. 1727 BAILEY (vol. II), To *Chuck* one under the Chin. 1762 MILLS *Syst. Pract. Husb.* I. 265 The share will be more inclined..if the wedge under the beam is loosened. 1815 J. SMITH *Panorama Sci. & Art* II. 525 Here the bracket.. denotes, that these two substances..form the compound written under it. 1862 THACKERAY *Philip* xxvii, Those scratches or dashes under her words, by which some ladies are accustomed to point their satire. 1888 'J. S. WINTER' *Bootle's Childr.* vii, A goodly crop of curly brown hair which he held under the pump..almost every morning.
**b.** Denoting the relationship of a horse to the rider, or of a ship to a person on board.
*a* 900 CYNEWULF *Elene* 1192 (Gr.), Þæs cyninges sceal mearh under modeȝum midlum ȝeweorðod. 1338 R. BRUNNE *Chron.* (1810) 183 Fightand on a gate, vndir him þei slouh his stede. 1485 CAXTON *Chas. Gt.* 210 Also that same day the hors of charles was slayn under hym. 1709 STEELE *Tatler* No. 17 ¶ 4 My Lord Galway had his Horse shot under him in this Action. 1720 DE FOE *Capt. Singleton* iii. (1840) 46 We might have some better vessels under us. 1795 *Ann. Reg., Hist.* 30 Three horses were killed under him. 1806 A. DUNCAN *Nelson* 15 His ship sunk under him. 1841 *Penny Cycl.* XXI. 492/1 Having had a horse shot under him.
**c.** = At a point just below (a part of the body).
*c* 1275 *Passion of our Lord* 388 in *O. E. Misc.* 48 Seþþe hi knowede and seyde, hayl gywene king, And smyten vnder þat ere, ne sparede hi no þing. *c* 1400 *Rom. Rose* 2097 He

touchide me Vndir the side full softly. *c* **1475** *RaufCoilȝear* 150 He..hit him vnder the eir with his richt hand. **1539** BIBLE 2 *Sam.* iii. 27 Joab..smote hym vnder yᵉ short rybbes yᵗ he dyed. **1585** T. WASHINGTON tr. *Nicholay's Voy.* III. x. 86 Breaches..gathered and made fast vnder the knee. **1604** SHAKS. *Oth.* I. ii. 5 Nine, or ten times I had thought t' haue yerk'd him here vnder the Ribbes. **1611**–[see FIFTH *a.* 1 a]. **1653** URQUHART *Rabelais* I. xxvii. 128 With a sound bounce under the hollow of their short ribs, he overturned their stomachs. **1886** ELWORTHY *W. Somerset Word-bk.* 500 I'll gi thee a nap under the ear.

**d.** Denoting position between the arm, etc., and the body.

**1377** LANGL. *P. Pl.* B. xv. 119 A peyre bedes in her hande and a boke vnder her arme. *c* **1480** HENRYSON *Fables, Lion & Mouse* 37 Ane Roll of paper in his hand he bair; Ane Swannis pen stikand vnder his eir. **1485** in *Yorkshire Deeds* (1909) 3 Lawrence..brought with him a small coferet under his arme and bar it hens. **1596** SPENSER *F. Q.* IV. vii. 24 And now he her away with him did beare Vnder his arme. **1602** *2nd Pt. Return fr. Parnass.* Prol., Stage Direction, Stagekeeper carrieth the boy away vnder his arme. **1721** KELLY *Scot. Prov.* 319 She is welcome that brings some Present under her Arm. **1820** KEATS *Cap & Bells* lxviii, Under one arm the magic book he bore. *c* **1850** *Arab. Nts.* (Rtldg.) 741 She shut the box, put it under her arm, and returned to the house.

**e.** Passing into the sense of 'in'.

**1812** SIR H. DAVY *Chem. Philos.* 285 It may be purified by ..passing it under water through shamois leather. **1827** FARADAY *Chem. Manip.* xv. (1842) 343 The transference of gas from vessel to vessel under mercury. **1855** *Orr's Circ. Sci., Inorg. Nat.* 215 The resulting lime..sets rapidly in a damp atmosphere, and even under water.

**5.** Denoting the relationship of persons: **a.** To something worn on the head. (In ME. esp. in conventional phrases.)

*Beowulf* 342 Word æfter spræc, heard under helme. *Ibid.* 1163 Þa cwom Wealhþeo forð gan under gyldnum beaȝe. *a* **1310** in Wright *Lyric P.* xvi. 52 With browen blysfol under hode. *c* **1400** *Emare* 303 Ther was noþer olde ny ȝynge, That kowþe stynte of wepynge, For þat comely vnþer kelle. **1508** DUNBAR *Poems* iv. 22 He takis the knythis in to feild, Anarmit vnder helme & scheild. *Ibid.* v. 4 Scho wes like a caldrone cruke cler vnder kellis. **1550** [see HOOD *sb.* 7]. **1667** MILTON *P. L.* III. 640 Under a Coronet his flowing haire In curles on either cheek plaid. **1825** BENTHAM *Offic. Apt. Maximized, Indic.* (1830) 38 Think now of the scene; ..culprit and judge under one hood. **1846** G. E. CORRIE in Holroyd *Mem.* (1890) xi. 241 There may be..more pride and hypocrisy under a close plain bonnet, than under a veil of silk. **1853** THACKERAY *Eng. Hum.* i. 17 What small men they must have seemed under these enormous periwigs.

**b.** To something carried or raised above the head, as a standard, etc. Hence in pregnant sense, denoting military service, nationality, etc.

*Beowulf* 1205 Siðþan he under seȝne sinc ealȝode. *c* **1500** [see STANDARD *sb.* I b]. **1517** *Reg. Privy Seal Scotl.* I. 451/1 William Turnbule..deit under umquhile our soverane lordis baner. *a* **1548** HALL *Chron., Edw. IV*, 243 Therle of Northumberlande, vnder whose standerd were..sixe thousande and seuen .c. men. **1552** [see BANNER *sb.*[1] 1 b]. **1596** DALRYMPLE tr. *Leslie's Hist. Scot.* (S.T.S.) I. 277 Wndir this croce, scotis men ar sure. **1611** COTGR. s.v. *Subhastation*, The auncient Romans vsed..to hold their Outcries [=auctions] vnder a kind of speare, or iauelin. **1667** MILTON *P. L.* VI. 533 Him soon they met Under spred Ensignes moving nigh. **1725** DE FOE *Voy. round World* (1840) 213 A small frigate-built vessel, under Spanish Colours. **1750** BEAWES *Lex Mercat.* (1752) 9 Very soon all the commerce of those parts was only carried on under French colours. **1769** [see BANNER *sb.*[1] 1]. **1852** [see STANDARD *sb.*[1] 1 b]. **1869** in *Cornh. Mag.* June (1918) 635 Some of the Colonies..may in process of time find themselves under the Stars and Stripes of the Flag of the United States.

**c.** *Naut.* Of ships, with reference to the sails, etc.

*c* **893**, **1508**–[see SAIL *sb.*[1] 3 d]. **1669** STURMY *Mariner's Mag.* I. ii. 17 Thus have you the Ship a trije under a Mizen. *Ibid.* 18 Thus you have the Ship..steering under all her Canvas. **1707** *Lond. Gaz.* No. 4380/3 The Firebrand..forc'd in under a Fore-course for the Light of St. Agnes. **1719** D'URFEY *Pills* III. 306 She lies a try under her Mizen. **1780** COXE *Russ. Disc.* 130 Drove 24 hours under bare poles. **1840** R. H. DANA *Bef. Mast* ix. 22 A large ship under top-gallant sails. **1885** *Law Times' Rep.* LIII. 54/1 The J. M. Stevens was proceeding under all sail close-hauled on the port tack.

**6.** With reference to something which covers, clothes, envelops, or conceals; passing into the sense of 'within'.

In ME. freq. in phrases: see quots. and GORE *sb.*[2] 2, LACE *sb.* 3, LINE *sb.*[1] 2 b, SHIELD *sb.* 1 b. *Under arms* (see ARM *sb.*[2] 5) is prob. an extension of this sense. For the fig. sense of *under a cloud* see CLOUD *sb.* 10 b. *Under water* (= flooded): see WATER *sb.*

*Beowulf* 1209 He under rande ȝecranc. *a* **1122** *O. E. Chron.* (Laud MS.) an. 688, He syððan..forðferde..under Cristes claðum. *a* **1225** *Leg. Kath.* 809 Schome ow is to schuderin lengre under schelde. **1382** WYCLIF *Jude* i. 6 Sothliche aungels..he reseruede..in euerelastinge boondis vndir derknesse. *c* **1386** CHAUCER *Frankl. T.* 381 Þis matere..Vnder his brest he baar it moore secree Than euere dide Pamphilus for Galathee. *c* **1400** *Emare* 250 Then sayde þat wordy vnþer wede. *Ibid.* 501 That semely vnþer serke. *c* **1402** LYDG. *Compl. Bl. Knt.* 64, I sawe ther Daphne closed under rynde. *c* **1450** HOLLAND *Howlat* 82 That is the plesant Pacok..Constant and kirklyk vnder his cler cape. **1579** W. WILKINSON *Confut. Fam. Love* Ep. Ded. * ij b, While the watchmen slept, many..vnder Lambes skinnes craftely crept into the sheepfold. **1599** GREENE *Orpharion* Wks. (Grosart) XII. 33 And vnder a faire face resteth a faithfull hart. **1621** T. WILLIAMSON tr. *Goulart's Wise Vieillard* 26 Our life may be compared to..the Moone,..often ecclipsed and vnder a cloud. **1775** FRANKLIN *Let.* in *Europ. Mag.* (1804) XLV. 349/2 Please to send your letters to him, under cover, directed to Mr. Alderman Lee. **1791** COWPER *Odyssey* VII. 357 There, under wither'd leaves, forlorn, I slept All the long night. **1798**, **1804** [see CO--R *sb.*[1] 2 d]. **1817** BOWDICH *Mission to Ashantee* ix. 375 It proceeds by ulcerating under the skin. **1859** *Habits of Gd. Society* 50 If you do not wear silk stockings under your boots. **1872** *Routledge's Ev. Boy's Ann.* 185/2 All addressed..to him under cover to the agents of his regiment.

*fig.* **1500–20** DUNBAR *Poems* xiii. 5, I tell ȝow this vndir confessioun.

**b.** Denoting the relationship of land to crops grown, or animals reared, on it: Planted, sowed, or stocked with; used for growing or rearing.

(*a*) **1569** *Reg. Privy Council Scot.* I. 676 Peciabill possessioun of the landis and stedingis of Cullard and Conege, under crop as it is. **1795** VANCOUVER *Agric. Essex* 53 The marshes which were formerly under grass, are now very generally under the plough. **1806** [see CROP *sb.* 8 b]. **1845** *Jrnl. R. Agric. Soc.* VI. II. 524, I put the ground..under early potatoes. **1868** *Ibid.* Ser. II. IV. II. 322 This field has been laid under grass. **1890** STANLEY *Darkest Africa* I. x. 232 The Manyuema had..five acres under rice, and as many under beans.

(*b*) **1799** [A. YOUNG] *Agric. Lincoln* 194 [The pasture] that had been under sheep [was] so greatly superior. **1891** *Pall Mall G.* 24 Aug. 2/2 Again, in Ross-shire, the area under deer has advanced..to a little more than one-half.

**7.** Denoting position at the bottom or foot of something, or beside it but at a lower level: By the side of, close by (a wood, town, etc.). Sometimes with implication of shelter or protection.

Also with abstract terms, esp. LEE *sb.*[1] 1, SHELTER *sb.* 2. *Under the wind*: see WIND *sb.*

*Beowulf* 211 Flota wæs on yðum, bat under beorȝe. *Ibid.* 710 Ða com of more under misthleoþum Grendel gongan. **971** *Blickl. Hom.* 211 Þæt wæter wæs sweart under þæm clife neoðan. *c* **1205** LAY. 27163 Þa he com in ane dale vnder ane dune, þer he gon at-stonden. *c* **1305** *Judas Iscariot* 70 in *E. E. P.* (1862) 109 So þat þis tuei schrewen..Adai ȝeode alone pleye vnder an orchard. *c* **1386** CHAUCER *Knt.'s T.* 1123 And dounward from an hille vnder a bente Ther stood the temple of Mars Armypotente. **1387** TREVISA *Higden* (Rolls) V. 329 Þat ryver renneþ under the citee of Wygan. *c* **1402** LYDG. *Compl. Bl. Knt.* 77, I sawe a litel welle, That had his course..Under a hille. **1495** *Cov. Leet Bk.* 563 Such grounde as the seid Maister had vnder the parke syde. *a* **1548** HALL *Chron., Edw. IV*, 201 So vnder a wooddes side, thei couertly espied them passe forward. **1585** T. WASHINGTON tr. *Nicholay's Voy.* II. i. 31 b, [We lay] seuen daies vnder the castle and fortresse called Capsali. *Ibid.* II. x. 44 b, The castle,..vnder which lieth a vallie very fertile. **1600** *1st Pt. Sir J. Oldcastle* IV. iv. 75 Hard vnder Islington wait you my comming. **1662** STILLINGFL. *Orig. Sacræ* III. iv. § 12 That part of Thessaly which lyes under the mountains Ossa and Olympus. **1720** DE FOE *Capt. Singleton* xi. (1840) 185 We were obliged to come to an anchor under a little island. **1751** LABELYE *Westm. Bridge* 28 The Carpenters began to make and erect, under the Surry Shore, 12 Frames of Timber. **1806** *Gazetteer Scotl.* (ed. 2) 402/2 Under the rock where the fowls build they row their boat. **1840** ALISON *Hist. Eur.* VIII. lxii. 365 Seeking refuge under any projecting ground from the intolerable musketry. **1842** LOUDON *Suburban Hort.* 625 Either in the open garden,..or under a wall.

**b.** In military and naval use.

**1677** *Lond. Gaz.* No. 1237/2 The slaughter would have been much greater, but that by the favor of the night they got under the Cannon of the Fort of Kiel. **1710** *Ibid.* No. 4731/2 The Duke of Anjou was encamped..under the Cannon of Lerida. **1805** in Nicolas *Disp. Nelson* (1846) VII. 167 *note*, At 2.5 The French Admiral's Ship under our Quarter had lost her foremast.

**8.** With verbs of motion, impulsion, etc., denoting change of place to a position below or beneath something.

*Beowulf* 403 Þa secg wisode under Heorotes hrof. *Ibid.* 820 Scolde Grendel þonan..fleon under fenhleoðu. *c* **888** K. ÆLFRED *Boeth.* xxxix. § 3 Hwa ne wundrað ðæs þæt sume steorran ȝewitað under þa sæ. *c* **1000** *Ags. Gosp.* Luke vii. 6 Ne eom ic wyrðe þæt ðu ga under mine þecene. *c* **1200** ORMIN 1551 And þurrh þatt tatt tu fullhtnesst hemm & unnderr waterr dippesst. *c* **1205** LAY. 8406 Tweien scalkes..scriðen under bordes & skirmden mid mæine. **13..** *E. E. Allit. P.* C. 179 A lodes-mon lyȝtly lep vnder hachches. **1382** WYCLIF *Luke* vii. 6, I am not worthi, that thou entre vndir my roof. **1585** T. WASHINGTON tr. *Nicholay's Voy.* II. xxiv. 65 The arcenal..hath neare an hundreth arches or vaultes to builde and hale the gallies vnder couert and drye. **1617** MORYSON *Itin.* I. 210 All which, at the ringing of this bell to prayer, went vnder the hatches. **1648** HEXHAM II, *Onderduycken*, to Dive vnder water, as in swimming. **1697** DRYDEN *Virg. Georg.* IV. 72 When Golden Suns appear, And under Earth have driv'n the Winter Year. **1702** ADDISON *Dial. Medals* (1726) 102 She thrusts a lighted torch under a heap of armour that lies by an Altar. **1806** *Med. Jrnl.* XV. 275 He admits that various active substances may be introduced under the cuticle. **1827** *Mirror* II. 254/1 Chance..led him under an apple-tree. **1892** *Photogr. Ann.* II. 251 Rude Boreas, who likes to let daylight under the focussing cloth.

**II.** In senses denoting subordination or subjection.

**9.** With reference to persons acting in a certain capacity, considered in relation to one holding a superior position or office.

*c* **893** K. ÆLFRED *Oros.* III. xi. 142 Þa þe under Alexandre fyrmest wæron. *c* **1000** *Rule of Chrodegang* vi, Se bisceop oððe se ðe under him ealdor is. *a* **1300** *Cursor M.* 16026 Þai..sent to pilate þair procuratur,..For he sett vte-ouer þam Vnder cesar þe king. *c* **1380** WYCLIF *Serm.* Sel. Wks. I. 316 So Syryne, þat was þere cheef undur þe emperour, bigan to make þis discripcion. *c* **1420** LYDG. *Assembly of Gods* 1259 Then made Vertu Frewyll baylle vndyr Reson. *c* **1425** *Eng. Conq. Ireland* 6 In that tym was prince in wales, Rys, Gryffynes son, vnder þe kyng of england. **1473** *Rental Bk. Cupar-Angus* (1879) I. 166 We hafe grantyt hym..to mak tenandis onder hym. **1531** *Dial. on Laws Eng.* II. xxxvi. 75 The pope is the vycar generall vnder god. **1546** *Yorks. Chantry Surv.* (Surtees) 348 The same prebendaries have vj vicars inducted under them. **1611** COTGR., *Soubcurateur*, ..one that hath the..charge of a thing vnder another. **1667** MILTON *P. L.* v. 695 Hee together calls..the Regent Powers, Under him Regent. **1761** *List Officers Army* 195/2 Capt. Sir Duncan Campbell, Bt. Staff-offi. la. under L. G. St. Clair. **1820** LAMB *Elia* I. *South-Sea House*, Deputy, under Evans, was Thomas Tame. **1849** MACAULAY *Hist. Eng.* i. I. 55 The King was, under Christ, sole head of the Church. **1854** R. S. SURTEES *Handley Cr.* vii, Betsey, a maid of all work, and a girl under her. **1891** E. PEACOCK *N. Brendon* I. 133 He had worked under Clark.

**b.** *Under God, Heaven*, etc., in parenthetic use. (Cf. GOD *sb.* 9 d.)

**1544** *Star Chamb. Cases* (Selden) II. 279 The ship.. wherof one John Goodlade..then vndir god was master. **1616** R. COCKS *Diary* (Hakl. Soc.) I. 199 Of his arivall there in our junck,..he under God saveing her. *a* **1704** LOCKE *Ess. Underst. St. Paul's Epist.* (1707) 17 This is the only safe Guide (under the Spirit of God..) that can be rely'd on. **1719** DE FOE *Crusoe* II. (Globe) 332 He..thank'd me that had, under God, given him and so many miserable Creatures their Lives. **1841** LYTTON *Night & Morn.* III. xi, The husband and wife..looked up to her as the author, under Heaven, of their happiness. *Ibid.* v. xix, It is from you, under Providence, that [etc.].

†**c.** = In addition to; besides. *Obs.*

*c* **1400** T. CHESTRE *Launfal* 48 For the lady bar..swych word, That sche had lemannys unther her lord. *c* **1440** *Gesta Rom.* i. 1 (Harl. MS.), Þis woman lovid by wey of synne an oþer knyȝt, vndir hire husbond. *Ibid.* v. 12 There was a knyȝt hadde a faire wife, þat tooke an oþer vndir him.

**d.** With reference to derivative rights or claims.

**1818** CRUISE *Digest* (ed. 2) II. 505 As to the grantee of the rent-charge, he was in under the first joint tenant who released. **1896** *Law Times* C. 410/1 The acts or defaults of any person other than himself and those claiming under him.

**10.** Denoting subordination to, or control by, a person or persons having or exercising recognized authority or command; occas. = in the service of.

*c* **950** *Lindisf. Gosp.* Matt. viii. 9 Ic..hæfo under mec ðeignas. *c* **1000** ÆLFRIC *Num.* iii. 9 Beon hiȝ þenas under Aarone and his sunum. *a* **1225** *Leg. Kath.* 223 He ane is to herien, þurh hwam & under hwam alle kinges rixleð. *c* **1230** *Hali Meid.* 31 For, beo hit nu, þat..[þu] habbe monie under þe, hirdmen in halle. **1382** WYCLIF *Matt.* viii. 9 For whi and I am a man..hauynge vndir me kniȝtis. *c* **1400** MAUNDEV. (Roxb) xxx. 133 Prestre Iohn has vnder him many kynges. *c* **1450** HOLLAND *Howlat* 133 For all statis of kirk that wnder Crist standis. **1495** *Act 11 Hen. VII*, c. 22 § 1 A maister Ship Carpenter taking the charge of the werke havyng men undre hym. **1538** STARKEY *England* I. i. 24 Now also vse your tyme, vnder so nobul a prynce, to the mayntenance..of the same. *a* **1548** HALL *Chron., Hen. V*, 38 While all was vnder one [king], no nacion durste..attempte warre against the Britons. **1639** A. WHEELOCKE in *Lett. Lit. Men* (Camden) 157, I could wish that our learned gentrie..would imploy some scholars to be under them..to compile a body of our Divinity. **1726** SWIFT *Gulliver* IV. iv, In my last voyage I was commander of the ship, and had about fifty Yahoos under me. **1779** *Mirror* No. 4, An uncle of my wife, who.. had obtained a very considerable office under government. **1838** W. BELL *Dict. Law Scot.* 168 The society is now under the keeper of the signet. **1849** MACAULAY *Hist. Eng.* i. I. 141 Favourable to the plan of reviving the old civil constitution under a new dynasty.

**b.** *spec.* Denoting relation to military commanders or political leaders: Led or commanded by; in the forces or following of.

**1297** R. GLOUC. (Rolls) 1332 Vor þe maistrie nis noȝt a kinges..Ac kniȝtes þat vnder him viȝteþ & ssedeþ hor blod. **1564** STAPLETON tr. *Staphylus' Apol.* Pref. 11 His wisedom ..he well declared..in the like seruice vnder the Catholike and vertuous Duke of Bauaria. **1599** SHAKS. *Hen. V*, IV. vii. 154 *King.* Who seru'st thou vnder? *Will.* Vnder Captaine Gower. **1612** T. TAYLOR *Comm. Titus* ii. 6 Let them now serue as voluntaries vnder the Captaine Iesus Christ. **1718** PRIOR *Poems Sev. Occas.* Ded., In the first Dutch War He went a Voluntier under the Duke of York. **1816** SCOTT *Old Mort.* xxxvi, I made my first campaigns under him. **1839** *Penny Cycl.* XIV. 347/2 On the 18th May, 1565, the Turks, under Mustapha Pacha,..landed on the island of Malta. **1855** MACAULAY *Hist. Eng.* xii. III. 204 He..had fought bravely under Monmouth on the Continent. **1861** M. PATTISON *Ess.* (1889) I. 45 The great communistic uprising under Wat Tyler in 1381.

**c.** Denoting relation to teachers or instructors: Subject to the instruction, direction, or guidance of.

*To sit under* (a preacher): see SIT *v.* 28. See also STUDY *v.* 1 c.

**1524** *Reg. Mag. Sig. Scot.* 200 The said M. Hary..has maid under him gude and perite scolaris now laitlie the tyme that he was maister of our scule. **1691** WOOD *Ath. Oxon.* II. 693 His first education in Grammar learning was under one Thom. Sibley. **1711** STEELE *Spect.* No. 154 ⁋ 2, I..had the finishing Part of my Education under a Man of great Probity. **1724** H. BEDFORD tr. *Life J. Barwick* App. 362 Under this Instructor he learnt the Art of blurting out crude Sermons. **1749** FIELDING *Tom Jones* VII. xii, There were likewise two Ensigns,..one of whom had been bred under an Attorney. **1808** SCOTT in Lockhart *Life* I. i. 43, I made some progress in Ethics under Professor John Bruce. **1837** K. H. DIGBY *Mores Cath.* VIII. vi. (1846) II. 594/2 He studied under Albert at Cologne and Paris. **1900** D. C. TOVEY in *Gray's Lett.* I. 3 *note*, Birkett was the tutor under whom Gray was admitted a Pensioner at Peterhouse.

**d.** = As a tenant of.

**1754** in *Nairne Peerage Evidence* (1874) 51 She lived under said lord Nairn very near his house.

**e.** = In the hands of (a doctor).

**1898** *Hutchinson's Arch. Surg.* IX. 382, I go once a week to Dr. Brown, but whether I am under him or he is under me I never can quite tell.

**11.** With names or designations of rulers, passing into the sense of 'during the reign or administration of', 'in the time or period of'.

*c* **888** K. ÆLFRED *Boeth.* i, He þa ȝemunde..þara ealdrihta þe hi under þam caserum hæfdon. ? *a* **900** *O. E. Chron.* (Parker MS.) an. 653, Her Middel-Seaxe onfengon under Peadan aldormen ryhtne ʒeleafan. *c* **950** *Lindisf. Gosp.* Luke iv. 27 Moniʒo hreafo weron..under [Helisaeo] ðæne witʒo. **1340** *Ayenb.* 12 Þe uerþe article belongeþ to his passion, þet is to zigge, þet he þolede dyaþ onder pouns pilate. *c* **1375** *Sc. Leg. Saints* ii. (*Paul*) 28 Quhen he come to rome, Wndir fell nero tholit dowme, And ded wes. **1445** in *Anglia* XXVIII. 277 What so evir we loste toforne vndir our princis fele By thi comforte..may soon be yolden ageyn. **1548–9** (Mar.) *Bk. Com. Prayer, Communion*, [He] was crucified also for vs vnder Pontius Pilate. **1565** Harding *Answ. to M. Ivelles Challenge* 41 b, Soter Byshop of Rome..who suffred martyrdom vnder Antoninus Verus the Emperour. **1618** Bolton *Florus* Ep. Ded. A 3 b, An heathen man, and living under Trajan the Emperour. **1756–9** Butler *Lives of Saints* (1821) XI. 105 Bishop Fisher, who was put to death for his religion under Henry VIII. **1807** Syd. Smith *Lett. Catholics* i. ₱ 12 There were as many persons put to death for religious opinions under the mild Elizabeth as under the bloody Mary. **1849** Macaulay *Hist. Eng.* iii. I. 280 The national wealth..was greater under the Tudors than under the Plantagenets. **1891** Farrar *Darkn. & Dawn* xxvi, He would have lost his head under Caligula.

**b.** Similarly with other nouns.

*a* **1400** *New Test.* (Paues) Heb. vii. 11 For vnder þat presthod þe pepel vnderfong þe lawe. **1641** J. Jackson *True Evang. T.* ii. 89 They are such beasts as while the Law was up,..furnished Gods Altar with Sacrifices, and now under the Gospell, our tables with meate. **1662** Stillingfl. *Orig. Sacræ* ii. vi. § 8 The Prophets under the old Testament, when they speak of things to come to pass in the New. **1688** Dryden tr. *Life Francis Xavier* i. 39 Overjoy'd, that under his Pontificate, a gate shou'd be open'd to the Gospel, in the Oriental Indies. **1807** Syd. Smith *Lett. Catholics* i. ₱ 8 Under the reign of his present Majesty. **1826** Lamb *Popular Fallacy* Wks. 1908 I. 368 But who can show it?.. Under what king's reign is it pretended?

**12.** Denoting subjection to power or force exercised by some person or persons: Beneath the rule or domination of; subject to.

*a* **950** *O. E. Chron.* (Parker MS.) an. 942, Burʒa fife..Dæne wæran ær, under Norðmannum nyde ʒebeʒde. *a* **1225** *Leg. Kath.* 1092 He is godd seolf, þe duste deað under him. **1297** R. Glouc. (Rolls) 9873 Hii..gret raunson him ʒeue, In þraldom as vnder him þere to bileue. *a* **1340** Hampole *Psalter* xvii. 43 Þou supplantid rysand in me vndire me. *c* **1400** Maundev. (Roxb.) xxix. 132 Cristen men schall be vnder þaim. **1517** Torkington *Pilgr.* (1884) 63 The havyn of Corfewe, whiche Cite and yle ys vnder the Venycianns. **1526** Tindale 1 *Cor.* xv. 27 It is manifest that he is excepted, which did putt all thynges vnder him. **1610** Healey *St. Aug. Citie of God* 122 What liues the citizens lastly led, vnder so huge a bed-roll of gods Guardians!

**b.** *Under the sea* (see quots.).

*Under the weather* (dial. and U.S.): see Weather *sb.*

**1627** Capt. Smith *Seaman's Gram.* ix. 40 When they would lie obscurely in the Sea, or stay for some consort, [they] lash sure the helme a lee, and so a good ship will lie at ease vnder the Sea as we terme it. **1867** Smyth *Sailor's Word-bk.* 706 *Under the sea*, a ship lying-to in a heavy gale, and making bad weather of it.

**13.** With abstract or other sbs. denoting authority or control, with or without specification of the person or persons exercising it.

Cf. Command *sb.* 3 d. Also in fig. phrases with Hand *sb.* 35 a, Foot *sb.* 30 c and 33, Thumb *sb.* 5 a *f, g*, Eye *sb.*[1] 6.

(*a*) *c* **888** K. Ælfred *Boeth.* xxxvi. § 1 Ðætte æfre swylc yfel ʒeweorðan sceolde under ðæs ælmihtʒan Godes anwalde. *c* **910** *O. E. Chron.* (Parker MS.) an. 901, Se wæs cyning ofer eall Ongelcyn butan ðæm dæle þe under Dena onwalde wæs. **971** *Blickl. Hom.* 99 Eaþmodʒiaþ eow sylfe under þære mihte Godes handa. *c* **1175** *Lamb. Hom.* 13 Murðhe sculen wunian on londe þet bið on griðe and on friðe under mire onwalde. *c* **1200** Ormin Introd. 35 To ben unnderr deofless þeowwdom. *c* **1340** Hampole *Pr. Consc.* 5884 Prelats..Sal acount yhelde in sere degre Of þair suggets undir þair powere. **1390** Gower *Conf.* I. 18 So that under the clerkes lawe Men sen the Merel al mysdrawe. **1399** — *Praise of Peace* 39 Of all the world to winne the victoire, So that undir his swerd it myht obeie. *c* **1450** *Merlin* xxviii. 576 The xix kynges..comaunded alle hem that were vnther theire Iustice that [etc.]. **1457** Harding *Chron.* in *Eng. Hist. Rev.* Oct. (1912) 744 Compleyntes of wrong alway in general Refourmed were, so vndyr his yerde egall. **1512** *Act* 4 *Hen. VIII*, c. 19 § 4 Every alien & stranger nott borne under the Kynges allegiance & not made Denyzen. *a* **1533** Ld. Berners *Gold. Bk. M. Aurel.* Z 5 b, Thou shalte tourne to be bonde to theim that are nowe under thy bondage. **1667** Milton *P. L.* iii. 242 Under his gloomie power I shall not long Lie vanquisht. **1754** A. Murphy *Gray's-Inn Jrnl.* No. 95, In all Ages the Managers of Play-houses have acquiesced under the Gallery-Jurisdiction. **1781–** [see Supervision 1]. **1817** Jas. Mill *Brit. India* II. v. iii. 412 He proposed that it should no longer act under the orders of that Presidency. **1850** *Tait's Mag.* XVII. 366/1 Banking operations come necessarily under its sphere. **1888** *Contemp. Rev.* July 36 A person who is under the direction of amateurish clerks.

(*b*) *c* **950** *Lindisf. Gosp.* Matt. viii. 9 Ic monn amm under mæht. [*c* **1000** *Ags. Gosp.* ibid., Soð lice ic eom man under anwealde.] *a* **1000** *Colloq. Ælfric* in Wr.-Wülcker 102 Forðam cild ic eom under gyrda drohtneinde. *a* **1300** *Cursor M.* 12117, Þou est vnder [lagh] and þar-in bunden, Bot i am ar þe lagh was funden. *c* **1400** *Rom. Rose* 4923 That he may er he hennes pace Conteyne vndir obedience Thurgh the vertu of pacience. **1565** Cooper *Thesaurus*, *Subiugo*,.. to bryng vnder yoke. **1615** Jackson *Creed* iv. iii. ix. § 1. 348 In the Fort..of the soule, where it hath euery..desire as it were vnder shot, or at..command. **1667** Milton *P. L.* ii. 322 To remaine In strictest bondage,..Under th'inevitable curb. **1682** Dryden *Medal* Ep. Whigs, Laws under which we were born. **1784** P. Wright *New Bk. Martyrs* 806/1 He..was at last taken..by three Moss-troopers, under no discipline. **1832** Ht. Martineau *Life in Wilds* Pref. 3 How the universe was formed and under what rules its movements proceed. **1846** Raikes *Life of Brenton* 125 The Santa Dorothea frigate, then under orders for England. **1890** Ld. Esher in *Law Times Rep.* LXIII. 734/1 Whenever that official acts under the rules ordinarily regulating his duties. **1892** *Photogr. Ann.* II. 397 It must be obvious how much the light is under control.

**b.** With words denoting guidance or direction.

*Under correction*: see Correction 1 b.

*a* **1575** tr. *Pol. Verg. Eng. Hist.* (Camden) I. 108 Thei camen home under the conduite of their lodesmanne Fergusius. **1598** Hakluyt *Voy.* Ep. Ded. ₱ 3 As..our skill in Nauigation hath hitherto bene very much bettered..vnder the Admiraltie of your Lordship. **1632–** [see Conduct *sb.*[1] 1 *β*]. *a* **1700** in *Cath. Rec. Soc. Publ.* (1911) IX. 336 She was both loved & fear'd by those y[t] had y[e] happines to be under her conduct. **1711** *Spect.* No. 67 ₱ 6 My eldest Daughter..has for some time been under the Tuition of Monsieur Rigadoon. **1794** Mrs. Radcliffe *Myst. Udolpho* xxxi, She saw herself at the approach of night under his guidance, among wild and solitary mountains. **1827** Faraday *Chem. Manip.* xxi. 546 Unless this be done by the experimenter, or under his particular directions, it should be left untouched. **1885** *Law Times* 23 May 63/1 A fourth edition..has just appeared under the editorship of Mr. Charles Burney.

**c.** With words denoting or implying subjection to, or being the subject of, (*a*) some form of handling or treatment, (*b*) consideration, trial, or notice.

(*a*) **1535**, **1659** [see Hand *sb.* 35 c]. *a* **1670** Hacket *Abp. Williams* ii. (1693) 28 The Subject which is now under the Quill is the Bishop of Lincoln. **1706** E. Ward *Wooden World Diss.* (1708) 61 He may with Justice boast, that very few die under his hands. *a* **1719** Addison *Virg. Georg.* Wks. 1721 I. 258 That Poem, which lay so long under Virgil's correction, and had his last hand put to it. **1792** Cowper *Let.* 26 Jan., But no laurels are to be won by sitting patiently under the knife of a surgeon. **1837** Disraeli *Venetia* i. xvi, As the Doctor was under the operation of the barber. **1843** *Blackw. Mag.* LIV. 616, I left him under the hands of his valet. **1884** *Marshall's Tennis Cuts* 234 He is..now under medical treatment.

(*b*) **1652** Needham tr. *Selden's Mare Cl.* 2 As to what concerns the point of Law, this Question falls chiefly under debate. **1664** *Extr. St. Papers Friends* Ser. iii. (1912) 214, I have had them thrice under private examination. **1677** Earl Essex in *E. Papers* (Camden) II. 112 The throwing ye man overboard, for w[hi]ch ye Master..of the ship will be brought under question. **1737** *Gentl. Mag.* VII. 660/2 Let me next suppose the Payment now under our Consideration to be made to the Bank. **1780** *Mirror* No. 102, It is not the character itself that falls under my observation. **1827** Faraday *Chem. Manip.* xii. 278 Any number of parts by volume of the acid under trial. **1849** *Tait's Mag.* XVI. 163/2 The first judge who comes under our notice is William Fitz-Osborne. **1892** *Photogr. Ann.* II. 198 The subject under discussion has nothing to do with chemicals.

**d.** *Under the plough*, employed as arable land. So *under cultivation, tillage*, etc.

**1795** [see 6 b]. **1805** R. W. Dickson *Pract. Agric.* I. 296 Land..under an arable system of cultivation. *Ibid.* 314 Soils..under tillage. **1833** Ht. Martineau *Brooke Farm* iv, Lands that have been under the plough for hundreds of years. **1862** Ansted *Channel Isl.* i. iii. (ed. 2) 37 Of this area, about 10,000 acres are under cultivation.

**e.** *Under steam*, etc. (Cf. 5 c.)

**1839** *Civil Eng. & Arch. Jrnl.* II. 475/2 She can scarcely fail to attain an uncommon speed under steam. **1860**, **1873** [see Steam *sb.* 7 d]. **1883** *Law Times Rep.* XLIX. 332/1 About to round Blackwall Point under a port helm.

**14.** With words denoting or implying restraint, confinement, or safe keeping.

*a* **900** Cynewulf *Elene* 485 (Gr.), In byrʒenne [he] bidende wæs under þeosterlocan. *a* **1300–** [see Lock *sb.*[2] 1 b]. **13..–** [see Key *sb.*[1] 1 b]. *c* **1386–** [see Arrest *sb.*[1] 9 b, 10]. **1495** *Cov. Leet Bk.* 569 Þat they be putte vnder suertie fro session vnto session. **1611** Florio, *Sottogardia*, vnder guard, keeping or custody. **1629** Wadsworth *Pilgr.* viii. 90 He left mee alone.., lockt vnder seuen doores. **1645** Howell *Twelve Treat.* (1661) 338 Their faculties have a kind of ubiquitary freedom, though the body be never so under restraint. **1689** *Sc. Acts Parlt.* (1875) XII. 50/2 The petitioner was sent for to be brought to the meeting under a gaurd [*sic*]. **1737** in *10th Rep. Hist. MSS. Comm.* App. I. 488 While he was Under confinement He liv'd very magnificently. **1799** *Hull Advertiser* 17 Aug. 2/4 No officer could be landed, the ship being under quarantine. **1841** Dickens *B. Rudge* 4 Sent under a strong guard to the tower. **1847** [see Restraint *sb.* 2 d].

**b.** With words denoting an obligation, compact, or formal engagement: Subject to, bound or constrained (legally or morally) by.

**1456** Sir G. Haye *Law Arms* (S.T.S.) 103 Cristin men that ar duelland in the mistrowand menis housis under malis suld be lele to thair malaris. **1538** Starkey *England* i. iv. 115 Certayn landys were gyuen out..to inferyor personys..vnder such condycyon that [etc.]. *a* **1548** Hall *Chron., Hen. VI*, 98 b, My Lorde of Winchester..hath subscribed with his awne hande, under the worde of priestehod, to stande at the aduise..of the persones abouesaied. **1626** C. Potter tr. *Sarpi's Hist. Quarrels* 185 He had particular Commandement from the King his Master, to oblige him vnder the Word of a King, to a neere Vnion with the Republique. **1712** Steele *Spect.* No. 362 ₱ 1 All who vend Wines should be under oaths in that behalf. **1790** Paley *Horæ Paul.* xi. § 1 As he was also under a promise to the church of Philippi to see them. **1818** Cruise *Digest* (ed. 2) IV. 488 A covenant to renew a lease, under the same rent and covenants as those contained in the original lease. **1834** Dickens *Sk. Boz, Steam Excurs.*, Mr. Samuel, the eldest, was an attorney, and Mr. Alexander, the youngest, was under articles to his brother. **1848** Mrs. Carlyle *Lett.* (1883) II. 26 This time I am under engagement to go. **1861** M. Pattison *Ess.* (1889) I. 47 Every master was under an obligation..to keep an iron helmet and harness.

**15.** With reference to physical weight or pressure. (Orig. in literal sense.) Also in fig. context.

*a* **1300** *Cursor M.* 6830 If þou find.. Vnder birthin his beist ligand, Help him. *a* **1400** *New Test.* (Paues) 2 Peter ii. 16 He spak not as resonable man, but as a doume beste þat vnder synne was ȝoked. **1591** Spenser *Ruins of Rome* 161 Th' earth vnder her childrens weight did grone. **1611** Bible *Exod.* vi. 6, I will bring you out from vnder the burdens of the Egyptians. **1667** Milton *P. L.* xii. 539 So shall the World goe on,.. Under her own waight groaning. **1714** Addison *Spect.* No. 559 ₱ 7 They wandered up and down under the Pressure of their several Burthens. **1794** Mrs. Radcliffe *Myst. Udolpho* xxvi, Her reason seemed to totter under the intolerable weight. **1827** Faraday *Chem. Manip.* xv. 374 The glass vessels intended to retain gases under pressure. **1842** Loudon *Suburban Hort.* 346 The health of the tree must decline under the load of..imperfectly nourished fruit. **1891** T. Hardy *Tess* iii, The cradle-rockers,..under the weight of so many children,..were worn nearly flat.

**b.** With words denoting pains, penalties, or similar consequences: Subject to the risk or certainty of incurring or suffering. Sometimes *ellipt.*

*c* **1449** [see Pain *sb.*[1] 1 b]. **1560** [see Penalty 2 d]. **1599** Sandys *Europæ Spec.* (1632) 112 Whom they charge under an high degree of mortall sinne and damnation..to appeach even their neerest and dearest friends. **1632** Lithgow *Trav.* ii. 49 Neither may they stay..all night vnder the paine of imprisonment. **1635** Pagitt *Christianogr.* i. iii. 56 Vndoubted verities, and to be believed under the Popes curse. **1665** in *Extr. St. Papers Friends* Ser. iii. (1912) 231 [They] shalbe vnder such penalties as the law may inflict vpon them. **1711** Steele *Spect.* No. 66 ₱ 5 Under Pain of never having an Husband. **1737** Challoner *Cath. Chr. Instr.* (1753) 123 Which is the Case of all who refuse..to comply with any Part of their Duty, to which they are obliged under mortal Sin. **1756** C. Lucas *Ess. Waters* I. 154 Of these, no subject was permitted to drink under severe penalties. **1820** Milner *Suppl. Mem. Eng. Cath.* App. 305 An obligation..under the guilt of a grievous sin. **1845** Lingard *Anglo-Saxon Ch.* II. ix. 67 He..forbade his sons, under their father's malediction, to molest them.

**c.** With words denoting something oppressive, distressing, or restrictive of free action: In the condition of suffering from, being afflicted or distressed by, etc.

Cf. the use of OE. *under* with words meaning 'grip or 'grasp'. With somewhat weakened force, the sense occurs frequently with certain words, as *contribution, difficulty, disadvantage, necessity, sentence.*

**1382** Wyclif *Gal.* iii. 10 Who euere ben of the workis of lawe, ben vndir curs. **1512** *Reg. Privy Seal Scotl.* I. 365/2 Thai stand now under accusatioun for crime of tresoun. **1569** *Reg. Privy Council Scot.* I. 662 [He] ressavit fra ilk ane..the sowme of thre pundis, and yit hes thame under danger of the rest. **1644–** [see Contribution 1 b]. **1663** J. Spencer *Prodigies* (1665) 335 The more modern Rabbins were under a despair of ..equalling the Traditional..Commentators upon their Law. **1688** Collier *Several Disc.* (1725) 369 The Publishers of it ..lay under Discountenance and Persecution from the civil Powers. **1711** *Spect.* No. 116 ₱ 7 If I was under any Concern, it was on the Account of the poor Hare. *Ibid.* ₱ 8 A noble Soul struggling under innumerable Pains and Distempers. **1750** Johnson *Rambler* No. 6 ₱ 6 Those that suffer under the dreadful symptom of canine madness. **1779** *Mirror* No. 8, It was with regret that the Editor found himself under the necessity of abridging the following letter. **1806–7** J. Beresford *Miseries Hum. Life* ii. x, If..it may afford you any consolation under the recollection of a calamity so dreadful. **1849** Macaulay *Hist. Eng.* v. I. 612 *note*, Wade was writing under the dread of the halter. **1869** Freeman *Norm. Conq.* III. xiv. 360 Harold was under the ban of Rome.

**d.** With reference to mental impressions: Possessed, swayed, or affected by.

**1667** Milton *P. L.* i. 313 Under amazement of their hideous change. **1683** [see Mistake *sb.* 2 a]. **1759** [see Impression 6 b]. **1779** *Mirror* No. 16, A man under the impressions I have described, will be led to look into himself. **1842** Lover *Handy Andy* xlvi, That Tom wouldn't hurt a fly, only 'under a mistake'. **1849** Macaulay *Hist. Eng.* v. I. 662 Evidence was produced which proved that Goodenough was also under the influence of personal enmity. **1875** Jowett *Plato* (ed. 2) I. 395 Are you under the impression that they will be better cared for..here? **1885** [see Misapprehension].

**e.** *ellipt.* = Under the influence of.

**1884** Thompson *Tumours of Bladder* 95 Some phosphatic deposits, which were removed..under ether. **1889** *Science-Gossip* XXV. 220/1 A fixed oil..is obtained from the seeds by expression under heat. **1892** Hugh Lane *Differ. Rheum. Dis.* (ed. 2) 72, I have seen these cases frequently treated.. under chloroform.

**III.** In senses implying that one thing is covered by, or included in, another.

**16.** Denoting that a thing is presented or observed in a certain form or aspect.

See also Kind *sb.* 13 b, Species 2.

*a* **1000** *Guthlac* 682 (Gr.), Eom ic þara twelfa sum, þe he ʒetreoweste under monnes hiw mode ʒelufade. *c* **1320** *Cast. Love* 657 Oþer God nis þen he þat..vnder vre wede vre kynde nom. *c* **1450** *Myrr. our Ladye* 189 This hympne ys spoken vnder ful fayre and darke examples. **1561** Rastell *Confut. Ivelles Serm.* (1565) 128 The people receiued under both kindes. **1586** in *Cath. Rec. Soc. Publ.* (1911) IX. 171 At w[ch] time vi or vii of the said company did communicate ..by receaving the sacrament under one kind only. **1659** Pearson *Creed* xii. 780 Life eternall may be looked upon under three considerations; as Initiall, as Partial, and as Perfectional. **1663** Bp. Patrick *Parab. Pilgr.* xxxvii, Bidding him to take great heed lest under the guise of this Humility..he proved unthankful for Gods favours. **1712** Addison *Spect.* No. 419 ₱ 7 When the Author represents any Passion, Appetite, Virtue or Vice, under a Visible Shape. **1713** — *Guard.* No. 101, The painter has represented his most Christian Majesty under the figure of Jupiter. **1774** Goldsm. *Nat. Hist.* VIII. 26 Some insects continue under the form of an aurelia not above ten days. **1817** Jas. Mill *Brit. India* II. v. vii. 608 Under the ignominious light in which imprisonment is regarded by the Indians. **1870** J. H. Newman *Gram. Assent* ii. viii. 307 We must contemplate the God of our conscience as a Living Being..under the aspect of this or that attribute. **1879** E. Waterton *Pietas Mariana Brit.* 225 The several types under which our Ladye was represented in England.

**b.** With words implying a specious or deceptive appearance. Also *ellipt.* = 'under the pretence of'.

See Colour *sb.*[1] 12 d, Cover *sb.* 3 d, Covert *sb.* 2 c, Guise *sb.* 5 b, Pretence *sb.* 3 b, 4, 6, Pretext *sb.*[1], Semblant *sb.* 2, Show *sb.*[1] 7 c, Veil *sb.*[1] 5.

**1607** SHAKS. *Timon* III. iii. 33 Like those that vnder hotte ardent zeale, would set whole Realmes on fire.

**c.** With suggestion of one thing being hidden or disguised beneath another: Beneath the form, guise, or concealment of.

*a* **1340** HAMPOLE *Psalter* cxxxix. 5 Þe snare is endles pyne, þat þai hid vndire delit of syn. **1382** WYCLIF *Pref. St. Jerome* vii. (1850) 70/1 Vndir name of Nynyue, [he] tellith helthe to Gentils. *c* **1400** *Destr. Troy* 11489 He thoght his falshed to feyne, vndur faire wordes. **1592** KYD *Sp. Trag.* III. x. 22 Vnder fained iest Are things concealde that els would breed vnrest. **1723** *Pres. St. Russia* II. 46 The Vagulitzes..have their own Language, and worship the Devil under their Idols. **1779** *Mirror* No. 27, A..friend of mine, whose real name I shall conceal under that of Wentworth. **1854** MRS. JAMESON *Commonpl. Bk.* (1877) 1 Extreme vanity sometimes hides under the garb of ultra modesty. **1857** PUSEY *Doctr. Real Presence* i. 156 A sacramental invisible presence of the Body and Blood of Christ, under the Bread and Wine.

**d.** *Under the name* (etc.) *of*, = by the name of. (See NAME *sb.* 13.)

**1641–2** LAUD *Diary* 20 Feb., There came a tall man to me, under the name of Mr. Hunt. **1662** *Extr. St. Papers Friends* Ser. II. (1911) 150 Seuerall Persons who are under the names of Quakers and other names of separacion now in the Goales of London and Middlesex. **1744** BERKELEY *Siris* § 268 The Egyptians..had..even deified her under the name of Isis. **1780** *Mirror* No. 80, The authors of those little essays which appear in the learned world under the title of *Advertisements*. **1817** JAS. MILL *Brit. India* II. v. ix. 704 Under the stile and title of a commutation, an additional window tax..was imposed. **1843** PEREIRA *Food & Diet* 120 Hard confectionary, sold under the names of Lozenges, Brilliants, Pipe, Rock, Comfits, Nonpareils. **1876** *Beneden's Anim. Parasites* 75 Naturalists had recognized some crustaceans under the name of *Ancei*.

†**e.** = In (a manner or fashion). *Obs. rare.*

**1523** in *Gentl. Mag.* (1785) II. 939/1 I..dyd christen the same childe under this manner. **1532** TINDALE *Exp. Matt.* v. (1550) 22 With greate payne they can suffry their grosse synnes to be rebuked vnder a fassion, as in a parable.

**17.** Denoting inclusion in a group, category, class, etc. † *Under* (*them*) *all*, in all, altogether.

*c* **960** ÆTHELWOLD *Rule St. Benet* xvii. (Schröer) 40 Ælc [psalm] on sundron and nan under anum gloria. *a* **1225** *Ancr. R.* 222 Þe oðer, & te ueorðe [temptation], ualleð under þe uttre. *c* **1290** *S. Eng. Leg.* I. 59/176 [Francis, Giles, and Bernard] and sethþe oþur þreo, So þat vnder heom alle sixe freres to-gadere weren i-brouȝt. **1297** R. GLOUC. (Rolls) 6998 Þe king..ȝef al so Tueie gode maners sein swithin þer to, þat wolde be tuenty vnder al. **1576** FLEMING *Panopl. Epist.* 352 *margin*, Under that word: lightening, thunder, ..mysts, fogges, earthquakes, &c. are to be understoode. **1585** T. WASHINGTON tr. *Nicholay's Voy.* IV. iii. 115 b, The Persians..whiche went vnder the armie of Darius. **1635** PAGITT *Christianogr.* I. ii. (1636) 43 Under these eight provinces all France is conteined. *a* **1662** HEYLYN *Cosmogr.* III. (1674) 173/2 Principal Cities of the whole at this present time under the notion of Cathay, are [etc.]. **1676** *Office Clerk of Assize* F iij, They shall speak without Oath unless the Fact be under Felony. **1711** ADDISON *Spect.* No. 21 ¶ 2 The rest are comprehended under the Subalterns. **1756** P. BROWNE *Jamaica* p. xxxiii, I have..distributed the species under their proper genera. **1793** SMEATON *Edystone L.* § 291 The fitting or adapting the parts of matter together, comes under no calculation in point of time. **1853** *Our Coal-Fields & Coal-Pits* 221 Many matters which would come under this head have already been incidentally mentioned. **1885** *Times* 6 Apr. 7 The owners of travelling booths and circuses come strictly under the class.

**b.** Denoting occurrence in a particular section or article of a literary work.

**1589** HAKLUYT *Voy.* To Rdr. ¶ 6 Vnder this title thou shalt first finde the old northerne Nauigations of our Brittish Kings. **1728** CHAMBERS *Cycl.* s.v. *Substraction*, Write the less Number under the greater,..as we have directed under *Addition*. **1783** *Encycl. Brit.* (ed. 2) X. 8307/2 Under the article Natural History, Sect. I. it is observed, that [etc.]. **1823** SCORESBY *Jrnl.* 280 The day of the present voyage under which these remarks are introduced. **1846** *Penny Cycl.* Suppl. II. 431 As explained under *House*,..it is frequently necessary [etc.]. **1879** E. WATERTON *Pietas Mariana Brit.* 221 As I have mentioned in the Series under Stowe.

**c.** *Under one*, in one, united(ly), conjointly, together, at one time. *Obs.* exc. *dial.*

Cf. Du. *ondereen*, together, pell-mell.

**1596** NASHE *Saffron Walden* Ep. Ded. B ij b, And so [I] leave them..outright to hang, draw, and quarter them al vnder one. **1611** COTGR. s.v. *Chemin, Tout d'un chemin*, all vnder one. **1642** D. ROGERS *Naaman* 170 So that he seeks his owne and his Masters advantage both under one. *a* **1667** C. HOOLE *School-Colloquies* (1688) 105 Come, I pray you, and you shall sup with us all under one. **1839–** in *Eng. Dial. Dict.* s.v. *Under* 2.

**d.** Of figures or angles in relation to the lines determining their size.

**1570** BILLINGSLEY *Euclid* II. def. i. 61 Rectangle parallelogrames which are comprehended vnder equal lines are equal the one to the other. **1660** BARROW *Euclid* I. prop. xlviii, The angle comprehended under those two other sides of the triangle. **1764** [see COMPREHEND *v.* 10]. **1798** HUTTON *Course Math.* II. 124 The rectangles under the sum and difference of the ordinates. **1854** TOMLINSON *Arago's Astron.* 167 The angle under which we see objects.

**18.** With words denoting protection, care, or benevolent interest.

See also AUSPICE 3, PROTECTION 1 b. To this sense may be assigned the apologetic phrases *under favour* (FAVOUR *sb.* 3 a), *leave*, *pardon*.

**971** *Blickl. Hom.* 41 Ne þurfon ȝe wenan þæt ȝe bæt orceape sellon, bæt ȝe under Drihtnes borh syllab. *c* **1230** *Hali Meid.* 7 Se seli sikernesse as ha was in, & mahte beon under Godes warde. *c* **1375** *Sc. Leg. Saints* iii. (*Andrew*) 943 Vndir ȝour proteccione to luf in contemplacione. *c* **1400** [see CARE *sb.*[1] 4]. **1470–85** [see SAFE-CONDUCT *sb.* 1]. **1550** *Reg. Privy Council Scot.* I. 84 Thair is diverse assurit personis.. sittis under assurance duelland within the boundes of the Merse. **1596** *Edward III*, v. i. 111 Vnder safe conduct of the Dolphins seale. **1692** E. WALKER tr. *Epictetus' Mor.* xxxvii, Methinks they've given enough, in that you live Under their prudent Care. **1711** ADDISON *Spect.* No. 106 ¶ 4 My worthy Friend has put me under the particular Care of his Butler. **1768** [W. DONALDSON] *Life Sir B. Sapskull* I. x. 105 To..institute an independant academy, under the auspices of that great name. **1803** SCOTT *Let.* in *Lockhart* (1837) I. xi. 392 The *mode* of telling the story approved by the French minstrel, under the authority of his Tomas. **1844** MRS. BROWNING *Drama of Exile* 32, I hold that Eden is impregnable Under thy keeping. **1866** [see PATRONAGE 3]. **1885** *Law Rep.* 14 Q.B.D. 867 Even if the plaintiff succeeds the action may have been defended under good advice.

**19.** Denoting a state or condition (frequently one imposed by implied circumstances).

In later use common with *circumstances* (see CIRCUMSTANCE *sb.* 4) and *conditions*. In parenthetical phrases, as *under these circumstances*, the sense passes into 'having regard to', 'taking account of'. For *under way* or *weigh* see the sbs.

*c* **1200** ORMIN Ded. 9 Þurrh þatt witt hafenn takenn ba An reȝhellboc to follȝhenn, Unnderr kanunnkess had & lif. *Ibid.* 10530 Unnderr Crisstenndom, & unnderr læfe o Criste. *c* **1205** LAY. 395 Assaracus heuede enne broþer, þe wes under wedlac iboren. **1428** *Munim. de Melros* (Bann. Cl.) 519, I wes requerit..for to wytnes vnder wryt þe thyng at wes determynyt befor me in iugement. **1490** CAXTON *Eneydos* xxvi. 93 Thou haste deliuerde me my traytour & peruerse enmye, vnder hope of loue & benyuolence. **1564** *Reg. Privy Council Scot.* I. 276 James Barry..quha allegeit him to be undir the King of Denmarkis wageis. **1581** RICH *Farew.* (1846) 58 She beyng under covert barne, your obligation is unpleadable. **1662** STILLINGFL. *Orig. Sacræ* II. v. § 1 A meer seducer was to be stoned to death under sufficient testimony. **1668** PEPYS *Diary* 7 July, Because of Fleet Bridge being under rebuilding. **1689** in *Sc. Acts Parlt.* (1875) XII. 76/1 Such persones as he hes already put under baile. **1712** ADDISON *Spect.* No. 349 ¶ 7 He died under a fixed and settled Hope of Immortality. **1720** WELTON *Suffer. Son of God* I. viii. 200 All things here are under a perpetual vicissitude and alteration. **1780** M. MADAN *Thelyph.* II. 61 Augustus rejected the testament of a man who died under a state of celibacy. **1817** JAS. MILL *Brit. India* II. v. vii. 607 He knew, under the sentiments which prevailed at home, by what a slender and precarious tenure he enjoyed his place. **1855** BAIN *Senses & Int.* II. i. § 11 The physical state of a muscle under contraction may be inferred from the details already given. **1884** DUNCKLEY in *Manch. Exam.* 26 May 6/2 Under the ballot it is as easy to vote as to pay a morning call.

**b.** *Under trust*, in a state of supposed safety. *Obs.* exc. *arch.*

**1545** in Tytler *Hist. Scot.* (1864) II. 349 The Lord Maclanis fader was cruellie murdressit under traist, in his bed. **1589** R. ROBINSON *Gold. Mirr.* (1851) 5 Then Mischief calde for treason vndertrust; Helpe now (quoth he) or els I am o're-throwen. **1609, 1818** [see TRUST *sb.* 5 a].

**20.** Denoting participation in the authoritative or confirmatory effect of a seal, signature, etc.: Authorized, warranted, or attested by.

See also HAND *sb.* 35 d, SEAL *sb.*[2] 1 c, SIGNET *sb.* 2, 3, SIGN-MANUAL 1.

**1338** R. BRUNNE *Chron.* (1810) 288 He kept his castels, his vitaile, his mone, Undere þe kyng seales. *a* **1400–50** *Alexander* 1845, I send to ȝowe my sawe vndir my sele wreten. **1417** [see SIGNET *sb.* 3]. **1460** in *Rec. City of Norwich* (1910) II. 94 If þe cloth be tokened and founde defauty under þe tokene. **1471** K. EDW. IV in *Rep. Hist. MSS. Comm., Var. Coll.* IV. 209 Yeven undir oure signet at oure Paleis of Westminster the xixth day of December. **1546** LANGLEY tr. *Pol. Verg. de Invent.* VII. iv. 135 b, Gregorie the nynth.. canonised Dominicke, and by his Bulle vnder Lead, allowed him for a sainct. **1551** in Feuillerat *Revels Edw. VI* (1914) 62 A warrante vnder the kinges Maiesties owne handes. **1592** in J. Morris *Troub. Cath. Forefathers* (1877) 23 And this averred by writing under all or most of his neighbours' hands. **1613** PURCHAS *Pilgrimage* (1614) 215 The bill of diuorce is.. deliuered to the woman before three credible witnesses, vnder their hands and seales. **1687** *Assur. Abby Lands* 120 Altho' we have empowered thee..by divers of our Letters, as well made under-Lead as in the Form of Breves. **1765–8** [see SIGNATURE *sb.* 1]. **1838** W. BELL *Dict. Law Scot.* 889 Under this seal commissions of tutory, gifts of bastardy,..are passed.

†**b.** *Under* (*the*) *name of*, = in the name of. (See NAME *sb.* 11 c.) *Obs.*

**1445** tr. *Claudian* in *Anglia* XXVIII. 265 His shrewde seruauntis..Pretendyng evir the Kyngis title..vndir his name þe wrongid. **1535** COVERDALE *Zech.* xiii. 3 Thou shalt dye, for thou speakest lyes vnder the name off the Lorde. **1585** T. WASHINGTON tr. *Nicholay's Voy.* I. x. 12 b, [He] coyned money vnder his name. **1596** SHAKS. *Tam. Shr.* IV. iii. 12 He does it vnder name of perfect loue.

**c.** Implying a statement or suggestion as to the authorship of a work.

**1662** STILLINGFL. *Orig. Sacræ* II. i. § 3 Who would ever undertake to prove..that Euclide was the undoubted Author of the *Geometry* under his name? **1712** P. METCALFE *Life St. Winefride* (1917) 5 Altho' the mention'd Author publish'd his Tomes under the Borrow'd Names of Alford, alias Griffith. **1802** MAR. EDGEWORTH *Moral T.*, *Forester* xvi, Our hero.. inserted his compositions, under a fictitious signature, in his master's newspaper.

**d.** = In accordance with (some regulative power or principle).

**1779** *Ann. Reg.*, *Chron.* 216/2 Numbers of them had been long supersedable, or intitled to their discharges under insolvent acts. **1867** FROUDE *Short Stud.* Ser. I. I. 47 Under this edict..more than fifty thousand human beings..were deliberately murdered. **1874** *Nairne Peerage Evidence* 169 That is the lady who was examined under a commission from this House? **1884** *Manch. Exam.* 16 Feb. 4/6 The first contested county election under the provisions of the Corrupt Practices Act.

**IV.** In senses which imply falling below a certain standard or level.

**21.** Beneath or below in point of worth or dignity.

*c* **888** K. ÆLFRED *Boeth.* xxxiii. § 5 Under hire selfre hio bið þonne, ðonne hio lufað þas eorðlican þing. *Ibid.* xxxvii. § 4 Hiora yfelnes awirpð hi under þa menniscan ȝecynd. *a* **1340** HAMPOLE *Ps.* xvii. 40 Til þa þat ere vndire me, þat is, ill men vndire me in merit bifor god. **1548** UDALL, etc. *Erasm. Par. Matt.* 100 b, This they thought a goodly prayse, although that it was farre vnder his maiestie. **1598** GRENEWEY *Tacitus, Ann.* III. i. 63 Tiberius and Augusta abstained from mourning in publicke: iudging it a thing vnder their maiestie.

**b.** Below the rank, standing, or level of.

**1610** B. JONSON *Alch.* II. vi, No, sir, shee 'll neuer marry Vnder a knight. **1632** MASSINGER & FIELD *Fatal Dowry* IV. i, Fight with Romont? No, I 'll not fight under a lord. **1650** FULLER *Pisgah* IV. vii. 123 Nothing under an Infinite can expleat and satiate the immortall minde of man. **1711** ADDISON *Spect.* No. 122 ¶ 9 It was too great an Honour for any Man under a Duke. **1822** LAMB *Elia* I. *Distant Correspondents*, No person, under a diviner, can..conduct a correspondence at such arm's length. **1847** L. HUNT *Men, Women, & B.* II. vii. 96 He uttered nothing under a gentility or a dulcitude.

**22.** Below, less, or fewer than (a specified number or amount).

*c* **1380** WYCLIF *Last Age Ch.* (1840) 30 Þat we ben undir þe hundrid ȝeere of .x. lettre I schewe schortly by Bede. **1530** TINDALE *Pract. Prelates* H iij, The Emperours host was vnder xx. thousande. **1557** NORTH *Gueuara's Diall Pr.* II. xi. 95 b, There was a lawe amongeste them, that no man should marye under three wiues. **1590** SIR J. SMYTH *Disc. Weapons* 6 b, In case they should compose smaller bands of 300 to an Ensigne, or vnder that number. **1601** R. JOHNSON *Kingd. & Commw.* (1603) 154 They receiue, some 1000. some 80. rubles a yeare, none vnder 70. **1664** P. HENRY *Diaries & Lett.* (1882) 155 That interdict lasted under 5. yeares. **1699** R. L'ESTRANGE *Erasm. Colloq.* (1725) 174 Sometimes ten, sometimes twelve, but never under six. **1745** H. WALPOLE *Lett.* (1857) I. 406 Repeated accounts make them under five thousand. ? **1800** WORDSW. *Andrew Jones* 28 Under half-a-crown, What a man finds is all his own. **1832** MACAULAY in Trevelyan *Life* (1876) I. 287 The voters are under 4,000 in number. **1855** — *Hist. Eng.* iv. IV. 624 The weight..proved to be under one hundred and fourteen thousand ounces.

**b.** Below, not having attained to (a specified age).

*c* **1400** MAUNDEV. (1839) xxvii. 278 The faireste Damyseles, that myghte ben founde undir the Age of 15 Zere. **1565** COOPER *Thesaurus* s.v. *Minor*, Vnder .xxv. yeres of age. **1570–4** BP. COX *Injunct.* in 2nd *Rep. Ritual Comm.* (1868) 406/2 Their chyldren and seruauntes..beyng of sixe yeres of age, and vnder twentie. **1658** HARRINGTON *Prerog. Pop. Govt.* Wks. (1700) 335 It is provided..that no man under thirty years of Age be capable of Magistracy. **1692** O. WALKER *Grk. & Rom. Hist.* 9 Then was Augustus under nineteen years old. **1729** JACOB *Law Dict.*, *Nonage*,..is all the Time of a Person's being under the Age of One and twenty; and, in a special Sense, where one is under Fourteen, as to Marriage, &c. **1825** T. HOOK *Sayings* Ser. II. II. 247 He is *under* fifty-seven. **1885** *Law Rep.* 10 P.D. 189 Till their only child should attain twenty-one, or die under that age.

**c.** At or for a less sum or lower price than (that specified).

*c* **1430** LYDG. *Min. Poems* (Percy Soc.) 107 'Thou scapst not here,' quod he, 'under ij. pence'. **1496** *Act 12 Hen. VII*, c. 6 They be sold far under the Price that they be worth. **1583** STUBBES *Anat. Abus.* II. Mi, You will not sell a sermon vnder a roiall, or a noble. **1592** *Arden of Feversham* II. ii. 76 But, were my consent to giue againe, we would not do it vnder ten pound more. **1712** STEELE *Spect.* No. 362 ¶ 1 They can have no advice for him under a Guinea. **1733** TULL *Horse-Hoeing Husb.* 142 *note*, Wheat was under Three Shillings a Bushel. **1831** JAMES *Phil. Augustus* III. i, I should suppose they would never free a knight of his renown under a ransom of ten thousand crowns.

**d.** In less time than (that specified).

**1632** J. HAYWARD tr. *Biondi's Eromena* 114 Great Fleets, which cannot be rigg'd under a great deale of time. **1639** W. MOUNTAGU in *Buccleuch MSS.* (Hist. MSS. Comm.) I. 280 We..can get none, neither can any be made under three weeks' time. **1711** ADDISON *Spect.* No. 102 ¶ 4 Flirts and Vibrations [of the fan]..that are seldom learned under a Month's Practice. **1726** LEONI *Alberti's Archit.* I. 29 Cato advises to dig the Stone in Summer..., and not to use it under two Years. **1728** FIELDING *Love in Sev. Masques* I. v, I shall hardly reduce it to any tolerable consistency under a fort-night's course of acids.

**e.** With less than; of less size, depth, etc., than.

**1570** FOXE *A. & M.* (ed. 2) I. 321/2 For commonly he neuer rode vnder a 1500 horses of Chaplaynes, Priestes, and other seruyng men waytyng vpon hym. **1702** *Eng. Theophrast.* 15 They will scarce believe that two and two make four, under a demonstration from Euclid. **1719–20** SWIFT *To Yng. Clergym.* Wks. 1727 II. II. 12, I remember several young men in this town, who could never leave the pulpit under half a dozen conceits. **1795** *Act 35 Geo. III*, c. 20 Sch. A, Ufers..under eight Inches square. **1867** SMYTH *Sailor's Word-bk.*, *Hand-lead*, a small lead..for sounding in rivers or harbours under 20 fathoms. **1883** *Rep. Channel Tunnel Comm.* App. Case li. 546 Barbarous orders..to sink every Spanish ship under 100 tons.

**f.** *ellipt.*, esp. in *and under*, *or under*, placed after statements of size, price, etc.

**1482** in *Eng. Hist. Rev.* XXV. 122 The firste and leeste soorte is of vj. ynchesse in lenghte and vndre. **1495** *Act 11 Hen. VII*, c. 61 § 1 To lette and demyse fermes ther for the terme of vij yere and undir. **1526** TINDAL *Matt.* ii. 16 All the chyldren,..as many as were two yere old and vnder. **1576** *Act 18 Eliz.* c. 6 In good Wheate after vjs. viijd. the Quarter or under. *c* **1580** in *Eng. Hist. Rev.* July (1914) 521 Yf you will by 100 Ballettes of woade together they will asshewre it to be good; yf you by under you shall bye it at your owne adventure. **1644** G. PLATTES in *Hartlib's Legacy* (1655) 211 When Barley is at two shillings the bushel, or under. **1670** in 12*th Rep. Hist. MSS. Comm.* App. V. 15 Courser [hangings]..your Honour may be served with from Flanders, att 18s. per stick or under. **1708** *Lond. Gaz.* No. 4422/7 The Commodore appear'd to be a Ship of 50 Guns, ..and the rest of 20 and under. **1797** *Encycl. Brit.* (ed. 3)

XVII. 432/1 Courses and topsails..for 44 gun ships and under. **1803** BEDDOES *Hygëia* XI. 40 Dr. C...estimates the infecting distance of patients in the plague at a foot or under. **1911** JACQUES in *36th Prov. Meeting Law Soc.* 263 Leaving property worth only £500 or under.

**23. a.** *Under age* (or † *years*), below the (legal) age of majority.

**1590** SPENSER *F. Q.* II. x. 64 Three sonnes he dying left, all vnder age. **1603** G. OWEN *Pembrokeshire* (1892) 22 William, who was then onder age. **1617** MORYSON *Itin.* I. 274 The Lords of Eriskin..vse to haue the keeping of the Prince of Scotland, being vnder yeeres. **1632** SHERWOOD, Under-yeares, *mineur, en bas age*. **1765–8** ERSKINE *Inst. Law Scot.* I. vii. § 1 But minority..includes all under age, whether pupils or *puberes*. **1821** KEATS *Cap & Bells* xxi, This was his page,.. Sent as a present, while yet under age, From the Viceroy of Zanguebar. **1843** JARMAN *Wills* (1881) I. xiv. 446 Under the old law..personalty was..disposable by the will of a person under age.

**b.** Below (a certain standard).

See also MARK *sb.*[1] 12 c, PAR *sb.*[1] 3 b, PROOF *sb.* 11.

**1615** W. LAWSON *Country Housew. Gard.* (1623) 30 Your graffe..will grow but to small purpose,..and lightly it will be vnder growth. **1661** WALTON *Angler* (ed. 3) ii. 52 So many Nets and Fish, that are under the Statute size. **1748** [see PROOF *sb.* 11]. **1799** COLERIDGE *Lett.* (1895) 271 The frost..was 20 degrees under the freezing point. **1825** J. NEAL *Bro. Jonathan* I. 364 Poor fatty! you know he's rather under par. **1857** MILLER *Elem. Chem., Org.* 121 If the spirit burned off and left the powder damp, it was considered under proof. **1875** E. C. STEDMAN *Victorian Poets* 275 The statement of Bulwer's preface is under the truth.

**c.** *Under* (one's) *breath*, in a low voice, in a whisper.

**1832** [see BREATH *sb.* 9 b]. **1883** WHITELAW *Sophocles, Oedipus Col.* 489 Pray, under breath, not lifting up thy voice. **1898** 'MERRIMAN' *Roden's Corner* xv. 155 'Oh, hang!' she added,..under her breath.

**V.** † **24.** Among. *Obs. rare.*

*c* **893** K. ÆLFRED *Oros.* IV. x. 196 Þa ne mehton þa senatus nænne consul under him findan þe dorste on Ispanie.. ʒefaran. *c* **1205** LAY. 915 Wet speke ʒe kempen vnder eou alle?

† **25.** During; in the time of. *Obs.*

Also *Sc.* † *under ane time*, at the same time.

*c* **893** K. ÆLFRED *Oros.* I. x. 46 Þa under þæm ʒewinne hie ʒenamon friþ wið þa wæpnedmen. **971** *Blickl. Hom.* 35 Þæt we sceolan under þæm feowertiʒeoþan ʒerime..syllan þone teoþan dæl ure worldspeda. *c* **1205** LAY. 32028 Vnder þissen uare-coste he sumnede ferde of alle þane monne þat he bi-ʒeten mihte. *c* **1425** *Eng. Conq. Ireland* 8 Vnder that tyme, Robert Steunes-son hym dyght to wend in-to Irland. **1533** BELLENDEN *Livy* I. ix. (S.T.S.) I. 51 Legatis war send on athir side vnder ane tyme desiring redres of all displeseris. **1597** J. PAYNE *Royal Exch.* 5 Now ys the tyme vnder lyfe to help one another; but when..breathe ys gon, neyther angells nor Apostles can geve any help. **1662** STILLINGFL. *Orig. Sacræ* II. vi. § 8 Not that these things should really be under Gospell times. *a* **1670** SPALDING *Troub. Chas. I* (1851) II. 396 Wnder speiking this Williame Forbes schootis the gentilman with ane pistoll deid.

† **b.** With demonstrative pronouns: During this or that time; meantime, meanwhile. *Obs.*

*c* **893** K. ÆLFRED *Oros.* II. ii. 66 He..him ʒehet ðæt he his rice wið hiene dælan wolde, & hiene under ðæm ofsloʒ. *a* **900** *O. E. Chron.* (Parker MS.) an. 876, Hie þa under þam hie nihtes bestælon..into Escanceaster. *a* **1122** *Ibid.* (Laud MS.) an. 1046, Ða wearð hit under þam þet þam cynge com word [etc.]. *c* **1205** LAY. 6433 Wnder þon hær com tidinde. *Ibid.* 9660 Vnder þan comen tiðende. *a* **1225** *Leg. Kath.* 1858 Under þis com þe þurs Maxence..aʒein to his kineburh. **1297** R. GLOUC. (Rolls) 2503 Þer come out of germaynie vnder þat..ssipes eiʒtetene. *a* **1300** *Floriz & Bl.* 635 The children awoken under thon.

**Under** (*v*·ndəɹ), *adv.* Forms: 1– under, 3–7 vnder (6 *Sc.* wnder), 4–5 vndyr, 5 vn-, undir, -dre, undur, owndir. [OE. *under*, = OS. *undar* etc.: see prec.]

**1.** Below, down below, beneath.

*Beowulf* 1417 Wæter under stod, dreoriʒ and ʒedrefed. *Ibid.* 2213 Stiʒ under læʒ eldum uncuð. *a* **900** *O.E. Martyrol.* 5 May 76 Se dæl þære circean..þær þæs hælendes fotlastas sindon under. *c* **1000** ÆLFRIC *Saints' Lives* IV. 393 He..het þa..fyr under betan. *c* **1250** *Gen. & Ex.* 3188 Moyses it folwede ðider it flet, And stod ðor ðe graue under let [= lay]. **13..** *Cursor M.* 377 (Gött.), He wroʒt..þe sky..wid watir schinand als cristall, þat es on hey, þat es vnder. **1390** GOWER *Conf.* I. 173 And under al aboute he seth The faire lusti floures springe. *c* **1400** MAUNDEV. (Roxb.) iv. 12 Men may see þare þe erthe of þe toumbe..stirre and moue, as þer ware a qwikke thing vnder. **1422** YONGE tr. *Secreta Secret.* 241 Yf the lyght mettis vndyr be, whan hit is defiet. **1535** COVERDALE *Gen.* xlix. 25 Helped..with blessynges of heauen from aboue, with blessinges of yᵉ depe yᵗ lyeth vnder. **1591** SPENSER *Vis. World's Vanity* 65 A sword-fish..in his throat him pricking softly vnder. **1648** CRASHAW *Poems* (1904) 152 Storme and Thunder Would sit under, And keepe silence round about thee. **1819** W. TENNANT *Papistry Storm'd* (1827) 48 At anes the bells baith up and under Begoud to rattle on like thunder. **1820** SHELLEY *The Cloud* 10, I wield the flail of the lashing hail, And whiten the green plains under.

**b.** With verbs expressing or implying movement.

† *To look under*, to look down (LOOK *v.* 44).

*a* **1120** *O. E. Chron.* (Laud MS.) an. 1083, Þa wreccan munecas laʒon onbuton þam weofode & sume crupon under. *c* **1400** *Destr. Troy* 1297 Þen the Troiens..Gird euyn to the Grekes with a grym fare,..Wondit of þe wightist, warpide hom vnder. **1539** BIBLE I *Kings* xviii. 23 Let them..laye hym on wodd, and put no fyre vnder. **1608** SYLVESTER *Du Bartas* II. iv. *Schism* 1012 Like as a Roach, or Ruff, or Gudgeon..Frisks to and fro, aloft and under dives. **1818** BYRON *Juan* I. cliii, There is the closet, there the toilet, there The antechamber—search them under, over. **1846** SOYER *Cookery* 176 Saw the rib bones asunder in the middle; pass your knife under.

**2.** In special senses: **a.** Beneath the rider.

*c* **1100** *O. E. Chron.* (MS. D) an. 1079, His hors wearð under of-scoten.

**b.** Lower down on a page, etc.

Chiefly in combs., as *under-mentioned, -named, -specified*; cf. also HEREUNDER *adv.* † *To seal under*: see SEAL *v.*[1] 4.

*c* **1362** [see UNDERWRITTEN *ppl. a.*]. **1474** *Cov. Leet Bk.* 390 These ben the names vnder folowyng of the Collectours. **1786** BURNS *Inventory* 74 This list,..I wrote it, Day an' date as under notit. **1892** *Photogr. Ann.* II. 257, I have designed a slide as under.

**c.** Below the garments; on the inner side of a garment.

*c* **1400** *Brut* clxxviii. 199 He..smote him wyþ a knyf; but þe false traitoure was armed vnder, so þat þe stroke myght done him none harme. **1457** *Sc. Acts Jas. II*, c. 13 Þat na woman weir..talys of vnsittande lenthe nor furryt vnder bot on þe haliday.

**d.** Of the sun, etc.: Below the horizon; set.

*c* **1489** CAXTON *Sonnes of Aymon* i. 46 Nyghe was the sonne vnder, and it was well aboute complyn tyme. *Ibid.* xiv. 346 Whan reynawd sawe all redy that yᵉ sonne was goon vndre, & that the nyght cam fast on. **1609** SKENE *Reg. Maj.* 104 He may cast the Proces, saying, that..it was made vnlawfullie vnder Sunne. **1850** R. G. CUMMING *Hunter's Life S. Afr.* (1902) 93/2 The sun was under before I laid him low. *Ibid.* 118/2 The moon was now under, and it was very dark. **1859** MEREDITH *R. Feverel* xxxiv, The sun was under.

**e.** Under water; submerged.

**1830–1873** [see GUNWALE b]. **1890** *Cent. Dict.* s.v. *Rail*, The vessel sailed rail under.

**f.** *Down under*, in the Antipodes.

**1899** *Westm. Gaz.* 1 June 5/1 He had once made 74 for Australia against England 'down under'.

**3. a.** Into a position or state of subjection or submission. (See also BRING *v.* 26, GET *v.* 71.)

*c* **1250** *Gen. & Ex.* 4041 Of ðe sal risen..a wond ðe sal smiten riʒt Moab kinges, and under don Al sedes kin ðis werld up-on. *a* **1300** *K. Horne* 1420 (Camb.), To schupe we mote draʒe; Fikenhild me haþ i-don vnder. **1390** GOWER *Conf.* I. 5 Love, which doth many a wonder And many a wys man hath put under. *Ibid.* 117, I that lawe obeie Of which the kinges ben put under. **1509** HAWES *Past. Pleas.* VI. (Percy Soc.) 26 It is alwaye at mannes pleasaunce To take the good and caste the evyll under. **1567** MAPLET *Gr. Forest* 1 Wherefore the Greekes call it Fickleforce, for that it can not be brought under. **1646** DRUMM. OF HAWTH. *Answ. to Objections* Wks. (1711) 214 We are not brought to such a Nonplus, and so under,..but that we dare both say and maintain, They proceed unjustly with us. **1723** *Lockhart Papers* (1817) II. 112 Both the contending partys did desire to promote unity and peace, provyded their opponents would knock under. **1791** *Ann. Reg., Chron.* 4* The fire was got under. **1852** MRS. STOWE *Uncle Tom's C.* xxix, I've begun now to bring them under. **1882** [see KNUCKLE *v.* 2].

**b.** In subjection or submission; in a subordinate or inferior position.

**13..** *K. Alis.* 3054 (Laud MS.), For no power, ne for no wonder, ʒitt ne weren we neuer vnder. *c* **1460** *Oseney Reg.* 19 Know he hym-selfe gilty,..And be he vndur to þe streyte veniaunce in þe last dome. **1463** G. ASHBY *Prisoner's Refl.* 292 The ryche slepeth, the pore laboreth vnder. **1480** *Robt. Devyll* 341 Nowe the people dyd wonder To se that all knyghtes to hym wer vnder. **1568** GRAFTON *Chron.* II. 330 Why should we then be so kept vnder lyke beastes and slaues? **1598** R. BERNARD tr. *Terence, Andria* I. i, How couldst thou know his nature,..whilst..awe and his master kept him vnder? **1611** BIBLE I *Cor.* ix. 27 But I keepe vnder my body, and bring it into subiection. **1647** N. BACON *Disc. Govt. Eng.* I. xvii. 54 The new stemme of Kingly power..sucked much from them, and kept them under. *a* **1700** EVELYN *Diary* 15 Aug. 1687, The King keeps them under by an army of 40,000 men.

**c.** *To go under*: see GO *v.* 93.

**4.** With preps. † **a.** *At under*, in an inferior place or position; in subjection. *Sc. Obs.*

**1375** BARBOUR *Bruce* VII. 365 For he ves put at vndir swa, That he ves left all hym allane. *c* **1425** WYNTOUN *Cron.* V. x. 2396 Dycius..held þaim euer at vnder ay. **1456** SIR G. HAYE *Law Arms* (S.T.S.) 36 Sum men wenis to be at outhe and abune that is at undir. **1500–20** DUNBAR *Poems* l. 23 He hes att warslingis beine ane hunder, ʒett lay his body nevir at wnder. **1573** J. TYRIE in *Cath. Tract.* (S.T.S.) 3 Sufficient to put at vnder the euill foundet fortres my aduersar hes buildede. **1652** URQUHART *Jewel* 197 The cruelty of whose perverse zeal, will keep the effects of his vertue still at under. **1677** GILPIN *Dæmonol.* (1867) 153 They kept them at under, as captives in a dungeon.

**b.** *From under*, from below.

**1535** COVERDALE *Amos* ii. 9, I destroyed his frute from aboue, and his rote from vnder. **1611** BIBLE *Ezek.* xlvii. 1 The waters came downe from vnder from the right side of the house.

**5.** Less in amount, etc.; lower in price.

**1574** W. BOURNE *Regiment for Sea* ii. (1577) 9 b, The Epacte sheweth the age of the Moone or chaunge day, within 12 houres under or over. **1632** LITHGOW *Trav.* IV. 137 The price of a virgin was too deare for him,..and widdowes were farre vnder.

**6.** *Under and over*, a gambling game with dice.

**1890** *Newcastle Even. Chron.* 26 Dec. 3/1 Fined..on a charge of playing 'under and over' with the dice and box.

† **Under**, *v. Obs.*⁻¹ [f. UNDER *adv.*] *trans.* To cast down, depress.

**1502** ATKYNSON tr. *De Imitatione* III. xxxviii. 227 As longe as the symple entent of his soule amonge all suche varyacyons is nat vndered, but dyrecte to me contynually.

**Under-** (*v*·ndəɹ), *prefix*[1], representing OE. *under-*, = OS. *undar-*, OHG. *untar-*, ON. *undir-*, etc. (see UNDER *prep.*). In OE. about eighty words with this prefix are recorded, but only fifteen or sixteen of these are of frequent occurrence. Of the total number about fifty are verbs, and twenty-five nouns, the adjectives being few and rare. In OHG. there are also many examples both of verbs and nouns, in ON. of nouns only; on the other hand there are few recorded examples in OS., and none in Gothic.

**2.** In OE. (as in OHG.) a considerable number of the compounds with *under-* were clearly suggested by Latin forms with *sub-* (*suc-*, etc.) and occur only as renderings of these, e.g. *underberan*, supportare, sustinere; *underbéged*, subjectus; *underbrǽdan*, *-bregdan*, substernere; *undercerrende*, subvertens; *undercuman*, subvenire. The frequency of such forms no doubt contributed greatly to establish the vogue of the prefix in ordinary use. The practice of rendering L. *sub-* by *under-* is extensively followed in the earlier Wycliffite version of the Bible, and gives rise to a large number of unique or unusual forms, as *underburn*, *-cry*, *-drench*, *-follow*, *-grow*, *-heave*, *-hile*, *-join*, *-laugh*, *-lead*, *-minister*, *-mow*, etc., which are illustrated below, together with some others occurring in the anonymous translation of the Pauline Epistles. Similar examples are occasionally found in other ME. translated texts, as *underorn*, *-slake* (q. v.), after L. *subornare*, *summitigare*.

**1382** WYCLIF *Nahum* ii. 13 And Y shal *vndre brenne [L. *succendam*] thi cartis of foure horsis. — *Gen.* xxxix. 14 Whanne Y hadde *vndercried [L. *succlamassem*],..he forsoke the mantil that I heelde. — *Luke* xxiii. 21 Thei vndircryeden [L. *succlamabant*], seyinge, Crucifie, crucifie him. — *Exod.* xv. 10 The see couerde hem; and thei ben *vnder dreynt [L. *submersi*] as leed in hidows watris. *a* **1400** *Pauline Ep.* (Powell) Gal. ii. 4 Þe false breþerene þe whyche *vndyrentredyn [L. *subintroierunt*] to spye oure freenesse þat we hafe in iesu crist. **1382** WYCLIF *Ps.* xxii. 6 Thi mercy shal *vnderfolewe [L. *subsequetur*] me alle the daʒis of my lif. *a* **1400** *Pauline Ep.* (Powell) 1 Tim. v. 24 Þe synnus of summe men ar schewyd opyn goande bifore to þe dome and of summe forsoþe þei vnderfolewyn [L. *subsequuntur*]. **1382** WYCLIF *Gen.* xxvi. 13 He ʒede profytynge and *vndurgrowynge [L. *succrescens*] to the tyme that he was maad hugeli greet. — *Exod.* xxiii. 5 If thow se an asse of hym that hatith thee lye vnder the charge,..thow shalt *vnderheue [L. *sublevabis*] with hym. — *Num.* xii. 14 Whether shulde she not..seuen days with reednes be *vnderhilid [L. *suffundi*]? — *Ps.* Prol., Heer also is taʒt..what bi penaunce be purchasid, whan he *vnderioyneth, 'I shal teche wicke men thi weies'. — *Ecclus.* xiii. 7 And *vnder laʒhende [L. *subridens*] hope he shal ʒyue, tellende to thee alle goodes. — *Ezek.* xxiii. 3 There the breestis..of hem ben *vndirled [L. *subacta*]. — *Ecclus.* xxxix. 39 Alle the werkes of the Lord [are] good; and ech werk in his hour shal *vndermynestren [L. *subministrabit*]. — 1 *Tim.* v. 10 If she vndirmynistride to men suffringe tribulacioun. *a* **1400** *Pauline Ep.* (Powell) Eph. iv. 16 On whom alle þe body is ..knyt to gydere by alle þe ioynture of *vndermynystracion [L. *subministrationis*]. **1382** WYCLIF *Ps.* xxxiv. 16 Thei *vndermouwiden [L. *subsannaverunt*] me with vndermouwing. — *Rom.* Prol., He writeth therfore to the Romaynes, the whiche..wolden with proud contencioun *vnderpoten either other. — *Gen.* xxvii. 36 Now secounde he hath *vnder rauyshide [L. *surripuit*] my benysoun. — 1 *Sam.* ii. 7 The Lord..mekith, and *vndurrerith [L. *sublevat*]. — *Acts* xxvii. 4 We *vndirsailiden [L. *subnavigavimus*] to Cypre, for that wyndis weren contrarie. — *Acts* xxvii. 17 The vessel *vndirsent [L. *summisso*], so thei were borun. *a* **1400** *Pauline Ep.* (Powell) Col. ii. 19 Þe hed, of whom alle þe body is bildid in to one þurgh coniunccions and *vnderseruyd [L. *subministratum*] þurgh þe bondys of charite. **1382** WYCLIF *Eph.* iv. 16 Al the body sett to gidere, and boundyn to gidere by ech ioynture of *vndirseruyng [L. *subministrationis*]. — *Deut.* xxxii. 22 Fier is *vndurtent [L. *succensus*] in my woodnes. — *Ps.* xvii. 9 Colis ben vndertend of hym. — *Dan.* viii. 3 Oo wether..hauynge heeʒ horns, and oon heeʒer than an other, and *vndrewexinge [L. *succrescens*]. — 1 *Sam.* Prol., Fro thens thei *vndurweuyden Sophym, that is, the book of Jugis. — *Gen.* xxvii. 37 Alle his britheren I haue *vndir ʒockid [L. *subjugavi*] to the seruyce of hym. — *Nehemiah* v. 5 We han vnder ʒokid our sonus and oure doʒtris in to seruage.

**3.** In combination both with verbs and with nouns various senses of the prefix were already developed in OE., and further variations have arisen in the later language, the starting-point for new developments being usually the Elizabethan period. In most of its senses *under-* can be freely employed to form new compounds, the meaning of which is obvious except when they are used in some special or technical connexion. In some of these general types *under-* is correlative to OVER-, and not infrequently the actual compound in *under-* is entirely due to the previous use of one in *over-*.

In the following sections a number of the more casual formations are given by way of illustration; those which have a more permanent character, or which for some reason require special treatment, are entered in their alphabetical places as main words. The uses which are most capable of giving rise to new formations, of which complete enumeration is impossible, are 4 a, 5, 6, 9, 10 a, b. Altogether the senses of the prefix may be classed under four heads:—

**I.** Denoting local position.

**4.** With verbs. The following variations are found in OE. and in the later language: **a.** Denoting action (or continuance of a state) carried on under or beneath something, as OE. *underberan* to support from below, *underdelfan* to dig beneath, *underetan* to eat away, to sap, *underiernan* to run beneath, etc., ME. *undercut, -dig, -grow, -hole, -mine, -pitch, -shore, -strew*, and the later *underbind, -brace, -build, -gird, -hew*, etc. **b.** Denoting the action of moving so as to be or to get under something, as OE. *underflówan* to flow under, *underhnígan* to descend beneath, *underscéotan* to pass under; ME. *undercreep*; also with causative force, as OE. *underbregdan* to spread under, *underdón* to put under, *understingan*, to thrust under, ME. *underput, -set.* Additions to this group are not frequent in the later language, but occur in *undercrawl, -dive, -run, -work*, and with slight variation of sense in *underpeep, -peer.* **c.** Rarely, the sense of 'from below' is found, as in *underpeep, -shine.*

In the dictionaries of Florio (1611) and Hexham (1647), *under-* is used in the above senses to form a number of compounds which are merely suggested by Italian forms in *sog-, sop-, sot(to)-* and Dutch in *onder-*, as *underbend, -knit, -loft, -mark, -note, -roof* (Florio), *underfume, -gripe, -lift, -press, -smoke* (Hexham). In addition to verbs, the following miscellaneous examples include instances of the ppl. adj. and agent-noun.

*c* 1900 *Buck's Handbk. Med. Sci.* VIII. 142 (Cent. Suppl.), The building is very solidly built, but *undercellared only. 1890 NASMITH *Cotton Spinning Mach.* x. 148 The '*under clearer' spring is attached to the roller beam. 1892 — *Students' Cotton Spinning* ix. 329 An underclearer D′, is sustained below the bottom front rollers. 1883 A. DOBSON *Old-World Idylls, Dead Letter* iii, Bonzes with squat legs *undercurled. 1828–32 WEBSTER, **Underditch*, v.t., to form a deep ditch or trench to drain the surface of land. 1904 *Nature* 13 Oct. 593/2 An *underfolded and underthrust knot of younger strata. *a* 1825 FORBY *Voc. E. Anglia*, **Under-grub*, to undermine. 1808 COLERIDGE *Lett., to T. Jeffrey* (1895) 537 When I first wrote it I *undermarked it. 1839 *Q. Rev.* LXIII. 415 No accuracy in *underpiling the platform is thus practicable. 1846 tr. *Port Royal Method Grk. Tongue* 8 The three *under-pointed [Greek vowels], ᾳ, ῃ, ῳ. 1864 KINGSLEY *Roman & T.* p. liv, We shall believe not merely in an over-ruling Providence, but (if I may dare to coin a word) in an *under-ruling one. 1800 HURDIS *Fav. Village* 132 Behold! where now he *undersaps the sward. 1846 LANDOR *Imag. Conv.* Wks. I. 472/2 One hath fallen the moment when he had reached the last step of the ladder, having *undersawed it for him who went before. 1877 BLACKIE *Wise Men* 119 The hidden working of the travelling fire That *underscoops the earth. 1879 LANIER *Poems, To B. Taylor* 2 To range, deep-wrapt, along a heavenly height, O'erseeing all that man but *undersees. 1885 W. K. PARKER *Mammalian Descent* vii. 169 We have a..ploughshare bone large and long in proportion to the..beam which it *undersplices. 1889 *Voice* (N.Y.) 28 Nov., A pure serious aim *undersweeps his work and comes out in it like a transfiguration. 1893 *Amer. Jrnl. Sci.* XLV. 306 (*heading*), *Underthrust Folds and Faults.

**d.** A noun of action with *under-* may have the same form as the verb, as *undercut, -gnaw, -hang, -lay, -lie, -lift, -mine, -run, -score, -spin, -thrust.*

1895 J. J. RAVEN *Hist. Suffolk* 1 The coast line has suffered, and still suffers, from the constant undergnaw of the German Ocean.

**5.** With nouns: **a.** In names of garments worn under other articles of clothing, found in OE. *underhwítel, -syrc*, but not common till the 16th century, when *undercap, -forebody, -frock, -garment, -girdle, -sleeve* occur. The following are examples of recent or less usual compounds.

Contrasted with OVER 8 c, and in modern use sometimes replaced by SUB- 3.

1895 *Daily News* 24 Dec. 6/3 The chiffon *under-bodice being visible between the two sides. 1611 FLORIO, *Sottomanto*, an *vnder-cloake, a Cassocke. 1894 'G. EGERTON' *Keynotes* 177 They [*sc.* trousers] ruck up at the knees, and show the end line of his *under-drawers quite plainly. 1859 *Habits of Gd. Society* iii. 144, I should like to know how often the advocates of linen change their own *under-flannel.

**b.** Denoting that the thing specified is either placed below something else, or is the lower in position of two similar things; the two cases are only clearly distinguishable when it is usual for the things to go in pairs. The use is very rare in OE. and ME., but begins to extend in the 16th century and is common from the 17th. When pairs of things are contrasted, *under-* becomes equivalent to *lower* (as *over-* to *upper*), and readily assumes an adjectival function: see UNDER *a.* 1 b.

1878 P. H. CARPENTER in *Quart. Jrnl. Microsc. Sc.* XVIII. 366, I shall shortly show that these second or *under basals are also present in the calyx of *Pentacrinus briareus.* 1889 *Science-Gossip* XXV. 261/1 A starling was found..having its *under-beak evidently shot off. 1611 COTGR., *Soupoultreau*, an *vnder-beame. 1862 in Veness *El Dorado* (1866) App. 140 An *under-box for a pump. 1707 MORTIMER *Husb.* 363 To rub off all the *Under-buds, leaving only a few near the top to draw up the Sap. 1738 CHAMBERS *Cycl.* s.v. *Letter*, Printers distinguish their letters into capital..or upper-case letters,..and minuscule, small, or *under-case letters. 1890 NASMITH *Cotton Spinning Mach.* Index, *Undercasings for carding machine. 1892 — *Students' Cotton Spinning* iv. 112 The relative position of the..knives and undercasing. 1690 C. NESSE *O. & N. Test.* I. 23 If the outside and the *underceiling..of this glorious room be so glittering. 1875 W. MCILWRAITH *Guide Wigtownshire* 7 Many of these smugglers had *under-cellars in their houses of concealment. 1611 FLORIO, *Sotto camera*, an *vnder-chamber. 1805 WORDSW. *Prel.* VI. 227 Her exulting outside look of youth And placid *under-countenance. 1852 MRS. CRAIK *Agatha's Husb.* xx. 281 He took out a paper, ..tore it open—tore likewise an *under-cover addressed to his wife. 1845 M. PATTISON *S. Langton* in *Lives Eng. Saints* vii. 124 A more honourable place..than the damp and dark *undercrypt. 1611 FLORIO, *Sottotazza*, an *vnder-cup of essay. 1897 *Daily News* 1 Jan. 6/6 After a diver has been down to examine the *under-fittings of the Delta. 1611 COTGR., *Beisle*, th' Orelop, or *vnder-hatches, of a ship. 1867 AUGUSTA WILSON *Vashti* xxxv, There were tears hanging.. on the long jet *under-lashes. 1841 *Florist's Jrnl.* (1846) II. 266 They are natives of the table land of Mexico,..wholly below the *underlimit of frost. 1611 FLORIO, *Sopalco*, an *vnder-loft, or sellar, or seeling. 1895 *Archæol. Æliana* XVII. II. 287 It has apparently been moved..for use as an *underpacking when the Early English arcade was built. 1855 *Poultry Chron.* II. 498 How again can they avoid mistakes when half the birds are hidden in dark *under-pens? 1730 A. GORDON *Maffei's Amphith.* 402 The Pedestal or *Under-Pilaster. 1871 tr. *Schellen's Spectr. Anal.* xxv. 87 This micrometer consists..of a sliding-plate,..[and] an *underplate on which the first plate travels. 1598 FLORIO, *Soppórtico*, an *vnderporch. 1839 CARLYLE *Lett.* (1904) I. 158 Chorley's under jaw went like the hopper or *under-riddle ..of a pair of fanners. 1883 GRESLEY *Gloss. Coal-m.* 234 **Under-rope* [= S-rope, the winding rope which passes round the under side of the drum]. *Ibid.* 268 **Under-seams*, lower or deeper coal seams. 1733 W. ELLIS *Chiltern & Vale Farm.* 128 The Drip of their Heads falling upon their *Under-shoots. 1883 F. DAY *Indian Fish* 28 Where large *under-sluices are present, fish can pass up such when open. 1843 *Civil Eng. & Arch. Jrnl.* VI. 265/2 A cross sheth..to be bolted down to the *undersole. 1877 RUSKIN *St. Mark's Rest* iv. (1894) 49 With such solid *under-support that, from 1480 till now, it stands rain and frost! 1902 *Westm. Gaz.* 29 Jan. 9/2 A large Government order for 2,100 *undertrucks and 150 complete wagons. 1822 J. PARKINSON *Outl. Oryctol.* 150 *note*, Attached to an operculum, or *undervalve.

**c.** Denoting position below a surface or covering, or at a depth. Examples of this occur from the 17th century, but are not common until the 19th.

1856 KANE *Arct. Expl.* II. i. 26, I hope that the *underbottom ice exceeds that height. 1892 MEREDITH *Poet. Wks.* (1912) 325 There chimed a bubbled *underbrew With witchwild spray of vocal dew. 1894 CROCKETT *Raiders* (ed. 3) 286 The rippling tide..swirling in the smooth places with an oily *underbubble. 1869 J. MARTINEAU in *Life* (1902) I. 446 How curiously the religious tendency..finds an *undercourse, and breaks out at unexpected points! 1858 CASWALL *Poems* 192 Up from the *underdepth unsearchable of primal Being. 1897 MARY KINGSLEY *W. Africa* 257 Hour after hour..we passed on, in the *under-gloom of the great forest. 1885 MABEL COLLINS *Ld. Vanecourt's Dau.* I. vi. 80 The light..brought out a warm *underglow in her hair. *a* 1825 FORBY *Voc. E. Anglia*, **Under-grup*, an under-drain; a concealed water course in wet soils. 1611 FLORIO, *Sottostanza*, an *vnder-lodging. 1856 RUSKIN *Mod. Paint.* IV. v. xv. § 2 The most fantastic..curves, governed by some grand *under-sweep like that of a tide. 1899 B. CAPES *Lady of Darkness* xviii. 151 There must be *underwarmth somewhere for the surface so to flower into colour.

**d.** Denoting something which is either covered (completely or partially) by, or is subordinate to, something of the same kind. An early example of this is *underwood* (1325), followed later by *undergrowth, -shrub* (*c* 1600). Other examples are mostly of recent date, and show considerable extension of the usage, as in *underfleece, -fur, -marking*, etc.

1866 SARTORIS *Week in French Country Ho.* (1902) 33 Working like a galley-slave in order to get the undergrainting of my picture done before coming over. 1873 E. SPON *Workshop Receipts* Ser. I. 420/1 The colour should be a trifle darker than the undergraining. 1901 *Smithsonian Rep.* 405 Where sheep have been allowed to graze..the undervegetation is destroyed. 1909 MRS. SMITH LEWIS *Codex Climaci Rescr.* Introd. p. xiii, The under-script of a palimpsest is seldom homogeneous.

**e.** With the sense of 'situated on the under side'.

1888 *Century Mag.* XXXVI. 703/1 Its head and back are blue, its throat and breast red, and its underfeathering white. 1902 CORNISH *Naturalist Thames* 45 The particoloured grey and yellow under-colouring of their wings.

**II.** Denoting inferiority in rank or importance.

**6. a.** With designations of persons, esp. of subordinate officers or officials. This use occurs in OE. in *undercyning, -diacon, -geréfa, -ládtéow, -þéow*, becomes common in ME., and is extensively employed from the latter part of the 16th century. The meaning is however as frequently expressed by SUB- 5 a and 6.

Examples of *under-* prefixed to a term of general import are rare, but *underman* occurs in the 14th cent., *underbeing, underfellow* in the 16th, *underswain* in the 17th.

1751 *Eng. Gazetteer* s.v. *Preston*, It..is governed by a mayor, recorder, 8 aldermen, 4 *under-aldermen. 1687 MIÈGE *Gt. Fr. Dict.* II, *Under-Brigadier, *Sou-Brigadier.* 1611 COTGR., *Soubchantre*, an *vnder-chaunter..inferiour to the head Chaunter. 1857 LIVINGSTONE *Trav.* (1861) 189 An imposing embassy from Masiko. It consisted of all his *underchiefs. 1888 'J. S. WINTER' *Bootle's Childr.* ii, All the 'lads'..had gone home for the night, with the exception of the *under-coachman. 1708 J. CHAMBERLAYNE *St. Gt. Brit.* (1710) 569 A Chief-Crier, Two *Under-Criers, Two Ushers. 1846 ETHERIDGE *Syrian Churches* 200 After which is read the Gospel in Syriac; an *underdeacon reading it in the vernacular Arabic. 1854 *Poultry Chron.* I. 265/1 Some competent feeder to look after the whole, and see that the *under-feeders..are constantly at work. 1891 *Daily News* 30 Nov. 6/6 The first footman..had an altercation with..an *under-footman. 1611 COTGR., *Subministrateur*,..an *vnderfurnisher, an inferior officer. 1876 E. A. ABBOTT in *Contemp. Rev.* June 141 To serve him as *under-gamekeeper. 1708 J. CHAMBERLAYNE *St. Gt. Brit.* (1710) 707 Edinburgh-Castle:..Master-Gunner,..6 *Under-Gunners. 1820 SCOTT *Abbot* iv, The famous university of Leyden, where they lack an *underjanitor. 1611 FLORIO, *Sequestratore*,..an *vnderiudge, an arbitrator. 1898 *Atlantic Monthly* LXXXII. 474 The cooks and the under-cooks, the laundresses, the *underlaundress. 1852 BAILEY *Festus* (ed. 5) 338 The more We feel of poesie do we become Like God in love and power,—*undermakers. 1818 MRS. SHELLEY *Frankenst.* ii. (1897) 6 Twice I actually hired myself as an *under-mate in a Greenland whaler. 1839 J. ROGERS *Antipopopr.* x. § 2. 253 We read nothing in Holy Scripture about the submediation or the *undermediators. 1868 HOLME LEE *B. Godfrey* xxiii. 122 Rebecca was the *under-nurse. 1771 LEDWICH *Antiq. Sarisb.* 223 He joined himself to..a tallow-chandler, as an *underpartner with him in the business. 1648 HEXHAM II, *Een Onder-Prioor*, an *Vnder-Priour. 1818 MOORE *Fudge Fam. Paris* vi. 32 Friends, whom his Lordship keeps in store, As *under-saviours of the nation. 1614 SELDEN *Titles Honor* 267 Earle, Churl, Thane, and *Underthane. 1559 AYLMER *Harborowe* L 2 b, Then must the hyghe Shrife be his frende: And the *vnderthefe (vndershrife I should saye) his man. 1748 MELMOTH *Fitzosborne Lett.* lvi. (1749) II. 79 All that numerous *undertribe in the commonwealth of literature. 1818 SCOTT *Hrt. Midl.* xiii, Just the post of *under-turnkey, for I understand there's a vacancy. 1706 PHILLIPS (ed. Kersey), *Sub-vicar*, an *Under-Vicar. 1611 COTGR., *Arriere-vasseur*, an vnder-vassall; or, an *vndervillaine. 1657 J. WATTS *Vind. Ch. Eng.* 125 The ministers are Christs *under-vine-dressers. 1854 *Poultry Chron.* I. 388/1 Abounding with game..which, by game-keepers and '*under-watchers', was..rigorously preserved.

**b.** With other nouns, in the sense of 'subordinate, subsidiary, minor'. An early instance of this is *underhelp* (1579); others, such as *underaccident, -action, -cause, -ministry*, etc., occur in the 17th cent. In later use the tendency is to employ either *sub-* (see SUB- 5 b, c, d) or an adjective, but A. Tucker *Light Nat.* (1768) has *under-aim, -plan, -scheme, -society, -species, -stage.*

1598 FLORIO, *Sottodistintione*, an *vnder-distinction, or subdistinction. 1711 SWIFT *Jrnl. Stella* 28 Apr. (1901) 203 All the *under-hints there are mine too. 1691 NORRIS *Pract. Disc.* 205 The Desire of Happiness..governs all the *undermotions of the Man. 1874 STUBBS *Const. Hist.* I. v. 100 The Lathe and the Rape may represent the *undershires of the Heptarchic kingdom. 1648 HEXHAM II, *Onder-vooght*, *Under-tuterage, or *Under-wardship.

**7.** With verbs, denoting reduction to (or acceptance of) an inferior or subordinate standing. Chiefly OE., as *underblegan* to subject, *underbúgan* to submit, *underþéodan* to subject, subjugate; and ME., as *undercast, -put, -thew.* See also *undershining, -sphere, -study, -sweat, -thrown.*

*Under-* is rarely employed in the sense of SUB- 9 (*b*); Florio (1611) has *under-appoint* rendering It. *sottodelegare.*

**III.** In figurative senses.

**8.** With verbs. **a.** In OE., various secondary meanings of *under-* are represented by such verbs as *under(be)ginnan* to begin or attempt, *underfón* to receive, *undergietan, -niman, -standan* to understand, *underséc̣an* to investigate. Several of these survive in ME., as *underfo, undergete, -nim, -stand, underseche*; and a few more are added, as *underfind, -grope, -take.* In later examples the sense is usually that of (secret) investigation, as *underfeel, -look, -search, -watch*, or of unobserved action, as *underhear.* In addition to the verbs some agent-nouns occur, as *under-dealer, -plotter, -puller.*

Florio (1611) renders It. *sottosapere, -ridere* by *under-know, -smile.*

**b.** From the end of the 16th cent. *under-* is used with verbs in the sense of 'below ( = at a lower rate than) another person', as in *underbid, -buy, -sell, -spend, -work.*

**c.** Occasionally the sense is 'to a point or degree below what is normal or customary', as in *undercooled, -hew.*

**d.** Very rarely, subordinate action is implied, as in *underlet* = sublet.

**9.** With nouns, denoting actions, etc., which lie or are kept beneath the surface or in the background. An early instance is *undercraft* (*c* 1400); others occur from the 17th cent., as *underdealing, -thought.* Modern instances are chiefly of an individual character.

1857 HEAVYSEGE *Saul* (1869) 421 Thine eyeballs roll, As if from some great *under-agitation. 1830 COLERIDGE *Church & State* (1839) 274 A sort of *under-consciousness blends with our dreams. 1876 T. HARDY *Ethelberta* xix, Simply an *underfeeling I have that [etc.]. 1863 BP. S. WILBERFORCE in *Life* (1882) III. 100 The curious *under-history of Trench's appointment to the archbishopric. 1817 COLERIDGE *Biog. Lit.* (1907) II. 207 There is a dull *underpain that survives the smart which it had aggravated. 1876 MRS. WHITNEY *Sights & Ins.* II. iii. 362 To me, who felt an *underpulse in all these things, there was a plain perception [etc.]. 1732 SIR C. WOGAN *Let. to Swift* 27 Feb., A very grave phiz that carried a wicked *undersneer. 1893 *Nation* (N.Y.) 29 June 475/3 The effect is artistic, while the *undersuggestion is scientific. 1805 WORDSW. *Prel.* VI. 558 Something of stern mood, an *under-thirst Of vigour seldom utterly allayed.

**b.** With words denoting sound of a subdued or subordinate character, esp. when produced or perceived at the same time as a louder or more distinct sound. (See also UNDERBREATH, -SONG, -STRAIN, -TONE, -TUNE, -VOICE.)

1904 E. RICKERT *Reaper* 10 He could hear the *underbeat of the surf on the rocks. 1863 IS. WILLIAMS *Baptistery* II. xxiv. (1874) 102 Or deep Gregorian chaunt of plaintive *underchime. 1893 E. H. BARKER *Wand. Southern Waters* 43 That continuous *undercry of the iron tongues. 1815 SCOTT *Guy M.* iv, She answered in the same tone of *under-dialogue. **1832** J. P. KENNEDY *Swallow B.* xxi, Ducks and geese,..with a sedate *under-gabble, like that of old burghers in conversation. **1892** MEREDITH *Poems, Spring* 134 But now the common life has come;..The grasses one vast *underhum. **1859** MRS. CRAIK *Romantic Tales* 182 The low, woman's voice, whose *under-melody,..lost amidst the tempests of life, was now needed to soothe its ending. *a* **1835** MRS. HEMANS *Poems, Flowers & Music* (1875) 572, I..caught an *under-music of lament in the stream's voice. **1876** MEREDITH *Beauch. Career* I. iii. 39 He quoted sayings..in which neither his ear nor Wilmore's detected the *underring Stukely was famous for. **1874** LANIER *Poems, Corn* 28 Fragmentary whispers, blown From *undertalks of leafy souls unknown. **1872** T. HARDY *Under Greenw. Tree* I. i, Dick Dewy..continued his tune in an *under-whistle.

**IV.** Denoting insufficiency or defect.

**10. a.** With verbs. From the latter part of the 16th cent., by contrast with OVER- 27, *under-* is prefixed to verbs to imply that the action falls below the usual or proper standard, and thus acquires the sense of 'at too low a rate', 'too low', 'too little', 'insufficiently'. Early instances are *underprize, -value,* others of slightly later date are *underbuy, -charge, -rate, -reckon, -sell,* etc. Subsequently the use becomes extremely common, especially in the sense of 'insufficiently, not enough', and occurs frequently with pa. pples. and ppl. adjs. Examples of vbl. sbs. (cf. b) are also included in the following illustrations.

**1885** *Pall Mall G.* 14 Feb. 3/2 The..over-worked and *under-accommodated class of reporters. **1862** *Lond. Rev.* 16 Aug. 141 Another baker will make his loaves originally of short weight, and will then *underbake them **1901** *Scotsman* 5 Mar 7/8 *Under-ballasted vessels were..a source of danger to themselves. *Ibid.*, Accidents to British ships..due to *under-ballasting. **1882** *St. James' Gaz.* 3 Apr. 5/2 The Cantabs were slightly *underboated this year **1725** *Fam. Dict.* s.v. *Brewing*, This is generally attributed to their *under-boiling their strong Worts. **1889** *Boy's Own Paper* 3 Aug. 700/2 My boat being considerably *under-canvassed, the weather was rarely too bad for me to make a start. **1866** *Ecclesiologist* XXVII 220 The reproach usual in French provincial towns, of being lamentably *under-churched. **1737** WATERLAND *Eucharist* 202 But there may be danger of *under-commenting, as well as of interpreting too high. **1861** MRS. BEETON *Bk. Househ. Managem.* xxxviii. 893 If the patient be allowed to eat vegetables, never send them up *undercooked. **1892** *Photogr. Ann.* II. 259 It might have been printed from a much *under-developed negative. **1889** *Anthony's Photogr. Bull.* II. 155 We lose the strength..by over-timing and *under-developing. **1778** [W. H. MARSHALL] *Minutes Agric., Digest* 134 Whose Farm is for ever understocked, *under-dunged, and under-tilled! **1856** MISS YONGE *Daisy Chain* II. vi. 393 He has been *under-educated,..and is not very brilliant. **1648** T. HILL *Spring of Grace* 11 We are apt to overgrieve or *undergrieve at crosses. **1866** ODLING *Anim. Chem.* 144 Strongly suggestive of these animals being, so to speak, *under-lunged. **1778** [W. H. MARSHALL] *Minutes Agric., Digest* 66 Re-load *under-made Hay. **1847** HELPS *Friends in C.* I. iv. 67 An ugly phantom of a caricature. which..*under-mimics its wisdom, over-acts its folly. **1884** *Spectator* 4 Oct. 1298/2 If..only the pure Milesian race should own the soil..the country would be *under-populated **1882** *Garden* 25 Feb. 135/3 Use manure water freely..to all [ferns] that are *under-potted. **1849** MAURICE *Let.* in *Life* (1884) II. 9 A misunderstanding, contraction or *under-realising of the truths of God's Absolute, Fatherly Love. **1776** ADAM SMITH *W. N.* I. x. I. (1869) I. 105 In point of pecuniary gain..they..are generally *under-recompensed. **1884** *Manch. Exam.* 16 Oct. 5/1 We are told that the counties are enormously *under-represented **1881** *Daily Tel.* 20 Oct., An absurdly *under-rigged steamer. **1844** H. STEPHENS *Bk. Farm* II. 673 The *under-ripened seed of the bad season of 1841 produced the good crop of potatoes of 1842. **1832** *Nat. Philos., Electric.* ii. § 49. 13 (L. U. K.), In a deficiency of fluid, or in matter *under-saturated. **1786** *Trans. Soc. Arts* IV. 102 The land was *under seeded. **1872** H. W. BEECHER *Lect. Preach.* iv. 109 Some men *under-sleep, and some over-sleep; some eat too much, and some too little. **1900** *Christian* 15 Nov. 9/1 We frequently have to pay..excess on delivery of *understamped letters. **1778** Under-tilled [see *under-dunged* above]. **1889** *Anthony's Photogr. Bull.* II. 227 The negative was so badly *undertimed as to be useless. **1861** O. W. HOLMES *Pages fr. Old Vol. Life* (1891) 9 They are very commonly pallid, *undervitalized, shy, sensitive creatures. **1832** *Prop. Reg. Instr. Cavalry* III. 99 The Troop Leaders may know whether to over-wheel or *under-wheel *ellipt.* **1628** FELTHAM *Resolves* II. xxviii. 89, I hold it a greater iniurie to bee ouer-valued, then vnder. **1847** C. BRONTE *Jane Eyre* vii, The under..or the over dressing of a dish.

**b.** With nouns, in the sense of 'insufficient, deficient, defective', contrasted with OVER- 29. Examples occur in the 17th cent. in *underprice, -rate, -value, -wages,* and are not uncommon in later use, though less frequent than the verbal forms.

**1895** *Westm. Gaz.* 8 Aug. 2/1 What the world is suffering from is under-production of everything and *under-consumption. **1891** *Lancet* 14 Mar. 624/2 Cases..of under-growth, and *underdevelopment. **1892** *Photogr. Ann.* II. 59 When from..under-development, only a poor slide results. **1895** *Pop. Sci. Monthly* July 380 The result is always over-eating and *under-exercise. **1861** M. ARNOLD *Pop. Educ. France* 11, I shall proceed to point out..some inconveniences of *under-government. **1899** PATTEN *Developm. Eng. Th.* vi. 382 Overnutrition as well as *undernutrition weakens the body. *c* **1900** *Buck's Handbk. Med. Sci.* VI. 158 (Cent. Suppl.), The foul air..makes a direct escape,..providing..it meets or passes no compartment on its way in which *under-pressure exists. **1887** *Pall Mall G.* 28 Feb. 1/2 Over production may exist in manufactures owing to *under production of crops. **1894** *Westm. Gaz.* 14 Sept. 1/3 More important ..is the *under-representation of the big societies. **1864** RUSKIN in *Daily Tel.* 31 Oct., An *under-supply of wages and an over-supply of labourers. **1883** GRESLEY *Gloss. Coal-m.* 268 * *Under ventilation*, too little air circulating in a mine.

**c.** With adjectives *under-* is rarely employed as the opposite of OVER- 28, except when directly suggested by the latter, e.g. *under-scrupulous* as the converse of *over-scrupulous*; *underhonest* (Shaks.) in contrast to *overproud*; *under-ripe*, etc.

**11.** In words formed with *under-* the stress is variable. Normally it falls on the stem in verbs (including participles in predicative use) and on the prefix in nouns, adjectives, and attributive participles, with a secondary stress on prefix or stem respectively, whenever form or sense makes a double stressing natural or necessary. Even in verbs, however, the prefix naturally takes either the main or an equal stress whenever it becomes emphatic through contrast either with the simple verb or with a compound in OVER-.

**12.** Compounds in which the two parts are not felt to be distinct are written as one word without a hyphen. In other formations the use of the hyphen is variable, and depends to a great extent on the form or the frequency of the word. Complete separation of the prefix, common in older usage, is now restricted to instances in which *under* may be taken as an adjective. Examples of these have been included under the compounds, as no clear distinction can be drawn between the two.

**Under-** (*v*·ndəɹ), *prefix*[2], originating in the coalescence of the preposition UNDER with a following noun, the compound being then usually employed as an adj. or adv., as UNDERFOOT, -GROUND, -HAND, -STAIRS, -WATER. In attributive use these compounds have the stress on the prefix.

Purely adjectival formations, as *under-celestial* (Florio), *-natural* (1642), *-proficient* (1703), are rare. An unusual type occurs in UNDERGRADUATE.

**1892** *Daily News* 1 Feb. 2/3 The Indian season being.. dull in consequence of *under-average grain crops. **1854** *Poultry Chron.* I 288/2 It is obvious that..an '*under-cover show' has..manifest advantages over an exposed one. **1899** KIPLING *Stalky* 83 By some accident of *under-floor drafts. **1886** *Pall Mall G.* 24 Aug. 4/2 The substitution for the old *under-guard lever of the 'snap', or spring action for opening the breech. **1876** T. HARDY *Ethelberta* ii, Everything turned upon whether the postmaster..would be in his *under-government manner. **1887** MEREDITH *Ballads & P.* 149 Some *undermountain narrative he tells. **1894** *Daily News* 3 Sept. 4/1 The work of real difficulty is..the *under-river portion of the tunnel. **1897** MARY KINGSLEY *W. Africa* 301 A bridge across an *under-swamp river.

**U·nder-aby:ss.** (UNDER-[1] 5 c.) **1662** GLANVILL *Lux Orient.* xiv, They are disposed of into those black under-abysses. **U·nder-a·ccident.** (UNDER-[1] 6 b.) *c* **1630** H. R. *Mythomystes* A 3, Nor in the vnder-Accidents, but in the Essentiall Forme, of true Poesy.

**Undera·ct,** *v.* [UNDER-[1] 10 a.] *trans.* To perform inefficiently or inadequately; *spec.* to act (a part) insufficiently.

*a* **1623** BUCK *Rich. III*, I. (1646) 9 Faulconbridge was appointed Admirall, with Commission to take or sinke all Ships he met;..who did not under act it, but made many depredations on the Coasts. **1775** ASH, *Underact*.., to perform in a manner below what is required or expected. **1847** MACREADY *Remin., Diary & Lett.* (1875) II. 293 The play was so underacted by the people engaged in it, that it broke down under their weight. **1899** *Daily News* 4 Dec. 6/6 It was reserved for Mr. Coghlan to underact the part.

**U·nder-a·ction.** [UNDER-[1] 6 b, 10 b.]

**1.** Subordinate or subsidiary action, as in the plot of a play or poem.

**1697** DRYDEN *Æneis* Ded. ¶ 1 The least and most trivial episodes, or under-actions, which are interwoven in it, are parts either necessary or convenient to carry on the main design.

**2.** Insufficient or defective action; less than normal activity.

**1887** *Buck's Handbk. Med. Sci.* IV. 656 Correction of underaction and overaction of muscles, nerves, and their central reflex apparatus.

**U·nder-a·ctor.** [UNDER-[1] 6 a.] A subordinate actor or agent.

**1723** BLACKMORE *Alfred* Pref. 46 The chaste, discreet, and honourable Characters of the chief Heroe and other under-Actors. **1771** GOLDSM. *Hist. Eng.* IV. 79 Some of the under actors, seized with fear or remorse, resolved to prevent the execution by a timely discovery. *a* **1797** H. WALPOLE *Mem. Geo. II* (1822) I. 199, I take leave of the reader, to add this person's portrait to those of the under-actors.

**U·nder-a·dmiral.** (UNDER-[1] 6 a: cf. Du. *onder-admiraal*, G. *unteradmiral*.) **16..** *Black Bk. Admiralty* (Rolls) I. 17 If hee hath an under-admirall (or rear-admirall). **1729** JACOB *Law Dict., Vice-Admiral*, an under Admiral at Sea. **U·nder-adve·nturer.** (UNDER-[1] 6 a.) **1607** in *E. India Co. Crt. Bks.* II. 48 (MS.), Any man coming in as an under-adventurer under any of the forenamed 50 adventurers.

**Under-a·ge,** *a.* and *sb.* [See UNDER *prep.* 22 b and UNDER-[2].]

**1.** *adj.* Not of full age; youthful, immature.

**1594** NASHE *Unfort. Trav.* Wks. (Grosart) V. 52 Farre bee it my vnder-age argumentes should intrude themselues as a greene weake prop to support so high a building. **1612** WEBSTER *White Devil* I. ii, I myself have loved a lady, and pursued her with a great deal of under-age protestation. **1876** T. HARDY *Ethelberta* xli, As secret as if I were some under-age heiress to an Indian fortune.

**†2.** *sb.* The time during which a person is under age; minority. *Obs.*

**1613-8** DANIEL *Coll. Hist. Eng.* (1626) 28 The Duke..recouers his peace, and the Castle of Thuilliers taken from him in his vnder-age. **1641** EARL MONM. tr. *Biondi's Civil Wars* III. 147 The underage and weaknesse of his succeeding sonne. **1649** BP. HALL *Cases Consc.* IV. i. (1654) 289 Neither do the Roman doctors generally hold otherwise this day in case of an under-age

So **Undera·gedness.** *rare*—°.

**1648** HEXHAM II, *Onbejaertheyt*, Vnder-agednesse.

**U·nder-a·gency.** [UNDER-[1] 6 b.] The office of an under-agent.

**1856** LEVER *Martins of Cro' M.* xxviii, I told him I'd hold the under-agency till he named some one to succeed me.

**U·nder-a·gent.** [UNDER-[1] 6 a.] A sub-agent.

**1677** GILPIN *Demonol.* (1867) 191 The woman Jezebel..was Satan's under-agent. **1679** EVERARD *Popish Plot* 2, I askt her..who were the leading-men in the contrivance, and who the Under-agents to carry it on? **1711** ADDISON *Spect.* No. 225 ¶ 3 Discretion..is like an Under-Agent of Providence, to guide and direct us in the ordinary Concerns of Life. **1733** T. STEWARD *Ordination Charge*, You [*sc.* clergymen] are made Ministers of Christ, and, as I may say, his Under-Agents. **1805** WORDSW. *Prelude* XIII. 273 Words are but under agents in their souls. **1883** *Manch. Guard.* 15 Oct. 5/3 The Earl of Dalhousie was driving near Carnoustie with his under agent.

**U·nder-aid,** *sb.* (UNDER-[1] 6 b.) **1579** TOMSON *Calvin's Serm. Tim.* 212/2 The woman is rather giuen to the man for an vnder ayde. **1611** COTGR., *Soubs-aide*, an vnder Aid; the Aid which tenants pay vnto their mesne Lord [etc.]. **Under-ai·d,** *v.* (UNDER-[1] 4 a.) **1613-8** DANIEL *Coll. Hist. Eng.* (1626) 23 Robert..is said to have under-aided Roul secretly, of purpose to make him friend his designes. **U·nder-air.** (UNDER-[1] 5 b.) **1833** TENNYSON *Miller's Dau.* xix, I heard,..When all the under-air was still, The low voice of the glad new year. **1905** *Westm. Gaz.* 16 Jan. 1/3 A dust of snow is in the under-air of the streets.

**Undera·nged,** *ppl. a.* (UN-[1] 8.) **1817** KIRBY & SP. *Entomol.* xxiii. II. 353 The wings of many male butterflies..are distinguished by a remarkable apparatus..for keeping them steady and underanged in their flight.

**Undera·rch,** *v.* [UNDER-[1] 4 a.] *trans.* To lie under, or support, as an arch; to span with an inverted arch.

**1611** FLORIO, *Subbarcare*, to bow vnder as a bow, to vnder arch, to vnder vault. **1827** MONTGOMERY *Pelican Isl.* I. 148 One sevenfold circle, That spanned the horizon, meted out the heavens, And underarched the ocean.

†**Under-area·r,** *v* [UNDER-[1] 4 a.] *trans.* To suborn. **1502** ARNOLDE *Chron.* 174 Also al thei..whiche such false witnesse in-bryng or vnder-areren in cause of matrimony. **U·nder-a·rgue,** *v.* (UNDER-[1] 10 a.) **1645** RUTHERFORD *Tryal & Tri. Faith* (1845) 55 We are not either to over-argue or to under-argue, neither to faint nor despise.

**U·nder-arm,** *a.* [UNDER-[2].]

**1.** *Cricket.* = UNDERHAND *a.* 1 c, d.

**1816** in Box *Cricket* (1877) 33 The ball may be twisted by the usual mode of under-arm bowling. **1882** *Daily Tel* 19 May, This brought on Humphreys, slow under-arm bowler.

**2.** *Swimming.* Of a stroke: Made with the arm below the level of the body. Also *ellipt.*

**1905** *Times* 10 Aug. 10/4 Burgess,..using his favourite under-arm stroke,..went off at a good pace. **1906** *Westm. Gaz.* 18 Aug. 9/2 After the second hour he varied his stroke for a while to the underarm

**Under-a·rming,** *a.* [UNDER-[2]] Worn under the armour. *c* **1611** CHAPMAN *Iliad* VIII. 341 Then put she on her ample breast her under-arming tire, And on it her celestial arms.

**U·nderback.** *Brewing.* [UNDER-[1] 5 b.] A vessel placed below the mash-tub or mash-tun to receive the raw wort when let out from this. (See also UNDERBECK.)

**1635** *Toke* (Kent) *Estate Acc.* (MS.) fol. 178 Underbacks in the bruehouse. **1686** in *Essex Rev.* (1906) XV. 173 One mashing tubb, and underback. **1725** *Fam. Dict.* s.v. *Brewing*, When all is run out into the Receiver, or Under-Back, lade or pump out your second Liquor. **1763** *Museum Rust.* I. 203 The first wort is then let out in a small stream into the underback. **1830** M. DONOVAN *Dom. Econ.* I. 159 When the tap has been set, and the worts are allowed to run from the mash-tun, the transparent liquor is received into a large vessel called the underback. **1887** *Pall Mall G.* 25 Oct. 6/1 A huge display of saccharometers, hydrometers,..false bottoms, copper underbacks, and live steam injectors

**b.** (See quot.)

**1875** KNIGHT *Dict Mech.* 2679/2 The name *underback* is also applied to a similar vessel in a vinegar factory.

**U·nder-bai·liff** (UNDER-[1] 6 a: cf. MDu. *onder-bailliu*, Du. *-baljuw*.) **1621** ELSING *Debates Ho. Lords* (Camden) 33 The undersheriff knewe not that he was the Kinges servaunte; nor the underbaylliffes. **1631** *Star Chamb. Cases* (Camden) 118 The underbayliffes come into the roome. **Under-ba·lance.** (UNDER-[1] 10 b: cf. Da. *underbalance*, Sw. *-balans* deficit.) **1641** *Decay of Trade* 1 The profit or losse which is made by the over or underbalance of our Forraigne Trade. **U·nder-ba·rber.** (UNDER-[1] 6 a.) **1666** HARRISON in Bedloe *Popish Plot* (1679) 16 He answered, The King's Under-Barber, Phillips **U·nder-bea·dle.** (UNDER-[1] 6 a.) **1679** BEDLOE *Popish Plot* 9 The under Beadle of White-Chappel-Parish. **1755** JOHNSON, *Subbeadle*, an under beadle.

**Underbea·r,** *v.* Now *rare.* [OE. *underberan*: see UNDER-[1] 4 a, and BEAR *v.*]

**1.** *trans.* To sustain, suffer, endure. Also *absol.*

*c* **950** *Rit. Eccl. Dunelm.* (Surtees) 13 *Subportantes invicem*, underbearað bitvien. *a* **1050** *Liber Scintill.* v. (1889) 24 Mid ge ·ylde underberende [L. *supportantes*] gemænelice & forgyfende eow sylfum. **1340** *Ayenb.* 84 Uirtue makeþ wynne heuene..and alle þe kueades of þe wordle onderbere and gledliche þolye. **1382** WYCLIF *Ecclus* xii. 14 If forsothe thou bowe doun, he shal not vnderbern [L. *supportabit*]. *a* **1400** *Pauline Ep.* (Powell Col. iii. 13 Onderberande oþþer oþer and forgifande. *Ibid.* Heb. xiii. 22, I preye ȝou..þat ȝee vndyrbere [L. *sufferatis*] pacyently þe word of solace. **1595** SHAKS. *John* III. i. 65 Get thee gone, And leaue those woes alone, which I alone Am bound to vnder-beare. *a* **1634** CHAPMAN *Alphonsus* IV. i. 183, I am not able for to underbear

The weight of sorrow which doth bruise my soul. **1697** CONGREVE *Mourn. Bride* IV. vii, All pains and tortures That ..dire revenge can think Shall he accumulated under-bear. **1888** G. YOUNG tr. *Sophocles* 265 My misery No mortal but myself can underbear.

**2.** To sustain, support, bear up.

**1382** WYCLIF *Ezra* vi. 3 Cirus the king demede..that thei putte groundis vnderberende [L. *supportantia*] the heiȝte of sixti cubitus. **1593** NASHE *Christ's T.* F iij, I will corroborate my Crosse Giant-like, to vnder-beare the Atlas burthen of her insolences. **1595** PEELE *Anglorum Feriæ* 202 Show the way To help to underbear with grave advice The weighty beam whereon the state depends. *a* **1618** RALEIGH *Rem.* (1644) 154 The first would soon be broken from their bodies, were they not underborn by many branches.

†**3.** To introduce, apply. *Obs.*⁻¹

**1382** WYCLIF *2 Peter* i. 5 Forsothe ȝe vndir beringe, or ȝeuynge, al cure [L. *curam omnem subinferentes*], mynistre in ȝoure feith vertu.

**4.** To trim round the lower part.

**1599** SHAKS. *Much Ado* III. iv. 20 Cloth a gold..set with pearles,..and skirts, round vnderborn with a blewish tinsel.

Hence Underbea·ring *vbl. sb.*

**1593** SHAKS. *Rich. II*, I. iv. 29 Wooing poore Craftes-men, with the craft of soules, And patient vnder-bearing of his Fortune. **1598** FLORIO, *Sopportatione*, a toleration,..a suffring, a supporting, an vnderbearing. **1600** SURFLET *Countrie Farme* VI. vi. 737 To vines so planted there neede no propping or vnderbearing.

†**U·nderbeard.** *Obs.*⁻¹ (UNDER-¹ 5 b: cf. BEARD *sb* 8.)

**1753** *Chambers' Cycl.* Suppl., *Beard*, or under-beard, called also *chuck*, of a horse.

**Underbea·rer.** Now *dial.* and *U.S.* [UNDER-¹ 4 a. Cf. BEARER *sb.* 1 c.] One who assists in carrying the coffin at a funeral.

**1700** S. SEWALL *Diary* 23 Mar., She is buried...The underbearers were honest men. **1755** JOHNSON, *Underbearer*, in funerals, those that sustain the weight of the body, distinct from those who are bearers of ceremony, and only hold up the pall. **1777** BRAND *Pop. Antiq.* iii. 35 St. Jerom..informs us, that Bishops were what in modern Language we call Underbearers at her Funeral. **1859** GEO. ELIOT *A. Bede* xl, All th' under-bearers and pall-bearers as I'n picked for my funeral are i' this parish and the next to't. **1885** *Century Mag.* July 394/1 The 'underbearers', who carried the coffin,.. were provided with plain gloves.

**U·nderbea:ring,** *ppl. a.* [UNDER-¹ 8 a.] Unassuming.

**1802** R. MANT *Mem. Warton* in *W.'s Poet. Wks.* I. p. ci, He was, as a friend of his once described him to me, the most under-bearing man existing.

**Underbeck,** var. of UNDERBACK.

**1764** *Museum Rust.* II. xcviii. 326 Large fats, or vats, (containing..wood ashes) with under-becks. **1828** *Hull Rockingham* 14 June 84/2 Three large guile tubs, several mash tubs and under becks. **1839** *Hist. Chesterfield Antiq.* 274 The instrument used in brewing, which is now called by some a betony, and by others an underbeck.

**U·nderbed.** (UNDER-¹ 5 b: cf. Du. *onderbed*, G. *unterbett*, Sw. *underbädd*.) **1648** HEXHAM II, *Onder-bedde*, an Vnderbed. **1827** STEUART *Planter's G.* (1828) 275 The thickness of the mass of roots and earth together, from the upper part of the collar, to the underbed of the roots. **U·nder-be·ing.** (UNDER-¹ 6 a.) **1587** GOLDING *De Mornay* v. 65 As we can not imagine God without his actions, so can wee not consider..any other underbeeings that proceede from thence.

†**Underbei·t,** *v. Obs.* [UNDER-¹ 4 a.] *trans.* To work under. Hence †**Underbeiting** *vbl. sb.*

**1670** PETTUS *Fodinæ Reg.* 88 And if any Miner of his own underbeit his Neighbours Meer, that then he shall fill his Underbeitings with such as he got out.

**U·nder-be·lly.** (UNDER-¹ 5 c.)

**1607** TOPSELL *Four-f. Beasts* 20 Vnderneath the common belly, there was a skinne like a bagge or scrip, wherin she keepeth..her young ones,..so that the same vnderbelly is her best remedie..to preserue her young ones.

**U·nder-be·velling.** [UNDER-¹ 5 b.] (See quots.)

**1754** [see STANDING *ppl. a.* 6]. **1846** A. YOUNG *Naut. Dict.* 33 The bevelling of a timber implies the angle contained between two of its adjacent sides: if an acute angle, it is termed an under bevelling (or bevel). **1875** KNIGHT *Dict. Mech.* 278/2 A *standing* beveling is made on the outside; an *under* beveling is one on an inner surface of a frame of timber.

**Underbi·d,** *v.* [UNDER-¹ 8 b, 10 a. Cf. Da. *underbyde*, Sw. *-bjuda*.]

†**1.** *trans.* To value at a lower rate; to undervalue.

**1593** NASHE *Christ's T.* 67 When hee hath resolued to prize himselfe..so great, and some man (as proude as himselfe) comes and vnderbids him. **1645** RUTHERFORD *Tryal & Tri. Faith* (1845) 99 Oh, we under-bid, and undervalue that Prince of love, who did overvalue us.

**2.** *intr.* To make too low an offer.

**1611** COTGR., *Mesoffrir*, to vnderbid; to offer lesse for a thing then tis worth. **1679** DRYDEN *Limberham* II. i, Before George, Son Limberham, you'll spoil all, if you under-bid so.

**3.** *trans.* To outbid (a person); to supplant by making a better offer.

**1677** MIÈGE *Fr. Dict.* II, To under-bid one. **1694** CONGREVE *Double Dealer* III. v, 'Tis only an inhancing the price of the Commodity, by telling you how many Customers have underbid her. **1864** LOWELL *Study Wind.* (1886) 124 Strepsiades striving to underbid him in demagogism.

**b.** *spec.* To supplant by making a lower offer; to offer services, labour, or goods at lower wages or prices than (another).

**1825** J. NEAL *Bro. Jonathan* II. 78 A pauper, who[m]..the Major had got for a coachman by underbidding everybody else. **1871** MILL *Pol. Econ.* IV. vii. § 7 II. 378 It is also to be protected against being underbid for employment by a less highly paid class of labourers. **1878** JEVONS *Prim. Pol. Econ.* 131 No tradesman or manufacturer likes to see himself underbid by those who offer better goods at lower prices.

Hence **Underbi·dding** *vbl. sb.* and *ppl. a.*

**1642** D. ROGERS *Naaman* 142 That we might bee dispensed within our underbidding of the price which God calls for. *Ibid.* 146 To take out of thine heart this slavish, base, and unbeteaming and underbidding nature. **1900** *Contemp. Rev.* July 128 We must abolish competition, preventing underbidding by fixing prices.

**U·nderbi·dder.** [UNDER-¹ 10 b.] One who offers a price next below the highest bid.

**1883** *Daily News* 13 July 3/6 Mr. H. Stevens..in this case was the underbidder at 600*l.*, the book being bought by Mr. Quaritch for 605*l.*

**Underbi·ll,** *v.* *U.S.* [UNDER-¹ 10 a.] *trans.* To bill or enter (goods) at less than the actual amount or value. Also **Underbi·lling** *vbl. sb.*

**1888** *Boston* (Mass.) *Jrnl.* 13 Apr. 3/3 The Interstate Commerce Commission has been investigating..the matter of underbilling. **1889** *Advance* (Chicago) 17 Jan., The bribing of a railroad servant to underbill goods or in some other way to give an advantage to a shipper.

**U·nder-bi·llow.** (UNDER-¹ 5 c.) **1608** CHAPMAN *Byron's Consp.* IV. i. 29 His high spirit That stoops to fear, less than the poles of heaven, Should doubt an under-billow of the sea.

†**Underbi·nd,** *v. Obs.* [UNDER-¹ 4 a. Cf. MDu. and Du. *onderbinden*, MHG. and G. *unterbinden* (OHG. *untarpintan*), MSw. and Sw. *underbinda*, Da. *underbinde*.] *trans.* To bind by a fastening placed beneath; also, to bind down, keep down firmly.

**1538** ELYOT, *Subligo*, to vnderbynde. **1600** FAIRFAX *Tasso* XIX. xviii, But the good prince his hand more fit for blowes With his huge weight the Pagan vnderbound. **1647** HEXHAM I, To Vnderbind, *onder-binden.* [Also in Bailey and Ash.]

**U·nder-bi·shop.** (UNDER-¹ 6 a. Cf. MDu. and Du. *onderbisschop*, OIcel. *undirbiskup*, G. *unterbischof.*) **-bi·shopric.** (UNDER-¹ 6 b.) **1574** *Life 70th Abp. Canterb.* To Rdr. D 2 Then followeth the Lorde suffraganes, which euery vnderbishoppe may haue vnder him. *Ibid.* C 8 Somwhat they strained at the vnderbishoprikes. **Underbi·te,** *v.* (UNDER-¹ 10 a.) **1876** P. G. HAMERTON *Etching & Etchers* 427 It is better to underbite a plate in the darks than to overbite it, because if underbitten in these lines it is easily darkened afterwards by rebiting.

**Under-bi·tted,** *ppl. a. north. dial.* [UNDER-¹ 4 a.] Earmarked in a special manner.

Cf. mod. U.S. *under-bit* (a semicircular earmark indicating ownership), and *under-bitten* ppl. a.

**1555** *Knaresb. Wills* (Surtees) I. 69 To my doughter..a browne rigged cowe, under bytted of bothe eyres. **1899** in *Cumbld. Gloss.* 381/2 Cheviot ewe, under bitted both ears.

†**Under-blade-lurker.** *Obs.* [UNDER-².] The subscapular muscle. **1683** SNAPE *Anat. Horse* IV. xviii. (1686) 180 The second Puller or Drawer back of the shoulder is the *subscapularis*, the under-blade-lurker.

**U·nder-board,** *sb.* [UNDER-¹ 5 b and UNDER *a.* 1 b.] The lower of two boards forming an organ bellows or wind-chest.

**1781** *Encycl. Brit.* (ed. 2) VIII. 5747/1 [In] the church-organ..the sound-board..is composed of two parts, the upper board..and the under board. **1845** STIMPSON *Gt. Organ B'ham* 8 Directly over the under-board is situated the upper-board, which is perforated with holes to correspond with those in the under-board.

†**U·nderboard,** *adv. Obs.* [UNDER-².]

**1. a.** Under the table. Also *fig.*

*a* **1548** HALL *Chron., Hen. VI*, 99 b, When the greate fire of this discencion..was thus..vtterly quenched out, and laied vnder boord. **1620** GATAKER *Marriage Duties* 46 Like those that climbe and take paines to get nuts, which hauing crackt and eaten the kernell out of, they cast the shels vnder-bord. **1642** D. ROGERS *Naaman* 309 [They will] be idle otherwise, as they were at their worke never well, till they have drunk themselves underboord.

**b.** Under deck.

**1588** PARKE tr. *Mendoza's Hist. China* 118 They do make their dwellinges in ships,..where they haue their..families under borde to defende them from the sunne and rayne.

**2.** In an underhand or secret manner; clandestinely; not openly or honestly. (Opposed to *above-board.*)

**1581** GOSSON *Plaies Confuted* F 5, [Thus] to shake off the yoake of seuerer discipline..is to iuggle vnder boarde. **1590** NASHE *Pasquil's Apol.* I. B iij b, My Reformer doth nothing but play the Iugler, he packs vnder-boord, and shewes not how farre forth the Archb. hath affirmed it. *a* **1603** T. CARTWRIGHT *Confut. Rhem. N. T.* (1618) 641 The better to discouer your ligier-demain and your playing vnder-board. **1664** H. MORE *Myst. Iniq.* 445 Then shall that Wicked one be revealed (who has dealt under-board hitherto with his Conspirators). **1703** *Secr. Policy of Jansenists* 6 It play'd now no more underboard.

**U·nder-bo·dy.** [UNDER-¹ 5 b, c.]

**1.** † **a.** The lower part of a woman's dress. *Obs.*

**1621** BRATHWAIT *Times Cvrtaine Drawne* D 4, About the May pole while she tripps, Downe fell her vnder-bodie from her hipps. **1621** — *Nat. Embassie* 204.

**b.** *U.S.* A corset-cover; underwaist.

**2.** The underside of an animal's body.

**1879** J. BURROUGHS *Locusts & W. Honey* 128 A dog..will manœuvre round the porcupine till he..fastens on his quill-less underbody.

**3. a.** *Naut.* The part of a ship's hull which is below the water-line.

**1895** *Westm. Gaz.* 6 Sept. 7/2 A coat of black composition ..has been given to the underbody of Valkyrie.

**b.** The under portion of the body of a vehicle.

**1904** *Daily Chron.* 6 Sept. 6/7 The wagons..were lifted bodily at the end of a trace of chains, hooked to the underbody of the vehicle.

**U·nderborn,** *ppl. a.* [UNDER-¹ 10 a.] Born with insufficient development.

**1884** D. GRAY *Homesick* in *Home in Poetry* (N. Y.) 162 The winter is decrepit, underborn.

**U·nder-bough.** [UNDER-¹ 5 b.] One of the lower boughs or branches of a tree. Also *fig.*

**1523** FITZHERB. *Husb.* § 135 And than the vnder bowes wolde be cutte awaye. **1626** BACON *Sylva* § 532 It is certain that timber trees in Coppice-woods grow more upright and more free from under-boughs, than those that stand in the fields. **1642** FULLER *Holy & Prof. St.* II. xxii. 143 These under-boughs grow from the same root with the top-branches. *a* **1661** — *Worthies, Wilts.* III. (1662) 153 His father,.. a fortunate Gentleman in all his Children,..some of his under-boughs out-growing the top-branch. **1814** WORDSW. *Excurs.* v. 148 The roof upheld By naked rafters intricately crossed, Like leafless underboughs, in some thick wood.

**U·nder-bow·ser.** [UNDER-¹ 6 a.] An under-bursar. *a* **1659** CLEVELAND *Rustick Ramp.* Wks. (1687) 458 The Under-Bowser's House, standing over against the Fish-market.

**U·nder-boy.** [UNDER-¹ 6 a.] A boy belonging to the lower or under-school.

**1843** THACKERAY *Fitz-Boodle P., Mr. & Mrs. Berry* i, Here, under-boy, take my coat. **1856** J. RICHARDSON *Recoll.* I. iv. 96 If the under boy refuses or declines to obey, he is punished by blows at the discretion of his tyrant.

**Underbra·ce,** *v.* [UNDER-¹ 4 a.] *trans.* To fasten together underneath.

**1791** COWPER *Iliad* III. 440 The broider'd band That underbraced his helmet at the chin.

**U·nderbreath,** *sb., a.,* and *adv.* [UNDER-¹ 9 b and UNDER-².]

**1.** *sb.* A low subdued tone; a whisper.

**1844** MRS. BROWNING *Rime Duchess May* III. x, I said in underbreath,—All our life is mixed with death. **1884** H. R. HAWEIS *Musical Life* 175 All the point was taken out of it [a story] because I had to hurry over it and end in a guilty kind of underbreath.

**b.** Whispered rumour.

**1880** MEREDITH *Tragic Com.* ii, She heard things related of Alvan by the underbreath.

**2.** *adj.* Low-toned, whispered.

**1853** H. LUSHINGTON *Italian War* (1859) 259 Rather extravagant in his liberalism, and given to underbreath confessions of conspiracy. **1874** AYLWARD in Manning *Ess. Relig. & Lit.* III. 106 The audience was greatly excited, and under-breath communications were made.

**3.** *adv.* In an undertone or whisper.

**1865** SWINBURNE *Chastelard* v. i. 177 Small broken oaths ..And underbreath some praise of Ashtaroth Sighed laughingly.

**U·nder-brea·thing,** *ppl. a.* (UNDER-¹ 4 a. Cf. prec.) **1760–72** H. BROOKE *Fool of Qual.* (1792) IV. 26 A kind of under-breathing bustle, and whispering commotion.

[In the earlier Wycliffite version of 2 Macc. vii. 5 *vndirbrethinge* is used to render L. *spirantem*; the translator probably read *suspirantem* (cf. UNDER-¹ 2).]

**U·nderbred,** *ppl. a.* and *sb.* [UNDER-¹ 10 a.]

**1.** Of inferior breeding or upbringing; wanting in polish or refinement; vulgar: **a.** Of persons.

**1650** B. *Discolliminium* 50 Our late..under-bred Committee-men. **1706** FARQUHAR *Recruiting Officer* v, Pray, Sir, dunna be offended at my Sister, she's something underbred. **1771** GOLDSM. *Haunch Venison* 37 An under-bred, fine-spoken fellow was he. **1825** T. HOOK *Sayings* Ser. II. III. 154 The boisterous mirth of the under-bred village belle. **1885** *Spectator* 30 May 715/1 All the gentlemen and ladies he has to do with are just a little underbred.

*Comb.* **1824** SCOTT *Redgauntlet* ch. vi, Behind a long table ..sat a smart, underbred-looking man.

**b.** Of manners or conduct.

**1796** MME. D'ARBLAY *Camilla* III. 209 The under-bred positiveness of her father. **1840** WILLIS *Loiterings* II. 161 His underbred politeness of insisting on following his host. **1849** C. BRONTE *Shirley* vii, His somewhat underbred manner and aspect.

**2.** Of animals: Not pure bred; of inferior strain.

**1890** 'R. BOLDREWOOD' *Col. Reformer* (1891) 337 Australian horses..seem wretched underbred creatures.

**b.** *sb.* An underbred animal (esp. a horse).

**1880** *Encycl. Brit.* XII. 198/1 When the thoroughbred is but cantering, the underbred will be doing his utmost. **1897** *Times* 11 Mar. 12/2 At recent shows in Ireland he thought there were more under-breds than 15 or 20 years ago.

**U·nder-bree·ding,** *vbl. sb.* (UNDER-¹ 10 b. Cf. prec.) **1673** *Ess. Educ. Gentlewom.* 22 Doubtless this under-breeding of Women began among Heathen and Barbarous People. **1850** *Bentley's Misc.* Sept. 234 Some of the lords and ladies ..used to..ridicule Mrs. Rawlings before her face, and when they were gone, criticise her underbreeding.

**U·nder-bridge.** Also *dial.* -brigg. [UNDER-¹ 5 c.] A bridge spanning an opening beneath a road or railway.

**1828** CARR *Craven Gloss.*, *Under-brigg*, an arch under a road to open a communication between two fields. **1876** *Encycl. Brit.* IV. 284/2 The over and under bridges of railways. **1891** *Daily News* 19 June 6/1 The state of the under-bridges throughout the [railway] system.

**U·nder-bright.** [UNDER-¹ 5 c.] (See quots.)

**1824** CARR *Craven Gloss.* 119 *Under-breet*, a bright light appearing under the clouds in the horizon. **1867** SMYTH *Sailor's Word-bk.* 705 *Under-bright*,..the strong light which sometimes appears below clouds near the horizon.

†**Underbri·ng,** *v. Obs.* [UNDER-¹ 4 b and 8. Cf. Du. *onderbrengen*, G. *unterbringen*.]

**1.** *trans* To bring into subjection.

*c* **1320** *Cast. Love* 1316 For whon þe world was furst wrouȝt, He haþ him vnder-i-brouȝt [*v.r.* underbrowght]. *c* **1440** *Eng. Conq. Irel.* 91 Smyrte agayn the bolde, meke wyth ham that weryn vndyr-broght.

**2.** To bring in surreptitiously.

**1382** WYCLIF *Gal.* ii. 4 For false britheren vndirbrouȝt yn, the whiche priuely entriden for to aspie oure liberte.

**U·nderbrush,** *sb.* [UNDER-¹ 5 c.] Shrubs and small trees forming the undergrowth in a forest.

Originally and chiefly *U.S.*; common from *c* 1845.

*a* 1813 A. Wilson *Foresters* Poet Wks. (1846) 256 Here piles of logs like furnaces appear, The rows of underbrush rage far and near. 1840 R. H. Dana *Bef. Mast* xix, The next thing was to clear away the underbrush, and have fair play at the trees. 1888 Stevenson *Black Arrow* vi, It was a tall grove of oaks, firm under foot and clear of underbrush.

Hence **U·nderbrush** *v. trans.*, to clear of underwood. Also *fig.*

1865 P. B. St. John *Snow Ship* vi, A thorough good chopper, after the land is underbrushed, will, in eight days, on an average, fell the trees. 1896 *Home Missionary* (N.Y.) Jan. 461 The minister..begins to underbrush and cut down the giant sins that have grown on such fat soil.

**Underbui·ld,** *v.* [Under-[1] 4 a, 10 a.]

**1.** *trans.* To build under, as a means of strengthening or supporting; to underpin. Also *intr.*

1610 Holland *Camden's Brit.* 185 In the underbuilding, pinning and propping up of their pits. 1653 Blithe *Eng. Improver Impr.* To Rdr., I shall a little by way of Reparation in some parts underbuild, and some lean-to, or less necessary, quite pull down of the old work. 1828 Owen & Blakeway *Hist. Shrewsbury* II. 245 A stone-mason..proposed to cut away the lower parts of the infirm pier, and to underbuild it with free stone. 1861 Smiles *Engineers* II. 322 Directing him to cut away the injured part of the pillar, in order to underbuild it.

**2.** To build or pile up under one.

1627 May *Lucan* viii. P 6 b, Fire brought, not vnderbuilt great Pompey takes.

**3.** To fall below in respect of building.

1847 Disraeli *Tancred* i. iv, It was built by the first duke of the second dynasty, who was always afraid of underbuilding his position.

**U·nder-bui:lder.** [Under-[1] 6 a.] An assistant or subordinate builder. Also *fig.*

1651 Jer. Taylor *Holy Dying* Ded. (1719) A viij b, It is enough for me to be an under-builder in the House of God. 1658-9 Sir H. Vane in *Burton's Diary* (1828) III. 177 Now shall we be under-builders to supreme Stuart? 1841 Trench *Parables* 185 The great master builder was about to take down the temporary scaffolding.., and this..the under builders were setting themselves to resist.

**U·nder-buoy.** (Under-[1] 5 b.) 1793 Smeaton *Edystone L.* § 152 He..proposed to fix an under-buoy..nine fathoms under the surface of the sea.

† **Underburn,** *v.*[1] (See Under-[1] 2.)

**Underbu·rn,** *v.*[2] [Under-[1] 10 a.] *trans.* To burn insufficiently. Also **U·nderburnt** *ppl. a.*

1841 *Civil Eng. & Arch. Jrnl.* IV. 341/2 The loss from over-burning, from under-burning and other accidents [to bricks]. 1844 H. Stephens *Bk. Farm.* I. 555 An underburnt as well as an over-burnt tile is bad.

**U:nderbu·ry,** *v.* [Under-[1] 8 b.] *trans.* To bury for lower charges than (another).

1753 H. Walpole *Lett.* (1857) II. 337 G—d d—n the bishops. ..So they will hinder my marrying...I'll be revenged! I'll buy two or three acres of ground, and..underbury them all!

**U·nderbush,** *sb.* [Under-[1] 5 c.] Underwood, underbrush.

1891 Stevenson *South Seas* iv. ii, Smoke rose in the green underbush. 1897 Mary Kingsley *W. Africa* 114 Pretty trailing lycopodium climbing..over the cardamoms which abound in the under-bush.

Hence **U·nderbush** *v. trans.*, = Underbrush *v.*

1886 *Nature* 21 Jan. 269/2, I was watching a coolie underbushing in the bush.

**U·nder-bu:tler.** (Under-[1] 6 a.)

1611 Cotgr., *Soubscelerier*, an vnder Butler. 1708 J. Chamberlayne *St. Gt. Brit.* (1710) 651 The Establishment of..the said Hospital [of Chelsea includes]..2 Under-Butl[ers] at 5*l.* each. 1821 C. Butler *Hist. Mem. Cath.* III. xxxvi. 238 He himself was, for some time, under-butler in Gray's-inn. 1837 Miss Braddon *Like & Unlike* i, The under-butler was over fifty.

**U:nderbuy·,** *v.* [Under-[1] 8 b, 10 a.] *trans.* To buy at less than the actual value, or for less than another. Hence **Underbuy·ing** *vbl. sb.*

*a* 1614 Fletcher *Valentinian* ii. iv, Madam ye have a witty woman. *Mar.* Two Sir, Or else ye underbuy us. *c* 1630 Sanderson *Serm.* (1681) II. 274 The underbuying of commodities far below the worth.

**U·ndercap.** [Under-[1] 5 a.] A cap worn under another; ? a night-cap.

1531 *Rec. St. Mary at Hill* 43 Item, two olde Caps and two ondercaps, x d. 1547 in Feuillerat *Revels Edw. VI* (1914) 11, vij vnder Cappes or nyght Cappes to the same of Crymsin Satten. 1651 in *Verney Mem.* (1907) I. 480, 6 serge undercapps and 6 Browne callico under-capps. 1825 Jamieson *Suppl.*, *Hoomet*,..a child's under cap.

**U·nder-ca:pitalled,** *ppl. a.* [Under-[1] 10 a.] Not furnished with sufficient capital.

1794 *Monthly Rev.* XV. 185 Many facts here stated fully prove that the country is under-capitalled. 1804 *Crit. Rev.* Ser. iii. I. 382 An habitually lower rate of profit than can be accepted by the merchants of under-capitaled countries.

† **U·nder-ca:ptain.** *Obs.* [Under-[1] 6 a.] A captain subordinate to another.

In quots. 1526 = 'centurion'.

1442 *Rolls of Parlt.* V. 60/1 All these saide Shippes.. to obey suche rewle..as be their Capitayne and undre Capitayns shall to hem be ordeyned. *c* 1450 *Harl. Contin. Higden* (Rolls) VIII. 453 That he delyvered..the castell.., when he was undercapiten, to the kynge of Fraunce. 1526 Tindale *Acts* xxi. 32 The hye captayne..toke soudiers and vndercaptynes. [*Ibid.* 33 When they sawe the vpper captayne, etc.] *Ibid.* xxvii. 11 The vndercaptayne beleved the gouerner..better then..Paul. 1550 Crowley *Way to Wealth* 641 He woulde not harken to the right aduice of Achior hys vndercaptaine. 1614 Raleigh *Hist. World* iii. 112 He lost fame and high reputation as easily againe, by meanes of some sleight injury done to them by his under-Captaines. 1648 Gage *West Ind.* x. (1655) 35 Also there were other Gentlemen, that were Under-captains, but a small number.

**U·nder-ca:rriage.** (Under-[1] 5 b.)

1794-6 W. Felton *Carriages* (1801) I. 49 The fore or under carriage, united to the upper carriage by the perch-bolt. 1886 Elworthy *W. Somerset Word-bk.* 813 The under-carriage [of a wagon]..includes all the framework which supports the body.

**U·nderca:rry.** [Under-[1] 5 c.] The movement of water beneath the surface.

1894 Crockett *Raiders* x. 94 The Seahorse..came swiftly, swaying with the undercarry of the sea into the harbour mouth.

**Under-ca·rve,** *v.* [Under-[1] 4 a.] *trans.* To cut away from below or from behind.

1904 Lethaby *Mediæval Art* i. 15 At Baalbec the frieze ..has become a band of carving..under-carved so that the light falls through it as through a trellis.

**U·nder-ca:rved,** *ppl. a.* [Under-[1] 4 a.] Carved below or lower down.

1616 B. Jonson *Forest, To C'tess of Rutland* 85 There like a rich and golden pyramede, Borne up by statues, shall I reare your head, Aboue your vnder-carued ornaments.

**U·ndercast,** *sb. Mining.* (Under-[1] 5 c.)

1883 Gresley *Gloss. Coal-m.* 266 *Undercast*, an air course or wind road carried underneath a wagon way or other road. 1886 J. Barrowman *Sc. Mining Terms* 69 *Undercast*, the lower of two air courses at an air crossing.

† **Underca·st,** *v. Obs.* [Under-[1] 5 b, 7, 8. Cf. MDa. and Da. *underkaste*, MSw. *undir-*, Sw. *underkasta.*]

**1.** *trans.* To cast down; to make subject, subdue.

*a* 1340 Hampole *Psalter* viii. 7 All thyngis þou vndirkast vndir his fete. 1382 Wyclif *Wisd.* xviii. 22 In wrd hym that ouertrauailede hym, he vndircaste. *a* 1395 Hylton *Scala Perf.* ii. xxxvii. (W. de W. 1494), Thenne forsakyth he vtterly hymself & vndercastyth hym holy to Jhesu. 1483 *Cath. Angl.* 259/2 To Ondyr cast, *subicere, subiectare.* *a* 1618 Sylvester *Mysterie of Myst., The Father* 7 Under All things, not under-cast: Over all things, not over-plac't.

**b.** To subject *to* a penalty.

1382 Wyclif *Exod.* xxi. 21 If..he [*sc.* a servant] lyue over a day, or two, he shal not be vndurcast to that peyne.

**2.** To cast under or below.

*c* 1440 *Pallad. on Husb.* iii. 1155 Of vines that forwepe,.. the fattest roote away they tere,..And aisel kene is vnderkest in ground.

**3.** To consider, reflect.

1489 *Barbour's Bruce* v. 552 (Edin. MS.), Till he..Intill hys hart gan undercast [*Camb. MS.* vmbecast] That the King had in custome ay For to ryss arly ilk day.

**U·nder-cause.** [Under-[1] 6 b.] A subordinate or secondary cause.

1645 Rutherford *Tryal & Tri. Faith* (1845) 385 In regard of irresistible efficacy and success, under-causes..are but idol-causes. 1768-74 Tucker *Lt. Nat.* (1834) I. 591 No more than a declaration or record of the causes in act, and operations of under-causes flowing from them.

†**Under-cele·stial,** *a. Obs.*[-1] [Under-[2].] Subcelestial. 1640 Bp. Reynolds *Passions* xl. (1647) 529 Creeping alwayes like those under-cælestial Orbes into another motion.

**U·nder-cha:mberlain.** (Under-[1] 6 a.)

13.. *K. Alis.* 246 (Laud MS.), She clepeþ to hir ane sweyn, Þat is hire vnder chaumberleyn. 1607 Cowell *Interpr.* s.v., Vnder-chamberlaine of the Exchequer. 1642 C. Vernon *Consid. Exch.* 44 The two Vnder-Chamberlaines bee both the Chamberlaines Deputies for the Recept. 1729 Jacob *Law Dict.* s.v. *Chamberlain*, There are also Under Chamberlains of the Exchequer, who make Searches for all Records in the Treasury.

**U·nder-cha:mbress.** (Under-[1] 6 a.) *c* 1450 in Aungier *Syon* (1840) 292 The sexteyne, and undersexteyn, the treseres and undertreseres, the chambres and under-chambresse.

**U·nder-cha:ncellor.** (Under-[1] 6 a.) 1707 *Lond. Gaz.* No. 4382/3 They write from Lemberg, That the Primate and the Under-Chancellor of the Crown arrived..last Month.

**U·nderchange.** [Under-[1] 2.] (See quot.)

1589 Puttenham *Eng. Poesie* iii. xv. (Arb.) 183 The Greekes call this figure *Hipallage* the Latins *Submutatio*, we in our vulgar may call him the vnderchange but I had rather haue him called the Changeling.

**U·nder-chap.** [Under-[1] 5 b.] The lower jaw.

1607 Topsell *Four-f. Beasts* 29 Their vnderchappe doeth in a deformed manner stretch foorth it selfe beyond the vpper, as it is in many fishes. *a* 1608 Dee *Relat. Spir.* i. (1659) 78 He striketh him with an yern,..griping his brain and underchaps, and so he fell down and disappeared. 1774 Goldsm. *Nat. Hist.* V. 382 The stork..produces no other noise than the clacking of its under chap against the upper. 1802 Paley *Nat. Theol.* xxiii, The skin which lies between the under chaps.

**U·ndercharge,** *sb.* (Under-[1] 10 b.) 1864 Webster, *Under-charge*, a charge less than is usual or suitable.

**U:ndercha·rge,** *v.* [Under-[1] 10 a.]

Florio (1611) has *Sottocaricare*, to vnder-charge.

**1.** *trans.* To impose insufficient charges on; to charge (a person, etc.) too little; to make an inadequate charge for (a thing).

1633 Strafford *Lett. & Disp.* (1739) I. 223 They have swallowed down this Maxim, that the Revenue of this Crown must ever be rather over than undercharged. 1712 Prideaux *Direct. Ch.-wardens* (ed. 4) 57 If any be overcharged, or others undercharged, the Ordinary will condemn the Wrong done. 1747 *Gentl. Mag.* 99/1 Any defraud in houses undercharg'd, the persons, &c. to pay double rates. 1864 Webster s.v., To undercharge goods or services. 1895 *Daily News* 15 Mar. 5/6 He affirmed that so far from overcharging India, India was undercharged

**2.** To fill or furnish with less than the average charge.

1794 R. J. Sulivan *View Nature* II. 23 A body that has lost part of its natural quantity, is said to be undercharged, or negatively electrified. 1881 J. C. Maxwell *Electr. & Magn.* I. 40 If the quantity of fluid in the body is..less [than that required], the body is said to be Undercharged.

Hence **U·ndercha:rged** *ppl. a.*

1815 J. Smith *Panorama Sci. & Art* II. 180 There is an attraction exerted between the overcharged extremity of one magnetic body, and the undercharged extremity of the other. 1834 J. S. Macaulay *Field Fortif.* 193 When it is required to determine the charge of an undercharged mine, the same rule may be followed.

**U·nder-chord.** [Under-[1] 5 b.] (See quot.)

1890 *Cent. Dict.* s.v. *Major*, According to this view, the major triad of C is called the *over-chord* of C, and the minor triad of F is called the *under-chord* of C, etc.

**Underci·rcle,** *v.* [Under-[1] 4 a.] *trans.* To pass round below.

1668 Culpepper & Cole *Barthol. Anat.* i. xiv. 34 A broad Membranous and thin Ligament,..arising from the Peritonæum which the Midriff undercircles.

**U·nder-ci:tizen.** (Under-[1] 6 a.) 1711 Addison *Spect.* No. 179 ⁋ 7 The next that mounted the Stage was an Under-Citizen of the [city of] Bath.

**U:ndercla·d,** *ppl. a.* [Under-[1] 10 a.] Insufficiently clad or clothed. Also *fig.*

1622 T. Scott *Belg. Pismire* 81 With vs the only glory is to be gay, and the greatest shame to be under-clad. 1647 N. Ward *Simple Cobler* 77 Not long since, I met with a book, the best to mee I ever saw;..yet under favour, it was somewhat underclad. 1896 *Voice* (N.Y.) 27 Aug. 4/6 The underfed, underclad, and needy millions.

**U:ndercla·ssman.** *U.S.* [Under-[1] 6 a.] A junior student; a sophomore or freshman.

1896 F. Cohen & Eliz. Boyd *Vassar* 53 Other much prized delicacies which tantalize the underclassmen as they pass by.

**U·nderclay.** [Under-[1] 5 b.] A bed of clay beneath a stratum, now *spec.* under a seam of coal.

1661 J. Childrey *Brit. Baconica* 58 The rains that fall, wash by degrees the uppermost mould down into the Valleys, ..but leaves the underclay behind. 1840 [see Underclift]. 1845 Lyell *Trav. N. Amer.* I. 84, I was curious to know whether the *Stigmariæ* would be found here in the underclays. 1867 Smyth *Coal* 25 The floor, thill, or seat..of the coal is an underclay, generally good for fire-brick.

**U·nder-clerk.** (Under-[1] 6 a. Cf. MDu. *onderclerc*, Du. *-klerk.*)

1393 *Test. Ebor.* (Surtees) I. 185 To the paresch clerk xij[d], and to the onder clerk vj d. 1426-7 *Rec. St. Mary at Hill* 64 Þe rode lofte & þe vndir clerkes chambre. 1450 *Rolls of Parlt.* V. 195/1 John Browne, undir Clerk of oure Kechyn. 1516 *Will R. Peke of Wakefield* 4 June (MS.), To the clarke iiij d, to the under-clarke ij d. 1611 Cotgr., *Soubdespensier*, an vnder Cater, or an vnder Clerke of a kitchin. 1670 Clarendon *Hist. Reb.* xiv. § 73 An Under-Clerk for writing Letters and Commissions. 1708 J. Chamberlayne *St. Gt. Brit.* (1710) 573 Clerks of the Jurat, or Under-Clerks of the Treasury. 1779 *Mirror* No. 37, Certain concurring circumstances..placed him as an under-clerk in a counting-house. 1837 B. D. Walsh *Aristoph., Knights* iv. i, I'll ask but..to..serve you as your under-clerk in actions. 1841 Thackeray *Gt. Hoggarty Diamond* ii, We under-clerks all thought it was a fine thing to sit at a desk by oneself.

**U·ndercliff.** [Under-[1] 5 b or Under-[2].]

**1.** A terrace or lower cliff formed from landslips caused by the action of rain and sea.

[1781 Worsley *Isle of Wight* 211 The country below this range of cliffs, is called, by the inhabitants, Under Cliff, or Under Way.] 1829 Phillips *Geol. Yorks.* 89 A very extensive slip of the superior heights, forming an 'undercliff'. 1865 J. H. Bennet *Winter Medit.* (ed. 3) i. iv. 60 A small amphitheatre, formed on the coast-line or undercliff of the mountains of southern Europe. 1880 *Daily Tel.* 23 Sept., The gradual movements along the undercliffs in the Isle of Wight.

**2.** (See quot. and next.)

1883 Gresley *Gloss. Coal-m.* 267 *Undercliff*, argillaceous shale forming the floor of many coal seams in this coal-field.

**U·nderclift.** (Under-[1] 5 b.) 1840 W. Logan in *Trans. Geol. Soc.* Ser. ii. VI. 491 In South Wales, immediately below every regular seam of coal,..lies a bed of clay, which is commonly called underclay, underclift, understone.

**Underclo·se,** *v.* (Under-[1] 5 a.) *c* 1440 *Pallad. on Husb.* ii. 94 The first is good ij fote & half or thre Feet depe to turne vp alle, but diligent Thou be lest balkis vndirclosed be [*L. ne crudum solum..fossor includat*].

**U·ndercloth.** (Under-[1] 5 b. Cf. MDu. *ondercleet*, Du. *-kleed*; MHG. *underkleit*, G. *unterkleid.*)

*c* 1440 *Promp. Parv.* 511/1 Vnder clothe, of a bedde, *lodix.* 1452 *Maldon* (Essex) *Court Rolls* Bundle 31, No. 2[r] (MS.), An olde materas, two pilewys, A vnder clothe of old towylle. 1532-3 *Durham Househ. Bk.* (Surtees) 157, 16 ulnæ pro 2 mappis vocatis underclothez pro tabula domini. 1552-3 *Inv. Ch. Goods, Staffs.*, It[e]m ij underclothes for alters, on cope, ij corporases with a case. 1570 *Bury Wills* (Camden) 156 One bed..withe a vndercIothe, and my best coverlet.

**U·ndercloth,** *v.* [f. Undercloth-ing.] *trans.* To provide with underclothing.

1857 *Putnam's Monthly Mag.* Mar. 244/1 We were, one and all, stoutly underclothed with flannel. 1904 G. B. Shaw *Comm. Sense Municipal Trading* 70 If you have to choose between underclothing your daughter comfortably [etc.].

**U:ndercloˑthed,** *ppl. a.* [Under-[1] 10 a.] Insufficiently clothed.

1890 *Lancet* 17 May 1056/1 No one was either underfed, underclothed,..or overworked. 1895 P. Hemingway *Out of Egypt* i. i. 9 Women, underclothed and overpainted.

**U·nderclothes.** (Under-[1] 5 a.)

1884 May Crommelin *Brown-Eyes* xviii, Letters A. H. embroidered on the little underclothes I wore.

**U·ndercloˑthing.** [Under-[1] 5 a.] Clothing worn below the upper or outer garments, esp. next to the skin. Also *fig.*

1835 T. Mitchell *Acharn. of Aristoph.* 1061 *note*, Used also of veils, and women's underclothing. 1866 Rogers *Agric. & Prices* I. xxii. 572 Linen for two purposes—for under-clothing, and for the table. 1878 Spurgeon *Treas. Dav.* Ps. cix. 29 Where sin is the underclothing, shame will soon be the outer vesture.

**U·ndercoat.** [UNDER-1 5 a, c.]

**1.** A coat worn beneath another. Also *fig.*

**1648** HEXHAM II, *Een Onder-rock*, an Vnder-coate. *a* **1680** BUTLER *Rem.* (1759) II. 449 A Pettifogger is an under-Coat to the Long-robe, a Kind of a coarse Jacket, or dirty daggled Skirt and Tail of the long-Robe. **1683** *Lond. Gaz.* No. 1797/4 In a new-fashion'd Campaign Coat of sad colour'd Frize,.. his under-Coat of grey Stuff turned. **1723** *Ibid.* No. 6150/3 His Under-Coat of a fine light Colour.

†**2.** A woman's underskirt; a petticoat. *Obs.*

**1741** RICHARDSON *Pamela* (ed. 3) I. 50, I bought two Flanel Under-coats, not so good as my..fine Linen ones. **1759** *Ann. Reg., Chron.* 73/2 She was stript of all her cloaths to her shift and under-coat. **1858** H. BAIRD *Poet. Lett.* Ser. I. 52 (Devon dial.).

**3.** The under layer of hair or down in certain long-haired animals.

**1840** DALLAS *Syst. Nat. Hist.* II. 447 The hair [of the goat] covers an undercoat of fine soft woolly down. **1884** *Field* 6 Dec. (Cassell's), The dog looked fresh and well..though lacking undercoat.

**Undercoat(e,** varr. UNDERCOT *v.*

**U·nder-colle·ctor.** (UNDER-1 6 a.)

**1475** *Rolls of Parlt.* VI. 152/1 The Collectours..deputed and ordeyned the maire and Aldermen..to be their under-collectours. **1570** FOXE *A. & M.* (ed. 2) I. 10/1 Which Sanction was also practised..agaynst the Popes collectors and vnder-collectors. **1572** *Act 14 Eliz.* c. 7 *Preamble*, Great Deceits done..by Under-Collectors of the Tenths and Subsidies of the Clergy.

**U·nder-co·lour.** (UNDER-1 5 c.) **1611** FLORIO, *Sotto colore*, vnder-colour. **1891** *Cent. Dict.*, *Under-color*, color beneath the exterior or surface color [as in feathers or fur].

**U·nder-co·loured,** *ppl. a.* (UNDER-1 10 a.)

**1777** H. WALPOLE *Let. to R. Jephson* 17 Oct., In landscape-painting some parts must be under-coloured to give the higher relief to the rest. **1870** *Spectator* 20 Aug. 993 We have steadily asserted that France was outnumbered, and now believe that our statements were under-coloured.

**U·nder-comma·nder.** (UNDER-1 6 a.) **1617** PURCHAS *Pilgrimage* (ed. 3) 588 The Gouvernour was an Abassine, with Seuen other vnder-Commanders, all renegado-Mahumetanes.

**U·nder-condi·tion.** [UNDER-1 6 b.] A subordinate condition or estate.

**1681** *Whole Duty Nations* 23 The Messiah then..must rest in a very low and under-condition of small, private, and particular Assemblies of his servants.

†**U·nder-conduct.** *Obs.*—1 [UNDER-1 5 c.] A subterranean conduit.

**1624** WOTTON *Archit.* 24 Wee should..Digge Wels and Cesternes, and other vnder-conducts and conueiances.

**U·nder-co·nstable.** (UNDER- 6 a.) **1647** HAWARD *Crown Rev.* 38 Deputy to the under Constable. Fee *per diem*, 12.d.

**Underconstumble,** var. UNDERCUMSTUMBLE *v.*

**U·nder-cook.** (UNDER-1 6 a. Cf. MDu. *onder-coc*, Du. *-kok*, G. *unterkoch*, Da. *underkok*, Sw. *-kock.*)

**1598** FLORIO, *Sotto cuoco*, an vnder-cooke. **1620** (*title*), The Historie of Frier Rush: how he came to a house of Religion to seeke seruice, and..was first made vnder Cooke. **1660** BLOUNT *Boscobel* 35 Col. Carlis the while being but Under-cook..made the fire and turn'd the Collops in the pan. **1734** BERKELEY in Fraser *Life* (1871) vi. 227 On breaking up of the Duke's kitchen, one of his under-cooks may be got. **1809** MALKIN *Gil Blas* x. iii. ¶ 10 The cook, the under-cook, and the scullion. **1900** *Daily News* 9 Oct. 5/1 An under-cook, aged 55, who had served 39 years in a boys' orphanage.

**U·ndercooled,** *ppl. a.* [UNDER-1 8 c.] (See quot.)

**1902** *Encycl. Brit.* XXVIII. 568/1 It is generally possible to cool a liquid several degrees below its normal freezing-point without a separation of crystals...A liquid in this state is said to be 'undercooled', or 'superfused'.

**U·nder-coo·per.** (UNDER-1 6 a.) **1745** in W. Thompson *R. N. Advoc.* (1757) 5 Mr. William Thompson (now an under Cooper in your Office).

**U·nder-corre·ct,** *v.* (UNDER-1 10 a.) **1831** BREWSTER *Optics* xliii. 368 In which the flint lens either over corrects or under corrects the colours of the crown glass lens.

†**Underco·t,** *v. Sc. Obs.* Also -coat(e. [UNDER-1 5 a, with obscure second element: cf. QUAT *sb.*1] *intr.* To suppurate or fester inwardly.

**1584** HUDSON *Du Bartas' Judith* II. 182 To Medciners, the medcine vailed not; So sore the poisond plague did vndercot. **1591** R. BRUCE *Serm.* T ij b, The outwarde scroofe, suppose it appeareth to be whole when the inward is festered auaileth nothing, bot maketh it to vndercoate again. **1637** RUTHERFORD *Lett.* I. cxl. (1664) 275 These..cannot have but such a peace with God, as will undercot and break the flesh again. **1669** R. FLEMING *Fulfilling Script.* I. (1726) 77 Too soon letting out of a sore may cause it undercot and gather new matter. **1727** P. WALKER *Biog. Presbyt.* (1827) I. 226 A slight Way of Healing indeed, which now is undercotted, and seems to be incurable.

Hence †**Underco·tted, Underco·tting** *ppl. adjs.*

**1636** RUTHERFORD *Lett.* (1664) 315, I finde old sores bleeding of new; so dangerous..is an undercotted conscience. **1637** *Ibid.* 222 My dumb sabbaths are undercotting wounds.

†**U·nder-cou·nter.** *Fencing. Obs.* (UNDER-1 5 b + COUNTER *sb.*5)

**1692** SIR W. HOPE *Fencing-Master* (ed. 2) 73 The contraries to the parade and slipping of under-counter. *Ibid.* 78 The second way is just done as you play under-counter.

**U·nder-cou·rtier.** (UNDER-1 6 a.) **1709** STEELE *Tatler* No. 78 ¶ 5 This Gentleman seems to have the true Spirit, without the Formality of an Under-Courtier.

**U·nder-co·vering.** (UNDER-1 5 a, c.)

**1483** CAXTON *Gold. Leg.* 131/2 Of hys skynne was made to the kyng of Perses a vndercoueryng. **1902** HANNAN *Textile Fibres of Commerce* 213 The downy under-covering of the Cashmere goat.

**U·nder-co·vert.** [UNDER-1 5 b, c.]

**1.** A covert of undergrowth.

**1805** WORDSW. *Prelude* III. 433 A primeval grove,..[Not] indigent of songs warbled from crowds In under-coverts.

**2.** *Ornith.* One of the small close feathers on the under-side of the wing or tail.

**1817** STEPHENS in Shaw *Gen. Zool.* X. I. 259 Tail like the wing-coverts, with its under-coverts white. **1895** *Funk's Standard Dict.* s.v. *Wing-covert*, Feathers..of the lining of the wing are called *under-coverts*.

†**U·ndercraft.** *Obs.* [UNDER-1 9 and 6 b.]

**1.** Hidden or secret craft or cunning.

*c* **1400** *Pilgr. Sowle* I. xxii. (1859) 27 If thou be vnwise how that thy sowle asayled is with synne and vndercraft.

**2.** A sly, underhand trick.

**1691** NORRIS *Pract. Disc.* 11 Are not..the little Under-crafts of the Plebeian all put into Motion by this Spring? **1765** STERNE *Tr. Shandy* VII. xix, 'Tis an undercraft of authors to keep up a good understanding amongst words, as politicians do amongst men.

**3.** *attrib.* Belonging to inferior crafts.

**1723** DK. WHARTON *True Briton* No. 59. 23 Dec. 2/1 The Under-Craft Traders; such as Tide-waiters, Tidesmen, and Supernumeraries.

**Under-cra·wl,** *v.* (UNDER-1 4 b.) **1844** MRS. BROWNING *Lost Bower* xvii, Under-crawling, overleaping Thorns that prick and boughs that bear, I stood suddenly astonied.

**Undercree·p,** *v. Obs.* exc. *dial.* [UNDER-1 4 b and 8 b. Cf. OE. *undercréopan.*]

**1.** *intr.* To creep in (stealthily).

**1382** WYCLIF *Deut.* xv. 9 Be war lest perauenture vndur crepe [L. *subrepat*] to thee a wickid thouȝt. *c* **1407** LYDG. *Reson & Sens.* 6226 For age, or they taken kepe, Lyche a thefe wil vnderkrepe, And appallen the beaute.

**2.** *trans.* To creep in beneath. Also *fig.*

*a* **1440** *Found. St. Bartholomews* (E.E.T.S.) 40 And now hath vndircrept them necligence, charite chyillith. **1558** PHAER *Æneid* VI. Qj b, That seat, men say, do Fansies keepe, And Dreames vncertaine dwell, and euery leafe they vndercreepe. *c* **1597** HARINGTON *On Play* in *Nugæ Ant.* (1804) I. 227 The olde wall standes by the helpe of that ivey that was the first cawse of rottinge and undercreepinge the fowndacion thearof. **1615** CHAPMAN *Odyss.* IX. 587, I then, Choosing myself the fairest of the den, His fleecy belly under-crept. **1642** H. MORE *Song of Soul* III. iii, When we that stately wall had undercrept, We straightway found our selves in Dizoie.

**b.** *fig.* To subvert secretly; to outdo by craft or stealth; to undersell in trade.

**1592** in R. W. Cochran-Patrick *Records Mining in Scotl.* (1878) 59 And thairby sum persones seikand thair avin commoditie myndis to vndercrepe my rycht and tytill. *Ibid.* 61. **1602** in H. Foley *Rec. Eng. Prov. Soc. Jesus* (1875) I. 10 He approved it for better policy to undercreep the Scottish agents here. **1623** SIR J. ELIOT in Forster *Life* (1864) I. 169 Now, for the price, others under-creep us, and so forestall our markets.

**c.** To evade, escape.

*a* **1618** RALEIGH *Prerog. Parl.* (1628) 34 Surely my Lord, it is a greater treason (though it vndercrepe the law) to teare from the Crowne the ornaments thereof.

Hence **Undercree·ping** *vbl. sb.* and *ppl. a.*

**1398** TREVISA *Barth. De P. R.* XIII. xix. (Bodl. MS.), Bi vndercreping and..preuey rennynge of water erþe is ywasted somme and somme. **1847** HALLIWELL, *Undercreeping*, mean; pitiful; in an underhand way. *Somerset.* (Also 1863- in south-western glossaries.) **1893** W. RAYMOND *Gentleman Upcott's Dau.* ix. (E.D.D.), Above everything he hated undercreeping.

**Undercre·st,** *v.* [UNDER-1 4 a.] *trans.* To support as on a crest.

**1607** SHAKS. *Cor.* I. ix. 72, I meane to stride your Steed; and at all times To vnder-crest your good Addition, To th' fairenesse of my power.

**U·ndercroft.** [UNDER-1 5 b or c + CROFT *sb.*2] The crypt of a church; an underground vault or chamber.

In early use app. limited to the crypt of Canterbury Cathedral.

**1395** in Legg & Hope *Inventories* (1902) 99 Prope altare beate Marie dicte ecclesie Cant. in Criptis que under croft vulgariter nuncupatur. **1601** F. GODWIN *Bps. of Eng.* 50 The monkes..buried it [the body] immediately in the vnder-craft. **1631** WEEVER *Anc. Funeral Mon.* 202 This murdered Bishop was buried first in the vndercroft of the Church. *Ibid.* 213. **1640** SOMNER *Antiq. Canterb.* 175 Let me now leade you to the Undercroft. A place fit..to keepe in memory the subterraneous Temples of the Primitives in the times of persecution. **1772** S. DENNE *Hist. Rochester* 61 From this chapel you descend into the under croft. **1790** PENNANT *London* 330 This undercroft, as these sort of buildings were called, had in it several chauntries and monuments. **1839** *Civil Eng. & Arch. Jrnl.* II. 250/1 The body of the church might be made to stand upon an under-croft. **1865** MORRIS *Jason* XV. 1021 Now went those maids, groping with outstretched hand Betwixt the pillars of the undercroft. **1869** FREEMAN *Norm. Conq.* III. xiii. 292 A vaulted undercroft supported the hall.

†**Undercro·p,** *v. Obs.* [UNDER-1 8 a.] *trans.* To question stealthily; to sound.

**1596** FORMAN *Diary* (Halliw.) 27 When I com home, Henry Pepper cam to me craftely to undercrop me.

**U·ndercrust.** (UNDER-1 5 b.)

**1738** SWIFT *Pol. Conversat.* 158 If you please, my Lord, a Bit of Undercrust. **1764** FOOTE *Mayor of G.* I, I don't think I have eat a bit of under-crust since we have been married. *fig.* **1893** *Advance* (Chicago) 13 July, The real teacher knows that shallowness is often due to a second 'undercrust' which he must break.

**Undercumsta·nd,** *v. dial.* [Alteration of *understand.*] To understand.

**1824** CARR *Craven Dial.* 39. **1840** HALIBURTON *Clockm.* Ser. III. iii. 39 Six bottles of iced champaigne,..then two dollars for tickets, makes a total of twenty-five dollars; do you undercumstand? **1869**- in northern dial. glossaries.

**Undercumstu·mble,** *v. dial.* Also -con-. [Alteration of prec.] To understand.

**1854** MISS BAKER *Northampt. Gloss.* 368. **1865** MISS BRADDON *Sir Jasper* xxx, Why the gentleman required a boat and a bark is more than I can underconstumble.

**U·ndercu·rrent,** *sb.* and *a.* [UNDER-1 5 b or c.]

**1.** A stream or current of water, air, etc., flowing beneath the upper current, or below the surface. Also *fig.* of Time.

**1683** T. SMITH in *Phil. Trans.* XIV. 565 My conjecture is, that there is an under-current, whereby as great a quantity of water is carried out, as comes flowing in. **1687** NORRIS *Coll. Misc.* (1699) 110 Time shall no more her under-current know, But one with great Eternity shall grow; Their streams shall mix. **1762** *Phil. Trans.* LII. 448 Recourse is had to the notion of an under-current. **1830** LYELL *Princ. Geol.* I. 181 The descending water sinks down and forms an under-current. **1878** HUXLEY *Physiogr.* xx. 346 Part of this air then returns as an undercurrent.

**b.** In hydraulic gold-mining, a settling-box additional to the main sluice.

**1877** RAYMOND *Statist. Mines & Mining* 95 The company has this season added a series of under-currents near the point where the washings empty into the river.

**2.** *fig.* An activity, force, tendency, etc., of a suppressed or underlying character.

**1817** COLERIDGE *Biog. Lit.* I. i. 23 Our genuine admiration of a great poet is a continuous under-current of feeling. **1860** TYNDALL *Glac.* I. xvi. 115 That undercurrent of emotion which surrounds the question of one's personal safety. **1878** BOSW. SMITH *Carthage* 371 That gift of humour, that genuine under-current of the soul.

**3.** *attrib.* or as *adj.* That runs or flows out of sight; concealed, hidden; suppressed.

**1855** TENNYSON *Maud* I. XVIII. viii, My heart more blest than heart can tell, Blest, but for some dark undercurrent woe. **1896** *Daily News* 9 Apr. 3/2 There was a good deal of under-current protest.

**U·ndercut,** *sb.* [UNDER-1 5 b and 4 d.]

**1.** The under-side of a sirloin of beef.

**1859** *Habits of Gd. Society* v. 223 The sirloin has an upper and an under cut, about which tastes differ. **1890** MRS. BEETON *Cookery Bk.* 165 The undercut, or fillet of a sirloin, is best eaten when hot.

**2.** *U.S.* A cut made in the trunk of a tree on the side towards which it is intended to fall.

Several other technical senses are recorded in recent American dictionaries.

**1883** *Harper's Mag.* Jan. 201/1 In about an hour the undercut had approached the heart of the tree.

**Undercu·t,** *v.* [UNDER-1 4 a and 8 b.]

†**1.** *trans.* To cut down or cut off. *Obs.*

**1382** WYCLIF *Isaiah* xxxviii. 12 Kut of is as of a weuere my lif; whil ȝit I weuede, he under kutte me.

**2.** To cut (away) below or beneath.

**1598** FLORIO, *Sottotagliare*, to vnder-cut. **1725** *Fam. Dict.* s.v. *Turfing Spade*, Its of very great Use to some to undercut the Turf, after it is mark'd out with the Trenching Plough. **1881** J. GEIKIE *Prehist. Europe* 71 Cliffs of homogeneous composition are often undercut by streams. **1883** GRESLEY *Gloss. Coal-m.* 135 *Hole*, to undercut a seam of coal, &c., by chipping away the coal. &c., with a *pick*.

**b.** *spec.* To cut or carve so as to leave the upper or exposed portion larger than the under or hidden part.

**1874** RUSKIN *Val D'Arno* (1886) 141 He has undercut his Madonna's profile..too delicately for time to spare. **1875** SIR T. SEATON *Fruit-Cutting* 61 You must now commence to back carve the whole; that is to say, to undercut the leaves, stems, and branches.

**c.** *Golf.* To strike (a ball) below the centre, causing it to rise high in the air. **1891** *Cent. Dict.*

**3.** To supplant by working for lower wages or payment, or by selling at lower prices.

**1884** *Manch. Exam.* 30 July 5/2 We do not want the Post Office to 'undercut' private agencies at the expense of the national taxpayer. **1886** MRS. LYNN LINTON in *Fortn. Rev.* Oct. 500 They are able to undercut the men, and can afford to work for less.

**U·ndercut,** *ppl. a.* [f. prec.] Cut or carved so as to have material removed from beneath the surface. (Cf. prec. 2 b.)

**1793** SMEATON *Edystone L.* § 39 The hole was somewhat under-cut; so that, when the lead was poured in, the whole together would make a sort of dovetail engraftment. **1853** ROCK *Ch. of Fathers* III. I. 111 Their slight open skreen-work looks but a frame for the deeply undercut thin foliage roving every where about it. *a* **1878** SIR G. SCOTT *Lect. Archit.* (1879) II. 187 They are most wonderfully carved, the leaves being so much undercut as in places to be quite detached.

**Undercu·tter.** [f. UNDERCUT *v.*] One who undercuts; a tool or machine for undercutting.

**1891** *Engineer* 16 Jan. 59/3 [Patent for] An expanding reversible Undercutter.

**Undercu·tting,** *vbl. sb.* [f. UNDERCUT *v.*] The action of the verb in various senses; the result of cutting away below.

**1613-39** I. JONES in Leoni *Palladio's Archit.* (1742) II. 45 The under cutting of the Corona too, is simple. *Ibid.*, Many times the Ancients did carve the Undercutting of the Corona, with Leaves. **1836** PALGRAVE *Cal. & Inv. Exchequer* I. p. xxi, The ground [of the seal] is grained, and the undercutting and fillagree are so deep [etc.]. **1853** RUSKIN *Stones Ven.* III. ii. 89 Elaborate backgrounds,..together with useless undercutting, and over-finish in subordinate parts. **1877** RAYMOND *Statist. Mines & Mining* 37 This will allow an undercutting of the old works from 800 to 1,000 feet.

†**Under-dark,** *a. Obs.* [UNDER-1 2, after L. *subobscurus.*] Somewhat dark; darkish.

**1382** WYCLIF *Lev.* xiii. 26 If..thilke spice of lepre were vnder derk, he shal recluse hym seuen daies.

†**Under-datary.** *Obs.*—1 (UNDER-1 6 a.) **1670** G. H. *Hist. Cardinals* III. III. 320 He confirm'd Monsignor the

Under-Datary likewise. **Under-dauber.** (UNDER-1 6 a.) 1667 JER. TAYLOR *Dissuas. Popery* II. I. ii. 64 That truth.. will..cast down this new mud-wall, thrown into a dirty heap by M. W. and his under-dawber M. S. **Under-dead.** (UNDER-1 5 c.) 1648 HERRICK *Hesper., Death of Sparrow*, Are not here..all flowers,..Met in one Hearce-cloth, to ore-spred The body of the under-dead? **†U·nderdeal.** *Obs.*—1 [UNDER-1 6 b.] Discomfiture. 1553 ASCHAM *Germany* Wks. (1904) 144 He..should haue had that countrey his onely refuge, if that in warre he had come to any vnderdele.

**†Underdea·ler.** *Obs.*—1 [UNDER-1 8 a.] An underhand dealer or agent.

1682 SOUTHERNE *Loyal Brother* v, All underdealers, as procurers, and retailers of pleasure.

**†Underdea·ling,** *vbl. sb. Obs.* [UNDER-1 9.] Underhand or secret action.

1649 MILTON *Eikon.* xii. 122 He..mentions not that by his underdealing to debaush Armies heer at home..hee had brought the Parlament into..a diffidence of him.

**Under-debauchee.** (UNDER-1 6 a.) 1676 ETHEREDGE *Man of Mode* IV. i, A dozen such good men as you would be enough to atone for..all the under-debauchees of the town.

**U·nder-deck.** [UNDER-1 5 b. Cf. Du. *onderdek*, G. *unterdeck*, Da. *underdæk*, Sw. *-däck*.] The lower deck of a vessel. Also *attrib.*

1826 SCOTT *Provinc. Antiq. Scot.* 73 Each inhabitable space was crowded like the underdeck of a ship. 1867 SMYTH *Sailor's Word-bk.* 705 *Under deck*, the floor of a cabin, or 'tween decks. 1872 TALMAGE *Serm.* 43 Allow your appetites and passions only an under-deck passage.

**U·nder-degree·d,** *a.* [UNDER-1 6 b.] Of lower degree; of inferior rank.

1748 RICHARDSON *Clarissa* (1811) IV. 48 The reputation of persons of birth must not lie at the mercy of every under-degreed sinner.

**†Underde·lve,** *v. Obs.* [UNDER-1 4 a, after L. *suffodĕre*. Cf. Du. *onderdelven*.] *trans.* To dig under; to undermine by digging.

*c* 1000 ÆLFRIC *Saints' Lives* xxxii. 204 Sum eac underdealf þa duru mid spade. *c* 1000 *Ags. Gosp.* Luke xii. 39 He wacode, and ne ʒeþafode þæt man his hus underdulfe. 1382 WYCLIF *Gen.* xlix. 6 In her owne wil thei vndurdelueden the wal. *a* 1400 *Pauline Ep.* (Powell) Rom. xi. 3 Lord þey haue slayn þi prophetis; þey haue vndyrdolue þyn auteris. *c* 1440 *Promp. Parv.* 511/1 Vnder delvyn, *suffodio.*

Hence **†Underde·lving** *vbl. sb.*, **Underdo·lven** *ppl. a. Obs.*

1382 WYCLIF *Ps.* lxxix. 17 The tend vp thingis with fyr, and the vnder doluen. *c* 1440 *Promp. Parv.* 511/1 Vnder deluynge,..*subfossura, subfossio.*

**U·nder-de·vil.** (UNDER-1 6 a.) 1659 R. WILDE *Poems* (1870) 8 He raised of armed sprites—Elves, goblins, fairies, Quakers, and new lights,—To be his under-devils. 1801 STRUTT *Sports & Past.* III. ii. 118 Beelzebub seems to have been the principal comic actor, assisted by his merry troop of under-devils.

**†Underdi·g,** *v. Obs.* [UNDER-1 4 a.] *trans.* = UNDERDELVE *v.*

1382 WYCLIF *Ezek.* xxxvi. 35 Citees desert and destitute and vndirdiggid. 1548 PATTEN *Exped. Scotl.* B vj, Ye Castel, whose walles were so thick..that it was not an easy matter sone to vnderdig them. 1580 HOLLYBAND *Treas. Fr. Tong*, *Sarfouir*,..to vnderdig or vndermine. 1600 SURFLET *Countrie Farme* III. iv. 430 So soon as they growe, they must be.. clensed from weedes, and vnderdigd.

**U·nder-dip,** *a. Mining.* [UNDER-1 5 c.] Lying below the level of the bottom of the engine-pit. Also const. *of.*

1839 URE *Dict Arts* 975 What is not included, is termed the under-dip coal. *Ibid.* 994 Under-dip workings have been already executed more than an English mile under-dip of the engine-pit bottom. 1886 J. BARROWMAN *Sc. Mining Terms* 69 Under-dip coals.

**U·nder-dish.** (UNDER-1 5 b.) 1653 GREAVES *Seraglio* 111 A deep Purcelain dish covered, standing upon a flat under-dish of the same mettal. **U·nder-distri·butor.** (UNDER-1 6 a.) 1708 J. CHAMBERLAYNE *St. Gt. Brit.* (1710) II. III. 512 There are also several Under-Distributors employ'd [by the distributors of stamped vellum].

**Underdi·ve,** *v.* [UNDER-1 4 b.] *trans.* To dive down into.

1615 CHAPMAN *Odyss.* II. 198 How is it, O my son, that you alive This deadly-darksome region underdive?

**Underdo·,** *v.* [UNDER-1 10 a.]

**1.** *intr.* **a.** To refrain from full action.

1611 B. JONSON *Catiline* II. iii, You ouer-act when you should vnder-doe.

**b.** To do less than is requisite or necessary.

1622 F. MARKHAM *Bk. War* II. vii. 67 He [*sc.* the corporal] must equally vnderstand both how to obey and how to command, and therwithal it must be mixt with such a temperance, that he must neither ouerdoe nor vnderdoe, lest he utterly undoe. 1642 W. PRICE *Serm.* 8 We would not cry, that Preacher overdoes, this underdoes, and that goes too farre, this falls short. 1681 GREW *Musæum* I. iv. iv. 79 Nature is so intent upon finishing her Work, that she may be observ'd much oftener to over do, than under do. 1710 PRIDEAUX *Orig. Tithes* ii. 121 He may either overdoe, and give too much,..or he may underdoe and give too little. 1739 J. TRAPP *Righteous Over-much* 5 We may..under-doe, and be defective.

**2.** *trans.* To do, or deal with, insufficiently or imperfectly.

1716 DERHAM *Phys.-Theol.* To Reader A vij, In the former of which I fear he will think I have as much under-done, as in the latter over-done, the Matter. 1776 ADAM SMITH *W. N.* I. v. (1869) I. 47 They sometimes overdo the business, and sometimes underdo it. 1886 MRS. HUNGERFORD *Mental Struggle* iii, Once or twice..it struck me that you were rather under-doing it. 1888 RICKABY *Mor. Philos.* 77 Doing right is opposed to overdoing the thing, and to underdoing it.

**b.** To act (a part) inadequately. Also used *attrib.*

1748 RICHARDSON *Clarissa* VII. 401 Thou must, however, own a good deal of blunder of the over-do and under-do kind, with respect to the part thou actedst. 1754 — *Grandison* I. xv. 95 Can I do it, if I place him in the light of a Lover, and not..underdo his character as such? *a* 1770 JORTIN *Serm.* (1771) I. v. 87 A disposition and behaviour which may be overdone as well as underdone.

**c.** *spec.* To cook insufficiently. (Cf. UNDERDONE *ppl. a.*)

1864 WEBSTER. 1894 *Westm. Gaz.* 1 Jan. 7/2 An adept at underdoing the meat and overdoing the potatoes.

Hence **U·nderdo·er.**

1753 RICHARDSON *Grandison* V. ix. 45 These overdoers, my dear, are wicked wretches. What do they, but make religion look unlovely, and put underdoers out of heart?

**U·nder-do·ctor.** (UNDER-1 6 a.) 1639 DRUMM. OF HAWTH. *Consid. to Parl.* Wks. (1711) 187 That it shall be lawful for the school-boys..to take the schools against their masters, ..and in their places appoint new doctors, under-doctors, masters, for the space of twenty days.

**U·nderdog.** Orig. *U.S.* [UNDER-1 5 b; cf. *top-dog* TOP *sb.*1 32.] The beaten dog in a fight; *fig.* the party overcome or worsted in a contest; one who is in a state of inferiority or subjection.

1887 *Daily Tel.* 30 Apr. 3/3 There is an indefinable expression in his face and figure of having been vanquished, of having succumbed, of having been 'under-dog' as the saying is. 1892 *Daily Chron.* 23 June 5/2 The mission of the Democratic party is to fight for the under-dog.

**Underdone,** *ppl. a.* (Stress var.) [UNDER-1 10 a, or f. UNDERDO *v.*] Of meat: Insufficiently cooked; left slightly raw after cooking.

1683 TRYON *Way to Health* 111 That it [*sc.* roast flesh] be neither over nor under-done, but of the two, it is better that it be under-done. 1798 *Spirit Public Jrnls.* (1799) II. 202, I shall give an account of every dinner I eat,..whether under or over-done. 1807 JANE AUSTEN *Lett.* (1884) I. 315 A boiled leg of mutton, underdone even for James. 1842 DICKENS *Amer. Notes* x, A plate of underdone roast-beef. 1874 H. W. PULLEN *Mod. Christianity* (1876) 65 You..make quite as much fuss, if the mutton is under-done.

*transf.* 1837 BARHAM *Ingol. Leg.* Ser. I. *Spectre of Tappington*, A little ferret-faced woman with underdone eyes.

**U·nder-dose,** *sb.* (UNDER-1 10 b.) 1822–7 GOOD *Study Med.* (1829) IV. 592 Given in a full dose, they destroy the life instantly; but, in an under-dose, the circulation is continued feebly.

**U·nderdo·se,** *v.* [UNDER-1 10 a.]

**1.** *trans.* To dose (a person) insufficiently; to administer too small a dose to.

1740 CHEYNE *Regimen* p. liv, Nature will,..by acute and intolerable Pains from Hunger, apprize him at least in some time, if he has under-dos'd her.

**2.** To give in insufficient doses.

1744 *Phil. Trans.* XLIII. 216 On the contrary, I was rather induced to think, that it had..been usually under-dosed.

**Underdo·tted,** *ppl. a.* [UNDER-1 4 a.] Marked with a dot or dots beneath.

1874 *Ripon Ch. Acts* (Surtees) 68 *note*, These three words under-dotted. 1897 ANNE PAGE *Afternoon Ride* 96 The message conveyed by letters under-dotted in a newspaper.

**†U·nder-dou·ble.** *Obs.* [UNDER-1 6 b: cf. *subdouble* s.v. SUB- 10.] = SUBDUPLE. Also **†Under-doubled** *ppl. a. Obs.*

*c* 1430 *Art of Nombryng* (E.E.T.S.) 16 It shewithe that a nombre componede was the quadrat, and his rote a digit last founde with vnder-double other vndirdoubles. *Ibid.*, Neþer to sette the doublede forwarde nether the vnder doublede.

**U·nder-down.** [UNDER-1 5 c.] The down below the outer feathers of birds.

1842 J. B. FRASER *Mesopot. & Assyria* xv. 363 Cold winters ..have every where the effect of lengthening the hair or fleece of animals, or of supplying them with an under-down. 1857 DUFFERIN *Lett. High Lat.* (ed. 3) 42 Where the eider ducks ..build nests with the soft under-down plucked from their own bosoms.

**U·nder-drain,** *sb.* [UNDER-1 5 c.] An underground drain.

1805 R. W. DICKSON *Pract. Agric.* I. 151 Where under-drains are formed for taking off the water below the footways. 1868 *Rep. U. S. Commissioner Agric.* (1869) 354 The longitudinal underdrains are to be made of broken stones, and are to be filled up to the level of the surface.

**Underdrai·n,** *v.* [UNDER-1 4 a.] *trans.* To drain by means of underground trenches.

1805 R. W. DICKSON *Pract. Agric.* I. 13 Those clayey soils where water stagnates on the surface of the ground, and.. cannot be removed by the more general modes of under-draining. 1832 *Scoreby Farm Rep.* 13 in *Husb.* III (L.U.K.), The land was..completely underdrained with tiles. 1898 *Yearbk. U. S. Dept. Agric.* 318 If it is not underdrained in all wet spots, [surface draining] should be the first work done.

Hence **Underdrai·ner.**

1832 *Scoreby Farm Rep.* 25 in *Husb.* III (L.U.K.), The great enemy to underdrainers, the mole.

**U·nder-drai·nage.** [UNDER-1 5 c.] Underground drainage.

1810 *Sporting Mag.* XXXV. 23 The System of under-drainage..in the neighbourhood of Edgwarebury. 1898 *Yearbk. U. S. Dept. Agric.* 504 A proper system of under-drainage.

**U·nder-draught.** [UNDER-1 5 c.] An under-current.

1853 KANE *Grinnell Exp.* xxxvi. (1856) 330 Our log-line ..showed still a marked under-draught toward the south.

**Underdraw·,** *v.* (ʊndəɹ-, ʊ·ndəɹ-). [UNDER-1 4 a, 10 a.]

**1.** *trans.* To mark by lines drawn underneath.

1799 ANNA SEWARD *Lett.* (1811) V. 195 The motto you will find underdrawn in the lines which suggested my design.

**2.** To cover (the inside of a roof or the under-side of a floor) with boards or with lath and plaster.

Hence dial. *underdrawing*, a ceiling.

1843 WORDSW. *Prose Wks.* (1876) III. 201 The interior of it has been..made warmer by underdrawing the roof, and raising the floor. 1865 *Spectator* 22 Apr. 435 The mud walls bulging in here and out there; the roof of thatch, and not underdrawn.

**3.** To represent or depict inadequately.

1865 MRS. H. WOOD *M. Arkell* I. xvi. 282 The sufferings described..were underdrawn rather than the contrary. 1890 *Academy* 3 May 300/2 One seems to be overdrawn, while the other is underdrawn.

**4.** To draw from a bank-account so as to leave a reserve. Also *absol.*

1898 *Times* 12 July 13/4, I..generally underdrew so as to leave a margin.

**†Underdrawn,** *ppl. a. Obs.*—1 (Meaning obscure; perhaps an error for *undrawn.*)

1581 *Knaresb. Wills* (Surtees) I. 141, I give to Henry Pott seaven kie,..one oxe,..and fower stottes under drawen.

**U·nderdress,** *sb.* [UNDER-1 5 a.]

**1.** Underclothes; a set of underclothing.

1785 BURNS *Mauchline Wedding* 17 But modest Muses only *think* What ladies' underdress is On sic a day. 1856 KANE *Arct. Expl.* II. xvii. 181 Each man had a woollen underdress.

**2.** A dress or gown worn beneath another; a part of a gown so made as to present the appearance of being worn in this way.

1861 *Archaeologia* XXXIX. 250 The sleeves of his doublet are cloth of gold; the under-dress is of a lavender gray. 1897 *Daily News* 23 Jan. 6/3 The under-dress, which showed in front, had three slashes of velvet at the sides.

**U·nderdre·ss,** *v.* [UNDER-1 10 a.] *intr.* To dress too plainly.

1908 R. BAGOT *A. Cuthbert* xxvi. 339 Miss Cuthbert assured her that there was no greater mistake than to under-dress on occasions such as this.

**Underdressed,** *ppl. a.* (Stress variable.) [UNDER-1 10 a.] Too plainly dressed.

*a* 1784 JOHNSON in Mrs. Piozzi *Anecd.* (1786) 109 No person (said he one day) goes under-dressed till he thinks himself of consequence enough to forbear carrying the badge of his rank upon his back. 1853 MRS. GORE *Dean's Daughter* xxvii, [She] ventured to whisper that Mrs. Hargreave had a sadly provincial air—that she was under-dressed, and a dowdy. 1861 MRS. BEETON *Bk. Househ. Managem.* 10 As a general rule..it is better to be under-dressed than overdressed.

**U·nderdrift.** [UNDER-1 5 c.] An undercurrent; *fig.* a tendency beneath the surface of things.

1849 CUPPLES *Green Hand* xiv, Either she [the ship] stood still, or she'd caught some eddy or under-drift. 1891 *Daily News* 12 Jan. 215 Thus the underdrift of things is in favour of an easier money market.

**U·nder-dru·dgery.** (UNDER-1 6 b.) 1624 MIDDLETON *Game at Chess* III. i, I'd make him do all under-drudgery.

**U·nder-earth,** *sb.* [UNDER-2.]

**1. a.** The earth or soil lying below the surface.

1765 *Museum Rust.* IV. 157 To defend the roots of my young trees from the damp, raw under-earth.

**b.** *Mining.* (See quot.)

1883 GRESLEY *Gloss. Coal-m.* 267 *Underearth*, a hard bastard fireclay forming the floor of a seam of coal.

**2.** The regions below the earth.

1878 GLADSTONE *Homer* iv. 56 Tartaros..standing to the Under-earth as the heaven stands to the Upper..world-surface. 1896 *Boston* (Mass.) *Youth's Companion* 10 Dec. 659/2 The economical resources of the underearth were the goals of the first practical studies of the rocks.

**U·nder-ea·rth,** *a.* [UNDER-2.] Subterranean, underground.

1592 NASHE *P. Penilesse* K 3, The vnder-earth spirits, are such as lurk in dens and little cauernes of the earth. 1613 PURCHAS *Pilgrimage* II. i. 104 Philip the Tetrarch..first found out this under-earth passage. 1662 J. CHANDLER *Van Helmont's Oriat.* 322 Paracelsus reducing all things into an under-earth off-spring. 1816 BYRON '*Could I remount*' 23 The under-earth inhabitants—are they But mingled millions decomposed to clay?

**†Under-earthly,** *a. Obs.* = prec.

1598 SYLVESTER *Du Bartas* II. ii. I. *Ark* 281 No hoorded waues Of ayrie clouds or vnder-Earthly caues.

**Under-ea·ten,** *ppl. a.* [UNDER-1 4 a.] Eaten away or eroded below.

1877 TENNYSON *Harold* I. ii, The sea may roll Sand.., not the living rock Which guards the land,..Except it be a soft one, And undereaten to the fall.

**U·nder-edge.** (UNDER-1 5 b.) Also *attrib.*

1683 MOXON *Mech. Exerc., Printing* xxiv. ⁋ 19 With the under-edge of the bottom of the Brayer. 1733 TULL *Horse-hoeing Husb.* xxiv. 394 Its Under-edge..will stand upon the prick'd Line *e f.* 1797 *Encycl. Brit.* (ed. 3) XVII. 395/1 The under edge of the false keel. 1883 GRESLEY *Gloss. Coal-m.* 267 *Underedge stone*, the floor of an iron-stone mine.

**U·nder-engra·ver.** (UNDER-1 6 a.) 1656 CROMWELL in *Antiq. Rep.* (1808) II. 408 Thomas Symon, Sole chiefe Engraver,..by his sufficient deputy or under-engraver [etc.].

**U·nder-e·nter,** *v.* [UNDER-1 10 a.] *trans.* To enter at less than the actual quantity.

1692 in Picton *L'pool Munic. Rec.* (1883) I. 300 All salt.. shall be measured, and a reasonable proporcion thereof taken ..if ye entrey be right, but if underentred, then ye town officers to take so much of ye said salt.

**†U·nderer.** *Obs.*—1 [f. UNDER *adv.*] An inferior; one of lower rank.

*c* 1449 PECOCK *Repr.* III. xvii. 393 How ellis myȝte..haue be ordeyned..suche statis in the church to be in subordinacioun of vndrers and ouerers.

**U·nder-escheа·tor.** (UNDER-1 6 a.) 1543 tr. *Acts*, 5 *Edw. III*, c. 4 B ij, Item it is enacted that no shyriffe, vnder-eschetour, baylyffe of fraunchises,..shall [etc]. **U·nder-espi·al.** (UNDER-[1] 6 a.) **1820** SCOTT *Abbot* xxiv, His loyal and faithful service as under-espial.

**U·nder-e·stimate,** *sb.* [UNDER-[1] 10 b.] Too low an estimate (of value, expense, etc.).

**1882** *Cornh. Mag.* Feb. 169 He sets a high value on wealth, combating..the stoical underestimate of its importance. **1895** *Bible Soc. Record* (N.Y.) Dec. 178/2 The statements..are underestimates rather than overestimates.

**U·nder-e·stimate,** *v.* [UNDER-[1] 10 a.]

1. *trans.* To estimate at too low an amount, quantity, number, etc.

**1812** *Q. Rev.* VIII. 329 He states the annual consumption ..at..from three to four hundred, evidently with no disposition to under-estimate the amount. **1869** TOZER *Highl. Turkey* II. 24 [He] seems to have greatly under-estimated the height.

2. To rate or rank too low; to undervalue.

*a* **1850** CALHOUN *Wks.* (1874) I. 73 It is not my aim..to underestimate the great power and influence [of the press]. **1882** FARRAR *Early Chr.* II. 96 Exactly as St. James neither ignores nor underestimates faith, so neither does St. Paul ignore nor underestimate the value..of good works.

Hence **U·nder-estima·tion.** (1891–.)

**U·nder-expo·se,** *v. Photogr.* [UNDER-[1] 10 a.] *intr.* and *trans.* To give too little exposure (to).

**1890** *Anthony's Photogr. Bull.* III. 287 The best negatives are not those taken the quickest; sooner over expose, than under expose.

**Under-exposed,** *ppl. a.* (Stress var.) *Photogr.* [UNDER-[1] 10 a.] Of a sensitized plate or film: Having received too short an exposure to light.

**1861** in *Wylde's Circ. Sci.* (1865) I. 162 This is an..advantage when the picture is under-exposed. **1878** ABNEY *Photogr.* 81 An under-exposed picture will develop very slowly.

**U·nder-expo·sure.** *Photogr.* [UNDER-[1] 10 b.] Insufficient exposure to light.

**1873** E. SPON *Workshop Receipts* Ser. I. 255 If the negative is deficient in density,..it is the result of under-exposure. **1892** *Photogr. Ann.* II. 90 Rodinal..gives much softer negatives than quinol, especially in cases of under-exposure.

† **Underf,** *a.*: see UN-[1] 3.

**U·nder-face.** (UNDER-[1] 5 b.) **1869** SWINBURNE *Ess. & Stud.* (1875) 346 A large priestly head,..a heavy lax lustful under-face. **U·nder-fa·ction.** (UNDER-[1] 6 b.) **1642** FULLER *Holy & Prof. St.* v. xi. 405 Thus is it given to all Heresies to break out into under-factions. **1667** *Decay Christian Piety* xi. ¶ 4 'Tis abundant evidence how much Christianity loses by these contests of under factions. **U·nder-fa·ctor.** (UNDER-[1] 6 a.) **1623** *St. Papers, Col.* 168 A purser's mate or underfactor. **U·nder-fa·culty.** (UNDER-[1] 6 b.) *a* **1628** PRESTON *Serm. bef. His Maj.* (1630) 81 How many impediments doth he finde in the vnder-faculties? *a* **1685** OTWAY *Epist. to Duke* 101 And there methinks, Fancy sits Queen of all; While the poor under Faculties resort, And to her sickly Majesty make Court. **U·nder-fa·lconer.** (UNDER-[1] 6 a.) **1660** FULLER *Mixt Contempl.* (1841) 252 He was preferred one of the King's underfalconers. **1825** SCOTT *Betrothed* xxiii, Blaming alternately the carelessness of the under-falconer, and the situation of the building.

**U·nderfall,** *sb.* [UNDER-[1] 5 b.] A foot-hill slope.

**1857** *Smith's Dict. Grk. & Rom. Geog.* II. 1274/2 The underfalls of the Alps that are thrust forward towards the plain. **1883** *Standard* 8 May 4/8 The last 'underfalls' of the..plateau terminate to the North of Tonquin.

**Under-fa·ll,** *v.* (UNDER-[1] 4 b.)

Prob. *trans.*, to fall under (the hands, etc.).

**1614** RALEIGH *Hist. World* IV. i. § 1. 157 It commonly falleth out with euery man of marke..that they vnder-fall, and perish, by the hands and harmes, which they least feare.

**Underfang,** var. UNDERFONG *v. Obs.*

**U·nder-fa·rmer.** (UNDER-[1] 6 a.)

**1609** T. COCKS *Diary* (1901) 77/5 Rec' of the vnderfermer of Bramblinge,..ijs vjd. *a* **1751** BOLINGBROKE *Refl. St. Nation* Wks. 1754 III. 160 All who served, cheated the public,..from the commissioners of the treasury down to the under-farmers and the under-treasurers. **1890** SETON-KARR *Cornwallis* vi. 131 A law..defining the extent of the legal coercion which landholders might exercise over under-farmers.

**U·nder-fea·ture.** [UNDER-[1] 6 b.] A minor feature in a landscape; a small elevation.

**1879** *Cassell's Techn. Educ.* IV. 115/2 All the small outlying features, such as hillocks or ridges;..the details of these 'under-features' [are] sketched in. **1900** *Daily News* 10 Mar. 5/6 The whole..Division, which was lying in front of the enemy's left, concealed by an underfeature.

**Underfed,** *a.* and *sb.* (Stress var.) [UNDER-[1] 10 a.] Insufficiently fed or nourished.

**1835** SIR J. ROSS *Narr. 2nd Voy.* xli. 545 We were often far underfed. **1868** M. COLLINS *Sweet Anne Page* I. 67 The boys were not starved, but certainly under-fed.

*transf.* **1893** *Month* July 326 Places..overstocked with labour or underfed with orders.

b. As *sb.* An underfed person.

**1893** *Advance* (Chicago) 1 June, And Growler's so stuffed now he needs to divide his rations with under-feds.

† **U·nder-fee.** *Obs.* (UNDER-[1] 6 b + FEE *sb.*[2])

**1594** R. ASHLEY tr. *Loys le Roy* 56 Wherehence are come the termes of fees and vnderfees, of vassals and vndervassals. *Ibid.* 117 b, The Nobilitie of the countrie are bound to go to the warre, by the fees, and vnderfees which they possesse.

**U·nderfeed,** *a.* [Cf. next, 2.] Of furnaces: Fed with fuel from below. (In recent use.)

**U·nderfee·d,** *v.* [UNDER-[1] 10 a, 4 a.]

1. *trans.* To feed insufficiently; to stint in food.

**1659** GAUDEN *Tears Ch.* III. xxviii. 363 The Fanaticks strive to underfeed and starve it to a despicable feeblenesse. **1842** A. COMBE *Physiol. Digest.* ix. (1845) 75 Underfeeding and great mortality of the poor. **1861** GOLDW. SMITH *Inaugural Lect.* 32 The folly of overworking and underfeeding the labourer.

2. To feed with fuel from below.

**1904** *Jrnl. Franklin Inst.* Dec. 439 He was convinced that the fundamental principle of underfeeding was a success.

† **Underfee·l,** *v. Obs.* [UNDER-[1] 8 a.] *trans.* To examine, pry into, quietly or secretly.

**1600** HOLLAND *Livy* 639 The young man .. practised secretly to underfeele and sound his mind. **1630** J. TAYLOR (Water P.) *Bawd* Wks. II. 92/1 The Priest..wil know her disposition,..and craftily vnderfeele her policies. **1654** GATAKER *Disc. Apol.* 81 Emissaries, who,..to underfeel and undermine men, repair to them with counterfeit errands.

**Underfeet**: see UNDERFOOT *adv.*

**U·nder-fe·llow.** (UNDER-[1] 6 a.) *a* **1586** SIDNEY *Arcadia* II. viii, A principall officer..Who with no more civilitie (though with much more busines then those under-fellowes had shewed) beganne..to put interrogatories unto him.

**Under-fiend.** [UNDER-[1] 5 b.] One of the fiends under the earth.

**1607** SHAKS. *Cor.* IV. v. 98, I will fight Against my Cankred Countrey, with the Spleene Of all the vnder Fiends.

**U·nder-fi·lling.** *Arch.* (UNDER-[1] 5 c.)

**1624** [see SUBSTRUCTION 1].

**Underfi·nd,** *v.* Now *dial.* [UNDER-[1] 8 a. Cf. Du. *ondervinden.*] *trans.* To perceive, understand.

*c* **1200** *Vices & Virtues* 99 3if hie cumeð fram mannen, hie cann hwatliche underfinden, an hwos half he is icumen. *a* **1300** *Cursor M.* 3664 If mi fader þat es now blind Mai mi fallace oght vnderfind, I dred me sare, for benison He sal me giue his malison. **1320–30** *Horn Ch.* 623 Þe kni3t toke a schaft in hand, & horn wele vnder-fand, Þat he couþe ride. *a* **1800** PEGGE *Suppl. Grose, Underfind*, to understand. Derb. **1877** *N.W. Linc. Gloss.* 263 He was here last neet, I underfind.

**U·nder-fired,** *ppl. a.* [UNDER-[1] 4 a, 10 a.]

1. Supplied with fuel from below.

**1890** D. K. CLARK *Steam Engine* I. 74 The furnace of an egg-end stationary boiler, under-fired, burning coal.

2. Insufficiently fired or baked. **1891** *Cent. Dict.*

**U·nder-flame.** (UNDER-[1] 5 b, 6 b.)

**1631** SIR L. CARY *Elegy on Donne* 44 To make us know the Crosse, and value it, (Although we owe that reverence to that name Wee should not need warmth from an under flame.) **1830** TENNYSON *Arab. Nts.* 91 Dark-blue the deep sphere overhead..Grew darker from that under-flame.

**U·nderflood.** (UNDER-[1] 6 b.) **1615** CHAPMAN *Odyss.* XVII. 606 But every fountain hath his underfloods.

**Under-floo·r,** *v.* [UNDER-[1] 4 a.] *trans.* To provide with, or form, a floor or under-floor.

**1778** *Phil. Trans.* LXVIII. 890 The method of underflooring I have also applied..to a wooden stair-case. **1884** COUES *Key N. Amer. Birds* (ed. 2) 155 The basitemporal and parasphenoid bones which underfloor the whole skull.

**U·nderflow,** *sb.* [UNDER-[1] 5 c.] An undercurrent. Also *fig.*

**1854** S. DOBELL *Balder* xxiv. 169 That underflow and substance wherein the future heaves. **1875** CROLL *Climate & T.* viii. 133 An underflow of polar water south into the Atlantic.

**Underflow·,** *v.* [UNDER-[1] 4 a, b. Cf. OE. *underflōwan.*]

1. *intr.* To flow beneath.

**1610** HOLLAND *Camden's Brit.* II. 45 It looketh downe to the underflowing sea. **1647** HEXHAM I.

2. *trans.* To flow in under (something).

**1872** DIXON *Switzers* v. 45 The waters..underflowed the beams, and lifted the strong habitations.

† **Underfo,** *v. Obs.* Pa. t. 1–4 (5) -feng (4 -fenge), 3–4 -ueng, 4 -uinge, 5 -fynge; 4 -fang, -vong, 4–5 -fong(e. Pa. pple. 1–2 -fangen, 4–5 -fongen (4 -un, -yng), 3–6 -fonge, 4 -uonge, -venge. [OE. *underfōn*, = MDu. *ondervaen*, OHG. *untarfâhan*, MHG. *undervâhen*. See UNDER-[1] 8 a and FANG *v.*[1]]

1. *trans.* To receive (a thing); to have (something) given to one; to come to have or possess.

*c* **888** K. ÆLFRED *Boeth.* xiv. § 3 Eala þæt hit is god..þæt mon micelne welan hæbbe, nu se næfre ne wyrð orsorg þe hine underfehð. **962–3** *Laws Edgar* Suppl. 1 Þa Godes þeowas, þe þa sceattas underfoð þe we Gode syllað. *c* **1040** *Bidding Prayer* in *Eng. Hist. Rev.* Jan. (1912) 10 For ealle þa saula þe fulluht under-fengan. *c* **1200** *Trin. Coll. Hom.* 97 Þis dai is bicumelich time husel to underfon. *c* **1275** *Sinners Beware* 317 in *O. E. Misc.* 82 To day ye schuleþ y-frede And vnder-fo luþre mede. **1340** *Ayenb.* 101 Alle oure broþren ..þet byeþ children of holy cherche, be þe byleaue þet hi onderuinge ine cristnynge. *c* **1400** *Brut* 13 And Guentolen ..vndirfonge feautes & homages of all þe men of þe land. *a* **1513** FABYAN *Chron.* 4 Of the peas that hath been vnderfonge, Both by great othes, and eke by maryage.

b. To receive willingly; to accept.

*c* **1000** *Ags. Psalter* (Spelman) vi. 9 Drihten 3ebed min he underfeng. *c* **1175** *Pater Noster* in *Lamb. Hom.* 65 God wule hit underfon, Wenne ic for3eue min hating. *c* **1205** LAY. 10141 For þe king wolde wel don, & Cristes la3en vnderfon. *a* **1225** *Leg. Kath.* 982 Þu..underfest þe an half & dustest adun þe oðere. *a* **1300** *Cursor M.* 2700 His læren [was] nineti and nine þat day Þai vnder-fang þis neu lai.

c. To admit into a receptacle; to conceive.

*a* **1100** in Napier *O. E. Glosses* I. 3819 [*Cadaver*] *receptet*, ..underfo. *c* **1175** *Lamb. Hom.* 77 Þu scald underfon an child in þi wombe. *c* **1275** *XI Pains of Hell* 236 in *O. E. Misc.* 153 Vurþer, her his on oþer put..Seoue duren þer beoþ on, Þe saulen for to under-fon. **1379** *Glouc. Cath. MS. 19* No. 1, Lib. I. iii. fol. 2 Whenne thy duodene hath vnderfongyng & receyved the fode out froo the mawe gutte.

d. To have understanding of or skill in.

*a* **1300** *Cursor M.* 1519 Cubal [*v.r.* Tobal] þer broþer first vnderfang Music, þat es þe sune o sang.

2. To take in hand; to undertake.

*c* **893** K. ÆLFRED *Oros.* II. ii. 66 Romulus æfter þiosan underfeng Cirinensa 3ewinn. *c* **897** — *Gregory's Past. C.* xxi. 161 Ðonne hie ðara eorðlicra monna heortan underfoð to læronne. *c* **1000** ÆLFRIC *Numb.* xi. 17 Hi3 underfoð þis folc mid þe, þæt þu ne si ana 3ehefe3od. **1399** GOWER *Praise of Peace* 264 The heved above hem hath noght undirfongen To sette pes, bot every man sleeth other.

3. To receive (a person); to admit to one's presence, society, or friendship; to accept.

**924–5** *Laws Edward* 10 Ne underfo nan man oðres mannes man butan þæs leafe þe he ær fyli3de. *c* **1000** *Ags. Gosp.* Matt. x. 40 Se þe eow underfehð, he underfehð me. *c* **1200** ORMIN 12936 Þatt Godd iss rædi3 tunnderrfon Þatt follc þatt rihht himm foll3heþþ. *c* **1250** *Gen. & Ex.* 1679 And a maiden was hire bi-tagt, Zelfa bi name...Iacob gan hire under-fon. **13..** *K. Alis.* 7046 (Laud MS.), Þise vnderfongen þe Emperoure, And duden to hym al honoure. **1382** WYCLIF *Rom.* 1st Prol., The Lord..not onli 3ee wolden not resceyuen, but also 3ee slowen; whom we vnderfongen.

b. To receive in a specified manner.

*a* **1122** *O. E. Chron.* (Laud MS.) an. 1022, Æðelnoð biscop for to Rome & wæs under-fangen þær fram Benedicte..myd mycclum wurðscipe. *c* **1200** *Trin. Coll. Hom.* 141 Ure drihten underfeng eadmodliche ane sinfulle wimman and forgiaf hire hire sinnen. *c* **1230** *Hali Meid.* 41 He vnderfeð bliðeliche, & bicluppeð swoteluche, þe alre laðlukest. *c* **1290** *Beket* 1367 in *S. Eng. Leg.* I. 145 Þo seint thomas to Rome cam, faire he was onder-fonge. *a* **1330** *Roland & V.* 87 Þemperour was glad y-wis, & vnderfenge wiþ miche blis Sir charls þe king. **1387** TREVISA *Higden* (Rolls) I. 239 At his comynge he schulde wiþ þre manere worschippe be vnderfonge. *c* **1400** *Brut* 9 And when Brut wyste whens þei were, he þo vndirfong hem with mychel ioy in-to his Shepys. *c* **1425** *Eng. Conq. Ireland* 8 Þe bisshop well wyrshipfully vndrefynge [*v.r.* vndyrfonge] Macmorgh.

c. *spec.* To receive at baptism.

**1362** LANGL. *P. Pl.* A. I. 74 Holi church Icham...Ich þe vndurfong furst and þi feiþ þe tau3te. **1377** *Ibid.* B. XI. 113 On holicherche I þou3te, Þat vnderfonge me atte fonte.

4. To receive by way of hurt or harm; to undergo, suffer.

*c* **1000** ÆLFRIC *Numb.* xiv. 34 On feowerti3um 3earum 3e underfoð eowere unrihtwisnissa, þæt 3e witon mine wrace. *c* **1175** *Lamb. Hom.* 119 Vre drihtnes..þrowunge þe he for moncunne underfeng. *a* **1225** *Leg. Kath.* 2234 Streche forð þine swire scharp sweord to underfonne. *c* **1250** *Gen. & Ex.* 480 Lamech dro3e is arwe ner, And letet fle3en of ðe streng, Caim unwarde it under-feng. *a* **1325** *MS. Rawl. B. 520* fol. 53 Þat he þat hat vnderfonge þe harmes habbe bref of wast.

5. To reprove, rebuke. *rare*—[1].

*c* **1400** *Brut* 138 Þe Erchebisshope..vnderfonge [*v.r.* vndirtoke] him of his Wickednesse.

**U·nderfold,** *sb.* (UNDER-[1] 5 c.) *a* **1618** SYLVESTER *Job Triumph.* III. 286 Earths surface yeelds him corn & fruits for food, Her under-folds, some burning Sulphury flood.

**Underfo·ld,** *v.* [UNDER-[1] 8 a.] *trans.* To wrap up, hide, conceal.

**1612** W. PARKES *Curtaine-Dr.* (1876) 42 Thou hast often fingered my Curtaine, and beene content therewith to shadow and vnderfold many black and vgly disguises.

† **Underfollow** *v.*: see UNDER-[1] 2. So **Underfollowing** *ppl. a. Sc. Obs.*

**14..** *Acta Parlt. Scot.* (1844) I. 711/2 And sa of vnderfollowand [L. *de subsequentibus*], that is to say of subarmigeris..[etc.].

† **Underfo·ng,** *v. Obs.* Pa. t. 4 -fanged, -id, -fonged. [UNDER-[1] 8 a + FANG *v.*[1] Cf. UNDERFO *v.* and MDu. and Du. *ondervangen*, MLG. *undervangen*, G. *unterfangen.*]

1. *trans.* = UNDERFO *v.* 1.

*c* **1175** *Lamb. Hom.* 51 Hwenne þu scrift underuongest of þe sunnen þe þu idon hauest. *c* **1200** ORMIN 11112 Forr tunnderrfanngenn Crissttenndom & fulluhht unnderr Criste. *a* **1300** *K. Horn* 345 (Harl. MS.), Shame þe mote by shoure, Ant euel hap to vnderfonge. *c* **1350** *Will. Palerne* 5259 To vnder-fonge in fee al þat faire reaume. *c* **1400** *St. Alexius* (Trin.) 44 Þo þis child to cherche com, To vnderfonge cristendom. *c* **1430** *Syr Gener.* (Roxb.) 3075 At the last we shal vndirfong For oure reward grete maugre. **1553** BECON *Reliques of Rome* (1563) 253 Al y[t]..giuen or vnderfongen in way of simonie. **1579** SPENSER *Sheph. Cal.* Nov. 22 If thou ..lust light virelayes, And looser songs of loue to vnderfong.

b. = UNDERFO *v.* 1 b.

*a* **1225** *Ancr. R.* 38 Swete lefdi seinte Marie,..vnderuong mine gretunge mid ten ilke Aue. **13..** *Guy Warw.* (A.) 1015 Ich vnder-fong þis present, & þonke hir þat it hider sent; Hir druerie ich vnder-fong. **1362** LANGL. *P. Pl.* A. III. 208 Þe pope and his prelates presentes vnderfongen. *c* **1400** *Prymer* in Maskell *Mon. Rit.* (1846) II. 107 God, to whom it is propre to be merciful,..vndirfonge oure preieris.

c. To comprehend; to conceive.

*a* **1300** *Cursor M.* 1542 For-þi lete god þam lijf sua lang þat þai moght seke and vnderfang þe kynd o thinges þat þan were dern. *Ibid.* 10354 A maiden child noght þar-to lang O þe þi wijf sal vnder-fang.

2. = UNDERFO *v.* 3.

*a* **1175** *Cott. Hom.* 239 Þer beoð anu 3eredie þe were3ede gastes, þe hine uniredlice underfangeð mid stiarne swupen. *a* **1225** *Ancr. R.* 190 Nedlunge 3e moten underuongen me...Hwose underuongeð me gledliche, & makeð me ueire chere [etc.]. **13..** *Coer de L.* 743 The kyng comaunded..In strong presoun they schuld be done. His jayler hem gan underfong, And took Kyng Rychard be the hond. *a* **1400–50** *Alexander* 2793 (Dublin MS.), And erls of our empire..Karyn þaim to sir Alexander,..And he þaim fair vnderfongez & feffys þaim in Landes. *c* **1440** *Gesta Rom.* I. 226 (Harl. MS.), Be thow tornid to me, thow synfulle soule, and I shalle vnderfonge the. **1553** BECON *Reliques of Rome* (1563) 253 That no man vndirfong or take any folke into his house.

3. = UNDERFO *v.* 2.

*c* **1330** *Amis & Amil.* 1255 Yif thou this bataile vnderfong, Thou schalt haue an euentour strong. *c* **1400** *Rom. Rose* 5710 He vndirfongith a gret peyne That vndirtakith to drynke vp seyne. **1430–40** LYDG. *Bochas* Prol. 35 To underfong this labour they him prey. *a* **1500** MEDWALL *Nature* (Brandl) II. 32 Hard yt wyll be for vs..Agayn them warre or batayll to vnderfong. ? **1525** *La Conusaunce Damours* (Pynson) c j, Our ornate Chaucer other bokes amonge In his lyfe dayes dyd vnderfonge To translate..the sayd story.

**4.** = UNDERFO *v.* 4. *rare*⁻¹.

1382 WYCLIF *Rev.* Prol., What sche [*sc.* the church] schal suffre in this present tyme, and what sche schal vndurfonge in tyme to come.

**5.** To seduce, entrap, overcome.

1579 SPENSER *Sheph. Cal.* June 103 Thou..that by trecheree Didst vnderfong my lasse, to wexe so light. 1596 — *F. Q.* v. ii. 7 With his powre he..makes them subiect to his mighty wrong; And some by sleight he eke doth vnderfong. 1614 J. DAVIES (Heref.) *Eclogue* 117 For, time will vnderfong vs; and our voice Woll woxon weake.

**6.** To surround, enclose. *rare*⁻¹.

1599 NASHE *Lenten Stuffe* 14 They haue towres vpon them sixteene: mounts vnderfonging and enflancking them.

Hence †**Underfo·nging** *vbl. sb. Obs.*

1340 *Ayenb.* 37 Þe ontrewe reuen..þet..rekeneþ more ine dedes and ine spendinge an lesse ine onderuonginge and ine rentes. *c* 1400 LOVE *Bonavent. Mirr.* (1908) xiv. 90 His souereyn mekenes in the vnderfongynge of his baptisme.

**U·nderfoot,** *a.* [Attrib. use of UNDERFOOT *adv.*]

**1.** Lying under the foot or feet. Also *spec.* (see later quots.).

1596 NASHE *Saffron Walden* K 4, The strange vntraffiqu't phrases,..as of incendarie for fire,..an vnder foote abiect for a shooe or a boote. 1824 MACTAGGART *Gallovid. Encycl.* 454 *Underfit* peats, peat turf, digged beneath the foot not in the common way of cutting them of a *breest.* 1844 H. STEPHENS *Bk. Farm* II. 318 In the under-foot wheel, the horses draw by means of trace-chains and swing-tree.

**2.** Inferior, abject, low, downtrodden.

1594 NASHE *Unfort. Trav.* B 1 b, Euerie vnder-foot souldior had a distenanted tun, as Diogenes had his tub to sleepe in. 1641 MILTON *Reform.* II. 90 The most dejected, most underfoot and downe-trodden Vassals of Perdition. 1645 — *Tetrach.* 17 What a stupidnes then is it, that..wee should deject our selvs to such a sluggish and underfoot Philosophy. 1831 CARLYLE *Sart. Res.* II. iii, My Schoolmaster, a downbent, brokenhearted, underfoot martyr.

**Under foot, underfoo·t,** *adv.* Also underfeet. [UNDER *prep.* 4 (cf. FOOT *sb.* 33), UNDER-². Cf. MDu. *ondervoet(e.*]

**1.** Beneath the foot or feet; on the ground: **a.** With vbs., esp. *tread.* (Also in fig. use: cf. 2.)

*a. c* 1200 ORMIN 2561 Forr ȝho tradd deofell unnderrfot Þwerrt ut onn alle wise. *c* 1400 *Hymns Virg.* (1867) 12 To felle oure foomen vndir foote. *c* 1475 *Mankind* 199 in *Macro Plays* 8 Yt doth my soull myche yll, To se þe flesch prosperouse, & þe soull trodyn wnder fote. 1560 DAUS tr. *Sleidane's Comm.* 30 b, Yet is not theyr authoritie so decaied herby that euery man may treade it vnder foote. 1596 SHAKS. *Tam. Shr.* v. ii. 122 Katerine, that Cap of yours becomes you not, Off with that bable, throw it vnderfoote. 1603 DEKKER *Wonderfull Yeare* Wks. (Grosart) I. 107 His lockes that hang wantonly dangling, troden in durt vnderfoote. 1678 WANLEY *Wonders Little World* IV. viii. 374 His Wife..overthrew the Table, and tumbled down all the Provision under-foot. 1708 T. WARD *Eng. Ref.* IV. (1815) 429 [He] Stamp'd underfoot a crucifix, As Hollanders are wont to do When on Japonian shore they go. 1802 MRS. GUTHRIE *Tour through the Taurida* 64 Instead of effecting this adhesion by the pressure of cylinders, it is done..by treading them underfoot for a few hours. 1868 MORRIS *Earthly Par.* (1870) I. I. 349 A fair ivory image of the god That underfoot a golden serpent trod.

*β.* 1539 BIBLE (Great) *Isaiah* xiv. 19 As a dead coarse that is troden vnder fete. *c* 1620 MORYSON *Itin.* IV. (1903) 496 The Empire..of the Greekes..hath beene vtterly abolished, and the people haue beene troden vnderfeete. 1641 BURROUGHS *Sions Joy* 33 They sought to cast shame upon the Saints,..trampling them underfeete as dirt. 1760 *Impostors Detected* II. ii. I. 170 Sacred relicks trampled under feet! 1857 HOLLAND *Bay Path* xxix, Her memory..trodden under feet by malice, prejudice, and superstition.

**b.** In other constructions.

1599 E. WRIGHT *Voy. Earl Cumbld.* 22 in *Cert. Errors Navig.*, Some licked with their tongues..the boardes vnder feete. 1603 HOLLAND *Plutarch's Mor.* 1225 Lysitheus mounting upon the bord, laied him along on the floore, and there under-foot dispatched him. 1667 MILTON *P. L.* IV. 700 Underfoot the Violet, Crocus, and Hyacinth with rich inlay Broiderd the ground. 1802 MRS. GUTHRIE *Tour through the Taurida* 203 They [*sc.* skins] are next worked under-feet in an infusion of oak-leaves in warm water. 1850 TENNYSON *In Mem.* xcv, By night we linger'd on the lawn, For underfoot the herb was dry. 1880 L. WALLACE *Ben-Hur* I. i, Dried leaves in occasional beds rustled underfoot.

**c.** *Naut.* (See FOOT *sb.* 33 b.)

**d.** Down below; underneath; underground.

1840 CARLYLE *Heroes* iii. (1904) 96 The obscure sojourn of dæmons and reprobate is underfoot. 1886 STEVENSON *Kidnapped* xxvi, Coming to the edge of the hills [we] saw the whole Carse of Stirling underfoot.

**2.** *fig.* In(to) a state of subjection or inferiority.

*c* 1205 LAY. 11693 For þis lond..he hit hæfde al vnder fot. *a* 1225 *Ancr. R.* 40 Ȝif me worpen mid him al þe world under vet. *c* 1290 *Beket* 1995 in *S. Eng. Leg.* I. 163 Ake nolde it god þat holi churche onder fote were so. 1340 *Ayenb.* 85 Ac uirtue areréþ þane man an heȝ, and him deþ þe wordle onderuot. 1390 GOWER *Conf.* I. 7 Tho was the vertu sett above And vice was put under fote. 1422 YONGE tr. *Secreta Secret.* 172 He ne holdyth hym not y-lowet ne vndyrfote of the dyssayses whyche he hathe escapid. 1508 FISHER 7 *Penit. Ps.* xxxviii. Wks. (1876) 52 She enhaunced herselfe ferre aboue the derknes of synne puttynge vnderfote thoccasyon of it. 1583 GOLDING *Calvin on Deut.* cxxxvi. 833, I sawe that that man was nothing vnder foote, and as for myselfe I was in extreme neede. 1891 MEREDITH *One of our Conq.* xxxiii, No, not he the man to have pity of women underfoot!

†**3.** Below the real or current value. *Obs.*

1594 *Death of Usurie* 12 The man beeing driuen to distresse, sels his corne farre vnder foote. 1600 HOLLAND *Livy* 591 The very same plot of ground whereon hee was encamped, happened at the same time to be sold: not underfoot, but at the full price. *a* 1654 SELDEN *Table-T.* (Arb.) 64 When men did let their Land underfoot, the Tenants would fight for their Landlords.

**4.** Quietly, secretly. *rare*⁻¹.

1860 GEN. P. THOMPSON *Audi Alt.* III. cxxxiv. 102 But it is not the same with the minor martyrdoms. A store of these is cherished under foot.

**Underfoo·t,** *v.* [UNDER-¹ 4 a.] *trans.* To provide with (new) footings or bases.

1870 *Baines' Hist. Lancs.* II. 27 In 1815 some of the pillars of the N. aisle having given way,..they were all skilfully underfooted and restored.

†**Under-forebody.** *Obs.*⁻¹ (UNDER-¹ 5 a.) 1547 in Feuillerat *Revels Edw. VI* (1914) 10 Longe garmentes narrowe of clothe of golde,..vnderforebodyes, colers & vndersleves of clothe of syluer. **U·nder-form.** (UNDER-¹ 6 b.) 1637 C. DOW *Answ. to H. Burton* 203 Vulgar Christians and the under-forme or ranke of Professors. †**U·nder-foud.** *Obs.* (UNDER-¹ 6 a.) 1576–7 in Balfour *Oppressions in Orkney & Shetl.* (1859) 58 The Underfowde (quhilk is the baillie of the parochin or yle).

**U·nder-frame.** [UNDER-¹ 5 b.] The substructure of a railway-carriage, forming the frame on which the body rests.

1855 D. K. CLARK *Railway Mach.* I. 266 The underframe is the foundation of the vehicle, as the frame is that of the locomotive. 1889 G. FINDLAY *Eng. Railway* 105 The underframes of these carriages are constructed of steel.

So **U·nder-fra·ming.**

1862 *Chambers's Encycl.* III. 93 The body of the Coach is made by one set of workmen, the under-framing by another. 1898 *Daily News* 11 Oct. 8/1 We have acquired a sufficient store in our own reservoirs, stowed away in the under-framing.

**Under-frei·ght,** *v.* (UNDER-¹ 8 d.)

1769 FALCONER *Dict. Marine* (1776), *Sous fréter*, to underfreight a ship, or hire her out to a second person, after having contracted for her freight with the proprietor.

**U·nder-fringe.** (UNDER-¹ 5 b.) 1859 TENNYSON *Geraint & Enid* 544 Broad-faced with under-fringe of russet beard. **U·nder-frock.** (UNDER-¹ 5 a.) 1547 in Feuillerat *Revels Edw. VI* (1914) 11, viij vnderfrockes..of blewe Satten. **U·nder-fur.** (UNDER-¹ 5 d.) 1895 *Funk's Standard Dict.* 1898 *Guide Mammalia* 70 A thick woolly under-fur.

**Under-fur,** *a. Sc.* [UNDER-².] (See quot. and FURROW *sb.* 1 *a*, quot. 1523.)

1743 MAXWELL *Sel. Trans. Soc. Improv. Agric. Scot.* 34 Sow the Rye above the Dung, plow it down with an ebb Fur, (which is termed under-fur Sowing).

**U·nder-fu·rnish,** *v.* (UNDER-¹ 8 a.) 1697 R. COLLIER *Ess. Mor. Subj.* I. (1703) 158 Can we suppose that God would underfurnish man for the state he designed him?

**Underga·ng,** *v. Obs.* exc. *dial.* [OE. *undergangan*, = MDa. *undergange*, Sw. *-ganga.*] = UNDERGO *v.* (in various senses).

*c* 1000 ÆLFRIC *Gram.* xxxvii. (Z.) 217 Ic undergange, *subeo.* *c* 1200 ORMIN 10661 Me birrþ beon fullhtnedd att tin hannd, Þin blettsinng tunnderrganngenn. 1425 *Munim. de Melros* (Bann. Cl.) 544 Tyll wndirgang asyse of purale of þe marchis debatabil. *a* 1470 HARDING *Chron.* CXLII. xii, His defautes all to mend..And vndirgange all his punycioun. 1743 RELPH *Poems* (1747) 94 Fie, Roger, fie—a sairy lass to wrang, And let her aw this trouble undergang. 1855– in Yorks. and Lancs. dial. glossaries.

Hence **Underga·nging** *vbl. sb. Obs.* exc. *dial.*

*a* 1300 *E. E. Psalter* xl. 10 For man of mi pees..In wham mikel hoped I,..Mikled vndergangingе [*v. rr.* -gange, undergoing] ouer me. 1855– in Yorks. dial. glossaries.

**U·nder-gao·ler.** (UNDER-¹ 6 a.) 1534 MORE *Comf. agst. Trib.* III. Wks. 1246 We forget with our foly, both ourselfe and our gayle, and our vnder gaylers, aungelles and deuilles both, and our chief gayler god. 1627 R. BERNARD *Isle of Man* 111 Now the Chiefe Gaoler..hath with him three Vnder-Gaolers to looke well to the Prisoners.

**U·nder-ga·rdener.** (UNDER-¹ 6 a.)

1687 NORRIS *Coll. Misc.* 112 So 'tis in Eden, let me but have An under-gardener's place, 'tis all I crave. 1710 SWIFT *Mem. Change Q. Anne's Ministry* ¶ 20 The letter..was delivered him by an under-gardener. 1830 MISS MITFORD *Village* Ser. IV. III. 109 His elder brother, Tom, could take an under-gardener's place directly. 1865 J. H. INGRAHAM *Pillar of Fire* xiv. 170 This venerable man..was followed by not less than fifty under-gardeners.

**U·nder-ga·rment.** (UNDER-¹ 5 a.)

1530 PALSGR. 285/2 Undergarment for a woman, *seurcot.* 1547 in Feuillerat *Revels Edw. VI* (1914) 11 Gownes or vndergarmentes of playne clothe of Syluer. 1615 G. SANDYS *Trav.* 68 Their vnder-garments (which within doores are their vppermost) do little differ from those that be worne by the men. 1831 SCOTT *Ct. Rob.* xiv, Over these under-garments was flung a rich velvet cloak. 1864 MRS. CARLYLE *Lett.* (1883) III. 207 A good supply of woollen under-garments. 1872 EARL PEMBROKE & G. H. KINGSLEY *S. Sea Bubbles* i. 29 Every kind of sail being hoisted, from new white canvas to the under garments of the lady passengers.

**U·nder-ga·rnished,** *ppl. a.* (UNDER-¹ 4 a.) 1596 *Edw. III,* I. ii. 159 These ragged walles,..like a cloake, doth hide From weathers Waste the vnder garnisht pride. **U·nder-gear.** (UNDER-¹ 5 a.) 1883 *Atlantic Monthly* Sept. 365/1 Their undergear hanging out on a pole from an upper window, in full sight of passers-by. **U·nder-ge·neral.** (UNDER-¹ 6 a.) 1698 *Lond. Gaz.* No. 3367/2 His Majesty has appointed the General of Great Poland, and the Under-General of Lithuania as his Commissioners. 1702 LUTTRELL *Brief Rel.* (1857) V. 162 The under general of Lithuania has cut in peices 500 Suedish horse. **U·nder-ge·ntleman.** (UNDER-¹ 6 a.) 1766 GOLDSM. *Vicar* ix, We found our landlord, with a couple of under-gentlemen and two young ladies.

†**Under-get,** *v. Obs.* [UNDER-¹ 4 b.] *trans.* To catch up with, overtake.

1390 GOWER *Conf.* I. 197 Hire Schip..stinte noght, er it..hath the vessell undergete, Which Maister was of al the Flete.

**Undergi·rd,** *v.* [UNDER-¹ 4 a. Cf. Flem. *ondergorden* 'subcingere' (Kilian).] *trans.* To secure or fasten from the under-side, as by a rope or chain passed underneath.

In actual use chiefly in renderings or echoes of Acts xxvii. 17 ὑποζωννύντες τὸ πλοῖον.

1526 TINDALE *Acts* xxvii. 17 We..had moche worke to come by a boote, which they toke vppe, and vsed helppe vndergerdynge the shippe. 1611 FLORIO, *Soccingere*, to vnder-guirt, or guird. 1702 ECHARD *Eccl. Hist.* (1710) 325 They undergirt the ship to secure it from splitting. 1857 DUFFERIN *Let. High Lat.* 20 By undergirding the ship with chains, St. Paul fashion, the leaks were partially stopped.

*fig.* 1848 H. ROGERS *Ess.* (1874) I. vi. 292 The infirmity of human nature requires to be 'undergirded' by all sorts of supports. 1874 HOLLAND *Mistr. Manse* 3 Its fragments build and undergird The songs and stories we rehearse.

Hence **Undergi·rding** *vbl. sb.* and *ppl. a.*

1868 H. BUSHNELL *Serm. Living Subj.* (1872) 218 That which is the undergirding import and reality of second death. 1895 *Advance* (Chicago) 17 Oct. 546/2 The preacher himself needs them..for the undergirding of his own convictions.

**U·nder-gi·rder.** (UNDER-¹ 5 b.) 1875 JOWETT *Plato* (ed. 2) III. 148 The undergirders of a trireme. **U·nder-gi·rdle.** (UNDER-¹ 5 a.) *c* 1532 DU WES *Introd. Fr.* in *Palsgr.* 906 The under gyrdell, *le demy chaint.* 1648 HEXHAM II, *Een Onder-gordel*, an Vnder-girdle.

**U·nder-glaze,** *a.* and *sb.* [UNDER-².]

**1.** *Under-glaze painting*, the process of painting on pottery before the application of the glaze.

1883 *Harper's Mag.* July 259/1 The underglaze painting of pottery. 1885 *Encycl. Brit.* XIX. 643/2.

**b.** *absol.* as *sb.* in the same sense.

1882 *Worcester Exhib. Catal.* iii. 4 Plaques painted in under-glaze. 1884 *American* VII. 217 The mysteries of 'overglaze' and 'underglaze'.

**2.** Of colours: Used in, adapted for, this method of decoration.

1883 *American* VII. 119 The good effects of underglaze colors depend so essentially upon the firing. 1885 *Encycl. Brit.* XIX. 643/2 The soft subdued colours of the under-glaze pigments.

**U·ndergo,** *sb.* [UNDER-¹ 5 a.] (See quot.)

1876 HOLLAND *Seven Oaks* x. 123 They were blue undergoes—in other words blue flannel shirts.

**Undergo** (vndəɹgōᵘ·), *v.* [Late OE. *undergán* (f. *under-* UNDER-¹ 4 b + *gán* GO *v.*), = MDu. *ondergaen* (Du. *-gaan*), OHG. *untarkân* (MHG., MLG., LG. *undergân*, G. *untergehen*), Da. *undergaa*, Sw. *undergå.*]

†**1.** *trans.* To work under, so as to impair or destroy; to undermine. *Obs.*

*c* 1000 *Sax. Leechd.* III. 444 Ne sy la nan eorðcund cyning mid ȝitsunge to þæm swiþe undergan. *a* 1300 *E. E. Psalter* xvi. 14 Ris vp, lauerd; forcome him swa, And als-swa him vnderga [L. *subverte*]. *c* 1315 SHOREHAM VII. 622 Ac þo þe deuel hyt aspyde þat man hym scholde þer abyde..He þouȝte gyle al onder-go. 1642 D. ROGERS *Naaman* 146 Be [thou] affraid lest thou shouldest undergo thy selfe in purchasing the pearle.

†**b.** To deceive, get the better of. *Obs.*

*c* 1250 *Gen. & Ex.* 1147 Ðis maidenes redden sone ðor-on..Hu he miȝten vnder-gon Here fader, ðat he ne wore ðor gon. *a* 1380 *St. Paula* 479 in Horstm. *Altengl. Leg.* [1878] 33 Þou hast me gyled and vndur-gone [L. *circumvenisti*].

†**c.** To get under, search below. *Obs.*⁻¹

1605 VERSTEGAN *Dec. Intell.* Verses by Author, That all men seeke all what they may to know; Yea Tyme in his own cours to vndergo.

†**2.** To submit *to* (do something). *Obs.*⁻¹

*c* 1200 ORMIN 2527 Þatt ȝho wass rædiȝ tunnderrgan Drihhtiness will to follȝhenn.

†**b.** To accept, admit, allow. *Obs.*⁻¹

*c* 1315 SHOREHAM VII. 187 Ȝet oure by-leaue wole onder-gon Þat þyse þre beþ ryȝt al on.

**c.** To be subject to, to serve. *rare.*

1586 G. WHITNEY *Emblems* 223 Here, man who first should heauenlie thinges attaine,..First, vndergoes the worlde with might, and maine. 1864 BROWNING in *Mem. Tennyson* (1897) II. i. 16 The new metre is admirable, a paladin's achievement. ..So have you made our language undergo you.

†**3.** To go or pass under. *Obs.*

*c* 1220 *Bestiary* 691 in *O. E. Misc.* 22 And tus adam he under-ȝede, reisede him up, and al mankin. *a* 1575 tr. *Pol. Verg. Eng. Hist.* (Camden No. 29) 37 Howbeit, hoping eyther to winne it by assault, or compell it to yeelde, they undergoe the wall. *c* 1611 CHAPMAN *Iliad* VI. 444 Better my shoulders underwent the earth, than thy decease. 1627 MAY *Lucan* V. I 4, That day the sea seem'd mountaines topps t' oreflow, And yeilding earth that deluge t' vndergoe.

†**b.** To sink below (one's sight). *Obs.*

1614 GORGES *Lucan* IX. 386 Thy sight the North-starre vndergoes,..And each starre, that is most of light, Seemes (by the sea) hid from thy sight.

†**4.** To occupy oneself with; to investigate. (Also with *of.*) **b.** To get knowledge of. *Obs.*

*c* 1250 *Gen. & Ex.* 1160 Nv bi-oueð us to wenden a-gen And of abraham song under-gon. *c* 1290 *S. Eng. Leg.* I. 353/273 His lettre he sende, þat he scholde of swuche þingue onder-go [*v.r.* scholde such þing vndergo]. *c* 1330 *Amis & Amil.* 603 Yif..ani wight of all þi kinne Might it vndergo, Al our ioie and worldes winne We schuld lese. *a* 1400 *Sir Beues* (MS. S.) 1514 That hors wel ȝerne vnder-ȝede That Beues nas not on is rigge.

**5.** To bear, endure, sustain, suffer, go through (pain, suffering, danger, etc.).

*a* 1300 *Cursor M.* 9748 And thol on me þe dom i sal, Þat he suld vnder-ga, yon thral. *c* 1375 *Sc. Leg. Saints* xxxviii. (*Adrian*) 243 For-þi mare ardent wes hi wil hard martirdome til vndirga. *c* 1400 *Apol. Loll.* 39 We wel þat þe bischops þat are neglecent in þis, vndir go þe same peyn. 1595 SHAKS. *John* IV. i. 135 Silence, no more; go closely in with mee, Much danger do I vndergo for thee. 1609 TOURNEUR *Funeral Poem Sir F. Vere* 216 If some were still so bold to undergoe his doome. 1666 in *Verney Mem.* (1907) II. 259 In that or other disappointments or crosses that your sister and I have undergone. 1711 *Spect.* No. 161 ¶ 5 They were..fit to undergo any Fatigues of bodily Labour. *a* 1770 JORTIN *Serm.* (1771) VII. xiii. 270 What security hath our

Church from undergoing the same fate? **1832** Ht. Martineau *Weal & Woe* ix. 124 His fine spirit was broken by the anxieties he had undergone. **1887** P. McNeill *Blawearie* 121 Soon all speculation anent the punishment we had to undergo was at an end.

*absol.* **1842** Tennyson *Godiva* 10 She Did more, and underwent, and overcame.

†**b.** To bear, sustain (a burden, etc.). *Obs.*

*c* **1460** *Oseney Reg.* 162 All charges to þe saide tithis longyng we..schalle bere and schall vndergoo for euer. *a* **1618** J. Davies *Witte's Pilgr.* ii. xvii, Though Atlas on him Heau'n impose, He that huge Burden, staidly undergoes! **1656** H. Phillips *Purch. Patt.* (1676) B 4 b, There may be an equality in the loss and charges, that so the burden may be the more easily undergone by both parties.

**6. a.** To subject or submit oneself, to be subjected, to (a law, inspection, examination, etc.).

*a* **1300** *Cursor M.* 9114 It semes wel..þat he wan merci of his mis..for þe scrift he vnder-yede. *c* **1315** Shoreham v. 152 Ope þe heȝe eȝtynde day He onder-ȝede þe gywen lay, And was ycircumcysed. *a* **1425** *Cursor M.* 12755 (Trin.), In watir baptized he alle þo þat wolde bapteme vndir go. **1594** Carew *Tasso* (1881) 18 They all agree to vnder go his lawes. *a* **1704** T. Brown *Two Oxford Scholars* Wks. 1730 I. 4, I must undergo an Examination. **1721** Strype *Eccl. Mem.* II. xxvi. 215 The Book of Public and Common Prayer, which about this time underwent a diligent inspection and reformation, by some of the bishops. **1817** Jas. Mill *Brit. India* II. v. v. 479 The danger to which this event might expose the expedition..underwent deliberation in the Council. **1844** H. H. Wilson *Brit. India* I. 547 On the 1st July several clauses again underwent examination.

**b.** To come or fall under, to experience; to have imposed on one.

**1599** Shaks. *Much Ado* v. ii. 57 Claudio vndergoes my challenge, and either I must shortly heare from him, or I will subscribe him a coward. *a* **1641** Bp. Mountagu *Acts & Mon.* (1642) 22 Those Elders, who..had seen and undergone the wars of Canaan. **1650** Earl Monm. tr. *Senault's Man bec. Guilty* 145, I foresee I cannot condemn this Action without under-going the jealousie of such. **1668** Hale *Rolle's Abridgm.* Pref. 2 It is a Posthumous work, which never underwent the last Hand or Pensil of the judicious Author. **1717** Lady M. W. Montagu *Let. to Miss S. Chiswell* 1 Apr., Every year thousands undergo this operation. **1774** Pennant *Tour Scotl. in* 1772 96 The castle has undergone its different sieges. **1827** D. Johnson *Ind. Field Sports* 155 The Hindoos every morning..undergo ablution. **1840** Dickens *Old C. Shop* xvi, It wouldn't do to let 'em see the present company undergoing repair. **1873** C. M. Davies *Unorth. London* (1876) 81, I made up my mind to undergo a Sunday morning service at one of these churches.

**c.** To experience, pass through (a change or alteration).

**1634** Milton *Comus* 841 She reviv'd And underwent a quick immortal change. **1711** Hearne *Collect.* (O.H.S.) III. 225, I know not what Alterations the Stone may have underwent. **1765** *Museum Rust.* IV. 339 After this has undergone a strong fermentation. **1825** J. Neal *Bro. Jonathan* I. 23 Seeing the error of his ways he had undergone a conversion. **1844** H. H. Wilson *Brit. India* III. 116 The situation of the British forces..had undergone a rapid improvement. **1884** L. J. Jennings *Croker Papers* I. iv. 116 His views underwent a very thorough change in course of time.

†**d.** To partake of, enjoy. *Obs. rare.*

**1603** Shaks. *Meas. for M.* i. i. 24 If any in Vienna be of worth To vndergoe such ample grace, and honour, It is Lord Angelo. **1604** — *Ham.* i. iv. 34 (Q 2), His vertues els be they..As infinite as man may vndergoe, Shall in the generall censure take corruption From that particular fault.

†**7.** To expose oneself to (risk). *Obs.*[-1]

*c* **1315** Shoreham i. 288 ȝet gret peryl hy vndergoþe þat cristneþ twyes enne.

**8.** To take in hand; to undertake. Now *rare.*

**1601** Shaks. *Jul. C.* i. iii. 123, I haue mou'd already Some certaine of the Noblest minded Romans To vnder-goe, with me, an Enterprize. **1605** Sylvester *Du Bartas* iii. ii. *Law* 291 Make me no excuse On thy..unworthinesse To under-goe so great a Businesse. **1655** Stanley *Hist. Philos.* i. 108 Since him a perfect Agent we may call, Who first considers what he undergoes. **1739** Tull *Horse-Hoeing Husb.* (1740) 252 [They] gave me such an Embarras, that if I had foreseen, I would not have underwent. **1817** Jas. Mill *Brit. India* II. v. viii. 670 Responsibility, thus limited, he had no objection to undergo.

†**b.** To perform or discharge (an employment, office, etc.). *Obs.* (Common in 17th c.)

**1609** Daniel *Civ. Wars* iv. xvii. 91 Hauing the chiefest actions undergone Both foreign and domestical of late. **1631** May tr. *Barclay's Mirr. Mindes* ii. 38 Few they are..able to undergoe perpetuall employment, and not confounded with the different face of businesse. **1667** Pepys *Diary* 11 Sept., [He is] a very young man to undergo that place. **1726** Ayliffe *Parergon* 266 It has been a Question among the Doctors, Whether an Executor may be compelled to undergo this Office?

†**9.** To go under or by, to bear (a name). *Obs.*

**1605** *Gunpowder Plot* in *Harl. Misc.* (Malh.) III. 26 Mr. Fawkes underwent the name of Mr. Percy's man. **1809** Malkin *Gil Blas* vii. xiv. ¶ 6 A large ape, which underwent the name of Cupid.

Hence **U·ndergo·ing** *ppl. a.*

**1610** Shaks. *Temp.* i. ii. 159, I haue..Vnder my burthen groan'd, which rais'd in me An vndergoing stomacke.

**U·nder-god.** (Under- 6 a. Cf. Du. *ondergod*, G. *untergott*, Sw. *undergud.*)

**1583** Golding *Calvin on Deut.* xlv. 270 As soone as we fall to bringing in of vndergoddes we forsake the liuing God. **1593** Nashe *Christ's T.* 20 The High-priest (the vnder-god of your Cittie). **1605** A. Wotton *Answ. Popish Pamph.* 47 You Papists..make our Sauiour, as it were an vnder God. **1712** Blackmore *Creation* v. 235 Of his own Substance does he Parts convey, Whose Motive Force the Under-Gods obey. **1891** F. W. Newman *Early Hist. Cdl. Newman* 20 This Power is an under-god...If we have no awe for this under-god, why [etc.].

**Undergo·er.** *rare.* [f. Undergo *v.*]

**1.** One who endures or is subjected.

**1601** Sir W. Cornwallis *Ess.* ii. xxxviii. A a 7 b, Dracoes lawes [were] very good for the behoulders, whatsoeuer they were for the vndergoers.

**2.** ? An assailant.

**1612** R. Daborne *Christian turn'd Turke* 869 All religious lawes Must suffer violence, your wife be exposed Vnto all vndergoers.

**Undergo·ing,** *vbl. sb.* [f. Undergo *v.*]

**1.** The action of the verb, in various senses.

*c* **1380** *E. E. Psalter* xl. 10 [see Underganging *vbl. sb.*]. *c* **1440** *Promp. Parv.* 511 Vndergoynge, *submeatus.* **1608** D. T[uvill] *Ess. Pol. & Mor.* 119 The prayse of hauing well conducted the course of one, is a bayte, which drawes them on to the vnder-going of another. **1612** W. Sclater *Christian's Strength* 9 What avails it..whether on the right hand, or on the left; by overgoing or undergoing; we be deprived of salvation? **1645** Bp. Hall *Rem. Discontents* Pref. 4 A meek undergoing of those sufferings. **1712** Berkeley *Pass. Obed.* Wks. 1871 III. 136 The undergoing an execution is worse than the hazard of a battle.

**2.** = Holing *vbl. sb.* 2.

**1883** Gresley *Gloss. Coal-m.* 135.

**Under-go·re,** *v.* (Under-[1] 4 a.) *c* **1611** Chapman *Iliad* xiv. 408 The dart did undergore His eye-lid, by his eye's dear roots, and out the apple fell. **U·nder-go·verness.** (Under-[1] 6 a.) **1669** E. Chamberlayne *Pres. St. Eng.* i. 317 Governess, Lady Francis Villiers, 400*l.* Under-governess, Mrs. Mary Kilbert, 150*l.* **1688** *Lond. Gaz.* No. 2355/4 The Lady Marchioness of Powis was Sworn by the Lord Chamberlain.., Lady Governess of their Majesties Children; And the Lady Strickland Under-governess. **U·nder-go·vernor.** (Under-[1] 6 a.) **1579** J. Stubbes *Gaping Gulf* D j b, By referring you to the proconsulates of Rome vnder that Empire: to the vndergouernors in the former monarchies. **1587** Golding *De Mornay* iii. 29 To be short, hee setteth downe some Gods as principall, some as meane, and othersome as vndergouernours. **U·ndergown.** (Under-[1] 5 a.) **1819** Scott *Ivanhoe* iv, Her dress was an under-gown and kirtle of pale sea-green silk.

**Undergra·d,** abbrev. of Undergraduate.

**1827** *Brasenose Ale* 16 Why, Undergrads, dine ye so early? **1853** 'C. Bede' *Verdant Green* vii. 63 The temporary sojourn that any undergrad has been forced to make there. **1884** Ornsby *Mem. J. R. Hope-Scott* I. 34 A brilliant Oxford undergrad of nineteen.

**U·ndergrade,** *a.* [Under-[2].] (See quot.)

**1884** Knight *Dict. Mech.* Suppl. 911/1 *Undergrade*, a term as applied to bridges synonymous with *deck* bridge in which the track is above the truss.

**Undergra·duate,** *sb.* and *a.* [Under-2.]

Also formerly written *under-graduate* and (rarely) *under graduate.*

**A.** *sb.* **1.** A student in a university who has not yet taken a degree, and thus is still below the academical standing of a graduate.

**1630** Laud *Wks.* (1854) V. 29, I think fourteen years is little enough for a bachelor of arts or undergraduate abroad. *a* **1670** Hacket *Abp. Williams* i. (1692) 20 He was an assiduous overseer and interlocutor at the afternoon disputations of the under graduates. **1721** Amherst *Terræ Filius* No. 33, The Thesis pitch'd upon by the excluding doctors for the undergraduates to moralize upon. **1850** Kingsley *A. Locke* I. xiii. 199 They have no influence over the rest of the under-graduates. **1882** Miss Braddon *Mt. Royal* I. i. 18 The traditionary college misdemeanours handed down from generation to generation of undergraduates.

**2.** *fig.* One imperfectly instructed, or as yet inexpert (*in* something).

*a* **1659** Osborne *Charac.* Wks. (1673) 624 Which is but the single and wild Opinion of some under-graduates in the Arts of Liveing. **1693** *Humours Town* 97 Thus far I myself have proceeded (that am yet an Under-graduate) in this admirable Science. **1748** Richardson *Clarissa* VII. lxxviii. 258 Now-and-then flitted in..subordinate sinners, under-graduates, younger than some of the chosen phalanx. **1795** Vancouver *Agric. Essex* 110 Here the under graduates in iniquity commence their career with deer stealing. **1832** *Edin. Rev.* LVI. 163 That Mr. Johnson..is still an under-graduate in modern German, will..be sufficiently apparent. **1897** P. Warung *Tales Old Régime* 88 The three who were undergraduates [in crime] muttered assent to the spokesman of the Three graduates.

**B.** *adj.* †**1.** Of lower degree; of inferior importance. *Obs.*

**1654** H. L'Estrange *Chas. I* (1655) 119 Sir Giles Allington fell also under censure for a sin of grand, though undergraduate abomination. **1659** — *Alliance Div. Off.* 437 It is ..to be supposed that in this consecration set forms were used, considering withal that they were assigned to undergraduate concernments.

**2.** Having the standing of an undergraduate; that is an undergraduate. Also *fig.*

**1685** in *Roxb. Ball.* (1885) V. 602 See here the minor Undergraduate Tool Takes his degree i' th' Doctor's flogging school. **1687** W. Sherwin in *Magd. Coll.* (O.H.S.) 216 There was a Cloth laid in the Hall for the undergraduate Fellow.

**3.** Of or belonging to an undergraduate; characteristic of undergraduates.

**1854** Faber *Growth in Holiness* xix. (1872) 387 There is something undergraduate about this levity. **1889** Gretton *Memory's Harkb.* 241 In my undergraduate days, one Ash Wednesday, there came down..a tornado of the tropics.

**4.** Consisting of undergraduates.

**1868** M. Pattison *Academ. Org.* iv. 109 The discipline of the undergraduate body is usually administered by the vicegerent.

Hence **Undergra·duatedom,** the body of undergraduates.

**1893** *Westm. Gaz.* 1 Mar. 3/3 He became an absentee, so as to remove the voice of undergraduatedom from the jurisdiction of the University.

**Undergra·duateship.** [f. Undergraduate *sb.* 1.] The condition or status of an undergraduate.

**1815** Whewell in Todhunter *Acc. Writ.* (1876) II. 12 Behold the end of my undergraduateship is at hand. **1850** Thackeray *Pendennis* lxx, Time, I think, has..rendered him a more accomplished rascal than he was during your undergraduateship. **1885** *Q. Rev.* Jan. 12 Mansel was rewarded for his laborious undergraduateship with a 'double-first'.

**U·ndergrass.** (Under-[1] 5 c.) **1838** Mrs. Browning *Seraphim* i. 144 The yew-tree bows its melancholy head, And all the undergrasses kills and seres.

†**Undergri·nd,** *v. Obs.* [Under *adv.*] *trans.* To grind by pressing on (something placed below).

**1598** Sylvester *Du Bartas* ii. i. iii. *Furies* 731 Like falling Towers o'rturned by the winde, That break themselves on that they under-grinde. **1608** *Ibid.* iv. iv. *Decay* 847 As with his weight, a hollow Rocky-Hill..Shivers it selfe on stones it under-grindes.

**Under-groa·n,** *v.* (Under-[1] 4 a.) *c* **1611** Chapman *Iliad* ii. 693 Earth under-groaned their high-raised feet.

†**Undergro·pe,** *v. Obs.* [Under-[1] 8 a] *trans.* To search into, to investigate; to learn.

? *a* **1412** Lydg. *Two Merch.* 351 And whan his freend the sothe gan vndirgrope Of this myscheef. **1412–20** — *Chron. Troy* iv. 4644 But he anon..Gan vndergrope, pleinly, what þei ment. **1447** Bokenham *Seyntys* (Roxb.) 28 The secunde yer of the forseyd pope, As be cronyculers I vndyrgrope, Fel a ful greuows dissencyoun. **1678** Littleton *Lat. Dict., Subtento*, to assay or try underhand, to under-grope.

**Undergrou·nd,** *adv.* [Under-[2].]

Also written *under-ground* and *under ground.*

**1.** Below the surface of the ground.

**1571** [see Ground *sb.* 8]. **1598** Florio, *Sotteraneo*, of or pertaining to things vnderground. *c* **1615** Sylvester *Job Triumphant* iii. 273 Mines and veinlings (vnder ground) Whence Silver's fetcht. **1684** T. Burnet *Theory Earth* i. 259 The..passage of the paradisiacal rivers under-ground or under-sea, from one continent into another. **1728** Chambers *Cycl.* s.v. *River*, Some Rivers bury themselves under Ground in the middle of their Course. **1780** Coxe *Russ. Disc.* 68 Their dwellings underground are similar to those of the Kamtchadals. **1850** Thackeray *Pendennis* xlvi, He..wished that lady..underground rather than there. **1878** Huxley *Physiography* 31 The laws which regulate the flow of water underground.

*Comb.* *c* **1720** C. Place in *Mem. W. Stukeley* (Surtees) I. 157 The old Giants are represented to us as underground-livers all of them. **1857** Henfrey *Bot.* § 634 They are Truffles, or underground-fruiting Fungi.

**b.** Governed by *from.* (Cf. From *prep.* 15 a.)

**1612** *Two Noble K.* Prol. 18 How will it shake the bones of that good man, And make him cry from under ground. **1697** Dryden *Virg. Georg.* iii. 820 Tisiphone, let loose from under Ground. **1872** Tennyson *Gareth & Lynette* 1386 Then sprang the happier day from underground.

**2.** *fig.* In secrecy or concealment; in a hidden or obscure manner.

**1632** *Star Chamb. Cases* (Camden) 104 If he had medled with St. Austin and the Fathers, and not medled so much with these workes underground, he might have knowen the difference betweene the Church of Rome and us. **1679** *Animadv. Sp. Five Jesuits* 16 Since they may still work under-ground, and not be discovered. **1709** Shaftesb. *Charac.* (1711) II. 269 Supplanting and Undermining may, in other Cases, be fair War: But in Philosophical Disputes, 'tis not allowable to work underground. **1820** Hazlitt *Lect. Dram. Lit.* 308 [Jeremy Taylor] does not dig his way underground, but slides upon ice. **1875** J. H. Newman *Let.* 29 Oct., The pains and achievements of an editor are emphatically underground and out of sight.

**U·nderground,** *a.* and *sb.* [f. prec.]

Also occas. written *under-ground.*

**A.** *adj.* = Subterranean *a.*

**1. a.** Found below the surface of the ground.

**1610** Holland *Camden's Brit.* 745 Vnder-grownd trees, or which haue lien a long time buried there. **1673** Ray *Journ. Low C.* 6 In Friesland..there are great numbers of these under-ground Trees found.

**b.** Growing, living, or developed underground.

**1757** *Phil. Trans.* L. 404 A compressed pod of the..Underground-Pea. **1807** Southey *Lett.* (1856) I. 417 Some Jerusalem or under-ground artichokes. **1842** Loudon *Suburban Hort.* 113 The most injurious of all underground larvæ. *Ibid.* 279 Tubers, or underground stems. **1875** Bennett & Dyer tr. *Sachs' Bot.* 673 The buds on underground rhizomes.

**c.** Dwelling underground or in the underworld.

**1833** Keightley *Fairy Mythol.* I. 314 A treasure which the underground-people must redeem at any price. **1866–7** Baring-Gould *Myths Mid. Ages* (1872) 216 The underground folk seek union with human beings.

**2.** Situated below the surface of the ground.

**1611** Cotgr., *Hypogee*, a vault, celler, or such like vnderground roome. **1664** Ingelo *Bentiv. & Ur.* ii. vi. 172 An under-ground Temple consecrated to Melancholy. **1665–6** *Phil. Trans.* I. 109 The Divine Structure of the under-ground World. **1774** Goldsm. *Nat. Hist.* VII. 353 The Mole-Cricket..at night..ventures from its under-ground habitation. **1823** P. Nicholson *Pract. Build.* 353 If a projected building is to have cellars, or under-ground kitchens. **1846** Mrs. A. Marsh *Father Darcy* II. i. 8 One of those long underground passages, used for communication between the different houses. **1878** Huxley *Physiogr.* 31 After slowly trickling through a long dark underground course.

**b.** In fig. context. (Cf. 4.)

**1675** Owen *Indwelling Sin* vi. (1732) 51 It will increase ..until it..makes it self an underground-passage, by some secret Lust that shall give a full Vent unto it. **1822** De Quincey *Confess.* 48 The stream of London charity flows in a channel..noiseless and underground.

**c.** *Underground railroad, railway,* (*a*) a railway running under the surface of the ground, esp. beneath the streets and buildings of a city; (*b*) *U.S.* The secret system by which slaves were enabled to escape to the Free States and Canada. (Also *u. line.*)

(*a*) **1834–6** P. BARLOW in *Encycl. Metrop.* (1845) VIII. 240/1 The under-ground Railways..in Newcastle, and its immediate vicinity. **1885** C. E. PASCOE *London of To-day* xiii. 137 The stuffy underground railway journey to Baker Street. (*b*) **1852** MRS. B. STOWE *Uncle Tom's C.* viii. 43 Till the gal's been carried on the underground line up to Sandusky or so. **1856** — *Dred* II. xxx. 318 An indefinite yet very energetic institution, known as the *underground railroad*. **1875** *N. Amer. Rev.* CXX. 67 More fugitives than ever came from the slave states, and the underground railroad was in fuller activity than before.

**3.** Carried on, taking place, underground.

**1709** T. ROBINSON *Nat. Hist. Westmorld.* Pref. A vj, The Inspection of Under-ground Projects of several Kinds. **1795** EARL DUNDONALD *Connex. Agric. w. Chem.* 171 The clay.. may be wrought by shafting and under-ground mining. **1831** T. HOPE *Ess. Orig. Man* II. 73 The earth-worm,..to whom a body dense and rigid..would only impede his underground progress. **1872** YEATS *Techn. Hist. Comm.* 218 The abandonment of ridges will render underground drainage even more necessary.

**b.** Worn while underground.

**1827** *Q. Rev.* XXXVI. 89 As soon as the men come to grass they repair to the engine-house, where they generally leave their underground clothes to dry. **1888** F. HUME *Mme. Midas* I. v, They arrayed themselves in underground garments.

**c.** Working, having control, underground.

**1852** *Eng. & Foreign Mining Gloss.* (1860) 60 *Overman*, an underground overlooker. **1871** *Daily News* 21 Sept., The underlookers, and the underground manager [of the colliery]. **1879** MISS JACKSON *Shropshire Word-bk.* 348 *Reeve*, the underground overlooker of the pits.

**d.** Adapted for use underground.

**1884** KNIGHT *Dict. Mech.* Suppl. 911/1 Stevens's underground engine.

**4.** *fig.* Hidden, concealed, secret.

**1677** GILPIN *Demonol.* (1867) 250 This is their help, that some secret underground hopes which they espy not, do revive, at least sometimes. **1848** KEBLE *Serm.* Pref. p. xlv, There may be an unseen, underground unity. **1886** GURNEY, etc. *Phantasms of Living* I. 538 We have already had numerous..instances of what may be called 'underground telepathy'.

**b.** Not open or public; concealed from or avoiding general notice.

**1820** J. W. CROKER *Diary* 12 Apr. in *C. Papers*, Brougham ..I believe has been for some time in underground communication with Carlton House. **1883** tr. *Kravchinsky's Underground Russia* 49 The inner life of Underground Russia.

**B.** *sb.* **1.** The region below the earth; the lower regions or underworld.

**1590** T. WATSON *Poems* (Arb.) 159 That..they may lament with guosts of vnder-ground. **1592** KYD *Sp. Trag.* I. vi. 1 Come we for this from depth of vnder ground? *a* **1618** SYLVESTER *Job Triumph.* III. 278 Beyond the bounds of Darkness Man hath pry'd And th' excellence of underground descry'd. **1887** *Scribner's Mag.* II. 449 The open spaces of the underground may..be divided into several distinct classes.

**b.** An underground space or passage.

**1594** KYD *Cornelia* II. i. 377 Those seas..Returne to springs by vnder-grounds. *c* **1611** CHAPMAN *Iliad* XV. 176 This Jupiter, and I, And Pluto, God of under-grounds. **1884** *Daily News* 24 Sept. 3/2 The financial success..had not been such as to encourage costly exploration in unknown undergrounds.

**2. a.** Underlying ground or soil; subsoil.

So Du. *ondergrond*, G. *untergrund*.

**1812** SIR J. SINCLAIR *Syst. Husb. Scot.* I. 231 A dry, free soil, on a sound under-ground or bottom. **1897** *Allbutt's Syst. Med.* III. 10 The underground of houses in certain localities being infiltrated with the virus [of rheumatic fever].

**b.** Ground lying at a lower level or below trees.

**1842** *Proc. Berw. Nat. Club* II. 7 Rushes and..marsh thistles filled up the under ground. **1878** MRS. OLIPHANT *Primrose P.* II. 124 The mossy underground beneath the firs.

**3.** An underground railway.

**1887** DOYLE *Study in Scarlet* (1892) 28 A third class carriage on the Underground.

Hence **U·ndergrou·nder, -grou·ndling.**

Also *underground* v., to place or lay under ground (1891 *Cent. Dict.*).

**1868** *Once a Week* 18 Jan. 66/1 The Metropolitan railway (the undergroundlings). **1882** *Belgravia* July 67 That the aëronauts had the advantage of the undergrounders.

**U·nder-grove.** (UNDER-[1] 5 b, 5 d.)

**1731** J. TRAPP tr. *Virg., Eclogues* I. 35 But that above all other Citys tow'rs, As the tall Cypress o'er the Under-Grove. **1798** WORDSW. '*A Whirlblast*' 6, I sat within an undergrove Of tallest hollies. **1820** KEATS *Isabella* xiii, Though Dido silent is in under-grove. *a* **1851** MOIR *Birth of Flowers* xiii, The undergrove Glow'd bright with rhododendron flowers.

**Undergrowe**, obs. var. UNDERGROWN.

**Undergrow·ing,** *ppl. a.* [UNDER-[1] 4 a, 8 a.]

*Undergrowing* should prob. be read in the gloss. (*a* 1400) in *Rel. Ant.* I. 6 *Frutex*, undirglowyng.

†**1.** Arising, occurring. *Obs.*—[1]

*a* **1440** *Found. St. Bartholomew's* (E. E. T. S.) 16 But dyuerse vndirgrowynge ympedymentys, and, at the last, lettyng the Article of deith, that he wold had fulfillid he myght nat.

**2.** Growing beneath trees, etc.; growing up from below.

**1598** *Sidney's Arcadia* III. 349 Sitting her downe vnder one of them, and making a posie of the fayre vndergrowing flowers. **1616** W. BROWNE *Brit. Past.* II. i. 17 On his legs Like fetters hang the vnder growing Segs.

**U·ndergrowl.** (UNDER-[1] 9 b.) *c* **1848** J. KEEGAN *Leg. & Poems* (1907) 480 'Och, you thief of the world!' cried the woman, in a kind of under growl. **1895** MEREDITH *Amazing Marriage* xxxii, The shaking of her gown and the snarl in the undergrowl sounded insatiate.

**Undergrow·n,** *ppl. a.* [UNDER-[1] 4 a, 10 a.]

**1.** Imperfectly grown or developed.

*c* **1386** CHAUCER *Prol.* 156 She hadde a fair forheed. It was almoost a spanne brood I trowe, For hardily she was nat vndergrowe.

†**2.** Showing signs of puberty. *Obs.*

**1601** HOLLAND *Pliny* I. 345 As well men as women-kind,.. when they are come to fourteene yeares of age, and be undergrowne. **1609** — *Amm. Marcell.* XXVI. iii. 287 He had put forth a sonne of his, scarce undergrowne, unto a Sorcerer.

**3.** Furnished with an undergrowth.

**1895** *Westm. Gaz.* 14 Aug. 3/1 A thicket of thorn trees, undergrown with long dried-up grass.

**U·ndergrowth.** [UNDER-[1] 5 d, 10 b.]

**1.** A growth of plants or shrubs under trees or other tall vegetation; brushwood, underwood.

**1600** SURFLET *Countrie Farme* VI. x. 744 There must good regard be taken euery where, what plants of branches or vndergrowth are dead. **1667** MILTON *P. L.* IV. 175 The undergrowth Of shrubs and tangling bushes. **1794** VANCOUVER *Agric. Cambridge* 117 In this parish is found some very good woodland..; the undergrowth is cut once in fourteen years. **1822** SHELLEY tr. *Calderon's Mag. Prodig.* I. 3 This intricate wild wilderness of trees..and undergrowth of odorous plants. **1884** Q. VICTORIA *More Leaves* 308 The tangled undergrowth of fern, &c. is almost like a jungle.

**b.** The shorter stems of certain cultivated plants.

**1765** *Museum Rust.* IV. 457 What is commonly called under-growth [of flax], may be neglected as useless. **1865** *Pall Mall G.* 3 July 5/2 Much of what farmers call the under-growths or under-stems of wheat are not coming into ear at all.

**2.** A growth of (shorter and finer) hair or wool underlying the outer fur or fleece.

**1641** BEST *Farm. Bks.* (Surtees) 20 Such sheepe as have their wooll thus risen, have, without question, a goode undergrowth. **1879** *Encycl. Brit.* X. 709/1 This undergrowth [of the Cashmere goat]..is beautifully soft and silky.

**3.** The condition of being undergrown or undersized; imperfect growth.

**1891** *Lancet* 14 Mar. 624/2 Cases of heart disease,..of undergrowth, and underdevelopment.

**U·nder-gua·rdian.** (UNDER-[1] 6 a.) **1554** *Dial. on Laws Eng.* II. xlii. 135 The sherif shal make such vndergardeins for the which they will aunswere. **1611** COTGR., *Soubcurateur*, an vnder Gardian. **U·nder-ha·bit.** (UNDER-[1] 5 a.) **1771** *Ann. Reg., Chron.* App. 216/2 The Knights companions in the full habit of the order,..the Knights elect in the under-habits of their order.

†**Under-ha·le,** *v. Obs.*—[1] [UNDER-[1] 4 a.] *trans.* To under-run.

**1615** *Admiralty Court of Oyer & Terminer 76* No. 10, Underhale the cable.

**U·nder-ha·mmer.** [UNDER-[1] 5 b.] In a pianoforte: (see quot. 1860).

**1840** [see HOPPER[1] 9]. **1845** G. DODD *Brit. Manuf.* IV. 160 The key acts on the 'grasshopper', and the 'grasshopper' on the 'under-hammer'. **1860** RIMBAULT *Pianoforte* 396 *Underhammer*, a hinged lever..to which the hopper is adjusted; used in upright pianofortes.

**Underha·nd,** *adv.* [UNDER-[2]. Cf. MDu. *onderhande(n)* by degrees, slowly; Du. *onderhandsch* secret, private; Da. *underhaanden* secretly, privately.]

†**1. a.** In (or into) subjection; under rule or command. *Obs.*

*a* **900** *Daniel* 71 Hie..ʒelæddon..Israela cyn on eastweʒas ..under hand..hæðenum deman. *a* **1000** in Thorpe *Laws* (1840) II. 218 *note*, Æʒhwæðer ʒa bisceope underhand. *a* **1300** *Cursor M.* 6442 Þis ilk folk was vntelland, Þat moyses had vnder hand. *Ibid.* 7057 Labdon þan had þam vnder-hand, Was ouerman aght yeir lastand.

†**b.** In (one's) possession or power. *Obs.*

*a* **1200** in Kemble *Codex Dipl.* (1846) IV. 268 Ðat lond ðat Berric hauede under hande. *c* **1200** in Thorpe *Dipl. Angl. Sax* (1865) 581 Alle þinge þe hi under honde habben buten þat lond. **1297** R. GLOUC. (Rolls) 2984 Þo he adde þe luþer king agag vnder honde, He let him hewe to peces.

†**c.** In hand; in course of doing. *Obs.*

*c* **1400** *Ywaine & Gaw.* 3478 This batayl wil he undertake, And he haves yit in other land Ful felle dedes underhand. **1693** *Mem. Ct. Teckely* IV. 26 Which made the People have a suspicion that there was a Design under hand, but it could not be discovered.

†**2. a.** *Archery.* (Meaning uncertain.) *Obs. rare.*

**1545** ASCHAM *Toxoph.* II. (Arb.) 126 Those that be lytle brested and big toward the hede..be fit for them whiche shote vnder hande. *Ibid.* 164 A byg brested shafte [is bad] for hym that shoteth vnder hande..: a little brested shafte for him yat shoteth aboue ye hande. ?**15..** *Robin Hoode & Qu. Kath.* xxix. (Percy MS.), Loxly puld forth a broad arrowe, He shott it vnder hand.

**b.** (See quot. 1834.)

**1721** S. SEWALL *Diary* 18 Nov., Went to the Funeral... The Sight was awfull to see the Father, and then the daughter underhand by four. **1834** MRS. BRAY *Warleigh* xx, The coffin..was borne 'underhand', as it is called in Devonshire, that is, carried by bearers, about a foot from the ground, by napkins passed through the coffin-rings.

**c.** (See quot.)

**1771** LUCKOMBE *Hist. Print.* 502 The Light and Easy, or Heavy and Hard Running in of the Carriage. Thus.., the Press goes light and easy under Hand, or it goes heavy or hard under Hand. **1888** JACOBI *Printers' Vocab.* s.v.

**d.** With the hand held below; *spec.* in *Cricket* (see UNDERHAND *a.* 1 c).

**1828** in Box *Cricket* (1868) 77 The ball must be bowled.. and delivered underhand with the hand below the elbow. **1885** *Graphic* 14 Feb. 166/1 He..drew out a pair of steel handcuffs, which he..threw up and caught underhand in the air.

**3.** In a secret, covert, or stealthy manner; by secret means; quietly or unobtrusively.

Common from *c* 1580; formerly often written as two words (β), or with hyphen (γ).

α. **1538** ELYOT, *Suppilo*, to steale vnderhand [**1545** vnder hande] or craftily. **1580** CAMPION in Allen *Martyrdom* (1908) 22 Neither can I tell who altered his determination saving God, to whom vnderhand I then humbly praied. **1615** G. SANDYS *Trav.* 215 The rest being put to the sword, saue those that were vnderhand saued by the Sidonians. **1654** GATAKER *Disc. Apol.* 44 Being underhand backed and fed with money by two Tenants. **1684** W. HEDGES *Diary* (Hakl. Soc.) I. 148 He told me that Mr. Richard Frenchfeild was, underhand, a great favorer of ye Interlopers. **1733** NEAL *Hist. Purit.* II. 605 His Majesty was underhand preparing for war. **1792** BURKE *Corr.* (1844) III. 375, I should not be surprised if he did all he could, underhand, to lessen you in the opinion..of those who employ you. **1814** SCOTT *Wav.* lxiv, Bailie Macwheeble provided Janet underhand with meal for their maintenance. **1894** STEVENSON & L. OSBOURNE *Ebb Tide* vii, Approaching that island underhand like eavesdroppers and thieves.

β. **1545** [see α]. **1577** HOLINSHED *Chron.* II. 305/1 The same Stigand was an helper vnder hande for king William to atteyne the Crowne. **1611** TOURNEUR *Ath. Trag.* III. iii, He does it under hand, out of a reseru'd disposition to doe thee good without ostentation. **1653** H. COGAN tr. *Pinto's Trav.* x. 31 He..used the interposure of a Man born in the country, who under hand went to the fishermen. **1726** CAVALLIER *Mem.* I. 103 Commonly we liv'd by the Assistance of our Friends, who under Hand supplied us in our Marches, with Bread and other Necessaries.

γ. **1583** BOWES & DAVISON in *B.'s Corr.* (Surtees) 336 He laboureth under-hand to work a peace betwen the duke and Gowrie. **1639** S. DU VERGER tr. *Camus' Admir. Events* 221 Meane time he under-hand advertises Appollinaire to go always well accompanied. **1683** *Lond. Gaz.* No. 1807/3 They begin very much to suspect that..he does under-hand encourage the Turks to the War. **1705** tr. *Bosman's Guinea* 362 These Gentlemen..agree under-hand with those who sell the Slaves. **1748** *Anson's Voy.* II. iii. 148 In appearance to acquiesce in this resolution, whilst he endeavoured under-hand to give it all the obstruction he could. **1818** SCOTT *Br. Lamm.* xx, That friend..was labouring hard under-hand to consolidate a band of patriots.

†**4.** = UNDERFOOT *adv.* 3. *Obs.*—[1]

**1617** MORYSON *Itin.* III. 55 If he bring his Horse thither, those that are to buy him, are such crafty knaues,..as he shall be forced to sell his Horse vnder hand.

**U·nderhand,** *a.* and *sb.* [f. prec.]

**A.** *adj.* (In predicative use *underha·nd.*)

**1.** †**a.** *Archery.* Used in shooting 'under hand'. (Cf. UNDERHAND *adv.* 2 a.)

**1545** ASCHAM *Toxoph.* II. (Arb.) 126 Thus the vnderhande [shaft] must haue a small breste, to go cleane awaye oute of the bowe.

**b.** Made with the hands kept below the level of the body.

**1705** tr. *Bosman's Guinea* 129 Paddling the Water with an under-hand stroke.

**c.** *Cricket.* Of bowling: Performed with the hand held under the ball and lower than the shoulder or (formerly) the elbow. (Cf. UNDERARM *a.* 1 and UNDERHAND *adv.* 2 d.)

**1850** 'BAT' *Cricket Man.* 33 By the underhand method of bowling, the ball..went directly to the wicket. **1867** *Lillywhite's Cricketers' Comp.* 8 Underhand bowling is almost extinct. **1905** *F. Sugg's Cricket Annual* 47 It is very essential that he should cultivate the under-hand throw.

**d.** Using underhand bowling.

**1848** W. N. HUTCHINSON *Dog-breaking* ii. 13 Similar to the swing of an under-hand bowler at cricket. **1851** LILLYWHITE *Guide to Cricketers* 68 He is a capital under-hand bowler and a dangerous bat.

**2.** Secret, clandestine, surreptitious. Also *absol.*

**1592** NASHE *P. Penilesse* G ij b, All under-hand cloaking of bad actions with Common-wealth pretences. **1621** ELSING *Debates Ho. Lords* App. (Camden) 149 It was ordered ..that..the sollicitor should goe with the officer, whoe had the warrant, and showlld searche all underhand workers' howsses. **1649** *Nicholas Papers* (Camden) 139 The former endeavouring by underhand treaties to undermyne him. **1678** WANLEY *Wond. Lit. World* v. ii. § 59. 471/1 Manuel..was an underhand enemy to the Western Christians, and an open enemy to the Turks. **1712** ADDISON *Spect.* No. 550 ¶ 1 Several indirect and underhand Practices. **1823** SCOTT *Quentin D.* i, These turbulent cities..never failed to find underhand countenance at the Court of Louis. **1868** FREEMAN *Norm. Conq.* (1877) II. ix. 366 Their influence must have been exercised in a purely underhand way. **1892** STEVENSON & L. OSBOURNE *Wrecker* x, A new element of the uncertain, the underhand, perhaps even the dangerous.

**b.** Of persons: Not straightforward.

**1842** J. H. NEWMAN *Lett.* (1891) II. 393, I am often accused of being underhand and uncandid. **1858** LYTTON *What will He do?* I. xvi, You could not mean to be sly and underhand.

**3.** Not open or obvious; unobtrusive; quiet.

**1600** SHAKS. *A. Y. L.* I. i. 142, I had my selfe notice of my Brothers purpose heerein, and haue by vnder-hand meanes laboured to disswade him from it. **1656** EARL MONM. tr. *Boccalini's Advts. fr. Parnass.* I. xxxviii. (1674) 50 By this handsom under-hand dealing, I have reduced the formerly ruinous..State..into the condition that now it is. **1824** MISS FERRIER *Inher.* xxiv, For, as she observed, in an underhand way, there was no disputing with a man who held the key of the post-bag. **1856** RUSKIN *Mod. Paint.* IV. v. iv. § 14 The most subtle moves of a game of chess,..which are, in dim, underhand, wonderful way, bringing out their foreseen and inevitable result.

**4.** Held in, manipulated by, the hand.

**1706** BAYNARD in Sir J. Floyer *Hot & Cold Bath* II. 274 He went..with Crutches, and was in six or eight times Bathing so much reliev'd as to walk with an underhand Stick. **1786** ABERCROMBIE *Gard. Assist.* 136 Ridge out melons in underhand glasses.

**5.** *Mining.* Worked from above downwards.

**1877** RAYMOND *Statist. Mines & M.* 226 Fifteen men were engaged in underhand stoping from the top of winze No. 3.

**B.** *sb.* 1. An underhand ball; underhand bowling. 1866 LE FANU *All in Dark* I. xxxiii. 282 He handles the willow pretty well, and would treat you to a tolerably straight, well pitched slow underhand. 1885 FINCH-HATTON *Advance Australia!* 338 All display a precocious talent for round-hand bowling, very different to the sneaking underhand affected by the uneducated youth of Great Britain.

2. A position of inferiority. 1886 STEVENSON *Kidnapped* xii, I paid the less attention to this, for I knew it was usually said by those who have the underhand.

**Underha·nded,** *adv.* and *a.* [f. prec.]

**A.** *adv.* 1. = UNDERHAND *adv.* 3. 1825 COBBETT *Rur. Rides* (1830) I. 342 The Quakers have been urging it on, underhanded. 1857 DICKENS *Little Dorrit* II. xx, You are reproaching me, under-handed, with having nobody but you to look to.

2. (Cf. UNDERHAND *a.* 1 c.) *c* 1822 *Laws of Cricket* in *Q. Rev.* (1884) CLVIII. 471 The ball must be delivered underhanded, not thrown or jerked.

**B.** *adj.* (In attributive use *u·nderha·nded.*)

1. = UNDERHAND *a.* 2. 1806 [implied in UNDERHANDEDLY *adv.*]. 1853 DICKENS *Bleak House* xxxvii, Under-handed charges against John Jarndyce. 1865 — *Mut. Fr.* I. ix, Dark deep underhanded plotting. 1884 *Harper's Mag.* Feb. 395/2 Life seemed to go on in an underhanded, secret way.

b. = UNDERHAND *a.* 2 b. 1865 DICKENS *Mut. Fr.* II. vii, That's an underhanded mind, Sir. 1899 MRS. F. H. BURNETT *Willoughby Claim* vi, You confounded, sneaking, underhanded little thief!

2. Short of 'hands'; undermanned. 1834 COLERIDGE *Table-t.* 4 Jan., If that country could be brought to maintain a million more of inhabitants, Norway might defy the world:..but it is much under-handed now. 1858 FROUDE *Hist. Eng.* III. 143 He was still underhanded, and entreated assistance. 1874 S. WILBERFORCE *Ess.* II. 97 The clergy are utterly underhanded.

3. *dial.* Undersized. 1856 P. THOMPSON *Hist. Boston* 728 A little, underhanded fellow. 1868- in Yks. and Cumb. glossaries.

4. Placed or printed below. 1884 *American* VIII. 347 Many of the caricatures were originally published in connection with the 'poem', which is underhanded.

Hence **U·nderha·ndedly** *adv.*; **-ha·ndedness.** 1806 *Feltham's Resolves* I. 106 To applaud virtue would procure us far more honour, than underhandedly seeking to disparage her. 1884 TENNYSON *Becket* Prol., All left-handedness and under-handedness. 1886 *Athenæum* 11 Sept. 335/1 A great deal of indirectness—not to say underhandedness. 1891 H. C. HALLIDAY *Someone must Suffer* III. xii. 213 You had acted underhandedly and deceived him.

† **Underha·nding,** *vbl. sb. Obs.* [UNDER-[2].] The action of taking in hand. 1639 T. DE GRAY *Expert Farrier* To Rdr., Thou wilt be much bettered and enabled in thy underhanding.

**U·nderhang,** *sb.* (UNDER-[1] 4 d. Cf. UNDERHANGING *vbl. sb.*) 1903 *Smart Set* IX. 8/2 He was a short man,..with the underhang of jaw which tells of indomitable perseverance.

† **Underha·ng,** *v. Obs.*[—1] [UNDER-[1] 4 a.] *trans.* To hang, suspend. 1603 HOLLAND *Plutarch's Mor.* 1064 This saying of Antisthenes,..that a man is to be provided either of wit to understand, or else of a with to under-hang himselfe.

**U·nderha·nging,** *vbl. sb.* [UNDER-[1] 4 a. Cf. UNDERHUNG *ppl. a.*] Projection, protrusion (of the lower jaw). 1842 YOUATT *Dog* iv. (1845) 99 A second cross considerably lessens the underhanging of the lower jaw. 1876 T. BRYANT *Pract. Surg.* (ed. 2) I. 545 In some cases complete underhanging of the jaw is present.

**U·nderha·nging,** *ppl. a.* [Cf. prec.] Having a prominent lower jaw. 1865 MRS. CRAIK *Christian's Mistake* ii. 41 Her full-lipped, underhanging mouth.

**U·nder-ha·ngman.** (UNDER-[1] 6 a.) 1611 SHAKS. *Cymb.* II. iii 135 Thou wert dignified enough.. to be stil'd The vnder Hangman of his Kingdome.

† **Under-hat.** *Obs.*[—1] [UNDER *prep.*] Some gambling game. 1629 *Maldon* (Essex) *Documents* Bundle 210, No. 3, They went to plaie at a game with shillings and testers called vnder hatt.

**U·nderhead.** [UNDER-[1] 6 a.]

1. A subordinate official. 1599 LEWKENOR *Contarini's Commw. Venice* 163 These heads & vnderheads are all elected by lot. 1876 *Whitby Gloss.* 205/2 *Underheeads*, minor officials.

† 2. A person of inferior intelligence. *Obs.* 1643 SIR T. BROWNE *Relig. Med.* I. § 55 Wiser discretions .. offend without a pardon; whereas under heads may stumble without dishonour. 1686 W. DE BRITAINE *Hum. Prud.* xix. 86, I find by experience, that under Heads and narrow Souls by Industry..work Wonders.

So † **U·nder-hea·ded** *a.*, of inferior intellect or parts. *Obs.*[—1] 1646 *Crashaw's Steps to Temple* Pref. A 4 It were prophane but to mention here..those under-headed Poets, Retainers to seven shares and a halfe.

† **Underhea·r,** *v. Obs.* [UNDER-[1] 8 a, after obs. It. *sottoudire* (cf. L. *subaudire*).] To overhear. *c* 1570 *The Bugbears* v. ii. 4, I wold not that the maydes ..In theis so waightie matters shold hap to vnderhear vs. [1598 FLORIO, *Sottoudire..*, to vnderheare, or as we say to ouerheare.]

† **Underheave**: see UNDER-[1] 2.

**U·nderhea·ven.** (UNDER-[1] 5 b.) 1598 CHAPMAN *Contn. Marlowe's Hero & Leander* v. 173 The yellow issue of the skie Came trouping forth, ielous of crueltie To their bright fellowes of this vnder heauen. 1719 OLDISWORTH *Callipædia* I. 117 When from the Azure Summit awful Jove Beheld this Under-heav'n and World of Love.

† **Underhei·ld,** *a. Obs.*[—1] [UNDER-[1] 7; the second element is related to HIELD *v.*] Subject. *a* 1300 *Cursor M.* 907 And þou, womman,..sal be to man vnder-heild, To him þi buxumnes to yeild.

**U·nderhelp.** (UNDER-[1] 6 b.) 1579 TOMSON *Calvin's Serm. Tim.* 927/2 If we say I haue a wise teacher,..all this is but an vnder help.

**Underhew·,** *v. rare.* [UNDER-[1] 4 a and 8 c.]

1. *trans.* To undercut, undermine. 1523 LD. BERNERS *Froiss.* I. 675 They..myned and vnder hewed the walles. [1611 FLORIO, *Sottotagliare*, to vnder-cut or hew.]

2. *U.S.* To hew (timber) in such a manner that it contains less than the proper number of cubic feet. 1847 WEBSTER (citing S. S. Haldeman).

**Underhid,** *ppl. a.* (UNDER-[1] 4 a.) 1387-8 T. USK *Test. Love* I. vi. (Skeat) l. 72 The underhidde malice and the rancour of purposing envye.

**U·nder-hill.** *rare.* [UNDER-[1] 6 b.]

1. A lower hill. 1687 NORRIS *Coll. Misc.* (1699) 52 Say sacred Mount, what meant thy Trance, And you small under-hills, why did you skip and dance?

2. *attrib.* (Meaning uncertain.) *a* 1722 LISLE *Husb.* (1757) 332 He had lost many a pound by not buying coarse or under-hill hay at the first hand of the year for their ewes.

**U·nderhi·ve,** *v.* [UNDER-[1] 10 a.] *trans.* To place (bees) in too small a hive. 1634 C. BUTLER *Fem. Mon.* 86 The Bees may doo wel enough in a middle-sized Hive: for beeing under-hived, they will cast soomwhat the sooner. 1707 MORTIMER *Husb.* 207 Rather under-hive a Swarm, than over-hive them.

**U·nderhold,** *sb.* [UNDER-[1] 5 b.] The hold obtained by a wrestler who gets his arms below those of his opponent. 1895 *Funk's Stand. Dict.*

† **Underho·ld,** *v. Obs.*[—1] [UNDER-[1] 8 d.] *intr.* To hold land by a sub-tenure. 1594 R. ASHLEY tr. *Loys le Roy* 55 b, The Gentlemen in France possesse, in high, base, and meane iustice,..Principalities, and Peereships patrimoniall: with vassalls holding, and vnderholding of them, bound by faith, and homage.

So † **U·nderho·lder,** a subtenant. *Obs.* 1605 CAMDEN *Rem.* 94 Noted..as men of least account, and as all, or most vnderholders specified in that Booke.

**Underho·le,** *v.* [UNDER-[1] 4 a.] *trans.* or *intr.* To undermine; *spec.* (in coal-mining), to undercut. Also **Underho·ling** *vbl. sb.* 1398 TREVISA *Barth. De P. R.* XIII. xix. (Bodl. MS.), Vnder hoolinge and vnder crepinge and wastinge vnder brymmes..is icleped Alluuio. 1891 *Cent. Dict.* (as U.S. mining-term).

**Under-honest,** *a.* (UNDER-[1] 10 c.) 1606 SHAKS. *Tr. & Cr.* II. iii. 133 You shall not sinne, If you doe say, we thinke him ouer proud, And vnder honest.

**U·nderho·rsed,** *a.* (UNDER-[1] 10 a.) 1860 *Cornh. Mag.* Dec. 689 Why won't he get something able to carry him?..It's the stupidest thing in the world to be under-horsed. 1887 *Illustr. Lond. News* 24 Sept. 360/2 That such an institution [*sc.* the fire-brigade]..should..be underhorsed and undermanned.

**U·nder-ho·rsing,** *vbl. sb.* (UNDER-[1] 10 b.) 1839 LEVER *H. Lorrequer* xiv. 108 The dreadful state of the roads,..the frequency of accidents latterly from under-horsing, &c.

**U·nder-hou·semaid.** (UNDER-[1] 6 a.) 1796 MME. D'ARBLAY *Camilla* III. 44 Nanny, the under house-maid, now joining them. 1862 MRS. CRAIK *Mistress & Maid* xxii, The only face..that she was honestly glad to see..was the under-housemaid. 1896 MRS. CAFFYN *Quaker Grandmother* 131 She returned sadly and fell on the under-housemaid.

**Underhu·ng,** *ppl. a.* (In attrib. use *u·nderhung.*) [UNDER-[1] 4 a.]

1. Having the lower jaw projecting beyond the upper, or coming unusually far forward. 1683 *Lond. Gaz.* No. 1800/4 Lost.., a red fallow Colour'd dun Bull-Bitch,..with a black Muzle under-hung. 1774 GOLDSM. *Nat. Hist.* II. v. 91 Those whose upper and under row of teeth are equally prominent, and strike directly against each other, are what the painters call under-hung. *c* 1815 JANE AUSTEN *Persuas.* xv, He..must lament his being very much under-hung, a defect which time seemed to have increased. 1861 HUGHES *Tom Brown at Oxf.* ii, [He] had got the trick which many underhung men have of compressing his upper lip.

b. Projecting beyond the upper jaw. 1809 MALKIN *Gil Blas* XI. iv. ¶ 4 Wagging his under-hung jaw in a paroxysm of humour-stricken ecstasy. 1868 DARWIN *Anim. & Pl.* I. i. 38 Bull-dogs..after two or three generations..lose the under-hung character of their lower jaws. 1899 *Allbutt's Syst. Med.* VIII. 235 The jaw heavy and sometimes underhung.

2. *Mech.* Suspended on an underlying support; *spec.* of a sliding-door which moves on a rail placed below it. (Opposed to OVERHUNG *ppl. a.* 3.) 1855 D. K. CLARK *Railway Mach.* I. 207/1 Engine. Cylinders underhung, castings in two pieces bolted together.

**Underi·ded,** *ppl. a.* (UN-[1] 8.) 1603 KNOLLES *Hist. Turks* (1621) 37 The Turkes attending vpon the Sultan could not walke in the streets vnderided. 1611 FLORIO, *Inderiso*, vnderided, not mocked.

† **Unde·ringness.** *Obs.* [UN-[1] 10, 12: see DERE *v.*] Harmlessness, innocence. *a* 1300 *E. E. Psalter* xxv. 11 In min underandnesse gane am I. *Ibid.* xl. 13, etc.

**U·nder-i·nstrument.** (UNDER-[1] 6 b.) 1673 [R. LEIGH] *Transp. Reh.* 70 Those who were but accessaries and under-instruments of our late troubles.

**Underi·vable,** *a.* [UN-[1] 7 b.]

1. That cannot be derived (*from* a source). 1640 TORRIANO (*title*), The Italian Tutor, With an Alphabet of primative and originall Italian words, underiveable from the Latin. 1884 tr. *Lotze's Logic* 24 Red and yellow seem to be still more essentially different and underivable one from the other.

† 2. Not transferable. *Obs.*[—1] 1643 PRYNNE *Sov. Power Parl.* III. 78 Whose personall Prerogatives..being incommunicable, underivable to any other, and peculiar to himselt alone, he can transferre no such protection to others.

**Underi·vative,** *a.* (UN-[1] 7 + DERIVATIVE *a.* 2.) 1656 JEANES *Fuln. Christ* 116 The fulnesse agreeable to Christ, as God, is underivative, without a cause. 1856 DOVE *Logic Chr. Faith* 258 Truths which are original and underivative.

**Underi·ved,** *ppl. a.* [UN-[1] 8.] Not derived or drawn *from* a source; primary, original. *c* 1630 SANDERSON *Serm.* (1681) II. 307 Because of the eternity of His own being, and that from Himself, and underived from any other. 1660 R. COKE *Justice Vind.* 5 If it be absolute and underived, then how can it be rational? 1719 WATERLAND *Vind. Christ's Div.* 289 To be able to distinguish between a delegated, and a supreme underived Power. 1799 KIRWAN *Geol. Ess.* 485 It must have had calcareous earth underived from shell fish. 1850 McCOSH *Div. Govt.* III. i. 289 Suppose that man had been a self-existent underived being like God. 1860 PUSEY *Min. Proph.* 468 Life specially belongs to God, since He alone is Underived Life.

b. Of words. (See DERIVE *v.* 10 b.) 1668 WILKINS *Real Char.* 303 That kind of word..is stiled an Adverb; which may be distinguished into Derived and Vnderived. 1827 *Q. Rev.* XXXV. 191 This not more useful than abused verb,..underived as it is from any parent or adjunct dialect. 1841 LATHAM *Eng. Lang.* 261 All, in respect to Verbs in general, which the Etymologist has to determine, is whether they be Derived or Underived.

Hence **Underi·vedly** *adv.*; **Underi·vedness.** 1644 BP. MAXWELL *Prerog. Chr. Kings* i. 19 It is underivedly, primarily, and natively in the Communitie. 1850 F. W. NEWMAN *Phases* ii. 51 This derivation of the Son and Spirit and the underivedness of the Father alone. 1886 *Mind* Jan. 39 What is that subjective necessity..? It is..not its underivedness in any one's mind, not its priority in time.

**U·nder-jaw.** [UNDER-[1] 5 b.] The lower jaw or mandible. 1687 A. LOVELL tr. *Thevenot's Trav.* I. 22 Mahomet the second having taken Constantinople,..beat off the under jaw of one of those heads. 1762 STERNE *Tr. Shandy* V. xxxviii, Touching his under-jaw with the thumb. 1774 GOLDSM. *Nat. Hist.* II. v. 91 The under jaw in a Chinese face falls greatly more backward than with us. 1802 PALEY *Nat. Theol.* xii. § 2. 238 The retired under jaw of a swine. 1868 *Rep. U. S. Commissioner Agric.* (1869) 329 [The female trout] has a less-projecting under-jaw.

**Underjawed,** *ppl. a.* (Stress var.) [f. prec.] Having a protruding lower jaw; underhung. 1772 LADY MARY COKE *Jrnl.* 25 Jan., He is under jaw'd and his chin advances a considerable way. 1812 SHAW *Gen. Zool.* II. 495 Under-jawed Mysticete. 1864 *Realm* 2 Mar. 1 Her mouth, which, slightly underjawed, loses in softness what it gains in piquancy.

**U·nder-jo·bbing,** *ppl. a.* [UNDER-[1] 6 b.] Doing subordinate work. 1697 BENTLEY *Phal.* (1699) 329 Some under-jobbing Assistant, of a low sordid Spirit.

**U·nderkeel.** *U. S.* ? *Obs.* [UNDER-[1] 5 b, with obscure second element.] 'A cut on the under side' of an animal's ear as a mark of ownership. 1783 *Maryland Jrnl.* 4 Feb. (Thornton), A crop in [a cow's] left ear, and an underkeel in her right. 1784 *Ibid.* 27 Jan., The right ear a crop and slit, the left a slit and underkeel.

† **Underkee·p,** *v. Obs.* [UNDER-[1] 4 a.] *trans.* To keep under or in subjection. 1590 SPENSER *F. Q.* III. vii. 33 He lightly lept Vpon the beast, that with great cruelty Rored, and raged to be vnder-kept. 1591 — *Tears Muses* 77 Learned Impes..They vnderkeep, and with their spredding armes Doo beat their buds.

**U·nderkee·per.** [UNDER-[1] 6 a.]

1. An assistant keeper of a forest, park, etc.; an under-gamekeeper. 1502 *Privy Purse Exp. Eliz. York* (1830) 29 To the undrekeper of Swalowfeld for the bringing of iij bukkes 1589 in *Essex Rev.* (1906) XV. 65 [Another deer was] given away by the underkeeper to his freends. 1622 LD. E. MOUNTAGU in *Buccleuch MSS.* (Hist. MSS. Comm.) I. 257 The Forest of Rockingham..where Sir Francis Fane is under-keeper. 1682 *Secr. Serv. Money Chas. & Jas.* (Camden) 58 Henry Lowin, underkeeper of New Lodge Walk within Waltham Forrest. 1826 SCOTT *Woodst.* xxxii, The horses are at the under-keeper's hut. 1891 C. JAMES *Rom. Rigmarole* 172 One of the under-keepers carried a little bamboo arrangement.

2. A subordinate custodian or warder. 1598 FLORIO, *Sotto custode*, an vnder-keeper. 1612 SIR T. BODLEY in Macray *Ann. Bodleian* (1880) 408 Ye keeper of the vniversitie Library, with his vnderkeeper. 1637 *Documents agst. Prynne* (Camden) 69 The Keeper or Under-Keeper of the Castle of Lancaster. 1679 *Hist. Jetzer* 37 He waited till the Under-keeper [of the jail] came in. 1710 *Douglas' Æneis* Pref., Under-Keeper of the Advocates Library. 1760-72 H. BROOKE *Fool of Qual.* (1809) II. 119 Sir, said the under-keeper [of the jail], there are few men now at liberty, near so wealthy as this gentleman.

† **U·nder-kind.** *Obs.* [UNDER-[1] 6 b.] A subspecies; an inferior or lower kind. 1571 GOLDING *Calvin on Ps.* lxxii. 1 It is expedient to descende from the general kynd to the underkynd 1587 — *De Mornay* 15 We reduce the particulars to an vnderkind, the vnderkinds to an vpperkind. 1671 DRYDEN *Even. Love* I. i, I would use thee like an under kind of Chymist, to blow the coals.

**U·nder-king.** [UNDER-[1] 6 a. Cf. Du. *onderkoning*, G. *unterkönig*, ON. *undirkonungr* (Sw. *underkonung*, Da. *-konge*).] A prince or ruler subordinate to a chief king.

*c* 950 *Lindisf. Gosp.* Matt. x. 18 Hia ȝesellas forðon iuih in ȝemotum..& to under-cyningum..fore meh. *c* 1060 *O. E. Chron.* (MS. C) an. 1056, Swa þæt Griffin swor aðas þæt he wolde beon Eadwarde kinge hold underkingc. *c* 1175 *12th Cent. Hom.* (1909) 22 Underkyng is ihaten þe under þam casere rixæð. *c* 1205 LAY. 31340 Cadwalan..nom him to rede ..þat he aȝain wolde..and bi-teche Penda, þe wes his under-kinge, folc and his ferde. 1387 TREVISA *Higden* (Rolls) VI. 275 He put out Egbertus þe sone of Alcmundus þe underkyng. *a* 1513 FABYAN *Chron.* v. cxl. 125 This kyngedome..and the kynges therof, namyd vnder-kynges. 1587 GOLDING *De Mornay* viii. 110 From the great Monarks we come to the Kings of seuerall Nations, and from them to vnderkings of Prouinces. 1867 FREEMAN *Norm. Conq.* I. ii. 26 Each having its own Ealdorman or Under-King, though united under one supreme chief. 1874 GREEN *Short Hist.* i. § 3 (1882) 18 The under-kings of Essex and East-Anglia received the creed of their overlord.

**U·nder-ki·ngdom.** (UNDER-[1] 6 b.)

1581 SIDNEY *Apol. Poetrie* (Arb.) 63 Where you shal haue Asia of the one side, and Affrick of the other, and so many other vnder-kingdoms. 1859 TENNYSON *Merlin & V.* 581 Thro' all The hundred under-Kingdoms that he sway'd. 1877 FREEMAN *Norm. Conq.* I. App. 774 Cnut, like Charles, established a system of under-kingdoms.

**U·nder-la·bourer.** (UNDER-[1] 6 a.)

*a* 1667 JER. TAYLOR *Serm.* Wks. 1831 IV. 140 You are the ministers of Christ's priesthood, under-labourers in the great work of mediation and intercession. 1690 LOCKE *Hum. Und.* To Rdr., 'Tis Ambition enough to be employed as an Under-Labourer in clearing the Ground a little. 1704 NORRIS *Ideal World* II. vii. 350 The proper office of this agent intellect, to serve as an under-labourer to that which is patient. 1836 KEBLE *Serm.* viii. (1848) 219 We, indeed, as Priests of the second order, are but under-labourers in that most holy cause.

**Underlai·d,** *ppl. a.* (Stress var.) [UNDER-[1] 4 a. Cf. UNDERLAY *v.*]

1. Laid or placed under or below.

*a* 1100 in Napier *O. E. Gloss.* I. 3518 *Suppositis..torribus*, of under ledum..brandum. 1552 HULOET, Vnder layed, *suffundatus*. 1598 FLORIO, *Soffondato*, vnderlaide or laid vnder. 1647 HEXHAM I.

2. Furnished with an under layer or support; strengthened from below; fitted or supplied underneath (*with* something). Chiefly *fig.*

*c* 1530 *Hickscorner* D iv, Therwith can you cloute me a payre of botes?..I wolde haue them well vnderlayd and easlye. 1618 BP. HALL *Contempl.*, *O. T.* XII. viii, That mans faith is well underlaid, that upholds it selfe by the Omnipotency of God. 1650 TRAPP *Comm. Deut.* iii. 6 Surely, every man in his best estate, or when best underlaid, is altogether vanity. 1658 J. HARRINGTON *Oceana* 91 If a Common-wealth have been introduced at once,..you are certain to find her under-lay'd with this as the main foundation. 1712 BUDGELL *Spect.* No. 379 ¶ 12 The Floor of the Vault was all loose, and under-laid with several Springs. 1820 SHELLEY *Witch Atl.* liii, They framed the imperial tent..Of woven exhalations, underlaid With lambent lightning-fire.

b. Const. *by* (what underlies).

1850 ANSTED *Elem. Geol., Min.*, etc. § 906 Seams of coal ..underlaid by a seam or bed of fire-clay. 1893 SIR H. HOWORTH *Glacial Nightmare* II. 463 That the coal-beds.. are overlaid by drift I have no doubt; that they are also underlaid by it seems to be most doubtful.

3. *Printing.* Of type, etc.: Raised by means of an underlay.

1771 LUCKOMBE *Hist. Print.* 362 These Underlaid Words standing higher than the rest of the Matter. 1880 *Scribner's Mag.* May 42/2 This addition to the plate springs it up in every part underlaid, so that the surface fairly meets the inking rollers.

†4. Of a horse: ? Strong-limbed. *Obs.*

1674 *Lond. Gaz.* No. 892/4 A strong underlaid Brown Bay Nag. *Ibid.* No. 909/4 A truss well underlaid Horse.

**U·nder-land.** (UNDER-[1] 5 b, c.) 1874 HOLLAND *Mistr. Manse* v, Down in to wonderland—Down to the under-land Go, oh go! 1877 A. DOBSON *Prov. Porcelain, To Greek Girl*, From under-lands of Memory.

**Underla·p,** *v.* [UNDER-[1] 4 a.] To extend some way beneath. Hence **Underla·pping** *ppl. a.*

1867 DK. ARGYLL *Reign of Law* iii. 141 The feathers of a bird's wing are made to underlap each other. *c* 1900 *Buck's Handbk. Med. Sci* IV. 680 (Cent. Suppl.), The margin of the underlapping side is sutured to the deep surface of the overlapping side.

**U·nder-law·yer.** (UNDER-[1] 6 a.) 1638 T. NABBES *Covent Garden* I. ii, What's his profession? An under-Lawyer, an Attourney.

**U·nderlay,** *sb.* [UNDER-[1] 4 d.]

†1. (See quot.) *Obs.*

1589 PUTTENHAM *Eng. Poesie* III. xix. (Arb.) 211 Ye haue another sort of repetition...The Greeks call him *Epizeuxis*, the Latines *Subiunctio*, we may call him the *vnderlay*.

2. a. A piece added to the sole of a shoe.

1612 *Pasquil's Night-cap* (1877) 25 She could line her shoes with vnder-laies, So cunningly, that few the fault did spie.

b. = EKE *sb.*[1] 2 b.

1641 BEST *Farm. Bks.* (Surtees) 63 They will or within a monethes space worke downe to the bottome of the hive, and then must yow give them an underlay. There is in an underlay usually five wreathes, viz., one for the hive to stand within, and fower belowe; yow are to putte in an underlay two spelles.

c. A piece inserted as a prop or support, esp. so as to make one part level with another.

1683 MOXON *Mech. Exerc., Printing* ii. ¶ 1 Presses [should] have..an even Horizontal Floor to stand on, That when the Presses are set up their Feet shall need no Underlays. *Ibid.* xxiv. ¶ 1 The aforesaid Battens will also keep these Underlays from working out.

d. *Printing.* A piece of paper or cardboard placed under type, cuts, or plates, to raise these to the required level.

1683 MOXON *Mech. Exerc., Printing* xxiv. 291 He tries thicker or thinner Vnder-lays till he have evened the Vnder-lay with the Face of the Letter. 1688 HOLME *Armoury* III. 118/2 Underlays, are small slips of Scabbord put under letters. 1824 J. JOHNSON *Typogr.* II. xv. 521 They will be found to sink a little from the repeated impressions, consequently the cuts will require an additional underlay. 1880 *Scribner's Mag.* May 43/1 He puts a proper underlay under every cut..that contains much black surface, and fairly braces it to resist hard impression.

3. *Mining.* = DIP *sb.* 5, HADE *sb.*[2] (See quots. 1831–55, and cf. UNDERLIE *sb.*)

1831–3 *Encycl. Metrop.* (1845) VIII. 203/1 The underlay of a lode is a term used to denote the direction of its inclination with regard to the horizon. 1855 [J. R. LEIFCHILD] *Cornwall* 101 The dip of a lode..being its inclination from a perpendicular line, or its underlay. 1880 C. C. ADLEY *Rep. to Pioneer Mining Co., Lim.* 2 Oct. 1 A small shaft will also be sunk,..following the underlay of the lode.

*attrib.* 1850 WEALE *Dict. Terms*, *Underlay shaft*, a shaft sunk on the course of a lode. 1882 *U. S. Rep. Prec. Met.* 461 The mine is entered by an underlay or inclined shaft 150 feet deep.

**Underlay·,** *v.* [OE. *underlecgan* (see UNDER-[1] 4 a and LAY *v.*), = MDu. and Du. *onderleggen*, MHG. *underlegen* (G. *unter-*), MSw. *undirläggia* (Sw. *underlägga*), MDa. and Da. *underlægge*.]

1. *trans.* To support by placing something beneath; to furnish *with* something laid below. Also *fig.*

*c* 897 K. ÆLFRED *Gregory's Past C.* xix. 143 Ðonne bið se elnboȝa underled mid pyle & se hnecca mid bolstre. *c* 1000 ÆLFRIC *Hom.* II. 144 Þa bæd he hi anre sylle, þæt he mihte þæt hus on ða sæ healfe mid þære underlecgan. *c* 1250 *Gen. & Ex.* 3388 He is under-leiden wið an ston, Til sunne him seilede in ðe west. 1555 EDEN *Decades* (Arb.) 327 They vnderlaye them with grasse. 1577 B. GOOGE *Heresbach's Husb.* II. (1586) 60 They vse to set the heads vnderlaying them with a Tileshard. 1658 A. FOX *Würtz' Surg.* II. xiv. 110 You ought not to stitch any wounded Finger,..but underlay it with little splinters. 1679 MOXON *Mech. Exerc.* ix. 157 If the Board be too thin, they underlay that Board upon every Joyst with a Chip. 1726 LEONI *Alberti's Archit.* II. 10 b, Another way of making the weight slip along..is by underlaying it cross-ways with Rollers. 1851 *Athenæum* Oct. 1049/1 Their project of underlaying the sea with electric wires.

b. To furnish with a lining or backing.

1502 *Acc. Ld. High Treas. Scot.* II. 302 Franch tanne to be ane cote to Jacob..v quartaris demy ostad to underlay the bordoring of it.

†c. To furnish (shoes) with additional solingpieces or heel-plates. Also in fig. context. *Obs.*

*c* 1530 [see UNDERLAID *ppl. a.* 2]. 1583 STUBBES *Anat. Abus.* II. F 4, If the sooles be naught (as they be indeede) yet must they be vnderlaied with other peeces of leather, to make them seeme thicke. 1587 TURBERV. *Epit.* 190 b, The heeles they vnderlay With clouting clamps of steele. 1632 HOLLAND *Cyrupædia* 181 The Medes use..such a kind of shooes, as they might underlay closely and out of sight. 1661 K. W. *Conf. Charac.* To Rdr. (1860) 1 Should I, like an vnthrifty cobler, haue vnderlayed the rotten soles of these now worn out buskings, with the new and costly leather of applause. 1681 W. ROBERTSON *Phraseol. Gen.* 1272 To underlay a shoe, *suppingere*.

*fig.* 1592 NASHE *Four Lett. Confut.* 7 Then wil I bind my selfe prentise to a Cobler, and fresh vnderlay all those writings of mine that haue trodde awrie. 1603 DEKKER *Wonderfull Yeare* E 3 b, Being a pollitike cobler, and remembring what peece of work he was to vnderlay. ? 1622 FLETCHER *Love's Cure* v. iii, Our souls have trode awry in all mens sight, We'll underlay 'em, till they go upright.

d. *Printing.* To place paper or cardboard under (type, etc.) in order to raise to the required level for printing.

1683 MOXON *Mech. Exerc., Printing* xxiv. 291 If any Wooden Letters..are too Low, (as they generally be) he Vnder-lays them. 1880 *Scribner's Mag.* May 42/2 The pressman underlays the plate, by pasting on its under side bits of paper of suitable size. 1888 JACOBI *Printers' Vocab.*, *Underlay*, the process of making-ready under type or cuts.

2. To place (something) beneath.

*c* 1000 ÆLFRIC *Gram.* xxviii. (Z.) 167 *Subpono*, ic underlecge. *c* 1440 *Promp. Parv.* 511/1 Vnderleyyn, *idem quod* underputtyn. 1573 TWYNE *Æneid* XII. Nnj, A tower stronge..the prince..had built alone, And choules [? *read* roules] had vnderlayd [L. *subdideratque rotas*]. 1683 MOXON *Mech. Exerc*, *Printing* xxii. ¶ 10 If a Page be too big for his Grasp, he underlays the Slice of a Galley.

b. To put underground, to bury.

Used punningly with allusion to sense 1 c.

1639 *Conceits, Clinches*, etc. (1860) 40 If any aske why this same stone was made? (Know) for a cobler newly underlayd Here for his overboasting.

†3. To make subject; to submit. *Obs.*

*a* 1300 *E. E. Psalter* viii. 7 Þou vnderlaide [L. *subjecisti*] alle þinges Vnder his fete. *a* 1300 *Cursor M.* 18266 Sin þou þe king o blis werraid And sua þi-self has vnder-laid. 1382 WYCLIF *Jer.* xxvii. 12 Vnderleith [L. *subjicite*] ȝoure neckus vnder the ȝoc of the king of Babyloyne.

4. To lie under or beneath; = UNDERLIE *v.* 3.

1591 SPENSER *Virg. Gnat* 99 Ne cares he if the..glistering of golde, which vnderlayes The summer beames, doe blinde his gazing eye. 1611 COTGR., *Haulse*, the vnderlaying of a shooe, or peece of leather that vnderlayes it. 1799 KIRWAN *Geol. Ess.* 178 In the south of France it occurs reposing on granite, and underlaying basalt. *Ibid.*, In the Altaischan mountains it sometimes underlays argillite. 1826 E. IRVING *Babylon* II. VII. 227 Our brethren and friends, who still underlay the curse. 1861 DASENT *Burnt Njal* I. Introd. p. xxviii, [The right of duel] underlaid all their early legislation.

5. *intr. Mining.* To slope, incline from the perpendicular; = UNDERLIE *v.* 5.

1728 *Phil. Trans.* XXXV. 403 The Sides of the Load.. constantly underlay either to the North or South. 1802 J. MAWE *Min. Derby* Gloss. s.v., When a vein *hades*, or inclines from a perpendicular line, it is said to underlay. 1855 [J. R. LEIFCHILD] *Cornwall* 101 A lode which underlays towards the north.

**Underlay·er**[1]. [f. prec. Cf. Du. *onderlegger*, G. *unterleger*.]

†1. An underlying part or thing; a base or support. *Obs.*

In quot. 1609 applied allusively to a woman.

*a* 1592 GREENE & LODGE *Looking Gl.* I. ii. 255 The Nutmeg ..is, saith one Ballad,..an vnderlayer to the braines. 1609 *Ev. Woman in Hum.* I. i, Ist not some vnderlayer, some she Cammell that will beare as much of her belly, as three beastes on their backes? 1702 BOYER *Dict. Royal* II, Underlayer,..(a piece of Wood to shore up any thing,) *une Etaye, un Etançon*. 1775 ASH, *Underlayer*.., that which is laid under to bear up any thing.

†2. A cobbler. *Obs.*[−1]

1692 R. L'ESTRANGE *Fables* I. cccci. 375 How many Underlayers,..when they could not live upon their Trade, have rais'd themselves from Cobbling to Fluxing?

3. *Mining.* 'A perpendicular shaft sunk to cut the lode at any required depth.'

1850 WEALE *Dict. Terms.*

**U·nderlay·er**[2]. [UNDER-[1] 5 b.] A lower layer; a substratum.

1896 *Daily News* 15 Dec. 2/2 The carpets are of heavy velvet pile on an underlayer of elastic felt and cork. 1904 W. P. KER *Dark Ages* 198 Rodulphus represents the permanent underlayer of medieval absurdity above which Gerbert rises so eminently.

**Underlay·ing,** *vbl. sb.* [f. UNDERLAY *v.*] The action of the verb, or the result of this.

1611 [see UNDERLAY *v.* 4]. 1648 HEXHAM II, *Ondersetsel van pileernen*, the Vnderlaying or the Ground-worke of pillars. 1683 MOXON *Mech. Exerc., Printing* xxiv. ¶ 1, I am loath to name the Vnder-laying of the Feet, because at the best it is but a Botch, and Subjects the whole Press to an unstable position. 1802 J. MAWE *Min. Derby* Gloss., *Hade*, the underlaying or inclination of the vein. 1882 SOUTHWARD *Pract. Printing* (1884) 429 In underlaying we put a piece of paper..under the type.

**U·nderleaf.** [UNDER-[1] 5 b.]

1. A variety of cider-apple. Also *attrib.*

1707 MORTIMER *Husb.* 540 The Underleaf..is a very plentiful bearer, hath a Rhenish Wine flavour. *Ibid.* 575 The best sorts for Cyder are found to be..the Olive Underleaf Apple [etc.]. 1786 ABERCROMBIE *Arrangem.* p. xi. in *Gard. Assist.*, Apples valued principally for Cyder..[include] Underleaf.

2. The under surface of a leaf.

1873 TRISTRAM *Moab* xviii. 353 The charm of the silvery [poplar] underleaf twinkling in the breeze.

**U·nder-lease,** *sb.* [UNDER-[1] 6 b.] A lease granted by a lessee; a sub-lease.

1702 BOYER *Dict. Royal* I, *Soubail*, .. an under-lease. 1730 *Act* 4 *Geo. II*, c. 28 § 6 Those Leases cannot by Law be renewed without a Surrender of all the Under-Leases. 1803 *Act* 43 *Geo. III*, c. 75 § 4 It may be for the Benefit of such Persons that Leases, or Under-Leases, should be made of such Estates. 1839 *Penny Cycl.* XIII. 378/2 Where the property is transferred for a part of the original term only, the transfer is called an under-lease, and the under-lessee is not liable to the original lessor. 1885 *Law Times* 7 Mar. 335/2 The underlease contained a covenant that if the underlessee..should..assign the underlease [etc.].

**Underlea·se,** *v.* [UNDER-[1] 8 d.] *trans.* To sublet by an underlease. Also *absol.*

1819 REES *Cycl.* XXXV. s.v. *Tenure*, The takers having the liberty..to under-lease to other tenants. 1885 *Law Times* LXXIX. 233/1 A large plot of ground is leased for a term of 999 years. A part of this is underleased for 990 years.

**U·nder-lea·ther.** (UNDER-[1] 5 b. Cf. MDu. *onderleder*, G. *unterleder*, Sw. *underläder*.)

1569 *Wills & Inv. N. C.* (Surtees, 1835) 307 Eleuen dakers of vnderleathers xxvj *s.* *l*, ij daker of soles x *l*, vij dakers of ouerlethers xvj *l* x *s*. 1611 COTGR., *La sollette d'un esperon*, the vnder leather of a spurre. 1845 G. DODD *Brit. Manuf.* IV. 100 The shoes may have scarcely any 'under-leathers' to keep the 'uppers' together.

**U·nder-le·gate.** (UNDER-[1] 6 a.)

1426 LYDG. *De Guil. Pilgr.* 2752 Seyn Peter..Hath mad yow..Hys vnderlegatys, ther to stonde, To kepe the passage.

**†U·nderle·gged,** *a. Obs.*[−1] [UNDER-[1] 10 a.] = UNDERLIMBED *a.*

1681 *Lond. Gaz.* No. 1566/4 A Brown Bay Gelding,..his neather-lip a little falling, and under-Legg d behind.

**†Underlegger.** *Obs.* [UNDER-[1] 5 b + *legger* LEDGER *sb.*] Some kind of oar.

1405 *For. Acc. 39* last membr., ij orys vocat' underleggers. 1406 *Exch. Acc.* 44/9 Remi vocati underleggers.

**U·nderlessee·.** (UNDER-[1] 6 a.)

1730 *Act* 4 *Geo. II*, c. 28 § 6 The Under-Lessees shall hold and enjoy the Messuages. 1839, 1885 [see UNDERLEASE *sb.*].

**U·nderle·t,** *ppl. a.* [UNDER-[1] 4 a.] Let in or inserted beneath.

1884 *Harper's Mag.* Aug. 347/2 Window-curtains of pale greenish-white satin, with underlet appliqués of other palehued silks.

**Underle·t,** *v.* [UNDER-[1] 8 c, d.]

1. *trans.* To let at an amount or rental below the true or full value.

1677 CAPELL in *Essex Papers* (Camden) II. 128 Ormond.. abusing King in underletting the excise to the value of 300,000 lbs. per annum. 1751 JOHNSON *Rambler* No. 103 ¶ 14 He..knows how much one man's cellar is robbed by his butler, and the land of another underlet by his Steward. 1791 *Rep. Comm. Thames-Isis Navig.* 24 The Two Pound Locks, Tolls, &c. at Ifley and Sandford..were previously much under-let. 1868 ROGERS *Pol. Econ.* xiii. 181 Agricultural land in England is rather under than over let. 1874 GREEN *Short Hist.* vi. § 5 (1876) 320 The land indeed had been greatly underlet.

**2.** To let to a sub-tenant; to sublet.

**1819** REES *Cycl.* XXXVII. s.v. *Underletting*, That tenants should have the power of underletting or assigning the farms. **1841** *Penny Cycl.* XXI. 400/1 The merchant may load with his own goods or those of others, or he may underlet the ship altogether. **1872–4** in Jefferies *Toilers Field* (1892) 253 No allotment, or any part thereof shall be under-let or exchanged.

Hence **Underle·tter** (Smart, 1836); **Underle·tting** *vbl. sb.*

**1819** REES *Cycl.* XXXVII. s.v., By a subset or underletting there, the principal tenant or tacksman is not changed. **1883** *Law Times* 27 Oct. 433/1 Covenants against assignments and underlettings without the landlord's consent.

**U·nder-le·vel.** [UNDER-[2].] (See quots.)

**1852** *Eng. & Foreign Mining Terms* (1860) 66 *Underlevel drift*, a drift driven from the pumping-pit to un-water dip workings. **1883** GRESLEY *Gloss. Coal-m.* 267 *Under-level*, winning the ironstone by driving drifts into the hill-sides, &c., instead of sinking shafts.

**U·nder-le:ver,** *a.* (UNDER-[1] 5 c.) **1892** GREENER *Breech-Loader* 68 Guns..with under-lever snap action.

**U·nder-lid.** [UNDER-[1] 5 b.]

**1.** The lower lid of the eye.

**1611** COTGR., *Soucille*, th' vnder-lid of the eye. **1859** MEREDITH *R. Feverel* xxxix, Her underlids worked. **1903** *Smart Set* IX. 12 His under-lids were puffy and discolored.

**2.** A lid placed under another.

**1907** J. H. PATTERSON *Man-Eaters of Tsavo* xi. 122 Opening a tin of biscuits.., and not being able to pull off the under-lid with his fingers.

**U·nderlie,** *sb. Mining.* [UNDER-[1] 4 d.] = UNDERLAY *sb.* 3. Also *attrib.*

**1778** W. PRYCE *Min. Cornub.* 80 The underlie or inclination of the Lode. **1818** W. PHILLIPS *Geol.* 106 When the underlie is towards the north, the strata are universally elevated on that side. **1855** [J. R. LEIFCHILD] *Cornwall* 100 The curvatures and irregularities in the underlie of lodes. **1875** J. H. COLLINS *Metal Mining* 36 The chief advantage of an underlie shaft.

**Underlie·,** *v.* [OE. *underlicgan* (f. UNDER-[1] 4 a + *licgan* LIE *v.*[1]), = MDu. and Du. *onderliggen*, MHG. *underligen*, G. *unterliegen*, MSw. *undirliggia*, Da. *underligge.*]

†**1.** *trans.* To be subject or subordinate to (a person or thing); to submit to or be controlled by.

Also (quot. 1382) const. *to* in place of earlier dative.

*c* **897** K. ÆLFRED *Gregory's Past C.* xxviii. 189 Ða underðieddan mon sceal læran..ðæt hi him [*sc.* their superiors] eaðmodlice underlicgen. *c* **1000** ÆLFRIC *Saints' Lives* i. 155 Heo [*sc.* the soul] bið atelic þurh leahtras ʒif he him underlið. *c* **1375** *Sc. Leg. Saints* xxvii. (*Machor*) 807 Mony printeise þat redy were Til vndirly his dyscypline. **1382** WYCLIF *Heb.* xiii. 17 Obeye ʒe to ʒoure prouostis, or prelatis, and vndir-ligge [L. *subjacete*] to hem. *a* **1500** in *Ratis Raving*, etc. 16 All elyk wnder-lyis vanite, and drawis till a law place downwart. **1536** BELLENDEN *Cron. Scot.* (1821) I. 205 The king..condiscendit to thir desiris; sa the said Donald come..at Dounstafage to underly his will. **1594** CAREW *Tasso* (1881) 92 But mongst our selues,..[I say] That others vnderly you, [who] safely might Cull out some ten to patronize her right.

**2.** To submit or be subjected to; to have (or allow to be) imposed on one; to undergo or suffer under: **a.** a punishment, penalty, accusation, etc.

Very common in older Sc. use: cf. next. Also (quot. 1382) const. *to* in place of dative.

*c* **960** *Rule St. Benet* xxxii. 56 Ʒif he betan nele, underlicgge he rihtlicre þreale. *a* **1300** *Cursor M.* 6691 Qua smites his thain wit a wand,..If he liue ouer a dai or tuin, þe lauerd sal vnderli na pain. *Ibid.* 22206 Þan sal all þaa..underli sa waful wrake. **1382** WYCLIF *Exod.* xxi. 31 The sone forsothe and the douʒter if it smyte with horn, to the lijk sentence he shal vnderligge. *c* **1400** *Apol. Loll.* 19 Þus it semiþ al onli in effect an heretik schuld vnderly þe curse of þe kirk. **1442** *Reg. Mag. Sig.* 64/1 Till underly the charge of ath breking. **1456** SIR G. HAYE *Law Arms* (S.T.S.) 275 Sa that..the accusour be oblist to underly the payne of talyoun. **1540** *Rec. Elgin* (1903) I. 52 [He] is content to vnderlie the sentence of the bailzeis. **1593** G. HARVEY *Pierce's Super.* Answ. Let., They that would rather vnderly the reproche of obscuritie, than ouercharge their mediocritie. **1612** J. DAVIES (Heref.) *Muse's Sacr.* Wks. (Grosart) II. 66/2 Praying for patience still to vnder-ly The heauie waight of this Worlds iniurie. **1678** SIR G. MACKENZIE *Crim. Laws Scot.* I. xxi. § 4 (1699) 112 [He] shall incur and underly the pain and punishment of death. **1819** SCOTT *Ivanhoe* xxvii, This defiance hath already been sent to thee by thy sewer; thou underliest it, and art bound to answer me. **1857** J. W. DONALDSON *Chr. Orthod.* 259 He underlies also the graver charge of intentional misrepresentation. **1882** O'DONOVAN *Merv Oasis* I. xv. 254 Since my last visit to the Russian lines I had underlain a ban.

**b.** *Sc.* the law. (Common 16–17th c.)

**1453** *Extr. Aberd. Reg.* (1844) I. 403 To ansueir and underlie the law. **1507** *Reg. Privy Seal Scotl.* 205/2 To underly the law for the said slauchter. *a* **1578** LINDESAY (Pitscottie) *Chron. Scot.* (S.T.S.) I. 51 To underly the law for sic crymes. **1678** SIR G. MACKENZIE *Crim. Laws Scot.* I. xi. § 16 (1699) 67 His Forefaulture could not fall to the King, upon a simple Denunciation for not appearing to underly the Law. **1752** J. LOUTHIAN *Form of Process* (ed. 2) 37 There to underly the Law for the Crime foresaid. **1838** W. BELL *Dict. Law Scot.* 489 To appear and underlie the law.

†**c.** *Sc.* (and *north.*) a charge or burden. *Obs.*

*c* **1400** *Rule St. Benet* (Verse) 1012 Who salbe meke,..Bus hald þam-self vile & worthy Al maners of charch to vnderly. **1473** *Reg. Cupar Abbey* I. 183 Tha sal gane to the monk myre of Coupergrange, and thar tak thar feuale, vndyrlyand al chargis of the wenyng of the myre. **1475** *Ibid.* 203 He sal ondyrly and kep our conyngar fra all scath and peryl. **1565** in Hay Fleming *Mary Q. of Scots* (1897) 495 He onderlyis charge and expensis for the keping of the said Castell. **1622** BRUCE in *Serm.*, etc. (1843) 131 To show..how unable I am to undertake and underly such a journey and charge.

**3.** To lie under or beneath; to subtend.

Esp. in *Geol.* of strata lying under others.

*a* **1600** HOOKER *Eccl. Pol.* VIII. i. § 2 In a figure triangle.. the self same Line is both a Base and also a Side;..a Base if it chance to be the bottom and underly the rest. **1830** LYELL *Princ. Geol.* I. 398 These deep-seated igneous formations must underlie all the strata containing organic remains. **1861** L. L. NOBLE *Icebergs* 139 The dark-blue inland hills..underlie a sky of unutterable beauty. **1881** *Nature* XXIV. 497 They must be everywhere underlain by the..Middle Coal Measures.

**b.** *fig.* To form a basis or foundation to; to exist beneath the surface-aspect of.

In common use from *c* 1860.

**1856** KINGSLEY *Misc.* (1859) II. 13 Let the details go for what they are worth; the idea, the spirit which underlies them, is still invaluable. **1866** J. MARTINEAU *Ess.* I. 46 Must a false postulate underlie the whole fabric? **1873** SYMONDS *Grk. Poets* x. 308 Theocritus..fully felt the charm which underlies the facts of rustic life.

†**4.** *intr.* To lie below ground; to be buried.

**1648** HERRICK *Hesper., Death of Sparrow*, She..for this dead which under-lies, Wept out her heart. **1739** in J. O. Payne *Rec. Eng. Cath.* (1889) 54 Here underlyes William Plowden honourably and very anciently descended.

**5.** *Mining.* = UNDERLAY *v.* 5.

**1778** W. PRYCE *Min. Cornub.* 80 Some Fissures do not alter much from a perpendicular; and some do underlie a fathom in a fathom. **1800** *Ann. Reg., Chron.* 436 It dips or underlies south, one foot in a fathom. **1855** [J. R. LEIFCHILD] *Cornwall Mines* 100 Instances..in which veins of almost every description dip or underlie in almost every direction. **1899** *Daily News* 3 Nov. 2/6 The vein underlies west 10 degrees from the vertical.

**Underlie,** obs. Sc. var. WONDERLY *a.*

**U·nderli·er.** [f. UNDERLIE *v.*]

**1.** Something that lies under.

**1542** *Acc. Ld. High Treas. Scot.* VIII. 74 Deliverit to him to be underlyaris laid dowbill under the jeit of velvet, thre elnis blak sating. **1640** G. ABBOTT *Job Paraphr.* 522 The weight of which burthen he is not well advised who seeketh not to support by some firme under-lyer.

**2.** *Mining.* (See quot.)

**1778** W. PRYCE *Min. Cornub.* 144 They sink the same Shaft deeper in the body of the Lode, upon its inclination or underlie; whence the Shaft becomes, and bears the name of, an Underlier.

**U·nder-lieute·nant.** (UNDER-[1] 6 a. Cf. Du. *onderluitenant*, G. *unterlieutenant.*) **1691** *Lond. Gaz.* No. 2700/3 One under Lieutenant, one Aid-Major..killed. **1730** BAILEY (fol.), *Sublieutenant*, an under Lieutenant.

**U·nderlife.** [UNDER-[1] 5 c.] A life beneath the surface or on a lower level.

**1847** *Edin. Rev.* Jan. 32 On looking more closely into Hume's underlife. **1865** MRS. WHITNEY *Gayworthys* xxiii, The underlife that never had been spoken—that lay between these three. **1878** STEWART & TAIT *Unseen Univ.* vii. § 242. 245 What we are driven to is not an under-life resident in the atom but rather a Divine overlife. **1888** *Harper's Mag.* Apr. 753/2 Paris; and the university, with its wild under-life, —some debts, some follies.

**U·nderlift.** [UNDER-[1] 4 d.] A raising (or rising) from below.

**1867** H. BUSHNELL *Mor. Uses Dark Th.* (1869) 367 The tremendous underlift of its humble, once dejected people.

**U·nderlight.** (UNDER-[1] 5 c.) **1876** GLADSTONE in Morley *Life* (1903) II. 550, I see that eastward sky of storm and of underlight. **U·nderli·king,** *vbl. sb.* (UNDER-[1] 10 b.) **1581** MULCASTER *Positions* xxxix. 215, I feare nothing so much, as the ouerliking of forreine, and so consequently some vnderliking at home, which will neuer let them staye.

**U·nderli·mbed,** *a.* [UNDER-[1] 10 a.] Having legs too slender in proportion to the body.

**1686** *Lond. Gaz.* No. 2142/4 A blackish brown Gelding.., long straight Legs, somewhat under-limbed. **1695** *Ibid.* No. 3091/4 A red Roan,..under Limb'd,..and flat Rib'd. **1751** GIBSON *Dis. Horses* 18 When he happens to be underlimb'd, it is reckoned a great fault. **1833** M. SCOTT *Tom Cringle* xvi, A pair of well polished hessian boots,..which by adhering close to his legs gave him..the appearance of being underlimbed. **1835** BURNES *Trav. Bokhara* (ed. 2) I. 132 All the horses appeared to be under-limbed.

**U·nderline,** *sb.* [UNDER-[1] 5 b, c.]

**1.** The line of the lower part of the body (of an animal).

**1886** C. SCOTT *Sheep-farming* 173 The back should be level and evenly covered with meat,..the underline straight. **1899** *Jrnl. R. Agric. Soc.* Mar. 18 Her back and underline were nearly parallel.

**2. a.** A line drawn below words printed or written. **b.** *pl.* A set of ruled guiding-lines placed under paper that is being written on.

**1888** E. M. GALLAUDET *Life T. M. Gallaudet* 23 It is written on unruled paper, with a most careful regard for lines and margins, suggesting the use of underlines.

**3.** A line at the bottom of a play-bill announcing the piece to be performed next. **1891** *Cent. Dict.* s.v.

† **U·nderline,** obs. var. UNDERLING *a.* 1.

**1750** ELLIS *Country Housew.* 2 Such Underline small Kernels make more Bran and less Flower than better Wheat does. *Ibid.*, The Underline or Blighted, or other Wheat Ears.

**Under-line,** *adv. rare*[—1]. [UNDER-[2].] Below the level of the sea.

**1605** CHAPMAN, etc. *Eastward Hoe* II, Tost from one waue to another; Now vnder-line; Now ouer the house.

**Underli·ne,** *v.*[1] [UNDER-[1] 4 a + LINE *v*[1]] *trans.* To furnish with an underlining; to form an underlining to. Also *fig.*

**1545** RAYNALD *Byrth Mankynde* 8 This ryme vnderlyneth all the hole cauyte,..or amplytude of the belly. *a* **1639** WOTTON *Reliq.* (1651) 86 By a meer chance, in appearance, though under-lined with a providence, they had a full sight of the Queen Infanta. **1834** WRANGHAM *Homerics* 9 So quick his raft Ulysses made; And floor'd the deck, by spars combined, And with long battens under-lined.

**Underli·ne,** *v.*[2] [UNDER-[1] 4 a + LINE *v.*[2] Cf. Du. *onderlijnen.*]

**1.** *trans.* To mark (words, etc.) with a line or lines drawn underneath; to underscore. (Cf. ITALICIZE *v.*)

**1721** STRYPE *Eccl. Mem.* (1822) II. xi. 579 There is also another memorial..with lines drawn under many of the words and sentences, and a note of Secretary Cecyl's hand, that what was so underlined was to be put in cypher. **1771** LUCKOMBE *Hist. Print.* 361 A Proof sheet printed Black, with the words to be printed Red under lined. **1856** DICKENS *Lett.* (1880) I. 423, I find myself underlining words constantly. **1901** *Athenæum* 24 July 119/1 Titles of books are printed in italics, though not underlined in the MS.

**b.** *fig.* To emphasize, esp. in utterance.

**1880** *Times* 10 Nov. 9/1 A passage that was not intended by the speaker to refer to Ireland..was seized upon and underlined by an appreciative audience. **1887** *Daily News* 15 Nov. 5/7 Madame Chaumont's tendency to 'underline' everything..is certainly no less apparent now than it was in former years.

**2.** To announce (a play) by an underline.

**1895** *Funk's Stand. Dict.* s.v., Faust is underlined for Thursday. **1900** *Westm. Gaz.* 27 Oct. 1 Mr. Stephen Phillips's historical play..is underlined for production.

Hence **U·nderlined** *ppl. a.*

**1866** MEREDITH *Vittoria* xxvii, He wrote a few underlined words entreating Vittoria to grant an immediate interview. **1888** HON. MORTEN *Sk. Hosp. Life* 35 An underlined note of warning.

**Underlinea·tion.** [f. prec., after *interlineation.*] The action or result of underlining.

*a* **1814** *Masquerade* I. i. in *New Brit. Theatre* I. 223 It is like Italics in print, or underlineation in writing, and always means more than meets the ear. **1864** *Realm* 17 Feb. 2 This extract Mr. Cobden copied, with the due amount of underlineation.

**U·nderli·nen.** [UNDER-[1] 5 a.] Underwear, underclothing made of linen or similar material.

**1862** *Eng. Wom. Dom. Mag.* IV. 237/1 Talking of underlinen, we must not forget the pretty white petticoats. **1882** CAULFEILD & SAWARD *Dict. Needlework* 506 Underlinen is made of a variety of materials. **1883** 'ANNIE THOMAS' *Mod. Housewife* 66 A 'set of underlinen' for children.

**U·nderling,** *sb.* and *a.* Forms: 2– underling (3–7 vnder-, 4 vndir-); 2 undur-, 4–6 vnderlyng (5 vndir-, vndyr-); 4 undur-, 4–6 underlynge; 3–4 onderling, -lyng. [Early ME., f. UNDER *adv.* 3 + -LING.]

**A.** *sb.* **1.** One who is subject or subordinate to another; in later use *esp.* a subordinate agent or official, an understrapper.

*c* **1175** *Leg. Nathan* in *E. E. Hom.* (1917) 89 Heo..ʒet synden underlinges, for þan þe heo heora hlaford belæwden. *c* **1200** *Trin. Coll. Hom.* 179 Þe riche þe ben louerdinges struien þe wrecche men, þe ben underlinges. *a* **1225** *Ancr. R.* 198 Þet child þet ne buhð nout his eldre; vnderling, his prelat; paroschian, his preost. *c* **1275** LAY. 22472 Alcus hehte þe king: he hadde mani onderlyng. *c* **1315** SHOREHAM *Poems* III. 176 Þou ne a-nourest god aryʒt, Ac dest is onderlynges. **1390** GOWER *Conf.* III. 128 The sterres..worchen manye sondri thinges To ous, that ben here underlinges. *c* **1400** *Laud Troy Bk.* 2640 My lord,..I am ʒoure knyght and ʒoure vndirlyng. *a* **1470** HARDING *Chron.* XXXIX. iv, Emman.. reigned in all kynde of tiranny, For whiche he was deposed, as an vnderlyng. **1553** T. WILSON *Rhet.* Pref. A iv, What manne..would not rather loke to rule like a lord, then to lyve lyke an underlynge? **1576** FLEMING *Panopl. Epist.* 226 The seruice that an underling..oweth to his Lord..is neither greeuous nor tedious. **1619** W. SCLATER *Exp. 1 Thess.* (1630) 259 Compare thy selfe with superiours, rather then with vnderlings in Grace. **1693** *Apol. Clergy Scot.* 102 In the next Paragraph he mentions Mr. Cant, whom he names underling to Mr. Hamilton. **1727** DE FOE *Prot. Monast.* 9 To hear the Daughter..take up her Father in his Discourse, as if he had been an Idiot or an Underling. **1796** LD. SHEFFIELD in *Ld. Auckland's Corr.* (1862) III. 357 What chance have we..when the House of Commons is filled with moneyed men, speculators, and underlings in office? **1847** EMERSON *Repr. Men, Napoleon*, He undoubtedly felt..an impatience of fools and underlings. **1878** STUBBS *Const. Hist.* III. xviii. 136 The work of an underling who hoped to secure his own promotion.

*transf.* **1614** RALEIGH *Hist. World* I. III. xii. 153 Epaminondas ..gaue vnto Thebes, which had euer-more beene an vnderling, ..the highest command in Greece.

**b.** A branch, plant, etc., growing under, or less strongly than, another; a small or weakly plant, animal, or child. Now *dial.*

**1688** R. HOLME *Armoury* II. 84/2 The Cyons..are underlings, or small twigs of a years growth. **1787** W. H. MARSHALL *Norfolk* II. 148 When one of them has got the superiority so far as to overhang the other, it is generally right to take the underling away. **1842** C. W. JOHNSON *Farmer's Encycl.* 1255 Of the Weeds called Underlings, or such as never rise in the Crop:..These are groundsel [etc.]. **1854** MISS BAKER *Northampt. Gloss.* s.v., The least thriving in a litter of pigs, or brood of chickens, is frequently called 'a poor little underling'. Fruit or vegetables smaller than the rest of the crop are called underlings.

**2.** In predicative use, passing into *adj.*: Subject, subordinate (*to* a person, etc.).

? **1370** *Robt. Cisyle* 55 He was to alle men undurlynge, So lowe was never ʒyt no kynge! *c* **1440** *Promp. Parv.* 511/1 Vnderlynge, *subditus, infimus.* *c* **1450** *Mirk's Festial* 187 Þeras he was befor..prowde of hert, aftyr he was lowe and vndyrlyng to al Godys seruantys. **1549** COVERDALE, etc. *Erasm. Par. 1 Cor.* xi. 30 b, Albeit the husbande be the wiues gouernour, yet is he vnderlyng and subiect to Christe his lorde and maister. **1598** MARSTON *Sco. Villanie* VIII, Can our Soule Be underling to such a vile controule? **1613**

PURCHAS *Pilgrimage* (1614) 187 Lilis..would not be vnderling, and Adam would not endure her his equall. **1647** N. BACON *Disc. Govt. Eng.* I. xlvii. 124 A league of cohabitation should be made between the two Swords, though the spirituall were for the present underling.

**b.** Similarly in attributive use.

**1615–6** BOYS *Wks.* (1629) 135 The Lord of all submitted himselfe to the gouernment of his supposed father, and vnderling mother. **1657** J. WATTS *Vind. Ch. Eng.* 265 We underling Shepheards and Pastours may imitate our Paramount Shepheard and Pastour. **1693** *Apol. Clergy Scot.* 104 The underling Pedlars amongst the Presbyterians may write what they please. **1714** POPE *Lett.* (1735) I. 205 There are indeed, a Sort of underling Auxiliars to the Difficulty of a Work, call'd Commentators and Critics. **1764** FOOTE *Patron* I, By..underling bards, that he feeds; and broken booksellers, that he bribes. **1802–12** BENTHAM *Ration. Judic. Evid.* (1827) IV. 577 The underling sort of lawyer whom the judge punishes every day without scruple.

**B.** *adj.* **1.** Undersized, small, weak. (Cf. UNDERLINE *a.*)

*a* **1722** LISLE *Husb.* (1757) 410 The underling hog put up with the rest, is longest a fatting. **1742** *Lond. & Country Brewer* III. (ed. 2) 172 Seven Quarters of these underling Kernels. **1788** W. H. MARSHALL *Yorks.* II. 72 [The flax] remains weak, short, and underling. **1840** in *Jrnl. R. Agric. Soc.* (1841) II. I. 120 Many short or underling straws, as they are here [*sc.* Pusey, Berks.] called.

**2.** Low-growing.

**1830** MACGILLIVRAY *Withering's Brit. Plants* II. 548 In gardens and other cultivated lands, it often proves a most troublesome underling weed.

**3.** Trivial, unimportant.

**1804** SOUTHEY in Robberds *Mem. W. Taylor* (1843) 481 While they can employ me more to their own advantage in little underling works.

**U·nderli·ning,** *sb.* [UNDER-[1] 5 c.] A lining placed under something; the inner lining of a garment. Also *fig.*

**1580** HOLLYBAND, *Vn haulse*, the vnderlining of a shoe. **1631** BRATHWAIT *Eng. Gentlew.* 176 When the Moath shall be your vnderlining, and the Worme your couering. **1897** *Daily News* 16 Jan. 6/5 An underlining of fine soft flannel makes them suitable for even the coldest weather.

**Underli·ning,** *vbl. sb.* [f. UNDERLINE *v.*[2]] The action of drawing lines below words, etc.; a line or lines so drawn.

**1864** WILLIAMS & SIMMONDS *Engl. Commerc. Corresp.* 1 Underlinings too are frequent,..so as to catch the eye more readily. **1891** MEREDITH *One of our Conq.* xxxi, She begged Captain Dartrey, in double under-linings of her brief words, to mount the stairs.

**U·nderlip.** [UNDER-[1] 5 b. Cf. Du. *onderlip*, G. *unterlippe*, Sw. *underläpp*, Da. *underlæbe*.]

**1.** The lower lip of a person, animal, or insect.

**1669** HOLDER *Elem. Speech* 25 The Tongue and under-Lip.. are moveable. *a* **1735** ARBUTHNOT *State Learn. Lilliput* Misc. Wks. 1751 I. 145 At that he put out his Under-Lip. **1737** CHALLONER *Cath. Chr. Instr.* (1753) 71 His Tongue a little advanced on his Under-lip. **1826** KIRBY & SP. *Entomol.* III. xxx. 124 These maxillæ of larvæ were regarded..as parts of the under-lip, on each side of which they are situated. **1855** TENNYSON *Maud* I. ii. 9 An underlip, you may call it a little too ripe, too full. **1882** 'F. ANSTEY' *Vice Versâ* i, His big underlip drooped rather weakly.

**b.** *spec.* (See quot.)

**1908** *Animal Managem.* 32 'Upperlip' and 'underlip' are the names used to denote white skin at the edges of the lips [of horses].

**2.** In an organ-pipe: (see quots.).

**1852** SEIDEL *Organ* 78 The under lip, on the foot, and immediately below the language. **1875** KNIGHT *Dict. Mech.* 1709 The *foot* is an inverted cone, formed in a similar manner, and having a corresponding indentation, called the *under lip.*

**† U·nderli·ve,** *v. Obs.* [UNDER-[1] 8 b.] *refl.* To live in a manner unworthy of oneself.

**1655** FULLER *Ch. Hist.* III. vi. § 37 No wonder then, if easily they did over-grow others in wealth, who basely did underlive themselves in all convenient accommodations. **1682** SIR T. BROWNE *Chr. Mor.* I. § 24 They who are merely carried on by the Wheel of such Inclinations are..rather lived than living, or at least underliving themselves.

**U·nderlook,** *sb.* [UNDER-[1] 9.] A covert look or glance.

**1821** T. MOORE *Diary* 2 July, She said it was..the peculiarity of a sort of under look he used to give that produced this effect upon her. **1889** HOWELLS *Hazard New Fort.* IV. viii, She said, with an underlook at her husband.

**Underloo·k,** *v.* [UNDER-[1] 4 b.]

**1.** *trans.* To look at, or inspect, from beneath.

**1682** HICKERINGILL *Black Non-Conf.* iii. 14 They would be Shepherds and feed his Sheep, and anoint them for the Scab, and underlook them. **1873** MRS. WHITNEY *Other Girls* xviii, The place where they could lean in between the trees, and overlook and underlook the shining tumult.

**2.** To miss seeing by looking too low.

**1802** BEDDOES *Hygëia* II. 56 Do they not *underlook* that sole essential condition to happiness, the inward state?

**U·nderloo·ker.** [UNDER-[1] 6 a.]

**1.** *Mining.* A subordinate to the manager, who has the superintendence of the miners and workings.

**1871** *Daily News* 21 Sept., Amongst the number were.. the underlookers, and the underground manager. **1885** *Law Times* LXXIX. 119/2 No person was..to blast coal without the charge having been inspected by the underlooker.

**2.** A subordinate overseer.

**1885** *Manch. Exam.* 9 Jan. 5/1 An underlooker..being struck by a shuttle which flew out of a loom.

**U·nderlout,** *a.* and *sb. Obs.* exc. *dial.* Forms: 3–5 underloute (4–5 -lowte), 4–6 underlout (4–5 -lowt), 4 underlote, -lut(te, 4–6 -lute. (Also 3–5 vnder-, 4–5 vndir-, vndyr-, etc.) [Related to OE. *underlútan*: see UNDER-[1] 4 a and LOUT *v.*[1] The second element may be a. ON. *lútr* adj., bending, stooping.]

**† A.** *adj.* Subject, subservient, submissive. Freq. const. *to. Obs.*

*a* **1300** *Cursor M.* 678 Þe bestes boud him all aboute, Als to þair lauerd vnderloute. *c* **1325** *Metr. Hom.* 109 Underlout til thaim was he, Als god child au til elderes be. *a* **1340** HAMPOLE *Psalter* xvii. 11 He made aungels vndirelout til man kynd. **1434** MISYN *Mending of Life* 117 In þe flesch if þou be tempyd, make it sugett, þat þe spiryt be not vndirlowt. *c* **1450** *Mirour Saluacioun* 787 Sho was..devoute To fulfille godis wille all gyven and vnderloute. **1513** DOUGLAS *Æneid* XIII. iii. 71 The chance of kyngis standis onderlout, To mekill dreid ay subiect. **1583** MELBANCKE *Philotimus* Aa iv b, Barbulas..was now at the checke of his vnderlout vassaile.

**B.** *sb.* **1.** One who is subject or subordinate to another; an underling or servant; an inferior. Now *dial.* (see later quots.).

*a* **1300** *Cursor M.* 3705 Þi breþer be þin vnderlute [*Gött.* -lout], And alle þat wonnes þe a-boute. *Ibid.* 18206 Þe erthis werld..has ben ai Vr vnderlut als to þis dai. *c* **1340** HAMPOLE *Pr. Consc.* 3877 Yhit may þai graunt Of þair power pardon aparty Til þair hawen underloutes anly. *c* **1400** *Apol. Loll.* 2 To wham Austeyn, Jerom, and Gregor tak awey þe name of þe bischop, or heldarman, þat he may be correctid of wnderlowtis. *c* **1440** *Alph. Tales* 223 Sho made hur selfe..so grete ane vnderlowte, þat ilkone vggid with hur. *a* **1470** HARDING *Chron.* xxx. viii, Then stande he moste in parell to bee slain, Or els putte doune right by his vnderloute. **1684** MERITON *Yorks. Dial.* 61 Thou's nut think that Ile be thy Underlout. **1790** GROSE *Prov. Gloss.*, *Under-lout*, a drudge in an inferior capacity. **1877** PEACOCK *N. W. Linc. Gloss.* 264 *Underlout*, (1) a lazy servant-boy. (2) The least boy on a farm. (3) The weakest beast in a herd. **1886** COLE *S. W. Linc. Gloss.* 158 *Underlout*,..the weaker pig in a sty,..the smaller and weaker trees in a plantation.

**† 2.** Some part of a ship. *Obs. rare.*

**1295–6** *Acc. Exch. K. R.* 5/20 m. 1 In vno ligno ad vnderloute cum quatuor aliis lignis ad scalmas..ix. s. vj. d. **1546** *Acc. High Treas. Scot.* VIII. 486 Quhilk he debursit upoun the calfating, dok casting, putting in of the underlute of the said Lyoun and outred of hir to the raid.

**† Underlou·t,** *v. Obs. rare.* [(1) = OE. *underlútan*; cf. prec. (2) f. prec.] **a.** *intr.* To be subject, to submit. **b.** *trans.* To make subject.

*a* **1400** *Pauline Ep.* (Powell) Heb. xiii. 17 Obesche ȝee to ȝoure prouostis and vndyrloute ȝee [L. *subjacete*] to þem. *c* **1440** *Promp. Parv.* 511/1 Vnderlowton, *subjicio, subjecto.*

**U·nderlow.** [UNDER-[1] 6 b.] One of the lower classes at Ushaw College, Durham.

**1837** in *Ushaw Mag.* Dec. (1904) 262 The Catechism Exam. of the High and Low Fig. and Underlows. **1896** *Ibid.* Mar. 33 All the classes, from Divinity to Underlow.

**† U·nderly,** *a. rare. Obs.* [f. UNDER *a.* or *adv.*]

**1.** Subordinate; inferior, low.

**1648** SYMMONS *Vind. Chas. I*, 3 Themselves were then but poor fellows of an underly condition. **1674** N. FAIRFAX *Bulk & Selv.* Ep. Ded., Such an underly Shrub in Knowledge, and unthrifty Sucker in Philosophy as I am.

**2.** In a low state of health.

**1715** STORY *Life*, etc. (1747) 502 Her Brother..was still very weak and underly.

**† U·nderly,** *adv. Obs.* [f. UNDER *adv.* + -LY[2]] At a lower level.

**1671** GREW *Anat. Plants* vii. § 17 The Seed-Branch..is presently divided into two main Branches, and those two into other less; whereof some underly, others aloft, run along the Coat.

**U·nderlye.** (UNDER-[1] 5 b.) **1887** *Encycl. Brit.* XXII. 203/2 It may be skimmed off the underlye.

**Underly·ing,** *vbl. sb. Mining.* [f. UNDERLIE *v.* 5.] Declination from the perpendicular.

**1778** W. PRYCE *Min. Cornub.* 80 This underlying varies much in different Lodes.

**Underly·ing,** *ppl. a.* [UNDER-[1] 4 a, or f. UNDERLIE *v.*] Lying under or beneath.

**1611** COTGR., *Subiacent*, subiacent, vnder-lying. **1615** G. SANDYS *Trav.* 289 This appeared more warlike, to behold from aboue the vnderlying country. **1616** W. BROWNE *Brit. Past.* II. ii. 42 Thence they beheld an vnderlying Vale. **1850** TENNYSON *In Mem.* ii, The stones That name the under-lying dead. **1865** LUBBOCK *Preh. Times* 303 In the pits at Amiens this bed is generally distinct from the underlying gravels. **1884** *Leisure Hour* June 345/2 They were stripping the tough hide and underlying blubber.

*fig.* **1852** MRS. STOWE *Uncle Tom's C.* xxxvi, A deep underlying spirit of cautiousness. **1882** FARRAR *Early Chr.* I. 321 The identity of phraseology does but serve to bring into prominence the underlying differences.

**U·nderma·n.** *rare.* [UNDER-[1] 6 a. Cf. ON. *undirmaðr* (Norw. *undermann*, Da. *-mand*), G. *untermann*, a subject, vassal.] An inferior or subordinate man.

**13..** *Peter & Paul* 65 in Horstm. *Altengl. Leg.* (1881) 77 Prelates and maisters þat þaire vndirmen so felli faisters Wiþ chidinge. *a* **1661** HOLYDAY *Juvenal* (1673) 152 You under-men (say'st thou) are our base rout, Whose parents country no man can find-out. **1905** *N. & Q.* 9th Ser. III. 273 These [heralds] were so expensive,..that a set of undermen arose, who acted in their stead.

**U·nder-ma·nager.** (UNDER-[1] 6 a.) **1748** RICHARDSON *Clarissa* VII. Concl. 419 They were compelled, for subsistence-sake, to enter themselves as under-managers at.. another house. **1894** *Northumberland Gloss.* 517 The manager or under-manager of a pit.

**U·nderma·nned,** *ppl. a.* [UNDER-[1] 10 a.] Not furnished with a sufficient number of men; short-handed; under-staffed.

**1867** SMYTH *Sailor's Word-bk.* 706 *Under-manned*, when a ship has an insufficient complement. **1889** *Boston Mission. Herald* June 236 These are all wide-reaching centers, and every one is undermanned. **1900** [see UNDERMASTED].

**U·nderma·nning,** *vbl. sb.* [UNDER-[1] 10 a.] The fact of furnishing, or being furnished with, too few men or 'hands'.

**1890** *Nature* 3 April 520/2 [They] cannot get on with their work on account of the undermanning of the Department. **1901** *Empire Rev.* I. 431 Caused by faults of organisation, rather than by undermanning.

**U·nder-ma·rshal.** (UNDER-[1] 6 a.) **1670** BLOUNT *Law Dict.* (1691), *Submarshal*, is an Officer in the Marshalsea... He is otherwise called Vnder-Marshal. **1753** HANWAY *Trav.* VI. lxxxii. (1762) I. 373 Monsieur Nariskin,..now under-marshal to the empress, had a coach. **U·nder-ma·rshalman.** (UNDER-[1] 6 a.) **1763** *Ann. Reg.*, *Chron.* 70/1 Four king's under-marshalmen on horseback.

**U·nderma·sted,** *ppl. a.* [UNDER-[1] 10 a.] (See quot. 1841.)

**1594** DOWNTON in Hakluyt *Voy.* (1599) II. II. 201 She was much vndermasted, and vndersailed, yet she went well for a ship that was so foule. **1627** CAPT. SMITH *Seaman's Gram.* ii. 15 If either too small or too short, she is vnder masted or low masted. **1674** PETTY *Disc. Dupl. Proportion* 29 The chief cause why short, bluff, undermasted Vessels sail cheaper than others. **1841** TOTTEN *Naval Text-book* (1862) 437 *Under-masted*, or *under-sparred*,..applied to vessels which have masts under the usual dimensions. **1867** SMYTH *Sailor's Word-bk.* 706. **1900** SIR W. KENNEDY *Life Sailor* xiii. 202 She was nothing else than an undermasted, undermanned coal-hulk.

**U·nderma·ster.** [UNDER-[1] 6 a. Cf. MDu. and Du. *ondermeester*, MLG. *undermêster*, MHG. *undermeister*.]

**1.** A subordinate instructor; esp. in schools, a master or teacher below the head-master.

By Wyclif used to render L. *pædagogus*.

**1388** WYCLIF *Gal.* iii. 24 And so the lawe was oure vndirmaister in Crist. *Ibid.* 25 Aftir that bileue cam, we ben not now vndur the vndurmaistir. **1561** in H. B. Wilson *Hist. Merchant Taylors' Sch.* (1814) 14 The high maister..shall say to the ussher,..I have chosen you to be the chief ussher or under maister of this schoole. **1598** FLORIO, *Sottomaestro*, an vnder master, an vsher of a schoole. **1709** *Ir. Act 8 Anne* c. 3 § 16 Several protestant school-masters..do entertain such persons..to be ushers, under-masters, or assistants. **1784** JOHNSON 13 June in *Boswell*, They were written by one Lewis, who was either under-master or an usher of Westminster-school. **1862** MRS. H. WOOD *Mrs. Hallib.* I. iv, [He] was earning his own living as an under-master in a school. **1875** JOWETT *Plato* (ed. 2) I. 250 Masters and under-masters of choruses.

**2.** A subordinate director or supervisor. *rare.*

**1688** *Lond. Gaz.* No. 2322/3 The Under-Master of the Horse. **1703** *Ibid.* No. 3914/4 The Earl of Marr served as Carver,..and Sir William Enstruther, Baronet, as under Master Houshold.

**† U·ndermatch,** *sb. Obs.* [UNDER-[1] 10 b.] One who is no match for another; an inferior rival.

*a* **1661** FULLER *Worthies, Denbigh* (1662) 34 He was no contemptible Historian, but I confess an under-match to Doctor Hackwell. **1769** GOLDSM. *Hist. Rome* (1786) I. 281 Claudius Nero..appearing an under-match for the cunning of the Carthaginian general.

**Underma·tch,** *v.* [UNDER-[1] 10 a.]

**1.** *trans.* To undervalue by comparison.

**1571** GOLDING *Calvin on Ps.* lx. 10 He passeth foorth to the forreiners, whom hee far undermatcheth to his owne people.

**2.** To unite or bestow in marriage below the proper rank or condition.

**1639** S. DU VERGER tr. *Camus' Admir. Events* 39 There is none that so jealously preserve their Nobility, as the German, nor more feare to undermatch themselves. **1708** CIBBER *Lady's Last Stake* III, Dispose of the Child as soon as you can; rather under-match her, than not at all. **1831** SCOTT *Ct. Rob.* xviii, A damsel..would think herself heinously undermatched, if wedded to a gallant whose fame in arms was yet unknown.

**† Underma·tched,** *ppl. a. Obs.* [UNDER-[1] 10 a.] Not equal to another; inferior.

**1642** FULLER *Holy & Prof. St.* II. iv. 60 He tyrannizeth not over a weak, and undermatched Adversary. **1765** JOHNSON *Shakespeare's Cymb.* II. iii. *note*, His argument is just and well enforced...As for rudeness, he seems not to be much undermatched.

**U·ndermath.** [UNDER-[1] 5 c: cf. *aftermath.*] An undergrowth of grass, etc.

**1881** G. ALLEN *Vignettes* xii. 119 Ferns..grow in the tangled shady undermath of the banks and thickets.

**† U·ndermeal.** *Obs.* Forms: 1 undernmæl, 4–5 vnder-, undermele (5 -mel), 6–7 vndermeale. [OE. *undernmǽl*: see UNDERN *sb.* and MEAL *sb.*[2]]

**1.** The time of undern; in later use esp. the early part of the afternoon. Also *attrib.*

*Beowulf* 1428 Ȝesawon..on næshleoðum nicras licgean, ða on undernmæl oft bewitiȝað sorhfulne sið. *c* **1000** ÆLFRIC *Saints' Lives* XXX. 319 Þa an undern-mæl spræcon hi betwux him þær-inne. *c* **1386** CHAUCER *Wife's T.* 875 Ther walketh now the lymytour hym self In vndermeles and in morwenynges. *c* **1400** *Trevisa's Higden* V. 373 Rosamunda in an undermele tyde [L. *meridiano tempore*] bonde..faste þe kynges swerd þat was on slepe. *c* **1440** *Promp. Parv.* 511/1 Vndermele, *postmeridies, postmesimbria.*

**b.** An afternoon nap; a siesta. Also *attrib.*

**1426** LYDG. *De Guil. Pilgr.* 9044 To leyn hym softely On Fether beddys, mad ful wel, For to slepe hys vndermel. **1589** NASHE *Greene's Menaphon* Pref. (Arb.) 15 The blacke pot; which makes our Poets vndermeale Muses so mutinous, as euerie stanzo they pen after dinner, is full poynted with a stabbe. **1599** — *Lenten Stuffe* Ep. Ded., Hee hath dinde at a tauerne, and slept his vnder-meale at a bawdy house. *Ibid.* 11 The forty yeares vndermeale of the seauen sleepers.

**2.** An afternoon meal.

c 1440 *Promp. Parv.* 511/1 Vndermele,..*merarium.* 1530 PALSGR. 285/2 Under mele, *ressigner.* 1586 *Withals' Dict.* (1599) 57/2 Another greater supper or vndermeale was made redie for them. 1614 B. JONSON *Barth. Fair* IV. ii, I thinke I am furnish'd for Catherne peares, for one vnder-meale.

**U·ndermea·ning.** (UNDER-[1] 9.) 1846 TRENCH *Mirac.* xxxiii. 455 We must continue to see an under-meaning..in all this. 1865 RUSKIN *Sesame* ii. § 93 Have you ever considered what a deep undermeaning there lies..in our custom.

**U·nder-mea·sure,** *sb.* (UNDER-[1] 10 b.) 1596 [see UNDERWEIGHT].

**U·nder-mea·sure,** *v.* [UNDER-[1] 10 a.] *trans.* To measure insufficiently or not to the full amount.

1672 GREW *Idea Philos. Hist. Plants* § 4 It is impossible to Measure, what we See not. And since we are most likely to under-measure [etc.]. 1845 DISRAELI *Sybil* III. i, Many's the morn we work for nothing,..and many's the good stint they undermeasure.

**U·nder-mea·ted,** *ppl. a.* [UNDER-[1] 10 a.] Underfed.

1653 J. TAYLOR (Water P.) *Journ. Wales* (1859) 6 He was a beast, had beated been and cheated; Too much hard over rid and under meated.

**Under-me·ntioned,** *ppl. a.* [UNDER *adv.* 2 b.] Named or noted below or in a place beneath.

1640-1 *Kirkcudbr. War-Comm. Min. Bk.* (1855) 10 The Commissioners undermentionit are appoyntit in ilk paroche. 1683 in Picton *L'pool Munic. Rec.* (1883) I. 330 We present the persons undermentioned for absenting from divine service. 1818 THOMSON *Lond. Disp.* 644 Oil of rosemary.. is chiefly used in the under-mentioned preparations. 1875 CROLL *Climate & T.* xx. 332 The number of years required by the undermentioned rivers.

**Under-metal:** see METAL *sb.* 7.

**U·nder-mi·ller.** (UNDER-[1] 6 a.) 1825 JAMIESON, *Gude-will*,..the proportion of meal..which is due to the under-miller. 1843 *Rep. Trial by Jury, Magistrates Jedburgh*, etc. 37 The under-miller always drew the multure.

**Undermi·nable,** *a.* [f. UNDERMINE *v.*] Capable of being undermined.

1622 DONNE *Serm.* Wks. 1839 VI. 228 So underminable is the love of this world which determines every minute. 1679 C. NESSE *Antid. agst. Popery* Ded. 2 Seated upon a rock that is unaccessible and not underminable.

**U·ndermine,** *sb.* [UNDER- 4 d, 5 c. Cf. next.]

†**1.** An underground excavation. *Obs.*

1599 HAKLUYT *Voy.* II. 86 They put fire in the vndermines, weening to haue cast downe the wall. 1610 HOLLAND *Camden's Brit.* I. 650 Under-mines or caves of very great widenesse. 1629 *Descr. S'hertogenbosh* 36 We made an vndermine through the walls of the Towne.

†**2.** A submerged mine. *Obs.*

1682 *Roxb. Ball.* (1885) V. 519 But thou, buoy'd up with Providence Divine, Shall float above, and fear no undermine.

**3.** An undermining movement.

1898 *Daily News* 12 May 8/4 The Bishop..said there was a very strong undermine of disloyalty to the Church.

**Undermi·ne,** *v.* Forms: *α.* 4-6 undermyne, 5- -mine, 7 -moine (also 4-6 vnder-, 4-5 vndir-, 5 vndyr-). *β.* 5 vndermynden, 6 -mynde, 6-7 vnder-, underminde, 7-8 (9 *dial.*) undermind. [UNDER-[1] 4 a + MINE *v.* Cf. Du. *ondermijnen*, older Da. *undermine*; also MDu. *ondermineren*, Da. *underminere*, Sw. *-era*, G. *unterminiren.*

In 15th cent. texts *undermyne* or *-mine* is occasionally miswritten for *undernim.*]

**1.** *trans.* To dig or excavate beneath, to make a passage or mine under (a wall, etc.), esp. as a military operation; to sap.

*α.* 13.. *Coer de L.* 4721 The Crystene the walles undermyne. 1382 WYCLIF *Jer.* li. 58 The wal of Babilon..with vndermynyng shal be vndermyned. *c* 1450 *Contin. Brut* 577 And after, [they] vndermynet þe walles and þe toures, and sette shores vndernethe. *a* 1548 HALL *Chron., Hen. V*, 45 Knowyng that their walles were vndermyned and shortely like to fal. 1582 N. LICHEFIELD tr. *Castanheda's Conq. E. Ind.* I. ix. 22 It is a verye great Citie, placed..so that it cannot be undermined. 1616 J. LANE *Contn. Sqr.'s T.* VII. 397 To lead his men safe to the walled towne, which vndermoine hee shoold. 1618 BOLTON *Florus* (1636) 181 Undermining their port Pireus, and more than six Walls of theirs. 1726 LEONI *Alberti's Archit.* I. 68 When the foundation is ..on a rock, it will be in vain to think of undermining it. 1776 G. SEMPLE *Building in Water* 40 We had no other Way to break it, but by undermining it, and then break it off in Pieces. 1834 MARRYAT *P. Simple* xxi, We must undermine the gate, O'Brien; we must pull up the pavement until we can creep under. 1848 DICKENS *Dombey* vi, Buildings that were undermined and shaking, [were] propped by great beams of wood.

*β.* *c* 1440 *Promp. Parv.* 511/1 Vndermyndyn, *idem quod* vnderdelvyn. 1513 DOUGLAS *Æneid* VIII. xi. 38 Sum vndermyndand the ground with a hoill. 1571 LESLIE *Hist. Scot.* (Bann. Cl.) 101 [They] under myndit the neddir sole of the yett of Dunbartane. *a* 1644 *Spottiswoode Misc.* (1844) I. 146 In the late warrs..the churches [were] undermynded and fired. 1828- in dial. glossaries (Yks., Linc., Surrey).

**b.** *absol.* To make excavations or mines.

1382 WYCLIF *Exod.* xxii. 2 If a theef brekynge an hows, or were foundun vndurmynynge. 1412-20 LYDG. *Chron. Troy* II. 6335 Þei..turnen vp so doun Boþe wal & tour..Þat no þing stood, so þei vnder-myne. 1601 HOLLAND *Pliny* II. 467 Necessarie it is..to undermine a great way by candlelight, & to make hollow vaults under the mountains. 1646 H. P. *Medit. Seige* 60 It is an usuall practice to under-mine, and when they have brought the Mine unto the Works, to blow it up with powder. 1685 TRAVESTIN *Siege Newheusel* 34 This day we began to undermine on the side attackt by the Troops of Brunswick.

**c.** In fig. context.

*c* 1400 *Beryn* 3480 Ye wend..þat ye had hym engyned; But yee shul fele in every veyn þat ye be vndirmyned, And I-brou3t at ground. 1559 AYLMER *Harborowe* C ij b, These ..be..the pik-axes to vnder mynde the state. 1601 SHAKS. *All's Well* I. i. 130 Man setting downe before you, will vndermine you, and blow you vp. 1668 DRYDEN *Tyrannic Love* III. i, Yet fierceness suits not with her gentle kind; They brave assaults, but may be undermined. 1794 BURKE *Corr.* (1844) IV. 254 As yet, the house is not fallen; but it is completely undermined. 1855 MOTLEY *Dutch Rep.* VI. i. III. 409 Religious fanaticism had undermined the bulwark almost as soon as reared. 1875 JOWETT *Plato* (ed. 2) V. 363 The fair superstructure falls because the old foundations are undermined.

**2. a.** Of water: To work under and wash away (ground, etc.).

1398 TREVISA *Barth. De P. R.* XV. lxxxii. (Bodl. MS.), Þe parties of ilondes beþ ywasted, & vndermyned wiþ betinge of watres. 1562 PILKINGTON *Expos. Abdyas* Pref. 5 A strong heady streame, undermining great hygh bankes. 1610 HOLLAND *Camden's Brit.* 676 The riveret Alen..undermineth the ground and once or twice hideth himselfe. 1707 MORTIMER *Husb.* 5 Alder makes an extraordinary Fence against Rivers and Streams, and preserves the Banks from being undermined by the Water. 1784 *Cook's Voy.* IV. ix. II. 464 By undermining and washing away those parts that lie exposed to the surge of the sea. 1855 *Orr's Circ. Sci., Inorg. Nat.* 155 The stream..relieving the gloom of the naked rocks, and at the same time tending to undermine them. 1860 TYNDALL *Glac.* I. xv. 101 The glacier..is incessantly undermined,..till at length the projecting mass.. tumbles into the lake.

*absol.* 1858 MACDONALD *Phantastes* xiii. 148 The springing waters were dammed back into his soul, where, finding no utterance, they..swelled, and undermined.

**b.** Of animals: To burrow under or in; to make insecure, to cause to fall, through burrowing; also, to form (a passage) by burrowing.

1526 *Pilgr. Perf.* (W. de W. 1531) 55 Catche these lytell foxes, whiche with dyggynge of theyr dennes vndermyndeth our vynes. 1567 MAPLET *Gr. Forest* 92 He hath his cabbage [=den] in the yearth with two contrary wayes vndermined to enter into it. 1579 LYLY *Euphues* (Arb.) 109 In a shorte space, there was a Towne in Spayne vndermined with Connyes. 1629 DAVENANT *Albovine* III. i, When she [*sc.* the mole] undermines the earth. 1697 DRYDEN *Virg. Georg.* IV. 355 Lizards..a dark Retreat Have found in Combs, and undermin'd the Seat. *a* 1704 T. BROWN *Declam. Adverbs* Wks. 1720 I. 45 All Thessaly had in the twinkling of a Shoeing-horn been certainly undermin'd by Lobsters.

**c.** *Path.* To erode beneath the surface.

1879 *St. George's Hosp. Rep.* IX. 254 Hip-joint..surrounded with œdema and undermined by sinuses. 1898 *Hutchinson's Arch. Surg.* IX. 111 The chronic infective inflammations..which ulcerate to a slight extent whilst they undermine widely.

**3.** *fig.* (Cf. 1 c.) To work secretly or stealthily against (a person); to overthrow or supplant by underhand means.

*α.* 1430-40 LYDG. *Bochas* IV. Prol. (1554) 99 b, Fortune could him vndermine That al hys wisedome stode in none auayle. 1535 COVERDALE *Gen.* xxvii. 36 He maye well be called Iacob, for he hath vndermined me now two tymes. 1561 T. NORTON tr. *Calvin's Inst.* IV. xviii, To beguile and vndermine an other man, al men know to be vnlawfull. 1633 P. FLETCHER *Purple Isl.* II. xviii, Whose pleasing sweetnesse..Doth oft the Prince himself with witch'ries undermine. 1768 WANLEY *Wond. Lit. World* v. i. § 100. 468/1 Rodolphus..being undermined by his brother Matthias, was forced to surrender to him..Hungary and Bohemia. 1759 ROBERTSON *Hist. Scot.* III. Wks. 1851 I. 237 Some of his rivals he secretly undermined. 1775 ADAIR *Amer. Ind.* 91 The religious advantages and arguments by which the French used to undermine us with the Indians. 1849 MACAULAY *Hist. Eng.* ii. I. 197 Those who had assailed and undermined him began to struggle for the fragments of his power. 1876 HOLLAND *Seven Oaks* xiv. 200 Are you to sit tamely down and be undermined?

*β.* 1530 PALSGR. 767/1 Medyll nat with hym,..for surely he wyll undermynde the. 1596 SPENSER *F. Q.* V. vi. 32 He was nothing valorous, But with slie shiftes and wiles did vnderminde All noble Knights. 1613 JACKSON *Creed* II. vii. § 7 Yet are they easily to be vnderminded by Sathan. 1663 GERBIER *Counsel* 103 If he be a Master workman, whom they will..suspect to have a design to underminde and supplant them. 1869- in *Eng. Dial. Dict.* (Yks., Lanc., Linc.).

*absol.* 1584 LYLY *Sappho* I. iii. 26 Where we suspect, we vndermine. 1712 BLACKMORE *Creation* VII. 349 The ambitious statesman labours dark designs, Now open force employs, now undermines.

†**4.** To underlie and spoil. *Obs.*[−1]

1430-40 LYDG. *Bochas* I. x. (1544) 21 b, Some fresh floures haue a full bitter rote And lothsom gal can suger eke vndermine.

**5.** To persuade or win over, to tamper with or pervert, by subtle means. Also *absol.*

1457 HARDING *Chron.* in *Eng. Hist. Rev.* Oct. (1912) 747 His language..so benygne was and trewe it vndyrmyned Thair hertes hole to loue hym at thair myght. 1522 SKELTON *Why not to Court?* 434 So he dothe vndermynde, And such sleyghtes dothe fynde, That the kynges mynde By hym is subuerted. 1579 LYLY *Euphues* (Arb.) 85 Ferardo..desired him to kepe silence, vntil he had vndermined hir by subtiltie. 1664 DRYDEN *Rival Ladies* IV. iii, She undermin'd my Soul With Tears. 1671 MILTON *P. R.* I. 179 The Father..Ventures his filial Vertue, though untri'd, Against whate're may ..Allure, or terrifie, or undermine.

†**6. a.** To ascertain, or inquire, in a secret or underhand manner. *Obs.*

*a* 1575 tr. *Pol. Verg. Eng. Hist.* (Camden No. 36) 56 Cæsar undermining their counsels throughe his Captives. *Ibid.* 80 When as Agricola hadd..undermined the purpose of his adversaries. 1596 NASHE *Saffron Walden* 82 He hath been noted..very suspitiously to vndermine, whither any man knew such a fellow.

†**b.** To question (a person) guilefully. *Obs.*

1581 [A. GILBY] *Test. 12 Patriarchs* 58 b, He wil talke guilefully with thee, and vndermine thee to doe thee a shrewde turne. 1599 HAKLUYT *Voy.* II. I. 266 There was a Dutch Jesuite..sent vnto them, to vndermine and examine them.

**7.** To weaken, injure, destroy or ruin, surreptitiously or insidiously.

*α.* 1569 (*title*), A Bull graunted by The Pope..to vndermyne ..Allegeance to the Quene. *a* 1596 *Sir T. More* I. ii. 69, I pray ye,..Goe not aboute to vndermine my life. 1641 J. JACKSON *True Evang. T.* II. 146 It is no fault..to undermine fraud with fraud. 1699 BURNET *39 Art.* xviii. 174 Which strikes at the Foundation, and undermines the Truth of all Revealed Religion. 1732 BERKELEY *Alciphr.* i. § 2 A dangerous sort of men that would undermine received principles and opinions. 1771 *Junius' Lett.* lix. 272 Who is he, that has made it the study..of his life, to undermine and alter the whole system of jurisprudence? 1850 MERIVALE *Rom. Emp.* ix. (1865) I. 384 The authority of the nobles as a class had been completely undermined. 1884 RUSKIN *Pleas. Eng.* 16 These controversies vexed and shook, but never undermined, the faith they strove to purify.

*β.* 1565 STAPLETON tr. *Staphylus' Apol.* 152 To vnderminde Christendom. 1694 R. BURTHOGGE *Reason* 110 The Ground of this underminded, and the nature of the Divine Omnipresence represented. 1726 CAVALLIER *Mem.* Ded. p. iv, Their Civil and Religious Liberties, which after having been artfully underminded by several preceding Princes, were at last totally subverted.

**b.** To weaken or destroy (the health or constitution) by degrees; to sap.

1812 CRABBE *Tales* II. 417 Augmented pay procured him decent wealth, But years advancing undermined his health. 1843 R. J. GRAVES *Syst. Clin. Med.* xxv. 319 Mercury may be given..in such a manner as gradually to undermine the constitution. 1860 J. M. CARNOCHAN *Operat. Surg.* 61 The constitution became..undermined [by ostitis].

Hence **Undermined** *ppl. a.*

1844 *P. Parley's Ann.* V. 13 The undermined bank of some river. 1899 *Allbutt's Syst. Med.* VIII. 801 On examination of the undermined skin and granulations.

**Undermi·ner.** [f. UNDERMINE *v.* So Du. *ondermijner.*]

**1.** One who undermines; a sapper.

1519 HORMAN *Vulg.* 257 b, Vndermynars ouerthrewe the walle. 1556 WITHALS *Dict.* (1562) 79/1 An vnderminer, *cunicularius.* 1610 HOLLAND *Camden's Brit.* I. 400 A frame or engin..under which the pioners and underminers had their ingresse and egresse. 1658 OSBORNE *Jas. I*, 34 These underminers..intended in their calculation the destruction of the house of Lords. 1802 JAMES *Milit. Dict.*, *Underminer*, a sapper.

*fig.* 1601 SHAKS. *All's Well* I. i. 131 Blesse our poore Virginity from vnderminers and blowers vp. 1654 'PALAEMON' *Friendship* 28 He that is an underminer of the Foundation must of necessity ruine the Superstructure.

**2.** A secret or insidious assailant, subverter, destroyer, etc.

1564 PALFREYMAN *Baldwin's Mor. Philos.* (1600) 129 b, The whole broode of..secret vnderminers, hipocrits, and double dealers. 1571 GOLDING *Calvin on Ps.* xxvi. 4 Neyther will I come in company with undermyners. 1608 D. T[UVILL] *Ess. Pol. & Mor.* 60 b, There are another kinde of cunning vndermyners. 1656 BAXTER *Reformed Pastor* III. ii. § 4 Nor suffer underminers or persecutors to scatter them. 1693 SOUTH *Serm.* 96 No one is bound to look upon..his underminer..as his friend. *a* 1734 NORTH *Lives* (1826) I. 386 At court there are always a sort of underminers who [etc.]. 1838 LYTTON *Calderon* i, To..his foes, his underminers—he assumed a yet greater frankness.

**b.** Const. *of* (the thing or person assailed).

1598 DALLINGTON *Meth. Trav.* B ij, The Iesuites, vnderminders and inveiglers of greene wits. 1650 HUBBERT *Pill Formality* 70 In all ages there have been underminers of the power of godliness in a secret way. *a* 1674 CLARENDON *Surv. Leviath.* (1676) 113 The neglect of Justice is an infallible underminer..of that security. *a* 1715 BURNET *Own Time* (1766) I. 403 A secret enemy to their interest and an underminer of it. 1768-74 TUCKER *Lt. Nat.* (1834) 412 A concealed infidel, a secret underminer of things sacred. 1802 MME. D'ARBLAY *Let.* 14 Mar., Depression, that cruel underminer of every faculty that makes life worth sustaining. 1879 JOS. COOK *Marriage* 8 Do you stand here, underminers of the family life, and gaze into the eyes of these women!

**Undermi·ning,** *vbl. sb.* [f. as prec.]

**1.** The action of digging under, excavating, eroding, etc. Also in fig. contexts.

*c* 1380 WYCLIF *Serm.* Sel. Wks. I. 277 Þis housebondis hous is his bodi, þat his soule is kept ynne; and undirmynyng of þis hous mai be don on two maneres. *c* 1440 *Promp. Parv.* 511/1 Vnder myndynge (*P.* vndermynynge), *idem quod* vnderdeluynge, *supra.* 1598 BARRET *Theor. Warres* V. i. 124 Fortes are wonne..by battery,..by vndermining, and such like. 1629 PRYNNE *Anti-Armin.* 78 By the vndermining of which alone, the whole superstruction..[is] vtterly subuerted. 1679 C. NESSE *Antichrist* 37 Their worshipping of saints [is] ..no better then real underminings of the sacred foundation. 1692 BENTLEY *Boyle Lect.* 271 The banks..jagged and torn by..the silent underminings of waves. 1726 CAVALLIER *Mem.* IV. 342 They came by underminding as far as the brink of the Ditch. 1833-4 J. PHILLIPS *Geol.* in *Encycl. Metrop.* (1845) VI. 705/1 The most characteristic effect of a cascade, is that ceaseless undermining of its base and sides. 1897 *Allbutt's Syst. Med.* II. 765 There are ulcers with but slight undermining of their edges.

†**b.** An excavation or mine. *Obs.*[−1]

1572 R. H. tr. *Lauaterus' Ghostes* 73 These [spirits] wander vp and down in caues and vnderminings.

**2.** The action of insidiously plotting, assailing, subverting, etc.; an instance of this.

1433 LYDG. *St. Fremund* 559 By vndirmynyng, this was his menyng; Affter Fremund he to be crownyd kyng. 1530 PALSGR. 285 Undermyndyng, *subornation.* 1571 GOLDING *Calvin on Ps.* lii. 5 He had..betrayed the giltlesse Preestes by treason and undermyning. 1600 NASHE *Summer's Last Will* F 3 b, Familiaritie and conference, That were the sinewes of societies, Are now for vnderminings onely vsde.

1667 *Decay Chr. Piety* ii. ¶ 5 The frauds and underminings, the busie scramblings for little parcels of earth. 1709 [see UNDERGROUND *adv.* 2]. 1841 DICKENS *Barn. Rudge* xxiv, We can't bear the plotting and undermining that takes place. 1904 *Brit. Med. Jrnl.* 17 Sept. 638 An undermining of strength that lessens resisting power.

**Undermi·ning,** *ppl. a.* [f. as prec.]

1. That excavates or erodes beneath a surface.

1617 MORYSON *Itin.* III. 160 Ireland hath neither singing Nightingall,..nor vndermining Moule. 1664 INGELO *Bentiv. & Ur.* VI. 219 Those great Hills..would have been worn away ..and..their high Tops would have been levell'd by the undermining Streams. 1853 KANE *Grinnell Exp.* viii. (1856) 57 The glacier, thus exposed to a saline water base..and to an undermining wave action,..is of course speedily detached. 1882 FLOYER *Unexpl. Baluchistan* 121 It has now probably been carried away piecemeal, for it was then perilously near the undermining river.

b. In fig. contexts.

1661 COWLEY *Cromwell* Wks. 1906 II. 352 No Guards can oppose assaulting Ears, Or undermining Tears. *a* 1665 J. GOODWIN *Filled w. the Spirit* xiv. (1670) 412 The Gospel.. hath cast down..many a strong hold..; it is of an undermining nature. 1711 ADDISON *Spect.* No. 124 ¶ 7 There are others who are Moles through Envy...I have already caught two or three of these dark undermining Vermin. 1858 J. MARTINEAU *Stud. Chr.* 271 Huge piles of curious learning,.. which..may detain men from search after the living rock, or notice of the undermining flood.

2. Insidiously subversive or destructive.

1583 MELBANCKE *Philotimus* R iv b, Vndermining easinge droppers..haue wroughte this estraungment betwene vs. 1616 R. C. *Times' Whistle* (1871) 44 Honours now are purchased by stealth Of vndermining bribes. 1679 *Roxb. Ball.* (1883) IV. 552 The Malice, and the restless Hate, Of Undermining Foes. 1709 STANHOPE *Paraphr.* IV. 35 Undermining Arts of Disputers and Deceivers. 1849 CLARIDGE *Cold Water Cure* 173 There are many sufferers from this undermining malady. 1860 GEO. ELIOT *Mill on Floss* v. ii, Instead o' whispering in corners, in that plotting, underminding way.

Hence **Undermi·ningly** *adv.*

*c* 1590 LADY BACON in J. Spedding *Bacon's Lett.* (1862) III. v. 113 He commonly opened underminingly all letters sent to you from counsel or friends. 1601 DEACON & WALKER *Spirits & Divels* To Rdr. 8 Which these men..vnderminingly haue publisht in print, without any..authenticall priuiledge.

**U·nder-mi·nister,** *sb.* [UNDER-[1] 6 a.] † An underling, subordinate, assistant.

1543 tr. *Act 2 Edw. III*, c. 7 To enquire of shiriffes,.. constables, and all other ministers,.. and of their vndermynysters. 1633 T. STAFFORD *Pac. Hib.* II. iv. 155 All Fees ..needfull for any of the sayd Officers, or Vnder-ministers.

† **Under-minister,** *v.*: see UNDER-[1] 2.

**U·nder-mi·nistry.** [UNDER-[1] 6 b.] Subordinate service or office.

1651 JER. TAYLOR *Serm. for Year* II. xxi. 272 That we should do all the under-ministeries we can in this great work. 1660 — *Ductor* III. iv. rule 5 § 2 The division of Ecclesiastical charges, the appointment of under-ministeries in the Church.

**U·ndermirth.** [UNDER-[1] 9.] A comic underplot.

1635 SHIRLEY *Coronation* Prol., There doth flow No undermirth, such as doth lard the scene For course delight.

**Undermo·ney,** *v.* [UNDER-[1] 4 a.] *trans.* To take by means of bribery.

*a* 1661 FULLER *Worthies, Suffolk* III. (1662) 65 He took the two Forts,..but whether they were undermined or undermonied it is not decided:

**U·nder-mo·ral.** (UNDER-[1] 6 b.) 1712 ADDISON *Spect.* No. 369 ¶ 15 Besides this great Moral,..there are an Infinity of Under-Morals which are to be drawn from the several parts of the Poem.

**U·ndermost,** *a.* and *adv.* [UNDER *adv.* + -MOST.]

1. *adj.* Holding the lowest place or position.

1555 EDEN *Decades W. India* Contents (Arb.) 45 The Antipodes whiche inhabite the vndermost halfe of the baule of the earth. *a* 1585 SIDNEY *Arcadia* III. ii, The fall is greater from the first to the second, then from the second to the vndermost. 1665 BUNYAN *Holy Citie* 171 This Jasper is said to be one of the Foundations, and that too the first and undermost. 1771 *Encycl. Brit.* III. 46 The advantage gained will be always equal to twice the number of pulleys in the moveable or undermost block. 1797 HOLCROFT tr. *Stolberg's Trav.* II. xlvii, The scenes were of three partitions: the undermost of marble,..and the upper of..wood. 1838 T. THOMSON *Chem. Org. Bodies* 986 A force sufficient to counterbalance this attraction of the undermost film.

b. *absol.* The bottom.

1876 MRS. WHITNEY *Sights & Ins.* II. xiii. 429 Living.. with keen, conscious pain at the undermost of everything.

2. Predicative, or as *adv.* In the lowest or lower place or position.

1617 J. TAYLOR (Water P.) *Obs. & Trav. fr. Lond. to Hamburgh* Wks. (1630) 85/2 A good featherbed vndermost, with cleane sheets...another featherbed vppermost. 1665 *Phil. Trans.* I. 45 These Crucibles are laid sloaping, eight undermost, and seven above them. 1709 BERKELEY *Th. Vision* § 115 It is inverted, because the heels are uppermost and the head undermost. 1781 *Phil. Trans.* LXXI. 391 Upon.. holding it with the snow undermost, the whole of it adhered. 1825 SCOTT *Talism.* iii, The assailant..flung himself above the struggling Saracen, and..kept him undermost. 1855 MACAULAY *Hist. Eng.* xiv. III. 396 The party indeed which had then been undermost was now uppermost.

† **Undermow,** *v.*: see UNDER-[1] 2.

† **Undermye,** *v. Obs.*—[1] [UNDER-[1] 4 a.] *trans.* To undermine.

The second element, which rhymes with *sleye* 'sly', may be MYE *v.* in a forced sense.

*c* 1330 R. BRUNNE *Chron. Wace* (Rolls) 3432 Mynours þey hadde ynowe, & sleye, Þe wal to perce & undermye.

**Undern** (*v*·ndəɹn), *sb. Obs.* exc. *arch.* and *dial.* Forms: *α.* 1–5, 9 **undern** (2 **unnderrn-**), 3 **vn-**, 4 **ondarne**, 3, 5 **on-**, 4–5 **underne**, 4 **undirne**, 5 **-dyrne**, 4–5 **undorne**, 5 **-dorn**, 4 **undurn**, 4–5 **undurne**, 7 *dial.* **aandorn**, 9 *dial.* **andern**; 4–5 **onderen**, 4–5 (9) **underen** (4–5 **-on**); 2–5 **undren**, 4 **undrin**, **-on**, **-un**, 5 **oundron**, **undrone**, 9 *dial.* **andren**; *Sc.* **ontron**, **auntrin**, **antrum**, **andrum**, etc. *β.* 1–5 **under** (4 **undur**, 4–5 **-yr**), 4–5 **vndre**; 4 **ondre**, **honder-**, 6 **ander-**; *dial.* 7 **oneder**, 7, 9 **aunder**, **ownder**, 9 **ounder**, **oander** (ōnder), **andra**, etc.; 8–9 **oandurth**. [Common Teutonic: OE. *undern*, = OFris. *unden*, *ond* (older NFris. *undern*; mod. *unnern-e*, *ünjern*, *onner-n*, *önner*), OS. *undorn*, *undern* (MLG. *undern*, LG. *unden*, *ünner*; MDu. *onderen*, *-ern*, *-er*, Du. dial. *onder*), OHG. *untarn*, *-orn*, *undorn* (MHG. *undarn*, *-ern*, G. dial. *undern*, *untern*, *unnern*, *onnern*, etc.), ON. *undorn*, *undarn* (Norw. dial. *undonn*, *ondaan*, *undaal*, etc., Sw. dial. *undarn*, *-dun*, Da. dial. *unden*, *unnen*), Goth. *undaurn-* (in *undaurnimats* ἄριστον); the relationships of the stem are doubtful. In all the Germanic languages the meaning shows a parallel development to that traceable in English; where the word survives it usually denotes either midday or afternoon or a meal taken at these times.

With some variation of form, *undern* is common in OE. and ME. down to the 15th cent.; in later use it is restricted to dialects of the north-midland and northern counties and the south-west of Scotland. In addition to the forms given above, some northern dialects exhibit (from the 17th c.) variants with a prefixed *d-*, as *downdrens*, *daundren*, *downder*, etc. (*Eng. Dial. Dict.* s.v. *Downdrins*). The OE. *ær undern* also survived in dialect use, and appears as *earnder*, *eender*, etc. (see YEENDER), while OE. *ofer undern* appears in the 15th c. as *orendron*, *ornedrone*, in the 17th as *orndorn*, *arndern*, and later as *ournder*, *orntren*, etc. (*Eng. Dial. Dict.* s.v. *Undern*). Both of these have equivalents in mod. N. Fris. (dialect of Sylt), viz. *irönner*, *irner* forenoon and *aurönner*, *aurner* afternoon.]

†**1.** The third hour of the day; the time at or about 9 o'clock in the morning. In ecclesiastical use = tierce. *Obs.*

*α.* *a* 900 *O. E. Martyrol.* 3 May 72 On þa þriddan tid dæᵹes, þæt is on undern. *c* 1000 *Sax. Leechd.* II. 140 Sele drincan on þreo tida, on undern, on middæᵹ, on non. *c* 1200 *Trin. Coll. Hom.* 117 Riht to-genes þe undrene;..þo com a dine of heuene. *c* 1250 *Kent. Serm.* in *O. E. Misc.* 33 Þat ferst uut-yede bi þe Moreghen;..so ha dede at undren and at midday also. 13.. *Sir Beues* (A.) 4168 Þus to gederes þai gonne dinge Fram prime til vnderne gan to ringe. 1338 R. BRUNNE *Chron.* (1810) 18 Bituex vnderon & noen was þe feld alle wonnen. 1382 WYCLIF *Acts* ii. 15 Whanne it is the thridde our of the day, or vndirne. 1470–85 MALORY *Arthur* XI. ii. 574 They lay to gyders vntyl vndorne on the morn. [1855 ROCK in *N. & Q.* XI. 150/1 The high mass..for Sunday was celebrated immediately after undern or tierce.]

*β.* *a* 1122 *O. E. Chron.* (Laud MS.) an. 540, Steorran heo ætewdon ful neh healfe tid ofer under. *a* 1225 *Leg. Kath.* 2496, I Nouembres moneð, þe fif & twentuðe dei, & Fridei, onont te under. *a* 1310 in Wright *Lyric P.* xii. 41 In marewe men he sohte, At under mo he brohte. *c* 1315 SHOREHAM II. 72 Crucyfige! crucifige! Gredden hy at ondre. 13.. *E. E. Allit. P.* A. 513 Aboute vnder, þe lorde to marked tos & ydel men stande he fyndez þer-ate. *c* 1450 *Mirk's Festial* 66 A husband-man ȝede..at pryme, and eftsones at vndyr, and efte at myddAy,..and hyryd men to his vyneȝorde.

†**b.** *High undern* (see HIGH *a.* 11). Also *half*, *whole undern* (see quot. *c* 1440). *Obs.*

*c* 960 *Rule St. Benedict* xlviii. 74 From ærmorᵹenne oð heane undern [L. *ad tertiam plenam*]. *c* 1275 *Passion of our Lord* 657 in *O. E. Misc.* 56 At þon heye vndarne a witsuneday. 1303 R. BRUNNE *Handl. Synne* 4059 Come þou home at hygh vndurne, And no lenger yn þe felde soiurne. 13.. *Floriz & Bl.* 555 Bi þat hit was undern hiȝ, Floris was þe brigge niȝ. 1390 GOWER *Conf.* II. 250 He..lay..Til it was undren hih and more. *c* 1440 *Pallad. on Husb.* VI. 226 Half vndron hath but ix [feet]; High vndron vj. *Ibid.* VII. 254 Half vndern viij, hool vndern v. [=L. *hora tertia* and *hora quarta*].

†**c.** With addition of *dayes* (also *day*) or *of the day*. *Obs.*

*c* 1122 *O. E. Chron.* (Laud MS.) an. 1122, Þa wearð swiðe mycel wind fram þa undern dæies to þa swarte nihte. *a* 1225 *Ancr. R.* 24 Seoue psalmes..siggeð abuten undern deies. *c* 1290 *Beket* 2445 in *S. Eng. Leg.* I. 176 A-boute onderne of þe daie to þis holi bones heo come. *c* 1386 CHAUCER *Nun's Pr. T.* 402 Stille he lay Til it was passed vndren of the day. *c* 1400 MAUNDEV. (Roxb.) xxxiii. 149 Þai will hyde þam in þe erthe fra vndrun of þe day til efter noone. *c* 1425 *Cast. Persev.* 138 in *Macro Plays* 81 Loke þat ȝe be þere be-tyme,.. for we schul be onward be vnderne of þe day. *a* 1500 *E. E. Misc.* (Warton Cl.) 10 At under day to skole I was i-sete.

†**2.** The sixth hour of the day; midday. *Obs.*

*a* 1300 *Cursor M.* 16741 Bi þis was vndren [*Laud MS.* vnder] on þe dai, Þat mirckend al þe light. 13.. *Gosp. Nicodemus* 657 At vnderon was þis done, omang þam wex it mirk. *c* 1380 WYCLIF *Wks.* (1880) 41 Late lewid freris seie ..for prime, tierce, vndern & noon, for eche of hem seuene pater nostris. 1382 — *John* iv. 6 Sothli the our was, as the sixte, or vndurn. *c* 1440 *Promp. Parv.* 511/1 Vnderne.. *submeridianum*, *submesimbria*. 1493 *Festivall* 7 An husbounde man went in to his gardeyn or vyne yerde at pryme and ayen at vndren or myddaye. (Cf. *Mirk's Festial* 66.)

**3.** The afternoon or evening. Now *dial.*

*α.* 1470–85 MALORY *Arthur* VII. xix. 242 Vpon the morowe he took his hors and rode vn-tyl vnderne,..and bitoke his hors to the dwarf, and commaunded hym to watche al nyghte. 1811 W. AITON *Surv. Ayrs.* Gloss. 693 *Ontron*, evening. 1858 MORRIS *Def. Guenevere*, etc. 206 Summer cometh to an end; Undern cometh after noon.

*β.* *c* 1480 *Childe of Bristowe* 235 in Hazl. *E. P. P.* I. 119 Betwene mydday and under ther cam a blast of lightnyng and dunder. 1674 RAY *N. Co. Words*, *The Aunder*, or as they pronounce it in Cheshire, Oneder; The afternoon. 1684 MERITON *Yorks. Dial.* 46 To Morn ith' Ownder we mun dod our Sheep. *c* 1746 J. COLLIER (Tim Bobbin) *View Lanc. Dial.* (1775) 16 Th' last oandurth boh one me Measter had lik't o killt meh. 1820 R. WILBRAHAM *Cheshire Gloss.* 49 *Ownder*, or *Aunder*, the afternoon. 1828 CARR *Craven Gloss.* I. 13 *Aunder*, afternoon. Nearly extinct in Craven. 1841 HARTSHORNE *Salop. Ant.* 525 *Owwnder*, the evening... A word in general acceptation on the banks of the Severn, betwixt Shrewsbury and Bridgenorth. 1879–81 MISS JACKSON *Shropsh. Word-bk.* 309 In places where this term obtains the day is divided into morning, middle of the day, *önder*, and night.

**4.** *dial.* A light or intermediate meal, esp. one taken in the afternoon. (Cf. ANDERS-MEAT.)

1691 NICOLSON in Ray *N. Co. Words* 139 *Aandorn*, Merenda. 1866–86 in Lincolnsh. glossaries (in forms *andern*, *andren*, *andra*, *andrew*). 1880 C. H. POOLE *Gloss. Stafford* 17 *Ounder*,..an afternoon tea. 1887 DARLINGTON *S. Chesh. Gloss.* 278 *Oanders*, the afternoon meal, often sent out in harvest time to the labourers in the fields. 1887 *Suppl. Jamieson* s.v. *Andrum* and *Antrum*.

**5.** *attrib.*, as *undern-bell*, *-song* [OE. *-sang*, *-song*]. See also UNDER-MEAL, UNDERN-TIDE, -TIME.

*a* 1400 *Sir Beues* 2250 So sted Beues in þat þring, Til noun [*v.r.* vndern] belle be-gan to ring. 1478–9 in Peck *Desiderata Curiosa* (1732) I. VI. 36 That no Person..set ther Corn to sale afore the Hour of Ten of the Bell, or els the Undernone [*sic*] Bell be rongyng. [1853 ROCK *Ch. of Fathers* III. II. 180 Every Sunday before undern-song or tierce.]

† **Unde·rn,** *a. Obs.* [OE. *undyrne*: see DERN *a.*] Not hidden; open.

*a* 1225 *Juliana* 75 ȝe schulen..reopen ripe of þat sed þat ȝe her seowen, þat is underne ȝeld of wa, oðer of wunne.

**Underna·me,** *v.* [UNDER *adv.* 2 b.] *trans.* To name or specify below.

1632 W. LITHGOW *Trav.* III. 101 These Cities seuen (I undername) did striue, Who first brought Homer to the world aliue.

**Underna·med,** *ppl. a.* [UNDER *adv.* 2 b.] Named or specified below.

1599 HAKLUYT *Voy.* I. 162 The declaration of the rest is proroged vntill a certayne terme vndernamed. 1603 *Philotus* F 4 b, The printer..hes..printit sindrie vther delectabill Discourses vndernamit. 1660 in *Buccleuch MSS.* (Hist. MSS. Comm.) I. 312 The persons undernamed. *c* 1770 *Rolls of Parlt.* II. 433/1 Which of the ancestors of the said William had the Woods undernamed.

**Under-na·tural,** *a.* [UNDER-[2].] Falling below what is natural.

1647 N. WARD *Simple Cobler* 49 Peoples prostrations of these things..are..under-naturall noddaries.

**Underneath,** *prep.*, *adv.*, *a.*, and *sb.* Forms: 1 **underneoðan**, **-nyðan**, 2 **-næðen**, 4 **-neþen**, 5 **undernethen**, **-nethyn**; 4 **underneþe**, **-nueþe**, **-neyþe**, 4–6 **undernethe**, **-neth**, 6– **underneath**. (Also 4–7 **vnder-**, 5 **vndir-**, **vndur-**, **vndyr-**, 5–6 **undre-**, 6 *Sc.* **wndir-**). [OE. *underneoðan* (f. UNDER *prep.* and *adv.* + NETHEN *adv.*), = older Da. *underneden*.]

**A.** *prep.* **1.** Beneath or below (in local position).

*c* 893 K. ÆLFRED *Oros.* III. ix. 134 Ðær wearð Alexander þurhscoten mid anre flan underneoðan oþer breost. *a* 1122 *O. E. Chron.* (Laud MS.) an. 1070, Hi..namen þa þet fotspure þe wæs undernæðen his fote. *c* 1375 *Cursor M.* 2380 (Fairf.), Abraham..come and lendid..vnder-neyþe a faire valay. *c* 1400 MAUNDEV. (Roxb.) xiii. 57 Vndreneth it es a well. *c* 1450 LOVELICH *Grail* xlvi. 129 Whanne that he say kyng Mordrayn On the Erthe liggen..vnder-nethen here hors feet. 1470–85 MALORY *Arthur* IV. xvi. 362 Vndernethe that castel they sawe a knyghte standynge. *a* 1533 LD. BERNERS *Huon* lix. 203 Vnderneth it was the porte. 1591 SPENSER *Mother Hubberd* 1322 The wicked weed..From vnderneath his head he tooke away. 1678 BUTLER *Hud.* III. i. 1116 He..Insconc'd himself as formidable As could be underneath a Table. 1697 DRYDEN *Virg. Georg.* III. 597 If a swarthy Tongue Is underneath his humid Palate hung, Reject him. 1728 YOUNG *Love Fame* III. 118 Tho' Phoebus and the nine for ever mow, Rank folly underneath the scythe will grow. 1817 SHELLEY *Rev. Islam* v. 2185 Underneath thy feet writhe Faith, and Folly, Custom, and Hell, and mortal Melancholy. 1879 S. C. BARTLETT *Egypt to Pal.* xx. 436 The immense quarries directly underneath the city.

**b.** *fig.* Under the form, cover, protection, authority, etc., of (something).

1390 GOWER *Conf.* I. 258 Bot undernethe such a jape He hath so for himselve schape, That [etc.]. *a* 1470 HARDING *Chron.* Pref. (1812) p. vii, Vndirnethe ȝoure fadirs magnificence He durste nought so haue lette hys righte fall doun. 1495 *Rolls of Parlt.* VI. 465/1 Dyvers Leesses..hath be made..undrenethe the Seales in these parties of old tyme used. 1560 DAUS tr. *Sleidane's Comm.* 437 Whether Christ is to be worshipped vnder the forme of bread and wine, whether Christ be wholly vnderneath either kinde. 1845 MAURICE *Mor. Philos.* in *Encycl. Metrop.* II. 627/1 The truths which lay underneath its false worship.

**2.** In subordination or subjection to; under the power or control of.

1375 BARBOUR *Bruce* v. 475 Schir amery..That wes vardane of þe land Vnder-neth þe Ynglis kyng. *c* 1440 *Alph. Tales* 88 A virtuos man..had vndernethe his gouernance in a monasterie ccc wommen. *Ibid.* 514 He had many servandis vnder-nethe hym. 1538 BALE *God's Promises* II, Beynge thy subject, he is undreneth thy cure, Correct hym thu mayest. 1546 *Yorks. Chantry Surv.* (Surtees) 348 The chantor..hath a vicare indowyd underneth hym. 1597 SHAKS. 2 *Hen. IV*, IV. iv. 10 Till these Rebels..Come vnderneath the yoake of Gouernment. 1651 N. BACON *Disc. Govt. Eng.* II. xxvii. 205 A man underneath many Passions, but above fear. 1667 DRYDEN & DAVENANT *Tempest* III. iii, When underneath my power my foes have truckl'd. 1822 SHELLEY tr. *Calderon's Mag. Prodig.* II. 34 Philosophy, thou canst not even Compel their causes underneath thy yoke.

**b.** Below the level of; inferior to.

**1587** GOLDING *De Mornay* Pref. 6 The least creatures which lie farre vnderneath man.

†**3.** Subject to, under (a condition). *Obs.*

*c* **1440** *Alph. Tales* 333, I will grawnt þe a plyte of my gown vnder-nethe a condicion, at þou sall not hurte me.

†**4.** Below, less than (in amount.) *Obs.*

**1455** *Paston Lett.* I. 355 Ther can noon be gete here.. undrenethe iijs. the yerde at the lowest price. **1528** in W. H. Turner *Select. Rec. Oxford* (1880) 57 Above the somme of vjs, and..under nethe the seyd somme.

**B.** *adv.* **1.** Down below; at an underlying or lower point or level.

*c* **1000** ÆLFRIC *Exod.* xxix. 12 And þu nymst cealfes blod mid þinum fingre,..and ӡitst þæt oðer undernyðan. *a* **1325** *MS. Rawl. B. 520* fol. 32 b, So þat þis statut ne portenez noӡt to..grete troen [= trees], ware fore [*sic*] hit be cler vnder nueþe. *c* **1375** *Sc. Leg. Saints* i. (*Peter*) 526 Þe hound.. schot on symeon..And to þe ӡerde hym vndirnethe Ruschit. **1387** TREVISA *Higden* (Rolls) V. 123 Constantine..made peynte the signe and tokene of þe crosse.., and he made write undirneþe, 'Þis is þe signe and tokene' [etc.] *c* **1400** *Destr. Troy* 9998 Till the sun in his sercle set vndernethe. **1489** CAXTON *Faytes of A.* I. xvii. 27 Wher the watre is lest and most low,..there in trauers ought to be sett a route of folke wel horsed and another in like wyse vndrenethe. **1526** *Pilgr. Perf.* (W. de W. 1531) 268 Lyke as they yt wrestleth be somtyme aboue, & somtyme vnderneath. **1560** DAUS tr. *Sleidane's Comm.* 24 b, The floore vnderneth was covered with clothe of Arras. **1615** G. SANDYS *Trav.* 259 The streetes are..vaulted vnderneath for the conueiance of the sulledge. **1657** R. LIGON *Barbadoes* 43 Leaving it hollow underneath for Ventiducts. **1747** WESLEY *Prim. Physick* (1762) 118 If they heal too soon, and a Matter gather underneath. **1791** COWPER *Odyss.* XIX. 552 So thick it was, and underneath, the ground With litter of dry foliage strew'd profuse. **1850** TENNYSON *In Mem.* c, I climb the hill: from end to end Of all the landscape underneath [etc.]. **1860** TYNDALL *Glac.* II. i. 232 The lines of light converged by the ripples upon the sand underneath.

*fig.* *c* **1374** CHAUCER *Boeth.* III. pr. v. (1868) 75 Ryӡt on þat same side nounpower entriþ vndirneþ þat makeþ hem wreches. **1390** GOWER *Conf.* II. 232 Bot undernethe he was bethoght In what manere he mihte aspie Achilles fro Deïdamie. **1509** HAWES *Past. Pleas.* XI. (Percy Soc.) 40 In an example..the poetes do wryte; And underneth the trouth doth so shroude. **1659** MILTON *Lett. Ruptures Commonw.* Wks. 1851 V. 404 If such a Union as this be not accepted on the Army's part, be confident there is a single Person underneath. **1674** CAMPION *Art Descant* I. 4 A fourth above is the same that a fifth is underneath, and a fourth underneath is as a fifth above.

**b.** Below or beneath other clothing.

*c* **1386** CHAUCER *Can. Yeom. Prol.* 5 A man that clothed was in clothes blake And vnder-nethe he wered a white surplys. *c* **1394** *P. Pl. Crede* 695 Ӡif he haue vnder-neþen whijt, þanne he aboue wereþ Blak. **1596** SPENSER *F. Q.* V. ix. 10 On his backe [was] an vncouth vestiment,..And vnderneath his breech was all to torne. **1856** tr. *Vehse's Mem. Court of Austria* I. 124 He wore a suit of black armour,..and underneath a shirt of close mail.

**c.** Lower down on a sheet of paper, etc.

**1389** in *Eng. Gilds* (1870) 3 Eche of hem had sworen on þe bok to perfourme þe pointz vndernethe wryten. *c* **1550** in Feuillerat *Revels Q. Mary* (1914) 250 Certayne sutes of apparell as be heare vndernethe mentyoned. *a* **1577** SIR T. SMITH *Commw.* II. xxv. (1589) 102 He..delieureth vp the examination which he tooke of him, and vnderneath the names of those whom he hath bound to giue euidence. **1653** W. RAMESEY *Astrol. Restored* 106 On the head of the fourth column you find *magnitude*, intimating that by the Figures underneath..is shewn the magnitude of each star. **1743** W. EMERSON *Fluxions* 33 Then I take the Sum of the Terms..and set this Sum..underneath.

**2.** On the under side.

**1776** WITHERING *Bot. Arr. Vegetables* I. 697 Leaves..with little scales and fringed appendages underneath. **1812** *New Bot. Garden* i. 7 The leaves..not shining or hoary underneath. **1820** SHELLEY *Prometh. Unb.* I. 442 They come Blackening the birth of day with countless wings, And hollow underneath, like death.

**C.** *adj.* **1.** Underhand; secret. *rare.*

**1747** *Mem. Nutrelian Crt.* II. 118 This..causes him to determine, by a sly, underneath cunning, to work that virtuous youth ruin. **1899** in *Eng. Dial. Dict.* (Leeds dial.).

**2.** Situated below.

**1894** *Daily News* 9 Mar. 5/4 In an underneath room, printers..will be seen printing some..newspapers.

**D.** *sb.* That which is in the lowest place; the under part or side.

**1676** MOXON *Print Lett.* 33 You must make up the Top and Underneath with straight lines. **1855** tr. *Labarte's Arts Mid. Ages* viii. 310 The underneath of his dishes. **1887** RUSKIN *Præterita* II. 159 For all other rivers there is a surface, and an underneath. **1889** MRS. LYNN LINTON *Thro' Long Night* II. 215 She read the underneath of the cards.

**U·nderness.** [f. UNDER *adv.*] The state or condition of being below a given mark or limit.

**1864** RUSKIN in *Daily Tel.* 31 Oct., An under-supply of wages and an over-supply of labourers...On what do this underness and overness of supply depend?

**U·nder-ni·ceness.** (UNDER-[1] 10 b.) **1748** RICHARDSON *Clarissa* VI. xxx. 107 Over-niceness may be under-niceness. Have you not such a proverb?

†**Underni·m,** *v. Obs.* Forms: (see UNDER-[1] 8 a and NIM *v.*). [OE. *underniman* (f. *under-* UNDER-[1] 8 + *niman* NIM *v.*), = OS. *undarniman* (to interrupt), MDu. and Du. *ondernemen*, OHG. *untarneman* (MHG., MLG. *undernemen*, G. *unternehmen*).]

**1.** *trans.* To take into the mind (or sense): **a.** To understand, comprehend, perceive; to feel. Also const. *that.*

*c* **1000** *Ags. Gosp.* Matt. xix. 12 Ne underfoð ealle menn þis word...Undernyme, se þe undernyman mæge. *a* **1023** WULFSTAN *Hom.* lviii. (1883) 305 Man mæg swiðe eaðe witan, se ðe hit underniman wile, þæt hit eallunga riht nis [etc.]. *c* **1200** *Trin. Coll. Hom.* 11 Ac ich wile seӡen, undernimeð hit, hwat makeð swilch letten. *c* **1230** *Hali Meid.* 19 Ne underneomeð nawt, quoð he, þis ilke word alle. *c* **1250** *Gen. & Ex.* 1553 Quan ysaac it under-nam ðat esau to late cam. **13..** *E. E. Allit. P.* C. 213 He ossed hym by vnnynges þat þay vnder-nomen, Þat he was flawen fro þe face of frelych dryӡtyn. *c* **1386** CHAUCER *Sec. Nun's T.* 243 Whan that he the sauour vndernoom, Which that the Roses and the lilies caste. *c* **1400** *St. Alexius* (Laud 463) 199 Sone he it vndernom, þat he to a borugh com, þat mychel was.

**b.** To receive by instruction; to learn.

*c* **1000** ÆLFRIC *Saints' Lives* xxix. 76 He..folӡode paule.. and deoplice under-nam drihtnes lare æt him. *c* **1200** *Trin. Coll. Hom.* 83 For þat þe hie undernomen þe wise lore of ionan þe prophete. *a* **1225** *Leg. Kath.* 117 Hire feder hefde iset hire earliche to lare, & heo..undernom hit se wel þet nan nes hire euening.

**2.** To take upon oneself; to undertake.

*c* **1000** ÆLFRIC *Hom.* I. 590 Ӡif þu leornian wille hu þæt ӡewurðan mæge, þonne undernim ðu leorning-cnihtes hiw. *c* **1175** *Lamb. Hom.* 55 Bute weo hes [= them] halden we doð sunne, and uwilc mon hes undernim to halden wel. *c* **1205** LAY. 26734 We..þis feht habbeoð under-numen buten Arðures rede. *a* **1225** *Ancr. R.* 202 Pusillanimitas, þet is, to poure iheorted..eni heih þing to undernimen. **1340** *Ayenb.* 83 Non ne is aryӡt preus..þet ne ys hardy and zyker to greate þinge ondernime. *c* **1425** *Seven Sages* (P.) 2858, I am comen For were that thou havest undirnome, For to helpe the.

**b.** *absol.* To undertake a journey; to travel.

*c* **1205** LAY. 8067 Al þat freoliche folc..þene daie heo vndernomen, & to Lundene heo comen. *c* **1325** *Orfeo* 441 With ryght gode wille they can out gon...So long they have undernome, That to Crassens they were ycome.

**3.** To reprove, rebuke.

Occas. miswritten or misprinted *undermyn(e, -mine.*

*c* **1250** *Gen. & Ex.* 2727 Ðis on wulde don ðe toðer wrong; And moyses nam ðer-of kep,..And vndernam him ðat it aӡte awold. *a* **1325** *Prose Psalter* xxxiv. 19 Hij vndernimmeden me wyþ vnder-nyminge, & gnaisted vp me wyþ her teþe. *c* **1380** WYCLIF *Wks.* (1880) 292 Ech man schulde bi þe lawe of þe gospel vndirnyme ech broþer þat synneþ aӡens him. *c* **1425** *Orolog. Sapient.* vi. in *Anglia* X. 373/21 Wheþer þy seruaunte..dorste be so bolde forto reprehende & vndirnime ..his lorde. *c* **1449** PECOCK *Repr.* I. xvii. 97 He comith not to liӡt, that hise werkis ben not vndernome.

*absol.* *a* **1400** *New Test.* (Paues) 2 Tim. iv. 2 Vndernyme þou, & byseche, & blame þou in eferich pacyence & in techynge. *c* **1449** PECOCK *Repr.* Prol. 2 Wherbi he canne schewe and proue it to be a defaute for which he vndirnymeth and blameth.

**b.** Const. *of* (a fault, etc.).

*c* **1320** *Cast. Love* 1420 He among hem com, And of misbileue he hem vndernom. **1377** LANGL. *P. Pl.* B. v. 115 Who-so vndernymeth me here-of I hate hym dedly after. **14..** HOCCLEVE *Min. Poems* 126/455 What art thow now presumptuous become, And list nat of thy mis been vndirnome? *a* **1450** *Knt. de la Tour* (1868) 87 As the wiff of Amon, that undernam not her husbonde of his foly. *a* **1470** H. PARKER *Dives & Pauper* (W. de W. 1496) IV. vii. 169/1 Byfore all the monkes he undername the cellerer of his pryde.

**c.** *refl.* To convict (oneself).

**1502** ARNOLDE *Chron.* (1811) 208 If otherwise he can not the lawe of the Lorde he reproueth and vndernymeth himself to be noo priest of his Lorde.

**4.** To take or catch, esp. secretly or unawares; to surprise.

*c* **1175** *Lamb. Hom.* 151 Monie kunnes men foleӡeden ure drihten,..summe to kunnen if heo mihten him mid sunne undernime. *a* **1225** *Leg. Kath.* 122 Modie meistres & feole fondeden hire ofte..for to underneomen hire. *c* **1250** *Gen. & Ex.* 2135 Ic rede ðe..To..gaderen coren, ðat ðin folc ne wurð vnder-numen, Quan ðo hungri ӡere ben forð-cumen. **13..** *Guy Warw.* (A.) 613 And he of mi loue vnder-nome were ..Me þenke y no myӡt it him nouӡt werne. **1340** *Ayenb.* 173 þe dyeaþ ssel come þet ofte ondernimþ þane zeneӡere huer he ne nimþ none hede.

**b.** To take away by stealth. (Also OE.)

**1483** CAXTON *Gold. Leg.* 45 He supplanted me of my patrymonye and now..he hath undernome from me my blessyng.

**5.** To receive into one's hands or charge.

**13..** *St. Gregory* 174 in Herrig's *Archiv* LVII. 61 Þe kniӡt þat leuedi vnder nom And ladde hire forþ wiþ moche honour. *c* **1325** *Orfeo* 306 To his owne lady wel ny he come, And hur wel ny had undernome;..His owe lady, dam Erodysse.

†**Underni·mmer.** *Obs.* [f. prec.]

**1.** A taker-up or supporter.

*a* **1400** in *Eng. Gilds* (1870) 350 Non of þe for-seyde fowre and twenty ne shal..be tellere ne vndurnemere of wordes in harmynge of þe fraunchyse of þe town.

**2.** One who reproves or rebukes.

**1382** WYCLIF *Prov.* xiii. 18 Who forsothe assenteth to the vndernymere, shal ben glorified. *c* **1449** PECOCK *Repr.* IV. vi. 452 These vndirnymers and blamers beren an hond to the clergie, that [etc.]. *Ibid.* v. xv. 565 Alle the seid ouer myche vndirnemers and blamers.

†**Underni·mming,** *vbl. sb.* [f. as prec.] The action of reproving or rebuking; a reproof, rebuke.

*a* **1325** *Prose Psalter* xliii. 16 Þou settest vs..vndernimyng and scorne to hem þat ben in our cumpas. **1382** WYCLIF *Ps.* xxxvii. 15, I am maad as a man not herende; and not havende in his mouth aӡen vndernemyngus. *c* **1449** PECOCK *Repr.* II. xvii. 253 Se ӡe that in ӡoure vndirnymyng ӡe bere ӡou discreetli.

†**Undernone**: see UNDERN *sb.* 5.

**U·ndernote.** [UNDER-[1] 9 b.] A subdued note; an undertone or suggestion.

**1820** SHELLEY *Prometh. Unb.* IV. 189 Listen too, How every pause is filled with under-notes. **1857** W. COLLINS *Dead Secret* III. iii, There was an under-note of pleasure running through its tones. **1873** SYMONDS *Grk. Poets* viii. 257 The deep under-note of good sense and wisdom which gives eternal value to the jests of Aristophanes.

**Under-no·ted,** *pa. pple.* (UNDER *adv.* 2 b.) **1891** *Cent. Dict.* **1902** *Trans. Glasgow Archæol. Soc.* IV. II. 303 Collation of certain identities of line and alliteration between the poems as undernoted.

†**Undern-tide.** *Obs.* Also undertide. [OE. *underntid*: see UNDERN *sb.* and TIDE *sb.*]

**1.** = UNDERN *sb.* 1.

α. *c* **900** tr. *Bæda's Hist.* IV. xxii. (1890) 328 Oftost his bendas..onlesde wæron from underntide, þonne mon mæssan oftost singeð. *c* **1000** *Ags. Gosp.* Matt. xx. 3 Þa he ut-eode embe undern-tide. *a* **1300** *Cursor M.* 985 Adam..was wroght at vndern tide, At middai eue draun of his side. *c* **1350** *Lybeaus Disc.* 810 Than seyde Gyfroun,..To all thys y graunte well, Thys day at underne-tyde.

β. *a* **1075** *Rule of Chrodegang* xviii, To þære undertide se halӡa gast com ofer þa apostolas. *c* **1160** *Hatton Gosp.* Matt. xx. 3 Þa he ut-eode ymbe under-tide [etc.]. *c* **1175** *Lamb. Hom.* 91 Hit is undertid, hu mihte we on þissere tide beon fordrencte? *a* **1225** *Ancr. R.* 400 Þe soðe sunne iðe undertid was forði istien on heih. *a* **1300** *Cursor M.* 21931 It sal him last ful littel quil. For if it be at vnder tide, It sal noght to þe none abide. **13..** *Sir Beues* (A.) 1756 Þus þai leide on in boþe side Be-twene midmorwe & vndertide. *c* **1325** *Orfeo* 74 The maydenes..lete hur slepe tyl after none, That the undertyde was agone. *a* **1513** FABYAN *Chron.* VII. ccxxvii. 256 At Notyngham from the morne to the vndertyde, the ryuer of Trent was so fordryd..yt men went ouer drye. [Cf. Trevisa *Higden* (Rolls) VII. 446–7.]

**2.** = UNDERN *sb.* 2.

*a* **1300** *Cursor M.* 19830 Þan was it vnderntide [*Trin. MS.* vndirtide] o þe dai,..þat petre went him for to prai. **1387** TREVISA *Higden* (Rolls) VII. 23 In an undertyde [*v.rr.* under-, hondertyde; L. *hora meridiana*], while kyng Edgar lay on his bed. **1398** — *Barth. De P. R.* VIII. xxviii. (Tollem. MS.), The sonne is red in þe dawnynge, þen he schineþ in þe morow tide, and he is hoot in þe undornetide [L. *in meridie*] and pale at even.

**Undern-time.** *Obs.* exc. *dial.* and *arch.* Also 4–6 vnder-, 5 vndyrtime. [OE. *underntima*: see UNDERN *sb.* and TIME *sb.*] = prec.

α. *c* **1000** in Bouterwek *Cædmon* (1854) p. ccxiv, On underntiman Crist wæs þurh þara Iudea dom to deaþe fordemed. *c* **1200** ORMIN 19458 An daӡӡ att unnderrn time I fir þeӡӡ sæӡhenn Godess Gast. *c* **1250** *Gen. & Ex.* 2269 It was vndren time or more, Om cam ðat riche louerd ðore. *a* **1300** *Cursor M.* 25538 Suet iesu, at vndrin time [*c* **1375** vnder-time]..Sufferd ..Dintes sare and smert. **1387** TREVISA *Higden* (Rolls) VII. 421 In þat book he radde priveliche in þe underne tymes [L. *meridianis horis*].

**1853** ROCK *Ch. of Fathers* III. x. 473 St. Beda died a little after undern-time or tierce-song hour. **1887** *Suppl. Jamieson* s.v. *Andrum*, The afternoon or early evening repast;..called also..*anterin-time*.

β. *c* **1375** [see *a* 1300 above]. *a* **1450** *Le Morte Arth.* 2807 Hys strength shulld wex in suche a space, From the vndyrtyme tylle none. **1495** *Trevisa's Barth. De P. R.* XVIII. xxiv. 783 Whan gete ben meuyd after the vnder tyme they drynke the more water. **1590** SPENSER *F. Q.* III. vii. 13 He comming home at vndertime, there found The fairest creature, that he euer saw.

**U·nder-o·fficer.** [UNDER-[1] 6 a. Cf. Du. *onderofficier*, G. *unterofficier*, *-offizier*, Da., Norw., and Sw. *underofficer*.] A sub-officer.

*c* **1400** *Pilgr. Sowle* (Caxton, 1483) III. iv. 53 Confedered and entendyd with other suche brybours, which e that were your vnder offycers. ? *c* **1425** *Lucidarie* (1909) 29 Hedes & vndirofficeres of hooly chirche. **1555** EDEN *Decades* (Arb.) 112 He spake to al the vnder officers sharplye. **1598** BARRET *Theor. Warres* II. i. 22 Vnto whom the souldiers and vnder-officers are to obey. **1626** JACKSON *Creed* VIII. xxix. § 5 Whether Pilate himselfe did write this title, or caused it to be written by some under-officer of the court. **1658–9** LD. FALKLAND in *Burton's Diary* (1828) IV. 154 Major-general Overton might have been committed by the general as an under-officer. **1708** *Lond. Gaz.* No. 4472/1 Bezeredi, with several of his Under-Officers,..divulged it to the common Soldiers. **1796** *Instr. & Reg. Cavalry* (1813) 121 Two under officers are sent from the rear division. **1876** BANCROFT *Hist. U. S.* V. xiii. 470 All officers and under-officers were obliged to appear at his head-quarters.

Hence **U·nder-o·fficered** *a.*[1], furnished with under-officers.

**1844** THACKERAY *B. Lyndon* vi, The Prussian army..was officered and under-officered by native Prussians.

**U·nder-o·fficered,** *a.*[2] [UNDER-[1] 10 a.] Insufficiently furnished with officers.

**1887** in *Gladden's Parish Probl.* 368 Most schools are under-officered. **1897** *Daily News* 19 May 5/6 The Greek regiments are much under-officered.

**Undero·gating,** *pres. pple.* [UN-[1] 10.] Without losing dignity.

**1808** SCOTT *Marm.* VI. Introd. 44 The heir..That night might village partner choose; The Lord, underogating, share The vulgar game of 'post and pair'.

**Undero·gatory,** *a.* (UN-[1] 7.) **1648** BOYLE *Seraph. Love* (1659) 132 The Apostle,..to create in us Apprehensions, underogatory from what we shall possesse,..removes our thoughts from all we Do Enjoy.

**U·nder-opi·nion.** [UNDER-[1] 10 b.] Too low an estimate of a person.

**1629** EARLE *Microcosm.* (Arb.) 79 Nothing threatens him so much as great expectation, which he thinks more prejudiciall, then your vnder-opinion.

**U·nder-orb.** (UNDER-[1] 6 b.) **1591** SYLVESTER *Du Bartas* I. iv. 350 Th' under-Orbs..Each by himselfe an oblique course doth slide.

†**Undero·rn,** *v. Obs.*—[1] [UNDER-[1] 2.] *trans.* To suborn.

*a* **1325** *MS. Rawl. B. 520* fol. 31 Þe schirreue..þoru his frendes..procurez þe contreie ant underornez.

**Under-over man**: see VIEWER 1 b.

**U·nderpai·d,** *ppl. a.* (UNDER-[1] 10 a.)

**1846** *Mechanic's Mag.* 4 July 7 Services..so notoriously underpaid by the government. **1866** W. COLLINS *Armadale*

I. ii, The shopman gave warning on the ground that he was underfed as well as underpaid.

**U·nderpart**, *sb.* [Under-[1] 5 b, 6 b. Also Under *a.* 1 b.]

1. A lower part or portion.

1662 Wase *Lat. Dict., Subtundo*, to knock, or beat the under-part of any thing. 1731 P. Miller *Gard. Dict.* s.v. *Leaves*, Their Leaves..have shot out young Plants from their under-Parts. 1797 *Encycl. Brit.* (ed. 3) XVII. 394/2 From the upper part of the lower deck to the under part of the main rail. 1825 Jamieson, *Fair-grass*,..said to be [so] denominated from the whiteness of the under part of the leaf.

b. *spec.* A part of the under-side of the body (of a bird or animal).

1783 Latham *Gen. Synop. Birds* II. 362 The under parts wholly white. 1815 Stephens in *Shaw's Gen. Zool.* IX. I. 21 The rest of the under parts dirty yellow. 1873 J. E. Taylor *Half-hours in Green Lanes* iv. 126 You could see their..black breasts and white underparts.

2. A subordinate part in action, esp. a minor rôle in a play; one who acts a subordinate part.

1679 Dryden *Troilus & Cress.* Pref. ¶ 20 Making Œdipus the best and bravest person, and even Jocasta but an under-part to him. 1693 — *Juvenal* (1697) p. lxxix, In the famous Pastoral of Guarini,..where Corisca and the Satyre are the Under-parts. 1711 Addison *Spect.* No. 7 ¶ 1 My Friend, I found, acted but an under Part at his Table. 1746 Francis tr. *Hor., Sat.* I. ix. 98 You should have a Man of Art; One who might act an under-part. 1780 J. Berington *State Eng. Catholics* 66 Plot was set up against plot, all of them under-parts of the same grand drama. 1822–7 Good *Study Med.* (1829) V. 490 The kidneys play merely an under-part, and are only secondarily affected.

3. A subordinate part or portion; a subdivision.

1711 Shaftesb. *Charac.* III. 113 Our religious Pastors.. have quitted their substantial Service, and uniform Division into Parts and Under-Parts. 1715 Pope *Iliad* Pref. ¶ 9 Nor is this..only in the principal Quality which constitutes the Main of each Character, but even in the Under-parts of it.

† **Under-pa·rt**, *v. Obs.*[−1] [Under-[1] 8 c.] *trans.* To subdivide.

1626 B. Jonson *Staple of N.* I. v, The foure Emissaries.. haue full parts: and then one part Is vnder-parted to a couple of Clarkes; And there's the iust diuision of the profits.

**U·nder-pa·ssion.** (Under-[1] 9 and 6 b.)

1711 Steele *Spect.* No. 208 ¶ 1 The Under-Passion (as I may so call it) of a noble Spirit, Pity. 1818 Keats *Endym.* III. 179 Thy starry sway Has been an under-passion to this hour.

U·nder-pay, *sb.* (Under-[1] 10 b.) 1851 Mayhew *Lond. Labour* II. 304/1 Over-work makes under-pay and under-pay makes over-work.

**U·nder-pay·**, *v.* (Under-[1] 10 a.)

1861 Ld. Brougham *Brit. Const.* xix. 316 There can be no worse economy..in any State than underpaying such functionaries as judges. 1899 *Daily News* 1 Feb. 5/1 The Post Office is having much trouble with people who under-pay their letters.

**Underpee·p**, *v.* [Under-[1] 4 b, c.] **a.** *trans.* To peep under. **b.** *intr.* To peep from under.

1611 Shaks. *Cymb.* II. ii. 20 The Flame o' th' Taper Bowes toward her, and would vnder-peepe her lids, To see th' inclosed Lights. 1827 Hood *Hero & Leander* lxi, Yet you might gaze twice Ere Death it seem'd, and not his cousin, Sleep, That through those creviced lids did underpeep.

**Under-pee·r**, *v.* [Under-[1] 4 b.] *trans.* and *intr.* To peer under.

1589 Puttenham *Eng. Poesie* III. vi. 128 Within they are stuffed full of browne paper and tow, which the shrewd boyes vnderpeering, do guilefully discouer and turne to a great derision. 1614 B. Jonson *Barth. Fair* II. v, Are you under-peering, you Baboon? up off my Hose, an you be Men.

**U·nder-peo·pled**, *ppl. a.* (Under-[1] 10 a.)

*a* 1687 Petty *Pol. Arith.* Pref. (1690) a 1 b, There is no Trade nor Employment for the People, and yet..the Land is under-peopled. 1707 Arbuthnot *Serm. on Union* 8 This is the chief Cause why Scotland..is underpeopled. 1776 Adam Smith *W. N.* I. ix. (1904) I. 102 A new colony must always, for some time, be..more underpeopled..than the greater part of other countries. 1834 Ht. Martineau *Moral* I. 24 The question is not now, as it was when the country was underpeopled. 1862 *Q. Rev.* Apr. 510 A valuable acquisition to any underpeopled colony.

**U·nder-pe·tticoat.** (Under-[1] 5 a.)

1625 K. Long tr. *Barclay's Argenis* I. xv. 41 She..herselfe comes, having onely put on an under-petticoate. 1670 in *12th Rep. Hist. MSS. Comm.* App. V. 21 Plaine black skirts,..and the under pettycoatt very richly laced. 1716 Lady Montagu *Let. to C'tess of Bristol* 22 Aug., Like a poor town lady of pleasure..with..a ragged under-petticoat. 1762 Sterne *Tr. Shandy* v. vii, Her bed-gowns, and comfortable under-petticoats.

Hence **U·nder-pe·tticoated** *a.*

1748 Richardson *Clarissa* VII. lxxviii. 257 They were all slip-shoed; stockenless some; only under-petticoated all.

† **Underpi·ght**, *pa. t.* and *pa. pple. Obs.* [Under-[1] 4 a: see Pitch *v.*[1]] Supported from below; propped up. Also *fig.*

*c* 1375 *Cursor M.* 7495 (Fairf.), Here-til þou art ful ʒing; ʒone mon wiþ strenght is vnder-piʒt and þou lered neuer atte fiʒt. 1377 Langl. *P. Pl.* B. XVI. 23 Pieres..bad me toten on þe tree...With þre pyles was it vnder-piʒte I perceyued it sone. 14.. Lydgate in *MS. Soc. Antiq.* 134 (Halliwell), And undirpyʒte this mancyoun ryalle, With seven pileris. 1549 Coverdale, etc. *Erasm. Par. Rom.* 11 Nor yet repent we our glory, with hope wherof we for this present tyme are aduaunced & vnderpyght. *Ibid., Gal.* 12 By the obseruaunce of this lawe then were menne so long stayed and vnderpyght.

**Underpi·n**, *v.* [Under-[1] 4 a + Pin *v.* 3.]

1. *trans.* To support or strengthen (a building or other structure) from beneath, *spec.* by laying a solid foundation below the ground-level, or by substituting stronger or more solid for weaker or softer materials.

1533 *MS. Rawl. D.* 776 fol. 131 Vnder pynnyng the Grownde plattes of the said wharff. 1583–4 in Willis & Clark *Cambridge* (1886) III. 22 To Mr. Stokes..for stone, and vnderpynnyng the whalles of the schooles. *c* 1700 in *Essex Rev.* (1906) XV. 170, I underpinned the side of the dwelling house. 1776 G. Semple *Building in Water* 65 We underpinned that West End of it, where we found that there was nothing supporting the upper Work, but the Bond of the Stones. 1833 Loudon *Encycl. Archit.* § 234 All the window and door frames to be properly bedded..and the sills underpinned. 1886 Willis & Clark *Cambridge* I. 24 A facing added to the decayed clunch by way of under-pinning it.

b. *fig.* To support, corroborate.

1522 More *De Quat. Noviss.* Wks. 76/1 It is better to.. thinke on some better thing the while, than to geue eare therto & vnder pinne the tale. *a* 1619 Fotherby *Atheom.* Pref. p. vi, I am called to vnder-pinne those foure maine Corner-stones. 1646 Saltmarsh *Groanes for Liberty* 9 Was it unlawfull..to underpin Episcopacy with some Texts of Scripture? 1866 De Morgan in *Athenæum* 2 Sept. 312/3 If so, away goes free will for good and all; unless, indeed, we underpin our system with the hypothesis [etc.]. 1884 *American* VIII. 294 These powers..might underpin the first lien on the property.

2. To form a base or support to.

1878 Bosw. Smith *Carthage* 148 Above the precipitous cliffs that underpinned the mountain was a broad plateau.

**U·nder-pi·nner**[1]. [Under-[1] 6 a + Pinner[2].] A subordinate pound-keeper.

1599 *George a Greene* E 4, I am vnder pinner of a towne, And..I shall be turned out of mine office.

**Under-pi·nner**[2]. [f. Underpin *v.*] A support or prop; *fig.* a leg.

1859 Bartlett *Dict. Amer.* (ed. 2) 493 *Underpinners*, the legs, which in English flash language are called pins. 1861 Reade *Cloister & H.* xliii, The underpinners gave way, and the tower suddenly sank away from the walls.

**Underpi·nning**, *vbl. sb.* [f. as prec.]

1. The action of supporting or strengthening a building, etc., from beneath. (See Underpin *v.* 1.)

1489 in Dugdale *Monast.* (1821) III. 359/2 Paid for a grounsell for the kechyn wall and for underpynnyng and leiyng in of the same, xv d. 1493–4 *Rec. St. Mary at Hill* 198 Payd for vndyrpynyng of Mastres Atclyffe ys pewe, vj d. *Ibid.*, Payd..for vndyrpynny[n]g of þe newe pewys. 1528 *MS. Acc. St. John's Hosp., Canterb.*, Paid to a tyler for stanchonyng, dobyng, & vnderpynnyng of the store house. 1707 Mortimer *Husb.* 304 Underpinning for the Bricklayer to dig the Foundation..is a Penny a foot. 1842 Gwilt *Archit.* Gloss. 1049. 1883 Gresley *Gloss. Coal-m.* 267 *Underpinning*, building up the walling of a pit-shaft to join that above it.

2. The materials or structure used for giving support to a building from beneath.

1538 Elyot, *Substructio*, vnderpynnynge or groundyng of a house. 1601 Holland *Pliny* II. 575 When Cambyses.. burnt all before him, as farre as to the very foundation and underpinning of the Obeliske. 1668 Wilkins *Real Char.* 256 Foundation,..Base, Bottom, fundamental, underpinning. 1741 *Phil. Trans.* XLI. 852 [The houses] were all, in a manner, rocked quite off from their Underpinnings. 1789 *Massachusetts Spy* 16 July 3/4 A new frame of a barn, uncovered,..was taken by a whirlwind from its underpinning. 1894 Howells *Traveller fr. Altruria* 112 The sod was backed up against the wooden under-pinning.

b. *fig.* A support or prop.

1589 R. Harvey *Pl. Perc.* 3 They are like to daunce after his pipe, and set themselues vpon a miry pinne,..till his vnderpinning will faile him, I doubt. 1656 *Artif. Handsom.* 71 Those grosse Solœcismes of Art, which by unseasonable ..affectations (as so many pitifull props and underpinnings) strive in vain to skrew and set up lapsed and tottering age. 1774 Burke *Sp. Amer. Tax.* Wks. 1842 I. 160 That this house..is itself held up only by the treacherous under-pinning and clumsy buttresses of arbitrary power. *a* 1894 in *Sunday Reform Leaflets* (Columbus) Sept. 6 The moral underpinning requisite to sustain the superstructure of man's rights.

**U·nderpitch**, *a. Arch.* (See quot.)

1875 *Encycl. Brit.* II. 466 When the main longitudinal vault of any groining is higher than the cross or transverse vaults which run from the windows, the system of vaulting is called underpitch groining.

**U·nderpi·tched**, *ppl. a.* (Under-[1] 10 a.)

1677 Plot *Oxfordsh.* 274 Roofs..whereof some are flat or under-pitched,..others due proportion'd, or over-pitched.

**Underpla·nt**, *v. rare.* [Under-[1] 2, 4 a.] *trans.* † **a.** To supplant. *Obs.* **b.** (See later quots.) Hence † **Underpla·nter**, a supplanter. *Obs.*

In OE., other senses of L. *supplantare* are rendered by *underplantian*.

*c* 1200 *Trin. Coll. Hom.* 151 Iacob on boc leden is icleped on englisse under-plantere of fule custumes [L. *supplantator viciorum*],..and rithliche.., for he under-plantede [L. *supplantavit*] fule custumes..mid his clenliche lifiode. 1538 Elyot, *Supplantare*,..to vnderplante or set a tree or vyne. 1598 Florio, *Sotto piantare*, to vnder-plant, to vnderset, to vnderprop. 1909 *Cent. Dict.* Suppl., *Underplant*,..to plant (young trees) under an existing stand.

**U·nderplay**, *sb.* [Under-[1] 9.]

1. An underlying or hidden motion or action.

1845 J. Martineau *Ess.* (1890) I. 63 The under-play of a living enthusiasm beneath the dry matter of the composition. 1862 R. Vaughan *Eng. Nonconformity* 224 The king was a party to this underplay.

2. *Card-playing.* (See quot. 1863.)

1850 *Bohn's Handbk. Games* 21. 1863 'Cavendish' *Whist* (ed. 5) 42 Underplay is keeping up the winning card, generally in the second round of a suit, by leading a low card, though holding the best.

**U·nderplay·**, *v.* [Under-[1] 8 b, 10 a.]

1. *refl.* To play below one's ability.

1733 Ld. Harvey in *Craftsman* No. 376, No person is ever known to flatter at this game [*sc.* chess], by underplaying himself.

2. *intr.* To play a low card, though holding a high one of the same suit, in hope of later advantage. (Also used *trans.*)

1850 *Bohn's Handbk. Games* 21 To underplay, he wins the trick with the ace, and returns the small one. 1863 'Cavendish' *Whist* (ed. 5) 42 Experienced players frequently endeavour to obtain the entire command of their suit by underplaying.

**U·nderplot.** [Under-[1] 6 b and 9.]

1. A (dramatic or literary) plot subordinate to the principal plot, but connected with it.

1668 Dryden *Dram. Poesy* ¶ 24 There may be many actions in a play..; but they must all be subservient to the great one, which our language happily expresses in the name of under-plots. 1684 T. Burnet *Theory Earth* I. 146 Such affairs are but the little under-plots in the tragicomedy of the world. 1711 Addison *Spect.* No. 40 ¶ 3 The skilful Choice of an Under-Plot. 1779 Sheridan *Critic* II. ii, I have laid my under-plot in low life. 1847 *Westm. Rev.* XLVII. 62 The greater part of the underplot was by the inferior writer. 1873 Symonds *Grk. Poets* ix. 300 The under-plots of many plays..are not sufficiently subordinated to the main design.

2. An underhand scheme or trick.

1668 Etheredge *She wou'd if she cou'd* III. i, We cannot be long without some Underplots in this Town. 1711 Addison *Spect.* No. 170 ¶ 12 They still suspect an Under-Plot in every female Action. *a* 1845 Hood *Lamia* vi. 62 Canst swear she is..No cheating underplot—no covert shape, Making a filthy masquerade of nature?

**U·nder-plo·tter.** [Under-[1] 8 a.] An underhand schemer.

1728 Ramsay *Bonnie Lass & Looking-Glass* 36 If you're opprest By Parasites with fause Design, Then will sic faithfu' Mirrors best These Underplotters countermine.

**U·nderply.** [Under-[1] 5 b.] (See quot.)

1883 Gresley *Gloss. Coal-m.* 267 *Underply*, a band or division of the upper portion of a thick seam of coal.

† **Underpoi·se**, *v. Obs.*[−1] [Under-[1] 10 a.] *trans.* To underweigh, undervalue.

1602 Marston *Ant. & Mel.* Induct., His worth being much underpoised by the uneven scale, that currants all thinges by the outwarde stamp of opinion.

**U·nder-po·led**, *ppl. a.* [Under-[1] 10 a.]

1. Provided with poles of insufficient height.

1707 Mortimer *Husb.* 136 If..you find a Hop over or under-poled, you may..place another Pole in its place.

2. Not stirred sufficiently. Cf. Pole *v.* 7.

1881 Raymond *Mining Gloss.*, *Under-poled copper*, copper not poled enough to remove all sub-oxide.

**U·nderposed**, *ppl. a.* [Under-[1] 4 a.] Placed beneath for support.

*a* 1656 Ussher *Power Princes* II. (1661) 172 The power doth not depart from the Lord; but he useth it by an underposed hand.

**U·nder-posse·ssor.** (Under-[1] 6 a.) 1653 Jer. Taylor *Serm. for Year* I. xvii. 230 The disposing them into portions of inheritance, the assignation of charges and governments, ..are the reserves of the superior right, and not to be invaded by the under-possessors. **U·nder-pow·er.** (Under-[1] 6 b.) 1805 Wordsw. *Prelude* I. 152 General Truths, which are themselves a sort Of..Under-powers, Subordinate helpers of the living mind.

**U·nderprai·se**, *v.* (Under-[1] 10 a.)

1698 Dryden *Ep. to Motteux* 52 In underpraising thy Deserts, I wrong. 1842 Mrs. Browning *Bk. of Poets* ii. ¶ 7 We must not underpraise Surrey to balance the overpraise we murmur at.

**U·nder-pre·ntice.** (Under-[1] 6 a.) 1632 Massinger *City Madam* I. i, Emploiment..Fitting an under-prentice, or a footman.

**U·nder-price**, *sb.* [Under-[1] 10 b. Cf. Sw. *underpris.*] A price below the standard or usual price; an inadequate payment.

1611 Cotgr., *Non-prix*, an vnder value, or vnderprice. 1727 Bailey (vol. II), To *Under-work*, to work for an Under-price. 1770 Langhorne *Plutarch* III. 268 He was selling a considerable estate, which he wanted a friend to have at an under-price. 1771 W. Evans tr. *Welshman's Candle* 399 At under-price men's lands I often bought. 1807 Southey *Espriella's Lett.* II. 354 To advertise in newspapers which.. insert their notices at an under-price. 1862 Mayhew *Lond. Labour* II. 344/2 The employers of these cab-drivers are as willing to receive it at an underprice.

**U·nder-pri·ce**, *v.* [Under-[1] 8 b, c.]

1. *trans.* To price lower than the value.

1756 H. Walpole *Let. to Montagu* 14 Oct., If you had offered ten pounds for a set of Pelhams, perhaps I should not have thought you had underpriced them.

2. To undercut (one) in price.

1890 *Daily News* 31 Dec. 7/2 Brown, in answer to the charge, said the prosecutor had underpriced him.

**U·nderpriced**, *ppl. a.* [Under-[1] 10 a.] Selling at less than the usual price(s).

1851–61 Mayhew *Lond. Labour* III. 210/2, I next went to work at a under-priced hatter's,..but I was disgusted with the price paid for labour.

**U·nderpriest.** (Under-[1] 6 a. Cf. ON. *undirprestr*, Du. *onderpriester.*) *c* 1200 Ormin 1146 Forr bisscopp & forr unnderrpreost, & forr þe follkess nede. *Ibid.* 10882.

**Underpri·nt**, *v.* [Under-[1] 4 a, 10 a.]

1. *trans.* To print or stamp from below or on the under side.

1598 Florio, *Soppresso*,..beaten vnder, drowned, boulged, vnder-printed. 1626 *Impeachm. Dk. Buckhm.* (Camden) 62 Subscribed per me,..and..sealed with a seale of reade wax, under-printed upon.

2. To print (an engraving or photograph) with insufficient depth or distinctness.

*c* 1865 *Wylde's Circ. Sci.* I. 154/1 It is better that the positive should be over, rather than under-printed. 1885

*Longm. Mag.* VI. 490 A series of book-illustrations that were over-printed in Paris and under-printed in London.

**Underpri·ze,** *v.* [UNDER-[1] 10 a.] *trans.* To prize too little; to undervalue.

**1596** SHAKS. *Merch. V.* III. ii. 129 How farre The substance of my praise doth wrong this shadow In vnderprising it, so farre [etc.]. **1598–9** B. JONSON *Case is Altered* III. iii, If I mistake not, He scorns to have his worth so underprised. **1647** H. MORE *Cupid's Conflict* l, Nor while I live, heed I what man doth praise Or underprize mine unaffected layes. **1665** WITHER *Lord's Prayer* 116 How is it neglected and underprized, as a Form of Prayer fitting none but Ideots and Children! **1889** SKRINE *Mem. Thring* 52 Boys thought their own genius under-prized.

**U·nder-profi·cient.** (UNDER-[2].) **1703** S. PARKER tr. *Eusebius' Eccl. Hist.* VI. 103 Such Crowds of Scholars daily throng'd to his Lectures..that he was at last oblig'd to assign the Instruction of the Under-Proficients to Heraclas.

**Underpro·mpt,** *v.* (UNDER-[1] 4 a.) *a* **1548** HALL *Chron., Edw. V*, 2 b, Slipper youthe [must be] vnderprompted with elder counsaill. **U·nder-pro·mpter.** (UNDER-[1] 6 a.) **1779** SHERIDAN *Critic* Dram. Pers., Under Prompter: Mr. Phillimore. *Ibid.* II. i, [Stage direction.] Enter Under Prompter.

**Under-proof:** see UNDER *prep.* 23 b.

**U·nderprop,** *sb.* [UNDER-[1] 5 b.] A prop or support placed under a thing. Usu. *fig.*

**1579** TOMSON *Calvin's Serm. Tim.* 45/1 The Monkes, &.. all those iolly vnderprops of that Romish Antichrist. **1602** BRETON *Mother's Blessing* D 3, Faiths strong pillars need no vnderprops. **1629** H. BURTON *Truth's Triumph* 264 An vnder-proppe or basis supporting and sustaining vs. **1826** W. E. ANDREWS *Crit. Rev. Fox's Bk. Mart.* II. 204 Cranmer,..this pillar and underprop of the reformation.

**Underpro·p,** *v.* [UNDER-[1] 4 a.]

**1.** *trans.* To support with a prop or props; to keep firm or upright with some form of material support. (Common in 17th c.)

**1534** MORE *Comf. agst. Trib.* I. Wks. 1162/2 Some haue I sene euen in their last sicknes set vp in their death bed vnderpropped with pillous. **1591** HARINGTON *Orl. Fur.* XXVII. lxix, One took him napping,..And underprop't his saddell with foure stakes And so from under him his courser takes. **1637** HEYWOOD *Pleas. Dial.* ii. Wks. 1874 VI. 124 Had you not rather..To see the trees full branches vnderpropt Laden with ripe fruit? **1699** J. POTTER *Antiq. Greece* III. xx. II. 161 It was frequent also for Sea-men, underpropping their Ships with their Shoulders, to thrust them forwards into the Sea. **1726** LEONI *Alberti's Archit.* II. 129 Underprop the Architrave with a strong arch. **1810** CRABBE *Borough* xi. 100 A mirror crack'd, With table underpropp'd, and chairs new-back'd. **1851** C. L. SMITH tr. *Tasso* XI. lxxxv, They who guided it their force applied To underprop it.

**b.** In fig. context.

**1532** MORE *Confut. Tindale* III. Wks. 473/1 But Tyndall perceiuing..howe fieble hys building is that he setteth therupon, hath therfore..vndershoren, & vnderpropped it with certayn strong postes made of rotten redes. **1581** J. BELL *Haddon's Answ. Osor.* 34 b, Our deepe Devine doth underproppe his lazie Monckerie upon these pillars. **1633** T. STAFFORD *Pac. Hib.* (1821) I. xi. 75 The effect thereof was, to implore ayde of that Egyptian Reed, to underprop their ruinous and almost rotten Building. **1645** RUTHERFORD *Tryal & Tri. Faith* 23 This doctrine is a..Pillar, to under prop the Chamber in Hell, which they call Purgatory.

**2.** *fig.* To support or sustain; to maintain. (Very common *c* 1550–1675.)

**1513** MORE *Rich. III*, Wks. 39/1 Childehood must be maintained by mens authoritye, & slipper youth vnderpropped with elder counsayle. **1561** T. NORTON *Calvin's Inst.* III. 255 To vnderprop and strengthen this faith with y^e^ signes of the good wil of God towarde it selfe. **1593** SHAKS. *Lucr.* 53 Within whose face Beautie and Vertue striued, Which of them both should vnderprop her fame. **1647** DIGGES *Unlawf. Taking Arms* § 2. 22 This art..of underpropping their reputation. **1695** BLACKMORE *Pr. Arth.* VI. 360 He could th' unstable People's Tumults stop, And a declining Kingdom underprop. **1738** WARBURTON *Div. Legat.* I. 47 He thought fit to underprop it with his heavenly God, the Leviathan. **1773** BERRIDGE *Chr. World Unmasked* (1805) 199 Moses is called in hastily to underprop his master Jesus. **1827** POLLOK *Course T.* v. 882 Leagues..on purpose made to underprop Iniquity, and crush the sacred truth. **1849** THOREAU *Week Concord River* Wedn. 300 Let such pure hate still underprop our love.

*refl.* **1571** GOLDING *Calvin on Ps.* iii. 3 Assone as he hath underpropped himselfe with assurance of comfort.

*absol.* **1596** *Edward III*, III. v. 78 Yet marble courage still did vnderprop.

**3.** To form a prop or support to (something).

*c* **1590** MARLOWE *Faustus* vii. 32 Know that this Citie stands vpon seuen hilles That vnderprops the groundworke of the same. *a* **1661** HOLYDAY *Juvenal* (1673) 56 He had yet forsooth a statue or two, particularly one of Cheiron, which underpropp'd his table. **1672** MARVELL *Reh. Transp.* I. 133 There is nothing more natural than for the Ivy to be of opinion..that the Church cannot hold up longer than It underprops the Walls. **1794** G. ADAMS *Nat. & Exp. Philos.* III. xxxi. 261 One considerable use of the wedge, is to raise up the beam of a house, to underprop it, when a floor gives way. **1830** TENNYSON *Arab. Nts.* 145 Six columns..underpropt a rich Throne of the massive ore. **1836** BUCKLAND *Geol. & Min.* xv. § 5 (1837) I. 360 The transverse plates..underpropping their flattest and weakest part.

Hence **Underpropped, -propping** *ppl. adjs.*

**1614** D. DYKE *Myst. Self-Deceiving* 45 There is no sinne, but we may..fall into, if Gods vnderpropping hand withdraw it selfe. **1632** LITHGOW *Trav.* I. 6 O heauy vnder-prop'd wrongs. **1655** FULLER *Ch. Hist.* IX. vi. § 1 The old underpropped Scaffolds overladen with people, suddenly fell down.

**U·nder-propo·rtion,** *v.* (UNDER-[1] 10 a.)

**1813** SOUTHEY *Nelson* I. 129 That fatal error of under-proportioning the force to the service.

**U·nder-propo·rtioned,** *ppl. a.* (UNDER-[1] 10 a.)

**1697** COLLIER *Ess. Mor. Subj.* I. (1703) 26 To make scanty and under-proportioned returns of civility. **1813** G. EDWARDS *Meas. True Pol.* 86 It is underproportioned to the capacity..and abilities of the nation.

**U·nder-proposi·tion.** (UNDER-[1] 6 b.) **1691** NORRIS *Pract. Disc.* 113 Taking the argument for, I shall think myself further concern'd only to justify the Under-Proposition.

**Underpro·pper.** [f. UNDERPROP *v.*] One who or that which supports or sustains. †Also *spec.* (see SUPPORTASSE).

**1532** MORE *Confut. Tindale* Wks. 473/1 This vnderpropper is not very proper for to beare vp his bilding. **1583** MELBANCKE *Philotimus* K ij, The strongest vnderproppers of her princely state. **1655** CROMWELL *Let. to Goodson* Oct. (Carlyle), That Roman Babylon, of which the Spaniard is the great underpropper. **1664** H. MORE *Myst. Iniq.* I. i. 1 For which reason they..style the chief Authour and underpropper thereof..by the name of Antichrist. **1740** CIBBER *Apol.* (1756) I. 43, I had a third chance..of becoming an under-propper of the state.

**Underpro·pping,** *vbl. sb.* [f. as prec.] The action of supporting with props, etc.; also *concr.*, that which serves to underprop.

**1586** T. B. *La Primaud. Fr. Acad.* I. 391 Mauger all the power and under-propping, which he receiveth from the wicked. **1592** NASHE *P. Penilesse* 17, I will not, by the vnderpropping of confutation, seeme to giue the idle witted aduersary so much encouragement. **1628** FELTHAM *Resolves* II. xix. 61 [The soul] rests full, in her owne approuement, without the weake Worlds reedy vnder-propping. **1658** A. FOX *Würtz' Surg.* II. xiv. 107 Such Wounds must be helped with underproppings and bolsters. **1726** LEONI *Alberti's Archit.* II. 129 Let this underpropping be run up as fast as possible.

**U·nder-pro·spect.** (UNDER-[1] 5 b.) *a* **1586** SIDNEY *Arcadia* I. x, A pleasant valley (of either side of which high hils lifted up their beetle-browes, as if they would over looke the pleasantnes of their under-prospect). **Underpry·,** *v.* (UNDER-[1] 4 b.) **1600** HOLLAND *Livy* 1073 Two Embassadors ..sent rather as spies to under-prie and to learne somwhat as touching those points.

†**Underpu·ll,** *v. Obs.* [UNDER-[1] 8 a.] *intr.* To work secretly; to act in matters without appearing to do so.

**1697** COLLIER *Ess. Mor. Subj.* II. (1703) 142 Covetousness ..engages honour in the most scandalous intrigues, and makes it under-pull to cheats and sharpers. *a* **1734** NORTH *Life Ld. Guilford* (1742) I. 24 His Lordship,..during his Incapacity to practise aboveboard, was contented to under-pull, as they call it, and managed diverse Suits for his Country Friends and Relations.

**Under-pu·ller.** [Cf. prec.] A secret agent.

**1682** T. FLATMAN *Heraclitus Ridens* No. 69, But 'tis great pity this Scribler be not made an Under-puller in the Work of defending the City-Charter against the King. **1698** FRYER *Acc. E. India & P.* 388 Underpullers to these are the Shopkeepers, whose Mercurial Parts are fitted to put off the worst Wares. *a* **1734** NORTH *Examen* II. iv. § 138 For the King is this..Ridiculer, and this Fellow, Fitzharris, his Underpuller.

†**U·nderput,** *sb. Obs.*[—1] [UNDER-[1] 4 d.] A mistress.

**1607** MIDDLETON *Michaelmas Term* III. i, Is she but your underput, master Lethe? *Let.* No more, of my credit;.. when all comes to all, 'tis but a plain pung.

†**Underpu·t,** *v. Obs.* [UNDER-[1] 4 b, 7.]

**1.** *trans.* To put (one thing) under (another); to place or set beneath.

*c* **1220** *Bestiary* 669 Rennande cumeð a ȝungling, raðe to him luteð, his snute him under puteð. **1382** WYCLIF *Gen.* xxviii. 18 [Jacob] took the stoon, the which he hadde vnderput to his heed. — *Exod.* xxvi. 21 Two stakis to eche table shulen be vnderput. *c* **1480** HENRYSON *Orpheus & Eurydice* 630 (Bann. MS.), Now pray we god..That he wald vndirput his haly hand Of mantenans, and gife ws forss to stand.

**b.** To furnish with something placed under, esp. as a support.

**1387–8** T. USK *Test. Love* II. vii. (Skeat) l. 72 Hadden they ben underput with any helpes, they had not so lightly falle. *c* **1475** *Promp. Parv.* (K.) 511/2 Vnder puttyn, or beryn up, ..*suffulcio*. *c* **1611** CHAPMAN *Iliad* XXI. 342 As a caldron, underput with store of fire,..up leapes his wave aloft.

**2.** To put under the power or control of; to place in subjection; to subject. Const. *to*.

*c* **1374** CHAUCER *Boeth.* I. pr. vi. (1868) 28 þat þou byleuest þat þe gouernynge of it nis nat subgit ne vnderput to þe folie of þise happes auenterouses. *a* **1400–50** *Alexander* 5402 Synches I hiȝt; And to my powere vndire-putt is all þe playn werd. *c* **1456** PECOCK *Bk. of Faith* (1909) 217 If it like to oure Lord God that he submitte and undirputte alle Cristen personys to resoun and fre wil. **1559** *Mirr. Mag., Hen. VI*, xiv, Wheron the rest depende and vnderput remayne.

**b.** To lower (the voice).

**1382** WYCLIF *Prov.* xxvi. 25 Whan he shal vndirputte [L. *submiserit*] his vois, ne ȝiue thou credence to hym.

**3. a.** To put or take fraudulently. **b.** To substitute.

*c* **1400** in Trevisa *Higden* (Rolls) VII. 133 Som men seiþ.. þat sche underput [L. *supposuisse*] to hir self lyenge in childebedde þe forseide Swane. *Ibid.* 137. *Ibid.* 149 He was..deposed, and anoþer i-ordeyned and underput [L. *subrogatus*].

Hence †**Underpu·tting** *vbl. sb. Obs.*

**1387–8** T. USK *Test. Love* I. ix. (Skeat) l. 62 Though thou be put to serve the ilke jewel duringe thy lyfe, yet is that no servage of underputtinge, but a maner of travayling plesaunce. *c* **1440** *Promp. Parv.* 511/2 Vnder puttynge,..*subposicio*. **1611** FLORIO, *Supposta*, an vnderputting or setting.

**Underpu·tter.** [f. UNDERPUT *v.*] †A pander, a procurer.

**1608** *Yorksh. Trag.* I. ii, My second sonne must be a promooter, and my third a theefe, or an vnderputter, a slaue pander.

**U·nderqua·lified,** *ppl. a.* (UNDER-[1] 10 a.) **1624** HEYWOOD *Gunaik.* III. 119 Each heroick and well disposed Ladie, or woman lower degreed and underqualified. **1847** H. BUSHNELL *Chr. Nurt.* II. ii, They are almost all disqualified, or under-qualified. **U·nder-queen.** (UNDER-[1] 6 a.) **1839** BAILEY *Festus* 186, I am but here the under-queen of beauty.

**Underquo·te,** *v.* [UNDER-[1] 8 b.] *trans.* To quote a lower price than.

**1891** *Engineer* 20 Feb. 156 In some instances merchants have been underquoting makers to the extent of 2s. 6d. to 5s. a ton. **1897** *Westm. Gaz.* 9 Sept. 8/1 The American competitors..are always ready to underquote the official prices.

**U·nder-ra·nger.** (UNDER-[1] 6 a.) **1685** *Secr. Serv. Money Chas. & Jas.* (Camden) 104 To..Lieut. of Waltham forrest, ..for the underkeepers and underrangers within the said forest. **1738** BIRCH *Milton* M.'s Wks. I. p. i, Our Author's Grandfather..was an Under-ranger or Keeper of the Forest of Shotover.

**U·nder-rate,** *sb.* [UNDER-[1] 10 b.] A rate lower than the true or proper one.

**1631** WEEVER *Anc. Funeral Mon.* 240 Being valued..at a fauourable and farre vnder-rate. **1693** G. STEPNEY in *Dryden's Juvenal* viii. (1697) 195 The worthless Brute is from New-Market brought, And at an under-rate in Smith-Field bought. **1712** HEARNE *Collect.* (O.H.S.) III. 477, I highly commend your Resolution of not letting Copies go at Under-Rates. **1748** RICHARDSON *Clarissa* VI. 255 Tho' her conscience permitted her to take them [clothes] at such an under-rate.

**U·nder-rate,** *a.* [UNDER-[2].] Inferior, subordinate.

**1709** SWIFT *Let. to Hunter* 12 Jan., The Whigs carry all before them, and how far they will pursue their victories we underrate Whigs can hardly tell. **1776** BENTHAM *Fragm. Govt.* Wks. 1843 I. 282 This deficiency is no other than what an underrate workman might easily supply.

**U·nderra·te,** *v.* [UNDER-[1] 10 a.]

†**1.** *trans.* To depreciate, lower. *Obs. rare.*

*a* **1623** BUCK *Rich. III*, III. (1646) 90 Dispatching Doctor William Warkam..to under-rate his credit with those Princes. **1649** LOVELACE *Poems* 69 He..under-rates himself below mankinde.

**2.** To assess or tax († lower or) too low.

**1641** *Rates for Poll-money*, Such as are under-rated of what they were in the former Subsidies. **1753** *Act 26 Geo. II*, c. 17 § 14 As often as they shall find any Person..to have been under-rated.

**3.** To rate or estimate at too low a value or worth; to undervalue.

**1650** E. WILLIAMS *Virgo Triumphans* 3 Though Mr. Bullocke be pleased to under-rate it [*sc.* wheat] at halfe the crowne the bushell. **1712** STEELE *Spect.* No. 272 ¶ 1 [She] so over-valued her self and under-rated all her Pretenders. **1774** JEFFERSON *Autobiog.* App., Wks. 1859 I. 126 We do not, however, mean to underrate those aids. **1831** D. E. WILLIAMS *Life & Corr. Sir T. Lawrence* II. 393 In the following passage, Sir Thomas..greatly under-rates his own talents. **1869** TOZER *Highl. Turkey* II. 337 [They have] underrated the views of their opponents.

*refl.* **1854** WHATELY *Common-pl. Bk.* (1864) 150 And one condition, I think, of forgiveness is to appear, or at least pretend to underrate yourself. **1863** COWDEN CLARKE *Shaks. Char.* x. 246 Helena's affection prompts her to *over*rate the man she loves, and to *under*rate herself.

**4.** To under-estimate in amount or extent.

**1691** NORRIS *Pract. Disc.* 35 He made an interest with his Lord's Debtors, by under-rating their Accounts. **1802** PLAYFAIR *Illustr. Hutton. Th.* 348 If we call it one fourth of the whole surface, its extent is certainly not under-rated. **1844** KINGLAKE *Eothen* iii, I had enormously misjudged its distance and underrated its height. *a* **1862** BUCKLE *Misc. Wks.* (1872) I. 358 Nearly every author I have seen, underrates the consumption of wheat in England during the middle ages.

Hence **U·nderra·ting** *vbl. sb.* and *ppl. a.* Also **U·nderra·tement.**

**1599** DANIEL *Musoph.* Wks. (1602) C ij b, Bring not downe the prizes of the minde With vnder-rating of your selues so base. **1708** *Brit. Apollo* No. 76. 1/1 Affront him not by an Under-ratement of his Merits. **1721** E. ERSKINE *Wks.* (1791) 78/1 It implies low and under-rating thoughts of ourselves.

**Underrea·ch,** *v.* [UNDER-[1] 4 a, 8 a.]

†**1.** *trans.* To stretch below. *Obs.*

**1578** BANISTER *Hist. Man* VII. 90 [The] Membran to all the ribbes..and to the whole brest bone vnderreached, and coueryng the bodyes of the Vertebres.

**2.** To entrap or defraud by stealth. *rare*[—1].

*a* **1652** BROME *Mad Couple* II. i, Your hopes are vaine..in seating mee here to overreach or underreach any body.

**U·nder-rea·der.** (UNDER-[1] 6 a.) **1706** PHILLIPS (ed. Kersey), *Sub-Reader*, an Under-Reader in one of the Inns of Court. **U·nder-realm.** (UNDER-[1] 6 b.) **1591** SYLVESTER *Yvry* 481 When Nile and Euphrate, as her under-Realms, Through fruitfull Plains roul'd tributary streams. **U·nder-recei·ver.** (UNDER-[1] 6 a.) **1579** *Reg. Privy Council Scot.* III. 143 Collectour-generall of the thriddis of benefices.., and..his under ressaver. **1651** in Peterkin *Orkney & Zetl.* (1822) I. 104 One to be chamberlain thereof and another to be under receiver of the rents.

**U·nder-re·ckon,** *v.* (UNDER-[1] 10 a.)

**1629** BP. HALL *Serm.* Wks. 1837 V. 354 So Suidas underreckons it by seven years. **1655** STANLEY *Hist. Philos.* I. 29 Laertius under-reckons him to have lived but eighty seven years. *Ibid.* 35 This lustration of the Citty, Eusebius under-reckons. **1876** *Whitby Gloss.* 205 *Under-reckon'd*, pp. undervalued.

**U·nder-re·gion.** (UNDER-[1] 5 b.) **1727** WATTS '*Eternal Wisdom*' iv, Those Under-regions of the Skies Thy num'rous Glories show.

**U·nder-re·nted,** *ppl. a.* (UNDER-[1] 10 a.)

**1801** *Farmer's Mag.* Nov. 448 A small piece of ground may serve as an object of convenience, seldom of profit, unless it is under-rented. **1898** *Westm. Gaz.* 17 Mar. 2/3 An independent valuer..reported that Mr. Morris was under-rented to the extent of £82 a year!

**U·nder-re·nting,** *vbl. sb.* (UNDER-[1] 10 b.) *a* **1635** NAUNTON *Fragm. Reg.* (Arb.) 22 One Carwarden..presented her with a paper, shewing how she was abused in the under-renting of her Customes.

**U·nder-ri·pe,** *a.* (UNDER-[1] 10 c.)
1707 MORTIMER *Husb.* 127 You must be very cautious.. that neither the Stalk nor Seed be under-ripe. 1778 [W. H. MARSHALL] *Minutes Agric.* 22 Aug. 1776, As I mean..to sow pea-beans for the sake of the halm,..I will, at all events, cut them under-ripe.

**U·nder-roa·rer.** (UNDER-[1] 6 a.) 1713 *Guardian* No. 124 ¶ 2 'Tis my Request, that I may be instituted his Under-roarer in this University, Town, and County of Cambridge.

**U·nder-roa·st,** *v.* (UNDER-[1] 10 a.)
1584 COGAN *Haven Health* 116 Mutton, contrarie to veale, should be rather vnder rosted than ouer. 1732 MANDEVILLE *Enq. Origin Honour* p. viii, It is wrong to under-roast Mutton for People who love to have their Meat well done. 1899 *Westm. Gaz.* 24 July 3/1 If it tastes of the raw berry (as Egyptian coffee generally does), it is under-roasted.

**U·nder-robe.** (UNDER-[1] 5 a.)
1725 POPE *Odyss.* v. 297 An under robe, unbound, In snowy waves flow'd glitt'ring on the ground. 1797 HOLCROFT tr. *Stolberg's Trav.* (ed. 2) IV. xci. 37 He..appeared in his underrobe. *a* 1802 *Duel of Wharton & Stuart* I. iii. in Scott *Minstrelsy*, Say, have you got no armour on? Have you no under robe of steel? 1907 *Westm. Gaz.* 6 Sept. 10/2 An under-robe of very rich purple cloth.

**U·nder-rogue.** (UNDER-[1] 6 a.) 1706 E. WARD *Wooden World Diss.* (1708) 58 Were it not for this Under-Rogue, and his Superiors, he would be a very rich Fellow.

**U·nder-ro·lling,** *ppl. a.* [UNDER-[1] 4 a.] Having an underswell.
1745 P. THOMAS *Jrnl. Anson's Voy.* 114 We found a large under-rolling sea.

**U·nder-roof.** (UNDER-[1] 5 b.) 1611 FLORIO, *Sotto cielo*, an vnder-roofe or testerne. 1830 TENNYSON *Dying Swan* i, The plain was..open to the air, Which had built up everywhere An under-roof of doleful gray. **U·nder-room.** (UNDER-[1] 5 b.) 1597 [see UNCHILDLY *a.*]. 1603 DANIEL *Def. Rhime* H 3 b, My ignorance, that hath set me in so lowe an vnder-roome of conceipt with other men.

**Under-roo·ted,** *ppl. a.* (UNDER-[1] 4 a.)
1485 CAXTON *Chas. Gt.* 210 The bowes & leues, wyth whyche the leues [? *read* speres] were planted and vnder-roted.

**U·nder-row·er.** [UNDER-[1] 6 a, after Gr. ὑπηρέτης, f. ὑπό under + ἐρέτης rower.] (See quots.)
1647 TRAPP *Comm. 1 Cor.* iv. 1 *Ministers of Christ* Gr. *Under-rowers* to Christ the Master pilot. 1655 FULLER *Ch. Hist.* IX. vii. § 23. 1796 J. BENSON in R. Treffry *Mem.* (1840) 221 The ministers of the Gospel..are under-rowers in that vessel of which Christ is the Pilot.

**U·nder-ru·ler.** (UNDER-[1] 6 a.) 1625 SANDERSON *Serm.* I. 120 At His command Moses striketh the rulers; and at Moses his command, the under-rulers must strike..those that had offended.

**U·nderrun,** *sb.* [UNDER-[1] 5 b.] An under-current.
1894 *Pall Mall Mag.* Nov. 381 You may..watch her little shape soar to the underrun of a billow. 1898 *Geogr. Jrnl.* March 291 The discovery of the underrun of the Hudson.

**Underru·n,** *v.* [UNDER-[1] 4 a, b. Cf. OE. *underirnan.*]

**1.** *trans.* To run, flow, or pass beneath.
1594 KYD *Cornelia* IV. ii. 47 Those braue Germains..Beheld the swift Rheyn vnder-run mine Ensignes. 1681 T. FLATMAN *Heraclitus Ridens* No. 13 (1713) I. 86 These fruitful Meadows came to be stock'd and under-run with those subterranean Inhabitants, vulgarly called Moles. 1799 W. TOOKE *View Russian Emp.* I. 157 The granite is under-run by schistose earth. 1855 MAURY *Phys. Geog. Sea* i. § 14 One part of it underruns the Gulf Stream. 1880 BLACKMORE *Mary Anerley* III. vii. 94 A scowl of dark vapour came over the headlands, and under-ran the solid snow-clouds.
*fig.* 1882 W. B. WEEDEN *Soc. Law Labor* 68 The principle ..underran all these modifications.

**2.** *Naut.* **a.** To overhaul or examine (a cable, etc.) on the under side, *spec.* by drawing a boat along under it.
1547 *Admiralty Crt. Oyer & Terminer* 73 No. 21, They toke ye kabyll in the botts hed and under rynned ye kabyll tyll yt was a pyke. 1633 T. JAMES *Voy.* 79 We vnder-run our small Cable. 1667 LD. BROUNCKER *Let. to Pepys* 3 July, Not only in my own opinion is the chain broke,..yet we could nether spare hands nor lighter to underrunn it. 1745 P. THOMAS *Jrnl. Anson's Voy.* 156 They..underran the Cables by which..[the ship] rode. 1798 *Hull Advertiser* 25 Aug. 3/2 The harbour..is..very rocky, the bottom so much so as to make it necessary to under-run every cable. 1834 MARRYAT *P. Simple* viii, Oblige me by under-running the guess warp. 1867 SMYTH *Sailor's Word-bk.* 706.

**b.** (See quot.)
1769 FALCONER *Dict. Marine* (1780), *To under-run a tackle*, is to separate the several parts of which it is composed, and range them in order, from one block to the other.

**c.** To pull in (a net or trawl) in order to clear it of the catch and reset it.
1883 JONCAS *Fisheries Canada* 30 As soon as the seals are caught in the meshes, the men under-run the nets. 1897 KIPLING *Capt. Cour.* 101 Underrunning a trawl means pulling it in on one side of the dory, picking off the fish, rebaiting the hooks, and passing them back to the sea again.

**3.** In *pa. pple.* (See quot. 1855.)
1855 *Jrnl. R. Agric. Soc.* XVI. I. 9 Cut away all hoof that is separated from the sensitive parts, or, as a shepherd would say, as much as is 'under-run'. 1908 *Animal Managem.* 337 Any horn [of an ox-hoof] which is underrun should be removed.

**U·nder-ru·nner.** [UNDER-[1] 4 b, 10 b.]

**1.** *Printing.* (See quot. 1888.)
1882 SOUTHWARD *Pract. Printing* (1884) 249 Underrunners ..are very unsightly and should be avoided. 1888 JACOBI *Printers' Vocab.*, *Under runners*, continuation of side-notes run under the foot of the page in a similar manner to a footnote.

**2.** *Cricket.* A batsman who makes too few runs for his hits.
1903 *Windsor Mag.* Sept. 394/1 Marshall, a confirmed under-runner at the best, was so nervous..that he crawled between the wickets.

**U·nder-ru·nning,** *ppl. a.* (UNDER- 4 a.) *a* 1586 SIDNEY *Arcadia* II. xvii, Her teares falling into the water, one might have thought, that she began meltingly to be metamorphosed to the under-running river.

† **Under-sail,** *v.*: see UNDER-[1] 2.

**U·nder-sai·led,** *ppl. a.* (UNDER-[1] 10 a.) 1594 [see UNDER-MASTED *ppl. a.*].

† **U·nder-sa·ker.** *Obs.*[−1] [UNDER-[1] 6 b.] A small variety of cannon.
1678 EARL ORRERY in *Cal. Ormonde MSS.* (N.S.) IV. 104 The lesser guns, as sakers and under-sakers.

**Under-salley:** see SALLY *sb.*[2], quot. 1688.
1668 [STEDMAN] *Tintinnalogia* (1671) 3 Next, that he [a young ringer] know how to Ring Round, or Under-Sally.

**U·nder-satisfa·ction.** (UNDER-[1] 6 b.) 1748 RICHARDSON *Clarissa* (1811) II. 65 That a person who has any over-ruling passion, will compound by giving up twenty secondary or under-satisfactions,..in order to have that gratified. 1871 MRS. WHITNEY *We Girls* v. 96 The work was getting on; that was such an undersatisfaction.

**U·nder-saw·yer.** [UNDER-[1] 6 a.] A subordinate or inferior person. (Cf. TOP-SAWYER.)
1865 DICKENS *Mut. Fr.* I. xii, There were no top-sawyers, every passenger was an under-sawyer.

† **Undersay·,** *v. Obs.* [UNDER-[1] 8 a.] *trans.* To say by way of answer.
1579 SPENSER *Sheph. Cal.* Sept. 91 They saye they con to heauen the high way, But by my soule I dare vndersaye, They neuer sette foote in that same troade.

**U·nder-school.** [UNDER-[1] 6 b. Cf. MDu. *onderscole.*] A (or the) lower or junior school.
1629 WADSWORTH *Pilgr.* iii. 15 After which time..the Students of the three vnder schooles go vp to those of the vpper. *a* 1633 W. AUSTIN *Medit.* (1635) 226 Such Societies are not Separations from the great Congregation, but parts of it, and as it were so many Vnder-schooles. 1843 THACKERAY *FitzBoodle P.*, *Mr. & Mrs. Berry* i, It was agreed that it [*sc.* the combat] should take place behind the under-school in the shade.

**U·nderscore,** *sb.* [UNDER-[1] 4 d.] A line drawn below (a word, etc.).
1901 *Phonetic Jrnl.* 4 May 288/1 The correct way of representing italicized words..is to use the underscore.

**Undersco·re,** *v.* [UNDER-[1] 4 a.] *trans.* To draw a score or line beneath; to underline.
1771 LUCKOMBE *Hist. Print.* 249 [They] either underscore the word, or make some other token, which may inform the Compositor of the Author's intention. 1838 LYTTON *Alice* XI. v, The notice to Howard, with the name of Vargrave underscored, was still on the panels. 1874 BLACKIE *Self-Cult.* 35 Underscore these distinctly with pen or pencil.
*fig.* 1891 W. S. GILBERT *Rosencrantz & G.* III, He who doth so mark, label, and underscore his antic speeches.
Hence **Undersco·red** *ppl. a.*, **-sco·ring** *vbl. sb.*
1847 KINGLAKE *Eothen* viii. 101 *note*, The underscoring of the word 'ancient', is by the writer of the letter. 1865 *Sat. Rev.* 4 Mar. 243 The underscored passages in the favourite sermon. 1871 LOWELL *Study Wind.* (1886) 165 An emphasis out of place..reminds one of the underscorings in young ladies' letters.

**U·nder-scribe.** (UNDER-[1] 6 a.) 1610 B. JONSON *Alch.* I. ii, No cheating Clim-o'the-Clovghs,..Nor any melancholike vnder-scribe, Shall tell the Vicar.

† **Underscri·ber.** *Obs.* [Cf. UNDER-[1] 4 a, and older Du. *onderschrijver.*] One whose name is written or given below; a subscriber to a document.
1681 in Grant *Burgh Sch. Scot.* (1876) II. iii. 136 We underscribers, keepers of Latin Schools, bind and oblige ourselves, that [etc.]. 1687 *Lond. Gaz.* No. 2270/3 In Testification hereof, we Underscribers..Subscribed as followeth. *c* 1785 J. BROWN (Haddington) *Sel. Rem.* (1807) 235 We underscribers having formed ourselves into a Society.

**U·nderscrub.** [UNDER-[1] 5 d.]

**1.** An undergrown or insignificant person.
1822 *Blackw. Mag.* XI. 362* The less you have to do with the Cockney underscrubs the better.

**2.** Undergrowth; brushwood.
1894 J. GEIKIE *Gt. Ice Age* (ed. 3) 455 The underscrub being composed chiefly of hazels and occasional birches. 1895 *Daily News* 21 May 6/3 They had been unable to commence cultivation until a clearance had been made of the underscrub.
Hence **U·nderscru·bbery**, a collection of underscrubs.
1851 G. W. CURTIS *Nile Notes* xxv. 116, I saw the Commander assisting the confused crowd of under-scrubbery out of the boat, with his kurbash or whip.

**U·nder-sea,** *sb. rare*[−1]. [UNDER-[1] 5 b.] An underlying sea.
1621 G. SANDYS *Ovid's Met.* XI. (1626) 220 High Tmolus with a steepe ascent vnfolds His rigid browes, and vnder-seas beholds.

**U·nder-sea,** *a.* [UNDER-[2]. Cf. Du. *onderzee-*, G. *untersee-(boot).*]

**1.** Situated or lying below the sea or the surface of the sea; submarine.
1613 PURCHAS *Pilgrimage* V. xiii. 511 The saltnesse of the sea some ascribe..to vnder-earth or under-sea fires of bituminous nature. 1851 *Chamb. Jrnl.* 27 Dec. 411 Mr. Wheatstone first conceived the possibility of an under-sea telegraph in 1837. 1861 L. L. NOBLE *Icebergs* 256 The noises of the waves at play in the long, concealed, under-sea piazzas.

**2.** Intended for use below the surface of the sea.
1901 *Westm. Gaz.* 27 Aug. 5/3 The new submarines will be as good as..any under-sea vessel yet constructed.

**Undersea·,** *adv.* [UNDER-[2].] Below the sea or its surface.
1684 [see UNDERGROUND *adv.* 1]. 1890 R. BRIDGES *Achilles in Scyros* 2 This rocky isle, That far from undersea riseth to crown Its flowery head above the circling waves.

**Undersea·rch,** *v. rare.* [UNDER-[1] 4 a, b, 8 a.] To search or seek under or into; to investigate.
1609 DANIEL *Civ. Wars* III. iv, Whil'st th' vnder-searching water, working-on, Beares (proudly) downe, all that was idly don. 1648 HEXHAM II, *Ondertasten*, to Examine, or Vndersearch.

**U·nder-sea·ted,** *ppl. a.* (UNDER-[1] 4 a.)
*c* 1611 CHAPMAN *Iliad* XV. 208 All The under-seated Deities that circle Saturn's fall, Had heard of me.

**U·nder-se·cretary.** (UNDER-[1] 6 a. Cf. G. *untersecretär*, Sw. *undersekreter.*)
Used esp. as the specific title of a secretary immediately subordinate to, or ranking below, a principal secretary of state.
1687 MIÈGE I, *Sou-Secretaire*, an Vnder-Secretary. 1692 LUTTRELL *Brief Rel.* (1857) II. 372 Said, Mr. Poultney goes undersecretary to Ireland. 1764 in *10th Rep. Hist. MSS. Comm.* App. I. 376, I have known a great many under-secretaries. 1841 *Penny Cycl.* XXI. 176/2 Each [secretary] is assisted by two under-secretaries of state. 1876 BANCROFT *Hist. U. S.* III. xiii. 191 Consulted through the under-secretaries, Franklin gave advice on the conduct of the..war.
Hence **U·nder-se·cretaryship.**
1687 MIÈGE *Gt. Fr. Dict.* II. 1859 LEVER *Dav. Dunn* lxiii, He might..mayhap have held some Lordship of This or Under-Secretaryship of That.

**U·nder-sect.** (UNDER-[1] 6 b.) 1653 JER. TAYLOR *Serm. for Year* I. xxii. 277 The whole religion which..hath been rent into innumerable sects, and under-sects. 1682 T. FLATMAN *Heraclitus Ridens* No. 65, What the Under-sects might have claim'd upon the score of their wanting Opportunity only ..to do Mischief. **U·nder-see·dman.** (UNDER-[1] 6 a.) 1615–6 BOYS *Wks.* (1622) 203 The Preacher is not properly the sower, but the seedcod, at most an vnderseedman.

† **Undersee·k,** *v. Obs.* Also 4 onderzeke. [OE. *undersēcan* (see UNDER- 8 a and SEEK *v.*), = OLFrank. *undersuocan* (Du. *onderzoeken*), MHG. *undersuochen* (G. *untersuchen*), Sw. *undersöka*, Da. *-søge.*] *trans.* To search into; to investigate; to seek out.
*c* 897 K. ÆLFRED *Gregory's Past. C.* xiii. 79 Ðæt is ðæt hie ðara ðing ðe him underðiodde bioð..inweardlice undersece. 13.. *Guy Warw.* (A.) 1838 Wiþ þat come Sadok prikeing, Þe douke Segyn vnder-secheing. 1340 *Ayenb.* 184 Huo þet heþ þise yefþe, he onderzekþ þe redes þet me him yefþ, and þengþ mid greate beþenchinge..yef me him ret wel.

**Underse·ll,** *v.* [UNDER-[1] 8 b, 10 a. Cf. Da. *undersælge*, Sw. *-sälja.*]

**1.** *trans.* To sell at a lower price than (another person); to cut out by selling at a lower rate.
1622 MALYNES *Anc. Law-Merch.* 230 The striuing of making commodities, and to vndersel one another, are dangerous. 1677 YARRANTON *Eng. Improv.* 115 Whereby the Manufacture is always cheaply done, and thereby hath the advantage of sending it to foreign Markets, and under-sell others. 1713 *Mercator* No. 9/1 The French being able to Underwork us, will also Undersell us. 1799 J. ROBERTSON *Agric. Perth* 213 The price of labour will become so enormous that we shall soon be undersold in every market. 1849–50 ALISON *Hist. Eur.* XIV. xcv. § 96. 192 England, which can easily undersell India in cotton manufacture,..finds its cultivators undersold by Poland and America with grain. 1884 *Law Times Rep.* 31 May 421/1 The defendants are selling cheaper materials and underselling the plaintiffs.

**b.** *transf.* (Said of the thing sold.)
1757 *Refl. Importation Bar-Iron* 12 The American Iron will always greatly undersell the British at Market. 1792 A. YOUNG *Trav. France* 262 England buys the French cotton, and works it into fabrics that undersell those of France.

**2.** To sell (a commodity) at too low a price. Also *fig.*
1647 N. WARD *Simple Cobler* 47 Just it is that such as undersell them, should not re-inherit them in haste. 1662 PETTY *Taxes* 20 The farmer for haste is forced to under-sell his corn. 1692 LYTTELTON in *Hatton Corr.* (Camden) II. 169 As to my pictures,..I doubt those of more esteeme will not be very ready money, unlesse mitily undersold. 1817 MILL *Brit. India* II. v. iv. 469 They accused the Presidency of underselling the lands. 1854 PATMORE *Angel in Ho.*, *Betrothal* 99 But lofty honours undersold Seller and buyer both disgrace.
Hence **Underse·ller; Underse·lling** *vbl. sb.* and *ppl. a.*
1672 PETTY *Pol. Anat.* (1691) 75 The Interest must enflame the price of Irish Commodities, and consequently give to other Nations the means of underselling. 1842 J. F. WATSON *Ann. Pennsylv.* (1877) I. 242 All prices were alike;..there was no motive to run about town to seek out undersellers. 1863 WYNTER *Subtle Brains*, etc. 377 The under-seller, however, manages to turn out from ninety-four to ninety-six [loaves]. 1899 *Westm. Gaz.* 16 Feb. 2/3 We doubt if the underselling foreigner could be kept out by such artificial manipulations of the market.

**U·nder-sense.** (UNDER-[1] 9.) 1805 WORDSW. *Prelude* VII. 735 To him who looks In steadiness, who hath among least things An under-sense of greatest. 1859 D. MASSON *Brit. Novelists* i. 60 Apart from the allegoric undersense..the romance is praised as a really interesting story. **U·nder-se·quence.** (UNDER-[1] 6 b.) 1863 'CAVENDISH' *Whist* (ed. 5) 19 Sequences which do not head a suit in a hand are called under sequences. *Ibid.* 24 When an under sequence is formed by intermediate cards.

**U·nder-se·rvant.** (UNDER-[1] 6 a.)
1548 ELYOT, *Subministrator*, an vnder seruaunt. 1630 tr. *Camden's Hist. Eliz.* IV. 132 One of the ordinary sort of men,.. hauing beene..an vnder-seruant in the Queenes stable. 1679 BP. CROFT *Coll. Jesuits* 3 The remaining Dwellers in the House..were but Under-Servants. 1768 *Phil. Trans.* LIX. 10 An under-servant in a gentleman's kitchen. 1809 MALKIN *Gil Blas* III. iii. ¶ 4 The steward..loves to see the under-servants creeping and crawling at his feet. 1871 W. ALEXANDER *Johnny Gibb* xlv, I ken my place better nor be forespoken by ony oon'er-servan'.

**Underse·rve,** *v.* [UNDER-¹ 8 a, 10 a. Cf. *underserve* s.v. UNDER-¹ 2.]

†**1.** To be subservient (to). *Obs.*

**1611** SPEED *Hist. Gt. Brit.* IX. vii. § 1 Things which did but onely vnder-serue, and conduce to the..principall end.

**2.** To serve insufficiently.

**1710** PALMER *Proverbs* 147 He, that over-works a servant to day, must be content to be under-serv'd to morrow.

**U·nder-se·rvice.** [UNDER-¹ 6 b.] Service of an inferior kind; subordinate service.

**1598** FLORIO, *Sumministratione*, a subministration,..an vnderseruice. **1641** MILTON *Ch. Govt.* II. Wks. 1851 III. 149 But were it the meanest under-service, if God by his Secretary conscience injoyn it, it were sad for me if I should draw back. **1760–72** H. BROOKE *Fool of Qual.* (1809) III. 4 Will you not suffer a sister..who may assist in the under-services to the servants of our Master?

**U·nderset,** *sb.* [UNDER-¹ 5 b, 6 a.]

†**1.** *Sc.* = UNDERSETTLE. *Obs. rare.*

**1509** *Reg. Privy Seal Scotl.* 285/1 To be haldin and to be had to him and his assignais,..subtenentis and undersettis under thaim in all or in parte. *Ibid.* 288/1.

**2.** *Mining.* A lower vein of ore.

**1747** HOOSON *Miner's Dict.* S 2 b, These Levells are called Sets, as the first is the Top-Set, the second which is found out by Sinking through the Deadness, is called the Under-Set.

**3.** An undercurrent. (See first quot.)

**1815** BURNEY *Falconer's Marine Dict., Under-set*, a motion of the water beneath the surface, produced by the wind impelling the upper part directly upon the shore of a bay, whereby the water..necessarily takes a direction contrary to the wind,..below the surface. **1867** SMYTH *Sailor's Word-bk.* 706 The *resaca*, or underset, is particularly dangerous on those beaches where heavy surf prevails.

**Underse·t,** *v.* [UNDER-¹ 4 a, etc. Cf. MDu. *ondersetten* (Du. *-zetten*), MLG. *undersetten*, MHG. *undersetzen* (G. *unter-*), MDa. *undersætte.*]

**1.** *trans.* To support or strengthen by means of something (esp. of the nature of a post or prop) placed beneath; to prop up.

*c* **1220** *Bestiary* 640 Ðe hunte haueð biholden ðis,..Saȝeð ðis tre and under-set, o ðe wise ðat he mai bet. *a* **1225** *Ancr. R.* 254 A treou þet wule uallen, me underset hit mid on oðer treou, & hit stont feste. **13..** *Seuyn Sages* (W.) 2101 We schulle the ymage so undersette, That we ne schal hit nothing lette. **1398** TREVISA *Barth. De P. R.* XVII. clxiv. (Bodl. MS.), Ofte it nedeþ to vndersette it wiþ a pelere or a poste. *c* **1425** *St. Eliz. of Spalbeck* in *Anglia* VIII. 115/28 Hir sistres..lifte vp and vndir-sette hir..wiþ two pilouès. **1477–9** *Rec. St. Mary at Hill* (1905) 90, ij postes of tymbir to vndirsette the kechyng. **1513** MORE *Rich. III* (1883) 9 The kynge liftinge vppe himself and vndersette with pillowes. **1555** WATREMAN *Fardle Facions* II. x. 214 Thei make theim ..rounde cotages of wickres, or of Felte vndersette with smothe poles. **1600** SURFLET *Countrie Farme* I. x. 48 He shall prepare props..to vnder set his vines. **1678** [BP. J. WILLIAMS] *Hist. Gunp. Treason* 22 A Bag of Powder..that they underset the Pan with. **1841** *Civil Eng. & Arch. Jrnl.* IV. 379/1 The base..has been underset with two pillars of solid masonry. **1842** FRANCIS *Dict. Arts* s.v., The Custom House, London, was underset some years ago, a new foundation having been made to it without the superstructure being disturbed.

*absol.* **1538** in *Lett. Suppression Monast.* (Camden) 181, x of them hewed the walles abowte, amonge the whych ther were 3 carpentars: thiese made proctes to undersette wher the other cutte away.

**b.** To serve as a support to. Also *absol. rare.*

*c* **1330** R. BRUNNE *Chron. Wace* (Rolls) 284 Þe hil was so hey, as men hit leet [*v.r.* lette], þat heuen (men seye) hit vnder-feet [*v.r.* vnder sette]. *c* **1400** *Lanfranc's Cirurg.* 110 Þo boonys þat vndir setten ben clepid ossa mendosa. **1609** DANIEL *Civ. Wars* VIII. xxvi, She had of fatall Lancaster Seene all the pillars crusht and ruined, That vnder-set it.

†**c.** To support or sustain by assistance. *Obs.*

**1388** WYCLIF *Eccl.* iv. 10 If oon fallith doun, he schal be vndurset [L. *fulcietur*] of the tothere. **1398** TREVISA *Barth. De P. R.* XII. ix. (Tollem. MS.), Whan þe fader and þe moder wexeþ olde and feble, þan þe ȝonge crowes under-setteþ hem and rereþ hem with hire owen wynges.

**d.** To act upon, furnish, fasten, etc., with something placed beneath. *rare.*

*a* **1547** SURREY *Æneid* II. 50 Capys..wild it to drown, or vnderset with flame The suspect present of the Grekes deceit. **1599** *Minutes Archdeaconry Colchester* (MS.) fol. 238 He and they did vndersett the churchdore. *c* **1618** MORYSON *Itin.* IV. 381 The ringe of her dore is all Couered with tape or linnen cloth (and in some places vndersett with a small sticke).

**2.** *fig.* To support, sustain, or strengthen.

**1395** PURVEY *Remonstr.* (1851) 86 Bi here owne statute,.. vndirset with ful strong oth and peynis. *a* **1470** H. PARKER *Dives & Pauper* (W. de W. 1496) A v b/2 Whan youth is vndersette with richesse, & is at his owne rule without drede of punysshyng. **1538** TINDALE *Exp. 1st Ep. John* v. 72 Yf oure soules be truely vnderset wyth sure hope. **1579** W. WILKINSON *Confut. Fam. Love* 38 Vnles the Lord vnderset them, their fall is..greeuous. **1605** RALEIGH *Introd. Hist. Eng.* (1693) 74 Our most renowned Kings have been best underset with Counsel. **1670** CUDWORTH *Serm.* 1 *John* ii. 3–4 (ed.2) 85 If we would but vnderset it [truth] with the Holinesse of our Hearts. **1871** L. MORRIS *Songs Two Worlds, Wand. Soul* xxxiii, The archetypes which underset the world With one broad perfect Law.

**3.** To set or place (a thing) under something else.

*a* **1340** HAMPOLE *Psalter* xxxvi. 25 When a rightwis has fallen he sall not be hurt, for lord vndirsettis his hand. **1388** WYCLIF *Gen.* xlix. 15 Isachar..vndirsettide his schuldre to bere. **1535** COVERDALE 1 *Kings* vii. 30 Vpon the foure corners there were proppes molten,..vnderset vnto the kettell. **1587** GOLDING *De Mornay* xxi. 376 Iulian the Apostata did vnderset his shoulder, to shore vp the seruice of the false Gods. **1611** SPEED *Hist. Gt. Brit.* VI. xxiii. § 9. 113 His monyes, whereon he sometimes formed a Trophy.. vndersetting the word Vict. Brit. **1898** E. GLANVILLE *Kloof Bride* xvii, While Miles pressed the rock forward, Hans kept it from swinging back by undersetting a stone.

†**b.** To place in subjection. *Obs.*⁻¹

**1422** YONGE *Secreta Secret.* 146 If þou wilt submyt or vndreset al thyngis to the, submyt thy-selfe to reysone.

†**4.** *Sc.* To beset. *Obs.*⁻¹

*c* **1470** HENRY *Wallace* IX. 796 With Sotheroun sone we sall be wndirset.

**5.** To sublet.

**1804** MAR. EDGEWORTH *Ennui* viii, These middle-men will underset the land, and live in idleness.

Hence **U·nderset** *ppl. a.*

**1833–4** J. PHILLIPS *Geol.* in *Encycl. Metrop.* (1845) VI. 588 In Swaledale the united thickness of the underset chert and underset lime..is nearly constant. **1865** LIVINGSTONE *Zambesi* xvii. 344 It contrives to pop its underset mouth directly over the unlucky victim.

**Underse·tter.** [f. UNDERSET *v.*] One who or that which supports or upholds. Also *fig.*

*c* **1400** *Lanfranc's Cirurg.* 110 Þe whiche þat beþ vndire-setterys to þo bonys þat beþ y-clepyde *nerualia*. *c* **1430** *Pilgr. Lyf Manhode* II. cxxvi. (1869) 123 J am to orguill an vnder-settere and a susteynour by especial. **1537** BIBLE (Matthew's) 1 *Kings* vii. 30 In yᵉ foure corners were vndersetters vnder the lauatorye. **1651** N. BACON *Disc. Govt. Eng.* II. vi. 60 Outward Power, and Honourable places, are but under-setters, or props to this Gourd of Prelacy. **1697** JOS. WOODWARD *Relig. Soc.* ii. (1701) 28 Undersetters, whom gain and the promises of court-favour had brought over to their party.

**Underse·tting,** *vbl. sb.* [f. as prec.]

**1.** A support or prop; a supporting or sustaining structure. Also *fig.*

**1388** WYCLIF *Ezek.* xli. 26 In the litle vndursettyngis of the porche. *c* **1440** *Promp. Parv.* 448/1 Schore, undur settynge of a thynge þat wolde falle, *suppositorium*. **1587** GOLDING *De Mornay* ix. 149 Their opinion was, that God was afore the World, howbeit not in time, but in order and by way of vndersetting only. **1624** WOTTON *Archit.* 32 They haue all their Vnder-settings, or Pedistals, in height a third part of the whole Columne. **1841** *Penny Cycl.* XIX. 253/1 The rock was supported by an under-setting of masonry.

**2.** The action of placing under, or of supporting by something placed under; underpinning.

*c* **1440** *Promp. Parv.* 511/2 Vndersettynge, *idem quod* vnderputtynge. **1598** FLORIO, *Soggiontione*, an vndersetting or ioining vnderneath. **1842** FRANCIS *Dict. Arts, Under-setting*, the supporting a wall or edifice..after the lower part has been removed.

**U·nderse·ttle.** *Obs.* exc. *Hist.* Also 3 -setle, 5 *Sc.* undirsettill, -sedell, wndersedyll, 6 *Sc.* vndersittell. [f. UNDER-¹ 6 a + *-settle*, *-setle*, repr. OE. *-setla* (see COTSETLA), f. *set-*, root of SIT *v.*] One who occupies a house (or part of one) held by another; a subtenant.

**1235–52** *Rentalia Glaston.* (Somerset Rec. Soc.) 108 Si famulus vel famula vel undersetles venerint, quisque dabit ob. per diem. **1326** in *Court Baron* (Selden Soc.) 146 [Strangers coming from without, who hire houses from divers persons and hold nothing of the lord,..called] Undersettles. **1476** *Peebles Burgh Rec.* (1872) 178 Grantand to..George Robyson fwll power to mak rasonabyll tenandis and wndersedyllis. **1480** *Exchequer Rolls Scotl.* IX. 30 De dicto loco de Farnele de anno elapso pro uno undirsettill,..xx s. **1510** in C. Rogers *Coldstream Chartul.* (1879) 58 With power to mak subtenentis and vndersittellis. **1607** *N. Riding Rec.* (1884) I. 95 Leon. Marshall of Ravensworth [presented] for keeping an undersettle for the space of a moneth. **1612** *Ibid.* 266 John Herdman..for keeping an undersettle in the house wherein one Will. Dynnis now dwelleth. **1781–** *Parish Terriers, Welton* (Yks.), For every messuage or cottage.. six pence and for every under-settle three pence.

So **U·nderse·ttler; U·nderse·ttling** *vbl. sb., ppl. a.*

**1576** *E. Worsely's MS. Surv. Mannor of Felsted, Essex* 47 It was granted to one John Lord..by vertue of a coppy of undersetling made thereof to the said John. *Ibid.* 147 Every tenant customary commonly called an Undersetling tenant. **1794** W. HUTCHINSON *Hist. Cumbld.* I. 163 *note*, The tenants are subject to pains..for taking in inmates or undersettlers.

**U·nder-sew·er.** (UNDER-¹ 6 a.) **1669** *Lond. Gaz.* No. 414/2 Segnior Potoski the under Sewer to the Crown.

**U·nder-se·xton.** (UNDER-¹ 6 a.)

*c* **1450** [see UNDER-CHAMBRESS]. **1722** DE FOE *Plague* (1756) 105 Under-Sexton of the Parish of St. Stephen...By Under-Sexton, was understood at that Time Grave-digger and Bearer of the Dead. **1829** LYTTON *Devereux* II. ii, I was ..the under-sexton of St. Paul's, Covent-Garden.

†**Undershad,** *pa. pple. Obs.* [UNDER-¹ 4 a; the second element may be *shod.*] Faced at the bottom.

**1528** *Lett. & Pap. Hen. VIII*, IV. II. 2228 The brayes about the towne [Calais] to be mended and heythed and under shadd with stone or brike.

**Undersha·pen,** *ppl. a.* [UNDER-¹ 10 a.] Insufficiently or imperfectly formed.

**1859** TENNYSON *Enid* 412 His dwarf, a vicious under-shapen thing, Struck at her with his whip.

**U·nder-she·pherd.** (UNDER-¹ 6 a.)

**1636** MASSINGER *Bashful Lover* III. i, I am no glutton, but an under-shepherd. **1669** PENN *No Cross* xii. § 8 [The Clergy] could be but Ministers, Stewards, and Under-Shepherds. *a* **1711** KEN *Hymnotheo* Poet. Wks. 1721 III. 385 Each Pastor,..Choice Under-Shepherds carefully ordain'd. **1826** MISS MITFORD *Village* Ser. II. (1863) 468 He had a pet sheep-dog, (for..he occasionally acted as under-shepherd). **1876** S. C. J. INGHAM *White Cross*, etc. xlvii, [The rector] had little idea of the true motive power which sustained his under-shepherd.

**U·ndershe·riff.** Forms: (see SHERIFF). [UNDER-¹ 6 a: cf. SHERIFF 2.] A deputy sheriff.

*a.* *a.* **1431** in Raine *Scriptores tres* (Surtees) App. p. ccxxi, Ye shall noon hafe to be your undershireve or clerk that was undershyreve or any of the Shyreves clerkes the last yere passed. **1452–3** *Paston Lett.* Suppl. (1901) 48 He schall non undirshireve, ne non othir officer make. **1535** COVERDALE 1 *Esdras* vi. 7 The vnder shreue in Syria and Phenices. **1558** in Strype *Eccl. Mem.* (1721) III. lxii. 457 The officers of this town..and the undershereve. **1631** LENTON *Charact.* G 3 b, An Vndershriefe..is the feare and terror of all debtors. *a* **1658** CLEVELAND *Poems, Young Man to Old Wom.* 35 Like Aldermen, or Under-shrieves With Canvas Backs, and Velvet-Sleeves.

*β.* **1444** *Rolls of Parlt.* V. 108/1 No Sherryff, ne Under Shereff, ne Clerk of the Sherryff. **1501** *Plumpton Corr.* (Camden) 159 Which Inpanell the sayd William Rossell had of the underschereffe of Nottingham. **1589** R. PAYNE *Briefe Descr. Ireland* 5 There is a sheriffe of euerie countie, with vndersheriffes. **1632** MASSINGER *City Madam* v. ii, An Under-sheriffe,..being well paid, will serve An extent on Lords or Lowns land. **1665** *Extr. St. Papers Friends* Ser. III. (1912) 240 The Bishop of Durham..nominates both high sheriffs and under sheriffs. **1723** in Harris *Life Ld. Hardwicke* (1847) I. 130 He made a speech at the gallows, and delivered a paper to the undersheriff. **1769** WESLEY *Jrnl.* 13 July, The Under-Sheriff had promised the use of the Town-hall. **1835** *App. Munic. Corpor. Rep.* III. 1991 (Nottingham), Officers of the corporation..[include] Two Sheriffs. An Under-Sheriff, who is also Steward. **1877** BURROUGHS *Taxation* 327 The under-sheriff cannot perform the duties of collector.

Hence **Undersheriffry, Undersheriffship, Undersheriffwick,** the office of an undersheriff.

*a* **1613** OVERBURY *A Wife*, etc. (1638) M 7 b, His honesty and learning bring him to Under-Shriveship. **1620** J. WILKINSON *Coroners & Sherifes* 50 All emoluments..to the office of sherifwicke or undersherifwicke belonging. **1625** BACON *Ess., Praise* (Arb.) 357 The Cardinals of Rome..call all Temporall..Emploiments, *Sbirrerie*; which is, Vnder Sheriffries;..Though many times, those Vndersheriffreries doe more good, then their High Speculations. [**1666** BP. PARKER *Platonic Philos.* 17 Being raised above the little concernments and under-Shreiveries of this life (as the Cardinals of Rome are pleased to stile all secular employments).] **1782** BURKE *Let. Penal Laws Rom. Cath.* Wks. 1792 III. 527 The exclusion from the law,..from sheriff-ships, and under-sheriff-ships. **1845** LD. CAMPBELL *Chancellors* I. 512 He declined a handsome pension.., which he could not hold without resigning his under-sheriffship.

**Undershi·ne,** *v.* [UNDER-¹ 4 c.] *trans.* To shine from below.

**1844** MRS. BROWNING *A Portrait* 11 A forehead fair and saintly, Which two blue eyes undershine.

**U·ndershi·ning,** *ppl. a.* [UNDER-¹ 7.] Of inferior brightness.

**1581** MULCASTER *Positions* xxxviii. 174 We haue besides her highnes as vndershining starres, many singuler ladies.

**U·ndershirt.** (UNDER-¹ 5 a. Cf. NFris. *onnersjürt*, Da. *underskjorte*, Sw. *-skjorta.*)

**1648** HEXHAM II, *Een Onder-hemde*, an Vnder-shirt. **1856** EMERSON *Eng. Traits, Aristocr.*, Older than all epics and histories, which clothe a nation, this undershirt sits close to the body. **1903** S. BROWN in F. W. H. Myers *Hum. Personality* I. 38 There was a sum of money in an inside pocket of his undershirt.

**Undershoe,ing**: see UNDERSOLING.

†**Undershoot,** *a. Obs. rare.* = UNDERSHOT *a.* 1.

**1602** CAREW *Surv. Cornwall* I. 26 b, So the imprisoned water payeth the ransome of dryuing an vnder-shoote wheele for his enlargement. **1678** *Patent Office* No. 208. 1 To Retayne Back Water of all sorts of Mills and..to make Vndershoote to serve Overshoote Mills.

**U·ndershoo·t,** *v.* [UNDER-¹ 10 a.] *trans.* and *intr.* To shoot short (of) or too low (for). Also *fig.*

*a* **1661** FULLER *Worthies, Lincoln.* II. (1662) 151, I believe they overshoot the Mark, who make it a Miracle, they undershoot it who make it Magick. **1874** J. W. LONG *Amer. Wild-fowl.* i. 24 The rib should be..sufficiently elevated at breech to prevent under-shooting. **1883** *Cent. Mag.* Aug. 492/1 The sportsman of unsteady nerve..is apt to undershoot. **1885** HORNADAY 2 *Yrs. in Jungle* xviii. 199, I..fired at his temple...Fool that I was, I undershot the brain because the elephant was below me.

**Undersho·re,** *v.* [UNDER-¹ 4 a. Cf. Du. and Flem. *onderschoren.*]

**1.** *trans.* To prop up; to support or strengthen with shores. Also in fig. context.

**1393** LANGL. *P. Pl.* C. XIX. 47 Ne were hit vnder-shored, certes hit sholde nat stande. *c* **1440** *Promp. Parv.* 511/1 Vndersettyn, or vnderschoryn, *fulcio, suffulcio.* **1532** MORE *Confut. Tindale* III. Wks. 473/2 He sheweth himself as wise, as one that lest hys rotten house should fall, wold.. pull vp ye groundsel to vndershore the sides with the same. **1583** H. HOWARD *Defensative* B iij b, A sillye proppe to vndershore the ruines of olde Adams walles. **1608** TOPSELL *Serpents* 72 To vnder-shore the ruinous walls. **1726** LEONI *Alberti's Archit.* II. 129 Undershore it with Levers made of strong beams. **1867** SMYTH *Sailor's Word-bk.* 706 *To undershore*, to support or raise a thing by putting a spar or prop under it.

**2.** *fig.* To support, strengthen, sustain.

*c* **1500** MEDWALL *Nature* (Brandl) 327 Yf ye wyll vndershore Hys croked old age. **1571** GOLDING *Calvin on Ps.* xxxvii. 34 The faithful..being undershored by him should not suffer themselves too bee drawen hither and thither. **1610** HEALEY *St. Aug. Citie of God* XVIII. xl. 729 The citizens of Babilon..know not which to beleeue. But we haue a diuine historie to vnder-shore vs. **1665** BUNYAN *Holy Citie* Pref. p. iv, Here is neither paint to adorn thy wrinkled face, nor Crutch to uphold or undershore thy shaking, tottering, staggering Kingdom of Rome.

**U·nder-sho·rtening,** *vbl. sb.* (UNDER-¹ 4 a.) **1814** *Monthly Mag.* XXXVIII. 212 The higher the eye above the level of the mirror, the greater is the under-shortening. **1815** *Ibid.* LXXVI. 120 Under-shortening is to be acquired only by fatiguing discipline.

**U·ndershot,** (*ppl.*) *a.* (and *sb.*). [UNDER-¹ 4 a.]

**1.** Driven by water passing under.

*Undershot wheel*, a water-wheel turned by force of water acting on the lower part of the wheel. *Undershot mill*, a mill worked by an undershot wheel.

1610 R. VAUGHAN *Water-Workes* P 3, To plant an vndershot-mil vpon a Riuer. 1660 R. D'ACRES *Art Water-drawing* 28 The close bucketted wheels..are of three sorts, the close bucketted under-shot, which receive their charge below [etc.]. 1759 *Phil. Trans.* LI. 125 The undershot-wheel was taken off the axis, and..an overshot wheel..was put into its place. 1805 BREWSTER *Ferguson's Lect.* I. 81 Water mills are divided into breast mills, undershot mills, and overshot mills. 1872 H. W. BEECHER *Lect. Preaching* viii. 149 If you have a great, full strong stream,..then the wheel is made under-shot.

**b.** *sb.* An undershot wheel or mill.

1705 S. CARPENTER *Let.* in Penn & Logan *Corr.* (1870) I. 233 After it has passed through the saw-mill it comes to the corn-mill, an undershot, and grinds very well. 1759 *Phil. Trans.* LI. 137 All those that receive the impulse or shock of the water, whether in an horizontal, perpendicular, or oblique direction, are to be considered as undershots.

**2.** Having the lower jaw or teeth projecting beyond the upper; underhung.

1881 V. SHAW *Bk. Dog* 39 *Undershot*, the lower incisor teeth projecting beyond the upper, as in Bulldogs. 1884 *Live Stock Jrnl.* Aug. 130 The second prize-winner is leggy, with straight shoulders, not good face, and is undershot.

† **Undershre·d,** *v. Obs.*—0 [UNDER-1 4 a.] *trans.* To cut away below.

1545 ELYOT, *Subluco*, to vndershreade boughes, that the lyght may come vnder the tree.

**U·ndershrie:valty.** [UNDER-1 6 b.] The office of an undersheriff; undersheriffship.

1836 SMART. (Hence in later Dicts.)

**Undershrieve(ry,** varr. UNDERSHERIFF(RY.

**U·ndershrub.** [UNDER-1 5 d.] A small or low-growing shrub; *spec.* in *Bot.*, a plant having a shrubby base. (Cf. SUBSHRUB.)

1598 FLORIO, *Soffrutice*, any maner of vndershrub. 1633 FORD *'Tis Pity* V. iii, If I must totter like a well-growne Oake, Some vnder shrubs shall in my weighty fall Be crusht to splitts. 1658 ROWLAND tr. *Moufet's Theat. Ins.* 1086 Indeed every shrub and under-shrub is eaten by Worms. 1718 OZELL tr. *Tournefort's Voy.* I. 173 The Stalk ..is full of Branches from the very bottom, ligneous, and comes to be an Under-Shrub. 1731 MILLER *Gard. Dict.* s.v. *Abrotanum*, It is used in Gardens as an Under-shrub. 1794 G. ADAMS *Nat. & Exp. Philos.* I. x. 429 At last the under-shrubs and trees put forth in their order. 1830 LINDLEY *Nat. Syst. Bot.* 57 *Haloragæ*... Herbaceous plants or under-shrubs, often growing in wet places. 1897 J. E. WILLIS *Flower. Pl. & F.* I. 165 Such low-growing shrubby plants as heather..are termed undershrubs.

Hence **U·ndershru:bby** *a.* (Cf. SUBSHRUBBY.)

1777 S. ROBSON *Brit. Flora* 117 Wild-thyme Cistus. Stem undershrubby, leaves oblong. 1786 ABERCROMBIE *Gard. Assist.* 189 The young side shoots of under-shrubby evergreens.

**Undershut,** *ppl. a.* [UNDER-1 4 a, 10 a.]

†**1.** Imperfectly shut. *Obs.*—1

1632 J. HAYWARD tr. *Biondi's Eromena* 17 So vigilant was the villanous Prodotima, who (expecting him, with the doore under-shut) suddenly leade him the way in.

**2.** *Mech.* (See quot.)

1875 KNIGHT *Dict. Mech.* 2680/2 *Under-shut-valve*, one placed beneath the sole-plate of a pump or other object, and not upon it; shutting underneath by an upward motion.

**U·nderside.** Also under-side, under side. [UNDER-1 5 b and UNDER *a.* 2 b. Cf. Du. *onderzijde*, Da. *underside*, G. *unterseite*.] The under or lower side or surface.

*a.* 1680 MOXON *Mech. Exerc.* x. 190 A Seat..having an Iron Pin fastned on either end the underside of it. 1704 *Phil. Trans.* XXV. 1625 The back or underside of the Leaves. 1768–74 TUCKER *Lt. Nat.* (1834) II. 459, I cannot conceive that surface separated from the table without an underside distinguishable from the upper. 1802 JAMES *Milit. Dict.* s.v. *Gun-carriage*, The underside of the gun. 1890 *Science-Gossip* XXVI. 215/1 The under-side of the wings was a blackish-brown.

*fig.* 1866 GEO. ELIOT *Ess.* (1884) 321 Comfort, which is the under-side or lining of all pleasure. 1876 *Fortn. Rev.* Jan. 108 Fear is the underside or wrong side of zeal.

*β.* 1738 CHAMBERS *Cycl.* s.v. *Subscapularis*, Spreading itself under the whole convex, or under side of it. 1794 W. CURTIS in *Bot. Mag.* VIII. 272 The blossoms have been of a sulphur colour, shaded..especially on the under side. 1835 J. DUNCAN *Beetles* 169 The legs and under side of the abdomen are reddish yellow. 1884 BOWER & SCOTT *De Bary's Phaner.* 476 At a greater distance from the stem the under side usually has the advantage.

**U·ndersight.** (UNDER-1 10 b.) 1894 H. DRUMMOND *Ascent Man* 13 The reason..is not oversight, but undersight.

**Undersi·gn,** *v.* [UNDER-1 4 a.] *trans.* To sign one's name below (a writing).

1580 HOLLYBAND *Treas. Fr. Tong*, *Soubsigner*, to vndersigne. 1770 SCRAFTON *Indostan* (ed. 2) 80 These words were written in his own hand, at the beginning of the Treaty, and were undersigned by him.

Hence **Undersigner, Undersigning** *vbl. sb.*

1611 FLORIO, *Sottoscrittione*, a subscription, an vnder signing or writing. 1753 *Scots Mag.* XV. 19/1 The undersigner has the honour to present..copies of the decrees. 1800 COLERIDGE *Piccolom.* II. ii, All rests upon his undersigning.

**Undersi·gned,** *ppl. a.* [Cf. prec. and SUBSIGNED *ppl. a.*] Whose signature is appended to a document, etc. Freq. *absol.* (in sing. or pl.).

1643 in J. M. Stone *Faithf. unto Death* (1892) 174, I, the undersigned,..am about to-day to lay down my life..in defence of the Roman Catholic Church. 1824 SYD. SMITH *Sp.* Wks. 1859 II. 201/1 We, the undersigned, being clergymen of the Church of England. 1845 in Claridge *Cold Water Cure* (1849) 12 We, the undersigned British and Americans, ..deem it our duty [etc.]. 1868 DICKENS *Lett.* (1880) II. 384 The undersigned is in his usual brilliant condition.

**U·nder-si:nging,** *vbl. sb.* (UNDER-1 9 b.) 1382 WYCLIF *Ps.* 3rd Prol., Ei3tety and ei3te forsothe seiden the salmys, and two hundrid the vndersinging. 1886 *Good Words* 308 A lark—a hundred larks are in the sky, A myriad birds an undersinging make. **U·nder-si:nner.** (UNDER-1 6 a.) 1684 OTWAY *Atheist* I, Good, pretty, little, Under-sinners,.. that a Man may fool away an Hour or two withal very comfortably.

†**U·nder-si:tter.** *Obs.* [UNDER-1 6 a. Cf. UNDERSETTLE.] One occupying part of another's house; a sub-tenant or lodger. Also *fig.*

1580 *Procl. Q. Eliz.* 7 July, For the offences in this part of increase of many indwellers, or as they be commonly termed Inmates, or vndersitters. 1607 *Proclamations Jas. I* (1609) 162 The letting of part of Houses and Chambers to Inmates and Undersitters. 1609 TUVILL *Vade-mecum* (1629) 18 Vertue cannot endure to be an vnder-sitter to any.

**U·nder-size,** *sb.* (UNDER-1 10 b.) 1791 W. GILPIN *Forest Scenery* II. 236 If such a distance as this..were painted on a larger scale than common,..we might be tempted to forget it's under-size.

**U·nder-size,** *a.* [UNDER-2.] = next 2.

1820 SCORESBY *Acc. Arctic Reg.* II. 254 Seldom more than two harpoons are struck into an under-size whale. *Ibid.* 419 The diminished value of under-size bone.

**U·ndersi·zed,** *ppl. a.* (In attrib. use *u·nder-sized.*) [UNDER-1 10 a.]

†**1.** Inadequately employed. *Obs.*—1

1657 GAUDEN *J. Watts' Scribe & Let. Answ.* Pref. ¶ j, His great abilities..were indeed much under-sized as to his auditory and employment.

**2.** Below the proper or ordinary size.

1706 *Lond. Gaz.* No. 4244/3 Each undersiz'd [Galloway] to be allow'd half a Stone for every Inch under. 1747 *Frauds & Abuses Coal Trade* (ed. 3) 20 The like Abuse, practised.. by undersized Sacks. 1825 T. HOOK *Sayings* Ser. II. I. 319 Mr. Abberly's undersized man-servant..delivered a note to Louisa. 1851 KINGSLEY *Yeast* xiii, The ill-looks of the young girls surprised him much;..the majority seemed under-sized, under-fed. 1884 T. F. R. CARR in *Fish. Exhib. Lit.* XI. 425 Fishermen..should be compelled to riddle the mussels..and return the undersized to the scalps.

**U·nder-skin.** (UNDER-1 5 b.) 1653 R. SANDERS *Physiogn.* a 4 b, Open it [*sc.* a peony], and take the flowers forth from that rinde or underskin, which represents the brain-pan.

†**U·nder-ski·nker.** *Obs.* (UNDER-1 6 a: see SKINKER 1.)

1596 SHAKS. *1 Hen. IV*, II. iv. 26 This peniworth of Sugar, clapt euen now into my hand by an vnder Skinker. 1631 HEYWOOD *2nd Pt. Fair Maid of West* IV, Ile see and I can be entertained to my old trade of drawing wine: if't be but an under skinker, I care not. [1867 SMYTH *Sailor's Word-bk.* 706 *Under-skinker*, assistant to the purser's steward.]

**U·nder-skirt.** [UNDER-1 5 a.] A skirt worn under another, a petticoat; also, a foundation over which drapery or an overskirt is disposed.

1861 MRS. RIDDELL *City & Suburb* (1862) 90 (H.), She.. affected flounces and many petticoats, wearing as many as eight or ten underskirts. 1883, 1884 [see OVERSKIRT]. 1907 H. WYNDHAM *Flare of Footlights* xix, Nearly all the latter ..displayed a greater amount of silk underskirt than seemed altogether necessary.

**U·nder-sky.** (UNDER-1 5 b.) 1830 TENNYSON *Dying Swan* iii, Floating about the under-sky,..the coronach stole..afar. 1870 MORRIS *Earthly Par.* III. IV. 87 From this dull rainy under-sky and low. **Undersla·ke,** *v.* (UNDER-1 2.) *c* 1440 *Pallad. on Husb.* II. 434 As oyl lauryne is lentiscyne of take, Whos rigour hoot water most vnderslake [gl. *summitigare*].

**U·nder-sleeve.** [UNDER-1 5 a.] A sleeve, esp. one of light material, worn below another.

1547 in Feuillerat *Revels Edw. VI* (1914) 10 Longe garmentes of playne clothe of Syluer,..thupper & nether Baces & thunder sleves of clothe of golde. 1560 — *Revels Q. Eliz.* (1908) 21 Undersleves of Damaske Bawdekyn. 1631 A. TOWNSHEND *Alb. Triumph* 13 The Labells of the sleeues,.. the vnder sleeues. 1861 *Archaeologia* XXXIX. 250 The under-sleeve is grey puffed with white. 1893 GEORGIANA HILL *Hist. Eng. Dress* II. 257 Fastening on with elastic or tape those uncomfortable undersleeves.

†**U·nderslops.** *Obs.* (UNDER-1 5 a.)

1737 OZELL *Rabelais* II. 72 Drawers or Under-slops are worn now by some.

†**Undersmall,** *a. Obs.*—1 [? UNDER-1 2 or WONDER *adv.*] Extremely small.

*c* 1530 *Judic. Urines* III. xviii. 60 b, They be bodys vnder-small as duste.

†**U·ndersock.** *Obs.* [UNDER-1 5 a.] A stocking.

1556 *Richmond. Wills* (Surtees) 190 One payr of sloppes of crayncoloryde fustyane, and the vndersokes belongynge the sayme.

**U·ndersoil.** [UNDER-1 5 b.] Subsoil.

1707 MORTIMER *Husb.* 315 A Planter or Raiser of Trees ought to consider the under Soil, as well as the superficies of the Earth. 1863 BATES *Nat. Amazon* I. 25 The difference in colour from the superficial soil..is owing to their being formed of the undersoil, brought up from a considerable depth.

**U·nder-so:ling.** (UNDER-1 5 b.) *c* 1440 *Promp. Parv.* 184/2 Galache, or galoche, vndyr solynge of mannys fote (.. *K.* vndirshone, *H.* vnderschoyinge), *crepita.* **U·nder-so:mething.** (UNDER-1 6 a.) *a* 1718 PARNELL *Allegory on Man* 18 Jove talk'd of breeding him on high, An under-something of the sky.

**U·ndersong.** [UNDER-1 9 b.]

**1.** A subordinate or subdued song or strain, esp. one serving as an accompaniment or burden to another. Freq. *transf.* of natural sounds.

1579 SPENSER *Sheph. Cal.* Aug. 128 And Willye is not greatly ouergone, So weren his vndersongs well addrest. 1593 DRAYTON *Ecl.* ix. G 3 b, When now at last..Was poynted who the Roundelay should singe And who againe the vndersong should beare. 1613–6 W. BROWNE *Brit. Past.* II. iii. 1028 He thus began..To prayse his love: his hasty waves among The frothed rockes, bearing the under-song. 1697 DRYDEN *Virg., Past.* III. 86 The challenge to Damœtas shall belong: Menalcas shall sustain his under-song. 1710 PHILIPS *Pastorals* vi. 8 As eldest, Hobbinol, begin; And Languet's Under-Song by Turns come in. 1795 COLERIDGE *To J. Cottle* 24 Th'unceasing rill..Murmurs sweet undersong 'mid jasmin bowers. 1820 KEATS *Lamia* II. 200 While fluent Greek a vowel'd undersong Kept up among the guests. 1885 RUNCIMAN *Skippers* 196 The hoarse undersong from the dim distance.

**2.** *fig.* An underlying meaning; an undertone.

1631 R. H. *Arraignm. Whole Creature* xviii. 326 Which is still as the conclusive undersong to the discanting of my larger Ditty. 1641 J. JACKSON *True Evang. T.* III. 183 Iobs sorrowfull Messengers make it their under song of sad tidings. 1818 KEATS *Let.* Wks. 1889 III. 141 If there is any fault in the Preface it is not affectation, but an undersong of disrespect to the public. 1886 HALL CAINE *Son of Hagar* II. xv, Beneath the chorus of their hearts' joy there was an undersong of discord.

**U·nder-so:rcerer.** (UNDER-1 6 a.) 1678 BUTLER *Hud.* III. i. 300, I..Prepar'd..His Under-Sorcerer t' ingage.

**U·nder-sort.** (UNDER-1 6 b.)

1655 T. WHITE *Grounds Obed. & Govt.* viii. 48 Of the Authority given to an absolute Governour; and of under-sorts of Governement. 1697 COLLIER *Ess. Mor. Subj.* I. 116 What if the under Sort of People should take the Hint, and practice upon it. 1828 CARR *Craven Gloss.*, *Undersort*, the vulgar.

**U·ndersoul.** (UNDER-1 6 b.) 1868 H. BUSHNELL *Mor. Uses Dark Th.* (1869) 350 The under-soul, the man, the everlasting, divinely moral personality. 1887 H. R. HAWEIS *Christ & Chr., Light of Ages* I. i. 4 The Oversoul, which is Divine Mind or God, embraces the Undersouls in all flesh. **U·ndersound.** (UNDER-1 9 b.) 1847 C. BRONTË *Jane Eyre* xxv, The gale still rising, seemed to my ear to muffle a mournful undersound. 1860 RUSKIN *Unto this Last* iv. § 82 No air is sweet that is silent; it is only sweet when full of low currents of under sound. **U·nder-so:vereign.** (UNDER-1 6 a.) *a* 1680 CHARNOCK *Attrib. God* (1834) II. 582 All under-sovereigns are..to be obedient to his orders. **Undersow·,** *v.* (UNDER-1 10 a.) 1650 W. BROUGH *Sacr. Princ.* (1659) 73 Let me prudently observe what each parcell of ground will best bear, that I may not over-cloy some, and undersow others.

†**Underspa·r,** *v. Obs.* [UNDER-1 4 a.] *trans.* To force up by means of a spar thrust underneath.

1577 STANYHURST *Descr. Ireland* in *Holinshed* I. 14/2 Vndersparring the gates, and bearing vp the dormitorie doore, they stabbed the adulterer.

**U·nder-spa·rred,** *ppl. a.* [UNDER-1 10 a.] Of vessels: Inadequately furnished with spars.

1841 [see UNDERMASTED].

†**U·nderspea·k,** *v. Obs.*—1 [UNDER-1 10 a.] *trans.* To come short in speaking of.

1635 A. STAFFORD *Fem. Glory* 119 If in this rude speech of mine I have over-talked my selfe, or under-spoken thee, impute it to my..doting yeares.

**Underspe·cified,** *ppl. a.* (UNDER *adv.* 2 b.)

1544 *Extr. Aberd. Rec.* (1844) I. 209 The ressett of this woll vnderwrittin, fra the personis vnderspecifeit. 1561 *Reg. Privy Council Scot.* I. 188 The quhilk day..comperit the gentilmen underspecifiit. 1682 *Papers rel. Scots in Poland* (1915) 136, I resaved..all as here underspecified.

**Under-spe·nd,** *v.* (UNDER-1 8 b.) *a* 1661 FULLER *Worthies, Lincoln* (1662) 168 When his friend [called] for half a pint of Wine, Mr. Sutton for a Gill, under-spending him a Moity.

**U·nder-sphere,** *sb.* (UNDER-1 5 b.)

1630 DRUMM. OF HAWTH. *Shadow of Judgem.* 4 The.. Raine-bow-sparkling Arch of Diamond cleare Which crownes the azure of each vnder spheare. *c* 1631 SIR L. CARY *Elegy on Donne* 86 He conquer'd rebell passions, rul'd them so, As under-spheares by the first Mover goe.

**Undersphe·re,** *v.* (UNDER-1 7.) 1652 URQUHART *Jewel* 162 The imputation, which they deserve for having been in so bad company, and undersphering themselves to the bodies of those vaster orbs.

**U·nderspin.** [UNDER-1 4 d.] A backward spin on a ball while in motion.

1901 *Westm. Gaz.* 13 Aug. 2/3, I do not see that photographs..'prove decisively that a golf ball, truly hit, develops underspin'.

†**Underspo·re,** *v. Obs.*—1 [UNDER-1 4 a + *spore* SPUR *sb.*1 8.] *intr.* (cf. UNDERSPAR *v.*).

*c* 1386 CHAUCER *Miller's T.* 279 Get me a staf, that I may vnderspore, Whil þat thou, Robyn, heuest of the dore.

**Underspre·ad,** *v.* (UNDER-1 4 a.)

1609 HOLLAND *Amm. Marcell.* 131 By that time it grew to be faire day-light, the skie all over was under-spread with a feeling, as it were, of yron harneis. 1857 EMERSON *Monadnoc* 296 Every morn I lift my head, See New England underspread.

**U·nderspring.** [UNDER-1 5 c.]

**1.** *attrib.* Having springs beneath.

1837 W. B. ADAMS *Carriages* 84 The simplest kind of four-wheeled spring vehicle for one horse is called an Underspring Phaeton.

**2.** An underlying fountain.

1851 MRS. BROWNING *Casa Guidi Wind.* I. 956, I feel how nature's ice-crusts keep the dint Of undersprings of silent Deity.

**Undersprou·t,** *v.* (UNDER-1 4 a.) 1584 HUDSON *Du Bartas' Judith* IV. (1608) 58 As the painefull plowman.. crops his hedge to make it vnder-sprout.

**Under-spurleather**: see SPUR-LEATHER 2.

**U·ndersta·ff,** *v.* (UNDER-1 10 a.) 1894 *Westm. Gaz.* 12 Sept. 2/2 The way in which the employers..had overworked him and understaffed his station. **U·ndersta·ffed,** *ppl. a.* (UNDER-1 10 a.) 1891 *Sat. Rev.* 7 Nov. 516 The country abounds with small churches understaffed.

**U·nderstair(s.** [UNDER-2.]

**1.** *attrib.* Situated below stairs; humble.

1616 T. ADAMS *Soul's Sickness* 61 Liuing in some vnderstaire office, when he would visite the countrey, he borrowes some Gallants cast sute of his seruant.

**2.** A space below a staircase.

1730 A. GORDON *Maffei's Amphith.* 290 There are two Under-stairs, which form Rooms.

† **Understa·nd**, *sb.* *Obs. rare.* [f. the vb.]
**1.** Understanding; knowledge.
*a* 1300 *Cursor M.* 9326 'Ne i herd neuer,' he said, 'in land Men sua herd of vnder-stand'. 1444 *Extr. Aberd. Rec.* (1844) I. 10 It was cum til his vnderstand that Marioune..hes complaynit to the lorde of Erole that [etc.].
**2.** Support, basis.
1580–90 J. STEWART *Poems* (S.T.S.) II. 149 Flie Sir, from sic, and lerne to vnderstand. Stand quhair ȝe vill, firm be ȝour vnderstand.

**Understa·nd**, *v.* Forms: (see STAND *v.*). [OE. *understondan*, *-standan* (UNDER-[1] 8 a), = OFris. *understonda*, MDa. *understande*, MSw. *undi(r)standa*, OIcel. (as a foreign word) *undirstanda*. Cf. MLG. *understân* to understand, to step under, MDu. *onderstaen* (Du. *-staan*), MHG. *understân*, *-stên* (G. *unterstehen*), to take upon oneself, to venture, presume, etc. With a different prefix, the same use of *stand* appears in OE. *forstandan*, OS. *farstandan*, OHG. *far-*, *firstantan* (*firstân*), and MHG. *verstân*, *-stên* (G. *verstehen*), MDu. *verstaen* (Du. *-staan*).

In the 15th and 16th cents. three forms of the past pple. were current, viz. (*a*) the original *understanden* (also *-stonden*), in use till about 1550; (*b*) the reduced form of this, *understande* (*-stonde*), *-stand* (*-stond*), common till about 1575, and surviving into the 17th cent.; (*c*) the new form *understanded* (*-stonded*), very common from about 1530 to 1585. The occurrence of *understanded* in the Thirty-Nine Articles, xxxv, in the phrase 'understanded of the people', has given rise to recent echoes of it, especially in journalistic use. The modern form *understood* came into use in the latter part of the 16th cent., and was usual by 1600.]

**I.** *trans.* **1.** To comprehend; to apprehend the meaning or import of; to grasp the idea of.
*c* 888 K. ÆLFRED *Boeth.* xxxix. § 8 Se godcunda foreþonc hit understent eall swiðe rihte, þeah..we ne cunnon þæt riht understandan. *c* 1000 ÆLFRIC *Hom.* I. 188 Wæs seo ealde æ swiðe earfoðe and diȝle to understandenne. *a* 1225 *Leg. Kath.* 1013 Liht to ure lare, þet tu mahe stihen to understonden in him godes muchele strencðe. *c* 1290 *S. Eng. Leg.* I. 11/343 Þe Aumperour þis onder-stod, þei he heþene were. 1340–70 *Alex. & Dind.* 609 Ȝe ne vndurstonde nouht þat stounde þe storie of þis wordus. 1387–8 T. USK *Test. Love* III. iii. (Skeat) l. 77 If these thinges be wel understonde, I wene that non inconvenient shalt thou fynde betwene goddes forweting and liberte of arbitrement. *a* 1450 *Mirk's Festial* 3 Whech noyse God hymselfe schall know and vndyrstond. 1523 [COVERDALE] *Old God* (1534) P v, The multytude of dyuerse ceremonyes..not being vnderstanded nor perceyued of the comen sorte..of people. 1548 R. HUTTEN *Sum of Diuinitie* E 4 b, The sentence shal be better understande if it be changed into a comparyson to an other. 1600 J. PORY tr. *Leo's Africa* III. 155 A man may much more easily vnderstand the text then the exposition thereof. 1667 MILTON *P. L.* XII. 376 Now clear I understand What oft my steddiest thoughts have searcht in vain. 1733 BERKELEY *Th. Vision* § 27, I have considered and endeavoured to understand your remarks. 1815 JANE AUSTEN *Emma* ix, One half of the world cannot understand the pleasures of the other. 1891 FARRAR *Darkn. & Dawn* xxi, The young prince saw that they were in possession of something more divine than the world could understand.
*refl.* *c* 1275 in *O. E. Misc.* 45/297 Peter a-non þer-after hyne vnderstod Hwat his louerd hedde iseyd.

**b.** To be thoroughly acquainted or familiar with (an art, profession, etc.); to be able to practise or deal with properly.
1533 ELYOT *Cast. Helthe* (1541) A ij, The science of phisicke, ..beyng well vnderstande, truely experienced, and discretely ordred. 1622 J. TAYLOR (Water P.) *Farew. Tower-bottles* A 4, When Vpland Trades-men thus dares take in hand A wat'ry buis'nesse, they not vnderstand. 1681 CHETHAM *Angler's Vade-m.* xxxix. (1689) 252, I will not deny but that (as the times phrase it) I understand something of eating. 1727 A. HAMILTON *New Acc. E. Ind.* II. 93 He..understood a small Sword excellently well, but [was] not much versed in Merchandize or foreign Commerce. 1768 EARL CARLISLE in Jesse *Selwyn & Contemp.* (1843) II. 292 Get somebody who understands it to taste it [*sc.* claret] for you. 1823 SCOTT *Quentin D.* xxvi, Galeotti..understood his own profession too well to let that ignorance be seen. 1859 *Habits Gd. Society* v. 221 Thomas, bring that fowl to me; Mr. Jones [who is trying to carve it] seems not to understand it.

**c.** To apprehend clearly the character or nature of (a person). Also *refl.*
1587 GOLDING *De Mornay* v. 57 God then conceyued and vnderstood himselfe; and it must needes be that he vnderstood himselfe seeing that the chiefest wisedome is to know ones selfe. 1588 KYD *Househ. Philos.* Wks. (1901) 267 So that the seruaunt, if you will rightly vnderstand him, is..a liuely and seueral instrument of action. 1846 MRS. A. MARSH *Father Darcy* II. viii. 137 It is my misfortune to be little understood; but our praise is not of men, but of God. 1876 PARKER *Paraclete* I. ix. 142 We cannot understand Christ until we understand Moses, nor can we understand the spirit until we understand Christ.

†**d.** *refl.* (*a*) To know one's place, or how to conduct oneself properly. (*b*) To be in possession of one's senses or faculties. *Obs.*
(*a*) 1602 SHAKS. *Ham.* I. iii. 96 You doe not vnderstand your selfe so cleerely, As it behoues my Daughter, and your Honour. 1687 MIÈGE, To understand himself, to know how to carry himself, *savoir se conduire.* 1745 J. MASON *Self-Knowledge* I. iii. (1758) 32 Nothing is more common than to say, when a Person does not behave with due Decency towards his Superiors, such a one does not understand himself.
(*b*) 1696 AUBREY *Misc.* 136 He was an Hundred Years old when my Friend was with him; and yet, did understand himself very well.

**2.** To comprehend by knowing the meaning of the words employed; to be acquainted with (a language) to this extent.
*a* 1000 *Colloq. Ælfric* in Wr.-Wülcker 100 Sprec us æfter urum andȝyte þæt we maȝon understandan þa þing þe þu specst. *c* 1250 *Gen. & Ex.* 2210 Wende here non it on his mod, Oc Iosep al it under-stod. *c* 1275 in *O. E. Misc.* 56/668 Eueruych þer vnderstod his icunde speche. *a* 1300 *Cursor M.* 232 Þis ilk bok es translate..For the loue of Inglis lede.. For the commun at understand. *a* 1384 CHAUCER *H. Fame* II. 2 Now herkeneth, euery maner man That englissh understonde kan. *c* 1400 MAUNDEV. (Roxb.) xxix. 131 Neuer þe latter þai wate noȝt whare þai myght aryfe, and also þai schuld noȝt vnderstand þer langage. 1535 COVERDALE *Gen.* xi. 7 Let vs..confounde their tonge euen there, yᵗ one vnderstonde not what another saieth. *c* 1595 CAPT. WYATT *Dudley's Voy.* (Hakluyt Soc.) 40 All theire conference was in the Indian tounge, which our Captaine nor anie of his companie did understande. 1613 PURCHAS *Pilgrimage* (1614) 250 The Arabike I vnderstand not. 1659 in *Burton's Diary* (1828) IV. 6 Seeing we all understand not French, let us take his word; that is English. 1716 HEARNE *Collect.* (O.H.S.) V. 314 He does not understand Latin. 1719 DE FOE *Crusoe* II. (Globe) 351 The Spaniards, two of whom understood English well enough. 1842 TENNYSON *Vision of Sin* v. 16 An answer peal'd.., But in a tongue no man could understand.

**b.** To grasp the meaning or purport of the words (or signs) used by (a person).
*a* 1225 *Leg. Kath.* 1641 Beo nu þenne, Porphire, stille & understont me. *a* 1300 *Cursor M.* 2260 Bot sua he mengud þam þair mode, þat naman oþer vndirstode. *c* 1386 CHAUCER *Man of Law's T.* 520 A maner latyn corrupt was hir speche, But algates ther by was she vnderstonde. *a* 1533 LD. BERNERS *Huon* lx. 208 Thus they compleynyd them one to another, and Huon, who was nere them, vnderstode them well. 1566 STAPLETON *Ret. Untr. Jewell* III. 110 b, To praie, it was not requisit he should be vnderstanded, For that was done..by sighynges. 1595 SHAKS. *John* IV. ii. 237 Thou didst vnderstand me by my signes. 1667 MILTON *P. L.* XII. 58 Forthwith a hideous gabble rises loud Among the Builders; each to other calls Not understood. 1687 A. LOVELL tr. *Thevenot's Trav.* I. 61 When he eats he speaks to no body, but makes himself be understood by signs to the mute Buffoons. 1838 LYTTON *Leila* II. i, 'Thou understandest me, father?' 'I do. I know your pious heart and well-judging mind.' 1848 THACKERAY *Van. Fair* lvi, Pretending to understand little George when he spoke regarding them.
*refl.* *c* 1395 *Plowman's T.* 792 Yet he jangleth as a jaie, And understont him selfe no thing. 1618 FLETCHER *Woman Pleas'd* IV. i, What Treason's that? does this fellow understand Himself?

**c.** *To understand each other*, to be in agreement or collusion; to be confederates.
1663 *Extr. St. Papers Friends* Ser. II. (1911) 171 The Quakers..with all other Sects are fully agreed in this business and doe perfectly understand each other. 1675 *Essex Papers* (Camden) 24 Its so apparent..that they understand one another. 1853 R. S. SURTEES *Sponge's Sp. Tour* vii, 'You trust me,' replied Leather,..with a look as much as to say, 'we understand each other'.

**3.** To comprehend as a fact; to grasp clearly, to realize. Chiefly with clause as object.
*c* 1000 ÆLFRIC *Saints' Lives* xxv. 178 Under-stand be ðam hu se ælmihtiȝa god hi ealle ȝesceop..of nahte. *c* 1012 WULFSTAN *Hom.* (1883) 156 Understandað eac..þæt deofol þas þeode nu fela ȝeara dwelode. *a* 1200 *Vices & Virtues* 19 Vnderstandeþ, alle ðe ðis radeþ oðer ihereð,..þe muchele ðolemodnesse of us on ðese liue. *a* 1225 *Ancr. R.* 66 So þe ueond, þurh hire word, understod anonriht hire wocnesse. *a* 1300 *Cursor M.* 4249 Sir putifar wel vndirstod þat ioseph was o gentil blod. *Ibid.* 14874 Quat he was þai noght vnderstode. *c* 1315 SHOREHAM I. 652 Nou onderstand: þe signe her Fourme hys of wyne and brede. 1390 GOWER *Conf.* I. 140 And understond that al this peine..Is schape al only for thi pride. *c* 1425 LYDG. *Assembly of Gods* 2040, I cowde nat vndyrstande Where he became, but sodenly As he came, he went. 1486 *Bk. St. Albans* d ij, Understonde ye that a Goshawke shulde not flie to any fowle. 1535 COVERDALE *John* viii. 27 Howbeit they vnderstode not, that he spake of the father. 1558 BP. WATSON *Seven Sacram.* xxi. 132 He hath often tymes with his reason vnderstande..what God hath commaunded and the goodnes of it. 1597 HOOKER *Eccl. Pol.* v. lxvii. § 4 Thus much they knewe, although as yet they vnderstoode not perfectly to what effect or issue the same would come. 1710 ADDISON *Whig Exam.* 14 Sept. ᴾ 3 This Œdipus, you must understand,.. was son to a King of Thebes. 1781 COWPER *Expost.* 159 They..could not understand That sin let loose speaks punishment at hand. 1819 SHELLEY *Cenci* IV. i. 101 Tell her to come; yet let her understand Her coming is consent. 1867 H. SPENCER *First Princ.* (ed. 2) I. iv. § 23. 70 You now understand..what has disabled the partridge.

†**b.** With reflexive pronoun. *Obs. rare.*
*c* 1175 *Lamb. Hom.* 35 For-þi leofemen understondet eouseluen þa hwile ȝe mahten: Nis þas weorld nawiht. *c* 1320 *Cast. Love* 1131 A! Mon, nim ȝeme and vnderstond þe Hou fynliche in herte God loueþ þe.

†**c.** To ascertain the purport of (a letter, etc.) by perusal and consideration. *Obs.*
1389 *Eng. Gilds* (1870) 50 We fulliche vndirstondend ȝour lettres sent to vs,..do ȝow openliche to wetyn [etc.]. *c* 1400 *Brut* II. 318 The which lettres, whan þe kyng..had seyn & vndirstonden, he had grete compassioun. 1430–40 LYDG. *Bochas* VIII. xxv. (1558) 16 b, Your letters red and plainly vnderstande. 1502 ARNOLDE *Chron.* (1811) 14 We haue understand the charter the whiche the Lorde Herry..made to yᵉ citezens of London in thes wordes. 1523 LD. BERNERS *Froiss.* I. xiv. 14 Whan all the cases and dedis that the kyng had done..were red, and wel understand.

**4. a.** To grasp as a fixed or established fact or principle; to regard as settled or implied without specific mention.
*c* 1055 *Byrhtferth's Handboc* in *Anglia* VIII. 304 Þis ylce understand be þam oðrum daȝum. *c* 1400 LOVE *Bonavent. Mirr.* (1908) 9 It is to vndirstonde..as for a principal and general rule..that [etc.]. 1523 FITZHERB. *Husb.* § 156 Than it is to be vnderstande, what goodes a man shall take with hym. 1553 EDEN *Treat. New Ind.* (Arb.) 8 The lyke is to be vnderstande of Popingiayes and spyces. 1667 MILTON *P. L.* I. 662 Warr then, Warr Open or understood must be resolv'd. 1854 *Poultry Chron.* II. 363 It must be also understood that no alteration can be made in the prices.

**b.** To have knowledge of, to know or learn, by information received. (Now merged in next.)
Freq. in *to give* or † *do* (one) *to understand*: see DO *v.* 22 c, GIVE *v.* 29 c.
*a* 1131 [see DO *v.* 22 c]. ? *a* 1200 in Kemble *Cod. Dipl.* IV. 218, I do ȝowe to understonden ðat I wolle ðat ðe prestes.. haue euere soke and sake ouere alle heore men. *a* 1300 *Cursor M.* 12342 To þe leones coue he yod, Þar he þe quelpes vnder-stod. *Ibid.* 19919 Quen þai vnderstod His cuming, son gain him þai yod. *c* 1350 *Will. Palerne* 5262 Whan þe worþi william..hade vnderston[d] þe tidinges to þende, to þe menskful messageres he made glad chere. *c* 1385 CHAUCER *L. G. W.* Prol. 470 Now wole I seyn what penaunce thow schalt do For thyn trespace, & vndyrstonde it here. 1423 JAS. I *Kingis Q.* cxxvii, My son, I..vnderstond, Be thy reherse, the matere of thy gref. 1482 *Cely Papers* (Camden) 128, I wndyrstonde be Robard Eryke that ȝe hafe ij fayr hawkes. 1560 DAUS tr. *Sleidane's Comm.* 401 b, I require you that you wyll make a direct aunswer..and let me understande it tomorrowe. 1585 T. WASHINGTON tr. *Nicholay's Voy.* I. xv. 16 b, The great displeasure he would take, when he should vnderstand the great dammage which the Turks had done. 1611 B. JONSON *Catiline* IV. iv, I vnderstand by Quintus Fabius Sanga,..you haue beene lately Sollicited against the Common-wealth. 1664 MRS. HUTCHINSON *Mem. Col. Hutchinson* (1806) 428 When the colonell's wife understood her husband's bad accommodation.

**c.** To take or accept as a fact, without positive knowledge or certainty; to get as an impression or idea; to believe. Chiefly with obj. clause.
1751 PALTOCK *P. Wilkins* II. x. 112 As I understand your great Ancestor would have come into it,..but for the Ragams. 1788 COWPER *Let. to Lady Hesketh* 6 May, The General, I understand by his last letter, is in town. 1825 T. HOOK *Sayings* Ser. II. I. 217, I understood from Mr. Abberly..that I should find him, if I called at this time of the day. 1829 SCOTT *Anne of G.* xxxiv, They understood it was his wish to observe incognito. 1858 *Congressional Globe* 18 Feb. 752/1, I understand the gentleman from Illinois to give way. *The Chairman.* The Chair understands not. 1885 'MRS. ALEXANDER' *At Bay* vii, It was understood she had made an engagement to go to India.

**5.** To take, interpret, or view in a certain way.
*c* 1000 *Ags. Psalter* xxi. 2 Ne understand þu hit me to unrihtwisnesse. *c* 1000 ÆLFRIC *Saints' Lives* xxv. 472 Æwfestlice understandende be ure ealra æriste. *c* 1175 *Lamb. Hom.* 75 Þis word..mon mei understonden on þro wise. *a* 1300 *Cursor M.* 337 Bot þou sal noght vndirstand þat he wroght al his werc wit hand. *c* 1340 HAMPOLE *Pr. Consc.* 4425 Þe dragon es understanden þe fende..And þe thred part of þe sternes bright Er cristen men undirstanden right. *c* 1425 WYNTOUN *Cron.* VIII. xi. 1928 (Cott. MS.), Þir wordis in to propyrte Al þus may vndirstandyn be. ? *a* 1533 FRITH *Answ. More* (1548) A 2 b, I shewed hym that it was not necessary, that the words shulde so be vnderstonde as they sownde. 1566 *Pasquine in Traunce* 107 That which Christ speaketh ..of many false Prophets..may be vnderstand to be the sundry sectes of Monkes and Fryers. 1581 J. BELL *Haddon's Answ. Osorius* 188 b, The Major must be understanded, that Paule treated not of the cause..but of the execution and effect of predestination. 1645 *Docq. Lett. Pat. at Oxf.* (1837) 257 Which Forces shalbe vnderstoode to be in the nature of Posse Comitatus. 1662 STILLINGFL. *Orig. Sacræ* II. iv. § 8 Some understand the first words..that he was not born a Prophet. 1772 *Lett. Junius* lxviii. (1788) 343 You, Lord Mansfield, did not understand me so. 1835 T. MITCHELL *Acharn. of Aristoph.* 339 *note*, Elmsley understands this word in its legal sense. 1860 WARTER *Sea-board* II. 492, I do not quite know how Miss Bremer..intended these words to be understood.

**b.** Const. *by.* (In passive passing into the sense of 'is signified'.)
*c* 1340 HAMPOLE *Pr. Consc.* 1681 Bi þe name of ded may be tane, And understanden ma dedes þan ane. 1377 LANGL. *P. Pl.* B. XII. 257 By þe po feet is vnderstonde. Excecutoures, fals frendes. *c* 1400 *Apol. Loll.* 69 By þis man is vnderstondyn feynar þat is fals, and lufiþ his synne. 1456 SIR G. HAYE *Law Arms* (S.T.S.) 10 All the cristin men that war undirstandin be the grene blude. 1484 CAXTON *Fables of Æsop* I. i, By the cok is to vnderstonde the fool whiche retcheth not of sapyence. 1502 *Ord. Crysten Men* (W. de W. 1506) I. iii. 34 By the coniuracyon the whiche is made unto the lefte ere is understande that he ought to put out of us all euyl thoughtes. 1561 DAUS tr. *Bullinger on Apoc.* (1573) 123 b, We read..that there was an Aungell of Grece, and an Aungell of Persia, and that by them yᵉ whole people are vnderstand. 1578 BANISTER *Hist. Man* I. 19 You shall heare what space is to be vnderstanded by the name of Necke. 1600 SHAKS. *A. Y. L.* IV. iii. 95 *Ros.* What must we vnderstand by this? *Oli.* Some of my shame. 1651 C. CARTWRIGHT *Cert. Relig.* I. 296 Estius..saith that Chrysostome and his followers by sacrifice then understand..Baptisme. 1727 DE FOE *Syst. Magic* I. I. (1840) 24 After this story no man need inquire what the world understood by the magicians and astrologers and wise men of those days. 1758 tr. *Juan & Ulloa's Voy.* (1772) I. 440 The llama, to which the Indians added the name of runa, to denote an India sheep; that beast being now understood by the *runa-llama.* 1865 RUSKIN *Sesame* i. § 3 We do not understand by this advancement, in general, the mere making of money.

**c.** Const. *of.*
1549 LATIMER *1st Serm. bef. Edw. VI* (Arb.) 22 The forsayd words of Paul are not to be vnderstande of all scriptures. 1581 J. BELL *Haddon's Answ. Osor.* 43 b, He demaundeth of us, what is to be understanded of those Sacramentes which we doe reteine. 1705 ADDISON *Italy* 110 Which is true, if understood only of the Rivers of Italy. 1861 PALEY *Aeschylus* (ed. 2) *Prometh.* 898 *note*, This is to be literally understood of the gadfly's sting.

†**d.** *To understand*, to wit, namely. *Obs.*
1579 J. DEE *Diary* (Camden) 5 To my heires and assignes for ever, to understand, Mr. Bullok and Mr. Taylor.

†**e.** To mean, to imply. (Cf. 12 b.) $Obs.^{-1}$
1617 MORYSON *Itin.* I. 227 Distant from Ierusalem some fiue miles, (in Turky I alwaies vnderstand Italian miles).

†**6. a.** To give heed to, attend to. *Obs.*

c 1000 ÆLFRIC *Saints' Lives* xxiii b 186 Þæt ʒeswinc his syðfætes ne understandende..[he] arn. c 1275 *O. E. Misc.* 90/8 Þu ert help in engelaunde. Vre stephne vnderstonde. c 1320 *Cast. Love* 953 3if þou wole me louen and vnderstonde, I chul þe bringe in-to þin owne londe. c 1400 tr. *Secreta Secret., Gov. Lordsh.* 48 Gouerne hem wyth goodnesse, and vnderstonde hem wyth debonertee.

†**b.** To receive, accept. *Obs.*

c 1200 *Trin. Coll. Hom.* 99 Ech þe understandeð þat holi husel unwurðliche, he understant him seluen eche pine. *Ibid.* 167 Þis holie maiden..stehȝ þis dai..in to þan heuenliche bure, þar heo was wurðliche understonden. c 1250 *Gen. & Ex.* 2275 Al ðo briðere..bedden him riche present,..And he leuelike it under-stod. c 1275 *O.E. Misc.* 90/3 Haly thomas of heoueriche Alle apostles eueliche Þe Martyrs þe vnderstonde. c 1300 *Havelok* 2814 And siþen shal ich under-stonde Of you..Manrede, and holde oþes boþe. c 1375 *Cursor M.* 2132 (Fairf.), Þe king..comanded þorou-out his lande men sulde him mensk and vnderstande.

†**c.** To conceive. *Obs.*—[1]

c 1200 *Trin. Coll. Hom.* 21 Þu shalt understonde [*Lamb. Hom.* 77, underfon] child on þine innoðe.

**7.** To recognize or regard as present in thought, though not expressly stated or mentioned; to supply mentally. Chiefly *Gram.*

1530 PALSGR. 342 Whan we use 'they' or 'them', understandyng femynin substantyves, they use ever *elles.* 1533 MORE *Answ. Poysoned Bk.* Wks. 1057/2 Though those wordes wer out, yet they be such as the sentence wold well require to repete and vnderstande. a 1704 T. BROWN *Sat. Ancients* Wks. 1720 I. 15 The Ancient Romans said *Saturam* understanding *Lancem.* 1861 PALEY *Aeschylus* (ed. 2) *Seven agst. Thebes* 249 *note,* Understand χαρίζοιο ἄν, or something to that effect, suppressed by aposiopesis.

**b.** In pa. pple.: Implied, though not expressed.

1580 LYLY *Euphues* (Arb.) 419 You resemble in your sayings the Painter Tamantes, in whose pictures there was euer more vnderstoode then painted. 1581 J. BELL *Haddon's Answ. Osor.* 200 Admit this also that god's name is not expressed, yet have ye not taught us that it is not understanded here. 1631 GOUGE *God's Arrows* v. § 1. 410 Circumstantiall words, which are as bonds to knit word to word, it leaveth to be understood. 1669 MILTON *Acced. Grammar* 59 A Noun and Pronoun with a Participle exprest or understood. 1754 R. NEWTON *Char. Theophrastus* 238 Here is an ellipsis of the substantive; which Lambert Bos hath not supply'd, and therefore I will venture to do it by ὁδὸν understood. 1817 MILL *Brit. India* II. IV. v. 192 An exception in favour of the Nabob was, from standing usage, so much understood, that to express it had appeared altogether useless. 1835 T. MITCHELL *Acharn. of Aristoph.* 675 *note,* The verb σκόπει or ὅρα is here understood. 1872 *Punch* 13 July 19/2 In order that any matter of business should be perfectly intelligible, nothing should be 'understood'.

*fig.* 1858 HOGG *Shelley* II. 417 There was an ellipsis of his waistcoat; it was not expressed, but understood.

†**8. a.** In passive: To be informed, advised, or (so) minded. *Obs.*

c 1275 *O. E. Misc.* 52/518 We beoþ vnderstonde þes ilke swike seyde..Ich wile þene þridde day aryse from deþe to lyue. 1297 R. GLOUC. (Rolls) 9300 3if þou seist it vor noble kunne, þou nart noȝt wel vnderstonde, Vor ich was þe kinges sone, þou wost wel, of þis londe. c 1440 *Pallad. on Husb.* III. 196 Tho thre wol multiplie, As semeth me, in euery maner lond; Yet Columelle is so not understonde.

†**b.** To plan, devise. With refl. dative. *Obs.*—[1]

1297 R. GLOUC. (Rolls) 8877 Þe king vor ire eritage him gan vnderstonde To bringe roberd is sone..in is warison þere.

**9.** To stand under. †Also *spec.*, to support or assist; to prop up.

13.. *Northern Passion* 1751 (Addit. MS.), Sayne Iohn hir body [*v.r.* Cristis word wel] vndir stude. [1591 SHAKS. *Two Gent.* II. v. 31 Why, stand-vnder: and vnder-stand is all one. 1601 — *Twel. N.* III. i. 90 My legges do better vnderstand me sir, then I vnderstand what you meane.] a 1611 CHAPMAN *Iliad* v. 687 Alcander, and a number more, he slew, and more had slain, If Hector had not understood. 1615 — *Odyss.* IV. 346 To let him reach the shore Of ships and tents before Troy understood. 1632 HEYWOOD *1st Pt. Iron Age* v. i, Thy rude hand Would lift a shield, thou canst not vnder stand. 1883 *Academy* 16 June 419/2 A full set of collations 'understands' the text.

**II.** *intr.* **10.** To have comprehension or understanding (in general or in a particular matter).

c 1000 ÆLFRIC *Hom.* I. 302 [Þam men] is ȝemæne mid nytenum, þæt he ȝefrede; mid englum, þæt he understande. c 1012 WULFSTAN *Hom.* (1883) 161 Eall þæt syndon micle and eȝeslice dæda, understande se ðe wille. 1297 R. GLOUC. (Rolls) 2221 Sire king,..3if þou wolt understonde, Deol þou miȝt abbe in þin herte of þin kunde londe. 1340 *Ayenb.* 56 Huanne þe glotoun geþ in to þe tauerne..he..speçþ wel and onderstant; huan he comþ ayen, he heþ al þis uorlore. c 1380 WYCLIF *Serm.* Sel. Wks. II. 13 3it 3e knowun not, ne undirstonden; 3it 3our herte is blyndid. 1456 SIR G. HAYE *Law Arms* (S.T.S.) 13 The quhilk lettis to have perfyte resoun..to understand rychtwisly. 1530 PALSGR. 767/2 For as farre as I can understande, it is so. 1587 GOLDING *De Mornay* v. 55 Albeit that of the things which are in this world, some vnderstand, and some vnderstand not;..all of them are appoynted to some certeyne end. 1613 FLETCHER, etc. *Hon. Man's Fort.* v. i, All women that on earth do dwell thou lov'st, Yet none that understand love thee again. 1648 MILTON *Ps.* lxxxii. 17 They know not nor will understand, In darkness they walk on. 1746 FRANCIS tr. *Horace, Epist.* I. xiv. 64 By my Advice, let each with chearful Heart, As best he understands, employ his Art. 1781 COWPER *Conversat.* 430 Man's heart had been impenetrably seal'd,..Had not his Maker's all-bestowing hand Giv'n him a soul, and bade him understand. 1850 TENNYSON *In Mem.* xcvii. 36 She dwells on him with faithful eyes, 'I cannot understand: I love'.

**b.** Const. *about,* †*of.* †Also with refl. dative.

c 1000 ÆLFRIC *Hom.* I. 10 Englas..ne maȝon fulfremedlice understandan ymbe God. a 1225 *Ancr. R.* 210 Nis..no mon þet ne mei understonden him of his sunnen nomeliche. c 1375 [see 10 c]. c 1477 CAXTON *Jason* 42 b, Certes gentil knight I knowe wel my self & vnderstonde of this marchandyse. 1860 W. COLLINS *Woman in White* I. xv. 187 You quite understand about that little matter of business being safe in my hands? 1892 J. H. MCCARTHY *1001 Days* II. 7, I understood about precious stones, and I had reason to hope that I should not do badly in the business.

†**c.** To know how *to* do something. *Obs.*

a 1300 *Cursor M.* 24792 Willam basterd..conquerur was gode, And for to warrai [c 1375 of þe were he] vnderstode. 1723 *Pres. St. Russia* I. 337 A Hatchet, which their Carpenters understand to handle with more Skill than those of any Nation whatsoever.

†**11.** To have knowledge or information, to learn, *of* something. *Obs.*

13.. *Cursor M.* 19919 (Gött.), Quen he of his comming vnderstode, Sone he ras and gain þaim him ȝode. a 1400 *Octouian* 1589 Anoon the kyng..dede hem alle to vntherstonde Of the Soudanes fyght. 1401 in Ellis *Orig. Lett.* Ser. II. I. 22 We do yow to understonde of tydynges the weche we have yherd of Owein Glyndor. 1509 *Mem. Hen. VII* (Rolls) 435 Howbe that ye wold merveł in case that ye understode of al the maters that hathe passyd. 1573 L. LLOYD *Marrow of Hist.* (1653) 116 The Philosopher..having understood of his mothers death. 1629 in Ellis *Orig. Lett.* Ser. II. III. 256, I was gladde to understande of your life and health, which this bearer..made knowen unto me. 1561 *Reg. Privy Counc. Scot.* Ser. III. I. 5, I shall not know nor understand of any maner of thing..against his Majesties persone..bot I shall lett and withstand the same.

†**b.** To get news, receive intelligence. *Obs.*—[1]

1574 HELLOWES *Gueuara's Fam. Ep.* (1577) 58 Pyrrhus..was the first that inuented Currers or Posts: and in this case he was so vigilant, that..in one day he vnderstood from Rome,..and in five out of Asia.

**12. a.** In parenthetic use (chiefly *I understand*): To believe or assume, on account of information received or by inference.

1297 R. GLOUC. (Rolls) 133 Þe kyng of norþhomberlond was king, ich vnderstonde, Of al þe lond biȝonde homber. a 1352 MINOT *Poems* vii. 92 Þe teres he lete ful rathly ren Out of his eghen, I vnderstand. 1390 GOWER *Conf.* I. 10 For thilke tyme, I understonde, The Lumbard made non eschange. c 1440 *Generydes* 16 Hire fader was a man of grete powre, And kyng of aufrike as I vnderstonde. c 1460 *Merita Missæ* 197 Thow ned the to fyght, I vndeyrstonde, With youre flesche, and with the fende. 1508 KENNEDIE *Flyting w. Dunbar* 345 Thow lufis nane Irische, elf, I vnderstand, Bot it suld be all trew Scottis mennis lede. 1592 *Arden of Feversham* IV. iv. 4 He is coming from Shorlow as I vnderstand. 1642 H. MORE *Song of Soul* I. ii. 52 You are Heavens Privy-Counsellour I understond. 1898 'MERRIMAN' *Roden's Corner* xii. 124 Mr. Wade..was, he understood, distantly related to the mother.

†**b.** To speak *of* (= to mean) something. *Obs.*—[1]

c 1425 *Craft Nombrynge* (E.E.T.S.) 4 Neuer-þe-les wen he says *Prima significat vnum &c.*,..he vndirstondes noȝt of þe first figure of euery rew.

†**13.** To be subject *to* one. *Obs. rare.*

? a 1200 in Kemble *Cod. Dipl.* IV. 193 Icc hate..ðæt alcc ða ðeȝnes of ðam landen hinnenforð understande to ðan abbod. c 1320 *Cast. Love* 246 He is þorw riht þeuwe and þral, To whos seruise he vnderstod with-al.

†**14.** To give heed, attend, listen, *to* one. *Obs.*

a 1200 *Moral Ode* 227 Vnderstondeð nu to me, edi men and arme, Ich wulle tellen of helle pin. 13.. *Guy of Warw.* 1292 Lordinges, þan seyd þe douk Otoun, Under-stond to mi resoun. a 1325 *Prose Psalter* liv. 1 Here myn oreisoun, and ne despise þou nouȝt my praiere, vnder-stonde to me, and here me. c 1450 *Merlin* xxxii. 633 Vndirstonde to me, and I shall telle the thy dreme.

**Understa·ndable,** *a.* Also 5 ondirstandabille. [f. prec. + -ABLE.]

**1.** That can be understood; intelligible.

c 1475 *Cath. Angl.* 260/1 (MS. A), Ondirstandabille, *intelligibilis.* 1577 HOLINSHED *Chron.* II. 735/1 Their language was vnknowne, and not vnderstandable to any man that coulde bee brought to talke with them. 1584 R. SCOT *Discov. Witchcr.* XII. xxi. 228 Whether the words of the charme be understandable or not, it skilleth not. 1625 A. GILL *Sacr. Philos.* Pref., Faith is a supplie of reason in things understandable, as the imagination is of sight in things that are visible. 1651 BAXTER *Inf. Baptism* 82 Otherwise we might pervert all Scripture, and none of it would be understandable. a 1670 SPALDING *Troub. Chas. I* (1851) II. 294 This vncouth act, scarss wnderstandabill, bred gryte feir and perturbatioun.

1799 SOUTHEY in *Life* (1850) II. 34, I suffer a good deal from illness, and in a way hardly understandable by those in health. 1832 *Examiner* 84/2 Putting the law in a readable and understandable shape. 1870 RUSKIN *Lect. Art* (1875) 73 There are two of the Puritans, whose work if I can succeed in making clearly understandable to you.., it is all I need care to do.

†**2.** Able to understand; capable of understanding.

1382 WYCLIF *Ecclus.* iii. 32 The wis herte and vnderstandable shal abstenen hymself from synnes. 1587 GOLDING *De Mornay* vi. 93 Theodorus..hath termed them, the substantiall Vnderstanding, the Vnderstandable substance, and the Fountayne of Soules. 1654 GAYTON *Pleas. Notes* IV. 197 The daughters of those mothers..are forward and understandable of womens matters, sooner than other children.

Hence **Understa·ndableness.**

Also, in recent use, *understandably* adv.

1656 tr. *T. White's Peripat. Inst.* 198 The Understandableness of a thing, or the quiddity, the whatnesse.

†**Understa·ndant.** *Obs.*—[1] [f. as prec. + -ANT.] An understanding person.

c 1400 *Secreta Secret., Gov. Lordsh.* 51 God..make his riches to abounde largely in the soules of wyse men, & gif graces to vnderstondantz & studiauntz.

**Understa·nder.** [f. as prec. + -ER.]

**1.** One who understands; one who has knowledge or comprehension (*of* something).

c 1430 *Pilgr. Lyf Manhode* II. xxi. (1869) 84 To good vnderstonderes it is the more gracious and the more plesaunt. 1456 SIR G. HAYE *Law Arms* (S.T.S.) 13 The thrid part of the understandaris of the faith. 1502 ATKYNSON tr. *De Imitatione* III. xlviii. 236, I am the inwarde techer of trouth, sercher of mannes hert, the vnderstander of mannes thought. 1577 FULKE *Confut. Purg.* 413 If you have not a better vnderstander, then you are a rule giuer, your rule is false. 1613 HEYWOOD *Braz. Age* II. ii, In Greece springs The fountaines of Diuine Phylosophy, They are all vnderstanders. 1677 GILPIN *Dæmonol. Sacra* II. 214 Some are pleased to be accounted Vnderstanders by others, and rest in such high words, as a badge of Knowledge. 1721 R. BALLE *Let.* in *Athenæum* 5 April (1902) 435/1 By th' understanders of sculpture, t'was att Florence esteemed next to the Duke's Veneri. 1855 PUSEY *Doctr. Real Presence* Note S. 527 Those among you who are yet called Catechumens or hearers, could be hearers, when it was being read: could they be understanders too?

†**2. a.** A leg or foot. **b.** A boot or shoe. *Obs.*

1583 MELBANCKE *Philotimus* U iij, She leuieth her army of huge boisterous hobs, wel beseming for their vnderstanders to bee the offspringe of Giauntes. 1749 J. RAY *Hist. Reb.* (1758) 135 They also borrow'd all the Shoes and Boots they could meet with; so that many were depriv'd of their Understanders.

†**3.** A spectator standing on the ground or floor *spec.* in a theatre. *Obs.*

1633 SHIRLEY *Contention Honour & Riches* C, When you ..make the understanders in Cheapside wonder to see ships swimme upon mens shoulders. 1646 — *Doubtful Heir* Prol., No shews, no dance, and what you most delight in, Grave understanders, here's no target fighting.

**4.** *poet.* A supporter, upholder.

1875 BROWNING *Aristoph. Apol.* 113 Strong understander of our common life, Staple sustainment of morality.

†**Understa·ndible,** var. UNDERSTANDABLE *a.*

1638 CHILLINGW. *Relig. Prot.* I. ii. § 103. 91 As to be understandible is a condition requisite to a Judge, so is not that alone sufficient to make a Judge.

**Understa·nding,** *vbl. sb.* [f. the vb. + -ING [1]. Cf. MSw. *undirstandning,* Icel. *-staðning.*]

**1.** (Without article.) Power or ability to understand; intellect, intelligence. Sometimes spec. = c.

a 1050 *Liber Scintill.* lxxxi. (1889) 221 Se þe þa on andȝyte inran understandincȝe [L. *intelligentiæ*] onfehþ. a 1300 *Cursor M.* 320 Minning es to [*v.r.* þe] fader cald, þe sune es vnderstanding tald. c 1340 HAMPOLE *Pr. Consc.* 605 Man when he is til worshepe broght Right understandyng has he noght. 1393 LANGL. *P. Pl.* C. XII. 300 Ac þese lewede laborers of lytel vnderstondynge Selde fallen so foule and so deepe in synne As clerkes of holy churche. 1422 tr. *Secreta Secret., Priv. Priv.* 135 By witte and connynge of vndyrstondynge a man may well chese the goode and lewe the ewill. c 1460 *Wisdom* 245–6 in *Macro Plays* 43 The iijde parte of þe soule ys 'wndyrstondynge'; For by wndyrstondyng I be-holde wat Gode ys In hym selff. 1531 ELYOT *Gov.* III. xxiv, To perceyue more playnly, what thinge it is that I call understandynge. It is the principall part of the soule. 1587 GOLDING *De Mornay* v. 55 The beginner of all ends is vnderstanding, and in the most of these there is no vnderstanding. 1621 BURTON *Anat. Mel.* I. i. II. x. 40 Vnderstanding is a power of the Soule, by which we perceiue, know, remember, and Iudge. 1667 MILTON *P. L.* IX. 1127 For Understanding rul'd not, and the Will Heard not her lore. 1716 HEARNE *Coll.* (O.H.S.) V. 338 This Nibb is a man of so little understanding that he was never known to laugh. 1759 ROBERTSON *Hist. Scot.* III. Wks. 1813 I. 245 Darnley was not superior to his father in understanding. 1779 *Mirror* No. 64, I found a perfect equality of understanding and of importance. 1821 SHELLEY *Epipsych.* 162 Love is like understanding, that grows bright, Gazing on many truths. 1894 A. BIRRELL *Ess.* xi. 131 He had not enough understanding to obfuscate it by drink.

**b.** *Of understanding,* intelligent, capable of judging with knowledge. Similarly *of some, of no, understanding.*

1428 *Munim. de Melros* (Bann. Club) 520 At þe quhilk day þe saide assis askyt mar help of men of vndirstandyng. 1535 COVERDALE 1 *Kings* iii. 12 Beholde, I haue geuen the an hert of wyszdome and vnderstondynge. 1537 BIBLE (Matthew) *Wisd.* xii. 24 They wente astraye..as chyldren of no vnderstandynge. 1600 HAKLUYT *Voy.* III. 21 And what danger that were,..each man of reason or vnderstanding may iudge. 1613 SHAKS. *Hen. VIII,* V. iii. 135 Men of some vnderstanding, And wisedome. 1772 *Boston Gazette* 3 Aug. 2/2 Men of understanding..view the Governor's Speech..as an impertinent sophistical Piece of Toryism.

**c.** With *the*: The faculty of comprehending and reasoning; the intellect.

1388 WYCLIF *Mark* xii. 33 That he be loued..of al the vndurstondynge, and of al the soule. 1620 T. GRANGER *Div. Logike* 108 The Vniuersall notions of the vnderstanding. 1663 BP. PATRICK *Parab. Pilgrim* (1687) 180 It cannot exercise the Understanding without provoking the passions. 1690 LOCKE *Hum. Und.* I. i. § 1 The Understanding, like the Eye,..takes no notice of it self. 1701 NORRIS *Ideal World* II. iii. (1704) 128 The business of the understanding can be no other than to understand. 1754 EDWARDS *Freed. Will* I. ii. 12 Then the Understanding must be taken in a large Sense, as including the whole Faculty of Perception or Apprehension. a 1859 DE QUINCEY *Knocking at Gate in Macb.* Wks. 1860 XIV. 192 The mere understanding..is the meanest faculty in the human mind, and the most to be distrusted. 1872 MORLEY *Voltaire* 5 Manifold ways, of all of which the emotions can give good account to the understanding.

†**d.** Mind, purpose, intent. *Obs. rare.*

1382 WYCLIF 1 *Pet.* iii. 8 Alle of oon vndirstondinge, or wille [L. *unanimes*]. 1531 ELYOT *Gov.* III. iv. (1883) II. 220 In euery couenaunt, bargayne, or promise aught to be..one playne understandinge or meaning betwene the parties.

**2.** The intellectual faculty as manifested in a particular person or set of persons.

1382 WYCLIF *Phil.* iv. 7 The pees of God..kepe 3oure hertis and vndirstondingis in Crist Jhesu. 1387-8 T. USK *Test. Love* I. Prol. (Skeat) l. 31 Right so..the understanding of Englishmen wol not strecche to the privy termes in Frenche.

*c* **1400** MAUNDEV. (1839) xvii. 186 So moche hathe the Erthe in roundnesse..aftre myn opynyoun and myn undirstondynge. *c* **1450** *Mirk's Festial* 228 Here ys no mencyon of our lady by semyng to mony mennys vndyrstondyng. **1535** COVERDALE 2 *Macc.* ii. 30 He that begynneth to wryte a story for the first, must with his vnderstondinge gather the matter together. **1576** FLEMING *Panopl. Epist.* 190 Haue these stately aduauncements of flourishing fortune, so blinded thine understanding? **1615** G. SANDYS *Trav.* 59 Auicen..reproueth..that saying of our Sauiour..as being weake and ill fitted to vulgar vnderstandings. **1666** BP. PARKER *Free & Impart. Censure* (1667) 77 A huge lushious stile..rather loaths and nauceats a discreet understanding, than informs and nourishes it. **1726** SWIFT *Gulliver, Brobdingnag* vii, It gave him..a very mean opinion of our understandings. **1769** ROBERTSON *Chas. V*, I. Wks. 1813 V. 167 Her understanding, always weak, was often disordered. **1815** SCOTT *Guy M.* xv, The idea of parting from Miss Lucy..had never once occurred to the simplicity of his understanding. **1874** CARPENTER *Ment. Phys.* I. ii. § 88. 98 Those who have obtained most influence over the understandings of others.

† **3.** Signification, meaning, sense. *Obs.*

13.. *Cursor M.* 14753 (Gött.), Vr lauerd Iesus þaim gaue ansuer, Bot þai ne wist quat vnderstanding it bar. **1340** *Ayenb.* 222 Huo þet ine þo onderstondinge yelt oþer acseþ zuiche dette, he ne zeneȝeþ naȝt. **1375** BARBOUR *Bruce* IV. 236 [Fiends] mak ay thair ansuering In-till dowbill vndirstanding, Till dissaf thame that will thame trow. *c* **1400** tr. *Secreta Secret., Gov. Lordsh.* 51 When ȝe haue fully þe vnderstondynges of þe sentences,..þanne shal ȝe pursewe fully..ȝoure purpos desiryd. **1424** *Paston Lett.* I. 13 Billes ..makyng mension and bering this undyrstondyng that the seyd William..schuld be slayn. *c* **1500** *Melusine* 364 There were ryche pictures where as were fygured many a noble hystory, and the wrytyng vndernethe that shewed the vnderstandyng of it. **1538** CROMWELL in Merriman *Life & Lett.* (1902) II. 152 As they be taught euery sentence of the same by rote ye shall expounde..the understandyng of the same vnto them. **1589** PUTTENHAM *Engl. Poesie* (Arb.) 189 Single words haue their sence and vnderstanding altered and figured many wayes. **1613** PURCHAS *Pilgrimage* (1614) 259 He and his fellowes were sent by..the Iewes, to learne the vnderstanding of some obscurer places of their law. **1635** *Gram. Warre* C 10 b, *Pasco* receiued two vnderstandings, 'to feed' and 'to bring vp'. **1728** CHAMBERS *Cycl.*, *Intendment of Law*, the Understanding, Intention, and true Meaning of the Law.

† **b.** Reference or application (*to* something).

**1433** *Rolls of Parlt.* IV. 451/2 Þat þis said worde Cloth.. have relation and understondyng to hole Clothes.

**4.** † **a.** Intelligence, information. *Obs.*

**1473** WARKW. *Chron.* 7 [He] had understondynge that Kynge Edwarde was in a vilage. *a* **1562** G. CAVENDISH *Wolsey* (1893) 242 His servaunts .. havyng understandyng of my lord's departyng awaye,..began to grudge. **1585** T. WASHINGTON tr. *Nicholay's Voy.* I. xvii. 19 b, The day before he had vnderstanding, that the Frigate..was of Malta.

**b.** Comprehension *of* something. *rare.*

**1548** ELYOT s.v. *Intellectus*, To atteyn to the knowlage or vnderstandyng of a thyng.

**5.** *A good* (or † *right*) *understanding*, amicable or friendly relations (between persons).

**1649** CROMWELL *Let.* 8 March (Carlyle), I trust there will be a right understanding between us, and a good conclusion. **1703** STEELE *Tender Husb.* v. i, I love to promote among my Clients a good Understanding. **1725** DE FOE *Voy. round World* (1840) 213 We came..to a better understanding about the frigate. **1762** in *10th Rep. Hist. MSS. Comm.* App. I. 323 To cultivate a good understanding between the two countries. **1833** HT. MARTINEAU *Loom & Lugger* I. iii. 37 The little hope there was of establishing a good understanding between the Coast Guard and the people. **1868** E. EDWARDS *Ralegh* I. xii. 230 Ralegh strove to bring about a good understanding between Essex and Cecil.

*transf.* **1765** STERNE *Tr. Shandy* VII. xix, 'Tis an undercraft of authors to keep up a good understanding amongst words, as politicians do amongst men.

**b.** A mutual arrangement or agreement of an informal but more or less explicit nature.

**1812** LADY GRANVILLE *Lett.* (1894) I. 43 They have, I hear, what is called, come to an understanding. **1860** TYNDALL *Glac.* I. xxiii. 164 With this understanding we parted for the night. **1876** BLACK *Madcap Violet* xv, I think it is better we should have a distinct understanding about that.

**c.** *spec.* (See quot.)

**1826** *Oxberry's Dram. Biog.* V. 97, 20 guineas per week and an understanding at Covent-garden. [*Note*] By this is meant, certain emoluments..that shall increase the real amount of her salary.

**6.** *slang* or *colloq.* **a.** *pl.* Foot-wear; boots or shoes.

**1822** MRS. NATHAN *Langreath* I. 29 They have been seen in the act of adapting their nethermost understandings to the costume of the more wealthy. **1838** JAS. GRANT *Sk. Lond.* 87 His toes began to peep out between the soles and uppers of his 'understandings'—as he sometimes facetiously called his boots. **1874** *Slang Dict.* 333 Men who wear exceptionally large or thick boots, are said to possess good understandings.

**b.** *pl.* Legs or feet.

**1828** *Lancet* 22 March 920/1 His plump, well-formed, little 'understandings' twinkling in the lustre of black silk hose. **1844** 'JONATHAN SLICK' *High Life N. York* II. 58 She had on a short petticoat that showed a..considerable chunk of understandings. **1856** 'STONEHENGE' *Brit. Rur. Sports* 381/2 Discount was..the perfection of a strong, well-bred horse,..if only his understandings had been sound.

**Understa·nding,** *ppl. a.* [f. as prec + -ING [2].]

**1.** Of persons (or animals): Possessed of understanding; having knowledge and judgement; intelligent.

Very common in the 17th century.

*c* **1200** *Trin. Coll. Hom.* 121 Ðe man is understondinde, þe him seluen cnoweð and gode leueð. **1338** R. BRUNNE *Chron.* (1810) 35 He was boþe gode & wys in alle his dedis, & right vnderstandyng, to help at alle nedis. **1382** WYCLIF *Deut.* iv. 6 A wise puple and an vndirstondynge! *c* **1440** *Promp. Parv.* 511 Vnderstondynge, or wytty, *intelligens.* **1535** COVERDALE *Deut.* iv. 6 What a wyse and vnderstondinge folke is this? **1613** WITHER *Abuses Stript* II. ii. O 5 b, A selected Crew,..the Wisest, The Vnderstanding'st, yea, and the Precisest Of a whole Empire. **1634** SIR T. HERBERT *Trav.* 29 A modest and understanding Gentleman. *Ibid.* 90 An Elephant (an vnderstanding beast). **1681** OTWAY *Soldier's Fort.* v. i, Aristotle..was an understanding fellow. **1711** ADDISON *Spect.* No. 42 ¶ 6 The more understanding Part of the Audience immediately see through it and despise it. **1772** PRIESTLEY *Inst. Relig.* (1782) I. 377 There were among them many..understanding persons. **1817–8** COBBETT *Resid. U.S.* (1822) 167 One of the most understanding and most worthy men I ever had the honour to be acquainted with. **1875** JOWETT *Plato* (ed. 2) I. 132 The Athenians are an understanding people.

*absol.* **1650** GENTILIS *Considerations* 194 So that..we may say, that the understandingest doth command by cunning, the most rash by violence.

**b.** Const. *in* (a matter, etc.). Now *rare* or *Obs.*

**1612** BACON *Ess., Of Judicature* (Arb.) 458 An ancient Clearke, skilful in presidents, .. and vnderstanding in the businesse of the Court. *c* **1643** LD. HERBERT *Autobiog.* (1824) 35 Howsoever he was very understanding in all other things, he was noted yet to be of a very high mind. **1732** LORD TYRAWLY in *Buccleuch MSS.* (Hist. MSS. Comm.) I. 381 My Captain, who is a very understanding fellow in these matters. **1755** *Mem. Capt. P. Drake* I. ii. 19 A very understanding Man in the Business of Cow-stealing.

**2.** Of the mind, etc.: Endowed with intelligence; intellectual.

**1382** WYCLIF 1 *Kings* iii. 12 I haue..ȝeuen to thee a wise herte and an vndurstondynge [L. *sapiens et intelligens*]. **1398** TREVISA *Barth. De P. R.* V. xxviii. (Bodl. MS.), Kinde ȝeueþ to man vndirstonding instrumentes according to his vertues. **1539** BIBLE (Great) 1 *Kings* iii. 9 Geue therfore vnto thy seruaunt an vnderstandyng hert. **1581** J. BELL *Haddon's Answ. Osor.* 141 Mans will and the understandyng parte of his soule. **1662** H. MORE *Antid. Ath.* III. i. § 2 Some free subtile understanding Essence distinct from the brute Matter. **1681** FLAVEL *Meth. Grace* xxiii. 401 The understanding faculty like a dial is enlightened with the beams of divine truth shining upon it. **1827** POLLOK *Course T.* III. 636 Be wise, Ye fools! be of an understanding heart. **1853** F. D. MAURICE *Proph. & Kings* v. 78 The understanding heart of Solomon led him to revere as well as to suspect himself.

**b.** Of speech: Displaying intelligence. *rare*[-1].

**1635** J. TAYLOR (Water P.) *Very Old Man* C, Loves Company, and Vnderstanding talke.

† **3.** Capable of being understood; intelligible. *Obs.*

**1387–8** T. USK *Test. Love* I. Prol. (Skeat) l. 56 By thilke thinges that ben made understonding here to our wittes. *c* **1400** tr. *Secreta Secret., Gov. Lordsh.* 93 All þare-by is vnderstandant, and neghys negh, þat þat ys remued of farre.

**Understa·ndingly,** *adv.* [f. prec. + -LY [2].] In a comprehending or intelligent manner; with understanding. † Also, so as to be understood.

*a* **1340** HAMPOLE *Psalter* xlviii. 12 For he wroght not vndirstandan[d]ly he is likynd..til vnwise bestis in vnwisdome. *c* **1400** tr. *Secreta Secret., Gov. Lordsh.* 101 Besily and vnderstandandly y amonest þe, and gyues þe good conseill. **1580** HOLLYBAND *Treas. Fr. Tong, Entendiblement*, vnderstandingly, learnedly. **1602** FULBECKE *Pandects* 55 It is more plainlie and understandinglie opened by hime in these wordes. **1649** F. ROBERTS *Clavis Bibl.* 46 Still fix your thought upon the Occasion and Scope of every Book, when you would peruse them understandingly. **1697** HUMFREY *Righteousn. God* I. 6 This Learned Man hath..understandingly exprest the very thing as it is. **1754** EDWARDS *Freedom Will* IV. viii. 248 A Work of his almighty Power,..upheld understandingly, and on Design, as much as if no other had been made but that. **1833** *New Monthly Mag.* XXXVIII. 154 His was one of those clear eyes which see beauty understandingly. **1850** *Fraser's Mag.* XLI. 524 The young people began to look very understandingly at each other. **1890** MARY E. WILKINS *Far-away Melody* 16 They had studied the Bible faithfully, if not understandingly.

† **Understa·ndingness.** *Obs.* [f. as prec. + -NESS.] The state or condition of having understanding; the faculty of understanding.

*a* **1628** F. GREVILLE *Poems* (1633) 60 In Mans youth, perchance, Fame multiplies Courage, and actiue vnderstandingnesse. **1662** J. CHANDLER *Van Helmont's Oriat.* 25 In the understandingness of the understanding.

**U·ndersta·te,** *v.* [UNDER-[1] 10 a.] *trans.* To state below what is correct or warrantable. Also *absol.*, to make an understatement.

**1824** MACKINTOSH *Sp. Ho. Comm.* 1 June, Wks. 1846 III. 430 A pious and amiable woman,..anxious rather to understate facts. **1850** GROTE *Greece* II. lxiv. VIII. 252 *note*, I have understated the number of lives in danger. **1874** GLADSTONE in *Contemp. Rev.* Oct. 673 In commenting on over-statement, I do not seek to understate.

† **U·nder-sta·ted,** *a. Obs.* [UNDER-[1] 10 c.] Of too low or poor an estate.

*a* **1661** FULLER *Worthies, Bedford.* I. (1662) 118 Sir Henry, though heir to his Brother Richard after his death; yet perceiving himself over-titled or rather under-stated, for so high an honour,..declined the assuming thereof.

**U·nderstatement.** [UNDER-[1] 10 b. Cf. UNDERSTATE *v.*] A statement which falls below the truth or fact.

**1799** *Monthly Rev.* XXVIII. 528 Stating at the lowest its own populousness and produce, and..favouring a similar understatement by its neighbours. **1877** MORLEY *Crit. Misc.* Ser. II. 330 Mr. Mill's remarks..involve a distinct understatement.

**U·nderstay,** *sb.* (UNDER-[1] 5 b.) *a* **1603** T. CARTWRIGHT *Confut. Rhem. N. T.* (1618) 729 That prop and vnderstay of our faith..is cleane ouerthrown. **Understay·,** *v.* (UNDER-[1] 4 a.) **1679** A. LOVELL *Indic. Univ.* 39 To prop or understay the Vine. **Understee·r,** *v.* (UNDER-[1] 4 b.) **1573** TWYNE *Æneid* x. E e j, In sight she deare apeerd With left hand couching waues, and smoth herself she vndersteerd [L. *subremigat*]. **U·nder-stem.** (UNDER-[1] 5 b.) **1853** RUSKIN *Stones Ven.* II. ii. § 6. 17 It is delightful to see how he has rooted the whole leaf in the strong rounded under-stem. **1868** *Rep. U.S. Commissioner Agric.* (1869) 94 The European species..is found upon low plants, gnawing the under-stems. **U·nderstep,** *sb.* (UNDER-[1] 5 b.) **1610** J. ROBINSON *Justif. Separat.* iii. 10 That by it, as by an understep, he might climb up..into the throne of iniquity. **Underste·p,** *v.* (UNDER-[1] 10 a.) **1843** *Blackw. Mag.* LIV. 652 Were such phraseology allowable, we should say that the sphere has understepped itself.

**U·nder-stew:ard.** (UNDER-[1] 6 a.)

**1472–3** *Rolls of Parlt.* VI. 35/1 Depute and understeward to John Erle of Wilteshire. **1483** *Act 1 Rich. III*, c. 6 § 1 No Steward, Under-Steward,..nor other Minister of such Courts of Pipowders. **1667** in Pettus *Fodinæ Reg.* (1670) 39 One Vnder-Steward to recide at the Mines. **1708** J. CHAMBERLAYNE *St. Gt. Brit.* (1710) 226 The Under-Steward of Westminster is likewise an Officer of great Note.

Hence **U·nder-stew:ardship.**

**1472–3** *Rolls of Parlt.* VI. 35/1 The said Office of understewardshipp.

† **Understi·pre,** *v. Obs.*[-1] [UNDER-[1] 4 a: see STIPER.] *trans.* To prop up, support.

The variant *understipen* corresponds to WFris. *stypje.*

*a* **1225** *Ancr. R.* 142 Heo wuneð under þe chirche, ase uorte understipren [*v.r.* understipen] hire, ȝif heo wolde uallen.

**U·nder-stock,** *sb. arch.* (UNDER-[1] 5 b.) **1821** SCOTT *Kenilw.* xxxi, His shoes being of white velvet; his understocks (or stockings) of knit silk.

**U:ndersto·ck,** *v.* (UNDER-[1] 10 a: cf. next.)

**1765** *Museum Rust.* IV. 267 The same ill consequences attend either over or under-stocking a farm with all other cattle. **1771** A. YOUNG *Northern Tour* IV. 272 If it be asked, why farmers..so much understock themselves.

**U:ndersto·cked,** *ppl. a.* (UNDER-[1] 10 a.)

**1670** SIR T. CULPEPPER *Necess. Abating Usury* 32 His farme is understocked, ill fenced, and out of heart. **1733** TULL *Horse-Hoeing Husb.* xiv. 166 The Ground may be.. understock'd with Plants. **1792** A. YOUNG *Trav. France* 489 For the country..to import so immensely, shews how wretchedly they are understocked with sheep. **1846** MCCULLOCH *Acc. Brit. Empire* (1854) I. 561 Farms in all parts of Britain are decidedly understocked.

**U·nder-sto:ckings.** (UNDER-[1] 5 a.) **1605** *Knaresb. Wills* (Surtees) I. 252 One paire of white under stockines. **1648** HEXHAM II, *Onder-koussen*, Vnder or Nether-stockins.

**Understone:** see quot. s.v. UNDERCLIFT.

**Understoo·d,** *pa. pple.* and *ppl. a.* [f. UNDERSTAND *v.*]

† **1.** Being made known or patent. *Obs.*[-1]

**1576** LAMBARDE *Peramb. Kent* 152 This done and vnder stoode to the Archbishop, she was by him appointed to S. Sepulcres.

**2.** Comprehended; thoroughly known.

**1605** SHAKS. *Macb.* III. iv. 124 Augures, and vnderstood Relations, haue..brought forth The secret'st man of Blood. **1661** BOYLE *Style of Script.* 48 By the light of understood Scriptures to penetrate the sense of the obscurer ones. *a* **1700** EVELYN *Diary* 12 Oct. 1677, The gardens are large,..and the husbandry part made very convenient and perfectly understood.

**3.** Agreed upon; assumed as known or fixed.

**1607** in W. H. Hale *Prec. in Causes of Office* (1841) 9 He doth now confesse that it was an understood part of his therein. **1833** HT. MARTINEAU *Fr. Wines & Pol.* iii. 33 There had been established a tolerably steady rate of understood value. **1853** MRS. GASKELL *Ruth* xxiii, It was an understood thing that no one was to be ill or tired..without leave asked. **1897** MARY KINGSLEY *W. Africa* 317 Each chief takes a certain understood value in goods as a commission for himself.

**4.** *Gram.* Implied though not expressed.

**1848** J. T. WHITE *Xenophon's Anab.* Notes 38 Observe the adverb between the article and the understood noun, supplying the place of an adjective.

**U·nderstrain.** (UNDER-[1] 9 b.) ? **1802** COLERIDGE *Happy Husband* 22 A more precipitated vein Of notes, that..leave their sweeter understrain, Its own sweet self.

**U·nderstra·pper.** [f. UNDER-[1] 6 a + STRAP *v.* Cf. STRAPPER [1] 2.] An underling; a subordinate agent; an assistant. (In common use from *c* 1710.)

*a* **1704** T. BROWN *Walk round Lond., Thames* Wks. 1709 III. III. 60 Every Wapping Understrapper, that has but a Congregation of old Women to hold himself forth to. **1753** SMOLLETT *Ct. Fathom* xxix, I desire you will order him and this barber, who is his understrapper, to be examined on the spot. **1842** THACKERAY *Fitz-Boodle's Conf.* Wks. 1869 XXII. 211 Let one of your understrappers correct the spelling and the grammar of my papers. **1894** BLACKMORE *Perlycross* 297 The meanest..understrapper of the 'Private Enquiry Firm'.

**U·nderstra·pping,** *a.* [Cf. prec.] Of a subordinate or inferior character or standing.

**1762** STERNE *Tr. Shandy* VI. xvii, I..have as great a share ..of that under-strapping virtue of discretion as the best of you. **1793** J. WILLIAMS *Calm Exam.* 45 The understrapping and base members of the awful mystery [of the law].

**U·nderstra·tum.** [UNDER-[1] 5 c.] An underlying stratum or layer; a substratum.

**1733** TULL *Horse-Hoeing Husb.* xx. 290 These Drags draw them sometimes into larger Heaps, leaving the Under-Stratum bare betwixt them. **1783** *Encycl. Brit.* (ed. 2) X. 8307/1 However great differences there may be among the under strata. **1807** VANCOUVER *Agric. Devon* (1813) 19 The soil and understrata of Little Torrington. **1886** *19th Cent.* Sept. 421 There is a vast and virtuous understratum in society which really loves the right.

**U·nderstream.** (UNDER-[1] 5 c.) **1830** TENNYSON *Poems* 125 The glistering sands that robe The understream. **1883** *Pall Mall G.* 26 July 7/1 As the understreams formed by the Horseshoe Falls rise to the surface.

**Understrew·,** *v.* [UNDER-[1] 4 a.] *trans.* To strew or spread beneath; *fig.* to cast under foot.

1382 WYCLIF *Luke* xix. 36 Thei vndir strewiden [L. *substernebant*] her clothis in the weye. 1471 RIPLEY *Comp. Alch.* Ep. i. in Ashm. (1652) 109 So that old ranckors understrewed, Tempestuous troubles and wretchednes shall cease. 1589 FLEMING *Virg. Georg.* III. 46 T' vnderstrew or spread the bare ground with..Handfuls of ferne.

**U·nderstrife.** *poet.* [UNDER-[1] 5 b.] Strife carried on upon the earth.

c 1611 CHAPMAN *Iliad* xx. 138 We soon shall..send them to heaven, to settle their abode With equals, flying understrifes.

**Understri·ke,** *v.* [UNDER-[1] 4 a, b.]

†**1.** *trans.* To let down (the sails of a ship). *Obs.*

1615 CHAPMAN *Odyss.* XVI. 474 Amphinomus in port display'd The ship arrived, her sails then under-stroke.

**2.** To strike (from) below.

1844 MRS. BROWNING *Lady Geraldine's Courtship* xlvii, For the root of some grave earnest thought is understruck so rightly As [etc.].

Hence **U·nderstri·king** *ppl. a.*

1880 A. J. HIPKINS in Grove *Dict. Mus.* II. 647/1 For understriking grand pianos..and for upright pianos. *Ibid.* 712/1 Both overstriking and understriking apparatus.

**U·nderstroke,** *sb.* (UNDER-[1] 5 b.) 1837 WHEELWRIGHT tr. *Aristophanes, Birds* III. i, By their feet the geese with understrokes As 'twere with shovels, threw it in the hods.

**Understro·ke,** *v.* [UNDER-[1] 4 b. Cf. G. *unterstreichen,* Da. *understrege.*] *trans.* To underline, underscore.

1732 SWIFT *Let. to Duchess of Queensbury* 20 Mar., You have understroaked that offensive word, to shew that it should be printed in italic.

**U·nderstu·dy,** *sb.* [f. next.] An actor or actress who studies a superior performer's part in order to be able to take it if required; also, the study of a part for this purpose. Also *transf.*

1882 *Society* 7 Oct. 13/2 His place during his absence..having been filled by his understudy. 1884 G. MOORE *Mummer's Wife* xv, The girl who..had been entrusted with the understudy. 1887 LANG *Myth, Ritual & Relig.* I. 336 There is a..tendency for gods to double their parts, or rather,..for each part to have its 'under-study'.

**Understu·dy,** *v.* [UNDER-[1] 7.]

**1.** *trans.* To study (a part or character) in order to be able to take the place of a principal actor or actress if necessary.

1874 *Slang Dict.* 333 Some actors of position..have always other and inferior..artists understudying their parts. 1880 *Theatre* Oct. 207 She was selected to understudy the characters of the stars.

**2.** To act as understudy to (a principal actor or actress).

1884 G. MOORE *Mummer's Wife* xv, Some one must understudy Serpolette. 1894 CROCKETT *Play Actress* ix, She has to understudy Rose Sargeant and play her parts when that lady's temper is out of order.

*transf.* 1893 *Westm. Gaz.* 23 June 5/2 (Racing), Watercress had no difficulty in understudying La Flêche last week.

Hence **U·nderstu·died** *ppl. a.*

1880 *Temple Bar* March 321 An under-studied Part.

**Understu·ffed,** *ppl. a.* (UNDER-[1] 4 a.) 1573 *Arte of Limning* A iij, A litle borde..couered with a calues skin raysed or vnderstuffed with wolle or floxe or else vnstuffed.

†**Understu·mble,** *v. colloq. Obs.* [Alteration of UNDERSTAND *v.*, after STUMBLE *v.* Cf. UNDERCUMSTUMBLE *v.*] *trans.* To understand.

c 1681 HICKERINGILL *Trimmer* vi. Wks. 1716 I. 386 Oh! ho! I begin to understumble you, Edad, I will not tell you. 1738 SWIFT *Polite Conv.* 105, I understumble you, Gentlemen.

†**Undersubscri·be, -scri·ve,** *v. Sc. Obs.* [UNDER-[1] 4 a.] *intr.* To subscribe to a document.

α. 1565 *Reg. Privy Council Scot.* I. 363 We, the Erlis..and Baronis undirsubscrivand. 1605 in *Abst. Protocols Town Clerks of Glasgow* (1896) II. 115 With expres consent ..of the counsall and deikinis of the said burght wndirsubscriveand. 1644 *Reg. Privy Counc. Scotl.* Ser. II. VIII. 97 In presence of me, notar publict undersubscryvand, and witnesses efternamet.

β. 1573 *Reg. Privy Council Scot.* II. 310 We undersubscriband to be bundin and obleist [etc.]. 1642 *Declar. Lords & Comm., To Gen. Assemb. Ch. Scot., Lond.* 12 Divers other undersubscribing. 1708 *Lond. Gaz.* No. 4430/6 We,..the Noblemen..of the Shire of Ayr undersubscribing.

Hence †**Undersubscri·ber.** *Obs.*

1681 W. KER, etc. (*title*), A Blasphemous and Treasonable Paper emitted by the Phanatical Under-subscribers. 1726 SHELVOCKE *Voy. round World* 39 We under subscribers, Officers, seamen and others. 1799 MITCHELL *Scotticisms* 88 We the under subscribers; Sc.—Subscribers, undersigned.

**U·nder-su·cking,** *ppl. a.* [UNDER-[1] 4 a, b.] **a.** Sucking from below. **b.** Sucking down.

1611 SPEED *Hist. Gt. Brit.* VII. xxxvii. § 2. 335 Yᵉ blossoms of vnder-sucking plants. *a* 1885 CHR. G. ROSSETTI *Poems* (1904) 144/2 Who sinks, uplift from the undersucking silt To set him on Thy rock.

**U·nder-suit.** (UNDER-[1] 5 a.)

1598 *Sidney's Arcadia* III. 361 Hauing..first put on a sleight vnder-sute of mans apparell. *a* 1661 FULLER *Worthies, Hampsh.* II. (1662) 8 He..put off his Robes of State, resigning his Office:..no danger of catching cold, his own Under-suit was so well lined, having gotten a fair Estate ..in Sussex. 1696 *Lond. Gaz.* No. 3204/3 The Knight Elect ..being in his Under-Suit of the Order, of Cloth of Silver,.. was..conducted..to the Chapter-house.

**U·nder-su·rface.** (UNDER-[1] 5 b.)

Also freq. as two words: see UNDER *a.* 2 b.

1733 TULL *Horse-Hoeing Husb.* xxv. 404 The Under-surface of the Limbers..parallel..to the Upper-surface..of the Beam. 1836–9 *Todd's Cycl. Anat.* II. 861/2 The pro-sternum or under-surface of the prothorax. 1853 MARKHAM *Skoda's Auscult. & Percuss.* 214 Murmurs are produced at the aortic valves, when their under-surfaces are roughened.

†**Undersustenta·tion.** *Obs.* (UNDER-[1] 5 c.) 1650 ELDERFIELD *Tythes* 180 The bottome foundation fails, and the whole frame must be left to sink and ruine with it for want of sustenance, or undersustentation. **U·nder-swain.** (UNDER-[1] 6 a.) 1644 QUARLES *Sheph. Orac.* iii, She..Cast am'rous eyes on every under-swaine. **U·nderswa·rd.** (UNDER-[1] 5 c.) 1883 G. ALLEN *Colin Clout's Cal.* 182 Stiff wiry knot-grass forming..a ragged undersward.

**U·nderswea·rer.** [UNDER-[1] 6 a.] One who supports another by oath.

1724 SWIFT *Drapier's Lett.* iv. Wks. 1761 III. 77 The infamous Coleby, one of his under-swearers at the Committee of Council.

**Underswea·t,** *v.* (UNDER-[1] 7 + SWEAT *v.* 6 b.)

1888 *Times* (weekly ed.) 18 May 7/4 The English Jews complain that they are 'undersweated'. 1896 *Globe* 15 Dec., The German toy-makers who undersweat the world.

**U·nderswell.** [UNDER-[1] 5 c.] A swell below the surface; an undercurrent.

1849 *Tait's Mag.* XVI. 760 This placid springtime of life had a strong underswell of sorrow. 1894 *Cycl. Rev. Current Hist.* (Buffalo, N.Y.) IV. 733 A certain insistence of tone which gives note of a strong underswell of feeling and purpose.

†**Under-swordfish.** *Obs.* = HALF-BEAK.

1681 GREW *Musæum* I. v. i. 87 The Head of the Under-Sword-Fish.

**Underta·kable,** *a.* [f. UNDERTAKE *v.* + -ABLE.] Capable of being undertaken.

1638 CHILLINGW. *Relig. Prot.* Ded., It was undertakable by a man of very mean..abilities.

†**U·ndertake,** *sb. Obs.* [f. next.] An undertaking, enterprise.

1647 SPRIGGE *Anglia Rediv.* IV. ix. 295 The spoyle of the Castle, which cannot be avoyded in extreame undertakes against it. 1676 *Doctrine of Devils* To Rdr., I shall say no more in vindication of the undertake.

**Undertake** (ʌndəɹtēⁱ·k), *v.* [f. UNDER-[1] 8 a + TAKE *v.*, after UNDERNIM *v.* Cf. MSw. *undertaka.*]

**I.** *trans.* †**1. a.** To take by craft, to entrap; to overtake, seize upon. *Obs.*

c 1200 ORMIN 10314 Forrþi þatt teȝȝ haffdenn niþ Wiþþ himm..& wolldenn unnderrtakenn himm Off summwhatt, ȝiff þeȝȝ mihhtenn. 1470–85 MALORY *Arthur* IX. xxxvii. 400 So sire Tristram endured there grete payne, for sekenesse had vndertake hym.

†**b.** To reprove, rebuke, chide. *Obs.*

1377 LANGL. *P. Pl.* B. XI. 89 'Wher-of serueth lawe,' quod lewte, 'if no lyf vndertoke it, Falsenesse ne faytrye'. 1387 TREVISA *Higden* (Rolls) II. 133 He wente to Scotlonde wiþ grete indingnacioun, for Wilfrede vndertook hym for he hylde vnlawfulliche Esterday. c 1400 *Pilgr. Sowle* I. xix. (1859) 19, I haue ful oftymes for thy mysdedys undertake the. c 1440 *Gesta Rom.* lxv. 290 Whan he was come, the Emperour vndirtoke hym of the cryme that he did to Guy. 1480 CAXTON *Chron. Eng.* cliii, And he wold dysherite the good erle..for encheson that he undertoke hym of his wikkedness. 1691 tr. *Emiliane's Frauds Rom. Monks* (ed. 3) 53 When he was in the company of Monks, who were not Reformed,.. he would undertake them in a high manner, yea, with Insolence it self.

†**2. a.** To accept, receive willingly. *Obs.*

*a* 1250 *Ancr. R.* 114 He..underueng [*Titus MS.* undertoc] hit edmodliche. *a* 1300 *Cursor M.* 917 And þou, man, þat has vndertaken þi wijf red, and min for-saken, Ne sal þou nawight þar wit win. *Ibid.* 9064 Yee rede me nu, for drightin sake, Your consail wil i vndertak. 1303 R. BRUNNE *Handl. Synne* 9984 For he wulde nat men hyt forsoke, But þat alle men hyt vndyrtoke. 1338 — *Chron.* (1810) 60 Þe barons said, ..Þare trespas we vndertake opon alle our fee.

†**b.** To receive; to have given. *Obs.*

13.. *Cursor M.* 4642 (Gött.), I wil þat he here vndir-take All þe worschip of mi land. 1393 LANGL. *P. Pl.* C. I. 98 And boxes ben broght forþ i-bounden with yre, To vndertake þe tol of vntrewe sacrifice In menynge of miracles. 1623 LISLE *Ælfric on O. & N. Test.* Introd., Moses,..who wrote as God himself directed..while he abode with God upon Mount Sinai..& undertook [OE. orig., *underfeng*] his law.

†**c.** To receive into the mind; to hear. *Obs.*

13.. *St. Alexius* 54 in Horstm. *Altengl. Leg.* (1881) 175 His fadir sette him sone to boke And wele clergie he vndirtoke. 1382 WYCLIF *Ecclus.* ii. 2 Bowe in thyn ere, and vndertac [L. *suscipe*] the wrdis of vndirstonding. 1596 SPENSER *F. Q.* v. iii. 34 Whose voice so soone as he did vndertake, Eftsoones he stood as still as any stake.

†**3.** To understand. *Obs.*

*a* 1300 *Cursor M.* 307 And be þe hette þou vnderta þe hali gost comms of hem tua. *Ibid.* 2050 Noe wit þat mantil woke, His sun hething he vnder-toke. *a* 1400–50 *Alexander* 2967 Sone þis gouernour of grece is of þis gaude ware,..& vndiretuke he touched of him-selfe. c 1440 *York Myst.* xxiii. 23 Ȝe cowde noght vndyr-take The tales þat I ȝou tolde. c 1510 MORE *Picus* Wks. 10/1 While she spake of the seconde death and euerlasting: & he vndertoke her of the first death & temporal.

**4.** To take upon oneself; to take in hand.

Sometimes contextually 'to enter upon, begin'.

*a* 1300 *Cursor M.* 4644, I wil him do at vnder-tak þe wardanscipp of al mi land. *Ibid.* 4795, I am all redi bun Our aller nedes vnder ta. *a* 1340 HAMPOLE *Psalter* xxiv. 7 A ȝoungman dredis noght to vndirtake þe peril þat he is slane in. c 1374 CHAUCER *Troylus* II. 807 He which þat no þyng vnder-taketh No þyng ne acheueth. 1404 in Ellis *Orig. Lett.* Ser. II. I. 20 The same cuntrees have undertake the seges of hem til thei ben wonnen. c 1489 CAXTON *Sonnes of Aymon* xxvi. 549 Telle me..what he sayeth of this quarell that ye have vndertake. 1597 HOOKER *Eccl. Pol.* v. liv. § 6 The.. offices of that mysticall administration..which he voluntarily vnder-tooke. *a* 1628 PRESTON *Effectual Faith* (1630) 8 Therefore they vndertake the businesse, they goe about the enterprize, and it comes to naught. 1654 GATAKER *Disc. Apol.* 53 [They] are readie to undertake more than they are able to undergo, or to go through with. 1717 LADY M. W. MONTAGU *Let. to Pope* 1 April, I have gone a journey not undertaken by any Christian for some hundred years. 1781 COWPER *Table-T.* 284 They, that fight for freedom, undertake The noblest cause mankind can have at stake. 1831 SCOTT *Ct. Rob.* xviii, What is the enterprise too bold to be undertaken on such a condition! 1847 MARRYAT *Childr. N. Forest* xvii, I hope you will undertake the post which I now offer you. 1874 GREEN *Short Hist.* vi. § 4 (1882) 306 Colet..was the first to undertake the reform of the Church.

*ellipt.* 1605 CAMDEN *Rem.* 3 If any one would vndertake the honour and precedence of Britaine before other Realmes in serious manner. 1655 STANLEY *Hist. Philos.* III. 37 His friends..desired him to æstimate it at 50. minæ, promising to undertake the sum.

**b.** Const. *to* with inf. (Sometimes implying a solemn pledge or promise: cf. next.)

*a* 1300 *Cursor M.* 3409 Now es god at vnder tak þe store tell [*Gött.* stori to tell] of ysaac. c 1385 CHAUCER *L. G. W.* Prol. 71, I ne haue nat vndyr-take As of the lef a-gayn the flour to make. 1390 GOWER *Conf.* I. 151 He..seith that he wol undertake Upon hire wordes forto stonde. c 1440 *Generydes* 3175 Among your knyghtez all that ther is on Shall vnder take to Answer for this lande. 1494 in *Lett. Rich. III & Hen. VII* (Rolls) I. 389 Diuers noble personnes hanne enterprised and undertaked to hold a justis roiall. 1560 DAUS tr. *Sleidane's Comm.* 259, I wold first vndertake to geue ye charge vpon thennemy wᵗ ii legions. 1591 SHAKS. *Two Gent.* III. ii. 38 Then you must vndertake to slander him. 1637 W. SALTONSTALL *Eusebius' Constantine* 26 Constantine had undertooke..to free the Christians from his tyranny. 1667 MILTON *P. L.* IV. 935, I alone first undertook To wing the desolate Abyss. 1712 BLACKMORE *Creation* v. 281 That matter..in the immense from endless ages strove, The Stagyrite thus undertakes to prove. 1754 SHEBBEARE *Matrimony* (1766) II. 259 Without this Power the Mother-in-Law would scarce have undertook to have trafficed in the commerce of a Son committed to her care. 1821 SCOTT *Kenilw.* xxvi, Wayland and she followed in silence the deputy-usher, who undertook to be their conductor. 1860 TYNDALL *Glac.* I. xxi. 150 A porter..undertook to conduct me to one of the adjacent glaciers.

**c.** To give a formal promise or pledge *that*; to take upon oneself to promise or affirm; to venture to assert.

c 1375 *Sc. Leg. Saints* vii. (*Jacob*) 606 Wil þu vndirta þat I and þai þat are with me, In gud fath sal vnschait be? 1393 LANGL. *P. Pl.* C. XXI. 20 Loue haþ vndertake That þis iesus of hus gentrise shal Iouste in peers Armes. c 1450 *Mirk's Festial* 13 He wold vndyrtake þat þay schuld want ryght noght of hor mette. 15.. *Adam Bel* cxxx, I dare vndertake for them That true men they shal be. 1530 PALSGR. 767/2, I dare undertake that he hath sayd nothynge but he wyll parforme it. *a* 1548 HALL *Chron., Edw. IV,* 230, I..vndertake, that this communicacion shal sorte, and come to suche an effecte, that [etc.]. 1617 MORYSON *Itin.* II. 63 Sir Richard Moryson (..whom he would vndertake to be as worthy in his profession, as any of his time). *a* 1649 WINTHROP *New Eng.* (1825) I. 145 Mr. Maverick came and undertook that the offenders should be forthcoming. *a* 1715 BURNET *Own Time* (1766) II. 49 He undertook to me, that the King should ask me no question. 1829 SCOTT *Anne of G.* xxxi, I have ridden ..to present you with this letter,..having undertaken to your father that it should be delivered without delay. 1895 *Funk's Stand. Dict.* s.v., I'll undertake I can run faster than you.

**d.** *I (dare) undertake,* added to a statement.

1362 LANGL. *P. Pl.* A. XI. 108 Þei two, as Ich hope.., Schul wisse þe to Dowel, I dar vndertake. ? *a* 1366 CHAUCER *Rom. Rose* 175 Wel coude he peynte, I vndirtake, That sich ymage coude make. *a* 1400 *Pistill of Susan* 208 Ȝit schal troupe hem a-taynt, I dar vnder-take. 1447 BOKENHAM *Seyntys* (Roxb.) 18 The fals goddys doth ye forsake,..Wych be not ellys, I undyrtake, But gold or sylvyr, stonys or tre. c 1480 HENRYSON *Fables, Lion & Mouse* 128 Thy fals excuse..Sall not auaill ane myte, I vnderta. 1821 SCOTT *Kenilw.* i, You have gallants among you, I dare undertake, that have made the Virginia voyage.

**e.** With ellipse of inf. or obj. clause.

c 1440 *Generides* 7006 A rich woman I shal you make, That dar I wel vndretake. 1638 *Hamilton Papers* (Camden) 2 They [were] injoyned to dou ther best, and to goe presentely home, which they undertuck. 1651 *Nicholas Papers* (Camden) 257 Hee himselfe goes into Plimouth till all the articles be confirmd by Act of Parliament, which they have undertaken.

†**f.** To guarantee to cure. *Obs.*

1479 *Stonor Lett.* (1919) II. 88 And [=if] he may kepe him alive till Tuesday none, he will undertake him. 1480 *Ibid.* 100 The ffesicion wolle do his cunnyng uppon me, but undertake me he wol not.

†**g.** To be surety for. *Obs.*[−1]

1597 SHAKS. *Lover's Compl.* 280 Lending..credent soul to that strong-bonded oath That shall prefer and undertake my troth.

**5.** To take in charge; to accept the duty of attending to or looking after.

c 1300 *Havelok* 377 [They] seyden, he moucthe hem [*sc.* the children] best loke, Yif þat he hem vndertoke. c 1330 R. BRUNNE *Chron. Wace* (Rolls) 13112 Þe kyng dide his prisons loke Wiþ wardeyns þat hem vndertoke. 1382 WYCLIF *Ps.* iii. 6, I sleep, and was a slepe, and ful out ros; for the Lord vndertoc me. c 1440 *Gesta Rom.* lxi. 251 (Harl. MS.), Thow shalt bid me..to kepe welle thi suster...And I shalle thenne vndir-take hir. 1613 SHAKS. *Hen. VIII,* II. i. 97 To th' water side I must conduct your Grace: Then giue my Charge vp to Sir Nicholas Vaux, Who vndertakes you to your end. 1629 DONNE *Serm.* 308 The Holy Ghost undertakes every man amongst us and would make every man fit for Gods service. 1658 *Whole Duty Man* Pref. A 8, If a Physician should undertake a patient that were in some desperate disease, and by his skill bring him..out of it. 1795 *Jemima* I. 60 Mrs. Wellon declared her readiness to undertake her. 1814 BYRON *Lett.* (1875) 436, I am going to be married... Miss Milbanke is the good-natured person who has undertaken me. 1846 TRENCH *Mirac.* xiii. (1862) 240 He was rather chasing away diseases..than Himself undertaking them. 1892 'H. S. MERRIMAN' *Slave of Lamp* xv, It fell to Hilda's lot to undertake the Frenchman.

**b.** To engage with, enter into combat with.

1470–85 MALORY *Arthur* XIX. x. 788 Syre Vrre..and sir

Alphegus..encountred to gyders for veray enuy, and soo eyther vndertook other to the Vtteraunce. **1616** B. Jonson *Cynthia's Rev.* v. iv, Sir, he shall yeeld you all the honor of a competent aduersarie, if you please to vnder-take him. **1667** Denham *Direct. Paint.* I. xvi. 4 As if in our reproach, the Wind and Seas Would undertake the Dutch, while we take ease.

**c.** To take in hand to deal with (a person).

**1601** Shaks. *Twel. N.* I. iii. 61 By my troth I would not vndertake her in this company. Is that the meaning of Accost? **1655** Fuller *Ch. Hist.* IV. iv. § 32 The King casually coming thither.., undertook the Priest himself, though we never read before of his Majesties disputing. **1683** Cave *Ecclesiastici, Athanasius* 58 An ancient Confessor,..unskill'd in the Tricks and Methods of disputing,.. offered himself to undertake him.

† **6.** To assume, take to oneself. *Obs.*

**1596** Shaks. *Tam. Shr.* IV. ii. 106 You are like to Sir Vincentio. His name and credite shal you vndertake. **1596** Warner *Alb. Eng.* x. lv. (1602) 243 Whilst she, in France, did vndertake our royall Armes and Stile. **1608** Topsell *Serpents* 115 It changeth..alwayes into the colour of that which is next it, except red and white, which colours it cannot easily vndertake.

**7.** To conduct the funeral of.

**1900** *Blackw. Mag.* Jan. 97/1 Urijah..gave a notable proof of his filial affection, by gracefully and successfully 'undertaking' his father.

**II.** *intr.* † **8.** To enter upon, commit oneself to, an enterprise. *Obs.*

*c* **1386** Chaucer *Prol.* 405 Hardy he was and wys to vndertake. *c* **1470** Henry *Wallace* v. 532 He was the man that pryncipall wndirtuk, That fyrst compild in dyt the Latyne buk. **1603** B. Jonson *Sejanus* IV. iii, No ill should force the subject undertake Against the sovereign. **1639** S. Du Verger tr. *Camus' Admir. Events* 215 The sonne-in-law undertakes against the father in law, and the brothers are at division.

**9.** To give a pledge or promise; to enter into a compact or contract.

*c* **1475** *Rauf Coilȝear* 572 Schir Rolland..left the Coilȝear to cum, as he had vndertane. **1608** [see Underwrite *v.* 2 *absol.*]. **1667** Milton *P. L.* x. 74 The worst on mee must light,..for so I undertook Before thee. **1671** — *P. R.* II. 129, I, as I undertook,..Have found him.

**10.** To become surety or security, to make oneself answerable or responsible, *for* a person, fact, etc.

**1548** Elyot, *Spondere pro aliquo*, to vndertake for one. **1586** J. Hooker *Irel.* in *Holinshed* II. 131/1 He brought also his two other brethren, for whome he had vndertaken. **1588** Shaks. *Tit. A.* I. i. 436 But on mine honour dare I vndertake For good Lord Titus innocence in all. **1607** Topsell *Four-f. Beasts* 323 He..confessed hee would vndertake for the Wolfe, if they would set him at liberty. **1655** M. Casaubon *Enthus.* (1656) 204 It shall not trouble me, who undertake not for the truth of it. **1690** Locke *Toleration* ii. Wks. 1727 II. 277 You undertake for the Success of this method, if rightly used. **1713** Arbuthnot *John Bull* III. v, She..undertook for her brother John's good behaviour. **1770** Langhorne *Plutarch* (1879) II. 865/2 It was he who had principally undertaken for the obedience of the Argives. **1817** Jas. Mill *Brit. India* II. IV. v. 162 Clive undertaking for his security, Dooloob Ram joined the camp. **1880** Froude *Bunyan* 69 His friends undertook for his appearance when he should be required.

**b.** To engage oneself in a promise *for*.

*a* **1715** Burnet *Own Time* I. 393 As there was no reason that..any discontents could be carried so far as to a general rising, which these men undertook for. **1790** Bruce *Source Nile* I. 260, I sailed with..three passengers, instead of one, for whom only I had undertaken. **1827** Hallam *Const. Hist.* vi. I. 367 Bacon..laughed at the chimerical notion, that private men should undertake for all the commons of England.

**11.** *colloq.* To carry on the business of a funeral undertaker. (Cf. 7.) **1891** *Cent. Dict.*

† **Underta·kement.** *Obs. rare.* [f. prec. + -ment.] An undertaking.

**1678** Gale *Crt. Gentiles* (ed. 2) IV. III. iii. 48 For what is the Psalmists intent and undertakement, but to demonstrate Gods infinite prescience. **1681** Flavel *Meth. Grace* xxiv. 419 In all..undertakements the people of God so earnestly beg direction and counsel from him.

**Underta·ken,** *ppl. a.* [f. Undertake *v.*]

† **1.** Attended to, made safe. *Obs.*—[1]

*c* **1440** *Pallad. on Husb.* I. 203 Eke as the grape is grene and wol not shake, Vpbynde hit softe, and hit is vndirtake.

**2.** Taken in hand; enterprised.

*a* **1592** Greene *Selimus* 2354 With willing heart great Tonombey hath left..my father's court, To aid thee in thy undertaken war. **1608** *Relat. Trav. W. Bush* C 2 b, Where he had so great a wager, as the venture of his life, in the performance of his vndertaken voyage. **1661** Baxter *Last Work Believer* Wks. 1830 XVIII. 35 May we not trust Him in his undertaken office? **1782** J. Brown *Nat. & Rev. Relig.* v. i. 383 God was constantly preparing to demand his undertaken satisfaction from his Son.

**Undertaker** (*v*·ndəɹteɪkəɹ). [f. Undertake *v.*]

† **1.** One who aids or assists; a helper. *Obs.*

In early quots. rendering L. *susceptor*.

**1382** Wyclif *Ps.* iii. 4 Thou forsothe, Lord, art myn vndirtakere. *Ibid.* liii. 6 The Lord is vndertakere of my soule. *c* **1450** tr. *De Imitatione* III. xviii. 85 In God, þe consolacion of poure & þe undertaker of meke men. **1612** *Two Noble K.* I. i. 78, I hope..some God hath put his mercy in your manhood Whereto hee'l infuse powre, and presse you forth Our undertaker. **1634** Sir T. Herbert *Trav.* 223 Columbus.. repaires to some Christian Princes for his vndertakers. **1645** Rutherford *Tryal & Tri. Faith* 56 If believers have not Christ for their undertaker to bring them to glory, to intercede for them.

† **2.** A rebuker, reprover. *Obs.*—[1]

*c* **1430** *Pilgr. Lyf Manhode* II. civ. (1869) 114, I wole haue noon vndertakere [F. *repreueur*], no maister ne techere.

**3.** One who undertakes a task or enterprise. Also const. *of* (the thing attempted).

*c* **1400** *Destr. Troy* 3789 He was..falsest in his fare, and full of disseit, Vndertaker of treyne. **1500–20** Dunbar *Poems* lxxxi. 87 Schir Johne Kirkepakar, Off many cures ane michtie vndertaker. **1595** Raleigh *Discov. Guiana* (1596) 21 Neither could any of the forepassed vndertakers, nor Berreo himselfe discover the country. **1603** Daniel *Def. Ryme* H 3, May wee not..suspect these great vndertakers, lest they haue conspired with enuy to betray our proceedings. **1647** N. Bacon *Disc. Govt. Eng.* I. xvii. 55 That was like some enterprises that owe more to extremity of occasion, then to the courage of the undertaker. *a* **1680** Butler *Rem.* (1759) I. 236 The Devil was the first o' th' Name,..Who was the first bold Undertaker Of bearing Arms against his Maker. **1712** E. Cooke *Voy. S. Sea* 251 All Attempts fail'd, either by the Death of the Undertakers, or some other Accidents. **1779** Johnson *L. P., Pope* Wks. IV. 28 Perhaps no extensive and multifarious performance was ever effected within the term originally fixed in the undertaker's mind.

† **b.** Const. *to* with inf. *Obs.*

**1601** Holland *Pliny* II. 594 Wee find it expressely set downe, That the undertaker to build a house at a certaine price, shall use no mortar under three years of age. **1634** Rainbow *Labour* (1635) 40 Let the..Constables..be the undertakers to draine..this fenny..ground. **1684** T. Burnet *Theory Earth* I. 214 Those projectors of immortality, or undertakers to make men live to the age of Methusalah.

† **c.** One who takes up a challenge. *Obs.*

**1601** Shaks. *Twel. N.* III. iv. 349 Nay, if you be an vndertaker, I am for you.

**4.** *Hist.* **a.** One who undertook to hold crown lands in Ireland in the 16th and 17th centuries.

**1586** *Acts Privy Counc.* (N.S.) 208 A letter to the Lord Deputie of Irelande..in the favor of Mr. Smithwicke,..that he might be accepted into the nomber of those that were Undertakers for landes in that Realme. **1589** R. Payne *Descr. Irel.* 10 The worsser sorte of vndertakers which haue seignories of her Maiestie, haue done much hurt in the countrie. **1617** Moryson *Itin.* II. 26 The hatred which the Geraldines bare to those English Vndertakers..which possessed their Ancestors lands. **1633** T. Stafford *Pac. Hib.* I. x. (1821) 121 A Castle..appertaining to Master Edward Gray, an Vndertaker. **1642** in Rushw. *Hist. Coll.* (1692) I. III. 417 The Cities of London-Derry, and Coleraign,..and some other places and Castles which were for the present gallantly defended by the British undertakers. **1778** *Phil. Surv. S. Irel.* 311 The occupier of the ground..was unable to pay the fines, and therefore dispossessed by the wealthy undertaker. **1827** Hallam *Const. Hist.* xviii. II. 738 These lands in the counties of Cork and Kerry..were parcelled out among English undertakers at low rents. **1888** E. Lawless *Ireland* xxxiii. 229 Something like a regular stampede of men ambitious to call themselves undertakers, began to cross over from the larger to the smaller island.

**b.** One of those who in the reigns of Jas. I, Chas. I, and Chas. II undertook to influence the action of Parliament, esp. with regard to the voting of supplies.

**1620** Jas. I *Sp.* in Rushw. *Hist. Coll.* (1659) I. 23, I was in my first Parliament a Novice; and in my last there was a kind of beasts called Undertakers, a dozen of whom undertook to govern the last Parliament. **1668** Pepys *Diary* 14 Feb., The House is..quite mad at the Undertakers, as they are commonly called,..that are brought over to the Court, and did undertake to get the King money. **1670** Marvell *Corr.* Wks. (Grosart) II. 314 His Majesty, fortified by some undertakers of the meanest of our House, threw up all as nothing. *a* **1734** North *Examen* III. vi. § 38 At such Times, a Sort of People stept in, called Undertakers, who would answer that all should be smooth and well in Parliament. **1738** Bolingbroke *Patriot., Idea of Patriot King* (1749) 180 Let our great doctors in politics..compare the conduct of Elizabeth in this respect with that of her successor, who endeavoured..to manage his parliament by undertakers. **1827** Hallam *Const. Hist.* vi. I. 365 Neville, and others who, like him, professed to understand the temper of the commons, and to facilitate the king's dealings with them, were called undertakers.

**c.** One of those Lowland Scots who attempted to colonize the Island of Lewis towards the end of the 16th century.

**1819** Scott *Leg. Montrose* ix, He mentioned the celebrated settlement of the Fife Undertakers, as they were called, in the Lewis.

**5.** One who undertakes to carry out work or business for another; a contractor; † a collector or farmer of taxes. Now *rare*.

**1602** in Moryson *Itin.* (1617) II. 242 So soone as any contract is made with the vndertakers, wee send an abstract thereof vnto your Lordship. **1612** in *10th Rep. Hist. MSS. Comm.* App. I. 604 One yt that hath inritched himselfe..by having been one of the principall undertakers of ye greate farme of salte. **1670** Eachard *Cont. Clergy* 118 An ordinary bricklayer, or carpenter (I mean not your great undertakers and master-workmen). **1688** in *Cal. Treas. Papers* 28 The further answer of the present undertakers for the Tynne Farme. **1710** *Lond. Gaz.* No. 4651/2 An Agreement is concluded with Undertakers for furnishing the Magazines..with Forage. **1751** McDouall *Inst. Laws Scot.* 393 If one give Commission to demolish a house, which the undertaker believes to belong to him. **1778** Pryce *Min. Cornub.* 237 The halvans of halvans are mostly dressed by an undertaker for so much in the pound sterling of the money they produce. **1817** Scott in *Lockhart* (1839) V. 226 The other point is, to take care that the undertakers in their anxiety for employment do not take the job too cheap. **1833** *1st Rep. Comm. Employment Childr., Western District* 2 There is a class of workmen [in Birmingham] called undertakers, who receive the material from the master manufacturer, and undertake to get it wrought up.

**b.** One who makes a business of carrying out the arrangements for funerals.

**1698** *Pres. St. Trade* in Chester Waters *Parish Reg.* (1883) 52 The furnishing of funerals by a small number of men called undertakers. **1706** Phillips (ed. Kersey), *Pollinctor*, an Embalmer of Dead Bodies..; an Undertaker. **1708** Swift *Wks.* (1755) II. I. 164, I was sent, sir, by the company of undertakers,..and they were employed by the honest gentleman, who is executor. **1728** Young *Love of Fame* v. 505 While rival undertakers hover round, And with his spade the sexton marks the ground. **1768** Goldsm. *Good-n. Man* I. i, His appearance has a stronger effect on my spirits than an undertaker's shop. **1822** Byron *Vis. Judgem.* xii, He's buried; save the undertaker's bill, Or lapidary scrawl, the world is gone For him. **1884** F. M. Crawford *Rom. Singer* I. 55 You must look as solemn as an undertaker.

**6.** † **a.** One who engages in the serious study of a subject or science. *Obs.*

**1605** Bacon *Adv. Learn.* I. iv. § 7 Those [School-men].., as they are,..are great undertakers indeed, and fierce with darke keeping. **1654** Hobbes *Lib., Necess., & Chance* (1841) 250 He who will speak with some of our great undertakers about the grounds of learning, had need either to speak by an interpreter, or to learn a new language. **1682** Wheler *Journ. Greece* v. 356 There is another Greek,..an Undertaker in Physick too, who understands Scholastick Greek a little. **1695** Woodward *Nat. Hist. Earth* II. 71 To free the Enquiry from the Perplexities that some Undertakers have encumber'd it withall.

**b.** One who embarks on, or takes part in, some business enterprise. Now *rare*.

**1615** E. S. *Britaines Buss* E 2, I confesse the private gaine to euery Vndertaker before propounded may seeme too great to be hoped for. *a* **1661** Fuller *Worthies, Cumb.* I. (1662) 228, I understand two small manufactures are lately set up therein;..and I wish that the Undertakers may not be disheartned with their small encouragement. **1677** W. Hubbard *Narrative* II. 5 Some of the first Undertakers were encouraged once more to try the verity of their hopes. **1752** *Phil. Trans.* XLVII. 500 The mine, which was formerly wrought on,..yielded vast profit to the undertakers. **1776** Adam Smith *W. N.* IV. ii. (1904) II. 52 The undertaker of a great manufacture. **1799** Young *Agric. Lincoln.* 149 It has long been the common practice for the undertakers of this culture to hire grass land. **1828** *Act* 9 *Geo. IV*, c. 98 (*title*), The Undertakers of the Navigation of the Rivers Aire and Calder. **1848** Mill *Pol. Econ.* 479 The difference between the interest and the gross profit remunerates the exertions and risks of the undertaker.

† **c.** One who undertakes the preparation of a literary work. *Obs.*

**1685** Dryden *Sylvæ* Pref., Ess. (ed. Ker) I. 269, I hope it will not be expected from me, that I should say anything of my fellow undertakers in this Miscellany. **1704** Swift *T. Tub* Auth. Pref. ¶ 3 The undertaker himself will publish his proposals with all convenient speed. **1787** J. Adams *Wks.* (1854) IX. 552, I was told by a bookseller that he was about getting it translated into Dutch. But I doubt whether any of these undertakers will proceed. **1800** *Monthly Mag.* VIII. 878 It seems natural to expect..some patronage of a translation, which must else be a mere sacrifice of toil and time to the English undertaker.

† **d.** A book-publisher. *Obs.*

**1697** Evelyn *Numism.* p. lxxiii, Finding it so miserably deformed through the confident undertakers, the phrase was expunged at Bentley's request. **1707** Hearne *Collect.* (O.H.S.) II. 31 Mr. Wasse..has so swell'd his Salust.. yt the undertaker is quite weary. **1762** H. Walpole *Vertue's Anecd. Paint.* (1782) V. 261 His performances by no means deserved to be condemned as they were by the undertakers, and the performer laid aside. **1823** J. Badcock *Dom. Amusem.* p. iv, The duty of rapid revision was imposed upon the Editor..by the undertakers.

† **e.** A producer of an opera or play; a manager, impresario. *Obs.*

**1711** Addison *Spect.* No. 5 ¶ 7 The undertakers [of the opera] being resolved to spare neither Pains nor Mony, for the Gratification of the Audience. *c* **1720** in *Buccleuch MSS.* (Hist. MSS. Comm.) I. 367 The undertaker..has treated me ill..; I never heard a sound of his trifling songs till Monday se'nnight last. **1740** Cibber *Apol.* III, I laid it down as a settled Maxim, that no Company could flourish while the chief Actors and Undertakers were at variance.

† **7.** One who acts as security or surety *for* another.

**1601** B. Jonson *Poetaster* Ded., I send you this peece of what may liue of mine; for whose innocence, as for the Authors, you were once a noble and timely vndertaker. *a* **1652** Brome *Eng. Moor* Epil., Now let me be a modest undertaker For us the players, the play and the playmaker. **1677** J. Owen *Justif.* xi. 349 Considering the Person and Grace of this Undertaker or Surety. **1706** Phillips (ed. Kersey), *Sponsor*, Surety, an Undertaker for another.

† **b.** *spec.* A baptismal sponsor. *Obs.*

**1645** Ussher *Body Div.* (1647) 422 Of the vowes and promises which we in our child-hood made by those who were undertakers for us. **1673** Cave *Prim. Chr.* I. x. 326 A venerable old Deacon who had been the Undertaker for him at his Baptism. **1697** Burghope *Disc. Relig. Assemb.* 126 We are brought to Christ by the charitable help of our parents and undertakers.

Hence (from 5 b) **U·ndertakerish, -takerlike, -takerly** *adjs.* Also **U·ndertakery.**

**1861** Wynter *Soc. Bees* 136 An attendant in sable habiliments..and with an *undertakerish eye and manner. **1857** Dickens *Dorrit* I. v, One *undertaker-like Cupid had swung round on his own axis. **1876** Meredith *Beauch. Career* xix, You introduced me..to that *undertakerly old Tomlinson. **1869** G. J. Chester *Transatl. Sk.* 240, I had also a sideways view of a large patent-coffin shop...Americans, generally, are great in the matter of *undertakery.

**U·ndertaking,** *vbl. sb.* [f. as prec. + -ing [1].]

**1.** † **a.** Enterprise, energy. *Obs.*

**1375** Barbour *Bruce* IX. 484 Bot he wes outrageous hardy, And of so hye vndirtaking, That he neuir had none abasing Of multitude of men. *c* **1400** tr. *Secreta Secret., Gov. Lordsh.* 111 Þe Persiens & þe Turkeys..er right coraious men, and of gret vndertakynge.

**b.** An action, work, etc., undertaken or attempted; an enterprise.

*c* **1425** Wyntoun *Cron.* VIII. 3138 Þat þai brocht sone till ending Be sum tressonable vndirtaking. **1598** Florio, *Suscettione*, an enterprise, a taking of a thing in hand, an vndertaking. **1602** Shaks. *Ham.* II. i. 104 This is the very extasie of Loue, Whose violent property..leads the will to desperate Vndertakings. 1647 CLARENDON *Hist. Reb.* I. § 23 He did not upon the Suddain comprehend the consequences, which would naturally attend such a rash undertaking. 1669 STURMY *Mariner's Mag.* I. ii. 3 Disastrous Periods have ended their Undertakings. 1707 MORTIMER *Husb.* 148 The Farmer is to consider..the Cost and Charges of such a Stock: that so he may suit his Undertaking to his Purse. 1780 S. J. PRATT *Emma Corbett* (ed. 4) I. 196, I am engaged in a very unthrifty undertaking. 1809 COLERIDGE *Friend* (1865) 8 In the preceding number I named the present undertaking an experiment. 1841 W. SPALDING *Italy & It. Isl.* I. 383 Not unfit preparatives for such extravagant undertakings. 1880 L. STEPHEN *Pope* iii. 62 Both sides took a pride in supporting the great literary undertaking which he [*sc.* Pope] had now announced.

**c.** The action of taking in hand.

1600 HAKLUYT *Voy.* III. 185 They, who..are well able to spare that which is required of each one towardes the vndertaking of this adventure. 1634 W. TIRWHYT tr. *Balzac's Lett.* 108 The time of the yeare being as yet somewhat troublesome, for the undertaking thereof, you will rather reserve it. 1640 BP. HALL *Episc.* Ep. Ded. 2 I sate downe, and waited for the undertaking of some abler pen.

**d.** *spec.* The business or occupation of a funeral undertaker. Also *attrib.*

1850 THACKERAY *Pendennis* xlvii, So Pen..asked about the undertaking business and how many mutes went down with Lady Estrich's remains. 1862 *Macm. Mag.* June 150 In the way of business..nothing seems stirring, except it be the undertaking trade.

†**2. a.** The action of lifting up; support. *Obs.*

1382 WYCLIF *Ps.* cvii. 9 Myn is Manasses; and Effraym the vndertaking [L. *susceptio*] of myn hed.

†**b.** Reproof, rebuke. *Obs.*

*c* 1430 *Pilgr. Lyf Manhode* I. iv. (1869) 3 Bi whiche cloumben wel swiftliche in to þilke citee þilke þat weren of hise folke,..with oute vndertakinge of any. *c* 1440 *Promp. Parv.* 461/2 Snybbynge, or vndyrtakynge, *deprehencio.*

**3.** A pledge or promise; a guarantee or surety.

?*a* 1400 *Morte Arth.* 3187 Of this vndyrtakynge ostage are comyne. 1702 C. MATHER *Magn. Chr.* I. v. (1852) 75 All who dare not submit their children to be baptized by the undertaking of god-fathers. *c* 1800 PEGGE *Anecd. Eng. Lang.* (1814) 338 'Give an Undertaking,' i. e. a Security. 1848 THACKERAY *Van. Fair* lxiv, Three hundred pounds a year, which he proposed to pay to her on an undertaking that she would never trouble him. 1879 M. PATTISON *Milton* 91 In each successive pamphlet he reiterates his undertaking to redeem his pledge of a great work.

**U·ndertaking,** *ppl. a.* Now *rare.* [f. as prec. + -ING[2].]

†**1.** Ready to undertake an enterprise, task, etc., esp. one involving some danger or risk; enterprising, bold. *Obs.*

?*a* 1400 *Morte Arth.* 2723 In ȝone okene wode an oste are arrayede, Vndir-takande mene of thiese owte londes. *c* 1410 *Master of Game* (MS. Bodl. 546) Prol., Men ben bettre rydyng,..and more vndirtakynge, and bettir knowynge of alle contreys and of alle passages. 1456 SIR G. HAYE *Law Arms* (S.T.S.) 60 His men war bathe wys, and hardy, and undertakand. 1614 RALEIGH *Hist. World* v. iii. § 12. 486 A thousand men, vnder .. an vndertaking and expert Captaine. 1655 FULLER *Ch. Hist.* IX. iii. § 41 Rome..entertaining, and rewarding him as a man of a daring, and undertaking spirit. 1671 tr. *Palafox's Conq. China* xiii. 261 The General, who was very ambitious, undertaking, and successful. 1713 STEELE *Englishm.* No. 24. 157 Daring and undertaking Fellows have ever been the Darlings of the Populace.

*transf.* 1561 T. HOBY tr. *Castiglione's Courtyer* III. Hh iij b, Inventions, merry conceites, vndertaking enterprises, sports [etc.].

†**b.** ?Engaged in literary work. (Cf. UNDERTAKER 6 c.) *Obs.*

1761 STERNE *Tr. Shandy* IV. xx, See!—if he has not galloped full among the scaffolding of the undertaking critics!

†**c.** Prepared to act as publishers. *Obs.*

1822 SCOTT *Nigel* Introd. Epist., Their power of annoying the public will be soon limited by the difficulty of finding undertaking booksellers.

**2.** Pledged, bound by promise.

1786 A. GIB *Sacred Contemplations* I. II. i. 85 For these he became an undertaking Surety as their Covenant-head.

Hence **U·nderta·kingly** *adv.*, responsibly.

1665 J. SERGEANT *Sure Footing* 39 What Certainty can we undertakingly promise to weaker heads, that is, to the Generality of Mankind?

**U·nderta·lk,** *v.* (UNDER-[1] 10 a.) 1736 HERVEY *Mem.* (1848) I. 109 Those..used to say he undertalked his capacity, that his conception was much superior to his utterance.

**U·nderta·xed,** *ppl. a.* (UNDER-[1] 10 a.) 1706 ARBUTHNOT *Serm. Edinb.* Wks. 1751 II. 184 The Party of the North and West, who are under-tax'd.

**U·ndertea·cher.** (UNDER-[1] 6 a.)

1581 MULCASTER *Positions* xl. 230 Prouided that he.. hasard not..his childrens profit vpon any absolute vnderteacher. 1607 in *Hist. Wakefield Gram. Sch.* (1892) 67 A fitt underteacher or usher to be chosen. 1847 C. BRONTË *J. Eyre* v, She looked, indeed, what I afterwards found she really was, an under-teacher. 1878 B. HARTE *Man on Beach* 75 At last..the underteachers..revealed themselves in their true colours.

**U·nderte·ller.** (UNDER-[1] 6 a.) 1694 LUTTRELL *Brief Rel.* (1857) III. 368 Mr. Squibb, an underteller [in the Exchequer], is also dead. **U·nderte·nancy.** (UNDER-[1] 6 b: cf. next.) 1766 BLACKSTONE *Comm.* II. viii. 136 The widow is immediate tenant to the heir, by a kind of subinfeudation or under-tenancy.

**U·nder-te·nant.** [UNDER-[1] 6 a.] A tenant holding land or premises from another tenant; a subtenant.

1546 in W. H. Turner *Select. Rec. Oxford* (1880) 185 Yf the undertenant be honest. 1582 *Ibid.* 422 Undertenants commonly called inmakes. 1612 DAVIES *Why Ireland*, etc. 276 To settle and secure the Under-Tenannts; to the End, there may be a repose and establishment of euery Subiects Estate; Lord and Tenant. 1666 in *10th Rep. Hist. MSS. Comm.* App. V. 23 The said Henry and his undertenants had been in peaceable possession thereof for four yeares. 1704 *Lond. Gaz.* No. 3990/4 The Manor of Lizard,..in the Possession of George Caning Esq., or his Under-Tenants. 1766 BLACKSTONE *Comm.* II. viii. 123 A third incident to estates for life relates to the under-tenants or lessees. 1804 MAR. EDGEWORTH *Ennui* v[iii], These fellows..live in idleness, whilst they *rack* a parcel of wretched under-tenants. 1872 FROUDE *Short Stud.* (1878) II. 556 He had no intention that the undertenant should be protected against himself.

*transf.* 1809 MALKIN *Gil Blas* x. v. ⁋ 7 They..exalted him to a level with the under-tenants of Olympus.

†**Undertend** (to kindle): see UNDER-[1] 2.

**U·nderte·nure.** (UNDER-[1] 6 b.)

1611 COTGR., *Subinfeudation*, a subinfeoffing; the creating of an vnder tenure, or tennancie in fee. 1775 JOHNSON *West. Isl.* Wks. X. 476 We were told of a particular mode of undertenure. The tacksman admits some of his inferior neighbours to the cultivation of his grounds, on condition that [etc.].

**U·nder-terre·strial,** *a.* [UNDER-[1] 10 c; rendering F. *soubterrain.*] Below what is earthly.

1603 [see SUPERCELESTIAL *a.* 2 b].

†**U·nder-thaw.** (UNDER-[1] 5 b.) 1726 WOODWARD *Nat. Hist. Earth* Introd. 151 The Thaw underneath is frequently considerably advanc'd..before any Thing like a Liquation or Thaw is perceived, above, at the Surface. This the Country People call a Ground, or Under-Thaw.

†**U·nder-the·saurer.** *Obs.* [UNDER-[1] 6 a.] An under-treasurer.

1534 CROMWELL in Merriman *Life & Lett.* (1902) I. 373 Suche patentes and grauntys as your highnes and..your father..haue grauntyd vnto..your undertesawrer of your exchequer. 1536–7 *Act* in Bolton *Stat. Irel.* (1621) 104 So as the said underthesaurer be one.

†**Underthew,** *v. Obs.*[—1] [UNDER-[1] 7: cf. THEW *v.*] *trans.* To subject, subdue.

13.. *K. Alis.* 1406 (Laud MS.), Me þinkeþ wel grete wondre Þat he miȝth, wiþ so fewe, Al þe werlde hym vnder þewe.

**U·nderthing.** [UNDER-[1] 6 b.]

**1.** A lower or inferior thing.

1611 BEAUM. & FL. *Philaster* I. i, My womans strength Is so o'recharg'd with danger..that these under-things Dare not abide in such a troubled sea.

**2.** *pl.* Under-clothing.

1864 E. A. PARKES *Pract. Hygiene* 354 If..woollen underthings are worn, the perspiration is sufficiently absorbed.

**U·nderthi·nk,** *v.* [UNDER-[1] 10 a, 4 b.]

†**1.** *trans.* To think too little of, to underestimate.

*a* 1623 BUCK *Rich. III* (1646) 52 Charles..was so..overweening of his owne..judgement, that he under-thought all mens else.

**2.** *intr.* To think insufficiently.

1711 SHAFTESB. *Charac.* III. 301 They might rather thank themselves, for having under-thought, or reason'd short, so as to rest satisfy'd with a very superficial Search.

**3.** *trans.* To penetrate under by thinking.

1886 A. WEIR *Hist. Basis Mod. Europe* (1889) 491 Man.. can to some degree return upon his thought, can to some extent underthink the conditions of cognition.

**U·nder-tho·rough,** *adv.* [See UNDER *prep.* and THOROUGH *sb.* 3.] Under furrow.

1733 W. ELLIS *Chiltern & Vale Farm.* 223 This is half Under-thorough, and half Over, and exceeds all others except Drilling.

**U·nderthought.** (UNDER-[1] 9.)

1601 B. JONSON *Poetaster* IV. i, Carrie not too much vnderthought betwixt your selfe and them. 1886 *Athenæum* 6 Feb. 192 Without any disturbing underthought. 1898 WEYMAN *Castle Inn* i, Until he had put it beyond question that she had no underthought.

†**Underthra·st,** *pa. pple. Obs.*[—1] [UNDER-[1] 4 a: see THREST *v.*] Suppressed.

?1402 QUIXLEY *Ballade* xi. in *Yorks. Archæol. Jrnl.* (1908) XX. 45 Who euil doth, he mon be vnderthrast.

†**Underthrow·n,** *pa. pple. Obs.*[—1] [UNDER-[1] 7.] Subjected, made subject.

1387–8 T. USK *Test. Love* III. viii. (Skeat) l. 51 Thus fil man un-to lykenesse of unresonable bestes; and with hem to corrupcion and unlusty apetytes was he under-throwen.

**Undertide,** var. UNDERN-TIDE *Obs.*

**U·ndertide.** (UNDER-[1] 5 b.) 1851 MRS. BROWNING *Casa Guidi Wind.* I. 56 The arrowy undertide Shoots on and cleaves the marble as it goes. 1883 in Butler *Bible Work* I. 597 The undertide that bears all up and sweeps all along.

**U·nderti·ded,** *a.* (UNDER-[1] 4 a.) 1855 BAILEY *Mystic* 95 The bells may clang, Still pendulous in those undertided towers.

**Undertie·,** *v.* [UNDER-[1] 4 a.] *trans.* To tie beneath. Also *spec.* (see quot. 1894).

1552 HULOET, Vndertye, *subligo.* 1648 HEXHAM II, *Onderbinden*, to Vndertye. 1894 *Outing* XXIV. 258/2 The wings are under-tied, as are all our home-made flies; that is, the wings cover the point of the hook.

**Under-time,** var. UNDERN-TIME.

**U·ndertint.** (UNDER-[1] 5 c.)

1885 RUSKIN *Præterita* I. ii. 48 It was done..in grey undertints of Prussian blue and British ink. 1889 *Athenæum* 12 Jan. 56/3 These clear golden and rosy undertints and sub-tones of grey.

**U·nder-ti·tle.** (UNDER-[1] 5 b.) 1687 NORRIS *Coll. Misc.* (1699) 166 A Picture that..wants an under-title to discover whose it is.

**Undertoe,** erron. var. UNDERTOW.

**Undertone,** *sb.* Also under-tone, under tone. [UNDER-[1] 5 c, 9, 9 b, 10 c.]

**1.** A low or subdued tone: **a.** of utterance.

1806 SURR *Winter in Lond.* II. 44 ''Tis very strange!' said Edward in an under tone of voice. 1819 KEATS *Lamia* II. 281 'Fool!' said the sophist, in an under-tone, Gruff with contempt. 1853 KINGSLEY *Hypatia* xv, All this was uttered rapidly, and in a wheedling undertone. 1886 W. J. TUCKER *E. Europe* 79 Hearing a low, monotonous..voice chanting a dirge in an undertone.

**b.** of sound. Also *attrib.*

1833 [see UNBLISSFUL *a.*]. 1853 KANE *Grinnell Exp.* vii. (1856) 52 With it came a strange undertone accompaniment, a not discordant drone. 1855 KINGSLEY *Westw. Ho!* xxiii, If beyond the silence we listen for the faintest undertones, we detect a stifled, continuous hum of insects.

**2.** *fig.* **a.** An underlying tone (*of* feeling, etc.); a subordinate or unobtrusive element; an undercurrent.

1861 TULLOCH *Eng. Purit.* II. 211 The undertone of sentiment in the Elizabethan Church. 1879 FARRAR *St. Paul* II. 180 Throughout all these high reasonings..there runs an undertone of controversy.

**b.** A subdued or underlying tone of colour.

1891 *Cent. Dict.* s.v., There was a subtle undertone of yellow through the picture.

**c.** The general basis of Exchange or market dealings in any stock or commodity.

1897 *Daily News* 2 Feb. 3/7 Stocks were irregular...The undertone was firm. 1902 *Times* 29 July 11/2 Maize has had a weak undertone during the entire session.

**3.** A tone (of health, etc.) below the normal.

1872 H. W. BEECHER *Yale Lect. Preaching* viii. 220, I have sometimes had a whole month of undertone, because I let go and ran clear down.

Hence **U·ndertone** *v. trans.*, to accompany as an undertone; **U·ndertoned** *ppl. a.*[1], expressed in an undertone.

1861 MEREDITH *Evan Harrington* xxx, His hasty undertoned questions. 1873 W. S. MAYO *Never Again* xi. 145 Low harmonics Undertone the music's roll. 1876 GEO. ELIOT *Dan. Der.* VII. lvi, She uttered this with the same undertoned decision.

**U·nderto·ned,** *ppl. a.*[2] [UNDER-[1] 10 a.] Defective in tone.

1849 *Athenæum* 3 Nov. 1114/1 Its production appeared to be of an extemporaneous character,—much in it was undertoned. 1888 G. WILSON *Centen. Confer. Missions* I. 96 The influence of a faithless under-toned Missionary on the Church at home is appalling.

**U·ndertow.** [UNDER-[1] 5 c.] A sea-current below the surface of the water, moving in a contrary direction to that of the surface current.

1817 *Sporting Mag.* L. 221 A current,..at times counteracted by means of a strong opposing 'undertow', as it is called. 1829 MARRYAT *F. Mildmay* xix, The recoil of the sea, and what is called by sailors the undertow, carried him back again. 1877 HUXLEY *Physiogr.* xi. 172 The water bursts with great force upon the land, and then sweeps back, as a powerful 'undertow' to the sea.

*transf.* and *fig.* 1840 GEN. P. THOMPSON *Exerc.* (1842) V. 232 There is always a strong 'under-tow', as the Americans would call it, of honest and well-disposed men in such situations. 1879 JEFFERIES *Wild Life* 41 The weathercock will sometimes point in precisely the opposite direction, obeying the 'undertow' of the gale.

**U·nder-tra·der.** (UNDER-[1] 6 a.) 1677 OTWAY *Cheats of Scapin* I. i, The great Rooks and Cheats allow'd by publick authority ruin such little Under-traders as I am.

†**Undertra·nch,** *v. Obs.* [UNDER-[1] 4 a: see TRANCH *v.*] *trans.* To carve (a porpoise).

1508 *Bk. Keruynge* (W. de Worde) A 1 b, Vndertraunche yᵉ purpos. [Hence in later works.]

†**U·nder-tra·verse.** *Obs.*[—1] (UNDER-[1] 5 b: see TRAVERSE *sb.* 16 β.)

1598 BARRET *Theor. Warres* v. i. 125 The place or roome for the artillery in the vnder Travesse or flanker.

**Undertrea·d,** *v.* [UNDER-[1] 4 a. Cf. MDu. *ondertreden*, MLG. *undertreden*, MDa. *undertræde*, MHG. *under-*, G. *untertreten.*] *trans.* To tread under foot; to subdue or subjugate.

1525 in Ellis *Orig. Lett.* Ser. III. II. 75, I doubte not but that he will assist..to vndre treade them that they shall not nowe lift vppe their hedds. 1558 PHAER *Æneid* I. A 4 b, Great warre in Italy haue he shall, ere he the people wyld May vndertread. *a* 1618 SYLVESTER *Mem. Mortalitie* II. lv, Wasps break the Web, Flies are held fast and hurt: The Guilty quit, the Guiltlesse under-trod. 1859 WHITTIER *Rock in El Ghor* iv, Unchanged the awful lithograph Of power and glory undertrod.

**U·nder-trea·surer.** (UNDER-[1] 6 a.)

Chiefly as the designation of the officer immediately subordinate to the Lord High Treasurer of England (TREASURER 1 b): see also CHANCELLOR 3.

1447 *Shillingford Lett.* (Camden) 7 There was myche peeple, lordes and other, my Lord Tresorer, under Tresorer, ..and many strangers. 1521 WOLSEY in *St. Papers Hen. VIII*, I. 74 Sir Thomas More, your Undre Treasourer. 1610 HOLLAND *Camden's Brit.* I. 283 William Essex, Vndertreasurer of England under King Edward the Fourth. 1642 C. VERNON *Consid. Exch.* 33 The Vnder-Treasurer or Vice-Treasurer [of the Exchequer] was not knowne till the time of King Hen. 7. 1710 in *Lond. Gaz.* No. 4668/3 They shall receive an Order, signed by the Treasurer and Under-Treasurer of the Exchequer. 1764 GOLDSM. *Hist. Eng. in Lett.* (1782) IV. 109 Harley..was appointed chancellor of the exchequer, and under-treasurer. 1823 *Gentl. Mag.* Feb. 176/1 Chancellor and Under Treasurer of his Majesty's Exchequer. 1863 H. COX *Instit.* III. vii. 696 He now holds..the office of Under-Treasurer.

So **U·nder-trea·suress.** *rare.*

*c* 1450 [see UNDER-CHAMBRESS].

**Undertrea·t,** *v.* [UNDER-[1] 10 a.] *trans.* To treat with too little respect.

1721 CIBBER *Refusal* II. i, She that has no Resentment at all, may be under-treated as long as she lives, I find.

†**Under-treble.** *Obs.* [UNDER-[1] 6 b.] = SUBTRIPLE. So †**Under-triplat, -triple.** *Obs.*

1430 *Art of Nombryng* (E.E.T.S.) 17 That triplat is to be put under the .3 next figure..And the vnder-trebille vnder the trebille. *Ibid.*, And than most thow fynde a digit..the whiche withe his vnder-triplat..sittethe away all that is ouer his hede. *Ibid.* 18 It is open that the nombre proposede was a cubike nombre, And his rote a digit founde last with the vnder-triples.

**U·ndertro·dden,** *ppl. a.* [f. UNDERTREAD *v.*] Downtrodden.

1594 NASHE *Unfort. Trav.* C j b, I was no common squire, no vndertrodden torchbearer.

**Undertru·mp,** *v.* [UNDER-[1] 10 a.] *trans.* and *intr.* To follow one's partner in trumping, but with a lower card.

1863 'CAVENDISH' *Whist* (ed. 5) 61, I should throw away a small trump, undertrumping y, in order to keep two winning queens.

**Undertru·ss,** *v.* (UNDER-[1] 4 a.) 1703 S. PARKER tr. *Eusebius' Eccl. Hist.* VIII. 157 Some planted Face to Face with their Feet off the Ground, and their Bodies undertruss'd with Chains. **U·nder-tub.** (UNDER-[1] 5 b.) 1606 SYLVESTER *Du Bartas* II. iv. II. *Magnificence* 1139 As in Grape-Harvest..A willing Troup.., dancing in the Must, To th' under-Tub a flowry showr doe thrust. **U·ndertune.** (UNDER-[1] 9 b.) 1865 SWINBURNE *Poems & Ball., August* 26 In the mute August afternoon They trembled to some undertune Of music. 1897 KIPLING *Capt. Cour.* 49 A steady undertune to the 'click-nick' of the knives in the pen. **U·nder-tu·nic.** (UNDER-[1] 5 a.) 1819 SCOTT *Ivanhoe* iv, An under tunic of dark purple silk. 1880 L. WALLACE *Ben-Hur* 379 An undertunic not unlike those of the enemy.

**U·nderturf,** *a.* [UNDER-[2].] Of earth or soil: Situated or found below the turf.

1675 EVELYN *Terra* (1676) 14 The fatness of this Under-turf Mould. 1695 WOODWARD *Nat. Hist. Earth* I. 12 That blackish Layer of Earth or Mould which is called by some Garden-Earth, by others Vnder-turf-Earth. 1765 *Museum Rust.* IV. 156 A tree..round the roots of which some underturf earth was piled.

**Undertu·rn,** *v.* [UNDER-[1] 4, 7.]

†1. *trans.* To overturn, overthrow. *Obs.*

1382 WYCLIF *Deut.* vii. 5 The auters of hem vndurturneth [L. *subvertite*], and brekith togidres the ymagis. — *Ezek.* xxvi. 12 Thei shulen vndirturne thi..housis.

2. To turn under ground; to bury.

1600 SURFLET *Countrie Farme* v. viii. 670 Those..doe presently thereupon bestow an earing vpon such ground, and so vnderturne the said stubble and weedes.

**U·nder-tu·tor.** (UNDER-[1] 6 a.) 1702 BOYER *Fr. Dict., Sougouverneur*,..an Vnder-tutor. 1843 J. BOUVIER *Law Dict. U.S.* s.v., In every tutorship, there shall be an under-tutor, whom it shall be the duty of the judge to appoint. **U·nder-twig.** (UNDER-[1] 5 b.) 1768–74 TUCKER *Lt. Nat.* (1834) II. 319 The impulse of covetousness or lust of fame, and that under twig of it, vanity. 1805 R. W. DICKSON *Pract. Agric.* I. 135 To make the side of the hedge to slope inwards a little above, which gives to the under-twigs a freshness they could not otherwise be made to attain. **U·nder-ty·rant.** (UNDER-[1] 6 a.) 1648 HEYLIN *Relat. & Observ.* I. 25 Our Generall and Army, with their under-Tyrants the Grandees. **U·nder-u·sher.** (UNDER-[1] 6 a.) 1561 in H. B. Wilson *Hist. Merchant-Taylors' Sch.* (1814) 15 Ther shalbe also in the said schoole two underusshers.

**U·ndervalua·tion.** [UNDER-[1] 10 b.] The action of undervaluing.

1. †a. Reduction or decline in value. *Obs.*[-1]

1622 MALYNES *Anc. Law-Merch.* 482 The vnderualuation of our moneys, causeth no more commodities to be brought into the Realme than is carried out.

b. Valuation at too low a figure; inadequate monetary valuation.

1653 in Somers *Tracts* I. 523 That the said Inventory doth contain all the Goods.., without any wilful Omission or Undervaluation. 1825 HONE *Every-day Bk.* I. 1461 Another person said he was willing to give three hundred for it. This undervaluation was decisive. 1885 *Manch. Exam.* 22 July 5/1 Suggestions as to the best mode of preventing undervaluations.

2. Insufficient appreciation or estimation; depreciation, disparagement.

1626 JACKSON *Creed* VIII. xxviii, In this their undervaluation of his person and paines, they did portend their posterities disesteeme of..the Lord himself. 1681 *No Protestant-Plot* 6 Having been so unhappy as to have heard him spoken of with too much disregard, and undervaluation. 1851 DE QUINCEY *Ld. Carlisle on Pope* Wks. 1859 XIII. 20 The first error was..no more than an undervaluation of the truth.

**U·nderva·lue,** *sb.* [UNDER-[1] 10 b.]

1. Insufficiency in worth. *rare*[-1].

1605 BACON *Adv. Learn.* I. To King § 3 What defects and vndervalewes I finde in such particular actes.

2. An inadequate monetary value; an amount or price below the real value.

1611 COTGR., *Non-prix*, an vnder value, or vnderprice. 1631 T. POWELL *Tom All Trades* 3 Poverty sells all at an vnder value. 1690 CHILD *Disc. Trade* 101 We shall buy Ships..for half their cost, which under value in purchase will be a present clear profit to England. 1737 LD. HARDWICKE in Harris *Life & Lett.* (1847) I. 362 A bishop..calling in his tenants to fill up leases at an undervalue. 1769 WARBURTON *Lett. to Hurd* (1809) 438 The magnificent set of Chelsea China..she took care should not go at an undervalue. 1829 SOUTHEY *Sir T. More* (1831) II. 163 Persons who buy..because they are tempted by the undervalue at which it is offered. 1885 *Law Times Rep.* LII. 648/2 Shaw knew that he was buying at an undervalue.

†3. An under-estimate of worth or importance; = UNDERVALUATION 2. *Obs.*

1615 A. STAFFORD *Heav. Dogge* 35 Diogenes knew his owne deserts, and was neerer the ouer then the undervalew of himselfe. 1654 WHITLOCK *Zootomia* 345 That gentlewoman that inverted the undervalue of Marriages Maxime, 'next to no wife a good wife the best'. 1680 J. AUBREY *Brief Lives* (1898) I. 302 He did not care for chymistrey, and was wont to speake against them with undervalue.

**U·nderva·lue,** *v.* [UNDER-[1] 10 a.]

†1. *trans.* To rate as inferior in value *to*. *Obs.*

1596 SHAKS. *Merch. V.* II. vii. 53 Or shall I thinke in Siluer she's immur'd Being ten times vndervalued to tride gold. 1612 in *10th Rep. Hist. MSS. Comm.* App. I. 602 Which entertainment they could not afford him, for that thei would not undervalewe themselves to yᵉ Spanishe greatenes.

2. To rate at too low a monetary value. Also *fig.*

1599 *Minutes Archdeaconry Colchester* fol. 257 b (MS.), Dominus, eo quod constat that the goods ar vndervalued, dyd appoynt the same goods to be again apriced. 1619 FLETCHER *Knt. Malta* v. i, How much you undervalue your own price, To give your unbought self, for a poor woman? 1765 *Museum Rust.* IV. 68 In your note..I observe you think the price of the corn undervalued. 1885 *Law Times* 7 Feb. 269/1 There was a strong reason why Mr. Thomas should over-value rather than under-value the goods.

b. To reduce or diminish in value; to make of less value or worth.

1622 MALYNES *Anc. Law-Merch.* 385 It followeth that the Siluer is vnderualued, and the Gold aduanced. 1692 C. O'K[ELLY] in *Irish Narr.* (Camden) 69 What undervalued it [*sc.* the coinage] most was the little esteem the great ones about court shewed for it. 1709 STEELE *Tatler* No. 61 ⁋ 4 'Tis such silly Starts and Incoherences which undervalue the beauteous Sex. 1866 ROGERS *Agric. & Prices* I. xi. 179 The currency has been undervalued by the fraudulent issue.

†c. To fall short of in value. *Obs.*

1657 J. SERGEANT *Schism Dispach't* 182 What follows is such pittiful stuff, as would under-value the worth of a piece of paper to vouchsafe it a confute.

3. To estimate or esteem too low; to value or appreciate insufficiently; to depreciate.

1611 FLORIO, *Sottostimare*, to vnder-value or esteeme. 1620 GATAKER *Spirituall Watch* 114 These that so highly ouerprize their owne priuate deuotions, as thus to vnder-value the publike assemblies of Gods Saints. 1653 W. RAMESEY *Astrol. Restored* To Rdr. 17 Vertue..wanting preferment, and truth riches, shall be disrespected and undervalued. 1713 ARBUTHNOT *John Bull* III. i, Extolling their own good qualities, and undervaluing those of others. 1771 *Junius Lett.* lv. (1788) 302 A vain man does not usually compare himself to an object which it is his design to undervalue. 1824 MISS MITFORD *Village* Ser. I. 210 We shall have a fine sunshiny day to-morrow,—a blessing not to be undervalued. 1884 CHURCH *Bacon* iii. 59 He was no mere idealist or recluse to undervalue or despise the real grandeur of the world.

*refl.* 1621 BURTON *Anat. Mel.* I. ii. III. xv, Schollers..haue store of gold, but know not the worth of it, they vnder-value themselues. 1822 HAZLITT *Table-T.* Ser. II. 341 He who undervalues himself is justly undervalued by others.

Hence **U·nderva·lued** *ppl. a.*

1628 QUARLES *Argalus & P.* I. 30 So rare a Branch, whose undervalued worth Brings greater glory to the Arcadian Land, Then can the dull Arcadians understand. 1661 BOYLE *Style of Script.* (1675) 89 His so much undervalued Parables ..comprise important prophecies.

**U·nderva·luer.** [f. the vb.] One who undervalues or esteems too lightly; a depreciator.

1651 BAXTER *Inf. Bapt.* 258 What judgements have befaln the undervaluers of God's works. 1690 C. NESSE *O. & N. Test.* I. 361 All our under-valuers shall in time know it. 1804 *Ann. Rev.* II. 233 What was called the jacobinism of Great Britain, that is the confederacies of undervaluers of church and king. 1824 *New Monthly Mag.* XI. 465 The civic classes, no undervaluers of good cheer.

**U·nderva·luing,** *vbl. sb.* [f. as prec.] The act of estimating at too low a value.

1636 SANDERSON *Serm.* (1681) II. 65 Your under-valuing of me..hath made that glorying now necessary for me. 1661 LOWTHER in *Extr. St. Papers Friends* Ser. II. (1911) 117 To the undervalewing of his Majesties Authorety. 1697 BURGHOPE *Disc. Relig. Assemb.* 167 A manifest undervaluing of Christ. 1831 E. IRVING *Exp. Rev.* I. 85 Against all such undervaluings I present these words of the Eternal and Unchangeable. 1871 R. H. HUTTON *Ess.* I. 129 Even in the highest of the prophetic strains there is perhaps an undervaluing of Nature.

**U·nderva·luing,** *ppl. a.* [f. as prec.] That undervalues; depreciatory.

1639 SALTMARSH *Policy* I. cxi. 93 If any have had a poore and undervaluing conceit of you. 1648 JENKYN *Blind Guide* iv. 88 Those undervalewing expressions. 1691 tr. *Emiliane's Frauds Rom. Monks* (ed. 3) 412 This Notion..of the Protestants was so far from giving me an undervaluing Conceit of them [etc.]. 1863 COWDEN CLARKE *Shaks. Char.* vi. 148 To write a flippant, undervaluing word of one of Shakespeare's characters.

Hence **Underva·luing-like** *a.*; **-va·luingly** *adv.*

1637 HENSHAW *Medit.* (1639) 18 Not slightly and undervaluingly to speake of other mens vertues. 1707 NORRIS *Treat. Humility* vi. 289 To lessen and vilify himself, and speak..very undervaluingly of his own worth. 1782 J. BROWN *Nat. & Rev. Relig.* II. i. 117 He uttered several undervaluing like words to his mother.

**U·nderva·ssal.** (UNDER-[1] 6 a.) 1594 [see UNDERFEE]. 1611 COTGR., *Arriere-vassal*, an vnder-vassall. 1918 *Times' Lit. Suppl.* 21 Mar. 135/2 Legal reforms which protected the under-vassals from the arbitrary use of seignorial jurisdictions. **Underva·ulted,** *ppl. a.* (UNDER-[1] 4 a.) 1843 *Civil Eng. & Arch. Jrnl.* VI. 127/1 If not undervaulted, it may be freed from damp by..furnace slag. **U·nder-vau·lting.** (UNDER-[1] 5 c.) 1823 BUCKLAND *Reliq. Diluv.* 115 These undervaultings have for the most part been entirely filled up. **U·nderverse.** (UNDER-[1] 5 b.) 1579 E. K. *Gloss. to Spenser's Sheph. Cal.* Aug., Perigot maketh hys song in prayse of his loue, to whom Willy answereth euery vnder verse. **U·nder-vest.** (UNDER-[1] 5 a.) 1813 SCOTT *Trierm.* III. xviii, With nought to fence his dauntless breast But the close gipon's vnder-vest. 1883 LD. LYTTON *Life Lytton* I. 47 A delicate pink silk kerchief, carelessly folded to answer the purpose of our modern undervest.

**U·nderviewer.** *Mining.* [UNDER-[1] 6 a.] An underlooker.

1881 *Instr. Census Clerks* (1885) 84 Miner: Viewer, Under-Viewer, Underlooker. 1885 *Manch. Exam.* 6 Aug. 4/7 The houses of the underviewer and of one of the men.

**Un-de·rvished,** *a.* (UN-[1] 9.) 1884 BROWNING *Ferishtah, Eagle* 1 Dervish—(though yet un-dervished, call him so No less beforehand).

**U·ndervoice.** (UNDER-[1] 9 b.) 1810 SHELLEY *Zastrozzi* vii. Pr. Wks. 1888 I. 42 'Ah!' replied Matilda, in an under-voice, 'look in that bed'. 1836 R. HOWITT *Gipsy King* III. lxv, Whilst many an undervoice is soft From many a talking dame. **U·nderwa·ges.** (UNDER-[1] 10 b.) 1669 STURMY *Mariner's Mag.* I. ii. 15 Lame and decrepit Fellows preferred..by Serving for Under-Wages. 1835 URE *Philos. Manuf.* 327 Volunteering to work at under-wages from necessity. **U·nder-wai·stcoat.** (UNDER-[1] 5 a.) 1794 MRS. OPIE in Brightwell *Memorials*, etc. (1854) 42 His green coat and crimson under-waistcoat. 1826 SOUTHEY *Vind. Eccl. Angl.* 251 The blessed Arnulph of the hedgehog skin underwaistcoat. 1838 LYTTON *Alice* II. ii, His black coat neatly relieved in the evening by a white underwaistcoat. 1863 *N. & Q.* 3rd Ser. III. 50 In some parts of Yorkshire.. an underwaistcoat or 'Jersey' is called a 'singlet'. **U·nder-walk.** (UNDER-[1] 6 b.) 1651 DAVENANT *Gondibert* Pref. ⁋ 29 Those compositions of second beauty I observe in the Drama to be the under-walks. 1673 BP. S. PARKER *Reproof Reh. Transp.* 10 Plots, and Scenes, and Walks, and underwalks. **U·nder-ward.** (UNDER-[1] 5 b.) 1826 SCOTT *Woodst.* viii, Wildrake passed through the under-ward or court. **U·nder-wa·rden.** (UNDER-[1] 6 a.) 1375 BARBOUR *Bruce* IV. 400 The vndirwardane arivit was With thre batis. 1611 COTGR., *Sou[b]gardien*, an vnder Warden, vnder Keeper. 1819 SCOTT *Leg. Montrose* xiii, A lackey of the Marquis of Argyle, and occasionally acting as under-warden. **U·nder-warp.** (UNDER-[1] 5 b.) 1668 CULPEPPER & COLE *Barthol. Anat.* Introd., Others said that the Groundwork or underwarpe of the Parts is Seed. **Underwa·sh,** *v.* (UNDER-[1] 4 a.) 1538 ELYOT, *Subluere*, to vnderwashe, as water, whyche runneth lowe vnder a banke or hylle. **Under-wa·tch,** *v.* (UNDER-[1] 8 a.) 1654 GAYTON *Pleas. Notes* IV. xi. 244 Every step being under-watch'd with Dragons.

**U·nderwa·ter,** *sb.* [UNDER-[1] 5 c, 5 b.]

1. Water below the surface of the ground. Also *fig.*

1637 RUTHERFORD *Lett.* cxl. (1664) 275 False under-water not seen in the ground of an enlightned conscience, is dangerous. 1703 BP. NICOLSON *Misc. Acc.* (1877) 6 The Church-yard strangely (considering the Discents on each hand of it) infested with Under-water. 1805 R. W. DICKSON *Pract. Agric.* II. 296 Where the under stratum is clay, and there is no under water. 1866 GREGOR *Banffshire Gloss.* 203.

2. Water entering a vessel from beneath.

1645 RUTHERFORD *Tryal & Tri. Faith* 229 The Anchor is broken, or she taketh in under-water, or the Sail is torn.

3. = UNDERTOW. (*Cent. Dict.* citing Herschel.)

**U·nderwa·ter,** *a.* [Attrib. use of the phr. *under water*: see UNDER *prep.* 2, UNDER-[2].]

1. Placed, situated, carried on, etc., under water.

1627 MAY *Lucan* IV. G ij b, Some from the rocke, some from the shore oppose, Vulteius found this vnder-water traine. 1674 PETTY *Disc. Dupl. Proportion* 117 The further Truth whereof doth appear in the Under-water-Air within the Vessels of Water-Divers. 1832 *Planting* 109 in *Husb.* (L.U.K.) III, The wood..is esteemed for under-water-work, as piles, pipes, pumps, sluices. 1886 *Pall Mall G.* 7 Sept. 2/1 It is not sufficient to lay down the finest system of underwater mines. 1894 *Westm. Gaz.* 21 Feb. 6/1 A new underwater vessel which might be either a gunboat or an ordinary cargo steamer.

2. *spec.* In ships: Situated below the water-line.

1882 *Nature* XXV. 261 The ships would be secured against sinking by an under-water deck. 1889 WELCH *Text Bk. Naval Archit.* i. 8 The under-water part of the hull.

**U·nderwave.** (UNDER-[1] 5 b.) 1838 MRS. BROWNING *Soul's Travelling* viii, When you hearken to the grave Lamenting of the underwave. 1895 A. NUTT in Meyer tr. *Voy. Bran* I. 232 An under- instead of a cross-wave locale appearing for the first time.

†**Underwax,** *v.*: see UNDER-[1] 2.

**U·nderwea·pon.** (UNDER-[1] 6 b.) 1646 H. LAWRENCE *Comm. Angells* 109 Unlesse this stone and sling, these underweapons, be mannaged by the name of God.

**U·nderwear.** [UNDER-[1] 5 a.] Underclothing; also, the fact of wearing, or of being worn, as underclothing.

1880 *Scribner's Mag.* 213 The general want of underwear was not so cruelly felt as had been feared. 1885 T. M. COAN *Ounces of Prevention* (1888) 10 Robust persons will get along well enough with the ordinary 'mixed underwear'.

†**Underweave,** *v.*: see UNDER-[1] 2.

†**U·nderwee·ning.** *Obs.* [UNDER-[1] 10 b.] Under-estimation (of self or *of* something).

1574 tr. *Marlorat's Apocalips* 16 The words that he [*sc.* St. John] set here..sauor of a certayne singular vnderweening. 1682 SIR T. BROWNE *Chr. Mor.* III. § 25 But the greatest underweening of this Life is to undervalue that, unto which this is but exordial.

**Underweigh·,** *v.* [f. the phr. *under weigh*: see WEIGH *sb.*] *intr.* To get under weigh.

1891 *Times* 25 Nov. 12/5 Witness at once underweighed and went to the rescue.

**U·nderweight.** [UNDER-[1] 10 b; UNDER *prep.* 23 b. Cf. Da. *undervægt*, Sw. *-vigt*, Du. *ondergewigt*, G. *untergewicht*.] Insufficient weight; deficiency in weight.

1596 BACON *Max. & Use Com. Law* II. (1635) 8 Tradesmen of all sorts, selling with under weights or measures. 1647 N. WARD *Simple Cobler* 30 They never complain of me for giving them hard measure, or under-weight. 1864 R. A. ARNOLD *Cotton Fam.* 470 The underweight of these bales made the stock seem larger than it really was. 1894 *Boston Arena* June 44 The minutest difference of overweight or underweight in the coin.

*attrib.* **1890** *Daily News* 22 Feb. 5/4 The first cost of the restoration of all underweight coins.

† **U·nderwind.** *Obs.* (UNDER-[1] 5 b.)

**1726** WOODWARD *Nat. Hist. Earth* Introd. 129 The North of England, where the Natives are wont to ascribe these Phænomena to what they call an Under-Wind, or Vapour ascending from the Bottom.

**U·nderwing.** [UNDER-[1] 5 b and UNDER-[2].]

**1.** A wing placed under, or partly covered by, another.

**1535** COVERDALE 2 *Esdras* xii. 29 Thou sawest two vnder-winges vpon the heade that is on the right syde. **1801** SOUTHEY *Thalaba* III. xxxiii, The admiring girl survey'd His out-spread sails of green; His gauzy underwings. **1826** KIRBY & SP. *Entomol.* III. 380 The part..in many cases is connected with the posterior basal margin of the under-wings.

**2.** Used *attrib.*, with adjs. of colour, to designate various species of moths.

**1749** WILKES *Eng. Moths & Butterflies* 2 The great yellow-underwing moth. *Ibid.* 17 The willow red-underwing moth. *Ibid.* 23, 33. **1826** KIRBY & SP. *Entomol.* III. xxxi. 272 A red under-wing-moth (*Noctua pacta*). **1882** *Proc. Berw. Nat. Club* IX. 559 One captured a Yellow Underwing Moth.

**b.** *ellipt.* = Underwing moth.

**1819** SAMOUELLE *Entomol. Compend.* 418 *Noctua Myrtilli.* The beautiful yellow Underwing. **1832** RENNIE *Consp. Butterfl. & M.* 51 The Pearl Underwing (*Agrotis æqua*). **1871** DARWIN *Desc. Man* II. xi. I. 394 The common yellow under-wings (Triphæna).

**3.** *attrib.* Situated beneath the wings.

**1896** *Daily News* 10 Jan. 6/7 The brightly-tinted varieties, ..lined like the underwing feathers of tropical birds.

**U·nderwit.** [UNDER-[1] 6 a, 10 b.]

**1.** A poor or inferior kind of wit.

**1655** SHIRLEY *Politician* Ded., Some abuses of the common theatres (which were not so happily purged from scurrility and under-wit—the only entertainment of vulgar capacities).

**2.** A person of defective understanding; a half-witted person.

Used as a surname in the Duke of Newcastle's *Country Captain* (1649).

**1682** T. FLATMAN *Heraclitus Ridens* No. 52 (1713) II. 75 Having often met with some of the Under-wits of that Panel, who threatened what their Foreman could have done. **1900** *Everybody's Mag.* III. 513/2 He was a single man, and many said an underwit.

**U·nder-witch.** (UNDER-[1] 6 a.) **1678** BUTLER *Hud.* III. I. 282, I found th' Infernal Cunning-man, And th' Under-witch, his Caliban.

**U·nder-wi·tted,** *a.* [UNDER-[1] 10 a.] Of inferior or defective understanding; half-witted.

**1683** KENNETT *Erasm. on Folly* 18 Cupid..is an under-witted whipster. *Ibid.* 125 The Athenian Commander..was a little underwitted. **1856** HAWTHORNE *Eng. Note-bks.* (1870) I. 424, I rather think it [*sc.* a child] was under-witted, and could not talk.

**U·nderwood.** [UNDER-[1] 5 d. Cf. MSw. *undirvidh.*]

**1.** Small trees or shrubs, coppice-wood or brush-wood, growing beneath higher timber trees.

*a* **1325** *MS. Rawl. B. 520* fol. 32 b, Þat te heiwes [=high-ways]..ben..ilargiste, Þer ase is wode, hegges oþer buskes ore vnderwode. *c* **1380** *Antecrist* in Todd *Three Treat. Wyclif* (1851) 119 His taile is likenyd to a cedre, [þat] wexyng in to heȝþe passiþ oþer vnderwod. **1467–8** *Rolls of Parlt.* V. 575/2 Every persone or persones, which have bought eny Tymbre, Woode or Underwode. **1480** *Cov. Leet Bk.* 415 The people..throwen down & beren away the vnderwode of þe seid Priour. **1512** *Act 4 Hen. VIII*, c. 18 § 17 Underwode growyng uppon the seid landes. *a* **1596** *Sir T. More* (Malone Soc.) Add. i. 65 Thinke when an oake falls, vnderwood shrinkes downe, And yet may liue,though brusd. **1642** FULLER *Holy & Prof. St.* II. xiii. 100 This underwood serves for supplies to save timber from burning. **1669** WORLIDGE *Syst. Agric.* (1681) 93 In a few years you may observe many fair Trees to steal up amongst the Under-wood. **1733** W. ELLIS *Chiltern & Vale Farm.* 128 The Underwood will be fit to fell in..fifteen Years. **1794** MRS. RADCLIFFE *Myst. Udolpho* xliv, At a deep recess of the forest,..so overgrown with underwood that they proceeded with difficulty. **1827** O. W. ROBERTS *Voy. Centr. Amer.* 64 Our way..was nearly free from underwood or any material impediment. **1882** 'OUIDA' *Maremma* I. 46 She made her way through the dense underwood.

*attrib.* **1796** W. H. MARSHALL *Planting* II. 51 Its branches ..very much resemble those of the Beech:..especially in the shrubby underwood state.

**b.** *fig.*

*a* **1637** B. JONSON *Underwoods* To Rdr., I am bold to entitle these lesser poems, of later growth, by this [name] of Underwood, out of the analogie they hold to the Forest in my former booke. **1693** DRYDEN *Juvenal* Ded. (1697) p. xxxiv, But these are the Under-Wood of Satire, rather than the Timber-Trees. **1863** COWDEN CLARKE *Shaks. Char.* ix. 230 It is from among the underwood of these stately productions..that we bring to remembrance gems of practical wisdom.

**2.** With *a* and pl. A quantity or stretch, a special kind, of woody undergrowth.

**1541** *Act* 33 *Hen. VIII*, c. 39 All woodes and vnderwoodes, belonging to your office. **1581–2** *Catal. Anc. Deeds* (1906) V. 484 Breers, brembles, bushes and underwoodes. **1607** J. NORDEN *Surv. Dial.* III. 140 Therefore must the Surueyor be heedful..to note what trees are among the underwoods. **1646** J. HALL *Horæ Vac.* 101 Great Oakes breake their own branches and neighbouring underwoods. **1708** *Lond. Gaz.* No. 4475/3 Posting the..Granadiers among the Thickets of an Underwood. **1766** GOLDSM. *Vicar* iv, Our little habitation was..sheltered with a beautiful underwood behind. **1847** EMERSON *Poems, Humble-bee* 29 Rover of the underwoods. **1867** LADY HERBERT *Cradle L.* i. 5 Enormous groves of date-palms.., with an underwood of poinsettias.

*fig. a* **1637** B. JONSON (*title*), Underwoods; consisting of divers poems. [Cf. 1 b.]

**3.** The wood underlying a veneer.

**1862** *Catal. Internat. Exhib., Brit.* II. No. 3411, The veneering..will bear an immense amount of heat or damp before it will strip from the underwood.

Hence **U·nderwoo·ded** *a.*

**1861** ROSSETTI in Ruskin *Life* (1899) 277 A rich sweet country, beautifully wooded, underwooded, and sloped.

**U·nderwork,** *sb.* [UNDER-[1] 5 c, 9, 10 b.]

†**1.** An under-current. *Obs.*[−1]

**1610** G. FLETCHER *Christ's Vict.* I. lvi, So curiously the underworke did creepe,..That afar off the waters seem'd to sleepe.

**2.** A structure placed under or supporting something; a substructure.

**1624** WOTTON *Elem. Archit.* 79 The Couer, or Roofe,..[if] too heauy,..will suffer a vulgar obiection of pressing too much the vnder-worke. **1772** T. SIMPSON *Vermin-Killer* Introd., The rain forces its way through, and rots the underwork [of the thatch]. **1776** G. SEMPLE *Building in Water* 18 The Under-work of the second Pier. **1890** W. J. GORDON *Foundry* 158 As packed for export, it goes into a flat case..and takes up little more room than its underworks.

**3.** †**a.** Work done at lower rates. *Obs.*[−1]

**1624** T. SCOTT *Belgic Souldier* E 3, There are so many of all Trades, who confound one another by vnderworke and indirect abuses, that [etc.].

**b.** Subordinate or inferior work.

**1645** MILTON *Colast.* 26 To bee put to this under-work of scowring and unrubbishing the low and sordid ignorance of such a presumptuous lozel. **1708** ADDISON *Pres. State War* 20 You will find most of those that are proper for War absolutely necessary for..carrying on the Underwork of the Nation.

**c.** Underhand or secret work.

**1814** D'ISRAELI *Quarrels Auth.* III. 294 The Tyrant himself had an openness, quite in contrast with the dark under-works of his Satellites.

**Underwo·rk,** *v.* [UNDER-[1] 8 a, 8 b, 10 a.]

†**1. a.** *intr.* To work secretly; to take clandestine measures. *Obs.*

**1504** *Plumpton Corr.* (Camden) 186 It is sayd that ye be lesse forward, & they underworketh falsly. **1603** B. JONSON *Sejanus* Argt., He raiseth in private a new instrument,.. and by him underworketh, discovers the other's counsels.

† **b.** *trans.* To work against secretly; to seek to undermine or overthrow. *Obs.*

**1595** SHAKS. *John* II. i. 95 But thou from loving England art so farre, That thou hast vnder-wrought his lawfull King. **1613–8** DANIEL *Coll. Hist. Eng.* (1626) 45 His delay yeelds the King time to..vnder-worke his enemies. **1627** ABP. ABBOT *Narr.* in Rushworth *Hist. Collect.* (1659) I. 440 He will underwork any man in the World, so that he may gain by it. **1659** RUSHW. *Ibid.* 4 He did first under-work his Voyage to Guienna.

**2.** †**a.** To spend too little work on; to leave unfinished. *Obs.*

**1691** NORRIS *Pract. Disc.* 228 There is no Artist, but will perform to the utmost of his Skill, provided it be as easy for him to make his Piece compleat, as to under-work it.

**b.** To impose too little work upon.

**1882** MISS BRADDON *Mt. Royal* I. iii. 78 Besides, he is not underworked.

**c.** *intr.* To do too little work.

**1902** G. HOWELL *Labour Legislation* xlii. 499 The man that under-works is as bad as the man that under-pays.

**3.** *trans.* To work for less wages than (another).

**1695** *Whether Preserving Protest. Relig. was Motive of Revolution* 17 Who by their frugal and parsimonious Living would be able..to underwork and undersell them. **1713** *Mercator* No. 9/1 The French being able to Underwork us, will also Undersell us.

**U·nder-wo·rker.** [UNDER-[1] 6 a.] An assistant or subordinate worker.

**1701** SWIFT *Contests Nobles & Comm.* iv, An usurping populace is..a meer underworker, and a purchaser in trust for some single tyrant. **1709** SACHEVERELL *Serm.* 15 Aug. 10 There must be Co-operators, Partners, and Under-workers in it. **1744** YOUNG *Nt. Th.* VII. 415 Want and convenience, under-workers, lay The basis, on which love of glory builds.

**U·nderwo·rking,** *sb.* [UNDER-[1] 9 a.] Action of a secret or unapparent nature.

**1613–8** DANIEL *Coll. Hist. Eng.* (1621) 26 Skornes, conspiracies and vnder-workings. **1679** EVERARD *Prot. Princes Europe* 20 The Emissaries of Rome have been the Instruments of the underworkings which have raised this War. **1811** MRS. GRANT in *Mem. & Corr.* (1844) I. 286 The underworkings of petty envy and malignity. **1833** MILL *Lett.* (1910) I. 45 Men who are now gaining..a considerable and increasing influence..over the underworkings of our government.

**U·nderwo·rking,** *ppl. a.* [UNDER-[1] 8 a, 4 a.] Working or acting in a secret or unapparent manner; also *lit.*, working beneath.

**1605** DANIEL *Philotas* II. iii. *Chorus* C vj, There dost thou struggle..Against some underworking pride that must Supplanted be. **1679** C. NESSE *Antid. agst. Popery* 87 He gives them up to the strong delusions of this under-working beast. **1818** MILMAN *Samor* 283 Deep echoed out From th' underworking caverns. **1883** *Century Mag.* XXVI. 373/2 As a strong character in underworking motive, Squire Gaylord seems to be his best.

**U·nder-wo·rkman.** (UNDER-[1] 6 a.)

**1608** WILLET *Hexapla Exod.* 724 The chiefe workeman doth the principall worke himselfe, and the other by his ministers and vnderworkemen. **1651** C. CARTWRIGHT *Cert. Relig.* I. 142 As an Architect, or the like chiefe workman, doth..appoint under-workmen where they shall imploy themselves. **1708** SWIFT *Sent. Ch. Eng. Man* Wks. 1755 II. I. 78 Under-workmen, who are expert enough at making a single wheel in a clock, but are utterly ignorant how to adjust the several parts. **1771** LUCKOMBE *Hist. Print.* 8 An Under-workman in the Printing-House at Harlem.

**U·nderworld.** [UNDER-[1] 5 b, c. Cf. Du. *onderwereld*, G. *unterwelt*, Da. *underverden.*]

**1.** The sublunary or terrestrial world.

**1609** DANIEL *Civ. Wars* VIII. xxx, The glory of that Mightinesse..That ouer-spreds..This vnder-world. *a* **1616** BEAUM. & FL. *Bonduca* III. ii, Loud Fame calls ye, Pitch'd on the topless Apenine, and blows To all the underworld. **1700** ROWE *Amb. Step-Mother* I. i, Thou, like the God thou serv'st, shall shine aloft, And with thy influence rule the under world. *a* **1719** ADDISON tr. *Virgil's Fourth Georgic* Wks. 1721 I. 19 When th' under-world is seiz'd with cold and night. **1822** SHELLEY *Chas. 1st* II. 140 For a king bears the office of a God To all the under world.

*fig.* **1694** ATTERBURY *Serm.* (1726) I. 173 Their Way was ..to look down with Pity and Contempt upon a poor deluded Under-World. **1795** WOLCOT (P. Pindar) *Liberty's last Squeak* III. Wks. 1812 III. 425 Our Lords on high, Who call the under-world of man, An ass ish, mulish, packhorse clan.

**2.** The abode of the departed, imagined as being under the earth; the nether world.

**1608** DAY *Hum. out of Br.* I. i, Since proud Anthonio..Is in his iourney towards th' vnderworld. **1713** C'TESS WINCHELSEA *Misc. Poems* 18 When to the Under-world despis'd he goes, A pamper'd carcase on the Worms bestows. **1858** BIRCH *Anc. Pottery* I. 365 Few Argive representations, except that of the Danaids in the under-world,..are given on vases. **1871** TYLOR *Prim. Cult.* I. 311 The western Hades, the underworld of night and death.

**b.** A region below the surface of the earth; a subterranean or underlying area.

**1885** *Daily News* 4 Nov., The extent to which the under-world in the Potteries is honeycombed with coal mines. **1886** WINCHELL *Walks Geol. Field* 56 Shall we venture among the dangers of the oceanic under-world?

**3.** The Antipodes; also, the part of the earth beyond the horizon.

**1847** TENNYSON *Princ.* IV. 27 Fresh as the first beam glittering on a sail, That brings our friends up from the under-world. **1868** KINGSLEY *Christmas Day* 34 New patriarchs of the new-found underworld. **1890** 'R. BOLDREWOOD' *Col. Reformer* (1891) 154 A shining sail came from the under-world and swept placidly towards the city.

**4.** A sphere or region lying below the ordinary one. Also *fig.*, a lower, or the lowest, stratum of society, etc.

**1859** MISS A. B. EDWARDS *Hand & Glove* vi. 54 Slowly I sank away, lower and lower, into the under-world of darkness and dreams. **1894** *Harper's Mag.* Mar. 630 The mysterious processes which go on under the influence of the bacteria in this underworld of life. **1899** F. T. BULLEN *Way Navy* 25 The begrimed company of toilers..in the underworld of engines and boilers [in a ship].

**Underwri·te,** *v.*[1] [UNDER-[1] 4 a, after L. *subscrībĕre* SUBSCRIBE *v.* Cf. OE. *underwritan.*]

In Langl. *P. Pl.* A. XI. 255 *vndirwriten* is apparently an error for the variant *vnwriten.*

**1.** *trans.* To write (words, figures, etc.) below something, esp. after other written matter.

*c* **1430** *Art Nombryng* 3 The nombre to be addede is that þat sholde be addede therto, and shalle be vnderwriten. *Ibid.*, It is convenient that the lesse nombre be vnderwrit, and the more addede. **1578** LYTE *Dodoens* 310 Euphorbium prepared in manner as shalbe vnder written, purgeth..slymie flegmes. **1611** SPEED *Hist. Gt. Brit.* IX. xiv. 614/2 The said Author, obseruing the scope of those lines,..doth vnderwrite and annex this Stanza. **1670** G. H. *Hist. Cardinals* I. III. 86 His business is to under-write answers to all Petitions. **1709** *Tatler* No. 74 ¶ 11 Each Subscriber should underwrite his Reason for the Place he allots his Candidate. **1753** RICHARDSON *Grandison* VI. xlix. 298, I will entreat her to vnderwrite her mind on this subject. **1882** *Act* 45 & 46 *Vict.* c. 61 Sched. I The bill..should be annexed, or a copy of the bill and all that is written thereon should be underwritten.

†**b.** To write, subscribe, sign (one's name) below, or at the end of, a document, etc. *Obs.*

**1569** in Strype *Ann. Ref.* (1709) I. lv. 566 That we, whose names are by ourselves underwritten, do acknowledge [etc.]. *a* **1593** MARLOWE *Edw. II*, v. ii, Our behoofe will beare the greater sway When as a kings name shall be vnder writ. **1616** B. JONSON *Devil an Ass* III. iii, I haue enough on't! for an hundred pieces? Yes, for two hundred, vnder-write me, doe. Your man will take my bond? **1682** SCARLETT *Exchanges* 61 The Acceptant, when he accepts, must underwrite his Name. **1793** GIBBON *Misc. Wks.* (1814) II. 493 When the subscription is proposed, I shall underwrite my name for, at least, six copies.

†**c.** *absol.* To become surety. *Obs.*

*c* **1650** HIGFORD *Instit.* (1658) 17 For the most part the borrowers of money..are engaged one for another...Those that stand engaged for you; you must underwrite for them also.

†**2.** To subscribe (a document) with one's name.

**1557** *Order of Hospitalls* C 7 b, Warrants..underwritten by the Thresorer..what shall be paid to any such Pencioner wekly. **1623** in Foster *Eng. Factories Ind.* (1908) II. 320 The agreement mad betwixt us was underwrytten and sealed. **1655** FULLER *Ch. Hist.* VIII. i. § 4 No importunity could prevail with him to underwrite this will. **1682** in *Lond. Gaz.* No. 1782/1 One part thereof Signed by such Servant, and also Under-written or Endorsed with the Name and Hand-writing of such Magistrate. **1713** *Guard.* No. 39, I shall not retract any advertisement till I see those verses, and I'll choose what to believe then, except they are underwritten by his nurse. **1748** RICHARDSON *Clarissa* (1811) VI. 365 A letter..signed by his Lordship,..and underwritten by myself.

*absol.* **1608** in Birch *Crt. & Times Jas. I* (1848) I. 84 His brother, whom..he hath now sent for up to undertake and underwrite with him.

**b.** *spec.* To subscribe (a policy of insurance) thereby accepting the risk of insurance. Also *absol.*

**1622** MALYNES *Anc. Law-Merch.* 102 If one be bound, and two or more do put their hand and seale, and vnder-write, and seale the said Bill as Principals. *Ibid.* 166 The custome

..doth impose the losse vpon those Assurors which did first vnderwrite. **1703** *Lond. Gaz.* No. 3940/4 Whosoever..hath underwritten any Policy of Insurance on the Ship Samuel. **1755** MAGENS *Insurances* I. 7 If this be declared when the Insurance is made, the Insurers..will never refuse to underwrite. **1766** W. GORDON *Gen. Counting-ho.* 21 If you underwrite a policy mentioning..the sum underwrote. **1809–11** COMBE *Syntax* XXV. 417 The Policies remain'd secure, Waiting for arms of signature; For what brave spirit e'er would fight 'em When nobody would underwrite 'em. **1876** F. MARTIN *Hist. Lloyd's* 365 Both non-underwriting members and annual subscribers are..forbidden to underwrite any policy of insurance.

**c** *absol.* To carry on the business of insurance.

**1784** LD. MACARTNEY in *Burke's Corr.* (1844) III. 27 The impossibility of men's fairly acquiring great wealth, in a short time, who neither lend, trade, play, nor under-write.

**3.** To set one's name to, subscribe to (a decision, statement, etc.); to agree to or confirm by signature. Also *fig.*

**1606** SHAKS. *Tr. & Cr.* II. iii. 137 Worthier then him selfe.., vnder write in an obseruing kinde His humorous predominance. **1633** G. HERBERT *Temple, Ch. Porch* xxiv, Man is a shop of rules, a well-truss'd pack, Whose every parcell under-writes a law. **1656** EARL MONM. tr. *Boccalini's Advts. fr. Parnass.* I. lxxvii. 161 All the Assembly had already underwritten the reformation, when Thales put them in mind [etc.]. **1678** BUTLER *Hud.* III. iii. 148 All which they took in Black and White, And cudgel'd me to under-write. *a* **1853** MRS. OPIE in Brightwell *Life* (1854) 49, I could, with a safe conscience, underwrite all that he there relates.

†**b.** *intr.* To subscribe or agree *to* something.

**1643** QUARLES *Loyal C.* 16 In case Papists should largely under-write to your Propositions,..would you not accept it?

**4.** †**a.** To guarantee to subscribe or contribute (a certain sum of money, etc.). *Obs.*

**1623** HERIOT in *Mem.* App. III. (1822) 72 All my stock and adventures in the East India Company,..wherein I did underwrite one thousand pounds. **1642** *Lanc. Tracts Civ. War* (Chetham Soc.) 62 Such moneyes and plate as Mr. Thomas Case..shall underwrite for the defence of Lancashire. *a* **1692** POLLEXFEN *Disc. Trade* (1697) 99 The last Stock was underwrit by Vertue of a Charter granted Anno 1657. **1705** R. BEVERLEY *Virginia* I. iv. (1722) 90 The Subscription-Money did not come in with the same readiness, with which it had been underwritten.

*absol.* **1680** R. L'ESTRANGE *Citt & Bumpkin* (ed. 3) 3 Masters underwrit for their Children, and Servants, Women for their Husbands.

**b.** *spec.* To agree to take up, in a new company or new issue (a certain number of shares if not applied for by the public).

**1889** LINDLEY *Company Law* 761 A promoter of a company who had agreed to underwrite 10,000 shares. **1896** *Times Law Rep.* (1897) XIII. 570 The Globe Company shall underwrite, or procure to be underwritten,..the first issue of 250,000 shares.

**c.** To support by a guarantee of funds.

**1890** *Spectator* 22 Nov., Many of the usual holders of great sums of money have of late been 'underwriting' great industrial enterprises.

†**5. a.** To undertake or guarantee in writing *to* do something. *Obs.*

**1621** in Foster *Eng. Factories Ind.* (1906) I. 346 The Ballochs..whoe underwrot to carry the last yeares caphila to Mando. **1642** *Propos. conc. Rais. Horse*, etc. 5 Whosoever..shall underwrite to furnish and maintain any number of Horse. **1644** VICARS *God in Mount* 163 Persons..who had..under-written to lend horse, and moneyes.

†**b.** To guarantee or promise *that*. *Obs.*

**1838** CALHOUN *Wks.* (1874) III. 237 Pass the bill, and I underwrite that we shall never have again to complain of a surplus.

Hence **U·nderwri·ting** *ppl. a.*

**1876** F. MARTIN *Hist. Lloyd's* 364 All underwriting members pay..an entrance fee of £100.

**U·nderwri·te,** *v.*[2] *rare.* [UNDER-[1] 10 a.]

**1.** *trans.* To describe in too low an aspect.

**1723–4** DK. WHARTON *True Briton* No. 69 II. 589 Who has under-wrote his Character, and represented him in faint and unbecoming Colors.

**2.** *refl.* To fall below (oneself) in writing.

**1766** *Monthly Rev.* XXXIV. 407 An author capable of so strangely under-writing himself.

**U·nderwri·ter.** [f. UNDERWRITE *v.*[1]]

†**1.** A subscriber to, or shareholder in, a mercantile venture. *Obs.*

**1616** in *Buccleuch MSS.* (Hist. MSS. Comm.) I. 250 For your venture in the East India Company I know not what to say...It's thought the King might do well to call to all the underwriters for a supply.

**2.** One who underwrites an insurance policy; *spec.* one who carries on an insurance business, esp. of shipping.

**1622** MALYNES *Anc. Law-Merch.* 166 The later vnderwriters of the Assurors do not beare any part of the losse, but make restitution of the *Premio.* **1713** STEELE *Englishm.* No. 53. An Abuse crept into the World for the Advantage of the Under-writers. **1791** BENTHAM *Panopt.* 71 He would get underwriter's profit by me; but let him get that and welcome. **1833** MARRYAT *P. Simple* (1863) 281 The plate presented me by the merchants and underwriters of Lloyd's. **1874** BURNAND *My Time* vii. 65 The fearful gales..had resulted in serious losses to the underwriters.

†**3.** One who appends his name to a writing; a subscriber. *Obs.*

*a* **1639** WOTTON in *Reliq.* (1651) 458, I have now no more to say, but that while the foresaid report shall be false, The under-writer is Truly yours H. Wotton.

**4.** A subordinate writer or clerk.

**1654** TAYLOR *Real Pres.* 288 Part of these words which Bellarmine, and from him the under-writers object. *c* **1710** CELIA FIENNES *Diary* (1888) 262 Under them is the 60 Clerks and other under writers.

**5.** One who engages to take up a certain number of company shares (see UNDERWRITE *v.*[1] 4 b.)

**1889** LINDLEY *Company Law* Index s.v., Difference between underwriter and person agreeing to place shares. **1897** *Times Law Rep.* XIII. 570 If..underwriter substitutes could not be procured, the Globe Company remained underwriter.

**Underwri·ting,** *vbl. sb.* [f. as prec.]

**1.** The action of writing beneath, *esp.* of appending one's name to a document; also, that which is so written.

**1598** FLORIO, *Sottoscrittione*, a subscription, a signing, an vnderwriting. **1622** MALYNES *Anc. Law-Merch.* 166 The later vnderwriters of the Assurors..reserue onely..10s. for their vnderwriting in the policie of Assurance. **1642** (*title*), That Great Expedition for Ireland By way of underwriting proposed by both Houses of Parliament..is heere Vindicated.

**2.** *spec.* **a.** The action or practice of (marine) insurance; the business of an underwriter. Also *attrib.*

**1775** ASH, *Underwriting*, the act of insuring by writing the name under certain conditions. **1887** *Daily News* 26 Jan. 6/4 The Union Marine Insurance Company show an underwriting income of 172,133*l.* **1905** *Times* 13 Sept. 2/6 One of the blackest years in the history of underwriting.

**b.** The action of agreeing to take up shares (see UNDERWRITE *v.*[1] 4 b). Freq. *attrib.*

**1895** in *Times Law Rep.* (1897) XIII. 156 Underwriting letter for ordinary shares. **1897** *Ibid.* 569 An underwriting agreement..between the two companies.

**U·nderwri·ting.** [UNDER-[1] 5 b.] Writing lying below other writing; the first writing in a palimpsest.

**1858** WISEMAN *Last Four Popes, Gregory XVI*, v. 305 It was this underwriting that Mai scanned with a sagacious eye.

**Underwri·tten,** *ppl. a.* [UNDER-[1] 4 a: cf. UNDERWRITE *v.*[1]]

**1.** Of words, statements, etc.: Written (out), expressed in writing, below or beneath; following upon, coming after, what is already written.

**1389** in *Eng. Gilds* (1870) 22 Deuouteliche we begynnen þis fraternite by þes ordynaunces vnderwriten. **1450–80** tr. *Secreta Secret.* Prol. 3 On of his Epistelis is here vndir writene, which he sent to Alexandre. **1483** *Rolls of Parlt.* VI. 240/1 All things said..and remembred in the said Rolle, and in the tenour of the same underwritten. **1568** GRAFTON *Chron.* II. 352 And al these Justices were commaunded to set to their handes to the questions under written. *a* **1586** SIDNEY *Arcadia* I. xix, Lalus..was by him answered in the underwritten sort. **1656** EARL MONM. tr. *Boccalini's Advts. fr. Parnass.* II. vi. (1674) 142 These under-written Articles were..penned..and sworn unto. **1667** *Protests Lords* I. 37, I, whose name is underwritten, do [etc.]. **1721** STRYPE *Eccl. Mem.* II. xviii. 389 She..writ English very well, as appears by her letter under-written. **1769** WESLEY *Wks.* (1831) XIII. 211 We, whose names are under-written,..are resolved [etc.]. **1874** SWINBURNE *Bothwell* IV. iv, His young child kneeling,..And the word underwritten of his prayer.

*absol.* **1683** W. HEDGES *Diary* (Hakl. Soc.) I. 113 The underwritten is Coppy of Capt. Minchin's affirmation. **1712** STEELE *Spect.* No. 431 ᴘ 2, I was sent for to see the Lady who sends you the Underwritten.

**2.** Of things or matters: Specified or set down in writing below, etc.

**1423** *Coventry Leet Bk.* 48 Ric. Hyckelyng & his felows..sayn, þat thes ffeldys vndurwryton owtȝ to be comyn from Lammas. **1455** *Rolls of Parlt.* V. 295/2 In certayn sommes of money undrewreten. **1497** *Naval Acc. Hen. VII* (1896) 309 The Stuff takle..and Abillamentes of warre vndrewrytyn. **1512** *Act 4 Hen. VIII*, c. 19 § 9 The Collectoures ..in maner underwritten to be..appoynted. **1545** *Reg. Privy Council Scot.* I. 3 To be sauld to the Franche army upoun the prices underwrittin. **1617** MORYSON *Itin.* III. 12 Let a Traueller obserue the vnderwritten things. **1669** STURMY *Mariner's Mag.* II. 115 These Years in the first Column under-written..are all Leap-years. **1747** in *Nairne Peerage Evidence* (1874) 81 The debts and sums of money underwritten viz. **1829** COOPER *Good's Study Med.* (ed. 3) IV. 268 Mr. Buchanan also directs the underwritten injection to be used. **1883** PICTON *L'pool Munic. Rec.* I. 10 From the date of the grant of this deed..you may take the underwritten tolls, that is to say [etc.].

**3.** Of persons: Whose names are written or signed below, etc..

**1425** *Munim. Melros* (Bann. Cl.) 544 Þe qwylke assyse was thir personis wnder wrytyn. **1483** in *Somerset Med. Wills* (1901) 238 The sadde discrecion of myn executours underwretyn. **1552–3** in Feuillerat *Revels Edw. VI* (1914) 94 Those persones be alredy furnyshed so yᵗ yt nedyth not to provyde but only for these vnderwrytten. **1772** *Ann. Reg., Chron.* 74/2 We the underwritten liverymen.

*absol.* *a* **1704** T. BROWN *Let. Oxford Taylor* Wks. 1711 IV. 253 We the under-written.., having maturely consider'd the Purport of your Charge [etc.]. **1809** BAWDWEN *Domesday Bk.* 413 The under-written have not paid the King's tax as they ought.

†**Underwroo·t,** *v. Obs.* [UNDER-[1] 4 b.] *trans.* To burrow under; to undermine.

*a* **1272** *O. E. Misc.* 97/123 Hit stont vppon a treowe mote. ..Ne may no Mynur hire vnderwrote, ne neuer false þene grundwal. *a* **1300** *Cursor M.* 23281 Þar wormes sal þaim vnder wrote In bale wit-vten hope and bote.

†**Underyawde,** app. for *-yode*, gone or passed under. *Obs.*—[1]

*c* **1557** ABP. PARKER *Ps.* I iv b, Ungodlynes in folyshnes, his tong hath under yawde.

†**Underye·te,** *v. Obs.* Forms: 1 -ȝytan, 3 -ȝiten; 2 -ȝeite, 3–4 -ȝete; *3rd sing.* 2–3 -ȝit. *Pa. t.* 1 -ȝeat, -ȝet, 3 -ȝeat, -ȝæt, 3–4 -ȝat, -ȝet, 5 -yate, -gat; *pl.* 1 -ȝeaton, -ȝeton, 3–4 -ȝete(n. *Pa. pple.* 1 -ȝiten, 3–4 -ȝite, -ȝete. [OE. *underȝietan*: see UNDER-[1] 8 a and GET *v.*]

**1.** *trans.* To get to know, to become aware of, to ascertain, to observe (a fact).

*c* **893** K. ÆLFRED *Oros.* III. vii. 112 Þa Crece þæt þa underȝeaton,..hie þa ealle wið hiene ȝewin up ahofan. *c* **1066** *O. E. Chron.* (MS. C) an. 1066, Þa Eadwine eorl and Morkere eorl þæt underȝeaton, þa coman hi þyder. *a* **1250** *Owl & Night.* 1055 Þe louerd þat sone vnderȝat. *c* **1290** *Beket* 1194 in *S. Eng. Leg.* I. 140 Seint thomas it vnder-ȝat and þare-with ne paid him nouȝt. *a* **1300** *Floriz & Bl.* (Camb. MS.) 556 Ac longe ne miȝte hi hem wite þat hi neren vnderȝete. *a* **1330** *Otuel* 1351 Þo garsie it vnder-ȝat, He was swiþe sori for þat.

**b.** With clause as object.

*c* **1000** ÆLFRIC *Saints' Lives* xxxi. 762 Þa underȝet se halȝa wer þurh haliȝne gast þæt hit se sylfa deofol wæs. *a* **1175** *Cott. Hom.* 231 Him a þance befell to underȝeite wa ..him were frend oðer fend. *c* **1200** *Trin. Coll. Hom.* 197 Wanne þe neddre hit underȝit þat hie sechen after hire, hie warneð hire wið hem. *c* **1205** LAY. 15028 Nu vnder-ȝat Uortimer his sune, Þet he hefde atter inomen. **1297** R. GLOUC. (Rolls) 2227 Þe londes abouten vs abbeþ wel under ȝite þat þer nis no volc bileued þat lond vor to wite. **13..** *Sir Beues* (A.) 1514 Þat hors wel sone vnder-ȝit, Þat Beues nas nouȝt vpon is rigge.

**2.** To perceive, observe (a person or thing); to catch sight of.

*c* **1000** ÆLFRIC *Judges* xvi. 3 Hwæt, þa Samson heora syrwunga underȝeat. *c* **1205** LAY. 1811 Brutus & his gode folc under-ȝeten þeos feondes. *a* **1225** *Ancr. R.* 150 Helle mucheres, þet robbeð al þe gold-hordes þet heo muwen underȝiten. *c* **1305** *Pilate* 200 in *E. E. P.* (1862) 116 Whan þu vnderȝete..þe gywene falshede, Whi naddestou ispeke þer aȝe? **13..** *Sir Beues* (A.) 4354 Beues at þe mete sat. He be-held and vnder-ȝat Al is fon, þat were þer oute.

**3.** To learn or know the character of; to understand the meaning of.

*c* **1000** *Ags. Gosp.* Matt. vii. 16 Fram hyra wæstmun ȝe hi underȝytað. *a* **1240** *Lofsong* in *O. E. Hom.* I. 215 Me ne hit underȝit nout er þen me hit leose. **13..** *Seven Sag.* (P.) 3151 The child was wys,..And nadde wyt of the Holy Gost, And wat thay sayden he undirgat.

†**Underyoke,** *v.*: see UNDER-[1] 2.

**U·nder-zeal.** (UNDER-[1] 10 b.) **1841** CARLYLE *Heroes* i. (1904) 40 King Olaf has been harshly blamed for his over-zeal;..I should have blamed him far more for an under-zeal!

**U·nder-zea·lot.** (UNDER-[1] 6 a.) **1682** T. FLATMAN *Heraclitus Ridens* No. 70 (1713) II. 181 Those crafty Knaves..do usually drop their Under-Zealots, when the success does not answer expectations.

**Undescanted,** *ppl. a.* (UN-[1] 8 c.) **1573–80** TUSSER *Husb.* (1878) 23 Leaue Princes affaires undeskanted on.

**Undesce·ndable,** *a.* (UN-[1] 7 b.) **1877** TENNYSON *Harold* I. i, Steam'd upward from the undescendable Abysm.

**Undesce·nded,** *a.* (UN-[1] 8.) **1701** DE FOE *Trueborn Eng.* I. 169 Yet who the Heroe was, no Man can tell...The silent Record Blushes to reveal Their Undescended Dark Original.

**Undescri·bable,** *a.* (UN-[1] 7 b and 5 b.)

**1728** ELIZA HEYWOOD tr. *Mme. de Gomez's Belle A.* (1732) II. 201, I have heard it reported, resumed the Marquis with an undescribable Agitation, that he was..in love with a Spanish Lady. **1768** STERNE *Sent. Journ.* 217, I felt such undescribable emotions within me. **1818** BYRON *Ch. Har.* IV. liii, Let these describe the undescribable. **1860** EMERSON *Cond. Life* v. (1861) 116 Graces and felicities not only unteachable, but undescribable.

Hence **Undescri·bably** *adv.*

**1792** CHARLOTTE SMITH *Desmond* II. 149 She is in love!—Oh! undescribably in love. **1818** MAR. EDGEWORTH *Let.* 8 Apr., You..will understand..how undescribably and exquisitely it is mixed with pain and pleasure.

**Undescri·bed,** *ppl. a.* [UN-[1] 8.]

**1.** Not described; not expressed in words.

**1575** T. CARTWRIGHT *2nd Reply to Whitgift* 446 As the Lord set forth the one, so he left nothing vndescribed in the other. **1600** PORY *Leo's Africa* 11 A description of places vndescribed by John Leo. **1697** COLLIER *Ess. Mor. Subj.* I. (1703) 32, I had rather leave it undescribed, than be forced to give it its proper character. **1837** CARLYLE *Fr. Rev.* III. II. i, It is a change such as History must beg her readers to imagine, *un*described. **1851** RUSKIN *Stones Ven.* (1874) I. Pref. p. vi, The reader will find..that the buildings ..have been hitherto undescribed.

**b.** *spec.* Not yet scientifically described. (Cf. NONDESCRIPT *a.* 1.)

*c* **1680** *Enquiries* 2/1 Have you any undescribed Plants, or others of special note? **1768** PENNANT in *Phil. Trans.* LVIII. 94 We believe this species to have been undescribed. **1817** KIRBY & SP. *Entomol.* xxi. II. 221 Two or three Brazilian species in my cabinet, that seem undescribed. **1890** *Science-Gossip* XXVI. 76/2 A very beautiful species of Metopidia, which I believe to be undescribed.

**2.** Not marked off or delineated.

**1852** BAILEY *Festus* (ed. 5) 475 The Atlantean axis of the world And all the undescribed circumference.

**Undescrie·d,** *ppl. a.* (UN-[1] 8.)

**1595** DANIEL *Civ. Wars* III. xl, Within rests more of feare, More dread of sad euent yet vndiscride, Than..I would there were. **1611** SHAKS. *Wint. T.* IV. iv. 669 Muffle your face,..that you may..to Ship-boord Get vndescry'd. **1642** SLINGSBY *Diary* (1836) 83 He comes close up to yᵉ town undiscry'd. **1722** WOLLASTON *Relig. Nat.* iii. 49 Who can tell at what undescried fields of knowledge even men may at length arrive? **1830** TENNYSON *Isabel* 22 Right to the heart and brain, tho' undescried. **1855** BROWNING *Men & Wom.* II. *In Three Days* iv, But years must teem with change untried,..With an end somewhere undescried.

**Undescri·ptive,** *a.* (UN-[1] 7.)

**1744** *Essay on Acting* 16 The Sentiment is languid, unintelligible and undescriptive. **1827** *Westm. Rev.* Oct. 431 The title..is altogether undescriptive of the contents..of the work. **1883** *Fortn. Rev.* July 42 It is undescriptive of such limitations..as were imposed by the Treaty of Paris.

†**Undescri·ved,** *ppl. a. Obs.* [UN-[1] 8.] Undescribed. **1435** MISYN *Fire of Love* 86 Þat lyght vndescryuyd with qwos fayrnes þa ar rauischyd.

**Unde·secrated,** *ppl. a.*

(Un-1 8.) **1865** *Sat. Rev.* 21 Oct. 527/1 They..will leave nothing undesecrated by their ribald impertinence. **1884** F. Harrison *Choice Bks.* (1886) 250 Conventual edifices still.. undestroyed and undesecrated.

**Undese·rt.** (Un-1 12 and 5 b.)
**1587** Golding *De Mornay* xxvii. 492 This infinite Godhead is not to recompence..our vndesert otherwise than with desert. **1841** Hor. Smith *Moneyed Man* III. vii. 180, I felt..my own total undesert, my inexcusable presumption.

**Undese·rted,** *ppl. a.* (Un-1 8.) [**1775** Ash.] **1792** Wordsw. *Descr. Sk.* 146 The mazes of a wood In which a cabin undeserted stood. **1892** Ld. Lytton *King Poppy* Prol. 32 That undeserted garden of the gods.

**Undese·rve,** *v.* [Un-1 14.] *trans.* To fail to deserve. Also *absol.*
**1621** Quarles *Div. Poems, Esther* vii, The blaze of Honour, Fortune's sweet excesse, Doe vndeserue the name of Happinesse. **1650** Gentilis *Considerations* 73 Where they doe not undeserve wanting the use of reason, wee should merit in rightly using it. **1721** Cibber *Heroic Daughter* II. Sp. 23 Let us not..undeserve the Grace by new false Fears. **1757** Mrs. Griffith *Lett. Henry & Frances* (1767) II. 277 There are certain base natures, which not deserving favours before hand, are sure to undeserve the more they receive. **1894** Ld. Rosebery in *Daily News* 3 May 6/6, I am inclined to think that..Government have done nothing so far to undeserve that welcome.

**Undeserved,** *ppl. a.* [Un-1 8.]
†**1.** Without having deserved it; undeserving.
*c* **1374** Chaucer *Troylus* III. 1021 O were it leful þat I pleyne of þe, That vndeserued suffrest Ialousie. **1390** Gower *Conf.* III. 13 Some comen to the dole In happ, and.. Drinke undeserved of the beste. **1412–20** Lydg. *Chron. Troy* I. 2407 And vndeserued [*sc.* of me] ben to me so trewe, þat I ensure vpon my feith [etc.]. *a* **1536** *Calisto & Melib.* A vj b, Yet vndeseruyd now thou comyst hydyr. **1593** Kyd *Let. to Puckering* Wks. (1901) p. cviii, Atheisme,..which I was vndeserved chargd withall.

†**b.** Without reason; unjustly. *Obs.*—1
?*c* **1570** *Bugbears* III. iv. 8 Vnderservde [*sic*] a thowsand tymes I wysh to see hym deade.

**2.** Not deserved or merited (*a*) as a reward, favour, etc., (*b*) as a punishment, harm, etc.
(*a*) **1390** Gower *Conf.* I. 43 Bot as the whiel aboute went He yifth his graces undeserved. *c* **1450** *Myrr. our Ladye* 132 That was hys othe, to gyue hymselfe to vs, A greate gyfte and vndeserued. **1551** Robinson tr. *More's Utopia* I. (1895) 20 Your great gentlenes to me, of my part vndeserued. **1596** Shaks. *Merch. V.* II. ix. 40 Let none presume To weare an vndeserued dignitie. **1631** Gouge *God's Arrows* I. § 33. 54 The whole cause therfore resteth in God; even in his free grace, and undeserved love. **1722** Wodrow *Corr.* (1843) II. 681 The undeserved kindness you have heaped on me. **1825** Scott *Talism.* xxiii, Permit me rather to express..my gratitude for..this undeserved generosity. **1855** Macaulay *Hist. Eng.* IV. 459 He was widely known by the very undeserved appellation of Honest Tom.
(*b*) **1513** More *Rich. III*, Wks. 62 What speke we of losse, his vtter spoile and vndeserued distruccyon. **1590** Spenser *F. Q.* I. ii. 26 Hart of flint would rew The vndeserued woes and sorrowes, which ye shew. **1644** Milton *Areop.* (Arb.) 61 The removal of an undeserved thraldom upon lerning. **1777** Sheridan *Sch. Scand.* IV. i, He was a merchant in Dublin, but has been ruined by a series of undeserved misfortunes. **1849** Eastwick *Dry Leaves* 63 The undeserved injuries and insults which had been heaped on the Amirs. **1896** W. K. Leask *H. Miller* ii. 39 Undeserved denunciations of the dangers of Chartism.

**Undese·rvedly,** *adv.* [Un-1 11; cf. prec.]
**1.** Without having deserved (to suffer); without contributory fault or demerit; unjustly.
In group (*a*) referring to the subject of the clause or concept, in (*b*) to the object of the action.
(*a*) **1549** Coverdale, etc. *Erasm. Par. 1 Pet.* i. 3 Where you suffre suche thynges vndeseruedly, you shall..receyue a great fruyte of your fayth. **1583** Melbancke *Philotimus* U iv b, With these daungers vndeseruedlye was noble Bellerophon distreste. **1652** Gaule *Magastrom.* 289 Iulian ..so died,..cursing..the Star-gazers and himselfe, for adhering to them, not undeservedly. **1712** Steele *Spect.* No. 474 ⁋ 6 A yearly Relief of my undeservedly necessitous Neighbours. **1809–10** Coleridge *Friend* (1865) 29 That I may have attracted notice to a writer undeservedly forgotten. **1877** E. Venables in *Dict. Chr. Biog.* I. 291/1 Whose reputation for orthodoxy was not undeservedly low.
(*b*) **1560** Daus tr. *Sleidane's Comm.* 264 [He] therfore ascribeth vnto vs Tyranny, extortion and disturbaunce of the Clergie, but vndeseruedly. **1597** A. M. tr. *Guillemeau's Fr. Chirurg.* 51/1 Oftentimes Princes vndeseruedlye punishe theire Chyrurgians. **1625** Hart *Anat. Ur.* I. iv. 43 He had wrongfully and vndeseruedly bene offended with me. **1656** Earl Monm. tr. *Boccalini, Pol. Touchstone* (1674) 269 A perfect Braggadochio, [they]..do not undeservedly personate ..by a Spaniard. **1901** *Athenæum* 27 July 115/1 This curt reference makes undeservedly light of Mr. Langley's immense labours.

**2.** Without desert or merit; in an unmerited degree.
In (*b*) referring to the object of the action.
(*a*) **1610** Healey *St. Aug. Citie of God* 620 There were kings in Israel, for some..predictions of theirs, may not undeservedly be called Prophets. **1651** Hobbes *Govt. & Soc.* iv. § 1. 58 The same Law..is also wont to be called Divine, nor undeservedly. **1712** Steele *Spect.* No. 302 ⁋ 5 Many of the prevailing Passions of Mankind do undeservedly pass under the Name of Religion. **1771** Luckombe *Hist. Print.* 464 The great number of Boxes which they undeservedly occupy. **1835** *Court Mag.* VI. 55/1 S. Filippo Neri has a high character, and not undeservedly.
(*b*) **1603** Florio *Montaigne* I. li. 167 Vnworthily and vndeservedly to bestow on whom we list the..loftiest titles. **1700** Dryden *Fables* Ded., One of those Athletick Brutes whom undeservedly we call Heroes.

**Undese·rvedness.** [Un-1 12.] **a.** The quality of being undeserved. **b.** Want of desert.
**1611** Speed *Hist. Gt. Brit.* IX. xix. 713/2 The reuerence of the man, or vndeseruednesse of his wrongs, moued so the affection of the Oxford Academians, that [etc.]. **1646** Jenkyn *Remora* 16 Ponder it in the..unexpectednesse, undeservednes, manner of bestowing it. **1711–2** R. Newton *Serm.* (1784) 458 If much be due..on account of the Greatness of our Blessing, how much more is due when we consider the Undeservedness of it? *a* **1834** J. Martin *Disc.* iv. 54 That consciousness of sin and undeservedness which every one feels.

**Undese·rver.** [Un-1 12.] One who is not deserving (*of* something); an unworthy person.
**1597** Shaks. 2 *Hen. IV*, II. iv. 406 The vndeseruer may sleepe, when the man of Action is call'd on. **1630** Massinger *Picture* IV. i, Too great an honour For such an undeserver. **1709** Mrs. Manley *Secret Mem.* (1720) III. 247 Since her Widowhood, she has been the perpetual Mark of ..a Croud of Undeservers. **1721** Cibber *Cæsar* v. Sp. 12 Hence,..Ye undeservers of Pharsalian Honour!

**Undese·rving,** *vbl. sb.* [Un-1 13.] Want of desert or merit.
**1598** Florio, *Immerito*, vnworthines, vndeseruing. *a* **1635** Sibbes *Confer. Christ & Mary* (1656) 24 When any temptation cometh for our unworthinesse, and our undeserving. **1711** M. Henry *Hope & Fear Balanced* 14 Let us keep up an humble Sense of our own Vndeservings and Ill-deservings. **1906** Quiller-Couch *Mayor of Troy* xi, They came contritely, conscious of their undeserving.

**Undese·rving,** *ppl. a.* [Un-1 10, 5 d.]
**1.** Not deserving (something good); lacking desert or merit; unworthy. Also const. *of.*
**1549** Coverdale, etc. *Erasm. Par. Jas.* ii. 30 b, He yt hath..preferred the vndeseruing rich man before the deseruing pore man. **1591** Shaks. *Two Gent.* III. i. 7 When I call to minde your gracious fauours Done to me (vndeseruing as I am). **1647** Cowley *Mistr., Discovery* iv, One would give with lesser grief, To an undeserving Beggar than a Thief. **1725** Pope *Odyss.* XV. 335 Mingling with the suitors' haughty train, Not undeserving, [I may] some support obtain. **1748** G. White *Serm.* (MS.), So should we love others, though undeserving of our Love. **1796–7** Jane Austen *Pride & Prej.* xlix, Wickham is not so undeserving, then, as we have thought him. **1821** Shelley *Adonais* xxiv, Whose sacred blood..Paved with eternal flowers that undeserving way. **1847** Harris *Life Ld. Hardwicke* I. 8 Such influences.. certainly were not..undeserving of attention.
*absol.* **1713** *Guardian* No. 4 ⁋ 1 Fame..promiscuously bestowed on the Meritorious and Undeserving. **1749** Fielding *Tom Jones* II. v, We are liable..to confer our choicest favours often on the undeserving.

**b.** With direct object.
**1603** Daniel *Panegyric Congratulatory* xxv, There is no accesse By grosse corruption, bribes cannot effect For th' vndeseruing any offices. **1796** Mme. D'Arblay *Camilla* V. 515 [It] makes me..feel undeserving my own hopes! **1860** Mrs. Clive *Why Paul Ferroll killed his Wife* xii, Creatures undeserving respect, incapable of goodness.

**2.** Not deserving (harsh treatment, etc.); guiltless, innocent. Also with direct object.
*a* **1586** Sidney *Arcadia* II. x, I was caried..to doo my best to destroy this sonne..undeserving destruction. **1598** R. Bernard tr. *Terence, Phormio* I. v, I hard you long since accuse vs all vndeseruing. **1697** Dryden *Æneis* VIII. 763 If your hard decrees..Have doomed to death his undeserving head. **1796** Mme. D'Arblay *Camilla* III. 59 Unused to, because undeserving control. *Ibid.* 404 Thou must linger on, then, in captivity, thou poor little undeserving sufferer! **1865** Conington tr. *Horace, Odes* I. xvii. (ed. 3) 21 Lest Cyrus ..His passion on your chaplet wreak, Or spoil your undeserving dress.

†**3.** Undeserved, unmerited. *Obs.*—1
**1588** Shaks. *L. L. L.* V. ii. 366 My Ladie..In curtesie giues vndeseruing praise.

**Undese·rvingly,** *adv.* [Un-1 11.]
**1.** Without possessing desert or merit; unworthily.
**1552** Huloet, Vndeseruyngelye, *immerito.* **1611** Cotgr., *Indignement*, vnworthily, vndeseruingly,..without merit. **1653** *Nissena* 118 Abusing the authority wherewith he was undeservingly intrusted. **1695** Ld. Preston *Boeth.* III. 116 For they who are praised & applauded undeservingly, must needs..be ashamed.

**2.** Without having done wrong; innocently.
**1645** Milton *Tetrach.* 56 He suffer'd..in his comon wealth some to bee undeservedly rich, others to bee undeservingly poore. **1781** G. Johnston *Hist. J. Juniper* II. 43 That state of happiness, from which she had so undeservingly fallen.

**Undeseuered**, obs. var. Undissevered.

†**Undesiccable,** *a.* (Un-1 7 b; see Desiccate *v.*) *a* **1425** tr. *Arderne's Treat. Fistula*, etc. 13 A fistule is nozt ellez þan ane vlcus vndesiccable, and for it is vndesiccable, þerfore by consequens it is vncurable.

**Unde·signated,** *ppl. a.* (Un-1 8.) **1795** Seward *Anecd.* (ed. 2) II. 183 The miseries of an idle and undesignated life. **1875** Whitney *Life Lang.* iii. 44 Linguistic changes..produced for the designation of conceptions before undesignated.

**Undesi·gned,** *ppl. a.* [Un-1 8.] Not designed or intended; unintentional.
**1654** Earl Orrery *Parthen.* (1676) 9 Having begg'd Ambixules pardon for an undesign'd wrong. **1745** Fielding *Tom Jones* XI. vii, The most undesigned word, the most accidental look,..will be misconstrued. **1790** Paley *Horæ Paul.* ii. § 2 Such coincidences may fairly be stated as undesigned. **1847** J. J. Blunt *Undesigned Coincidences* III. iii. 235 Confirmed as a matter of fact..by an undesigned coincidence. **1872** Yeats *Growth Comm.* 40 A result undesigned but of great moment followed the policy.

**Undesi·gnedly,** *adv.* [Un-1 11: cf. prec.] Without design or intention; unintentionally.
**1687** Boyle *Martyrd. Theodora* xi. 120 Having been, though undesignedly, so..accessory to the early loss of a life. **1768–74** Tucker *Lt. Nat.* (1834) II. 679 It is better they should do good undesignedly..than not to do it at all. **1829** I. Taylor *Enthus.* x. 299 Insensibly and undesignedly and from the operation of various causes. **1884** *Law Times* 20 Sept. 345 It is this aspect..on which 'W. B.' seems, perhaps not altogether undesignedly, to have thrown most light.

**Undesi·gnedness.** [f. Undesigned *ppl. a.*] The quality of being undesigned.
**1768–74** Tucker *Lt. Nat.* (1834) II. 87 The very essence of chance consists in undesignedness, and deviation from rule. **1794** Paley *Evid.* II. vii, The undesignedness of the agreements..demonstrates that [etc.].

**Undesi·gning,** *ppl. a.* [Un-1 10.]
**1.** Not designing or planning. *rare.*
**1673** *Remarques Humours Town* 4 That careless and undesigning way of living now in use. **1685** Boyle *Eng. Notion Nat.* vii. 260 What..happens to deliberating or designing, and..to inanimate or undesigning beings.

**2.** Having no ulterior or selfish designs; free from designing or underhand motives.
**1697** Collier *Ess. Mor. Subj.* II. (1703) 164 Children.. believe others as kind and undesigning as themselves. **1748** Richardson *Clarissa* (1811) II. xix. 130 An undesigning, open heart. **1796** Mme. D'Arblay *Camilla* III. 316 Unsuspicious as she was undesigning, [she] thanked the Baronet for his message. **1866** Geo. Eliot *Ess.* (1884) 336 The undesigning ignorant poor.

**b.** *transf.* Of things.
**1709** in *Lady M. W. Montagu's Lett.* (1887) I. 47 'Tis a plain undesigning truth, your friendship is the only happiness of my life. **1779** J. Moore *View Soc. Fr.*, etc. (1789) II. liv. 44 An open manner, and undesigning civility, distinguish the German character. **1860** Dickens *Uncom. Trav.* xvi, Of such undesigning aspect is his guileless yard now.

**Undesirabi·lity.** (Un-1: cf. next.) **1870** Miss Broughton *Red as Rose* I. 22 Quite affected by her lover's description of his own undesirability. **1885** *Manch. Exam.* 25 Feb. 5/2 The undesirability of leaving Berber in his rear.

**Undesi·rable,** *a.* and *sb.* [Un-1 7 b.]
**a.** *adj.* Not to be desired; objectionable.
**1667** Milton *P. L.* IX. 824 So to..render me more equal, and perhaps, A thing not undesireable, somtime Superior. *a* **1768** Secker *Serm.* (1770) I. v. 113 It will provoke the better Part of their Inferiors to think ill of them, which is a very undesirable Thing. **1813** Lamb in *Gentl. Mag.* June 618/1 A little excess in that article is not undesirable in youth. **1887** Ruskin *Præterita* II. 142 A porter's lodge, where undesirable visitors could be stopped.

**b.** *sb.* An undesirable thing or person.
**1883** *Athenæum* 20 Jan. 81/3 Why not, then, connect.. 'glanders' and 'gluttony' as undesirables, at once? **1900** *Daily News* 12 Nov. 7/5 Having among her passengers 42 'undesirables', deported from Capetown.

Hence **Undesi·rableness.**
**1675** Owen *Indwelling Sin* xi. (1732) 137 It casts Death and undesirableness upon them all. *c* **1815** Jane Austen *Persuas.* ii, The undesirableness of any other house..for Sir Walter. **1886** *Athenæum* 20 Feb. 267/2 The doctrine of the utter unreality and undesirableness of all life.

**Undesi·rably,** *adv.* (Un-1 11.) **1890** *Retrospect Med.* CII. 36 An undesirably large amount of glycerin. **Undesi·re,** *sb.* (Un-1 12.) **1880** W. S. Blunt *Love Sonnets of Proteus* xciv, One winter's discontent..[has] brought me to this pass of undesire. †**Undesi·re,** *v. Obs.* (Un-2 3.) *a* **1395** Hylton *Scala Perf.* II. xli. (W. de W. 1494), He that hath ones sothfastly feled it,..he maye not vndesyre it.

**Undesi·red,** *ppl. a.* [Un-1 8.]
**1.** Not asked or requested; uninvited.
**1470–1** *Rolls of Parlt.* VI. 233/1 Uncompelled, unstirred or undesired soo to doo. **1509** Fisher *Funeral Serm. C'tess Richmond* Wks. (1876) 302 He prayed vndesyred of ony. **1598** Florio, *Ingerire*,..to offer himselfe vndesired. **1634** Sir T. Herbert *Trav.* 123 Mahomet-Ally-beg vndesired, bolted out, that he knew his Master..stood more affected to no one Prince..then to our King.

**2.** Not desired or wished for; unsought.
**1599** T. M[oufet] *Silkwormes* 38 Striuing no lesse to be deliuered Than Thisbe did from vndesired life. **1617** Moryson *Itin.* III. 45 As the Poet saith, *Ignoti nulla Cupido*: Unknowne, undesired. **1697** Dryden *Æneis* II. 902 Your gift was undesired, and came too late. **1751** Johnson *Rambler* No. 175 ⁋ 2 The knowledge of crimes intrudes uncalled and undesired. **1850** Mrs. Carlyle *Lett.* (1883) II. 112 Walked in Mrs. N—, of all undesired people! **1877** Mrs. Oliphant *Makers Flor.* v. 133 Filippo set his active mind to work to get rid of his undesired partner.

Hence **Undesi·redly** *adv.*
**1845** T. W. Coit *Puritanism* 276 Those who are undesiredly tender of Puritan reputation.

**Undesi·ring,** *ppl. a.* (Un-1 10.)
**1693** Dryden *Persius* V. 161 Money to despise, And look on Wealth with undesiring Eyes. **1728–46** Thomson *Spring* 676 Away they fly, Affectionate, and undesiring bear The most delicious morsel to their young. **1880** Meredith *Tragic Com.* (1881) 88 The convalescent is receptive and undesiring, or but very faintly desiring.

**Undesi·rous,** *a.* (Un-1 7.)
Chiefly const. *of* (also *that, to*).
**1654–66** Earl Orrery *Parthen.* (1676) 289 That vice would render me as unworthy, as undesirous to live. **1670** *Devout Commun.* (1688) 15 The qualms of undesirous Communicants. **1787** Jefferson *Writ.* (1859) II. 230 This hasty measure has embarrassed England, undesirous of war if it can be avoided. **1860** Ruskin *Mod. Paint.* V. IX. i. § 11 To a being undesirous of it, and hating it, revelation is impossible. **1879** *Athenæum* 13 May, Forcing the crude productions of his mind on an undesirous world.

**Undesi·rously,** *adv.*, **-ness.** (Un-1 11, 12; cf. prec.) **1587** Fleming *Contn. Holinshed* III. 1320/2 Therefore these knights by the authoritie of darkenes verie vndesirouslie are compelled to depart from whence they came. **1668** Howe *Bless. Righteous* (1825) 261 An undesirousness or indifferency of spirit towards the eternal glory.

**Undesolved**, obs. var. Undissolved.

**Undespai·red,** *ppl. a.* (Un-1 8.) **1412–20** Lydg. *Chron. Troy* IV. 3323 þis was hir hope, fully deuoide of drede, Vndispeired in ther oppinioun.

**Undespai·ring,** *ppl. a.* (Un-1 10.)
**1730** Thomson *Sophonisba* I. i, Mean time the dauntless, undespairing youth Lay in a cave conceal'd. **1757** Dyer *Fleece* IV. 601 'Twas there Perils and conflicts inexpressible

Anson, with steady undespairing breast, Endur'd. **1824** CARLYLE in Froude *Life* (1882) I. 233 Who is it that has struggled for me..with undespairing diligence? **1847** FR. A. KEMBLE in *Rec. Later Life* (1882) III. 313 That faith which alone can bear us undespairing over the earth.

**Undespi·sed,** *ppl. a.* (UN-[1] 8.) *c* **1550** *Vertuous Scholehous* H iij b, He wyll haue wedlock kept pure and vndespised. **1579** FULKE *Heskins' Parl.* 76 That they may haue a principall and vndespised sanctification. **Undespi·sing,** *vbl. sb.* [UN-[1] 13.] † Lack of (self-) depreciation. *c* **1400** LOVE *Bonavent. Mirr.* (1908) 304 They that dreden not god..thoruȝ her owne wickednesse and vndespisynge in soule taken hit and eten hit. **Undespoi·led,** *ppl. a.* (UN-[1] 8.) **1846** WORCESTER (citing Scott). **1881** JOWETT *Thucyd.* I. 53 Their fields will be still untouched, and their goods undespoiled. **Undespo·ndent,** *a.* (UN-[1] 7.) **1876** LOWELL *Among my Bks.* Ser. II. 119 Such a life as his through all those sorrowing but undespondent years. **Undespo·nding,** *ppl. a.* (UN-[1] 10.) **1818** HALLAM *Mid. Ages* (1872) II. 271 The appearance of a Nero so undesponding. **Undespo·tic,** *a.* (UN-[1] 7.) **1820** BENTHAM *Lib. Press* Wks. 1843 II. 286/2 The difference between a despotic government and an undespotic one. **1888** BRYCE *Amer. Commw.* I. 343 So undespotic an instrument as the Federal Constitution of 1789. **Unde·stined,** *ppl. a.* (UN-[1] 8.) **1827** [see UNCOMPASSIONED *ppl. a.*].

**Undestroy·able,** *a.* (UN-[1] 7 b.)

*a* **1420** *Wycliffite Bible* Wisd. ii. 23 For whi God made man [vnable to be distried; *margin*] vndistriable. **1533** GAU *Richt Vay* 67 Of it cummis ane vndistroyabil power and heil in ye body. **1678** CUDWORTH *Intell. Syst.* 70 The substance of matter and body..is the only thing in the world that is uncorruptible and undestroyable. **1846** RUSKIN *Mod. Paint.* III. I. iv. § 9 A trace of feeling..undestroyable by any reasoning.

**Undestroy·ed,** *ppl. a.* (UN-[1] 8.)

*c* **1450** LOVELICH *Merlin* 9886 Al the Lordschepis..That this Lond defenden schal evere with-al Vndistroyed. **1523** [COVERDALE] *Old God* (1534) C j, Beel contynued afterwardes in babylon..as long as that proud kyngdom dyd stonde vndestroied. **1598** DRAYTON *Heroical Ep.* 31 How can that beauty yet be vndestroyd, That yeares haue wasted? **1637–50** ROW *Hist. Kirk* (Wodrow Soc.) 54 A principal act wes concluded, and also remains undestroyed in the Books..of this Kirk. **1758** *Elaboratory laid Open* 273 The leaving too much [sulphur] undestroyed. **1826** MISS MITFORD *Village* Ser. I. II. 245 The shrubs and flowering trees are undestroyed. **1886** WILLIS & CLARK *Cambridge* II. 383 The original windows..with the cusps still undestroyed, may still be seen.

**Undestru·ctible,** *a.* (UN-[1] 7, 5 b.) [**1775** ASH.] **1807** *Ann. Rev.* V. 589 All good is progressive, prolific, and undestructible. **1872** W. R. GREG *Enigmas of Life* iv. 157 Men in whose nature Love is as undestructible as Thought. **Undeta·chable,** *a.* (UN-[1] 7 b.) **1871** MRS. WHITNEY *Real Folks* xvii, [He] attached himself to her forthwith in a most undetachable and determined manner. **1898** *Harper's Mag.* XCVI. 681 Every machine also must have a maker's number stamped on some undetachable part. **Undeta·ched,** *ppl. a.* (UN-[1] 8.) [**1775** ASH.] **1877** RAYMOND *Mines* 449 The particles showed plainly..these grayish colors undetached from the more white quartz. **Undetai·nable,** *a.* (UN-[1] 7 b.) **1630** DONNE *Serm.* 249 Christ was and I am..undetainable in the state of Death. **Undetai·ned,** *ppl. a.* (UN-[1] 8.) **1795** COLERIDGE *Æolian Harp* 39 Full many a thought uncall'd and undetain'd..Traverse my indolent and passive brain. **Undete·ctable,** *a.* (UN-[1] 7 b, 5 b.) **1863** *Cornh. Mag.* VII. 345 Substances which may cause death and yet be undetectable, with certainty, in the body.

**Undete·cted,** *ppl. a.* (UN-[1] 8.)

*a* **1593** MARLOWE *Ovid's Elegies* III. v. 84 But woods and groues keepe your faults vndetected. **1663** BOYLE *Usef. Exp. Nat. Philos.* II. v. ii. 124 Undetected properties might in many others..be discovered. **1749** JOHNSON *Irene* III. ii, Strange! that this gen'ral fraud from day to day Should fill the world with wretches undetected. **1825** LD. COCKBURN *Mem.* (1856) 206 Which show how much inaccuracy may sometimes pass undetected. **1862** LYTTON *Str. Story* I. 194 The gift..is stored, unknown to the possessor, undetected by the common observer.

**Undete·ctible,** *a.* (UN-[1] 7, 5 b.) **1802–12** BENTHAM *Ration. Judic. Evid.* (1827) IV. 16 On a variety of undetectible, though false, pretences. **1877** LE CONTE *Elem. Geol.* (1879) 229 In the strata the quantity is so small as to be undetectible. **Undeteriorated,** *ppl. a.* (UN-[1] 8.) **1856** RUSKIN *Mod. Paint.* IV. v. xi. § 2. 130 The most delicate sculptures if executed in good marble will remain for ages undeteriorated.

**Undete·rminable,** *a.* [UN-[1] 7 b and 5 b.]

† **1.** Incapable of being terminated; unending. *Obs.*

**1581** J. BELL *Haddon's Answ. Osor.* 444 Albeit the thing it selfe..be past, and yᵉ tyme thereof determined: yet doth the power..thereof remaine unmoveable, sure, and undeterminable beyond all ages. **1605** CHAPMAN *All Fools* v. ii. 358 Lastly, for continuance of the horne, it is undeterminable till death. **1622** DONNE *Serm.* xvi. (1640) 160 He..considers farther..the inevitable, the irreparable, and for all that, undeterminable torments of hell.

† **b.** = INDETERMINABLE *a.* 1. *Obs.*

**1633** EARL MANCH. *Al Mondo* (1636) 32 An undeterminable desire of more than present life can yeeld. **1653** H. MORE *Conject. Cabbal.* (1713) 12 This vast Capability of things was unsettled, fluid, and, of it self, undeterminable as Water.

**2.** = INDETERMINABLE *a.* 3 and 3 b.

**1588** J. HARVEY *Disc. Probl.* 44 The certaine Locall region ..lurketh stil undetermined, yea, and undeterminable to, in my poore conceite. **1644** MILTON *Divorce* (ed. 2) II. xxi. 78 It doth all one as if it sent back the matter undeterminable at law, and intractable by rough dealing [etc.]. **1692** RAY *Disc.* III. ix. (1732) 397 This is absolutely uncertain and undeterminable. **1754** GOODALL *Exam. Lett. Mary Q. Scots* Introd. 28 More might have been expected from so high a pretender to reason..than to conclude the question to be undeterminable. **1872** W. S. SYMONDS *Rec. Rocks* viii. 301 The fish remains are scanty and undeterminable.

† **3.** = INDETERMINABLE *a.* 2. *Obs.*

*a* **1639** WOTTON in Gutch *Coll. Cur.* I. 217 The fight was.. surely undeterminable without the death of one of the chiefest. **1670** G. H. *Hist. Cardinals* I. II. 54 Profound and undeterminable Disputes.

**Undete·rminate,** *a.* [UN-[1] 7 and 5 b.]

† **1.** = INDETERMINATE *a.* 2. *Obs.*

**1603** HOLLAND *Plutarch's Mor.* 768 Thus would not he admit, or leave any thing..infinit and undeterminate; but adorne nature with proportion, measure, and number. **1690** LOCKE *Hum. Und.* II. xvii. § 10 As if this line of number were extended both ways to an unconceivable, undeterminate, and infinite length.

† **2.** = INDETERMINATE *a.* 2 b. *Obs.*

**1649** JER. TAYLOR *Gt. Exemp.* Disc. vi. II. § 9 He, under an undeterminate reproof, intended those that were such. **1664** H. MORE *Myst. Iniq.* 213 Any determinate conception does more vigorously..affect the mind than what is more general and undeterminate. **1736** BUTLER *Anal.* II. viii. 276 Owing to Half-views,..and to undeterminate Language.

† **3.** = INDETERMINATE *a.* 5. *Obs.*

**1668** H. MORE *Div. Dial.* I. xx. (1713) 42 To know a free Agent, which is undeterminate to either part, to be so undeterminate, and that he may choose which part he will.

**4.** = INDETERMINATE *a.* 3 and 4. Now *rare.*

**1767** A. YOUNG *Farmer's Lett. to People* 162 This undeterminate provision for the poor makes them depend on the parish for all. **1813** T. BUSBY *Lucretius* I. I. Comm. p. xxii, The argument is derived from that which is undeterminate. **1863** D. WILSON *Preh. Ann.* (ed. 2) I. iv. 128 Caverns..of undeterminate age.

† **Undete·rminated,** *ppl. a.* (UN-[1] 8; cf. prec.) **1641** EARL MONM. tr. *Biondi's Civil Wars* III. 156 Betweene two and three thousand; an undeterminated number. **1653** H. MORE *Antid. Ath.* II. v. § 6 Changing the fluid and undeterminated Matter into shapes so comely and symmetrical.

**Undete·rminately,** *adv.* (UN-[1] 11 and 5 b.)

**1571** GOLDING *Calvin on Ps.* iv. 10 The name of (citie) is put undeterminately, too the intente [etc.]. **1588** FRAUNCE *Lawiers Log.* I. vi. 33 b, If the generall bee but indefinitely, simply, or undeterminately put downe. **1670** H. STUBBE *Plus Ultra* 95 When we speak undeterminately of the Sinus, we understand those of the brain. **1681** H. MORE *Exp. Dan.* iv. 112 What was spoke more at large and more undeterminately..may here..be more punctually defined.

**Undete·rminateness.** (UN-[1] 12 and 5 b.)

**1653** H. MORE *Conject. Cabbal.* (1713) 184 What Moses may mean by the mobility of the Waters, Plotinus has expressed by..the Indefiniteness or Undeterminateness of Matter. **1656** tr. *T. White's Peripat. Inst.* 232 Quantity implying a kind of undeterminatenesse and confusion.

† **Undetermina·tion.** *Obs.* (UN-[1] 12 and 5 b.)

*a* **1631** DONNE *Serm.* Wks. 1839 IV. 289 Though I do withdraw myself from the woeful uncertainties and irresolutions and undeterminations of the Court. *a* **1676** HALE *Prim. Orig. Man.* (1677) 61 The undetermination, incertainty, and unsteadiness of the operation of his Faculties.

**Undete·rmined,** *ppl. a.* [UN-[1] 8 and 5 b.]

**1.** Not authoritatively decided or settled; not brought to an end by decision.

**1442** in *Proc. King's Council Irel.* (Rolls) 275 Many grete tresons..stonde yet vndetermyned. *a* **1513** FABYAN *Chron.* VII. ccxxviii. 257 The pope gaue suche a defuse sentence in this mater yᵗ he left yᵉ stryfe vndetermyned and vnassoyled. **1541** *Act* 33 *Hen. VIII*, c. 39 Thinges nowe..dependinge before them vndiscussed and vndetermined. **1628** COKE *On Litt.* (1629) 40 b, Hanging the voucher and vndetermined, the wife of the feoffee brings her action of dower. **1698** LUTTRELL *Brief Rel.* (1857) IV. 396 To leave the points undetermined to the arbitration of King William. **1771** LUCKOMBE *Hist. Print.* 1 It long remained an undetermined point..concerning the place. **1825** *Art Brewing* (ed. 2) 127 The question, therefore, still remains undetermined. **1885** SIR L. W. CAVE in *Law Rep.* 15 Q. B. D. 327 The question..was discussed and left undetermined in the case of Reg. *v.* Robson.

**b.** Not definitely settled or fixed; still subject to alteration or uncertainty.

**1668** [see UNCONSENTED]. **1697** DRYDEN *Virg. Georg.* I. 30 Thou, whose undetermin'd State Is yet the Business of the Gods' Debate. **1736** BUTLER *Anal.* I. iv. (1834) 88 Which miseries are, beforehand, just as contingent and undetermined as their conduct, and left to be determined by it. **1779** FORREST *Voy. N. Guinea* 171 All the charts..leave the north coast of Waygiou undetermined by a dotted line. **1831** SCOTT *Ct. Rob.* xxxiii, I vow..that the combat was yet within the undetermined doom of Providence, when [etc.]. **1862** SPENCER *First Princ.* I. v. § 29 (1875) 102 That conception of disorder, or undetermined order, which underlies every superstition.

**2.** Not definitely ascertained or identified; uncertain, doubtful.

**1588** [see UNDETERMINABLE *a.* 2]. **1697** BENTLEY *Phal.* (1699) 191 Though the date be undetermined, it might fairly be presumed to be more recent than He. **1794** R. J. SULIVAN *View Nat.* I. 435 Onyx, an undetermined transparent gem. **1839** DE LA BECHE *Rep. Geol. Cornw.*, etc. viii. 223 A few casts of one or two undetermined species. **1884** HIGGS *Magn. Dyn. Electr. Mach* 269 Where ρ, the only quantity remaining unexplained, represents the undetermined factor.

**3.** Not definitely limited or restricted in meaning or application; indefinite, vague.

**1611** FLORIO *World of Words* Rules 640 The Preterpluperfect or vndetermined tence. **1656** tr. *Hobbes' Elem. Philos.* 21 Some names are of certain and determined, others of uncertain and undetermined signification. **1705** BERKELEY *Cave of Dunmore* Wks. 1871 IV. 506 Such undetermined expressions as wide, narrow, deep. **1769** SIR J. REYNOLDS *Disc.* ii. (1778) 47 By precepts only, which will always be fleeting, variable and undetermined.

**4.** Not restrained within limits; left free or open.

**1627** MAY *Lucan* Ep. Ded., The vast strength and forces of the Prince gaue him too absolute and vndetermined a power. **1697** CONGREVE *Mourn. Bride* II. viii, Not so the mind, whose undetermined view Revolves, and to the present adds the past. **1712** ADDISON *Spect.* No. 412 ᴾ 2 Such wide and undetermined Prospects are..pleasing to the Fancy. **1818** SHELLEY *Let. to Peacock* 5 June, The mountains are wide and wild, and the whole scenery broad and undetermined.

**5.** Not determined or fixed in respect of character, action, etc.

*a* **1676** HALE *Prim. Orig. Man.* (1677) 74 Possibly Matter it self undetermined to any particular form, or under any particular constitution. **1712** ADDISON *Spect.* No. 458 ᴾ 2 False Modesty..is only a general undetermined Instinct. **1754** EDWARDS *Freed. Will* II. ix. 83 A Self-determining Power in the Understanding,..independent, undetermined by any Thing prior to its own Acts and Determinations.

**6.** Undecided, irresolute.

**1718** POPE *Iliad* XV. 595 How long on these cursed confines will ye lie, Yet undetermined or to live or die? **1796** MME. D'ARBLAY *Camilla* III. 110 Perceiving him undetermined, [she] called forth all her artillery of eloquence. **1862** BORROW *Wales* I. 1 We were undetermined for some time with respect to where we should go.

**Undete·rred,** *ppl. a.* (UN-[1] 8.)

**1607** TOPSELL *Four-f. Beasts* 203 If their rage proceede vndeterred,..forth they go into the woods. *c* **1765** FALCONER *Demagogue* 55 The fearless muse..True to herself, advances, undeterr'd By the rude clamours. **1814** WORDSW. *Excurs.* VI. 321 Who, by humiliation undeterred, Sought for his weariness a place of rest. **1846** TRENCH *Mirac.* xviii. 306 Step by step he had advanced,..undeterred by opposition.

**Undete·sting,** *ppl. a.* (UN-[1] 10.) **1736** THOMSON *Liberty* V. 293 Who these indeed can undetesting see?—But who unpitying? **Undethro·nable,** *a.* (UN-[1] 7 b.) **1835** in H. Martineau *Soc. in America* (1837) III. 69 Like an Asian monarch,..unimpeachable, undethronable. **1848** LOWELL *Biglow P.* I. v, Justice, venerable with the undethronable majesty of countless æons. **Undetra·ctingly,** *adv.* (UN-[1] 11.) **1661** BOYLE *Style of Script.* (1675) 156 As little.. as the water of a diamond can be undetractingly painted.

**Undeve·loped,** *ppl. a.* (UN-[1] 8.)

**1736** THOMSON *Liberty* IV. 224 Where undevelop'd lay The future wonders that enrich'd mankind. **1817** LADY MORGAN *France* VIII. (1818) II. 381 Those profounder feelings.. remained cold and undeveloped. **1850** GROTE *Greece* II. lxvii. VIII. 459 Of all this, the undeveloped germ doubtless existed in the previous epic..composition. **1897** MARY KINGSLEY *W. Africa* 659 A black man is no more an undeveloped white man than a rabbit is an undeveloped hare.

**Unde·viated,** *ppl. a.* (UN-[1] 8.) **1889** *Anthony's Photogr. Bull.* II. 40 The undeviated ray DE, drawn parallel to SA.

**Unde·viating,** *ppl. a.* [UN-[1] 10.] Showing no deviation; maintaining the same course; steady, constant: **a.** Of conduct, character, etc.

**1732** ARBUTHNOT in Aitken *Life & Wks.* (1892) 138 The undeviating pravity Of his Manners. **1763** GOLDSM. *Misc. Wks.* (1836) I. 526 Rational entertainment and undeviating candour. **1808** SCOTT in *Lockhart* I. i. 59 Stern, steady, and undeviating industry. **1841** MISS MITFORD in L'Estrange *Life* (1870) III. viii. 123 Whose kindness is, and has been, constant and undeviating.

**b.** In other applications.

**1784** COWPER *Task* v. 37 With such undeviating and even force He severs it away. *Ibid.* VI. 127 The race Of the undeviating and punctual sun. **1826** *Art Brewing* (ed. 2) 7 Undeviating and powerful causes of destruction or fermentation. **1874** SAYCE *Compar. Philol.* i. 11 Language..obeys undeviating laws of its own.

**Unde·viatingly,** *adv.* (UN-[1] 11; cf. prec.)

**1812** J. HENRY *Camp. agst. Quebec* 10 A simple tale of truth, which he undeviatingly throughout his book adheres to. **1854** W. OSBURN *Mon. Hist. Egypt* I. i. 7 Its [*sc.* the Nile's] course is undeviatingly from south to north. **1894** *Educat. Rev.* June 77 Their demands agree substantially, though not undeviatingly.

**Unde·vil,** *v.* [UN-[2] 4 b and 6.]

**1.** *trans.* To free from demoniacal possession.

**1632** QUARLES *Div. Fancies* I. xi, Whenas our blessed Saviour did un-devill The Man possest, the Spirits..Entred the Swine. **1655** FULLER *Ch. Hist.* x. iv. § 55 The Boy.. would not be undeviled by their Exorcisms. **1890** TALMAGE *From Manger to Throne* 81 Mouth of cavern, where madman was undevilled.

**2.** To deprive of the qualities of a devil.

**1726** DE FOE *Hist. Devil* II. iii. (1840) 199 If we should take away his invisibility too, we should undevil him quite.

Hence **Unde·villing** *vbl. sb.*

**1653** A. WILSON *Jas. I*, 108 Some Romish Priests..tampering with their Exorcisms, to the undevilling of the boy.

**Unde·vious,** *a.* (UN-[1] 7.) **1777** MELMOTH *Cato* (ed. 2) I. 206 So shall thy steps..Undevious tread in virtue's paths divine. **1804** EUGENIA DE ACTON *Tale without Title* III. 206 He is not so impertinent as to put them out of their undevious path. **Unde·viously,** *adv.* (UN-[1] 11; cf. prec.) **1813** T. BUSBY *Lucretius* I. II. 256 But did they undeviously descend, Nor contact nor concussion would ensue. **Undevi·sable,** *a.* (UN-[1] 7 b.) **1858** CARLYLE *Fredk. Gt.* III. xiv, Quirks did not prove undevisable on behalf of the Kaiser.

**Undevi·sed,** *ppl. a.* [UN-[1] 8.]

**1.** Not assigned by will.

**1766** BLACKSTONE *Comm.* II. xxxii. 515 The undevised surplus of the estate shall go to the next of kin. **1875** POSTE *Gaius* II. (ed. 2) 239 The undevised or lapsed portion..goes ..to the devisee..of the remainder of the heritage.

**2.** Not planned or intended.

**1894** H. GARDENER *Unoff. Patriot* 37 With long and undevised breaks in the continuity of sound and sense.

† **Undevote,** obs. var. UNDEVOUT *a.*

*a* **1300** *Cursor M.* 28368 Vn-deuote in my praier Seruid i haue a-but þe autere. *a* **1340** HAMPOLE *Psalter* xlix. 17 Whi þou vndeuot, takis my haly testament thurght þi filed mouth?

**Undevo·ted,** *ppl. a.* (UN-[1] 9, 5 b.) **1647** CLARENDON *Hist. Reb.* II. § 36 The lords Say and Brook (two popular men, and most undevoted to the Church, and in truth to the whole Government). † **Undevo·tely,** obs. var. UNDEVOUTLY *adv.*

† **Undevo·tion.** *Obs.* (UN-[1] 12 and 5 b.)

*c* **1340** HAMPOLE *Prose Treat.* (1876) 10 Of new prechynge þat es vanyte and vndevocyone. *c* **1386** CHAUCER *Pars. T.* ᴾ 649 Thanne comth vndeuocion thurgh which a man is blent. **1502** *Ord. Crysten Men* (W. de W. 1506) II. xv. 122 Undeuocyon and foulenes of spyryte unto us is foreboden. **1565**

JEWEL *Repl. Harding* 14 Priuate Masse..came in afterwarde by the negligence and vndeuotion of the people.

**Undevou·red**, *ppl. a.* (UN-[1] 8.) **1661** *Peacham's Compl. Gent.* 235 The only Baron that is left undevoured by time of those eight. **1827** POLLOK *Course T.* v. 79 Undevoured By spurious appetites, she found enough.

**Undevou·t**, *a.* (UN-[1] 7 and 5 b.)

*a* **1395** HYLTON *Scala Perf.* II. xlii. (W. de W. 1494), It is bothe olde & drye, vndeuoute & vnsauery in itselfe. *c* **1430** *Hymns Virgin* (1867) 89 Þan þi bodi þat was rank & Vndeuout, Of alle men is bihatid. **1502** ATKYNSON tr. *De Imitatione* I. xxv. 178 So vndeuout & remysse in the seruyce of god. **1575** FENTON *Gold. Epist.* (1582) 96 No other thing is the religious man vndeuout, than a candel dead. **1656** JEANES *Fuln. Christ* 70 Men come with as..undevout thoughts and affections to a sermon, as to a play. *a* **1701** MAUNDRELL *Journ. Jerus.* (1707) 136 The Greeks being seemingly the most undevout..of any sort of People in the Christian World. **1746** YOUNG *Nt. Th.* IX. 771 An undevout astronomer is mad. **1829** CARLYLE *Misc.* (1857) II. 48 Destitute of Religious reverence,..undevout both in heart and head. **1874** H. R. REYNOLDS *John Bapt.* v. § 1. 301 Sceptical and supercilious, frivolous and undevout.

*absol.* **1561** T. NORTON *Calvin's Inst.* III. 309 If he had willed, of the vndeuout he mighte haue made deuoute.

† **Undevou·t**, *v. Obs.* (UN-[2] 6.) *c* **1440** *Jacob's Well* 283 Abraham kecche awey flyes fro þe sacryfyse; Ry3t so, kacche out flyes þat vndeuoutyth thou3t.

**Undevou·tly**, *adv.* (UN-[1] 11.)

**1377** LANGL. *P. Pl.* B. Prol. 98 Here messe and here matynes and many of here oures Arn don vndeuoutlych [C. I. 126 vndeuotlich]. *c* **1380** WYCLIF *Wks.* (1880) 167 Be þe masse seide..schortly & vndewoutly, litel sauour of holynesse schal men fynden wiþ hem. *c* **1440** *Jacob's Well* 281 Whanne þou slawly, & vndeuoutly, & heuyly,..doost ony good dede. **1509** BARCLAY *Shyp of Folys* 203 In prayeng thou bokest vnmanerly Spuynge vp thy prayers: god wot vndeuoutly. **1647** HEXHAM I, Vndevoutely, *ongodtsdienstelick*.

**Undevou·tness.** (UN-[1] 12; cf. prec.) *c* **1440** *Jacob's Well* 294 Þe synnes of þe herte arn..dulhed, vndeuowtnesse, wanhope [etc.]. **Undew·ed**, *ppl. a.* (UN-[1] 8.) *c* **1440** *Pallad. on Husb.* VII. 237 Now flouring grapes wilde vndewed [L. *sine rore*] strie In sunne. **Undew·y**, *a.* (UN-[1] 7.) *c* **1440** *Ibid.* v. 139 To x sester old wyn, v pound inslake Of violet vndewy. **1771** *Ann. Reg., Poetry* 242 O may thy sun..Parch with unusual heat th' undewy ground.

**Unde·xterous, -trous**, *a.* (UN-[1] 7 and 5 b.)

**1688** MRQ. HALIFAX *Lady's New-years Gift* (ed. 2) 59 You must be very undextrous if when your Husband shall resolve to be an Ass, you do not take care he may be your Ass. **1781** JUSTAMOND *Priv. Life Lewis XV*, I. 162 This was not surely undextrous management. **1840** CLOUGH *Dipsychus* II. iv. 63 If the occasion coming should find us undexterous, incapable.

**Unde·xterously**, *adv.* (UN-[1] 11; cf. prec.) **1848** THACKERAY *Van. Fair* lxv, 'She hasn't a friend in the world,' Jos went on, not undexterously. **Undia·demed**, *a.* (UN-[1] 9.) **1846** WORCESTER (citing Milman). **1879** MEREDITH *Egoist* II. 109 Movements of similarity..in crowned and undiademed ladies. **Undiagno·sed**, *ppl. a.* (UN-[1] 8.) **1854** E. A. PARKES *Pract. Hygiene* 426 Many of the diseases of nutrition, which..are yet undiagnosed. **Undia·phanous**, *a.* (UN-[1] 7.) **1666** BOYLE *Orig. Forms* 231 Swarms of little Metalline and Undiaphanous Bodies, shining in the water.

**Undicta·ted**, *ppl. a.* (UN-[1] 8.)

*a* **1797** H. WALPOLE *Mem. Geo. II* (1847) I. xi. 361 Undictated by religion as those Bills were,..they breathed the very essence of it. **1804** *Ann. Rev.* II. 275 These letters have not so unaffected, uninspired, undictated an appearance as the earlier. **1873** MOZLEY *Univ. Serm.* viii. (1876) 189 It is ..His own free and undictated choice.

**Undi·eted**, *ppl. a.* (UN-[1] 8.) **1649** *Markham's Country Contentm.* (ed. 6) I. xix. 109 The best cock undyeted, not being able to encounter with the worst cock that is dyeted. **1855** SMEDLEY *Occult Sciences* 128 Undieted by ambrosia and nectar. † **Undiffa·ded**, *ppl. a.* (UN-[1] 8: cf. DEFADE *v.*) *c* **1430** LYDG. *Min. Poems* (Percy Soc.) 178 Roosys reede, Medlyd with lilies..Fresshe undiffadid. † **Undi·fference**, *v. Obs.*—[1] (UN-[1] 14, 15; app. for DIFFERENCE *v.* 4.) **1654** GAYTON *Pleas. Notes* III. xi. 144 Whether a man may abdicate his reason..for a time, and discover..no reasonable Acts, whereby a man should not undifference him from a Beast. **Undi·fferenced**, *ppl. a.* (UN-[1] 8.) **1859** SIR W. HAMILTON *Lect.* (1877) II. xxxv. 295 Abstracting from differences, and attending to resemblances, we arrive at naked or undifferenced existence. **1865** *Edin. Rev.* Apr. 346 The transgressors included..cadets bearing their arms undifferenced. **Undi·fferencing**, *ppl. a.* (UN-[1] 10.) **1624** CHAPMAN *Homer's Hymn Hermes* 1006 Thus..Hermes lived, Who truly help'd but few, but all deceived With an undifferencing respect. *a* **1661** FULLER *Worthies, Essex* I. (1661) 320 Some Sciolists will boast to distinguish bones of Beasts from Men by their Porosity, which the learned deride as an undifferencing difference. † **Undi·fferency**. *Obs.*—[1] (UN-[1] 12, 15; app. misused for 'partiality'.) **1583** GOLDING *Calvin on Deut.* cii. 627 A continuall holding on so as no vndifferencie may be perceiued nor any diuersitie of weightes and ballances nor any respect of persons. † **Undi·fferent**, *a. Obs.*—[1] [UN-[1] 7, 5 b.] = INDIFFERENT *a.*[1] I. *c* **1400** *Destr. Troy* 3915 The fourme of þo freikes was..Right suche as the syre,.. Vndifferent to deme fro þere dere fader.

**Undiffere·ntiated**, *ppl. a.* (UN-[1] 8 and 5 b.)

In very common use from *c* 1875.

**1862** H. SPENCER *First Princ.* I. iv. § 26 (1867) 96 That undifferentiated substance of consciousness which is conditioned anew in every thought. **1879** G. ALLEN *Colour Sense* iii. 27 Simple undifferentiated animal tissue.

**Undi·g**, *v.* [UN-[2] 5 b.] *trans.* To exhume, or open again, by digging.

**1641** *Termes de la Ley* 87 Neverthelesse the Coroner ought to undigge the body out of the ground. **1824** MISS MITFORD *Village* Ser. I. I. 165 One is tempted to send for the sexton and the undertaker, to undig the grave.

**Undi·genous**, *a. rare*—[1]. [f. L. *und-a* wave.] Produced by aqueous action.

**1799** KIRWAN *Geol Ess.* 221 All stratified mountains were considered as secondary, and called undigenous (flotzgebirge).

† **Undige·st**, *ppl. a. Obs.* [UN-[1] 8 b and 5 b.] Undigested. Also *fig.*

**1398** TREVISA *Barth. De P. R.* XVII. i. (Bodl. MS.) fol. 186 b/2, Leues springeþ sone for moche watry humoure vndigeste. **1456** SIR G. HAY *Gov. Princes* Wks. (S.T.S.) II. 126 Quhen it ressavis mare na it was wont to, that remaynis in the stomak undegest and rawe. **1513** DOUGLAS *Æneid* XI. iv. 63 This haisty deid [= death], sa ondegest. *Ibid.* vii. 104 A man nocht indegest [*v.r.* vndegest], bot wys and cald. **1570** LEVINS *Manip.* 92 Vndigest, *inconcoctus*. **1590** BARROUGH *Meth. Physick* I. x. (1596) 13 If the wine be yet vndigest, and do flow in the stomacke. **1623** HART *Arraignm. Ur.* I. iv. 17 The urine may be thin, crude, and undigest or raw.

**Undige·stable**, *a.* (UN-[1] 7 b and 5 b.) **1612** SELDEN *Illustr. Drayton's Poly-olb.* xvii. 271 He was so besieged with continuall & vndigestable incentiues of the Clergy.

**Undige·sted**, *ppl. a.* [UN-[1] 8 and 5 b.]

**1.** Not brought to a mature or proper condition by natural physical change.

**1528** PAYNELL *Salerne's Regim.* b j b, Fleme is vndigested bloudde. *Ibid.* B iv b, The vndigested & rawe humours are y[e] cause of opilations. **1586** T. B. *La Primaud. Fr. Acad.* I. 201 When we behold the sunne through thicke clouds and undigested vapors, we see it not cleere. **1634** SIR T. HERBERT *Trav.* 168 Vpon Mount Taurus, where wee exposed our heated bodies to vndigested vapours which easily penetrated vs. **1700** BLACKMORE *Job* 10 Deform'd he lay, disfigur'd, cover'd o'er With running boyls and undigested gore. **1738** GRAY *Tasso* 58 Further they pass, where ripening minerals flow, And embryon metals undigested glow.

**2.** Of food, etc.: Not digested in the stomach.

**1597** A. M. tr. *Guillemeau's Fr. Chirurg.* 27 b/2 When as the stomacke is burthened with anye cruditye of vndigested meat or drincke. **1620** VENNER *Via Recta* viii. 166 It is the hurtfullest thing to the body, to ingest meat vpon meat vndigested. **1693** DRYDEN, etc. *Juvenal* IV. (1697) 60 Thy own third Story smoaks, while thou, supine, Art drench'd in Fumes of undigested Wine. **1808** *Med. Jrnl.* XIX. 22 She then took an emetic, which brought up some green undigested stuff. **1892** H. LANE *Differ. Rheum. Dis.* (ed. 2) 87 Undigested food giving rise to acute gastritis.

*fig.* *c* **1610** *Women Saints* 122 Verie bitter speaches.. such as swelling and vndigested discord is wonte to belke oute. **1855** MACAULAY *Hist. Eng.* xiv. III. 460 His reading, too, though undigested, was of immense extent. **1890** *Daily News* 2 June 5/5 Trusts have found favour with the public, and have relieved financiers of much undigested stock.

**3.** Not reduced to order or harmony; not properly arranged or regulated; chaotic; confused.

**1598** FLORIO, *Indigésto*, vndigested, vnpollished. **1621** SANDYS tr. *Ovid's Met.* I. (1626) 1 One face had Nature, which they Chaos nam'd: An vndigested lump. **1633** P. FLETCHER *Purple Isl.* I. xxxix, When that great Power ..Brought into act this undigested Ball. **1665** in *Surtees Misc.* (1860) 263 The Treasury and Registry are undigested into order. **1866** J. B. ROSE tr. *Ovid's Met.* I One dull unvaried face Of matter undigested. **1884** *Manch. Exam.* 17 Sept. 4/6 A crude and undigested mass of useless rubbish.

**b.** Of discourse, ideas, etc.

**1655** *Nicholas Papers* (Camden) II. 282 Thus haue I made you a most broken vndigiested discourse. **1692** WASHINGTON tr. *Milton's Def. People* Pref., M.'s Wks. 1851 VIII. 11 The undigested and immethodical bulk of his Book. **1742** WEST *Let.* in *Gray's Poems* (1775) 147 At least a volume of undigested observations. **1792** BURKE *Corr.* (1844) IV. 35 What signifies their sputtering out a few hasty and undigested invectives? **1839** HALLAM *Lit. Eur.* II. I. II. 35 *note*, The whole was published in an undigested, incoherent, and sometimes self-contradictory paragraph.

†**Undige·stible**, *a. Obs. rare.* (UN-[1] 7 and 5 b.) **1611** COTGR., *Indigestible*, vndisgestible; which cannot, or will not, be disgested. **1613** PURCHAS *Pilgrimage* (1614) 696 The chaine holding him..and by his vndigestible nature deuouring the deuourer. **Undige·sting**, *ppl. a.* (UN-[1] 10.) **1725** *Fam. Dict.* s.v. *Nicotiana*, The Indians use it to comfort a weak and undigesting Stomach. **1865** KINGSLEY *Lett.* (1878) II. 215 Not a mere formula to be swallowed by the undigesting reason. †**Undige·stion.** *Obs.* (UN-[1] 12, 5 b.) *c* **1450** LYDG. *Secrees* 1252 That vndigestion..Causith ofte sithe by processe that they deye. **1650** W. D. tr. *Comenius' Gate Lat. Unl.* § 292 Of rawness or undisgestion com belchings, hickoping and windie rumbling. **Undi·gged**, *ppl. a.* (UN-[1] 8.) **1580** LUPTON *Sivqila* 25 For what is it to sowe seede uppon the.. greene swarde, unplowed or undigged? **1633** SALTONSTALL tr. *Ovid's Tristia* III. xii. (1637) F j b, I see the snow melt with the Sunne, The undigged water now begins to run.

† **Undi·ght**, *v. Obs.* [UN-[2] 4, 4 b.]

**1.** *trans.* To divest (of clothing, armour, etc.); to disarray, strip. Also *refl.* and with *of*.

*a* **1400** *Sir Beues* (E.) 2064 Beues anon þo doun ly3te, And þe palmere hym vndy3te. *c* **1400** *Laud Troy Bk.* 7030 The stedis..ar vndight and set in stable. *Ibid.* 10348 Ector.. wolde not him vndyght Off his armure & his a-tire. **1611** FLORIO, *Disornare*, to disadorne, to vndight.

**2.** To unfasten, undo; to unclench or open.

**1590** SPENSER *F. Q.* I. iii. 4 From her faire head her fillet she vndight, And laid her stole aside. *Ibid.* III. v. 31 His mayled haberieon she did vndight. **1633** P. FLETCHER *Purple Isl.* x. xxxvi, When she deignes those precious bones undight, Soon heav'nly notes from those divisions flow.

**Undi·ght**, *ppl. a. dial.* or *arch.* [UN-[1] 8 b.]

**1.** Not adorned, decked, or put in order.

**1555** *Richmond. Wills* (Surtees) 86, xxxvij dight dishes viij[d]; xviij undight dishes viij[d]. **1558** PHAER *Æneid* VI. Q ij, His hoary bushe and beard both overgrown and foule vndight. **1593** DRAYTON *Ecl.* viii. 98 Sayth she, I may not stay till night, And leaue my summer hall vndight. **1811** WILLAN in *Archaeol.* XVII. 162 *Undight*, undressed, or undecked. **1817** SHELLEY *Rev. Islam* IX. xxxvi, Her dark deep eyes, her lips,..her locks undight.

**2.** *Sc.* Unwinnowed. (See DIGHT *v.* 14 e.)

**1574** *Reg. Privy Council Scot.* II. 341, xvi bollis of beir or thairby undicht in the said Archibaldis barne.

**Undi·ghted**, *ppl. a.* (UN-[1] 8.) Undressed. **1673** WEDDERBURN *Voc.* 21 (Jam.), *Lana rudis*, undighted wool.

†**Undi·gne**, *a. Obs.* [UN-[1] 7, 5 b.] Unworthy.

*c* **1315** SHOREHAM I. 425 Þi bileaue of ihesu crist His nou al weuerinde, Vndigne. **1340–70** *Alex. & Dind.* 745 For þe dedus undingne þat 3e don alle..3e schulle be..put in paine for euere. *c* **1400** *Rule St. Benet* (Prose) vii. 13 Þu sal þinke in þi herte þat tu es vndinge to gode dede. *a* **1470** HARDING *Chron.* CXIII. xvii, His barons, for cause he was vndigne, Made hym his crowne for to resigne.

Hence † **Undi·gnely** *adv.*, unworthily. *Obs.*

*c* **1315** SHOREHAM I. 601 For, wo þat hy3t takeþ ondygneliche, Hys iugement he gna3eþ.

**Undi·gnified**, *ppl. a.* [UN-[1] 8.]

**1.** Of clergy: Not holding a position of dignity; not ranking as a dignitary. ? *Obs.*

**1689** *Apol. Fail. Walker's Acc.* 24 All this by the Service ..attributed to one of their undignify'd Clergy. **1776** ENTICK *London* I. 95 A great number of the undignified clergy. **1833** ALISON *Hist. Eur.* I. iii. 125 The great body of the undignified ecclesiastics.

**2.** Not dignified *by* or *with* something; undistinguished.

**1716** SWIFT *Further Acc. E. Curll* Wks. 1755 III. I. 154 An undignified scribler of a sheet and half. **1744** J. HARRIS *Coll. Voy. & Trav.* I. Ded., I have also chosen the greatest ..Body of Men undignified with Titles. **1779–81** JOHNSON *L.P., Prior* Wks. III. 134 Through the reigns of William and Anne no prosperous event passed undignified by poetry. *a* **1821** [see UNBENEFITED].

**3.** Lacking in dignity of manner, etc.

**1782** V. KNOX *Ess.* iii. (1819) I. 18 The undignified vivacity of nations which have been taught by their philosophy to degrade human nature. **1836** HOR. SMITH *Tin Trump.* I. 14 Deep and genuine emotion..is never undignified, never ungraceful. **1880** M[c]CARTHY *Own Times* xli. III. 233 He sometimes ran the risk of seeming undignified.

Hence **Undi·gnifiedly** *adv.*

**1856** FABER *Creator & Creature* I. ii. (1858) 70 Facts which seem so undignifiedly familiar. **1859** F. FRANCIS *Newton Dogvane* xxx, Sneaking,..undignifiedly, out of the gate.

**Undi·gnify**, *v.* [UN-[2] 6 c.] *trans.* **a.** To deprive of ecclesiastical dignity. ? *Obs.* **b.** To make undignified.

**1702** DE FOE *Reform. Manners* Pref. 1 All our Clergy are undignified and suspended at a Blow. **1768** *Woman of Honor* I. 224 Selfishness, which not only undignifies them, but endangers their..interest. **1840** MILMAN *Hist. Chr.* I. 185 His father's humble station..had..still farther undignified the person of Jesus to the mind of his fellow-townsmen. **1867** HOWELLS *Ital. Journ.* iii. 33 Modern civilization has not crossed the castle moat, to undignify its exterior with any visible touch of the present.

**Undi·ked, -dyked**, *ppl. a.* (UN-[1] 8, 9.) *c* **1611** CHAPMAN *Iliad* XV. 311 The Greeks found time to get Beyond the dike and th' undik'd pales. **1870** MORRIS *Earthly Par.* IV. 261 Woodbine, and the odorous virgin's-bower, Hung in great heaps about that undyked tower. **Undila·pidated**, *ppl. a.* (UN-[1] 8.) **1830** SCOTT *Demonol.* viii. 229 Their comparatively undilapidated revenue. **Undila·table**, *a.* (UN-[1] 7 b, 5 b.) **1862** MEADOWS *Man. Midwifery* 173 The os [uteri]..is still very undilatable. **1863** BATES *Nat. Amazon* iii. I. 102 The undilatable jaws..also distinguish them from other snakes. **Undila·ted**, *ppl. a.* (UN-[1] 8.) [**1775** ASH.] **1862** A. MEADOWS *Man. Midwifery* 243 If the parts are undilated and unyielding. **Undi·latory**, *a.* (UN-[1] 7, 5 b.) **1802–12** BENTHAM *Ration. Judic. Evid.* (1827) I. 471 This undilatory, unexpensive..mode of redress.

**Undi·ligent**, *a.* (UN-[1] 8 and 5 b.)

**1547** BALDWIN *Mor. Philos.* 111 Those which be vndiligent, carelesse, and sluggish. **1570** LEVINS *Manip.* 69 Vndiligent, *incurius*. **1649** JER. TAYLOR *Gt. Exemp.* I. Disc. iv. 122 He that is apt to be angry..may at some time or other be surprized when his guards are undiligent. *a* **1684** LEIGHTON *Comm.* I Pet. iii. 19–21 Why wear you out the day of grace ..as uncertain of Christ, yea, as undiligent after Him, as you were long ago? **1886** RUSKIN *Præterita* II. ix. 330 Though perfectly well-behaved, he was undiligent and effectless.

Hence **Undi·ligently** *adv.*

**1645** MILTON *Tetrach.* Wks. 1851 IV. 209 Cameron.., commenting this place not undiligently, affirmes that [etc.].

†**Undilu·cidated**, *ppl. a. Obs.* (UN-[1] 8.) **1635** PERSON *Varieties* I. 23 Ferdinando Oviedes..leaveth that question undilucidated. **1638** SIR T. HERBERT *Trav.* (ed. 2) 14 The mountaines, without doubt, abound with..mineralls, which for want of search are yet undilucidated. **Undilu·te**, *ppl. a.* [UN-[1] 8 b.] = next. **1876** BRISTOWE *The. & Pract. Med.* (1878) 657 Undilute liquid extract of opium.

**Undilu·ted**, *ppl. a.* (UN-[1] 8.)

**1756** F. HOME *Exper. Bleaching* 89 If..the oil of vitriol remains, in some parts, undiluted, the cloth is corroded into holes. **1791** COWPER *Odyss.* IX. 343 When thus the Cyclops.. had quaff'd Much undiluted milk. **1860** PIESSE *Lab. Chem. Wonders* 14 An atmosphere of undiluted oxygen. **1873** ROLFE *Phys. Chem.* 159 A concentrated solution of..undiluted blood.

**Undi·m**, *a.* (UN-[1] 7.) *c* **1838** MRS. BROWNING *An Island* xxvii, The undim Unsetting Godlight.

**Undimi·nishable**, *a.* (UN-[1] 7 b and 5 b.)

**1653** H. MORE *Conject. Cabbal.* 145 It being no object of sense but of intellect, and being also impassible and undiminishable. **1661** RUST *Origen's Opin.* 43 By an unchangeable and undiminishable necessity of Nature. **1817** SHELLEY *Pr. Athan.* II. ii. 12 Sharing that undiminishable store. **1844** EMERSON *Ess., Character* P 1 Character is of..undiminishable greatness. **1893** R. T. JEFFREY *Visits Calvary* 436 Out of His..undiminishable fulness, thou mayest receive.

Hence **Undimi·nishableness.**

**1653** H. MORE *Antid. Ath.* III. xvi. *heading*, By reason of the undiminishableness of their magnitude.

**Undimi·nished**, *ppl. a.* (UN-[1] 8.)

**1587** GOLDING *De Mornay* iii. 34 He..should be fayne to set downe his whole treatises vndiminished. **1641** MILTON *Ch. Govt.* II. 64 While he keeps them about him undiminisht and unshorn. **1693** DRYDEN *Juvenal* X. 443 Sergius, who a bad Cause bravely try'd, All of a Piece, and undiminish'd Dy'd. **1762** FALCONER *Shipwr.* II. 485 Now the sounding cord,

Updrawn, an undiminish'd depth explor'd. **1820** C. R. Maturin *Melmoth* xxx, With fading sight but undiminished feeling. **1891** Farrar *Darkn. & Dawn* xlix, Thrasea..set out on his return to Rome with undiminished cheerfulness.

**Undimi·nishing,** *ppl. a.* (Un-[1] 10.) [1828 Webster.] **1882** H. S. Holland *Logic & Life* (1885) 291 A permanent and undiminishing gladness of soul.

**Undi·mmed,** *ppl. a.* (Un-[1] 8.)
**1723** A. Hill *Hen. V*, III. i. 26 When Your great Father shall perceive Your Flame, Burning, undimn'd. **1839** Bailey *Festus* 187 Thou art as the cloudless moon, Undimmed and unarrayed. **1871** Macduff *Mem. Patmos* xiv. 186 The strong frame, the vigorous pulse, and undimmed eye.

**Undi·mpled,** *ppl. a.* (Un-[1] 8.) [1775 Ash.] **1821** Scott *Pirate* x, The little lake lay in profound quiet; its surface undimpled. *c* **1872** G. H. Kingsley *Sp. & Trav.* v. (1900) 110 The clear brown water,..undimpled by the sign of a fish.

† **Undimy.** *Obs.*—[1] [ad. med.L. *undimia*, *udimia*, ad. Gr. οἴδημα Œdema.] An impostume.
**1562** Bullein *Bulwarke, Dial. Sorenes & Chir.* 10 b, Apostumacions, of Fleume or Melancholie, have ioined unto them these names, as undimies, knottes.

**Undine** (*v*·ndīn). Also ondine. [ad. mod.L. *Undina* (Paracelsus *De Nymphis* etc., Wks. 1658 II. 391), f. L. *unda* wave. Hence also G. *undine*, F. *ondine* (whence the *a*-forms), *ondin*.] A supernatural female being, imagined as inhabiting the water; a nymph. Also *attrib.*

(The following early instance is based upon the variant *Undena* also employed by Paracelsus:—1657 Pinnell tr. Crollius *Philos. Reformed* i. 26 To the Water there belongs Nimphs, Undens, Melosyns.)

α. **1821** *Tales Landlord, Fair Witch Glas Llyn* III. 207 The ondines rich in the spoils of pearls and coral from the deep bed of ocean. **1865** Lecky *Ration.* (1878) I. i. 42 The Cabalists believed in the existence of spirits of nature, embodiments..of the four elements, sylphs, salamanders, gnomes, and ondines.

β. **1837** Hallam *Hist. Lit.* I. vii. § 19 Nature..is peopled with spiritual beings,.. the silvains (sylphs), undines, or nymphs, gnomes and salamanders. **1867** Augusta Wilson *Vashti* vi, Their foaming cataracts braided glittering spray into spectral similitude of Undine tresses and Undine faces.

**Undi·ned,** *ppl. a.* (Un-[1] 8.)
**1500–20** Dunbar *Poems* xxii. 14 The gentill goishalk gois vndynd. **1544** Betham *Precepts War* I. lxxvii. E j b, His souldiours whych were wyllynge to fyght, fastyng and vndyned. **1596** Danett tr. *Comines* (1614) 35 Neuer was so plentifull a marriage feast, but some departed vndined. **1602** L. Lloyd *Confer. Lawes* 55 They should goe away vndined for that day. **1837** Carlyle *Fr. Rev.* I. vii. v, Dined or undined, they march with one heart. **1865** — *Fredk. Gt.* xix. iv. VIII. 146 This gallop home of the undined Generals.

**Undi·nnered,** *ppl. a.* (Un-[1] 8.) **1799** *Spirit Pub. Jrnls.* III. 322 Leave me uncurl'd, undinner'd, here to mourn.

**Undi·nted,** *ppl. a.* (Un-[1] 8.)
**1606** Shaks. *Ant. & Cl.* II. vi. 39 To part with vnhackt edges, and beare backe Our Targes vndinted. **1636** R. Durham in *Ann. Dubrensia* (1877) 56 With what nimble pace Your coursers poasted, ore th' undinted face O' th' earth. **1863** Baring-Gould *Iceland* 231 To our right lay..the undinted snow.

**Undi·ocesed,** *a.* (Un-[1] 9.) **1641** Milton *Reform.* I. 22 He that will mould a modern Bishop into a primitive, must yeeld him to be..undiocest, unrevenu'd, unlorded. **Undiplo·maed,** *a.* (Un-[1] 9.) **1790** J. Williams *Shrove Tuesday* 28 Authoritative Oafs combine to teize Unhappy Oaflings —undiploma'd Curs. **Undiploma·tic,** *a.* (Un-[1] 7. Cf. G. *undiplomatisch*.) **1831** Carlyle *Sart. Res.* III. iii, The most undiplomatic and unstrategic of these [men.] **1853** Lytton *My Novel* II. ii, The dark eyes..went right into Frank's unprotected and undiplomatic heart.

**Undi·pped,** *ppl. a.* [Un-[1] 8.]
**1.** Not dipped (in a liquid).
**1648** G. Daniel *Eclog* ii. 160 A Qvill soe low, soe yet vndipt, to cope with these well-mention'd worthyes. **1692** Dryden *Cleomenes* IV. i, Like Achilles, Thou hadst a soft Egyptian heel undipt, And that has made thee mortal. **1868** Geo. Eliot *Sp. Gipsy* 18 A fountain near,..Where timorous birds alight,..And fly away again with undipped beak. **1886** *Daily News* 13 Oct. 3/4 They will during the dipping season guard the undipped sheep.

**2.** *spec.* Unbaptized.
**1693** (*title*), Semper idem:..Dedicated to undipt John [*sc.* Tillotson]. **1821** Lamb *Elia* I. *Valentine's Day*, The consigner of undipt infants to eternal torments. **1880** Ruskin *Fathers have told us* I. i. 28 That undipped people may be as good as dipped if their hearts are clean.

† **Undire·ct,** *a. Obs.* [Un-[1] 7.] = Indirect *a.*
*a* **1592** Greene *Selimus* 929 His brethren both..Do seeke the Empire while your grace doth liue, And that by vndirect sinister meanes. **1614** Latham *Falconry* (1633) 80 When through our disorder & vndirect courses, we haue wrought their vnsoundnes, we forget to looke backe. **1652** J. Wright tr. *Camus' Nat. Paradox* II. 45 Those, who by oblique and undirect wayes do seek to accomplish their pretensions.

**Undire·ct,** *v.* [Un-[1] 14.] *trans.* To misdirect, lead astray. **1647** Fuller *Gd. Th. in Worse T.* 100 Some English People on the Sea side..who make false fires to undirect Seamen in a Tempest.

**Undire·cted,** *ppl. a.* (Un-[1] 8 and 5 b.)
**1596** Spenser *St. Irel.* Wks. (Globe) 617/1 The realme was left, like a shipp in a storme,..unruled, and undirected of any. **1692** Bentley *Boyle Lect.* 103 To make out, how matter by undirected motion could..fall..into such a curious formation of humane bodies. **1762** Sterne *Tr. Shandy* VI. xxxv, Listlessness, with her lax fibre and undirected eye, sat quietly down beside him. **1822** Lamb *Elia* I. *On Some Old Actors*, A veering undirected goodness of purpose. **1882** Minchin *Unipl. Kinemat.* 108 Any quantity which has merely magnitude but not direction is called an undirected, or scalar, quantity.

†**Undire·ctly,** *adv. Obs.* (Un-[1] 11, 5 b.) **1535** in Strype *Eccl. Mem.* (1721) I. App. lxiv. 158 That neither of both parties shal give any help..against the other, directly or undirectly, secretly or openly, to the invasor. **1550** Baldwin *Mor. Philos.* II. v. K ij, Lyfe iudgeth vndirectly of deathe. **Undisa·bled,** *ppl. a.* (Un-[1] 8.) **1705** J. Collier *Ess. Mor. Subj.* III. *Pain* 6 Why then should we suppose the Touch continues entire and undisabled? **1875** Kinglake *Crimea* (1877) V. i. 237 The survivors of the first line who remained undisabled. **Undisappoi·ntable,** *a.* (Un-[1] 7 b.) **1871** Ruskin *Fors Clav.* v. 15 The straightforward and undisappointable effort to advance. **Undisappoi·nted,** *ppl. a.* (Un-[1] 8.) **1750** *Rambler* No. 3 *motto*, Undisappointed in designs, With native honours virtue shines. **Undisa·rmed,** *ppl. a.* (Un-[1] 8.) **1648–9** *Eikon Bas.* 130 Nor shall they be long undisarmed and undestroyed. **1879** Froude *Cæsar* 349 Pompey was still undisarmed.

**Undisba·nded,** *ppl. a.* (Un-[1] 8.)
**1641** *Nicholas Papers* (Camden) 32 If any soldiours be kept together..undisbanded, it will rayse jelousies. **1649** Milton *Eikon.* x. 92 There were 8000 Irish Papists which he refus'd to disband,..and so kept them undisbanded [etc.]. *a* **1754** Carte *Hist. Eng.* (1755) IV. 373 There was at that time a body of 5000 foot, part of their army undisbanded. **1810** *Monthly Rev.* LXII. 495 Some events are too complex to be wholly transacted in the presence of an undisbanded chorus. **1860** Forster *Grand Remonstr.* 166 The pay of the five undisbanded troops of the Northern army.

**Undisbu·rdened,** *ppl. a.* (Un-[1] 8.) **1659** O. Walker *Oratory* 11 The mind travelling with many conceptions at once (undisburdened of any) must needs be much surcharged.

†**Undisce·rnable,** *a. Obs.* [Un-[1] 7 b and 5 b.] = Undiscernible *a.* (Common in 17th c.)
**1586** Hooker *Disc. Justif.* § 23, I doe not meane..that building vndiscernable by mortall eyes,..but Ispeake of the visible Church. *a* **1633** W. Austin *Medit.* (1635) 139 Let us (then) not will, or strive to ascend to Honour..by secret and undiscernable meanes. **1656** Jeanes *Fuln. Christ* 229 If we take but a drop of the sea, it makes some diminution, though it be unsensible, and undiscernable. **1710** *Tatler* No. 205 ¶ 5 How undiscernable [is] the Transition from one to the other! **1794** G. Adams *Nat. & Exp. Philos.* IV. xliii. 169 The primordial threads, or first principles of the texture, are utterly undiscernable.

Hence †**Undisce·rnableness.** *Obs.*
**1645** Hammond *View Infallibility* (1646) 141 Your answer to the undiscernablenesse of errours. **1654** Whitlock *Zootomia* 536 Compared with which..the Stateliest Pallaces lessen into undiscernablenesse.

†**Undisce·rnably,** *adv. Obs.* (Un-[1] 11: cf. prec.)
**1594** Nashe *Unfort. Trav.* H ij b, By the mathematicall experimentes of long siluer pipes..vndiscerneablie conuaid..into their small throats. **1642** Milton *Apol. Smect.* 54 If they for lucre use to creepe into the Church undiscernably. **1690** Locke *Hum. Und.* II. xxxi. § 15 The sensible Ideas..are most commonly very near and undiscernably alike.

**Undisce·rned,** *ppl. a.* (Un-[1] 8 and 5 b.)
**1529** More *Dyaloge* II. ix. 57 b/2 Standyng as they do vnknowen and vndyscerned. *a* **1625** Fletcher *Captain* IV. iv, Bring me to a place Where undiscerned of her self I may Feed my desiring eyes. **1653** Holcroft *Procopius, Vand. Wars* II. 41 The plot was undiscerned by any: For though many were engaged in it, yet none..revealed it. **1703** Rowe *Ulysses* II. i, Warriors from my Fleet Who undiscern'd..and by Stealth Late came ashore. **1784** Cowper *Task* III. 242 If his word..reveal Truths undiscern'd but by that holy light, Then all is plain. **1819** Shelley *Peter Bell 3rd* v. iii, But he in shadows undiscerned Trusted.
*absol.* **1898** Meredith *Odes Fr. Hist.* 16 She had..Forgot her faith in the Great Undiscerned.

Hence **Undisce·rnedly** *adv.*
**1660** N. Ingelo *Bentiv. & Ur.* (1682) II. 61 The traiterous dispositions..in their own breasts; which though they might lurk more undiscernedly before, will then be sure to shew what they are. **1665** Boyle *Occas. Refl.* v. x. 185 Death has undiscernedly stoll'n upon them, and unawares intruded into their Studies. **1734** Falle *Jersey* (ed. 2) vi. 243 Others lavish theirs [*sc.* grants] out so wantonly and undiscernedly, that to be ev'n loaded with them is no argument of Merit.

**Undisce·rnible,** *a.* [Un-[1] 7 and 5 b: cf. Undiscernable *a.*] = Indiscernible *a.*
**1624** Gataker *Transubst.* 162 Not by running into a corner..but by becoming undiscernible by them. **1706** Stanhope *Paraphr.* III. 384 Albeit the manner of working be undiscernible yet the Work it self can be none but God's. **1768–74** Tucker *Lt. Nat.* (1834) I. 618 Minute particles, undiscernible with a microscope. **1837** Ht. Martineau *Soc. Amer.* III. 18 Where men, knowing how undiscernible consequences are,..abide them without fear. **1873** Proctor *Expanse Heaven* 270 Those other stars separately undiscernible, which produce the milky light of the galaxy.

Hence **Undisce·rnibleness.**
**1646** Hammond *Sinnes* 4 The levity and undiscerniblenesse of the matter. **1743** J. Ellis *Knowl. Div. Things* ii. 84 Because of their Remoteness, Subtilty, and Undiscernibleness, it cannot know them adequately.

**Undisce·rnibly,** *adv.* [Un-[1] 11 and 5 b: cf. Undiscernably *adv.*] = Indiscernibly *adv.*
**1655** Jer. Taylor *Repentance* v. § 5 Disc. (1674) 685 While one habit lessens, another may undiscernibly increase. **1681** Flavel *Right Man's Ref.* 183 The angels..working secretly and undiscernibly, but very effectually. **1802** *Eng. Encycl.* VI. 118/2 The ideas..are very near, and undiscernibly like. **1862** Geo. Eliot *Romola* II. v, It is probable that his imperious need of ascendancy had burned undiscernibly.

**Undisce·rning,** *sb.* [Un-[1] 13.] Want of discernment.
**1711** Steele *Spect.* No. 157 ¶ 1 The Ignorance and Undiscerning of the Generality of Schoolmasters. **1850** Browning *Christmas Eve* VII. 14 Far alike from thriftless learning And ignorance's undiscerning.

**Undisce·rning,** *ppl. a.* (Un-[1] 10 and 5 b.)
**1589** Nashe *Pref.* in Greene *Menaphon* (Arb.) 8 Which being the effect of an vndescerning iudgement, makes drosse as valuable as gold. **1643–5** Milton *Divorce* II. xii, That power the undiscerning Canonist hath improperly usurpt. **1673** *Lady's Calling* I. ii. § 5 These sophisticators of divinity desire the most undiscerning auditors. **1711** Pope *Temple of Fame* 297 Thus..fickle Fortune.., undiscerning, scatters crowns and chains. **1751** Johnson *Rambler* No. 164 ¶ 6 He is on one side censured by undiscerning malice,..and idolized on the other by ignorant admiration. **1812** Crabbe *Tales* x. 132 All are appropriate—bog, and marsh, and fen, Are only poor to undiscerning men. **1849** Macaulay *Hist. Eng.* vii. II. 240 Intemperate and undiscerning as was his zeal for the Declaration.

Hence **Undisce·rningly** *adv.*
**1707** W. Caroll *Let. Dr. Prat* 10 Not upon the 10th Chap. of that Essay, as this Gentleman very undiscerningly has it.

**Undischa·rgeable,** *a.* (Un-[1] 7 b.) **1587** Golding *De Mornay* xx. 354 These are so farre off from amounting to a discharge, that they turne to a huge heape of worse and more vndischargeable bonds.

**Undischa·rged,** *ppl. a.* [Un-[1] 8.]
**1.** Unpaid; not cleared off or settled.
**1585** Abp. Sandys *Serm. Rom. xiii. 8–13* xi. 181 What should we say but..confesse that wee haue left that debt of loue..vndischarged? **1611** Cotgr., *Insolu*, vnpayed, vndischarged, vndefrayed. *a* **1639** Spottiswood *Hist. Ch. Scot.* (1655) 336 Some private accounts, that rested undischarged at his parting forth of the Countrey. **1723** *Lond. Gaz.* No. 6183/2 The said four Exchequer Bills (which are all that are now standing out and undischarged). **1800** *Misc. Tr.* in *Asiat. Ann. Reg.* 34/2 The arrears have accumulated..and the claims of the government remain undischarged. **1908** Atton & Holland *King's Customs* 16 The long-standing claims of the Aquitaine mayors were still undischarged.

**2.** Not set free or dismissed; not released from office, liability, etc.
**1603** B. Jonson *Sejanus* v. iii, Those [cohorts] we must Hold still in readiness and undischarged. *a* **1671** Ld. Fairfax *Mem.* (1699) 125 Being yet undischarged of my place, they set my name in way of course to all their papers. **1834** Coleridge *Let.* in *Sotheby's Sale Catalogue* 20 Nov. (1899) 17, I know myself an undischarged debtor. **1888** *Pall Mall G.* 6 Mar. 2/1 He was duly adjudicated a bankrupt;..he paid nothing.., and is at present undischarged.

**3.** Not relieved *of* something.
**1670** *Devout Commun.* (1688) 27 An unfixed heart, undischarged of worldly thoughts.

**4.** Not accomplished or carried out.
*c* **1705** Pope *Jan. & May* 473 For whate'er work was undischarg'd a-bed, The duteous knight in this fair garden sped. **1881** *Atlantic Monthly* XLVIII. 380 Fulfilling important..functions which would otherwise go undischarged.

**5.** Not fired off.
**1798** S. & Ht. Lee *Canterb. T.* II. 46 Throwing down the remaining pistol undischarged. **1812** J. Henry *Camp. agst. Quebec* 130 A drunken sailor returned to his gun swearing he would not forsake it while undischarged.

**6.** Not unloaded (*from* a vessel).
**1864** Williams & Simmonds *Engl. Commerc. Corresp.* 225 Tincal undischarged from the country steamer at the Ghat.

**Undi·sciplinable,** *a.* (Un-[1] 7 b and 5 b.)
*a* **1652** J. Smith *Sel. Disc.* vi. i. (1821) 183 God..would not make us so undisciplinable in divine things. **1676** Hale *Contempl.* II. (1677) 97 Such [boys] as are undisciplineable, are after some years of probation sent away to Mechanical Imployments. **1749** Smollett *Gil Blas* XII. vi, I imagined that the pedagogues..would find their Latin thrown away, believing one at his age undisciplinable. **1815** Simond *Tour Gt. Brit.* I. 371 How can you expect to succeed with this undisciplinable spirit. **1860** Pusey *Min. Proph.* 52 The..wild ass of the east, is heady, unruly, undisciplinable.

**Undi·scipline.** (Un-[1] 12 and 5 b.)
**1827** Scott *Napoleon* Introd., Amidst debauchery and undiscipline. **1840** Alison *Hist. Europe* (1859) VIII. 668 The undiscipline of part of the Hungarian force. **1889** Gore *Rom. Cath. Claims* x. 162 This undiscipline in doctrine is at least no worse than undiscipline in morals.

**Undi·sciplined,** *ppl. a.* [Un-[1] 8. Cf. G. *undisciplinirt*, Sw. *odisciplinerad*.]
**1.** Not subjected to discipline; untrained.
**1382** Wyclif *Wisd.* xvii. 1 For these the vndisciplyned soulis erreden. — *Ecclus.* v. 14 Lest thou be take in an vndisciplined wrd, and thou be confoundid. **1596** Spenser *F. Q.* VI. v. 1 Like this wyld man, being vndisciplynd. **1602** Warner *Alb. Eng.* Epit. (1612) 357 The Warr-intricated Romaines vtterly left Britaine to the vndisciplind Britons. **1665** J. Spencer *Vulg. Proph.* 46 Their undisciplin'd mind is unable to disabuse it self by an appeal to some sober and enduring principles. **1736** Berkeley *Disc.* Wks. 1871 III. 415 The savage state of undisciplined men, whose minds are nurtured to no doctrine. **1796** Coleridge *Destiny of Nations* 137 She was quick to mark The good and evil thing, in human love Undisciplined. **1841** W. Spalding *Italy & It. Isl.* I. 19 The passions of the people were then nearly as undisciplined. **1892** Westcott *Gospel of Life* 285 The fancies of undisciplined enthusiasm.

**2.** *spec.* Not properly subjected or submissive to military discipline.
**1718** Prior *Solomon* II. 728 Loose and undisciplin'd the Soldier lay. **1792** Gouv. Morris in Sparks *Life & Writ.* (1832) II. 177 The French troops are extremely undisciplined. **1846** H. W. Torrens *Rem. Milit. Hist.* 240 The army..as yet wholly undisciplined by those to whom..new and unwonted authority had been delegated. **1878** Bosw. Smith *Carthage* i. 37 The discipline which he enforced on the most undisciplined of his army.

Hence **Undi·sciplinedness.**
**1661** Boyle *Style of Script.* 55 Generous Horses, [acting]..not out of Undisciplinednesse, but purely out of Metall. **1888** Abp. Benson in *Life* (1899) II. 209 The undisciplinedness of the spirit which despised 'the day of small things'.

† **Undisciplinous,** *a. Obs.* (Un-[1] 7.) **1382** Wyclif *Ecclus.* xxiii. 17 To the vndisciplynous speche [L. *indisciplinatæ loquelæ*] vse not thi mouth. **Undisclo·se,** *v.* [Un-[1] 14.] *trans.* To keep concealed. **1601** Daniel *Delia* xxxvi, The halfe blowne Rose,..Whilst yet her tender bud doth vndisclose That full of beautie, tyme bestowes vpon her.

**Undisclo·sed,** *ppl. a.* [Un-[1] 8.]

**1.** Not revealed or made known.

**1571** Golding *Calvin on Ps.* vi. 6 The grace of God being yet undisclosed before the comming of Christ. **1648** Hexham ii, *Ongeopenbaert*, Vnrevealed, Vndiscovered, or Vndisclosed. **1814** Byron *Lara* i. xxiii, Whate'er there be between you undisclosed, This is no time [etc.]. **1880** Muirhead tr. *Ulpian* xxv. § 17 *note*, It is doubtful whether he could take under a secret and undisclosed trust.

**2.** Unhatched. (Cf. Disclose *v.* 1 b.)

**1581** T. Howell *Deuises* H j, Counte not the byrds that vndisclosed bee. **1744** Thomson *Summer* 260 The sweet task,..where to wrap In what soft beds their young, yet undisclos'd, Employs their tender care. **1817** Kirby & Sp. *Entomol.* xxvii. II. 503 They place a guard over the cells of those [bees yet] undisclosed.

**Undisco·loured,** *ppl. a.* (Un-[1] 8.)

**1666** Boyle *Orig. Forms & Qual.* 318 An undiscolour'd mixture of syrup of Violets. **1814** Wordsw. *Excurs.* v. 164 Fixed aloft A faded hatchment hung, and one by time Yet undiscoloured. **1847** H. Rogers *Ess.* (1874) I. v. 237 The severest raillery..flows on in a stream undiscoloured by one particle of malevolence. **1876** Miss Broughton *Joan* xxvii, A face unswollen, undiscoloured by any tears.

**Undisco·mfitable,** *a.* (Un-[1] 7 b.) *a* **1555** Philpot in *Exam. & Writ.* (Parker Soc.) 351 But those things are so undisconfitable..that for want of good argument [etc.].

**Undisco·mfited,** *ppl. a.* Also 4-5 *Sc.* vndisconfit, wndiscumfyt. (Un-[1] 8.)

*c* **1374** Chaucer *Boeth.* i. met. iv. (1868) 12 He may holde hys chiere vndiscomfited. **1375** Barbour *Bruce* iii. 274 Thai that wald Thar hartis wndiscumfyt hald. **1523** Ld. Berners *Froiss.* I. cclix. 384 They..fought..and so helde themselfe vndiscomfited the space of ii. houres. **1856** Mrs. Browning *Aur. Leigh* i. 775 That..undiscomfited Look steadfast truths against Time's changing mask.

**Undisconti·nued,** *ppl. a.* (Un-[1] 8.)

**1629** Donne *Serm.* (1839) V. 253, I shall have..an unintermitted, an undiscontinued Sight of God. **1702** S. Parker tr. *Cicero's De Finibus* ii. 125 For a true Blessedness of Life ..is as Lasting and as Undiscontinu'd as Wisdom. **1719** Jas. the Pretender *Let.* in *Pearson's Catal.* (1894) 33, I hope God will bless at last my undiscontinued efforts. **1818** Bentham *Ch. Eng.* 47 The test above brought to view ..consisting of the undiscontinued assortment of quotations.

**Undisco·rdant,** *a.* (Un-[1] 7.) **1819** Wordsw. '*Departing Summer*' 21 Wide is the range, and free the choice Of undiscordant themes. **Undisco·rding,** *ppl. a.* (Un-[1] 10.) *c* **1630** Milton *At a Solemn Musick* 17 That we..with undiscording voice May rightly answer that melodious noise. **1742** G. West *Instit. Order of Garter* (1807) 109 Attuning to the sweet harmonious spheres Their undiscording lyres.

**Undiscou·rageable,** *a.* (Un-[1] 7 b.)

**1571** Golding *Calvin on Ps.* xxii. 2 Such an one as was vndiscorageable in undertaking troubles. **1684** *Gilby's Test. 12 Patriarchs* B 8 b, My heart was stout, my mind unmoveable, and my stomach undiscourageable. **1865** H. Bushnell *Vicar. Sacr.* ii. iv, His..upright, impartial, passionless, undiscourageable rule. **1882** H. C. Merivale *Faucit of B.* III. ii. xv. 94 She had watched..the fair Emily's patient and undiscourageable angling.

**Undiscou·raged,** *ppl. a.* (Un-[1] 8.)

*a* **1628** F. Grevil *Life Sidney* xiv. (1652) 167 My yet undiscouraged Genius. **1642** in *Chas. I's Wks.* (1662) II. 201 Your Parliament, whose constant and undiscouraged Endeavours..have passed through Difficulties unheard-of. **1773** *Cook's 1st Voy.* I. Introd. p. xii, Mr. Banks however returned, undiscouraged, from his first expedition. **1859** H. Kingsley *G. Hamlyn* xiv, He, nevertheless, held on his way undiscouraged. **1898** G. W. Steevens *Egypt in 1898* xvii. 203 The practical, undiscouraged Englishman.

**Undiscou·rsed,** *ppl. a.* (Un-[1] 8.) *a* **1670** Hacket *Abp. Williams* i. (1693) 130 We would submit to all with indefinite and undiscoursed Obedience. *Ibid.* ii. 217.

**Undisco·verable,** *a.* (Un-[1] 7 b and 5 b.)

**1642** Quarles *Observ. Princes & States* lxxvi, It is the height of a provident Commander..to keepe his owne designes undiscoverable to the Enemy. **1688** Boyle *Final Causes Nat. Things* ii. 79 Among the ends of God, which he thought undiscoverable by us. **1768–74** Tucker *Lt. Nat.* (1834) II. 79 The multitude of events..produced by the concurrence of undiscoverable causes. **1841** Myers *Cath. Th.* iv. § 36 What..portion of such Plan it is, is at present undiscoverable by us. **1885** *Law Times* 11 Apr. 420/2 The undiscoverable flaw constituted a breach of such warranty.

Hence **Undisco·verableness.**

**1656** Jeanes *Fuln. Chr.* 383 His riches are said to be unsearchable,..which Epithet denoteth the undiscoverableness of them by the light of nature.

**Undisco·verably,** *adv.* (Un-[1] 11 and 5 b.)

**1645** Milton *Tetrach.* Wks. 1851 IV. 228 He..permitted by accident the evil of them who divorc't against the laws intention undiscoverably. **1680** Cotton *Compl. Gamester* (ed. 2) 12 How neatly and undiscoverably he managed his tricks. **1892** Zangwill *Bow Mystery* 171 To assassinate secretly, mysteriously, unintelligibly, undiscoverably.

**Undisco·vered,** *ppl. a.* [Un-[1] 8 and 5 b.]

†**1.** Uncovered, exposed. *Obs.*[−1]

**1542** Boorde *Dyetary* viii. (1870) 247 When..you do slepe, let not..your handes, nor fete,..lye bare vndyscouered.

**2.** Undisclosed, unrevealed; not cleared up.

*a* **1542** Wyatt *Psalm*, '*Oh happy ar they*' 20 As adder freshe new stryppid from his skin, nor in his sprite is owght vndiscoverd. **1576** Fleming *Panopl. Epist.* 64 All your loue is apparant and manifest unto me.., and neuer a part or parcel thereof left undiscouered. **1611** Shaks. *Wint. T.* v. ii. 130 This Mysterie remained vndiscouer'd. **1697** Tutchin *Search Honesty* v, In whose Bigg Bellies undiscover'd lye The Fate of Kings. **1867** M. Arnold *A Wish* vii, The future and its viewless things—That undiscover'd mystery.

**3.** Not discovered, found, or come upon.

**1555** Eden *Decades* (Arb.) 285 What parts of the baul of the earth remained yet vndiscouered. **1602** Shaks. *Haml.* iii. i. 79 The vndiscouered Countrey, from whose Borne No Traueller returnes. **1676** Glanvill *Ess.* vii. 1 In that immense undiscover'd Abyss, that was beyond both the Old World, and the New. **1769** E. Bancroft *Guiana* 2 If we may be allowed to form an idea of things undiscovered, by the immense variety..of its Animal and Vegetable Productions. **1806** Lamb *Mr. H—* ii. Wks. 1908 II. 758 Some yet undiscovered Otaheite. **1850** Tennyson *In Mem.* xl, My paths are in the fields I know, And thine in undiscover'd lands. **1894** H. Nisbet *Bush Girl's Rom.* 171 They were not so pleased to hear that their cash was as yet undiscovered.

**b.** Not ascertained or made out.

**1707** Mortimer *Husb.* A 2 b, The detecting of specious and prevailing Errors,..so as to clear the way to what remains undiscovered. **1793** Beddoes *Calculus* 273 The grasses (of which the product is variable from undiscovered causes). **1855** Brewster *Newton* II. xxvii. 408 Those inspired doctrines which alone can throw a light over the dark ocean of undiscovered truth.

**4.** Not found out; unobserved, undetected.

**1593** Shaks. 2 *Hen. VI*, iii. i. 369 Full often Hath he conuersed with the Enemie, And vndiscouer'd, come to me againe. **1669** Sturmy *Mariner's Mag.*, *Penalties & Forfeit.* 4 Goods..that shall be Exported, and escape undiscovered unto the Officers of the Customs. **1697** C. Leslie *Snake in Grass* (ed. 2) 308 The Quakers take it very ill to suppose that Jesuits cou'd Preach among them undiscover'd. **1725** De Foe *Voy. round World* (1840) 63 A little cape which kept us perfectly undiscovered. **1798** S. & Ht. Lee *Canterb. T.* II. 101 Let me fly undiscovered. **1890** *Retrospect Med.* CII. 310 In order to guard against the possibility of leaving a perforation undiscovered.

**Undisco·vering,** *ppl. a.*: see Un-[1] 5 d.

†**Undiscree·t,** *a. Obs.* [Un-[1] 7 and 5 b. Cf. MDu. *ondiscreet.*] = Indiscreet *a.* (Common *c* 1400–1650.) **a.** Of persons.

**1382** Wyclif *Ecclus.* xxxi. 23 Waking, and colere, and anguysh to an vndiscreet man. *c* **1400** tr. *Secreta Secret., Gov. Lordsh.* 116 He þat hauys a greet wombe, ys vndiscreet, foltysch, proud. **1482** *Monk of Evesham* (Arb.) 97 He was lyght of behauyng and ondyscrete as in eatyng and drynkyng. **1549** Latimer *3rd Serm. bef. Edw. VI* (Arb.) 77 We are noted to be rassh, and vndiscrete in our preachynge. **1584** R. Scot *Discov. Witchcr.* xiv. viii. (1886) 311 Into what follie and madnes vaine hope may drive undiscreete and unexpert men. **1676** Hobbes *Iliad* 308 What need we, like two women in the street,..to rail and scoff? Who, say they true or false, are undiscreet. *a* **1704** T. Brown *Wks.* (1709) III. ii. 116 My Despair proceeded not from the same Motive, as that of the undiscreet Lucretia.

*absol.* **1535** Coverdale *Ecclus.* xxvii. 12 Yf thou be amonge the vndiscrete. **1595** Daniel *Civ. Wars* i. l, This publique course..compassion drawes; Especially in cases of the great, Which worke much pitty in the undiscreat.

**b.** Of actions, conduct, etc.

*c* **1340** Hampole *Prose Tr.* 17 He..by vndiscrete trauellynge turnes þe braynes in his heuede. **1420–2** Lydg. *Thebes* iii. 3114 Thorgh vndiscret and hasty gredynesse. *c* **1440** *Jacob's Well* 99 Be-cause of þin vndyscret dyspysing it doth hym vnworschip. **1529** More *Dyaloge* iv. Wks. 276/2 Some of them may haue som time either ouer feruent mynd or vndiscrete zele. **1579** Lyly *Euphues* (Arb.) 133 By which their vndiscreet dealing, they are like those sicke men which reiect the..cunning Phisition. **1640** Fuller *Joseph's Coat* 182 The flames of ill-tempered and undiscreet zeal. **1694** *Gracian's Courtier's Orac.* 50 Blind passion, undiscreet engagement, imprudent haste, fool-hardiness.

†**Undiscree·tly,** *adv.* [Un-[1] 11: cf. prec.] = Indiscreetly *adv.* (Common *c* 1450–1650.)

*c* **1380** Wyclif *Sel. Wks.* III. 362 For ȝif þei cursen undiscretly,..þanne þei cursen hemsilf first. *c* **1440** *Jacob's Well* 262 Whanne þou behotyst myche thyng vndyscretly, and doost noȝt þi behest. *c* **1491** *Chast. Goddes Chyld.* 21 Suche men unresonably and undyscretly encline to the rest and commodyte of the body. **1539** Elyot *Cast. Helthe* 63 Put to the heed vndiscretely, it hurteth both the heed and the eies. **1579** Fulke *Heskins' Parl.* 201 Dionyse the Charterhouse Monke, whom he matcheth vndiscretely with Cyrill. **1618** *Barnevelt's Apol.* G ij b, Seeing both the words and meaning thereof are much different from that which they vndiscreetely coyne. **1698** *Phil. Trans.* XX. 75 'Tis very necessary for them to forbear much drinking undiscreetly. **1704** *Collect. Voy.* (Churchill) III. 680/2 Heated with strong Liquor, [he] reply'd undiscreetly.

†**Undiscree·tness.** *Obs.* [Un-[1] 12: cf. prec.] = Indiscreetness.

**1542** Udall *Erasm. Apoph.* 295 b, He gravely restreigned and staied the heddie undiscretenesse of the oratours. **1587** Golding *De Mornay* xi. 181 The fault is in thyne owne vndiscreetnesse, and not in their nature. **1647** Hexham i. s.v.

**Undiscre·te,** *a.* (Un-[1] 7, 5 b.) **1862** Beveridge *Hist. Ind.* II. iv. iv. 119 Eternal matter, undiscrete, destitute of parts.

†**Undiscre·tion.** *Obs.* [Un-[1] 12 and 5 b.] = Indiscretion.

*a* **1395** Hylton *Scala Perf.* i. xxviii. (W. de W. 1494), Therfor they by undescrecion oft sithes ouertraueyle her witts. **1420–2** Lydg. *Thebes* iii. 3449 3oure-silf to drowne in torment & in woo..Is gret foly and vndiscreccioun. **1563** Harding *Answ. to M. Ivelles Challenge* To Rdr. (1565) 4 b, The note of vndiscretion shall remaine to them.

**Undiscri·minated,** *ppl. a.* (Un-[1] 8 and 5 b.) **1768** Gibbon *Misc. Wks.* (1814) V. 569 All M. de Buffon's witnesses appear levelled by an undiscriminated equality.

**Undiscri·minating,** *ppl. a.* (Un-[1] 10, 5 b.)

*a* **1800** Cowper *Odyss.* (ed. 2) xxii. 298 Hurl the spear At once with undiscriminating aim Against them all. **1844** H. H. Wilson *Brit. India* III. 440 The undiscriminating nature of their outrages. **1871** Freeman *Hist. Ess.* Ser. i. iv. 87 Morris writes in a spirit of undiscriminating admiration.

Hence **Undiscri·minatingly** *adv.*, **-ness.**

**1866** Geo. Eliot *F. Holt* xvi, They encourage a coarse undiscriminatingness. **1894** *Athenæum* 27 Oct. 574/1 The bookworm swallows all printed matter undiscriminatingly.

†**Undiscu·rrent,** *a. Obs.* (Un-[1] 7.) *a* **1529** Skelton *Bk. 3 Fools* Wks. 1843 I. 200 Shee is so debylyte, colde,..vnnaturall, and vndyscurrente, for the coldenes that is in her.

**Undiscu·rsive,** *a.* (Un-[1] 7.) **1633** T. Adams *Exp. 2 Peter* ii. 2 It is an inconsiderate, undiscoursive applyment of themselves to anothers will, without waighing the goodnesse or fitnesse of the action. **1874** Lewes *Probl. Life & Mind* I. 141 Enough here to define it [*sc.* knowledge] as lapsed or undiscursive Intelligence. **Undiscu·ssable,** *a.* (Un-[1] 7 b and 5 b.) **1861** Dickens *Gt. Expect.* viii, She said it finally and in..an undiscussable way.

**Undiscu·ssed,** *ppl. a.* (Un-[1] 8 and 5 b.)

In older use (15–17th c.) chiefly in the sense of 'undecided, unsettled': see Discuss *v.* 4.

*c* **1340** Hampole *Pr. Consc.* 5697 Þe lest thoghtes þat thurgh use had yhe In þe dome sal noght undiscussed be. **1439** *Rolls of Parlt.* V. 17/1 Which Assise hangyng undiscussed, ye same Phelip desired often tymes [etc.]. *a* **1513** Fabyan *Chron.* v. cxvi. 90 Not without great stryfe had atwene hym and his sayde vncle,..whereof at this day some deale was vndiscussyd. **1567–9** Jewel *Def. Apol.* (1611) 458 This matter notwithstanding it had beene much beaten thorow the world, yet lay still vndiscussed. **1610** Healey *St. Aug. Citie of God* 561 This question wee touched at in our third booke, but left it undiscussed. **1643** Prynne *Sov. Power Parl.* i. (ed. 2) 31 That the Parliament should not depart so long as any Petition..hangeth undiscussed or undecided.

[**1775** Ash.] **1818** Cobbett *Resid. U.S.* (1819) 294 There remains a very important part of the subject yet undiscussed. **1898** S. Evans *Holy Graal* 30 The question was left undiscussed and unsettled.

**Undisea·sed,** *ppl. a.* [Un-[1] 8.]

†**1.** Free from discomfort or trouble. *Obs. rare.*

*c* **1450** *Life St. Cuthbert* (Surtees) 6881 Þar was nane wery, alde ne ȝyng,..Þai come to Rypoun all vndyseesed. **1535** Coverdale *Dan.* vi. 2 Aboue these he set thre prynces,..that the lordes might geue accomptes vnto them, and the kynge to be vndiseased.

**2.** Not affected by or suffering from disease.

**1746** Young *Nt. Th.* ix. 1804 Where reason (un-diseas'd with you) runs mad, And nurses folly's children as her own. **1807** Southey *Espriella's Lett.* (1808) II. 322 Undiseased parts will not convey any remarkable impression to the examiner. **1879** H. Spencer *Data of Ethics* xv. 277 Scientific knowledge of organic actions that are undiseased.

**Undisfi·gured,** *ppl. a.* (Un-[1] 8.)

**1720** Pope *Iliad* xxiv. 509 Yet undisfigured, or in limb or face, All fresh he lies. *a* **1873** Lytton *Pausanias* i, Severe and early training..had left, undisfigured by superfluous flesh, the grand proportions [etc.]. **1897** Miss Kingsley *W. Africa* 223 Their teeth..undisfigured by filing.

**Undisfulfi·lled,** *ppl. a.* (Un-[1] 8.) **1823** Bentham *Not Paul* 285 So long as the predictor lived, it [*sc.* the prediction] would remain good and undisfulfilled.

**Undisgra·ced,** *ppl. a.* (Un-[1] 8 and 5 b.)

**1748** Chesterf. *Lett.* cxlvii. (1792) II. 24 If Shakespeare's genius had been cultivated, those beauties..would have been undisgraced by those extravagancies. **1812** Byron *Ch. Harold* ii. xciii, So may our country's name be undisgraced. **1820** Keats *Hyperion* ii. 344 Hyperion, Our brightest brother, still is undisgraced.

**Undisgui·sable,** *a.* (Un-[1] 7 b.)

**1673** R. Head *Canting Acad.* 89 Their speech is undisguisable. **1804** Southey in Robberds *Mem. W. Taylor* (1843) I. 501 Your language is as undisguisable as my face. **1862** Mrs. Oliphant *Last of Mortimers* iv. v, Blushing in the most violent undisguisable way.

**Undisgui·se,** *sb.* (Un-[1] 12.) **1804** *Europ. Mag.* XLV. 339/2 He told her with equal undisguise, but more warmth, that [etc.]. **1869** *Pall Mall G.* 9 Aug. 11 The bitter candour and reckless undisguise of Heine.

**Undisgui·se,** *v.* [Un-[2] 4.] *trans.* To strip of, or free from, a disguise. Also *refl.* and *absol.*

**1638** Mayne *Lucian* (1664) A iv, Who stopt the mouthes of Oracles,..undisguised their Delusions [etc.]. *Ibid.* 390 As soon as I undisguise him, I shall know the truth. **1655** tr. *Sorel's Com. Hist. Francion* iii. 60 You promis'd..to undisguise your selfe, and give me a real account of your more particular Adventures. **1671** Crowne *Juliana* v, Madam, undisguize, and let the Duke affront you if he dares. **1700** Motteux *Quix.* i. iv. iv, The Curate advis'd him to return it, telling him that he might now undisguise himself. **1871** B. Taylor *Faust* (1875) I. iii. 53 Now, to undisguise thee, Hear me exorcise thee.

**Undisgui·sed,** *ppl. a.* (Un-[1] 8.) **a.** Of things.

*a* **1500** *Chaucer's Dreme* 1450 The prince,..in plaine English undisguised, Hem shewed hole his journeye. **1656** [see Unartificial *a.* 2]. **1663** Bp. Patrick *Parab. Pilgr.* vii, The naked and undisguised practice of real Godliness. **1697** Collier *Ess. Mor. Subj.* i. (1709) 165 By parity of Reason, we may court undisguised Ruin. **1726** Pope *Odyss.* xvii. 18 The very truth I undisguised declare. **1828** Lytton *Pelham* III. iii, A friendly dinner, a family meal, are things from which I fly with undisguised aversion. **1873** Holland *A. Bonnic.* i. 19 With ingenuous and undisguised wonder.

**b.** Of persons.

**1671** Milton *P. R.* i. 357 Whom thus answer'd th' Arch Fiend now undisguis'd. **1727** De Foe *Syst. Magic* i. iii. (1840) 79 He did not walk about in person, undisguised and open,..and acting like himself. **1796** Mme. D'Arblay *Camilla* III. 383 The declared and undisguised pursuer of her favour. **1827** Pollok *Course T.* viii. 137 Each,..undisguised, was what his seeming showed.

Hence **Undisgui·sedness.**

**1814** Shelley in Hogg *Life* (1858) II. 494 It proves..the sincerity, undisguisedness, of your passion.

**Undisgui·sedly,** *adv.* (Un-[1] 11; cf. prec.)

**1611** in *10th Rep. Hist. MSS. Comm.* App. I. 548, I desire your Lo[rdship] should undisguisedly bee informed of ye truthe how things heere passe. **1805** *Ann. Rev.* III. 308 This corn-bill undisguisedly..undertakes to increase the price of necessary food. **1875** Poste *Gaius* i. (ed. 2) 154 All power was undisguisedly absorbed by the emperor.

**Undisgui·sing,** *ppl. a.* (Un-[1] 10.) **1813** Shelley *Q. Mab* v. 187 Those duties..Are bought and sold as in a public mart Of undisguising selfishness. *Ibid.* ix. 42 Crime..Unblushing, undisguising. **Undisgu·sting,** *ppl. a.* (Un-[1] 10.) **1755** Young *Centaur* i. Wks. 1757 IV. 115 Rendering them ..undisgusting, and palateable to all the rational part of mankind. **Undishea·rtened,** *ppl. a.* (Un-[1] 8.) **1827** Hallam *Const. Hist.* xiv. II. 432 To this one object..the whole of his heroic life was directed with undeviating, undisheartened firmness. **1877** W. R. Cooper *Egyptian Obelisks* xx. (1878) 104 Undisheartened by this want of success, he waited till the fall of the Nile. **Undisho·nested**, *ppl. a.* (Un-1 8.) **1631** T. Powell *Tom All Trades* 5 While your Land is of virgin reputation, while it is chast, and vndishonested.

**Undisho·noured**, *ppl. a.* (Un-1 8.)

**1590** Shaks. *Com. Err.* II. ii. 148 I liue distain'd, thou vndishonoured. **1613** Beaum. & Fl. *Honest Man's Fort.* I. i, Then you were So noble, that I durst have trusted your Embraces.., And yet come from you—undishonor'd. **1638** Brome *Antipodes* III. vii, In money I tender him double satisfaction, With his own wares again unblemished, undishonor'd. **1726** Pope *Odyss.* XXII. 350 Still undishonour'd or by word or deed Thy house, for me, remains. **1850** Thackeray *Pendennis* lviii, The name of Pendennis..was left undishonoured behind us. **1881** Swinburne *Mary Stuart* III. i, I had rather die Thus undishonoured.

**Undisinhe·ritable**, *a.* (Un-1 7 b.) *a* **1631** Donne *Sermons* i. (1634) 35 The undisinheritable sonnes of God.

**Undisjoi·ned**, *ppl. a.* (Un-1 8.) *a* **1800** Cowper *Odyss.* (ed. 2) v. 431 While yet the planks sustain This tempest undisjoin'd, I will abide A suff'rer on the raft. **Undisjoi·nted**, *ppl. a.* (Un-1 8.) **1631** Weever *Anc. Funeral Mon.* 778 An ashie dry carkasse.., whole and vndisioynted. **Undislocated**, *ppl. a.* (Un-1 8.) [**1775** Ash.] **1876** Mrs. Whitney *Sights & Ins.* xxix. 286 The wonder was that she..had come off with undislocated vertebræ. **Undislo·dged**, *ppl. a.* (Un-1 8.) [**1775** Ash.] *a* **1847** Chalmers *Bridgewater Treat.* (1853) I. i. 64 Moral rectitude still undislodged from its empire. **Undisma·ntled**, *ppl. a.* (Un-1 8.) [**1775** Ash.] **1830** Wordsw. *Elegiac Musings* 28 Oh! severed too abruptly,..Rapt in the grace of undismantled age. **1871** Browning *Pr. Hohenst.* 117 The fort which caps the crag, All undismantled of a turret-stone. **Undismay·able**, *a.* (Un-1 7 b.) *a* **1586** Sidney *Arcadia* III. viii, Neither could danger be dreadfull to Amphialus his undismayable courage.

**Undismay·ed**, *ppl. a.* (Un-1 8.)

**1615** G. Sandys *Trav.* 83 His body (hers) she imbrac't: and undismaide, Betweene his lips, her cleauing soule conuaide. **1667** Milton *P. L.* II. 432 With reason hath deep silence and demurr Seis'd us, though undismaid. **1712** Blackmore *Creation* III. 227 But undismay'd we face the intrepid foe. **1798** Mathias *Purs. Lit.* 7 England is still prepared, and alert,..and bold, and undismayed. **1823** Scott *Quentin D.* xxii, His look was composed and undismayed. **1855** Singleton *Virgil* II. 402 He undismayed remains, His high-souled foe awaiting.

**Undisme·mbered**, *ppl. a.* (Un-1 8.) **1758** J. Dalrymple *Ess. Feudal Property* (ed. 2) 50 The extent of the residue of the fief remaining undismembered. **Undismi·ssed**, *ppl. a.* (Un-1 8.) *a* **1800** Cowper *Iliad* (ed. 2) XXIII. 5 Their valiant band Still undismiss'd Achilles thus bespake.

**Undisobli·ging**, *ppl. a.* [Un-1 10 + Disoblige *v.* 1 b.] †Not causing disconnexion.

**1715** Broome in Pope *Iliad* I. 235 *note*, All this he would have expatiated upon with Connexions of the Discourses,.. and the most easy,..undisobliging Transitions.

**Undisonant**, *a.* *rare*—1. [f. It. *undisono*, ad. L. *undisonus*.] Making the noise of waves.

**1592** R. D. *Hypnerotomachia* 3 b, Their current..still augmented by other undissonant [It. *undisoni*] torrents.

**Undiso·rdered**, *ppl. a.* (Un-1 8.) **1805** Wordsw. *Prelude* III. 154 If things viewed By poets in old time..May in these tutored days no more be seen With undisordered sight. **1847** De Quincey *Sp. Mil. Nun* Wks. 1853 III. 13 Spanish diet and youth leave the digestion undisordered. **Undispa·raged**, *ppl. a.* (Un-1 8.) **1636** Heywood *Love's Mistress* III. i, Thus undisparag'd, Phœbus leaves the place. **1770** Langhorne *Plutarch* (1879) II. 905/2 Demosthenes..left none of the actions of the King of Macedon undisparaged. **Undispa·tchable**, *a.* (Un-1 7 b.) **1853** Mrs. Gore *Dean's Daughter* II. vi. 143 Devoting weeks and months to despatch of undespatchable business.

**Undispa·tched**, *ppl. a.* [Un-1 8.]

†**1.** Not having one's business completed. *Obs.*

*c* **1610** Sir J. Melvil *Mem.* (Bann. Cl.) 101 Being yet at Paris on dispatched, I rasauit wretingis to com in Scotland. **1684** *Col. Rec. Pennsylv.* I. 109 They have been soe long un-Dispacht of the Buisness proposed.

**2.** Not settled or disposed of.

**1614** Raleigh *Hist. World* II. (1634) 435 This..had caused many men's private businesses to lie undispatched. **1628** in *Buccleuch MSS.* (Hist. MSS. Comm.) I. 267 Your wardenship when I found undispatched I would not let longer to stick. **1721** Strype *Eccl. Mem.* II. I. xvi. 134 Which [bill] was..sent up to the lords' house, where it lay undispatched.

**3.** Not deprived of life; not killed outright.

**1589** Warner *Alb. Eng.* VI. xxxii. 142 But not long His Father moned vndispatcht alike for death and wrong. **1888** Stevenson *Black Arrow* 71 Here and there..horse or man rolled, undespatched, in his agony.

**Undispa·tching**, *ppl. a.* (Un-1 10.) **1648** *Petit. Eastern Assoc.* 4 The tedious Suspensions of the undispatching Parliament. **Undispe·llable**, *a.* (Un-1 7 b, 5 b.) **1839** Lady Lytton *Cheveley* viii, All of which plunged his wife into an undispellable fit of sulk.

**Undispe·lled**, *ppl. a.* (Un-1 8.)

[**1775** Ash.] **1860** Bp. S. Wilberforce *Addr. Ordination* 105 Delusion on our part and undispelled darkness on theirs. **1877** *In Mem. J. M. Charlton* 2 The shadows of the grave remained undispelled.

†**Undispe·nded**, *ppl. a.* (Un-1 8.) *a* **1483** *Liber Niger* in *Househ. Ord.* (1790) 82 The chaundelers truelye..to bringe to the pantrey the remanentes undispended.

†**Undispe·nsable**, *a. Obs.* [Un-1 7 b, 5 b.]

**1.** = Indispensable *a.* 2.

**1559** Bp. Cox in Strype *Ann. Ref.* (1709) I. App. xxii. 51 Your Majesty's learned and godly clergy..do think this commandment of God to be undispensable. *a* **1600** Hooker *Eccl. Pol.* VII. xiv. § 4 Things whereunto everlasting, immutable, and undispensable observation did belong. **1651** Hobbes *Leviath.* II. xxviii. 164 The Punishment of the transgression of a Law undispensable. **1672** H. More *Brief Reply* Pref. a 3 This..could never affright me into the neglect of so undispensable a duty.

**2.** = Indispensable *a.* 1.

**1609** Bible (Douay) *Gen.* xvi. comm., The Catholique doctrin..sheweth how pluralitie of wives was..especially since Christ altogether unlawful and undispensable. **1649** Milton *Eikon.* ix. 84 He was bound..by a most strict and undispensable Oath to preserve that Order.

**3.** = Indispensable *a.* 3.

**1658** T. Wall *Charact. Enemies Ch.* 27 Religion being.. the undispensable prop of States.

So †**Undispe·nsably** *adv. Obs.*

*a* **1676** Hale *Prim. Orig. Man.* I. iii. (1677) 81 Some determinate *ubi* or *situs*..is undispensably necessary to every created individual Body.

**Undispe·nsed**, *ppl. a.* [Un-1 8.] Not absolved or released by dispensation. Also *absol.*

*a* **1300** *Cursor M.* 28367 In dedly sin i tok vnscriuen Myn orders.., And..vn-despensed sang i messe. **1604** Tooker *Fabrique Ch.* 47 He..doth not onely seeke being vnqualified and vndispensed with to procure vnto himselfe two diuerse Ecclesiasticall dignities. **1863** Bp. Wilberforce in *Life* (1882) III. 87 Then the undispensed are bound, because the dispensed are released. **1902** *Academy* 24 May 526/1 Even undispensed, such [convent] vows do not invalidate a marriage subsequently contracted.

**Undispe·nsing**, *ppl. a.* [Un-1 10.] Not giving dispensation.

**1643–5** Milton *Divorce* II. iv, Under such an undispencing covenant as Moses made with them,..[this] cannot give quiet to the brest of any intelligent man.

**Undispe·rsed**, *ppl. a.* (Un-1 8, 5 b.)

*c* **1586** C'tess Pembroke *Ps.* (1823) LXXXIX. iv, What one thy foe did undisperst abide? **1621** Quarles *Div. Poems, Esther* Medit. xviii. M 3 b, The Sunne (whose beames so bright And vndispers'd, are too-too much refin'd For view). **1673** Hickeringill *Greg. F. Greyb.* 284 There is or at least was such a nation undispersed. **1860** Ellicott *Life Our Lord* vii. 327 Still followed by the yet undispersed Eleven, our Lord now leaves that upper room.

**Undispe·rsing**, *ppl. a.* (Un-1 10.) **1837** Carlyle *Fr. Rev.* II. I. ii, To..serve any undispersing Assemblage with musket-shot, or whatever shot will disperse it. †**Undispi·teous**, *a. Obs.*—1 (Un-1 7.) *a* **1500** *Chaucer's Dreme* 676 Save onely a looke piteous Of womanhead undispiteous That she shewed in countenance. **Undispla·ced**, *ppl. a.* (Un-1 8.) **1802–12** Bentham *Ration. Judic. Evid.* (1827) I. 570 The audience in the court remaining undisplaced. **1881** Ld. Rayleigh in *Nature* XXV. 66 An eye applied to the prism sees the disks undisplaced as a whole. **Undisplay·ed**, *ppl. a.* (Un-1 8.) **1822** Byron *Heaven & Earth* I. iii, Their flashing banners,..Yet undisplay'd, Save to the Spirit's all-pervading eye. **Undisplea·sed**, *ppl. a.* (Un-1 8.) *a* **1500** *Chaucer's Dreme* 925 He would forgive all old trespace And undispleased be of time past. **1631** A. Townshend *Alb. Triumph* 13 Sit not secure, nor thinke in ease Still vndispleas'd, your selues to please.

†**Undispo·ned**, *ppl. a. Sc. Obs.* (Un-1 8.)

**1488** *Acta Dom. Conc.* (1839) 93/1 Gif þar be ony of þar gudis in place ondisponit apoun. **1530** *Reg. Privy Seal Scot.* II. 66/1 The tua merk land and ane half..wer in his handis ..undisponit to ony personis. *a* **1651** Calderwood *Hist. Kirk* (1843) II. 299 The reteaning of them in her owne hands, undisponed to qualifeid persouns, is ungodlie.

†**Undispo·se**, *v. Obs.* [Un-1 14 and 5 b.] *trans.* = Indispose *v.* (in various senses).

*c* **1380** Wyclif *Sel. Wks.* I. 218 But make we no general reule to undispose men on þe dai, whanne þei shulden do workes of li3t. *c* **1400** *Apol. Loll.* 14 Þat is dedely synne, bi þe wilk a man..vndisposiþ himsilf to tak part of þe merits of þe kirk. *c* **1430** Lydg. *Min. Poems* (Percy Soc.) 23 The wolf..Saide he maade his water unholsom, His tender stomake to hinder and undispose. **1777** Potter *Æschylus, Persians* Introd. 458 The poet..indirectly undisposing his countrymen to a continuation of the war.

**Undispo·sed**, *ppl. a.* [Un-1 8, 8 c, 5 b.]

†**1.** Unfitted; unprepared; unqualified. *Obs.*

*c* **1380** Wyclif *Wks.* (1880) 191 To maken men wery & vndisposid to studie goddis lawe. **1421** Hoccleve *Min. Poems* xxiii. 546 He mischeeueth Where as he wende han recouered be; Vndisposid to dye, sterueth he. *c* **1449** Pecock *Repr.* III. v. 308 If eny man be..vndisposid vnscapabili, lete him abstene and forbere that he come not into prelacie endewid.

†**2.** Disordered; out of condition. *Obs.*

*c* **1380** Wyclif *Sel. Wks.* I. 104 Þus þis lond is undisposid bi þree enemyes of a man. *Ibid.* II. 348 Man þat þus contrarieþ himsilf mut nedis be undisposid bi synne. **1599** Davies *Immort. Soul* II. ccclxxvii, The Soule to such a body knit, Whose inward senses vndisposed bee. **1645** Quarles *Sol. Recant.* xii. 6 Then shall the sinews silver cord be los'd ..: The undispos'd And idle liver's ruby fountain dri'd.

†**3.** Of death: For which one is not prepared.

**1421** Hoccleve *Min. Poems* xxiii. 474 Lest þat heere-aftir y..In-to lyke peril haaste may and hye Of vndisposid sodein deeth. *c* **1425** *Orolog. Sapient.* v. in *Anglia* X. 359/23, I wepe for þe harmes of vndisposed dethe.

†**4.** Ill-disposed; unfriendly; adverse. *Obs.*

**1456** *Rolls of Parlt.* V. 451/1 Your said Besecher, by the untrewe synfull procuryng of the said undisposed persones, ..was endited of Treason. **1472** *Coventry Leet Bk.* 384 If eny mysdoers, or persones vndisposid, be the occasion of eny supportacion. **1621** Quarles *Div. Poems, Esther* xvii, Some curse Fate, Others blaspheme the name of heau'n, and rate Their vndisposed Starres.

**5.** Not disposed of; not put to any purpose.

**1483** *Rolls of Parlt.* VI. 260/2 The residue of the said money, goodes, and catalles..undistributed and undisposed. **1653** Hartlib *Discov. Divis. Land* (title-p.), The Fens and other Waste and undisposed Places in England and Ireland. **1711** *Lond. Gaz.* No. 4946/3 The several Quantities of Tin.. remaining undisposed. **1827** Hallam *Const. Hist.* xviii. II. 770 The house took care..to prevent the recurrence of an undisposed surplus.

**b.** With *of.* (Now usual; cf. Dispose *v.* 8.)

**1626** B. Jonson *Staple of N.* I. ii, Emissarie Westminster's vndispos'd of yet. **1667** in *10th Rep. Hist. MSS. Comm.* App. V. 29 Other lands undisposed of, now remaining in his Majestie's disposall. **1743** Pope *Last Will* Wks. 1751 IX. 270 All the residue and remainder to be considered as undisposed of, and to go to my next of kin. **1803** tr. *P. Le Brun's M. Botte* III. 124 That preference which would have made him ..choose her, if her heart had been undisposed of. **1893** *Bailey's Mag.* Oct. 282/2 Finding himself with some undisposed-of stock.

**6.** Not inclined or willing, indisposed (*to* or *to do* something).

**1590** Shaks. *Com. Err.* I. ii. 80, I shall breake that merrie sconce of yours That stands on tricks, when I am vndispos'd. **1597** Hooker *Eccl. Pol.* V. lxviii. § 10 Because the greater part is carelesse and vndisposed to ioine with them. **1650** Baxter *Saints' R.* I. vii. (1662) 86 That I conceive the reason also, why we are more undisposed to those secret duties.

Hence **Undispo·sedness.**

**1600** Surflet *Countrie Farme* III. xxxviii. 504 There hapneth..vnto it [*sc.* the plum-tree] an vndisposednes, through the fault of the gardener. **1658** A. Fox tr. *Würtz' Surg.* II. xii. 95 A rottenness, which you may know by the Patients breath,..and his daily undisposedness. **1675** Baxter *Cath. Theol.* II. I. 114 Can no man,..notwithstanding the undisposedness of his Will, yet so far..prevail against his undisposedness, as [etc.]?

**Undispo·sing**, *ppl. a.* (Un-1 10.) *c* **1400** Love *Bonavent. Mirr.* (1908) 132 He that taketh mete or drynke wilfully knowynge that it is contrarie to hym and vndisposynge to bodily hele. †**Undisposi·tion.** *Obs.* (Un-1 12, 5 b.) *c* **1400** *Apol. Loll.* 28 Wan Crist..may not..hele þe folk for þer..vndisposicoun, and vnabilite to reseyue. *c* **1449** Pecock *Repr.* III. v. 308 In indisposid persoones bi her vndisposicioun oonli thei ben..occasiouns of vicis. **Undispri·vacied**, *ppl. a.* (Un-1 8.) **1869** Lowell *Cathedral* 224 He can find a fireside..By throngs of strangers undisprivacied.

**Undispro·ved**, *ppl. a.* (Un-1 8.)

**1579** J. Stubbes *Gaping Gulf* A iij, I will aunswere such.. peruerse reasons as shall be lefte vndisproued in thys my proofe. **1614** Jackson *Creed* III. v. § 3 Arguments unrefuted, and probable pledges of God's Spirit undisproved. **1838** Mrs. Browning *The Sleep* iii, What do we give to our beloved? A little faith all undisproved. **1841** Wiseman *Remarks on Lett. fr. Palmer* 84, I therefore..consider it to stand as yet undisproved.

†**Undispu·nged**, *ppl. a. Obs.* (Un-1 8.) *a* **1670** Hacket *Abp. Williams* II. (1693) 120 The Court did all vote..that the Defence should remain undispunged.

**Undisputable**, *a.* Now *rare.* [Un-1 7 b and 5 b.] = Indisputable *a.* 1.

**1598** Sylvester *Du Bartas* II. ii. IV. *Columnes* 218 Undisputable Art, and fruitfull skill, Which with new wonders all the World shall fill. **1650** Bulwer *Anthropomet.* 254 Whereof there passe for current many undisputable examples. **1699** Burnet *39 Art.* i. 40, I think it is safer to build upon sure and undisputable grounds. **1886** *New Princeton Rev.* Sept. 156 A wealth of undisputable evidence is at hand.

**Undisputably**, *adv.* (Un-1 11 and 5 b.) **1706** E. Ward *Wooden World Diss.* (1708) 107 Our Ships of War are undisputably the best in the World. **1762** [see Undisputedly.]

**Undispu·ted**, *ppl. a.* [Un-1 8 and 5 b.]

**1.** Not disputed or argued *with.* *rare*—1.

**1570** Foxe *A. & M.* (ed. 2) 2034/2 So in the end, the bishop making to our ambassadours good countenaunce,..dismissed them vndisputed wythall.

**2.** Not disputed or called in question.

*a* **1625** Fletcher *Nice Valour* IV. i, That if my anger chance let fall a stroke,..Yet it may pass unmurmur'd, undisputed. *a* **1698** Temple *Ess. Pop. Discontents* Wks. 1720 I. 261 This Moral Principle..is certainly the most undisputed. **1732** Berkeley *Alciphr.* VI. § 5 If a man assent to the undisputed books, he is no longer an infidel. **1781** Cowper *Truth* 527 Let heathen worthies..Possess, for me, their undisputed lot. **1844** Kinglake *Eothen* viii, Her superiority over all others..remained undisputed. **1866** Geo. Eliot *F. Holt* Introd., A man who..held a position of easy, undisputed authority.

**Undispu·tedly**, *adv.* [Un-1 11: cf. prec.] Without dispute or question.

**1778** Hume *Hist. Eng.* (new ed.) I. 200 The reigning prince, provided he be of the royal family, passes undisputedly [**1762** undisputably] for the legal sovereign. **1821** Byron *Let. to Murray* 7 Feb., The Georgics are indisputably, and, I believe, undisputedly, even a finer poem than the Æneid. **1896** *Cent. Mag.* Feb. 590 He is undisputedly one of the first Latinists of our time.

**Undispu·ting**, *ppl. a.* (Un-1 10.) **1827** Pollok *Course T.* IX. 49 Inquiring still..to know their duty, When known, with undisputing trust..performing.

**Undisqui·eted**, *ppl. a.* (Un-1 8.)

**1627** May *Lucan* VIII. O v b, If you, O Parthians, vndisquieted I euer left. **1649** *Test. conc. J. Boehme* ii. 7 The two ..witnesses..have remained in their Graves undisquieted by the Babylonians. **1863** H. Allon *Mem. J. Sherman* Introd. 6 He..spake with the power and passion of full and undisquieted conviction.

**Undisse·mbled**, *ppl. a.* [Un-1 8.]

**1.** Not feigned or pretended; genuine.

**1651** Baxter *Inf. Bapt.* 97 A reall undissembled Faith. **1697** Collier *Ess. Mor. Subj.* I. (1703) 170 An infallible proof of a natural and undissembled goodness. **1748** Melmoth *Fitzosborne Lett.* lv. (1749) II. 73 Tell me then, with the same undissembled sincerity [etc.]. **1804** Larwood *No Gun Boats* 10 Caparisoned for undissembled Field-of-Battle contest.

**2.** Not disguised or concealed; evident.

**1671** Milton *Samson* 400 She purpos'd to betray me, and (which was worse Then undissembl'd hate) with what con tempt [etc.]. **1751** Smollett *Per. Pic.* lxxvi, Emilia..listened to his protestations with undissembled pleasure. **1814** Scott *Wav.* xxix, Callum..enjoyed, with undissembled glee, the ridiculous figure of Mr. Cruickshanks. **1850** Hawthorne *Scarlet L.* xi, The anguish in his inmost soul, and the undissembled expression of it in his aspect.

Hence **Undisse·mbledness.**

**1681** Kettlewell *Chr. Obed.* III. viii. 301 The sincerity and undissembledness of our faculties.

**Undisse·mbling**, *ppl. a.* (Un-1 10.)

**1613** Zouche *Dove* 28 Helen in her undissembling glasse, Viewing the wrinckles which her age had wrought. **1727** Thomson *Summer* 904 The Heart Of Innocence, and undissembling Truth. **1788** Cowper *Let. to S. Rose* 29 March.

Be assured of an undissembling welcome. **1830** E. E. CROWE *Hist. France* I. 259 The same frank and undissembling temper..made speedy enemies of those whom he disliked.

**Undisse·mblingly,** *adv.* (UN-[1] 11; cf. prec.)
**1585** CARTWRIGHT in R. Browne *Answ.* 87 If there were but in euery church one truely and vndissemblingly faithfull. **1607** HIERON *Wks.* I. 296 To professe truely and vndissemblingly a dependance onely vpon Christ. **1621** SANDERSON *Serm.* I. 184 Hadst thou not a faithful counsellour.., if thou wouldst but have conferred with him..undissemblingly?

**Undisse·vered,** *ppl. a.* (UN-[1] 8.)
α. **1521** FISHER *Wks.* (1876) 332 Though all theyr workes be vndiuyded & vndeseuered one from another. **1598** STOW *Surv.* 164 They found..the Corps of a woman, whole of skin, and of bones vndeseuered.
β. **1548** PATTEN *Exped. Scot.* G iv b, If they doo assaile vndisseuered, no force can well withstond them. **1556** OLDE *Antichrist* 45 A constant vndisseuered faithe.

†**Undissi·mulate,** *a. Obs.*[−1] (UN-[1] 7.) **1652** COTTERELL tr. *Calprenède's Cassandra* I. 21 That warlike, franck, and undissimulate people. **Undissi·mulated,** *ppl. a.* (UN-[1] 8.) **1776** S. J. PRATT *Pupil of Pleas.* (1777) I. 189 Real, undissimulated love. **1779** G. KEATE *Sketches fr. Nat.* (ed. 2) II. 27 All tenderness and undissimulated nature.

**Undi·ssipated,** *ppl. a.* (UN-[1] 8.)
**1661** BOYLE *Scept. Chem.* I. 41 That it may not appear absurd to conceive, that such little primary Masses..may remain undissipated. **1733** *Phil. Trans.* XXXVIII. 7 Capable of..conveying the tender medullary Substance..safe, unhurt, and undissipated to the several Organs. **1779** *Ann. Reg., Hist.* 52/2 If the reduction..of France was the object, the war against her might be pursued with undissipated force. **1830** LD. GRANVILLE in *Life* (1905) I. i. 17 Although you say that it is such an undissipated season.

†**Undi·ssoluble,** *a. Obs.*[−1] (UN-[1] 7 and 5 b.) **1587** GOLDING *De Mornay* xv. 264 Now..the Soule of Man is very like the Godhead;..Vniforme, Vndissoluble, and euermore of one sorte. **Undissolu·tion.** (UN-[1] 12.) **1662** J. CHANDLER *Van Helmont's Oriat.* 267 Under the co-resemblance of immortality, and undissolution.

**Undisso·lvable,** *a.* [UN-[1] 7 b and 5 b.] = INDISSOLUBLE *a.*
(*a*) **1611** COTGR., *Indissoluble*, indissoluble,..vndissolueable. **1622** T. SCOTT *Belg. Pismire* 64 God hath bound vs together by an vndissolueable band of necessitie. **1656** OSBORNE *Adv. Son* 57 This requires Love to be ushered into this undissolveable noose, by Discretion. **1702** ROWE *Tamerl.* III. i, That holy Knot, which ty'd once, all Mankind Agree to hold Sacred, and Undissolvable.
(*b*) **1705** T. GREENHILL *Art Embalming* 153 The Sands..over-whelm Passengers.., who..are thro' the power of the hot Sun..so dry'd, they become..for ever undissolvable. **1756** F. HOME *Exper. Bleaching* 268 There remained half a grain of powder that was undissolvable by the spirit.

**Undisso·lved,** *ppl. a.* [UN-[1] 8.]
**1.** Not dissolved by loosening, undoing, annulling, dismissing, etc.
**1535** *Act 27 Hen. VIII*, c. 26 § 15 Every suche celle shalbe ..ondyssolvyd..as yf this Acte had never be made. **1598** DRAYTON *Heroical Ep.* 23 b, By that firme and vndissolued knot, Betwixt the neighboring French, and bordering Scot. **1649** MILTON *Eikon.* v. 45 As necessity of affaires call'd them, so the same necessity should keep them undissolv'd, till that were fully satisfi'd. **1833** KEBLE *Serm.* vi. (1848) 127 Those members of the Church also believe..the oaths and obligations..undissolved and indissoluble. **1856** FROUDE *Hist. Eng.* I. 166 By the law he could not have formed a second engagement so long as the first was undissolved.
**2.** Not broken up; not dissolved by natural decay.
**1603** KNOLLES *Hist. Turks* (1621) 54 [Andronicus' body] is yet there vndissolued to be seene. **1615** CHAPMAN *Odyss.* XII. 594 The mast torn down Tore her up piece-meal, and for me to drown Left little undissolved. **1759** JOHNSON *Rasselas* xlvii, It is commonly supposed that the Egyptians believed the soul to live as long as the body continued undissolved.
**3.** Not reduced to a soft or liquid state; unmelted.
**1674** tr. *Scheffer's Lapland* iii. 8 The snows which as well in Summer as Winter continue undissolved. **1694** SALMON *Bate's Dispens.* (1713) 150/1 That which remains undissolv'd ..is the acid or saline Part of the Sulphur. **1765** A. DICKSON *Treat. Agric.* (ed. 2) 377 Some things are digested..by some animals, that pass thro' others sound and undissolved. **1807** T. THOMSON *Chem.* (ed. 3) II. 461 The dissolved portion having the properties of a resin; the undissolved, of asphaltum. **1868** *Amer. Naturalist* I. 39 Ice accumulates..during the winter, and lies undissolved until late in spring.

**Undisso·lving,** *ppl. a.* (UN-[1] 10.)
**1712** BLACKMORE *Creation* v. 351 A coherent, undissolving chain Of causes and effects. **1726** THOMSON *Winter* 657 Where undissolving from the first of time Snows swell on snows amazing to the sky. **1805** WORDSW. *Waggoner* IV. 105 A moving shroud To form, an undissolving cloud.

**Undistai·ned,** *ppl. a.* (UN-[1] 8.)
**1565** COOPER *Thesaurus* s.v. *Incolumis*, To keepe his good name vndisteyned. **1622** WITHER *Philarete* G ij b, I know her Maker will Keepe her vndistained still. **1625** QUARLES *Sion's Sonn.* xvii. 3 Vnblemisht, vndistayned with a spot.

†**Undista·sted,** *ppl. a. Obs.* (UN-[1] 8; cf. DISTASTED *ppl. a.* 2.) **1607** DANIEL *Introd. Poems* Wks. (Grosart) I. 14 There will be found therein, that which..will sufficiently allow T' an vndistasted iudgement fit delight.

**Undiste·mpered,** *ppl. a.* (UN-[1] 8.)
*c* **1589** *Theses Martinianæ* 4 Hee might sitte long enough vndistempered in his chaire for vs. **1634** SIR T. HERBERT *Trav.* 79 See how mischiefe appeares in a louely and vndistempered Scene. *a* **1698** TEMPLE *Ess. Pop. Discontents* Wks. 1720 I. 266 Some Parliament that..shall be cool and undistemper'd from those Heats of Faction. **1814** WORDSW. *Excurs.* v. 487 With undistempered and unclouded spirit.

**Undiste·nd,** *v.* (UN-[2] 3.) **1868** BROWNING *Ring & Bk.* II. 1502 Had Guido..Cloven each head..In one clean cut..—Bidding, who pitied, undistend the skulls.

**Undisti·lled,** *ppl. a.* (UN-[1] 8.)
**1600** SURFLET *Countrie Farme* III. lxix. 593 The very water of the vine alone vndistilled doth the like. **1652** FRENCH *Yorksh. Spa* vii. 67 The two first spoonfuls, which were distilled, and the rest undistilled that remained. **1771** *Phil. Trans.* LXI. 125, I found, that..tin distilled or sublimed ..would produce finer colours than any solution..of tin, unsublimed or undistilled.

**Undisti·nct,** *a.* [UN-[1] 7 and 5 b.]
**1.** = INDISTINCT *a.* 3.
**1495** *Trevisa's Barth. De P. R.* v. xxiii. h vij/1 Men that ben kyndely dombe ben deef, and they haue voys & all vndystyncte. **1555** EDEN *Decades* (Arb.) 367 Sum yelowe, and sum of vndistinct colours. **1853** MISS MULOCK *Avillon*, etc. II. 274 The image of a dim and undistinct divinity.
†**2.** = INDISTINCT *a.* 1. *Obs.*
**1534** MORE *Treat. Passion* Introd., One vndiuisable & vndistinct infinit almighty god. **1610** HEALEY *St. Aug. Citie of God* 13 It doth not proue the persons vndistinct, because so they both do joyntly indure like pains. **1631** WEEVER *Anc. Funeral Mon.* 74 The Church will haue them to be of an vndistinct excellence.

**Undisti·nction.** (UN-[1] 12, 5 b.) **1647** HEXHAM I, Vndistinction, *onverscheydenheydt*. **1662** J. CHANDLER *Van Helmont's Oriat.* Prayer, Tis true indeed, that thou wilt be worshipped by men in the Spirit, but not in such a manner that it may remain in the undistinction of the first object. **Undisti·nctive,** *a.* (UN-[1] 7, 5 b.) *c* **1860** DICKENS *Reprinted Pieces* (1866) 220 As undistinctive Death will come here, one day, sleep comes now. **1888** STOPFORD BROOKE in *Life & Lett.* (1917) II. 398 Undistinctive praise and blame.

†**Undisti·nctly,** *adv. Obs.* [UN-[1] 11, 5 b.] = INDISTINCTLY *adv.* 1.
**1548** ELYOT, *Indistinctè*, vndistinctely. **1597** HOOKER *Eccl. Pol.* v. lxviii. § 9 To consider..their sundry ouer-sights, first, in equalling vndistinctly crimes with errours. **1602** FULBECKE *1st Pt. Parall.* 100 Yet our law punisheth undistinctly and without difference, the immature electing of any of these. **1706** STEVENS I, *Indistintamente*, undistinctly.

†**Undisti·ngued,** *ppl. a. Obs*[−1]. [UN-[1] 9.] Undistinguished. **1398** TREVISA *Barth. De P. R.* VIII. xvi. (1495) v. vij/2 Shappes of thynges whiche ben vnknowen in derknesse and vndystyngued. **Undisti·nguish,** *v. rare*[−1]. [UN-[2] 3.] *trans.* To make undistinguishable. **1690** NORRIS *Refl. Hum. Life* (1695) 132 One Glance whereof shall..undistinguish the greatest Doctor from the most ignorant Peasant.

**Undisti·nguishable,** *a.* [UN-[1] 7 b and 5 b.]
**1.** Incapable of being made out or discerned; imperceptible.
**1590** SHAKS. *Mids. N.* II. i. 100 The queint Mazes in the wanton greene, For lacke of tread are vndistinguishable. **1645** MILTON *Tetrach.* 19 The Form by which the thing is what it is, is oft so slender and undistinguishable. **1768** H. WALPOLE *Hist. Doubts* 92 One does not learn any language ..with a good, nay, undistinguishable accent, between Christmas and Easter. **1816** SCOTT *Old Mort.* xxxvi, The city and port..became undistinguishable in the distance. **1872** BLACK *Adv. Phaeton* xii. 171 Two almost undistinguishable figures pacing along.
**2.** Incapable of being distinguished or discriminated; of which the different elements cannot be distinguished or recognized; inseparably alike.
**1679** DRYDEN *Troil. & Cress.* Pref. ⁋ 26 It has been prov'd already that confus'd passions make undistinguishable characters. **1693** *Humours Town* 128 Drunken Rakes, and dirty Beau's,..besides a number of undistinguishable Mob. **1794** GISBORNE *Walks Forest* III. 9 Where sunk the parting orb, and with the sky In undistinguishable splendor join'd. **1802–12** BENTHAM *Ration. Judic. Evid.* (1827) V. 662 Hope and fear..run into one another and are undistinguishable. **1860** PUSEY *Min. Proph.* 124 The locust [-swarm]..becomes in a few hours one undistinguishable, putrifying, heaving mass.
**b.** Const. *from.* (Common in recent use.)
**1686** PLOT *Staffordsh.* 380 Altogether undistinguishable from the best French wines. **1833–4** J. PHILLIPS *Geol.* in *Encycl. Metrop.* (1845) VI. 674/2 The badger (probably undistinguishable from the common European species). **1870** J. H. NEWMAN *Gram. Assent* I. v. 112 That apprehension..may become almost undistinguishable from an inferential acceptance of the great truth.
†**3.** Indiscriminate. *Obs. rare.*
**1702** *Eng. Theophrast.* 86 An undistinguishable Facility shall never fail of meeting with an undistinguishable Infidelity.
Hence **Undisti·nguishableness.**
**1727** BAILEY (vol. II). **1843** MILL *Logic* I. iii. § 11. 93 Resemblance, when it exists in the highest degree of all, amounting to undistinguishableness, is often called identity. **1878** E. WHITE *Life in Christ* (ed. 3) III. xx. 289 The undistinguishableness of generic difference in character.

**Undisti·nguishably,** *adv.* [UN-[1] 11 and 5 b.]
†**1.** Without distinction or difference. *Obs.*
**1671** BARROW *Serm.* Wks. 1687 I. 427 So that righteousness and mercifulness..are in Scripture-expression..undistinguishably put one for the other. **1710** *Tatler* No. 270 ⁋ 5 Gold and silver galloon upon hats..being undistinguishably worn by Soldiers, Esquires [etc.].
**2.** So as to be undistinguishable.
*a* **1691** BOYLE *Hist. Air* (1692) 248 Whilst the liquor was hot ..they would swim together undistinguishably in the liquor. **1705** T. GREENHILL *Art Embalming* 138 The Humour.. assumes no visible Body, but undistinguishably mixes with the pure Air. **1780** BENTHAM *Princ. Legisl.* x. § 27 In many instances the desire of pleasure and the sense of pain run into one another undistinguishably. **1869** MCLAREN *Serm.* Ser. II. xii. 213 A faint ethereal echo..which blends undistinguishably with its parent sound.

**Undisti·nguished,** *ppl. a.* [UN-[1] 8 and 5 b.]
**1.** Not separated or kept distinct.
**1598** FLORIO, *Indistinto*, vndistinct, vndistinguished, confused. **1647** COWLEY *Mistress, Bathing* v, Her Beauties.. will mixt and undistinguish't ly, With all the meanest things that dy. **1760** STERNE *Serm. Yorick* vii. (1784) 197 The undistinguished offers of his services. **1792** WORDSW. *Descrip. Sketches* 161 Where afar rich orange lustres glow Round undistinguished clouds, and rocks. **1879** J. TODHUNTER *Alcestis* 10 If Zeus arms to smite thee,..let us stand one undistinguished mark For his stern thunder!
**b.** In which no distinction is made or can be observed.
**1608** SHAKS. *Lear* IV. vi. 278 (Q 2), O vndistinguish't space of womans wit. **1666** BOYLE *Orig. Forms & Qual.* 30 Nor must we look upon the Universe that surrounds us as upon a moveless and undistinguish'd Heap of Matter. **1727** THOMSON *Summer* 347 A dazling deluge reigns; and all From pole to pole is undistinguish'd blaze. **1814** BYRON *Address Caledonian Meeting* 17 The lowly brave,..Who sleep beneath the undistinguish'd sod. **1851** TRENCH *Poems* 155 Like undistinguished Night, darkening the skirts of Eve.
**c.** Not distinguished *from* or *by* something.
**1612** CHAPMAN *Rev. Bussy d'Ambois* IV. i. 86, I grieve that virtue lives so undistinguish'd From vice in any ill. **1693** DRYDEN *Juvenal* III. 291 Their Habits (undistinguish'd by Degree) Are plain, alike. **1784** COWPER *Task* I. 592 Blest he, though undistinguish'd from the crowd By wealth or dignity, who dwells secure. **1823** SCOTT *Quentin D.* xxxvii, The noise..was of a character so undistinguished by any peculiar or precise sound, that [etc.]. **1882** FARRAR *Early Chr.* I. 491 The majority are only known to us as names, sometimes undistinguished by a single incident.
**2.** Not made distinct to perception: **a.** Indistinct, confused. Now *rare.*
**1595** DANIEL *Civ. Wars* II. lxviii, Where diuers-speaking zeale, one murmure findes In vndistinguisht voice to tell their mindes. **1611** FLORIO, *Inarticolata voce*, an vndistinguished voice. **1678** DRYDEN *All for Love* V. i, Some undistinguish'd Words she inly murmur'd. **1781** J. RIPLEY *Sel. Orig. Lett.* 62 Standing upon the bank of a river, muttering undistinguished prayers. **1814** SCOTT *Lord of Isles* II. xxx, Flush'd is his brow,..And undistinguish'd accents broke The awful silence ere he spoke.
**b.** Not clearly perceived or discerned.
**1814** JANE AUSTEN *Mansfield Park* xxxviii, Finding herself undistinguished in the dusk. **1821** SCOTT *Kenilw.* xxxvii, Mixing with the crowd, [he] stood in some degree an undistinguished spectator..of the masque.
**3.** Not marked by any distinction; not noted or elevated above others.
**1600** E. BLOUNT tr. *Conestaggio* 6 Being vndistinguished, and allyed for money with some Noblemen of the countrey. *a* **1643** W. CARTWRIGHT *Poems, No Drawing of Valentines* Wks. (1651) 242 Cast not in Chloe's Name among the Common undistinguish'd Throng. **1693** CONGREVE in *Dryden's Juvenal* XI. (1697) 283 Who..tho' a Knight, 'mongst common Slaves now stands Begging an Alms, with undistinguisht hands. **1757** W. WILKIE *Epigon.* II. 31 Hissing amidst the Spartan ranks it came, And struck a youth of undistinguish'd name. **1800** *Asiatic Ann. Reg.* 26/2 He remained undistinguished for any thing, except the infamous action, in which [etc.]. **1875** JOWETT *Plato* (ed. 2) I. 140 Would not their sons grow up to be distinguished or undistinguished according to their own natural capacities?

**Undisti·nguishing,** *ppl. a.* [UN-[1] 10.]
**1.** Making no distinction or difference; not discriminating: **a.** Of persons, personal attributes, etc.
**1599** SANDYS *Europæ Spec.* (1629) 229 The blunt and undistinguishing witts of the vulgar. **1641** 'SMECTYMNUUS' *Answ.* § 16 (1653) 67 If it be a fault in the impetuous, and undistinguishing Vulgar. **1712** ADDISON *Spect.* No. 291 ⁋ 7 A sower undistinguishing Critick. **1776** GIBBON *Decl. & F.* vi. I. 160 *note*, The undistinguishing compiler has buried these interesting anecdotes under a load of trivial and unmeaning circumstances. **1836** J. GILBERT *Chr. Atonem.* iii. 102 There is still addressed to undistinguishing minds another objection. **1871** BLACKIE *Four Phases* i. 129 The superficial undistinguishing eye of the general public of Athens.
**b.** *transf.* Of things.
**1665** MANLEY *Grotius' Low C. Wars* 205 There was none of them so imprudent, as to trust their Lives and Fortunes to the undistinguishing Sword of a Forreign Conquerour. **1753** W. ROBERTS *Looker-On* No. 36, These furious advocates ..are at issue with all governments..and would involve them all in one undistinguishing ruin. **1821** SOUTHEY *Vis. Judgem.* XI. 19 In undistinguishing battle, Or by pestilence stricken, they fell. **1847** G. HARRIS *Life Ld. Hardwicke* II. 230 Numbers of people..were sacrificed to the undistinguishing vengeance of the victorious army.
**c.** Const. *of.*
**1811** *Henry & Isabella* I. 259 Our..dog.., haply undistinguishing of crimes and evils, kindly fawned upon me.
**2.** Of actions, etc.: Marked by want of distinction or discrimination; indiscriminate.
*a* **1677** BARROW *Serm.* xxxvi. Wks. 1686 III. 403 Benefits would not be scattered among the crowd of men with so promiscuous and undistinguishing a freeness. **1710** STEELE *Tatler* No. 204 ⁋ 7 An undistinguishing Application of Sounds of Honour. **1782** ELIZ. BLOWER *Geo. Bateman* II. 60 But don't you think the ridicule rather too undistinguishing? **1853** RUSKIN *Stones Ven.* III. 104 That opposition was..intemperate, undistinguishing and incautious. **1892** LOUNSBURY *Stud. Chaucer* III. vii. 201 We need not make it an object of undistinguishing depreciation.

**Undisti·nguishingly,** *adv.* [UN-[1] 11: cf. prec.] Without distinction or discrimination.
**1665** J. SERGEANT *Sure Footing* 159 To alledge Authorities undistinguishingly..is such a wild proceeding. **1725** *Fam. Dict.* s.v. *Mixing Colours*, 'Till you see it perfectly and undistinguishingly mix'd together. **1780** MRS. COWLEY *Belle's Stratagem* II. i, Her behaviour is undistinguishingly polite to her husband, and all mankind. **1830** MACKINTOSH *Eth. Philos.* Wks. 1846 I. 89 For a time the work was admired more undistinguishingly than its literary character warrants. *a* **1871** GROTE *Eth. Fragm.* v. (1876) 139 No man can blindly and undistinguishingly follow every immediate impulse.

**Undisto·rted,** *ppl. a.* (UN-[1] 8.)
**1647** H. MORE *Song of Soul* To Rdr. B 3 b, The undistorted suggestions of his own heart. **1662** STILLINGFL. *Orig. Sacræ* III. i. § 15 Those more refined..spirits who went only upon principles of pure and undistorted reason. **1814** *Monthly Rev.* LXXIII. 480 In a series of plays which imprint the leading events on the memory in an..undistorted manner. **1881** C. A. YOUNG *Sun* 33 If the planet's edge were..sharp and definite, and the sun's limb undistorted.
**Undisto·rting,** *ppl. a.* (UN-[1] 10.) **1823** *Monthly Rev.* CI. 513 A mirror so sincere and so undistorting.

**Undistra·cted,** *ppl. a.* [UN-[1] 8.]

† 1. Not drawn apart by dissension. *Obs.*—1
*a* 1649 Drumm. of Hawth. *Hist. Jas. V*, Wks. (1711) 100 To turn the Imperial Crown Hereditary to his own House, which, Germany being all of one Mind and undistracted, he could never have brought to pass.

† 2. Not drawn aside or perverted; genuine, real.
1656 Stanley *Hist. Philos.* v. ii. 149 That there is a credible undistracted concurrence, is manifest from Menelaus. *Ibid.*, Such is undistracted phantasy. *a* 1659 Osborne *Charac.*, etc. (1659) 126 Valour and Cowardice, both strangers, if not Contrary to the Practice of undistracted Nature.

3. Not diverted or interrupted by other occupations or interests.
1648 Boyle *Seraph. Love* (1659) 106 He was pleas'd..to admit him to a yet Closer, more Immediate, and more Undistracted Communion with himself. 1683 *Brit. Spec.* 121 By undistracted Prayers to renew their Courage and Patience in their Apostolical Employment. 1817 Coleridge *Biogr. Lit.* ii. (1907) I. 30 In order to devote himself, an entire and undistracted man, to the instruction..of his fellow-citizens. 1871 Liddon in *Life & Lett.* (1904) 155, I..require an amount of undistracted thought which I never get here.

b. Const. *by*.
1759 Robertson *Hist. Scot.* ii. Wks. 1813 I. 112 Undistracted by those cares..which occupy and oppress other men. 1852 M. Arnold *Self-Depend.* v, Undistracted by the sights they see, These demand not [etc.].

4. Not drawn aside or away *from* something.
1833 Lamb *Elia* ii. *Barrenness Mod. Art*, [With] her soul undistracted from Theseus—Ariadne is still pacing the solitary shore. 1862 Lytton *Str. Story* I. 87 Some one..by whom your thoughts would have been undistracted from the channels into which your calling should concentrate their flow.

Hence **Undistra·ctedness**.
1660 Boyle *New Exp. Phys. Mech.* Pref. p. viii, That calmness of Minde, and undistractedness of Thoughts, that are wont to be requisite to Happy Speculations. 1886 *Athenæum* 7 Aug. 166/3 The impression..as a whole is one of undistractedness and elegance.

**Undistra·ctedly**, *adv.* [Un-1 11: cf. prec.] Without distraction.
1648 Boyle *Seraph. Love* iv. (1663) 26 The affections of one being at liberty, to devote themselves more undistractedly to God. 1687 — *Martyrd. Theodora* iv. (1703) 56 The great advantage of serving God more undistractedly. 1806 A. Duncan *Nelson* 66 The attention of every captain could almost undistractedly be paid to the condition of his..ship. 1872 Benson in A. C. Benson *Life* (1899) I. 349 The work in God's Church to which I should devote myself undistractedly.

**Undistra·cting**, *ppl. a.* (Un-1 10.) *a* 1684 Leighton *Exp. Lect. Psalm xxxix*, iii. Wks. 1805 II. 375 It were good we used more easy and undistracting diligence, for increasing of these treasures. **Undistrai·ned**, *ppl. a.* (Un-1 8.) *a* 1400-50 *Alexander* 2779 It semed no3t 3oure seruand sire, vndistreyned Vn-to 3our mekill maieste þis mater to write. 1475 *Aberdeen Reg.* (1844) I. 34 The said Johne his landis and gudis..to be vncompellit, vndistrengeit..be ony juge. **Undistrau·ght**, *ppl. a.* (Un-1 8 b.) 1773 J. Ross *Fratricide* iv. 528 (MS.), His senses Yet undistraught remain. 1874 J. Thomson *City Dreadf. Nt.* xxi. iii, The keen wolf-hound sleeping undistraught.

**Undistre·ssed**, *ppl. a.* (Un-1 8.)
1582 in J. H. Pollen *Acts Eng. Martyrs* (1891) 28 He sought for honours uncorrupt, and undistressed joys. 1591 Harington *Orl. Fur.* xxv. lxxiv, He..sweares that when his Prince were undistrest, The siege quite raised [etc.]. 1614 Sylvester *Parlt. Vertues Royall* 191 When for som pretence Hee hath betraid..his Prince Or yeelded-up som un-distressed Place. 1772 *Test Filial Duty* I. 122 She was sensible an undistressed heroine would make a very uninteresting figure. 1807 Wordsw. *White Doe* vii. 205 She..Received the memory of old loves, Undisturbed and undistrest. 1897 *Westm. Gaz.* 9 Mar. 2/2 Thousands of pounds go to the relief of undistressed land.

**Undistri·buted**, *ppl. a.* (Un-1 8.)
1483 [see Undisposed *ppl. a.* 5]. 1802-12 Bentham *Ration. Judic. Evid.* (1827) II. 508 The keeping of the rule of action ..in one immense and unorganic mass, undistributed. 1869 Gladstone *Juv. Mundi* viii. 280 Their journeys are usually undistributed and instantaneous. They set out, and..arrive.

b. *Logic.* (See Distribute *v.* 6.)
1827 Whateley *Logic* (ed. 2) 93 You will then have either the middle Term undistributed, or an illicit process. *Ibid.* 96 Another..is an allowable mood in the third Figure; but in the first it would have an undistributed middle. 1864 Bowen *Logic* vii. 193 It is a Negative with an undistributed Predicate.

† **Undistrou·bled**, *ppl. a. Sc. Obs.* (Un-1 8.)
1456 Sir G. Haye *Law Arms* (S.T.S.) 29 The quhilkis has maid trouble that was clere undistroublit. 1466 *Acta Dom. Audit.* (1839) 5/1 To kepe & defend þe saide elisabeth vndistrublit..in tyme tocum. 1561 *Reg. Privy Council Scot.* I. 183 To be unharmit, unvexit, unmolestit, and undistrublit.

**Undistru·stful**, *a.* (Un-1 7.) 1654 R. Codrington tr. *Iustine* ii. 44 [They] had not only undistrustful but delightful feastings together. 1865 Mrs. Whitney *Gayworthys* xxiii, There were hearts weary often, but undistrustful. **Undistu·rbable**, *a.* (Un-1 7 b, 5 b.) 1577 Knewstub *Confut.* (1579) 61 b, An everlasting fast standing Jerusalem,..the which is the very true vndisturbable Kingdome. 1883 T. M. Healy in *Pall Mall G.* 28 Dec. 2/1 Then in turn the new Act becomes perfect, final, and undisturbable.

**Undistu·rbed**, *ppl. a.* [Un-1 8, 5 b.] Not disturbed or interfered with.

1. In predicative use.
It is doubtful whether *vndistrobbed* in *Alexander* 3418 (see Undisturbled *ppl. a.*) belongs here, or is an error for *vndistrobled* = Undistroubled *ppl. a.*
*a* 1610 Healey *Epictetus* (1636) 70 So shall thy thoughts remaine undisturbed. 1622 in Foster *Eng. Factories Ind.* (1908) II. 73 Wee shall not be undisturbed till the one or other of us have given some kind of sattisfaxione. 1712 Addison *Spect.* No. 381 ¶ 4 His Imagination is always clear, and his Judgment undisturbed. 1794 S. Williams *Vermont* 90 When undisturbed, this animal is without any ill scent. 1807 [see Undistressed]. 1876 Bancroft *Hist. U. S.* I. Introd. 2 Even the enemies of the state..have liberty to express their opinions undisturbed.

b. Const. *by*, † *with*.
1635-56 Cowley *Davideis* i. 80 Where their vast Court the Mother-waters keep, And undisturb'd by Moons in silence sleep. 1674 *Jackson's Recant.* D 4, On that day the Roads are most quiet, being undisturbed with great quantities of People. 1796 Mme. D'Arblay *Camilla* IV. 258 Undisturbed by the various noises around him. 1827 Lytton *Falkland* i. 36, I am undisturbed by a single intruder. 1875 Jowett *Plato* (ed. 2) I. 373 Like the sleep of him who is undisturbed even by the sight of dreams.

2. In attrib. use: a. Of things, places, or persons.
1627 May *Lucan* v. H 4 b, Shee vtters from an vndisturbed brest Fain'd words with no confused murmure flowing. 1692 Bentley *Boyle Lect.* 108 All the parts of an undisturb'd fluid. 1728 Eliza Heywood tr. *Mme. de Gomez's Belle A.* (1732) II. 272 To retire from Court; and in some safe and undisturb'd Retreat..pass the remainder of my days. 1819 Keats *Fame* 12 The undisturbed lake has crystal space. 1898 J. T. Fowler *Durh. Cath.* 33 The undisturbed grave-covers of the bishops buried beneath.

b. Of conditions, courses of action, etc.
1647 Clarendon *Hist. Reb.* i. § 162 A full, entire, and undisturbed Peace. 1728 Eliza Heywood tr. *Mme. de Gomez's Belle A.* (1732) II. 105 This Night was pass'd..in all the Charms of an undisturbed Tranquillity. 1765 Blackstone *Comm.* I. 197 By a long and undisturbed descent from his ancestors. 1862 Ansted *Channel Isl.* iv. xxii. (ed. 2) 538 Undisturbed possession during thirty years is a good title. 1884 *Manch. Exam.* 17 May 4/7 The volumes..are left to undisturbed repose on the shelves of our public libraries.

Hence **Undistu·rbedness**.
1649 Rainbow *Funeral Serm. 29 May* 25 They have health, leisure and undisturbedness of understanding. 1718 *Entertainer* No. 34. 229 None has given us a truer idea of.. Moderation, Calmness and Undisturbedness.

**Undistu·rbedly**, *adv.* [Un-1 11: cf. prec.] Without being disturbed; tranquilly, quietly.
1647 H. More *Song of Soul* Notes 350 For infinite animadversion can discern all things unmixtly and undisturbedly. 1683 Cave *Ecclesiastici* Introd. p. lxxi, The Gentiles undisturbedly brought their Sacrifices..to their Images. 1768-74 Tucker *Lt. Nat.* (1834) I. 517, I expect..that the healed will accompany me as undisturbedly as the unwounded along our future progress. 1842 F. E. Paget *Milford Malvoisin* 94 She..slept as calmly and undisturbedly as the infant at her breast. 1877 Lady Brassey *Voy. Sunbeam* xix, Ravens croak, and pigeons coo, as undisturbedly as if..in the deepest woodland solitude.

**Undistu·rbing**, *ppl. a.* (Un-1 10.) 1607 Markham *Cavel.* ii. (1617) 123 Letting him goe and come continuall with easie, soft, and vndisturbing mouings. 1814 Wordsw. *Excurs.* viii. 161 The punctual stars..in the firmament of heaven Glitter—but undisturbing, undisturbed. *a* 1851 Moir *Poems, Angler* ii, At his feet..An undisturbing spaniel lay. † **Undistu·rbled**, *ppl. a. Obs.* (Un-1 8.) *a* 1400-50 *Alexander* 3418 The passage shall..plane be & opyn, þe Comers oute of athir coste to cayre vndistourblett [*v.r.* vndistrobbed].

† **Undi·t**, *v. Obs.* [Un-2 3.] *trans.* To open (up). Also *fig.*
*a* 1225 *Leg. Kath.* 1821 Ne we nusten hwet we duden a3et he undutte us, & tahte us treowe bileaue. *c* 1275 in *O. E. Misc.* 153/234 Vurþer þer his on oþer put þat ne cumeþ neuer vndut. *c* 1300 *Childhood Jesus* 1038 þo Jhesu crist was i gon, vndut was þe Ouene a non.

**Undiu·rnal**, *a.* (Un-1 7.) 1832 Lytton *Eugene A.* iv. vii, The solemn and undiurnal mood..was reflected back in hues so gentle. 1837 — *E. Maltrav.* ix. v, The novel glow of Ernest's undiurnal and stately thoughts. **Undive·rging**, *ppl. a.* (Un-1 10.) 1795 Coleridge *Lett.* (1895) 139 The wisdom of making Self an undiverging Centre. † **Undive·rsificated**, *ppl. a. Obs.* (Un-1 8.) 1659 H. More *Immort. Soul* i. ii. 11 The Idea of a meer Undiversificated Substance. **Undive·rsified**, *ppl. a.* (Un-1 8.) 1684 T. Burnet *Theory Earth* i. 291 To conceive it [*sc.* matter] undivided, undiversified, and unmov'd. 1862 *Mem. R. Craig* ix. 170 The life.. is generally of a very uniform and undiversified character.

**Undive·rted**, *ppl. a.* [Un-1 8.]

1. Not turned aside.
1665 Boyle *Occas. Refl.* iv. ix. 57 Though these Grounds have not any patent Passages, whereby to derive Water and Fatness from the River, and therefore must suffer the greatest part of it to run by them undiverted. *a* 1711 Ken *Psyche* Poet. Wks. 1721 I. 205, I was ambitious of that Height, To gain of Heav'n an undiverted Sight. 1794 Mathias *Purs. Lit.* (1798) 313 By a patient continuance and undiverted attention to academical studies. 1859 Miss Mulock *Dom. Stories* (1862) 124 Her mind, undiverted from the past by any charms of the present, became dead to all outward impressions. 1859 I. Taylor *Logic in Theol.* 308 Such persons find it difficult to read their Bible in undiverted remembrance of what it is.

2. Not entertained or amused.
1792 G. Wakefield *Mem.* 8 The reader, however, may not be undiverted with its unaffected simplicity and pathos.

**Undive·rtible**, *a.* (Un-1 7, 5 b.) 1856 Mrs. Browning *Aur. Leigh* vi. 21 Even so direct, So sternly undivertible of aim, Is this French people. 1880 *Daily Tel.* 4 Mar., The true and undivertible highroads of Eastern traffic. **Undive·rtibly**, *adv.* (Un-1 11, 5 b.) 1865 Bushnell *Vicar. Sacrif.* v. 81 A few of the passages that persist most undivertibly in this kind of testimony.

**Undive·rting**, *ppl. a.* (Un-1 10.)
1697 Collier *Ess. Mor. Subj.* ii. (1703) 195 The charms of authority made Cato aver that old age was none of the most undiverting periods of life. 1754 Shebbeare *Matrimony* (1766) II. 260 These accounts might furnish out a Novel not undiverting and certainly useful. 1859 *Sat. Rev.* 12 Mar. 293/1 A character not altogether undiverting.

**Undive·sted**, *ppl. a.* (Un-1 8.) 1753 Richardson *Grandison* (1781) V. xxxvi. 223, I cannot be so great, so undivested, ..as you can be! 1853 Mrs. Moodie *Life in Clearings* 154 The animals undivested of their harness were browsing peacefully. **Undive·stedly**, *adv.* (Un-1 11, 15.) 1748 Richardson *Clarissa* (1811) II. x. 64 As undivestedly as possible of favour or resentment.

**Undivi·dable**, *a.* (and *sb.*). Now *rare.* [Un-1 7 b, 5 b.] Incapable of being divided; indivisible.
1548 R. Hutten *Sum of Diuinitie* I 3 b, A person is an undeuidable substaunce in vnderstandyng. 1594 Carew *Huarte's Exam. Wits* 97 In respect of which selfe qualitie, Galen tearmeth them vndiuidable. 1617 Hieron *Wks.* II. 215 Hee knew iustification and sanctification to be vndiuidable. 1650 Earl Monm. tr. *Senault's Man bec. Guilty* 82 Eternity..in it's undividable unity. 1831 T. Hope *Ess. Orig. Man* I. 48 Since mere space is undividable in parts separate from each other.

b. As *sb.* An indivisible thing.
*a* 1739 Jarvis *Quix.* ii. iv. viii. (1749) 351 Reducing the undivideables into money, he shared it among his company.

**Undivi·dably**, *adv. rare.* (Un-1 11: cf. prec.) 1611 Cotgr., *Indivisiblement*, indiuisibly, vndiuidably. *a* 1641 Bp. Mountagu *Acts & Mon.* (1642) 472 Schisme and heresie are not the same thing, nor ever incident undividably to the same parties.

**Undivi·ded**, *ppl. a.* [Un-1 8 and 5 b.]

1. Not divided, separated, or broken up into parts.
*c* 1412 Hoccleve *De Reg. Princ.* 4469 The blessid trinite, Whiche þat euery man of cristen byleeue Knoweth an vndyuyded vnite. 1480 *Cov. Leet Bk.* 442 And so ye togeder, as on holy body vndevided, to sewe for the redresse therof. 1553 Eden *Treat. New Ind.* (Arb.) 16 Theyr fete..hauing fyue toes like hoeues vndeuided. *c* 1620 Robinson *Mary Magd.* 952 A robe hee wore, like to his essence, pure; That vndiuided; vndeuided hee. 1662 Stillingfl. *Orig. Sacræ* iii. ii. § 18 Some of them [*sc.* particles] are more undivided then others are. 1780 *Mirror* No. 100, One great undivided impression, or an uninterrupted chain of congenial events. 1837 P. Keith *Bot. Lex.* 374 The feet..are single and undivided, as in the horse. 1869 Tozer *Highl. Turkey* II. 152 One unbroken level, which..presents an undivided area of dry and yellow soil.

b. Not separated or parted from each other.
1521 [see Undissevered *ppl. a.*]. *c* 1600 Shaks. *Sonn.* xxxvi, We twomust be twaine, Although our vndeuided loues are one. 1626 Bacon *Sylva* § 752 There have been some Men, that have had their Teeth undivided, as of one whole Bone. 1760-72 H. Brooke *Fool of Qual.* (1809) IV. 34 In death we will be undivided. 1822 Shelley *Epitaph* 1 These are two friends whose lives were undivided.

2. Not divided by disagreement or dissension.
*c* 1440 Lydg. *Hors, Shepe & G.* 510 Vndevided with herte, will & thouht To doon her office as nature hath hem wrouht.

3. Not divided between persons; shared or held jointly or in common. Also quasi-*adv.*, jointly.
1544 tr. *Littleton's Tenures* 67 They ought by the lawe to occupy suche landes and tenementes in comon, and vndeuyded to take the profytes in comon. 1660 R. Coke *Power & Subj.* 1 To suppose..all men to be equal, and to have a common and undivided Right to all things. 1713 C'tess Winchelsea *Misc. Poems* 243 Your unentailed, your undivided Air, Where no Proprietor was ever known. 1817 Shelley *Rev. Islam* ix. xxix, Let those..Insult with careless tread, our undivided tomb. 1877 Raymond *Statist. Mines & Mining* 247 It..is owned by Lewis Reese and Co.,..who hold an undivided half interest.

b. Not divided between different objects; concentrated on, devoted to, directed towards, one object; whole, entire.
1746 Hervey *Refl. on Flower Garden* 81 Be it thy one undivided Aim to glorify Him! 1779 *Mirror* No. 13, Where the undivided attention has leisure to brood over the few.. objects which surround him. 1856 *N. Brit. Rev.* XXVI. 261 A course of study..sufficient to occupy the undivided time of the longest life. 1876 Bancroft *Hist. U.S.* I. Pref., The present revision, to which a solid year of close and undivided application has been devoted.

c. Not shared by others; confined to one person.
1867 Pearson *Hist. Eng.* I. 39 The success of Agricola, showed that the country was not too large for an undivided command. 1878 Bosw. Smith *Carthage* 177 On his own undivided responsibility, he crossed the straits.

Hence **Undi·videdness**.
1889 Abp. Benson in *Life* (1899) II. 283 To illustrate the undividedness of the Church of Wales and England.

**Undivi·dedly**, *adv.* [Un-1 11: cf. prec.] In an undivided manner; without division.
1539 *Act 31 Hen. VIII*, c. 1 § 1 Dyuers..haue lyke righte ..in the same maners,..jointly or in common undevidedly togither with other. 1624 Gataker *Transubst.* 107 Under them all and each particle of them undividedly remaining. 1681 Flavel *Meth. Grace* vi. 122 Christ is offered to us in the Gospel, intirely and undividedly, as cloathed with all his offices. 1704 Norris *Ideal World* ii. xii. 438 This universal nature which so undividedly communicates itself to all that is intellectual. 1848 Mill *Pol. Econ.* ii. viii. § 1. 347 The case in which the produce of land and labour belongs undividedly to the labourer. 1887 Bp. W. How in *Mem.* (1898) 225 Pray for me that God will give me grace..to be more undividedly His.

† **Undivi·dible**, obs. var. Undividable *a.* 1569 J. Sanford tr. *Agrippa's Van. Artes* 65 b, Betweene the *Atomi*, that is undiuidible parts.

† **Undivi·dual**, *a. Obs. rare.* [Un-1 7 and 5 b.] Indivisible; = Individual *a.* 1.
1603 J. Davies (Heref.) *Microcosmos* 195 Shee is Prides second selfe, or other name, Monsters distinct, yet vndiuiduall. *a* 1661 Fuller *Worthies, Worc.* iii. (1662) 172 Indeed true courage and courtesie, are undividuall Companions.

**Undivi·nable**, *a.* (Un-1 7 b, 5 b.) 1611 Cotgr., *Indivinable*, vndiuinable, most obscure, not to be ghessed at. 1858 Carlyle *Fredk. Gt.* vi. iii. (1872) II. 159 He..was complimentary to a degree,—for reasons undivinable to Wilhelmina.

**Undivi·ne**, *a.* (Un-1 7 and 5 b.)
1685 H. More in Norris *Theory of Love* (1688) 191 It were a thing Disangelical, if I may so speak, and undivine. 1732 Berkeley *Alciphr.* v. § 19 If divines are quarrelsome, that is not so far forth as divine, but as undivine and unchristian. 1837 Carlyle *Misc. Ess.* (1888) V. 161 With force of genius she represses..her Undivine Idea. 1860 Ruskin *Unto this Last* (1862) 134 All attempt at concealment implies some practice of the opposite, or undivine science.

**Undivi·ned**, *ppl. a.* (Un-¹ 8.) 1852 Bailey *Festus* 500 The sunsmile of Salvation beamed..Unrecognized—unrecked of —undivined. 1880 'Vernon Lee' *Stud. Italy* III. ii. 122 An obscure youth with undivined talents. **Undivi·nelike**, *adv.* (Un-¹ 7 c.) 1649 Milton *Eikon.* xvii. Wks. 1851 III. 465 How undivinelike writt'n, and how like a worldly gospeller.., posterity no doubt will be able to judge.

**Undivi·nely**, *adv.* [Un-¹ 11.]

†1. In a manner unbefitting a divine. *Obs.*

1618 Daniel *Coll. Hist. Eng.* 182 The Bishop of Hereford ..concludes most undevinely, that an aking..Head of a Kingdome was of necessity to be taken of. 1657 J. Watts *Vind. Ch. Eng.* 110 You not onely inartificially but undivinely say From the University, whereas every good gift is from above, as the Apostle saith.

2. In a manner which is not divine.

1884 *Congregational Year Bk.* 65 There was nothing so undivinely merciless as the divine beauty of Greece.

**Undivi·ning**, *ppl. a.* (Un-¹ 5 d.) 1848 Lytton *Harold* ix. vii, Undivining the solemnity of the appointed snare.

†**Undivi·sible**, *a. Obs.* (Un-¹ 7 and 5 b.)

1495 *Trevisa's Barth. De P. R.* xix. cxxiii. mm iij/2 That nombre is par that is departyd in euen nombres alwaye vnto one that is vndiuysible. 1533 More *Wks.* 1131/2 For he seeth..that the soule is vndiuisible and is in euery part of the body, and in euery part it is whole. 1561 T. Norton *Calvin's Inst.* I. 7 Let Epicure answer me, what meting of vndiuisible bodies..bringeth to passe [etc.].

**Undivo·rceable**, *a.* (Un-¹ 7 b.) 1825 Coleridge *Aids Refl.* (1848) I. 205 From the same reluctance to abandon the too dear and undivorceable Eve. 1884 *Encycl. Brit.* XVII. 86 The musical moiety undivorceable from the literary half. **Undivo·rced**, *ppl. a.* (Un-¹ 8.) 1744 Young *Nt. Th.* v. 1057 These dy'd together; Happy in ruin! undivorc'd by death! [Also in recent use.] **Undivo·rcing**, *sb.* (Un-¹ 12.) 1644 Milton *Divorce* (ed. 2) II. ix. 51 Questionlesse this were a hardheartednesse of undivorcing, worse then that in the Jews. **Undivo·rcing**, *ppl. a.* (Un-¹ 7.) 1643 Milton *Divorce* 13 Made the thrall of heavines and discomfort by an undivorcing Law of God, as he erroneously thinks.

**Undivu·lged**, *ppl. a.* (Un-¹ 8.)

1605 Shaks. *Lear* III. ii. 52 Tremble thou Wretch, That hast within thee vndiuulged Crimes Vnwhipt of Iustice. 1854 J. S. C. Abbott *Napoleon* (1855) I. xxxi. 477 He..listened, with emotions undivulged, to the acclamations of seventy thousand voices. 1883 A. Dobson *Fielding* vi. 167 A secret that, to this day, remains undivulged.

**Undi·zened**, *ppl. a. rare.* (Un-¹ 8.) 1601 Holland *Pliny* II. 298 The peasants..forbid their wiues..to carie their rockes and distaves undizened or bare.

**Undo** (vndū·), *v.* [OE. *an-*, *on-*, *undón* (see Un-² 3 and Do *v.*), = OFris. *un(d)dua* (WFris. *ont-*, *ûntdwaen*), MDu. and Du. *ontdoen*, OS. *an(t)dôn*, *-duan* (MLG. *entdôn*), OHG. *anttoan*, *in(t)duon*, etc. (MHG. *entuon*).]

The absence or scarcity of material illustrating senses 1 and 3 in the 17th and 18th centuries is remarkable; the evidence suggests that, in these senses, the word was revived or reintroduced into literary use by Scott.

I. 1. *trans.* To unfasten and open: a. A door, gate, or window.

c 893 K. Ælfred *Oros.* vi. i. 254 Þa wearð eft Ianes duru andon,..þeh þær nan ȝefeoht þurhtogen ne wurde. c 1000 *Ags. Psalter* (Thorpe) xxiii. 7 Undoð nu eowre ȝeatu,..and onhlidað þa ecan ȝeata. 11.. *Grave* 20 in *Anglia* V. 290 Nefst ðu nenne freond..Ðæt æfre wndon ðe wule ða dure. c 1175 *Lamb. Hom.* 5 Þet faire ȝet me hat hit, &..nefre ouer xii monþe nis hit undon bute to dei. c 1250 *Gen. & Ex.* 603 Arches windoȝe undon it is, ðe Rauen ut-fleȝ. c 1325 *Lai le Freine* 183 The porter of the abbay aros,..The chirche dore he vndede. c 1386 Chaucer *Miller's T.* 541 The wyndow she vndoth, and that in haste. 1412-20 Lydg. *Chron. Troy* iv. 4691 We for fer dar nat issen oute, Nor be so bolde to vndone a gate. 1520 in *Collect.* (O. H. S.) I. 100 Vndo your dore. 1581 A. Hall *Iliad* vi. 114 The dores of gold she doth vndoe, vnfolded, rich and large. 1801 Scott *Eve St. John* xvii, The door she'll undo, to her knight so true. 1821 — *Kenilw.* xxxii, The Earl undid the lattice, and stepped out. 1841 Dickens *Barn. Rudge* ix, Undo the shop window, that I may get in that way. 1880 Mrs. Parr *Adam & Eve* II. 63 She undid the gate, and held it half open.

*absol.* a 1300 *K. Horn* 1069 (Camb. MS.), He com to þe gateward...Horn bad undo softe. 1390 Gower *Conf.* I. 243 This Geta cam thanne ate laste Unto the dore and seide, 'Undo'. c 1425 *Seven Sages* 1410 (P.), At hys dore he wolde inne,..He schof ther-onne and bade undo.

b. A box, sack, bale, etc.

c 1000 Ælfric *Gen.* xlii. 27 Þa undyde hira an his sacc. a 1300 *Cursor M.* 5004 Þai..did þair fardels be vndon. c 1315 Shoreham I. 2148 He seȝ a bok was fast ischet;..Ne myȝte hy no man ondo. c 1350 *Will. Palerne* 4846 Þe clerk þanne deliuerli vndede þo letteres. c 1412 Hoccleve *De Reg. Princ.* 1112 Vn-to his cofre he dressith hym in hye;..He it vndoth, and opneth. c 1450 *Mirk's Festial* 85 Then made he men to vndo þe tombe. 1465 *Paston Lett.* II. 293, I sende yow..iij. tracle pottes of Geane;..they weer never ondoo syns that they come from Geane. 1535 *Act 27 Hen. VIII*, c. 14 § 4 Which packes..be not vndone nor opened at their arriual within the portes. 1573 Baret *Alv.* O 114 To vndooe, or open a letter sealed. 1853 M. Arnold *Scholar Gipsy* xxv, [The] Tyrian trader..on the beach undid his corded bales.

*fig.* a 1300 *Sarmun* xxxvi. in *E. E. P.* (1862) 5 Vn-do þin hert þat is iloke wiþ couetise. a 1310 in Wright *Lyric P.* xviii. 58 Swete Jhesu,..Undo myn herte ant liht ther-yn. 1596 Drayton *Legends* iii. 106 What is that Man, by whom thou art controll'd, Or hath the Key of Reason to vndoe thee?

†c. To open by unlocking or uncovering. *Obs.*

a 1122 *O. E. Chron.* (Laud MS.) an. 656, Ȝif hwa hit hælt, S. Petre mid heofne keie undo him heofenrice. a 1300 *Cursor M.* 6611 Þaa holes, quen þai þam vndid, Þai fand bot wormes creuland emid. *Ibid.* 6725 If animan vndus a pitt, And siþen wil it noght ditt.

†2. To open (the mouth or eyes). *Obs.*

a 1000 *Kentish Gloss.* in Wr.-Wülcker 62 *Aperientur* [*labia mea*], siont ondone. c 1000 Ælfric *Hom.* I. 548 He undyde his muð, and hi lærde. c 1055 *Byrhtferth's Handboc* in *Anglia* VIII. 317 Þæt he undo his eaȝan. c 1175 *Lamb. Hom.* 121 Imong alle þere pine..ne undude he nefre ene his muð. c 1250 *Gen. & Ex.* 3971 Balaam it spureð and smit ðor-on; And god vndede ðis asses muð. 1297 R. Glouc. (Rolls) 7185 He gan as he awoke of slepe is eyen þo vndo. c 1420 *Lay Folks Mass Bk.* 82 Lorde un-do my lyppis. c 1430 *Syr Gener.* (Roxb.) 684 Yit a litle his eyen he vndede.

3. To unfasten by untying or by releasing from a fixed position; to unfix. Also in fig. context.

c 950 *Lindisf. Gosp.* John i. 27 Ðæs ic ne am wyrðe þætte ic undoe [*Rushw.* ondoe] his ðuong scoes. c 1000 Ælfric *Hom.* I. 572 On ðære ylcan nihte Godes engel undyde þa locu ðæs cweartermes. c 1250 *Gen. & Ex.* 2114 Ne was non so wis man in al his lond, ðe kude vn-don ðis dremes bond. 13.. *Cursor M.* 17357 (Gött.), [Þai] vndid þair lock all wid þe kay. 1382 Wyclif *Mark* i. 7 Of whom I..am not worthi for to vndo, or vnbynde, the thwong of his schoon. c 1440 *Promp. Parv.* 365/1 Ondoon, or ondo lokys or speryngys, *aperio*. c 1450 *Mirk's Festial* 248 Oure lady aperet..yn þe prison, and vndyd his bondes. 1542 Udall *Erasm. Apoph.* 230 b, Writhen..with so diffuse a knotte, that noman could vndooe it. c 1586 C'tess Pembroke *Ps.* (1823) lxviii. ii, The prisoners chaines are by his hands undone. 1605 Shaks. *Lear* v. iii. 309 Pray you vndo this Button. 1683 Moxon *Mech. Exerc.*, *Printing* iv. 44 The Cheeks may..receive the Head..without un-doing the Cap and Winter. 1805 Scott *Last Minstrel* v. xxii, Some friendly hand Undo the visor's barred band! 1818 Byron *Juan* I. cxxxvii, Do pray undo the bolt a little faster. 1868 Morris *Earthly Par.* (1870) I. I. 431 She..turned the box round,..undid The clasp, and fearfully raised up the lid.

b. To unfasten the clothing of (a person).

1633 Rowley *Match at Midn.* iv, Wid[ow]. Alas! you will undo me. *Alex.* No, no, I will undo myself, look ye. 1841 Dickens *Barn. Rudge* ix, Having undone her mistress, as she phrased it (which means, assisted to undress her). 1899 T. M. Ellis *3 Cat's-Eye Rings* 90 'Now undo me. I shall get into bed.' 'Yes, my lady.'

†4. To unbind; to release or free from a bond, bandage, covering, etc. *Obs.*

c 930 *Laws Athelstan* i. 23 Beon þreo niht, ær mon þa hond undo. c 950 *Durham Rit.* 42 From allvm vsiȝ..synnvm..vndo. c 1250 *Gen. & Ex.* 581 Ilc wateres springe here strengðe undede. c 1290 *S. Eng. Leg.* I. 34/30 Nov, he seide, we schullen iseo..Ȝweþer he þe mai a-ȝein me vndo. a 1300 *Cursor M.* 14970 A moder ass yee sal þar find, And yee hir sal vn-do Vte of hir band. c 1380 *Sir Ferumb.* 1310 Oundo þis prysouns on & on;..þey schulleþ out of þis sory won. c 1400 *Melayne* 785 The kynge vndid his hede alle bare. 1513 Douglas *Æneid* vi. vi. 45 Sche,..with that word, the branch schew and vndid, That preualie ondir hir clok wes hid.

†5. a. To remove, take away; to detach, cut off.

c 1275 Lay. 19205 Merlyn hadde al his craft ondo of þan kinge. 1340 *Ayenb.* 106 Þe yefþe of wysdom, þet uestneþ.. þe herte in god,..þet hi ne may by ondo ne to-deld. 1513 Douglas *Æneid* iv. xii. 117, I man Vndo this hair, to Pluto consecrait.

†b. To cut up (an animal). *Obs.*

13.. *Gaw. & Gr. Knt.* 1327 Quykly of þe quelled dere a querre þay maked,..& didden hem derely vndo. c 1400 *Master of Game* (MS. Digby 182) xxxiii, Þenne he shulde charge whome hym lyste to vndo þe deere. 1486 *Bk. St. Albans, Hunting* e iii, When ye haue slayn the boore.., Ye shall vndo hym vnflayne when he shall be dight.

†c. To cut open; to open with a knife. *Obs.*

c 1440 *Anc. Cookery* in *Househ. Ord.* (1790) 451 Take pykes, and undo hom on the bale. c 1440 *Pallad. on Husb.* I. 601 Al esely me may vndo the skyn With prickyng of a nelde or of a pyn. a 1450 Myrc *Par. Pr.* 99 Teche the mydwyf that scho hye For to vndo hyre wyth a knyf, And for to saue the chyldes lyf. 1672 Walker *Paræm.* 34 Undone, as ye would undoe an Oyster. 1688 J. Grubb in *Roxb. Ball.* (1888) VI. 726 George undid the Dragon just as you'd undo an oyster.

†6. *intr.* To go apart; to open; to become unfastened, come undone. *Obs.*

1122 *O. E. Chron.* (Laud MS.), Se wolcne undide on fower healfe and faht þær to ȝeanes. c 1300 *Harrow. Hell* 138 (Harl. MS.), Helle gates y come nou to, ant y wole þat heo vndo. c 1500 in Hazlitt *E. P. P.* III. 109 At the dore I will assaie, If it will undoe. 1548 in S. Haynes *St. Papers Cecil* (1740) 99 The Lady Elizabeth heryng the Pryvie-Lock undo, ..ran out of hir Bed.

II. 7. *trans.* To annul, cancel, rescind (something done, effected, or decided on); to reduce to the condition of not having been done, effected, decided, etc.

c 970 in Birch *Cartul.* (1887) III. 417 Þet hyra nan næ undo þe ic to ðam haliȝum mynstrum binnan þære byrig ȝedon hæbbe. a 1122 *O. E. Chron.* (Laud MS.) an. 656, Leidon þa Godes curs..[on him] þe ani þing undyde þæt þær wæs ȝedon. 1123 *Ibid.* an. 1123, He sæde þone cyng þæt hit wæs to ȝeanes riht,..ac se cyng hit nolde undon. c 1250 *Gen. & Ex.* 3014 Pharaon wroð herte on hard, And vndede hem ðat forward. 1297 R. Glouc. (Rolls) 5692 He vndude alle þe luþer lawes þat me huld biuore, & gode lawes broȝte vorþ. c 1315 Shoreham I. 1669 For þet compleþ þet spoushod..Þat hyt ne may be ondon. c 1400 *Beryn* 3355 For I have made a bargeyn, þat may nat be vndo. 1495 *Act 11 Hen. VII*, c. 56 § 2 Provided alweys that this present acte extend not..to undo eny your lettres patentes. a 1533 Ld. Berners *Gold Bk. M. Aurel.* (1546) B viij, Julius Cesar ..adnulled and vndyd all that Sylla hadde made. 1605 Shaks. *Macb.* v. i. 75 What's done, cannot be vndone. 1651 Hobbes *Leviath.* II. xix. 96 The diligent appearance of a few of the contrary opinion undoes to day, all that was concluded yesterday. 1680 Baxter *Answ. Stillingfl.* l. 72 And what Princes do, they have power to undo. 1709 Addison *Tatler* No. 108 ¶ 5 To disappoint and undo what the most refined Spirits have been labouring to advance. 1768 Tucker *Lt. Nat.* II. I. xiv. 196 Annihilating time and space, undoing past events or producing contrary ones. 1820 Shelley *Œd. Tyr.* I. 384 With a little common sense, ..Only undoing all that has been done. 1873 Dixon *Two Queens* xxii. viii, No one could recall a case in which the peers had undone the finding of a grand jury.

*absol.* 1440 *Bone Flor.* 1511 He seyde, Thou haste wychyd me,..Undo or thou schalt abye. 1577-82 Breton *Floorish upon Fancie* Wks. (Grosart) I. 6/1 To doo, and vndoo too, so that they may obtaine Their mistresse looue. 1593 Shaks. *3 Hen. VI*, II. vi. 105 Warwicke as our Selfe, Shall do, and vndo as him pleaseth best. 1697 Vanbrugh *Prov. Wife* I. i, Methinks, they do and undo, and make but bad work on't. 1803 Wordsw. *Sonn. Liberty* xxii. 3 One man..Raised up to sway the world, to do, undo.

b. To reverse the doing or making of (some material thing or effect) so as to restore the original form or condition.

1426 Lydg. *De Guil. Pilgr.* 11328 Tel me..Why makestow, & vndost ageyn Thy werk [*sc.* mats] so offte sythe a day? 1606 Shaks. *Ant. & Cl.* II. ii. 210 Whose winde did seeme To gloue the delicate cheekes which they did coole, And what they vndid did. 1632 Sanderson *Serm.* I. 309 He never knoweth the end of his work: what he doth now, anon he must undo. 1679 Moxon *Mech. Exerc.* vii. 125 It is sometimes used when Carpenters have committed error in their work, and must undo what they did, to mend it. 1797 *Encycl. Brit.* (ed. 3) XVI. 484/1 It will not stop till it has turned as often as the end *m* has been twisted, and now all the twist will be undone. 1853 *Arab. Nts.* (Rtldg.) 572 He went up..to the workmen, and..made them..undo all they had yet finished. 1866 Geo. Eliot *F. Holt* i, She liked to insist that work done without her orders should be undone from beginning to end.

8. To destroy; to bring to naught; to do away with; to take away, remove. Now *rare.*

c 950 *Lindisf. Gosp.* Mark xiv. 58 Ic undoe *vel* ic toslito [L. *dissolvam*] tempel. c 1175 *Lamb. Hom.* 7 Ne swincke þu nefre swa muchel, a hit bið undon. c 1250 *Gen. & Ex.* 3902 Quat stungen man so saȝ ðor-on, ðat werk him sone al was vn-don. a 1275 in *O. E. Misc.* 101 Hwenne deþ heom lat to þe murehþe þat neuer ne byþ undon. 13.. *E. E. Allit. P.* B. 562 Hym rwed þat he hem vp-rerde.., & efte þat he hem vndyd, hard hit hym þoȝt. 1382 Wyclif *Matt.* v. 17, I came not to vndo the lawe, but to fulfille. c 1425 *Eng. Conq. Ireland* 94 Thay comen ayeyn hym..for to mak hym turne ayeyne; other, to vndo hym ryght yn the watyr. c 1440 *Pallad. on Husb.* I. 284 Vnhusbondynge vndoth fertilite. c 1482 J. Kay in Gibbon *Crusades*, etc. (1870) 135 To undoo and subuerte the holy cytee of Rome. 1573 Tusser *Husb.* (1878) 73 Look daily well to them, least dogs vndoo them. 1638 Sir T. Herbert *Trav.* (ed. 2) 303 The Bannyan is..so innocent, as not to undoe the silliest vermin. 1669 Pepys *Diary* 31 May, Having done now so long as to undo my eyes almost every time that I take a pen in my hand. 1703 Rowe *Fair Penit.* I. i, Nor tell him that which will undo his Quiet. 1788 *Trifler* No. 14. 186 This hypothesis however is undone by the manifest design and order displayed through the whole creation. 1871 Jowett *Plato* I. 499 The love of Aristogeiton and the constancy of Harmodius had a strength which undid their power.

b. To destroy in respect of means or position; to ruin. †Also (*refl.*) with (*out*) *of.*

1390 Gower *Conf.* I. 193 Thurgh the conseil of you tuo I stonde in point to ben undo. 1477 *Paston Lett.* III. 199, I beseche yow that I maye have an assyngnement of suche dettes..; ffor..I sholde ellys wylfully ondoo myselffe. 1483 Caxton *G. de la Tour* C v b, For a lytel thynge ye haue vndo yow. 1531 *Star Chamb. Cases* (Selden) II. 187 Extending vtterly to defame, inpouerisshe and vndoo your seid oratours. 1573 Tusser *Husb.* (1878) 24 The rich it compelleth to paie for his pride; the poore it vndoeth on euerie side. 1612 *Two Noble K.* III. vi. 137 Our Folly has undon us. 1687 A. Lovell tr. *Thevenot's Trav.* I. 32 It is never heard in Turkie, that a man hath undone himself by House-keeping. 1712 Arbuthnot *John Bull* II. iii, A foolish and negligent husband, who..was undone by his wife's elopement from him. 1798 S. & Ht. Lee *Canterb. T.* II. 15 A single error undid him. 1852 Miss Yonge *Cameos* I. i. 5 England had been well-nigh undone by them, when the spirit of her greatest king awoke. 1867 Morris *Jason* II. 81 For surely mayst thou lean upon me, when..a king with wrong Would fain undo thee.

(*b*) 1621 J. Taylor (Water P.) *Unnat. Father* Wks. (1630) 136/2 He was enticed to vndoe himselfe out of all his earthly possessions. 1628 Gaule *Pract. The.* 4 He hath quite vndone himselfe of Money, Wit [etc.].

c. To injure (a person) seriously. *rare.*

1530 Palsgr. 767/2, I undo one by any..hurt done to his person by reason of any stroke. 17.. *Christmas Ba'ing* xxi. in *Skinner's Misc. Poet.* (1809) 130 An't had na been for Davy Mair, The rascals had ondune him.

d. To ruin by seducing. Also *absol.* Now *rare.*

1612 Shelton *Quix.* I. iii. 16 Doing many wrongs, sollicit-ing many widdowes, vndoing certaine maidens. a 1695 Prior '*Whither would my passion run*' i, Losing Her I am undone, Yet would not gain Her to undo Her. 1792 Wolcot (P. Pindar) *More Money* II. ix, As Darkness oft turns Pimp to undo a belle. 1809 Malkin *Gil Blas* II. vii. ¶ 14 In my eyes he was created to undo.

9. To explain, interpret, expound. Now *rare.*

Sometimes with suggestion of sense 3.

a 1300 *Cursor M.* 4474 Said ioseph,..I sal vn-do þe wel þi sueuen. *Ibid.* 12206 Vndos me first quat es alpha. ? a 1366 Chaucer *Rom. Rose* 9 Macrobes, That..vndothe vs the auysioun That whilom mette kyng Cipioun. 1393 Langl. *P. Pl.* C. III. 40 Dauid vn-doþ hit hym-self, as þe doumbe sheweþ. c 1450 *St. Cuthbert* (Surtees) 680 Ga in my blissing þi mayster to, He sall þis dreeme þe vndo. 1581 Pettie *Guazzo's Civ. Conv.* II. (1586) 82, I praie you.. vndo me the knot of this Gentrie, which I see to be verie intricate. 1618 Fletcher *Women Pleas'd* IV. i, Here may be so much wit (though much I fear it) To undo this knotty question. 1654 Whitlock *Zootomia* 252 Commend them to such as can undo a Text (as they tearm it) with as much ease as a bow-knot. 1833 Tennyson *Two Voices* 232 In seeking to undo One riddle, and to find the true.

**Undo**, obs. variant of Undone *ppl. a.*

**Undo·able**, *a.* (Un-¹ 7 b.) 1865 Carlyle *Fredk. Gt.* xviii. ii. VII. 113 'Difficult, not undoable,' persists the King.

**Undoch(t**: see Undought.

†**Undo·cible**, *a.* [Un-¹ 7, 5 b.] = Indocible.

1653 R. Sanders *Physiogn., Moles* 17 He is undocible and stubborn. 1668 H. More *Div. Dial.* I. xxxi. (1713) 69 You see..that I am not altogether an undocible Auditor of Metaphysicks. 1702 De Foe *Reform. Manners* 52 The hardn'd Guilt undocible appears. **1722** — *Col. Jack* (1840) 157 A negro..perfectly untractable, undocible.

†**Undo·cile,** *a. Obs.* (Un-[1] 7 and 5 b.) **1656** Cowley *Pindar. Odes, Plagues Egypt* 241 What Blindness..did there e'er Like this undocil King's appear? **1703** *Secret Policy Jansenists* (ed. 2) 25 They give out they are Undocil, but the truth is, they are not Instructed.

**Undo·ck,** *v.* [Un-[2] 5.] *trans.* To take (a ship) out of a dock; sometimes *spec.*, to launch.

**1750** *Naval Expos.* 15 On docking and undocking Ships. **1804** *Trans. Soc. Arts* XXII. 277 Enabling large ships to be docked, suspended, and undocked, the same spring tides. **1897** *Westm. Gaz.* 30 Sept. 5/2 Before the *Lynx* could be docked it was necessary to undock..another destroyer.

**Undo·cked,** *ppl. a.* (Un-[1] 8 + Dock *v.*[1])

**1677** *Lond. Gaz.* No. 1231/4 A light dun Colt,..three years old,..undockt. **1802** [see Uncropped 2]. **1859** F. Mahony *Rel. Father Prout* 375 Remotest posterity..would enjoy thy book undocked of its due proportions.

**Undo·ctor,** *v.* (Un-[2] 6 b.) [1598 Florio, *Disdottorare*, to vndoctor, to degrade a doctor.] **1833** Mrs. Carlyle in Froude *Carlyle, First Forty Years* II. 353 My brother-in-law is a paragon of the class,..but he is so by..undoctoring himself. **Undo·ctored,** (*ppl.*) *a.* (Un-[1] 8, 9.) **1803** in *Spirit Pub. Jrnls.* VII. 370 No diploma did he bring from Jutland, but came undoctored and undubbed. **1882** *Med. Temp. Jrnl.* L. 85 It would be much better to use the spirit undoctored. **Undo·ctrinal,** *a.* (Un-[1] 7.) **1863** Geo. Eliot *Romola* xxv, Brave undoctrinal lovers of a sober republican liberty, who preferred fighting to arguing. **Undo·ctrined,** *ppl. a.* (Un-[1] 7.) **1869** Blackmore *Lorna Doone* i. (1891) 3 Any boy, soever small and undoctrined. **Undo·cumented,** *ppl. a.* (Un-[1] 8.) **1883** *Boston Herald* 12 May 2 During such undocumented period. **1888** *Athenæum* 4 Aug. 153/2 The inexact and undocumented synthesis of the insufficient student.

**Undo·er** [1]. [f. Undo *v.* + -er [1].]

†**1.** An expounder, interpreter. *Obs.*

**1382** Wyclif *Jas.* Prol., So also of interpretouris, or vndoeris, in to Latyn speche thei were turned treuly. *c* **1440** *Promp. Parv.* 365 Ondoar, or expownare, *expositor, interpres.*

**2.** One who opens or unfastens. *rare.*

*c* **1440** *Promp. Parv.* 365/1 Ondoare, or opynnare of thyngys schet or closyd.., *apertor.*

**3.** A destroyer, wrecker, ruiner.

*c* **1440** *Promp. Parv.* 365/1 Ondoare, or dystroyare, *destructor.* **1456** Sir G. Hay *Gov. Princes* Wks. (S. T. S.) II. 101 Thus ar the tymes of somer and wynter bathe doare and undoare to all erdly thing that growis under the hevyn. **1567** Drant *Horace, Ep.* i. xv. E vj, Th' vndoer, tempest, and the hell of al the shambles then. **1598** R. Bernard tr. *Terence, Adelphos* v. iii, Loe heere at hand the common corruption and vndoer of our children. **1633** Heywood *Eng. Trav.* iv, This my customary comming hither, Hath bin to base and sorded purposes: To..be mine owne vndoer. **1796** C. Anstey *Pleaders' Guide* (1803) 171 Sure Law was made to be the undoer Of just such Nincompoops as you are! **1844** Mrs. Browning *Drama of Exile* 423, I now confess myself thy death And thine undoer. **1885** R. L. & F. Stevenson *Dynamiter* 161 Greed..has been your undoer.

**b.** *spec.* One who ruins a woman; a seducer.

**1703** Rowe *Fair Penit.* iv. i, Think, whom I shou'd devote to Death and Hell, Whom Curse, as my Undoer, but Lothario. **1760–72** H. Brooke *Fool of Qual.* (1809) II. 49, I awakened..in the arms of my cruel and accursed undoer. **1847** Lytton *Lucretia* ii. xiv, The child of..your betrayer, your undoer, stands between the daylight and your son.

**Undo·er** [2]. *rare*⁻¹. [Un-[1] 12.] One who does not act or perform.

**1628** Feltham *Resolves* ii. 232 Hope without Action is a barren vndooer.

**Undo·ffed,** *ppl. a.* (Un-[1] 8.) *c* **1440** *Alph. Tales* 173 And so [the priest] þe shone lefte vndofte vnto his servand did þaim off. **1854** Miss Baker *Northampt. Gloss.*, *Undoffed*, undressed. 'He hasn't been undoffed this two days.' **Undogma·tic,** *a.* (Un-[1] 7.) **1857** Pusey *Doctr. Real Presence* i. 108 Melancthon's mind however was undogmatic. **1894** Drummond *Ascent Man* 9 Of all men the Evolutionist..must be humble, tolerant, and undogmatic. **Undogma·tical,** *a.* (Un-[1] 7.) **1863** *Q. Rev.* CXIV. 571 It was only on the most dogmatic of all sciences..that he lived for the purpose of making all teaching undogmatical.

**Undo·ing,** *vbl. sb.*[1] [f. Undo *v.*]

†**1.** Exposition; interpretation. *Obs.*

*a* **1330** *Seuyn Sages* (W.) 2352 He scholde..brenge a besaund to offring, And of his sweuen have undoing. **1382** Wyclif *Gen.* xl. 8 And Joseph seide to hem, Whether not of God is the vndoyng? *c* **1425** Wyntoun *Cron.* iv. xxvi. 2576 Discripcion is wrytynge In til our propyr vndoynge. *c* **1440** *Promp. Parv.* 365/1 Ondoynge, or expownynge, *exposicio.*

**2.** The action of opening, unfastening, taking apart, loosening, etc.

*c* **1375** *Sc. Leg. Saints* vi. (*Thomas*) 477 Of þat ee þe vndoynge Is of oure harte & vndirstandinge. *a* **1400** *Pauline Ep.* (Powell) 1 Cor. vii. 27 If þou art bowndyn to a wif, seeke þou not vndoyng. *c* **1440** *Promp. Parv.* 365/1 Ondoynge, or opynynge of schettellys, or sperellys, *apercio.* **1486** *Bk. St. Albans, Hunting* e iii, Now of thage & undoyng of the boore. **1598** Florio, *Disciolare*,..to put off hose and doublet without vndoing of points. **1613** Purchas *Pilgrimage* (1614) 484 The heeles of their shooes are seldome pulled vp, to saue labour of vndoing them. **1897** *Allbutt's Syst. Med.* II. 912 They all bring about a loosening of the framework of..nervous matter...The muscular system also..shows a like undoing.

**3.** The action of bringing to nought, destroying, or ruining; the fact of being so dealt with; the state of being undone; also (with *a*), an instance of this.

Quotations under (*a*) illustrate the active, those under (*b*) the passive, use of the word.

(*a*) **1398** Trevisa *Barth. De P. R.* x. iii. (Tollem. MS.), It is þe leste party and laste in undoynge of the body. **1423** *Rolls of Parlt.* IV. 198/2 In hy undoyng to the Kynges Liege peple, and ayenis the ordenaunce and statuts. *c* **1440** *Promp. Parv.* 365/1 Ondoynge, or dystroyynge, *dissipacio, destruccio.* *c* **1475** *Golagros & Gaw.* 497 May nane do thame na deir with vndoyng. **1598** Florio, *Sfaccimento*, a defacing,..a defeasance, an vndoing. **1617** Hieron *Wks.* II. 358 If thou leauest out the manner of doing, this is an vndoing to thy doing. **1671** Flavel *Fount. Life* v. 13 An Undoing to him in point of Reputation.

(*b*) *c* **1400** *Laud Troy Bk.* 9125 The Grekes were in point of vndoyng: Ne hadde ther comen ther riche kyng. **1415** Sir T. Grey in *43rd Rep. Dep. Kpr. Rec.* (1882) 583 Hit has broghte me to þis shame and undoyng. **1503–4** *Plumpton Corr.* (Camden) p. cxiii, Sir Roger Hastings is at the point of undoinge, because hee hath not money to pay where he ought to pay. **1577** tr. *Bullinger's Decades* ii. vi. 171/1 Neither doest thou read that the state..of the Israelites was euer at any time in greater daunger and peril of vndooing. **1614** R. Tailor *Hog hath lost Pearle* iv, How many country Clyents then might rest, Free from vndooing! *a* **1716** South *Serm.* (1744) XI. viii. 183 He that ventures to be a surety for another, ventures an undoing for his sake.

**b.** With possessive pronoun or genitive.

Chiefly in passive sense.

**1377** Langl. *P. Pl.* B. xv. 589 Danyel of her vndoynge deuyned and seyde [etc.]. *c* **1440** *Jacob's Well* 127 He took redyly þo ȝiftes, & þat was cause of his vndoyng. **1478** *Paston Lett.* Suppl. (1901) 151 Now he ys upon hys makyng by vertues governance, or undoyng to the contrarye. **1562** Pilkington *Expos. Abdias* Pref. 16 They saved your lyves and goods, not seeking your undoinge when it laye in their handes. **1609** Holland *Amm. Marcell.* 353 For, exposed he was..to the accesse of as manie as sought the undoing of others. **1679** J. Goodman *Penit. Pard.* ii. i. (1713) 157 His undoing was his making, and his misfortune proved his recovery. **1740** Richardson *Pamela* (1824) I. 64 You see your undoing has been long hatching. **1823** Byron *Juan* xiv. lxxxv, The latter works its own undoing. **1852** Thackeray *Esmond* iii. ix, He was not the first that has..brought about his own undoing.

**c.** In the phrase *to* (one's) *undoing.*

?**1456** *Paston Lett.* Suppl. (1901) 59 Thei wuld put alle juparte up on me to myn utter ondoyng. **1526** *Pilgr. Perf.* (W. de W. 1531) 97 b, Lest he gete helpe of thy superyour, & so vanquysshe yᵉ to thy vtter vndoynge. *a* **1548** Hall *Chron., Edw. V*, 5 b, Whiche..might abuse the name of his commaundemente to any of our vndoyng. **1621** Elsing *Debates Ho. Lords* (Camden) App. 138 By that meanes all his creditors came upon him to his utter undoinge. **1641** W. Hakewill *Libertie of Subject* 83 That desperate motion that had been made against them to all their utter undoings. **1883** Whitelaw *Sophocles, Ajax* 402 But me the child of Zeus..plagues To my undoing.

**4.** A cause of ruin or destruction.

**1390** Gower *Conf.* III. 229 Which was to him his undoinge. *a* **1450** *Knt. de la Tour* (1906) 60 Adam..beleued his wyff, the whiche was dethe and vndoyng to hym and her, and to us all. **1576** in Feuillerat *Revels Q. Eliz.* (1908) 414 It is an accion of accompt..like to be the vtter vndooing both of him and his. **1605** Chapman *All Fools* ii. i. 197 It had beene her undooing t' have hime seene. **1659** Rushw. *Hist. Coll.* i. 420 The Soldiers brake out into great disorders..; they were a terror to all, and an undoing to many. **1727** Gay *Begg. Op.* i. iv, Mary-bone and the Chocolate-houses are his Undoing. **1818** Scott *Hrt. Midl.* xxiii, She will tell the truth, if it should be the undoing of her. **1871** Freeman *Norm. Conq.* (1875) III. xiii. 264 The marriage of Emma had well nigh been the undoing of England.

**5.** The action of reversing, annulling, etc.

**1540** *Act 32 Hen. VIII*, c. 30 § 1 The said judgementes..shall stande..without any reuersell or vndooyng of the same. **1611** Cotgr., *Rompement*,..a cancelling, dissoluing, infringing, vndoing. **1650** B. *Discolliminium* 16 Our Trade of doing, and undoing, will be endlesse. **1866** J. H. Newman *Let. to Pusey* 36 He..became man, that by what way the disobedience arising from the serpent had its beginning, by that way also it might have an undoing. **1891** J. Winsor *Columbus* ii. 50 When Isabella decreed the undoing of Columbus's kidnapping exploits.

**Undo·ing,** *vbl. sb.*[2] *rare*⁻¹. [Un-[1] 12.] The omission or neglect of doing; non-performance.

**1587** Golding *De Mornay* ii. 25 To speake properly, we must not seeke whence commeth the doing of euill, but whence commeth the vndoing of good.

**Undo·ing,** *ppl. a.* [f. Undo *v.*] Ruinous, destructive.

**1654** Tuckney *Death Disarmed* 33 It is an undoing gain to break their arm by catching at a feather. **1681** Flavel *Meth. Grace* xvi. 305 Little do such men know how..they put an undoing cheat upon their own souls for ever. **1793** Anna Seward *Lett.* (1811) III. 292 The present fashion of head-dress..has an undoing influence upon youth and beauty.

**Undo·ingness.** *rare*⁻¹. [Un-[1] 12.] Inaction.

**1640** O. Sedgwick *Christs Counsell* 192 Forgetfulnesse keeps us..in an estate of barrennesse and undoingnesse.

**Undome·stic,** *a.* [Un-[1] 7.]

**1.** Not caring for, not pertaining to, home life or duties.

**1754** Richardson *Grandison* V. lviii. 385 That wives and daughters were never more faulty, more undomestic, than at present. **1806** R. Cumberland *Mem.* (1807) II. 281, I am very rarely called off by avocations of an undomestic kind. **1857** Dufferin *Lett. High Lat.* (ed. 3) 5 The undomestic Mr. Ebenezer Wyse.

**2.** Unlike a home; lacking the character of a home.

**1798** Coleridge *Lett.* (1895) 265 When the tears rolled out of my eyes, and this naked, undomestic room became again visible. **1883** *Century Mag.* Oct. 859/1 As undomestic a looking pile of brick and mortar as was ever put together.

**Undome·sticate,** *v.* (Un-[2] 6 a.) **1754** Richardson *Grandison* I. xlvii. 326 The turn our Sex take in *un*-domesticating themselves. **1799** Han. More *Strict. Mod. Syst. Fem. Educ.* xvi, Clubs..generate..every temper and spirit which tends to undomesticate. **Undome·sticated,** *ppl. a.* (Un-[1] 8.) **1847** Webster (citing Chalmers).

**Undo·ne,** *ppl. a.*[1] [Un-[1] 8 b. Cf. OFris. *ondan* (NFris. *ündōn*), MDu. *ongedaen* (Du. *-daan*), MHG. *ungetân* (G. *-than, -tan*).]

**1.** Not done; unaccomplished, uneffected.

*a* **1300** *Cursor M.* 13176 His comandment was noght vn-dun, For he was heued and þat als sun. *c* **1380** Wyclif *Wks.* (1880) 90 He mot leue goddis comaundement vndon. *c* **1440** *Jacob's Well* 114 ȝif..þou leve vnsayd or vndo þat is nedefull..þanne is it dedly synne. *a* **1450** Myrc *Par. Pr.* 1187 Hast þou any pylgrimage laft vn-do When þou were i-ioynet þer-to? **1535** *Act 27 Hen. VIII*, c. 25 Euery parishe..shal lose & forfait .xx.s. for euery moneth, in whiche it is omitted and vndone. **1585** T. Washington tr. *Nicholay's Voy.* iii. xxi. 110 [They] goe on such pilgrimage, leauing vndone al other houshold or common affaires. **1678** Butler *Hud.* iii. ii. 160 The Publick Business is undone, Which still the longer 'tis in doing, Becomes the surer way to Ruine. **1706** Prior *Ode to the Queen* xix, Nought done the Hero deem'd, while ought undone remain'd. **1759** Johnson *Rasselas* xxx, I must not ..leave at last undone what I came hither only to do. **1791** Mrs. Radcliffe *Rom. Forest* iv, They went out of the shop together, leaving my horse's shoe undone. **1847** Helps *Friends in C.* I. 5 If I leave it undone, some one else will do it to my mind. **1871** Macduff *Mem. Patmos* vi. 74 The sword completed what the fire had left undone.

**b.** As *sb.* That which is not done.

**1872** Ruskin *Arrows of Chace* (1880) II. 208 The condemnation..is all for the *undones* and not for the *dones.*

**2.** Not done *away*, not removed.

**1679** C. Nesse *Antichrist* 204 While this Vail and face of Covering is undone away.

**Undo·ne,** *ppl. a.*[2] [f. Undo *v.*]

**1.** Brought to decay or ruin; ruined, destroyed.

Chiefly predicative, but the attributive use was not infrequent in the 17th and was common in the 18th century.

**1340** *Ayenb.* 136 Hueruore his bodi is ondo, and his inwyt uolueld. *a* **1400–50** *Alexander* 1472 We ere dredles vnd one, bot driȝten vs help. *a* **1450** *Mirk's Festial* 192 He..ȝaf hym all to foly aftyr, and laft hit neuer til he wer vndon. **1484** Caxton *Fables of Æsop* ii. ix, Many one is vndone and lost for faulte of obedyence. *a* **1542** Wyatt in *Tottel's Misc.* (Arb.) 85 When her store was stroyed with the floode: Then weleaway for she undone was cleane. **1573** Tusser *Husb.* (1878) 91 Keepe hop from sunne, and hop is vndunne. **1608** Middleton *Trick to catch Old One* iii. i, That Witgood is a riotous, undone man. **1646** P. Bulkeley *Gospel Covt.* i. 48 The low and undone condition they have brought themselves into by their sins. *a* **1687** Petty *Pol. Arith.* (1690) 89 England commonly beareth the whole burthen, and charge, whereby many in England are utterly undone. **1724** Swift *Drapier's Lett.* ii, We are all undone if Wood's halfpence must pass. **1749** Fielding *Tom Jones* xvii. iv, I am the most miserable undone Wretch upon Earth. **1810** Crabbe *Borough* xiv. 14 Blaney, a wealthy heir at twenty-one, At twenty-five was ruin'd and undone. **1839** Dickens *Nickleby* lvi, I am undone. Whichever way I turn, I am undone. *a* **1864** Ferrier *Grk. Philos.* (1866) I. xii. 348 A soul without justice..is a soul undone.

**2.** Unfastened, untied, detached, etc.

**1565** Cooper *Thesaurus*, *Vincla resoluta*, loosed or vndoone. **1806–7** J. Beresford *Miseries Hum. Life* vi. xxxvi, The outer bandage of a hurt in your bridle-hand coming undone. **1884** W. S. Gilbert *Princess Ida* ii, Let all your things misfit, and yourselves At inconvenient moments come undone.

Hence **Undo·neness.** *rare*⁻¹.

**1835** R. M. McCheyne *Addit. Rem.* (1847) 35 Under a sense of undoneness, to flee for refuge to the Saviour.

**Undoo·med,** *ppl. a.* (Un-[1] 8.) [1775 Ash.] **1813** Byron *Giaour* xvi, Unfit for earth, undoom'd for heaven. **1821** Scott *Pirate* xix, Visitor bold,..Who hast hither presumed, —Ungifted, undoom'd, Thou shalt not depart.

**Undo·se,** *a. rare.* [ad. L. *undōs-us*, f. *unda* wave. Cf. Sp. and Pg. *undoso*, It. *ondoso.*]

†**1.** Of the pulse: Having beats of unequal strength. *Obs.*

**1707** Floyer *Physic. Pulse-Watch* 138 Generally an undose Pulse is a degree of slow Pulses from weak Spirits. **1758** *Phil. Trans.* L. 524 The pulse..was sometimes heavy and undose.

**2.** *Ent.* (See quot.)

**1826** Kirby & Sp. *Entomol.* IV. xlvi. 271 *Undose*, having undulating nearly parallel broader depressions which run into each other.

†**Undo·sous,** *a. Obs.*⁻⁰ (Cf. prec. and -ous.)

**1623** Cockeram i, *Vndosous*, full of surges and waues. **1644** *Vindex Anglicus* 6 [in list of pedantic words].

**Undo·tted,** *ppl. a.* (Un-[1] 8.) **1830** Lindley *Nat. Syst. Bot.* 101 Pinnated resinous undotted leaves. **1891** *Science-Gossip* XXVII. 95/1 The stonechat and whinchat seem to have dotted and undotted eggs with almost equal frequency.

**Undou·ble,** *v.* [Un-[2] 6.]

**1. a.** *trans.* To take out of a doubled or folded state; to straighten out. **b.** *intr.* To become unfolded or straight.

**1611** Florio, *Sdoppiare*, to vndouble, to vnfold. **1683** Moxon *Mech. Exerc., Printing* xxiv. ¶ 15 As he comes to a Token-sheet, he un-doubles that, and smooths out the Crease. **1730** A. Gordon *Maffei's Amphith.* 363 Then undoubling the Rope,..I extended the Rope with a Pin. **1850** Thackeray *Pendennis* lviii, The dirty fist..was obliged to undouble itself. **1889** *Advance* (Chicago) 14 Nov., To Jim's surprise, the fists undoubled, and no angry words came.

**2.** *Chess.* To move (pawns) so that one no longer stands directly in front of the other.

**1868** *Illustr. Lond. News* 25 Aug. 187 By this advance Dr. Lange undoubles and consolidates the Pawns on the Q's side, and thus adds greatly to the strength of his game.

**Undou·bled,** *ppl. a.* (Un-[1] 8.) **1598** Barret *Theor. Warres* iii. i. 40 The od file or rank which resteth vndoubled, may..close vp shoulder to shoulder.

**Undou·btable,** *a.* (and *adv.*). [Un-[1] 7 b, 5 b.] That cannot be doubted; indubitable.

*c* **1425** *St. Christina* Prol. 40 in *Anglia* VIII. 119 As wee haue leeryd be ful certeyne and vndoutabil tellynge. **1529** More *Dyaloge* iv. Wks. 265/1 That the gospell he had preached, was the plain, sure and undoubtable trouth. **1611** Cotgr., *Indubitable*, vndoubtable. **1665** J. Sergeant *Sure Footing* 233 How can their Authority ever come to be undoubtable or certain? **1815** LAMB *Lett.* (1888) I. 284 Let me..mention that my brother..has picked up an undoubtable picture of Milton. **1870** *Daily News* 21 Oct., The leading facts..I have..from an undoubtable source.

†**b.** As *adv.* = next. *Obs.*

*c* **1440** *Alph. Tales* 196 Þat þou may trow vndowtable at þe rysyng of deade folk sall be trew. **1513** DOUGLAS *Æneid* VI. v. 56 Anchises get!..Discend vndowtable of the goddis blude.

**Undou·btably,** *adv.* ? *Obs.* [UN-[1] 11, 5 b: cf. prec.] Without doubt; indubitably.

*c* **1425** *St. Eliz.* in *Anglia* VIII. 107/26 Þoos þinges þat I perceyued vndoutably with myn eyen. *c* **1449** PECOCK *Repr.* I. v. 26 Hise iij. parties schal conferme vndoutabli al what is seid here. *a* **1513** FABYAN *Chron.* VII. ccxxi. 244 Where thou sayest..that Gregory myght..haue confirmed all things vndowtably with this worde,..that is sothe.

**Undou·bted,** *ppl. a.* and *adv.* [UN-[1] 8, 8 c, 5 b.]

**1.** Not held doubtful in respect of fact.

*c* **1460** FORTESCUE *Abs. & Lim. Mon.* v. (1885) 119 But we must holde it for vndouted, þat ther mey no reaume prospere..vndir a poure kynge. **1487** HEN. VII in *Ep. Acad. Oxon.* (1898) II. 514 Yff ye will take hym as fore a scolare, as we hold it undowted ye wyll nott do. **1590** SWINBURNE *Testaments* 191 If it be certaine and vndoubted, that the testament is written or subscribed with the testators owne hand. **1634** SIR T. HERBERT *Trav.* 81 The mighty Army and vndoubted threats of the King. **1757** W. WILKIE *Epigon.* Pref. p. iv, This is his undoubted privilege; and I have no intention to break in upon it. **1791** COWPER *Judgm. Poets* 36 Adorning May..With June's undoubted right. **1839** T. MITCHELL *Frogs of Aristoph.* Introd. p. xci, It is the undoubted business of learned men to profit by those hints.

**2.** Of persons: Not called in question in respect of status or character.

*c* **1460** *Brut* II. 514 The general Counsel of Basil deposed Eugeny, which was only Pope & vndoubted. **1568** GRAFTON *Chron.* II. 643 King Richard the seconde was the true and vndoubted heyre to the valiant Conquerour. **1593** SHAKS. 3 *Hen. VI*, v. vii. 6 Three Dukes of Somerset, threefold Renowne, For hardy and vndoubted Champions. **1659** PEARSON *Creed* (1839) 173 It is true, at first he was subject ..to his reputed father and undoubted mother. *a* **1718** PRIOR *Power* 464 He made Me to his Crimes undoubted Heir. **1751** EARL ORRERY *Remarks Swift* (1752) 14 She was ..the concealed, but undoubted wife of Dr. Swift. **1827** SCOTT *Surg. Dau.* iv, Mr. Gray is an undoubted judge.. what person will best suit him as a professional assistant.

**3.** Not affected or impaired by doubt; absolute, complete.

**1489** *Cov. Leet Bk.* 536 Wherin ye may be..ioyous and haue full trust and vndoubted affiance therunto. **1560** DAUS tr. *Sleidane's Comm.* 182 Wherof..the Bisshops legat hath put him into an undoubted hope. **1813** SHELLEY *Q. Mab* IX. 82 Those delicate and timid impulses..with undoubted confidence disclosed The growing longings of..love.

**4.** About the nature of which no doubt is entertained; accepted as true, certain, or genuine.

**1513** MORE *Rich. III*, Wks. 61/1 This is his own countenance,..yᵉ sure vndoubted image..of that noble Duke. **1577** HANMER *Anc. Eccl. Hist.* 56 The undoubted writings of Clement are apparent. **1665** J. SPENCER *Vulg. Proph.* 42 That natural wisdom,..of which the true prophets of God gave such undoubted evidences. **1710** BERKELEY *Princ. Hum. Knowl.* § 10 An undoubted truth, which they can demonstrate beyond all exception. **1808** L. MURRAY *Eng. Gram.* I. 199 An historian of undoubted credit. **1897** J. W. CLARK *Barnwell* Intr. 13 Relics of undoubted authenticity.

†**b.** Similarly with *of*. *Obs.*

**1683** D. A. *Art Converse* 40 'Tis an undoubted of truth, that the greatest swearers are commonly the greatest liars.

†**5.** As *adv.* = UNDOUBTEDLY *adv.* 1. *Obs.*

Common in the early part of the 16th cent.

*a* **1500** *Coventry Corpus Chr. Pl.* I. 395 Ondowtid sche ys cum of hy parrage. **1523** FITZHERB. *Husb.* § 146 Vndouted a woman can-not gette her lyuynge honestely with spynnynge on the distaffe.

Hence **Undou·btedness.**

**1691** W. NICHOLLS *Answ. Naked Gospel* Pref. C j, When he has full assurance of the undoubtedness of the Testimony.

**Undou·btedly,** *adv.* [UN-[1] 11, 5 b; cf. prec.]

**1.** Without or beyond any doubt; indubitably, assuredly, certainly.

?*a* **1500** *Chester Pl.* xiii. 180 Our sonne he is,..And blynde was borne undowtedlye. **1551** T. WILSON *Logike* (1580) 37 By searchyng euery borough he shall haue his purpose vndoubtedly. **1585** T. WASHINGTON tr. *Nicholay's Voy.* IV. xxxv. 158 b, They (quoth he) are vndoubtedly condemned by nature. **1662** STILLINGFL. *Orig. Sacræ* II. i. § 3 The Records under the name of Moses were undoubtedly his. **176.** WILKES *Corr.* (1805) III. 13 This is undoubtedly the handsomest compliment that has been paid to his present majesty. **1838** JAMES *Louis XIV*, I. 164 He was, however, undoubtedly a man of much courage. **1874** GREEN *Short Hist.* iii. § 6 (1882) 147 The influence which the Friars undoubtedly exerted.

**b.** Used to introduce a sentence.

**1521** WOLSEY in *St. Papers Hen. VIII*, VI. 85 And ondowgtydly, by all apparance, He shall prove a very wyse man. **1596** *Edward III*, II. ii. 20 Vndoubtedly, then, some thing is a misse. **1663** COWLEY *Cutter Coleman St.* II. vii, Undoubtedly they had a Hand in't. **1765** *Museum Rust.* IV. 185 Undoubtedly the farmers will think the charges of this feed too great. **1834** J. H. NEWMAN *Par. Serm.* I. i. 2 Undoubtedly He may prescribe the terms on which He will give it. **1878** SEELEY *Stein* II. 160 Undoubtedly this refusal was honourable to him.

†**2.** In a manner which removes or rejects all doubt; positively, decidedly. *Obs.*

**1513** *Life Hen. V* (1911) 182 When this..Kinge was vndoubtedly acertained of his phisicions that the time of his resolucion approached. **1584** R. SCOT *Discov. Witchcr.* III. xix. 56 They affirme undoubtedlie, that the divell plaieth Succubus to the man. **1638** R. BAKER tr. *Balzac's Lett.* (vol. II) 36, I..assure you most undoubtedly, that [etc.].

**1653** H. MORE *Antid. Ath.* I. ii. § 3 The thing that it doth thus resolvedly and undoubtedly reject.

**Undou·btful,** *a.* [UN-[1] 7.]

†**1.** Not mixed with or qualified by doubt; firm, sure. *Obs.*

*c* **1450** *Oseney Reg.* 161 Vndowtefull feith to þese presente writynges to ȝeve. **1508** FISHER 7 *Penit. Ps.* li. Wks. (1876) 94 He promyseth very true and vndoubtefull hope to hymselfe of the desyre that he asketh. *a* **1626** W. SCLATER *Exp. Rom.* iv. (1650) 134 Sure..to us, in respect of our apprehension, and undoubtful perswasion.

**2.** Not admitting of doubt; free from any dubiety; positive, certain.

**1533–4** *Act* 25 *Hen. VIII*, c. 22 § 2 The laufull matrimonie ..shall be..taken for vndoubtfull, trewe, sincere, and perfecte. **1619** W. SCLATER *Exp.* 1 *Thess.* (1630) 22 Is the cleannesse of the outward life an vndoubtful euidence of the cleannesse of the heart? **1655** tr. *Sorel's Com. Hist. Francion* XII. 25 To render the affair more criminal and undoubtful, I came hither. **1856** MRS. BROWNING *Aur. Leigh* III. 539 A girl of doubtful life, undoubtful birth.

**3.** Not feeling doubt; certain (*of* something).

**1613** FLETCHER, etc. *Hon. Man's Fortune* I. i, Our husbands might have lookt into our thoughts, And made themselves undoubtfull. **1773** J. ROSS *Fratricide* v. 630 (MS.), And ..Justice bids go on Undoubtful of his patronizing pow'r.

Hence **Undou·btfulness.**

**1619** W. SCLATER *Exp.* 1 *Thess.* (1630) 241 Some Foole I haue heard boasting of vndoubtfulnesse for the matter of their owne saluation.

**Undou·btfully,** *adv.* [UN-[1] 11; cf. prec.] † Without doubt; indubitably.

**1628** VERSTEGAN *Dec. Intell.* ii. 51 Such as so persuade themselues are therin vndoubtfully deceiued. **1629** LYNDE *Via Tuta* 251 Little can be said of any certainty, or as vndoubtfully true.

**Undou·bting,** *ppl. a.* (and *adv.*). [UN-[1] 10.]

†**1.** *Sc.* Undoubted; also *adv.*, undoubtedly. *Obs.*

*c* **1400** *Sc. Trojan War* II. 2887 At his moder he gan Inquere Quho was his fader vndowtand. **1552** ABP. HAMILTON *Catech.* (1884) 4 It is undoutand ane synfull..thing to varie and discord in materis of our faith.

**2.** Harbouring no doubts; confident.

**1735** BERKELEY *Free-think. in Math.* § 1 Asserting with such undoubting assurance things so easily disproved. **1788** V. KNOX *Winter Even.* xi. (1790) II. 71 When any man speaks with the assurance of undoubting conviction. **1810** SCOTT *Lady of L.* I. xxxiii, Again returned the scenes of youth, Of confident undoubting truth. **1828** WEBSTER s.v., An undoubting believer. **1870** BRYANT *Iliad* IV. I. 112 All this I know in my undoubting mind.

Hence **Undou·btingness.**

**1857** M. PATTISON *Ess.* (1889) II. 404 We can turn the history of a foreign people into doctrine..with a rapidity and undoubtingness which fail us when we attempt our own. **1871** W. G. WARD *Ess. Philos. Theism* (1884) I. 14 The mere undoubtingness of an assent..arises from mere accident.

**Undou·btingly,** *adv.* [UN-[1] 11; cf. prec.]

**1.** Without harbouring any doubts; unhesitatingly; with confidence.

*c* **1400** *Sc. Trojan War* II. 788 He lay befor þe gret altere.. Wndoutandly [L. *indubitanter*] þe dede bydand. **1742** RICHARDSON *Pamela* IV. 337, I..shall then be able to let you know all my Sentiments..more undoubtingly, as I shall be more improv'd by Years. **1802** MRS. E. PARSONS *Myst. Visit* II. 9 Neither did she consign him over undoubtingly to guilt and shame. **1882** H. S. HOLLAND *Logic & Life* iv. 62 We know undoubtingly what good is, and what evil is.

†**2.** *Sc.* Undoubtedly. *Obs.*[—1]

**1552** ABP. HAMILTON *Catech.* (1884) 64 Undoutandly the abhominabil abusioun of the name of God..bringis apon vs the vengeance of God.

† **Undou·btly,** obs. var. UNDOUBTEDLY *adv.*

**1487** HEN. VII in *Ep. Acad. Oxon.* (1898) II. 517 Oure extent in thys partie shalbe undowtly executed. **1539** TAVERNER *Erasm. Prov.* (1552) 48 Undoutly, nothynge is more hurtfull to a man, then selfe loue is.

† **Undou·btous,** *a. Obs.*[—1] [UN-[1] 7.] Undoubtful, undoubted.

*c* **1374** CHAUCER *Boeth.* v. pr. i. (1868) 149 Syn it nis nat to douten of þe þinges folwynge whan euery side of þi disputisoun shal be stedfast to me by vndoutous [L. *indubitata*] feiþ.

**Undou·ght.** *Sc.* Now *rare* or *Obs.* Forms: 6 wn-, 7 vn-, undought; 6 wn-, vn-, 8 undocht, 7 vndoght; 6 vndoche, 7 undoch. [UN-[1] 12 + DOUGHT *sb.* or *a.* Cf. NFris. *ündöght* worthless person; WFris. *on-, ûnducht* corrupt or morbid matter; obs. Flem. *ondocht* a worthless kind of crab (Kilian).] An ineffective worthless person. (Cf. WANDOUGHT.)

**1508** KENNEDIE *Flyting w. Dunbar* 508 Tak the a fidill, or a floyt & geste, Wndought [*v.r.* vndocht], thou art ordanyt to not ellis! *a* **1583** MONTGOMERIE *Flyting* 454 (Tullib. MS.), Let nevir þis vndoche [*v.rr.* vndoght, vndought] of evill doing Irk. **1636** W. SCOT *Apol. Narr.* (1846) 239 Mr. George Grahame, the undought of Bishops. **1679** in Wodrow *Hist. Suff. Ch. Scot.* (1828) IV. 501 Mr. Brown being removed, they will have little to do to trample upon the poor undought that is left behind. **1721** RAMSAY *Poems* Gloss., *Undocht*, or *wandocht*, a silly weak person.

† **Undou·ghty,** *a. Obs.* [UN-[1] 7. Cf. MDu. *onduchtich, -dochtich*, MLG. *undochtich*, MHG. *untuchtic* (G. *untüchtig*), MDa. and Da. *udygtig*.] Lacking in good qualities; worthless, bad, vile.

*a* **1225** *Juliana* 4 (Royal MS.), Maximian þe modi keiser.. wið unmeð muchel hird & unduhti duheðe. *c* **1460** *Towneley Myst.* xxiv. 367 Now thise dyse that ar vndughty for los of this good, here I forswere hertely. **1570** *Satir. Poems Reform.* xxiv. 43 Deir sall ȝe by ȝone foule vnduchtie deid.

† **Undow·ed,** *ppl. a. Obs.* [UN-[1] 8 + DOW *v.*[2]] Unendowed.

*c* **1380** WYCLIF *Sel. Wks.* III. 357 As þis power were in vein ȝif þe Chirche were undowid. **1596** WARNER *Alb. Eng.* XI. lxii. (1597) 288 How seldome Women come vndow'd with.. answerable Faults to these. **1648** HEXHAM II, *Onbegaeft*, Vndowed, or Vngifted.

**Undow·ered,** *ppl. a.* (UN-[1] 8.)

**1803** GODWIN *Chaucer* II. xlvi. 378 The other [religion] humble, naked and undowered. **1830** D'ISRAELI *Chas. I*, III. viii. 161 His celebrated but undowered daughter. **1876** MISS BRADDON *Dead Men's Shoes* I. ii. 27 He.., if Nature's bounties are to be counted as a heritage, is not undowered.

**Undow·ned,** *a.* (UN-[1] 9 + DOWN *sb.*[2]). **1657** LOVELACE *Poems* (1864) 251 When thy undown'd face mov'd the Nine to shake.

**Undra·g,** *v.* (UN-[2] 4 b.) **1809** MAR. EDGEWORTH *Ennui* iii, When we had dragged and undragged, and came up with Paddy, we found him..mending some of his tackle.

**Undra·goned,** *a.* (UN-[1] 9.) **1868** BROWNING *Ring & Bk.* VI. 1772 The officious priest would personate Saint George For a mock Princess in undragoned days.

**Undrai·nable,** *a.* [UN-[1] 7 b.]

**1.** Incapable of being drained dry; inexhaustible.

**1611** COTGR., *Inespuisable*,..undraynable, which cannot be dryed vp, or laden dry. **1627** J. CARTER *Plain Expos.* 108 Your heauenly Father,..The undrainable Fountaine of all goodnesse. **1652** J. WRIGHT tr. *Camus' Nat. Paradox* I. 6 A very plentiful and almost undreinable source of riches. **1842** TENNYSON *Œnone* 113 Overflowing revenue..from labour'd mines undrainable of ore.

**2.** Incapable of being freed from water by means of draining.

**1852** HENFREY *Veget. Europe* 181 Parts..irreclaimable to cultivation..being either steep arid slopes of the hills or undrainable bogs. **1884** *Harper's Mag.* Apr. 761/1 Undrainable or undrained..surfaces.

**Undrai·ned,** *ppl. a.* (UN-[1] 8.)

**1573** TUSSER *Husb.* (1878) 114 The fen and the quamire,.. Which yeerelie vndrained..annoieth the meadowes that thereon doo but. **1697** DRYDEN *Æneis* III. 921 The..fenny lake, undrained by Fate's decree. **1761** STERNE *Tr. Shandy* IV. xxxi, A fine, large, whinny, undrained, unimproved common. **1812** *Examiner* 11 May 292/1 Ill-cultivated and undrained soils. **1898** *Allbutt's Syst. Med.* V. 350 In some cases of small empyema, even when undrained.

**Undrama·tic,** *a.* [UN-[1] 7.]

**1.** Lacking the essential qualities of drama.

**1754** A. MURPHY *Gray's Inn Jrnl.* No. 94, The following Lines..are certainly very inartificial and undramatic. **1805** *Ann. Rev.* III. 621 As works of literary art, these dialogues are dull and undramatic. **1861** GEO. ELIOT in Cross *Life* (1885) II. 289 These less known undramatic tales of want.

**2.** Not gifted with or exhibiting dramatic power; not adapted for the production of drama.

**1769** *Garrick's Vagary* 10 Procuring the Stage's deliverance from the many undramatic Beasts of Lumber. **1821** BYRON *Let.* Jan., Wks. 194/2 Many people think my talent essentially undramatic. **1870** LOWELL *Among my Bks.* Ser. I. (1873) 205 Goethe affirmed, that..Shakespeare was too undramatic for the German theatre.

**b.** Unable to appreciate drama.

**1836** T. HOOK *G. Gurney* i, English audiences, who are..as undramatic in their notions as methodists.

**3.** Not written in the form of drama.

**1840** L. HUNT in *Dram. Wks. Wycherley*, etc. (Rtldg.) p. xxxv, Congreve's undramatic prose writings are few.

So **Undrama·tical** *a.*, **Undrama·tically** *adv.*

**1829** BEDDOES *Let.* Feb., in *Poems* (1851) p. lxxx, The play is too long;..the second [act] dull and *undramatical. **1827** SIR H. TAYLOR *Autobiog.* (1885) I. 97 If I were to write another play at this rate, I might die *undramatically before the fifth act. **1901** M. PEMBERTON *Pro Patria* XX. 223, I told him, undramatically, that I was the man.

**Undra·pe,** *v.* (UN-[2] 4.) **1869** *Sat. Rev.* 30 Jan. 140/1 Our own women are encouraged to undrape themselves for show and not for comfort.

**Undra·ped,** *ppl. a.* [UN-[1] 8.] Not furnished or covered with draperies; nude, naked.

**1814** *Monthly Rev.* LXXIII. 531 He observes that those.. intend to incur the contemplation of the undraped figure. **1866** *Athenæum* 24 Nov. 676/3 He made of the little, lively, happy fellow, a joyous, undraped child.

*fig.* **1870** BURTON *Hist. Scot.* lxii. (1873) V. 373 Although his indulgence in drinking was..undraped by any outward cover of decorum.

**Undra·peried,** *a.* (UN-[1] 9.) **1802** MME. D'ARBLAY *Diary* 4 May, My feet in their native, undraperied state. **1837** HAWTHORNE *Twice-told T.* (1851) I. vi. 95 The unplastered walls, the naked woodwork, and the undraperied pulpit.

**Undraw·,** *v.* [UN-[2] 3.]

†**1.** *trans.* To draw out, withdraw. *Obs.*

*c* **1400** *Trevisa's Higden* (Rolls) V. 373 Rosamunda..bonde so faste þe kynges swerd..þat it myȝte not be undrawe [*MS.* γ. y-drawe] out of þe scaberke.

**2.** To draw back (esp. a curtain); to unfasten by pulling.

**1677** MIÈGE II, To Undraw the curtains, *ouvrir les rideaux*. **1744** YOUNG *Nt. Th.* VII. 813 Death's inexorable hand Draws the dark curtain close; undrawn no more. *Ibid.* 1107 Angels undrew the curtain of the throne. **1791** MRS. RADCLIFFE *Rom. Forest* iv, The door was held by two strong bolts. Having undrawn these, it disclosed a flight of steps. **1839** LADY LYTTON *Cheveley* (ed. 3) III. iii. 71 He undrew the window curtain, and sat in the window. **1872** J. L. SANFORD *Estimates Eng. Kings, Jas. I*, 324 In the cause of the Palatine..the purse-strings of the English people would have been willingly undrawn.

**3.** *intr.* To move back on being pulled.

**1794** MRS. RADCLIFFE *Myst. Udolpho* xxxiii, Emily presently heard..the heavy chain fall, and the bolts undraw of a small postern door. **1845** BROWNING *How they brought the News* 3 'Good speed!' cried the watch, as the gate-bolts undrew.

Hence **Undraw·ing** *vbl. sb.*

**1797** MRS. RADCLIFFE *Italian* xix, She distinguished the undrawing of iron bars.

**Undraw·n,** *ppl. a.*[1] [UN-[1] 8.]

†1. ?That has never drawn a plough. *Obs.*
1527 *Lanc. Wills* (Chetham Soc.) I. 32 A heffur in calf and ij bolokks of the best sort undrawen.
2. a. Not disembowelled.
1562 Turner *Herbal* II. 25 At the tyme of yeare the feldefares fede only of Iuniper berries the people Eate the feldefares undrawen.
b. Unmilked.
1820 Shelley *Prometh. Unb.* II. ii. 90 Noontide would come, And thwart Silenus find his goats undrawn.
3. Not drawn from a receptacle; untapped.
a 1595 Southwell *Christs Bloody Sweat* 3 Fat soil, full spring, sweet olive, grape of bliss,..Untill'd, undrawn, unstamp'd, untouch'd of press. 1809 Byron *Bards & Rev.* 636 Beer undrawn, and beards unmown. 1868 R. Buchanan *Tragic Dramas, Wallace* I. iii, Even at the first assault,.. A drop of blood undrawn, the dastard fled.
4. Not drawn, dragged, or pulled along, out, etc. Also with *forth*.
1667 Milton *P. L.* vi. 751 Forth rush'd with whirl-wind sound The Chariot of Paternal Deitie,..Wheele within Wheele undrawn. 1730 *Act 3 Geo. II*, c. 25 § 11 The same Names shall be..returned to the former Box or Glass, there to be kept with the other Names remaining at that Time undrawn. 1760 Sterne *Tr. Shandy* iv. *Slawkenb. T.*, Was there in the great arsenal of chance, one single engine left undrawn forth to torture your curiosities? 1837 Lytton *Athens* II. 219 Lamenting..that his sword was as yet undrawn against the invader. 1899 *Westm. Gaz.* 16 June 2/1 The casting-line should be of the finest undrawn gut.
b. Of a lottery: cf. Draw *v.* 34.
1730 Fielding *Author's Farce* I. i, A Benefit-Ticket in an un-drawn Lottery.
5. Not delineated or depicted.
1742 Young *Nt. Th.* II. 621 The Death-bed of the just! is yet undrawn By mortal hand.

**Undraw·n**, *ppl. a.*[2] [f. Undraw *v.*] Drawn back, withdrawn.
1748 Richardson *Clarissa* (1811) III. iii. 30, I have told thee what were my transports, when the undrawn bolt presented to me my long-expected goddess.

**Undrea·ded**, *ppl. a.* (Un-[1] 8.)
1535 *Aberdeen Reg.* (Jam.), And cam nocht to be ondreyd be him thairof. 1647 Stanley *Poems, Europa* 11 Oh whither sacred Bull? who art thou, say! That through undreaded flouds canst break thy way. 1692 Ray *Disc.* 239 A dreadful indeed, but by thee formerly undreaded sentence. 1784 Cowper *Task* II. 811 Vice parries wide Th' undreaded volley with a sword of straw. 1834 *Tait's Mag.* I. 338/2 Death, undreaded, approached; and the spirit departed. a 1873 Lytton *Pausanias* i, The unexpected, and not undreaded, approach of the great Pausanias.

**Undrea·dful**, *a. rare.* [Un-[1] 7.]
†1. Having no dread; unapprehensive (*of*). *Obs.*
c 1400 *Comm. Luke* i. 13 (MS. Bodl. 143), þe deuels cruelte is best ouercomon bi vndredeful feiþ. 1648 Herrick *Hesper.*, *Christian Militant*, A man prepar'd against all ills to come, ..Undreadfull too of courtly thunderclaps.
2. Not causing dread.
1611 Florio, *Informidabile*, vndreadfull, not terrible.
So **Undrea·dfully** *adv.*, † without dread or fear.
c 1430 *Life St. Katherine* (Roxb. Club) 34 She made vppon hir self þe token of þe crosse and vndredfully went vnto þe paleys. a 1440 *Found. St. Bartholomew's* (E.E.T.S.) 55 For cause, yn rycchynge of thy-self othir men thou spoylid vndredfully, now thou begynnyst to nede.

**Undrea·ding**, *ppl. a.* (Un-[1] 5 d, 10.) 1745 Eliza Heywood *Female Spect.* III. 171 By them we sleep securely, undreading all Incursions and foreign Depredations. 1750 Collins *Ode Superstit. Highlands* 166 They.., Along th' Atlantic rock, undreading, climb. 1830 Tennyson *Grasshopper* I. 16 Unknowing fear, Undreading loss.

**Undrea·med, -drea·mt**, *ppl. a.* [Un-[1] 8, 8 c.]
1. Not apprehended (even) in a dream or dreams; not imagined or thought of.
1611 Shaks. *Wint. T.* iv. iv. 578 A Course more promising, Then a wild dedication of your selues To vnpath'd Waters, vndream'd Shores. 1827 Moore *Alciphron* iii. 278 A light Leading to undreamt happiness. 1880 E. White *Cert. Relig.* 48 That Voice which..lifted up men's thoughts to heights undreamed before.
2. With *of*. (Cf. Dream *v.*[2] 1.)
1636 Pagitt *Christianography* (ed. 2) II. 40 Ecclesiasticks were unexempted, and deposing of Kings was then undreamed of. 1674 Boyle *Excell. Theol.* II. v. 213 Even practical inventions..by undreamed of discoveries may be brought to lose the general reputation they had. 1802 Coleridge *Dejection* v, A new Earth.., Undreamt of by the sensual and the proud. 1860 Ruskin *Unto this Last* ii. (1896) 65 In some far-away and yet undreamt-of hour. 1880 Geo. Eliot in Cross *Life* (1885) III. 406 The great, once undreamed-of change in my life.

**Undrea·ming**, *ppl. a.* (Un-[1] 10.) 1831 Lamb *Elia* II. *Ellistoniana*, The days when, undreaming of Theatres and Managerships, thou wert a scholar. 1850 L. Hunt *Autobiog.* ii. 41 The most real of all things, and our only undreaming time. **Undrea·my**, *a.* (Un-[1] 7.) 1849 Lytton *Caxtons* II. i, My love for study..was a vigorous, wakeful, undreamy love. **Undre·ggy**, *a.* (Un-[1] 7.) 1720 T. Boston *Fourfold State* (1784) 12 Man had a life of pure delight and undreggy pleasure in this state.

†**Undrei·gh**, *a. Obs. rare.* [Un-[1] 7 + *dreigh* Dree *a.* Cf. ON. *údrjúgr* (Norw. *udrjug*, Sw. *odryg*, Da. *udrøi*) falling short, insufficient.]
1. ?Lacking in diligence; slack.
a 1310 in Wright *Lyric P.* xii. 41 To hem he sayde an heh, That suythe he[m] wes undreh, so ydel forte stonde.
2. Not tedious or tiresome.
a 1400 in *Hampole's Wks.* (1895) I. 80 Þi dayes sal be vndregh, þat þe na sorow schende.

**Undre·nched**, *ppl. a.* (Un-[1] 8.) 1627 May *Lucan* ix. R 3 b, You slowly seeing Cynosure, suppose Her vndrench'd carre into the Ocean goes. 1794 Campbell tr. *Medea Antist.* II. 16 The blade, undrenched in blood's eternal dye.

**U·ndress, undre·ss**, *sb.* [Un-[1] 12.]
1. Partial or incomplete dress; dress of a kind not ordinarily worn in public; dishabille. Also (esp. of men), informal or ordinary dress, as distinct from that worn on ceremonial or special occasions.
a. Of women.
The common use during the 18th century.
1685 Crowne *Sir C. Nice* iv, To-day the beauty lyes ambush'd in undresses, the hair pin'd up in papers. a 1704 T. Brown *Pleasant Lett. to Gent.* Wks. 1709 III. II. 15 How he surpriz'd a famous Miss of the Town, dining at her Lodgings in an Undress. 1767 *Lond. Gaz.* No. 10716. 2/1 The Ladies to wear black Silk or Velvet...Undress, white or grey Lustrings [etc.]. 1785 Sarah Fielding *Ophelia* I. viii, The night-gowns and common undresses were grown familiar to me. 1821 Scott *Kenilw.* xxii, Where she sat.. adorned with all that Janet's art, and a rich and tasteful undress, could bestow. a 1847 [see Dishabille 2].
b. Of men.
1683 Dryden *Life Plutarch* 94 Here you are led into the private lodgings of the hero; you see him in his undress. a 1700 Evelyn *Diary* 4 Feb. 1685, He had ben on the bed, but was now risen and in his undresse. 1767 *Lond. Gaz.* No. 10716. 2/1 The Men to continue in Black full trimmed; ..Undress, light grey Frocks. 1821 Scott *Kenilw.* xxxii, Varney..had changed his splendid attire, and now waited on his patron in a very modest and plain undress. 1853 R. S. Surtees *Sponge's Sp. Tour* viii, There are few more difficult persons to identify than a huntsman in undress.
c. *Mil.* and *Naval*: Dress or uniform authorized to be worn on ordinary occasions, as distinguished from *full* or *service dress*.
1748 Smollett *R. Random* xx, To get into [Captain] O'Donnell's apartment, while he was abroad in an undress, and examine his sword. 1783 *Ann. Reg., Chron.* 193/2 Undress. Admiral's. A blue cloth frock, with blue cuff and blue lappels. 1829 S. Haigh *Sk. Buenos Ayres & Chile* 123 The soldiers wore what I supposed was their undress; it consisted of a military cap, a poncho, and sandals of hide. 1849 Lever *Con Cregan* v, A young officer, in a cavalry undress. 1857 *Dress Regul. Army* 28 Scarlet Undress... Blue Undress. 1879 *Unif. Reg.* in *Navy List* July (1882) 487/2 Trowsers, without lace.—As in undress.
2. *transf.* and *fig.*
(*a*) 1684 T. Burnet *Theory Earth* I. 141 'Tis very useful ..to look often upon such bare draughts as shew us nature in an undress. 1692 Dryden *Cleomenes* iv. i, This famine has a sharp and meagre face: 'Tis death in an undress of skin and bone. c 1705 Pope *Imit. Eng. Poets, Cowley's Garden* 6 Where Lilies smile in virgin robes of white, The thin Undress of superficial Light. 1853 Is. Williams *Baptistery* I. xi. (1874) 138 Such Basil's Pontic home, .. beautiful in nature's stern undress.
(*b*) 1797 *Monthly Mag.* III. 493/1 When we are able to attend the author in the sequestered scenes of life, and contemplate the undress of his mind. 1825 *Examiner* 738/2 We now and then detected a little colloquial undress in the female dialogue. 1886 Pater *Appreciations* (1890) 127 When he writes (still in undress) he does but take the 'friendly reader' into his confidence.
3. *attrib.* Constituting an undress; worn when in undress; *spec.* in *Mil.* and *Naval* use (see 1 c).
1829 Marryat *F. Mildmay* vii, The officers in their undress uniform. 1844 *Regul. & Ord. Army* 132 When Officers attend in Uniform as spectators at the Review,..they are not to appear in Blue Frock-Coats or Undress Jackets. 1894 Mrs. Dyan *Man's Keeping* (1899) 238 The Collector of Poggulpore's portly form, in very much undress garb. *fig.* 1806 W. Taylor in Robberds *Mem.* (1843) II. 135 The simple, idiomatic, undress, conversational tone of Lessing's blank verse.

**Undre·ss**, *v.* [Un-[2] 4.]
1. *refl.* To divest (oneself) of clothing.
1596 Shaks. *Tam. Shr.* Induct. ii. 119 Madam vndresse you, and come now to bed. 1674 J. B[rian] *Harv. Home* iv. 29 T' undress themselves they all see cause, And call'd to come they seldome use to pause. 1712 *Spect.* No. 506 ¶ 5 A French Woman offering to undress and dress herself before the Lover. 1788 Gibbon *Decl. & F.* l. V. 184 Undress thyself, thy aunt..is without a garment. 1853 *Arab. Nts.* (Rtldg.) 149 She then undressed herself and went to bed.
b. *intr.* To take off one's clothes.
a 1625 Fletcher *Noble Gent.* II. ad fin., What are you mad, to make me Dress, and undress,..Because you find me plyant? a 1721 Prior *Truth & Falsehood* 25 Falsehood more leisurely undrest, And laying by Her tawdry vest, Trick'd her self out in Truth's array. c 1755 in B. Ward *Hist. St. Edmund's Coll.* (1893) 302 It is always one of the Masters Business to be present while they are undressing. 1841 Lane *Arab. Nts.* I. 121 In cold weather, the bather undresses in the former. 1885 *Law Rep.* 10 P. D. 93 She lay down on the bed in her clothes, and for three hours refused to undress.
†c. *refl.* and *intr.* To change one's dress. *Obs.*
1760–72 H. Brooke *Fool of Qual.* (1809) IV. 83 If such a fine gentleman could condescend to undress himself, you might come..as a person who wanted hire. 1769 Lady Mary Coke *Jrnl.* 15 June, Being engaged to dine at the Imperial Ambassador's at Kensington I undressed and set out at four o'clock.
2. *trans.* To divest or strip (a person) of clothes.
1615 G. Sandys *Trav.* 67 Women stand prepared to vndresse her. 1732 Lediard *Sethos* II. ix. 282 He caus'd him to be undress'd in his presence. 1796 Mme. D'Arblay *Camilla* V. 453 She resisted being undressed, and was seized with an aguish shivering fit. 1838 [Mrs. Maitland] *Lett. fr. Madras* (1843) 206 The ayah undressed me as quickly as she could. 1885 R. Buchanan *Annan Water* ii, We must undress the child at once and put him to bed.
b. In fig. uses.
1633 P. Fletcher *Poet. Misc., Ps. lxiii*, ii, Till I slumber, and death shall undresse me, Thus will I sing. 1668 Bp. Hopkins *Serm., Vanity* (1685) 143 It is childish to quarrel at that hand which undresses us..only to lay us to sleep. a 1734 North *Examen* Pref. (1740) p. i, The present Writer hath chosen..to undress a filthy Libel not long since published. 1883 G. Moore *Modern Lover* (1887) 75 He was conscious that Lord Seaton was undressing him with a look, and already knew that his clothes had come from Halet's.
c. To strip *of* something.
1641 Milton *Ch. Govt.* II. Wks. 1851 III. 177 The protestant religion..must undresse them of all their guilded vanities. a 1699 J. Beaumont *Psyche* xvi. xvii, Disrobe me of my Beauty, and unty My closest veins; undress me of my skin.
d. To dress scantily or lightly.
1818 *La Belle Assemblée* XVII. 75/1 She shrunk from the gaze on that display which mamma had undressed her in.
†3. To undo or disarrange (the hair). *Obs.*
1598 Florio, *Scapigliare*,..to vndresse or vntie ones head or haires. 1601 Weever *Mirr. Mart.* B ij b, The baulme-sweet breathing of the aire..diuides each haire, each plight vndresses. 1652 Crashaw *Carmen Deo Nostro, Epiphanie* (Close), Thus he undresses His sacred unshorn tres[s]es.
4. To remove the dressing from (a wound).
1651 Davenant *Gondibert* I. vi. xxxiv, His hands the duke's worst-order'd wounds undress And gently binde.
Hence **Undre·sser**. *rare.*
1611 Cotgr., *Desapareilleur*, an vndresser; a maker vnreadie; a disorderer. 1658 Cokaine *Epithalamium* Poems 134 The fearfull Virgin's lead away;..And her undresse[r]s tell next morn, What she must rise.

**Undre·ssed**, *ppl. a.* [Un-[1] 8, 8 c.]
I. Not dressed by trimming, putting in order, or preparing in some way.
1. Of the hair. (Cf. Dress *v.* 13 b.)
1445 tr. *Claudian* in *Anglia* XXVIII. 281 Gallia fers with heere vndressid stode with a coler of price, Holdyng in hande ij. dartys to gider. 1598 Florio, *Scapigliata*, desheueled, vnkembd, vndrest about the head.
b. *fig.* Inelegant, unkempt.
1588 Shaks. *L. L. L.* iv. ii. 17 To show as it were his inclination after his vndressed, vnpolished..fashion.
c. Of a horse: Ungroomed.
1731 Fielding *Grub St. Op.* I. ix, Have I not left my horses undrest, to whet thy knives?
2. †a. Of places (or things) in respect of orderly appearance or arrangement. *Obs.*
1530 *Nottingham Rec.* III. 364 [He] suffreth the merkett places to be vndressed. 1611 Cotgr., *Taudis*,..a foule, sluttish, vnhandsome, or vndressed roome. 1635 *Boston Rec.* (1877) II. 4 That all the wood..shall bee gathered up, and layd or heaped in pyles,..upon the forfeyture of 6s. for every load left undressed up. 1649 G. Daniel *Trinarch., Rich. II*, ccxxxix, Ashes flew about The vndrest Hearth, and the ill house-wif'd roome Lay all on heaps.
b. Of a shop-window. (Cf. Dress *v.* 8.)
1883 Miss Broughton *Belinda* II. vii, In the haberdashers' undressed windows..are to be seen nothing but bare boards and skeleton stands.
3. a. Of textile fabrics or materials. (Cf. Dress *v.* 13 g and 11.)
1535 *Act 27 Hen. VIII*, c. 13 § 1 Whiche white clothe.. shalbe..solde for lesse price..then thei shuld be vndressed. 1557 N. T. (Genev.) *Matt.* ix. 16 No man peceth an olde garment with a pece of new clothe and vndressed. 1617 Moryson *Itin.* III. 274 Strict Lawes are made..that the web vndressed be viewed by three skillfull men, and be marked according to the goodnes. 1670 R. Coke *Disc. Trade* 3 The Exportation of our White and Undrest Clothes. 1763 *Act 4 Geo. III*, c. 26 (*heading*), The Importation of..rough and undressed Flax. 1834 McCulloch *Dict. Commerce* (ed. 2) 646, Undressed hemp imported in 1831.
b. Of skins or leather. (Cf. Dress *v.* 13 f.)
1808 Scott *Marm.* v. v, The hunted red-deer's undress'd hide Their hairy buskins well supplied. 1853 Kane *Grinnell Exp.* v. (1856) 38 A black-locked Esquimaux, enveloped in an undressed seal-skin. 1898 *Daily News* 2 Dec. 5/1 The bindings in undressed morocco which mellows with age.
c. Of stone or wood. (Cf. Dress *v.* 11.)
1846 *Hull & Lincoln Railway Bill* 11 All undressed materials for the repair of public roads. 1854 H. Miller *Sch. & Schm.* (1858) 101 Flat undressed stones lay thick amid the rank grass. 1893 Earl Dunmore *Pamirs* I. 22 Piers composed entirely of undressed logs.
4. Of wounds or sores. (Cf. Dress *v.* 10.)
1597 A. M. tr. *Guillemeau's Fr. Chirurg.* 45 b/2 Simple Fractures, we keep sometimes sixe or seaven dayes vndressed. 1669 Earl Orrery *Parthen.* (1676) 781 Those slight hurts I had received, were still undrest. 1747 Doddridge *Col. Gardiner* 12 The poor Patient's Wound being still undressed. 1782 J. Warton *Ess. Pope* II. ix. 102 With their wounds undressed and putrifying. 1848 T. Aird *Christian Bride* III. xxxii, That I may know if, still his wounds undressed, 'Tis safe to move him farther on his way.
5. Of grounds, trees, etc. (Cf. Dress *v.* 13 c.)
1611 Bible *Lev.* xxv. 5 Thou shalt not..gather the grapes of thy Vine vndressed. — *2 Esdras* xvi. 78 Like as a field is..left vndressed. 1697 Dryden *Virg. Past.* II. 104 Thy vineyard lies half-pruned, and half-undressed. 1780 A. Young *Tour Irel.* I. 264 Crossing some of this undressed ground, we came to the point of a hill. 1813 Scott *Rokeby* II. xvii, Untrimm'd, undress'd, neglected now, Was alley'd walk and orchard bough.
6. Of food. (Cf. Dress *v.* 13 a.)
1647 Cowley *Mistress, Answ. Platonicks* 10 Beasts..taste those pleasures as they do their food; Undrest they tak't. 1714 *Advt.* in *Westm. Gaz.* 18 Mar. (1909) 2/3 If any.. bring with them their own Provisions for Eating, undressed, ..they may have them dress'd after their own way. 1771 Goldsm. *Haunch of Venison* 21 So I cut it [*sc.* venison], and sent it to Reynolds undrest. 1806 A. Hunter *Culina* (ed. 3) 220 A dish, that..differs very little from the flesh of an undressed lobster. 1832 R. & J. Lander *Exped. Niger* I. i. 22 The chief was eating an undrest onion.
II. 7. Not covered or invested with clothing; unclothed, naked (or nearly so).
1613 W. Browne *Brit. Past.* I. iv. 474 To see misfortune spending Her utmost rage on Truth, dispisde, distressed,

Unhappy, unrelieved, yet undressed. 1649 MARVELL in Lovelace *Poems* (1904) 5 The Ladies..all in mutiny though yet undrest Sally'd. 1749 FIELDING *Tom Jones* I. iii, He.. now..recollected his being undressed, and put an end to her terrors by desiring her to stay without the door. 1815 L. SIMOND *Tour Gt. Brit.* I. 3 The women highly dressed, or rather highly undressed, in extremely thin draperies. 1892 *Daily Tel.* 28 Apr. 3/2 What I would consider..indecent is a naked woman which represents an undressed woman.

*fig.* 1754 WARBURTON *Bolingbroke's Philos.* ii. 102 You catch his First Philosophy..undressed, and without a rag of form, but flaunting and fluttering in Fragments.

**8.** Not properly or fully dressed; wearing informal dress or undress.

1605 CHAPMAN *All Fooles* I. i. 73 Undressed, sluttish, nasty, to their husbands, Spung'd up, adorn'd, and painted to their lovers. 1668 PEPYS *Diary* 31 Mar., Took up my wife and Deb., and to the Park, where, being in a hackney, and they undressed, was ashamed to go into the tour. 1693 W. BOWLES in *Dryden's Juvenal* v. (1697) 96 Thus Blest, must Trebius to his Levees run,..Break off sweet Slumbers, drowsie, and undrest, To shew his Zeal. 1753 RICHARDSON *Grandison* (1781) II. iv. 42 You came, though undressed, with your sword on. 1792 A. YOUNG *Trav. France* 213 The orchestra powerful, yet..the musicians all so dirty and undressed. 1859 *Habits of Gd. Society* iii. 155 To be 'undressed' is to be dressed for work and ordinary occupations.

**b.** *transf.* Not of a dressy character; not requiring formal or full dress.

1798 JANE AUSTEN *Northang. Abb.* v, Neither at the upper nor lower rooms, at dressed or undressed balls, was he perceivable. 1809 MALKIN *Gil Blas* I. xv. ¶ 3 Plain cloths.. I threw aside with contempt, as thinking them too undrest.

**Undre·ssing,** *vbl. sb.* [f. UNDRESS *v.*] The action of taking off (one's own or another's) clothes.

1677 MIÉGE *Fr. Dict.* II. s.v., The Undressing of one. 1741–3 WESLEY *Jrnl.* (1749) 60 Our children were always put into a regular method of living,..as in dressing, undressing, changing their linen, etc. 1789 GOUV. MORRIS *Diary* 27 May, So we have the whole performance of undressing and dressing except the shift. 1824 BYRON *Juan* XVI. xi, But next to dressing for a rout or ball, Undressing is a woe. 1866 KINGSLEY *Herew.* xiv, The queen-countess' chamber, where a solemn undressing of that royal lady..took place.

*attrib.* 1697 POTTER *Archæol. Græca* I. 40 The Undressing-room. 1862 E. FALKENER *Ephesus* I. iv. 93 The large room at the back might be the apodyterium, or undressing-room.

**Undret,** obs. variant of HUNDRED.

**Undrie·d,** *ppl. a.* (UN-[1] 8.)

*c* 1440 *Pallad. on Husb.* XII. 454 Elm & asshe ydried beth rigent, And while they beth vndried, so curuable [etc.]. 1565 COOPER, *Insiccatus*,..vndried. 1683 MOXON *Mech. Exerc., Printing* xxiv. ¶ 10 Least his Weight pressing it cause the un-dryed Inck to Set-off. 1707 MORTIMER *Husb.* 139 Four pounds of undried Hops, thorough ripe. 1798 S. & HT. LEE *Canterb. T.* II. 372 The tears of apprehension were yet undried on the cheeks of Emily. 1801 *Farmer's Mag.* Apr. 215 An half boll of dried (about 8 pecks and a half of undried) bear.

**Undri·lled,** *ppl. a.* (UN-[1] 8.) [1775 ASH.] 1837 CARLYLE *Fr. Rev.* III. I. iv, All Paris shall..have itself enrolled. Unarmed,..and undrilled; but desperate. 1864 E. SARGENT *Peculiar* I. 17 A mob of undrilled, uneducated Africans.

†**Undrincled,** *ppl. a.*: see UN-[1] 3.

**Undri·nkable,** *a.* (UN-[1] 7 b.)

1611 COTGR., *Imbuvable*, vndrinkable, vnfit to be drunke of. 1826 DISRAELI *V. Grey* VI. i, We..refrain from refreshing our bodies with that sanctified and most undrinkable fluid. 1880 GEIKIE *Phys. Geog.* iii. 107 Should he taste some of this ..water he would find it salt and undrinkable.

Hence **Undri·nkably** *adv.*

1894 *Pall Mall Mag.* Nov. 455 It [*sc.* coffee] was not undrinkably bad.

**Undri·nking,** *vbl. sb.* (UN-[1] 13.) 1692 [see UNEATING *vbl. sb.*]. **Undri·vable,** *a.* (UN-[1] 7 b.) 1873 LYTTON *Ken. Chillingly* I. v, If it be hard to drive a common pig.., a hog in armour is indeed undrivable.

**Undri·ven,** *ppl. a.* [UN-[1] 8 b and 15. Cf. OE. *undrifen.*] Not forced on by driving.

1615 BP. HALL *Contempl., O. T.* x. vi, When maintenance and honour calls him, hee goes vndriuen. 1697 DRYDEN *Æneis* x. 499 The doubtful rack of heav'n Stands without motion, and the tyde undriv'n. 1748 RICHARDSON *Clarissa* (1811) I. 214 It shall sooner burst than voluntarily, uncompelled, undriven, dictate a measure that shall cast a slur.. upon them. 1892 M. DODS *John* II. xiii. 195 To stand before life as independent, unfettered, undriven men.

**b.** Of snow: (App. for DRIVEN *ppl. a.* 2).

1833 DISRAELI *Cont. Flem.* v. xxii, Its [Sunium's] columns against a dark cloud looked like undriven snow. 1865 GOSSE *Land & Sea* 195 The purity of the undriven snow.

**Undroo·ping,** *ppl. a.* (UN-[1] 10.)

1736 THOMSON *Liberty* v. 79 Whate'er..An ample generous Heart, undrooping Soul, And firm tenacious Valour can bestow. 1814 WORDSW. *Excurs.* VI. 1128 Bright garland form they for the pensive brow Of their undrooping Father's widowhood. 1854 J. D. BURNS *Vis. Prophecy* 121 Whose undrooping eye can keep Watch over His beloved.

**Undro·pped,** *ppl. a.* (UN-[1] 8.) 1798 COLERIDGE *Nightingale* 105 His fair eyes, that swam with undropped tears. **Undro·ssy,** *a.* (UN-[1] 7.) 1708 J. PHILIPS *Cyder* II. 228 Her wat'ry Skirts are edg'd With lucid Amber, or undrossy Gold. 1716 POPE *Iliad* VIII. 53 Of heaven's undrossy gold the god's array Refulgent, flash'd intolerable day.

**Undrow·ned,** *ppl. a.* [UN-[1] 8.] Not drowned, in various senses.

(*a*) 1573 TUSSER *Husb.* (1878) 104 To prouide ye of meadow for hay; if fennes be vndrowned, there cheapest ye may.

(*b*) 1610 SHAKS. *Temp.* II. i. 237 'Tis as impossible that hee's vndrown'd, As he that sleepes heere, swims. *Seb.* I haue no hope That hee's vndrown'd. *a* 1684 LEIGHTON *Com.* 1 *Pet.* iii. 21 (1849) II. 240 What availed it wicked Ham, to outlive the flood,..to be kept undrowned in the waters? 1849 ALISON *Hist. Eur.* II. viii. § 36 Such..as were thrown undrowned upon the shore. 1858 CARLYLE *Fredk. Gt.* v. vii. (1872) II. 128 Gundling..breaks a big hole in the ice, and scarcely..can be got out undrowned.

(*c*) 1838 [MRS. MAITLAND] *Lett. fr. Madras* (1843) 222, I was in hopes..I might be able to make out some of their tunes undrowned by their..accompaniments. 1861 GEO. ELIOT *Silas M.* i, A village where many of the old echoes lingered, undrowned by new voices.

**Undru·gged,** *ppl. a.*[1] (UN-[1] 8.) 1868 BROWNING *Ring & Bk.* VI. 1452 You lay down undrugged, I see. 1874 TYNDALL *Fragm. Sci.* (1879) II. x. 221 Out of the conflict of vanities his words emerge wholesome and strong, because undrugged by dogma. **Undru·gged,** *ppl. a.*[2] (UN-[2] 4 b, 8.) 1868 BROWNING *Ring & Bk.* II. 919 While Guido was left go and get undrugged.

**Undru·nk,** *ppl. a.* [UN-[1] 8 b, c.]

**1.** Not swallowed by drinking; not drunk.

1637 HEYWOOD *Pleas. Dial.* ii. Wks. 1874 VI. 124 The wine that men At merry meetings jovially downe poure, Is happier far, than what (vndrunke) growes soure. 1796 MME. D'ARBLAY *Camilla* II. 47 Feeling her chagrin almost intolerable, [she] quitted the room with her tea undrunk. 1897 *Daily News* 2 June 7/3 Kaiser's health undrunk. Odd omission at a Hamburg banquet.

**2.** Not drunk *to.* (Cf. DRINK *v.*[1] 13 b.)

1618 HOLYDAY *Marr. Arts* III. v, These Noune-Adiectiues of the Fœminine gender sit all this while vn-drunke to.

**Undru·nken,** *ppl. a.* [UN-[1] 8 b. Cf. (in sense a) ON. *údrukkinn*, (in sense b) MDu. and Du. *ongedronken*, MHG. *ungetrunken.*]

**a.** Not affected by drinking; not partaking of drink. **b.** = UNDRUNK *ppl. a.* 1.

*c* 897 K. ÆLFRED *Gregory's Past C.* xl. 295 He..sua micle bet his agen dysig oncnew sua he undruncenra wæs. *a* 1275 *Prov. Ælfred* 459 Drunken & vndrunkin, eyþer is wisdome wel god. *a* 1400–50 *Bk. Curtasye* III. 787 in *Babees Bk.*, In þe lordys cupp þat leuys vndrynken, Into þe almesdisshe hit schalle be sonken.

**Undry·,** *v.* [UN-[2] 7.] *intr.* To lose dryness.

*c* 1440 *Pallad. on Husb.* XI. 70 Ek there is warm & drie Ablaqueate hem that they may vndrie.

**Undry·ing,** *ppl. a.* (UN-[1] 10.) 1541 R. COPLAND *Galyen's Terap.* 2 B j, The salues that are layde to the sayde vlceres must be more vndryeng than they that are layd to a syngle sore. **Undu·b,** *v.* (UN-[2] 3 + DUB *v.*[3] 2.) 1812 J. H. VAUX *Flash Dict., Undub*, to unlock, unfasten, &c.

**Undu·bbed,** *ppl. a.* [UN-[1] 8.]

**1.** Not invested with dignity or title.

1602 [?SIR J. ROE] in *Donne's Wks.* (1912) I. 403, I know What made his Valour, undubb'd, Windmill go, Within a Pint at most. 1803 [see UNDOCTORED]. 1894 STEVENSON *Songs of Travel, Woodman* x, I..climb Where no undubbed civilian dares, In my war harness, the loud stairs Of honour.

**2.** Not having the comb and gills removed.

1855 *Poultry Chron.* III. 429/1 To know whether the game chickens..are to be dubbed or undubbed. 1867 TEGETMEIER *Poultry Bk.* 139 In these combats an undubbed bird is at fearful disadvantage.

**Undu·bitable,** *a.* Now *rare.* [UN-[1] 7 b and 5 b.] = INDUBITABLE *a.*

1643 PRYNNE *Sov. Power Parl.* II. 59 b, This their ancient undubitable oft-enjoyed Right and Priviledge. 1664 H. MORE *Myst. Iniq.* 207 A sense of things..so coherent with undubitable Principles. 1816 BENTHAM *Chrestom.* 208 To judge from the undubitable etymologies of the two words.

**Undu·bitably,** *adv.* Now *rare.* [UN-[1] 11 and 5 b.] = INDUBITABLY *adv.*

1660 R. COKE *Power & Subj.* 38 Extorting it [*sc.* dominion] from their rightful Kings in whom it undubitably was. 1709 MRS. MANLEY *Secret Mem.* (1720) I. 219 That to be well receiv'd, it is undubitably necessary to become useful to those we would recommend ourselves to. 1778 STEEVENS in *Shaks. Wks., Tit. A.* VIII. 561 The performances on which the seal of Shakespeare is undubitably fixed. 1890 *Retrospect Med.* CII. 133 The beneficial effect of the operation was thus undubitably established.

†**Undu·bitate,** *a. Obs.* [UN-[1] 7 and 5 b.] = INDUBITATE *a.*

1482 CAXTON *Polycron.* VIII. xiii. 406 b, To depose them that were scysmatykes, and to chose one very heede and vndubytate pope. *a* 1548 HALL *Chron., Hen. IV*, 15 An vndubitate kyng, crouned and anoynted by the spiritualtie. 1590 BARROUGH *Meth. Physick* IV. xi. (1596) 243 This shalbe a great and vndubitate signe to you. 1611 SPEED *Hist.* IX. xix. § 26 The vndubitate heire to Richard Plantagenet.

So † **Undu·bitately** *adv.* = INDUBITATELY *adv.*

*a* 1548 HALL *Chron., Edw. IV*, 249 My hope is with a sure anchor grounded, and myne inwarde conceipte vndubitatly resolued. *Ibid., Hen. VII*, 31 b.

**Undu·cal,** *a.* (UN-[1] 7.) 1824 MOORE *Mem.* (1853) IV. 161 The Duke of Montrose's most un-ducal letter. **Undu·chess,** *v.*, **Undu·chessed,** *ppl. a.* (UN-[2] 6 b.) 1819 *Metropolis* III. 239 How it would mortify my pride if I was, at a future period, to be un-Duchessed! 1887 BROWNING *Parleyings, D. Bartoli* xiv, That a fervid youth..loved, as boyhood can, The unduchessed lady.

**Undue** (*v*ndiū·), *a.* [UN-[1] 7 + DUE *a.*, after OF. *indeu*, L. *indēbitus.*]

**1.** Not properly owing or payable.

1387 TREVISA *Higden* (Rolls) VIII. 241 For þe pope greved þe chirches of Engelond wiþ taxes and wiþ paiementis undewe and uncustemable. 1818 COLEBROOKE *Obligations* 98 It was not undue, though payment might have been postponed. 1843 CARLYLE *Past & Pr.* II. xii, My Lord of Clare, coming to claim his *undue* 'debt' in the Court at Witham.

**2.** Not appropriate or suitable; improper. Also of times, etc.: Unseasonable.

1398 TREVISA *Barth. De P. R.* II. xix. (1495) 45 Also in an undewe manere the deuyll coueyted highnes that fell not for hym. 1436 *Pol. Poems* (Rolls) II. 176 Thow this proverbe be homly and undew, Yet be liklynesse it is for soth fulle trew. *c* 1440 *Jacob's Well* 165 Whan playes arn hantyd in vndewe places & in vndewe tyme. 1541 *Act* 33 *Hen. VIII*, c. 21 § 1 Culpeper and she met..at an vndue houre of a leuen a clocke in the night. 1585 T. WASHINGTON tr. *Nicholay's Voy.* I. xvii. 19 Wee woulde not at an vndue houre enter amongest the Turkes armie. 1641 SIR E. DERING *Sp. on Relig.* (1642) 77 Throwing that overboard which is adventitious, borrowed, and undue. 1680 W. ALLEN *Peace & Unity* Pref. p. lx, Our undue separations, and unchristian Contentions. *a* 1716 BP. O. BLACKALL *Wks.* (1723) I. 250 It is a Sin to omit the holy Duty, and it is likewise a Sin to perform it in an undue manner. 1774 J. BRYANT *Mythol.* I. 344 They seem to have been aware, that they were guilty of an undue representation. 1865 KINGSLEY *Herew.* xxi, Men-at-arms.., who would, on due or undue cause shown, hunt men while he hunted game. 1875 JOWETT *Plato* (ed. 2) V. 58 The undue awarding of honours is the ruin of states.

**3.** Not in accordance with what is just and right; unjustifiable; illegal.

*c* 1400 *Apol. Loll.* 11 If þe pope..graunt or behi3t ani swilk þingis..for vndeu cause and oþer vndeu cause and vnpertinent. *c* 1440 *Jacob's Well* 99 3if þou do it..wyth exces of vndewe mesure, wyth a strong wyll to sle,..it is dedly synne. 1456 *Coventry Leet Bk.* 293 Diuers subbaillifs of this Cite afore this han made many vndue returnes of preceptes directed..vnto theym. 1598 FLORIO, *Iritto*, vnlawfull, vndue, vnfit, vnright. 1622 BACON *Hen. VII*, 14 Which proceeding being even at that time taxed for vigorous and undue [etc.]. 1660 R. COKE *Justice Vind.* Ep. Ded. 7 Such miscreants..had by undue ways devoured the patrimony of the Church. 1692 LUTTRELL *Brief Rel.* (1857) II. 601 Irish letters say, divers persons were committed for undue practices. 1783 BURKE *Rep. Aff. India* Wks. XI. 149 Complaints against the inferiour collectors of the Landed Revenue, stating their undue and vexatious exactions.

**b.** In special contexts.

(*a*) 1477 EARL RIVERS (Caxton) *Dictes* iij b, To gadre money..by subtyl extorcion or other undewe meanes. 1534 *Act* 26 *Hen. VIII*, c. 2 Without gile, fraude, or other vndew meane. 1621 ELSING *Debates Ho. Lords* (Camden) App. 136 Those innes..that have benne lately erected by his undue meanes. 1676 HALE *Contempl.* II. 132 Frauds, and Plots, and Underminings, and Undue Means.

(*b*) 1687 BP. CARTWRIGHT in *Magd. Coll. & Jas. II* (O.H.S.) 134 The Election was undue. 1736 *Gentl. Mag.* VI. 440/1 The Petition..complaining of an undue Election and Return for the City of Coventry. 1764 T. HUTCHINSON *Hist. Mass.* I. (1765) 62 This election was immediately determined..to be undue..[and] a warrant issued for a new.

(*c*) 1735 BOLINGBROKE *On Parties* 122 Thus He acquired an undue Influence over the Elections. 1772 *Junius' Lett.* Ded. p. viii, Long parliaments are the foundation of the undue influence of the crown. 1854 *Act* 17 & 18 *Vict.* c. 102 (*title*), An Act to..amend the Laws relating to Bribery, Treating, and undue Influence at Elections.

†**c.** Of persons: Acting unjustly. *Obs.*[—1]

*a* 1400 *Pistill of Susan* 236 Hir domus men vnduwe do hir be withdrawen.

**4.** Going beyond what is appropriate, warranted, or natural; excessive.

*a* 1684 LEIGHTON *Comm.* 1 *Pet.* iv. 8 (1849) II. 350 [Love] delights not in the undue disclosing of brethren's failings. 1739 *Hist. Works of Learned* I. 137 He seems to own they are both chargeable with some Instances of undue Warmth and Zeal. 1780 COWPER *Progr. Error* 269 Pleasure admitted in undue degree, Enslaves the will. 1814 CHALMERS *Evid.* i. 21 An undue advantage has been given to that argument. 1865 TYLOR *Early Hist. Man.* i. 2 An undue confidence in the statements of ancient writers. 1893 TRAILL *Soc. Eng.* Introd. p. xiv, The undue prominence formerly given..to these matters has produced a reaction.

Hence **Undue·ness.** *rare.*

1653 W. A[LLEN] (*title*), An Answer..in which..the Undueness of mixt Communion is declared. 1680 — *Peace & Unity* Pref. p. xxxv, I shall..argue the undueness of their practise that withdraw..upon the foresaid ground.

**Unduely,** obs. f. UNDULY *adv.*

**Undu·g,** *ppl. a.* (UN-[1] 8 b, c.)

1657 W. RAND tr. *Gassendi's Life Peiresc* III. 34 The remainder [of the epitaph] being as yet..undug up. *c* 1730 WALDRON *Descr. Isle of Man* Wks. (1731) 188 Their Turf lay in the Bowels of the Earth undug for. 1775 S. J. PRATT *Liberal Opin.* xliii. (1783) I. 256 There may be still an undug mine of knowledge. 1844 MRS. BROWNING *Drama of Exile* 1149, I feel your steps..strike A sense of death to me, and undug graves! 1894 *Outing* XXIV. 427/2 In the few drills of undug potatoes which the improvident Casey had left.

**Undu·ke,** *v.* (UN-[2] 6 b.) 1611 FLORIO, *Sducare*, to vnduke. 1663 PEPYS *Diary* 12 Dec., He hath letters from France that the King hath unduked twelve Dukes. 1893 *Westm. Gaz.* 10 Mar. 3/2 Is it the Duke of Devonshire un-Duked?

**Undulant** (*v*·ndiŭlănt), *a.* [ad. L. **undulant-*, *undulans*: cf. next, and Sp. *undulante*, F. *ondulant.*] Moving after the manner of waves; rising and falling like waves.

Hence, in recent use, *undulancy*, wave-like motion.

1830 MAUNDER *Dict.* 1834 LD. HOUGHTON *Tour Greece* 138 Whose sweet undulant murmur the homeless mariner hearkened, Over the undulant sapphire. 1862 SIR H. TAYLOR *St. Clement's Eve* II. ii, Sea-spirits..Gliding and lapsing in an undulant dance. 1896 HOWELLS *Impress. & Exp.* 215 The lesser craft that plied upon the many channels of the meadows..seemed to sail upon their undulant grasses.

**b.** *Undulant fever*, Malta fever.

1897 M. L. HUGHES *Medit. Fever* i. 3 *note*, During epidemics of undulant or enteric fevers.

**U·ndular,** *a.* [ad. L. type **undulār-is*: cf. next.] Wavy, undulating. Hence **U·ndularly** *adv.*

1738 CHAMBERS *Cycl.* s.v. *Muscle*, They contract themselves into an undular kind of surface. 1805 T. WEAVER tr. *Werner's Ext. Charact. Fossils* 275, 1. Spherically..2. Undularly.

†**U·ndulary,** *a. Obs.*[—1] [ad. L. type **undulāri-us*, f. *unda* wave: cf. next.] Coming in waves.

1646 SIR T. BROWNE *Pseud. Ep.* VII. xvii. 377 The blasts and undulary breaths thereof maintaine no certainty in their course.

**Undulate** (*v*·ndiŭlĕt), *a.* [ad. L. *undulāt-us* diversified as with waves, f. *unda* wave. Cf. Sp. *undulado*, F. *ondulé.*]

**1.** Furnished with wave-like markings.

1658 PHILLIPS, *Undulate*, Chamolet wrought, or painted like waves. 1661 LOVELL *Hist. Anim. & Min.* Isagoge, The cramp-fish,..raie undulate and oculate. 1706 PHILLIPS (ed. Kersey), *Undulate*, or *Undulated*, made in fashion of Waves, as watered Stuffs and the Grain of Wainscot.

**2.** *Bot.* and *Zool.* = UNDULATED *ppl. a.* 1.

Also comb., as *undulate-convex*, *-serrate*, etc.

a. *Bot.* 1760 J. LEE *Introd. Bot.* I. xii. (1765) 28 *Undulate*, waved, as in *Gloriosa*. 1821 W. P. C. BARTON *Flora N. Amer.* I. 91 Leaves..entire, but undulate and irregular on the margin. 1870 HOOKER *Stud. Flora* 305 Margins cartilaginous and undulate when dry.

b. *Zool.* 1826 KIRBY & SP. *Entomol.* IV. 290 *Undulate*,.. when fasciæ, strigæ, lines, &c. curve into alternate sinuses resembling the rise and fall of waves. *Ibid.* 293 *Undulate*, ..when the surface rises and falls obtusely, not in angles. 1846 DANA *Zooph.* (1848) 167 Surface a little undulate.

**Undulate** (*v*·ndiŭleᵗt), *v.* [ad. L. type **undulāt-* (cf. prec.), ppl. stem of **undulāre*, f. *unda*. Cf. Sp. and Pg. *undular*, It. *ondulare*, F. *onduler*.]

**1.** *intr.* To move in, or after the manner of, waves; to have a wave-like motion.

1664 POWER *Exp. Philos.* I. 69 The former Experiment of the Snail,..whose Animal Spirits never begin to undulate till she begin to move. 1721 BAILEY, To *Undulate*, to roll as waves do. 1796 H. HUNTER tr. *St.-Pierre's Stud. Nat.* (1799) II. 41 The..swallow is continually skimming along their surface, undulating like the waters of a lake. 1820 SHELLEY *To M. Gisborne* 120 The ripe corn under the undulating air Undulates like an ocean. 1869 J. PHILLIPS *Vesuv.* ix. 253 The water undulates, the land vibrates.

b. *transf.* Of sound, etc.

1760–72 H. BROOKE *Fool of Qual.* (1809) IV. 158 An universal shout..followed and undulated after our company. 1784 COWPER *Task* I. 175 Tall spire, from which the sound of cheerful bells Just undulates upon the list'ning ear. 1818 SHELLEY *Rosalind* 833 The light serene Of smiles, whose lustre bright and soft Beneath lay undulating there.

c. To float *on* waves. Also *fig.*

1813 H. & J. SMITH *Horace in Lond.* 24 He undulates on Ocean's swell. 1891 T. HARDY *Tess* xix, She undulated upon the thin notes [of the harp] as upon billows.

**2.** *trans.* a. To cause to move, esp. to rise and fall, after the manner of waves.

1669 HOLDER *Elem. Speech* 47 It may very well be, that Breath vocalized, i.e. vibrated or undulated, may in a different manner affect the Lips. 1725 *Fam. Dict.* s.v. *Hot-bath*, Like a Fomentation, which..by gently shaking and undulating the Fibres, helps forwards those animal Motions. 1865 *Intell. Observ.* Sept. 84 A snail-leech..attaching its suckers to the glass vessel in which it is confined, and..undulating the intervening portion of the body. 1873 LELAND *Egypt. Sketch-Bk.* 135 The first dancing of all Ghawâzi is simply moving about to the music and undulating the body.

b. To invest with the form or appearance of a wavy or rippling surface.

1730 A. GORDON *Maffei's Amphith.* 351 The red..and yellow Coverings of the Theatre, reflected back on the Assembly of Spectators,..undulating the whole with their Colours. 1804 SHAW *Gen. Zool.* V. 419 The body is obliquely undulated by twelve lines of the same colour. 1843 tr. *Custine's Empire of Czar* I. 216 It is for man to build mountains, when nature has not undulated the surface of the earth.

**3.** *intr.* To present a wavy surface or outline.

1833 L. RITCHIE *Wand. by Loire* 255 The vast plain undulates in hills and valleys. 1849 RUSKIN *Sev. Lamps* v. § 13. 149 There is not one of the arches the same in height as another; their tops undulate all along the wall. 1866 GEO. ELIOT *F. Holt* i, A..masculine face, with rich brown hair..undulating beside each cheek.

b. To have the effect of waves to the eye.

1888 H. W. PARKER *Spirit of Beauty* 220 Silks of changing hues that undulate like a purple sunset on a billowy sea.

**Undulated** (*v*·ndiŭleᵗtėd), *ppl. a.* [Cf. prec. and UNDULATE *a.*]

**1.** Formed into a waved surface or outline; arranged in a series of wave-like curves.

1623 COCKERAM I, *Vndulated*, made like the waues of the Sea. 1673 GREW *Anat. Trunks* I. i. § 31 Next there is an undulated Ring of other Lymphæducts. 1753 *Chambers' Cycl.* Supp. s.v. *Leaf*, *Undulated leaf*, that whose..edges are necessitated to rise and fall in a regular manner. 1783 *Phil. Trans.* LXXIII. 181 The bridge has taken an undulated form, and the rail on each side is curiously scolloped. *a* 1853 PEREIRA *Polarized Light* (1854) 117 A series of rods disposed horizontally in an undulated form, so as to represent a system of plane waves. 1873 J. TOMES *Dental Surg.* (ed. 2) 7 The inferior edge of the lower jaw..is undulated.

b. Of ground, hills, etc. (Cf. UNDULATING 2 b.)

1821 T. NUTTALL *Arkansa* 11 A deeply undulated country. 1845 E. WARBURTON *Crescent & Cross* I. 15 An amphitheatre of finely undulated hills. 1893 SIR H. HOWORTH *Glacial Nightmare* I. 59 A small elevated plain, slightly undulated.

**2.** Furnished or diversified with wavy markings.

1664 EVELYN *Sylva* xxv. 65 The Roots of this [Box] Tree ..do furnish the..Cabinet-makers with pieces rarely undulated. 1706 PHILLIPS [see UNDULATE *a.* 1]. 1787 [see 2 b]. 1798 *Lond. Gaz.* 20 Nov., A Chief undulated Argent, thereon Waves of the Sea. 1811 SHAW *Gen. Zool.* VIII. 469 Yellowish Green Parrakeet, undulated above with brown.

b. *spec.* In the names of birds or fishes.

1785 LATHAM *Gen. Synop. Birds* III. 333 Undulated Flycatcher. 1787 *Ibid.* Suppl. 225 Undulated Trumpeter;..the plumage..of a pale reddish brown, beautifully undulated with black. 1803 SHAW *Gen. Zool.* IV. 223 Undulated Coryphene. 1811 *Ibid.* VIII. 469 Undulated Parrakeet.

**U·ndulately**, *adv.* [f. UNDULATE *a.*] In a wave-like manner.

1872 H. C. WOOD *Fresh-Water Algæ* (1874) 144 End lobes ..sinuately or undulately cut at the apex.

**U·ndulating**, *ppl. a.* [f. UNDULATE *v.*]

**1.** Moving after the manner of waves; rising and falling in (or like) waves.

1711 POPE *Temple Fame* 446 Thro' undulating air the sounds are sent. 1758 REID tr. *Macquer's Chym.* I. 268 From these cracks will issue undulating flames. 1816 SIR H. DOUGLAS *Milit. Bridges* 70 The intervals must be considerable, and the balks be laid from boat to boat only, to admit of an undulating motion. 1820 W. IRVING *Sketch Bk.* I. 12 To watch the gently undulating billows, rolling their silver volumes. *a* 1874 in Coues *Birds N. W.* 113 Its flight is in undulating lines, like the Crossbill's.

b. *transf.* Of sounds.

1700 DRYDEN *Ovid's Met.* XII. 60 Whence all Things.. thither bring their Undulating Sound. 1712 BLACKMORE *Creation* VII. 101 Mark how the spirits..Seize undulating sounds, and catch the vocal air. 1844 KINGLAKE *Eothen* i. 6 Those well-undulating tones [of speech] which belong to the best Osmanlees.

c. *fig.* Exhibiting variations comparable to the rising and falling of waves.

1815 BENTHAM *Springs of Action* Wks. 1843 II. 202 The maintenance of discipline among the undulating and tumultuous multitude. 1849 DE MORGAN *Trigonometry & Double Algebra* 1 Trigonometry contains the science of continually undulating magnitude. 1898 P. MANSON *Trop. Diseases* x. 182 Those cases [of Malta Fever] with well-marked waves of fever he calls 'undulating'.

**2.** Forming a series of wave-like curves.

1728 CHAMBERS *Cycl.* s.v. *Muscle*, The Fibres..contract themselves into a wavy undulating kind of Surface. 1799 KIRWAN *Geol. Ess.* 369 The strata are parallel to each other, horizontal or undulating. 1846 ELLIS *Elgin Marb.* II. 23 The undulating flow given to every part of the drapery. 1884 BOWER & SCOTT *De Bary's Phaner.* 366 The endodermis.. only differs..in the undulating bands on its radial walls.

b. Of grounds, hills, etc.: Presenting a succession of gently rounded heights and hollows.

1794 PIOZZI *Synon.* II. 353 The wavy corn floats very beautifully upon the undulating downs. 1815 ELPHINSTONE *Acc. Caubul* III. i. 351 It is an undulating plain, about twenty-five miles long. 1832 G. DOWNES *Lett. Cont. Countries* I. 451 The luxuriance of the region, into whose leafy and beautifully undulating bosom we were now to be immerged. 1873 MRS. BROOKFIELD *Not a Heroine* II. 162 Soft, undulating distant hills.

Hence **U·ndulatingly** *adv.*

1796 KIRWAN *Elem. Min.* (ed. 2) I. 85 In some places it was dark grey, and undulatingly slaty. 1835 *Blackw. Mag.* XXXVII. 341 The..line of thesky, that..plays undulatingly from and into the..deeper tones of the river's visible bed.

**Undulation** (*v*ndiŭlēᵗ·ʃən). [ad. med. or mod. L. **undulātio*: cf. UNDULATE *a.* and *v.*, and Sp. *undulacion* (Pg. *-ação*), F. *ondulation*, It. *ondulazione*.]

**1.** The action of moving in a wave-like manner; a gentle rising and falling in the manner of waves.

1646 SIR T. BROWNE *Pseud. Ep.* III. xv. 142 Those animals, whose bodies consist of..annulary fibers, and move by undulation, that is, like the waves of the Sea. 1664 POWER *Exp. Philos.* I. 36 Their motion is..restless and constant, with perpetual undulations and wavings, like Eels or Snakes. 1707 FLOYER *Physic. Pulse-Watch* 267 The undulation of the Spirits towards the Brain produces all our Sensations. 1762 FALCONER *Shipwreck* I. 308 Soon this transient undulation o'er The sea subsides. 1820 KEATS *Hyperion* III. 132 His golden tresses..Kept undulation round his eager neck. 1854 OWEN in *Orr's Circ. Sci.*, *Org. Nat.* I. 228 Whales and porpoises progress by bounding movements or undulations in a vertical plane. 1875 MANNING *Mission H. Ghost* iv. 106 We are as unstable as.. the restless undulation of the water.

*transf.* 1777 JOHNSON *Lett.* I. 389 Mrs. * * grows old, and has lost much of her undulation and mobility.

b. A wave-like motion of the air, ether, etc., as in the propagation of sound or light.

1658 PHILLIPS s.v., Undulation of the air. 1672 *Phil. Trans.* VII. 5148 The other Secondary Affections of Winds; as their Undulation,.. Opposition, etc. 1728 CHAMBERS *Cycl.* s.v. *Sound*, A Wave or Undulation of Air. 1764 REID *Inquiry* iv. § 1. 117 Each undulation must be made up of the advance and recoil of innumerable particles of elastic air. 1802 YOUNG in *Phil. Trans.* XCII. 21 The undulations of green light being nearly in the ratio of 6½. 1870 H. SPENCER *Princ. Psych.* I. I. iii. 47 Those minute agents that terminate the nerves of the retina are acted on by luminiferous undulations.

*Comb.* 1838 WHEWELL in Todhunter *Acc. Writ.* (1876) II. 269 A curious..paper upon the theory of the rainbow treated undulation-wise.

c. *transf.* Of sound.

1668 DRYDEN *Ess. Dram. Poesy* ? 3 Those little undulations of sound..still seeming to retain somewhat of their first horror. 1705 ADDISON *Italy* 42 Two parallel Walls that beat the Sound back on each other, till the Undulation is quite worn out. 1791 MRS. RADCLIFFE *Rom. Forest* xi, The notes floated on the air in soft undulations. 1851 FROUDE *Short Stud.*, *Homer* (1867) II. 166 The actions of men.. crumble away into the softer undulations of prose.

†d. *spec.* (See quot.) *Obs.*⁻¹

1676 GREW *Musæum, Anat. Stomach* vi. 25 Vndulation, is when the Contraction is made in several parts of the Stomach successively.

**2.** A wave-like curve or a series of these; an undulating curvature or sweep.

1670 EVELYN *Sylva* (ed. 2) 119 The Root of the wilder sort [is] incomparable for its crisped undulations. 1803 SHAW *Gen. Zool.* IV. 497 Scales..edged with yellow, so as to form numerous obliquely transverse undulations over the whole body. 1846 CARPENTER *Man. Phys.* 186 Minute tubuli,.. exhibiting numerous minute undulations, and sometimes more decided curvatures, in their course. 1875 SIR T. SEATON *Fret-Cutting* 36 How..you will turn or bend the stalks, so as to give a natural undulation and appearance to the whole work.

**3.** The fact of forming or presenting a series of rounded heights and hollows; an undulating rise and fall of level.

1798 S. & HT. LEE *Canterb. T.* II. 441 For many a mile, with graceful undulation, wandered the high road. 1835 WILLIS *Pencillings* I. xxiv. 167 A continual undulation of rock and sand.

b. An instance of this; also, a single rise and fall of this nature.

1823 RUTTER *Fonthill* 86 The undulations of the surface occasionally give a beautiful variety to the scene. 1878 HUXLEY *Physiogr.* 214 Here the strata..have been thrown into a succession of gentle undulations.

**Undula·tionist.** [f. prec. + -IST.] One who holds the undulatory theory of light.

1834 WHEWELL in Todhunter *Acc. Writ.* (1876) II. 194 We undulationists do not conceive that we are in many points inferior to our adversaries. 1881 *Nature* XXIV. 382/1, I suppose that in the ordinary language of undulationists the velocity of light means..the velocity with which an individual wave travels.

**U·ndulative**, *a. rare*⁻⁰. = UNDULATORY *a.*

1860 WORCESTER (citing Fletcher).

**Undula·to-**, comb. form of UNDULATE *a.*, used in some botanical terms, as *undulato-rugose*, *-striate*.

1829 LOUDON *Encycl. Plants* (1836) 1027 *Stromatosphæria deusta*;..rigid spreading thick undulato-rugose. 1866 *Treas. Bot.* 1191/1 Undulato-striate.

**Undulatory** (*v*·ndiŭlătəri), *a.* [ad. mod.L. type **undulātōri-us*: cf. UNDULATE *v.* and -ORY. So Sp. and Pg. *undulatorio*, It. *ondulatorio*, F. *ondulatoire*.]

**1.** Of motion: Characterized by successive rise and fall after the manner of waves.

1728 CHAMBERS *Cycl.* s.v. *Undulation*, The Undulatory Motion of the Air, is supposed the..Cause of Sound. 1759 *Phil. Trans.* LI. 531 The motion here appeared to be very deep, and was rather undulatory than tremulous. 1832 BREWSTER *Nat. Magic* iv. (1833) 78 A tempest at sea is imitated, by having the sea on one slider, and the ships on other sliders, to which an undulatory movement is communicated. 1879 R. H. ELLIOT *Written on Forehead* xvi, The translator..tells us that breadth across the hips..would give an undulatory motion to their walk.

b. Exhibiting, or acting with, undulating motion.

1794 R. J. SULIVAN *View Nat.* I. 169 An elastic fluid.. would cause an undulatory diffusion of the luminous particles. 1813 J. THOMSON *Lect. Inflam.* 525 This air.. gives an elastic undulatory sensation to the fingers. 1882 *Gd. Words* June 382 Vast masses of white cumulus clouds ..piled up as in great undulatory breaking billows.

c. *Undulatory theory* (also *hypothesis*, † *system*), the theory that light consists in an undulatory movement of an elastic medium pervading space.

1802 YOUNG in *Phil. Trans.* XCII. 13 That prepossession which I before entertained for the undulatory system of light. 1827–8 HERSCHEL in *Encycl. Metrop.* (1845) IV. 449 General Statement of the Undulatory Theory of Light. 1834 MRS. SOMERVILLE *Connex. Phys. Sci.* xxi. 190 These intervals determine the lengths of the waves on the undulatory hypothesis.

**2.** = UNDULATING *ppl. a.* 2 and 2 b.

1796 MORSE *Amer. Geog.* I. 220 The other moccasin snake is..of a pale grey, sky-coloured ground, with brown undulatory ringlets. 1845 DARWIN *Voy. Nat.* xiv, In wooded undulatory districts. 1853 G. JOHNSTON *Nat. Hist. E. Bord.* I. 51 An undulatory rising ground. 1884 in H. Thompson *Tumours Bladder* 94 The deep limit of the growth is clearly defined, convex, undulatory or lobular in character.

**3.** *fig.* = UNDULATING *ppl. a.* 1 c.

1897 M. L. HUGHES *Medit. Fever* 99 The remittent..type of pyrexia of the undulatory or malignant varieties.

**Undu·ll**, *a.* (UN-¹ 7.) *c* 1400 *Destr. Troy* 13908 To the noise oponone neghit þe kyng..With a dart vndull. **Undu·ll**, *v.* (UN-² 6 a.) 1654 WHITLOCK *Zootomia* 477 Poetry ..is a most musicall Modulator of all Intelligibles,..undulling their Grossenesse. **Undu·lled**, *ppl. a.* (UN-¹ 8.) [1775 ASH.] 1837 MANGAN *Poems* (1903) 265 His laughing flowers are Undulled by tears. 1899 MACKAIL *Life Morris* II. 337 His own admiration was undulled by their complete..fraternity. **Undu·llness.** (UN-¹ 12.) 1793 T. TWINING in *Recreat. & Stud.* (1882) 180 His admirable sense, and undulness of conversation.

**Undulo·se**, *a.* [Cf. next and -OSE.] = next.

1889 *Q. Jrnl. Geol. Soc.* May 342 The curvature of the twin-lamellæ, which is accompanied by..a marked 'undulose' extinction.

**Undulous** (*v*·ndiŭləs), *a.* [ad. mod.L. type **undulōs-us*: cf. UNDULATE *v.* and -OUS. So Sp. and Pg. *unduloso*, F. *onduleux*.] Of an undulating nature. Hence (in recent use) **U·ndulously** *adv.*

1728 CHAMBERS *Cycl.* s.v. *Undulation*, The adjoining Liquid ..forms the first undulous Circle. 1862 LYTTON *Str. Story* xvii, A vague, dusky vapour, undulous, and coiling like a vast serpent. *Ibid.* lxx, Beyond stretch undulous pastures. 1869 BLACKMORE *Lorna D.* lxv, He felt the undulous readiness of her volatile paces under him.

**Unduly** (*v*ndiū·li), *adv.* [UN-¹ 11: cf. UNDUE *a.*]

**1.** Without due cause or justification; without proper regard to right and wrong; unrightfully, improperly.

1399 LANGL. *Rich. Redeles* II. 124 Þus ȝe derid hem vnduly with droppis of anger. 1426 AUDELAY *Poems* (Percy Soc.) 35 Aȝayns the order of holé cherch and Goddys ordenawns This dole is undeulé dalt, hit maketh dystans. 1477 EARL RIVERS (Caxton) *Dictes* 44 b, Nether is nothing so [un]couenable to a king as to coueyte vnduely the goodes of his peple. 1598 FLORIO, *Indebitamente*, vndulie, vnlawfullie. 1657 in Picton *L'pool Munic. Rec.* (1883) I. 214 The same Ley shalbe denyed and not paid, being unduly taxed. 1687 *Reason. Toleration* 33 Unless it can be prov'd that it is for the Common Good,..the Penal Laws are unduly made. 1721 STRYPE *Eccl. Mem.* III. xix. 161 Remitting and relaxing to all persons..all the fruits and profits from the same taken, however unduly. **1796** Mme. D'Arblay *Camilla* III. 394 She could only feel reproach from a conquest, unduly, unfairly and uningenuously obtained. **1844** Mrs. Browning *Lost Bower* ix, While beyond,.. Malvern hills, for mountains counted Not unduly, loom a-row.

**b.** Irregularly.

**1660** Jer. Taylor *Ductor* III. iv. rule 16 § 4 Alexander the third.. was a schismatical Pope,.. and unduly elected.

†**2.** Without due care or industry; badly; not in the right way. *Obs.*

**1423** *Rolls of Parlt.* IV. 255/2 All the werk of Brauderie so undwely made as above. **1444** *Ibid.* V. 108/1 Divers Sherryffs.. unduely and yvell and untruely served the Kyng and his poeple. **1477** Earl Rivers (Caxton) *Dictes* 35 b, Many erre by cause they seke her [*sc.* Wisdom] vnduely and blame her without cause.

**3.** More than is due or proper; excessively.

*a* **1779** Warburton *Serm.* Wks. 1788 V. 431 The mechanism of the body,.. when unduly agitated either by sensation or reflection. **1841** Myers *Cath. Th.* IV. § 19. 276 Unquestionably External evidences.. have been unduly magnified. **1869** Freeman *Norm. Conq.* (1875) III. xiii. 281 On such mere backslidings William had never been unduly harsh.

**Undu·mpish,** *v.* (Un-[2] 6; see Dumpish *a.*) *a* **1661** Fuller *Worthies, Stafford.* III. (1662) 47 When Queen Elizabeth was serious.. and out of good humour, he could un-dumpish her at his pleasure.

**Undu·nged,** *ppl. a.* (Un-[1] 8.)

*c* **1440** *Pallad. on Husb.* II. 152 Vndonged sleck wole make hem lene, as preue is. **1733** Tull *Horse-hoeing Husb.* 73 Wider and narrower Spaces, more or less Hoed, dung'd and undung'd. **1763** Mills *Pract. Husb.* II. 351, I perceived no .. difference.. between the dunged and the undunged beds.

**Undur,** var. of Undern *Obs.*

**Undu·rable,** *a.* (Un-[1] 7 b and 5 b.)

*c* **1550** Coverdale *Bk. Death* I. viii. 28 Among all thinges, most vndurable and most frayle is mannes lyfe. **1600** Surflet *Countrie Farme* III. xlix. 530 A rawe, weake,.. vndurable, and soone souring licour. **1650** Arnway *Tablet* 107 All unmeasurable vice is undurable. **1721** R. Keith tr. *T. à Kempis, Vall. Lillies* xxx. 93 All temporal Things are defective and undurable. **1886** Dicey *England's Case* 65 As undurable as Grattan's Constitution of 1782.

Hence **Undu·rableness.**

**1648** Hexham II, *Ongedurigheyt*, Vndurablenesse. **1691** T. H[ale] *Acc. New Invent.* 7 Its undurableness and doubtful efficacy.

†**Undu·re,** *v. Obs.*[−1] [f. Un-[2] 6 a + L. *dūr-us* hard.] *trans.* To crumble, break up.

*c* **1440** *Pallad. on Husb.* III. 1174 And pocion forsayd in sum mesure Half ful be don, quik erthe among vndure [L. *resolvas*] As ly is made.

**Undurn(e,** varr. Undern *Obs.*

**Undu·st,** *v.* [Un-[2] 4 b.] *trans.* To clear from dust; to wipe clean.

**1611** Florio, *Dispoluerâre*, to vndust. **1654** W. Montague *Dev. Ess.* II. vi. § 3. 121 When we frequently dress up the Altar of our hearts, and undust it from all these little foulnesses. **1884** in *N. & Q.* 14 June 466/1 The piece [a play] has been unearthed, or rather undusted, by Mr. Thicke.

**Undu·sted,** *ppl. a.* [Un-[1] 8.]

**1.** Not sprinkled with dust.

**1648** Hexham II, *Onbestoven*, Vndusted.

**2.** Not freed from dust; left dusty.

**1862** Thornbury *Turner* I. 308 The old Greek books, long undusted, are brought out. **1868** *Dublin Univ. Mag.* Aug. 124/2 Dr. Johnson wrote a tragedy, but.. suffered it to moulder on his undusted shelves.

**Undu·teous,** *a.* (and *adv.*). [Un-[1] 7.]

**1.** Undutiful; also *adv.*, undutifully.

**1598** Shaks. *Merry W.* v. v. 240 This deceit looses the name of craft, Of disobedience, or vnduteous title. **1645** Milton *Tetrach.* Wks. 1851 IV. 260 Perpetually unsociable, unpeacefull, or unduteous. **1694** Dryden *Love Triumph.* I. i, I.. must condemn This carriage, as unduteous to your father. **1745** *Matrimony pro & con* 7 What! teach a Child unduteous to behave? **1848** Lytton *Harold* XI. viii, Why this dispute? —why this unduteous discord?

**2.** *spec.* = Inofficious *a.* 1 b. *rare*[−1].

**1861** Maine *Anc. Law* vii. 215 A new remedy.. called.. 'The Plaint of an Unduteous Will,' directed to the reinstatement of the issue in inheritances, from which they had been unjustifiably excluded.

**Undu·tiful,** *a.* [Un-[1] 7.]

**1.** Contrary to the spirit of duty.

**1582** (*title*), A Particular Declaration.. of the undutifull and traiterous Affection borne against her Maiestie by Edmond Campion. **1647** Clarendon *Hist. Reb.* II. § 58 The Old Man .. with some bitterness put his Son in mind of his Undutyful carriage towards him. **1697** Luttrell *Brief Rel.* (1857) IV. 169 Undutifull words, which were.. spoken by him of the King. **1870** J. Bruce *Life Gideon* xx. 368 Gideon's.. undutiful because unbelieving demeanour.

**2.** Lacking in the observance of duty.

**1593** Shaks. 3 *Hen. VI*, v. v. 33, I know my dutie, you are all vndutifull. **1623** Gouge *Serm. Extent God's Provid.* § 7 Such undutifull servants as take occasion from their masters .. weaknesse. **1641** Tatham *Distracted State* II. i, And y'ave proved The most undutiful'st of all her children. **1700** T. Brown *Amusem. Ser. & Com.* viii. (1709) 81 Many Citizens Wives had hard Hearts, Undutiful Husbands, and Disobedient Children. **1748** Richardson *Clarissa* (1811) I. xli. 312 Come not near us, if you resolve to be undutiful. **1831** *Society* I. xii. 178 She.. begged him to remonstrate with the undutiful girl. **1849** Macaulay *Hist. Eng.* vi. II. 117 The King in reply sharply reprimanded his undutiful Councillors.

**Undu·tifully,** *adv.* (Un-[1] 11: cf. prec.)

**1583** Babington *Commandm.* (1590) 216 These boiling hearts not bearing iust reproofe, vnduetyfullie haue often.. repined at their authoritie. **1643–5** Milton *Divorce* II. xvi, It justifies a man in so doing, that nothing is done undutifully to father or mother. **1693** *Dryden's Juvenal* IV. (1697) 79 The Fish had long in Cæsar's Ponds been fed, And from its Lord undutifully fled. **1824** Scott *St. Ronan's* xviii, He had a son who most undutifully laughed at all this. **1849** Macaulay *Hist. Eng.* iv. I. 457 The guilt of having acted undutifully and disrespectfully towards France.

**Undu·tifulness.** (Un-[1] 12.)

**1549** Cheke *Hurt Sedit.* (1569) F iv b, The haie.. hath bene by mens ydlenesse and vndutifulnesse, let alone vntouched. **1571** Dk. Norfolk in *14th Rep. Hist. MSS. Comm.* App. IV. 574, I confesse my unduetifullnes nowe hath blotted the same. **1662** Hibbert *Body Divinity* I. 278 Not to answer when called, is incivility in most, and it is undutifulness in some. **1742** Fielding *J. Andrews* II. vi, He had seen such examples of undutifulness happen from the too early generosity of parents. **1825** T. Hook *Sayings* Ser. II. I. 168 The extraordinary undutifulness of his child. **1876** Miss Yonge *Womankind* xvi, Opposition or undutifulness are fatal blots in a Christian character.

**Undu·ty.** *rare.* (Un-[1] 12.) **1594** H. Walpole in *Cath. Rec. Soc. Publ.* V. 266 For which my vndutye I humbly crave pardon. *Ibid.* 267. **Undwe·llable,** *a.* (Un-[1] 7 b.) **1382** Wyclif *Jer.* vi. 8 Be taȝt, Jerusalem,.. lest þar auenture I sette thee desert, a lond vndwellable. **1611** Florio, *Inhabitabile*, vnhabitable, vndwellable.

**Undwe·lt,** *ppl. a.* [Un-[1] 8 b, c.] Not dwelt *in*; † uninhabited.

*c* **1550** Cheke *Matt.* xii. 44 He commeth and findeth it vndwelt in, swept, and trimmd. **1613** W. Browne *Brit. Past.* I. i. 635 If beautie wanting lovers long should stay, It like an house undwelt in would decay. **1674** Marvell *Ball. Ld. Mayor & Aldermen* ii, Whilst their churches [are] unbuilt, And their houses undwelt.

**U·ndy,** *a. Her.* [Anglicized f. Undee *a.*] Wavy.

**1592** Wyrley *Armorie* 9 The sonne of Thomas went away with his ancestors marke without distinction (being vndie golde and red). **1611** Cotgr., *Vndé*,.. in Blason, vndie, or wauie. **1728** Chambers *Cycl.*, *Undee*, or Undy, in Heraldry. See *Wavy.* **1780** *Encycl. Brit.* (ed. 2) V. 3588/1 Vert, a Chief undy Or. **1880** *Encycl. Brit.* XI. 694/1 A bend undy or wavy is not a mere bend with a wavy edge, but the whole bend is in waves.

**Undye·,** *v.* (Un-[2] 3.) **14..** Lydg. in *MS. Soc. Antiq.* 134 fol. 1 (Halliwell), Blakke into white may not be undyed, Ne blood infecte with corrupcioun.

**Undye·d,** *ppl. a.* (Un-[1] 8.)

**1538** Elyot, *Abaphus*, vndied or vncoloured. **1570** Levins *Manip.* 50 Undyed, *non tinctus.* **1603** J. Davies (Heref.) *Extasie* Wks. (Grosart) I. 91/2 Thou shalt haue powre to crush the crownes of kings.., and yet thy hands vndide. *a* **1618** Raleigh *Rem.* (1661) 191 About fourscore thousand undrest and undied cloaths. **1807** Wordsw. *White Doe* VII. 58 A hood of mountain-wool undyed. **1880** L. Wallace *Ben-Hur* 32 An unbleached, undyed blanket.

**Undy·ing,** *ppl. a.* [Un-[1] 10.] That does not die; immortal.

*a* **1300** *Cursor M.* 18620 He ras.. Bath godd and man als he was ar, Vndeiand [*Trin.* Vndyinge] nu for euermar. **1608** Beaum. & Fl. *Four Plays in One* III. Wks. 1912 X. 337 And [I] wish heartily, That firm affection.. May take as deep undying root.. Betwixt my Daughter Casta, and your goodness. **1667** Milton *P. L.* VI. 739 Driven down To chains of Darkness, and th' undying Worm. **1816** Byron *Siege Cor.* xv, They fell devoted, but undying. **1887** Morris *Odyss.* XI. 133 Unto the Gods undying of the widespread heavenly home. *absol.* **1821** [see Unborn *ppl. a.* 3]. **1891** Morris (*title*), The Story of the Glittering Plain,.. or the Acre of the Undying.

**b.** *transf.* Of feelings, etc.

*c* **1765** Falconer *Occas. Elegy* 31 No more.. Shall.. hopeless Love impart undying pain. **1816** Byron *Ch. Har.* III. c, By heavenly feet thy paths are trod,—Undying Love's. **1885** 'Mrs. Alexander' *Valerie's Fate* v, The undying interest ever felt by kindly women in a question of love or marriage.

Hence **Undy·ingly** *adv.*, **Undy·ingness.**

*a* **1864** Hawthorne *Septimius* (1872) 33 That strange idea of undyingness which had recently taken possession of him. **1881** Miss Braddon *Asph.* II. 282 He remembered how devotedly,.. undyingly, he had once loved.. Madeline.

**Une,** obs. Sc. var. Oven.

†**Une,** *v. Obs.* [ad. L. *ūnīre* (= It. *unire*, OF. and mod.F. *unir*, Sp. and Pg. *unir*), f. *ūn-us* one.] *trans.* To unite.

*c* **1400** *Beryn* 3724 The hole science of al surgery Was vnyd, or the chaunge was made of both hir eye, With many sotill enchauntours. *c* **1450** *Myrr. Our Ladye* 104 So.. had yt bene vnpossyble that thys worde.. shulde haue bene touched .. but yf yt had bene vned to mannes body. **1526** *Pilgr. Perf.* (W. de W. 1531) 295 This is how the hole ymage of god, memory, vnderstandynge and wyll, be vned and ioyned to god. **1534** More *Treat. Passion* Wks. 1348/2 He is not by the spirite of god vnyd with holy saintes as a liuely membre of Christes.. body. **1538** Bale *God's Promises* III. C ij, O most myghtye gouernour of thy people,.. that of two maketh one, vnynge the Jews with the gentyles in one churche.

*refl.* **1533** tr. *Erasmus' Com. Crede* 69 b, It vned or dyd knytte itselfe into one hypostase or persone.

**b.** In Sc. use in pa. pple.

Perh. in some instances ad. L. *ūnīt-us*: see Unite *ppl. a.*

**1456** Sir G. Hay *Gov. Princes* Wks. (S.T.S.) II. 133 Than is the naturale hete unyt in the body. **1529** *Reg. Privy Seal Scot.* II. 49/2 The barony of Wester Ferny with certane uther landis and officis annexit and unit thairto. **1568** *Peebles Burgh Rec.* (1872) 73 The said prebendarie of the Rude and Halie Bludealtare, baith vnit in ane. **1615** *Reg. Great Seal Scot.* 543/1 Quhilk deanrie is unit and incorporat to the patrimonie of the said colledge.

Hence † **Un·ing** *vbl. sb. Obs.*

**1545** Douglas in *St. Papers Hen. VIII*, V. 418, I sal.. be glade to set fordvart the uneing off thir two Relmis.

†**Une,** app. an obs. var. of Even *adv.*

*c* **1400** *Destr. Troy* 1545 The walles vp wroght.. Fro the vrthe vpward vne of a mesure. *Ibid.* 5529 He was made as a mon fro þe myddell vp, And fro the nauyll by-neithe, vne an abill horse.

**Unea·ger,** *a.* (Un-[1] 7.) **1819** Keats *Lamia* I. 218 Like a young Jove with calm uneager face. **1844** Ld. Houghton *Mem. Many Scenes* 186 A youth.. with calm, uneager face.

**Unea·gled,** *a.* (Un-[1] 9.) **1858** [see Uncrossed 1].

**Uneais,** Sc. var. Uneaths *adv. Obs.*

**Unea·red,** *ppl. a. Obs.* exc. *arch.* [Un-[1] 8 + Ear *v.*[1]] Unploughed, untilled.

*c* **1000** Ælfric *Gloss.* in Wr.-Wülcker 147 *Rus*, unered land. *c* **1440** *Pallad. on Husb.* II. 15 The balkis that they calle vnered lond. **1558** *Reg. Cupar Abbey* (1890) II. 268 [He] sall ere.. Robertsonis land for this instant crope, safar as is vnerit. *c* **1600** Shaks. *Sonn.* iii, Where is she so faire whose vn-eard wombe Disdaines the tillage of thy husbandry?

**Unea·rned,** *ppl. a.* [Un-[1] 8.]

**1.** Not earned by merit or desert; unmerited or undeserved (as reward or punishment).

*c* **1200** *Trin. Coll. Hom.* 33 Deflen.. bireueden him [Adam] alle his riche weden, þat waren unerned giue, and undeð-licnesse. **1599** Shaks. *Mids. N.* v. i. 439 If we haue vnearned lucke, Now to scape the Serpents tongue, We will make amends ere long. **1796** Mme. D'Arblay *Camilla* II. 383 The sufferings, so utterly unearned by fault or by folly, of a sister so dear to her. **1805** Wordsw. *Prelude* VI. 168 Such dispositions then were mine unearned By aught, I fear, of genuine desert.

**2.** Not earned by labour; not worked for.

**1667** Milton *P. L.* IX. 225 Casual discourse.. intermits Our dayes work brought to little,.. and th' hour of Supper comes unearn'd. **1708** J. Philips *Cyder* I. 374 Wilt thou.. rather chuse To lye supinely, hoping Heav'n will.. give thee Bread unearn'd? **1799** Coleridge *Ode to Duchess of Devonsh.* 17 Rich viands.. Were yours unearned by toil. **1850** Grote *Greece* II. lxii. VIII. 53 This anticipation of an unearned salary. **1873** Hamerton *Intell. Life* I. iii. 11 One of the unearned gifts of nature.

**b.** *Unearned increment*, such increase in the value of land or property as takes place without labour or expenditure on the part of the owner.

**1873** J. S. Mill in *Dissert. & Discuss.* (1875) IV. 299 The detention by the State of the unearned increment of rent. **1884** in A. Cawston *Street Improv. London* (1893) 115 The increased value, the unearned increment of this property.

**Unea·rnest,** *a.* (Un-[1] 7.)

**1542** Udall *Erasm. Apoph.* 332 Al ye whyle [he] pronounced suche an hainous matier wt an unearnest countenaunce. **1548** — *Erasm. Par. Luke* xii. 105 Except that euen those veraie thinges.. be possessed of vs after an vnearnest sorte. **1611** Florio, *Disferuorare*, to make vnearnest, to coole. **1877** Abp. Benson in *Life* (1899) I. 435 The state of things in which she wrote was.. very unearnest in many ways.

**Unea·rth,** *v.* [Un-[2] 5 and 6.]

**1.** *trans.* To dig out of the earth, to exhume; to disclose by the removal of earth.

*c* **1450** *Mirour Saluacioun* (Roxb.) 7 When he his fadirs body efter deth vnherthid. **1626** T. H[awkins] *Caussin's Holy Ct.* 67 As Diamonds buryed in a Dunghill, which if once you vn-earth,.. will set the sunne before your eyes. **1798** Wordsw. *Simon Lee* 75, I chanced to see This old Man doing all he could To unearth the root of an old tree. *a* **1845** Barham *Ingol. Leg.* Ser. III. *Knight & Lady*, His cane,.. which he used.. when unearthing his worms and his grubs. **1877** Huxley *Physiogr.* 209 When the ruins were first unearthed, the upper floor stood much higher.

**b.** To force out of a hole or burrow.

**1622** Mabbe tr. *Aleman's Guzman d'Alf.* I. 48 Hee was jealous, that the Foxe was now vn-earthed. **1730** Thomson *Autumn* 475 The sly destroyer of the flock.. from his craggy winding haunts unearth'd. **1818** Scott *Rob Roy* xii, We will join the rest.. and see their luck at unearthing the badger. **1844** H. H. Wilson *Brit. India* III. 39 One man .. dug a hole in the ground deep enough to give him shelter, .. [but] he was speedily unearthed.

*transf.* **1841** Lever *C. O'Malley* cxii, Oh, it's you, is it?— at last! so I've unearthed you, have I?

**c.** To free from, to clear by removal of, earth.

**1663** Davenant *Siege of Rhodes* I. 31 Away! unchain the Streets, unearth the Ports! Pull down each barracade!

**2.** *fig.* To bring to light; to disclose, reveal, discover, etc. (Freq. from *c* 1860.)

**1820** Byron *Blues* ii, *Scamp.* They have merit, I own... *Ink.* Then why not unearth it in one of your lectures? **1863** Cowden Clarke *Shaks. Char.* xii. 308 You may trust a woman to unearth a plot. **1883** Stevenson *Silverado Sq.* 114 What would I not have given to unearth a letter..?

**3.** *fig.* To free from earthly qualities.

**1765** J. Brown *Chr. Jrnl.* 286 O to be unearthed, unselfed, that I may be like him!

Hence **Unea·rthed** *ppl. a.*[1]; **Unea·rthing** *vbl. sb.* and *ppl. a.*

**1612** *Two Noble K.* v. i. 58 Thou mighty one,.. whose havocke in vaste Feild Vnearthed skulls proclaime. **1870** Morris *Earthly Par.* III. IV. 21 An unearthed blind mole.. Was wandering there. **1876** Fox Bourne *Locke* II. xv. 527 To invent,.. with much.. material of his own unearthing, the art of logic. **1897** *19th Cent.* Aug. 276, I got to regard a resurrection man as.. an unearthly because unearthing demon.

**Unea·rthed,** *ppl. a.*[2] [Un-[1] 8.] Not buried; not carried into the ground.

**1513** Douglas *Æneid* VI. ii. 145 Vnerdit lyis of new the deid body. *Ibid.* v. 62. **1905** *Elect. World & Engin.* 18 Feb. 339 (Cent. Suppl.), Giving over 14,000 volts between the unearthed conductors.

**Unea·rthliness.** (Un-[1] 12; cf. next.)

(*a*) **1860** Pusey *Min. Proph.* 569 A picture of our Lord's humility and of the unearthliness of His kingdom. **1896** G. A. Simcox in *Academy* 22 Feb. 150/3 The world.. liked him all the better for the elegant unearthliness of his aspect.

(*b*) **1867** H. Macmillan *Bible Teach.* ii. 33 There was a coldness and unearthliness about it.. which repelled.. me.

**Unea·rthly,** *a.* [Un-[1] 7.]

**1.** Rising above what is characteristic of earth; exalted, sublime; celestial.

**1611** Shaks. *Wint. T.* III. i. 7 O, the Sacrifice. How ceremonious, solemne, and vn-earthly It was i' th' Offring? **1795** Coleridge *Refl. Place of Retirem.* 24 The inobtrusive song of Happiness, Unearthly minstrelsy! **1855** Brimley *Ess.* (1858) 304 [An] almost unearthly intensity of faith, love, and resignation. **1876** H. W. Pullen *Mod. Christianity* 73

Having made choice of an unearthly Guide, you should be content to follow Him along unearthly paths.

**2.** Not belonging to this earth; supernatural, mysterious, ghostly. (Cf. Sc. *wanearthly*.)

*a* **1802** *Tamlane* xxxv. in Scott *Minstrelsy*, How shall I thee knaw Amang so many unearthly knights? **1828** Lytton *Pelham* II. x, A mysterious and unearthly communion of the soul with the beings of another world. **1871** L. Stephen *Playgr. Eur.* ii. 82 There is something almost unearthly in the sight of enormous spaces of hill and plain.

**b.** Of sounds or voices.

**1808** Scott *Marm.* II. Introd., In the bittern's distant shriek, I heard unearthly voices speak. **1846** Mrs. A. Marsh *Father Darcy* II. xi. 183 The unearthly sound..immediately ceased. **1890** 'R. Boldrewood' *Col. Reformer* (1891) 150 The half-heard music is full of unearthly cadences.

**c.** *colloq.* Not appropriate to anything earthly; absurdly early or inconvenient.

**1865** Mrs. Carlyle *Lett.* (1883) III. 267 Your starting from the Gill at an unearthly hour. **1891** Mrs. Riddell *Mad Tour* 63 In the streets of Cologne at that unearthly hour in the morning.

**Unea·se,** *sb.* [Un-[1] 12. Cf. Wanease *sb.*] Want or lack of ease; discomfort; uneasiness.

App. not in use in the 18th cent., and not common in the 19th till about 1880.

*a* **1300** *Cursor M.* 29091 Discipline..in askes and in hare, And weping and vneses lair. *c* **1400** *Rom. Rose* 3102 Thanne seide I, ser, not you displease To knowen of myn gret vnnese. *a* **1450** *Knt. de la Tour* (1906) 152 That none other creatoure aught not to be ameruailed to suffre displesaunce and vnese, whanne so high a lady suffered..so gret sorw and tribulacion. **1523** Ld. Berners tr. *Froiss.* I. cxlvi. 174 We haue endured moche payne and vnease. **1593** Nashe *Christ's Tears* 13 More and more thou addest to my vnease. **1632** Lithgow *Trav.* vii. 327 In this unease Of tackling Boards, we so the way make short. **1676** Hobbes *Iliad* Pref. (1686) 3 Such unease, as in a Coach a man unexpectedly finds in passing over a furrow. **1828** Carr *Craven Gloss.*, *Unease*, uneasiness. **1857** Sir F. Palgrave *Norm. & Eng.* II. 458 The unease thereby occasioned was exceedingly enhanced.. when general belief superadded [etc.]. **1894** J. Knight *D. Garrick* vii. 109 A tendency to self-consciousness with a consequent unease was a fault of his style.

† **Unea·se,** *v. Obs.* [Un-[2] 4.] *trans.* To incommode, trouble, distress.

*c* **1400** *Laud Troy Bk.* 14481 Vnnethes of vs is any That we nare wounded or vnhesed. *c* **1440** *Pallad. on Husb.* III. 562 Cannetes old ek tyme is now to wede, And of to kytte hit that their roote vneseth. **1464** *Rolls of Parlt.* V. 568/1 The comon people..is gretely uneased therby. *c* **1590** J. Stewart *Poems* (S.T.S.) II. 195 Not, Sir, till vneis 3ow, Bot mening to meis 3ow.

**Unea·seful,** *a.* (Un-[1] 7.)

**1515** in Ellis *Orig. Lett.* Ser. II. I. 266 Forsomuche as the Quene-is lyeng here is uneasfull and costelye, by occasion of farre cariage of every thing. **1567** Drant *Horace, Ep.* xii. E iij, For thou this drosse, vneasefull drosse, doste sette but little by. **1840** Lowell *The Moon* 28 Howe'er its waves above May toss and seem uneaseful.

Hence **Unea·sefulness.**

**1661** Rust *Origen's Opin.* 74 If this gentler smart and uneasefulness will not reclaim them.

**Unea·sily,** *adv.* [Un-[1] 11.]

† **1. a.** With difficulty on account of discomfort; only with pain or suffering. *Obs.*

*c* **1290** *Beket* 2211 in *S. Eng. Leg.* I. 170 With luytel aise he mi3te sitte, and ful on-aisi-liche ride, And on-aisiliche ligge also. **1535** Stewart *Cron. Scot.* (Rolls) II. 534 Vneselie thocht that he mycht ryde or go,..Than vp he rais rycht fraklie on his feit. **1600** Hakluyt *Voy.* III. 54 It was.. counted a place very hardly and vneasily to be inhabited for the great colde.

† **b.** Not in any easy or simple manner; with difficulty or trouble. *Obs.*

**1600** E. Blount tr. *Conestaggio* 232 Where (although vneasily)..they might imbarke and descend. **1669** Sturmy *Mariner's Mag.* A. 4, I might haply appear..monstrous to the eye of the World, and uneasily escape submersion. **1725** Sloane *Jamaica* II. 17 They are uneasily kept from apes and squirrels.

**2.** In an uneasy or uncomfortable manner; in such a way as to cause discomfort.

In older use (*a*) of physical uneasiness.

(*a*) **1377** Langl. *P. Pl.* B. xiv. 232 He goth to cold beddynge, And his heued vn-heled vn-esiliche I-wrye. *a* **1425** tr. *Arderne's Treat. Fistula*, etc. 38 Þai slepe vnesely; þai ar made heuy als wele in mynde as in body. **1550** Thomas *Ital. Dict.*, *Distretto*, straictly or vneasilie. **1621** J. Taylor (Water P.) *Sir G. Nonsence* Wks. (1630) Aa 1 b, Resting vneasily on a banke of Sicamores. **1822–7** Good *Study Med.* (1829) I. 211 Concentrated jellies..sit more uneasily on a weak stomach, than meat..in a solid form.

(*b*) **1863** Mrs. Oliphant *Salem Chapel* iv. 30 Mr. Vincent stood uneasily at a corner when he was brought into the apartment. **1887** Miss Betham-Edwards *Next of Kin Wanted* II. xi. 140 He..hemmed and ha'd uneasily.

† **3.** Without ease; awkwardly. *Obs.*—[0]

**1611** Cotgr., *Inhabilement*,..vnweldily, vneasily, vnhandsomely.

**Unea·siness.** [Un-[1] 12.]

† **1.** The quality of being troublesome. *Obs.*

**1387** Trevisa *Higden* (Rolls) VII. 331 He commaundede to put out Lanfranc out of Normandye for his unesynes [L. *pro sua importunitate*]. **1712** in J. J. Vernon *Par. & Kirk Hawick* (1900) 100 The s[ai]d day compeared Bessie Pasley..for her uneasiness among her nighbours.

† **2.** Difficulty; difficult nature or character.

**1594** R. Ashley tr. *Loys le Roy* 73 b, The vneasinesse of the places where he made his Conquests. **1645** Ussher *Body Div.* 271 Frowardnesse, and uneasinesse to be intreated. **1691** T. H[ale] *Acc. New Invent.* 38 Very apt to gather Filth, and of no less uneasiness when fouled to be thoroughly cleansed again.

† **b.** Unwillingness, reluctance. *Obs.*

*a* **1715** Burnet *Own Time* II. viii. (1897) I. 374 The king.. charged him to tell him the truth. The other did it, though not without some uneasiness. **1737** Whiston *Josephus, Hist.* IV. iii. § 3 The Roman garrisons,..partly out of their uneasiness to take such trouble,..did little or nothing.

† **c.** Unpleasantness; ill feeling. *Obs.*

*a* **1734** North *Lives* (1826) III. 366, I mentioned before some uneasinesses between the doctor and his seniors about elections. **1771** Ledwich *Antiq. Sarisb.* 42 The Prelate stiffly refused, and thereby created much uneasiness between Henry and Pope Paschal.

**3.** Discomfort, trouble, or anxiety, as affecting one's circumstances or welfare. Also (with pl.), an instance of this.

**1599** Shaks. *Hen. V*, II. ii. 27 There's not I thinke a subiect That sits in heart-greefe and vneasinesse Vnder the sweet shade of your gouernment. **1658** *Whole Duty Man* vii. § 9 An abundant amends for all the uneasiness and hardship thou canst suffer in the way. **1681** J. Scott *Chr. Life* I. i. 8 Short intermissions of the pains and uneasinesses of a wretched Life. **1740** Richardson *Pamela* I. 13 But, may-be, without these Uneasinesses to mingle with these Benefits, I might be too much puffed up. **1805** A. Knox *Rem.* (1834) I. 29 When we wish to rise above worldly uneasiness.

**b.** Physical discomfort (falling short of actual or definite pain).

**1665** Boyle *Occas. Refl.* II. xiv. 235 Having sadly Experienc'd the uneasiness of Sickness. **1709** *Phil. Trans.* XXVI. 491 The Cause of this Peeping in the Shell, I take to be from some Uneasiness the young Bird may find there. **1774** Goldsm. *Nat. Hist.* (1776) II. 55 The infant's cries are sufficient indications of the uneasinesses it must at every interval endure. **1815** J. Smith *Panorama Sci. & Art* II. 446 With nearly all persons who have breathed this gas, not the least uneasiness or languor subsequently remains. **1862** A. Meadows *Man. Midwifery* 220 Pain in the seat of injury, followed by a general sense of uneasiness and distension.

**c.** Mental discomfort; anxiety, apprehension.

**1682** Norris *Hierocles* 60 There is a necessity therefore of Impatience and Uneasiness, and that our misery be augmented from the ignorance of our selves. **1709** Lady M. W. Montagu *Let. to Miss A. Wortley* 8 Aug., Till then I shall be in terrible uneasiness. **1756** Cowper *Wks.* (1837) XV. 291, I have lately been under some uneasiness at your silence. **1844** Kinglake *Eothen* xviii, My coming from an infected city did not cause him the least uneasiness. **1885** 'Mrs. Alexander' *At Bay* iv, The next day brought Glynn a few lines..which struck him as expressing more uneasiness than was intended.

**Unea·stern,** *a.* (Un-[1] 7.) **1760–2** Goldsm. *Cit. W.* li, Unnatural, un-Eastern,..would be the whole cry. **1838** Thackeray *Major Gahagan* iv, The phraseology peculiar to my own country..is so uneastern.

**Unea·sy,** *a.* [Un-[1] 7.]

**1.** Not conducing to ease or comfort; productive of physical discomfort. Also in fig. context. † Occas. const. *to* (a person).

*c* **1290** *Beket* 1446 in *S. Eng. Leg.* I. 148 Swiþe on-aisi [*v.r.* unese] was is brech a-boute for-to ride. **1398** Trevisa *Barth. De P. R.* XVII. clxix. (Bodl. MS.), Whete þat groweth in vnmoderat tyme & vnesy wedre & tyme is vnperfite. **1601** Holland *Pliny* II. 265 If the skin be newly fretted off by wearing some uneasie shoes. **1660** N. Ingelo *Bentiv. & Ur.* II. (1682) 21 Golden fetters are as uneasie as those of Iron. **1713** *Guardian* No. 32 ⁋ 7 [He] appeared in Cloths, that were so strait and uneasy to him, that he seemed to move with Pain. **1748** *Anson's Voy.* II. v. 183 The heat in..the tropics must be much more troublesome and uneasy. **1820** Keats *Hyperion* II. 64 Above her, on a crag's uneasy shelve, ..Shadow'd Enceladus. **1860** Hawthorne *Marb. Faun* viii, A minute's walk will transport the visitor from the small, uneasy lava stones.

† **b.** Causing mental discomfort or disquietude; unpleasant, disagreeable. *Obs.*

Very common in 18th cent., freq. with *to*.

**1483** *Gower's Conf.* (Caxton) v. 459 Wherof it is y^t^ he conceyueth That ylke vnesy [*orig.* unsely] maladye, The which is cleped jelousye. **1669** Earl Orrery *Parthen.* (1676) 790 Till I knew my Fate..I should be in Horrors, whose visible Effects were the least uneasie part of them. **1691** Stillingfleet *Charge* 52 Nothing will be more uneasie to me, than to be forced to make use of any Severity against you. **1744** Johnson *Let. to J. Levett* 3 Jan., Not to have the satisfaction of waiting upon [you]..will be a great and uneasy disappointment. **1788** Charlotte Smith *Emmeline* (1816) IV. 240 The anxiety of Delamere..is uneasy even to me. **1798** — *Yng. Philos.* IV. 209 My mother,..I thought, wished..to conceal something from me; that something then must be uneasy.

**c.** Characterized by absence of ease or comfort; suggesting or manifesting want of ease in body or mind.

*a* **1513** Fabyan *Chron.* VI. clxxii. 167 Alurede, beynge thus ouerset in multytude of enemyes,..ladde an vncertayne lyfe, and vneasy. **1590** Spenser *F. Q.* I. v. 36 Where was a Caue.. Deepe, darke, vneasie, dolefull, comfortlesse. **1647** Clarendon *Hist. Reb.* II. § 55 They..made the residence of any amongst them very uneasy, and very insecure, who were but suspected by them not to wish well to their Proceedings. **1667** Milton *P. L.* I. 295 His Spear..He walkt with to support uneasie steps Over the burning Marle. **1748** *Anson's Voy.* II. v. 184 That uneasy and suffocating sensation. **1780** *Mirror* No. 88, I soon found my situation at the university a very hard and uneasy one. **1846** Mrs. A. Marsh *Father Darcy* II. iii. 75 He sank into an uneasy slumber. **1893** Tout *Edw. I*, 54 The surgeons exchanged uneasy whispers.

† **2.** Of persons: Troublesome, annoying, disagreeable, unaccommodating (*to* others). *Obs.*

**1387** Trevisa *Higden* (Rolls) I. 87 Euere þei beeþ vnesi [L. *inquieti*] to hir owne neiheboures oþer to strong [=strange] men. *c* **1400** *Pilgr. Sowle* (Caxton, 1483) IV. xxxiv. 83 Shirreues shold speke for the peple, so that they be nought mysfaren ne ouercharged with ouer sore seruyce ne by vnesy lordes. **1652** *Nicholas Papers* (Camden) 291, I am much afraid that Mr. Attorney will be very unquiet with his associates and uneasy to the K[ing] in council. **1678** Dryden *All for Love* II. i. 26, I kept you far from an uneasie Wife. *a* **1715** Burnet *Own Time* II. xii. (1897) I. 481 He was cynical in the whole administration, and uneasy to the king in every thing. **1737** Whiston *Josephus, Antiq.* I. xviii. § 4 Not caring to be uneasy to his son,..he resolved to be silent.

† **b.** Unfriendly; on bad terms. *Obs.*—[1]

**1725** P. Walkden *Diary* (1866) 15, I..discoursed them concerning the division that is among them, and they both own they had been uneasy, but were now reconciled.

† **c.** Displeased, dissatisfied. *Obs.*

*a* **1715** Burnet *Own Time* III. vii. (1900) II. 125 The king was uneasy at this, and sent them several very angry messages. *Ibid.* xvii. 449 The king seemed to be so uneasy with him, that he was glad to send him away from the court.

**d.** Uncompromising, rigid.

**1819** Byron *Juan* I. lxii, Ladies even of the most uneasy virtue Prefer a spouse whose age is short of thirty.

**3.** Not easy or simple; difficult, hard, troublesome. Now *rare*. (Common in 17th c.)

In first quot. = 'having difficulty'.

**1398** Trevisa *Barth. De P. R.* v. vi. (Tollem. MS.), The thycker and more trowbled spirite that a man hathe, the uneasyer [L. *tanto difficilior*] and the feblier of syghte he is. *Ibid.* VI. xx. (Bodl. MS.), In olde menne abstinence of mete is eth and esy, and in 3onge menne & children hard and vnesye. **1570** Levins *Manip.* 108 Vneasy, *difficilis*. **1591** Savile *Tac. Hist.* I. xxi. 50 By lewdenesse and craft (a matter not vneasy) [he] bare it away from good men. **1614** Raleigh *Hist. World* I. III. 139 About this time the Spartans beganne to perceive how uneasie a thing it would bee to maintaine the warre against men as good as themselves. **1663** Boyle *Consid. Usef. Nat. Philos.* II. (1664) 348 To keep the rectified Spirit..is more uneasie, than any thing but trial would make one think. *a* **1724** in *Ramsay's Tea-t. Misc.* (1733) I. 22 If I can but get it [*sc.* a sword] drawn, Which will be right uneasy. **1851** Helps *Comp. Solit.* iii. 37 By a not uneasy diversion of mind, I turned to another branch. **1900–1** in *Eng. Dial. Dict.*

**b.** Const. with inf. (active or passive).

(*a*) *a* **1548** Hall *Chron., Edw. IV*, 241 The kyng of England answered, that the tounes of Flanders were..verie uneasie to bee kepte when they were conquered. **1603** H. Crosse *Vertues Commw.* (1878) 45 A way vneasie to be trackt, hard to finde. **1666** Boyle *Orig. Forms & Qual.* 268 Much more elaborate, and therefore more uneasie to be restored, then that of many other Concretes.

(*b*) **1570** Buchanan *Admonitioun* Wks. (S.T.S.) 26 It is not vneasie to persave..that yai meane..ye deid of ye King. **1594** Sylvester *Monodia* 82 Till time..had worne away Her sorrowe's edge, uneasie to allay. **1621** Quarles *Div. Poems, Esther* Wks. (Grosart) II. 58/2 To him there's nought vneasie to atchieue. **1690** T. Burnet *Theory Earth* II. 163 It will be very uneasie to give a satisfactory account ..of the regeneration. **1819** Scott *Ivanhoe* ii, 'The road will be uneasy to find,' answered Gurth.

† **c.** Of ways, etc.: Difficult to traverse on account of ruggedness, steepness, or other obstacles. *Obs.*

**1550** T. Hoby *Trav.* (1902) 46 It is a very uneasie waye by the reason of the great quantitie of great and sharpe stones that are upon yt. **1604** E. G[rimstone] *D'Acosta's Hist. Indies* IV. vi. 221 As he strived to gette vp a way which was somewhat rough and vneasie, hee was forced to lay holde vpon a braunch. **1697** Dryden *Æneis* XI. 458 The flood, constrained within a scanty space, Roars horrible along the uneasy race. **1756** Nugent *Gr. Tour, Italy* III. 38 Gentlemen..are in the wrong to choose to travel there in winter, for the ways are uneasy at that time, and dangerous.

† **d.** Difficult to handle. *Obs.*—[0]

**1611** Cotgr., *Inhabile*,..vnweldie, vneasie, vnhandsome.

**4.** Uncomfortable or disturbed in mind; anxious, apprehensive.

**1680** Burnet *Rochester* Pref. A 5 b, He..seemed not uneasie at my frequent Visits. **1693** in *Verney Memoirs* (1907) II. 486 Nothing but the want of your blessing can make me uneasie, for otherwise I am perfectly happy. **1719** De Foe *Crusoe* II. (Globe) 362 The Spaniard..found himself very uneasy in the Night, and could by no Means get any Sleep. **1748** *Anson's Voy.* II. ix. 230 We began to be uneasy for her safety. **1782** Miss Burney *Cecilia* v. i, It contributed to render her thoughtful and uneasy. **1832** Ht. Martineau *Ireland* 38 His countenance brightened,..but he still seemed uneasy till he had put one question. **1859** W. Collins *Q. of Hearts* I. 117, I was..as anxious and as uneasy as our guest.

**b.** Suffering physical discomfort.

**1725** N. Robinson *Th. Physick* 276 If he be very restless and uneasy, let the following Prescriptions be exhibited.

**c.** Of animals: Restless, unsettled.

**1855** *Poultry Chron.* II. 449/2 Should they not be fed at regular intervals, it will tend to make them uneasy and discontented. **1897** 'Mrs. Rayner' *Type-writer Girl* xix, Like ..restless Spanish sheep in spring, when they herd and leap, uneasy to be driven to their pastures in the mountains.

**d.** *transf.* Of things: Moving in a disturbed or unquiet manner.

**1816** L. Hunt *Rimini* III. 61 Scattering smiles on this uneasy earth. *c* **1860** H. Stuart *Seaman's Catech.* 62 Weights at the extremities cause a ship to be uneasy in a seaway. **1894** Crockett *Raiders* 103 The upper arch of the cave is not less than forty feet above the floor of uneasy water.

**5.** Quasi-*adv.* Uneasily.

**1596** Mascall *Govt. Cattle* 120 Let your axeltrees..fill close the nathes of the wheeles, for when they gaggle or shake, they goe vneasie. **1597** Shaks. 2 *Hen. IV*, III. i. 31 Vneasie lyes the Head, that weares a Crowne. **1684** *Contempl. St. Man* II. viii. (1699) 226 You..will perswade your self, that you never laid so uneasie in your whole Life before. **1807** Southey *Espriella's Lett.* I. 176 The farmer told him it was but an uneasy-going beast. **1862** Thackeray *Philip* xxviii, [So] thinks the general, rolling uneasy on the midnight pillow.

**Unea·table,** *a.* (Un-[1] 7 b.)

**1611** Cotgr., *Immangeable*, vneatable, vnfit to be fed on. **1775** Adair *Amer. Ind.* 16 The..Indians..formerly reckoned it [*sc.* opossum] as..uneatable an animal, as a hog. **1798**

W. BLAIR *Soldier's Friend* 16 Biscuits would..be preferable: a loaf becomes mouldy and uneatable in a few days. **1861** MUSGRAVE *By-roads* 12 A dreary breadth of sand hills, dotted with tufts of uneatable herbage and rank weeds. **1876** MRS. WHITNEY *Sights & Ins.* xviii, We got an uneatable dinner (having blundered upon a wrong hotel).

Hence **Unea·tableness.**

**1869** *Trans. Entom. Soc.* I. 21 Thus showing that the spines were not the cause of the uneatableness of the larvæ.

**Unea·ten,** *ppl. a.* [UN-¹ 8 b. Cf. ON. *ú-etinn*, MDu. *ongeëten* (Du. *-gegeten*), MLG. *ungegeten*, MHG. *ungeëzzen*, *-gëzzen* (G. *ungegessen*).] Not eaten; left undevoured.

*c* **1290** *St. Brendan* 301 in *S. Eng. Leg.* I. 227 Al ore couent nis nouȝt here, ake muche it hath vn-ete [*v.r.* for moche del is un-y-ete]. *c* **1375** *Sc. Leg. Saints* vii. (*James Min.*) 682 For nothire wes lewit in þat towne hwnde, na catte,..vnhetyne, be þis wes done. *c* **1450** *Bk. Hawking* in *Rel. Ant.* I. 307 Of thees fleschys loke that she have good plente ech day, so that sche leve sum what uneton. **1611** BEAUM. & FL. *King & No King* III, Therefore I will out-swear him and all his followers, that this is all that's left uneaten of my sword. **1630** J. TAYLOR (Water P.) *Siege Jerus.* Wks. 15/1 From out their throats they tear the meat in haste, Halfe eaten, halfe vneaten. **1791** COWPER *Odyss.* VIII. 582 A huge brawn, of which uneaten still Large part and delicate remain'd. **1868** *Rep. U. S. Commissioner Agric.* (1869) 297 The remains of the uneaten leaves must be carefully taken away.

**Unea·th,** *a.* *Obs.* or *arch.* Forms: (see quots.) [OE. *unéaðe*, *-ieðe*, etc.: see UN-¹ 7 and EATH *a.*] Difficult, hard, troublesome, distressing.

*a* **900** *Andreas* 205 Nis þæt uneaðe eallwealdan gode to ȝefremmanne on foldweȝe. *c* **1000** ÆLFRIC *Saints' Lives* xiii. 247 Þa cwæð dauid him to: Uneaðe me is ðis. *c* **1050** *Voc.* in Wr.-Wülcker 444 *Molestus*, unyþe. *a* **1200** *Moral Ode* 181 Nis na sullic þech hom bo wa and hom bo uneade [*v.r.* uneaðe]. *c* **1205** LAY. 2259 Corineus wes un-eðe, & wa on his mode.

**1570** LEVINS *Manip.* 213 Vneathe, *difficilis*. **1590** SPENSER *F. Q.* IV. x. 39 An altar of some costly masse, Whose substance was vneath to vnderstand. **1629** H. BURTON *Truth's Triumph* 210 The..hare..makes many doubles,..that vneath it is for the most sagacious pursuer to..finde her out. **1647** H. MORE *Song of Soul* II. liii, But what's within, uneath is to convey To narrow vessels that are full afore. *Ibid.* lxxxv. **1714** CROXALL *Another Orig. Canto Spenser* xii, Where Freres and Monks swarm round, that it uneath May seem 'mongst them to live. **1767** MICKLE *Concubine* II. xxxvii, Uneath it is long Habits to expell. **1799** SCOTT *Covenanter's Fate* xxii, 'I fear me,' quoth he, 'uneath it will be To match thy word with deed'.

**Uneath** (*vnī·þ*), *adv.* Now only *arch.* Forms: *α.* 1–3 uneaðe (3 -æðe), 2–3 uneðe (2 -ieþe), 3 on-, 4 uneþe, 4–6 unethe (4–5 on-), 6 *Sc.* on-, uneith, 6– uneath. *β.* 3–5 unneþe (3 -eæþe, -eðe, onneþe), 4–6 (9) unnethe (5 onnethe, unnythe); 3 unneaðe, -eaþe, 4 onn(y)eaþe, 6–7 unneath, 7 unneeth. *γ.* 4–7 uneth (5–6 oneth), 4 unneþ, 4–7 unneth. (Also 3–7 vn-.) [OE. *unéaðe*, f. *un-* UN-¹ 11 b + *éaðe* EATH *adv.*]

**1.** Not easily; (only) with difficulty; scarcely, hardly.

In very common use from *c* 1300 to *c* 1600. Usually denoting limitation of the power to act in the way desired or intended, so that the sense of 'scarcely' becomes the prominent one.

*c* **888** K. ÆLFRED *Boeth.* v. § 3 Uneaþe ic mæȝ forstandan þine acsunga. *Ibid.* xxxix. § 4 Uneaðe hire cymð ænig mon of, ȝif he ærest an cemð. *c* **950** *Lindisf. Gosp.* Matt. xix. 23 Forðon wlonc uneaðe *vel* hefiȝ innȝeongas in ric heofna. *a* **1000** *Colloq. Ælfric* in Wr.-Wülcker 96 Hwylon forlidenesse ic þolie.., uneaþe cwic ætberstende. ? *a* **1050** *O. E. Chron.* (MS. C) an. 1040, He..astealde þa swiðe strang ȝyld, þæt man hit uneaðe acom. *c* **1205** LAY. 31438 Mucchel del heo sloȝen of þan mon-weorede, and þe king Penda uneðe gon anwende. *a* **1250** *Owl & Night.* 1605 Þu me hauest sore igremed..Þat ic may vnneþe speke. **13..** *Sir Beues* (A.) 884 So mani arwes to him þai sende, Unneþe a miȝte him self defende. *c* **1369** CHAUCER *Dethe Blaunche* 712 As I yow telle Vnnethe myght y lenger duelle. **1382** *Pol. Poems* (Rolls) I. 267 Unnethe may prestes seculers Gete any service for thes frers. *c* **1440** *Generydes* 977 So sorowfull he was That he onnethe myght speke to the kyng. *Ibid.* 4946 [He] was..sore for-bled that vnnethe myght he stonde. *a* **1450** *Knt. de la Tour* (1906) 9 Making suche noise that unnethe thei might haue herde the thundre. **1542** UDALL *Erasm. Apoph.* 338 b, Whiche did asmuche benefite to the commenweale, as uneth any penne maye wryte. **1578** LYTE *Dodoens* v. lxxiv. 641 The blades are cut almost euery day harde by the grounde,..and therefore it can vnethe or scarsely growe vp. **1601** HOLLAND *Pliny* II. 90 Thyme seed lyeth so close, that unneth or hardly it can be found. **1631** GOUGE *God's Arrows* I. § 70. 117 There was so grievous a mortality of people, as the quicke might unneath burie the dead. *a* **1656** USSHER *Ann.* (1658) 395 His army grew so loaden with the spoile..that they were unneeth able to march above five mile a day. **1739** G. WEST *Abuse Trav.* xliii, A small river, that full slow did glide, As it uneath mote find its watry path For stones and rubbish. **1805** SCOTT *Last Minstrel* VI. xxix, The standers-by might hear uneath, Footstep, or voice,..Through all the lengthen'd row. **1834** HARE *Guesses* (1848) 346 Man's hard, clencht mouth, whence words uneath do slip.

**b.** Scarcely, hardly, barely (in respect of extent, amount, degree, etc.).

*c* **1200** *Trin. Coll. Hom.* 33 Þeues..wundeden him swiðe sore, and forleten him unneðe liues. **1297** R. GLOUC. (Rolls) 1421 After him was gayus [emperor] vif ȝer vnneþe. *c* **1300** *Seyn Julian* (Ashm. MS.) 178 Þat led þat bolynde was, vnneþe it þoȝte hire warm. *c* **1374** CHAUCER *Anel. & Arc.* 135 On him is al hir thought, Þat wele vnneþe of mete tooke she keepe. **1390** GOWER *Conf.* I. 364 The remenant of folk aboute Unethe stonden eny doute To werre ech other and to slee. *c* **1430** *Two Cookery-bks.* 44 Put hem in a panne.., & vnneþe ony grece in þe panne. **1484** CAXTON *Fables of Alfonce* i, I haue lyued lenger than thy self haste & vnnethe I haue gete half a frend. **1542** UDALL *Erasm. Apoph.* 296 Uneth any tree [is] more goodly to beholde afarre of then the cypres tree. **1596** FITZ-GEFFREY *Sir F. Drake* (1881) 58 Honour enmoves her to attempt the flight, And wave her feathers (unneath taught to flie). **1606** N. BAXTER *Sidney's Ourania* D ij, Ignorant, lewde, Uneth with one drop of Nectar bedewde.

†**c.** With accompanying negative. *Obs.*

**13..** *Guy Warw.* (A.) 254 He no dar his loue keþe, No sen hir wel vnneþe. **1362** LANGL. *P. Pl.* A. v. 100 Al my breste bolleþ for bitter of my galle; May no suger so swete aswagen hit vnneþe. *c* **1400** MAUNDEV. (1919) xxii. 128 Fissches..casten hem self to the see banke of þat yle, so gret plentee..þat noman may vnnethe see but fissch. **1412–20** LYDG. *Chron. Troy* I. 3392 Wel onethe he ne myȝt endure Hym to dismembre. **1477** *Paston Lett.* III. 175 The causey ..is so over flowyn that ther is no man that may onethe passe it. **1559** *Primer* in *Priv. Prayers* (1851) 90, I dare not unneth make my prayers unto thee, for thou art angry with me. **1600** FAIRFAX *Tasso* v. xxxiv, And further ads,..That none offence could greater be vneath, And yet the place the fault did aggrauate.

†**d.** *ellipt.* with *but.* (Cf. BUT *conj.* 7.) *Obs.*

**1601** WEEVER *Mirr. Mart.* C 2 b, A vile contagious mist which can vnneath But pestilence or worse diseases breede.

†**e.** *erron.* Almost. *Obs. rare.*

**1590** SPENSER *F. Q.* I. xi. 4 A roaring hideous sound That ..seemd vneath to shake the stedfast ground. **1600** FAIRFAX *Tasso* IV. lix, Thus causelesse hatred, endlesse is vneath.

†**2. a.** Reluctantly, unwillingly. *Obs.*

*c* **900** tr. *Baeda's Hist.* II. ii. 100 Þa ȝeðafodan þæt uneaðe þa his ȝesacan. *c* **1000** ÆLFRIC *Gen.* xxxiii. 11 Ic bidde þe, þæt þu onfo þissa laca..Þa underfeng he hiȝ uneaðe. *a* **1200** *Moral Ode* 189 We ȝeueð uneðe [*v.r.* uneaðe] for his luue a stuche of ure brede. **1382** WYCLIF *Gen.* xxxiii. 11 Vnneth, the brother compellynge, takynge [he] seith, Goo we togideres.

†**b.** In difficult circumstances; in hardship. *Obs.*

**1591** SPENSER *F. Q.* I. ix. 38 Is then uniust to each his due to giue?..Or let him die at ease, that liueth here vneath? *a* **1592** GREENE *Selimus* I. 375 The gray-beard..liu'd at ease, while others liu'd vneath.

†**3.** Scarcely, in respect of time; only just. *Obs.*

*c* **1000** ÆLFRIC *Gen.* xxvii. 30 Uneaðe Isaac ȝeendode þas spræce, þa Iacob ut eode. *c* **1205** LAY. 16397 Vn-neæðe [*c* 1275 onneþe] wes þis spel isæid to þan ende, þa iseȝen heo Hængest halden ouer dune. *a* **1225** *Leg. Kath.* 1993 Þis wes uneaðe iseid, þet an engel ne com: *a* **1300** *Cursor M.* 11685 Vnnethe had he said þe sune, Quen þe tre it boghed dune. **1382** WYCLIF *Gen.* xxvii. 30 Vnneth Ysaac had fulfillid the word, and Jacob goon out, Esau com. *a* **1400–50** *Alexander* 4185 Vnneth his prayer was past, quen purid all þe cloudis. **1513** BRADSHAW *St. Werburge* I. 1227 Whan kynge Vulfer approched his castell And vnneth was entred into his hall. **1556** J. HEYWOOD *Spider & Fly* lxxiv. 83, I was no soner returnd vnneth, Ere I had..judgement of deth.

†**Unea·ths,** *adv.* *Obs.* Forms: *α.* 3 uneðes, 4 uneþes, 4–6 unethes (5–6 -is), 5 onethes (-ys), anedes, 6 uneathes. *β.* 2–3 unneðes, 4 unneþes (-is, -ys, -us), 4–6 unnethes (4–5 -is, 5 -ys), 5 onnethis. *γ.* 4 uneths, 4–5, 7 unneths. *δ.* *north.* and *Sc.* 4 unees, 4–5 un(n)ese, 5 onnese, un(h)es, unnes, wnes, 5–6 uneis, 6 uneais. [f. prec. + -s.]

**1.** = UNEATH *adv.* 1.

*α, β, γ.* *c* **1200** *Trin. Coll. Hom.* 179 Unneðes hie winnen ȝiet here louerdes rihttes. *c* **1220** *Bestiary* 134 He..nimeð vnneðes ðurȝ, for his fel he ðer leteð. *c* **1250** *Gen. & Ex.* 2341 He dede halle ut ðe toðere gon, And spac un-eðes, so e gret. *a* **1300** *Cursor M.* 12686 Hes knes war bolnd sua þat he ne moght vnnethes ga. *Ibid.* 20982 Vneths he bar lif a-way. *c* **1330** R. BRUNNE *Chron. Wace* (Rolls) 1176 Byhinde, bifore, on þeym þei cam, Vneþes any a-wey þer nam. *c* **1380** WYCLIF *Wks.* (1880) 22 Þei wolen travaile..so bisily þat vnneþis may þei at reste seie metenes or masse. **1450** *Paston Lett.* I. 124, I..have so wesshe this litel bille with sorwfulle terys, that on-ethes ye shalle reede it. **1482** *Monk of Evesham* iv. (Arb.) 23 In a voyce onethys audybille and noo thyng intelligibille. *c* **1520** BARCLAY *Jugurth* (1557) 7 b, Vnnethes coude he with moche paine induce him therto. *c* **1530** LD. BERNERS *Arth. Lyt. Bryt.* (1814) 135 Rockes..of suche heyght, that..the toppe of them myght vnnethes be sene. **1590** SPENSER *F. Q.* II. vi. 1 Vneathes it can refraine From that, which feeble nature couets faine. **1621** BP. MOUNTAGU *Diatribæ* 22 For unneths shall we finde a man..but hath a tang one of these two wayes. **1635** HEYWOOD *Hierarchy* IX. 579 He lifts at juggs.., but they..Had been so well fill'd, that he vnneths may Aduance them..to his head.

*δ.* *a* **1300** *Cursor M.* 1648 Al ar þai worthþi for to wite, vnnes es ani funden quite. *c* **1375** *Sc. Leg. Saints* xix. (*Christopher*) 247 Þe lytil barne..wox [h]euiare mare & mare, þat vnese oure þe watir he wane. *c* **1400** *Ywaine & Gaw.* 342 There sal cum slik slete and rayne, That unnese sal thou stand ogayne. *c* **1450** *St. Cuthbert* (Surtees) 282 Þar was a grete clernes of lyght,..Vnnes þar on men luke myght. *c* **1475** *Rauf Coilȝear* 157 He start vp stoutly agane—vneis micht he stand. **1500–20** DUNBAR *Poems* lxxii. 45 Vneis with lyf he mycht sustene That croune.

**2.** = UNEATH *adv.* 2 a.

**1388** WYCLIF *Gen.* xxxiii. 11 Vnnethis, while the brothir compellide, he resseyuede, and seide, Go we to gidere.

**3.** = UNEATH *adv.* 3.

*a* **1300** *Cursor M.* 8159 Vnnethes [*Gött.* vnese] had he monid his mode, Þat a lem fra þe wandes stode. *c* **1340** HAMPOLE *Pr. Consc.* 476 For unnethes es a child born fully þat it ne bygynnes to..cry. **1388** WYCLIF *Gen.* xxvii. 30 Vnnethis Isaac hadde fillid the word, and..Esau cam.

**Unea·ting,** *vbl. sb.* (UN-¹ 13.) **1692** R. L'ESTRANGE *Fables* l. 51 They..that take Eating and Drinking, and Un-Eating, and Un-Drinking,..to be the Great Bus'ness of Mankind. **Une·bbing,** *ppl. a.* (UN-¹ 10.) **1652** BENLOWES *Theoph.* VII. xc, Flouds of unebbing joyes from Thee do rowl. **1822** BYRON *Juan* VII. lxviii, Oh, glorious laurel! since for one sole leaf,..Of blood and tears must flow the unebbing sea.

**Une·briate,** *a.* [UN-¹ 7, 5 b.] **a.** Unintoxicating. **b.** Unintoxicated. **1853** LYTTON *My Novel* IV. xvii, There were.. unebriate liquors, pressed from cooling fruits. *Ibid.* VI. xxii, Forth, unebriate, unpolluted, he came from the orgy. **Unecclesia·stical,** *a.* (UN-¹ 7), **-ally,** *adv.* (UN-¹ 11.) **1766** STERNE *Tr. Shandy* IX. iv, Most un-ecclesiastically did the Corporal do it. **1834** MOZLEY *Lett.* (1885) 40 Newman and all his party declare it to be quite unecclesiastical. **1870** F. R. WILSON *Ch. Lindisf.* 41 Carham Church is another of the unecclesiastical buildings. **Une·choed,** *ppl. a.* (UN-¹ 8.) **1601** SIR W. CORNWALLIS *Ess.* II. xlii, Speach and reason.. loue trafficke and exercise, the former of which is vnecchoed without company. **Une·choing,** *ppl. a.* (UN-¹ 10.) **1817** MOORE *Lalla R.*, *Veiled Proph. Khorassan* 486 The.. Priestess, whose light bound Came like a spirit o'er th' unechoing ground. **1823** J. WILSON *Marg. Lyndsay* ix. 66 There was..no sound in the misty and unechoing air.

**Uneclı·psed,** *ppl. a.* (UN-¹ 8.)

**1649** RAWLINS in Lovelace *Poems* (1904) 8 More bright Then the first day in 's uneclipsed light, Is thy Lucasta. *a* **1657** R. LOVEDAY *Lett.* (1663) 180 Till the uneclipsed Sun shall chase keen winter before his victorious rayes. **1764** *Phil. Trans.* LIV. 106 A full digit of the Sun, or more, remained uneclipsed. **1827** POLLOK *Course T.* VI. 357 The moon..grew black and dark, Unclouded, uneclipsed. **1882** *Nature* XXV. 573 Various phenomena observed on the uneclipsed sun.

*fig.* **1675** tr. *Camden's Hist. Eliz.* III. 269 Her Glory..she retained intire to herself and uneclipsed. **1683** in *Lond. Gaz.* No. 1856/5 An uninterrupted, uneclips'd Monarchy. **1824** GALT *Rothelan* IV. vii, Increasing the lustre of your own hitherto unclouded and uneclipsed renown.

**Unecono·mical,** *a.* (UN-¹ 7), **-ally,** *adv.*, **-alness.** **1816** BENTHAM *Chrestom.* Wks. 1843 VIII. 117 As to uneconomicalness. **1840** HERSCHEL *Ess.* (1857) 109 The abandonment of ancient methods as comparatively inefficient and uneconomical. **1881** *Nature* XXIV. 137 It would work.. not so uneconomically as to be..fatal to the proposed use.

**Une·dge,** *v.* [UN-² 4.] *trans.* To take the edge off; to blunt. Also *fig.*

*a* **1614** FLETCHER *Valentinian* I. iii, Here our weapons And bodies..Are both unedg'd and old with ease and women. **1638** MAYNE *Lucian* (1664) 71 Least despaire should lessen their flame, or unedge their desires. **1718** D'URFEY *Grecian Heroine* v. i, About good Kings, I grant there is a..sacred Virtue That would unedge the Sword of Treachery.

**Une·dged,** *a.* (UN-¹ 9.) **1799** LAMB *J. Woodvil* in *Lett.* (1837) I. 126 To instruct raw youth in..practice of the unedg'd players' foils. **Une·dible,** *a.* (UN-¹ 7 and 5 b.) **1884** *Imp. Dict.* (citing H. Miller). **1894** *19th Cent.* XXXVI. 421 We reposed under a spreading tree, a wild unedible fig.

**Une·dified,** *ppl. a.* (UN-¹ 8.)

**1618** FLETCHER *Women Pleas'd* IV. i, This un-edified ambling, hath brought a scourge upon us. **1644** MILTON *Areop.* (Arb.) 59 Our Ministers..frequented with such an unprincipl'd, unedify'd, and laick rabble. **1740** SOMERVILLE *Hobbinolia* II. 261 In Shoals they come, Neglected, feeless Clients, nor return Unedify'd. **1815** LAMB *Lett.* (1888) I. 298 My zeal is great against the unedified heathen. **1859** SALA *Tw. round Clock* (1861) 58 Not wholly, I trust, unedified by the cursory view we have taken of Babylon the Great.

**Une·difying,** *ppl. a.* (UN-¹ 10, 5 b.)

Also *unedifyingly* adv. (Webster, 1847).

**1641** BP. HALL *Answ. Vind. Smect.* ii. 19 Bringing in loud Musick; uncouth, and unedifying Anthems. **1698** NORRIS *Pract. Disc.* (1707) IV. 2 Those that think and know most, being remarkable for speaking least, which makes their conversation so insignificant and unedifying. **1722** WODROW *Corr.* (1843) II. 649 Matters are yet before sub-committees, and tedious, unedifying debates cast up. **1834** BECKFORD *Italy* II. 309 It was not unedifying to witness the solemnity ..with which these devotions were performed. **1881** W. R. SMITH *Old Test. in Jew. Ch.* i. 10 Finding much that seems .., at first sight, positively unedifying.

**Une·dited,** *ppl. a.* (UN-¹ 8, 5 b.) **1829** *Q. Rev.* XXXIX. 368 The unedited Poem on the Superstitions of the North. **1834** J. AKERMAN (*title*), Descriptive Catalogue of Rare and Unedited Roman Coins. **Une·ducable,** *a.* (UN-¹ 7 b, 5 b.) **1884** *Contemp. Rev.* May 685 The sufferer, unless utterly uneducable, is directed to a suitable dietary. **Une·ducate,** *a.* *Obs.* exc. *Sc.* [UN-¹ 8 b.] Uneducated. **1592** KYD *Sol. & Pers.* I. iii. 141 O harsh, vn-edicate, illiterate pesant. **1871** W. ALEXANDER *Johnny Gibb* xxxv, An inhaudin, unedicat taupie chiel.

**Une·ducate,** *v.* (UN-² 3.)

**1838** R. MUDIE *Man his Phys. Struct.* ii. 66 That system which uneducates the physical powers of the child. **1851** SPENCER *Soc. Stat.* xxvi. § 10. 355 A government can educate in one direction only by *un*educating in another.

**Une·ducated,** *ppl. a.* (UN-¹ 8.)

**1588** SHAKS. *L. L. L.* IV. ii. 17 After his vndressed, vnpolished, vneducated..fashion. *a* **1676** M. HALE *Prov. for Poor* Pref., The multitude of Poor, and necessitous, and uneducated persons. **1780** *Mirror* No. 106, His mind was as empty and uneducated as that of Drexelius. **1847** PRESCOTT *Peru* (1850) II. 348 His uneducated mind had no relish for..intellectual recreation. **1879** B. TAYLOR *Stud. Germ. Lit.* 87 He was wholly uneducated, could not read and write.

Hence **Une·ducatedness.**

**1825** BENTHAM *Offic. Apt. Maximized, Indic.* (1830) 59 Uneducatedness..operating in extenuation of moral guilt.

**Unee·rily,** *adv.* *Sc.* [UN-¹ 11.] †Fearlessly.

*c* **1375** *Sc. Leg. Saints* xliii. (*Cecilia*) 379 Þai brethire þane vnerely Sad to be prefet opynly [etc.].

†**Une·ffable,** *a.* [UN-¹ 7, 5 b.] = INEFFABLE *a.*

*c* **1400** *Comm. Luke* i. 20 (MS. Bodl. 143), Þe heuenly & vneffable natiuyte of crist. **1548** UDALL, etc. *Erasm. Par. John* 26 Therfore there is felt an vneffable strength & efficacie. **1575–85** ABP. SANDYS *Serm.* 264 Yea, inestimable & vneffable was the loue of our gratious Lord. **1614** RALEIGH *Hist. World* I. i. 1 God, whom the wisest men acknowledge to be a Power vneffable. **1689** *Contempl. St. Man* II. iv. (1699) 160 The Joy and Happiness of God, must needs be infinite and uneffable.

**Uneffa·ceable,** *a.* (UN-¹ 7 b and 5 b.) **1611** [see UNDEFACEABLE *a.*]. **1851** [J. B. HUME] *Poems Early Years* 169 A fragment of a sculptur'd stone..; there it lies Apart and uneffaceable.

**Uneffa·ced,** *ppl. a.* (Un-1 8.)
[1775 Ash.] 1792 V. Knox *Serm.* ii. 46 If we have received a good impression, let us bear it away uneffaced to our graves. 1816 Byron *Siege Cor.* iv, Unnamed accusers.. Within the 'Lion's mouth' had placed A charge against him uneffaced. 1864 Pusey *Lect. Daniel* 564 Its own unchanging brightness..uneffaced, undimmed, uninjured.

**Uneffe·cted,** *ppl. a.* (Un-1 8.)
1592 Kyd *Span. Trag.* iii. iv. 80 One onely thing is vneffected yet, And thats to see the Executioner. 1653 Whitelocke *Jrnl. Swed. Emb.* (1772) I. 75 Butt the buisnes was delayed, and uneffected, to Whitelocke's great discouragement. 1846 Worcester (citing C. B. Brown).

**Uneffe·ctible,** *a.* (Un-1 7.) 1646 Earl Monm. tr. *Biondi's Civil Wars* ix. 167 Moved by her womanish anger to practise uneffectible Chimæra's, she lost her Honour. **Uneffe·ctive,** *a.* (Un-1 7 and 5 b.) 1670 C. Gataker in *Gataker's Antid. Errour* Ep. Ded. A iij, The Stars, Skie, Air, or other Elements, which are all..uneffective upon the wills of men. *a* 1676 Hale *Prim. Orig. Man.* iv. vii. (1677) 351 Yet a Law or Rule or Order is a dead, unactive, uneffective thing of it self. **Uneffe·ctless,** *a.* [Un-1 7.] Not ineffective. 1607 Topsell *Four-f. Beasts* 347 This I haue proued vneffectlesse for this disease, and also much auaileable for any other inward sickenesse.

† **Uneffe·ctual,** *a. Obs.* [Un-1 7 and 5 b.] = Ineffectual *a.* (Common *c* 1550–1660.)
1548 Udall, etc. *Erasm. Par. John* i. 7 Moses..brought a lawe vneffectuall, sharpe, and hard. 1590 Swinburne *Testaments* 240 The testament made by feare is vneffectuall. 1620 Gataker *Mariage Praier* 13 The vndue manner of the repairing euen of such to Gods board, maketh those holy things vnfruitfull and vneffectuall vnto them. 1668 R. Steele *Husbandman's Calling* v. 117 They shall go to Hell for their uneffectual knowledge.

So † **Uneffe·ctually** *adv.*, † **Uneffe·ctualness.**
1661 Baxter *Mor. Prognost.* ii. xxxiii. 55 Nor [shall] an uncertain Evil be *uneffectually resisted by a certain greater Mischief. 1598 Florio, *Inefficacia*, *vneffectualnes. 1651 Baxter *Inf. Bapt.* 319 His..reasons of the uneffectualness of baptism to some. 1663 Boyle *Usef. Exp. Nat. Philos.* ii. 228 Having found the uneffectualness of ordinary Remedies,.. he resolved to try a sympathetick Medicine.

†**Uneffe·ctuous,** *a. Obs.* (Un-1 7.) 1549 W. Wycherley in *Lansd. MS. 2*, fol. 63 b, About two monethes past he vsed.. a sworde vnconsecrated, and therefor vneffectuouse. **Uneffe·minate,** *a.* (Un-1 7.) 1606 Drumm. of Hawth. *Answ. Chall. Knts.* Wks. (1711) 233 Men, overcome with Women, are made..far inferior to the Valour of uneffeminate Knights. **Uneffe·minate,** *v.* (Un-2 6 a.) 1631 Quarles *Samson* Wks. (Grosart) II. 144/2 That strength of Nature..with her manly bounty did begin To uneffeminate his smoother chin. **Uneffe·minated,** *ppl. a.* (Un-1 8.) [1775 Ash.] 1813 T. Busby *Lucretius* II. v. p. xxvii, Uneffeminated by luxury, his naked body braved the boisterous winds. †**Unefferyde** (= *un-yfurred*), obs. var. Unfurred *ppl. a.* 1531 *Rec. St. Mary at Hill* (1905) 44 Item, iiij parteletes of velvett,..two feryd with Cony and two vnefferyde. **Uneffica·cious,** *a.* (Un-1 7 and 5 b.) 1742 *Johnson's Debates* (1787) II. 264 Mocking her calamities with unefficacious friendship. **Uneffi·giated,** *ppl. a.* (Un-1 8: cf. Effigiate *v.*) 1747 Carte *Hist. Eng.* I. 44 A great unshapen uneffigiated pillar or obelisk. **Uneffu·sed,** *ppl. a.* (Un-1 8.) [1775 Ash.] 1827 G. S. Faber *Sacr. Calend. Prophecy* (1844) III. 236 The contents of the still uneffused seventh vial.

† **Une·gall,** *a. Obs.* [Un-1 7, 5 b: cf. WFris. *on-*, *ûnegael*, and Unequal *a.*] Unequal. Also † **Une·gally** *adv.*, † **Une·galness.**
1508 Fisher *7 Penit. Ps.* li. Wks. (1876) 104 Is not my waye good and egall, & yours shrewed nought & more *vnegall [L. *prava*]. 1589 Puttenham *Eng. Poesie* i. xx. (Arb.) 57 Not onely because mens estates are vnegall, but for that also vertue it selfe is not in euery respect of egall value. 1541 R. Copland *Galyen's Terap.* 2 D ij b, After the pustule is broken there commeth an vlcere dyscoloured with fretyng *vnegally. 1589 Puttenham *Eng. Poesie* ii. iii. (Arb.) 81 He must be sometimes swift, sometimes slow, sometime vnegally marching. 1561 T. Norton *Calvin's Inst.* iv. 98 It behoued that he shoulde shewe that there is no *vnegalnesse betwene vs and them in those good thinges.

**Unege·sted,** *ppl. a.* (Un-1 8.) 1616 T. Adams *Serm.* Wks. (1629) 1053 The former crudities vndigested, vnegested, hauing the greater force, turne the good nutriment into themselues. **Unegoti·stically,** *adv.* (Un-1 11.) 1854 E. G. Holland *Mem. Badger* vii. 91 Unegotistically do I record the simple fact. † **Une·gual(ly,** varr. Unegal(ly. 1542 Udall *Erasm. Apoph.* 48 b, Thou and I do carke & feare for a..life of *vnegual valour [=value]. 1553 T. Wilson *Rhet.* 101 b, Unegual examples commende muche the matter. 1548 Udall, etc. *Erasm. Par. Luke* xiv. 127 b, To trye the hasarde of battayle with powers..*vnegually matched.

**Unela·borate,** *a.* (Un-1 7 and 5 b.)
1663 Boyle *Usef. Exp. Nat. Philos.* ii. v. vi. 159 Either simples, or cheap, or unelaborate Galenical mixtures. 1688 — *Final Causes Nat. Things* ii. 44 Most of them..are of such easy and unelaborate contextures. 1747 Warburton in *Shakespeare's Wks.* VII. 349 The work of brief nature, i.e. of hasty, unelaborate nature. 1819 Wordsw. *To Rev. Dr. Wordsw.* 34 Whether the rich man's sumptuous gate Call forth the unelaborate sounds [etc.]. 1853 Ruskin *Stones Ven.* III. ii. 106 The comparatively Hebraized and unelaborate idiom.

**Unela·borated,** *ppl. a.* (Un-1 8 and 5 b.) 1817 Coleridge *Biog. Lit.* xvii. (1907) II. 38 Simple and unelaborated expressions. 1850 Carlyle *Latter-day Pamph.* ii. (1872) 21 The materials of human virtue..lie yet unelaborated and stagnant in..[their] souls. **Unela·psed,** *ppl. a.* (Un-1 8.) 1805 *Ann. Rev.* III. 307 The average unelapsed term of a lease being three years and a half.

**Unela·stic,** *a.* (Un-1 7 and 5 b.)
1728 Chambers *Cycl.* s.v. *Elasticity*, The Difference between Elastic and Unelastic Bodies. 1764 Reid *Inquiry* vi. § 21 Are the small vessels distended with some redundant elastic or unelastic fluid? 1826 Kirby & Sp. *Entomol.* IV. xlvi. 259 A hard unelastic substance like wood. 1861 Beresf. Hope *Eng. Cathedr. 19th C.* 14 An unelastic law of parochial subdivision and endowment.

Hence **Unelasti·city.** (Webster, 1847.)

**Unela·ted,** *ppl. a.* (Un-1 8.)
1710 Palmer *Prov.* 236 How happy shou'd we be, if we cou'd..bear prosperity with a steady unelated mind. 1758 Johnson *Idler* No. 11 ⁋ 10 To make man unshaken by calamity, and unelated by success. 1885 *Soc. in London* 285 Unelated by the memory of past successes.

**Une·lbowed,** *ppl. a.* (Un-1 8.)
1732 Pope *Ep. Bathurst* 242 Is there a Lord..Whose table, Wit, or modest Merit share, Unelbow'd by a Gamester, Pimp, or Play'r? 1814 Wordsw. *Excurs.* ix. 130 Unelbowed by such objects as oppress Our active powers. 1866 Seeley *Ecce Homo* xii. 135 When the Roman cannot walk the Via Sacra unelbowed by Greeks and Syrians.

†**Une·ld.** *Obs.*$^{-1}$ [Un-1 4 b.] Weak or miserable old age. *a* 1300 *E. E. Psalter* lxx. 18 Til in un-elde and alder-elde, God, ne forlete me in un-welde. **Unele·ct,** *v. rare*$^{-1}$. (Un-2 3.) 1570 Foxe *A. & M.* (ed. 2) 362/2 One Iohn Blund was elected, who..was also repealed and vnelected agayne.

**Unele·cted,** *ppl. a.* (Un-1 8.)
1581 Sidney *Apol. Poetrie* (Arb.) 20 In these my not old yeres.., hauing slipt into the title of a Poet, [I] am prouoked to say somthing vnto you in the defence of that my vnelected vocation. 1607 Shaks. *Cor.* ii. iii. 207 You should haue ta'ne th' aduantage of his Choller, And pass'd him vnelected. 1621 G. Sandys *Ovid's Met.* v. (1626) 97 Then, vnelected, rudely stept forth one, Who sung the Giants warre. 1836 E. Howard *R. Reefer* vi, The agonies of a new-born infant, under the torture of eternal fire, because it had died unelected. 1866 *Sat. Rev.* 8 Sept. 286/1 The privilege of.. telling the unelected many [etc.].

**Unele·ctive,** *a.* (Un-1 7.) 1666 Bp. S. Parker *Free & Impart. Censure* (1667) 161 The Issues of a necessary and unelective cause. *a* 1676 Hale *Prim. Orig. Man.* iii. v. (1677) 274 An ignorant, unknowing, unelective Principle. **Unele·ctric,** *a.* [1775 Ash.] 1876 Blackmore *Cripps* xxvii, To do all this required some hours with a mind so unelectric.

**Unele·ctrified,** *ppl. a.* (Un-1 8.)
1747 *Gentl. Mag.* 200/2 Six being addled eggs, among which was one unelectrified egg. 1771 *Phil. Trans.* LXI. 654 A small unelectrified ball. 1867 Noad *Text Bk. Electricity* 207 In its natural or unelectrified state the natural electricities..are in equilibrium.

**Unele·ctrify,** *v.* (Un-2 6 c.) 1760 *Phil. Trans.* LI. 900 After unelectrifying the bottle, it was set again upon the stand of wood. **Unele·ctrized,** *ppl. a.* (Un-1 8.) 1761 *Phil. Trans.* LIII. 84, I placed myself on an electric stand, and, being well electrised, threw my hat to an unelectrised person. †**Une·led,** *ppl. a. Obs.* [f. Un-1 8 + OE. *ǽlan* to burn: cf. Anneal *v.*] Unbaked. *c* 1440 *Pallad. on Husb.* ix. 103 A potters potte vneled wol alete..Yf eny sprynge of water ther wole rise.

† **Une·legant,** *a. Obs.* [Un-1 7 and 5 b.] = Inelegant *a.*
1570 Levins *Manip.* 26 Vnelegant, *inelegans.* 1611 Florio, *Inelegante*, vnelegant, without grace. 1666 Dryden *Ann. Mirab.* Pref., I hope they are neither improper nor altogether unelegant in Verse. 1711 *Spect.* No. 67 ⁋ 18 Concluding.. that the Person who collected them is a Man of no unelegant Taste. *a* 1768 Secker *Serm.* (1771) VII. xv. 343 Possibly in some of these Books you meet with Expressions..which appear unelegant and singular.

So † **Une·legantly** *adv. Obs.*
1603 Holland *Plutarch's Mor.* 517 Neither seemeth he unelegantly and besides the purpose..to have expressed as much in this verse. 1659 O. Walker *Oratory* 23 Transitions ..are not unelegantly ushered in, by the Orators making Interrogations himself. 1758 Jortin *Erasm.* I. 142 It was no wonder if they wrote it ill and unelegantly.

**Uneleme·ntary,** *a.* (Un-1 7.) *a* 1706 Evelyn *Hist. Relig.* (1850) I. 185 Things unelementary, incorporeal, and consequently immortal. †**Une·lementated,** *ppl. a.* (Un-1 8.) *Ibid.* I. 156 That they could tell us how to unite an unelementated substance with corporeal matter.

**Une·levated,** *ppl. a.* (Un-1 8.)
1627 W. Sclater *Exp. 2 Thess.* (1629) 243 Nature, I mean, vneleuated aboue itselfe, and vnaltered by grace. 1690 Shadwell *Am. Bigot* i, Thou hast a gross unelevated fancy. 1774 *Trinket* 198 A soul unelevated by nature, or worn down by art. 1877 F. H. Laing *Bacon's Philos. Exam.* 7 So unelevated a philosopher as the materialist Mill.

† **Une·ligible,** *a. Obs.* [Un-1 7 and 5 b.] = Ineligible *a.*
1690 Locke *Hum. Und.* i. iii. § 13 Unavoidable punishment, great enough to make the transgression very uneligible. 1709 Shaftesb. *Charac.* (1711) II. 141 He himself may.. endeavour the utmost Prolongment of his own un-eligible State. 1775 Adair *Amer. Ind.* xx. 187 [The] state of celibacy; which to many of them is as uneligible, as it was to the Hebrew ladies.

**Uneli·minable,** *a.* (Un-1 7 b and 5 b.) 1876 *Contemp. Rev.* XXVIII. 800 The uneliminable element of dualistic relation and difference.

**Une·loquent,** *a.* (Un-1 7 and 5 b.)
1565 Cooper *Thesaurus* s.v. *Incolo*, A rude style without eloquence: vneloquent. 1603 Florio *Montaigne* iii. x. 605 If they once conceive a hatred against an Orator.., the next day he becommeth barbarous and vneloquent. 1642 Gauden *Serm.* 63 Innocence is often timorous, uneloquent, unexpert. 1885 Pennell *Fishing* 241 The foregoing description, however uneloquent, may give..a faint idea of what every lover of the sport feels on rising and hooking a salmon.

**Une·loquently,** *adv.* (Un-1 11, 5 b; cf. prec.)
1611 Cotgr., *Indisertement*, vneloquently. 1792 A. Young *Trav. France* (1794) I. i. 124 He speaks ungracefully, and uneloquently. 1836 J. Gilbert *Chr. Atonem.* ix. 412 We give many of you credit..for kindly deeds, and for recommending them not uneloquently.

**Unelu·cidated,** *ppl. a.* (Un-1 8.) [1775 Ash.] 1845 *Encycl. Metrop.* II. 742/1 The most diligent research has left many things obscure and unelucidated. **Unema·ncipated,** *ppl. a.* (Un-1 8.) [1775 Ash.] 1841 Lane *Arab. Nts.* I. 63 Unemancipated slaves..become the property of his heirs. 1875 Maine *Hist. Inst.* vii. 223 The home-staying, unemancipated son..is preferred to the others. **Unema·sculated,** *ppl. a.* (Un-1 8.) [1775 Ash.] 1791 Cowper *Iliad* xxiii. 474 Borne by his unemasculated steeds Of Trojan pedigree. 1888 *Pall Mall G.* 6 June 6/1 If it becomes law with its main provisions unemasculated.

**Unembacelled,** obs. var. Unembezzled.

**Unemba·lmed,** *ppl. a.* (Un-1 8.) *c* 1730 Waldron *Descr. Isle of Man* Wks. (1731) 144 A human Body, unembowelled, unembalmed. 1800 in *Spirit Pub. Jrnls.* IV. 294 Yet one shall moulder unembalmed to dust. **Unemba·nked,** *ppl. a.* (Un-1 8.) [1775 Ash.] 1807 Britton *Lincoln* 547 He conjectures there may be..200,000 [acres] of commons, wastes, and unembanked salt marshes. 1894 *Daily News* 2 July 5/2 The Thames, unpurified and unembanked.

**Unemba·rrassed,** *ppl. a.* [Un-1 8.]
1. Not encumbered, hampered, or impeded. (In lit. or fig. uses.)
1708 *Diss. Drunkenness* 31 Temperance, how clean and unembarrassed it keeps the Senses! 1717 Berkeley in Fraser *Life* (1871) 551 [The church of] St. Spiritus [is] very neat and unembarrassed [with ornament]. 1796 *Instr. & Reg. Cavalry* (1813) 201 The movements of the second line to conform to that of the first are free and unembarrassed. 1836 J. Gilbert *Chr. Atonem.* ix. (1852) 296 Not a single doctrine could remain unembarrassed with doubt. 1884 *Manch. Exam.* 6 Oct. 5/2 To be left to pursue an unembarrassed course in [governing] Egypt.
2. Not confused or constrained; free, at ease.
1746 Yorke in G. Harris *Life Ld. Hardwicke* (1847) II. 235 The second [ballad] is entitled, 'The Unembarrassed Countenance'. 1762 Foote *Liar* i. i, He is as unimbarrassed, easy, and fluent..as if he really believed what he said. 1786 *Beckford's Vathek* (1868) 73 His gait was unembarrassed and noble. 1850 Thackeray *Pendennis* xxix, The young man was perfectly easy and unembarrassed. 1897 *Harper's Mag.* Apr. 726 Declining the unembarrassed entreaties.., I despatched my inquiries and fled.

**Unemba·rrassedly,** *adv.* (Un-1 11; cf. prec.) 1873 Miss Broughton *Nancy* iii, Looking frankly and unembarrassedly up into his face. **Unemba·rrassing, -ment:** see Un-1 10 and 12. **Unemba·ttled,** *ppl. a.* (Un-1 8.) 1615 G. Sandys *Trav.* 233 The walls..vnimbattald, and sheluing on the outside. 1876 T. Hardy *Ethelberta* (1890) 366 The square unembattled tower of Knollsea Church.

**Unembe·llished,** *ppl. a.* (Un-1 8.)
1630 Fanshawe *Pastor Fido*, etc. (1648) 228 Let no darke corner of the land Be unimbellisht with one Gemme. 171. Eusden in Addison *Cato* A.'s Wks. 1721 I. 266 Such energy of sense might pleasure raise, Tho' unembellish'd with the charms of phrase. *a* 1763 Shenstone *Past. Ode Lyttleton* 148 And Grenville..prais'd these unembellish'd woods. 1805 Wordsw. *Prelude* iii. 108 Earth, nowhere unembellished by some trace Of that first Paradise whence man was driven. 1862 'Shirley' (J. Skelton) *Nugæ Crit.* ix. 416 A literal and unembellished account of the fact.

**Unembe·zzled,** *ppl. a.* (Un-1 8.)
1546 *Inv. Ch. Goods* (Surtees) 87 One chalice of sylver.. and also two bells..savely to be kept unspoiled, unembecyled, and sold. 1553 *Ibid.* 88 To..kepe unspoiled, unembacelled and solde. 1643 Chas. I in Carte *Coll.* (1735) 165 That the houses, chattels and other estates..be saved harmless,..that so they may be found unimbezzeled. 1744 Eliza Heywood *Female Spect.* No. 3 (1748) I. 120 We should leave it as intire and unembezzled as we received it.

**Unembi·ttered,** *ppl. a.* Also 8–9 unim-. (Un-1 8.)
α. *a* 1711 Ken *Hymns Evang.* Poet. Wks. 1721 I. 102 Bless'd are the Meek,..Who unimbitter'd, the injurious treat. 1748 Hervey *Medit.* (ed. 4) II. 69 Those happy Regions, where Delights, abundant and un-imbittered flow. 1816 Scott *Antiq.* xvi, While the tear can drop unimbittered by any painful recollection.
β. 1744 Young *Nt. Th.* vii. 296 They drink the Stream ..un-embitter'd With Doubts, Fears, fruitless Hopes. 1786 *Francis the Philanthropist* II. 92 Our parting..was however unembittered by any apprehensions. 1834 Whewell in Todhunter *Acc. Writ.* (1876) II. 176, I am to have them unembittered by that part of the business.

**Unembo·died,** *ppl. a.* Also unim-. [Un-1 8.]
1. Not invested with a body; incorporeal.
1662 Glanvill *Lux Orient.* xiii. (1682) 104 To urge, that there are..purely unembodied Spirits in the Universe. 1719 De Foe *Crusoe* ii. (Globe) 363, I am satisfied our Spirits embodied have a Converse with..the Spirits unembodied. *a* 1766 Mrs. F. Sheridan *Nourjahad* (1767) 196 He felt as it were unimbodied, and an involuntary adjuration burst from his lips. 1848 R. I. Wilberforce *Incarnation* xii. 393 The natural intercourse of the mind with its unembodied Creator. 1855 Milman *Lat. Chr.* xiv. iii. VI. 468 Matter ..subsisted potentially only,..unembodied, immaterial.
2. Not embodied, in various senses.
1760 *Ann. Reg., Chron.* 189 The charge of pay and cloathing for the unembodied militia. 1841 Miall in *Nonconf.* I. 17 A mere theory,..an abstract unembodied principle.

**Unembow·elled,** *ppl. a.* (Un-1 8.) *c* 1730 [see Unembalmed]. **Unembow·ered,** *ppl. a.* (Un-1 8.) [1775 Ash.] 1814 Wordsw. *Excurs.* vii. 55 All unembowered And naked stood that lowly Parsonage. **Unembra·ceable,** *a.* (Un-1 7 b.) 1859 G. Meredith *Poet. Wks.* (1912) 92 The bride..Scarcely faceable, Quite unembraceable!

**Unembra·ced,** *ppl. a.* (Un-1 8.)
[1775 Ash.] 1792 *Elvina* II. 83 [They] took their departure, unattended,—unembraced,—unregretted. 1853 Talfourd *Castilian* v. iii, It is hard To leave her unembraced, yet on a moment Hangs the last issue. 1867 Morris *Jason* x. 272 Another monster..raised aloft his crest Against her unembraced tender breast.

**Unembroi·dered,** *ppl. a.* (Un-1 8.) 1649 Lovelace *Poems* (1904) 136 Naked as their own innocence, And unimbroyder'd from Offence. **Unembroi·led,** *ppl. a.* (Un-1 8.) 1759 H. Walpole *Let. to Mann* 13 Sept., An opportunity of embrolling the little of Europe that remains unembroiled.

**Unement,** obs. form of Ointment.

**Unemo·lumented,** *a.* (Un-1 9.) 1810 Bentham *Offic. Apt. Maximized, Def. Econ.* (1830) 126 The expense..they have been at in obtaining their unemolumented seats.

**Unemo·tional,** *a.* (Un-1 7.)
Frequent from *c* 1880; hence also, in recent use, *unemotionalism, unemotionalness.*

1876 Geo. Eliot *Dan. Der.* lxii, Lapidoth..thought of all that this inscription signified with an unemotional memory. 1887 Miss Braddon *Like & Unlike* x, He was the most unemotional young man Colonel Deverill had ever encountered.

Hence **Unemoˈtionally** *adv.*

1884 *Athenæum* 12 Jan. 52/1 The aged cynic, whose ungrateful task it is to regard them unemotionally. 1894 Du Maurier *Trilby* II. 202 He unemotionally, dispassionately, wished himself dead.

**Unemoˈtioned,** *a.* (Un-1 9.) 1817 W. Godwin *Mandeville* III. v. 98 The dry, sarcastic, unemotioned..way in which he detailed them [*sc.* anecdotes]. **Uneˈmperor,** *v.* (Un-2 6 b.) 1642 Fuller *Holy & Prof. St.* v. xviii. (1841) 427 Prince Manuel..in vain opposed this decree, alleging this to be the ready way for his father to un-emperor himself.

**Unemphaˈtic,** *a.* and *sb.* (Un-1 7.)

1800 *Monthly Mag.* X. 317 An emphatic syllable is long; an unemphatic syllable, short. 1836–7 Sir W. Hamilton *Lect. Metaph.* xxi. (1859) II. 19 The participle *knowing* is too vague and unemphatic to be employed. 1874 Blackie *Self-Cult.* 74 The general action..languid and unemphatic.

**b.** As *sb.* An unstressed syllable.

1815 *Monthly Mag.* XXXIX. 118 The regular arrangement of their longs and shorts,..their emphatics and unemphatics.

So **Unemphaˈtical** *a.* (Worcester, 1846, citing Brown), **-ically** *adv.* (Webster, 1847).

**Unempiˈrically,** *adv.* (Un-1 11.) *a* 1849 Poe *Eureka* Wks. 1865 II. 137 This result is in the fullest keeping with that which I have reached unempirically. **Unemployˈ.** (Un-1 12.) 1887 F. W. Newman in Sieveking *Mem.* (1909) x. 241 Unless..the causes of Un-Employ be removed, we must calculate on frightful disorder. 1891 [see Ptochology].

**Unemployˈable,** *a.* and *sb.* (Un-1 7 b.)

Common in recent use; hence *unemployability.*

1887 *St. James's Gaz.* 22 Dec. 4/1 Persons who are unemployed because they are unemployable. 1900 *Q. Rev.* Jan. 174 The class of the casual labourer or the unemployable.

**Unemployˈed,** *ppl. a.* and *sb.* Also 7–8 unim-. [Un-1 8.]

**1.** Not put to use; not applied to some end or purpose.

1600 Surflet *Countrie Farme* ii. iii. 205 Wherefore it behooueth that the vnimploied or fallow ground..be first well cleansed from stones. 1665 in De Foe *Plague* (1754) 53 Till their Coaches..have stood unemploy'd by the Space of five or six Days after such Service. 1748 Chesterf. *Let.* 16 Feb., Every moment may be put to some use, and that with much more pleasure than if unemployed. 1826 Kirby & Sp. *Entomol.* III. 363 The real instrument of suction, which when unemployed is retracted within the tubulet. 1882 Child *Ballads* Advt. p. vii, No becoming means has been left unemployed.

**2.** Not engaged in any work or occupation; idle; *spec.* temporarily out of work.

1667 Milton *P. L.* iv. 617 Other Creatures all day long Rove idle unimploid, and less need rest. 1677 Yarranton *Eng. Improv.* 61 Admit there be in England and Wales a hundred thousand poor people unimployed. 1740 Cibber *Apol.* (1756) I. 167, I remember him three times for some years unemploy'd in any theatre. 1824 Miss L. M. Hawkins *Annaline* I. 40 Being unemployed they amused themselves and others with conjectures. 1860 Ruskin *Unto this Last* iii. § 54 The vexed question of the destinies of the unemployed workmen. 1887 [see Unemployable].

**b.** *absol.* or as *sb.*

1882 *Pall Mall G.* 10 May 3/2 The genuine total abstainers among the unemployed. 1900 H. Lawson *On Track* 108 Here I've been mooning round like an unemployed for three weeks.

**c.** Pertaining to, connected with, unemployed persons.

1844 Stocqueler *Handbk. Brit. India* 49 During this interval he draws the unemployed salary of three hundred rupees per mensem. 1895 *Daily News* 19 Aug. 5/2 Twenty-four per cent. of its 10,000 members received unemployed benefits.

**Unemployˈment.** (Un-1 12.)

In common use from *c* 1895 (cf. Unemploy). Also *attrib.* with *insurance, problem,* etc.

1888 *Science* XI. 192/1 The chief purpose of the inquiry was to ascertain..the extent of unemployment generally. 1894 *Liberal* 1 Dec. 67/2 These figures..represent the normal unemployment of the State.

**Unempoiˈsoned,** *ppl. a.* (Un-1 8.) [1775 Ash.] 1791 Charlotte Smith *Celestina* (ed. 2) II. 27 Till I..can see you, with all those delicious hopes unempoisoned. **Unempowˈered,** *ppl. a.* (Un-1 8.) 1731 A. Hill *Adv. Poets* Ep. p. vi, The Poet,..unimpower'd to act greatly Himself, asserts his Fire in describing the Great Actions of others.

**Uneˈmpt,** *v. dial.* [Un-2 9.] *trans.* To empty, to unload.

1798 J. Jefferson *Let. to J. Boucher* 19 Mar. (MS.). 1847– in dial. glossaries (midland and western).

**Uneˈmptiable,** *a.* (Un-1 7 b.) 1594 Hooker *Eccl. Pol.* ii. i. § 4 A drop of that vnemptiable Fountaine of wisdome. 1882 Farrar *Early Chr.* I. 286 The unemptiable fountain of Divine wisdom. †**Uneˈmptible,** *a. Obs.* (Cf. prec. and Empt *v.*) 1656 Jeanes *Fuln. Christ* 229 An indeficient fullnesse, an inexhaustible fountaine, unemptible treasures.

**Uneˈmptied,** *ppl. a.* (Un-1 8.)

1624 Massinger *Renegado* iii. iii, There is not a vein of mine which yet is Unemptied in his service but..should freely open. 1655 Vaughan *Silex Scint., Rules & Lessons* xvii, Admire his ways Who fils the world's unempty'd granaries! 1810 Southey *Kehama* xxiv. xx, Yielding to the bony hand The unemptied cup, he moved toward the Throne. 1818 Byron *Ch. Har.* iv. lxx, An unceasing shower..With its unemptied cloud of gentle rain.

**Uneˈmulative,** *a.* (Un-1 7.) 1775 'J. Collier' *Mus. Trav.* (ed. 2) 68 The vulgar restrictions which reason imposes upon unemulative minds. **Unenaˈbled,** *ppl. a.* (Un-1 8.) 1801 Southey *Thalaba* v. xxiii, No eye of mortal man, If unenabled by enchanted spell, Had pierced those fearful depths. **Unenaˈcted,** *ppl. a.* (Un-1 8.) 1802–12 Bentham *Ration. Judic. Evid.* (1827) II. 587 Unpromulgated, and unenacted, and spurious laws. 1843 Keble in *Newman's Corr.* (1917) 232 The unenacted leanings and tendencies of a particular generation. **Unenaˈmelled,** *ppl. a.* (Un-1 8.) 1851 G. A. Mantell *Petrifact.* iii. 253 [Teeth having] an unenamelled triangular space. 1889 *Anthony's Photogr. Bull.* II. 128, I prefer the prints unenamelled. **Unenaˈmoured,** *ppl. a.* (Un-1 8.) [1775 Ash.] 1791 Huddesford *Salmag.* (1795) 14 There Townsend threads the pleasing maze: Ah who can unenamoured gaze! †**Unenaˈrrable,** *a. Obs.* (Un-1 7 b and 5 b.) 1382 Wyclif 2 *Cor.* ix. 15, I do thankingis to God vpon the vnenarrable, or that may not be told, 3ifte of hym. 1382 — 1 *Pet.* i. 8 In gladnesse vnenarrable. **Unenchaˈnt,** *v.* (Un-2 3.) 1654 Gayton *Pleas. Notes* iv. ix. 237 Where by this time the Don is unenchanted from sleep.

**Unenchaˈnted,** *ppl. a.* Also 7 uninchanted. (Un-1 8.)

1634 Milton *Comus* 395 But beauty..hath need the guard Of dragon watch with uninchanted eye. *a* 1644 Quarles *Sol. Recant.* x. 11 The rash reproving mouth of fools are arm'd Like unenchaunted serpents, if not charm'd. 1791 Cowper *Odyss.* x. 399 Amaz'd I see thee with that potion drench'd, Yet unenchanted. 1810 *Monthly Mag.* XXIX. 149 It requires ascetic virtue..to remain unenchanted by the glare.

**Uncloˈsed,** *ppl. a.* Also unin-. (Un-1 8.)

1676 *Rector's Bk., Clayworth* (1910) 20 Such as had grounds still unenclosed. 1712 Blackmore *Creation* vii. 700 In the dark and undistinguish'd Space, Unfruitful, unenclos'd and wild of Face. 1776 Adam Smith *W. N.* i. xi. 214 In waste and uninclosed lands, any person who discovers a tin mine, may mark out its limits. 1809 Pinkney *Trav. France* 67 Being situated in an unenclosed country. 1867 Latham *Black & White* p. ix, A country two-thirds of which are uninclosed. 1898 Taunton *Eng. Black Monks* I. 108 Unenclosed nuns doing God's work in the world.

**Unencoˈmpassed,** *ppl. a.* (Un-1 8.) [1775 Ash.] *a* 1822 [? Shelley] '*There is no work*' 16 A brain unencompassed with nerves of steel. 1848 Pusey *Paroch. Serm.* I. viii. (1873) 152 His Own All-encompassing, Unencompassed Love. **Unencouˈnterable,** *a.* (Un-1 7 b.) 1590 T. Fenne *Frutes* 73 b, Philip King of Macedon having by..experience found out the unincounterable force thereof. **Unencouˈntered,** *ppl. a.* (Un-1 8.) [1775 Ash.] 1821 Scott *Pirate* ii, He was then most sure to wander unencountered and unobserved. **Unencouˈraged,** *ppl. a.* (Un-1 8.) [1775 Ash.] 1854 E. Forbes in Geikie *Mem.* xv. (1861) 554 Tastes that might have speedily perished if unobserved and unencouraged. **Unencouˈraging,** *ppl. a.* (Un-1 10.) 1844 Stocqueler *Handbk. Brit. India* 277 They are, however, in an awkward and unencouraging position. 1858 Polson *Law & L.* 105 To the junior part of the bar..Lord Kenyon was unencouraging and ungracious. **Unencroaˈching,** *ppl. a.* (Un-1 10.) *a* 1628 F. Greville *Sidney* (1652) 208 Judicious..Favorites of unincroaching Monarchs.

**Unencuˈmbered,** *ppl. a.* Also 8–9 unin-. (Un-1 8.) **a.** In pred. use and const. *with* or *by.*

α. 1722 De Foe *Plague* (1754) 22 Such People as were unincumbred with Trades and Business. 1800 *Asiat. Ann. Reg., Hist. Ind.* 13/2 His forces now consisting of light horse only, unincumbered by artillery or heavy baggage. 1877 Mrs. Oliphant *Makers Flor.* iv. 117 He is unincumbered by any restrictions.

β. 1727 Thomson *Britannia* 208 Unencumber'd with the Bulk immense Of Conquest. 1822 Scott *Nigel* x, His address was gallant, free, and unencumbered either by pride or ceremony. 1866 Geo. Eliot *F. Holt* iv, His small legs, unencumbered by any other drapery than his black silk stockings.

**b.** Without const., in predicative or attrib. use.

*c* 1725 Somerville *Martial's Epigr.* xlvii. 6 An estate,..unincumber'd left, and free from debt. 1781 Cowper *Truth* 22 Heav'n's easy, artless, unincumber'd plan. 1818 Syd. Smith *Wks.* (1867) I. 235 This seems a very spirited, unincumbered way of passing through life. 1856 Kane *Arct. Expl.* I. xvi. 188 My first impulse was to move..with an unencumbered party. 1884 Sir E. Fry in *Law Rep.* 25 Ch. Div. 581 Jeffery was the unencumbered lessee..of all the other plots.

Hence **Unencuˈmberedness.**

1891 *Atlantic Monthly* Feb. 182/2 To step jauntily along in airy unencumberedness.

**Unencuˈmbering,** *ppl. a.* (Un-1 10.) [1775 Ash.] 1824 Landor *Imag. Conv.* II. 330 They would lose..no graceful and unencumbering ornaments of life. 1861 Sir F. Palgrave *Norm. & Eng.* III. 306 The archers,..arrayed in a light and unincumbering garb. **Unencyˈsted,** *ppl. a.* (Un-1 8.) [1775 Ash.] 1885 *Encycl. Brit.* XIX. 855/2 In rare cases sporulation has been observed in unencysted Gregarinidea. †**Uneˈnd,** obs. var. of An-end *adv.* 1559 *Mirr. Mag., Northumb.* xvii, Whereas the folke drew to me stil vnend.

**Unendaˈngered,** *ppl. a.* Also 7 unin-. (Un-1 8.)

*a* 1658 Cleveland *Rustick Rampant* Wks. (1687) 409 These Impieties being once allowed, there can be neither Peace, Society nor Government amongst Men safe and unindangered. 1746 Young *Nt. Th.* ix. 1191 Un-endanger'd in health, wealth, or fame. 1814 Wordsw. *Excurs.* iii. 523 See, rooted in the earth,..The unendangered myrtle.

**Unendeaˈred,** *ppl. a.* (Un-1 8.) 1667 Milton *P. L.* iv. 766 Not in the bought smile Of Harlots, loveless, joyless, unindeard. **Unendeaˈvoured,** *ppl. a.* (Un-1 8.) 1656 Earl Monm. tr. *Boccalini's Advts. fr. Parnass.* 167 Nothing was left unindeavoured, neither by himself, nor by other Princes. **Unendeaˈvouring,** *ppl. a.* (Un-1 10.) 1831 Carlyle *Sart. Res.* ii. iv, The as yet unendeavouring, unattaining young gentleman.

**Uneˈnded,** *ppl. a.* Now *rare.* [Un-1 8: cf. OE. *ungeendod.*]

**1.** Not made to end or stop; having no limit or bounds; continued, lasting, infinite.

*c* 1250 *Gen. & Ex.* 3518 For if ðu it ȝernes and ȝisse, ðu tines vn-ended blisce. 1340–70 *Alex. & Dind.* 751 Bochours ben þei echon ȝour body to dismembre, & euerich pinchen his part þere paine is vnended. 1382 Wyclif *Job* xxii. 5 For thi myche malice, and thi wickidnessis vnendid. *c* 1400 tr. *Secreta Secret., Gov. Lordsh.* 84 Thes er tho þat out soght, and disputyd..of full, of voyde, of endyd, of vnendyd. 1522 Vaus *Rudiment. Gram.* Bb ij b (Jam.), *Infinitivo modo.* On-endyt or determyt mode to nowmyr or persone. 1596 *Edw. III*, ii. i. 139 Wherefore talkest thou of a period To that which craues vnended admiration?

**2.** Not brought to an end or conclusion; unfinished, incomplete.

1382 Wyclif *Wisd.* iv. 5 Forsothe braunchis vnendid [1388 vnperfit] shul be to-broken. 1471 *Sc. Acts, Jas. III* (1814) II. 101/1 Al materis..þat ar now opynit in þis present parliament & vnendit. 1535 Stewart *Cron. Scot.* (Rolls) II. 414 Rycht weill ȝe ken..Oure interpryiss wnendit is and done. 1591 Sparry tr. *Cattan's Geomancie* 235 The sute shall be for unmoueable goods, and shall not last long unended. 1805 *Monthly Mag.* XX. 43 It would probably have remained unended for a long time.

**Uneˈnding,** *ppl. a.* [Un-1 10.] Endless.

1661 Feltham *Resolves*, etc. (ed. 8) 378 When we think we have progress'd far in the un-ending Circles of laborious Science. 1729 Madden *Themistocles* iv. i. 50 Have I not sworn at the conscious Shrines Unending Faith to Xerxes? 1767 Goldsm. *Vic. W.* xxix, When our bliss shall be unutterable, and still, to crown all, unending. 1813 Shelley *Q. Mab* ii. 73 Countless and unending orbs In mazy motion intermingled. 1875 Clodd *Childhood of Religions* ii. 28 How Frost and Fire had fierce unending battle.

Hence **Uneˈndingly** *adv.*, **Uneˈndingness.**

1674 N. Fairfax *Bulk & Selv.* 165 You can no wayes..say, This half is unbeginningly, and that unendingly. 1845 Bailey *Festus* (ed. 2) 39 Though a thousand worlds..were elanced Each minute into life unendingly. 1881 *Brit. Q. Rev.* Oct. 499 The theory of the literal unendingness of even moral perdition.

†**Unendliche,** *adv.*: see Un-1 3. †**Uneˈndly,** *a. Obs.* [Un-1 7: cf. Endly *a.*] Unending. *a* 1586 Sidney *Arcadia* iii. i, Shall..faith and loue be rewarded with mortall disdaine, bent to vnendly reuenge? **Unendoˈrsed,** *ppl. a.* (Un-1 8.) 1682 Scarlett *Exchanges* 196 When he makes his Bills..or accepts of unendorsed Bills. 1886 *Times* 20 Aug. 9/6 Recommendations unendorsed by Government.

**Unendowˈed,** *ppl. a.* Also 7 unin-. (Un-1 8.)

1647 Clarendon *Hist. Reb.* i. § 142 A man rather..unindowed with any notable virtues, than..transported with any vitious inclinations. 1709 Pope *Jan. & May* 550 Reflect what truth was in my passion shewn, When unendow'd, I took thee for my own. 1790 [see Unconsecrated]. 1819 Crabbe *T. of Hall* ix. 42 That every beauty..Must be by him, if unendow'd, resign'd. 1866 Geo. Eliot *Ess.* (1884) 348 The claims of the unendowed multitude of working men.

**Unendueˈd,** *ppl. a.* (Un-1 8.)

1647 Clarendon *Hist. Reb.* v. § 341 A sufficient Instance how unendued Men were with that Spirit and Courage, which was requisite. 1855 Pusey *Doctr. Real Presence* Note i. 106 Things unendued with reason. 1862 Ellicott *Destiny Creature*, etc. ii. (1865) 28 Individuals that belong to lower genera unendued with foresight and reason.

**Unenduˈrable,** *a.* (and *sb.*). Also 7 unin-. [Un-1 7 b.]

**1.** Incapable of enduring; †impatient *of.*

1630 *R. Johnson's Kingd. & Commw.* 79 In battell they are fearlesse,..and in service unindurable of temporizing. 1879 *Cassell's Techn. Educ.* I. 314 If it be soft, broken granite ..will prove a useless because an unendurable surface.

**2.** That cannot be endured; insufferable.

1801 Southey *Thalaba* xii. xviii, No eye could penetrate That unendurable excess of light. 1853 Kane *Grinnell Exp.* xxxiv. (1856) 303 The sensation most unendurable..is a pain between the eyes and over the forehead. 1880 'Ouida' *Moths* x, This ceaseless sense of unendurable reproach.

**b.** *sb.* An insufferable person.

1826 F. Reynolds *Life & Times* II. 84 That my friend Andrews may not be considered as one of these *unendurables*, I will yet add another short anecdote of him.

Hence **Unenduˈrabiˈlity.**

1858 Carlyle *Fredk. Gt.* v. viii, Some excessive pressure of that lisping snuffling unendurability. 1862 *Ibid.* xii. xi, Such injustices and unendurabilities.

**Unenduˈrably,** *adv.* [Un-1 11: cf. prec.] In an unendurable manner or degree.

1832 Southey *Hist. Penins. War* III. 103 That sovereignty ..would become unendurably tyrannical. 1867 Augusta Wilson *Vashti* xxvii, My ardent lover would be too unendurably miserable separated from me. 1890 'R. Boldrewood' *Col. Reformer* (1891) 177 The routine life..would be unendurably dull.

**Unenduˈring,** *ppl. a.* (Un-1 10.) [1775 Ash.] 1814 Wordsw. *Excurs.* ix. 6 The stars Of azure heaven, the unenduring clouds. 1855 Milman *Lat. Chr.* xiv. viii. VI. 573 The architectural..conquests of Justinian were but partial and unenduring.

**Unenergeˈtic,** *a.* (Un-1 7 and 5 b.)

1805 A. Knox *Mem.* I. 6 The cold, low, unenergetic notion of it..is really below Cicero in moral matters. 1850 Thackeray *Pendennis* ii, He is a very good boy, rather idle and unenergetic. 1878 Seeley *Stein* III. 532 A man of this unenergetic character..has no colour.

**Uneˈnervated,** *ppl. a.* (Un-1 8.) 1766 in *Hansard Parl. Debates* (1813) XVI. 286 The supreme law with me shall ever be to maintain, unrelaxed and unenervated, the fundamentals of the constitution. 1854 J. S. C. Abbott *Napoleon* (1855) I. x. 174 We shall found a colony there unenervated by the curse of slavery. **Unenfeeˈbled,** *ppl. a.* (Un-1 8.) 1648 Hexham ii, *Ongekrenckt*, Vnweakned, or Vn-enfeebled. 1814 Wordsw. *Excurs.* vii. 208 The comeliness of unenfeebled age. 1878 E. Jenkins *Haverholme* 78 The new doctrine is, that the Crown has a sacred trust..to preserve the Regal prerogative unenfeebled. **Unenfoˈrceable,** *a.* (Un-1 7 b.) 1868 Benjamin *On Sales* (1884) 530 The terms of the bargain included a wager that rendered it illegal: quaere—unenforceable. 1885 *Law Times* 10 Jan. 183/1 A covenant to build or repair would be unenforceable as against an assignee even with notice.

**Unenfoˈrced,** *ppl. a.* Also 7 unin-. (Un-1 8.)

1607 Hieron *Wks.* I. 220, I will let you see how this doctrine ariseth kindly and vn-enforced from this scripture. 1625 K. Long tr. *Barclay's Argenis* ii. vi. 80 By a slow and uninforced inhibition of the old discipline. 1646 Earl Monm. tr. *Biondi's Civil Wars* ix. 177 The Duke of Orleans would not, unenforced, yeeld to any Pacification. 1832 Moore *Mem.* (1854) VI. 267 Sifting both sides and leaving nothing unenforced on either. *a* 1861 Sir F. Palgrave *Norm. & Eng.* III. 363 A formal..submission..unenforced by the sword.

Hence **Unenfo·rcedly** *adv.*

1617 Hieron *Wks.* II. 165 Foure points doe very kindly and vnenforcedly spring out of this place.

**Unenfra·nchised,** *ppl. a.* (Un-[1] 8.)

[1775 Ash.] 1832 A. W. Fonblanque *Eng. under 7 Administr.* (1837) II. 292 The identity of interest of the enfranchised, and unenfranchised. 1878 Bosw. Smith *Carthage* 62 The long..struggle between the privileged Patricians and the unenfranchised plebeians.

**Unenga·ged,** *ppl. a.* Also 7–8 unin-. [Un-[1] 8.]

†**1.** Unimpeded. *Obs.*[−1]

1653 Gauden *Hierasp.* To Rdr. 2 b, From which free and un-ingaged prospect both he and they may..behold the later..changes in exterior matters of Religion.

**2.** Not bound or committed in any way (esp. by a pledge or promise).

*a* 1656 Bp. Hall *Modest Offer* 2 Both the Houses of Parliament..stand yet free, and unengaged to any part. 1697 Collier *Ess. Mor. Subj.* I. (1703) 110 'Tis my humble Opinion, that they should keep their Inclinations unengaged. 1757 W. Wilkie *Epigon.* v. 148 The truce subsists with all the rest; are we Alone excepted, unengag'd and free?

**b.** *spec.* Not bound by an engagement or promise to marry; not betrothed.

1702 Vanbrugh *False Friend* III. i, His Behaviour wou'd engage any thing that were unengag'd. 1709 Mrs. Manley *Secret Mem.* I. 217 He was handsome, he was young:..She was innocent and uningag'd. 1814 Scott *Wav.* lviii, An alliance, which to an unengaged person,..holds out too many charms to be lightly laid aside. 1877 Sir H. Taylor *Autobiog.* (1885) I. 218 He consented to our seeing more of one another on an unengaged footing.

†**3.** Not committed to a special view or opinion; unprejudiced. *Obs.*

1653 Milton *Hirelings* Wks. 1851 V. 338 If it suffic'd..to convince..the uningag'd of other Nations in the justice of your doings. 1663 J. Spencer *Prodigies* (1665) 401 Persons of more free and un-ingaged minds, and that use not to believe without asking themselves *why*.

**4.** Not hired.

1654 Dorothy Osborne *Lett.* (1888) 293 He is commended to me..for a most excellent servant...I'll keep him unengaged till I hear from you. 1889 Gunter *That Frenchman* xiii, She chances to find an unengaged cab.

**5.** Not occupied or busied (*in* something).

1712 Pope *Lett.* (1735) I. 187 If your Thoughts are unengaged, I shall explain myself further. 1759 Johnson *Rasselas* xlv, The activity of Rasselas did not leave much time unengaged. 1800 Mrs. Hervey *Mourtray Fam.* II. 78 Her companion, who wandered about..unengaged in any pursuit. 1819 Crabbe *T. of Hall* IV. 187, I took a trip, But duty none, in a relation's ship; Thus, unengaged, I felt my spirits light.

**b.** Disengaged *from*.

1805 Emily Clark *Banks of Douro* II. 300 The first moment she was unengaged from Minette and Lady Archdale, she resolved to go and see them.

**c.** Not occupied or involved in fighting.

1806 A. Duncan *Nelson* 39 The ships..were..unengaged in the contest. 1895 A. Forbes in *Daily News* 18 Feb. 6/3 Mr. Herbert, in his redoubt in the centre of the Grivitza heights, remained unengaged until 4 p.m.

**6. a.** Not appropriated or allocated to a particular purpose.

*a* 1732 Swift (J.), When we have sunk the only unengaged revenues left, our incumbrances must remain perpetual.

**b.** Not assigned to a person.

1751 Smollett *Per. Pic.* xci, Some profitable places were at that time vacant, and, as far as he knew, unengaged. 1755 Johnson *Let. to Richardson* 3 Feb. in *Pearson's Catal.* (1900) 44 If you have any parts of the Universal History yet unengaged I know a gentleman desirous of giving his assistance.

**Unenga·ging,** *ppl. a.* (Un-[1] 10.)

1749 Chesterf. *Lett.* (1774) I. 429 Without them, your learning will be pedantry,..and your figure..awkward and unengaging. 1768–74 Tucker *Lt. Nat.* (1834) II. 592 The one [life] is pleasant, easy, smooth, and dispatchful; the other unengaging, toilsome, stiff. 1895 Kath. Simpson *Yorks. Stories* 92 Too ugly and unengaging to be able to boast of a lover.

**Unengendered,** *ppl. a.* (Un-[1] 8.) 1776 S. J. Pratt *Pupil of Pleas.* (1777) I. 159 At present, this is only in embrio,..unformed, unengendered.

**Un-E·nglish,** *a.* [Un-[1] 7.]

**1.** Not English in character; lacking the qualities regarded as typically English.

1633 Prynne *Histrio-m.* 546 So unmanly, degenerous and un-English (if I may so speake) in their whole conversation. 1745 H. Walpole *Let. to H. S. Conway* 27 May, This is so un-English, or so un-heroic, that I despair of you! 1763 *Ann. Reg., Chron.* 89/2 One of the members..called the attack 'a horrid un-English act'. 1803 Mackintosh *Def. Peltier* Wks. 1846 III. 286 Though deserted by the un-English Government of England, they asserted their own ancient character. 1848 in *Life A. Fonblanque* (1874) 225 The un-English practice of secret voting will be resorted to. 1872 Yeats *Growth Comm.* 308 A false patriotism that thought it un-English to wear foreign fabrics.

**2.** Not English by occupation or possession.

1738 *Gentl. Mag.* 427/1 Such beauties..are,..save at Finedon, hardly found On English or un-English ground. 1902 *Daily Chron.* 18 July 5/4 With Delagoa Bay the only harbour still un-English passes into England's power.

**Une·nglish,** *v.* (Un-[2] 6 a.) 1745 H. Walpole *Lett.* (1846) II. 55, I would not for the world be so unenglished as to do otherwise. 1786 *Microcosm* (1787) 23 Having thus unenglished himself, let him get his advertisement drawn up.

**Une·nglished,** *ppl. a.* [Un-[1] 8.] Not translated into English.

*c* 1546 Joye in Gardiner *Declar.* 52 b, He layd on scriptures wryten and vnwryten, englyshed and vnenglyshed as thicke as hayle. 1620 Bp. Hall *Hon. Marr. Clergy* III. ii. (1628) 794 We..returne his [epistle]..to the next hand; whereto I am no whit beholding for leaving it vn-Englished. 1650 Fuller *Pisgah* v. xix. 174 Such passages (which for me shall goe unenglished) being found frequent therein.

**Unengra·ven,** *ppl. a.* (Un-[1] 8 b.) [1775 Ash.] 1831 Carlyle *Sart. Res.* II. iv, I undertook to compose his Epitaph;..which however..still remains unengraven.

**Unengro·ssed,** *ppl. a.* (Un-[1] 8.) 1681 *Lond. Gaz.* No. 1633/4 There is now published a Printed List of all such Fines as remain uningrossed.

**Unenjoy·able,** *a.* (Un-[1] 7 b.)

*a* 1797 H. Walpole *Geo. II* (1822) I. 195 A very few years of unenjoyable power. 1850 Robertson *Serm.* Ser. III. vi. (1864) 92 Life is an unenjoyable Canaan. 1869 Tozer *Highl. Turkey* I. 90 How empty and unenjoyable life would be without the range of European ideas.

**Unenjoy·ed,** *ppl. a.* Also 7 unin-. (Un-[1] 8.)

1643–5 Milton *Divorce* II. i, A good man who finds himself consuming away in a disconsolate and uninjoy'd matrimony. 1684 T. Burnet *Theory Earth* I. 322 We cannot suppose the better [parts] to lie as desarts, uninjoy'd and uninhabited. 1757 Mrs. Griffith *Lett. Henry & Frances* (1767) II. 245 The pleasure..which you have suffered to pass by, unheeded, unenjoyed. 1827 Pollok *Course T.* III. 229 The spectre..threatened..to blast it unenjoyed.

**Unenjoy·ing,** *ppl. a.* (Un-[1] 10.)

1697 Creech *Manilius* IV. 10 The more we have, the meaner is our Store; The unenjoying craving Wretch is poor. 1799 Coleridge *Ode to Duchess of Devonsh.* 18 Nor could you see The unenjoying toiler's misery. 1851 Robertson *Serm.* Ser. II. 15 The shadow of our own melancholy unenjoying national character. 1866 Geo. Eliot *F. Holt* i, When..her face looked bitter, restless, and unenjoying, like her life.

Hence **Unenjoy·ingly** *adv.*

1844 Browning *Colombe's Birthday* II. 106 Hurry one's feast down unenjoyingly At the snatched breathing-intervals of work?

**Unenla·rged,** *ppl. a.* (Un-[1] 8.) 1741 Watts *Improvement Mind* I. xvi. 219 These unenlarged souls are in the same manner disgusted with the wonders which the microscope has discovered. 1805 Foster *Ess.* (1806) I. 58 Under the habitual..influence of one individual..of unenlarged views. 1844 Mrs. Browning *Lett. R. H. Horne* (1877) II. 24 You had better leave the notice unenlarged.

**Unenli·ghtened,** *ppl. a.* Also 7 unin-. [Un-[1] 8.]

**1.** Not illuminated or lit up.

1662 Boyle *Spring of Air* II. i. 22 For the Corpuscles of Light that permeate that space may be so numerous, as to leave no sensible part of it un-inlightned. 1789 *Phil. Trans.* LXXX. 8 During the time..when evidently we were turned towards the unenlightened side. 1803 *Ibid.* XCV. 152, I mentioned the probability that there existed..unenlightened stars (if I may be allowed the expression) that have ever remained in eternal darkness. 1833–4 J. Phillips *Geol.* in *Encycl. Metrop.* (1845) VI. 715/2 The Phlegrean Fields,..unenlightened either by the rising or the setting sun.

*fig.* 1774 *Trinket* 165 Faces unenlightened with the smile of friendship.

**2.** Not mentally illuminated; uninstructed.

*a* 1656 Bp. Hall *Rev. Unrevealed* § 8 A conceit, that would have sounded very strangely in the ears of our unenlightened forefathers. 1768–74 Tucker *Lt. Nat.* (1834) II. 638 The unenlightened Canadian takes pride in singing while tortured by his conquerors. 1797 Mathias *Purs. Lit.* II. 5 *note*, Such unenlightened and ignorant men as myself. 1865 M. Arnold *Ess. Crit.* v. 189 A strong, dogged, unenlightened opponent of the chosen people. 1882 Farrar *Early Chr.* II. 342 Imperfect, narrow-minded and unenlightened Christians.

**b.** Uninformed *on* some matter.

1829 Scott *Anne of G.* xxxi, The old King was..still strangely unenlightened on the difference of her taste from his own.

**3.** Marked by lack of enlightenment.

1792 A. Young *Trav. France* I. Pref. p. iv, Unenlightened practices exist, and want improvement. 1870 Lowell *Among my Books* Ser. I. (1873) 148 Political or other doctrines which seem to us barbarous and unenlightened.

**Unenli·ghtening,** *ppl. a.* (Un-[1] 10.) 1768 Pennant *Brit. Zool.* I. 193 Commentators, after loading whole pages with unenlightening learning, leave us..in the dark. **Unenli·sted,** *ppl. a.* (Un-[1] 8.) [1775 Ash.] 1840 J. H. Newman *Ch. of Fathers* ix. 153 Yet unenlisted in God's army.

**Unenli·vened,** *ppl. a.* (Un-[1] 8.)

1692 Atterbury *Serm.* 29 May (1726) I. 31 That Majestick Plainness and Simplicity of Thought which goes through it, Unadorn'd by Words, Unenliven'd by Figures. *c* 1765 Beattie *Ep. to Blacklock* 57 The cautious, slow, and unenlivened eye. 1817 Coleridge *Biog. Lit.* (1907) I. 169 The distorting medium of his own unenlivened and stagnant understanding. 1893 Liddon *Life Pusey* I. xiv. 330 Their intercourse was not unenlivened by differences of opinion.

**Unenli·vening,** *ppl. a.* (Un-[1] 10.) 1774 *Trinket* 158 My ideas are more unenlivening than the desolate prospect that inspires them. 1835 A. C. Dick *Church Polity* vii. 194 [He] falls into..an unenlivening coldness of address. **Unenno·bled,** *ppl. a.* (Un-[1] 8.) [1775 Ash.] 1830 *Westm. Rev.* Oct. 300 The..deeds of the unennobled patriot-soldier. 1863 *Q. Rev.* CXIII. 469 The unennobled inhabitants of the provinces that were to be annexed to Russia. **Unenou·nced,** *ppl. a.* (Un-[1] 8.) 1859 Sir W. Hamilton *Lect.* (1877) I. xvi. 286 It remains unenounced and unknown.

**Unenqui·red,** *ppl. a.* (Un-[1] 8 c.) *a* 1818 M. G. Lewis *W. Ind.* (1834) 367 He left their complaints unenquired into.

**Unenqui·ring,** *ppl. a.* (Un-[1] 10.)

1813 Lamb *Play-house Mem.* Wks. 1908 I. 202, I love the unenquiring gratitude of such spectators. 1850 Marsden *Early Purit.* (1853) 65 He is a son of the church because he is unenquiring. 1862 M. Hopkins *Hawaii* 373 It demands..unenquiring condemnation and unpitying punishment.

Hence **Unenqui·ringly** *adv.*

1841 Myers *Cath. Th.* III. § 50. 191 They give themselves up..unenquiringly to mere traditions concerning it. 1862 M. Hopkins *Hawaii* 350 The American missionaries..threw themselves unenquiringly..into a crusade against the prevailing licentiousness.

**Unenri·chableness.** (Un-[1] 7 b, 12.) *a* 1816 Bentham *Offic. Apt. Maximized, Introd. View* (1830) 19 The French [language, with]..its scantiness, unenrichableness, and intractability.

**Unenri·ched,** *ppl. a.* Also 8 unin-. (Un-[1] 8.)

1723 Dk. Wharton *True Briton* No. 55. II. 473 That he died un-inriched by the Plunder of his Fellow Subjects. 1786 Mrs. Piozzi *Anecd. of Johnson* Pref. 7 The great parent of African plenty,..unenriched by any extraneous waters. 18.. Wordsw. *Michael* 19 A story—unenriched with strange events. 1864 *Realm* 11 May 5 He has preferred to remain ..unenriched by the events which have enriched..others.

**Unenro·lled,** *ppl. a.* (Un-[1] 8.) [1775 Ash.] 1837 Carlyle *Fr. Rev.* I. v. ix, Unenrolled men deposit their arms, ..and receive 'nine francs.' 1881 Jowett *Thucyd.* I. 27 The treaty allows any unenrolled cities to join either league.

**Unensla·ve,** *v.* (Un-[2] 3.) 1644 *Prerogative Anatomized* 1 That the deceived people..may see the necessitie..to uninslave their soules, persons and estates, from Ecclesiasticall ..tyrannie. **Unensla·ved,** *ppl. a.* (Un-[1] 8.) 1691 Norris *Refl. Cond. Hum. Life* Ep. Ded. A vj b, If I happen to bring over here and there an ingenuous and uninslaved Spirit,..I shall not think my Labour ill bestow'd. 1705 Addison *Remarks on Italy* 108 By Thee She sits a Sov'reign, Unenslav'd and Free. **Unensna·red,** *ppl. a.* (Un-[1] 8.) *a* 1711 Ken *Hymnotheo* Poet. Wks. 1721 III. 186 No Danger found them unprepar'd, They kept their Spirits un-ensnar'd. 1860 Mozley *Univ. Serm.* vii. (1877) 155 Free and unensnared souls. **Unensou·led,** *ppl. a.* (Un-[1] 8.) 1860 Pusey *Min. Proph.* 41 When..they were lifeless bodies, unensouled by His grace.

**Unentai·led,** *ppl. a.* (Un-[1] 8.)

1713 C'tess Winchelsea *Misc. Poems* 243 Your unentailed, your undivided Air, Where no Proprietor was ever known. 1784 R. Bage *Barham Downs* II. 315 His unentailed estates are to be sold. 1827 Lytton *Pelham* iii, The whole of his unentailed property..he bequeathed to her.

**Unenta·ngle,** *v.* Also 7 unin-. [Un-[2] 3.] *trans.* To disentangle.

1610 Donne *Pseudo-martyr* 226 It is impossible to..vnentangle our consciences by any of those Rules. 1655 tr. *Sorel's Com. Hist. Francion* IV. 13 All this was intermingled ..in a more than a barbarous confusion, which was so uneasie to unintangle [etc.]. 1887 Bowen *Æneid* VI. 29 Dædalus.. of himself unentangled the woven trick of the grove.

Hence **Unenta·ngler.** *rare*[−1].

1610 Donne *Pseudo-martyr* 345 The late vn-entangler of perplexities,..who vndertakes to cleare so many cases, which Nauarrus and many others left in suspence.

**Unenta·ngled,** *ppl. a.* Also 7–8 unin-. (Un-[1] 8.)

*a* 1586 Sidney *Arcadia* III. ix, So I in simple course, and unentangled minde, Did suffer drousie lids mine eyes..to blinde. 1622 S. Ward *Christ All in All* (1627) 36 He had now nothing left but..Christ, whom hee..would now with vnlimed and vnentangled wings flye vnto. 1647 Clarendon *Hist. Reb.* VII. § 218 He was unintangled with any Acquaintance or Friends. *a* 1715 Burnet *Own Time* I. (1766) I. 124 To keep the thread of the narration in an unintangled method. 1779–81 Johnson *L. P., Collins*, That this man..passed always unentangled through the snares of life, it would be.. temerity to affirm. 1842 J. B. Fraser *Allee Neemroo* I. 20 Its rider, shot forward from its back,..fortunately unentangled by its harness. 1901 H. W. Holden *Justif.* 96 We may be free indeed to follow the Lord..unentangled and unembarrassed by any other will.

**Une·nted,** *ppl. a.* [Un-[1] 8 + late L. *ent-*, *ens*: see Ens.] Not endowed with being. 1657 Reeve *God's Plea* 241 God.. out of..an unshapen un-ented Nothing hath set up..this specious and spacious Universe. **Une·nterable,** *a.* (Un-[1] 7 b.) 1650 Fuller *Pisgah* 366 That mysterious place being unenterable..save [for] the high-Priest alone.

**Une·ntered,** *ppl. a.* [Un-[1] 8.]

**1.** Not recorded by an entry in a book.

1482 in *Charters, etc. Edinb.* (1871) 168 Gudis..enterit in the tovnis bukis, togidder with the eschete of the sammyn quhare it beis fundin vnenterit. 1554–5 in Feuillerat *Revels Q. Mary* (1914) 169, xij elles of white & blewe sarcenet..left out vnentred in the boke of the same [masque]. 1763 *Brit. Mag.* IV. 174 The makers of cyder or perry..shall enter ..the mills,..and other places to be made use of,..under the penalty of 25*l.* for using any unentered place.

†**2.** Not initiated or introduced. *Obs.*

1548 Udall, etc. *Erasm. Par. Luke* i. 7 A people not vtterly vntraded or vnentred in his discipline, but somwhat prepaired already. 1642 Milton *Apol. Smect.* 45 In the Greek tongue most of them unletter'd, or unenter'd to any sound proficiency in those Attick maisters of morall wisdome.

**3.** *Sc. Law.* Not formally admitted.

1711 in *Nairne Peerage Evidence* (1874) 142 [They are] not to lye out themselves unentered in the superiority to their prejudice. 1868 *Act* 31 & 32 *Vict.* c. 101 § 6 The rights and remedies competent to a superior against his vassal lying out unentered.

**4.** Of hounds: Not yet put into a pack.

1896 *Sportsman* 10 July 4/1 In young unentered hounds the Eamont were first and Boddington second.

**5.** Not gone into; not penetrated.

1775 Warton *Hist. Eng. Poetry* I. i. 20 *note*, This cavern.. remained closely shut and unentered for many ages. 1821 Byron *Cain* II. ii, The intelligences I have seen Round our regretted and unenter'd Eden.

**Une·ntering,** *ppl. a.* (Un-[1] 5 d and 10.) 1583 *Reg. Privy Council Scot.* III. 603 For keping of his guides and cattell unentering in the said forrest. 1801 Southey *Thalaba* IX. xxxii, The evening sun Pour'd his unentering glory on the mist, And it was night below. †**Une·nterpen,** *v. Obs.*[−0] (Un-[2] 3: see Enterpen *v.*) 1647 Hexham I. (Birds), To unenterpen a Hawke, *Een Valck ontwerren.* 1671 Skinner s.v., The hawk unenterpenneth. **Une·nterprise:** see Un-[1] 12.

**Une·nterprising,** *ppl. a.* (Un-[1] 10.)

Also *unenterprisingly* adv. (Webster, 1847).

1777 Robertson *Hist. Amer.* II. ¶ 11 A maxim under which the ignorant and unenterprising shelter themselves in every age. 1791 Burke *Th. French Aff.* Wks. VII. 29 Under a lazy and unenterprising prince. **1855** Macaulay *Hist. Eng.* xviii. IV. 235 He would not again be told that he was a timid and unenterprising commander.

**Unentertai·ned,** *ppl. a.* (Un-¹ 8.) **1628** Wither *Brit. Rememb.* ii. 1647 The Mother was constrain'd To let her child depart unentertain'd. **1669** Earl Orrery *Parthen.* (1676) 737 These Generals..afforded me Particulars, which never left me unentertained. **1754** Fielding *Voy. Lisbon* 27 July, A man must..have been..duller than Cibber is represented in the Dunciad, who could be unentertained with him a little while.

**Unentertai·ning,** *ppl. a.* (Un-¹ 10.) **1697** Collier *Ess. Mor. Subj.* ii. (1703) 38 If he is silent and unentertaining to a visiter, the spleen is his excuse. **1748** Melmoth *Fitzosborne Lett.* xlvii. (1749) II. 20 His conversation is unentertaining: for..all that he utters is delivered with labour and hesitation. **1796** *Hist. Ned Evans* II. 118 The ceremony of adoption being somewhat singular it may not be unentertaining to relate it. **1837** Syd. Smith *2nd Let. to Singleton* ¶ 21 The idea of abandoning this taxation..is not unentertaining.

Hence **Unentertai·ningly** *adv.*, **-ness.** **1740** Gray *Let. to West* 25 Sept., Last post I received a very diminutive letter. It made excuses for its unentertainingness. **1847** Webster, *Unentertainingly.* **1886** Ruskin *Præterita* I. v. 146 A conceited and unentertainingly troublesome little monkey.

**Unenthra·lled,** *ppl. a.* Also 7 uninthrall'd. (Un-¹ 8.) **1649** Milton *Eikon.* Pref., Wks. 1851 III. 335 It must needs be ridiculous to any judgement uninthrall'd, that they..should in this one particular outstripp all precisianism. **1809–10** Coleridge *Friend* (1818) III. 172 Observation, unaided, but at the same time unenthralled, by partial experiment. **1851** Trench *Poems* 153, I know not any, unenthralled of sorrow.

**Unenthu·siastic,** *a.* (Un-¹ 7.) Also, in recent use, *unenthusiastically* adv. **1805** A. Knox *Rem.* (1834) I. 38 There is nothing supposed here, which the..unenthusiastic Addison does not..admirably describe. **1865** Trollope *Belton Est.* xxviii, He had been calm, unenthusiastic, and reasonable.

**Unenti·ced,** *ppl. a.* (Un-¹ 8.) [**1775** Ash.] **1823** in *Spirit Pub. Jrnls.* 102 Who scorned to share it with him; unenticed By shame's imperial bait.

**Unenti·re,** *a.* Also 7 unin-. (Un-¹ 7.) *a* **1618** J. Davies (Heref.) *Witte's Pilgr.* Wks. (Grosart) II. 50/2 The Elements,..in firme accord, mine ende conspire:..Which well agrees to make me vnintire. **1702** S. Parker tr. *Cicero's De Finibus* iii. 177 Representing Vertue as Unentire and Abortive.

**Unenti·tled,** *ppl. a.* Also 8 unin-. (Un-¹ 8.) *a* **1768** Secker *Serm., Gal. vi. 15* (1771) V. 396 That State is undoubtedly a bad one;..unintitled to Pardon of Sin. **1832** Scott *Redgauntlet* Introd., Persons totally unentitled to..such a distinction, were presented to the unfortunate Prince. **1869** Tanner *Clin. Med.* (ed. 2) 171 A boy appropriating a nicety to which he was unentitled.

**Unento·mbed,** *ppl. a.* (Un-¹ 8.) **1697** Dryden *Æneis* vi. 508 Think'st thou thus unintomb'd to cross the Floods,..And visit, without leave, the dark abodes? **1823** J. G. Todd *Strila* 156 All gory and mangled he hung unentombed.

**Unentomolo·gical,** *a.* (Un-¹ 7.) **1807** Kirby *Let.* in K. & Spence *Entomol.* (1856) App. 579 Occupied with unentomological affairs. **1817** Kirby & Sp. *Entomol.* xvi. II. 10 Unentomological observers..might easily mistake one kind of insect for another.

**Unentra·nce,** *v.* (Un-² 3.) **1834** Sir H. Taylor *Artevelde, Elena* 278 As that common day advanced His heart was wholly unentranced.

**Unentrea·table,** *a.* Also unin-. (Un-¹ 7 b.) **1561** Daus tr. *Bullinger on Apoc.* (1573) 97 Corrupt Preachers..haue..borne men in hand that God is an unintreatable Rhadamantus. **1581** J. Bell *Haddon's Answ. Osor.* 478 b, The Pope..did with unentreatable bloudthyrstynes rushe upon good and godly ministers. **1611** Cotgr., *Inexorable*, inexorable, vnintreatable.

**Unentrea·ted,** *ppl. a.* In 7 unin-. (Un-¹ 8.) **1601** Munday & Chettle *Death Earl Huntington* ii. ii, A gallant crue Of courtly maskers.., Before whome, vnintreated, I am come. **1641** Earl Monm. tr. *Biondi's Civil Wars* i. 22 The doing of what of himself, as King, he ought unintreated to have done. *a* **1652** Brome *New Acad.* ii. ii, Will you turne Match-maker For others unintreated?

**Unentre·nched,** *ppl. a.* (Un-¹ 8.) **1641** Earl Monm. tr. *Biondi's Civil Wars* iv. 63 What doth Charles deserve, who..durst not confront him, whilst unintrench'd, hee stood ready to receiue him. **1716** Pope *Iliad* II. 332 An army that lay unfortify'd and unintrench'd.

**Unenu·merable,** *a.* (Un-¹ 7 b.) **1895** *Westm. Gaz.* 12 June 3/1 The countless triumphs.., the unenumerable charms.

**Unenu·merated,** *ppl. a.* (Un-¹ 8.) [**1775** Ash.] **1837** Moloney *Forestry W. Africa* 198 Wood and timber imports...Unenumerated.

**Unenve·nomed,** *ppl. a.* (Un-¹ 8.) **1767** S. Paterson *Another Trav.* II. 134 Disarm them of their stings!—that henceforward they may be all dartless unenvenomed buz. **1831** Trelawny *Adv. Younger Son* III. 322 The rejection, unenvenomed by ministers, was not offensive.

**Une·nviable,** *a.* and *sb.* (Un-¹ 7 b.) **1641** Milton *Animadv.* Pref. 3 Their hopes of ascending above a lowly and unenviable pitch in this life. **1797** Mrs. A. M. Bennett *Beggar Girl* (1813) II. 205 All the unenviables of her situation recurred to her mind. **1849** Macaulay *Hist. Eng.* vi. II. 143 He now daily proved that he was well entitled to this unenviable reputation. **1885** C. E. Pascoe *Lond. of To-day* 262 The church..which has earned an unenviable notoriety in connection with..Ritualistic practices.

Hence **Une·nviably** *adv.* **1854** Huxley in *Life* (1900) I. 47 One of that class unenviably distinguished in the war-time as a 'donkey frigate'.

**Une·nvied,** *ppl. a.* [Un-¹ 8, 9.]

†**1.** Not mixed with envy. *Obs.*—¹ **1390** Gower *Conf.* I. 7 Tho was ther unenvied love, Tho was the vertu sett above And vice was put under fote.

**2.** Not made the object of envy; not regarded with envious feelings. **1615** Chapman *Odyss.* xvii. 285 Why thou vnenuied Swaine, Whither dost thou leade..this most nasty begger? *a* **1667** Cowley *Ess., Dangers Hon. Man*, Why you may stay, and live unenvyed here. **1725** Pope *Odyss.* xiv. 452 Let us..here, unenvy'd, rural dainties taste. **1741** Richardson *Pamela* III. 216, I shall..injoy, unenvied, the Favour of my dear Papa and Mamma. **1831** Wordsw. *Primrose of Rock* 33 Let myriads of bright flowers, Like Thee, in field and grove Revive unenvied.

**3.** Not enviously desired or grudged. **1645** Symonds *Diary* (Camden) 274 My witt, That seekes no higher prise, Than in unenvyed shades to sett. **1667** Milton *P. L.* ii. 23 Mee..this loss, Thus farr at least recover'd, hath much more Establisht in a safe unenvied Throne. **1713** Berkeley in *Guard.* No. 62 ¶ 1 To draw a secret unenvied Pleasure from a thousand Incidents over-looked by other Men. **1816** Scott *Antiq.* xviii, Martin Waldeck..often regretted bitterly the labours and sports of his unenvied poverty. **1905** J. B. Bury *St. Patrick* ii. 17 To be a decurion..in the days of Calpurnius and his father was..an unenvied dignity.

Hence **Une·nviedly** *adv.* **1738** R. Whatley *Lett. & Applic.* vii, A Right Reverend Prelate,..unenviedly possest of one of the most eminent stations.

**Une·nvious,** *a.* (Un-¹ 7.) **1656** Cowley *Pindar. Odes, 2nd Olympique* x, Fortune's free gifts as freely to impart With an Unenvious hand, and an unbounded Heart. **1746** Akenside *Hymn to Naiads* 67 You too, O Nymphs, and your unenvious aid The rural powers confess. **1754** Secker *Serm.* (1771) xi. 287 We shall be far surer of finding these upright, unenvious,..compassionate, than others, who have not equal inducements. **1838** Lytton *Alice* v. iii, Caroline gazed with honest but not unenvious admiration at the fairy form. **1881** *Fortn. Rev.* Feb. 199 The only unenvious people in Europe.

So **Une·nviously** *adv.* **1896** *Daily News* 13 June 5/6 Though the naval architects may look never so unenviously at the developement of the German fleet.

**Une·nvying,** *ppl. a.* (Un-¹ 10.) **1741** Richardson *Pamela* III. 242 They all yield to her the Palm, unenvying. **1820** Shelley *Prometh. Unb.* ii. ii. 97 Delightful strains..which charm To silence the unenvying nightingales.

**Unenwo·ven,** *ppl. a.* (Un-¹ 8 b.) **1871** Swinburne *Songs bef. Sunrise, Mentana* 83 Lycoris, with hair unenwoven.

**Une·pilogued,** *a.* (Un-¹ 9.) **1773** Goldsm. *Stoops to Conq.* Epil., And now with late repentance, Un-epilogued the Poet waits his sentence.

**Unepi·scopal,** *a.* [Un-¹ 7.]

**1.** Not controlled by bishops; not episcopalian in character or government. **1659** Gauden *Tears Ch.* ** 2 He never set up any soveraign and unepiscopal Presbytery as an Idol or Moloch. **1863** A. Blomfield *Mem. Bp. Blomfield* I. xi. 298 The High-Church party..looked with dislike..upon any display of friendly feeling towards an un-episcopal Church.

**2.** Not pertaining to or befitting a bishop. *a* **1661** Fuller *Worthies, Wilts.* iii. (1662) 150 If any say, this was an un-episcopal act; know, he did it not as Bishop, but as Lord Treasurer. **1716** M. Davies *Athen. Brit.* III. 34 They could not have pleas'd the Dissenters..better, than by such Un-episcopal Ravings. **1889** Gretton *Memory's Harkb.* 55 The sayings and doings of his early unepiscopal days were remembered. **1897** J. W. Clark *Barnwell* Introd. 20 The Bishop lost his temper, and used very unepiscopal language.

Hence **Unepi·scopally** *adv.* **1886** *Manch. Exam.* 6 Jan. 3/1 The unepiscopally explicit declaration.

**Une·pitaphed,** *a.* (Un-¹ 9.) **1827** Pollok *Course T.* iii. 434 To live unknown..: to die unpraised, Unepitaphed! **1858** M. Arnold *Merope* 779 Those dead unepitaph'd, who lie In the stone coffins at Orchomenus.

**Une·quable,** *a.* (Un-¹ 7 and 5 b.) **1692** Bentley *Boyle Lect.* viii. 261 March and September..are..the most unsettled and unequable of seasons. **1748** Hartley *Observ. Man* i. i. § 3. 108 Unequable and irregular Motions of the Heart and Bowels. **1763** *Phil. Trans.* LIII. 245 The true (or unequable) motions of the Sun, Moon, and nodes. **1825** J. Nicholson *Operat. Mechanic* 45 The unequable motion of the piston moved in the common way by a crank. **1855** Faber *Growth in Holiness* xvii. 306 We are fluctuating and unequable in our very fears.

Hence **Une·quably** *adv.* **1834** Mrs. Somerville *Connex. Phys. Sci.* iii. (1840) 20 As the planet moves unequably in its orbit. *a* **1849** Poe *Eureka* Wks. 1865 II. 180 We have now reached a point from which we behold the Universe as a spherical space, interspersed, unequably, with clusters.

**Une·qual,** *sb.* [Un-¹ 7, 12; cf. next.]

**1.** *pl.* Persons who are not on an equality with each other in respect of rank or social standing. **1600** W. Watson *Decacordon* (1602) 51 It is an act of great humility..neither to striue for the last or first word, or place taking amongst not much vnequals. **1667** Milton *P. L.* viii. 383 Among unequals what societie Can sort, what harmonie or true delight? **1768** *Woman of Honor* II. 56 Such is generally the end of that society among unequals. **1875** Poste *Gaius* i. (ed. 2) 40 The law of Persons considers men as unequals.

**2.** *pl.* Things that are not equal to each other in kind, magnitude, etc. **1611** W. Sclater *Key* (1629) 149 An Antithesis of things diuers;..secondly, a comparison of vnequals. *a* **1653** Gouge *Comm. Heb.* iii. 2 Unequals may be compared in quality and likeness, though not in equality. **1719** Whiston *Elem. Euclid* 6 If to Unequals you add Equals, the Wholes will be unequal. **1789** T. Taylor *Proclus* II. 17 Let a be equal to b, and add to each the unequals c, d.

**Une·qual,** *a.* and *adv.* [Un-¹ 7 and 5 b: cf. the earlier Unegall (Unegually) and Inequal.]

**1.** Not equal in amount, size, quality, etc.

**a.** Of two or more things or persons in comparison with each other. **1565** Cooper *Thes., Calami dispares*, vnequall reedes, one smaller then an other. **1570** Billingsley *Euclid* i. post. v. 7 If to vnequall thinges ye adde equall thinges, the whole shall be vnequall. **1607** J. Davies (Heref.) *Summa Totalis* Wks. (Grosart) I. 14/2 Then, if his Will and Prayer vnequall be, How shall we equall make his Properties? **1653** Blithe *Eng. Improver Imp.* 197, I..onely advise that if your horses be unequall for height, then place the highest formost. **1693** T. Creech in *Dryden's Juvenal* xiii. (1697) 328 Ev'ry Age relates That equal Crimes have met unequal Fates. **1743** Francis tr. *Hor., Odes* i. xxxiii. 16 With sportive cruelty she binds Unequal forms, unequal minds. **1784** Astle *Orig. & Progr. Writing* 79 The Rustic capitals were bold, negligent, unequal. **1836** W. C. Taylor *Anc. Hist.* xvi. § 1. 372 Tarraconensis was divided into two unequal portions by the river Iberus. **1860** Tyndall *Glac.* i. xiv. 95 Three stakes..would, I think, move with unequal velocities. **1861** J. S. Adams *5000 Musical Terms* 104 Compositions written for both male and female voices are said to be for unequal voices.

**b.** With abstract sbs. in the singular. **1593** Shaks. *3 Hen. VI*, iii. ii. 159 Shee did corrupt frayle Nature..To shape my Legges of an vnequall size. **1651** Hobbes *Leviath.* i. viii. 34 The Experience of men equall in age, is not much unequall, as to the quantity. **1710** *Tatler* No. 235 ¶ 1 That unequal Love by which Parents distinguish their Children from each other. **1780** Cowper *Progr. Error* 560 Halting on crutches of unequal size. **1827** Jarman *Powell's Devises* II. 265 There seems to be no solid ground for treating with such unequal regard the two objects of the testator's bounty. **1838** Lytton *Calderon* i, The courtiers one by one approached the marquis, who received them with very unequal courtesy. **1908** *Animal Managem.* 185 The more unequal the balance of weight carried the greater the risk of injury.

**c.** Of single persons or things. *a* **1677** Barrow *Math.* x. 233 That will be called unequal, which contains in it another..and some thing besides. **1829** Scott *Anne of G.* xxxv, Surely..a match with one so unequal in birth..was too monstrous to be mentioned? **1887** Bowen *Æneid* i. 475 Ill-starred youth, for Achilles unequal match in the fight.

**d.** Of numbers: Odd; not even. **1697** Dryden *Virg. Past.* viii. 105 Thrice bind about his thrice devoted Head,..Unequal numbers please the Gods. **1807** Robinson *Archæol. Græca* v. x. (1827) 447 The gods were supposed to be pleased with unequal numbers.

**2.** †**a.** Of things: Inadequate, insufficient. *Obs.* **1582** Bentley *Mon. Matrones* iii. 278 Continue, O God, such goodnesse towards me,..which doo here..appeale..to accept mine vnequall thanks for the same. **1646** Sir T. Browne *Pseud. Ep.* Pref., Authority..which the privacie of our condition, and unequall abilities cannot expect. **1676** Dryden *Aurengz.* i. i. 74 Those Rebel-Sons, who dare..To sway his Empire with unequal Skill And mount a throne which none but he can fill. **1736** Gray *Statius* i. 5 From out the gazing host Young Pterelas with strength unequal drew, Labouring, the disc, and to small distance threw.

**b.** Not equal or adequate *to* some task, etc. (Occas. with inf. or vbl. sb.) *a* **1694** Tillotson *Serm.* (1743) VII. 1991 We are very unequal to our religion, if we make a doubt of these things. **1776** Gibbon *Decl. & F.* ii. (1782) I. 60 Four of them were immediately rejected as unequal to the burden. **1802** Marian Moore *Lascelles* II. 99, I was unequal to personally opposing that dear friend. **1816** Scott *Old Mort.* xxxiii, Unequal..to arrange his own thoughts into suitable expressions. **1855** Macaulay *Hist. Eng.* xii. III. 229 Avaux had given it as his opinion that Richard Hamilton was unequal to the difficulties of the situation. **1885** 'F. Anstey' *Tinted Venus* 111 Imagination was unequal to the task.

**3.** Exhibiting inequality in some respect; varying, variable: **a.** In movement or action. **1565** Cooper, *Inæquabilis percussus venarum*, vnequall pulse. **1655** Culpepper, etc., *Riverius* viii. ii. 181 After an unequal Pulse, he fell into a Palpitation and an Asthma, and so died. **1715** tr. *Gregory's Astron.* (1726) I. 463 The Motion of this Body which is in its own Nature unequal, ought to be reduced to an equality. **1799** in *Spirit Pub. Jrnls.* III. 271 The gratitude of the depredator of Hibernia walked forth with unequal pace by the side of his emoluments. **1821** Scott *Kenilw.* xxxiv, Her step was not only slow, but even unequal.

**b.** In extent, amount, duration, etc. **1591** G. Fletcher *Russe Commw.* (Hakl. Soc.) 112 By means of an unequall partition of the people and parishes. **1593** Fale *Dialling* 40 By an unequall houre is meant the 12 part of the day whether it be short or long. **1656** Earl Monm. tr. *Boccalini's Advts. fr. Parnass.* i. xxiv. (1674) 26 Is it not..able to make a man die for anger,..in so unequal a thirst, to drink still the same measure? **1684** Earl Roscom. *Ess. Transl. Verse* 234 If you will unequal Numbers try, Their Accents on odd Syllables must lie. **1815** Stephens in *Shaw's Gen. Zool.* IX. i. 6 Tail very long, unequal, the outer feathers the shortest: tip black. **1836** Macgillivray *Trav. Humboldt* xxi. 302 The climate..is marked by an unequal distribution of heat at different periods of the year.

*spec.* **1816** R. Jameson *Char. Min.* (ed. 2) 204 Unequal tourmaline..is a nine-sided prism, having seven alternating planes on one extremity, and three on the other.

**c.** In surface: Uneven, undulating. **1613** Purchas *Pilgrimage* viii. iii. 624 The unequall Seas, which might amaze the hearer, and amate the beholder. **1686** tr. *Chardin's Trav. Persia* 79 The Country it self is unequal; full of Hills.., Valleys and Plains. **1718** Prior *Solomon* ii. 5 The perplexing and unequal Ways, Where Study brings Thee. **1732** Munro *Anat. Bones* 131 This Bone is extremely ragged and unequal. **1796** Mme. D'Arblay *Camilla* I. 4 The parsonage-house.., beautifully situated in the unequal county of Hampshire. **1826** Kirby & Sp. *Entomol.* xlvi. IV. 270 *Unequal*, having very slight and indeterminate excavations. **1852** Bailey *Festus* (ed. 4) 342 Shining upon it like the quiet moon Illustrating the obscure unequal earth.

**d.** In character, condition, quality, etc. **1703** Rowe *Fair Penit.* iv. i. 1259 With what unequal Tempers are we form'd? **1799** S. & Ht. Lee *Canterb.*

*T.* (1800) III. 147 Her spirits were often unequal from the delicate state of her health. **1811** SCOTT *Let.* in *Lockhart* (1837) II. xi. 364 The unknown author of a fine, but unequal poem, called *Albania.* **1897** GRANT DUFF *Notes from Diary* (1911) 81 No man writes above himself; but most men are very unequal.

†**4. a.** Not characterized by equal or fair treatment; inequitable, unjust, unfair. *Obs.*

**1535** COVERDALE *Ezek.* xviii. 25 Are my wayes vnright, o ye house of Israel? Are not youre wayes rather vnequall? *a* **1578** LINDESAY (Pitscottie) *Chron. Scot.* (S.T.S.) I. 66 His unequall punisching of innocencie. **1606** SHAKS. *Ant. & Cl.* II. v. 101 To punnish me for what you make me do Seemes much vnequall. **1620** E. BLOUNT *Horæ Subs.* 531 It is a thing both vnequall and vniust to insnare the people with multitude of Lawes. **1647** J. TAYLOR *Lib. Proph.* Ep. Ded. 12 Yet it will be unequall to say, that he who owns this Doctrine preaches it lawfull. **1761** HUME *Hist. Eng.* I. x. 205 To lend [money] at exorbitant and unequal interest.

†**b.** Of persons: Acting, or disposed to act, unfairly or unjustly. *Obs.*

**1588** GREENE *Pandosto* (1607) 15 Iealousie is an vnequall Iudge. **1605** B. JONSON *Volpone* III. ii, You are vnequall to me, and how ere Your sentence may be righteous, yet you are not. **1628** FELTHAM *Resolves* II. xxiii. 75 Few againe are so iust, as that they seeme not to some vnequall. *a* **1721** PRIOR *Ess. Opinion* Wks. 1907 II. 195 You will find him always uncertain,.. an Unequal Parent and a froward Master. **1725** POPE *Odyss.* XIV. 73 Far hence is by unequal Gods remov'd That man of bounties!

*transf.* **1613** PURCHAS *Pilgrimage* (1614) 629 The sword, the vnequallest arbiter of equity, is now made vmpire. **1630** R. N. tr. *Camden's Hist. Eliz.* I. 111 She.. admonished her,.. saying that the times were vnequall and maligne, and malice blinde. **1743** FRANCIS tr. *Hor., Odes* II. x. 4 And when you hear the tempest roar, Press not too near th' unequal shore.

**5.** In which the two sides or parties are not on equal terms, or have not equal advantage.

**1552** ELYOT, *Impar certamen*, in contencion, or in gameyng, where is an vnequall matche. **1591** SHAKS. 1 *Hen. VI*, v. v. 34 A poore Earles daughter is vnequall oddes, And therefore may be broke without offence. **1604** BACON *Apol.* Wks. 1879 I. 437, I doubted his words would have so unequal a passage above theirs that should charge him. **1671** MILTON *Samson* 346 Himself an Army, now unequal match To save himself against a coward arm'd At one spears length. **1748** ANSON *Voy.* III. x. 416 This was much short of her value, but the impatience of the Commodore.. prompted them to insist on so unequal a bargain. **1795** MME. D'ARBLAY *Camilla* III. 390 She had entered the world, by a sudden and most unequal marriage. **1833** HT. MARTINEAU *Cinnamon & Pearls* v. 92 The colony will not long fulfil its part in this unequal bargain. **1856** KANE *Arct. Expl.* II. xx. 205, I left my own tired dogs.., and took from them their only team in unequal exchange.

**b.** *esp.* Of combats or contests.

**1654** FULLER *Two Serm.* 4 The next verse presents an unequall combat between armed power.. and naked Innocence. **1697** DRYDEN *Æneis* IX. 542 Or desperate should he rush and lose his life, With odds oppressed, in such unequal strife? *c* **1750** SHENSTONE *Ruin'd Abbey* 56 My pinnace.. shuns Th' unequal conflict, and declines the deep. **1817** SHELLEY *Rev. Islam* VI. xiv, Then the combat grew Unequal but most horrible. **1878** DAVIDSON *Inverurie & Garioch* ix. 317 The struggle with England which ensued was necessarily an unequal one.

†**c.** Disproportionate, excessive. *Obs.*

**1704** SWIFT *Battle of Bks.* ¶ 10 Which, yielding to the unequal Weight, sunk down to the very Foundation. **1717** POPE *Eloisa* 195 Unequal task! a passion to resign, For hearts so touch'd,.. so lost as mine.

**6.** *Comb.*, as *unequal-lengthed, -lobed, -sided, -tempered, -valved.*

**1853** R. S. SURTEES *Sponge's Sp. Tour* lv, The *unequal-lengthed candles of the previous night's illumination. **1851** G. A. MANTELL *Petrifact.* v. § 2. 433 Two genera.. which are characterised by their *unequal-lobed tail. **1725** W. HALFPENNY *Sound Building* 19 An *unequal-sided Groin. **1856** HENSLOW *Dict. Bot. Terms* 208 *Unequal-sided*, when opposite sides are not symmetrical. **1885** J. E. TAYLOR *Brit. Fossils* 243 The shells are frequently unequal-sided. **1703** MOXON *Mech. Exerc.* 169 Heavy *unequal tempered Stuff. **1822** J. PARKINSON *Outl. Oryctol.* 187 An irregular, adherent, *unequal-valved bivalve.

**7.** *adv.* or quasi-*adv.*

**1602** SHAKS. *Ham.* II. ii. 493 (Q 1), Vnequall matcht, Pirrhus at Priam driues. **1663** GERBIER *Counsel* 50 To cause the foundation.. to be.. laid, without leaving any toutchings, since walls new begun on them will settle more unequal than those [etc.]. **1700** S. WESLEY *Epist. Poetry* 12 Of Chaucer's Verse we scarce the Measures know, So rough the Lines, and so unequal flow. **1853** MARKHAM *Skoda's Auscult.* 266 Unequal-bubbling dull râles.

**Une·qualable**, *a.* (UN-[1] 7 b.)

**1648** BOYLE *Seraph. Love* (1659) 129 Christ.., whose love to God is questionlesse Filiall and unequalable. **1799** SOUTHEY *Lett.* (1856) I. 87 Milton and Shakspeare,.. the two unequalable men. **1870** CARLYLE *New Letters* (1904) II. 263 Our welcome continues to be unsurpassable, or indeed unequallable.

†**Unequa·lity.** *Obs.* [UN-[1] 12 and 5 b.] = INEQUALITY.

**1541** R. COPLAND *Guydon's Quest. Chirurg.* M iv, Whan it is seen that it [sc. the pulse] alyeneth to vnequalyte.. the veyne ought to be stopped. **1587** GOLDING *De Mornay* ii. 20 When.. wee see an equalitie of good behauior in an vnequality of degrees of people. **1623** COCKERAM II, Vnequalitie, or contrary to a thing, *anomalie.* **1720** *Temple's Ess., Govt.* Wks. I. 106 The first must overturn whenever there happens any unequality [1680 inequality] in the Balance. **1770–4** *A. Hunter's Georg. Ess.* (1803) I. 289 Hence an unequality of the crop.

**Une·qualized**, *ppl. a.* (UN-[1] 8.)

**1596** FITZ-GEFFREY *Sir F. Drake* (1881) 69 A vowed votarie to honour still, Vnequaliz'd by valours chiefest peeres. **1822** J. PARKINSON *Outl. Oryctol.* 69 The terminations of unequalized pentagons and hexagons. **1880** EARLE *Philol. Eng. Tongue* (ed. 3) § 239 Its application is unequalized even within the four seas.

**Une·qualled**, *ppl. a.* (UN-[1] 8.)

**1622** FLETCHER *Sea Voy.* IV. i, Do ye like wealth, and most unequal'd beauty? **1639** SIR W. BERKELEY *Lost Lady* I. i, I will relate the story of his Unequal'd suffrings. **1667** MILTON *P. L.* IX. 983 Chiefly assur'd.. of thy so true, So faithful Love unequald. **1746** FRANCIS tr. *Hor., Sat.* II. ii. 38 No; 'tis th' unequall'd beauty of its train Deludes your eye. **1794** R. J. SULIVAN *View Nat.* I. 177 Why should there be.. such unequalled heats, and such unequalled evaporation? **1841** MISS MITFORD in L'Estrange *Life* (1870) III. viii. 120 Our ancestors were rare architects. Their painted glass and their carved oak are unequalled. **1872** YEATS *Techn. Hist. Comm.* 81 Buildings which are unequalled for grandeur.

**b.** Const. *by.*

**1769** GOLDSM. *Hist. Rome* (1786) II. 103 An act of unequalled heroism by anything that had hitherto appeared in Rome. **1796** MORSE *Amer. Geog.* II. 19 A violence and noise unequalled by the loudest cataracts. **1829** *Chapters Phys. Sci.* 64 The battering-ram.. exerted a force which in some respects rendered it unequalled by our battering cannon. **1869** TOZER *Highl. Turkey* II. 124 A panorama.. unequalled.. by any view in Greece.

**Une·qually**, *adv.* [UN-[1] 11: cf. UNEQUAL *a.*]

**1.** In an unequal manner; not equally or evenly.

**1548** ELYOT, *Inæqualiter*, vnequally. **1563** GOLDING *Cæsar* VII. (1565) 208 b, The Romanes were vnequallye matched, both in place and number. **1611** BIBLE 2 *Cor.* vi. 14 Be ye not vnequally yoked together with vnbeleeuers. **1665** MANLEY *Grotius' Low C. Wars* 417 All this Region is divided, though somewhat unequally, between wild Beasts, and these Savage men. **1726** MONRO *Anat. Bones* 149 The square-bone is unequally concave... Its.. Edge is unequally ragged. **1776** GIBBON *Decl. & F.* I. (1782) I. 23 That great peninsula [Spain], at present so unequally divided between two sovereigns. **1831** BREWSTER *Optics* iv. 40 Rule for finding the principal focus.. for a glass unequally convex. **1880** GEIKIE *Phys. Geog.* iv. 284 The rocks.. are worn down unequally.

†**2.** Unfairly, unjustly. *Obs.*

**1596** SPENSER *F. Q.* VII. vii. 14 Damning all Wrong.. Which any of thy creatures doe to other (Oppressing them with power, vnequally).

**Une·qualness.** [UN-[1] 12: cf. UNEQUAL *a.*]

**1.** The quality of being unequal.

**1550** BALE *Image Both Ch.* II. xxi. Nnn iij b, As for the vnequalnesse of length in yᵉ furlongs & cubits [etc.]. **1561** T. HOBY tr. *Castiglione's Courtyer* IV. (1577) T vij b, Bestowing promotions and honors according to the vnequalnesse of desertes. **1652** FRENCH *Yorksh. Spa* xiii. 102, I forbid much variety of meats, because of the unequalness of their concoction. **1698** ATTERBURY *Serm.* (1737) IV. 308 This unequalness in acting.. will draw upon a man the suspicion of hypocrisy. **1776** *Ann. Reg.* 148 Notwithstanding the unequalness of the wind.. he only missed the target three times. **1880** *Wood's Guide Steam-Engine Indicator* (title-p.), Geometrical Sketch, showing the Cause of Unequalness.

†**2.** Lack of equity; unfairness. *Obs.*

**1628** tr. *Mathieu's Powerfull Favorite* 126 The vapours of his way-ward disposition, of his distrust and vnequalnesse. **1695** *Def. Vind. Deprived Bps.* 98 The very unequalness of it [*sc.* a contract] would be in Equity a strong Presumption.

**Uneque·strian**, *a.* (UN-[1] 7.) **1846** H. W. TORRENS *Rem. Milit. Hist.* 21 A remarkable proof of the unequestrian habits of the Greek. **Unequia·ngular**, *a.* (UN-[1] 7.) **1805** R. JAMESON *Char. Min.* 41 These lateral edges are either equiangular as in the icosahedron,.. [or] unequiangular as in topaz. **Unequia·xed**, *a.* (UN-[1] 9, 5 b.) *a* **1853** PEREIRA *Polarized Light* (1854) 164 In a very large proportion of cases the axes are not all equal, and these crystals are said to be unequiaxed. **1877** LE CONTE *Elem. Geol.* (1879) 185 A plastic mass, with unequiaxed foreign particles disseminated through it. **Unequila·teral**, *a.* (UN-[1] 7, 5 b.) **1662** J. BARGRAVE *Pope Alex. VII* (1867) 120, I have in my cabinet another triangular unequilateral.. loadstone. **1761** *London & Environs* IV. 145 Nineteen unequilateral arches.. supported the street above. **Unequili·brated**, *ppl. a.* (UN-[1] 8.) [**1775** ASH.] **1833** HERSCHEL *Ess.* (1857) 50 The.. constant fluctuation of an unequilibrated ocean. **1895** W. H. HUDSON *Spencer's Philos.* 97 Remaining exposed to surrounding forces that are unequilibrated. **Unequi·pped**, *ppl. a.* (UN-[1] 8.) [**1775** ASH.] **1895** HARDY in *Harper's Mag.* Mar. 569 The miserable struggle in which he had been engaged thus unequipped.

**Une·quitable**, *a.* (UN-[1] 7 and 5 b.)

**1647** DIGGES *Unlawf. Taking Arms* IV. 99 Not all, but in an unequitable proportion. **1662** J. BARGRAVE *Pope Alex. VII* (1867) 82 For very feare of falling into the legate's displeasure, who they knew was averse to such unequitable designs. **1726** AMHERST *Terræ Fil.* II. App. 169 It is almost as unjust and unequitable.. as it would be to act.. against any such authority. **1759** STERNE *Tr. Shandy* II. xvii, A cunning contexture of dark arts and unequitable subterfuges. **1844** THIRLWALL *Greece* VIII. lxi. 101 This would seem perhaps not unequitable.

Hence **Une·quitably** *adv.*

**1649** [F. ROUS] *Bounds Publ. Obed.* 61 They being unequitably deriv'd upon us. **1750** SECKER *Eight Charges* (1771) 126 Any Part of it, which is illegally or unequitably seized.

†**Une·quity.** *Obs. rare.* [UN-[1] 12 and 5 b.]

**a.** Iniquity, wickedness. **b.** Unfairness.

*c* **1380** WYCLIF *Wks.* (1880) 394 If it was vnequite.. for to leue þe prechynge of goddis worde,.. hou myche more vnequite and wronge to god & man is it [etc.]. **1382** — *Rom.* iii. 5 If oure wickidnesse, or vnequyte, comende the riȝtwysnesse of God. **1598** FLORIO, *Inequità*, vnequitie.

**Une·quivalve(d)**, *a.* (UN-[1] 7, 9, and 5 b.) **1788** J. BARBUT *Genera Vermium* 42 The shell unequivalve, of a hard consistency. **1822** J. PARKINSON *Outl. Oryctol.* 179 A regular unequivalved, inequilateral bivalve.

**Unequi·vocal**, *a.* (UN-[1] 7 and 5 b.)

In common use from about 1795.

**1784** COWPER *Task* v. 653 In the deed, The unequivocal authentic deed, We find sound argument. **1791** NEWTE *Tour Eng. & Scot.* 236 In the Highlands.. men of years.. are struck with the most unequivocal proofs of depopulation. **1838** THIRLWALL *Greece* xlii. V. 213 He.. aided him in several acts of unequivocal hostility against his country. **1858** SEARS *Athan.* III. v. 294 This.. is here asserted by the Apostle in most unequivocal language. **1871** EARLE *Philol. Eng. Tongue* 340 An adjectival form which should be unequivocal.

Hence **Unequi·vocalness.**

**1846** WORCESTER (citing Godwin).

**Unequi·vocally**, *adv.* (UN-[1] 11.)

**1794** PALEY *Evid.* I. vii, The descent of Christ from David, ..his resurrection,.. are unequivocally referred to. **1800** MRS. HERVEY *Mourtray Fam.* III. 26, I hope.. to receive a line from you, unequivocally to contradict it. **1844** THIRLWALL *Greece* lxvi. VIII. 467 Still the good-will of the early emperors was unequivocally manifested. **1884** EARL SELBORNE in *Law Times Rep.* 10 May 313/2 Such an intention.. might have been expected to be made unequivocally clear.

**Unera·dicable**, *a.* (UN-[1] 7 b and 5 b.) **1818** BYRON *Ch. Har.* IV. cxxvi, This uneradicable taint of sin, This boundless upas. **Unera·dicated**, *ppl. a.* (UN-[1] 8.) [**1828–32** WEBSTER.] **1861** J. G. SHEPPARD *Fall Rome* vi. 323 The uneradicated influences of heathen taste. **1871** ALABASTER *Wheel of Law* 41 The believers in it.. will still have their souls contaminated with uneradicated evil. **Unera·s(e)able**, *a.* (UN-[1] 7 b and 5 b.) **1826** MRS. SHELLEY *Last Man* II. 156 Now in words unerasable.. the knowledge went forth. **1853** G. JOHNSTON *Nat. Hist. E. Bord.* I. 233 The coloured unerasable stain cries out for yet unavenged blood. **Unera·sed**, *ppl. a.* (UN-[1] 8.) **1760–72** H. BROOKE *Fool of Qual.* (1809) IV. 65, I discerned some unerased traces of the image ..of my God. **1821** BYRON *Two Foscari* I. i, *Lor.* It is written thus. *Bar.* And will you leave it unerased? **Unera·sible**, *a.* (UN-[1] 7.) **1811** SHELLEY *St. Irvyne* i, Grief, in unerasible traces, sate deeply implanted on the front of the outcast. **Unera·sing**, *ppl. a.* (UN-[1] 10.) **1820** SHELLEY *Prometh. Unb.* III. iii. 160 Where ever lies, on unerasing waves, The image of a temple built, above. †**Unerrabi·lity.** (UN-[1] 12 and 5 b; cf. next.) **1628** PRYNNE *Brief Survay* 14 Hee doeth ..likewise apply this Popish Position.. euen to iustifie the vnerrabilitie of these his Deuotions.

†**Une·rrable**, *a. Obs.* [UN-[1] 7 b and 5 b.] = INERRABLE *a.*

**1616** SHELDON *Mirac. Antichrist* vii. 142 This puddle of Pope Ioane, whereout the ignominy of your vnerrable See is so liuely discouered. **1664** H. MORE *Myst. Iniq.* xviii. 67 The ancient Types.. already made use of by his choice who was unerrable. **1715** M. DAVIES *Athen. Brit.* I. Pref. 12 Those sole unerrable Records of the Holy Scriptures.

Hence †**Une·rrableness.** *Obs.*

**1645** HAMMOND *View Infallibility* (1646) 186 Concluding the truth of all their assertions from the unerrablenesse of the asserter. **1667** *Decay Chr. Piety* xvi. ¶ 3 The danger of presuming upon the unerrableness of a guide.

**Une·rrancy.** (UN-[1] 12 and 5 b.)

**1646** J. HALL *Horæ Vac.* 7 Hee takes the best course.. that narrowly heeds upon what principles both parties build.., so long as no man can challenge an unerrancy. **1891** F. G. LEE *Sinless Concept.* 66 Unerrancy belonged alone to the Church Universal.

**Une·rring**, *vbl. sb.* (UN-[1] 13.) **1709** STRYPE *Ann. Ref.* 247 He was in Judgment for the unerring of General Councils.

**Une·rring**, *ppl. a.* [UN-[1] 10 and 5 b.]

**1.** Making no error or mistake; not going or leading astray in judgement or opinion.

*c* **1660** SOUTH *Serm.* (1697) I. 254 They believed his Miracles upon the Credit of constant unerring Tradition. **1697** DRYDEN *Virg. Georg.* IV. 565 With sure Foresight, and with unerring Doom, He sees what is, and was, and is to come. **1732** CHALLONER (*title*), The Unerring Authority of the Catholic Church in matters of Faith. **1795** SOUTHEY *Joan of Arc* IV. 324, I know this vision sent From Heaven, and feel of its unerring truth. **1844** H. H. WILSON *Brit. India* I. 565 The unerring principles of political economy. **1875** JOWETT *Plato* (ed. 2) I. 32 The unerring guides of ourselves and of those who were under us.

*absol.* **1813** COLERIDGE *Remorse* III. ii. 36, I breath'd to the Unerring Permitted prayers.

**2.** Corresponding with the utmost exactness or closeness to some standard or aim.

**1665** GLANVILL *Def. Van. Dogm.* 39 The unerring exactness we find in Animal formations. **1684** J. S. *Profit & Pleas. United* 166 Therefore I thought fit to lay down such Unerring Rules, as [etc.]. **1710** PRIOR *Examiner* 7 Sept., The Works of learned Men are weighed here by the unerring Ballance of Party. **1775** TYRWHITT *Chaucer's Cant. T.* IV. 91 An operation, which every Ballad-monger in our days ..is known to perform with the most unerring exactness. **1819** SCOTT *Leg. Montrose* xiv, The Son of the Mist again led the way, with an unerring precision. **1861** BUCKLE *Civiliz.* (1873) II. viii. 434 We may trace with unerring certainty the steps [etc.].

**3.** Not going astray from the intended mark; certain, sure: **a.** Of missiles or other weapons.

**1621** G. SANDYS *Ovid's Met.* XII. (1626) 240 With that, th' vnerring dart.. [he] flung. **1712** *Spect.* No. 527 ¶ 3 Procris ..made her Husband.. a Present of an unerring Javelin. *c* **1743** FRANCIS tr. *Hor., Sec. Poem* 12 Goddess, whose unerring dart Stops the lynx, or flying hart.

**b.** Of aim, agents or agencies, etc.

**1697** DRYDEN *Æneis* XII. 712 One dart he drew, And with unerring aim, and utmost vigour, threw. *c* **1709** PRIOR *2nd Hymn Callimachus* 127 Thy unerring Hand elanc'd Another, and another Dart. **1743** FRANCIS tr. *Hor., Odes* V. v. 9 By the unerring wrath of Jove, Unerring shall his vengeance prove. **1801** SCOTT *Glenfinlas* ii, How matchless was thy broad claymore, How deadly thine unerring bow! **1849** EASTWICK *Dry Leaves* 46 He was considered an unerring shot. **1855** *Orr's Circ. Sci., Inorg. Nat.* 112 Occasionally striking with unerring aim at its prey.

**Une·rringly**, *adv.* (UN-[1] 11; cf. prec.)

**1645** TOMBES *Anthropol.* 15 A power to interpret Scriptures unerringly. **1746** HERVEY *Reflect. Flower Gard.* 76 Know, that God is unerringly wise. *a* **1774** TUCKER *Lt. Nat.* (1834) II. 399 It does imply an exact discernment.., so as to distinguish unerringly what lies within its compass, and what does not. **1826** SYD. SMITH *Wks.* (1859) II. 104/2

They first learn it practically and unerringly. **1873** Earle *Philol. Eng. Tongue* (ed. 2) § 239 Here is a distinction which is unerringly observed by the most rustic people.

**Une·rringness.** (Un-[1] 12.)
**1670** Vaughan *Rep.* (1677) 139 If any man thinks that a person..must submit in all, or any of these, to the implyed discretion and unerringness of his Judge. **1866** Meredith *Vittoria* vii, The result corroborated his devotional belief in the unerringness of his own powerful intuition.

**Uneru·pted,** *ppl. a.* (Un-[1] 8.) [1775 Ash.] **1802** Playfair *Illustr. Hutton. Th.* 69 A subterraneous or unerupted lava. **1833** Lyell *Princ. Geol.* III. 107 These unerupted newer Pliocene lavas of Sicily.

**Unesca·pable,** *a.* (Un-[1] 7 b and 5 b.)
**1614** Donne *Lett.* (1651) 197 In this particular, I am under an unescapable necessity, as [etc.]. *c* **1625** — *Serm.* Wks. 1839 VI. 70 She exposes herself to an imminent and (for any thing she knew) an unescapable danger of death. **1832** L. Hunt *Redi's Bacchus in Tuscany* 135 Gall of the satiric poet, Gall from out his blackest well, Shuddering, unescapeable. **1886** W. Graham *Soc. Problem* 243 A power more subtle and all-compelling and unescapable than that of the sword.

Hence **Unesca·pableness; -ably** *adv.*
**1610** Donne *Pseudo-martyr* 353 With how much curiositie and unescapablenesse their formes of Abiuration vnder oath are exhibited? **1882** *Gd. Words* Apr. 174 With a certain twinkle at the back of his eye,..full, unescapably full of fun.

**Uneschew·able,** *a.* (Un-[1] 7 b and 5 b.)
*c* **1374** Chaucer *Boeth.* v. pr. i. (1868) 151 Þilke ordre procedynge by an vneschewable byndynge to-gidre. **1513** Douglas *Æneid* xi. xiv. 102 He..schuke in hand hys oneschewabill speir. **1542** in *Harl. Misc.* (1745) IV. 509/2 Ther came a sodeyne and piteous Calamyte or Miserye vneuitable or uneschuable. **1602** Carew *Cornwall* 124 b, If an vneschewable destiny had not haltered him to that aduancement. **1870** W. H. Gillespie *Being & Attributes God* (1871) iv. ii. 149 Our dread but uneschewable topic.

Hence **Uneschew·ably** *adv.*
*c* **1374** Chaucer *Boeth.* v. pr. iii. (1868) 157 Yif þat he deme þat þei ben to comen vneschewably.

**Unesco·rted,** *ppl. a.* (Un-[1] 8.)
**1774** *Trinket* 45 The chits knew I must attend them, for it was not safe to go unescorted. **1805–6** Cary *Dante, Inf.* viii. 127 Passing the circles, unescorted, comes One. **1898** Rider Haggard *Dr. Therne* i. 13 Now, quite alone and unescorted, she was on her way to Mexico City.

**Unescu·tcheoned,** *a.* (Un-[1] 9.) **1814** Wordsw. *Excurs.* vi. 412 Their bones.., With unescutcheoned privacy interred Far from the family vault.

**Unespie·d,** *ppl. a.* (Un-[1] 8.)
*c* **1374** Chaucer *Troylus* iv. 1457 It is ful hard to halten vn-espied Byfore a crepul for he kan on þe craft. **1542** Udall *Erasm. Apoph.* 81 No faulte of the bodye maye escape vnespied. **1596** Spenser *F. Q.* vi. x. 11 He..in the couert of the wood did byde, Beholding all, yet of them vnespyde. **1653** H. Cogan tr. *Pinto's Trav.* xix. 67 He got up close to this Junk, and..boarded her on a sudden unespied. **1697** Dryden *Æneis* ix. 786 The second shaft came swift and unespied, And pierced his hand. **1742–3** *Observ. Methodists* 8 Of all other Religions every man enjoys the free Exercise..unquestioned and unespied. **1831** Scott *Ct. Rob.* xxvi, Nothing, however, in a palace, passes altogether unespied. **1842** Browning *Through the Metidja* ii, Through the desert..Do I glide unespied as I ride?

**Unessay·ed,** *ppl. a.* (Un-[1] 8.)
**1642** in Clarendon *Hist. Reb.* iv. § 266 They cannot leave any means unessayed for their relief. **1686** Jas. II *Sp. Edin.* 29 Apr. in *Lond. Gaz.* No. 2135/3 [He] will leave nothing unessayed that may promote a work so beneficial. **1742** *Col. Rec. Pennsylv.* IV. 601 The French, who will leave no methods unessay'd to corrupt their fidelity. **1778** Miss Burney *Evelina* lxxiv, Remains there one resource unessayed? **1855** Singleton *Virgil* II. 299 Lest aught there had been or of crime, or craft, Unhazarded or unessayed.

**Une·ssence,** *v.* [Un-[2] 4.] *trans.* To deprive of essence or essential properties.
**1642** T. Case *God's Rising* (1644) 8 The Enemies of Gods truth and people would..not un-scepter him only, but unessence him. **1659** Revett in Lovelace *Poems* (1904) 212 While we sustain the losse that him gone Vn-essenc'd in the separation. **1822** Lamb *Elia* i. *Distant Correspondents,* Not only does truth, in these long intervals, unessence herself, but [etc.].

**Unesse·ntial,** *a.* and *sb.* [Un-[1] 7 and 5 b.]
**1.** Possessing no essence or substance; immaterial.
**1667** Milton *P. L.* ii. 439 The void profound Of unessential Night receives him next. **1727** Thomson *Summer* 81 Prime Chearer, Light!..Without whose vesting Beauty, all were wrapt In unessential Gloom. **1768–74** Tucker *Lt. Nat.* (1834) I. 666 Ask me by what authority of history I prove that Regulus had any notion of..the unessential nature of justice. **1827** Pollok *Course T.* iii. 412 Most unsubstantial, unessential shade, Was earthly Fame.

**2.** Not pertaining to or affecting the essence of a matter; unimportant.
*a* **1656** Bp. Hall *Beauty & Vnitie Ch.* Wks. 1837 V. 245 Neither difference of time, nor distance of place,..nor any unessential error, can bar our interest in this Blessed Unity. **1716** Addison *Freeholder* No. 39 ⁋ 5 Those, who differed from him in the unessential Parts of Christianity. **1748** Melmoth *Fitzosborne Lett.* (1763) 169 So far is he from thinking it unessential, that he acknowledged it as the only separation which distinguishes them from prose. **1838** Arnold *Hist. Rome* (1845) I. 166 A form..as unessential as the crowd's acceptance of the king at an English coronation. **1873** M. Arnold *Lit. & Dogma* (1876) 166 This excludes as unessential much of the criticism which [etc.].

**b.** *absol.* That which is not essential.
**1840** Carlyle *Heroes* iv. (1904) 139 He distinguishes what is essential, and what is not; the unessential may go very much as it will. **1841** Myers *Cath. Th.* iii. § 33. 120 Who is to determine..the limit of the Unessential?

**3.** *sb.* An unessential thing or feature.
**1828–32** Webster s.v., Forms are among the unessentials of religion. **1876** Stainer & Barrett *Dict. Mus.* 444/2 *Unessentials,* notes not forming a necessary part of the harmony. Passing, auxiliary, or ornamental notes. **1882** *Nature* XXVI. 523 A general conception..is arrived at by abstracting the essentials and neglecting the unessentials.

Hence **Unesse·ntially** *adv.*
[1847 Webster.] **1856** Olmsted *Slave States* 182 With a climate so unessentially dissimilar.

**Unesta·blish,** *v.* [Un-[2] 3.] To disestablish.
**1649** Milton *Eikon.* xxvii. 215 In order to which the Parlament demanded of the King to un-establish that Prelatical Government. **1834** W. P. Wood *Let.* in Stephens *Hook* (1878) I. 261 Where we find a Church established we ought not to lend any assistance towards *un*establishing.

**Unesta·blished,** *ppl. a.* [Un-[1] 8.]
**1.** Not established or firmly settled.
**1646** Sir T. Browne *Pseud. Ep.* 227 [A conclusion] clapt up from petitionary foundations and principles unestablished. **1744** Young *Nt. Th.* vi. Pref., This great fundamental truth, unestablish'd, or unawaken'd in the minds of men. **1776** Mickle *Camoens' Lusiad* Introd. 154 A work which claims poetical merit, while its reputation is unestablished. **1873** M. Arnold *Lit. & Dogma* xi. § 3. 346 A notion unestablished, not resting on observation and experience.

**2.** *spec.* **a.** Of churches or religious bodies: (see Establish *v.* 7).
**1885** Abp. Benson in *Life* (1899) II. 496 The difference of court made no difference to the union even of an established Church, and how can it..do so for an unestablished Church? **1887** *Pall Mall G.* 4 Oct. 1/1 Her communion embraces Churches established, unestablished, and disestablished.

**b.** Of employees or employment: Not included in the regular staff or establishment.
**1890** *Pall Mall G.* 7 July 5/2 Sanction..to..increase the minimum wage to postmen (including unestablished men). **1894** *Daily News* 15 Sept. 6/3 Within the same time 'unestablished situations'..have been given to 1,110 soldiers.

**Unesta·blishment.** (Un-[1] 12.) **1776** S. J. Pratt *Pupil of Pleas.* (1777) I. 182 Shall I once again confess to you.. my unestablishment in the maxims of thy Preceptor?

**Unestee·med,** *ppl. a.* (Un-[1] 8.)
*c* **1550** Cheke *Matt.* xiii. 57 Theer is not a propheet..vnesteemed but in his own contree. **1561** T. Norton *Calvin's Inst.* i. 18 The Hebrue tong lay not onely vnestemed, but almost vnknowen. **1616** Drumm. of Hawth. *Madrigals, Rose,* O Show of Showes! of vnesteemed Worth. **1852** Bailey *Festus* (ed. 4) 473 In thy voice The warning and foreknowledge unexplained, Not unesteemed. **1858** Carlyle *Fredk. Gt.* ii. xii. I. 167 An unesteemed creature, who strove to make his time peaceable in this world.

† **Une·stimable,** *a. Obs.* [Un-[1] 7 b and 5 b.]
**1.** = Inestimable *a.* 1.
**1542** Udall *Erasm. Apoph.* 172 *marg.,* A learned kyng [is] an vnestimable treasure. **1548** — *Erasm. Par. Luke* xxiv. 183 b, Beyng enkiendled with the vnestimable fyer of charytee & loue towardes mankynd. **1577** tr. *Bullinger's Decades* 210/1 Some by warre haue..vnestimable riches with verie little losse or no dammage at all. **1628** tr. *Mathieu's Powerfull Favorite* 102 Here all the world laments the vnestimable losse of the bookes of Cornelius Tacitus.

**2.** = Inestimable *a.* 3.
**1654–66** Earl Orrery *Parthen.* (1676) 694 There can hardly be a higher evincement how unestimable most Worldly things deserve to be. *a* **1670** Hacket *Abp. Williams* i. (1692) 41 None are so unestimable..as those fickle-fancy'd men, whose friendships will hold no longer then Pliny's peaches.

**Unestra·nged,** *ppl. a.* (Un-[1] 8.) [1775 Ash.] *a* **1851** Moir *Poems, Highl. Return* viii, Four years had lapsed in absence, ..but his heart was unestranged.

† **Une·te,** *a. Obs.* [OE. **unǽte* (cf. *micel-, oferǽte*), f. pret. stem of *etan* to eat.] Without eating.
**1387** Trevisa *Higden* (Rolls) I. 405 The men may dure longe vnete, And loueþ wel comune mete.

**Unete·rnal,** *a.* (Un-[1] 7.) [1775 Ash.] **1862** F. Hall *Hindu Philos. Syst.* 254 That which exists, and is destroyed at a given time, is..uneternal and perishable.

**Uneth(e, -ethes**: see Uneath(s *adv.*

**Unethe·rial,** *a.* (Un-[1] 7.) [1775 Ash.] **1847** Bushnell *Chr. Nurt.* ii. iii. (1861) 283 This unetherial and undiffusive kind of bliss. **Une·thic,** *a.* [Un-[1] 7.] = next. **1871** Tylor *Prim. Cult.* I. 370 An imagination so little in keeping with his unethic nature jars upon the reader's mind.

**Une·thical,** *a.* (Un-[1] 7.)
**1871** Tylor *Prim. Cult.* II. 94 The savage, unethical doctrine of continuance. **1879** Spencer *Data of Ethics* xi. § 68. 187 Ethics has to recognize the truth, recognized in unethical thought, that egoism comes before altruism. **1882** *Pall Mall G.* 15 July 4/2 The intermingling of so unethical a people with..societies of European blood.

Hence **Une·thicalness.**
**1886** W. S. Lilly in *Fortn. Rev.* 591 How can we predicate ethicalness or unethicalness of a thing?

**Uneupho·nious,** *a.* (Un-[1] 7.) **1880** Burton *Reign Q. Anne* I. i. 36 The uneuphonious name of Godolphin has been traced..to certain words of Celtic origin. **Un-Europe·an,** *a.* (Un-[1] 7.) **1849** Eastwick *Dry Leaves* 81 The un-European officers might..take the lead. **1870** Kingsley *At Last* x, Around were..all appliances of European taste, even luxury: but in a house utterly un-European. **Uneva·cuated,** *ppl. a.* (Un-[1] 8.) **1612** Woodall *Surg. Mate* Wks. (1653) 201 Some cholerick matter remaineth behinde in the right-gut yet unevacuated.

**Uneva·dable,** *a.* Also -evadeable, -evadible. (Un-[1] 7 b, 7, and 5 b.)
**1839** De Quincey *Casuistry* Wks. 1862 VII. 272 The.. downright unevadable pressures of realities. **1857** Toulmin Smith *Parish* 367 Efficient action on this matter was formerly unevadible. **1869** Rossetti *Mem. Shelley* p. liv, [A] deadly, and, at last, unevadeable discovery.

**Unevane·scent,** *a.* (Un-[1] 7.) **1802–12** Bentham *Ration. Judic. Evid.* (1827) I. 597 Signs of an unevanescent and imperishable nature. **Unevange·lic,** *a.* [Un-[1] 7.] = next. **1857** Baden Powell *Chr. without Judaism* 219 Engrafting on it an unevangelic formalism most alien from its spirit.

**Unevange·lical,** *a.* (Un-[1] 7.)
**1648** *Eikon Bas.* xii. 103 Which..un-evangelicall Zeal is too like that of the rebuked Disciples. **1661** Prynne *Unbish. Tim.* (ed. 3) 81 An unevangelical, malignant, or Romish Spirit. **1710** T. Godwin *Life Bp. Stillingfleet* 28 Their unevangelical and destructive doctrines. **1842** Manning *Serm.* xvii. (1848) I. 249 They are looked upon as carnal, legal, unevangelical rites. **1881** W. R. Smith *Old Test. in Jew. Ch.* i. 7 This point of view is..unprotestant, unevangelical.

**Uneva·ngelized,** *ppl. a.* (Un-[1] 8.)
[1775 Ash.] **1813–5** *Proc. Ch. Miss. Soc.* IV. 519 If the Heathen, un-evangelized, be considered as objects of salvation. **1884** J. Parker *Apost. Life* II. 135 The Church.. would see every unevangelised country..typified in this Macedonian man.

**Uneva·porate,** *ppl. a.* (Un-[1] 8 b.) **1864** Lowell *Fireside Trav.* 174 Faith and Awe survive there unevaporate. **Uneva·porated,** *ppl. a.* (Un-[1] 8.) **1829** Bentham *Offic. Apt. Maximized, Militia* (1830) 6 Hostility from the small, still unevaporated, remnant of the savage race. **1890** *Nature* 11 Sept. 481/2 The natural salts..with which the unevaporated residue of water becomes saturated.

**Une·ven,** *a.* [OE. *unefen* (f. *un-* Un-[1] 7 + *efen* Even *a.*), = OFris. *oniovn* (WFris. *on-, ûneven,* NFris. *unëven,-īven*), MDu. and Du. *oneven, -effen,* MLG. *uneven,* OHG. *uneban* (MHG. and G. *uneben*), ON. and Icel. *ú-, ójafn* (Norw. *ujamn,* Sw. *ojemn,* Da. *ujevn*).]
**1.** Unequal; not properly corresponding or agreeing. Now *rare.*
*a* **900** Cynewulf *Crist* 1460 Hu þær wæs unefen racu unc ȝemæne! *a* **1225** *Ancr. R.* 312 Ure blod..aȝean his blode þet he shedde for us were ful unefne chaunge. *a* **1340** Hampole *Psalter* xlii. 1 My consciens and my ȝernynge is vneuen til þairs. **1390** Gower *Conf.* II. 279 Thou tellest forth, Hou that hire weyhte of love unevene Is unto thin. *c* **1450** *Myrr. our Ladye* 104 Yf it were vneuen to the tother, or faylynge in eny thynge that an other had. *a* **1470** H. Parker *Dives & Pauper* (W. de W. 1496) vii. xi. 293/1 By wyckednesse of false couetyse in the people men ben uneuen in rychesse. **1596** Spenser *F. Q.* vi. v. 9 So forth they traueld an vneuen payre,..A saluage man matcht with a Ladie fayre. **1609** J. Davies (Heref.) *Holy Roode* Wks. (Grosart) I. 8/2 What diff'rence is betweene those Hymnes diuine!..They are as Fame, and Shame, no lesse vneu'n. **1669** Boyle *Contn. New Exp.* i. (1682) 40 Two pipes of Glass very uneven in length. **1885** *Manch. Exam.* 14 July 4/5 Stands are very uneven, and the size of the plant varies from 2 in. to 3½ ft.

**b.** Of numbers: Odd. Also of things: Making up, or marked by, an odd number.
**1577** B. Googe *Heresbach's Husb.* i. (1586) 35 Which Plinie accounteth to haue vneauen corners as Pease hath. **1598** Florio, *Disparo,* vneeuen, or od in number, vnequall. **1613** Purchas *Pilgrimage* (1614) 173 Nothing ought to be eaten by euen numbers, but by vneuen, wherewith God is pleased. **1615** G. Sandys *Trav.* 78 Let rauisht Poets drinke thrice three, Of whom the vneuen Muses be Belou'd. **1728** Chambers *Cycl.* s.v. *Number,* The Sum, or the Difference, of two uneven Numbers, makes an even Number. **1771** Luckombe *Hist. Printing* 265 According to the folio either of an even, or uneven page. **1875** Jowett *Plato* (ed. 2) I. 485 Then the triad or number three is uneven. **1888** Jacobi *Printers' Vocab., Uneven pages,* pages with odd folios, such as 1, 3, 5, etc.

† **2.** Unequitable, unfair, unjust: **a.** Of acts, etc.
*c* **1380** Wyclif *Wks.* (1880) 316 Summe ben too wel fed bi vneuene partyng of here goodis. **1398** Trevisa *Barth. De P. R.* xix. cxxi. (1495) 922 For euen and vneuen dedes that here ben doon. **1585** Abp. Sandys *Serm.* ii. 40 If merchaunts ..doe inriche themselues by impouerishing others, through deceitfull shifts, the common wealth suffereth dammage by their vneuen dealings. **1613** J. Fletcher *Christ's Bloody Sweat* 11 By courses indirect and lawes vn-euen, Of will and sensuall lust.

† **b.** Of persons, etc. *Obs.*
*c* **1400** *Apol. Loll.* 104 Þei are vnfeiþful to þer souereyns, vn euyn to þer lowar. *a* **1500** *Ratis Raving* Prol. 60 He saw ..rychtwysmen and god-lyk baith, With wykyt men & wnewyne lyk scaith. **1581** J. Bell *Haddon's Answ. Osor.* iii. 392 They are in this their partition, so parciall and vneuen dealers, that they will not leaue to Christ, the whole cleansing of the guilt. **1611** Speed *Hist. Gt. Brit.* ix. xxi. 780/2 N. D. with his vneuen hand (euer ouerhard to shadow the truth). **1641** Milton *Animadv.* 7 Sir Francis Bacon.. complaines of the Bishops uneven hand over these Pamflets.

**3.** Diverging from a straight or exactly parallel position. (In early quots. *fig.*)
**1390** Gower *Conf.* I. 30 Thei hemself divide And stonden out of reule unevene. *Ibid.* II. 126 Among the vices..Ther is yit on..Which al this world hath set unevene. **1639** Ld. Digby *Lett. conc. Relig.* (1651) 90 And lines many times that at first appear parallels to the eie..prove apparently uneven. **1683** Moxon *Mech. Exerc., Printing* xxiv. ⁋ 15 If..the sides of the Sheet lye uneven upon the Tympan-sheet. **1862** Miss Braddon *Lady Audley* i, The windows were uneven.

**4.** Not smooth or level; irregular, broken, rugged.
**a.** Of ground, etc.
*c* **1275** in *O. E. Misc.* 75/88 Þe weyes beoþ vn-euene, Wiþ wepynde stefne To helle he schulle þenne. **1565** Cooper s.v. *Inæquabilis,* An open place beyng high and low, or vneuen. **1577** Googe tr. *Heresbach's Husb.* i. 42 b, Beastes and Poultry..with tramplyng and skraping wyll make it rugged and uneven. **1596** Shaks. *1 Hen. IV,* ii. ii. 26 Eight yards of vneuen ground, is threescore & ten miles afoot with me. **1618** J. Taylor (Water P.) *Penniless Pilgr.* E 4, The way so vneuen, stonie, and full of bogges. **1653** W. Ramesey *Astrol. Restored* 91 Aquaries [governs] Hilly and uneven places. **1746** in *10th Rep. Hist. MSS. Comm.* App. I. 440 As we march'd, all the way up hill, and over very uneven Ground, our men were greatly Blown. **1774** Goldsm. *Nat. Hist.* (1776) I. 290 In it [*sc.* the sea-bottom] we find the same uneven surface that we do upon land. **1858** Hawthorne *Fr. & It. Note-bks.* (1871) II. 199 On the verge and within the crater of an extinct volcano, and therefore..as uneven as the sea in a tempest.
*fig.* **1592** Shaks. *Rom. & Jul.* iv. i. 5 Vneuen is the course,

I like it not. a 1596 Sir T. More IV. v. 4 You see the floore of greatnesse is uneuen.

b. In general use.

1398 Trevisa Barth. De P. R. IV. iii. (1495) e vj b/1 The vtter partyes ben vneuyn wyth holownes sonke and had partes areryd. 1590 Spenser F. Q. I. viii. 48 For one of them was like an Eagles claw,..The other like a Beares vneuen paw. 1599 Hakluyt Voy. II. 162 The sorting together of Wools of seueral natures,..which causeth cloth to cockle and be uneven. 1683 Moxon Mech. Exerc., Printing xvii. P 2 [He] cuts out what may remain in the bottom of the Shanck by reason of the un-even breaking. 1712 J. James tr. Le Blond's Gardening 140 Its Bark is somewhat rugged and uneaven. 1798 S. & Ht. Lee Canterb. T. II. 431 The uneven writing..proved that it was sent while the young man was still fluctuating between life and death. 1810 Crabbe Borough xxii. 178 The sun-burnt tar ..And bank-side stakes in their uneven ranks. 1855 Poultry Chron. III. 522/1 The upper part of the cell..being more convex; therefore, the comb is very uneven.

*absol.* 1796 Kirwan Elem. Min. (ed. 2) I. 157 Fracture, fine or coarse splintery, which sometimes pass into the uneven of a fine grain.

c. *transf.* and *fig.* (of immaterial things, sounds, style, etc.).

OE. unefn, unemn, occurs in similar uses.

(a) 1596 Shaks. 1 Hen. IV, I. i. 50 Farre more vneuen and vnwelcome Newes Came from the North. 1603 — Meas. for M. IV. iv. 3 In most vneuen and distracted manner, his actions show much like to madnesse. 1649 Lovelace Poems (1864) 114 Where is a joy uneven, There never, never can be Heav'n. 1719 De Foe Crusoe I. (Globe) 159 Such is the uneven State of human Life. 1763 Scrafton Indostan iii. (1770) 76 The uneven temper of the Soubah could never long retain its disguise. 1885 J. J. H. Burgess Shetland Sketches, etc. i. 48 He..went away down to the house, feeling very sorrowful, and mad, and altogether uneven.

(b) 1608 Willet Hexapla Exod. 50 The horses euill and vneuen going proceedeth of his owne lamenes.

(c) 1668 Culpepper & Cole Barthol. Anat. III. ix. 150 Not only with cold Air, but with any other uneven noise, passing through their Mouth into their Ears. 1731 Pope Ep. Burlington 143 Light quirks of Music, broken and uneven. 1811 W. R. Spencer Poems Ded., His strain is weak, his voice uneven.

(d) 1763 J. Brown Poetry & Music vi. 111 Homer is equal, large, flowing, and harmonious; Eschylus is uneven, concise, abrupt, and rugged.

5. *Comb.*, as *uneven-carriaged*, *-numbered*, *-roofed*.

1670 Brooks Wks. (1867) VI. 342 A rotten heart, is a very uneven-carriaged heart. 1882 Contemp. Rev. Aug. 234 The 16 alternate or uneven-numbered sections in all townships. 1887 Hissey Holiday on Road i. 3 Weather-stained outbuildings, lichen-laden and uneven-roofed.

**Une·ven**, *adv.* [OE. unefne (f. un- Un-1 11 b + efne Even adv.), = MDu. onevene, -effene (obs. Du. oneven), OS. unefno, MLG. unevene, -even, MHG. unebene, -eben.] = Unevenly adv.

c 1000 Ags. Ps. (Thorpe) cxl. 9 Swa unefne is eorþe þicce. c 1275 in O. E. Misc. 86/1 Weole, þu art awaried þing, vneuene constu dele. a 1300 Cursor M. 24178 Þou..folus þam þat þe wald fle, And lues all þat letthes þe, þis part vneuen es delt. 1390 Gower Conf. I. 9 So stant the pes unevene parted. 1500-20 Dunbar Poems lxxxi. 96 The ballance gois vnevin.

**Une·ven**, *v.* [Un-2 6 a.] To make uneven.

c 1440 Pallad. on Husb. x. 100 For eny thyng no beest vppon hit trede; Vneven hit they wolde, hit is to drede.

**†Une·venly**, *a. Obs.* [Un-1 7: cf. OE. unefenlic various, diverse.]

1. Incomparable.

a 1225 Ancr. R. 410 Þeo blisse þet he ȝerkeð ham..is unefenlich to alle worldes blissen.

2. Unequal; ill-matched.

c 1425 Eng. Conq. Irel. 30 Reymond & hys men—thogh they fewe wer, they wer nat feynt—with vneuenly host wenten out & assembled wyth ham. 1513 Douglas Æneid XII. iv. 147 This ilk bargane Semyng..To be ane rycht onevynly [v.r. vneuinly] interprys.

3. Uneven; not level.

1683 J. Reid Scots Gard'ner I. iii. 11 Though the ground be unevenly, yet you must hold the chain level.

**Une·venly**, *adv.* [Un-1 11.]

†1. Unfairly, unjustly. *Obs.*

1382 Wyclif Gen. xvi. 5 And Saray seide to Abram, Vneuenlie thow dost aȝens me. c 1400 Apol. Loll. 74 Scho may sey þat Sara seid to Abraam, Þu dost vneuenly aȝens me.

2. In an uneven or unequal manner; not regularly, uniformly, or smoothly.

1398 Trevisa Barth. De P. R. VIII. xvi. (1495) 143 b, Though it seme somtyme þat he meue vneuenly, swyfter other slower in comparison to other thynges. 1412-20 Lydg. Chron. Troy I. 2242 And þus sche stood in a Iupardye Of Loue and Schame, in maner of a traunce, Vn-euenly hanged in balaunce. 1557 Recorde Whetst. iij b, Euen nombers vneuenly, are suche nombers as maie bee diuided into 2 equalle partes, whiche are odde numbers. 1570 Billingsley Euclid II. Introd. 60 In this booke are set forth the powers of lines, deuided euenly and vneuenly. 1638 Rawley tr. Bacon's Life & Death (1650) 60 The same Abundance unevenly placed, is in like manner hurtfull. 1668 H. More Div. Dial. I. xxxiv. (1713) 77 To harbour such unconceivable Notions, that lie so unevenly in every Man's Mind but your own. 1704 Dict. Rust. s.v. Waggons, Therefore the lesser the Wheel is, the heavier and more unevenly and jogging they go. 1839 De la Beche Rep. Geol. Cornwall, etc. xi. 318 An opening between the unevenly-fractured surfaces of a fissure. 1879 R. K. Douglas Confucianism iv. 95 A chair which..stands unevenly on its feet, is useless as a support.

†3. Not in equal proportion. *Obs.*—1

c 1440 Pallad. on Husb. XII. 234 Oyldreggis watertemprid euenly..Or old vryne admyxt vneuenly With water partis too.

**Une·venness.** [f. Uneven a.]

1. Inequality, discrepancy, difference.

1398 Trevisa Barth. De P. R. IX. iii. (Tollem. MS.), Solstitium is moste uneuennesse of day and nyȝte. 1622 Malynes Anc. Law-Merch. 487 Hee findeth twentie two ..peeces or thereabouts, because of the vneuennesse of the sheyre. 1659 Gentl. Calling (1660) 18 The great unevenness that is..between Gentlemen and their Inferiors. 1884 Bower & Scott De Bary's Phaner. 44 The subsequent various unevenness of height..arises through the growth of the cells.

2. The quality or fact of being uneven in form.

1398 Trevisa Barth. De P. R. IV. iii. (1495) e vj b/1 Roughnesse is not elles but an vneuynnesse in an harde thynge. Ibid. iv. e viij/2 Contrary humours werke contraryousnes and vneuynnesse with roughnes in the vtter parte of the body. 1560 Whitehorne Arte Warre (1588) 49 b, Also the vneuennesse of the ground saueth them, for that euery litle hillocke, or high place,..letteth the shotte thereof. 1577 B. Googe Heresbach's Husb. III. (1586) 115 His cheekebones would be euen and small, for..the vneuennes of the Cheekes will make him headstrong. 1634 Sir T. Herbert Trav. 51 Hils of stupendious height and vneuennesse to ascend. a 1688 Cudworth Immut. Mor. (1731) 200 We plainly observe much..Unevenness and Inequality in the Lines, and Bluntness in the Angles. 1772 Ann. Reg., Nat. Hist. 82/2 Which extreme agitation and whirling, I presume, must be owing to the unevenness of the rocky bottom. 1853 Markham Skoda's Auscult. 3 The finger must be always used whenever, through unevenness of the surface, the pleximeter cannot be well applied. 1880 Blackw. Mag. Feb. 243/1 The painful unevenness of the principal roadways.

b. An instance of this; an inequality; a rough or rugged part, place, or feature.

1597 A. M. tr. Guillemeau's Fr. Chirurg. 12 b/2 If there remayne anye small splinter thereone, or other vnevennes. 1664 H. More Myst. Iniq. 297 To phansy one and the same Hill for some little unevennesses in it to be more then one. 1680 Tides (MS. Bodl. Add. A. 202) fol. 3 In deep Rivers the surface conceales these unevenesses. 1728 Chambers Cycl. s.v. Filing, The..File..serves to take off the Unevennesses of the Work, left by the Hammer, in Forging. 1753 Phil. Trans. XLVIII. 88 An horizontal thin edge, which scooped up and carried off the little unevennesses of the turfy ground. 1849 Eastwick Dry Leaves 140 There was not the slightest jag or unevenness—a tolerable proof of the sharpness of the sword.

c. In various figurative uses.

1636 B. Jonson Discoveries Wks. (1641) 98 They would not have it run without rubs, as if that stile were more strong and manly, that stroke the eare with a kind of unevenesse. 1652 Gaule Magastrom. 255 Saturne was pressed with unevennesse or roughnesse, either in leaping or speaking. 1707 Reflex. upon Ridicule 319 The whimsical Unevenness of some People ruins the pleasure of Conversation. 1779 Johnson L. P., Dryden Wks. II. 427 Such is the unevenness of his compositions, that [etc.]. 1805 Med. Jrnl. XIV. 395 The unevenness of disposition, the convulsive sobs and strong paroxysms of weeping. 1882 L. Keith Alasnam's Lady III. 105 Di hardly noticed the unevenness of her mood.

†3. Unfairness, injustice. *Obs.*

a 1470 H. Parker Dives & Pauper (W. de W. 1496) 293/1 Goodes of this worlde ben called rychesses of uneuenesse and of wyckednesse.

**Uneve·ntful**, *a.* (Un-1 7.)

1800 Mrs. Hervey Mourtray Fam. I. 7 There is little to keep up its energy in the uneventful tenour of domestic life. 1862 Gifts & Graces xxv. 249 There is little to tell, for their uneventful lives are gliding on as usual. 1890 W. J. Gordon Foundry 167 We have said enough to show that its story has not been uneventful.

Hence **Uneve·ntfully** *adv.*, **-fulness**.

1865 Cornh. Mag. Apr. 405 The two next days passed quietly and uneventfully. 1872 Howells Wedding Journ. (1892) 192 They rattled uneventfully down..by rail. 1878 Grosart H. More's Poems Introd. p. ix, The uneventfulness outwardly of the 'Life' accounts for the few facts given.

**†Une·vesed**, *ppl. a. Obs.* (Un-1 8.) ?14.. Lat.-Eng. Voc. (MS. Harl. 2257), Intonsus, vnclipped, vneuesed.

**Une·vidence.** *rare*—1. (Un-1 12.) a 1676 Hale Prim. Orig. Man. I. i. (1677) 10 So full of unevidence and uncertainty, so full of precarious and imaginary Postulata.

**Une·videnced**, *ppl. a.* (Un-1 8.) [1775 Ash.] 1842 G. S. Faber Prov. Lett. (1844) II. 53 The unevidenced Popish Innovations advocated by my two opponents. 1892 J. Tait Mind in Matter 234 The impression [made] on the illiterate mind by the unevidenced assertion of miracles.

**Une·vident**, *a.* (Un-1 7 and 5 b.)

c 1400 Apol. Loll. 9 As þis consonaunt is vnknowen to þe japer, so þis fendly marchaundy is vneuident to þe feiþful peple knowend þis. 1570 Levins Manip. 69 Vneuident, ineuidens. 1629 H. Burton Truth's Triumph 165 The actuall faith hee cals a firme and certaine, but vneuident assent. 1651 Hobbes Leviath. II. xxv. 134 Rash and unevident Inferences. a 1670 Hacket Abp. Williams I. (1692) 197 We conjecture at unevident things by that which is evident.

**Unevide·ntial**, *a.* (Un-1 7.) 1826 G. S. Faber Diffic. Romanism (1853) 117 Arbitrary exertion of more unevidential dogmatic authority.

**†Une·vitable**, *a. Obs.* [Un-1 7 b and 5 b.] = Inevitable a.

1539 Elyot Cast. Helthe 59 They receyue in medicine that, whiche shall ingender..vneuitable destruction vnto al the body. 1594 J. King Funeral Serm. (1599) 677 Let his dead ..corpse adde one more [instruction] vnto you of common & vneuitable mortalitie. 1621 G. Sandys Ovid's Met. VI. (1626) 113 His haste th'vneuitable bowe o're-took, And through his throte the deadly arrow strook. 1656 W. Montague Accompl. Wom. 59 We have put on black, because mourning is unevitable, since we must needs bewaile our husbands. 1711 W. King Heathen Gods & Heroes xiii. 38 [Pluto] bound them with unevitable Chains.

So **†Une·vitably** *adv.*, inevitably. *Obs.*

1623 in Rushw. Hist. Coll. (1659) I. 142 Seeing we..cannot but foresee and fear lest the like may..unevitably bring such peril to your Majesties Kingdoms.

**†Une·vitated**, *ppl. a. Obs.* (Un-1 8.) 1621 G. Sandys Ovid's Met. XII. (1626) 240 With that, th'vnerring dart at Cycnus [he] flung. Th'vneuitated on his shoulder rung.

**Unevo·lved**, *ppl. a.* (Un-1 8.)

[1775 Ash.] 1831 Landor Wks. (1846) II. 633, I held down a branch And gathered her some blossoms...So crisp were some, they rattled unevolved. 1884 Congregational Year Bk. 93 Nature..holds in her bosom, unsolved and unevolved, the problems and the germs of all the philosophies.

**Unexa·ct**, *a.* [Un-1 7 and 5 b.] = Inexact a.

1758 Maclaine Mosheim's Eccles. Hist. I. 407 note, Dr. Mosheim's account of the time of Nestorius's death is perhaps unexact. 1776 S. J. Pratt Pupil of Pleas. (1777) I. 153 How is it that so scrupulous a man in point of equity is so unexact a correspondent? 1862 'Shirley' (J. Skelton) Nugae Crit. ii. 137 The literalness of an unpoetic intellect.. is always comparatively sterile and unexact.

So **Unexa·ctness**, inexactness. *rare*—1.

1677 Gilpin Demonol. II. ix. 389 Satan here plays upon the unexactness of the Translation.

**Unexa·cted**, *ppl. a.* (Un-1 8.)

1609 Tourneur Funerall Poem Sir F. Vere 23 All that I speak is unexacted, true and free. 1697 Dryden Virg. Georg. I. 196 All was common, and the fruitful Earth Was free to give her unexacted Birth.

So **Unexa·ctedly** *adv.*

c 1642 Observ. his Majesty's late Answer 18 The father doth all his offices meritoriously, freely, and unexactedly.

**Unexa·cting**, *ppl. a.* (Un-1 10.) 1862 Milman in Proc. Roy. Soc. XI. p. xv, A seat in Parliament, independent even on generous and unexacting friendship. 1884 Mrs. Coote Sure Harvest 24 The most unselfish, unexacting old lady I ever knew. **Unexa·ggerable**, *a.* (Un-1 7 b.) 1818 Q. Rev. XVIII. 41 Gongora's exaggerating and unexaggerable style.

**Unexa·ggerated**, *ppl. a.* (Un-1 8.)

1770 Armstrong Misc. II. 272 In some places natural and unexaggerated representations of life are not felt. 1812 Q. Rev. VIII. 329 A mass of immediate evil..of which the unexaggerated report might almost startle our belief. 1861 Mill Repr. Govt. (1865) 34/1 It would be..ungenerous to offer this..as an unexaggerated picture of the French people.

**Unexa·ggerating**, *ppl. a.* (Un-1 10.) 1825 Ld. Cockburn Mem. (1856) 332 Calm, clear, and unexaggerating, he went into all the details with precision.

**Unexa·lted**, *ppl. a.* (Un-1 8.)

1611 Florio, Innessaltato, vnexalted. 1648 Hexham II, Ongehooght, Vnlifted up, or Vn-exalted. 1746 Young Nt. Th. IX. 755 Who sees it unexalted, and unaw'd? 1805 Wordsw. Prelude XIII. 243 Not unexalted by religious faith, Nor uninformed by books.

**Unexa·minable**, *a.* (Un-1 7 b.) 1641 Milton Reform. I. Wks. 1851 III. 4 The lowly, alwise, and unexaminable intention of Christ. 1890 Abp. Benson Let. in Life (1901) 373 She had read your book carefully, and I daresay knew it (in an unexaminable sort of way).

**Unexa·mined**, *ppl. a.* (Un-1 8.)

1495 Act 11 Hen. VII, ii. § 3 As often as eny suche of the seid mysdoers..departen unexamyned and unpunysshed. 1526 Pilgr. Perf. (W. de W. 1531) 132 That no worde passe out vntryed, & nothynge entre vnexamyned. 1568 Grafton Chron. II. 765 Watching that no man shoulde..passe vnserched nor vnexamined. 1620 Southampton Court Leet Rec. (1907) III. 582 The teachinge of a Stranger vnexamined and vnripe of yeres. 1684 T. Burnet Theory Earth I. 285 Those manuscripts that are yet unexamin'd in these parts of Christendom. 1747 Richardson Clarissa (1811) II. 268 More pride and vanity than I could have thought had lain in my unexamined heart. 1779 Johnson L. P., Watts Wks. IV. 187 He has left neither corporeal nor spiritual nature unexamined. 1875 Scrivener Lect. Text N. Test. 14 To leave the great mass of copies wholly unexamined.

**Unexa·mining**, *ppl. a.* (Un-1 10.)

1682 in Lond. Gaz. No. 1714/6 A means to ferment the Factious Un-examining Vulgar into Rebellious Heats. 1748 Richardson Clarissa (1811) IV. 213 Which concealed itself from my unexamining heart under the specious veil of humility. 1809-10 Coleridge Friend (1837) I. 163 The unexamining and boisterous youth of the world. 1835 Willis Pencillings I. 90, I passed them with the same lost unexamining..feeling which I cannot overcome in this place.

**Unexa·mpled**, *ppl. a.* [Un-1 8.] Having no preceding or similar example; unprecedented, unparalleled.

1610 Holland Camden's Brit. I. 724 David King of Scots, who with his unexampled cruelty had made this country almost a wildernesse. a 1676 Hale Prim. Orig. Man. IV. iv. (1677) 325 This admirable..production of such a Nature unexampled before. 1763 Wilkes Corr. (1805) I. 75 Your lordship's unexampled care of his majesty's youth. 1816 J. Scott Vis. Paris (ed. 5) 176 With unexampled ability and villainy, he fashioned the people to suit his views. 1855 Bain Senses & Int. III. iv. § 24 This is an extreme case, but not unexampled in the history of the world.

**Unexa·sperating**, *ppl. a.* (Un-1 10.) 1855 Milman Lat. Chr. XIV. vii. VI. 549 The most quiet, uninsulting, unexasperating satire. **Une·xcavated**, *ppl. a.* (Un-1 8.) [1775 Ash.] 1874 Withrow Catacombs (1877) 20 Some unexcavated spaces have been observed traced in outline. **Unexcee·ded**, *ppl. a.* (Un-1 8.) 1813 T. Busby Lucretius I. I. Comm. p. xii, The comparison .. is conceived with unexceeded vigour.

**Unexce·lled**, *ppl. a.* (Un-1 8.)

a 1800 Cowper Iliad (ed. 2) v. 193 Say, Pandarus! Thy bow, thy shafts, thy fame Unrivall'd here, in Lycia unexcell'd, Where are they now? 1821 Huish George III, Introd. 3 Unexcelled as a father, unshaken as a friend. 1874 H. H. Cole Catal. Ind. Art S. Kens. Mus. 216 The textile fabrics of India..remain unexcelled by other countries.

**Unexce·lling**, *ppl. a.* (Un-1 5 d.) 1844 Mrs. Browning Dead Pan xxxvii, Shame!.. To think God's song unexcelling The poor tales of our own telling. **Unexce·ptable**, *a.* (Un-1 7 b.) 1702 C. Mather Magn. Chr. III. ii. 33/1 Waiting, till God might furnish him with Unexceptable Opportunities, for his..Preaching of the Gospel.

**Unexce·pted**, *ppl. a.* (Un-1 8 and 8 c.)

1614 B. Jonson Barth. Fair Induct., Hee that will sweare, Ieronimo, or Andronicus are the best playes, yet, shall passe vnexcepted at, heere. 1710 Prideaux Orig. Tithes ii. 46 The Precedent doth become of unexcepted authority. 1813 Chalmers Posth. Wks. (1849) VI. 172 There is no getting away from..His ceaseless, from His unexcepted agency. 1852 BAILEY *Festus* (ed. 4) 265 Progress is nature's unexcepted law.

**Unexce·pting,** *ppl. a.* (UN-[1] 10). 1716 M. DAVIES *Athen. Brit.* II. 410 A rising Clergyman..seem'd to excuse that..Prelate's Prophetick Vein, or even exempt it from his unexcepting Censure. 1870 J. BRUCE *Life of Gideon* xxii. 401 There is a general and unexcepting revival..within his heart, even of all such graces.

**Unexce·ptionable,** *a.* [UN-[1] 7 b.]

1. To whom, or to which, no exception can be taken; perfectly satisfactory or adequate.

a. Of persons.

1664 INGELO *Bentiv. & Ur.* VI. 276 All which I have said was done in the Presence of unexceptionable Witnesses. 1699 T. BAKER *Refl. Learn.* iii. 27 Cicero tho the most unexceptionable [authority] has not escaped their censure. 1740 CIBBER *Apol.* (1756) I. 48 Not even the Revolution..has been able to furnish us with unexceptionable statesmen. 1796 MME. D'ARBLAY *Camilla* II. 193 She affectionately embraced the unexceptionable Lavinia. 1868 FREEMAN *Norm. Conq.* (1877) II. ix. 431 There was now no such unexceptionable rival to oppose to the Norman.

b. Of material things. (Rare before 19th c.)

1681 FLAVEL *Meth. Grace* xvi. 301 The blood of Christ..; 'tis unexceptionable blood, being..untainted by sin. 1756–7 tr. *Keysler's Trav.* (1760) II. 425 This statue..is in all its parts unexceptionable. 1835 BROWNING *Paracelsus* v. 455 *Fest.* This cell? *Par.* An unexceptionable vault: Good brick and stone. 1852 H. ROGERS *Ecl. Faith* 168 Questionable as was the entertainment for the mind, that for the body was unexceptionable.

c. Of character, conduct, style, taste, etc.

1697 C. LESLIE *Snake in Grass* (ed. 2) 359 And the Lives of these Seperatists were as un-exceptionable as any of the Quakers. 1716 M. DAVIES *Athen. Brit.* III. 31 His English style is unexceptionable. 1742–3 *Johnson's Debates* (1787) II. 503 The authority of this man, my Lords, cannot indeed be urged as unexceptionable and decisive. 1794 S. WILLIAMS *Vermont* 183 The most unexceptionable evidence ought to be produced. 1826 F. REYNOLDS *Life & Times* II. 126 His taste was unexceptionable, and his judgment was never sullied by prejudice. 1848 MILL *Pol. Econ.* II. xv. § 1. 478 Lending his capital on unexceptionable security. 1884 *Law Rep.* 9 App. Cases 558, I am..of opinion that rule 32 is unexceptionable.

2. Admitting of no exception. *rare*—[1].

1871 RUSKIN *Fors Clav.* vii. 9 That being the, alas, almost unexceptionable lot of human creatures.

Hence **Unexce·ptionabi·lity.**

1837 *Chambers's Jrnl.* 8 July 192 Morals of pure unexceptionability. *a* 1849 POE *Whipple*, etc., Wks. 1864 III. 388, I—with a very partial modification of the imagery..—may elevate the passage into unexceptionability.

**Unexce·ptionableness.** (UN-[1] 12.)

1669 H. MORE *Exp. 7 Epist.* Pref. a vij b, If it had been accompanied with other parts of his Exposition of these Epistles that had had the like unexceptionablenesse. 1712 *H. More's Antid. Ath.* III. x. *heading*, A reflection on the unexceptionableness of these Instances for the proof of Spirits. 1753 RICHARDSON *Grandison* (1781) II. xiv. 151 My Lord..modestly hinted at the unexceptionableness of his own character. 1823 BENTHAM *Not Paul* 229 In order to have the clearer view of the plan..., from which will be seen the unexceptionableness of it.

**Unexce·ptionably,** *adv.* [UN-[1] 11.]

1. In an unexceptionable manner; beyond criticism or objection.

1662 H. MORE *Antidote agst. Atheism* vi. 58 Wee'l betake our selves to..what is more unexceptionably stringent and forcing. 1718 *Free-thinker* No. 141 (1733) III. 178 It is very rare to find a Glass, that does Justice unexceptionably to Objects, in every nice Circumstance. 1740 RICHARDSON *Pamela* II. 328 It will not be an easy Task to behave unexceptionably to him. 1827 SOUTHEY *Hist. Penins. War* II. 626 The Junta of Cadiz had obtained their power unexceptionably. 1859 GEO. ELIOT *A. Bede* xvii, Let all people who hold unexceptionable opinions act unexceptionably.

2. = UNEXCEPTIONALLY *adv.*

1719 J. T. PHILLIPS tr. *Thirty-four Confer.* 89 All your Religious Women who assist at the Performances of Pagod Ceremonies, are unexceptionably great Whores. 1799 *Monthly Rev.* XXX. 507 Such is not unexceptionably the character of all treatises; such ill consequences do not obtain universally. 1806 BLOOMFIELD *Wild Flowers* 106 It has generally and almost unexceptionably appeared a subject of little promise.

**Unexce·ptional,** *a.* [UN-[1] 7.]

1. = UNEXCEPTIONABLE *a.* 1 c.

1775 MME. D'ARBLAY *Early Diary* (1889) II. 10 She bears an unexceptional character. 1805 *Ann. Rev.* IV. 730 We ..secretly retain a higher esteem for the stimulant and unusual, than for the quotidian accuracy of regular unexceptional composition. 1877 W. S. GILBERT *Foggerty's Fairy* (1892) 62 The duty is extremely light, and the county society unexceptional.

2. Admitting of, subject to, no exception.

1844 KINGLAKE *Eothen* xxix, Declaring that the orders received from Constantinople were imperative, and unexceptional. 1883 SIR H. COTTON in *Law Rep.* 24 Chan. Div. 332, I should think that that would, almost as an unexceptional rule, be of the greatest possible advantage to the infant.

**Unexce·ptionally,** *adv.* [UN-[1] 11.] Without exception.

1866 RUSKIN *Crown Wild Olive* (1873) 68 So completely and unexceptionally is this so, that [etc.]. 1871 W. G. WARD *Ess. Philos. Theism* (1884) I. 50 That which I have habitually and unexceptionally experienced, I regard as contingent.

† **Unexce·ptioned,** *ppl. a. Obs.*—[1] [UN-[1] 8.] = UNEXCEPTIONABLE *a.* 1. 1704 T. BAKER *Act at Oxf.* II. ii. 12 A Gentleman unexception'd in Person, Temper, and Estate.

**Unexce·ptive,** *a.* (UN-[1] 7.) 1856 *N. Brit. Rev.* XXVI. 54 An unexceptive Christian belief. 1860 I. TAYLOR *Ess.* i. 118 The Rights of Man..are universal and unexceptive.

**Unexcha·nged,** *ppl. a.* (UN-[1] 8.) 1618 in W. Foster *Eng. Factories in India* (1906) I. 8 And we compelled to leave a whole chest of ryalls and three ingotts unexchanged. 1777 BURKE *Let. to Sheriffs of Bristol* Wks. III. 143 If..we..contend that you may justly reserve for vengeance, those who remain unexchanged.

**Unexci·sed,** (*ppl.*) *a.*[1] [UN-[1] 8, 9.]

1. Not subjected to an Excise or tax.

*c* 1740 I. H. BROWNE *Pipe of Tobacco* v. 20 Come to thy poet..And let me taste thee unexcis'd by kings. 1861 *Sat. Rev.* 23 Nov. 532 So all the benefits of a free press, unstamped, unexcised, may be altogether thrown away.

2. Not appointed to a post in the Excise.

1820 BYRON *Juan* III. xciii, All are not moralists, like Southey,..Or Wordsworth unexcised, unhired.

**Unexci·sed,** *ppl. a.*[2] [UN-[1] 8.] Not excised or cut out.

1871 T. H. GREEN *Introd. Pathol.* 203 The inflammatory changes..in the unexcised cornea of the opposite eye.

**Unexci·table,** *a.* (UN-[1] 7 b and 5 b.)

1839 LD. CLARENDON in Maxwell *Life & Lett.* (1913) I. 155, I am of a mature age, unexcitable temperament. 1859 CORNWALLIS *New World* I. 297 He did the work simply as a means of living, and he liked it because it was dry and unexcitable. 1895 *Outing* XXVI. 432/1 During this battle royal, the other fish had darted away, and..only the unexcitable sturgeon was to be seen.

Hence **Unexcitabi·lity.**

1885 E. G. PARRY *Suakin* ix. 215 The extreme unexcitability of temperament of these people.

**Unexci·ted,** *ppl. a.* [UN-[1] 8.]

1. Not mentally stirred or moved.

1735 LD. LYTTELTON *Lett. fr. Persian in Eng.* iii, The human brutes, who, unexcited by any rage or sense of injury, could spill the blood of others. 1850 ROBERTSON *Serm.* Ser. III. ix. (1857) 133 Remember Him pausing to weep.., unexcited, while the giddy crowd around Him were shouting 'Hosannas to the Son of David!' 1856 KANE *Arct. Expl.* I. xvii. 202 A more unexcited inspection showed us..that their numbers were not as great.

2. Not affected by outward influence.

1746 *Phil. Trans.* XLIV. 734 There is an Endeavour by the nearest unexcited Non-electric to restore the Æquilibrium. 1839 G. BIRD *Nat. Philos.* 399 To produce upon an unexcited eye the sensation of a colour corresponding to that of the wafer. 1856 FROUDE *Hist. Eng.* II. 26 [Protestantism] sprung up spontaneously, unguided, unexcited, ..among the masses of the nation.

**Unexci·ting,** *ppl. a.* (UN-[1] 10.)

1833 J. H. NEWMAN *Arians* I. § 1. 20 Judaism..indisposed the mind for the severe and unexciting mysteries..of the Catholic faith. 1861 MILL *Repr. Govt.* 37 Uncivilized races ..are averse to continuous labour of an unexciting kind. 1885 'MRS. ALEXANDER' *At Bay* viii, He had..led a quiet, busy life, humbly useful, but unexciting.

b. *spec.* of diet.

1880 BARWELL *Aneurism* v. 44 If an aneurismal patient..have a dry, unexciting diet. 1888 P. FURNIVALL *Phys. Training* 3 Substantial, nourishing solids, with simple unexciting fluids.

**Unexclu·ded,** *ppl. a.* (UN-[1] 8.) 1780 [see UNCOUNTERBALANCED]. 1814 WORDSW. *Excurs.* v. 542 [The sun] doth dispense His beams; which, unexcluded in their fall,..Have gently exercised a melting power. **Unexclu·ding,** *ppl. a.* (UN-[1] 10.) 1822 LAMB *Elia* II. *Detached Th. on Bks.*, I can read almost anything. I bless my stars for a taste so catholic, so unexcluding. **Unexclu·sive,** *a.* (UN-[1] 7.) 1831 SIR W. HAMILTON *Discuss.* (1852) 222 Muench's unexclusive views have found favor with Mayerhoff. 1862 J. MARTINEAU *Ess., Sci. Nescience & Faith* (1866) 189 To the Infinite, as unexclusive, every thing affirmative belongs. **Unexclu·sively,** *adv.* (UN-[1] 11, 5 b.) 1814 WORDSW. *Excurs.* IX. 392 From culture, unexclusively bestowed On Albion's noble Race in freedom born. 1841–2 SIR W. HAMILTON *Diss.* in *Reid's Wks.* (1846) 886/1 *note*, Mr. Stewart..is wrong in stating, unexclusively, that Reid's writings were anterior to Kant's. **Unexclu·siveness.** (UN-[1] 12.) 1818 BENTHAM *Mem. & Corr.* Wks. 1843 X. 498 Though I should prefer universality on account of its simplicity and unexclusiveness. 1861 MILL *Repr. Govt.* 157 A government equally democratic in its unexclusiveness, but better organized in other important points.

**Unexco·gitable,** *a.* (UN-[1] 7 b and 5 b.)

1592 R. D. *Hypnerotomachia* 81 b, Her virgineall aspects, exceedingly beautified with a comely grace and unexcogitable elegancie. 1614 RALEIGH *Hist. World* I. ii. § 1. 24 Wherein can man be said to resemble his vnexcogitable power and perfectnesse? *c* 1624 CHAPMAN *Hymn Hermes* 158 Unexcogitable thoughts in act Putting.

**Unexco·gitated,** *ppl. a.* (UN-[1] 8.) *a* 1706 EVELYN *Hist. Relig.* (1850) I. 23 Moreover, this unexcogitated division would also have been illimited. **Unexcommu·nicate(d,** *ppl. a.* (UN-[1] 8, 8 b.) 1588 UDALL *Demonstr. Discipline* (Arb.) 82 If they had not throwne out the incestuous person, he had remayned still vnexcommunicated. 1680 *Answ. Stillingfleet's Serm.* 15 Every one that dies Un-excommunicate in the Parish. **Unexco·rticated,** *ppl. a.* (UN-[1] 8.) 1725 *Fam. Dict.* s.v. *Diahexapte*, Take Juniper-Berries unexcorticated, and Bay-berries excorticated.

† **Unexcu·sable,** *a. Obs.* [UN-[1] 7 b and 5 b.] = INEXCUSABLE *a.*: a. Of persons.

Chiefly in a religious or moral sense, after Rom. ii. 1 (Gr. ἀναπολόγητος, L. *inexcusabilis*).

1382 WYCLIF *Rom.* ii. 1 For which thing thou ert vnexcusable, thou ech man that demest. *a* 1425 *St. Elizabeth of Spalbeck* in *Anglia* VIII. 118/39 Þou, man, arte vnexcusabil, if so quik argumentz..stir þe not to strengthe of feith. *c* 1561 VERON *Free-will* 47 That they may..be made unexcusable agaynst the day of iudgement. 1583 GOLDING *Calvin on Deut.* i. 4 Therefore are we too unexcusable if we cannot tell what God saith to us there. 1642 G. MOUNTAGU in *Buccleuch MSS.* (Hist. MSS. Comm.) I. 298 To leave them altogether unexcusable, [he] sent them a licence ..for their absence. 1685 BAXTER *Paraphr. N. T.* Matt. x. 17 That both Jews and Gentiles..may..be unexcusable in their sin.

b. Of faults, offences, etc.

1550 LATIMER *Last Serm. bef. Edw. VI*, Sermons (1580) 113 b, An irremissible sinne, an vnexcusable sinne. 1602 T. FITZHERBERT *Apol.* 12 Whereby their martyrdome was far more glorious,..then the iniury donne vnto them vnexcusable. 1659 BP. WALTON *Consid. Considered* 3 The unexcusable negligence of the Greek church. 1685 J. SCOTT *Chr. Life* II. i. 32 As gross and unexcusable a Stupidity as if [etc.].

Hence † **Unexcu·sableness**; **-ably** *adv. Obs.*

1611 COTGR., *Inexcusablement*, vnexcusably. 1647 CLARENDON *Hist. Reb.* I. § 25 The Prince Electour..had unexcusably, and directly against his Advice, incurred the Ban of the Empire in an Imperial Dyet. *a* 1660 HAMMOND *Serm.* xii. Wks. 1684 IV. 642 We will..rip up to you the unexcusableness of the heathen ignorance in general.

**Unexcu·sed,** *ppl. a.* (UN-[1] 8.) *c* 1650 *Don Bellianis* 84 Get you out of my Persepolis..unless you will here dye, unheard, and unexcused. **Unexcu·sing,** *ppl. a.* (UN-[1] 10.) 1853 RUSKIN *Stones Ven.* II. 199 Scripture History..sets down with unmoved and unexcusing resoluteness the virtues and errors of all men of whom it speaks. 1858 MISS MULOCK *Th. ab. Wom.* 275 With a resolute, uncompromising, unexcusing veracity. † **Unexcu·ssed,** *ppl. a.* (UN-[1] 8.) 1660 STANLEY *Hist. Philos.* IX. (1687) 540/1 Concerning all these, he delivered most proper Sciences, leaving nothing unexcussed. **Unexe·cutable,** *a.* (UN-[1] 7 b and 5 b.) 1794 EARL MALMESBURY *Diaries & Corr.* III. 223 The instructions..were nearly unexecutable. 1850 GROTE *Greece* II. lx. VII. 455 Though sensible of the wisdom of his advice, the generals thought it wholly unexecutable.

**Une·xecuted,** *ppl. a.* (UN-[1] 8.)

1585 T. WASHINGTON tr. *Nicholay's Voy.* II. xiii. 48 b, There was no kind of..cruelty by them left vnexecuted. 1606 SHAKS. *Ant. & Cl.* III. vii. 45 You therein..leaue vnexecuted Your owne renowned knowledge. 1741–2 GRAY *Agrippina* 155 Why do I waste the fruitless hours In threats unexecuted? 1790 PENNANT *London* (1813) 140 A vast plan, left unexecuted on account of the unhappy times. 1850 GROTE *Greece* II. lxiv. VIII. 253 The duty remained unexecuted, and the seamen..were left to perish unassisted. 1863 H. COX *Instit.* II. viii. 499 The Court directs the cancellation of unexecuted agreements.

**Une·xecuting,** *ppl. a.* (UN-[1] 10.) 1770 *Lee's Alexander* I. i, Curse on this weak, unexecuting arm!

† **Unexe·mplar,** *a. Obs.* [UN-[1] 7.] = next 2.

1685 J. L. *Papist Mis-represented & Repr.* 76 If some,..by their unexemplar lives, prove a scandal to their profession.

**Unexe·mplary,** *a.* [UN-[1] 7.]

† 1. Unexampled, unprecedented. *Obs.*

1649 in Ellis *Orig. Lett.* Ser. II. III. 340 To give you some relation of the sad and unexemplary murther of our Soveraign. 1704 in *Lond. Gaz.* No. 4058/1 Your Majesty's unexemplary Piety. 1730 SWIFT *Vind. Ld. Carteret* Wks. 1761 III. 186 He hath in a most unexemplary manner led a regular domestic life.

2. Not exemplary; not to be taken as a model.

1699 SHAFTESB. *Inquiry conc. Virtue* I. ii. 3 Nothing horrid or unnatural, nothing unexemplary, nothing destructive of..natural affection. 1894 *Daily News* 5 Feb. 3/3 A staunch upholder of that unexemplary husband [*sc.* George IV] in his long contest with his wife.

† **Unexe·mpled,** obs. var. UNEXAMPLED *ppl. a.*

1611 SPEED *Hist. Gt. Brit.* IX. i. § 18 His eies, which now beheld in a stranger, so strange and vnexempled kindnes. 1640–6 SIR J. CULPEPPER in Rushw. *Hist. Coll.* III. (1692) I. 35 There are some worthy Gentlemen..that carried themselves ..with great wisdom and unexempled moderation.

**Unexe·mplified,** *ppl. a.* (UN-[1] 8.)

*a* 1634 CHAPMAN *Rev. for Honour* IV. i. 184 Dismiss these tyrannous instruments of death And cruelty unexemplified. 1681 OWEN *Design Impend. Judgm.* To Rdr. A 2 b, There is an unexemplified Neglect in calling the Inhabitants of it unto Repentance. 1755 JOHNSON *Dict.* Pref. C j b, It is remarkable that, in reviewing my collection, I found the word 'Sea' unexemplified.

**Unexe·mpt,** *ppl. a.* [UN-[1] 8 b.] = next. 1634 MILTON *Comus* 685 Scorning the unexempt condition By which all mortal frailty must subsist. **Unexe·mpted,** *ppl. a.* (UN-[1] 8.) 1636 PAGITT *Christianogr.* (ed. 2) II. 40 Ecclesiasticks were unexempted, and deposing of Kings was then undreamed of. 1643–5 MILTON *Divorce* II. xiii, How can the..Law of God..require an unexempted and impartiall obedience to all her decrees,..and yet [etc.]. **Unexe·mpting,** *ppl. a.* (UN-[1] 10.) 1837 CARLYLE *Fr. Rev.* I. III. iv, Is there not Calonne's..universal, unexempting Landtax, the sheet-anchor of Finance? **Une·xercise.** (UN-[1] 12.) 1640 BP. REYNOLDS *Passions* xiii. 129 By reason of the volubility of the minde joyned with an infirmity and unexercise of memory.

**Une·xercised,** *ppl. a.* [UN-[1] 8.]

1. Not employed or made use of; not put in force or practised.

*c* 1374 CHAUCER *Boeth.* II. pr. vii. (1868) 56 Þat is to seyn, þat list þat or he wex olde, His uertue þat lay now ful stille ne sholde nat perisshe vnexercised in gouernaunce of comune. 1526 *Pilgr. Perf.* (W. de W. 1531) 86 Let neuer ony parte of thy good day passe and scape the vnexercysed. 1562 J. SHUTE *Cambini's Turk. Wars* 19 A place wherein no filthie exercise was left unexercised. 1635 BRATHWAIT *Arcad. Pr.* 19 Their Comitiall courts like desarts, wilde and unexercised. 1671 CLARENDON *Hist. Reb.* IX. § 42 The enemy left no manner of barbarous cruelty unexercised that day. 1796 MME. D'ARBLAY *Camilla* II. 278 Her judgment and penetration had been wholly unexercised. 1893 FAIRBAIRN in Selbie *Life* vii. (1914) 247 Certain faculties would remain unexercised.

2. Not taking exercise; remaining inactive; not put in motion; left unmoved or unstirred.

1562 TURNER *Baths* 6 Some other [men]..eat euell and vnholsome meates,..and then being vnexercised..make much euill humours. 1607 TOPSELL *Four-f. Beasts* 273 Be not afraid..of this sluggish and vnexercised people, for..they stir not out of the City. 1624 WOTTON *Archit.* I. 3 That it [*sc.* air] be not..vndigested, for want of sunne, not unexercised for want of winde.

3. Of persons: Not accustomed or prepared by training or practice; untrained.

1577 tr. *Bullinger's Decades* I. iii. (1592) 24 Whereby we gather, that the scripture is difficult or obscure to the vnlearned, vnskilfull, vnexercised, and malicious..wils. 1623

Bingham *Xenophon, Comp. Wars*, An vnexercised Souldier is alwaies raw, though he haue serued neuer so long. *a* 1653 Gouge *Comm. Heb.* xii. 5 This teacheth us..to fit and prepare ourselves for tryals. An unexercised man will not dare to enter into the list. 1702 Echard *Eccl. Hist.* (1710) 599 Some few..being unprepared and unexercised, through fear and frailty, fell away. 1768–74 Tucker *Lt. Nat.* (1834) I. 377 Unexercised in their understandings and unpractised in the ways of men. 1802 Lamb *Cooke's Rich. III*, Wks. 1908 I. 47 Breaking out into..plaudits at its own success, like an unexercised noviciate in tricks.

*transf.* 1587 W. Fowler *Wks.* (S.T.S.) I. 16 With my vnexcercised style [to] debaise suche graces.

**Unexe·rted,** *ppl. a.* (Un-1 8.)

1675 Traherne *Chr. Ethics* 347 Without its exercise it remaineth unexerted, is wholly vain. 1708 *Brit. Apollo* No. 88. 1/2 The Faculties of the Soul lie Dormant and Unexerted. 1790 Han. More *Relig. Fash. World* (1791) 181 To prevent the total stagnation of unexerted principles.

**Unexha·led,** *ppl. a.* (Un-1 8.) 1703 *Phil. Trans.* XXIII. 1433 The little Water which remained unexhaled.

**Unexhau·sted,** *ppl. a.* [Un-1 8 and 5 b.]

**1.** Not emptied or drained of contents.

1648 Boyle *Seraph. Love* (1659) 87 His Plenty being so unexhausted a spring of goods. 1652 E. Benlowes *Theoph.* vii. xc, Floods of unebbing joyes..Thou dost exhibit in an unexhausted bowl! 1704 *Phil. Trans.* XXV. 1786 As the Vibrations in the unexhausted Receiver were a little contracted. 1721 Ramsay *Prospect of Plenty* 245 Neptune's unexhausted bank has store Of endless wealth. 1833–4 J. Phillips *Geol.* in *Encycl. Metrop.* (1845) VI. 756/2 An unexhausted fountain of melted matter.

**2.** Not used up, expended, or brought to an end.

1602 Lodge *Josephus, Antiq.* vi. xiv. 149 Whatsoeuer they be that spend their many and vnexhausted labours in their seruice. 1656 Cowley *Pindar. Odes, 2nd Olympique* vii, In the Lands of unexhausted Light. *a* 1704 T. Brown *Mr. H. Silly* Wks. 1711 IV. 249 Thy Tenants,..With deep and unexhausted Woe, Lament their Generous Master dead. 1827 Jarman *Powell's Devises* II. 77 Such unexhausted interest..belongs to the heir as real estate undisposed of. 1857 Dufferin *Lett. High Lat.* (ed. 3) 112 Having separated into two streams, the unexhausted torrent again recommenced its march. 1878 Jevons *Prim. Pol. Econ.* 93 Tenant right consists in giving the tenant a right to claim the value of any unexhausted improvements.

**Unexhau·stible,** *a.* Also 7 -able. [Un-1 7, 7 b, 5 b.] = Inexhaustible *a.*

1656 Earl Monm. tr. *Boccalini's Advts. fr. Parnass.* i. xv. (1674) 18 His own so unexhaustible riches which he had accumulated. 1683 Tryon *Way to Health* 345 From the divine Principle..doth arise and flow, as from an unexhaustible Fountain, all Friendly Qualities. 1690 in *Cath. Rec. Soc. Publ.* IX. 359 Ye unexhaustable purse of Gods divine providence. 1779 Johnson *L. P., Butler*, If unexhaustible wit could give perpetual pleasure, no eye would ever leave half-read the work of Butler.

**Unexhau·stion.** (Un-1 12.) *a* 1741 Tull *Horse-hoeing Husb.* (1822) 151 There unexhaustion is more effectual than dung. **Unexhi·bited,** *ppl. a.* (Un-1 8.) [1775 Ash.] 1862 Thornbury *Turner* I. 262 Nor can I affix a certain date to the unexhibited 'Squally Weather'. **Unexi·l(e)able,** *a.* (Un-1 7 b.) 1592 Nashe *Strange Newes* E iv, A thousand more such vnexileable ouer-thwart merrimentes.

**Unexi·stence.** (Un-1 12 and 5 b.)

1593 Nashe *Christ's T.* P 2 b, Some there be that fantasie phylosophicall probabilities of the Trinities vnexistence. 1623 Cockeram i, *Vnexistence*, not being. 1828 *Blackw. Mag.* Sept. 300/1 Can it be that thou art numbered among forgotten things—unexistences! 1854 Cdl. Wiseman *Fabiola* ii. viii. 179 Had he melted into unexistence?

**Unexi·stent,** *a.* (Un-1 7 and 5 b.)

1682 Sir T. Browne *Chr. Mor.* iii. xiii. (1716) 97 A Retrograde cognition of times past..is more satisfactory than a suspended Knowledge of what is yet unexistent. 1723 Blackmore *Alfred* Pref. p. xlv, Only empty Phantasms, and the unexistent Creatures of human Invention. 1746 Young *Nt. Th.* ix. 812 Are there..those to whom Unseen and unexistent, are the same?

**Unexi·sting,** *ppl. a.* (Un-1 10.)

1785 Anna Seward *Lett.* (1811) I. 18 What you tell us is an unexisting circumstance. 1804 — *Mem. Darwin* 33 It is surely better to recede, even at the church-porch, than to plight at it's altar the vow of unexisting love. 1834 Mrs. Jameson *Visits & Sk.* (1839) I. 138 There are those who regard..the unknown as the unexisting.

†**Une·xorable,** *a. Obs.* [Un-1 7 b and 5 b.] = Inexorable *a.*

1577 *Fruites of Prayer* H 5 b, If God were (in a maner) vnexorable. 1608 Bp. J. King *Serm. 5 Nov.* 12 Is your malice vnexorable as the graue? Deepe and bottomles as hell? *a* 1641 Bp. Mountagu *Acts & Mon.* (1642) 422 They were..unexorable against malefactors for breach of the Law.

Hence †**Une·xorableness.** *Obs.*

1611 Florio, *Inessorabilita*, vnexorablenesse.

**Une·xorcised,** *ppl. a.* (Un-1 8.)

*c* 1750 Shenstone *Ruin'd Abbey* 174 That their dishonour'd corse..Must sleep with brutes..in marle unexorcis'd! 1854 Milman *Lat. Chr.* iii. vii. (1864) II. 152 She is possessed by a devil, who had been swallowed in the unexorcised lettuce. 1860 Froude *Hist. Eng.* VI. 306 That spectre remained unexorcised in all its shadowy terror.

**Unexpa·nded,** *ppl. a.* (Un-1 8.)

1664 Power *Exp. Philos.* ii. 110 The Quicksilver,..overpowring the Atmosphærical or unexpanded Ayr, falls down. 1712 Blackmore *Creation* vi. 290 So every fœtus bears a secret hoard, With sleeping, unexpanded issue stor'd. 1796 Withering *Brit. Plants* (ed. 3) III. 657 Leaves, and especially the unexpanded heads, with a good deal of woolliness. 1854 Hooker *Himal. Jrnls.* I. vi. 163 Most of its flowers drop unexpanded from the tree. 1887 W. Phillips *Brit. Discomycetes* 358 The unexpanded cups somewhat like a *Cucurbitaria*.

**Unexpa·nsive,** *a.* (Un-1 7 and 5 b.)

1846 Grote *Greece* (1862) II. 332 These bodies were close and unexpansive. 1862 T. A. Trollope *Marietta* I. xv. 271 By nature an unexpansive man. 1869 Lecky *Europ. Mor.* I. 433 The Jewish religion was essentially conservative and unexpansive.

†**Unexpe·ct,** *ppl. a.* [Un-1 8 b.] Unexpected.

1633 P. Fletcher *Elisa* i. xl, Not unexpect thou com'st to claim thy due.

**Unexpe·ctable,** *a.* (Un-1 7 b and 5 b.)

1598 Barret *Theor. Warres* i. ii. 9 Brought through manifold daungers, and vnto vnexpectable euents. 1604 T. Wright *Passions* v. § 4. 289 The difficulty of obtayning that we desire..rendreth the thing desperate and consequently vnexpectable. 1664 Ingelo *Bentiv. & Ur.* v. 30 The concatenation of like Successions..seems to make the end of sinning almost unexpectable. 1749 Byrom *Rem.* (1857) II. ii. 489 Your brother's journey to Smithills was indeed unexpectable. 1825 Bentham *Offic. Apt. Maximized, Indic.* (1830) 27 One of the most unexpectable of all incidents. 1863 Hawthorne *Our Old Home* (1879) I. 260 Our kind friend kept bringing out one unexpected and wholly unexpectable thing after another. 1892 *Graphic* 16 Apr. 478/1 Where the unexpected, or rather unexpectable, occurred.

**Unexpe·ctant,** *a.* (Un-1 7 and 5 b.)

1811 Wordsw. *Epist. to Beaumont* 209 Not unexpectant that by early day Our little Band would thrid this mountain-way. 1881 E. F. Poynter *Among the Hills* II. 84 Abashed by the unexpectant calm that met her.

**Unexpecta·tion.** (Un-1 12 and 5 b.) 1611 Florio, *Inn-aspettatione*, vnexpectation. 1650 Bp. Hall *Balm of Gilead* vii. § 1 As every other evill, so this [loss] especially is aggravated by our unexpectation.

**Unexpe·cted,** *ppl. a.* (Un-1 8 and 5 b.)

*a* 1586 Sidney *Arcadia* i. v, In such an unexpected mischiefe. 1597 A. M. tr. *Guillemeau's Fr. Chirurg.* 50/1 Because of vnexpected accidentes, he is blamed, disdayned and diffamed. 1634 Sir T. Herbert *Trav.* 5 An vnexpected violent gust. 1651 Hobbes *Leviath.* ii. xxviii. 162 The unexpected addition is no part of the Punishment. 1733 Berkeley *Let.* Wks. 1871 IV. 204 This circumstance, not foreseen, occasions an unexpected delay. 1781 Gibbon *Decl. & F.* xxx. (1787) III. 147 Stilicho..suddenly repressed, by his unexpected presence, the enemy. 1825 Scott *Talisman* iii, His attention was suddenly caught by an unexpected apparition. 1860 Maury *Phys. Geog.* xviii. § 750 The most unexpected discovery of all.

*absol.* 1884 in *Littell's Living Age* April 125/2 He is very great in the art of the unexpected. 1891 Bartlett *Fam. Quots.* (ed. 9) 701 The unexpected always happens.—A common proverb. 1892 [see Unexpectable].

**Unexpe·ctedly,** *adv.* (Un-1 11, 5 b; cf. prec.)

1605 Drayton *Idea* li, Calling to mind..How things still unexpectedly have run, As it please the Fates. 1693 Dryden *Juvenal* (1697) p. xxii, A most Bountiful Present, which..came most seasonably and unexpectedly to my Relief. 1774 Pennant *Tour Scotl. in 1772*, 283 A seat beautifully wooded, gracing most unexpectedly this almost treeless tract. 1825 Scott *Talisman* xxiii, Engaged in subduing the angry feelings which had been so unexpectedly awakened. 1869 Tozer *Highl. Turkey* II. 220 We found ourselves close to the beach.., on which we unexpectedly emerged.

**b.** With adjs. or advs.

1818 Scott *Rob Roy* xxvi, We took a kind farewell of this unexpectedly zealous friend. 1850 Mrs. Carlyle *Lett.* (1883) II. 123 She arrived yesterday unexpectedly early. 1877 Lady Brassey *Voy. Sunbeam* xviii, Rejoicing that we had..a fresh fair wind, so unexpectedly soon.

**Unexpe·ctedness.** (Un-1 12 and 5 b.)

1614 Tomkis *Albumazar* iv. ii, This man admires the vnexpectednesse Of my returne. 1654 Earl Orrery *Parthen.* (1676) 74 You should haue lessen'd my ruine, at least of one misery, which is the suddenness and unexpectedness of it. 1725 Watts *Logic* iii. iv. § 8 This will plainly prove that he describes the Unexpectedness of his Appearance. 1804–6 Syd. Smith *Mor. Philos.* (1850) 378 The unexpectedness of the news excites..the feeling of surprise. 1893 McCarthy *Red Diamonds* III. 221 An adventure stranger in its ironic unexpectedness than anything which had befallen him.

**Unexpe·cting,** *ppl. a.* (Un-1 10, 5 d.) 1632 Lithgow *Trav.* i. 7 The harmlesse innocent, vnexpecting euill, may suddenly bee surprised. 1831 James *Phil. Augustus* I. ii, The cold unexpecting fixedness of his companion's features. **Unexpe·ctingly,** *adv.* (Un-1 11.) 1801 Eliz. Helme *St. Margaret's Cave* xx, Thus unexpectingly meeting with a stranger..had the most sensible effect upon the good old man. †**Unexpe·diency.** *Obs.* (Un-1 12 and 5 b.) 1607 T. Sparke *Brotherly Persuasion* 7 Some inconuenience, and vnexpediencie in some of the things commaunded.

†**Unexpe·dient,** *a. Obs.* [Un-1 7 and 5 b.] = Inexpedient *a.*

*c* 1449 Pecock *Repr.* ii. v. 163 For ellis the sacramentis of Crist weren vnleeful, vnexpedient, and vnprofitable. *c* 1520 Barclay *Jugurth* (1557) A ij b, Neuertheles so to do it is vnbehouefull and vnexpediente. 1583 Golding *Calvin on Deut.* xxiii. 134 For this kinde of speach were vnexpedient if to make images were..lawfull. 1643 Quarles *Loyall Convert* Wks. (Grosart) I. 142/2 What is unexpedient in the one, is lawfull in the other. 1655 Fuller *Ch. Hist.* ix. ii. § 25 Others did condemne the present excommunication.. as unexpedient. *a* 1768 Secker *Serm.* (1770) II. 180 For their Abuse doth not of Necessity make our Use of them unlawful, nor possibly sometimes unexpedient.

**Unexpe·ditated,** *ppl. a.* (Un-1 8.) 1598 Manwood *Lawes Forest* xvi. 97 b, The forfaiture..onely for the keeping of Mastiues within a Forrest vnexpeditated. 1885 M. Collins in *Eng. Illustr. Mag.* 586/1 Some Commoners claimed a right to keep certain dogs unexpeditated. **Unexpe·lled,** *ppl. a.* (Un-1 8.) [1775 Ash.] 1811 Byron *Hints fr. Hor.* 240 He.., unexpelled perhaps, retires M.A.

**Unexpe·nded,** *ppl. a.* (Un-1 8.)

1571 *Act* 13 *Eliz.* c. 4 § 9 Any Part thereof..founde to be owing and unexpended. [1775 Ash.] 1818 Scott *Br. Lamm.* xviii, Computing how long..the provisions which had been unexpended might furnish forth the Master's table. 1855 Pusey *Doctr. Real Presence* Note R. 365 That which is eaten is unexpended. 1884 *Act* 47 & 48 *Vict.* c. 73 § 5 The unexpended balances of certain votes for navy services.

**Unexpe·nsive,** *a.* [Un-1 7 and 5 b.] = Inexpensive *a.*

1642 Milton *Apol. Smect.* Wks. 1851 III. 305 Providence ..hath ever bred me up in plenty, although my life hath not bin unexpensive in learning, and voyaging about. 1727 Thomson *Britannia* 204 Then cherish this, this unexpensive power,.. By lavish Nature thrust into your hand. 1770 Langhorne *Plutarch* (1879) I. 74/2 His sacrifices..consisting chiefly of..simple and unexpensive things. 1834 Ht. Martineau *Farrers* ii. 21 Mr. Farrer eschewed luxuries, except a few of the most unexpensive. 1859 Mill *Lett.* (1910) I. 233 Neither they nor the Tories wish to make elections unexpensive.

Hence **Unexpe·nsively** *adv.*, **-ness.**

1815 Jane Austen *Emma* xxv, Keeping little company, and that little unexpensively. 1825 Carlyle *Schiller* (1845) App. 285 Add to this the unexpensiveness to me of such a town as Weimar.

†**Unexpe·rience,** *sb. Obs.* [Un-1 12 and 5 b.] = Inexperience.

1611 Florio, *Imperitia*, vnskilfulnesse, vnexperience, ignorance. 1617 Bp. Hall *Quo Vadis?* x, To recant that which my vn-experience hath..written in praise of the French education. 1691 Hartcliffe *Virtues* 61 Ignorance and Unexperience makes men bold and foolhardy. 1755 *Mem. Capt. P. Drake* I. xiii. 93 He offered to appoint me his second Lieutenant, which I declined accepting, on account of my Unexperience in maritime Affairs.

**Unexpe·rience,** *v.* [Un-1 14.] *trans.* To fail to experience.

1603 Harington in *Nugæ Ant.* (1804) I. 336 Nor did I.. unexperience her love and kyndness on manie occasions.

**Unexpe·rienced,** *ppl. a.* [Un-1 8 and 5 b.]

**1.** Not furnished with, or taught by, experience; not skilled or trained in this way.

1569 Underdown *Ovid's Invect. Ibis* Pref. A vj b, If you wil bear with mine vnexperienced iudgemente. 1608 Willet *Hexapla Exod.* 273 No man will commit his.. bodie to an vnexperienced physitian. 1678 Otway *Friendship in F.* iv. i, Her natural and unexperienc'd tenderness exceeded practis'd charms. 1751 Johnson *Rambler* No. 175 ¶ 10 Credulity is the common failing of unexperienced virtue. 1793 Holcroft tr. *Lavater's Physiog.* i. 16 Shades scarcely discernible to an unexperienced eye. 1822 Chisholm in Good *Study Med.* (1829) II. 213 Let the young and unexperienced practitioner guard himself against it. 1860 A. L. Windsor *Ethica* iii. 146 An unexperienced hand might have expected [etc.].

**b.** Const. *in.*

1599 Hakluyt *Voy.* II. ii. 138 Our English Surgeons (for the most part) be vnexperienced in hurts that come by shot. 1620 E. Blount *Horæ Subs.* 85 To be vnexperienced in the first, argues much disability for the latter. 1654 tr. *Martini's Conq. China* 211 He quickly dispersed them, being wholy unexperienced in Military Discipline. 1760–72 H. Brooke *Fool of Qual.* (1809) IV. 27 My..child here, is unexperienced in the world. 1771 Smollett *Humph. Cl.* Oct. ii, Unexperienced as I am in the commerce of life.

**c.** *absol.* (with *the*).

1622 Peacham *Compl. Gent.* xvi. 200 If it be the common Law of Nature, that the learned should..instruct the ignorant, the experienced, the vnexperienced. 1665 Boyle *Occas. Refl.* iv. xix. 125 Whatever the unexperienc'd may imagine. 1742 *Johnson's Debates* (1787) II. 100 By these arts I have known the young and unexperienced kept in suspence. 1810 Crabbe *Borough* xxiii. 87 The unexperienced and the inexpert.

**2.** Not known or felt by experience.

1698 Norris *Pract. Disc.* IV. 89 A new and altogether unexperienc'd State and way of Life. 1721 Perry *Daggenh. Breach* 69 My Work was in a Method entirely new, and unexperienc'd by those Persons appointed to carry on the same in my Absence. 1756 *Monitor* No. 27. I. 239 The towers.. gave me an unexperienced delight, as I had never seen such a place before. 1844 Disraeli *Coningsby* ix. v, There was ..no unexperienced scene or sensation of life to distract his intelligence.

Hence **Unexpe·riencedness.**

1654 Gayton *Pleas. Notes* i. viii. 30 Whereat he vapoured extremely, shaking his head at the fellows unexperiencednesse. 1727 Bailey (vol. II) s.v., *Unskilfulness.*

†**Unexpe·rient,** *a. Obs. rare.* [Un-1 7 and 5 b.] Inexperienced.

1597 Shaks. *Lover's Compl.* 318 The naked and concealed feind he couerd, That th'vnexperient gaue the tempter place. 1750 Carte *Hist. Eng.* II. 638 Errors and oversights.. proceeding..from unexperient ignorance.

**Unexpe·rimented,** *ppl. a.* [Un-1 8.]

†**1.** Inexperienced; unskilled. *Obs.*

1598 Barret *Theor. Warres* i. i. 1 My selfe, and other country Gentlemen, vnexperimented in such martiall causes. 1622 R. Hawkins *Voy. S. Sea* 152 To commend such charges to men vnexperimented in their profession. 1635 J. Hayward tr. *Biondi's Banish'd Virg.* 162 So ignorant and unexperimented in all wylinesse..as to discover her love.

**2.** Not tried, known, or ascertained by experiment.

1594 R. Ashley tr. *Loys le Roy* 78 b, The diligence of the auncients, who haue left nothing vnsearched, and vnexperimented. 1674 R. Godfrey *Inj. & Ab. Physic* 54, I cannot but..wonder, that any persons should be so stupidly idle, and vain, to publish unexperimented Processes. 1839 B. H. Smart *Way out of Metaph.* 51 We may..apply it to similar particulars remaining unexperimented. 1870 Lowell *Study Wind.* 194 Whether equally so to the most distant possible heathen or not was unexperimented.

†**Unexpe·rt,** *a. Obs.* [Un-1 7 and 5 b. Cf. MDu. *onexpert.*]

**1.** = Inexpert *a.*

*a* 1425 tr. *Arderne's Treat. Fistula*, etc. 55 Lewed men and vnexperte men calleþ al þe infirmitez bredyng in þe lure emeroydez, or pilez, or fics. 1509 Barclay *Shyp of Folys* (1570) ¶¶ v, If ye consider the scarcenes of my wit, and my vnexpert youth. 1598 Barret *Theor. Warres* ii. i. 23 The expert souldier loth to obey the vnexpert Captaine. 1639 G. Daniel *Ecclus.* xxxiv. 25 Ignorance is vnexpert, and the Face Of smiling Error leads to Wickedness. **1698** FRYER *Acc. E. India & P.* 269 The Men here being unexpert how far the Friendly Offices [etc.].

**b.** Const. *of* or *in*.

(*a*) *a* **1440** *Found. St. Bartholomew's* (E.E.T.S.) 62 Vtterly vnexpert of mannys cownsell and helpe. *c* **1520** BARCLAY *Jugurth* 32 b, Theyr felowes whiche were fereful and unexpert of suche chaunces of warre. *a* **1548** HALL *Chron., Hen. VI*, 150 b, Nor of diligence, studie, and businesse, she was not vnexperte. **1635** HEYWOOD *Hierarchy* VI. 393 A Barbarian,..Unexpert of your Greekish plenitude. *a* **1689** MRS. BEHN *Mem. Crt. K. Bantam* (1722) II. 295 A pure Celibate, and altogether unexpert of Women.

(*b*) **1526** *Pilgr. Perf.* (W. de W. 1531) 274 They that be vnexperte in suche spirituall swetnesse. **1551** ROBINSON tr. *More's Utop.* II. (1895) 121 Yf they should be al together newe and fresh and vnexperte in husbandrie. **1629** WADSWORTH *Pilgr.* 35 Wee were young and vnexpert in sea fight. **1684** J. S. *Profit & Pleas. United* 166 Such Uner[r]ing Rules, as will..perfect the unexpert therein. **1778** [W. H. MARSHALL] *Minutes Agric., Observ.* 159 A man unexpert in boxing the Compass.

**c.** *ellipt.* in special sense.

*a* **1586** SIDNEY *Arcadia* III. v, Not doubting the easie conquest of an unexpert virgin. **1623** WODROEPHE *Marrow Fr. Tongue* 322/2 If a Woman be a Virgen, shee is vnexpert.

**2.** Of things: Untried. *rare*[−1].

*c* **1510** BARCLAY *Mirr. Gd. Manners* (1570) B v, When thou shalt ought do of unexpert or newe.

Hence † **Unexpe·rtly** *adv.*, **-ness.** *Obs.*

**1538** LATIMER *Rem.* (Parker Soc.) 398 If affection do reign in me, then I will not; if ignorance and unexpertness, then I cannot. **1565** COOPER, *Imperite*, vnexpertly: vnskilfully. **1598** FLORIO, *Imperitia*, vnskilfulnes, vnexpertnes. **1611** COTGR., *Imperitement*,..vnlearnedly; vnexpertly.

† **Une·xpiable,** *a. Obs.* [UN-[1] 7 b and 5 b.] = INEXPIABLE *a.* 1.

**1606** BP. J. KING *Serm.* Sept. 46 The fault is unexpiable; the blood of martyrdome cannot wash out this spot. **1657** TRAPP *Comm. Esther* ii. 10 This lyeth upon them as a punishment for their unexpiable guilt.

**Une·xpiated,** *ppl. a.* [UN-[1] 8 and 5 b.] = INEXPIATED *a.*

**1681** EARL ROSCOMMON *Poems* (1721) 6 The Bar..Stain'd with the (yet unexpiated) Blood Of the brave Strafford. **1809** MALKIN *Gil Blas* x. i. ⁋ 4 It gives me the horrors..to think of my unexpiated murders. **1873** SYMONDS *Grk. Poets* vii. 190 Orestes..has..unexpiated crimes of father and of grandsire to atone for.

**Unexpi·red,** *ppl. a.* (UN-[1] 8.)

**1570** WALSINGHAM in *Wills Doctors' Comm.* (Camden) 70 All my leases, or so many of them as then shall remayne unsoulde and unexpired. **1635** QUARLES *Embl.* v. x. 281 She ..begs th' untimely date Of unexpired thraldome, to release Th' afflicted Captive. **1659** *Knaresb. Wills* (Surtees) II. 240 Yeares of a lease..which are yet uncome and unexpired. **1778** [W. H. MARSHALL] *Minutes Agric., Observ.* 191 The unexpired term of the lease. **1859** J. LANG *Wand. India* 27 The unexpired portion of their leave having been cancelled. **1883** D. C. MURRAY *Hearts* xxiii. (1885) 189 The unexpired lease of the theatre was supposed to be worth a thousand.

**Unexplai·nable,** *a.* [UN-[1] 7 b and 5 b.] Inexplicable.

*a* **1711** KEN *Hymnotheo* Poet. Wks. 1721 III. 357 Each Plant, Worm, Mite, Pebble we behold, Strange Wonders unexplainable enfold. **1858** MRS. OLIPHANT *Laird of Norlaw* II. 88 The unconscious, unexplainable poetic elevation of the lad. **1875** WHITNEY *Life Lang.* x. 195 Facts which for the time seem unexplainable by ordinary means.

Hence **Unexplai·nably** *adv.*, inexplicably.

**1899** SOMERVILLE & ROSS *Experiences Irish R. M.* 247 At last we came, unexplainably, into smooth water.

**Unexplai·ned,** *ppl. a.* (UN-[1] 8.)

**1721** AMHURST *Terræ Filius* No. 31, All their doctrines are generally embrac'd whilst unexplained and unexamined. **1784** COWPER *Task* II. 58 Fires from beneath, and meteors from above, Portentous, unexampled, unexplain'd. **1842** MANNING *Serm.* (1848) 10 The great and unexplained fall of the 'sons of God'. **1879** *St. George's Hosp. Rep.* IX. 706 A rule, subject doubtless to no few unexplained exceptions.

Hence **Unexplai·nedly** *adv.*

**1811** MISS L. M. HAWKINS *C'tess & Gertr.* II. 366 These insular situations,..where nothing can occur unexpectedly and unexplainedly, without..carrying an inflammable train.

**Unexpla·natory,** *a.* (UN-[1] 7.) **1816** BENTHAM *Chrestom.* Wks. 1843 VIII. 171 The arbitrary and unexplanatory denomination given to them. **1847** C. BRONTË *J. Eyre* xxxiii, The hasty and unexplanatory reply. † **Une·xpliable,** *a. Obs.* [UN-[1] 7 b, 5 b.] = INEXPLE(A)BLE *a.* **1658** J. JONES *Ovid's Ibis* 15 The Belides sieve [may be] the unexpliable desires of the soule.

† **Une·xplicable,** *a. Obs.* [UN-[1] 7 b and 5 b.]

**1.** = INEXPLICABLE *a.* 2.

**1532** MORE *Confut. Tindale* Wks. 542/1 Which places of themselfe all olde holy doctours confesse for diffuse and almost unexplicable. **1644** DIGBY *Nat. Soul* Pref. ⁋ 5 Later Philosophers..haue filled their bookes..with vnexplicable opinions, out of which no account of nature can be given. **1656** EARL MONM. tr. *Boccalini's Advts. fr. Parnass.* I. lxxvii. 100 Justice being oppressed by the unexplicable ambition of potent men. **1803** *Ann. Rev.* I. 275 What remains unexplicable in the conduct of public men is not solved by conjecture. **1815** *Monthly Mag.* XXXVIII. 111 Many hundred words obsolete, unexplicable, barbarous,.. will be dislodged.

**2.** = INEXPLICABLE *a.* 1.

**1615** G. SANDYS *Trav.* 225 Him Minos doomes To durance, in vnexplicable roomes. *a* **1624** R. CRAKANTHORP *Vigilans Dormitans* xix. (1631) 313 By most admirable and unexplicable fraud & subtilty. **1675** EVELYN *Terra* (1676) 61 Mould to entertain the Fibers, which else you will find to mat in unexplicable intanglements.

Hence † **Une·xplicableness.** *Obs.*

**1712** *H. More's App. Antid. Ath.* 185 The unexplicableness of a Spirit's moving Maker is no greater argument [etc.].

**Une·xplicated,** *ppl. a.* (UN-[1] 8.) **1666** BOYLE *Orig. Formes & Qual.* Pref. B 6 b, Qualities..which have been by the Schooles either left Unexplicated, or Generally referr'd, to..Incomprehensible Substantiall Formes. **1698** LOCKE *Let. to Molyneux* 6 Apr., To have..unravell'd to you that which lying in the lump unexplicated in my mind I scarce yet know what it is my self.

**Unexpli·cit(ly,** *a.* and *adv.* (UN-[1] 7, 11, 5 b.) [**1775** ASH, *Unexplicit.*] **1831** SCOTT *Ct. Rob.* xxvi, So unexplicitly expressed,..that it was by no means easy to conceive the meaning of what he said. **1838** SIR W. HAMILTON *Logic* xvii. (1866) I. 319 Very brief and unexplicit in his treatment of this subject. **1852** JAMES *Pequinillo* II. 211 It was briefly and unexplicitly that he explained himself.

**Unexploi·ted,** *ppl. a.* (UN-[1] 8.) **1888** *Pall Mall G.* 3 Sept. 2/1 Developing the wonderful resources of their unexploited continent. **Unexplo·rable,** *a.* (UN-[1] 7 b, 5 b.) **1859** T. S. HENDERSON *Life E. Henderson* 149 The guide, who regarded the region not only as unexplored, but unexplorable.

**Unexplo·red,** *ppl. a.* (UN-[1] 8.)

**1697** DRYDEN *Æneis* IV. 600 No female Arts or Aids she left untry'd, Nor Counsels unexplor'd, before she dy'd. **1700** — *Sigism. & Guiscardo* 678 Under thy friendly Conduct will I fly To Regions unexplor'd. **1751** JOHNSON *Rambler* No. 137 ⁋ 7 The unexplored abysses of truth. **1824** MISS L. M. HAWKINS *Annaline* III. 65 They had led him round through an unexplored country. **1884** J. GILMOUR *Mongols* xviii. 225 The spirit which prompts men to..seek out unexplored knowledge.

**Unexplo·sive,** *a.* (UN-[1] 7, 5 b.) *a* **1828** SIR W. CONGREVE (Worcester, 1846). **1866** [see INEXPLOSIVE *a.*] **1884** *Contemp. Rev.* Nov. 617 Guns firing solid, and therefore unexplosive, shot. **Unexpo·rtable,** *a.* (UN-[1] 7 b.) **1827** P. CUNNINGHAM *N. S. Wales* II. 103 Paper-money..being unexportable, and consequently only available for home use.

**Unexpo·sed,** *ppl. a.* [UN-[1] 8.]

**1.** Not brought to light; not shown up.

**1703** MRS. CENTLIVRE *Beau's Duel* II. ii, Would they take my advice, no fop..shou'd 'scape unexposed. **1741** WATTS *Improv. Mind* I. v. § 8 (1801) 55 They will endeavour..to render it useless by their censures, rather than suffer..the little mistakes of the author to pass unexposed. **1817** COBBETT *Taking Leave* 29 While her infamous press was revelling in unexposed falsehoods and calumnies.

**2.** Not rendered open, subject, or liable, *to* something.

*a* **1691** BOYLE *Hist. Air* (1692) 82 A place unexposed to the moon's light. **1769** E. BANCROFT *Guiana* 17 The white inhabitants..are unexposed to the rays of the sun near midday. **1814** WORDSW. *Excurs.* IV. 757 Existence unexposed To the blind walk of mortal accident. **1865** NEALE *Hymns Paradise* 10 Unexposed to change and chance.

**3.** *Photogr.* (See EXPOSE *v.* 3.)

**1892** *Photogr. Ann.* II. 229 The principal constituent of an unexposed dry plate is silver bromide.

**Unexpo·stulating,** *ppl. a.* (UN-[1] 10.) **1819** SHELLEY *Cenci* II. ii. 150 Her mother scared and unexpostulating. **Unexpou·ndable,** *a.* (UN-[1] 7 b.) **1611** COTGR., *Inexplicable*,.. vndisplayable, vnexpoundable. **1835** *Court Mag.* VI. 230/1 In spite of legal interdictions and unexpoundable acts of parliament. **1844** *North Brit. Rev.* I. 147 Dark sayings and unexpoundable dogmas. **Unexpou·nded,** *ppl. a.* (UN-[1] 8.) **1648** HEXHAM II, *Onbeduydet*, Vnexpounded. **1651** JER. TAYLOR *Serm. for Year* II. xxii. 279 When we are to choose our doctrine,..we take that which is in the plain unexpounded words of Scripture. **1826** SCOTT *Woodst.* xiv, 'As gospel unexpounded by a steeple-man,' said the Independent. **Unexpre·ss,** *a.* (UN-[1] 7.) **1851** CARLYLE *Sterling* I. iv, The express schoolmaster is not equal to much at present—while the *unexpress*..is so busy.

† **Unexpre·ssable,** *a. Obs.* [UN-[1] 7 b.] = UNEXPRESSIBLE *a.*

**1548** G. WISHART tr. *Conf. Fayth* xxii, We exulte and rejoyce with a myrth unexpressable in wordes. *a* **1586** SIDNEY *Arcadia* III. x, As well consorted partes to such an unexpressable [1621 unexpressible] harmonie. **1607** HIERON *Wks.* I. 468 Now she..still beggeth with Him by sighes vnexpressable. **1652** *Eliza's Babes* 75 A felicity that fils our hearts with an unexpressable delight. **1683** E. HOOKER *Pordage's Mystic Div.* Pref. 70 To the..unexpressabl refreshing of the..faithful Servants of Christ. *c* **1721** MRQ. TULLIBARDINE in *10th Rep. Hist. MSS. Comm.* App. I. 126 Those who find their account in unexpressable confusion.

**Unexpre·ssed,** *ppl. a.* (UN-[1] 8 and 5 b.)

**1561** T. NORTON *Calvin's Inst.* I. Pref., So that he do with an vnexpressed Fayth (as they cal it) submit hys mynde to the iugement of the Chirch. **1611** BEAUM. & FL. *Maid's Trag.* III, And you will feel so unexprest a joy In chast embraces, that you will indeed appear another. **1659** EVELYN tr. *Gold. Bk. Chrysostome* Ep. Ded. A x j, The Ellipsis, and Defects of Verbs and Nouns unexpressed. **1676** *Life Father Sarpi* in *Brent's Counc. Trent* 8 All their regular orders continued with professions as yet unexprest. **1813** BYRON *Corsair* III. xv, His thoughts..; deep, dark, and unexprest, They bleed within..his breast. **1876** FOX BOURNE *Locke* I. vi. 273 By its unexpressed terms all the courtiers and politicians..were to be well bribed.

So **Unexpre·ssedly** *adv.*

**1561** T. NORTON *Calvin's Inst.* III. 173 It is not enough, if a man vnexpressedly beleue..: but he requireth an expressed acknowleging of Gods goodnesse.

**Unexpre·ssible,** *a.* (and *sb.*). Now *rare* or *Obs.* [UN-[1] 7 and 5 b.] = INEXPRESSIBLE *a.*

**1621** [see UNEXPRESSABLE *a.*, quot. *a* 1586]. **1626** DONNE *Serm.* 746 That unexpressible worke of the Redemption. **1675** TRAHERNE *Chr. Ethics* 73 The first of these is occasioned by a secret and unexpressible agreement of tempers. **1731** *Hist. Litteraria* II. 267 The many, almost unexpressible, Calamities he suffered, during his Captivity. **1826** SOUTHEY *Vind. Eccl. Angl.* 177 An unexpressible, uncomparable, unimaginable stench..filled that whole place of darkness.

**b.** *sb.* = INEXPRESSIBLE *sb.* 2.

**1810** S. GREEN *Reformist* I. 92 No, we called 'em 'fie-for-shames', 'unexpressibles', 'inspeakables'; for 'small-clothes' has been long out of wogue.

Hence **Unexpre·ssibleness.** Also **-ibi·lity.**

**1649** AMBROSE *Media* iii. (1652) 56 The Infiniteness, and unexpressibleness of God's Bounty. *a* **1672** STERRY *Freed. Will* (1675) 7 The unexpressibleness of the Divinity, and the Divine Vnity. **1816** BENTHAM *Chrestom.* Wks. 1843 VIII. 117 Of impracticability, in this case two causes present themselves..: viz. uncognoscibility and unexpressibility.

**Unexpre·ssibly,** *adv.* Now *rare* or *Obs.* [UN-[1] 11 and 5 b.] = INEXPRESSIBLY *adv.*

**1634** BP. HALL *Char. Man* (1635) 47 Till then your condition..is unexpressibly wofull. **1668** H. MORE *Div. Dial.* III. xvi. 411 Tumbling them down into the pit of Hell, there to be eternally and unexpressibly tormented. **1702** ECHARD *Eccl. Hist.* (1710) 598 Which meeting with a person of his age,..must needs be unexpressibly burdensome.

**Unexpre·ssive,** *a.* [UN-[1] 7 and 5 b.]

† **1.** = INEXPRESSIVE *a.* 1. *Obs.*

**1600** SHAKS. *A. Y. L.* III. ii. 10 Run, run Orlando, carue on euery Tree, The faire, the chaste, and vnexpressiue shee. **1629** MILTON *Hymn Nativ.* xi, Harping in loud and solemn quire, With unexpressive notes to Heav'ns new-born Heir. **1637** — *Lycidas* 176 So Lycidas..hears the unexpressive nuptiall Song, In the blest Kingdoms meek of joy and love.

**2.** = INEXPRESSIVE *a.* 2.

**1755** *World* No. 150. V. 81 If the device had been a triple-crown, it would not have been unexpressive. **1816** BENTHAM *Chrestom.* 109 In so far as it simply fails of being subservient to those purposes, it is unexpressive—simply unexpressive. **1851** W. R. GREG *Creed Christendom* xv. 227 Exhausting superlatives, even to unexpressive and wearisome satiety.

So **Unexpre·ssively** *adv.*, **-ness.**

[**1846** WORCESTER, *Unexpressively.*] **1885** *Athenæum* 21 Mar. 369/2 She is distinguished from the other muses by the unexpressiveness of her name.

† **Unexprimable,** *a. Obs.* [UN-[1] 7 b and 5 b.] Inexpressible.

**1632** LITHGOW *Trav.* I. 9 An infinite treasure, of vnexprimable vertues. **1727** [DORRINGTON] *Philip Quarll* 222 The two Indians..with unexprimable Activity leapt in it.

**Unexpu·gnable,** *a.* [UN-[1] 7 b and 5 b.] = INEXPUGNABLE *a.*

**1382** WYCLIF *Ezek.* xxxii. 12 Alle thes folkis ben vnexpugnable, or mowen not be ouercomen. **1388** — 2 *Macc.* xii. 21. **1533** BELLENDEN *Livy* II. iv. (S.T.S.) I. 140 He began to edifie ane strang toure..quhilk be municioun and straitnes of þe ground apperit Vnexpugnabil. **1608** CHAPMAN *Byron's Conspir.* Plays 1873 II. 225 Their owne strengths Are not so sure and vnexpugnable But that [etc.]. **1653** H. COGAN *Diod. Sic.* 70 Arabia is a country unexpugnable to a forraign enemy. **1831** SCOTT *Ct. Rob.* xxiv, A safe and unexpugnable barrier of the empire against the Saracens.

† **Unexpui·sable,** *a. Obs.* [ad. F. *inépuisable.*] Inexhaustible.

**1623** LISLE *Ælfric on O. & N. Test.* Preface b 2 b, That vnexpuisable, that vnwastable light, .. which they had of old time shining..in their sepulchers.

**Unexpu·nged,** *ppl. a.* (UN-[1] 8.) [**1775** ASH.] **1826** MALTHUS *Popul.* (ed. 6) II. 457 If the statute..were to remain unexpunged.

**Une·xpurgated,** *ppl. a.* (UN-[1] 8.)

**1882** FARRAR *Early Chr.* II. 516 Even in the unexpurgated passages of the Amsterdam edition. **1889** HAMERTON *French & Eng.* 315 Young maids and old maids read Shakspeare in unexpurgated editions.

**Unexte·nded,** *ppl. a.* [UN-[1] 8 and 5 b.]

**1.** Not extended or stretched out.

**1648** HEXHAM II, *Ongereckt*,..Vnreached, or Vnextended. **1697** CONGREVE *Mourn. Bride* III. vi, Think on to-morrow, when thou shalt be torn From these weak, struggling, unextended arms. **1712** BLACKMORE *Creation* VII. 75 See his right hand he unextended keeps. **1757** JOHNSON *Let. to C. O'Connor* 9 Apr. in *Boswell*, Of these provincial and unextended tongues, it seldom happens that more than one are understood by any one man.

**2.** *spec.* Having no extension.

**1674** N. FAIRFAX *Bulk & Selv.* 33 Nor is All-fillingness any more unextended,..because 'tis not thing enough to be recht out. **1678** CUDWORTH *Intell. Syst.* I. i. § 20. 20 Aristotle..did suppose Incorporeal Substance to be unextended, and as such, not to have Relation to any place. **1764** REID *Inquiry* vii. 210, I appeal to any man of common sense, whether extension can be in an unextended subject. **1803** *Monthly Mag.* XV. 322 If..spirit be defined an active sensitive unextended formless substance. **1860** MANSEL *Proleg. Log.* (ed. 2) 49 An unextended colour is therefore a purely negative notion.

So **Unexte·ndedly** *adv.*, **-ness.**

**1674** N. FAIRFAX *Bulk & Selv.* 16 If..Gods eternity not be an everlasting now, and his immensity an unbounded unextendedness. **1678** CUDWORTH *Intell. Syst.* I. v. 823 Such considerations..as tend directly to prove, that there is something unextendedly incorporeal.

**Unexte·nuated,** *ppl. a.* (UN-[1] 8.)

**1778** JOHNSON *Shakespeare's Othello* I. iii. 80 *note*, The main, the whole, unextenuated. **1823** SOUTHEY *Hist. Penins. War* I. 237 The whole transaction was a business of pure, unmingled treachery, unprovoked, unextenuated. **1844** R. H. HORNE *New Spirit of Age* I. 150 Licentious works, which are unredeemed and unextenuated by any one sincere passion.

**Unexti·nct,** *a.* (UN-[1] 7 and 5 b.)

? **1622** FLETCHER *Love's Cure* III. ii, Be there but one spark Of fire remaining in him unextinct, With my discourse I'll blow it to a flame. **1678** CUDWORTH *Intell. Syst.* I. iv. § 18. 312 Their arcane Theology remained more or less amongst them unextinct to the last. **1820** SHELLEY *Ode to Naples* 168 Be man's high hope and unextinct desire The instrument to work thy will divine!

**Unexti·nguishable,** *a.* [UN-[1] 7 b and 5 b.] = INEXTINGUISHABLE *a.* **a.** Of fire or flame (also *fig.* and *transf.*).

**1642** *Forerunner of Rev.* in *Select. fr. Harl. Misc.* (1793) 274 The duke's fire of his anger and fury being unextinguishable. **1654** COKAINE *Dianea* IV. 351 Perceiving the flames unextinguishable, and defence impossible. **1762** FALCONER *Shipwr.* III. 169 There, all unquench'd by cruel fortune's ire, It glows with unextinguishable fire. **1860** PUSEY *Min.*

*Proph.* 375 We see the arrow with the unextinguishable fire, ready to be discharged.

**b.** Of feelings, qualities, actions, etc.

**1656** JEANES *Fuln. Christ* 156 A ground of unconquerable comfort, and unextinguishable joy. **1697** COLLIER *Ess. Mor. Subj.* II. (1709) 14, I must repeat, That this Earnestness..is an unextinguishable Desire. **1760–72** H. BROOKE *Fool of Qual.* (1809) III. 52 The people's inseparable and unextinguishable share in the legislative power. **1815** J. CORMACK *Abol. Fem. Infanticide Guzerat* viii. 143 The ardent and unextinguishable zeal of female character. **1873** MOZLEY *Univ. Serm.* (1876) 201 The doctrine which..declares most unextinguishable war with materialistic ideas of the Deity.

**c.** Of laughter. (After the Homeric ἄσβεστος γέλως, *Iliad* I. 599, *Odyss.* VIII. 326.)

**1658** SIR T. BROWNE *Gard. Cyrus* ii. 42 That famous network of Vulcan, which..caused that unextinguishable laugh in heaven. **1801** MAR. EDGEWORTH *Angelina* iii, The milliner ..burst into uncontrollable and..unextinguishable laughter. **1842** MRS. BROWNING *Grk. Chr. Poets* iii. ¶5 That unextinguishable laughter which is the laughter of gods or poets.

Hence **Unexti·nguishableness; -ably** *adv.*

*a* **1660** HAMMOND *Hell Torments* i. Wks. 1684 I. 615 So the Unextinguishableness of the one must be answered with the durableness of the other. **1775** JOHNSON, *Unquenchableness*, unextinguishableness. **1779** — *L. P.*, *Hammond*, Hammond..was unextinguishably amorous, and his mistress inexorably cruel.

**Unexti·nguished,** *ppl. a.* [UN-¹ 8 and 5 b.] Not extinguished, quenched, or put out: **a.** Of fire or light (also *fig.*).

**1697** DRYDEN *Æneis* VI. 601 The souls whom that unhappy flame invades..Lament too late their unextinguished fire. **1730** in Willis & Clark *Cambridge* (1886) I. 230 One of yᵉ Candles..happen'd..to fall down unextinguish'd. **1757** W. WILKIE *Epigoniad* VIII. 241 The seeds of fire, Which unextinguish'd glow in ev'ry pyre. **1817** SHELLEY *Rev. Islam* Ded. xiv, Two tranquil stars..That burn from year to year with unextinguished light. **1858** HAWTHORNE *Fr. & It. Note-bks.* II. 175 The comet was already visible amid the unextinguished glow of twilight.

**b.** Of feelings, etc. (Cf. UNEXTINGUISHABLE *a.*)

**1700** DRYDEN *Sigism. & Guisc.* 732 If thou hast remaining in thy Heart Some Sense of Love, some unextinguish'd Part Of former Kindness. **1757** W. WILKIE *Epigoniad* VII. 198 But burning still the unextinguish'd pain, The shore he left. **1800** COLERIDGE *Talleyrand to Ld. Grenville* 71 Your merit self-conscious..keeps you up, Unextinguish'd and swoln. **1858** SEARS *Athan.* III. x. 331 There is conflict between the Holy Spirit..and our own unextinguished selfishness.

**Une·xtirpated,** *ppl. a.* (UN-¹ 8.)

**1663** BOYLE *Usef. Exp. Nat. Philos.* II. i. 10 That I might be sure there was not the least part of the spleen left unextirpated. **1792** HORSLEY *Serm.* xl. (1816) III. 221 Taking offence at the sin which remains as yet unextirpated. **1802–12** BENTHAM *Ration. Judic. Evid.* (1827) IV. 189 So long as that system of abominations remains unextirpated. **1867** PUSEY *Eleven Addresses* xi. (1908) 142 Our besetting sins, still unextirpated.

**Unexto·rted,** *ppl. a.* (UN-¹ 8.) **1711** SWIFT *Examiner* No. 25 ¶5 The free unextorted addresses sent some time before from every part of the kingdom. **1755** COWPER *To Delia* 20 The soul's affection can be only given Free, unextorted, as the grace of heaven. **Unextra·ctable,** *a.* (UN-¹ 7 b.) **1659** FULLER *App. Inj. Innoc.* II. IV. 44 The Animadvertor now proceeds to a new Intimation of mine, utterly unextractable from my words. **Unextra·cted,** *ppl. a.* (UN-¹ 8.) **1630** *R. Johnson's Kingd. & Commw.* 37 Selling their Sugars unextracted from the Cane. **1879** *Pall Mall Budget* 12 Sept. 24 One passage is too characteristic of the writer to be left unextracted. **Unextra·vagating,** *ppl. a.* (UN-¹ 10.) **1865** J. GROTE *Explor. Philos.* I. 105 It is impossible to find words un-extravagating in this respect.

† **Une·xtricable,** *a. Obs.* [UN-¹ 7 b and 5 b.] = INEXTRICABLE *a.*

**1659** H. MORE *Immort. Soul.* II. ii. 126 Which supposition we shall finde involved in unextricable difficulties. *a* **1677** BARROW *Serm. Ps. cxlv. 9* Wks. 1686 III. 402 Many times the World is rescued from confusions, and distractions unextricable by any visible wit or force.

**Unextru·ded,** *ppl. a.* (UN-¹ 8.) [**1775** ASH.] **1808** BENTHAM *Sc. Ref.* 100 More..there may be..as yet lying unextruded in the womb of time.

**Uney·ed,** *ppl. a.* [UN-¹ 8.] Unobserved, unperceived, unseen.

*a* **1616** FLETCHER *Wit at Sev. Weapons* II. ii, A pair of Lips, oh that we were uney'd, I could suck Sugar from 'em. **1654** E. JOHNSON *Wonder-wrkg. Provid.* 164 Many thousands uneyed of mortal man. **1820** L. HUNT *Indicator* No. 23 (1822) I. 184 The maiden..Kept not her bloom uneyed Which now a veil must hide. **1852** BAILEY *Festus* (ed. 4) 500 Pure and mere autocracy, unchecked—Unled—uneyed—ruled with a random hand.

**Uneymable**: see UNAIMABLE *a. Obs.*

**Uneyment,** obs. Sc. var. OINTMENT.

**Unfa·bled,** *ppl. a.* (UN-¹ 8.) [**1775** ASH.] **1809** SYD. SMITH *Wks.* (1859) 142 They are more amusing than plain, unfabled precept. **1853** C. BRONTE *Villette* xxvii, Not thickly, as the diamonds were scattered in the valley of Sindbad, but sparely, as those gems lie in unfabled beds. **Unfa·bling,** *ppl. a.* (UN-¹ 10.) **1797** *The College* 33 Shall the unfabling Muse the tale pursue? † **Unfa·bricate,** *ppl. a. Obs.* (UN-¹ 8 b.) **1630** J. TAYLOR (Water P.) *Epigr.* xxxvi. Wks. II. 266/1, I could wish man were vnfabricate, His faults he doth so much exaggerate.

**Unfa·ce,** *v.* [UN-² 4.] *trans.* To strip of a facing or disguise; to expose the face of.

**1611** FLORIO, *Suisare*, to vnface, to disuisage. **1640** SIR J. CULPEPPER in Rushw. *Hist. Coll.* III. (1692) I. 34 Unface these, and they will prove as bad Cards as any in the Pack. **1886** *Cheshire Gloss.* 374 To 'unface sand' would be to dig away all the soil so as to expose a face of sand.

**Unfa·ceable,** *a. dial.* [UN-¹ 7 b.] **a.** (See quot. *a* 1825.) **b.** Unattractive in features.

*a* **1825** FORBY *Voc. E. Anglia*, *Unfaceable*, unreasonable; indefensible. **1899** CROCKETT *Kit Kennedy* xxxiii, I hae seen mony queer-lookin' and unfaceable ministers.

**Unfa·ceted,** *ppl. a.* (UN-¹ 8.) **1893** E. A. BUTLER *Househ. Ins.* 327 A pair of simple, rounded, unfaceted eyes. **Unfa·ce·tious,** *a.* (UN-¹ 7.) **1831** [see INFICETE *a.*]. **Unfa·ct.** (UN-¹ 12.) **1887** *North Star* 3 Dec., The astounding statement..was an unfact. **1890** *Cath. News* 4 Oct. 6/4 We will call this an evangelical unfact. **Unfa·ctious,** *a.* (UN-¹ 7.) **1834** DE QUINCEY *Autob. Sk.* Wks. 1854 II. 220 The pure-hearted and unfactious champions of liberty. **1853** BP. S. WILBERFORCE in *Life* (1881) II. 170 Temperate, reasonable, and unfactious in their conduct. **Unfa·dable,** *a.* (UN-¹ 7 b.) **1626** BP. HALL *Contempl. O. T.* XXI. iv, A crowne incorruptible, unfadable.

**Unfa·ded,** *ppl. a.* (UN-¹ 8.)

? *a* **1550** in *Dunbar's Poems* (S.T.S.) 327 O fair sweit blossum, .. Vnfaidit bayth of cullour and vertew! **1697** DRYDEN *Æneis* XI. 101 A lovely flower, New cropt by virgin hands,..Unfaded yet. **1782** MISS BURNEY *Cecilia* I. iii, Her cheeks..unfaded by bad hours and continual dissipation. **1821** SHELLEY *Ginevra* 81 The flowers upon my bridal chamber strewn Will serve unfaded for my bier.

† **Unfa·dging,** *ppl. a. Obs.* [UN-¹ 10.] Not going properly; intractable.

**1629** T. ADAMS *Medit. Creed* Wks. 1120 The potter may erre in framing his vessel, and so in anger dash the vnfadging clay against the walles.

**Unfa·ding,** *ppl. a.* (UN-¹ 10.)

**1652** BENLOWES *Theoph.* XII. xlii, Such suppling balm As might vain trophies turn to an unfading Palm. **1738** GRAY *Propertius* III. 9 Let on this head unfading flowers reside. **1816** SOUTHEY *Poet's Pilgr.* I. 216 The vallies with perpetual fruitage blest, The mountains with unfading foliage drest. **1869** RUSKIN *Q. of Air* i. § 5 The real atmosphere, calm in its dominion of unfading blue.

**b.** In figurative use.

**1665** BOYLE *Occas. Refl.* Sect. iv. iv. 73 We should.. receive unfading Honours, and uncloying Delights. **1728** RAMSAY *Bonny Kate* viii, His pleasure each moment shall blossom Unfading, gets her for his mate. **1765** TUCKER *Lt. Nat.* (1834) II. 312 He might have excited sensations, ideas, and intelligence,..permanent, unfading, and unsatiating. **1820** SCOTT *Monast.* xxxii, By His holy Word, that unfading and unerring lamp of our paths.

Hence **Unfa·dingly** *adv.*, **Unfa·dingness.**

*a* **1672** STERRY *Rise, Race & Royalty Kingd. God* (1683) 211 All flourish together *unfadingly in the person of Christ. **1806** MOORE *Epist.* v. 44 That..The rose and the stream.. Should still be before me, unfadingly bright. **1658** PHILLIPS, *Immarcescence*, *unfadingness. **1797** POLWHELE *Hist. Devonsh.* I. 160 That its use..was known to the Phenicians will appear probable, when we consider the unfadingness of their purple. **1860** PUSEY *Min. Proph.* 91 Graces beyond nature, in their manifoldness, completeness, unfadingness.

† **Unfai·lable,** *a. Obs.* [UN-¹ 7 b and 5 b.]

**1.** = INFALLIBLE *a.* 2 a.

*c* **1425** *St. Eliz. of Spalbeck* in *Anglia* VIII. 108/15 Stronge and vnfaylabil preef of hool and clene virginite. *Ibid.* 113/41 Bi an vnfaillabil clock. **1553** EDEN *Treat. New Ind.* (Arb.) 10 Moste certayne..demonstracions of Geometrye, and vnfayleable experymentes. **1623** BP. HALL *Gt. Impostor* Wks. (1625) 509 Trust them not, till you haue tried them by that vnfaileable rule of righteousnesse. **1673** O. WALKER *Educ.* 49 [Religion] is a principle, universal, perfect, unfailable.

**2.** Incapable of failing; sure, reliable.

*c* **1450** HOLLAND *Howlat* 383 Of Scotland the wer wall,.. Our fais force to defend, and vnfalȝeable. **1553** *Short Catech. Edw. VI*, 38 b, Christ, the author, earnest and vnfailable pledge of theyr fayth. **1643** TRAPP *Comm. Gen.* xvii. 7 The sure or unfailable mercies of David. **168.** in Somers *Tracts* I. 276 That He left there one to be Heir of His Grace and Spirit, in a perpetual unfailable Succession.

Hence † **Unfai·lableness; -ably** *adv. Obs.*

**1555** EDEN *Decades W. Ind.* (Arb.) 350 By the degrees is *vnfaylably measured the hole circumference of the lande and sea. **1641** BP. HALL *Def. Humble Remonstr.* viii. 71 This is perpetually and unfailably done by us. **1624** — *Peacemaker* Wks. (1625) 538 Euery where extolling..the assurance and *vnfailablenesse of that comfort. **1644** — *Serm.* Rem. Wks. (1660) 137 He takes all beleevers into the partnership of this comfortable unfailablenesse.

**Unfai·led,** *ppl. a.* (UN-¹ 8.) **1827** POLLOK *Course T.* v. 523 When, on the glittering dews of orient life, Shone sunshine hopes, unfailed, unperjured then.

**Unfai·ling,** *ppl. a.* (and *adv.*). [UN-¹ 10.]

**1.** Not failing or giving way.

*a* **1400** *Sir Perc.* 1474 Thair scheldis were un-failande. **1648** BP. HALL *Serm.* Wks. 1808 V. 545 Hereby..are we freed from the sense of the second death and the sting of the first, to the unfailing comfort of our souls. **1653** BLITHE *Eng. Improver Impr.* 129 An unfailing Prevention of Crows, Rooks, or Daws from Corn. **1718** POPE *Iliad* XV. 551 Some god..Has, from my arm unfailing, struck the bow. **1798** S. & HT. LEE *Canterb. T.* II. 554 May you deserve that love, is the prayer of your unfailing friend. **1827** POLLOK *Course T.* x. 2 My God! my Father! my unfailing hope!

**2.** Never giving out or coming to an end; unceasing, constant, continual.

**1382** WYCLIF *Ecclus.* xxiv. 6, I made in heuenus, that vnfailende liȝt shulde springe. **1435** MISYN *Fire of Love* 38 Þi swetnes.., þat end art of syghing, of desire begyninge, þe ȝate of ȝernynge vnfaylinge. *c* **1450** *Myrr. our Ladye* 180 But thow in thyne vnfaylynge fayrenesse..shuldest abyde vndepartably in his moste loued loue. **1784** COWPER *Tiroc.* 316 This fond attachment..Maintains its hold with such unfailing sway, We feel it ev'n in age. **1832** LYTTON *Eugene A.* I. i, He found a pure and unfailing delight in watching the growth of their young minds. **1855** [J. R. LEIFCHILD] *Cornwall* 127 An unfailing bank of bituminous bullion. **1876** BANCROFT *Hist. U. S.* I. x. 29 A country.. watered by unfailing rivers.

**3.** Infallible, positive, certain. † Also as *adv.*

*c* **1400** *Sc. Trojan War* II. 273 Quharfor wnfalȝeand ar we Mayd rytht certeyn þat it shall be. **1553** WOOD tr. *Gardner's True Obed.* To Rdr. A ij b, The vndoubted truth of gods vnfailing word. **1849** MACAULAY *Hist. Eng.* vii. II. 164 The event of battles, indeed, is not an unfailing test of the abilities of a commander. **1853** KANE *Grinnell Exp.* xxix. (1856) 240 This frost-smoke is an unfailing indication of open water. **1862** A. MEADOWS *Man. Midwifery* 76 One almost unfailing test may be here mentioned, namely, chloroform.

† **4.** As *adv.* Without fail, unfailingly. *Obs.*

*c* **1425** WYNTOUN *Cron.* IX. xxi. 2146 (Cott. MS.), Off Marche þe xxv. day, Wnfaillande þat [*sc.* the Annunciation] sal be ay.

Hence **Unfai·lingness.**

*c* **1630** SANDERSON *Serm.* II. 307 The stability, unchangeableness, and unfailingness of Gods counsels. *a* **1656** BP. HALL *Serm.* Wks. 1837 V. 576 We may be so much the more infallibly assured..by how much we do more know his unfailingness, his unchangeableness.

**Unfai·lingly,** *adv.* [UN-¹ 11: cf. prec.] Without fail; in all cases or circumstances.

*c* **1400** *Sc. Trojan War* II. 319 Fra Gregeois þat shall ay but les Be holden ay wnfalȝeandly [*v.r.* wnfenȝeandly; L. *inviolabiliter*]. **1436** *Pol. Poems* (Rolls) II. 191 God wote, we have nede, Unfayllyngly, unfeynynge, and unfeynte, That concience for slought you not atteynte. **1833** ARNOTT *Physics* (ed. 5) II. 8 If the colds of winter arrive too early, they unfailingly produce the wintry scene. **1888** H. MORTEN *Hospital Life* 26 He was..unfailingly patient with the querulous babes.

**Unfai·n,** *a.* Now *arch.* and *dial.* [OE. *unfægen* (f. *un-* UN-¹ 7 + *fægen* FAIN *a.*), = ON. *úfeginn* (Norw. *ufegen*).] Not glad or delighted; ill-pleased, sorry; reluctant.

*a* **1300** *Cursor M.* 3591 Quen þai it [*sc.* eld] haue þai are vnfayn, And wald ha youthed þan again. **1338** R. BRUNNE *Chron.* (1810) 100 He seged bi þat coste þe kastelle of Tenkere...Þe Courthose was vnfayn, him þenk it a trespas. *c* **1400** *Destr. Troy* 12107 All þe folke were vnfayn, & of fyn will To haue reft hir the rynke. *a* **1450** *Le Morte Arth.* 2691 They made hem Redy to that Rese, There-fore was fele folke vnfayne. **1535** STEWART *Cron. Scot.* (Rolls) II. 43 Force it wes the Romanis for till fle, And leif the feild, thocht tha war rycht vnfane. *a* **1600** *Flodden F.* xiv. in Child *Ball.* III. 355 If Lancashire and Cheshire be fled and gone, Of those tydings wee may be vnfaine.

**1846** *Whistle-Binkie* II. 11 Though o' him the men were a' rede and unfain, The lasses aye leuch when they met him again. **1876** *Whitby Gloss.* **1881** *Macm. Mag.* XLIII. 234 As she told, The hearers were unfain to hear.

**Unfai·nt,** *a.* (UN-¹ 7.)

**1436** [see UNFAILINGLY]. **1486** *Bk. St. Albans, Her.* Fj, Durable & unfaynt in his kyngys battaylle [he] shall be. **1586** FERNE *Blaz. Gentrie* 148 Dyamond [is] vnfaint and durable.

† **Unfai·nted,** *ppl. a. Obs.* (UN-¹ 8.)

*c* **1425** *St. Cath. of Senis* in *Anglia* VIII. 187 Alwey and wiþ vnfeyntyd herte she spake of god. *a* **1539** COVERDALE *Ghostly Ps.* cxxix. Wks. (Parker Soc.) II. 577, I wyll abyde the Lorde paciently; My soule loketh for hym unfaynted.

**Unfai·nting,** *ppl. a.* (UN-¹ 10.)

**1615** G. SANDYS *Trav.* 167 And o that I could retaine the effects which it wrought, with an vnfainting perseuerance! **1691** *Andros Tracts* II. 297 With inviolate Integrity, excellent Prudence, and unfainting Diligence. **1850** S. DOBELL *Roman* vi, Thou who in thy breast didst carry The fate of worlds unfainting. **1852** BAILEY *Festus* (ed. 4) 274 Some with wings Like an unfainting rainbow.

**Unfai·ntly,** *adv.* (UN-¹ 11.)

*c* **1425** *St. Cath. of Senis* in *Anglia* VIII. 186/27 Vnsuffurabil labours, vnfeyntly borne. **1844** MRS. BROWNING *Catarina to Camoens* xvi, Since with saintly Watch unfaintly Out of heaven shall o'er you lean Sweetest eyes.

**Unfai·r,** *a.* [OE. *unfæger* (f. *un-* UN-¹ 7 + *fæger* FAIR *a.*), = ON. *úfagr* (Norw. *ufager*), Goth. *unfagrs*.]

† **1.** Not fair or beautiful; uncomely; disfigured; ugly. *Obs.*

*Beowulf* 727 Him of eaȝum stod liȝȝe ȝelicost leoht unfæȝer. *c* **888** K. ÆLFRED *Boeth.* xli. § 4 Sio ȝefrednes ..ne mæȝ ȝefredan hwæðer he bið þe blæc þe hwit, ðe fæȝer ðe unfæȝer. **971** *Blickl. Hom.* 111 [Him] þincð his neawist laþlico & unfæȝer. *c* **1050** *Voc.* in Wr.-Wülcker 530 *Larbata*, se unfæȝera. *a* **1300** *Cursor M.* 22509 Þe sun þat es sa bright..It sal becum þan ful vnfair, Dune and blak sum ani hair. **13..** *Gaw. & Gr. Knt.* 1572 Þe froþe femed at his mouth vnfayre bi þe wykez. *a* **1400–50** *Alexander* 4864 Rochis & rogh stanes, rokkis vnfaire. *c* **1449** PECOCK *Repr.* v. xii. 548 In oon maner of sumwhat foul or vnfair schap and in oon maner of poor and symple colour. *a* **1500** *Ratis Raving* I. 1722 Þis eild is wnfair of fassoun, And failȝes of perfectioun. **1648** HEXHAM II, *Onschoon*, Vnfaire, or Vnbeautifull.

† **b.** Wicked; evil, bad. *Obs.*

**13..** *E. E. Allit. P.* B. 1801 He was corsed for his vnclannes,..Done doun of his dyngnete for dedez vnfayre. **1375** BARBOUR *Bruce* I. 123 For wnfayr thingis may fall, perfay, Als weill to-morn as ȝhisterday. *Ibid.* XV. 123 Bot I trow falsat euirmar Sall haue vnfair and euill ending.

**2.** Not fair or equitable; unjust: **a.** Of actions, conduct, etc.

**1713** BERKELEY *Hylas & Phil.* II. Wks. 1871 I. 319 This shifting, unfair method of yours. **1746** WESLEY *Princ. Methodist* 5 If indeed it were so abridged as to alter the Sense, this would be unfair. **1798** S. & HT. LEE *Canterb. T.* II. 98 This conclusion appeared so unfair,..that she burst into tears. **1854** E. FITZGERALD *Lett.* (1889) I. 229 There was a very unfair Review in the Athenæum. **1890** 'R. BOLDREWOOD' *Col. Reformer* (1891) 185 Riding a well-bred powerful horse, which evidently made little of his somewhat unfair weight.

**b.** Of persons, the mind, etc.

**1724** WATERLAND *Farther Vind. Christ's Div.* ii. § 15. 57 Sometimes they complain of me as very unfair to take an Advantage of an Opinion of theirs. **1736** BUTLER *Anal.* II. vi. 315 Opportunity to an unfair mind of explaining away ..that evidence. **1812** SCOTT *Let. to Byron* July in *Lockhart*, I do not know the motive would make me enter into controversy with a fair or an unfair literary critic. **1855** TENNYSON *Maud* I. xiii, Who shall call me ungentle, unfair.

**c.** *spec.* Not paying the usual rate of wages.

**1886** *Pall Mall G.* 22 Oct. 10/2 To give their printing contract..to what was known in the trade as an 'unfair house'. **1888** JACOBI *Printers' Vocab.*, *Unfair offices*, this term is applied by society hands generally to those printing offices where the existing scale of prices is not recognized.

**3.** Of the wind: Unfavourable.

**1801** in Nicolas *Disp. Nelson* (1845) IV. 299 If the wind proved fair..they should be sent up the harbour, but if unfair, no time would have been lost. **1802** *Naval Chron.* VIII. 433 The wind being unfair at S.W.

**4.** Not fitting or corresponding exactly.

**1869** SIR E. REED *Shipbuild.* xix. 415 That drifting unfair holes would be considered bad work. **1874** THEARLE *Naval Archit.* 58 Great precautions are..necessary to prevent unfair seams in the subsequent operations of laying the deck.

† **Unfai·r,** *adv. Obs.* [UN-1 11 b: cf. prec.] In a rough, disorderly, or untidy manner.

*a* **900** *Genesis* 2063 Gripon unfæȝre under sceat werum scearpe garas. *a* **1400–50** *Alexander* 555 Cloudis clenely to-clefe, clatird vn-faire. *c* **1400** *Destr. Troy* 13891 With the remnond full rade he rixlit unfaire. *c* **1480** HENRYSON *Test. Cres.* 163 Atouir his belt his lyart lokkis lay Felterit vnfair.

**Unfai·r,** *v.* [UN-2 6 a.] *trans.* To deprive of fairness or beauty.

*c* **1600** SHAKS. *Sonn.* v, Those howers..Will play the tirants to the very same, And that vnfaire which fairely doth excell.

**Unfai·rly,** *adv.* [UN-1 11.]

**1.** In an unfair manner; inequitably, unjustly.

**1713** BUTLER *Let. to S. Clarke* i. (1716) 8 If I have..in any respect argu'd unfairly, I assure you it was without design. *a* **1768** SECKER *Serm.* (1771) VII. xiii. 283 To use even those unfairly, who have used us so, is very bad: but to use any one unfairly, because Another hath used Us so, is..monstrously wicked. **1796** [see UNDULY 1]. **1848** KINGSLEY *Yeast* ii, Argemone..fancying herself, and not unfairly, very intellectual. **1877** HUXLEY *Physiogr.* 84 It might, therefore, not unfairly be assumed that the carbonic acid..would tend to settle down in a stratum near the ground.

**2.** By unfair or foul means.

**1791** MRS. RADCLIFFE *Rom. Forest* v, There were strong reasons to believe he came unfairly to his end.

**Unfai·rness.** [UN-1 12: cf. OE. *unfægernes.*] Lack of fairness or equity; injustice.

**1713** BENTLEY *Remarks Disc. Free-Think.* xlv. II. 33 We may observe from this Passage..the unfairness and malignity of our Writer. **1796** MME. D'ARBLAY *Camilla* IV. 387 [They] have a certain instinctive sense of its unfairness. **1833** BURTON *Eccl. Hist.* xx. 192 The unfairness which looks for different results in the second century from those which are produced in the nineteenth. **1875** JOWETT *Plato* (ed. 2) IV. 232 He is occasionally playing both parts himself, and even charging his own arguments with unfairness.

**Unfai·th.** [UN-1 12.] Lack of faith or belief, esp. in religion.

**1415** HOCCLEVE *To Sir J. Oldcastle* 247 For thyn vnfeith men maken many mones. **1826** MISS MITFORD *Village* Ser. II. 272 At the end of one of her daily professions of unfaith in gipsies and their predictions. **1859** TENNYSON *Merl. & V.* 386 Faith and unfaith can ne'er be equal powers: Unfaith in aught is want of faith in all. **1870** SWINBURNE *Ess. & Stud.* (1875) 81 Another form of bastard belief, another cross-breed between faith and unfaith.

**Unfai·thful,** *a.* [UN-1 7.]

**1.** Not having the proper religious faith; infidel, unbelieving. Also *absol.*

**1382** WYCLIF *1 Cor.* vii. 12 If ony brothir haue an vnfeithful..wyf, and sche consentith for to dwelle with hym, leue he..hir not. **1388** — *Ps.* l. 15, I schal teche wickid men thi weies; and vnfeithful men schulen be conuertid to thee. **1456** SIR G. HAYE *Law Arms* (S.T.S.) 106 Thai landis that the unfaithfull men haldis. **1534** MORE *Treat. Passion* Wks. 1341/2 Justinus..writing of our faith in his second Apologye to the vnfaithful Emperour Antonius. **1560** BIBLE (Genev.) *2 Esdras* xv. 4 For euery vnfaithful shal dye in his vnfaithfulnes. **1643–5** MILTON *Divorce* I. viii, The author of a generall divorce between the faithfull and unfaithfull seed. **1667** — *P. L.* XII. 481 What will betide the few, His faithful, left among th' unfaithful herd, The enemies of truth? **1768–74** TUCKER *Lt. Nat.* (1834) II. 484 Whatever supernatural virtue or nutritive faculty the priest has infused into the bread, are verily..received by the unfaithful. **1800** *Asiat. Ann. Reg., Misc. Tr.* 334/1 Therefore he who follows Mahommedanism and..violates this treaty, so comporting himself like the unfaithful [etc.].

† **b.** Not in accordance with faith; irreligious.

**1549** *Compl. Scot.* i. 22 Mony ignorant pepil hes confermit ane ymaginet onfaythtful opinione in ther hede.

**2.** Not keeping good faith; acting falsely or treacherously. Also *absol.*

*c* **1400** *Destr. Troy* 714 Vnfaithfull freke, with þi fals cast, Þat such a lady belirt. **1530** PALSGR. 328/1 Unfaythfull of promesse, *desloyal*. **1549** CHEKE *Hurt Sedit.* L j, Shall they not truly saye the subiectes to be more vnfaithfull in disobedience, than other subiects worse ordered be. **1600** SHAKS. *A. Y. L.* IV. i. 199, I will thinke you the most patheticall breake-promise..that may bee chosen out of the grosse band of the vnfaithfull. **1620** in Foster *Eng. Factories Ind.* (1906) I. 209 Theis Pegu factors were fownde to be royotous, vitious and unfaithfull. *a* **1729** CONGREVE *Ovid's Art of Love* III. 63 The prince so far for piety renown'd, To thee, Eliza, was unfaithful found. **1803** WELLESLEY in Owen *Desp.* (1877) 331, I propose to view this transaction as the combined offence of two unfaithful servants. **1832** HT. MARTINEAU *Demerara* iii. 35, I should be unfaithful if I had ever promised either.

**b.** *transf.* Of things.

*a* **1586** SIDNEY *Arcadia* III. xii, The unfaythfull armour yeelding to the swoordes strong-guided sharpenesse. **1615** G. SANDYS *Trav.* 2 A sea tempestuous and unfaithfull, at an instant incensed with sudden gusts. **1669** DRYDEN *Tyrannic Love* I. i, I..Did first the depth of trembling Marshes sound, And fix'd my Eagles in unfaithful ground. **1726** LEONI *Alberti's Archit.* I. 35 Sea-sand..is..unfaithful in supporting great Weights. **1779** SHERIDAN *Monody on Garrick* 14 As Fancy, oft,..Has view'd by shadowy Eve's unfaithful Gloom, A weeping Cherub on a Martyr's Tomb. **1831** JAMES *Phil. Augustus* I. v, One of those people whose lips—those ever unfaithful guardians of the treasures of the heart—are peculiarly apt to murmur..unconsciously. **1842** TENNYSON *Love & Duty* 91 With quiet eyes unfaithful to the truth.

**c.** Not following an original, not translating or translated, faithfully; incorrect, inexact.

*a* **1697** AUBREY *Lives* (1898) II. 174 He was a learned man,..but is much blamed for his unfaithfull quotations. **1724** A. COLLINS *Gr. Chr. Relig.* 163 The Septuagint seems the work both of ignorant and unfaithful Translators. **1776** MICKLE tr. *Camoens' Lusiad* Introd. 130 The unfaithful and unpoetical version [of the Lusiad] of Fanshaw. **1798** FERRIAR *Illustr. Sterne*, etc. 91 Burton has spoiled this passage by an unfaithful translation. **1855** MACAULAY *Hist. Eng.* xix. IV. 332 An unfaithful interpreter of the sense of the nation. **1864** PUSEY *Lect. Daniel* 379 To which act this writer probably alluded in his unfaithful paraphrase, 'chrism shall be removed'.

**d.** *spec.* Not faithful in wedlock.

**1828** WEBSTER s.v., An unfaithful husband or wife. **1841** W. SPALDING *Italy & It. Isl.* II. 147 Galeotto Manfredi,..having married Francesca Bentivoglio,..not only was unfaithful to her, but treated her with cruelty.

**3.** Of conduct: Characterized by want of good faith; not honest or upright.

**1565** COOPER s.v. *Perfidia*, To be deceiued by ones treacherie and vnfaithfull dealing. *Ibid.* s.v. *Infidus*, An vnfaithfull league that will not long be kepte. **1651** JER. TAYLOR *Serm. for Year* xxiii. 292 Lying or craftinesse, and unfaithful usages, robs a man of the honour of his soul. **1680** OTWAY *Orphan* IV. vi, I might think with Justice most severely Of this unfaithful dealing with your Brother. **1704** TRAPP *Abra-Mulé* II. i. 451 Spies..who for hope Of a Reward, will give the Sultan notice Of such unfaithful Dealing. **1866** GEO. ELIOT *F. Holt* v, Your father..was, as I understand, a man whose walk was not unfaithful.

**Unfai·thfully,** *adv.* [UN-1 11.] In an unfaithful manner; with lack of good faith.

**1340–70** *Alisaunder* 239 And Philip unfaithfully þe faire coste had, Arisba in exile euer was after. **1491** *Act 7 Hen. VII*, c. 22 *Preamble*, The seid John unfeithfully and untruly suffred the bringer of the seid writing to goo at his plesure. *c* **1545** LD. MORLEY *Hyst. Massuccio* fol. 2 b, You haue been vnfaithefully, vniustly and falsely [accused]. **1579** E. K. *Spenser's Sheph. Cal.* June, Argt., He is nowe forsaken vnfaithfully. **1607–12** BACON *Ess., Counsel* (Arb.) 316 The daunger of being vnfaithfullie councelled. **1679** EVERARD *Popish Plot* 5 Sir Robert most unfaithfully..discovered all to Colonel Talbot. **1722** WOLLASTON *Relig. Nat.* vi. § 19 (1724) 144 He, who acts unfaithfully, acts against his promises and ingagements.

**Unfai·thfulness.** [UN-1 12.]

† **1.** Lack of faith; infidelity. *Obs.*

**1388** WYCLIF *2 Tim.* ii. 16 But eschewe thou vnhooli and veyn spechis, for whi tho profiten myche to vnfeithfulnesse. **1395** PURVEY *Remonstr.* (1851) 61 Unfeithful men that shulen be dampnid uttirli..if thei dien in unfeithfulnesse. **1526** *Pilgr. Perf.* (W. de W. 1531) 129 Therof foloweth somtyme infidelite or vnfaythfulnes. **1561** T. NORTON *Calvin's Inst.* I. 56 Whoso therfore wil beware of this vnfaithfulnesse, let him kepe alwayes in remembrance [etc.].

**2.** The quality of being unfaithful; lack of good faith or fidelity.

*c* **1480** HENRYSON *Test. Cres.* 570 Traisting in vther als greit vnfaithfulnes, Als vnconstant, and als vntrew of fay. **1532** in Ellis *Orig. Lett.* Ser. III. II. 251 As towchinge the onfaythfulnes..of Father Forest, I dyd wryte of unto my Lady Marcas of Penbroke. **1590** SWINBURNE *Testaments* 218 So the legataries and children of the deceased are often defrauded..by the vnfaithfulnesse of the executor. **1685** BAXTER *Paraphr. N. T.* Matt. xxv. 26–27 Unprofitableness and omission of duty, is damnable unfaithfulness in us that are but Stewards and Servants. **1737** in *10th Rep. Hist. MSS. Comm.* App. I. 493 It contains a clear Proof of the Unfaithfullness of a Person in whom Your Majesty has placed a Trust. **1752** CARTE *Hist. Eng.* III. 14 Henry was in the height of his resentment, at the unfaithfulness of his allies. **1842** J. B. FRASER *Allee Neemroo* II. 31 If you impute to me any unfaithfulness towards you, I swear that you are deceived. **1881** R. W. CHURCH *Cathedral & Univ. Serm.* v. (1892) 59 The taint..of insincerities, of treacheries, of unfaithfulnesses to light.

**b.** *spec.* (Cf. UNFAITHFUL *a.* 2 d.)

**1848** THACKERAY *Van. Fair* lxvi, Is it unfaithfulness to my husband? I scorn it and defy anybody to prove it. **1851** FROUDE *Short Stud.* (1867) II. 191 Nor, again, was unfaithfulness..conclusively fatal against a wife.

† **Unfaken,** *a.*: see UN-1 2.

**Unfalla·cious,** *a.* (UN-1 7, 5 b.) **1802–12** BENTHAM *Ration. Judic. Evid.* (1827) IV. 490 Shutting the door against an article of true and unfallacious evidence. **Unfalla·ciously,** *adv.* (UN-1 11.) **1852** BAGEHOT *Lit. Stud.* (1879) I. 69 Pope unfallaciously said, 'Once a heretic, always a heretic'.

**Unfa·llen,** *ppl. a.* [UN-1 8 b. Cf. G. *ungefallen*, ON. *úfallinn* (Norw. dial. *ufallen*).]

**1.** Not morally fallen.

**1653** H. MORE *Conject. Cabbal.* ii. 41 The natures..of the fallen and unfallen Angels, or good and bad Genii. **1679** J. C[HENEY] *Vind. Oaths & Swearing* 7 In Paradise it self,..while man was innocent and unfallen. **1740** CHEYNE *Regimen* 129 This..must be the Constitution..of the unfallen angelical State. **1825** COLERIDGE *Aids Refl.* (1848) I. 242 We may say, that in the unfallen rational agent, the will constitutes the law. **1848** KINGSLEY *Yeast* vi, Who am I to demand her all to myself? Her, the glorious, the saintly, the unfallen!

*fig.* **1759** YOUNG *Conject. Orig. Composition* 60 What we mean by Blank verse, is verse unfallen, uncurst.

**2.** Not fallen (in literal sense).

**1735** SOMERVILLE *Chase* I. 116 Fix'd as a mountain ash, that braves the bolts Of angry Jove; tho' blasted, yet unfall'n. **1878** GILDER *Poet & Master* 29 It was I who behold the sun's level light strike through the unfallen..leaves.

Hence **Unfa·llenness.**

**1876** W. BATHGATE *Deep Things of God* v. 79 A peerless perfect man,—albeit entirely Divine in his unfallenness.

† **Unfa·llible,** *a. Obs.* [UN-1 7 and 5 b.] = INFALLIBLE *a.* (Common *c* 1530–1620.)

**1529** MORE *Dyaloge* I. Wks. 168/2 If ye will..take a sure and vnfallyble way ye must..beleue and obey the churche. **1545** BRINKLOW *Compl.* 5 b, It is certen and vnfallible, that if we knock,..we shal be hard. **1592** R. D. *Hypnerotomachia* 82 b, Disposing my selfe to her sweete loue, with an unfallyble, obstinate, and firme resolution. **1614** LATHAM *Falconry* 68 These my friendlie admonitions, being grounded vpon the absolute truth of vnfallible experience. **1653** BLITHE *Eng. Improver Impr.* 145 A very Excellent Unfallible Remedy against Barrenness.

† **Unfa·llibly,** *adv. Obs.* [UN-1 11 and 5 b.] = INFALLIBLY *adv.*

**1542** UDALL *Erasm. Apoph.* 32 b, A feloe..who professed..to bee hable unfallibly..to fynd out & judge the naturall disposicion of any manne. **1567** DRANT *Horace, Ep.* I. i. C iij, The wyseman ames vnfalliblie. **1604** HIERON *Wks.* I. 547 A christian man may bee vnfallibly certaine of his saluation in his owne conscience. **1642** ROGERS *Naaman* 44 The Lord..beholds the effecting of the one, in the other, necessarily and unfallibly.

† **Unfa·llid,** *a. Obs.*[−1] [UN-1 7 and 5 b: see INFALLID *a.*] Infallible.

**1624** HEYWOOD *Captives* IV. i. in Bullen *O. Pl.* IV, By these tokens, These of her childhood most unfallid signes, I knowe her for my doughter.

**Unfa·llowed,** *ppl. a.* (UN-1 8.)

**1607** J. CARPENTER *Plaine Mans Plough* 102 Why man..is likened to the Earth, or to the unfallowed Land. **1634** RAINBOW *Labour* (1635) 40 Let not us bee that unfallowed ground where the Divell may sowe his tares. **1708** J. PHILIPS *Cyder* I. 549 Th' unfallow'd Glebe Yearly o'ercomes the Granaries with Store Of Golden Wheat.

**Unfa·lsified,** *ppl. a.* (UN-1 8.) **1687** MIÈGE II. s.v., Provided the Account be true and unfalsify'd. **1855** LEWIS *Cred. Early Rom. Hist.* xiv. § 2. II. 491 The current story..has descended..in a substantially unfalsified state.

**Unfa·ltering,** *ppl. a.* (UN-1 10.)

**1727** THOMSON *Summer* 299 With unfaultering accent to conclude That This availeth nought? **1744** AKENSIDE *Pleas. Imag.* I. 163 Thro' the tossing tide of chance and pain To hold his course unfaltering. **1825** SCOTT *Betrothed* xxix, He tells me of it with..an eye composed, an unfaltering tongue. **1862** 'SHIRLEY' (J. Skelton) *Nugæ Crit.* v. 233 The confident and unfaltering witness of the strong man, who goes to the stake with..a sense of triumph in his heart.

So **Unfa·lteringly** *adv.*

**1665** BOYLE *Occas. Refl.* I. iv. 169 Unfaultringly to traverse Adversitie's rough ways. **1850** MRS. SARAH ELLIS *Pique* (1875) 269 Lady Catherine turned away, and..unfalteringly approached the door. **1885** *Manch. Exam.* 9 Sept. 3/2 A character who is at once vividly human..and unfalteringly noble.

**Unfa·med,** *ppl. a.* (UN-1 8.)

**1606** SHAKS. *Tr. & Cr.* II. ii. 159 There's..none so Noble, Whose life were ill bestow'd, or death vnfam'd, Where Helen is the subiect. **1724** A. HILL *Prol. to Savage's Sir T. Overbury* p. xi, Young, and unfam'd, and but by Hope inspir'd. **1855** SINGLETON *Virgil* II. 346 Thus laid aside, unfamed here let him pass His life. **1887** HISSEY *Holiday on Road* 156 Some few whose names and deeds will dwell a little longer than the unfamed rest.

**Unfami·liar,** *a.* (UN-1 7.)

**1594** HOOKER *Eccl. Pol.* I. i. § 2 The matters which we handle seeme by reason of newnesse..darke, intricate, and vnfamiliar. **1648** HERRICK *Hesper., Oberons Feast* 4 Because thou prizest things that are Curious, and unfamiliar. *c* **1698** LOCKE *Cond. Underst.* § 32 (1754) 127 Abstruse and unfamiliar ideas which the mind is not yet throughly accustomed to. **1753** WARTON *Obs. Spenser's F. Q.* 141 It must be confest that his uncouth or rather unfamiliar language has deterr'd many from perusing him. **1829** LYTTON *Devereux* III. vi, His face did not seem unfamiliar to me. **1848** DICKENS *Dombey* xlix, Looking without interest or recognition at the unfamiliar walls around her. **1891** FARRAR *Darkn. & Dawn* xli, When Onesimus recovered full consciousness he did not recognise his unfamiliar surroundings.

Hence **Unfami·liarness.**

**1881** *Times* 17 May 4/6 A multitude of little changes of this kind..arouse a general sense of unfamiliarness.

**Unfamilia·rity.** (UN-1 12 and 5 b.)

**1755** JOHNSON *Dict.* Pref. C 2 How shall it be..recalled again..when it has once by disuse become unfamiliar, and by unfamiliarity unpleasing. **1861** MILL *Repr. Govt.* (1865) 62/2 The only serious obstacle is the unfamiliarity...But unfamiliarity is a disadvantage which..it only requires time to remove. **1880** MUIRHEAD *Gaius* IV. § 16 *note*, An inaccuracy, due..to his unfamiliarity with a procedure that had become a mere matter of history.

**Unfami·liarized,** *ppl. a.* (UN-1 8.)

**1775** S. J. PRATT *Liberal Opin.* xcvii. (1783) III. 211 Whenever the eye is struck with scenes to which it is unfamiliarised. **1817** COLERIDGE *Lay Serm.* 109 The plan itself would, I suspect, startle an unfamiliarized conscience. **1847–8** DE QUINCEY *Protestantism* Wks. 1858 VIII. 163 The gay mythologic religion of Greece..; that of Egypt, more revolting to unfamiliarised sensibilities.

† **Unfa·mous,** *a. Obs.* [UN-1 7 and 5 b.]

**1.** Not famous; unrenowned.

*c* **1384** CHAUCER *H. Fame* III. 56 Of the lettres oon or two Was molte away of euery name, So vnfamouse was wox hir fame. *a* **1560** PHAER *Æneid* X. D d 2 b, Let him dwell there, Vnfamous, free from wars, and honourlesse lead out his age.

**2.** Infamous, ill-famed.

*c* **1380** WYCLIF *Sel. Wks.* III. 357 Bi þes two unfamous lawes mai men wite whiche ben oþir. *c* **1489** CAXTON *Blanchardyn* xlviii. 186 Olde vnfamouse myschaunt, how arte thou soo folyshe..as for to wene to haue her. **1530** PALSGR. 328/1 Unfamouse, yvell named, *infame*. **1596** D. BLACK in Calderwood *Hist. Kirk Scot.* (1678) 337 To compear and answer for certain unreverent, unfamous and undecent speeches.

**Unfana·tical,** *a.* (UN-1 7.) **1826** COLERIDGE in *Lit. Rem.* (1836) III. 52 The prudential morals..that have characterized the unfanatical clergy since the Revolution in

1688 **1828** J. T. RUTT in *Burton's Diary* IV. 441 *note*, The signatures are 164, all quite unfanatical. **Unfa·nciable,** *a.* (UN-[1] 7 b.) **1669** EARL ORRERY *Parthen.* (1676) 796, I could not hinder myself from saying in unfanciable Transports [etc.].

**Unfa·ncied,** *ppl. a.* (UN-[1] 8.)

**1655** EARL ORRERY *Parthen.* I. I. 14 So many unfancy'd joyes disclose themselves. **1771** KELLY *Clementina* V. 62 Hence with his more than crocodile complaining,.. Let him teach tears of yet unfancy'd falshood. **1840** BROWNING *Sordello* I. 232 Till some growth, Unfancied yet, exuberantly clothe A surface solid now.

**Unfa·nciful,** *a.* (UN-[1] 7.) **1815** L. HUNT *Feast Poets*, etc. 48 There is something not inelegant or unfanciful in the conduct of Mr. Hayley's Triumphs of Temper. **1839** G. DARLEY *Beaum. & Fletcher's Wks.* (Rtldg.) p. xxiv, Ambitious fustian,..unfanciful extravagance.

**Unfa·nkle,** *v. Sc.* [UN-[2] 4 b.] *trans.* To unfetter, set free.

**1824** MACTAGGART *Gallovid. Encycl.* 113 The auld fowk left now closer draw, O' care their sauls unfankle.

**Unfa·nned,** *ppl. a.* (UN-[1] 8.) **1764** GOLDSM. *Trav.* 222 Their level life is but a mouldering fire, Unquench'd by want, unfann'd by strong desire. **1816** SCOTT *Old Mort.* xxxvii, Their zeal, unfanned by persecution, died gradually away.

**Unfanta·stic,** *a.* (UN-[1] 7.)

**1794** T. TAYLOR *Plotinus* Introd. p. xxv, Nature operates without knowledge in an unphantastic manner. **1842** LYTTON *Zanoni* 22 His wife was a daughter of quiet, sober, and unfantastic England. **1871** PALGRAVE *Lyr. Poems* 2 That unfantastic strain, Void of weak fever and self-conscious cry, ..What modern hand can try?

**Unfanta·stical,** *a.* (UN-[1] 7.) [**1775** ASH.] **1862** R. H. PATTERSON *Ess. Hist. & Art* 334 In any common-sense and unfantastical view of the matter.

**Unfa·rced,** *ppl. a.* (UN-[1] 8.)

**1725** *Fam. Dict.* s.v. *Potage*, They may be garnish'd with farc'd or unfarc'd Lettice. **1775** ASH, *Unfarced*.., not farced, not stuffed. **1890** CHILD *Ballads* IV. 232/2 C is a briefer, that is, an unfarced, form of B.

**Unfa·rcical,** *a.* (UN-[1] 7.) **1850** L. HUNT *Autobiog.* x. II. 25 Some of these comic actors..are as unfarcical as can be imagined in their interior.

†**Unfa·rdle,** *v. Obs.* [UN-[2] 4 b.] *trans.* To unload, unburden, discharge.

**1599** NASHE *Lenten Stuffe* H 3, Our Fisherman..vnfardled to the King his whole sachel of wonders. **1706** STEVENS I, *Desenfardelar*, to unfardle, to unpack.

**Unfarewe·lled,** *a.* (UN-[1] 9.) **1704** D'URFEY *Abrad. & Panth.* i. 15 The pangs she feels To part unfarwell'd to his gloomy cells, From her lov'd Abradate.

**Unfa·ring,** *ppl. a. Obs.* exc. *Sc.* Also *Sc.* 6 onfarrand, 9 on-, unfarrant. [UN-[1] 10.] Unattractive, unpleasant. Also †**Unfa·ringly** *adv. Obs.*

**1513** DOUGLAS *Æneid* IX. ix. 52 Wyth drawin swerd in hand, And quhite targat, onsemly and onfarrand. **1519** HORMAN *Vulg.* 57 b, He went with an vnfaryng chere [L. *vultu abducto*]. *Ibid.*, He loked vnfaryngly [L. *truci fuit aspectu*]. *c* **1530** tr. *Erasmus' Serm. Ch. Jesus* (1901) 38 So that it, whiche a lytle to fore semed unfarynge, waxeth amyable: whiche semed amyable, waxeth vnfarynge. **1818** HOGG *Hunt of Eildon* ii, O, man, ye're an unfarrant beast! **1887** *Suppl. Jamieson* 179 An onfarant body.

**Unfarme,** var. UNFERME *a. Obs.*

**Unfa·rming,** *ppl. a.* (UN-[1] 10.) **1797** J. WHITAKER in Polwhele *Trad. & Recoll.* (1826) II. 469, I have had cares and anxieties,..that you un-farming divines can hardly conceive.

**Unfarrant,** Sc. variant of UNFARING *ppl. a.*

**Unfa·rrowed,** *ppl. a.* (UN-[2] 4, 8.) **1842** TENNYSON *Walking to Mail* 92 We took them all, till she was left.., the Niobe of swine, And so return'd unfarrow'd to her sty.

**Unfa·shion,** *sb.* (UN-[1] 12.)

**1822** GALT *Sir A. Wylie* xxv, I have fallen in, notwithstanding the unfashion of my apparel, with some creditable acquaintance. **1876** MISS YONGE *Womankind* xiii, Sunday-schools were the fashion of one generation, then the unfashion.

**Unfa·shion,** *v.* [UN-[2] 4.] *trans.* To undo the fashion or make of.

**1569** J. SANFORD tr. *Agrippa's Van. Artes* 170 b, They rente our Sauioure Christe in peeces,..and..do facion and vnfacion him vnto what forme they liste. **1580** LUPTON *Sivqila* 23 Man..doth so disorder and unfashion himselfe, that you wyll not take hym that was laste yeare, to be hymselfe thys yeare. **1611** SPEED *Hist. Gt. Brit.* IX. ii. § 10 They to curry fauour with the Normans..altogether vnfashioned themselues to imitate them. **1631** QUARLES *Samson* Wks. (Grosart) II. 149/1 Our sinfull usage does unfashion What heaven hath made, and makes a new creation.

**Unfa·shionable,** *a.* and *sb.* [UN-[1] 7 b, 5 b.]

†**1.** Incapable of being fashioned or shaped; not admitting of a material form. *Obs.*

**1563** MAN *Musculus' Commonpl.* 47 They doe sinne in that they set forth to the invisible and unfashionable God an image of an olde man with a hore beard. **1607** HIERON *Wks.* I. 236 Thou, beeing a builder, when a stone breakes or is vnfashionable, throwest it from thee.

†**2.** Badly shaped or formed. *Obs.*

**1594** SHAKS. *Rich. III*, I. i. 22 Scarse halfe made vp, And that so lamely and vnfashionable, That dogges barke at me, as I halt by them. **1611** SPEED *Hist. Gt. Brit.* VI. v. § 6. 58 He was of stature tall, of complexion pale and wan, of body somewhat grosse and vnfashionable. **1638** STRAFFORD *Lett.* (1739) II. 197 The Pikes short and ill-headed, their Arms unfashionable and very little good. **1663** COWLEY *Cutter Coleman St.* Pref., The slight Reparations..of an Old and unfashionable Building.

**3.** Of actions, conduct, etc.: Not in accordance with the prevailing fashion.

**1648** BOYLE *Seraph. Love* (1659) 158 As Unfashionable as such a Profession may seem in a Gentleman not yet two and Twenty. **1693** LOCKE *Educ.* § 70 All the Actions of Childishness, and unfashionable Carriage, and whatever Time and Age will of it self be sure to reform. **1759** JOHNSON *Idler* No. 48 ¶ 8 They give the mind an unfashionable cast. **1776** ADAM SMITH *W. N.* I. ix. (1869) I. 101 It is there [*sc.* in Holland] unfashionable not to be a man of business. **1843** BETHUNE *Sc. Fireside Stor.* 16 She had herself been bred in the country where unfashionable revels of this kind are quite common.

**4.** Of persons: Not following the current fashion; not living in a fashionable way.

**1660** F. BROOKE tr. *Le Blanc's Trav.* 340 These unfashionable Doctors had mind on nothing but to satisfie their insatiable avarice. **1693** CONGREVE in *Dryden's Juvenal* XI. (1697) 290 Then, that Unfashionable Man am I, With me they'd starve for want of Ivory. **1704** STEELE *Tender Husb.* v. i, Let me come at the intruder on ladies' private hours—the unfashionable monster! **1766** [ANSTEY] *Bath Guide* i. 70 When Sim, unfashionable Ninny, In public calls me Cousin Jenny. **1865** DICKENS *Mut. Fr.* I. ix, They sat side by side, a hopelessly Unfashionable pair. **1890** *Spectator* 16 Aug., Far from the madding crowd of fashionable or unfashionable society.

**b.** *sb.* An unfashionable person.

**1822** [LADY BLESSINGTON] *Magic Lantern* 19 The crowds ..tempted me to stroll into that gay *rendezvous* of fashionables, as well as unfashionables. **1831** *Westm. Rev.* XIV. 436 The fashionables are almost uniformly witty and agreeable, the unfashionables stupid and disagreeable.

Hence **Unfa·shionableness.**

**1693** LOCKE *Educ.* § 184 Natural Unfashionableness being much better than apish, affected Postures. **1884** *Contemp. Rev.* July 102 All that people will see in this latter sort of work..will be its shapelessness, *plus* its unfashionableness.

**Unfa·shionably,** *adv.* [UN-[1] 11.] In an unfashionable manner; at variance with the prevailing fashion; so as to be unfashionable.

**1621** LADY M. WROTH *Urania* 122 Assuredly more there was of this Song, or else she had with her vnframed and vnfashioned thoughts, as vnfashionably fram'd these lines. **1683** OLDHAM *Wks.* (1686) 99 That sniveling Puritan, who spite of all the mode Would be unfashionably good. *a* **1704** T. BROWN tr. *Sylvius' Death Lucretia* Wks. 1709 III. II. 84 At thy Work among thy Maids unfashionably busy. **1797** J. LAWRENCE in *Monthly Mag.* XLVIII. 490, I..am most unfashionably unacquainted with all..the great post-roads and cross-roads. **1871** *Figure Training* 50 Her waist is not only unfashionably, but..almost disproportionately large.

**Unfa·shioned,** *ppl. a.* [UN-[1] 8.]

**1.** Not wrought into form or shape.

**1538** ELYOT, *Ineffigiatus*, vnfacyoned, withoute good proporcyon. **1561** T. NORTON *Calvin's Inst.* I. 38 When Moses sheweth that the very vnfashioned lump [of the world] was susteined in him [*sc.* the Spirit]. **1635** DONNE *Elegy* xv. 97 Countlesse multitudes Of formlesse curses, projects unmade up, Abuses yet unfashion'd. **1669** STURMY *Mariner's Mag.* b j, Go forth, thou shapeless Embryon of my Brain, Unfashion'd as thou art. **1712** *Spect.* No. 554 ¶ 9 Many a good natural Genius is lost, or lies unfashioned, like a Jewel in the Mine. **1764** GOLDSM. *Trav.* 330, I see the lords of human kind pass by.., By forms unfashion'd, fresh from Nature's hand. **1848** T. AIRD *Winter Day, Evening* 24 A cloudy confluence of unfashioned light.

†**2.** Not refined or polished; not made elegant or fashionable: **a.** Of persons. *Obs.*

**1606** DANIEL *Queen's Arcadia* 2509 Worthier people too, of subtler spirits, Then these vnfashion'd and vncomb'd rude swaines. **1673** DRYDEN *Marr. à la Mode* II. i, An unfashioned untravelled mere Sicilian is a *bête.* **1711** STEELE *Spect.* No. 154 ¶ 2 A sober modest Man was always looked upon by both Sexes as a precise unfashioned Fellow. **1821** MAR. & R. L. EDGEWORTH *Mem.* I. 75 She was a plump goodnatured unfashioned girl, with little knowledge of any sort and no accomplishments.

†**b.** Of things. *Obs.*

**1630** J. TAYLOR (Water P.) *Water Cormorant* Wks. III. 6/2 That Muld-Sack for his most vnfashion'd fashions Is the fit patterne of their transformations. **1670** DRYDEN *1st Pt. Conq. Granada* III. i, There's something roughly noble there, Which, in unfashion'd Nature, looks Divine. **1695** J. EDWARDS *Perfect. Script.* 436 Illiterate, blunt, unfashion'd language.

**Unfa·st,** *a.* Now *rare.* Also 4 unfest(e. [OE. *unfæst* (UN-[1] 7), = WFris. *on-*, *ûnfest*, MDu. and Du. *onvast*, MHG. *unvast*, MDa. *ufast*; OHG. *unfesti*, *-vesti* (MHG. *unveste*, G. *unfest*).]

**1.** Insecure.

*c* **888** K. ÆLFRED *Boeth.* xi. § 2 For þæm þe æ3þer is unfæst, 3e seo wyrd 3e seo 3esælð. *c* **897** — *Gregory's Past. C.* 37. *a* **1300** *E. E. Psalter* xvii. 40 Þou tobreddest mi gainges under me, And mi steppes noght unfest þai be. *Ibid.* xxvi. 4 Mi faas þat are, Þai are unfest and felle sare. **13..** *Prose Psalter* cviii. 23 (Dubl. MS.), Myn knowes beþ vnfast for fastyng. *c* **1584** T. MATHEW *Let.* in *Life Sir C. Hatton* (1847) 407 You be not the first, Sir,..that have found both friends unfast and neighbours unthankful. **1818** TODD, *Unfast*, not safe; not secure. **1883** R. W. DIXON *Mano* I. xiv. 45 Ah, could he but have rent shame's unfast cloak, And seen her heart.

**2.** Not close or tight.

**1648** HEXHAM II. s.v. *Leken*, To Leake as unfast Vessels.

Hence **Unfa·stness,** want of firmness. *rare.*

**1398** TREVISA *Barth. De P. R.* XVII. cl. (Bodl. MS.), Þat treen beþ scharp with pikes & þornes..comeþ of vnfastenes & vnsadnes of þe tre. **1616** T. ADAMS *Forest of Thorns* Wks. (1629) 1055 Hee would haue it [*sc.* thorniness] caused by the insoliditie and vnfastnesse of the Tree.

†**Unfa·st,** *v. dial. Obs.* [UN-[2] 3.] = next.

**1684** MERITON *Yorksh. Ale* Gloss. 112 To unfest is to untye or unloose.

**Unfa·sten,** *v.* Also 4 onvestne, 5 onfestyn. [UN-[2] 3 and 7.]

**1.** *trans.* **a.** To unfix; to deprive of firmness or fixity; to make loose or slack. Also *absol.*

*a* **1225** *Ancr. R.* 252 Al his attente is uorte unuestnen heorten & fort to binimen luue, þet halt men togederes. **1382** WYCLIF *Isaiah* xiv. 27 The Lord forsothe of ostes demede, and who shal moun vnfastnen? **1532** HERVET *Xenophon's Househ.* 55 b, Els the sonne drynge the erthe away from the rootes of the plante, shulde lewse and vnfasten it, and so kyll it. **1597** SHAKS. *2 Hen. IV*, IV. i. 209 Plucking to vnfixe an Enemie, Hee doth vnfasten so, and shake a friend. **1698** ATTERBURY *Serm.* (1737) IV. 316 He must take care not to..come within reach of anything that may anyways unfasten his resolutions. **1736** CARTE *Ormonde* II. 373 The design of this proposal was, first to unfasten him, and then to lay him totally aside.

**b.** To detach; to undo or release.

*c* **1440** *Promp. Parv.* 365/1 Onfestyn, *idem quod* on-losyn. *a* **1586** SIDNEY *Arcadia* II. viii, He had no sooner unfastned his hold, but that a wave forcibly spoiled his weaker hand of hold. **1633** T. JAMES *Voy.* 14 We vnfastened our Ship, and came to saile. **1667** MILTON *P. L.* II. 879 Then..every Bolt and Bar Of massie Iron or sollid Rock with ease [she] Unfast'ns. **1797** MRS. RADCLIFFE *Italian* xii, We will see whether my key cannot unfasten all the locks that hold it. **1860** WARTER *Sea-board* II. 459 Unfastening, as it were, the links that bound the people to their Parish Church. **1862** MISS BRADDON *Lady Audley* vii, Lady Audley was standing unfastening her dress. *a* **1873** LYTTON in *Life & Lett.* (1883) I. 289 The man began to unfasten the boat.

*fig.* **1655** tr. *Sorel's Com. Hist. Francion* II. 29 She.. prayed me to come to her house as soon as I could unfasten my self from my Mistresse.

**2.** *intr.* To become detached or loose; to open; *fig.* to separate.

*c* **1315** SHOREHAM *Poems* I. 2093 Nou lestne: 3ef þe oþer oþren so by-swykeþ, No mo3e hy nou3t onuestne. *c* **1430** *Pilgr. Lyf Manhode* I. cxxvi. (1869) 67 The bocle holt and keepeth faste the girdel that it vnfastne nouht. **1865** SWINBURNE *Atalanta* 91 From this time..My lips shall not unfasten till I die.

**Unfa·stenable,** *a.* (UN-[1] 7 b.) **1880** *Blackw. Mag.* Mar. 377/1 A belt not always unfastenable in a moment.

**Unfa·stened,** *ppl. a.* (UN-[1] 8.)

**1587** GOLDING *De Mornay* xxiii. 401 The Image of Serapis hung vnfastened in the ayre. **1611** SPEED *Theat. Gt. Brit.* (1614) 132/2 An Iland that removeth from place to place, as the winde forceth her spongeous and unfastened body. **1794** MRS. RADCLIFFE *Myst. Udolpho* xlii, She asked the housekeeper whether she was certain no door had been left unfastened. **1861** GEO. ELIOT *Silas M.* iv, Where could he be ..on such an evening, leaving..his door unfastened? **1897** MRS. E. L. VOYNICH *Gadfly* (1904) 69/2 The unfastened sleeve fell back, showing a series of..scars covering the arm.

**Unfasti·dious,** *a.* (UN-[1] 7.)

**1815** JANE AUSTEN *Emma* x, So prosing—so undistinguishing and unfastidious. **1822** LAMB *Elia* I. *Decay of Beggars*, Well fare the soul of unfastidious Vincent Bourne! **1865** *Sat. Rev.* 4 Feb. 141/2 An unfastidious taste is not offended by its style.

Hence **Unfasti·diousness.**

**1881** GRANT WHITE *Eng. Without & Within* 476 None the less, however, was I puzzled to account for the unfastidiousness of palate.

**Unfa·thered,** *a.*[1] [UN-[1] 9.]

**1.** Having no (known or acknowledged) father; illegitimate.

**1597** SHAKS. *2 Hen. IV*, IV. iv. 122 The people feare me: for they doe obserue Vnfather'd Heires, and loathly Births of Nature. **1726** POPE *Odyss.* XIX. 187 Thy port asserts thee of distinguish'd race; No poor unfather'd product of disgrace. **1856** MRS. BROWNING *Aur. Leigh* VII. 327 Marian's babe, her poor unfathered child. **1874** TROLLOPE *Lady Anna* i, She would be a penniless unmarried female with a daughter, her child would be unfathered and base.

**2.** Unfatherly. *rare*[−1].

**1778** LANGHORNE *Owen of Carron* XVIII. 2 And Moray, with unfather'd Eyes,..Attends his human Sacrifice, Without the Grecian Painter's Veil.

**3.** Of obscure origin; unauthenticated.

**1830** DE QUINCEY *Bentley* Wks. 1863 VI. 55 Unfathered rumours, rumours unacknowledged and untraceable. **1888** BRYCE *Amer. Commw.* III. ci. 419 Men are..therefore ready to trust their own fancies or some unfathered tale.

**Unfa·thered,** *a.*[2] [UN-[2] 4, 8.] Deprived of a father; made fatherless.

*a* **1586** SIDNEY *Arcadia* III. xvii, Iole had her owne father killed by Hercules..& yet ere long this..unfathered Lady could sportfully put on the Lions skin. *c* **1600** SHAKS. *Sonn.* cxxiv, Yf my deare loue were but the childe of state, It might for fortunes basterd be vnfathered.

**Unfa·therlike,** *a.* or *adv.* (UN-[1] 7 c.) **1610** HEYWOOD *Gold. Age* III. i, Haue not these ruthlesse and remorselesse eyes (Vn-father-like) beheld their panting hearts?

**Unfa·therly,** *a.* [UN-[1] 7. Cf. Du. *onvaderlijk*, MHG. and G. *unväterlich*, Da. *ufaderlig*, MSw. *ofaderelik*; also OE. *unfæderlice* adv.] Unbefitting a father.

**1621** J. TAYLOR (Water P.) *Unnatural Father* Wks. (1630) 138/1 So hee performed his last vnfatherly deed vpon her. **1621** LADY M. WROTH *Urania* 209 To tirie, if by his vnfatherly tortures, shee may bee wrought to leaue louing you. **1784** COWPER *Tiroc.* 866 Nature, pulling at thine heart, Condemns th' unfatherly, th' imprudent part.

Hence **Unfa·therliness.**

**1850** L. HUNT *Autobiog.* xxv. III. 285 No hell. No unfatherliness. No monstrous exactions of assent to the incredible.

**Unfa·thomabi·lity.** (UN-[1] 12; cf. next.) **1866** CARLYLE *Remin.* (1881) II. 331 To my private self his divine reflections and unfathomabilities seemed stinted..and uncertain.

**Unfa·thomable,** *a.* [UN-[1] 7 b.]

**1.** *fig.* Of feelings, qualities, conditions, etc.: Incapable of being fully ascertained, explored, exhausted, etc.

**1617** COLLINS *Def. Bp. Ely* II. ix. 404 Who are you then to gage hearts, which Hieremy sayes are vnfaddomable. **1663** BP. PATRICK *Parab. Pilgr.* xxvii, Thy Goodness is unfathomable, else we should have sunk long before this beyond the depth of it. **1719** YOUNG *Busiris* v. i, An earnest Of vast unfathomable woes to come. **1768–74** TUCKER *Lt. Nat.* (1834) I. 119 What their real sentiments may be I shall not pretend to guess, for they are an unfathomable sort of people. **1807–12**

BENTHAM *Ration. Judic. Evid.* (1827) II. 315 Subjected to an unfathomable mass of punishment. **1850** THACKERAY *Pendennis* iv, Her eyes..shone with tenderness and mystery unfathomable. **1891** MEREDITH *One of our Conq.* xxvi, Lady Cantor spoke to her of Dudley's unfathomable gloom.

**2.** Incapable of being fathomed or measured; unsoundable, immeasurable, vast:

**a.** Of space (esp. in depth).

*a* **1676** HALE *Prim. Orig. Man.* II. vii. (1677) 187 Not.. meerly by the Superficies of the Sea, but by its vast depth, which in some places is unfathomable. **1712** ADDISON *Spect.* No. 420 ¶ 3 Those unfathomable Depths of Ether. **1799** KIRWAN *Geol. Ess.* 479 The unfathomable abysses of the ocean. **1815** SHELLEY *Alastor* 373 On the unfathomable stream The boat moved slowly. **1851** MRS. BROWNING *Casa Guidi Wind.* I. 760 Ye may well look up surprised To those unfathomable heavens that feed Your purple hills! **1879** MISS BRADDON *Cloven Foot* iv, The long dazzling boulevards stretching into unfathomable distance before her eyes.

**b.** In fig. contexts. (Cf. 1.)

**1640** BP. HALL *Chr. Moder.* II. § 7. 47 These are indeed unfadomable depths in that Ocean, wherin we shall vainly hope to pitch our anchor. **1672** STILLINGFL. *Serm.* xii. (1673) 237 O the unfathomable Abysse of Eternity! **1712** ADDISON *Spect.* No. 309 ¶ 14 Sounding the unfathomable Depths of Fate, Free-will and Fore-knowledge. **1739** WESLEY *'Lo! God is here!'* v, Thou source and life of all! Thou vast, unfathomable Sea! **1820** SHELLEY *Fiordispina* 9 For thou the wonders of the depth canst know Of this unfathomable flood of hours. **1855** MACAULAY *Hist. Eng.* xxi. IV. 575 In truth the depths of this man's knavery were unfathomable. **1859** GEO. ELIOT *A. Bede* iii, An unfathomable ocean of love and beauty.

*absol.* **1831** CARLYLE *Sartor Res.* II. viii, Two little visual Spectra of men, hovering..in the midst of the Unfathomable.

**c.** *fig.* Of the eyes.

**1817** SHELLEY *Rev. Islam* VI. xxxviii, The sweet peace of joy did almost fill The depth of her unfathomable look. **1854** THACKERAY *Newcomes* xxx, Her unfathomable eyes were wells of gloom. **1882** 'OUIDA' *Maremma* I. 212 Her lustrous, unfathomable, star-like eyes.

Hence **Unfa·thomableness.**

**1690** NORRIS *Beatitudes* (1692) 133 The Unfathomableness of the great Dispensation of Mercy. **1832** tr. *Tour Germ. Prince* II. xii. 244 The immortal secret.., the unfathomableness of which had so tormented the '*élégants*' of the metropolis. **1872** GEO. ELIOT *Middlem.* III. xxiii, In Mr. Horrock there was certainly an apparent unfathomableness, which offered play to the imagination.

**Unfa·thomably,** *adv.* [UN-[1] 11; cf. prec.] To an unfathomable extent.

**1695** BLACKMORE *Pr. Arth.* VII. 61 A wide mouth'd Den, ..That downward goes unfathomably deep, Beneath the subterranean Vaults. **1771** SMOLLETT *Humph. Cl.* 3 Sept., A surprising body of pure transparent water, unfathomably deep in many places. **1820** SHELLEY *Witch Atl.* xlix, The tremulous stars sparkled unfathomably. **1833** HT. MARTINEAU *Briery Creek* i. 4 His grandfather appeared to him ..unfathomably wise.

**Unfa·thomed,** *ppl. a.* [UN-[1] 8.]

**1.** Of unascertained depth; unsounded.

**1628** FELTHAM *Resolves* II. xxvii. 85 [The river] at last.. inwaves it selfe in the vnfathom'd Ocean. **1634** MILTON *Comus* in Birch *Wks.* (1738) I. p. vii, Halfe his wast Flood the wide Atlantique fills, And halfe the slow unfadom'd Stygian Poole. **1723** MRS. CENTLIVRE *Stolen Heiress* v, Ope' earth, hide me in thy unfathom'd womb. **1757** GRAY *Elegy* xiv, Full many a gem of purest ray serene, The dark unfathom'd caves of ocean bear. **1813** SHELLEY *Q. Mab* IV. 95 The lovely silence of the unfathomed main. **1873** PROCTOR *Expanse Heav.* 302 He still saw that cloudy light which speaks of star depths as yet unfathomed.

**b.** In fig. context. (Cf. 2.)

**1623** MIDDLETON & ROWLEY *Sp. Gipsy* III. iii, A soul drown'd deep In the unfathom'd seas of matchless sorrows. **1683** NORRIS *Passions of Saviour* 5 Sing the unfathom'd depths of love. **1755** YOUNG *Centaur* iv, The first moment man quits hold of his Creator, he drops! In distraction and ruin, how unfathomed his fall! **1817** BYRON *Manfred* I. i. 243 By thy unfathom'd gulfs of guile,..I call upon thee! **1861** W. F. COLLIER *Hist. Eng. Lit.* 146 The unfathomed depths of the poet's mind.

**2.** *fig.* Not fully explored or known; unascertained; immense.

**1659** T. PECKE *Parnassi Puerp.* 181 Nature in the unfathom'd Stagyrite, Compos'd a Body, abject to the sight. **1688** PRIOR *Ode* vi, Man does with dangerous Curiosity These unfathom'd Wonders try. **1784** COWPER *Task* II. 538 When in him reside Grace, knowledge, comfort—an unfathom'd store. **1809** COLERIDGE *Friend* (1865) 61 If the mere acquiescence in truth, uncomprehended and unfathomed, were sufficient. **1897** *Atlantic Monthly* LXXIX. 35 That was the thought of the unfathomed might of man.

†**Unfa·thomless,** *a.* (UN-[1] 5 a.) **1673** JANEWAY *Heaven on E.* 20 Oh that I might lose myself..as a small drop in the unfathomless depth of his Love.

†**Unfa·tigable,** *a. Obs.* [UN-[1] 7 b and 5 b.] Indefatigable.

*c* **1550** *Clariodus* v. 1925 Apollo restless and unfatigabill. **1592** NASHE *P. Penilesse* F 2 b, As industrie and vnfatigable toyle rayseth meane persons..to high thrones of authoritie. **1622** MALYNES *Anc. Law-Merch.* 84 Which cannot be done without an vnfatigable industrie. **1627** *Lisander & Cal.* IX. 184 Hee seemed so unfatigable in his armes.

**Unfati·guable,** *a.* (UN-[1] 7 b.)

**1799** SOUTHEY *Songs Amer. Indians, Huron's Address to Dead* iii, Those are the unfatigueable feet That traversed the forest tract. **1805** — *Madoc* II. ix. 84 With fleet feet and unfatiguable. **1873** RUSKIN *Fors Clav.* xxxiii. 5 The waist elastic as a reed, and as unfatiguable.

**Unfati·gue,** *v.* [UN-[2] 4 b.] *refl.* To restore (oneself) from fatigue.

**1734** CAREY *Chrononhotonthologos* i, Fatigu'd with the tremendous Toil of War,..on downy Couch..Himself he unfatigues with gentle Slumbers. **1836** B. HALL *Schloss Hainfeld* i. 14 May I trust you will induce Mrs Hall to 'unfatigue' herself..in this Tadmore in the wilderness?

**Unfati·gued,** *ppl. a.* (UN-[1] 8.)

**1705** J. PHILIPS *Blenheim* 39 Over dank, and dry, They journey toilsome, unfatigu'd with Length Of March. **1775** S. J. PRATT *Liberal Opin.* vi. (1783) I. 19 Celebrated for volubility of conversation, and so unfatigued a continuer, that nothing human could ever come in for a word. **1860** HOLME LEE *Leg. Fairy L.* 93 He was again standing beside me, perfectly cool and unfatigued. **1879** SPENCER *Data of Ethics* x. § 65. 179 Sounds..which yield to unfatigued ears intense pleasure.

**Unfati·guing,** *ppl. a.* (UN-[1] 10.)

**1808** SCOTT in *Lockhart* I. i. 20 That imperceptible and unfatiguing exercise. **1822–7** GOOD *Study Med.* (1829) III. 473 Provided the patient passes a quiet and unfatiguing life. **1865** *Pall Mall G.* 31 Aug. 3/2 To accept scanty pay for monotonous but unfatiguing work.

**Unfa·tted,** *ppl. a.* (UN-[1] 8.) **1752** J. HILL *Hist. Anim.* 486 The pheasant..when in good condition..is little less than a common unfatted fowl.

**Unfau·lty,** *a.* (UN-[1] 7.)

**1548** UDALL, etc., *Erasm. Par. Matt.* xxi. 83 Whom because he had prouoked agaynst hym with well doynge, he made them not vnfaultye. **1587** *Mirr. Mag., Locrinus* iii, What meane I here th' unfaulty for to blame? **1628** WITHER *Brit. Rememb.* 289 b, In a Watch or Clocke When it is out of order once, or broke, The wheeles that are unfaultie move awry. **1645** MILTON *Tetrach.* 31 A Covnant therfore brought to that passe, is on the unfaulty side without injury dissolv'd. **1741** RICHARDSON *Pamela* (1824) I. xiv. 252 And glad I am that the poor unfaulty baby is so justly beloved by Mr. B—. **1855** SINGLETON *Virgil* II. 27 Be it allowed to me To pity my unfaulty friend's mishap.

**Unfa·vourable,** *a.* (and *sb.*). [UN-[1] 7 b.]

**1.** Not favourable, in various senses: **a.** Of persons, opinions, etc.

**1548** UDALL *Erasm. Par. Luke* xix. 147 The Pharisees ..thynke theimselues fortunate that they carry the deuill on theyre backes, ye roughest sitter possible and ye moste vnfauourable. **1678** SIR G. MACKENZIE *Crim. Laws Scot.* II. xxii. § i. (1699) 239 After a Crime is proved, the Pannel is most unfavourable. **1777** ROBERTSON *Hist. Amer.* II. ¶ 12 Talavera, at last, made..an unfavourable report to Ferdinand and Isabella. **1779** *Mirror* No. 32, He was pleased.. to communicate his opinions. The last I found generally unfavourable both of men and things. **1835** T. MITCHELL *Acharn. of Aristoph.* 200 *note*, The insertion of a choriambus.., viewed with an unfavourable eye by Bentley and Elmsley. **1890** *Retrospect Med.* CII. 45 The prognosis was unfavourable only in severe cases.

**b.** Of conditions, circumstances, times, etc. Also const. *to* or *for*.

**1748** *Anson's Voy.* I. viii. 77 These tempests.., though unattended by any other unfavourable circumstance, were yet rendered more mischievous to us by their inequality. **1766** SMOLLETT *Trav.* xi. I. 174, I have always found a cold and damp atmosphere the most unfavourable of any to my constitution. **1796** MME. D'ARBLAY *Camilla* III. 444 [She] thought the moment unfavourable for a tête-à-tête. **1846** MRS. A. MARSH *Father Darcy* II. xvi. 277, I must dispose of the outlaying estates in Northamptonshire, and these times are unfavourable. **1874** J. GEIKIE *Gt. Ice Age* xxiii. 302 In situations that would now be considered most unfavourable to their growth.

**c.** Of winds or weather.

**1788** GIBBON *Decl. & F.* xli. IV. 132 An unfavourable wind detained them four days. **1789** CHARLOTTE SMITH *Ethelinde* IV. 155 A successless hunt, the morning being frosty and unfavourable. **1820** W. SCORESBY *Acc. Arctic Reg.* I. 307 The winds were mostly unfavourable. **1865** CARLYLE *Fredk. Gt.* XIX. viii. V. 581 In spite of..the unfavorablest weather, it was..his fixed purpose to recapture Dresden.

†**d.** Of diseases, physical injuries, etc. *Obs.*

**1782** V. KNOX *Ess.* clxiii. (1819) III. 217 They were seized with an unfavourable small-pox. **1793** COWPER *Let. to J. Hill* 10 Dec., You mentioned..an unfavourable sprain that you had received. **1818** SCOTT *Hrt. Midl.* xxxiii, Her mind is totally alienated, which..is sometimes the consequence of an unfavourable confinement.

**2.** Of features or appearance: Ill-favoured.

**1776** E. TOPHAM *Lett. Edin.* 83 The men are large and disproportioned with unfavourable, long, and saturnine countenances. **1782** A. HIGHMORE *Ramble Coast Sussex* (1873) 47 She said I did not carry an unfavourable appearance. **1825** SCOTT *Talism.* v, With all this most unfavourable exterior, there was one trait in the features of both which argued alertness and intelligence.

**b.** Creating a bad impression.

**1817** JAS. MILL *Brit. India* II. IV. vi. 230 A procedure which bore a most unfavourable appearance.

**3.** *sb.* An unfavourable result.

**1838** DE MORGAN *Ess. Probab.* 42 But of these 36 throws, any one of the five unfavourables of the first throw may combine with any one of the second throw.

Hence **Unfa·vourableness.**

**1764** *Phil. Trans.* LIV. 105 The best account..of my observation, however imperfect through the unfavourableness of the weather. **1842** LOUDON *Suburban Hort.* 123 The unsuitableness of the soil, the unpropitiousness of the climate, and the unfavourableness of the seasons.

**Unfa·vourably,** *adv.* [UN-[1] 11.] In an unfavourable manner: **a.** In respect of opinion, statement, etc.

**1460** *Paston Lett.* Suppl. (1901) 63 Thei reporten you unfavorably and withoute credence, as men seyn, and some I have herd. *a* **1680** GLANVILL (J.), Bacon speaks not unfavourably of this. *a* **1768** SECKER *Serm.* (1771) V. xv. 335 There hath been..something or another that should not have been; else so many would not have judged..so unfavourably. **1816** SCOTT *Old Mort.* xv, If our summons is unfavourably received we will instantly attack. **1866** J. H. NEWMAN *Let. to Pusey* 86 That compromise of which our countrymen report so unfavourably from abroad.

**b.** In respect of circumstances, conditions, etc.

**1833** CARLYLE *Misc.* (1840) IV. 337 A richly endowed, unfavourably situated nature. **1846** MRS. A. MARSH *Father Darcy* II. ix. 151 His tones and gestures..contrasted unfavourably with the appearance either of Catesby or Winter. **1871** A. MEADOWS *Man. Midwifery* (ed. 2) 230, I believe it.. to compare very unfavourably with the death-rate of the supposed more formidable operation.

**Unfa·voured,** *ppl. a.* (UN-[1] 8.)

**1774** GOLDSM. *Nat. Hist.* II. 251 There was a time, when these unfavoured children of Nature, were the peculiar favourites of the great. **1796** [see UNCULTIVATED *ppl. a.* 1]. **1908** WALLACE *Children Chapel* 175 This diminished the reputation and profit of the unfavored players.

**Unfa·vouring,** *ppl. a.* (UN-[1] 10.) **1835** *Woman* II. 203 In an unfavouring soil, where many seeds are sown, we reap a full harvest of weeds. **1878** STEVENSON *Inland Voy.* 17 We still spread our canvas to the unfavouring air.

**Unfaysible,** obs. f. UNFEASIBLE *a.*

**Unfea·red,** *ppl. a.* [UN-[1] 8.]

†**1.** Not affected by fear; undismayed. *Obs.*

**1435** MISYN *Fire of Love* 100 Als þi saule criste truly has soght & vnferde & in sekynge wolde not cees. *c* **1475** *Cath. Angl.* 127/2 (A), Vn-Ferde, *vbi* hardy. **1600** FAIRFAX *Tasso* I. lii, Vnfear'd in fight, vntir'd with hurt or wound. **1611** B. JONSON *Catiline* IV. i, Though Heauen should speake, with all his wrath at once,..we should stand vpright, and vnfear'd. **1627** MAY *Lucan* II. 556 He yet vnfear'd, his anger doth retain.

**2.** Not regarded with fear; undreaded.

**1612** *Two Noble K.* I. ii. 71 A most unbounded Tyrant, whose successes Makes heaven unfeard. **1667** MILTON *P. L.* IX. 187 Nor nocent yet, but on the grassie Herbe Fearless unfeard he slept. **1796** COLERIDGE *Destiny of Nations* 146 That..herself Unfeared by Fellow-natures, she might wait On the poor labouring man with kindly looks. **1839** BAILEY *Festus* 291 It is the thing Unfeared and unforethought which tempts, betrays. **1868** MORRIS *Earthly Par.* (1870) I. II. 597 Till death unfeared at last shall come to me.

**Unfea·rful,** *a.* [UN-[1] 7.] Having no fear; fearless.

**1544** BETHAM *Precepts War* I. cxliii. G viij b, To chose souldyours whyche ben vnfearfull and couragious to encountre wyth theyr enemyes. *a* **1569** KINGESMYLL *Comf. Afflict.* (1585) E 6 Other notable women, that were so unfearefull to suffer moste sharpe death. **1603** BRETON *Mad World* Wks. (Grosart) II. 10/1 He..led me into his house, the doore open, as unfearefull of theeves, as vnprovided for strangers. **1784** *Unfortunate Sensibility* II. 155 Thou mayest enjoy thy full inheritance unfearful of the shafts of envy. **1850** ALISON *Hist. Eur.* (ed. 2) XIII. xc. 270 The humming-bird,..so quick in its motions, so unfearful of man. **1888** *Encycl. Brit.* XXIII. 313/2 The very fish..would glide, unfearful, between his [Thoreau's] hands.

**Unfea·rfully,** *adv.* [UN-[1] 11; cf. prec.] Fearlessly, resolutely.

*c* **1430** *Life St. Kath.* (1884) 33 Þe holy seruant..was ryght nought troubled, but vnferfully sche commended þe labour of hir chyualrye vnto our lord god. **1563** GOLDING *Cæsar* (1565) 81 b, Our enemies fought stoutly and unfearfullye. **1571** — *Calvin on Ps.* iv. 3 Unfearfully to despise whatsoever they wrought against him. **1615** G. SANDYS *Trav.* 270 The vndanted giuing or receiuing of wounds; and life so vnfearfully parted with.

**Unfea·ring,** *ppl. a.* (UN-[1] 10.)

**1796** *Monthly Mag.* II. 615 Him would the storm-vext Adriatic surge,..The wreck of shattering worlds, Unfearing smite. **1824** MISS MITFORD *Village* Ser. I. 18 In addition to these multifarious talents, he was ready, obliging, and unfearing. **1868** LYNCH *Rivulet* CLXI. viii, Down with unfearing heart I lie, And wait sleep's healing mystery.

Hence **Unfea·ringly** *adv.*

**1895** *Contemp. Rev.* Mar. 434 Unfearingly to allow the total severance of the bond.

**Unfeary,** var. UNFEIRIE *a. Sc.*

†**Unfea·sable,** *a. Obs.* [UN-[1] 7 b and 5 b.] = UNFEASIBLE *a.*

**1628** MEAD in Ellis *Orig. Lett.* Ser. I. III. 268 Their works seem now altogether unfeisable. **1640** SIR K. DIGBY in *Lismore Papers* Ser. II. (1888) IV. 133 All those wayes were not onely very difficult and peradventure vnfeazable [etc.]. **1673** *S'too him Bayes* 15 The bishop was a weak man, and laid an unfeisable design.

Hence †**Unfea·sableness**; †**Unfea·sably** *adv.*

**1612** WOODALL *Surg. Mate* Wks. (1653) 390 To brand it with pittiful inhibitions..and *unfeasablenesse [etc.]. **1678** CUDWORTH *Intell. Syst.* 682 Those small and pitiful attempts ..only showing the unfeisableness and impossibility thereof. **1638** JUNIUS *Paint. Ancients* 331 Workes..done by an unspeakable way of Art, delicatly, divinely, *unfeisably, etc. insinuate nothing els.

**Unfeasibi·lity.** (UN-[1] 12; cf. next.) **1655** FULLER *Hist. Camb.* 70 The failing is not in the unfeacibility of the Design, but in the accidentall defaults of the Vndertakers. **1839** CARLYLE *Chartism* ix, The matter..can at least solace itself with hope, and die gently, convinced of *un*feasibility. **1850** — *Latter-d. Pamph.* ii. 9 Nature..taught him the futility and unfeasibility of the system followed here.

**Unfea·sible,** *a.* (UN-[1] 7 and 5 b.)

**1527** *St. Papers Hen. VIII*, I. 247 As the discripcion.. shulde be to tedious..to rede, so the explicacion therof shulde be unfaysible unto me. **1648** J. BEAUMONT *Psyche* XVIII. ccxix, But seeing this unfeasible, the sight Redoubled her compassionate sorrows weight. **1657** G. STARKEY *Helmont's Vind.* 145 This Logick would make almost all Mechanicks to be impossible, if what ever you cannot do must straight be unfecible. **1673** O. WALKER *Educ.* (1677) 37 Harshnes is discovered in..enjoying things in themselves too difficult, unfesible, unsupportable. **1804** COLEBROOKE *Husb. Bengal* 35 Circumstances that render it unfeasible to enter these fields to select the ripe plants, without damaging the rest. **1886** *Brit. Med. Jrnl.* 12 June 1142/2 The use..is doubtless charming in theory,..but, in practice, it is unfeasible.

Hence **Unfea·sibleness.**

**1653** HOLCROFT *Procopius, Pers. Wars* II. 42 Seeing excessive undertakings ever are rewarded with unfaisibleness.

**Unfea·sted,** *ppl. a.* (UN-[1] 8.) **1636** HEYWOOD *Love's Mistress* I, Nor shall they part from hence with unfeasted eares. **1897** R. KEARTON *Nature & Camera* 51 The trippers had to return with .. their curiosity unfeasted. **Unfea·stful,** *a.* (UN-[1] 7.) † Non-festival. *a* **1564** BECON *Art. Chr. Relig.* xvii, Not on yᵉ feastful, nor on the vnfeastful, dayes only, but at al tymes.

**Unfea·stly,** *a.* [UN-[1] 7. Cf. G. *unfestlich.*] Not in festival trim.

*c* **1386** CHAUCER *Sqr.'s T.* 358 Hir liste nat appalled for to be Ne on the morwe vnfeestlich [*v.rr.* onfestelyche, vnfestly, etc.] for to se.

† **Unfea·t,** *a. Obs.*—[1] [UN-[1] 7.] Not well disposed; unfit.

*a* **1533** LD. BERNERS *Gold. Bk. M. Aurel.* (1535) C c iij b, They ar vnfete to do wel: & are holly disposed to do yl.

**Unfea·ther,** *v.* [UN-[2] 4 and 7.]

**1.** *trans.* To strip of feathers; to unplume.

**1483** *Cath. Angl.* 124/2 To vn-Fedyr, *expennare, explumare.* **1586** J. HOOKER *Hist. Irel.* in *Holinshed* II. 116/2 He so handled the matter, that he had vnfethered him of his best friends, aids, and helps. **1603** FLORIO *Montaigne* II. x. 236, I will love him that shall trace, or vnfeather me. *a* **1639** T. CAREW *Poems* Wks. (1824) 79 Love lent thee wings to flye, so hee Unfeather'd, now must rest with mee. **1681** RYCAUT tr. *Gracian's Critick* 183 None are here of those who can .. unfeather our Nests, whilst they enwrap us in the quilts. **1769** COLMAN *Oxonian in Town* I. 8 Ay, ay, we'll unfeather the whole nest in time.

**2.** *intr.* To lose the feathers.

**1849** J. A. CARLYLE tr. *Dante's Inf.* 202 When poor Icarus felt his loins unfeather by the heating of the wax.

**Unfea·thered,** *a.* [UN-[1] 9. Cf. OE. *ungefeðered*, MDu. *ongevedert*, G. *ungefiedert*, † *-federt*, older Da. *ufedret*, Sw. *ofjädrad.*]

**1.** Not provided or covered with feathers: **a.** Of birds, etc.

**1570** LEVINS *Manip.* 50 Vnfethered, *implumis.* **1605** A. WILLET *Hexapla Gen.* Ded., I .. haue brought forth my implumed and vnfeathered birds. **1653** JER. TAYLOR *Serm. for Year* I. Ep. Ded., They are like callow and unfeathered birds. **1697** DRYDEN *Virg. Georg.* IV. 745 Whose Nest some prying Churl had found, and thence, By Stealth, convey'd th'unfeather'd Innocence. **1780** COWPER *Sparrows in Trin. Coll.* 14 In hope of crumbs, Which kindly giv'n, may serve with food Convenient their unfeather'd brood. **1826** S. COOPER *First Lines Surg.* (ed. 5) 83 A roughness which is compared to the skin of an unfeathered goose. **1884** COUES *N. Amer. Birds* 86 Feathered Tracts and Unfeathered Spaces.

**b.** Applied generically to man.

*c* **1600** *Timon* v. iv. (1842) 86 A peripatetick is a two legd liuing creature, gressible, unfeathered. **1681** DRYDEN *Abs. & Achit.* I. 170 And all to leaue what with his Toil he won To that unfeather'd two-legg'd thing, a Son. **1754** WARBURTON *Bolingbroke's Philos.* i. 36 Ribaldry and ill language disgrace the *animal implume bipes*, the two-leg'd unfeathered Philosopher. **1817** BENTHAM *Parl. Reform* Introd. 213 The speeches of so many unfeathered bipeds. **1895** *Atlantic Monthly* LXXVI. 141/2 Such tastes .. have been known among the unfeathered tribes.

**2.** Of arrows: Not fitted with feathers.

**1611** COTGR., *Materas desempenné*, .. an vnfeathered quarrell. **1790** *Cook's Voy.* I. 75 But .. kneeling down, [he] shot an arrow, unfeathered (as they all are), near the sixth part of a mile. **1837** LYTTON *Athens* II. 122 Lycians with mantles of goat skin and unfeathered arrows of reed. **1860** MAURY *Phys. Geog.* (Low) iv. 103 The unfeathered arrows represent winds.

† **Unfea·tly,** *adv.* (UN-[1] 11.) **1548** UDALL *Erasm. Pref. Par. Luke* (∴) ij b, It was a thynge not vnfeactly ne vnskilfully spoken in the prouerbes of the Grekes, that [etc.]. **1611** COTGR., *Improprement*, .. vnaptly, vnfitly, vnfeatly.

**Unfea·tured,** *a.* (UN-[1] 9.)

**1693** DRYDEN *Juvenal* x. 308 A ropy Chain of Rhumes; a Visage rough, Deform'd, Unfeatur'd, and a Skin of Buff. **1810** L. HUNT *Politics & Poetics* 30 Nightmare, horrid mass! unfeatured heap! **1856** R. A. VAUGHAN *Mystics* XIII. iii, The starless, unfeatured night. **1892** STEVENSON *Across the Plains* 226 His whole unfeatured wilderness of an existence.

† **Unfea·ty,** *a.* (UN-[1] 7.) *Obs.* *a* **1586** SIDNEY *Arcadia* II. ii. (1598) 100 For his part, hee neuer saw more vnfeatie [1590 unfeatlie] fellowes then great clearks were.

**Unfeible,** obs. f. UNFEASIBLE *a.*

† **Unfe·ct,** *a. Obs.* [UN-[1] 7: cf. FECT *v.*] Uninfected. **1502** ATKYNSON tr. *De Imitatione* III. xxxviii. 227 Seldome suche persones be fre and vnfecte of the venym of theyr owne sekynge. † **Unfe·ctual,** *a. Obs.* [UN-[1] 7; cf. FECTUALLY *adv.*] Uneffectual, ineffective. **1549** COVERDALE, etc. *Erasm. Par. Gal.* 11 It was .. meete, that shadowes should gyue place to the truth; and the unfectuall, to that whiche was .. effectuall.

**Unfe·cundated,** *ppl. a.* (UN-[1] 8 and 5 b.)

[**1775** ASH.] **1857** GEO. ELIOT *Amos Barton* v, An unfecundated egg, which the waves of time wash away into nonentity. **1859** *Todd's Cycl. Anat.* V. 68/1 The mass of the yolk and the germ, in their unfecundated state.

**Unfe·d,** *ppl. a.* [UN-[1] 8 b. Cf. MDu. *ongevoedet, -voet*, Du. *-voed* unfed, unnourished; ON. and Icel. *ú-, óféddr* (Sw. *ofödd*, Da. *ufødt*) unborn.]

**1.** Not supplied or nourished with food.

*a* **1300** *Cursor M.* 12925 Iesus .. fasted fourti dais vn-fedd. *Ibid.* 19650 Thre dais liued he þar vnfedd. **1513** DOUGLAS *Æneid* IX. vi. 71 The empty lioun, lang onfed, .. Trubland the fald full of sylly schep. **1579** SPENSER *Sheph. Cal.* May 44 Shepeheards .. That playen, while their flockes be vnfedde. **1641** BEST *Farm. Bks.* (Surtees) 123 Carre-swannes, that are unfedde, are usually at 2s. 6d. a peece. **1687** DRYDEN *Hind & P.* III. 195 Some sons of mine .. Have sharply tax'd your converts, who unfed Have follow'd you for miracles of bread. **1737** *Gentl. Mag.* VII. 570/1, I wonder'd, why his oxen stray'd, His sheep and heifers pine'd unfed. **1853** KANE *Grinnell Exp.* xlviii. (1856) 442 Now the half-tutored, unfed Esquimaux dog would eat a goat, bones, skin, and for aught I know, horns. **1868** MORRIS *Earthly Par.* (1870) I. II. 565 Upon his perch the falcon sat Unfed.

*transf.* **1890** 'R. BOLDREWOOD' *Col. Reformer* xxvii, The diet .. became wellnigh intolerable: the flaccid unfed meat, .. the milkless tea [etc.].

**2.** *fig.* Not supplied with necessary material, support, etc.

*a* **1625** FLETCHER & SHIRLEY *Lover's Progr.* IV. i, She that is forfeited to lust must dye, That humour being unfed. **1664** DRYDEN & HOWARD *Indian Queen* IV. ii, I shou'd .. like an unfed stream run on and dye. **1697** DRYDEN *Æneis* XI. 101 A lovely Flow'r, New cropt by Virgin Hands, .. Unfaded yet, but yet unfed below. **1816** BYRON *Ch. Har.* III. xliv, Even as a flame unfed, which runs to waste With its own flickering. **1883** *Jrnl. Educ.* XVIII. 148 A church unfed from the public table.

**Unfee·ble,** *a.* (UN-[1] 7.) **1547** SALESBURY *Dict.* C iv, *Dilesc*, unfeble. **1569** J. SANFORD tr. *Agrippa's Van. Artes* lviii. 83 b, Sinners with the faithfull had already entred into the Churche, the feeble with the unfeeble.

**Unfee·d,** *ppl. a.* [UN-[1] 8.] Not rewarded with, or engaged by, a fee; unpaid.

**1605** SHAKS. *Lear* I. iv. 142 Then 'tis like the breath of an vnfeed Lawyer, you gaue me nothing for't. *a* **1628** DABORNE *Poor-man's Comf.* II. (1655) C 4, Now he's as speechlesse, as an unfeed Atturney. **1709** GARTH *Dispens.* (ed. 6) v. 39 Vaunt now no more the Triumph of your Skill, But, tho' unfeed, exert your Arm, and kill. **1802–12** BENTHAM *Ration. Judic. Evid.* (1827) IV. 419 But it is .. the honest interest of the unfeed judge, that .. the truth shall come to light. **1850** BLACKIE *Æschylus* I. 148 And why walks Grief, an unfee'd page, with thee?

**Unfee·dable,** *a.* (UN-[1] 7 b.) **1867** RUSKIN *Time & Tide* iii. § 10 Have you considered what is to be done finally with the unfeedable mouths? **Unfee·ding,** *ppl. a.* (UN-[1] 10.) **1585** ABP. SANDYS *Serm.* xviii. 316 What can .. the vnfeeding pastor, the vniust iudge, .. aunswere in that day but pleade guiltie? **1610** BP. HALL *Apol. Brownists* xxvii. (1627) 596 The necessary patterne of an vnteaching pastor, or an vnfeeding teacher.

**Unfeel**: see UNFELE *a.* and UN-[2] 3.

**Unfee·lable,** *a.* [UN-[1] 7 b.]

† **1.** Unable to feel; insensible. *Obs.*

*c* **1400** LOVE *Bonavent. Mirr.* (1908) 243 Sche was all out of hir self and vnfelable made, as half dede. **1568** TURNER *Herbal* III. 51 The Nux methel is poyson and maketh num or vnfelable .. It maketh vnfelable the head.

**2.** Incapable of being felt; impalpable. *rare.*

**1611** COTGR., *Impalpable*, impalpable, vnfeelable. **1632** J. DOD *Ten Sermons*, etc. 269 This Christ, .. in whom we behold God which is invisible, and touch him which is vnfeelable.

**Unfee·ling,** *vbl. sb.* [UN-[1] 13.] Lack of feeling.

**1603** FLORIO *Montaigne* II. xii. 285 Indolencie or vnfeeling of paine. **1805** *Monthly Mag.* XIX. 657 The rapacity, the selfish unfeeling, the low cunning of Odysseus.

**Unfee·ling,** *ppl. a.* [UN-[1] 10 and 5 d.]

**1.** Having no feeling or sensation, insensible; *fig.* not sensitive to impressions, etc.

*c* **1000** *Sax. Leechd.* II. 264 Yfele swilas unfelende. *a* **1300** *Cursor M.* 24426 Quen i sagh þus all thinges .. Vnfeland for þair lauerd murn, Moght i me noght for-ber. *c* **1430** *Life St. Kath.* (1884) 31 For þay wot not hem self þat þay are [offended] whyl þay are bot vnfelyng matere. **1590** SHAKS. *Com. Err.* II. i. 103 Vnfeeling fools can with such wrongs dispence. **1593** — *2 Hen. VI*, III. ii. 145 Fain would I go to chafe his palie lips, .. And with my fingers feele his hand, vnfeeling. **1619** J. TAYLOR (Water P.) *Kicksey Winsey* Wks. (1630) 42/1 They must not take me for a Stupid asse, That I (vnfeeling) will let these things passe. **1760–72** H. BROOKE *Fool of Qual.* (1809) IV. 127 [He] pressed his lips to the pale and unfeeling lips. **1780** COWPER *Progr. Error* 528 So one .. Woo'd an unfeeling statue for his wife. **1846** TRENCH *Mirac.* iv. 36 When he blesses, it is men; but when he smites, it is an unfeeling tree. **1876** BLACKIE *Songs Relig. & Life* 223 All my weeping can recall her never, Back from the cold unfeeling sod!

**b.** Const. *of, to*, or with direct object.

**1744** ELIZA HEYWOOD *Female Spect.* No. 3 (1748) I. 113 It is sure a pleasure which no words can paint!—No heart unfeeling it conceive! **1748** THOMSON *Cast. Indol.* II. liv, But should to fame your hearts unfeeling be, .. Then hear [etc.]. **1760–72** H. BROOKE *Fool of Qual.* (1809) II. 119 They appeared so cheerful and unfeeling of their own wretchedness.

**2.** Devoid of kindly or tender feelings; uncompassionate, unsympathetic.

**1596** SHAKS. *Merch. V.* IV. i. 63 This is no answer thou vnfeeling man, To excuse the currant of thy cruelty. **1598–9** B. JONSON *Case is Altered* v. iii, O heauen! can it be? That men should liue with such vnfeeling soules, Without or touch or conscience of religion? **1734** POPE *Ess. Man* IV. 319 The broadest mirth unfeeling Folly wears, Less pleasing far than Virtue's very tears. **1781** GIBBON *Decl. & F.* (1787) III. xxx. 167 *note*, The bloody actor is less detestable than the cool unfeeling historian. **1818** SCOTT *Rob Roy* xviii, I was neither a false lover nor an unfeeling son. **1883** FROUDE in *Mrs. Carlyle's Lett.* III. 204 John Carlyle .. had been rough and unfeeling.

*absol.* **1742** GRAY *Prospect Eton Coll.* 94 The tender [groan] for another's pain; Th' unfeeling for his own.

**Unfee·lingly,** *adv.* (UN-[1] 11; cf. prec.)

*c* **1374** CHAUCER *Troylus* II. 19 Ek þough I speke of loue vnfelyngly, No wondir is. **1753** T. CIBBER *Lives Actors, Booth* 74 The first has been unfeelingly mouthed and ranted throughout. **1768** STERNE *Sent. Journ., Dwarf*, The German turn'd his head back, look'd down upon him as Goliah did upon David—and unfeelingly resumed his posture. **1902** *Monthly Rev.* Aug. 187 'Bid your minnie good-bye, lad,' said Robin, not unfeelingly.

**Unfee·lingness.** [UN-[1] 12.]

**1398** TREVISA *Barth. De P. R.* VI. xxv. (Tollem. MS.), Austyne sayeþ þat slep is a kyndely unfelingenesse [L. *insensibilitas*] comen to þe body and to þe soule. **1583** BABINGTON *Commandm.* (1590) 99 When wee .. headlong in vnfeelingnesse runne on. **1598** FLORIO, *Insensibilità*, sencelesnes, vnfeelingnes. **1766** MRS. CARTER *Lett.* (1809) III. 285 Surely it implies rather the want of philosophical pride and unfeelingness. **1780** *Mirror* No. 101, A warm remonstrance against the inhumanity of parents, the unfeelingness of age, and the injustice of the world. **1853** ROBERTSON *Serm.* Ser. IV. xvi. (1876) 209 Would it not be coarse unfeelingness to treat such customs with anything but respect. **1895** *Pop. Sci. Monthly* Sept. 654 The same predominance of self .. is said to reappear in the .. unfeelingness of children.

**Unfei·gned,** *ppl. a.* (and *adv.*). Forms: (see FEIGN *v.*). [UN-[1] 8.]

**1.** Not feigned, pretended, or simulated; sincere, genuine, true, real.

*a.* *c* **1374** CHAUCER *Anel. & Arc.* 289 Verraylye yee slee me with þe peyne þat may yee see vnfeynid on myn huwe. *c* **1440** *Pallad. on Husb.* v. 194 Of vnfeyned curage [L. *sponte*] Of been therto wole come a multitude. **1494** *Act* 11 *Hen. VII*, c. 18 Or ellis he have such unfayned siknes, letting or diseas that he may not .. come to do his personell attendaunce. **1526** *Pilgr. Perf.* (W. de W. 1531) 99 b, Neuer eate ne drynke out of due tyme, except .. vnfayned nede compell the. **1577** GRANGE *Golden Aphrod.* L j, Neither passed this tedious tyme .. without vnfayned ioyes & vnspeakeable pleasure. **1649** BP. REYNOLDS *Hosea* ii. 68 Profession of faith, unfained, and sincere Repentance was made before Baptisme. **1712** STEELE *Spect.* No. 402 ¶ 2, I have an unfeigned Love of Virtue. **1778** MISS BURNEY *Evelina* lxxxii, I need not tell you what unfeigned joy accompanied our meeting. *a* **1859** MACAULAY *Hist. Eng.* xxiii. (1861) V. 82 Keppel .. looked up with unfeigned admiration to a master whom he had been accustomed .. to consider as the first of living men.

*β.* *c* **1375** *Sc. Leg. Saints* xliii. (*Cecilia*) 528 Of conscience gud & clere, & fath vnfenȝet. **1562** WINȜET *Wks.* (S. T. S.) I. 2 Ane Exhortatioun .. For vnfenȝeit reformation of doctrine and maneris. **1609** HUME in *Wodrow Soc. Misc.* (1844) 585 So I wische to God that .. the Prince's wrathe mycht be appeazed, .. and his unfainzed favour reconcealed.

**2.** Of persons or the heart: Honest or sincere in feeling or action.

*c* **1374** CHAUCER *Troylus* II. 839, I loue oon which is most ententyf To seruen wel vnwery or vnfeyned. *c* **1400** *Rom. Rose* 7363 As it were in a pilgrimage Lyke good and hooly folk vnfeyned. **1525** LD. BERNERS *Froiss.* II. clxx. 195/2 Whan .. his companyons .. herde hym speke those wordes, they parceyued well howe he spake them with all his herte vnfayned. **1573** BARET *Alv.* V 126 Your unfeined, trusty, and assured friend. **1613** W. BROWNE *Brit. Past.* I. iv. 301 Succour a seely maid, that doth implore Aide, on a bended heart, unfain'd and meeke. **1647** N. BACON *Disc. Govt. Eng.* I. iv. 16 Of fained friends, becomming unfained foes to the Britons. **1696** (*title*), Some Seasonable and Modest Thoughts .. Concerning the Scots East India Company, by an unfeigned and hearty Lover of England.

† **3.** As *adv.* Without feigning; honestly. *Obs.*

**1463–7** *Paston Lett.* Suppl. (1901) 81, I shal and do pray God dayly to sende you such one .. that wil drede and faithfully unfeyned love you. *a* **1529** SKELTON *Ware the Hauke* 81 But the fawconer vnfayned Was much more febler brayned. **1550–3** *Decaye Eng.* in *Supplic.* (1871) 100 And then vnfayned, as we do thynke, we sholde haue corne ynough.

**Unfei·gnedly,** *adv.* [UN-[1] 11.] In an unfeigned manner; without feigning or pretence; sincerely, honestly.

*a.* **1526** *Pilgr. Perf.* (W. de W. 1531) 77 b, He must subdue & meke hym selfe in very treuth vnfaynedly. **1577** tr. *Bullinger's Decades* 564 Then shall wee like true penitents vnfeignedly reuerence & dread the Lord. **1628** WITHER *Brit. Rememb.* II. 1231 And if unfainedly we practise thus He doth of safety also warrant us. **1686** HORNECK *Crucif. Jesus* xiv. 308 Both parties do unfeignedly, and without guile, or fraud, or equivocation, declare themselves willing .. to perform the things agreed upon. **1763** BURKE *Corr.* (1844) I. 51, I am very unfeignedly glad to hear from you. **1825** SCOTT *Betrothed* xix, If you will speak unfeignedly, you must .. allow [etc.]. **1891** FARRAR *Darkn. & Dawn* xxiii, She rejoiced .. unfeignedly at the boy's recovery.

*β.* **1552** ABP. HAMILTON *Catech.* (1884) 56 Quhasaevir luffis God with trew lufe unfenyetlie. **1573** *Satir. Poems Reform.* xlii. 774 Quha feiris God vnfenȝeitlie Of that sweit word will neuer Irk.

**Unfei·gnedness.** [UN-[1] 12.] The quality of being unfeigned; sincerity, etc.

**1535** COVERDALE *1 Chron.* xxx. 17, I knowe .. that vnfaynednes is acceptable vnto the. **1561** T. NORTON *Calvin's Inst.* III. 299 That by prouing them yᵗ be his he may haue a triall of their vnfainednesse. **1628** WITHER *Brit. Rememb.* v. 941 Lord, remember thou, That with unfainednesse, I beg thee, now, To keepe me alwayes mindfull of thy love. *a* **1684** LEIGHTON *Comm. 1 Peter* ii. (1693) 468 His feet strive to keep pace with his Tongue, which gives evidence of its unfainedness.

**Unfei·gning,** *ppl. a.* (UN-[1] 10.)

*c* **1400** [see UNFEIGNINGLY *adv.*]. **1436** [see UNFAILINGLY *adv.*]. **1791** COWPER *Iliad* x. 488 With unfeigning truth Simply and plainly will I utter all. **1791** — *Odyss.* XXI. 247 He then, convinced Of their unfeigning honesty, began.

**Unfei·gningly,** *adv.* (UN-[1] 11.)

*c* **1400** *Sc. Trojan War* II. 580 Dyomed has furst sworne þe pees Wnfenȝheandly [*v.r.* wnfenȝeand] to hold. *a* **1568** *Bannatyne MS.* (Hunterian Club) 623 To yow .. Unfenyeandlie with hairtlie lufe .. I me commend.

**Unfei·rdy,** *a. Sc. rare.* [UN-[1] 7 + *feirdy* able, active.] **a.** Awkward, clumsy. **b.** (See quot.)

*c* **1590** J. STEWART *Poems* (S.T.S.) II. 9/58 Than sall It pertlie occupie the place, Thocht it be framd with my vnferdie fyle. **1866** EDMONSTON *Orkney Gloss.* 136 *Unfierdy*, unwieldy, overgrown.

**Unfei·rie,** *a. Sc.* Also 6 vn-, onfery, vnfeire, 8 unfiery, 8–9 unfeary, 9 onfeirie. [UN-[1] 7.] Inactive; incapable of exertion.

**1513** DOUGLAS *Æneid* x. xiv. 70 Thocht the violens of his sayr smart Maid hym onfery [*v.r.* vnfery]. **1535** STEWART *Cron. Scot.* (Rolls) III. 437 Cruikit he wes, vnfeire of his cors. *a* **1736** T. WHITTELL *Poems* (1815) 170 But Sawney grew weary,..Being auld, and unfeary, and fail'd of his strength. *a* 1779 GRAHAM *Writings* (1883) II. 32 The auld beast being unfiery o' the feet, she fundred. 1806 R. JAMIESON *Pop. Ball.* II. 171 Thoch auld onfeirie and lyart I'm now. 1809 SCOTT *Let.* in *Lockhart* II. vii. 263 Coursing is my only and constant amusement, and my valued pair of four-legged champions..wax old and *unfeary*.

**Unfe·le,** *a. Obs.* exc. *dial.* Forms: 1–2 unfæle (2 unn-), 3 unfeale; 2–3 unfele (vn-), 3–4 unvele (vnuele, onvele), 9 *Sc.* and *north.* onfeel, unfeil. [OE. *unfǽle*, f. *un-* UN-[1] + *fǽle* good, FELE *a.*[2]] Bad, evil, wicked; wretched, miserable, unpleasant.

*a* 900 *Genesis* 723 Hit wæs þeah..menniscra morð, þæt hie to mete dædon ofet unfæle. *c* 1000 ÆLFRIC *Gloss.* in Wr.-Wülcker 108 *Satiri, uel fauni*,..unfæle men, wudewasan, unfælewihtu. *c* 1000 *Ags. Gosp.* Mark vi. 49 Hi wendon þæt hit unfæle [*c* 1160 un-fele] gast wære. *c* 1200 *Trin. Coll. Hom.* II. 79 ȝif þe unfele man his wille folȝeð and ..teð him to unwrenches. *c* 1205 LAY. 22018 Neh þere sæ stronde is a mære swiðe muchel; þat water is un-fæle. *a* 1250 *Owl & Night.* 1003 Þat lond is grislich & vnuele. *Ibid.* 1381 He is vnvele and forbroyde. *c* 1290 *S. Eng. Leg.* I. 468/231 Þe sarazins onvele weren fulle of nyþe and hete. 13.. *R. Gloucester's Chron.* (Rolls) App. G. 39 Þe moder his þrote carf, þo was heo vnfele. *c* 1400 *Laud Troy Bk.* 8830 The while that he hadde his hele, Ther he sclow Gregeys as vn-vele. 1825 JAMIESON, *Onfeel*,..unpleasant, disagreeable, implying the idea of coarseness or roughness; as, 'an onfeel day', 'onfeel words', &c. Teviotd. 1894 *Northumberland Gloss.* 756.

**Unfeli·citous,** *a.* (UN-[1] 7 and 5 b.) 1802–12 BENTHAM *Ration. Judic. Evid.* (1827) IV. 487 In principle, the arrangement [is]..correct, howsoever in the application misguided and unfelicitous. 1876 M. COLLINS *Midnight to Midn.* III. viii. 136 Let us predict for them premature and unfelicitous exit into the land of scoundrels.

**Unfe·lled,** *ppl. a.* (UN-[1] 8.)

1543 *Act* 35 *Hen. VIII*, c. 17 § 1 There shall be left standing and unfelled..twelve Standils or Storers of Oak. 1593 MARLOWE tr. *Lucan* I. 448 In vnfeld woods, and sacred groues you dwell. *c* 1611 CHAPMAN *Iliad* VI. 68 Nor, like the king of men, Let any scape unfell'd. 1839 CARLYLE *Chartism* x, Where Canadian Forests stand unfelled. 1883 *Harper's Mag.* Feb. 435/2 Couriers are out summoning.. the wood-choppers to leave the half-cut tree unfelled.

**Unfe·llied,** *a.* (UN-[1] 9.) 1885–94 R. BRIDGES *Eros & Psyche* March xxix, Melicertes drave His chariot..with swift unfellied wheel. **Unfe·llow,** *v.* (UN-[2] 6 b.) 1856 MRS. BROWNING *Aur. Leigh* v. 552 Death quite unfellows us, Sets dreadful odds betwixt the live and dead.

**Unfe·llowed,** *a.* (UN-[1] 9.)

1597 *Prayers* in *Liturg. Serv. Q. Eliz.* (Parker Soc.) 671 So shall..the faithful [be] encouraged to repose in thy unfellowed Grace. 1634 FORD *Perk. Warbeck* IV. i, The English general returns A sensible devotion from his heart..to this unfellowed grace. 1649 ARNWAY *Tablet* 22 If it be high treason against the Allmightie, to severe so unfellow'd a Paire. 1887 MEREDITH *Ballads & P.* 104 Every second man, unfellowed, Took the strokes of two, and gave.

**Unfe·llow-like,** *a.* (UN-[1] 7 c.) 1608 HIERON *Defence* III. 19 An act of abasement..such as convinceth us..to be of an inferior and unfellowlike condition, with Christ at his table. † **Unfe·lon,** *a. Obs.* (UN-[1] 7.) *a* 1300 *Cursor M.* 6040 Þan sent drightin a litel beist, O toth es noght vnfelunest. **Unfelo·niously,** *adv.* (UN-[1] 11.) *a* 1634 CHAPMAN & SHIRLEY *Chabot* III. ii, If traitorous pride..Were sentenc'd unfeloniously before, I'll burn my books.

**Unfe·lt,** *ppl. a.* (UN-[1] 8 b. Cf. Du. *ongevoeld*, G. *ungefühlt*.)

*a* 1586 SIDNEY *Astr. & Stella* Sonn. xxiv, Let him, depriu'd of sweet but vnfelt ioyes,..grow in only folly rich! 1595 DANIEL *Civ. Wars* V. xcvii, Whilst Talbot..Carries his vnfelt age as if forgot. 1607 CHAPMAN *Bussy d'Ambois* III. ii, O, 'tis a subtle knave; how like the plague Unfelt he strikes into the brain of man. 1681 DRYDEN *Abs. & Achit.* I. 693 Thus, form'd by Nature, furnish'd out with Arts, He glides unfelt into their secret hearts. 1742 GRAY *Adversity* 8 Purple Tyrants vainly groan With pangs unfelt before, unpitied and alone. 1814 WORDSW. *Excurs.* IV. 456 Nor is its power Unfelt among the sedentary fowl That seek yon pool. 1883 PARKER *Apost. Life* II. 192 He was writhing in an unfelt and unknown agony.

*absol.* 1886 A. WEIR *Hist. Basis Mod. Europe* (1889) 487 Few have been destitute of some theory respecting the unseen and unfelt.

Hence † **Unfe·ltly** *adv. Obs.*

1605 SYLVESTER *Du Bartas* II. iii. III. *Law* 107 Into his brest he blowes A banefull ayre, whose strength unfeltly flowes Through all his veins.

**Unfe·lt,** *v.* (UN-[2] 4 b.) 1611 FLORIO, *Disfeltráre*, to vnfelt. 1655 W. DU GARD tr. *Comenius' Gate Lat. Unl.* 135 Having unfelted the hair [the barber] partly polleth it with scisers.

**Unfe·minine,** *a.* [UN-[1] 7, 5 b.] Not in accordance with, or appropriate to, female character.

1757 MRS. GRIFFITH *Lett. Hen. & Frances* (1767) IV. 30, I ..continue still..averse to the unfeminine Vanity of a literary Name. 1796 MME. D'ARBLAY *Camilla* III. 301 What a lesson is this to youthful females against..the false brilliancy of unfeminine popularity! 1849 MACAULAY *Hist. Eng.* vi. II. 69 She had..two brilliant eyes, the lustre of which, to men of delicate taste, seemed fierce and unfeminine. 1875 MRS. RANDOLPH *Wild Hyacinth* I. 14 Why should it be wrong and unfeminine for us to do anything except dress, and read novels, and play the piano?

Hence **Unfe·minineness.**

1856 MISS YONGE *Daisy Chain* I. vi, If those high purposes should..grow out into eccentricities and unfemini[ne]nesses, what a grievous pity it would be! 1876 — *Womankind* i. 7 She becomes ridiculous.., and renders him averse to the culture to which he erroneously ascribes her unfeminineness.

**Unfemi·nity.** (UN-[1] 12.) 1863 COWDEN CLARKE *Shaksp. Char.* viii. 197 He has retained the two women from the remotest charge of unfeminity. **Unfe·minize,** *v.* (UN-[2] 6 c.) 1886 MISS MULOCK in *Gd. Words* 313/2 These young students seem to go through the ordeal..without being unfeminized. 1895 F. ADOLPHUS *Mem. Paris* 296 The example offered by the English is unfeminising France. **Unfe·nce,** *v.* (UN-[2] 4.) *a* 1716 SOUTH *Serm.* (T.), Whensoever it shall please God to unfence it [*sc.* a vein or artery], and let in some sharp disease or distemper upon it.

**Unfe·nced,** *ppl. a.* [UN-[1] 8.]

1. Undefended, unprotected.

1548 ELYOT, *Immunitus*, not defended, not fortified, vnfensed. 1585 HOLINSHED *Hist. Scot.* in *Chron.* II. 408/2 Iedworth [is] a towne which after the manner of the countrie is vnwalled and vnfensed, but onelie with the strength of the inhabitants. 1646 J. HALL *Horæ Vac.* 90 When a man is in earnest, he stands upon his guard; in mirth he lies open unfenc't. 1654 tr. *Martini's Conq. China* 115 The Chineses ran all away.., leaving the whole shore unfenced to their landing. 1791 COWPER *Odyssey* XI. 316 Though puissant Heroes both, in spacious Thebes, Unfenced by towers, they could not dwell secure. 1867 MORRIS *Jason* VI. 331 For the unfenced head, Where we have been, soon rests among the dead.

2. Not provided with, or enclosed by, a fence or fences.

1608 *Presentment* in *Essex Rev.* XV. 46 The churchyard is unfensed, the windows unglazed. 1623 LISLE *Ælfric on O. & N. Test.* Ded. xviii, This three-cornerd Ile on ev'ry side, Unfens'd, undelv'd, ungardined. 1725 *Fam. Dict.* s.v. *Melonry*, These take in three Ridges, only the outermost Ridge lies to the South unfenced. 1794 MISS BERRY *Jrnl.* (1865) I. 448 The country, tho' not without trees, is..perfectly open and unfenced and unditched. 1847 LONGF. *Evang.* I. i. 9 Orchards and cornfields Spreading afar and unfenced o'er the plain. 1885 *Law Rep.* 14 Q.B.D. 918 The footpath ran over an open moor and was unfenced.

b. Not provided with a ledge, guard, or the like.

1683 MOXON *Mech. Exerc.*, *Printing* xxiv. ⁋ 11 He might draw too great a body of Inck to the unfenced sides; so that the Inck would be subject to run off. 1894 *Daily News* 4 July 3/3 Machine after machine was found thus unfenced, the workpeople being too indifferent to take the trouble of putting them on.

† **Unfe·ncible,** *a. Sc. Obs.* In 6 -fensabil. [UN-[1] 7.] Incapable of defence.

1513 DOUGLAS *Æneid* IX. xii. 16 Lyke as ane rageand wyld tygyr onstabill Amang the febill bestis onfensabill. 1536 BELLENDEN *Cron. Scot.* (1821) I. 239 The agit and febill personis, that war left at hame as unfensabil bodyis.

† **Unfe·nded,** *ppl. a. Obs.*—[1] (UN-[1] 8.) 1576 GASCOIGNE *Steele Gl.* (Arb.) 76 Some other ranne, before the greedy woolfe, And left the folde, vnfended from the fox. **Unfe·nestrated,** *ppl. a.* (UN-[1] 8.) 1884 C. B. KELSEY *Dis. Rectum* vii. 209 A good, fresh, unfenestrated drainage-tube.

**Unfenȝeit**(lie, obs. Sc. ff. UNFEIGNED(LY.

† **Unfe·re,** *sb. Obs.* [Cf. next, and ON. *úfœ́ra* fem., *úfœ́ri* neut., a state of trouble or difficulty.] Infirmity, weakness.

*a* 1300 *Cursor M.* 3556 Sir ysaac þat dughti man, Vnfere and eld a-pon him ran.

† **Unfe·re,** *a. Obs.* Also 3–4 unfer, 3 onver, -viere, vnueren. [OE. *unfére* (= ON. and Icel. *ú-*, *ófœrr*, Norw. *ufør*, MSw. and Sw. *oför*): see UN-[1] 7 and FERE *a.*] Infirm, weak, unfit for or incapable of exertion. Also *absol.*

*a* 1060 *O. E. Chron.* (MS. C) an. 1055, Tremerig se Wylsca biscop., wæs Æþelstanes biscopes ȝespelia syððan he unfere wæs. *c* 1205 LAY. 6780 Þa iwærð þe king vn-fere [*c* 1275 on-ver]. *Ibid.* 11079 Þa iwærð his fader vnueren [*c* 1275 onviere]. *c* 1250 *Gen. & Ex.* 2810 In hise bosum he dede his hond, Quit and al unfer he it fond. *a* 1300 *Cursor M.* 3507 His fader þat old was and vnfere. 13.. *Ibid.* 13262 (Gött.), Þe vnfer fast tille him þai soght. *c* 1325 *Metr. Hom.* (MS. Ashm. 42) fol. 158 b, A man vnfere þat nouther might speke ne here. *c* 1400 *Destr. Troy* 1357 Childer..of chere febill, Wyth olde ffolke vnfere. *Ibid.* 13618, I am febyll and vnfere, fallyn into elde.

Hence † **Unfe·reness,** infirmity. *Obs.*

*a* 1300 *Cursor M.* 20744 He on hir bere laid his hand, Þarof vnfernes son he fand.

† **Unferme** (also 6 -farme), obs. var. UNFIRM *a.*

*c* 1450 tr. *De Imitatione* III. lxiv. 149 In þe þerfor I sette all my tribulacion,..for I finde all vnferme & vnstable, what euere I beholde oute of þe. 1483 CAXTON *Gold. Leg.* 84/1 Theuangelyste was not so unferme but that he myght gete for hys syght that saynt andrewe gate for hym so lyghtly. *a* 1542 WYATT in *Anglia* XIX. 427, I..fele my bonis consume and wax vnfarme By dayly rage.

**Unferme·ntable,** *a.* (UN-[1] 7 b.) 1844 H. STEPHENS *Bk. Farm* II. 131 Filling the paunch with unfermentable matter.

**Unferme·nted,** *ppl. a.* (UN-[1] 8 and 5 b.)

1663 BOYLE *Usef. Exp. Nat. Philos.* II. ii. 40 The volatile salt of unfermented urine. 1731 ARBUTHNOT *Aliments* v. (1735) 123 All such Vegetables must be unfermented, for Fermentation changes their Nature. 1799 G. SMITH *Laboratory* I. 430 To make the wine keep unfermented. 1834 *Brit. Husb.* I. 250 (L.U.K.), The effect of unfermented dung on.. crops. 1886 AXON *Ann. Manchester* 217 An unfermented wine for sacramental use.

**Unfe·rtile,** *a.* and *sb.* (UN-[1] 7 and 5 b.)

1596 *Edward III*, I. ii. 151 The ground..Seemes barrayne, sere, vnfertill. 1620 MARKHAM *Farew. Husb.* (1625) 24 That barren and unfertile earth,..which is overrunne only with whinnes. 1661 J. CHILDREY *Brit. Bacon.* 51 These unfertile beds do intersect each other. 1792 *Resid. France* (1797) I. 121 Unfertile, neglected vallies and hills. 1818 COLEBROOKE *Import Colonial Corn* 104 The permanent improvement of poor and unfertile land. 1865 W. G. PALGRAVE *Arabia* II. 244 A not unfertile strip of coast.

*fig.* 1616 R. C. *Times' Whistle* (1871) 110 The abortive issue of my vnfertile braine. 1667 *Decay Chr. Piety* xix. ⁋ 12 Peace is not..such a sapless unfertile thing. 1866 WHIPPLE *Char. & Charac. Men* 54 The thought..would not come into that unfertile brain.

b. *sb.* An unfertile egg.

1891 *Bazaar* 20 Feb. 269/3 Purchasers should always make sure that unfertiles will be replaced before giving their orders. *Ibid.*, I returned the unfertiles carriage paid.

Hence **Unfe·rtileness, Unferti·lity.**

1611 COTGR., *Infecondité*,..vnfertilnesse, vnfruitfulnesse. 1888 *19th Cent.* June 834 The unfertility of the soil. 1899 MARY KINGSLEY *W. African Stud.* xi. 279 The unfertility of the greater part of their country.

**Unfe·rtilized,** *ppl. a.* (UN-[1] 8.) [1775 ASH.] 1893 TUCKEY *Amphioxus* 37 A nucleus..in the unfertilized [eggs] ..was always quite plainly to be seen. **Unfe·rvency.** (UN-[1] 12.) 1787 J. BROWN in Mackenzie *Life* (1918) 285, I see ..such unfervency, and unconcern,..in all that I have done.

**Unfery,** obs. f. UNFEIRIE *a. Sc.*

† **Unfe·st,** *v. Obs.* [UN-[2] 4 b + *fest* FAST *v.*[1]] *trans.* To unfasten; to untie.

*a* 1225 *Ancr. R.* 218 He..makeð him swuðe sterne,..uorte uonden ȝete ȝif he muhte hire luue touward him unuesten. *c* 1330 R. BRUNNE *Chron. Wace* (Rolls) 651 Loke þy schip be vnfest, & þy folk be al prest. 1790 GROSE *Prov. Gloss.*, *Unfest*, to untie.

**Unfe·stival,** *a.* (UN-[1] 7.) 1603 HOLLAND *Plutarch* 599 But a sacrifice, where no god is present,..is profane, unfestivall, impious. **Unfe·stive,** *a.* (UN-[1] 7.) 1844 THACKERAY *Greenwich Whitebait* Wks. 1899 XIII. 615 Sudden gusts of genius unknown in the quiet unfestive state.

**Unfe·stly**: see UNFEASTLY *a.*

**Unfe·tched,** *ppl. a.* (UN-[1] 8 c.) *c* 1611 CHAPMAN *Iliad* XIX. 196 Our friends by Hector slaine,..lie vnfetch [*sic*] off. 1616 J. LANE *Contn. Sqr.'s T.* x. 430 Distroienge all and some, that stood in 's way, nor left hee one vnfetchd vp.

**Unfete**: see UNFEAT *a. Obs.*

**Unfe·tid,** *a.* (UN-[1] 7.) 1754 *Phil. Trans.* XLVIII. 829 Which must therefore be the effect of unfetid putrefaction.

**Unfe·tter,** *v.* [UN-[2] 4 b. Cf. G. *entfesseln*.] To free from fetters; to remove the fetters from.

1362 LANGL. *P. Pl.* A. III. 134 Heo ȝeueþ þe Iayler Gold and grotes..To vn-Fetere þe False. *c* 1400 *Gamelyn* 613 The shirreue unfetered him right sone anone. *c* 1412 HOCCLEVE *De Reg. Princ.* 2399 To prison he gooth; he gette no bettre, Til his mainpernour his arrest vnfettre. 1485 CAXTON *Paris & V.* (1868) 81 He sayd to the freres that they shold unfeter the doulphyn. 1598 FLORIO, *Scatenare*, to vnchaine, to vnfetter, to vnshakle. 1611 COTGR., *Destraver*, to vnshackle, vngyue, vnfetter. 1748 SMOLLETT *R. Random* xxvii, Captain Oakum..ordered the fellow to be unfettered. 1799 COLERIDGE *Devil's Thoughts* xi, He saw the same Turnkey unfetter a man, With but little expedition.

b. In fig. contexts or uses.

*c* 1374 CHAUCER *Troylus* II. 1216 She..gan hire herte vnfettre Out of disdaynes prison but a lyte. *a* 1470 HARDING *Chron.* CXI. vii, Fyftye batayls and syx he smote, Somtyme the worse, and somtyme had the better;..Lyke as fortune his cause leste vnfeter. 1627 SANDERSON *Serm.* I. 280 As for whatsoever other hank thou mayst think thou hast over him,..he can..easily unfetter himself from them all. 1671 WOODHEAD *St. Teresa* I. xx. 136 Whom she desires to see unfettered from the prison of this life. 1766 BLACKSTONE *Comm.* II. 345 The transcendent power of parliament is called in..to unfetter an estate. 1830 HERSCHEL *Study Nat. Phil.* 8 It unfetters the mind from prejudices of every kind. *c* 1860 FABER *Hymn, Desire of God* v, And the langour of love captive hearts can unfetter.

Hence **Unfe·ttering** *vbl. sb.* and *ppl. a.*

*a* 1653 BINNING *Serm.* (1845) 189 To bring along a Deliverer unto your spirits, for the..unfettering of them from the chains of fleshly lusts. 1824 MISS L. M. HAWKINS *Mem.*, etc. I. 257 Too much of the spirit of John Knox, or something equally unfettering. 1854 J. B. PATON in *Life* iii. (1914) 33 Those words which should for ever consecrate us to His unfettering service.

**Unfe·ttered,** *ppl. a.* [UN-[1] 8: cf. Sw. *offjettrad*.] Not confined or restrained by fetters. Chiefly in fig. use: Unrestrained, unrestricted.

1601 DONNE *Progr. Soul* I. xviii, To an unfetterd soules quick nimble hast Are falling stars, and hearts thoughts, but slow pac'd. 1697 DRYDEN *Æneis* Ded., Ess. (ed. Ker) II. 220 Now, if a Muse cannot run when she is unfettered, it is a sign she has but little speed. 1748 SMOLLETT *R. Random* xxiv, One of my fellow captives who was unfettered. 1787 BURNS *Let. to Moore* 15 Feb., The unfettered wild flight of native genius. 1855 PRESCOTT *Philip II*, II. i. (1857) 193 A people accustomed from infancy to the unfettered exercise of their faculties. 1879 FROUDE *Cæsar* x. 117 He was left unfettered to act at his own discretion.

b. Const. *by*.

1800 *Asiat. Ann. Reg.*, *Chron.* 14/1 He took a new estate, unfettered by conditions, and subject only to the quit rents. 1850 TENNYSON *In Mem.* xxvii, I envy not the beast that takes His license..Unfetter'd by the sense of crime.

**Unfeu·dal,** *a.* (UN-[1] 7.) *c* 1815 JANE AUSTEN *Persuas.* xv, Feelings..too strict to suit the unfeudal tone of the present day. **Unfeu·dalize,** *v.* (UN-[2] 6 c.) 1837 CARLYLE *Fr. Rev.* II. v. v, The Austrian Kaiser answers that his German Princes..cannot be unfeudalised. **Unfeu·dalized,** *ppl. a.* (UN-[1] 8.) 1801 HELEN M. WILLIAMS *Sk. Fr. Rep.* I. vi. 57 The lavish produce of the earth unfeudalized, and untythed. 1874 *Act* 37 & 38 *Vict.* c. 94 § 9 A personal right to land under an unfeudalized conveyance. **Unfeu·ed,** *ppl. a. Sc.* (UN-[1] 8.) 1819 *Aberdeen Jrnl.* 20 Jan. (Jam.), The unfeued and unproductive property. 1871 W. ALEXANDER *Johnny Gibb* xliv, Half-a-dozen acres of the unfeued land. **Unfe·vered,** *ppl. a.* (UN-[1] 8.) 1864 SIR A. DE VERE *Tr. & Cr.* 4 Had I been worthy of the love you gave,..My bed had been unfever'd as my grave.

† **Unfew** *a.*: see UN-[1] 3.

**Unfezable,** var. UNFEASABLE *a. Obs.*

**Unfi·brous,** *a.* (UN-[1] 7.) 1768–74 TUCKER *Lt. Nat.* (1834) I. 395 That small mixture of unfibrous matter, which may serve as an integument. **Unfi·ckle,** *a.* (UN-[1] 7.) 1802 MARIAN MOORE *Lascelles* II. 233 Frank, ingenuous, and unfickle in his behaviour. **Unficti·tious,** *a.* (UN-[1] 7.) 1836 *Todd's Cycl. Anat.* I. 799/2 Scott's touching picture.. has had many unfictitious counterparts. 1858 CARLYLE *Fred. Gt.* IV. xiii, For work is of an extremely unfictitious nature. **Unfie·ry,** *a.* (UN-[1] 7.) *c* 1611 CHAPMAN *Iliad* VII. 84 But you are earth and water all, which..Have framed your faint unfiery spirits. **Unfi·ght,** *v.* (UN-[2] 3.) 1720 T. GORDON *Humourist* I. 3 Fighting Battles and unfighting them in the same Paper. **Unfi·ghting,** *ppl. a.* (Un-[1] 10.) **1678** Rymer *Trag. Last Age* 27 The Spectators were some sort of feminine unfighting fellows. *a* **1704** T. Brown *Wks.* (1720) IV. 37 Their General gone, the rest like Lightning fly, A cheap unfighting Herd. **1747** in *Gentl. Mag.* XVII. 234 Descants upon unfighting captains at sea. †**Unfi·gurate,** *a. Obs.* (Un-[1] 7.) *a* **1752** R. Erskine in Fisher *Mem.* (1765) 115 Christ is the second Adam, the real unfigurate head of the human body. **Unfi·gurative,** *a.* (Un-[1] 7.) **1780** Bentham *Princ. Legisl.* x. § 4 The sense it bears on these occasions may be styled its literal or unfigurative sense. **1871** Macduff *Mem. Patmos* xxi. 287 St. Peter's unfigurative Epistle.

**Unfi·gured,** (*ppl.*) *a.* [Un-[1] 8 and 9.]

**1.** Not expressed in, or employing, figurative speech.

**1577** tr. *Bullinger's Decades* IV. i. 534/2 The vnfigured and vnrecouered promises..in the Psalmes. **1783** Blair *Lect.* I. xv. 317 What we call the moral, is the unfigured sense or meaning of the Allegory. **1827** G. S. Faber *Sacr. Cal. Prophecy* (1844) I. 8 The unfigured language of highly cultivated nations. **1904** Dowden *Browning* 68 A plain, unfigured and uncoloured style.

**2.** Not marked with a numerical figure or figures.

**1596** Nashe *Saffron Walden* F 2 b, Hee..in halfe a quire of paper..hath left the Pages vnfigured. **1873** H. C. Banister *Music* 62 It is understood that the unfigured notes bear Triads. *Ibid.* 287 All the Unfigured Basses.

**3.** Not including figures of persons, etc.

**1624** Wotton *Elem. Archit.* 96 In vnfigured paintings the noblest is, the imitation of Marbles, and of Architecture it selfe.

**b.** Not (yet) depicted by a figure.

**1822** J. Parkinson *Oryctology* 244 *Nautilus*, an unfigured species deeply umbilicated. **1869** D. G. Elliot (*title*), The new and heretofore unfigured Species of the Birds of North America.

**4.** *Logic.* Of a syllogism: Not belonging to one of the usual figures.

**1838** Sir W. Hamilton *Logic* App. (1860) IV. 350 The Unfigured Syllogism, or that in which the terms compared do not stand to each other in the reciprocal relation of subject and predicate. **1864** Bowen *Logic* viii. 244 Reducing all Mediate Inference to what he calls the Unfigured Syllogism.

**Unfi·lamentous,** *a.* (Un-[1] 7.) **1831** R. Knox *Cloquet's Anat.* 472 The white and unfilamentous cord..behind the rest of the nerve. **Unfi·lched,** *ppl. a.* (Un-[1] 8.) **1818** Byron *Juan* I. clxv, Nothing so dear as an unfilch'd good name!

**Unfi·led,** *ppl. a.*[1] *Obs.* exc. *dial.* [Un-[1] 8 + File *v.*[2]] Undefiled; unfouled.

*c* **1200** *Trin. Coll. Hom.* 133 Ure drihten him shop of eorðe þat was unfiled. *a* **1300** *E. E. Psalter* xvii. 33 Mi God unfiled es his wai. *a* **1340** Hampole *Psalter* xvii. 35 God þat beltid me wiþ vertu, & sett vnfiled my way. **1435** Misyn *Fire of Love* 44 Faynnes of þi mynde..sall make þe beloued if it to lufe of hym onely þou kepe vnfilyd. *a* **1470** Harding *Chron.* cxxvi. iii, Clothes and meate and beddyng newe vnfiled, Wyne also and ale she gaue. **1513** Douglas *Æneid* II. ii. 153 Be the hie goddis abuife,..And by the faith wnfilit, ..Gif it with mortale folkis ma fundin be. **1583–4** *Burgh Rec. Edinb.* (1882) IV. 321 That thai keip the said nichtbouris quheitt..vnfylet. **1791–** in *Eng. Dial. Dict.*

**Unfi·led,** *ppl. a.*[2] [Un-[1] 8 + File *v.*[1]] Not reduced or smoothed by filing; *fig.* unpolished, rude.

**1590** Spenser *F. Q.* III. vii. 30 He was all armd in rugged steele vnfilde, As in the smoky forge it was compilde. **1633** Wither *Juvenilia, Sat. King* 342 Pardon me, and daigne a gracious eye On this my rude unfil'd Apologie. **1641** W. Cartwright *Royal Slave* Epil., The unfil'd Author..Fears yet he may miscarry. **1774** W. Mason *Heroic Postscript to Chambers* 12 Each glittering orb the sacred features bore Of George.., Unfil'd, unsweated, all of sterling weight.

**Unfi·led,** *ppl. a.*[3] [Un-[1] 8 + File *v.*[3]] Not arranged in or as in a file; not placed on a file.

**1571** Campion *Hist. Irel.* v. (1633) 15 Of this people therefore severally by themselves I must intreate. Yet none otherwise then as they stand unfiled. **1864** Trevelyan *Compet. Wallah* (1866) 36 Codes and translations of codes, and letters of every size and age, filed and unfiled.

**Unfi·lial,** *a.* (Un-[1] 7.)

Also *unfilially* adv. (Webster 1864), *unfilialness.*

**1611** Shaks. *Wint. T.* IV. iv. 417 You offer him..a wrong Something vnfilliall. **1648** Boyle *Seraphic Love* (1659) 121 To preserve them from the Contagion of Sinne, or Cure them of the unfilial habitudes of it. **1756** Foote *Eng. fr. Paris* II, Ungrateful, unfilial wretch! so soon to trample on his ashes. **1803** Wordsw. '*When I have borne*' 8 Verily, in the bottom of my heart, Of those unfilial fears I am ashamed. **1880** Moule *Chinese Stories* v. 78, I charged him with unfilial conduct in compelling his mother..to connive at idolatry.

†**Unfi·ling,** *ppl. a.* (Un-[1] 10 + File *v.*[2]) *a* **1400** *New Test.* (Paues) 1 Peter iii. 4 (p. 215), þat þat is hydde wiþ-inne in mans herte..in vnfilynge reste (of here body & soule).

**Unfi·ll,** *v.* [Un-[2] 3. Cf. obs. Flem. *ontvullen.*] *trans.* †**a.** To stop, break off. *Obs.* **b.** To empty.

**1486** *Bk. St. Albans, Hunting* e vj b, To fulfill or vnfill eche maner of chaas The hunt euermoore in his mowth that worde he haas. **1607** Tourneur *Rev. Trag.* II. ii, Thy veines are sweld with lust, this shall unfill 'em. **1611** Cotgr., *Desemplir*, to emptie, or vnfill.

**Unfi·llable,** *a.* Now *rare.* (Un-[1] 7 b.)

*a* **1340** Hampole *Psalter* c. 7 Wiþ proude eghe & vnfilabil [L. *insatiabili*] hert. **1382** Wyclif *Prov.* xxvii. 20 Helle and perdicioun neuere ben fulfild; and the eȝen of men vnfillable. **1456** Sir G. Haye *Law Arms* (S.T.S.) 27 Ane unfillable gredy appetite. *c* **1475** *Cath. Angl.* 130/2 Vnfylabylle, *insaciabilis.* *c* **1610** *Women Saints* 178 Ouergoing that vnsatiable greedynes of euill, with vnfillable desire of goodnes. **1890** *Brit. Med. Jrnl.* 2 Aug. 293 Places which had hitherto seemed unfillable by the pigmies of our later days.

**Unfi·lled,** *ppl. a.* [Un-[1] 8, 8 c. Cf. OE. *ungefylled*, Du. *ongevuld*, G. *unausgefüllt.*]

**1.** Not filled; not made full.

**1584** Cogan *Haven Health* ccxiv. 201 That it were better to eate fine meates first, and grosser meates afterward, if perchance any corner were left vnfilled. **1601** Shaks. *Twel. N.* II. iii. 7 A false conclusion: I hate it as an vnfill'd Canne. **1646** Crashaw *Sospetto d'Herode* xlii, A cursed Feast, Which Harpyes, with leane Famine feed upon, Unfill'd for ever. **1755** Johnson, *Unstuffed*, unfilled, unfurnished. **1837** Carlyle *Fr. Rev.* I. VII. i, Our mouths, unfilled with bread, are to be shut, under penalties? **1893** *Spectator* 15 Apr. 471/1 The Colonies..possess great properties in their unfilled lands.

**b.** With *up.*

*c* **1640** J. Smyth *Lives Berkeleys* (1883) II. 380 Hee..being within less then his length of an old Colepit unfilled up. **1817** J. Scott *Paris Revisit.* (ed. 4) 105 That their capacities ..did not seem to be improved,—that much of them remained unfilled up.

†**2.** Unfulfilled. *Obs.*

*c* **1400** *Apol. Loll.* 34 So is no man worþi to mak a letter or title of his to go by vnfillid. **1651** Baxter *Inf. Bapt.* 296 Those to whom that Promise is yet unfilled.

**Unfi·lleted,** *ppl. a.* (Un-[1] 8.) [1775 Ash.] **1802** Coleridge *Picture* 158 The hand Holds loosely its small handful of wild-flowers, Unfilleted, and of unequal lengths. **1868** Swinburne *Ess. & Stud.* (1875) 363 The heavy straying flakes of unfilleted hair. †**Unfilling(like,** (*ppl.*) *a. Obs.* [Un-[1] 10, 7 c.] Insatiable. *a* **1300** *E. E. Psalter* c. 6 With proud egh and un-fillandlike [*v.r.* un-filland] hert. **Unfi·lm,** *v.* (Un-[2] 4 b.) **1839** Bailey *Festus* 16, I will.. unfilm them, That so thou mayst not dally with the blind. **1871** Palgrave *Lyr. Poems* 115 The callow bird unfilm'd his fervent eyes. **Unfi·ltered,** *ppl. a.* (Un-[1] 8.) [1775 Ash.] **1896** *Pop. Sci. Monthly* April 857 The resulting unfiltered stream of bacteria.

**Unfi·ndable,** *a.* (Un-[1] 7 b.)

**1791** Bentham *Mem. & Corr.* Wks. 1843 X. 248 Hampstead is the road you must take, as the other would be unfindable. **1859** Green *Lett.* (1901) 32 Lady of my dream, unfindable among human flesh and blood. **1895** *Athenæum* 17 Aug. 224/3 [A book] not unfindable, scarce though it be.

**Unfi·ne,** *a.* (Un-[1] 7; cf. MDu. *onfijn*, MHG. *unvin*, G. *unfein*, Da. *ufin.*)

*c* **1400** Maundev. (Roxb.) 149 Pissemyres..disseuerez þe fyne gold fra þe vnfyne. **1566** Drant *Horace, Sat.* II. iii. G j b, If one..drincke nothing but vinaiger, vntastie and vnfyne. **1687** Montague & Prior *Hind & P. Transv.* 26 Thou hast brought us Wine, Sour to my tast, and to my Eyes unfine. *a* **1700** B. E. *Dict. Cant. Crew, Foul Wine*, when it stinks; also when unfine. **1762** H. Walpole *Let. to Montagu* 8 June, The birth-day was far from being such a show; empty and unfine as possible. **1793** Sir J. Dinely *Methods to get Husbands* 7 Your convenient legs, younger than mine, Can nimbly travel in weather unfine.

†**Unfi·ned,** *ppl. a. Obs.* [Un-[1] 8 + Fine *v.*[3]] Unrefined, unpurified.

*a* **1500** *Colkelbie Sow* III. 857 (Bannatyne MS.), So long as it lay on the ground, It was vnfynit as fruct nevirmoir found. **1606** W. Crashaw *Rom. Forgeries* 33 This is new and vnfined wine put into this old vessell. **1611** Cotgr., *Balluque*, gold ore, or gold vnfined. **1628** Feltham *Resolves* I. lxxxix. 83 In drinking the Wine, that is yet vnfined.

**Unfi·ngered,** (*ppl.*) *a.* [Un-[1] 8 and 9. Cf. (in sense 2) older Flem. *ongevingert.*]

**1.** Not provided with fingers.

**1603** J. Davies (Heref.) *Extasie* Wks. (Grosart) I. 91/1 Not haire, but golden wire drawne like the Twist The Spider spins with her vnfing'red fist.

**2.** Not touched with the fingers; unhandled.

**1811** W. R. Spencer *Poems* 190 When sighs of seraph lovers Breathe upon th' unfinger'd wire. **1839** Barrie *Window in Thrums* 173 The few shillings..remained unfingered.

†**Unfi·nified,** *ppl. a. Obs.* (Un-[1] 8.) **1609** W. M. *Man in Moone* (1849) 26 No friend to the barber it should seeme by his rusticall, overgrowne, and unfinified beard. **Unfi·nish.** [Un-[1] 12.] Want of finish; unfinished state. **1831** Fr. A. Kemble *Rec. Girlhood* (1878) III. 26 Found the stage in a state of unfinish. **1875** Pitt-Rivers *Evol. Culture* (1906) 34 A celt..somewhat rougher, and showing evidence of unfinish.

**Unfi·nishable,** *a.* (Un-[1] 7 b.)

*a* **1739** Jarvis *Quix.* I. I. i, He commended in his author the concluding his book with a promise of that unfinishable adventure. **1835** Motley *Corr.* (1889) I. iii. 59, I thought..of strange, unfinished, unfinishable buildings. **1878** T. Sinclair *Mount* 166 Faust..ever remains a torso unfinishable.

**Unfi·nished,** *ppl. a.* (Un-[1] 8.)

**1553** in Feuillerat *Revels Q. Mary* (1914) 150 The same.. surseased and were lefte of vnfynysshed. **1590** Shaks. *Com. Err.* III. ii. 173 The chaine vnfinish'd made me stay thus long. **1671** Milton *Samson* 1027 That inward gifts Were left for hast unfinish't. **1714** R. Fiddes *Pract. Disc.* I. 144 We haue so great a work lying unfinish'd upon our hands. **1797** S. & Ht. Lee *Canterb. T.* (1799) I. 373 The recital he was about to make remained unfinished. **1865** Dickens *Mut. Fr.* II. i, Here, another unfinished street already in ruins. **1887** Bowen *Æneid* IV. 77 She..Speaks, then leaves unfinished the speech already begun.

Hence **Unfi·nishedness.**

**1887** *Pall Mall G.* 22 Jan. 4/1 There is an appearance of hurry and unfinishedness about some [pictures].

**Unfi·nishing,** *vbl. sb.* (Un-[1] 13.) **1642** Milton *Apol. Smect.* § 8 Their noble deeds, the unfinishing whereof already surpasses what others before them have left enacted.

**Unfi·red,** *ppl. a.* [Un-[1] 8.]

**1.** Not set on fire; unignited.

**1590** Sir J. Smyth *Disc. Weapons* 18 b, With the powder next vnto the bullets vnfired. **1623** Massinger *Bondman* IV. ii, *Marullo.* We'll right ourselves..*Gracculo.* And not leave One house unfired. **1664** Evelyn *Sylva* 102 It is continually to be fed with short and fitting wood, that no part remains unfir'd. **1756** *Demi-Rep* 14 Chaste as unfired coals they seem. **1781** *Phil. Trans.* LXXI. 248 No less than 40 large grains of unfired powder were driven through the screen. **1849** James *Woodman* ix, The abbey itself was still unfired.

*fig.* **1729** T. Cooke *Tales*, etc. 24 The human Brute, who view'd her Charms unfir'd. *a* **1788** Earl Nugent *Ep. Visct. Cornbury* 154 Such gifts she to the happy few imparts,..To heads unfir'd by youth's tumultuous rage.

**2.** Not subjected or exposed to fire.

**1791** Cowper *Iliad* XXIII. 1092 Then, last, Achilles in the circus placed A pond'rous spear and cauldron yet unfired. **1888** *Archaeol.* LI. I. 52 These un-fired bricks lasted perfectly well.

**3.** Of a gun: Not discharged by firing.

**1892** Greener *Breech-Loader* 200 If one barrel is fired repeatedly without discharging the other, it is advisable to take out the unfired cartridge occasionally. **1902** *Daily Chron.* 16 Apr. 7/6 The starboard gun remained unfired.

**Unfi·rm,** *a.* [Un-[1] 7 and 5 b; cf. Infirm *a.* and the earlier form Unferme.]

**1.** Of a loose or soft consistency; incompact.

**1592** Shaks. *Rom. & Jul.* v. iii. 6 The Churchyard..Being loose, vnfirme with digging vp of Graues. **1625** K. Long tr. *Barclay's Argenis* II. ii. 71 Further onward the water very deepe, and the ground unfirm. **1683** Tryon *Way to Health* 95 What is the reason that most Veal is so unfirm and like a Jelly? **1726** Leoni *Alberti's Archit.* II. 117 b, When the banks of a River are unfirm, its channel will be stopt up with shelves. **1866** J. B. Rose tr. *Ovid's Met.* 1 Unfirm the earth, unbuoyant was the wave.

†**2.** Unsteady, flighty. *Obs.*

**1601** Shaks. *Twel. N.* II. iv. 34 Our fancies are more giddie and vnfirme..Then womens are.

†**3.** Weak; wanting in strength or power; feeble, infirm, invalid. *Obs.*

**1616** Surfl. & Markh. *Country Farme* III. ix. 345 A subiect of a more feeble and vnfirme nature than the graft it selfe. **1660** Jer. Taylor *Ductor* III. v. rule viii. § 8 For without it, it [*sc.* marriage] is not only inauspicious and unlucky, but illegal, unfirm and insufficient.

**4.** Not firmly placed or planted; insecure; unstable, unsteady; liable to slip or fall.

**1697** Dryden *Æneis* x. 397 Now take the time, while staggering yet they stand With feet unfirm. **1761** Earl Pembroke *Milit. Equitation* (1778) 58 Depend upon it those people are not only ignorant and unfeeling, but also very unfirm in their seat. **1771** Mrs. Griffith *Hist. Lady Barton* III. 20 His supplicating eye..may change my unfirm purpose. **1809** *Susan* I. 176 Our best resolutions are, however, unfirm.

**Unfi·rmamented,** *ppl. a.* (Un-[1] 8.) **1843** Carlyle *Past & Pr.* III. viii, Burying itself..in the waste unfirmamented seas. **1865** Mrs. Whitney *Gayworthys* xliii, He had touched unfirmamented space.

**Unfi·rmly,** *adv.* (Un-[1] 11, 5 b. Cf. Unfirm *a.*)

**1633** Ford *Broken H.* IV. ii, Like tempest-threatened trees, unfirmly rooted. **1822–7** Good *Study Med.* (1829) II. 418 The child walks unfirmly, as though stepping over a threshold.

**Unfi·rmness.** (Un-[1] 12, 5 b; cf. Infirmness.) **1566** *Act 8 Eliz.* c. 8 § 1 Fenne Groundes, because of their rottennesse, unfirmnes, moysture and wateryshnes [etc.]. **1828** Webster. **Unfi·shable,** *a.* (Un-[1] 7 b.) **1873** G. C. Davies *Mount. & Mere* ii. 8 The other side was so shallow and muddy that it was unfishable. **1891** A. Lang *Angling Sk.* 98 The loch is almost unfishable. **Unfi·shed,** *ppl. a.* (Un-[1] 8.) **1863** Johns *Home Walks* 47 The main reason why unfished waters are most productive, is that they are then more plentifully stocked. **1883** in N. Okoshi *Fisheries Japan* 26 In his unfortunate country [*sc.* Ireland] they had at present over 2500 miles of unfished coast. **Unfi·shlike,** *a.* (Un-[1] 7 c.) **1874** Wood *Nat. Hist.* 621 A creature so unfishlike that its real position..was long undecided.

**Unfi·st,** *v.* [Un-[2] 4 b.] *trans.* To unhand.

**1692** [J. Smith] *Scarron.* 85 You goodman Brandy-face, unfist her; How durst you keep my wife?—your sister.

**Unfi·t,** *a.* (and *adv.*). [Un-[1] 7 and 5 b.]

**1.** Of things: Not fit, proper, or suitable *for* some purpose or end. † Also const. *to* (a person).

In quot. 1709 app. 'badly fitting'.

**1548** Udall, etc. *Erasm. Par. John* i. 11 b, For there is no tyme nor place vnfit or vnconuenient for to learne those thynges whiche pertayne to euerlastynge welth. **1584** in *Cath. Rec. Soc. Publ.* V. 82 The Earle..gave the poore man many..opprobrious wordes, unfytte and unseemely for a man of that howse and blod. *a* **1658** Lovelace *Poems* (1904) 191 He that dares this, nothing to him's unfit. **1697** Dryden *Virg. Georg.* IV. 190 Lord of few Acres, and those barren too; Unfit for Sheep or Vines, and more unfit to sow. **1709** *Lond. Gaz.* No. 4551/4 He wears..a brown Drugget Coat and Wastecoat..very unfit for him. **1785** Cowper *Let. to Newton* 19 Mar., The sideboard-table..was equally unfit for my purpose. **1812** Crabbe *Tales* xiii. 351 Those duties were to her unfit, Nor would her spirit to her tasks submit. **1827** Faraday *Chem. Manip.* v. (1842) 151 Mortars of wood, marble, or iron, are unfit for ordinary laboratory service. **1884** Thompson *Tumours of Bladder* 71 In cases considered temporarily unfit for operation through exhaustion, etc.

**b.** Without prepositional const.

**1545** Ascham *Toxoph.* (Arb.) 118 An vnfit and staffysh bow. *a* **1586** Sidney *Arcadia* II. xxix, Because of the unfit election she had made. **1604** E. G[rimstone] *D'Acosta's Hist. Indies* VI. xiv. 460 Although these buildings were great, yet were they commonly ill appoynted and vnfit. **1661** Rust *Origen's Opin.* 78 If old age it self can make the Soul quit her unfit tenement. **1711** in *Nairne Peerage Evidence* (1874) 133 Rendered the same unfit and in human probability impossible. **1863** Hawthorne *Our Old Home* (1879) 317 The anxious fidelity with which they discharged their unfit office.

**c.** Const. with inf. (active or passive).

*a* **1586** Sidney *Arcadia* I. xiii, A place for pleasantnes, not unfitte to flatter solitarinesse. **1611** Cotgr., *Imbuvable*, vndrinkable; vnfit to be drunke of. **1651** Hobbes *Leviath.* II. xxix. 173 There be other [diseases], not so great; which neverthelesse are not unfit to be observed. **1697** [see 1 a]. **1710** Lady M. W. Montagu *Let. to Mr. W. Montagu* Aug., There are a thousand things, not ill in themselves, which custom makes unfit to be done. **1879** Harlan *Eyesight* viii. 117 The flame..is never steady, and is unfit to read by.

**2.** Of persons (or other agents): Not fitted, suited, or adapted for some end or action. Also *Comb.* (in *unfit-like*) and *absol.*

**1551** T. Wilson *Logike* D j, We see many dull wittes for lernyng, and muche vnfit that waie. **1577** tr. *Bullinger's Decades* (1592) 510 To giue an vnfitte man orders,..is that kinde of sin which we doe call anothers sin. **1782** J. Brown *Nat. & Rev. Relig.* II. i. (1796) 105 In propagating the gospel by so unfit-like instruments. **1818** Cruise *Digest* (ed. 2) III. 128 A person unknown and unfit..may happen to have the same, under an estate of inheritance. **1882** *Nonconf. & Indep.* 10 Oct. 986/1 The survival of the unfittest, instead of the fittest.

b. Const. *to* (chiefly with inf.) or *for*.

(*a*) **1586** T. B. *La Primaud. Fr. Acad.* (1589) 111 It maketh him good for nothing,..slothfull, and unfit to every good thing. **1630** Prynne *Anti-Armin.* 136 This makes them.. open rebels against God, vnfit to take his word or name within their lips. **1645** Milton *Colast.* Wks. 1851 IV. 349 The unfittest man that could bee to offer at a comment upon Job. **1747** H. Walpole *Lett.* (1846) II. 201, I am the unfittest person in the world to give you any satisfaction on this head. **1816** Byron *Ch. Har.* III. xii, But soon he knew himself the most unfit Of men to herd with Man. **1863** H. Cox *Instit.* I. vii. 91 Men who are morally or intellectually unfit to be jurors.

(*b*) **1594** Shaks. *Rich. III*, I. ii. 109 *Rich.* He was fitter for that place then earth. *An.* And thou vnfit for any place, but hell. **1660** R. Coke *Power & Subj.* 73 Being of all mortal men the most unfit for a Churchman. **1697** Dryden *Virg. Georg.* III. 102 Then release the Cow, Unfit for Love, and for the lab'ring Plough. **1736** Berkeley *Disc.* Wks. 1871 III. 413 Monsters, utterly unfit for human society. **1855** Macaulay *Hist. Eng.* xv. III. 584 In order that one man might fill a post for which he was unfit. **1880** Dixon *Windsor* IV. i. 2 He was a man unfit for such a trust.

**3.** Not physically fit.

Usually const. *for* or with infinitive.

**1665** in *Verney Mem.* (1907) II. 251, I grow every day more unfit for such a Jorney. *a* **1718** Prior *Amaryllis* 24 The furious heat forbids the reaper's toil. Both beast and men for work are now unfit. **1798** S. & Ht. Lee *Canterb. T.* II. 428 The Marquis was very unfit for a journey when he left Naples. **1856** Kane *Arct. Expl.* II. i. 26, I am myself so disabled..as to be entirely unfit..to do any work.

**4.** As *adv.* Unfitly.

**1653** J. Taylor (Water P.) *Cert. Trav. uncert. Journ.* 8 Sometimes the wits and tongues do, most unfit, Travell, when tongues do run before the wit.

**Unfi·t,** *v.* [Un-² 6.] *trans.* To render unfit; to disqualify.

**1611** Florio, *Disadattare*, to vnfit, to disorder. **1665** Boyle *Occas. Refl.* II. x. (1848) 128, I..esteem'd sickness more formidable for its unfitting me to learn. **1690** Norris *Beatitudes* (1692) 80 Consider again, How much causless..Anger unfits us for all the Parts of Divine Worship. **1779** *Mirror* No. 16, It may disqualify the mind for the more active..scenes of life, and unfit it for the enjoyments of ordinary society. **1847** Helps *Friends in C.* (1851) I. 36 To have erred in one branch of our duties does not unfit us for all the rest. **1898** 'Merriman' *Roden's Corner* vi. 57 Those whose birth and education unfit them for such pursuits.

**Unfi·tly,** *adv.* [Un-¹ 11.] In an unfit or unsuitable manner; unfittingly, inappropriately.

**1561** T. Norton tr. *Calvin's Inst.* I. xiii. 37 b, Least if I bryng foorth any thyng vnfittly, it should geue occasion..to the malicious to cauill. **1632** Massinger & Field *Fatal Dowry* III. i, Wherein hath Charalois Unfitly so demean'd himself? **1676** Jas. Cooke *Marrow Chirurg.* I. III. vii. 590 There are chaps of the Lips and other parts, which if neglected or unfitly dressed, may turn Cancerous. **1788** Gibbon *Decl. & F.* lx. VI. 128 Their military talents were unfitly recompensed by the lucrative offices of judges and treasurers. **1807** G. Chalmers *Caledonia* I. III. vii. 393 It is, however, unfitly interpolated, by the editor, as a continuation of the *Chronicon Pictorum*.

b. In the phr. *not unfitly*.

**1586** T. B. *La Primaud. Fr. Acad.* I. 160 The answer also of an Egyptian was not unfitlie made to one that asked him what he caried there folded. **1615** Crooke *Body of Man* 541 Thence also they are not vnfitly called by a Poet..The leaues of the Eye. **1695** J. Edwards *Perfect. Script.* 236 They..are not unfitly translated *aprons*. **1710** Berkeley *Princ. Hum. Knowl.* § 108 The steady consistent methods of nature may not unfitly be styled the Language of its Author. **1853** Ruskin *Stones Ven.* II. vi. 215 The three architectures may..not unfitly receive their names from those nations by whom they were carried to the highest perfection.

**Unfi·tness.** [Un-¹ 12.]

**1.** Want of fitness (in various senses).

*a* **1586** Sidney *Arcadia* III. xxiv, Having impatiently borne the delay of the nights unfitnesse, this morning he gat up. **1624** in Ellis *Orig. Lett.* Ser. I. III. 173, I represented to her the unfitnesse of the seventh article. **1643–5** Milton *Divorce* I. i, What greater..unfitnes of mind then that which hinders ever the solace..of the married couple. **1736** Butler *Anal.* I. iii. 69 A Proof from Fact..which is deduced from..the Fitness and Unfitness of Actions. **1750** tr. *Leonardus' Mirr. Stones* 31 A bad commixture..sometimes happens..from the unfitness of the place, which gives a diversity to stones. **1824** Southey *Sir T. More* (1831) II. 94 There is a natural unfitness in distant dominion. **1863** Cox *Instit.* III. iii. 636 The rule..has no respect to the fitness or unfitness of the persons.

b. Const. *for*, or *to* with inf.

**1619** in Foster *Eng. Factories India* (1906) I. 70 The unfitnesse of those comodityes for the Dabulleers. **1631** Gouge *God's Arrows* III. § 22. 223 Mans unworthinesse and unfitnesse to appeare in Gods sight. **1750** Secker *Eight Charges* (1771) 124, I have too much Cause, in every Thing, to be sensible of my own Unfitness to direct. **1811** *Regul. & Orders Army* 283 The Causes of their unfitness for further Military Service. **1885** *Manch. Exam.* 18 Mar. 5/2 There was..evidence of his unfitness to take care of himself.

**2.** With pl. An instance of lack of fitness.

**1645** Milton *Tetrach.* Wks. 1851 IV. 193 Law..cannot make equal those inequalities, it cannot make fit those unfitnesses. **1674** N. Fairfax *Bulk & Selv.* 32 If they could be brought in without other unfitnesses.

**Unfi·tted,** *ppl. a.* [Un-¹ 8.]

**1.** Not adapted or suited; unfit.

**1592** in Ellis *Orig. Lett.* Ser. III. IV. 109, I am come upp raggedlie suted and clothed, unfittedst to geve duetiefull attendance on Royall presence. *a* **1625** Fletcher *Hum. Lieut.* II. iv, How yet unripe we were, unblown, unharden'd, Unfitted for such fatal ends. **1794** S. Williams *Vermont* 351 Such a code is wholly unfitted to the uncorrupted state of the people. **1809** Kendall *Trav.* I. i. 7 A scene, that was not unfitted to leave on the mind a..respectful impression. **1873** Symonds *Grk. Poets* x. 340 Unfitted, perhaps, by temperament for the most impassioned lyrics, Tennyson delights in minutely finished pictures.

**2.** Not provided with something suitable.

**1606** Chapman *Gentl. Usher* IV. iv, If it be nothing but the jarre Of your unfitted fancie that procures Your wilfull coynesse.

**3.** Not fitted up or out; not properly furnished.

**1708** *Lond. Gaz.* No. 4414/3 Some [ships] in the Peer are yet unfitted. **1908** *Animal Managem.* 269 If for military reasons long journeys have to be made in unfitted trucks.

**4.** Not adjusted by fitting.

**1895** *Pall Mall G.* 1 Feb. 5/2 Nations that have not arrived at the artificial prettiness of finely-fitted dress had best be content with the natural beauty of unfitted.

Hence **Unfi·ttedness.**

**1654** Gayton *Pleas. Notes* III. v. 94 The Actors were privately to be tried upon the Stage, that upon the insufficiency of the persons, or unfittednesse, the men might be chang'd. **1870** Hales *Longer Eng. Poems* 112 This sense of his unfittedness to perform as yet a poet's high duties.

**Unfi·tting,** *ppl. a.* [Un-¹ 10, 5 d.] Not fitting or suitable; unbecoming, improper.

Apparent earlier examples, when verifiable, have proved to be errors for *unsitting*. Cf. the note to Fitting *ppl. a.*

**1590** Greene *Orl. Fur.* I. i. 220 Least little brooking these vnfitting braues, My cholar ouer-slip the law of Armes. **1631** Weever *Anc. Funeral Mon.* 318 These Canons did not continue long at Ottebam, the scituation of the place being vnfitting. **1656** Earl Monm. tr. *Boccalini's Advts. fr. Parnass.* II. lxviii. (1674) 221 A thing which..is altogether unfitting to be named. **1687** in *Magd. Coll. & Jas. II* (O.H.S.) 103 He was unfitting by reason of his Immorality. **1771** Burke *Prosecut. Libels* Wks. 1842 II. 493 This is an unfitting, it is a dangerous, state of things. **1853** Abp. Thomson *Laws Th.* (ed. 3) Pref. p. v, Some account of the exact position which this work pretends to occupy..may not be an unfitting introduction to its pages.

b. Const. *for*, or with direct object.

**1591** *1st Pt. Troub. Raigne K. John* (1611) B j b, These thoughts are farre vnfitting Fauconbridge. *a* **1593** Marlowe *Ovid's Elegies* III. i. 40 Small doores vnfitting for large houses are. **1603** Florio *Montaigne* I. xxxix. 125 Qualities mis-seeming his place, and unfitting his calling. **1660** R. Coke *Power & Subj.* 71 Lest..the seamen should be forgetful, and unfitting for naval warfare. **1849** Rock *Ch. of Fathers* I. v. (1903) I. 293 What so unfitting the solemnity of soul..at a burial service?

Hence **Unfi·ttingness.**

**1861** *Macm. Mag.* June 134 Colour or form which represents an unfittingness would be likely to become itself an unfittingness.

**Unfi·ttingly,** *adv.* (Un-¹ 11.)

**1637** Abp. Laud *Sp. Star-Chamber* 14 June 24 That clause being unfittingly expressed, we thought fit to passe it over. **1656** W. Montague *Accompl. Wom.* 101 It were to be ill advised..to be so unfittingly pitifull to insolence or detraction. **1828** Scott *F. M. Perth* xiii, Men who have matched unfittingly become careless in the choice of those whom they love.

**Unfi·tty,** *a.* Now *dial.* [Un-¹ 7.] Unfit. **1613** Withers *Juvenilia, Abuses* I. x, For, 'tis a shame to speake How wonderfull vnfitty and how weake This ignorance makes most of vs. **1837–** in s.w. glossaries (s.v. *Unvitty*).

**Unfi·x,** *v.* [Un-² 3 and 7.]

**1.** *trans.* To undo from a fixed state or position; to unfasten, loosen.

**1597** Shaks. *2 Hen. IV*, IV. i. 208 Plucking to vnfixe an Enemie, Hee doth vnfasten so, and shake a friend. **1605** — *Macb.* I. iii. 135 That suggestion, Whose horrid Image doth vnfixe my Heire. **1775** Ash, *Unfix*,..to loosen, to make less fast. **1804** J. Grahame *Sabbath* 554 Storms that loudly threaten to unfix Islands. **1854** H. Miller *Sch. & Schm.* (1858) 438 Unfixing the haulser from the stem, and bringing it aft to the stern, we commenced hauling.

b. *spec.* in military use.

**1802** James *Milit. Dict.*, *To unfix*, in a military sense, to take off, as Unfix Bayonet, on which the soldier disengages the bayonet from his piece, and returns it to the scabbard. **1813** *Examiner* 10 May 303/2 Two men lost their bayonets, whilst in the act of unfixing them. **1859** F. A. Griffiths *Artill. Man.* (1862) 13 Unfix Swords (or bayonets).

**2.** *fig.* To unsettle; to render uncertain or doubtful.

**1650** R. Stapylton *Strada's Low C. Wars* I. 6 Neither gold,..nor the noise of War,..could any way unfix his mind. **1663** J. Spencer *Prodigies* (1665) 211 Now one Negative instance will appear..of far more force to unfix a pretending Rule, then two Affirmative to establish it. **1802** Paley *Nat. Theol.* xxvi. Wks. (1834) 548/2 By unfixing those motives which promote exertion, or by relaxing those habits which engender patient industry. **1849** Macaulay *Hist. Eng.* viii. II. 322 The shock which had overturned his early prejudices had at the same time unfixed all his opinions.

**3.** *intr.* To become unfixed; to lose fixity.

**1844** Hood *Forge* II. 417 But the ruthless talons refuse to unfix. **1863** Reade *Hard Cash* II. 57 As the blood escaped, his eye unfixed, and the pupils contracted and dilated.

**Unfi·xable,** *a.* (Un-¹ 7 b.) **1831** T. Hope *Ess. Orig. Man* I. 26 The fleeting perceptions of that fugitive and unfixable present. **1832** Coleridge *Self-knowledge* 7 Dark fluxion, all unfixable by thought.

**Unfi·xed,** *ppl. a.* [Un-¹ 8.]

**1.** Not fixed in a definite place or position; unfastened, loose, free.

**1598** Sylvester *Du Bartas* II. ii. IV. *Columnes* 131 The Criticall and double-sexed Seven, The Number of th' unfixed Fires of Heav'n. **1660** Jer. Taylor *Ductor* I. iii. rule i. § 5 It is like a fire-stick, which..being gently mov'd gives a volatile and unfixed light. **1721** Ramsay *Morning Interview* 93 Her unfix'd eyes with various turnings range. **1787** Jefferson *Writ.* (1859) II. 99 The Count of Vergennes has..had a very severe attack of what is deemed an unfixed gout. **1805** Loudon *Improv. Hot-Houses* 65 A stripe of cloth..is left unfixed at top. **1837** Dickens *Pickw.* iii, There was a low cinder fire in a rusty unfixed grate. **1844** *Regul. & Ord. Army* 260 All Guards are to parade, with shouldered Arms, and unfixed Bayonets.

†b. Of persons: Not restricted by office to one or a special place. *Obs.*

**1661** *Papers on Alter. Prayer-bk.* 10 Generall unfixed Bishops, like the Evangelists or Apostles,..and the fixed Bishops of Parochial Churches. **1685** Baxter *Paraphr. N. T.* 1 Tim. iii. 7 The Ministerial Work was..Indefinite, by Itinerant, or unfixed Men.

**2.** *fig.* **a.** Unsettled, uncertain, undetermined; fluctuating, variable.

**1654** Z. Coke *Logick* Pref., To guid the intricate and perplexed thoughts of the unfixed people through the great Labyrinth of Time. **1697** J. Potter *Antiq. Greece* I. ix. (1715) 48 It appears to have been unfix'd and arbitrary. **1763** Johnson 21 July in *Boswell*, He is totally unfixed in his principles, and wants to puzzle other people. **1826** E. Irving *Babylon* I. III. 197 Which..doth exactly determine the time of this trumpet which otherwise would have been unfixed. **1862** Ansted *Channel Isl.* III. xix. (ed. 2) 440 The orthography is not only unfixed, but..is varied.

*absol.* **1844** Mrs. Browning *Vis. Poets* clix, The tones.. throbbed betwixt The incomplete and the unfixed.

b. Unstable; lacking permanency.

**1669** Boyle *Notes Atmospheres* in *Contn. New Exp.* I. 196 The weights themselves..are commonly made of Brass (a Metal very unfixt).

†**3.** Not properly fitted. *Obs.*—[1]

**1643** Chas. I in *Tregaskis' Catal.* (1907) 6 So many recovered men of that Regiment as are able to march, divers of whom have unfixed muskets.

Hence **Unfi·xedness.**

**1668** J. Corbet *Sec. Disc. Relig. Eng.* § xix. 44 Christianity it self would be much endangered in a state of Ataxy and unfixedness. **1707** Norris *Treat. Humility* ii. 53 The unfixedness and dissipation of his spirit. **1754** Edwards *Freed. Will* III. v. 174 There is a vast Indistinctness and Unfixedness in..very many of the Terms. **1840** Mill *Ess.* (1859) 65 That entire unfixedness in the social position of individuals.

**Unfi·xing,** *ppl. a.* (Un-¹ 10.) **1810** Crabbe *Borough* III. 38 Who sought a readier way the heart to move Than by faint dalliance of unfixing love. **Unfi·xity.** (Un-¹ 12.) **1856** Bagehot *Biog. Studies* (1880) 19 A certain unfixity of opinion. **Unfla·gged,** *ppl. a.* (Un-¹ 8 and Flag *v.*[1]) **1608** Heywood *Lucrece* v. vii, Yet grow our lofty plumes unflagg'd with blood.

**Unfla·gging,** *ppl. a.* (Un-¹ 10.)

**1715** South *Serm.* IV. i. 4 With a continued, unflagging Vigor of Expression. **1860** Froude *Hist. Eng.* VI. 395 A purpose..which he pursued with unflagging energy. **1891** E. Peacock *N. Brendon* II. 347 Her unflagging spirits were a great consolation.

So **Unfla·ggingly** *adv.*

**1858** *Lit. Churchman* 15 May 186/2 A hundred pages, in which the 'view' of this writer is unflaggingly pursued. **1883** *Contemp. Rev.* Sept. 331 Forces that are constantly and unflaggingly at work.

†**Unflain,** *ppl. a. Obs.* [Un-¹ 8 b.] = Unflead *ppl. a.*

*c* **1320** *Sir Tristr.* 468 ȝond liþ a best vnflayn, Atire it as þou wold. **1486** *Bk. St. Albans* e iij, Ye shall vndo hym vnflayne when he shall be dight.

**Unfla·ky,** *a.* (Un-¹ 7.) **1675** Han. Woolley *Gentlew. Comp.* 162 Green ginger;..the better sort is unfleaky. **Unfla·me,** *v.* (Un-² 4.) **1635** Quarles *Embl.* III. Prol. 22 Where neither..doubt afflicts, nor baser fear Unflames your courage in pursuit. **Unfla·ming,** *ppl. a.* (Un-¹ 10.) **1644** Nye *Gunnery* xlvi. (1647) II. 24 Dispart your peece with a lighted and unflaming wax candle.

**Unfla·nked,** *ppl. a.* (Un-¹ 8.)

**1553** Brende *Q. Curtius* III. 25 It was the thing that he doubted moste, that they..should inuade the open side of his battaile whiche lay vnflancked towardes them. **1756** Home *Douglas* III. iii. 40 Water-wafted armies, whose chief strength Lies in firm foot, unflank'd with warlike horse. **1870** *Milit. Engineering* I. v. 33 The points selected for assault should be, if possible, unflanked parts of the work.

**Unfla·ttened,** *ppl. a.* (Un-¹ 8.) [1775 Ash.] **1884** McLaren *Spinning* 178 Four feet of yarn in its natural state unrubbed and unflattened. **Unfla·tterable,** *a.* (Un-¹ 7 b.) **1640** D. Cawdrey *Commission for Assise* (1641) 9 Such as Chrysippus would have all earthly Judges: Incorrupt, unflatterable. **1647** Trapp *Comm. Matt.* xxii. 16 He was *inadulabilis*, unflatterable.

**Unfla·ttered,** *ppl. a.* (Un-¹ 8.)

**1634** Habington *Castara* I. (Arb.) 47 Time mocks our youth; and..brings us to unflattered age. *Ibid.* II. 76 Retir'd like Princes from the noise of men, To breath a while unflatter'd. **1742** Young *Nt. Th.* II. 631 In vaults, thin courts of poor unflatter'd kings. **1789** T. Twining *Aristotle's Treat. Poetry* 352 The unsoftened and unflattered character of Achilles. **1845** Darwin in F. Darwin *Life* (1887) I. 333 At which I ought to be much flattered and unflattered.

**Unfla·ttering,** *ppl. a.* (Un-¹ 10.)

**1581** Sidney *Apol. Poetrie* (Arb.) 62 They that delight in Poesie it selfe, should..looke themselues in an vnflattering Glasse of reason. **1651** Sherburne *Salmacis* 283 The Neighbouring Lake,..In whose unflattering Mirrour, every Morn, She Counsell takes how best her self t'adorn. **1704** Norris *Ideal World* II. iii. 257 A faithful and unflattering representation of his beloved object. **1823** Byron *Juan* IX. x, To you the unflattering Muse deigns to inscribe Truths, that you will not read in the Gazettes. **1873** H. Rogers *Orig. Bible* ii. (1875) 96 A plan so unflattering to man's self-righteousness.

So **Unfla·tteringly** *adv.*
**1874** *Fortn. Rev.* Feb. 246 Our most popular poet..unflatteringly compares them to 'broken lights'.

**Unflaw·ed,** *ppl. a.* (UN-¹ 8.)
**1665** HOOKE *Microgr.* 97 A very solid and unflaw'd piece of cleer white Marble. **1817** SCOTT *Harold* VI. vii, Firm was that faith,—as diamond stone Pure and unflaw'd. **1856** RUSKIN *Mod. Paint.* IV. v. ix. § 7 Furnishing light, broad, and unflawed pieces to serve for slates upon the roof.

†**Unflea·d,** *ppl. a. Obs.* [UN-¹ 8 + *flea* FLAY *v.*] Not flayed or skinned.
**1580** BLUNDEVIL *Horsemanship* III. 32b, Two sheepesheads vnfleade. **1647** HERRICK *Noble Numb., Thanksgiving for House* 22 A little Byn, Which keeps my little loafe of Bread Unchipt, unflead. **1654** GAYTON *Pleas. Notes* III. x. 142 Such a beardlesse boy as the unflead goatheard.

**Unflechand**: see UNFLICHING *ppl. a. Obs.*

**Unfle·cked,** *ppl. a.* (UN-¹ 8.) **1865** J. THOMSON *Sunday up River* VI. iii, White-robed, my own white dove unflecked. **1883** STEVENSON *Silverado Sq.* 4 Although the upper sky was still unflecked with vapour.

**Unfle·dge,** *v.* (UN-² 4.)
**1598** FLORIO, *Spennacchiare*,..to vnfeather, to vnfledge, to vnplume. **1809** MALKIN *Gil Blas* x. x. ⁋ 33 For fear he should unfledge me, by taking away my livery.

†**Unfle·dge,** *a. Obs.* [UN-¹ 7.] = next.
**1581** NEWTON tr. *Seneca's Plays* Pref., Mine I confess to be an unflidge nestling, unhable to flye. **1603** HOLLAND *Plutarch's Mor.* 570 The nightingales instruct their yoong birds in song, insomuch as those which be taken unfledge out of the nest,..never afterwards sing so well.

**Unfle·dged,** *ppl. a.* Also 7–8 unfletch'd, 7 unfletcht. [UN-¹ 8.]
**1.** Not yet furnished or covered with feathers; callow; unfeathered. Also in fig. context.
**1611** SHAKS. *Cymb.* III. iii. 27 We poore vnfledg'd Haue neuer wing'd from view o' th' nest. **1717** *Poem Birthday K. George*, Now boldly dare, With unfletch'd Wings, Nobly to soar. **1752** FOOTE *Taste* I. i, This superannuated Beldame gapes for flattery, like a nest of unfledg'd crows for food. **1821** SCOTT *Kenilw.* ix, The two-legged and unfledged species called mankind. **1890** *Science-Gossip* XXVI. 19/2, Two unfledged birds lying dead at the base of the wall.
**b.** *poet.* Of an arrow: = UNFEATHERED *a.* 2.
**1752** YOUNG *Brothers* II. i, Nor can he feather there his unfledg'd shaft But from ambition's wing.
**2.** Of things: Not fully developed; still in a crude or imperfect state.
**1615** BRATHWAIT *Strappado* (1878) 50 You that..betake to worser parts Your vnfledg'd fancies. **1649** G. DANIEL *Trinarch., Hen. V*, xxxvii, Vnfledg'd Witt Imp't from the ragged Sarcill Chaucer drop't. **1790** SIR J. REYNOLDS in Leslie & Taylor *Life & Times* (1865) II. x. 592 Newly hatched, unfledged opinions. **1851** MRS. BROWNING *Casa Guidi Wind.* II. 270 Alas, poor people, of an unfledged will!
**3.** Of persons: Immature, inexperienced, undeveloped in knowledge, etc.
**1602** SHAKS. *Ham.* I. iii. 65 But doe not dull thy palme, with entertainment Of each vnhatch't, vnfledg'd Comrade. **1669** DRYDEN *Prol. to Wild Gallant reviv'd* 14 By such degrees, while knowledge he did want, Our unfletch'd Author writ a Wild Gallant. **1712** ADDISON *Spect.* No. 305 ⁋ 15 This Society of unfledged Statesmen. **1769** *Junius Lett.* xxv. (1788) 159 The unfledged race of ensigns, who infest our streets. **1824** DOYLE in Fitz-Patrick *Life* (1880) I. 314 To stare with wonder..at what appears strange only because it is unknown to some unfledged traveller or essayist.
**4.** Pertaining to, characteristic of, youth and inexperience.
**1611** SHAKS. *Wint. T.* I. ii. 78 In those vnfledg'd dayes, was my Wife a Girle. **1760–72** H. BROOKE *Fool of Qual.* (1809) III. 134, I am but as a bird from the nest, and this is the first of my unfledged excursions. **1809** MALKIN *Gil Blas* x. x. ⁋ 42 My unfledged youth might lead him to take me for some graceless little truant. **1881** *World* 28 Dec., She has lost the innocence of unfledged girlhood.

**Unflee·ce,** *v.* (UN-² 4.) **1609** DEKKER *Ravens Alm.* D 2 The Clergie..shall haue thin cheekes, for euerie body shall fleece or rather vnfleece them. **Unflee·ced,** *ppl. a.* (UN-¹ 8.) *c* **1825** MOORE *Country Dance & Quad.* 98 Yet unfleeced by funding blockheads, Happy John Bull..had..'Money in both pockets'. **Unflee·ting,** *ppl. a.* (UN-¹ 10.) *a* **1640** JACKSON *Creed* x. iii. § 1 The original controversy..plainly propounded in constant or unfleeting terms. **1811** W. R. SPENCER *Poems* 49 Painting,..whose magic-gifted hand Can..raise unfleeting visions of the past. **Unfle·nched,** *ppl. a.* (UN-¹ 8.) **1820** SCORESBY *Acc. Arctic Reg.* II. 32 Leaving one ship with..two whales and a half unflenched.

**Unfle·sh,** *v.* [UN-² 4.] *trans.* To strip of flesh. Hence **Unfle·shing** *vbl. sb.*
**1598** FLORIO, *Scarnare*, to vnflesh, to pare the flesh from the bones. **1611** *Ibid.*, *Scarnatura*, any vnfleshing. **1683** E. HOOKER *Pordage's Mystic Div.* Pref. 25 When the inexorable Messenger..shal come..and uncloath and unflesh him too. **1894** BARING-GOULD *Deserts S. France* I. 190 A body had been deliberately unfleshed before it was laid in its last habitation.

**Unfle·shed,** *ppl. a.*¹ [UN-¹ 8 + FLESH *v.*] Not yet stimulated by tasting flesh; *fig.*, untried, inexperienced, new. Also *absol.*
**1542** UDALL *Erasm. Apoph.* 280, I wil never present an hoste unto yᵉ high capitaine of Roome..unfleashed on their enemies. **1611** SPEED *Theat. Gt. Brit.* 125/1 Some..who (like unflesht souldiers) gaue ouer their enterprise without further hope. **1635–56** COWLEY *Davideis* III. 499 With some less Foe thy unflesht valour try. **1692** DRYDEN *Cleomenes* v. ii, As a generous, unfleshed hound, that hears From far the hunters' horn and cheerful cry. **1748** RICHARDSON *Clarissa* VII. 409, I am no unfleshed novice; this [duel] is a sport, that..I love as well as my food. **1833** LYTTON *Godolphin* 8 Percy's heart was full of enterprise and the unfleshed valour of inexperience. **1895** MEREDITH *Amazing Marriage* ix, Customary phrases of the unfleshed in folly.

**Unfle·shed,** *ppl. a.*² [f. UNFLESH *v.*, or UN-¹ 8.] **a.** Stripped of flesh. **b.** Not covered with flesh.
**1607** W. BARKSTED *Mirrha* D 4 b, Nor let the dead repine, ..let the vnflesht thronges..be glad. **1795** SOUTHEY *Vis. Maid Orleans* I. 99 Behold this skull, These eyeless sockets, and these unflesh'd jaws. **1864** LOWELL *Fireside Trav., At Sea*, May it be long before Professor Owen is comforted with the sight of his unfleshed vertebræ.

**Unfle·shly,** *a.* (UN-¹ 7.)
**1855** PUSEY *Doctr. Real Presence* 335 For if some unfleshly quality of a body be opposed to us, surely..it will not have blood. **1861** READE *Cloister & H.* l, Those unfleshly eyes, with which they say the very air is thronged.
Hence **Unfle·shliness.**
*a* **1859** DE QUINCEY *Posth. Wks.* (1891) I. 186 Without the idea of holiness and unfleshliness, eternity..cannot sustain itself.

**Unfle·shy,** *a.* (UN-¹ 7.) **1612** J. DAVIES (Heref.) *Muse's Sacr.* Wks. (Grosart) II. 13/1 At gastly Deaths vnfleshy feet. †**Unfle·t,** *ppl. a. Obs.*—¹ (UN-¹ 8 b + FLEET *v.*²) **1688** R. HOLME *Armoury* III. 335/1 Dairy People..make.. Flet and unflet Milk Cheese.

**Unfletch'd,** obs. var. UNFLEDGED.

†**Unfle·xible,** *a. Obs.* [UN-¹ 7 and 5 b.] = INFLEXIBLE *a.*
*a* **1586** SIDNEY *Arcadia* III. xv, Falsly accounting an unflexible anger, a couragious constancie. **1611** SPEED *Hist. Gt. Brit.* IX. viii. § 44. 498 Seeing the Pope vnflexible, and vnsensible of so many Christians calamitie. **1677** GILPIN *Demonol.* (1867) 152 Some spirits are unfixed and volatile. ..Others are tenacious and unflexible.

†**Unfli·ching,** *ppl. a. Obs.* [UN-¹ 10.] Unflinching. *a* **1340** HAMPOLE *Psalter* ii. 9 þou sall gouern þaim.. in stabile and vnflichand [*v.r.* unflechande] rightwisnes. **Unfli·ckering,** *ppl. a.* (UN-¹ 10.) **1856** MRS. BROWNING *Aur. Leigh* III. 173 With fixed unflickering outline of dead heat. **1884** *Pall Mall G.* 23 June 16/2 A steady and unflickering light.

**Unfli·nching,** *ppl. a.* (UN-¹ 10.)
**1728** MORGAN *Algiers* II. v. 315 The Valour and Resolution of the unflinching Knights. **1814** SCOTT *Lord of Isles* VI. xxvi, Unflinching foot 'gainst foot was set. **1846** MRS. A. MARSH *Father Darcy* II. ix. 145 A fresh element of resolute, unflinching, persevering determination. **1882** *Macm. Mag.* XLV. 372 Yet he is..determinedly persevering, unflinching as a foe.
Hence **Unfli·nchingly** *adv.*
**1833** COLERIDGE *Table-t.* 5 Feb., Oh! for a great man.. who could..unflinchingly put it into act! **1879** CHR. G. ROSSETTI *Seek & F.* 236 The more unflinchingly we abide by this truth, the keener will our spiritual faculty become.

**Unfloa·table,** *a.* (UN-¹ 7 b.) **1880** 'MARK TWAIN' *Tramp Abr.* I. 231 The floating of iron cable-chains and other unfloatable things. **1884** LD. BLACKBURN in *Law Rep.* 9 App. Cases 409 That natural impediment renders the stream at that spot practically unfloatable. **Unflo·ck,** *v.* (UN-² 6 b.) **1611** FLORIO, *Disgreggiare*, to scatter, to vnflocke. **1778** H. BROOKE *Contending Brothers* v. vi, It were pity that birds of such a feather should be unflock'd. **Unfloo·r,** *v.* (UN-² 4.) **1589** PUTTENHAM *Arte Eng. Poesie* III. xix. (Arb.) 230 They beate downe the walles, they vnfloored the loftes, they vntiled it. **1611** COTGR., *Desplanché*, ..vnfloored, or, whose floore is taken vp. **Unfloo·red,** *ppl. a.* (UN-¹ 8.) **1816** in Hone *Every-day Bk.* (1825) I. 572 The upper story is unfloored. **1897** *Daily News* 26 Nov. 8/5 A tiny unfloored, corrugated iron shanty. **Unflou·red,** *ppl. a.* (UN-¹ 8.) [**1775** ASH.] **1795** in *Spirit Pub. Jrnls.* IV. 229 With surly face and head unflour'd. **Unflou·rished,** *ppl. a.* (UN-¹ 8.) **1486** *Bk. St. Albans, Her.* a j b, Adam the begynnyng of man kynde was as a stokke vnsprayde and vnfloreshed. **Unflou·rishing,** *ppl. a.* (UN-¹ 10.) **1782** BAKER *Biog. Dramatica* III. 92 The Edinburgh theatre, at that time in no unflourishing condition. **Unflow·er,** *v.* (UN-² 4.) **1610** G. FLETCHER *Christ's Vict.* I. lxxxv, Bring..all your silver flaskets,.. That I may soone unflow'r your fragrant baskets, To strowe the fields with odours. **Unflow·ered,** *ppl. a.* (UN-¹ 8.) **1648** HEXHAM II, *Ongebloemt*, vnflowred, or without Flowers. **1775** ASH, *Unflowered*..., not flowered, not ornamented with flowers. **Unflo·wn,** *ppl. a.* (UN-¹ 8 b.) [**1775** ASH.] **1791** COWPER *Iliad* IV. 137 He chose a dart Unflown, full-fledged.

**Unflu·ctuating,** *ppl. a.* (UN-¹ 10.)
**1723** BLACKMORE *Alfred* IV. 129 In the Steerage they preside, And, tho' in Storms, unfluctuating guide The agitated State. **1823** DE QUINCEY *Lett. Educ.* i. 1 That you had the priceless blessing of unfluctuating health. **1858** NORTON *Topics* 243 The tax must be..unfluctuating in amount. **1896** *N. Amer. Rev.* Dec. 743 A sound unfluctuating currency.

**Unflu·ent,** *a.* (UN-¹ 7.) **1605** SYLVESTER *Du Bartas* I. vi. 29 Poure vpon my faint vn-fluent tongue The sweetest hunnie of th' Hyantian Fount. **1659** O. WALKER *Instruct. Oratory* 25 The first making the language dull and slow; the other,..abrupt, and unfluent. **Unflu·rried,** *ppl. a.* (UN-¹ 8.) **1854** CDL. WISEMAN *Fabiola* (1855) 287 She completed, unflurried, the preparations for supper. **Unflu·sh,** *v.* (UN-² 7.) **1866** M. ARNOLD *Thyrsis* xvii, The west unflushes, the high stars grow bright.

**Unflu·shed,** *ppl. a.*¹ [UN-¹ 8 + FLUSH *v.*¹ 2.] Of game: Not driven up.
**1769** *Stratford Jubilee* I. i, There will be rare poaching for experienced sportsmen among unflush'd game.

**Unflu·shed,** *ppl. a.*² [UN-¹ 8 + FLUSH *v.*²] Not flushed in colour.
[**1775** ASH.] **1860** LD. LYTTON *Lucile* II. i. § 16. 4 That pale cheek for ever by passion unflush'd. **1868** H. BUSHNELL *Moral Uses Dark Th.* (1869) 217 We see it in a laying out of white, unflushed by mortal sympathy.

**Unflu·ted,** *ppl. a.* (UN-¹ 8.) [**1775** ASH.] **1843** *Civil Eng. & Arch. Jrnl.* VI. 270/2 The columns are unfluted. **1854** tr. *Hettner's Athens & Peloponnese* 46 Pieces of friezes,..and unfluted drums of pillars. **Unflu·tterable,** *a.* (UN-¹ 7 b.) **1871** MRS. WHITNEY *Real Folks* viii, The quiet, unflutterable gray bonnet calmly horizontal. **Unflu·xile,** *a.* (UN-¹ 7.) **1757** tr. *Henckel's Pyritol.* 349 Crude, unmetallic, unfluxile earth. **Unfoa·led,** *ppl. a.* (UN-¹ 8.) **1863** MISS BRADDON *Aurora Floyd* xiii, Winning future Derbys..with colts that are as yet unfoaled. **Unfoe·d,** *a.* (UN-¹ 9.) **1586** WARNER *Alb. Eng.* III. xviii, Augustus..was Emperour alone; In whose unfoed Monarchie our comon health was knowen.

**Unfoi·led,** *ppl. a.*¹ [UN-¹ 8 + FOIL *v.*¹]
†**1.** Not injured, marred, or impaired. *Obs.*
**1579–80** NORTH *Plutarch* (1595) 242 When the golden and vnfoiled age remained yet whole..at Rome. *a* **1640** JACKSON *Creed* x. viii. § 3 The Naturalist..hunts after the truth with fresh unfoiled scent. **1691** RAY *Creation* II. (1692) 22 To let in [to the eye] the Light and Colors unfoiled and unsophisticated by any inward Tincture.
**2.** Not overcome, beaten, or baffled.
**1587** T. HUGHES *Misfort. Arthur* v. i. 31 For had impatient ire indu'rde abuse,..I mought haue liu'd in forreine coastes vnfoilde. **1600** SIR F. VERE *Comm.* 93 Their footmen (which were old trained souldiers, and to that day unfoiled in the field). **1672** TEMPLE *Ess., Govt.* Wks. 1720 I. 107 The usurped Powers..thought themselves secure in the Strength of an unfoiled Army of above Sixty Thousand Men.

†**Unfoi·led,** *ppl. a.*² *Obs.* [UN-¹ 8 + FOIL *v.*³] Unploughed.
**1611** COTGR., *Terre vierge*, ground that is whole or vnfoyled; good ground that was neuer plowed.

**Unfoiled,** *ppl. a.*³ [UN-¹ 8 + FOIL *v.*⁴] Not coated or backed with foil.
**1640** in Entick *London* (1766) II. 165 Glass-plates, or sights for looking-glasses, unfoiled. **1731** *Phil. Trans.* XXXVII. 155 The second Speculum may have a Part unfoil'd. **1761** *Ibid.* LII. 561 By reflexion from the unfoiled part of the speculum.

**Unfo·ld,** *v.*¹ Forms: 1 unfealdan, 3 unuolden, 3–6 un-, vnfolde (5 onfolde), 4– unfold (4–7 vn-), 6–7 vnfould; 5 *north.* vnfald(e, 6, 8 *Sc.* unfauld. [OE. *unfealdan* (f. *un-* UN-² + *fealdan* FOLD *v.*¹), = MDu. and Du. *ontvouden, -vouwen* (eastern MDu. *-volden, -valden*), G. *entfalten.*]
**1.** *trans.* To open or unwrap the folds of; to spread open; to expand; to straighten out.
*c* **890** WÆRFERTH tr. *Gregory's Dial.* 333 Þa boc..unlysan & unfealdan. *c* **1000** *Ags. Gosp.* Luke iv. 17 Sona swa he þa boc unfeold, þa funde he [etc.]. *c* **1205** LAY. 10544 Æuere his writen he vnfeold þer he forð ferde. **13..** *Coer de L.* 4809 Hys baner anon was unfolde, The Sarezynes anon gan behold. **1338** R. BRUNNE *Chron.* (1810) 284 Bot if þe bulle vnfolden were red among vs here, ȝour hote salle be holden. **1377** LANGL. *P. Pl.* B. XVII. 176 Þe paume hath powere..to vnfolde þe folden fuste. *a* **1400–50** *Alexander* 3027 Bald bernes on bent banars vnfaldis. *c* **1450** LOVELICH *Grail* xxxvi. 462 Whanne this body he hadde beholde, Anon the clothes he dyde on-folde. **1530** PALSGR. 767/2, I unfolde any thyng that is folded up togyder, *Je desploye. Ibid.*, Unfolde this clothe. *a* **1553** UDALL *Roister D.* III. iv, No lesse..Than this letter purporteth, which ye haue vnfolde. **1663** DAVENANT *Siege of Rhodes* Wks. (1672) 8 Sweeter then Buds unfolded in a Shower. **1697** DRYDEN *Æneis* VI. 393 Strife, that shakes Her hissing tresses, and unfolds her snakes. **1743** FRANCIS tr. *Hor., Odes* IV. xv. 5 Phœbus.. warn'd me..Not to unfold my little sail. **1784** COWPER *Task* IV. 153 The pattern grows, the well-depicted flow'r..Unfolds its bosom. **1828** SCOTT *F. M. Perth* xix, Come now,.. unfold your arms from about my patient. **1841** T. R. JONES *Anim. Kingd.* 399 One of the snails unfolds from the right side of its neck..a wide sacculus.
**b.** *transf.* or *fig.*
**1390** GOWER *Conf.* II. 24 For I ne mai my wit unfolde To find o word of that I mene. **1603** KNOLLES *Hist. Turks* (1621) 540 Unfolding his troupes (that standing there, they might at more libertie use their swords). **1633** G. HERBERT *Temple, Dawning* 3 Unfold thy forehead gather'd into frowns. **1744** AKENSIDE *Pleas. Imag.* I. 73 Till in time.. What he admired and loved, his vital smile Unfolded into being. **1839** THIRLWALL *Greece* VI. 253 As these thoughts had been nourished and unfolded in himself by the recent change in his fortunes.
**c.** To open (the eyes or lips); to open (a gate, etc.) upon hinges.
*a* **1325** in Horstm. *Altengl. Leg.* (1878) 144 Adam his eiȝen vnfeld; & seþþen his sone he biheld. **1620** SHELTON *Quix.* I. IV. xix. 518 He would not once vnfold his lips, vntill he might see what would be the period of his disgrace. **1667** MILTON *P. L.* IV. 381 Hell shall unfould..her widest Gates. **1801** SOUTHEY *Thalaba* VI. xvi, The gates of iron, by no human arm Unfolded, turning on their hinges slow. **1896** DE VINNE *Moxon's Mech. Exerc.* 410 He..unfolded the frisket and tympan.
**d.** *refl.* (Also in fig. use.)
**1779** *Mirror* No. 22, Her voice seemed to unfold itself in singing, to suit every musical expression. **1821** SHELLEY *Epipsych.* 480 An atom of th' Eternal, whose own smile Unfolds itself. **1891** FARRAR *Darkn. & Dawn* xxxv, The whole world had turned..to thorns; would some new rosebud now unfold itself among them?
**2.** To disclose or reveal by statement or exposition; to explain or make clear.
*a* **1050** *Liber Scintill.* xxxviii. (1889) 140 Ȝeþancu unrihtwisnysse [hi] unfealdað. *a* **1225** *Ancr. R.* 100 Þis is a cruel word...Hit is bilepped & bihud, ac ich hit wulle unuolden. *a* **1250** *Prov. Ælfred* 659 Al he bi-fulit his frend, Þen he him vnfoldit. **13..** *E. E. Allit. P.* B. 1563 Calle hem alle to my cort.., Vnfolde hem alle þis ferly þat is bifallen here. **1426** LYDG. *De Guil. Pilgr.* 10962 At the grete Iugement Wher tassyses shal be holde, Al couert falsenesse to vnfolde. *c* **1475** *Partenay* 5124 The holy fader wondred on that he told, Off tho merueles that ther [he] gan vnfold. **1595** *Locrine* I. i. 83, I will vnto you all vnfold Our royall mind and resolute intent. **1658** FLECKNOE *Epigr. & Enigm. Char.* 1 Clearly unfolding and explicating the notions of her minde. **1693** *Humours Town* 38, I will only unfold it to you as the nature of the thing is. **1782** PRIESTLEY *Matt. & Spir.* I. Pref. p. xxxii, His system is..perhaps the same..if he would distinctly unfold it. **1817** JAS. MILL *Brit. India* II. v. ix. 689 In a speech..[he] unfolded the causes and extent of the national calamities. **1875** JOWETT

*Plato* (ed. 2) IV. 239 The brethren whose mysteries I am about to unfold to you are far more ingenious.

*refl.* **1602** SHAKS. *Ham.* I. i. 2 Nay answer me: Stand & vnfold your selfe. **1637** B. JONSON *Sad Sheph.* II. v, What riddle is this? unfold your selfe, deare Robin. **1831** CARLYLE *Sart. Res.* II. v, The self-secluded unfolds himself in..free, glowing words.

**3.** To disclose or lay open to the view; to display. Also *fig.*

*c* **1374** CHAUCER *Boeth.* IV. met. v. (1868) 132 Whi þat boetes þe sterre vnfoldiþ his ouer swift arisynges. **1590** SHAKS. *Mids. N.* I. i. 146 Briefe as the lightning in the collied night, That (in a spleene) vnfolds both heauen and earth. **1713** BLACKMORE *Creation* I. 430 The hollow vales their smiling pride unfold. **1812** S. ROGERS *Columbus* XII. 32 To other eyes shall Mexico unfold Her feathered tapestries, and roofs of gold. **1872** JENKINSON *Guide Eng. Lakes* (1879) 91 When the steep part of the journey is accomplished a lovely prospect is unfolded.

*refl.* **1837** W. IRVING *Capt. Bonneville* III. 76 From this lofty eminence, a vast and magnificent prospect unfolds itself.

**4. a.** To unwrap; to take out of something folded.

**1553** BRENDE *Q. Curtius* 190 Vnfolding his wound,..[he] shewed his legge vnto them. **1827** SCOTT *Chron. Canongate* v, Then was unfolded, out of many a little scrap of paper, the reserved sum of fifteen shillings.

**b.** To release, let go.

In Beaum. & Fl. *Faithf. Shepherdess* II, 'vnfould' is an error for 'infold' or 'enfold': see note to UN-[1] 5 b.

**1633** P. FLETCHER *Purple Isl.* XII. xlviii, These suppliant hands..Will never let thee loose, will never more unfold thee.

**5.** *intr.* To open (up or out); to spread out or expand; to become patent or plain, etc.

(*a*) *c* **1350** *Libeaus Desc.* 2091 As he set þus in halle, Out of þe stone walle A window faire unfelde. **1697** DRYDEN *Æneis* X. 1 The Gates of Heav'n unfold; Jove summons all The Gods to Council. **1715** POPE *Iliad* IV. 1 And now Olympus' shining gates unfold. **1725** — *Odyss.* IX. 533 Seest thou these lids that now unfold in vain? **1746** FRANCIS tr. *Horace, Epist.* I. xviii. 122 Ears, that unfold to every Tale, Intrusted Secrets ill conceal. **1828** SCOTT *F. M. Perth* xix, But the fingers do unfold. **1887** BOWEN *Æneid* III. 94 The gates unfold of the shrine.

(*b*) *c* **1586** C'TESS PEMBROKE *Ps.* (1823) LXXXI. i, Let joyfull songes to god unfold. **1601** SHAKS. *Twel. N.* I. ii. 19 Mine owne escape vnfoldeth to my hope. **1725** POPE *Odyss.* XII. 240 Now all at once tremendous scenes unfold. **1759** ROBERTSON *Hist. Scot.* II. Wks. 1813 I. 139 The queen's scheme began gradually to unfold. **1833** TENNYSON *Eleanore* v, I see thy beauty gradually unfold. **1858** SEARS *Athan.* III. i. 256 A system of infinite truth, which is to unfold through the ages.

(*c*) *a* **1649** CRASHAW *Carmen Deo Nostro, To C'tess of Denbigh*, Unfold at length, unfold fair flowre. **1813** SCOTT *Rokeby* VI. i, That morning sun has three times seen The flowers unfold on Rokeby green. **1862** THACKERAY *Philip* xvi, The pony-chaise unfolded into a noble barouche. **1875** BENNETT & DYER tr. *Sachs' Bot.* 175 The position of the leaves in the lateral buds before unfolding.

**Unfo·ld,** *v.*[2] [UN-[2] 4 b + FOLD *v.*[2]] *trans.* To release (sheep) from a fold or folds.

**1530** PALSGR. 768/1 It is tyme to unfolde our shepe. *a* **1613** OVERBURY *A Wife*, etc. (1638) 172 She dares goe alone and unfold sheepe i'th'night. **1781** COWPER *Retirem.* 397 The boy, who..Unfolds his flock.

†**Unfo·ldable,** *a. Obs.* [UN-[1] 7 b.] Incapable of being unfolded.

**1611** COTGR., *Inexplicable*, inexplicable, vnfouldable. *a* **1641** BP. MOUNTAGU *Acts & Mon.* (1642) 420 The sense is marred, intricate, unfoldable.

**Unfo·lded,** *ppl. a.*[1] [UN-[1] 8 + FOLD *v.*[1]] Not folded or arranged in folds.

**1683** MOXON *Mech. Exerc., Printing* xxii. ᴘ 10 Folding in the un-folded corners. **1695** *Lond. Gaz.* No. 3047/4 Part of them is Unfolded, so as to be useful to all Gentlemen and others conversant in the Mechanicks. **1860** DICKENS *Uncomm. Trav.* ix, A pretty large prayerbook in an unfolded pocket-handkerchief.

**Unfo·lded,** *ppl. a.*[2] [UN-[1] 8 + FOLD *v.*[2]] Not enclosed in a (sheep) fold.

**1589** GREENE *Menaphon* (Arb.) 44 So long we..forget our labours, that both our flockes shall be vnfolded. **1641** BEST *Farm. Bks.* (Surtees) 14 Men cannot leave their sheepe unfolded soe longe as there is any corne in the field. **1832** J. BREE *St. Herbert's Isle* 81 Th' unfolded flocks that o'er them bleat. **1856** MRS. BROWNING *Aur. Leigh* II. 602 A lamb's small shadow.., Unfed, unfolded!

**Unfo·lded,** *ppl. a.*[3] [f. UNFOLD *v.*[1]] Opened out or up; *fig.* displayed, revealed.

**1602** FULBECKE *Pandects* 29 Though the parties will, doe appeare in a secret will,..yet consent is onely verified in an expresse & vnfolded wil. **1629** H. BURTON *Truth's Triumph* 212 Euery beleeuer must haue..a cleare, explicite, and vnfolded faith in Christ. **1697** CONGREVE *Mourn. Bride* II. v, The iron gates..are still wide stretch'd..And staring on us with unfolded leaves. **1784** COWPER *Task* VI. 280 From shop to shop Wandering, and littering with unfolded silks The polished counter. **1820** SHELLEY *Liberty* iv, Like unfolded flowers beneath the sea.

**Unfo·lder.** [f. UNFOLD *v.*[1]] One who, or that which, unfolds, in various senses of the word.

**1611** COTGR., *Expliqueur*, an explicator, vnfolder, explainer. **1651** BAXTER *Inf. Bapt.* 240 Himself was an accurate unfolder of truth. **1728** THEOBALD *Double Falsehood* I. ii, Is your Father yet moved in the Suit, who must be the prime Unfolder of this Business? **1797** *Monthly Mag.* III. 264 Both copyists and unfolders [of papyrus rolls] are injudiciously paid by the month. **1845** TRENCH *Huls. Lect.* VII. 115 The unfolder of all the nobler and higher life of the world. **1871** MACDUFF *Mem. Patmos* ix. 119 The sudden appearance..of the Unfolder of the roll.

**Unfo·lding,** *vbl. sb.* [f. UNFOLD *v.*[1]] The action of the verb, in various senses.

**1483** *Cath. Angl.* 121/1 An vn Foldynge, *explicio, deuolucio.* **1538** ELYOT, *Replicatio*, a replycation or vnfoldynge of a thynge. **1599** MINSHEU *Span. Gram.* 80 The farther unfolding of this language. **1615** HIERON *Wks.* I. 653 Death..is (as it were) the vnfolding of the net, or the breaking open of the prison doore. **1646** P. BULKELEY *Gospel Covt.* I. 121 The time of unfolding [of the blessings] is not yet come. **1760–72** H. BROOKE *Fool of Qual.* (1809) IV. 45 The growth and unfolding of any common vegetable from..the seed. **1794** MRS. RADCLIFFE *Myst. Udolpho* i, He watched the unfolding of her infant character with anxious fondness. **1843** MANNING *Serm.* I. 276 The springing or unfolding of a stately tree. **1873** TRISTRAM *Moab* ii. 26 The sudden unfolding [to view] of the Dead Sea basin.

**Unfo·lding,** *ppl. a.*[1] [f. UNFOLD *v.*[1] 5.] That unfolds, discloses, or develops.

**1762** FALCONER *Shipwr.* II. 285 The sailors..Attend th' unfolding brails at his command. **1798** S. & HT. LEE *Canterb. T.* II. 355 The gay delights of unfolding nature. **1814** WORDSW. *Excurs.* VI. 855 It was the season of unfolding leaves. **1862** 'SHIRLEY' (J. Skelton) *Nugæ Crit.* ii. 107 The unfolding acts of a great drama.

**Unfo·lding,** *ppl. a.*[2] [f. UNFOLD *v.*[2]]

**1.** Indicating the time for unfolding sheep.

**1603** SHAKS. *Meas. for M.* IV. ii. 218 Looke, th' vnfolding Starre calles vp the Shepheard.

**2.** Coming out of the fold.

**1821** CLARE *Vill. Minstr.* I. 13 Raising the bleatings of unfolding sheep.

**Unfo·ldment.** [f. UNFOLD *v.*[1]] The process of unfolding.

**1850** D. THOMAS *Crisis of Being* iv. 64 Matter is..the unfoldment of ideas. **1884** *Christian World* 11 Sept. 688/2 All that is asked..is your co-operation..in its unfoldment.

**Unfo·ldress.** [f. UNFOLDER.] A female unfolder.

**1577** STANYHURST *Descr. Ireland* Ep. Ded. in *Holinshed* I. 1 b/1 The learned haue..adiudged an hystorie to be..the vnfoldresse of treacherie.

**Unfo·ldure.** [f. UNFOLD *v.*[1]] Unfolding.

**1837** C. LOFFT *Self-formation* I. 254 The relaxation and expansion and gentle unfoldure of the mind.

**Unfo·liaged,** *ppl. a.* (UN-[1] 8.) **1795** ANNA SEWARD *Lett.* (1811) IV. 91 The pale unfoliaged ruins of Castle Dinas Bran. **1804** — *Mem. Darwin* 123 There, indeed, we see rocks piled on rocks, unfoliaged and frowning. *a* **1843** SOUTHEY *Comm.-pl. Bk.* (1851) IV. 86 The ash is still unfoliaged. **Unfo·liated,** *ppl. a.* (UN-[1] 8.) **1859** A. NESBITT in *Archaeol.* XXXIX. 105 Two segmental unfoliated arches, on which rests a circle, also unfoliated. *a* **1878** SCOTT *Lect. Archit.* (1879) I. 176 The use..of moulded unfoliated capitals.

**Unfo·llowed,** *ppl. a.* (UN-[1] 8.)

**1508** [see UNACCUSED *ppl. a.*]. **1596** DANETT tr. *Comines* VIII. vi. 332 The Estradiots..forsooke their men of armes, who by means thereof were vnfollowed. **1630** J. TAYLOR (Water P.) *Trav.* Ded., I shall hereafter sacrifice whole Hecatombs..at the shrine of your vnfellowed and vnfollowed vertues. **1825** *Q. Rev.* XXXIV. 75 This example remained unfollowed by England for almost a century. **1864** E. SARGENT *Peculiar* I. 121 We will allow Peculiar Institution to quit this room free and unfollowed.

**Unfoo·l,** *v.* (UN-[2] 6 b.)

**1598** SHAKS. *Merry W.* IV. ii. 120, I, but if it proue true (Mr. Page) haue you any way then to vnfoole me againe. **1632** STRAFFORD in *Life* (1892) 301 The sooner wee vnfoole ourselues of this errore, the sooner wee shall learne to know our selues. **1635** QUARLES *Embl.* II. iii. 5 Will no plump fee Bribe thy false fists..T'unfool whom thou hast fool'd?

**Unfoo·lish,** *a.* (UN-[1] 7.) **1603** FLORIO *Montaigne* 561, I daylie heare fooles utter unfoolish wordes. **1885** *Sat. Rev.* 3 Jan. 12/2 The foolisher sort of a very unfoolish people.

**Unfoo·t,** *v.* [UN-[2] 4.] *trans.* To wash or wear away the foot of.

**1758** BORLASE *Nat. Hist. Cornw.* 66 Vast masses of cliff, which the sea has unfooted. *Ibid.* 109 The contiguous strata have been unfooted..many times.

**Unfoo·ted,** *ppl. a.* [UN-[1] 8.] Not trodden by the feet (of man); untraversed.

**1818** KEATS *Endym.* I. 77 Some unfooted plains Where fed the herds of Pan. **1839** BAILEY *Festus* 338 And oft, at night, ..We would breathe ourselves amid unfooted snows. **1895** MEREDITH *Amazing Marriage* xxx, Calamity hung around, with the future an unfooted wilderness.

†**Unfoo·tsore,** *a. Sc. Obs.* (UN-[1] 7.) *c* **1480** HENRYSON *Fables, Two Mice* 15 Ane tyme quhen scho wes full and vnfute sair. *c* **1500** *Priests of Peblis* 5 Thrie Preists..sat richt soft and vnfutesair. **Unfo·raged,** *ppl. a.* (UN-[1] 8 + FORAGE *v.* 1.) *a* **1649** DRUMM. OF HAWTH. *Hist. Jas. IV*, Wks. (1711) 75 By fighting in England, he kept his own Country unforaged. **Unforba·de,** *ppl. a.* (UN-[1] 8 b.) **1844** MRS. BROWNING *Vis. Poets* ccxlii, Nor know I if the man who prayed Rose up accepted, unforbade. **Unforbea·rance.** (UN-[1] 12.) **1699** SHAFTESB. *Char.* (1711) II. 150 The Injurys we do our-selves, by Excess and Unforbearance. **Unforbea·ring,** *ppl. a.* (UN-[1] 10.) **1820** T. MITCHELL *Aristoph.* I. 113 A ranting, storming, unforbearing fellow.

**Unforbi·d,** *ppl. a.* [UN-[1] 8 b.] = next.

**1667** MILTON *P. L.* VII. 94 If unforbid thou maist unfould What wee..aske. **1827** POLLOK *Course T.* VIII. 350 He..took all joys, Forbid and unforbid, as impulse urged. **1869** LOWELL *Winter Evening Hymn to Fire* vii, Nicotia..We worship, unforbid of thee.

**Unforbi·dden,** *ppl. a.* (UN-[1] 8 b.)

**1535** COVERDALE *Acts* xxviii. 31 Teaching those thinges ..with all boldnesse, vnforbydden. **1611** FLORIO, *Inuietato*, vnforbidden. **1648** HEXHAM II, *Ongeboden*,..Vnforbidden. **1819** SHELLEY *Cenci* IV. iv. 29 All was prepared by unforbidden means Which we must pay so dearly, having done. **1861** GEO. ELIOT *Silas M.* x, To..take up his old quarters unforbidden, and swagger as usual.

Hence **Unforbi·ddenly** *adv.*, **-ness.**

**1665** BOYLE *Occas. Refl.* V. ix. 179 This unforbiddenness they think sufficient to evince, that the Sumptuousness..is not absolutely..Sinful. **1860** ELLICOTT *Life Our Lord* viii. 387 When..love..may hereafter unforbiddenly direct itself to the ascended Lord.

†**Unforbo·den,** obs. var. UNFORBIDDEN *ppl. a.* Cf. MDu. and Du. *onverboden*, MHG. and G. *unverboten.*

**1534** TINDALE *Acts* xxviii. 31 Teachynge those thinges.. with all confidence, vnforboden.

**Unfo·rced,** *ppl. a.* [UN-[1] 8.]

**1.** Not compelled or constrained.

**1598** SYLVESTER *Du Bartas* II. ii. *Colonies* 513 Being fed.. With wholesome Fruits of an un-forced soyl. **1624** HEYWOOD *Gunaik.* V. 231 Artimesia..unforced and uncompeld followed the expedition of Xerxes against Greece. **1697** DRYDEN *Æneis* XI. 654 Why thus, unforced, should we so tamely yield? **1741** RICHARDSON *Pamela* III. 248 He will judge us according to the unforced and unbyassed Use we make of that Light. **1805** WORDSW. *To the Daisy* 52 Unforced by wind or wave To quit the Ship for which he died. **1884** *19th Cent.* Mar. 436 The unforced zeal and docility of the horse.

**b.** Of plants: Not produced out of season.

**1868** *Daily News* 8 July, Some of the fuchsias..would have borne comparison with any unforced flowers of their class.

**2.** Not pushed beyond the natural limits; not produced by exertion or effort; easy, natural.

**1604** SHAKS. *Oth.* II. i. 239 This granted (as it is a most pregnant and vnforc'd position) who stands so eminent..as Cassio do's? **1665** J. SPENCER *Vulg. Proph.* 52 All the great Prophets..delivered themselves in a natural and unforc'd order of words. **1717** ADDISON tr. *Ovid's Met.* III. Notes, Wks. 1721 I. 242 This is one of Ovid's finished stories. The transition to it is proper and unforced. **1790** PALEY *Horæ Paul.* xii. § 2 Here we have a fair unforced example of coincidence. **1850** IRVING *Goldsmith* i. 17 The unforced humour, blending so happily with good feeling and good sense. **1883** D. C. MURRAY *Hearts* ix, His objections..were unforced and genuine.

**3.** Requiring or involving no physical exertion.

**1643** DENHAM *Cooper's H.* 42 With such an easie and unforc't ascent. **1765** STERNE *Tr. Shandy* VIII. xix, By an unforced compression..of his cap with the thumb and the two forefingers.

Hence **Unfo·rcedly** *adv.*; **Unfo·rcedness.**

**1632** G. SANDYS *Ovid's Met.* XIII. Notes 451 This may vnforcedly admit of the former interpretation. **1664** H. MORE *Myst. Iniq.* 261 The naturalness and unforcedness of this Imbibition shall be made good. **1696** M. HENRY *Life P. Henry* iv. Wks. 1853 II. 647/1 Such a distribution as the matter did most easily and unforcedly fall into.

**Unfo·rcible,** *a.* [UN-[1] 7.]

**1.** Lacking force or power.

**1597** HOOKER *Eccl. Pol.* V. lxv. § 9 Wee cannot thinke that the signe which our new baptized foreheads did there receiue, is either vnfit or vnforcible. **1754** A. MURPHY *Gray's Inn Jrnl.* No. 90, Pieces..unforcible in Sentiment, and destitute of Character.

**2.** Incapable of being forced or enforced.

**1611** COTGR., *Inforçable*, vnforcible, vnexpugnable, impregnable. **1649** MILTON *Tenure Kings* 39, I wish them ..not to compell unforcible things in Religion especially.

**Unfo·rcibly,** *adv.* (UN-[1] 11.) **1831** SCOTT *Ct. Rob.* v, So I did express myself,..and, as I trust, not altogether unforcibly. *c* **1890** A. MURDOCH *Yoshiwara Episode* 8 Which ..illustrates not unforcibly what a glorious thing the.. system is for the capitalist.

**Unfo·rdable,** *a.* (UN-[1] 7 b and 5 b.)

**1611** FLORIO, *Inguazzabile*, vnwadable, vnfoordable. **1649** TAYLOR *Gt. Exemp.* ii. § 21 When he is to pass a sudden or unfordable flood. **1732** LEDIARD *Sethos* II. VII. 58 Their excursions..over unfordable rivers. **1834** PRINGLE *Afr. Sk.* 187 A very heavy rain..swells the river to an unfordable size. **1868** *Rep. U.S. Commissioner Agric.* (1869) 351 Many of the unfordable streams are still crossed by flat-boat ferries.

*fig.* *a* **1641** BP. MOUNTAGU *Acts & Mon.* (1642) 25 Many deep hidden mysteries, and unfordable.

Hence **Unfo·rdableness.**

**1652** HEYLYN *Cosmogr.* II. 193 The unfordablenesse of the River.

**Unfo·rded,** *ppl. a.* (UN-[1] 8.) **1697** DRYDEN *Virg. Georg.* III. 396 He..contemns Unruly Torrents, and unforded Streams. **Unforebo·ded,** *ppl. a.* (UN-[1] 8.) **1818** COLEBROOKE *Import Colonial Corn* 58 In the event of ultimate failure of accustomed supplies not unforeboded. **1863** B. TAYLOR *H. Thurston* III. 284 A power,..as welcome as it was unforeboded, had usurped her life. **Unforebo·ding,** *ppl. a.* (UN-[1] 10.) **1725** POPE *Odyss.* II. 212 Unnumber'd birds glide through the aërial way, Vagrants of air, and unforeboding stray. **1863** MRS. OLIPHANT *Chron. Carl. I. Salem Ch.* xvi. 146 She could see the half-awakened girl starting up,..unforeboding of evil. **Unforego·ne,** *ppl. a.* (UN-[1] 8 b.) **1844** MRS. BROWNING *Vis. Poets* cxlii, The life lay coiled unforegone Up in the awful eyes alone. **Unfo·reign,** *a.* (UN-[1] 7.) **1718** QUINCY *Compl. Disp.* 36 The Amalgamation of Metals..[is] not unforeign to this Head. **Unforeknow·able,** *a.* (UN-[1] 7 b.) **1678** CUDWORTH *Intell. Syst.* I. v. 710 Predictions of Future Events, otherwise unforeknowable to men. **1697** J. SERGEANT *Solid Philos.* 447 These, and a thousand other Unforeknowable Mischances.

**Unforekno·wn,** *ppl. a.* (UN-[1] 7 b.)

**1667** MILTON *P. L.* III. 119 Foreknowledge had no influence on their fault, Which had no less prov'd certain unforeknown. *a* **1680** CHARNOCK *Attrib. God* (1834) I. 561 No man can certainly prove that anything is unforeknown to him. **1882** ARMSTRONG *Garl. fr. Greece* 95 Nor unforeknown it comes.

**Unfore·nsic,** *a.* (UN-[1] 7.) **1858** CARLYLE *Fredk. Gt.* VIII. iv. II. 323 Fancy the hurry-scurry, the unforensic attitudes and pleadings! **1883** *Edin. Rev.* Jan. 245 The turn of his mind did not lead him astray into unforensic rhetoric.

**Unforesee·,** *v.* [UN-[1] 14.] To fail to foresee.

*a* **1670** HACKET *Abp. Williams* (1693) I. 171 The Lord Keeper did not unforesee how far this Cord might be drawn.

**Unforesee·able,** *a.* (UN-[1] 7 b.)

Also, in recent use, *unforesee·ableness, -ably.*

**1672** SOUTH *Serm.* (1717) V. 300 By such unlikely and unforeseeable Ways does Providence sometimes bring about its great Designs. **1802–12** BENTHAM *Ration. Judic. Evid.* (1827) I. 205 The suddenly put and unforeseeable question. **1877** MORLEY *Crit. Misc.* Ser. II. 377 The source of continual and unforeseeable improvements.

**Unforesee·ing,** *ppl. a.* (UN-[1] 10, 5 d.) 1602 DANIEL *Cleopatra* I. F iiij, My vnforeseeing weakenesse must intoome My Countries fame and glory with my fall. 1690 CHILD *Disc. Trade* Pref. A 7 b, May we not think that some..People in the World may be as un-foreseeing as this Gentleman pretends to be? 1755 *Man* No. 4. 3 An indulgent but unforeseeing parent. 1801 SOUTHEY *Thalaba* IV. xv, Later years..teach me to regret Youth's unforeseeing indolence. 1886 SWINBURNE *Misc.* 130 The unforeseeing security of a charmed and confident happiness.

*absol.* 1855 SINGLETON *Virgil* I. 94 Ne'er storm of rain Hath to the unforeseeing scathful proved.

**b.** Const. with object.

1871 M. COLLINS *Marq. & Merch.* II. iv. 112 Amy, unforeseeing anything of this sort, had been doing what she thought was her duty.

Hence **Unforesee·ingly** *adv.*

1611 FLORIO, *Improuistamente*, vnprouidedly, suddainely, vnforeseeingly. 1832 CHALMERS *Pol. Econ.* iii. 96 This sum ..might have been imprudently or unforeseeingly vested in the manufacture of luxuries.

**Unforesee·n,** *ppl. a.* (UN-[1] 8 b. Cf. MDu. *onvoresien*, Du. *onvoorzien*; MHG. *unvorsên*.)

1651 HOBBES *Leviath.* IV. xliv. 334 By reasoning from the un-foreseen mischances. 1667 MILTON *P. L.* II. 821 Through dire change Befalln us unforeseen, unthought of. 1725 BERKELEY *Proposal* Wks. 1871 III. 228 Unforeseen difficulties may arise. 1778 EARL CARLISLE in Jesse *Selwyn & Contemp.* (1844) III. 302 In case nothing unforeseen happens. 1836 W. IRVING *Astoria* III. 132 Unless some unforeseen contingency should render a modification necessary. 1875 WHITNEY *Life Lang.* vii. 127 The unforeseen consequence of an external addition.

Hence **Unforesee·nly** *adv.*, **-ness.**

1853 G. J. CAYLEY *Las Alforjas* I. 104 A peasant appeared unforeseenly, and offered to carry me across. 1897 *Daily News* 21 Sept. 4/7 The 'unforeseenness' of the cycle is its worst reproach in towns.

**Unforesho·rtened,** *ppl. a.* (UN-[1] 8.) 1846 WORCESTER (citing Godwin). 1866 HERSCHEL *Familiar Lect. Sci.* v. § 19. 194 So as to be seen unforeshortened from the star. **Unfo·reskinned,** (*ppl.*) *a.* (UN-[1] 9 or UN-[2] 4.) 1671 MILTON *Samson* 1100 The glory of Prowess..won by a Philistine From the unforeskinn'd race. **Unforesta·lled,** *ppl. a.* (UN-[1] 8.) 1657 J. HOWE in H. Rogers *Life* (1836) 74 They shall meet with unforestalled judgments. 1658 OSBORNE *Adv. Son* Wks. (1673) 178 Unforestalled by a like custom.

**Unfo·rested,** *ppl. a.*[1] [UN-[1] 8.] Not covered with forest; not included in a deer-forest.

1885 *Pall Mall G.* 11 Mar. 4/2 One class of incident..on unforested ground when in quest of deer. 1897 *Outing* XXIX. 357/2 The snowskate..is better adapted to an un-forested, or partially forested, hilly country.

**Unfo·rested,** *ppl. a.*[2] [UN-[2] 6 b, 8.] Deprived of forest, or of the status of a forest; deforested.

1502 ARNOLDE *Chron.* (1811) 19 That alle the wareyn of Stanes wyth the apertinaunce be unwareyned and vnforested for euermore. 1881 C. MORRISON *Hist. School Geog.* II. 58 Sherwood Forest in Notts,..now almost unforested.

**Unforethou·ght,** *ppl. a.* (UN-[1] 8 b, c.) 1601 DANIEL *Civ. Wars* VI. vii, This unfore-thought-on accident confounds All their dessignes. 1839 [see UNFEARED *ppl. a.* 2]. **Unforeto·ld,** *ppl. a.* (UN-[1] 8 b.) 1846 WORCESTER (citing *Ec. Rev.*). 1853 RUSKIN *Stones Ven.* II. iv. § 71 A silence has followed them, not unforetold. **Unforewa·rned,** *ppl. a.* (UN-[1] 8.) 1651 CLEVELAND *Poems* 38 The Devill sure such language did atchieve, To cheat our un-fore-warned Grandam Eve. 1667 MILTON *P. L.* v. 245 This let him know, Least.. he pretend Surprisal, unadmonisht, unforewarnd. 1814 WORDSW. *Excurs.* VII. 685 All unforewarned, The household lost their pride and soul's delight.

**Unfo·rfeit,** *a.* [UN-[1] 7.] Unforfeited.

1631 CHAPMAN *Cæsar & Pompey* I. ii. 156 That most strangely Would put..powers (Unforfeit by my fault) in others' wills. 1742 YOUNG *Nt. Th.* III. 96 This group Of bright ideas, flow'rs of Paradise, As yet unforfeit!

**Unfo·rfeitable,** *a.* (UN-[1] 7 b.)

1648 NETHERSOLE *Problems* I. 3 Their rights ought..to be ..unforfeitable. *a* 1754 CARTE *Hist. Engl.* (1755) IV. 62 Conveying an actual right..unforfeitable by any act of their father. 1874 W. R. GREG *Rocks Ahead* 45 Short of declaring this peasant's farm inalienable,..unforfeitable for any negligence,..—how is he to keep it?

**Unfo·rfeited,** *ppl. a.* (UN-[1] 8.) 1596 SHAKS. *Merch. V.* II. vi. 7 To keepe obliged faith vnforfaited. 1663 COWLEY *Verses Sev. Occas., To Royal Society* 3 All that Human Knowledge which has bin Unforfeited by Mans rebellious Sin. **Unfo·rgeable,** *a.* (UN-[1] 7 b.) 1837 LOCKHART *Scott* III. x. 332 Stamped with the unforgeable seal of truth and nature. 1889 *Pall Mall G.* 30 Dec. 2/3 There is..no difficulty in the way of making a practically unforgeable note.

**Unfo·rged,** *ppl. a.* [UN-[1] 8.]

**1.** Not fashioned at the forge.

*c* 1374 CHAUCER *Former Age* 49 Vnforged was the hawberke and the plate.

**2.** Not forged or counterfeit; genuine.

1610 BP. CARLETON *Jurisd.* 102 You dare not auouch them to be vnforged. 1628 FORD *Lover's Mel.* III, A letter printed From my vnforg'd relation. 1804 *Europ. Mag.* XLV. 367/2 We have as much reason to doubt the existence of any un-forged manuscript upon this subject.

**Unforge·tful,** *a.* (UN-[1] 7), **-ness** (UN-[1] 12). 1632 LITHGOW *Trav.* VI. 285 A grateful and vnforgetfull Frier. 1850 BLACKIE *Æschylus* I. 111 For vengeance unforgetful, From their graves they call. 1888 MACKEY *Life Bp. Forbes* ix. 76 The bishop's unforgetfulness of those to whom honour is due.

**Unforge·ttable,** *a.* Also -getable. (UN-[1] 7 b.)

1806 *Ann. Rev.* IV. 608 The unforgettable scenes of this fine poem. 1856 EMERSON *Eng. Traits* i. 5 Wisdom, wit, and indignation that are unforgetable. 1873 M. ARNOLD *Lit. & Dogma* (1876) 173 In single sentences, which have their ineffaceable and unforgettable stamp.

Hence **Unforge·ttably** *adv.*

1871 CARLYLE in Mrs. Carlyle *Lett.* (1883) II. 242 Jean's look unforgettably sad and grand. 1899 MACKAIL *Life Morris* I. 213 The powerful..face impressed itself unforgettably even on those who saw it but once.

**Unforge·tting,** *ppl. a.* (UN-[1] 10.) 1777 POTTER *Æschylus, Prom. Bd.* 33 The triple Fates and unforgetting furies. 1867 HOWELLS *Ital. Journ.* 95 The latest witness of God's unforgetting justice.

**Unforgi·v(e)able,** *a.* (UN-[1] 7 b.)

Sometimes spec. with *sin*, in allusion to Matt. xii. 31.

1548 R. HUTTEN *Sum of Diuinitie* H 3 b, Euerye persecution of the Gospell is not to be iudged synne unforgyueable. 1550 LATIMER *Last Serm. bef. Edw. VI*, Wks. (Parker Soc.) I. 250 This sin it was that he thought to be unforgiveable. 1832 SOUTHEY *Hist. Penins. War* III. 195 Bad as his conduct was, it would be his own fault if he made it unforgiveable. 1851 CARLYLE *Sterling* I. vii, This is what it would have been the unforgivable sin to swerve from and desert. 1885 *Manch. Exam.* 17 June 4/7 The circumstances..ought to stamp it as an unforgivable offence.

Hence **Unforgi·v(e)ably** *adv.*

1890 *Pall Mall G.* 15 May 2/3 All these books sin unforgiveably against the scientific sense. 1897 'MRS. RAYNER' *Type-writer Girl* xxi. 243, I have never acted.. grossly and unforgivably wrong.

**Unforgi·ven,** *ppl. a.* [UN-[1] 8 b. Cf. (in sense 2) OE. *unforgifen*, MDu. *onvergeven*.]

†**1.** *Sc.* Without any remission. *Obs.*

1425 *Sc. Acts Jas. I* (1814) II. 12/1 Ande quha sa..be fundyn fautyfe sal pay ane vnlaw..vnforgevin. 1442 *Extr. Aberdeen Rec.* (1844) I. 7 The said Master Jhon sal pay to kyrk werk xl s. vnforgiffin. 1510 *Ibid.* 81 Ane amerciament of viii s. vnforgiven. *a* 1578 LINDESAY (Pitscottie) *Chron. Scot.* (S.T.S.) II. 242 Nane sould eit flesche on frydayes.. vnder the paine of xx poundis on forgivin for the first fault. 1622 *Extr. Aberdeen Rec.* (1848) II. 378 The counsallour.. sall pay for ilk dayis absence..twelff schillingis, money vnforgiven.

**2.** Not forgiven. Also *absol.*

1565 HARDING *Confut. Apol. Ch. Eng.* v. vii. 251 b, That temporall satisfaction, which after the sacrament of penaunce is left vnforgeuen. 1737 CHESTERF. *Epitaph Q. Charlotte* 18 To her own offspring mercy she denied, And unforgiving, unforgiven died. 1796 MME. D'ARBLAY *Camilla* V. 409 To present herself..undemanded and unforgiven at Etherington, she thought impossible. 1819 SHELLEY *Cenci* IV. i. 89 As she shall die unshrived and unforgiven. 1845 BAILEY *Festus* (ed. 2) 226 And thou wilt then be wretcheder than I;—The unforgiving than the unforgiven.

**Unforgi·veness.** [UN-[1] 12.] = UNFORGIVINGNESS.

1611 FLORIO, *Imperdonanza*, vnforgiuenesse. 1748 RICHARDSON *Clarissa* VII. 118 They are sufficiently cleared from every imputation of unforgiveness. 1797 MRS. A. M. BENNETT *Beggar Girl* (1813) I. 65 He became notorious for ingratitude to his friends, and unforgiveness of his enemies. 1829 *Westm. Rev.* XI. 276 Adding at that fearful moment the expression of his unforgiveness and his hate. 1870 T. ERSKINE *Unconditional Freeness Gospel* vii. 153 We cannot have confidence in any one who, we think, regards us with unforgiveness.

**Unforgi·ver.** (UN-[1] 12.) 1748 RICHARDSON *Clarissa* (1811) VII. 26, I hope, however, that these unforgivers..were always good, dutiful, passive children to their parents.

**Unforgi·ving,** *ppl. a.* (UN-[1] 10.)

1713 ROWE *Jane Shore* IV, Accursed Jealousy! O merciless, wild and unforgiving Fiend! 1784 COWPER *Task* II. 247 Chatham..Secur'd it by an unforgiving frown. 1828 SCOTT *F. M. Perth* xi, I have brought the vengeance of an unforgiving devil upon this helpless creature. 1880 'OUIDA' *Moths* II. 165 We are an unforgiving race.

*absol.* 1819 SHELLEY *Cenci* V. iii. 105 Canst Thou forgive even the unforgiving? 1845 [see UNFORGIVEN 2].

Hence **Unforgi·vingness.**

1748 RICHARDSON *Clarissa* VII. xlvii. 184 That cruelty and unforgivingness, which..have no example. 1850 L. HUNT *Autobiog.* II. xi. 55 An extraordinary mixture of ..good nature with unforgivingness. 1887 MARY BURT *Browning's Women* 52 Unforgivingness beyond a certain limit is a base crime.

**Unforgo·t,** *ppl. a.* [UN-[1] 8 b.] = next.

1653 J. TAYLOR (Water P.) *Cert. Trav. Uncert. Journey* 15 But to them all my thanks is unforgot. *a* 1847 ELIZA COOK *Old Barn* iv, Delight that is still unforgot. 1870 MORRIS *Earthly Par.* III. IV. 372 Many a tale yet unforgot.

**Unforgo·tten,** *ppl. a.* (UN-[1] 8 b. Cf. MDu. and Du. *onvergeten*, MHG. *unvergezzen*, G. *unvergessen*.)

1813 BYRON *Giaour* 103 Clime of the unforgotten brave! *a* 1822 SHELLEY *Triumph Life* 209 The great, the unforgotten,—they who wore Mitres and helms and crowns. 1850 HAWTHORNE *Scarlet L.* xviii, The foe that would win over again his unforgotten triumph.

**Unfo·rk,** *v.* [UN-[2] 5, 6 b.]

**1.** *trans.* To remove from a fork.

1598 FLORIO, *Disforcare*, to vnforke. 1611 *Ibid.*, *Sforcinato*, vnforked, vnhooked.

**2.** To make straight or plain.

1654 Z. COKE *Logick* (a j), It unforks Oracles, making them Toothless. 1657 TOMLINSON *Renou's Disp.* Pref., Their Enigmatical expressions unforked and unvailed.

†**Unforla·tit,** *ppl. a. Sc. Obs.* [UN-[1] 8 + MDu. *verlaeten* to draw off, rack (wine).] Not drawn off from one vessel into another.

1513 DOUGLAS *Æneid* v. Prol. 53 Bot my propyne..[is] Vnforlatit, not jawyn fra tun to tun. *Ibid.* Direction 90 Onforlatyt, new from the berry run.

†**Unforle·t,** *ppl. a. Sc. Obs.* [UN-[1] 8 b. Cf. OE. *unforlæten*.] Not abandoned or given up.

1513 DOUGLAS *Æneid* XI. xi. 16 Ne this luf, suythly, is nocht cummin of new,..Bot of ald kyndnes lang tyme vnforleyt.

**Unforlo·rn,** *ppl. a.* [UN-[1] 8 b. Cf. OFris. *onforloren* (unforfeited), MDu. and Du. *onverloren*, MHG. *unverlorn* (G. *-loren*), older Da. *uforloren*.]

**a.** Not lost. **b.** Not bereft (*of*).

1567 *Gude & Godlie B.* (S.T.S.) 146 Zit keipit scho hir madinheid vnforlorne. 1635 J. HAYWARD tr. *Biondi's Banish'd Virg.* 13 Yet was hee alive, and as yet unforlorne of either sense or memory.

†**Unfo·rm,** obs. var. INFORM *a.* or UNFORMED *ppl. a.* ? *a* 1400 in *MS. Lincoln A i 17* fol. 276 b, Whilom when a man was noghte, Bothe vnfourme and vn forthe broghte.

**Unfo·rm,** *v.*[1] [UN-[2] 4.] *trans.* To divest of (a special) form; to make formless. Also *absol.*

1621 G. SANDYS *Ovid's Met.* II. (1626) 35 How great our act! how is our powre display'd! Vnform'd a Woman, and a Goddesse made. 1704 *Hymn Victory* xvi, He never form'd a proper Scheme, But they unform'd it all again. *a* 1822 SHELLEY in Medwin *Life* II. 169 It was easier to form, than unform or reform. 1876 GLADSTONE in *Contemp. Rev.* June 12 It has formed Christian nations; or at least, has not un-formed them. 1882 *Pall Mall G.* 14 June 5/1 It unforms his style, and produces scrappy..sentences.

**Unfo·rm,** *v.*[2] [UN-[2] 5.] *trans.* To rouse (a hare) from its form.

*a* 1773 in Ruddiman *Coll. Pieces* (1773) 277 Such with the beagle rise, at dusky morn,..Unfourm the hare close squatted in her bush.

**Unfo·rmal,** *a.* [UN-[1] 7, 5 b.] = INFORMAL 1.

*c* 1449 PECOCK *Repr.* I. ii. 9 Thei schulden not be..so ruyde and vnformal and boistose in resonyng. 1597 MORLEY *Introd. Mus.* 81 Your fift, sixt, and seuenth notes be wilde and vnformall, for that vnformall skipping is condemned in this kinde of singing. 1661 CAMPION *Counterpoint* 109 This passage from the flat to the sharp would be unformal. 1678 SIR G. MACKENZIE *Crim. Laws Scot.* II. xxiii. § 4 (1699) 249 Often times they return unformal verdicts. 1799 H. MITCHELL *Scotticisms* 87 The contract was unformal.

**b.** = INFORMAL *a.* 1 b.

1825 CATH. STANLEY *Jrnl.* in *Mem.* (1879) 211 The unpunctual [people] are easy, good-tempered, unfussy,..unformal. 1858 M. PATTISON *Ess.* (1889) II. 328 The rude independence of character, which was generated by that free and unformal life.

Hence **Unfo·rmally** *adv.*

1597 MORLEY *Mus.* 86 Your seuenth and eighth notes, wherein you fal..so vnformallie to B fa ♭ mi backe againe.

**Unfo·rmalized,** *ppl. a.* (UN-[1] 8 a *c.*) 1853 C. BRONTE *Villette* xix, He listened so kindly, so teachably; unformalized by scruples.

**Unfo·rmed,** *ppl. a.*[1] [UN-[1] 8 and 5 b. Cf. MDu. *ongeformet*, *-vormet* (Du. *-vormd*), MHG. *ungeformet* (G. *-formt*), NFris. *ünfuaremd*.]

**1.** Not formed or fashioned into a regular shape; not invested with any definite form.

*a* 1340 HAMPOLE *Psalter* xxxii. 9 Þai ere fourmyd of vnfourmyd matere. 1382 WYCLIF *Deut.* xxvii. 6 Thow shalt bild there vp an auter..of stonus vnfourmed and vnpolishid. 1599 DANIEL *Musoph.* 951 Who..knows..What words in th' yet unformed Occident, May come refin'd with th' accents that are ours? 1621 G. SANDYS *Ovid's Met.* XV. 406 [He] sees Their bodies limme-lesse: these vnformed things In time put forth their feet, and after, wings. 1651 HOBBES *Leviath.* I. xii. 55 The unformed matter of the World, was a God, by the name of Chaos. 1712 ADDISON *Spect.* No. 309 ¶ 2 His Passage through the Regions of unformed Matter. 1825 *Bull-baiting* II. in *Houlston Tr.* I. No. 28. 6 His head so torn and mangled, that it appeared nothing but a frightful unformed mass of blood. 1855 *Poultry Chron.* II. 571/1 Those amateurs who, like myself, prefer..the breast small and unformed. 1877 CAIRD *Philos. Kant* II. i. 203 While matter altogether unformed is a mere abstraction.

**b.** *transf.* Of immaterial things: Not brought to a definite or properly developed state; crude.

1689 *Andros Tracts* II. 195 They would..endeavour to prevent what ill effects an Unform'd Tumult might produce. 1736 BUTLER *Anal.* I. v. 86 Mankind is left, by Nature, an unformed, unfinished Creature. 1774 REID *Aristotle's Logic* vi. § 2 (1788) 144 Every science is in an unformed state until its first principles are ascertained. 1857 BUCKLE *Civiliz.* I. xiv. 832 The chemical department of mineralogy is in an unformed and indeed anarchical condition. 1880 SAYCE *Introd. Sci. Lang.* viii. II. 188 The rude and unformed Bushman and the polished Finnic [language].

**c.** *fig.* Of persons (or the mind): Not developed by education or training; unpolished.

1711 ADDISON *Spect.* No. 66 ¶ 2 You can't imagine how unformed a Creature it is. She comes to my Hands just as Nature left her. 1798 S. & HT. LEE *Canterb. T.* II. 12 On [him],..in the helplessness of an unformed mind, his sister threw herself. 1856 MISS YONGE *Daisy Chain* I. xx, Ethel was very queer and unformed, and could do nothing by herself. 1894 MRS. H. WARD *Marcella* I. 104 Very clever in some ways—and very unformed—childish almost—in others.

**2.** Not formed or made; uncreated.

*a* 1325 *Prose Psalter* (1891) 194 Vnfourmed is þe fader, vnfourmed is þe sone, vnformed is þe holi gost. *c* 1400 *Pilgr. Sowle* (Caxton, 1483) v. xiv. 107 God hymself is nature vnformed and vnwrought that yeueth nature fourmed to euery creature. 1611 COTGR., *Informé*,..also, vnformed, vnmade, vnfashioned. 1757 in 10*th Rep. Hist. MSS. Comm.* App. I. 313 If the New Ministry yet unformed, should subsist. 1794 R. J. SULIVAN *View Nat.* IV. 99 Would it not sound strangely to talk of a self-existent house, an uncaused pyramid, an unformed statue? *a* 1824 BYRON *Heav. & Earth* I. iii, He broke forth Into the dawn, which lighted not the yet Unform'd forefather of mankind. 1855 *Poultry Chron.* III. 195/2 Lime..is especially necessary for making the as yet unformed bones.

†**3.** *Unformed stars* (or *signs*): (see quots.). *Obs.*

1590 T. HOOD *Use Celestial Globe* 34 b, The vnformed starres about the Scorpion. 1638 CHILMEAD tr. *Hues' Treat. Globes* (1889) 53 This Constellation hath..three unformed..Starres. 1700 MOXON *Math. Dict., Unformed Signs*, such are those that are called Nebulous or Cloudy, scarce to be seen by the bare Eye or Instrument. 1764 J. FERGUSON *Lect.* 185 Those stars which lie between the figures of those imaginary animals, and could not be brought within the compass of any of them, were called unformed stars. 1810 VINCE *Elem. Astron.* 269.

† **Unfo·rmed**, *ppl. a.*² [UN-¹ 8.] = UNINFORMED *ppl. a.*

*c* 1400 *Destr. Troy* 760 Lest þe day vs be-daghe..And I vnformet in faith how I fare shall.

**Unfo·rmidable**, *a.* (UN-¹ 7 b and 5 b.)

1667 *Decay Chr. Piety* xi. ¶ 2 A guilt which nothing but our too familiar acquaintance with it could make unformidable. 1846 M'GEE *Gallery Irish Writers* 163 It was no unformidable degree of success which could call Clarendon against him. 1898 BODLEY *France* II. III. v. 235 When a minister thus retains his portfolio, it is because he is unformidable.

**Unfo·rmulated**, *ppl. a.* (UN-¹ 8.) 1866 *Spect.* 14 Apr. 406/1 The trustful, free, unformulated attitude of mind. 1899 MACKAIL *Life Morris* II. 115 The ambiguities of an unformulated creed.

**Unforsa·ken**, *ppl. a.* (UN-¹ 8 b.)

1648 HEXHAM II, *Onbegeven*, Vnforsaken. 1654 HAMMOND *Fundam.* viii. Wks. 1674 I. 290 Any sort of sins continued in or unforsaken. 1857 J. H. NEWMAN *Serm. Var. Occas.* vi. 100 Hearts polluted with mortal, unforsaken sin. 1864 PUSEY *Lect. Daniel* viii. 495 He..did not enter into a relation to His creature, only, of His own accord, Himself unforsaken, to end it.

**Unforsa·king**, *ppl. a.* (UN-¹ 10.) 1862 MRS. NORTON *Lady of La Garaye* Ded. 74 Towards thee their thoughts shall roam, Whose unforsaking faith time hath not riven.

**Unforsoo·k**, *ppl. a.* (UN-¹ 8 b.) 1838 MRS. BROWNING *Seaside Walk* v, Absent friends and memories unforsook.

**Unforswo·rn**, *ppl. a.* (UN-¹ 8 b.) 1636 MASSINGER *Gt. Dk. Florence* v. ii, *Cozimo.* You all conspire To force our mercy from us. *Charomonte.* Which giv'n up To aftertimes preserves you unforsworne. † **Unforthbrought**: see UNFORM *a.* † **Unforthi·nking**, *sb.* and *ppl. a. Obs.* (UN-¹ 12, 10.) 1483 *Cath. Angl.* 139/1 An vn Forthynkynge, *jnpenitencia*. *Ibid.*, Vn Forthynkynge, *jnpenitens*.

**Unfo·rtified**, *ppl. a.* (UN-¹ 8.)

1525 LD. BERNERS *Froiss.* II. clxx. 484 The lorde of the Towre was sore blamed..that he had lefte that place vnfortyfyed and vnprouyded. 1607 TOPSELL *Four-f. Beasts* 467 The which Beare..finding the den vnfortified..entred into the same. 1709 POPE *Ess. Crit.* 434 While their weak heads, like towns unfortify'd, 'Twixt sense and nonsense daily change their side. 1775 BURKE *Sp. Concil. Amer.* Wks. III. 64 Pouring down upon your unfortified frontiers a fierce and irresistible cavalry. 1849 GROTE *Greece* II. xlvii. (1862) IV. 170 Samos remained..unfortified, deprived of its fleet.

*fig.* 1602 SHAKS. *Ham.* I. ii. 96 It shewes..A Heart vnfortified, a Minde impatient. 1646 HAMMOND *Sinnes* 18 The will will be taken unfortified, and so..won to consent. 1705 COLLIER *Ess. Mor. Subj.* III. *Pain* 14 Persons of the tenderest Age, of the most unfortified Sex,..encountered the Fury of wild Beasts. 1802–12 BENTHAM *Ration. Judic. Evid.* (1827) V. 659 A mere pecuniary interest, unfortified by any admixture of sympathy. 1885 *Manch. Exam.* 4 Feb. 5/2 This opinion,..unfortified by legal sanction.

**Unfo·rtify**, *v.* (UN-² 3.)

1574 HELLOWES tr. *Gueuara's Fam. Ep.* (1577) 272, I commaund you..to discamp your camp, and to vnfortifie Tordisillas. 1603 FLORIO *Montaigne* II. xv. 359 A peaceable time will require we should vnfortifie them [*sc.* our houses].

† **Unfo·rtunable**, *a. Obs.* [UN-¹ 7 b, 5 b.] Unfortunate.

1509 BARCLAY *Shyp of Folys* (1570) 223 Which seeth and feeleth..That all his dedes are much unfortunable. 1567 PAYNELL tr. *Treas. Amadis of Gaule* 77 This manner of doing..is so unfortunable, and so farre out of reason. 1715 H. CAREY *Contrivances* (1729) 27 The Gentleman of this House, who was so unfortunable as to be kill'd by Thieves.

† **Unfo·rtunacy.** *Obs.* [UN-¹ 12, 5 b.] Lack of good fortune; an unfortunate occurrence.

*a* 1575 tr. *Pol. Verg. Eng. Hist.* (Camden Soc. 29) 124 The rumor was spred that the same was doone by therles assent, ..but in dede yt was the unfortunacy of king Henry. *a* 1662 HEYLYN *Laud* II. (1671) 312 The King he tacitly upbraids with the unfortunacies of his Reign by Deaths and Plagues.

**Unfo·rtunate**, *a.* and *sb.* [UN-¹ 7 and 5 b.]

**A.** *adj.* **1.** Of persons, etc.: Not favoured by fortune; meeting with bad fortune; suffering mishap or mischance; unlucky.

For examples of the superlative in *-est* see (*b*).

1530 PALSGR. 328/1 Unfortunate,..*malfortuné*. 1553 BRENDE *Q. Curtius* IV. 55 b, I haue learned to be vnfortunate, and it is often tymes a comforte of a mans calamitie to knowe his misshapp. 1577 tr. *Bullinger's Decades* 254 Hee was of all the Jewishe kinges..in his lyfe the most vnfortunate. 1652 *Nicholas Papers* (Camden) 315 He hath been not only unfortunate in most of his counsels but incompatible in business. 1680 *Charac. Town-Miss* (Hindley III) 5 She shall..fall a Sniveling and call herself the most unfortunate of Women. 1769 ROBERTSON *Chas. V*, II. Wks. 1813 VI. 81 It was late next morning before the fate of the unfortunate prince was known. 1804–6 SYD. SMITH *Mor. Philos.* (1850) 218 You travel for twenty or five-and-twenty miles over one of the most unfortunate, desolate countries under heaven. 1885 'MRS. ALEXANDER' *Valerie's Fate* vi, The unfortunate gentleman was well known...What a blow his death will be to..his partner!

*absol.* 1675 DRYDEN *Aurengz.* v. (1676) 72 Envious death will shun th'unfortunate. 1712 POPE *Lett.* (1735) I. 177 The Unfortunate of all People are the most unfit to be left alone. 1781 GIBBON *Decl. & F.* xxvii. (1787) III. 7 He was taught, by cruel experience, that every gate is shut against the unfortunate. 1825 SCOTT *Talism.* xx, To have doomed the unfortunate to death might have been severity, but had a show of justice.

(*b*) 1622 R. HAWKINS *Voy. S. Sea* 2 The *Revenge*, which was ever the vnfortunatest Ship the late Queenes Maiestie had. 1639 S. DU VERGER tr. *Camus' Admir. Events* 35 Tearming himselfe the unfortunatest of all lovers. 1840 DICKENS *Old C. Shop* xxix, I remember the time when he was the unluckiest and unfortunatest of men.

† **b.** Const. *of. Obs.*—¹

1611 SPEED *England, Wales* II. vii, The Townes for commerce,..two of them vnfortunate of their former greatnes.

**c.** In specific uses: (see quots.).

1785 GROSE *Dict. Vulg. T.*, *Unfortunate gentlemen*, the horse guards, who thus named themselves in Germany. 1796 — *Unfortunate women*, prostitutes. 1827 HARE *Guesses* Ser. I. (1847) 154 As a strumpet is become an unfortunate female. 1883 MISS BETHAM-EDWARDS *Disarmed* xxxviii, Alice Ashe, seamstress, unmarried, 'unfortunate'.

**2.** Marked by, or associated with, misfortune or mishap; disastrous, inauspicious. Also, in weaker sense: Untoward, unlucky, regrettable.

*a* 1548 HALL *Chron.*, *Hen. VI*, 178 What number of noble men haue ben..executed, sith that vnfortunate day. 1560 DAUS tr. *Sleidane's Comm.* 404 b, But after chaunced a time more unfortunate. 1600 HAKLUYT *Voy.* III. 318 They put themselues to sea, and with so slender victuals, that the end of their interprise became vnluckly and vnfortunate. 1626 D'EWES in Ellis *Orig. Lett.* Ser. I. III. 218 By reason of suspicion of irregularitie upon the unfortunate killing of a man some few yeares since. 1671 MILTON *Samson* 747 In some part to recompense My rash but more unfortunate misdeed. 1779 *Mirror* No. 33, But for this unfortunate weakness, Mr. Gold..would make one of the best of husbands. 1846 MRS. A. MARSH *Father Darcy* II. xxi. 354 Would not some link of connexion with this 'unfortunate business', as he styled it, be detected? 1885 'MRS. ALEXANDER' *At Bay* iii, Is it not unfortunate?..my father can not return till to-morrow. 1890 *Retrospect Med.* CII. 103 The word 'massage' seems rather an unfortunate one to apply to the procedure.

**B.** *sb.* **1.** One who is unfortunate; an unfortunate person.

1683 T. HOY *Agathocles* 23 But of the brave Unfortunates was none Whose glorious Suff'rings Philocles out-shone. 1697 BURGHOPE *Disc. Relig. Assemb.* 87 Out of pity to those unfortunates that are design'd for that place [*sc.* hell]. 1776 S. J. PRATT *Pupil of Pleas.* (1777) I. 206 You..appeared only in the light of a person..not allied to the parent of that dear unfortunate. 1801 *Monthly Mag.* II. 131 You will not be able to avoid pitying these unfortunates when they inform you that their souls are mortal. 1875 WHITNEY *Life Lang.* i. 2 These unfortunates are wont to be trained and taught by those who speak.

**2.** A fallen woman; a prostitute.

1844 HOOD *Bridge of Sighs* i, One more Unfortunate.. Gone to her death! 1866 ROGERS *Agric. & Prices* I. v. 118 Unfortunates committed to prison were in evil case.

**3.** *Irish.* An idiot.

1881 *Folk Lore Rec.* IV. 113 Do you see that 'innocent' or 'unfortunate' or 'object'?

† **Unfo·rtunate**, *v. Obs.* [UN-² 6 a.] *trans.* To make unfortunate or unlucky.

1602 CAREW *Cornwall* 101 b, By his dreery influence, [he] unfortunateth any birth that shal then casually befall. 1653 W. RAMESEY *Astrol. Restored* 317 An Eclipse of the Sun.. unfortunateth the Sea and the affairs thereof.

Hence † **Unfo·rtunating** *ppl. a.*

1647 LILLY *Chr. Astrol.* xxii. 131 If the unfortunating Planet be in the seventh.

**Unfo·rtunately**, *adv.* [f. UNFORTUNATE *a.*] In an unfortunate manner; unhappily, unluckily.

1548 ELYOT, *Infœliciter*, vnhappily, vnfortunately. 1560 DAUS tr. *Sleidane's Comm.* 282 b, The death of kinge Fraunces chaunced unfortunately for studentes. 1621 LADY M. WROTH *Urania* 536 Shee was..the vnfortunateliest married, and vnhappiest wife this Countrey had. 1651 HOBBES *Leviath.* 390 Sidney Godolphin, who..was unfortunately slain in the..late Civill warre. 1700 DRYDEN *Sigism. & Guiscardo* 630 She..Ev'n kept her Count'nance, when the Lid remov'd Disclosed the Heart, unfortunately lov'd. 1710 STEELE *Tatler* No. 204 ¶ 4 We use Words of Respect sometimes very unfortunately.

**b.** In parenthetic or detached use.

1706 E. WARD *Wooden World Diss.* (1708) 37 He might unfortunately have grown up to be a Pedant. 1779 *Mirror* No. 10, Unfortunately for us, we found with our friend a number of his jovial companions. 1827 FARADAY *Chem. Manip.* xviii. 472 Unfortunately this evil increases with the heat. 1874 J. GEIKIE *Gt. Ice Age* xiv. 183 These relics, unfortunately, have almost invariably been lost or mislaid.

**Unfo·rtunateness.** (UN-¹ 12 and 5 b.)

1561 T. HOBY tr. *Castiglione's Courtyer* IV. (1577) X ij b, Although it putteth them in afflictions, daungers, trauels, and..unfortunatenesse. 1608 T. MORTON *Preamb. Encounter* 123 The vnfortunatenesse of this his declamatorie calumniation. 1654 GAYTON *Pleas. Notes* II. xxv. 285 O the unfortunateness of this adventure! 1697 COLLIER *Ess. Mor. Subj.* I. 205 To play upon the Indigence..of another; and take an advantage from the Unfortunateness of his Condition. 1867 BP. WILBERFORCE *Let.* in *Life* (1882) III. 217, I cannot agree as to the unfortunateness of the language.

**Unfo·rtune.** Now *arch.* [UN-¹ 12, 5 b. Cf. WANFORTUNE.] Misfortune, mischance; bad luck.

*c* 1470 *Gol. & Gaw.* 1225 Quhan on-fortone quhelmys the quheil, thair gais grace by. 1483 CAXTON *Cato* g iij, Thys felawe mocqued..suche one now late of his unfortune and myserye. *a* 1533 LD. BERNERS *Gold. Bk. M. Aurel.* (1546) Ff iv, The calme seson moste sure, is the vigile of the more vnfortune. 1647 HEXHAM I. s.v., An unfortune that cold not be avoided. 1888 STEVENSON *Black Arrow* 164 What unfortune [ye have had], ye have noways deserved.

**Unfo·rtuned**, *a. rare.* [UN-¹ 9.] Connected with, visited by, misfortune.

*c* 1403 LYDG. *Temple of Glas* 389 Þuruȝ þe cruelte Of old Saturne, my fadur vnfortuned. 1909 R. BRIDGES *Virgil's Æneid* VI. 618 Sitteth and to eternity shall sit Unfortun'd Theseus.

**Unfossili·ferous**, *a.* (UN-¹ 7.) 1836 T. THOMSON *Min., Geol.*, etc. II. 193 The unfossiliferous stratified formations. 1882 GEIKIE *Geol. Sk.* 292 The rocks of Scotland are, as a whole, unfossiliferous. **Unfo·ssilized**, *ppl. a.* (UN-¹ 8.) 1846 WORCESTER (citing *Qu. Rev.*). 1848 OWEN in *Times* 14 Nov. 9/1 The carcase of such reptiles..in a recent or unfossilized state. 1887 MOLONEY *Forestry W. Africa* 127 Newer resins (unfossilized). **Unfo·stered**, *ppl. a.* (UN-¹ 8.) 1744 ARMSTRONG *Preserv. Health* II. 170 No youth of genius whose neglected bloom Unfoster'd sickens in the barren shade. 1847 C. BRONTË *J. Eyre* xiv, I was..partial to the unfledged, unfostered and unlucky. **Unfo·thered**, *ppl. a. Sc.* [UN-¹ 8.] Not foddered. 1725 RAMSAY *Gentle Sheph.* II. i, Like the pack-horse that's unfother'd And burden'd, [they] will tumble down faint.

**Unfou·ght**, *ppl. a.* [UN-¹ 8 b, 8 c; cf. next.]

**1.** Of persons: Not fought *with* or *for*.

1523 LD. BERNERS *Froiss.* I. xviii. 25 He toke mede and money of the Scottis, to thentent they myght departe pryuely by nyght, vnfoughte withall. 1586 J. HOOKER *Hist. Irel.* 148/1 in *Holinshed* II, Thinking it should be too great a dishonour vnto him to be bearded with a traitor, and to let him depart vnfought withall. 1619 FLETCHER, etc. *Knt. Malta* I. iii, Mountferrat should perceive my Sister had A Brother would not live to see her dye Unfought for. 1659 B. HARRIS *Parival's Iron Age* 211 Prince Rupert..might have gone away unfought with but that such counsell was too cold for so hot a stomach. [1822 SCOTT *Halidon Hall* I. ii. 9 If we leave it Unfought withal, it squares not with our honour.]

**b.** Not encountered in fight; without fighting.

1596 *Edward III*, III. iii. 139 These English faine would spend the time in words, That, night approching, they might escape vnfought. 1697 DRYDEN *Æneis* IX. 159 For fly they cannot, and, constrained to stay, Must yield unfought, a base inglorious prey.

**2.** Of battles, etc.: Not fought; uncontested.

1669 EARL ORRERY *Parthen.* (1676) 738 How many Battels ..had been unfought? 1807 WORDSW. *White Doe* III. 217 We yield (and can it be?) an unfought field! 1820 PRAED *Eve of Battle* 68 Anticipation fires his brain With fights unfought. 1898 *Westm. Gaz.* 6 June 2/2 We think that the constituency ought not to go unfought.

**Unfou·ghten**, *ppl. a.* Now *arch.* [UN-¹ 8 b. Cf. MDu. and Du. *ongevochten*, MHG. *ungevohten* (without fighting).] = prec.

1475 *Bk. Noblesse* (Roxb.) 47 Youre gret adversarie of Fraunce..fled and voided unfoughten at the said jorney of Senlis. *c* 1500 *Three Kings Sons* 89 In-asmoche as we haue ben so long vnfoughten with. ? 15.. *Battle of Otterburn* xli. in Child *Ball.* III. 297 If that I weynde..onfowghten awaye, He wolde me call but a kowarde knyght. *a* 1575 tr. *Pol. Verg. Eng. Hist.* (Camden No. 29) 140 He had sufferyd them..to passe by him unfoughten withal. 1811 SCOTT *Don Roderick* III. viii, But thou—unfoughten wilt thou yield to Fate? 1867 MORRIS *Jason* IX. 369 Soothly, have we no will to fight with thee If we may pass unfoughten.

**Unfou·lable**, *a.* (UN-¹ 7 b.) 1862 *Catal. Internat. Exhib.* II. No. 2796, Unfoulable anchor. 1884 *Health Exhib. Catal.* 82/1 Treated with our patent unfoulable enamel.

**Unfou·led**, *ppl. a.*¹ [UN-¹ 8 + FOUL *v.*¹] Not made foul or impure; undefiled.

*c* 1380 WYCLIF *Sel. Wks.* III. 388 Seynt Jame seis, For þis is a clene religioun,..to kepe a mon unfoulid fro þis worlde. *a* 1425 *Cursor M.* 19504 (Trin.), God him kepte..His hondes vnfouled of monnes blood. *a* 1470 HARDING *Chron.* LXXII. vii, Hir wyfehode..Afore that tyme euer was kept vnfouled. 1653 H. MORE *Antid. Ath.* II. xii. § 3 Light and Colours unfoul'd and unsophisticated by any inward tincture.

† **Unfou·led**, *ppl. a.*² *Sc. Obs.* [UN-¹ 8 + FOUL *v.*²] Unexhausted.

1535 W. STEWART *Cron. Scot.* (Rolls) II. 412 Kenethus than ..maid efter thame till go The freschest men [that] onfowllit wer in feild.

**Unfou·nd**, *ppl. a.* [UN-¹ 8 b, 8 c. Cf. ON. *ú-fundinn*, older Da. *ufunden*, Du. *ongevonden*.] Not found; undiscovered. Also with *out*.

1584 LYLY *Campaspe* v. ii, Content to lyue vnknowne, and die vnfounde. 1644 QUARLES *Barnabas & B.* (1651) 211 Being lost, hee seekes himselfe unfound, or findes himselfe unknowne. 1678 DRYDEN & LEE *Œdipus* I. i, But for the Murderer's self, unfound by Man, Find him ye Pow'rs Cœlestial and Infernal. 1721 RAMSAY *Content* 316 More than seventy years..I've sought this court, till now unfound by me. 1818 BYRON *Ch. Har.* IV. cxxiv, Unfound the boon, unslaked the thirst. 1895 RIDER HAGGARD *Heart of World* xi, Our eyes might behold the greatest of these cities, sought for many generations but as yet unfound.

(*b*) 1621 G. SANDYS *Ovid's Met.* II. (1626) 28 To farthest Earth affrighted Nilus fled; And there conceal'd his yet vnfound-out head.

**Unfou·nd**, *v.* (UN-² 3.)

*c* 1430 *Pilgr. Lyf Manhode* III. viii. (1869) 139 To a king it is thing reprouable..to vnfounde foundaciouns that hise auncestres hauen founded.

**Unfou·nded**, *ppl. a.*¹ [UN-¹ 8 + FOUND *v.*¹] Having no foundation or basis; chiefly *fig.*, groundless, unwarranted.

1648 HEXHAM II, *Ongegrondet*, Vngrounded, or Vnfounded. 1667 MILTON *P. L.* II. 829, I..one for all My self expose, with lonely steps to tread Th' unfounded deep. 1785 BURKE *Nabob of Arcot* Wks. IV. 282 These debts..[he] at one stroke expunged..as utterly irrecoverable; he might have added, as utterly unfounded. 1828 LYTTON *Pelham* I. xxxiv, I advance a claim not altogether new and unfounded. 1855 *Orr's Circ. Sci.*, *Inorg. Nat.* 129 Vague speculations and unfounded theories concerning the origin of things. 1883 *Law Rep.* 11 Q.B.D. 593 The imputation..was altogether unfounded and absurd.

Hence **Unfou·ndedly** *adv.*

1820 SCOTT *Monast.* xxvi, I should wish to know the author ..of all these suspicions, so unfoundedly urged against me. 1883 *Law Times Rep.* XLIX. 251/1 Bringing a civil action, however unfoundedly.

† **Unfou·nded**, *ppl. a.*² *Obs.* [UN-¹ 8 + FOUND *v.*³] Not numbed or powerless.

14.. *Sege Jerusalem* (E.E.T.S.) 35/618 Þei wynnen vp, whyȝtly þe walles to kepe, Fresche vnfounded folke.

**Unfo·xed**, *ppl. a.* [UN-¹ 8.] Sober. 1622 J. TAYLOR (Water P.) *Farewell to the Tower Bottles* A 2 b, Yet alwayes 'twas my chance in Bacchus spight, To come into the Tower, vnfox'd vpright. **Unfra·ctured**, *ppl. a.* (UN-¹ 8.) 1742 *De Foe's Tour Gt. Brit.* (ed. 3) I. 262 Its huge Bulk lies unfractur'd. **Unfra·grant**, *a.* (UN-¹ 7, 5 b.) **1858** HAWTHORNE *Fr. & It. Note-bks.* (1871) II. 211 Children ..exceedingly unfragrant, but very courteous and gentle. **1880** RUSKIN *Bible Amiens* i. (1884) 4 Extensive plains of useful and not unfragrant peat. **Unfra·grantly**, *adv.* (UN-¹ 11.) **1883** *Harper's Mag.* June 121/1 It fumed not unfragrantly. **†Unfrai·sted**, *ppl. a. Obs.* [UN-¹ 8.] Untried, inexperienced. ? *a* **1400** *Morte Arth.* 2736 Bot I ame bot a fawntkyne, vn-fraystede in armes. *Ibid.* 2861. **Unfra·m(e)able**, *a.* (UN-¹ 7 b.) **1594** HOOKER *Eccl. Pol.* I. xvi. § 6 The cause of..their disposition so vnframeable vnto societies wherein they liue. **1597** *Ibid.* v. ix. § 1 The matter which he hath to worke on is vnframable. **Unfra·m(e)ableness.** (UN-¹ 12.) **1648** SANDERSON *Serm.* (1653) 9 The unframableness of our nature, to the doing of anything that is good.

**†Unfra·me**, *sb.*: see UN-¹ 3.

**Unfra·me**, *v.* [UN-² 3.]

†**1.** *trans.* To distress, trouble. *Obs.*—¹

*c* **1250** *Gen. & Ex.* 1213 Wintres forð-wexen on ysaac, And ysmael was him vn-swac; Often it gan ysaac un-framen.

**2.** To take to pieces; to destroy. Also *fig.*

*a* **1548** HALL *Chron., Hen. V*, 46 All the bridges wer by his enemies broken and unframed. **1603** J. DAVIES (Heref.) *Microcosmos* Wks. (Grosart) I. 83/2 The Pynns, the Tenons, Beams, Bolts,..All which they marke when they doe it vn-frame. **1621** SANDERSON *Serm.* I. 179 The curse of God ..gnaweth asunder the pins and the joynts of the building, till it have unframed it, and resolved it into a ruinous heap. *a* **1716** SOUTH *Serm.* (1744) VIII. v. 129 Sin has unframed the fabrick of the whole man.

†**b.** To undo. *Obs.*

**1567** TURBERV. *Epit.*, etc. 82 b, Those two agreed with common voyce my bondage to vnframe.

**3.** To dislocate; to throw into confusion or disorder, to distract.

**1574** HELLOWES *Gueuara's Fam. Ep.* (1584) 109 You are much offended by manie slaunderers that deprave your doings, and unframe your attempts. **1603** J. DAVIES (Heref.) *Microcosmos* Wks. (Grosart) I. 55/1 Disastrous Richard second of that name,..Who did the forme of this State quite vnframe. **1668** OWEN *Mortif. Sin* ii. (ed. 3) 14 It unframes our Spirit; and thence is called the sin that so easily besets us. **1727** [DORRINGTON] *Philip Quarll* 87 This unexpected but lucky Adventure, like a sudden Surprize, unfram'd his Reason.

**Unfra·med**, *ppl. a.* [UN-¹ 8.]

**1.** Not formed or moulded, unfashioned.

**1548** UDALL, etc. *Erasm. Par. John* vi. 37 b, He fourmeth and fasshyoneth the rude and vnframed witte with certayne principles. **1591** SAVILE *Tacitus, Agricola* 238 To compose, though in rude and vnframed speech, a memory of our late thraldome. **1621** G. SANDYS *Ovid's Met.* I. (1626) 1 The Sea, the Earth, al-couering Heauen vnfram'd, One face had Nature, which they Chaos nam'd.

**2.** Not set or enclosed in a frame.

**1718** POPE *Lett.* (1737) 201 He lugg'd out the tatter'd fragments of an unframed picture. **1885** HOWELLS *Silas Lapham* (1891) I. 13 A large warped, unframed photograph.

**Unfra·nchised**, *ppl. a.* (UN-¹ 8.)

**1648** HEXHAM II, *Onbevrijdt*, Vnfreed, or Vnfranchized. [**1775** ASH.] **1832** A. W. FONBLANQUE *Eng. under 7 Administr.* (1837) II. 284 The honest elector will only derive from his suffrage a share..which his unfranchised neighbour will also enjoy. **1847** GROTE *Greece* II. xxxi. IV. 217 The memorable partnership..between Kleisthenês and the unfranchised multitude.

**†Unfra·ngible**, *a. Obs.* (UN-¹ 7 and 5 b.) **1601** DOLMAN *La Primaud. Fr. Acad.* (1618) III. 847 Iron, be it neuer so thin, is made vnfrangible by blowes. **1654** JER. TAYLOR *Real Pres.* 198 That body of Christ which is in heaven..being whole and impassible, and unfrangible. **Unfra·nk**, *a.* (UN-¹ 7.) **1861** C. W. S. BROOKS *Silver Cord* xxvi, Impertinent curiosity, and..unfrank conversation. **Unfra·nkable**, *a.* (UN-¹ 7 b.) **1819** SOUTHEY *Lett.* (1856) III. 106 The next question is how to transport them.., for they are of an unfrankable shape and texture.

**Unfra·nked**, *ppl. a.* (UN-¹ 8. Cf. G. *unfrankiert*, Da. *ufrankeret*, Sw. *ofrankerad*.)

*a* **1765** D. MALLET *Let.* in *Pearson's Catal.* No. 81 (1900) 50 My last letter was franked by Mr. Nugent. Perhaps that was the cause of its miscarriage. I therefore send this unfranked. **1809** SIR G. JACKSON *Diaries & Lett.* (1873) I. 3, I wondered..that a letter—an unfranked one, too—should follow me. **1843** CARLYLE *Past & Pr.* III. xv, Heavy Packets, most of them unfranked.

**Unfrate·rnal**, *a.* (UN-¹ 7.) **1865** CARLYLE *Fredk. Gt.* xx. v, A not unfraternal or unpatriotic procedure. **1879** FARRAR *St. Paul* I. 447 To them..he never utters one single disrespectful or unfraternal word. **Unfrau·dulent**, *a.* (UN-¹ 7.) **1590** SWINBURNE *Testaments* 237 To take of the goods..by the lawful & vnfraudulent gift of the testator.

**†Unfrau·ght**, *sb. Obs.*—¹ [UN-¹ 12.] Want of cargo or freight.

**1436** *Libel Eng. Policy* in *Pol. Poems* (Rolls) II. 191 And now so fele shippes thys yere there were, That moche losse for unfraught [*v.r.* unfreyght] they bare.

**Unfrau·ght**, *ppl. a.* (UN-¹ 8 b.)

**1587** TURBERV. *Trag. T.* (1837) 16 With manly minde, and mouth unfraught of feare. **1605** BACON *Adv. Learn.* II. To the King § 12 Mindes emptie & vnfraught with matter. **1650** ASHMOLE *Chym. Collect.* Prol. 15 Such Vagrants doubtless are empty and unfraught. **1709** *Brit. Apollo* II. No. 53. 2/1 Men of narrow Intellects are Unfraught with..Noble Ideas.

**†Unfrau·ght**, *v. Obs.* [UN-² 3.] *trans.* To unload, discharge.

**1559** *Mirr. Mag.* (1563) X ij, Suffiseth nowe this playnt.. Whereof my hart his bottome hath vnfraught. **1633** P. FLETCHER *Purple Isl.* VI. xix, Then thou deare swain, thy heav'nly load unfraught. **1773** J. ROSS *Fratricide* I. 413 (MS.), Meantime, unfraughting thus returning love, He to his Mother runs.

**†Unfray·ed**, *ppl. a. Sc. Obs.* [UN-¹ 8.] Undaunted. **1536** BELLENDEN *Cron. Scot.* (1541) 142 b/2 Thir men..went, with vnfrayit curage, to ye wallis. **1680** in *Proc. Soc. Antiq. Scot.* XLV. 249 Beliving in the sufficencie of a Saviour..quherby ye may stand unfraid befor his tribunall. **†Unfray·ned**, *ppl. a. Obs.*—¹ [UN-¹ 8.] Unasked. *a* **1275** *Ancr. R.* 333 Schrift ouh to beon willes, þet is, willeliche, iureined [*MS. C.* vnfreined]. **†Unfre·deable**, *a. Obs.* [UN-¹ 7 b + FREDE *v.*] Insensible; without feeling. *c* **1450** in *Alphita* (Anecd. Oxon.) 123 *note*, A fishe þat..yf fissher put his honde upon hit hit makeþ his honde onfredeabile.

**Unfree·**, *a.* [ME. *unfre* (UN-¹ 7), = MDu. *onvri* (Du. *onvrij*), OHG. *unfrî* (MHG. *unvrî*, G. *unfrei*), WFris. *on-*, *ûnfrij*, MDa. and Da. *ufri*, MSw. and Sw. *ofri*.]

†**1.** Ignoble, base. *Obs.*—¹

*c* **1320** *Sir Tristr.* 2727 Þou slouȝ his breþer þre In fiȝt: Vrgan and morgan vn-fre And moraunt, þe noble kniȝt.

**2.** Characterized by want of freedom.

**13..** *E. E. Allit. P.* B 1129 So if folk be defowled by vnfre chaunce,..he may polyce hym at þe prest, by penaunce taken. **1568** GRAFTON *Chron.* II. 120 The election beyng vnfree,..eche of them almost of necessitie must hate the other. **1849** KEMBLE *Saxons in Eng.* I. 203 Serfs by reason of unfree birth. **1882–3** *Schaff's Encycl. Relig. Knowl.* 2206 The State..must be invested with all power over industry, which thus may be called practically unfree.

†**3.** Not at liberty *to* do something. *Obs.*

*c* **1380** WYCLIF *Wks.* (1880) 284 ȝif lordis myȝte ȝeue here heritage to clerkis..þei were vnfree to helpe here soulis.

**4.** Not possessed of personal liberty; destitute of freedom.

*c* **1380** WYCLIF *Sel. Wks.* I. 363 And so, as myche as in hem is, þei have maad Crist unfree. **1587** GOLDING *De Mornay* xii. 207 If it be demaunded why God created man free, and not vnfree. **1602** J. DAVIES (Heref.) *Mirum in Modum* Wks. (Grosart) I. 28/1 Better vnfree (saist thou) then be so ill, But 'tis not ill at libertie to bee.

**1849** KEMBLE *Saxons in Eng.* I. 203 The children..of parents who are both unfree, or..of one unfree parent. **1865** KINGSLEY *Hereward* xx, All the folk, free and unfree, man and woman, were out on the streets. **1882** WEEDEN *Soc. Law Labor* 40 The savage is the most unfree man in the world.

*absol.* **1864** KINGSLEY *Roman & T.* 54 The custom of chiefs choosing..their companions-in-arms, from among the most valiant of the unfree. **1874** GREEN *Short Hist.* i. § 2 (1882) 13 A slave class, a class of the unfree.

**5.** Not holding the position of a free or privileged member of a corporation. *Obs.* or *arch.*

**1442** *Extr. Aberd. Rec.* (1844) I. 8 Item, that al the communytie, alsweile vnfree as free men, be sworne to rise..in the defence of the toune. **1459–60** *Cal. Anc. Rec. Dublin* (1889) 303 Thay be put out of ther franches and ymad unfre. **1574** in *10th Rep. Hist. MSS. Comm.* App. V. 423 None of the inhabitance of Galway, free or onfree, yonge or old. **1608** in Gross *Gild Merch.* (1890) I. 150 *note*, Anie Englishe borne subiect beinge vnfree or no member of this ffellowshippe. **1687** LUTTRELL *Brief Rel.* (1857) I. 407 The lord mayor might drink to one as sherif free or unfree of the citty. **1717** in J. J. Vernon *Par. & Kirk Hawick* (1900) 205 Payd..for the bells tolling at the buriall of every unfree person within the said toun.

**6.** Not free of duty, tax, or impost; not exempt from commercial restrictions.

**1678** SIR G. MACKENZIE *Crim. Laws Scot.* I. xxvi. § ii. (1699) 130 The Customers Officers were about to poynd some unfree goods. **1684** *Lond. Gaz.* No. 1916/1 No such Clause or Provision as makes Free Goods to become Unfree when Laden and taken in Unfree Ships.

**Unfree**, *v.* [UN-² 6 a.] *trans.* To make unfree; to deprive of freedom.

*c* **1380** WYCLIF *Sel. Wks.* III. 431 Also oblishyng of men unfreeþ hem to God.

**Unfree·d**, *ppl. a.* (UN-¹ 8.)

**1565** *Reg. Privy Council Scot.* I. 423 How lang that evir the said Thomas remanit in Ingland unfred or put to libertie. **1648** HEXHAM II, *Onbevrijdt*, Vnfreed, or Vnfranchized. **1715** POPE *Iliad* II. 213 Shall beauteous Helen still remain unfreed? **1852** M. ARNOLD *Summer Night* 50 Death in their prison reaches them Unfreed, having seen nothing, still unblest. **1873** W. MORRIS *Love is Enough* 127 Few folk as friends shall unfreed Pharamond meet.

**Unfree·dom.** (UN-¹ 12.) *c* **1380** WYCLIF *Wks.* (1880) 286 Þe moste vnfredom is vnfredom of synne, for þat makiþ a man seruaunt..to þe fend. **1884** *Athenæum* 12 Apr. 465/3 Slavery as distinct from unfreedom died out very early [in England]. **†Unfree·holder.** *Sc. Obs.* (UN-¹ 12.) **1507** *Extr. Aberd. Rec.* (1844) I. 436 [Selling of ale] be fre folkis, and..be vnfrehaldaris.

**†Unfree·ly**, *a. Obs* [UN-¹ 7.] Not beautiful.

*a* **1300** *Cursor M.* 8082 Þair muthes wide, þair eien brade, Vn-freli was þair face made! *c* **1450** HOLLAND *Howlate* 56 Quhy is..My forme and my fetherem vnfrely, but feir? *Ibid.* 851. *a* **1568** STEWART in *Bannatyne MS.* (Hunter. Club) 397/35 Fast vnfrely fowll flobbis, And bubillis full lyk.

**Unfree·man.** Now *arch.* [f. UNFREE *a.* 5.] One who is not a freeman of a corporation.

**1445** in *Charters*, etc. *Edinb.* (1871) 67 Of strangearis and of vnfremen. **1480** *Newcastle Merch. Vent.* (Surtees) I. 3 The ackit [= act] of collarying of an unfremans gudes. **1511** *Burgh Rec. Edinb.* (1869) I. 134 Pakkis of lint..brocht to the samyn be vnfremen and strayngeris. **1584** in *10th Rep. Hist. MSS. Comm.* App. V. 433 Any goodes that apertayned to unfreemen (as it is termed). **1627** in Irving *Hist. Dumbarton.* (1860) 476 Gif ony freeman byis the same..for the use and behoof of an unfreeman..or wt unfreemanis moneyis to the unfreemanis behoof. **1707** *Lond. Gaz.* No. 4306/1 The Duties to be paid by the Unfreemen Importers of Coals into the Port..of Great Yarmouth. **1788** *Faculty Decisions* II. 30–1 (E.D.D.), That the three saddlers should be discharged to pack and peel with unfreemen. **1824** SCOTT *Redgauntlet* ch. x, I am not a person to pack or peel with Jacobites, and such unfreemen as poor Redgauntlet. **1876** GRANT *Burgh Sch. Scot.* 141 The supplying of instruction to the son and daughter of every burgess and unfreeman.

**†Unfree·ness.** *Obs.* (UN-¹ 12.) **1648** HEXHAM II, *Onvryigheydt*, Vnfreenesse, or Subjection. **1657** THURLOE in *State Papers* (1742) VI. 281 The three great men professinge their great unfreenes to act,..sayd, that [etc.].

**Unfree·ze**, *v.* [UN-² 3 and 7.]

**1.** *trans.* To cause to thaw.

**1584** HUDSON *Du Bartas' Judith* IV. 196 Loues firy dart Could neuer vnfriese the frost of her chast hart. **1598** FLORIO, *Disghiacciare*, to vnfreese, to thaw. **1651** OGILBY *Æsop* (1665) 11 Such Trumpeters would blood turn'd Ice unfreeze. **1879** MISS BIRD *Lady's Life Rocky Mount.* I. 280 Eggs, butter, milk,..have to be unfrozen.

*fig.* **1637** N. WHITING *Albino & Bellama* 36 Such quickning heat..That thawd his voyce, and did unfreeze his tongue. **1670** BROOKS *London's Lament.* 41 God by fiery tryals will unfreeze the frozen graces of his people. **1862** THORNBURY *Turner* II. 125 At an age when..he could not unfreeze himself into hospitality.

**2.** *intr.* To become thawed. Also *fig.*

**1662** J. DAVIES tr. *Olearius' Voy. Ambass.* 64 The cold having..pierc'd to the Centre of the earth, it must have leasure to unfreeze. **1746** W. HORSLEY *Fool* (1748) I. 234, I wish he would put off his Amour to the ensuing May, when the Virgin Heart unfreezes.

**Unfree·zing**, *ppl. a.* (UN-¹ 10.) **1775** T. SMITH *Jrnl.* (1849) 279 It has been a wonder of a winter, so moderate and unfreezing. **1897** *Outing* XXIX. 555 Ghastly in its shroud of snow and the blackness of unfreezing waters about it.

**†Unfreight**, *sb.*: see UNFRAUGHT *sb.*

**Unfrei·ght**, *v.* (UN-² 3.) **1580** H. GIFFORD *Gilloflowers* 36 Unfraight the shippe of all unlawfull wares. **Unfrei·ghted**, *ppl. a.* (UN-¹ 8.) [**1775** ASH.] **1854** PATMORE *Angel in Ho.* I. viii. 5 [I] Breathed with a heart unfreighted.

**†Unfreme**: see UN-¹ 3.

**Un-French**, *a.* (UN-¹ 7.)

**1830** MISS MITFORD *Our Village* Ser. IV. 74 A step..so un-French, so un-English. **1850** N. HAWTHORNE *Amer. Note-bks.* (1883) 380 This poor little Frenchman,..eating our most un-French victuals. **1878** E. FITZGERALD *Lett.* (1889) I. 423 Alfred [de Musset] appears to me a fine Fellow, very un-French in some respects.

**Un-French**, *v.* [UN-² 6 a.] *trans.* To translate from French. **1605** GAYWOOD in *Sylvester's Du Bartas* Pref. Sonn., Whom..loue to Heau'n and vs, Mou'd to vn-French his learned labours thus. **Unfre·nchified**, *ppl. a.* (UN-¹ 8.) **1784** P. OLIVER in *T. Hutchinson's Diary* (1886) II. 400 Be sure, return unfrenchified in thought, word, and deed. **1833** T. HOOK *Love & Pride, Marquess* vii, Following the extremely unfrenchified fashion.

**Unfre·nchify**, *v.* (UN-² 6 c.)

**1598** FLORIO, *Sfranciosato*,..vnfrenchifide. **1814** *Edin. Rev.* Sept. 297 We are glad..to have the assistance of a Parisian..to help to unfrenchify them.

**Unfre·nzied**, *ppl. a.* (UN-¹ 8.) **1805** in *Spirit Pub. Jrnls.* IX. 243 In thy calmer and unfrenzied hour.

**Unfre·quency.** Now *rare* or *Obs.* (UN-¹ 12, 5 b.)

**1611** COTGR., *Infrequence*, vnfrequencie, solitarinesse. **1662** GLANVILL *Lux Orient.* 133 This may be the reason of the unfrequency of their appearance. **1753** MISS COLLIER *Art Torment.* 224 The frequency of corporal punishments, and the unfrequency of rewarding men. **1802–12** BENTHAM *Ration. Judic. Evid.* (1827) V. 708 The comparative unfrequency of criminative perjury. **1834** *Good's Study Med.* (ed. 4) IV. 397 A point, however, of less importance, from the unfrequency of their occurrence.

**Unfre·quent**, *a.* [UN-¹ 7 and 5 b.]

**1.** = INFREQUENT *a.* 3.

**1611** FLORIO, *Infrequente*, vnfrequent, seld, not frequent. **1712** STEELE *Spect.* No. 472 ¶ 1 This Misfortune is so very great and unfrequent, that one would think, an Establishment for all the Poor under it might be easily accomplished. **1793** COLERIDGE *Songs of Pixies* iii, Beneath whose foliage pale Fann'd by the unfrequent gale We shield us from the Tyrant's mid-day rage. **1824** MISS MITFORD *Village* Ser. I. 246 In those unfrequent frosts which destroy all vegetation. **1866** HOWELLS *Venet. Life* v. 63 The blond, unfrequent beauty of the German aliens.

**b.** With preceding negative.

**1665** BOYLE *Occas. Refl.* II. xiii. 230 As Deliriums and Phrensies are not unfrequent in Feavers. **1749** J. MASON *Numbers in Poet. Compositions* 57 This is a peculiar close, but not unfrequent in Milton. **1831** SCOTT *Ct. Rob.* vii, A personage not so unfrequent in the streets of Constantinople as to excite any particular notice. **1871** MILL *Pol. Econ.* (ed. 7) 200 There is, however, a not unfrequent case, in which the purpose of the borrower is different.

†**2.** = INFREQUENT *a.* 2. *Obs.*—¹

**1618** ROWLANDS *Sacred Mem.* 24 This place is solitary, vnfrequent; We are belated.

**Unfreque·nt**, *v.* [UN-¹ 14 or UN-² 3.] *trans.* To refrain or cease from frequenting.

**1598** FLORIO, *Disconuersare*, to vnfrequent, not to conuerse together. *Ibid.*, *Sconuersare*, to disaccompanie, to vnfrequent. **1708** J. PHILIPS *Cyder* I. 404 Glad to shun his hostile Gripe, They quit their Thefts, and unfrequent the Fields.

**Unfreque·nted**, *ppl. a.* (UN-¹ 8.)

**1588** SHAKS. *Tit. A.* II. i. 115 The Forrest walkes are wide and spacious, And many unfrequented plots there are. **1653** H. COGAN tr. *Pinto's Trav.* xlviii. 277 Not one appearing in the streets for the space of ten days, during which time all places were unfrequented. **1701** NORRIS *Ideal World* I. viii. 452 The straight and single, however unfrequented path of truth. **1779** FORREST *Voy. N. Guinea* 154 During our stay here we found the islands unfrequented. **1817** J. SCOTT *Paris Revisit.* (ed. 4) 275 Going round..by one of the more unfrequented walks, running through the woods. **1878** HUXLEY *Physiogr.* 189 There are no doubt many slight disturbances, in unfrequented districts.

Hence **Unfreque·ntedness.**

**1654** EARL ORRERY *Parthen.* (1676) 79 A Grove, whose unfrequentedness was fit for my melancholly. **1680** H. MORE *Apocal. Apoc.* 160 There would be a great deadness of Trade,..and so great unfrequentedness..would seize his principal Seat. **1727** A. HAMILTON *New Acc. E. Ind.* I. i. 5 The Unfrequentedness of the Coast between the Cape of Good Hope and Natal.

**Unfreque·nting**, *vbl. sb.* (UN-¹ 12.) **1620** *Southampton*

*Court Leet Rec.* (1907) III. 578 We fynde the vnfrequentinge therof doth breed a murmer. **Unfreque·nting,** *ppl. a.* [UN-1 10.] † Unfrequented. **1607** ROWLANDS *Famous Hist.* 46 Terry, Guy and Osile wanting guide, Did stay about the unfrequenting Wood.

**Unfre·quently,** *adv.* (UN-1 11 and 5 b. Usually with preceding negative.)

**1646** SIR T. BROWNE *Pseud. Ep.* 7 They like Judas desire death, and not unfrequently pursue it. **1674** BOYLE *Excell. Theol.* 196 'Tis not unfrequently so [prejudiced] by those, that mention him with an *Encomium.* **1794** R. J. SULIVAN *View Nat.* I. 397 Systematic philosophy..is not unfrequently involved in difficulty. **1845** LINDLEY *Sch. Bot.* iv. (1858) 35 Flowers white, unfrequently pink. **1893** *Law Times* XCV. 56/1 Negotiations..not unfrequently fall through on some point of disagreement.

† **Unfre·t,** *v.*1 *Obs.*—1 [UN-2 3 + FRET *v.*3] *trans.* To unbind, untie.

**1496** *Bk. St. Albans, Fishing* h j b, Unfrette hym thenne and lete hym drye in an hous roof in the smoke.

† **Unfre·t,** *v.*2 *Obs.* [UN-2 3 + FRET *v.*1] *trans.* To make smooth; to unknit.

**1594** GREENE & LODGE *Looking Gl.* III. i, To Ioppa will I flee, And for a while to Tharsus shape my course, Vntill the Lord vnfret His angry browes. **1601** CHESTER *Love's Mart.* xcix, O happie time since I with Nature met, My unmelodious Discord I vnfret.

**Unfre·tted,** *ppl. a.* [UN-1 8.]

**1.** Not eaten or worn away; unimpaired.

**1577** STANYHURST *Hist. Irel.* 91/1 in *Holinshed* I, At night againe he founde the Paper vnfretted, and musing thereof he beganne to poare on the writing. **1663** BOYLE *Usef. Exp. Nat. Philos.* II. iii. 84 Shewing that the shell was..eaten away,..but the thin skin..continu'd altogether unfretted. **1894** MRS. A. WEBSTER *Mother & Dau.* (1895) 30 She sees this [feature] fair, and that unfretted still.

**2.** Not vexed or worried.

**1870** E. PEACOCK *Ralf Skirl.* III. 47 When his mind was sufficiently unfretted. **1893** *Atlantic Monthly* Feb. 283 He is..unfretted by the cares of housekeeping.

**Unfri·able,** *a.* (UN-1 7 b.)

**1802** PALEY *Nat. Theol.* viii. (1819) 105 The elastic and unfriable nature of cartilage.

**Unfrie·nd,** *sb.* (and *a.*). Forms: (see UN-1 and FRIEND *sb.*). [ME. *unfreond, -frend,* = WFris. *on-, ûnfrjeon,* MDu. *onvrient* (Du. *-vriend*), MLG. *unvrund,* MHG. *unvriunt* (G. *unfreund*).]

**1.** One who is not a friend or on friendly terms; an enemy. In early use chiefly *Sc.* (sometimes in predicate without article), and in the 19th cent. app. revived by Scott.

*c* **1275** LAY. 5632 We sollen..slean houre onfrendes and wenden after Brenne. *Ibid.* 17612 Wend to oure onfreondes and drif heom of londe. *c* **1425** WYNTOUN *Cron.* VIII. xxvi. 3890 For he doutit þe gret mycht Off his vnfreyndis, and þare slycht. *a* **1475** ASHBY *Dicta Philos.* 885 Showe to al maner freindis grete honnour..And pardon freendes & vnfreendes errour. **1581** MULCASTER *Positions* xxxix. (1887) 213 Socrates..uniustely condemned by the furie of the people, and persuasion of his vnfreindes. **1600** W. WATSON *Decacordon* (1602) 125 Some night Crowes, or other vnfriends or backe friends that may be set on to incense against him. **1663** *Lauderdale Papers* (Camden) I. 127 His unfriends here had taken pains to procure..copies of the books. **1814** SCOTT *Wav.* xv, He is a very unquiet neighbour to his un-friends. **1835** GEN. P. THOMPSON *Exerc.* (1842) III. 158 With this reservation, there must be no unfriends. **1877** STUBBS *Med. & Mod. Hist.* (1886) 110, I am ready to stick to my friends and vote against my un-friends.

**b.** Const. *of, to.*

**1513** DOUGLAS *Æneid* IX. vi. 111 The day lycht, quhilk is to ws onfrend, Approchis neyr. *c* **1600** W. FOWLER *Wks.* (S.T.S.) I. 241/30 Thow, o atropos, vnfreind to hir, and to to freind to me. **1626** in Rushw. *Hist. Coll.* (1659) I. 253 That one near the Crown of England should..become an unfriend to our State. **1692** *Scotch Presbyterian Eloquence* (1738) 47 This Way will render us more formidable to our Enemies, and Unfriends to our Way. **1819** SCOTT *Leg. Montrose* vi, They are but unfriends to each other. **1888** *Spectator* 22 Dec. 1804 Mr. Courtney, certainly no unfriend of the Parnellites.

**2.** One who is not a member of the Society of Friends. Also *attrib.*

**1828** SOUTHEY *Ep. to A. Cunningham* 387 From such a barber, O unfriend Darton! was that portrait made. **1846** W. E. FORSTER in T. W. Reid *Life* (1888) I. 186 To make their movement a national one by adding the names of unfriend ladies to their committee.

**Unfrie·nd,** *v.* (UN-2 6 b.) **1659** FULLER *App. Inj. Innoc.* III. xxxj b, I hope, Sir, that we are not mutually Unfriended by this Difference which hath happened betwixt us.

**Unfrie·nded,** *a.* [UN-1 9.] Not provided with friends; friendless.

**1513** MORE *Rich. III* (1883) 55 In how much she is now in the more beggerly condicion, vnfrended and worne out of acquaintance. **1554** ASCHAM in Whitaker *Richmondshire* (1823) I. 275 That [time] when I, unfreinded and unknowne, came first to your lordshipp. **1601** SHAKS. *Twel. N.* III. iii. 10 A stranger, Vnguided, and vnfriended. **1656** JEANES *Mixt. Schol. Div.* 5 And how should they, who were but..poor unfriended persons, escape..so potent..a malice. **1735** POPE *Let.* Wks. 1751 IX. 195 He will be a friend and benefactor..to your un-friended, un-benefited Nation. **1772** *Test Filial Duty* II. 2 [I] cannot think that I am unfriended, unheeded. **1842** ROGERS *Burke's Wks.* Introd. I. 10 Barry (afterwards the well known painter, then an unfriended son of genius). **1875** HOWELLS *Foregone Concl.* 209 A man more than ordinarily orphaned and unfriended.

*absol.* **1804** W. L. BOWLES *Spir. Discov.* III. 120 Who stood a guardian angel in distress To the unfriended.

**b.** Const. *of.*

**1589** WARNER *Alb. Eng.* Prose Addit. 159 Fly Trayterous Æneas, fly vnfolowed and vnfriended of Elisa. **1725** POPE *Odyssey* IV. 631 Still on this desert Isle my fleet is moor'd; Unfriended of the gales. **1868** LANIER *Jacquerie* V. 18 That blade flew up..And left Lord Raoul unfriended of his weapon.

Hence **Unfrie·ndedness.**

**1821** *Tales Landlord, Fair Witch of Glas Llyn* III. 325 This sublime unfriendedness.

† **Unfrie·ndfully,** *adv. Obs.*—1 (UN-1 11.) **1513** DOUGLAS *Æneid* VI. i. 135 Hard fortoun has..The Troianis..persewit vnfreindfully [1553 vnfrendly]. **Unfrie·nd-like,** *a.* (UN-1 7 c.) **1797** LAMB *Let. to Coleridge* 7 April, I did not expect so long, so unfriend-like a silence. **Unfrie·ndlily,** *adv.* (UN-1 11.) **1864** W. J. LINTON *Claribel* II. ii, Your harsh words Unfriendlily apparel'd.

**Unfrie·ndliness.** (UN-1 12; cf. next.)

*a* **1684** LEIGHTON *Comm. 1 Pet.* ii. 11 (1693) 351 But by the troubles, and unfriendliness of the World he gains this. *a* **1768** SECKER *Serm.* (1771) V. iv. 71 Every Day we see those..return monstrous Acts of Injustice for slight Instances of Neglect or Unfriendliness. **1790** MME. D'ARBLAY *Diary* 20 May, I never diminished from the frank unfriendliness to the cause with which I began. **1861** GEO. ELIOT *Silas M.* ix, Not because of any unfriendliness, but because..courtesy is not a growth of such homes.

**Unfrie·ndly,** *a.* [UN-1 7. Cf. WFris. *on-, ûnfrjeonlik,* MDu. *onvriendelijc* (Du. *-lijk*), MHG. *unvriuntlîch* (G. *unfreundlich*).]

**1.** Not characteristic of a friend or friends; exhibiting dislike or hostility.

**1425** *Rolls of Parlt.* IV. 274/1 Þis delaye, of which were like to growe unease and unfrendely love betwene me and my said Cousyn. *a* **1513** FABYAN *Chron.* (1516) VII. 134/1 They mette with vnfrendely countenaunce, &..departyd with lytle loue or charyte. *a* **1548** HALL *Chron., Edw. IV,* 229 The French kyng..knewe by his espials..the vnfrendly departyng of the Duke of Burgoyn. **1663** BP. PATRICK *Parab. Pilgr.* xxxvii, Nor have you given me cause to be less your Friend than heretofore; unless it be by this unfriendly jealousie. **1757** FOOTE *Author* II, It was, d'ye see, a very unfriendly thing to make love to Becky in my absence. **1837** DE QUINCEY *Lake Poets, Coleridge,* Discoverers who would make a more unfriendly use of the discovery. **1898** *Westm. Gaz.* 21 Jan. 2/2 We are very much afraid that this would be looked upon by other countries as an 'unfriendly act'.

**2.** Not having the qualities or disposition of a friend; *esp.* unfavourably disposed, inimical, hostile.

**1483** *Cath. Angl.* 142/2 Vn Frendly, *inhumanus, inimicus.* **1553** ASCHAM *Germany* Wks. (1904) 127, I am not so vnaduised..nor you so vnfrendly to looke for so much from me. **1579** HARVEY *Letter-bk.* (Camden) 58 To his very unfrendly frende that procurid ye edition of his slender and extemporall devises. *a* **1616** BEAUM. & FL. *Wit at Sev. Weapons* V. i, Sure some unfriendly Messenger Is imploy'd betwixt you. **1629** in Foster *Eng. Factories India* (1909) III. 358 Our unfriendlie neighbours the Dutch. **1794** S. WILLIAMS *Vermont* 170 The Indians became unfriendly. **1836** THIRLWALL *Greece* III. 379 They put forward some of their partizans, who were not so notoriously unfriendly to him. **1884** CHURCH *Bacon* 18 His unsympathetic and suspicious, but probably not unfriendly relative.

**3.** Not propitious or favourable (*for* or *to*).

**1513** BRADSHAW *Lyfe St. Werburge* II. 1047 By fortune vnfrendly..Both horse and man fell to grounde sodendly. **1608** SHAKS. *Per.* III. i. 58 No light, no fire; the unfriendly elements Forgot thee utterly. **1707** *Curios. in Husb. & Gard.* 41 The Wind that blows from thence..is always unfriendly to Vegetation. **1784** *Phil. Trans.* LXXIV. 468 It must be supposed to have arisen from some unfriendly mixture in the tin, probably from Arsenic. **1805** DICKSON *Pract. Agric.* I. 406 It frequently happens that..a coarse, unfriendly, stiff soil, is brought up. **1815** JANE AUSTEN *Emma* xvi, The atmosphere in that unsettled state..which is..the most unfriendly for exercise. **1845** WHATELY in *Encycl. Metrop.* (1845) I. 225/1 Qualities unfriendly to each other are rarely combined.

**Unfrie·ndly,** *adv.* Now *rare.* [UN-1 11.] In an unfriendly manner.

*a* **900** *Genesis* 2689 Þu us leanast nu, unfreondlice fremena þancast. **1483** *Cath. Angl.* 142/2 Vn Frendly,..*inhumane, inhumaniter.* **1548** ELYOT, *Insequor,*..to speake vnfrendly agaynst one. **1553** [see UNFRIENDFULLY]. **1570** G. HARVEY *Letter-bk.* (Camden) 5, I delaied thus unfrendly. **1722** WOLLASTON *Relig. Nat.* vi. § 15 To covet to obtain what is another man's by just means, and with his consent,..has nothing surely that looks unfriendly upon truth, or is blameable, in it. **1757** W. THOMPSON *R. N. Advoc.* 46 [This] I leave to be determined by the..Wisdom of the Contracting Coopers that undermine one another unfriendly.

**Unfrie·ndship.** Now *arch.* [UN-1 12. Cf. MDu. *onvrientscap* (Du. *onvriendschap*), MLG. *unvruntschap,* OHG. *unvriuntscap* (G. *unfreundschaft*).] Unfriendliness; enmity.

*a* **1340** HAMPOLE *Psalter* xl. 10 In signe þat crist did til him nane vnfrendschip. *a* **1400–50** *Alexander* 2722 And if þou wirke þaim all þe wa & wrak at þou may, Þe mare vnfryndschip þarfore fall sall þe neuire. **1549** COVERDALE, etc. *Erasm. Par. Jas.* iv. 36 A Christian, if he assaye to haue frendshyp agayne with the worlde, doeth vtterly receaue vnfrendshyp with God. **1666** *Despautere's Gram. Instit.* D 8 b (Jam.), *Inimicitiæ,* unfriendship. **1819** SCOTT *Ivanhoe* i, An act of unfriendship to my sovereign person and royal wardrobe. **1897** LD. E. HAMILTON *Outlaws of Marches* xi, The auld unfriendship betwixt the twa houses.

† **Unfri·ght,** *a. Obs. rare*—1. [UN-1 7. Cf. AFFRIGHT *ppl. a.* and OE. *unforht.*] Unafraid.

*c* **1250** *Gen. & Ex.* 3713 Burȝes stronge and folc v(n)friȝt, stalwurði to weren here riȝt.

**Unfri·ghted,** *ppl. a.* (UN-1 8.)

**1611** B. JONSON *Catiline* V. vi, If..he alone, In so great feare of all men, stand vn-frighted. **1624** QUARLES *Job* xvii. 54 Who euer heard the voyce Of th' angry heauens, vnfrighted at the noyse? ? *c* **1730** RAMSAY *Thimble* 53 Could you unfrighted view hell's dismal shore? **1840** BROWNING *Sordello* VI. 629 To the soft small unfrighted bee.

**Unfri·ghtened,** *ppl. a.* (UN-1 8.)

**1675** CROWNE *Calisto* Prol. A. 4 b, These beautious Nymphs unfrightned too,..Their innocent delights pursue. **1835** W. IRVING *Tour Prairies* 259 He..fired, but without effect: the deer remained unfrightened. **1885** PENNELL *Fishing* (1889) 417 He then..renews his attentions to the still unfrightened fish above.

Hence **Unfri·ghtenedness.**

**1858** FABER *Foot of Cross* 138 The manifest unfrightenedness of a creature who has for the moment forgotten Him.

**Unfri·ghtful,** *a.* (UN-1 7.) **1837** CARLYLE *Fr. Rev.* I. VII. iv, Not unfrightful it must have been; ludicro-terrific, and most unmanageable. **Unfri·nged,** (*ppl.*) *a.*1 [UN-1 8, 9 + FRINGED *ppl. a.*] Not fringed; unadorned. **1646** JENKYN *Remora* 30 Plain and unfringed reformations..are poor, dry, dull things to such. † **Unfri·nged,** *ppl. a.*2 *Obs.*—1 [UN-1 8 + (IN)FRINGE *v.*] Not infringed. **1751** ELIZA HEYWOOD *Betsy Thoughtless* II. 234 She..thought it the privilege of youth to do whatever it listed, provided the rules of virtue were unfringed.

† **Unfrith:** see UN-1 3.

**Unfri·zzled,** *ppl. a.* (UN-1 8.) **1611** COTGR., *Drap d'or ras,* smooth, or unfrizeled cloth of Gold. **1765** STERNE *Tr. Shandy* VII. xxxviii, She had better have gone with it [= her hair] unfrizled.

**Unfro·ck,** *v.* [UN-2 4. Cf. F. *défroquer,* and UNGOWN *v.*]

**1.** *trans.* To strip (an ecclesiastic) of his frock as a sign of degradation; hence, to deprive of priestly function or office. Also **Unfro·cking** *vbl. sb.*

The second quotation is the only source for the common attribution of the term to Queen Elizabeth.

**1644** MILTON *Areop.* 30 It is not the unfrocking of a Priest ..that will make us a happy Nation. ? *a* **1750** *Forged Letter Q. Eliz.* in *Ann. Reg., Char.* (1761) 15/1 If you do not forthwith fulfil your engagement, by ——, I will immediately unfrock you. **1817** T. L. PEACOCK *Melincourt* I. 10 He took especial care that this..should not reach the ears of his bishop, who would infallibly have unfrocked him. **1857** TROLLOPE *Barchester T.* III. xvii. 296 Clergymen have been unfrocked for less than what you have been guilty of. **1884** *Nonconf. & Indep.* 22 May 505/3 Mr. Justice Stephen truly remarked, there was no power to unfrock him.

*refl.* **1822** *Q. Rev.* XXVIII. 41 Who had been first a Dominican friar, then, having unfrocked himself, a gardener. **1855** L. HUNT *Old Court Suburb* I. 150 Who had also been a prelate, but had unfrocked himself to become a statesman.

*absol.* **1808** E. S. BARRETT *Miss-led General* 85 He had unfrocked, that is, given over the cure of souls in this world.

**2.** *transf.* To unmask or expose.

**1876** BANCROFT *Hist. U. S.* VI. xxix. 74 Spain had the monkish Calderon..There no poet like Molière unfrocked hypocrisy.

Hence **Unfro·cked** *ppl. a.*

**1794** MATTHIAS *Purs. Lit.* (1798) 44, I love no atheist French Bishops, nor unfrocked grammarians in England. **1861** PEARSON *Early & Mid. Ages* 357 The unfrocked priest would of course be amenable to lay tribunals in future. **1880** DIXON *Windsor* III. xxiv. 245 On the unfrocked priest attempting flight, he..locked him in the Tower.

† **Unfro·ckify,** *v.* [UN-2 6 c.] = UNFROCK *v.* **1694** MOTTEUX *Rabelais* V. xxvii. 134 In Germany they pull down Monasteries and *unfrockifie* the Monks.

† **Unfrome,** var. *unfreme*: see UN-1 3.

**Unfro·nted,** *ppl. a.* [UN-1 8.] Not faced or confronted. **1615** BRATHWAIT *Strappado* 25 Hence Sergeants walk vnfronted (though they know it).

**Unfro·st,** *v.* [UN-2 4 b.] *trans.* To thaw. **1611** FLORIO, *Disghiacciáre,* to vnfrost, to thaw. **1853** KANE *Grinnell Exp.* xxxii. (1856) 275 We celebrated it by an extra dinner, a plum-cake unfrosted for the occasion.

**Unfro·sted,** *ppl. a.* (UN-1 8.) [**1775** ASH.] **1886** C. SCOTT *Sheep-farming* 45 The relative value of frosted and unfrosted turnips in the feeding of sheep. **1887** W. WESTALL *Her Two Millions* xxi, The lightness of his hair..as yet unfrosted with white. **Unfro·wardly,** *adv.* (UN-1 11.) **1859** TENNYSON *Pelleas & Ettarre* 612 Hath the great heart of knighthood in thee fail'd So far thou canst not bide, unfrowardly, A fall from him? **Unfro·wning,** *ppl. a.* (UN-1 10.) **1830** W. TAYLOR *Hist. Surv. Germ. Poetry* III. 5 O Jove, Canst thou, unfrowning, view his perfidy? **1888** A. S. WILSON *Lyric Hopeless Love* 123 Enough one solitary ray From thine unfrowning sky.

**Unfro·ze,** var. of next.

**1705** J. PHILIPS *Blenheim* 234 The Memphian Soldiery That swell'd the Erythræan Wave, when Wall'd The unfroze Waters marvellously stood. **1774** GOLDSM. *Nat. Hist.* (1776) I. 178 The ice..grown more bulky, by freezing, than the water, which remains unfroze.

**Unfro·zen,** *ppl. a.*1 [UN-1 8 b. Cf. Norw. *ufrosen,* Sw. *ufrusen,* MDu. (once) *ongevroren.*] Not frozen; not congealed by frost.

**1596** DALRYMPLE tr. *Leslie's Hist. Scot.* (S.T.S.) I. 31 Thair fatt..freises nocht frahand..bot certane dayes remanes vnfrossin lyke oyle. **1598** FLORIO, *Ingelido,* not frozen, vnfrozen. **1656** tr. *Hobbes' Elem. Philos.* xxviii. 354 The Wine which remains unfrozen in the midst will be very strong. *a* **1691** BOYLE *Hist. Air* (1692) 154 They..were obliged to dig about six foot deep in the ice, before they could come at unfrozen water. **1766** REID *Wks.* (1846) I. 45/1 The unfrozen water soon came to the temperature of the room. **1817** KIRBY & SP. *Entomol.* II. 451 Remaining unfrozen though exposed to the severest cold. **1860** TYNDALL *Glac.* II. xxiv. 360 The water..which has been carried down from the névé unfrozen.

**Unfro·zen,** *ppl. a.*2 [f. UNFREEZE *v.*] Released from frost; thawed.

**1633** P. FLETCHER *Purple Isl.* VI. lxviii, The flowres that.. in the Spring..Peep out again from their unfrozen tombe.

**Unfru·cted,** *a. Her.* [UN-1 9.] Not furnished with fruit.

**1688** R. HOLME *Armoury* II. 83/1 The branch is not to be so termed (unfructed, or without fruit) except it be thus made, and consist of nine leaves. *c* **1828** BERRY *Encycl. Her.* I. Gloss. s.v., Slips of laurel, bay, and the like, consist of three leaves, the sprig of five leaves, and the branch, being unfructed, of nine leaves.

† **Unfru·ctful**, obs. var. Unfruitful *a.* **1549** Coverdale, etc. *Erasm. Par. Eph.* v. 11 b, To doe fruictefull honeste offices of godlines,..and from henceforth be ashamed to haue adoe with the vnfructefull workes of darkenesse. **Unfru·ctify**, *v.* [Un-2 6 c.] *trans.* To render unfruitful. **1628** R. Hobart *Edw. II*, cclxiii, So may we see how God unfructifies A fruitfull land for mens impieties. **Unfru·ctifying**, *ppl. a.* (Un-1 10.) **1827** Montgomery *Pelican Isl.* iv. 55 While in the womb of earth their embryos tarried, Unfructifying, yet imperishable. **Unfructuo·sity.** (Un-1 12 and 5 b; cf. next.) **1884** *Manch. Exam.* 29 Mar. 4/8 The intellectual unfructuosity of the Royal stock.

**Unfru·ctuous**, *a.* [Un-1 7 and 5 b.]

†**1.** Producing no fruit; unfruitful. *Obs.*

**1382** Wyclif *Exod.* xxiii. 26 Ne thi loond shal be vnfructuous, ne bareyn. — *Job* xxiv. 20 Be he not in recording, but be to-trede as a tree vnfructuous. *c* **1400** *Pilgr. Sowle* (Caxton, 1483) iv. ii. 58 The trees..were bycomen wylde and vnfructuous.

**2.** *fig.* = Unfruitful *a.* 2. Now *rare*.

*c* **1380** Wyclif *Sel. Wks.* III. 29 My mouþ..þat bifore was filid þoru unfructuouse jangelingis. *c* **1430** Lydg. *Min. Poems* (Percy Soc.) 258 Ryot and dronkenesse, Unfructuous talkyng, intemperat diete. *c* **1450** tr. *De Imitatione* iii. ii. 65 Speke..þou, my lorde god, euerlastyng trouþe; lest I dye & be made unfructuouse. **1513** Douglas *Æneid* iv. Prol. 19 3our frute is bot vnfructuus fantasy. **1588** A. King tr. *Canisius' Catech.* 135 Be 3e nocht partakers of the vnfruictuous warkis of wickitnes. **1828** Scott *Jrnl.* 27 Feb., We had a final and totally unfructuous meeting. **1904** R. Bridges *Demeter* iii. 954 Unfructuous night Stifles her essence in her truthless heart.

Hence **Unfru·ctuously** *adv.*

**1827** Scott *Jrnl.* 6 May, Wrought again at Hoffmann—unfructuously I fear.

**Unfru·gal**, *a.* (Un-1 7 and 5 b.)

?**1629** T. Craufurd *Hist. Univ. Edinb.* (1808) 113 He was not given to the cares of the world, though not unfrugal. **1720** *Humourist* Ded. p. xvi, They will..restore us again to our unfrugal and unfortunate Ravings. **1780** Bentham *Princ. Legisl.* xvii. § 19 This punishment, it is evident, is in an eminent degree unfrugal. **1826** *Art of Brewing* (ed. 2) 29 Some..brewers adopt the following dangerous and unfrugal practice. **1846** Landor *Imag. Conv.* Wks. II. 113/1 Ladies who have been unfrugal of their favours.

**Unfrui·tful**, *a.* [Un-1 7. In early use after L. *infructuosus, infecundus*.]

**1.** Not producing offspring; barren.

**1388** Wyclif *Exod.* xxiii. 26 Neithir a womman vnfruytful, neither bareyn, schal be in thi lond. **1535** Coverdale *Judg.* xiii. 2 His wife was vnfruteful & bare him no children. **1577** B. Googe *Heresbach's Husb.* iv. (1586) 169 The vnfruitfull.., and the otherwise faultie, ought cheefely to be fatted. **1650** Bulwer *Anthropomet.* 233 They cur'd themselves, but became unfruitful and impotent. **1735** Berkeley *Querist* § 208 So many unhappy and unfruitful marriages.

**2.** *fig.* Not productive of good results; unprofitable, unremunerative.

*a* **1400** *New Test.* (Paues) Eph. v. 11 Þe vnfruytful werkes of darkenesse. *c* **1430** *Life St. Kath.* (1884) 47 What euer we do to oure goddes me thinkeþ hit is bot veyn and vnfruytfull. **1526** *Pilgr. Perf.* (W. de W. 1531) 76 b, The communycacyon was not onely vnfruytfull, but also moche euyll. **1593** Shaks. *Lucr.* 344 But in the midst of his unfruitful prayer,..Even there he starts. **1634** Sir T. Herbert *Trav.* 29 Conditions dishonourable and vnfruitfull. *a* **1718** Parnell *Donne's 3rd Sat. Versified* 4 To laugh or weep at sins might idly show Unheedful passion, or unfruitful woe. **1780** *Mirror* No. 72, The cold unfruitful virtues of monkish solitude. **1821** Scott *Pirate* x, It was a time of idle and unfruitful laughter. **1869** J. Martineau *Ess.* II. 250 This hint has not been permitted to remain unfruitful.

*absol.* **1781** Cowper *Truth* 500 She may..leave to mercy ..The worthless and unfruitful of mankind.

**3.** Of trees: Not bearing fruit. Also *fig.*

**1531** Tindale *Exp. 1 John* (1537) 94 He yt is cut from ye vynestocke..can not but abyde vnfruteful. **1846** J. Baxter *Libr. Pract. Agric.* (ed. 4) II. 177 The substratum ought to be dry,..otherwise trees planted will be liable to become ..unhealthy and unfruitful.

**4.** Of ground or seasons: Not yielding fruit or crops; unfertile, unproductive.

**1545** Brinklow *Compl.* 14 Moory ground, as is vnfruteful for corne or pasture. **1585** T. Washington tr. *Nicholay's Voy.* iii. xxi. 110 Manye desartes, sandye, wythered, vnfruitefull. **1615** G. Sandys *Trav.* 1 A hill not vnfruitfull in Oliues. **1653** W. Ramesey *Astrol. Restored* 228 The year shall be unseasonable,..unfruitful or scarce. *Ibid.* 284. **1712** Blackmore *Creation* ii. 197 Should but the sun his duty once forget,..Unfruitful earth her wretched fate would mourn. **1782** Martyn *Geog. Mag.* i. iii. I. 201 Mountains and rocks, interspersed with unfruitful plains. **1820** Wordsw. *River Duddon* v, Unfruitful solitudes, that seem to upbraid The sun in heaven.

*fig.* *a* **1586** Sidney *Arcadia* ii. xxix, She..besought him, not to cast his love in so unfruitfull a place.

**Unfrui·tfully**, *adv.* (Un-1 11; cf. prec.)

*c* **1450** tr. *De Imitatione* i. x. 11 We speke muche of suche þinges as we loue or desire...But allas! ofte tymes veinly & unfruytfully. **1529** *Supplic. Hen. VIII* (1871) 42 To lyue both wickedly towardes God, and also vnfrutefully towardes the worlde. **1583** Melbancke *Philotimus* M j b, Senior Mondaldo which neuer mispent time vnfruitfully. **1654–66** Earl Orrery *Parthen.* (1676) 568 Civilities were not unfruitfully placed. **1833** S. Hoole *Discourses* xiii. 171 We shall..praise him—not tremblingly and unfruitfully,..but joyfully and profitably.

**Unfrui·tfulness.** (Un-1 12; cf. prec.)

**1565** Cooper *Thesaurus, Infœcunditas*,..barrainenesse: vnfruitefulnesse. **1577** B. Googe *Heresbach's Husb.* iv. (1586) 158 The little Pullets, or Hennes,..both for their vnfruitfulnesse, and other causes. **1615** Bp. Hall *Contempl., O.T.* xi. v, The unfruitfulness of Hannah. **16..** Middleton, etc. *Old Law* ii. i, We judge Dotage complete then, as unfruitfulness In women at threescore. **1707** Mortimer *Husb.* 527 The great Point to be taken care of about Fruit Trees, which is the Unfruitfulness of them. **1764** H. Walpole *Otranto* i, I divorce her from this hour. Too long has she cursed me by her unfruitfulness. **1850** R. I. Wilberforce *Holy Baptism* 35 It is unreasonable..to complain of that unfruitfulness [of baptism] which results from their own neglect. **1873** B. Stewart *Conserv. Force* v. 140 The unfruitfulness of the earlier views.

† **Unfrui·ting**, *ppl. a.* [Un-1 10.] Barren. *a* **1300** *Cursor M.* 12257 A commament nu mak i here,..Þat þe vnfruitand þair frutes find. † **Unfrui·tous**, *a. Obs.* [Un-1 7.] = Unfructuous *a.* **1382** Wyclif *Eph.* v. 11 Vnfruytouse workes of derknessis. — *Tit.* iii. 14 Oure men lerne for to be bifore in good werkis,..that thei be not vnfruytouse.

**Unfru·strable**, *a.* (Un-1 7 b and 5 b.)

**1714** R. Fiddes *Pract. Disc.* ii. 239 Here is a fix'd and unfrustrable reward secur'd. **1791** W. Jay in *Autobiog.* (1855) vii. 74 Immutable in his nature, unfrustrable in his designs. **1832** Bp. Law *Charge to Clergy* (R.), An irresistible, or, what the schoolmen have called, an unfrustrable power.

So **Unfru·strably** *adv.* (Un-1 11.)

**1654** Owen *Doctr. Saint's Persev.* xii. 274 Those cloudy expressions of 'irresistibly' and 'unfrustrably'. **1754** Edwards *Freed. Will* ii. xii. 123 Such Means, as shall unfrustrably produce the End.

**Unfu·elled**, (*ppl.*) *a.* (Un-1 8, 9.)

**1687** *Death's Vis.* viii, But Let me Gaze on..That Boyling Ocean of Unfuel'd Fire. **1801** Southey *Thalaba* ii. ii, Before them in the vault, Blazing unfuel'd.., Ten magic flames arose. **1817** Coleridge *Lay Serm.* 61 It must be Seraphs..that can burn unfuelled and self-fed. *Ibid.* 102 Ill-fed, ill-clothed, and unfuelled winters.

**Unfulfi·lled**, *ppl. a.* (Un-1 8.)

**1382** Wyclif *Rom.* ix. 6 Sothli not that the word of God hath falle down, or failide vnfulfillid. **1526** *Pilgr. Perf.* (W. de W. 1531) 187 b, Than one iote or lettre of ye lawe of God sholde be vnfulfylled or founde vntrue. **1548** Udall *Erasm. Par. Luke* iii. 34 b, To the entente that he would leaue no one poynte of humilitee or of righteousnesse vnfulfilled. **1610** Healey *St. Aug. Citie of God* xvii. ii. 621 No part of the earthly promise was left vnfulfilled. **1676** Glanvill *Ess. Philos. & Relig.* i. 26 Had Authority prevail'd here,..Seneca's Prophesie had been an unfulfil'd Prediction. **1796** Mme. D'Arblay *Camilla* V. 459 Thou art come,..thy task unfulfilled, thy peace unearned. **1821** Shelley *Adonais* xlv, The inheritors of unfulfilled renown Rose from their thrones. **1879** B. Taylor *Germ. Lit.* 275 The promise of loftier development was not left unfulfilled.

**Unfulfi·lling**, *ppl. a.* (Un-1 10.) **1821** Shelley *Hellas* 973 Alas! for Liberty! If numbers, wealth, or unfulfilling years, Or fate, can quell the free! **Unfu·il**, *a.* (Un-1 7.) *c* **1450** *Mirk's Festial* 80 And fore bycause þat þylke nombyr may not be vnfulle, hit ys nedfull to chese on of þes men. **1598** Sylvester *Du Bartas* ii. i. *Handy-crafts* 540 Th' un-full Harmony Of uneven Hammers, beating diversly. **Unfu·lled**, *ppl. a.* (Un-1 8.) **1467** *Rolls of Parlt.* V. 621 That noo persone..carie..by yonde the See, any Wollen Yerne, nor untoked and unfulled Cloth. *Ibid.*, To bie rawe Clothes, untoked and unfulled. *c* **1550** Cheke *Matt.* ix. 16 No man doth lai on a patch of an vnfulled ragg on an old garment. **Unfu·lly**, *adv.* (Un-1 11.) *c* **1449** Pecock *Repr.* v. xv. 564 It is no nede forto seie ther of eny thing vnperfitli and vnfully..here.

† **Unfu·lyeit**, *ppl. a. Sc. Obs.* [Un-1 8.] Not exhausted or worn out.

**1508** Dunbar *Tua Mariit Wemen* 62 Birdis..ilk 3eir..fangis thame ane fresche feyr, vnful3eit, and constant. **1535** Stewart *Cron. Scot.* (Rolls) I. 71 We ar all fresche vnful3eit into feild.

**Unfu·med**, *ppl. a.* (Un-1 8.) **1667** Milton *P. L.* v. 349 She..strews the ground With Rose and Odours from the shrub unfum'd. **1891** *Anthony's Photogr. Bull.* IV. 117 It is often advisable to print..on unfumed paper. **Unfundame·ntal**, *a.* (Un-1 7.) **1638** Chillingworth *Relig. Prot.* i. ii. § 155. 114 This assertion..is neither a Fundamentall nor Vnfundamentall point of Faith. *a* **1711** Ken *Hymnotheo* Poet. Wks. 1721 III. 236 How tenderly God treats all Hearts sincere, Who tow'rds Mistakes unfundamental veer.

**Unfu·nded**, *ppl. a.* (Un-1 8.)

[**1775** Ash.] **1776** Adam Smith *W. N.* v. iii. II. 539 What is called the unfunded debt of Great Britain, is contracted in the former of those two ways. **1812** *Examiner* 4 May 285/1 The Unfunded Debt, up to the 5th of January 1812, amounted to fifty-two millions. **1879** F. Hitchman *Public Life Beaconsfield* I. vii. 415 That notable device for swelling the unfunded debt of the country.

**Unfu·nny**, *a.* (Un-1 7.)

**1858** Hogg *Life Shelley* I. 318 The application was..'haud illepidum', not unfunny. **1892** *Nation* (N.Y.) 30 June 489/1 It is most lugubriously unfunny.

**Unfu·r**, *v.* (Un-2 4.) **1598** Florio, *Spellicciare*, to vnskin, to vnfur. **1655** Moufet & Bennet *Health's Improv.* (1746) 295 To stir up Appetite, to unfur the Tongue and relish the Mouth. **Unfu·rbelowed**, *ppl. a.* (Un-1 8.) **1772** *Test Filial Duty* II. 64 My ruffles are short, and my aprons unfurbellowed. **Unfu·rbished**, *ppl. a.* (Un-1 8.) [**1775** Ash.] **1829** Scott *Anne of G.* iii, Near these, but..unfurbished and neglected, hung a helmet.

**Unfu·rl**, *v.* [Un-2 3.]

**1.** *trans.* To open or spread out (a flag or sail) to the wind.

**1641** Milton *Reform.* ii. 69 Such poor drifts to..ingage the unattainted Honour of English Knighthood, to unfurle the streaming Red Crosse. **1667** — *P. L.* i. 535 A Cherube tall: Who forthwith from the glittering Staff unfurld Th' Imperial Ensign. **1717** Prior *Alma* i. 489 Antonius fled from Actium's Coast,..His Sails by Cupid's Hand unfurl'd. **1795** in *Naval Chron.* III. 117 The royal standard was unfurled in the barge. **1836** W. Irving *Astoria* I. 87 They saw the sails unfurled, and that it was getting under way. **1860** Tyndall *Glac.* i. xvi. 105, I took the glorious banner thus unfurled as a sign of hope.

**b.** *transf.* and *fig.*

**1678** *Poor Robin's True Char. Scold* 4 When once her Flag of Defiance, the Tippet, is unfurl'd, she cares not a straw for Constable. **1711** Addison *Spect.* No. 102 ¶ 4 The next Motion is that of unfurling the Fan, in which are comprehended several little Flirts and Vibrations. **1796** *Mod. Gulliver* 226, I once more unfurled my umbrella, and away we went. **1840** Dickens *Old C. Shop* xvii, Codlin pitched the temple,..hastily unfurling the drapery and concealing Short therewith. **1884** *Harper's Mag.* Dec. 117/1 He takes the fan out, and unfurls it.

**2.** *intr.* To open to the wind.

**1813** Byron *Corsair* i. xvi, As marks his eye..the sails unfurling fast. **1854** Patmore *Angel in Ho., Betrothal* 119 As to the breeze a flag unfurls My spirit expanded.

Hence **Unfu·rled** *ppl. a.*, **Unfu·rling** *vbl. sb.*

**1647** N. Ward *Simple Cobler* 54, I am resolved to display my unfurled soule in your face. **1780** *Mirror* No. 102, The art which the ladies..used in the unfurling of their fans.

**Unfu·rlable**, *a.* (Un-1 7 b.) **1845** E. Warburton *Crescent & Cross* I. 188 The Arabs..reel with the staggering boat, and look fearfully up to the unfurlable sails.

**Unfu·rnish**, *v.* [Un-2 4.]

**1.** *trans.* To divest (a place, etc.) of men or other means of defence. Also const. *of*.

**1580** Hollyband *Treas. Fr. Tong, Se Desgarnir de son armée*,..to vnfurnish. **1591** Harington *Orl. Fur.* xxxi. xlix, Renaldo had six hundred men and more,..Though at this need his Princes turn to furnish, He soon agreed his own towns to unfurnish. **1600** E. Blount tr. *Conestaggio* vii. 225 He desired first to see the issue, before he woulde bee vnfurnished of his forces. **1686** Parr *Life Usher* 58 He was now forced to unfurnish this, as well as others, of its Souldiers and Ammunition. **1829** Sir W. Napier *Penins. War* vi. iii. II. 157 English troops should, without unfurnishing Lisbon, co-operate for the relief of Oporto.

†**b.** To make clear *of*; to depopulate. *Obs.*

**1603** Knolles *Hist. Turks* (1621) 292 Europe is unfurnished of the Turks, busied in the Caramanian warre. **1614** Markham *Cheap Husb.* i. viii. 50 This Pestilence..hath vtterly vnfurnished whole Countries.

**2.** To divest of furnishings or furniture; to dismantle.

**1598** Florio, *Sfornire*.., to vnfurnish, to disaray, to deface. **1598** W. Phillip tr. *Linschoten* 66/2 All their ships are brought into the riuer, and vnfurnished of tacklings. *a* **1638** Mede *Wks.* (1672) 174 When men account them the most religious to God-ward who do or would unfurnish the House of God most. **1662** J. Davies tr. *Mandelslo's Trav.* 108 His predecessour makes way for him,..unfurnishes the Palace, and leaves him only the Guards and the bare walls. **1707** *Lond. Gaz.* No. 4377/1 His Excellency dispatch'd Orders to Rome to forbid his House being unfurnish'd. **1886** P. Fitzgerald in *Art Jrnl.* 324/1 Among the incidents of a flitting, or of unfurnishing a house.

†**3.** To divest or deprive *of* something. *Obs.*

**1611** Shaks. *Wint. T.* v. i. 123 Thy speeches Will bring me to consider that, which may Vnfurnish me of Reason. *a* **1642** Sir W. Monson *Naval Tracts* v. (1703) 489/1 This will..unfurnish them of all Materials to fit out Fleets. **1664** T. Mun *Eng. Treas.* 112 To unfurnish the poor Prince of his provision.

†**b.** *spec.* To divest (a tree) of foliage. *Obs.*—1

**1712** J. James tr. *Le Blond's Gardening* 47 To raise..the Palisade itself,..would certainly unfurnish it at Foot.

**Unfu·rnished**, *ppl. a.* [Un-1 8.]

**1.** Not furnished, in various senses; unprovided, unequipped, unprepared.

(*a*) **1549** Cheke *Hurt Sedit.* (1569) F ij, Exeter..being in the middest of Rebelles, vnuittailed, vnfurnished, vnprepared, for so long a siege. **1592** Shaks. *Rom. & Jul.* iv. ii. 10 Go, be gone, we shall be much vnfurnisht for this time. **1599** — *Hen. V*, i. ii. 148 The Scot, on his vnfurnisht Kingdome, Came pouring like the Tyde into a breach. **1601** W. T. *Ld. Remy's Civ. Considerations* ix. *heading*, Ambassadours of Princes ought not to shew themselues bashfull and vnfurnished. **1638** T. Verney in *V. Papers* (Camden) 197, I need not putt downe tooles for euery tradesman, for I beleeue you will not send them unfurnished. **1734** Waterland *Doctr. Holy Trin.* vii. 396 [New servants] who..may be unfurnished for the Employ, or not well affected to his Person and Government. **1822** Shelley *Chas. I*, ii. 266 We want money, and my mind misgives me That for so great an enterprise, as yet, We are unfurnished. **1860** Froude *Hist. Eng.* V. 183 As the treasury was unfurnished, the lords..raised money by every possible shift.

(*b*) **1697** Collier *Ess. Mor. Subj.* i. (1703) 25 What though our Minds were poor, and unfurnished at first. **1731** Fielding *Grub St. Op.* i. ii, Whatever Nature hath done for him in another way, she hath left his head unfurnish'd. **1784** Cowper *Task* iv. 209 All the tricks That idleness has ever yet contriv'd To fill the void of an unfurnish'd brain. **1817** Coleridge *Biogr. Lit.* xvii. (1907) II. 43 An unfurnished or confused understanding.

**b.** Const. *of* or *with*.

(*a*) **1541** *Act* 33 *Hen. VIII*, c. 9 § 2 Other cities..remaine and be vnfurnished of artificers and craftes men before rehersed. **1625** Hart *Anat. Ur.* Ded. A iv, Some nations vnfurnished of frankincense, offer vp milke..to their gods. **1707** Norris *Treat. Humility* Pref. 3 So that..he may not be unfurnished of a competent consideration of the matter in hand. **1802** Lamb *J. Woodvil* i, Nor am I so unfurnish'd, as you think, Of practicable schemes.

(*b*) **1611** in *Essex Rev.* (1906) XV. 155 The sayd place is very muche hindred and unfurnyshed with a convenient Schole howse. **1691** T. H[ale] *Acc. New Invent.* 41 England being never to be supposed unfurnished with Lead, as bearing it within its own Bowels. **1791** Cowper *Iliad* xvii. 173 Chieftain of excelling form, But all unfurnish'd with a warrior's heart! **1833** Chalmers *Const. Man* v. (1835) I. 211 Because he is so unfurnished with the ideas of justice.

**2.** Of houses or apartments: Not provided with furniture, *spec.* not furnished by the landlord or person letting; requiring to be furnished by the tenant or occupant.

**1581** Anne Askew in Nicolas *Hatton's Life & T.* (1847) 223 This short warning and my unfurnished house, do ill agree. **1593** Shaks. *Rich. II*, i. ii. 68 Alacke, and what shall good old Yorke there see But empty lodgings, and vnfurnish'd walles. **1680** *Lond. Gaz.* No. 1553/4 A Fair House to be Lett Furnished or Unfurnished. **1769** *Phil. Trans.* LIX. 181 An unfurnished room of the Hospital. **1824** MISS L. M. HAWKINS *Annaline* II. 268 [He] pays for ships and houses,..the latter he would let if he could either furnished or unfurnished. **1885** [W. H. WHITE] *M. Rutherford's Deliv.* i. (1892) 11 McKay..had unfurnished apartments. *fig.* **1663** BUTLER *Hud.* I. i. 162 Such [cobwebs] as take Lodgings in a Head That's to be lett unfurnished.

**b.** Not fitted up; devoid of the usual fittings, tackle, etc.

**1608** SYLVESTER *Du Bartas* II. iv. *Schisme* 298 Chariots, unfurnisht and unharnest. **1623** *State Papers, Col., East Indies* (1878) 202 They utterly refuse unfurnished ships.

**c.** Destitute of foliage; defective in flesh.

**1712** J. JAMES tr. *Le Blond's Gardening* 151 If the Plant be crooked,..mishapen.., or very much unfurnish'd. **1893** *Kennel Gaz.* Aug. 217/3 The latter [dog] is also smart but quite unfurnished, and his feet are not good.

Hence **Unfu·rnishedness.**

**1647** BOYLE in Birch *Life* (1744) 82 Trying such experiments, as the unfurnishedness of the place..will permit me.

† **Unfu·rniture.** *Obs.* [UN-[1] 12 + FURNITURE 2.] Lack of intellectual equipment.

**1640** REYNOLDS *Passion* xxxvii. 481 [His] hesitancy and slownesse of resolution in matter of Learning proceeded not from any emptines or unfurniture. *Ibid.* xxxix.

**Unfu·rnitured,** *a.* (UN-[1] 9.) ? **1879** LOWELL *To W. L. Garrison* i, The place was dark, unfurnitured, and mean.

**Unfu·rred,** (*ppl.*) *a.* [UN-[1] 8, 9.]

**1.** Not lined or trimmed with fur.

*a* **1450** *Knt. de la Tour* (1868) 165 She clothed her in a cote hardy vnfurred, the whiche satte right streite upon her.

**2.** Not having or provided with fur.

**1830** MISS MITFORD *Village* Ser. IV. 80 The unfurred, unfeathered animals, who walk on two legs,..and are called rational. **1906** *Westm. Gaz.* 8 June 8/1 Unfledged birds, and un-furred baby mice.

**Unfu·rrowable,** *a.* (UN-[1] 7 b.) **1860** RUSKIN *Unto this Last* (1862) 167 Their desert kingdoms, bound with unfurrowable rock, and swept by unarrested sand.

**Unfu·rrowed,** *ppl. a.* (UN-[1] 8.)

**1566** DRANT *Horace, Sat.* iii. B 3 b, In feildes vnforowde frute is none, for brakes all over growes. *a* **1700** KEN *Hymnotheo* Poet. Wks. 1721 I. 67 The Wheels kiss lightly the unfurrow'd Air. **1721** RAMSAY *Content* 303 Unfurrow'd was her brow, her cheeks were smooth. **1791** COWPER *Odyss.* IX. 140 The unseeded and unfurrow'd soil. **1823** BYRON *Island* II. xi, The unreap'd harvest of unfurrow'd fields. **1859** GEO. ELIOT *A. Bede* xii, Such young unfurrowed souls roll to meet each other like two velvet peaches.

**Unfu·rthersome,** *a. Sc.* (UN-[1] 7.)

*c* **1820** HOGG *Tales & Sk.* (1836) II. 131 The snow had been accumulating all day, so as to render walking very unfurthersome. **1864** CARLYLE *Fredk. Gt.* IV. v. (1872) I. 310 Tearing off..his own full-bottom wig,..finding it unfurthersome for actual business in battle.

**Unfu·sed,** *ppl. a.* (UN-[1] 8.)

[**1775** ASH.] **1796** KIRWAN *Elem. Min.* (ed. 2) I. 396 Shorls, which are fusible at 95°, are ejected [from volcanos], unfused, and unaltered. **1875** WHITNEY *Life Lang.* vii. 123 As *donner-ai*, 'I shall give', when compared with..'I have to give', its unfused equivalent.

**Unfu·sible,** *a.* (UN-[1] 7 and 5 b.) **1758** REID tr. *Macquer's Chym.* I. 6 Earth, in general, with regard to its properties, may be distributed into *fusible*, and *unfusible*. **Unfu·ssy,** *a.* (UN-[1] 7.) **1825** CATH. STANLEY *Jrnl.* in *Mem.* (1879) 211 The unpunctual are easy, good-tempered, unfussy. **1862** H. R. REYNOLDS in *Life* vii. (1898) 185 The annual meeting will be made as quiet and unfussy as possible. **Unfu·zed,** *a.* (UN-[1] 9.) **1885** *Science* V. 74/2 Three unfuzed shells..were fired from the eighty-pounder.

**Unga·g,** *v.* (UN-[2] 4 b.)

**1705** ELSTOB in Hearne *Collect.* (O.H.S.) I. 109 Then he ungagg'd him. **1719** DE FOE *Crusoe* II. (Globe) 580 Having ..ungagg'd their Mouths. **1890** C. MARTYN *W. Phillips* 303 Here lips were ungagged when they were padlocked elsewhere for thirty years.

**Unga·ged,** *ppl. a.* [UN-[1] 8.] † Unentangled, free. **1617** CAMPION *Wks.* (1909) 181 Shall my wounds onely weepe, and hee vngaged goe? **Unga·gged,** *ppl. a.* (UN-[1] 8.) **1863** W. PHILLIPS *Speeches* viii. 226 They must be free and ungagged. **1887** *Pall Mall G.* 8 July 4/1 A free, public, ungagged meeting.

† **Ungai·n,** *sb. Obs.*—[1] [UN-[1] 12 + GAIN *sb.*[1] Cf. ON. *úgagn* (MSw. and Sw. *ogagn*, MDa. *ugavn*), Norw. dial. *ugjegna.*] Detriment, harm.

**13..** *St. Cristofer* 251 in Horstm. *Altengl. Leg.* (1881) 457 Þere rynnes bysyde þis heghe mountayne A water, þat turnes to mekill vngayne.

**Ungai·n,** *a.* Now chiefly *dial.* [UN-[1] 7 + GAIN *a.* Cf. ON. *úgegn* unreasonable, obstinate, MSw. *ogēn* unsuitable, unpleasant.]

**1.** Of ways: Not plain or direct.

*a* **1400** *Bone Florence* 1421 The lady seyde, We ryde ylle, Thes gates they are ungayne. **1426** AUDELAY *Poems* (Percy Soc.) 14 Therof the pepul wold be fayne, Fore to cum home azayne, That hath goon gatis ungayne, for defaute of lyȝt. **1613** BEAUM. & FL. *Cupid's Rev.* IV. i, Though she take th' ungain'st weas she can, I'll ne'er ha't fro' you. **1824** [CARR] *Craven Gloss.* 119 *Vngain*, round about, indirect. **1854** MISS BAKER *Northampt. Gloss.* s.v., An indirect roundabout road is an ungain one.

† **2.** Unsparing, severe; rough. *Obs.*

*c* **1400** *Destr. Troy* 1332 Ercules..Gird gomes vnto grounde with vngayn strokes. *c* **1425** WYNTOUN *Cron.* I. xi. 952 Thare reueris ragis for na rayne, Na muffis for na wedderis vngayne.

**3.** Unpleasant, disagreeable.

*a* **1425** *Cursor M.* 22751 (Trin.), Alas what shal þe synful say? vngeyn [*earlier MSS.* ungainand] þenne shal be his gamen. **1795** H. WALPOLE *Let. to Miss Berry* 28 Aug., The assemblage was not so ungain as I expected, for..there were several I knew. **1851** PALGRAVE *Normandy & Eng.* I. 312 The ungain character of Raoul Torta..has been clearly chronicled.

**4.** Awkward, inconvenient, troublesome, difficult. † *At ungain*, inconveniently.

*c* **1460** *Towneley Myst.* ii. 379 Bot this cors I wold were hid, For som man myght com at vngayn. **1553** BALE *Gardiner's De Vera Obed.* C iij b, Left hande mater is vngayne, and wicked what soo euer proceedeth of the fleshe. **1635** QUARLES *Embl.* I. xiii, How backward! how preposterous is the motion Of our ungain devotion! **1763** WESLEY *Compend. Nat. Philos.* (1784) I. II. i. § 2. 206 The joints by which they bend are nearly in the middle,..and the large bulk which they are to support, makes their flexure ungain. **1764** *Museum Rust.* II. 84 As they are ungain to empty on the cloth,..they are not much used. **1782** MISS BURNEY *Cecilia* IX. vi, But, Sir, that was but an ungain business..t' other morning. **1823–** in dialect glossaries. **1837** MARRYAT *Dog Fiend* iii, The ungain temper of his brute companion. **1893** P. H. EMERSON *Lagoon* xxxii. 168 Are you all alone in that wherry?..isn't she ongain for the bridges?

**5.** Unskilled, incompetent; good-for-nothing.

**1658** W. BURTON *Itin. Anton.* 229 Peutingers Military Tables, which the noble Mark Velser set forth, but corruptly (for how could it be otherwise after so long time, and so ungain Transcribers?). **1834** BECKFORD *Italy* II. 93 One of the most ungain, conceited professors of the art of murdering I ever met with. **1851** BORROW *Lavengro* III. 374 For fear that he should turn out what is generally termed ungain, my father determined to send him to sea.

**6.** = UNGAINLY *a.* 1.

**1709** MRS. MANLEY *Secret Mem.* (1720) III. 269 She look'd wholesome, ungain, and country. *Ibid.* IV. 72 What we see of her now is nothing but an old slatternly, ungain Thing. **1779** G. KEATE *Sk. fr. Nat.* (ed. 2) II. 66, I was..a pupil of the famous Marcel of Paris, though no one who now views my curved and ungain figure, would suppose it. **1835** BECKFORD *Recoll.* 108 One of the most ungain hobbledehoys I ever met with. **1844** *P. Parley's Ann.* V. 306 He is the most ungain and foolish loitering bird in our domain. *Comb.* **1834** J. J. HALLS *Life H. Salt* I. i. 15 A tall, thin, and somewhat ungain-looking young man.

**b.** Of movement, bearing, etc.

**1757** [E. PERRONET] *Mitre* I. xxxi, What ungain postures of deference, As void of manliness as sense! **1776** MME. D'ARBLAY *Let.* 2 Dec. in *Early Diary*, She..has a carriage the most ungain that ever was seen. **1820** L. HUNT *Indicator* No. 64 (1822) II. 95 Walking in the most ungain manner upon its hind legs. **1824** *Examiner* 1 Feb. 71/1 The position on her knees is ungain.

**Ungai·nable,** *a.* (UN-[1] 7 b.) **1661** PIERCE *Serm.* 29 *May* 35 The better protected your Peace will be from the ungainable enemies of each extream.

† **Ungai·nand,** *ppl. a. north.* and *Sc. Obs.* [UN-[1] 10.] Inappropriate, unbecoming, unsuitable.

*a* **1300** *Cursor M.* 12404 Quen iesus him sagh sa bese be Abute þis ilk vngainand tre. *Ibid.* 17248 For for to serue lauerds tuin It es vngainand to be-gin. **1493** in Laing *Abbey of Lindores* (1876) 181 Gyff thar be ony vnganand persons resett in the burgh..that thair persons..be removit the tovne. **1533** BELLENDEN *Livy* IV. v. (S.T.S.) II. 66 Þai faucht in place richt vnganand to batell, and mare vnganand to fle. **1562** WINȜET *Wks.* (S.T.S.) II. 59 It is weray iniust and vnganand, that we,..for the self veritie of the quheit, mot cheis the errour of fitches.

**Ungai·ned,** *ppl. a.* (UN-[1] 8.) **1606** SHAKS. *Tr. & Cr.* I. ii. 315 Men prize the thing vngain'd, more then it is. **1860** FROUDE *Hist. Eng.* V. 389 Thus it is that patriots and..reformers show in fairest colours when their cause is ungained.

† **Ungai·nful,** *a.*[1] *Obs.*—[0] = UNGAIN *a.* 4.

**1565** COOPER *Thesaurus*, *Incommodus*,..hurtfull: noysome: vngaynefull; unhandsome.

**Ungai·nful,** *a.*[2] (UN-[1] 7.)

**1599** DANIEL *Musoph.* 2 Fond man,..that thus dost spend ..In an ungainful art thy dearest days. **1647** BP. HALL *Account* Wks. 1808 I. p. xxxii, Sir Robert Drury,..hearing my errand, dissuaded me from so ungainful a change. **1803** A. SWANSTON *Serm. & Lect.* II. 231 Their conduct may be accounted for when they perform unfashionable or ungainful duties. **1849** ALFORD *Grk. Test.* I. Prol. 45 Those who carried on the by no means despised or ungainful business of fishermen.

† **Ungai·nfully,** *adv.*[1] *Obs.* [Cf. UNGAINFUL *a.*[1]] With discomfort; severely. *c* **1320** *Antichrist* 564 (MS. Cott. Vesp. A III), Ungainfulli þan sal þai quak, Þat alle þe erth it sal do scak. **Ungai·nfully,** *adv.*[2] [f. UNGAINFUL *a.*[2]] Unprofitably. **1593** NASHE *Christ's T.* Wks. (Grosart) IV. 93 Wherefore you Pilgrims,..vngainefully you consume good houres. **1611** COTGR., *Incommodement*,..vngainefully, vnprofitably. **Ungai·ning,** *ppl. a.* (UN-[1] 10.) *c* **1630** H. R. *Mythomystes* 24 All vngaining Sciences, that conduce not to worldly profit. **1807** *Monthly Mag.* XII. 579 The porcelain-makers of Paris..saunter in ungaining idleness. **Ungai·n-like,** *a.* [f. UNGAIN *a.*] Unsuitable. **1796** MME. D'ARBLAY *Camilla* IV. 166 It's ungain-like to speak for one's self.

**Ungai·nliness.** (UN-[1] 12; cf next.)

**1755** JOHNSON s.v. *Clumsiness*. **1848** L. HUNT *Town* iv. I. 182 There is an ungainliness in the lines we have just quoted. **1870** DICKENS *E. Drood* ix, His ungainliness gave him enough of the air of his simile to set Rosa off laughing.

**Ungai·nly,** *a.* [UN-[1] 7. Cf. Norw. dial. *ugjegnleg* vexatious, obstinate.]

**1.** Awkward, clumsy, ungraceful.

**1611** COTGR., *Saugrenu*, vntoward, vngainely, ill-fauoured. *a* **1700** B. E. *Dict. Cant. Crew*, *Blunderbuss*, a Dunce, an unganely Fellow. **1709** STEELE *Tatler* No. 193 ⁋ 3 Persons ..so very aukward and ungainly, that it is impossible to believe the Audience will bear them. **1752** MRS. DELANY in *Life & Corr.* (1861) III. 79 Her person is fine, her arms a little ungainly, and her voice disagreeable. **1814** SCOTT *Wav.* xxix, At length the tall ungainly figure and ungracious visage of Ebenezer presented themselves. **1878** E. JENKINS *Haverholme* 44 A man..with a slow delivery, ungainly gestures, an affected manner and accent.

† **2.** Unsuitable, improper. *Obs.*—[1]

*a* **1660** HAMMOND *Serm.* (1664) xiii. 217 Their Misusing of their knowledge to ungainly ends, as either ambition, superstition [etc.].

**Ungai·nly,** *adv.* [Cf. prec. and UNGAIN *a.*]

† **1.** Threateningly, terribly. *Obs.*—[1]

*a* **1200** *St. Marher.* 9 He..ȝeonede mid his wide geneow uppon hire ungeinliche.

† **2.** Improperly, unduly; unsuitably. *Obs.*

*c* **1400** *Destr. Troy* 9333 Oure godys, oure gold [are] vngaynly dispendit. *c* **1460** *Towneley Myst.* xvi. 160 Thus shuld ye not thrett vs, vngaynly to bete vs. **1548** ELYOT, *Incommodé*,..vngaynely,..vnhansomely, vneasyly.

**3.** In an ungainly manner; awkwardly, clumsily, ungracefully.

*a* **1661** FULLER *Worthies, Cambridge.* I. (1662) 150 A Camel passeth in the Latine proverb, either for gibbous and distorted, or for one that undertaketh a thing awkely or ungeenly. **1705** VANBURGH *Confed.* I. iii, Why dost thou stare, and look so ungainly; Don't I speak to be understood? **1854** MISS BAKER *Northampt. Gloss.*, *Skrauming*, spreading widely, stretching out the arms ungainly. **1896** *Westm. Gaz.* 9 May 2/1 Mr. Record-Breaker..waddles ungainly by, and is lost in the crowd.

**Ungai·nness.** [f. UNGAIN *a.*] Ungainliness.

**1727** BAILEY (vol. II), *Ungainness*,..Awkwardness. **189**[?] *Midl. Herald* 28 May (E.D.D.), Their [*sc.* cattle] lovely ungainness when at play.

**Ungainsai·d,** *ppl. a.* (UN-[1] 8.)

**1587** GOLDING *De Mornay* xv. 263 With consent of all the wyse men of olde tyme vngeinesaid of any. **1610** HOLLAND *Camden's Brit.* I. 365 The surname of *Doctor Irrefragabilis*, that is, the Doctor ungainsaid, as hee that could not bee gain-said. **1641** MILTON *Animadv.* § I. 11 The Pope may as well boast his ungainsaid authority.

**Ungainsay·able,** *a.* (UN-[1] 7 b.)

**1618** *Barnevelt's Apol.* G 3 The hypothesis makes the proposition of an ungainsayable truth. **1634** JACKSON *Creed* VII. iv. § 3 Many matters of fact..of which there can be no ungainsayable proof or demonstration. **1718** BP. HUTCHINSON *Witchcraft* 95 A Book that was Ungainsayable. **1890** GEN. BOOTH in *Daily News* 18 Nov. 6/5 In the first place the facts were ungainsayable.

Hence **Ungainsay·ably** *adv.*

Cf. the earlier UNAGAINSAYABLY.

**1637** *Declar. Pfaltzgrave's Faith* 35 Out of which vngainesayably followes, that also wee ought to haue no Images. **1702** C. MATHER *Magn. Chr.* III. III. (1852) 551, I wish that the ministers..may be as ungainsayably importunate..as Mr. Eliot was.

**Ungainsay·ing,** *ppl. a.* (UN-[1] 10.) **1681** J. SCOTT *Chr. Life* I. iii. 89 A full and ungainsaying Judgment.

**Ungai·nsome,** *a.* **-somely,** *adv.* (UN-[1] 7, 11.)

**1655** GURNALL *Chr. in Arm.* I. (1669) 497/1 They know not how to handle them [*sc.* tools], they go ungainsomly about the work, and cut all into Chips. **1832** LYTTON *Eugene A.* II. vi, 'Tis so ungainsome, and be d—d to it.

**Unga·llant,** *a.* (UN-[1] 7.)

**a.** **1710** SHAFTESB. *Charac.* (1711) I. 312 Nor is there any thing ungalante in the manner of thus questioning the Lady-Fancys. **1762** H. WALPOLE *Vertue's Anecd. Paint.* (1765) II. 128 Vandyck..was so ungalant as to dispute with her on the price of her picture.

**β.** **1731** GAY *Let. to Swift* 27 Apr., All my fear is, that you will give up me for her, which, after my ungallant declaration, would be very ungenerous. **1829** LYTTON *Devereux* I. i, It must not be supposed that Sir William Devereux was an ungallant man. **1863** 'OUIDA' *Held in Bondage* viii, True enough!..It is an ungallant admission.

*absol.* **1808** ELEANOR SLEATH *Bristol Heiress* V. 282 His behaviour was..a little upon the ungallant.

Hence **Unga·llantness.**

**1859** JEPHSON & REEVE *Brittany* 176 On my making him aware of his ungallantness.

**Unga·llantly,** *adv.* (UN-[1] 11: cf. prec.)

**1835** MARRYAT *Olla Podr.* xv, The doctor..ungallantly told his wife she might remain all night. **1865** TRISTRAM *Land of Israel* iv. 68 They had seen us indignantly chide one of our lads for ungallantly threatening them with the stick.

**Unga·llantry.** (UN-[1] 12.)

**1723** *Briton* No. 7 (1724) 29 That I in a private capacity may atone for the Ungallantry of my Brethren. **1891** *Pall Mall G.* 29 Oct. 2/1 Such ungallantry, while there were partners sitting out, being considered most reprehensible.

**Unga·lled,** *ppl. a.* (UN-[1] 8.)

**1590** SHAKS. *Com. Err.* III. i. 102 Supposed by the common rowt Against your yet vngalled estimation. **1602** — *Ham.* III. ii. 283 Why let the strucken Deere go weepe, The Hart vngalled play? **1621** G. SANDYS *Ovid's Met.* III. (1626) 45 Cadmus..a Heifer saw, by no man tended, Her neck vngall'd with groning seruitude. **1818** SCOTT *Hrt. Midl.* li, Her conscience was ungalled. **1868** GEO. ELIOT *Sp. Gipsy* 15 Men With limbs ungalled by armour.

**Unga·lling,** *ppl. a.* (UN-[1] 10.) **1744** ELIZA HEYWOOD *Female Spect.* IV. (1748) I. 208 Follies..exposed in the ungalling satire of genteel comedy! **Unga·mboling,** *ppl. a.* (UN-[1] 10.) **1788** H. WALPOLE *Let. to Mrs. H. More* 22 Sept., Your *gambols*, as you call them, after the most ungamboling peeress in christendom.

† **Unga·ng,** *v. Sc. Obs.* [f. *un-* UM- + GANG *v.*] *trans.* To surpass, go beyond.

**1768** ROSS *Helenore* II. 85 For it ungangs me sair gin at the last, To gang together binna found the best.

**Unga·ngrened,** *ppl. a.* (UN-[1] 8.) **1753** N. TORRIANO *Gangr. Sore Throat* 81 Those..think that by cutting,..they can more easily separate the gangrened from the ungangrened Parts. **Unga·rbed,** *ppl. a.* (UN-[1] 8.) **1848** BAILEY *Festus* (ed. 3) 199 A pure, cold..rayonnance As is the moon's of naked light, ungarbed In circumsphereal air. **Unga·rbished,** *ppl. a.* (UN-[1] 8 and GARBAGE *v.*) **1641** S. SMITH *Herring Buss Trade* 18 To sell them at sea ungarbished, salted or unsalted.

**Unga·rbled,** *ppl. a.* [UN-[1] 8.]

**1.** Not garbled, cleansed, or sifted; not selected or sorted out.

**1439** *Rolls of Parlt.* V. 32/1 Uppon peyne of forfaiture of the said Spiceries so yfound ungarbeled and unclensyd. **1483** *Act 1 Rich. III*, c. xi. § 1 They will not suffre any garbelyng of theym to be made but sell good and bad at so excessyf price togedyr ungarbeled. **1614** *St. Papers, Col., E. Indies* (1862) 294, 20 bags of ungarbled pepper. **1649** *Jrnl. Ho. Commons* VI. 304/1 An Act for Liberty to transport Spices ungarbled, was this Day read the Third time. **1859** R. F. BURTON *Centr. Afr.* in *Jrnl. Geog. Soc.* XXIX. 37 At the end of the rains..[the copal] is usually carried ungarbled to Zanzibar. *c* **1870** *Townend & Co.'s Circular Col. & For. Produce* s.v. *Coffee*, Mocha Coffee, ungarbled.

**2.** Of a fact or statement: Not mutilated or misrepresented.

**1721** AMHERST *Terræ Fil.* No. 41 (1726) 213 Some future unprostituted, ungarbled history of a rebellion. **1810** BENTHAM *Packing* (1821) 116 A jury of the original, the constitutional, the ungarbled, the uncorrupted stamp. **1834** H. N. COLERIDGE *Grk. Poets* (ed. 2) 141 It is not without parallel in the ungarbled writings of greater wits than Zoilus.

**Unga·rdened,** (*ppl.*) *a.* (UN-[1] 8, 9.) **1623** [see UNFENCED 2]. **Unga·rlanded,** (*ppl.*) *a.* (UN-[1] 8, 9.) **1828** WORDSW. *Triad* 108 The ringlets of that head Why are they ungarlanded? **Unga·rment,** *v.* (UN-[2] 4.) **1805** SOUTHEY *Madoc in Wales* I. v. 73 They..Ungarmented my limbs, and in a net..They laid and left me.

**Unga·rmented,** *ppl. a.* (UN-[1] 8.)

**1798** SOUTHEY *Joan of Arc* (ed. 2) IV. I. 245 And round her limbs ungarmented, the fire Curl'd its fierce flakes. **1818** SHELLEY *Rosal. & Helen* 477 'Tis..houseless Want in frozen ways Wandering ungarmented. **1866** J. B. ROSE tr. *Ovid's Met.* 73 Now tell..that thou hast viewed Dian ungarmented.

**Unga·rnered,** *ppl. a.* (UN-[1] 8.) **1850** TENNYSON *In Mem.* lxxii, Thro' clouds that drench the morning star, And whirl the ungarner'd sheaf afar. **1883** GOODE *Fish. Indust. U.S.A.* 10 Where the harvest of the sea is still, for the most part, ungarnered.

**Unga·rnish,** *v.* (UN-[2] 4.)

**1530** PALSGR. 768/1, I ungarnysshe, *je desgarnis*... Me thynke my cupborde is ungarnisshed nowe I wante my salte celler. **1598** FLORIO, *Sfregiare*, to vngarnish, to vndeck, to disadorne. **1848** DICKENS *Dombey* iii, When the funeral was over, Mr. Dombey ordered the furniture to be covered up..and the rooms to be ungarnished.

**Unga·rnished,** *ppl. a.* (UN-[1] 8.)

**13..** *E. E. Allit. P.* B. 137 The gome was vngarnyst with god men to dele. *c* **1400** *Pilgr. Sowle* (Caxton, 1483) v. i. 74 How durst ony wyght trowen..that he wold leuen his regne ..vngarnysed of his werkes. *a* **1548** HALL *Chron., Edw. IV*, 249 b, Thei shall..deplore, and lament their vngarnished estate, and naked condicion. **1591** SYLVESTER *Du Bartas* I. i. 291 A Heav'n..Un-garnished, un-gilt with Stars apparent. **1621** QUARLES *Div. Poems, Esther* viii, May my vngarnisht Quill presume so much, To glorifie it selfe. **1641** MILTON *Animadv.* § 4. 38 He that now for haste snatches up a plain ungarnish't present as a thanke-offering to thee. **1705** WATTS *Lyrick Poems* II. (1743) 144 Beauteous she lies;..Ungarnish'd; yet not blushing. **1800** WORDSW. *Michael* 19 A story..ungarnished with events. *a* **1847** ELIZA COOK *Christmas Song of Poor Man* ii, Some scrap, ungarnished, cold and scant. **1876** FOX BOURNE *Locke* II. xi. 189 Plain, ungarnished words were certainly the best.

**Unga·rrisoned,** *ppl. a.* (UN-[1] 8.)

**1660** MARVELL *Corr.* Wks. (Grosart) II. 18, I..hope to see your Town once more ungarrisond. *a* **1701** MAUNDRELL *Journ. Jerus.* (1721) 48 On the north side it has an old Turkish ungarrison'd Castle. **1813** *Edin. Rev.* XXI. 193 The frontiers were unguarded,..the forts dismantled or ungarrisoned. **1865** W. G. PALGRAVE *Arabia* II. 289 It is crowned by an old castle and tower.., now ungarrisoned.

**Unga·rter,** *v.* (UN-[2] 4 b.)

**1594** NASHE *Unfort. Trav.* Wks. (Grosart) V. 98 He that had then vngartered mee, might haue pluckt out my heart at my hams. **1607** MARKHAM *Cavel.* IV. (1617) 9 Which as soone as he doth, you shall immediately vngarter his legges. **1753** A. MURPHY *Gray's Inn Jrnl.* No. 31, Ungartering my Stockings, and pulling off my Wig. **1886** *Pall Mall G.* 2 Dec. 6 A native unbraceleting or ungartering himself.

Hence **Unga·rtering** *vbl. sb.*

**1785** G. A. BELLAMY *Apology* (ed. 3) II. 15 He loved his good fat capon;..and *ungartering*, as he called it.

**Unga·rtered,** (*ppl.*) *a.* [UN-[1] 8, 9.]

**1.** Not tied with or wearing a garter.

**1591** SHAKS. *Two Gentl.* II. i. 79 When you chidde at Sir Protheus, for going vngarter'd. **1607** *Puritan* II. i. 233 A man that would..go vngarterd, vnbuttend, nay, sir Reuerence, vntrust, to Morning Prayer. **1647** R. STAPYLTON *Juvenal* 68 Trebius, oblig'd, has that for which he must Break's sleep, and run ungarter'd and untrust. **1749** FIELDING *Tom Jones* IV. viii, Catching hold of her ungartered stocking. **1823** S. ROGERS *Italy* I. viii. 50 Gliding on, he comes Slip-shod, ungartered. **1828** LYTTON *Pelham* I. xxiv, Thornton..lounged idly in a chair, with one ungartered leg thrown over the elbow.

**2.** Not invested with the Order of the Garter.

**1845** DISRAELI *Sybil* IV. xiv, Ireland was not yet governed by the Duke of Fitz-Aquitaine, and the Earl de Mowbray was still ungartered.

**Un-Ga·sconated,** *ppl. a.* (UN-[2] 8.) **1658** R. BAKER tr. *Balzac's Lett.* I. iv. 102 You may..teach them to speak good French, now you are perfectly Vn-Gasconated.

**Unga·thered,** *ppl. a.* [UN-[1] 8. Cf. Du. *ongegaderd, -gegaard.*]

**1.** Not gathered or brought together; uncollected.

**1461** *Rolls of Parlt.* V. 495/1 Youre dettes remaynyng ungadered. **1481** *Coventry Leet Bk.* 478 Þer rested behynde vngadered..of þe seide hole somme xiij li. ix s. vj d. **1525** LD. BERNERS *Froiss.* II. cxvi. 332 A great parte of that money as than nat payde and vngadered. **1590** H. BARROW in *Confer.* i. 9 They being as yet vngathered to Christ. **1625** CHAS. I *Sp.* in Rushw. *Hist. Coll.* (1659) I. 177 Your love to me..you expressed by a Grant of Two Subsidies yet ungathered. **1851** *Buried City of East, Nineveh* vi. 93 Finding..the bundle of faggots for the evening fire yet ungathered. **1873** PROCTOR *Expanse Heav.* 191 Enormous quantities of as yet ungathered materials.

**b.** *spec.* (See quot.)

**1888** JACOBI *Printers' Vocab.*, *Ungathered*, books delivered to binders in sheets, i.e. not gathered into books.

**2.** Of flowers, etc.: Not gathered or culled; unpicked, unharvested.

**1592** DANIEL *Compl. Rosamond* I 3 b, Th' vngathred Rose, defended with the thornes. **1600** SURFLET *Countrie Farme* II. lxv. 412 If at this time there be found euer a combe vngathered and not pluckt away,..you must not therefore kill the Bees. **1697** DRYDEN *Virg. Past.* I. 51 We wonder'd..For whom so late th' ungather'd Apples hung. **1825** SCOTT *Talism.* xix, Is it not hard that..I should be doomed to see fade before me ungathered such a rich harvest of glory to God? **1850** TENNYSON *In Mem.* civ, This holly by the cottage-eave, To night, ungather'd, shall it stand. **1896** *Daily News* 4 Sept. 7/5 The barleys which are still ungathered will, it is feared, be spoilt for malting purposes.

**3.** Not drawn together.

**1615** G. SANDYS *Trav.* 63 Ouer all when they goe abroad they weare gownes..vngathered in the shoulders. **1690** C. NESSE *O. & N. Test.* I. 104 As a web of cloth is rolled up, only a little left at the end ungathered.

**Ungau·dy,** *a.* (UN-[1] 7.) **1795** SOUTHEY *Let. to G. C. Bedford* 29 Nov., The violet is ungaudy in the appearance. *a* **1834** COLERIDGE *To Thelwall* Poet. Wks. 1912 II. 1090 Ungaudy flowers that chastest odours breathe.

**Ungau·ged,** *ppl. a.* (UN-[1] 8.)

**1745** YOUNG *Nt. Th.* VIII. 671 A cask Unbroach'd by just authority, ungaug'd By temperance, by reason unrefin'd. **1872** GEO. ELIOT *Middlem.* iii, Dorothea..had looked deep into the ungauged reservoir of Mr. Casaubon's mind. **1881** M. A. LEWIS *2 Pretty G.* III. 207 There may be ungauged depths behind our chatter, and ungauged vanity behind your silence.

**Ungau·ntlet,** *v.* (UN-[2] 4.) **1846** LANDOR *Imag. Conv.* Wks. I. 144/2 The kings..ran against the chalice of poison,.. by which their own hands were..ungauntleted, undirked, and paralysed.

**Ungau·ntleted,** (*ppl.*) *a.* (UN-[1] 8, 9.)

**1800** COLERIDGE *Talleyrand to Ld. Grenville* 12 I'm no Jacobin foul,..That your Lordship's *un*gauntleted fingers need fear An infection! *a* **1876** M. COLLINS *Th. in Garden* (1880) II. 266 [He] offers his ungauntleted hand in knightly fashion to his old opponent.

**Ungay·ed,** *ppl. a.* (UN-[1] 8.) **1670** EACHARD *Cont. Clergy* 7 Getting by heart three or four leaves of ungay'd nonsense.

**Unga·zed,** *ppl. a.* (UN-[1] 8 c.)

**1818** MRS. SHELLEY *Frankenst.* xix, I lived ungazed at and unmolested. **1820** SHELLEY *Prometh. Unb.* II. iv. 5 The meridian sun, Ungazed-upon and shapeless. **1902** F. THOMPSON in *Academy* 12 Apr. 378/1 Ophir he saw, her longungazed at gold.

**Ungaze·tted,** *ppl. a.* (UN-[1] 8.) **1825** T. HOOK *Sayings* Ser. II. II. 352 An ungazetted commandery of Poyais.

**Ungea·r,** *v.* [UN-[2] 3, 4 b.]

**1.** *trans.* To unharness. Now *dial.*

*c* **1611** CHAPMAN *Iliad* XI. 536 And Nestor's squire, Eurymedon, the horses did ungear. [**1775** ASH, *Ungear*,..to unharness, to deliver from the gears.] **1825** BROCKETT *N. C. Words* s.v., Ungear the yoke. **1828** *Trial of W. Dyon & Son at York Assizes* 11, I was ungeering the horses. **1854** MISS BAKER *Northampt. Gloss.*, *Ungear*, to unharness; restricted to husbandry horses.

**2.** To disconnect the gearing of.

**1828** *Craven Gloss.* s.v., A mill is also said to be *ungeared*, when the water is turned off or the machinery displaced. **1852** MORFIT *Tanning & Currying* (1853) 118 The necessity of ungearing the pinion.

**Ungea·red,** *ppl. a.* (UN-[1] 8.) **15..** *Christ's Kirk* 167 Bot quhair thair gobbis wes vngeird They gat vpoun the gammis. **1588** *Wills & Inv. N. C.* (Surtees 1860) 329, vj geared yockes 4s, iiij yockes, ungeared, 6d, v geard forkes, 20d, ij forkes, vngeared, 6d.

†**U·nged,** *a.* *Her.* *Obs.* [Irreg. f. L. *ung-uis* or *ung-ula* hoof.] Represented with the hoofs of a different tincture from the animal itself.

**1562** LEGH *Armory* (1597) 51 b, He bereth Or, a Hart tripping Geules. If you should haue occasion to tel of his hornes, you should saie, he were attyred, and so likewise of the Bucke, and they are both vnged.

**Ungela·tinizable,** *a.* (UN-[1] 7 b.) **1809** *Phil. Trans.* XCIX. 338 Ungelatinizable oxide of animal substance. **1884** *Encycl. Brit.* XVII. 675/1 Gelatin..is converted into an ungelatinizable modification.

**Unge·lded, unge·lt,** *ppl. a.* (UN-[1] 8, 8 b.)

α. **1398** TREVISA *Barth. De P. R.* v. xxiii. (Bodl. MS.), Malis haue strenger senewes..þanne femalis.., and vngelded haue strenger þanne gelded. **1598** FLORIO s.v. *Integro*.

β. **1573** TUSSER *Husb.* (1878) 82 Ungelt of the best [sows] keepe a couple for store. **1607** MARKHAM *Cavel.* I. (1617) 68 The longer that a Colt goes vngelt, the thicker and fatter his head will growe. **1651** HOWELL *Venice* 124 What are their soldiers but..a multitude of unghelt Eunuchs? **1725** *Fam. Dict.* s.v. *Sow*, The Male [swine] ungelt being call'd a Boar.

**Unge·ndering,** *ppl. a.* (UN-[1] 10.) **1706** DE FOE *Jure Div.* XI. 260 The Froth of Envy! Vain ungendring Cloud, To beat the Minds of Fools, and move the Crowd.

**Unge·neral,** *v.* *rare.* [UN-[2] 6, 6 b.]

**1.** *trans.* To deprive of the rank of general.

*a* **1657** LOVEDAY *Lett.* (1663) 80 My Lord F. his house (retir'd thither to a private life since he ungenerall'd himself).

†**2.** To free from generality or vagueness. *Obs.*

*a* **1661** FULLER *Worthies, Wales* IV. (1662) 8, I doe not despair,..that having gained better intelligence,..these persons may be Un-general'd, and impaled in their particular Counties.

**Unge·neralized,** *ppl. a.* (UN-[1] 8.) **1843** MILL *Logic* II. iii. § 3 A number of..unexpressed, ungeneralized analogies.

**Unge·nerate,** *ppl. a.* [UN-[1] 8 b.] = next. **1546** LANGLEY tr. *Pol. Verg. de Invent.* I. iii. 5 They which contende that the worlde was vngenerate. *a* **1618** SYLVESTER *Mysterie of Myst., Holy-Ghost* 2 The Comforter, ay Uncreate, Unmade, Unborne, Ungenerate.

**Unge·nerated,** *ppl. a.* (UN-[1] 8 and 5 b.)

**1614** RALEIGH *Hist. World* I. iv. § 1. 66 He foresaw..that Millions of soules must haue beene vngenerated, and haue had no being, if the first number..had abode therein for euer. **1738** WARBURTON *Div. Legat.* App. 52 He must needs have made it ungenerated. **1861** STANLEY *East. Ch.* iii. 99 Ask a man how many oboli, he answers by dogmatising on generated and ungenerated being.

**Unge·nerative,** *a.* (UN-[1] 7.) **1733** THEOBALD *Shakspere's Meas. for M.* III. ii. 104 He is a motion ungenerative [1623 generatiue] that's infallible. **1854** MAURICE *Mor. & Met. Philos.* (ed. 2) vi. § 17 Justinian existed..to declare that the Greek Church and the Greek Empire were withered and ungenerative stocks. **Ungenero·sity.** (UN-[1] 12; cf. next.) **1757** MRS. GRIFFITH *Lett. Henry & Frances* (1767) II. 91, I..take it very unkindly that you will not recollect yourself a little, before you treat me with so much ingratitude and ungenerosity. **1886** STEVENSON *Kidnapped* xxiv, I could open my mouth upon neither [subject] without black ungenerosity.

**Unge·nerous,** *a.* [UN-[1] 7 and 5 b.]

**1.** Not generous or large-minded; illiberal: **a.** Of actions, conduct, etc.

**1641** MILTON *Ch. Govt.* II. iii, To start back..from the mixture of any ungenerous and unbeseeming motion. **1699** BENTLEY *Phalaris* 213, I will not say, how ungenerous a design this is, to leave his Sicilian Prince in the lurch. **1748** SMOLLETT *R. Random* xli, I recounted to him the ungenerous usage I had met with from Potion. **1796** MME. D'ARBLAY *Camilla* V. 514 The sense that now breaks in upon me of ungenerous..doubt. **1842** W. C. TAYLOR *Anc. Hist.* xvii. § 9 (ed. 3) 552 An ungenerous attack on the memory of the late emperor. **1882** MISS BRADDON *Mt. Royal* II. ix. 168 She had never harboured an ungenerous thought.

**b.** Of persons, disposition, etc. Also *absol.*

*a* **1704** T. BROWN *Eng. Sat.* Wks. 1730 I. 25 His ungenerous Father-in-law..discreetly hang'd himself. **1753** MISS COLLIER *Art Torment.* II. iii. (1757) 141 Bent upon defeating the purposes of ungenerous friends or relations. **1798** S. & HT. LEE *Canterb. T.* II. 350 The Duke too, though not a tender parent, had never been an unkind or ungenerous one. **1850** MRS. BROWNING *Sonn. fr. Portuguese* ix, Givers of such gifts as mine are, must Be counted with the ungenerous. **1874** MOZLEY *Univ. Serm.* ix. (1876) 195 An ungenerous temper may be easily fostered under the guise of generous condescension.

†**2.** Inferior or poor in quality. *Obs.*[—1]

**1744** *Phil. Trans.* XLIII. 163 A small armed Loadstone ..which, being reputed but of an ungenerous Nature, took up..barely 2 Ounces.

Hence **Unge·nerousness.**

**1757** MRS. GRIFFITH *Lett. Henry & Frances* (1767) I. 94 The poverty of my nature, and ungenerousness of my principles. **1892** R. W. CHURCH *Cathedral & Univ. Serm.* 61 The ungenerousnesses of the generous, the injustices of the just.

**Unge·nerously,** *adv.* (UN-[1] 11; cf. prec.)

**1722** WODROW *Corr.* (1843) II. 676 People very ungenerously take more liberty with him when he is not to answer for himself. **1775** SHERIDAN *Rivals* III. ii, I am ever ungenerously fretful. **1830** D'ISRAELI *Chas. I*, III. iii. 29 Charles.. felt that the Commons had ungenerously used him. **1855** MACAULAY *Hist. Eng.* xvi. III. 718 Halifax, who had.. been ungenerously and ungratefully persecuted by the Whigs. **1895** *Daily News* 29 May 3/6 [The horse] running ungenerously towards the finish, he was headed in the last few strides by Boxer.

**Unge·nial,** *a.* [UN-[1] 7.]

**1.** Not favourable to growth or development. Also const. *to*.

**1726** THOMSON *Winter* 718 Those sullen seas, That wash th' ungenial pole, will rest no more. **1796** W. H. MARSHALL *W. England* II. 100 The frequency of rain..renders West Devonshire,..in a wet season, ungenial to Agriculture. **1829** SOUTHEY *Sir T. More* II. 142 No plants will thrive in a cold and meagre soil, ungenial to their nature. **1856** EMERSON *Eng. Traits, Land* Wks. (Bohn) II. 21 Art..transforms a rude,..ungenial land into a paradise of comfort and plenty.

*fig.* **1768** [W. DONALDSON] *Life Sir B. Sapskull* II. i. 7 The citizen from the ungenial atmosphere of Watling-Street.

**b.** Of weather: Cold or wet; raw.

**1815** JANE AUSTEN *Emma* I, I did not quite like your looks on Tuesday, but it was an ungenial morning. **1885** *Manch. Exam.* 14 May 5/1 The ungenial weather has compelled the outdoor part of the programme to be abandoned.

**2.** Not agreeable or pleasant (*to* one).

**1796** MME. D'ARBLAY *Camilla* V. 243 She declined the excursion, as..ungenial to her feelings. **1822** LAMB *Elia* I. *Praise of Chimney-sweepers*, The rake..curses the ungenial fume, as he passeth. **1857** DUFFERIN *Lett. High Lat.* (ed. 3) 401 Henceforth, the words..can convey no cold or ungenial associations to my ears.

**b.** Not congenial or suited *to* the genius of.

**1871** EARLE *Philol. Eng. Tongue* 145 We must regard this ..as being a creation of the English speech-genius. To the Danish it is ungenial.

**3.** Not cheerful, jovial, or kindly.

**1796** MME. D'ARBLAY *Camilla* V. 38 [I] appeared to you too rigorous, too ungenial. **1867** LD. HOUGHTON in Brodrick, etc. *Ess. Reform* 48 An ungenial German, ignorant of our language and offensive to our manners. **1870** LOWELL *Among Bks.* Ser. I. 237 The Puritans had their faults. They were narrow, ungenial. **1889** GRETTON *Memory's Harkb.* 25 He was of a somewhat ungenial, crusty temperament.

Hence **Ungenia·lity.**

**1859** G. WILSON *Mem. E. Forbes* iv. (1861) 109 A deep, quiet enthusiasm..which his ungeniality of nature could not prevent being contagious.

**Unge·nially,** *adv.* (UN-[1] 11; cf. prec.)

**1858** CARLYLE *Fredk. Gt.* x. iii. II. 609 The Crown-Prince reports to Papa, in a satirical vein, not ungenially. **1889** SWINBURNE *Study Jonson* 85 He shows himself ungenially observant and contemptuously studious of his models.

**Unge·nitured,** *a.* (UN-[1] 9.) **1603** SHAKS. *Meas. for M.* III. ii. 184 This vngenitur'd Agent will vn-people the Prouince with Continencie.

**Ungentee·l,** *a.* Also 7 ungenteile, -iel, 7–8 ungentile. [UN-[1] 7 and 5 b.] Not genteel: **a.** Of manners, habits, employments, etc.

*a.* **1633** PRYNNE *Histrio-m.* Ep. Ded., Yet I hope I shall finde no such ungenteile, discourteous entertainment. **1642** FULLER *Holy & Prof. St.* v. xiv. 413 Drinking is..a most ungentile quality, fit to be banished to rogues and rags. **1691** E. RAWSON in *Andros Tracts* I. 68 The Buffoonry and Railery of such ungentiel Pens. **1711** J. GREENWOOD *Eng. Gram.* 110 It is counted ungentile and rude to say, Thou dost so and so.

*β.* **1683** MOXON *Mech. Exerc., Printing* xii. ¶ 1 Some Letter-Cutters..scorn to use a Forge, as accounting it..Ungenteel for themselves to officiate at. **1716** M. DAVIES *Athen. Brit.* I. 180 Bale bestows another ungenteel Sarcasm upon this great Armach. **1778** EARL MALMESBURY *Diaries & Corr.* I. 211 His person was awkward, and his dress ungenteel. **1811** *Sporting Mag.* XXXVIII. 93 It is considered ungenteel to cut the pastry. **1898** WATTS-DUNTON *Aylwin* IV. ii, Have I not often told you the reason why I..missed my high vocation in ungenteel comedy?

**b.** Of persons.

**1676** SHADWELL *Libertine* II, Thou art the most ungenteel Knight alive: use your Ladies civilly, for shame. **1712** *Spect.* No. 404 ¶ 6 Iras is ugly and ungenteel, but has Wit and good Sense. **1749** FIELDING *Tom Jones* I. x, [The half-pay officer] was not ungenteel, nor entirely void of Wit. **1813** JANE AUSTEN *Lett.* (1884) II. 172 She is a large, ungenteel woman, with self-satisfied and would-be elegant manners. **1844** THACKERAY *Barry Lyndon* ix, With this sum of money ..we were enabled to make no ungenteel figure.

Hence **Ungentee·lness.**

**1706** STEVENS I, *Desalino*,.. sluttishness, ungenteelness. **1723** *Briton* No. 11 (1724) 50 Philander discovers some Ungenteelnesses in his Manner and Behaviour. **1727** *Art of Speaking in Publick* 81 The indecency and ungenteelness of clamour and noise.

**Ungentee·lly,** *adv.* Also 7 ungenti(le)ly. (UN-[1] 11; cf. prec.)

**1666** PEPYS *Diary* 6 Aug., My Lord..did treat her thereupon very rudely and ungenteely. **1673** BP. S. PARKER *Reproof Reh. Transp.* 452 You might have done very honestly, but yet very ungentily. **1709** STRYPE *Ann. Ref.* I. 505 And further, very ungenteely,..Dorman..charged his Adversary with no less than Eighty Two Lyes. **1825** WATERTON *Wand. S. Amer.* I. ii. (1879) 132 Parson Evans, the Welshman, was treated most ungenteelly by an enraged spirit. **1875** W. ALEXANDER *Ain Folk* 115 After you felt that you had been ungenteelly treated.

†**Ungentilesse.** *Obs.* (UN-[1] 12.) **1390** GOWER *Conf.* II. 30 Wher was ther evere such a knyht, That so thurgh his ungentilesce..Ayein his trowthe brak his stevene?

**Ungenti·lify,** *v.* (UN-[2] 6 c.) **1614** in Birch *Crt. & Times Jas. I* (1848) I. 299 It is propounded that all these should be disarmed or ungentilified, unless they will give twenty or thirty pounds for confirmation of their gentry.

**Ungenti·lity.** (UN-[1] 12 and 5 b.)

**1822** LAMB *Old Actors* Wks. 1908 I. 849 Miss Pope, a gentlewoman ever, to the verge of ungentility. **1871** W. ALEXANDER *Johnny Gibb* xxxii, At the *ungentility* of which saying Miss Birse looked shocked.

**Unge·ntilize,** *v.* (UN-[2] 6 c.) **1637** W. SALTONSTALL *Eusebius' Constantine* 36 Such as had beene ungentiliz'd, and degraded from their Gentility.

**Unge·ntle,** *a.* Forms: (see UN-[1] and GENTLE *a.*). [UN-[1] 7.]

†**1.** Of persons, their birth, family, etc.: Not gentle or belonging to a family of position; not distinguished by birth. Also *absol.* *Obs.*

*c* **1374** CHAUCER *Boeth.* II. pr. iv. (1868) 41 Som man haþ grete rycchesse, but he is ashamed of hys vngentil lynage. **1387** TREVISA *Higden* (Rolls) III. 415 [He] putte adoun meny gentil men, and putte ungentil men in here stede. *c* **1440** *Promp. Parv.* 365/1 On-gentylle of kynne, *ignobilis, degener.* *Ibid.* 365/2 On-gentyl be fadyr, and moder, *ybridus.* **1486** *Bk. St. Albans, Her.* A j, How gentilmen shall be knowyn from vngentill men. *a* **1533** LD. BERNERS *Gold. Bk. M. Aurel.* (1546) H viij, But for all he was not called vngentyll, nor infamed, nor traytour. **1594** R. ASHLEY tr. *Loys le Roy* 56 b, Of noble, and vnnoble, of gentlemen, and vngentle. **1648** HEYLIN *Relat. & Observ.* I. 23 Gentle or ungentle, I write to all. **1688** R. HOLME *Armoury* III. 68/2 The Ungentle is bound..to keep silence whilst a Gentleman speaks.

**2.** Of persons: Not possessing the attributes or characteristics of good birth; unchivalrous; discourteous, unmannerly. Now somewhat *arch.*

**1411–2** HOCCLEVE *De Reg. Princ.* 3300 He dredde hym.. The peple hym wolde han for a proude man deemed, And vngentil. *c* **1450** CAPGRAVE *Life St. Aug.* 44, I aspied wel þat I must chere men þat cam on-to me with mete and drynk, for if I ded not, I schuld be hald on-gentil. **1562** LEGH *Armory* Pref. ¶ iv, The second sort are vngentile gentlemen. **1593** MARLOWE *Edw. II*, IV. ii, Sith the vngentle king Of Fraunce refuseth to giue aide of armes To this distressed Queene his sister heere. **1653** J. TAYLOR (Water P.) *Short Relat. Long Journ.* (1859) 22 Quoth I, I doubt I must bee necessitated to take up my lodging in the field: to which the said ungentle gentlewoman..gave me a finall answer, that I might if I would. **1688** SHADWELL *Sqr. Alsatia* II, Belfond, thou art the most ungentle Knight alive. **1829** CUNNINGHAM *Brit. Paint.* I. 344 They aided him in the resolution..of making his escape from such crushing patronage and ungentle company. **1872** TENNYSON *Gareth & Lynette* 738 Too well I know thee, ay—The most ungentle knight in Arthur's hall.

*transf.* **1398** TREVISA *Barth. De P. R.* XII. xxxvii. (Tollem. MS.), The lapwynke is ungentel [1535 most filthy] and unclene.

**b.** *absol.* and as *sb.*

**1562** LEGH *Armory* Pref. ¶ iij b, I beseche your honours, to dayne to be patrones of this my woorke, against the middle finger poyntinges of the vngentiles. *Ibid.*, The first wherof are gentel vngentile.

**c.** Not appropriate to or befitting one of gentle birth or breeding.

**1565** JEWEL *Reply Harding* (1611) 160 This seemeth to be a very simple argument, and a grosse vngentle opinion of the simplicity of the people. **1590** SPENSER *F. Q.* III. i. 67 For nothing would she lenger there be stayd, Where so loose life, and so vngentle trade Was vsd of Knights and Ladies seeming gent. **1642** MILTON *Apol. Smect.* Wks. 1851 III. 270 Whereof not to be sensible,..argues both a grosse and shallow judgement, and withall an ungentle, and swainish breast. **1823** SCOTT *Quentin D.* x, According to the rules of woodcraft, he held it ungentle to interfere with the game attacked by another hunter. **1861** MEREDITH *Evan Harrington* xxx, They had seen her ungentle training in a dozen little instances.

**3.** Not gentle in action; rough, harsh, unkind, violent: **a.** Of persons or disposition.

**1509** FISHER *Funeral Serm. C'tess Richmond* Wks. (1876) 307 Were not she an vnkinde and vngentyl moder? **1561** T. NORTON *Calvin's Inst.* III. 202 The iudge that threatneth that he wil be vnappeasable to them that be to rigorous and ungentle. **1628** WITHER *Brit. Rememb.* II. 1835 To travell farre, and finde Those prove ungentle, whom you hoped, kinde. **1693** DRYDEN *Ovid's Met.* I. 876 Her Head to her ungentle Keeper bow'd, She strove to speak. **1763** G. COLMAN *Posth. Lett.* (1820) 256 Pray hint this to him, but let him not be ungentle with Sterne. **1837** HT. MARTINEAU *Soc. in America* III. 117 Men are ungentle, tyrannical. **1849** MACAULAY *Hist. Eng.* vi. II. 47 His temper, naturally ungentle, had been exasperated by his domestic vexations. **1872** CALVERLEY *Fly Leaves* (1903) 7 She had gone from the ken of ungentle men!

**b.** *fig.* Of things.

**1551** ROBINSON tr. *More's Utopia* I. (1895) 62 Moyses lawe, thoughe it were vngentle and sharpe,..punnyshed thefte by the purse, and not wyth deathe. **1596** SHAKS. *1 Hen. IV*, V. i. 13 You haue..made vs doffe our easie Robes of Peace, To crush our old limbes in vngentle Steele. *a* **1649** CRASHAW *Carmen Deo Nostro, Mary Magd.* xxvii, Such Teares the suffring Rose that's vext With ungentle flames does shed. **1812** BYRON *Ch. Har.* I. xxiii, Vain are the pleasaunces on earth supplied; Swept into wrecks anon by Time's ungentle tide!

**c.** Of actions, language, etc.

**1603** DEKKER & CHETTLE *Grissil* 2022 Why must my babes beare this vngentle doome? **1649** JER. TAYLOR *Gt. Exemp.* Disc. iii. § 15 When two seas meet, the billows contest in ungentle embraces. **1726** POPE *Odyss.* XVII. 548 His shoulderblade receiv'd th' ungentle shock. **1779** *Mirror* No. 43 ¶ 2 Every better feeling, warm and vivid; every ungentle one, repressed or overcome. **1846** KEBLE *Lyra Innoc.* (1873) 180 Jesus in His babes abiding Shames our cold ungentle ways. **1890** DOYLE *White Company* xxviii, Taken aback at this ungentle speech,..Alleyne stood [etc.].

†**Unge·ntled,** *ppl. a.* (UN-[2] 6 a, 8.) ? **1584** SIDNEY *Disc. Def. Earl of Leicester* Misc. Wks. (1829) 269 Even of charity sake he should..not leave him not only ungentled, but fatherless. †**Unge·ntlefy,** *v.* (UN-[2] 6 c.) **1595** R. JOHNSON *Maroccus Extaticus* 10 The state of gentlemen that have ungentlefied..themselves by buying and selling.

**Unge·ntleman,** *v.* [UN-[2] 6 b.] *trans.* To deprive of the standing or character of a gentleman. Also *refl.*

**1671** F. PHILIPPS *Reg. Necess.* 204 A man disenabled, or ungentleman'd by reason of his Fathers attainder of Treason. **1713** *Gentl. Instructed* III. vi. (ed. 5) 419 Some tell me home-breeding will ungentleman him. **1719** DE FOE *Serious Refl.* ii. 58 The minute he does that, he ungentlemans himself. **1752** CHESTERF. *Let.* Misc. Wks. 1777 II. 558, I..am persuaded, that you do not give into this *cochonnerie*, which ungentlemans every body.

**Unge·ntlemanlike,** *a.* and *adv.* [UN-[1] 7 c.]

**A.** *adj.* **1.** Of character, actions, etc.: Not befitting or natural to a gentleman.

**1592** NASHE *Four Lett. Confuted* H 1 b, Neither was I.. pincht with any vngentleman-like want, when I inuented Pierce Pennilesse. **1652** WADSWORTH tr. *Sandoval's Civ. Wars Spain* 363 Hee was mightily condemned by all that saw or heard of that ungentleman-like action. **1728** *Lett. fr. Fog's Jrnl.* 21 Dec. 1/1, I cannot conceive the Cause from whence that base, that unworthy, that Un-Gentleman-like Quality [*sc.* avarice] should arise. **1800** MAR. EDGEWORTH *Limerick Gloves* iv, Complaining of the ungenerous and ungentlemanlike behaviour in the grocer. **1884** *Macm. Mag.* Nov. 12/2 Work just as dirty, and tricks just as ungentleman-like.

**2.** Not resembling a gentleman.

**1718** *Free-thinker* No. 126, The most Illiberal, Ungentlemanlike, Members of Society. **1749** CHESTERF. *Lett.* 15 May (1774) I. cl. 413 They come home, the unimproved, illiberal, and ungentleman-like creatures, that one daily sees them. **1814** JANE AUSTEN *Mansfield Park* xli, Ungentlemanlike as he looked.

**B.** *adv.* Not after the fashion of a gentleman.

**1664** PEPYS *Diary* 14 July, My Lord Chancellor..said that I did most ungentlemanlike with him. **1687** SETTLE *Refl. Dryden* 74 Do not deal so unnaturally and ungentleman like, to treat so honourable a man..so rudely. **1823** SCOTT *Quentin D.* xxiii, How unkingly, unknightly, ignobly, ungentleman-like, he hath conducted himself towards us.

Hence **Unge·ntlemanlikeness.**

**1848** J. H. NEWMAN *Loss & Gain* I. iv. (1853) 201, I have behaved quite rudely to the Puseyites sometimes, and then been ashamed of my ungentlemanlikeness.

**Unge·ntlemanliness.** (UN-[1] 12; cf. next.) **1828** *Q. Rev.* XXXVIII. 560 A charge of bigotry, intolerance, calumny, and ungentlemanliness. **1877** MISS YONGE *Cameos* III. xxxii. 329 The ungentlemanliness of the Tudor.

**Unge·ntlemanly,** *a.* (UN-[1] 7.)

**1562** LEGH *Armory* 122 There are nyne rebatings of armes, which for nyne sondry vngentilmanly dedes done, are resembled as hereafter followeth. **1614** B. JONSON *Barth. Fair* I. iii, What an vnmercifull companion art thou to quit thy lodging at such vngentlemanly houres! **1684** OTWAY *Atheist* v, It is an opportunity I should make no ungentlemanly use of. **1741** RICHARDSON *Pamela* (ed. 3) I. 84, I can stoop to the ordinariest Work of your Scullions,..sooner than bear such ungentlemanly Imputations. **1825** T. HOOK *Sayings* Ser. II. III. 303 This letter produced an abusive, vulgar, and ungentlemanly answer. **1881** W. G. WARD *Ess. Philos. Theism* (1884) II. 286 They thought it thoroughly ungentlemanly so to speak in the presence of ladies.

Hence **Unge·ntlemanly** *v.*

**1834** MEDWIN *Angler in Wales* II. 117 There were some ungentlemanlying themselves, by giving it against the horse.

**Unge·ntlemanly,** *adv.* (UN-[1] 11.)

**1572** BOSSEWELL *Armorie* 12 b, The rebatinge of Armes for diverse vngentle deedes vngentlemanly donne. **1603** HOLLAND *Plutarch's Mor.* 179 They..so defraud and cousin them ungentlemanly of their parents love. **1713** S. SEWALL *Diary* 24 Apr., [She] said Mr. Alford had done ungentlemanly by her. **1819** *Metropolis* II. 207 He speaks ungentlemanly loud, as all sailors do.

†**Unge·ntlemanny,** *a.* *Sc. Obs.* [UN-[1] 7.] = UNGENTLEMANLY *a.*

**1667** SIR R. MORAY in *Lauderdale Papers* (1885) II. 42 How ungentlemanny a thing it is to use a lady rudely. **1770** BP. FORBES *Jrnl.* (1886) 315 No man dare say he has ever been guilty of a dirty or ungentlemanny Action.

**Unge·ntleness.** [UN-[1] 12.]

†**1.** Lack of good breeding or manners; discourtesy; boorishness. *Obs.*

**1387–8** T. USK *Test. Love* II. ii. (Skeat) l. 132 And therfore, he that wol ben gentil, he mot daunten his flesshe fro vyces that causen ungentilnesse. **1470–85** MALORY *Arthur* VIII. xxxviii. 332 For your curtosy and gentilnes I shewed you vngentilnesse, & that now me repenteth. *a* **1533** LD. BERNERS *Gold. Bk. M. Aurel.* II. xv. (1536) 150 The whiche forgettynge is as straunge to be in him that serueth, as vngentilnes in the ladye that is serued. *a* **1577** SIR T. SMITH *Commw. Eng.* (1609) 131 It is taken for vngentlenes and dishonor, ..if any gentleman doe take any other gentlemans seruant [etc.]. **1600** SHAKS. *A. Y. L.* V. ii. 83 You haue done me much vngentlenesse, To shew the letter that I writ to you.

**2.** Meanness of birth. *rare*—[0].

**1552** HULOET, Vngentlenes of bloude, *ignobilitas.*

**3.** Harshness, roughness, unkindness.

**1548** PATTEN *Exped. Scotl.* Pref. d ij, It was too muche vngentlenes and inhumanitie sure in suche a case too be shewed. **1598** FLORIO, *Inhumanita*, inhumanitie, vngentlenes. **1623** COCKERAM II, *Vngentlenes*, inclemencie. **1716–20** *Lett. fr. Mist's Jrnl.* (1722) I. 231 There runs through the Male Line an odd Ungentleness of Temper. **1871** SMILES *Charac.* ix. (1876) 240 Their own crossgrained ungentleness. **1889** F. C. KOLBE *Minnie Caldwell* iv. 30 Whatever ungentleness or unkindness she had shown.., had proceeded from thoughtlessness, not ungenerosity.

**Unge·ntlewomanlike,** *a.* (UN-[1] 7 c.) **1789** ANNA SEWARD *Lett.* (1811) II. 295 Vulgarisms, of most ungentlewomanlike choice, and most unscholar-like frequency.

**Unge·ntly,** *adv.* [UN-[1] 11.] In an ungentle manner; unkindly; roughly; discourteously, rudely.

*c* **1440** *Jacob's Well* 200, I seyde of hym vnkyndely, vndewly, vngentylly, vnwysely, folyly, & perylously. **1483** *Vulgaria abs Terentio* 25 Thow hast seruyd me vngentilly. **1523** [COVERDALE] *Old God* (1534) D j, It shall make the sorye..to see that Paule..was so vnkyndly and vngently entreated. **1575** VAUTROLLIER *Luther on Ep. Gal.* 210 Paule handleth you very vngentely, he calleth you foolish,..and disobedient to the truth. **1621** BP. MOUNTAGU *Diatribæ* 25 In this poynt you are to be taxed deeply, for dealing vngently and vnthankfully with your much admired..Joseph Scaliger. **1655** tr. *Sorel's Com. Hist. Francion* IV. 23 It was not by these people alone that I was..so ungently intreated. **1822** LAMB *Gentle Giantess* Wks. 1909 I. 269, I have seen these shy gownsmen..ungently neglecting the delicacies of her polished converse. **1860** RUSKIN *Unto this Last* i. (1896) 12 The servant who, gently treated, is ungrateful, treated ungently, will be revengeful.

**Unge·nuine,** *a.* *rare.* (UN-[1] 7 and 5 b.)

**1665** J. WEBB *Stone-Heng* (1725) 178 Making ungenuine and false Translations. **1698** JER. COLLIER *Immor. Stage* i. 18 His best Plays are almost alwaies Modest...His Amphitrio, excepting the ungenuine Addition, is such. **1883** *Schaff's Encycl. Relig. Knowl.* 2400 The writings that had been declared ungenuine.

Hence **Unge·nuineness.**

**1848** FR. A. KEMBLE *Rec. Later Life* (1882) III. 328 There is an element of ungenuineness about her. **1866** FELTON *Anc. & Mod. Gr.* I. v. 84 Internal evidence of ungenuineness or genuineness, founded on mere style.

**Ungeogra·phical,** *a.* (UN-[1] 7.) **1702** C. MATHER *Magn. Chr.* I. i. (1852) 41, I would not quote any words of Lactantius,..because of their being so ungeographical. **1873** W. CORY *Lett. & Jrnls.* (1897) 301 They say things wildly ungeographical. **Ungeome·tric,** *a.* [UN-[1] 7.] = next. **1789** [see UNARITHMETIC *a.*].

**Ungeome·trical,** *a.* (UN-[1] 7.)

**1570** BILLINGSLEY *Euclid* XII. prop. xviii. 385 A notable Error, which among..vngeometricall Masters and Doctors hath..been vpholden. *a* **1696** SCARBURGH *Euclide* (1705) 13 Of all our late Transformers of Euclide, He is the most Ungeometrical in Demonstration. **1788** T. TAYLOR *Proclus* p. cvii, The testimony of the first mathematicians..against the unlawfulness of this ungeometrical invasion.

Hence **Ungeome·tricalness.**

**1690** LEYBOURN *Curs. Math.* 771 For they that object against Him an Ungeometricalness in the Hypothesis, have not yet solv'd his Problem.

**Un-Ge·rman,** *a.* (UN-[1] 7.) **1830** CARLYLE *Richter Again* Ess. 1840 II. 298 Even the Un-German part of the public. **1855** GEO. ELIOT in Cross *Life* (1885) I. 374 Lessing's 'Laocoon'—the most un-German of all the German books that I have ever read. **Unge·rmanism.** (UN-[1] 12.) **1858** CARLYLE *Fredk. Gt.* VI. v. II. 61 Friedrich Wilhelm.. snorting contempt on 'Ungermanism (*Undeutschkeit*)'. **Unge·rminated,** *ppl. a.* (UN-[1] 8.) **1899** J. R. GREEN *Soluble Ferments* ii. 19 The diastase..of ungerminated grain.

**Unge·t,** *v.* [UN-[2] 3.]

**1.** *trans.* To cause to be unbegotten.

**1775** SHERIDAN *Rivals* II. i, I'll disown you, I'll disinherit you, I'll unget you! **1788** COLMAN *Ways & Means* III. 47 I'll disclaim him, I'll discard him,..I'll unget him,..That's disinherit him.

**2.** To give up possession of.

**1893** *Daily News* 14 July 2/7 Having got the conviction, how was he to unget it?

**Unget-a·t-able,** *a.* (Un-¹ 7 b.)
**1862** H. Marryat *Year in Sweden* II. 204 The lusus more usually refers to some ungetatable new fashion. **1886** W. J. Tucker *E. Europe* 2 The country swarms with quiet, retired, remote, cheap, and un-get-at-able towns. **1897** *Outing* XXX. 271/1, I always have the feeling..that we do not know him at all. He seems so unget-at-able.

**Unge·ttable,** *a.* (Un-¹ 7 b.) **1554** *Extr. Aberd. Reg.* (1844) I. 282 [If the sum is] vngettable of his office, thai oblissis thame..to releiff him therof.

**Ungho·stly,** *a.* [Un-¹ 7. Cf. (in sense 1) MDu. *ongeestelijc*, MHG. and G. *ungeistlich*.]

**1.** Unspiritual.
**1526** Tindale 1 *Tim.* iv. 7 Cast awaye ungostly and olde wyves fables. **1535** in *Lett. Suppress. Monast.* (Camden) 78 The mayntenans of the busshope and his ungostly spirituall officers. **1565** Stapleton *Fortr. Faith* 94 Martin Luther the first preacher of this vnghostely ghospell. **1822** T. L. Peacock *Maid Marian* 219 The abbot of Rubygill picked up the..arrow..with a very unghostly malediction on the sender. **1864** Carlyle *Fredk. Gt.* xvii. ii. IV. 524 Whom the Pompadour has brought with her as henchman, or *un*ghostly counsellor.

**2.** Not belonging to a ghost.
**1888** *Daily Tel.* 26 Jan. (Cassell's), A most unghostly-looking pair of boots.

**Ungho·stly,** *adv. rare*⁻¹. [Un-¹ 11. Cf. prec. 1.] † Unspiritually.
*a* **1400–50** *Alexander* 4430 Ȝoure grete garisons of gold vngastly ȝe spende In bigging of burgis & bilding of toures.

**Ungi·bbet,** *v.* (Un-² 3.) **1747** W. Horsley *Fool* (1748) II. 195 When..you become a sincere Penitent,..you shall be fairly ungibbetted again, and exposed to the Public View. **Ungi·ddy,** *a.* (Un-¹ 7.) **1615** Brathwait *Strappado* (1878) 158 If I had liu'd in Phaeton his daies, When with vngiddy course he rul'd the Sun. **1904** E. Nesbit *Phœnix & Carpet* ii. 28 When..they were ungiddy enough to look about them, they were out of doors.

**Ungi·fted,** (*ppl.*) *a.* [Un-¹ 8, 9.]

**1.** Having no spiritual or intellectual gifts.
**1637** Ld. Wariston *Diary* (S.H.S.) 276 Thou knouest thy servant,..hou ungifted, unfit, unready. **1655** tr. *Sorel's Com. Hist. Francion* x. 16 We ought not to believe such an ungifted Prophet as he is. **1712** Arbuthnot *Hist. John Bull* ii. i. 7 A hot-headed, ungifted, unedifying Preacher. **1850** Robertson *Serm.* Ser. iii. iii. Introd. (1857) 33 The Eternal Word spoke..to those who were uninspired and ungifted. **1891** Farrar *Darkn. & Dawn* xvi, While he was still young and beautiful, and not ungifted.

**b.** Not gifted *with* something.
**1831** Palmerston in Francis *Opinions & Policy* (1852) 176 The conduct of a child ungifted with reason. **1861** Beresf. Hope *Eng. Cathedr. 19th C.* ii. 41 The man ungifted with architectural tact.

**2.** Having received no gifts; giftless.
*a* **1631** Donne *Lett.* (1639) A 4 b, Pure Virtue; an ungifted Deity..without Oblation, Altar, or Temple. **1791** Cowper *Odyss.* xv. 258 He..will himself enforce Thy longer stay, That thou may'st not depart Ungifted. **1822** Milman *Mart. Antioch* 19 The sad priests of all our Gods do sit Round their cold altars and ungifted shrines. **1887** Bowen *Æneid* v. 304 This festival day None of the number around me shall go ungifted away.

Hence **Ungi·ftedness.**
**1646** Mayne *Serm. agst. False Proph.* 35 The ungiftednes of the persons, who have drawn this reproofe upon us.

**† Ungi·g,** *v. Obs.*⁻¹ [Un-² 3 + Gig *v.*¹ (?).] *trans.* To unravel, extricate.
**1686** F. Spence tr. *Euvremont's Misc.* Pref. C 3 In a Comedy nothing is so unmercifully insupportable as to ungigg or explicate the Intrigue by a Miracle.

**Ungi·ld,** *v.* (Un-² 4.) Also **Ungi·lding** *vbl. sb.* (also *attrib*).
**1611** Cotgr., *Dedorer*, to vngild. **1641** Milton *Animadv.* Wks. 1851 III. 238 By all this wee may conjecture, how little wee neede feare that the unguilding of our Prelates will prove the woodening of our Priests. **1651** Stanley *Poems* 209 Night began to ungild the skies. **1743** Young *Nt. Th.* v. 174 Vice sinks in her allurements, is ungilt, And looks, like other objects, black by night. **1873** Spon *Workshop Rec.* Ser. i. 205/2 Iron and steel articles are ungilt..by dipping them into [etc.]. *Ibid.*, Removing the gold from articles.. which cannot be submitted to the ungilding bath.

**Ungi·ldated,** *ppl. a.* (Un-¹ 8 a.) **1890** Gross *Gild Merch.* I. 49 Ungildated merchants could purchase..exemption from the many restrictions.

**Ungi·lded,** *ppl. a.* [Un-¹ 8.] = next.
**1674** Dryden *Prol. at Opening of New House* 7 You, who each Day can Theatres behold, Like Nero's Palace, shining all with Gold, Our mean ungilded Stage will scorn, we fear. **1688** *Lond. Gaz.* No. 2329/4 A good Quantity of all sorts of Pictures, and Frames gilded and ungilded. **1815** Kirby & Sp. *Entomol.* iii. (1816) I. 67 Terms..not strictly applicable to ungilded pupæ. **1872** Holmes *Poet Breakf.-t.* ii, A.. chamber..obliged to content itself with ungilded daylight.

**Ungi·lt,** *ppl. a.* (Un-¹ 8 b. Cf. ON. and Icel. *ú-*, *ógylldr*.)
**1444** *Test. Ebor.* (Surtees) II. 112, I wil yᵗ William my sone haue..vj sponis gilt, a dosen vngilt. **1497** *Naval Acc. Hen. VII* (1896) 98 Halberdes gilt in a chest, 1; Halberdes vngilt in the same Chest, xx. **1532–3** *Act 24 Hen. VIII*, c. 13 It shall be lefull for him to weare..a horne tipped or flewed with siluer, gilte or vngilte. **1591** Sylvester *Du Bartas* i. i. 291 A Heav'n..Un-garnished, un-gilt with Stars apparent. **1692** *Lond. Gaz.* No. 2806/4 A large gilt Plate for the Bread and a large Cup ungilt. **1812** *Monthly Rev.* LXVII. 529 They..forbad any other than..gondolas unvarnished, ungilt, undecorated. **1866** G. Stephens *Runic Mon.* I. 183 The staves are carved on the ungilt back.

**† Ungi·lt,** *v. Obs. rare.* [Un-² 4.] = Ungild *v.* *a* **1533** Ld. Berners *Golden Bk. M. Aurel.* Prol. (1536) A ij b, Bycause that there was none yll that did vngylt it. **1580** Hollyband *Treas. Fr. Tong*, *Desdorer*, to vngilt.

**Ungiltyf,** obs. variant of Unguilty *a.* 1.

**Ungi·nned,** *ppl. a.* (Un-¹ 8 + Gin *v.*² 2.) *a* **1858** in Homans *Cycl. Comm.* 436/2 An acre of ground will produce about 600 lbs. of unginned cotton.

**Ungi·rd,** *v.* [Un-² 4, 4 b. Cf. MDu. *on(t)-gorden* (Du. *ont-*), OHG. *ingurten*, *-curten* (MHG. *engürten*, G. *entgürten*).]

**1.** *trans.* and *refl.* To divest of, or free from, a girdle or girth.
In OE. (quot. *c* 900) also with instr. (of the thing) as well as acc. (of the person).
*c* **900** tr. *Baeda's Hist.* iii. xiv. (1890) 196 Se cyning þonne ..ongyrde hine þa his sweorde & sealde his þegne. *c* **1000** Ælfric *Saints' Lives* xxx. 409 Se casere..het hine ungyrdan and bewæpnian. **14..** in Wr.-Wülcker 578 *Discingo*, to ungyrd. **1530** Palsgr. 768/1, I ungyrde a horse. **1548** Udall, etc. *Erasm. Par. John* xxi. 117 For thou vngirdedst or gyrdest thy self at thyne owne wil and pleasure. **1568** Grafton *Chron.* II. 391 As he stoode at the Barre, the Lord Neuel was commaunded..to vngyrde him. **1601** Holland *Pliny* II. 301 Let the man come,..and after he hath ungirt himselfe, gird her about the middle with his owne girdle. **1611** Bible *Gen.* xxiv. 32 The man..vngirded his camels.
*fig.* **1593** Nashe *Christ's T.* E iv b, The resplendent..buildings of your Temple, (like a Drum), shal be vngirt & vnbraced. **1825** Macaulay *Ess.*, *Milton* (1897) 5 The sportive exercises for which the genius of Milton ungirds itself.

**2.** To release, or take off, by undoing a belt or girth.
**1485** Caxton *Chas. Gt.* 158 Rychard..descended fro hys hors for to vngyrde and lose hys sadle. **1623** Bp. Hall *Contempl.*, *O. T.* xix. iii, Was not this he that advised Benhadad, not to boast in the putting on his armour, as in the ungirding it. **1641** J. Jackson *True Evang. T.* i. 63 How many..in the hot sun-shine of prosperity have ungirt and cast off that cloake. **1810** Scott *Lady of L.* vi. xxii, When mourns thy tribe thy battles done,..Thy sword ungirt ere set of sun! **1848** Bp. A. Jolly *Observ. Sunday Services* (ed. 4) 293 We must..never ungird our armour.
*fig.* **1601** Shaks. *Twel. N.* iv. i. 15, I prethee now vngird thy strangenes, and tell me.

Hence **Ungi·rding** *vbl. sb.*
**1639** J. Corbet (*title*), The Ungirding of the Scottish Armour: or, an Answer to the Informations [etc.].

**Ungi·rded, † ungi·rd,** *ppl. a.* [Un-¹ 8 or Un-² 8.] = Ungirt *ppl. a.*
**1382** Wyclif 1 *Kings* xx. 11 Ne glorye euenly the gird as the vngird. **1387** Trevisa *Higden* (Rolls) VIII. 213 Þe abbot and þe chanouns of Osenay..com barefoot and barelegged and ungerd [*v.r.* ungurd] þorugh Londoun. *c* **1449** Pecock *Repr.* ii. i. 135 That a man wole were a girdel, or that he wole go vngerd. **1490** Caxton *Eneydos* xxiv. 89 [She was] alle vngyrde, and vpon her knees, as a vassall that doeth homage to his lorde. **1523** Fitzherb. *Surv.* 31 b, He shalbe vngirde and his heed vncouered. **1565** Cooper, *Recinctus*, vngirded. **1865** W. G. Palgrave *Arabia* II. 42 His attendants caught up their swords where they lay ungirded for prayer. **1867** Augusta Wilson *Vashti* xxx, Her white merino *robe de chambre* was partially ungirded.

**Ungi·rdle,** *v.* [Un-² 4, 4 b.] = Ungird *v.*
**1618** Bolton *Florus* ii. iv. 132 For Æmilius having the victory, ungirdled them in the Capitoll. **1629** J. Maxwell tr. *Herodian* (1635) 141, I command my souldiers to ungirdle you; and divest you of all Military Attire.

**Ungi·rdled,** *ppl. a.* (Un-¹ 8 or Un-² 8.)
**1611** Florio, *Discinto*, vngirt, vngirdled. **1834** Lytton *Pompeii* i. iii, Loosening to a yet more luxurious ease his ungirdled tunic. **1867** Myers *St. Paul* (1908) 23 Oceans ungirdled of the ocean-stream. **1887** Bowen *Æneid* iv. 518 One foot all unsandalled, her robe ungirdled, she stands.

**Ungi·rlish,** *a.* (Un-¹ 7.) **1850** Lynch *Theoph. Trinal* v. 80 Are not..these last lines a little ungirlish? **1863** [Miss M. Roberts] *Denise* I. 92 Her new acquaintances thought her odd and ungirlish.

**Ungi·rt,** *ppl. a.* [Un-¹ 8 b or f. Ungird *v.* Cf. OFris. *un-*, *ongert*, MDu. *ongegort* (Du. *-gord*), MHG. (and G.) *ungegürtet*.]

**1.** Not girded or wearing a girdle; having the girdle or belt undone, slackened, or removed.
**1297** R. Glouc. (Rolls) 10826 Vn-hosed & bareuot & vngurt al so. **13..** *Coer de L.* 4153 Out com the wardayn Orgayl, And an hundryd knyghtes.., Barefoot, ungyrt, withouten hood. *c* **1380** *Sir Ferumb.* 1943 Bar-fot þou most go, Al open-her, & eke oungerte. *c* **1400** *Gamelyn* 215 Barfoot and vngirt Gamelyn In came. **1550** Thomas *Ital. Gram.*, *Discinto*, vngyrte. **1586** Ferne *Blaz. Gentrie* 109 The idle and sluggish person..goeth loose and vngirt. **1604** *Littleton's Tenures* C 2 b, When the Tenaunt shall make Homage to his Lord, he shall be vngirt, and his head vncouered. *a* **1658** Cleveland *Old Gill* vi, She has always the Squirt, She is loose and ungirt. **1700** J. Tyrrell *Hist. Eng.* II. 835 Prince Lewis coming Barefoot and Ungirt from his own Pavillion. *a* **1822** Shelley *Fragm. Elegy Death Adonis* 18 Aphrodite..is wandering through the woods, 'Wildered, ungirt, unsandalled. **1850** Rossetti *Blessed Damozel* ii, Her robe, ungirt from clasp to hem.

**† b.** In proverbial use. *Obs.*
**1596** Spenser *F. Q.* iv. v. 18 Fie on the man, that did it first inuent, To shame vs all with this, 'Vngirt vnblest'. **1635** Quarles *Embl.* iii. xiii, Am I a fitting Guest..With hands and face unwash'd, ungirt, unblest? **1690** C. Nesse *O. & N. Test.* I. 451 Here, if ever, doth that proverb Ungirt, Unblest, hold true.

**2.** *fig.* **a.** Deprived or destitute *of* something.
*c* **1412** Hoccleve *De Reg. Princ.* 3653 Dignite had ben vnlaced And vngirt of honour, nad vertu be.

**b.** Not drawn together; left loose or incompact; not braced up for action.
**1579** Spenser *Sheph. Cal.* Ep. Ded., What in most English wryters vseth to be loose, and as it were vngyrt, in this Authour is..strongly trussed vp together. **1644** Milton *Divorce* (ed. 2) Pref. A 4 b, Let him bethink him withall how he will soder up the shifting flaws of his ungirt permissions. **1670** *Devout Commun.* (1688) 27 If I go with a loose, ungirt spirit, I cannot instantly entertain my Lord. **1878** Emerson *Sov. Ethics* Wks. (Bohn) III. 381 Our later generation appears ungirt, frivolous, compared with the religions of the ..Calvinistic age.

**† Ungi·rt,** *v. Obs.* [Un-² 4 b.] = Ungird *v.*
**1598** Florio, *Discingere*,..to vnguirt. **1612** R. Daborne *Christian turn'd Turke* 1275 The Muffty..girds his sword: then sweares him on the Mahomet's head, vngirts his sword [etc.]. **1661** Morgan *Sph. Gentry* iv. i. 5 He ungirteth himself of his Sword, and..to God offereth it there.

**Ungi·rth,** *v.* [Un-² 4 b.] *trans.* To free from a girth; to release or remove by undoing a girth.
**1580** Hollyband *Treas. Fr. Tong*, *Descengler vn cheval*, to vngirth a horse. **1760–72** H. Brooke *Fool of Qual.* (1792) IV. 180 Two knavish wags came, and, ungirthing his saddle, supported it on either hand. **1787** W. Taylor *Scots Poems* 100 You hear, an e'en ungirth their laigen. **1820** Scott *Monast.* ix, Ye may ungirth your horses,..and dismiss.

**Ungi·rthed,** (*ppl.*) *a.* [Un-¹ 8, 9.] Not provided with, or secured by, a girth. Also *fig.*
**1628** Feltham *Resolves* ii. ix. 24 Many times, honest Industry spends a man more, then the vngirthed Solaces of a sensuall Libertine. **1813** Scott *Rokeby* vi. *note*, The major..clapped the saddle, ungirthed as it was, upon his horse. **1901** *Westm. Gaz.* 13 Aug. 8/2 If..there had been a saddle thrown upon the pony, it was ungirthed.

**Ungi·ve,** *v.* [Un-² 7, 3. Cf. obs. Flem. *ontgheven* to fail, Du. (*zich*) *ontgeven* to yield, desist.]

**1.** *intr.* To give way, to relax; to lose tenacity or firmness. Now *dial.*
**1523** Fitzherb. *Husb.* § 25 Make it in greatter hey-cockes, and to stande so one nyght or more, that it maye vngiue and sweate. **1655** Fuller *Ch. Hist.* ii. ii. § 40 That Religion which is rather suddenly parched up, then seasonably ripened, doth commonly ungive afterwards. **1670** Evelyn in *Phil. Trans.* V. 1063 When the wheels will not turn round because of the clay and over-much moisture, it is a signe, that 'tis not fit for cultivation, until it ungive, and be dry. *c* **1700** in *Bell's Anc. Poems* (1857) 19 Who thinks that love doth live In beauty's tempting show, Shall find his hopes ungive, And melt in reason's thaw. **1854** Miss Baker *Northampt. Gloss.* 369 Gingerbread losing its crispness, and salt or any other substance relaxing from the humidity of the atmosphere, are said to ungive. **1881–** in *Eng. Dial. Dict.* s.v. (Lancs., Chesh., Leics., Bedford, Hants).

**† 2.** *trans.* To relax; to yield or give up. *Obs.*
**1645** Lightfoot *Comm. Acts* vi. 104 It is a daring that deserves castigation in him,..that hee should..deny the puritie of the Greeke text, before hee will ungive any thing of his owne groundlesse opinion. **1655** Fuller *Hist. Cambr.* 118 He was over-frozen, in his Northern Rigour, and could not be thaw'd, to ungive any thing of the rigidnesse of his Discipline.

**Ungi·ven,** *ppl. a.* [Un-¹ 8 b. Cf. ON. and Icel. *ú-*, *ógefinn* (MSw. *ogivin*), MDu. *ongegeven*, MHG. *ungegeben*.]

**† 1.** Not given in marriage. *Obs.*
*c* **1330** R. Brunne *Chron. Wace* (Rolls) 6545 Gentil damysels vngyuen, þat able to mennes companye were þryuen.

**2.** Not given or bestowed as a gift; not imparted.
**1511** *Acc. Ld. High Treas. Scot.* IV. 253 To hald in ungewin the Kingis goune..quhilk the King ordanit to be gewin. **1542** Udall *Erasm. Apoph.* 230 b, Fortune leaft nothyng vngeuen to hym. *a* **1586** Sidney *Arcadia* iii. viii, Philanax himselfe could haue wished the blow vngiuen, when he saw him fal. **1600** Sir R. Cecil *Lett.* (Camden) 62, I beleeve that office wilbe for a while vngeuen. **1662** H. Hibbert *Body Divinity* i. 172 Sometimes men take offence ungiven. **1713** Mrs. Centlivre *Wonder* ii. i, What proof remains ungiven of his love? **1768–74** Tucker *Lt. Nat.* (1834) I. 63 Neither let him harbour such an overweening conceit of his own ungiven strength. **1818** Colebrooke *Obligations* 48 By the Hindu law, whatever has been given by mistake, must be considered as ungiven.

**3. a.** Not given *over*; unsurrendered.
*a* **1670** Spalding *Troub. Chas. I* (1850) I. 272 It [*sc.* the castle] wes not long on-givin over.

**b.** Unaddicted *to* something.
**1876** *Whitby Gloss.* 206. **1897** *Westm. Gaz.* 2 Mar. 2/1 Silent of speech, morose of nature, not ungiven to beer.

**Ungi·ving,** *ppl. a.* (Un-¹ 10.)
**1682** Dryden *Epil. Unhappy Favourite* 8 Courtiers living on the Rents Of the three last ungiving Parliaments. **1692** Dryden *Cleomenes* iii. ii, In vain at shrines the ungiving suppliant stands. **1737** Hervey *Mem.* (1848) xxviii. II. 251 The costive nature of the King's ungiving spirit. **1829** Lamb *Gypsy's Malison* 14 So sang a wither'd Beldam.., And bann'd the ungiving door.

**Ungla·ciated,** *ppl. a.* (Un-¹ 8.) **1883** *Science* I. 270/2 The average production..is nearly twice as large in the glaciated as in the unglaciated portion.

**Ungla·d,** *a.* [OE. *unglæd* (Un-¹ 7 + Glad *a.*) = ON. *úglaðr* (MSw. *ogladh*, Norw. and Da. *uglad*).] Not glad or joyful; unhappy, sorry.
*c* **888** K. Ælfred *Boeth.* vi, Þon wyrð heo swiðe hraðe ungladu, þeah heo ær gladu wære on to locienne. **13..** *Guy Warw.* (A.) 1554 Now haþ Gij miche sorwe made, For his felawes he is vnglade. *c* **1350** *Will. Palerne* 2106 He..goþ to þemperour of grece vnglad at his herte. **1390** Gower *Conf.* III. 370, I..sih my colour fade, Myn yhen dymme and al unglade. *c* **1412** Hoccleve *De Reg. Princ.* 4081 At the last, Men þinke shullen þei to mochil haue had, And of þis worldys muk be ful vnglad. **1470–85** Malory *Arthur* x. iii. 499 Whanne this crye was made many knyghtes were gladde and many were vngladde. **1536** Bellenden *Cron. Scot.* (1821) II. 128 The Scottis wer not unglaid thairof. **1620** Shelton *Quix.* ii. x. 60 Don Quixote..beheld with vnglad..eyes her that Sancho call'd Queene and Lady. **1648** Hexham ii, *Onblijde*, Vnglad, Vnjoyfull. **1819** Lamb *Sonn.*, *Work* 8 Sabbathless Satan! he who his unglad Task ever plies mid rotatory burnings. **1873** Dixon *Two Queens* ix. iv. II. 119 Max had been as loth to let him go, as he had been unglad to see him come.

**† Ungla·d,** *v. Obs.* [Un-² 6 a. Cf. ON. *úgleðja*.] *trans.* To afflict, distress.

1390 GOWER *Conf.* II. 317 O thou, which alle love ungladest, And art ensample of alle untrewe. *c*1430 *Syr Gener.* (Roxb.) 9202 The first assaute that euer thei made, Gwynan thei gan to vnglade.

**Ungla·ddened,** *ppl. a.* (UN-$^1$ 8.)

*a* 1851 MOIR *Lament of Selim* i, The soul Of him whose days ungladden'd roll On, month by month. 1861 J. G. SHEPPARD *Fall Rome* iii. 148 A howling wilderness, ungladdened by the sight of 'Flocks, or herds'.

†**Ungla·dly,** *a. Obs.*$^{-1}$ [UN-$^1$ 7; cf. OE. *unglædlic* morose.] Of the eyes: Dull.

*c* 1450 *Bk. Hawking* in *Rel. Ant.* I. 301 At his eyen thu mayst perceve [it], for his eyen woll be derke, and ungladly.

**Ungla·dly,** *adv.* [UN-$^1$ 11.] Without gladness (†or brightness.)

*a* 1225 *Ancr. R.* 338 Hwon ich hit do,..oðer ich hit do ungledliche,..oðer lete wel þerof. 1486 *Bk. St. Albans, Hawking* C iv b, When yowre hawke is encombred in the bowillis ..hir Eighen will be derke and she will looke ungladli. 1902 *Westm. Gaz.* 25 Jan. 1/3 Men and women who know their Asia and are now returning to it ungladly.

**Ungla·dness.** [UN-$^1$ 12.] Want of gladness (†or good spirits).

*a* 1300 *Cursor M.* 15545 Time sal cum þat yee Sal yur vngladnes þat es nu haf turnd in to gle. *c* 1450 *Bk. Hawking* in *Rel. Ant.* I. 304 A man may knowe by the ungladnesse after the chear that he maketh. [1486 *Bk. St. Albans, Hawking* C iv, A man may knaw by the chere and vngladnes of an hawke this infirmyte.]

**Ungla·dsome,** *a.* (UN-$^1$ 7.) 1558 PHAER *Æneid* III. I j, Than hauen at Drepanus I tooke, in that vngladsome shore [L. *illætabilis ora*]. **Ungla·moured,** *ppl. a.* (UN-$^1$ 8.) 1891 T. HARDY *Tess* x, However terrestrial and lumpy their appearance just now to the mean unglamoured eye.

**Ungla·zed,** *ppl. a.* [UN-$^1$ 8. Cf. (in sense 2) MDu. *ongeglaset.*]

**1.** Not glazed or having a smooth shining surface.

1599 A. M. tr. *Gabelhouer's Bk. Physicke* 43/2 Combure it to poulder in an vnglazede pot. 1612 WOODALL *Surg. Mate* Wks. (1653) 211 Put these into an earthen pan unglazed. 1694 SALMON *Bate's Dispens.* (1713) 497/2 Lemery heats an unglazed Pot or Crucible red hot. 1744 BERKELEY in Fraser *Life* (1871) viii. 300 Tar-water is best made in glazed earthen vessels;..it is finer and clearer when so made than if in unglazed crocks. 1799 G. SMITH *Laboratory* I. 95 Then take an unglazed pot, or a large crucible. 1844 NOAD *Electricity* (ed. 2) 160 These porous jars..are now composed of the thinnest unglazed biscuit ware. 1874 H. H. COLE *Catal. Ind. Art S. Kens. Mus.* 208 Made of common red clay, unglazed.

**2.** Not filled in with glass; lacking glass windows.

1608 *Presentment* in *Essex Rev.* XV. 46 The churchyard is unfensed, the windows unglazed. *a* 1721 PRIOR *Down-Hall* xxxvii, O now a low ruin'd white Shed I discern, Untyl'd and unglaz'd; I believe 'tis a Barn. 1816 *Q. Rev.* XVI. 346 Unglazed windows, balconies, and lattices,—shops without windows. 1862 LYTTON *Str. Story* I. 215 The cornice of the ceiling rested on pilasters, within which the compartments were formed into open unglazed arches.

†**U·ngle.** *Obs.* [ad. F. *ongle* (cf. ONGLE) or L. *ungula* UNGULA.]

**1.** A claw, nail, or hoof.

1480 CAXTON *Myrr.* II. iv. 70 The gryffons wylde..whiche easily bere a man away..whan he may sease hym with his clawes and vngles. 1491 — *Vitas Patr.* (W. de W. 1495) I. xlviii. 93/2 The ungles or nayles of his fete and hondes weren merueyllously longe. 1566 ADLINGTON *Apuleius* 39 We fleade of the skinne..of the beare..and kept his ungles whole. 1657 TOMLINSON *Renou's Disp.* 457 It hath bifidous ungles like a Goat.

**2.** A hooked instrument of torture.

1483 CAXTON *Gold. Leg.* 122/2 The tormentes of the pryson, the naylles, the vngles, the streynynge combes of yron.

**3.** A morbid growth in the eye; = UNGULA 2.

1590 BARROUGH *Meth. Physick* I. xxxvi. (1596) 59 Somtime..another vngle ariseth in the other corner [of the eye].

**4.** *Geom.* = UNGULA 4.

1669 WALLIS in Rigaud *Corr. Sci. Men* (1841) II. 508 He proceeds to a sum of squares to find the solid ungula, or the moment of that plane; and so to the sums of cubes, to find the moment of that ungle, and so on.

**Unglea·ned,** *ppl. a.* (UN-$^1$ 8.) [1775 ASH.] 1858 in *Homans' Cycl. Commerce* 1775/1 Scarce a field [has been] left ungleaned. 1869 RUSKIN *Q. of Air* § 157 Remnants of tradition..which remain ungleaned.

**U·ngled,** *ppl. a. Her.* [f. UNGLE. Cf. F. *onglé.*] = UNGULED.

1675 WOOD *Life* (O.H.S.) II. 311 A lyon rampant sable ungled and lang'd gules. 1684 *List Military* 11 Vnicorn passant, argent, armed, ungled. 1722 A. NISBET *Syst. Her.* I. 333 A stag..attired and ungled, Or. 1892 *Daily Tel.* 12 July 5/1 A cock..armed or 'ungled'.

†**Unglee.** *Obs.*$^{-1}$ [UN-$^1$ 12.] Sadness. *a* 1300 *Cursor M.* 24120 (Edin.), Bot for na bod þat he me mad, Ne moht he min vngle ma [= make] glad. **Ungli·ttering,** *ppl. a.* (UN-$^1$ 10.) 1813 *Monthly Rev.* LXX. 458 The unglittering dilation of their stanzas. 1868 GEO. ELIOT *Sp. Gipsy* I. 54 The time of sweet serenity When colour glows unglittering. **Unglo·be,** *v.* (UN-$^2$ 3.) 1611 FLORIO, *Disglobare*, to vnglobe, to make vnround. 1855 PATMORE *Angel in Ho.* II. Prol. 3 The beast [*sc.* the hedge-hog], Found stock-still.. And feigning so to be deceased,..Unglobed himself. **Ungloo·med,** *ppl. a.* (UN-$^1$ 8.) 1737 GREEN *Spleen* 700 With look ungloom'd by guile, And wearing Virtue's livery-smile.

**Unglo·rified,** *ppl. a.* (UN-$^1$ 8.)

*a* 1395 HYLTON *Scala Perf.* I. xliii. (MS. Bodl.), Þe resoun was maad cleer and bri3t..as parfytli as a soule in a bodi vnglorifyed my3te haue. 1533 MORE *Answ. Frith* Wks. 839/1 But I am sure glorified or vnglorified, yf hee sayed it hee is able to dooe it. 1597 HOOKER *Eccl. Pol.* v. xliii. § 3. 90 Least God should be any way vnglorified, the greatest part of our dayly seruice they know consisteth..in much varietie of Psalms and Hymnes. 1653 W. RAMESEY *Astrol. Restored* 10 So long as we carry this earthy Tabernacle about us unchanged and unglorified. 1876 MRS. OLIPHANT *Curate in Charge* II. ii. 34 The triumphant sunshine..leaving not an inch even of the common high road unglorified.

**Unglo·rify,** *v.* (UN-$^2$ 6 c.)

*a* 1740 WATTS *Remnants of Time*, etc. § 21 Forbid it, O my God, that ever I should be so unhappy as to unglorify.. my Saviour, or my Sanctifier. 1751 R. SHIRRA in *Remains* (1850) 75 The Word should as it were unglorify himself. 1873 BROWNING *Red Cott. Nt.-cap* III. 145 Unglossed was shrubbery, unglorified Each copse, so wealthy once.

**Unglo·rious,** *a.* Now *rare.* [UN-$^1$ 7 and 5 b. Cf. MDu. *onglorioos.*] = INGLORIOUS *a.*

In earliest quots. rendering L. *inglorius.*

1382 WYCLIF *Job* xii. 19 He bringeth the prestis of hem vnglorious, and the beste men of wrshipe he supplauntith. — *Isaiah* lii. 14 So vnglorious shal ben among men his si3te. *c* 1400 *The Brut* ccxxvii. 298 Þe same vnglorious Philip wiþdrowe him, wiþ þe residue of al his peple. *c* 1450 *Myrr. our Ladye* 183 Tho aungels,..made vngloryous for thyr wyckednes, felle from glory. 1663 COWLEY *Ess. in Verse & Pr., Virg. Georg.* 46 In the next place, let Woods and Rivers be My quiet, though unglorious destiny. 1744 ARMSTRONG *Preserv. Health* III. 13 Needlessly to brave Unglorious dangers. 1882 FROUDE *Carlyle* II. 153 Something should be found..neither unglorious nor unprofitable.

**Unglo·ry,** *v.* [UN-$^2$ 4.] To deprive of glory.

1626 LAUD *Serm. Ps. lxxiv. 22*, 16 Wee must not looke that God should Arise to help vs, if wee arise to oppose and vnglorie him. 1655 SHIRLEY *Politician* III. i, The triumph he Expected..Will be ungloried in our sudden match.

**Unglo·ss,** *v.* (UN-$^2$ 4.) 1873 [see UNGLORIFY *v.*]. **Unglo·ssaried,** *a.* (UN-$^1$ 9.) 1887 W. BEATTY-KINGSTON *Music & Manners* II. 341 Why has he been thus branded, dateless and unglossaried. 1894 J. R. C. HALL *Anglo-Saxon Dict.* Pref., I do not profess to have searched unglossaried matter. **Unglo·ssed,** *ppl. a.*$^1$ (UN-$^1$ 8 and GLOSS *v.*$^1$) 1866 MORRIS *Ayenbite* Pref., Editors have left the word unglossed. **Unglo·ssed,** *ppl. a.*$^2$ (UN-$^1$ 8 and GLOSS *v.*$^2$) 1802 H. MARTIN *Helen of Glenross* III. 293 Her errors you saw unveiled, unglossed. 1862 MRS. H. WOOD *Channings* xxiv, Tell me..the simple truth, unglossed over. **Unglo·ssing,** *ppl. a.* (UN-$^1$ 10.) 1827 LAMB in Hone *Table-bk.* I. 488 The honest unglossing pages of the homely Newgate Ordinary. **Unglo·ssy,** *a.* (UN-$^1$ 7.) 1822 GOOD *Stud. Med.* IV. 693 A dull or unglossy white diffused over the body. 1854 H. MILLER *Sch. & Schm.* xxi. 438 The dull, unglossy coat given..by the agencies of friction and water.

**Unglo·ve,** *v.* [UN-$^2$ 4 and 7.]

**1.** *trans.* To divest of a glove or gloves.

*c* 1430 *Pilgr. Lyf Manhode* IV. xliii. (1869) 196 Weel þou wost þe name of þe gloouen...A fool þou were whan þou vnglooueedest þee of hem. 1611 FLORIO, *Disguantare*, to vngloue. 1624 MASSINGER *Parl. Love* II. iii, See, I dare touch this hand, And without adoration unglove it. *a* 1625 FLETCHER & SHIRLEY *Lover's Progress* II. i, *Cla.* 'Tis said you can tell fortunes to come. *Lan.* Yes Mistris and what's past, Unglove your hand. 1823 SCOTT *Quentin D.* xii, The King, ungloving his right hand, courteously handed the Countess Isabelle and her kinswoman to their apartment. 1861 *Eng. Wom. Dom. Mag.* III. 142 He laid the hand which he had ungloved upon his heart.

**2.** *intr.* To remove a glove or gloves. Also *fig.*

1797 MRS. A. M. BENNETT *Beggar Girl* (1813) IV. 212 The earl, on every occasion a complete courtier, got out to unglove to Mrs. Woudbe. 1855 LYNCH *Rivulet* LXVI. iii, The covered buds ungloving Seem with offered hand to greet.

Hence **Unglo·ving** *vbl. sb.*

1818 KEATS *To Lady at Vauxhall* 4 Snared by the ungloving of thine hand. 1873 T. W. HIGGINSON *Oldport Days* v. 129 The turning of her head, the ungloving of her hand.

**Unglo·ved,** *ppl. a.* (UN-$^1$ 8.)

1626 BACON *New Atl.* (1650) 26 Holding forth his Hand ungloved, and in Posture of Blessing. 1626 BRETON *Fantastickes* Wks. (Grosart) II. 8/1 It is now March,..and the faire hands must not be vngloued. 1802 COLERIDGE *Lett.* (1895) 417, I..would shake hands with them ungloved. 1844 W. IRVING in *Life & Lett.* (1866) III. 359 On one hand is a black glove; the other hand, ungloved, is small. 1888 A. K. GREEN *Behind Closed Doors* v, She had laid her ungloved hand upon his arm.

**Unglo·zed,** *ppl. a.* (UN-$^1$ 8.) 1377 LANGL. *P. Pl.* B. IV. 145 Late 3owre confessoure, sire Kynge, construe þis vnglosed.

**Unglue·,** *v.* [UN-$^2$ 3 and 7.]

**1.** *trans.* To free from the binding or adhesive effect of glue; to detach or make loose in this way.

1548 ELYOT, *Reglutino*, .. to vnglewe. 1598 FLORIO, *Sgommare*, to vngum, to vnplaister, to vnglue. 1686 AGLIONBY *Painting Illustr.* i. 29 Being Vexed at the Suns ungluing some Pictures of his. 1703 R. NEVE *City & C. Purchaser* 277 To prevent..Brick-walls from Ungluing the Joynts of the Pannels. 1718 OZELL tr. *Tournefort's Voy.* I. 130 Their Strings or Filaments separate..in parcels, as if they had been glued together at first, and now were unglued. 1859 MORLEY *Mem. Bartholomew Fair* i. 12 There was a young man..whose head stuck to his left hand. He was unglued at St. Bartholomew's establishment. 1872 T. HARDY *Under Greenw. Tree* I. v, That there instrument [a fiddle] will be unglued and spoilt in ten minutes.

**b.** *transf.* To open (the eyes) after sleep.

1606 DEKKER *Seuen Deadly Sinnes* Wks. (Grosart) II. 31 Another..arriu'de at one of the Gates, before any Porters eyes were vnglewd. 1682 N. O. *Boileau's Lutrin* IV. 207 But yet the Noise that had unglew'd their eyes Could not perswade the Sluggish Chanons rise. 1728 SWIFT *Jrnl. of Mod. Lady* 42 She stretches, gapes, unglues her eyes, And asks if it be time to rise.

**c.** *fig.* To detach, separate, dissolve.

1619 HIERON *Wks.* I. 641 Happy were it for vs if the meditation of this point..were able to vnglue and vntwist our affections, which are so neerely tyed vnto it. 1649 BP. HALL *Cases Consc.* IV. ii. (1654) 307 Heresie and Infidelitie, which are enough to unglew all naturall and civill relations betwixt father and son. 1675 HOBBES *Odyssey* (1677) 130 Your death.., for which Age shall prepare you, and your soul unglew Insensibly. 1831 SYD. SMITH in Lady Holland *Mem.* (1855) II. 314 Where is it to end? Are all political agglutinations to be unglued? 1897 HALL CAINE *Christian* IV. iii, Unless we unglue ourselves from the vanities which imperil our existence.

**2.** *intr.* To lose cohesion; to become detached.

1693 EVELYN *De la Quint. Compl. Gard.* II. 112 Otherwise they are apt to unglue, that is, to separate cleverly from the part where they are Graffed, in great Storms of Wind. 1703 R. NEVE *City & C. Purchaser* 29 When ever the Joints shall happen to unglue.

Hence **Unglu·ing** *vbl. sb.*

1591 PERCIVALL *Sp. Dict.*, *Desengrudamiento*, vngluing. 1623 COCKERAM I, *Reglutination*, an vngluing. 1703 R. NEVE *City & C. Purchaser* 277 Yet neither of these ways will prevent their ungluing in some Houses.

**Unglue·d,** *ppl. a.* (UN-$^1$ 8.) 1694 STRYPE *Mem. Cranmer* II. xv. 206 They had Leaves put in as Additions to the Book, some glewed, and some unglewed. **Unglu·tinate,** *v.* [UN-$^2$ 3.] = UNGLUE *v.* 1 c. 1683 PETTUS *Ess. Metallick Words* s.v. *Load-stone*, To be kept from..moist places, which do unglutinate, and so destroyes or subdues their Virtues.

**Unglu·tted,** *ppl. a.* (UN-$^1$ 8.)

1813 BYRON *Corsair* II. viii, For Seyd's unglutted eye Would doom him ever dying—ne'er to die! 1847 LYTTON *Lucretia* II. viii, The two inheritors of a revenge unglutted by the grave. 1897 RHOSCOMYL *White Rose Arno* 46 His eyes all hell with unglutted murder.

†**Ungly,** erroneous f. UGLY *a.* and *adv.*

*c* 1400 *Apol. Loll.* 55 But wo is þe..biginning of þis þus gret iuel, I drede ungly to sey. *a* 1513 FABYAN *Chron.* v. cix. 83 Such an vngly nombre of multytude of monkes.

**Ungnaw·ed,** *ppl. a.* (UN-$^1$ 8.) 1836 F. MAHONY *Rel. Father Prout* (1859) 376 Thy MSS. have come down to us.. ungnawed by the tooth of Time. 1881 DARWIN *Veg. Mould* 80 Ungnawed petioles had not become more decayed near the base than elsewhere. **Ungnaw·n,** *ppl. a.* (UN-$^1$ 8 b.) *a* 1560 PHAER *Æneid* VIII. Y 3 To thee he trembling shooke, and left his bones begonne ungnawn. 1648 HEXHAM II, *Ongeknaeght*, Vngnawne. 1775 ASH, *Ungnawn.*

†**Ungne·de,** *a. Obs.* [UN-$^1$ 7: cf. OE. *ungnieðe.*] Unsparing, liberal.

*a* 1300 *Cursor M.* 9933 Þat castel brightnes sua vngnede, Oueral þat curt on lenght and brede. *a* 1400 *Pistill of Susan* 276 Grete god,..of gyftes vngnede.

**Ungnement,** obs. form of OINTMENT.

†**Ungo·,** *v. Obs.*$^{-1}$ [UN-$^2$ 7. Cf. MDu. *ontgaen* (Du. *-gaan*), LG. *und-, untgân*, MHG. *ent-, engân* (G. *entgehen*), to escape, fail, etc.] *intr.* To pass away, perish.

*c* 1450 *Hymns Virgin* (1867) 121 They schalle se heuyn vngo, And þe erthe schall also.

**Ungoa·ded,** *ppl. a.* (UN-$^1$ 8.) [1775 ASH.] 1817 LADY MORGAN *France* VI. (1818) II. 130 Ungoaded by the necessities of a commercial existence. 1873 W. CORY *Lett. & Jrnls.* (1897) 313 A..creaking wheel turned by an ungoaded, tall, lean ox.

**Ungo·d,** *v.* [UN-$^2$ 6 b. Cf. Du. *ontgoden*, G. *entgöttern.*] To deprive of the qualities or position of deity; to undeify. (Common *c* 1640–1740.)

1627 WREN *Serm. bef. King* 17 Feb. 33 All slight and unawful Expressions..Vngodding him no lesse..then does rash and unadvised blasphemie. 1655 GURNAL *Chr. in Arm.* II. 61 Though men cannot come to pull God out of his throne, and un-god him. 1677 [see UNCHRISTED *ppl. a.*]. 1708 O. DYKES *Eng. Prov. & Refl.* (1709) 243 Attempting saucily to rival, to insult, or to ungod his Creator. *a* 1750 T. GORDON *Another Cordial* (1751) II. 293 The Jew crucifies his Saviour, the Socinian and Mahometan ungod him. *a* 1834 COLERIDGE in *Lit. Rem.* (1839) IV. 224 A consistent Socinianism..in ungodding the Saviour must deify cats and dogs. 1892 *Gospel Watchman* Dec. 191/1 God..will be dethroned and ungodded before it shall come to pass.

*refl.* 1672 VILLIERS (Dk. Buckhm.) *Rehearsal* IV. ii, For fair Parthenope, Gods would, themselves, un-god themselves to see. 1685 J. SCOTT *Chr. Life* II. vii. § 1 Which would be to destroy his own Being, and un-god himself.

Hence **Ungo·dding** *vbl. sb.*

1656 BEAKE in *Burton's Diary* (1828) I. 59 It is a crime that deposes the majesty of God himself,..the ungodding of God. 1678 CUDWORTH *Intell. Syst.* I. iv. § 20. 381 His Ungodding of the Sun, Moon and Stars. 1716 M. DAVIES *Athen. Brit.* II. 407 What a horror the Primitive Christians had of the Notions, of Ungodding our Saviour.

†**Ungo·dded,** *ppl. a. Obs.* [UN-$^1$ 8: see GOD *v.* 2.] Not spiritually united with God.

1579 W. WILKINSON *Confut. Fam. Love* B iij b, They are . vnrenewed, vngodded, vnsent. 1660 H. MORE *Myst. Godl.* VI. xii. 248 What the ungodded or unilluminated men ..preach and teach. 1687 DRYDEN *Hind & P.* III. 742 Thus men ungodded may to places rise.

**Ungo·ddess,** *v.* [UN-$^2$ 6 b.] *trans.* To deprive of the status of a goddess.

1760 MURPHY *Way to Keep Him* I. i, They whisk about the Town,..as if they were treated at home like so many Goddesses, though every body knows possession has ungoddessed them all long ago. 1797 MRS. A. M. BENNETT *Beggar Girl* (1813) III. 290 Fortune..was at this moment most unmercifully ungoddessed. 1837 CARLYLE *Fr. Rev.* III. v. iv, What articulate words poor Mrs. Momoro.. uttered, when she had become ungoddessed again.

†**Ungo·derly,** *a. Obs.* [UN-$^1$ 7; the second element is obscure.] Squalid, filthy.

13.. *E. E. Allit. P.* B. 145 Þow art a gome vngoderly in þat goun febele. *Ibid.* 1092 [Christ] nolde neuer towche O3t þat was vngoderly oþer ordure was inne.

**Ungo·dlike,** *a.* (UN-$^1$ 7 c.)

*a* 1652 J. SMITH *Sel. Disc.* viii. (1660) 364 But alas, such an ungodlike Religion as this can never be owned by God. 1684 T. BURNET *Theory Earth* I. 165 This, I confess, seems to me..a way of working very un-God-like. 1729 W. REEVE *Serm.* 149 The pleasures at God's right hand must be tasteless to an ungodlike filthy spirit. 1854 P. FAIRBAIRN *Typol. Script.* (ed. 2) I. II. ii. 218 How cheering to know this ungod-like state of disorder and confusion is not to be perpetual. **1869** GLADSTONE *Juv. Mundi* vii. 211 It did not assign to deity that most ungodlike quality, respect of persons.

**Ungo·dlily,** *adv.* (UN-[1] 11.)
**1583** J. FIELD *Godly Exhort.* C j b, Being thus vngodlilie assembled, to so vnholy a spectacle. **1645** PAGITT *Heresiogr.* (1647) 66 Ungodlily alledging the..Scriptures. **1674** *Govt. Tongue* 114 'Tis but an ill essay of that reverence and godly fear, to use that very ungodly so irreverently and ungodlily as men now do. **1860** PUSEY *Min. Proph.* 413 Israel..slaying ungodlily Him who was by nature His Begotten Son.

**Ungo·dliness.** (UN-[1] 12: cf. next.)
**1526** TINDALE *Rom.* i. 18 For the wrath of god of heven apereth agaynst all vngodlynes and vnrightewesnes. *Ibid.* xi. 26. **1555** EDEN *Decades W. Ind.* (Arb.) 58 He dyd not keepe silence of so wicked an vngodlynesse. **1642** L. HUGHES (*title*), Certain Grievances: or, the Popish Errors and Ungodlinesse of the Service-book plainly laid open. **1671** BARROW *Duty & Reward Charity* 21 Performing such acts, is a good sign of true Piety; and omitting them, is a certain argument of ungodliness. **1742** YOUNG *Nt. Th.* III. 165 Oh! the curst ungodliness of zeal! **1865** C. J. VAUGHAN *Plain Words* x. (1866) 183 The recollection of His love in contrast with our ungodliness.

**Ungo·dly,** *a.* [UN-[1] 7. Cf. MDu. *ongodelijc* (Du. *ongoddelijk*), MHG. *ungötlich* (G. *ungöttlich*), (M)Da. *ugudelig*, MSw. *ogudhlik* (Sw. *ogudlig*).]
**1.** Of persons: Not fearing or reverencing God; irreligious, impious, wicked.
**1526** TINDALE *Rom.* v. 6 Christ dyed for vs which were vngodly. **1587** GOLDING *De Mornay* xx. 358 There is also a certeine Religion,..and the vngodlyest man that is cannot scape from it. *a* **1613** OVERBURY *A Wife*, etc. (1614) H 4 b, The charitable man dreames of building Churches, but starts to thinke the vngodly Courtier will pull them down again. **1653** HOLCROFT *Procopius, Pers. Wars* II. 48 His son succeeding him, being the ungodlyest man living. **1698** NORRIS *Pract. Disc.* IV. 180 Which justifies a certain English Phrase..wherein we use to call a Man of a Wicked Life, an Vngodly Man. **1731** WATERLAND *Script. Vind.* II. 100 Shimei was an ungodly wretch. **1849** JAMES *Woodman* ii, The admission into her own private chamber of such very ungodly personages as Mars and Venus.
*absol.* **1526** TINDALE 1 *Pet.* iv. 18 Yf the righteous scasly be saved: where shall the vngodly and the sinner appere? **1535** COVERDALE *Zeph.* iii. 5 But the vngodly will not lerne to be aszshamed. **1631** GOUGE *God's Arrows* I. § 12. 17 Of the godlies exemption from the ungodlies destruction. **1738** WESLEY *Ps.* I. iv, But no Success th' Ungodly find. **1825** J. NEAL *Bro. Jonathan* I. 24 While he was rebuking the ungodly. **1847** S. AUSTIN *Ranke's Hist. Ref.* III. 385 He did not doubt that the ungodly, as well as the pious, partook of the body and blood of Christ.
*transf.* **1595** SHAKS. *John* III. i. 109 Let not the howres of this vngodly day Weare out the daies in Peace.
**b.** Of the stomach: Gluttonous, greedy.
*c* **1746** J. COLLIER (Tim Bobbin) *Goose* 78 You must not Pamper your ungodly Belly. **1746** AINSWORTH (ed. 2) I, An ungodly gut, *venter improbus.* **1828** [CARR] *Craven Gloss.*, *Ungodly*, insatiable, or squeamish and nice; used of the stomach or guts.
**2.** Of actions, etc.: Not in accordance with the will or law of God.
**1526** [see UNGODLY *adv.*]. **1555** EDEN *Decades* (Arb.) 109 They sayde it was vngodly to feyght ageynst any, not beinge prouoked. **1577** GOOGE *Heresbach's Husb.* 15 Let hym in no wyse suffer them..to vse filthy or vngodly speache. **1617** WOODALL *Surg. Mate* Pref., Wks. (1639) 6 Wherefore it were a very ungodly thing..to forbid a Surgeon to learne all, or any thing that concerneth his calling. **1671** MILTON *Samson* 898 Gods unable To acquit themselves and prosecute their foes But by ungodly deeds. **1851** LONGFELLOW *Gold. Leg.* IV. *Refectory*, Were Peter Damian still upon earth, To be shocked by such ungodly mirth. **1864** PUSEY *Lect. Daniel* i. (1876) 3 The moral law..strongly condemned forgery even when not ungodly.
**3.** *colloq.* Outrageous, dreadful.
**1887** STEVENSON *Merry Men, Olalla*, The wind['s]..ungodly and unintermittent uproar, would not suffer me to sleep.

**Ungo·dly,** *adv. Obs.* exc. *arch.* [UN-[1] 11. Cf. MDu. *ongod(e)like* (Du. *ongoddelijk*), MHG. *ungöttlich*, MSw. *ogud(e)like* (Sw. *ogudligt*).] = UNGODLILY *adv.* (Common in 16th c.)
**1526** TINDALE *Jude* 15 To rebuke..all their vngodly dedes, which they haue vngodly committed. [Also in later versions.] **1533** FRITH *Judgm. Tracy* Pref., But this I dare boldly professe, that his godly sayinges are vngodly handled. **1564** *Brief Exam.* A iij, All true Godly men, may Godly vse those rites, which wicked men haue abused, howesoeuer vngodly. **1606** G. WOODCOCK *Hist. Iustine* I i 2, Leontius.. being made Emperor, ruled most ungodly eleuen years.

**Ungo·dmothered,** *a.* (UN-[1] 9.) ?**1714** *Widow of Watling Street* I. i, You Half Christened Katomites—ungodmothered varlets. **†Ungo·ingable,** *a. Obs.*[−1] [UN-[1] 7 b.] Impossible to traverse. **1482** *Monk of Evesham* (Arb.) 39 Sothly to owre semyng the lengthe of thys fyrste place afore seyde was on goyngable. **Ungo·ld,** *v.* (UN-[2] 4.) **1637** N. WHITING *Albino & Bellama* 28 Saturne's exilde, Jove awes this massie Ball, And now the Iron age un-goldeth all.

**Ungon,** obs. var. ONION.

**Ungo·ne,** *ppl. a.* [UN-[1] 8 b.]
**1.** Not (yet) gone or departed. † *To keep ungone* (Sc.), to keep from going.
*c* **1475** *Rauf Coilȝear* 661 ȝit was the King in the hall, And mony gude man with all, Vngane to the meit. **1597** in *Archpriest Controv.* (Camden) I. 2 Mr. Gwyn tould me that fissher was vngone at his comyng from London. **1638** SIR E. STANHOPE in *Strafford's Lett.* (1739) II. 239 A Letter ..to intreat me to meet him the next Day, and if he were ungone, to bring my Son John with me. **1657** *Rec. Burgh Lanark* (1893) 160 To keip their prenteissis, servands, and childrin ungone avaiging on the Lordes day. **1824–77** in dialect glossaries (Yks., Linc.).
**†2.** Untraversed. *Obs.*[−0]

**1611** FLORIO, *Inuio sentiere*, an vngone, vntroden or vncouth path.

**Ungoo·d,** *a.* Now *rare.* [OE. *ungód* (UN-[1] 7), = MDu. *ongoet* (older Du. *ongoed*), MLG. *ungût* (LG. *ungôd*), OHG., MHG. *unguot* (G. *ungut*), ON. *úgóðr* (Norw. dial. *ugod*).] Not good; evil, bad; wicked.
*c* **1000** *Sax. Leechd.* III. 184 Seldan he bið eald, ungodan deaðe he swylt. *Ibid.* 188. *c* **1200** ORMIN 16739 Forrþi þatt teȝȝre dede iss all Unngod & all unnclene. *Ibid.* 17056. *a* **1300** *E. E. Psalter* i. 1 In strete of sinfulle noght he stode, Ne sat in setel of storme un-gode. *c* **1305** *Judas Iscariot* 22 in *E. E. P.* (1862) 107 Loþ hem was..a bern to norischie, so liþer and vngod. **1390** GOWER *Conf.* I. 20 The vice of hem that ben ungoode Is no reproef unto the goode. *c* **1445** PECOCK *Donet* 37 Þat þing whiche resoun knowiþ..to be bad, or vngood. *c* **1485** *Digby Myst.* (1882) IV. 675 His synows.. Are brokyn sonder by payns vngude! **1904** C. N. & A. M. WILLIAMSON *Princess Passes* xii, You have been so good to us; don't be ungood now.
**b.** *absol.* or as *sb.*
*a* **1250** *Owl & Night.* 129 Al so hit is bi þan vngode þat is icumen of fule brode. *Ibid.* 1364 Vor nys a worlde þing so god þat ne may do sum vngod. *a* **1568** in *Bannatyne MS.* (Hunter. Cl.) 203/86 Vngud and gud sall fair,..Bot richteous gud..lestis for euir mair. **1885** L. OLIPHANT *Sympneumata* 248 For universal good, and for suppression of the ungood.

**†Ungoo·dlihead.** *Obs.*[−1] [UN-[1] 12: cf. next.] Lack of goodness.
**1430–40** LYDG. *Bochas* VI. iii. (1554) 150 b, She her cours gan varye..To shewe her malice and ungoodlyhed.

**†Ungoo·dly,** *a. Obs.* [UN-[1] 7. Cf. MDu. *ongoedelijc-* (Du. *ongoedelijk*), MLG. *ungûtlik*, *-gôtlik*, MHG. *unguotlich*, *-güetlich* (G. *ungütlich*).]
**1.** Lacking goodness; bad, wicked: **a.** Of persons.
**1390** GOWER *Conf.* I. 293 He is that ilke ungoodlieste Which many a lusti love hath twinned. *Ibid.* II. 338 Ha, thou ungoodlich ypocrite. **1432** *Paston Lett.* I. 32 The whiche lak or defaulte mighte be caused by ungodely or unvertuous men. **1472** *Coventry Leet Bk.* 374 Wher ther be diuers and many vagabundes, and vngoodly & ille disposed persones. **1553** BECON *Reliques of Rome* (1563) 159 This is yᵉ goodly Godlye Catholyke doctrine wherwith the vngoodly vngodly Papists infecte the mindes of such Christians as are simple.
**b.** Of actions, language, etc.
**1390** GOWER *Conf.* II. 333 Which thing, mi Sone, I thee forbede, For it is an ungoodly dede. **1412–20** LYDG. *Chron. Troy* III. 3352 Epistrophus..Rebuked hym in vngoodly wyse. **1455** T. BECKINGTON *Corr.* (Rolls) II. 342 That I sholde haue vttered and seid vngoodly langage touchynge yor noble persone. **1530** in W. H. Turner *Select. Rec. Oxford* (1880) 84 For his ungoodly maner so then usid to the comyssarie [he] did send hym to prison.
**2.** Uncomely; unhandsome.
**1495** *Trevisa's Barth. De P. R.* v. xiii. 42 Yf the nose lackyth, all yᵉ other dele of yᵉ face is yᵉ more vngoodly & vnsemely. **1519** HORMAN *Vulg.* 14 b, No man that..hath a mahayme or a blemmysshe, that maketh hym vngoodly, shall take orders. **1549** COVERDALE, etc. *Erasm. Par.* 1 *Cor.* 34 Suche [parts] as seme vngoodly, to them ioyne we some comly vesture.

**†Ungoo·dly,** *adv. Obs.* [UN-[1] 11. Cf. MDu. (and obs. Du.) *ongoedelike*, MLG. *ungûtliken*, *-gôtliken*, MHG. *unguotlîche*, *-güetlîche*.]
**1.** In an uncomely manner. *rare.*
*a* **1300** *Cursor M.* 18404 Þar come ouerthuert A wreche man, vngodli gert, On his schuldres a croice he bar.
**2.** Badly, wrongly, improperly; roughly or rudely.
*c* **1380** WYCLIF *Wks.* (1880) 339 And þus is þat man contrite of synne, þat he vngodeli to god haþ don. **1426** LYDG. *De Guil. Pilgr.* 3952, I..ful vngoodly spoke now, Wher-off I repente sore. **1450** *Paston Lett.* I. 158 He tolde H. his part how that he levid ungoodly in puttyng awey of his wyff, and kept an other. **1475** *Bk. Noblesse* (Roxb.) 5 That noble and trew knyght,..ayenst all manhode ungoodely entretid, died in prison. **1526** TINDALE *Matt.* xxii. 6 The remnaunt toke his servauntes and entreated them vngoodly and slewe them. **1545** ASCHAM *Toxoph.* (Arb.) 50 Good thinges ungoodlye vsed, are not good.

**Ungo·red,** *ppl. a.*[1] [UN-[1] 8.] Unpierced.
**1604** SHAKS. *Ham.* v. ii. 261 (Q. 2), I..will no reconcilement, Till..I haue a voyce and president of peace To [keep] my name vngord [**1623** vngorg'd]. **1647** HEXHAM I, Vngored, *ondoorsteken.*

**†Ungo·red,** *ppl. a.*[2] [UN-[1] 8.] Unbloodied.
**1605** SYLVESTER *Du Bartas* II. iii. *Vacation* 288 Yet one might behold Bright swords and shields, and plumed helms of gold Un-goard with bloud.

**Ungo·rge,** *v.* (UN-[2] 3.)
**1601** CHETTLE & MUNDAY *Death Earl Huntington* v. ii. L j b, But when thou dost vngorge thee, grant me this, Thou power those poysons on the head of Iohn.

**Ungo·rged,** *ppl. a.* (UN-[1] 8.)
[**1623**: see UNGORED [1].] **1700** DRYDEN *Theod. & Hon.* 213 The Hell-hounds, as ungorg'd with Flesh and Blood, Pursue their Prey. **1743** FRANCIS tr. *Hor., Odes* III. iv. 79 On Tityus' liver shall the vulture feed With rage ungorged.

**Ungo·rgeous,** *a.* (UN-[1] 7.) **1837** CARLYLE *Fr. Rev.* II. IV. viii, The ignominious Royal Procession..sweeps along there, in most *un*gorgeous pall. **Ungo·spel,** *a.* [UN-[1] 12 b.] Unevangelical. **1649** H. LAWRENCE *Some Consid.*, etc. 75 Can that Ordinance be legall, and servile, and ungospell? **1653** PRYNNE *Gospel-plea* 33 Which ungospell practises I wish they would first reforme. **Ungo·spel,** *v.* (UN-[2] 6 b.) **1847** H. BUSHNELL *Chr. Nurt.* II. vii. (1861) 376 Confessing shortcomings and defeats..enough to ungospel all the gospel promises. **Ungo·spelized,** *ppl. a.* (UN-[1] 8.) **1706** *Acc. Soc. Propag. Gospel* 57 They had addressed the Remoter ungospelized Plantations. **1721** S. SEWALL *Diary* 16 Feb., The Money for Gospellizing ungospellized places. **Ungo·spelled,** *a.* (UN-[1] 9.) **1674** N. FAIRFAX *Bulk & Selv.* 8 That thread-bare Question, which did so much gravel the ungospel'd world. **1902** SKRINE *Pastor Agnorum* 193 The sick that need the physician, the ungospelled poor.

**Ungo·spel-like,** *a.* (UN-[1] 7 c.)
**1574** *Life 70th Abp. Canterb.* Pref. E 4 That so the open mouth off the Lewde Papist might bee stopped from..the approuing of suche vngospellike legends. **1641** MILTON *Ch. Govt.* II. iii, The..tyranny of an undue, unlawfull and ungospellike jurisdiction. **1674** PENN *Urim & Thummim* (title-p.), The opposite plea of Samuel Grevill..in his ungospel-like discourse.

**Ungo·t,** *ppl. a.* Also 5 vnget. [UN-[1] 8 b.]
**1.** Not acquired, obtained, or won.
*c* **1400** *Sege Jerus.* (E.E.T.S.) 68/1169 Ay wer þe ȝates vnget till two ȝeres ende: So longe þey souȝt hit by sege, or þey þe cite hadde. **1601** DANIEL *Civ. Wars* VI. xlvii, Whilst Sommerset with maine endeuour lay To get his giuen but vngot gouernment. **1611** COTGR., *Vuarisons*,.. corne, grasse..standing, or vncut, vngot.
**2.** Unbegot.
**1603** SHAKS. *Meas. for M.* v. i. 141 Your Substitute, Who is as free from touch, or soyle with her As she from one vngot.

**Ungo·tten,** *ppl. a.* Also 5 vngettyn, -getyn. [UN-[1] 8 b.]
**1.** Unbegotten.
**1435** MISYN *Fire of Love* 14 For nouþer þe substanc of þe sone som-tyme vngetyn myȝt be called,..with-oute an onely gettyn sone of þe self. **1470–85** MALORY *Arthur* VI. i. 571 He that shal sytte there is vnborne and vngoten. **1548** PATTEN *Exped. Scotl.* A vij, Astyages..was..admonished yᵗ he shoulde be ouercommen by a nephew of hys as yet then vngotten & vnborne. **1599** SHAKS. *Hen. V*, I. ii. 288 And some are yet vngotten and vnborne, That shal haue cause to curse the Dolphins scorne.
**2.** Not acquired, obtained, or won.
*a* **1548** HALL *Chron., Hen. VI*, 107 b, The Frenchemen.. seyng the strong fortres was ungotten,..fetched a compasse about. **1600** PALFREYMAN *Baldwin's Mor. Philos.* 135 b, They that indeuour to get theyr husbandes or wiues by deceipts & charmes, may lightly get them, but better vngotten. **1628** FELTHAM *Resolves* I. xlviii. 45 Let her wander, in a wearied sollicitude, after vngotten plenty. **1775** ASH, *Ungotten*,..not gotten, not gained. **1876** GEO. ELIOT *Dan. Der.* xxiii, To carry the map of an ungotten estate in your pocket is a poor sort of copyhold. **1883** GRESLEY *Gloss. Coal-m.* 197 Solid or ungotten coal forming the roof of a roadway.

**Ungo·vernable,** *a.* (and *sb.*). [UN-[1] 7 b.] That cannot be governed; uncontrollable.
**a.** Of persons (or animals).
**1673** [R. LEIGH] *Transp. Reh.* 112 Such ungovernable cattle as conscientious savages. **1680** DRYDEN *Ovid's Ep.* Pref. (ad fin.), So wild and ungovernable a poet cannot be translated literally. **1725** DE FOE *Voy. round World* (1840) 312 The fellows were so rude, so ungovernable and unbounded in their hunting after gold. **1768** BOSWELL *Corsica* ii. (ed. 2) 135 A lawless and ungovernable rabble of banditti. **1829** SCOTT *Anne of G.* xxv, The abbess..will have an ungovernable penitent under her charge. **1849** MACAULAY *Hist. Eng.* v. I. 592 These animals..became ungovernable as soon as they heard a gun fired. **1855** *Ibid.* xvii. IV. 101 The fiercest and most ungovernable part of the..population.
*sb.* **1810** BYRON *Let. to H. Drury* 3 May, I have been with ..governors and ungovernables.
**b.** Of temper, passion, etc.
**1676** HALE *Contempl.* I. 341 Men pretending to greatness of wit and learning, but in truth of haughty and ungovernable spirits. **1741** RICHARDSON *Pamela* II. 36 This strange wayward Heart of mine, that I never found so ungovernable and awkward before. **1781** GIBBON *Decl. & F.* xxxi. (1787) III. 251 The ungovernable spirit of a Barbarian host, impatient of peace or discipline. **1843** BETHUNE *Sc. Fireside Stor.* 100 He fell into a most ungovernable passion. **1876** T. HARDY *Ethelberta* (1890) 400 As if by an ungovernable impulse, Ethelberta broke into laughter also.
**c.** Of things.
**1773** COOK *Voy. S. Pole* II. ii. (1777) I. 205 Having unshipped the rudder, which rendered her ungovernable. **1839** FR. A. KEMBLE *Resid. in Georgia* (1863) 58 The stiff and ungovernable hair. **1852** HAWTHORNE *True Stories* iii. (1879) 22 That..ungovernable wonder the wind.
Hence **Ungo·vernableness.**
**1673** *Lady's Calling* I. ii. § 13 The ungovernableness of a woman. **1701** COLLIER *M. Aurel.* (1726) 96 You'd best murther your general, and add villany to your ungovernableness. **1751** ELIZA HEYWOOD *Betsy Thoughtless* I. 103 Lamenting the ungovernableness of youth. **1853** RUSKIN *Stones Ven.* II. App. 393 The ungovernableness of its colour (changing in the furnace). **1882** *Pall Mall G.* 20 June 2/1 As much an illustration of misgovernment as of our ungovernableness.

**Ungo·vernably,** *adv.* (UN-[1] 11; cf. prec.)
**1682** NORRIS *Hierocles* 134 Demeaning themselves ungovernably in all fortunes. **1764** GOLDSM. *Trav.* 314 Heavens! how unlike their Belgic sires of old! Rough, poor, content, ungovernably bold. **1810** CRABBE *Borough* iii. 42 Accuse me not that I..think the passions,..Strong as they are, ungovernably strong. **1855** MACAULAY *Hist. Eng.* xix. IV. 357 He had..been turned out of office in a way which had made him ungovernably ferocious. **1882** M. DODDS *Genesis* 195 A nature..whose passions raged ungovernably.

**Ungo·verned,** *ppl. a.*[1] [UN-[1] 8.] Not brought under government or control; uncontrolled: **a.** Of disposition, feelings, actions, etc.
**1591** SHAKS. *Two Gentl.* IV. i. 45 Some of vs are Gentlemen, Such as the fury of vngouern'd youth Thrust from the company of awfull men. **1622** MISSELDEN *Free Trade* 73 It now remaineth briefely to show the Too Loose Vse thereof, by Vngouerned Trade. **1667** MILTON *P. L.* XI. 514 When themselves they vilifi'd To serve ungovern'd appetite. **1712** STEELE *Spect.* No. 290 ¶ 1 The ungoverned Passions of such as are enamoured of each other. **1781** GIBBON *Decl. & F.* xviii. (1787) II. 95 Unable to withstand the ungoverned fury of the populace. **1839** FR. A. KEMBLE *Resid. in Georgia* (1863) 14 The furious and ungoverned execration which all reference to the possibility..draws down upon those who suggest it. **1846** MRS. A. MARSH *Father Darcy* II. x. 165 There was..something so violent and ungoverned in her temper and feelings.

**b.** Of persons, animals, or things.

**1594** SHAKS. *Rich. III*, IV. iv. 392 Thou.., Vngouern'd youth. **1606** CHAPMAN *Gentl. Usher* IV. iii, For mad men, By paynes vngouernd, have no sense of payne. **1628** in Foster *Eng. Factories India* (1909) III. 198 Our people for the most part being heedlesse, ungoverned, without discipline and order. **1719** DE FOE *Crusoe* I. (Globe) 348, I knew they were a Parcel of refractory, ungovern'd Villains. **1725** POPE *Odyss.* VIII. 199 Ill bear the brave a rude ungovern'd tongue. **1791** COWPER *Iliad* XXIII. 585 Thrown.. From his seat,.. his ungovern'd steeds have roam'd away. **1827** POLLOK *Course T.* V. 1052 The Tartar hordes, that roamed.., Ungoverned, southward to the wondrous Wall.

†**Ungo·verned,** *ppl. a.*[2] [UN-[2] 6 b.] Deprived of the position of governor. **1654** GAYTON *Pleas. Notes* IV. 230 Ungovern'd, Uncardinall'd, Unlorded, Outed of all his hopes.
**Ungo·verning,** *ppl. a.* (UN-[1] 10.) **1823** J. F. COOPER *Pioneers* xxxi, The ungoverning feeling that caused the violence of the youth had passed away.

**Ungow·n,** *v.* [UN-[2] 4.] **a.** *refl.* To deprive (oneself) of a gown. **b.** *trans.* = UNFROCK *v.*

**1789** COWPER *Let. to Lady Hesketh* 31 Jan., I had a thousand times rather be as poor as all poets are, than you should ungown yourself to prevent it. **1895** *Westm. Gaz.* 30 Jan. 5/3 She said he had gone out cursing her and then assisted in God's house, but she had no wish to ungown him.

**Ungow·ned,** *ppl. a.* (UN-[1] 8.)

**1611** SPEED *Hist. Gt. Brit.* IX. ix. § 59 To whose importunity the proud Legate would not condiscend, vnlesse all the Bishops.., vngowned and vnshod, should humbly craue absolution. **1721** AMHERST *Terræ Fil.* No. 50. 267 Sure of being mobb'd and insulted by whole crowds of the ungown'd and ungown'd rabble. **1827** POLLOK *Course T.* VIII. 69 Ungowned, unbeneficed, Uncorpulent.

**Ungra·ce.** (UN-[1] 12. Cf. WANGRACE[1].) **1430–40** LYDG. *Bochas* V. xxii. (1554) 137 b, Ungrace and youth made hym for to erre. **1871** JOWETT *Plato* I. 512 Ungrace and love are always at war with one another.

**Ungra·ced,** *ppl. a.*[1] (UN-[1] 8.)

**1595** DANIEL *Civ. Wars* IV. iv, Can England see the best that shee can boast, Ly thus vngract, undeckt, and almost lost? **1603** DRAYTON *Bar. Wars* IV. lxii, Merit goes vnregarded and vngrac'd. *a* **1618** SYLVESTER *Du Bartas* II. Ded. to Essex 14 Daign [thou] to grace my yet vngraced Muse. **1735** THOMSON *Liberty* I. 265 Unadorn'd your hills; Ungrac'd your lakes. **1769** CHURCHILL *Rosciad* 884 To epithets [he] allots emphatic state, Whilst principals, ungrac'd, like lacqueys wait. **1867** JEAN INGELOW *Story of Doom*, etc. 52 Her eyes..looked One moment in the ungraced lover's face. **1889** SKRINE *Mem. Thring* 42 The plain, ungraced, ungifted nature, without destiny or distinction.

**b.** Const. *by* or *with.*

**1768** *Woman of Honor* I. 60 A woman of honor though ungraced with a coronet in her family. **1781** COWPER *Table-T.* 378 Courage, ungrac'd by these, affronts the skies. **1862** H. AIDÉ *Carr of Carrlyon* II. 165, I see..all the deformity ungraced by anything save love.

**Ungra·ced,** *ppl. a.*[2] [UN-[2] 4, 8.] Deprived or stripped *of* something.

**1602** MARSTON *Antonio's Rev.* I. ii, Poore Maria must appeare ungrac't Of the bright fulgor of gloss'd majestie.

**Ungra·ceful,** *a.* (UN-[1] 7.)

**1667** MILTON *P. L.* VIII. 218 Nor are thy lips ungraceful, Sire of men, Nor tongue ineloquent. *a* **1732** T. BOSTON *Crook in Lot* (1805) 11 The cause of the uneasy and ungraceful walking of the lame. **1751** EARL ORRERY *Remarks Swift* (1752) 111 These real ornaments, like his hair, were thin and ungraceful. **1821** SCOTT *Kenilw.* xiv, His stature low, his limbs stout, his bearing ungraceful. **1849** MACAULAY *Hist. Eng.* iii. I. 356 The front, though ungraceful, was lofty and richly adorned. **1871** KENNEDY *Lat. Gram.* 467 In Versus Elegiacus a final trisyllable is rare and ungraceful.

**Ungra·cefully,** *adv.* (UN-[1] 11: cf. prec.)

**1661** COWLEY *Cromwell* Wks. (1669) 74 This Man was wanton and merry (unwittily and ungracefully merry) with our sufferings. **1711** STEELE *Spect.* No. 151 ¶ 7 He has been..ungracefully noisy at such a Time. **1748** CHESTERF. *Lett.* (1774) I. 299, I shall judge of your parts by your speaking gracefully or ungracefully. **1827** LYTTON *Pelham* xiv, In person, Vincent was short and ungracefully formed. **1868** BROWNING *Ring & Bk.* V. 914 Men say I battled ungracefully enough.

**Ungra·cefulness.** (UN-[1] 12; cf. prec.)

**1658** PHILLIPS, *Inconcinnity*, Ungracefulness. **1673** *Lady's Call.* I. i. ¶ 11 Whether it were from the ungracefulness of the thing,..I shall not determin. **1782** SIR J. REYNOLDS *Disc.* xi. (1825) 75/1 The child..appeared to observe only the ungracefulness of the persons represented. **1835** LYTTON *Rienzi* II. iii, Habituated to the ungracefulness of an unlettered pride. **1867** RUSKIN *Time & Tide* xix. § 115, I cannot help what taint of ungracefulness you..may feel that I incur in speaking..of myself.

**Ungra·cious,** *a.* [UN-[1] 7 and 5 b. Cf. (in sense 5) MDu. *ongracioos.*]

†**1.** Of persons: Devoid of spiritual grace; graceless, reprobate, wicked. *Obs.*

In ME. also const. with inf. (quot. 1362).

*a* **1225** *Ancr. R.* 368 Þauh clennesse..beoð ȝeouen of grace, vngraciuse stondeð þer to-ȝeines. *c* **1330** R. BRUNNE *Chron.* (1810) 103 Þris þat alle mot se þe light on Roberd toke, Vngracious man was he, þris he it forsoke. **1362** LANGL. *P. Pl.* A. x. 206 False folke..Vn-Gracios to gete loue or eni good elles. *c* **1420** LYDG. *Assembly of Gods* 754 He seyde he shuld haue..With Vyce to do a myghty strong batayll; Of vngracious gastes he bryngeth a long tayll. **1461** *Paston Lett.* II. 59 Ther is an ongracious felaschip of hem and a fals. **1523** LD. BERNERS *Froiss.* I. clxxxii. 217 These myscheuous peple chose hym that was moost vngracyoust of all other. *Ibid.*, Ther were a certayne of the same vngracyous peple bytwene Parys and Noyon. **1579** LODGE *Defence of Poetry* 19 The Angels haue sinned in heauen,..emong ye holy apostles vngratious Iudas. *a* **1638** MEDE *Wks.* (1672) 203 Let him..take heed of familiar and friendly converse with lewd, prophane and ungracious company. **1693** DRYDEN *Juvenal* x. 545 To the Gods alone Our future Offspring, and our Wives are known; Th'audacious Strumpet, and ungracious Son. **1771** FOOTE *Maid of B.* I, Well, you ungracious young dog, and what is become of the poor wench? **1793** BURKE *Conduct Minority* Wks. 1842 I. 623 The consequences are most logically..drawn from the premises..by that wicked and ungracious faction.

*transf.* **1820** SOUTHEY *Wesley* II. 256 At baptism, it was customary not to dip the right arm,..that he might strike a more deadly and ungracious blow therewith.

†**b.** Of actions, conduct, etc.: Characterized by gracelessness, or wickedness. *Obs.*

**1415** SIR T. GREY in *43rd Rep. Dep. Kpr. Rec.* 582 This vngracius and mescheffus gouernaunz. *c* **1485** *Digby Myst.* (1882) IV. 649 Cruell Iewes! what mad yow so bold To commyt þis Crym most vngraciose? *a* **1548** HALL *Chron.*, *Hen. VI*, 104 Inquisicion was made of the authors of this ungracious conjuracion. **1593** SHAKS. *Rich. II*, II. iii. 88 That word Grace, In an vngracious mouth, is but prophane. **1634** SIR T. HERBERT *Trav.* 70 Their sonnes vngracious life opposed their best contentments. **1683** D'URFEY in *Roxb. Ball.* (1888) V. 246 Let Perkin his ungracious error see, And Toney 'scape no more the Triple-Tree.

†**2.** Unfortunate, unlucky, unfavourable. *Obs.*

**1387** TREVISA *Higden* (Rolls) IV. 289 He was most ungracious in homeliche þinges, and happy in oþer þinges. **1398** — *Barth. De P. R.* XII. xxxvii. (Bodl. MS.), Amonge dyuynours here [*sc.* owls'] voice is vngracious. **1445–50** METHAM *Wks.* 152 The .xv. day ys noght spedeful to be-gynne ony werke vp-on, for yt ys ongracyus. **1515** *Scottish Field* 349 in *Chetham Misc.* (1856) II, They had gotten them a ground Most ungracious of other Upon the toppe of a high hill. *c* **1550** CHEKE *Let.* in *Athenæum* 28 Aug. (1909) 237/3 Until I be mended of my ungracious disease. **1600** HOLLAND *Livy* II. xlix. 78 Then set they forward on their journey,.. taking the ungracious and unluckie way,..untill at length they came to the river Cremera. *a* **1634** CHAPMAN *Rev. for Honour* I. i. 42 To give the noble weasand, Which has the steel defied, to th' hanging mercy Of the ungracious cord.

†**3.** Rude; unmannerly. *Obs.*

**1534** MORE *Comf. agst. Trib.* II. Wks. 1187/1 Her husband said also that it were lytle synne..to choppe of that vnhappye head of hers, that caryed suche an vngracious tong therin. *c* **1550** *Vertuous Scholehous* B ij b, Thou vsest vngracious wordes, cursest thy good husbande. **1601** SHAKS. *Twel. N.* IV. i. 51 Vngracious wretch, Fit for the Mountaines, ..Where manners nere were preach'd. **1606** — *Tr. & Cr.* I. i. 92 Peace you vngracious Clamors, peace rude sounds.

†**b.** Of low birth and manners. *Obs.*[−1]

**1584** LODGE *Alarum agst. Vsurers* (Hunter. Cl.) 23 Doeth the Weesell loue the Cockatrice? Or gentle borne, such as bee vngratious?

**4.** Not held in favour; unacceptable; disliked.

**1598** FLORIO, *Sgrato*, vngratious, nothing acceptable. **1671** CLARENDON *Hist. Reb.* XI. § 149 Prince Rupert, at that time, was generally very ungracious in England. **1761** HUME *Hist. Eng.* III. l. 95 Abbot's principle of liberty, and his opposition to Buckingham, had always rendered him very ungracious at court.

**b.** Unpleasant and unappreciated.

**1807** *Med. Jrnl.* XVII. 317 However ungracious the task is, I conceive it necessary to correct mistake. **1844** H. H. WILSON *Brit. India* II. 115 The ungracious duties inseparable from his office. **1884** *L'pool Mercury* 21 June 5/3 It is an ungracious duty to preach saving habits when times are bad.

**5.** Ungraceful, unattractive.

**1647** CLARENDON *Hist. Reb.* IV. § 122 His Person, and manner of Speaking, were ungratious enough. **1695** DRYDEN *Du Fresnoy's Art Painting* 23 Show no parts which are ungracious to the Sight, as all fore-shortnings usually are. **1762–71** H. WALPOLE *Vertue's Anecd. Paint.* (1786) I. 181 It was difficult to ascertain the period when one ungracious form jostled out another. **1775** T. SHERIDAN *Art Reading* I. 4 The best scholars often..disgraced beautiful composition by an ungracious delivery. **1807** SIR R. WILSON *Jrnl.* 7 May in *Life*, A religion so ungentlemanlike mean and ungracious that I would sooner be a pagan.

**6.** Lacking in condescension, courtesy, or affability: **a.** Of actions.

**1745** H. WALPOLE *Lett.* (1846) II. 78 An ungracious parallel between the mercenary views of..the regiment-factors,.. with the disinterested behaviour of my Lord Kildare, was drawn. **1780** *Mirror* No. 103, An overture of mine towards a reconciliation.., which met with a very ungracious reception. **1844** KINGLAKE *Eothen* xii, Whilst the amber is at your lips, there is nothing ungracious in your remaining silent. **1868** DICKENS *Lett.* (1880) II. 400 Refusal on my part would be too ungracious. **1890** *Lancet* 29 Nov. 1151 It would be ungracious to conclude without expressing my gratitude to our distinguished colleagues.

**b.** Of persons. Also *fig.* of a country.

**1752** YOUNG *Brothers* III. i, Nor in my brother let it pass for virtue, That, as he is, ungracious he would seem. **1819** SHELLEY *Cyclops* 117 Ah! no; they live in an ungracious land. **1849** MACAULAY *Hist. Eng.* v. I. 654 The meek and affable duchess turned out an ungracious and haughty queen. **1864** TENNYSON *Aylmer's Field* 247 Take it,..tho' his gift; For I am more ungracious ev'n than you, I care not for it either.

**Ungra·ciously,** *adv.* [UN-[1] 11; cf. prec.]

†**1.** With ill fortune; unfortunately, unhappily.

*c* **1330** R. BRUNNE *Chron.* (1810) 223 To Chestrefeld ilkon þei com vngraciously. Þe kyng did þam spie.., assailed þam in þe toun. **1387** TREVISA *Higden* (Rolls) VI. 193 Eiþer of hem hadde hymself so ungraciousliche, þat me woste nevere wheþer of hem hadde worse spede. **1533** FRITH *Judgem. upon Tracy* Wks. (1573) 81/2 And verely the iudgement of this cause came out of season, & euer vngraciously vnto our Canonistes. **1578** *Chr. Prayers* in *Priv. Prayers* (Parker Soc.) 454 We have learned of thee, how ungraciously [L. *infeliciter*] we be born of the first Adam.

†**b.** Injuriously, severely. *Obs.*

*c* **1450** HOLLAND *Howlat* 840 He cryid: 'Allace,..I am vngraciously gorrit, baith guttis and gall!' *c* **1520** SKELTON *Magnyf.* 2270 Some rybbys of the motton be so ranke That they wyll fyre one vngracyously in the flanke.

†**2.** Gracelessly; wickedly, wrongfully. *Obs.*

**1377** LANGL. *P. Pl.* B. XV. 129 Þis þat with gyle was geten, vngraciouslich is spended. *a* **1400** *Partonope* 6432 'Allas,' þoȝte he, 'howe vn-gracyously To my loue haue I gouerned me!' *c* **1520** SKELTON *Magnyf.* 2295 And so vngracyously thy dayes thou hast spent, That thou arte not worthy to loke God in the face. **1581** NOWELL & DAY in *Confer.* I. (1584) F ij, Hee hath most vngratiously broken the vowe made to God in Baptisme. **1645** GATAKER *God's Eye on Israel* 44 Tho they ungratiously and ungratefully..demand of him, wherein he had loved them.

**3.** Not with a good grace; not pleasantly or agreeably.

**1664** JER. TAYLOR *Diss. from Popery* ii. § 4. 99 That a wicked person..can ease and take off the punishment..by any external good work done ungraciously, is a piece of new Divinity. **1823** GRACE KENNEDY *Father Clement* i. 18 Permission was always so unwillingly and so ungraciously given, that it was a penance to ask it. **1849** MACAULAY *Hist. Eng.* ii. I. 227 The treasurer..was induced..to become, unwillingly indeed and ungraciously, an agent in those transactions. **1894** H. NISBET *Bush Girl's Rom.* 95 'I'll do that also,' grumbled Timothy, somewhat ungraciously.

**4.** Unbecomingly; with lack of manners, discourteously.

**1736** WARBURTON *Alliance* I. v. 51 They are,..I know not why, ungraciously ashamed of their Pedigree. **1791** BOSWELL *Johnson* (1904) II. 627 *note*, It were to be wished, that he..had not followed the example of Dr. Adam Smith in ungraciously attacking his venerable *Alma Mater*, Oxford. **1829** SCOTT *Anne of G.* xxix, His 'fleecy care' seemed actually to be under the influence of his music, instead of being ungraciously insensible to its melody.

**Ungra·ciousness.** [UN-[1] 12; cf. prec.]

†**1.** Gracelessness, reprobacy, wickedness. *Obs.*

**1509** BARCLAY *Shyp of Folys* (1570) 219 Yet trouble thou not by thy vngraciousnes Suche as are good and liue in righteousnes. **1571** GOLDING *Calvin on Ps.* Ep. Ded. 3 The verye welsprings of all error, hipocrisie, and ungraciousnes. **1612** BRINSLEY *Lud. Lit.* xxiv. (1627) 268 Who cannot indure to see sluggishnesse or idlenesse in any, much lesse any ungraciousnesse. **1658** T. WALL *Charact. Enemies Ch.* 34 Dost thou see a man,..in contempt of goodness, to be a graduate in ungraciousness. **1742** RICHARDSON *Pamela* IV. 353 Can those Persons be surpris'd at the Ungraciousness of their Children?

†**2.** Unfortunate or wretched state. *Obs.*[−1]

**1578** J. STOCKWOOD *Serm. 24 Aug.* 89 Complaintes of the vngraciousnesse and vnhappinesse of schollers.

**3.** Lack of courtesy or pleasantness.

**1836** KEBLE *Let.* in Liddon *Pusey* (1893) I. 428 It was a great piece of ungraciousness, my not telling you sooner how much I am obliged to you. **1864** TENNYSON *Aylmer's F.* 245 O pardon me, I seem to be ungraciousness itself. **1884** *Contemp. Rev.* July 150 To surrender the hand of a woman ..after a great deal of hesitation and ungraciousness.

**Ungrada·ted,** *ppl. a.* (UN-[1] 8.) **1859** RUSKIN *Two Paths* App. v. 270 Colour ungradated is wholly valueless.

**Ungra·ded,** *ppl. a.* [UN-[1] 8.]

**1.** Not laid out with or in proper gradients.

**1879** MISS BIRD *Lady's Life in Rocky Mount.* 219 Golden City..is ungraded, with here and there a piece of wooden sidewalk. **1885** *Atlantic Monthly* April 467/1 These roadways, ungraded, unsewered, and unpaved.

**2.** Not classified by grades.

**1884** *Pall Mall G.* 14 Aug. 11/1 Sales have been made of ungraded wheat..at 75 c.

†**Ungra·duate,** *v. Obs.* [UN-[2] 4.] *trans.* To degrade. **1633** T. ADAMS *Exp. 2 Peter* iii. 3 Alas, that man should degenerate and ungraduate himselfe to a childe.

**Ungra·duated,** *ppl. a.* [UN-[1] 8.]

**1.** That has not graduated; having no University degree.

**1783** H. WALPOLE *Let. to Earl Strafford* 12 Sept., I am glad at least that they have ungraduated assessors. **1802–12** BENTHAM *Ration. Judic. Evid.* (1827) V. 120 Your learned brethren, and their ungraduated fellow-practisers, the barristers of the present time. **1867** SEEBOHM *Oxford Reformers* 6 Another Oxford Student,..yet ungraduated in divinity, not even in deacon's orders.

**2.** Not graded or regularly arranged.

**1841** MYERS *Cath. Th.* III. § 4. 11 So ungraduated an estimate of Duty as this. **1899** *Allbutt's Syst. Med.* VII. 363 These [limbs] being..raised and set down in a brusque and characteristically ungraduated fashion.

**Ungra·ft,** *v.* (UN-[2] 3.) **1600** SURFLET *Countrie Farme* III. v. 432 You must also take graftes and graft them in other plum trees, .. and not to vngraft siences to transplant them. †**Ungra·ft,** obs. var. of next. **1598** SYLVESTER *Du Bartas* II. i. I. *Eden* 525 A plenteous Orchard planted rare With un-graft Trees.

**Ungra·fted,** *ppl. a.* (UN-[1] 8.)

**1657** AUSTEN *Fruit Trees* II. 175 Fruit trees that are ungrafted (wild trees). **1766** *Compl. Farmer* s.v. *Fence*, If they have proceeded from apple-kernels, they may remain ungrafted. **1795** *Phil. Trans.* LXXXV. 293 The bearing branches of some old ungrafted pear-trees. **1905** HAGGARD *Gard. Year* 235 An ungrafted bush of..the common stock.

†**Ungrai·ned,** *a. Obs.*[−1] [UN-[1] 9.] Seedless. *c* **1440** *Palladius on Husb.* III. 1121 Vngreyned grape in high iocundite Me may suppe of. †**Ungrai·ned,** *ppl. a.*[1] *Obs.* [UN-[1] 8.] Not dyed in grain. **1502** ARNOLDE *Chron.* (1811) 193 The Subside of Cloth as wel in greine as vngreyned. **Ungrai·ned,** *ppl. a.*[2] [UN-[2] 4, 8.] Not reduced to separate grains. **1884** E. F. KNIGHT *Cruise Falcon* I. xv. 266 When the maize arrived..we found it was ungrained. **Ungrai·ning,** *vbl. sb.* [UN-[2] 4, 8.] (See quot.) **1839** URE *Dict. Arts* 613 *Ungraining* [of gilt work] consists in rubbing the whole work with shave-grass, to remove any granular appearance.

†**Ungrai·th,** *a. Obs.* [UN-[1] 7. Cf. ON. *úgreiðr* (Norw. *ugreid*).] **a.** Unready. **b.** Not straightforward; perverse.

*a* **1310** in Wright *Lyric P.* xxxvi. 99 Vol of merci thou art ay, al ungreythe icham to the to go. *a* **1400** *Pistill of Susan* 293 Vmbeloke ȝou, lordes; suche lawes ben leiþ;..Aȝein to þe ȝild-halle, ȝe gomes vngreiþ.

**Ungrai·thed,** *ppl. a. Obs.* exc. *dial.* (Un-1 8.) *c* **1290** *Beket* 2200 in *S. Eng. Leg.* I. 169 Þat bodi..Al on-greiþet [*v.r.* ungreithed] to leggen it in [the grave] heo heiȝeden bliue. **1876** *Whitby Gloss.* 206/1 *Ungraith'd*, not yet furnished or equipped; unadorned.

† **Ungrai·thly,** *adv. Obs.* Also 4 vngretli, 5 vngraidly. [Un-1 11.] Badly, improperly. *a* **1300** *Cursor M.* 24504 On him mi hefd i scock, and said. Vngretli, leif sun, er þou graid! *c* **1400** *Destr. Troy* 7615 As folis, þat folily hade..Myche gold & goodes vngraidly dispendit. *c* **1460** *Towneley Myst.* x. 341, I that thus haue vngrathly gone, And vntruly taken apon Mary, that dere darlyng. *Ibid.* xxvii. 100.

**Ungra·mmared,** *a.* (Un-1 9.) **1837** Fr. A. Kemble *Rec. Later Life* (1882) I. 119 Uncultivated men, unlettered, and ungrammared.

**Ungramma·tic,** *a.* [Un-1 7.] = next. **1806** Anna Seward *Lett.* (1811) VI. 258 All modes of phraseology within the limits of the immodest, the disgusting, and the ungrammatic. **1850** Browning *Christmas Eve* xxii. 30 Fourthly, the English is ungrammatic.

**Ungramma·tical,** *a.* [Un-1 7 and 5 b.]

**1. a.** Not in accordance with the rules of grammar. **1654** Jer. Taylor *Real Pres.* § 5. 88 [To] expound it in a sense which suffers a violence and a most unnatural, ungrammatical torture. **1679** Dryden *Troil. & Cress.* Pref. ¶ 1 Of those [words] which we understand, some are ungrammatical, others coarse. **1749** Chesterf. *Let.* 5 Dec., His diction was not only inelegant, but frequently ungrammatical, always vulgar. **1821** Lamb *Elia* I. *Mrs. Battle on Whist*, She called it an ungrammatical game. **1848** Thackeray *Van. Fair* xxxii, French..of a very ungrammatical sort. **1883** *Law Rep.* 11 Q. B. Div. 614 A defining section, confused and ungrammatical.

**b.** Not observing the rules of grammar. **1859** *Habits of Gd. Society* iii. 155, I am wondering whether everybody arranges his wardrobe as our ungrammatical nurses used to do ours. **1871** Earle *Philol. Eng. Tongue* 412 So they (the ungrammatical people) made a plural *this-e*.

**2.** At variance with correct rule or method. **1851** Ruskin *Mod. Paint.* I. ii. ii. ii. § 12 Some really ungrammatical and false picture of the old masters. **1903** G. Baldwin Brown *Arts Early Eng.* II. viii. 327 The enrichment of the wall surfaces..is..in parts quite ungrammatical.

Hence **Ungramma·ticalness.** **1698** *Christ Exalted* § xi. 9 Omitting several Blunders of Ungrammaticalness. **1803** *Gentl. Mag.* LXXIII. i. 145 To vindicate the dialect of London..from the imputation of vulgarisms and ungrammaticalness.

**Ungramma·tically,** *adv.* (Un-1 11.) **1727** Boyer *Dict. Royal* ii. **1737** *Gentl. Mag.* VII. 13/2 As A. P. has very weakly, as well as unliterally and ungrammatically translated. **1763** Bp. Lowth *Introd. Eng. Gram.* 32 *note*, Some Writers have used *Ye*, as the Objective Case.., very improperly and ungrammatically. **1860** Huxley in *Life* (1900) I. 214 Some of the..articles being absolutely ungrammatically written.

**Ungra·ntable,** *a.* (Un-1 7 b.) **1784** R. Bage *Barham Downs* II. 258 'You shall be allowed to give and grant it, out of your own free will.'..'Ungrantable,' says Sir George. **1794** Ld. Macartney *Wks.* (1807) II. 326 A court artifice to elude an ungrantable demand.

**Ungra·nted,** *ppl. a.* (Un-1 8.) **1570** Levins *Manip.* 50 Vngranted, *inconcessus*. **1660** Bonde *Scut. Reg., Hist. Phaeton* 12 He wisht..His suites ungranted. **1697** Dryden *Æneis* ix. 377 This only from your goodness let me gain; (And, this ungranted, all rewards are vain). **1828** P. Cunningham *N. S. Wales* (ed. 3) II. 333 The local administration..having the sole disposal of the ungranted lands. **1870** Morris *Earthly Par.* IV. iv. 385 He some day might..turn away from that ungranted kiss.

**Ungra·pple,** *v.* (Un-2 4 b.) **1611** Cotgr., *Desagrafer*, to vnclaspe, vngraple, vnhaspe. *a* **1642** Sir W. Monson *Naval Tracts* ii. (1704) 246/2 Our Barks were forc'd to ungraple and fall off. **1653** Urquhart *Rabelais* i. xlii. 188 The Monk going about to ungrapple his vizor, let go his hold of the bridle.

Hence **Ungra·ppler.** **1891** C. E. Norton tr. *Dante, Hell* xxii. 119 The heat was a sudden ungrappler.

**Ungra·sp,** *v.* (Un-2 3.) **1621** Bp. Mountagu *Diatribæ* 328 He might haue knowne..yt Popes vse neuer to vngraspe what they haue griped. *a* **1784** C. Dunster in Chambers *Illustr. Worcester* (1820) 555 Have I not seen at thy command, Avarice herself ungrasp her hand?

**Ungra·spable,** *a.* (Un-1 7 b.) **1741** Richardson *Pamela* I. Introd. p. xxvi, A beautiful Girl of Sixteen, who..had not, yet, reach'd ungraspable Roundness. **1822** Pollok in D. Pollok *Life* (1843) 129 The ungraspable spectres of the night. **1853** Cdl. Wiseman *Ess.* II. 305 Of all slippery phrases in controversy, a metaphorical one is the most ungraspable. **1880** 'Mark Twain' *Tramp Abroad* I. 168 How ungraspable is the fact that real men ever did fight in real armour.

**Ungra·sped,** *ppl. a.* (Un-1 8.) **1743** Young *Nt. Th.* iv. 241 Its value vast, ungraspt by minds create. **1897** Mather *Ruskin* (ed. 5) p. xvii, Even though the truth burdening the style remains vague and is ungrasped by the reader. **Ungra·sping,** *ppl. a.* (Un-1 10.) **1855** Faber *Growth in Holiness* viii. 128 Humility..makes us unanxious, ungrasping,..and calm.

† **Ungra·te,** *a.* and *sb. Obs.* [Un-1 7 and 5 b.]

**1.** Unpleasant, disagreeable; = Ingrate *a.* 1. **1550** Crowley *Inform. & Petit.* 469 To passe ouer the days of theyr youth in vngrate seruitude. **1646** R. Baillie *Lett.* (Bann. Cl.) II. 364 It's a marvell to me if these men should allwayes prosper, their wayes are so impious, unjust, ungrate, and every way hatefull. **1656** *Artif. Handsom.* 46 Impertinent and ungrate must that superstition be.

**2.** Ungrateful; = Ingrate *a.* 3. (In later use *Sc.*) *a* **1548** Hall *Chron., Hen. VII*, 12 Kyng Henry..thought it..necessary..to forgett the vngrate offence agaynst the duke of Briteyne commytted. *Ibid.* 26 b, So vngrate people were they to their souereigne lorde. **1561** T. Hoby tr. *Castiglione's Courtyer* i. (1577) C vi, To discouer the deceytes of an ungrate woman, who..neuer agreeth hir tong wyth hyr minde. **1606** Marston *Sophonisba* ii. ii, But, Carthage, fie! It cannot be ungrate, faithlesse through feare. **1697** G. Keith *2nd Narr. Proc. Turner's Hall* 6 Judge..whether they be not a very ungrate People. **1720** A. Petrie *Rules Good Deportm.* (1877) 24 It is rude and ungrate to leave a House..without your taking Leave of the Master and Mistress. **1767** Meston *Poems* 196 Ye Muses, who were never yet ungrate, When you your benefactors deed relate.

**b.** *sb.* An ungrateful person; an ingrate. *c* **1400** *Destr. Troy* 13944 Þan he..told hym full tyte, þat Telagon he was, His son,..Þat þou gate on þi gamyn, as vngrate felle. **1596** Dalrymple tr. *Leslie's Hist. Scot.* I. 122 A murthirer, a dum, or vngrate to his parents. **1689** *Gt. Bastard, Protector of Little One* 5 It was indeed the true Motive that induc'd this Vngrate to ruin them. **1720–1** *Lett. fr. Mist's Jrnl.* (1722) II. 118 The Sweetness of my Lips, which that Ungrate too oft has praised.

**Ungra·teful,** *a.* [Un-1 7 and 5 b.]

**1.** Not feeling or displaying gratitude. **1553** Brende *Q. Curtius* x. 216 The Macedons..confessyng them selues bothe wicked and vngrateful for depriuynge him of anye name wherof he was worthye. **1587** *Mirr. for Mag., Albanact* lxii, If you ungratefull mindes doe beare, What meaneth death to let mee linger here. **1621** in Foster *Eng. Factories Ind.* (1906) I. 354 Such base ungratfull slaves they bee. **1697** Dryden *Æneis* iv. 529 All, symptoms of a base ungrateful mind, So foul, that which is worse, 'tis hard to find. **1740** Richardson *Pamela* II. 356 If it was, I must be the ungratefullest Person in the World, because I am the most obliged Person in it. **1813** Scott *Rokeby* iv. xx, Ungrateful to God's clemency, That spared me penitential time. **1875** Jowett *Plato* (ed. 2) III. 206 That I am ungrateful I wholly deny.

*absol.* **1675** Dryden *Aurengz.* iv. (1676) 64 Th' ungrateful does a more ungrateful find. **1690** *The Great Scanderbeg* 82 The Ungrateful despises my flame with a cruel obstinacy. **1829** Lytton *Devereux* i. i, He could not persuade his lips to repeat a sarcasm hurting even the dead or the ungrateful.

*spec.* **1785** Grose *Dict. Vulgar T.*, *Ungrateful man*, a parson, who at least once a week abuses his best benefactor, i. e. the devil.

**b.** Of actions, etc.: Displaying lack of gratitude. *a* **1586** Sidney *Arcadia* iii. iv, By ungratefull scorning the ornaments of Nature, am I now piping in a shadow? **1641** Prynne *Antipathie* 9 O perfidious, ungratefull Councell and swasion of this Prelate. **1700** Prior *Carm. Sec.* xxxv, Nor let the Muses, with ungrateful Pride, The Sources of their Treasure hide. **1799** *Med. Jrnl.* I. 220 Asserting, that contemporary writers received his works with an ungrateful silence. **1825** Scott *Betrothed* xix, These sentiments..I have combated..as being..ungrateful to you.

**c.** *transf.* Of soil, trees, etc.: Not responding to cultivation. **1681** Dryden *Abs. & Achit.* i. 12 A soil ungrateful to the Tiller's care. **1732** Pope *Ess. Man* ii. 181 As fruits, ungrateful to the planter's care, On savage stocks inserted, learn to bear. **1788** Gibbon *Decl. & F.* l. V. 178 Their ungrateful soil refused the labours of agriculture. **1842** Borrow *Bible in Spain* xxiii, The land is ungrateful and barren. **1864** Trevelyan *Compet. Wallah* (1866) 288 The labourers in this ungrateful vineyard.

**2.** Unpleasant, disagreeable, distasteful. **1596** Davies *Orchestra* 19 [To] tell..How she illudes.. Th'vngratefull loue which other Lords began. **1641** *Vind. Smectymnuus* iii. 53 It is in his power to save himselfe and us this ungrateful labour. **1691** Hartcliffe *Virtues* 178 For a Man to praise or dispraise himself is ungrateful, and quickly cloyes the hearer. **1753** Hanway *Trav.* (1762) v. lxxi. I. 320 Monopolies..are generally ungrateful to the people of a free state. **1776** Gibbon *Decl. & F.* xii. I. 325 The ungrateful rumour reached his ears. **1836** J. Gilbert *Chr. Atonem.* ix. (1852) 281 Even the kindness.., though not ungrateful, will not excite the proper working of esteem.

**b.** Of taste or smell, or of things in respect of these. **1597** Gerarde *Herbal* i. xxviii. 34 These roots haue a strong..smell, and somewhat an vngratefull taste. **1612** Woodall *Surg. Mate* Wks. (1653) 307 Laudanum is best to be taken in a Pill, because of his ungrateful tast. **1663** Bp. Patrick *Parab. Pilgr.* xxviii, Good wine which..is rendred ..acid and ungrateful to our palate. *a* **1682** Sir T. Browne *Tracts* (1683) 12 That which we now have is of an ungratefull odour. **1725** Sloane *Jamaica* II. 17 The Nuts..are then tosted,..and made into an ungrateful drink. **1753** Hanway *Trav.* v. lx. (1762) I. 279 The reeds through which we passed sent forth an ungrateful stench. **1846** Mrs. A. Marsh *Father Darcy* II. ii. 69 There he sat—endeavouring to touch the ungrateful food. **1897** *Allbutt's Syst. Med.* III. 465 By which certain foods are recognised, consciously or not, as grateful or ungrateful.

**c.** Of sounds. **1659** O. Walker *Instruct. Oratory* 24 Too many Consonants or Vowells comming together are to be avoided, as causing an ungrateful sound. **1690** C. Nesse *O. & N. Test.* I. 16 Some sounds..are very harsh and ungrateful. **1759** Goldsm. *Polite Learn.* ii, It was the poet who harmonized the ungrateful accents of his native dialect. **1850** Tennyson *In Mem.* xxxviii. 12 Then are these songs I sing of thee Not all ungrateful to thine ear.

**Ungra·tefully,** *adv.* [Un-1 11 and 5 b.]

**1.** Harshly, unpleasantly, disagreeably. **1581** Sidney *Apol. Poetrie* (Arb.) 42 Telling of a man, whose belouęd Lambe was vngratefullie taken from his bosome. **1693** Dryden *Juvenal* (1697) p. lxxxi, It tickles aukwardly with a kind of pain;..we are pleas'd ungratefully, and, if I may say so, against our liking. **1698** Hearne *Duct. Hist.* (1714) I. 385 Cæsar..returned to Rome and triumphed, though a little ungratefully to some of Pompey's friends. **1712** Arbuthnot *John Bull* ii. v, The musick..sounded more ungratefully in her ears than the noise of a screech-owl.

†**2.** Without due return or gratitude. *Obs.*—1 **1593** Nashe *Christ's T.* P 1 b, Vngratefully hath God giuen thee long peace and plenty, since..thy peace and plentie hath begotte more sinnes then warre euer hearde of.

**3.** With lack of gratitude. *a* **1625** Fletcher *Hum. Lieutenant* iii. vi, I am not greedy of your lives and fortunes, Nor do I gape ungratefully to swallow ye. **1692** Washington tr. *Milton's Def. Pop.* M.'s Wks. 1738 I. 537 Yet these very men did a great part of the People ungratefully desert in the midst of their undertaking. **1737** in *10th Rep. Hist. MSS. Comm.* App. I. 493 A Person in whom your Majesty has placed a Trust and who has so Ungratefully abused that Trust. **1798** Pennant *Hindoostan* II. 47 He continued in employ till 1754, when he was ungratefully superseded. **1856** *N. Brit. Rev.* XXVI. 195 Having been coldly and (as he thought) ungratefully treated by the Whig leaders.

**Ungra·tefulness.** [Un-1 12 and 5 b.]

**1.** = Ingratitude 1. **1581** Sidney *Apol. Poetrie* (Arb.) 20 They goe very neer to vngratfulnes, to seek to deface that which..hath been the first light-giuer to ignorance. **1599** Sandys *Europæ Spec.* (1632) 247 Those graces and blessings, which vngratefulnesse would not acknowledge. **1631** Gouge *God's Arrows* i. § 20. 27 O the ungratefulnesse of the wicked in the world! **1734** Chalkley *Jrnl.* Wks. (1766) 271 A Youth..went out hastily..as I was showing the Ungratefulness of the first [*sc.* disobedience], much more of the last. **1896** *Cincinnati* (Ohio) *Sunday Sch. Jrnl.* Apr. 237/1 The ungratefulness of people to those who have helped them.

**2.** Unpleasantness; disagreeableness. *rare.* *a* **1680** Glanvill in *Disc., Serm., & Rem.* (1681) 338 He (considering the ungratefulness of the Message..) diverts another way, and flees towards Tarshish. *a* **1688** Cudworth *Immut. Mor.* (1731) 54 The Gratefulness and Ungratefulness of Tastes and Smells.

† **Ungra·tely,** *adv. Obs.* [Un-1 11 and 5 b.] Ungratefully. **1548** Elyot, *Ingratè*, vngrately, vnthankefully. *c* **1614** Sir W. Mure *Dido & Æneas* ii. 412 A woman..My mariage most vngrately hath disdain'd.

**Ungra·tified,** *ppl. a.* (Un-1 8.) **1613** Fletcher, etc. *Hon. Man's Fort.* i. i, By the justice now Of thine own rule,..I should turn thee away ungratified For all thy former kindness. **1728** Eliza Heywood tr. *Mme. de Gomez's Belle A.* (1732) II. 17 That Request being refused, he made his escape privately, resolving that the Queen should not be long ungratified. **1779** Johnson *L. P., Waller* Wks. II. 269 The poem of Davis, which..seldom leaves the ear ungratified. **1821** Byron *Sardanap.* i. ii. 582 Leaving thy subjects' eyes ungratified. **1865** Trevelyan *Cawnpore* 67 No whim ungratified, every propensity cherished and pampered. **1894** H. Nisbet *Bush Girl's Rom.* 263 He had not a wish left ungratified.

**Ungra·tifying,** *ppl. a.* (Un-1 10.) **1697** Collier *Ess. Mor. Subj.* iii. (1703) 115 Envy is of all others the most ungratifying and disconsolate passion. **1885** *Law Times* 3 Jan. 172/2 It will not be ungratifying to have the statute more authoritatively expounded.

† **Ungra·titude.** *Obs.* [Un-1 12 and 5 b.] Ingratitude; ungratefulness. *a* **1548** Hall *Chron., Edw. IV*, 249 b, That the sequele thereof, maie rather turne..to an vngratitude, than to a rewarde. *Ibid., Rich. III*, 34 b, All these vngratitudes and vndeserued vnkindnes I..suffered pacientelie. **1621** Lady M. Wroth *Urania* 29, I..neuer could be wonne to thinke of harming him, whose vngratitude I beleeu'd sufficiently would one day burden him. **1685** J. Fraser *Let.* in *Academy* 21 Oct. (1876) 408/2 The Princess..giving a Reprimand for their ungratitud, dismissed them.

† **Ungra·ve,** *a. Obs.* (Un-1 7.) **1609** J. Davies (Heref.) *Holy Roode* Wks. (Grosart) I. 7/1 Now thinke..thou seest those hounds of hell,..With vngraue gate, to runne doe him compell. **1642** in Clarendon *Hist. Reb.* v. § 276 Sure,..the Penner of that Declaration inserted that ungrave and insolent expression,..without the consent..of both Houses. *a* **1674** Clarendon *Surv. Leviath.* 73 A very bold and ungrave wresting of Scripture.

**Ungra·ve,** *v.* [Un-2 5.] *trans.* To take out of the grave; to disinter. **1664** J. Wilson *Commenius* ii. i, I scorn to raze Thy monument, or to ungrave thy dust. **1788** Mickle *Eskdale Braes* ix, As the spectres, ungrav'd, glide along. **1849** Rock *Ch. of Fathers* II. vi. 179 *note*, The unknown bishop whose body was as late as A. D. 1827, ungraved in Durham cathedral. **1866** R. Morris *Ayenb.* 61 *margin*, The beast Hyane, who ungraves dead men's bodies and eats them.

**Ungra·ved,** *ppl. a.* [Un-1 8.] Unburied. *a* **1547** Surrey *Æneid* iv. 832 His realme, nor life desired may he brooke; But fall before his time, ungraved amid the sandes. **1635** Pagitt *Christianogr.* i. 131 After his death..he was ungraved and kept above ground 5 yeares. **Ungra·velled,** *ppl. a.* (Un-1 8.) **1611** W. Austin *Paneg. Verses* 3 in Coryat *Crudities*, To him that farre and neere hath travaild, Gone & retourned, his wit ungraveld. **1616** [see Undashed *ppl. a.* 1]. **Ungra·velly,** *a.* (Un-1 7.) **1655** Moufet & Bennet *Health's Improv.* 213 The most clear, transparent, thin-skind, ungravelly [apples].

**Ungra·vely,** *adv.* (Un-1 11.) **1607** Shaks. *Cor.* ii. iii. 233 His present portance, Which most gibingly, vngrauely, he did fashion After the ineuterate Hate he beares you. **1698** *Christ Exalted* Ep. A 4 The Doctor, whom you have very ungravely treated, as an Heterodox wild Monster.

**Ungra·ven,** *ppl. a.* Also 4 vngraue. [Un-1 8 b. Cf. (M)Du. *ongegraven* unburied, undug.]

**1.** Not engraved or carved. **1377** Langl. *P. Pl.* B. iv. 130 That..Rome-renneres [take].. no siluer ouer see,..Noyther graue ne vngraue. **1611** Florio, *Inscolpito*, vncarued, vngrauen. **1651** Stanley *Poems* 169 The oaks that most obdurate are Shall..by themselves ungraven wear My verse upon their leaves and rind. **1855** M. Arnold *Balder Dead* ii. 165 Young men who died Too soon for fame, with white ungraven shields.

† **2.** Unburied, uninterred. *Obs.* *c* **1400** *Laud Troy Bk.* 11104 Kyng Priamus Thought.. Where he myght saue Ector his sone Vngrauen with-oute corrupcione. *c* **1425** Wyntoun *Cron.* v. x. 2590 Mony a day Vngraiffin [*v.r.* vngrawyn] outwith þe erd he lay.

**Ungrayhair,** *v.* (Un-2 4.) **1639** Fuller *Holy War* iii. xxix. 160 Whilest his old wife plucked out his black hairs.., his young one ungray-haired him. **Ungra·ze,** *v.* [Un-2 4.] *trans.* To render unfit for grazing. **1661** Feltham *Resolves* (ed. 8) II. xlvi. 273 No crowded throngs need fill our Law-Tribunals; nor armed Troops ungraze our fruitful fields. **Ungrea·se,** *v.* (Un-2 4.) **1611** Cotgr., *Desgraisser*, to vnfatten; vngrease. **1799** G. Smith *Laboratory* I. 436 To ungrease Wine in less than twenty-four hours.

**Ungrea·sed,** *ppl. a.* (Un-1 8.)

*c* **1440** *Jacob's Well* 260 As a carte-qweel, drye & vngrecyd, cryeth lowdest of oþere qwelys. **1663** Boyle *Usef. Exp. Nat. Philos.* II. v. xiv. 250 The grating of an ungreased cartwheele upon the axle-tree. **1668** Shadwell *Sullen Lovers* IV, What a vile noise he makes, worse than..a coach-wheel ungreas'd. **1783** Latham *Gen. Syn.* IV. 687 Having a creaking harsh kind of note, somewhat like..an ungreased axle-tree. *a* **1894** Stevenson *Lay Morals*, etc. (1911) 247 A creaking of ungreased axles had been heard.

**Ungrea·sing,** *vbl. sb.* (Un-2 4, 8.) **1883** R. Haldane *Workshop Receipts* Ser. II. 321/1 The cleansing or separation of the peritoneal membrane, a portion only of which has been removed by the 'ungreasing' at the slaughter-house.

† **Ungrea·t,** *a. Obs.* In 6 *Sc.* **ongrit.** [Un-1 7.] Small.

**1549** *Compl. Scotl.* xiv. 113 And als it vas as ongrit blythnes to sa mony..tounis quhilkis hed randrit them..to Annibal.

**Un-Gre·cian,** *a.* (Un-1 7.) **1847** Leitch tr. *C. O. Müller's Anc. Art* § 206. 171 The reliefs on sarcophagi..did not come into general use until this period, through the influence of un-Grecian ideas. **1859** E. Masson *Winer's Gram. N. T. Diction* I. Introd. 14 Peculiarities manifestly derived from an un-Grecian source.

**Ungree·able,** *a. Obs.* exc. *dial.* [Un-1 7 b.] Disagreeable.

**1550** *Chaucer's Boethius* I. met. i. 220 b, Myne vnpytous lyfe draweth alonge vngreable dwellinges [L. *ingratas moras*]. **1580** E. Knight *Trial Truth* 4 b, This doctrine is so vngreeable vnto the children of pride, as [etc.]. **1886** Cunliffe *Rochdale Gloss.* 94 *Ungreeable*, disagreeable.

† **Ungree·ing,** *ppl. a. Obs.* [Un-1 10.] Unfitting. **1560** J. Heywood *Seneca's Thyestes* Translatour to Bk., Though thou slender volume be, Vngreeyng gyfte for state of honour guest.

**Un-Gree·k,** *sb.* and *a.* [Un-1 12 and 7. Cf. (in sense 1) Du. *Ongriek*, G. *Ungrieche* (Luther), older Da. *Ugræke*.]

**A.** *sb.* One who is not a Greek. *rare.*

**1535** Coverdale *Rom.* i. 14, I am detter both to the Grekes, and to the vngrekes.

**B.** *adj.* Not Greek in character; not in accordance with Greek ideas or habits.

**1846** Keightley *Notes Virg.* 332 Supplying..a totally un-Latin *secundum*, in Greek a κατά, which is for the most part quite as un-Greek. **1853** Whewell *Grotius* III. 221 The slaughter of the Thebans, who had surrendered, was an un-Greek massacre. **1871** Jowett *Plato* II. 38 One of the most remarkable conceptions of the Republic [of Plato], because un-Greek in character.

**Ungree·n,** *a.* (Un-1 7: cf. OE. *ungréne*, Du. *ongroen*, MHG. *ungrüene*.) *c* **1400** *Rom. Rose* 4749 May devoide of al delite With seer braunches, blossoms vngrene. **1838** Mrs. E. B. Browning *Seraphim* II. 32, I see her vales, ungreen Where steps of man have been! **Ungree·nable,** *a.* (Un-1 7 b.) **1882** [see Greenable *a.*].

**Ungree·ted,** *ppl. a.* (Un-1 8. Cf. OE. *ungegrét*, MDu. *ongegroetet*, MHG. *ungegrüezet*.)

**1611** Florio, *Insalutato*, vnsaluted, vngreeted. **1648** Hexham II, *Ongegroetet*, Vnsaluted, or Vngreeted. *a* **1849** Poe *Angel of Odd* Wks. 1864 IV. 285 My premeditated rudeness in passing her by ungreeted. **1877** Talmage *Serm.* 322 This Young Man was not ungreeted when he came back.

**Ungree·ting,** *ppl. a.* (Un-1 10.) **1855** M. Arnold *Haworth Churchyard* 142 Faces ungreeting and cold. **Ungrega·rious,** *a.* (Un-1 7.) **1829** Southey in *Corr. w. C. Bowles* (1881) 173 Which would infallibly have made me a Beguine, ..if I was not a most ungregarious animal. **1884** Augusta Wilson *Vashti* xi, They appeared as gravely silent and ungregarious as Sphinxes.

† **Ungrete**: see Un-1 3.

**Ungretli**, obs. var. Ungraithly *adv.*

† **Ungrie·ffulness.** *Obs.*—1 (Un-1 12.) **1553** Grimalde *Cicero's Offices* III. (1558) 118 As they who measure thyngs meete to bee desired eyther by pleasure or ungrieffulnes. **Ungrie·ve,** *v.* (Un-2 4 b.) **1589** Warner *Alb. Eng.* VI. xxix. 129 For you were booteles then to gesse how to vngreeue my smart. **Ungrie·ved,** *ppl. a.* (Un-1 8.) **1676** Hobbes *Iliad* I. 397 Ay me, (said Thetis) would you could here rest Unhurt, ungriev'd. **1837** Verlander *Vestal*, etc. 74 And joy'st thou in the life unliv'd?..the griefs ungriev'd? **Ungrie·ving,** *ppl. a.* (Un-1 10.) **1837** Praed *Drachenfels* 142 If the blinded tribes..Could but have caught one bright brief glance Of that ungrieving countenance.

† **Ungrie·ving,** *pres. pple. Sc. Obs.* [Un-1 5 d.] Without grieving, distressing, or injuring.

*c* **1375** *Sc. Leg. Saints* xxxiii. (*George*) 517 Vngrewand hyme mare þan he Had dronkyne pyment & clarre. **1456** Sir G. Haye *Law Arms* (S.T.S.) 162 How may than a man do till othir sik dissait, ungrevand God?

† **Ungri·ght,** *ppl. a. Obs.* [Un-1 8 b: see Grutch *v.*] Ungrudgingly; readily.

*c* **1400** *Destr. Troy* 8868 Priam..grauntid vngright with a good chere. *a* **1400–50** *Bk. Curtasye* 751 in *Babees Bk.*, Þo Coke assayes þe mete vngryȝt.

**Ungri·ndable,** *a.* (Un-1 7 b.) **1840** Carlyle in A. H. Stirling *Life Stirling* (1912) iii. 50 Windmills..to grind.. sunbeams, or some other entirely ungrindable substance. † **Ungrith**: see Un-1 3. **Ungri·zzled,** *ppl. a.* (Un-1 8.) **1858** Motley *Corr.* (1889) I. 311 Having thick, brown, ungrizzled hair and beard. **Ungroa·ning,** *ppl. a.* (Un-1 10.) **1821** Byron *Sardanap.* I. ii. 265 Enough For me, if I can.. glide Ungroaning to the tomb. **Ungroo·med,** *ppl. a.* (Un-1 8.) **1864** Sala in *Daily Tel.* 26 Feb., Their horses as ungroomed, and their hair as unkempt as usual. **Ungro·pable,** *a.* (Un-1 7 b.) **1558** Phaer *Æneid* VI. R iij b, Through his hands he flies Like wind vngropable, or dreames.

**Ungrou·nd,** *ppl. a.* [Un-1 8 b.]

**1.** Not ground in a mill; not crushed or reduced to powder.

**1488** *Acta Dom. Conc.* (1839) 98/2 Half a boll of malt vngrond, price xs. **1623** Fletcher & Rowley *Maid in Mill* v. ii, Shall the sayls of my love stand still? Shall the grists of my hopes be unground? **1631** Gouge *God's Arrows* II. § 24. 163 Some of them did eate the corne as it was unground. **1722** De Foe *Col. Jack* (1840) 300 A hundred sacks of unground malt. **1760** *Ann. Reg.*, *Chron.* 192/2 A duty of 1d. ½ ..shall be paid on every bushel of malt, whether ground or unground, which [etc.]. **1805** Dickson *Pract. Agric.* I. 211 The trials which Dr. Hunter made with ground and unground bones. **1882** *U. S. Rep. Prec. Met.* 603 The mill is then stopped, [and] the water drained off from the unground sand and mercury.

**2.** Not sharpened, smoothed, or worn down by grinding.

**1611** Cotgr. s.v. *Morfil*, The edge side of a new and vnground knife. **1793** *Phil. Trans.* LXXXIII. 92 The swinging level.., fixed to the tube of the telescope,..is unground. **1865** Tylor *Early Hist. Man.* viii. 193 The finding of hundreds of unground implements. **1893** *Athenæum* 25 Mar. 382/2 The palæolithic or unground stage of the implement-maker's art.

**Ungrou·ndable,** *a.*; **-ably,** *adv.* (Un-1 7 b, 11.) **1395** Purvey *Remonstr.* (1851) 84 The noveltees of this Innocent, ..that ben ungroundable and unlicli to be sothe. *c* **1449** Pecock *Repr.* I. xviii. 104 Rather he schal be schamed that he hath it bifore so vngroundabili holde, and withoute suficient evidence thereto.

**Ungrou·nded,** *ppl. a.* [Un-1 8. Cf. MDu. *ongegrondet*, *-gront* (Du. *-grond*), G. *ungegründet*, Da. *ugrundet*, Sw. *ogrundad*.]

**1.** Not based or established *in* something.

*c* **1380** Wyclif *Wks.* (1880) 38 Euyle lawis vngroundid in holy writt & reson. *c* **1380** — *Sel. Wks.* III. 351 Þus love ungroundid in God..mut nedis faile. **1426** Audelay *Poems* (Percy Soc.) 25 Ȝe beth ungroundid in grace.

**2.** Having no real basis or justification; unfounded, groundless.

*c* **1380** Wyclif *Wks.* (1880) 337 If he had not couetise of worldly goodis..he shuld..leue al siche rownyng þat is ungrundid. **1597** Hooker *Eccl. Pol.* v. lxii. § 16 A few men's new, ungrounded, and as yet unapproved imagination. **1629** H. Burton *Truth's Triumph* 291 Humane deuices, and labyrinths of vngrounded distinctions. **1672** Newton in *Phil. Trans.* VII. 5084, I shall refer him to my former Letter, by which that conjecture will appear to be ungrounded. **1728** R. Morris *Ess. Anc. Archit.* 70 The Executions of their own ungrounded Fancies. **1782** Priestley *Corrupt. Christianity* I. I. 30 Nothing can appear..more ungrounded. **1863** E. V. Neale *Anal. Th. & Nat.* 58 Thus the whole operation appears either useless or ungrounded.

**3.** Of persons: Not properly instructed or informed (*in* something).

*c* **1449** Pecock *Repr.* Prol. 3 Therfore to ech such vngroundid and vnredy and ouer hasti vndirnymer and blamer y seie [etc.]. **1581** Mulcaster *Positions* iii. 11 It is a sufficient argument..of an vngrounded learner, if his error be in speeche. **1646** P. Bulkeley *Gospel Covt.* II. 111 If any be ignorant and ungrounded in the doctrine of grace. **1670** Baxter *Cure Ch. Div.* 168 The pitiful case of the ignorant and ungrounded, and troubled sort of religious persons.

**Ungrou·ndedly,** *adv.* [Un-1 11.] Without any ground or basis.

**1550** Bale *Apol.* 84 b, That putteth he in here, vngroundedly, doubtfully, hypocritically, and vtterly agaynst hymselfe. **1593** Nashe *Strange Newes* B j, They that are vngroundedly offended at any thing in 'Pierce Pennilesse'. **1624** Bedell *Lett.* iii. 59 Many things there be in Poperie ..to my conceit weakely and vngroundedly affirmed. **1692** Ray *Disc.* III. ix. 343 The event shews how ungroundedly and erroneously. [Also in recent use.]

**Ungrou·ndedness.** [Un-1 12.] The quality or state of being ungrounded: **a.** Of persons.

**1628** Bp. Hall *Old Relig.* Ded. ¶ 8 b, The cause..was, their vngroundednes in the points of Catechisme. **1652** Gaule *Magastrom.* 28 Away, then, with that excuse, from the folly, errour, and ungroundedness of the artsmen!

**b.** Of opinions, statements, etc.

**1637** Bastwick *Litany* III. 7 Besides the impiety, vanity, and ungroundednes of it, let us looke..into the needlesnesse and unprofitablenes of it. **1688** Steele *Old Age* 284 The folly and ungroundedness of this Imagination, is obvious. **1804** *Ann. Rev.* II. 296 We mention this..to expose the utter ungroundedness of the writer's speculation.

**Ungrou·ped,** *ppl. a.* (Un-1 8.) [**1775** Ash.] **1853** Ruskin *Stones Ven.* II. vii. § 8. 238 That palace; ..its capitals are all different and ungrouped. **Ungrow·,** *v.* (Un-2 7.) **1598** Florio, *Discrescere*,..to vngrow, to diminish, to wane. **1648** Hexham II, *Onwassen*, to Vngrowe, to Waxe lesse.

**Ungrow·n,** *ppl. a.* [Un-1 8 b.] Not yet grown up or fully grown; immature.

**1592** Shaks. *Ven. & Ad.* 526 No fisher but the ungrown fry forbears. **1596** — *1 Hen. IV*, v. iv. 23 With lustier maintenance then I did looke for Of such an vngrowne Warriour. **1633** P. Fletcher *Purple Isl.* VI. iv, A narrow compasse best my ungrown Muse impounds. **1880** Miss Broughton *Sec. Th.* I. i, The Squire; his half-grown daughters..; [and] his ungrown son.

**Ungru·bbed,** *ppl. a.* (Un-1 8.) *c* **1374** Chaucer *Former Age* 14 Vn-koruen and vn-grobbed lay the vyne.

**Ungru·dged,** *ppl. a.* (Un-1 8.)

*a* **1631** Donne *Div. Poems*, *Cross* 31 For when that Crosse ungrudg'd, unto you stickes, Then are you to your selfe, a Crucifixe. **1822** Lamb *Elia* I. *Decay of Beggars*, Theirs were the only rates..ungrudged in the assessment. **1877** Blackie *Wise Men* 345 Loved and lover grow, By mutual breathing in of excellence, Ungrudged, unstinted.

**Ungru·dging,** *ppl. a.* (Un-1 10.)

**1768–74** Tucker *Lt. Nat.* (1834) II. 218 Such perfect ungrudging resistance both of pleasure and pain..being impracticable. **1823** Lamb *Elia* I. *Decay of Beggars*, Cheap monument of no ungrudging hand. **1890** *Science-Gossip* XXVI. 178/2 The provisions gathered by their sisters with ungrudging generosity.

Hence **Ungru·dgingness.**

**1885** J. Martineau *Types Ethic. Th.* I. I. 58 Plato speaks of the world as the product of the divine ungrudgingness.

**Ungru·dgingly,** *adv.* (Un-1 11.)

Common from *c* 1860.

*a* **1631** Donne *Elegies* xi. 67 Receive from him that doome ungrudgingly, Because he is the mouth of Destiny. **1822** Lamb *Elia* I. *Roast Pig*, I am one of those, who freely and ungrudgingly impart a share..to a friend. *a* **1862** Buckle *Misc. Wks.* (1872) I. 15 Let that honour be paid freely, ungrudgingly, and with an open and bounteous heart. **1887** *Spectator* 15 Oct. 1392 His gifts and graces must be ungrudgingly admitted.

**Ungtment,** obs. form of Ointment.

**Ungual** (ʋ·ŋgwăl), *a.* and *sb.* [f. L. *ungu-is* nail, claw + -al. Cf. Ungueal *a.*]

**A.** *adj.* **1.** *Anat.* **a.** Pertaining to, connected with, a nail or claw; esp. *ungual phalanx*, the terminal bone in the digits of the hand or foot.

**1834** Roget *Anim. & Veg. Phys.* I. 405 To the last joint, which is often termed the *ungual bone*, there is usually attached either a nail, a claw, or a hoof. **1836** *Penny Cycl.* V. 22/2 An external thick condyle, with which the ungual phalanx is articulated. **1898** A. S. Packard *Entomol.* 101 The ungual joint is wanting in the weevil Anoplus.

**b.** *Ungual bone*, a lachrymal bone.

**1888** *Cassell's Encycl. Dict.* s.v. *Lachrymal*.

**2.** *Path.* Affecting the nail.

**1872** T. Bryant *Pract. Surg.* 450 Ungual exostosis..is a bony outgrowth from the extreme phalanx of the great toe.

**B.** *sb.* An ungual phalanx, claw, or bone.

In recent use.

**Unguarantee·d,** *ppl. a.* (Un-1 8.) **1855** Milman *Lat. Chr.* XIV. i. VI. 396 The faith and hope unguaranteed by any earthly mediator. **1864** Smiles *G. & R. Stephenson* 305 Stephenson..avoided holding unguaranteed railway shares.

**Ungua·rd,** *v.* [Un-2 4.]

**1.** *trans.* To strip of a guard or edging.

**1598** Florio, *Disfrangiare*, to vnfringe,..to vngard.

**2.** To deprive of a guard or defence; to lay open to attack.

**1745** Fielding *Tom Jones* v. v, Some well-chosen presents from the philosopher so softened and unguarded the girl's heart, that a favourable opportunity became irresistible. **1801** Ireland *Nuptiæ Sacræ* 128 Every man, by degrees, will unguard the virtue of his house, hitherto sacred. **1847** Lytton *Lucretia* 64 She accepted the intimacy held out to her, not to unguard herself, but to lay open her opponent.

**b.** *Whist*, etc. To expose (a high card) to the risk of loss by discarding a lower and protecting card.

**1862** 'Cavendish' *Whist* (1864) 95 Trick v.—*a* unguards his queen of spades. **1887** McIntosh *Mod. Whist* 81 It is better to blank an ace than unguard king or queen.

**Ungua·rdable,** *a.* (Un-1 7 b.) **1690** *Def. Dr. G. Walker* 14 Yet this boldly asserted impregnable Fortress hath an unguardable Breach.

**Ungua·rded,** *ppl. a.* [Un-1 8.]

**1.** Not furnished with, or protected by, a guard; left undefended or open to attack, spoliation, etc.

*a* **1593** Marlowe *Ovid's Elegies* III. iv. 26 Few loue what others haue vnguarded left. **1626** Mead in Ellis *Orig. Lett.* Ser. I. III. 250, I hear some of opinion that the Duke likes not so unguarded a place. **1697** Dryden *Æneis* XII. 817 He views the unguarded city from afar, In careless quiet, and secure of war. **1741–2** Gray *Agrippina* 5 Alone, unguarded and without a lictor. **1781** Gibbon *Decl. & F.* xxxi. III. 193 His troops..occupied the unguarded passes of the Apennine. **1824** Miss L. M. Hawkins *Annaline* III. 40 [He] made off and left the door unguarded. **1869** Tozer *Highl. Turkey* I. 208 We used to ride..through the country unarmed and unguarded. **1885** *Manch. Exam.* 13 Jan. 5/3 A small body..entered the town by an unguarded gate.

**b.** In fig. contexts.

**1673** [R. Leigh] *Transp. Reh.* 39 This is Momba's and De Groot's doings, to leave this passage open and ungarded. *a* **1704** T. Brown *Sat. agst. Woman* Wks. 1730 I. 56 Thus all the unguarded passes of his mind she'll try.

**c.** *transf.* In chess or card-playing: Not protected by other pieces or cards.

**1808** *Hoyle's Game of Chess* 46 *note*, Your knight will then defend your king's pawn, otherwise unguarded. **1862** 'Cavendish' *Whist* (1864) 95 Queen singly guarded may make a trick, but the ten of clubs unguarded cannot.

**2.** Not on one's guard; not taking heed or exercising caution. Chiefly *fig.*

**1640** Fletcher, etc. *Coronat.* IV. i. ad fin., I..have not A thought so much unguarded, as to be won From my truth, and innocence. **1697** Dryden *Æneis* XII. 1058 Rais'd on the Stretch, young Turnus aims a blow, Full on the Helm of his unguarded Foe. *a* **1763** W. King *Polit. & Lit. Anecd.* (1819) 44 Sir Robert [Walpole] was frequently very unguarded in his expressions. **1796** Mme. D'Arblay *Camilla* IV. 185 The unsuspicious frankness of an unguarded, because innocent nature. **1840** Lady Lyttelton *Corr.* (1912) 298 Such a new thing for her to dare to be unguarded in conversation with anybody. **1881** Jowett *Thucyd.* I. 186 The general who..never loses an opportunity of striking at an unguarded foe.

**b.** Of times: Characterized by the absence of guard or caution.

**1680** Otway *Orphan* I, I'll yet possess her love, Wait on and watch her loose unguarded hours. **1776** Gibbon *Decl. & F.* xii. I. 336 An active enemy..must, in the end, discover some feeble spot or some unguarded moment. **1855** Macaulay *Hist. Eng.* xv. III. 596 It is highly probable that his mother..took a fatal advantage of some unguarded hour, when he was irritated by finding his advice slighted.

**c.** Of expressions, actions, etc.: Incautious, imprudent; careless.

**1714** S. OCKLEY in *Lett. Lit. Men* (Camden) 350 If a person should..upon the account of an unguarded expression.. suffer a capital sentence. **1751** EARL ORRERY *Remarks Swift* ix. (1752) 114 A picture..drawn in too loose a garment, and too unguarded a posture. **1827** LYTTON *Falkland* 37, I have watched feeling in its unguarded sallies. **1835** — *Rienzi* x. vii, Their gestures were vehement and unguarded. **1849** MACAULAY *Hist. Eng.* vii. II. 163 Every unguarded word uttered by him was noted down.

**3.** Not protected, screened, or fenced off, by some arrangement or device.

**1771** LUCKOMBE *Hist. Print.* 240, *d, f, l*, when they stand with their beaks unguarded,..run as great a hazard [of being broken]. **1784** COWPER *Task* IV. 469 Ev'ry twentieth pace Conducts th' unguarded nose to such a whiff Of stale debauch. **1844** NOAD *Electricity* (ed. 2) 80 Decomposing water by current alone, and with unguarded poles. **1872** HOWELLS *Wedding Journ.* (1892) 177 The road.., next the precipice, is unguarded by any sort of parapet. **1900** *Westm. Gaz.* 2 May 6/3 Dust or gas..ignited by an unguarded lamp.

Hence **Ungua·rdedness.**

**1825–9** MRS. SHERWOOD *Lady of Manor* IV. xxvii. 282 That sort of unguardedness which consists in supposing all around one to be well-intentioned. **1887** *Women's Union Jrnl.* 15 Dec. 94 A moment of optical unguardedness, when ..eye-glasses lay on a table before him.

**Ungua·rdedly,** *adv.* [UN-[1] 11.] In an unguarded manner; incautiously, uncircumspectly.

**1713** BERKELEY *Guard.* No. 3 ¶ 1 Whatever Clergymen, in Disputes against each other, have unguardedly uttered. **1746** WESLEY *Princ. Methodist* 40 But how little did I profit by begging your Excuse, suppose I had spoken a Word unguardedly? *a* **1813** in J. Thomson *Lect. Inflam.* 477 The same spunge having been unguardedly used for different sores. **1886** *Manch. Exam.* 19 Oct. 5/5 The Bishop spoke unguardedly and without due premeditation.

**U·ngueal,** var. of UNGUAL *a.* 1.

**1835–6** *Todd's Cycl. Anat.* I. 289/2 The ultimate or ungueal phalanges. **1851** MANTELL *Petrifactions* ii. § 3. 116 The ungueal or claw-bones are large and strong.

**Unguent** (*ʌ·ŋgwĕnt*), *sb.* Also 5 vngwent, 6–7 vnguent. [ad. L. *unguent-um*, f. *unguĕre* to anoint. Cf. F. *onguent*, It., Sp., Pg. *unguento*.] An ointment or salve.

*c* **1440** *Pallad. on Husb.* IV. 147 Or madifie hit so in oil lauryne, Let drie hem, sowe hem, vp by oon assent They wol, and haue odour like her vnguent. **1448–9** J. METHAM *Amoryus & Cleopes* 1500 For had not a bene that precyus vngwent, He had be slayn and on pecys rente. **1563** T. GALE *Antidot.* II. 7 Unto whiche I haue also added no smal number of vnguents. **1624** HEYWOOD *Gunaik.* III. 131 Forgetting the Physitions with all their drugges, unguents, and emplasters. **1656** J. SMITH *Pract. Physick* 66 Unguents for scaldings must be made so that they stick not too fast. **1720** POPE *Iliad* XXIII. 229 Celestial Venus hover'd o'er his head, And roseate unguents, heav'nly fragrance! shed. **1778** LIGHTFOOT *Flora Scot.* II. 618 The buds yield a yellow resinous unguent. **1857** MAURICE *Ep. St. John* x. 162 Oils and unguents in the East had a virtue which we do not commonly attach to them. **1887** BOWEN *Æneid* III. 280 Bared and anointed shoulders with glistening unguent stream.

*attrib.* **1894** *Daily News* 13 Dec. 8 A small unguent bottle, only slightly damaged, was in this part of the building.

**b.** *fig.* or in fig. context.

**1596** FITZ-GEFFREY *Sir F. Drake* (1881) 19 Soules sweet Emplastrum, unguent of the eyes. *a* **1625** FLETCHER & MASS. *Elder Bro.* v. i, Your festred reputation, which no Balm or gentle Unguent could ever make way to. *a* **1683** OWEN *Two Discourses Holy Spirit* (1693) 62 An Unction, an Unguent from the Holy One. **1838** JAMES *Louis XIV*, I. 257 There was no unguent which made the wheels of their foreign policy move so rapidly as gold.

**c.** *spec.* (See quot.)

**1867** *Ure's Dict. Arts* (ed. 6) III. 971 *Unguents*, the name given by engineers to the greases applied to the bearing parts of machinery.

**U·nguent,** *v.* [f. prec. Cf. L. *unguent-āre*, It. *-are*.] *trans.* To treat with an unguent; to anoint.

**1656** S. HOLLAND *Zara* (1719) 42 When they found their Ears unguented with warm water. **1657** TOMLINSON *Renou's Disp.* 689 A Medick should be Unguented, that is, Perfumed. **1819** *Metropolis* III. 194 Brushing, perfuming, unguenting, and twisting about the hair.

**Unguenta·rian.** *rare.* [-IAN.] = UNGUENTARY *sb.* 1.

**1657** TOMLINSON *Renou's Disp.* 123 Plaisters..bought in unguentarians shops. **1894** *Yellow Bk.* I. 81 The admirable unguentarians of Bond Street.

‖ **Unguenta·rium.** *Archæol.* [L. *unguentārium* (*vās*), f. *unguent-um* UNGUENT *sb.*] A vessel for holding ointment; an unguentary.

**1859** R. HUNT *Guide Mus. Pract. Geol.* (ed. 2) 85 Vases, bowls, lamps, unguentaria, amphoræ. **1888** *Pall Mall G.* 22 Aug. 5/2 Besides the unguentaria, there are..specimens of the early Phœnician glass.

**U·nguentary,** *sb.* and *a.* Now *rare.* [ad. L. *unguentārius, -a, -um* (adj. and sb.), f. *unguentum* ointment. Cf. It. and Sp. *unguentario*, OF. *ung-, onguentaire*.]

**A.** *sb.* **1.** A maker of or dealer in (perfumed) ointment; a perfumer.

**1382** WYCLIF *Exod.* xxx. 25 An oynement maad with the werk of ungwentarye [1388 a makere of oynement]. **1483** CAXTON *Gold. Leg.* 64 b/2 He shal also take your doughters and make them his unguentaryes. **1609** BIBLE (Douay) *Exod.* xxx. 25 Thou shalt make the holie oile of unction, an ointment compounded by the arte of an unguentarie. **1684** tr. *Agrippa's Van. Arts* xc. 313 In stead of Alchymists, Cacochymists;..in stead of Unguentaries, Victuallers.

**2.** = UNGUENTARIUM.

**1911** *Sotheby's Sale Catal. Egypt. Antiq.* 87 An Unguentary, shaped as a Gazelle with its legs tied together.

**B.** *adj.* Adapted for use in, suitable for, having connexion with, ointments.

**1657** TOMLINSON *Renou's Disp.* 273 Which Hippocrates calls myrepsicum, that is, unguentary, from its suavity. **1846** WORCESTER (citing *Gent. Mag.*). **1891** *Cent. Dict.*, *Unguentary vase*, a small vase for unguents.

**Unguenti·ferous,** *a.* [See UNGUENT *sb.* and -(I)FEROUS. Cf. It. *unguentifero*.] Producing ointment.

**1844** T. MEYRICK *Fam. St. Richard*, etc. 95 The saints who are called 'Elæophori' or 'unguentiferous'.

**U·nguentous,** *a. rare.* [f. UNGUENT *sb.* + -OUS.]

**1.** Smeared with ointment; greasy.

**1654** GAYTON *Pleas. Notes* III. ii. 73 His bed was full of holes, so that the Flocks broke through the breaches, and stuck all about his fulsome and unguentous Body.

**2.** Of the nature of ointment.

**1684** tr. *Bonet's Merc. Compit.* XIX. 833 Unguentous things hinder transpiration. **1819** *Metropolis* III. 151 His unguentous compound has not hindered a spoke from being put into his wheel.

†**Unguenty.** *Obs.*[−1] (See quot.)

*c* **1720** W. GIBSON *Farrier's Dispens.* xv. (1734) 284 *Unguentum Album*, called by the common people, Unguenty.

**Ungue·rdoned,** *ppl. a.* Now *poet.* (UN-[1] 8.)

**1433** *Rolls of Parlt.* IV. 424/2 Suche as have so served and be unguerdonned. *c* **1477** CAXTON *Jason* 47 b, As your trewe louer and humble seruaunt vnguerdonned I shal goe withdrawe me into som deserte. **1611** COTGR., *Inguerdonné*, vnguerdoned, vnrecompenced. **1813** SCOTT *Rokeby* VI. xii, Unguerdon'd, I would give with joy The father's arms to fold his boy. **1855** SINGLETON *Virgil* II. 25 No one of this company By me unguerdoned shall depart.

**Ungue·ssable,** *a.* (UN-[1] 7 b.)

**1832** MISS MITFORD *Our Village* Ser. v. 278 An old bonnet,..so twisted..that its pristine shape was unguessable. **1865** *Dublin Univ. Mag.* I. 266 There are passages ..the meaning whereof..is to me unknowable, unguessable. [Common in recent use.]

**Ungue·ssed,** *ppl. a.* [UN-[1] 8 and 8 c.]

†**1.** Unexpected, unlooked-for. *Obs.*

*c* **1400** *Comm. Luke* (MS. Bodl. 143) i. 7 God ordeyned þat ioon was born of fadir & modir of old age,..þat bi vngessid birþe of child a graciousere ȝifte shulde enfourme hem.

**2.** Not solved or known by guessing.

**1590** SPENSER *F. Q.* I. ix. 7 For whither he through fatall deepe foresight Me hither sent, for cause to me vnghest, Or [etc.]. **1805** SCOTT *Last Minstrel* v. xvii, But cause of terror, all unguess'd, Was fluttering in her gentle breast. **1837** LYTTON *Athens* I. 50 The frequent operation of causes unrecognised, unforeseen, unguest. **1900** *Pilot* 22 Sept. 358/2 An explanation of its mysterious and once unseen and unguessed processes.

**b.** Not guessed *at*, not dreamt *of*.

**1746** ELIZA HEYWOOD *Female Spect.* No. 22 (1748) IV. 203 By what unseen, unguessed at means, are frequently the greatest events brought about! **1838** LYTTON *Zicci* xiv, Art thou some itinerant mountebank, or some unguest-of friend? **1876** MISS YONGE *Womankind* xiii, The best endeavours.. are often frustrated by some unguessed-at peril.

**Ungue·stlike,** *a.* or *adv.* (UN-[1] 7 c or 11 b.) **1645** MILTON *Tetrach.* Wks. 1851 IV. 207 He cast his eye unlawfully and unguestlike upon Herodias.., the wife of Philip.

**U·nguical,** *a. rare.* [f. L. *unguic-ulus* (see next) + -AL.] = UNGUAL *a.* 1.

**1833** SIR C. BELL *Hand* (1834) 106 These unguical bones, or bones of the claws.

†**U·nguicle.** *Bot. Obs.* [ad. L. *unguiculus*, dim. of *unguis* nail, claw.] A part of a leaf or petal resembling a nail or claw.

**1657** TOMLINSON *Renou's Disp.* 375 Medlers, which are of a moderate magnitude, with late heads, discreted with five unguicles or leafes. **1796** H. HUNTER tr. *St.-Pierre's Stud. Nat.* (1799) II. 95 The unguicle..is always clearer [in colour] than that of the rest of the petal.

**Ungui·cular,** *a. rare.* [f. as prec + -AR.] = UNGUAL *a.* 1.

**1826** KIRBY & SP. *Entomol.* III. xxxii. 307 The last or unguicular joint..is on both sides fringed with long hairs.

**Unguiculate** (*ʌŋgwi·kiŭlět*), *a.* and *sb.* [ad. mod.L. *unguiculāt-us* (Ray, 1693), f. L. *unguiculus* UNGUICLE. Cf. F. *ung-, onguiculé*.]

**1.** *Bot.* Of petals: Having an unguis or claw.

**1802** R. HALL *Elem. Bot.* 193 *Unguiculate*,..clawed. **1830** LINDLEY *Nat. Syst. Bot.* 34 Their..many-celled fruit, and unguiculate petals. **1861** BENTLEY *Man. Bot.* 454 Petals.. imbricate, generally unequal and unguiculate.

**2.** *Zool.*, etc. Ending in, assuming the form of, a nail or claw: **a.** Of the limbs of animals.

**1826** KIRBY & SP. *Entomol.* III. xxx. 138 Those of the former..resemble the second class of unguiculate prolegs, except in the defect of claws. **1852** DANA *Crust.* I. 252 Tarsus not unguiculate. **1881** MIVART *Cat* 472 Their digits are also unguiculate and never sheathed in horny hoofs.

**b.** Of other organs or parts.

**1826** KIRBY & SP. *Entomol.* III. xxviii. 30 Mandibles cheliform or unguiculate. **1851** S. P. WOODWARD *Mollusca* 102 The operculum is described as..Claw-shaped, or unguiculate. **1872** COUES *N. Amer. Birds* 25 A bill is..unguiculate (clawed), when strongly epignathous.

**3.** *Zool.* Of quadrupeds: Furnished with nails or claws; belonging to the order *Unguiculata*.

**1839** HALLAM *Hist. Lit.* IV. viii. § 16 Quadrupeds he [*sc.* Ray] was the first to divide into ungulate and unguiculate, hoofed and clawed. *a* **1847** *Todd's Cycl. Anat.* III. 843/2 In all unguiculate Mammalia the tarsal bones are well developed. **1877** COUES *Fur Anim.* iv. 117 Causing the feet to appear slender.., though they are relatively stouter than in many unguiculate animals.

**b.** *sb.* An unguiculate quadruped.

**1840** *Cuvier's Anim. Kingd.* 42 Among the unguiculates the first is Man. *a* **1847** *Todd's Cycl. Anat.* III. 236/2 Those Unguiculates which have the front teeth trenchant.

**Ungui·culated,** *ppl. a.* [f. as prec. + -ED.]

**1.** = prec. 2.

**1752** J. HILL *Hist. Anim.* 110 The Lacerta,..with five unguiculated toes to each foot. **1819** SAMOUELLE *Entomol. Compend.* 192 *Antennæ* moniliform,..*maxillæ* unguiculated. **1841** *Penny Cycl.* XXI. 424/1 The external jaw-feet are.. sometimes unguiculated at the end. **1861** HULME tr. *Moquin-Tandon* II. III. i. 69 The toes free, flat, and unguiculated.

**2.** = prec. 3.

**1834** M'MURTRIE *Cuvier's Anim. Kingd.* 224 As the Marsupialia..are parallel to the other unguiculated Mammalia. **1851** G. F. RICHARDSON *Geol.* 336 Rodentia (or Gnawers).— Form a natural order of unguiculated animals.

**U·nguicule.** *rare*[−1]. [ad. L. *unguicul-us*.] A finger-nail.

**1694** MOTTEUX *Rabelais* v. xx, Your Taciturnity..discovers that..you have..scalptiz'd your heads with frequent applications of your Unguicules. [Not in Fr. original.]

**Ungui·dable,** *a.* (UN-[1] 7 b.) **1822** BEWICK *Mem.* 6 My father began by telling him that I was so very unguidable that he could not manage me. **1896** *Westm. Gaz.* 12 May 4/1 [The vessel,] in the absence of much wind, was almost unguidable. **Ungui·dably,** *adv.* (UN-[1] 11.) **1837** CARLYLE *Fr. Rev.* I. II. vi, Beautiful invention; mounting heavenward, so beautifully,—so unguidably!

**Ungui·ded,** *ppl. a.* [UN-[1] 8.] Not guided in a particular path or direction; left to take one's own course or way.

**1585** ABP. SANDYS *Serm.* xix. 341 The ship cannot keepe hir right course vnguided but will fall vpon euerie sande. **1633** FLETCHER & SHIRLEY *Night-Walker* IV. i, *Ha.* The world's a Labyrinth, where unguided men Walk up and down to find their weariness. **1674** BOYLE *Grounds Corpusc. Philos.* 3 The material parts being able by their own unguided motions, to cast themselves into such a system. **1726** POPE *Odyss.* XX. 441 Unguided hence my trembling steps I bend. **1801** SOUTHEY *Thalaba* I. xviii, Not by Heaven unseen, Nor in unguided wanderings, hast thou reach'd This secret place. **1856** KANE *Arct. Expl.* II. xxi. 211 The dogs speed from hut to hut, almost unguided by their drivers. **1891** T. HARDY *Tess* ii, An unguided ramble into its recesses in bad weather.

**b.** *fig.* Of action, conduct, etc.: Undirected, uncontrolled.

**1597** SHAKS. 2 *Hen. IV*, IV. iv. 59 Th' vnguided Dayes, And rotten Times, that you shall looke vpon. **1651** HOBBES *Leviath.* I. viii. 37 Passions unguided, are for the most part meere Madnesse. **1711** STEELE *Spect.* No. 167 ¶ 1 The unhappy Force of an Imagination, unguided by the Check of Reason and Judgment. **1760–72** H. BROOKE *Fool of Qual.* (1809) III. 136 He..has left his own household unchastened and unguided. **1856** FROUDE *Hist. Eng.* II. 26 It [Protestantism] sprung up spontaneously, unguided, unexcited,.. among the masses of the nation. *a* **1880** GEO. ELIOT *Leaves fr. Note-bk., Ess.* (1884) 364 They are not left to their own unguided rashness, or their own unguided pusillanimity.

Hence **Ungui·dedly** *adv.*

**1660** tr. *Amyraldus' Treat. conc. Relig.* II. i. 153 To discharge all his actions at randome, and permit his natural appetites to run unguidedly at a venture. **1885** E. F. BYRRNE *Entangled* I. xi, Her tongue spoke strangely and unguidedly.

**Ungui·ferous,** *a. rare*[−1]. [f. L. *ungui-s* nail, claw + -FEROUS.] Bearing nails or claws.

**1826** KIRBY & SP. *Entomol.* III. 137 The remaining description of unguiferous prolegs..are those of certain *Diptera*.

**U·nguiform,** *a.* [f. as prec. + -FORM.] Having the form of a nail or claw; claw-shaped.

**1726** MONRO *Anat. Bones* 137 These unguiform Bones compose the anterior internal Parts of the Orbites. **1815** KIRBY & SP. *Entomol.* iv. (1816) I. 140 Armed with two unguiform mandibles. **1843** HUMPHREYS *Brit. Butterflies* 36 With simple claws furnished with an unguiform appendage. **1866** R. TATE *Brit. Mollusks* iv. 83 The shell..is unguiform.

**Ungui·lded,** *a.* (UN-[1] 9.) **1858** J. S. BREWER *Mon. Francisc.* Pref. p. xvii, For the unguilded population who resided in the suburbs..there were no such advantages. **Ungui·leful,** *a.* (UN-[1] 7.) **1630** I. CRAVEN *Gods Tribunall* (1631) 33 In the day when an vnguilefull Israelite shall not faile of a Testimoniall.

**U·nguilite.** *Geol.* [f. L. *ungui-s* nail + -LITE.] Gompholite.

**1799** KIRWAN *Geol. Ess.* 246 It alternates with unguilite (Nagel fluhe) in Swisserland..and in Bavaria.

**Ungui·llotined,** *ppl. a.* (UN-[1] 8.) **1837** CARLYLE *Fr. Rev.* I. II. viii, There too an unruly Linguet, still unguillotined,..can emit his hoarse wailings.

† **Ungui·ltihead.** *Obs.* = UNGUILTINESS.

*a* **1470** H. PARKER *Dives & Pauper* (1493) IV. xix. N vij b/1 The prest moste take hede whether his vngiltyede is openly knowen or is in doute.

**Ungui·ltily,** *adv.* (UN-[1] 11.)

*a* **1634** CHAPMAN *Alphonsus* I. Plays 1873 III. 211 Thus am I wrong'd, God knows, unguiltily. **1861** TRENCH *Comm. Ep. Churches Asia* 119 All of us, by careless walking,..are in danger of unconsciously, but not unguiltily, being the same. **1891** MEREDITH *One of our Conq.* xxvi, Unguiltily tainted, in herself she was innocent.

**Ungui·ltiness.** (UN-[1] 12.)

**1535** COVERDALE *Job* vi. 29 Be indifferent iudges, and considre myne vngyltinesse. **1571** GOLDING *Calvin on Ps.* xvii. 1 It is lawfull for us to protest our ungiltynesse before God. *a* **1634** CHAPMAN *Alphonsus* v. 60 Great Emperor,..Your Conscience knows my hearts unguiltiness. *a* **1680** BUTLER *Rem.* (1759) I. 301 Their approved Liberty of Conscience, and Unguiltiness of Faith.

†**Ungui·ltless,** *a. Obs.*[−1] (UN-[1] 15.)

*c* **1320** *Sir Tristr.* 2144 Vngiltles er ȝe In swiche a sclaunder brouȝt.

**Ungui·lty,** *a.* Forms: (see UN-[1] 4 c and GUILTY *a.*). [UN-[1] 7.]

**1.** Not guilty; guiltless; innocent: **a.** Of persons.

*c* 893 [see below]. *c* 1374 CHAUCER *Troylus* III. 1018 Is þis an honour to þi deite That folk vngiltyf [*v.r.* ongilti] suffren here Iniure? 1388 WYCLIF *Num.* xiv. 18 Doynge awei wickidnesse and trespassis, and leeuynge no man vngilti. *c* 1440 *Jacob's Well* 22 Fleeth hem, ȝif ȝe be vngylty, & leuyth hem, ȝif ȝe be gilty. 1558 PHAER *Æneid* II. C iv b, Whom by a treason false the Greekes..Ungiltie did condempne. 1599 BRETON *Miseries Manillia* Wks. (Grosart) II. 46/1 The Lord of lordes dooth knowe this tale to bee untrue, And her unguiltie. *a* 1634 CHAPMAN *Alphonsus* V. i. 220, I kill'd thy father, therefore let me die, But save the life of this unguilty Empress. 1736 THOMSON *Liberty* IV. 330 Rare to be seen, unguilty cities rise, Cities of brothers form'd. 1816 *Monthly Mag.* XLII. 430 Thou sea,..Receive for ever in thy dark abyss The unguilty Melicertes. 1860 TRENCH *Serm. Westm. Abb.* v. 53 The clothing..could only have been obtained at the cost of..the life of one unguilty.

*absol. c* 893 K. ÆLFRED *Oros.* IV. vii. 184 Ac hit God wræc on him..þæt hie mid hiera cucum onguldon þæt hie ungyltiȝe cwealdon. 13.. *Prose Psalter* ix. 30 (Dubl. MS.), He sitteþ in waytynges wyþ ryche men in preuytes þat he slee þe vngylty. 1553 LATIMER *Serm. Lord's Prayer* vi. (1562) 46 And so we acknowledge our selues to be offenders. For the vngilty nedeth no pardon. 1612 WOODALL *Surg. Mate* Wks. (1653) 146 The guilty and unguilty are censured both alike by the common sort. 1703 *Secr. Policy of Jansenists* 24 That I may not asperse the unguilty.

**b.** Of the hands, mind, blood, etc.

13.. *Prose Psalter* cv. 35 And hij..shadde blode nouȝt filed [*v.r.* vngilty blode]. 1382 WYCLIF *Gen.* xxxvii. 22 Kepe ȝe ȝoure hondes vngilti. 1595 DANIEL *Civ. Wars* I. xc, Stay here thy foote, thy yet vnguilty foote. 1605 — *Philotas* III. i, With th' assured Chear Of my unguilty Conscience. 1633 FORD *Broken H.* II. iii, Time can never On the white table of unguilty faith Write counterfeit dishonour. 1740 RICHARDSON *Pamela* I. 230 Surrendering up my Life, spotless and unguilty, to that merciful Being who gave it.

**c.** Of an animal. *rare*⁻¹.

1600 *Maides Metam.* I. in Bullen *O. Pl.* (1882) I. 109 And, hauing slaine it, rip his panting breast, And take the heart of the vnguiltie beast.

**2.** Guiltless or innocent *of* something.

*c* 1440 *Jacob's Well* 89 He of Baldac cryed, 'late be! late be! he is vngylti of þat mannys deth!' 1535 COVERDALE *Matt.* xxvii. 24, I am vngiltie of yᵉ bloude of this righteous man. 1577 GRANGE *Golden Aphrod.* E iij b, Sith I vnguiltie am thereof, I wil not seeke the same T'excuse. 1606 CHAPMAN *M. D'Olive* Plays 1873 I. 224 Keepe your cullour stiffe, vnguiltie of passion or disgrace. 1820 HOGG *Tales & Sk.* (1837) III. 96 He is as unguilty of the whole affair, as the child that is not after being born.

† **b.** Undeserving *of*. *Obs.*⁻¹

1596 W. SMITH *Chloris* (1877) 21 With patience bearing loues captiuitie, Themselves vnguiltie of his wrath alleaging.

† **3.** Not involving guilt. *Obs.*

*a* 1586 SIDNEY *Arcadia* III. x, This outward glosse, intitled Beautie, which it pleaseth you to lay to my (as I thinke) vnguiltie charge. 1662 J. CHANDLER *Van Helmont's Oriat.* 213 That now and then, the digestion beares the unguilty fault of the expulsive faculty.

**U·nguinal,** *a.* *Anat.* [Irreg. f. L. *ungui-s* nail, claw.] = UNGUAL *a.*

1860 MAYNE *Expos. Lex.* s.v. 1870 GILLMORE tr. *Figuier's Reptiles & Birds* ii. 59 A spur or nail..in which the anatomist discovered the elements of an unguinal phalanx.

† **U·nguinous,** *a.* *Obs.* [ad. L. *unguinōsus*, f. *unguin-*, *unguen* ointment.] Greasy, oily.

1601 HOLLAND *Pliny* II. 174 The powder entreth into those unguinous or oleous plasters which the Greeks call Liparas. 1603 — *Plutarch's Mor.* 675 The tortch staves made of them..are so fattie and unguinous.

‖ **Unguis** (*v·ŋgwis*). Pl. **ungues** (-*īz*). [L. *unguis* nail, claw, etc.]

† **1.** = UNGULA 2. *Obs.*

1693 [see UNGULA 2]. 1728 CHAMBERS *Cycl.* s.v. *Pannus*, The Pannus is an Excrescence..less hard and membranous than the Unguis.

**2.** *Bot.* The narrow part of a petal, by which it is attached to the receptacle.

1728 CHAMBERS *Cycl.* s.v., In preparing of Medicines, the *Ungues*..are pull'd off the Flowers. 1760 J. LEE *Introd. Bot.* I. iii. (1765) 7 Each Petal consists of *Unguis*, a Claw, which is the lower Part fastened to the Base. 1830 LINDLEY *Nat. Syst. Bot.* 284 The inner segments of the perianthium being petaloid, with the stamens proceeding from the top of their ungues. 1879 A. GRAY *Struct. Bot.* vi. § 4. 245 The expanded portion of a petal..is the *Lamina* or Blade; any much contracted base is the *Unguis* or Claw.

† **3.** A claw-shaped obstetrical instrument. *Obs.*⁻¹

1752 SMELLIE *Midwif.* Introd. p. xii, [Hippocrates] directs us to introduce the hand,..dividing the parts with an *unguis* fixed on the great finger.

**4.** *Zool.*, etc. A nail or claw.

*c* 1790 *Encycl. Brit.* (ed. 3) VI. 680/1 Tarsus, or foot.. Unguis, or claw. 1819 MACLEAY *Horæ Entomol.* I. 66 The size of their tarsi and ungues, and their comparatively small pectus. 1840 *Cuvier's Anim. Kingd.* 526 *Dasyus*..has the ungues of the two fore-feet..bifid, the others entire. 1884 COUES *N. Amer. Birds* 102 There it is always terminated by a hard, horny, unguis or 'nail', more or less distinct.

† **Ungul,** Anglicized f. next (in sense 4).

1670 *Phil. Trans.* V. 2006 He shews the Center of Gravity of all Arches of Circles, with their Superficial Vnguls.

‖ **Ungula** (*v·ŋgiŭlă*). [L. *ungula* claw, hoof, f. *unguis* nail, UNGUIS.]

† **1.** = ONYCHA, ONYX 2. *Obs.*

1382 WYCLIF *Ecclus.* xxiv. 21 [15], Galban, and vngula, and gutta [1388 vngula, and gumme].

† **2.** A morbid growth in the eye; = ONYX 3, PTERYGIUM 2 a. *Obs.*

*c* 1400 *Lanfranc's Cirurg.* 19 Vngula is a þing, þat bigynneþ bi þe nose & goiþ over þe iȝe til he keuere al þe iȝe. 1597 A. M. tr. *Guillemeau's Fr. Chirurg.* c ij b/1 When we desire to cut of[f] an Vngula. *Ibid.* c ij b/2 An Eye, in the which is an Vngula. 1693 tr. *Blancard's Phys. Dict.* (ed. 2), *Pterygium*,..a membranous Excrescence above the horny Tunic of the Eye, called *Unguis* and *Ungula*.

† **3.** = UNGUIS 3. *Obs.*⁻⁰

1693 tr. *Blancard's Phys. Dict.* (ed. 2), *Ungula*, a sort of hooked Instrument to draw a dead Fœtus out of the Womb.

**4.** *Geom.* (See quots.)

1710 J. HARRIS *Lex. Techn.* II, *Ungula*, in Geometry, is the Section of a Cylinder cut off by a Plane, which passes obliquely thro' the Plane of the Basse, and part of the Cylindric Surface. 1824–5 *Encycl. Metrop.* (1845) I. 362/1 A spherical wedge or ungula is that portion of the solid sphere, which is included between the same great semicircles, and has the lune for its base. 1843 *Penny Cycl.* XXV. 514/2 The hoof of a horse looks like the part of a cone which is separated from the part containing the vertex by an oblique plane. Hence such a solid is called an ungula.

‖ **Ungulata** (*vŋgiŭlē¹·tă*), *sb. pl.* [L. *ungulāta*, neut. pl. of *ungulātus*: see next.] The order or division of ungulate or hoofed animals.

1839 *Penny Cycl.* XIV. 352/2 The *Ungulata*, comprising the *Belluæ* and *Pecora*. 1872 MIVART *Elem. Anat.* 43 The spinous processes may be very much more prolonged, as in the Ungulata. 1891 W. H. FLOWER *Horse* i. 11 The group *Ungulata*, discarded by Linnæus, Cuvier, and others,..has been resuscitated of late years.

**Ungulate** (*v·ŋgiŭlět*), *a.* and *sb.* [ad. L. *ungulāt-us*, f. *ungula* hoof.]

**1.** Having the form of a hoof; hoof-shaped.

1802 R. HALL *Elem. Bot.* 193 Ungulate, or Hoof-shaped, *ungulatus*. 1858 W. CLARK *Van der Hoeven's Zool.* II. 634 Feet tridactylous, with all the toes insistent, ungulate. 1888 G. ALLEN in *Longm. Mag.* July 303 The slender and delicate ungulate feet of the gazelles and the chamois.

**2.** Of quadrupeds: Having hoofs.

The classification was introduced by Ray (1693).

1839 G. ROBERTS *Dict. Geol.* s.v., An ungulate quadruped. 1872 DARWIN *Orig. Spec.* (ed. 6) vii. 179 The competition.. must be between giraffe and giraffe, and not with the other ungulate animals. *Ibid.* xi. 302 The existing horse and certain older ungulate forms. 1875 C. C. BLAKE *Zool.* 32 The odd-toed division of ungulate Mammalia.

**b.** *sb.* An ungulate animal.

1842 BRANDE *Dict. Sci.*, etc. 1274/2. 1854 OWEN in *Orr's Circ. Sci.*, *Org. Nat.* I. 236 In the odd-toed or 'perissodactyle' ungulates. 1894 LYDEKKER *Roy. Nat. Hist.* II. 152 In all the Ungulates the limbs have entirely ceased to be used as organs of prehension.

So **U·ngulated** *a.* *rare*.

1822 GOOD *Study Med.* I. 174 Generally speaking, the tenderest food is that of the gallinaceous birds: then that of the ungulated quadrupeds. 1891 W. H. FLOWER *Horse* i. 11 The ungulated or hoofed animals, and the unguiculated.

**Ungulèd** (*v·ŋgiŭld*), *a.* *Her.* [f. L. *ungul-a* claw, hoof. Cf. UNGLED.] Of animals: Having the hoofs or claws of a different tincture from the body.

1572 BOSSEWELL *Armorie* II. 100 Two demye hyppotames, sable, armed and vnguled. 1610 GUILLIM *Heraldry* III. xiv. 130 He beareth Argent, a Stagge Tripping Proper, Armed and Vnguled. *a* 1695 WOOD *Surv. Oxford* (O.H.S.) III. 143 A lyon rampant sable, collered or, ungulèd and langed gules. 1728 CHAMBERS *Cycl.* s.v. *Unicorn*, An Unicorn seiant sable, armed and unguled, Or. 1763 *Brit. Mag.* IV. 238 Two bucks, proper, attired, and unguled, or. 1864 BOUTELL *Her. Hist. & Pop.* xvii. (ed. 3) 280 Two bulls arg., ..armed unguled, collared and chained. *Ibid.* xxi. 366 An ox gu., armed and unguled or.

**U·ngulìgrade,** *a.* *Zool.* [ad. mod.L. *unguligradus*, f. L. *ungula* claw + -*gradus* walking. Cf. F. *ongulograde*.] Walking on the tips of the digits.

1869 HUXLEY *Introd. Classif.* 146 *Unguligrade*, those animals which walk on the tips of the digits only, which are always hoofed. 1881 MIVART *Cat* 472 The Carnivora also are always digitigrade or plantigrade, never unguligrade.

**Ungulite** (*v·ŋgiŭlait*). *Palæont.* [f. L. *ungul-a*, UNGULA + -ITE ¹.] A Palæozoic brachiopod, the obolus. *Ungulite grit*: see OBOLITE.

1850 ANSTED *Elem. Geol.*, *Min.*, etc. § 980 A sandstone, or grit, distinguished by a remarkable fossil (the *Ungulite*) unknown in Western Europe. *Ibid.* Index, Ungulite grit. 1859 MURCHISON *Siluria* (ed. 3) xiv. 374 The little horny brachiopod, the Obolus or Ungulite, is so much more abundant than any other fossil, as to have induced Pander to give to the rock the name of Ungulite grit.

**Ungu·ll,** *v.* (UN-² 6 b.)

1652 BENLOWES *Theoph.* x. xxvi, Fawn, and betray, and Treasons self outdare,..But I'l ungull thy Minions.

**U·ngulous,** *a.* [f. UNGULA.] Pertaining to or resembling a hoof; ungulate. (Webster, 1879.)

**Ungu·m,** *v.* [UN-² 4 b. Cf. Du. *ontgommen*.] *trans.* To free from gum or from being gummed; *spec.* in the preparation of silk.

1598 FLORIO, *Sgommare*, to vngum, to vnplaister, to vnglue. 1839 URE *Dict. Arts* 142 As soon as the whole [of the silk] is completely ungummed, they [*sc.* the hanks] are taken out. 1901 B. PAIN *Another Englishwoman's Love-Lett.* xxv. 111, I kiss the label..until it comes ungummed.

Hence **Ungu·mming** *vbl. sb.*

1839 URE *Dict. Arts* 142 For the first [method of scouring silk], or the ungumming. 1883 R. HALDANE *Workshop Receipts* Ser. II. 39/1 Two operations are necessary [in silk-bleaching], 'ungumming' (*dégommage*) and 'boiling'.

**Ungu·mmed,** *ppl. a.*¹ [UN-¹ 8. Cf. Du. *ongegomd*.] Not smeared or treated with gum; free from gumming.

[1775 ASH.] 1799 G. SMITH *Laboratory* II. 80 An ungummed paper will stick very close to the top of your tongue. 1891 KIPLING *City Dreadf. Nt.* 95 He now takes up an ungummed *chupatti* and fits it carefully all round.

**Ungu·mmed,** *ppl. a.*² [f. UNGUM *v.*] Freed from gum; detached from being gummed.

1839 URE *Dict. Arts* 142 Into bags of coarse canvass.. about 25 lbs. or 35 lbs. of ungummed silk are enclosed.

**Ungu·tted,** *ppl. a.* (UN-¹ 8.) 1712 in J. J. Vernon *Par. & Kirk Hawick* (1900) 99 Thinking they [*sc.* herring] would spile if lying ungutted until ye Monday.

**Ungy·ve,** *v.* [UN-² 4 b.] *trans.* To free from gyves or fetters. Also *fig.*

1531 ELYOT *Gov.* II. vi, He..commaunded hym to be ungyued and sette at libertie. 1569 NEWTON *Cicero's Olde Age* 4, I haue knowen a great maignie..who were well pleased to be ungiued, loosed, and deliuered out of the yoke of their sensuall lustes. 1610 HEALEY *St. Aug. Citie of God* 310 Our intellect being ungived from the body, if it want the light of God's truth, it must needes lament and languish. 1831 CARLYLE *Sart. Res.* II. ix, My mind's eyes were now unsealed, and its hands ungyved.

**Ungy·ved,** *ppl. a.* [UN-¹ 8.] Not gyved or fettered; free.

1607 MARSTON *What You Will* II. i, Think'st thou a libertine, an vngiu'd breast Skornes not the shacklesse of thy enuious clogges? *c* 1850 LOWELL *Without & Within* vii, I envy him the ungyved prance By which his freezing feet he warms. 1892 'M. FIELD' *Sight & Song* 40 Intent upon her work, as though It were full liberty ungyved to go.

**Unhabil,** obs. Sc. var. UNABLE *a.*

† **Unha·bile,** *a.* *Obs.* [UN-¹ 7 and 5 b.] = INHABILE *a.*, UNABLE *a.*

1539 ELYOT in Ellis *Orig. Lett.* Ser. I. II. 117 Nowe althowgh very unmeete and unhabile, I have servyd the King.. truely and faithfully. 1567 *Sc. Acts*, *Mary* (1814) II. 573/1 Decerning thairfore .. his posteritie to be fra thine furth unhabile to bruik offices..within this Realme. 1660 JER. TAYLOR *Ductor* III. ii. rule 2 § 14 The offending person is bound in Conscience not to accept a benefice..to which by that censure he is made unhabile and unapt.

**Unha·bit,** *v.* [UN-² 4 b.] *trans.* To free from a habit; to disaccustom.

1650 FULLER *Pisgah* II. i. 64 So hard it is to unhabit mens mouths from old ill customs.

† **Unha·bit,** *ppl. a.* *Sc.* *Obs.* [UN-¹ 8 b.] Uninhabited. 1580 *Reg. Privy Council Scot.* III. 304 The said hous..remanis unhabite be him.

**Unha·bitable,** *a.* Now *rare*. [UN-¹ 7 b and 5 b.] Uninhabitable. (Common *c* 1550–1690.)

1382 WYCLIF *Jer.* ii. 6 Wher is the Lord, that..ladde vs ouer by desert, by the lond vnhabitable? 1388 — *Jer.* vi. 8 Lest.. Y sette thee forsakun, a loond vnhabitable [1382 vndwellable]. *a* 1485 FORTESCUE *Wks.* (1869) 486 He..made Babyloyne unhabitable. 1527 in Hakluyt *Voy.* (1599) I. 219 The..opinion, that vnder the line Equinoctiall for much heate the land was vnhabitable. 1555 EDEN *Decades* (Arb.) 297 That opinion .. touching the vnhabitable clime vnder the poles. 1615 G. SANDYS *Trav.* 90 Next vnto this stands Rhodes,..once couered with the sea, or at least an vnhabitable marish. *a* 1652 J. SMITH *Sel. Disc.* ix. 452 The soul of a wicked man becomes a very unhabitable and incommodious place to itself. 1702 C. MATHER *Magn. Chr.* I. v. (1852) 76 They that have made Britain more unhabitable than the Torrid Zone. 1733 SWIFT *On Poetry* 181 So Geographers in Afric-Maps..o'er unhabitable Downs Place Elephants for want of Towns. 1887 *Spectator* 15 Oct. 1381 The whole deep Northern fringe..is unhabitable and uninhabited except by a few savages.

Hence **Unha·bitableness.**

1661 BOYLE *Physiol. Ess.* (1669) 27 The Unhabitableness of the Torrid Zone. 1668 H. MORE *Div. Dial.* III. xxxiv. I. 523 *marg.*, Difficulties touching the Habitableness or Unhabitableness of the Planets.

† **Unha·bitated,** *ppl. a.* *Obs.*⁻⁰ [UN-¹ 8.] = next. 1648 HEXHAM II, *Een Onbewoont landt*, a land or country Vnhabitated.

† **Unha·bited,** *ppl. a.* *Obs.* [UN-¹ 8 and 5 b.] Uninhabited. (Freq. *c* 1500–1625.)

1490 CAXTON *Eneydos* xxii. 81 Goyng by longe wayes, dystroied, deserte & vnhabyted. 1491 — *Vitas Patr.* (W. de W. 1495) III. i. 317 b/2 We arryued a londe in a contree unhabyted. 1553 EDEN *Treat. New Ind.* (Arb.) 39 When Vesputius had entered into the Iland, he found it rude and vnhabited. 1585 T. WASHINGTON tr. *Nicholay's Voy.* II. xi. 45 b, The promontory is ful of ruines vnhabited. 1640 J. RUTTER *2nd Pt. Cid* III. i. 19 Ile seek some place unhabited by women. 1656 HEYLIN *Surv. France* 75 She will rather choose to leave her fine house unhabited.

**Unhabi·tual,** *a.* (UN-¹ 7.) 1864 LOWELL *Fireside Trav.* 60 A deacon..drinking in, with unhabitual ears, a song.. with a dash of libertinism. 1895 J. RAE *Life A. Smith* xx. 324 Smith's outbreak of very unhabitual irritation with Strahan.

**Unhabi·tuate,** *ppl. a.* [UN-¹ 8 b.] = next. 1815 MILMAN *Fazio* (1821) 28 This cataract of courtesy O'erwhelms my weak and unhabituate ears.

**Unhabi·tuated,** *ppl. a.* (UN-¹ 8.)

[1775 ASH.] 1796 MME. D'ARBLAY *Camilla* I. 227 Delighted to give, but unhabituated to any other exertion. 1834 COOPER *Good's Study Med.* (ed. 4) I. 632 Strangers, unhabituated to the climate and its diseases, suffer from remittents. 1898 P. MANSON *Trop. Diseases* iv. 89 A full dose of the drug which in the unhabituated would produce profound..narcosis.

**Unhable,** obs. var. UNABLE *a.* and *v.*

**Unha·cked,** *ppl. a.*¹ [UN-¹ 8 + HACK *v.*¹ Cf. MDu. *ongehact*, Sw. *ohackad*.] Not hacked or cut.

1595 SHAKS. *John* II. i. 254 With vnhack'd swords, and Helmets all vnbruis'd. 1606 — *Ant. & Cl.* II. vi. 38 To part with vnhackt edges, and beare backe Our Targes vndinted.

**Unha·cked,** *ppl. a.*² [UN-¹ 8, 9 + HACK *sb.*³ or *v.*³]

**1.** Not employed as a literary hack.

1778 *Heroic Ep. Unfort. Monarch* 2 A plain bard,..Unhack'd, unplac'd, amongst the venal quire.

**2.** Not made common or hackneyed.

1894 BARING-GOULD *Deserts S. France* I. Pref. p. vii, It is a country unhacked by ordinary tourists.

**Unha·ckled,** *ppl. a.* (UN-¹ 8.) 1853 HICKIE *Aristoph.* (1872) II. 424 My flax which I have left at home unhackled.

**Unha·ckneyed,** *ppl. a.* [UN-[1] 8.]
**1.** Not habituated by long practice; inexperienced. Const. *in*.

**1759** STERNE *Tr. Shandy* I. xi, In plain truth, he was a man unhackneyed and unpractised in the world. **1785** G. A. BELLAMY *Apology* III. 94, I was then unhackneyed in the villainies of mankind. **1814** SCOTT *Wav.* xxxii, He had a sort of naiveté and openness of demeanour, that seemed to belong to one unhackneyed in the ways of intrigue.
*absol.* **1796** MME. D'ARBLAY *Camilla* III. 112 Public amusements, to the young and unhackneyed, give entertainment without requiring exertion.

**2.** Not rendered commonplace or stale by frequent use or contact.

**1824** MISS MITFORD *Village* Ser. I. 93 Her English was racy, unhackneyed, proper to the thought to a degree that only original thinking could give. **1856** G. BRIMLEY *Ess.* (1858) 236 To open to her almost untried and certainly unhacknied regions of beauty. **1880** *Academy* 27 Nov. 390/1 His [picture]..shows a research after unhackneyed effects.

Hence **Unha·ckneyedness.**

**1884** SAINTSBURY in Ward *Eng. Poets* III. 218 There is almost always something novel in his dressing up of his images and a suggestive unhackneyedness in their expression.

**Unha·d,** *ppl. a. rare.* [UN-[1] 8 b.] Unobtained.

**1421** HOCCLEVE *Jereslaus' Wife* 111 With this addicion, þat he nat shal Wirke, my Conseil and assent vnhad. *c* **1449** PECOCK *Repr.* II. xi. 212 That the hool profite of remembring..be not lost and vnhad. **1876** *Whitby Gloss.* 206 *Unhad*, not yet obtained.

† **Unhadien,** *v.*: see UN-[2] 2.

**Unha·ft,** *v.* (UN-[2] 4.)

**1582** STANYHURST *Æneis* I. (Arb.) 21 The oars are cleene splintred, the helme is from ruther vnhafted. **1598** FLORIO, *Smanicare*,..to vnhaft, to vnhilt, to vnhandle. **1611** COTGR., *Desmanchement*, an vnhafting.

**Unha·fted,** (*ppl.*) *a.* (UN-[1] 8, 9.) **1894** BARING-GOULD *Deserts S. France* I. 145 Their rude stone axes,..unhafted.

**Unhail,** *a.*: see UNHALE *a.*

**Unhai·led,** *ppl. a.* (UN-[1] 8.)

**1715** ROWE *Lady Jane Grey* IV. i, Thro' a staring ghastly looking crowd, Unhail'd, unbless'd, with heavy heart he went. **1828** ALFORD in *Life* (1873) 31 Disappointment, and unhail'd success. **1832** TENNYSON *Lady of Shalott* 21 Unhail'd The shallop flitteth silken-sail'd. **1896** KIPLING *Seven Seas* 7 'Twixt seas unsailed and shores unhailed.

**Unhailsum,** obs. Sc. var. UNWHOLESOME.

**Unhai·r,** *v.* [UN-[2] 4 and 7. Cf. MDu. and Du. *ontharen*, MHG. *enthâren*.]
**1.** *trans.* To deprive (the head, etc.) of hair.

**1382** WYCLIF *Ezek.* xxix. 18 Eche heed maad ballid, and eche shuldre is vnheerid. **1598** FLORIO, *Disparuccare*, to pull off ones haire or perawig, to vnhaire. **1606** SHAKS. *Ant. & Cl.* II. v. 64 Ile vnhaire thy head, Thou shalt be whipt with Wyer. **1849** J. A. CARLYLE tr. *Dante's Inf.* 393 Even if thou unhair me, I will not tell thee who I am.

**b.** *Tanning.* To remove the hair from (a skin) by special processes.

**1845** G. DODD *Brit. Manuf.* Ser. v. 182 The hide is then spread out on the beam, and 'unhaired', that is, scraped with a knife till the hair is removed. **1880** *Times* 27 Sept. 12/6 The cost of unhairing, fleshing, and scudding all kinds of skins.

**2.** *intr.* To lose the hair; to become free of hair.

**1843** in Morfit *Tanning & Currying* (1853) 177 So that they [*sc.* the hides] may unhair without tainting. **1883** R. HALDANE *Workshop Rec.* Ser. II. 370/1 The hide is said to unhair in 24 hours.

Hence **Unhai·red** *ppl. a.*

**1852** MORFIT *Tanning & Currying* (1853) 20 The softened and unhaired skins. **1881** MORGAN *Contrib. N. Amer. Ethnol.* 127 Screens of willow matting or unhaired skins.

**Unhai·red,** *a.* [UN-[1] 9.] Hairless, beardless.

Suggested by Theobald (1733), and formally possible, but cf. UNHEARD *ppl. a.* 2.

**1595** SHAKS. *John* V. ii. 133 This vn-heard [*Th.* unhair'd] sawcinesse and boyish Troopes, The King doth smile at.

**Unhai·ring,** *vbl. sb. Tanning.* [f. UNHAIR *v.* 1 b.] The process of removing the hair from skins. Also *attrib.*

**1842** *Penny Mag.* 28 May 212/1 The operations of 'fleshing', of 'unhairing' and of 'graining' are..nearly alike in their general appearance. **1851–4** TOMLINSON *Arts & Manuf.* II. 30/1 A curved two-handled iron scraper, called the unhairing knife. **1897** C. T. DAVIS *Manuf. Leather* (ed. 2) 331 The goat-skins..then go on to the unhairing machine.. or to the unhairing beams.

**Unhai·ry,** *a.* (UN-[1] 7.) **1576** NEWTON *Lemnie's Complex.* 42 b, In their other partes their skinne is smothe and vnhayrye, because moysture is aboue heate.

**Unha·le,** *a. rare.* [UN-[1] 7. See HAIL *a.*, HALE *a.* 3.] †**a.** Unsalutary. *Obs.* **b.** Not hale or healthy.

**a.** **1483** *Gower's Conf.* (Caxton) I. 2122 [He] yaf suche counseyle Towarde his kyng, which was vnheyle. **b.** **1653** E. WATERHOUSE *Apol. Learn.* 74 No more then it follows that a wasted man must get a child unhail, because he himself is consumptive. **1828–32** WEBSTER, *Unhale*, a., unsound;..not healthy.

**Unhale,** obs. variant of UNWHOLE *a.*; dial. var. UNHELE *v.* **Unhalesom,** Sc. var. UNWHOLESOME.

**Unha·llow,** *v.* [UN-[2] 3. Cf. G. *ent-*, Du. *ontheiligen*, ON. *úhelga* (Sw. *ohelga*, older Da. *uhelge*).] *trans.* To deprive of a holy or sacred character; to profane. (Common *c* 1575–1660.)

**1535** COVERDALE *Isaiah* lvi. 2 He that taketh hede, y[t] he vnhalowe not the Sabbath. — *Zeph.* iii. 4 Hir prestes vnhalowe the Sanctuary. **1571** GOLDING *Calvin on Ps.* I. 8 Defylements that unhalowe the servis of God. **1628** WITHER *Brit. Rememb.* III. 1898 That I, for ever, may those paths refuse Which may unhallow, or pervert my Muse. **1645** MILTON *Tetrach.* Wks. 1851 IV. 192 Nothing more unhallows a man,..then a habit of wrath and perturbation. **1694** F. BRAGGE *Disc. Parables* xiv. 462 Pride, and vainglory, and self-esteem,..unhallow'd everything else that was good in him. **1821** LAMB *Elia* I. *Grace before Meat*, A sense of the co-presence of circumstances which unhallow the blessing. **1860** TRENCH *Serm. Westm. Abb.* xxix. 331 In a world where so much is ever seeking to unhallow our spirits, to render them common and profane.

**Unha·llowed,** *ppl. a.* [OE. *unhálgod* (and *ungehálgod*), f. UN-[1] 8 + HALLOWED *ppl. a.*]
**1.** Not formally hallowed or consecrated; left secular or profane.

*c* **1000** *Sax. Leechd.* I. 380 Nim eall swa fela dropena.. unhalȝodes eles. **1297** R. GLOUC. (Rolls) 7156 Ac vor þe chirche vn-halewed was, þeruore him was wo; He þoȝt lete it halwy. **1303** R. BRUNNE *Handl. Synne* 8609 3yf þyng vnhalewed were forgete, Þat yn holy cherche were lete, Or halewed þyng yn ouþer stede lay. *c* **1380** WYCLIF *Wks.* (1880) 69 Þei wolen suffre an auter vnhalwedid [*sic*], or a chirche or a chirche ȝerde suspendid. *c* **1440** *Jacob's Well* 16 Þey..þat..beryn awey, or stelyn holy cherche good out of ony oþer place vnhalwyd. **1532** MORE *Confut. Tindale* Wks. 375/1 Nowe wyll not Tyndal sette a strawe the more by the annoyntyng with holye oyle, then by smeryng with vnhalowed butter. **1587** in T. Norton *Calvin's Inst.* IV. xix. 492 *margin*, Men vnhallowed and vnconsecrated. **1797** S. & HT. LEE *Canterb. T.* (1799) I. 311 Let us beware how we deem that spot unhallowed which receives the ashes of the good! **1805** SOUTHEY *Madoc* I. xv, This night, Thy father's body..shall be..cast aside In some unhallowed pit, with foul disgrace.

**2.** Not having a hallowed or sacred character; unholy, impious, wicked: **a.** Of actions.

**1591** *Troub. Raigne K. John* xii. 88 His quarrell is vnhallowed, false, and wrong. **1626** JACKSON *Creed* VIII. xi. § 1 To adventure upon the pretended mysteries of some unhallowed art. **1656** MILTON *Lett. State* Wks. 1851 VIII. 361 That unhallow'd villany nefariously attempted upon the Person of our Agent. **1725** POPE *Odyss.* XII. 468 Six guilty days my wretched mates employ In impious feasting, and unhallow'd joy. **1813** SCOTT *Rokeby* VI. xviii, What ruth can Denzil claim from him, Whose thoughtless youth he led astray, And damn'd to this unhallow'd way? **1846** MRS. A. MARSH *Father Darcy* II. xvi. 271 She..felt her heart shudder with unhallowed pleasure, as she thought of the dreadful day of reckoning.

**b.** Of persons, the hands, tongue, etc.

**1588** SHAKS. *Tit. A.* V. iii. 14 Away Inhumaine Dogge, Vnhallowed Slaue. **1603** DRAYTON *Bar. Wars* V. xxxv, Vile traytors, hold of your vnhallowed hands. **1663** BP. PATRICK *Parab. Pilgr.* xvii, He cares not for being extolled by such unhallowed mouths. **1703** ROWE *Ulysses* I. i, The rude unhallow'd Railer's Tongue. **1765** GOLDSM. *Hermit* xxiv, Forgive a stranger rude,..Whose feet unhallow'd thus intrude Where Heaven and you reside. **1827** DISRAELI *V. Grey* VI. i. 272 Ye most unhallowed rogues.

**c.** Of places or things.

**1588** SHAKS. *Tit. A.* II. iii. 210 Why dost not..helpe me out, From this vnhallow'd and blood-stained Hole? **1634** MILTON *Comus* 757, I had not thought to have unlockt my lips In this unhallow'd air. **1651** HOBBES *Leviath.* IV. xliv. 339 Wherein every thing..(except the unhallowed Spittle of the Priest) hath some set form of Exorcisme. **1853** KINGSLEY *Hypatia* i, He had entered the unhallowed precincts, where devils still lingered about their ancient shrines.

Hence **Unha·llowedness.**

**1899** MRS. E. KENNARD *Morals Midlands* 399 It has shown me the unhallowedness of love that is not lawful.

**Unha·llowing,** *vbl. sb.* [f. UNHALLOW *v.*] The action of making unhallowed.

*c* **1554** BRADFORD *Hurt of Hearing Mass* (1580) C v, The prophanation and vnhallowyng, bothe of bodie and soule. **1571** GOLDING *Calvin on Ps.* lxxiv. 1 Beholding the horrible unhalowing of the Temple. **1645** USSHER *Body Div.* (1647) 242 The unhallowing or prophaneing of the Sabbath. *a* **1859** DE QUINCEY in Hogg *De Q. & Friends* (1895) 89 A sort of desecration and unhallowing analogous to the profanation of a temple.

**Unhallow-washed,** *ppl. a.* [UN-[1] 8.] Not sprinkled with holy water. **1614** SYLVESTER *Parl. Vertues Royall* 196 When, by mis-heed or by mis-hap, hee comes Un-hallow-washt into the Sacred Rooms. **Unha·loed,** *a.* (UN-[1] 9.) **1823** J. WILSON *Trials Marg. Lyndsay* xxxix, The evening sun sank..and left the sky open..to an unhaloed moon.

**Unha·lsed,** *ppl. a. Sc.* [UN-[1] 8 + HALSE *v.*[1] 3. Cf. ON. *úheilsaðr* (MSw. *ohelsadh*, MDa. *uhelset*).] Not greeted or saluted.

**1513** DOUGLAS *Æneid* IX. v. 141 Now hir I leif onhalsyt as I ryde. **1821** SCOTT *Pirate* xxi, It shall never be said that my kinswoman sat in her bower unhalsed.

**Unha·lter,** *v.* (UN-[2] 4 b. Cf. MDu. *onthalteren*.)

**1584** PEELE *Arraignm. Paris* IV. ii, I do know a cast.. that we would help t'unhalter them as fast. **1598** FLORIO, *Scapestrato*, vnbridled, vnhaltred, disintangled. **1611** COTGR., *Deschevestrer*, to vnhalter, or take off the halter from. **1816** J. WILSON *City of Plague* 287 Unhalter yon poor wretch—he must be carried Back to his prison.

**Unha·lting,** *ppl. a.* (UN-[1] 10.) **1832** L. HUNT *Poems* Pref. p. xlv, An unhalting and consistent narrative. **1852** ROCK *Ch. of Fathers* I. viii. III. 54 Holding..the true Catholic belief in the Eucharist, with a faith that was unhalting. **Unha·mmered,** *ppl. a.* (UN-[1] 8.) [**1775** ASH.] **1861** SIR W. FAIRBAIRN *Iron* 214 These results give a mean of 27·246 tons for the unhammered..steel.

**Unha·mper,** *v.*[1] [UN-[2] 5.] *trans.* To let out of a cage or hamper.

**1620** SHELTON *Quix.* II. xvii. 105 Ech of them striuing to get as farre from the Cart as they could, before the Lyons should be vnhampered.

**Unha·mper,** *v.*[2] [UN-[2] 3.] *trans.* To disengage; to set free, release.

**1648** J. BEAUMONT *Psyche* XX. xxxvi, Now all her Passions unhamper'd were, And every Bond to Libertie relented. **1675** WORTHINGTON *Self-Resignation* I. vi. 39 His mind is unhampered, disentangled, and set loose. **1831** LAMB *Hercules Pacificatus* 111 The varlets, glad to be unhamper'd, Made each a leg,—then fairly scamper'd.

**Unha·mpered,** *ppl. a.* [UN-[1] 8.] Unclogged, unimpeded. (Common from *c* 1850.)

*a* **1699** J. BEAUMONT *Psyche* IX. lxxxix, Their free unhamper'd Contemplations towre Up to the crest of their divine desires. **1724** E. ERSKINE *Serm.* Wks. (1791) 118 A full, free, and unhampered offer. **1882** BRYCE *Manitoba* 23 He would start unhampered by old conditions and preexisting enactments.

†**Unha·nced,** *ppl. a.* [UN-[1] 8.] Not raised or lifted up. **1582** STANYHURST *Æneis*, etc. (Arb.) 126 Therefor in houre iudicial The vngodlye shal vnhaunst remayne.

**Unha·nd,** *v.* [UN-[2] 4 b.] *trans.* To take the hand off; to release from one's grasp; to let go. Chiefly *arch.* in the imperative phrase *unhand me!*

**1602** SHAKS. *Ham.* I. iv. 84 Vnhand me Gentlemen: By Heau'n, Ile make a Ghost of him that lets me. **1655** tr. *Sorel's Com. Hist. Francion* VII. 22, I desired them to unhand me. **1687** MRS. BEHN *Lucky Chance* v, Unhand me, false deceiver, let me loose! **1748** RICHARDSON *Clarissa* (1811) II. 358 Unhand me this moment, or I will cry out for help. **1801** MAR. EDGEWORTH *Moral T.*, *Angelina* iv, Unhand my Angelina, or I shall die! **1860** SALA *Baddington Peerage* I. vii. 132 The surgeon unhanded his assistant, looking at him with a vexed and puzzled air.
*fig.* **1880** LANIER *Sunrise* 77 'Tis here thou canst unhand thy heart And breathe it free.

**Unha·ndcuffed,** *ppl. a.* (UN-[1] 8.) **1861** GEN. P. THOMPSON *Audi Alt. Part.* III. clxii. 178 They might as well say, allow men to go un-handcuffed, and [etc.]. **1894** *Daily News* 8 Dec. 7/1 The prisoner..was seen sitting..unhandcuffed. **Unha·ndicapped,** *ppl. a.* (UN-[1] 8.) **1879** MEREDITH *Egoist* xxxvi, How was he to compete with these unhandicapped men?

**Unha·ndily,** *adv.* (UN-[1] 11.)

**1706** STEVENS I, *Inabilmente*, unaptly, unhandily. **1775** ASH, *Unhandily*,..aukwardly. **1865** CARLYLE *Fredk. Gr.* XII. vi. IV. 163 St. Agnes Day falls but unhandily this year; and I think the Fair will..not be held. **1896** DE VINNE *Moxon's Mech. Exerc.*, *Printing* 421 The signature was put unhandily in the center of the line.

**Unha·ndiness.** [UN-[1] 12.]
**1.** Awkwardness, inexpertness.

**1706** STEVENS I, *Inhabilidad*, Inhability, Unhandiness, Incapacity. **1862** MISS YONGE *C'tess Kate* iii, Whether it were from the difference of height, or from Kate's innate unhandiness. **1889** *The Voice* (N. Y.) 19 Sept., From whom communications would be accepted,..if only some one would help their unhandiness with the pen.

**2.** Unmanageableness.

**1883** *Harper's Mag.* Aug. 449/1 The sloop rig..is so dangerous as to demand large crews to control its unhandiness. **1897** MARY KINGSLEY *W. Africa* 609 It was highly dangerous,..because of the violent storms..and the unhandiness of the native craft.

**Unha·ndled,** *ppl. a.* [UN-[1] 8. Cf. MDu. *ongehandelt*, OHG. *ungehandelôt*, MDa. *uhandlet* (not negotiated).]
**1.** Of horses, etc.: Not broken in; untamed.

**1558** *N. Co. Wills* (Surtees 1912) 12 My yong blacke hambling gelding unhandlyd. **1596** SHAKS. *Merch. V.* v. i. 72 A wilde and wanton heard Or race of youthful and vnhandled colts. **1639** T. DE GRAY *Expert Farrier* 302 Horses unhandled, to wit, in their youth. **1812** *Sporting Mag.* XXXIX. 68 Every description of horse, or mule, whether previously broke or unhandled. **1902** KIPLING *The Islanders* 21 Sons of the sheltered city — unmade, unhandled, unmeet — Ye pushed them raw to the battle.

**2.** Not dealt with or treated of.

**1613** SHAKS. *Hen. VIII*, III. ii. 58 Cardinall Campeius.. Ha's left the cause o' th' King vnhandled. **1657** TOMLINSON *Renou's Disp.* 79 The extraction of oyles is yet unhandled.

**b.** Untried, unemployed.

**1826** GALT *Last of Lairds* xi. 103 There's no a claw..the whilk Caption will leave unhandled.

**3.** Not touched with the hand. Also *fig.*

*a* **1657** R. LOVEDAY *Lett.* (1663) 218 Those [delights] that ..after an advantagious intermission return fresh and unhandled to the senses. **1745** ELIZA HEYWOOD *Female Spect.* No. 17 (1748) III. 258 The plumb unhandled lost its bloom. **1794** COLERIDGE *Lett.* (1895) 59, I, too, possessed the tender irritableness of unhandled sensibility.

**Unha·ndselled,** *ppl. a.* (UN-[1] 8.) **1837** EMERSON *Addr. Amer. Schol.* Wks. (Bohn) II. 182 Out of unhandselled savage nature..come at last Alfred and Shakespeare. *a* **1862** THOREAU *Maine W.* i. (1864) 70 Here was no man's garden, but the unhandselled globe.

**Unha·ndsome,** *a.* (and *adv.*) [UN-[1] 7. Cf. WFris. *on-*, *ûnhânsum* inexpert, unmanageable, Du. and Flem. *onhandzaam* (earlier *-saem*) intractable, unusable, older Da. *uhandsøm*.]
**1.** Not handsome, elegant, or graceful; faulty in appearance, form, or structure; plain, uncomely.

**1530** PALSGR. 328/1 Unhansome,..*mausade*. **1579** E. K. *Gloss to Spenser's Sheph. Cal.* Nov. 51 Not comed, that is rude and vnhansome. **1589** HORSEY *Trav.* (Hakl. Soc.) App. 343, I was placed in an howse verie unhandsoom [and] unholsoom. **1648** J. BEAUMONT *Psyche* XVI. clxxxix, Who ever thought the Rose or Lilie stood Guilty of course unhandsom Nakednesse, Because they never put on borrowed Hood? **1695** *Phil. Trans.* XIX. 152 This was formerly no unhandsom Structure, being built in the form of our Churches. **1781** P. BECKFORD *Hunting* (1802) 49, I could tell you that I have seen very good sport with very unhandsome packs. **1789** GIBBON *Autobiogr.* (1854) 43 A narrow, gloomy street, the most unfrequented of an unhandsome town. **1819** SCOTT *Ivanhoe* xiv, Both dressed in the ancient Saxon garb,..not unhandsome in itself. **1866** R. TATE *Brit. Mollusks* iv. 142 *Helix rotundata* is provided with not an unhandsome shell. **1895** SIR G. PARKER *Trail of Sword* viii, A large unhandsome house.

**b.** Of persons, their features, etc.

*a* 1586 SIDNEY *Arcadia* II. xix, I was glad I had done so good a deede for a Gentlewoman not unhandsome. 1631 A. TOWNSHEND *Albion's Tri.* 22, I was as loath to be brought vpon the Stage as an vnhansom Man is to see himselfe in a great Glasse. 1653 R. SANDERS *Physiogn.* 144 Socrates was the most nasty and unhandsom of all men living. 1709 MRS. MANLEY *Secret Mem.* (1720) II. 215 This spruce, affected, not unhandsome Lawyer had maid the Overture of his fair Person to Corinna. 1787 W. THOMSON tr. *Hist. Gt. Brit.* III. I. 121 Being generally well-shaped, and not unhandsome. 1826 *Q. Rev.* XXXIV. 331 It was hard to say whether he was more dunce or dwarf, more unlearned or unhandsome. 1887 ANNE ELLIOT *Old Man's Favour* II. i, A dark, unhandsome..face.

**c.** As *adv.* Unhandsomely.

1596 SPENSER *F. Q.* v. xii. 38 Such were these Hags, and so vnhandsome drest.

†**2.** Unhandy, inconvenient, ill-adapted. *Obs.*

1548 UDALL, etc. *Erasm. Par. John* ix. 67 The night (perdy) is unhansome to woorke in. 1567 PALFREYMAN *Baldwin's Mor. Philos.* To Rdr., If I should haue ioyned the said number of sentences to the whole sum of this treatise, it should..haue seemed..the more vnhandsome of the reader to be carried. 1608 TOPSELL *Serpents* 270 These kindes of Spyders haue..shorter feete, and more vnhandsome to worke or finish any Webbes in their Loomes. 1690 NESSE *O. & N. Test.* I. 451 A loose, discinct, and diffluent mind is unready, unnimble, unhandy, and unhandsome for Gods service.

†**3.** Inexpert, unskilful. *Obs.*[—1]

1604 SHAKS. *Oth.* III. iv. 151, I was (vnhandsome Warrior, as I am) Arraigning his vnkindnesse with my soule.

**4.** Unfitting, unbecoming, unseemly; discourteous, mean.

1645 CHAS. I in Ellis *Orig. Lett.* Ser. I. III. 317 The treuth is, that his unhansom quitting the Castell and Forte of Bristol, hath inforced me to put him off those Commands. 1658 in *Verney Mem.* (1907) II. 83 Let mee conjure you not to doe a thing soe unhandsom, soe unmanly. 1729 FRANKLIN *Ess.* Wks. 1840 II. 18 It is barbarously unhandsome that one should be the butt of the company. 1799 DUNDAS in Owen *Wellesley's Desp.* (1877) 700 It was an unhandsome proceeding upon their part. 1810 *Sporting Mag.* XXXVI. 234 What he thought unhandsome conduct on the part of the plaintiff. 1856 G. WILSON *Gateways Knowl.* (1859) 96 To employ one's tongue..to speak against itself is but unhandsome treatment of it.

**b.** Of expressions, language, etc.

1647 CLARENDON *Hist. Reb.* v. § 263 To countenance those unhandsome expressions..they had found a new way of exprobration. 1656 HOBBES *Six Lessons* Wks. 1845 VII. 331, I leave it to your consideration to whom belong..the unhandsome attributes you so often give me. 1704 *Lond. Gaz.* No. 3987/2 Their Commander, having used some unhandsome Expressions, was detained. 1732 NEAL *Hist. Purit.* I. 187 It was reported that some of the warmer Puritans had turned the Habits into ridicule, and given unhandsome language to them that wore them. 1814 JANE AUSTEN *Mansfield Park* xxi, Lest it should betray her into any observations seemingly unhandsome.

**c.** Not generous or liberal.

1800 MRS. HERVEY *Mourtray Fam.* III. 109 I'll take her without a sixpence; which, let me tell you, I think no unhandsome offer.

†**5.** Unfortunate; unhappy. *Obs.*

1633 FLETCHER & SHIRLEY *Night-Walker* I. i, I know she loves him..Beyond the Indies in his mouldy Cabinets, But 'tis her unhandsome fate. 1657 W. COLES *Adam in Eden* To Rdr., Sundry unhandsome dysasters have happened to the ruine of many.

†**6.** Unpleasant, nasty. *Obs.*

1660 JER. TAYLOR *Ductor* I. v. rule 8 § 28 Like unhandsome and ill-tasted physick, it is against nature in the taking and in its operating.

**Unha·ndsomely,** *adv.* [UN-[1] 11; cf. prec.]

†**1.** Not dexterously or cleverly; unskilfully. *Obs.*

1545 ASCHAM *Toxoph.* I. (Arb.) 89 And so the more stronge man not vsed to shote, shootes moost vnhansumlye. 1611 COTGR., *Faire le mibaudichon*, to doe a thing foolishly, or ill-fauouredly; vnhandsomely to goe about it. 1638 JUNIUS *Paint. Ancients* 100 The boy..did delight..to make oxen, horses, and men likewise, and..did it not unhandsomly.

**2.** Ungracefully, inelegantly.

1565 COOPER s.v. *Incompositus*, The verses runne vnhandsomely. *a* 1586 SIDNEY *Arcadia* I. xvii, About his middle he had..a long cloake of silke, which as unhandsomely, as it needes must, became the wearer. 1632 MASSINGER & FIELD *Fatal Dowry* IV. i, What fouler object in the world than to see a young, fair, handsome beauty unhandsomely dighted? 1670 OWEN *Disc.* vi. (1760) 82 A Man may have a Garment that may fit very ill, very unhandsomely, about him. 1705 COLLIER *Ess. Mor. Subj.* III. *Pain* 13 The Roman Gladiators..chose rather to receive a Cut than avoid it unhandsomely.

†**3.** Unfitly; inappropriately, awkwardly. *Obs.*

1548 ELYOT, *Incommodé*,..vngaynely,..vnh somely, vneasyly. 1573 BARET *Alv.* I 96 Verie Incommodiouslie, verie vnhandsomelie. 1649 JER. TAYLOR *Apol. Liturgy* § 92 This was not unhandsomely intimated by the word sometimes used by..the Greek church. 1651 C. CARTWRIGHT *Cert. Relig.* I. 290 These things do but very unhandsomely hang together. 1680 H. MORE *Apocal. Apoc.* 192 Lacqueyes..in querpo, which sutes not unhandsomly with the word σώματα, bodies.

**4.** Unfittingly, unbecomingly; illiberally, meanly.

1650 R. STAPYLTON *Strada's Low C. Wars* IV. 79 His Majesty..thought it best to do that, while his authoritie was intire, which perhaps necessity might unhandsomely inforce him to. 1668 DRYDEN *Tyrannic Love* IV. i, He raves, sir, and, to cover my disdain, Unhandsomely would his denial feign. 1700 in *Pennsylv. Hist. Soc. Mem.* IX. 4 A bill.. opposed and voted out—I think, very unhandsomely. 1709 STRYPE *Ann. Ref.* iv. 82 Dering..had charged him with neglect of religion, and unhandsomely and untruly told him [etc.]. 1839 HALLAM *Hist. Lit.* III. ii. § 61 This story Franklin, rather unhandsomely, appropriated to himself. 1855 MACAULAY *Hist. Eng.* xvii. IV. 55 He had poor relations; and the government..had most unhandsomely left them to his care.

**b.** Discourteously, rudely; without due respect or consideration.

1662 PEPYS *Diary* 5 Nov., My Lady Batten..complained ..of my wife's speaking unhandsomely of her. 1707 NORRIS *Treat. Humility* vi. 250 To know when he is handsomely or unhandsomely treated. 1759 STERNE *Tr. Shandy* I. xii, Bruised and mis-shapened with the blows which..some others have so unhandsomely given me in the dark. *a* 1781 R. WATSON *Philip II*, III. (1793) I. 378 They complained that their masters were rather used unhandsomely. 1817 KIRBY & SP. *Entomol.* xix. II. 170 They seize her, keep her in confinement, and treat her very unhandsomely.

**Unha·ndsomeness.** [UN-[1] 12.]

†**1.** Unhandiness; inconvenience. *Obs.*

1550 THOMAS, *Malageuolezza*, vnhandsomnesse, or difficultee. 1577 B. GOOGE *Heresbach's Husb.* II. (1586) 83 b, Such Uines as are ioyned with Trees, for the vnhandsomenesse, can not be thus handled.

**2.** Inelegance, uncomeliness, plainness.

*a* 1586 SIDNEY *Arcadia* II. xxii, The sweetnes of her countenance did give such a grace to what she did, that it did make hansome the unhansomnes. 1606 DEKKER *Sev. Sins* I. (Arb.) 11 Couered with two or three threed-bare Carpets.. to hide the vnhandsomnes of the Carpenters worke. 1658 *Whole Duty Man* xiii. § 7 First, for infirmities, be they either of body or mind, the deformity and unhandsomness of the one, or the weakness and folly of the other [etc.]. 1675 G. R. tr. *Le Grand's Man without Passion* 168 You carry nothing of less use about you then that which you employ to hide your unhandsomeness. 1873 MISS BROUGHTON *Nancy* I. 6 We reach our nadir of unhandsomeness in Ton Ton.

**3.** Unbecomingness; unfittingness.

1598 FLORIO, *Sgratia*, a disgrace, a gracelesnes or vnhandsomnes. 1611 COTGR., *Inconvenance*, a misbecomming, vnhandsomenesse, vnfitnesse, vnseemelinesse. 1653 JER. TAYLOR *Serm. for Year, Winter* ii. 26 Then we shall see things as they are, the evill circumstances and the crooked intentions, the adherent unhandsomenesse and the direct crimes. 1664 INGELO *Bentiv. & Ur.* VI. 350 When they Consider that Unhandsomness which will never cease to attend their unjust Prosperities. 1774 ADAM SMITH in Thomson *Life Cullen* (1832) I. 475 Bating the unhandsomeness of the practice,..in what manner does the public suffer by it? 1871 *Routledge's Ev. Boy's Ann.* June 338 The unhandsomeness of breakfasting upon one's offspring.

**Unha·ndsoming,** *vbl. sb.* (UN-[2] 6 a, 8.) 1592 NASHE *P. Penilesse* B iv b, Any thing that is said or doone to the vnhandsoming of their ambition, is straight wrested to the name of treason. 1593 G. HARVEY *Pierce's Super.* 180 Vnhandsoming of diuinityship, absurdifying of phrases.

**Unha·ndy,** *a.* [UN-[1] 7. Cf. WFris. *on-, ûnhandich*, Du. *onhandig*, LG. *unhandig*, Da. *uhændig*, Norw. *uhendig*, Sw. *ohändig.*]

**1.** Not easy to handle or manage; inconvenient, awkward, clumsy.

1664 ETHEREDGE *Love in Tub* II. iii, If she be not as kind as fair, But peevish and unhandy, Leave her. 1719 DE FOE *Crusoe* II. (Globe) 422 They took in Pieces all my clumsy unhandy Things. 1775 R. CHANDLER *Trav. Asia M.* (1825) I. 68 Our boat carried a large unhandy sail. 1778 [W. H. MARSHALL] *Minutes Agric., Digest* 47 Their being worked double made them unhandy. 1816 J. WILSON *City of Plague* II. v. 114 These swords are ugly and unhandy things. 1871 *Routledge's Ev. Boy's Ann.* Feb. 91 The very size and nature of the rig of many of the Spanish ships rendered them unwieldy and 'unhandy', as sailors call it. 1876 *N. Amer. Rev.* CXXIII. 32 An unhandy arrangement, which detracts from the value of the work.

**2.** Not skilful in using the hands; lacking in dexterity.

1669 SHADWELL *Royal Shepherd* I. i, O fie, Urania! how unhandy art thou! Sir, let me practise my little skill in surgery Upon you. 1726 SWIFT *Gulliver* III. ii, Yet in the common actions and behaviour of life, I have not seen a more clumsy, awkward, and unhandy people. 1798 W. HUTTON *Life* 6 Being hurt at seeing the nurse unhandy, she would do the work herself. 1850 GROTE *Greece* II. lx. (1862) V. 288 The Akarnanian darters..were for this reason unhandy with their missiles. 1876 TREVELYAN *Macaulay* (1883) I. 123 He was unhandy to a degree quite unexampled in the experience of all who knew him.

*fig.* 1683 KENNETT *Erasm. on Folly* 32 Wise men were so awkward and unhandy in the ordering of publick affairs.

**Unha·ng,** *v.* [UN-[2] 3. Cf. Du. *onthangen.*]

**1.** *trans.* To take down from a hanging position.

1399 LANGL. *Rich. Redeles* III. 293 For ho so þus leued his lyff to the ende..My3te seie þat he sawe..Þat heuene were vnhonge out of þe hookis. *c* 1430 *Pilgr. Lyf Manhode* I. cxxiv. (1869) 66 From thennes the scauberk she vnheeng and brouhte it. *c* 1532 DU WES *Introd. Fr.* in *Palsgr.* 941 To unhange, *despendre.* 1598 FLORIO, *Disimpiccare*, to vnhang. 1614 W. BROWNE *Sheph. Pipe* I. B 2 b, Wicked Swaines, that beare me spight,..Of my fold will draw the pegges,.. Or vnhang my Weathers bell. 1630 J. TAYLOR (Water P.) *Trav.* Wks. III. 82/1, I pray the let vs make hast, and put the Waggon vnder the Gibbet, to see if we can vnhang and saue him. 1722 DE FOE *Col. Jack* v, They unhanged a small copper, and brought it off. 1769 *Lloyd's Even. Post* Sept.–Oct. 319/2 A Butcher's wife..was endeavouring to unhang a joint of meat. 1856 SMETHAM in Beardmore *Smetham* (1906) 26 Unhanging a Turner from the wall of a distant room, he brought it to the table. 1888 A. NUTT *Holy Grail* 40 No knight should..unhang the shield till Galahad should come.

*fig.* 1616 HIERON *Wks.* II. 24 It was not inough..for our Sauiour to take them off, & (as it were) to vnhang them from the world, unlesse He did also fixe them other-where.

**b.** *Naut.* To remove (a rudder) from its fastening.

1600 HAKLUYT *Voy.* III. 552 Their cables do oftentimes breake, and their ruthers are vnhanged,..by reason the shippes doe ride but in little water. 1691 T. H[ALE] *Acc. New Invent.* 49 They were forced to unhang the Rudder, and new hang it again. 1772–84 *Cook's Voy.* (1790) III. 796 We..found the Tamar lying between the island and the main, having unhung her rudder. 1799 *Naval Chron.* II. 568 The rudder of the Isis was unhung.

**c.** To divest of hangings. *rare*—[0].

1719 BOYER *Dict. Royal* II, To Unhang a Room, *détendre la Tapisserie d'une Chambre.*

**2.** To undo the hanging of (a person).

1829 SOUTHEY *Pilgrim to Compostella* III. 54 So, with all honours that might be, They gently unhang'd Pierre. 1837 HAWTHORNE *Twice-told T.* (1851) I. vii. 134 And hanging the nigger wouldn't unhang the old gentleman!

**Unha·nged,** *ppl. a.* [UN-[1] 8. Cf. Sw. *ohängd.*] Not (yet) executed by hanging. (Cf. UNHUNG *ppl. a.* 2.)

*c* 1440 *York Myst.* xxxii. 186 Þou on-hanged harlott, hark what I saie. 1525 LD. BERNERS *Froiss.* II. ccxviii. [ccxiv.] 674 It is pytie these vnthriftes be vnhanged or drowned, for tellyng of suche lies. 1596 SHAKS. I *Hen. IV*, II. iv. 144 There liues not three good men vnhang'd in England. 1786 BURNS *Twa Dogs* 228 They..Pore owre the devil's pictur'd beuks;..An' cheat like ony unhanged blackguard. 1821 SCOTT *Kenilw.* v, Some evil fortune dogs the heels of that unhanged rogue Lambourne. 1848 THACKERAY *Van. Fair* li, We may abuse a man as much as we like, and call him the greatest rascal unhanged—but do we wish to hang him therefore? 1899 T. M. ELLIS *Cat's-eye Rings* 78 Through this unhanged fiend..my mother was one day..murdered.

*transf.* 1834 *Tait's Mag.* I. 54/1 The advent of the Whigs to power..has been a decided godsend to the trading advocates of unhanged abuses.

**Unha·nging,** *vbl. sb.* [UN-[1] 13.] Omission of hanging (a gate). *a* 1500 *Bk. of Brome* (1886) 166 3e shall enquere 3ef yer is ony mane yat hath no3te hangyd his fal-3ates,..the whiche on-hangyng hath be noyans to hys neyburs. **Unha·ngingly,** *adv.* [UN-[1] 11.] † Disconnectedly. *c* 1449 PECOCK *Repr.* IV. iv. 441 For elles this clausul..hadde be seid vnpertynently and vnhangingli fro the materis of the clausulis folewing and afore going.

†**Unha·p,** *sb. Obs.* [UN-[1] 12. Cf. ON. *úhapp* (Icel. *óhapp*, Norw. dial. *uhapp*), and WANHAP.]

**1.** Misfortune, mishap.

*a* 1225 *Ancr. R.* 180 Mislikunge wiðuten—ase sicnesse, meseise, scheome, vnhep. *c* 1325 *Body & Soul* 257 in *Map's Poems* (Camden) 343 What eyleth the, thou grimli gaast? That me thus breidest of myn unhap. *c* 1384 CHAUCER *H. Fame* 89 [To] shelde hem fro pouerte and shonde And fro vnhappe and eche disese. 1412–20 LYDG. *Chron. Troy* III. 5099 For of þe cite, sothly, and þe toun, His vnhap were endeles ruyne. *c* 1440 *Gesta Rom.* xxxiii. 129, I have thorow vnhappe slayn a man. *c* 1489 CAXTON *Sonnes of Aymon* i. 38 Your sone is ded by grete unhappe. 1523 LD. BERNERS *Froiss.* I. 521 This was the ende of yuan, or Owen, of Wales,.. slayne by great vnhap and treason. *a* 1586 SIDNEY *Arcadia* II. xvi, Sometime to visit that place, where first she was so happy as to see the cause of her vnhap.

**2.** With pl. A misfortune or mishap.

*c* 1230 *Hali Meid.* 29 Ne mei na worldlich unhap bireauen ham hare weole. *a* 1250 *Owl & Night.* 1267 Naueþ mon no sikerhede þat he ne may wene & adrede þat sum vnhap neih him beo. 13.. *E. E. Allit. P.* B. 892 Þay wern wakned ..Of on þe vglokest vnhap þat euer on erd suffred. 1390 GOWER *Conf.* II. 36 Thei..to the god for helpe criden Of suche unhappes as betyden. *c* 1440 *York Myst.* xviii. 152 That no myscheue on hym betyde, Nor none vnhappe. 1559 *Mirr. Mag.* (1562) A vj, Al which unhappes that they were not foreseene, I was in fault.

**3.** *attrib.* or as *adj.* = UNHAPPY *a.*

1509 HAWES *Past. Pleas.* (Percy Soc.) 82 Now all my desteny Unhap and happy, upon you doth growe. *Ibid.* 137 This unhap love had his mynde so broken.

†**Unha·p,** *v. Obs.*[—1] [f. prec.] *intr.* To bring misfortune.

*c* 1560 A. SCOTT *Poems* xxxiv. 123 Quhair [*v. r.* For] hurdome ay vnhappis With quenry, canis, and coppis.

**Unhap'ly,** obs. var. UNHAPPILY *adv.*

†**Unha·ppen,** *a. Obs.* [UN-[1] 7: cf. ON. *heppinn* fortunate, Norw. *uheppen* unfortunate; and see UNHEPPEN *a.*] Unfortunate, miserable, wretched.

13.. *E. E. Allit. P.* B. 573 And al was for þis ilk euel, þat vn-happen glette. 13.. *St. Erkenwolde* 198 in Horstm. *Altengl. Leg.* (1881) 270 One þe vnhapnest hathel þat euer one erthe 3ode. 1535 STEWART *Cron. Scot.* (Rolls) I. 528 Than da by da tha waittit on thair tyme, For to commit that curst vnhappin cryme.

**Unha·ppen,** *v.* (UN-[1] 14 or UN-[2] 7.) 1805 *Ann. Rev.* III. 270 The past cannot unhappen. 1876 MRS. WHITNEY *Sights & Ins.* II. xxxiii. 628 Had I been letting things happen that couldn't unhappen any more, ever?

**Unha·ppily,** *adv.* [UN-[1] 11. Cf. ON. *úheppiliga* (Norw. dial. *uheppelege*).]

**1.** Unfortunately, unluckily; by misfortune or mischance; regrettably.

*c* 1374 CHAUCER *Troylus* v. 937 But he was slayn..Vnhappyly at Thebes al to rape. *c* 1400 *Destr. Troy* 7104 Þen vnhappely hys hest he hastid to do, Þat angart hym after angardly sore. *c* 1430 *Syr Gener.* (Roxb.) 7351 Jewel vnhappelie hidre did hir bring, For now he hath an euel ending. 1558 in Feuillerat *Revels Q. Mary* (1914) 251, I ame not able to ryde..by reason of a strayn which I have vnhappelie mett with. 1576 LAMBARDE *Peramb. Kent* 138 b, I delyver suche only as lying in my waye doe offer them selues, and suche as..I haue not vnhappily lighted vpon. 1609 DANIEL *Civ. Wars* IV. lvii, Worc'ster (who had escap'd vnhappily His death in battel) on a Scaffold dies. 1647 CLARENDON *Hist. Reb.* I. § 51 That War in which the King was so unhappily engaged against Spain. 1738 in *Nairne Peerage Evidence* (1874) 42 Whereas John Nairne..was unhappily seduced..to join in the rebellion.

**b.** Used parenthetically or in loose construction.

*a* 1586 SIDNEY *Arcadia* III. xxviii, She saw, as he lifted up his armes.., about one of them, unhappily, tied a garter. 1603 SHAKS. *Meas. for M.* I. ii. 160 *Lucio.* With childe, perhaps? *Claudio.* Vnhappely, euen so. 1649 *Bounds Publ. Obed.* 2 The first Treatise, in which (and the unhappilier, to give foundation to practicable errors) they.. mistake principles. **1697** BENTLEY *Phal.* (1699) 109 He had unhappily forgot it, when he writ this Epistle. **1728** *Col. Rec. Pennsylv.* III. 327 By being unhappily in the Company of those who committed it. **1796** MME. D'ARBLAY *Camilla* III. 388 But to all that was thus most fascinating to others, she joined unhappily all that was most dangerous for herself. **1849** MACAULAY *Hist. Eng.* iv. I. 460 Unhappily the splendid qualities of John Churchill were mingled with alloy of the most sordid kind. **1890** *Retrospect Med.* CII. 340 But when this is unhappily not to be accomplished, a partial removal has obviously prolonged life.

**2.** With evil fortune or mischance; evilly, miserably, wretchedly.

*c* **1375** *Sc. Leg. Saints* xxxiv. (*Pelagia*) 179, I..þat has nocht anerly my-selfe Sonkyne in syne vnhapely. **1390** GOWER *Conf.* I. 54 And ate laste unhappely This Hert his oghne houndes slowhe. **1412–20** LYDG. *Chron. Troy* IV. 1489 Achilles axeþ how it is Amonge Grekis, & clerly how it stood...'Certis,' quod he, 'ful vnhappily'. **1509** BARCLAY *Shyp of Folys* (1570) 20 But these lewde caitifs.., liuing vnhappily, In shame they liue, and wretchedly they dye. **1596** in *10th Rep. Hist. MSS. Comm.* App. I. 76 At the last maist unnaturally and unhappilie..fell out the lamentable slauchter of the saidis vmquhill James Stirling. **1605** SHAKS. *Lear* I. ii. 157, I promise you, the effects he writes of, succeede vnhappily. *a* **1658** LOVELACE *Poems* (1904) 134 Ah Victory! unhap'ly wonne, Weeping and Red is set the Sun. **1667** MILTON *P. L.* x. 917, I..unweeting have offended, Unhappilie deceav'd. **1779** WARNER in Jesse *Selwyn & Contemp.* (1844) IV. 300 The giddy girl who married unhappily. **1781** COWPER *Charity* 632 If, unhappily deceiv'd, I dream, And prove too weak for so divine a theme.

**b.** Unsuccessfully.

**1533** BELLENDEN *Livy* I. xv. (S.T.S.) I. 86 Þe Sabynis faucht vnhappely in þis last battall. **1654** tr. *Martini's Conq. China* 55 So as if any fought unhappily, .. the Governors hardly ever escaped alive. **1831** SCOTT *Ct. Rob.* xiii, One of those simple persons who manage so unhappily what they mean for civilities, that those to whom they are addressed receive them frequently in another sense.

† **3.** Mischievously, maliciously. *Obs.*

**1509** HAWES *Past. Pleas.* XVIII. (Percy Soc.) 85 What man on live can use suche governaunce..but right pryvely Behinde his backe some sayth unhappely? **1549** CHALONER *Erasm. on Folly* G iij, They thynke unhappeliest in their herts, whan they speake smotheliest with their toungs. **1660** J. S. *Andromana* III. iii, I know you always talk'd unhappily, And if your heart dare do what's ill, I know it can well teach your tongue excuses.

† **b.** Unfavourably. *Obs.*[−1]

**1613** SHAKS. *Hen. VIII*, I. iv. 89 You are a Churchman, or Ile tell you Cardinall, I should iudge now vnhappily.

† **4.** Unpleasantly near the truth; shrewdly. *Obs.*

**1577–82** BRETON *Toyes Idle Head* Wks. (Grosart) I. 33/2 The iust occasion why, God knowes: and I, perhappes, can gesse vnhappily. **1584** LYLY *Campaspe* v. iv, *Alex.* Think you not, Hephestion, that she wold faine be commaunded? *Hep.* I am no thought catcher, but I gesse vnhappily. **1602** SHAKS. *Ham.* IV. v. 13 Which..Indeed would make one thinke there would be thought, Though nothing sure, yet much vnhappily.

† **5.** Unfitly; unskilfully. *Obs.*

**1602** BRETON *Wonders worth Hearing* To Rdr., A few odde Wonders, that being vnhappily set downe, might passe away a little idle time to looke on. **1704** SWIFT *T. Tub* Pref., My genius being conceived to lie not unhappily that way. **1726** — *Gulliver* III. iv, On the contrary, I never knew a soil so unhappily cultivated.

**6.** Without happiness or pleasure.

**1687** MIÉGE *Gt. Fr. Dict.* II, He lives very unhappily with her, *il vit fort mal avec elle.* **1814** JANE AUSTEN *Mansfield Park* ii, Fanny..grew up there not unhappily among her cousins. **1848** THACKERAY *Van. Fair* xxxvi, A village ..where little Rawdon passed the first months of his life, not unhappily, with a numerous family of foster-brothers.

**Unha·ppiness.** [UN-[1] 12.]

**1.** Misfortune, mishap, ill luck.

**1470–85** MALORY *Arthur* VII. vii. 221 Vnhappely he hath donne this day thorou myshappe;..and other dedes he dyde beforne ryght merueyllous and thorou vnhappynes. **1509** HAWES *Past. Pleas.* XVI. (Percy Soc.) 70 Now have I tolde you all the veray trouthe Of my wofull chaunce and great unhappynesse. **1561** T. NORTON *Calvin's Inst.* II. iii. 17 b, Whose feete are swyfte to shedde bloude, in whose wayes ys sorrowe and vnhappynesse. **1621** WITHER *Motto, Nec Habeo* C 1 b, I haue not that vnhappinesse, to be A Rich Mans Sonne. **1651** HOBBES *Gov. & Soc.* Ep. Ded., Yet the naturall right of Preservation..will not admit it to be a Vice, though it confesse it to be an Unhappinesse. *a* **1701** MAUNDRELL *Journ. Jerus.* 17 March 1697, It was our unhappiness to have..a very violent storm of Thunder, and Rain. **1753** CIBBER *Lives Poets* I. 18 Lamenting the unhappiness of a fluctuating language, that buries in its ruins even genius itself. **1872** TENNYSON *Gareth & Lynette* 1204, I..here lie thrown by whom I know not, all thro' mere unhappiness—Device and sorcery and unhappiness.

**b.** Unfavourable character.

**1704** *Collect. Voy.* (Churchill) III. 639/2 The Unhappiness of the Climate.

† **2.** Evil, wrong-doing, mischief. *Obs.*

*c* **1485** *Digby Myst.* (1882) II. 627 Thys traytour..That doth this vnhappynes a-gayns all! **1526** *Pilgr. Perf.* (W. de W. 1531) 242 b, Manasses was as the pyt and synke of all fylth & synne and vnhappynesse. **1548** UDALL, etc. *Erasm. Par. John* vii. 57 Readye to be hiered to do all unhappinesse. **1606** HOLLAND *Sueton.* 156 *margin*, Such as would play Bo-peepe and hide themselves when they had done some unhappinesse. *a* **1625** FLETCHER *Love's Pilgrimage* II. ii, A wild boy, That for the fruits of his unhappiness, Is faign to seek the wars.

**3.** The condition of being unhappy in mind.

**1722** WOLLASTON *Relig. Nat.* vi. (1724) 143 No doubt there is to every wrong and vitious act a suitable degree of unhappiness and punishment annext. **1791** BOSWELL *Johnson* an. 1758, As easy and pleasant a state of existence, as constitutional unhappiness ever permitted him to enjoy. **1842** A. COMBE *Physiol. Digestion* (ed. 4) 201 Hence..too often arise indifference and unhappiness between those whom Nature has formed..to suit each other. **1861** MILL *Utilit.* ii. 10 By unhappiness is intended, pain and the privation of pleasure. **1895** ROSA BAUGHAN *Palmistry* 27 A star on Venus means unhappiness caused by love.

**Unha·ppy,** *a.* [UN-[1] 7.]

**1.** Of persons (or animals): Causing misfortune or trouble (to oneself or others); objectionable or miserable on this account.

To some extent passing into sense 2.

*a* **1300** *Cursor M.* 3637 Ful lath me ware, þat he þat blissing fra þe bare, Vnhappi wreche has he ben ai. *c* **1375** *Sc. Leg. Saints* xxxvi. (*Baptista*) 736 For cowaitise a man, vnhappy & wnwyse, dalf vpe his graf be nichtirtale. **1470–85** MALORY *Arthur* VII. vii. 221 He is an vnhappy knaue, and vnhappely he hath donne this day thorou myshappe. *c* **1489** CAXTON *Sonnes of Aymon* viii. 194 Lete vs goo assaylle thise vnhappy folke of the kynge Charlemagne. *c* **1518** SKELTON *Magnyf.* 1374, I haue brought Vnto Magnyfycence a full vngracyous sorte, For all hokes vnhappy to me haue resorte. **1585** T. WASHINGTON tr. *Nicholay's Voy* I. xix. 22 b, An vnhappie souldier of Prouence..declared vnto the Turkes the weakest places of the castle. **1607** G. WILKINS *Miseries Enforced Marriage* K 1, I am sure they are greater sinners, That made this match, and were vnhappy men, For they caus'd all, and may heauen pardon them. *a* **1614** FLETCHER *Valentinian* v. ii, *Lici.* He is poyson'd...*Lyci.* Who? *Lici.* The wretch Aretus, That most unhappy villain. **1624** DARCIE tr. *Du Moulin's Heraclitus* vi. 41 There is nothing more hard to find in this world than a good woman, a good Mule, and a good Goat, being three vnhappie beasts. **1770** HARRIS in *Priv. Lett. Ld. Malmesbury* (1870) I. 192 He was an unhappy sot, and last week shot himself through the head. **1828** SCOTT *F. M. Perth* x, These unhappy Highland clans are again breaking into general commotion.

† **b.** *Sc.* Ill-natured; bad-tempered. *Obs.*[−1]

**1756** MRS. CALDERWOOD in *Coltness Collect.* (Maitl. Cl.) 127 Indeed he was so unhappy, (which signifies ill-nature in Scots,) that she durst never ask anything at him he was not pleased to tell her.

**2.** Of persons: Unfortunate, unlucky, ill-fated; miserable in lot or circumstances. Also, in later use, wretched in mind.

**1375** BARBOUR *Bruce* III. 291 Bot he the mar be wnhappy, He sall eschew it in party. *c* **1400** *Destr. Troy* 2689 A! nobill Troye, þe noy þat neghis þe at hond!..A! vnhappy hegh kyng, what hardship is to the! *c* **1440** *Promp. Parv.* 365/2 On-happy, *infortunatus, infelix.* **1470–85** MALORY *Arthur* VI. x. 198 Who that vseth peramours shalle be vnhappy, and all thyng is vnhappy that is aboute hem. **1523** FITZHERB. *Husb.* § 144 He is an vnhappy man or woman, that..woll chose the worst parte. **1587** GOLDING *De Mornay* xvi. 295 The most parte..come to this point, that man is the most vnhappiest of liuing wights. **1600** J. PORY tr. *Leo's Africa* II. 70 This unhappie king beeing utterly driuen to dispayre,..in the night time road foorth of the citie. **1655** FULLER *Ch. Hist.* III. vi. § 40. 86 Endless it were to reckon up the indignities offered unto these Jews. ..A people equally unhappy at feasts, and at frays. **1726** SWIFT *Gulliver* II. viii, The seamen might conjecture some unhappy mortal to be shut up in the box. **1794** MRS. RADCLIFFE *Myst. Udolpho* xxvii, Some unhappy person, who, having been plundered by his banditti, was brought hither a captive. **1849** MACAULAY *Hist. Eng.* iv. I. 432 In the midst of this splendour,..the unhappy woman gave herself up to an agony of grief. **1900** *Longm. Mag.* Mar. 450 He fully agreed that her mother must not be made unhappy.

*absol.* **1647** COWLEY *Mistr.*, *Sleep* iv, Thou scorn'st th' Unhappy; and the Happy, Thee. **1762** STERNE *Tr. Shandy* v. i, Pity the unhappy, said a devout, venerable, hoary-headed man. **1839** CARLYLE *Chartism* viii, A tear at least is due to the unhappy.

**b.** Const. *in* (some respect).

**1604** SHAKS. *Oth.* III. iv. 102 Sure, there's some wonder in this Handkerchiefe, I am most vnhappy in the losse of it. **1634** SIR T. HERBERT *Trav.* 221 Vnhappiest in this, that their owne Nation forgot them quite. **1711** ADDISON *Spect.* No. 164 ⁋ 1 Constantia was..very unhappy in a Father, who ..took delight in nothing but his Money. **1770** HARRIS in *Priv. Lett. Ld. Malmesbury* (1870) I. 201 They have been unhappy in another fire at Wilton.

**c.** Unsuccessful; apt to make mistakes.

**1651** WITTIE tr. *Primrose's Pop. Err.* I. 45, I have observed that no man is more unhappy than those physicians, that note their medicines out of books. **1662** STILLINGFL. *Orig. Sacræ* I. iii. § 9 He is as unhappy a person in Philology, as any that have pretended so much acquaintance with it. **1711** MRS. LONG *Let. to Swift* 18 Nov., That I may clear my meanings, which are always far from offending my friends, however unhappy I may be in my expressions.

**d.** Of places: Subject to, suffering from, misfortunes or evils.

**1591** SPENSER *Ruins Time* 146 Seemes, that that gentle Riuer..From my vnhappie neighborhood farre fled. **1667** MILTON *P. L.* I. 268 Wherefore..call [we] them not to share with us their part In this unhappy Mansion? **1697** DRYDEN *Virg. Georg.* II. 308 And such a country could Acerræ boast, Till Clanius overflowed the unhappy coast. *Ibid.* IV. 751 Th' unhappy Climes, where Spring was never known. **1846** MRS. A. MARSH *Father Darcy* II. iv. 92 You! —have you ventured to our unhappy house? **1849** MACAULAY *Hist. Eng.* iv. I. 498 The bands which oppressed and wasted these unhappy districts.

**3.** Of things: Associated with, bringing about or causing, misfortune or mishap; disastrous.

*c* **1386** CHAUCER *Man of Law's T.* 204 Infortunat ascendent tortuous,..O fieble Moone, vnhappy been thy paas. **1390** GOWER *Conf.* I. 236 Sche tok out thilke unhappi scherte. *Ibid.* 326 At thilke unhappi freisshe welle. **1420–2** LYDG. *Thebes* I. 821 Of whom the weddyng..Vnhappy was and passing odious, Infortuned and vngracious. **1470–85** MALORY *Arthur* II. xviii. 97 Thenne Balyn smote hym ageyne with that vnhappy swerd. **1523** LD. BERNERS *Froiss.* I. cccxl. 216/2 This vnhappy wether for the englisshmen fell well for them in the cyte. **1607** *Peele's Jests* 14 The Gentleman was..disturbed in thought at this unhappy accident. **1652** HOWELL *Giraffi's Rev. Naples* II. 142 An unhappy Bullet came and killed one of the principall of the Black-coats that was in Arms. **1711** ADDISON *Spect.* No. 125 ⁋ 7 It is very unhappy for a Man to be born in such a stormy and tempestuous Season. **1796** MME. D'ARBLAY *Camilla* III. 18, I am shocked to find you informed of this unhappy transaction. **1837** LOCKHART *Scott* III. iii. 110 His friend was aware that he had an unhappy propensity to drinking. **1891** FARRAR *Darkn. & Dawn* lxiii, An unhappy and accidental collision between the jealous cohorts led to a battle.

**b.** Inauspicious; foreboding evil.

**1533** BELLENDEN *Livy* I. viii. (S.T.S.) I. 47 Numa schewe in his Calendar sic dayis as wer happy and sic dayis as war unhappy. **1590** SPENSER *F. Q.* II. vi. 44 Death is for wretches borne vnder vnhappie starre. **1638** RAWLEY tr. *Bacon's Life & Death* (1650) 11 The Black-Bird is reported to be..one of the longest livers: An unhappy Bird, and a good singer. **1814** SOUTHEY *Roderick* VI. 90 The spurious race Whom in unhappy hour Favila's wife Brought forth for Spain.

**c.** Infelicitous; unsuccessful.

**1719** SWIFT *To Yng. Clergyman* Wks. 1755 II. II. 3 Neither is it rare to observe among excellent..divines a certain ungracious manner, or an unhappy tone of voice. **1779** JOHNSON *L. P.*, *Rochester* Wks. II. 199 His imitation of Horace on Lucilius is not inelegant or unhappy.

**4.** Of conditions: Marked by misfortune or mishap; miserable, wretched.

**1390** GOWER *Conf.* III. 59 Helas, that evere was I bore, That this unhappi destine So wofulli comth in be me! **1484** CAXTON *Fables of Æsop* II. viii, In the vnhappy and Infortunat tyme men ought not to be despayred. **1509** HAWES *Past. Pleas.* XVI. (Percy Soc.) 68 Sayeng to him, my chance and desteny Of al other is the moste unhappy. **1585** T. WASHINGTON tr. *Nicholay's Voy.* I. xv. 16 The end of his moste vnhappye life. *Ibid.* IV. xxvii. 146 Through hunger [he] was..to die an vnhappie death. **1600** BRETON *Pasquil's Madcappe* D 3 b, If they be met with in their going home, I can not pitty their vnhappy speede. **1712** BLACKMORE *Creation* III. 325 You oft declaim on man's unhappy fate. **1794** MRS. RADCLIFFE *Myst. Udolpho* xxx, Her mind deeply impressed with the unhappy fate of this object, she forgot all her faults. **1838** FR. A. KEMBLE *Resid. in Georgia* (1863) 13, I have never been among them to judge what faculties their unhappy social position leaves to them unimpaired. **1878** BROWNING *La Saisiaz* 30 Life thus owned unhappy, is there supplemental happiness..in life to come?

† **5.** Causing or involving trouble or mischief; objectionable, evil; naughty. *Obs.*

**1474** *Paston Lett.* III. 121 Wherffor I sende yow herwith yowr rynge, and the onhappy muskeball. **1529** MORE *Dyaloge* IV. Wks. 259/2 Moreouer the vnhappy dedes of y[t] sect must nedes be imputed to the sect selfe. **1585** T. WASHINGTON tr. *Nicholay's Voy.* III. xvii. 102 They are also full of diuers vnhappy vices. *a* **1618** RALEIGH *Rem.* (1664) 110 The world..never gave you but an unhappy welcome—a hurtful entertainment. **1678** CUDWORTH *Intell. Syst.* 420 It seems to be but like to Womens frighting of Children from doing unhappy tricks.

† **b.** Unfavourable, poor. *Obs.*

**1765** *Museum Rust.* IV. xxviii. 125 A very proper grass to cultivate on such unhappy soils, where hardly any other grass..will grow at all.

**6.** *Comb.*, as *unhappy-faced, -happy, -looking, -witted* adjs.

**1591** SPENSER *M. Hubberd* 49 For both were craftie and vnhappie witted. *a* **1618** SYLVESTER *Funeral Elegie Dr. Hill's Wife* 185 (Her first and last) unhappy-happy Boy, Which cost her life. **1863** W. C. BALDWIN *Afr. Hunting* ix. 378 An odd unhappy-looking springbuck or two. **1876** GEO. ELIOT *Dan. Der.* xxviii, That unhappy-faced woman.

† **Unha·ppy,** *v. Obs.* [UN-[2] 6 a.] *trans.* To make unhappy or unfortunate.

**1593** SHAKS. *Rich. II*, III. i. 10 You haue mis-led a Prince, ..A happie Gentleman in Blood, and Lineaments, By you vnhappied, and disfigur'd cleane. **1605** SYLVESTER tr. *Paradox agst. Libertie* 410 In our selues doth rest That which vnhappieth vs, and that which makes vs blest. **1653** E. LLOYD *Let.* 28 July (MS. Ashmole), I admire you..should for any By-end vnhappie your selfe and stepdame your children.

**Unha·rassed,** *ppl. a.* (UN-[1] 8.) [**1775** ASH.] **1796** P. L. COURTIER *Pleas. Solitude* (1802) 58 The solitary haunt, by foe unharassed more! **1883** 'ANNIE THOMAS' *Mod. Housewife* 30 'We must retrench!' we said.., and in those unharassed days we said it cheerfully enough. † **Unha·rborough,** *v. Obs.* [UN-[2] 5.] = next. **1611** FLORIO, *Disalbergare*, to dislodge, to vnharborough.

**Unha·rbour,** *v.* [UN-[2] 5.] *trans.* To dislodge (a deer) from covert or shelter.

**1576** TURBERV. *Venerie* 100 An Hart and a Bucke [are] likewise reared, rowsed, and vnharbored. **1582** STANYHURST IV. (Arb.) 100 The heard deare dooth stray from mounten vnharbourd. **1686** R. BLOME *Gentl. Recreat.* II. 83/1 Your Hounds should not all be uncoupled until the Hart is unharboured by the Harbourer. **1721** *Phil. Trans.* XXXI. 167 After you unharbour a Moose, he will run a Course of 20, or 30 miles, before he..comes to a Bay. **1797** *Sporting Mag.* IX. 264 Mr. Sturt's stag hounds unharboured a hind at Maggot-Hill Wood. **1823** SCOTT *Quentin D.* ix, To the devil with the discourse, for the boar is unharboured. **1856** STONEHENGE *Brit. Rural Sports* 109 The regular pack being held at hand.., ready to be laid on when the hart or hind is 'unharboured'.

**b.** *transf.* and *fig.*

**1593** *Sidney's Arcadia* III. (1922) II. 29 Your compassion makes me open my hart to you, and leave unharboured mine owne thoughts. **1647** N. WARD *Simple Cobler* 44, I am sure.. it was never storyed that *Salus Populi* began with *Majestas Imperii*, unlesse *Majestas Imperii* first unharbour'd it, and hunted it to a stand. **1768** FOOTE *Devil* I, Advance! now let us unharbour the rascal! **1771** R. CUMBERLAND *West Indian* II. vi, I'll unlodge him, I'll unharbour him, I warrant. **1824** SCOTT *St. Ronan's* iv, Clara..is a little wilful; and I believe your ladyship must take the task of unharbouring her into your own hands.

Hence **Unha·rbouring** *vbl. sb.*

1591 R. TURNBULL *Exp. St. James* 102 These..house themselues by the vnharbouring..of the poore. 1686 R. BLOME *Gentl. Recreat.* II. 83/1 The Chase of the Hart or Stag; and first the Vnharbouring him. 1897 D. H. MADDEN *Diary W. Silence* 30 The rest of the company made ready to assist at the unharbouring of the hart.

**Unha·rboured,** *a.* [UN-1 8.]

1. Having no shelter or refuge.

*c* 1450 *Cov. Myst.* (Shaks. Soc.) 403 Ye had no pete on seke nor lame...Unherborwed men ye servyd the same.

2. Affording no shelter; wild.

1634 MILTON *Comus* 423 She that has that..May trace huge Forests, and unharbour'd Heaths.

†**Unha·rd,** *a. Obs.* [UN-1 7. Cf. ON. *úharðr*, obs. Flem. *onherd*, OHG. *unherti.*] Soft.

*a* 1300 *Cursor M.* 24502 Quen i sa moght kis þat suete, þe vnharder was mi harm. 1552 HULOET, Vnharde, *edurum.* 1570 LEVINS *Manip.* 31 Unhard, *mollis.*

**Unha·rden,** *v.* (UN-2 6 a.)

1552 HULOET, Vnharden, *eduro.* 1611 FLORIO, *Discallire*, to suple, to vnharden. 1879 BROWNING *Ivan Ivanovitch* 243 Ivan Ivanovitch, 'Tis you unharden me.

**Unha·rdened,** *ppl. a.* (UN-1 8.)

*fig.* 1590 SHAKS. *Mids. N.* I. i. 35 Messengers Of strong preuailment in vnhardned youth. 1608 H. CLAPHAM *Errour Right Hand* A 4 If thine heart be vn-hardned, it will easily ioyne with mee. 1619 [see UNHATCHED 2]. 1747 RICHARDSON *Clarissa* (1811) II. 26 After you have heard what your friends shall further urge in his behalf, unhardened by clandestine correspondencies. 1792 MME. D'ARBLAY *Diary* V. 390 The few unhardened in crimes. 1821 SOUTHEY in *Life A. Bell* (1844) III. 630 Preserving his heart the while unstained and unhardened. 1846 LANDOR *Imag. Conv.* Wks. I. 249/2 The studious, the enthusiastic, the unhardened in politics.

*lit.* 1835–6 *Todd's Cycl. Anat.* I. 349/1 An intermediate layer of unhardened epiderm. 1884 F. J. BRITTEN *Watch & Clockm.* 6 Unhardened springs do not accelerate.

**Unha·rdiness.** (UN-1 12.) 1611 FLORIO, *Sbaldanza*, vnboldnesse, vnhardinesse. 1893 *Mod. Rev.* April 252 A hundred generations of unhardiness and want of power.

†**Unha·rdle,** *v. Obs.*—1 [UN-2.]

The second element is app. f. OF. *hardel* m. or *hardelle* f., either in the sense of 'troop, company', or of 'cord, leash' (cf. F. *harde* leash for hounds). In the former case the sense is 'to break up, disperse'; in the latter, 'to unleash, uncouple'. Either meaning is suitable to the context.

13.. *Gaw. & Gr. Knt.* 1697 Hunteres vnhardeled bi a holt syde, Rocheres roungen bi rys, for rurde of her hornes.

**Unha·rdy,** *a.* (UN-1 7.)

1377 LANGL. *P. Pl.* B. Prol. 180 [They] helden hem vnhardy and here conseille feble. *c* 1386 CHAUCER *Reeve's T.* 4208, I wil arise, and auntre it by my fayth: Vnhardy is vnseely, thus men sayth. 1430–40 LYDG. *Bochas* IV. viii. (1554) 105 Nother heauenly gods nor fortune blind of syght Wer both vnhardy tattempt agein his might. 1539 TAVERNER *Erasm. Prov.* (1545) 79 With sluggers or unhardy persons, it is alwayes holy daye. 1611 SPEED *Hist. Gt. Brit.* IX. xi. § 5. 555/1 Neither yet was he vnhardie in Arms. 1671 MILTON *P. R.* III. 243 The wisest, unexperienc't, will be ever..Irresolute, unhardy, unadventrous.

**Unha·rmed,** *ppl. a.* (UN-1 8.)

1340–70 *Alex. & Dind.* 227 And y bi-hote ȝou her vnharmed to leue. *c* 1400 *Beryn* 1804 Howe shuld o sely lombe, a-mong wolvis weld, And scapen vn-i-harmyd? 1456 SIR G. HAYE *Law Arms* (S.T.S.) 164 He sall seurly cum and gang unharmyt of me or ony of myn. 1513 DOUGLAS *Æneid* I. Prol. 51 Thocht I offend, onhermit is thine fame. 1582 STANYHURST *Æneis* II. (Arb.) 64 Wasd for this (moother) that mee throgh danger vnharmed You led? 1667 DRYDEN & DAVENANT *Tempest* II. (1670) 25 *Prosp.* No courage can resist 'em. *Hip.* How then have you, Sir, Liv'd so long unharm'd among them? 1687 [see next]. 1791 COWPER *Odyss.* V. 197, I will also give New raiment for thy limbs, and will dispatch Winds after thee to waft thee home unharm'd. 1855 MACAULAY *Hist. Eng.* xiii. III. 327 Here he might possibly have remained unharmed and harmless, had not an event..made his enemies implacable. 1886 HALL CAINE *Son of Hagar* III. vi, What a mercy we're safe and unharmed.

**Unha·rmful,** *a.* (UN-1 7.)

1538 ELYOT, *Innocuus*, vnharmefull, he that doth none harme. 1548 UDALL, etc. *Erasm. Par. John* i. 9 b, This is he..whose vnharmefull blood defended the children of Israel. 1594 CAREW *Tasso* (1881) 87 That hungry teene of gold, and thirst withall Of mine vnharmefull blood. 1615 CHAPMAN *Odyss.* II. 138 And..hold unharmful on your wished way. 1687 DRYDEN *Hind & P.* I. 299 Themselves unharmful, let them live unharm'd, Their jaws disabl'd, and their claws disarm'd. 1855 SINGLETON *Virgil* I. 162 Often have malignant stepdames..mingled drugs and not unharmful spells.

**Unha·rmfully,** *adv.* (UN-1 11.) 1888 *Contemp. Rev.* Nov. 676 To grapple unharmed and unharmfully with the very deepest problems of our being.

**Unha·rming,** *ppl. a.* (UN-1 10.)

1795 SOUTHEY *Joan of Arc* VII. 162 Again he thrust the spear; At once Dunois on his broad buckler met The unharming stroke. 1835 LYTTON *Rienzi* x. iv, Dangerous tools they were, but without the workman they may rust unharming. 1852 KINGSLEY *Andromeda* 149 A fiery rainfall, unharming, Sparkled and gleamed.

**Unharmo·nic,** *a.* (UN-1 7 and 5 b.)

1694 PEPYS *Let.* in *Academy* 9 Aug. (1890) 110/1 There is a decent and not unharmonick playnesse in it. 1810 S. GREEN *Reformist* II. 20 The unharmonic squalling of a ballad-singer.

**Unharmo·nious,** *a.* [UN-1 7 and 5 b.]

1. Not sounding in harmony; unmelodious.

*a* 1634 CHAPMAN *Rev. for Honour* II. i. 224 These sounds are unharmonious. 1727 SWIFT *Let. Eng. Tongue* Wks. 1755 II. I. 188 Such harsh unharmonious sounds, that none but a northern ear could endure. 1753 R. CLAYTON *Jrnl. fr. Cairo to Mt. Sinai* 4 The noisy sonnets of our Eastern friends, who ..designed these their unharmonious vociferations as a compliment. 1832 G. DOWNES *Lett. Cont. Countries* I. 139 Some country-seats, one of which bears the unharmonious name, Gutsch. 1859 R. F. BURTON *Centr. Afr.* in *Jrnl. Geog. Soc.* XXIX. 266 An unharmonious chorus of collective voices.

b. Not yielding or producing harmonious sounds.

1742 YOUNG *Nt. Th.* III. 89 Transfixt by fate,..How from the summit of the grove she fell, And left it unharmonious! 1784 COWPER *Task* III. 734 Wholesome airs,..And groves, if unharmonious, yet secure From clamour. *a* 1861 T. WOOLNER *My Beautiful Lady, Night* i, What trite old folly unharmonious sages..write..Of sin original and growing crime!

2. Not exhibiting harmony or agreement.

1667 MILTON *P. L.* XI. 51 Those pure immortal Elements that know No gross, no unharmoneous mixture foule. 1796 MRS. M. ROBINSON *Angelina* I. 125 Pardon me..for the impertinence of supposing that your enlightened mind can for a moment be unharmonious. 1805 LOUDON *Improv. Hot-Houses* 38 Walls and flues covered with white plaster, the raw glare of which..has a harsh and unharmonious effect. 1846 GROTE *Greece* ix. (1862) II. 246 The distinct and unharmonious elements of which the population..was made up. 1876 BERNSTEIN *Five Senses* 120 The cause of the harmonious or unharmonious relation between colours.

**Unharmo·niously,** *adv.* (UN-1 11; cf. prec.)

[1775 ASH.] 1783 BLAIR *Lect.* I. xix. 393 [There is] little beauty in the construction of his sentences, which are frequently suffered to drag unharmoniously. 1856 FROUDE *Hist. Eng.* I. 262 Factions nearly equal in number, though unharmoniously composed.

**Unha·rmonize,** *v.* (UN-2 6 c.) 1797 MRS. A. M. BENNETT *Beggar Girl* (1813) III. 67 It was not in the power of sir Jacob or his companion entirely to unharmonise her mind. **Unha·rmonized,** *ppl. a.* (UN-1 8.) [1775 ASH.] 1803 MARY CHARLTON *Wife & Mistress* III. 144 This promised interview was now the only circumstance she looked forward to, ere she quitted this unharmonized society. 1873 SYMONDS *Grk. Poets* xii. 417 Fragments of primitive..superstition unharmonized with the serene element of the Hellenic spirit. **Unha·rmonizing,** *ppl. a.* (UN-1 10.) 1851 W. R. GREG *Creed of Christendom* xi. 152 Those single, unharmonizing discrepant texts. 1865 PUSEY *Truth Eng. Ch.* 42 The Holy Synod approved the letter..as..in no wise unharmonizing with the inspired Scriptures. **Unha·rmony.** (UN-1 12, 5 b.) 1832 GEN. THOMPSON *Exerc.* (1842) 101 A marvellous blunder,..which..caused all ancient music to flounder in a mass of unharmony. 1866 R. CHAMBERS *Ess.* Ser. II. 189 That unharmony of opinion which so often makes social life uncomfortable.

**Unha·rness,** *v.* [UN-2 4, 4 b. Cf. Du. and Flem. *ontharnassen* to disarm ('exarmare', Kilian).]

1. *trans.* To divest of armour. Also *fig.*

*c* 1435 *Torr. Portugal* 302 Blythe then wase that lady jent, For to on-harnes Torrent. 1549 COVERDALE, etc. *Erasm. Par. Col.* ii. 6 Then declared he them freely and playnly to be ouercommen and vnharnysed, when..he caryed vs aboute as it were in a triumphe. 1552 HULOET, Vnharnayes *exarmo.* 1802 JAMES *Milit. Dict.*, *Unharnessed*, disarmed divested of armour or weapons of offence.

2. To free (horses, etc.) from harness; to unyoke. Also *fig.* and (in recent use) *absol.*

1611 COTGR., *Desharnacher*, to vnharnesse, or vntrap; to take off the furniture from a horse. 1643–5 MILTON *Divorce* II. xxi, When two unfortunately met are by the Canon forc't to draw in that yoke..till death unharnesse 'em. 1697 DRYDEN *Virg. Past.* II. 96 The sweating steers, unharnessed from the yoke, Bring, as in triumph, back the crooked plough. 1746 *Phil. Trans.* XLIV. 296 The Carter drove him home; but, as soon as he had unharnessed him, the poor Creature.. dropp'd down dead immediately. 1799 *Hull Advertiser* 2 Feb. 2/4 A number of respectable inhabitants unharnessed the cattle from his carriage. 1852 GROTE *Greece* II. lxxi. IX. 203 Xenophon unharnessing a waggon-bullock.., immediately offered sacrifice. 1894 *Westm. Gaz.* 10 June 5/1 He had to leave off helping to unharness the horse.

Hence **Unha·rnessing** *vbl. sb.*

1856 LEVER *Martins of Cro' M.* xv, Grooming, and shoeing, and unharnessing went on with..noise and merriment.

**Unha·rnessed,** *ppl. a.*1 [UN-1 8.]

†1. Not ornamented or trimmed. *Obs.*

1488 *Acc. Ld. High Treas. Scot.* I. 83 A belt of crammassy hernessit with gold and braid;..a belt of gold vnharnessit.

2. Not provided with or wearing armour.

*a* 1513 FABYAN *Chron.* VII. 308 Kynge Rycharde,..with a fewe accompanyed & vnharnaysed, shulde comme to ye Frenshe Kynges tent. 1562 PILKINGTON *Expos. Abdyas* 55, 300 naked men unharnessed,..vanquished them all. 1586 HOOKER *Conq. Irel.* I. xlii. 28/1 in *Holinshed*, As in combates in England, so they being vnharnessed, did fight with their swords or weapons in the open sight of the people. 1721 RAMSAY *Poems* 397 Ungeard, naked, not clad, unharness'd.

3. Not fitted with, or put into, harness.

1608 SYLVESTER *Du Bartas* II. iv. *Schisme* 298 Chariots, unfurnisht and unharnest. 1697 DRYDEN *Æneis* IX. 425 Unharnessed chariots stand along the shore. 1791 COWPER *Iliad* II. 950 Beside the chariots stood the unharness'd steeds Cropping the lotus.

b. Not adapted for industrial use.

1903 KIPLING *5 Nations* 57 Watching unharnessed rapids wasting fifty thousand head an hour.

**Unha·rnessed,** *ppl. a.*2 [f. UNHARNESS *v.*]

1. Released from harness.

1676 HOBBES *Iliad* 212 The horses, that me brought, unharnessed Attend me at the foot of Ida hill. 1725 POPE *Odyss.* VI. 103 The mules unharness'd range beside the main. 1859 DICKENS *Holly Tree* i. (1899) 31, I had the honour of leading one of the unharnessed post-horses.

*fig.* 1867 MACGREGOR *Voy. Alone* ii. 29, I reclined unharnessed in the cabin, reading intently.

2. Divested of armour.

1664 BUTLER *Hud.* II. II. 49 Where now arriv'd, and half unharnest, To carry on the work in earnest, He stopp'd.

**Unha·rped,** *ppl. a.* (UN-1 8.) 1859 F. K. HARFORD *Martyrs of Lyons & V.* 26 Song unharp'd on Seraph's golden strings. **Unha·rried,** *ppl. a.* (UN-1 8.) 1871 FREEMAN *Norm. Conq.* xvii. IV. 80 The coast..remained unharried by either friends or enemies. 1889 *Daily News* 10 Apr. 5/1 You will leave his nest unharried.

**Unha·rrowed,** *ppl. a.* (UN-1 8.)

1573 TUSSER *Husb.* (1878) 88 Not onely thy peason, but also thy beanes, Unharrowed die, being buried in clay. *a* 1722 LISLE *Husb.* (1752) 118 Let the furrows lie unharrowed for some time. 1778 [W. H. MARSHALL] *Minutes Agric., Observ.* 103 A belt across the middle [of the field], left experimentally unharrowed.

**Unha·rvested,** *ppl. a.* [UN-1 8.]

1. From which no harvest is taken.

1867 MORRIS *Jason* II. 731 In what strange wain Hast thou crossed o'er the green and restless plain Unharvested of any? 1868 *Rep. U. S. Commissioner Agric.* (1869) 428 The method..of turning the hogs into an unharvested field when commencing to fatten. 1879 BUTCHER & LANG *Odyssey* 77 The perilous gulfs of the unharvested sea.

2. Not reaped or brought in.

1874 J. W. LONG *Amer. Wild-fowl* xvi. 198 They feed upon the previous season's waste and unharvested grain.

**Unha·sp,** *v.* [UN-2 4 b.] *trans.* To free from a hasp or catch; to unfasten; *fig.* to disclose.

13.. *E. E. Allit. P.* B. 688 Me bos..alle myn atlyng to abraham vn-haspe bilyue. 1598 *Mucedorus* Epil. 22 Enuie, spit thy gall;..Vnhaspe the Wicket where all perijureds roost. 1615 J. TAYLOR (Water P.) *Urania* i, Eternall God, which.. at the doomefull day will once vnhaspe Th' acusing booke of Subiects and of Kings. 1810 SCOTT *Lady of L.* VI. xii, While bolt and chain he backward roll'd, And made the bar unhasp its hold. 1895 *Chamb. Jrnl.* XII. 781/1 Old Hird unhasped the door in the corner.

**Unha·sped,** *ppl. a.* (UN-1 8.) 1856 HAWTHORNE *Snow Image*, etc. (1879) 221 By some accident, it had been left unhasped. 1894 BARING-GOULD *Kitty Alone* II. 35, I will leave the door of my stores open—unhasped. **Unha·ste.** (UN-1 12.) 1879 DESHLER *Afternoons w. Poets* 8 'Cultivate the virtue of patience,' he replied with imperturbable unhaste. 1893 BLISS CARMAN *Low Tide on Grand Pré* 54 The noiseless secret Of Eternity's unhaste. **Unha·sted,** *ppl. a.* (UN-1 8.) 1854 S. DOBELL *Balder* iii. 13 The unhasted life That plods with equal step the wonted way.

**Unha·sting,** *ppl. a.* (UN-1 10.)

Also, in recent use, *unhastingness.*

1839 CARLYLE *Chartism* iv, Perseverance, unhasting unresting diligence,..characterise this people. 1872 MORLEY *Voltaire* 287 That grave and unhasting dignity, which is the life of history. 1891 W. TUCKWELL *Tongues in Trees* 151 Unhasting yet unresting chroniclers of fleeting time.

**Unha·sty,** *a.* (UN-1 7.) 1590 SPENSER *F. Q.* I. iii. 4 One day nigh wearie of the yrkesome way, From her vnhastie beast she did alight. 1651 JER. TAYLOR *Serm. for Year* II. xv. 192 He is a perfect man..who hath..so unhasty and wary a spirit, as that he decrees upon no act before he hath considered maturely.

**Unha·t,** *v.* (UN-2 4, 7.)

1611 FLORIO, *Disberettare*, to vncap, to vnhat. 1879 H. SPENCER *Ceremonial Inst.* vi. 134 Unhatting on the knees when the host is carried by, occurs still in Catholic countries. 1883 *Academy* 30 June 460/1 To the latter we must often unhat as to the oldest of acquaintances.

**Unha·tched,** *ppl. a.*1 (UN-1 8 + HATCH *v.*1)

1601 HOLLAND *Pliny* I. 298 Whiles the chick is unhatched and within the egge. 1794 MORSE *Amer. Geog.* 169 The young cuckow..immediately sets about clearing the nest of the young sparrows, and the remaining unhatched eggs. 1854 BADHAM *Halieut.* 186 Many [tunny-fish]..drop their unhatched posterity about, wherever they may happen to reside. 1872 DARWIN *Orig. Spec.* (ed. 6) iv. 68 The hard tip to the beak of unhatched birds, used for breaking the egg.

*fig.* 1602 SHAKS. *Ham.* I. iii. 65 But doe not dull thy palme, with entertainment Of each vnhatch't, vnfledg'd Comrade. 1635 PAGITT *Christianog.* 223 Papall Indulgences were then unhatched. *a* 1639 T. CAREW *Poems* Wks. (1824) 85 Though niggard Time left much unhatch'd by deeds.

† **Unha·tched,** *ppl. a.*2 *Obs.* [UN-1 8 + HATCH *v.*2] Unhacked; unstained.

1601 SHAKS. *Twel. N.* III. iv. 257 *Vio.* I pray you sir what is he? *To.* He is knight dubb'd with vnhatch'd Rapier. 1619 FLETCHER *Knt. Malta* II. v, Tender, and full of fears our blushing Sex is, Unhardned with relentless thoughts; unhatcht With bloud, and bloudy practice.

**Unha·tted,** *a.* (UN-1 9.)

1832 MISS MITFORD *Village* Ser. v. 197 Frederick of Prussia's unhatted soldier. 1847 HELPS *Friends in C.* I. ii. 31 A great, unhatted, uncravated, bearded man. 1893 *Westm. Gaz.* 22 Apr. 2/3 He was unhatted, but he leant forward with a graceful bow.

b. *spec.* (See HAT *sb.* 3.)

1880 *Sat. Rev.* 25 Dec. 808/1 Bembo..in his pleasant, unregenerate, because still unhatted, days.

**Unhau·nted,** *ppl. a.* [UN-1 8.]

†1. Not practised or used. *Obs.*—1

1533 BELLENDEN *Livy* III. (S.T.S.) I. 298 Nocht knawand ..quhy þe thing (þat was sa mony ȝeris afore vnhantit and out of consuetude) was brocht agane in vse.

2. Not frequented; lonely, solitary.

1568–9 *Act 11 Eliz.* in Bolton *Stat. Irel.* (1621) 369 Enormities that have followed of the disordered trade of aliens to creekes and unhaunted portes. 1581 J. BELL *Haddon's Answ. Osor.* 349 b, Nor were they sojourning then in ye Cities, or Townes. But coucht close..in unhaunted woodes and fennes. 1617 CAMPION *Wks.* (1909) 181 We both will sit in some vnhaunted shade. 1659 W. CHAMBERLAYNE *Pharonnida* IV. 94 Like beauteous flowers, which vainly waste the scent Of odors in unhaunted desarts.

3. Not haunted *by* (or *of*) something.

1818 COBBETT *Pol. Reg.* XXXIII. 162 [They] can lay their heads on their pillows unhaunted by the apprehension of seeing him no more. 1819 KEATS *Indolence* ii, Unhaunted quite of all but—nothingness. 1866 HOWELLS *Venet. Life* ii. 21 Unhaunted by any pang for the decay that afterwards saddened me.., I glided on.

Hence **Unhau·ntedness.**

1611 FLORIO, *Infrequenza*, vnhauntednesse.

**Unhau·nting,** *vbl. sb.* (UN-1 13.) 1538 ELYOT, *Insolentia*, seldomnes of vse in any thynge, vnhauntynge of a place. †**Unha·ving,** *vbl. sb. Obs.*—1 (UN-1 13.) *c* 1449 PECOCK *Repr.* I. xvi. 89 For harme which y haue knowen come bi defaut and the vnhauying and the vnknowing of this..consideracioun.

**Unha·zarded,** *ppl. a.* (Un-[1] 8.)
**1588** Howard in Laughton *State Papers Defeat Armada* (1894) I. 288 There shall be nothing either neglected or unhazarded, that may work their overthrow. **1649** Milton *Eikon.* v. Wks. 1851 III. 376 He..hath himselfe left nothing unhazzarded to keep three [kingdoms]. **1671** — *Samson* 809 Here I should still enjoy thee day and night,..Whole to my self, unhazarded abroad. **1855** [see Unessayed].

**Unha·zarding,** *ppl. a.* (Un-[1] 10.) **1807** Southey *Espriella's Lett.* III. 75 Their habits of patient and unhazarding industry ensure success.

**Unha·zardous,** *a.* (Un-[1] 7.)
**1682** Dryden *Dk. Guise* Epist. A ij b, 'Tis enough, my Lord, that your own Part was neither obscure in it, nor unhazardous. **1802–12** Bentham *Ration. Judic. Evid.* (1827) II. 227 It is in the honest and unhazardous task of recollection that he employs himself. **1891** T. Hardy *Tess* xiii, The fact..lent Tess's..position, by its fearsomeness, a far higher fascination than it would have exercised if unhazardous.

**Unhea·d,** *v.* [Un-[2] 4. Cf. MDu. *onthoveden, onthoofden* (also Du.), MLG. *enthoveden*, MHG. *enthoubeten, -houpten* (G. *enthaupten*).]

**1.** *trans.* To behead (a person).
*c* **1375** *Sc. Leg. Saints* i. (*Peter*) 377 For, lo, as I vnhevdyt wes,..þe thrid day, as I sad to þe, I am resine. *Ibid.* xxxi. (*Eugenia*) 432 Scho..gert þe lord þe ȝerle ta, &..At hyr tysinge gert hyme vnhed. *a* **1704** T. Brown *Wks.* (1720) II. 260 You..did not only dare to uncrown, but to unhead a Monarch. *a* **1734** North *Exam.* iii. vii. § 98 (1740) 580 Legs and Arms lay scattered about, Heads undressed, and Bodies unheaded.

**2.** To deprive or divest of a head, top, or end.
**1611** Florio, *Scapezzare*, to vntop, to vnhead, to shred or lop trees on the top. **1725** *Fam. Dict.* s.v. *Verjuice*, And when you have a mind to have your Verjuice you must unhead the Barrel, and you will find it very good. **1778** W. Pryce *Min. Cornub.* 98 They often meet with a Cross-Gossan, which..unheads and breaks off the continuity of the Lode they work upon. **1843** Tizard *Brewing* 473 When steam is not to be had, stinking casks need unheading.

**Unhea·ded,** *a.* [Un-[1] 9.] Destitute or devoid of a head, in various senses.
(*a*) **1586** J. Hooker *Hist. Irel.* 94/1 in *Holinshed* II, The most part of those arrowes, which were shot ouer the walles, were vnheaded. **1600** J. Pory tr. *Leo's Africa* Introd. 36 A kinde of small slender dartes or pikes, some whereof are headed with some kinde mettall, the residue being unheaded.
(*b*) **1608** Topsell *Serpents* 609 This monster..nor man nor dragon is.., But man unlegged, and snake unheaded.
(*c*) **1607** *Puritaine Widdow* v. iv. 8 Such is the blind besotting in the state of an vnheaded woman thats a widdow. **1673** Temple *Obs. United Prov.* Wks. 1720 I. 16 The People were enraged, but awed and unheaded.

†**Unhea·l.** *Obs.* [OE. *unhǽlu, -o, unhǽl* (Un-[1] 12 + Heal *sb.*), = OHG. *unhailî, -heilî* fem. Cf. MDu. (rare) and Du. *onheil*, MLG. *unheil*, OHG. *unhail, unheil* (also MHG., G.), Goth. *unhaili* neut.] Want of health or soundness; infirmity, trouble, misfortune.
*c* **700** *Laws of Ine* § 56 Ȝif mon hwelcne ceap ȝebyȝeð, & he þonne onfinde him hwelce unhælo on [etc.]. *c* **893** K. Ælfred *Oros.* iv. iv. 164 Þa ðe þær on unhæle wæran. *c* **950** *Lindisf. Gosp.* Matt. iv. 23 Hælend..hælde all unhælo & all untrymnise in folce. *c* **1000** *Rule of Chrodegang* vii, Þæt nan ne beo aspelod..butan hwa for unhæle..ne maȝe. *c* **1200** *Trin. Coll. Hom.* 33 Ðos word sede þe engel..naht for englen unhele þe habbeð eche hele, ac far mannen unhele. *a* **1225** *Leg. Kath.* 1064 He..healde halte & houerede, & euch unheale. *a* **1300** *Cursor M.* 8137 Mikel on him he had vn-hele, Thritti yere had ben mesel. *c* **1386** Chaucer *Doctor's T.* 116 Saue Enuye allone That sory is of oother mennes wele And glad is of his sorwe and his vnheele. *c* **1450** Holland *Houlate* 254 It neidis nocht to renewe all myn vnhele.

**Unheal,** var. Unhele *v.*

**Unhea·lable,** *a.* [Un-[1] 7 b.] Incapable of being healed; incurable.
**1382** Wyclif *Ecclus.* xxviii. 30 Lest parauenture..thi fallyng be vnheleable in to the deth. — *Isaiah* xiv. 6 The Lord to-brosede the staf of vnpitous men..with an vnheleable plage. **1611** Cotgr., *Incurable*,..vnhealeable. *a* **1661** Fuller *Worthies, Warwick.* iii. (1662) 125 He in his Youth was afflicted with an unhealable Sprain in his Hip. **1795** Coleridge *Let. to Southey* 135 Of innovation they see dreadful..and unhealable consequence. **1862** Thackeray *Philip* xx, In the midst of feuds unhealable. **1891** F. W. Newman *J. H. Newman* p. vi, A most painful breach, through mere religious creed, broke on me.., and was unhealable.
*absol.* **1837** Carlyle *Fr. Rev.* ii. v. xii, Lafayette indites his emphatic Letter..against Jacobinism; which..will not heal the unhealable.

**Unhea·led,** *ppl. a.* (Un-[1] 8. Cf. NFris. *unhialed*, Du. *ongeheeld*, MHG. *ungeheilet*, G. *-heilt*.)
*a* **1225** *Ancr. R.* 328 Forði he iwende awei unhealed..ut of þe temple. **1398** Trevisa *Barth. De P. R.* vii. liv. (Bodl. MS.), But if he leue one [hemorrhoid] vnheled it is perile. *a* **1425** tr. *Arderne's Treat. Fistula*, etc. 44 If þe fynger..of any man haue be long vnheled of vnwise cure. **1500–20** Dunbar *Poems* xc. 22 Off tuenty woundis, and ane be left unhelit Quhat awalis the leiching of the laif? **1573** Baret *Alv.* V 142 Unhealed, vncured. **1647** Hexham i, Vnhealed, *ongenesen*. **1795** Helen M. Williams *Lett. on France* I. 251 Whom the tyrants had dragged to prison, while the wounds were yet unhealed, which he had received in defending his country. **1846** Trench *Mirac.* xxxi. (1862) 444 Their condemnation was..that, being unhealed, they counted themselves whole. **1884** R. W. Church *Bacon* vi. 154 The wounds of Ireland were unhealed.

†**Unhea·lful,** *a. Obs.* [Un-[1] 7.] Unwholesome. *c* **1400** tr. *Secreta Secret., Gov. Lordsh.* 79 Þay ar vnhelfull, as þes stondyng waters. *Ibid.*, Waters..hote and vnhelfull.

**Unhea·lth.** [Un-[1] 12: cf. Unheal.] Want of health; weak or poor health.
*c* **1000** *Ags. Gosp.* Luke v. 31 Ne beþurfon læces þa ðe hale synd, ac þa ðe unhælþe habbaþ. *a* **1050** *Liber Scintill.* xxviii. (1889) 107 Maneȝa..menn þurh win lichaman unhælþe mæste togæderetugan. *a* **1200** *Moral Ode* 323 Ac þer nis hunger ne þurst ne deð, ne vnhelþe ne elde. *a* **1250** *Prov. Ælfred* 113 in *O. E. Misc.* 108 Þenne cumeþ elde, and vnhelþe. **1551** Parry in *Macm. Mag.* XLV. 454 Her Grace's unhealth hath made it [her hand] weaker, and so unsteady. **1826** Coleridge in D. Campbell *Life* (1894) 267 *note*, I am at present sadly below even my par of health, or rather unhealth. **1853** Kingsley *Misc.* I. 316 The spokesman..of all the unrest and unhealth of sensitive young men for many a year after.

**Unhea·lthful,** *a.* [Un-[1] 7.]

**1.** = Unhealthy *a.* 1.
**1580** Sidney *Ps.* xxii. i, My God,..from me why is thy presence taken? Soe farre from seeing mine unhealthfull eyes. **1600** Surflet *Countrie Farme* i. xv. 95 They be small, alwaies leane, vnhealthfull, and their flesh of small relish. **1683** Tryon *Way to Health* 202 These latter sort of People ..are certainly the most unhealthful men in the World. ? **1737** Bolingbroke *Study Hist.* vii, Charles the second: an unhealthful youth. **1768–74** Tucker *Lt. Nat.* (1834) II. 81 Many come into the world maimed, weakly, and unhealthful.
*absol.* **1660** R. Coke *Power & Subj.* 164 That you may never in the same manner judge rich and poor,..the healthful and unhealthful.

**b.** Of life, growth, etc.
**1595** in Ellis *Orig. Lett.* Ser. iii. IV. 124 In my declyninge and unhealthfull yeres. **1612** T. Taylor *Comm. Titus* i. 13 Of an vnhealthfull..and painfull life men are so weary, as they would seeke for death. **1786** Abercrombie *Gard. Assist.* 247 Any plants of an infirm, unhealthful, stunted..growth. **1831** Willis *Poem Brown University* 88 Unhealthful fires burn constant in his eye. **1895** *Atlantic Monthly* Mar. 340 The bark peels away in strips, leaving them in white unhealthful nakedness.

**2.** = Unhealthy *a.* 2.
**1598** Florio, *Insalubre*, vnholsome, vnhealthfull. **1653** W. Ramesey *Astrol. Restored* 303 The Winter following will be very unhealthful and obnoxious to all creatures. **1683** Dryden *Life Plutarch* in *P.'s Lives* I. 5 Being also expos'd to the winds which blew from that quarter, the town was perpetually unhealthful. **1756** C. Lucas *Ess. Waters* I. 36 All countries where stagnant waters abound must be unhealthful. **1784** Cowper *Task* iv. 363 The unhealthful East, That breathes the spleen, and searches ev'ry bone Of the infirm. **1841** Myers *Cath. Th.* iii. § 50. 193 Such Rest..is sweeter far than any which unhealthful indolence..can supply. **1865** Mrs. Whitney *Gayworthys* xxiii, There was truly something in the air that had made the place unhealthful to her.

**Unhea·lthfully,** *adv.* (Un-[1] 11.) **1677** Miége ii. s.v., To live somewhere unhealthfully. **1846** Worcester.

**Unhea·lthfulness.** [Un-[1] 12.] Unhealthiness: **a.** Of persons.
**1589** Puttenham *Eng. Poesie* i. viii. (Arb.) 33 Horace.. was thought meete..to be Secretarie of estate,..which neuerthelesse he refused for his vnhealthfulnesse sake. **1611** Cotgr., *Indisposition*, .. vnhealthfulnesse. *a* **1676** Whitelocke *Memorials* (1732) 378 Which occasioned sir Thomas Widdrington to..excuse himself..because of his unhealthfulness. **1727** Bailey (vol. II), *Sickliness*, Unhealthfulness.

**b.** Of places, climate, etc.
**1598** Florio, *Insalubrita*, vnhealthfulnes. **1626** Bacon *Sylva* § 786 *margin*, Experiment Solitary, touching the Healthfulnesse or Vnhealthfulnesse of the Southern wind. **1677** in *Misc. Cur.* (1708) III. 246 The Town lying in a bottom, ..the Air may be infected, and contribute to its unhealthfulness. **1757** J. H. Grose *Voy. E. Indies* 48 Bombay, in fact, had long born an infamous character for unhealthfulness. **1802** *Naval Chron.* VIII. 147 The unhealthfulness of Madagascar. **1897** Bryce *Impress. S. Africa* 2 Its unhealthfulness is a factor of prime importance.

**Unhea·lthily,** *adv.* (Un-[1] 11.)
**1644** Milton *Divorce* (ed. 2) Pref. A 2, Which..puffs up unhealthily a certaine big face of pretended learning. **1673** Kirkman *Unlucky Citizen* x. 171 She..lived poor and unhealthily, wanting and miserably. **1807** Sir R. Wilson in *Life* (1862) II. 302 His face was very pale and unhealthily full. **1876** Miss Yonge *Womankind* xxxi, When a child is dressed cumbrously or unhealthily because it is the fashion.

**Unhea·lthiness.** [Un-[1] 11.] The quality or condition of being unhealthy: **a.** Of persons, etc.
**1634** Sir T. Herbert *Trav.* 25 Doubtlesse their too much farcinating..acted rather their vnhealthinesse. **1727** Bailey (vol. II), *Unhealthiness*,.. sickliness, unhealthful Quality or Condition. **1789** W. Buchan *Dom. Med.* (1790) 7 One great source of the diseases of children is, the unhealthiness of parents. **1828–32** Webster s.v., The unhealthiness of trees or other plants. **1851** Hawthorne *Twice-told T.* I. vi. 107 A certain unhealthiness in the mind of the boy.

**b.** Of places, climate, etc.
**1666** Sancroft *Lex Ignea* 51 To scatter the Cloud of the last years unhealthiness. **1697** Dampier *Voy.* I. 224 Whether it was the badness of the Water, or the unhealthiness of the Town was the cause of it we did not know. **1773** *Cook's Voy.* iii. xi. III. 728 In less than a week, we were sensible of the unhealthiness of the climate. **1871** Napheys *Prev. & Cure Dis.* i. viii. 205 Hence the unhealthiness of brilliantly lighted apartments. **1898** *Jrnl. Sch. Geog.* (U.S.) Oct. 300 The chief..cause of the unhealthiness of the city.

**Unhea·lthsome,** *a.* Now *rare.* [Un-[1] 7.]
The spelling with *-same* in quots. 1597–9 is due to the Dutch origin of the translations (after Du. *-saem*).

**1.** Unwholesome.
**1544** Betham *Precepts War* ii. xxxviii. K vij, To make the water noysome and vnhealthsome to thyne enemies. **1599** A. M. tr. *Gabelhouer's Bk. Physicke* 378/1 Experience also hath taught the same to defende any man from vnhealthsame ayre. **1621** *Henryson's Fables* (1832) 50 Unhealthsome meat is of ane sairie Mouse. *a* **1860** J. Younger *Autobiog.* (1881) 130 No corn in these years was substantial; all meal black 'mattened' and unhealthsome.

**2.** Unhealthy.
**1597** A. M. tr. *Guillemeau's Fr. Chirurg.* 23/1 In aged persons, and in those which are vnhealthsame of bodye. *Ibid.* 52/1 Those which..have binn badlye nourished, we call vnhealthsame poeple.

Hence **Unhea·lthsomeness.** ? *Obs.*
**1613** Purchas *Pilgrimage* (1614) 688 The aire is vnholesome. But what vnhealthsomenesse can there be found, where God is found?

**Unhea·lthy,** *a.* [Un-[1] 7.]

**1.** Of persons, etc.: Not possessed of good health; weak or sickly in health. **b.** *Path.* Not in a sound or healthy condition; diseased, morbid. Also *absol.*
**1611** Cotgr., *Mal-sain*,..sicklie, crazie, vnhealthie. **1813** J. Thomson *Lect. Inflam.* 424 When they exceed this, and take on a growing disposition, they are then unhealthy. **1825** T. Hook *Sayings* Ser. ii. II. 61 A watering-place, one of the most fashionable resorts for the idle and unhealthy. **1862** A. Meadows *Man. Midwifery* v. ii. 181 They are apt to take on afterwards unhealthy inflammation. **1877** W. Roberts *Spontaneous Generation* 22 We know that when a wound becomes unhealthy, as surgeons term it, the discharges become offensive.

**2.** Of places, climate, etc.: Prejudicial or hurtful to health; insalubrious; unwholesome.
**1595** in Hakluyt *Voy.* (1600) III. 587 The towne was situated in a waterie soile,..very vnhealthy as any place in the Indies. **1616** W. Browne *Brit. Past.* ii. i. 785 Then mists from marishes,..From standing pooles and fens were following Unhealthy fogs. **1739** Labelye *Piers Westm. Bridge* 72 The opposite Shore,..cover'd with unhealthy Ooze and Filth. **1740** in *10th Rep. Hist. MSS. Comm.* App. I. 275 That very unhealthy and dangerous climate. **1806** *Med. Jrnl.* XV. 17 It was now the most unhealthy season of the year. **1827** Scott *Chron. Canongate* iv, There never was a trade so unhealthy yet, but men would fight to get wark at it. **1884** in Cawston *Street Improv. London* (1893) 108 We bought shops and warehouses on just the same terms as we bought unhealthy dwellings.

**3.** *fig.* (See Healthy *a.* 3.)
**1821** Lamb *Elia* i. *Imperfect Sympathies*, I do feel the differences of mankind, national or individual, to an unhealthy excess. **1849** W. S. Mayo *Kaloolah* v. (1850) 39 He had set himself..against what his good sense led him to pronounce an unhealthy..excitement.

**4.** *Comb.*, as *unhealthy-looking* adj.
**1890** L. C. D'Oyle *Notches* 98 We steamed away again, through a swampy and unhealthy-looking country. **1890** *Retrospect Med.* CII. 318 The skin is usually described as dusky,..unhealthy looking, or yellowish.

†**Unhea·r,** *v. Obs.*[−1] [Un-[1] 14.] *trans.* To hear not; to refuse to hear.
*a* **1300** *Cursor M.* 28793 Certes vr lauerd..for na riche man to here, Vn-hers he pouer man praier.

**Unhea·rable,** *a.* (Un-[1] 7 b.) **1483** *Cath. Angl.* 184/1 Vn-Hereabylle, *in-audibilis*.

**Unhea·rd,** *ppl. a.* [Un-[1] 8. Cf. NFris. *unhiard*, ON. and Icel. *ú-, óheyrðr* (Sw. *ohörd*, Da. *uhørt*); also OE. *ungehéred* (in sense 2), MDu. *ongehoort* (Du. *-hoord*), MLG. *ungehôrt*, OHG. *ungehôret* (MHG. *-hôrt, -hœrt*, G. *-hört*).]

**1.** Not caught or apprehended by the sense of hearing; not heard.
*a* **1300** *Cursor M.* 25182 Or ai vm-quil vr bon es right, Bot vnherd thoru vr aun plight. *c* **1450** *Myrr. our Ladye* 51 He that wyttyngly leuyth oughte of these holy houres vnsayde & vnharde..he synneth deadly. *Ibid.* 294 The prayer..may not be vnherde. **1595** Shaks. *John* iv. ii. 137 But if you be a-feard to heare the worst, Then let the worst vn-heard, fall on your head. **1616** W. Browne *Brit. Past.* ii. i. 789 Clamour grew dumb, unheard was shepheard's song, And silence girt the woods. **1667** Milton *P. L.* i. 395 Their childrens cries unheard, that past through fire. *Ibid.* iii. 645 He drew not nigh unheard. **1742** Young *Nt. Th.* iii. 337 To see what we have seen? Hear, till unheard, the same old slabber'd tale? **1796** Mme. D'Arblay *Camilla* V. 66 The energy of Melmond made her approach unheard. **1842** J. Wilson *Chr. North* I. 89 Not unheard, although scarcely noticed, was the cry of the curlew. **1894** Mrs. Dyan *Man's Keeping* (1899) 143 Craving..for the sound of the long-unheard familiar tones.

**b.** Of persons: Not heard in self-defence or entreaty; not listened to.
**1595** Daniel *Civ. Wars* iii. xxii, Neuer shall this poore breath of mine consent That he..Should here be iudgd vnheard, and vnaraignd. **1606** Shaks. *Ant. & Cl.* iii. xii. 24 This if shee performe, She shall not sue vnheard. **1607** — *Cor.* v. i. 43. **1655** in *Verney Mem.* (1907) I. 538, I will not condemn you unheard. **1718** Prior *Solomon* ii. 720 Unheard the injur'd Orphans now complain. **1760** [see Unconvicted]. **1805** Scott *Last Minstrel* v. xxiii, Unheard he prays;—the death-pang's o'er! Richard of Musgrave breathes no more.

**2.** Not before heard of; unknown, new, strange.
*c* **1375** *Sc. Leg. Saints* l. (*Catherine*) 845 With wnhard pane Sa fellounly scho sall be slaane. **1382** Wyclif *Esther* xvi. 13 For Mardoche..with newe maner and vnherd engynes ful out askide [Haman] in to deth. **1459** *Rolls of Parlt.* V. 346/1 His fals and traiterous ymaginations,..compassed by the most unherd meanes. **1535** Coverdale *2 Macc.* iv. 13 The Heithenish & straunge conuersacion, brought in thorow the vngracious and vnherde wickednesse of Iason. **1586** A. Day *Eng. Secretary* i. (1625) 23 A huge wonder, of the vnheard secrets neuer before reported of. **1658** Cokaine *Trappolin* iv. ii, Some unheard malady Vnknown unto the world before. **1677** Yarranton *Eng. Improv.* 7 Notwithstanding all these strange, and unheard Inconveniences, yet they will not quit their Station. **1746** Francis tr. *Horace, Art of Poetry* 68 A new-discover'd Theme.., unheard in ancient Times. **1813** Shelley *Q. Mab* vii. 165 Humbly He came,.. His name unheard, Save by the rabble of His native town.

**b.** More usually with *of.* (Common from *c* 1600.)
Hence, in recent use, *unheard-of-ness*.
**1592** Greene *Groat's W. Wit* (1617) 35 If wofull experience may moue you (Gentlemen) to beware, or vnheard of wretchednes intreat you to take heed. **1615** G. Sandys *Trav.* 145 Inflicting vnheard-of tortures on the patient Christians. **1699** Bentley *Phalaris* 170 The Phrase was then so new and unheard of, that it puzzled a whole City. **1752** in *10th Rep. Hist. MSS. Comm.* App. I. 308 An Arminian who governed with unheard of Despotism. **1790**

BURKE *Fr. Rev.* 20 This new, and hitherto unheard-of bill of rights. **1848** THACKERAY *Van. Fair* lxvii, She tended him through a series of unheard-of illnesses. **1891** FARRAR *Darkn. & Dawn* xv, From the first he broke out into unheard-of extravagance.

**Unhea·ring,** *ppl. a.* (UN-[1] 10.)
**1785** BURKE *Sp. Fox's E. Indian Bill* Wks. IV. 41 The cries of India are given to seas and winds to be blown about ..over a remote and unhearing ocean. **1828** *Lights & Shades* II. 106 My own close, unhearing, unseeing condition. **1894** *Outing* XXIV. 461/2 The inexorable mandate .. resounded in our unhearing ears.

**Unhea·rse,** *v.* (UN-[2] 5. The exact sense is doubtful.)
**1596** SPENSER *F. Q.* v. iii. 37 He..from him reft his shield, and it renuerst, .. And himselfe baffuld, and his armes vnherst. **Unhea·rsed,** *ppl. a.* (UN-[1] 8.) **1809** LAMB *To a River*, etc. ii, In thy channel,..Deep immersed, and unhearsed, Lies young Edward's corse. **1813** HOGG *Queen's Wake* Concl. xxxviii, The Border chiefs, that long had been In sepulchres unhearsed and green.

**Unhea·rt,** *v.* [UN-[2] 4. Cf. MDu. *ontherten*, MHG. and G. *entherzen*.] *trans.* To deprive of heart; to dishearten. Also **Unhea·rted** *ppl. a.*
**1593** *Pass. Morrice* (1876) 76 My..sences gon, my bodie haue vnharted: so that I liue aliue, as being dead. **1607** SHAKS. *Cor.* v. i. 49 Yet to bite his lip, And humme at good Cominius, much vnhearts mee. **1650** *Let. Cens. & Redargution Lilburne* Verses, Which scorn the Son of Noble Jonathan, As a desponding, poore unhearted man. **1830** CARLYLE *Richter & De Stael* Ess. 1840 II. 431 It is probable she knows only the French (un-souled and un-hearted) Shakspeare.

†**Unhea·rt's-ease.** *Obs.* (UN-[1] 12.)
**1470** *Paston Lett.* II. 405 Wretyn with onhertes ease the Monday next aftir Relike Sonday. *c* **1530** LD. BERNERS *Arth. Lyt. Bryt.* (1814) 70 It is a great shame for you .. thus to suffre payne and vnhertes ease.

**Unhea·rtsome,** *a.* *Sc.* and *north.* (UN-[1] 7.)
**1637** RUTHERFORD *Lett.* I. clxxix. (1664) 347 It is an unheartsom thing to see our Father & mother agree so ill. **1752** E. ERSKINE *Serm.* Wks. 1871 III. 440 A melancholy unheartsome habitation would this be. **1876** *Whitby Gloss.* 206/2 *Unheartsome*,..without affection. **1897** CROCKETT *Lochinvar* xxi, An uncanny and unheartsome journey.

**Unhea·rty,** *a.* [UN-[1] 7.]
†**1.** Faint-hearted, spiritless. *Obs.*
*c* **1440** *Promp. Parv.* 237/2 Hertles, or vnherty, *vecors*. *c* **1482** J. KAY tr. *Caoursin's Siege of Rhodes* P 12 They had not..to fyghte wyth men of Asea..couwerdes and unherty as women.
**2.** Not hearty or cordial.
**1583** MELBANCKE *Philotimus* X ij b, I..salute thy ingratitude with an vnhartie greeting. **1621** *First & Second Bk. Discipl.* 11 Such as embraced the true religion..were not onely unheartie friends, but..great hinderers. **1784** J. BROWN *Hist. Brit. Ch.* (1823) II. v. 188 Most of the English either declined serving in the invasion, or were very unhearty in it.
**3.** *Sc.* Listless, dispirited; in poor condition.
*a* **1698** J. FRASER *Mem.* (1738) 136, I..lost my Assurance, Peace, and Strength, and became very unhearty and indisposed. **1825** JAMIESON *Suppl.*

**Unhea·ted,** *ppl. a.* (UN-[1] 8.)
*a* **1691** BOYLE (J.), Neither salts, nor the distilled spirits of them can penetrate the narrow pores of unheated glass. **1768** STERNE *Sent. Journ.* I. 78 Submitting the offer, and themselves with it, to be sifted..by an unheated mind. **1843** *Civil Eng. & Arch. Jrnl.* VI. 304/1 A blast of atmospheric air, in the natural or unheated state. **1883** *World's Cycl. Sci.* 15 As attraction is weak in the gases of the Earth's atmosphere—comparatively unheated.

**Unhea·ven,** *v.* (UN-[2] 5.)
**1609** J. DAVIES (Heref.) *Holy Roode* Wks. (Grosart) I. 28/1 Vnheau'n your selues, ye holy Cherubins, And giue attendance on your Lord, in Earth. **1659** GAUDEN *Tears Ch.* II. xxviii. 242 How should all men..be..unsainted,unheavened, ..if these men might not have their wills. **1844** L. HUNT *Our Cottage* 97 Heav'n..held us flimsy triflers—gnats i' the sun—Made but for play, and so to die, unheav'n'd.

**Unhea·venly,** *a.* (UN-[1] 7.)
**1752** LAW *Spirit of Love* I. (1766) 21 To remove every Thing that is unheavenly, gross, dark, from every Part of this fallen World. **1823** MOORE *Loves of Angels* Introd. 61 Still fair and glorious, he but shone Among those youths th' unheavenliest one. **1893** J. PULSFORD *Loyalty to Christ* II. 230 He feels that he is very unheavenly, very unworthy.

**Unhe·dged,** (*ppl.*) *a.* (UN-[1] 8, 9.)
**1648** HEXHAM II, *Onbeheymt*, Vnhedged, or Vnfenced. **1743** YOUNG *Nt. Th.* v. 741 Our needful knowledge, like our needful food, Unhedg'd, lyes open in life's common field. **1855** LEWES *Goethe* I. 98 The botanist despairs of flowers on the unhedged plains of France. **1868** MORRIS *Earthly Par.* (1870) I. I. 345 The fair abode..o'erlooked, across the road, Unhedged green meads.

**Unhee·d,** *v.* [UN-[1] 14.] *trans.* To pay no heed to, to disregard. (Cf. UNHEEDING *ppl. a.* 2 *b.*)
**1847** *Illustr. Lond. News* 17 July 39/2 The girl..began to unheed his solicitations. **1856** J. PULSFORD *Jesus Revealing Heart of God* (ed. 2) 19 He unheeds the charges brought against him.

**Unhee·ded,** *ppl. a.* (UN-[1] 8.)
**1611** COTGR., *Improuueu*, vnprouided for,..vnheeded, vnthought vpon. **1660** BOYLE *New Exp. Phys. Mech.* xxxviii. 320 Whether it were due to any unheeded accident, or to the exsuction of the Air. **1736** GRAY *Statius* i. 21 He..scornful flung th' unheeded weight Aloof. **1748** *Anson's Voy.* III. v. 336 A good meal was neither an uncommon nor an unheeded article. **1817** SHELLEY *Prometh. Unb.* II. iv. 26 Pain, whose unheeded and familiar speech Is howling. **1864** PUSEY *Lect. Daniel* (1876) 326 Only one or two raised an unheeded doubt.
**b.** In predicative use.
**1682** CREECH *Lucretius* IV. 126 The fleeting Images, Unseen,..unheeded, cease. **1709** PRIOR *Henry & Emma* 666 Succeeding Years their happy Race shall run; And Age unheeded by Delight come on. **1783** CRABBE *Village* I. 293 His drooping patient,..long unheeded, knows remonstrance vain. **1824** MISS L. M. HAWKINS *Annaline* II. 221 [She] left them when she found that her warning to take rest passed unheeded. **1875** JOWETT *Plato* (ed. 2) I. 33 He cannot let the thought..pass away unheeded and unexamined.
Hence **Unhee·dedly** *adv.*
**1818** BYRON *Ch. Har.* IV. lxiii, And such the frenzy,..that, beneath the fray, An earthquake reel'd unheededly away! **1821** SHELLEY *Epipsych.* 421 Day, and Storm, and Calm,.. Treading each other's heels, unheededly.

**Unhee·dful,** *a.* [UN-[1] 7.] Heedless.
**1570** LEVINS *Manip.* 186 Vnheedful, *incautus*. **1591** SHAKS. *Two Gentl.* II. vi. 11 Vn-heedfull vowes may heedfully be broken. **1631** HEYLIN *St. George* 28 Some secret venome, which the unheedfull Reader may swallow unawares. **1740** CIBBER *Apol.* (1756) I. 175 He so often lost the value of them by an unheedful confidence. **1782** ELIZ. BLOWER *Geo. Bateman* II. 171 The glassman, unheedful of his threats, picked up the half-crown. **1804** J. GRAHAME *Sabbath* 25 The toil-worn horse,..Unheedful of the pasture. **1842** TENNYSON *Gardener's Dau.* 261 As once we met Unheedful, tho' beneath a whispering rain [etc.].
So **Unhee·dfully** *adv.*; **Unhee·dfulness.**
**1591** SHAKS. *Two Gentl.* I. ii. 3 Would'st thou then counsaile me to fall in loue? *Luc.* I Madam, so you stumble not *vnheedfully. **1586** W. WEBBE *Eng. Poetrie* (Arb.) 91 Such errours doo happen..by *vnheedefulnes, when one escapeth them by negligence. **1603** BRETON *Packet Mad Lett.* II. lxxxv, I know you..therefore doe thus kindly touch the hurt of vnheedfulnesse.

†**Unhee·dily,** *adv.* [UN-[1] 11.] Heedlessly.
**1596** SPENSER *F. Q.* IV. x. 13 Whose manner was all passengers to stay,..Through which some lost great hope vnheedily. **1603** FLORIO *Montaigne* II. xxxv. 428 Beseeching her, that she wold not so vnheedily loose her self. **1629** H. BURTON *Truth's Triumph* 301 If vnheedily thou hast fallen vpon the same rockes. **1720–1** *Lett. fr. Mist's Jrnl.* (1722) II. 270 Anything that has the Name of it deceives them, who unheedily take the Title for the Reality.

†**Unhee·diness.** *Obs.* [UN-[1] 12.] Unheedfulness, heedlessness.
**1486** *Lichfield Gild Ord.* (1920) 21 That the seid summe.. by vnhedynes, blame, and neglygens of kepers..ys now diminysshed. **1576** NEWTON *Lemnie's Complex.* 23 b, Them yᵗ be phlegmatick, they helpe forward, to slouth,..sleapines, rechlesse vnheedynes. **1607** R. WILKINSON *Serm. at Whitehall* 9 She sailes not, but by sounding, lest by her vnheedines she runne her selfe aground. *a* **1641** BP. MOUNTAGU *Acts & Mon.* (1642) 276 The wicked practices..whereto, through unheedinesse the two young men had given great fomentation.

**Unhee·ding,** *ppl. a.* [UN-[1] 10, 5 d.]
**1.** Not giving heed; heedless, inattentive.
*pred.* **1737** GLOVER *Leonidas* VI. (1810) 111 Some torn deer, which..Had roam'd, unheeding, in the secret shade. **1816** BYRON *Parisina* x, All silent and unheeding now, With downcast eyes and knitting brow. **1848** MRS. GASKELL *Mary Barton* ix, He sat down by the fire in his wet things, unheeding.
*attrib.* **1791** COWPER *Iliad* XVI. 424 Lambs, which haply some unheeding swain Hath left to roam at large the mountains wild. **1817** SHELLEY *Rev. Islam* III. x, These words had fallen on my unheeding ear. **1872** BLACK *Adv. Phaeton* xxvi. 355 Groups of unheeding trees and streams.
**2.** Const. *of*, or with direct object.
(*a*) **1795** *Fate of Sedley* II. 198, I ramble over the country unheeding of the storm. **1840** T. HOOK *Fitzherbert* II. vi. 153 To pull the rose unheeding of the thorn.
(*b*) **1798** SOUTHEY *Joan of Arc* (ed. 2) I. I. 124, I sat in silence,..unheeding and unseeing all Around me. **1835** LYTTON *Rienzi* I. iii, Waving his hand to the smith, and unheeding his brandished weapon. **1892** GUNTER *Miss Dividends* xi, Then, unheeding his proffered aid, Erma descends from the carriage.
Hence **Unhee·dingly** *adv.*, heedlessly.
**1787** *William of Normandy* II. 126 All the secrets..I unheedingly trusted him with. **1834** LYTTON *Pilgr. Rhine* xix, He passed..unheedingly.

†**Unhee·dy,** *a.* *Obs.* [UN-[1] 7.] Unheedful.
**1579** E. K. *Gloss to Spenser's Shepherd's Cal.* April 26 His præsumptuous and vnheedie hardinesse. **1590** SHAKS. *Mids. N.* I. i. 235 Nor hath loues minde of any iudgement taste: Wings and no eyes, figure, vnheedy haste. **1631** MILTON *Epit. Marchioness Winchester* 38 So have I seen som tender slip..Pluck't up by som unheedy swain. **1656** HOBBES *Six Lessons* Wks. 1845 VII. 222 So much is unheedy learning a hinderance to the knowledge of the truth. **1787** *William of Normandy* II. 9 He again set off for his unheedy voyage.

†**Unhee·r,** *a.* *dial.* *Obs.* [?OE. *unhéore*, *-hére*, etc., fierce.] (See quot.) **1691** RAY *N. Co. Words* (ed. 2) 78 *Unheer*, adj., impatient. [Hence in Bailey (1721), etc.]

**Unheind,** var. UNHEND *a.* *Obs.*

**Unhei·red,** *ppl. a.* (UN-[2] 4 and 8.) *c* **1611** CHAPMAN *Iliad* v. 25 If the God..Had not (in..pittie of his Sire, To leaue him vtterly vnheird) giuen safe passe to his feet.

**Unhe·ld,** *ppl. a.* (UN-[1] 8 b: cf. UNHOLDEN.) **1612** WARNER *Alb. Eng.* XI. lxv. 279 If amorous Hopes, or Hopes vnheld to him from me had past. **1827** POLLOK *Course T.* v. 661 Forgetful, she leaves him [*sc.* her infant] a while unheld.

**Unhele,** *sb.*: see UNHEAL.

**Unhe·le,** *v.* *Obs.* exc. *dial.* Forms: 1 unhelan, 2–3 unhelen, 4–6 vnhele, 4–6, 9 *dial.*, unhele (4 oun-), 6 *Sc.* vnheild-, 6–7 vnheale, 7–8, 9 *dial.*, unheal, 8 unheel, 9 *dial.* unhale. [OE. *unhelan* (UN-[2] 3 + HELE *v.*): cf. MDu. *onthelen*, MHG. *enthelen*, and UNHILL *v.*]
**1.** *trans.* To uncover (something) so as to display or make visible; hence *fig.*, to discover, reveal, make patent or known. Also *refl.*
*c* **1000** *Ags. Gosp.* Luke xii. 2 Nis nan þing oferheled, þe ne beo unheled. *c* **1200** *Trin. Coll. Hom.* 77 Seinte poul.. minegeð us..þat we..cumen festliche to ure saule leche and unhelen him ure saule wundes. *a* **1225** *Ancr. R.* 150 Al so god dede þet wule adeaden forworpeð hire rinde, þet is, unheleð hire. *c* **1330** *Arth. & Merl.* 2689 (Kölbing), þe king.. ladde him fram & gan his priuete vnhele, & bad, þat he it schuld hele. **1387** TREVISA *Higden* (Rolls) VIII. 161 Here he is i-hud, but he is unheled. **1483** CAXTON *Gold. Leg.* 249/1 Netheles the body of saynt laurence was discouerd and unheled by ygnorance. **1530** TINDALE *Practice Prelates* H vij, Thou shalt not vnhele ye secretes of thy brothers wyffe. **1590** SPENSER *F. Q.* II. xii. 64 Then suddeinly both would themselues vnhele.
**2.** To uncover so as to leave open or exposed; to strip of covering or (freq.) roofing material.
*a* **1225** *Ancr. R.* 58 Auh þe dom is ful strong upon ham þet unhelieð þene put. **1387** TREVISA *Higden* (Rolls) I. 367 Þere was a welle in þat lond..alle wey i-heled; and ȝif it were vnheled, þe welle wexe and adrenche al þe lond. **1393** LANGL. *P. Pl.* C. xx. 301 Yf hus hous be vnheled and reyne on hus bedde. *c* **1440** *Pallad. on Husb.* II. 56 Yet wol this werk the roote..Vnhele or kerue, and cold hit after quelle. **1501** DOUGLAS *Pal. Hon.* II. xlv, I kneillit law, and vnheildit my heid. **1551** *Southampton Court Leet Rec.* (1905) I. 28 Robarde foster hathe vnhellyde partte off thomas cupers housse. **1604** MARSTON *Malcontent* II. iii. D ij b, Would I were forcde To burne my fathers Tombe, vnheale [*v.r.* vnhill] his bones.., rather than this. **1610** G. FLETCHER *Christ's Tri.* II. ix, Thear should the Swallowe see..the grave vnheale his face, To let the living from his bowels creepe. **1730** BUDGEN *Passage of Hurricane fr. Bexhill* 9 Mr John Collier had..the ridging of the house unheeled. **1741** *Phil. Trans.* XLI. 852 It presently unhealed the House we were in. **1848** in *Eng. Dial. Dict.* s.v. *Unheal* (Wilts, Dorset, Som., Devon). **1891** T. HARDY *Tess* xlvii, They were busily 'unhaling' the rick, that is, stripping off the thatch.
†**b.** In pa. pple. Of the head: Uncovered. *Obs.*
**1377** LANGL. *P. Pl.* B. XIV. 232 He goth to cold beddynge, And his heued vn-heled vn-esiliche i-wrye. *a* **1400–50** *Alexander* 3450 Hire hede vn-helid was on hiȝe & hild all in trissis.
Hence **Unhe·ler**; **Unhe·ling** *vbl. sb.*
*c* **1430** *Pilgr. Lyf Manhode* III. xvii. (1869) 144 This hand is an vnmakere of howses, and an *vnhelere and brekere of cofres. **1398** TREVISA *Barth. De P. R.* v. xxvii. (Bodl. MS.), In acutis [febribus] *vnheling and puttinge oute of bare armes is tokene of deep. **1640** in *Archæol. Cant.* (1902) XXV. 8 His mother being then in distress, by reason of the unhealing of her house by the late severe time.

**Unhe·lm,** *v.* [UN-[2] 4, 7. Cf. Du. *onthelmen*.]
**1.** *refl.* and *trans.* To divest (oneself or another) of a helmet.
*refl.* *c* **1400** *Pilgr. Sowle* (Caxton, 1483) IV. xxxviii. 66 This knyght..vnhelmed hym, and come before the kynge. *c* **1468** in *Archaeol.* (1846) XXXI. 338 Then the Duke unhelmed hyme, and..chargid pece in paine of deth. **1587** HOLINSHED *Chron.* (ed. 2) III. 825/1 When the iusts were doone, the king & all the other vnhelmed them, & rode about the tilt. **1632** J. HAYWARD tr. *Biondi's Eromena* 100 Striving to unhelme himself.., he taking his brothers hand, would needs kisse it. **1801** STRUTT *Sports & Past.* III. i. 124 The laws of the tournament permitted any one of the combatants to unhelm himself at pleasure. **1866** LAWRENCE *Sans Merci* xli, The five kings..unhelmed themselves to quench their thirst.
*trans.* **1470–85** MALORY *Arthur* x. lxxxvi. 565 Thenne they vnarmed them. And whanne syre Launcelot was vnhelmed, sir Tristram and syr Palomydes knewe hym. **1525** LD. BERNERS *Froiss.* II. clxviii. 468 Eche of them strake other on their helmes...With yᵗ ataynt the lorde of saynt Pye was vnhelmed. **1587** HUGHES *Misfort. Arthur* v. i, Vnhealme his luckelesse head, set bare his face. **1819** SCOTT *Ivanhoe* xii, The marshals..unhelmed him by cutting the laces of his casque. **1848** LYTTON *Harold* XII. ix, They unhelmed another corpse.
**2.** *intr.* To take off one's own helmet.
**1865** J. M. LUDLOW *Epics Mid. Ages* II. 228 Nor will she let William in till he has unhelmed.

**Unhe·lmed,** (*ppl.*) *a.*[1] [f. prec., or f. UN-[1] 9 + HELM *sb.*[1]] **a.** Divested of a helmet. **b.** Not covered by, or not wearing, a helmet.
[**1775** ASH.] **1795** SOUTHEY *Joan of Arc* v. 26 The Maid, her brows in reverence vnhelm'd,..Knelt to his prayer. **1805** — *Madoc in Azt.* xxii. 5 The victors,..With unhelm'd heads, reclining on their shields. **1834** BECKFORD *Italy* II. 317 Here,..bare-headed and unhelmed, kneel the figures [etc.]. **1868** MORRIS *Earthly Par.* (1870) I. I. 20 By his side unhelmed, but armed, stood one.

**Unhe·lmed,** (*ppl.*) *a.*[2] [UN-[1] 8, 9 + HELM *sb.*[2] or *v.*[2]] Unguided, ungoverned.
**1628** FELTHAM *Resolves* II. xxiv. 78 As if hee were an imperfect Prince, that leaueth an vnhelmed State. **1794** COLERIDGE *Relig. Musings* 126 Embattling Interests on each other rush With unhelmed rage.

**Unhe·lmet,** *v.* [UN-[2] 4.] = UNHELM *v.* **1823** SCOTT *Quentin* xv, He was compelled to dismount,..and unhelmet himself.

**Unhe·lmeted,** *a.* (UN-[1] 9.)
**1823** SCOTT *Quentin D.* xxii, His head was unhelmeted, but he wore the rest of his ponderous and bright armour. **1870** RUSKIN *Lect. Art* vi. 153 Next you have Athena, again unhelmeted and crowned with leaves.

†**Unhe·lp,** *sb.* *Obs.* [UN-[1] 12. Cf. MLG. *unhulpe* disadvantage.] Absence of help; hindrance.
*c* **1449** PECOCK *Repr.* I. xviii. 108 Manie lettis and manye vnhelpis and manye lackis of helpis. **1483** *Cath. Angl.* 182/2 Vn Helpe, *irrefugium*. **1598** FLORIO, *Disaiuto*, hinderance, vnhelpe, let.

**Unhe·lp,** *v.* [UN-[2] 3. Cf. MDu. *onthelpen*, MLG. *enthelpen*.] *trans.* To deprive of help; to hinder.
**1598** FLORIO, *Disaiutare*, to vnhelpe, to hinder, to disfauour. **1845** T. W. COIT *Puritanism* 118 They would help him, if thereby they might unhelp Churchmen.

**Unhe·lpable,** *a.* (UN-[1] 7 b.) **1886** *Illustr. Lond. News* 5 June 597/3 The most unhelpable creature possible.

**Unhe·lped,** *ppl. a.* (UN-[1] 8.)
**1388** WYCLIF *Wisd.* xii. 5 Fadris and modris, autours of soulis vnhelpid. **1598** DRAYTON *Heroic Ep.* 6 That poore king, of al these hopes preuented, Vnhard, vnhelp'd. **1720** POPE *Iliad* XVII. 580 Unhelp'd we stand, unequal to engage The force of Hector. *a* **1784** T. ADAM *Poor Man's Guide* (1788) 13 Your case is as much unhelped as if there was not one promise there. **1853** RUSKIN *Stones Ven.* III. ii. 53 Let

him consider..how many living souls may have been left uncomforted and unhelped by him. **1888** Bryce *Amer. Commw.* II. 531 Nor will the opposite party always accept the proffered help..; sometimes it hopes to win unhelped.

**Unhe·lpful,** *a.* [Un-[1] 7.]

**1.** Unable to help; not rendering help.

**1593** Shaks. *2 Hen. VI*, III. i. 218 Euen so my selfe bewayles good Glosters case With sad vnhelpefull teares, and with dimn'd eyes. **1643–5** Milton *Divorce* II. xvii, A blamelesse creature,..to whose ease you cannot adde the tithe of one small atome, but by letting alone your unhelpfull surgery. **1856** Miss Yonge *Daisy Chain* I. xvii, Standing unhelpful, when the others were busy bringing in the benches. **1880** Swinburne *Stud. Shaks.* 62 As yet the one contemporary book..remains..inaccessible and unhelpful to students.

**2.** Helpless, shiftless. Also *absol.*

**1855** I. Taylor *Restor. Belief* (1856) 290 The luckless, the unhelpful, the feeble,..receive such help as their several cases call for.

Hence **Unhe·lpfulness.**

**1626** Bp. Hall *Contempl., O. T.* XXI. v, To take vengeance ..for this cold unhelpfulnesse to his distressed Church.

**Unhe·lping,** *ppl. a.* (Un-[1] 10.)

**1604** E. Hake (*title*), Of Golds Kingdome and this Unhelping Age. **1645** W. Jenkyn *Stil-Destroyer* 35 View them as usefull and efficacious, not as idle and unhelping. **1861** [Mrs. A. J. Penny] *Romance Dull Life* xiii. 98 Others of the family came in with kind words and offered help... Poor Constance, alone, sat silent and unhelping.

†**Unhe·lpless,** *a. Obs.*[−1] [Un-[1] 5 a.] Helpless. **1681** Crowne *Hen. VI*, IV. 45 Whilst I with as unhelpless tears bewail The good Man's injuries.

†**Unhe·lply,** *a. Obs.*[−1] [Un-[1] 7. Cf. Da. *uhjelpelig*, Sw. *ohjelplig* irremediable; Norw. *uhjelpelig* unserviceable.] Unhelpful.

**1408** tr. *Vegetius' Art War* (MS. Digby 233) fol. 216/2 Al þat is helpliche to hym is vnhelpliche to þe.

**Unhe·mmed,** *ppl. a.* [Un-[1] 8.]

**1.** Unconfined, unrestrained.

*a* **1400–50** *Alexander* 2835 For-þi hoo with þi hatness & þi vn-hemmyd wittes, Avale of þi vanyte.

**2.** Not furnished with a hem.

**1561** in *Inuentaires de la Royne Descosse* (Bannatyne Club) 24 Aucht serviottis of vnhemmit great lyning. **1611** Florio, *Inorlato*,..vnhemmed. **1889** *Daily News* 13 July 3/3 The new little Redfern capes..with their triple row of unhemmed cloth.

†**Unhe·nd,** *a.*, *sb.*, and *adv.* [Un-[1] 7.]

**1.** Of persons: Discourteous, impolite; ungentle, rude, rough.

*c* **1205** Lay. 28826 Ne durste nauere nan vn-hende þas kinges hus isechen. *a* **1300** *Cursor M.* 9023 Bot mistru nan ..þat i Thinc sai o womman wilani, If i sua did i war vnhind [*v.r.* vnhend]. *Ibid.* 28426 Gains godd i haue bene vn-hende, þat i wit-halden ha my tende. *c* **1330** R. Brunne *Chron. Wace* (Rolls) 16022 But longe er hit was brought til ende, He was slayn wyþ folk vnhende. *c* **1380** *Sir Ferumbras* 1965 Þar-after schalt þow wende..And take þe kyng þat is ounhende. *a* **1450** *Le Morte Arth.* 1081 Off foo ne frend, the sothe to say, So vn-hend of thewis is ther none. *absol. c* **1460** *Towneley Myst.* xx. 642 My comforth from care may ye sone wyn, If ye happely may hent that vnheynde.

**2.** Of acts, words, etc.: Unfitting, improper.

*c* **1205** Lay. 13265 Þe frume wes vnhende & al swa wes þe ænde. *c* **1225** *Ancr. R.* 204 Mid luue speche, cos, unhende gropunges, þet beoð heaued sunnen. *a* **1300** *Cursor M.* 27734 Vnheind talking, o dede vtrage,..Hurtes grett, and sclander and tene. ? *c* **1400** *Emare* 445 The old qwene spakke wordus unhende. *c* **1425** *Cast. Persev.* 2030 in *Macro Pl.* 138 Þis day ȝe dyth a good defens! Whyl Mankynde is in good entent, His þoutis arn vn-hende.

**b.** *sb.* Trouble, mischief.

**1377** Langl. *P. Pl.* B. xx. 185 'Sire euel-ytauȝte elde,' quod I, 'vnhende go with the!'

**3.** *adv.* Improperly; unfaithfully.

**1338** R. Brunne *Chron.* (1810) 259 Ȝe sette a certeyn þing, at ȝour boþe assent,..Þou brak þat certeynte wikkedly & vnhende.

†**Unhe·ndly,** *adv. Obs.* [Un-[1] 11.] Discourteously, rudely, roughly; improperly.

*a* **1225** *Leg. Kath.* 2117 He..het, on hat heorte, unhendeliche neomen hire. **1297** R. Glouc. (Rolls) 8540 He it vorsok vnhendeliche & in vaire manere none. *c* **1350** *Will. Palerne* 492 Now witterly ich am vn-wis..Þus vn-hendly & hard mi herte to blame. *c* **1400** *Destr. Troy* 6729 He hurlet forth vnhyndly, harmyt full mony.

**Unhenge,** obs. f. Unhinge *v.*

**Unhe·nt,** *pa. pple.* [Un-[1] 8 b.] Untaken.

*c* **1350** *Will. Palerne* 1671, I kan bi no coyntyse knowe nouȝ þe best, how ȝe mowe un-hent or harmles a-schape.

**Unhe·ppen,** *a. north. dial.* [Un-[1] 7 + dial. *heppen* tidy, handy, a. ON. *heppinn* (Norw. *heppen*) lucky, dexterous. Cf. Norw. *uheppen.*] **a.** Untidy, slatternly. **b.** Ungainly, etc.

**1790** Grose *Prov. Gloss.*, *Unheppen*, slatternly. **1824** [Carr] *Craven Gloss.* 119 *Unheppen*, unbecoming, uncomfortable, indecent, untidy. **1855–** in *Eng. Dial. Dict.* (Yks., Linc.). **1880** Tennyson *Village Wife* xvi, An' Lucy wur laäme o' one leg,..Straänge an' unheppen Miss Lucy!

**Unhe·ralded,** *ppl. a.* (Un-[1] 8.)

**1845** Neale *Euphratean Angels* iv. in *Seatonian Poems* (1864) 7 Yet not unheralded by fear, The End of all things shall draw near. **1871** Macduff *Mem. Patmos* xxiii. 315 A prey to the disquieting thought of the unheralded footfall. [Freq. in recent use.]

**Unhe·rd,** *v.* [Un-[2] 5, 6 b, 7.]

**1.** *trans.* To disperse or separate (cattle, etc.) from a herd.

**1611** Florio, *Smandrare*, to let out of the fold or pen, to vnherd, to scatter cattle. *a* **1641** Suckling *Brennoralt* I. i, When I had..at length unhearded the proud Deer, The Currs have snatch'd him up.

**2.** *intr.* To break away from the common herd.

**1661** Boyle *Style of Script.* (1675) 175 The..title of a wit, which they hope to acquire by unherding and keeping out of the road.

**Unhe·rded,** *ppl. a.* (Un-[1] 8.) [**1775** Ash.] **1891** in C. Roberts *Adrift in America* 241 It is my opinion, after experience.., that unherded sheep do much better than those which are closely looked after. **Unhere·ditary,** *a.* (Un-[1] 7.) **1823** Lamb *Elia* II. *Child Angel*, As if to explore its path in those its unhereditary palaces. **1848** J. O'Donovan tr. *Four Masters* III. 2299 Countless numbers..were buried in strange places and unhereditary churches.

**Unhe·ritable,** *a.* [Un-[1] 7 b.]

†**1.** Incapable of being heirs. *Obs.*[−1]

**1553** in Holinshed *Chron.* (1577) II. 1717/1 Thereby you [are] iustly made illegitimate and vnheritable to the Crowne Imperiall of thys Realme.

**2.** Uninheritable.

[**1775** Ash.] *a* **1854** H. Reed *Lect. Brit. Poets* (1857) 384 The glory of Shakspeare's name began and ended with himself, his own unheritable self.

†**Unhe·rited,** *ppl. a. Obs.* [Un-[1] 8.] Uninherited. **1542** *Test. Ebor.* (Surtees) VI. 128 An erle or an erles sone and heyre,..his landes beinge unherited. *Ibid.*, A knyghte havinge his lands unherited. †**Unhe·rly,** *a. Obs.*[−1] [repr. OE. *unhéorlic*, *unhíerlic* (-*hýrlic*), fierce, savage, dismal.] Repulsive. *c* **1325** *Metr. Hom.* 129 Riht als leper mas bodi Ugli, and lathe, and unherly.

**Unhero·ic,** *a.* and *sb.* (Un-[1] 7.)

**1732** Ld. Peterborow *Let.* in *Pope's Wks.* (1751) VIII. 164 If the translator of Homer find fault with this unheroic disposition. **1745** [see Un-English *a.* 1]. **1840** Carlyle *Heroes* v. (1904) 177 Hollow Formulism, gross Benthamism, and other unheroic atheistic Insincerity. **1881** P. Brooks *Candle of Lord* 169 The heroic moments in all of our most unheroic lives.

*absol.* and *sb.* **1843** Carlyle *Past & Pr.* IV. i, The Unheroic of such volumes. *Ibid.*, An Alexandrian Library of Unheroics.

**Unhero·ical,** *a.* [Un-[1] 7.] = prec. **1635–56** Cowley *Davideis* III. Note 1, I call it Nobe..; for (methinks) Nob is too unheroical a Name. **1718** J. Trapp tr. *Virgil* (1735) I. Pref. p. xlix, Nor can I forbear thinking..that the Figure which Vulcan makes..is a little improper, and unheroical. **Unhero·ically,** *adv.* (Un-[1] 11.) **1834** Beckford *Italy* I. 39 We procured comfortable though not magnificent apartments, and slept most unheroically sound. **1876** Emerson *Lett. & Soc. Aims* i. 63 The brains are so marred, so imperfectly formed, unheroically. **Unhe·roism.** (Un-[1] 12.) **1845** Carlyle *Cromwell* (1871) I. 72 Search not for the secret of Heroic Ages..among their falsities, their greedy quackeries and *un*heroisms! **1871** J. S. Brewer *Eng. Stud.* (1881) 267 Shakspeare in his unheroism and in his realism was exhibiting..the growing tendency of his own age.

†**Unhersumness**: see Un-[1] 3.

**Unhese,** obs. f. Unease.

**Unhe·sitating,** *ppl. a.* (Un-[1] 10.)

**1753** Francis *Constantine* IV. 48 Answer me: speak; unhesitating speak. **1823** Scott *Quentin D.* xxiii, I, who have the advantage of your unhesitating devotion, have done you foul and ungrateful wrong. **1862** 'Shirley' (J. Skelton) *Nugæ Crit.* vii. 295 He can discover..little or nothing that can command his clear and unhesitating assent.

Hence **Unhe·sitatingness.**

**1876** Meredith *Beauch. Career* xl, Unhesitatingness was the warrior virtue of her desire.

**Unhe·sitatingly,** *adv.* [Un-[1] 11.] Without hesitation; confidently; promptly.

**1829** S. H. Cassan *Lives Bps. Bath & Wells* 15 *note*, Such alienations have been unhesitatingly made. **1853** Kane *Grinnell Exp.* xliii. (1856) 396 They [snowbirds] alight on the decks, and come unhesitatingly to our very feet. **1877** Mrs. Oliphant *Makers Flor.* iv. 103 All the critics..take his opinion unhesitatingly on this point.

**Unhew·ed,** *ppl. a.* [Un-[1] 8. Cf. MHG. *ungehouwet.*] = next.

**1382** Wyclif *Josh.* viii. 31 Thanne Josue bilde vp..an auter of stonus vnhewid, the whiche yren hath not towchid. **1612** Drayton *Poly-olb.* ix. 421 With a bended knee On th' unhew'd altar laid. **1644** Bulwer *Chiron.* 5 If Man were disarmed of this native weapon..the expression of his Tongue would be very weake and unhewed.

**Unhew·n,** *ppl. a.* [Un-[1] 8 b. Cf. MDu. *on-*, MHG. *ungehouwen*, ON. *úhǫgginn* (MDa. *u-*, Sw. *ohuggen*).]

**1.** Not hacked or cut with weapons.

*a* **1400–50** *Alexander* 1945 Besely we shapid Out of þe handis vn-hewyn of oure hatill fais.

**2.** Not hewn or cut into shape; not fashioned or shaped by hewing.

**1382** Wyclif *Josh.* viii. 31 (MS. Douce 369), An auter of stones vnhewen þe whiche eiren haþ not touchid. **1651** Hobbes *Leviath.* IV. xlv. 359 A Stone unhewn has been set up for Neptune. **1797** Mrs. Radcliffe *Italian* xviii, The walls, of unhewn marble, were high and strengthened by bastions. **1804** *Ann. Rev.* II. 191 An unhewn log of wood..decorated with red feathers. **1857** Dufferin *Lett. High Lat.* (ed. 3) 309 This fringe of unhewn timber that lined the beach. **1887** Bowen *Æneid* III. 688 Pantagia's harbour, a gorge in the unhewn stone.

**b.** *fig.* Unpolished, rough, rugged.

**1659** Pell *Impr. Sea* 44 Ignorant, knotty, illiterate, and unhewn Sailors. **1687** Montague & Prior *Hind & P. Transv.* Wks. 1907 II. 18, I hate such a rough unhewen Fellow as Milton. **1703** Mrs. Centlivre *Beau's Duel* IV. i, I hope the world will distinguish the difference between a rough, unhewn soldier, and a polish'd Gentleman. **1850** Marsden *Early Purit.* iii. 71 Cartwright is described as unhewn and awkward.

**Unheyle,** obs. var. Unhale *a.*

**Unheynd,** var. Unhend *a. Obs.*

**Unhi·d,** *ppl. a.* [Un-[1] 8 b.] Not hid; unconcealed.

*a* **1300** *Cursor M.* 26617 O sin þat opin es and kid Tak open penance and vn-hid. *a* **1400–50** *Alexander* 3437 Bot ȝour harmes were vnhid I held noȝt myne athis. *c* **1430** *Pilgr. Lyf Manhode* I. xxxv. (1869) 22 It is bettere the keyes..ben hid than unhyd. **1648** Hexham II, *Ongeborgen*, Vnhid, or Vncovered.

**Unhi·dden,** *ppl. a.* (Un-[1] 8 b.)

**1599** Shaks. *Hen. V*, I. i. 86 The seueralls and vnhidden passages Of his true Titles to some certaine Dukedomes. **1829** H. Miller in *Sch. & Schm.* xx. (1858) 439 All around we saw extended the complete sphere,—unhidden above from Orion to the Pole. **1868** Morris *Earthly Par.* I. I. 379 All unhidden once again they saw That peerless beauty.

**Unhi·de,** *v.* [Un-[2] 3.] *trans.* To make unhidden; to lay open; to disclose, reveal.

*a* **1300** *Cursor M.* 7230 Drunkennes oft mai bitide Dos man his consail to vn-hide. *c* **1375** *Sc. Leg. Saints* i. (*Peter*) 283 For dowt his craft vnhid suld be, He kest his bukis in þe se. *c* **1400** *Rom. Rose* 2168 If that ye wole so long abide Tyl I this Romance may vnhide. *c* **1420** *Anturs of Arth.* 328 (Douce MS.) Þe wyndes, þe weders, þe welkene vnhides; Þene vnclosed þe cloudes. **1535** Stewart *Cron. Scot.* (Rolls) III. 431 Quhen tha saw him nakit and wnhid, With bludie woundis.., tha..weipit full soir. **1580** Hollyband *Treas. Fr. Tong*, *Descacher*, to vnhide. **1631** P. Fletcher *Piscatory Eclog.* v. xiv, If thou desir'st my help, unhide the sore. **1676** Hobbes *Iliad* 59 Whilst in stooping he his flank unhides, Agenor quickly his advantage spyes. **1880** J. Nicol *Poems & Songs* 126 To thee the sea her secret oft unhides.

**Unhi·deable,** *a.* (Un-[1] 7 b.) **1606** Sylvester *Du Bartas* II. iv. II. *Magnificence* 1256 A light so bright, set in such eminence (Un-hideable by envious Arrogance, Under the Bushell of black Ignorance). **Unhi·debound,** *a.* (Un-[1] 7.) **1667** Milton *P. L.* x. 601 Which here..all too little seems To stuff this Maw, this vast unhide-bound Corps.

**Unhi·ded,** *ppl. a.*[1] [Un-[1] 8.] Of land: Not divided into hides.

**1867** *Chronicle* 10 Aug. 470/1 At 120 acres the hide..only one-tenth of England would be left unhided. But..the real proportion of hided to unhided land was only as 1 to 2.

**Unhi·ded,** *ppl. a.*[2] [Un-[2] 4, 8.] Deprived of hide; skinned.

*a* **1658** Lovelace *Poems* (1904) 179 Is not this finer far Then walk un-hided, when that every Stone Has knock'd acquaintance with your Anckle bone?

**Unhi·gh,** *a. rare.* [Un-[1] 7, after OE. *unhéah*, *-hêh.*] Wanting in height.

**1838** Longf. *The Grave* ii, Thy house..is unhigh and low [*orig.* unheh and lah]. *Ibid.*, The heel-ways are low, The side-ways unhigh [*orig.* unheȝe].

†**Unhi·ght,** *v. Obs.* [Un-[2] 3.] *trans.* To deprive of grace or beauty.

**1387** Trevisa *Higden* (Rolls) I. 11 Ȝif I..vnhiȝte [L. *decolorarem*] so noble a matire with grisbaitinge. **1398** — *Barth. De P. R.* IX. xxv. (Tollem. MS.), Nyȝte schulde nouȝt be all unhyȝte [L. *indecora*] by absence of þe sonne.

†**Unhi·ghted,** *ppl. a. Obs.*[−1] [Un-[1] 8.] Not invested with beauty.

**1629** T. Adams *Med. Creed* Wks. 1138 Through the chinkes of an vnhighted flesh, we may read a neglected soule.

†**Unhi·ghtness.** *Obs.* [Un-[1] 12.] Impairment; uncomeliness.

**1398** Trevisa *Barth. De P. R.* VII. iii. (Bodl. MS.), Þe heed [suffereth] in heere þereof with..vnhiȝtenes þat phisicians clepen furfurisca. *Ibid.* VII. xvii, Suche an vnhiȝtenes in þe yȝe comeþ of blood.

**Unhila·rious,** *a.* (Un-[1] 7.) **1879** F. W. Robinson *Coward Consc.* I. iv, He laughed in an odd, unhilarious fashion.

†**Unhi·ll,** *v. Obs.* [Un-[2] 3 + Hill *v.*[1]]

**1.** = Unhele *v.* 1.

*c* **1200** *Trin. Coll. Hom.* 69 Synnes on dede and on speche unhileð hem seluen. *c* **1250** *Gen. & Ex.* 1912 If he saȝ hise breðere mis-faren, His fader he it gan vn-hillen & baren. *a* **1300** *Cursor M.* 26585 Noght wit wordes fayr and slight Agh þou for to plane þi plight, Þat mai þi derf dedis dill, Bot openli þou þam vnhill. **13..** *E. E. Allit. P.* B. 1628 Goddes gost is þe geuen.., & þou vnhyles vch hidde þat heuen kyng myntes. **1388** Wyclif *Ecclus.* xlvii. 16 He was fillid with wisdom,..and his soule vnhilide the erthe. **1482** Caxton *Trevisa's Higden* 369 Here he is hyd, but he is vnhyled, for name dureth euermore.

**2.** = Unhele *v.* 2. Also *refl.*

*a* **1250** *Ancr. R.* 58 (Trin. MS.), [If anyone] unhulede þe put & beast fel þerin. *a* **1300** *E. E. Psalter* xxviii. 9 Vn-hil thickenesses sal he swa. *a* **1340** Hampole *Psalter* cxviii. 18 Vnhil myn eghen & i sall bihalde wondirthyngis of þi laghe. *a* **1375** *Joseph Arim.* 515 Þer weoren hedes vn-huled, helmes vphaunset. **1388** Wyclif *2 Sam.* vi. 20 The kyng of Israel ..vnhilynge hym silf bifor the handmaidis. *c* **1440** *Promp. Parv.* 364/2 Oncuryn, or on-hyllyn, *detego, discooperio.* **1604** [see Unhele *v.* 2.] **1611** Cotgr.,..*Descouvrir*, to vncouer, vnhill, denude.

**b.** In pa. pple. = Unhele *v.* 2 b.

**13..** *Gosp. Nicod.* 169 His heued vnhyld, on knese he kneled. *c* **1400** *Gamelyn* 87 His howses were vnhiled; and ful yuel dight. **1470–85** Malory *Arthur* XIV. viii. 644 A passynge old man..; his sholders were naked & vnhylled.

**3.** To remove (a covering).

**1388** Wyclif *Ruth* iii. 4 Thou schalt..vnhile the cloth, with which he is hiled.

**Unhind,** var. Unhend *a. Obs.*

**Unhi·nderable,** *a.* (Un-[1] 7 b.) **1678** Cudworth *Intell. Syst.* 429 God made..the whole World it self Perfect and Vnhinderable. **1894** *Advance* (Chicago) 1 Mar., Nothing could be more natural or more unhinderable. **Unhi·nderably,** *adv.* (Un-[1] 11.) **1678** Cudworth *Intell. Syst.* 482 Because all things are by him Connected together, and proceed from him unhinderably.

**Unhi·ndered,** *ppl. a.* (Un-[1] 8. Cf. MDu. *ongehindert*, *ongehendert* (Du. *ongehinderd*), MHG. (MLG., G.) *ungehindert*, MSw. *ohindraþer*, *ohindrat*, etc. (Sw. *ohindrad*), MDa. (Da.) *uhindret.*)

**1615** T. Adams *Blacke Devill* 30 The vnhindred force of the wind. **1703** Clarke *Evid. Nat. & Rev. Relig.* II. iv. (1738) 260 Virtue,..with all its full Effects and Consequences unhindered. **1839** ALFORD in *Life* (1873) 11 Flowing in one full, unhindered stream. **1856** R. A. VAUGHAN *Mystics* I. 361 The unhindered service of the state of glory.

**Unhi·ndering,** *ppl. a.* (UN-[1] 10.) **1839** BAILEY *Festus* 28 In her [*sc.* Fiction's] loving and unhindering lap Voluptuously lulled, we dream.

**Unhi·nge,** *v.* [UN-[2] 3.]

**1.** *trans.* To take (a door, etc.) off the hinges; to remove the hinges from; to open in this way.

**1616** A. RICH *Cabinet* 96 A house, whose chambers are full of cobwebbes; the dores vnhindged. **1634** W. WOOD *New Eng. Prosp.* (1865) 106 Our hogges having found a way to unhindge their barne doores. **1644** QUARLES *Sheph. Orac.* x, The arme that shall unhenge Th' incestuous gates of Sodom. **1674** *Jackson's Recantation* A 2, I..perswaded my self that the Machinations of my Brain were able to unhinge the Poles. **1775** MRS. DELANY *Life & Corr.* Ser. II. (1862) II. 108 That may still be done, and yᵉ box none the worse for it, or you may unhinge it and keep it in the top.

*fig.* **1633** G. HERBERT *Temple, Sunday* vii, As Samson bore the doores away, Christs hands, though nail'd, wrought our salvation, And did unhinge that day.

**b.** *transf.* To unlock, unclose, open.

**1624** QUARLES *Job* XV. 16 Would any..try a fall with Angels, and preuaile? Or with a Hymne, vnhinge the strongest Iayle? **1865** A. J. MUNBY *Verses New & Old* 185, I will not once..Unhinge my jaws to speak again.

**2.** To unsettle, unbalance, or disorder (the mind, brain, etc.).

**1612** SHELTON *Quix.* II. xlvi. 303 The powerfull force of Loue Oft doth vnhinge the soule. **1663–70** SOUTH *Serm.* (1715) IV. 306 Why should I then unhinge my Brains? **1690** NESSE *O. & N. Test.* I. 60 Until another bad bargain happen..to unhinge his spirit again. **1764** H. WALPOLE *Otranto* iv, Theodore..has unhinged the soul of Manfred. **1793** *Friendly Address to Poor* 13 These plays..serve only to unhinge and disorder their minds. **1867** BAKER *Nile Trib.* xii. (1872) 215 The nerves of Mahomet were completely unhinged. **1885** *Law Times* 7 Feb. 270/2 Study..had unhinged the deceased's mind.

**b.** With personal object. Also in weaker sense: To upset.

**1631** MABBE *Celestina* xvii. (1894) 254 The Blockhead hath swallowed the bayte; hee hath let her unhinge him. **1681** H. MORE *Postscr. Glanvill's Sadducismus* 50 The Soul of Samuel might indeed have..so unhinged her, that she had been fit for nothing. **1719** DE FOE *Crusoe* II. (Globe) 320 One Blow from unforeseen Providence unhing'd me at once. **1782** MISS BURNEY *Cecilia* IV. vi, The effort..has unhinged me for a fortnight! **1855** BAIN *Senses & Int.* III. iii. § 13 Some constitutions are rendered more alert and active by excitement, others are unhinged. **1888** MISS BRADDON *Fatal Three* I. v, The very mention of sickness..had unhinged him.

**c.** To unsettle (opinions, etc.), to render uncertain or doubtful. Also with personal object.

**1719** DE FOE *Crusoe* II. (Globe) 320 But in the Middle of all this Felicity, one Blow from unforeseen Providence unhing'd me at once; and..drove me [etc.]. **1770** PRIESTLEY in *Phil. Trans.* LX. 197 The following experiments..quite unhinged me again, and left me as much at a loss as ever. **1782** — *Matt. & Spir.* I. p. xxviii, When persons' minds are unhinged with respect to their opinions. **1831** BLAKEY *Free-will* 28 Calculated..to unhinge our opinions on matters highly important to our interests. **1856** DOVE *Logic Chr. Faith* VI. § 4. 352 Does any such fact unhinge our moral convictions?

**3.** To deprive of stability or fixity; to throw into confusion or disorder.

**1664** LYTTELTON in *Hatton Corr.* (Camden) 37 Which wee doubt will unhinge all that trade we thought soe well settled. **1674** N. FAIRFAX *Bulk & Selv.* 149 Our bounded wills not being of strength enough to unhinge Gods unbounded power. **1709** T. ROBINSON *Vind. Mosaick Syst.* Introd. 5 To entertain such..Ideas of God..would certainly unhinge the Foundation of all Religion. **1760** *Ann. Reg., Hist. War* 15/2 Any motion of his threatened to shake and unhinge the whole scheme of his defence. **1796** MRS. M. ROBINSON *Angelina* I. 2 The extravagance of sordid connections..have so unhinged my finances. **1886** *Daily News* 10 Dec. 2/4 The supplies are coming in very irregularly and unhinge the trade.

**b.** *esp.* To unsettle (some established order of things).

**1679** *Hist. Jetzer* Pref. A j b, That Principle which obliges them to unhinge, and overturn all Government. **1688** LUTTRELL *Brief Rel.* (1857) I. 468 Restoring things to their old legall foundation, which hath been the work of some years past to unhinge. **1718** *Free-thinker* No. 42. 306 The Luxury of a Nation does likewise unhinge the Publick Peace and Tranquillity. **1788** JEFFERSON *Writ.* (1859) II. 372 The old system is unhinged, and no new one hung in its place. **1812** *Examiner* 24 Aug. 533/2 Wages that unhinged all that order in society.

**4.** To detach, separate, or dislodge *from* something. † Also const. *of*.

**1655** FULLER *Ch. Hist.* XI. xvii. 145 These unhinge the day off from any Divine Right. **1680** C. NESSE *Church Hist.* 463 Thus God by this providence unhing'd him of his Romish religion. **1713** BLACKMORE *Creation* I. 233 And hills unhing'd from their deep roots depart. **1764** *Mem. G. Psalmanazar* 14 Some other avocations..unhinged me from my method oftener than I wished. **1788** WESLEY *Wks.* (1872) VI. 447 Whenever the mind is unhinged from God. **1861** GEO. ELIOT *Silas M.* ii, Minds that have been unhinged from their old faith and love.

Hence **Unhi·nging** *vbl. sb.*

**1661** FELTHAM *Resolves* (ed. 8) I. iii. 181 The unhindging of the whole frame of Government. **1678** *Yng. Man's Call.* 72 The unhinging of the whole man from things of nobler worth toward God. *a* **1704** T. BROWN *Wks.* (1709) III. II. 97 It portends..the unhinging of his Polish Majesty, or the beating of Prince Eugene out of Italy. **1850** HT. MARTINEAU *Hist. Peace* II. v. vi. 313 The unhinging of society. **1886** *Athenæum* 4 Dec. 742/1 The outcome of an entire unhinging of his system caused by physical fear.

**Unhi·nged,** *ppl. a.* [f. prec.]

**1.** Thrown into confusion; unsettled, disordered.

**1719** DE FOE *Crusoe* II. (Globe) 509, I might by my loose and unhing'd Circumstances be the fitter to embrace a Proposal for Trade. **1778** PRINGLE *Gunnery* 23 The unhinged state of this part of the mixed mathematics. **1835** MARRYAT *Olla Podr.* i. 5 Society is unhinged, and every one is afraid to offer an opinion. **1811** CHALMERS *Let.* in *Life* (1851) I. 243 The moral constitution of our nature is unhinged. **1895** J. A. NOBLE in *Contemp. Rev.* Apr. 490 A person whose intellectual, moral, or emotional sanity was unhinged.

**b.** *spec.* Of persons or the mind.

**1732** J. WHALEY *Poems* 213 Shall the Mind lie unhing'd by each mad flight? **1757** FOOTE *Author* I, Last winter..I cou'd have made as good a speech upon any subject,..but I am all unhinged, all. **1811** LAMB *Shaks. Trag.* Wks. 1908 I. 131 Tokens of an unhinged mind. **1836** MARRYAT *Japhet* xxx, I never felt more nervous or more unhinged.

**2.** Deprived of hinges; taken off the hinges.

**1824** W. IRVING *T. Trav.* I. 14 An unhinged window-shutter. **1824** GALT *Rothelan* II. IV. iv. 130 Bearing the corpse of a man on an unhinged door.

**Unhi·ngement.** [f. as prec.] The act of unhinging; the fact of being or becoming unhinged.

**1817** CHALMERS *Astron. Disc.* vii. 251 A melancholy unhingement in the constitution of man. **1857** J. HAMILTON *Less. fr. Gt. Biog.* 203 The disciples were beginning to recover from..the unhingement of old hopes. **1886** SYMONDS *Renaiss. It.* VII. viii. 130 The unhingement of his reason.

**Unhi·nted,** *ppl. a.* (UN-[1] 8.) **1889** C.C.R. *Up for Season* 16 New novels unprinted, new scandals unhinted Before.

**Unhi·pped,** *a.* (UN-[1] 9.) **1847** L. HUNT *Men, Women, & B.* I. xiv. 278 The most melancholy, hipped, unhipped generation, that ever walked.

**Unhi·red,** *ppl. a.* (UN-[1] 8. Cf. older Du. *ongehuurt* (Du. *ongehuurd*), Sw. *ohyrd*.)

**1617** MORYSON *Itin.* To Rdr., I wrote at leasure, giuing (like a free and vnhired workeman) much time to pleasure. **1653** MILTON *Hirelings* Wks. 1851 V. 348 And who unhir'd will be so hardy as to say, that [etc.]? **1821** SCOTT *Kenilw.* iv, There..is thy morning wage—thou shalt not say thou hast been my guide unhired. **1852** MUNDY *Antipodes* (1857) 203 There were..three hundred of them unhired at the Immigrant Dépôt.

**Unhisto·ric,** *a.* (UN-[1] 7; cf. next.)

**1862** 'SHIRLEY' (J. Skelton) *Nugæ Crit.* iii. 177 Only a rash and unhistoric mind can affirm that [etc.]. **1874** WITHROW *Catacombs of Rome* (1877) 535 A new, unscriptural, and unhistoric method.

**Unhisto·rical,** *a.* [UN-[1] 7.]

**1.** Not in accordance with history.

**1611** SPEED *Hist. Gt. Brit.* IX. viii. § 9 So partiall and vnhistoricall is the report of one,..who faines [etc.]. **1830** *Gentl. Mag.* C. II. 139 It is perfectly unhistorical to suppose that [etc.]. **1852** BUNSEN *Hippolytus & Age* II. 160 The notion of a merely historical revelation by written records is as unhistorical as it is unintellectual. **1877** J. NORTHCOTE *Catacombs* I. v. 89 The thoroughly unhistorical way in which these few subjects are dealt with.

**b.** Not versed in history.

**1865** W. G. PALGRAVE *Arabia* II. 22 Perhaps the unhistorical prophet had in mind some confused idea [etc.].

**2.** Not possessed of a historical character; not having actually occurred.

**1848** JAS. SMITH *Voy. & Shipwr. Paul* 252 Such circumstances..are unhistorical, and are..omitted by the Evangelist who wrote historically. **1882** FARRAR *Early Chr.* II. 13 The supposed fact is unhistorical, but the remark shows [etc.].

So **Unhisto·rically** *adv.*

Also, in recent use, *unhistoricalness*.

**1887** *Athenæum* 13 Aug. 206/3 We have unhistorically applied the word 'German' as the designation of one particular language of the group.

**Unhistrio·nic,** *a.* (UN-[1] 7.) **1837** CARLYLE *Fr. Rev.* III. vi. vi, 'What is passing?' repeats Collot, in the unhistrionic Cambyses' vein.

**Unhi·t,** *ppl. a.* (UN-[1] 8 b.)

**1513** DOUGLAS *Æneid* VI. xiv. 87 Quha wald the, gret Cato, leif vnhit? **1595** RALEIGH *Discov. Guiana* (1596) 97 The woods are so thicke..as a mouse cannot sitte in a boate vnhit from the banke. **1601** B. JONSON *Poetaster* To Rdr. 26 Whilst I, at whom they shot, sit here shot-free, And as vnhurt of enuy, as vnhit. **1889** 'MARK TWAIN' *Yankee* xiii, They all looked unhit, and said they didn't know.

**Unhi·tch,** *v.* [UN-[2] 4 b.]

**1.** *trans.* To detach (*from* a practice).

**1622** MABBE tr. *Aleman's Guzman d'Alf.* I. I. i. 10 From which terrible griping..nothing can vn-hitch them but deaths flesh-hooke.

**2.** To detach (a horse, etc.) by undoing a fastening: **a.** From a vehicle, plough, or the like.

**1706** STEVENS I, *Destravar*, to unhitch. **1862** B. TAYLOR *Home & Abroad* Ser. II. II. iv. 91 While the younger children unhitched and watered the horses. **1884** J. GILMOUR *Mongols* i. 2 My Chinese carter,..unhitching his two mules [from the cart], went off and left me in the encampment.

*absol.* **1887** I. R. *Lady's Ranche Life Montana* 150 So he helped me to unhitch, and I led the horses, while he dragged the buggy across.

**b.** From something to which its head is tied.

**1883** *Harper's Mag.* Aug. 386/2, I went out and unhitched the horse, and drove straight home.

**3.** To detach or unfasten (a thing).

**1876** WHYTE MELVILLE *Katerfelto* xxviii. 315 He unhitched his bridle from the garden palings. **1891** COTES *2 Girls on Barge* 27 With silent alacrity I unhitched the lamp. **1901** *Westm. Gaz.* 24 Oct. 7/3 A detachment of the men unhitched the long ladders.

**Unhi·ve,** *v.* [UN-[2] 5.] *trans.* To turn out of a hive.

**1729** MADDEN *Themistocles* I. i. 2 These armed Millions, that, like some vast Swarm,..unhiv'd have left their Home To seek new Seats of Empire. **1736** NEAL *Hist. Purit.* III. Pref. p. ix, Having unhived a numerous swarm of labouring bees. **1879** BROWNING *Ivan Ivanovitch* 71 Fancies, swarms that stung like bees unhived.

**Unhoa·rd,** *v.* [UN-[2] 5.] *trans.* To take or bring out of a hoard.

**1667** MILTON *P. L.* IV. 188 As a Thief bent to unhoord the cash Of some rich Burgher. **1721** AMHURST *Terræ Fil.* No. 12 (1726) 60 Every old hunks and miser unhoarded his dear treasure. **1797** *Monthly Rev.* XXIII. 569 Much coin has been reimported, and much unhoarded.

**Unhoa·rded,** *ppl. a.* (UN-[1] 8.) *a* **1683** OLDHAM *Rem.* (1684) 99 His unconfin'd unhoarded Store Was still the vast Exchequer of the poor. **Unhoa·rding,** *ppl. a.* (UN-[1] 10.) **1695** LOCKE *Further Consid. Value Money* 54 They would still be..greater losers than their unhoarding Neighbours.

**Unho·bble,** *v.* (UN-[2] 4 b.) **1881** *Chequered Career* 335 Unhobble the spare horses. **1887** W. S. S. TYRWHITT *New Chum in Queensland Bush* ix. 179 The horses are now unhobbled, saddled and bridled. **Unhoe·d,** *ppl. a.* (UN-[1] 8.) **1733** TULL *Horse-hoeing Husb.* (Dublin ed.) 72 A Hoed Plant of Corn will have Twenty or Thirty Stalks,..where an unho'd Plant..will have only Two or Three Stalks. **1872** *Pall Mall G.* 22 Aug. 5 His roots cannot be left unhoed,..or his corn uncut. **Unho·gged,** *ppl. a.* (UN-[1] 8.) **1886** KIPLING *Departm. Ditties*, etc. (1899) 100 With your mane unhogged and flowing.

† **Unho·ld,** *a.* (and *sb.*). *Obs.* [OE. *unhold* (f. UN-[1] 7 + HOLD *a.*), = MDu. *onhout*, Flem. (Kilian) *onhoud*, OS., OHG., G. *unhold*, MLG., MHG. *unholt*; MSw. *ohulder* (*ohwl*, *ohull*), MDa. *uhuld*.]

**1.** Unfaithful; disloyal; false.

*c* **1000** ÆLFRIC *Hom.* II. 556 Se unholda ðeowa wearð ða aworpen on þam yttrum þeostrum. *c* **1395** *Plowman's Tale* 473 Hir servaunts be to hem unhold, But they can doublin hir rentall To bigge hem castels.

**2.** Of persons: Exhibiting dislike or hostility; unfriendly, hostile.

*c* **900** tr. *Bæda's Hist.* II. xii. (1890) 132 Swa..he him þa sætunge þa ʒewearonode þæs unholdan cyninges [*L. regis sibi infesti*]. *c* **1050** *O. E. Chron.* an. 1040 (Tiberius B. i), Him wæs þa unhold eall þæt his ær ʒyrnde. *c* **1320** *Sir Tristr.* 936 Marke schuld ȝeld vnhold..Þre hundred pounde of gold.

**b.** Of events: Troublesome, disastrous.

*a* **1310** in Wright *Lyric P.* iv. 24 He mai..sore ben fered on folde, Lest he to harmes helde, ant happes hente un-holde.

**3.** *absol.* or as *sb.* An enemy or foe.

*a* **1200** *Moral Ode* 36 (Lamb. MS.), Monies monnes sare iswinc habbeð oft unholde. *a* **1225** *Ancr. R.* 222 Vnholde uor-ureten þe strencðe of his soule, & he hit nout nuste.

† **Unho·lden,** *ppl. a.* [UN-[1] 8 b. Cf. MDu. and Du. *ongehouden* (dial. *ongeholden*, *-halden*), MLG. *ungeholden*, MHG. and G. *ungehalten*.]

**a.** = UNBEHOLDEN 1. **b.** Not kept; unobserved.

*c* **1380** WYCLIF *Serm.* Sel. Wks. I. 309 Here it semeþ þat þes prestis ben moche unholden to seculer lordis. *a* **1425** *Cursor M.* 18736 (Trin.), Þe lawe he helde wondir wel Vnholden lafte he neuer a del.

**Unhole,** obs. f. UNWHOLE *a.*

**Unho·lily,** *adv.* (UN-[1] 7. Cf. UNHOLY *a.*)

**1561** T. NORTON *Calvin's Inst.* III. 221 So is it vnlawfull that it be vnholily profaned by the vncleannesse of the inhabitantes. **1619** W. SCLATER *Exp. 1 Thess.* 439 Men of corrupt mindes,..if they be elected,..shall be saued, how euer holily, or vnholily they liue. **1647** J. VICARS *Coleman-st. Conclave Visited* B ij b, The sad..breach, which is..most unholily made by..Sectaries. **1754** EDWARDS *Freed. Will* IV. ii, It is impossible for Him to act unrighteously and unholily. **1898** *Advance* (Chicago) 16 June 808/2 Before their imaginations were unholily stirred by these pages.

**Unho·liness.** [UN-[1] 12.]

**1.** The quality of being unholy; lack of holiness or sanctity.

**1534** MORE *Treat. Passion* ii. Wks. 1311/2 The vyces of vicious folke in Christes church, can not lette, but that hys catholike church..is for their vnholynes, his holy catholyke churche. **1597** HOOKER *Eccl. Pol.* V. lxxiv. § 2 She is not..in respect of any vnholinesse forbidden entrance into the Church. **1645** MILTON *Tetrach.* 36 Where an unfit mariage administers continual cause of hatred and distemper, there..cannot choose but much unholines abide. **1675** BROOKS *Gold. Key* Wks. 1867 V. 195 Adam's holiness was as natural..to him as any way of unholiness can be natural..to us. **1845** CORRIE in *Encycl. Metrop.* II. 880/1 All that blindness of heart, all that unholiness of affections,..which issue in overt acts of sin. **1871** FARRAR *Witn. Hist.* i. 11 Let us..beware that in us unholiness do not cloud the spiritual eye.

**2.** Applied to the Pope: cf. HOLINESS 2.

**1682** G. TOPHAM *Rome's Tradit.* 204 No sooner did the news of that bloody Butchery arrive his Unholiness [Gregory XIII], but [etc.].

**Unholl,** obs. f. UNWHOLE *a.*

**Unho·llow,** *a.* (UN-[1] 7.) **1548** UDALL, etc. *Erasm. Par. John* 117 b, The sepulchre..was cut out of an whole sound vnholow rocke of stone. **1611** FLORIO, *Inuacuo*, vnempty, vnhollow. **Unho·llowed,** *ppl. a.* (UN-[1] 8.) **1609** DOULAND *Ornith. Microl.* 22 Make it hollow in the middle, leauing the ends of it vnhollowed. **1913** R. HARRIS *Boanerges* xxxi. 301 The hollow oak is higher in sanctity than the unhollowed tree.

**Unho·lpen,** *ppl. a.* Now *arch.* [UN-[1] 8 b. Cf. MDu. (and Du.) *ongeholpen*, MHG. *ungeholfen*; Sw. *ohulpen*.] = UNHELPED *ppl. a.*

**1382** WYCLIF *1 Esdras* ix. 11 But for the multitude is gret, and the time winter, and wee moun not vnholpen stonde. **1390** GOWER *Conf.* II. 189 'The lif is suete', and that he kepeth, So that the feith unholpe slepeth. *c* **1440** *Gesta Rom.* 121 (Add. MS.), She woll leve none vnholpen that crieth to her hertly. **1485** CAXTON *Chas. Gt.* (1881) 174 God forbede..that I leue hym vnholpen. **1545** BRINKLOW *Lament.* 88 Ye ..leaue..the presoned vnholpen. **1568** T. HOWELL *Arb. Amitie* (1879) 70 Thou hast the forme that cut the wound, of my vnholpen paine. **1608** DOD & CLEAVER *Expos. Prov.* xi–xii. 183 Neuer any was left unholpen, that sought help at his hand. **1864** SWINBURNE *Atalanta* 1674 These shall lie

Dead, unbeloved, unholpen. **1870** Morris *Earthly Par.* III. IV. 224 The maddening fear that burned Round his unholpen heart.

**Unho·ly,** *a.* and *sb.* [OE. *unhálig* (f. *un-* Un-1 7 + *hálig* Holy *a.*), = NFris. *unhilleg*; older Fl. (Kilian) *onheyligh*, MDu. *onheilich* (rare), Du. *onheilig*; ON. *úheilagr* (MDa. and Da. *uhellig*, Sw. *ohelig*).]

**1.** Not holy; impious, profane, wicked: **a.** Of persons.

*c* **1000** *Lambeth Ps.* xlii. 1 Toscead intingan minne of unhaliȝre þeode. **1362** Langl. *P. Pl.* A. Prol. 3 In Habite of an Hermite vn-holy of werkes. **1526** Tindale 2 *Tim.* iii. 2 The men shalbe..vnthankfull, vnholy, churlisshe. **1607** Shaks. *Cor.* v. vi. 119 Will you be put in minde of his blinde Fortune..by this vnholy Braggart? **1685** Baxter *Paraphr. N. T.* Matt. xxv. 26 To confess God's holy Government, and yet to be unholy, is to be self condemning. **1738** Wesley *Ps.* v. ii, In Souls unholy and unclean Thou never canst delight. **1817** Shelley *Rev. Islam* x. xlvii, Unholy men, Feasting like fiends upon the infidel dead. **1833** Carlyle *Misc.* (1857) III. 287 To lodge the whole unholy Brotherhood ..in separate cells of the Bastille!

*absol.* **1526** Tindale 1 *Tim.* i. 10 The lawe is..geven..to synners, to vnholy and vnclean. **1667** Milton *P. L.* xi. 106 Hast thee, and..drive out the sinful Pair, From hallowd ground th' unholie. **1873** Symonds *Grk. Poets* vii. 192 The idea of Nemesis quelling the insolent and smiting the unholy.

**b.** Of acts, things, etc.

**1382** Wyclif 2 *Tim.* ii. 16 Schonye thou vnhooli and veyn spechis. **1390** Gower *Conf.* II. 363 (MS. A), If he pourchace By wey of thefte unholy thing. **1526** Tindale *Heb.* x. 29 He..which..counteth the bloud off the testament as an vnholy thynge. **1591** Shaks. *Two Gent.* iv. iii. 30 To keepe me from a most vnholy match. **1632** Milton *L'Allegro* 4 In Stygian Cave forlorn 'Mongst horrid shapes, and shreiks, and sights unholy. **1653** Jer. Taylor *Serm. for Year* iv. 50 If things that are lawfull may yet be unholy in this sense; much more are unlawfull things most unholy in all senses. **1717** Pope *Eloisa to Abelard* 224 Far other dreams my erring soul employ, Far other raptures, of unholy joy. **1791** Cowper *Odyss.* xxii. 479 Unholy is the voice Of loud thanksgiving over slaughter'd men. **1842** Manning *Serm.* x. (1848) I. 135 Cultivation of mind, refinement,..are often found in men of the unholiest passions. **1885** 'Mrs. Alexander' *Valerie's Fate* v, There is nothing so awful, so unholy as a mere marriage of expediency.

**2.** *colloq.* Awful, dreadful. (Cf. Ungodly *a.* 3.)

**1865** Dickens *Mut. Fr.* iv. iii, An unholy glare..shone in the eyes of Mr. Wegg. **1883** D. C. Murray *Hearts* xxxiv. (1885) 288 He had arrived..at a rather unholy sort of hour. **1899** E. Phillpotts *Human Boy* 35 Trelawny had called him an 'unholy bounder'.

**3.** *sb.* An unholy person or thing.

**1831** Carlyle *Sart. Res.* iii. xi, How many other Unholies has your covering Art made holy, besides this Arabian Whinstone! **1837** — *Fr. Rev.* i. i. ii, All Phenomena of the spiritual kind: Dignities, Authorities, Holies, Unholies!

**Unho·ly,** *v.* [Un-2 3.] *trans.* To make unholy. Hence **Unho·lied** *ppl. a.*

*a* **1555** Philpot in Coverdale *Lett. Mart.* (1564) 238 You haue bene sanctifyed and made pure through the truth, take hede you be not vnholied and defyled. **1603** Drayton *Bar. Wars* i. vi, Thou shouldst to them haue layd the Holy Word, And not thy hand to the unholyed Sword. **1649** Heylin *Relat. & Observ.* ii. To Rdr., O wretched unholied men! What are they that thus commit Burglary in the Sanctum Sanctorum of Gods Providence?

**Unho·med,** *ppl. a.* (Un-1 8 and Un-2 8.) **1839** Bailey *Festus* xxvii. 334 [The day] shall shew itself With all its little tyrannous .. deeds, Unhomed and clear. **1884** *Advance* (Chicago) 13 Mar., In no state of the Union are there more un-homed young men. **Unho·melike,** *a.* (Un-1 7 c.) **1852** Mundy *Antipodes* (1857) 194 The untidy and un-homelike look of the half-cleared fields. **1886** *Athenæum* 8 May 621/2 The same large room with the dreadful shadows and unhomelike furniture. **Unho·melikeness.** (Un-1 12.) **1858** Hawthorne *Fr. & It. Note-bks.* (1872) I. 57 The ugliness, shabbiness, unhome-likeness of a Roman Street. **1869** Jos. Butler, etc. *Women's Work* i. 10 The unhomelikeness of the abodes of the richest single men..is pitiable.

**Unho·meliness.** (Un-1 12; cf. next.)

*c* **1440** *Relig. Pieces fr. Thornton MS.* (1914) 12 Ypocrisy and vnhamlynes, and oþer [sins] þat ofte ere sene amanges prowde men. **1879** Miss Keary *Doubting Heart* III. 120 Such signs..only seemed to bring out more prominently the stately unhomeliness of the place.

**Unho·mely,** *a.* (Un-1 7.)

**1871** *Athenæum* 4 Mar. 280 Everything in the picture is neglected and unhomely and coarse. **1882** *Pall Mall G.* 31 Aug. 4 He does not chafe..because the hotels are so unhomely. **1892** Stevenson *Across the Plains* 185 This unhomely, rugged turret-top of submarine sierras.

**Unho·mish,** *a.* (Un-1 7.) **1858** Mrs. Gore *Heckington* viii, The unhomeish home of her aunt. **1880** T. Hodgkin *Italy & Inv.* I. i. v. 298 Nor drinks he, wandering, from un-homish streams. **Unhomogene·ity.** (Un-1 12.) **1862** E. B. Denison in *Guardian* No. 882, The founder..and his advocates declare that porosity and unhomogeneity are unavoidable [in bells].

**Unhomoge·neous,** *a.* (Un-1 7.)

**1823** Herschel in *Encycl. Metrop.* (1845) IV. 449 Bodies of unhomogeneous density. **1865** W. G. Palgrave *Arabia* I. 369 Without taking into account healthier but unhomogeneous admixtures. **1899** *Speaker* 11 Nov. 134/1 The native races of Africa are at present utterly unhomogeneous.

† **Unho·ne.** *Obs.*−1 [Un-1 12 + Hone *sb.*2] Absence of delay; haste.

*a* **1400–50** *Alexander* 5530 And he vnhurt with mikill vnhone [*read* -hoine] he to his ost wynes.

**Unho·nest,** *a.* *Obs.* exc. *arch.* or *dial.* [Un-1 7 and 5 b.]

In senses 2 and 3 very common in the 16th cent.

**1. a.** Physically or morally objectionable, offensive, or unpleasant; indecent, filthy, vile.

**13..** *K. Alis.* 6472 Bothe byfore and eke byhynde, They haveth clothyng unhonest. *a* **1350** *St. Philip & Jas.* 21 in Horstm. *Altengl. Leg.* (1881) 52 Blastes out of his mouth he blew, þat war so euyl and vn-honeste, þai destryd oft both man and beste. **1526** *Pilgr. Perf.* (W. de W. 1531) 283 The membres of our body that be moost vnhonest and moost rebellynge to our reason. **1542** Udall *Erasm. Apoph.* 152 b, Whatsoever thyng wer not of it self unhonest, he affermed not to bee unhoneste in open presence. **1633** P. Fletcher *Purple Isl.* viii. xx, His shamefull parts, that shunne the hated light, Were naked left; (ah foul unhonest sight!).

**b.** Uncomely, unhandsome.

**1382** Wyclif 1 *Cor.* xii. 23 And tho membris that ben vnhonest, han more honeste. **1398** Trevisa *Barth. De P. R.* v. lxvi. (Bodl. MS.), If a man is withoute heed heere, he is yholde þe more vnhoneste.

**c.** Unseemly, unbecoming, improper.

*a* **1400–50** *Bk. Curtasye* 96 in *Babees Bk.*, While þou holdes mete in mouþe, be war To drynke, þat is an [vn]honest char. **1502** Arnolde *Chron.* (1811) 277 Item that the bookis and vestmentis bien broken and vnhonest for dyuine seruice. **1542** Udall *Erasm. Apoph.* 89 b, It was not a thyng unhonest for one to carrye a gammonde of bakon in his hande. **1568** Grafton *Chron.* II. 234 They dayly chaunged there apparel, sometime long and wide, and at another tyme, cutted short.., and altogether vnsemely and vnhonest.

**2.** Of actions, language, etc.: **a.** Morally unfitting or unbecoming; unseemly, immodest, lewd.

**13..** *E. E. Allit. P.* B. 579 Alle illez he hates..; But non nuyez hym..As harlottrye vnhonest, heþyng of seluen. *c* **1380** Wyclif *Sel. Wks.* III. 29, I dreede to telle holy wordis wiþ my foule mouþ, fillid wiþ unhoneste wordis. **1456** Sir G. Haye *Law Arms* (S.T.S.) 142 Thair undertaking was in the begynnyng unhonest, unlefull. *c* **1475** *Babees Bk.* 99 Whenne yee er sette, take noone vnhoneste tale. **1502** *Ord. Crysten Men* (W. de W. 1506) iv. xvi. Tij, Yf in songes vnhonest, & tryfylles, & talkynges of langage, he swereth god. **1598** Grenewey *Tacitus, Ann.* iv. xii. (1622) 107 Domitius Afer..laid to her charge that she lead an vnhonest life with Furnius. **1607** Dekker *Jests to make you Merry* Wks. (Grosart) II. 302 To this vnhonest pleasure, is begot a companion repentance. **1645** Ussher *Body Div.* 279 This commandement [is] broken by..taking delight in hearing unhonest things.

**b.** Dishonourable, discreditable.

*c* **1400** *Apol. Loll.* 100 A wowe is..vnwise, wan it is only about temporal þingis, or vnhonest, or vnprofitable to soule hele. *c* **1440** *Alph. Tales* 41 What profettis þi frenship vnto me, when þu desyris me for to do for þe þat þing þat is vnhoneste? *a* **1470** *Dives & Pauper* (W. de W. 1496) iv. xviii. 181/2 The suget shal not..do ony thyng unryghtfull & unhonest. **1540** Cromwell in Merriman *Life & Lett.* (1902) II. 254 There is daunger of vnhonest condicions or of Discontentement at departing. **1587** Fleming *Contn. Holinshed* III. 1384/1 My case is hard, but yet am I not so desperat as to reuenge it vpon my selfe, which must needs be the euent of so vnhonest and vnpossible an enterprise. **1614** Raleigh *Hist. World* iii. x. § 5. 116 He brought an vnhonest message to his owne Countrimen. **1649** Canne *Snare Broken* 14 An oath is unlawfull when..we promise any thing that is unjust or unhonest. **1825** Brockett *N. C. Words, Unhonest,* dishonourable, dishonest. Stated in Todd's John. to be obsolete; but it is not so in the North.

**3.** Of persons: **a.** Not honourable, respectable, or of good repute; acting in a dishonourable or discreditable manner. Also *absol.*

**1382** Wyclif *Ecclus.* xxxvii. 13 With the dredful trete [not] of bataile,..with the vnhonest, of bateile. **1388** — *Prov.* xxv. 8 Whanne thou hast maad thi frend vnhonest. *c* **1400** tr. *Secreta Secret., Gov. Lordsh.* 64 Kepe þy most noble saule hegh,..þat ys geuyn to þe, noght to be maad vnhonest by þe, but to be enhyed and glorifyed. *a* **1548** Hall *Chron., Hen. IV*, 16 b, This false father in lawe, this untrew, unhonest and perjured persone. **1586** A. Day *Eng. Secretary* i. (1625) 32 These and such like, as confounders of all ciuility,..are confirmed to be vnhonest. **1610** Healey *St. Aug. Citie of God* 462 Some ambitious unhonest fellow. **1624** Burton *Anat. Mel.* (ed. 2) iii. ii. 442 Of a majesticall presence, but peradventure imperious, vnhonest, selfewill'd.

**b.** Bad or immoral in character or conduct; disreputable.

*c* **1422** Hoccleve *Min. Poems* 218/63 To goode wommen that it be no shame, Al thogh þat thow vnhonest wommen blame. **1456** Sir G. Haye *Law Arms* (S.T.S.) 190 Gif a man fyndis ane unhonest foule creature hafand conversacioun with his wyf. **1536** Cromwell in Merriman *Life & Lett.* (1902) II. 28 They shall not geve theymself to drinking and ryote sitting all daye at Tables or cardes playng.. and specially with vnhonest and vnthryftye persons. **1574** Hellowes *Gueuara's Fam. Ep.* (1577) 60 All which were in their liues very vnhonest, and in their gouernement very offensiue. **1621** Burton *Anat. Mel.* i. ii. iv. i, If a Nurse be mishapen, vnchast, vnhonest, impudent, drunke,..the child..will be so too. **1640–1** *Kirkcudbr. War-Comm. Min. Bk.* (1855) 35 George cryit—Unhonest Beoche and adulterous Beoche.

**4.** Dishonest (in respect of dealings with others).

**a.** Of actions, gain, etc. (Also *dial.* as *adv.*)

**1583** Fulke *Def. Tr. Script.* iii. (1843) 195 This scornful replier..is so accustomed to false and unhonest dealing. **1607** Markham *Cavel.* iii. (1617) 35 To give a false colour to their owne knowledges,..or..to get vnhonest polling pence to their own purses. **1628** Feltham *Resolves* ii. xxxv. 109 Vnworthines is euer the end of vnhonest Deceit. *a* **1670** Spalding *Troub. Chas. I* (1850) I. 109 The purches of there bischoprikis be brybes, thair vnhonest dealling in civill barganes. **1730** *St. Trials* I. 315 The Earl as well abusing the King's Favours,..as bearing unhonest Friendship, in Conference with Sir Thomas concerning that Imployment. **1901** 'Zack' *Dunstable Weir* 48 What wud it feel like to come by the money unhonest?

**b.** Of persons.

**1545** Ascham *Toxoph.* (Arb.) 20 Honest fletchers and bowyers do not so, and they that be vnhonest, oughte..to amende them selues. *a* **1586** Sidney *Arcadia* ii. xv, The old man.. folowed his suite with all meanes of vnhonest seruants, large promises [etc.]. **1603** Breton *Dial. Pith & Pleas.* Wks. (Grosart) II. 13/2 How vnhonest is that labourer, who will not worke for his wages? **1645** in J. Wilson *Annals of Hawick* (1850) 65 In calling of him..ane runnigat beggar,.. and ane false unhonest thief. **1825–** in dial. glossaries (N.Cy., Yorks., Lancs., Linc.).

**Unho·nestly,** *adv.* ? *Obs.* [Un-1 11, 5 b.]

**1.** In an unbecoming manner; indecorously.

*c* **1380** Wyclif *Sel. Wks.* II. 193 Trowe we not þat Crist dide here dispitously or unhonestly, spittynge in þis mannis face? *c* **1400** Maundev. (Roxb.) xxvi. 123 When þai hafe eten, þai wype þaire hend on þaire clathez vnhonestly. **1502** Arnolde *Chron.* (1811) 278 Item that the chircheyard is vnhon[e]stly kepte.

**2.** With dishonour; disgracefully; discreditably, dishonourably; dishonestly.

**1382** Wyclif 2 *Macc.* ix. 1 In the same tyme Antiochus turnyde aȝein vnonestly [L. *inhoneste*] fro Perse. *c* **1449** Pecock *Repr.* 325 As into this point, that he therbi be iust or uniust,.. doing honestli or doing vnhonestli. **1535** Coverdale *Ecclus.* x. 34 Who so ordreth himself vnhonestly in riches, how moch more shal he behaue himself vnhonestly in pouerte? **1598** R. Bernard tr. *Terence, Adelphos* ii. i, I my selfe am very vnhonestly dealt withall. **1628** Feltham *Resolves* ii. ii. 5 As I would neuer doe any thing vnhonestly, so I would neuer feare the immateriall wind of censure, when it is done. **1648** Hexham ii, *Oneerbaerlick,* Vnhonestly, Dishonestly, or Impudently. **1721** Strype *Eccl. Mem.* II. 388 Most unhonestly slandering old Writings.

**3.** Indecently, immorally.

**1382** Wyclif 2 *Sam.* xiii. 2 The which for she was a mayde, hard to hym it semede, that eny thing vnhonestly [L. *inhoneste*] he shulde do with hir. *c* **1400** *Pilgr. Sowle* (Caxton, 1483) iii. x. 56 These it ben that so horrybly stynken,..for they haue liued ful vnhonestly in fowle lustes. **1486** *Rec. St. Mary at Hill* (1905) 12 Yf the same preest so chosen vnhonestly behave hym. **1535** Coverdale *Prov.* xii. 4 She that behaueth herself vnhonestly, is a corrupcion in his bones. **1597** Beard *Theatre God's Judgem.* (1612) 400 His Proctors wife, with whom..he acquainted himselfe ouer familiarly and vnhonestly. **1609** Bible (Douay) 2 *Sam.* xiii. 2.

**Unho·nesty.** *Obs.* exc. *dial.* [Un-1 12, 5 b.] Absence or lack of honesty (esp. in obsolete senses of that word).

*c* **1425** Wyntoun *Cron.* iv. xxv. 2356 Þat nane suld se Spot, fylth na vnhoneste Behind him in his doun falling. *a* **1470** *Dives & Pauper* (W. de W. 1496) viii. vi. 328/2 The bacbyter hath more lykynge to speke of other mennes defautes & of theyr unhonestes & synne. **1526** Tindale 2 *Cor.* iv. 1 We..have cast from vs the clokes of vnhonestie. **1586** A. Day *Eng. Secretary* ii. (1625) 22 Where Gentilitie is not all onely spotted, but in a manner couered and debased already with vnhonesty. **1600** Breton *Strange Fort. Two Princes* Wks. (Grosart) II. 4/1 Vnthankefulnesse is so neare to vnhonestie, as to auoid the touch of both. **1647** Hexham i, Vnhonesty or dishonesty, *oneerbaerheyt.* **1871** W. Alexander *Johnny Gibb* viii. 51 Sic creaturs [ye are] wi' oonhonesty.

† **Unho·nour,** *v.* *Obs.*−1 [Un-2 3.] *trans.* To dishonour.

**1382** Wyclif *John* viii. 49, I honoure my fadir, and ȝe han vnhonourid me.

† **Unho·nourable,** *a.* *Obs.* [Un-1 7.]

**1.** Not honourable; not deserving of honour.

*a* **1400–50** *Alexander* 2950 Sen þis vse is here vn-honourable, here I þam leue. **1456** Sir G. Haye *Law Arms* (S.T.S.) 280 He war a wikkit man of lyf, a tyran and unhonourable. **1548** Geste *Pr. Masse* 117 Why then shuld.. thee presence therof cause to honour his Godhed in the same, ther otherwyse unhonourable. **1599** Sandys *Europæ Spec.* (1632) 209 To trace out an unhonourable and fruitlesse life. **1635** [Glapthorne] *Lady Mother* iii. ii. in Bullen *O. Pl.* (1883) II. 161 We are noe peasants or unhonorable To be affronted with indignities.

**2.** Dishonourable, discreditable.

**1540** Sir T. Wyatt *Let. to Cromwell* 5 April, If it were so the King's pleasure, I would make him such company as should not be unhonourable to the King. **1595** Daniel *Civ. Wars* ii. xxiv, Th' vnhonourable meanes of safety, bade Danger accept, what Maiesty withstood. **1621** in Foster *Eng. Factories Ind.* (1906) I. 274 Unhonnorable action by breatch of his word and cowle.

† **Unho·nourably,** *adv.* *Obs.* [Un-1 11.] Dishonourably, discreditably.

**1553** Ascham *Germany* Wks. (1904) 159 Libertie in speakyng should be so mingled with..discretion, as no great person should be vnhonorably spoken vpon. **1560** Pilkington *Expos. Aggeus* (1562) 133 Mahomet..made him glad with money to bye peace unhonorably. **1589** Puttenham *Eng. Poesie* ii. xi[i]. (Arb.) 116 Dishonored be he, who meanes vnhonorably.

**Unho·noured,** *ppl. a.* (Un-1 8.)

*a* **1513** Fabyan *Chron.* vii. (1516) 103/1 The holye seruyce of God [was] lefte, and holye Churche vnworshyppyd & vnhonouryd, with many great enormyties. **1633** P. Fletcher *To my honoured Cousin W. R.* vii, Here among th' unhonour'd willows shade. **1697** Dryden *Æneis* xi. 314 The rest, unhonoured, and without a name, Are cast a common heap to feed the flame. **1718** Prior *Solomon* iii. 176 Unhonor'd from the Board The Crystal Urn, when broken, is thrown by. **1751** Gray *Elegy* xxiv, Mindful of th' unhonour'd Dead. **1849** Ruskin *Sev. Lamps* vi. § 3. 166 Those comfortless and unhonoured dwellings. **1891** Farrar *Darkn. & Dawn* xxxvi, The site of her sepulchre was left unhonoured and no mound was raised above her ashes.

**Unhoo·d,** *v.* [Un-2 4.] *trans.* To divest (*spec.* a hawk) of a hood or similar covering. Also *absol.*

(*a*) **1575** Turberv. *Falconrie* 79 At the ende of three dayes you may unhood hir and feede hir unhooded. **1652** Fuller *Holy & Prof. St.* v. xviii. 488 Like Hawks when they are first unhooded, and newly restored to the light. **1667** Dryden *Sir Martin Mar-all* v. iii, He's an ill Falconer that will unhood before the quarry be in sight. **1742** Somerville *Field Sports* 10 Falcner, take care,..And slily stalk; unhood thy Falcon bold. **1852** R. F. Burton *Falconry Valley Indus* vi. 65 The falconer unhoods her, places her upon the perch.

(*b*) **1601** HOLLAND *Pliny* I. 221 Perceiving after that he was unhooded that he served as a stalion to his own dam. **1608** SYLVESTER *Du Bartas, Job Triumphant* 615, I will not hide..[Leviathan's] Strength, nor seemly Symmetries. Who shall unhood him? **1629** MASSINGER *Picture* III. v, Enter servants with Mathias..blindfolded. *Acanthe*...I'll anon unhood him. **1797** MRS. RADCLIFFE *Italian* xii, [In] one of the lonely aisles..he unhooded the lamp. **1853** ROCK *Ch. of Fathers* III. x. 491 Among all that sea of heads, there is not one but is bared and unhooded. **1887** BROWNING *Parleyings, Apollo & Fates* 121 Unhook wings, unhood brows! Dost hearken?

*transf.* **1603** FLORIO *Montaigne* II. xii. 334 Some people ..who tooke pleasure to vnhood the end of their yard, and to cut off the fore-skin.

**b.** *fig.* or in fig. context.

**1648** BOYLE *Seraph. Love* (1660) 11 As it has hitherto been my not unprosperous task to unhood your soul, I shall now..shew her game to fly at. *c* **1681** HICKERINGILL *Trimmer* Wks. 1716 I. 356, I am forc'd to bring him to light, and unhood him, sometimes by some (otherwise unwelcome) Periphrasis. **1824** *New Monthly Mag.* X. 306 Thou unhood'st the stars, Shew'st their bright eyes. **1848** BOKER *Calaynos* III. iii, They two can put their restless heads together, Unhood their thoughts at every whim that flies. **1869** BLACKMORE *Lorna D.* xii, Tom Faggus himself was a quarry for the law, if ever it should be unhooded.

**Unhoo·ded,** *ppl. a.* [UN-1 8 or UN-2 8: cf. prec.] Not wearing, divested of, a hood. Also *fig.*

**1575** [see UNHOOD *v.* (*a*)]. **1614** LATHAM *Falconry* 32 Many of them will be more gentle..when they are vnhooded, then when they are hooded. **1730** RAMSAY *Fables, Lure* 63 [He] loos'd the falcon frae his hand. Unhooded, up she sprang with birr. **1795** SOUTHEY *Joan of Arc* VII. 140 A rude coat of mail Unhosed, unhooded, as of lowly line He wore. **1798** BLOOMFIELD *Farmer's Boy, Autumn* v. 269 In earliest hours of dark unhooded morn. **1848** LYTTON *Harold* IX. i, On a perch..sate his favourite Norway falcon, unhooded. **1868** ADAH I. MENKEN *Infelicia* 129 In the great strength of thy unhooded soul, pray for my weakness.

**Unhoo·dwink,** *v.* (UN-2 4.) *a* **1608** DEE *Relat. Spir.* I. (1659) 393 Least peradventure God unhood-wink and make open the sight of Satan. **1682** HICKERINGILL *Black Non-Conformist* Introd. C, The Popish methods of old, but not practicable now, people are generally unhoodwinkt. **1691** tr. *Emiliane's Frauds Rom. Monks* (ed. 3) 242 There is scarcely any way left to disabuse and unhoodwink them. **Unhoo·dwinked,** *ppl. a.* (UN-1 8.) **1657** W. BRAYNE in Thurloe *Coll. St. Papers* (1742) VI. 211 They haveing bin unadvisedly brought unhudwinckt through the fortifications of our harbour. **Unhoo·f,** *v.* (UN-2 3.) **1530** PALSGR. 768/1, I unhooffe a horse, I pull of his hooffe, *je dessole. Ibid.*, And you unhoofe this hors agaynst wynter, he is utterly marred. **1598** FLORIO, *Disonghiare*, to vn-naile, or to vnhoofe. **Unhoo·fed,** *ppl. a.* (UN-1 8.) **1709** SHAFTESB. *Charac.* (1711) II. 301 Ask not merely, Why Man is naked, why unhoof'd, why slower-footed than the Beasts?

**Unhoo·k,** *v.* [UN-2 4 b.]

**1.** *trans.* To detach from a hook; to disengage or unfasten in this way. Also *refl.*

**1611** COTGR., *Desaccrocher*, to vnhooke. **1662** J. BARGRAVE *Pope Alex. VII*, etc. (1867) 136 To break a fall, they will hang by the horns, and, when they have taken breath, they unhook themselves and take another leap. **1825** J. NICHOLSON *Operat. Mechanic* 132 If the wind should blow against the back sides of the said sails..the said bars or rods will be unhooked and set at liberty. **1856** LEVER *Martins of Cro' M.* 147 In an instant she had unhooked the heavy chain. **1878** T. HARDY *Ret. Native* v. viii, Venn unhooked the lantern and leaped down. **1892** [see UNHOOKER].

*fig.* **1640** C. HARVEY *Synagogue, Ch.-gate* iii, Unhook'd from him, we quickly turn aside. **1669** BARROW in Rigaud *Corr. Sci. Men* (1841) II. 70 My mind being indeed unhooked from these things. **1672** MARVELL *Reh. Transp.* I. 324 Striving to unhook himself hence, p. 152 of his Second Book, swallows it deeper.

**2.** To take out the hooks of (a dress). Also with personal object.

**1840** COCKTON *Val. Vox* xiii, The ladies [began] to unhook their dresses behind, in order to enjoy another small glass of gin. **1898** *Longm. Mag.* Aug. 366 She..remarked that..I must have my frock unhooked and be tried on. I submitted silently to be unhooked.

**3.** To disengage from a curved position.

**1865** DICKENS *Mut. Fr.* II. i, As she said it, she unhooked her arm.

Hence **Unhoo·ker.**

**1892** *Labour Commission* Gloss., *Unhookers*, old men or boys who stand on the plank connecting a ship with the dock and unhook the coal when it is in a stable position on the back of the men who carry it.

**Unhoo·ked,** *ppl. a.* (UN-1 8.)

**1600** in Hakluyt *Voy.* III 671 What more nimble spirits, Apter to byte at such vnhooked baytes, Gaine by our losse. **1897** *Outing* XXX. 220/2 Another instance will give an idea of how high an unhooked bass can leap when frightened.

**Unhoo·l,** *v. Sc.* [UN-2 5.] To disembody.

**1722** RAMSAY *Three Bonnets* IV. 19 A stalwart ghaist Whase stern and angry looks amaist Unhool'd their sauls.

**Unhool,** obs. f. UNWHOLE *a.*

**Unhoo·p,** *v.* (UN-2 4. Cf. Du. *onthoepen.*)

**1611** DONNE *Paneg. Verses* 36 in Coryate *Crudities*, When Merchants do unhoope Voluminous barrels. **1657** DAVENANT *Entertainment at Rutland House* 43 Let the sour Cynick live coopt; Let him quake in his thrid-bare Cloak Till he find his old Tub unhoopt. **1711** ADDISON *Spect.* No. 127 ¶ 10 To Unhoop the Fair Sex, and cure this fashionable Tympany that is got among them.

**Unhoo·pable,** *a.* (UN-1 7 b.) **1672** MARVELL *Reh. Transp.* I. 246 Instead of assuming your unhoopable jurisdiction, they are..satisfied with the abundance of their power. **1673** [R. LEIGH] *Transp. Reh.* 23 The unhoopable Tun of Heidelberg. **Unhoo·ped,** *ppl. a.* (UN-1 8.) **1861** DICKENS *Gt. Expect.* i, Like an unhooped cask upon a pole.

†**Unhope.** *Obs.* [UN-1 12. Cf. MDu. *onthope*, and WANHOPE *sb.*] Lack of hope; despair.

*a* **1225** *Ancren R.* 8 Þet ȝe muhten sone uallen..in desperaunce, þet is, in unhope. *a* **1240** *Sawles Warde* in *O.E. Hom.* I. 251 Ant tis ilke unhope is ham meast pine. **1477** EARL RIVERS (Caxton) *Dictes* H iv, Take not vnhope of that, that thou maist not amende.

**Unho·ped,** *ppl. a.* [UN-1 8. Cf. MDu. *ongehopet*, MDu. and Du. *-hoopt.*]

†**1. a.** Unexpected, unforeseen. *Obs.*

*c* **1374** CHAUCER *Boeth.* IV. pr. vi. (1876) 108 What so euere þou mayst sen þat is don in this world vnhoped, or vnwenyd. **1382** WYCLIF *Wisd.* xvii. 14 Forsothe to them sodeyn and vnhopid drede ouercam. *a* **1575** tr. *Pol. Verg. Eng. Hist.* (Camden 36) 185 [He was] amazed at this unhoped danger. **1697** DRYDEN *Æneis* x. 99 Did God, or Man, your Fav'rite Son advise, With War unhop'd the Latians to surprise?

†**b.** Unconceived, unimagined. *Obs.*

**1435** MISYN *Fire of Love* 15 Treuly it is not of gods vnpower þat he may not þe tech hym-self als he is in hym-self, bot for hys vnhopyd worþines.

**2.** Not anticipated with hope or desire; not hoped for. (Cf. 3.)

**1382** WYCLIF *Wisd.* v. 2 Thei..shul merueilen in the sodeynesse of the vnhopid helthe. **1561** T. NORTON *Calvin's Inst.* I. 19 Paul,..from a cruell and bloody enemy conuerted to a new man, with sodaine and vnhoped change. *a* **1586** SIDNEY *Arcadia* IV. (1629) 426 His other prisoners..he found increased by this vnhoped meanes. **1593** SHAKS. 3 *Hen. VI*, III. iii. 172 What are thy Newes?..*Margaret.* Mine such, as fill my heart with vnhop'd ioyes. **1660** DRYDEN *Astræa Redux* 140 The Prince of Peace would..confer A Gift unhop'd without the price of war. **1697** — *Æneis* v. 262 Chance aids their daring with unhop'd success. **1721** RAMSAY *Love's Cure* i, He spies A ship, which gives unhop'd surprise. **1728** ELIZA HEYWOOD tr. *Mme. de Gomez's Belle A.* (1732) II. 175 Kerme, who waited her Answer,..was so much transported at the unhoped Compliance of it, that [etc.]. **1820** L. HUNT *Indicator* No. 31 (1822) I. 245 What unhoped courage reanimates me!

**b.** In quasi-adverbial construction: Unexpectedly, beyond expectation.

**1667** MILTON *P. L.* x. 348 To Hell he now return'd, And ..unhop't Met who to meet him came, his Ofspring dear. **1734** THOMSON *Liberty* III. 453 The power resign'd, And all unhop'd the commonwealth restor'd, Amaz'd the public. **1791** COWPER *Odyssey* v. 491 Though Jove hath given me to behold, Unhop'd, the land again. **1810** SCOTT *Lady of L.* v. xvii, He falter'd thanks to Heaven for life, Redeem'd, unhoped, from desperate strife. **1830** W. TAYLOR *Hist. Surv. Germ. Poetry* II. 328 Like sons who meet unhop'd a father.

**3.** Not hoped († or looked) *for.*

**1598** R. BERNARD tr. *Terence, Andriæ* III. iv, I was the cause of the marriage that shall be made to day, euen quite vnhoped for of the old man. **1622** FLETCHER *Love's Cure* I. ii, A Temple..where I may give thanks For this unhop'd for blessing. **1697** DRYDEN *Æneis* IX. 939 Suddenly th' unhop'd for News was brought. **1725** POPE *Odyss.* v. 525 When ..These eyes at last behold the unhoped-for coast. **1749** FIELDING *Tom Jones* XVI. vi, Blifil having obtained this unhoped for acquiescence. **1825** SCOTT *Betrothed* Concl., Her unhoped-for union with Damian. **1857** DUFFERIN *Lett. High Lat.* (ed. 3) 406 These unhoped-for circumstances opened a new field to our explorations.

**Unho·pedly,** *adv.* (UN-1 11.) **1611** FLORIO, *Insperatamente*, vnhopedly. **1831** HOWITT *Seasons* 123 Was it that some faint pilgrim came Unhopedly to thee?

**Unho·peful,** *a.* [UN-1 7.]

**1.** Not affording grounds for hope; unpromising.

*c* **1450** *Mirour Saluacioun* 2871 For both thire sonnes tholed she the vnhopfulle bitternesse. **1599** SHAKS. *Much Ado* II. i. 392 And Benedick is not the vnhopefullest husband that I know. **1646** G. DANIEL *Poems* Wks. (Grosart) I. 73 More valewing encrease From this vnhopefull Impe, then all the Store Hee had beside. **1663** BOYLE *Usef. Exp. Nat. Philos.* II. iii. 67 The unhopefullest season of the year, the winter solstice. **1785** JEFFERSON *Corr.* Wks. 1859 I. 406 The lethargic character of their ambassador here gives a very unhopeful aspect to a treaty on this ground. **1858** H. BUSHNELL *Nat. & Supernat.* vi. (1864) 183 There is nothing in it unhopeful, nothing to accuse. **1890** *Spectator* 7 June, The chance of reading the great Minister a lesson in humility seemed not unhopeful.

**2.** Not feeling hope; despondent.

**1850** *Westm. Rev.* April 64 The fear which the mass, if uneducated and unhopeful, will always feel. **1858** CARLYLE *Fredk. Gt.* II. xiv. I. 180 Jobst tried..to do some governing; but finding all very anarchic, grew unhopeful.

Hence **Unho·pefulness.**

[**1737** BAILEY.] **1868** H. BUSHNELL *Mor. Uses Dark Th.* (1869) 346 They become, in this way, a kind of mystery of unhopefulness.

**Unho·pefully,** *adv.* (UN-1 11; cf. prec.)

**1840** LOWELL *Moon* 13 The sea..lay unhopefully alone, And lived but in an aimless seeking. **1861** *Sat. Rev.* 21 Dec. 639 Measuring its force and danger..more unhopefully than many of his contemporaries.

**Unho·ping,** *ppl. a.* (UN-1 10.)

*a* **1628** F. GREVIL *Wks.* (1870) IV. 267 In which unhoping time you must resolue [etc.]. **1738** G. LILLO *Marina* II. i, Or Jove restore to my unhoping eyes What his vindictive hand hath taken from me. **1866** CARLYLE *Remin.* (1881) II. 172, I was Thomas the Doubter, the unhoping. **1892** *Nation* (N.Y.) 28 Apr. 322/2 The latest of these unhoping encomiums on greatness deferred.

**b.** As pple. with object. (UN-1 5 d.)

**1748** RICHARDSON *Clarissa* (1811) III. 40 Unhoping..the success of their schemes in Solmes's behalf.

**Unho·pingly,** *adv.* [UN-1 11.] Inconceivably.

**1435** MISYN *Fire of Love* 36 Þat heet treuly sensibily swete smellynge vnhopingly [L. *inestimabiliter*], I was besy vnto þe..takynge of heuenly sounde.

**Unho·pped,** *ppl. a.* (UN-1 8. See HOPPED *ppl. a.*, and cf. G. *ungehopft.*) **1725** *Fam. Dict.* s.v. *Malt Liquor*, Hopp'd and unhopp'd Drinks. *Ibid.*, Unhopp'd Liquor. **1799** W. TOOKE *View of Russian Empire* I. 362 Brown beer and metheglin are more in use than..busa or white unhopped wheat-beer. **Unhori·zoned,** *ppl. a.* (UN-1 8.) **1811** MISS L. M. HAWKINS *C'tess & Gertr.* II. 121 The unhorizoned charity of him who bid us pray. **1888** LIGHTHALL *Yng. Seigneur* 122 A vista ocean-like and unhorizoned.

**Unho·rned,** *a.* (UN-1 9. Cf. Du. *ongehoorned*; older Da. *uhornet.*)

**1570** LEVINS *Manip.* 50 Vnhorned, *incornis.* **1607** TOPSELL *Four-f. Beasts* 233 There are two kindes of Goates,..the vnhorned are best for breed. **1621** G. SANDYS *Ovid's Met.* IV. (1626) 66 Thou 'rt seene in heauen;..And, when vnhorn'd, thou hast a Virgins face. **1648** HEXHAM II, *Ongehoornt*, Vnhorned, or without hornes.

**Unho·rse,** *v.* [UN-2 3. Cf. MDu. *ontorsen.*]

**1.** *trans.* To throw or drag (a person) from his horse, esp. in battle. Also in fig. context.

**1390** GOWER *Conf.* I. 368 He..smot him with a dethes wounde, That he unhorsed fell to grounde. **1412–20** LYDG. *Chron. Troy* IV. 2077 Menelay..to Troilus faste gan hym spede Fully avysed to vnhorsen hym anon. **1448–9** METHAM *Amoryus & Cleopes* 933 Qwat ys he yon,..that thus fersly iustyth to-day; That no knyght hym onhors may? **1530** PALSGR. 768/1, I unhorse a man by feates of armes in the felde, *Je rue jus.* **1563** GOLDING *Cæsar* 39 b, If any of them were sore wounded or vnhorsed, theis garded him about. **1607** CHAPMAN *Bussy d'Ambois* IV. i, He turn'd wild lightning in the lackeys' hands, Who, through their sudden violent twitch unhors'd him. **1668** R. STEELE *Husbandman's Calling* vi. (1672) 159 Neither wouldst thou be ridden at the Devil's pleasure if thou didst understand thyself: unhorse Satan quickly from off thy soul. **1724** DE FOE *Mem. Cavalier* (1840) 277 Ireton..was unhorsed and taken prisoner. **1756** tr. *Keysler's Trav.* I. 29 A large quantity of armour,..some for unhorsing an antagonist in a turnament. **1820** SCOTT *Monast.* xxiv, To me it is recommended, because it..unhorses the lazy monks that have ridden us so long, and spur-galled us so hard. **1843** JAMES *Forest Days* xx, And so you unhorsed the traitor, but could neither kill nor take him?

**b.** *fig.* To dislodge, overthrow, discomfit, nonplus.

**1577** *F. de L'isle's Legendarie* G vij, The Duke of Guise and his partakers..without the policie of the Queene mother, ..had at the same instant bene quite vnhorsed. **1602** J. RHODES *Answ. to Romish Rime* 519 So did all of Rome beside, Untill they grew to their full pride; And were of late unhorst agayne. **1656** EARL MONM. tr. *Boccalini's Advts. fr. Parnass.* I. lxxviii. (1674) 106 The trick of unhorsing people..by meer Words. **1680** C. NESSE *Church-Hist.* 280 The scruple..about his marriage became the occasion of unhorsing the Pope in England. **1825** SCOTT *Talism.* xxvi, Thou hast unhorsed me with that very word. **1845** DISRAELI *Sybil* (1863) 207 She did not deign even to notice the unhappy cavalier whom she had thus as it were unhorsed.

**c.** In passive: To be thrown from a horse.

**1583** MELBANCKE *Philotimus* X j b, He that rides with one girth, may feare to be vnhorst. *a* **1713** ELLWOOD *Autobiography* (1714) 72 If it [*sc.* the knife] should have been found..under my coat when I came to be Unhorsed. **1748** *Anson's Voy.* II. xii. 263 His horse..turning round suddenly rode off with his master, who was very near being unhorsed in the surprize. **1802** JAMES *Milit. Dict.*, *Unhorsed*, thrown from the saddle; dismounted.

†**2.** To help (one) to dismount. *Obs.*

**1530** PALSGR. 768/1, I unhorse a man, I sette hym bysyde his horse, *je desmonte. Ibid.*, Helpe to unhorse these ladyes.

**b.** *intr.* To dismount.

**1633** QUARLES in P. Fletcher *Poet. Wks.* (1909) II. 284 I lasht through thick and thinne, Dispatch'd my businesse, and return'd agen: I call'd the second time; unhors'd, went in.

**3.** To deprive of a horse. *rare.*

**1465** *Paston Lett.* II. 178 But I trow to gyte Dorlet ayen hys hors or els Mr Phylyp ys lyke to be unhorssyd ons, and we lyve all. **1651** in *Crawford Proclam.* (1910) II. 58 All tories not joining the army within 14 days to be unhorsed and counted traitors. **1837** W. IRVING *Capt. Bonneville* xii, A whip and a rope were left..by the robbers, as a taunt to the simpletons they had unhorsed.

**4.** To unharness the horses from (a carriage, etc.).

**1654** EARL MONM. tr. *Bentivoglio's Wars Flanders* 385 Coming to their Batteries they unhorst some of their Peeces. **1784** COWPER *Task* VI. 701 Others..unhorse The gilded equipage,..turning loose His steeds. **1829** SIR W. NAPIER *Penins. War* VI. iii, The artillery was unhorsed.

Hence **Unho·rsement**; **Unho·rsing** *vbl. sb.*

**1603** BP. HALL *Serm.* v. 13 If you ever therefore look to see..the unhorsing and confusion of that strumpet of Rome. **1884** TRAILL *New Lucian* 52 It was a moral unhorsement of the most dishonouring kind.

**Unho·se,** *v.* [UN-2 4. Cf. Flem. (Kilian) *onthosen.*] *trans.* To strip or divest of hose. Also *fig.* Hence **Unho·sing** *vbl. sb.*

**1483** CAXTON *Gold. Leg.* 161 b/2 Peter is as moche to saye as knowynge or unhosyng,..and therfore he was sayd unhosyng for he unhosed and dyd of his wyll fro his feet. *c* **1489** — *Sonnes of Aymon* xvi. 371 Whan mawgis had taken all this, he..vnhosed him. *c* **1532** DU WES in *Palsgr.* 942 To unhose, *deschausser.* **1598** FLORIO, *Scalciatura*, an vnshoing, vnhosing, vnbreeching. **1611** COTGR., *Deschausser*, ..to vnhose, or draw off hosen.

**Unho·sed,** *ppl. a.* [UN-1 8.] Not wearing hose.

**1297** R. GLOUC. (Rolls) 10826 And hii..To him come at gloucetre..Vn-hosed & bareuot & vngurt al so. **1594** R. ASHLEY tr. *Loys le Roy* 27 Without clothing, vnhosed, and vnshood. **1795** [see UNHOODED].

**Unho·spitable,** *a.* [UN-1 7 b, 5 b.] = INHOSPITABLE *a.* **a.** Of places.

**1601** SHAKS. *Twel. N.* III. iii. 11 Being skillesse in these parts: which to a stranger..often proue Rough, and vnhospitable. **1612** WEBSTER *White Devil* v. iii. 45 They have..divorst friends, and made great houses unhospitable. **1687** DRYDEN *Hind & P.* III. 612 No neighbouring Dorp, no lodging to be found, But bleaky plains, and bare unhospitable ground. **1703** ROWE *Ulysses* I. i, You..from th'unhospitable Dwelling drive Safety and friendly Peace. **1740**

CHEYNE *Regimen* 106 Our Earth has,..unfruitful Climates, unhospitable and uninhabited Regions. **1808** FORSYTH *Beauties Scotl.* V. 472 A cluster of unhospitable rocks.

**b.** Of persons.

*a* **1625** FLETCHER *Fair Maid Inn* II. i, *Serv.* Shall we kill him? *Alber.* No, I'll not be so unhospitable. **1641** J. SHUTE *Sarah & Hagar* (1649) 116 James and John..call'd for fire from heaven upon those unhospitable Samaritans. **1708** ROWE *Royal Convert* V. i, The Britons then shall join their Arms with yours, To drive out these unhospitable Guests. **1722** DE FOE *Plague* (1754) 163 They would be loth to have it remembered..how unhospitable, and how unkind they were. **1842** J. B. FRASER *Allee Neemroo* II. 289 The young man, unwilling to be rash or unhospitable. **1864** TROLLOPE *Can you forgive her?* xii, It cannot perhaps fairly be said that George Vavasor was an unhospitable man.

**c.** Of actions, character, etc.

**1625** K. LONG tr. *Barclay's Argenis* IV. ii. 237 To renounce your hospitality, were superfluous, when you have done first, by offering vnhospitable iniury. **1682** MRS. BEHN *City Heiress* 50 What Recompence can I make for so unhospitable usage? **1727** SWIFT *State Irel.* Wks. 1755 V. II. 168, I think it a little unhospitable..that..guests [etc.]. **1750** G. HUGHES *Barbados* 93 He lies concealed..till the next prey calls him forth to repeat his unhospitable talents. **1760** *Ann. Reg., Chron.* 66/1 The unhospitable custom of giving vails to servants.

Hence **Unho·spitableness.**

**1681** J. KETTLEWELL *Meas. Chr. Obed.* II. iv. 165 The Law against uncharitableness.., against unhospitableness.

† **Unho·spital,** *a. Obs.* [UN-[1] 7, 5 b.] Inhospitable.

**1570** LEVINS *Manip.* 15 Vnhospitall, *inhospitus.* *a* **1586** SIDNEY *Arcadia* I. ii, A civill warre..hath..disfigured the face of nature, and made it so unhospitall as now you have found it. **1615** G. SANDYS *Trav.* 39 First called Axenus, which signifieth vnhospitall: by reason of the coldnesse thereof, and inhumanity of the bordering Nations. *a* **1639** W. WHATELEY *Prototypes* I. xix. (1640) 174 Hee was hospital in that unhospitall citie.

† **Unhospita·lity.** *Obs.* [UN-[1] 12, 5 b.] Inhospitality. **1388** WYCLIF *Wisd.* xix. 13 Thei suffriden iustli,..for thei ordeyneden more abhomynable vnospitalite. **Unho·stile,** *a.* (UN-[1] 7.) **1705** J. PHILLIPS *Blenheim* 163 Of Pain impatient, the high prancing Steeds..Spurn their dismounted Riders; they expire Indignant, by unhostile Wounds destroy'd. **1825** R. WILSON *Sk. Hist. Hawick* 214 A House of Commons, formed of such materials,..would be unhostile to the security of property.

**Unhou·se** (ʊnhau·z), *v.* [UN-[2] 5. Cf. MDu. *onthusen*, WFl. *onthuizen*, MHG. *enthûsen*.] *trans.* To turn out of a house, habitation, or abode; to make houseless or homeless.

*a* **1375** *Joseph Arim.* 455 Þei come bi tholomers tentes, vnhoused hem sone, Token holliche his stor. **1598** SYLVESTER *Du Bartas* II. ii. *Colonies* 154 So one People doth pursue another; And scarce the second hath a first un-housed, Before a third him thence again have roused. **1633** P. FLETCHER *Purple Isl.* VII. i, Thirsil up starting from his fearlesse bed,..Unhous'd his bleating flock. **1643** [ANGIER] *Lanc. Vall. Achor* 8 If they peeped out of the houses, they were unhoused. **1759** SARAH FIELDING *C'tess of Dellwyn* II. 147 He was at once unwived, unhoused, and undone. **1795** MACNEILL *Scotland's Scaith* III. vi, What a change, unhoused and beggared, Starving. **1821** CLARE *Vill. Minstr.* I. 72 Unhous'd from beds of ling The fluskering pheasant took to wing. **1885** *Manch. Exam.* 13 July 5/5 Only 150 persons will be for the present unhoused.

*refl.* **1599** NASHE *Lenten Stuffe* 38 When he vn-houseth him, or hath cast off his shel, he..lookes as red as a Fox. **1606** J. RAYNOLDS *Dolarneys' Prim.* (1880) 123 The drowsie vapours, takes their sable flyghts, And bright Aurora, doth her selfe vnhouse. **1854** MILLER *Sch. & Schm.* xiii, We had very nearly unhoused ourselves ere our work was finished.

**b.** *fig.* or in fig. context.

**1594** DANIEL *Cleopatra* (Bang) 1323, I must myselfe force open wide a dore To let out life, and to vnhouse my spirit. **1625** MILTON *Death Fair Infant* 21 He..all unwares with his cold-kind embrace Unhous'd thy Virgin Soul from her fair biding place. **1690** C. NESSE *O. & N. Test.* I. 122 He that hath God for his house..can never be unhoused. **1727** DE FOE *Hist. Appar.* v. (1840) 45 Souls which have been encased in flesh, but being unhoused are now moving about. *a* **1814** *Sulieman* II. iii. in *New Brit. Theatre* II. 26 But for wine..This shatter'd shell of body had unhous'd Long since my soul.

Hence **Unhou·sing** *vbl. sb.*

In recent use also *attrib.*, as *unhousing scheme.*

**1809** R. LANGFORD *Introd. Trade* 72 Unhousing, Wharfage and Shipping, £2 2s. 1d. **1886** *Pall Mall G.* 22 Sept. 6/1 This scheme..will take five years to complete, so that the unhousing will be gradual.

**Unhou·sed,** *ppl. a.*[1] [UN-[1] 8. Cf. MDu. *ongehuset*, MLG. *ungehuset*, MHG. *-hûset*.]

**1.** Not provided with, not lodged in, a house; homeless.

**1604** SHAKS. *Oth.* I. ii. 26, I would not my vnhoused free condition Put into Circumscription, and Confine, For the Seas worth. **1623** MIDDLETON *More Dissemblers* IV. i, Th' unhous'd race of fortune-tellers. **1649** OGILBY *Virgil's Georgics* III. 370 Lybian Shepherds..unhous'd Cattel through vast Desarts lead. **1709** POPE *Lett.* (1735) I. 86 The faithful Dog,..Unfed, unhous'd, neglected, [lay] on the Clay. **1743** FRANCIS tr. *Hor., Odes* IV. xiv. 44 Whom unhoused Scythians fear, unconquer'd Spain obeys. **1830** CROLY *Geo. IV*, 283 Unhoused beggary, and the hideousness of civil bloodshed, combined and shaped themselves into a colossal power. **1860** LONGF. *Wayside Inn, K. Olaf* XVII. v, Every warlike Dane..Left..Unhoused the cattle. **1867** LEWES *Hist. Philos.* (ed. 3) II. 210 Their tottering architecture would have sheltered none whom Spinoza's visionary fabric left unhoused.

**2.** Not occupied by houses.

**1582** STANYHURST *Æneis* IV. (Arb.) 96 Heere ye sit embayed with Moors, with Syrtis vnhowsed [L. *inhospita Syrtis*]. **1611** COTGR., *Place*, a plaine and vnhoused ground.

**Unhou·sed,** *ppl. a.*[2] [f. UNHOUSE *v.*] Deprived of house or dwelling. Also *absol.*

**1621** SANDYS *Ovid's Met.* IV. (1626) 77 The gates still open stand..And as all Riuers run into the Deep: So all vnhoused Soules doe thither creep. **1886** *Pall Mall G.* 22 Sept. 6/1 This is a sufficient accommodation for the unhoused in this improvement.

**Unhou·sed,** *ppl. a.*[3] [UN-[1] 8: see HOUSE *v.*[2]] Not covered with a house or housing.

**1560** [see HOUSED *ppl. a.*[2]].

**Unhou·seled,** *ppl. a.* [UN-[1] 8.] Not having had the Eucharist administered.

**1532** MORE *Confut. Tindale* Wks. 377/2 Yet thynketh Tyndall that..the people were as good vnhowseled as howseled. **1602** SHAKS. *Ham.* I. v. 77 Cut off euen in the Blossomes of my Sinne, Vnhouzzled, disappointed, vnnaneld. **1819** SCOTT *Ivanhoe* xxx, Me..they suffer to die like the houseless dog on yonder common, unshriven and unhouseled. **1826** SOUTHEY *Vind. Eccl. Angl.* 500 He died, unhouselled, in his sins. **1865** E. BURRITT *Walk to Land's End* 334 The articulate plaint of some unhouseled spirit moaning for admission.

**Unhou·sewife.** (UN-[1] 12 b.) **1823** J. WELSH in *Love Lett.* (1909) I. 199 These 'reddings-up'..to my unhousewife perceptions..produce no other effects than confusion, discomfort, and dirt. †**Unho·vable,** *a. Obs. rare*[−0]. [UN-[1] 7 b. Cf. UNBEHOVABLE *a.*] Unfitting. **1570** LEVINS *Manip.* 3 Vnhouable, *impertinens.* †**Unho·ve.** *Obs. rare*[−1]. [UN-[1] 12 + HOVE *sb.*[2], probably after ON. *úhóf.*] Lack of moderation. *a* **1300** *Cursor M.* 28222 My breth [= anger] it wald be til vnhoue þat many man was won to droue. †**Unho·ven,** *ppl. a. Sc. Obs.* [UN-[1] 8 b: see HEAVE *v.* 3.] Unbaptized. *c* **1375** *Sc. Leg. Saints* xxxiv. (*Pelagia*) 115 He..byd þam þat vnhowine ware, þat þai suld ga þar gat but mare. **1456** SIR G. HAYE *Law Arms* (S.T.S) 204 Him behufit to be slayne or ellis to leve the barne unhovin. **Unho·ver,** *v.* [UN-[2] 5: see HOVER *sb.* 3.] *trans.* To dislodge from a hiding-place. **1827** *Sporting Mag.* XX. 104 Mr. Treby's harriers, assisted by his..terriers, unhovered an otter.

**Unhue,** *v.*: see WANHUE *v. Obs.*

**Unhu·lled,** *ppl. a.*[1] [UN-[1] 8.]

**1.** Not furnished with a hull or husk.

**1597** GERARDE *Herbal* I. xlviii. 68 These naked Otes..in Northfolke and Southfolke..are called unhulled and naked Otes. *a* **1722** LISLE *Husb.* (1752) 126 Seeds will not grow unhulled, or extra cotyledones.

**2.** Not freed from husk.

**1883** *Pall Mall G.* 27 Sept. 11/1 Sand and unhulled paddy are mixed with their morning and evening rice.

**Unhu·lled,** *ppl. a.*[2] [UN-[2] 4, 8.] Having the hull or husk removed.

**1656** J. SMITH *Pract. Physick* 84 Take the decoction of unhulled Barley. **1658** BROWNE *Gard. Cyrus* iii. 131 If Barley unhulled would grow.

**Unhu·man,** *a.* [UN-[1] 7, 5 b.]

**1.** Inhuman, inhumane, unmerciful, cruel: **a.** Of actions, etc.

*α.* **1549** *Compl. Scot.* xiv. 119 Ther for ȝe hef committit ane onhumain act. **1605** *London Prodigal* III. i. 185 That were vnchristian, and an vnhumane part. **1622** in Foster *Eng. Factories Ind.* (1908) II. 18 They..have..committed such unhumaine acts in murtheringe all they take. *a* **1660** *Contemp. Hist. Irel.* (Ir. Archæol. Soc.) I. 251 Unnaturall lust and unhumane crueltie.

*β.* **1646** HAMMOND *Tracts* Pref., Not only the most unchristian but unhuman practices. *a* **1716** SOUTH *Serm.* (1744) XI. ii. 39 Their insatiable avarice, and their unhuman and remorseless cruelty. **1796** MRS. M. ROBINSON *Angelina* III. 373 Against parental authority so unhuman, nature has some plea. **1871** BLACKIE *Four Phases* i. 36 A one-sided, unhuman, unworthy and altogether false assertion.

**b.** Of persons.

**1611** SPEED *Hist. Gt. Brit.* VI. xxxv. § 5. 136 He was flaied aliue by direction of this vnhumane King. **1663** SOUTH *Serm.* (1717) V. 101 Bleeding and dying at the Feet of Bloody, Unhuman Miscreants. **1700** RYCAUT *Hist. Turks* 333/2 That insolent and unhumane Robber. **1749** FIELDING *Tom Jones* VI. xi, All agreed that he was sent away pennyless..from the house of his unhuman father.

**2.** Not limited by human qualities or conditions; superhuman.

**1782** MME. D'ARBLAY *Let.* 6 Apr., [They] are neither plunged in the depths of misery, nor exalted to unhuman happiness. **1855** CDL. WISEMAN *Fabiola* I. ix. 49 Converted..by some means, so unhuman, so divine, as we shall never..forecast. **1856** R. A. VAUGHAN *Mystics* (1860) I. 100 This divorce between the virtues of daily life and certain other virtues which are unhuman. **1874** H. ROGERS *Orig. Bible* ii. 70 An argument for the unhuman character of the project.

**3.** Not pertaining to mankind.

**1885** G. ALLEN *Darwin* vii. 120 These curious and almost unhuman-looking objects [*sc.* palæolithic implements]. **1885** R. L. & F. STEVENSON *Dynamiter* 153 'How is this?' he cried, in a sharp, unhuman voice. 'Am I blind?'

Hence **Unhu·manness.**

**1885** L. OLIPHANT *Sympneumata* 275 The stamp of unhumanness which clings to the acts and operations of success.

**Unhu·man,** *v.* [UN-[2] 6 a.] *trans.* To make unhuman.

**1648** EARL WESTMORELD. *Otia Sacra* 129 And yet (as if unhuman'd) we By no means with each other can agree.

**Unhu·manize,** *v.* [UN-[2] 6 c.]

**1.** *trans.* To deprive of human virtues; to render inhuman or callous.

**1752** YOUNG *Brothers* III. i, Thy heart, how dead to every call of nature! Unson'd! unbrother'd! nay, unhumaniz'd! **1755** *Man* No. 24. 3 A life consisting entirely of..sensual delights, unhumanises the soul. **1807** J. BARLOW *Columb.* VI. 398 How long, deluding phantom, wilt thou blind, Mislead, debase, unhumanize mankind? **1852** HAWTHORNE *Blithedale Rom.* xviii, That cold tendency..appeared to have gone far towards unhumanizing my heart. **1860** I. TAYLOR *Spir. Hebrew Poetry* (1873) 124 The work of slaughter did not unhumanize those who effected it.

**2.** To deprive of human qualities.

**1800** *Monthly Mag.* X. 319 By endeavouring to sublimate his Jesus into a Jehovah, he unhumanizes the most lovely of characters.

Hence **Unhu·manized** *ppl. a.*

*c* **1780** PORTEUS *Serm.* (1799) II. vi. 140 Purity is ridiculed and set at nought, as a sour, unsocial, unhumanized virtue. **1805** FOSTER *Ess.* (1806) I. 207 The firmness..is accompanied..in a mere man of the world, with an unhumanized repulsive hardness. **1815** KIRBY & SP. *Entomol.* xiv. (1816) I. 434 The most ignorant and unhumanized of their race.

**Unhu·manly,** *adv.* (UN-[1] 11, 5 b.)

**1586** *Reg. Privy Council Scot.* IV. 118 The said Jonnett..maist cruellie and unhumanlie invadit and persewit hir. **1663** SOUTH *Serm.* (1717) V. 55 Charles I,..Unhumanly Imprison'd, and at length Barbarously Murder'd. **1868** H. BUSHNELL *Mor. Uses Dark Th.* (1869) 305 Acting in a style of frenzy so unhumanly foul and malign.

**Unhu·mble,** *a.* (UN-[1] 7.)

**1611** FLORIO, *Dishumile*, vnhumble, high minded. **1642** DAVENANT *Unfort. Lovers* Epil., An unhumble Epilogue. **1842** PUSEY *Crisis Eng. Ch.* 13 A Communion,..in this country, schismatic, and acting in a very unhumble and schismatic spirit. **1882** W. MORRIS in Mackail *Life* (1899) II. 77, I hope I am not quite unhumble.

Hence **Unhu·mbleness.**

*a* **1732** T. BOSTON *Crook in Lot* (1805) 117 Their condition will be brought to the lowest pass, but the unhumbleness of their spirits will remain.

**Unhu·mbled,** *ppl. a.* (UN-[1] 8.)

**1604** HIERON *Wks.* I. 498 The sawcines of an ignorant and vnhumbled heart. **1657** BAXTER *Agst. Quakers* 8 What an unhumbled people these are. **1671** MILTON *P. R.* III. 429 Unhumbl'd, unrepentant, unreform'd. **1704** *Faction Displ.* x, Uncheck'd by Fear, unhumbled by Disgrace. **1808** HAN. MORE *Cœlebs* xxiv. II. 3 A critical spirit..being a symptom of an unhumbled mind. **1846** G. S. FABER *Lett. Tractar. Secess.* 65 Or did he come to it in the unhumbled position of a modern Socinian..? **1904** P. FOUNTAIN *Gt. North-West* xxiv. 294 A flag..floating over its unhumbled sons.

*absol.* *a* **1732** T. BOSTON *Crook in Lot* (1805) 101 The removal of the cross is not a means to humble the unhumbled. *a* **1838** C. NEAT *Serm.* (1839) 129 The worldly-minded, the unhumbled, the prayerless.

Hence **Unhu·mbledness.**

*c* **1670** O. HEYWOOD *Diaries*, etc. (1881) II. 326 The unhumbledness and impenitency of most under open scandalls. **1737** J. WILLISON *Afflicted Man's Comp.* (1744) 46 It imports much Impenitency and Unhumbledness for sin.

**Unhumi·liated,** *ppl. a.* (UN-[1] 8.) **1856** RUSKIN *Mod. Paint.* IV. 248 Precipices..gathered after every fall into darker frowns and unhumiliated threatening. **Unhu·morous,** *a.* (UN-[1] 7.) **1881** *Athenæum* 17 Dec. 810/3 To treat the most dreadful of all crimes as a slight misdemeanour is..essentially unhumorous. **Unhu·morously,** *adv.* (UN-[1] 11.) **1768** *Woman of Honor* III. 229 Mrs. Arnold used, not quite unhumorously, to say [etc.].

**Unhu·ng,** *ppl. a.* [UN-[1] 8 b.]

**1.** Not furnished with hangings.

**1648** HEXHAM II, *Ongehangen*, Vnhung, or, not Hanged with hangings or tapistry. **1666** PEPYS *Diary* 2 Mar., [Sir P. Warwick] shewed me his house, which is yet all unhung, but will be a very noble house indeed.

**2.** Of persons: Not (yet) executed by hanging. (Cf. UNHANGED *ppl. a.*)

[**1775** ASH, *Unhung*,..not hanged.] **1840** DICKENS *Old C. Shop* lxvi, One of the greatest scoundrels unhung. **1875** W. S. GILBERT *Tom Cobb* II, To look upon you as the coolest scamp unhung. **1892** ZANGWILL *Childr. Ghetto* I. 206 The Emperor let the man go unhung.

**b.** Not hung up (for exhibition).

**1880** *Pall Mall G.* 28 Aug. 6/1 It is said that much good work [in painting] will remain unhung for want of room. *transf.* **1906** *Macm. Mag.* Feb. 302 Declaiming excitedly because some fragile painter is unhung at the Academy.

**Unhung,** pa. pple. of UNHANG *v.*

**Unhu·nted,** *ppl. a.* [UN-[1] 8.]

**1.** Not hunted in; not searched by hunting.

**1572** BOSSEWELL *Armorie* II. 94 A great Parke..that had remained vnhunted, duringe the time of foure mens ages. **1811** MISS L. M. HAWKINS *C'tess & Gertr.* 59 No part of England, but the extreme northern counties, was 'unhunted' in this search. **1883** R. BRIDGES *Prometh.* 1078 Skirting wide The unhunted forest. **1899** F. V. KIRBY *Sport Africa* xi. 118 In comparatively unknown and unhunted districts.

**2.** Not hunted or chased.

**1648** HEXHAM II, *Ongejaeght*, Vnhunted, or Vnchased. **1809** CAMPBELL *Gert. Wyom.* I. iii, The wild-deer arched his neck from glades, and then Unhunted sought his woods. *a* **1822** SHELLEY *Fragm.*, '*When soft Winds*' 4 Bold as an unhunted fawn.

**Unhu·ntsmanlike,** *a.* (UN-[1] 7 c.) **1607** MARKHAM *Cavel.* III. (1617) 9 When..I haue vn-Huntsman-like ridden in amongst the Dogges. **Unhu·rdled,** *a.* (UN-[1] 9.) *a* **1711** KEN *Ded.* Poet. Wks. 1721 I. 4 My Flock stray on the unhurdled Wild. **Unhu·rled,** *ppl. a.* (UN-[1] 8.) [**1775** ASH.] **1798** W. TAYLOR in Robberds *Mem.* (1843) I. 219 Not yet the great retributress has closed The book of fate—her unhurled lightnings glow.

**Unhu·rried,** *ppl. a.* (UN-[1] 8.)

**1768–74** TUCKER *Lt. Nat.* (1834) II. 547 There is a virtue in keeping one's self..unhurried in dangers or alluring pursuits. **1859** RUSKIN *Two Paths* i. 47 The noble person..deals with them in unalarmed intelligence and unhurried strength. **1876** MRS. WHITNEY *Sights & Ins.* II. xxvi. 540 It was built into ourselves, by our unhurried possession of it in restful hours. **1881** A. A. KNOX *New Playground* (1883) 9 Eight hours of bed, and an unhurried breakfast.

So **Unhu·rriedly** *adv.*

**1880** P. GILLMORE *On Duty* 349, I..then, unhurriedly, rode through the station.

**Unhu·rrying,** *ppl. a.* (UN-[1] 10.) **1768–74** TUCKER *Lt. Nat.* (1834) II. 537 Continual unhurrying activity in pursuit of some end.

**Unhu·rt,** *ppl. a.* (UN-[1] 8 b.)

*a* **1225** *Juliana* 31 Þe worldes wealdent þat wiste sein iuhan..unhurt ibe ueat of wallinde eoli. 1387 TREVISA *Higden* (Rolls) VII. 165 Sche passed unhert nyne brennynge cultres. *c* 1400 *Destr. Troy* 1264 His shafte all-to sheuerit, the shalke was unhurt. *c* 1440 *Alph. Tales* 25 If þine arm com vp vnhurte. *c* 1460 *Oseney Reg.* 144 And I and myne heyres that howse schall kepe vn-hurt, that hit be not..apeyred by owr vse. 1565 COOPER *Thesaurus, Indistrictus*, ..vnhurte: without scarre. 1597 A. M. tr. *Guillemeau's Fr. Chirurg.* 9 b/2 With the shott of a gunne, the first table was vnhurte. 1601 [see UNHIT]. 1647 CLARENDON *Hist. Reb.* II. § 7 They believed there [were]..no Persons of what Quality soever unconcerned and .. unhurt in them [*sc.* matters of religion]. 1676 HOBBES *Iliad* I. 397 Would you could here rest Unhurt, ungriev'd. 1718 PRIOR *Pict. Seneca Dying* 11 While unhurt, divine Jordain, Thy Work and Seneca's remain. 1755 YOUNG *Centaur* iv, His happiness is of so strong a constitution, that it can stand real calamities unhurt. 1818 [S. WESTON] *La Scava* 27 A statue of Venus, ..the legs and arms are broke, the nose unhurt. 1894 D. CAMPBELL *Coleridge* i. 12 [He] escaped unhurt from the fray.

**Unhu·rted,** *ppl. a.* [UN-1 8.] *Obs.* or *dial.* = prec.

1483 CAXTON *Gold. Leg.* 432/2 They had oute of the quarrye the forsayd ten men the whyche were founde unhurted. 1742 T. DE LA MAYNE *Love & Honour* 102 With Them familiar grown, unhurted dwell In unmolested Truce.

**Unhu·rtful,** *a.* (UN-1 7.)

1549 COVERDALE, etc. *Erasm. Par. 1 Cor.* 15 In vnhurtefull manners, playne, pure, and without all counterfaictyng. 1570 DRANT *Serm.* G vij, That..the Wolfe [might] become an vnhurtfull neighbour to the Lambe. 1603 SHAKS. *Meas. for M.* III. ii. 175 You imagine me to vnhurtfull an opposite. *a* 1680 BUTLER *Charac., Humorist*, A Humorist is..some out-lying Whimsie of Nature, that being tame and unhurtful is suffered to go at Liberty. 1712 BLACKMORE *Creation* IV. 175 Whence shoots..the falling star, And flames unhurtful hovering dance in air? 1753 RICHARDSON *Grandison* (1781) III. ix. 62 All that is wished for..is, that she may be made unhurtful. *a* 1806 H. K. WHITE *Poems* (1837) 136 When happy Superstition, gabbling eld, Holds her unhurtful gambols.

Hence **Unhu·rtfully** *adv.*, **Unhu·rtfulness.**

1549 COVERDALE, etc. *Erasm. Par 1 Cor.* vi. 15 b, Your vnhurtefulnes shal condemne theyr vnclennes. 1725 POPE *Let. to Swift* 14 Sept., To laugh at others as innocently and as unhurtfully as at ourselves.

**Unhu·rting,** *ppl. a.* (UN-1 10, 5 d.)

1613 W. BROWNE *Brit. Past.* I. iv. 74 As if she in her kinde (vnhurting elfe) Did bid me take such lodging as her selfe. 1814 *Monthly Mag.* XXXVII. 146 While the evening shower retires, Kindle thy unhurting fires. 1822 BEDDOES *Bride's Trag.* IV. i, Because I fold Mine arms like any man unhurt, unhurting.

† **b.** *Sc.* With object: Without violating.

1581 *Rec. Burgh Lanark* (1893) 84 Hie being chossing hie may, unhurtand his aith, refuis the samyn offece.

**Unhu·sbanded,** *ppl. a.* [UN-1 8.]

**1.** Not improved by husbandry; untilled, uncultivated: **a.** Of ground.

1538 ELYOT, *Incultus*, a place vnhusbanded or vntilled. 1601 R. JOHNSON *Kingd. & Commw.* (1603) 184 No foot of land is left vnhusbanded. 1628 ROBSON *News fr. Aleppo* 13 The vnhusbanded plaines, for many miles together blame their stupidity. 1654 EARL MONM. tr. *Bentivoglio's Wars Flanders* 134 Other little islands..are almost nameless, as being almost unhusbanded. 1894 *Pall Mall G.* 1 Nov. 2/3 Dwellers for the more part in remote, unhusbanded districts.

**b.** Of plants or trees.

1615 G. SANDYS *Trav.* II. 116 A desert producing here and there a few vnhusbanded Palmes. 1616 W. BROWNE *Brit. Past.* II. v. 341, I have beheld A widow vine,..Unhusbanded, neglected, all forlorne. 1620 BRINSLEY *Virgil* 43/2 The great brambles vnhusbanded (or vntrimmed, or not cut) but wilde. 1888 DOUGHTY *Arabia Deserta* II. 184, I went..to dig up off-sets of unhusbanded young palms.

**2.** Not provided with a husband.

[1775 ASH.] 1797 SOUTHEY *Eng. Ecl., Hannah* 19 She bore unhusbanded a mother's pains. 1879 MEREDITH *Egoist* xxxii, He considered himself to have been too lenient to the wine of an unhusbanded hostess.

†**Unhu·sbanding,** *vbl. sb. Obs.*-1 [UN-1 13.] Lack of husbandry. *c* 1440 *Pallad. on Husb.* I. 284 Vnhusbondynge vndoth fertilite. **Unhu·sbandly,** *adv.* (UN-1 11.) 1607 NORDEN *Surv. Dial.* v. 239, I see the hedges lye very vnhusbandly: a true note of few good husbands. **Unhu·shed,** *ppl. a.* (UN-1 8.) 1813 BYRON *Corsair* I. xiv, Still must each action to my bosom suit, My heart unhush'd, although my lips were mute!

**Unhu·sk,** *v.* [UN-2 5.]

**1.** *trans.* To divest of husk or shell; †to clean (a fish) of spines.

1598 FLORIO, *Diliscare*, to vnhuske or clense fish from bones. 1602 DOLMAN *La Primaud. Fr. Acad.* (1618) III. 812 It must bee beaten in a morter, to vnhuske it. 1665–6 *Phil. Trans.* I. 202, I have sown a little French Barley and Rice seed and am thinking on a way of un-husking them. *a* 1693 *Urquhart's Rabelais* III. xviii. 145 The Bean is not seen till..it be unhuskt. 1808–14 A. WILSON in *Poems & Lit. Prose* (1876) I. 288 Unhusking the seed from the burr in a twinkling. 1884 R. WALKER *Five Threes* 79 The nuts ..are then split open with an axe (not unhusked).

**2.** *fig.* To strip of a covering or disguise; to lay open, expose.

1596 NASHE *Saffron-Walden* S iv, I would we might know her, and see her vnhu[s]kt and naked once. 1607 TOURNEUR *Rev. Trag.* I. i, He began By policy to open and unhusk me About the time and common rumour. 1610 HEALEY *St. Aug. Citie of God* 390 All the good wee doe, comes from God, by whose pardon wee are unhusked of the old man, sinne. 1892 *Sat. Rev.* 17 Dec. 719/1 The 'Comic Spirit' may puzzle him...You have got but to unhusk and unshell it, and there it is.

Hence **Unhu·sking** *vbl. sb.*

1706 PHILLIPS (ed. Kersey), *Decortication*,..the peeling, or unhusking of Roots, Seeds, Fruits, &c. 1756 T. BIRCH *Hist. Royal Soc.* II. 78 The way used by them for the unhusking of rice.

**Unhu·sked,** *ppl. a.*1 [UN-1 8.] Not divested of the husk.

1769 E. BANCROFT *Guiana* 61 Resembling unhusked coffee-berries. 1787 JEFFERSON *Writ.* (1859) II. 196 To furnish you with some of the Piedmont rice, unhusked. 1859 R. F. BURTON in *Jrnl. Geog. Soc.* XXIX. 365 Upon journeys the African boils his holcus unhusked in an earthen basin. 1888 J. Q. BITTINGER *Hist. Haverhill* (N.H.) 360 The unhusked corn was piled in a heap,..and the huskers..sat around the fire on the floor.

**Unhu·sked,** *ppl. a.*2 [f. UNHUSK *v.*] Stripped of, taken out of, the husk.

1597 BP. HALL *Sat.* III. i, Could no vnhusked Akorne leaue the tree, But there was chalenge made whose it might bee. 1661 LOVELL *Hist. Anim. & Min.* 440 The diet of the sick ..: sparing, as unhusked barley, hydromel. 1708 OCKLEY *Saracens* I. 250 That sort of Provision..is either Barley, Rice, or Wheat, sodden and unhusk'd.

**Unhygie·nic,** *a.* (UN-1 7.) 1883 *Jrnl. Educ.* XVIII. 83 Unhygienic conditions in or about the building. 1897 *Allbutt's Syst. Med.* II. 315 When the heat is intense,.. the surroundings unhygienic. **Unhygie·nically,** *adv.* (UN-1 11.) 1861 J. H. BENNET *Winter Medit.* I. viii. (1875) 209 A densely populated city,..badly drained, and unhygienically built. 1897 *Daily News* 17 Sept. 6/7 Skirts will continue..dangerously and unhygienically to trail upon the ground. **Unhy·mned,** *ppl. a.* (UN-1 8.) 1851 MEREDITH *Poems, Pastorals* vii, All the flowers are falling! Falling unhymned.

**Unhynde,** var. UNHEND *a. Obs.*

**Unhypochondri·acous,** *a.* (UN-1 7.) 1683 E. HOOKER *Pref. Pordage's Mystic Div.* 13 All the name I desire is an honest good Fellow;..Unhypochondriacous, or toucht with the yellow. **Unhypocri·tical,** *a.* (UN-1 7.) 1862 CARLYLE *Fredk. Gt.* XI. iii. III. 61 My shrill Princess,..of a highly unhypocritical nature. **Unhypo·thecated,** *ppl. a.* (UN-1 8.) 1802 *Guineas an Incumbrance* 73 The unhypothecated part of the income tax. 1897 *Westm. Gaz.* 2 Oct. 6/3 The unhypothecated portion of the revenue. **Unhyste·rical,** *a.* (UN-1 7.) 1886 GURNEY, etc. *Phantasms of Living* II. 323 Accounts of..apparitions at death from educated and unhysterical witnesses.

**Uni-** (yū·ni), repr. L. *ūni-* combining form of *ūnus* one, a single, forming the first element in a number of words with the sense 'having, composed or consisting of, characterized by, etc., one (thing specified by the second element)'. The Latin prefix *ūni-* (before a vowel *ūn-*) was employed before or during the classical period in only a few terms, as *ūnicolor, ūnigena, ūnimanus, ūniversus, ūnanimus, ūnoculus* adjs.; *ūniversitās, ūnanimitās* sbs. In the post-classical and later language the prefix had a more extensive use, although the recorded instances are not very numerous; they are chiefly adjectival forms, as *ūnicalamus, ūnicaulis, ūnicornis, ūniformis, ūnigenitus, ūnijugus, ūniversālis, ūnivocus*, etc., *ūnanimis*. The earliest appearance of the element in English is naturally in words directly adopted from French or Latin, as UNANIMITY, UNICORN, UNIFORM *a.*, UNISON, UNIVERSAL *a.*, UNIVERSE, UNIVERSITY, etc. In more general use it first appears in words adapted from Latin compounds or modelled on these, as *univocate* (1432–50), *univocal* (1541), *unigenit* (*a* 1568); but it was not until the 17th c. that the prefix obtained much currency, when in addition to normal combs. as *unicolorate, unicornous, uniparous, unireme, univalve*, etc., such occasional formations as *unifoil, unifold, unipresence, unipresent* were coined on analogy with other numerical prefixes. In the 18th c. a comparatively small number of new compounds were adapted or formed, as *uniangulate, unicapsular, unigenous, unilocular, unisoil*, etc. In the 19th c. the element came to be freely employed in the formation of scientific and technical terms, especially in *Bot.* and *Zool.*, freq. after mod.L. formations as *unicapsularis, -cellularis, -foliatus, -labiatus, -lobatus, -nervatus, -nervus, -ovulatus, -sexus*, or adapted from F. terms as *unicursal, -cuspidé, -lobé, -nerve*. The second element in these compounds is thus naturally of Latin origin, but after the prefix had acquired a more extensive use it was not infrequently combined with English forms or words, and has been used occasionally in place of the Greek equivalent MONO-. (The use with English participial forms in *-ed* was not fully established until the 19th c.)

In scientific works the prefix is sometimes represented by the Arabic numeral, as *1-bracteate*, etc.

The older and more important combinations will be found in this Dict. in their alphabetical place as main words.

**1.** Forming adjectives with the general sense 'having, provided with, composed or consisting of, or characterized by one (thing specified or connoted by the second element)'. Many of these compounds are self-explanatory or are sufficiently explained by the quots., and in such cases no definition is added. **Unia·ngulate** *Bot.* **Uniarea·gerous** [-GEROUS] *Conch.*, having a single 'area'. **Uniarti·culate** *Ent.* and *Zool.*, having a single joint. **Uniauri·culate(d** *Zool.*, having a single auricle or auriculate process. **Uniba·sal, Unibra·cteate, -bra·cteolate. Unice·ntral** (see quots. and cf. *monocentric* MONO- 1). **Unicli·nal,** = MONOCLINAL *a.* (1879 Oldham *Geological Gloss.* 58). **Unico·rneal** *Zool.*, of an ocellus: having a single cornea. **Unico·state** *Bot.* and *Zool.*, having one rib. **Unicuira·ssed,** = *unipeltate*. **Unicu·spidate,** ending in one cusp or point. **Unide·ntate(d** *Zool.* and *Bot.*, having a single tooth-like serration. **Unidenti·culate** *Zool.* and *Bot.*, having but one denticulation. **Unidime·nsional,** of one dimension. **Unidire·ctional,** having or moving in one direction. **Uniequi·valent,** = UNIVALENT *a.* **U·nifaced,** of a coin (see quot.). **Unifa·cial** *Zool.* **Unifla·gellate** *Zool.*, of an infusorian: having but one flagellum. **Uniflo·rate, -flo·wered,** = UNIFLOROUS *a.* **Unifo·liate, -fo·liolate,** of leaves, etc.: consisting of one leaflet; of plants: characterized by or bearing leaves of this kind. **Uniglo·bular,** consisting of a single globular part; in quot. *absol.* **Unigu·ttulate,** marked with one drop-like spot. **Uniju·gate** *Bot.* **Unila·mellar, Unila·minar,** having one lamella, lamina, or layer. **Unili·near** *Math.*, affecting or involving but one line (see quot. 1851). **Unilo·bar, -lo·bate, -lobed. Unilo·bular** *Path.*, of cirrhosis: characterized by hypertrophy of single lobules; hypertrophic. **Unima·cular,** marked with a single spot. **Unime·dial,** coming through a single medium. **Unimo·dular** *Math.* **Unimu·ltiplex. Unimu·scular** *Zool.* **Unine·rvate, -nerved. Unio·vular, -o·vulate,** containing one ovule. **Unipe·ltate** *Zool.* (see 2). **Unira·diate(d. Uniramo·se, -ra·mous,** having or consisting of a single ramus or branch. **Unise·ptate** *Bot.* **U·nisexed,** consisting of members of one sex. **Unisoci·etary,** consisting of or characterized by one society or social order. **Unispi·culate,** having but one spicule. **Unispino·se,** having or bearing one spine. **Unisu·lcate,** having one groove or furrow. **Unitelegra·phic,** pertaining to a telegraph capable of being used by only one person at a time. **Unitenta·cular. Unite·rnary** *Cryst.* (see quot.). **Unitube·rculate. Uniungui·culate,** having one unguis or claw. **Univo·calized,** converted into a single voiced sound.

Various terms having little or no real currency have appeared in Dicts., etc., as *unicarinated, -lineated* (1840), *uniclinal* (1879), *unicarinate, -foliar* (1888), *uniforate, -foveate, -lamellate, -laminate, -loculate, -sepalous, -serrate, -serrulate, -spiral* (1891); etc.

1777 S. ROBSON *Brit. Flora* 4 *Uniangulate, having one angle, as in Stinking Sedge. 1850 W. KING *Permian Fossils* 142 Genus *Ismenia*. Diagnosis.—*Uni-areagerous...*Area*, both halves oblique to the hinge-margin, and to each other. 1819 SAMOUELLE *Entomol. Compend.* 99 Legs bifid, the last joint of the four anterior pairs..*uniarticulate. 1856 W. CLARK *Van der Hoeven's Zool.* I. 300 Tarsi uniarticulate, with single arcuate claw. 1835 KIRBY *Hab. & Inst. Anim.* II. xxii. 416 The *Cæcilia*, or blind serpent, too, is almost *uniauriculate. 1859 AGASSIZ *Ess. Classification* 338 Gasteropoda (Uniauriculate animals). Membranous heart with one auricle. 1839 *Penny Cycl.* XIV. 335/2 M. de Blainville divides the genus into three sections..; 2, consisting of *uniauriculated species (*Malleus normalis*). 1890 *Amer. Naturalist* May 406 *Unibasal pectoral and ventral fins. 1870 HOOKER *Stud. Flora* 387 Bog Asphodel,..pedicel *1-bracteate. *Ibid.*, Eriocauloneæ...Flowers minute., in involucrate heads, *1-bracteolate. 1864 SPENCER *Biol.* I. § 50. 137 Central development may be distinguished into *unicentral and *multicentral*, according as the product of the original germ develops symmetrically round one centre, or..in subordination to many centres. 1875 DOWDEN *Shakespere* 61 Assured that the organism is living, he fearlessly lets it develope itself in its proper mode, unicentral (as Macbeth) or multicentral (as King Lear). 1902 *Brit. Med. Jrnl.* No. 2154. 908 Cancers either started from one centre (unicentral or monocentral) or from many centres (multicentral or plurocentral). 1884 SEDGWICK & HEATHCOTE tr. *Claus' Zool.* 538 The*unicorneal ocelli are principally present in larval life. 1849 BALFOUR *Man. Bot.* 72 Reticulated Venation. 1. *Unicostate...A single rib or costa in the middle (midrib). 1852 DANA *Crust.* I. 335 Hand..faintly uni-costate towards lower part. 1842 *Penny Cycl.* XXIII. 82/1 *Unicuirassed Stomapods. 1883 FLOWER in *Encycl. Brit.* XV. 403/2 The *unicuspidate upper and lower front incisors. 1819 SAMOUELLE *Entomol. Compend.* 222 Antennæ with their internal base *unidentate. 1833 HOOKER in *Smith's Eng. Flora* V. I. 124 The lower [lobes of the leaves] ..frequently unidentate. 1856 W. CLARK *Van der Hoeven's Zool.* I. 357 Mandibles small, narrow, unidentate or edentulous. 1822 J. PARKINSON *Outl. Oryctol.* 201 *Ancilla olivula*: *unidentated at the base. 1828 STARK *Elem. Nat. Hist.* II. 266 Mandibles small, depressed, pointed and entire, or unidentated in the internal side. 1887 *Trans. Royal Soc. Edin.* XXXII. 637 Radula, two rows of teeth. 1 and 2, lateral teeth; 3, median tridenticulate; 5 and 4, central *unidenticulate. 1883 *C. S. Peirce's Studies in Logic* 156 Analogous reasoning would obviously apply to any portion of an *unidimensional continuum. 1883 *Knowledge* 13 July 25/1 Intermittent, *unidirectional currents in the brushes. 1894 *Athenæum* 9 June 745/3 Note on the Possibility of obtaining a Unidirectional Current to Earth from the Mains of an Alternating Current System. 1867 *Chambers' Encycl.* IX. 537/1 Monad or *Uniequivalent Elements (or Monads), one atom of which in combination is equivalent to..one atom of hydrogen. 1877 JEWITT *Half-hrs. among Eng. Antiq.* 139 Many of the early coins are *unifaced, i.e. one side is plain, while the other bears the device. 1846 Dana *Zooph.* iv. (1848) 65 A species, which usually has polyps only on one surface,—*unifacial. 1881 Carpenter *Microscope* (ed. 6) xi. § 419 Their simple *uniflagellate Monad (*Monas Dallingeri*). 1800 Mayne *Expos. Lex.* 1310 *Uniflorus*, Bot., having or bearing one flower: *uniflorate. 1845–50 Mrs. Lincoln *Lect. Bot.* App. 27 Pl. vii, Scape naked, *uni-flowered. Flower drooping, spathaceous. 1849 Craig s.v., *Unifoliate. 1881 *Jrnl. Linn. Soc.* XVIII. 291 These apparently unifoliate stems are long petioles. 1866 *Treas. Bot.* 1191/2 *Unifoliate*, **Unifoliolate*, when a compound leaf consists of one leaflet only; as in the orange-tree. 1872 Oliver *Elem. Bot.* ii. 130 Common Barberry,..with fascicled unifoliolate leaves. 1875 Bennett & Dyer tr. *Sachs' Bot.* 823 As in Duchesne's unifoliolate Strawberry. 1891 *Geol. Jrnl.* XLVII. 6 The structure of the zoœcia and of the dorsal surface is the same as in those with shorter nodes, so that we seem to have a series from the *uniglobular. 1887 W. Phillips *Brit. Discomycetes* 13 Sporidia elliptic, obtuse, *uniguttulate. 1849 Balfour *Man. Bot.* 79 When a pinnate leaf has one pair of leaflets, it is **unijugate*. 1861 Bentley *Man. Bot.* 168 The leaflets..are arranged along the sides of the rachis or common petiole in pairs, and according to their number, the leaf is said to be unijugate or one-paired,..bijugate, etc. 1875 Bennett & Dyer tr. *Sachs' Bot.* 315 A vein..is formed from the base towards the apex, dividing the *unilamellar lamina into right and left halves. 1876 Van Duyn tr. *Wagner's Gen. Pathol.* 466 In epithelial regeneration with *unilaminar epithelium. 1851 Sylvester in *Lond.* etc. *Phil. Mag.* Feb. 128 Accordingly this may be termed *unilinear-intersection contact, or more briefly, unilinear contact. 1870 Rolleston *Anim. Life* 29 Both the liver and the pulmonary organs [of the common ringed snake] are *unilobar, the left lung being merely represented by a rudimentary structure. 1839–47 *Todd's Cycl. Anat.* III. 310/1 In the Potoroo the left lung is *unilobate. 1851 G. F. Richardson *Geol.* 286 In the strata anterior to the lias, almost all the fishes had heterocercal or *unilobed tails. 1897 *Allbutt's Syst. Med.* IV. 170 In a less common variety [of cirrhosis of the liver] a finer network of new fibrous tissue tends to surround individual lobules (*unilobular). 1859 *Todd's Cycl. Anat.* V. [134]/1 The germinal vesicle is *unimacular in general in the small-yolked ova. 1802–12 Bentham *Ration. Judic. Evid.* (1827) III. 438 Constitutive of so many modifications or species of unoriginal evidence, we have *unimedial, bimedial, trimedial and so forth: in a word, multimedial evidence. 1866 Brande & Cox *Dict. Sci.*, etc. II. 378/1 The determinant formed from the coefficients.. is called the modulus of transformation, and when D is equal to unity the transformations are said to be **unimodular*. 1816 T. L. Peacock *Headlong Hall* ix, These thousand images, indeed, were but one; and yet the one was a thousand, a sort of *uni-multiplex phantasma. 1835 Kirby *Hab. & Inst. Anim.* I. viii. 237 The second [order of molluscans] is *Unimuscular, having only one such [attaching] muscle with one impression. 1875 Blake *Zool.* 241 If there be but one muscular impression on a valve, then it belongs to monomyary or unimuscular bivalve. 1866 *Treas. Bot.* 1191/2 **Uninervate*,..one-ribbed. 1891 *Nature* XLIII. 454/1 The linear, *uninerved leaves characteristic of the..genus *Asterophyllites*. 1904 *Brit. Med. Jrnl.* 17 Dec. 1644 A chapter is devoted to this subject [i.e. polysomatous terata] under the subheadings of *uniovular twins. 1857 A. Gray *First Less. Bot.* (1866) 235 **Uniovulate*, having only one ovule. 1845 *Encycl. Metrop.* XXV. 2 This genus [Squilla] belongs to the *Unipeltate family of the Stomapodous order. 1887 Sollas in *Encycl. Brit.* XXII. 416/2 Monaxon *Uniradiate Type (stylus).—By the suppression of one of the rays of an oxea, an acuate spicule or stylus results. 1828–32 Webster (citing *Encyc.*), **Uniradiated*, having one ray. 1888 Rolleston & Jackson *Anim. Life* 532 The first antenna is primitively *uniramose. 1890 *Microsc. Sci.* XXX. 109 Six pairs of (thoracic) appendages.., of which the first are long, slender, and uniramose. 1877 Huxley *Anat. Inv. Anim.* vi. 283 Entirely destitute of appendages, except a shorter anterior, *uniramous..pair of oar-like organs. 1866 *Treas. Bot.* 1192/1 **Uniseptate*, having but one septum or partition. 1875 Cooke *Fungi* 40 In other..species they [i.e. spores] are uniseptate. 1856 *Putnam's Mag.* Oct. 390/2 Besides, in England a bar-maid was highly respectable. How precious must be in this *uni-sexed fair! [= California]. 1835 L. Oliphant *Sympneumata* 286 The wise and sanguine..infer, both from the suffering and the capacities of present human nature, a future of new order in a *uni-societary world. 1900 *Proc. Zool. Soc.* 20 Feb. 138 Skeleton forming a rather regular reticulum of *unispiculate fibres. 1828 Stark *Elem. Nat. Hist.* II. 168 The Shrimp. Thorax behind, and on each side of the rostrum *unispinose. 1852 Dana *Crust.* I. 414 Emargination uni-spinose. 1819 Samouelle *Entomol. Compend.* 181 Thorax with a gibbous protuberance, *unisulcate above. 1853 Ure *Dict. Arts* I. 626 According to this improved plan of working, the wire of communication.. may be considered as a public word road, or an omnitelegraphic way; whereas, in contradistinction, the conductor, as heretofore used, may be considered a private word road, or a *unitelegraphic way. 1889 *Amer. Nat.* XXIII. 597 Microcampana is not the only *unitentacular Medusa found in the prolific waters of our Pacific coast. 1816 R. Jameson *Char. Min.* (ed. 2) 212 A crystal is named..*Uniternary, when there is one by one row, the other by three rows. 1852 Dana *Crust.* I. 122 Post-medial region with a small tubercle; intestinal *uni-tuberculate. 1856 W. Clark *Van der Hoeven's Zool.* I. 303 *Gyropus Nitzsch*.—Tarsi *uniunguiculate. 1876 Douse *Grimm's Law* App. 206 Our own familiarity with *univocalized consonants.

**b.** Prefixed to a sb. and forming a compound used attrib., as *uni-direction, -face, -rhyme, -soil.*

1778 [W. H. Marshall] *Minutes Agric., Digest* 18 A Unisoil Farm requires fewer Implements than a Polysoil Farm. 1859 E. Williams in *Cambrian Jrnl.* March 12 Four-lined unirhyme stanzas, of five or six syllables in a line. 1888 Bottone *Electr. Instr. Making* (ed. 2) 103 The uni-direction current machine. 1897 W. C. Hazlitt *Suppl. Coinage Europ. Continent* 17 A silver uniface bracteate of Otho I. 1900 *Engineering Mag.* XIX. 740 In some instances the engines are only uni-direction.

**2.** Forming sbs., as **Unia·xifer.** **U·nicell** *Bot.*, a unicellular plant (Jackson *Gloss. Bot. Terms*, 1900). **Unipe·ltate** (see quot.). **Unisty·list** [L. *stylus*] (see quot.). † **U·nitrine** [L. *trīn-us*], a unity in trinity. *Obs.* **Unitri·nity,** unity in trinity. **U·nitrope** (see quot.).

1869 *Student* II. 12 They [*sc.* polymerous leaves] will be *uniaxifers, biaxifers, etc.; multiaxifers, according as their meriphylls [= the space between two nodes of a leaf] are arranged along a single axis, or an axis ramified two, three, or more times. 1842 Brande *Dict. Sci.*, etc. 1275 *Unipeltates, [Cuvier's] *Unipeltata*, the name of a family of Stomapodous Crustaceans, comprehending those in which the carapace is composed of a single shield-like plate. *a* 1849 Poe *Marginalia* cxlii, He is as thorough a *unistylist as Cardinal Chigi, who boasted that he wrote with the same pen for half a century. 1605 Timme *Quersit.* ii. ii. 108 It hath pleased the omnipotent Creator to manifest & showe himselfe a *Unitrine or Triune. 1775 Adair *Amer. Ind.* 127 Her belief of the *uni-trinity, and tri-unity of the deity. 1910 A. B. Basset *Treat. Geom. Surfaces* 25 The reciprocal polar of a unode is called a *unitrope.

† **Uniable,** *a.* *Obs.*[—1] (Meaning obscure.)

*a* 1450 *Ten Comm. of Love* (MS. Fairfax 16, fol. 185 b), Consider that my conning is disable To write to you the figure vniable.

† **U·nial,** *a.* *Obs.*[—1] [f. Uni- + -al. Cf. OF. *uniel, unial* in Godef. *Compl.*] United into one.

1613 Sherley *Trav. Persia* 4 Those Countries, limitting vpon the King of Spaines vniall parts.

**Uniat, Uniate** (yū·niæt, -ėt). [ad. Russ. униятъ *uniyat*, f. унiя *uniya* union (spec. the united Greek and Roman Catholic Churches), f. L. *ūni-, ūnus* one.] A Russian, Polish, or other member of that part of the Greek Church which, while retaining its own liturgy, acknowledges the supremacy of the Pope and is in communion with the Roman Catholic Church; a United Greek.

1833 R. Pinkerton *Russia* 82 The inroads of the Uniats among the members of the Greek Church. 1863 Edwards *Polish Captivity* II. 61 As a Uniate he acknowledges the authority of the Pope. 1883 Beresf. Hope *Worship & Order* 127 The restoration of the uniates to Eastern communion.

**b.** *attrib.* or as *adj.* Of, adhering or pertaining to, or denominating the United Greek Church.

1855 *Pict. Chr. Heroism* 37 The Greek-uniat curé of Jansff. 1885 *Ch. Quarterly Rev.* Apr. 162 In Russia, the once powerful Uniat Church has declined. 1905 *Times* 22 Sept. 7 The much persecuted Uniate or Greek Catholic creed.

**Uniaxal** (yūni,æ·ksăl), *a.* [f. Uni- 1 + Axal *a.*] = Uniaxial *a.* Hence **Unia·xally** *adv.*

1829 *Nat. Philos., Polaris. Light* vii. 24 (L. U. K.), The whole system of rings will appear to be like the uniaxal system. 1866 B. Stewart *Heat* § 43 Crystals that are optically uniaxal. 1881 Glazebrook in *Phil. Trans.* CLXXIII. 595 The Surface of a Uniaxal Crystal.

**Uniaxial** (yūni,æ·ksiăl), *a.* [f. Uni- 1 + Axial *a.*]

**1.** *Optics* and *Crystall.* Having one optical axis.

1827–8 Herschel in *Encycl. Metrop.* (1845) IV. 520 When the two axes coalesce, or the crystal becomes uniaxial, the lemniscates become circles. *a* 1853 Pereira *Polarized Light* (1854) 176 The crystal possesses the singular property of being uniaxial for violet light and biaxial for red. 1888 Rutley *Rock-Forming Min.* 37 Uniaxial crystals.

**2.** *Bot.* and *Zool.* = Monaxial *a.*

1879 Rossiter *Dict. Sci.*, *Uniaxial development*: in all vertebrate animals, some molluscs and annulosa; in some of exogens, endogens, algæ, and fungi.

**Uniber,** error or mispr. for Umber *sb.*[1] 4.

1824 Meyrick *Ant. Armour* II. 99 The war helmet..shews the intermediate form of the uniber. 1844 James *Agincourt* I. 77 Shields, and pallets and unibers.

† **Unible,** *a.* *Obs. rare.* [ad. med.L. *ūnibilis* (Dief.), f. L. *ūnīre* to Unite. So Sp. and Pr. *unible*, It. *unibile*.] Capable of being united; unitable.

1559 Udall tr. *Geminus' Anat.* 3/1 A father, by whose grace we haue receaued a nature..vnible to the glorified bodie of his sonne Christ. 1683 Baxter *Dying Thoughts* 22 Either Souls are partible substances or not. If not partible, how are they unible?

**Unic,** obs. f. Unique *a.* and *sb.*

† **Unical,** *a.* *Obs. rare.* [f. L. *ūnic-us* Unique *a.* + -al.] Forming or consisting of one only; alone of its kind, unique.

1598 Sylvester *Du Bartas* ii. i. ii. *Impost.* 651 A body.. differing little from th' One unicall,..the onely-beeing Beeing. 1650 Charleton *Paradoxes* Prol. 26 The form or Essence of Verity, is unicall, single, and devoid of all Alterity.

Hence † **Unically** *adv.*, entirely, undividedly.

1689 G. Harvey *Curing Dis. by Expect.* v. 33 If..your confidence is so unically fixed on the Virtues of Steel.

**Unica·meral,** *a.* [f. Uni- 1 + Cameral *a.*] Having, consisting of, or characterized by one legislative chamber.

1853 F. Lieber *Civil Liberty & Self-Govt.* xxiv. 242 As a feature of Gallican liberty, must be mentioned here the unicameral system. 1890 *Century Mag.* Feb. 506/1 Georgia, Pennsylvania and New Hampshire abandoned the unicameral system after a short trial of it. 1894 Morley in *Daily News* 28 June 7/4 There is very little chance of our being ..what is called unicameral.

Hence **Unica·meralist,** an advocate of a unicameral system. Also **Unica·merist.**

1888 Earl of Pembroke in *Univ. Rev.* I. 101 The ideal of the unicamerists seems to me to be quite out of the region of practical politics. 1893 *Westm. Gaz.* 14 Feb. 1/3 Of course, I, as a Democrat, do not care for the two Chambers. I am a unicameralist.

**Unica·psular,** *a.* *Bot.* [ad. mod.L. *ūnicapsulār-is* (whence F. *unicapsulaire*): see Uni- and Capsular *a.*] Of a pericarp: Having a single capsule. Of a plant: Characterized by a pericarp of this kind.

Also *Zool.* = Monocyttarian *a.* (*Cent. Dict.* 1891).

1720 P. Blair *Bot. Ess.* ii. 52 Therefore Papaver is only an Unicapsular Plant. 1760 Lee *Botany* i. xv. 38 In respect to external Division, the Pericarpium is either..Unicapsular, ..as in Lychnis [etc.]. 1793 Martyn *Lang. Bot.* s.v., A Unicapsular pericarp.

**U·nicelled,** *a.* [Uni- 1.] Unicellular. 1877 Le Conte *Elem. Geol.* (1879) 154 The beautiful siliceous shells of diatoms (uni-celled plants).

**Unicellular** (yūni,se·liŭlăı), *a.* (and *sb.*). *Biol.* [ad. mod.L. *ūnicellulār-is* (whence also F. *unicellulaire*): see Uni- and Cellular *a.*]

**1.** Composed or consisting of, having, a single cell; said esp. of the organisms belonging to the primary divisions of the animal and vegetable kingdoms.

Also in recent use as *sb.*

1858 Carpenter *Veg. Phys.* § 35 The minute unicellular plants, known by the name of Diatomaceæ. 1875 Darwin *Insectiv. Pl.* xiv. 329 All the leaves contained unicellular and other Algæ. 1892 Mivart *Ess. & Crit.* II. 437 The distinction between unicellular and multicellular animals.

**2.** Characterized by the formation or presence of a single cell or cells.

1863 Dana *Man. Geol.* 747 Plants in passing from the unicellular state by growth lose in power. 1892 J. Tait *Mind in Matter* (ed. 3) 58 In the animal world colonies are the next approach of unicellular to multicellular organisation.

**Unicellula·rity.** [a. F. *unicellularité*, or f. prec. + -ity.] Unicellular condition or formation.

1896 G. W. Field tr. *Hertwig's Zool.* 21 The unicellularity of the lowest animals.

**Unicist** (yū·nisist). [f. L. *ūnic-us* one + -ist.]

**1.** A believer in the unicity of the Godhead.

1807 Coleridge in *Lit. Rem.* (1839) IV. 291 As understood by the modern Unicists. 1832 — *Table-t.* 4 Apr., The schoolmen would perhaps have called you Unicists: but your proper name is Psilanthropists.

**2.** *Med.* An advocate or adherent of the theory of unicity. Also *attrib.*

1890 Billings *Nat. Med. Dict.* II. 720. 1901 J. Ewing in *Jrnl. Exper. Med.* V. 483 Inclined to accept the unicist theory.

**Unicity** (yūni·siti). [ad. med.L. **ūnicitās* (whence F. *unicité*, It. *unicità*, Sp. *unicidad*), or f. L. *ūnic-us* one, unique: see -ity.]

**1.** The fact of being or consisting of one in number or kind; oneness.

1691 J. Howe *Wks.* (1834) 147/2 The most unquestionable unity or unicity of the Godhead. 1694 R. Burthogge *Reason & Nat. Spirits* 166 Composition is Unity, but simplicity is Unicity. 1817 Coleridge '*Blessed are ye that sow*' 55 For Unity or Unition, and indistinguishable Unicity or Oneness, are incompatible terms. 1849 Alford *Grk. Testament* I. 608 The καινότης of this commandment consists in its simplicity and (so to speak) unicity. 1880 C. I. Black *Proselytes of Ishmael* 301 What our so-called Unitarians teach is..the Unicity of the Godhead.

**b.** *Med.* The theory that syphilis is caused by only one kind of venereal virus.

1861 Bumstead *Ven. Dis.* 349 Some explanation..of what was called by its discoverer [Ricord] the 'unicity' of syphilis.

**2.** The fact or quality of being unique; unique nature or character.

1859 *Todd's Cycl. Anat.* V. 106/1 Bernard then goes on to prove, by the method of elimination, the unicity and propriety of this property of the pancreatic secretion. 1887 Saintsbury *Hist. Elizab. Lit.* 91 Which..gives The Faerie Queene its unique unicity, if such a conceit may be pardoned.

**Unick,** obs. f. Unique *a.*

**U·nicode.** [Uni- 2.] A telegraphic code in which one word or set of letters represents a sentence or phrase; a telegram or message in this.

1886 '*Unicode*': *The Universal Telegraphic Phrase-Book* Pref. p. iii, The 'Unicode' aims at..a low price. *Ibid.* p. v, The 'Unicode' word 'Obumbro'. 1897 *Westm. Gaz.* 20 Jan. 6/3 [He] gave evidence as to sending a unicode to both [persons]. 1899 *Daily News* 23 Dec. 5/3 The dispatch of messages in 'Unicode'.

**Unico·lor,** *a.* [L.; cf. F. *unicolore.*] Of a single uniform colour. Chiefly *Nat. Hist.*

1781 Pennant *Hist. Quadrup.* II. 482 Unicolor Shrew of an uniform dusky cinereous color. 1811 Shaw *Gen. Zool.* VIII. 538 Unicolor Lory, *Psittacus unicolor*.

**Unico·lorate,** *a.* *rare.* [f. L. *ūnicolor* + -ate [2].] Unicoloured, unicolorous.

1657 Tomlinson *Renou's Disp.* 302 Its flowers like Pease-bloom, but lesser, unicolorate and purpureous. 1826 Kirby & Sp. *Entomol.* IV. xlvi. 291 Unicolorate (*Unicolor*), when a surface is of one colour. 1837 Richardson *Fauna Bor.-Amer.* IV. 14 Cymindis Unicolor. Unicolorate Cymindis.

**Unicolorous** (yūnikɒ·lərəs), *a.* Also 7, 9 unicolourous. [f. L. *ūnicolor* + -ous.] Having only one colour; uniform in colour. Chiefly *Ent.*

1657 Tomlinson *Renou's Disp.* 197 Two unicolourous juices mixed together. 1843 Humphreys *Brit. Moths* II. 66 The wings rounded, destitute of markings, and unicolorous. 1894 *Naturalist* 226 All unicolorous black, instead of having the typical red elytra.

**Unico·lour,** *a.* [Cf. Unicolor.] = prec.

1860 *Proc. Zool. Soc.* 51 The fur of all parts of the body.. is unicolour, and of a lightish cinnamon-brown.

**Unico·loured,** *a.* [Uni- 1.] Unicolorous.

1811 Pinkerton *Petral.* II. 121 Others are spotted in infinite variety; and others, though rarely, are unicoloured. 1821 Meyrick & C. H. Smith *Costume Orig. Inhab.* 24 The uni-coloured robe of sky-blue. 1890 *Sat. Rev.* 5 Apr. 413/2 The uni-coloured thread that runs throughout my motley history.

**Unicorn** (yū·nikǭrn). Forms: 3–7 uni-, 4–6 uny-, 4–7 vni-, vnycorne (6 inny-, ine-; *Sc.* 5 iny-, owni-, 6 wnicorne); 4–5 vny-, 4–6 vni-, 5 unycorn, 5– unicorn (5–6 vnykorn, 6 vnykhorn). [a. AF., OF. (mod.F.) *unicorne* (= Pg. *unicorne*, Pg. and Sp. *unicornio*, It. *unicorno*), or directly ad. their source L. *ūnicorn-*, *ūnicornis* having one horn (also in late Lat. as sb.), f. *ūn-us* UNI- + *cōrnu* horn. Cf. late L. *ūnicornuus*, med.L. *unicornus*, *-(i)um* sbs., from the same source.

The word was corrupted in OF. to *licorne* (the usual form in mod.F.), *lincorne*, etc., It. *liocorno*, Pg. *(a)licorne*, etc.]

**I. 1.** A fabulous and legendary animal usually regarded as having the body of a horse with a single horn projecting from its forehead (cf. 2 *note*); the monoceros of the ancients.

The unicorn has at various times been identified or confused with the rhinoceros, with various species of antelope, or with other animals having a horn (or horns) or horn-like projection from the head. According to Pliny (*Nat. Hist.* VIII. xxi. § 31) it had a body resembling that of a horse, the head of a deer, the feet of an elephant, and the tail of a lion, with one black horn projecting 'two cubits' from the middle of the forehead.

The horn of this animal was reputed to possess medicinal or magical properties, esp. as an antidote to or preventive of poison: see UNICORN'S HORN.

*a* **1225** *Ancr. R.* 120 Mon wroð is wulf, oðer leun, oðer unicorne. **13..** *K. Alis.* 6710 (Bodl. MS.), ȝitt þou shalt habbe sex hundreþ Rinoceros..And two hundreþ vnicornes. *c* **1315** SHOREHAM *Poems* v. 113 Of hyre barme hyt was god game, Þer-inne þe vnicorn weks tame Þat er þan was so wylde. **1387** TREVISA *Higden* (Rolls) I. 159 Þere beeþ also ..vnycornes [L. *rhinoceros*], camels, pardes [etc.]. **1423** JAS. I *Kingis Q.* clv, The lufare vnicorne, That voidis venym with his euoure horne. *c* **1511** *1st Eng. Bk. Amer.* (Arb.) p. xxxiii/2 These vnicornes slee many Lyons, and the Lyon sleeth the vnicorne with subtylnes. **1590** SPENSER *F. Q.* II. v. 10 Like as a Lyon, whose imperiall powre A prowd rebellious Vnicorne defies. **1609** DEKKER *Gull's Horn-bk.* ii. 12 The Unicorne, whose horne is worth halfe a City. **1657** TRAPP *Comm. Job* xxxix. 9 This is the..Unicorn... A very fierce and strong creature it is; and now adayes very rare, but anciently more common. **1735** JOHNSON *Lobo's Abyssinia, Descr.* ii. 51 In the Province of Agaus, has been seen the Unicorn, that Beast so much talk'd of, and so little known. **1801** *Monthly Rev.* XXXV. 351 On the probability of the existence of an Unicorn. **1843** DE QUINCEY *Ceylon* Wks. 1859 XII. 8 The whole traditionary character of the unicorn as the antagonist..of the lion. **1895** J. G. MILLAIS *Breath fr. Veldt* 133 Any one who has seen a wild sable antelope galloping cannot fail to be struck by its resemblance to the unicorn.

**b.** Used in ME. versions of the OT. to render the Vulgate *ūnicornis* or *rhīnocerōs* (Gr. μονόκερως) as translations of Heb. ראם *rᵉ'em* (also רים *rēym*), and retained in various later versions (but translated by 'wild-ox' in the Revised Bible). See REEM.

*a* **1300** *E. E. Psalter* xxi. 22 (xxii. 21), Sauf me fra mouth of lioun es, And fra hornes of vnicornes mi mekenes. [Also versions *a* 1340–1611.] **1382** WYCLIF *Numb.* xxiii. 22 Whos strengthe is lijk to an vnycorn. [Also versions 1388–1611.] *c* **1580** SIDNEY *Psalms* XXII. xiii, Show to heare me, By aiding, when fierce Vnicornes come neere me. **1639** SIR W. MURE *Ps.* xxii, Wks. (S.T.S.) II. 89 From the hornes of vnicornes Thine eare (Lord) found I have. **1696** TATE & BRADY *Ps.* xxix. 6 They..leap, like Hinds that bounding go, Or Unicorns in youthful play.

**c.** In fig. or allusive use.

In quot. 1607 = 'a cuckold'.

**1509** BARCLAY *Shyp of Folys* 212 [Let] James of Scotlande.. haue the forwarde, haue ye no disdayne Nor indignation, for neuer kynge was borne, That of ought of warre can shewe the vnycorne. **1592** G. HARVEY *Four Lett.* 52 The only Vnicorne of the Muses. **1607** DEKKER *Northw. Hoe* IV. F j b, Fetherstone..it seemes makes her husband a vnicorne. **1826** GALT *Last of Lairds* vi. 53 Bridle the unicorn o' your impatience.

†**d.** Horn reputed to be that of the unicorn prepared as an embellishment or ornament. *Obs.*

*a* **1533** LD. BERNERS *Gold. Bk. M. Aurel.* (1559) Y ij b, It was of wood Libanus, and round about garnished with unicorne. **1599** PEELE *David & Bethsabe* H ij, Shee that in chaines of pearle and vnicorne, Leads at her traine the ancient golden world.

**2.** A figure, picture, or representation of this animal, esp. in *Her.* either as a charge or more usually as a supporter of the Royal Arms of Great Britain (or Scotland).

Usually depicted heraldically as having the head, neck, and body of a horse, the legs of a deer and the tail of a lion, with a straight and spirally twisted horn growing out of the forehead.

*c* **1400** *Emaré* 164 The fayr mayden her by-forn Was portrayed an vnykorn, Wyth hys horn so hye. **1488** *Acc. Ld. High Treas. Scot.* I. 85 A couering..browdin with thrissillis and a vnicorne. **1549** in Gage *Hengrave* (1822) 127, iij cuppes with a cover chased, with unicorns on the top. **1610** GUILLIM *Heraldry* VI. vii. 280 Supported by a Lion.. and an Vnicorne Luna, gorged with a Crowne. **1766** in Seton *Law Her. Scotland* (1863) 442 His Majesty's royal coat-of-arms supported on the right side by a unicorn with an imperial crown over the head. **1789** MRS. PIOZZI *Journ. France*, etc. II. 221 The family crest, a unicorn, made in white marble. **1813** *Gentl. Mag.* LXXXIII. 37/2 With supporters (lion and unicorn) of the Royal arms. **1875** W. MCILWRAITH *Guide Wigtownshire* 55 Here is an escutcheon bearing two unicorns and a lion rampant and the crown.

**3.** *Sc.* The specific designation of one of the pursuivants of the court of the Lyon King of Arms. See PURSUIVANT 1.

**1445** *Exchequer Rolls Scot.* V. 204 Quia Unicorn signifer regis illam terram habuit ex concessione regis. **1473–4** *Acc. Ld. High Treas. Scot.* I. 52 Item gevin to Vnicorne herald, ..to his expensis, xli. **1546** *Ibid.* IX. 33 To Petir Thomson, alias Unicorne pursevant. **1636** *Reg. Privy Council Scot.* Ser. II. VI. 605 The deceased George Wast, Unicorn pursuivant. **1662** *Ibid.* Ser. III. I. 259 Leyes..was charged by William Malcolm, Unicorn pursuivant, to compear this day. **1742** NISBET *Syst. Heraldry* II. IV. xvi. 171 As for Pursevants, they are also for most Part locally denominate, Unicorn only excepted. **1863** SETON *Law Her. Scotland* 38 As in the case of the Heralds, the Pursuivants are also six in number, and bear the names of Kintyre, Dingwall, Carrick, Bute, Ormond, and Unicorn.

**4.** A Scottish gold coin current in the 15th and 16th centuries at the value of 18 shillings Scots; so called from the figure of the unicorn stamped upon its obverse. Also *half unicorn*. Now *Hist.*

**1487** *Exchequer Rolls Scot.* IX. 549 In denariis aureis vocatis unicornys. **1500–20** DUNBAR *Poems* lxvi. 78 Vpon the heid of it is hecht Bayth unicornis, and crownis of wecht. **1538** *Aberd. Reg.* XVI. (Jam.), Ane vnicorn gud & sufficient gold. **1845** LINDSAY *Coinage Scot.* 137 The Unicorns generally weigh about fifty-eight grains,..the half Unicorns in proportion. **1887** E. BURNS *Coinage Scotl.* II. 151 The coinages of unicorns that took place under James V.

†**b.** Used *attrib.* as the designation of a weight, equivalent to about one-eighth of an ounce troy.

**1506** *Extr. Aberdeen Reg.* (1844) I. 434 Ane corss of gold, weyand half ane unce, and half ane unicorn weicht. **1560** *St. Giles Charters* (1859) p. xlvii, Foure vnce, ane half, and ane vnicorne weicht of gold.

**5.** *Astr.* A southern constellation lying between Canis Minor and Canis Major.

This constellation was noted by Hevelius in his *Prodromus Astron.* (1690) pp. 118, 294, under the name of *Monoceros*.

**1771** *Encycl. Brit.* I. 487/2 Hevelius's Constellations made out of the unformed Stars [include]..*Monocerus*, The Unicorn. **1868** LOCKYER *Guillemin's Heavens* (ed. 3) 382 The northern half of the Milky Way extends..to the Unicorn at the altitude of and near the belt of Orion.

**6.** A carriage, coach, etc., drawn by three horses, two abreast and one leader; now usually, a team of three horses so arranged. (Cf. 11 b.)

**1785** GROSE *Dict. Vulgar T.*, *Unicorn*, a coach drawn by three horses. **1800** MAR. EDGEWORTH *Belinda* xvi, She drove in her unicorn to Oakly-park. **1866** FREEMAN in *Life & Lett.* (1895) I. 342, I would put on the children's pony..in front of my two, so as to make an unicorn. **1889** *Evening News* 28 Aug 3/2 Their demands of 24*s.* for a single horse, 28*s.* for a pair, and 30*s.* for a 'unicorn'.

*transf.* **1860** R. F. BURTON *Centr. Afr.* xiii. II. 38 We crossed as usual on a 'unicorn' of negroids, the upper part of the body supported by two men, and the feet resting upon the shoulders of a third. **1887** *Cyclists' Tour. Cl. Gaz.* May 215/1 The unicorn..is made up of a[n]..ordinary bicycle front-wheel coupled to a..sociable.

**b.** Quasi-*adv.*

**1859** *Habits of Gd. Society* v. 200 You will seldom be called upon to drive tandem, unicorn, or four in hand. **1863** MISS BRADDON *Aurora Floyd* v, There were more lofty accomplishments than driving unicorn or shooting..game.

**II.** †**7.** The one-horned rhinoceros. *Obs.*

**1398** TREVISA *Barth. De P. R.* XIV. ix. (Bodl. MS.), [In] þat londe [*sc.* Ethiopia] beþ..þe rynocerota þat is þe vnicorne, a beste wiþ oon horne. *a* **1700** EVELYN *Diary* 22 Oct. 1684, I went..to see the Rhinoceros, or Unicorn, being the first that I suppose was ever brought into England.

**8.** As the name of a fish, shell, etc., having a projecting horn or horn-like process, or regarded as resembling the fabulous unicorn in some other respect. Cf. MONOCEROS 2 and 4.

A few examples other than those illustrated here are recorded in American Dicts. from 1891 onwards.

†**a.** (See quot.) *Obs.*

**1668** CHARLETON *Onomast.* 123 *Monoceros Clusii*, the little Vnicorn, or Sawfish.

**b.** The narwhal or sea-unicorn.

Named also *unicorn-fish*, *-whale*, and abbrev. UNIE.

**1694** *Marten's Voy. Spitzbergen* in *Acc. Sev. Late Voy.* II. 126 The Unicorn is but seldom seen in these parts. **1745** tr. *Egede's Descr. Greenland* 76 Among the different Kinds of Whales, some reckon the Unicorn, as they commonly call him,..but his right Name is Nar-Whale. **1823** W. SCORESBY *Jrnl.* 39 Here we saw a considerable number of 'unicorns' (narwals).

**c.** A unicorn-shell. (See 11.)

*c* **1711** PETIVER *Gazophyl.* VI. liii, Grass girdled Indian Unicorn, Cat. 263. A beautiful Shell and rarely met with.

**9.** *Zool.* A species having one horn.

**1822** J. PARKINSON *Outl. Oryctol.* 312 There appear to be three existing species of rhinoceroses:—1. That of India: a unicorn;..—2. That of the Cape: a bicorn.

**III. 10.** *attrib.* and *Comb.*, as *unicorn bone* (i.e. horn), *horse*, *-ivory*; *-crested*, *-like* adjs.

**1477** EARL RIVERS (Caxton) *Dictes* D iv, Ther is summe contre that a litil yuory or vnycorne bone is bought for a grete somme of gold. **1838** *Penny Cycl.* XII. 306/1 The ..Onager, figured..with a unicorn-like horn in the midst of its forehead. **1843** *Ibid.* XXVI. 3 Strabo..refers to Unicorn horses with the heads of deer. **1853** R. S. SURTEES *Sponge's Sp. Tour* xlix, The unicorn-crested gates, with tea-caddy looking lodges. **1856** KANE *Arct. Expl.* II. xiv. 141 The natives carried no arms but the long knife and their unicorn-ivory lances.

**11.** Special combs., chiefly in the names of animals, birds, fishes, plants, etc., which are characterized by a long projecting horn-like process or spine regarded as resembling the horn of the unicorn: **unicorn acanthurus** (see quot. and UNICORN-FISH *c*); **unicorn auk** (see quot.); **unicorn-bird**, the horned screamer, *Palamedea cornuta*; **unicorn file-fish** (see quot.); †**unicorn guard** *Fencing*, a guard in which the sword is advanced well to the front of the fencer; **unicorn hawk** (-**moth**), **hornbill** (see quots.); **unicorn-moth**, the North American moth, *Cœlodasys unicornis*; **unicorn narwhal**, = sense 8 b; **unicorn-plant** *U.S.*, a name for various North American plants, esp. *Martynia proboscidea*, the capsule of which terminates in two horn-like spines; **unicorn-root** *U.S.* (see quots.); **unicorn-shell**, a marine gasteropod having a horn-like lip projecting from the shell, now esp. one belonging to the genus *Monoceros*; **unicorn whale**, = sense 8 b.

**1803** SHAW *Gen. Zool.* IV. 374 *Unicorn Acanthurus. *Acanthurus Unicornis*. .. From the front proceeds a strong, conical, horn-shaped process. **1884** COUES *North Amer. Birds* 805 *Ceratorhina monocerata*. *Unicorn Auk. Horn-bill Auk. **1681** GREW *Musæum* I. § iv. ii. 65 The *Unicorne Bird [is]..Horned on his Forehead (with some likeness) as the Unicorne is pictur'd. **1863** BATES *Nat. Amazon* I. 277 The Curicáca..was soon joined by a unicorn bird..; whose harsh screams [etc.]. **1804** SHAW *Gen. Zool.* V. II. 399 *Unicorn File-fish. *Balistes Monoceros*... Immediately over the head..is a very strong..spine of considerable length. **1617** J. SWETNAM *Sch. Sci. Defence* 126 An other very sure and dangerous guard at the Backe-sword, called the *Vnicorne guard, or the fore-hand guard. **1711** WYLDE *Eng. Master Defence* 23 The Medium Unicorn or Center Guard, is made thus. **1832** J. RENNIE *Consp. Butterfl. & M.* 24 The *Unicorn Hawk (*Sphinx Convolvuli*, Linnæus) appears in September. **1834** T. BROWN *Butterflies & Moths* I. 96 Two fine males of the *Sphinx Convolvuli* (Unicorn Hawk-moth). **1811** SHAW *Gen. Zool.* VIII. 11 *Unicorn Hornbill. [*Buceros Monoceros*.]..The casque is prolonged in front into a kind of horn. **1891** *Cent. Dict.* s.v., Larva of *Unicorn-moth. **1813** BINGLEY *Anim. Biog.* (ed. 4) II. 1 The *Unicorn Narwal, or Sea Unicorn. **1796** MORSE *Amer. Geog.* I. 189 *Unicorn [plant] (*Aletris farinosa*). **1845–50** MRS. LINCOLN *Lect. Bot.* II. 110/1 *Helonias diœcia*, scape leafy...Unicorn plant. **1847** DARLINGTON *Amer. Weeds*, etc. (1860) 222 *M. proboscidea*..Long-beaked Martynia. Unicorn Plant. **1891** H. HERMAN *His Angel* 6 Woodbine, unicorn plant, and wild currant surged all about it. **1846** A. WOOD *Class-bk. Bot.* (1850) 559 *Helonias dioica*, Ph. (*Veratrum luteum*. Linn.) *Unicorn Root. **1847** WEBSTER, *Unicorn-root*, a popular name of two plants, viz. *Chamælirium Carolinianum* [= *Helonias dioica*], to which this name was first applied, and *Aletris farinosa*..; both used in medicine. **1891** *Cent. Dict.*, *Unicorn-root*, the blazing star, *Aletris farinosa*. *c* **1711** PETIVER *Gazophyl.* VI. lv, A *Unicorn Shell with Bugle Twirls. *Ibid.* VIII. lxxv, Small Unicorn-shell, with rugged Twirls and Waves between. **1888** *Cassell's Encycl. Dict.*, *Monoceros*,..Unicorn-shell; a genus of prosobranchiate gasteropods..peculiar to the west coast of America. **1668** CHARLETON *Onomast.* 168 *Balæna Monoceros*, *Vnicornu Marinum*, .. the *Vnicorn Whale. **1694** *Acc. Sev. Late Voy.* p. xix, The Monoceros or Unicorn Whale. **1858** BAIRD *Cycl. Nat. Sci.* 199/1 The.. unicorn whale, *Monodon Monoceros*, has no teeth in the lower jaw.

**b.** Attrib. in sense 6, as *unicorn carman*, *fashion*, *omnibus* (attrib.), *team*.

**1856** MORTON *Cycl. Agric.* II. 726 A unicorn team is two abreast and one in front. **1877** 'C. BEDE' *Figaro at Hastings* 47 Some [wagonettes] with four horses, some with three (unicorn fashion). **1884** 'R. BOLDREWOOD' *Melb. Mem.* i. 14 Frank Liardet is driving his unicorn omnibus team from the lonely beach. **1898** *Westm. Gaz.* 6 Sept. 1/3 A 'unicorn carman'..means 'one who drives three horses'.

†**12.** Passing into *adj.* Made a unicorn or cuckold (cf. sense 1 c above). *Obs.*[−1]

**1603** DEKKER *Wonderfull Yeare* E 4 The vnicorne cobler being ouer head and eares in sleepe.

**Unicorn-fish.** [Cf. UNICORN 8 b.] The narwhal or sea-unicorn, *Monodon monoceros*.

**1688** R. HOLME *Armory* IV. vii. (Roxb.) 324/1 For his Supporters he beareth a vnicorne fish, Argent, the fish or taile part, Azure: Horne, Hoofes, and finns, Or. **1752** J. HILL *Hist. Anim.* 314 Monodon. The Unicorn-fish, or Narwal. **1773** *Gentl. Mag.* XLIII. 220 The Jackulator Fish, the Unicorn Fish, the Trumpet Fish. **1812** J. WALKER *Ess. Nat. Hist.* 527 *Monodon Monoceros*. Linn...Scot. Unicorn Fish. **1860** WRAXALL *Life in Sea* i. 12 The Narwhal, or Unicorn-fish, attains a length of twenty or twenty-five feet.

**b.** (See quots.)

**1876** GOODE *Fishes of Bermudas* 17 The Bahama Unicorn-Fish is *Alutera scripta*. **1900** *Nature* 21 June 182/2 An example of the rare unicorn-fish (*Lophotes cepedianus*) from the Cape of Good Hope.

**c.** One or other of various fishes belonging to the genus *Acanthurus*. (Webster, 1911.)

**Unico·rnic,** *a. rare.* [f. prec. + -IC.] Resembling, having the form of, a unicorn.

**1881** R. BROWN *Unicorn* 14 A unicornic animal frequently appears in archaic art. **1885** — in *Academy* 28 Nov. 363/2 The familiar conventional unicornic representation.

**Unico·rnous,** *a. rare.* [f. L. *ūnicorn-is* (see UNICORN) + -OUS.] Having but one horn.

**1646** SIR T. BROWNE *Pseud. Ep.* V. xix. 261 The Rhinoceros, the Indian Asse, and the Unicornous Beetles. [Hence in Blount, Phillips, Bailey, etc.]

**Unicorn's horn.** Also † **unicorn horn.** [See UNICORN 1.]

**1.** A horn regarded as or alleged to be obtained from the legendary unicorn, but in reality that of the rhinoceros, narwhal, or other animal, freq. mounted or made into a drinking cup and employed as a preventive of or charm against poison.

*a.* **1451** *Lincoln Diocese Doc.* (1914) 51 A ryng of vnicorn horne. **1555** *Reg. Gild Co. Chr. York* (1872) 207, I give to Sir Thomas Chaloner, knyghte, my unicorn horne. *c* **1650** *Invent. Goods Chas. I* in Pegge *Curialia* (1806) IV. 122 An unicorn horn.

*β.* **1549** THOMAS *Hist. Italie* 80 b, Two fayre vnicornes hornes. 1564 BULLEYN *Dial. agst. Pest.* 74 A pece of a Unicornes horne, good against poison. 1603 LODGE *Treat. Plague* Wks. (Hunter. Cl.) IV. 61 The horne of that beast which..the simple sorte [call] vnicornes horne. 1687 *Lond. Gaz.* No. 2227/4 There will be exposed to Sale..considerable quantities of Drugs, Colours, and Unicorns Horns. 1728 CHAMBERS *Cycl.* s.v., What ordinarily passes among us for Unicorn's Horn,..we are assured by Pereyra..to be the Tooth of a large Fish of the Whale Kind. 1838 PRESCOTT *Ferd. & Is.* I. vii. 383 He is said to have kept a reputed unicorn's horn always on his table.

**b.** Narwhal's horn.

1856 KANE *Arct. Expl.* I. 412 A shaft of unicorn's horn.

†**2.** The material of this powdered or prepared as a drug and used medicinally, esp. as an antidote against poison. *Obs.*

1590 E. WEBBE *Trav.* (Arb.) 35 Some lewde Gunners ..gaue me poyson in drinke..; his Phisition..gaue me speadely Unicorns horne to drinke. 1631 JORDEN *Nat. Bathes* vii. (1632) 44 This volatill salt..is commonly very Diaphoreticke: & this it is which makes our..supposed Vnicornes horne to be in such esteeme. 1698 *New Descr. Moscovy* 21 Likewise some use the Powder to Antedote Poison, as the Vnicorns horne; this I hold to be the same with the Morse.

**3.** *Bot.* (See quot.)

1864 *Chambers's Encycl.* VI. 393 The root of *Helonias dioica* is used..as an anthelmintic...The plant..is called Starwort and Blazing Star, also Unicorn's Horn. [Cf. *unicorn-plant, -root* s.v. UNICORN II.]

‖ **Unicum** (yū·nikŏm). [L., neut. sing. of *ūnicus* UNIQUE *a.* So in G. and Du.] A unique example, specimen, or thing.

1885 *Daily Tel.* 14 July 5/3 Some picture, work of art, or old book, which is represented to him as being a 'unicum'. 1892 MRS. J. P. MORGAN tr. *Rubinstein's Conv. on Music* 26 The symphony in G minor (this *unicum* of symphonic-lyric).

**Unicursal** (yūnikɒ·ɹsăl), *a.* and *sb.* *Math.* [f. UNI- 1 + L. *cursus* course: see -AL.] **a.** *adj.* Having, traversing, or being on one course or path. **b.** *sb.* A unicursal curve.

1866 CAYLEY in *Proc. London Math. Soc.* April, A unicursal curve is nothing else than a curve with a deficiency D = 0. 1871 — *Math. Papers* (1895) VIII. 388 On the Transformation of Unicursal Surfaces. 1873 G. SALMON *Higher Plane Curves* ii. 29 If the coordinates can be expressed as rational functions of a parameter the curve has the maximum number of double points. Curves of this sort are called unicursal curves.

Hence **Unicursa·lity**; **Unicu·rsally** *adv.*

1887 *Amer. Jrnl. Math.* X. 24 In the unicursality-equation a cusp plays the role of an ordinary double-point. 1892 W. W. R. BALL *Math. Recreat.* 124 A figure is described unicursally when the whole of it is traversed in one route.

**Unicycle** (yū·nisəik'l). *U.S.* [f. UNI- 2 + CYCLE, after *bicycle, tricycle.*] A vehicle or conveyance having only one wheel; esp. a monocycle used by acrobats or for gymnastic displays.

1869 *The Velocipede* (N.Y.) April 76 Hemmings' Unicycle or 'Flying Yankee Velocipede'. 1884 KNIGHT *Dict. Mech.* Suppl. 913/1 *Unicycle*, a one-wheeled vehicle for propulsion by foot-power.

Hence **U·nicyclist**, one who rides a unicycle.

1881 *Sells Bros. Show-Bill*, Celebrated Russian Bicyclists, Unicyclists, and Roller Skaters.

**Unide·aed,** *a.* Also unidea'd. [UN-[1] 9.] Not furnished with an idea.

1752 JOHNSON in *Boswell* (1904) I. 166 Leaving his social friends, to go and sit with a set of wretched un-idea'd girls. 1822 SCOTT *Peveril* xxvii, A silly scrupulous unidea'd Puritan. 1888 *Jrnl. Educ.* May 242 The un-idea'd vulgarity of the lower middle classes.

**Unide·al,** *a.* [UN-[1] 7.]

†**1.** Of sounds or words: Expressing or conveying no idea. *Obs.*

1751 JOHNSON *Rambler* No. 184 ℙ12 However we amuse ourselves with unideal sounds. 1792 W. ROBERTS *Looker-On* No. 23 (1794) I. 324 A language..rich in the unideal terms of a raving philosophy.

†**2.** Destitute of, lacking in, ideas. *Obs.*

1751 JOHNSON *Rambler* No. 135 ℙ9 A short relief from the tediousness of unideal vacancy. 1801 *Phil. Trans.* XCI. 91 Un-ideal operations conducted without principle, purpose, or regularity.

**3.** Having or following no ideal.

1760 D. WEBB *Beauties of Painting* iv. 68 Those servile and unideal painters. 1856 EMERSON *Eng. Traits, Lit.* Wks. (Bohn) II. 113 The scholars have become un-ideal. They parry earnest speech with banter and levity. 1867 F. HARRISON *Choice of Bks.* (1886) 110 To be fierce is to be unideal, to be unideal is to be sanguinary.

**4.** Not marked by idealism; having no ideal character or features, etc.

1846 RUSKIN *Mod. Paint.* II. III. xiii. § 2 Unideal works of art..represent actual existing things. 1873 SPENCER *Stud. Sociol.* ix. (1877) 222 Instead of our practice being unideal, the ideas which guide it verge on the romantic. 1877 L. MORRIS *Epic Hades* III. 276 The bare And unideal aspect of the fields Which Spring not yet had kissed.

**Unide·alism, -ist.** (UN-[1] 12.)

Also, in recent use, *unidealistic* adj.

1870 J. GROTE *Exam. Utilit. Phil.* xvii. 273 Utilitarianism may be..either of an idealist or unidealist type. 1888 W. S. LILLY *Right & Wrong* (1890) iv. 121 The singular unidealism..of the English mind in respect of eternal and divine things.

**Unide·ntified,** *ppl. a.* (UN-[1] 8.)

1860 R. NOEL in *Vac. Tour.* 467 The site of a town or village unidentified presented itself within incredibly short distances. 1867 LATHAM *Black & White* 68 Of these graves 138,901 will be nameless and unidentified.

**Uni·dioma·tic,** *a.* (UN-[1] 7.)

*a* 1822 SHELLEY *Pr. Wks.* (1888) I. 395 The clear, and exact, but unidiomatic phrases of their native language. 1855 PUSEY *Doctr. Real Presence* 153 The interpretation of Bellarmin is inconsistent and unidiomatic. 1891 DRIVER *Introd. Lit. O. Test.* 445 An author who..translated the Aramaic idiom..into unidiomatic Hebrew.

**Uni·dle,** *a.* [UN-[1] 7.] Busy, industrious.

*a* 1586 SIDNEY *Astr. & Stella* Sonn. xxvi (Qo.[2]), For me, I doe Nature vnydle know. 1604 MARSTON *Malcontent* v. iii, Is he not a pretty dapper unydle gallant?

†**Unido·latrize,** *v.* *Obs.*[−1] (UN-[2] 6 c.) 1659 FULLER *App. Inj. Innoc.* I. 55 The Animadvertor..endeavouring to un-idolatrize the Brittains as much as he could. **Unido·latrous,** *a.* (UN-[1] 7.) 1841 WISEMAN *Remarks on Lett. Palmer* 6 To substitute an idolatrous, for an unidolatrous, worship. 1881 *19th Cent.* No. 49. 502 The two religions ..were both nominally monotheistic, and both unidolatrous.

**Unie** (yū·ni), abbrev. of UNICORN 8 b.

1874 A. H. MARKHAM *Whaling Cruise Baffin's B.* 137 A couple of narwhals, or as they are called by the whalers, 'unies' (unicorn abbreviated). 1878 — *Gt. Frozen Sea* v. 67 Another source of amusement..was chasing 'unies'.

**Unie,** *v.*: see UNY *v.*

**Unific** (yūni·fik), *a.* [ad. L. type *ūnificus*: see UNI- and -FIC.] That unifies or unites; producing unity.

1788 T. TAYLOR *Proclus* I. 118 A power collective of divisible natures, and unific of such as are multiplied. 1841 *Fraser's Mag.* XXIII. 130 The centre of unific power is the invisible. 1861 *Q. Rev.* CX. 394 That so-called unific principle..by which we are impelled to reduce all that we see and hear to unity. 1877 FARRAR *Days of Youth* xi. 105 The unific rectitude of a manly life.

**Unification** (yūnifikē¹·ʃən). [f. UNIFY *v.* (see -ATION), or a. F. *unification*, It. *unificazione.*] The action or process of unifying or uniting; reduction to unity or to a uniform system; the result of this.

*Unificationist*, sb. and a., has had some slight currency in recent use (1909-).

1851 GALLENGA *Italy* II. i. 25 The unification of Italy would thus be gradual and pacific. 1865 LECKY *Ration.* I. 231 A process of transformation or unification of religious ideas. 1880 E. KIRKE *Garfield* 46 The recent movement for the unification and preservation of nations.

So **U·nificator**, a unifier.

1870 *Contemp. Rev.* XV. 400 The people..proclaimed them in anticipation the 'unificators' of Italy.

**Unified** (yū·nifəid), *ppl. a.* [f. UNIFY *v.* + -ED[1].] That is or has been made into one from separate parts; united, combined, consolidated.

1862 F. HALL *Hindu Philos. Syst.* 178 The residual part..he is to consider as unified. 1882 *Standard* 30 Dec. 2/2 The Unified Debt fell about 1/8. 1883 *Fortn. Rev.* July 107 After the whole metropolis is under a unified authority.

**b.** Used absolutely or as *sb.*

1883 *Pall Mall G.* 30 Nov. 5/2 Egyptian Unifieds continued to rise yesterday. 1884 *Academy* 2 Aug. 74/1 Unification is pleasant to the unifier only, not to the unified.

**Unifier** (yū·nifəi,əɹ). [f. as prec. + -ER.] One who or that which unifies or unites; one who advocates unification in administration.

1867 SPENCER *First Princ.* II. iii. § 51 (ed. 2) 171 The derivative idea needed by Philosophy as the unifier of Science. 1881 *Echo* 2 Feb. 1/6 The Great Victor Emmanuel, the liberator and unifier of Italy.

**Unifilar** (yūnifəi·lăɹ), *a.* [f. UNI- 1 + L. *fīl-us* thread: see -AR[1].] Of a magnetometer or other magnetic instrument: Having or suspended by a single thread or fibre.

1856 KANE *Arct. Expl.* I. xiv. 153 We had a good unifilar [magnetometer]. 1873 J. C. MAXWELL *Electr. & Magn.* II. 119 The Unifilar Declinometer. 1879 THOMSON & TAIT *Nat. Phil.* I. I. § 435 In the unifilar torsion-balance.

**Uniflo·ral,** *a.* [UNI- 1.] = UNIFLOROUS *a.*

1849 CRAIG. 1861 BENTLEY *Man. Bot.* 212 A series of single-flowered axes (unifloral) arranged in the form of a raceme.

**Uniflorous** (yūniflōᵊ·rəs), *a.* *Bot.* [f. mod.L. *ūniflōr-us* (f. L. *ūn-us* UNI- + *flōr-, flōs* flower) + -OUS. Cf. F. *uniflore* (1753), Pg. *unifloro.*] Having or bearing only one flower.

1760 [see MULTIFLOROUS *a.*]. 1800 *Asiatic Ann. Reg.* 299/1 The hermaphrodite calyx is sometimes biflorous,.. sometimes uniflorous. 1881 *Jrnl. Linn. Soc.* XVIII. 353 Distinguished..by its unifoliate uniflorous stem.

†**U·nifoil.** *Obs.*[−0] [f. UNI- + FOIL *sb.*[1]] The plant one-blade, *Smilacina bifolia*.

1688 R. HOLME *Armoury* II. 58/1 He beareth Argent, an Unifoile Vert...Vnifoile or Vnfall. This is an Herb that never hath more then one leaf from a Root,..it is also called one blade. [Hence in Berry *Encycl. Her.* (*c* 1828), Elvin (1889), and in some recent Dicts. as a bearing in Heraldry.]

**Uniform** (yū·nifǫɹm), *sb.* [f. the adj. Cf. F., It., Sp., and Pg. *uniforme*, Du., G., Sw., and Da. *uniform* in sense 2.]

†**I. 1.** *In uniform*, in one body or flock. *Obs.*

1623 LISLE *Ælfric on O. & N. Test.* Ded. p. ix, Our sheepe shall feare no Wolfe, or suddaine storme; But goe and come all safe in vniforme.

**II. 2.** A distinctive dress of uniform cut, materials, and colour worn by all the members of a particular naval, military, or other force to which it is recognized as properly belonging and peculiar.

1748 in *Jrnl. Archæol. Soc.* (1847) II. 79 That no commission-officer or midshipmen do presume to wear any other uniform than what properly belongs to his rank. 1760 *Cautions & Adv. to Officers of Army* 123 You are..to consider what is to be furnished out of this last Sum, and that is your Regimentals or Uniform. 1802 JAMES *Milit. Dict.* s.v., Scarlet is the national uniform of the British army. *Ibid.*, Generally speaking each [corps] has an uniform within itself, yet this uniform, strictly considered, is a regimental. 1837 DICKENS *Pickw.* iv, Colonel Bulder, in full military uniform, on horseback. 1879 *Cassell's Techn. Educ.* III. 363 Insisting that none shall fight who do not wear the uniform of one of the armies engaged.

*fig.* 1768–74 TUCKER *Lt. Nat.* (1834) II. 121 Passion so commonly marches under the colours and in the uniform of reason,..that [etc.].

**b.** A distinctive uniform dress worn by the members of any civilian body or association of persons.

1837 DICKENS *Pickw.* ii, The proposed uniform, sir, of the Pickwick Club. 1885 'MRS. ALEXANDER' *At Bay* i, A good-looking boy in the polytechnique uniform. 1897 HALL CAINE *Christian* x, The girls were nearly all nurses, and they wore their nurse's uniform.

**c.** A single suit of this kind. †Also *pl.*, the separate garments composing this.

1783 *Ann. Reg., Chron.* 193/2 Such flag officers, however, as were provided with the uniforms were permitted to wear the same. 1814 SCOTT *Wav.* xvii, He had laid aside the Highland dress for the time, to put on an old blue and red uniform. 1834 MARRYAT *P. Simple* xxxviii, That is the reason why my uniforms are so shabby. I spoilt them then.

†**3.** A person wearing a uniform. *Obs.*[−1]

1786 MME. D'ARBLAY *Diary* Oct., I opened the eating-room door,..but saw to my surprise a party of uniforms.

**4.** *attrib.* **a.** In the sense 'pertaining to, forming (part of) a uniform', as *uniform case, clothes, coat.*

In some instances not clearly distinguishable from the adj. Cf. UNIFORM *a.* 2 c.

1807 P. GASS *Jrnl.* 188 We got a canoe from the natives, for which we gave an officer's uniform coat. 1825 in J. A. Heraud *Voy. Midshipm.* (1837) x. 179 Buy your..uniform clothes (two jackets and one coat) in London. 1852 THACKERAY *Esmond* II. xiii, An officer in a green uniform coat. 1889 HISSEY *Tour in Phaeton* 399 We pack our personal belongings in tin uniform cases.

**b.** In the sense 'wearing uniform; uniformed'.

1895 *Westm. Gaz.* 1 Jan. 4/3 Several uniform policemen watched the prosecutor and prisoners.

**Uniform** (yū·nifǫɹm), *a.* Also 6 vnifourme, 6–8 uniforme. [a. F. *uniforme* (14th c. in Godef., = It., Sp., Pg. *uniforme*), or ad. L. *ūniform-is*: see UNI- and FORM.]

**I.** Of things in respect of their own qualities or constitution.

**1.** Of one form, character, or kind; having, maintaining, occurring in or under, the same form always; that is or remains the same in different places, at different times, or under varying circumstances; exhibiting no difference, diversity, or variation.

1540 PALSGR. *Acolastus* A ij, One selfe and vniforme maner of teachynge of all those Grammaticalle ensygnementes. 1555 WATREMAN *Fardle Facions* I. v. 72 The ordre of Mariage emong the Egiptians is not vniforme. 1601 HOLLAND *Pliny* I. 161 This impression, that maketh either the foresaid uniforme likenesse, or confusion and varietie. 1662 *Extr. St. Papers Friends* Ser. II. (1911) 150 Wee would be glad that all our Subjects could be brought to agree in a uniforme Worship of God. 1710 PRIDEAUX *Orig. Tithes* ii. 127 From whence else should they have such a Uniform Usage but by a Uniform Tradition from them? 1780 BENTHAM *Princ. Legisl.* xiv. § 1 It is lost time to seek for an uniform base of agreement upon so essential an object. 1818 SCOTT *Br. Lamm.* xi, According to a uniform custom in remote places in Scotland. 1869 F. W. NEWMAN *Misc.* 224 A uniform franchise through the whole federation would have followed. 1891 *Law Times* XCII. 124/1 In Ireland the practice in this respect..was not uniform.

*absol.* 1606 SYLVESTER *Du Bartas* II. iv. II. *Magnif.* 1335 Cause of all Causes, Ocean of all Good,..The Uni-form, which gives all forms their Being.

**b.** Of persons (or personifications), their disposition, etc. Hence, exhibiting or preserving uniformity or consistency in respect of conduct or opinion; consistent.

1551 CRANMER *Answ. to Gardiner* I. 14 The churche of Rome..sheweth her selfe alway vniforme and consonaunt, to confound all the doctrine of Christe. 1647 H. MORE *Phil. Poems* II. lxxii, If he will his own fortunes overturn It cannot well be holp, we must be uniform. 1692 DRYDEN *St. Euremont's Ess.* 339 There is a man so uniform as to have nothing of Inequality and contrariety in his Actions. 1748 RICHARDSON *Clarissa* i. I. 3 Every-body pities you. So steady so uniform in your conduct. 1799 WELLINGTON in Gurw. *Desp.* (1834) I. 16 Of this uniform disposition abundant proofs have been afforded by each of the allies. 1822 SCOTT *Peveril* xlviii, For Buckingham's sins,..he is the regular and uniform sponsor.

†**c.** Of consent: Unanimous. *Obs.*

1559 in Strype *Ann. Ref.* viii. (1709) 116 We..have with one uniform consent set forth this short declaration. 1620 BRENT tr. *Sarpi's Counc. Trent* VIII. 745 An vniforme consent of Doctors.

**d.** Of clothing or dress: Of the same pattern, colour, and material amongst a number or body of persons.

Merging into an attrib. use of UNIFORM *sb.* (sense 4).

1746 in *Jrnl. Archaeol. Soc.* (1847) II. 77 That a uniform dress is useful and necessary for the commissioned officers. 1768 *Ann. Reg., Chron.* 63/1 The lappels and cuffs of the military uniform frocks, appointed to be worn by the lieutenants of his Majesty's fleet. 1783 *Ibid.* 193/2 The uniform clothing..worn by the flag officers. 1890 *Harper's Mag.* Feb. 333 The practice of clothing soldiers, by regiments, in one uniform dress.

**2.** Having or presenting the same appearance or aspect; exhibiting no, or little, diversity in respect of form, design, or dimensions; hence, having a plain, unbroken, or undiversified surface or exterior.

In the 17th–18th centuries freq. of buildings, etc.

*a* 1550 LELAND *Itin.* (1768) I. 107 The Church of S. Mary is excellent, newe, and uniforme yn work. 1621 in Kempe *Losely MSS.* (1836) 456 The church of St. Treguse ys..a very good one, were it uniforme. 1632 MASSINGER & FIELD *Fatal Dowry* III. i, All else about you, cap-a-pie, So uniform in spite of handsomeness, Shews such a bold contempt of comeliness. 1696 WHISTON *Theory of Earth* II. 115 Every such state of external Nature was even, uniform, and regular. 1723 CHAMBERS tr. *Le Clerc's Treat. Arch.* I. 59 Columns..ought not to have any Flutings; for ..plain uniform Columns carry..a better appearance. 1756 NUGENT *Gr. Tour, Netherl.* I. 299 The street called La Rue Royale, is one of the longest, straightest, and most uniform in Europe. 1784 COWPER *Task* VI. 178 All this uniform, uncolour'd scene, Shall be dismantled of its fleecy load. 1859 DARWIN *Orig. Spec.* iii. 73 The face of nature remains uniform for long periods of time. 1884 BOWER & SCOTT *De Bary's Phaner.* 110 The thickening mass is either uniform or pitted.

As *adv.* 1630 *R. Johnson's Kingd. & Commw.* 132 Paris.. is the greater, the uniformer built, and stronglier situate.

†**b.** *Bot.* Of flowers: (see quots.). *Obs.*

1693 *Phil. Trans.* XVII. 929 Such as have a Uniform Flower, as Senna, or such as have a difform or Papilionaceous Flower. 1704 J. HARRIS *Lex. Techn.* I, *Uniform Flowers* of Plants, the Botanists call such as are all round of the same Figure; or whose fore and back part, and whose right and left parts are exactly alike.

**c.** Of material things or colour.

In this group the sense sometimes becomes narrowed down to 'not mixed or blended'.

1756 BURKE *On the Sublime & Beautiful* III. xxvii, Nor ..is the power of black as black, or of white as white, so strong as when each stands uniform and distinguished. 1764 HARMER *Observ.* iv. § 27. 192 This mingled wine stands in opposition to new wine, which is, to the eye, an uniform liquor. 1823 SCOTT *Quentin D.* ii, His jerkin, hose, and cloak, were of a dark uniform colour. 1845 *Florist's Jrnl.* 261 Few gardens could boast an uniform luxuriant green among the plants. *c* 1860 FARADAY *Forces Nat.* 67 This piece of glass..being perfectly uniform in its internal structure.

**3.** Of motion, dimensions, etc.: Free from fluctuation or variation in respect of quantity or amount.

1559 W. CUNNINGHAM *Cosmogr. Glasse* 10 The sterres kepe one vniforme distance in mouing. 1597 HOOKER *Eccl. Pol.* v. lxix. § 2 The heauens..keepe in their motions vniforme celeritie. 1656 tr. *Hobbes' Elem. Philos.* III. xv. 156 Uniform [motion] is that by which equal Lines are alwayes transmitted in equal times. 1764 *Museum Rust.* IV. 58 We should find it in an uniform progression of encrease. 1796 WITHERING *Brit. Plants* (ed. 3) III. 879 Branches of a uniform breadth. 1860 MAURY *Phys. Geog.* (Low) xxii. § 883 The flow of heat from the sun is held to be uniform. 1879 THOMSON & TAIT *Nat. Phil.* I. I. § 20 Velocity..may be uniform, *i.e.* the same at every instant; or it may be variable.

**II.** Of things of the same class in respect of each other, or of one thing in relation to another or others of the same class.

**4.** Of the same form, character, or kind as another or others; agreeing or according with one another, conforming to one standard, rule, or pattern; alike, similar.

1548 W. THOMAS in Strype *Eccl. Mem.* (1721) II. App. v. 71 So because we have no neighbour of uniform religion, I determine we can find no friend, whose amity is to be trusted. 1594 HOOKER *Eccl. Pol.* IV. xiii. § 2 The only doubt is about the manner of their unity; how far churches are bound to be uniform in their ceremonies. 1637 SALTONSTALL *Eusebius' Constantine* 77 Thus the Emperours Edict discovered the Dens and uniforme Cages of these Heretickes. 1660 R. COKE *Power & Subj.* 222 The ceremonies of Edward's Reformation were more uniform than before. 1702 *Engl. Theophrast.* 263 Things Past, Present, and to Come, are strangely Uniform and of a Colour. 1762 KAMES *Elem. Crit.* (1833) 481 When two figures are composed of similar parts, they are said to be uniform. 1794 MRS. RADCLIFFE *Myst. Udolpho* xvi, My answers on the subject have been uniform. 1867 SMILES *Huguenots Eng.* i. 6 The copies sold having been compared with each other, were found to be exactly uniform. 1878 BRISTOWE *Th. & Pract. Med.* (ed. 2) 534 The symptoms of rupture of the heart are far from uniform.

†**b.** Of buildings. *Obs.*

1549 W. THOMAS *Hist. Italy* 207 Buildynges on bothe sides so fayre and vniforme. 1617 MORYSON *Itin.* III. 66 The houses are most of bricke,..and so vniforme, as if they had all beene built at a time, and by the same workemen. 1684 BURNET tr. *More's Utopia* 73 Their Buildings are good, and are so uniform, that a whole side of a Street looks like one House. 1700 in Picton *L'pool Munic. Rec.* (1883) I. 291 Ye buildings be handsome & uniform.

†**c.** Of persons. *Obs.*

In quot. referring to Matt. xxii. 11–13.

*a* 1626 BP. ANDREWES *Pattern Cath. Doctr.* (1630) 210 He that was not uniforme was punished.

†**d.** In agreement with, accordant *to*, something.

*a* 1586 SIDNEY *Arcadia* II. xii, So divers be the Elements disposed In this weake worke, that it can never be Made uniforme to any state reposed. 1669 in Willis & Clark *Cambridge* (1886) II. 557 Three outward dore cases shalbe arched..with freestone vniforme to the windowes. 1702 H. DODWELL *Apol.* § 19, I have shewn it agreeable to the severest Reasoning..to make his Death uniform to the rest of his Life.

**Uniform** (yū·nifǫɹm), *v.* [f. the adj. or sb. Cf. Sp. and Pg. *uniformar*, It. *uniformarsi.*]

**1.** *trans.* To make conformable *to.*

In a parody of pedantic language.

*a* 1586 SIDNEY *Wanstead Play* in *Arcadia* (1629) 622 Thus must I vniform my speech to your obtuse conceptions.

**2.** To make or render (a number of persons or things) uniform or alike; to bring or reduce to uniformity.

In later quots. with suggestion of sense 3.

*c* 1681 HICKERINGILL *Trimmer* iii. Wks. 1716 I. 372 We'll uniform you all, and make you all alike. 1708 T. WARD *Eng. Ref.* I. (1710) 64 To..Uniform the Multitude In Prayer, and joyn the jarring crowd. 1870 LOWELL *Study Wind.* (1871) 258 The more than Protean travesties which words underwent before they were uniformed by Johnson and Walker. 1887 *Harper's Mag.* July 280 It is a human device to uniform people into friends and enemies.

**3.** To dress in, put into, uniform. Cf. UNIFORMED *a.*, UNIFORMING *vbl. sb.*

1894 *Outing* XXIV. 78/2 Hull persisted in uniforming the militia after his own sweet will.

† **Unifo·rmable,** *a. Obs. rare.* [f. L. *ūniformis* UNIFORM *a.* + -ABLE.] Uniform.

1632 LITHGOW *Trav.* x. 474 Vniformable no; some of your Priests giue the Sacrament onely in Bread..; some in Wine without Bread, and some in both. 1653 BLITHE *Eng. Improver Impr.* 155 As easie..to cast or lot out thy Wood into an Artificial uniformable plot, as to do it rudely or confusedly.

**Unifo·rmal,** *a.* [f. as prec. + -AL.] Uniform, in various senses.

1573 [implied in next]. 1598 FLORIO, *Simbolo*,..an vniformall consent of sundry opinions. *a* 1608 DEE *Relat. Spir.* I. (1659) 4 All things shall be brought into an uniformal order. 1645 HERRICK *Descr. Woman* 11 Her comly nose with vniformall grace Like purest white stands in the middle place.

1848 BAILEY *Festus* (ed. 3) 206 One arrayed in white And one in uniformal black. 1888 D. MAGUIRE *Art Massage* ii. (ed. 4) 18 A uniformal friction on those parts of the body which are irregularly formed.

Hence **Unifo·rmally** *adv. rare.*

1573 BARET *Alv.* s.v. *C*, [The letter C] shoulde haue his proper sownd and euer to keepe the same vniformally in speaking, nor waueringly. 1603 FLORIO *Montaigne* III. ii. 491, I will present my selfe..every where vniformallie. 1624 GATAKER *Transubst.* 48 These being..uniformally recounted by three Evangelists.

**Uniformaliza·tion.** [f. next + -ATION.] The action of making or fact of being made uniform.

1805 *Ann. Rev.* III. 255 The uniformalization of tenures.

**Unifo·rmalize,** *v. rare.* [f. UNIFORMAL *a.* + -IZE.] *trans.* To make uniform; to reduce to a uniform system.

1805 *Ann. Rev.* III. 294 It is desirable to uniformalize the circulating medium of both countries. 1830 W. TAYLOR *Hist. Surv. Germ. Poetry* I. 161 By uniformalizing coins, weights, and measures.

**Uniforma·tion.** *rare.* [f. UNIFORM *a.* + -ATION.] The action of making uniform; reduction to uniformity.

1895 *Dublin Rev.* April 335 Not through the blunting, checking, or uniformation of thinking.

**U·niformed,** *a.* [f. UNIFORM *sb.* 2 + -ED.] Dressed in or wearing uniform. (Freq. *c* 1880–.)

1813 LADY LYTTELTON *Corr.* 12 Dec., Wednesday we dine at Count Romanzoff's—full-dressed, long-trained, uniformed. 1840 GEN. P. THOMPSON *Exerc.* (1842) V. 53 A uniformed agent of the law. 1895 MEREDITH *Amazing Marriage* xliii, A foreign army or tag-rag of uniformed rascals.

*fig.* and *transf.* 1864 LOWELL *Fireside Trav.* 154 We.. come out uniformed..with habits of thinking and doing cut on one pattern. 1892 *Nation* (N.Y.) 3 Mar. 176/1 The book is handsomely uniformed in Confederate gray.

**Unifo·rming,** *vbl. sb.* [f. UNIFORM *v.*]

**1.** The action of making or fact of being made uniform in some respect. *rare*$^{-1}$.

1700–1 GOUGH *Hist. Myddle* (1875) 115 The Twelvth Peiw ..Was a supernumerary Peiw at the uniforming of the seates.

**2.** The action of clothing in or providing with uniform or a uniform dress.

1891 *Harper's Mag.* March 647/1 In the uniforming of a community set apart for an unworldly purpose. 1897 *Daily News* 4 May 9/2 The uniforming of troops.

**Uniformist** (yū·nifǫɹmist). [f. UNIFORM *a.* + -IST.] An advocate of or believer in uniformity or a uniform system, esp. in respect of religious doctrine or observance.

1885 R. W. DIXON *Hist. Ch. Eng.* III. 465 He was..as staunch a Uniformist now, as..he had been a Nonconformist. 1891 *Athenæum* 15 Aug. 214/3 A strict uniformist with regard to the phonetics of Latin.

**Uniformitarian** (yū:nifǫɹmitēə·riăn), *sb.* and *adj.* [f. UNIFORMIT-Y + *-arian.*]

**A.** *sb.* **1.** *Geol.* One who maintains or accepts the theory that geological processes and phenomena have always been and still are due to causes or forces operating continuously and with uniformity. (Opposed to CATASTROPHIST or CONVULSIONIST.)

1840 WHEWELL *Philos. Induct. Sciences* I. p. xxxvi, The Catastrophist constructs Theories, the Uniformitarian demolishes them. 1860 HUXLEY *Darwiniana* Coll. Ess. 1893 II. 65 The most philosophical uniformitarian of the present day. 1891 SIR R. BALL *Ice Age* 173 It places the ice-sheet ..at the disposal of the geological uniformitarian.

**2.** An advocate of uniformity; a uniformist. *rare.*

1890 GILDERSLEEVE *Ess. & Stud.* 214 The Procrustean work of a miserable uniformitarian.

**B.** *adj.* **1.** *Geol.* Of or pertaining to, characteristic of or held by, uniformitarians.

1840 WHEWELL *Philos. Induct. Sci.* II. 135 The uniformitarian doctrine on this subject rests on most unstable foundations. 1869 HUXLEY in *Scientific Opinion* 21 April 464/3 The influence of uniformitarian views has been..favourable to the progress of sound geology. 1884 H. SPENCER in *Contemp. Rev.* July 25 The leading expositor of the uniformitarian theory in Geology.

**b.** In accordance with the theory of the uniformitarians; proceeding from geological uniformity.

1869 HUXLEY in *Scientific Opinion* April 487/1 All these irregular..catastrophes would be the result of an absolutely uniformitarian action.

**c.** Of persons: Holding or adhering to the theory or doctrines of the uniformitarians.

1864 BOWEN *Logic* ix. 301 The speculations of those whom Dr. Whewell calls the uniformitarian school of geologists. 1895 *Q. Rev.* April 386 The most influential uniformitarian geologist of our age.

**2.** Of or pertaining to, advocating or practising, uniformity in something.

1897 *Daily News* 12 July 6/3 The Puritanism of the intolerant, uniformitarian Presbyterians.

**Uniformitarianism** (yū:nifǫɹmitēə·riăniz'm). *Geol.* [f. prec. + -ISM.] The principles or doctrines held by the uniformitarian school of geologists; the theory of uniformity of action in the forces and processes of inorganic nature. (Opposed to CATASTROPHISM or CONVULSIONISM.)

1865 T. MARSDEN *Sacr. Steps Creation* 113 One is induced to ask, whether Uniformitarianism be mere Proselytism in the garb of Philosophy. 1894 *Nature* 26 July 290/1 The natural though exaggerated reaction into scientific uniformitarianism.

**Uniformity** (yūnifǭ·ɹmĭti). Forms: 5 **vniformite,** 6 **-ete,** 6–7 **-itie,** 7 **-ity, uniformitie,** 7– **-ity.** [a. F. *uniformité* (14th c., = It. *uniformità*, Sp. *uniformidad*, Pg. *-dade*), or ad. L. *ūniformitāt-*, *ūniformitās*, f. *ūniformis* UNIFORM *a.*: see -ITY. So also Du. *uniformiteit*, G. *uniformität.*] The quality of being uniform.

**1.** The fact or condition of having the same form or character as another or others; conformity amongst several things, parts, etc., to one form or character.

1432–50 tr. *Higden* (Rolls) III. 215 Zenon, whiche put euery synne to be of vniformite, so that he scholde synne as moche that did steyle chaffe as the man stelenge golde. 1513 DOUGLAS *Æneid* IX. iv. 39 To thir tua was a will in vnite, A lust, and mynd in vniformete. 1611 CORYAT *Crudities* 23 Such is the vniformity of almost al the houses of the same streete..that they are made alike both in proportion of workmanship and matter. 1614 RALEIGH *Hist. World* II. 543 The consent of those that have written thereof, being nothing neare to uniformity. 1630 *R. Johnson's Kingd. & Commw.* 132 Its attributes of a Winding river, and the five Bridges, sorting forsooth to uniformitie of streets. 1701 NORRIS *Ideal World* I. ii. 50 Whence should arise this specific uniformity in the natures of man..if not that they are all cast in one mould? 1756 BURKE *Subl. & B.* II. ix, Succession and uniformity of parts are what constitute the artificial infinite. 1815 J. SMITH *Panorama Sci. & Art* II. 601 Various differences in the depth, extent, or want of uniformity of the gravelly or clayey strata. 1854 *Poultry Chron.* II. 149/1 Quality, purity, beauty of plumage, and uniformity [in fowls].

**b.** Conformity to (or compliance with) one standard of opinion, practice, or procedure, esp. in respect of religion or religious observance.

*Act of Uniformity*, in *Eng. Hist.*, one or other of three Acts regulating public worship, passed in 1549 (21 Jan.), 1559, and 1662 respectively, which prescribed the use and acceptance of the Books of Common Prayer published in those years; esp. the Act (13 & 14 Charles II, c. 4) passed 19 May 1662, which also required the 'assent and consent' of the clergy to everything contained in the Book of Common Prayer; etc.

1549 *Act* 2 & 3 *Edw. VI*, c. 1 (*title*), An Acte for the Unyformytie of Service and Admynistracion of the Sacramentes throughout the Realme. 1552 ABP. HAMILTON *Catech.* Pref., To keip vniformitie and concord in setting furth to ye people the doctrine. 1611 BIBLE *Transl. Pref.* ¶ 13 When the father of their Church..findeth so great fault with them for their oddes and iarring; we hope the children haue no great cause to vaunt of their vniformitie. 1651 BAXTER *Inf. Bapt.* 147 His treatise against Uniformity. 1670 in Somers *Tracts* I. 21 All Uniformity (or Colour of it) was distasteful to the Independents. 1708 J. CHAMBERLAYNE *St. Gt. Brit.* I. III. i. (1710) 155 He must carry with him.. Letters Testimonial..from..Three..Reverend Divines, who ..can give a good Account of his Vertue, Uniformity, and Learning. 1830 D'ISRAELI *Chas. I*, III. v. 63 Lord Bacon considered that uniformity in religion was absolutely necessary. 1871 C. DAVIES *Metric Syst.* III. 79 Its adoption was therefore a great and important advance toward uniformity.

*Comb.* 1647 *Case Kingd.* 10 Till Vniformity-mongers be pointed at as the only Enemies of a State.

**c.** With *a* or *an.*

1560 DAUS tr. *Sleidane's Comm.* 125 b, Therfore is an vniformitie to be sought for, that maye be grounded vpon the sure foundation of Scripture. 1641 MILTON *Reform.* II. 17 This distinction of honour will bring forth a seemly and graceful uniformity over all the kingdom. 1705 NELSON *Fest. & Fasts* i. (ed. 3) 19 The great Council of Nice ordained there should be a constant uniformity in this Case. 1874 GREEN *Short Hist.* iii. § 3. 125 An uniformity of weights and measures was ordered to be enforced throughout the realm.

**2.** The condition of having, occurring in, or maintaining only one form or character; resemblance to or agreement with itself at all times or on all occasions; regularity in action or occurrence. Freq. const. *of.*

1577 HARRISON *England* II. iii. (1877) I. 73 For vniformitie of building, orderlie compaction, and regiment, the towne of Cambridge exceedeth that of Oxford..by manie a fold. 1739 BUTLER *Serm.* Wks. 1874 II. 217 There is a wonderful uniformity in the conduct of Providence. 1802 PALEY *Nat. Theol.* xxv. 482 Of the unity of the Deity, the proof is, the uniformity of plan observable in the universe. 1863 KINGLAKE *Crimea* I. 64 That branch of industry which seeks to give uniformity and mechanic action to bodies of men. 1875 JOWETT *Plato* (ed. 2) IV. 415 Genius is of all ages, and there is perhaps more uniformity in excellence than in mediocrity.

**b.** *spec.* in *Geol.* Cf. UNIFORMITARIAN(ISM.

1837 WHEWELL *Hist. Induct. Sci.* III. 609 The progress of physical geology will be better understood by attending to the doctrine of uniformity. 1869 HUXLEY in *Scientific Opinion* 28 Apr. 487/1 It is very conceivable that catastrophes may be part and parcel of uniformity.

**3.** The condition of having the parts similar in appearance; presentation of one regular or unvaried form on this account; similarity of appearance, design, structure, style, etc.; freedom from or lack of variety, diversity, or irregularity.

Regarded as either an artistic virtue or defect.

1625 BACON *Ess.* (Arb.) 547 Houses are built to Liue in, and not to Looke on: Therefore let Vse bee preferred before Vniformitie. 1642 FULLER *Holy & Prof. St.* III. vii. 168 Uniformity also much pleaseth the eye. 1686 PLOT *Staffordsh.* 360 The beauty of a structure..did not consist, as now, in uniformity; but in the greatest variety the Artist could possibly shew. 1753 HOGARTH *Anal. Beauty* iv. 22 Variety is more pleasing than uniformity, where the same end is answer'd by both. 1778 SHERIDAN *Camp* II. iii, The tents are all ranged in a straight line; now,..is there not a horrid uniformity in their infinite vista of canvas? no curve, no break. 1842 MRS. BROWNING *Bk. Poets* ii. Wks. (1904) 635/1 There is a difference between uniformity and monotony, and he [Marlowe] found it.

**b.** Unvaried or wearisome sameness; monotony, esp. *of* life.

1707 *Curios. in Husb. & Gard.* 64 Custom and Uniformity ..soon make the best Things seem dull and insipid. 1751 JOHNSON *Rambler* No. 167 ¶ 6 The uniformity of life must be sometimes diversified. 1819 SCOTT *Leg. Montrose* xvii, Men to whom the late uniformity of their military life had rendered any change of society an interesting novelty. 1860 W. COLLINS *Wom. White* I. W. H.'s Narr. viii, The dull uniformity of life at Limmeridge.

**4.** With *a* and pl. A particular instance of this condition; a uniform feature, law, etc.

1665 J. SPENCER *Prodigies* (ed. 2) 104 All kind of pretty Equalities and Uniformities, especially between Signs and Events. 1733 BERKELEY *Th. Vision Vind.* § 67 We must not, for the sake of uniformities or analogies, depart from truth and fact. 1864 BOWEN *Logic* xii. 412 Simple uniformities, such as are comprehended in a General Fact, may be merely accidental. 1867 BAKER *Nile Trib.* iii. 63, I measured the depth of some of the wells, and found a uniformity of forty feet.

**Uniformize** (yū·nifǭɹmәiz), *v. rare.* [f. UNIFORM *a.* + -IZE. Cf. F. *uniformiser*, Pg. *-izar*, med. L. *ūniformisāre.*] *trans.* To make uniform; to reduce to a uniform system. So **U·niformized** *ppl. a.*

Also, in recent use (1907), *uniformization.*

1866 G. STEPHENS *Runic Mon.* I. p. xiii, To translate the oldest runic inscriptions..into a modern uniformized 'Icelandic'. 1889 *Nature* Oct. 563 The formation of..an International Commission to fix units and uniformize methods.

**U·niformless,** *a.* [f. UNIFORM *sb.* + -LESS.] Lacking or not wearing uniform.

1863 W. H. RUSSELL *My Diary North & S.* I. 308 Great long-bearded fellows in flannel shirts and slouched hats, uniformless.

**U·niformly,** *adv.* Also 6–7 vni-, 7 uniformely. [f. UNIFORM *a.* + -LY [2].] In a uniform manner; with uniformity.

**1.** With or in conformity to one form or standard on the part of several; in the same way as others or another; without diversity of one from another.

In later use merging into sense 3, from which it is not always clearly distinct.

1549 W. THOMAS *Hist. Italy* 74 b, The one syde [of the street] is built of harde stone, all vniformely with faire glasen wyndowes. 1559 BP. C. SCOT in Strype *Ann. Ref.* (1709) I. II. App. x. 27 Common prayers, and the holie sacraments uniformly mynystred. 1617 MORYSON *Itin.* I. 182 The houses are vniformely, and very fairely built of free-stone. 1748 *Anson's Voy.* III. vii. 360 A hundred..were uniformly drest in the regimentals of the marines. 1847 C. BRONTE *J. Eyre* v, They were uniformly dressed in brown stuff frocks.

**2.** With uniformity in degree, quantity, or extent; in or with the same relative proportion; equally, equably.

1577 HARRISON *England* II. vi. (1877) I. 156 They giue it gentle heats..till it be drie, and in the meane while they turne it often, that it may be vniformelie dried. 1609 DOULAND *Ornithoparcus' Microl.* 78 A Consonance is a mixture of two Sounds falling into the eares vniformely. 1656 HOBBES *Six Lessons* Wks. 1845 VII. 282 Two movents, one uniform, the other uniformly accelerated. 1743 W. EMERSON *Fluxions* 109 The Space..would be uniformly discribed in a given Time. 1773 COOK *First Voyage* III. vi. III. 632 Their skins were so uniformly covered with dirt, that it was very difficult to ascertain their true colour. 1815 J. SMITH *Panorama Sci. & Art* II. 654 It is advisable to make the soil uniformly deep in every part. 1869 TYNDALL in *Fortn. Rev.* 1 Feb. 244 If..the plate be wedge-shaped, thickening gradually and uniformly from edge to back.

**3.** In a manner that is always the same; without variation or alteration; at all times or in every case alike; invariably.

1682 NORRIS *Hierocles* 11 By Law is understood the power of God as it always acts uniformly. 1736 BUTLER *Anal.* I. ii. Wks. 1874 I. 38 We find the consequences, which we were beforehand informed of, uniformly to follow. 1776 GIBBON *Decl. & F.* xiii. I. 375 The calm dignity which he uniformly affected. 1825 SCOTT *Talism.* xxvi, When once noticed, it uniformly made a strong impression on the spectator. 1863 E. V. NEALE *Anal. Th. & Nat.* 249 The judgments of our propositions are uniformly made by the verb 'to be'. 1891 *Law Times* XCII. 124/1 Since 1846 the Chancellorship has been uniformly held by Irish barristers.

**b.** Qualifying adjectives or adverbs.

1769 ROBERTSON *Chas. V*, XI. Wks. 1813 III. 329 An administration uniformly equitable and moderate. 1827 J. IVIMEY *Pilgr. 19th Cent.* iii. 59 'Was he uniformly successful in trade?'..'I cannot say that he was always successful; he was uniformly honourable.' 1842 J. WILSON *Chr. North* I. 245 Life has gone uniformly well with him. 1898 'MERRIMAN' *Roden's Corner* x, The result has been uniformly satisfactory.

**U·niformness.** [f. as prec.] Uniformity.

1579 W. WILKINSON *Confut. Fam. Love* Bij, That we might serue euen so the onely liuing God in..vniformenes of hart. 1581 MULCASTER *Positions* xlv. 296 The great varietie in teaching, which is now generally vsed, maye be reduced to some vniformnesse. 1710 BERKELEY *Princ. Hum. Knowl.* I. § 105. 151 Rules grounded on the Analogy, and Uniformness observ'd in the Production of Natural Effects.

**Unify** (yū·nifəi), *v.* [ad. med.L. *unificāre*, f. L. *ūni-* UNI-: see -FY. So F. *unifier* (14th c.), It. *unificare*, Sp. *unificar.*] *trans.* To make, form into, or cause to become one; to combine (two or more) *in* one; to join (one or more) *to* or *with* another or others so as to form one whole or unit; to unite, consolidate.

Rare in 18th c. (see the *ppl. a.*); frequent in recent use.

1502 *Ord. Crysten Men* (W. de W. 1506) I. vii. G iv, Yᵉ holy goost vnyeth & vnyfyeth al these membres of the holy chyrche in one. 1509 HAWES *Joyf. Med.* 6 Two tytles in one thou dydst well vnyfye. 1654 W. MONTAGU *Dev. Ess.* II. viii. 156 Let then all the pretenders to peace, procure to simplifie and unifie their desires by this single address to the will and order of God. 1656 BLOUNT *Glossogr.*, *Unifie*, ..to joyn or make one, as mariage doth Husband and Wife. [Hence in later Dicts.] 1802 COLERIDGE *Lett.* (1895) 404 A poet's heart and intellect should be..intimately combined and unified with the great appearances of nature. 1853 LYNCH *Self-Improv.* 3 Religion will..unify and glorify all his studies. 1884 *Manch. Exam.* 26 Mar. 5/1 The great effect of successive Reform Bills has been to unify the nation.

*absol.* 1817 COLERIDGE *Biog. Lit.* xiii. (1882) 144 It..dissipates, in order to re-create; or..at all events, it struggles to idealize and to unify. 1888 *Classical Rev.* Oct. 256/1 These Homeridæ..worked continuously.., adding and unifying, and so they produced the epics.

Hence **U·nifying** *vbl. sb.*

1681 BAXTER *Acc. Sherlocke* vi. 209 Distinguishing between the Unifying of the Society, and the uniting a single Member to that Society.

**U·nifying,** *ppl. a.* [f. prec. + -ING [2].] That unifies.

1681 BAXTER *Acc. Sherlocke* iv. 184 The Church hath its true, proper, specifying and unifying, that is, constitutive Government. 1751 HARRIS *Hermes* III. iv. (1765) 363 No where is this collecting and (if I may be allowed the expression) this unifying Power more conspicuous. 1775 — *Philos. Arrangem.* vii. 137 By virtue..of this combining, this unifying Comprehension. 1840 DE QUINCEY *Style* IV. (1860) 298 This great unifying event. 1881 MIVART *Cat* 376 The organ and vehicle of such unifying activity.

**Uni·genist,** *a.* [f. UNI-, after MONOGENIST.] Of or pertaining to monogeny; monogenistic.

1896 A. H. KEANE *Ethnology* vii. 156 Another argument in support of the unigenist doctrine against polygenist views.

† **Unigenit,** *a. Obs.*⁻¹ [ad. eccl. L. *ūnigenit-us.* Cf. OF. *unigenit.*] Only begotten.

*a* 1568 in *Bannatyne MS.* (Hunter. Club) 107/5 O vnigeneit Sone to God of micht!

**Unige·niture.** [f. as prec. + -URE.]

**1.** *Theol.* The fact of being the only-begotten Son.

1659 PEARSON *Creed* 278 Unigeniture being the foundation of his singular love. *Ibid.* 279 As primogeniture consisteth in prelation, so unigeniture in exclusion. 1691 E. TAYLOR *Behmen's Theos. Philos.* 369 The intire Will, and Divine Unigeniture.

**2.** The fact of being an only child; the practice of having only one child.

1887 *Edin. Rev.* Oct. 304 The Norman peasantry who secure the advantages of primogeniture by unigeniture.

† **Uni·genous,** *a. Geol. Obs.*⁻¹ [f. UNI- + Gr. γέν-ος kind, origin: see -OUS.] Of uniform structure. (Cf. MONOGENOUS *a.* 4.)

1799 KIRWAN *Geol. Ess.* 214 The unigenous limestone mountains of Carniola.

**Unigni·ted,** *ppl. a.* (UN-[1] 8.)

1773 *Phil. Trans.* LXIV. 27 The dark and unignited state of the great internal globe of the sun. 1784 *Ibid.* LXXV. 194 A very dense fume of unignited particles arises. 1856 FROUDE *Hist. Eng.* I. 28 Like a train of gunpowder, the isolated grains of which have..no effect on each other, while they remain unignited.

**Unihoded,** *ppl. a.*: see UN-[1] 3.

**Unila·biate,** *a.* [ad. mod.L. *ūnilabiāt-us*: see UNI- and LABIATE *a.*] (See quots.) Also **Unila·biated** *a.*

1731 BAILEY (ed. 2) II, *Unilabiated*, having but one lip, spoken of flowers. [Hence in Ash (1775), etc.] 1826 KIRBY & SP. *Entomol.* IV. 38 Some spiracles, however, are unilabiate, or have only one lip. 1847 ROYLE *Mat. Med.* 614 Corolla with outer limb 3-parted, the interior unilabiate.

**Unila·teral,** *a.* [ad. mod.L. *ūnilaterāl-is*, or f. UNI- + LATERAL *a.* Cf. F. *unilatéral* (1804), Sp. and Pg. *unilateral*, It. *-ale.*]

**I. 1. a.** *Bot.* Of a raceme or panicle: Having the flowers on one side of the peduncle. Also, of a cyme: Having a branch or axis on one side only.

1802 R. HALL *Elem. Bot.* 156 One-sided, or Unilateral, *unilateralis*, applied to a raceme with all the flowers inserted on one side. 1853 G. JOHNSTON *Nat. Hist. E. Bord.* I. 218 A coarse but productive species, distinguished readily by its unilateral panicle.

**b.** *Bot.* and *Zool.* Arranged or produced on one side of an axis or surface; directed or turned towards one side.

1870 HOOKER *Stud. Flora* 275 Disk hypogynous unilateral. 1876 tr. *Wagner's Gen. Pathol.* 118 The genital pores are unilateral. 1879 *Hardwicke's Science-Gossip* XV. 203/2 Its flowers are unilateral, as those of the forget-me-not.

**2.** Of or pertaining to, occurring on or affecting, one side of an organ or part.

*Unilateral horse-shoe* (see quot. 1843).

1843 YOUATT *Horse* (ed. 3) xxi. 424 The Unilateral, or one side nailed shoe. *Ibid.*, The unilateral shoe has this great advantage. 1877 M. FOSTER *Physiol.* III. vi. 456 The loss of voluntary movement which follows upon a unilateral section of the medulla. 1880 BASTIAN *Brain* iii. 57 The unilateral influence of Light.

**b.** *Path.* and *Med.* Affecting or developed on only one side of the body at the same time.

1876 DUHRING *Dis. Skin* 225 Zoster is almost invariably unilateral. 1879 P. SMITH *Glaucoma* 5 Hence the bilateral character of chronic glaucoma, and the unilateral acute attacks. 1893 A. S. ECCLES *Sciatica* 7 In the more common form, viz., unilateral sciatica.

**c.** *Phonetics.* Uttered or produced with the glottis open on one side only.

1867 ALEX. MELVILLE BELL *Visible Speech* 59 Uni-lateral formations. When the breath issues by only one side aperture in forming any 'divided' consonant, the modifier [etc.]. 1887 ELLIS in *Encycl. Brit.* XXII. 387/1 Voiced form or buzz of unilateral Welsh *ll.*

**3.** *Math.* (See latter quot.)

1884 SYLVESTER *Coll. Math. Papers* (1912) IV. 152 A unilateral simple equation. *Ibid.* 225 The Quadratic Equation of a form which I call unilateral, because the quaternion coefficients in it are supposed all to lie on the same side of the unknown quantity.

**II. 4.** Performed or undertaken by or on the part of one side; made, enjoyed, shared in, felt, etc., by only one person or party.

1802 W. WINDHAM *Let.* in *Windham Papers* II. 200 This communication..is in this way..unilateral, in which I may speak to you, without hearing anything in return. 1836 TURNBULL *Stubbes' Anat. Abuses* Pref. p. x, That the Editor may not be accused of an unilateral predilection for his *protegé*. 1885 *Times* 6 May 9 It is time to make him understand..that our relations with him cannot continue to be of this unilateral character.

**b.** *Law.* Made or entered upon by one party, esp. without reciprocal obligation on the part of another or others; binding or imposed upon one party only.

1802–12 BENTHAM *Ration. Judic. Evid.* (1827) II. 495 In the case of an unilateral deed, the scribe may be the party himself. 1826 G. J. BELL *Comm. Laws Scotl.* I. 334 Unilateral obligations and bonds. *a* 1859 AUSTIN *Jurispr.* (1879) I. 324 The promise..is, in the language of the jurists, a convention unilateral. 1875 POSTE *Gaius* III. 362 A unilateral Disposition is one made by a solitary principal disposer.

**c.** Of succession: Of or from one side or parent.

1881 *Times* 17 Jan. 4 Men may contract for reciprocal rights of cross or unilateral succession.

**5.** Dealing or concerned with, relating to, only one side of a subject; one-sided.

1830 *Edin. Rev.* LI. 531 The results of this uni-lateral.. mode of proceeding. 1838 SIR W. HAMILTON *Logic* xxx. (1866) II. 111 The unilateral and incompetent reasoning which I have here supposed in the case of time. 1873 MORLEY *Rousseau* II. 145 This is a unilateral view of the social contract, and omits the element of reciprocity.

**b.** *Logic.* (See quot.)

1864 BOWEN *Logic* vi. 170 In some cases, the Restriction.. and the Integration may be bilateral.., as affecting both Subject and Predicate;..or unilateral,..as affecting either the Subject only,..or the Predicate only.

Hence **Unilatera·lity**, the quality or character of being unilateral.

1844 DELANE in Dasent *Life & Corr.* (1908) I. 46 Unilaterality (there's a long word for you) is an essential ingredient in a printer's happiness. 1887 ELLIS in *Encycl. Brit.* XXII. 387/1 This unilaterality [of click] is insisted on by Salesbury. 1899 *Allbutt's Syst. Med.* VIII. 622 True zoster of the face characterized by unilaterality.

**Unila·terally,** *adv.* [f. UNILATERAL *a.* + -LY [2].] In a unilateral manner: **a.** *Bot.*, *Zool.*, and *Path.* On one side or surface only.

1830 LINDLEY *Nat. Syst. Bot.* 162 Flowers..often arranged unilaterally along the divisions of the cymes. 1852 DANA *Crust.* II. 1297 With several setæ at apex, which are unilaterally setulose. 1875 BENNETT & DYER *Sachs' Bot.* 463 The descending portions..joining others lower down either unilaterally or on both sides.

**b.** In respect of one side only; by means of or on the part of one side or party; one-sidedly.

1858 GLADSTONE *Homer* II. 297 But then such representations in Homer are not perseveringly, much less are they unilaterally, developed. 1875 POSTE *Gaius* I. Introd. (ed. 2) 8 A judgment..may be unilaterally penal, that is, may impoverish the defendant without enriching the plaintiff.

† **Uniliche,** *a.* and *sb. Obs.* [OE. *ungelīc* (see UN-[1] 7 and YLIKE *a.*), = MDu. *ongelijc* (Du. *ongelijk*, WFris. *on-*, *ungelyk*), MLG. *ungelīk* (LG. *unglīk*), OHG. *ungalīh* (MHG. *ungelich*, *unglich*, G. *ungleich*), ON. *úglíkr.*]

**A.** *adj.* Unlike; not of the same kind or condition; different; *spec.* incomparable, superior.

*c* 888 K. ÆLFRED *Boeth.* xxxiii. § 5 Ealle ȝesceafta þu ȝesceope him ȝelice, & eac on sumum ðingum unȝelice. 971 *Blickl. Hom.* 97 Þonne is unȝelic be þon ecan life. *a* 1100 in Napier *O. E. Glosses* I. 2325 *Dispari sexu*, unȝelicum

[*Brussels MS.* unilicum] hade. *a* **1200** *Moral Ode* 360 (Trin. MS.), Þar ben wuniinges fele elch oðer uniliche. *a* **1225** *Juliana* 60 An godd al mihti, al oðer unilich. *c* **1400** *R. Gloucester's Chron.* (Rolls) 815/268 He was..swiþe riche; Of richesse to fore alle oþere he was vniliche.

**B.** *sb.* = UNILIKE (q.v., quot. *a* 1250).

† **Uniliche,** *adv. Obs.* [OE. *ungelíce* (cf. prec.) differently, = OS. *ungilîko*, OHG. *ungelicho*, etc.] Incomparably.

*c* **1290** *St. Brendan* 143 in *S. Eng. Leg.* I. 223 Fairere hi beoþ þan ȝoure scheep, & grettere vnyliche. *a* **1400** *R. Gloucester's Chron.* (Rolls) 786/58 Ac þe oþer were strengore, & richore oniliche.

† **Unilike.** *Obs. rare.* [OE. *ungelíca*, = MDu. *ongelike*: cf. UNILICHE *a.*] One different from, or superior to, another.

*c* **1000** ÆLFRIC *Saints' Lives* vii. 28 Ic hæbbe oðerne lufiend, þinne unȝelican on æðelborennysse. *a* **1250** *Owl & Night.* 806 (Cott.), Þu seist þat þu canst fele wike Ac euer ich am þin unilike [*Jesus MS.* vnyliche].

**Unili·ngual,** *a.* [See UNI- 1 and LINGUAL *a.*, and cf. F. *unilingue.*] Pertaining to one language only; knowing or employing only one language.

Hence, in recent use, *unilingualism*.

**1866** VISCT. STRANGFORD *Select.* (1869) II. 18 In Crete, one of the most primitive and unilingual parts of the Levant. **1886** *Standard* 8 Oct. 5 A good linguist has a pull..over his unilingual contemporary. **1894** *Educat. Rev.* VII. 190 The unilingual method..advocated by pedagogical writers.

**Unili·teral,** *a.* [See UNI- 1 and LITERAL *a.*]

**1.** *Math.* (See quot.)

**1817** COLEBROOKE *Algebra*, etc. 185 Equation uniliteral, or involving a single unknown quantity.

**2.** Involving the use of, or consisting of, only one letter.

**1828–32** WEBSTER. **1863** TOWNSEND *Mod. Geom.* I. 2 The latter or uniliteral notation is generally the more convenient. **1892** C. TAYLOR *Witness of Hermas* 86 Examples of the uniliteral acrostic abound in the Sibylline Oracles.

**Unillu·med,** *ppl. a.* (UN-[1] 8.) **1796** COLERIDGE *Destiny of Nations* 161 Her full eye, now bright, now unillumed. **1869** TYNDALL in *Fortn. Rev.* 1 Feb. 143 The unillumed blackness of space.

**Unillu·minated,** *ppl. a.* [UN-[1] 8.]

**1.** Not spiritually or mentally enlightened.

**1579** W. WILKINSON *Confut. Fam. Love* B iij b, H. N. sayth of all preachers without his Familie, that they are vnilluminated. **1639** W. SCLATER *Worthy Commun.* 23 Thus surely may your dull Capernaites, and unilluminated men imagine. **1660** H. MORE *Myst. Godl.* VI. xii. 248 What the ungodded or unilluminated men..bring forth. **1798** *Brit. Critic* XI. 47 The hazard of being reputed the disciples of a very *unilluminated* school. **1858** H. BUSHNELL *Serm. New Life* 100 The unilluminated and superficial speculations of our times. **1882** FARRAR *Early Chr.* I. 454 To the eyes of the unilluminated heart the region in which Faith lives and moves is a dark cavern.

**2.** Not illuminated or lighted up. Also *fig.*

**1824** DE QUINCEY *Analects fr. Richter* Wks. 1860 XIV. 137, I saw the Form which still lightened as before, but left all around it unilluminated. **1874** tr. *Lommel's Light* 15 The back unilluminated surface of the body.

**Unillu·minating,** *ppl. a.* (UN-[1] 10.) **1882** A. AINGER *C. Lamb* 70 The very unilluminating notes of Johnson or Malone. **Unillu·mined,** *ppl. a.* (UN-[1] 8.) [**1775** ASH.] **1826** LAMB *Elia* II. *Pop. Fallacies* xv, Our ancestors..wintering in caves and unillumined fastnesses. **1892** 'M. FIELD' *Sight & Song* 54 A solid disc of unillumined brown. **Unillu·sory,** *a.* (UN-[1] 7.) **1853** LYTTON *My Novel* III. xxii, Always scrutinizing the domestic felicity..through a pair of cold unillusory barnacles. **Uni·llustrated,** *ppl. a.* (UN-[1] 8.) [**1775** ASH.] **1828** WEBSTER (citing Good). **1879** *Cassell's Techn. Educ.* II. 275/1 Better than the most impressive verbal description, unillustrated. **1883** *American* VII. 9 Heavy, unillustrated English magazines. **Unillu·strative,** *a.* (UN-[1] 7.) **1803** GODWIN *Chaucer* II. xlii. 282 It may not..prove..unillustrative of the history..of England. **1867** *Fortn. Rev.* Oct. 377 Certain lights, not unillustrative as well of the one side as of the other. **Unillu·strious,** *a.* (UN-[1] 7.) **1885** D. HANNAY in *Mag. Art* Sept. 448/1 A long and unillustrious line of successors. **1897** W. WATSON *Year of Shame, To Sultan*, It merged thee with the unillustrious herd.

**Unilo·cular** (yūni-), *a.* [f. UNI- + LOCULAR *a.* Cf. mod.L. *ūniloculāris* and F. *uniloculaire* (1771).] Having, consisting of, characterized by only one loculus (in various senses); one-celled.

**1753** *Chambers' Cycl.* Suppl. *App.*, *Unilocular*, in botany, is applied to a capsule having but one cell. **1762** *Phil. Trans.* LIII. 83 An oblong, oval striated unilocular seedvessel. **1815** W. WOOD *Gen. Conchol.* p. lx, The Paper Nautilus, the Cowries, the Olives, etc. are unilocular shells. **1860** PIRRIE *Surg.* 607 The unilocular cystic tumour. **1867** J. HOGG *Microsc.* II. ii. 376 The Polythalamia or Multilocular Rhizopods, in their earliest state are unilocular. **1899** *Allbutt's Syst. Med.* VIII. 634 A vesicle of H[erpes] Zoster at its height is a unilocular cavity.

Hence **Unilocula·rity,** unilocular character or formation.

**1819** LINDLEY tr. *Richard's Observ. Fruits & Seeds* 11 Unilocularity (provided there be no abortion) always establishes the unity of fruit. **1839** A. GRAY *Lett.* (1893) I. 150 The unilocularity of the anthers.

**Uni·maged,** (*ppl.*) *a.* (UN-[1] 8, 9.)

**1648** HEXHAM II, *Ongebeeldt*, Vn-imaged, without Figure or Image. **1775** ASH, *Unimaged*.., not imaged, not formed in the imagination. **1841** CLOUGH *Poems* (1862) 17 The bare conscience of the better thing Unfelt, unseen, unimaged. **1860** PUSEY *Min. Proph.* 153 Their great forefathers ..worshipped the un-imaged Self-existing God.

**Unima·ginable,** *a.* and *sb.* [UN-[1] 7 b, 5 b.]

**1.** *adj.* Incapable of being imagined; inconceivable, incomprehensible.

**1611** COTGR., *Inimaginable*, vnimaginable, vnconceiuable. *a* **1631** DONNE *Serm.* i. (1634) 30 Miserable, unexpressible, unimaginable, macerable condition, where [etc.]. **1655** H. MORE *App. Antid.* vii. 377 It is utterly unimaginable, but that there should be a Triangular distance in the midst of them. **1746** HERVEY *Medit., Refl. Flower Garden* 42 With what un-imaginable Complacency, does Justice rest satisfied! **1821** SCOTT *Kenilw.* vi, I shall thank him more for the love that has created such an unimaginable paradise, than for all the wonders it contains! **1878** P. BAYNE *Purit. Rev.* i. 7 To believe in an unseen and unimaginable Spirit.

**2.** *sb. pl.* = INEXPRESSIBLE *sb.* 2.

**1833** T. HAMILTON *Men & Manners* (1843) 391 The men.. rejoiced in snuff-coloured waistcoats and unimaginables.

Hence **Unima·ginableness.**

**1659** H. MORE *Immort. Soul* I. vi. 37 The unimaginableness of Points and smallest Particles. **1871** W. G. WARD *Philos. Theism* (1884) I. 17 That the unimaginableness of a proposition is incompatible with its truth.

**Unima·ginably,** *adv.* (UN-[1] 11; cf. prec.)

**1666** BOYLE *Orig. Forms & Qual.* II. ix. 395 It appear'd a ..heap of Corpuscles..unimaginably small. *a* **1672** STERRY *2nd Posth. Vol.* 331 The Righteousness..of God in Christ ..unimaginably outshineth ten thousand Suns. **1734** WATTS *Reliq. Juv.* 191 And thus..we unimaginably slide into a cordial Defence of the Cause. **1857** HAWTHORNE *Eng. Notebks.* (1870) II. 432 Hues..indescribably beautiful, and unimaginably, unless one can conceive of the colours of the rainbow [etc.]. **1883** *Harper's Mag.* June 115/2 Unimaginably frightful shapes.

**Unima·ginary,** *a.* (UN-[1] 7.) **1608** D. PRICE *Chr. Warre* 27 God ouercame more gloriously for you by a weake, small vnimaginarie, Charactericall armie. **1828** MACKINTOSH *Sp.* Wks. 1846 III. 490 One of their not unimaginary grievances.

**Unima·ginative,** *a.* (UN-[1] 7.) Also *absol.*

**1802** WORDSW. *Excurs.* II. 24 Ranging through the tamer ground Of these our unimaginative days. **1831** SCOTT *Ct. Rob.* xvii, Nor shall Anna Comnena, the soul of wit and genius, be chained to such an unimaginative log as yonder half barbarian. **1898** *Fortn. Rev.* LXIV. 300 To the unimaginative, all imaginative work must inevitably present a closed door.

Hence **Unima·ginatively** *adv.*, **-ness.**

**1850** *N. Brit. Rev.* XII. 320 Not contented with such a stretch of unimaginativeness. **1883** *Cornh. Mag.* April 456 The Roman, more unimaginatively, held to the bare fact of change.

**Unima·gine,** *v.* (UN-[2] 3.) *a* **1670** RUST *Disc. Truth* (1682) 170 He may as easily unimagine that Imagination.

**Unima·gined,** *ppl. a.* and *adv.* (UN-[1] 8.)

*a* **1548** HALL *Chron.*, *Hen. VI*, 103 A thyng discended from heauen, of theim vnsought, vnimagined and not deuised. **1649** LOVELACE *Poems* (1904) 69 The unimagin'd Woes..of the Hierarchy. **1736** BUTLER *Anal.* I. i. 20 A latent and..an unimagined unknown power of perceiving sensible objects. **1754** FRANCIS *Constantine* III. 36 What uninvented, unimagin'd Tortures Have I to dread? **1846** TRENCH *Mirac.* xvii. 276 His walking over the sea must have been altogether unimagined by them. **1884** CHURCH *Bacon* viii. 187 That hitherto unimagined empire of man over the powers and forces that encompassed him.

† **b.** *adv.* Unexpectedly. *Obs.*—[1]

**1614** W. B. *Philosopher's Banquet* (ed. 2) 254 When, vnimagined, the wench demaunded of him,..whether he [etc.].

**Unimbue·d,** *ppl. a.* (UN-[1] 8.) [**1775** ASH.] **1813** SHELLEY *Q. Mab* v. 152 A weak and inexperienced boy,..unimbued With pure desire and universal love. **1880** TROLLOPE *Life of Cicero* I. 202 He was..altogether unimbued with the humanity..of his brother.

† **Unime·te,** *sb. Obs.* [OE. *ungemet*: see UN-[1] 12 and IMET.] Immoderation, excess.

*c* **888** K. ÆLFRED *Boeth.* xl. § 3 He ne mæȝ nauþres unȝemet adrioȝan. *c* **1000** *Sax. Leechd.* II. 106 Þonne ȝeweaxeð on innan unȝemet wætan. *a* **1225** *Ancr. R.* 74 Urom soð hit slit te uals; vt of god into vuel, & from mesure into unimete.

† **Unime·te,** *adv. Obs.* [OE. *ungemete*, dat. of *ungemet*: see prec.] Immoderately, excessively.

*Beowulf* 2420 Him wæs ȝeomor sefa,..wyrd unȝemete neah. *Ibid.* 2721 Þeȝn unȝemete till. *c* **1000** *Ags. Ps.* (Thorpe) cxv. 2 Ic sylfa cwæð..þæt wæron ealle menn unȝemete lease. *c* **1205** LAY. 7393 Sixti scipen heo makeden vnimete [*c* **1275** onimete] muchele. *a* **1225** *Leg. Kath.* 738 Stoden on an half þeos meistres so monie, & unimete modi. **1300–1400** *R. Gloucester's Chron.* (Rolls) App. A. 15 Þe wynd..schouueþ & þrast þat al þe erþe quakiȝeþ & schakeþ onymete.

† **Unime·te,** *a. Obs.* [OE. *ungemǽte*: see UN-[1] 7 and IMETE *a.*] Immeasurable, vast; immoderate, excessive.

*a* **1122** *O.E. Chron.* an. 1115 (Laud MS.), Ðises ȝeares wæs swa strang winter..& wearð þurh þæt unȝemæte orf cwealm. *c* **1175** *Lamb. Hom.* 101 Unimete festen and to michel forhefednesse..macað þene mon un-halne. *c* **1205** LAY. 4964 Þe ferde wes swa muchel þat heo wes vnimete [*c* **1275** onimete]. *a* **1225** *Ancr. R.* 40 Þo þi swete blisfule sune underueng ðe in his vnimete blisse. *c* **1275** *Sinners Beware* 50 in *O. E. Misc.* 73 Chele and hete, And hunger vnymete.

Hence † **Unime·tely** *adv.*, immeasurably. *Obs.*

*a* **1225** *Ancr. R.* 398 Ne schal neuer heorte þenchen swuch seluhðe, þet ich nulle ȝiuen more uor þine luue, vnimeteliche and vnendliche more. *a* **1240** *Wohunge* in *O. E. Hom.* I. 281 Swa unimeteliche þu swanc and swa sare þat reade blod þu swattes.

**Uni·mitable,** *a.* ? *Obs.* (UN-[1] 7 b, 5 b.)

Very common in 17th century.

**1581** SIDNEY *Apol. Poetrie* (Arb.) 46 As the vnimitable Pindar often did. **1622** F. MARKHAM *Bk. War* Ep. Ded. A 3 b, As by his owne vnimitable pen is protested. **1683** KENNETT *Erasm. on Folly* 48 As they [*sc.* bees] give a model of in their unimitable Combs. **1695** J. EDWARDS *Perfect. Script.* Ded., You bore the..insults of the enemy with unimitable bravery. **1773** JOHNSON in *Shakespeare's Wks.* V. 508 But Falstaff unimitated, unimitable Falstaff, how shall I describe thee?

So † **Uni·mitably** *adv. Obs.*

**1622** PEACHAM *Compl. Gent.* x. 91 His sweetnesse and facilitie in a verse, vnimitably excellent. **1670** WALTON *Lives, Donne* 80 His fancy was unimitably high, equalled only by his great wit.

**Uni·mitated,** *ppl. a.* (UN-[1] 8.)

*c* **1610** *Women Saints* 185, I beseeche..you women doe not leaue this example vnimitated. *a* **1670** HACKET in Plume *Life* (1865) 171 The..perpetual sobriety of the primitive Christians began to be unimitated. **1773** [see UNIMITABLE *a.*]. **1837** CARLYLE *Fr. Rev.* I. III. viii, An excellent new-idea, which, in these coming years, shall not remain unimitated.

**Uni·mitating,** *ppl. a.* (UN-[1] 10.) **1748** RICHARDSON *Clarissa* (1811) VIII. 331 A spiteful, perverse, unimitating thing. **Uni·mitative,** *a.* (UN-[1] 7.) **1807** ANNA SEWARD *Lett.* (1811) VI. 334 The original unimitative compositions of James H. **1849** RUSKIN *Sev. Lamps* iv. § 2. 95 The Doric capital was unimitative. **1883** *Pall Mall G.* 8 Sept. 2/1 Among us unimitative but not unappreciative Britons. **Unimme·diate,** *a.*, **-ly,** *adv.* (UN-[1] 7, 11.) **1802–12** BENTHAM *Ration. Judic. Evid.* (1827) III. 362 In an unimmediate, though, for efficacy, not too remote way. **1816** — *Chrestom.* Wks. 1843 VIII. 91 Instruments of all kinds, whether applied immediately or unimmediately to use.

**Unimme·rgible,** *a.* [UN-[1] 7.] Insubmergible.

**1806** L. LUKIN (*title*), The Invention, Principles of Construction, and Uses of Unimmergible Boats. **1809** *Naval Chron.* XXI. 299 To make it..unimmergible,..casks..were ranged along. **1823** *Blackw. Mag.* XIV. 303 They met with an unimmergible buoyancy in this case.

**Unimme·rsed,** *ppl. a.* (UN-[1] 8.)

[**1775** ASH.] **1835** I. TAYLOR *Spir. Despot.* iv. 408 These good souls will not eat the Lord's loaf in company with the unclean and unimmersed commonalty of professed Christians. **1885** PENNELL *Fishing* 267 The effect of refraction kept the unimmersed portion of the fly fisher's figure practically out of sight.

**Uni·mmolated,** *ppl. a.* (UN-[1] 8.) **1855** PUSEY *Doctr. Real Presence* Note I. 115 We too shall be able to receive Him wholly in ourselves continually immolated unimmolated for us.

**Unimmo·rtal,** *a.* (UN-[1] 7.)

**1667** MILTON *P. L.* x. 611 They both betook them several wayes, Both to destroy, or unimmortal make All kinds. **1876** FARRAR *Marlb. Serm.* i. (1877) 5 Their unimmortal but sinless destiny being accomplished.

**Unimmo·rtalize,** *v.* (UN-[2] 6 c.) **1839** BAILEY *Festus* 336 They have well-nigh unimmortalized myself. **Unimmo·rtalized,** *ppl. a.* (UN-[1] 8 a *c.*) [**1775** ASH.] **1839** BAILEY *Festus* 10 But The shadowy giant alway thinned away, And I was fated unimmortalized.

**Unimmu·red,** *ppl. a.* [UN-[1] 8.] † Unwalled. (See IMMURE *v.* 1.)

**1615** G. SANDYS *Trav.* 155 The Iewes..began to reedifie the same [temple]; which yet was vnimmured for threescore and three yeares after.

**Unimpai·rable,** *a.* (UN-[1] 7 b.)

**1627** HAKEWILL *Apol.* (1630) 288 It is unimpareable like the light..of the sunne. **1647** CLARENDON *Contempl. Ps.* Tracts (1727) 504 From that unimpairable stock of thy mercies..blot out our offences. **1653** H. MORE *Conject. Cabbal.* (1713) 175 It being the lowest degree and shadow of Being; and not only immoveable, but undiminishable and unimpairable.

**Unimpai·red,** *ppl. a.* (UN-[1] 8.)

Before 1760 somewhat *rare*; in freq. use from *c* 1790.

**1583** GOLDING *Calvin on Deut.* 41 b, In such wise as God may holde still his right vnimpayred. **1628** LE GRYS tr. *Barclay's Argenis* 122 To him will I restore what they rob'd thee of, as I finde by them yet vnempayred. **1738** G. LILLO *Marina* II. ii, My youth yet unimpair'd By riot or disease. **1772** *Junius' Lett.* Ded. (1788) 7 When you leave the unimpaired, hereditary freehold to Your children. **1816** BYRON *Ch. Har.* III. v, Shapes which dwell Still unimpair'd, though old, in the soul's haunted cell. **1855** MACAULAY *Hist. Eng.* xx. IV. 532 She..repeated her part of the office with unimpaired memory. **1860** MOTLEY *Netherl.* II. I. 51 He had preserved the most unimpaired good-humour.

**Unimpa·radised,** *ppl. a.* (UN-[2] 5, 8.) **1601** W. PARRY *Trav. Sir A. Sherley* (1863) 4 A scruple..whether Man were (for transgression) ever unimparadized or no.

**Unimpa·rted,** *ppl. a.* (UN-[1] 8.)

**1655** (*title*), Natura Exenterata,..Whereunto are annexed, Many Rare, hitherto un-imparted Inventions. **1791** COWPER *Iliad* XI. 924 But brave Achilles shuts His virtues close, an unimparted store. **1824** SCOTT *St. Ronan's* xvi, That the knowledge which is unimparted is necessarily a barren talent.

**Unimpa·ssionate,** *a.* (UN-[1] 7.) **1845** MOZLEY *Ess.* (1878) II. 119 In proportion to the extent to which such a view obtains, worship must become necessarily unimpassionate and unadoring.

**Unimpa·ssioned,** *ppl. a.* (UN-[1] 8.)

**1744** THOMSON *Autumn* (ed. 4) 1070 Fancy then..Will.. Correct her Pencil to the purest Truth Of Nature, or, the unimpassion'd Shades Forsaking, raise it to the human Mind. **1778** MISS BURNEY *Evelina* xxiii, The cool eye of unimpassioned philosophy. **1802** COLERIDGE *Dejection* ii, A stifled, drowsy, unimpassion'd grief. **1876** T. HARDY *Ethelberta* xxvii, She would not go out of her way at a beck from a man whose interest was so unimpassioned.

**Unimpeachabi·lity.** (UN-[1] 12; cf. next.)

**1830** R. CHAMBERS *Life Jas. I*, I. iv. 119 Nations..too much disposed..to question the unimpeachability of their sovereigns. **1881** SALA in *Illustr. Lond. News* 19 Feb. 171 The unimpeachability of the arrangements.

**Unimpea·chable,** *a.* (UN-[1] 7 b.)

**1784** COWPER *Task* IV. 676 Merchants, unimpeachable of sin Against the charities of domestic life. **1794** BURKE *Sp. Acts Uniformity* Wks. 1842 II. 465 The unimpeachable integrity and piety of many of the promoters of this petition. **1830** MISS MITFORD *Village* Ser. IV. 189 He could..take Harry's dinner to the same place with unimpeachable honesty. **1848** DICKENS *Dombey* iv, Seeing what time it is by the unimpeachable chronometer. **1864** BOWEN *Logic* xii. 392 The testimony of one unimpeachable witness.

Hence **Unimpea·chableness.** Also **Unimpea·chably** *adv.*

1817 GODWIN *Mandev.* III. 188 The insinuations they threw out against the *unimpeachableness of his motives. 1866 GEO. ELIOT *F. Holt* iv, Mrs. Holt was not given to tears; she was much sustained by conscious unimpeachableness. 1821 LAMB *Confess. Delamore* Wks. 1908 I. 266 For more than five centuries, the current of our blood hath flowed *unimpeachably. 1883 *Manch. Exam.* 22 Dec. 5 The jury were aided by a luminous and unimpeachably fair summing up.

**Unimpea·ched,** *ppl. a.* [UN-1 8.]

†**1.** Not impeded or hindered. *Obs.*

*c* 1430 *Pilgr. Lyf Manhode* II. xcvi. (1869) 110 With hire cordes she withheeld me, of which j was not unenpeched.

**2.** Not assailed, accused, or called in question.

1583 GOLDING *Calvin on Deut.* xxxix. 235 Let vs glorifie him, and beware yt he remaine vnimpeached in his Maiestie. *c* 1611 CHAPMAN *Iliad* IX. 383 Many fair Achive princesses of unimpeached life. 1702 ROWE *Tamerl.* IV. i, While yet my Regal State stood unimpeach'd. 1790 COWPER *Let. to Bagot* 22 June, A person of most unimpeached veracity. 1823 BYRON *Siege Cor.* vii, When unimpeached for traitorous crime..He glittered thro' the Carnival. 1869 [see UNIMPLICATE]. 1871 JOWETT *Plato* IV. 158 The public and unimpeached use of anything for a year.

**Uni·mped,** *ppl. a.* (UN-1 8 + IMP *v.* 8.)

1603 DRAYTON *To Maiestie K. Jas.* A 3, Our early Muse.. Of her own strength which boldly thus presumes, That's yet vnimpt with any borowed plumes.

**Unimpe·ded,** *ppl. a.* (UN-1 8.)

1760 D. MALLET in Derrick *Lett.* (1767) II. 23 Much more so as..your access to them [is] unimpeded. 1795 SOUTHEY *Vis. Maid of Orleans* I. 79 Through the roof..The moonbeams enter'd..With unimpeded light. 1861 MILL *Repr. Govt.* 52 Whatever invigorates the faculties,..creates an increased desire for their more unimpeded exercise. 1878 Bosw. SMITH *Carthage* 388 It gave them an unimpeded landing, and a second base of operations in Africa.

Hence **Unimpe·dedly** *adv.*

Also, in recent use, *unimpededness.*

1846 POE *A. C. Mowatt* Wks. 1864 III. 43 The mere instruments by which she may effectively and unimpededly lay bare to the audience the movements of her own passionate heart.

**Unimpe·dible,** *a.* (UN-1 7.) 1677 GALE *Crt. Gentiles* III. II. 515 Where-ever there is passive Power there is impedibilitie: There is nothing ἀνεμπόδιστος, unimpedible, but God. **Unimpe·rative,** *a.* (UN-1 7.) 1817 BENTHAM *Parl. Reform* Introd. 102 A mere exercise of the unimperative faculty of deputation. **Unimpe·rious,** *a.* (UN-1 7.) [1775 ASH.] 1792 J. RICHARDSON *Fugitive* IV. iii, The merits of your most unimperious sex. **Unimpi·nging,** *ppl. a.* (UN-1 10.) 1800 COLERIDGE *Lett.* (1895) 326 Alfoxden would make two houses sufficiently divided for unimpinging independence. **Uni·mplicate,** *ppl. a.* [UN-1 8 b.] = next. 1869 BROWNING *Ring & Bk.* XI. 1287 She, unimpeached of crime, unimplicate In folly. **Uni·mplicated,** *ppl. a.* (UN-1 8.) 1822–7 GOOD *Study Med.* (1829) IV. 687 The sound parts remain unimplicated in the action. 1857 DE QUINCEY in 'H. A. Page' *Life* (1877) II. xvii. 56 The boy was quite unimplicated in any part of the case. **Unimpli·cit,** *a.* (UN-1 7.) 1673 MILTON *True Relig.* 16 Which must needs conduce much..to the general confirmation of unimplicit truth.

**Unimplo·red,** *ppl. a.* (UN-1 8.)

1667 MILTON *P. L.* IX. 22 If answerable style I can obtaine Of my Celestial Patroness, who deignes Her nightly visitation unimplor'd. *a* 1711 KEN *Hymnarium* Poet. Wks. 1721 II. 85 To Sinners thou..Grace unimplor'd benignly dost impart. 1746 YOUNG *Nt. Th.* IX. 904 We feel A sudden succour, un-implor'd, un-thought. 1806 JOHN HOGG *Poems* 31 [She was] Impatient to perform her offer made To Zara, unimplor'd. 1842 WORDSW. *Eccles. Sonn.* III. xxix, If sorrow for thy sin be dead, Guilt unrepented, pardon unimplored.

**Unimpo·rtance.** (UN-1 12.)

1751 JOHNSON *Rambler* No. 146 ⁋5 By such arts..does every man endeavour to conceal his own unimportance from himself. 1775 S. J. PRATT *Liberal Opin.* v. (1783) I. 15 The eye of a child converts every trifle into an object of entertainment, and every pretty unimportance, is esteemed a joyful acquisition. 1823 LAMB *Wks.* (1908) I. 286 The unimportance of the subject. 1879 R. K. DOUGLAS *Confucianism* iii. 66 To the succeeding millions of China it has been a matter of unimportance.

**Unimpo·rtant,** *a.* [UN-1 7.]

**1.** Unassuming, modest. *rare*—1.

1727 POPE *Let. to Swift* 8 Mar., A free, unimportant, natural, easy manner; diverting others just as we diverted ourselves.

**2.** Of no importance or moment.

1750 CHESTERF. *Let.* 1 Nov., Ransacking..the minute and unimportant parts of remote and fabulous times. 1798 S. & HT. LEE *Canterb. T.* II. 465 He was too unimportant to act on [the passions]..of any one around him. 1841 MIALL in *Nonconf.* I. 1 The ends they sought appeared too unimportant to justify the cost. 1869 FREEMAN *Norm. Conq.* xi. III. 53 Esegar and Bondig play not unimportant parts in the great struggles of the year.

*Comb.* 1841 CARLYLE *Heroes* iv. (1904) 129 There was not a more entirely unimportant-looking pair of people.

**Unimpo·rted,** *ppl. a.* (UN-1 8.) [1775 ASH.] 1784 R. BAGE *Barham Downs* II. 88 Two bottles of unimported wine.

†**Unimpo·rting,** *ppl. a.* [UN-1 10.] = UNIMPORTANT *a.* 2.

*c* 1625 BP. HALL *St. Paul's Combat* Wks. 1634 II. 449 If it be only matter of rite, or of unimporting consequence. 1642 FULLER *Holy & Prof. St.* III. xx. 206 Such Divines, who in unimporting controversies extract the probablest opinions from all Professions. 1658 T. WALL *Charact. Enemies Ch.* 40 Things of unimporting consequence.

**Unimpo·rtunate,** *a.* (UN-1 7.) 1755 YOUNG *Centaur* iii. Wks. 1757 IV. 174 These are the men, who..rush headlong into even unimportunate temptations. 1824 LANDOR *Imag. Conv.* I. 299 The demon of Socrates, not always unimportunate, followed Euripides. **Unimportuned,** *ppl. a.* (UN-1 8.) ? 1611–2 DONNE *Let. to Lady Carey* 23 Who ever ran To Danger unimportun'd. *a* 1631 — *Paradoxes* (1652) 27 To run into Death unimportuned is to run into the first condemned Desperateness. 1849 C. BRONTË *Shirley* xiii, [They] were suffered to keep details to themselves, unimportuned by the curiosity of their listeners. **Unimportu·nely,** *adv.* (UN-1 11.) 1657 EARL MONM. tr. *Paruta's Pol. Disc.* 42 Rather..to dissemble their injuries and suspitions, then by unimportunely revenging the one and asser-taining the other, put their affairs in greater danger.

**Unimpo·sed,** *ppl. a.* (UN-1 8.)

1642 MILTON *Apol. Smect.* 50 The very act of prayer and thanksgiving with those free and unimpos'd expressions..is the greatest decency that can be imagin'd. 1677 GILPIN *Demonol.* II. iv. 249 From the toleration of a private Opinion of some Doctors and unimposed, it obtained at last a Canon to make it Authentick, Publick Doctrine.

So **Unimpo·sedly** *adv.*

1647 BOYLE in Birch *Life* (1744) 80 The gallantry..of their own principles will carry them on unimposedly to do much more.

**Unimpo·sing,** *ppl. a.* [UN-1 10.]

†**1.** Not burdensome or oppressive. *Obs.*—1

1736 THOMSON *Liberty* v. 626 Beauteous Order reigns, Manly Submission, unimposing Toil.

**2.** Unimpressive.

1809 C. SIMEON in W. Carus *Life* (1847) 272 The slow unimposing voice. 1854 MILMAN *Lat. Christianity* VII. ii. III. 169 A grey haired man..of small unimposing stature. 1871 EARLE *Philol. Eng. Tongue* 421 A feature..unimposing in its appearance.

So **Unimpo·singly** *adv.*

1880 MISS BIRD *Japan* I. 15 The British Consulate, imposingly ugly;..the Union Church,..unimposingly so.

**Unimpou·nded,** *ppl. a.* (UN-1 8.) 1866 HOWELLS *Venetian Life* 5, I do not say that these cells are calculated to enamour the unimpounded spectator with prison-life. **Unimpow·ered,** *ppl. a.* (UN-1 8.) 1731 A. HILL *Adv. Poets* Epist. p. vi, The Poet..unimpower'd to act greatly Himself, asserts his Fire in describing the Great Actions of others. **Unimpre·gnate,** *ppl. a.* [UN-1 8 b.] = next. 1834 LD. HOUGHTON *Mem. Tour Greece* 140 Dumb forms, unimpregnate with vital emotion. 1849 LOWELL *Biglow P.* Ser. I. Poet. Wks. (1912) 226/2 Lads, unimpregnate with the more sublimated punctiliousness of Walton.

**Unimpre·gnated,** *ppl. a.* [UN-1 8.]

**1.** Not rendered pregnant.

1744 *Phil. Trans.* XLIII. 83 Nor can we conceive any Use of them while the Uterus is unimpregnated at any time. 1793 M. BAILLIE *Morb. Anat.* 269 The uterus in such cases is considerably larger than the unimpregnated size. 1862 A. MEADOWS *Man. Midwifery* 52 The nerve-tubules in the unimpregnated state. 1877 HUXLEY *Anat. Inv. Anim.* vii. 446 The unimpregnated, apterous, caterpillar-like females of the Lepidopterous genera Psyche and Solenobia.

**b.** Not fructified or made prolific.

1800 *Med. Jrnl.* III. 160 The remark, that a similar liquor had been found in unimpregnated eggs. 1842 J. BURNET *Reynold's Disc.* 33 Many young men of genius have disappeared like unimpregnated blossoms, flowery but fruitless.

**2.** Not impregnated (*with* some matter).

1772–3 T. PERCIVAL *Ess.* (1777) I. 59 An ounce and a half of Jamaica Rum, which was..unimpregnated with any astringent matter from the cask. 1790 *Phil. Trans.* LXXX. 372 A thick white turbid liquor, which was rendered clear by addition of unimpregnated oil of vitriol.

**Unimpre·ssed,** *ppl. a.* [UN-1 8.]

†**1.** Not subjected to restraint. *Obs.*—1

1743 YOUNG *Nt. Th.* v. 122 Thoughts uncontroul'd, and unimpress'd, the births Of pure election.

**2.** Not affected by feelings of respect or awe.

1861 [F. W. ROBINSON] *Under the Spell* I. 300 He did not mind her being 'un-impressed' by the knowledge that her father was only his tutor. 1896 MRS. CAFFYN *Quaker Grandmother* 110 Mossy did this sort of thing remarkably well. But Miriam was quite unimpressed.

**3.** Not bearing an impression.

1868 HERSCHEL in *People's Mag.* Jan. 63 Do the same with one side of the unimpressed square, and then apply the one square to the other,..the impression being between them.

**Unimpressibi·lity.** (UN-1 12; cf. next.)

1854 YONGE tr. *Athenæus* III. 966 When he found he could make no impression on the coldness and unimpressibility of the stone. 1889 SKRINE *Mem. Thring* 124 Heartiness in his own belief, and iron unimpressibility against the noise and flourishes of an enemy.

**Unimpre·ssible,** *a.* (UN-1 7.)

1828 L. HUNT *Byron & Contemp.* 26 She..was..absolutely unimpressible in that respect. 1856 KANE *Arct. Expl.* I. ii. 24 As stolid and unimpressible as one of our own Indians. 1878 Bosw. SMITH *Carthage* 44 The African was so unimpressible, and the Phœnician was so little disposed..to assimilate himself to his surroundings.

Hence **Unimpre·ssibleness.**

1830 ARNOLD *Let.* in Stanley *Life* (1858) I. 223 Thorough careless unimpressibleness beats one all to pieces.

**Unimpre:ssionabi·lity.** (UN-1 12; cf. next.)

1862 F. W. ROBINSON *Female Life in Prison* I. 80 This strange apathetic indifference, this unimpressionability.

**Unimpre·ssionable,** *a.* (UN-1 7 b.)

1847 C. BRONTË *J. Eyre* xxi, Unimpressionable natures are not so soon softened. 1850 THACKERAY *Pendennis* xv, Ah! what mad desires dashing up against some rock of obstruction or indifference, and flung back again from the unimpressionable granite! 1884 E. YATES *Recoll.* II. 201 [He] was..as unimpressionable as an oyster.

**Unimpre·ssive,** *a.* (UN-1 7.)

1796 GISBORNE *Walks Forest* (ed. 2) vi. 121 Does Truth, disclosed from heaven, .. her sacred shafts behold Bound unimpressive from the callous heart? 1828 P. CUNNINGHAM *N. S. Wales* (ed. 3) II. 314 The slovenly and unimpressive manner in which the witness is sworn. 1880 C. WICKSTEED in *S. Brooke's Life & Lett.* (1917) I. 330 Look at the men who pass into the shades of our theology—impassive, unimpressive shades!

Hence **Unimpre·ssively** (Webster, 1847), **-ness.**

1827 HARE *Guesses* Ser. I. 107 The accuracy and unimpressiveness of Algebraic characters. 1860 GEO. ELIOT in Cross *Life* (1885) II. 221 The variety is in some degree a cause of comparative unimpressiveness.

**Unimpri·son,** *v.* (UN-2 3.) 1817 COLERIDGE *Biog. Lit.* (1882) 263 No fly unimprisoned from a child's hand, could more buoyantly enjoy its element. **Unimpri·sonable,** *a.* (UN-1 7 b.) 1649 MILTON *Eikon.* 148 To imprison and confine by force..those two most unimprisonable things, our Prayers and that Divine Spirit of utterance that moves them.

**Unimpri·soned,** *ppl. a.* [UN-1 8 and UN-2 8.]

**a.** Not imprisoned. **b.** Released from prison.

1659 W. CHAMBERLAYNE *Pharonnida* I. 75 Her unimprisond Soul disrob'd of all Terrestrial thoughts. 1809–14 WORDSW. *Excurs.* IV. 106 The unimprisoned Mind May yet have scope to range among her own. 1820 BENTHAM *Liberty of Press* Wks. 1843 II. 283/1 To live unhanged, unsabred, unimprisoned. 1837 CARLYLE *Fr. Rev.* III. I. iv, That the King's Friends in Prison would burst out,..and, joined by the unimprisoned, ride roughshod over us all.

**Unimpri·soning,** *ppl. a.* (UN-2 3, 8.) 1820 E. IRVING in Froude *Carlyle* (1882) I. 86 Now it will be like the unimprisoning of a bird to come and let me have free talk. **Unimpro·priate,** *ppl. a.* (UN-1 8.) 1655 FULLER *Waltham Abbey* 8 An Abby and a Parsonage unimpropriate in the same place, are as inconsistent together, as good woods and an Iron Mill. **Unimprovabi·lity.** (UN-1 12; cf. next.) 1861 *Gd. Words* 432 The Boeotian dulness and unimprovability of the fatuous German king.

**Unimpro·vable,** *a.* (UN-1 7 b.)

*a* 1660 HAMMOND *Serm.* Wks. 1684 IV. 577 The principal faculty which is irrecoverably wanting in such, and by all teaching irreparable and unimproveable, is the power of numbring. *a* 1683 OLDHAM *Art of Poetry* Wks. (1684) II. 14 At first dash, as if before 'twere known, [he] Embarques you in the middle of the Plot And what is unimprovable leaves out. 1785 G. A. BELLAMY *Apol.* (ed. 3) III. 52 The 'Squire, however, remained totally unimprovable. 1790 *Act* 30 *Geo. III*, c. 50 To sell or alienate Fee Farm, and other unimproveable Rents. 1822 SCOTT *Nigel* xv, You show an absolute and unimprovable acquaintance with..mankind in general. 1847 GROTE *Greece* xxiv. III. 548 A people the most unprincipled and unimproveable of all.

Hence **Unimpro·vableness.**

1654 HAMMOND *Fundam.* xvi. 174 This must be imputed ..to their ignorance and unimproveableness in matters of knowledge.

**Unimpro·ved,** *ppl. a.*1 [UN-1 8.]

**1.** Not made better; not raised in quality.

1665 BOYLE *Occas. Refl.* I. ii. 163 Flowers (which, unimprov'd by Art, delight but whilst they are..fresh). *c* 1695 J. MILLER *Descr. New York* (1843) 41 The whole country, improved or unimproved, to belong to the King. 1764 GOLDSM. *Trav.* 230 From sire to son Unalter'd, unimprov'd the manners run. 1794 S. WILLIAMS *Vermont* 134 Man in the most simple, rude and unimproved state. 1858 GREENER *Gunnery* 4 This range being quite equal..to that of the late unimproved rifles. 1890 'R. BOLDREWOOD' *Col. Reformer* (1891) 247 A cheap unimproved property.

**2.** Not turned to use; not taken advantage of.

1781 COWPER *Truth* 524 He that scorns the noon-day beam, perverse, Shall find the blessing, unimprov'd, a curse. 1820 W. JAY *Prayers* 110 Those privileges, which, unimproved, will only augment our guilt. 1850 GROTE *Greece* lxi. VII. 533 They preferred leaving their victory unimproved, to the hazard of a general battle.

**3.** Not medically bettered.

1879 *St. George's Hosp. Rep.* IX. 466 One case was discharged 'unimproved',..but the others were all benefited.

†**Unimpro·ved,** *ppl. a.*2 *Obs.*—1 [UN-1 + IMPROVE *v.*1] Unreproved, uncensured.

1602 SHAKS. *Ham.* I. i. 96 Young Fortinbras Of vnimproued Mettle, hot and full.

**Unimpro·vement.** (UN-1 12.) 1757 MRS. GRIFFITH *Lett. Henry & Frances* (1767) I. 80 The visto of some absurd fellows unimprovement.

**Unimpro·ving,** *ppl. a.* (UN-1 10.)

1747 *Mem. Nutrebian Crt.* I. 206 While Gen Haragen was indulged in play, and idle unimproving amusements. 1788 V. KNOX *Winter Even.* lii. (1790) 378 If the idle were to lay aside such unimproving works. 1823 KEBLE *Serm.* iii. (1848) 48 It might be no unimproving exercise of self-denial, to men of refined judgments. 1883 *Academy* 15 Sept. 175/2 Many unimproving anecdotes of his proceedings still linger along the Spanish Main.

**Unimpu·gnable,** *a.* (UN-1 7 b.)

1832 MRS. GORE *Fair of May Fair* III. 278 His judgment was invaluable,..and unimpugnable at Lloyd's. 1857 DICKENS *Dorrit* II. xxxii, Solely supported by his unimpugnable calculations.

**Unimpu·gned,** *ppl. a.* (UN-1 8.)

[1775 ASH.] 1838 JAMES *Louis XIV*, I. 247 That all the arbitrary acts of his predecessor..should remain as unimpugned precedents in case of necessity. *a* 1857 R. A. VAUGHAN *Ess. & Rem.* (1858) I. 37 Thus did Origen.. attempt to retain the justice of God unimpugned.

**Unimpu·lsive,** *a.* (UN-1 7.)

[1775 ASH.] 1856 LEVER *Martins of Cro' M.* xiv. 138 The most suspectful, unimpulsive, and ungenerously-disposed of all natures, an old lawyer. 1886 RUSKIN *Præterita* I. iv. 112 The steady pains of her unimpulsive practice.

Hence **Unimpu·lsiveness.**

1860 TROLLOPE *Framley P.* xxv, Such a degree of unimpulsiveness as this.

**Unimpu·ted,** *ppl. a.* (UN-1 8.) 1723 POPE *Let. to Blount* 27 June, You must look on this as the first day I've been myself, and pass over the mad interval un-imputed to me. **Uninau·gurated,** *ppl. a.* (UN-1 8.) 1823 SCOTT *Quentin D.* Introd., An immense *assiètte* of spinage, not smoothed into a uniform surface, as by our uninaugurated cooks upon your side of the water.

**Uninca·rnate,** *a.* (UN-1 7.)

1687 *Death's Vision* 182 Blind to the World of Unincarnate Hosts! 1716 HUME *Sacr. Succession* 159 What God ..perform'd by heavenly un-incarnate angels. 1827 POLLOK *Course T.* v. 575 The spirits unincarnate. 1860 FABER *Bethlehem* 90 The unincarnate Saviour redeemed millions before His actual Incarnation.

So **Uninca·rnated** *ppl. a.*

1859 W. Anderson *Disc.* (1860) 146 The idea of the Unincarnated Eternal One.

**Unince·nsed,** *ppl. a.* (Un-1 8.)

1594 Carew *Huarte's Exam. Wits* x. 139 The flegmaticke vnincensed, haue their braine very cold and moist. *a* 1800 Cowper *Iliad* (ed. 2) v. 899 Jove! see'st thou, unincensed, these deeds of Mars? 1885 Swinburne *Stud. Victor Hugo* (1886) 84 The aspect of babies when unvexed and unincensed by any cross accident.

**Uni·nchoative,** *a.* (Un-1 7.) 1649 J. Ellistone tr. *Behmen's Epist.* 106 The soule (which ariseth..out of the Eternall un-inchoative Nature). 1691 E. Taylor *Behmen's Theos. Philos.* 367 What God is in his Eternal uninchoative Generation. **Unincide·ntal,** *a.* [Un-1 7.] Not marked by any incident. 1772 *Theatrical Biogr.* I. 147 [Parsons'] memoirs would be too unincidental, and consequently too unentertaining for a place here. 1853 Wilberforce in *Life* (1881) II. 194 The dead level plains of times of fat quietness and un-incidental ease. **Uninci·ted,** *ppl. a.* (Un-1 8.) 1648 Hexham II, *Ongehisset*, Vn-incited, or Vnsummoned. 1809–14 Wordsw. *Excurs.* v. 597 And unincited by a wish to look Into high objects farther than they may. **Unincli·nable,** *a.* (Un-1 7 b.) 1640 Walton *Life of Donne* in *D.'s Eighty Serm.* Pref., The King..perswaded M. Donne to enter into the Ministery, to which he appeared (and was) uninclinable. 1656 Hobbes *Liberty, Necess., & Chance* 9 Seeing that mans heart without the grace of God, is uninclinable to good. **Unincli·ned,** *ppl. a.* (Un-1 8.) 1729 Law *Serious C.* xvi. 291 They who..render themselves..unincln'd to observe rules and hours of devotion. 1740 Richardson *Pamela* II. 10 In which..you take Notice of my being uninclin'd to marry. **Unincli·ning,** *ppl. a.* (Un-1 10.) 1794 T. Taylor *Pausanias' Descr. Greece* III. 294 Of pure and uncontaminated order, and of uninclining power.

**Uninclu·ded,** *ppl. a.* (Un-1 8.)

1775 R. Chandler *Trav. Greece* (1825) II. 299 Lombardi was..unincluded in the general amnesty. 1802–12 Bentham *Ration. Judic. Evid.* (1827) III. 474 If any one of the possible modes of transcription were left unincluded in the penal consequences. 1855 W. H. Mill *Applic. Panth. Princ.* (1861) 234 Those who believe St. James the Just to be unincluded in the number of the twelve.

**Uninclu·sive,** *a.* (Un-1 7.) 1864 Pusey *Lect. Daniel* viii. 468 The word 'until'..is to be understood ideally of an unending, unclosed, uninclusive term. **Uninconve·nienced,** *ppl. a.* (Un-1 8.) 1829 *Encycl. Metrop.* (1845) VI. 291/1 Casemates..uninconvenienced by smoke.

**Uninco·rporate,** *a.* [Un-1 7.]

**1.** Unembodied.

1821 Byron *Sardanap.* IV. i, If there be indeed A shore where mind survives, 'twill be as mind, All unincorporate. 1866 Grote *Exam. Utilit. Phil.* iv. (1870) 62 He is writing as a true utilitarian about happiness in that unindividual, unincorporate, abstract notion of it.

**2.** = next 2.

1880 *Act* 43 & 44 *Vict.* c. 42 § 7 Where the employer is a body of persons corporate or unincorporate.

**Uninco·rporated,** *ppl. a.* [Un-1 8.]

**1.** Not incorporated or united *with*.

1715 Atterbury *Serm.* (1737) III. 128 They have continued unmixed, unincorporated with any of the nations..amidst whom they dwelt.

**2.** Not formed into a corporation.

1818 Hallam *Mid. Ages* (1819) I. 443 The arrangement of twenty-one trading companies had still left several kinds of artisans unincorporated. *Ibid.* III. 167 The representation of unchartered, or at least unincorporated boroughs. 1884 *St. James's Gaz.* 10 May 5/1 The regulation of proceedings brought against unincorporated clubs.

**Unincrea·sable,** *a.* (Un-1 7 b.)

1648 Boyle *Seraph. Love* i. (1659) 8 An..almost unincreaseable Elevation, and vastnesse of affection. 1698 Norris *Pract. Disc.* IV. 296 The Blessed God, whose Perfect and Unincreaseable Happiness makes him utterly uncapable of ..such a Love. 1872 Ruskin *Fors Clav.* xvi. 12 These..are your wealth, for ever—unincreasable. 1872 Bagehot *Physics & Pol.* 54 The unincreasable land being occupied.

**Unincrea·sed,** *ppl. a.* (Un-1 8.)

[1775 Ash.] 1824 Miss Mitford *Village* Ser. I. 273 There it stands,..unincreased and undiminished by a single brick. 1890 *Retrospect Med.* CII. 140 Even with the urine unincreased..there is a large drain upon the liquids.

**Unincrea·sing,** *ppl. a.* (Un-1 10.) 1587 Golding *De Mornay* vi. 72 To be short, he calleth him ye myndly speech,..vncorruptible, vnincreasing, vndecreasing,..and first beknowne after God. **Unincru·sted,** *ppl. a.* (Un-1 8.) 1880 Swinburne *Stud. Shaks.* 157 Unincrusted with any flake of dirt. **Uni·ncubated,** *ppl. a.* (Un-1 8.) 1859 Darwin *Orig. Spec.* vii. 217 Those first laid would have to be left for some time unincubated. 1891 *Science-Gossip* XXVII. 8 A nest..which contained four eggs unincubated.

**Uninde·bted,** *ppl. a.* (Un-1 8.)

1672 Dryden *Assignation* v. iv, So you shall still be innocent, and I Die blessed, and unindebted for my being. 1759 *Ann. Reg., Hist. War* 41/2 Unindebted to family or connections. 1781 Cowper *Table-t.* 525 Give me the line.. That, like some cottage beauty, strikes the heart, Quite unindebted to the tricks of art. 1846 Sir W. Hamilton *Diss.* in *Reid's Wks.* 891 Neither ignorant of, nor unindebted to, their writings. 1882 Saintsbury *Hist. French Lit.* III. vii. 380 He was..probably not unindebted to Descartes for the force and vigour of his reasonings.

Hence **Uninde·btedness.**

1866 *Times* 4 Jan. 8/4 If they shall have paid off their present debt, they will enjoy a confidence far stronger than that from simple unindebtedness.

**Uninde·nted,** *ppl. a.* [Un-1 8.]

**1.** Not marked with indentations.

1750 G. Hughes *Barbados* 133 Two unindented Seams crossing one another at Right Angles. 1828 Lytton *Pelham* III. v, The rest of the countenance was perfectly smooth and unindented. 1863 Tyndall *Heat* v. 160 The border finally becomes unindented.

**2.** Of type: Set up without indention.

1903 *Athenæum* 17 Jan. 78/2 Printed either in fourteen unindented lines, or with only the final couplet indented.

**3.** Not indentured.

1881 Stevenson *Not I & other Poems* (1898) 7 The pamphlet..Was planned and printed by A printer unindented.

**Uni·ndexed,** *ppl. a.* (Un-1 8.) 1832 Palgrave *Eng. Commw.* II. 124 These most valuable records..are still unindexed. 1856 Ruskin *Mod. Paint.* IV. v. ii. § 17 Over all this unindexed and immeasurable mass of treasure. **Uni·ndicated,** *ppl. a.* (Un-1 8.) [1775 Ash.] 1825 Coleridge *Aids Refl.* 148 *note*, The unprotrusive and unindicated convolutes of the Brain, that secrete honesty and commonsense. 1904 E. Gosse *Jer. Taylor* iii. 103 No temptation ..is allowed to pass unindicated or unreproved. **Unindi·ctable,** *a.* (Un-1 7 b.) 1861 Wynter *Soc. Bees* 29 The various hydro-carbons..escape in the form of thin unindictable vapour, of a highly obnoxious character. 1870 Lowell *Among my Bks.* Ser. I. 127 The unindictable Powers of Darkness. **Unindi·cted,** *ppl. a.* (Un-1 8.) [1775 Ash.] 1806 in *Spirit Pub. Jrnls.* X. 311 By unindicted thieves, alas! purloin'd.

**Unindi·fference.** [Un-1 12.] = next.

1665 Ever *Tryals per Pais* ix. 106 Where there is no unindifference or default in the Sheriff. 1824 Barnewall & Cresswell *Rep.* II. 104 The panel of tales having been quashed..on the ground of the unindifference of the sheriff.

**Unindi·fferency.** Now *arch.* [Un-1 12 + Indifferency 1.] Lack of impartiality.

1578 Whetstone *1st Pt. Promos & Cass.* IV. ii, Such grace woulde mee, with vnindifferencie tuch, To pardon him, that dyd commit a Rape. 1625 tr. *Boccaccio's Decam.* II. 26 His successe proved answerable to his hope, no unindifferencie appearing in their purposes. 1665 Ever *Tryals per Pais* ix. 106 In respect of the cause of unindifferency, or default of the Sheriff or other Officer that made the Return. 1844 *Judgm. Ld. Denman in O'Connell* v. *Queen* 7 Unindifferency or misconduct on the part of the sheriff.

**Unindi·fferent,** *a.* [Un-1 7.]

†**1.** Unequal, unfavourable. *Obs.*[−1]

1565 Golding *Cæsar* 209 When he saw howe thencounter was in an vnindifferent place..[he] sent to..his Lieuetenant.

**2. a.** Of persons: Not impartial or fair-minded; prejudiced. Now *arch.*

1571 Golding *Calvin on Ps.* xli. 3 The miserable man whom cruel and unindifferent persons surmise to bee forlorne. 1611 A. Munday *Brief Chron.* A 8, This vertuous..man, knowing Death to be an vnindifferent Executor. 1673 O. Walker *Educ.* 204 Unindifferent are those who are preingaged. 1852 *Fraser's Mag.* March 246/1 He may consequently be supposed, to use the language of the law, 'to stand unindifferent as he stands unsworn'.

†**b.** Of actions, etc.: Lacking in impartiality or fairness. *Obs.*

1583 Golding *Calvin on Deut.* xxxix. 231 Such vnindifferent dealing shall alwayes be taken for theft before God. 1600 Tate in Gutch *Coll. Cur.* I. 7 It may justly be thought unindifferent to nominate his own country for the place. 1602 Warner *Alb. Eng.* Epit. 378 Stomacking..the vnindifferent sharing of the Nordaine Bootie.

**3.** Not indifferent; concerned, interested.

1813 Lamb *Play-ho Mem.* Wks. 1908 I. 202 Those honest, hearty, well-pleased, unindifferent mortals above.

So **Unindi·fferently** *adv.*, unfairly.

1608 Hieron *Defence* II. 126 He..maie easely perceyve.. how unindifferently and unequally he sorteth us and Cochlæus togither.

**Uni·ndigent,** *a.* (Un-1 7.) 1830 T. Taylor *Argts. Celsus* 63 A corporeal worship cannot even be paid to these, because they are naturally unindigent. **Unindi·gnant,** *a.* (Un-1 7.) 1789 Anna Seward *Lett.* (1811) II. 299 A well-informed woman..will at once find these volumes..too vulgar for her unindignant endurance. 1800 G. Wakefield in *Mem.* (1804) II. 425 With unindignant apathy pass by Of Antijacobins the filthy stye? **Unindivi·dual,** *a.* (Un-1 7.) 1812 Coleridge in *Lit. Rem.* (1836) I. 351 In the abstract and, as it were, unindividual nature of the idea, self, or soul. 1892 *Pall Mall G.* 27 Apr. 2/3 A patient, thoughtful pianist,.. but almost altogether unindividual. **Unindivi·dualized,** *ppl. a.* (Un-1 8.) 1864 W. Shedd *Hist. Chr. Doctrine* II. 81 Original sin is the product of human will as yet unindividualized in Adam. 1882 Traill *Sterne* iv. 42 A completely colourless and unindividualized figure. **Unindu·ctive,** *a.* (Un-1 7.) 1855 Baden Powell *Ess.* 58 The 'catastrophic' hypothesis seems of an essentially uninductive nature. **Unindu·lged,** *ppl. a.* (Un-1 8.) [1775 Ash.] 1820 T. Mitchell *Aristoph.* I. p. lxxviii, To leave nothing unindulged, which could contribute to their gratification. 1847 *Ainsworth's Mag.* XII. 42 A luxury almost unindulged since she had been in England. **Unindu·lgent,** *a.* (Un-1 8.) 1743 Francis tr. *Horace, Odes* II. xvi, To Me, not unindulgent Fate Bestow'd a rural, calm Retreat.

**Unindu·strious,** *a.* (Un-1 7, 5 b.)

1599 Daniel *Musoph.* Wks. (1602) C iii b, So farre beyond the ordinarie course, That other vnindustrious Ages ran. 1612 Donne *Lett.* (1651) 122, I have [not] been..unindustrious in attempting that [*i. e.* to do good]. 1667 *Decay of Chr. Piety* xiii. ¶ 1 We cannot think it so sluggish or unindustrious an agent. 1693 W. Freke *Sel. Ess.* xxxiv. 216 It were..an unindustrious encroaching on the publick property to attain it. 1883 *Century Mag.* XXVI. 805 Hardly an industry, perhaps, or at any rate an unindustrious one. 1887 Rider Haggard *Jess* xxi, That intelligent but unindustrious race.

So **Unindu·striously** *adv.*

1648 Boyle *Seraph. Love* xvii. (1659) 115 Ev'n the Socinians..are not a little, or un-industriously sollicitous.

**Unine·briating,** *ppl. a.* (Un-1 10.) *a* 1861 T. Winthrop *Life in Open Air* xii. (1863) 96 Toasting each other in the uninebriating flow of our beverages.

**Uninfe·cted,** *ppl. a.* [Un-1 8.]

**1.** Not infected or tainted with sedition, heresy, vice, or the like. Also const. *by*, *with*.

1628 Le Grys tr. *Barclay's Argenis* 88 What dost thou stay for? Till there be nothing vninfected in Sicily. Art thou afraid to disturbe their scarce ripe preparations? 1678 Cudworth *Intell. Syst.* I. iv. § 36. 553 Neither was Plotinus himself..altogether uninfected with this Phantastick Conceit. *a* 1715 Burnett *Own Time* II. xiii. (1897) I. 535 By this means..all the outed ministers would be..kept from going round the uninfected parts of the kingdom. 1777 Robertson *Hist. Amer.* I. (1778) I. 8 Preserving them a separate people uninfected by idolatry. 1795 V. Knox *Spir. Despotism* § 29 As influence increases, the jealousy and vigilance of the uninfected part of the community should increase in proportion.

**2.** *spec.* Not infected with disease, poison, etc.

1625 K. Long tr. *Barclay's Argenis* II. xv. 111 Let us see, quoth hee, whether the Bracelet be uninfected. 1684 J. S. *Profit & Pleas. United* 16 Separating the infected, from the uninfected [cattle]. 1744 Armstrong *Preserv. Health* III. 31 Serene he bears the peevish eastern blast, And uninfected breathes the mortal South. 1813 J. Thomson *Lect. Inflam.* 485 If pains be taken to prevent intercourse between the infected and uninfected. 1890 *Retrospect Med.* CII. 292 The risk of leaving untreated a clot in the immediate neighbourhood of very virulent septic matter in the hope that it may remain uninfected.

**Uninfe·ctious,** *a.* (Un-1 7.) 1744 Birch *Life Boyle* 32 If he were given to any vice himself, he was careful..to render it uninfectious. **Uninfe·ft,** *pa. pple.* (Un-1 8 b.) 1869 R. Campbell *Austin's Jurispr.* I. 392 A. infeft can enforce his right against a persona in general; A. uninfeft, only against certas personas. **Uninfe·sted,** *ppl. a.* (Un-1 8.) 1670 Milton *Hist. Eng.* VI. 244 Nor was Devonshire and Cornwall uninfested on the shore. 1787 *Generous Attachment* IV. 8 The haunts uninfested by the voice of man. **Uni·nfiniteness.** (Un-1 12.) 1656 [? J. Sergeant] tr. *T. White's Peripat. Inst.* 230 Science..is only restrain'd by uninfinitenesse of the number of the objects.

**Uninfla·med,** *ppl. a.* [Un-1 8.]

**1.** Not set on fire.

1626 Bacon *Sylva* § 602 When any of those..Bodies come to bee Inflamed then they gather a much greater Heat, than others have un-inflamed. 1663 J. Spencer *Prodigies* 15 The more gross and uninflamed parts must sometimes needs interrupt our sight of that fire. 1743 Young *Nt. Th.* IV. 647 Rise odours sweet from incense uninflam'd? 1794 R. J. Sulivan *View Nat.* II. 163 That this inflammable body of coal should have remained uninflamed..seems highly improbable.

**2.** *fig.* Not emotionally warmed or excited.

1714 Young *Force of Relig.* II. 199 Oh! let thy thought o'er our past converse rove, And show one moment uninflam'd with love! 1846 Landor *Imag. Conv.* Wks. I. 204/2 You enunciate even these sentences,..the most seditious, uninflamed, unwarmed. 1876 Lowell *Among my Bks.* Ser. II. 235 So hard is it to escape..uninflamed by the tumult of partisanship which besets the doors.

**3.** *Path.* Not affected by inflammation.

1793 J. Hunter *Treat. Blood*, etc. (1794) 280 The uninflamed ear dried clear and transparent. 1813 Thomson *Lect. Inflam.* 75 That the circulation is slower in inflamed than in uninflamed arteries. 1866 Aitken *Pract. Med.* II. 911 Dry, imbricated scales..resting upon a perfectly uninflamed surface.

**Uninflammabi·lity.** (Un-1 12; cf. next.)

1826 Henry *Elem. Chem.* II. 553 The second class..are distinguished..by their uninflammability. 1843 *Civil Eng. & Arch. Jrnl.* VI. 210/2 To test their uninflammability, Mr. Nash had a bonfire..lighted on the roof.

**Uninfla·mmable,** *a.* (Un-1 7 b.)

1666 Boyle *Orig. Forms & Qual.* II. v. 325 To produce, out of two uninflammable Bodies, a third, that would be easily inflammable. 1674 — *Grounds Corpusc. Philos.* 25 Sulphur..abounds with an acid and uninflammable salt. 1756 C. Lucas *Ess. Waters* I. 52 Water is an uninflammable fluid. 1826 Henry *Elem. Chem.* I. 234 That one measure of hydrogen and oxygen gases..was rendered uninflammable by eight additional measures of hydrogen. 1897 F. J. Burgoyne *Library Construct.* 22 Some uninflammable non-conductor.

*fig.* *a* 1797 H. Walpole *Geo. II* (1847) III. iv. 97 Uninflammable as the times were, they carried a great mixture of superstition.

**Uninfla·ted,** *ppl. a.* (Un-1 8.) [1775 Ash.] 1861 *Times* 22 Oct., He is perfectly modest, unassuming, and uninflated.

**Uninfle·cted,** *ppl. a.* [Un-1 8.]

**1.** Not bent or deflected.

1713 Derham *Phys. Theol.* I. i. 13 An uninflected Ray [of light]. 1843 Griffith in *Trans. Linnæan Soc.* XIX. 198 The ordinary and uninflected membrane of the sac.

**2.** Not possessed of inflections.

1875 Whitney *Life Lang.* vii. 133 The original indefiniteness of uninflected languages.

Hence **Uninfle·ctedness.**

1875 Whitney *Life Lang.* xii. 239 The line which separates utter uninflectedness from a rude agglutination.

**Uninfli·cted,** *ppl. a.* (Un-1 8.) 1757 W. Wilkie *Epigon.* v. 151 While uninflicted hangs the fatal stroke. **Uni·nfluenceable,** *a.* (Un-1 7 b.) 1734 Bolingbroke *On Parties* Ded. p. xii, The uninfluenc'd and uninfluenceable Freedom of Elections.

**Uni·nfluenced,** *ppl. a.* [Un-1 8.] Not influenced or affected (*by* something).

1734 [see prec.]. 1748 *Anson's Voy.* III. vii. 363 Cool and uninfluenced by what they had drank. 1773 J. Allen *Serm. at St. Mary's, Oxford* 18 The unprejudiced, uninfluenced members of the holy Catholic Church. 1853 Kane *Grinnell Exp.* xii. (1856) 86 The pack seems as yet uninfluenced. 1880 Disraeli *Endym.* xliii, Lord Roehampton..will not.. be uninfluenced by the circumstances.

**Uni·nfluencing,** *ppl. a.* (Un-1 10.) 1813–21 Bentham *Wks.* (1843) VIII. 209 Uninfluential or uninfluencing circumstances. **Uni·nfluencive,** *a.* (Un-1 7.) 1816 Coleridge *Statesm. Man.* App. 32 A few, on whose convictions it will not be uninfluencive to know, that [etc.].

**Uninflue·ntial,** *a.* (Un-1 7.)

1661 Glanvill *Van. Dogm.* 191 Causes in our account the most palpable, may possibly be but uninfluential attendants. 1815 Wordsw. *Prose Wks.* (1876) II. 123 Those pretended treasures of antiquity..have been wholly uninfluential upon the literature of the Country. 1840 Gen. P. Thompson *Exerc.* (1842) V. 67 It is intimated in some far from uninfluential journals. **1882** Farrar *Early Chr.* I. 206 Would a writer so..powerful..have remained uninfluential and unknown?

Hence **Uninflue:ntia·lity.**

**1880** J. Cairns *Let.* in MacEwen *Life* (1895) 701 There has been a stronger tendency..to put the broader side..into visible uninfluentiality.

**Uninfo·rmative,** *a.* (Un-[1] 7.) **1837** C. Lofft *Self-formation* I. 129 The child is driven to learn everything from books..uninformative upon points of doubt.

**Uninfo·rmed,** *ppl. a.* [Un-[1] 8.]

**1.** Not informed, instructed, or enlightened on some matter or in some respect.

**1597** Sir R. Cecil in Ellis *Orig. Lett.* Ser. I. III. 45 His being a King not of many yeares..may happilie leave him uninformed of that course. **1644** Milton *Bucer on Div.* To Parlt. B 2 b, I..was not un-inform'd that divers..men testify'd their daily approbation of the book. **1667** — *P. L.* VIII. 486 Guided by his voice, nor uninformd Of nuptial Sanctitie and marriage Rites. **1725** Pope *Odyss.* VIII. 533 Who by Phœbus uninform'd, could..sing so well the woe? **1794** S. Williams *Vermont* 156 The uninformed spectator is struck with horror. **1796** Mme. D'Arblay *Camilla* IV. 328 She was uninformed he had propagated it. **1854** J. S. C. Abbott *Napoleon* (1855) I. xxvii. 436 Uninformed as to its contents. **1854** *Poultry Chron.* I. 260/2 Persons..totally uninformed on the subject.

*absol.* **1815** J. Cormack *Abol. Fem. Infanticide Guzerat* i. 5 This is a position, which the uninformed and the unintelligent alone will dispute. **1892** *Temple Bar* Oct. 185 Notwithstanding the abstract nature of his studies, Mr. Hopkins was a charming companion, even to the uninformed.

**2.** Uninstructed, uneducated, ignorant.

**1647** Clarendon *Hist. Reb.* II. § 98 They..obtained Proselytes of weak uninformed Ladies. **1745** Fielding *Tom Jones* VI. ii, So great a politician..must surely..find out what passes in the rude uninformed mind of a girl. **1791** Newte *Tour Eng. & Scot.* 372 Uninformed and credulous minds readily discover a similitude. **1825** Coleridge *Aids Refl.* 169 Even though the uninformed Heathens should not perish.

**b.** Marked by lack of enlightenment, information, or knowledge.

**1796** Gisborne *Walks Forest* (ed. 2) i. 14 Him uninform'd attachment to his chief..arranged Beneath Rebellion's standard. **1817** J. Scott *Paris Revisit.* (ed. 4) 114 In the vagueness of uninformed speculation. **1891** *Daily News* 5 Nov. 2/5 The bankers pledged themselves..with blind and uninformed confidence.

**3.** Not animated, enlivened, or inspired.

**1709** Swift *Vind. Bickerstaff* Wks. 1755 II. I. 172 If an uninformed carcase walks still about. **1711** Steele *Spect.* No. 33 ⁋ 12 Without this irradiating Power..her most perfect Features are Uninform'd and Dead. **1803** Wordsw. *Yew-Trees* 19 A growth Of..fibres serpentine upcoiling, and inveterately convolved,—Nor uninformed with Phantasy, and looks That threaten the profane.

†**4.** Unimproved by art. *Obs.*

**1748** Foote *Knights* I. Wks. 1799 I. 61 A raw boarding-school girl..with a mind unpolished, a figure uninformed.

**Uninfo·rming,** *ppl. a.* (Un-[1] 10.)

**1709** Mrs. Manley *Secret Mem.* (1720) II. 199 An Absence of Mind, and an uninforming Faculty. **1764** Goldsm. *Hist. Eng. in Lett.* (1772) II. 222 It would be..uninforming to relate all the preparations. **1812** Combe *Syntax, Picturesque* II, The mangled post thus long had stood, An uninforming piece of wood. **1901** C. A. Scott *Evang. Doctrine* ii. 28 The name of 'Protestant' is popular, accidental and uninforming.

**Uninfri·ngeable,** *a.* (Un-[1] 7. Cf. *uninfringible* there.) **1743** H. Walpole *Lett.* (1903) I. 368 Upon conditions uninfringeable, I will give you one [*sc.* a commission].

**Uninfri·nged,** *ppl. a.* (Un-[1] 8.)

**1610** Healey *St. Aug. Citie of God* 784 Yet this doth not barre them [*i. e.* the Romans] the name of a people..as long as they beare this our last definition vnin-fringed. **1663** Boyle *Usef. Exp. Nat. Philos.* II. ii. 60 Whether their strength be that way more uninfringed..then if they [*sc.* poisons] were taken in at the mouth. **1736** Franklin *Ess.* Wks. 1840 II. 281 Let us be vigilant to preserve them uninfringed, and free from encroachments. **1791** Cowper *Iliad* III. 128 He..insures The compact, to both parties, uninfringed. **1852** M. Arnold *Human Life* 4, I haue kept uninfringed my nature's law. **1871** Geo. Eliot *Middlem.* xxxvii, Here was a question of ties which left them uninfringed.

**Uninge·nious,** *a.* [Un-[1] 7.]

†**1.** = Uningenuous *a. Obs.*

**1638** Chillingw. *Relig. Prot.* I. iv. § 53. 220 Full of uningenious dealing with your adversary. **1656** Heylyn *Extraneus Vapulans* 20 Of Mr. Noye..(besides those uningenious passages of him which are still left standing) he telleth us also [etc.].

**2.** Lacking in ingenuity.

**1769** Burke *Obs. Late St. Nation* 8 These uningenious paradoxes and reveries without imagination. **1787** Bentham *Def. Usury* xiii. 183 The wounded pride of the uningenious herd. **1888** Doughty *Arabia Deserta* I. 244 Little cups..made, for the uningenious Arabs, in the West.

**Uningenu·ity.** [Un-[1] 12.] †Disingenuousness.

**1650** J. Weekes *Truth's Conft.* ii. 34 With as much disparagement and uningenuity, as likely can be in so many words. **1672** Clarendon *Ess.* Tracts (1727) 264 This uningenuity is still practised,..contrary to truth.

†**Uninge·nuous,** *a. Obs.* [Un-[1] 7.]

**1.** Not frank, candid, or open; disingenuous.

**1638** Chillingw. *Relig. Prot.* Answ. to Pref. 6 If beginings be ominous..D. Potter hath cause to look for great store of uningenuous dealing from you. **1670** Clarendon *Ess.* Tracts (1727) 189 The grossest and most uningenuous importunities of the most worthless men.

**2.** Ignoble, servile.

**1660** Jer. Taylor *Ductor* III. ii. rule 9 § 5 It is..an uningenuous subjection, to pay tribute for our meat and drink.

Hence †**Uninge·nuousness.** *Obs.*

**1644** Hammond *Vind. Christ's Reprehending Peter* 72, I cannot guesse what could be further added to prove the injustice and uningenuousnesse..of this answer.

†**Uninge·nuously,** *adv. Obs.* [Un-[1] 11.] Disingenuously.

**1656** Hobbes *Lib., Necess., & Chance* 4 To bring [such] arguments..is to deale uningenuously and fraudulently with his Readers. **1796** Mme. D'Arblay *Camilla* III. 394 A conquest, unduly, unfairly, and uningenuously obtained.

**Uningra·fted,** *ppl. a.* (Un-[1] 8.) **1830** Gen. P. Thompson *Exerc.* (1842) I. 289 [France] attempted..to make terms with ungrafted royalty. **1834** J. Brown *Lett. Sanctif.* i. 204 It is folly to look for good fruit on an ungrafted tree.

†**Uninha·bit,** *ppl. a. Sc. Obs.* [Un-[1] 8 b.] Uninhabited. *c* **1460** in *Bann. Cl. Misc.* (1855) III. 36 To seke void landis and unenhabyte.

**Uninha·bitable,** *a.* (Un-[1] 7 b. Cf. Unhabitable.)

**1448** *Extr. Aberd. Reg.* (1844) I. 401 The balyheis sal..tak doune the durris..of thaim [*sc.* houses], and mak thaim uninhabitable. **1574** Golding *Marlorat's Apocalips* 299 The countrie of Sichimie..is desert and vninhabitable by reason of extreme cold. **1610** Shaks. *Temp.* II. i. 37 Though this Island seeme to be..Vninhabitable, and almost inaccessible. **1662** J. Davies tr. *Mandelslo's Trav.* 281 They would needs know of him..how he came to that uninhabitable place. **1774** Pennant *Tour Scotl. in 1772*, 174 The far greater part of the country being uninhabitable by reason of the..mountains. **1837** Whewell *Hist. Induct. Sci.* I. 155 It was supposed that the space between the tropical circles must be uninhabitable from heat. **1884** *Law Times* 27 Sept. 359/2 The Manor House..being so dilapidated as to be almost uninhabitable.

Hence **Uninha·bitableness.**

**1669** Stillingfl. *Serm.* ix. (1673) 166 The opinion of the Ancients concerning the uninhabitableness of the torrid Zone. **1676** *Doctrine of Devils* 194 The Uninhabitableness of the middle Zone. **1839** Fr. A. Kemble *Rec. Later Life* I. 255 Eight dwelling houses, all in different states and stages of uninhabitableness.

**Uninha·bited,** *ppl. a.* (Un-[1] 8. Cf. Unhabited.)

**1571** Golding *Calvin on Ps.* lxv. 12 The same fatnesse spreadeth itselfe even into the uninhabited countries. **1647** Cowley *Mistr., Welcome* iii, Hast thou not found each womans breast..Either by Savages possest, Or wild, and uninhabited? **1670** R. Coke *Disc. Trade* 10 The Country too becomes thin and uninhabited. **1711** Addison *Spect.* No. 26 ⁋ 4 The present War had filled the Church with many of these uninhabited Monuments. **1794** Mrs. Radcliffe *Myst. Udolpho* xxxv, This chateau was uninhabited when St. Aubert and his daughter were in the neighbourhood. **1824** Miss L. M. Hawkins *Annaline* III. 193 The imposing stillness pervading these almost uninhabited regions. **1866** Geo. Eliot *F. Holt* i, We have been too poor to keep servants for uninhabited rooms.

Hence **Uninha·bitedness.**

**1727** Bailey (vol. II), *Wildness*,..uninhabitedness. **1884** *Chr. World* 12 June 434/4 The solitary uninhabitedness..was something awful in its impressiveness.

**Uninheritabi·lity.** (Un-[1] 12.) **1812** Coleridge in Southey *Omniana* II. 7 A most determined believer in the uninheritability of sin. **Uninhe·ritable,** *a.* [Un-[1] 7 b.] † Incapable of inheriting. **1611** Speed *Hist. Gt. Brit.* IX. xvi. 671/1 [They allege] that the said Richard was finally for treason attainted, and adiudged vninheritable. **1780** M. Madan *Thelyphthora* II. 13 If women..were not lawful wives in God's sight, then..the issue must be illegitimate, and, if so, uninheritable.

**Uninhu·med,** *ppl. a.* (Un-[1] 8.)

**1621** G. Sandys *Ovid's Met.* VII. (1626) 142 Dead corps, without the Dues of funerall, They weakly beare:..Or vninhum'd they lye. **1791** Cowper *Odyss.* XI. 84 Leave me not undeplored Nor uninhumed. **1835** *Oriental Ann.* 215 Thousands of carcasses..would not then lie uninhumed, scattering pestilence over the land.

**Unini·tiate,** *ppl. a.* [Un-[1] 8 b.] = next.

**1801** Southey *Thalaba* V. xxxvi, That, led by me, Feet uninitiate tread Your threshold, this atones! **1853** Kingsley *Hypatia* viii, The uninitiate vulgar..who revile such interpretations. **1874** Withrow *Catacombs* (1877) 532 The sacred mysteries hidden from the uninitiate and the unworthy.

**Unini·tiated,** *ppl. a.* (Un-[1] 8.) Also *absol.*

**1678** Cudworth *Intell. Syst.* I. v. 637 The Prophane and Uninitiated in the Mysteries. **1800** Whiter *Etymol. Magnum* 174 The uninitiated reader will perhaps be astonished. **1816** Bentham *Chrestom.* 55 Those..formularies, so appalling to every as yet uninitiated, and more particularly to the uninitiated juvenile eye. **1842** Dickens *Amer. Notes* i, What seemed to the uninitiated a serious journey. **1885** *Athenæum* 19 Dec. 800/2 One uninitiated in the mysteries of Scottish genealogies.

**Uninitia·tion.** (Un-[1] 12.) **1834** H. O'Brien *Round Towers* 303 Nor was it but on the plea of ignorance and un-initiation that he did ultimately obtain pardon. **1873** Mrs. Whitney *Other Girls* xv, She left no lee-way for uninitiation. **Uninje·ctable,** *a.* (Un-[1] 7 b.) **1830** R. Knox *Béclard's Anat.* 178 The sum of the capillary blood vessels, and their proportion to the solid and uninjectable substance. **Uninjurable,** *a.* (Un-[1] 7 b.) **1846** Mrs. Gore *Eng. Char.* I. 310 His soda-water..being uninjurable by street rumbling.

**Uni·njured,** *ppl. a.* (Un-[1] 8.)

**1578** R. L. in Whetstone *Promos & Cass.* A iij, I hould my paynes wel satisfyed, and Maister Whetston uninjured. **1634** Milton *Comus* 403 [To] let a single helpless maiden pass Uninjur'd. **1693** Prior *To Dr. Sherlock* 57 Untouch'd thy Tomb, uninjur'd be thy Dust. **1725** Pope *Odyss.* XI. 477 Heroes who uninjur'd stood Amidst a war of spears. **1797** Nelson in Nicolas *Disp.* (1845) II. 346 To put me on board the first uninjured Ship of the Line. *a* **1821** V. Knox *Serm.* Wks. 1824 VI. 171 Their own bosoms will be calm and serene, uninjured and uninjurious. **1884** *Fortn. Rev.* Jan. 50 The Indian tribes..uninjured by and uninjuring Western culture.

**Uni·njuring,** *ppl. a.* (Un-[1] 10, 5 d.) **1820** Milman *Fall of Jerusalem* 42 The pines..From their proud heads shake off the uninjuring tempest. **1884** [see prec.].

**Uninju·rious,** *a.* (Un-[1] 7.)

**1809** Coleridge *Friend* 155 The uninjurious and useful privileges of our English Nobility. *a* **1821** [see Uninjured]. **1866** Pusey *Mirac. Prayer* 32 A concentration of rain or its absence, uninjurious at other times, would ruin seed-time or harvest.

Hence **Uninju·riousness.**

**1860** Pusey *Min. Proph.* 374 Yea, foolishness itself is cloked under the name of uninjuriousness.

**Uninju·riously,** *adv.* (Un-[1] 11.) **1881** Sir W. Thomson in *Times* 2 Sept. 4/1 The charging [of a Faure cell] may be done uninjuriously, and with good dynamical economy [etc.]. **Uni·nked,** *ppl. a.* (Un-[1] 8.) **1637** Rutherford *Lett.* (1664) 290 What is harder then..to have blanks & uninked paper for assurance of Christ in real fruition or possession? **Uni·nn,** *v.* [Un-[2] 7.] *intr.* To leave an inn. **1602** Warner *Alb. Eng.* XII. lxxv. 312 The Gentle woman, hearing this, vn-Inn'd by day did peepe. **Uni·nnocence.** (Un-[1] 12.) **1593** Nashe *Christ's T.* F ij b, Thou shalt be my vninnocence, and whole summe of delinquishment. **Uninocu·lated,** *ppl. a.* (Un-[1] 8.) [**1775** Ash.] **1818** *Monthly Rev.* LXXXVII. 131 Mr. Koster..observes that the cow-pox was extensively contagious..among the uninoculated inhabitants. **1898** P. Manson *Trop. Diseases* 151 Afterwards the originally healthy and uninoculated mice also succumbed.

**Unino·dal** (yūni-), *a.* [See Uni- 1 and Nodal *a.*] Having one node or nodal point.

**1839** Lindley *Introd. Bot.* 160 The cyme of Monocotyledons appears to be typically uninodal. **1880** *Nature* XXI. 427 Long oscillations..due to uninodal waves. **1894** *Athenæum* 17 Feb. 216/3 Some Properties of the Uninodal Quartic and Quintic having a Triple Point.

**Unino·minal** (yūni-), *a.* [a. F. *uninominal* (1878): see Uni- 1 and Nominal *a.*]

**1.** Based on the principle of one member being separately elected by each constituency.

**1881** *Times* 12 Mar. 11 At present..the Chamber of Deputies is elected by what is called..the uninominal method of voting. **1884** *Pall Mall G.* 8 Nov. 1 The proposed uniformity of uninominal electoral districts.

**2.** Having or involving one name, *spec.* in *Nat. Hist.* **188**. [see *plurinominal* Pluri-].

**Uninqui·red,** *ppl. a.* (Un-[1] 8 c.) **1725** De Foe *Voy. round World* (1840) 224 Infinitely more [wealth] lay uninquired after, than had yet been known. **1826** Scott *Woodst.* xxviii, Some unhappy mistake, the grounds of which shall remain..uninquired into.

**Uninqui·ring,** *ppl. a.* (Un-[1] 10.)

**1804** *Ann. Rev.* II. 68 The uninquiring and contented ignorance with which he has beheld every thing. **1833** L. Ritchie *Wand. by Loire* 8 Wandering..through a foreign town, ignorant and uninquiring, without a plan. **1863** Whittier *Countess* 83 There..The native dweller..keeps, in uninquiring trust, The old, dull round of things.

**Uninqui·sitive,** *a.* (Un-[1] 7.)

**1609** Daniel *Civ. Wars* VI. xxxv, Go loose the links of that soule-binding chaine; Inlarge this vninquisitive Beliefe. *a* **1639** Wotton *Reliq.* (1651) 154 Of those..have I many times heard (not uninquisitive, I acknowledg..) how [etc.]. **1796** Horsley *Serm.* xi. (1816) I. 236 Their uninquisitive temper keeps them in a total ignorance about secondary causes. **1815** L. Hunt *Feast Poets* 34 So contented and uninquisitive had every body become. **1848** Thackeray *Van. Fair* xii, Mrs. Sedley was of so easy and uninquisitive a nature, that she wasn't even jealous. **1872** Tulloch *Ration. Theol.* I. 290 Uninquisitive, unreflecting faith.

**Uninscri·bed,** *ppl. a.* (Un-[1] 8.)

**1704** Pope *Windsor For.* 320 Make sacred Charles's tomb for ever known (Obscure the place, and un-inscrib'd the stone). **1837** Lytton *Athens* I. 325 Altars uninscribed to a particular god. **1859** G. Wilson *Mem. E. Forbes* vi. (1861) 173 The whole of the uninscribed leaves of the book.

**Uninspe·cted,** *ppl. a.* (Un-[1] 8.) [**1775** Ash.] **1858** in *Sat. Rev.* 27 Nov. 531/1 Those schools,..'whether Church or Dissenting,..inspected or uninspected'. **1895** *Westm. Gaz.* 11 Oct. 2/2 Any change that gave us uninspected drinking clubs for inspected public-houses.

**Uninspi·red,** *ppl. a.* (Un-[1] 8.)

**1690** Locke *Hum. Und.* IV. xix. § 11 All the truths..that men uninspired are enlightened with. **1707** E. Chishull (*title*), The great Danger and Mistake of all new uninspired Prophecies relating to the End of the World. **1715** Pope *Iliad* II. 220 Ulysses heard, nor uninspir'd obey'd. **1746** Young *Nt. Th.* IX. 439 No mortal, un-inspir'd, Has ever yet conceiv'd..How kind is God. **1831** Campbell *Lines on Poland* 5 A theme for uninspired lips too strong. **1846** J. E. Ryland *Life Foster* I. 3 Vivacity was merely physical and uninspired by sentiment. **1900** *Ch. Q. Rev.* Apr. 110 As though..Paul [were] on a level with any uninspired writer.

**Uninspi·ring,** *ppl. a.* (Un-[1] 10.)

Also, in recent use, *uninspiringly.*

**1815** J. Scott *Vis. Paris* 24 Monotonous in its character, and uninspiring in its tendency. **1859** Jephson & Reeve *Brittany* 268 The uninspiring region of railroads and metropolitan industry. **1896** *Harper's Mag.* XCIII. 17/2 Gazing ..over the uninspiring chimney-pots of New York, at the equally uninspiring Long Island station.

**Uninsta·lled,** *ppl. a.* (Un-[1] 8.) [**1775** Ash.] *a* **1856** H. Miller *Cruise Betsey* 353 The minister of Allness—uninstalled at the time in his new dwelling. **Uni·nstigated,** *ppl. a.* (Un-[1] 8.) [**1775** Ash.] **1846** Poe *Criticism* Wks. 1865 III. 22 A voluntary, that is to say, an uninstigated notice of the book. **Uni·nstituted,** *ppl. a.* (Un-[1] 8.) **1702** C. Mather *Magn. Chr.* II. vii. (1852) 144 Certain confessedly unscriptural and uninstituted rites. **1742** J. Willison *Balm of Gilead* iv. Wks. (1852) 404/2 Many are warping towards popery.., observing uninstituted festivals.

**Uninstru·cted,** *ppl. a.* [Un-[1] 8.]

**1.** Not instructed or informed; unenlightened, ignorant. Also const. *in*, or with clause.

**1598** Florio, *Inerudito*,..vntaught, vninstructed. **1660** Jer. Taylor *Ductor* II. iii. rule 10 § 12 By uninstructed is only meant such who have not heard, or could not learn. **1665** Boyle *Occas. Refl.* III. xx. 131 These are utterly uninstructed in the Laws. **1690** Dryden *Don Sebast.* III. i, That Fool intrudes,..uninstructed how to stem the tide. **1744** Harris *Three Treat.* Wks. (1841) 3 Not even what we do intentionally, if it proceed from mere will and uninstructed instinct. 1785 REID *Intell. Powers* II. xx. 326 The most uninstructed peasant. 1806 A. HUNTER *Culina* (ed. 3) 268 Women uninstructed in cookery and the management of a family. 1875 E. WHITE *Life in Christ* v. xxviii. 491 To build a credulous assent..on the authority of the uninstructed multitude.

*absol.* 1662 JER. TAYLOR *Fides Formata* (1663) 167 Faith .., if it be not followed,..damns deeper than the Hell of the Infidels and uninstructed.

**2.** Not furnished with instructions.

1892 *Spectator* 21 May 699/1 Its delegates will enter the Convention 'uninstructed'.

Hence **Uninstru·ctedness.**

1833 MONTGOMERY *Lect. Poetry* 333 That perpetual thraldom of uninstructedness (if I may coin such a negative). 1871 JOWETT *Plato* I. 170 These base fears and confidences originate in ignorance and uninstructedness.

**Uninstru·cting,** *ppl. a.* [UN-[1] 10.] = next. ? 1630 H. R. *Mythomystes* 45 Our common uninstructing fabulous rimes. 1642 MILTON *Apol. Smect.* 30 That Lordly and uninstructing jurisdiction which properly makes the Pope Antichrist. 1762 MILLS *Syst. Pract. Husb.* I. 441 The little differences in their methods may not be un-instructing.

**Uninstru·ctive,** *a.* (UN-[1] 7.)

1666 BOYLE *Orig. Forms & Qual.* II. vii. 369 That the present Discourse shall not be uninstructive to You. 1695 LOCKE *Hum. Und.* II. xx. § 18 (ed. 3) 123 Pain from captious uninstructive wrangling. 1764 REID *Inquiry* vi. § 15. 172 Facts less vague and uninstructive. 1839 DE LA BECHE *Rep. Geol. Cornwall*, etc. ii. 29 The sections near the Start Point are .. particularly uninstructive. 1849 MACAULAY *Hist. Eng.* vi. II. 104 His character was remarkable, and his history not uninstructive.

So **Uninstru·ctively** *adv.*

1816 *Edin. Rev.* Sept. 182 No great man has been..more uninstructively commended.

**Uni·nsulate,** *v.* [UN-[2] 3.] *trans.* To deprive of insulation.

1844 NOAD *Electricity* (ed. 2) 17 Let the metallic plate be replaced, and uninsulated by touching it with the finger. 1866 R. M. FERGUSON *Electr.* 54 When an insulated body is charged by being uninsulated.

**Uni·nsulated,** *ppl. a.* (UN-[1] 8.)

1794 *Phil. Trans.* LXXXIV. 266 The insulated and uninsulated parts of my high pointed rod. 1839 G. BIRD *Nat. Philos.* 204 Holding beneath and parallel to it..a second disc of metal, but uninsulated. 1884 C. G. W. LOCK *Workshop Receipts* Ser. III. 116/1 Uninsulated German silver wire.

**Uninsu·lted,** *ppl. a.* (UN-[1] 8.) 1747 CARTE *Hist. Eng.* I. 288 The Danes..left no part of the coast of England uninsulted. 1832 L. HUNT *Poems* Pref. p. xlv, The hearth of an uninsulted poverty. **Uninsu·lting,** *ppl. a.* (UN-[1] 10.) 1855 MILMAN *Lat. Chr.* XIV. vii. VI. 549 The most quiet, uninsulting, unexasperating satire.

**Uninsu·rable,** *a.* (UN-[1] 7 b.)

1864 T. S. WILLIAMS & SIMMONDS *Eng. Commerc. Corr.* 275 That vessel however being an American..was almost uninsurable here. 1884 *Law Times Rep.* LI. 248 The life.. is..uninsurable by reason of the assumed state of his health.

Hence **Uninsurabi·lity.**

Also, in recent use (1903), *uninsurableness*.

1884 *Law Times Rep.* LI. 244/2 Written opinions..as to the insurability or uninsurability of the life of.. Harvey.

**Uninsu·red,** *ppl. a.* (UN-[1] 8.)

1799 *Hull Advertiser* 16 Nov. 3/3 The tenant, who..will be a considerable sufferer, is uninsured. 1853 R. S. SURTEES *Sponge's Sp. Tour* lxix, Farmer Slyfield's stack-yard was fired.., and all its uninsured contents destroyed. 1891 C. JAMES *Rom. Rigmarole* 154 My boots..were in London; and my life was uninsured.

**Unintelle·ctive,** *a.* (UN-[1] 7.) 1837 C. LOFFT *Self-formation* I. 36 Scholarship without talent is..a mass of unintellective confusion—a mere chaos.

**Unintelle·ctual,** *a.* [UN-[1] 7.]

†**1.** Not endowed with intellect; unintelligent.

*a* 1676 HALE *Prim. Orig. Man.* IV. viii. (1677) 373 The rest of Mankind, or the unintellectual Creatures.

**2. a.** Not intellectually developed; dull.

1819 KEATS *Lines to Fanny* 14 My muse..Unintellectual, yet divine to me. 1872 LIDDON *Elem. Relig.* i. 13 They thought that the apostles had been unintellectual persons.

**b.** Not characterized by the presence of intellect.

1837 HALLAM *Hist. Lit.* I. viii. § 3 A sound..not unpleasing to all.., but monotonous, unintellectual. 1846 POE *A. C. Mowatt* Wks. 1865 III. 43 The forehead is..by no means an unintellectual one. 1856 *N. Brit. Rev.* XXVI. 129 It has become the fashion to decry such pleasures..as unintellectual.

Hence **Unintelle·ctualism, Unintellectua·lity.**

Also *unintellectually* adv. (Webster, 1847).

1850 *Tait's Mag.* XVII. 735/1 The very same characteristics of inertia, unintellectuality, and uncombiningness. 1880 W. L. COURTNEY in E. Abbott *Hellenica* 254 That theory of unintellectualism with which Epicurus started.

**Uninte·lligence.** (UN-[1] 12; cf. next.)

1634 BP. HALL *Contempl.*, *N. T.* IV. iv, His un-intelligence, was not more strange then his mis-construction. 1829 CARLYLE *Misc.* (1840) II. 228 From afar I heard say, that Unintelligibility was but the result of Unintelligence. 1891 ETHEL GLAZEBROOK *Dower of Earth* II. xv. 236 The general moroseness and unintelligence of the English race.

**Uninte·lligent,** *a.* [UN-[1] 7.]

**1.** Having no knowledge or understanding *of* something. *rare.*

1609 B. JONSON *Sil. Wom.* IV. iii. 572 My mistris is not altogether vn-intelligent of these things. 1611 SHAKS. *Wint. T.* I. i. 16 That your Sences (vn-intelligent of our insufficience) may..as little accuse vs. 1850 CARLYLE *Latter-d. Pamph.* iv. 23 With China, or some distant country, too unintelligent of us and too unintelligible to us.

**2.** Devoid of intelligence.

1664 H. MORE *Myst. Iniq.* xiii. 45 The Sun is..an Inanimate and unintelligent masse of flammeous matter. 1701 NORRIS *Ideal World* I. vi. 342 So we must suppose God.. as an unintelligent being, and also in the production of truth acting as an unintelligent agent. 1788 REID *Active Powers* IV. ix. 627 If this be so, what is unintelligent may be the cause of what is intelligent. 1802 PALEY *Nat. Theol.* ii. § 2 By the application of an unintelligent impulse to a mechanism previously arranged..the corn is ground. 1864 PUSEY *Lect. Daniel* viii. 554 Time,..the most spiritual of the unintelligent creatures of God.

**3.** Deficient in intelligence or intellect; dull, stupid. Also *absol.*

*a* 1676 HALE *Ep. to Son* (1684) 13 A sort of brain-sick, melancholy, unintelligent persons. 1703 MOXON *Mech. Exerc.* 95 Its use is..well known (even to the most unintelligent). 1791 COWPER *Odyss.* VI. 234 Neither base by birth thou seem'st, Nor unintelligent. 1815 [see UNINFORMED *ppl. a.* 1 *absol.*]. 1861 OLMSTED *Journ. & Expl. Cotton Kingd.* I. 44 Most of the company were of a very poor appearance, rude and unintelligent.

**b.** Marked by lack of intelligence.

1860 W. COLLINS *Wom. White* II. 267 My servant..is really attached to me, in his unintelligent way. 1869 TOZER *Highl. Turkey* I. 302 [A man] with..an unintelligent expression of countenance.

†**4.** Unintelligible. *Obs.*

1683 MOXON *Mech. Exerc.*, *Printing* xxii. ¶ 5 That I may be the less unintelligent to the Reader. 1756 MRS. CALDERWOOD in *Coltness Collect.* (Maitl. Club) 190 He was obliged then to have recourse to 'calling grace', and severall other unintelligent things.

**Uninte·lligently,** *adv.* (UN-[1] 11; cf. prec.)

1754 EDWARDS *Freed. Will* II. xiii. 134 Liable to act unintelligently and unreasonably. 1836 J. GILBERT *Chr. Atonem.* iv. 119 The doctrine..has been charged with exhibiting the Divine Being as implacable, most unintelligently. 1889 JESSOPP *Coming of Friars* v. 224 They knew how to..go through the services though unintelligently.

**Unintelligibi·lity.** (UN-[1] 12; cf. next.)

1665 GLANVILL *Scepsis Sci.* iv. 17 To credit the unintelligibility..of this union and motion. 1719 *T. Burnet's Theory Earth* (ed. 4) I. vii. 107 If we have truly prov'd..the Impossibility or Unintelligibility of it in all other ways. 1806–7 J. BERESFORD *Miseries Hum. Life* IV. i, Their own ruin.. must obviously be the direct consequence of their unintelligibility. 1866 FELTON *Anc. & Mod. Gr.* II. ii. 288 Lycophron, chiefly famous for his unintelligibility.

**Uninte·lligible,** *a.* and *sb.* [UN-[1] 7.]

**1.** Not intelligible; incapable of being understood. Also *absol.*

1616 BULLOKAR *Eng. Expos.*, *Vnintelligible*, which cannot be vnderstood. 1647 COWLEY *Mistr.*, *Womens Superstit.* i, Or I'm a very Dunce, or Womankind Is a most unintelligible thing. 1684 T. BURNET *Theory Earth* I. 259 The trajection..is to me, I confess, unintelligible. 1717 BERKELEY *Tour Italy* Wks. 1871 IV. 527 The ruins above ground are pretty unintelligible. 1796 MME. D'ARBLAY *Camilla* V. 516 This is..so incredible—so unintelligible! 1834 LAMB *Wks.* (1908) I. 454 Coleridge..had the tact of making the unintelligible seem plain. 1871 JOWETT *Plato* I. 26 He made an unintelligible attempt to hide his perplexity.

**b.** Of language, statements, etc., or persons in respect of such.

1651 HOBBES *Leviath.* I. xii. 53 Men..choose rather to confesse he is Incomprehensible,..than to..confesse their definition to be unintelligible. 1683 *Brit. Spec.* 40 Their Records also were preserved in the Greek Tongue and Characters .. unintelligible by the Vulgar. 1703 DE FOE *More Reform.* 41 To b' Unintelligible is a Crime. 1765 JOHNSON *Shakespeare's Plays* I. p. lxviii, Homer has fewer passages unintelligible than Chaucer. 1841 LANE *Arab. Nts.* I. 113 Where, taking a little of its water, she pronounced over it some unintelligible words. 1884 *Solicitors' Jrnl.* 8 Nov. 29/2 The prisoner..having an impediment in his speech, which made him unintelligible and unable to read it.

**c.** *sb.* An unintelligible thing.

1838 SOUTHEY *Doctor* cxlix. V. 176 As two negatives make an affirmative, it might be found that two unintelligibles make a meaning.

†**2.** Unintelligent. *Obs.*[−1]

1694 R. FRANCK *North. Mem.* 121 Nor has it any Claim or Title from the Lough Minever, as superstitiously surmiz'd by the unintelligible Inhabitant.

**Uninte·lligibleness.** [UN-[1] 12, or f. prec.]

†**1.** Lack of understanding. *Obs.*[−1]

1616 DONNE *Serm.* V. 466 God shall suffer him to settle.. in an insensibleness and an unintelligibleness..of his own Condition.

**2.** The quality or fact of being unintelligible; unintelligibility.

1678 ALLESTREE *Lively Oracles* viii. § 14. 201 We ordinarily have so much candor, as to impute their unintelligibleness to our own ignorance. 1736 BUTLER *Anal.* II. vii. 347 The obscurity or unintelligibleness of one part of a prophecy. 1754 EDWARDS *Freed. Will* II. ii. 38 The Thing in Question seems to be forgotten, or kept out of Sight, in a Darkness and Unintelligibleness of Speech. 1832 H. MELVILL in *Preacher* III. 222/1 If it is unintelligible, it is the unintelligibleness of the Scriptures, and not of the commentator. 1877 E. R. CONDER *Basis Faith* ii. 69 The supposed unintelligibleness..of the doctrine.

**Uninte·lligibly,** *adv.* (UN-[1] 11.)

1664 POWER *Exp. Philos.* Pref. 11 Motion may be both invisibly and unintelligibly slow, as well as swift. 1713 BERKELEY *Hylas & Phil.* II. (1725) 70 You talk unintelligibly, instead of forming a reasonable Hypothesis. 1794 MRS. RADCLIFFE *Myst. Udolpho* xxx, He..hurried unintelligibly over some lines, and..offered her a pen. 1808 L. MURRAY *Eng. Gram.* I. 413 The second occasion of our being apt to write unintelligibly. 1892 [see UNDISCOVERABLY].

**Uninte·nded,** *ppl. a.* (UN-[1] 8.)

1649 MILTON *Eikon.* xix. 173 By any pretentions in the Parlament, which are now prov'd false, and unintended. 1670 EACHARD *Cont. Clergy* 78 The ridiculous, senseless, and unintended use, which many of them make of concordances. 1740 CIBBER *Apol.* 117 The first unintended Favour. 1796 MME. D'ARBLAY *Camilla* I. 233 The youthful group was much diverted with this unintended exhibition. 1835 MILL *Diss. & Disc.* (1859) I. 153 The unintended good or evil which has followed from our actions. 1884 *Manch. Exam.* 4 Nov. 6/1 The debate very nearly suffered an unintended collapse.

So **Uninte·ndedly** *adv.*

1782 PAINE *Let. Abbé Raynel* (1791) 43 This declaration ..has led me unintendedly into a train of metaphysical reasoning. 1818 BENTHAM *Ch. Eng.* Introd. 34 The intimation thus..unintendedly afforded.

**Uninte·ntional,** *a.* [UN-[1] 7.]

**1.** Not done with, not arising from, intention.

Given by Johnson (1755) as employed by Boyle.

1782 V. KNOX *Ess.* I. 120 The infirmity of human nature which causes unintentional lapses in the duties of friendship. 1803 SYD. SMITH *Wks.* (1859) I. 28 A very unintentional encouragement to offences. 1883 J. GILMOUR *Mongols* xxiii. 285 The accused admitted the charge, but pleaded that it was unintentional.

**2.** Not acting with intention.

1838 JAMES *Robber* v, He had been an unintentional, and even an unwilling witness to [it]. 1851 KITTO *Hist. Palestine* v. iii. 125 Six cities,..to any one of which the unintentional man-slayer might hasten.

Hence **Unintentiona·lity.**

1780 BENTHAM *Princ. Legisl.* (1823) II. xiii. 8 In the case of unintentionality: where he intends not to engage..in the act. *a* 1859 AUSTIN *Jurispr.* (1863) II. xx. 110 Unintentionality, and innocence of intention, seem both to be included.

**Uninte·ntionally,** *adv.* (UN-[1] 11.)

1769 PENNANT *Brit. Zool.* III. 71 A spear..with which he afterwards committed parricide, unintentionally,..on his father Ulysses. 1849 MACAULAY *Hist. Eng.* x. II. 574 Those who..had unintentionally done him a great service. 1874 H. R. REYNOLDS *John Bapt.* i. § 6. 55 He unintentionally revealed the forgery.

**Uninte·ntioned,** *ppl. a.* (UN-[1] 8.) 1851 MRS. BROWNING *Casa Guidi Wind.* II. 11 As little children take up a high strain With unintentioned voices. **Uninte·ntness.** (UN-[1] 12.) 1670 CLARENDON *Contempl. Ps.* Tracts (1727) 651 There is not a greater obstruction to devotion than the unintentness upon the action they are at. **Unintercepted,** *ppl. a.* (UN-[1] 8.) 1646 EARL MONM. tr. *Biondi's Civil Wars* VII. 92 She had not time enough to keep the secret undiscover'd, and him unintercepted. 1814 R. HALL *Wks.* (1832) I. 288 The light..becomes stronger and clearer by an unintercepted converse with its object.

† **Uni·nteressed,** *ppl. a.* *Obs.* Also 8 -est. [UN-[1] 8.] = UNINTERESTED *ppl. a.* 1 and 2.

1647 DIGGES *Unlawf. Taking Arms* IV. 158 None can be named, who are uninteressed in the decision. 1688 NORRIS *Theory Love* I. v. 58 Although there cannot be a pure and uninterressed Malice. 1702 tr. *Le Clerc's Prim. Fathers* 153 This is rather a Panegyrick than an uninterest History.

Hence † **Uni·nteressedness.** *Obs.*

1702 *Eng. Theophrast.* 360 'Tis the Motive only that gives Merit to our Actions, and Uninteressedness that makes them perfect.

**Uni·nterest.** (UN-[1] 12.) 1890 *Tablet* 5 July 19 A few notes concerning the great antiquity of the..church..may not be of uninterest.

**Uni·nterested,** *ppl. a.* [UN-[1] 8.]

†**1.** Unbiassed, impartial. *Obs.*

*a* 1646 J. GREGORY *Posthuma, Episc. Puerorum* (1649) 107 By this uninterested disguis, the more to justifie the Celebrations. 1660 R. COKE *Power & Subj.* 49 Nor do I think that any uninterested casuist will deny [etc.].

†**2.** Free from motives of personal interest; disinterested. *Obs.*

1661 (*title*), A Relation of the business..concerning Bedford Levell,..by a person uninterested. 1704 N. N. tr. *Boccalini's Advts. fr. Parnass.* III. 191 What think you of uninterested Men, who value the Publick Good beyond their own private Interest? 1767 COWPER *Let.* Wks. 1837 XV. 17 You know me to be an uninterested person.

**3.** Unconcerned, indifferent.

1771 *Ann. Reg.* II. 253/1 He is no cold, uninterested, and uninteresting advocate for the cause he espouses. 1774 *Trinket* 54 In this amiable society can my heart be uninterested? 1823 BYRON *Juan* x. lxxiii, In the same quaint, Uninterested tone. 1850 THACKERAY *Pendennis* lvii, An almost silent but not uninterested spectator.

Hence **Uni·nterestedly** *adv.*, **-ness.**

1691 T. H[ALE] *Acc. New Invent.* 55 As to that Uninterestedness so pretended to by them. 1891 H. HERMAN *His Angel* 108 He looked upon the..crowds..uninterestedly.

**Uni·nteresting,** *ppl. a.* (UN-[1] 10.)

1769 BURKE *Observ. State of Nation* ¶ 4 Uninteresting barren truths which generate no conclusion. 1782 MISS BURNEY *Cecilia* VII. ix, Too much occupied..to..listen to such uninteresting discourse. 1840 HOOD *Up Rhine* 43 The banks of the Lower Rhine are of a very uninteresting character. 1869 TOZER *Highl. Turkey* II. 176 Writers, whose pages are..extremely uninteresting.

Hence **Uni·nterestingness.** Also **Uni·nterestingly** *adv.*

1793 W. ROBERTS *Looker-on* No. 82 My days pass serenely, but *uninterestingly. 1896 BLACK *Briseis* xvii, I'm sick of blue skies—skies that are monotonously and uninterestingly blue. 1794 *European Mag.* XXVI. 344 The *uninterestingness of genealogical detail. 1854 FABER *Growth in Holiness* viii. (1872) 129 The momentary dulness and uninterestingness of the things of God.

**Uninterme·diate,** *a.* (UN-[1] 7.) 1863 LD. LYTTON *Ring of Amasis* II. 232 His nerves..had forced into his service a new unintermediate sense. **Unintermi·ssion.** (UN-[1] 12.) 1681 BP. S. PARKER *Demonstr. Law of Nat.* 134 The continuation and unintermission of his Pain had tired out his Patience.

† **Unintermi·ssive,** *a.* *Obs.* (UN-[1] 7.)

1610 E. SKORY *Extract fr. Hist. Hen. IV of France* 5 Anxieties caused by vn-intermissiue infidelities. 1645 QUARLES *New Distemper* Wks. (Grosart) I. 150/2 The unintermissive continuance [of Episcopal government] for so many Ages. 1655 EARL ORRERY *Parthen.* II. III. 293 His first stroakes were so vnintermissiue and briske.

Hence † **Unintermi·ssively** *adv.*, **-ness.** *Obs.*

1655 EARL ORRERY *Parthen.* I. I. 3 Perceiveing the unintermissiuenes of his melancholy. **1656** *Ibid.* III. IV. 295 That admirable equalitie which this fair Princess had so unintermissively practised.

**Unintermi·tted,** *ppl. a.* (UN-[1] 8.)

**1611** COTGR., *Suyte*,..a succession, continuance, or vnintermitted course of things. **1651** T. STANLEY *Poems, Moschus* 48 The hoarse frogs unintermitted groan. **1738** *Gentl. Mag.* VIII. 581/2 His Application was unintermitted, his Head clear. **1751** JOHNSON *Rambler* No. 108 ⁋ 1 Some scorched with unintermitted heat. **1812** SHELLEY in Dowden *Life* (1887) I. 218 My desire is ardent and unintermitted. **1884** CHURCH *Bacon* ix. 220 Easy and unstudied as his writing seems, it was..the result of unintermitted trouble.

Hence **Unintermi·ttedly** *adv.*

*a* **1693** URQUHART *Rabelais* III. xvii. 140 A pair of Yarn Windles, which she nine times unintermittedly veered, and frisked about. **1861** MILL *Utilit.* v. 81 Unless the machinery ..is kept unintermittedly in active play. **1863** W. PHILLIPS *Speeches* iii. 51 This heart of mine which beats so unintermittedly in the bosom.

**Unintermi·ttent,** *a.* (UN-[1] 7.)

**1850** J. H. NEWMAN *Diffic. Anglic.* 130 Which has been in unintermittent traditionary error. **1883** J. GILMOUR *Mongols* 261 The unintermittent feasting lasts about a week.

Hence **Unintermi·ttently** *adv.*

**1875** *Wonders of Phys. World* I. iii. 100 Their ruins crumble unintermittently.

**Unintermi·tting,** *ppl. a.* (UN-[1] 10.)

**1661** FELTHAM *Resolves*, etc. 384 To procure an un-intermitting joy..is beyond a Solomon. **1709** MRS. MANLEY *Secret Mem.* (1720) IV. 195 In answer to her unintermitting Reproaches. **1777** ROBERTSON *Hist. Amer.* v. (1778) II. 117 All were ready to sink under the toils of unintermitting service. *a* **1818** M. G. LEWIS *Jrnl. W. Ind.* (1834) 4 The flashes of lightning were..unintermitting. **1890** *Retrospect Med.* CII. 368 The continuous roar..is..unintermitting.

Hence **Unintermi·ttingness.**

**1866** MRS. RITCHIE *Village on Cliff* xiv, His talk was a wonder of ingenuity and unintermittingness.

**Unintermi·ttingly,** *adv.* (UN-[1] 11; cf. prec.)

**1782** *Ann. Reg., Hist.* 85/2 An infinite number of rockets were unintermittingly thrown. **1809** PINKNEY *Trav. France* 164 The attention of the French Government is now unintermittingly occupied. **1885** J. PAYN *Talk of Town* I. 103 He now resolved to cultivate it [*i. e.* his father's favour] unintermittingly, and at any sacrifice.

**Unintermi·xed,** *ppl. a.* (UN-[1] 8).

**1595** DANIEL *Civ. Wars* I. vi, Vnintermixt with fiction's fantasies, I versify the truth. **1618** SIR S. D'EWES *Autobiog.* (1845) I. 110 An eternal and unintermixed happiness. **1630** DRUMM. OF HAWTH. *Hymn of Fairest Faire* 189 Those Bodies faire and greate Which faint not in their Course,.. Vnintermixt, which no disorder proue. **1720** WELTON *Suffer. Son of God* II. xxvii. 714 In Him, Alone, whose Love and Friendship is Pure, and un-intermixed.

**Uninte·rpolated,** *ppl. a.* (UN-[1] 8.) **1790** PORSON *Lett. to Travis* 277 [They] think that *authenticæ* means no more than genuine, uninterpolated. **1818** G. S. FABER *Horæ Mosaicæ* I. 350 It is found impossible to ascribe the uninterpolated Pentateuch to any author save Moses. **Uninterpo·sing,** *ppl. a.* (UN-[1] 10.) **1749** MELMOTH *Fitzosborne Lett.* xlviii. II. 13 To prove, that the supreme being remains an uninterposing spectator of what is transacted upon this theatre of the world.

**Uninte·rpretable,** *a.* (UN-[1] 7 b.)

**1625** PURCHAS *Pilgrims* II. 1456 Through the virtue of an uninterpretable name. **1729** G. ADAMS tr. *Sophocles, Antig.* IV. i. II. 56 An unknown Voice of Birds crying with an ill Fury, uninterpretable. **1879** THOMSON & TAIT *Nat. Phil.* I. I. § 385 Many formulae are at present obscure and uninterpretable. **1884** *Pop. Sci. Monthly* XXIV. 822 Figures of men and animals and uninterpretable signs.

**Uninte·rpreted,** *ppl. a.* (UN-[1] 8.)

**1662** HIBBERT *Body of Divinity* I. 218 Amen. It is..an Hebrew word, .. and .. remaines uninterpreted. *a* **1768** SECKER *Serm.* (1771) V. vii. 139 Combinations of several Words may come to have Meanings very different from what the Terms,..uninterpreted by Practice, would lead one to apprehend. **1848** E. A. LEATHAM *Charmione* (1858) II. 22 Attributing that uninterpreted gladness to..the sights and sounds of a spiritual world. **1895** *Educat. Rev.* Nov. 352 Unsorted and uninterpreted fragments.

**Uninte·rred,** *ppl. a.* (UN-[1] 8.)

**1648** *Hunting of Fox* 17 Left uninter'd for the Fox and other beasts to prey upon. *a* **1684** LEIGHTON *Com.* I *Pet.* iii. 19 Rotting above ground, as carcases uninterred. **1720** POPE *Iliad* XXII. 474 Unwept, unhonour'd, uninterr'd he lies! **1827** POLLOK *Course T.* VI. 258 By him lay the uninterred corpse. **1837** LYTTON *Athens* II. 161 Leaving the remainder uninterred he invited all..to examine the scene of contest.

**Uninte·rrogable,** *a.*, **-ated,** *ppl. a.* (UN-[1] 7 b, 8.) **1802–12** BENTHAM *Ration. Judic. Evid.* (1827) II. 295 His own ready-written and uninterrogable testimony. *Ibid.* I. 450 The mass of sworn but uninterrogated deposition called an affidavit. **1803** MARY CHARLTON *Wife & Mistress* III. 174 No one will question me upon the dark subject.., and uninterrogated, how could I endure to mention it!

**Uninterru·pt,** *ppl. a. Sc.* [UN-[1] 8 b.] = next. **1776** C. KEITH *Farmer's Ha'* lxiii, O here are joys uninterrupt', Far hence is pleasure's gangrene cup.

**Uninterru·pted,** *ppl. a.* and *adv.* [UN-[1] 8.]

**1.** Not interrupted or broken in respect of continuity or sequence; unintermittent, continuous.

**1602** WARNER *Alb. Eng.* XIII. lxxvi. 316 The euer mouing heauens vninterrupted rounde. **1647** CLARENDON *Hist. Reb.* I. § 5 The uninterrupted pleasures .. of twenty-two years Peace. **1709** ADDISON *Tatler* No. 192 ⁋ 6 An uninterrupted Friendship and Felicity. **1781** GIBBON *Decl. & F.* xxxi. III. 195 The uninterrupted succession of senators. **1849** COBDEN *Speeches* 29 An interval of several years of uninterrupted peace. **1880** MCCARTHY *Our Times* xl. III. 223 His career was one of uninterrupted success.

**b.** Not broken in surface; having no intervals between the parts.

**1791** NEWTE *Tour Eng. & Scot.* 58 The cascade..falls..in one uninterrupted sheet. **1822** J. PARKINSON *Outl. Oryctol.* 159 The margin [of the shell is]..uninterrupted and reflected. **1866** *Treas. Bot.* 1191/2 *Uninterrupted*, consisting of regularly increasing or diminishing parts, or of parts all of the same size.

**2.** Not disturbed or broken into; not interrupted *by* something.

**1657** CROMWELL *Sp.* in Somers *Tracts* (1811) VI. 367 A more free exercise, more uninterrupted by any hand of power. **1728** ELIZA HEYWOOD tr. *Mme. de Gomez's Belle A.* (1732) II. 63 The rest of our Voyage was..uninterrupted by the least cross Accident whatever. **1796** MME. D'ARBLAY *Camilla* V. 202 Mr. Tyrold would not suffer this scene to be long uninterrupted. **1854** *Poultry Chron.* II. 194/2 An uninterrupted day of rest. **1873** B. HARTE *Fiddletown* 7 The dwellings were..uninterrupted by shops.

**3.** *adv.* Without interruption; unhindered.

**1677** YARRANTON *Eng. Improv.* 3 That the Smacks and small Vessels may..fetch in Provisions and Naval Stores uninterrupted.

**Uninterru·ptedly,** *adv.* [UN-[1] 11; cf. prec.] Without interruption or break; continuously, connectedly.

**1665** SIR T. HERBERT *Trav.* (1677) 203 Where the Mountain uninterruptedly runs as far as Mergiana. *a* **1691** BOYLE *Hist. Air* (1692) 7 Having not the leisure to prosecute this discourse uninterruptedly. **1794** *Phil. Trans.* LXXXV. 39 In which case the following particles would exert their force uninterruptedly. **1826** F. REYNOLDS *Life & Times* II. 183 From that time..our intimacy has continued..uninterruptedly. **1875** JOWETT *Plato* (ed. 2) III. 4 That the Republic was written uninterruptedly and by a continuous effort.

**Uninterru·ptedness.** (f. UNINTERRUPTED.)

**1665** J. SERJEANT *Sure Footing* 106 The ever-continuance or uninterruptedness of Tradition. **1671** FLAVEL *Fount. Life* ii. 4 The Perpetuity and uninterruptedness thereof. **1791** WASHINGTON *Let.* Writ. 1892 XII. 46 My return to this place is sooner than I expected, owing to the uninterruptedness of my journey. **1834** J. W. CROKER in *C. Papers* 11 June, The musicians..spoiled that uninterruptedness (what a word) which was so beautiful yesterday. **1876** CARPENTER in *Contemp. Rev.* Jan., The Scientific Theist..looks at the uninterruptedness of this order [in Nature] as the highest evidence of its original perfection.

**Uninterru·ptible,** *a.* (UN-[1] 7.) *a* **1683** SIDNEY *Disc. Govt.* III. xxx. (1704) 361 An uninterruptible Line of Descent. **Uninterru·ptibleness.** (UN-[1] 12.) **1654** OWEN *Doctr. Saints' Persev.* Pref. Rdr. B j b, The uninterruptibleness of any Act of God. **Uninterru·pting,** *ppl. a.* (UN-[1] 10.) **1809** W. TAYLOR in Robberds *Mem.* (1843) II. 364 My imagination is rapidly learning..to exult in the uninterrupting character of rural scenery.

**Uninterru·ption.** (UN-[1] 12.)

**1647** CLARENDON *Hist. Reb.* III. § 65 To have Questioned ..the Seditious Riots..before the uninterruption and security had confirmed the People in all three. **1740** CHEYNE *Regimen* 47 To allow Time and Uninterruption from the natural Powers. **1744** WALDRON *Descr. Isle of Man* (ed. 2) 106 That Uninterruption and Solitude of the Sea, gave the Mermen..frequent Opportunities of visiting the Shore. **1808** G. EDWARDS *Pract. Plan* iii. 20 The enlargement and uninterruption of commerce.

**Uninterspe·rsed,** *ppl. a.* (UN-[1] 8.) **1887** BROWNING *Parleyings, Apollo & Fates*, Is age..so uninterspersed with good? **Uni·nterviewed,** *ppl. a.* (UN-[1] 8.) **1886** PHELPS *Burglars in Paradise* viii, The hitherto uninterviewed American citizen.

**Uninthralled, -intitled,** etc.: see UNEN-.

**Uninti·midated,** *ppl. a.* (UN-[1] 8.)

**1764** *Museum Rust.* II. lxxviii. 275 If I find your *Museum* that unintimidated receptacle which I hope it will appear to be. **1815** WRAXALL *Hist. Mem.* I. 361 Unintimidated by the clamours of Sir Fletcher's adherents. *a* **1849** H. COLERIDGE *Ess.* (1851) II. 60 The unbought, unintimidated suffrage of fame. **1876** BANCROFT *Hist. U.S.* III. xx. 305 Unintimidated by the prophecy.

**Uninto·xicating,** *ppl. a.* (UN-[1] 10.)

**1773** *Observ. State Poor* 57 This unintoxicating beverage. **1844** H. G. ROBINSON *Odes of Horace* I. xvii, Here shalt thou quaff.. The unintoxicating bowl Of Lesbian. **1876** TYNDALL *Fragm. Sci.* (1879) II. xii. 256 Unintoxicating grape-juice is converted into intoxicating wine.

**Uni·ntricated,** *ppl. a.* (UN-[1] 8.) *a* **1660** HAMMOND *Serm.* Wks. 1683 IV. 502 The fair open Campania of even, clear, unintricated designs. **Unintri·guing,** *ppl. a.* (UN-[1] 10.) **1755** *Monitor* No. 9. I. 72 The plain, disinterested, unintriguing man. **1771** H. WALPOLE *Vertue's Anecd. Paint.* IV. 5 In truth he was..a modest unintriguing man.

**Unintrodu·ced,** *ppl. a.* (UN-[1] 8.)

**1743** YOUNG *Nt. Th.* v. 89 Think not un-introduc'd I forc'd my way. **1813** *Examiner* 19 Apr. 250/1 The romping, ungainly, unintroduced girl of seventeen. **1897** MARY KINGSLEY *W. Africa* 6 When I have arrived..in a steamer or canoe, unexpected, unintroduced, or turned up equally unheralded out of the bush.

**Unintro·itive,** *a.* (UN-[1] 7.) **1819** COLERIDGE in *Lit. Rem.* (1836) II. 239 And then again, still unintroitive, [Banquo] addresses the witches. **Unintromi·tted,** *ppl. a.* (UN-[1] 8.) **1563** *Reg. Privy Council Scot.* I. 246 To.. keip the samyn [corn]..upoun the grund of the saidis landis, unintromittit with be ather of the saidis parteis. **Unintru·ding,** *ppl. a.* (UN-[1] 10.) **1796** MME. D'ARBLAY *Camilla* III. 300 She is there almost every night; only being unintruding, she is unnoticed. **Unintu·itive,** *a.* (UN-[1] 7.) **1842** SIR W. HAMILTON *Diss.* in *Reid's Wks.* 767 The unintuitive judgments.

**Uninu·clear** (yūni-), *a.* [UNI- I.] Having, or characterized by, one nucleus.

**1882** VINES tr. *Sachs' Bot.* 946 Treub..has observed the division of the nucleus..and finds that it takes place in the manner described..for uninuclear cells. **1896** *Allbutt's Syst. Med.* I. 71 In the boundary zone away from the cocci the uninuclear form [of leucocyte] predominated.

So **Uninu·cleate, Uninu·cleated** *adjs.*

**1885** E. RAY LANKESTER in *Encycl. Brit.* XIX. 862/1 Young uninucleate individual which has emerged from the cyst within the Tadpole, and will now multiply its nuclei. **1898** *Allbutt's Syst. Med.* V. 636 There are present in the blood numerous large uninucleated cells.

**Uninu·red,** *ppl. a.* (UN-[1] 8.)

*a* **1708** J. PHILIPS *Fall of Chloe's Jordan* 100 Protected mice The race exiguous, uninured to wet, Their mansions quit. *a* **1800** COWPER *Odyss.* (ed. 2) XXI. 182 Fatiguing, first, his hands Too delicate and uninured to toil. **1856** ALFORD *Quebec Chapel Serm.* III. 128 Uninured to the selfishness of this wicked world. **1880** SWINBURNE *Stud. Shaks.* 18 An incongruity..imperceptible to eyes uninured to the use of their spectacles.

**Uninva·dable,** *a.* (UN-[1] 7 b.) *a* **1711** KEN *Hymns Evang.* Poet. Wks. 1721 I. 32 Spreading a glorious Evangelick Light, And uninvadeable by ghostly Night. *a* **1806** ELIZ. CARTER in *Mem.* (1808) I. 36 My heart, which I thought so secure and so uninvadable.

**Uninva·ded,** *ppl. a.* (UN-[1] 8.)

[**1571–2** *Reg. Privy Council Scot.* II. 125 To be unhurt, unharmit, un-molestit invadit and in ony wayis persewit.] **1647** CLARENDON *Hist. Reb.* II. § 7 They believed there was no part of their Civil Government uninvaded by them. **1748** RICHARDSON *Clarissa* (1811) III. 165, I expect to be uninvaded in my retirements. **1769** SIR J. REYNOLDS *Disc.* ii. (1778) 36 Of this I shall speak with such latitude, as may leave the province of the professor uninvaded. **1830** TENNYSON *Kraken* 3 His ancient, dreamless, uninvaded sleep The Kraken sleepeth. **1885** O. CRAWFURD *Woman's Reputation* i, Our old England indeed, uninvaded by modern ideas.

**Uninva·lidated,** *ppl. a.* (UN-[1] 8.) **1813** *Monthly Mag.* XXXV. 217 The fact remains uninvalidated. **Uninvei·gled,** *ppl. a.* (UN-[1] 8.) **1687** tr. *Sallust* (1692) 38 Nor did he leave uninveigl'd the very Thieves and Robbers.

**Uninve·nted,** *ppl. a.* (UN-[1] 8.)

**1611** BEAUM. & FL. *King & No King* IV. ad fin., If that happen Then I..shall pull a heap Of strange yet uninvented sin upon me. **1667** MILTON *P. L.* VI. 470 Not uninvented that, which thou aright Beleivst so main to our success. **1680** OTWAY *Orphan* v, Rack me..with all your choicest torments,..and pains yet uninvented. **1754** [see UNIMAGINED]. **1875** JEVONS *Money* xxi. 283 It has grown spontaneously, uninvented, unauthorized by the legislature.

**Uninve·ntful,** *a.* (UN-[1] 7.) **1856** RUSKIN *Mod. Paint.* III. IV. xviii. § 13 The harsh outline and..uninventful blankness of the design.

**Uninve·ntive,** *a.* (UN-[1] 7.)

**1776** MICKLE tr. *Camoens' Lusiad* Dissert. 164/1 A most servile uninventive imitation of the sixth Eneid. **1783** BLAIR *Lect.* I. 349 Nature..appears, to his uninventive genius, exhausted by those who have gone before him. **1816** *Q. Rev.* XV. 71 One is of a dry and uninventive faculty. **1855** MILMAN *Lat. Chr.* XIV. iii. VI. 447 The inert and uninventive disciple of the Western philosophy.

Hence **Uninve·ntively** (Webster, 1847), **-ness.**

**1863** *Sat. Rev.* 14 March 335/2 The very grotesqueness and uninventiveness..which distinguished the illuminations of Tuesday.

**Uninve·rted,** *ppl. a.* (UN-[1] 8.) **1745** YOUNG *Nt. Th.* VIII. 1161 He follows nature (not like thee), and shews us An uninverted system of a man. **1865** J. HULLAH *Transition Period of Music* 217 There are..no less than six perfect cadences, in the direct or uninverted form.

**Uninve·sted,** *ppl. a.* (UN-[1] 8.)

[**1775** ASH.] **1802–12** BENTHAM *Ration. Judic. Evid.* (1827) V. 218 A man..uninvested with any coercive power. **1816** SCOTT *Old Mort.* xxii, Supposing the insurgents were to march onward and leave it [*sc.* a stronghold] uninvested. **1833** J. BURKE (*title*), A Genealogical and Heraldic History of The Commoners..uninvested with Heritable Honours.

**Uninve·stigable,** *a.* (UN-[1] 7 b, 5 b.)

*a* **1677** BARROW *Serm.* Wks. 1686 III. 464 We (to whom God's judgements are inscrutable, and his ways uninvestigable). **1691** RAY *Creation* I. (1692) 2 The Number of them being uninvestigable by us. **1768–74** TUCKER *Lt. Nat.* (1834) I. 582 Brought about by the courses of fortune dependent upon one another, to us accidental and uninvestigable. **1858** H. BUSHNELL *Serm. New Life* 31 The manner of the fact is uninvestigable and mysterious. **1866** — *Vicar. Sacr.* II. iv. 179 God is.., in some sense uninvestigable by us, both finite and subject.

**Uninve·stigated,** *ppl. a.* (UN-[1] 8.) **1816** SCOTT *Bl. Dwarf* iv, I am unwilling to leave a matter uninvestigated which [etc.]. **1862** MILLER *Elem. Chem., Org.* (ed. 2) iii. § 4. 244 It yields a liquid..the nature of which, however, is at present uninvestigated. **Uninve·stigating,** *ppl. a.* (UN-[1] 10.) **1802** *Noble Wanderers* I. 246 The secret of his heart was too visible to escape the uninvestigating eye. **Uninvi·dious,** *a.* (UN-[1] 7.) **1822** LAMB *Elia* I. *Decay of Beggars*, Theirs were the only rates uninvidious in the levy. **1865** F. OAKELEY *Hist. Notes* 3 Unpretending, uninvidious, and sufficient for the purpose. **Uninvi·diously,** *adv.* (UN-[1] 11.) **1678** CUDWORTH *Intell. Syst.* I. iii. 117 Intellectual Love..having an Infinite overflowing Fulnes and Fecundity, dispenses it self Uninvidiously.

**Uninvi·te,** *v.* [UN-[2] 3 or UN-[1] 14.] *trans.* To cancel or omit the invitation of (a person).

**1665** PEPYS *Diary* 26 Nov., So I made them uninvite their guests. **1873** MRS. WHITNEY *Other Girls* xviii, Without letting him answer, she turned..and sprang up the rugged stairway...But she had not uninvited him, after all.

**Uninvi·ted,** *ppl. a.* (UN-[1] 8.)

**1631** MASSINGER *Emperor East* IV. v, Thou uninvited guest,..I charge thee, leave me! **1665** BOYLE *Occas. Refl.* IV. xvii. 112 The great Advantage..of freeing themselves from uninvited Companions. **1702** VANBRUGH *False Friend* III. ii, That thought comes uninvited. Then, like an uninvited guest, let it be treated: Begone intruder. **1796** MME. D'ARBLAY *Camilla* IV. 183 [There] he had spent the night, though uninvited by its agitated owner. **1840** HOOD *Up Rhine* 241 Uninvited and unannounced, an unceremonious visitor stepped boldly into the room. **1882** MAYNE REID in *N. York Tribune* 21 June, All uninvited people would be looked upon as intruders.

Hence **Uninvi·tedly** *adv.*

**1669** EARL ORRERY *Parthen.* III. v. 11 Uninvitedly I came to participate in their Glory.

**Uninvi·ting,** *ppl. a.* (UN-[1] 10.)

**1686** PLOT *Staffordsh.* 301 That a man should thus long

after such uninviting things. **1690** BOYLE *Chr. Virtuoso* I. 102 That such Unlikely Men should so Succesfully preach so Uninviting a Doctrine. **1777** ROBERTSON *Hist. Amer.* VI. (1778) II. 151 He found every where the same uninviting country. **1821** LAMB *Elia* I. *Old Benchers I. T.*, His look was uninviting. **1894** MRS. DYAN *Man's Keeping* (1899) 60 The outside looked formidable and uninviting.

*Comb.* **1880** BEALE *Slight Ailm.* 172 Half a dozen unripe and very uninviting-looking apples.

**Uninvo·ked,** *ppl. a.* (UN-[1] 8.) **1718** ROWE tr. *Lucan* I. 125 Let Phœbus dwell Still uninvok'd in Cyrrha's mystick cell. **1809–14** WORDSW. *Excurs.* III. 753 The powers of song I left not uninvoked. **1849** GROTE *Greece* II. xlvii. VI. 123 That the god would help them, invoked or uninvoked.

**Uninvo·lved,** *ppl. a.* (UN-[1] 8.) **1793** V. KNOX *Lett. Yng. Noblem.* xxvii, So long as you preserve your own finances uninvolved. **1853** RUSKIN *Stones Ven.* II. 207 Loveliness of simple design and grace of uninvolved proportion.

‖ **Unio** (yū·nio). *Zool.* Pl. **unios** (‖ **uniones**). [L. *ūnio* a single large pearl (Pliny). Cf. UNION *sb.*[2]] A genus of freshwater bivalves typical of the family *Unionidæ*; a mussel belonging to this or a related genus, esp. one yielding pearls; a river-mussel, pearl-mussel.

**1824** *Encycl. Brit.* Suppl. V. 581/1 The second [family], *Uniodæ* [sic], will embrace Unio,..Anodonta, and Iridina. **1834** GRIFFITH tr. *Cuvier* XII. 387 Pearls..are more especially produced by the thick bivalve shells, such as the *uniones*. *Ibid.* 401 There is nothing to induce us to mention the Unio here, except [etc.]. **1851** S. P. WOODWARD *Mollusca* 41 Some of the unios thicken their umbones enormously. **1899** *Nature* 15 June 151/2 The washing out of loose pearls from the unios.

**b.** *attrib.* and *Comb.*, as *Unio-fisher*, *mollusc*, *-shaped*; Unio-beds (see quot. 1888).

**1861** P. P. CARPENTER in *Rep. Smithsonian Instit. 1860*, 259 *Unio*-shaped shells. *Ibid.* 263 The musk-rats..being nature's great Unio-fishers. **1882** *Proc. Berw. Nat. Club* IX. 506 Birds..picking up the large Unio molluscs in rivers. **1888** *Cassell's Encycl. Dict.*, *Unio-beds*,..certain beds in the Purbeck, characterized by the occurrence of species of Unio. **1897** *Quart. Jrnl. Geol. Soc.* Index 400/2 Unio-bed on Notowasaga River (Canada).

**Unio·cular,** *a.* [See UNI- and OCULAR *a.*, and cf. med.L. *ūnioculus.*] **a.** *fig.* Characterized by the use of one eye. **b.** Of or pertaining to, affecting, one eye. Cf. MONOCULAR *a.*

**a.** *a* **1830** *Edin. Rev.* LI. 531 The results of this unilateral, uni-ocular mode of proceeding. **b.** **1890** *Lancet* 28 June 1416/1 In two [cases] there was occasional lateral nystagmus; one uniocular. *a* **1901** F. W. H. MYERS *Human Personality* (1903) I. 479 Cases, where ciliary spasm..led to uniocular diplopia.

**U·nioid,** *a. Zool.* [f. UNI-O + -OID. Cf. UNIONOID *a.*] Resembling or shaped like (that of) a unio. **1861** P. P. CARPENTER in *Rep. Smithsonian Instit. 1860*, 268 Shells, with two Unioid teeth in each valve.

**Union** (yū·niən), *sb.*[1] Also 5–6 vnyon, 5–7 vnion. [a. F. *union* (12–13th c., = Sp. *union*, Pg. *união*, It. *unione*), ad. L. *ūniōn-em*, *ūnio* the number one, unity, uniting, etc., f. *ūnus* one.]

**I. 1.** The action of joining or uniting one thing to another or others, or two or more things together, so as to form one whole or complete body; the state or condition of being so joined or united; combination, conjunction: **a.** In non-physical sense or of abstract things.

*Hypostatic union*: see HYPOSTATIC *a.* 1.

**1432–50** tr. *Higden* (Rolls) V. 9 He ordeynede that water scholde be mixte with wyne in the chalice, to betoken the union of the churche un to Criste. *c* **1450** *Myrr. Our Ladye* 208 Conuenyently are deuoute wedlockes lykened vnto fayre trees, wherof the route ys suche vnyon of tow hartes. *Ibid.* 229 By whiche knyttynge..the godhed was vnyed vnto the manhed, and the very manhed vnto the godhed...And in this moste acceptable vnyon [etc.]. **1538** STARKEY *England* 41 The vnyon and coniunctyon of the body and soule togyddur. **1560** tr. *Fisher's Godly Treat. Prayer* F 5 b, The very true and sincere delectation, whiche groweth by a certayne vnion and perfect agreement..of our soules with almightie God. **1627** SIR J. FINCH in *Parl. Hist.* (1807) II. 224/2 This union of hearts, sir, is a greatness beyond that of the kingdom to which you are heir. **1651** HOBBES *Leviath.* II. xviii. 92 The strength of an Army [consisteth] in the union of their strength under one Command. **1667** MILTON *P. L.* IX. 966 Adam, from whose deare side I boast me sprung, And gladly of our Union heare thee speak, One Heart, one Soul in both. **1728** CHAMBERS *Cycl.* s.v. *Hypostatical*, The Union of the human Nature with the Divine. **1800** *Med. Jrnl.* IV. 334 By the union and investigation of several data, the truth may at last be discovered. **1841** MIALL in *Nonconf.* I. 1 The union of church and state. **1873** FREEMAN *Comp. Politics* ii. 49 The union of Roman and Teutonic elements.

**b.** Of persons or countries with reference to joint action or policy. Cf. 3.

**1608** W. WILKES *Sec. Memento for Magistrates* 59 Compleat union is of better consequence to the furtherance of religion. **1687** A. LOVELL tr. *Thevenot's Trav.* I. 78 The Janizaries swore the same Union with the Spahis. **1711** DK. MARLBOROUGH in *10th Rep. Hist. MSS. Comm.* App. I. 144, I haue no other views then what tend to the firmest union with his Lordship. **1817** SHELLEY *Rev. Islam* IX. xviii, The cold sneers of calumny were vain, The union of the free with discord's brand to stain.

**c.** In physical sense; *spec.* in *Surg.*, the growing together of the parts of a broken bone, lips of a wound, etc., in the process of healing.

**1631** H. C[ROOKE] *Expl. Instrum. Chirurg.* 13 To hold the lips of the wound..together till the vnion be perfected. **1704** J. HARRIS *Lex. Techn.* I. s.v., The Union of Atoms, or Particles which touch in a Plain: as in the Chrystallization of Salts, and other like Bodies. **1767** GOOCH *Treat. Wounds* I. 152 The time generally allowed for the union of wounds. **1815** J. SMITH *Panorama Sci. & Art* II. 341 This affinity or union, is always..of a chemical nature, for it is attended with the grand characteristic of chemical union, viz. it destroys the identity of the ingredients. **1842** LOUDON *Suburban Hort.* 287 To fit the scion to the stock in such a manner that the union of their inner barks..may be as close as possible. **1860** TYNDALL *Glac.* I. vii. 54 The moraine..formed by the union of the lateral moraines.

**d.** With *a* and pl. An instance or occasion of this. (Rarely in physical sense, see (*b*).)

In some instances not clearly separable from 7.

**1570** LEVINS *Manip.* 166 An Vnion, *vnio.* *c* **1600** SHAKS. *Sonn.* viii. 6 If the true concord of well tuned sounds, By vnions married, do offend thine eare. *a* **1653** BINNING *Serm.* Wks. (1735) 8/2 There was an Union made already in his first Moulding. **1679** SOUTH *Serm.* 167 The same [object] luckily hapning upon another [mind] of a Disposition..framed for it, is..greedily clasped into the nearest Unions and Embraces. **1781** COWPER *Charity* 122 While providence enjoins to ev'ry soul An union with the vast terraqueous whole. **1817** J. BRADBURY *Trav. Amer.* 331 A colony having an union of interest, and of course an union of action. **1871** JOWETT *Plato* III. 363 There is a union of qualities in him such as I have never seen in any other.

(*b*) **1826** S. COOPER *First Lines Surg.* (ed. 5) 281 In some instances [of compound fracture], only a partial union follows. **1842** LOUDON *Suburban Hort.* 281 Instances frequently occur of the inner bark of the scion being placed out of contact with that of the stock, and a union nevertheless ensues.

**e.** Without article, in prec. senses.

† *At union*, in union, united.

*c* **1483** H. BARADOUN in *Pol., Rel. & L. Poems* 289 Hertis ease & I be not at vnion. **1526** *Pilgr. Perf.* (W. de W. 1531) 284 b, In that all swetenesse and vnyon of loue and grace is signifyed. **1625** BACON *Ess., Friendship* (Arb.) 173 For in Bodies, Vnion strengthneth and cherisheth any Naturall Action;..And euen so is it of Minds. **1651** HOBBES *Govt. & Soc.* v. § 7. 79 This submission of the wills of all those men to the will of one man, or one Counsell, is then made, when each one of them obligeth himself by contract to every one of the rest,..this is called union. **1675** R. BURTHOGGE *Causa Dei* 39 The Soul in state of Union to the Body. **1738** R. GREY *Meth. Hebrew* p. v, The Line of Union called *Maccaph.* **1789** BELSHAM *Ess.* II. xli. 526 Persecution, said Mr. Fox, is a bond of union. **1800** tr. *Lagrange's Chem.* II. 114 Nitric solutions of mercury and silver..are themselves decomposed at the moment of union. **1847** MRS. A. KERR tr. *Ranke's Hist. Servia* 117 The league of independent chiefs..was on the closest terms of union with both these parties. **1849** LEVER *Con Cregan* xi, While a sharp wound in my neck..had just begun that process called 'union'. *a* **1881** A. BARRATT *Phys. Metempiric* (1883) p. xxv, The feeling of real invisible union among the spirits of all the universe.

**f.** Sexual conjunction; copulation. *rare.*

**1728** CHAMBERS *Cycl.* s.v. *Univocal*, Animals..produced by Univocal Generation, that is, by the sole Union or Copulation of a Male and Female of the same Species. **1799** *Med. Jrnl.* II. 321 A female rabbit..and..a buck..were allowed to caress each other whilst absolute union was prevented.

**2.** The uniting together of the different sections, parties, or individuals of a nation, people, or other body so as to produce general agreement or concord; the condition resulting from this; absence of dissension, discord, or difference in opinion or doctrine; unity.

*c* **1460** *Brut* II. 508 This Frederike..was long Emperoure, & differred for to be crowned at Rome because of þe Scisme; but after þat vnion was had, he was crowned with Emperial Diademe. *c* **1460** G. ASHBY *Dicta Philos.* 703 That kyng that maketh his Region To be obedient to his iuste lawe, That reigne peasibly in an vnyon. **1525** LD. BERNERS *Froiss.* II. ccxxxiii. 301 b/1 The vnyon of the churche I desyre, and I haue taken great payne therin. **1539** CROMWELL in Merriman *Life & Lett.* (1902) II. 230 Ye shal..bring a very vnion..bitwene all them there & conduce them to suche a knott as there shalbe perfite vnion amonges them without striffe. **1647** CLARENDON *Hist. Reb.* I. § 10 The Union, Peace and Plenty of the Kingdom. **1683** TEMPLE *Mem.* Wks. 1720 I. 480, I, that never had any thing so much at heart as the Union of my Country. **1828** SCOTT *F. M. Perth* xiii, Have I not thanks to pay to God, who has restored union to my family? **1841** BORROW *Zincali* I. iii. II. 271 However some of the Gitános may complain that there is no longer union to be found amongst them, there is [etc.]. **1849** MACAULAY *Hist. Eng.* i. I. 160 They were so far from being disposed to purchase union by concession that they objected to concession chiefly because it tended to produce union.

**b.** *Painting.* Agreement or harmony in respect of colour, design, etc.

**1704** J. HARRIS *Lex. Techn.* I, *Union* (a Term among Painters) is the mutual Agreeableness and Sympathy of the Colours in a Piece of Painting. **1728** CHAMBERS *Cycl.*, *Harmony*,..in the Ordonnance,..signifies the Union, or Connection between the Figures, with Respect to the Subject of the Piece. **1770** SIR J. REYNOLDS *Disc.* iii. (1778) 83 A figure..though deviating from beauty, may still have a certain union of the various parts.

**c.** *Horsem.* (See quots.)

**1753** *Chambers's Cycl.* Suppl. s.v. *Unite*, A horse is said to *unite*, or walk in union, when, in galloping, the hind quarters follow and keep time with the fore. **1884** E. L. ANDERSON *Mod. Horsem.* 110 That state of collection that we have styled the union. That is, the forces of the two extremities must be united as closely as is consistent with the maintenance of the pace.

**3. a.** *Scots Law.* The uniting into one tenantry of lands or tenements not lying contiguous. *Charter* or *clause of union* (see quot. 1765–8).

**1503** *Sc. Acts, Jas. V* (1814) II. 246 Anent landis..quhilk ..ar anext or vnit in ane halding or barony þat nochtwithstanding þe said anexation or vnion [etc.]. **1542** *Acc. Ld. High Treas. Scotl.* VIII. 117 The forfaltouris and unionis maid in the last parliament. **1578** *Reg. Privy Council Scot.* II. 693 Erectionis of baroniis, unionis or burghis in barony. **1693** STAIR *Instit.* II. ii. § 44. 221 The whole Lands lying contiguous are naturally Unite, and needs no Union. **1751** MCDOWALL *Inst. Laws Scot.* II. iii. I. 567 The union or erection into a barony of lands, lying in different shires. **1765–8** ERSKINE *Inst. Law Scotl.* II. iii. § 45 By a charter of union, i.e. by a charter in which the sovereign dispenses with the necessity of taking a separate seisin upon every discontiguous tenement. **1838** W. BELL *Dict. Law Scot.* 1020 The object of a charter, or clause of union.

**b.** *Eccl.* The uniting or combination of two or more churches or benefices into one. (Cf. UNITION a.)

**1529** *Act 21 Hen. VIII*, c. 13 § 11 If any person..procure ..any Licence or Licences, Union, Toleration or Dispensation, to receive and take any mo Benefices with Cure than is above limited. **1537** tr. *Latimer's Serm. bef. Convoc.* D j b, Some brought forth canonizations, some expectations, some pluralities and unions. **1545** *Act 37 Hen. VIII*, c. 21 A Unyon or Consolidacion of two Churches in one, or of a Churche and Chappell in one. **1607** COWEL *Interpr.*, *Vnion*, ..is a combining or consolidation of two Churches in one, which is done by the consent of the Bishop, the Patron, and the Incumbent. **1665** *Act 17 Chas. II*, c. 3 ¶ 3 The said Union shall take effect for every such Church or Chappell. **1713** E. GIBSON *Eccl. Law* 920 By the union, the two churches are become so much one, that a second benefice may be taken. **1796** PEGGE *Anonym.* (1809) 444 Consolidation, or the union of divers places in the person of one man, is a great obstacle to justice and equity. **1860** *Act 23–24 Vict.* c. 142 § 2 An Union of Two or more contiguous Benefices with one another.

**4.** The action of uniting, or the state or fact of being united, into one political body; esp. formation or incorporation into a single state, kingdom, or political entity, usually with one central legislature.

**a.** In general use.

**1547** J. HARRISON (*title*), An Exhortacion to the Scottes to conforme themselfes to the..godly Union betweene the two Realmes of Englande & Scotland. **1603** BACON *Briefe Discourse* B ij, And..leauing violent Vnions [of countries]: wee will consider onelye naturall Vnions. **1672** PETTY *Pol. Anat.* (1691) 35 Why was there ever a Union between England and Wales? **1729** T. INNES *Crit. Ess.* (1879) 67 That the Picts continued in possession..till their union in one kingdom with the Scots. **1754** FRANKLIN *Plan of Union* Wks. 1887 II. 351 The said commissioners..came to an unanimous resolution: That a union of the colonies is absolutely necessary for their preservation. **1848** W. H. KELLY tr. *L. Blanc's Hist. Ten Y.* I. 268 To the Belgians France could offer, as the price of a fraternal union, the substitution [etc.]. **1855** MOTLEY *Dutch Rep.* v. i. (1906) III. 95 Early in January, 1577, the celebrated 'Union of Brussels' was formed. **1888** *Encycl. Brit.* XXIII. 741/2 This success of the struggle for union gave the United States a date for the political..existence of the nation.

**b.** *Eng. Hist.* The uniting of the English and Scottish crowns in 1603, or parliaments in 1707; or of the parliaments of Great Britain and Ireland, dating from 1 Jan. 1801. (With *the* and capital.)

(*a*) **1603** BACON (*title*), A Briefe Discovrse, tovching the Happie Vnion of..England, and Scotland. **1604** *Proclam. Jas. I*, 20 Oct., The blessed Union, or rather reuniting of.. England and Scotland, vnder one Imperial crowne. *a* **1700** EVELYN *Diary* 25 Feb. 1671, Came to visit me one of the Lords Commissioners of Scotland for the Union. **1707** HEARNE *Collect.* (O. H. S.) II. 10 This day being the beginning of the Union of England with Scotland. **1712** Z. HAIG in J. Russell *Haigs* (1881) xii. 344 Prosperity to Scotland, and No Union! **1827** HALLAM *Const. Hist.* xvii. II. 696 The union closes the story of the Scots constitution. **1864** BURTON *Scot Abr.* I. 121 Scotland did not fully recover from the ruin of that conflict until the Union made her secure.

(*b*) **1798** *The Union* (ed. 4) 15 As..the Protestants become the majority of our people upon the establishment of the Union. **1829** SCOTT *Wav.* Gen. Pref., Miss Edgeworth..may be truly said to have done more towards completing the Union, than [etc.]. **1880** *Encycl. Brit.* XIII. 271 Carried in great measure by the same corrupt means as the constitution of '82 had been worked by, the Union earned no gratitude.

**5.** The joining of one person to another in matrimony; an instance or occasion of this, a marriage.

**1595** SHAKS. *John* II. ii. 446 This vnion shall do more than batterie can To our fast-closed gates. **1678** E. COOKE (*title*), Love's Triumph,—or, The Royal Union: A Tragedy. **1751** JOHNSON *Rambler* No. 167 ¶ 2 The happy event of a union in which caprice and selfishness had so little part. **1778** MISS BURNEY *Evelina* lxxix, He was himself of opinion, the sooner the union took place, the better. **1826** MISS MITFORD in L'Estrange *Life* (1870) II. xi. 239 The immediate union of the Princess Constance..to Don Pedro. **1841** THACKERAY *Gt. Hoggarty Diam.* viii, Her grandfather had been at the first very much averse to our union. **1879** FARRAR *St. Paul* II. 69 He pronounced against any voluntary dissolution of unions already existing between Pagans and Christians.

**II.** †**6.** The quality of being one in number; oneness; the fact or condition of consisting of, involving, or being restricted to, one person or thing only. *Obs.*

In quots. 1548 and *a* 1564 with reference to the partaking of the Communion by the priest only.

*a* **1513** FABYAN *Chron.* VII. ccxliv. 286 An other erronyous opynyon concernynge the vnyon of the Trynytie. **1548** GESTE *Pr. Masse* K viii, Thee prieste masse, whyche is rather an vnion then a communion. *a* **1564** BECON *Display. Popish Mass* Wks. II. 50 Ye call it a Communion, which is a partaking of many together; but ye might right well call it an vnion. For no man eateth and drinketh of the bread and wyne but you alone. **1564** HARDING *Answ. Jewel* 81 For euery multitude..contineweth one. And that whereof it is one, and is kepte in vnion or onenesse, it is necessary that it be one, elles [etc.]. **1652** BENLOWES *Theoph.* VIII. xxvii, Thus Holy, Holy, Holy's nam'd, to show A Ternion we in Union know.

† **b.** = MONAD *a.* 1 b. *Obs.*[−1]

**1565** B. GOOGE tr. *Palingenius' Zodiac* VII. U iij, As from the Union [L. *monas*] fyrst eche other number springs.

† **c.** A unique example. *Obs.*[−1]

1657 J. WATTS *Vind. Ch. Eng.* 48 But an Union, one such text, I mean, in all the Bible.

**7.** That which is united or combined into one; a body formed by uniting one thing to another or others, or several things together; a combination or compound.

1660 JER. TAYLOR *Worthy Commun.* Introd. 10 My purpose is..to gather together into an union al these several portions of truth. **1696** STANHOPE *Chr. Pattern* (1711) 2 What is a man the better for entring into the sublime mysteries of the Trinity, and being able to dispute nicely upon that adorable Union? **1807** J. E. SMITH *Phys. Bot.* 212 Carbonic acid gas, (which was formerly called fixed air, and is an union of oxygen and carbon).

**b.** A number, group, or body of persons or states joined or associated together for some common purpose or action; an association, league, or society; in later use esp. = TRADE-UNION.

(*a*) **1660** JER. TAYLOR *Ductor* III. iv. rule x. § 11 He is not to be reckoned as a Brother, or a relative in our religious friendship and union. **1736** BUTLER *Anal.* I. iii. 83 To separate from their adversaries, and to form an union among themselves. **1762** FALCONER *Shipwr.* II. 409 [The] sagacious statesman..darts around his penetrating eyes, Where Dangers grow and hostile unions rise. **1832** GEN. P. THOMPSON *Exerc.* (1842) II. 236 Once more to the Political Unions,.. don't endure it [*sc.* slavery]; but hold together like burrs. **1903** *Science* (N.Y.) 5 June 892/2 The International Union of the American Republics, popularly known as the Pan-American Union.

(*b*) **1833** *2nd Rep. Factory Com.* D 2. 39 Our spinners..said they had no fault to find..,but the union obliged them to turn out. **1848** MRS. GASKELL *M. Barton* viii, Block-printers is going to strike; they're getten a bang-up Union, as won't let 'em be put upon. **1878** JEVONS *Prim. Pol. Econ.* 65 It is certain that the increase of wages is not confined to those trades which have unions.

**c.** *spec.* A number of states or provinces united together or incorporated into one legislative confederacy; a confederation or federation; esp. the United States of America.

Sometimes in American use restricted to the Northern States which adhered to the Union in contradistinction to the eleven Southern States whose attempted secession from it led to the Civil War of 1861–5.

**1775** JEFFERSON *Let.* Writ. 1892 I. 491 So as to bring the Canadians into our Union. **1792** BELKNAP *Hist. New Hampsh.* III. 257 An important branch of the American union. **1817** J. BRADBURY *Trav. Amer.* 277 The separation of the States west of the Alleghanies from the Union. **1865** LOWELL *Wks.* (1890) V. 258 The South will come back to the Union. **1909** in R. H. Brand *Union of S. Africa* 142 The words 'the Union' shall be taken to mean the Union of South Africa as constituted under this Act.

**d.** A number of parishes united or incorporated together under one Board of Guardians for the administration of the poor laws; an area or sub-district so formed and administered.

**1834** *Act* 4–5 *Will. IV*, c. 76 § 26 Such Parishes shall thereupon be deemed a Union for such Purpose. **1837** MCCULLOCH *Acc. Brit. Empire* II. 639 The operation of Gilbert's Act in the unions formed under it. **1862** GLADSTONE *Sp.* in *Times* 29 Dec. 9/5 The bulk of the cotton manufacture was carried on in a region comprised within 27 Unions.

**e.** A textile fabric composed of two or more different materials woven together, esp. one containing cotton and linen, or cotton and some other material as wool, silk, or jute. Freq. *pl.*, kinds or varieties of goods or fabrics so woven, union-cloths.

**1844** G. DODD *Textile Manuf.* v. 167 A mixture of flax and cotton called 'union'. **1851** MAYHEW *Lond. Labour* I. 378/1 Then we had an Irish linen, an imitation, you know, a kind of 'Union', which we call double twist. **1893** *Photogr. Ann.* 284 Two or three yards of 'union', or white window blind material.

*pl.* **1851** MAYHEW *Lond. Labour* I. 376/2 Linen of good quality used to be extensively hawked, but from 1820 to 1825, or later..the hawkers got to deal in an inferior quality, 'unions' (a mixture of linen and cotton) glazed and stiffened. **1879** *Cassell's Techn. Educ.* IV. 387/2 A real Scotch carpet is all wool, but fabrics similar in appearance are made with cotton warps and worsted wefts, in which case they are called 'unions'. **1890** *Textile News* 20 Oct. (List Manufacturers), Manufacturer of black and coloured unions.

**8.** *Brewing.* One of a series of casks or vats used in the Union or Burton system of cleansing beer.

**1876** *Encycl. Brit.* IV. 275/2 When beer is cleansed..it is necessary to keep the casks or Unions full to the bung. **1897** W. J. SYKES *Brewing* 448 When a set of unions are cleansed, the swan-necks are first removed.

**III. 9.** That which unites or connects one thing to another; *techn.*, a device for connecting the ends of pipes or tubes, or for attaching a pipe to some other part; a coupling, pipe-coupling.

**1850** [see *union joint* in sense 12]. **1863** *Appleby's Handbk. Mach. & Iron Work* 59 Wrought-iron Wrenches for Hose Unions. **1864** *Riddel & Co.'s Catal.*, Steam and Valve Cocks, Brass Unions. **1889** *Daily News* 11 Feb. 4/7 Makers of cocks, taps, unions, and bar fittings are fairly busy.

**IV. 10.** In elliptical senses. **a.** = UNION-FLAG or UNION-JACK, either as (*a*) a separate flag (also † *Great union*), or (*b*) as inserted in the upper inner canton of the ensign; freq. in phr. *union down* or *downwards*, indicating an inverted position, with the union as if in the lower inner canton, when the flag is hoisted or flown on a vessel as a signal of distress or mourning.

(*a*) **1769** FALCONER *Dict. Marine* (1780) s.v. *Jack*, In the British Navy the jack is..a small union flag..; but in merchant-ships this union is bordered with a red field. **1812** *Ann. Reg., Gen. Hist.* 110 The proud old British Union floated triumphantly over it. **1849** C. STURT *Exped. Centr. Australia* I. 20 Some young ladies of the colony..had worked a silken union to present to Mr. Eyre. **1865** *N. & Q.* 18 Feb. 136/1 His majesty is depicted stepping from a barge with the Union hoisted at the stern.

(*b*) **1804** *Naval Chron.* XII. 144 The colours..were hoisted Union downwards. **1830** CAMPBELL *Dict. Mil. Sci.* s.v. *Colours*, The Red Cross of St. George in a White Field, with the Union in the Upper Canton. **1883** *Harper's Mag.* Jan. 321/1 The American flag..was by mistake hoisted 'union down'.

**b.** Short for *Union House, workhouse* (sense 12).

**1843** NEALE *Ball. & Songs for People* 16 We never built the unions Wherein they starve the poor. **1874** T. HARDY *Far fr. Mad. Crowd* xxx, I wonder sometimes if I am doomed to die in the Union.

**c.** (With capital.) The name at various Universities (orig. at Oxford and Cambridge) of a general club and debating society usually open to all members, or all undergraduates, of the University; also, the buildings or offices of such.

Originally short for *Union Society* or *Union Club*. Also used attrib., as *Union audience, rhetoric, speech.*

**1835** *Rep. Committee Oxford Union Soc.* 2 The Treasurer of the Union. **1853** THACKERAY *Eng. Hum., Congreve* (1858) 58 Before the passing of the Reform Bill, there existed at Cambridge a certain debating club, called the 'Union'. **1883** *Oxford Univ. Mag.* 24 Jan. 7/1 No more eloquent speech has been heard in the Union during the last three years. **1891** *Cal. St. Andrews Univ.* 315 The scheme for instituting a Students' Union in the University of St. Andrews. *Ibid.* 316 The general management of the Union.

**V.** Attrib. and comb., passing into adj.

**11. a.** In senses 4 b and 7 c, with the sense 'of or belonging to, promoting or advocating, adhering to or supporting (a particular) legislative union', as (*a*) *Union arms, colours, -maker, parliament*; esp. (*b*) in American use (see 7 c note), as *Union banner, league, man, planter*, etc.

(*a*) **1707** *Lond. Gaz.* No. 4374/1 On Two opposite Corners were the Union Arms. *Ibid.*, The Norton Galley hoisted the Union Colours. **1771** SMOLLETT *Humph. Cl.* To Phillips 8 Aug., During a sitting of the union parliament [at Edinburgh, 1707]. **1811** *Gen. Reg. & Orders of Army* 13 The first Standard, Guidon, or Colour of Regiments, which is the Union Colour. **1846** A. AMOS *Gt. Oyer of Poison.* 4 The union-maker, King James.

(*b*) **1863** BRIGHT *Sp. Amer.* 26 Mar. 127 Not Union planters only, but Secession planters began to bring in the produce. **1863** HAWTHORNE *Our Old Home* (1883) I. 23 The latest is now a gallant general under the Union banner. **1872** DE VERE *Americanisms* 280 The Union-men..or Federals..fought for the Union against rebellion. *Ibid.* 289 Loyal Leagues, as well as Union Leagues, were formed all over the country.

**b.** In general and miscellaneous use, as *union-band, canopy, vowel*, etc.

**1723** E. FENTON *Mariamne* III. vi, Such as good spirits are suppos'd to sing O'er saints, while death dissolves the union-band. **1785** [R. GRAVES] *Eugenius* II. xxxi. 188 A great many variegated roses..called union roses (as they unite the party distinctions of York and Lancaster). **1824** T. FENBY *Mulberry Tree* iii, The tree, Which love's union-canopy made. **1879** WHITNEY *Sanskrit Gram.* 78 All the simple vowels come to assume in certain cases the aspect of union-vowels, or insertions between root or stem and ending of inflection or of derivation.

**c.** In sense 7 b, as *Union-jobber, -smashing* vbl. sb.

**1841** *Penny Cycl.* XXI. 411/1 The many dishonest abstractions of their [Pension Societies'] funds, of which the mere Union jobbers are so often guilty. **1897** *Westm. Gaz.* 30 Aug. 1/3 A general policy of union-smashing.

**d.** In sense 7 e, as *union cloth, cord* (*braid*), *damask, diaper, goods*, etc.; also (of garments), 'made of union cloth or fabric'.

**1862** *Catal. Internat. Exhib., Brit.* II. No. 3995, Woollen and union cloths. **1867** *Ure's Dict. Arts* (ed. 6) III. 971 *Union goods*, cloths of a mixed character, as of flax and jute, or cotton and jute. **1868** *Chambers' Encycl.* X. 268/1 Many of the names used in the all-wool class are retained in this [*sc.* fabrics composed of wool and cotton], with the addition of the word 'union', as union merino, union shalloon, union damask, &c. **1882** CAULFEILD & SAWARD *Dict. Needlew.* 507 *Union cord*, a round white cord, made for stay-laces,..composed of both linen and cotton thread. *Ibid.*, Union Cord Braid, Union Diaper. **1896** *Godey's Mag.* Feb. 218/2 Union undergarments of silk or wool.

**e.** In senses 7 d, 10 b, as *union boy, man.*

**1846** (*title*), The Union and Parish Officer's Pocket Almanac and Guide. **1859** J. H. STEGGALL *Hist. Suffolk Man* i. 29, I was worse than any union boy with his hair polled. **1871** 'M. LEGRAND' *Cambr. Freshm.* 303 He's out o' the Union. ..The Union men break the stones on the roads.

**12.** Special combs.: **union bow** *Archery*, a bow made of two or more pieces united together; a backed or back bow (*Cent. Dict.* 1891); **union-grass**, one or other of the grasses belonging to the genus *Uniola* (ibid.); **Union House**, the poor-house or workhouse of a Poor Law union (cf. senses 7 d and 10 b, and *Union workhouse*); **union-joint** (see quots. and sense 9); **union nut**, (*a*) a nut used with a screw to unite one part to another; (*b*) the Australian timber-tree *Bosistoa sapindiformis*, or its wood; **union pear** (see quot.); **union-pump** (see quot.); **union-room** *Brewing*, the room containing the unions or cleansing vats; **union-rustic**, a British night-moth, *Apamea connexa* (*Encycl. Dict.* 1888); **union screw** (see quot. and *union joint*); † **union suit**, ? a set of mirrors; **union system** *Brewing* (see quots. and sense 8); **Union workhouse**, = *Union House*. See also UNION FLAG, JACK.

**1847** ALB. SMITH *Chr. Tadpole* xlvi, 'Anything new at the *Union House to-day, Mr. Mole?' **1893** *Daily News* 10 April 5/4 The Prince's inscription in the Dunmow Union House visitors' book. **1850** WEALE *Dict. Terms* 493 **Union screws* or *joints*,..the brass unions for connecting the elastic bore-pipe of the tender to the feed-pipe of the [locomotive] engine. **1867** J. HOGG *Microsc.* I. ii. 107 A finer [adjustment] is secured by a well made union-joint. **1838** *Civil Eng. & Arch. Jrnl.* I. 133/1 It..is attached to a ferrule by a *union nut and screw, and can be as easily removed. **1889** MAIDEN *Useful Pl.* 387 *Bosistoa sapindiformis*, *Union Nut. **1731** MILLER *Gard. Dict.* 6 U, The *Union Pear; otherwise call'd Dr. Uvedale's St. Germain. This is a very large long Pear, of a deep green Colour. **1860** J. HOGG *Fruit Man.* 217. **1875** KNIGHT *Dict. Mech.* 2681/2 **Union-pump*,..one in which the engine and pump are united in the same frame. **1886** 'BICKERDYKE' *Cur. Ale & Beer* 339 The *union-room.. [at Allsopp's] contains 1,424 unions, which can cleanse 230,688 gallons at one time. **1850** WEALE *Dict. Terms* 494 The feed-pipe is likewise attached to the lower end of the pump by a large *union screw. **1714** *Lond. Gaz.* No. 5214/3 All sorts of Coach Glasses, Chimney Glasses, Sconces, Dressing Glasses, *Union Suits, Dressing Boxes, swinging Glasses [etc.]. **1876** *Encycl. Brit.* IV. 275/2 There are three modes of cleansing—..2*d*, by running the beer into casks, and then allowing the yeast to work out through the bung holes; and 3*d*, on what is called the *Union, or Burton system, which is the second plan with some improvements. **1886** 'BICKERDYKE' *Cur. Ale & Beer* 333 When the fermentation has almost ceased, the beer is put into smaller vessels ..and the froth either works over the side or is skimmed off or, as in the 'union' system at Burton, works up through pipes. **1851** KINGSLEY *Yeast* xii, As he went on, talking wildly to himself, he passed the *Union Workhouse. **1863** FAWCETT *Pol. Econ.* IV. iv. 581 The inmates of the union-workhouse are subject to certain restraints.

Hence **U·nional** *a.*, of or pertaining to union or a union (esp. of countries); **U·nioned** *a.*, joined in union; **U·nioner** *U.S.*, an adherent of the Union during the American Civil War.

**1889** *Scott. Leader* 18 Apr. 6 If the Unionist has destroyed both the national and *unional sentiment in the Irish. **1905** *Q. Rev.* July 273 The Unional flag had been hauled down. **1787** J. BARLOW *Vision of Columbus* VI. 191 Great Washington arose in view, And *union'd flags his stately steps pursue. **1880** TOURGEE *Fool's Err.* vii. 31 The old *Unioner's report in regard to the doughty colonel.

**U·nion**, *sb.*[2] Now *arch.* Also 4 **vniune.** [ad. L. *ūniōn-em, ūnio* UNIO: cf. ONION *sb.* 7.

So called (acc. to Pliny *Nat. Hist.* IX. xxxv. § 56) because no two are exactly alike.]

A pearl of large size, good quality, and great value, esp. one which is supposed to occur singly.

Freq. in 17th c., esp. in allusion to or echoes of the story related of Cleopatra: see Pliny *loc. cit.* § 59. The following early instance is prob. of AF. origin: *c* **1305** *Land Cokayne* 89 Þer is saphir and vniune, Carbuncle and astiune.

**1592** *Soliman & Pers.* II. i, Then they play, and when she hath lost her gold, Erastus pointed to her chaine, and then she said: I, were it Cleopatraes vnion. **1599** HAKLUYT *Voy.* II. 5 Precious unions and costly spyces. **1635** HEYWOOD *Hierarchy* VII. 419 A Pendant Vnion to adorne her Eare, Rarer no Queene was euer seene to weare. **1694** MOTTEUX *Rabelais* IV. iv. 19 Between whose Septenary Links.. Rubies, Emeralds,..and Unions were alternatively set in. *a* **1700** EVELYN *Diary* 21 Feb. 1645, The other Union, that Cleopatra was about to dissolve and drink up.

*fig. a* **1672** P. STERRY *Posth. Wks.* (*c* 1680) II. 227 Pearls are called Unions, because they are ever found alone: a Saint's Pearl is his Union for a contrary Reason, because he is never found alone in his Spiritual Being or Beauty.

**b.** *attrib.* with *pearl*. Also *transf.*

**1656** BLOUNT *Glossogr.* s.v., Union Pearls..are the best sort of Pearl. [Hence in Phillips, Bailey, etc.] **1885** R. F. BURTON *Arab. Nts.* (1887) III. 67 This damsel, the mistress of moons, the union pearl.

† **U·nion**, *v. Obs. rare.* Also 5 **unyon.** [f. UNION *sb.*[1]] *trans.* To unite.

*a* **1470** HARDING *Chron.* ccxli. *heading*, The kynges tytle to all his londes, briefely reported, with a monicion to vnion Scotlande and Englande. **1475** *Bk. Noblesse* (Roxb.) 23 The countee of Mayne by Maryage was unyoned to the erledom of Angew.

**Union flag.** [UNION *sb.*[1] 4 b, 7 c.] **a.** The national flag or ensign, formerly of Great Britain, in later use (from 1801) of the United Kingdom of Great Britain and Ireland, formed by combining the crosses of St. George, St. Andrew, and St. Patrick, retaining the blue ground of the banner of St. Andrew. See UNION JACK, and UNION *sb.*[1] 10 a.

This flag was introduced to symbolize the union of the crowns of England and Scotland and was formed by surmounting the cross saltire of St. Andrew by the cross of St. George; the cross saltire of St. Patrick was added on the union of the parliaments of Great Britain and Ireland, when the whole flag was blazoned by Royal Proclamation (*Lond. Gaz.* 1 Jan. 1801), as follows: Azure, the Crosses saltires of St. Andrew and St. Patrick Quarterly per Saltire, counterchanged Argent and Gules; the latter fimbriated of the Second, surmounted by the Cross of St. George of the Third, fimbriated as the Saltire.

**1634** in Rymer *Fœdera* (1732) XIX. 549/1 None shall from henceforth presume to carry the Union Flag in the main Top or other part of their Ships, that is Saint George his Cross and Saint Andrews Cross joined together,..but that the same Union Flag be still reserved as an Ornament proper for our own Ships, and Ships in our immediate Service and Pay, and none other. **1681** in *English Hist. Rev.* Jan. (1911) 50 [An article forbidding] privateers to wear our Union flagg and jack. **1696** *Lond. Gaz.* No. 3190/3 Leaving the Command of the Fleet with my Lord Berkeley, who..has put up the Union Flag on Board the Britannia. **1724** C. JOHNSON *Hist. Pirates* 153 One of them struck the Union Flag on the Top of the Castle. **1769** [see UNION[1] 10 a]. **1829** MARRYAT *F. Mildmay* viii, A union flag is displayed at the mizen peak. **1844** *Regul. & Ord. Army* 48 The Union Flag or Jack being the distinctive flag or mark of an Admiral of the Fleet, when displayed at the main-top-gallant-mast-head. **1865** *N. & Q.* 11 March 208/2 The incorporation of the red saltier of St. Patrick into the Union Flag.

**b.** The flag of the federated colonies or provinces of the American Union.

**1776** *Pennsylv. Even. Post* 28 May 266/2 The Union Flag of the American States waved upon the Capitol.

**Unionic** (yūni̦ǫ·nik), *a.* [f. UNION *sb.*[1] + -IC.] Of or pertaining to, characteristic of, a Union or University Union Society; frequenting or debating at the Union.

**1855** *Househ. Words* 30 June 521, I breakfasted with jovial undergraduates... I heard old talk..of Unionic speakers eloquent. **1865** *Pall Mall G.* 13 April 10/1 The characteristics of Unionic eloquence. **1884** J. PAYN *Lit. Recoll.* 54 In Mr. Lewis's classification of his fellow-students, it was that of 'the Unionic Cantab.'

**Unionid** (yū·niǫnid). *Zool.* [a. mod. L. *Unionid-æ* (see def.), f. L. *unio* UNIO: see -ID[3].] A member of the *Unionidæ*, a large family of bivalve molluscs typified by the genus *Unio* of freshwater mussels; a unio.

**1861** P. P. CARPENTER in *Rep. Smithsonian Instit. 1860*, 263 The extreme forms of the Unionids.

**Unio·niform,** *a. Zool.* [f. mod.L. *Unio* UNIO: see -(I)FORM.] Belonging to or resembling the *Unionidæ*; unionoid.

**1868** R. TATE *App. to Woodward's Mollusca* 71 *Anthracosia* differs from *Unio*, to which genus the majority of the Unioniform shells have been referred.

**Unionism** (yū·nyəniz'm). [f. UNION *sb.*[1] + -ISM.] The principle or policy of union; combination in union as a system of social organization; advocacy of this. Cf. TRADE(S)-UNIONISM.

**1845** MIALL in *Nonconf.* V. 173 The gravest objections against congregational unionism. **1869** J. STIRLING *Trade Unionism* 21 To the unionist himself, the results of Unionism are no less hurtful. **1884** *Brit. Alm. & Comp.* 67 The growth of unionism among farm labourers.

**b.** *U.S.* Advocacy of, attachment or adherence to, a legislative union between states.

**1864** LOWELL *McClellan or Lincoln?* Pr. Wks. 1890 V. 157 The somewhat light Unionism of Mr. Pendleton. **1865** — *Reconstruct.* Ibid. 222 We do not mean to say that there is any very large amount of even latent Unionism at the South. **1883** *American* VI. 92 The obstinate Unionism of the mountaineer farmers.

**c.** Loyalty to or advocacy of the principles, views, or programme of the Unionist party of Great Britain and Ireland; the political tenets characteristic of a Unionist.

**1886** *Sat. Rev.* 5 June 763/2 Unionism has to deal with an enemy perfectly unscrupulous. **1889** MRS. BUXTON in O'Brien *Life Parnell* (1898) I. 220 We talked a little about Home Rule and the future of Ireland—my Unionism getting very shaky.

**Unionist** (yū·nyənist), *sb.* and *a.* [f. as prec. + -IST. Cf. F. *unioniste.*]

**A.** *sb.* **1.** An adherent of or believer in unionism as a political principle or system of organization; esp. one who advocates or supports the formation or maintenance of some particular legislative union.

Usually with initial capital in particularized sense.

**1799** *Monthly Rev.* XXX. 337 [Duigenan] is particularly severe in his criticisms on Lord Minto, a Brother Unionist. **1851** GALLENGA *Italy* 41 Nothing..has been more fatal to the cause of Italian federation than a departure from the views of the Unionists. **1887** MAHAFFY & GILMAN *Alexander's Empire* xxx. 286 There was a large nationalist party ..violently opposed to the unionists,..constantly asserting the right of every Greek state to legislate for itself. **1890** HATTON *By Order of Czar* II. i, [He] was above all things an Imperial Unionist, and would defend to the death the merest scrap of soil over which the flag had ever floated.

**b.** *U.S.* A supporter or advocate of the Federal Union of the United States of America; esp. one who during the Civil War of 1861–5 was opposed to Secession.

**1830** D. WEBSTER *1st Sp. on Foot's Res.* Wks. 1851 III. 259, I am a unionist, and, in this sense, a national republican. **1862** MOTLEY *Corr.* (1889) II. 94 The anti-slavery men became the Unionists, the slaveholders the Destructionists. **1883** *American* VII. 149 A Texas 'Unionist' is going to sue the United States for the value of his slaves.

**c.** *British Politics.* A member of the political party which advocated or supported maintenance of the parliamentary Union between Great Britain and Ireland; an opponent of Home Rule.

This party was formed in 1886 by the coalition of the Conservatives with those Liberals (Liberal Unionists: see LIBERAL *a.* 5) who were opposed to Gladstonian Home Rule. While the chief tenet of this party was the maintenance of the Union, its general policy and principles gradually became identified with those of the Conservative party.

**1886** LD. R. CHURCHILL *Sp. at Manch.* 3 March, Do you not think that such a party might be formed which might combine all that is best of the politics of the Tory, the Whig, or the Liberal?..Might we not call it the party of the Union? Members of that party might be known as Unionists. **1886** in *Pall Mall G.* 6 July 14/1 The opinion ..that..the Liberal Unionists are coming to signal grief... The Unionists have, indeed, pulled the chestnuts out of the fire for Lord Salisbury. **1893** *Times* 25 Apr. 11/1 A representative company of British Unionists to meet the Unionists of Ireland.

**2.** A member of a trade-union; a TRADE-UNIONIST.

**1834** *John Bull* 13 July 219/1 The cases on the Crown side were principally Unionists, charged with administering unlawful oaths. **1854** H. MILLER *Sch. & Schm.* xv. 327 The life of my friend was..pitched on a..higher tone than that of most of his brother unionists. **1879** T. H. S. ESCOTT *England* I. 282 The charges of conspiracy and violence brought against unionists and unionism.

**3.** One who desires or advocates the union of churches or congregations. Cf. REUNIONIST.

**1852** NEWLAND *Lect. Tractar.* 165 We are Tractarians or Unionists or whatever you may please to call us. **1866** G. TALBOT in E. Purcell *Life A. P. de Lisle* (1900) I. xv. 408, I think that the sympathy of the Unionists for the Greek Schism is a proof of want of sincerity. **1869** *Union Review* 311 The Unionist, whether he be a Roman or an Anglican.

**B.** *attrib.* passing into *adj.* **1.** Of or pertaining to, advocating or supporting, a legislative union, esp. that between Great Britain and Ireland.

**1816** SCOTT *Bl. Dwarf* xii, The Unionist courtiers, that have bought and sold old Scotland. **1848** DAUNT *Recoll. O'Connell* I. ii. 16, I spoke in reply to a Unionist effusion of Emerson Tennent's. **1863** DICEY *Federal St.* II. 187 The *Atlantic Monthly*..is..staunchly Unionist, and more or less anti-slavery. **1888** A. J. BALFOUR in *Times* 2 Oct. 10/1 The union of the Unionist party.

**b.** Of or belonging to the Unionists or Unionist Party. (Cf. A. 1 c.)

**1886** *Pall Mall G.* 3 July 4/1 The utter failure of the Unionist attack..at Stockton. **1890** RIDER HAGGARD *Beatrice* xviii, He knew the head Unionist whip very well. **1897** H. TENNYSON *Tennyson* II. 412 The large Unionist meetings throughout Great Britain.

**2.** Of or belonging to trade-unionism or trade-unionists.

**1879** H. SPENCER *Data of Ethics* xii. § 78. 211 The unionist principle that the better workers must not discredit the worse by exceeding them in efficiency. **1884** *Pall Mall G.* 11 Sept. 3/1 The success of the unionist movement.

**Unioni·stic,** *a.* [f. UNIONIST *sb.* + -IC.] Of or relating to, characteristic of, unionists; advocating, promoting, or favourable to union or unionism.

**1860** WORCESTER (citing Schaff). **1867** LD. ACTON *Lett.* (1906) 346 The Bishop of Mentz..has written a pamphlet decidedly unionistic. **1882–3** *Schaff's Encycl. Relig. Knowl.* II. 1683 When the unionistic measures of Bucer were being discussed. **1884** *American* VIII. 6 For this reason the simply unionistic feeling burned in the northwest.

**U·nionite.** *Min.* [Named by Silliman from its locality, *Unionville*, Pennsylvania.] = ZOISITE.

**1849** B. SILLIMAN in *Amer. Jrnl. Sci. & Arts* Ser. II. VIII. 384 Unionite..in general appearance..somewhat resembles scapolite or spodumene. **1855** *Orr's Circ. Sci., Geol.*, etc. 521 Antitomus Felspar, Soda Spodumene, Unionite.

**Unionize** (yū·nyənəiz), *v.* [f. UNION *sb.*[1] + -IZE.]

**a.** *trans.* To form into a union. *rare*[—1].

**1841** R. OASTLER *Fleet Papers* I. No. 23. 182 The breaking up of the old local, domestic, family system of self-government, by unionizing and centralizing society.

**b.** *esp.* To bring under trade-union rules or principles; to cause (persons) to become members of a trade-union.

Freq. since *c* 1900. Hence (in journalistic use) *Unionization*, *Unionized* ppl. a., *Unionizing* vbl. sb.

**1890** *Columbus* (Ohio) *Dispatch* 18 Nov., It has been decided by the Trades Council to take radical measures.. to unionize all work in the building trades. **1903** *Liberty Review* July 16 The servants have been unionised under the rules of the..Federation.

**Union Jack.** [f. UNION *sb.*[1] + JACK *sb.*[3]] Originally and properly, a small British union flag flown as the jack of a ship; in later and more general use extended to any size or adaptation of the union flag (even when not used as a jack), and regarded as the national ensign. See UNION FLAG a and UNION *sb.*[1] 10 a.

Written either with capitals or small initials.

**1674** *Lond. Gaz.* No. 924/1 To Charge..His Subjects.., That from henceforth they do not presume to wear His Majesties Jack (commonly called, The Union Jack) in any of their Ships or Vessels, without particular Warrant. **1694**, **1702** [see JACK *sb.*[3]]. **1801** *Union Magazine* Jan. 52 The Royal Union standard was hoisted on the Tower;..the Union Jack on the Parade. **1822** *Admiralty Order* in *Lond. Gaz.* No. 17871. 1893/1 We..authorize all His Majesty's subjects to hoist the Union Jack at the top-mast-head.., or at the fore-top-mast-head.., as a signal for a pilot. **1883** MRS. BISHOP *Golden Chersonese* 222 Everything was 'ship-shape',..a union jack over the desk, from which the liturgy was read, and a tiger-skin [etc.].

**b.** A figure or representation of this. Also *attrib.*

**1848** ALBERT SMITH *Chr. Tadpole* xxiv. 220 Quite unexpectedly they all produced union-jack pocket-handkerchiefs, at the same moment. **1856** MISS YONGE *Daisy Chain* I. xix, Harry used to write his name all over his—see—and draw union-jacks on it. **1886** *Pall Mall G.* 3 July 4/1 In Sunderland the Liberals have all taken to wear Union Jacks in their buttonholes.

Hence (with reference to the use of the union jack as a national flag) **Union Ja·ckery, Union Ja·ckist, Ja·ckite.** *nonce-words.*

**1886** *Pall Mall G.* 3 July 4/1 At Nottingham,..the Tory party is locally known as the Union Jackists. **1896** *Spectator* 7 March 342 The national outbursts of 'Union-Jackery' in the courts and music-halls. **1901** *Daily Chron.* 2 Dec. 10/2 Men who no doubt call themselves patriotic Union-Jackites and Big Englanders.

**U·nionoid,** *a.* and *sb. Zool.* [f. mod.L. *Union-* UNIO.] **a.** *adj.* Of or belonging to the *Unionidæ*; unioniform. **b.** *sb.* A unionid (*Cent. Dict.* 1891).

**1879** H. A. NICHOLSON *Palæont.* (ed. 2) I. 492 Unionoid Bivalves, with thick shells.

**Union pipes,** *sb. pl.* [? ad. Ir. *píob uilleann*, f. *píob* pipe + *uilleann*, gen. sing. of *uille* elbow.] A form of bagpipes in which the wind-bag is inflated by bellows worked by the elbow; Irish bagpipes.

**1851–61** MAYHEW *Lond. Labour* III. 163/1 The union pipes are the old Irish pipes improved. **1877** R. BELL *Early Ballads*, etc. 441 We first heard it sung in Malhamdale, Yorkshire, by..an old Dales'-minstrel, who accompanied himself on the union-pipes.

**Unipa·rient,** *a.* [See UNI- and PARIENT *a.*] = next 1.

**1822–7** GOOD *Study Med.* (1829) V. 227 [These signs] belong as frequently to the uniparient as to the multiparient, and hence are unentitled to attention. **1859** *Todd's Cycl. Anat.* V. 560/2 In Man, although generally uniparient, two or more follicles may..become matured about the same time.

**Uniparous** (yūni·pǎrəs), *a.* [f. mod.L. *ūniparus* (whence F. *unipare*, It. *uniparo*, Sp. *uniparo*): see UNI- and -PAROUS.]

**1.** Bearing or producing one at a birth; characterized by this kind of parturition.

**1646** SIR T. BROWNE *Pseud. Ep.* VI. vi. 298 For animals multifidous..there are but two that are uniparous, that is, Men and Elephants. **1662** PETTY *Treat. Taxes & Contrib.* xii. 58 'Tis also the second choice out of the young of multiparous Cattle taken in *specie*,..or else a Composition in Money for the Uniparous. **1744** MONRO *Compar. Anat.* 37 Those of the uniparous Kind have them placed between the posterior Extremities. **1787** *Phil. Trans.* LXXVII. 358 The females of the human species, though most commonly uniparous. **1839–47** *Todd's Cycl. Anat.* III. 315 The oviducts are shorter..in the uniparous Kangaroo,..than in the multiparous Opossums. **1856** GRINDON *Life* iv. (1875) 41 Rousseau ingeniously urges..that woman is a uniparous animal. **1859** OWEN *Lect. Classif. Mammalia* 56 The mastodons, megatheria,..and diprotodons, are uniparous.

**2.** *Bot.* Of a cyme: Having only one axis or branch; developing a single axis at each branching.

**1839** LINDLEY *Introd. Bot.* (ed. 3) 160 [An] axis of uniparous, that is one-peduncled, cymes. **1878** M. T. MASTERS *Henfrey's Bot.* 318 The inflorescence..is probably a uniparous scorpioid cyme. **1887** BENTLEY *Man. Bot.* (ed. 5) 215 The terms *helicoid* and *scorpioid* are thus used by us indifferently to indicate the same form of *unilateral*, *monochasial*, or *uniparous cyme.*

**Unipartite** (yūnipā·ɹtəit), *a. Math.* [See UNI- and PARTITE *a.*] Consisting of or involving a single part.

**1870** CAYLEY *Math. Papers* (1893) VI. 464 The quantic is unipartite, bipartite, tripartite, etc., according as the number of sets [of variables] is one, two, three, etc. **1890** *Nature* 20 Feb. 380/2 In the theory of the single system [of equations] the conceptions and symbolism..are based upon the properties of single integral numbers and their partitions into single integral parts. In this sense the former theory may be regarded as being unipartite.

**Uniped** (yū·niped), *sb.* and *a.* Also -pede (-pīd). [f. UNI- + L. *ped-*, *pēs* foot.]

**A.** *sb.* A person having only one foot (or leg); a one-footed creature.

**1801** SOUTHEY *Thalaba* iv. 218 *note*, There is said to be a nation of one legged men, and one of these unipeds is represented in a print, lying on his back, under the shade of his own great foot. **1846** *Blackw. Mag.* LX. 227 To wake up ten minutes afterwards an unsuffering uniped. **1863** C. M. SMITH *Dead Lock* 248 In all diseases of the toes..the liabilities of the uniped are but as five to ten compared with those of his two-legged brethren.

*fig.* **1897** *Contemp. Rev.* Oct. 536 The greater sort will escape one-sidedness by inventing some outlet for themselves, but the average will present us with an endless variety of quaint queer unipeds.

**B.** *adj.* Having only one foot (or leg); one-footed.

**1835** KIRBY *Hab. & Inst. Anim.* II. 125 [These] Molluscans ..are the only instance of a *unipede* structure in creation. **1866** R. CHAMBERS *Ess.* Ser. II. 206 An auctioneer..who.. sells off pots and pans, and small uniped tables.

**Unipe·rsonal,** *a.* [See UNI- and PERSONAL *a.* Cf. F. *unipersonnel* (in sense 2), Pg. *unipessonal.*]

**1.** Consisting of a single person or individual.

*c* **1810** COLERIDGE in *Lit. Rem.* (1838) III. 220 If there be a functionary of divine institution, synodical or unipersonal, who with the name of the 'Church' has the right [etc.].

**b.** Having, or existing as, one person.

Cf. TRI-PERSONAL *a.* and PERSON 7 a.

**1869** *Contemp. Rev.* XII. 450 The God of the Bible is neither unipersonal nor tripersonal in that sense of person. **1901** R. C. MOBERLY *Atonem. & Person.* viii. 172 [Not] one of them [*sc.* analogies]..go far towards enabling uni-personal man to enter into the consciousness of Tri-personality.

**2.** *Gram.* Of a verb: = IMPERSONAL *a.* 1. *rare.*

**1860** WORCESTER (citing Wells). [Hence in Webster (1864) and later Dicts.]

Hence **Unipe·rsonalist**, a believer in the unipersonality of the Deity (1846 Worcester, citing Faber); **Unipersona·lity**, existence in one person.

**1859** J. MARTINEAU *Ess. & Addr.* (1891) II. 389 If we set up as our essential a doctrine, like that of the Unipersonality of God. **1884** — in *Life* (1902) II. viii. 70.

**Unipe·talous,** *a. Bot. rare*[—1]. [ad. mod.L. *unipetal-us* (whence F. *unipétalé*): see UNI- and PETALOUS *a.*] (See quot.)

1849 J. H. Balfour *Man. Bot.* 178 A corolla rarely consists of one petal, and when this occurs..it depends on the abortion or non-development of others. Such a corolla is *unipetalous*.., a term quite distinct from monopetalous.

**Uni·phonous**, *a. rare*$^{-1}$. [f. Uni- 1, after Mono-, Polyphonous *adjs.*] Producing only one kind of note.

1832 *Westm. Rev.* Nov. (Cassell's), That uniphonous instrument the drum.

**Unipla·nar**, *a.* [See Uni- and Planar *a.*]

1. *Geom.* Having or characterized by coincident planes. *Uniplanar node* (or *point*), a form of node or conical point in which the tangent cone has become a pair of coincident planes; a unode.

1866 Brande & Cox *Dict. Sci.*, etc. II. 675 When this cone breaks up into two planes, the node is termed a biplanar node, and when these planes coincide, a uniplanar node. 1869 [see Uniplane]. 1889 *Cent. Dict.* s.v. *Dyadic*, *Uniplanar diadic*, a planar diadic in which the plane of the antecedents coincides with that of the consequents.

2. *Mech.* Of motion: Lying or taking place in, confined to, one plane; of or pertaining to such motion.

1882 Minchin (*title*), Uniplanar Kinematics of Solids and Fluids. *Ibid.* 1 By uniplanar motion, or one-plane motion, is understood in the following pages motion which takes place in one plane or parallel to one plane.

**U·niplane**, *a.* and *sb.* [Uni-.] **a.** *adj.* Forming or lying in one plane. **b.** *sb.* (See quot. 1869.)

1843 *Civil Eng. & Arch. Jrnl.* VI. 218/2 A pneumatic machine for casting, and a uniplane machine for composing. 1869 Cayley *Math. Papers* (1893) VI. 361 U..is a uniplanar-node, where the quadric cone becomes a coincident plane-pair; say, the plane is the uniplane.

**U·niplicate**, *a. rare*$^{-0}$. [f. Uni- 1, after Multiplicate *a.*] Having but one fold.

1840 Smart; and in later Dicts.

**Unipo·lar**, *a.* (and *sb.*). [See Uni- and Polar *a.* Cf. F. *unipolaire.*]

1. *Electr.* Produced by, proceeding from, one magnetic pole; exhibiting one kind of polarity.

1812 Sir H. Davy *Chem. Philos.* 168 There are substances that are imperfect conductors which are capable of receiving only one kind of electricity..and which M. Ehrman..has named unipolar bodies. 1873 J. C. Maxwell *Electr. & Magn.* II. 7 The property produced by magnetism in transparent bodies of twisting the plane of polarization of the incident light, is, like magnetism itself, a unipolar property. 1881 *Nature* XXIII. 616 To illustrate unipolar conductivity. *Ibid.* XXIV. 570 Whether it be not possible entirely to separate one from the other, and to produce what may be called a unipolar discharge. 1888 *Encycl. Brit.* XXIII. 330/1 The so-called 'unipolar' induction supposed to be due to the rotation of the earth.

**b.** Of apparatus: Having, or operating by means of, one magnetic pole. Also *ellipt.*

1876 *Nature* XIV. 263/2 A unipolar magnetic needle. *Ibid.*, The space through which a subsidiary magnet must be moved in order to restore the unipolar to its original position. 1883 *Daily News* 10 Sept. 2/2 The remarkable machine of Messrs. Siemens and Halske, called the unipolar machine. 1884 *Health Exhib. Catal.* 79/2 A true unipolar continuous current dynamo.

2. *Biol.* Of nerve-cells: Having one pole or fibrous prolongation; connected to the nerve-fibre by a single fibrous process.

1859 *Todd's Cycl. Anat.* V. 436/2 Those [ganglionic corpuscles] from which one tube proceeds are termed unipolar. 1873 A. Flint *Physiol. Man, Nerv. Syst.* i. 46 Unipolar cells exist in some of the lower orders of animals. 1880 Bastian *Brain* ii. 48 Unipolar nerve cells..are alleged to exist in the ganglia on the spinal nerves and elsewhere.

**b.** (See quot.)

1878 F. J. Bell tr. *Gegenbaur's Comp. Anat.* 597 If the rete remains broken up, then it is known as a diffuse, unipolar, or monocentric rete mirabile.

Hence **U:nipola·rity**, the condition or character of being unipolar. (Cf. F. *unipolarité.*)

1888 *Philos. Mag.* Ser. v. XXVI. 129 We do not believe that Ohm ever observed the phenomenon of unipolarity in strong sulphuric acid with [etc.].

**Uni·porous**, *a.* [Uni- 1. Cf. Polyporous *a.*] (See quot.)

1888 Dawson *Geol. Hist. Plants* 160 Wood-cells elsewhere called discigerous tissue, and to which I applied the terms uniporous and multiporous.

† **Unipre·sence.** *Obs.*$^{-1}$ [f. Uni- + Presence, after Omnipresence.] The fact, on the part of a number, of being present in one place. So † **Unipre·sent** *a. Obs.*$^{-1}$

1619 Lushington *Recant. Serm.* (1659) 77 The unipresence, or local union of body; 'in one place'. *Ibid.* 96 They were unanimous and unipresent.

**Unique** (yūnī·k), *a.* and *sb.* Also 7 unick(e, 7–8 unic. [a. F. *unique* († *unic* masc.), ad. L. *ūnic-us* (whence also Sp., Pg., It. *unico*) single, sole, alone of its kind, f. *ūnus* one. In early use also directly ad. L. *ūnicus*, and stressed on the first syllable.]

Regarded by Todd (1818) as 'an affected and useless term of modern times'.

**A.** *adj.* **1.** Of which there is only one; one and no other; single, sole, solitary.

1602 Dolman *La Primaud. Fr. Acad.* (1618) III. 639 Engendring one eternitie, and by an alone vnique action never disturbed, his linage full of understanding. *c* 1645 Howell *Lett.* II. xliv, He hath lost..his unic Son in the very flower of his age. 1677 Gale *Crt. Gentiles* iv. i. ii. 53 Divines, who make..right Reason the unic Criterion or Rule of moral Virtue.

1818 Todd, *Unique*, adj.,..sole;..without another of the same kind known to exist. 1861 Paley *Æschylus, Prometh.* (ed. 2) 39 The student will notice the unique example of στιχομυθία. 1873 Hamerton *Intell. Life* iii. iii. 87 A man ..who made Latin scholarship his unique intellectual purpose. 1882 Farrar *Early Chr.* II. 476 St. John instantly leaves the subject..to which he has made this unique and passing allusion.

2. That is or forms the only one of its kind; having no like or equal; standing alone in comparison with others, freq. by reason of superior excellence; unequalled, unparalleled, unrivalled.

In this sense readopted from French at the end of the 18th c. and regarded as a foreign word down to the middle of the 19th, from which date it has been in very common use, with a tendency to take the wider meaning of 'uncommon, unusual, remarkable'.

The usage in the comparative and superlative, and with advs. as *absolutely*, *most*, *quite*, *thoroughly*, *totally*, etc., has been objected to as tautological.

1618 W. Barclay *Well at King-horne* A vij, This is a soueraigne and vnicke remedie for that disease in Women. 1794 R. J. Sulivan *View Nat.* I. 3 A concentrated, and an unique aggregation of almost all the wonders of the natural world. 1809 R. K. Porter *Trav. Sk. Russia & Sweden* (1813) I. xxv. 285 As it was thoroughly *unique*, I cannot forbear presenting you with so singular a curiosity. 1842 J. P. Collier *Armin's Nest Ninn.* Introd., A relic.. not only *unique* in itself, but unprecedented in its kind. 1866 Liddon *Bamp. Lect.* v. (1867) 368 [Christ's] relationship to the Father..is absolutely unique. 1871 B. Taylor *Faust* (1875) II. ii. i. 84 A thing so totally unique The great collectors would go far to seek. 1885 *Harper's Mag.* April 703/1 When..these summer guests found themselves defrauded of their uniquest recreations.

**b.** Of persons.

1808 Foster *Contrib. Eclectic Rev.* (1844) I. 233 [Sir T. More] is a person so *unique* in the records of statesmen, that [etc.]. 1871 Blackie *Four Phases* 15 Such a unique mortal.. no man can describe. 1885 Mabel Collins *Prettiest Woman* xi, He believed this woman whom he loved to be unique.

**c.** *absol.* with *the*: (see quots.).

1767 *Phil. Trans.* LVIII. 26 All these are examples of the *unique*; that is, of quantities in a state that is..exclusive of all others. 1849 C. Bronte *Shirley* xxiii, She felt that Rose Yorke was a peculiar child—one of the unique.

† **3.** Formed or consisting of one or a single thing. *Obs.*$^{-1}$

*a* 1631 Donne *Lett.* (1651) 163 A Mathematique point, which is the most indivisible and unique thing which art can present.

**B.** *sb.* **1.** A thing of which there is only one example, copy, or specimen; esp., in early use, a coin or medal of this class.

1714 R. Thoresby *Diary* 23 June, My Lord showed me some unics and other valuable curiosities. 1730 A. Gordon *Maffei's Amphith.* 47 It..may be an Unic, for what we know as yet. 1774 *Gentl. Mag.* XLIV. 8 A coin, which I have reason to think is a Unic. 1826 Disraeli *V. Grey* ii. viii, Mr. Vivian Grey had promised his Lordship, who was a collector of medals, an unique which had never yet been heard of. 1872 O. W. Holmes *Poet Breakf.-t.* iii. 89 A unique, sir, and there is a pleasure in exclusive possession.

† **b.** Something of which only one is possessed by a person or persons. *Obs. rare.*

1783 H. Walpole *Let. to C'tess Upper Ossory* 20 June, Lady Pembroke having lent them a servant besides their own unique. 1806 Surr *Winter in Lond.* III. 170 This Belcher girdle was not old; but being an *unique*, it had been..constantly in use.

2. A thing, fact, or circumstance which by reason of exceptional or special qualities stands alone and is without equal or parallel in its kind.

1768 *Phil. Trans.* LVIII. 215 When I presented this map to the Academy..it was looked upon as an Unique. 1781 *Gentl. Mag.* LI. 280/2 The dedication [of a volume of Sermons] being an *unique* in its kind. 1794 Paley *Evid.* ii. ix. iii. ad fin., The propagation of Christianity..is an *unique* in the history of the species. 1835 *Tait's Mag.* II. 651 It is.. an *unique* in English biography. 1838 De Quincey *Lamb* Wks. 1858 IX. 156 Of Lamb's writings..some were so memorably beautiful as to be uniques in their class. 1844 *N. Brit. Rev.* I. 124 A conflict, that stands out from all shadow of parallelism—a wild originality—a terrible unique.

**b.** A person of this class.

1758 *Case of Authors Stated* 14 He presumes, that he, this *Unic*, must therefore appear in the same stupendous Magnitude to every body else. 1782 Cowper *Let.* Nov., Wks. (1876) 121 He is a man much to my taste, and quite an unique in this country. 1802 Mrs. E. Parsons *Myst. Visit* IV. 145, I trust that he though very good, is not an unique. 1813 *Examiner* 22 Feb. 122/2 Those..charms of manner, which constitute an *unique*. 1866 Alger *Solit. Nat. & Man* ii. 65 The peculiar endowment in which he so far surpasses others as to be an insulated unique.

**Uni·quely**, *adv.* [f. prec. + -ly 2.]

1. Exclusively, solely; only.

1820 T. Mitchell *Aristoph.* I. 13 It is a picture uniquely Greek, to have a person of his rank in life giving such a debtor and creditor account of his intellectual pleasures as Dicæopolis does. 1893 Saltus *Mme. Sapphira* 182 She had married him uniquely to go into society. 1893 *Nation* (N.Y.) 28 Sept. 220/1 That distinction he can still boast to be his uniquely.

**b.** By itself alone; separately.

1885 Leudesdorf *Cremona's Proj. Geom.* 43 Therefore $D_1$ must coincide with $D'$, since the three points $A'B'C'$ determine uniquely the fourth point which forms with them a harmonic range.

2. To a unique degree or extent; so as to be unique; singularly, especially, pre-eminently.

1846 Darwin in *Life & Lett.* (1887) I. 345, I sent you a uniquely laudatory epistle. 1881 H. W. Nicholson *From Sword to Share* vii. 41 The climate is simply and uniquely perfect. 1886 W. J. Tucker *E. Europe* 310 The uniquely-shaped and quaintly-coloured furniture.

**Uni·queness.** [f. as prec. + -ness.] The fact or condition of being unique or unequalled; unique quality or character; an instance of this; a unique fact or circumstance.

1820 Coleridge *Lett., Convers., &c.* I. 152 The contra-distinction between the Shakespearian and the Greek Drama, and its still remaining uniqueness. 1874 H. R. Reynolds *John Bapt.* i. § 1. 4 So a great man loses something of his sublimity and uniqueness as we come close to him. 1880 Bertha Thomas *Violin-Player* II. x. 231 The novelty, the uniqueness of the scene. 1897 D. W. Forrest *Christ of Hist. & Exper.* v. 205 The uniquenesses of Christ are manifold and indubitable.

**Uni·quity.** [Irreg. f. Unique *a.* + -ity, prob. after *antiquity*.] = prec. (Cf. Unicity 2.)

Also, in recent use (1917), = a unique book.

1789 H. Walpole *Let.* 20 July, As rarities, a collector would give ten times more for them: and *uniquity* will make them valued more than the charming poetry. 1793 — *Let.* 17 Sept., I lament that the summer is over; not because of its uniquity, but because you two made it so delightful to me. 1862 B. Taylor *Home & Abr.* Ser. ii. 399 The originality, the uniquity, of the place. 1886 E. Randolph *Mostly Fools* II. i. 16 The idea..is unique, and uniquity, if I may permit myself the expression, is what we must aim at. 1898 *Atlantic Monthly* LXXXII. 495/1 The lateness..of the bird's appearance, together with what a certain scholarly friend of mine would have called his 'uniquity'.

**Unireme** (yū·nirīm). [f. Uni- + L. *rēm-us* oar, after *bi-*, *quadri-*, *trireme*, etc.] An ancient vessel or galley having one bank of oars.

1699 J. Potter *Antiq. Greece* iii. xiv. II. 135 [A ship] betwixt an Vnireme, and Bireme, consisting of a Bank, and a half. 1799 Charnock in *Naval Chron.* I. 134 The Uniremes ..had only one row of oars. 1900 *Athenæum* 18 Aug. 221/3 The thing shown is meant for a unireme.

**Un-I·rish**, *a.* (Un-[1] 7.) 1842 Lover *Handy Andy* ix, The youth endeavoured to become un-Irish in everything. 1854 Grace Greenwood *Haps & Mishaps* 108 An awkward effort at enjoyment and amusement, un-Irish and lamentable in the extreme. **Un-I·rishly**, *adv.* (Un-[1] 11.) 1830 Moore *Mem.* (1854) VI. 135 They wisely and un-Irishly chose the money.

† **Uni·rked**, *ppl. a. Sc. Obs.* (Un-[1] 8.)

1513 Douglas *Æneid* xiii. xi. 35 The Eneadanis all of his menȝe Ithandly and onyrkyt luiffit haue I. 1533 Bellenden *Livy* iv. xiv. (S. T. S.) II. 99 Horsmen..fresche and vnirkit of lauboure.

**Uni·ron**, *v.* (Un-[2] 4 and 4 b.)

1611 Florio, *Disferrare*, to vniron, to vnshooe a horse. *Ibid.*, *Sferrare*, to vniron, to free or deliuer from out irons or bondes. [1863 Sala *Captain Dangerous* II. i. 18 Captain Handsell had me unironed.]

**Uni·roned**, *ppl. a.* (Un-[1] 8.)

*c* 1430 *Pilgr. Lyf Manhode* i. cviii. (1869) 57 A burdoun yrened weyeth more than thilke that is vnyrened. 1788 Holcroft tr. *Baron Trenck* (1886) II. 21, I was thus left four days in peace, unironed. 1880 *New Virgin.* I. 57 Unironed shirts and coats.

**Unirra·diated**, *ppl. a.* (Un-[1] 8.) 1806 Symmons *Life of Milton* 544 (Jod.), A mind not unirradiated with the golden visions of fancy. 1816 Coleridge *Lay Serm.* (Bohn) 342 The understanding..unirradiated by the reason and the spirit. **Uni·rrigated**, *ppl. a.* (Un-[1] 8.) 1878 Browning *Poets Croisic* 83 Our Academic clodpoles must be dense Indeed to stand unirrigated still. 1883 *Standard* 31 Aug. 4/6 The unirrigated tracts between the head waters of the.. rivers. **Uni·rritant**, *a.* (Un-[1] 7.) 1822–7 Good *Study Med.* (1829) V. 120 We should employ the unirritant tonics. **Uni·rritated**, *ppl. a.* (Un-[1] 8.) 1649 Earl Monm. tr. *Senault's Use Passions* (1671) 83 Bulls..do little unirritated. 1793 T. Beddoes *Lett. Darwin* 71, I do not understand why in an irritable state of the body, the iris should be unirritated. **Uni·rritatedly**, *adv.* (Un-[1] 11.) 1869 Browning *Lett.* Ser. ii. (1907) I. 34 Yours unirritatedly, R. B.

**Uni·rritating**, *ppl. a.* (Un-[1] 10.)

Also *unirritatingly* (Webster, 1847).

1797 Abernethy *Surg. Ess.* 98 The abscess at last became ..un-irritating to the constitution. 1839–47 *Todd's Cycl. Anat.* III. 613/2 The smooth and unirritating condition of the inner surface of the deserted shell. 1896 Mrs. Caffyn *Quaker Grandmother* 20 Sin is a chastener that conduces to unirritating niceness.

† **Unirroo·ted**, *ppl. a. Obs.* [f. Un-[1] 8 c + *y-rooted*, pa. pple. of Root *v.*[2] Cf. Unrooted *ppl. a.*] Not rooted out or eradicated.

1600 Tourneur *Transf. Metam.* lviii, Not hable to endure His heart should knowledge of such harme immure An houre, and th' wrong rest vnirrooted out.

**Uniserial** (yūnisīə·riăl), *a.* Chiefly *Bot.*, *Zool.*, etc. [See Uni- and Serial *a.*] Arranged in, consisting of, one series or row; characterized by this kind of form or arrangement.

1839 *Proc. Berw. Nat. Club* I. 198 Suckers uniserial. 1859 *Todd's Cycl. Anat.* V. 290/1 In those genera in which these processes form a single line the gills are said to be uniserial. 1872 H. A. Nicholson *Palæont.* 325 The teeth are conical and uniserial.

**Uniseriate** (yūnisīə·riĕt), *a. Bot.* and *Zool.* [See Uni- and Seriate *a.*] = prec.

1846 Dana *Zooph.* (1848) 215 With cellules interruptedly uniseriate, and occasionally biseriate. 1872 H. C. Wood *Fresh-w. Algæ* 68 Cells uni-seriate. 1887 W. Phillips *Brit. Discomycetes* 243 Sporidia uniseriate.

Hence **Unise·riately** *adv.*

1848 Dana *Zoo.* 133 Upper margin uniseriately tuberculate.

**Unisexual** (yūnise·ksiuăl), *a.* [ad. mod.L. *unisexual-is* (F. *unisexuel* (1812), Pg. *unisexual*): see Uni- and Sexual *a.*]

1. Of one sex; having the essential generative or

reproductive organs of one or other sex developed or present in individuals: **a.** *Bot.* Of flowers: In which either the stamens or pistils are absent or suppressed. Also, of plants: Characterized by flowers of this kind; = DICLINOUS *a.*

**1802** R. HALL *Elem. Bot.* 193 *Unisexual*,..having one sex. **1828** STARK *Elem. Nat. Hist.* II. 461 The last three classes [of plants]..have the flowers thus disposed, and are hence named unisexual. **1839** LINDLEY *Sch. Bot.* 16 In particular species the stamens are found in one flower, and the pistil in another..; such plants are called unisexual. **1854** S. THOMSON *Wild Fl.* 62 These unisexual blossoms being either the production of the same individual plant, or of separate individuals of the same species. **1872** OLIVER *Elem. Bot.* II. 169 Burnet Sanguisorb,..with..unisexual flowers.

*Comb.* **1877** *Nature* 26 April 548/1 A unisexual-flowering plant.

**b.** *Zool.* Of animals or their organs.

In *Ent.* of certain agamic broods of *Aphides*: consisting of the female sex only (*Cent. Dict.* 1891).

**1830** R. KNOX *Béclard's Anat.* 29 The organs of generation present all the varieties, unisexual, without copulation, hermaphrodite [etc.]. **1861** HULME tr. *Moquin-Tandon* II. I. 47 In a great number of animals the sexes are separated and placed on distinct individuals: these are said to be unisexual. **1877** DARWIN *Forms of Fl.* Introd. 2 The males and females of ordinary unisexual animals.

**2.** Pertaining or restricted to one sex; *U.S.* esp. of colleges or schools.

**1885** L. OLIPHANT *Sympneumata* 182 The relationship of person which would maintain in a painful activity the currents of the decaying unisexual layers of either frame. **1886** *Century Mag.* June 326/1 One final provincialism of the mind there is, which a unisexual college certainly never would have any power to eradicate. **1904** *Daily Chron.* 14 Oct. 6 The present unjust system of unisexual punishments.

Hence **Unise·xually** *adv.*

**1891** *Cent. Dict.* s.v., Animals unisexually developed. **1901** *Nature* 10 Jan. 252/1 Not that spontaneous variations are always inherited unisexually.

**Unisexua·lity.** *Bot.* and *Zool.* [f. prec. + -ITY.] The state or condition of being unisexual.

**1830** LINDLEY *Nat. Syst. Bot.* 155 The unisexuality of the flowers of both genera. **1877** HUXLEY *Anat. Inv. Anim.* i. 67 There is some reason to suspect..that unisexuality is the result of the abortion of the organs of the other sex, in males and females respectively. **1898** *Pop. Sci. Monthly* July 298 Asexuality passes through bisexuality into unisexuality.

**Unisi·licate.** *Min.* [UNI- 2.] (See quot. from Dana.) Also *attrib.*

**1879** RUTLEY *Stud. Rocks* x. 140 In chemical composition the garnets are essentially unisilicates of different sesquioxides and protoxides. **1879** DANA *Man. Min.* (ed. 3) 242 In the Unisilicates, one molecule of silicon is combined with two of an element in the protoxide state..; or with two-thirds of a molecule in the sesquioxide state. *Ibid.*, Among the species referred to the Unisilicates there are some that vary from the unisilicate ratio.

**Uni·solated,** *ppl. a.* (UN-[1] 8.) **1886** *Jrnl. R. Microsc. Soc.* VI. 47 The unisolated hyoid muscles of the frog.

**Unison** (yū·nisən, -zən), *sb.* and *a.* Also 6 unisonne, vnisone, unizon (vnisson), 7 unisone. [a. OF. *unison* (Oresme), later and mod.F. *unisson* (16th c.), or ad. late L. *unison-us* (whence It., Sp., and Pg. *unisono* (also as *sb.*), It. †*unissono*, Sp. *unison*) of the same sound as something else, f. L. *ūni-* UNI- and *sonus* SOUND *sb.*[3]]

The apparently early example in the *York Mystery Plays* xxv. 262 is probably a scribal error for 'vrysoune' (= orison).

**A.** *sb.* **1.** *Mus.* and *Acoustics.* **a.** A sound or note of the same pitch as another; also loosely, a note taken as a starting-point from which intervals are reckoned. Now *rare*, or taken as *transf.* from b.

**1574** F. KETR. *A. Le Roy's Instr. Lute* 17 You must..haue recourse to an other stryng, that maketh the vnisson with that. **1609** DOULAND *Ornithoparcus' Microl.* 17 An Vnison is..a Voyce so qualified, that it neither tendeth to depth nor to height. **1660** BOYLE *New Experiments Phys. Mech.* 211 A string tun'd (as Musicians speak..) to an Unison with it. **1694** HOLDER *Harmony* iv. 54 By Unison is meant, sometimes the Habitude or Ration of Equality of two Notes compared together, being of the very same Tune. Sometimes (as here) for the given single Note to which the Distance, or the Rations of other Intervals are compared. **1728** CHAMBERS *Cycl.* s.v. *Interval*, Unisons, 'tis plain, cannot possibly have any Variety. **1881** *Nature* XXIV. 358 When the higher note has reached a point about half-way between unison and the octave note.

*transf.* **1677** *Phil. Trans.* XVIII. 840 Not the whole of that other string doth thus tremble, but the several parts severally, according as they are Unisons to the whole.

*fig.* **1760–72** H. BROOKE *Fool of Qual.* (1792) I. 181 The muscles of Harry's expressive countenance, like an equally-tuned instrument, uttered unisons to every word he heard.

**b.** Identity in pitch of two or more sounds or notes; the agreement or consonance of the sounds of two or more bodies vibrating at equal rates; the relation of two notes of the same pitch reckoned as one of the musical 'intervals'.

**1575** GASCOIGNE *Weedes* Wks. 1907 I. 381 At Musickes sacred sounde, my fansies eft begonne, In concordes, discordes, notes and cliffes, in tunes of unisonne. **1596** BATHE *Brief Introd. Skill of Song* C, A concord is diuided into an Vnizon, Third, Fift, Sixt [etc.]. **1626** BACON *Sylva* § 103 The Diapason or Eight in Music is the sweetest Concord; insomuch as it is in effect an Unison. **1694** [see a]. **1728** CHAMBERS *Cycl.* s.v. *Octave*, The most simple Perception the Soul can have of true Sounds, is that of Unison. **1749** J. MASON *Numbers in Poet. Comp.* 21 Those [metrical] Feet..are in Proportion of the Unison in Musick...And they are said to answer to the Unison. **1806** CALLCOTT *Mus. Gram.* II. i. 90 The Unison,..although it cannot properly be reckoned an Interval, is always considered as such. **1873** BANISTER *Music* § 103 Two, or more, perfect 5ths, perfect 8ves, or perfect unisons, are forbidden between the same two parts. **1896** W. G. WOOLCOMBE *Pract. Work Physics* III. Pref., The nearest approach to unison between two musical notes.

**c.** A combination of melodies at the same pitch (or, loosely, one or more octaves apart) in different parts, i. e. performed by different voices or instruments. Also in fig. context.

In quot. 1730 used loosely for each of such melodies (in this case on different sets of strings of the same instrument: cf. *unison string* in 5).

[**1724** *Short Explic. For. Wds. in Mus. Bks.*, *Unissono*, a Unison...This word is also used when in Symphonies of Songs Two Violins both play the same Thing, or the Violin and Song, or the Bass and Song, &c.] **1730** in *Abridgm. Specif. Patents, Music* (1871) 1 A new invented harpsichord upon which (having only two sets of strings) may be performed either one or two unisons, or two unisons & one octave together. **1795** MASON *Ch. Music* i. 82 Every ear felt the stupendous effect both of unison and harmony. **1799** KOLLMANN *Ess. Mus. Composition* iii. 18 In Unisons, or passages where all instruments play the same melody, though in different Octaves. **1855** PUSEY *Doctr. Real Presence* 721 When the Holy Spirit..swept over the discordant strings of human tongues and thoughts..and blended all their varying notes into one holy unison of truth. **1869** OUSELEY *Counterp.* xiv. 83 When the number of parts exceeds four, unisons may be used.

**d.** In the phrase *in* (..) *unison* (in sense b or c).

**1616** W. BROWNE *Brit. Past.* II. ii. 546 Not suffering her shrill waters, as they run, Tun'd with a whistling gale in unison. **1749** J. MASON *Numbers in Poet. Comp.* 21 Two Strings of equal Length (supposing their respective Tensions and Thickness to be equal) being put in Motion, will be in Unison, or give exactly one and the same Sound. **1765** STERNE *Tr. Shandy* VII. xliii, The nymphs joined in unison, and their swains an octave below them. **1795** MASON *Ch. Music* iii. 208 What old Calvin meant to be sung in unison, they chose should be performed in counterpoint, or in four parts. **1856** MRS. C. CLARKE tr. *Berlioz' Instrument.* 32 To violoncellos..is ordinarily given the part of the double bass, which they double in the octave above or in unison. **1873** HALE *In His Name* vi. 58 As the three voices, in strict unison, closed the little song.

*transf.* **1828** SCOTT *F. M. Perth* xxvii, The cry from the numberless boats..rose in wild unison up to the Tom-an-Lonach. **1876** HOLLAND *Seven Oaks* xi. 149 'Not at all,' was responded almost in unison.

**e.** *ellipt.* for 'unison string' (see 5).

**1820** *Q. Mus. Mag.* II. 306 He tried the octaves, and found them..all flat..; the unisons, generally speaking, were in tune. **1889** [see *unison-tuning* in 5].

**2.** A single unvaried tone; a monotone. ? *Obs.*

**1609** DOULAND *Ornithoparcus' Microl.* 26 The prayers.. are read in an Vnison. **1742** POPE *Dunc.* IV. 612 Lost was the Nation's Sense, nor could be found, While the long solemn Unison [*sc.* a yawn] went round.

**3.** A union or combination of concordant sounds; a united and unanimous declaration or utterance.

**1806** WORDSW. '*Loud is the Vale*' 3 A mighty unison of streams! Of all her Voices, One! **1871** PALGRAVE *Lyr. Poems* 135 That cry has been heard By a nation's unison swelled.

**4.** *fig.* **a.** Something perfectly agreeing or consonant with another; an utterance or expression of perfect agreement or assent; something that responds sympathetically as a string tuned to a corresponding note. Now *rare* or *Obs.*

**1650** BULWER *Anthropomet.* 63 A forehead which keeps its natural magnitude is one of the Unisons of the face. **1658** GURNALL *Chr. in Arm.* II. 205 Adam indeed had such a righteousnesse made to his hand, his heart and the Law were unisons. **1702** C. MATHER *Magn. Chr.* III. III. (1852) 539 He thought that ministers and market-men were not unisons. **1796** ELIZA HAMILTON *Lett. Hindoo Rajah* (1811) II. 218 The tender sigh..in vibrating on the ears of Miss Ardent, seemed to touch some pleasant unison, that overspread her countenance with a smile. **1812** COLERIDGE in *Lit. Rem.* (1836) I. 375 To make the intellectual faith a fair analogon or unison of the vital faith.

**b.** Exact or perfect agreement, concord, or harmony; harmonious combination or union.

**1654** WHITLOCK *Zootomia* 454 Physitians..are at Discord the best, but at Unisons the worst; for they do all so disagree [etc.]. **1674** PLAYFORD *Skill Mus.* A 5, Friendship the Vnison of well tun'd Hearts. **1744** THOMSON *Summer* (ed. 5) 1375 Social Friends, Attun'd to happy Unison of Soul,.. Now call'd abroad enjoy the falling Day. **1796** MME. D'ARBLAY *Camilla* I. 4 This exemplary couple was bound to each other by the most perfect unison of character. **1819** KEATS *Vis. Hyperion* I. 418 Nor could my eyes And ears act with that unison of sense Which marries sweet sound with the grace of form. **1858** SEARS *Athan.* ix. 77 Thence life and health spread through our animal frames, restoring them to a unison with divine laws. **1871** FARRAR *Witn. Hist.* v. 183 That beautiful unison of noble manhood, stainless womanhood, joyous infancy, and uncontaminated youth.

†**c.** *At unison* (also *at.. unisons*), = next. *Obs.*

**1665** GLANVILL *Scepsis Sci.* xiii. 76 Reason and Faith are at perfect Unisons. **1772** *Test Filial Duty* II. 173 The sensations of friendship have not enough of fire in them, to warm the heart into that proper temperature, requisite to render it at unison with the delirium of lovers. *Ibid.* 238 Set all my affections at unison.

**d.** *In unison*, in agreement or harmony, concordant, consonant, harmonious. Freq. *in unison with.*

**1780** COWPER *Parrot* 36 Each character in ev'ry part Sustain'd with so much grace and art, And both in unison. **1782** V. KNOX *Ess.* xxviii. ¶ 8 It is the more tranquil style which is most frequently in unison with our minds. **1815** JANE AUSTEN *Emma* xli, It was all in unison; words, conduct, discretion and indiscretion told the same story. **1836** W. IRVING *Astoria* I. 287 A mode of redress perfectly in unison with the character of the man. **1860** PUSEY *Min. Proph.* 26 Dumb inanimate nature seems to rejoice and to be in unison with our sense of joy. **1879** FARRAR *St. Paul* I. 312 When such allies were in unison..it was easy to strike a deadly blow at the Nazarenes.

**5.** *attrib.*: **unison stop,** (*a*) in an organ, a stop of the same pitch as the diapasons; (*b*) in a harpsichord (see quot. 1896); **unison string,** in a pianoforte or other instrument, a string tuned to the same pitch as another (or, loosely, to a pitch an octave higher); **unison tune,** a tune to be sung in unison, as distinct from harmony or 'parts'; **unison-tuning,** the tuning of strings (of a pianoforte, etc.) in unison.

**1840** *Penny Cycl.* XVI. 493/1 Trumpet and Oboe stops, being what are called *unison stops,..take their lengths from the open diapason. **1896** A. J. HIPKINS *Pianoforte* 122 *Unison Stop*, properly the second foundation register in a harpsichord; the shorter of the unison strings in a double keyboard one, and sounding on the lower keyboard only. **1685** BOYLE *Effects Motion* vii. 80 A certain impulse of Air, made by one of the *Unison-strings of a musical Instrument, may suffice to produce a visible motion in another. **1732** BERKELEY *Alciphr.* III. § 4, I feel an affection in my soul, like the trembling of one lute, upon striking the unison strings of another. **1896** [see *unison stop* above]. **1869** *Pall Mall G.* 7 July 12/2 Mr. John Goss, Mr. E. J. Hopkins, and Mr. J. Baptiste Calkin have composed *unison tunes for this volume. **1889** BRINSMEAD *Hist. Pianoforte* 186 The same plan as that for learning the *unison-tuning may be adopted for the octave, but care must be taken that the unison of the note is tuned afterwards.

**B.** *adj.* †**1.** Sounding at once or together. *Obs.*[−1]

**1582** STANYHURST *Æneis* III. (Arb.) 73 Thus God Apollo cryed; but wee with an vnison outcrye..demaunded, what place God Phœbus apoincted.

†**b.** *fig.* United and consenting, as the pronouncement of a number of persons; expressing complete agreement; unanimous, concordant, consonant, harmonious. *Obs.*

**1650** W. CHARLETON *Paradoxes* Prol. f 4 b, By the unisone vote of the multitude. **1651** H. L'ESTRANGE *Answ. Mrq. Worcester* 51 Is the Church of Rome so unison, so all of a piece, as to afford no jarres? *a* **1662** HEYLYN *Laud* II. (1671) 447 The first branch [of a Bill] was carried in the Negative by..an Unison-consent in the Lords then present. **1760–2** GOLDSM. *Cit. W.* xxx, I only beg you'll endeavour to make your souls unison with mine.

†**c.** Concordant or consonant *to* something. *Obs.*

**1710** R. WARD *Life H. More* 234 Some Circumstances.., or Particulars of his Writings, are not so unison to my Slower Faculties. **1760–72** H. BROOKE *Fool of Qual.* (1792) V. 10 This doctrine sounded unison to the secret feelings of our young Englishman.

†**d.** Like-sounding; equivalent. *Obs.*[−1]

**1759** STERNE *Tr. Shandy* I. xix, Tristram!—Melancholy dissyllable of sound! which, to his ears, was unison to Nincompoop.

**2.** *Mus.* and *Acoustics.* Identical in pitch; singing, sounding, etc., in unison; unisonal, unisonous. Now *rare* or *Obs.*

**1614** JACKSON *Creed* III. xviii. § 4 As a string, though untouched, and unable to begin motion of itself, will yet raise it selfe to an vnison voice. **1622** PEACHAM *Compl. Gent.* xi. 104 Two Lutes of equall size being laid vpon a Table, and tuned Vnison, or alike in..any..string; the one stricken, the other untouched shall answer it. **1667** MILTON *P. L.* VII. 599 All sounds on Fret by String or Golden Wire Temper'd soft Tunings, intermixt with Voice Choral or Unison. **1694** HOLDER *Harmony* iv. 51 The Unison Concord..is no Space or Interval, but an Identity of Tune. **1721** A. MALCOLM *Treat. Mus.* 580 When Two Voices sing together one Song, 'tis more agreeable that they be 8ve than *unison* with one another, in every Note. **1893** S. GEE *Auscult. & Percussion* (ed. 4) I. iii. 69 A unison vibration, convibration, or consonance of the wall is required to the production of tone.

**Unisonal** (yuni·sŏnăl), *a.* *Mus.* [f. prec. + -AL.] = UNISONOUS *a.* 1.

**1728** R. NORTH *Mem. Music* (1846) 66 All was plain-song, that is counterpoint unisonall. **1865** *Reader* 19 Aug. 214 The unisonal female-voice choruses. **1882** *Amer. Missionary* Mar. 70 Their general style is recitative and chorus, though a few are pure solos or unisonal measures. **1898** *Record* 4 Nov. 1084/2 In spite of one's own loving reverence for unisonal singing.

Hence **Uni·sonally** *adv.*, in unison.

**1882** *Standard* 20 Feb., A passage of broken quavers.. given out unisonally by the full orchestra. **1887** *Ch. Times* 4 March (Cassell's), Tenors and basses burst in unisonally.

**Uni·sonance.** *rare.* [ad. L. type **unisonantia* (whence Sp. and Pg. *unisonancia*), f. med.L. *unison-us*: see UNISON.] Agreement or identity of sounds (see quots.).

**1728** CHAMBERS *Cycl.* s.v. *Concord*, Unisonance, then, being the Relation of Equality between the Tunes of two Sounds, all Unisons are Concords, and in the first Degree. *Ibid.* s.v. *Unison*, What constitutes Unisonance, is the Equality of the Number of Vibrations of the two sonorous Bodies in equal Times. [Hence in Webster (1828–32), etc.]

**Unisonant** (yuni·sŏnănt), *a.* [f. L. *ūni-* UNI- + *sonant-*, *sonans* (see SONANT *a.*), after *dissonant*, etc. Cf. F. *unissonant.*] Of the same pitch or sound; unisonal, unisonous. Also in fig. context.

**1801** BUSBY *Dict. Mus.*, *Unisonus*, or *Unisonant*, an epithet applied to those sounds which are..in unison with each other. **1834** MRS. SOMERVILLE *Connex. Phys. Sci.* xvii. (1836) 168 If two bottles be..tuned by filling them with such a quantity of water as will render them unisonant with two tuning-forks which differ in pitch. **1886** LINSKILL *Haven under Hill* II. ix. 115 The mystic, moving, unisonant harmony that was stirring and breaking upon her own soul.

† **Unisone·ity.** *Obs.*⁻¹ [f. as next + -(E)ITY.] A state of agreement or concord; unanimity.

**1663** WATERHOUSE *Fortesc. Illustr.* 414 The Lawes of Nations do affirm the nature of it [*sc.* marriage] to a Vnisoneity, as appears in the Digest.

**Unisonous** (yuni·sŏnəs), *a.* [f. late L. *unison-us* (see UNISON) + -OUS.]

**1.** *Mus.* Of the same pitch for the different voices or instruments; composed, performed, or rendered in unison or in octaves, and not in parts; unisonal.

**1781** WARTON *Hist. Eng. Poetry* III. 171 These apt notes [to sing the Psalms with] were about forty tunes, of one part only, and in one unisonous key. **1789** BURNEY *Hist. Mus.* III. 389 Nothing now but syllabic and unisonous psalmody was authorised in the Church. **1818** *Blackw. Mag.* III. 65 The Psalms being set to simple or unisonous melodies, to render them fit for public service. **1867** *Contemp. Rev.* IV. 190 Their deadness took the form of a drawling unisonous singing of the old tunes. **1894** *Times* 11 June 9/5 The player's left hand.. was audibly less at home than the right in the unisonous finale.

**2.** Exhibiting agreement, concord, or sameness of character or nature; concordant.

**1812** SHELLEY *Let. to Miss Hitchener* 29 Jan., Minds unisonous in reason and feeling. **1851** GALLENGA *Italy* II. xii. 415 The patriots are uniform, methodical in their transactions, unisonous in their demands. **1858** GLADSTONE *Homer* I. 34 The voice of the Homeric poems is in this respect.. unisonous,.. and not multiform.

† **Unisound.** *Obs. rare.* [Alteration of UNISON *sb*: see UNI- and SOUND *sb.*³] A unison.

**1763** *Ann. Reg., Misc.* 192/2 By dividing the musical notes into six, as nature directs, the unisound will fall on the seventh note. *Ibid.* 193/1 [The notes] *i, j, s, d*, are likewise unisounds to *f, z, t*, alike.

† **U·nisounding,** *ppl. a.* *Obs.*⁻¹ [See UNI-.] Having only one sound.

**1620** H. FITZ-GEOFFERY *Certain Elegies* A 8 b, Fennor, with his Vnisounding Eare word.

**Uni·ssued,** *ppl. a.* (UN-¹ 8.)

**1667** *10th Rep. Hist. MSS. Comm.* App. V. 57 He may be recompenced.. out of the pay of the said Sir James Midleton unissued. **1703** *Lond. Gaz.* No. 3890/3 Several of the Debentures.. do remain still unissued. **1898** *Daily News* 12 Oct. 9/3 A large block of unissued shares.

**Unit** (yū·nit), *sb.* (and *a.*). Also 6–8 **unite.** [f. L. *ūn-us* one; the ending was probably suggested by *digit* and *composit(e.*

Introduced by Dee, who thus draws attention to the form in his *Math. Pref.* (1570) *iij *marg.*, Note the worde, Vnit, to expresse the Greke Monas, and not Vnitie: as we haue all, commonly, till now, vsed.]

**1.** *Math.* A single magnitude or number regarded as an undivided whole and as the ultimate base of all number; *spec.* in *Arithmetic*, the least whole number; the numeral 'one', represented by the figure 1. Cf. UNITY 1 b.

*α.* **1570** DEE *Math. Pref.* *iij, Number, we define, to be, a certayne Mathematicall Summe, of Vnits. And, an Vnit, is that thing Mathematicall, Indiuisible, by participation of some likenes of whose property, any thing, which is in deede, or is counted One, may reasonably be called One. **1575** RECORDE *Gr. Artes* Y iij b, An Improper Fraction,.. that is to saye, a fraction in forme, which in dede is greater than an Unit. **1654** J. EYRE *Exact Surveyor* 12 In the ordinary use of this [Decimal] Chain, for measuring and plotting, you may take onely notice of Units and Primes. **1669** STURMY *Mariner's Mag.* VII. xxxiv. 51 The Characteristick of any Logarithme must consist of an Unit less than the given Number consisteth of Digits or Places. **1728** CHAMBERS *Cycl.* s.v. *Number*, Cardinal Numbers [are] those which express the Quantity of Units; as, 1, 2, &c. **1794** CUNN *Doctr. Fractions* 62 Repetends that begin at the same place, whether at Units, Primes, Seconds. **1832** HOOD *Ode to J. Hume* i, Units, Tens, Hundreds, Thousands, Millions. **1838** DE MORGAN *Ess. Probab.* 33 Write down as many numbers, reckoning downwards, as there are units in the number. **1875** *Encycl. Brit.* II. 527/1 [In arithmetical notation] the figure placed furthest to the right has the same significance as when it stands alone, *i. e.* it represents units.

*β.* **1588** A. KING tr. *Canisius' Catech.* i ij, Compte.. swa mony epactis as yair is vnites in ye golden nombre. **1597** BLUNDEVIL *Exerc.* (ed. 2) I. vii. 12 Such [numbers] as cannot bee divided but that there will remaine some odde unite, those are called Primes. **1669** W. SIMPSON *Hydrol. Chym.* 226 The great variety the number seven doth produce by the various transposition of its unites. **1679** MOXON *Math. Dict.* 162 An Unite is the beginning of Number, and.. receiveth no division in Numbers, even as a Point in Magnitudes. **1726** LEONI *Alberti's Archit.* II. 89/1 If, as some affirm, the unite be no number, but only the source of all others.

† **b.** Without article: = UNITY 1 b. *Obs.*

**1717** *Phil. Trans.* XXX. 618 The Logarithm of Unite is nothing; and.. the nearer any Number is to Unite, the nearer will its Logarithm be to 0. **1823** JEFFERSON *Writ.* (1830) IV. 364 In the proportion of a million at least to unit.

**c.** Any determinate quantity, dimension, or magnitude adopted as a basis or standard of measurement for other quantities of the same kind and in terms of which their magnitude is calculated or expressed.

A large number of special units adopted in technical and scientific use are recorded in some recent Dicts.

**1738** CHAMBERS *Cycl.* s.v. *Degree*, Thus, a Degree, as being the integer or unite, is denoted by °. **1816** PLAYFAIR *Nat. Phil.* II. 209 Hitherto, the distance of the Sun from the Earth has served as the unit, by which we have measured all other distances in the planetary system. **1825** JEFFERSON *Autobiog.* Wks. 1859 I. 52 The necessity of establishing a standard of value with us, and of the adoption of a money Unit. **1854** RONALDS & RICHARDSON *Chem. Technol.* (ed. 2) I. 253 The loss of heat from these sources has been estimated.. at about 7 units of heat per hour per square foot. **1867** NOAD *Text Bk. Electricity* 201 The unit of a current conveys a unit of electricity through the circuit in a unit of time. **1870** F. L. POPE *Electric Tel.* iii. (1872) 25 The ohm is a unit of resistance, in the same manner that an inch is a unit of length, or a pound a unit of weight. **1886** RUSKIN *Præterita* I. 323 Musical people.. have not yet fixed their unit of time.

*Comb.* **1892** *Nation* (N.Y.) 15 Dec. 459/1 The hopeful earnestness with which Mr. Norman offers his unit-of-weight system as a panacea for the cure of all financial ills.

**d.** A substance adopted as a standard by which the specific gravity of various bodies is estimated.

**1829** *Chapters Phys. Sci.* 169 As water is taken as the unit for solids and liquids, so is atmospheric air for gases. **1869** GILL *Chem. for Sch.* xxii. 274 Dalton.. adopted it [*sc.* hydrogen] as the unit or standard of atomic weight.

**e.** (See quots. and REPEAT *sb.* 4 b.)

**1855** R. N. WORNUM *Anal. Ornament* 18 Units of repetition, or repeats of irregular shapes, arranged diagonally. *Ibid.* 19 As it is in this case the group that is repeated, the group of figures becomes the pattern or unit of repetition.

**2.** A single individual or thing regarded as a member of a group or number of things or individuals, or discriminated from these as having a separate existence; one of the separate parts or members of which a complex whole or aggregate is composed or into which it may be analysed.

**1642** H. MORE *Song of Soul* II. I. ii. 55 In number, measure, weight, he all things made; Each unite he dissevers by his Art. **1690** LOCKE *Hum. Und.* II. xii. § 6. 74 Which collective Ideas of several Substances thus put together, are as much each of them one single Idea, as that of a Man, or an Unite. **1716** M. DAVIES *Athen. Brit.* II. To Rdr. 13 Some few Despicable Unadditionable Units or Unitarians. **1739** HUME *Hum. Nat.* I. II. ii, 'Tis evident, that existence in itself belongs only to unity, and is never applicable to number, but on account of the unites, of which the number is composed. **1817** SCOTT *Rob Roy* xxxi, The unit of that life.. was for ever withdrawn from the sum of human existence. **1856** MERIVALE *Rom. Emp.* xl. IV. 459 Our history becomes a review of the affairs of a vast unit, the aggregate of a multitude of smaller members. **1872** H. C. BASTIAN *Begin. Life* I. 216 Before a nucleus is evolved.., the simple living unit (*plastide*) is able to assimilate nutritive material and grow.

**b.** That division or section of a collective body or whole which is regarded as the lowest or least to have a distinctive existence; such a division or group of individuals considered as a basis of formation or administration.

**1847** GROTE *Greece* II. xxviii. IV. 68 The village is a fraction, but the city is an unit. **1861** MAINE *Anc. Law* v. 126 The unit of ancient society was the Family. **1888** BRYCE *Amer. Commw.* II. 224 The county remained the practically important unit of local administration, the unit to which the various functions of government were aggregated.

**c.** In military or naval use.

**1876** VOYLE & STEVENSON *Milit. Dict.* 446/1 In military organization, the term unit is applied to that single portion upon which any part of an army, regiment, &c. is formed. Thus a company is the unit of a regiment; a battery, that of a brigade of artillery. **1893** *Infantry Drill* p. xxiii, [A] Battalion [is] the unit of infantry. **1899** *Times* 14 Oct. 9 A waterproof bag which is left at the base.. on a unit going into action.

**3.** *attrib.*, passing into *adj.*, with the general meaning 'of, pertaining or equivalent to, (that of) a unit; produced or caused by a unit; consisting of, containing, or forming a unit or units'.

A large number of special collocations, chiefly of a scientific or technical nature, are given in some recent Dicts.

**a.** In sense 1 c, chiefly in *Electr.*, as *unit coil, current, force, jar, measure, pole*, etc.

**1839** NOAD *Electricity* i. 31 A very useful little electrical instrument.. for registering the exact quantity of electricity given to a Leyden phial from the machine; it is called the unit jar. **1842** BRANDE *Dict. Sci.*, *Unit jar*.. announce[s] by its repeated discharges, which may be counted, the number of them which have passed into the larger jar. **1844** NOAD *Electricity* (ed. 2) 53 The value of the unit measure. **1866** R. M. FERGUSON *Electr.* 17 A magnetic needle of unit size and strength. **1867** NOAD *Text Bk. Electricity* 201 A circuit of unit resistance. *Ibid.*, The unit current flowing through a conductor unit of length will exert the unit force on the unit pole at the unit distance. **1867** BRANDE & COX *Dict. Sci.*, etc. III. 899/1 *Unit coil*,.. a standard measure used by electricians for expressing the amount of resistance experienced in a given electrical circuit. **1873** J. C. MAXWELL *Electr. & Magn.* II. 3 The unit-pole is a pole which points north, and is such that, when placed at unit distance from another unit-pole, it repels it with unit of force. **1876** P. G. TAIT *Rec. Adv. Phys. Sci.* (ed. 2) xiv. 357 Unit force is.. that force which, whatever be its source, produces unit momentum in unit of time. **1884** KNIGHT *Dict. Mech.* Suppl. 913/2 *Unit and safety valve*, one exposing 1 square inch to the force of the steam.

**b.** In general use.

**1896** R. G. MOULTON *Lit. Study Bible* xi. 258 These Unit Proverbs exhibit two varieties. **1897** *Daily News* 9 Feb. 3/4 Was the scheme to be organized on brigade, battalion, or unit lines? *Ibid.*, The unit system of organization. **1898** *Engineering Mag.* XVI. 104 A plant of a certain size may be run by a unit-body of men. **1898** SIR W. CROOKES in *Daily News* 8 Sept. 6/1 The consumption of wheat per head of the population (unit consumption) was over 6 bushels per annum.

**4.** As *adj.* Having the distinct or individual existence of a unit; individual.

**1870** J. H. NEWMAN *Gram. Assent* I. i. 7 All things in the exterior world are unit and individual;.. the mind contemplates these unit realities as they exist. *a* **1881** A. BARRATT *Phys. Metempiric* (1883) 115 If the unit minds were parts or modes of this absolute mind.

**Unit,** variant of UNITE *sb.*

**Unitable** (yūnəi·tăb'l), *a.* [f. UNIT-E *v.* + -ABLE.] That can be united; capable of union.

**1653** H. MORE *Antid. Ath.* (1662) 151 The Plantal faculty of the Soul whereby she is unitable to this terrestrial body. **1659** — *Immort. Soul* III. xiv. 481 That Order of immaterial Creatures which we call Souls, vitally unitable with the Matter. **1678** CUDWORTH *Intell. Syst.* 565 Such Beings or Spirits Incorporeal.. are Vitally Unitable to Bodies. **1707** *Vulpone* 22 The Offer of the Scots to Unite the Nations in such things as they are Unitable. **1854** OWEN in *Orr's Circ. Sci., Org. Nat.* I. 166 When fractured, the broken parts.. are not unitable.. from within.

Hence **Unitabi·lity.**

**1863** tr. *Dorner's Person of Christ* III. 280 The real unitability of the divine and human.

† **Uni·tage.** *Obs.*⁻¹ [f. as prec. + -AGE.] The action of uniting; union.

**1641** *Dial. Rattlehead & Roundh.* 4 You can find no means to conjoyn an vnity? *Rattleh.* Only perversnesse in the vnitage of your circular opinions.

**Unital** (yū·nităl), *a.* [f. UNIT or UNIT-Y + -AL.] That unites; causing or producing unity or union; of the nature of a unit; unitary.

**1860** W. J. C. MUIR *Pagan or Chr.* 82 The nave grandly predominates over the aisles, without there being any unital element common to both. **1882** J. B. STALLO *Concepts & The. Mod. Physics* 20 In nature there is a great unital, continuous and everlasting process of development. **1894** *Forum* March 34 To give to each one-tenth of its capital stock.. a single director, is open to the objection that it prevents unital control.

**Unitarian** (yūnitē·riăn), *sb.* and *a.* [Partly, in theol. use, f. mod.L. *unitari-us* (1656: f. L. *ūnitās* UNITY) + -AN, partly f. UNIT-Y *sb.* + -*arian*. So F. *unitarien* a. and sb. Cf. UNITARY *a.*]

**A.** *sb.* **1.** *Theol.* One who affirms the unipersonality of the Godhead, especially as opposed to an orthodox Trinitarian; *spec.* a member or adherent of a Christian religious body or sect holding this doctrine.

Usually with initial capital.

**1687** [? S. NYE] *Brief Hist. Unitarians* 109 The Polonian Unitarians were.. zealous.., the Unitarians of Transylvania were more moderate. *Ibid.* 117 The Unitarians, vulgarly called Socinians. **1697** STILLINGFL. *Disc. Trinity* 22 Our Vnitarians own the Ebionites as their Predecessors. **1705** T. EMLYN *Vind. Worship Christ* 1/1 Mr. B. flatters himself upon this head, as tho he had quite baffled the Cause of the Unitarians. **1782** PRIESTLEY *Corrupt. Chr.* I. I. 8 Eusebius [had] prejudice against the unitarians of his own time. **1787** HAWKINS *Life Johnson* (ed. 2) 233 In his religious principles he [Dr. E. Barker] professed himself an unitarian. **1813** J. ADAMS *Wks.* (1856) X. 50 The dissenters of all denominations in England, and, especially, the Unitarians, are cowed. **1837** HT. MARTINEAU *Soc. Amer.* III. 279 The Unitarians, the religious body with which I am best acquainted. **1889** *Ch. Q. Rev.* April 35 We may roughly state these three conceptions [of Christianity] as (1) the Unitarian, which conceives of Christ as an exalted human teacher merely; (2) the Protestant,.. (3) the Catholic.

**b.** In wider use, as applied to any non-Christian monotheist, esp. a Mohammedan.

**1708** OCKLEY *Saracens* 227 Abu Obeidah sent Abdo'llah Ebn Kort with an Express to Omar.. begging his Prayers and some fresh Recruits of Vnitarians (a Title they glory in, reckoning themselves the only Asserters of the Unity of the Deity). **1788** GIBBON *Decl. & F.* lix. VI. 105 His preachers .. called aloud on the unitarians, manfully to stand up against the Christian idolaters. **1819** W. J. FOX *Lect.* iv. Wks. 1865 I. 211 Five different classes of Unitarians, who are out of the pale of Christianity. **1909** G. K. CHESTERTON *Orthodoxy* viii. 249 The real Unitarians who with scimitar in hand have laid waste the world.

**2.** One who believes in or favours some theory or system based upon unity: **a.** *Philos.* (See quot. and MONIST). *rare.*

**1836–7** SIR W. HAMILTON *Metaph.* xvi. (1859) I. 295 The Realists or Substantialists are again divided into Dualists, and into Unitarians or Monists, according as they are, or are not, contented with the testimony of consciousness to the ultimate duplicity of subject and object in perception.

**b.** In miscellaneous uses.

**1847** EMERSON *Poems, Blight* 27 The old men studied magic in the flower.. And an omnipotence in chemistry, Preferring things to names, for these were men, Were unitarians of the united world. **1865** MANSFIELD *Salts* 254 A compound, which even by the unitarians, must be called a double salt. **1904** *Brit. Med. Jrnl.* 10 Sept. 572 In this toxin-antitoxin discussion there has been a tendency to ascribe to us the position of 'unitarians' in contradistinction to the 'pluralists'.

**c.** An advocate of national or political unity; one who supports the union of several states into one confederation under a central government.

**1862** *Times* 9 April, Garibaldi.. said all great Italians had been unitarians. **1865** *Cornh. Mag.* Aug. 249 As a unitarian and partisan of centralization he hurled anathemas at all autonomous cities and provinces. **1882–3** in *Schaff's Encycl. Relig. Knowl.* III. 2422/2 There is also a political party in Buenos Ayres.. devoted to centralization in government, called Unitarians.

**B.** *adj.* **1.** *Theol.* Of or pertaining to, connected with, the Unitarians or their doctrines; of the nature of, characteristic of, Unitarianism.

**1687** [? S. NYE] *Brief Hist. Unitarians* 36 The Unitarian Doctrine has been reduced so low by the Persecutions of Rome [etc.]. **1691** W. NICHOLLS *Answ. Naked Gospel* 101 Whilst Faustus kept close in Italy, the Unitarian Cause was carried on by others. **1705** EMLYN (*title*), Vindication of the

Worship of the Lord Jesus Christ on Unitarian Principles. **1782** PRIESTLEY *Corrupt. Chr.* I. 1. 8 What could this be but the proper unitarian doctrine? **1819** M. STUART *Lett. to W. E. Channing* 144 The younger preachers of Unitarian sentiments. **1824** LONGF. in *Life* (1891) I. v. 52 Our little Unitarian Society at Bowdoin. **1889** *Ch. Q. Rev.* April 35 The Unitarian conception of our Lord's Person and Office.

**b.** Of persons: Accepting, professing, or advocating the doctrines of Unitarianism; belonging to a religious body or sect of Unitarians.

**1691** W. NICHOLLS *Answ. Naked Gospel* 96 The most remarkable of this sort of Unitarian Hereticks. ? **1765** [W. HOPKINS] *Attempt* (title-p.), A Friendly Dialogue between a common Unitarian Christian and an Athanasian. **1793** KIPPIS *Biog. Brit.* (ed. 2) V. 596 Dr. Bennet..laid himself open to the strictures both of Trinitarian and Unitarian Divines. **1815** W. J. FOX *Serm.* 38 The general character of Unitarian professors and converts. **1876** FOX BOURNE *Locke* II. xii. 240 Thomas Firmin..the excellent unitarian merchant.

**c.** In wider use (see A. 1 b).

**1780** WESLEY *Hymn*, '*Sun of unclouded righteousness*' iii, Stretch out thy arm, thou triune God, The Unitarian fiend expel, And chase his doctrine back to hell.

**2.** Of or pertaining to, involving, based or founded upon, characterized by, unity (in various senses); unitary: **a.** *Philos.* Monistic. *rare.*

**1836–7** SIR W. HAMILTON *Metaph.* xxiii. (1859) II. 78 He would..be forced to admit one or other of the unitarian conclusions of materialism or idealism.

**b.** Of systems, theories, etc.

**1845** LOWELL *Lett.* (1894) I. 102 My system is fully as unitarian as your own. **1875** *Encycl. Brit.* I. 460/2 These two theories, the one dualistic, the other unitarian, strangely foreshadow the discoveries of modern dynamics. **1893** *19th Cent.* Aug. 249 Under the unitarian system we no longer divide the molecule.

**c.** Advocating, promoting, or directed towards national unity, union, or centralization in government or administration.

**1865** *Morn. Star* 10 Feb., The King of Unitarian Italy. **1877** *Academy* 10 Nov. 1/1 The unitarian movement of twenty years later differed..from the revolution which enthroned the triumvirate at Rome.

**Unitarianism** (yūnitēᵊ·riăniz'm). [f. prec. + -ISM. So F. *unitarianisme.*]

**1.** *Theol.* Belief in or affirmation of the unity of God; esp. the tenets, principles, or views of the Unitarians; Unitarian doctrine or beliefs.

**1698** F. B. *Modest Censure* 22 The Missionary Fathers have not more ways..of gaining Converts in China,..than these men have of winning over people to Unitarianism. **1792** (*title*), Reasons for Unitarianism; or the Primitive Christian Doctrine...By a Welsh Freeholder. **1815** W. J. FOX *Serm.* 39 The success of Unitarianism speaks in its favour. **1874** HUXLEY in *Sci. & Cult.* (1881) 94 That hypothesis respecting the Divine nature which is termed Unitarianism by its friends and Socinianism by its foes. **1876** GLADSTONE in *Contemp. Rev.* June 17 Considerable changes seem to have taken place in the scheme of Unitarianism.

*transf.* **1823** COLERIDGE *Table-t.* 1 Jan., The Turks have no church; religion and state are one; hence there is..no mutual support. This is the very essence of their Unitarianism.

**2. a.** *Philos.* = MONISM 1. **b.** Any unitarian or unitary system or theory. **1891**– in recent Dicts.

**Unita·rianize**, *v.* [f. as prec. + -IZE.] **a.** *trans.* To make Unitarian. **b.** *intr.* To become Unitarian; to adopt Unitarianism. Hence **Unita·rianized** *ppl. a.*

**1846** WORCESTER (citing *Ec. Rev.*). **1893** J. MARTINEAU in *Life* (1902) II. 191 For its support it depends on a people long Unitarianised.

**U·nitarist.** [f. UNITAR-Y + -IST.] An advocate of a unitary system of government; *spec.* a supporter of the unity of Italy.

Also, in recent use (1910), *unitarism.*

**1862** *Parthenon* 26 July 398 Was Cavour, up to the time of the treaty of Villafranca, 'Unitarist' or Federalist? **1882** *Contemp. Rev.* Sept. 465 The Constitutional Monarchists of Italy are naturally Unitarists.

**Unitary** (yū·nitări), *a.* [f. UNIT *sb.* or UNIT-Y [1] + -ARY [1]. Cf. F. *unitaire* sb. and a., It. *unitario* sb., f. mod.L. *unitari-us* UNITARIAN.]

**1.** *Crystallography.* (See quot.)

**1816** R. JAMESON *Char. Min.* (ed. 2) 211 A crystal is named Unitary, when it experiences only a single decrement by one row.

**2.** Of or pertaining to, characterized by, based upon, or directed towards, unity.

**1847** *Tait's Mag.* XIV. 560 The parcelled and the associative systems...With the latter the economies of unitary habitation..might be obtained. **1871** LOWELL *Study Wind.* (1886) 221 The national and unitary tendencies of the people. **1893** *Contemp. Rev.* 799 The unitary movement in the latter country [*sc.* Italy].

**b.** *Philos.* Of or pertaining to, proceeding from, involving, unity of being or existence. Also *absol.*

*a* **1842** CHANNING *Perfect Life* (1888) 64 Man loves the Universal, the Unchangeable, the Unitary. **1885** J. MARTINEAU *Types Eth. Th.* I. 86 Every attempt at unitary deduction of a universe by predicamental logic. **1893** C. B. UPTON *Bases Relig. Belief* 298 A unity of substance which ..connects every part with the unitary life of the whole.

**3.** Of the nature of a unit; having the separate existence or individual character of a unit. Of sounds: Simple, uncompounded.

**1861** LOWELL *E Pluribus Unum* Pr. Wks. 1890 V. 49 The United States are not a German Confederation, but a unitary and indivisible nation. **1875** WHITNEY *Life Lang.* iv. 56 We have altered their original unitary sounds. **1881** HUXLEY in *Nature* XXIV. 345 An indivisible unitary archæus dominating..the parts of the organism.

**b.** *Philos.* Of being or personality.

**1865** J. GROTE *Explor. Philos.* I. 88 Whether..we are to be considered as having a locally distributable, or on the other hand concentrated and unitary, feeling self. **1886** *Encycl. Brit.* XXI. 379/1 Indirect proofs of a universe of pure and unitary Being. *a* **1901** F. W. H. MYERS *Human Personality* (1903) I. p. xxvi, Each man is at once profoundly unitary and almost infinitely composite.

**c.** Serving as a unit of measurement or calculation.

**1889** *Sci. Amer.* LX. 304/1 A wind pressure of 1,200 pounds for the same unitary distance is allowed for.

**4.** Of or pertaining to a unit or units; esp. in *Chem.*, and *spec.* as denominating a theory or system in which the molecules of all bodies are regarded as units.

**1865** MANSFIELD *Salts* 137 The unitary theory of the substitution of the two halves of the hydrogen of water. **1867** BLOXAM *Chem.* Index 675 Unitary definitions, 256. **1880** CLEMENSHAW *Wurtz' Atomic Theory* 84 This was at that time—perhaps improperly—called the unitary system.

**b.** Of an alphabet, etc.: Consisting or composed of single letters or symbols for each sound.

**1874** ELLIS *Eng. Pronunciation* IV. 1338 His 'unitary' arrangement. *Ibid.* 1339 Professor Whitney's Unitary Alphabet.

**c.** *Arith.* A modification of the 'rule of three,' by which, the value, extent, etc., of one unit being first determined, that of any number is found by multiplication.

**1877** J. HAMBLIN SMITH *Arithmetic* 164 The Unitary Method..is rapidly displacing the Rule of Three. **1908** HALL & STEVENS *School Arith.* 135 The process is known as Reduction to the Unit, or the Unitary Method.

**5.** Forming a unit *with* something.

**1868** LOWELL *Among my Bks.* Ser. I. Wks. 1890 III. 26 [Shakespeare] seems in some strange way unitary with human nature itself.

Hence **U·nitariness.**

**1865** J. GROTE *Moral Ideals* (1876) 27 [Must not] the plant ..have..a sort of feeling to the extent of its unitariness of organization? [Also, in recent use, *unitarily* adv.]

**Unite** (yū·nəit, yunəi·t), *sb. Numism.* Also **unit.** [f. pa. pple. of UNITE *v.* Cf. UNITY [2].

Named in allusion to the Union of the Crowns under James I, coins of the original issue bearing on the obverse the inscription *Faciam eos in gentem unam* (Ezek. xxxvii. 22). The β-form is prob. due to assimilation with UNIT *sb.*]

An English gold coin first issued by James I in 1604, originally current at the value of 20 shillings, and raised in 1611 to 22 shillings. Cf. BROAD *sb.* 4, BROAD-PIECE, and JACOBUS.

Different issues of this coin were denominated the *laurel* (LAUREL *sb.* 4) and the *sceptre* (SCEPTRE *sb.* 3) after the distinguishing feature of each, and these terms were also used attrib. with *unite.*

α. **1604** *Proclam. Coynes* 16 Nov., One piece of Gold of the value of Twentie shillings sterling, to be called The Vnite, stamped on the one side with our Picture formerly vsed, with this Stile [etc.]. **1611** *Proclam. Alteration Prices of Gold* 23 Nov., The piece of Gold called the Vnite [to be current] at xxij.s. **1612** R. RICART *Maire of Bristowe's Kal.* (Camden) 65 In which purse were 100 vnites of gould, amountinge to the summe of 110 [li]. **1726** S. M. LEAKE *Nummi Brit. Hist.* 90 A Pound weight of Crown Gold 22 Carracts fine, and two Carracts Allay into 41 l, by Tale, to wit, into Unites at 20 s. **1763** [see BROAD *sb.* 4]. **1898** GERTR. B. RAWLINGS *Story Brit. Coinage* 77 A triple unite was also coined, but at the Oxford mint only.

β. **1736** FOLKES *Gold Coins* 6, 2 Ja. 1. Sovereign or Units, vulgarly called Scepters. **1853** HUMPHREYS *Coin-Coll. Man.* II. 471 The principal gold coins in the early part of the reign [of Charles I] were—the unit, or broad-piece (20 shillings), with its half and quarter.

†**b.** As the name proposed for certain silver coins (see quots.). *Obs.*

**1691** LOCKE *Lower. Interest* Wks. 1714 II. 79 He proposes that his Silver Vnite..should go for 75 Pence. **1695** LOWNDES *Rep. Ess. Amend. Silver Coins* 62 One Piece which may be called the Sceptre or the Silver-Unite.

†**Unite**, *pa. pple.* and *ppl. a. Obs.* [ad. late L. *ūnīt-us* (whence also It. *unito*, Sp. and Pg. *unido*, F. *uni*), pa. pple. of L. *ūnīre*: see the vb.] Combined or formed into one; conjoint, united. (Latterly *Sc.*)

**1422** YONGE tr. *Secreta Secret.* 143 By lewte and trowthe and feyth the Pepill byth vnyette [*sic*], Citteis fulfillid, and mayntenyd lordshuppis. **1460** *Rolls of Parlt.* V. 381/2 Londes and Tenementes..that were unyte or annexed to the same Duchie. **1542** HEN. VIII *Declar. Scots* in *Compl. Scot.* 199 Two or mo of one astate might be rulers in one countrie vnite as this Isle is. *a* **1548** HALL *Chron., Hen. IV*, 2 By the whiche mariage..the redde Rose was vnite and joyned with the white Rose. **1605** *Play of Stucley* 1508 in Simpson *Sch. Shaks.* (1878) I. 219 That Spain and Portingale shall be unite. **1647** H. MORE *Song of Soul* II. App. lxxxiii, A cluster of small starres unite These Meteors some do deem. **1693** STAIR *Inst.* II. ii. § 18. 201 When Lands are rightly Unite or Erected in Barronies. **1721** WODROW *Corr.* (1843) II. 595 The body of the ministers are joint and unite.

**b.** In attributive use.

**1613** HEYWOOD *Silver Age* III. i, My charm, Which gods and devils gave unite consent To be infract. **1632** LITHGOW *Trav.* IV. 133 [He] reduced all the Empire of Greece, to a vnite tranquilitie. **1675** R. FLEMING *Short Acc. Doctr. Rom. Ch.* 2 A continual visibility of the Church, as an unite body.

**Unite** (yunəi·t), *v.* Also 5–6 unyte. [f. *ūnīt-*, ppl. stem of post-Aug. L. *ūnīre*, to join together, make one, f. *ūnus* one. Cf. UNE *v.*, UNY *v.*]

**1.** *trans.* To combine or join (one or more things) *to* or *with* another or others, to bring or put together (separate or divided things), so as to form one connected or contiguous whole; to form or incorporate into one body or mass; to make or cause to be one: **a.** In non-physical connexion or union.

In early examples used as pa. t. and pa. pple. active without final -*d*: cf. prec.

**1432–50** tr. *Higden* (Rolls) VI. 289 Egberte prevaylynge in that batelle, unyte to his realme the realmes of the marches. **1513** DOUGLAS *Æneis* x. Prol. 26 Set our natur God hes to hym vnyte. **1560** DAUS tr. *Sleidane's Comm.* 16 That he take no counsel to vnite Thempire to his house and posteritie. *c* **1630** MILTON *At a Solemn Music* 27 Till God ere long To his celestial consort us unite, To live with him. **1651** HOBBES *Leviath.* II. xix. 96 Where the publique and private interest are most closely united. **1728** CHAMBERS *Cycl.* s.v. *General*, By retaining only those Qualities, and uniting them into one Idea, they have another, more general Idea. **1781** GIBBON *Decl. & F.* xxviii. III. 73 A wealthy and noble senator, who united the sacred characters of pontiff and augur, with the civil dignities of proconsul of Africa. **1825** SCOTT *Betrothed* xix, Before the *fiançailles* had united his troth with that of Eveline Berenger. **1839** MURCHISON *Silur. Syst.* I. xxvi. 333, I attribute the discrepancy to my having united observations made on both flanks of the river. **1882** MRS. PITMAN *Mission L. Greece & Pal.* 174 The strongest wish of the Cretans is that they should be united to Greece.

*absol.* **1713** BLACKMORE *Creation* VII. 273 The mind..does distinguish here, and there unite.

*refl.* **1818** SCOTT *Hrt. Midl.* xviii, Here our story unites itself with that part of the narrative which [etc.].

**b.** In physical connexion or union.

In quot. 1602 in figurative context.

**1597** SHAKS. 2 *Hen. IV*, IV. i. 222 Our Peace will (like a broken Limbe vnited) Grow stronger. **1602** MARSTON *Antonio's Rev.* V. i, Be gratious, observation, to our sceane, For now the plot unites his scattred limbes. *a* **1700** EVELYN *Diary* 23 May 1645, The whole Chapell..and roofe are full of precious stones united with the mouldings. **1738** GRAY *Tasso* 61 The parent sun's warm powers..In one rich mass unite the precious store. **1788** SIR J. REYNOLDS *Disc.* (1789) 22 Much smoothness, and uniting the colours, is apt to produce heaviness. **1800** tr. *Lagrange's Chem.* II. 46 A salt which crystallizes in small needles united together. **1846** BRITTAN tr. *Malgaigne's Man. Oper. Surg.* 244 Sanson made his incision..,and united the wound from before backwards. **1867** PITT-RIVERS *Evol. Culture* (1906) 67 A..breast-piece of armour..composed of seals' teeth, set like scales, and united with string.

*refl.* **1788** LEMPRIÈRE *Classical Dict.* s.v. *Cælus*, Saturn.. deprived his father of the organs of generation, as he was going to unite himself to Terra.

**c.** To combine or amalgamate into one body; to bring together or consolidate (an army).

**1591** SHAKS. 1 *Hen. VI*, IV. i. 164 Vnite Your Troopes of horsemen, with his Bands of foote. **1599** HAKLUYT *Voy.* II. 69 The English and French, with forces and mindes vnited, sayled ouer into Africa. **1647** CLARENDON *Hist. Reb.* VIII. § 153 All those forces..being united with Manchester. *Ibid.*, The King..not believing that the enemy could be so soon united. **1802** JAMES *Milit. Dict.* s.v. *Battle*, You should unite all your force, examine the advantage of the ground [etc.]. **1840** THIRLWALL *Greece* VII. 369 [If] the forces of Greece..had been united and well directed.

**d.** To join or clasp (hands), esp. in the marriage ceremony. (Cf. 2 b.)

**1602** SHAKS. *Ham.* III. ii. 170 Since..Hymen did our hands Vnite comutuall, in most sacred Bands. **1817** SHELLEY *Rev. Islam* V. xlviii, Now unite Thine hand with mine. **1820** SCOTT *Monast.* xxxvii, A house of the village, where next day their hands were united by the Protestant preacher.

**e.** *Horsem.* To cause (a horse) to move with the hind- and fore-quarters in union or agreement. (Cf. 5 d, UNION *sb.*[1] 2 c, and F. *unir.*)

**1884** E. L. ANDERSON *Mod. Horsem.* 110 To unite a horse at a walk, the rider will press his legs against the sides of the animal, and, carrying back the forces of the forehand, prevent an increase of the speed by a corresponding operation of the hand.

**2.** To make one in feeling or thought; to cause to agree; to combine or join (persons) together in action or interest, or for some special purpose.

**1547** J. HARRISON *Exhort. Scottes* hiv b, Remember (I besech you..) how that by this calling of vs into this vnitie, ..he woulde also vnite & ioyne vs in one religion. **1565** COOPER *Thesaurus* s.v. *Vnitas, In vnitatem venire*, Plin., to be vnited:..to be no more at variance. **1593** SHAKS. 2 *Hen. VI*, I. i. 23 If Simpathy of Loue vnite our thoughts. **1599** [see 1 c]. **1647** CLARENDON *Hist. Reb.* VIII. § 84 A general who might unite all those northern counties in his service. **1649** *Nicholas Papers* (Camden) 155 The meanes to unite the heartes of all the sober Royalysts. **1709** PRIDEAUX *Lett.* (Camden) 202 His interest with the northern protestants may be of great use to unite them with the Church of England. **1791** COWPER *Odyss.* XXIV. 567 Let mutual amity..Unite them, and let wealth and peace abound. **1817** SHELLEY *Rev. Islam* XII. xxiii, The fond and long embrace which did their hearts unite. **1857** BUCKLE *Civiliz.* I. xii. 661 Men of all tastes..were on this point united as by a common bond.

*refl.* **1594** HOOKER *Eccl. Pol.* I. x. § 1 This was the cause of mens vniting themselues at the first in politique societies. **1648** MILTON *Ps.* lxxxiii. 19 Themselves against thee they unite And in firm union bind. **1706** PHILLIPS (ed. Kersey) s.v. *Province*, Provinces..that made a firm Alliance,..by which they united themselves, so as never to be divided.

**b.** To join (persons) in marriage. Also *refl.*

**1728** CHAMBERS *Cycl.*, *Marriage*, a..Contract, by which a Man is join'd and united to a Woman. **1871** R. ELLIS tr. *Catullus* lxiv. 21 Then did a father agree Peleus with Thetis unite him. **1882** MISS BRADDON *Mt. Royal* II. vi. 119 She wants to see the two people she loves best on earth united.

**3.** Of persons (or things): To have, possess, or

exhibit (qualities, etc.) in union or combination; to combine (features usually regarded as distinct).

**1796** H. HUNTER tr. *St.-Pierre's Stud. Nat.* I. 52 We shall seek that [specific character] of each plant..in it's grain, which, as being the principle, must unite every thing proper for it's expansion. **1798** FERRIAR *Illustr. Sterne*, etc. ii. 38 A specimen of D'Aubigné's style, which unites the severe and the ludicrous. **1824** *Encycl. Brit. Suppl.* II. 111/1 Uniting in himself all the vices of..a Barbary despot. **1864** BRYCE *Holy Rom. Emp.* xii. (1875) 195 The Emperor..was also the East Frankish King, uniting in himself, to use the legal phrase, two wholly distinct 'persons'. **1871** FREEMAN *Norm. Conq.* xviii. IV. 143 The sons of Ealdgyth united the blood of the two greatest houses in England.

**4.** *intr.* Of persons, personifications, states, etc.: To enter into association, alliance, combination, or union; to join together or *with* others for some common purpose; to combine *in* some action or *to* do something; to act in concert or agreement.

**1613** SHAKS. *Hen. VIII*, III. ii. 1 If you will now vnite in your Complaints,..the Cardinall Cannot stand vnder them. **1670** CLARENDON *Hist. Reb.* XIII. § 58 The Presbyterians of Lancashire..nobody imagined to be..unwilling to unite and join with the royal party. **1749** FIELDING *Tom Jones* VIII. xiv, All united at last, to drive out that king. **1787** WASHINGTON *Lett.* Writ. 1891 XI. 183 Is it best for the States to unite or not to unite? **1847** MRS. A. KERR tr. *Ranke's Hist. Servia* 22 Now it was necessary that all should unite in direct conflict against a common enemy. **1890** *Retrospect Med.* CII. 343 Teachers and text-books have all united in impressing upon us the necessity of the greatest care in handling tar.

**b.** Of hearts or minds: To become one in feeling or sentiment. *poet.* or *rhet.*

**1766** FORDYCE *Serm. Yng. Wom.* (1767) II. x. 101 With mind only can mind unite. **1781** COWPER *Ep. Lady Austen* 32 When minds, that never met before, Shall meet, unite, and part no more. **1817** SHELLEY *Rev. Islam* VI. xxxix, Few were the living hearts which could unite Like ours.

**c.** To join in marriage *with* another.

**1755** JOHNSON, *To Join*, v.n.,..to unite with in marriage. **1866–7** BARING-GOULD *Curious Myths* (1872) 216 A man.. unites with a woman of the underground race.

**5.** To form one material whole or body; to become one; to be joined together, or *to* or *with* others; to combine physically; to coalesce; *spec.* in *Chem.*, to combine by chemical affinity or attraction.

**1667** MILTON *P.L.* XII. 382 From my Loynes Thou shalt proceed, and from thy Womb the Son Of God most High; So God with man unites. **1690** LOCKE *Hum. Und.* II. xxiii. § 26 Let but a sharp cold come, and they unite, they consolidate, these little atoms cohere. **1716** POPE *Iliad* V. 375 Where to the hip the inserted thigh unites. **1794** R. P. KNIGHT *Landscape* I. 194 To lead..the prying sight To where component parts may best unite. **1826** S. COOPER *First Lines Surg.* (ed. 5) 292 When not too severely contused, they will be found to live and unite to the surrounding parts. **1835** J. DUNCAN *Beetles* (Nat. Lib.) 213 There are two broad stripes..on each wing-case, which unite behind. **1871** A. MEADOWS *Man. Midwifery* (ed. 2) 54 The tubes.. sometimes remaining throughout single, but at other times dividing and uniting again.

(*b*) **1800** tr. *Lagrange's Chem.* I. 303 They form together a triple salt,..which proves that they exercise a reciprocal attraction, in virtue of which they unite. **1807** T. THOMSON *Chem.* (ed. 3) II. 103 In this way it [water] unites to lime. **1867** BLOXAM *Chem.* 1 Chemical attraction is the force which causes different kinds of matter to unite, in order to form a new kind of matter.

**b.** Of naval or military forces, etc.: To form one combined or conjoint body.

*a* **1700** EVELYN *Diary* 5 May 1692, The Eastern wind so constantly blowing, gave our fleete time to unite. **1748** *Anson's Voy.* I. vii. 75 The time drew near, when the squadron would be separated never to unite again.

**c.** Of immaterial things or in non-physical connexion.

**1795** in Cruise *Digest* (1818) III. 228 Their heirship is *unitas juris*: the whole body of the coheirs, however numerous, must unite to constitute the heir. **1809** COLERIDGE *Friend* 142 The nature of the Earth and the nature of the Mind unite to make the contrary impossible. **1822** BYRON *Vis. Judgem.* lxvi, The next world; where unite All the costumes since Adam's.

**d.** *Horsem.* (See quot. and cf. 1 e above.)

**1753** *Chambers' Cycl.* Suppl. s.v., A horse is said to *unite*, or walk in union, when, in galloping, the hind quarters follow and keep time with the fore.

**Uni·ted,** *ppl. a.* [f. prec.]

**1.** Put or joined together; combined, connected, made one. (Cf. also sense 4.)

**1552** HULOET, Vnited, *vnitus*. **1663** BP. PATRICK *Parab. Pilgr.* xiii, They will teach those united hearts the greatest Love. **1671** MILTON *Samson* 1110 [They] durst not with their whole united powers In fight withstand me. **1706** PRIOR *Ode to Queen* xiii, Unmov'd the Two united Chiefs abide. **1796** WITHERING *Brit. Plants* (ed. 3) I. 340 Anthers 5, narrow, united. **1804** *Gazetteer Scot.* (1806) 541 The united streams of the Dochart and Lochy. **1839** T. MITCHELL *Frogs of Aristoph.* p. xcviii, A poem at least of equal length with the Iliad and Odyssey united. **1865–6** CAYLEY *Math. Papers* (1893) VI. 9 If two points of a unicursal curve have an $(\alpha, \alpha')$ correspondence, the number of united points is $= \alpha + \alpha'$.

**2.** Of, belonging to, or produced by two or more persons, agents, or things in union or combination; conjoint, joint.

*a* **1586** SIDNEY *Arcadia* II. xxvi, Their united rage was now growne..to a crossing one of another. **1647** CLARENDON *Hist. Reb.* VIII. § 235 They could not..support the war any longer against the united power of the rebels. **1697** DRYDEN *Virg., Georg.* IV. 242 All, with united Force, combine to drive The lazy Drones from the laborious Hive. **1797** MRS. RADCLIFFE *Italian* ix, With sudden strength, he burst from their united hold. **1820** R. PEEL in *Croker Papers* (1884) I. 177 The united voice of King, Lords, and Commons. **1847** MRS. A. KERR tr. *Ranke's Hist. Servia* 257 The united consent of all Europe would have been the most desirable. **1856** KANE *Arct. Expl.* I. xxiii. 300 Our united estimate assigned to it an elevation of from 2500 to 3000 feet. **1871** JOWETT *Plato* II. 174 Incapable of united action by reason of sedition.

**b.** Constituted or formed by, resulting from, the union of two or more parts or sections.

Freq. in the titles of churches, societies, etc., formed by the union or reunion of bodies or sections which had seceded or were formerly separate, e.g. United Free Church of Scotland, United Methodist Free Church, United Secession Church: cf. 4.

**1697** DRYDEN *Æneis* IV. 145 One common kingdom, one united line. **1833** JAS. DAVIDSON *Brit. & Rom. Rem. Axminster* 25 Where, forming a junction with its fellow ['trackway'], the united road leads through the town. **1835** [T. JACKSON] *Man. Sects & Heresies* 112 In 1829 the two bodies were rejoined under the name of the United Secession Church. **1847** MRS. A. KERR tr. *Ranke's Hist. Servia* 284 The united army took up its position close by the mouths of the Morawa.

**c.** *Bot.* Of a flower (see quot. 1829).

**1807** J. E. SMITH *Phys. Bot.* 396 In this genus the Pistil of the united flower scarcely produces seed. **1829** T. CASTLE *Introd. Bot.* 92 When the stamens and pistils are both, as usual, in one flower, it is called perfect or united.

**d.** *Horsem.* (See UNITE *v.* 1 e and 5 d.)

**1884** E. L. ANDERSON *Mod. Horsem.* 139 When the horse will continue the united trot without the aid of the reins. *Ibid.*, The horse will be practised in keeping the united form at the walk.

†**3.** Forming or conferring union. *Obs.*[−1]

**1598** SHAKS. *Merry W.* IV. vi. 51 That you'l procure the Vicar To stay for me at Church...And in the lawfull name of marrying, To giue our hearts vnited ceremony.

**4.** Special collocations in the names of states, corporate bodies, or persons allied, associated, or joined together in a union or confederation.

*United Brethren*, the Moravians. *United Colonies*, † (*a*) the four colonies which formed the New England Confederation (see CONFEDERATION 2); (*b*) the thirteen North American colonies which revolted against Great Britain and formed the original Republic of N. America (see UNION *sb.*[1] 3 c and 7 c, and cf. UNITED STATES 1 *b*). *United Greek*, a member of the United Greek Church (see quot. 1863), a Uniat. *United Irishman*, a member of the Society of United Irishmen, a political association, originally formed to promote union between Protestants and Catholics, which became a separatist secret society and took part in organizing the rebellion of 1798. *United Presbyterian*: (see PRESBYTERIAN *a.* 1 c). *United Provinces*, the seven northern provinces of the Netherlands, allied together principally by the Union of Utrecht in 1579, and subsequently developing into the kingdom of Holland (cf. UNITED STATES 1 a).

**1586** *Acts Privy Counc.* (N. S.) 190 The knowen subjectes ..of the Unyted Provinces. **1617** MORYSON *Itin.* III. 92 The States of the vnited Provinces. **1643** in Winthrop *New Eng.* (1826) II. 101 They..do..conclude that they all be..called by the name of the United Colonies of New England. **1677** W. HUBBARD *Narrative* (1865) II. 252 The Commissioners of our United Colonyes. **1702** C. MATHER *Magnalia* IV. iv. 177 It had not been so long before the Names of Presbyterian and Congregational, had been melted down into that One of United Brethren. **1775** *Pennsylv. Even. Post* 21 Dec. 587/1 Captain Coit, in an armed schooner of the United Colonies, lately chased a transport. **1777** R. WATSON *Philip II*, XXIV. II. 406 Although this event gave great satisfaction to the people subject to the Spanish government, it was not likely to produce any change in the sentiments, or conduct of their neighbours in the United Provinces. **1791** in W. Tone *Autobiog.* (1826) I. 368 We have agreed to form an association to be called 'The Society of United Irishmen'. **1799** J. ADAMS *Wks.* (1854) IX. 4 He is doubtless a United Irishman. **1837** LOVER *Rory O'More* I. x. 214 An extended palm which..exchanged with him the grip of the United Irishman. **1849** ROCK *Ch. of Fathers* I. ii. I. 90 The United or orthodox Greeks. **1863** *Chambers' Encycl.* V. 88/1 The United Greek Church comprehends those Christians who, while they..observe the general discipline of the Greek Church,..are yet united with the Church of Rome. *Ibid.*, The United Greeks.

**b. United Kingdom**, the kingdom of Great Britain, or esp. (after the union with Ireland in 1801) of Great Britain and Ireland. Abbrev. *U.K.*

**1737** *Gentl. Mag.* VII. 609/1, I have more Reason to oppose it, than any Man in this House, by perhaps than any Man in the United Kingdom. **1800** *Act* 39 & 40 *Geo. III*, c. 67. 359 The said Kingdoms of Great Britain and Ireland shall.. be united into one Kingdom, by the name of The United Kingdom of Great Britain and Ireland. **1832** *Act* 2 & 3 *Will. IV*, c. 75 § 1 That part of the United Kingdom called Great Britain, and..that part of the United Kingdom called Ireland.

**c.** *United Irishism*, the views or principles of the United Irishmen.

**1800** W. DRENNAN in *Microscope* March 134 He fears that political and religious schism, that White-Boyism,.. Catholicism, United-Irishism may..change into Patriotism. **1844** P. HARWOOD *Hist. Irish Reb.* 120 Munster was..the only province of Ireland not deeply leavened with Defenderism or United Irishism.

**Uni·tedly,** *adv.* [f. UNITED *ppl. a.* + -LY[2].] In a united manner; so as to be united; in union or combination, together; with agreement or concurrence of thought or action on the part of several.

**1603** FLORIO *Montaigne* I. xxvii. 93 Our mindes haue jumped so vnitedly together. **1641** LD. DIGBY *Parl. Sp.* 9 Feb. 7 All the Vertue of this House, how unitedly soever collected. **1697** *State Philadelph. Soc.* 8 Though they meet..to implore the good Spirit of God Unitedly. **1762** tr. *Busching's Syst. Geog.* V. 491 Both unitedly pay eighty-six rixdollars. **1788** *Trifler* No. 16. 214 The various pleasures and inconveniences of which..we had unitedly participated. **1835** *Fraser's Mag.* XI. 494 Our possession of power, and our belief in the truth of our own religious professions, cannot, even when taken unitedly, justify us. **1865** PUSEY *Truth Eng. Ch.* 6 To resist unitedly an inroad upon our common faith.

**Uni·tedness.** [f. as prec. + -NESS.] The state or quality of being united; union.

**1636** DRUMM. OF HAWTH. *Fam. Ep.* Wks. (1711) 151 So harmonious an Unitedness, as hath so long continued between us. **1652** BENLOWES *Theoph.* VIII. xlv, Be ever-ever-ever blest, ô Trine! Ever Unitednesse divine! **1679** KING in *Spirit of Popery* 37 Harmony and Unitedness in things. **1864** PUSEY *Lect. Daniel* viii. 498 The assurance of a deathless unbroken unitedness with God. **1894** G. GRIFFITH tr. *Fouard's St. Paul* xii. 296 An act of thanksgiving for the spirit of unitedness now restored among them.

**United States.**

**1.** The proper name or distinctive title of a confederacy, federation, or union of States.

In later use freq. construed as a singular.

**a.** The kingdom or republic of Holland, = the United Provinces (UNITED *ppl. a.* 4). Also *attrib.* Now *rare* or *Hist.*

**1617** MORYSON *Itin.* III. 94 The Territory of Utrecht is also associated under the same United States. *c* **1622** FLETCHER & MASSINGER *Barnavelt* V. iii, in Bullen *O. Pl.* II. 306 Do you hold the United States so tame to feare him? **1665** MANLEY *Grotius' Low C. Wars* 929 By the publick and private colloquies of the United States people. **1779** HERVEY *Nav. Hist.* II. 168 The United States, overwhelmed with the expence of the war,..were extremely desirous of an accommodation.

**b.** The Republic of North America. Abbrev. *U.S.* or *U.S.A.* (Cf. STATE *sb.* 31 c, d, and *United Colonies* UNITED *ppl. a.* 4 a.)

**1781** J. ADAMS *Fam. Lett.* (1876) 403 You will never have peace while the Britons have a company of soldiers at liberty within the United States. **1781–8** in Bryce *Amer. Commw.* (1888) I. 569 The style of this Confederacy shall be, 'The United States of America'. **1812** EARL OF LIVERPOOL in *Examiner* 11 May 292/2 The United States had assumed a very warlike attitude. *a* **1817** T. DWIGHT *Trav. New Eng.*, etc. (1821) I. 18 The United States have been regarded by this class of men as fair game. **1888** *Encycl. Brit.* XXIII. 759/1 The United States..was anxious to establish what Great Britain was not disposed to grant.

*attrib.* **1840** (*title*), United States Digest. **1843** *Penny Cycl.* XXVI. 13/2 The officers of the United States navy. **1875** JEVONS *Money* xix. 246 The United States government.

**c.** In other applications (see quots.).

**1864** *Chambers's Encycl.* VI. 734 New Granada (since 1858 the official designation has been The Granadian Confederation, and since 1862, The United States of Colombia). **1890** *Hazell's Annual* 64/2 That the provinces of Brazil, united by federation, compose the United States of Brazil.

**2.** The form of English spoken in the United States of North America or regarded as distinctly American. *To talk United States*, to use strong language, to express oneself forcibly.

**1891** E. ROPER *Track & Trail* ix. 134 Most of the ladies spoke decided 'United States'; one was 'Dutch',..and one..had a decided British accent. **1898** HAMBLEN *Gen. Manager's Story* x. 134 If he made any disparaging comments..I vowed to myself that I'd talk United States to him if I lost my job by it.

Hence **United-Sta·tesian** *a.*, of or belonging to the United States of America; *sb.*, an inhabitant or citizen of the United States.

Also *United Statesman* (1850), and, in recent use, *United Stateser*.

**1892** *N. & Q.* 8th Ser. II. 146/2 To an outsider, say a Frenchman or a United-Statesian. **1897** *Westm. Gaz.* 26 Aug. 3/3 The secret of the American or rather United-Statesian race.

†**Uni·tely,** *adv. Obs.* [f. UNITE *ppl. a.* + -LY[2].] Unitedly.

**1602** LD. MOUNTJOY *Let.* in Moryson *Itin.* (1617) II. 213 The Lyst of the Forces here in Ireland, being vnitely considered. **1614** CORNWALLIS in Gutch *Coll. Cur.* I. 164 That we might all unitely..cast ourselves at his Majesty's feet. **1677** GALE *Crt. Gentiles* IV. 247 Unitie..hath all numbers in it singularly and unitely.

†**Uni·tement.** *Obs.*[−1] [f. UNITE *v.* + -MENT.] The fact or condition of being united; union.

**1631–2** N. FERRAR *Story Bks. Little Gidding* (1899) 169 The hope of better serving God and the firmer unitiment [*sic*] unto him.

†**Uni·teness.** *Obs.* [f. as prec. + -NESS.] Unitedness.

**1639** LD. DIGBY, etc. *Lett. conc. Relig.* (1651) 132 Conformity and uniteness of minde. **1684** J. RENWICK in *Biogr. Presbyt.* (1827) II. 261 The Uniteness of my Heart unto you.

**Uniter** (yunəi·təɪ). [f. UNITE *v.* + -ER[1]. Cf. UNITOR and It. *unitore*.] One who or that which unites; a uniting agency or quality.

**1587** GOLDING *De Mornay* vi. 79 The Vniter, and the thing Vnited. **1605** BACON *Adv. Learn.* I. vii. § 1 Uniters of states and cities. **1633** T. ADAMS *Exp. 2 Peter* i. 7 Friendship is a great uniter. **1700** J. BROME *Trav. Eng.* 199 James..became the Happy Uniter of the two Crowns. **1724** SWIFT *Drapier's Lett.* iv, Money..hath..been the great uniter of a most divided people. **1746** HERVEY *Medit. Flower Garden* 29 The Ocean is the grand Vehicle of Trade, and the Uniter of distant Nations. **1840** CARLYLE *Heroes* iv, The Priest..presides over the worship of the people; is the Uniter of them with the Unseen Holy. **1852** LYNCH *Lett. Scattered* (1872) 299 How could we love God the bereaver, if He were not the uniter also?

†**Uni·terable,** *a. Obs.*[−1] [UN-[1] 7 b.] That cannot be repeated. **1682** SIR T. BROWNE *Chr. Mor.* III. § 23 To play away an uniterable life.

**Uniting** (yunəi·tiŋ), *vbl. sb.* [f. UNITE *v.* + -ING[1].] The action of the verb; union; an instance or occasion of this.

**1548** ELYOT, *Vnitas*, vnitee, vnityng or ioygnyng of two thynges or mo together. **1559** *Fabyan's Chron.* 567/2 The vnitinge of the twoo houses of Yorke and Lancaster. **1581** T. ROGERS *St. Aug. Praiers* xvi. (1597) 66 That vnspeakable ..vniting togither of thy Godhead and manhood in one person. **1615** CROOKE *Body of Man* 379 These vnitings are not alwayes after one manner. **1651** HOBBES *Leviath.* II. xxii. 122 All uniting of strength by private men. **1712** J. JAMES tr. *Le Blond's Gardening* 172 Cavities or Stones.. hinders their uniting with the Ground. **1778** in Picton *L'pool Munic. Rec.* (1886) II. 211 A Bill..for the uniting the kingdom of Ireland with this kingdom. **1841** LANE *Arab. Nts.* I. 125 The uniting of two persons in marriage.

*attrib.* **1713** BERKELEY in *Guardian* 5 Aug., That benevolent uniting instinct implanted in human nature. **1714** in *Jrnl. Friends Hist. Soc.* (1918) 29 Truth..broke through for our..comfort, soe 'twas an Uniting time.

**b.** The place where two or more things unite or join. *rare*⁻¹.

**1728** R. MORRIS *Ess. Anc. Archit.* 81 The Joint is..apt to discover the Grains of each Wood at the uniting.

**Uni·ting,** *ppl. a.* [f. as prec.] That unites or joins.

*a* **1635** SIBBES *Confer. Christ & Mary* (1656) 92 That Spirit of God..is a uniting spirit. *a* **1653** BINNING *Serm.* Wks. (1735) 11/2 Christ is the uniting Principle. **1713** BLACKMORE *Creation* VI. 420 The sportive flood..with uniting tides.. wanton clasps the intercepted soil. **1817** SHELLEY *Rev. Islam* II. xlvi, Then..shall all the kinds Of evil, catch from our uniting minds The spark which must consume them. **1826** HENRY *Elem. Chem.* I. 192 When the uniting wire was perpendicularly opposite to the north pole of the suspended needle. **1895** *Athenæum* 6 July 8/3 A book of impressions without any uniting idea.

Hence **Uni·tingly** *adv.*

**1728** R. MORRIS *Ess. Anc. Archit.* p. iv, Inroads daily made..unitingly conspire, to destroy..its Beauties.

**Unition** (yuni·ʃən). Also 6 unycion. [ad. late L. *ūnitiōn-*, *ūnitio*, n. of action f. L. *ūnīre*: see UNITE *v.* Cf. OF. *unition, unicion*, It. *unizione.*] The action of uniting; the fact or condition of being united; union, conjunction, junction.

†**a.** Of ecclesiastical benefices. *Obs.*

**1511–2** *Act* 3 *Hen. VIII*, c. 17 § 14 The appropriacion, unycion, or consolidacione of the same Patronage..to the seid Abbot & Convent. **1564** PARKER *Corr.* (Parker Soc.) 214 This is to require you, if upon the understanding of the matter ye shall see cause to give out such an unition [of a benefice and a chapel], to grant it. **1587** HARRISON *England* II. i. (1877) I. 21 The vnition of two [livings] in one man.

†**b.** Of material substances or bodies. *Obs.*

**1543** TRAHERON *Vigo's Chirurg.* III. i. vi. 93 The curation.. is accomplisshed..by vnition, or coniunction of seperated or soundred partes. **1587** HARRISON *Desc. Brit.* in Holinshed *Chron.* I. 78/1 After whose vnition with the aforesaid water, they run on as one till they meet with the Clothie. **1613** M. RIDLEY *Magn. Bodies* 78 To cause these Magneticall bodies to..turne away, to the end that they may better.. dispose themselues to a conuenient and naturall vnition. *c* **1644** W. CHAMBERLAYNE *Pharon.* II. iii. 255 Death's large gripe did take Whole troops..,and in 's march prevents The unition of unrallied regiments. **1699** *Phil. Trans.* XXI. 140 This Unition of Bones at their articulations. **1738** BRACKEN *Farriery Impr.* (1757) II. 244 Motion hinders Unition in Wounds.

**c.** Of abstract things, persons, etc., in non-physical or ideal union.

**1584** *Leycesters Commonw.* 24 By this breach wyth Fraunce, we stand alone..wythout anie great vnition or friendship abrode. **1629** H. BURTON *Truth's Triumph* 106 That is the most singular..vnity, which consists not by vnition, but existeth by eternity. *a* **1680** GLANVILL *Sadducismus* I. (1681) 174 The unition of Spirit with Matter. **1709** T. ROBINSON *Vind. Mosaick Syst.* 21 The Seminal Forms being by a vital Unition conjoined to their Material Vehicles or Bodies. **1733** WATTS *Philos. Ess.* III. (1734) 85 The Union or rather Unition of a particular Soul and particular Body. **1816** [see UNICITY]. **1871** W. H. GILLESPIE *Argt. Being & Attrib. God* IV. iii. (ed. 5) 159 The attributes, whose unition yields us this Holiness. **1873** B. GREGORY *Holy Catholic Ch.* xvi. 187 The ultimate unition and universal inclusiveness of the Church.

**d.** Of man and (*to* or *with*) the Deity. Now *rare.* Sometimes distinguished from *union* (see quot. 1681).

**1635** JACKSON *Creed* VIII. 79 This part of the nature wounded..was first to bee perfectly cured, and throughly purified by personall unition to the Sonne of God. **1681** FLAVEL *Method of Grace* v. 94 There must be an unition before there can be a union with Christ. Union is to be conceived efficiently as the work of God's spirit, joyning the believer to Christ; and union is to be conceived formally, the joyning itself of the persons together. **1782** J. BROWN *Nat. & Rev. Relig.* III. ii. 232 Christ..signified his unition of his people into one mystical body with himself. **1784** — *Hist. Brit. Ch.* (1823) I. 343 Their regeneration and spiritual unition to him. **1845** BAILEY *Festus* (ed. 2) 323 The summit-flower of all created life Is its unition with Divinity.

**U·nitism.** *rare*⁻¹. [f. UNIT *sb.* + -ISM.] = MONISM 1 b.

**1850** W. SMITH *Conf. Faith* I. in *Thorndale* (1857) 488 He [*sc.* Seckendorf] would coin the term *Unitism* as a simple opposite to the generally received *Dualism*.

**Uniti·stic,** *a.* [f. UNITY: see -IST and -IC.] Of or pertaining to, believing in, a theory of unity.

**1888** T. K. CHEYNE in *Jewish Q. Rev.* Oct. 77 A unitistic critic. *Ibid.* 82 From a decided separatist [he] became as decided a maintainer of the unitistic view of the Book of Zechariah.

**Unitive** (yū·nitiv), *a.* [ad. late L. *ūnītīv-us* (Quicherat), f. L. *ūnit-*, ppl. stem of *ūnīre*: see UNITE *v.* and -IVE. Cf. F. *unitive, -if* (15th c.), Sp., Pg., and It. *unitivo.*]

**1.** Having the property or effect of uniting; serving to unite or cause union; characterized by or involving union.

Freq. *c* 1643–*c* 1670, esp. in the writings of H. More.

**1526** *Pilgr. Perf.* (W. de W. 1531) 285 b, For loue..is unityue, that is to saye, it disposeth and draweth all thynges that it ruleth, to peace & vnite. **1647** H. MORE *Song of Soul* Notes 136/2 The unitive power of the Intellect. **1660** JER. TAYLOR *Ductor* II. i. rule i. § 33 That all laws which are commonly called Natural are most reasonable, they are perfective of Nature, unitive of Societies. **1678** CUDWORTH *Intell. Syst.* 162 The ground of magical fascination is one vital unitive principle in the universe.

*a* **1834** COLERIDGE in *Lit. Rem.* (1839) IV. 26 Christ, the head, and by his Spirit the bond, or unitive *copula* of all. **1845** J. H. NEWMAN *Ess. Developm.* 337 The very nature of a true philosophy relatively to other systems is to be polemical, eclectic, unitive. **1893** PATMORE *Relig. Poetæ* 99 Genius consists wholly in the possession of the divine faculty of synthetic or unitive apprehension.

†**b.** Of a person. *Obs. rare*⁻¹.

**1651** H. MORE *Second Lash* in *Enthus. Tri.*, etc. (1656) 195 Thou art so unitive a soul, Phil,..that thou wouldst not stick to match chalk and cheese together.

**c.** *Anat.* Of fibres: (see quots.).

**1875** HAYDEN *Dis. Heart* 31 Luton describes the fibres of the ventricles [of the heart] as common and proper. The former are the 'unitive' fibres of Gerdy. *Ibid.* 32 The posterior 'unitive' fibres pass from the posterior segments of the auriculo-ventricular zones..to the right edge of the heart.

**2.** Having the quality or attribute of uniting spiritually to the Deity.

*a* **1659** ROUS *Heav. Univ.* (1702) 160 Until that I shall arrive to the unitive union of the Father. **1675** O. WALKER *Paraphr. St. Paul* 94 The institution of the unitiue vertue of the Sacrifices. **1855** PUSEY *Doctrine of Real Presence* 312 This introduction [of the body of Christ under these species]..is not an action bringing (adductive of) the Body of Christ, nor simply unitive. **1855** BAILEY *Mystic*, etc. 58 That blessed secret, unitive and divine,..which us Ones with the heavens. **1879** L. SHEPHERD tr. *Guéranger's Liturg. Year* I. 389 This unitive power of the Eucharist.

**b.** *spec.* in *unitive life, way*, etc., applied to the third and final stage of spiritual advancement.

**1649** JER. TAYLOR *Gt. Exemp.* Disc. i. § 9 All the eminencies and spirituall riches of the unitive life. *Ibid.* Disc. iii. § 26 Concerning the very same thing which the old Divines call the unitive Way. **1687** NORRIS *Coll. Misc.* (1699) 341 Seraphic love, and this with Contemplation, makes up that which the Mystic Divines stile the Unitive way of Religion. **1716** M. DAVIES *Athen. Brit.* I. 237 The Purgative, Illuminative and Unitive Conditions of the Mind. **1749** LAVINGTON *Enthus. Meth. & Papists* (1754) 146 By the purgative and illuminating Way, she attains to the Unitive. **1830** *For. Rev. & Cont. Misc.* V. 318 The purgative, illuminative, and unitive stages of devotion. **1848** BAILEY *Festus* (ed. 3) 208 The soul..Lay lulled in glory, and in unitive Life with divinity. **1899** W. R. INGE *Chr. Mysticism* i. 10 Strictly, the unitive road (*via*) leads to the contemplative life (*vita*).

Hence **U·nitively** *adv.*; **U·nitiveness.**

**1664** H. MORE *Myst. Iniq.* 322 The consideration of the collectiveness and unitiveness of..[these] types. **1678** CUDWORTH *Intell. Syst.* 307 Jupiter who conteineth the Vniverse, and All things within himself, Vnitively and Intellectually. *Ibid.* 582 The First of these is sometimes said to be..'All things Vnitively,' The Second..'All things Intellectually.' **1812–29** COLERIDGE in *Lit. Rem.* (1838) III. 147 The corrupt will cannot..be unitively subordinated to the reason. **1865** NEALE *Hymns Paradise* 68 Whom, embracing unitively, Thou shalt love with perfect will.

**U·nitize,** *v. rare.* [f. UNIT *sb.* + -IZE.] *trans.* To form into a unit; to unite or make one.

**1849** [implied in next]. **1860** WORCESTER (citing *Ch. Reg.*). **1893** J. PULSFORD *Loyalty to Christ* II. 320 [Christ] is the head of every principality and power..to subdue all things to Himself, and to unitise highest and lowest.

So **U·nitized, U·nitizing** *ppl. adjs.*

**1849** SEARS *Regeneration* III. xii. (1859) 239 The governing and unitizing principle of all endeavour. **1873** *Contemp. Rev.* XXI. 269 The rapid immediate advance of unitized societies.

†**Uni·tor.** *Obs.*⁻¹ [f. UNITE *v.* + -OR.] = UNITER.

**1602** WARNER *Albion's England* XIV. 339 Seaueenth Henry, the Vnitor of those Flowers that long dissented.

**U·nitude.** *nonce-word.* [f. UNI- or UNIT, after *multitude*: see -TUDE.] The character of being one.

**1851** SPENCER *Soc. Stat.* 18 It hints that the first principle of a code for the right ruling of humanity in its state of multitude, is to be found in humanity in its state of unitude.

**Unity**[1] (yū·nĭti). Forms: 4–6 **vnite, vnyte,** 4–7 **unite,** 5–6 **unyte;** 4 **vnitee, vnytee,** 6 **unitee;** 5 **vnytie,** 6 **unytie,** 5–6 **vnytye, vnitye,** 5–7 **vnitie,** 6–7 **unitie, vnity** (7 **vnitty**), 7– **unity.** [a. AF. *unite*, OF. *unite, uniteit* (*c* 1200), F. *unité* (= Sp. *unidad*, Pg. *unidade*, It. *unità*), or ad. L. *ūnitāt-*, *ūnitās* oneness, sameness, agreement, f. *ūn-us* one: see -ITY.]

**I. 1.** The fact, quality, or condition of being, comprising, or consisting of one in number; oneness, singleness. Freq. of the Deity, and in early use in the phr. *in unity.*

Used *spec.* in *Philos.* and *Metaph.* to express the negation of multiplicity of being or existence; individuality, identity (see Baldwin *Dict. Philos. & Psychol.*).

*a* **1300** *Cursor M.* 6342 Þis wandes takens persons thre, And an-fald godd in vnite. *c* **1325** *Spec. Gy Warw.* 429 Wid þe fader, and wid þe sone, And wid þe holi gost in vnite. *c* **1380** WYCLIF *Serm.* Sel. Wks I. 383 Two passen fro unyte. **1398** TREVISA *Barth. De P. R.* XIX. cxvi. (1495) 921 The one and vnyte of nombre..: therby is fygure and lyknesse of the vnyte of our lorde god. *c* **1532** DU WES *Introd. Fr.* in *Palsgr.* 1023 The blessed Trinite thre persones in unite. **1594** HOOKER *Eccl. Pol.* I. ii. § 2 Our God is one, or rather very oneness, and meere unitie. **1606** SHAKS. *Tr. & Cr.* V. ii. 141 If there be rule in vnitie it selfe, This is not she. **1621** T. BEDFORD *Sin unto Death* 6 The singular number doth not alwayes imply an individuall vnitie. **1690** LOCKE *Hum. Und.* II. vi. § 1 Amongst all the Ideas we have,..there is none more simple than that of Unity, or One. **1725** WATTS *Logic* (1736) 245 The Unity and Spirituality of the Godhead. **1766** BLACKSTONE *Comm.* II. 433 The notion of an unity of person between the husband and wife. **1844** KINGSLEY *Lett.* (1878) I. 117 Perfect unity in extreme multiplicity. **1864** BOWEN *Logic* ix. 292 A question often involves a real duplicity under a seeming unity. *a* **1881** A. BARRATT *Phys. Metempiric* (1883) 106 *A priori* a spacial principle of unity seems as reasonable as a temporal.

**b.** *Math.* The condition of the unit or number one; the numeral one regarded abstractly as the basis of number in reckoning or calculation.

**1570** BILLINGSLEY *Euclid* VII. i. 184 Vnitie is that, whereby euery thing that is, is sayd to be on. **1657** HOBBES *Absurd Geom.* 2 The excesse of the rising proportion above subtriple is the same which unity hath to the six times the number of termes after o. **1709–29** V. MANDEY *Syst. Math., Arith.* 6 Unity measures every number by the number itself; so 1 measures 7 by 7. **1831** BREWSTER *Optics* iv. 28 Take 1 part or unity from the same scale. **1869** J. H. SMITH *Elem. Algebra* 50 The quotient is unity when the Dividend and the Divisor are equal. **1885** WATSON & BURBURY *Math. Th. Electr. & Magn.* I. 232 Taking unity as the combining number for hydrogen.

**c.** A quantity, magnitude, or substance regarded as equivalent to the number one in calculation, measurement, or comparison.

**1728** CHAMBERS *Cycl.*, *Measure*, in Geometry, any certain Quantity assumed as one, or Unity, to which the Ratio of other..Quantities is express'd. **1797** *Encycl. Brit.* (ed. 3) XVII. 659/1 The most convenient way..would be to consider the weight of the standard as unity. **1801** *Monthly Rev.* XXXV. 525 The ten millionth part of the..distance ..was taken as the unity of measure. **1816** PLAYFAIR *Nat. Phil.* II. 287 If the mass of Jupiter be supposed unity. **1836** BRANDE *Chem.* (ed. 4) 220 Others adopt oxygen as unity, in which case hydrogen becomes one-eighth of that unit. **1880** HAUGHTON *Phys. Geog.* iii. 138 If we call the Gulf Stream unity, we may form an approximate estimate of the other four systems of circulation.

**2.** An instance of this: †**a.** = UNIT *sb.* 1. *Obs.*

*c* **1425** *Craft Nombrynge* (E. E. T. S.) 22 Reken ten for on vnite. *Ibid.* 28 Loke how mony vnityes ben in þe nounbre þat comes of þe multiplicacioun of þe 2 digittes. **1543** RECORDE *Arith.* 119 b, In that place of vnities dothe appere only 7. **1587** FLEMING *Contn. Holinshed* III. 1490/2 The residue..being multiplied by vnities, doo make vp the complet number of three score and twelue. **1630** WINGATE *Arith.* I. i. 15 The Integers, or intire Vnities. **1669** STURMY *Mariner's Mag.* III. ii. 129 Because the Angle CAB is a Right Angle,..I therefore only put an Unity before the second Term. **1837** WHEWELL *Hist. Induct. Sci.* I. 250 His objections to geometry and arithmetic are founded on abstract cavils concerning the nature of points, letters, unities.

**b.** One separate or single thing, quality, etc.; something which is complete or entire in itself, or is regarded as such.

**1587** GOLDING *De Mornay* ii. 16 The foresayd most single and alonly One, abyding still one in it selfe, bringeth foorth all the other vnities. **1598** MARSTON *Sco. Villanie* I. iv. (1599) 187 Sylenus now is old, I wonder, I, He doth not hate his triple venerie...Me thinkes a vnitie were competent. *a* **1600** EDMONDS *Observ. Cæsar's Comm.* 38 The life and strength of a multitude consisteth in vnities. **1681** *Whole Duty Nations* 7 He himself is the prime Unity and Universality. **1828** CARLYLE *Misc.* (1840) I. 319 The clear view of it as an indivisible Unity. **1847** EMERSON *Repr. Men, Swedenborg* Wks. (Bohn) I. 317 The unities of each organ are so many little organs, homogeneous with their compound. **1889** MIVART *Orig. Hum. Reason* 46 They are apprehensions of abstract qualities grouped round a unity.

**II. 3.** The quality or condition of being one in mind, feeling, opinion, purpose, or action; harmonious combination together of the various parties or sections (*of* the Church, a state, etc.) into one body; concord or harmony amongst several persons or between two or more.

In the usage with *a* (†*an*) the meaning tends to become concrete (see *b*).

*c* **1325** *Poem temp. Edw. II* (Percy) xxii, Among men of religioun Is non unite. *c* **1380** WYCLIF *Serm.* Sel. Wks. II. 226 Þis unite shulden men have bi þe lore of Jesus Crist, and þanne shulden þei be of o wille. *c* **1425** WYNTOUN *Cron.* IX. viii. 942 That tyme at Bulone..Wes a tretis of vnyte Betuix þe Franche and Inglismen. **1460** CAPGRAVE *Chron.* (Rolls) 294 Be this mene was the unite of the Cherch lettid. **1560** DAUS tr. *Sleidane's Comm.* 123 The Germains within them selues shold..come to some vnitie & concord. **1590** GREENE *Never too late* (1600) 42 Vnitie is the essence of amitie. **1606** SHAKS. *Tr. & Cr.* I. iii. 100 The vnity and married calme of States. **1647** TRAPP *Comm. Rom.* xv. 6 (1656) 652 It is recorded to the high commendation of the Church of Scotland, that for this 90 years and upwards they have kept unity. **1738** WESLEY *Ps.* CXXXIII. i, When Brethren all in One agree; Who knows the Joys of Unity! **1776** PAINE *Com. Sense* 49 'Tis not in numbers but in unity that our great strength lies. **1830** D'ISRAELI *Chas. I*, III. v. 62 Laud..contemplated establishing unity by uniformity. **1854** MILMAN *Lat. Chr.* IV. iv. II. 99 No sooner has Anglo-Saxon Britain become one (no doubt her religious unity must have contributed..to her national unity) than [etc.]. **1878** STUBBS *Const. Hist.* III. xviii. 221 The king's death at once broke up the unity of the Court.

(*b*) **1460** CAPGRAVE *Chron.* (Rolls) 120 Edgare..mad a very unite of all the vii. kyngdammes. *a* **1466** *Hist. Coll. Cit. Lond.* (Camden) 116 The same yere..the general conselle was endyd, and a unyte made in Hooly Chyrche, and oo pope chosynne. *a* 1500 *Bale's Chron.* in *Six Town Chron.* (1911) 145 The king..and divers lordes..agreed and ther made a full unyte and peas betwene the dukes of york and somerset. 1577 HOLINSHED *Chron.* I. 286/2 Diuerse offers were made on both partes..for an vnitie to haue beene had betwixte the two Princes.

**b.** Freq. in adverbial phr. *at* or † *in unity*, in agreement, concord, or harmony; at one.

*c* 1374 CHAUCER *Troylus* III. 29 Ye holden regne and hous in vnite. 1390 GOWER *Conf.* III. 194 So schal I live in unite With every man. *c* 1430 LYDG. *Lyke thyn Audience* i, Yf yow wilt lyffe in pease and vnite. *c* 1450 BURGH *Secrees* 1520 These Sustrys Cheyned in parfight vnyte, departe may not by natural resoun. 1535 COVERDALE *Ps.* cxxi, Ierusalem is buylded as a cite, that is at vnitie in it self. *a* 1619 FOTHERBY *Atheom.* II. x. § 4 (1622) 308 An Vnity is alwayes at vnitie with it selfe, and neuer varieth from it selfe. 1662 PLAYFORD *Skill Mus.* I. v. 18 To guide his Voyce in unity to the sound of the Instrument. 1671 BAXTER *Holiness* lxiv. 18 It plainly sheweth that they are very much at unity in the main. 1714 in *Jrnl. Friends Hist. Soc.* (1918) 27 Leaving our family and friends in great love and Unity. 1768 STERNE *Sent. Journ., Dwarf*, The old French officer would have set me at unity with myself. 1825 *Q. Rev.* XXXII. 369 No Italian city or state was at unity in itself. 1871 JOWETT *Plato* I. 56 The bad..are never at unity with one another or with themselves.

**c.** Agreement or accord between things.

1393 LANGL. *P. Pl.* C. IV. 338 As adiectif and substantyf vnite asken, Acordaunce in kynde, in cas and in numbre. *Ibid.* 398. 1593 SHAKS. *Lucr.* 1558 These contraries such unity do hold, Only to flatter fools and make them bold. 1611 — *Wint. T.* V. ii. 35 There is such vnitie in the proofes.

†**d.** Agreement or concurrence *with* something.

1760 J. WOOLMAN *Journal* vii. (1900) 146 Some Friends.. expressed their willingness to have it read; which being done, many expressed their unity with the proposal.

**4.** The fact of forming or being united into one body or whole; union (of two or more persons or things, or of one *with* another); rarely, physical union or connexion; † conjunction of two or more things.

1387 TREVISA *Higden* (Rolls) V. 9 By tokene þe onynge and þe unite of Crist and of holy chirche. 1472–3 *Rolls of Parlt.* VI. 23/1 Entierly desiryng..the unyte of the nobles and other his subgettes. 1483 CAXTON *Gold. Leg.* 255 b/2 The unyte and assemble of the flesshe of oure lord and of oure lady. 1565 ALLEN *Defence Purg.* xvii. 283 Which forme of argument serued the Arians against the consubstantiall vnitye of God the father, and his son our sauiour. 1578 TIMME *Calvin on Gen.* 76 Herein we see a true image of our unitie with the Son of God. 1597 A. M. tr. *Guillemeau's Fr. Chirurg.* 11/2 The synnuish filamentes which have a vnitye and fasteninge with the Pericranium. 1611 TOURNEUR *Ath. Trag.* I. ii, The unitie of Families is a worke of loue and charitie. 1651 HOBBES *Leviath.* II. xvii. 87 This is more than consent, or concord; It is a reall Unitie of them all, in one and the same Person. 1796 BURKE *Regic. Peace* i. 43 In this unity and indivisibility of possession are sunk ten..wealthy provinces. 1801 HAMILTON *Wks.* (1886) VII. 186 They have approved the unity of the legislative power in one branch. 1871 R. W. DALE *Commandm.* i. 23 That our Lord claimed for himself a mysterious unity with the Father. 1880 J. CAIRD *Philos. Relig.* v. 157 The unity of subject and object..is implied in every act of thought.

†**b.** A meeting or assembly of people. *Obs.*—1

*a* 1470 HARDING *Chron.* CLXXXVII. ii, In cytees al he helde wel vnitees, Great iustes ay, and ioyous tournementes.

**c.** A body formed by union, esp. *the Unity of the* (Moravian) *Brethren*. In later quots. *ellipt.*

1780 LA TROBE tr. *Cranz's Hist. Brethren* 67 Twenty-four ministers of the Unity of the Brethren. *Ibid.* 353 Every actual member of the Unity that is desirous of taking the benefit of this act. 1814 WM. BROWN *Hist. Propag. Christianity* II. 124 This, by the synods of the Brethren's church, is vested solely in the Elders' Conference of the Unity. 1865 J. GILL *Banished Count* xxv. 262 The affairs of the Unity called the Count..to the Continent.

**5.** The quality or fact of being one body or whole, esp. as made up of two or more parts; an undivided whole, as distinct from its parts.

1390 GOWER *Conf.* I. 37 If a man were Mad al togedre of o matiere Withouten interrupcioun, Ther scholde no corrupcioun Engendre upon that unite. 1398 TREVISA *Barth. De P. R.* v. ii. (Bodl. MS.), Yf the vertu is ilette..þe vnyte & ioynyng of alle þe body to falleþ. 1533 GAU *Richt Vay* (S.T.S.) 57 He is wordine man and sua is spousit with the halie chrissine kirk in to ane body the quhilk vnite S. Paul ..callis ane greit halie secreit thing [etc.]. 1583 MELBANCKE *Philotimus* P iv b, The coniunction of manye in an vniforme vnitie. 1813 SHELLEY *Q. Mab* IV. 144 Every grain Is sentient both in unity and part. 1850 ROBERTSON *Serm.* Ser. III. iv. (1857) 57 In proportion as you rise from lower to higher life, the parts are more distinctly developed, while yet the unity becomes more entire. 1875 JOWETT *Plato* (ed. 2) V. 69 [Plato] does not insist, as in the Protagoras, on the unity of the virtues.

†**6.** The quality of being of one kind; uniformity of substance or appearance. *Obs.*

1638 JUNIUS *Paint. Ancients* 119 To vary the unitie of a stone by inserting such spots into the crust as were not by nature.

**7.** As a literary or artistic quality: **a.** Agreement of the various parts of which something is composed so as to form a whole which exhibits singleness of design or effect; combination or arrangement which produces this, or the effect so produced.

1712 ADDISON *Spect.* No. 267 ¶ 3 Aristotle himself allows, that Homer has nothing to boast of as to the Unity of his Fable. 1756 J. WARTON *Ess. Pope* I. iii. 101 Horace observed a strict method, and unity of design, in his epistle to the Pisones. 1783 BLAIR *Lect.* I. 216 The second quality of a well-arranged sentence, which I termed its Unity. 1808 L. MURRAY *Eng. Gram.* I. 430 But most of all, in a single sentence, is required the strictest unity. 1864 PUSEY *Lect. Daniel* i. 11 Amid apparent want of unity on the surface of the Book, there is a real unity in the whole, resting on the unity of the plan of the writer. 1874 R. TYRWHITT *Sketch. Club* 272 Unity in a picture is the sympathy of its groups or parts.

**b.** One or other of the three principles of the Aristotelian canon of dramatic composition as adopted and expanded by the French classical dramatists, according to which a play should consist of one main action, represented as occurring at one time (i.e. one day) and in one place. Also in loose application.

1668 DRYDEN *Ess. Dram. Poesy* Ess. (Ker) I. 38 The famous Rules, which the French call *Des Trois Unitez*, or, the Three Unities, which ought to be observed in every regular play. [1682 SHEFFIELD (Dk. Buckhm.) *Ess. Poetry* 12 The Unites of Action, Time, and Place.] 1712 ADDISON *Spect.* No. 267 ¶ 2 Homer to preserve the Unity of his Action hastens into the Midst of Things. 1789 BELSHAM *Ess.* I. ii. 18 The diction of these plays is lofty,..the unities strictly preserved. 1816 SCOTT *Old Mort.* xxxvii, It is fortunate for tale-tellers that they are not tied down like theatrical writers to the unities of time and place. 1859 TROLLOPE *Bertrams* xvi, Two years..; it is a terrible gap in a story, but in these days the unities are not much considered. 1878 O. W. HOLMES *Motley* iv. 24 A series of incidents..flung together with no more regard to the unities than [etc.].

*transf.* 1821 LAMB *Elia* I. *My Relations*, Nature hath her unities, which not every critic can penetrate.

**c.** *transf.* (See quot.)

1861 WHYTE MELVILLE *Good for Nothing* xvi, Those functionaries in white hats and red waistcoats, who with singular attention to 'the unities,' adopt the very colours of the Post-office Directory and Court Guide.

**8.** Freedom from or absence of diversity or variety; unvaried nature *of* (some quality or thing).

Not always clearly distinct from sense 1.

1802 PALEY *Nat. Theol.* xx. (1819) 314 What we have first to notice is unity of purpose under variety of expedients. 1824 MISS MITFORD in L'Estrange *Life* (1870) II. ix. 176 ['Our Village'] is..a series of sketches..with some story intermixed, and connected by unity of locality, and of purpose. 1841 MYERS *Cath. Th.* III. § 48. 184 Amidst all this variety, what unity of spirit and of aim is there in the Bible! 1884 F. TEMPLE *Relat. Relig. & Sci.* vi. 164 The unity of plan..pervading any great class of animals..seems to point to unity of ancestry.

**b.** Singleness of aim, purpose, or action.

1836 HOR. SMITH *Tin Trump.* I. 5 There is a simplicity and unity in despotism which is not without its advantages. 1848 W. H. KELLY tr. *L. Blanc's Hist. Ten Y.* II. 176 The grand principle of unity in power. 1866 GEO. ELIOT *F. Holt* i, She had thought that the possession of this child would give unity to her life.

**9.** *Law.* (See quots.)

1607 COWELL *Interpr., Vnitie of possession*,..in the Ciuill lawe,..a ioynt possession of two rights by seuerall titles. 1691 BLOUNT *Law Dict.* s.v. *Possession*, If the Lord purchase the Tenancy held by Heriot service, the Heriot is extinct by Unity of Possession. 1766 BLACKSTONE *Comm.* II. 180 The properties of a joint estate are derived from it's unity, which is fourfold; the unity of interest, the unity of title, the unity of time, and the unity of possession. 1818 CRUISE *Digest* (ed. 2) III. 104 It was held clearly that this common was extinguished by the unity of possession. 1858 LD. ST. LEONARDS *Handy-bk. Prop. Law* xxv. 189 Unity of possession—that is, where the land and the right exercised over it are in the same person.

† **U·nity** [2], obs. var. of or error for UNITE *sb.*

1604 in Rymer *Fœdera* (1715) XVI. 605/2 One Peece of Gold.., to be called The Unitie. 1643 BAKER *Chron., Jas. I*, 147 Ordayning the peice called the Vnity..to bee currant now for two and twenty.

**Univalent** (yūni·vălĕnt), *a.* *Chem.* [f. UNI- + L. *valent-em*, pr. pple. of *valēre* to be worth.] Having a valency of one; having the combining power of one atom of hydrogen or other radical.

Also, in recent Dicts. (1891–), *univalence, univalency*.

1869 *Eng. Mech.* 19 Nov. 222/1 A univalent body can only join its single atom to a single atom of a univalent body. 1872 WATTS *Dict. Chem.* VI. 243 Chlorine is univalent in argentic chloride. 1893 *19th Cent.* Aug. 249 Each atom of potassium ..is univalent, and has the same valency as one atom of hydrogen.

**Univalve** (yū·nivælv), *a.* and *sb.* *Nat. Hist.* [See UNI- and VALVE *sb.*[1] Cf. F. *univalve* (1752), It. and Pg. *univalve*, It. and Sp. *univalvo*, mod.L. *univalvis*.]

**A.** *adj.* **a.** *Conch.* Of molluscs: Having a shell consisting of one valve. Of shells: Composed of a single valve or piece.

1661 LOVELL *Hist. Anim. & Min.* A 7 b, Fishes, which.. are, turbinate,..bivalve,..or univalve. 1752 J. HILL *Hist. Anim.* 115 The first [series of shellfish] containing those formed of only one piece; this I shall call the simple ones; others have called them univalve ones. 1774 *Phil. Trans.* LXV. 46 The smallest univalve or testaceous animal of any such kind. 1816 W. SMITH *Strata Ident.* 27 Bivalve shells [are] most common to the thick beds; univalve to the thin. 1851 G F. RICHARDSON *Geol.* viii. 230 When they have a shell it is thin, fragile, and univalve. 1872 W. S. SYMONDS *Rec. Rocks* vi. 181 A univalve mollusk.

**b.** *Ent.* Having one valve.

Also in recent use in *Zool.* and *Bot.*

1826 SAMOUELLE *Direct. Collect.* 54 Proboscis [of *Diptera*] (rarely wanting) univalve.

**B.** *sb.* *Conch.* A univalve mollusc or shell.

1668 WILKINS *Real Char.* 129 Venus Shell..being of near affinity to the Univalvs. 1683 *Phil. Trans.* XIV. 507 Distinction of shells into Univalves, Bivalves, and Turbinated. 1755 *Gentl. Mag.* XXV. 32/2 When a shell, therefore, is found to be a Univalve. 1785 *Phil. Trans.* LXXV. 342 The univalves..have the intestine reflected back. 1832 LYELL *Princ. Geol.* II. 110 Aquatic univalves usually attach their eggs to leaves and sticks. 1854 KINGSLEY *Lett.* (1878) I. 411 The crevices of the highest rocks..have their peculiar little univalves. 1879 tr. *Semper's Anim. Life* 41 Animals.. as low in the scale as the Amphibia or Univalves.

Hence **Univa·lved, Univa·lvular** *adjs.*, *Bot.* having or consisting of one valve.

Also, in recent Dicts. (1891–), *univalvate*.

1823 CRABB *Technol. Dict.*, **Univalved*,..one-valved; an epithet for a pericarp. 1857 A. GRAY *First Less. Bot.* (1866) 235 *Univalved*, a pod of only one piece after dehiscence. 1793 MARTYN *Lang. Bot.*, *Folliculus*,..a follicle, a *univalvular pericarp. 1830 LINDLEY *Nat. Syst. Bot.* 294 Those species of Panicum whose outer flower is univalvular. 1849 BALFOUR *Man. Bot.* § 530 The pericarp becomes divided into different pieces, which are denominated valves, the fruit being univalvular, bivalvular,..&c. according as there are one, two, or many valves.

**Universal** (yūnivɔ̄·ɹsăl), *a.* (*adv.*) and *sb.* Forms: *α.* 4–5 vni-, 5 unyuersel, 4 universiel (-uersele). *β.* 4–5 uny-, 5–6 vnyuersal, 5 -all, 4–7 vniuersal (5 -ale, -versale), 6–7 -all, vniversal(l, 5–6 universalle, 6 -uersalle, 6–7 uniuersal(l; 4, 6– universal. See also VARSAL *a.* and VERSAL *a.* [a. OF. *universel, universal* (12–13th c.; F. *universel*, = It. *universale*, Sp. and Pg. *universal*), or ad. L. *ūniversāl-is* (post-Aug.), f. *ūniversus*: see UNIVERSE and -AL [1]. The sb. occurs in OF. *universal* (1372), in F. (17th c.) in pl. *universaux* universals (see B. 1), F. *universel* (16th c.) the universe, It. *universale*.

Early examples in verse exhibit stressing on the second or fourth syllable.]

**A.** *adj.* **1.** Extending over, comprehending, or including the whole of something specified or implied; prevalent over all.

Contexts in which the reference is to the whole of a particular community are numerous, esp. in groups b and c.

Freq. the adj. develops a more or less specialized sense, as in *universal grammar, root, succession*; see also 14.

*c* 1374 CHAUCER *Boeth.* v. pr. iv. (1868) 165 Resoun surmounteth ymaginacioun and comprehendeþ by an vniuersel lokynge þe commune spece þat is in þe singuler peces. *c* 1386 — *Pars. T.* ¶ 292 His contricioun...shal been vniuersal [*Camb. MS.* vnyuersel] and total, this is to seyn, a man shal be verray repentaunt for alle hise synnes. 1390 GOWER *Conf.* III. 77 Ther felle wondres many on Of terremote universiel. 1398 TREVISA *Barth. de P. R.* (W. de W. 1495) II. xii. 39 By an vnyuersall excellence the hygher angellis ben areryd abouea subieccion. 1555 EDEN *Decades* (Arb.) 45 Of the vniuersall carde and newe worlde. *Ibid.* 211 After my vniuersall description of the historie of the Indies. 1557 RECORDE *Whetst.* Rr iij b, These rootes therefore bee called vniuersalle rootes, because thei are the rootes..of the whole compounde nomber. 1597 BLUNDEVIL *Exerc.* III. I. xv. (ed. 2) 150 The Moone..cannot shadow all the Earth, and therefore the Eclipse of the Sunne cannot be vniuersall. 1630 J. TAYLOR (Water P.) *Jack a Lent* Wks. 118/1 The knauery of the Baker is vniuersal, in Asia, Europa, Afrike, and America. 1647 CLARENDON *Hist. Reb.* I. § 32 The loudest and most universal rejoycing over the whole Kingdom. 1697 DRYDEN *Æneis* VIII. 194 What further force can stay The victor troops from universal sway? 1736 BUTLER *Anal.* II. vi, As neither the iewish nor christian Revelation have been universal. 1751 HARRIS *Hermes* Wks. (1841) 120 How few, then, must be those who know grammar universal; that grammar which..only respects those principles that are essential to them all? 1765–8 ERSKINE *Inst. Law Scot.* III. viii. § 1 This kind of succession is called universal; and may be defined, the right of an heir or executor to enter upon the estate which belonged to a person deceased at the time of his death. 1784 COWPER *Task* IV. 204 The slope of faces.. Relax'd into an universal grin. 1822 BYRON *Vis. Judgem.* xxvii, The gate flew Asunder, and the flashing of its hinges Flung over space an universal hue Of many-colour'd flame. 1860 TYNDALL *Glac.* II. i. 226 This is now the universal belief. 1891 FARRAR *Darkn. & Dawn* xxiv, The day was kept as a universal holiday.

**b.** Affecting or involving the whole of something specified or implied; *spec.* in *Path.* (see quot. 1876).

*c* 1412 HOCCLEVE *De Reg. Princ.* 2295 Gretter cheerte He hadde of the profet vniuersel Than of hym self. *a* 1425 tr. *Arderne's Treat. Fistula*, etc. 64 Without dout it schal cure perfitely, vniuersale purgacions goyng afore. *a* 1475 ASHBY *Active Policy* 772 The vniuersal And the comyn wele of this Region. 1542 BOORDE *Dyetary* xxxvi. (1870) 297 They the whiche haue the Palsye, vnyuersall or pertyculer, must beware of anger. 1560 DAUS tr. *Sleidane's Comm.* 108 The Emperour doth establyshe a vniuersall peace throughout Germany. 1611 SHAKS. *Wint. T.* v. ii. 100 If all the world could haue seen't, the Woe had beene vniuersall. 1656 EARL MONM. tr. *Boccalini's Advts. fr. Parnass.* II. vi. (1674) 140 In Germany, and in universal concerns, there appears but one only Commonwealth.., but many in particulars. 1697 DRYDEN *Virg. Georg.* III. 827 At length [Tisiphone] strikes an Universal Blow; To Death at once whole Herds of Cattle go. 1734 POPE *Ess. Man* IV. 114 God sends not ill; if rightly understood, Or partial Ill is universal Good. 1754 SHERLOCK *Disc.* (1759) I. 11 Are you alone exempt from this common, this universal Blindness? 1826 DISRAELI *V. Grey* VI. i, The battle was general, the overthrow universal. 1876 DUHRING *Dis. Skin* 52 When an eruption involves the whole surface, it is said to be universal. 1878 BROWNING *La Saisiaz* 44 What a preferable state were universal happiness?

**c.** Proceeding from the whole body or number; committed, given, made, etc., by all without exception of the persons to whom there is reference or allusion.

1586 DAY *Eng. Secretary* II. (1625) 41 The vniuersall sentence of the whole boord. 1611 CORYAT *Crudities* 627 The vniuersall suffrage of all the learned. 1663 BP. PATRICK

*Parab. Pilgr.* xxxviii, His title and claim unto our universal obedience. 1687 A. Lovell tr. *Thevenot's Trav.* II. 30 Baron..discharged that Office [of Consul] with honour and universal Approbation. 1701 Swift *Contests Nobles & Comm.* v, For a house of commons to lose the universal favour of the numbers they represent. *a*1800 Cowper *Odyss.* (ed. 2) xxiv. 598 Forefathers, whose exploits Have shared so long, such universal praise. 1844 H. H. Wilson *Brit. India* III. 432 An almost universal insurrection of the Bhils. 1871 Freeman *Norm. Conq.* xvii. IV. 91 The English visitors were the objects of universal attention, of universal admiration. 1871 Jowett *Plato* II. 185 The universal voice of mankind is saying that [etc.].

† **d.** Applied to the whole body. *Obs.*—¹

1725 *Fam. Dict.* s.v. *Fomentation*, A Bath is universal, and therefore never made use of to Horses, because of their large Size.

**2.** Qualifying (in senses 1 and 1 a) agent-nouns, personal designations, or titles; freq. in *universal bishop*, esp. (now *Hist.*) as a title assumed by or given to some of the Popes.

*c*1380 *Antecrist* in Todd *Three Treat. Wyclif* 118 Oo bischop þat wole be clepid vnyuersal bischop. 1483 Caxton *Cato* a ij b, God is the unyuersel commaunder of alle our production. 1552 Abp. Hamilton *Catech.* (1884) 38 The universal Lord of all this world. 1582 T. W[ilcox] *B. de Loque's Disc. Ch.* 73 Saint Peter was not an vniuersall Apostle, nor a soueraigne and high bishoppe ouer all the Churche. 1606 Shaks. *Ant. & Cl.* III. xiii. 71 To heare frome me you had..put your selfe vnder his shrowd, the vniuersal Landlord [*sc.* Julius Cæsar]. 1632 Lithgow *Trav.* x. 474 Boniface the third obtained of Phocas..to be called vniuersall Bishop. 1667 Milton *P. L.* III. 317 Here shalt [thou] Reigne Both God and Man, ..Anointed universal King. 1728 Chambers *Cycl.* s.v. *Oecumenical*, Supposing the Title *Oecumenic* to imply Universal Bishop, or Bishop of all the World. 1784 Cowper *Task* VI. 449 The universal Father's love. 1818 Shelley *Homer's Hymn to Earth* 1 O universal Mother, who dost keep From everlasting thy foundations deep! 1876 Freeman *Norm. Conq.* xxiv. V. 391 He became universal landlord, but he did not cease to be universal ruler.

**b.** In legal use (*spec.* in *Scots Law*): Of or in respect of the whole estate or property.

1669 in W. M. Morison *Dict. Decis.* (1807) 16167 His executor and universal legatar. 1702 *London Gazette* No. 3806. 6 His Majesty has..appointed the Prince of Frise to be his Universal Heir. 1765–8 Erskine *Inst. Law Scot.* III. ix. § 6 Where a settlement is made by the deceased of the whole or the *universitas* of his moveable estate, the person gratified is called universal legatee. 1790 in *Nairne Peerage Evidence* (1874) 99 The said Marg^t Mercer to be my sole executor and universal intromitter.

**c.** *Scots Law.* Succeeding to an estate by a universal, as distinct from a singular, title.

1681 Stair *Inst.* xxvi. 92 Heirs in Law are called Universal Successors, .. [because] they do wholly represent the defunct. 1838 Bell *Dict. Law Scot.* 951 In this sense the two terms of *singular successor* and *universal successor* are opposed to each other.

**3.** Of or pertaining to the universe in general or all things in it; existing or occurring everywhere or in all things; occas., of or belonging to all nature. Chiefly *poet.* or *rhet.*

1390 Gower *Conf.* III. 91 Yit withouten eny forme Was that matiere universal, Which hihte ylem. 1637 Milton *Lycidas* 60 Her inchanting son Whom Universal nature did lament. 1643 Swan *Spec. Mundi* (ed. 2) 213 These things..are but in particular seas,..where a generall and universall cause may be much hindered. 1731 Bolingbroke *Let. to Swift* 2 Aug., The first epistle, which considers man..relatively to the whole system of universal being. 1738 Gray *Propertius* III. v. 18 That first, eternal, universal Cause. 1819 Shelley *Peter Bell 3rd* v. viii, On the universal sky. 1823 S. Rogers *Italy, St. Mark's Place* 165 Subtle, invisible, And universal as the air. 1848 R. I. Wilberforce *Doctr. Incarnation* xi. (1852) 267 The Universal Mind which pervades all things.

**b.** *poet.* as an epithet of Pan.

1667 Milton *P. L.* IV. 266 While Universal Pan Knit with the Graces and the Hours in dance Led on th' Eternal Spring. 1809 Wordsw. '*O'er the wide earth*' 3 A Godhead, like the universal Pan. 1820 Shelley *Witch Atlas* ix, And universal Pan, 'tis said, was there.

**c.** Of language, etc.: Adopted, (intended to be) used, understood, etc., everywhere or by all nations; freq. = Latin.

1652 Urquhart *Jewel* 24 Bringing all these words within the systeme of a Language, which..may..be intituled The Universal Tongue. 1653 — *Logopandect.* 13 So can there be no Universal Language but this I am about to divulge unto the world. *Ibid.*, The Universal Alphabet therefore must be first conceived. 1668 Wilkins *Real Char.* 13 A Real universal Character. 1756 Mrs. Calderwood in *Coltness Collect.* 131 The universall language so much wished for. 1793 Martyn *Lang. Bot.* Pref. p. xiii, The advantage which is derived from speaking and writing one universal language. 1818 Hazlitt *Eng. Poets* i. 2 Poetry is the universal language which the heart holds with nature and itself. 1836 (*title*), Universal Character; or, Manner of Writing intelligible to the Inhabitants of every Country. 1885, 1890 [see Volapük].

**d.** *Mil.* Of stores: (see quot.).

1876 Voyle & Stevenson *Milit. Dict.* 446/2 *Universal*.. is applied to certain stores of a general pattern, such as the saddlery and harness now in use in the army.

† **4.** Not going into details or particulars; general. *Obs.*—¹

*c*1430 *Lanfranc's Cirurg.* 5 (MS. Addit.), Chap. j of broken bonys an vniuersel word.

† **5. a.** Of a council: General, œcumenical (see Council 2). *Obs. rare.*

1432–50 tr. *Higden* (Rolls) V. 241 A cownsayle universalle of vj^c and xxx^ti bischoppes hade at Calcedonia.

† **b.** Made up of, inclusive of, all. *Obs.*—¹

1585 T. Washington tr. *Nicholay's Voy.* II. vi. 36 Many fair fountaines, which after a long..course do come altogether into an vniuersall flood [Fr. *vn vniuersel fleuve*].

† **6.** Of persons: Preserving the same attitude *to* all. *Obs.*—¹

*c*1450 in Aungier *Syon* (1840) 269 The presidente..owethe to be unyuersal to al and not parcial.

**7.** Of the church: Of, belonging to, or including all persons; consisting of the whole body of Christians; = Catholic *a.* 5.

1483 Caxton *Cato* b ij, Our moder chyrche unyuersall. 1509 *Paternoster, Ave & Creed* (W. de W.) a iij, I trowe in y^e holy goost, holy chirche Unyversall [etc.]. 1552 Abp. Hamilton *Catech.* (1884) 3 The haly spreit quhilk is ane daily techeour and governour of the hail universal kirk. 1620 T. Granger *Div. Logike* 227 Euen the vniuersall Church may erre. 1645 Ussher *Body Div.* (1647) 187 The Catholick Church, that is, God's whole or universall Assembly. 1663–70 South *Serm.* (1715) IV. 281 The Universal Christian Church. 1807 J. Crook (*title*), The Universal Church; an Essay on Nature, as the Universal Basis of Truth, Perfection, and Salvation. 1893 Liddon, etc. *Life Pusey* I. 417 The Ancient Fathers..bring the thought of particular Churches into community with the thought of the Universal Church when outwardly united.

**8.** Constituting or forming, existing or regarded as, a complete whole; entire, whole. **a.** Of the world, earth, etc.

Common in 16th c.; now somewhat *rare.* See Varsal *a.* 1.

1470–85 Malory *Arthur* v. i. 160 That noble empyre whiche domyneth vpon the vnyuersal world. 1480 Caxton *Myrr.* Prol. 4 b, The situacion..of the firmament, and how the vnyuersal erthe hangeth in the myddle of the same. 1513 Douglas *Æneid* VI. xii. 10 By his power myndit is our all This meikle body clepit vniuersall. 1527 R. Thorne in Hakluyt *Voy.* (1589) 253 This Card, though little, conteineth the vniuersall whole world. 1649 Quarles *Virgin Widow* II. i, 'Twas for nothing in the universal world but for killing a rich Patient. 1667 Milton *P. L.* v. 154 Thine this universal Frame, Thus wondrous fair. [Hence in Blackmore *Creation* v. 657, Cowper *Retirement* 90.] *Ibid.* VII. 257 With joy and shout The hollow Universal Orb they fill'd. 1823 W. Faux *Mem. Days* 212, I would live no where else in all the universal world. 1859 Darwin in *Life & Lett.* (1887) II. 169 Now I care not what the universal world says.

**b.** In general use.

1502 Atkynson tr. *De Imitatione* IV. xviii. (1893) 282 All the vniuersall people prayse the. 1559 W. Cunningham *Cosmogr. Glasse* 48 At midde day through the vniuersal yere. 1585 T. Washington tr. *Nicholay's Voy.* III. iii. 73 b, Their order vniuersall is distributed in tenths. 1603 Daniel *Def. Ryme* G 3 b, Euery Rymer in this vniuersall Iland. 1615 G. Sandys *Trav.* 113 Neither cement nor wood was imploied thorowout the vniuersall fabricke. 1667 Milton *P. L.* I. 541 The universal Host upsent A shout that tore Hells Concave. 1830–1860 in Thornton *Amer. Gloss.* (1912) s.v., The Universal Yankee nation. 1871 Blackie *Four Phases* i. 27 The political importance..had been blazoned forth before universal Greece.

**9.** Of persons: Instructed or learned in all or many subjects; having an extensive knowledge or experience; widely accomplished; interested in or devoted to a great variety of subjects; having a wide range of interests or activities. Also of the mind or disposition.

1520 *Caxton's Chron. Eng.* IV. 32 b/2 He [Adrian] was an vnyuersall man almost in all scyences. 1540 J. Heywood *Four P. P.* B ij, Why be ye so vniuersall, That ye can do what so euer ye shall. 1631 Weever *Anc. Funeral Mon.* 383 One William West, a Canon of Saint Pauls,..a good companion, a man vniuersall, affable, and curteous. 1679 Dryden *Pref. to Troylus & Cress.* ad fin., Shakespeare had an universal mind. *a*1700 Evelyn *Diary* 5 Mar. 1673, This gentleman is a very excellent and universal scholar. *Ibid.* 19 July 1691, I never knew a man of a more universal and generous spirit. *a*1715 Burnet *Own Time* II. x. (1897) I. 427 He was..very universal in all other learning. 1749 Smollett *Gil Blas* XI. v, He sets up for an universal man, because he has a small tincture of every science. 1829 Lytton *Devereux* II. vi, Don Saltero is a universal genius. 1833 Coleridge *Table-t.* 17 Feb., Shakspeare is universal, and in fact has no manner. 1841 D'Israeli *Amen. Lit.* III. 178 With a universal mind Rawleigh was eager after universal knowledge.

**b.** Not limited or restricted to any particular branch or class of work, etc. † *Attorney universal*, an Attorney-General. *Obs. Universal maid*, a maid of all work, a general servant.

1637 J. Bastwick (*title*), The Answer..to the Information of Sir John Bancks, Knight, Atturney universall. 1770 R. Weston (*title*), The Universal Botanist and Nurseryman, etc. 1840 Thackeray *Shabby-genteel Story* iii, She had been in the kitchen helping Becky, the universal maid.

**c.** Embracing or covering all (or a great variety of) subjects, branches of knowledge, etc.

1638 R. Baker tr. *Balzac's Lett.* (vol. II) 39 His knowledge is so universal, and comprehends such an infinite number of things that one cannot touch upon any point where he is not ready for you. 1688–9 (*title*), The Universal Intelligence. 1690 Locke *Hum. Und.* IV. iii. § 28 For wherever we want that, we are utterly uncapable of universal and certain Knowledge. 1786 (*title*), The Fashionable Magazine,..being a Compleat Universal Repository of Taste, Elegance, and Novelty for both Sexes. 1821 A. Jamieson (*title*), Universal Science, or the Cabinet of Nature and Art. 1841 [see sense 9]. 1861–5 (*title*), Beeton's Dictionary of Universal Information. 1882–4 (*title*), Universal Instructor; or, Self-Culture for All.

† **10.** With pl. sbs. All, every one, regarded collectively as a body or whole. *Obs. rare.*

1530–1 *Act 22 Hen. VIII*, c. 14 His lyberall and free habytations resortes and passages to and fro the vniuersall places of this realme. 1563 *Homilies* II. *The Sacrament* II. 458 b, Wherfore, let vs all vniuersall and singuler, beholde our owne maners and lyues, to amend them.

**11.** *Logic.* Applicable to, extending or relating to, involving, the whole of a class or genus, or all the individuals or species forming it; *spec.* of a proposition: Predicable of each of the things denoted by the subject. Opposed to *particular.*

1551 T. Wilson *Logike* G viii, The first proposition must be vniuersall euer, or els it is not good. 1606 Bryskett *Civ. Life* 124 That sense is busied about things particular, and..onely things vniuersall are knowne. 1650 Hobbes *Hum. Nat.* v. 50 The appellations that be universal, and common to many things, are not always given to all the particulars. 1697 tr. *Burgersdicius' Logic* I. xvii. 66 Cause efficient is divided into universal and particular. Universal is that which concurrs with other causes. 1725 Watts *Logic* (1726) 36 This sort of universal Ideas, which may either be considered as a Genus, or a Species, is call'd Subaltern. *Ibid.* 147 An universal Proposition is when the Subject is taken according to the whole of its Extension. 1842 Abp. Thomson *Laws Th.* 64 As to Quantity, judgments are either Universal, Particular, or Singular. 1885 J. Martineau *Types Eth. Th.* I. I. ii. § 8. 201 What is there 'universal' in this geometrical equation?

**b.** Applicable to, operative or valid in, all cases. Of a law or rule (cf. General *a.* 5 b).

1583 Melbancke *Philotimus* R j b, Yet the vniuersallest Axiomes haue their cautions. 1651 Hobbes *Leviathan* II. xxvi. 148 Naturall Lawes being Eternall, and Universall, are all Divine. 1667 Sprat *Hist. R. Soc.* 247 A universal Standard, or measure of Magnitudes, by the help of a Pendulum. 1687 P. Ayres *Lyric Poems* (1906) 309 This Universal Remedy, To hope and live. 1728 Chambers *Cycl.* s.v. *General*, A *General* Rule, *q. d.* an universal Rule. 1747 Wesley *Prim. Physick* (1762) p. xxvii, It comes the nearest an Universal Medecine. 1839 Dickens *Nickleby* ix, As there is no reason to suppose that she was a solitary exception to a universal rule. 1884 tr. *Lotze's Metaph.* 117 The validity of Universal laws. 1890 'R. Boldrewood' *Col. Reformer* (1891) 317 Compelled to employ that only universal solvent, a cash payment.

† **12.** Of motion or action: Constant, continual, perpetual. *Obs. rare.*

1588 Shaks. *L. L. L.* IV. iii. 305 Why, vniuersall plodding poysons vp The nimble spirits in the arteries. 1604 E. G[rimstone] *D'Acosta's Hist. Indies* III. vi. 137 [The comet] mooved daily with an vniversal motion, from East to Weast.

**13.** Of implements, machines or their parts, etc.: Adjustable to all conditions or requirements; not restricted to one fixed type of operation, but capable of variety of work; adapted to various purposes, sizes, forms, etc.

Freq. *universal joint*, a joint or coupling which permits of free movement in any direction of the parts joined, *spec.* one which does this in such a way that one of the connected parts conveys rotary action to the other.

A number of other instances in purely technical use are recorded in Knight's *Dict. Mech.* (1875) and *Suppl.* (1884), and recent Dicts. (1891–).

1676 Hooke *Helioscopes* 14 The Universal Joynt for all these manner of operations. 1688 Holme *Armoury* III. 373 Pendant Dials.., commonly called Equinoctial or Universal Dials, are most used by Sea-Men and Travellers. 1700 Moxon *Math. Instr.* s.v., [The] Universal Equinoctial Dial ..finds the Latitude and Hour of the day and most propositions on the Globe. 1815 J. Smith *Panorama Sci. & Art* I. 111 The stop and fence of the universal plough. 1825 J. Nicholson *Operat. Mechanic* 324 On the end, *n*, of the spindle P,..is screwed occasionally an universal chuck for holding any kind of work which is to be turned. 1829 *Nat. Philos., Mechanics* II. xiii. 62 (L. U. K.), Hooke's universal joint is a very simple and effectual method of transferring rotation from one axis to another. 1881 Raymond *Mining Gloss., Universal train*, a roll train having adjustable horizontal and vertical rolls, so as to produce sections of various sizes. 1888 Jacobi *Printers' Vocab., Universal machine*, a jobbing platen machine—for steam or treadle.

**14.** Special collocations: **universal arithmetic**, † **mathematics**, algebra; **universal suffrage**, a suffrage extending to the whole of a community, esp. one in virtue of which all male persons over twenty-one years of age, except lunatics, aliens, and criminals, have the right to vote for representatives to a legislative (usually parliamentary) assembly; hence *universal suffragist*; **universal umbel** (see quot.).

1720 Raphson, etc. (*title*), *Universal Arithmetick: or, a Treatise of Arithmetical Composition and Resolution. Translated from the Latin [of Newton's *Arithmetica Universalis* (1707)]. 1826 *Encycl. Metrop.* (1845) I. 524/2 The title *Universal Arithmetic* very inadequately expresses the nature, objects, and extent of this department of Analysis. 1673 J. Kersey *Algebra* b 3, The learned Works of which [they]..proclaim their rare Talents in *Universal Mathematicks. 1752 (*title*), The Elements of Universal Mathematics, or Algebra; to which is added, a Specimen of a Commentary on Sir Isaac Newton's Universal Arithmetic. 1706 De Foe *Jure Div.* v. 3 The Land divided, Right to rule divides, And *universal Suffrage then provides. 1798 [see Suffrage 10 b]. 1817 Cobbett *Pol. Reg.* XXXII. 226 That, as to Universal Suffrage, you cannot help calling it universal impracticability. 1857 D. P[useley] *Rise Australia*, etc. 69 Even absolutism with its attendant evils would..be preferable to universal suffrage. 1822 *Blackw. Mag.* XII. 156 If they come back *Universal Suffragists. 1834 Mar. Edgeworth *Helen* xxxv, It is curious that.. Louisa Castlefort, should be obliged..to..turn ultra liberale, or an universal suffragist. 1760 J. Lee *Introd. Bot.* I. viii. (1765) 17 The Umbel that bears the Umbellula on its Footstalks, is called an *universal Umbel.

**15.** Quasi-*adv.* **a.** Universally; in all places. **b.** With universal power. *rare.*

1524 in *Acta Parlt. Scot.* (1875) XII. 40/2 Þat Justice

Airis be halden universale throu oute þe Ralme. **1759** MASON *Caractacus* 86 What, if Cæsar aims To lord it universal o'er the world.

**16.** *absol.* with *the.* **a.** The whole of, all of (something expressed or implied); *spec.* in *Logic* and *Philos.*, the whole class or genus, as distinct from the individuals comprising it.

*c* **1374** CHAUCER *Boeth.* v. pr. iv. (1868) 165 For resoun is she þat diffinisseþ þe vniuersel of hir conseite ryȝt þus. **1551** T. WILSON *Logike* I i b, From the vniuersall to the particular, the argument goeth well. **1818** COLERIDGE *Friend* (ed. 2) I. 269 The ideas of the Necessary and the Universal. **1865** MOZLEY *Mirac.* ii. 46 The universal as a law and the universal as a proposition are wholly distinct. **1871** JOWETT *Plato* I. 265 Tell me what virtue is in the universal.

†**b.** *By* or *in the universal*, in respect of, or with reference to, the whole class; in general terms; generally. *Obs.*

**1552** LATIMER *Serm.* (1562) 127 Suche a maner of speakyng is vsed in the scripture, to speake by the vniuersall: meaning a great numbre, but yet not all: only those that be giltie. **1628** SPENCER *Logick* 206 Both of these distinct formes are one, and the same thing in the generall, or vniversall.

†**c.** The whole community; the people in general. *Obs.*

**1676** in *Brent's Counc. Trent* p. lxx, Which hath produced ..a most intense desire of the conservation of their good Servant, and in the universal a more glorious fame to see.. so singular a favour.

†**17.** *In universal*: **a.** As a body or whole; collectively. **b.** In respect of every thing or part; entirely, wholly. *Obs.*

**1387–8** T. USK *Test. Love* II. xiii. (Skeat) l. 70 At the ginninge of the worlde, every thing by him-selfe was good; and in universal they weren right good. **1615** in *Buccleuch MSS.* (Hist. MSS. Comm.) I. 168 The Spaniard interdicteth Trade to the East Indies in universal, and the Hollanders but to a part.

**B.** *sb.* **1.** *Logic* and *Philos.* That which is predicated or asserted of all the individuals or species of a class or genus, or of many things which are regarded as forming a class; an abstract or general concept regarded either as having an absolute, mental, or nominal existence; a universal proposition; a general term, notion, or idea. Chiefly in *pl.* and opposed to *particulars* or *singulars.*

In mediæval Scholastic philosophy the nature of universals gave rise to the great controversy which resulted in the division of the Schoolmen into Realists, Nominalists, and Conceptualists, according to their respective theories.

*sing.* **1553** EDEN *Treat. New Ind.* (Arb.) 9 A perticuler proueth no vniuersall. **1692** BENTLEY *Boyle Lect.* 141 It is merely a notional and imaginary thing, an abstract universal, which is properly nothing, a conception of our own making. **1697** tr. *Burgersdicius' Logic* I. i. 3 A universal is that which is apt..to be predicated of many things, as *man, horse, plant,* &c. **1728** CHAMBERS *Cycl.* s.v. *Predicable*, Thus Animal is an Universal, with regard to Man and Beast. **1751** *Phil. Trans.* XLVII. 314 The business of natural philosophy is..to note down facts,..and..to collect their proper universal, by a fair..induction. *Ibid.* A new collection of constant and similar facts affords an higher universal. *pl.* **1606** BRYSKETT *Civ. Life* 124 As the hand is apt to take hold of all instruments; so is this power or facultie apt to apprehend the formes of all things, from whence grow the vniuersals. *a* **1676** HALE *Prim. Orig. Man.* (1677) 28 For Universals are but Notions and *Entia Rationis.* **1725** WATTS *Logic* (1726) 36 Some of these Universals are Genus's, if compared with less common Natures. **1794** BURKE *On Petition of Unitarians* Wks. 1842 II. 474 No rational man ever did govern himself, by abstractions and universals. **1837** HALLAM *Hist. Lit.* I. iii. § 67 The long controversies between the Realists and Nominalists concerning the nature of universals. **1860** ABP. THOMSON *Laws Th.* (ed. 5) § 62 Universals..or those general properties which many things share alike, and which are acquired by the mind only by abstracting from the things that exhibit them. **1889** MIVART *Orig. Hum. Reason* 43 General ideas, or 'universals', only arise in our mind after we have experienced corresponding groups of sense-impressions.

†**b.** *pl.* Items of general information or news.

**1650** HOWELL *Lett.* III. 3 This Letter runs upon Univerșalls, because I know your Lordship hath..a spacious understanding, which comprehends the whole world.

†**c.** Abstract magnitude or volume. *Obs.*

**1674** N. FAIRFAX *Bulk & Selv.* 66 Universal, or boak, as taken in the Mathematicks.

**2.** That which is universal; esp. one who or that which is universally powerful, potent, current, etc.

**1556** OLDE *Antichrist* 49 For that cause this honour ought to be graunted to the bishop of Constantinople, that he maye be called the universall of all prelates and the bishop of bishoppes. **1709** MRS. MANLEY *Secret Mem.* (1720) III. 122 Omnipotent Gold has a Power so extensive, that we presume we are not guilty of Hyperbole..in representing it, as the grand Universal. **1855** MILMAN *Lat. Chr.* XIV. vii. VI. 528 The primitive word for 'father' is so nearly an universal, that [etc.].

†**3.** The universe. *Obs.* (common 1600–1625).

**1569** J. SANFORD tr. *Agrippa's Van. Artes* 65 b, It is no lesse folie to saye that, in the universall, is but one worlde alone. **1591** SPARRY tr. *Cattan's Geomancie* 23 So the Earth ..resteth in the middle of the whole vniuersall. **1613** CHAPMAN *Rev. Bussy d'Ambois* III. iv. 72 Hee that striues t'inuert The Vniuersals course with his poore way. **1628** FELTHAM *Resolves* II. lviii. 168 There is a secret chaine in Nature, which drawes the Vniversall to revenge a vice.

†**4.** A medicament or remedy affecting the whole body or system. *Obs.*

**1656** J. SMITH *Pract. Physick* 119 Gallen commends a Bath after Universals. **1694** SALMON *Bate's Dispens.* Pref. A 4 b, Russel's Powder...that Fam'd Universal, which for these twenty-five Years last past has obtain'd a general Reputation..in a manner through the whole World. *Ibid.* I. xvii. 793/2 If it be used for a Gonorrhœa,..Universals ought to be premised, that the Body may be cleansed as much as may be.

‖ **Universa·lia,** *sb. pl.* ? *Obs.* [L., neut. pl. of *ūniversālis*: see prec.] An official letter or proclamation issued by one in authority to all the states or nobles of Poland, esp. one convening the national diet. Also erron. as *sing.* (quot. 1772).

**1708** *Lond. Gaz.* No. 4429/7 The Grand General has..publish'd his Universalia, to exhort the Confederate Estates to continue firm in their Adherence to each other. **1763** *Brit. Mag.* IV. 551 The Primate..dispatches his universalia to the several provinces. **1772** *Hartford Merc.* Suppl. 18 Sept. 4/1 General Haddick is going to publish an Universalia.

**Universa·lian,** *a. rare.* [f. UNIVERSAL *a.* + -IAN.] Universalist, universalistic.

**1853** E. G. HOLLAND *Mem. J. Badger* xi. (1854) 205 [Calvinism's] bold premises were the foundation of the plea of its opposite extreme,—the Universalian statement.

**Unive·rsalism.** [f. as prec. Cf. F. *universalisme.*]

**1.** The fact or quality of being concerned with or interested in all or a great variety of subjects; universality of knowledge.

*c* **1827** COLERIDGE in *Blackw. Mag.* (1882) CXXXI. 119 The all-meaningness and thin-blown bladdery universalisms of the lectures. **1838** *New Monthly Mag.* LIV. 132 The full-blown facility of modern universalism. **1877** MORLEY *Crit. Misc.* Ser. II. 247 That weak kind of universalism which nullifies some otherwise good men.

**2.** *Theol.* The beliefs or special views held by the Universalists; the doctrine of universal salvation or redemption.

**1805** J. SPAULDING (*title*), Universalism Confounds and Destroys Itself. **1840** G. S. FABER *Christ's Disc. Capernaum* 224 A tremendously wide and long enduring Apostasy..is.. rhetorically spoken of in terms which literally import Universalism. **1864** J. DONALDSON *Crit. Hist. Chr. Lit. & Doctr.* I. 37 Heathen Christianity..proclaimed all men alike in God's sight. Paul was the preacher of this universalism. **1871** MOZLEY *Univ. Serm.* v. (1876) 112 The waves of universalism..cannot possibly shake the seat of distributed power and government.

**3.** The fact or condition of being universal in character or scope; universality.

**1840** T. GORDON tr. *Menzel's Germ. Lit.* III. 288 Poetical Universalism.—Herder. **1882** *Athenæum* 14 Oct. 490/1 It is, indeed, somewhat doubtful whether the religion of Rome did not approach universalism almost as much as Islam. **1883** FAIRBAIRN *City of God* III. i. 230 This is..the universalism of Jesus Himself... He belongs to humanity, not to Israel. *Ibid.* 240 The universalism of the person has its counterpart in the universalism of the words.

**Unive·rsalist,** *sb.* and *a.* [f. as prec. + -IST. Cf. F. *universaliste*, G. *universalist.*]

**A.** *sb.* **1.** *Theol.* One who believes or maintains the doctrine that redemption or election is extended to the whole of mankind and not confined to a part of it; *spec.* in *U.S.*, a member of a sect or Church holding this doctrine.

**1626** tr. *Parallel* A ij, The error of the Vniuersalists is too vniuersally dispread. **1648** O. HOWE (*title*), The Vniversalist examined and convicted, destitute of plaine Sayings of Scripture. **1684** BURNET *Trav.* i. (1750) 58 Some Assertors both in Geneva and Switzerland, who denied the Imputation of Adam's Sin, and asserted the Universality of Christ's Death, together with a sufficient Grace given to all Men...These came to be called Universalists. **1728** CHAMBERS *Cycl.* s.v., The Arminians are particularly denominated Universalists. **1773** WESLEY *Wks.* (1872) X. 425 Bishop Ridley, Hooper, and Latimer..were firm Universalists. **1805** J. SPAULDING *Universalism* 150 These Universalists pretend to be the foremost in extolling the grace of God. **1853** BP. S. WILBERFORCE *Let.* in *Life* (1881) II. 211 That you therefore do.. revive the old doctrine of the Universalists. **1861** *Contrib. Eccl. Hist. Connecticut* 278 Attempts..to gather a congregation of Universalists for public worship.

†**2.** A believer in or maintainer of the universality of the Roman Catholic Church. *Obs.*[−1]

**1644** FEATLY *Roma Ruens* 29 To this poynt I earnestly desire particular satisfaction, which I have not yet received from any Roman Catholike, or universalist (as they would be called).

**3.** One who in respect of a specified thing acts with universality or uniformity. *rare.*

**1677** GILPIN *Demonol.* III. xx. 172 A true Christian should be a perfect Universalist, he should be universally against all Sin, and universally for All Duty.

†**4.** One who uses universals or universal propositions. *Obs.*[−1]

**1680** BAXTER *Answ. Stillingfl.* Pref. A 3 Universallists, that can prove me to be an Ass, because I am an Animal.

**5.** One who is supposed to have, or pretends to, a knowledge of all things; a person who is devoted to many subjects or sciences, as opposed to a *specialist*; a universal scholar.

**1713** BENTLEY *Freethinking* iii. 11 A modern Free-thinker is an Universalist in Speculation; any Proposition whatsoever he's ready to decide. **1800** in *Spirit Pub. Jrnls.* IV. 154 All subjects were alike to this universalist. **1830** S. H. CASSAN *Bps. Bath & Wells* II. 172 He was an Universalist in the best sense of the word; and not a smatterer in various sciences. **1881** *Nature* XXIV. 356 The gold of a universalist is apt to shrink down into dross when tested in the crucible of a specialist.

**b.** One who has many occupations, interests, etc.

**1801** *Sporting Mag.* XVIII. 104 You'll find I'm an universalist; i.e. a *Professor* of all trades.

**6.** One who regards something as a whole and not from one particular point of view.

**1892** E. C. STEDMAN *Nat. Poetry* iv. 142 The best critic, then, is the universalist, who sees the excellence of either phase of expression according as it is natural to one's race and period.

**B.** *adj.* Universalistic.

**1819** *Universalist Mag.* 21 Aug. 32/3 Pastor of the First Independent Church of Christ, called Universalist, in Philadelphia. **1859** ALLIBONE *Dict. Eng. Lit.* I. 109 Ballon, Rev. Hosea,..a prominent Universalist minister. **1877** J. E. CARPENTER tr. *Tiele's Hist. Relig.* 89 The universalist monotheism of the Gospel, which has entirely broken down the bounds of nationality.

**Universali·stic,** *a.* [f. prec. + -IC.]

**1.** *Theol.* Of or pertaining to, characteristic of, Universalism or the Universalists.

**1847** R. W. HAMILTON *Rewards & Punishm.* vii. 389 A strong defence of the universalistic doctrine. **1887** E. JOHNSON *Antiqua Mater* 219 The Gnostics, sharing the universalistic aspirations of the time.

**2.** Of, pertaining or extending to, including or affecting, the whole of something, esp. the whole of mankind; inclined to be universal in scope or character. Also *transf.*

*Universalistic Hedonism*, Utilitarianism.

**1872** *Contemp. Rev.* XIX. 664 A..syncretion of Egoistic and Universalistic Hedonism. **1878** MORLEY *Diderot* II. 207 Holbach is a universalistic and not an egoistic Hedonist. **1882** *Athenæum* 11 Feb. 184/1 The universalistic tendencies of the great empires. **1886** *Encycl. Brit.* XX. 370/1 Universalistic religious communities: Islâm, Buddhism, Christianity.

**Universality** (yūnivəɪsæ·lĭti). [a. F. *universalité*, OF. *universaliteit* (14th c.; = It. *universalità*, Sp. *-idad*, Pg. *-idade*), or ad. late L. *ūniversālitās* (Boethius), f. L. *ūniversālis*: see UNIVERSAL *a.* and -ITY.]

**I. 1.** The fact or quality of extending over, existing in, or belonging to the whole (of something expressed in or implied by the context); esp. extension, occurrence, prevalence, or diffusion throughout the whole world, everywhere, or in all things.

*c* **1374** CHAUCER *Boeth.* v. pr. v. (1868) 169 Þat is..þat resoun lokeþ and comprehendiþ by resoun of vniuersalite [L. *in ratione universitatis*], boþe þat þat is sensible and þat þat is ymaginable. **1587** GOLDING *De Mornay* 351 All men knowe, that cheefly Auerrhoes vrgeth the eternitie of the World, and the vniuersalitie of one onely Mynd. **1589** PUTTENHAM *Eng. Poesie* I. ix. (Arb.) 38 The Nobilitie and dignitie of the Art considered aswell by vniuersalitie as antiquitie. **1624** H. MASON *Art of Lying* ii. 25 Persons claimeth..Universality, Antiquity, and Consent, for this..vpstart fancie of their owne. **1686** *Caldwell Papers* (Maitl. Cl.) I. 168 The French language, being, because of its universalitie, so very necessarie for converse. **1707** MORTIMER *Husb.* 501 The Planting of Fruit-Trees;..and the Advantages of it, which consist.. in the Universality of it, there being hardly any Soil, but one sort..or other may be raised on them. **1760–72** H. BROOKE *Fool of Qual.* (1809) IV. 78 God..cannot depart from..that universality of essence, by and in which alone all essences subsist. **1811** PINKERTON *Petral.* p. xxxvi, Experiments more and more evince the universality of iron. **1879** FARRAR *St. Paul* II. 266 He has shown the universality of guilt, and the universality of grace.

**b.** Of a church or religion, esp. Roman Catholicism: Extension to the whole world or all men.

Freq. in 17th cent.; now *rare* or *Obs.*

? **1559** A. P. tr. *Vincent of Lirins' Golden Treatise* (title-p.), The antiquitie, and vniuersalitie, of the Catholicke Religion. **1574** WHITGIFT *Def. Aunsw.* ii. 106 This strengthneth the Papistes vniversalitie. **1608** WILLET *Hexapla Exod.* 551 Vniuersalitie and multitude..is no good rule to know the right church..by. **1691** SIR T. P. BLOUNT *Ess.* 90 That thing call'd *Vniversality*, is so slight an Evidence of Truth, that even Truth it self is asham'd of it. **1728** CHAMBERS *Cycl.* s.v., The Catholicks assert the Universality of their Church, both as to Time, and Persons. **1730** J. DENNE (*title*), Want of Universality no just Objection to the Truth of the Christian Religion. **1874** GREEN *Short Hist.* ix. § 1 He dismissed with contempt the accepted test of universality.

†**c.** Of persons with reference to power or authority (see UNIVERSAL *a.* 2). *Obs.*

**1620** T. GRANGER *Div. Logike* 228 Gregory pronounced the same of Iohn Patriarch of constantinople affecting vniuersalitie. **1661** MORGAN *Sph. Gentry* III. vii. 67 The pope, who hath usurped the Universality, will have his triple Crown, to signifie his dominion over the Universe.

**2.** The fact or quality of extending or applying to, affecting or prevailing among, all the members of a class of persons or things; relation to or inclusion of all individuals, cases, or instances.

**1577** HARRISON *England* II. xix. (1877) I. 307 If a man may presentlie giue a ghesse at the vniuersalitie of this euill. **1634** *T. Norton's Calvin's Inst.* Table of Contents, The universality of the promises of salvation maketh nothing against the doctrine of the predestination of the reprobate. **1695** J. EDWARDS *Perfect. Script.* 342 The universality of the slaughter. **1764** HARMER *Observ.* ii. § 17. 75 The tents of the Arabs are with great universality black. **1771** SIR J. REYNOLDS *Disc.* iv. (1778) 113 He might have seen it in an instance or two; and he mistook accident for universality. **1829** GEN. P. THOMPSON *Exerc.* (1842) I. 132 Closely connected with the universality of suffrage, is the opportunity of its frequent exercise. **1873** HOLLAND *A. Bonnic.* ix. 162 The universality of the influence which they [*sc.* religious revivals] exert during the time of their highest activity.

**b.** Of laws, etc., esp. with reference to validity.

**1712** BERKELEY *Pass. Obed.* Wks. 1871 III. 138 The universality of this mathematical rule. **1747** *Gentl. Mag.* 120/2 That we are not sure of the universality of this law. **1855** BREWSTER *Newton* I. xiii. 381 Every new comet, every new planet,..proclaims the universality of Newton's philosophy. 1874 CARPENTER *Ment. Phys.* II. xvi. 634 The universality of the Law of Gravitation.

†**3.** The study or contemplation of things from a general point of view. *Obs. rare.*

1605 BACON *Adv. Learn.* I. v. § 5 Another error..is, that after the distribution of particular arts and sciences, men haue abandoned vniuersalitie, or *Philosophia prima. Ibid.* II. To the King § 6 If any man think philosophy and universality to be idle studies, he doth not consider that all professions are from thence served and supplied.

**4.** The quality or character of extending to or comprehending all or (more usually) a great variety of subjects; unbounded or very great versatility *of* (mind, genius, etc.).

1765 H. WALPOLE *Vertue's Anecd. Paint.* III. 11 The following [pictures] by Streater.. show the universality of his talent. 1818-9 LADY MORGAN *Autobiog.* (1859) 203 His gigantic labours..indicate the universality of the highest order of mind. 1824 MISS MITFORD *Village* Ser. I. 17 A man..of that peculiar universality of genius which forms..a handy fellow. 1871 'M. LEGRAND' *Cambr. Freshm.* 112 The universality of my friend's mind.

**b.** Capacity for, knowledge of, interest in, all or many things or pursuits; width or extensiveness of understanding, knowledge, or sympathy.

1831 CARLYLE *Sart. Res.* II. iv, Whereby..the vague universality of a Man shall find himself ready-moulded into a specific Craftsman. 1855 HAWTHORNE *Eng. Note-bks.* (1870) I. 375 Perhaps there may be a universality in his face. 1856 R. A. VAUGHAN *Mystics* I. 7 One quality in Gower I have always especially liked,—his universality. 1862 *Macm. Mag.* 240 The universality of the heart, which enables them to feel for, and make allowances for all. 1900 E. HOLMES *What is Poetry?* 65 Universality, not individuality, is of the essence of the poet's genius.

**c.** The fact of knowing everybody or a large number of persons; extensiveness *of* (acquaintance).

1791 PAINE *Rights of Man* 89 By the universality of his acquaintance. 1838 TICKNOR in *Life*, etc. (1876) II. ix. 182 He added, that he himself had never seen him so as to know him..; a curious fact, considering Roger's own universality.

**II. 5.** The entire or whole body or number, the whole, *of* the people, a nation, mankind, etc., regarded collectively; also, the bulk or mass *of* the people. Now *arch.* (Cf. UNIVERSITY 2.)

1561 T. NORTON *Calvin's Inst.* I. 7 Shall the whole vniuersalitie of the world be without this prerogatiue? 1588 *Copy of a Letter* in *Harl. Misc.* (1809) II. 82 The universality of the people through the realm. 1655 *Theophania* 77 The vast frame of the world may be shaken, and the universality of nature suffer a change. 1673 *Essex Papers* (Camden) I. 65 Ye Universallity of their Clergie,..& all their Merchants. 1680 H. MORE *Apocal. Apoc.* 163 One mighty City.. consisting of the University of Cities considered as one. 1709 STRYPE *Ann. Reformation* ii. 72 So averse did the universality of the nation stand against popery. 1737 L. CLARKE *Hist. Bible* VI. 356/1 Innumerable Acclamations.. by the Universality of the People. 1874 GREEN *Short Hist.* iv. § 5. 203 The consent of the prelates, earls, barons, and universality of the realm.

†**b.** The whole world; the universe. *Obs. rare.*

*a* 1586 SIDNEY *Arcadia* III. x, What madd furie can ever so enveagle any conceipte, as to see our mortall..selves to have a reason, and that this universalitie (whereof we are but the lest pieces) should be utterly devoide thereof? 1593 Q. ELIZ. *Boeth.* III. pr. xii. 72 That God was he that ruld the vniuersalitie by the raynes of goodnes.

†**c.** The whole people or state; the people in general. *Obs.*

1614 RALEIGH *Hist. World* v. iii. 496 The Common happinesse of the vniuersalitie. 1644 [H. PARKER] *Jus Populi* 18 The Parliament differs many wayes from the rude bulk of the universality. 1675 *Machiavelli's Prince* xvii, Exorbitant mercy has an ill effect upon the whole universality.

†**d.** The whole subject; a matter or subject regarded generally or as a whole. *Obs.*—1

1726 LEONI *Alberti's Archit.* II. 5/1, I shall speak first of those wherein this particular Art is most concerned; and as for the others, which relate to the universality, they shall serve by way of epilogue.

**6.** *pl.* Something which extends to all the members of a class; a general statement or description, a generality. *Obs.*

*a* 1591 H. SMITH *Sinful Man* (1592) A 5 To the Heathen hee shewed vniuersalities and antiquities. 1608 D. T[UVILL] *Ess. Pol. & Mor.* 9 Simple men; who..beeing vnable to iudge, or conceiue of vniuersalities, suffer themselues..to be wholly guided by their externall sense. 1629 H. BURTON *Truth's Triumph* 210 The deceitful man loueth to walke in vniuersalities or generalities. 1647 JER. TAYLOR *Lib. Proph.* ix. 162 If you can..determine those great questions which consist much in universalities, then also you may determine the particulars.

†**b.** A universal medicine or remedy; a panacea. *Obs.*—1

1756 TOLDERVY *Hist. 2 Orphans* IV. 126 Men who..poyson you with universalities, medicines that are generally ineffectual, and of whose formations they are quite unacquainted.

†**7.** A collective whole or body, as distinct from one of the parts of which it is composed. (Cf. 5.)

1622 BRETON *Strange Newes* C 3 b, Neare the chiefe Citie of Nullibi, in an vniuersalitie, in stead of an Vniuersitie,.. there was a deepe studient in the secrets of Nature. 1642 *View Print. Book int. Observat.* 8 Kingdome or *Regnum* denotes an universalitie or body collected. [1875 POSTE *Gaius* II. com. (ed. 2) 290 As single things can be bequeathed, so can a universality.]

†**8.** Something which exists everywhere or in all things; a universal being. *Obs.*—1

1681 *Whole Duty Nations* 7 He himself is the prime Unity and Universality.

**Universaliza·tion.** [f. next + -ATION.] The action of the verb; the fact or process of becoming universal.

1798 *Monthly Rev.* XXVI. 538 A language already so general must, for that very reason, tend to universalization. 1840 G. S. FABER *Christ's Disc. Capernaum* 225 [A] sentence, which..would have changed this Apparent Universalization into Real Generalization. 1886 W. GRAHAM *Social Problem* 13 A universalisation of the practice [of striking] over the entire field of labour.

**Universalize** (yūnivə·rsăləiz), *v.* [f. UNIVERSAL *a.* + -IZE. Cf. F. *universaliser*, It. *-izzare*, Pg. *-isar.*]

**1.** *trans.* To make or render universal; to give a universal character to; to extend to all the members of a class; to apply or appropriate to a class of things, as distinct from the individuals composing it.

1642 H. MORE *Song of Soul* II. II. iii. 7 Can souls that be thus universalis'd, Begot into the life of God e're dy? 1664 — *Apology* 552, I do not speak of the English Church,..but of..the Reformed Churches in General—so Universalized were my thoughts in that Meditation. 1840 L. HUNT *Seer* 73/1 Their ideal of a face, let them try to universalise it as they can, is a French one. 1855 MILMAN *Lat. Chr.* XIV. iii. VI. 463 The conception by the senses is confused,..till abstracted, analysed, at once universalised and individualised by the intelligence. 1876 L. STEPHEN *Eng. Th. 18th C.* I. 323 We must, then, universalize our terms.

*absol.* *a* 1853 ROBERTSON *Lect.* ii. (1858) 185 It is thus that the poets universalize and unite. 1871 FRASER *Life Berkeley* iii. 77 We cannot even perceive without universalizing.

†**2.** To imbue with general (in contrast to specific) properties. *Obs.*—1

1676 *Princ. Chymists Lond.* 59 Salts distilled from the Soots of Chymnies, arising from different Woods, notwithstanding their Alteration by the Ambient Air, and their being (by that Medium) in some measure Universallized.

**3.** To make of universal application; to bring into universal use.

1809 *Crit. Rev.* XVI. 499 He must universalize in his empire the given religion which he prefers. 1829 BENTHAM *Justice & Cod. Petit.* 102 In the case of circuit business this source of misdecision is purposely established and universalised. 1845 MAURICE *Mor. Philos.* in *Encycl. Metrop.* II. 603/1 To universalize the system of Plato. 1891 [F. C. S. SCHILLER] *Riddles Sphinx* 183 If the law of evolution could be really and completely universalized.

**b.** To extend or spread over the whole expanse.

1813 JEFFERSON *Writ.* (1830) IV. 186 To complete and universalize the desolation of the globe. 1875 W. R. GREG *Misc. Ess.* vi. (1882) 144 Our sewerage system shall be universalized and perfected.

Hence **Unive·rsalized** *ppl. a.*; **Unive·rsalizing** *vbl. sb.* and *ppl. a.* Also **Unive·rsalizer**, one who makes universal.

1651 H. MORE *Second Lash* in *Enthus. Tri.*, etc. (1656) 179 A free divine *universalized spirit is worth all. 1691 NORRIS *Pract. Disc.* 64 The unselfish universalized nature of God. 1871 R. H. HUTTON *Ess.* I. 169 The fourth gospel is essentially a universalised Judaism. 1895 W. M. RAMSAY *St. Paul* xvi. § 3. 375 A distinct step towards the Universalised Church. 1853 E. G. HOLLAND *Mem. J. Badger* xviii. (1854) 372 The active theological minds..may fall under two general classifications which..we may call the centralizers and *universalizers. 1811 BENTHAM *Panopt. Corr.* Wks. 1843 XI. 161 An engine for the *universalising of Protestantism. 1891 [F. C. S. SCHILLER] *Riddles Sphinx* 183 The first case will evidently not bear universalizing. 1836 G. S. FABER *Prim. Doctr. Election* II. iii. 306 The attentive reader..will readily perceive their palpably *universalising tenor. 1851 *Fraser's Mag.* XLIII. 150 A kind of vagabondizing, universalizing philanthropy.

†**Unive·rsaller.** *Obs.*—1 [f. UNIVERSAL *a.* + -ER [1].] One who believes that something is universal; a universalist.

1626 W. FENNER *Hid. Manna* (1652) 44 Thou that are an Universaller of Grace.

**Universally** (yūnivə·rsăli), *adv.* Also 4 vniuersalliche, 5 vniuerselly, 6 -allye, -allie. [f. as prec. + -LY [2].] In a universal manner.

**1.** In every case or instance.

1398 TREVISA *Barth. De P. R.* XVI. ii. (Bodl. MS.), Grauel ..also..haþ vniuersalliche kinde of druynge and of clensinge. 1530 PALSGR. Introd. p. xvi, That thyng happeneth in the soundyng of thre of theyr vowelles onely,..and that nat universally, but onely so often as [etc.]. 1544 *Exhort.* in *Priv. Prayers* (1851) 565 Universally in all our affairs, whatsoever shall befall unto us. 1613 PURCHAS *Pilgrimage* (1614) 130 The fat and bloud being vniuersally forbidden them for food. 1625 N. CARPENTER *Geogr. Del.* I. iii. 66 This proportion is not to be taken vniuersally, but commonly for the most part. 1755 MAGENS *Insurances* II. 189 All Insurances on expected Gains [etc.]..are universally forbid. 1781 GIBBON *Decl. & F.* xxxviii. (1787) III. 588 Under the empire of Charlemagne, murder was universally punished with death. 1809 COLERIDGE *Friend* 28 Such a Rule, if it were universally established, would encourage the arrogant. 1871 MOZLEY *Univ. Serm.* vi. (1876) 122 It would not be true..to say that use was universally accompanied by beauty.

**2.** So as to include every individual of a group or number; without exception of any.

*c* 1412 HOCCLEVE *De Reg. Princ.* 2454, I wolde that the hye degree Of Chiualrie vniuersally Bare vp his hede. 1496 *Act 12 Hen. VII*, c. 6 Wollen Clothe,..by making wherof.. the pover pepull have moste universally their leving. 1561 T. NORTON *Calvin's Inst.* III. 210 Not one or two of them, but all the Scholemen vniuersallye. 1590 GREENE *Never too late* (1600) 9 Women are vniuersally *mala necessaria*, wheresoeuer they be eyther bred or brought vp. 1618 BOLTON *Florus* (1636) 141 Spaine never had a disposition to rise universally against us. 1662 STILLINGFL. *Orig. Sacræ* III. i. § 11 It is hardly conceivable..how mankind should universally agree in some common sentiments. 1709 STEELE *Tatler* No. 46 ¶ 1 The Zealots..fell universally into this Emperor's Policies. 1798 S. & HT. LEE *Canterb. T.* II. 133 A splendid entertainment, to which the English strangers were universally invited. 1847 G. HARRIS *Life Ld. Hardwicke* II. 33 The whole nation was universally against it. 1869 TOZER *Highl. Turkey* II. 308 They are almost universally malevolent.

**3.** With extension to every part of a definite whole; in every part or place; everywhere.

*c* 1430 HOCCLEVE *Min. Poems* 46 The sonne, of whom hir light Shee [*sc* the moon] takith, & it vniuerselly Yeueth vn-to the world whan it is nyght. 1577 HOLINSHED *Chron.* II. 362/1 Murreyn of cattel beganne..so vniuersally in all places, that no towne nor village escaped free. 1664 H. MORE *Myst. Iniq.* xvi. 58 Which implies that the Church has a right..to be universally spred over the face of the Earth. 1664 H. POWER *Exp. Philos.* I. 61 They are universally diffused throughout all Bodies in the World. 1750 tr. *Leonardus' Mirr. Stones* p. ix, An age when Superstition universally prevailed. 1796 H. HUNTER tr. *St.-Pierre's Stud. Nat.* V. 188 The opinion..is universally propagated over all the Nations. 1846 *J. Baxter's Libr. Pract. Agric.* (ed. 4) I. 15 It is an element universally present in nature. 1871 C. DAVIES *Metric Syst.* III. 275 We have universally the Winchester bushel. 1872 RAYMOND *Statist. Mines & Mining* 15 Universally distributed through the vein.

†**4.** So as to affect the whole or every part of something expressed or implied; all over. *Obs.*

*c* 1485 *Digby Myst.* (1882) IV. 1357 He suffered patiently.. To be woundid vniuersally with scowrges, nayles, & spere. 1580 BLUNDEVIL *Horsemanship* III. 72 If he be vexed with an ague, or with anie other disease, vniuersallie hurting his bodie. 1734 tr. *Rollin's Anc. Hist.* (1827) IX. 154 The whole city continued universally in flames. 1758 J. S. *Le Dran's Observ. Surg.* (1771) 36 The Child seemed to be universally swelled. 1793 *Minstrel* II. 159 The storm.. universally chilled her frame. 1805 EMILY CLARK *Banks of Douro* II. 280 She trembled so universally, that Lucy gave her some..water to drink.

†**b.** Inclusively, all together. *Obs.*—1

1673 CAVE *Prim. Chr.* III. i. 221 Himself, family, and house [were] universally burnt to ashes.

**5.** *Logic* and *Metaph.* In relation to all the members of a class or genus; in the manner of a universal proposition or concept (see UNIVERSAL *a.* 11).

1551 T. WILSON *Logike* G vi b, The argument is euermore made from the generall, to the kynde vniuersally. 1620 T. GRANGER *Div. Logike* II. vi, The predicate is in the Subiect vniuersally, that is, in euery subiect of the same kind. 1678 CUDWORTH *Intell. Syst.* 67 The Essences of singular Bodies ..being Abstracted from those Bodies themselves, are consider'd Universally. 1697 tr. *Burgersdicius' Logic* I. xxxi. 122 The enunciation universally first is only that in which the predicate agrees or convenes with the subject. 1725 WATTS *Logic* II. ii. (1726) 152 Mankind..generally have an Inclination to magnify their Ideas, and to talk roundly and *universally* concerning any thing they speak of. 1825 WHATELY *Logic* in *Encycl. Metrop.* (1845) I. 200/1 The term 'necessary to life' is affirmed of food, but not universally; for it is not said of every kind of food.

**b.** In relation to, in respect of, all the things or subjects of the same class or kind.

1660 BOYLE *New Exp. Phys. Mech.* Pref. p. xiii, Being almost universally a Linguist. 1741 KAMES *Decis. Crt. Sess. 1730-52* (1799) 37 The defender's possession of the estate subjected him universally to the predecessor's debts.

**6.** With respect to every individual of a class; by, among, to, etc., all the persons concerned.

1647 CLARENDON *Hist. Reb.* II. § 51 Which was a design willingly heard, and universally grateful. 1667 MILTON *P. L.* IX. 542 Thy Celestial Beautie.., there best beheld Where universally admir'd. 1726 SWIFT *Gulliver* II. vii, I could not avoid reflecting how universally this talent was spread, of drawing lectures in morality..from the quarrels we raise with nature. 1765 *Museum Rust.* IV. 344 Rye is generally (nay universally, I think) allowed to be a better bearer than wheat. 1804 *Med. Jrnl.* XII. 397 As to my third assertion, its truth is so universally known, that all proof is unnecessary. 1838 DE MORGAN *Ess. Probab.* 167 These tables..are almost universally used by the assurance offices. 1875 W. S. HAYWARD *Love agst. World* 5 He was universally respected in the county.

**7.** With adjs. or pa. pples. (Sometimes hyphened.)

1656 COWLEY *Praise of Pindar* Notes iv, The Fabulous, but universally received Tradition. 1675 OWEN *Indwelling Sin* v. (1732) 43 The constant keeping of the Soul in an universally holy Frame. *a* 1700 EVELYN *Diary* 13 July 1654, We all din'd at that..universally-curious Dr. Wilkin's. 1818 COBBETT *Pol. Reg.* XXXIII. 180 The chief reason of this universally evil effect. 1869 DUNKIN *Midn. Sky* 8 The universally-known seven stars in Ursa Major. 1890 *Science-Gossip* XXVI. 30/1 The universally received opinion.

**Unive·rsalness.** [f. as prec. + -NESS.] The quality of being universal; universality.

1561 T. NORTON *Calvin's Instit.* III. 310 The vniuersalnesse of ye promise. 1587 GOLDING *De Mornay* Pref. xxx, The vniuersalnesse of this consent. 1642 H. MORE *Song of Soul* II. I. ii. 46 They'll object Gainst th' universalnesse of this clear notion. *a* 1680 CHARNOCK *Attrib. God* (1834) I. 56 The universalness of his knowledge. 1880 SCHAFF *Person of Christ* 158 The universalness of his character and mission. 1888 *Longm. Mag.* July 255 The apparent universalness of what is presented to them in quantity.

†**Unive·rsalty.** *Obs.*—1 [f. UNIVERSAL *a.* + -TY [1].] Universality.

1567 MAPLET *Gr. Forest* 29 Not onely intending an Aegemonie which we onely promised and is but the chiefest part, but an vniuersaltie which is ye whole.

**Universa·nimous,** *a. nonce-wd.* [Irreg. f. L. *ūnivers-us* universal + *animus* mind.] Universally or completely unanimous.

1862 LOWELL *Biglow P.* Ser. II. ii. ¶ 2 Though the learned

are not agreed as to the particular dialect employed by Theocritus, they are universanimous..as to its rusticity.

**Universa·rian.** *rare*⁻¹. [Cf. next and -ARIAN.] One who belongs to the universe in respect of knowledge (see quot.).

1880 *Times* (weekly ed.) 16 April, If a mind open to new ideas, no matter whence they come, is to be termed 'cosmopolite', then every thinking being must be a universarian.

**Unive·rsary,** *sb.* and *a. rare.* [f. L. *ūnivers-us* UNIVERSAL *a.* or *ūnivers-um* UNIVERSE *sb.*]

†**A.** *sb.* The whole body or number *of* something. *Obs.*⁻¹

*a* 1604 HANMER *Chron. Ireland* (1633) 205 He injoyned the collegiat Vicars of Kilkenny to celebrate the universary and aniversary of the reverend fathers his predecessors.

**B.** *adj.* Of or pertaining to, open to, all.

1816 in *N. & Q.* 9th Ser. XII. (1903) 365/2 This first Stone of the Royal Universary Infirmary for Children.

**Universe** (yū·nivəɹs). Also 5 vniuerse, 6 -uers, 7 univers. [a. F. *univers* (12th c.; = Sp., Pg., It. *universo*), ad. L. *ūniversum* sb., the whole world, orig. neut. sing. of *ūniversus* all taken collectively, universal, f. *ūnus* UNI- and *versus*, pa. pple. of *vertĕre* to turn.]

†**1.** *In universe*, universally, of universal application. *Obs.*⁻¹

*c* 1374 CHAUCER *Troylus* III. 36 Ye folk a lawe han sette in vniuerse; And þis know I by hem þat loueres be, Þat whoso stryueth with 3ow hath þe worse.

**2.** The whole of created or existing things regarded collectively; all things (including the earth, the heavens, and all the phenomena of space) considered as constituting a systematic whole, esp. as created or existing by Divine power; the whole world or creation; the cosmos.

1589 PUTTENHAM *Eng. Poesie* II. xi. (Arb.) 111 The Roundell or spheare..for his ample capacitie doth resemble the world or vniuers. 1596 SPENSER *Hymn Heav. Beauty* 31 Looke on the frame Of this wyde vniuerse, and therein reed The endlesse kinds of creatures. 1611 B. JONSON *Catiline* I. i, O for a clap of thunder now, as loud As to be heard throughout the universe, To tell the world the fact. 1656 COWLEY *Davideis* I. 800 Dull Earth with its own Weight did downwards pierce To the fixt Navel of the Universe. 1738 SWIFT *Pol. Conversat.* 63, I wou'dn't touch a Man's Flesh for the Universe. 1796 H. HUNTER tr. *St.-Pierre's Stud. Nat.* I. 149 That active power of Nature which fills the Universe. 1817 BYRON *Manfred* II. ii. 111 She had..The quest of hidden knowledge, and a mind To comprehend the universe. 1843 *Penny Cycl.* XXVI. 18/1 *Theory of the Universe*,.. what is known of the general arrangement of planets, stars, etc. and of their connexion with one another. 1871 MORLEY *Carlyle* in *Crit. Misc.* Ser. I. 216 The same sense of the puniness of man in the centre of a cruel and frowning universe.

**b.** With *a* and pl. Also const. *of* (something).

1667 MILTON *P. L.* II. 622 A Universe of death, which God by curse Created evil. 1805 WORDSW. *Prelude* XIV. 160 To.. substitute a universe of death For that which moves with light and life informed. 1837 CARLYLE *Fr. Rev.* I. I. ii, To Newton and to Newton's Dog Diamond, what a different pair of Universes! 1872 MOZLEY *Mirac.* (ed. 3) Pref. p. xxvi, These two schools of minds live indeed in different universes.

**c.** *transf.* and *fig.*

*Less universe* (quot. 1674) = MICROCOSM I.

1674 MILTON *P. R.* IV. 459 As..harmless, if not wholsom, as a sneeze To mans less universe. 1728 CHAMBERS *Cycl.* s.v. *University*, They are call'd Universities, or Universal Schools, by reason the four Faculties are supposed to make the World or Universe of Study. 1821 SHELLEY *Epipsych.* 589 Into the height of Love's rare Universe. 1847 J. KIRK *Cloud Dispelled* iv. 67 His conduct is false, and will be denounced as such by the universe of mind. *a* 1854 H. REED *Lect. Brit. Poets* ii. (1857) 62 To trace the associations between the universe of sense and the spiritual life within us. 1871 E. F. BURR *Ad. Fidem* xv. 299 A universe of light and color—a universe of sound.

**d.** *Universe of discourse*: (see quot. 1896).

1881 J. VENN *Symbolic Logic* vi. 128 We must be supposed to know the nature and limits of the universe of discourse with which we are concerned... If we are talking of ordinary phenomena we must know whether we refer to them without limit of time and space. 1896 'L. CARROLL' *Symbolic Logic* I. II. iii. 14 The Genus, of which [the] Terms [of a Proposition] are Species, is called its 'Universe of Discourse'.

**3.** The world or earth, esp. as the place of abode of mankind or as the scene of human activities.

1630 *R. Johnson's Kingd. & Commw.* 134 Such a bridge, that without exception, it may worthily be accounted the admirablest Monument, and firmest erected Collosseum (in that kinde) of all the Vniverse. 1687 T. BROWN *Saints in Uproar* Wks. 1720 I. 89 No People in the Universe know better. 1704 (*title*), The Present State of the Universe. 1765 BLACKSTONE *Comm.* I. 6 A land, perhaps the only one in the universe, in which political or civil liberty is the very end and scope of the constitution. 1791 HAMPSON *Mem. J. Wesley* III. 96 [Wesley] took the universe for his parish. 1820 SHELLEY *Prometh. Unb.* IV. 339 Who all our green and azure universe Threatenedst to muffle round with black destruction.

**b.** *transf.* The inhabitants of the earth; mankind in general.

1742 *Johnson's Debates* (1787) II. 222 The decline of that power which has so long intimidated the universe. *Ibid.* 230 That wisdom..which..the greatest part of the universe will remember with gratitude. 1774 GOLDSM. *Retal.* 31 Here lies our good Edmund,..Who, born for the universe, ..to party gave up what was meant for mankind. 1843 CARLYLE *Past & Pr.* III. viii, 'Go to,..thou shalt pay due debt!' shouts the Universe to them.

Hence **U·niverseful,** as many or as much as the universe will hold.

1891 J. ORR *Chr. View of God & World* (1893) 374 A whole universeful of other spiritual beings.

**Universitarian** (yūnivəɹsitēə·riăn), *a.* [f. as next + *-arian.*] Of or pertaining to, characteristic of, obtaining in, a university.

1834 F. MAHONY in *Fraser's Mag.* X. 317/1 Awfully ludicrous were the dying convulsions of the old universitarian system. 1858 *Almae Matres* 44 No wars between privileges collegiate and universitarian. 1872 MRS. OLIPHANT *Mem. Montalembert* II. 44 The desire that this universitarian teaching should be above reproach.

Hence **Universita·rianism,** the educational method or system characteristic of or prevailing in a university; advocacy of or preference for this.

1889 *Jrnl. Educ.* 1 Sept. 479/1 At the risk of being accused of classicism, or universitarianism, I must confess that I do believe in a certain amount of classical work.

**Unive·rsitary,** *a. rare.* [f. UNIVERSIT-Y + -ARY¹. Cf. F. *universitaire* (1835).] Of the nature of, having the character of, a university.

1889 *Cath. News.* 26 Oct. 5 The half-ecclesiastical, half-universitary French College of Tunis.

‖**Unive·rsitas.** *Scots Law.* [L.: see next.] The whole (of an estate or inheritance).

1765–8 [see UNIVERSAL *a.* 2 b]. 1838 W. BELL *Dict. Law Scot.* 467 Things, in their nature heritable, may become moveable by being made part of a moveable *universitas.* 1888 LD. MACNAGHTEN in *Law Rep. Ho. Lords* XIII. 383 The legacies are to be paid out of the universitas of the testator's estate.

**University** (yūnivə̄·ɹsĭti), *sb.* Forms: 6 vniuersite, 5 -versite, 5–6 -uersitee, 4–5 vnyuersite(e, 5–6 -uersyte(e; 5–7 vniuersitie (6 *Sc.* wni-), 6 -tye, vnyuersytye, -tie, 7 vniuersity, -versity, 6–7 universitie, 7– university. See also VARSITY, VERSITY. [a. AF. *université*, *universeté*, *univercyté*, OF. *universitei*, *universiteit*, *université* (13th c.; mod.F. *université*, = Pr. *universitat*, It. *università*, Sp. *universidad*, Pg. *-idade*; also in sense 1 MDu. *universitet*, MDu. and Du. *universiteit*, MG., MLG. *universitête*, MHG. *universitêt*, G. *universität*, Dan., Sw. *universitet*):— L. *ūniversitāt-*, *ūniversitās*, (1) the whole, entire number, universe, (2) in later and mediæval Latin (chiefly in legal use), a society, company, corporation, or community regarded collectively; f. L. *ūniversus* (see UNIVERSE).]

**I. 1.** The whole body of teachers and scholars engaged, at a particular place, in giving and receiving instruction in the higher branches of learning; such persons associated together as a society or corporate body, with a definite organization and acknowledged powers and privileges (esp. that of conferring degrees), and forming an institution for the promotion of education in the higher or more important branches of learning; also, the colleges, buildings, etc., belonging to such a body.

Sometimes, especially in former use, synonymous with *college*: see COLLEGE *sb.* 4 c.

*c* 1300 *St. Edmund* in *S. Eng. Leg.* I. 438/256 So þat he bigan at Oxenford of diuinite, So noble aloused þer nas non in al þe vniuersite. *Ibid.* 439/278 He bigan so deope desputi of þe trinite, Þat gret wonder me hadde þurf al þe vniuersite. *c* 1384 ? WYCLIF *Wks.* (1880) 157 Heþene mennus lawis and worldly clerkis statutis ben red in vnyuersitees. *c* 1400 *Rom. Rose* 6769 At Parys..he had..The accorde of the vniuersite, And of the puple as semeth me. *c* 1425– [see COLLEGE *sb.* 4]. *c* 1450 *Godstow Reg.* 438 The house..that Robert of Staunton held of the vnyuersite of Oxenford. 1509 FISHER *Funeral Serm. C'tess Richmond* Wks. (1876) 301 The studyentes of bothe the vnyuersytees. 1579 W. WILKINSON *Confut. Fam. Love* 40 They labour to put out [the eyes of this land (the Vniuersityes I meane). 1644 MILTON *Educ.* 3 This place should be at once both School and University. 1661 LAMPLUGH in *Extr. St. Papers Friends* Ser. II. (1911) 126 University, Town and Country are far more active and vigilant then before. 1702 LUTTRELL *Brief Rel.* (1857) V. 145 A patent..for founding an university.., to be called king Williams university. 1725 BAILEY *Erasm. Colloq.* (1733) 259 Are you going to Louvain to see the University? 1785 J. ADAMS *Wks.* (1854) IX. 530 He is anxious to study some time at your university [= Harvard College] before he begins the study of law. 1840 CARLYLE *Heroes* v. (1858) 305 Universities are a notable, respectable product of the modern ages. 1856 STANLEY *Sinai & Pal.* x. 364 The great Jewish university which rendered Tiberias for three centuries the metropolis of the race. 1868 M. PATTISON *Academ. Org.* 46 The university of the chancellor, masters, and scholars, is one corporation, and each of the colleges distinct and independent societies.

**b.** *fig.* and *transf.*

1595 *Locrine* III. iii, I think you were broght vp in the vniuersitie of bridewell; you haue your rhetorick so ready at your toongs end. 1607 HIERON *Wks.* I. 386 To be admitted into that great vniuersitie, where He, which is the doctour of the chaire, Christ Iesus, will [etc.]. 1615 (*title*), A Catalogue or Table of all the Arts and Sciences read and taught in this University of London. 1652 BENLOWES *Theoph.* II. xiii, Man,..by infusion wise;..Chanc'llor install'd of Eden's University. *c* 1852 J. GIBSON in *Biog.* (1911) iii. 28 He looked upon Rome as the great University of Sculpture. 1863 MISS BRADDON *Aurora Floyd* xxxi, In the London universities of crime. 1890 'R. BOLDREWOOD' *Col. Reformer* (1891) 215 None of these young gentlemen was absolutely necessary at that ovine university [= a sheep-station.]

†**2.** The whole body, aggregate, or number *of* creatures, persons, things, etc.; = UNIVERSALITY 5.

1382 WYCLIF *Tobit* viii. 19 That the vnyuersite of Jentilis knowe, for thou art God alone in al erthe. ? 1402 QUIXLEY in *Yorksh. Archæol. Jrnl.* (1908) XX. 50 To all þe worldes vniversitie This balade be ensample and myrrour. *c* 1449 PECOCK *Repr.* II. xvi. 243 In al the hool vnyuersite of thingis and of beingis. 1494 *Hylton's Scala Perf.* II. xlvi. (W. de W.), Al thise gracyous knowynges felid in a soule of the vnyuersitee of al creatures. *c* 1510 MORE *Picus* Wks. 18/2 If any part of the whole vniuersitye of creatures were destroyed. 1563 MAN *Musculus' Commonpl.* 29 b, All that compasse of the whole universitie of thinges and times. 1581 W. FULKE in *Confer.* III. (1584) O iv b, The vniuersitie of faithfull doeth pray. 1604 T. WRIGHT *Passions* VI. 304 The vniversity of Beastes, foules, and fish. 1659 H. THORNDIKE *Wks.* (1846) II. 483 If in all Scripture..a Church signify the university of Christians. 1677 GALE *Crt. Gentiles* IV. 180 The Communitie or Universitie of the Multitude. [1862 G. LONG tr. *Th. M. Aurelius Anton.* p. lxxvi, The gods will do whatever is best and consistent with the university of things.]

*fig.* 1382 WYCLIF *Jas.* iii. 6 Oure tunge is fijr, the vniuersite of wickidnesse [L. *universitas iniquitatis*]. 1526 *Pilgr. Perf.* (W. de W. 1531) 76 b, Yᵉ tonge is but a small thynge, ..but it is (sayth the sayd apostle) the vniuersite of all euyls.

†**b.** Without const. The whole of something; all things, etc.; universal nature. *Obs.*

*c* 1374 CHAUCER *Boeth.* v. pr. iv. (1868) 165 Þe eye of intelligence is hey3er for it sourmounteþ þe environynge of þe vniuersite and lookeþ ouer þat by pure subtilite of þou3t. 1382 WYCLIF *2 Macc.* xiv. 35 Thou, Lord of vnyuersitee, or of alle creatures. 1387–8 T. USK *Test. Love.* I. ix. (Skeat) l. 46 Man is mad of al the foure elementes. Al universitee is rekened in him alone. 1432–50 tr. *Higden* (Rolls) II. 205 For God knowethe how euery thynge awe to be create, and how he scholde dispose the pulcritude of the vniversite in hit. 1502 *Ord. Crysten Men* (W. de W. 1506) I. iv. D iij, By the nombre of seuen..vnyuersyte to vs is sygnyfyed. 1610 HEALEY *St. Aug. Citie of God* 314 Where ever they live, they may finde a god the governor and father of all university.

†**c.** The universe; = UNIVERSALITY 5 b. *Obs.*

1494 *Hylton's Scala Perf.* II. xlvi. (W. de W.), Our lorde Jhesu maker & keper of al this fayr vnyuersitee. 1591 SYLVESTER *Du Bartas* I. i. (1641) 5/1 In Six dayes [God] formed..All things contain'd in th' Universitie. 1598 T. BASTARD *Chrestoleros* (1880) 6 Man is a little world and beares the face And picture of the Vniuersitie. *a* 1619 FOTHERBY *Atheom.* II. x. § 1 (1622) 299 This Vnity: which they make the onely cause of the whole vniuersity. 1642 H. MORE *Song of Soul* I. ii. 13 Physis is the great womb From whence all things in th' University Yclad in divers forms do gaily bloom.

†**d.** The whole people; = UNIVERSALITY 5 c.

1677 GALE *Crt. Gentiles* III. I. v. 181 That the first invention ..of Laws may be committed to prudent men; and yet the.. confirmation of them appertain to the universitie or common multitude.

**e.** *Law.* (See quot. 1832.)

1832 AUSTIN *Jurisprudence* II. p. xli, Such universities of rights and duties (or such complex aggregates of rights and duties) as arise by universal succession. 1861 MAINE *Anc. Law* 178 Without this fact there is no university of rights and duties.

†**3.** *Your university*, the collective whole of the members of a body, group, or company of persons specifically addressed in some formal or official document. Also pl. in Sc. use. *Obs.*

Chiefly in renderings of the common phrase *Noverit universitas vestra.*

*c* 1400 *Brut* cli. 163 To alle Cristen peple..Iohn, by the grace of God, kyng of Engeland, gretyng to 3our vniuersite. 1416 *Munim. de Melros* (Bann. Cl.) 539 Wit yhoure vniuersite þat [etc.]. 1500 *Cartular. St. Nicholai Aberdon.* (New Spald. Cl.) I. 76 Till all ande sindry.., gretinge in gode euirlesting. 3oure vniuersiteis sall wit ws..till hafe consentit [etc.]. 1543 *Test. Ebor.* (Surtees) VI. 161 Knowe your universitie, that I..do make my last will of certayne my landes. *c* 1596 in *Abstr. Protocols Town Clerks of Glasgow* (1897) V. Pref. 16 To all and sindry..gretyng... Wittis your universiteis that [etc.].

†**4. a.** A body or company of persons associated together for some purpose. *Obs.*⁻¹

1471 CAXTON *Recuyell* (Sommer) 617 Hit is leefful þ[a]t an vnyuersite answere not alway to one maister.

†**b.** A body or class of persons regarded collectively; esp. an aggregate of persons forming a corporate body or society, a corporation. *Obs.*

1607 COWELL *Interpr.*, *Vniversitie*, is by the Ciuill lawe any bodie politicke, or corporation. 1643 PRYNNE *Sov. Power Parl.* App. 159 Although kings doe die, the people in the mean time (as niether any other Universitie) never dyeth. 1678 SIR G. MACKENZIE *Crim. Laws Scot.* I. i. § 7 (1699) 11 A collective Body of People, or university, such as a Burgh or Incorporation. [1755 MAGENS *Insurances* II. 40 The Prior and Consuls..of the University of the Shippers and Merchants..of this City of Seville. 1776 A. SMITH *W. N.* I. x. I. 148 All such incorporations [of trades] were antiently called universities. *Ibid.*, The university of smiths, the university of tailors, &c. 1843 *Penny Cycl.* XXVI. 22/2 The universities or corporate bodies at Rome.]

**II.** †**5.** Extension to the whole (*of* something); = UNIVERSALITY 1. *Obs. rare.*

1553 ASCHAM in *Lett. Lit. Men* (Camden) 18 My trust is ye will not judge me unconstant, for this universitie in choice of my living. 1677 GALE *Crt. Gentiles* III. II. iv. 270 Al perfection importes some kind of universitie. *Ibid.* 271 Now God having the whole of essence in himself must necessarily have an universitie of perfection.

**III.** *attrib.* and *Comb.* (in sense 1).

**6. a.** Simple attrib., passing into adj. use (rarely with hyphen): Of, pertaining or belonging to, characteristic of, prevailing or obtained at, a University or Universities, as *University course*, *court*, *education*, *learning*, *lecture*, *library*, etc.

1379 *Rolls of Parlt.* III. 69/1 Son College appellez Mokel

Universite Hall en Oxenford. **1589** R. HARVEY *Pl. Perc.* (1590) 17 He will..praise him, that he is not infected with.. Vniuersitie learning. **1602** *2nd Pt. Return Parnass.* IV. v. 1806 Few of the university pen plaies well. **1606** DEKKER *News fr. Hell* F 3 b, Ibis Homere, that hath laine sick seuenteen yeers together of the Vniuersitie plague, (watching and want). *a* **1628** F. GREVIL *Sidney* (1652) 199 Lest.. she might be constrained to..labour the compassing of disorderly ends, by a Mechanicall kinde of University Canvasse. *a* **1700** EVELYN *Diary* 5 Mar. 1673, University lectures and erudition. **1708** J. CHAMBERLAYNE *St. Gt. Brit.* I. III. (1710) 302 [The] University Library [Cambridge]. **1726** R. NEWTON (*title*), University Education; or, an Explication and Amendment of the Statute which [etc.]. **1783** *Encycl. Brit.* (ed. 2) X. 8753/2 The jurisdiction of the university-courts in criminal matters. **1868** *Rep. U.S. Commissioner Agric.* (1869) 140 Students enter upon the university course with a certain preparation. **1871** J. PLACE (*title*), University Tests, and their Abolition, Considered in a Letter [etc.]. **1895** RASHDALL *Univ. of Europe* II. II. 325 Another essential qualification for a University town..is facility of access.

**b.** That is (or has been) a member of a University; educated or studying at a University, as *University chum, man*, etc.

**1580** SPENSER *Three Proper Lett.* Wks. (1912) 619/1 Some learned, and well aduized Uniuersitie man. **1641** R. BROOKE *Eng. Episc.* II. vii. 111 They thinke the wayes of Gods Spirit are free, and not tied to a University man. **1706** PHILLIPS (ed. Kersey), *Servitour*,..a poor University-Scholar that attends others for his Maintenance. **1755** *Man* No. 13. 4 An university chum of mine. **1868** M. PATTISON *Academ. Org.* 2 Even University men themselves betray..an impression that something should be done.

**c.** With the names of officials, etc., attached to or connected with a University, as *University auditor, lecturer, librarian, orator* (see ORATOR 5), *preacher, register*, etc.

**1589** NASHE in Greene *Menaphon* (1610) A iv b, That royall erection of Trinitie Colledge, which the Vniuersity Orator.. aptly termed *Colonia deducta*. **1614** J. CHAMBERLAIN in *Crt. & Times Jas. I* (1848) I. 305 The University Orator, Nethersole,..is taxed for calling the prince *Jacobissime Carole*. **1631** MILTON (*title*), On the University Carrier who sicken'd in the time of his vacancy. *a* **1700** EVELYN *Diary* 10 July 1669, The *Terræ filius* (the Universitie Buffoone). **1708** J. CHAMBERLAYNE *St. Gt. Brit.* I. III. (1710) 298 The Custos Archivorum, or University-Register. **1800** *Cambr. Univ. Cal.* 6 University Officers [include] Chancellor, ..High Steward,..Vice-Chancellor [etc.]. **1882** *Addenda Corpus Stat. Univ. Oxon.* 882/2 The University Auditor appointed under the provisions of the Statute. **1893** *Glasgow Univ. Calendar* 19 Lecturers, Demonstrators, or University Assistants.

**d.** With past or pres. pples., chiefly in locative combs., as *University-bred, -taught, -trained*; *-going* adjs.

**1846** LD. CAMPBELL *Chancellors* cxxi. (1857) VI. 2 The common-place progress of a high-born, university-bred barrister. **1879** J. C. MORISON *Gibbon* 11 The two greatest historians..were not university-bred men. **1898** *Edin. Rev.* Jan. 121 The university-going class among the Roman Catholic community.

**7.** Special combs., as **University cap**, the academical cap worn by the members of a University, a square cap or 'mortar-board'; **University chair**, the chair or office of a University professor; **University Chest**, at Oxford and Cambridge, the funds of the University, or the office which receives and administers these; **University extension**: (see EXTENSION 9 g); **University sermon**, a sermon preached before the members of a University, usually by a specially nominated or appointed person.

**1772** NUGENT *Hist. Fr. Gerund* I. 73 Heads stuck in *university-caps. **1831** CARLYLE *Sart. Res.* III. x, They sometimes invert the hat, and wear it brim uppermost, like a University-cap. **1883** *N. & Q.* 15 Dec. 469/1 The University or 'Trencher' Cap. **1711** SHAFTESB. *Charac.* III. 287 He finds these Subjects..appropriated to the School, the *University-Chair, or Pulpit. **1717** E. MILLER *Acc. Univ. Camb.* 177 Neither the Vice-chancellor.., or the *University Chest, get one Farthing of Money by it. **1870** *Addenda Corpus Stat. Univ. Oxon.* II. 800 The Curators of the University Chest. **1827** *Oxford Guide* 56 In the Long Vacation there are no *University sermons.

Hence † **Unive·rsity** *v.*, to provide or endow with a University; **Unive·rsityless** *a.*, having no University; **Unive·rsityship**, the state or condition of being a University; status as a University.

**1682** *Loyal Satirist* in Somers *Tracts* (1812) VII. 69 Pembroke may be visited, and Manchester *universitied. **1655** FULLER *Hist. Camb.* 21 As for Scotland, it was *University-less till [etc.]. *Ibid.* 35 The *University-ship of Cambridge, is to be accounted from her original constitution.

† **Uni·vocacy.** *Obs.*[−1] [f. post-cl. L. *ūnivoc-us* (see next) + -ACY.] Univocal quality; oneness or sameness of character.

**1658** SIR T. BROWNE *Gard. Cyrus* 135 The Æquivocall production of things under undiscerned principles, makes a large part of generation, though they seem to hold a wide univocacy in their set and certain Originals.

**Univocal** (yuni·vŏkăl), *a.* and *sb.* Also 6 vnyuocal(le. [f. post-cl. L. *ūnivoc-us* having one meaning (f. L. *ūni-* UNI- + *vōc-, vōx* VOICE *sb.*) + -AL. So It., Sp., Pg. *univoco*, F. *univoque* (see UNIVOQUE).]

**A.** *adj.* **1.** † **a.** Of symptoms, signs, etc.: Indicative of, signifying, or denoting one thing; certain or unmistakable in significance. Chiefly *Med. Obs.*

**1541** COPLAND *Guydon's Quest. Chirurg.* Q iij b, Fyrste than in procedynge..to the knowlege of the vnyuocal sygnes. *Ibid.*, The sygnes of lepry aswel equyuocalles as vnyuocalles. **1706** PHILLIPS (ed. Kersey), *Univocal Signs* (in Surgery) are certain Accidents or Signs of the Fracture of the Scull,..distinguish'd from others termed Equivocal. **1738** WARBURTON *Div. Legat.* I. 5 No less illustrious, but more univocal Marks of Truth, that God hath been pleased to impress upon his Dispensations. **1783** POTT *Chirurg. Wks.* II. 405 Though this be one symptom,..yet it is not an univocal or infallible one.

**b.** Of terms, etc.: Having only one proper meaning or signification; admitting or capable of a single interpretation or explanation; of which the meaning is unmistakable; unambiguous.

Opposed to EQUIVOCAL *a.* 2. Now esp. in *Logic*.

**1656** [? J. SERGEANT] tr. *T. White's Peripat. Inst.* 285 The same name would signifie God and a Creature, in the same signification, and would be univocall. **1661** MORGAN *Sph. Gentry* I. vi. 88 The crown and horn are in the sacred scripture univocal expressions of glory and dignity. **1671** BAXTER *Holiness* xxviii. 9 It is but Analogically called either *Holiness* or *Morality*, and not in a proper or univocal sense. **1725** WATTS *Logic* I. iv. § 6 Univocal words are such as signify but one idea, or at least but one sort of thing. **1774** REID *Aristotle's Logic* i. § 3. 4 An explication of what is meant by univocal words, what by equivocal. **1843** MILL *Logic* I. ii. § 8 A name is univocal, or applied univocally with respect to all things of which it can be predicated in the same sense. **1865** GROTE *Plato* I. xvii. 500 The different significations of the same word: the univocal and the equivocal. **1892** *Tablet* 28 May 848 Declaring in terms which are simply univocal [etc.].

† **c.** *Mus.* (See quot.) *Obs. rare*[−0].

**1801** BUSBY *Dict. Mus.*, *Univocal*, the epithet applied by Ptolemy to the octave and its replicates. [Hence in some later Dicts.]

† **2.** Uniform, homogeneous; not exhibiting variation or deviation; confined to one kind or nature.

Freq. in the latter half of the 17th c., esp. in the writings of Jeremy Taylor; in some instances it is difficult to determine the precise sense.

**1615** CROOKE *Body of Man* 28 A dead or mortified part.. may not be called a part but equiuocally, because it hath not an vniuocall forme with the whole. **1647** JER. TAYLOR *Lib. Proph.* xiii. 201 When the actions and perswasions of a sect ..are univocall. **1653** — *Serm. for Year* I. xx. 255 The joyes of religion are not univocal but productive of..præternatural pleasures. **1662** J. CHANDLER *Van Helmont's Oriat.* 156 So, from the univocall, simple, and homogeneall immortall minde, should so many properties and inclinations of men badly be fetched. **1727** WARBURTON *Tracts* (1789) 87 But Truth..is of much cooler Contemplation; as paying its Court to the Understanding only, by affording a regular View of its simple univocal Original.

† **3.** Of or belonging to, characteristic of, things of the same name or species; esp. in *univocal generation*, normal or regular generation between male and female members of the same species. *Obs.*

**1638** JACKSON *Creed* IX. viii. § 3 He which is as truly the Son of God..must needs be as absolutely eternal as the Deity,..otherwise the generation should be equivocal and imperfect, not univocal. **1660** R. COKE *Justice Vind.* 6 Creatures..generated and produced from univocal generation or production, that is, from the coition of male and female of the same species. **1708** *Brit. Apollo* No. 2. 2/1 Generation is Univocal: That is, a Species can be no otherwise naturally formed than by a seminal Production. **1748** *Phil. Trans.* XLV. 656 Thus do these Principles..never deviate further than is consistent with univocal Generation. **1822** J. FLEMING *Philos. Zool.* I. 23 A process which is termed Univocal or Regular Generation.

† **b.** Of actions, causes, etc. *Obs.*

*a* **1640** J. BALL *Answ. to Can* (1642) I. 132 That which is spoken of causes univocall, necessary and proper. **1669** FLAVEL *Husb. Spiritualized* viii. 76 Grace in it self.. cannot be the proper univocal cause of any evil effect. **1697** tr. *Burgersdicius' Logic* I. viii. 27 Action univocal is that by which the action produces an effect of its own species; action æquivocal, of a diverse.

† **4.** Made, uttered, etc., with or as if with one voice. Of consent, etc.: Unanimous. *Obs.*

**1615** J. STEPHENS *Satyr. Ess.* 242 Hee..is never free of the Company..till hee hath drunke out his Apprentise-hood among the grand Masters; and then with an vnivocall consent, hee may commend his Wares. *a* **1734** NORTH *Lives* III. 114 They bellowed and roared with univocal noise, not only in the city but all over England. *a* **1734** — *Exam.* III. vii. § 61 (1740) 548 It was their univocal Declaration, that [etc.].

**B.** *sb.* A univocal term or word.

**1728** CHAMBERS *Cycl.* s.v., Univocals..are defined by Aristotle to be those Things whose Name is common, and the Reason corresponding to the Name..the same. **1788** T. TAYLOR *Proclus* I. p. ii, If infinite men, horses, and a multitude of other univocals, are produced in an infinite time. **1822-7** *Good's Study Med.* (1829) I. 407 Regius, arquatus, aurigo, are not indeed univocals, but very clearly equivalents.

**Uni·vocally,** *adv.* [f. prec. + -LY [2].]

**1.** So as to mean only one thing or species; in one and the same sense; with one meaning or signification; hence, unmistakably, unambiguously.

**1593** T. BELL *Motives Romish Faith* (1605) 110 If matrimony be a sacrament properly and vnivocally so called. **1626** JACKSON *Creed* VIII. viii. § 2 The generall definition..of a servant is univocally the same, (1) in legall servants, (2) in servants to sin [etc.]. **1638** CHILLINGW. *Relig. Prot.* I. vi. § 42. 363 You have not set down cleerely and univocally what you mean by it. **1677** GALE *Crt. Gentiles* III. II. iii. 248 That nothing can predicate univocally of God and the Creature is most evident. **1728** CHAMBERS *Cycl.* s.v. *Predicable*, A Predicable is a Nature which may be predicated univocally of all things to which it is common. *c* **1790** REID *Let.* Wks. 1846 I. 75/2 The same word may be applied to different things in three ways:..Univocally, when the things are species of the same genus [etc.]. **1842** SIR W. HAMILTON in *Reid's Wks.* (1846) I. 205/2 If the names..were to be employed univocally—*i.e.*, to denote always things the same or similar. **1874** *Contemp. Rev.* XXIV. 788 As if every tyro in theology did not know that not even 'being' could be predicated univocally of God and of any creature.

† **2.** By members of the same species; regularly, normally. (Cf. UNIVOCAL *a.* 3.) *Obs.*

*a* **1676** HALE *Prim. Orig. Man.* II. ix. (1677) 207 Animals which are perfect and univocally generated. **1704** RAY *Creation* (ed. 4) II. 372 All Creatures are generated Univocally by Parents of their own kind. **1728** CHAMBERS *Cycl.* s.v. *Equivocation*, The Moderns..hold that all Animals, nay and Vegetables too, are Univocally produced.

**3.** With one voice; unanimously.

**1671** J. WEBSTER *Metallogr.* xviii. 255 Therefore the.. Secretaries of this Philosophy do univocally testifie, that [etc.]. **1862** *Temple Bar Mag.* VI. 171 All bellowed out univocally that the sole object..was to drive dull care away.

† **Uni·vocalness.** *Obs.*[−1] [-NESS.] = UNIVOCATION.

**1697** J. SERGEANT *Solid Philos.* 26 The Univocalness which I assert to the word (Cognition) and (Notion) is such a one as is taken from their Radix (Nosco).

† **Uni·vocate,** *a. Obs.*[−1] [f. post-cl. L. *ūnivocus* UNIVOCAL *a.*: see -ATE [2].] Of one sound or pronunciation.

**1432-50** tr. *Higden* (Rolls) II. 161 The langage of Normannes is oon and vnivocate [L. *univoca*] allemoste amonge theyme [*sc.* Englishmen] alle.

† **Univocation.** *Obs. rare.* [ad. late L. *ūnivocātiōn-*, *ūnivocātio* (Quicherat), noun of action f. **ūnivocāre* (see UNIVOCAL *a.*). Cf. F. *univocation*, Sp. *univocacion*, Pg. *univocação*, It. *univocazione*.] Oneness or identity of name or meaning.

*a* **1610** G. FLETCHER *Israel Redux* (1677) 13 This univocation of Tartar Cities with those of Israel..doth plainly shew that the Israelitish People have been there. **1693** SOUTH *Animadv. Sherlock's Bk.* (ed. 2) 242 Since no one Thing can agree both to God and the Creature, by a perfect Univocation. **1728** CHAMBERS *Cycl.* s.v., The School-men have long disputed about the Univocation of Being.

**Univo·ltine,** *sb.* and *a.* [ad. F. *univoltin, -tain*, f. *uni-* UNI- + It. *volta* turn, time.] **a.** *sb.* One of a breed of silkworms which produces a single brood in a year. **b.** *adj.* Having but one brood each year.

**1874** J. GEOGHEGAN *Parl. Rep. Silk in India* 118 That this insect [*sc.* a silkworm] has quite changed its period of existence.., and from a multivoltine become a univoltine [*sic*]. **1883** G. WATT *Econ. Prod. India* III. 66 In Upper India and in Kashmir the univoltine worms are those usually reared. **1892** *Chambers's Encycl.* IX. 453/1 The *B*[*ombyx*] *mori* is univoltine or annual.

† **Univoque,** *a. Obs.*[−1] In 6 vnyuoke. [a. F. *univoque*: see UNIVOCAL *a.*] = UNIVOCAL *a.* 1 a.

**1541** R. COPLAND *Guydon's Quest. Chirurg.* Q ij, They.. shulde ryght dylygently beholde theym & considre the vnyuoke sygnes and equyuokes also. And nat for one onely token gyue theyr sentences, but by many conuenaunces, and specyally vnyuokes.

† **Uniw·are,** *adv. Obs.* In 4 vn-, onywar, oniwar. [UN-[1] 11 b and 7: cf. UNAWARE and UNWARE.] Unaware, unawares; esp. in phr. *on uniware* = at unaware(s).

**1297** R. GLOUC. (Rolls) 1966-7 Þis prince al an onywar [*v.rr.* al vn ywar, al in on oniwar] toward hom drou. Hii come aȝen him onywar [*v.r.* on oniwar] & slowen him al vor noȝt. *Ibid.* 2927, 3261, 3501, 4328, etc.

† **Uniwa·res,** *adv. Obs.*[−1] In 3 unȝewares. [f. as prec. + -S. Cf. UNAWARES, UNWARES.] Unawares.

*a* **1200** *Vices & Virtues* 19 Speded ȝeu, forðan ȝure ændedai neihȝeð, and cumð unȝewares al swa þief be nihte.

† **Unja·cobitize,** *v.* [UN-[2] 6 c.] *trans.* To detach from the Jacobite cause. **1719** OZELL tr. *Misson's Mem.* 138 Now their Castles in the Air being overturn'd, they begin to be Unjacobitiz'd.

**Unja·ded,** *ppl. a.* (UN-[1] 8.)

[**1775** ASH.] **1779** J. MOORE *View Soc. Fr.* (1789) I. iii. 23 My head undisturbed with wine, and my spirits unjaded by play. **1876** MISS YONGE *Womankind* xix, The freshness of her unjaded mind. **1880** J. NICHOL *Byron* 71 A public taste as yet unjaded by..imaginative descriptions of foreign scenery.

**Unja·gged,** *a.* (UN-[1] 9.) **1728** BRADLEY *Dict. Bot.* s.v. *Jacobæa*, This unjagged Ragwort hath..Leaves lying next the Root, not jagged or divided at all. **Unjai·led,** *pa. pple.* (UN-[2] 5, 8.) **1630** J. TAYLOR (Water P.) *World's Eighth Wonder* Wks. II. 62 For Eolus..With winds vniayled came at vnawares, And greenefaced Neptune with defiance dares.

**Unja·rring,** *ppl. a.* (UN-[1] 10.)

**1624** T. ADAMS *The Temple* 31 God who..hath put vs in the right & vniarring harmony of truth. **1651** H. L'ESTRANGE *Answ. Mrq. Worcester* 52 A grave Author hath cull'd out..303 oppositions amongst the Marquis his unjarring Catholiques. **1880** S. LANIER *Poems* (1884) 8 The wave-serrate sea-rim sinks unjarring, unreeling.

**Unjau·ndiced,** *ppl. a.* (UN-[1] 8.) [**1775** ASH.] **1792** COWPER *Lines to Darwin* v, But we..Can gaze on even Darwin's wit With an unjaundic'd eye. **1804** COLLINS *Scrip. scrap.* 161 Men of Merit and Sense..Behold its Promotion with unjaundic'd Eyes. **1879** MALLOCK *Is Life Worth Living?* 19 To the unjaundiced eye nothing is more clear than that happiness [etc.]. **Unjau·nty,** *a.* [UN-[1] 7.] †Ungenteel. **1671** MRS. BEHN *Forc'd Marriage* II. ii, 'Tis the most unjanty humour that ever I saw; I, I, he is my rival. **1687** SETTLE *Refl. Dryden* 41 It being something Drydenish, Illnatured and unjauntee.., to fair well, and cry Roastmeat, especially to a Husbands face.

**Unjea·lous,** *a.* (UN-[1] 7.)

Also, in recent use, *unjealously* adv.

**1673** CLARENDON *Relig. & Policy* x. (1811) II. 706 The gentle and unjealous temper of the King. **1789** E. DARWIN *Bot. Gard.* II. 8 And three unjealous husbands wed the dame. **1824** MISS MITFORD *Village* Ser. I. 121 A pure and unjealous delight that made its own happiness. **1850** L. HUNT *Autobiog.* II. x. 23 The poet, though not unjealous of his dignity. **1876** S. LANIER *Poems, Clover* 2 My large unjealous Loves.

**Unjea·loused,** *ppl. a.* (UN-¹ 8.) **1710** T. BLACKWELL *Schema Sacra* Pref. p. ii, Incorporating himself with an unjealoused Creature. **Unje·sting,** *ppl. a.* (UN-¹ 10.) **1885** RUSKIN *Pleas. Eng.* 108 The unjesting Lombards. **1894** *Athenæum* 23 June 800/1 Until one longs for a dull, unjesting page or two. †**Unje·suited,** *ppl. a. Obs.* [UN-¹ 8.] Not influenced by Jesuits. **1659** GAUDEN *Tears Ch.* III. xxiv. 346 If the unjesuited Papists could have found in their hearts.. to apply to that Reformation of Religion [etc.]. **1716** M. DAVIES *Athen. Brit.* III. *Diss. Drama* 8 The said Servant left most of the Estate to the Un-Jesuited Knight's Lady. **Unjew·ish,** *a.* (UN-¹ 7.) **1822** *Monthly Mag.* LIII. 125 No other Protestant nation..keeps the sabbath in so unjewish and unscriptural a manner. **1892** ZANGWILL *Childr. Ghetto* I. 208 Keeping a dog is an un-Jewish trait. **Unjo·bed,** *ppl. a.* [UN-¹ 8.] Not reproved. **1732** J. WHALEY *Poems* 165, I with gracious Furlo bless'd Unjob'd can Sport and Play. **Unjo·gging,** *ppl. a.* (UN-¹ 10.) **1748** A. HILL in Mrs. Barbauld *Life Richardson* (1804) I. 129 The unjogging slide of something..that paces their lame understanding smoothly on.

**Unjoi·n,** *v.* Now *rare.* [UN-² 3.]

**1.** *trans.* To detach from being joined; to disjoin, sever, separate.

**1340** *Ayenb.* 107 He him uestneþ zuo ine god þet no þing ne may him to parti ne onioyni. *c* **1374** CHAUCER *Boeth.* v. pr. iii. (1868) 159 It byhoueþ..þat þe lynage of mankynde.. ben departed and vnioyned from hys welle and faylen of hys bygynnynge. **1400** *Destr. Troy* 939 Jason..gyrd of his hede, Vnioynis the Jamnys þat iuste were to-gedur. **1538** ELYOT, *Disiungo*, to vnioyne, to separate. **1583** GOLDING *Calvin on Deut.* xxi. 127 Euen by vnioyning the thinges that God had ioyned. **1603** J. DAVIES (Heref.) *Microcosmos* 107 It glues together states, that Warres vnioin'd. **1878** T. HARDY *Ret. Native* I. iii, When folks are just married 'tis as well to look glad o't, since looking sorry won't unjoin 'em.

**b.** *intr.* To become unjointed or detached.

*a* **1533** LD. BERNERS *Gold. Bk. M. Aurel.* (1536) T iv, My sinewes dry..: the ioyntes vnioyne asonder, and mi spirites are troubled.

**2.** *trans.* To separate the parts of; to take apart. Also *fig.*, to undo.

**1340–70** *Alisaunder* 294 Stones stirred they þo & stightlich layde On hur engines full gist to ungome [*read* unjoine] þe walles. **1377** LANGL. *P. Pl.* B. XVIII. 255 But ihesus rise to lyue,..conforte al his kynne.., And al þe iuwen ioye vnioignen & vnlouken. *c* **1430** *Pilgr. Lyf Manhode* II. cxlviii. (1869) 135 In Iacob and Esau thou hast seyn the figure: I sawede hem and vnioyned hem.

†**3.** *intr.* To rejoin, make answer. *Obs.*

*c* **1400** *Destr. Troy* 824 Than Jason vnioynid to the gentill speche:—Lord, and it like you, longe am I here!

Hence **Unjoi·ning** *vbl. sb.*

**1589** PUTTENHAM *Eng. Poesie* III. xi. (Arb.) 173 This alteration is sometimes by..ioyning or vnioyning of sillables. **1598** FLORIO, *Diuulsione*, a diuulsion, vnioyning, cutting.

**Unjoi·ned,** *ppl. a.* (UN-¹ 8.)

**1538** ELYOT, *Incompactum*, vnioyned, or yll ioyned. **1595** DANIEL *Civ. Wars* II. xci, Nor my teares without thine are fullie teares, For thus vnioyn'd, sorrow but halfe appeares. *a* **1600** HOOKER *Eccl. Pol.* VII. xxi. § 2 In respect of them, who being as yet unjoined unto this conspiracy, may be haply somewhat stayed. **1615** MARKHAM *Eng. Housewife* II. iv. 111 Gather the butter together into one intire lumpe and body, leauing no peeces thereof seuerall or vnioyned.

**Unjoi·nt,** *v.* [UN-² 3.]

**1.** *trans.* To sever the joints of; to disjoint, to dislocate.

**1390** GOWER *Conf.* II. 10, I wolde I were unjoynted Of every lime. *a* **1547** SURREY in *Tottel's Misc.* (Arb.) 17 Vnhappy hand, it had been happy time for me, If..vnioynted hadst thou be. **1561** T. NORTON *Calvin's Inst.* II. 115 Like to the partes of a house vnioynted and fallen downe. **1579** SPENSER *Sheph. Cal.* Mar. 52 Thilke same vnhappye Ewe..vnioynted both her bones. **1609** HOLLAND *Amm. Marcell.* 161 This old Ram, being unjoynted and taken in pieces, for easier carriage. **1646** FULLER *Wounded Consc.* 101 In case his Leg be set, he flings, flounces, and flies out, unjoynting it again. **1723** *Pres. St. Russia* I. 63 The Houses..are wholly made of Timber notched in on the four Corners, which they can unjoint in a few Hours. **1762** *Phil. Trans.* LII. 509 Hence it proceeded up the nave..to the pulpit, which it unjointed. *a* **1878** W. CARLETON *Farm Ballads* (1893) 84 The mechanic Had well-nigh unjointed the stove-pipe. **1903** A. ADAMS *Log Cowboy* xi, The steer's leg had been unjointed in swinging him around.

†**b.** To carve (*spec.* a curlew or bittern). *Obs.*

*c* **1470** *Hors, Shepe & G.* (Roxb.) 33 A curlew unioynted. **1508** W. DE WORDE *Bk. Keruynge* B j b, Vnioint that bytture. [Hence in later works.] **1821** G. LAMB *Catullus* I. 139 Let me see a fowl unjointed, When your table next is spread.

**2.** *fig.* To sever, separate, disunite.

**1561** NORTON & SACKV. *Gorboduc* I. i, Eche chaunge of course vnioynts the whole estate. **1577** HANMER *Anc. Eccl. Hist.* 239 In as much as the subtletye of sophisters, fonde quirckes,..seuered also, and as it were vnioynted the membres of Christ. **1612** DONNE *Progr. Soule, 2nd Anniv.* 133 None can these lines or quantities unjoynt, And say this is a line, or this a point. **1624** MIDDLETON *Game at Chess* IV. ii, Hast thou..Unjointed the fair frame of peace? **1671** MILTON *Samson* 177, I hear the sound of words, thir sense the air Dissolves unjointed e're it reach my ear.

**3.** *intr.* To come asunder.

**1826** *Acc. Loss Wesleyan Missionaries* (ed. 2) 18 The wreck began to unjoint.

Hence **Unjoi·nted** (also 6 vnioynte) *ppl. a.*

**1541** R. COPLAND *Guydon's Quest. Chirurg.* L iv b, To stay and conpryme the places dissolued, and confort the natural heate of the membre vnioynte. **1561** T. NORTON *Calvin's Inst.* I. 54 In a ruine they sought for an vpright building, and for strong ioyntes in an vnioynted ouerthrow. **1591** FLORIO *2nd Fruites* 129 Shee is some what crooke backt, shee hath one shoulder vnioynted. **1614** RALEIGH *Hist. World* Pref. A j, The unioynted and scattered frame of our English affaires.

**Unjoi·nted,** *a.* [UN-¹ 9.]

**1.** *fig.* Lacking due connexion or cohesion; unconnected, incoherent.

**1588** FRAUNCE *Lawiers Log.* Ded. ¶ 4 Neyther himselfe can well understand his unjoynted discourse, nor the hearers conceave his uncohærent jangling. **1596** SHAKS. *1 Hen. IV*, I. iii. 65 This bald, vnioynted Chat of his. *a* **1610** HEALEY tr. *Theophrastus* (1636) 37 Their tedious unjoynted tales. **1687** *Reflect. Hind & Panther* 35 To renew the old way of fighting with Sand-bags, the true Emblem of his unjoynted, incoherent Stuff.

**2.** Not furnished with, or connected by, joints.

**1681** GREW *Musæum* I. ii. 161 Upon his Shoulders he hath two immovable or unjoynted Horns. **1774** *Phil. Trans.* LXV. 7 The columns..are of the simple, or unjointed species. **1826** KIRBY & SP. *Entomol.* III. 520 A short, tapering, unjointed bristle. **1854** OWEN in *Orr's Circ. Sci.*, *Org. Nat.* I. 183 They may be simple, unjointed, firm, bony spines. **1877** HUXLEY *Anat. Inv. Anim.* vii. 399 Two minute unjointed styles.

**Unjoi·nting,** *vbl. sb.* [f. UNJOINT *v.*] The action of disjointing or dislocating.

**1598** FLORIO, *Dislogatione*, an vniointing of any lim or joint. **1603** — *Montaigne* II. xxxi. 410 These spraines, and vnjoyntings of lims. **1639** FULLER *Holy War* v. xxx. 284 The cause, first of the unjoynting, and then of the finall ruine..of many worthy States.

**Unjo·lly,** *a.* (UN-¹ 7.) **1791–3** *Spirit Public Jrnls.* (1799) I. 419 In dusty schools forlorn, Amongst..books unjolly. **1856** WHEWELL in *Life* (1881) 458, I look at this prospect with horror. Besides, the mere sitting so long will be 'awfully unjolly'. **Unjo·lted,** *ppl. a.* (UN-¹ 8.) **1777** SHERIDAN *Trip Scarb.* Prol., The cramm'd glutton snores, unjolted, home. **Unjo·stled,** *ppl. a.* (UN-¹ 8.) **1831** SCOTT *Ct. Rob.* ix, Do you feel that I have not left you unjostled by my advance to these squadrons of yours? **Unjou·rnalized,** *ppl. a.* (UN-¹ 8 *c.*) **1843** MOORE *Mem.* (1856) VII. 359 Much of late has been left unjournalised by me. †**Unjou·rneyed,** *ppl. a. Sc. Obs.*⁻¹ [UN-¹ + JOURNEY *v.* 6.] Not adjourned. **1542** in *Origines Par. Scotiæ* (1854) II. I. 310 [To go and come to the King] vnarrestit, vniornait, vncallit, vnpersewit. **Unjo·vially,** *adv.* (UN-¹ 11.) **1607** MIDDLETON *Phœnix* II. ii, Lady—what, so unjovially departed? **Unjoy·ed,** *ppl. a.* (UN-¹ 8.) **1837** VERLANDER *Vestal*, etc. 74 And joy'st thou in..the joys unjoy'd? the griefs ungriev'd?

**Unjoy·ful,** *a.* (UN-¹ 7.)

**1340–70** *Alisaunder* 1161 Menne..wer..By iustes unioyfull iugged too death. *c* **1374** CHAUCER *Boeth.* II. pr. v. (1868) 47 Certys þilke þinges..shullen ben vnioyeful to þe. **1709** STEELE *Tatler* No. 16 ¶ 2 This unjoyful Set of People, who are always Enemies to those in Possession of the good Opinion of the Company. **1837** CARLYLE *Fr. Rev.* III. I. viii, A squalid unjoyful Figure. **1868** LYNCH *Rivulet* CLII. ii, Not with unjoyful care Nor with unpraiseful prayer We live below.

**Unjoy·fully,** *adv.* (UN-¹ 11; cf. prec.)

**1553** BALE *Vocacyon* Pref. 4 By his Regall power..was I.. confirmed and not all vnioyfully receiued of ye people. **1831** JAMES *Phil. Augustus* III. iii, There were but two beings ..to whom that peal sounded unjoyfully.

**Unjoy·ous,** *a.* (UN-¹ 7.)

Also, in recent use (1891–), *unjoyously* adv.

**1645** MILTON *Tetrach.* 62 It must needs bee both unjoyous and injurious to any perceaving person so detain'd. **1712** STEELE *Spect.* No. 406 ¶ 8 The wat'ry Length of these unjoyous Moors. **1797** *Monthly Mag.* III. 536/1 The aspect of the new moon was only unjoyous to those who owed money. **1829** LYTTON *Devereux* II. ii, A coarse, yet not unjoyous, spirit of reckless debauchery. **1857** HAWTHORNE *Eng. Note-bks.* (1870) II. 216 All looking unjoyous, and as if they had no home nor parents' love.

**Unju·dge,** *v.* [UN-² 6 b.] *trans.* To deprive of the office of judge.

**1633** T. ADAMS *Exp. 2 Peter* ii. 9 If he be not at leisure to do this, it is time to unjudge him.

**Unju·dged,** *ppl. a.* (UN-¹ 8.)

**1647** HEXHAM I, Vnjudged, *ongeoordeelt.* **1709** SHAFTESB. *Charac.* (1711) II. 424 Never can the Form be of real force where it is uncontemplated, unjudg'd of, unexamin'd. **1718** PRIOR *Solomon* II. 722 Causes unjudg'd disgrace the loaded File. **1837** CARLYLE *Fr. Rev.* I. v. ix, The morning has worn itself into noon: and he is still unjudged! **1859** GEN. P. THOMPSON *Audi Alt.* lxxxvii. II. 57 The American colonel who is claiming his millions of dollars..for some unjudged complaint.

**Unju·dge-like,** *a.* (UN-¹ 7 c.) **1644** MILTON *Divorce* II. xi. (ed. 2) 53 What more un-Judge-like, more un-Magistrate-like, and in warre more un-commander-like? **1792** WOLCOT (P. Pindar) *Ode Ld. Lonsdale* 114 While Erskine..Tears to un-judgelike grins, the hanging Graces. **Unju·dging,** *ppl. a.* (UN-¹ 10.) **1679** J. GOODMAN *Penit. Pard.* I. iii. (1713) 65 Those strong, but unjudging faculties,..have an inclination to such things. **1712** BLACKMORE *Creation* III. 644 You may..with a different cant the unjudging ear amuse. **Unju·dicable,** *a.* (UN-¹ 7 b.) **1678** CUDWORTH *Intell. Syst.* 897 These Sovereign Legislative Powers, may be said to be Absolute also,..as being..Un-Judicable or Un-Censurable by any Humane Court.

**Unjudi·cial,** *a.* (UN-¹ 7, 5 b.)

**1599** *Warn. Faire Wom.* I. 34 You have..Some odd ends of old jests scrap'd up together, To tickle shallow unjudicial ears. **1867** *Sat. Rev.* 6 Apr. 436/2 A vigour which almost reaches vehemence, but which is never unscholarlike or unjudicial. **1894** *Daily News* 15 June 3/3 Infusing into it a very unjudicial amount of sentiment and passion.

**Unjudi·cially,** *adv.* (UN-¹ 11, 5 b; cf. prec.)

*a* **1628** F. GREVIL *Sidney* xv. (1652) 198 Not truly active, but rather passive vaine, to imprison and release unjudicially. **1884** *Spectator* 16 Feb. 210/2 Afraid of having the law which they have interpreted so passionately and unjudicially, reviewed in a really judicial spirit.

**Unjudi·cious,** *a.* ? *Obs.* (UN-¹ 7, 5 b.)

**1614** SYLVESTER *Bethulia's Rescue* III. 459 O! unjudicious Judges, will you thus Give Law to God? *a* **1624** BP. M. SMITH *Serm.* (1632) 71 Feare not vniudicious and impudent iudgement of the multitude. *a* **1674** MILTON *Hist. Eng.* III. Wks. 1851 V. 100 Prosperous to win a field; but to know the end and reason of winning, unjudicious and unwise. **1725** *Fam. Dict.* s.v. *Lucatellus*, The Sanders is a very unjudicious Ingredient, since it cannot answer any End as a Balsamick. **1776** MICKLE tr. *Camoens' Lusiad* 139 *note*, An unjudicious mixture of sacred and profane mythology and history.

**Unjui·ced,** *ppl. a.* [UN-² 4, 8.] Deprived of juice; squeezed out. *a* **1652** BROME *City Wit* IV. i, Every man lov'd his Fortune, squeez'd it, and when it was unjuic'd, farewell kind heart. **Unjui·cy,** *a.* (UN-¹ 7.) **1712** BLACKMORE *Creation* VII. 418 From unjuicy limbs without a root.. leafy branches shoot. **Unju·mpable,** *a.* (UN-¹ 7 b.) **1886** *Horse & Hound* 4 Dec. 742 A fine fox..ran..by the side of the unjumpable bottom.

**Unju·st,** *a.* [UN-¹ 7, 5 b; cf. Du. *onjuist.*]

**1. a.** Of persons: Not acting justly or fairly; not observing the principles of justice or fair dealing. Also const. *to.*

**1382** WYCLIF *Heb.* vi. 10 Sothli God is not vniust, that he forȝete ȝoure workis. **1549** CHEKE *Hurt Sedit.* (1569) D iij b, Shall they be thought not vniust, who..misvse and waste the same vngodlye? **1568** GRAFTON *Chron.* II. 400 An vniust and unprofitable Prince. **1603** SHAKS. *Meas. for M.* v. i. 302 The Duke's vniust, Thus to retort your manifest Appeale. **1664** in *Verney Mem.* (1907) II. 208 You would bee very unjust to your sonne. **1729** BUTLER *Serm.* Wks. 1874 II. 16 [Men] are as often unjust to themselves as to others. **1781** COWPER *Expost.* 56 He saw his people..avaricious, arrogant, unjust. **1841** LANE *Arab. Nts.* I. 74 In the beginning of his reign [he was] an unjust monarch. **1876** J. PARKER *Paracl.* II. xix. 354 To compare the universal with the limited is to be unjust to both.

*absol.* **1382** WYCLIF *1 Pet.* iii. 18 Crist oonys dyede for oure synnes, he iust for vniuste. **1593** SHAKS. *Lucrece* 285 Foul hope and..fond mistrust; Both which, as servitors to the unjust, So cross him [etc.] **1667** MILTON *P. L.* XI. 455 Th' unjust the just hath slain, For envie. **1781** COWPER *Expost.* 268 Cry to the proud, the cruel, and unjust. **1847** EMERSON *Repr. Men, Plato*, False opinion respecting the just and unjust.

**b.** Of actions, etc.: Not in accordance with justice or fairness.

*c* **1400** *Destr. Troy* 12965 This Forenses..prayet, þat he might ryde..To Ioyne with Engest for his vniust werkes. **1549** *Compl. Scot.* 2 [They] intendit ane oniust veyr..contrar our realme. *a* **1586** SIDNEY *Astr. & Stella* v. x, I lay then to thy charge vniustest tyrannie. **1611** BIBLE *Prov.* xxviii. 8 By vsurie and vniust gaine. **1697** DRYDEN *Virg. Past.* I. 93 Are we condemned by fate's unjust decree, No more..our homes to see? **1766** KAMES *Princ. Equity* (1767) 6 An action that we ought not to do is termed unjust; and the omission of what we ought to do is also termed unjust. **1858** J. B. NORTON *Topics* 156 Every case of annexation has been most manifestly unjust. **1890** *Retrospect Med.* CII. 399 It would be unjust not to refer..to the excellent results obtained by Pawlik and Byrne.

*absol.* **1659** RUSHWORTH *Hist. Coll.* I. Ep. Ded., The Law ..puts a Difference betwixt Good and Evil, betwixt Just and Unjust. **1733** POPE *Ess. Man* III. 269 So drives Self-love, thro' just and thro' unjust, To one Man's pow'r.

**2.** Not upright or free from wrong-doing; faithless, dishonest. Also const. *of* or *to.* Now *rare.*

*c* **1500** *Communycacyon* (W. de W.) B ij, But lorde though I haue ben uniuste..I hope to rube awaye the ruste With repentaunce and grace of the. **1526** TINDALE *Luke* xvi. 8 The lorde commended the uniust stewarde because he had done wysly. *a* **1593** MARLOWE *Massacre Paris* II. v. 686 Thou trothles and vniust, what lines are these? **1603** KNOLLES *Hist. Turks* (1621) 958 Their king accounted unjust of his word; who [etc.]. **1651** HOBBES *Leviath.* I. xv. 71 When a Covenant is made, then to break it is Unjust. **1766** GOLDSM. *Vicar* xxxi, Else nothing could have ever made me unjust to my promise. **1857** TROLLOPE *Barchester T.* xxxix, Mr. Plomacy was not quite happy in his mind, for he thought of the unjust steward.

†**3.** Improper; incorrect. *Obs.*

*a* **1533** LD. BERNERS *Gold. Bk. M. Aurel.* (1546) Q vj b, They..leaue the iuste trauayle, and take vniuste idelnesse. **1586** A. DAY *Eng. Secretary* II. (1625) 98 Would they not thinke you, straight proclaime against vs the vniust name of Christians. **1613** PURCHAS *Pilgrimage* II. viii. 143 Beda giveth an uniust interpretation of their name. **1713** STEELE *Guard.* No. 17 ¶ 1 The unjust taste they have who affect that way of pleasure.

†**4.** Irregular; inexact; inaccurate. *Obs.*

**1602** J. DAVIES (Heref.) *Mirum in Modum* Wks. (Grosart) I. 22/2 The Sea through vaines and Arteries of the Earth, Creeps through her Corpes,..And then returnes with windings most vniust. **1612** W. COLSON *Gen. Tresury* 246 Because of the vniust fractions in the said table..the said proofe will be found somewhat vniust, but tollerable.

**Unju·stice.** [UN-¹ 7, 5 b.]

**1.** = INJUSTICE. *Obs.* exc. *Sc.*

**1532** MORE *Confut. Tindale* Wks. 579/2 An occasion to lay the weght of their iust damnacion, to the vniustice of gods eternal ordinaunce. **1569** UNDERDOWN *Ovid's Invect. Ibis* E iiij, Pausanias therefore much moued with the kings vniustice,..slewe hym. **1626** R. HARRIS *Hezekiah's Recovery* (1630) 4 He intimated that Ingratitude was a kinde of Vnjustice. **1687** STANLEY *Hist. Philos.* (ed. 2) XIII. 933/1 His unjust deeds will come to the ears of the avengers of Unjustice. **1704** J. GIBBS *Sev. Divine Treat.* (ed. 3) 103 All the Infidelity and Unjustice of Unbelievers. **1871** W. ALEXANDER *Johnny Gibb* xvii, To dee 'im nae oonjustice, we sall suppose that he only deliver't the laird's orders.

†**2.** (See quot. and JUSTICE *sb.* 8.) *Obs.*⁻¹

*a* **1661** FULLER *Worthies, Essex* I. (1662) 323 Rose Allin.., who being in her Calling,..was intercepted by Iustice, or rather un-justice Tyrrell, who with a Candle most cruelly burnt her wrists.

**Unju·stifiable,** *a.* (UN-[1] 7 b, 5 b.) In very frequent use from *c* 1760.
**1641** CLARENDON *Hist. Reb.* I. § 117 Their unjustifiable designs and pretences. **1674** *Essex Papers* (Camden) 262 Being resolved never to doe any Thing unjustifyable. **1716** HEARNE *Collect.* (O. H. S.) V. 324 An intolerable and unjustifyable Injury. **1748** HARTLEY *Observ. Man* II. ii. § 34. 171 They did nothing unjustifiable. **1849** MACAULAY *Hist. Eng.* vii. II. 178 That even..Russell had gone to unjustifiable lengths against the government. **1879** TROLLOPE *Cousin Henry* xi, They had been hard words—quite unjustifiable unless [etc.].

Hence **Unju·stifiableness.**
**1653** MANTON *Exp. James* ii. 24 The unjustifiableness of that faith which is without works. **1728** R. MORRIS *Ess. Anc. Archit.* 91 The Unjustifiableness of Proceedings of this nature. **1745** J. MARCHANT *Expos. Gen.* xix. 66/2 The Unjustifiableness of the Means dissecrates the Means. **1853** RUSKIN *Stones Ven.* III. i. § 14. 9 In proportion to the unjustifiableness of its introduction, was the extravagance of the form it assumed.

**Unju·stifiably,** *adv.* [UN-[1] 11.]
[**1755** JOHNSON.] **1758** SECKER *Serm. 5 Nov.* (1771) 355 Censuring the legal Constitution of any Government, because they, who rebel against it, behave unjustifiably. **1796** MORSE *Amer. Geog.* I. 116 That part of Florida which they had cruelly and unjustifiably seized three years before. **1834** JAMES *J. Marston Hall* xxi, That liberty of which they have been most unjustifiably deprived. **1883** RUSKIN in *Westm. Gaz.* 8 Aug., My friends flatter me unkindly and unjustifiably.

**Unju·stified,** *ppl. a.* [UN-[1] 8.]
†**1.** Not brought to justice; not punished or executed. *Obs.*
*c* **1340** HAMPOLE *Pr. Consc.* 5871 At þat day..loverds alswa [shall give account] of þair meigne þe whilk þai lete uniustifyed be. **1564** *Reg. Privy Council Scot.* I. 306 He wald haif sauffit the sone of ane theif, being his tennent, unjustifiit, allegeand [him]..to be his awin. **1596** DALRYMPLE tr. *Leslie's Hist. Scot.* II. 202 Gif it be won, nocht ane in the castel, except the king sal chaip vniustifiet.
**2.** Not brought into a state of justification.
**1651** BAXTER *Inf. Bapt.* 308 If they have not *Jus in re*, then they are still unpardoned, and unjustified. **1661** *Papers Alter. Prayer-bk.* 104 Those that by living in open sin, do shew themselves to be unjustifyed. **1701** BEVERLEY *Glory of Grace* 51 Let him be Unjustifyed still. **1828** WEBSTER (citing J. M. Mason).
**b.** Not cleared from a charge or imputation.
**1678** DRYDEN *All for Love* IV. iv, I go Unjustifi'd, for ever from your sight.
**3.** Not made exact or accurate.
**1671–2** T. MARSHALL in Hart *Notes Cent. Typogr. Oxf.* 166, I haue examined yᵉ unjustifyed Paragon Greek matrices.
**4.** Not proved to be right or proper; unwarranted. In frequent use from *c* 1885.
**1685** BOYLE *Enq. Notion Nat.* iv. 97 The boldness of these unjustified paradoxes. **1849** COBDEN *Speeches* 27, I hope I may not be considered as unjustified by precedent. **1885** *Law Times* 23 May 62/1 The plaintiff's conduct..was unjustified.

**Unju·stify,** *v.* (UN-[2] 6 c.) **1646** HAMMOND *Tracts* 31 In the same proportion that any such act of sin doth unjustify, it doth unsanctify also. **1654** WARREN *Unbelievers* 250 No following sin shall unjustifie him.

**Unju·stly,** *adv.* [UN-[1] 11, 5 b.]
**1.** In an unjust manner; contrary to the principles of justice.
**1382** WYCLIF 1 *Pet.* ii. 19 If for conscience of God ony man suffrith sorewes,..suffringe vniustly. **1529** MORE *Suppl. Souls* Wks. 291/1 He concludeth..who that iustlye punishe a priest by the temporal law, is vniustly troubled agayn in the spirituall law. *a* **1557** in *Tottel's Misc.* (Arb.) 141 Here lieth vnhappy Harpelus,..By Phillida vniustly thus Murdred with false disdaine. **1604** ROWLANDS *Looke to it* 8 Suff'ring the Iust vniustly be opprest. **1651** HOBBES *Leviath.* II. xxii. 122 It is evident enough, that they have done unjustly. **1722** WOLLASTON *Relig. Nat.* vi. (1724) 138 Even the desire of obtaining any thing unjustly is evil. **1783** HAILES *Antiq. Chr. Ch.* iv. 79 Rutilius..was unjustly banished. **1860** PUSEY *Min. Proph.* 314 To judge unjustly, absolving the guilty, condemning the innocent. **1891** FARRAR *Darkn. & Dawn* lxvi, Unjustly suspected of a disloyal intention.
†**2.** Improperly; incorrectly. *Obs.*
**1612** SELDEN *Illustr. Drayton's Poly-olb.* iv. 73 This accompt..White of Basingstoke (although ayming to be accurat) uniustly followes. **1755** *Phil. Trans.* XLIX. 222 Whose upper surface is strictly a horizontal plane, and not convex,..as is always, tho' very unjustly, painted.

**Unju·stness.** [UN-[1] 12.] Injustice.
*c* **1449** PECOCK *Repr.* I. xviii. 106 The vniustnes of iuging which is ȝouun upon me y knowe better than the vniustnes of iugingis doon vpon othere. **1586** A. DAY *Eng. Secretary* I. (1625) 67 The indignity, vniustnesse, wickednesse,..that thereof ensueth. **1599** CROMPTON *Mansion of Magnan.* L l b, The vniustnesse of this man to his Lord. **1622** MABBE tr. *Aleman's Guzman d'Alf.* II. 9 He shall therein..giue me iust cause to suspect the vniustnesse of his intent. **1670** PENN *Truth Rescued* 62 The Unreasonableness and Unjustness of such Arbitrary Proceedings. **1757** MRS. GRIFFITH *Lett. Hen. & Frances* (1767) I. 48, I interdict you..from the unjustness of any satyr against our sex. **1879** C. GEIKIE *Eng. Reform.* xix. 330 The unjustness of a wholesale confiscation. **1887** L. OLIPHANT *Episodes* 211 The unjustness of my suspicions.

†**Unk,** *pron. Obs.* In 3 unc (*Orm.* unnc), unke. [OE. *unc*, dat. and acc. of *wit* we two, = NFris. *unk, onk*, OS. *unc*; Goth. *ugkis* (also acc. *ugk*); ON. *okkr*.] Us two, both of us.
*c* **1200** ORMIN Ded. 27 Unnc birrþ baþe þannkenn Crist Þatt itt iss brohht till ende. *c* **1205** LAY. 23626 For þi hit is betere bi-twixen unke seoluen to-dælen and to-dihten þis kine-lond mid fihte. *a* **1225** *Leg. Kath.* 1515 Swa þe cnotte is icnut bituhhen unc tweien. *a* **1275** *Prov. Alfred* 583 Mine daȝis arren nei done, and we sulen unc to-delen.

**Unkaimed, -kamed:** see UNCOMBED.

**Unkard(ness,** dial. varr. UNKED(NESS.
Cf. *unkward* in Skinner (1671) s.v., and dial. *unkert*.
**1727** BAILEY (vol. II), *Unkardness*, Solitariness, Loathsomeness. **1787** GROSE *Prov. Gloss.*, *Unkard*, awkward. **1788** W. H. MARSHALL *Yorksh.* II. Gloss. s.v., A servant is *unkard* on his first going to a fresh servitude. **1855–91** in Whitby and Gloucester glossaries.

**Unkea·med,** obs. variant of UNKEMBED.
**1600** J. LANE *Tom Tel Troth* 369 Pyning Enuie..With..withered face, and with vnkeamed haire. **1697** *View Penal Laws* 260, 2000 Tods of unkeamed Wool.

**U·nked, u·nkid,** *a.* Now *dial.* Forms: α. 4–5 vnkid (4 -kidd, 5 -kidde), vnkyd (4 -kydd, 6 -kydde), vnkud, 8–9 unkid. β. 4 vnkede, 5– unked, 8–9 unket. [ME. *un-kidd*, f. UN-[1] + pa. pple. of KITHE *v.* Cf. UNCO, UNCOUTH, UNKARD, UNKETH, and UNQUOD *adjs.*]
**1.** Not made known or revealed; unknown, unfamiliar, strange.
*a* **1300** *Cursor M.* 6920 He-self has berid him and hidd In a priue sted vn-kydd. *c* **1375** *Sc. Leg. Saints* xxxi. (*Eugenia*) 90 Oure treuth to þaim wes vnkid. *a* **1400** *R. Gloucester's Chron.* (Rolls) 7247 Þe kinges were of engelond of vnkunde [*MS. C.* vnkede] sede. *c* **1465** *Eng. Chron.* (Camden, 1856) 2 Not onli for deuocion, but also forto se the newe and unkid solennite. **1540** HYRDE tr. *Vives' Instr. Chr. Wom.* (1541) 47 The women were taken with an unked kynd of franzy. **1583** *Abstract of Acts, Canons, etc. temp. Q. Eliz.* 70 A phisition..must not minister after any vnked maner, but [etc.]. **1825** BROCKETT *N. C. Words, Unket, Unkid*, strange, unusual. **1894–6** in Northumb. and Warw. glossaries.
**2.** Awkward or troublesome through being unfamiliar or unknown.
**1634** C. BUTLER *Eng. Gram.* Pref., So powerful is the tyrant custom..that..this little change..will seem to some harsh and unked at the first. **1810** S. GREEN *Reformist* I. 89, I, who never has handled a needle, will make but an unked kind of business of it. **1815** MRS. PILKINGTON *Celebrity* I. 131 It is but an unked kind of way for a stranger to find.
**b.** Causing awkwardness or unpleasantness.
**1860** HUGHES *T. Brown at Oxf.* xviii, I hopes as you don't think I be any ways unked 'bout this here quire-singin'.
**3.** Unfamiliarly lone or dreary; lonely, dismal, forbiddingly dull.
**1706** PHILLIPS (ed. Kersey), *Unked*,..Solitary, Lonely. **1727** HEARNE *Diary* 11 Nov., W[hi]ch way (a strangely unked, solitary walk) I had never went..before. **1790** COWPER *Let. to Mrs. Throckmorton* 21 Mar., Weston is sadly unked without you. **1825** JENNINGS *Observ. Dial. W. Eng.* 148 Late at night a rawd along All droo a unket ood. **1869** BLACKMORE *Lorna D.* xiii, The place was unkid and lonesome, and the rolling clouds very desolate.
**b.** Of persons: Feeling lonely, dull, or depressed.
**1760** MISS TALBOT *Let. to Mrs. E. Carter* 8 May, Mr. Okey gone to his apprenticeship, and I a little *unkit* for want of my scholar. **1795** H. WALPOLE *Let. to Miss Berry* 2 Sept., I am very unked without you. **1854** MISS BAKER *Northampt. Gloss.* s.v., Old people suffering from the loss of friends will frequently say they feel very unkid.
**4.** Disagreeable, unpleasant, unnatural, eerie.
**1800** *Gentl. Mag.* Feb. 107 [In Oxon.] every thing that is unfortunate, or unlucky, or not as it could be wished, is *unked*. **1864** CHR. G. ROSSETTI *Jessie Cameron* v, By her hut..they would not pass at night, Lest they should hear an unked strain Or see an unked sight. **1884** *Standard* 6 Sept. 2/1 The..lapping of the waters evoke[s] a weird feeling that is somewhat, as the West Country people called it, *unked*.
Hence **U·nkedness.** *rare.*
**1796** CHARLOTTE SMITH *Marchmont* I. 232 The unketness of the place. **1838** LADY LYTTELTON *Lett.* (1873) 235, I..had a wretched unkedness of a morning at the Inn. **1905** *Eng. Dial. Dict.* s.v.

**Unked:** see UNCKED *a. Obs.*

**Unkee·led,** *ppl. a.* [UN-[1] 8.]
**1.** Not sailed upon; not traversed by ships.
**1807** J. BARLOW *Columb.* I. 526 Their waves unkeel'd, their havens unexplored.
**2.** Not furnished with a keel.
*a* **1844** CAMPBELL *Napoleon & Brit. Sailor* 35 A wherry..uncompass'd, and unkeel'd. **1870** HOOKER *Stud. Flora* (1884) 289 The glabrous unkeeled sepals.

**Unke·mbed,** *ppl. a.* Now *rare.* Forms: α. 4, 6–7 vnkemd (7 unkem'd), 5 vnkemmyde, 6 *Sc.* vnkemmit, 6–7 vnkemmed (9 un-). β. 5 vnkembyd, 6 -keembd, 7 -kembed, -kemb'd, -kembd. [UN-[1] 8. Cf. ON. *úkembdr*, MHG. *ungekembet*.] Uncombed, unkempt.
**1390** GOWER *Conf.* III. 260 Hire her hangende unkemd aboute. **1483** *Cath. Angl.* 202/1 Vn kembyd,..*jncomptus, impexus*. **1542** UDALL *Erasm. Apoph.* 80 b, He brought theim foorth vnkembed & vnpiked, without cotes. **1565** GOLDING *Ovid's Met.* I. (1590) 16 Hir haire unkemd about hir necke downe flaring. **1627** MAY *Lucan* VI. 585 Laden she is with long vnkemmed haires. **1693** DRYDEN *Juvenal* III. 121 His once unkem'd, and horrid Locks. **1697** *View Penal Laws* 267, 1000 Tods of unkemb'd Wool. **1824** CARR *Craven Gloss.*, *Unkemmed*, [**1828** *Unkemb'd*,] uncombed. **1860** KAY-SHUTTLEWORTH *Scarsdale* II. 28 Ungroomed, and unkemmed strings of 'gals'.
*fig.* **1577** tr. *Bullinger's Decades* I. i. 13/1 In these plaine and simple, not darke and vnkemmed books, is comprehended the ful doctrine of godlynes.

**Unke·mpt,** *ppl. a.* [UN-[1] 8 b: cf. prec. and older Flem. *ongekempt*.]
**1.** Of hair, etc.: Uncombed.
**1742** SHENSTONE *Schoolmistr.* ii, Oft-times [they]..For Hair unkempt..are sorely shent. **1825** LD. COCKBURN *Mem.* (1856) 268 The bur in the throat,..the unkempt locks. **1843** CARLYLE *Past & Pr.* III. x, It is forever indispensable for a man to fight: now with Necessity,..tangled Forests, unkempt Cotton.
**b.** Having the hair uncombed or dishevelled.
**1748** THOMSON *Cast. Indol.* I. lxi, Unkempt, and rough, of squalid face and mein. **1812** BYRON *Ch. Har.* I. xvii, Though shent with Egypt's plague, unkempt, unwashed. **1877** BLACK *Green Past.* xlv, Tall, uncouth, unkempt fellows..seated on a bench smoking.
*transf.* **1864** MISS BRADDON *Doctor's Wife* i, The horse had a rakish, unkempt look about the head and mane.
**c.** Neglected; not cared for; untrimmed; rough.
**1867** D. G. MITCHELL *Rural Stud.* 1 A wild, unkempt, slatternly farm. **1879** DIXON *Windsor* II. xx. 207 Their filthy habits and unkempt attire.
*fig.* **1861** J. BROWN *Horæ Subs.* Ser. II. 370 In that formidable and unkempt nature..lay the delicacy..of a gentleman.
†**2.** *fig.* Of language: Inelegant, unrefined; rude. (Cf. INCOMPT *a.*, UNCOMBED *ppl. a.* 2.) *Obs.*
**1579** SPENSER *Sheph. Cal.* Nov. 51 To well I wote..howe my rymes bene rugged and vnkempt. **1590** — *F. Q.* III. x. 29 Thy offers base I greatly loth, And eke thy words vncourteous and vnkempt. **1606** N. BAXTER *Sidney's Ourania* D 2 Our Spokes beene blunt,..Vnable in Mysteries to know the sooth; Vnkempt, vnpolished, ignorant, lewde.
Hence **Unke·mptness.**
**1876** *World* V. 16 Untidyness and unkemptness [of a garden]. **1900** *Scribner's Mag.* Sept. 297/2 The foul unkemptness of the natives.

**Unke·nned,** *ppl. a.* Chiefly *Sc.* and *north.* Now *arch.* or *dial.* [UN-[1] 8. Cf. NFris. *ünkänd*, Norw. *ukjend*, Da. *ukendt*, Sw. *okänd*, Du. *ongekend*. See also UNKENT *ppl. a.*]
**1.** Unknown; strange.
*a* **1300** *Cursor M.* 28474 Wit womman knaun and vnkend. *c* **1375** *Sc. Leg. Saints* xvi. (*Magdalene*) 891, I ame scho..Þat here þe thretty vintir ay til al men has vnkennyt bene. *c* **1400** tr. *Secreta Secret., Gov. Lordsh.* 84, I aiugyd þat þey [*sc.* secrets] sholde noght be vnkennyd to þy worthy myghtynesse. *a* **1440** *Sir Eglam.* 843 A grype..Hur yonge sone awey..bare Yn-to a cuntre unkende. *c* **1475** *Rauf Coilȝear* 247, I am wonder wa to cum quhair I am vnkend. **1535** STEWART *Cron. Scot.* (Rolls) II. 115 Quhat movit thame it is wnkend to me. **1591** SYLVESTER *Du Bartas* I. iii. 1160 Let me..among the Great un-kend, My rest of dayes in the Calm Countrey end. **1632** J. HAYWARD tr. *Biondi's Eromena* 193 Both of us altogether unkend and quite forgotten. **1721** RAMSAY *Keitha* 37 Ye unkend pow'rs wha water haunt or air. **1785** BURNS *To W. Simpson* vii, She lay like some unkend-of isle. **1814** SCOTT *Wav.* xviii, For the..trouble which he had..to an unkenn'd degree.
**2.** Undescried, unperceived; unexplored.
**1592** DANIEL *Compl. Rosamond* 422 Witnesse the world, wherein is nothing rifer, Then miseries vnken'd before they come. *a* **1680** BUTLER *Rem.* (1759) I. 417 No Ship in the Day time, can pass unken'd. **1747** [G. RIDLEY] *Psyche* xxiv. in *Museum* III. 88 Unkenn'd of her, he raught the embroider'd Bank. **1890** Æ. PRINCE *Palomide* 25 Deep in trackless, unkenned ways.
Hence **Unke·nnedness.**
**1896** FLORA A. STEEL *Face of Waters* I. vi, There was a strange unkennedness about their would-be familiarity.

**Unke·nnel,** *v.* [UN-[2] 5.]
**1.** *trans.* To dislodge (a fox) from its hole; to start. Also in fig. context, and *absol.*
**1576** TURBERV. *Venerie* 100 An Hart or a Bucke is flayed,..an Hare started, and a Fox vnkennelled. **1598** SHAKS. *Merry W.* III. iii. 172 Ascend my Chambers..: Ile warrant wee'le vnkennell the Fox. **1632** B. JONSON *Magn. Lady* I. i, Your fox there, Unkennell'd with a choleric, ghastly aspect,..Would run their fears to any hole of shelter. **1679** C. NESSE *Antichrist* 105 The great fox that hath so long spoild the vines of Christs vineyard shall be unkennel'd. **1703** (*title*), The Fox with his Fire-Brand unkennell'd and Insnar'd. **1753** FOOTE *Eng. in Paris* I. i, Did I tell you what a Chace she carry'd me last Christmas Eve? We unkennel'd at —. **1825** *Eng. Life* I. 216 We unkennelled Reynard capitally. **1852** MISS YONGE *Cameos* I. xxvii. 221 Vowing he would unkennel the young fox,..John sent his troops into Scotland.
**b.** *intr.* To come out of a hole or lair.
*c* **1760** in T. C. Croker *Pop. Songs Irel.* (1839) 223 Ten minutes past nine was the time o' the day, When Reynard unkennelled. *c* **1820** S. ROGERS *Italy, Banditti* 59 He comes slowly forth, Unkennelling.
**2.** *fig.* To force or drive out from a place or position; to dislodge; to bring to light.
**1612** WEBSTER *White Devil* V. i, I'le unkennell one example more for thee. **1630** J. TAYLOR (Water P.) *Jack a Lent* Wks. (1630) 116/2 The wet Fishmongers..vnkennell the salt Eeles from their brinie Ambuscadoes. **1670** COTTON *Espernon* I. IV. 149 Hunting, and every where unkennelling the Savoyards,..who had possess'd themselves of most of the best Cities of Provence. **1743** YOUNG *Nt. Th.* v. 969 A precious pack of votaries Unkennell'd from the prisons. **1749** FIELDING *Tom Jones* XV. v, Where is she?..I'll unkennel her this instant. Shew me her chamber. **1809** SOUTHEY *Lett.* (1856) II. 131, I am in want of the 'Annual Letters from Paraguay';..by that time, if they are in England, I may hope to unkennel them. **1818** MOORE *Fudge Fam. Paris* VI. 25 Lucky the dog that first unkennels Traitors and Luddites now-a-days. **1839** *Times* 10 June, It is their interest to unkennel this knavery.
*refl.* **1602** SHAKS. *Ham.* III. ii. 86 If his occulted guilt Do not it selfe vnkennell in one speech, It is a damned Ghost that we haue seene.
**3.** To let (hounds) out of a kennel. Also *fig.* and in fig. context.
**1607** DEKKER *Wh. Babylon* C 4, Shee shall bee torne, Euen ioynt from ioynt: to haue her baited wel,..wee will vnkennell hell. **1628** WITHER *Brit. Rememb.* Pref. 157, I can unkennell such an eager packe Of deep-mouth'd Hounds. **1840** KEIGHTLEY *Hist. Roman Empire* I. iii. 63 The baleful pack of informers was unkennelled, and their victims..were hunted to death. **1861** DIXON *Pers. Hist. Bacon* vi. § 1 Blount..unkennels..a pack of needy ruffians eager for any service.

Hence **Unke·nnelled** *ppl. a.*$^1$; **Unke·nnelling** *vbl. sb.*

**1589** WARNER *Alb. Eng.* VI. xxxiii. 144 Like *vnkenneld Cerberus the crooked Tyrant swore. *a* **1653** G. DANIEL *Idyll., Landskip* 7 Vnkennell'd Fury (deep-mouth'd) rings Liberty lodg'd; and Chas'd it quite away. **1687** DRYDEN *Hind & P.* I. 152 Thou first Apostate to Divinity, Unkennel'd range in thy Polonian Plains. **1700** S. PARKER *Six Philos. Ess.* 48 The poor unkennell'd Fryars.. are ready to bear me out in my Assertion. **1600** J. B. (*title*), A Toile for Two-legged Foxes, wherein their noisome properties, their hunting and *vnkenelling,..is liuelie discouered. **1602** *2nd Pt. Return Parnass.* II. v. 829 What sir, do you meane at the vnkennelling, vntapezing, or earthing of the Fox?

**Unke·nnelled,** *ppl. a.*$^2$ [UN-$^1$ 8.] Not provided with a kennel.

**1838** ELIZA COOK *Old Pincher* ix, Unkennelled and chainless, yet truly he served.

**Unke·nning,** *ppl. a. Sc. rare.* [UN-$^1$ 10.] Unknowing, ignorant.

*c* **1375** *Sc. Leg. Saints* xl. (*Ninian*) 98 Fore scorne it ware gret to se þe thechure [=teacher] suld vnkennand be. **1788** J. MACAULAY *Poems* 130 Unkenning how to carp or mourn, Their joy to spoil. *a* **1870** in Rogers *Scottish Minstrel* 488/2 Unkennin' o', uncarin' for, cauld care or crosses stern.

**Unke·nt,** *ppl. a.* Chiefly *north.* and *Sc.* [UN-$^1$ 8 b.]

†**1.** Undirected, untaught. *Obs.*—$^0$

**1570** LEVINS *Manip.* 67 Vnkent, untaught, *incorrectus.*

**2.** Unknown. (Cf. UNKENNED *ppl. a.* 1.)

**1579** SPENSER *Sheph. Cal.* To his Bk. i, Goe little booke: thy selfe present, As child whose parent is vnkent. **1613** W. BROWNE *Brit. Past.* I. i, I..sought [not] for bay,..But as a Swaine unkent fed on the plaines. **1647** TRAPP *Comm.*, 1 *John* iii. 1 Princes unknown are unrespected; Unkent, unkist, as the Northern Proverb hath it. **1790** A. SHIRREFS *Poems* 174 Unkent to a',.. Ae night I bade the cruel place adieu. **1807**– in dialect use (*Eng. Dial. Dict.*).

**Unke·pt,** *ppl. a.* Also 4 *north.* unkepide, 5 (*Sc.* 6) unkepit; etc. [UN-$^1$ 8, 8 b.]

**1.** Not attended to; not tended or looked after; neglected.

*c* **1340** HAMPOLE *Prose Tr.* 28 If þou..latis þame [*sc.* the feet] spill for defaute of kepynge—unarayede, unkepide, and noghte tente to as þam aughte for to be,—thou pleses Hym noghte. *c* **1440** *Pallad. on Husb.* XII. 57 Lond vnkept and insolent. *c* **1450** *St. Cuthbert* (Surtees) 514 Sho hir childe saw vnkepyd, And wante þat he was wonte to haue. **1469** *Cal. Anc. Rec. Dublin* (1889) 336 That they goo to noon other labore and lewe the gye rope unkepit. **1600** SHAKS. *A. Y. L.* I. i. 9 He keepes me rustically at home, or (to speak more properly) staies me heere at home vnkept. **1611** FLORIO, *Incustodito*, vnkept, not looked vnto.

**b.** Unguarded, undefended.

*c* **1400** *Destr. Troy* 1085 The kyng had no knawlache..Of the folke so furse,.. For-þi vnkeppit were þe costes all þe kythe ouer. **1611** FLORIO, *Suadata*, open, vnkept, free for all men.

**2.** Not observed or obeyed; disregarded.

*c* **1380** WYCLIF *Wks.* (1880) 38 Certis þei..maken hem..to leue holy writt vnstudied, vnknoud & vnkept. *c* **1440** *Jacob's Well* 154 He..is for-sworn, for truthe vnkept & othe brokyn is all on. **1513** DOUGLAS *Æneid* IV. x. 61 Allace! vnkeipit is the trew cunnand. **1594** HOOKER *Eccl. Pol.* IV. xiv. § 5 Many things generally kept heretofore, are now .. vnkept and abolished euerywhere. **1623** SANDERSON *Serm.* (1632) 151 Lawes..are farre better vnmade, then vnkept.

**3.** Not stored up.

**1842** TENNYSON *Will Waterproof* 97 Whether the vintage, yet unkept, Had relish fiery-new.

†**Unker,** *pron. Obs.* [OE. *uncer* (gen. of *wit* we two), = OHG. *unker, uncher*, OS. *unkero*, Goth. **ugkara*, ON. *okkarr* (Icel. *okkar*).] Of us two.

In quot. *a* 1300 apparently for *inker* 'of you two'.

*c* **1205** LAY. 23665 And whaðer unker he geð abake:.. beo he in ælche londe iqueðe for ane sconde. *a* **1250** *Owl & Night.* 151 Hwy neltu fleon into [þe] bare And schewi hweþer unker beo Of brihtur hewe of fayrur bleo. *a* **1300** *Havelok* 1882 Roberd! William! hware ar ye? Gripeth eyþer unker a god tre.

†**U·nker,** *poss. a. Obs.* [OE. *uncer* (cf. prec.), = OS. *unka*, ON. *okkarr.*] Belonging to us two.

*c* **1200** ORMIN Ded. 80 Þeȝȝ shulenn lætenn hæþeliȝ Off unnkerr swinnc, lef broþerr. *c* **1205** LAY. 8891 Ilæst ich habbe þe..al þet ich þe bi-hehte bi-foren vnkere cnihten. *a* **1250** *Owl & N.* 1689 Ah hit wes vnker uoreward..Þat we [etc.].

**Unke·rchiefed,** *a.* (UN-$^1$ 9.) [1775 ASH.] **1781** COWPER *Truth* 137 With bony and unkerchief'd neck. **1812** CARY *Dante, Purg.* XXIII. 95 [Lest] The unblushing dames..bare Unkerchief'd bosoms to the common gaze. *a* **1851** MOIR *Poems, Highl. Ret.* xi, Before him she reclined In half unkerchief'd loveliness. **Unke·rnelled,** *a.* (UN-$^1$ 9.) **1673** BP. S. PARKER *Reproof Reh. Transp.* 189 An empty and unkernel'd shell. **1827** POLLOK *Course T.* IX. 972 Nor failed [Satan] to misadvise his..faith, by false unkerneled promises.

**Unkert, Unket,** dial. varr. UNKARD, UNKED *a.*

†**Unketh,** *a. Obs.* Also 3–4 onekeþ, 4–5 unkythe. [var. ME. *uncoth*: see UNCOUTH *a.* and cf. UNKED.] Unknown, strange.

*a* **1275** *Prov. Ælfred* 535 in *O. E. Misc.* 133 Elde cumid to tune, mid fele unkeþe costes. **1297** R. GLOUC. (Rolls) 6758 Mid lute onekeþ folc to engelond he drou. *c* **1400** *Destr. Troy* 3325 Weikenes of women may not wele stryve, ..And nomely in an unkythe lond nedys hom so. *c* **1510** *Lytell Geste Robyn Hode* 24 (W. de W.), To dine I have no lust, Till I have some bold Baron, Or some unketh guest. **1577** HOLINSHED *Chron., Hist. Scotland* I. 297/1 Many strange wonders and vnketh sightes were seene in the dayes of this Alexander the thyrde.

Hence †**U·nkethness.** *Obs.*

**1564** HAWARD tr. *Eutropius* x. 108 This unkethenesse of passinge greate good fortune, and successe in his affairs.

**Unkeuer(e,** obs. variants of UNCOVER *v.*

**Unke·vel,** *v.* [UN-$^2$ 4 b.] *trans.* To ungag.

*c* **1300** *Havelok* 601 He stirten boþe up to the knaue,.. Vnkeueleden him, and swiþe unbounden.

**Unkey·,** *v.* (UN-$^2$ 4; cf. KEY *v.*)

**1751** LABELYE *Westm. Bridge* 22 Upon unkeying any one of the Arches the whole Bridge would fall. **1828** SPEARMAN *Brit. Gunner* (ed. 2) 183 [No. 3] keys and unkeys the left hand cap-square of the gun-carriage. **1840** *Civil Eng. & Arch. Jrnl.* III. 402/1 The labour..of removing the wheels from the axles, which in the keying and unkeying is known to be very troublesome. **1859** F. A. GRIFFITHS *Artill. Man.* (ed. 8) 179 No. 1 attends to the pawls and commands, keys, and unkeys keep chain.

**Unki·cked,** *ppl. a.* (UN-$^1$ 8.) **1732** LADY MARY MONTAGU & LD. HERVEY *Verses to Pope* 69 If..Unwhipt, unblanketed, unkick'd, unslain, That wretched little carcase you retain.

**Unkid,** var. of UNKED *a.*

**Unkillabi·lity.** (UN-$^1$ 12; cf. next.) **1835** LADY LYTTON *Diary* in L. Devey *Life* (1887) 102 My nature must be a happy mixture of asbestos, cast iron, and feline unkillability.

**Unki·llable,** *a.* (UN-$^1$ 7 b.) **1878** P. BAYNE *Purit. Rev.* x. 409 Of all the unkillable lies..this is perhaps the most toughly immortal. **1885** *Daily News* 14 July 2 The chickens are so hardy as to be unkillable by the ordinary diseases.

**Unki·lled,** *ppl. a.* (UN-$^1$ 8.)

**1535** STEWART *Cron. Scot.* (Rolls) I. 586 All his men..That levand war on lyfe that tyme vnkeild. **1547** *Homilies* I. *Obedience* I. N i b, Take away Kynges, Princes, Rulers,..no man shall slepe in his awne house or bed vnkylled. **1608** *Yorksh. Trag.* I. ix. 215, I repent now that one is left unkill'd; My brat at nurse. **1662** HIBBERT *Body Divinity* I. 197 If he see a snake unkilled, he fears a mischief. **1707** MORTIMER *Husb.* 45 Leave no Weeds or Turfs of Grass unkilled or unbroke with your Harrows. **1802** H. MARTIN *Helen of Glenross* I. 146 Scream ladies; for our pistols are fired, and we unkilled. **1842** THACKERAY *Sultan Stork* Wks. 1898 V. 738 Nor of the latter did there remain any unkilled (if I may coin such a word). **1901** G. DOUGLAS *Ho. w. Green Shutters* 264, I have let him get away unkilled.

**Unki·lling,** *ppl. a.* (UN-$^1$ 10.) **1651** W. JANE Εἰκων Ακλαστος 171 The instruments of Rebells are harmles, and vnkilling. **Unki·lned,** *ppl. a.* (UN-$^1$ 8.) **1658** tr. *Porta's Nat. Magic* VI. vii. 183 Fill an earthen pot with unkill'd lime. **1890** GEN. BOOTH *Darkest England* Pref., If the bricks were merely unkilned clay.

**Unki·nd,** *a.* [UN-$^1$ 7. Cf. OE. *uncynde, ungecynde* (ME. *unicunde* UN-$^1$ 3), Norw. *ukyndt.*]

†**1.** Strange, foreign. *Obs.*

*c* **1250** *Gen. & Ex.* 2302 Iosep..hem..taȝte wel, And hu he sulden hem best leden, Quene he comen in vnkinde ðeden. **1297** R. GLOUC. (Rolls) 7247 Vor þre kinges were of engelond of vnkunde [*v.r.* vnkynde] sede. *a* **1400** *Northern Passion* 1554 (Camb. MS.), A vnkynd man sone gan þai mete.

**2. a.** Of the weather or climate: Not mild or pleasant; ungenial. Now *dial.* or *arch.*

*a* **1300** *Frag. Pop. Sci.* (Wright) 168 He ne mai nevere thanne come bote the weder uncunde beo. *c* **1325** *Poem temp. Edw. II* (Percy Soc.) lxxvi, Wederyng..Cold & unkynde. *c* **1330** R. BRUNNE *Chron. Wace* (Rolls) 16541 Al þe folk wyþ tempest vnkynde Were slayn. **1580** LYLY *Euphues* (Arb.) 465 So vnkinde a yeare it hath beene in England, that [etc.]. **1733** TULL *Horse-Hoeing Husb.* xii. 145 Favourable Years will cure the Smut, as *unkind* ones will cause it. **1775** JOHNSON *West. Isl.* Wks. X. 488 The climate is unkind and the ground penurious. **1813** C. MARSHALL *Gardening* (ed. 5) xviii. 294 A fourth bed..would be a greater advantage as to size, especially if the weather is unkind. **1876, 1881** in Surrey and Radnor glossaries (s.v. *Kind*).

†**b.** Physically unnatural; contrary to the usual course of nature. *Obs.*

**1435** *Cov. Leet Bk.* 181 Yif he be necligent & mysrule his Iron, that he wirkithe, be onkynd hetes or elles in oder maner. *c* **1440** *Promp. Parv.* 365/2 On-kyynd, or nowȝt after cowrs of kynde, *innaturalis.* **1546** PHAER *Bk. Children* (1553) X ij b, A soueraine medycyne for burning and scaldyng, and all vnkynde heates. **1601** HOLLAND *Pliny* II. 167 They doe quench and allay thirst, and coole unkind heat. **1603** J. DAVIES (Heref.) *Microcosmos* 53 That by their service that fire might not vade, Which vnkinde coldnesse else might overlade.

**c.** Naturally bad or hurtful; unfavourable or unsuitable; untoward. Also const. *for* or *to*. Now *dial.* (esp. of soil).

*c* **1425** LYDGATE *Assem. Gods* 1023 Sensualyte..sewe the felde with hys vnkynde seede. *c* **1450** LOVELICH *Grail* xxxvi. 595 That beste wolde..ony man qwelle that there-offen ete, it is so vnkynde, And þerto so hot. **1541** R. COPLAND *Galyen's Terap.* 2 A iv b, Whiche is..commune to the curatyons of vnkynde humoures. **1609** C. BUTLER *Fem. Mon.* ii. B 8 b, The East-wind being cold..is verie vnkind for Bees. **1682** W. HEWER *Let. to Pepys* 13 May, A very unfortunate and unkinde disaster. **1762** MILLS *Pract. Husb.* I. 19 The blue, white, and red clay, if strong, are all unkind. **1767** A. YOUNG *Farmer's Lett. to People* 16 The constitutions..of several countries in Europe, which are unkind to the cultivation of the earth. **1877**– in dialect glossaries, etc. (*Eng. Dial. Dict.*). **1879** MISS JACKSON *Shropshire Word-bk.* 169 *Gall*,..a stiff, wet, 'unkind' place in plough-land.

**d.** Of animals: Not thriving or naturally tending to do so. Now *dial.*

**1814** G. HANGER *To all Sportsmen* 13 Whenever a horse looks unkind in his coat. **1834** SOUTHEY *Doctor* cxliv, If ever he attempts to fatten an unkind beast.

**e.** *dial.* (See quot.)

**1866** BROGDEN *Linc. Gloss.* 216 *Unkind*, rough or crooked. These poles are very unkind.

†**3. a.** Lacking in natural gratitude or willingness to acknowledge benefits; ungrateful. *Obs.*

*c* **1290** *S. Eng. Leg.* I. 204/156 Ȝwane þov hast boþe bodi and soule iȝyuen us bi þine liue, Saunt faille we ne beoth nouȝt so onkuynde þat we it nellez ȝelde þe bliue. **1338** R. BRUNNE *Chron.* (1810) 62 Malcolme..ȝit on Inglond ran, Þe kyng had him auanced, he was an vnkynd man. **1377** LANGL. *P. Pl.* B. v. 437 Ȝif any man..helpeth me at nede, I am vnkynde aȝein his curteisye. **1422** YONGE tr. *Secreta Secret.* 205 He is an onkynde man that denyeth hym to haue recevid a good dede. *c* **1450** *Mirk's Festial* 26 Þat scho was vnkynde to hym þat suffred so moche for hur. **1509** BARCLAY *Shyp of Folys* (1570) 85 These vnkinde caytiues will scantly him honour. **1576** LAMBARDE *Peramb. Kent* 276 Whiche..inestimable benefites..if any man..acknowledge not, he is to to vnkinde. **1649** J. TAYLOR (Water P.) *Western Voy.* 6 The Redeemer of unkinde mankinde.

*absol.* **1382** WYCLIF *Wisd.* xvi. 29 The hope of the vnkinde as cold ijs shal flowen. **1526** TINDALE *Luke* vi. 35 He is kynde vnto the vnkynde.

†**b.** Lacking in filial affection or respect; undutiful. *Obs.*

*a* **1300** *Cursor M.* 28270 Vn-kynd i was..Gayn fader & moder. **1303** R. BRUNNE *Handl. Synne* 1072 Ȝyf þou euer ..On fadyr or modyr leydest þyn hand,..swyche a chylde ys kalled vnkynde. **1380** *Lay Folks Catech.* (Lamb. MS.) 710 Vnkende men..helpe not here eldrys as þey schuld do. **1595** DANIEL *Civ. Wars* I. lxxxix, O! whither dost thou tend my vnkind sonne? What mischiefe dost thou go about to bring To..Thy mother countrey?

†**c.** Devoid of natural goodness; vile, bad, wicked, villainous. *Obs.*

**1297** R. GLOUC. (Rolls) 2379 Þere he kudde wat he was vnkunde ssrewe & quoynte. **13..** *Guy Warw.* (A.) 4382 Þou me hast bitreyd,..þou fel treytour, vnkinde blod. **1377** LANGL. *P. Pl.* B. v. 276 Thow art an vnkynde creature; I can þe nouȝte assoille, Til þow make restitucioun. **1430–40** LYDG. *Bochas* VIII. xxv. (1494) E iij b/2, Late men beware euer of vnkynde blode. *c* **1460** *Towneley Myst.* xxiv. 192 Then noy vs nomore of this noyse; you carles vnkynde, who bad you call me? **1529** S. FISH *Supplic. Beggers* (1871) 4 Let vs then compare the nombre of this vnkind idell sort, vnto the nombre of the laye people. **1590** SPENSER *F. Q.* III. ii. 43 For they, how euer shamefull and vnkind, Yet did possesse their horrible intent. **1602** *2nd Pt. Return fr. Parnass.* IV. ii. 1705 Thou slimie sprighted vnkinde Saracen.

†**d.** Of a worse kind; degenerate. *Obs.*

**1340** *Ayenb.* 188 Þe zone ssel by ylich þe uader oþer he is onkende be zaynte peter. **1398** TREVISA *Barth. De P. R.* XII. xxvi. (Tollem. MS.), Þe lenger he lyueþ þe more he scheweþ þat his owen kynde is unkynde. **14..** *Voc.* in Wr.-Wülcker 577/41 *Degener*, vnkynde. **1483** *Cath. Angl.* 203/1 To be vn Kynde, or to go oute of kynde, *degenerare.*

†**e.** Uncharitable, ungenerous. *Obs.*

**1303** R. BRUNNE *Handl. Synne* 6788 For ful comunly shalt þou fynde Ofte ryche men vnkynde. **1377** LANGL. *P. Pl.* B. x. 29 Þilke þat god moste gyueth, leste good þei deleth, And moste vnkynde to þe comune þat moste catel weldeth. *Ibid.* XI. 206 Euery man helpe other,..And be we nouȝte vnkynde of owre catel ne of owre kunnynge neyther.

†**4.** Of actions: Contrary to nature, unnatural, *esp.* unnaturally bad or wicked. *Obs.*

*c* **1250** *Gen. & Ex.* 449 Bigamie is unkinde ðing, On engleis tale, twie-wifing. **1297** R. GLOUC. (Rolls) 852 Many kundemen of þis lond mid king leir hulde also, Vor þe vnkende [*v.r.* vnkynde] suikedom þat is doȝtren adde ido. *c* **1320** *Sir Tristr.* 2758 Vnkinde were ous to kis As kenne. **1377** LANGL. *P. Pl.* B. XIII. 356 Þorw coueityse and vnkynde desyrynge. *c* **1480** HENRYSON *Fables, Trial of Fox* 809 Fy! Couetice, vnkynd and venemous. **1592** GREENE *Philomela* Wks. (Grosart) XI. 131 If such vnlawfull lust, such vnkinde desires,..procures so great losse. **1606** SYLVESTER *Du Bartas* II. iv. I. *Tropheis* 1232 Cowardly treason,..Un-kinde Rebellion. **1656** COWLEY *Davideis* III. 204 Their too much Wealth, vast, and unkind does grow.

†**5.** Unnaturally cruel, severe, or hostile. *Obs.*

**1340–70** *Alex. & Dind.* 540 Vn-kinde kiþe ȝe ȝou to kille ȝour children. *a* **1375** *Joseph Arim.* 242 He tolde hem..of heore fadres bi-fore þat he fond vn-kuynde. *c* **1400** *Brut* 245 Wiþ sir Andrew of Herkela, þat is callede þe vnkynde out-putter. *c* **1440** *Gesta Rom.* lxvii. 306 (Harl. MS.), My fadir is so vnkynde, þat he woll not pay my raunsom for me. **1513** DOUGLAS *Æneid* I. i. 44 Full deip ingravin in hir breist vnkynd [was] The jugement of Paris. **1635** R. JOHNSON *Hist. Tom a Lincolne* (1828) 117 Making thyselfe unkinde and monstrous in murthering of thy mother. **1659** HAMMOND *On Ps.* cxxxvii. 7 When our unkind neighbours the Edumæans were so forward to joyne their hands with our enemies.

**6.** Lacking in kindness or kindly feeling; acting harshly or ungently to others. Also *absol.*

**1362** LANGL. *P. Pl.* A. I. 166 Beo no men hardore þen þei,.. Vn-kuynde to heore kun and to alle cristene. **1393** *Ibid.* C. XX. 216 Beo vnkynde to þyn emcrystene, and..The holygost huyreþ þe nat. **1509** FISHER *Funeral Serm. C'tess Richmond* Wks. (1876) 307 Were not she an vnkynde & vngentyl moder? **1523** FITZHERB. *Husb.* § 11 His neyghbours be vnkynde, if they wyll not lende this yonge housbande parte of this sede. *a* **1550** in *Early XVI Cent. Lyrics* lxv. 71 The turtle doue is not vnkinde to him that loues her so. **1602** SHAKS. *Ham.* III. i. 101 To the Noble minde, Rich gifts wax poore, when giuers proue vnkinde. **1645** in *Verney Mem.* (1904) I. 422 Censured by the world to be the most unkind and unnatural brother. **1675** DRYDEN *Aurengz.* I. i. 428 That Man..Has been to you unkind, to me unjust. **1738** WESLEY *Ps.* v. iii, The Hearts unkind, and Hearts untrue, Are both abhor'd by Thee. **1796** MRS. J. WEST *Gossip's Story* II. 169 She tried to recal the dear unkind by tears, and soft complaints. **1820** SHELLEY *Hymn Mercury* lii, What mean you to do With me, you unkind God?

*transf.* **1802** WORDSW. '*Bright Flower*' 15 Thou wouldst teach him how to find..A hope for times that are unkind. **1875** MORRIS *Æneid* XII. 144 Thee only..I love of all who e'er have come Into the unkind bed of Jove from out a Latin home. **1885** R. BRIDGES *Eros & Psyche* Apr. xxiv, Ascending many a mile Over the long brown slopes and crags unkind.

**b.** Of actions, speech, etc.: Characterized by want of kindness.

*c* **1400** *Destr. Troy* 1452 What myschefe befell, Þere no cause was to ken but vnkynd wordes. *c* **1586** C'TESS PEMBROKE *Ps.* (1823) LV. iii, Then I would have borne with patient cheere An unkind part from whom I know unkind. **1596** SPENSER *F. Q.* VI. xi. 24 In charge of one..who with vnkind disdaine..her did much molest. **1601** SHAKS. *Jul. C.* III. ii. 187 This was the most vnkindest cut of all. **1647**

CLARENDON *Hist. Reb.* I. (1702) I. 6 The abrupt, and unkind breaking off the Two first Parliaments. **1710** STEELE *Tatler* No. 246 ⁋ 1 The Word Imperfection would not carry an unkinder Idea than the Word Humanity. **1796** MME. D'ARBLAY *Camilla* III. 432 If she persisted in such unkind and unnatural conduct. **1810** LAMB *Wks.* (1908) I. 78 This was the unkindest blow of all. **1891** FARRAR *Darkn. & Dawn* xxx, A mistress who never addressed to them an unkind word.

†**Unki·ndfully**, *adv. Obs.* (UN-[1] 11.) *c* **1500** *Communycacyon* (W. de W.) C j, Without cause ofte thou arte wrothe Unto thy frendes unkyndfully.

† **Unki·ndhead.** *Obs.* [f. UNKIND *a.*] Unnatural conduct; ingratitude; baseness.

**1297** R. GLOUC. (Rolls) 765 þis leir..plainede of þe unkundhede [*v.rr.* vnkuinde-, vnkyndehede] of is doȝter gornorille. *Ibid.* 2392, etc. **1303** R. BRUNNE *Handl. Synne* 5093 Yn sum man, vnkyndehede ys so rank þat [etc.]. *Ibid.* 6508 þarfore..spende weyl þyn owne þyng, þat þou fal nat yn auaryce: Of vnkyndhede hyt cumþ, þat vyce.

**Unkindhea·rted**, *a.* (UN-[1] 9.) **1759** STERNE *Tr. Shandy* I. x, He was not an unkind-hearted man, and every case was more pressing..than the last.

**Unki·ndled**, *ppl. a.* (UN-[1] 8.)

*a* **1513** FABYAN *Chron.* VII. 648 In this yere began a grudge to growe.., but it was keept vnkyndelyd duryng yᵉ lyfe of yᵉ duke. **1535** COVERDALE *Job* xx. 26 An vnkyndled fyre shal consume him. **1717** POPE *Iliad* XI. 239 The unkindled lightning in his hand he [*sc.* Jove] took. **1742** YOUNG *Nt. Th.* I. 111 They live! they greatly live a life on earth Unkindl'd,unconceiv'd. **1809** COLERIDGE *Friend* 161 My feelings ..and imagination did not remain unkindled in this general conflagration. **1865** DICKENS *Mut. Fr.* I. xiii, The unkindled lamp stood on the table.

Hence **Unki·ndledness.**

**1869** ABP. BENSON in *Life* (1901) 116 The yellow wax lights on the Altar stood in their irrational, legal, unkindledness.

**Unki·ndliness.** (UN-[1] 12; cf. UNKINDLY *a.*)

*c* **1470** HENRY *Wallace* IX. 347 We fand nane in that art, That proffryt ws sic wnkyndlynes. **1587** GOLDING *De Mornay* xvii. 308 His wrath..cannot bee kindled against nature.., but against the faultinesse and vnkindlynesse that are in nature. **1627** HAKEWILL *Apol.* II. § 3. 133 The vnkindlinesse of the weather now..hurtfull to the fruites. **1668** H. MORE *Div. Dial.* II. ix. 223 The..unkindliness of the Season. **1763** MILLS *Pract. Husb.* I. 206 The uncommon.. unkindliness of the soil. **1797** LAMB *Let. to Coleridge* 7 Apr., Clear from the imputation of unkindliness (a word, by which I mean the diminutive of unkindness). **1859** TENNYSON *Merlin & V.* 735 Kill'd with inutterable unkindliness.

**Unki·ndling**, *ppl. a.* (UN-[1] 10.) **1818** MILMAN *Samor* II. 108 As summer meteor,..Waning into the dull unkindling air.

**Unki·ndly**, *a.* [repr. OE. *ungecyndelic*, or in later use f. UN-[1] 7 + KINDLY *a.*]

†**1. a.** Morally unnatural; unnaturally wicked or vile. *Obs.*

*a* **1225** *Ancr. R.* 116 Vor hondlunge, oðer eni velunge bitweone mon & ancre is..unkundelich þincg. *a* **1300** *Cursor M.* 27966 Vnkindli sin and sodomite, Austin cals al suilk delite. **1418** *26 Pol. Poems* xiv. 84 Vnkyndely synne and shameles haunted. *a* **1450** *Knt. de la Tour* (1868) 102 The deuell slow all, for as moche as they vsed unkindely werke. **1590** SPENSER *F.Q.* II. x. 9 Their owne mother..gan abhorre her broods vnkindly crime. **1614** SYLVESTER *Little Bartas* 905 Besides th' unkindly slaughter Of his owne Selfe, by his owne Sons soon after.

†**b.** Unnatural in respect of relations or dealings with others. *Obs.*

**1456–70** in *Acta Parlt. Scotl.* (1875) XII. 27/1 Thynkand it onkyndle tyll thole ane nominatioun of lardschipe of sic ane man. *a* **1513** FABYAN *Chron.* VII. 642 After this vnkyndly warre had duryd by the space of vi. monethes. **1591** *Troub. Raigne K. John* (1611) 68 Vnkindly rage, more rough than northern wind, To clip the beautie of so sweete a flower! **1605** SYLVESTER *Du Bartas, Sonn. Late Peace* iv, War's unkindly quarrels. **1647** N. WARD *Simple Cobler* 15 How unseasonable and unkindely it is, to interturbe the State and Church with these Amalekitish onsets.

†**2.** Unnatural in respect of physical qualities or actions. *Obs.*

*a* **1300** in *E. E. P.* (1862) 10/104 þe þing þat bodi no flesse naþ non..vnkundlich þing ded sal don. *c* **1375** *Cursor M.* 26253 (Fairf.), þe man þat mengis wiþ vnkindeli best his flesshe luste to fulfille. **1390** GOWER *Conf.* I. 264 Thilke unkendeli peines Thurgh whiche Envie is fyred ay. *a* **1500** *Flower & Leaf* 413 Salades, which they made hem ete, For to refresh their greet unkindly hete. **1555** WATREMAN *Fardle Facions* 324 Lest therby the vnkindlie couplings against kinde, passe also at lengthe vnto men. **1611** GUILLIM *Heraldry* III. xxv. 179 The shape of the Leopard bewraieth his vnkindly birth. **1639** T. DE GREY *Expert Farrier* II. xxi. (1656) 628 Unkindly and unnatural heats given him by most violent and intemperate riding.

**b.** Of weather, soil, etc.: Unnaturally bleak or cold; unfavourable to growth or comfort; inclement.

**14..** in *Tundale's Vis.* (1843) 154 Mych of oure welth hase wastud awey With grete darthe..And unkyndle wedurs. **1535** W. STEWART *Cron. Scot.* (Rolls) III. 43 In..Hungar and cald, and wnkyndlie distres. **1579** SPENSER *Sheph. Cal.* Jan. 26 My life bloud friesing with vnkindly cold. **1652** GAULE *Magastrom.* 332 We had not a more unkindly summer, for many yeeres, in respect of extraordinary cold. *a* **1684** LEIGHTON *Wks.* (1835) I. 109 A tender plant in a strange unkindly soil. **1763** MILLS *Pract. Husb.* I. 188 The land continued unkindly and sour. **1775** *Phil. Trans.* LXVI. 282 The summers are often so unkindly, that their wheat is blighted while in ear. **1850** ROBERTSON *Serm.* Ser. III. iii. (1857) 36* The unkindly climate of their birth. *a* **1864** HAWTHORNE *Amer. Note-bks.* (1868) I. 282 Besides the bleak, unkindly air.

**c.** Not answering to its (or their) proper kind; not properly conditioned, developed, or thriving. Now *dial.* or *arch.*

*c* **1400** *Destr. Troy* 8523 Ho was vnkyndly to knaw of hir kyd frendis, So disfigurt of face & febill of hew. **1587** GOLDING *De Mornay* xvii. 313 In vs only there is such an vnkindly and Bastardly Nature, that [etc.]. **1601** HOLLAND *Pliny* I. 225 Kine, Buls, and Oxen are not to be despised as unkindly, although they looke but illfavouredly. **1616** BRETON *Invective agst. Treason* Wks. (Grosart) I. 4/1 [To] make theyr bread, of an vnkindly Branne; which seeming Wheate, is but a Hellish weede, sown by the Devill. **1790** *Trans. Soc. Arts* VIII. 32 [These] Peas..ripen later, and become so unkindly that the pods..never fill. *c* **1813** MRS. SHERWOOD *Stories Ch. Catech.* xxxiv. 357 Lopping off..a dead leaf, or unkindly branch. **1887–8** in Cheshire and Somerset glossaries (applied to plants or animals).

†**d.** Prejudicial to health; not developing in a natural healthy manner. *Obs.*

*a* **1649** DRUMM. OF HAWTH. *Hist. Jas. V*, Wks. (1711) 114 He was troubled by an unkindly Medicine. **1667** MILTON *P. L.* IX. 1050 Grosser sleep Bred of unkindly fumes. **1797** UNDERWOOD *Disorders Childhood* II. 117 An oozing of blood from the part, after an unkindly separation of the cord. **1822–7** GOOD *Study Med.* (1829) IV. 99 The exciting causes [of madness]..are..unkindly child-bed [etc.]. *Ibid.* V. 583 It [*sc.* opium] proved a cordial to him through the whole of this tedious affection, without a single unkindly concomitant.

†**3.** Not of the same kind; strange. *Obs.*

**1560** ROLLAND *Seven Sages* 23 Vnkyndlie Captanes ouirthrawis And commoun welth doun drawis. **1591** SYLVESTER *Du Bartas* I. v. 765 Th' infamous Bird that layes His Bastard Egges within the nests of other, To have them hatcht by an unkindely Mother.

†**4. a.** Lacking natural affection. **b.** Cruel, malicious. *Obs.*

**1590** SPENSER *F. Q.* I. i. 26 To see th' vnkindly Impes.. Deuoure their dam. **1591** — *Tears Muses* 15 Her loued Twinnes,..whom her vnkindly foes The fatall Sisters, did for spight destroy.

**5.** Devoid of kindness; unkind.

**1805–6** CARY *Dante, Inf.* XXI. 97, I to my leader's side adhered, mine eyes..bent On their unkindly visage. **1827** SCOTT *Surg. Dau.* vii, He was conscious of unkindly, if not hostile, feelings towards his old companion. **1862** LYTTON *Str. Story* 132 That gentle heart could not bear one unkindlier shade between itself and what it loved.

**Unki·ndly**, *adv.* [repr. OE. *ungecyndelice*, or in later use f. UN-[1] 11 + KINDLY *adv.*]

†**1. a.** With unnatural immorality or impropriety. *Obs.*

*a* **1225** *Ancr. R.* 50 Ne of tollinde lokunges, ne lates, þæt summe,..weilawei! unkundeliche makieð. *a* **1300** *Cursor M.* 28495 Wit womman seke vmquile haue i And vnkyndeli don licheri. *c* **1386** CHAUCER *Pardoner's T.* 485 Lo how þat dronken loth vnkyndely Lay by his doughtres two vnwityngly. *c* **1400** *Destr. Troy* 13820 Now full hard..is þi hegh lust, þat þou couetus vnkyndly to couple with me. **1579** [see UNKINGLY *adv.*]. **1602** WARNER *Alb. Eng.* XIII. lxxvi. 315 Vnkindly though Nature it is defaced so in some, As that by often sinning Sinne an habette doth become.

†**b.** With unnatural enmity, harshness, or cruelty. *Obs.*

*c* **1300** *Beket* (Percy Soc.) 1540 The Kyng..sende him word that him thoȝte..That hi wolde him so moche misdo uncundeliche and wouȝ. **1535** COVERDALE 2 *Macc.* xv. 2 O do not so cruelly and vnkyndly [1611 barbarously], but halowe yᵉ Sabbath daye. **1547** J. HARRISON *Exhort. Scottes* h j b, That you..should thus vnkindly, vnnaturally, and vnchristenly bathe youre swoordes in eche others blode. **1598** SYLVESTER *Du Bartas* II. i. IV. *Handy-crafts* 7 Envious Cain His (better) Brother doth vnkindly brain. **1605** *Ibid.* iii. IV. *Captains* 833 Lo there, another valiant Champion.. His onely Daughter doth unkindly kill.

†**c.** Contrary to right feeling or conduct; improperly; ungratefully. *Obs.*

**1380** *Lay Folk's Catech.* (L.) 952 [To] be euer sory..for he haþ greuyd god so vnkendely. **1393** LANGL. *P. Pl.* C. IV. 264 Vnkyndely þow, conscience, consailedest hym þennes, To lete so hus lordshup for a lytel moneye. *c* **1440** *Promp. Parv.* 365/2 On-kyndely yn herte, *ingratanter, acaride.* **1470–1** *Rolls of Parlt.* VI. 233/1 Unnaturelly, unkyndly and truly entendyng his destruccion. **1567** *Gude & Godlie B.* (S.T.S.) 65 Lat nocht my hart vnkyndlie depart, From the rycht lufe of thy mercie. **1588** SHAKS. *Titus* v. iii. 104 Lastly, [I was] my selfe vnkindly banished.

†**2.** Unsuitably. *Obs. rare.*

*c* **1300** *Havelok* 1250 Goldeborw..wende she were bi-swike, þat she were yeuen un-kyndelike. **1362** LANGL. *P. Pl.* A. x. 177 Summe..For Couetise of Catel vnkuyndeliche beoþ maried.

†**b.** Contrary to the usual course of nature; at variance with natural conditions. *Obs.*

**1390** GOWER *Conf.* I. 292 Unkindeliche he was transformed, That he which erst a man was formed Into a womman was forschape. **1426** LYDG. *De Guil. Pilgr.* 3530 But ye wolden ..Tourne vnkyndely my wyn In-to blood, folk for to drynke. **1541** R. COPLAND *Galyen's Terap.* 2 B j, There must be had delyberacyon, to knowe yf all the party dyscoloured and hardened vnkyndly ought to be cut. **1615** W. LAWSON *Country Housew. Gard.* (1626) 8 Who did euer know a tree so vnkindly splat, come to age? **1667** MILTON *P. L.* III. 456 All th' unaccomplisht works of Natures hand, Abortive, monstrous, or unkindly mixt,..fleet hither. **1703** ROWE *Fair Penit.* I. i, You mourn unkindly by your self, And rob me of my Partnership of Sadness. **1766** *Compl. Farmer* s.v. *Malt*, The malt..appears shrivelled, and often is unkindly hard.

**c.** Badly, unsuccessfully.

**1763** MILLS *Pract. Husb.* III. 128 Kiln-drying is apt to make wheat grind unkindly. **1811** *Self Instructor* 516 Umber is..very greasy, and mixes unkindly with water-colours. **1887** *Daily News* 21 July 2/4 Fanfare remained a staunch favourite to the end. He, however, ran very unkindly.

**3.** In an unkind or unkindly manner; with marked want of kindness.

*c* **1384** CHAUCER *H. Fame* I. 295 How he betrayed hir allas, And lefte hir ful vnkyndely. **14..** *Sir Beues* (C.) 1448 That he tolde me not, when he went, Iwysse, he dud onkyndely, verament. *c* **1489** CAXTON *Sonnes of Aymon* xvii. 397 The whiche Reynawde kepeth..for his prysoner not vnkyndely. **1590** SHAKS. *Mids. N.* III. ii. 183 But why vnkindly didst thou leaue me so? **1603** KNOLLES *Hist. Turks* (1621) 114 Vnkindly to cast him off that had so honorably vsed him in like extremitie. **1695** LD. PRESTON *Boeth.* II. 55 She hath looked unkindly upon thee. **1768** STERNE *Sent. Journ., Snuff-box*, I treated him most unkindly; and from no provocations. **1828** SCOTT *F. M. Perth* x, 'You will not deal so unkindly with us, cousin,' replied the gentle Monarch. **1889** B. WHITBY *Awakening Mary Fenwick* II. 45 Don't haul me over the coals so unkindly.

*Comb.* **1605** SYLVESTER *Du Bartas* II. iii. II. *Fathers* 480 Among them all..you shall not finde Such an example, where (unkindly-kinde) Father and Son so mutually agree. *a* **1699** J. BEAUMONT *Psyche* XII. v, Nor could unkindly-courteous He resist The huging of his Spouse's seeming Friend.

**4.** With dissatisfaction or resentment.

Freq. in the phrase *to take* (..) *unkindly.*

**1562** GRESHAM in Burgon *Life* (1839) I. 448 Assewring yow, I doo take it very unkindelye at your handes. **1607** SHAKS. *Timon* III. vi. 39, I hope it remaines not vnkindely with your Lordship, that I return'd you an empty Messenger. **1635** *Argt. Pastoral of Florimene* 6 Florimene desires Dorine not to take it unkindly, if [etc.]. **1725** DE FOE *Voy. round World* (1840) 91 Nothing to be had but for ready money; which our men took so unkindly,..that [etc.]. **1771** *Junius Lett.* l. (1788) 270 The only letter I ever addressed to the King was..unkindly received.

**Unki·ndness.** [UN-[1] 12.]

†**1.** Unnatural conduct; absence of natural affection or consideration for others. *Obs.*

*a* **1300** *Cursor M.* 13018 þis herod..vnkendnes kidd ful rjf, He reft his broþer philipp his wijf. **1362** LANGL. *P. Pl.* A. III. 280 Vnkuyndenesse is Comaundour and kuyndenesse is Banescht. **1380** *Lay Folks Catech.* (L.) 938 Yf he kepe hem [*sc.* the commandments] not he doþ to god more vnkendenesse þan ony broþer may do to anoþer. *c* **1400** *Beryn* 1354 He cursid his grete vnkyndnes To foreȝit his modir. **1477** *Rolls of Parlt.* VI. 173/1 The grett offences, unkyndnese and mysbehavyngs, that..Nevell hath doon. *a* **1513** FABYAN *Chron.* I. xv. (1811) 15 The vnkyndnesse of his ii. doughters, consyderynge theyr wordes to hym before spoken and sworne. **1570** *Homilies* II. *Wilful Rebellion* I. (1640) 282 So farre doth their unkindnesse, unnaturalnesse, wickednesse..excell anything..that can be expressed.

†**b.** Uncharitableness; niggardliness. *Obs.*

**1377** LANGL. *P. Pl.* B. XVII. 263 Diues deyed dampned for his vnkyndenesse Of his mete & his moneye to men that it neded.

†**2.** Ingratitude, unthankfulness. *Obs.*

**1340** HAMPOLE *Pr. Consc.* 5587 Agayne þam sal Crist allege sone,..And reherce his benefices,..To reprove þam of þair unkyndenes. **1380** *Lay Folks Catech.* (L.) 946 Yf we with-stond þat lord þat made vs..we do þe most vnkendenesse þat may be wroȝt. *c* **1450** *Mirk's Festial* 113 Saynt Barnard yn Cristys person makyth gret waymentacyon for þe vnkyndenesse þat he sethe yn men. **1483** CAXTON *Gold. Leg.* 362/2 We receyue dayly many bienfaites of this cyte and it sholde be a grete unkyndnes to us yf we socoured it not in this grete nede. **1531** ELYOT *Gov.* II. xiii, The moste damnable vice..is ingratitude, commenly called unkyndenesse. **1585** ABP. SANDYS *Serm.* 189 After that God had thus set forth his great goodnesse towardes them, hee chargeth them with their great vnkindenesse towards him. **1605** SHAKS. *Lear* III. ii. 16, I taxe not you, you Elements with vnkindnesse. I neuer gaue you Kingdome, call'd you Children.

†**b.** A flock (of ravens). *Obs.*—⁰

*c* **1452** in *Trans. Philol. Soc. 1907–10*, III. 52 Vnkyndenys of rauynnys. **1486** *Bk. St. Albans* f vj.

**3.** The fact of being unkind; unkind action or treatment.

*c* **1374** CHAUCER *Anel. & Arc.* 292 My self I mourdre with my prevy thoght For sorowe and routhe of your vn-kyndnesse. **1390** GOWER *Conf.* II. 299 This Emperour al that he tolde Hath herd, and thilke unkindenesse He seide he wolde himself redresse. *c* **1491** *Chast. Goddes Chyld.* 12 Trouth fynde they nowhere but wronges detraccyons and unkyndenes. **1535** COVERDALE *2 Macc.* xiv. 30 When Machabeus sawe that Nicanor beganne to be churlish vnto him.. he perceaued that soch vnkyndnes came not of good. **1594** R. WILSON *Coblers Proph.* III. iii, Know you not, vnkindnes kills a woman? **1621** J. TAYLOR (Water P.) *Unnat. Father* Wks. (1630) 136/2 Ruing his vnkindnesse to his Wife. **1651** HOBBES *Leviath.* I. vi. 27 Some Weep for the losse of Friends; Others for their unkindnesse. **1742** GRAY *Eton* 76 The stings of Falshood those shall try, And hard Unkindness' alter'd eye. **1784** COWPER *Task* VI. 627 Attachment..proof alike Against unkindness, absence, and neglect. **1825** SCOTT *Talism.* xx, Eloquent in urging her own defence, the Queen was far more so in pressing upon Richard the charge of unkindness. **1882** 'OUIDA' *Maremma* I. 69 Joconda feared no scorn and unkindness on the score of her birth.

**b.** An instance of this; an unkind action.

**1505** in *Mem. Hen. VII* (Rolls) 266 The which the kynge ..takithe for a grete onkyndnes. **1555** BRADFORD *Let.* in Foxe *A. & M.* (1583) 1661/1 All those vnkyndnesses, rudenes, &c., whereof you accuse your selfe. **1606** SHAKS. *Ant. & Cl.* I. ii. 138 Why then we kill all our Women. We see how mortall an vnkindnesse is to them. **1660** *Trial Regic.* 133, I hope he will think it no unkindnesse in me. **1809–14** WORDSW. *Excurs.* VI. 776 Her uncharitable acts, I trust, And harsh unkindnesses are all forgiven. **1860** EMILY EDEN *Semi-attached Couple* xiii, A series of small unkindnesses is very offensive indeed.

**4.** Unkindly feeling; ill-will, enmity, hostility. Now *rare* or *Obs.*

*c* **1400** *Destr. Troy* 144 With a course of vnkyndnes he caste in his thoghte, The freike vpon faire wise ferke out of lyue. **1465** in *10th Rep. Hist. MSS. Comm.* App. V. 302 The tyme of thar unkyndnesse other warre with the citie. **1562** *Child. Marr.* 203 By which did growe an vnkindnes betwene them. **1588** *Marprel. Epist.* (Arb.) 38 Because the gamesters..wan all his monie at trey trip [he] tooke such vnkindenes at the alehouse that [etc.]. **1624** CAPT. SMITH *Virginia* III. 52 This bred some vnkindnesse betweene our two Captaines. **1658** JER. TAYLOR *Let.* in *12th Rep. Hist.*

*MSS. Comm.* App. V. 5 If ever you have .. heard of any overtures of unkindness betweene them. *a* 1700 EVELYN *Diary* 24 Apr. 1692, Unkindness betweene the Queene and her sister. 1823 SCOTT *Quentin D.* vii, I will bestow another to wash away unkindness. 1825 — *Betrothed* xviii, He died when we were in unkindness with each other.

†5. Unnatural character or quality. *Obs.*

1502 *Ord. Crysten Men* (W. de W. 1506) I. vii. F iv b, By this artycle we sholde knowe the mysery & ryght unkyndenesse of humayne condycyon. *a* 1513 FABYAN *Chron.* v. cxxiv. 104 Whan the Embassade..had shewyd ye vnkyndnesse of this warre with the ieopardyes that myght ensue of ye same.

**Unki·ndred,** *a.* (UN-1 7.) 1700 SHIPPEN *Hymn to Sun* x, in Rowe *Amb. Step-Mother* III. ii, Conscious of superior birth [It] Despises this 'unkindred earth. 1804 EUGENIA DE ACTON *Tale without Title* III. 75 Their souls, unkindred, can never understand our language. 1865 *Spectator* 14 Jan. 42 Not quite unkindred to this fact is the other. **Unki·ndredly,** *a.* (UN-1 7.) 1748 RICHARDSON *Clarissa* (1811) VI. 381 What an implacable..set of wretches are those of her unkindredly kin. †**Unki·ndship.** *Obs.* [UN-1 12.] Unkindness. 1390 GOWER *Conf.* I. 263 As he which thurgh unkindeschipe Envieth every felaschipe.

**Unki·ng,** *v.* [UN-2 6 b. Cf. MDu. *ontconingen*, Du. *ontkoningen*, G. *entkönigen*.]

1. *trans.* To deprive of the position of king; to depose from sovereignty. (Common in 17th c.)

1578 *Paradise Dainty Devices* L ij, Such toile do thei sustain, That often tymes of God thei wishe, to be unkyngde again. 1602 MARSTON *Ant. & Mel.* IV, That very word Unkings me quite, makes me vile passions slave. 1684 E. PELLING *Serm. 30 Jan.* 20 They may crown them or unking them as they think fit. 1711 *Pol. Ballads* (1860) II. 100 These men do design To un-king the Queen and keep out the Right Line. 1784 COWPER in Hayley *Life* (1809) II. 158 Government therefore is bound to interfere, and to un-king these tyrants. 1815 *Q. Rev.* XIII. 489 Having.. escaped unhanged when they were unkinged, they started up again to perform the part of princes in the new revolutionary drama. 1870 LOWELL *Study Wind.* (1871) 216 Some passion which the churchyard smothered while the Stuarts were yet unkinged.

*fig.* 1638 SUCKLING *Aglaura* I. i, There was with me fresh Rebellion, And reason was almost unking'd agen. 1731 *Gentl. Mag.* I. 168 The comic muse Unkings your Cupid, or obstructs his views. 1818 MILMAN *Samor* v. 463 Thou.. hast unking'd Thy stately soul within the wreathing arms Of that fair Saxon.

*absol.* 1644 MAXWELL *Prerog. Chr. Kings* 3 [That] the Pope.. by this indirect power..may King and unking at his pleasure. 1646 BP. MAXWELL *Burd. Issach.* 18 Every individual Person is..to punish, to dethrone, to un-King, to kill, &c.

b. *refl.* To divest (oneself) of royal status or character; to abdicate.

1647 N. WARD *Simple Cobler* 54, I would honour their very heeles, that would..teach me..to king it better, when they saw me unkinging myselfe and kingdome. 1689 *Advantages of Present Settlement* 22 If a king..ruine his people..he so far Unkings himself. 1700 J. TYRRELL *Hist. Eng.* II. 794 [King John] thereby..Unking'd himself. 1859 J. MARSHALL *Hist. Scott. Eccl. & Civ. Affairs* 290 Charles's concessions had been in vain. He had unkinged himself.

2. To deprive (a country) of a king.

1647 *Old Ballads* (Percy Soc.) 86 They may thus..Un-king our state, un-church us too. 1820 BYRON *Mar. Fal.* v. i. 437 A wife's dishonour unking'd Rome for ever. 1883 *Harper's Mag.* June 139/1 An empire, unkinged to-night, sees to-morrow a new king.

**Unki·ngdomed,** *ppl. a.* (UN-2 8.) 1611 SPEED *Hist. Gt. Brit.* IX. vi. 463 Hee was not vnking'd, though vnkingdom'd.

**Unki·nged,** *ppl. a.*1 [f. UNKING *v.*] Deprived of the position or authority of king; deposed from kingship. Also *absol.*

1593 SHAKS. *Rich. II*, IV. i. 220 God saue King Henry, vn-King'd Richard sayes. 1611 [see prec.]. 1818 MILMAN *Samor* XI. 196 Then gaz'd the unking'd, then cried out the fallen. 1837 CARLYLE *Fr. Rev.* I. I. iv, There must thou enter, naked, all unking'd. 1845 FORD *Handbk. Spain* II. 947 Ferdinand..dismissed,..a prisoner and unkinged.

**Unki·nged,** *ppl. a.*2 [UN-1 8.] Not raised to the dignity of king. 1855 BAILEY *Mystic, Spir. Leg.* 82 Fair thorn, as yet unkinged, Unsanctified by woes of brow divine. **Unki·nger.** [f. UNKING *v.*] One who deposes a king. 1656 S. H. *Gold. Law* 24 It unking'd him, and King'd his unkingers in point of Power. **Unki·nglike,** *a.* (UN-1 7 c.) 1611 SHAKS. *Cymb.* III. v. 7 For our selfe To shew lesse Soueraignty then they, must needs Appeare vn-Kinglike. 1892 TENNYSON *Akbar's Dream* 60 To drive A people from their ancient fold of Faith, And wall them up perforce in mine—unwise, Unkinglike.

**Unki·ngly,** *a.* [UN-1 7. Cf. ON. *ókonungligr*.]

1. Unbecoming to a king; not in accordance with the position or character of a king.

1600 HEYWOOD *2nd Pt. Edw. IV*, Wks. 1874 I. 100 Edward of England, these are vnkingly words. 1658 OSBORNE *Q. Eliz.* 12 An Art lost in these latter times, or thought unkingly. *a* 1661 HOLYDAY *Persius* (1673) 310 When cruel lust..moves..fierce kings To act unworthy and unkingly things. 1702 ROWE *Tamerl.* I. i, With most un-kingly baseness, H' has ta'en the advantage of their absent arms. 1765 BURKE *Tracts on Popery Laws* Wks. 1812 V. 250 [Louis XIV] had recourse..to an unkingly denial of the fact which made against him. 1853 TRENCH *Proverbs* 41 He was about, in somewhat unsoldierly and unkingly fashion, immediately to retire. 1880 SHORTHOUSE *J. Inglesant* xii, To introduce Popery..by ways the most unkingly and perfidious.

2. Unlike a king.

1718 POPE *Iliad* XIV. 90 What shameful words (unkingly as thou art) Fly from that trembling tongue and timorous heart?

**Unki·ngly,** *adv.* [UN-1 11. Cf. ON. *ókonungliga*, MHG. *unkünecliche*.] In an unkingly manner; unlike a king.

1412-20 LYDG. *Chron. Troy* I. 3770 He vnkyngly of verray malys souȝt Ageynes vs firste occasioun. 1579 STUBBES *Gaping Gulf* C 5 Rychard [II]..fell amourous most vnkindlye and vnkingly with a french girle but eyght yeeres of age.

†**Unki·ngship.** *Obs.*-1 (UN-1 12.) *a* 1700 EVELYN *Diary* 30 May 1649, Un-kingship was proclaim'd, and his Majesty's statues thrown down. **Unki·nlike,** *a.* (UN-1 7 c.) 1869 BLACKMORE *Lorna D.* xi, It would be a sad and unkinlike thing for you to despise our dwelling-house. †**Unki·nsman.** *Obs.*-1 (UN-1 12.) 1606 SYLVESTER *Du Bartas* II. iv. *Tropheis* 1216 With an un-kinsman's kisse (un-loving Lover) The Brother shall his Sister's shame discover. **Unki·rsened,** *ppl. a. dial.* [UN-1 8.] Unchristened. *a* 1779 GRAHAM *Writings* (1883) II. 136 A cock, a cat, or some unkirsen'd creature. 1824 J. TELFER *Border Ball.* 65 It was unkirsent blood. 1873- in *Eng. Dial. Dict.* s.v.

**Unki·ss,** *v.* (UN-2 3.)

1562 A. BROOKE *Romeus & Jul.* 843 A thousand times she kist, and him vnkist agayne. 1593 SHAKS. *Rich. II*, v. i. 74 Let me vnkisse the Oath 'twixt thee, and me. 1634 FORD *Perk. Warbeck* v. iii, That man, that shall vnkisse This sacred print next. 1653 W. HEMINGS *Fatal Contract* III. ii, With this kiss..Unkiss the kiss that seal'd it on thy lips.

**Unki·ssed,** *ppl. a.* Also 4-7 unkist, etc. [UN-1 8. Cf. Du. *ongekust*, Sw. *okysst*.] Not kissed; without being kissed.

1390 GOWER *Conf.* II. 92 Ofte he goth to bedde unkist. *a* 1400 *Hymns Virg.* (1867) 80 We schulen go vnkist boþe at þe dore & at þe gate. *a* 1542 WYATT '*What should I say?*' 28 And thus betraide, Or that I wiste Farewell, unkiste! *a* 1592 GREENE *Jas. IV*, I. ii, I cannot abide a full cup unkissed. 1852 WHITTIER *April* 11 Round the boles of the pine-wood the ground-laurel creeps, Unkissed of the sunshine. 1870 MORRIS *Earthly Par.* III. IV. 53 She sighed as those sweet sounds did fall From her unkissed lips.

†b. In the phrase *unknown* (*unknowe* or *uncouth*), *unkissed*. *Obs.*

1374 CHAUCER *Troylus* I. 809 Vnknowe vnkyst and lost þat is vn-sought. 1401 *Pol. Poems* (Rolls) II. 59 On old Englis it is said, unkissid is unknowun. 1562 J. HEYWOOD *Prov. & Epigr.* (1867) 148 Unknowen vnkist, and beyng knowen I weene, Thou art neuer kist, where thou mayst be seene. 1579 E. K. *Ded. to Spenser's Sheph. Cal.* § 1 Our new Poete, who for that he is vncouthe (as said Chaucer) is vnkist, and vnknown to most men, is regarded but of few. *c* 1592 NASHE *Mar-Martine* xxii, Thou caytif kerne, vncouth thou art, vnkist thou eke sal bee. 1624 BP. MOUNTAGU *Immed. Addr.* 119, I would gladly see and know, by what warrant I on Earth so vncouth and therefore vnkist,..can say unto them, Holy Peter, blessed Paul, pray for mee. *a* 1697 AUBREY *Lives* (1898) II. 254 He..ransackt the MSS. of the church of Hereford (there were a great many that lay uncouth and unkiss). [1897 V. HUNT (*title*), Unkist, Unkind!]

†**Unki·the,** *v.* *Obs.*-1 [UN-2 3.] *intr.* To disappear, vanish. *a* 1300 *Cursor M.* 11438 Fra þai come þar als suith, Þe stern it hid and can vnkyth. **Unkna·ve,** *v.* (UN-2 6 b.) 1746 W. HORSLEY *Fool* (1748) II. 9 By pursuing their Master's Instructions, [they] make it their Business to unknave him. **Unknea·ded,** *ppl. a.* (UN-1 8.) *c* 1631 T. CAREW *Elegy Death Donne* 4 Why yet dare we not trust Though with unkneaded dowe-bakt prose thy dust. **Unkne·lled,** *ppl. a.* (UN-1 8.) *a* 1770 CHATTERTON *Battle of Hastings* II. 556 And sowles unknelled hover'd oer the bloude. 1818 BYRON *Ch. Har.* IV. clxxix, Without a grave, unknell'd, uncoffin'd, and unknown.

**Unkni·ght,** *v.* [UN-2 6 b.] *trans.* To divest of knighthood; to depose from the rank of knight. Hence **Unkni·ghting** *vbl. sb.*

1623 in Birch *Crt. & Times Jas. I* (1848) II. 439 Francis Mitchell, that was unknighted the last parliament. *a* 1661 FULLER *Worthies, Yorks.* III. (1662) 207 Another author unknighteth him, allowing him only a plain Esquire. 1844 *P. Parley's Ann.* V. 251 By St. George, I will unknight thee. 1856 DORAN *Knights* xxx. 489 Knights, irregularly made so, were unknighted with little ceremony. *Ibid.* 490 There are fewer examples of unknighting in this country than in France.

**Unkni·ghted,** *ppl. a.* [UN-1 8.] Not raised to the rank of knight; not invested with knighthood.

1631 in Birch *Crt. & Times Chas. I* (1848) II. 99 Ere long they will bring all the unknighted lords into play. *a* 1661 FULLER *Worthies, Camb.* I. (1662) 168 Indeed, I..cannot believe that he was Un-knighted so long. 1892 *Verney Mem.* I. 205 Mr. Badnage..remained unknighted.

**Unkni·ghtlike,** *adv.* (UN-1 7 c.) 1872 TENNYSON *Gareth & Lynette* 1122 Forth that other sprang, And, all unknightlike, writhed his wiry arms Around him.

**Unkni·ghtly,** *a.* [UN-1 7.]

1. Not appropriate to a knight or to knighthood.

*c* 1412 HOCCLEVE *De Reg. Princ.* 2286 Of suche vnknyghtly trikkes he nat roghte. 1423 JAS. I *Kingis Q.* lv, The crueltee of that vnknyghtly dede. 1586 FERNE *Blaz. Gentry* 161 Lewes..had so vnknightlye a regarde..of Armes, that [etc.]. 1611 GUILLIM *Heraldry* II. vi. 56 Base and vnknightly actions and qualities, deserue a base and vnknightly chastisement. 1664 BUTLER *Hud.* II. I. 832, I here..free you from th' Unknightly Jail. 1704 D'URFEY *Tales, Abradatus & P.* I. 12 The dire reward that did belong To him that Acted such unknightly wrong. 1828 SCOTT *F. M. Perth* viii, The unknightly advantage which yonder rascal had taken of his stumbling horse. 1860 GEN. P. THOMPSON *Audi Alt. Part.* III. cxlii. 123 A foreign force..threatening to sack, unless unknightly and degrading terms were complied with.

2. Unlike a knight; not having the qualities of a knight.

1596 SPENSER *F. Q.* VI. iii. 35 Vnknightly Knight,..Loe I defie thee. 1813 BYRON *Ch. Har.* Pref., Add., It has been stated, that..he is very unknightly, as the times of the Knights were times of Love, Honour, and so forth. 1842 TENNYSON *Morte d'Arth.* 120 Ah,..untrue, Unknightly, traitor-hearted!

**Unkni·ghtly,** *adv.* [UN-1 11.] In an unknightly manner.

*a* 1586 SIDNEY *Arcadia* III. xviii, They helde playe against the rest, though the two brothers unknightly helped them. 1859 TENNYSON *Geraint & Enid* 723 The brute Earl..unknightly with flat hand, however lightly, smote her on the cheek.

**Unkni·t,** *v.* [OE. *uncnyttan* (UN-2 4 b).]

1. *trans.* To untie or undo (a knot or something tied).

*c* 1000 *Ags. Gosp.* Luke iii. 16 Þæs ic ne eom wyrþe þæt ic hys sceo-þwancg uncnytte. *c* 1200 *Trin. Coll. Hom.* 137 Ich nam noht ne forðen wurðe þat ich un-cnutte his sho þuong. 1387 TREVISA *Higden* (Rolls) II. 43 So þat þe more wynd he wol haue, he wil vnknette þe mo knottes. *c* 1430 *Syr Gener.* (Roxb.) 7091 Hir kerchef lift vp wold he Hir visage there forto see; Tho thoght he hir kerchefe to vnknyt. 1530 PALSGR. 768/1 Unknyt my gyrdell, I praye you. 1547 in *Leland's Collect.* (1774) IV. 321 Then tooke he the said Rope, and..tyed himselfe by the Right Legg, .. and after ..unknet the Knot, and came downe again. 1615 G. SANDYS *Trav.* 66 Tying on her silken buskins with knots easily not vnknit. 1675 HOBBES *Odyssey* (1677) 147 Binde me you must upright, both hand and foot, And so as I may not the knot unknit.

b. In figurative contexts (with *knot* or *bond*).

*a* 1225 *Leg. Kath.* 1150 Ich habbe uncnut summe of þeos cnotti cnotten. *c* 1374 CHAUCER *Boeth.* v. pr. iii. (1868) 154 þat som men wenen þat þei mowen assoilen & vnknytten þe knot of þis questioun. 1387-8 T. USK *Test. Love* III. vi. (Skeat) l. 129 Thilke falsheed..hath unknit the bond of understanding reson bytwene wil and the herte. *c* 1407 LYDG. *Reson & Sens.* 3202 Wher so as her [*sc.* Venus's] sort was set, The knot never was vnknet. *c* 1430 *Life St. Kath.* (1884) 44, I haue spoused me to hym in a bonde þat neuer schal be vnknytte. 1561 NORTON & SACKV. *Gorboduc* IV. ii, Whan thus I sawe the knot of loue vnknitte. 1596 SHAKS. *1 Hen. IV*, v. i. 15 Will you againe vnknit This churlish knot of all-abhorred Warre? 1850 W. R. WILLIAMS *Religious Progress* IV. (1854) 82 Demoralization that unknits the bonds of obligation.

†c. To ungird (oneself). *Obs.*-1

*a* 1500 in *Three 15th Cent. Chron.* (Camden) 111 Ther he shall unknyte hym, and his swerde..shall offer to God and to Holy Churche moste devowtly.

d. To disjoint, disunite; to unclasp. *rare.*

1580 HOLLYBAND *Treas. Fr. Tong* s.v. *Desnouer*, To vnknitte a bone, to put out of ioynte. 1582 STANYHURST *Æneis* II. (Arb.) 58 Thee ioyncturs vnknit, with an horribil hurring Pat fals thee turret. 1726 LEONI *Alberti's Archit.* I. 15 Rain..loosens and unknits all the Nerves of the Building. 1856 RUSKIN *Mod. Paint.* III. IV. xviii. Concl. 339 If again petty jealousies..prevail to unknit their hands from the armoured grasp.

e. To smooth out. *rare*-1.

1596 SHAKS. *Tam. Shr.* v. ii. 136 Fie, fie, vnknit that threatning vnkinde brow.

2. *fig.* a. To disperse, dissolve, undo, destroy; to relax or weaken. Also *absol.*

1377 LANGL. *P. Pl.* B. XVIII. 213 So god..suffred to be solde to see þe sorwe of deyinge, The which vnknitteth al kare & comsynge is of reste. *c* 1412 HOCCLEVE *De Reg. Princ.* 2564 Al-thogh a kyng haue habundance of myght In his land, at his lust knytte & vnknytte. *a* 1500 *Ragman Roll* 151 in Hazl. *E. P. P.* I. 76 Weyr he unknytte, al this worldes rychesse Ne myghte noghte yow two knyttyn in feir. 1551 T. WILSON *Logike* 3 Logike is bound..to knit true arguments and unknit false. 1592 LYLY *Gallathea* III. i, I feele my thoughts vnknit. 1642 CHAS. I *Let. to both Ho. Parl.* 7 Ambitious spirits, that may disjoynt and unknit his Majesty and this House. 1655 VAUGHAN *Silex Scint., Match* ii, Shut out all distractions That may unknit My heart. *c* 1837 WORDSW. '*Ah why*' 5 Where for ages they have lain ..With life's best sinews more and more unknit.

b. To separate, sever, detach.

1388 WYCLIF *Job* vi. 17 Thei schulen be vnknyt fro her place. *a* 1395 HYLTON *Scala Perf.* I. xii. (MS. Bodl. 592), þis spirit wole vnknytte and vndo ih'u fro þe soule: & þerfore it is not of god. *c* 1412 HOCCLEVE *De Reg. Princ.* 1658 Þanne is to hem an helle hire mariage, Þanne þei desyren for to be vnknyt.

3. *intr.* To become unknit, in various senses.

1574 HELLOWES *Gueuara's Fam. Ep.* (1577) 187 It is a sore that neuer openeth, and a bonde that neuer vnknitteth. 1609 C. BUTLER *Fem. Mon.* v. F 3 b, Then may you bid them farewel: for presentlie they begin to vnknit, and to be gone. 1677 *Gov. Venice* 6 The private Magistrates are as it were the Nerves and Bones..; and the Council of Ten are the ligaments, hindring the parts from unknitting. 1748 THOMSON *Cast. Indol.* I. xxiii. For whomsoe'er the villain takes in hand, Their joints unknit, their sinews melt apace. 1870 *Pall Mall G.* 10 Dec. 12 The lady's eyebrows unknit, and wintry smiles break from the grey eyes.

Hence **Unkni·tting** *vbl. sb.*

1382 WYCLIF *Nahum* ii. 10 Herte feylynge, and vnknyttynge of smale knees. 1545 *Act 37 Hen. VIII*, c. 21 § 2 Without any dissolucion, undoinge, unknittinge, or repeale of them. 1611 COTGR., *Desnouement*, an vntying, vnknitting, vnbinding (of knots).

**Unkni·t,** *ppl. a.* [UN-1 8 b.] Not knit together or closely united.

1607 MARKHAM *Cavel.* I. xviii. 73 His ioynts being tender and vnknit. *a* 1625 FLETCHER *Fair Maid of Inn* III. i, The petty brawls..shall, like tender unknit joynts, Fasten again together of themselves. 1809-14 WORDSW. *Excurs.* III. 914 Let us..Leave this unknit Republic to the scourge Of her own passions. 1860 MOTLEY *Netherl.* vii. (1868) I. 465 A loose, disordered and unknit state needs no shaking, but propping.

**Unkni·tting,** *ppl. a.* (UN-1 10.) 1587 GOLDING *De Mornay* x. 165 [Aristotle] sayth that the knitting parts, .. the bones, the skin, the sinewes,..may be made of the mixing togither of the elements, and that the vnknitting parts, as the Head, the Leg, the Arme,..cannot. **Unkno·ck,** *v.* (UN-2 3.) 1680 MOXON *Mech. Exerc.* xii. 203 Its Office is to knock and unknock the Wedge in the Puppets.

**Unkno·t,** *v.* (UN-2 3. Cf. G. *entknoten*.)

1598 FLORIO, *Sgroppare*, to vntie, to vnknot. 1623 COCKERAM II, Not to be vnknotted, *inenodable*. 1866 MISS A. CARY *Ball. & Lyrics* 54, I saw my Charley The..shawl from his neck Unknot, with a quick, wise cunning. **1891** *Daily News* 8 July 4/8 The man..who hoards string, unknotting it..from parcels.

*refl.* **1880** *Daily News* 27 Nov. 2/8 This remarkable worm ..has the power of unknotting himself.

**Unkno·tted,** *ppl. a.* (Un-[1] 8.)

**1642** H. More *Song of Soul* To Rdr., All homogeneall, simple, single,..unknotted, uncoacted. **1744** Mrs. Delany *Life & Corr.* (1861) II. 291 You ask me how many pounds of thread I have got for you; do you mean knotted or unknotted? **1756** Dyer *Fleece* iii. 58 Even, unknotted, twine will praise your skill. **1892** Yeats *C'tess Kathleen* iii. 51 The green things love unknotted hearts and minds.

**Unkno·tty,** *a.* (Un-[1] 7.)

**1621** G. Sandys *Ovid's Met.* x. (1626) 198 Vnknottie Firre, the solace-shading Planes, Rough Chesnuts. **1622** Mabbe tr. *Aleman's Guzman d'Alf.* ii. 348 The wooll of the Mattresses..[was] kept vnknotty, and soft.

**Unknow·,** *v.*[1] [Un-[1] 14.]

**1.** *trans.* Not to know (something); to fail to recognize or perceive. Also *absol.*

*c* **1380** Wyclif *Serm.* Sel. Wks. I. 160 Þou art maister in Israel, and ȝit þou unknowist þes þingis. **1382** — 1 *Cor.* xiv. 38 If ony man vnknowith, he schal be vnknowen. *c* **1400** *Apol. Loll.* 61 Þoo þat vnknawen þe riȝtwisnes of God. *c* **1532** Du Wes *Introd. Fr.* in *Palsgr.* 942 To unknowe, *descognoistre.* **1646** Sir T. Browne *Pseud. Ep.* 41, I hardly beleeve, he hath from elder times unknowne the verticity of the loadstone. **1709** Mrs. Manley *Secret Mem.* (1720) III. 252 [He] is obliged to turn his Eyes, as if to unknow, or at least must take no notice of it here. **1871** Swinburne *Hertha* 19 Love or unlove me, Unknow me or know.

†**2.** To be ignorant *that*, etc. Also *intr.* with *of.*

**1382** Wyclif 1 *Cor.* x. 1, I nyle ȝou for to vnknowe, for [1388 that] alle oure fadris weren vndir cloude. [Also 1 *Kings* xxii. 3, *Rom.* i. 13.] *a* **1400** *Pauline Ep.* (Powell) 2 Cor. i. 8 We wil not ȝou to vnknowe, breþere, of oure tribulacyoun. **1709** Mrs. Manley *Secret Mem.* (1720) II. 58 Sure these seem to unknow that there is a certain Portion of Misery.. allotted to all Men.

**Unknow·,** *v.*[2] [Un-[2] 3.] *trans.* To cease to know, to forget (what one has known). Also *absol.*

*a* **1586** Sidney *Arcadia* iii. v, She..rather wished to unknowe what she knewe, then to burden her hart with more hopeles knowledge. **1627** S. Ward *Happiness of Practice* 31 Such..shall soone vnknow that which they know [to be good]. **1697** J. Sergeant *Solid Philos.* b 2, His Method of Unknowing all that Nature had taught him. **1782** Paine *Let. Abbé Raynel* (1791) 50 There is no possibility..of the mind *un*knowing any thing it already knows. **1859** I. Taylor *Logic in Theol.* 270 Unless I might unknow what I have come to know. **1865** J. Grote *Explor. Philos.* i. 243 We have got to unsee and unknow much further back than this, if [etc.].

**Unknow,** variant of Unknowe *ppl. a. Obs.*

**Unknowabi·lity.** (Un-[1] 12; cf. next.) **1863** Mill *Lett.* (1910) I. 272 The doctrine of unknowability. **1871** R. H. Hutton *Ess.* I. 28 The unknowability of the primal Cause.

**Unknow·able,** *a.* and *sb.* (Un-[1] 7 b.)

*c* **1374** Chaucer *Boeth.* iii. met. vii. (1886) 47 Liggeth thanne stille al owtrely vnknowable, ne fame ne maketh yow nat knowe. **1456** Sir G. Hay *Bk. Knighthood* Wks. (S.T.S.) II. 16 The quhilkis ar unknawable till..unworthy personis. **1653** H. More *Antid. Ath.* i. iv. § 3 He is a very Novice in Speculation that does not acknowledge that to be unknowable. **1678** Cudworth *Intell. Syst.* i. iv. § 31. 471 There is something of God Vnknowable and Incomprehensible by all Mortals. **1740** Cheyne *Regimen* 35 If we dropt both substances, as unknown and unknowable Things at present. **1754** Edwards *Freed. Will* ii. xii. 119 If there be any Truth which is absolutely without Evidence, that Truth is absolutely unknowable. **1818** F. Hall *Trav. Canada & U.S.* 28 Indeed privacy..seems quite unknown, and unknowable to the Americans. **1873** Morley *Rousseau* II. 90 Men.. will be thankful not to waste life in guessing evil about unknowable trifles.

**b.** *absol.* (with *the*). That which cannot be known. (Common from *c* 1860.)

**1823** *Monthly Rev.* CI. 447 Here, again, the author professes to know the unknowable. **1867** Lewes *Hist. Philos.* I. p. cxv, We always hope that the Unknown is not also the Unknowable.

**c.** As *sb.* An unknowable thing.

**1725** Watts *Logic* i. vi. § 1 To distinguish well between Knowables and Unknowables. **1733** — *Philos. Ess.* i. xii, In every Age..there will be some Unknowables and Insolvables. **1874** B. P. Browne *Philos. H. Spencer* ii. 41 (Stand.), Mr. Spencer's argument proves an unexplainable, not an unknowable.

Hence **Unknow·ableness.**

**1664** N. Ingelo *Bentiv. & Ur.* ii. vi. 367 The unknowableness of the manner of this Union. **1697** J. Sergeant *Solid Philos.* 301 The Unknowableness of Real Essences. **1856** Ruskin *Mod. Paint.* IV. 81 The great religious painters rejoiced in that kind of unknowableness. **1886** Jane Lee *Faust* p. xxxiii, The unknowableness of the nature of things.

†**Unknow·e** (also 5–6 -know, 6 *Sc.* -knaw), obs. variants of Unknown *ppl. a.*

For the phrase *unknowe, unkissed,* see Unkissed *ppl. a.*

**1340–70** *Alex. & Dind.* 382 We holden hit a vertu..Among þe men of our march mercy vnknowe. *c* **1350** *Lybeaus Disc.* 71 Than may ye wete a rowe, 'The fayre unknowe', Sertes so hatte he. **1387** Trevisa *Higden* (Rolls) I. 87 Þan were þe Parthi as it were..vnknowe amonge men of the est londes. **1430–40** Lydg. *Bochas* viii. xiv. (1558) 9 b, A knight vnknowe angelyke of vysage. *c* **1440** *Gesta Rom.* i. 2 (Harl. MS.), Þat she euer pursuyd for my deth, þat is vnknowe to me. **1513** Douglas *Æneid* vi. ii. 52 Virgyne, na kynd of pane may rise Vnknaw to me.

So †**Unknow·ed** *ppl. a. Obs.*

*c* **1380** *Sir Ferumb.* 3847 If þar comeþ any ounknowed man. *c* **1380** [see Unkept *ppl. a.* 2].

†**Unknow·ing,** *vbl. sb.* [Un-[1] 13.] Ignorance.

**1340** Hampole *Pr. Consc.* 194 In myrknes of unknawyng þai gang. *Ibid.* 5741 Ne mene þou noght Of my freyle unknawynges of thoght. *c* **1380** Wyclif *Sel. Wks.* I. 159 So Nichodeme..for þis unknowinge..axide þis questioun. *c* **1449** Pecock *Repr.* i. xvi. 89 The vnhauyng and the vnknowing of this..consideracioun. *c* **1450** Lovelich *Grail* lii. 775 That I haue don be vnknowenge, Of forȝevenesse I preye ȝow. **1556** Olde *Antichrist* 127 b, What other thing shal we cal this, but the most grosse unknowing of God?

**Unknow·ing,** *ppl. a.* [Un-[1] 10, 5 d.]

**1.** Not knowing; not possessed of knowledge; uninformed, ignorant.

*c* **1315** Shoreham v. 148 Al one-knowynge þaȝ hy were, Hy makede ioye. **1386** *Rolls of Parlt.* III. 225/2 Owre lyge Lordes comaundement to symple and unknouuing men. **1435** Misyn *Fire of Love* 48 Bot þis ar vnknawand, for vertew of contemplatife þai knaw not. **1538** G. Browne in Ware *Hist. Coll.* (1681) 3 The People of this Nation be zealous, yet blind and unknowing. **1612–3** C. Brooke *Elegy* Poems (1872) 175 Those baser mindes, vnknowing, sensuall, rude. **1649** Bp. Hall *Cases Consc.* vi. (1654) 45 The matter may be intricated by passing through many perhaps unknowing hands. **1725** Pope *Odyss.* xx. 56 Man on frail unknowing man relies. **1760–72** H. Brooke *Fool of Qual.* (1809) IV. 27 My..child..is unexperienced in the world, quite unknowing and unknown. **1845** Hirst *Com. Mammoth,* etc. 89 Winds that pilfer from unknowing flowers Their balmy breaths. **1871** H. Macmillan *True Vine* vi. 249 It..does what it does in simple, perfect, unknowing dependence upon the will of God.

*absol.* **1718** J. Chamberlayne *Nieuwentijdt's Relig. Philos.* p. xx, [They] pass amongst the Unknowing for great Mathematicians. **1833** Disraeli *Cont. Flem.* i. i, Our instructors are the unknowing and the dead. **1876** *Nature* 2 Nov. 17/1 Undated..works..may be palmed off on the unknowing as the genuine product of the current year.

**2.** Without knowledge, ignorant, *of* something.

In frequent use from *c* 1700.

*a* **1300** *Cursor M.* 28313 O godds godes..haue i ben vnknauand. *c* **1400** *26 Pol. Poems* 149 All that lyuen..Shall dye, vnknowyng of her day. *a* **1450** *Knt. de la Tour* (1868) 159 That is gret pite..to be vncunnynge and vnknowynge of hym selff. **1542** Udall *Erasm. Apoph.* 16 The residue wer vnknowyng of this thyng. **1691** Wood *Ath. Oxon.* I. 587 [He was] simple, and unknowing of matters of State. **1740** Richardson *Pamela* II. 270 She had found out a Match for me,..and had..brought me into the Lady's Company, unknowing of her Design. **1844** [see 2 c]. **1869** Freeman *Norm. Conq.* III. xii. 242 He laid his hand on the chest, while still unknowing of all that was in it.

**b.** With direct object.

**1382** Wyclif *Gal.* iv. 8 ȝe, vnknowynge God, seruyden to hem that weren not goddis. **1460** Capgrave *Chron.* 110 Sche went unknowyng hir tyme fro Seynt Petirs onto Lateran. *c* **1500** *Melusine* v. 27 He..rode apas vnknowing the way. **1760–2** Goldsm. *Cit. W.* xxii, Mankind wanders, unknowing his way, from morning till evening. **1830** Tennyson *Grasshopper* i. 16 Unknowing fear, Undreading loss, A gallant cavalier. **1847** T. D'Arcy McGee *Art MacMurrogh* p. x, When, unknowing facts, they [*sc.* historians] lay down suppositions in their place.

**c.** With objective clause.

*c* **1425** *St. Elizabeth* in *Anglia* VIII. 147 Not vnknowynge þat oure lorde couerde þe naked of oure firste fader and moder after hir falle. *c* **1465** *Eng. Chron.* (Camden, 1856) 62 Unknowyng the said peple wherfore it was. **1542** Udall *Erasm. Apoph.* 182 b, Thou art not unknowyng that we are now conquerours. **1697** Dryden *Æneis* vi. 236 Æneas went Sad from the cave,..Unknowing whom the sacred Sibyl meant. **1748** Richardson *Clarissa* (1811) III. i. 2 They were all working for me,..unknowing that they did so. **1820** Scott *Monast.* xxv, Driven by calamity, and unknowing where my course is bound. **1844** Kinglake *Eothen* xii, Unknowing of all geography, unknowing where he was, or whither he might go.

**d.** With inf. (alone or preceded by *how,* etc.).

**1666** Dryden *Ann. Mirab.* xcvi, The Kingly beast..slowly moves, unknowing to give place. **1697** — *Virg. Georg.* iv. 126 Unknowing how to fly, And obstinately bent to win or dye. **1700** — *Wife of Bath's T.* 100 Lest surpriz'd, unknowing what to say, Thou damn thy self. **1746** Francis tr. *Horace, Art of Poetry* 51 In one grand Whole unknowing to unite Those different Parts. **1771** Goldsm. *Hist. Eng.* II. 204 Unknowing whether to ascribe their misfortunes to ..sorcery, or to a celestial influence. **1801** Southey *Thalaba* v. 170 Unknowing whitherward to bend his way, He stood. **1812** J. Henry *Camp. agst. Quebec* 46 The huge animal.. seemed unknowing which way to run.

†**3.** In absolute construction. *Obs.*

**1451** *Paston Lett.* I. 198 He thought that ye and James Gresham had do it un malyce,..your moders unknowyng. **1483** *Vulgaria abs Terentio* 20 He hyde nott fro me that.. odyr doo, vnknowynge theire faders. *c* **1500** *Melusine* xxiv. 171 They came & lodged them a leghe nygh to the Calyphes oost, vnknowyng the paynemes of it.

**4.** As quasi-*adv.* = Unknowingly *adv.*

**1382** Wyclif *Acts* xvii. 23 Therfore which thing ȝe vnknowynge worschipen, this thing I schewe to ȝou. **1470–85** Malory *Arthur* x. lxxix. 554 There syr Tristram vnknowyng smote doune kyng Arthur. **1721** Amherst *Terræ Fil.* (1726) 101 See..what mischiefs ye might do unknowing. **1743** Francis tr. *Hor., Odes* v. iii. 6 Have I swallow'd the gore of a viper unknowing? **1852** Kingsley *Andromeda* 250 From afar, unknowing, I marked thee.

**5.** Unknown *to* (a person). Chiefly in absolute const., = without the knowledge of. *Obs.* exc. *dial.*

*c* **1400** *Destr. Troy* 11318, I..neuer comynd in þis case vnknowing to you. **1462** *Paston Lett.* II. 119 It is not on knowyng to you that [etc.]. **1513** Bradshaw *St. Werburge* i. 2677 A seruaunt..pryuely hydde it,..Vnknowynge to Werburge. **1577** Grange *Golden Aphrod.* I iv b, He..sodenly departed (vnknowing to the Ladies). **1617** Collins *Def. Bp. Ely* (1628) 302 When he praied for his children, vnknowing to them. **1643** E. Symmons *Loyal Subjects Belief* Ep. Ded., Unknowing, I beleeve, to them in particular, some others did intend [etc.]. **1886–91** in Somerset and Devon glossaries.

Hence **Unknow·ingness.**

**1493** *Festivall* 23 b/1 Vnknowyngnesse shalle not exscuse you at yᵉ day of dome. **1872** H. Bushnell *Serm. Living Subj.* 211 The unknowingness, the innocence, the sweet simplicity of childhood.

**Unknow·ingly,** *adv.* [Un-[1] 11: cf. prec.] Without knowledge, ignorantly; unintentionally. Also const. *to* (a person).

**1340** *Ayenb.* 175 Huanne me zeneȝeþ wytindeliche, me zeneȝeþ more ynoȝ þanne onknawyndliche. *c* **1440** *Promp. Parv.* 366/1 On-knowyngly, *ignoranter.* *a* **1500** *Ratis Raving* i. 904 Better to be styll Than say vnknawandly thar tyll. **1641** Sir E. Dering *Sp. on Relig.* 22 Nov. 70, I speake it not unknowingly. **1697** *Dryden's Virg. Past.* Preface (1721) I. 97 The Roman Historian..falls, unknowingly, into a Verse not unworthy Virgil himself. **1709** Shaftesb. *Charac.* (1711) II. 89 An Eye..fails not to shut together, of its own accord, unknowingly to us. **1768–74** Tucker *Lt. Nat.* (1834) I. 595 Made unknowingly to work out the advantage of fellow-creatures, whereof we have not the least knowledge. **1807** Wordsw. *White Doe* ii. 100 Leaning on a lance Which he had grasped unknowingly. **1871** Freeman *Hist. Ess.* Ser. i. iii. 213 Nations and parties learn to shape themselves unknowingly.

†**Unknow·ledge.** *Obs.* [Un-[1] 12.]

**1.** Unacknowledgement.

*a* **1300** *Cursor M.* 27833 O couaitise..cums..fals wittnesing, Vnknaulage, manath, and lesing.

**2.** Absence or want of knowledge; ignorance. *Your unknowledge,* unknown to you.

*c* **1450** *Cov. Myst.* (Shaks. Soc.) 121 For unknowlage he is desesyd. **1470** *Paston Lett.* II. 393, I have betyn the mater for yow, your onknowleche, as I told hyr. **1483** *Sc. Acts, Jas. III* (1814) II. 166 At thay may not excuse thame of the vnknawlege of thir articlis. **1593** Nashe *Christ's T.* F ij b, Your pretence of vnknowledge or ignorance.

†**Unknow·ledged,** *ppl. a.* [Un-[1] 8.] Unacknowledged.

*c* **1445** Pecock *Donet* 96 Þat no svnne be left bihinde for vnknowen and vnknowlechid. **1598** *Mucedorus* v. ii. 104 Condemne not..My rude behauiour, so compeld by Nature, That manners stood vnknowledged. **1603** B. Jonson *The Satyr* Wks. (Rtldg.) 537/2 For which bounty to us lent, Of him unknowledg'd, or unsent, We prepared this compliment.

†**Unknow·ledging.** *Obs.* [Un-[1] 12.] Ignorance. *Unknowledging to,* without the knowledge of.

**1357** *Lay Folks Catech.* 73 Nane sal excuse tham Thurgh unknalechyng for to kun tham. ? **1530** in Ellis *Orig. Lett.* Ser. iii. II. 229 The sayd Dean,..vnknowlegyng to..the surveyor of Hampton Corte,..hathe..dygyd uppe by the rootts xxxv. of my..ffeyrest elmes.

**Unknow·n,** *ppl. a.*[1] and *sb.* [Un-[1] 8 b. Cf. OE. *ungecnawen.*]

**A.** *adj.* **1.** Not known; strange, unfamiliar: **a.** Of places.

**13..** *Cursor M.* 1170 (Gött.), I sal be flemed for mi sinne, In vnknaun land to duell ine. **13..** *E. E. Allit. P.* B. 1679 He..carfully is out-kast to contre vnknawen. *a* **1440** *Sir Eglam.* 917 As sche were of an unknowen londe. **1586** T. B. *La Primaud. Fr. Acad.* i. 71 As if he should undertake to.. walke through unknowen places without a guide. **1638** in *Verney Mem.* (1907) I. 90 Some unknown place in the world. **1697** Dryden *Virg. Georg.* iii. 532 So vast a Space Of Wilds unknown..Allures their Eyes. **1790** Cowper *Odyss.* xxiv. 344 The fishes of the unknown deep. **1844** H. H. Wilson *Brit. India* II. 402 The armies..beheld countries previously unknown. **1853** M. Arnold *Scholar Gypsy* xiv, Where o'er thy unknown grave..white flowering nettles wave.

**b.** Of persons.

For the phrase *unknown, unkissed,* see Unkissed.

**13..** *Cursor M.* 12131 (Gött.), Ani man, vnknauen or cuth. **1382** Wyclif 1 *Cor.* xiv. 38 Forsothe if ony man vnknowith, he schal be vnknowen [Vulg. *ignorabitur*]. *c* **1386** Chaucer *Friar's T.* 99, I am vnknowen as in this contree. *c* **1440** *Alph. Tales* 175 Ane vnknowen man sittand on a hors. *c* **1449** Pecock *Repr.* 53 He schal be vnknowen of God forto be eny of hise. **1526** Tyndale *Acts* xvii. 23, I founde an aultre wher in was written: vnto the vnknowen god. **1555** Eden *Decades* (Arb.) 49 It had byn better for hym to haue byn obscure and vnknowen. **1622** J. Taylor (Water P.) *Sir G. Nonsence* To Nobody, The narration of the Vnknowne Knight. **1676** Ray *Corr.* (1848) 123 An unknown person, who sent me a letter without a name. **1718** *Free-thinker* No. 4. 25 The Discourse..turned upon the Unknown Fair. **1797** S. & H. Lee *Canterb. T.* (1799) I. 364 To Lothaire the lord of St. Aubert was personally unknown. **1846** Mrs. A. Marsh *Father Darcy* II. x. 164 Mr. Keyes..was a man quite unknown about town. **1885** 'Mrs. Alexander' *At Bay* iv, Unknown, doubtful Americans, neither rich nor highly-placed are beyond the pale.

**c.** Of things or facts.

*Unknown quantity,* orig. a term of algebra (see quots. 1676, 1728, and cf. Quantity 12); also freq. in figurative use.

*c* **1330** R. Brunne *Chron. Wace* (Rolls) 2757 [They] caste þer armes of, þe vnknowen, And armede hem eft wyþ here owen. *c* **1374** Chaucer *Former Age* 6 Onknowyn was þe quyerne and ek the melle. *c* **1450** *Myrr. our Ladye* 158 Then oure lady..was sturred in her harte wyth vnspecable & vnknowen gladnesse. **1509** Fisher *Wks.* (1876) 297 It is not vnknowen how studyously she procured Iustyce to be admynystred. **1568** Grafton *Chron.* II. 180 A man of vnknowen or low birth. **1622** S. Ward *Life of Faith* (1627) 51 Death is the knownest and vnknownest thing in the world. **1669** Sturmy *Mariner's Mag.* iv. i. 138 Many times the Ship is carried away by unknown Currents. **1676** Glanvill *Ess.* iii. 15 The degree of Composition in the unknown Quantity of the Æquation. **1728** Chambers *Cycl.* s.v. *Equation,* The Root of an Equation, is the Value of the unknown Quantity in the Equation. *a* **1768** Secker *Serm.* (1770) IV. xviii. 387 Their having a real, though unknown, Subserviency to valuable Ends. **1827** Faraday *Chem. Manip.* xv. 389 As the whole volume of gas introduced is unknown, and the specific gravity is as yet unknown. **1885** 'Mrs. Alexander' *At Bay* vi, For some reasons unknown very little was said of the occurrence in the newspapers.

**d.** Const. *to* (*unto,* †*till*) or †*of* (= by).

**1340** Hampole *Pr. Consc.* 7694 Na thyng..tylle him unknawen es. **1399** Langl. *Rich. Redeles* iii. 263 It is not vnknowen to kunnynge leodis. **1486** *Paston Lett.* III. 328

What pleasur ye maie do to the Kings Grace..is not to you unknowen. **1578** LYTE *Dodoens* 5 Straunge herbes..vnknowen of the common people. ? **1600** C. PERCY in *Shaksp. Cent. of Praise* 38 Anything..that may bee unknown unto you. **1670** PETTUS *Fodinæ Reg.* 11 That Mine, which was afterward discovered..in that Countie (as yet unknown to the Societie). **1738** GAY *Propertius* III. 65 Happy the youth, and not unknown to Fame. **1823** H. J. BROOKE *Introd. Crystallogr.* 231 A crystal whose primary form is unknown to us. **1866** GEO. ELIOT *F. Holt* Introd. 16 These things are often unknown to the world.

**e.** With *of*. (Cf. KNOW *v.* 18 b.)

**1606** G. WOODCOCK *Lives Emperors* in *Hist. Ivstine* G g 2 When nature did hatch such euils as were vnknowne of to the whole world. **1839** MARY HOWITT *Boy of Southern Isle* I. xx, Some unknown-of isle. **1864** PUSEY *Lect. Daniel* ii. 94 It is..one strange, unknown-of, God, whom he shall recognise.

**2.** In absolute const.: Without it being known (*to* one), without the knowledge *of* (some one).

**1390** GOWER *Conf.* II. 169 Diane his dowhter he begat Unknowen of his wif Juno. **1423** JAS. I *Kingis Q.* xlv, Bewailling myn infortune.., Vnknawin how or quhat was best to doon. *c* **1450** *Mirk's Festial* 207 Scho..was þer þrytte ȝere vnknowon of all men wythout mete oþir drynke. **1483** CAXTON *G. de la Tour* I j, Two prestes unknowen of her cam wher as she was alone. **1523** LD. BERNERS *Froiss.* I. 74 The kyng..was ther unknowen of his ennemyes. **1590** SHAKS. *Com. Err.* IV. ii. 48 Thus he vnknowne to me should be in debt. **1606** — *Ant. & Cl.* II. vii. 84 Being done vnknowne, I should haue found it afterwards well done. **1672** WISEMAN *Wounds* I. viii. 74 The Patient, unknown to me, pursued his intention. **1761** MRS. F. SHERIDAN *Sidney Bidulph* III. 106 He stole, unknown to anybody, on board a ship. **1820** KEATS *Isabella* xi, All close they met,..Unknown of any, free from whispering tale. **1823** SOUTHEY *Hist. Penins. War* I. 77 An agent..was employed to negociate it unknown to the Spanish embassador. **1898** 'MERRIMAN' *Roden's Corner* iii, The terrible distress..going on unknown to us in our very midst.

†**3. a.** Ignorant (*of*), unskilled *in*. *Obs.*

*a* **1300** *Cursor M.* 11809 þis herods..[was] O carles costes al til vnknauin. *c* **1475** *Rauf Coilȝear* 127 Sen ellis thow art vnknawin, To mak me Lord of my awin. **1653** W. RAMESEY *Astrol. Restored* 3 We see thereby the folly of such..gain-sayers of what they are altogether unknown in.

†**b.** Not recognizing, owning, acknowledging, or confessing. *Obs.*

*a* **1300** *Cursor M.* 18796 Of vn-man-hede es it draun, To be again god dede vn-knaun. *Ibid.* 28288 Ic ha made vous oft vn-right, And halden þam efter my might, þe gode vous ic am vn-knaun. *c* **1375** *Ibid.* 26666 (Fairf.), þat is þou art vnknawen of ani man synnis bot þine awen.

**B.** *sb.* **1.** An unknown person: **a.** With *the*. *The Great Unknown* (quot. 1825), the author of the Waverley Novels.

**1597** in Salusbury & Chester *Poems* (1914) 79 To the Honorable minded vnknowne, the Name-lesse wisheth..perpetuall happines. **1652** LOVEDAY *Hymen's Præludia* 8 The faire Unknowne found enough in his Noble looks to claime respect. **17..** WATTS *Hymn*, '*Who dares*' iv, When shall we see the Great Unknown, And in his presence stand? **1774** *Trinket* 70 The charming unknown turned his eyes on me. **1825** R. WILSON *Sk. Hist. Hawick* 51 The powerfully superior mind of the Great Unknown. **1834** DICKENS *Sk. Boz, Boarding-ho.* i, The distinguished unknown who condescends to play the 'swell' in the pantomime.

**b.** With *an*, *this*, etc., or pl.

**1611** SHAKS. *Cymb.* IV. iv. 43, I am asham'd To looke vpon the holy Sunne,..remaining So long a poore vnknowne. **1686** tr. *Agiatis or Civ. Wars Lacedemonians* 71 To unite her self to that Unknown, whom she prefers before me. **1709** MRS. MANLEY *Secret Mem.* (1720) IV. 140 I'll never run after the Cant of a Letter from an unknown again. *a* **1774** GOLDSM. tr. *Scarron's Com. Romance* (1775) II. 160 He immediately recollected his unknown by her person. **1839** W. IRVING *Wolfert's R.* (1855) 45, I have only to find out this amiable Unknown, to wed her, and be happy! **1902** ELIZ. BANKS *Newspaper Girl* 214 Looking at the bodies of the unfortunate unknowns.

**2. a.** With *the*: That which is unknown.

**1656** STANLEY *Hist. Philos.* VIII. (1687) 433/2 From which proceedeth Opinion..to the false and unknown. **1759** B. PORTEUS *Death* 300 When my Soul starting from the dark unknown Casts back a wishful look. **1816** CHALMERS *Let.* in *Life* (1851) II. 65 Running into the dark unknown of legal perplexities. **1876** T. HARDY *Ethelberta* xxxv, Losing the indefinite interest of the unknown, it acquired the charm of a riddle.

**b.** An unknown state or condition.

**1837** CARLYLE *Fr. Rev.* I. IV. i, A new omnipotent Unknown of Democracy was coming into being.

**3.** *Math.* An unknown quantity

**1817** H. T. COLEBROOKE *Algebra*, etc. 63 The demonstration is by resolution of a quadratic equation involving several unknown. **1890** A. MARSHALL *Princ. Economics* p. xi, His equations are neither more nor less in number than his unknowns.

†**Unknown,** *ppl. a.*[2] *Obs.*[—1] [var. of *on-*, *aknown*: see ACKNOW *v.* 4 d.] In a state of acknowledgement or confession.

*a* **1300** *Cursor M.* 26094 þe toþer pont es scrift o muth To mak to preistes vr costes cuth; Of al vr plight to be vnknaun, Wit will to bete þat we ha schaun.

**Unknow·nly,** *adv. rare.* [f. UNKNOWN *ppl. a.*[1]] In an unknown manner; mysteriously.

**1611** FLORIO, *Isconosciutamente*, vnknowenly. **1644** QUARLES *Sheph. Orac.* vi, Just then it open'd; and th' enclosed Grain Unknownly vanish't; and then, clos'd again.

**Unknow·nness.** [f. UNKNOWN *a.*] The quality of being unknown.

**1619** W. SCLATER *Exp.* 1 *Thess.* (1630) 398 The vnknownnesse, and suddennesse of Christs comming. **1675** tr. *Camden's Hist. Eliz.* (ed. 3) II. 252 They stood in no Fear at all of Pirates, by reason of..the Unknownness of that Sea. **1864** N. HAWTHORNE *S. Felton* (1883) 383 Soon they would all drop away,..all leaving him in blessed unknownness to adopt new temporary relations. **1899** *Outlook* 15 Apr. 364/2 Her studies..appeal by the very unknownness to English readers.

**Unknow·nst,** dial. var. (see -ST) of UNKNOWN *ppl. a.* 2 (*c*).

**1837** LOVER *Handy Andy* iii, By the powers! I'll pop in a ball *onknownst* to him. **1887** HALL CAINE *Deemster* xxiii, It'll be unknownst to the law as we are..innocent.

**Unko,** var. UNCO *a.* **Unkunning, -yng,** varr. UNCUNNING *Obs.* **Unkward:** see UNKARD *a.* **Unkyt,** ME. var. UNCUT.

**Unla·belled,** *ppl. a.* (UN-[1] 8.)

**1844** KINGLAKE *Eothen* xii. 175 A little while you are free, and unlabelled, like the ground that you compass; but Civilization is coming. **1890** W. J. GORDON *Foundry* 166 The reels are turned over, and their unlabelled ends exposed.

**Unla·biate,** *a.* (UN-[1] 7.) **1835–6** *Todd's Cycl. Anat.* I. 265/2 Two unlabiate and edentate mandibles.

**Unlabo·rious,** *a.* (UN-[1] 7.)

**1644** MILTON *Areop.* (Arb.) 54 The Parlament, whose command perhaps made all things seem easie and unlaborious to them. **1750** MRS. CARTER *Johnson's Rambler* No. 44 ₱ 7 Does she [*sc.* Religion] lead her votaries through flowery paths, and bid them pass an unlaborious life? **1809** *Edin. Rev.* XIV. 4 The simple and unlaborious plenty which reigned among the scattered inhabitants. **1863** LD. LYTTON *Ring Amasis* I. 260 Those wandering but not unlaborious days.

Hence **Unlabo·riousness.**

**1642** J. CARYL *Wks. of Ephesus Expl.* 21 Unlaboriousnesse..is the buriall of our workes.

**Unla·boured,** *ppl. a.* [UN-[1] 8.]

†**1.** Not cultivated by study. *Obs.*

*c* **1450** BURGH *Secrees* 1516 These Sevene Sustryn..The nyne musys blame shal in maneere, That they vnlabouryd stant on my partye.

**2.** Of land: Unworked, untilled, uncultivated.

**1473** *Reg. Cupar Abbey* I. 201 Gif thar be ony..that levis ony his land..onlaboryt. *a* **1513** FABYAN *Chron.* VII. ccxix. 241 He destroyed the lande..in suche wyse, that .ix. yeres after..the lande laye vnlabored and vntylled. **1586** T. B. *La Primaud. Fr. Acad.* I. 166 Good ground becommeth unfruitfull,..the more it is left unlaboured. **1684** T. BURNET *Theory Earth* I. 243 Seeing it..had a soil so fruitful, a new unlabour'd soil. **1708** J. PHILIPS *Cyder* I. 115 Let thy Ground Not lye unlabour'd. **1804** *Europ. Mag.* XLV. 60/2 Gallia mourns..Unpeopled cities, and unlabour'd plains.

**3.** Not obtained or brought about by labour; *esp.* attained or accomplished in an easy or natural manner; spontaneous.

**1631** SIR W. CORNWALLIS *Disc. Seneca* Ll 6 b, When goodnes was vnlabored excellency. **1697** DRYDEN *Virg. Past.* IV. 33 Unlabour'd Harvests shall the Fields adorn. **1797** *Monthly Mag.* III. 538 Of the translation itself we shall only observe, that it is natural and unlaboured. **1853** RUSKIN *Stones Ven.* II. viii. 369 Their perfect, pure, unlaboured naturalism. **1882** *Homiletic Monthly* July 599 Such inspirational and unlabored success was built on a firm basis of general study.

†**4.** Left unapproached or uninfluenced. *Obs.*[—1]

**1644** LAUD *Wks.* (1854) IV. 147 The judge at Chester (altogether unknown to me and unlaboured by me) did say [etc.].

**5.** Not subjected to, free from, labour.

**1598** GRENEWEY *Tacitus, Descr. Germanie* ii. 261 Horses, which are..maintained in those woods.., white, vnbacked, or vnlaboured. **1765** BEATTIE *Judgm. Paris* 514 The bower of bliss..be thine, Unlabour'd ease, and leisure's careless dream.

**Unla·bouring,** *ppl. a.* (UN-[1] 10.)

**1619** SIR J. SEMPIL *Sacrilege Handled* 57 Paul had..onely to iustifie, that he and Barnabas might liue vnlabouring, as well as other Apostles. **1791** COWPER *Odyss.* XXI. 488 A bard Unlabouring strains the chord to a new lyre. **1795** COLERIDGE *To Jos. Cottle* 18 Ere aught of perilous ascent you meet, A mead of mildest charm delays th' unlabouring feet. **1810** T. L. PEACOCK *Genius of Thames* 77 Where Lechlade sees thy current strong First waft the unlaboring bark along.

**Unla·ce,** *v.* [UN-[2] 3.]

**1.** *trans.* To undo the lace or laces of (a piece of armour, clothing, etc.); to unfasten, or loosen in this manner.

**13..** *Coer de L.* 3171 A knyght hys armes gan unlace. **1388** WYCLIF *Mark* i. 7 Y am not worthi to..unlace his schoone. *c* **1400** *Beryn* 2426 He vnlacyd his mantell. **1470–85** MALORY *Arthur* I. xxiii. 69 He vnlaced his helme and gate hym wynde. **1590** C'TESS PEMBROKE *Antonie* 1593 His armor he vnlaste, and cast it of. **1652** C. B. STAPYLTON *Herodian* 129 His Purple Coat he 'gins for to Unlace. *c* **1696** PRIOR *Love Disarmed* 12 Her Boddice half way She unlac'd. **1731** SWIFT *Poems, Nymph going to Bed* 24 The lovely goddess Unlaces next her steel-rib'd bodice. *a* **1861** T. WOOLNER *My Beautiful Lady, Night* x, I wonder whether She now her braided opulent hair unlace. **1885** *Law Rep.* 15 Q. B.D. 360 The belts..could be removed from the shafting altogether by being unrivetted or unlaced. **1888** J. PAYN *Myst. Mirbridge* viii, She instantly busied herself..in unlacing her boots.

**b.** In fig. context, or *transf.*

*c* **1400** *Beryn* 67 [He] pryuelich vnlasid his both eyen liddes, And lokid hir in the visage. *c* **1422** HOCCLEVE *Min. Poems* 224/231 The feruence Of loue..Was qweynt, & loues knotte was vnlaced. **1593** G. HARVEY *Pierce's Super.* 69 Thou mightest haue knowen him, that can Vnbutton thy vanity, and Vnlase thy folly. *a* **1699** J. BEAUMONT *Psyche* XVI. xvii, Unlace my nerves, and try My finest tenderest membranes to unpin.

**c.** *Naut.* (See quot. 1769.) Also *absol.*

**1669** STURMY *Mariner's Mag.* I. ii. 16 The Wind blows a fresh Gale...Unlease your Bonnets. **1769** FALCONER *Dict. Marine* (1780), *Délacer la bonnette*, to unlace or take off the bonnet from the foot of a sail. **1777** COOK *Second Voyage* III. ii. II. 18 [To] unlace that part of the sail from the yard which is between the tack and mast-head. **1886** R. C. LESLIE *Sea-painter's Log* iii. 41 With bonnet-pieces..made to unlace instead of reef.

**2.** To free or relieve (a person, the body, etc.) by undoing a lace or laces. Also *refl.* and *absol.*

*c* **1350** *Will. Palerne* 3200 þe quen kauȝt a knif & komli hire-selue william & his worþi fere swiftli vn-laced out of þe hidous hidus. *a* **1400** *Sir Perc.* 786 Gawayne doun lyghte, Unlacede the rede knyghte. *c* **1440** *York Myst.* xxxi. 42 My lorde, vn-lase you to lye, Here schall none come for to crye. *a* **1524** W. CORNYSHE in *Early XVI Cent. Lyrics* lxii. 45 Ther wyth reuyued sche, and her smalle wast ful fast vnlast. *a* **1586** SIDNEY *Arcadia* II. xii, She lay for dead, till I helpt with vnlasing her. **1648** HERRICK *Hesper.* (title), Upon Julia's unlacing her self. *c* **1680** *Roxb. Ball.* (1891) VII. 459 Do no less, then undress, and unlace, all a-pace. **1725** *Fam. Dict.* s.v. *Swoon*, To make him lie on his Back, to unbutton or unlace. **1889** *Spectator* 9 Nov. 635/1 Showin' their tongues Or unlacin' their lungs, For divle one symptom the docther disparages.

*transf.* *c* **1440** *Pallad. on Husb.* VII. 26 If al the lond attonys rody grete, Enclyne, and thonke vnlaced so for hete. **1762** STERNE *Tr. Shandy* VI. xi, As if he had snatched the occasion of unlacing himself with a few more frolicsome strokes at vice, than the straitness of the pulpit allowed.

†**3.** To cut up or carve (in later use *spec.* a rabbit); to cut off in carving. *Obs.*

**13..** *Gaw. & Gr. Knt.* 1606 A wyȝe þat was wys vpon wod craftez, To vnlace þis bor lufly bigynnez. *c* **1460** J. RUSSELL *Bk. Nurture* 410 Furst, vn-lace þe whynges, þe legges þan in sight. *c* **1486** *Bk. St. Albans* F vij b, A Cony vnlaceedde. **1508** W. DE WORDE *Bk. Keruynge* A j b, Vnlace that cony. **1618** BRETON *Court & Country* Wks. (Grosart) II. 13/1 A Trencher must not be laid, nor a..Capon carued, nor a Rabbet vnlaced out of order. *a* **1661** HOLYDAY *Juvenal* (1673) 78 'Tis no small difference, with what gesture men Of art vnlace a hare and spoil a hen. **1687** J. SHIRLEY *Accomp. Ladies Rich Closet Rarities* 52 In unlacing a Coney, Turn the belly upwards, cutting the belly-pieces from the kidneys. **1771** MRS. HAYWOOD *New Present for Maid* 269 To unlace a Rabbit.

†**4.** To disentangle, unravel. *Obs.*[—1]

*c* **1374** CHAUCER *Boeth.* III. pr. xii. (1868) 105 Scornest þou me..þat hast so wouen me wiþ þi resouns, þe house of didalus so entrelaced, þat it is vnable to ben vnlaced.

†**5.** *fig.* **a.** To undo or destroy; to deprive *of* something. *Obs.*

*c* **1412** HOCCLEVE *De Reg. Princ.* 2456 Of his honour, vntrouthe a knyght vnlaceth. *Ibid.* 3652 Dignite had ben vnlaced And vngirt of honour. **1577** GRANGE *Golden Aphrod.*, etc. Q j b, Milesian maydes, your steppes I mean to trace, And as Lucrecia did, my lyfe for to vnlace. **1604** SHAKS. *Oth.* II. iii. 194 What's the matter That you vnlace your reputation thus.

†**b.** To disclose, reveal. *Obs.*

**1567** PAINTER *Pal. Pleas.* II. xiii. (1890) II. 301, I purpose, then, to vnlace the dissolute lyues of three Amorouse Dames. **1577** GRANGE *Golden Aphrod.*, etc. R iv b, Wherefore if my penne were able, well might I here vnlace my loyaltie. **1582** STANYHURST *Æneis* Ded. (Arb.) 7 Yt may bee..I shal bee occasioned..too vnlace more of theese mysteries.

†**c.** To relax or loosen; to set free. *Obs.*

**1610** G. FLETCHER *Christ's Tri.* II. xlii, An intire embrace That no satietie can ere unlace. **1639** FULLER *Holy War* II. iv. 48 These Hospitallers afterwards getting wealth, unlaced themselves from the strictnesse of their first Institution.

**6.** To strip of lace.

**1598** FLORIO, *Disfrangiare*, to vnfringe, to vnlase.

**Unla·ced,** *ppl. a.* [f. prec. or UN-[1] 8.]

**1. a.** Having a lace or laces undone or slackened. **b.** Not laced; with lace(s) unfastened.

**1447** BOKENHAM *Seyntys* (Roxb.) 277 Whan the gospel shulde be Red..evere ryht up stude she Wyth slevys unlaced. *a* **1529** SKELTON *E. Rummyng* 133 Some wenches come vnlased, Some huswyues come vnbrased. **1582** STANYHURST *Æneis* IV. (Arb.) 113 Her self..standing neere the halloed altars, Naked in her oane foote, with frock vnlaced aparralyd. **1601** HOLLAND *Pliny* II. 308 Women..with their haire hanging loose about their eares, vngirt, vnlaced, and vnbraced. **1827** POLLOK *Course T.* VIII. 91 Unscutcheoned all,..Unlaced, uncoroneted, unbestarred. **1871** *Figure Training* 79, I had never..been suffered to remain unlaced one instant longer than was absolutely necessary.

†**2.** Cut up, carved. *Obs.*[—1]

**1602** *2nd Pt. Return Parnass.* IV. i. 1526 Sometimes a messe of stewd broth will do well, and an vnlac'd Rabbet is best of all.

**Unlach,** obs. Sc. variant of UNLAW.

†**Unla·ckable,** *a. Obs.* [UN-[1] 7 b.] Indispensable. *c* **1449** PECOCK *Repr.* I. ix. 44 Thilk leernyng..is necessarie and vnlackeable to Cristen men. †**Unla·ckably,** *adv. Obs.* [UN-[1] 11.] Indispensably. **1449** PECOCK *Repr.* I. vii. 35 Ellis he were not vnlackeabli necessarie to Cristen men. **Unla·ckeyed,** *ppl. a.* (UN-[1] 8.) **1784** COWPER *Task* II. 652 To her who, frugal only that her thrift May feed excesses she can ill afford, Is hackney'd home unlackey'd. **Unla·cquered,** *ppl. a.* (UN-[1] 8.) [**1775** ASH, *Unlackered*, not lackered.] **1833** CARLYLE *Misc.* (1872) V. 124 The brow of brass, behold how it has got all unlacquered.

**Unla·de,** *v.* [UN-[2] 4. Cf. OE. *onhladan*, OHG. *intladen*, MHG., MLG., G. *entladen*, MDu. and Du. *ontladen*.] To unload.

**1.** *trans.* To take a load off (a horse, cart, etc.).

**1398** TREVISA *Barth. De P. R.* XVIII. xxviii. (Bodl. MS.), þei leyeþ..þe stikkes and wood bitwene his legges and þies and drawiþ hem home..and vnladeþ and dischargeþ hym þanne. *c* **1489** CAXTON *Sonnes of Aymon* iii. 103 Thenne they vnladed theyr somers & theyr cartes. **1494** *Cov. Leet Bk.* 557 To drive his Cart laden with Otes into þe Croschepyng & there to vnlade the seid Cart. **1622** FLETCHER *Span. Cur.* II. i, I have the mony ready, and I am weary...Pray ye Sir, unlade me. **1695** CONGREVE *Mourn. Muse Alexis* 6 Thither, let all th' industrious Bees repair, Unlade their Thighs, and leave their Hony there. **1760–72** H. BROOKE *Fool of Qual.* (1809) III. 64 Some arose, and unladed two asses of the creels..they carried.

*fig.* a **1592** T. WATSON *Tears of Fancie* xlii, Vnlade me of the burthen..enuious fates..Haue heapt vpon me.

**b.** To take the cargo out of (a ship). Also in fig. context.

c **1489** CAXTON *Sonnes of Aymon* 525 As they vnladed the ship. **1555** EDEN *Decades* (Arb.) 240 The port..is so..commodious to defraight or vnlade shyppes, as [etc.]. **1586** B. YOUNG *Guazzo's Civ. Conv.* IV. 194 b, If you thinke..your stomacke will not serue you to vnlade all the ship, let me helpe you. **1642** MILTON *Apol. Smect.* 36 He must cut out large docks and creeks into his text to unlade the foolish frigate of his unseasonable autorities. **1693** *Lond. Gaz.* No. 2838/2 They are now Unlading her, but the Goods are very much Damnified. **1781** GIBBON *Decl. & F.* xxiv. (1787) II. 443 Fourscore vessels were gradually unladen. **1864** TENNYSON *En. Ard.* 812 He..help'd At lading and unlading the tall barks. **1871** KINGSLEY *At Last* ii, Along the beach a market.., with canoes drawn up to be unladen.

*refl.* **1666** DRYDEN *Ann. Mirab.* ccc, The vent'rous Merchant..Shall here unlade him, and depart no more. **1860** GEO. ELIOT *Mill on Floss* I. xii, Where the black ships unlade themselves of their burthens.

**c.** To unburthen or relieve by the removal or discharge of something. Chiefly *fig.* and const. *of*.

**1581** J. BELL *Haddon's Answ. Osor.* 263 b, To unlade you of some cholericke humours. c **1600** CHALKHILL *Thealma & Cl.* (1683) 127 Cattel gan to low Homewards t'unlade their milky bags. **1688** *Pulpit-Sayings* 29 When a Man unlades himself of all his Sins. **1703** ROWE *Fair Penit.* I. i, Let me unlade my Breast. **1898** WATTS-DUNTON *Aylwin* VII. iii, Unlading the mind of the trash previously called knowledge.

**2.** To discharge (a cargo, etc.) from a ship.

**1427–8** *Rec. St. Mary at Hill* 68 For cariage of ij lode fro Cambregges key, ladyng & vnladyng, xiiij d. **1542–3** *Act* 34 & 35 *Hen. VIII*, c. 9 § 4 That no persone..doo caste or unlade out of any..ship..Balast rubbishe gravell or any other wracke. **1590** WEBBE *Trav.* (Arb.) 19 We vnladed our bourthen at Narre. **1612** in *10th Rep. Hist. MSS. Comm.* App. V. 467 Goodes to be discharged, unladen, or brought in. **1661** GODOLPHIN *View Admir. Jurisd.* Introd. b 3 b, A Lighter, or Skiff, or the Ships Boat into which part of the Cargo is unladen for the lightning of the Ship. **1722** DE FOE *Plague* (1754) 246 They would not suffer them..to unlade their Goods upon any Terms whatever. **1725** POPE *Odyss.* XVI. 375 They moor the vessel and unlade the stores. a **1864** HAWTHORNE *Amer. Note-bk.* (1868) I. 164 Huge trunks and bandboxes [were] unladed and laded. **1884** *Harper's Mag.* June 52/1 All cargoes must be unladed between sunrise and sunset.

**b.** To discharge or get rid of; to put off or lay down (a burden, etc.); to unpack or bring forth. Chiefly *fig.*

**1591** SPENSER *Daphn.* lxx, There will I..the huge burden of my cares vnlade. **1599** CHAPMAN *Humorous Days Mirth* F 4 b, Forth and vnlade the poyson of thy tongue. **1639** J. SHIRLEY *Maid's Rev.* II. i. D 3, Ere you let fall words of welcome, Let me unlade a treasure in your eare. **1812** CRABBE *Tales, Arabella* 283 When all inquiries had been duly made, Came the kind friend her burthen to unlade. **1821** LAMB *Elia* I. *Imperfect Sympathies*, He..unlades his stock of ideas in perfect order.

**3.** *absol.* To discharge a cargo or cargoes.

**1547** *Privy Council Acts* (1890) II. 466 If he unladed there, he might cary the vytayles a good wey after by the river. **1568** GRAFTON *Chron.* II. 567 The ships..were forced to vnlade at Douer. **1666** *Lond. Gaz.* No. 69/2 A large Swede..is likewise arrived with Deales, and is to unlade in this Harbor. **1774** E. JACOB *Faversham* 15 Where the great Vessels used to unlade. **1796** MORSE *Amer. Geog.* II. 24 Large ships may..lade and unlade close to the ware houses. **1863** SUSAN WARNER *Old Helmet* xxxv, At Tonga she was detained a week and more, unlading and taking in stores. **1879** FARRAR *St. Paul* II. 405 The wharfs where the barges..were accustomed to unlade.

**b.** To discharge a burden, contents, etc. Also *fig.*

**1629** MASSINGER *Picture* IV. ii, You may safer run vpon The mouth of a cannon, when it is vnlading. **1717** BULLOCK *Wom. a Riddle* I. i, What adventure is this you are so full of? come, unlade, unlade. **1862** GOULBURN *Pers. Relig.* III. viii. (1873) 226 While caravans were unlading or making up their complement of passengers.

†**4.** *trans.* To discharge (a fire-arm). In quot. *fig.*

**1649** G. DANIEL *Trinarch., Rich. II*, ccxliii, Thus overcharg'd & yet vnwilling to Vnlade Himselfe by the first Match that came.

Hence **Unla·ding** *ppl. a.*

**1607** CHAPMAN *Bussy d'Ambois* III. ii. 38 I'll..so thump his liver, That, like a huge unlading Argosy, He shall confess all.

**Unla·den,** *ppl. a.* [UN-[1] 8 b.] Unloaded.

? **1802** FORSTER *Arabian Nights* (1839) 393/1, I was returning from Balsora with my camels unladen, which I had conducted thither with goods to be embarked for India. **1820** SHELLEY *Witch Atl.* lxviii, The wizard-maiden..with an eye serene and heart unladen. **1849** EASTWICK *Dry Leaves* 70 Send no camels unladen, if you have wherewith to lade them.

**Unla·ding,** *vbl. sb.* [f. UNLADE *v.*] The action of unloading or discharging.

**1428–9** *Rec. St. Mary at Hill* 70 Also paid..for þe caryage & ladyng & vnladyng, ix d. **1627** J. TAYLOR (Water P.) *Navy of Land Ships* Wks. (1630) 82/1 The often returnes, lading and vnlading of this ship. **1691** *Lond. Gaz.* No. 2656/2 That no such..Vessel shall be above Ten days in Unlading. **1726** LEONI *Alberti's Archit.* I. 75 b, For the more easy unlading of the Shipping. **1818** *Sporting Mag.* II. 161 Hogarth has already given the picture of the unlading of a stage coach. **1849** EASTWICK *Dry Leaves* 210 Affording great facilities for the unlading or shipment of cargoes.

**b.** *attrib.*, as *unlading place, port, time*.

**1611** FLORIO, *Sbarco*,..[an] vnlading place for ships. **1681** *Cal. Treas. Bks.* 7 The books of the unlading port. **1755** MAGENS *Insurances* I. 48 The customary unlading Places in that Port. **1884** J. PARKER *Apost. Life* III. 61 We must have landing places, and unlading times,..in life.

**Unla·dyfied,** *ppl. a.* (UN-[2] 6 c.) **1612** N. FIELD *Wom. a Weathercock* V. ii, Know That I am married to this gentleman...What ease I find being unladified!

**Unla·dylike,** *a.* (UN-[1] 7 c.)

**1824** MISS MITFORD *Village* Ser. I. 229 A very discreditable and unladylike partiality, of which I am quite ashamed. **1856** WHYTE-MELVILLE *Kate Coventry* i. 4 She said it was improper and unladylike, and even unfeminine.

**Unlage,** obs. variant of UNLAW.

**Unlai·d,** *ppl. a.* and *sb.* [UN-[1] 8 b. Cf. ON. *úlagðr*; also Du. *ongelegd*, G. *ungelegt* (of eggs).]

**1.** Not laid, placed, or set.

**1468–9** *Paston Lett.* Suppl. (1901) 124 The lenger that it [*sc.* the roof-tile] lythe unleyd the wers it wyll be. **1570** LEVINS *Manip.* 197 Vnlayd, *non positus*. **1597** HOOKER *Eccl. Pol.* V. lvi. § 5 The first foundation of the world being as yet vnlayd. **1656** OSBORNE *Adv. Son* Lett.. Wks. 1722 I. B 5, The severest Curse remaining in the custody of Fortune, yet unlaid upon me. **1872** *Daily News* 12 Aug., The spot where the final stone of the great structure yet hung unlaid.

**b.** ? Laid out (as a corpse); laid in the grave.

c **1635** B. JONSON *Underwoods, Petition Chas. I*, Parts of me they judg'd decay'd; But we last out still unlay'd.

**c.** Of a hedge: (see LAY *v.*[1] 6 b).

**1868** *Rep. U.S. Commissioner Agric.* (1869) 255 If..the shoots are cut toward the bottom growth of the wood as downward in an unlaid one, or against the leaning direction of the layers in a laid hedge.

**2.** Of spirits: Not laid by exorcism.

**1611** SHAKS. *Cymb.* IV. ii. 278 *Guid.* Ghost vnlaid forbeare thee. *Arui.* Nothing ill come neere thee. **1634** MILTON *Comus* 434 No evil thing that walks by night,..Blew meager Hag, or stubborn unlaid ghost,..Hath hurtfull power o're true virginity. **1780** BURKE *Œcon. Reform* Wks. III. 297 Ghosts of unlaid accountants, haunt the houses. **1806** MOORE *Epist.* VIII. i, Pagan spirits, by the Pope unlaid. **1831** WORDSW. '*The forest huge*' 11 The feudal Warrior-chief, a Ghost unlaid, Hath still his castle. **1888** (*title*), Unlaid Ghost: a Study in Metempsychosis.

**3.** Not laid *open, out*, etc.

**1608** SHAKS. *Per.* I. ii. 89 How many worthy princes' bloods were shed, To keep his bed of blackness unlaid ope. **1674** N. FAIRFAX *Bulk & Selv.* 62 Though they be unlaid out in themselves, they may be laid out by body laid in.

**4.** Not covered or plated *with* something.

**1648** HEXHAM II, *Ongebleckt*, Vnlaid with plates of Lettine.

**5.** In technical uses, e.g. of a rope (see LAY *v.* 37), of paper (see LAID *ppl. a.*), etc.

In recent dicts.

**6.** *sb.* A blanket made from untarred wool. *Sc.*

a **1869** J. YOUNGER *Autobiog.* (1881) iv. 38 He rolled up his pipes, bag and all, in the blankets above him..—which bag imparted that election-dinner stain to her best white unlaids.

**Unla·me,** *a.* [UN-[1] 7.] † Wholly free. a **1300** *Cursor M.* 21045 [John] was o lust vn-lame. **Unla·med,** *ppl. a.* (UN-[1] 8. Cf. MLG. *ungelemt*.) c **1470** *Gol. & Gaw.* 442 Sauand my senyeoury fra subiectioun, And my lordscip vn-lamyt, withoutin legiance. **1839** CARLYLE *Chartism* iii. (1840) 23 His unlamed right-hand,..is not this defined to be 'the sceptre of our Planet'?

**Unlame·nted,** *ppl. a.* (UN-[1] 8.)

**1595** DANIEL *Civ. Wars* I. xx, A tyrant loth'd,..Poysoned he dies, disgrac'd, and vnlamented. **1626** MASSINGER *Rom. Actor* V. ii, Such as governed only by their will..unlamented fall. **1647** CLARENDON *Hist. Reb.* I. § 115 He died unlamented by any, bitterly mentioned by most. **1717** POPE *Elegy Unfort. Lady* 43 Thus unlamented pass the proud away. **1818** SHELLEY *Rosal. & Helen* 231, I watched..My husband's unlamented tomb. **1896** *Pop. Sci. Jrnl.* L. 277 The old systems that lie unlamented in their graves.

**Unlampoo·ned,** *ppl. a.* (UN-[1] 8.) [**1775** ASH.] **1828** SOUTHEY *To A. Cunningham* 36 Extend those laws Till every chimney its own smoke consume, And give thenceforth thy dinners unlampoon'd. **Unla·nced,** *ppl. a.* (UN-[1] 8.) **1593** G. HARVEY *Pierce's Super.* 26 Where..the filthiest corruption of abhominable villany [may] passe vnlaunced. **1643** FULLER *Serm.* 27 Mar. 7 Sometimes Chirurgions leave their ulcers unlaunch't [*sic*].

†**Unland,** *sb. Sc. Obs.* [UN-[1] 12. Cf. OE. *unland*, ON. *úland*, WFris. *onlân*, *unlân*, MDu. *onlant* (Du. *onland*), MLG. *unlant*, LG. and G. *unland*.] Unarable land.

**1573–4** *Reg. Mag. Sig. Scot.* 577/2 Terras arabiles *lie corneland*, terras non arabiles *lie unland*. **1611** *Ibid.* 230/2 Cum..parca, pratis, wardis (*lie unland* seu *tedderingis*) et silvis apud idem.

**Unla·nd,** *v.* [UN-[2] 4.] *trans.* To deprive of land.

a **1661** FULLER *Worthies, Monmouth.* IV. (1662) 51 But one Bishop..more unlanded Llandaff in one, than all his Predecessors endowed it in four hundred years.

**Unla·nded,** *a.* [UN-[1] 9.] Not possessed of land.

**1488** *Sc. Acts, Jas. IV* (1814) II. 207/1 The gudis movabill belanging to the pure vnlandit folkis. **1530** *Extr. Aberd. Reg.* (1844) I. 138 Ilk gentilman landit ij^c lib., ilk gentilman vnlandit ij^c markis. **1581** MULCASTER *Positions* xxxix. 199 Either rich or poore: landed or vnlanded. **1633** FORD *Love's Sacr.* IV. i, The sallow-colour'd brat Of some unlanded bankrupt. **1668** SEDLEY *Mulberry Gard.* III. ii, Give your estate where you please, so you will but settle your affection upon me,..and the like artillery of unlanded lovers. **1884** *Pall Mall G.* 2 April 2/1 The rights of the unlanded millions.

**Unla·ndmarked,** *a.* (UN-[1] 9.) **1870** LOWELL *Among my Bks.* Ser. I. 124 The unlandmarked deep of speculation.

**Unla·nguaged,** *a.* [UN-[1] 9.]

**1.** Not gifted with speech.

**1654** DAVENANT in Earl Monm. *Bentivoglio's Warrs Flanders* b 1 b, The ceaseless nature of your Kindness then, Still ready to inform un-languag'd Men, Deserves less Praise [etc.]. **1850** H. BUSHNELL *God in Christ* i. 11 There is no difficulty in perceiving how our two unlanguaged men will proceed.

**2.** Not expressed in articulate speech.

**1846–8** LOWELL *Biglow P.* Ser. I. ii. Introd. Let., The unlanguaged prattlings of infants. **1860** FABER *Bethlehem* 100 To what numberless unlanguaged and unsung Magnificats did not all this give rise.

**Unla·nterned,** *ppl. a.* (UN-[1] 8.) **1826** LAMB *Elia* II. *Pop. Fallacies* xv, It has a sombre cast,..derived from the tradition of those unlantern'd nights.

**Unla·p,** *v.* Now *rare*. [UN-[2] 4.]

**1.** *trans.* To uncover by withdrawing a cloth or the like. Also *refl.* and *fig.*

**13..** *E. E. Allit. P.* A. 214 As schorne golde schyr her fax þenne schon. On schylderez þat leghe vnlapped ly3te. c **1440** *York Myst.* xxx. 256 Vnlappe yow belyve wher ye lye. **1656** BAXTER *Reformed Pastor* 369 If a cripple do but unlap his sores. **1664** MRS. HUTCHINSON *Mem. Col. Hutchinson* (1806) 441 Satisfied with this, they did not unlap the body. **1809** MAR. EDGEWORTH *Manœuvring* xv, The influence of her..prettiness, joined to the power of my mother's irresistible address, have almost lapped me in elysium...But ..I unlapped myself. **1886–** in dial. glossaries, etc. (Yks., Lancs., Chesh.).

**2.** To unfold; to spread open. Also *intr.*

a **1400–50** *Alexander* 1932 Þire princes, sone as þe pistill was put þam in hand,..Vn-lappis li3tly þe lefe & þe line redes. **1501** DOUGLAS *Pal. Hon.* Prol. 37 The dasy and the maryguld vnlappit, Quhilks all the nicht lay with their leuis happit. **1586** W. TRAVERS *Supplic. Privy Council* (1612) 23 Tapestrie which,..being vnlapt and laid open, sheweth plainely to the eye all the worke that is in it.

**3.** To detach in a strip or flap.

**1834–6** *Encycl. Metrop.* (1845) VIII. 103/2 A curve traced by the extremity of the thread *FC*, unlapped from the circumference. *Ibid.*, Let the acting face of the tooth *b* be formed by unlapping a thread from its circumference.

Hence **Unla·pping** *vbl. sb.*

**1839** URE *Dict. Arts*, etc. 233 In the course of the lapping and unlapping of such a length of webs.

**Unla·psed,** *ppl. a.* (UN-[1] 8.) **1668** H. MORE *Div. Dial.* IV. vii. 26 His Dominion..over Angels, whether lapsed or unlapsed. **1740** CHEYNE *Regimen* 297 Unlapsed, tried and purified angelical Hierarchies. **Unla·rded,** *ppl. a.* (UN-[1] 8.) **1748** CHESTERF. *Lett.* 22 Feb., Speak the language.. purely, and unlarded with any other. **Unla·rge,** *a.* [UN-[1] 7.] † Not generous in giving. **1483** *Cath. Angl.* 208/2 Vn Large, *illeberalis*. **Unlasci·vious,** *a.* (UN-[1] 7.) **1593** NASHE *Strange Newes* E 3 There is no other unlascivious use or end of poetry but to..magnifie vertue.

**Unla·sh,** *v.* [UN-[2] 4 b.]

**1.** *trans.* To detach or release by undoing a lashing.

**1748** SMOLLETT *R. Random* xxvi, Our hammocks..were immediately unlashed. **1850** R. G. CUMMING *Hunter's Life S. Afr.* (1902) 102/2 Returning to the waggons, I commenced to unlash from the side of one of these a shovel. **1862** *Catal. Internat. Exhib.* II. No. 2659, Improved systems of unlashing..ships' boats. **1879** FARRAR *St. Paul* IX. xliii. II. 379 They began to unlash the boat and lower her into the sea.

**2.** To undo or untie (a lashing).

**1853** SIR H. DOUGLAS *Milit. Bridges* (ed. 3) 67 Nos. 1 and 3 unlash the [Pontoon] Lashings. **1870** *Milit. Engineering* 347 At the word *Unlash*, each man stoops down, and casts off the lashing in front of him.

**Unla·shed,** *ppl. a.* [UN-[1] 8.] Not scourged. **1761** CHURCHILL *Rosciad* 500 Actors, unlash'd themselves, may lash mankind. †**Unla·st,** *v. Obs.*—[1] [UN-[1] 14.] *intr.* To fail to last. (A misunderstanding of L. *indurare*.) a **1300** *E. E. Psalter* lxxxix. 6 It wites als gresse areli at dai;..At euen doun es it broght, Un-lastes, and welkes, and gas to noght.

**Unla·sting,** *ppl. a.* (UN-[1] 10.)

**1585** ABP. SANDYS *Serm.* ix. 146 Mans life is as vnlasting as a flower. **1790** A. WILSON *Epist. to A. Clarke* Poet. Wks. (1846) 48 Struggling hard for base unlasting pelf.

**Unla·tch,** *v.* [UN-[2] 3.]

**1.** *trans.* To undo the latch or catch of (a door, etc.); to unfasten in this way.

**1642** H. MORE *Song of Soul* I. i. 60 Then stiller whispering winds dark visions unlatch. **1697** DRYDEN *Æneis* VI. 704 Mean time my worthy wife..The door unlatch'd. **1822** BYRON *Werner* IV. i. 434 Who..Unlatch'd the door of death for thee. **1873** MISS BROUGHTON *Nancy* I. 54 Unlatching the gate in the fence. **1890** *Anthony's Photogr. Bull.* III. 200 The bellows is closed up, it is now allowed to fall open, when unlatched, by a catch on the side and top.

**b.** *intr.* To become, or admit of being, thus unfastened.

**1871** B. TAYLOR *Faust* (1875) I. i. ii. 12 The gate of gold no more unlatches. **1875** BLACKMORE *A. Lorraine* xviii, The gate at this end unlatches.

**2.** *trans.* To unlace (shoes). Cf. LATCHET 1 c.

**1880** L. WALLACE *Ben-Hur* 253 Another unlatched Ben-Hur's Roman shoes.

**Unla·tched,** *ppl. a.* [UN-[1] 8.] Not fastened by a latch. **1888** *Daily News* 5 Dec. 7/5 An unlatched window. **1901** *Munsey's Mag.* XXV. 435/1 [He] had left the flat door unlatched. † **Unla·ted,** *ppl. a. Sc. Obs.* [UN-[1] 8.] Undisciplined. a **1449** in Bower *Fordun's Scotichron.* (1759) II. 376 The unlatit woman the licht man will lait. **Unla·thed,** *ppl. a.* (UN-[1] 8.) **1854** H. MILLER *Sch. & Schm.* (1858) 44 A mud floor below, and an unlathed roof above. †**Un-La·tin,** *a. Obs.*—[1] [UN-[1] 7.] = next. **1675** T. TULLY *Let. to Baxter* 2 Only I beg your leave to English it for the sake of your un-latine Readers. †**Unla·tined,** *a. Obs.* [UN-[1] 9.] Not acquainted with Latin. **1550** HARINGTON tr. *Cicero's Bk. Friendship* (1562) Pref. A iij b, How so euer it [*sc.* this translation] shalbe lyked of the learned, I hope it shalbe allowed of the vnlatined. **1570** DEE *Math. Pref.* A iij b, Being vnlatined people, and not Vniuersitie Scholers. **Unla·tinize,** *v.* (UN-[2] 6 c.) **1836** *Penny Cycl.* V. 325 Published..by Conrad Aslacus (we cannot unlatinize Gassendi's name). **1847** DE MORGAN *Arith. Bks.* p. viii, Why the unlatinizing process should..be practised by the learned only. **Unla·tticed,** *ppl. a.* (UN-[1] 8.) **1820** SCOTT *Abbot* ix, An unlatticed aperture gave him the view of the demolished garden.

**Unlauch**, obs. Sc. form of Unlaw.

**Unlau·dable,** *a.* (Un-1 7 b. Cf. Illaudable.) 1550 Thomas *Ital. Dict., Dispregeuole,* shamefull or vnlaudable. 1673 *Lady's Call.* ii. i. § 12 Some very unlaudable qualities of a woman. 1826 *Q. Rev.* XXXIV. 451 Playing small games,..an innocent and not unlaudable pastime.

Hence **Unlau·dableness.**

1744 [Garrick] *Essay on Acting* 26 A farther Confirmation of the Unlaudableness of such Proceedings.

**Unlau·gh,** *v.* (Un-1 3.) 1532 More *Confut. Tindale* Wks. 684/1 Tindall must of reason gyue vs leaue to laugh at hys proude inuented folye. And I shall find hym fower suerties..that at what tyme hereafter he proue himselfe a true prophete, I shall vppon reasonable warning onlaughe agayn it al. 1637 J. Williams *Holy Table* 153 You must unlaugh again this foolish Laughter. †**Unlau·ght,** *ppl. a. Obs.*—1 [Un-1 8 b + *laght*, obs. pa. pple. of Latch *v.*1] Unseized, untaken. c 1400 *Destr. Troy* 3237 The Troiens.. Lefte noght vnlaght þat lykyng was in.

†**Unlau·ghter-mild,** *a. Obs.*—1 [Un-1 7: cf. ON. *hlátr-mildr*, Da. *lattermild*, prone to laugh.] Not given to laughter or mirth.

a 1300 *Cursor M.* 3283 Had he noght rested bot a thrau, O maidens sagh he cum on raw; Þe formast was vnlaghter milde, Hir semed na wight to be wilde.

**Unlau·nched,** *ppl. a.* (Un-1 8.) [1775 Ash.] 1810 Byron *Occas. P., Nurse's Dole* 3 The good ship Argo..still unlaunch'd from Grecian docks. 1863 P. Barry *Dockyard Econ.* 128 To allow the unlaunched ship to remain and rot. **Unlau·relled,** *ppl. a.* (Un-1 8.) 1812 Byron *Ch. Har.* i. xci, Thus unlaurel'd to descend in vain, By all forgotten. 1856 Merivale *Rom. Emp.* xliii. V. 63 The Marcomanni.. had kept Tiberius himself at bay, and sent him back unlaurelled across the Danube. **Unla·ving,** *ppl. a.* (Un-1 10.) 1834 Lytton *Pompeii* i. vii, Those who took only the cold bath..withdrew into that graceful..building..to shame the unlaving posterity of the south. **Unla·vish,** *a.* (Un-1 7.) 1728 Thomson *Spring* 733 Unlavish Wisdom never works in vain. **Unla·vished,** *ppl. a.* (Un-1 8.) 1743 Shenstone *Elegies* xix. 12 He blam'd..My time, unlavish'd in pursuit of pow'r.

**U·nlaw,** *sb.* [OE. *unlagu* (Un-1 12), = ON. *úlög* (pl.), Icel. *ólög*, Norw. *ulag*, Sw. *olag*, MDa. *ulog* (Da. *ulov*).]

1. Illegal action; illegality.

After the early 14th cent. only in occasional Sc. use, but revived by recent writers.

1008 *Laws Ethelred* (Liebermann) I. 236 Þæt man rihta laȝe up-arære & ælce unlaȝa ȝeorne afylle. a 1200 in Kemble *Cod. Dipl.* IV. 195 Ich nelle suððen ðat man hym eny unlawe beode. 1297 R. Glouc. (Rolls) 9705 Ȝuf..eni man made is apel, ȝuf me dude him vnlawe. a 1300 *Cursor M.* 19196 Þe lauerd þat bidd þe man wit-stand, Vnlau it es to tell in land. 1303 R. Brunne *Handl. Synne* 8795 Ȝyf þou dedyst euer þat vnlawe, A man oute of holy cherche to drawe. 1318 *Sc. Acts Parlt.* (1844) I. 471 Torth & noun raysoun quod dicitur wrang et unlaw. 14.. *Ibid.* 347/2 Bot þai hald na court of lyfe and lym bot of jniur and vnreson þat is to say wrang and vnlaw. 1609 Skene *Reg. Maj., Stat. Robt. I,* 23 Sa lang as he or his preloquutour defends tort and non reason, that is, wrang and vnlach (that is to haue done na iniurie, nor vnreason agains the Law).

1871 Freeman *Norm. Conq.* xxi. IV. 620 This state of things was what our fathers called *unlaw.* 1876 *Ibid.* xxii. V. 52. 1881 Pusey (*title*), Unlaw in Judgements of the Judicial Committee of Privy Council. 1883 Bp. E. H. Browne *Serm. Reading Congress* 15 The conflict between law and unlaw, between Christianity and irreligion.

†b. An evil custom or habit. *Obs.*—1

a 1225 *Juliana* 72 Bireowseð ower sunnen,..leaueð ower unlahen.

†2. *Sc.* A fine or amercement; a penalty. *Obs.*

1424 *Sc. Acts, Jas. I* (1814) II. 5/1 Quha sa euer be conuickit.., he sall pay xl. s. for þe vnlaw. 1459 in *Laing Charters* (1899) 37 Syndry unlawis amerciamentis and all uther fautis. 1496 *Acta Dom. Conc.* II. 2 Ane unlaw of xl s. 1541 *Rec. Elgin* (1903) I. 65 The baxstaris for thair falt salbe punist..with viii s. of vnlaw. 1613 in *Northern N. & Q.* I. 74 Under the payne of ane vnlaw of ane pound Fleymis. 1678 Sir G. Mackenzie *Crim. Laws Scot.* i. xix. § 15 The Unlaw to be ten Pound. 1732 J. Louthian *Form of Process* 273 Fines, Amerciaments, or Unlaws inflicted upon Offenders,..are sometimes ordained wholly to be paid to the King. 1767 in Craig & Laing *Hawick Tradition* (1898) 243 [He] is not worth the King's unlaw, being on the Parish Roll or Poors List.

**Unlaw,** *v.* [f. prec., or Un-2 3, 7.]

†1. *trans.* (also *absol.*) To fine, amerce. *Sc. Obs.*

14.. in *Sc. Acts Parlt.* (1844) I. 710/2 Item..to his [*sc.* the justice's] clerk for jlk man vnlawit or sald, ij s. 1491 [see the vbl. sb.]. 1508 *Reg. Privy Seal Scotl.* I. 244/2 That nane of ȝow presume to call, geif sentence, unlaw,..the said Johnne. 1564 *Reg. Privy Council Scot.* I. 307 [He] wes unlawit in the soum..of ane thowsand markis. 1613 in R. M. Fergusson *A. Hume* (1899) 199 The counsall ..have..unlawit the said Adam..for his said offence. 1678 Sir G. Mackenzie *Crim. Laws Scot.* ii. xiii. § 3 A Barron may unlaw for Absence, for ten Pounds. 1710 in J. J. Vernon *Par. & Kirk Hawick* (1900) 203 [They] were each of them.. fyned and onlawed in egregious ryotts. 1732 J. Louthian *Form of Process* 295 The several Sheriff Deputes,..if any be absent,..are unlawed in 100 Merks each.

†b. *intr.* To pay a fine. *Obs.*—1

1692 in W. Hector *Judic. Rec. Renfrew* (1876) 54 Ilk ane o' them ought to unlaw to the Pror.-Fiscal.

2. *trans.* To annul (a law). Also *refl. rare.*

1644 Milton *Areop.* (Arb.) 76 That also..no law can possibly permit, that intends not to unlaw it self. 1654 Cromwell *Sp.* 12 Sept. (Carlyle), Of what assurance is a Law to prevent so great an evil, if it lie in the same Legislature to unlaw it again?

Hence **Unlaw·ing** *vbl. sb.*

1491 *Acta Dom. Audit.* (1839) 164/1 Þe vnlawing of þe said alexr. blare. 1511 *Reg. Privy Seal Scotl.* I. 351/2 That thai desist..fra all..unlawing, forfaltin and proceding agains the said David. 1651 N. Bacon *Disc. Govt. Eng.* ii. xxvii. 213 The King hath a power of Lawing, and Unlawing in Christs kingdome.

**Unlaw·ed,** *ppl. a.* [Un-1 8.]

1. (See Law *v.* 3, Expeditate *v.*)

1598 Manwood *Laws Forest* xvi. 92 The owners..are to be amerced 3s. for the keeping of such Dogges vnlawed. 1659 *Termes de la Ley* 163 b/2 A privilege to keep Doggs within the Forrest unlawed without punishment. 1685 Brady *Hist. Eng.* App. 142 (tr. *Charter of Forests*), He whose Dog at such time shall be found unlawed. 1913 *Contemp. Rev.* Oct. 560 It was considered a great honour to be allowed to keep unlawed dogs for pleasure of the chase.

2. Exempt from law.

1880 *Mem. J. Legge* 291 Miracle is not an unlawed interference.

**Unlaw·ful,** *a.* and *adv.* [Un-1 7, 11 b.]

1. Contrary to law; prohibited by law; illegal.

a 1300 *Cursor M.* 29516 Þat cursing tald vn-laghful es Þat ordir wantes and right-settnes O lagh. 1398 Trevisa *Barth. De P. R.* ix. xxvi. (Bodl. MS.), It was iholde vnlawefulle to goo more wey one þe seturdaie. c 1430 *Syr Gener.* (Roxb.) 3024 Here ye thes vnlawful reasouns Mi lord the Soudon seith vs among. 1475 *Cov. Leet Bk.* 418 Vnlaufull & hurtfull ordenaunces made by the seid dyers. *Ibid.*, Vnlaufull othes and wrytynges. 1515 in W. H. Turner *Select. Rec. Oxford* (1880) 13 William Flemynge usith..unlawfull mesures, that is to seye, an unlawfull yerde. 1581 [see next]. a 1613 Overbury *A Wife*, etc. (1614) B 4 b, Some lawfull things to be auoyded are, When they occasion of vnlawfull be. 1652 Needham tr. *Selden's Mare Cl.* 449 Anie other prohibited places and unlawful Ports whatsoever, in the Kingdoms of Denmark, Sweden, and Norway. 1667-8 Marvell *Corr.* Wks. (Grosart) II. 239 The unlawfull meetings of Papists and Non-conformists. 1805 Southey *Madoc in W.* xv. 131 Becket did excommunicate thy sire For his unlawful marriage. 1891 Farrar *Darkn. & Dawn* liv, A fresh edict..which declared Christianity to be an unlawful religion.

b. *Unlawful assembly*: (see quots. 1581, 1841).

1485 *Rolls of Parlt.* VI. 287/2 Maintenance, Imbracerie, Riotts, or unlawfull Assemblie. 1549 *Act Edw. IV*, c. 5 (*heading*), An Acte for the punyshment of Unlawfull Assemblyes. 1581 Lambarde *Eiren.* i. xix. 175 An Vnlawful Assembly is, ye company of three persons (or more) gathered togither to doe..an vnlawfull acte. 1651 Hobbes *Leviath.* ii. xxii. 123 It is not a set number that makes the Assembly Unlawfull, but such a number [etc.]. 1664 *Act 16 Chas. II*, c. iv. 9 Every person who shall..suffer any such Conventicle, unlawfull Assembly or Meeteing aforesaid to be held in his or her House. 1714 *Act Geo. I*, c. 5. 5 Any such unlawful, riotous, and tumultuous Assembly. 1841 *Penny Cycl.* XX. 17/1 It is an unlawful assembly when great numbers of people meet together with such circumstances of behaviour as to raise the fears of their fellow-subjects, and to endanger the public peace.

c. Of offspring: Illegitimate.

1606 Shaks. *Ant. & Cl.* iii. vi. 7 All the vnlawfull issue, that their Lust Since then hath made betweene them. 1833 Disraeli *Cont. Flem.* i. i, The unlawful children of ignorance and expediency.

2. Not permissible; contrary to moral standards or spiritual principles.

?c 1475 *Knight Curtesy* 120 (Ritson), The knight..Which with your lady was talkinge Of love unlawfull pryvely. 1526 *Pilgr. Perf.* (W. de W. 1531) 45 They profyte moche in ye refreynynge..of vnlawfull pleasures. 1590 Shaks. *Com. Err.* v. i. 51 Hath not else his eye Stray'd his affection in vnlawfull loue? 1601 — *All's Well* iii. v. 73 May be the amorous Count solicites her In the vnlawfull purpose. 1641 J. Jackson *True Evang. T.* iii. 206 That Anabaptisticall..tenet..that all warres were utterly unlawfull under the Gospel. 1751 Johnson *Rambler* No. 178 ¶ 4 The allurements of unlawful pleasure. 1827 Lytton *Falkland* 81 How fearful, how selfish, how degrading, is unlawful love! 1849 Macaulay *Hist. Eng.* vii. II. 244 He cannot be accused of having deviated from the path of right in search.. of unlawful pleasure.

3. Of persons: Not obeying the law; acting or ruling illegally.

1429 *Rolls of Parlt.* IV. 344/1 Unlaweful hunters of Forestes, Parkes or Warennes. ?1536 Anne Boleyn in *Harl. Misc.* (1809) III. 62 Mine offence being so lawfully proved, your Grace is at liberty..to execute worthy punishment on me as an unlawful wife. 1581 *Satir. Poems Reform.* xliv. 319 Moyses forbad ȝou to giue the nichbouris vyf To the vnlauchful husbandis cumpanie. 1603 Shaks. *Meas. for M.* iv. ii. 16, I haue beene an vnlawfull bawd. 1643 Prynne *Sov. Power Parl.* i. (ed. 2) 49 These Lawes..are the Acts of the..Courts themselves, which are lawfull; not of the usurping King, who is unlawfull. 1859 Dickens *T. Two Cities* ii. i, The unlawful opener of a letter was put to death.

4. Contrary to rule; irregular.

1729 T. Cooke *Tales*, etc. 208 The same Word in the Greek and Latin likewise has unlawful Degrees of Comparison. 1836 J. R. Major *Guide Grk. Trag.* 117 In Iambic verse it is unlawful to divide the anapæst between two words.

†5. As *adv.* = next. *Obs.*

1477 in *Surtees Misc.* (1890) 27 William Bacon holdes ij dogges unlawefull.

**Unlaw·fully,** *adv.* [Un-1 11.]

1. In an unlawful manner; illegally.

a 1310 in Wright *Lyric P.* xvi. 53 That he wolde..Me lede to my lyves ende, unlahfulliche in lyhte. 1393 Langl. *P. Pl.* C. iv. 290 As þe sauter sheweþ by suche as ȝeuen mede, þat vnlawfulliche lyuen, hauen large honden. 1414 *Rolls of Parlt.* IV. 57/1 The processe of myn outelawery was unlawfully made. 1456 Sir G. Haye *Law Arms* (S.T.S.) 134 Injure or violence unlauchfully usurpit. 1549 Cheke *Hurt Sedit.* (1569) D iij b, If their goodes..shall unlawfully and vnorderly..be spoyled. 1653 *Urquhart's Logopandecteision* H iij b, Unlawfully-acquired goods. 1685 Baxter *Paraphr. N. T.*, Mark i. 44 The unlawfully called and bad priests. 1710 *Act 9 Anne* c. 16 If any Person..shall unlawfully attempt to kill, or shall unlawfully assault..one of the most Honourable Privy Council. 1824 Mackintosh *Sp. Ho. Comm.* 1 June, Wks. 1846 III. 401 Whether a British subject has been lawfully or unlawfully condemned to death. 1844 Kinglake *Eothen* xxv, The Mahometan authorities..were conscious of having acted unlawfully.

2. Illegitimately.

1552 Elyot, *Illegitimi*, vnlaufully begotten, bastardes. 1596 Dalrymple tr. *Leslie's Hist. Scot.* (S.T.S.) I. 132 Athir Bastardis, or vnlawfollie gottin and borne. 1603 Shaks. *Meas. for M.* iii. i. 196 Rather..then my sonne should be vnlawfullie borne. 1711 Addison *Spect.* No. 203 What Part I, being unlawfully born, may claim of the Man's Affection who begot me. 1755 Johnson, *Illegitimate*, unlawfully begotten; not begotten in wedlock.

**Unlaw·fulness.** [Un-1 12.]

†1. Unlawful (or disloyal) conduct. *Obs.*

c 1500 *Melusine* i. 14 Ye ne oughte to retche ne care more of the vnlawfulness [F. *desleaulté*] & falshed of oure fader. 1531 Tindale *Exp. 1 John* (1537) 53 That the Englyshe calleth here vnryghteousnesse the Greke called Anomia, vnlawfulnesse or breakynge ye lawe. 1613 Purchas *Pilgrimage* (1614) 28 The Formall part of sinne, being nothing else but a deformitie..and vnlawfulnesse in our naturall condition.

2. The quality of being unlawful; illegality.

1593 *Sidney's Arcadia* iii. (1922) II. 48 Now that love.. had awaked her spirits, and perchance the very unlawfulnes of it had a litle blowne the coale. 1631 Gouge *God's Arrows* i. § 18. 25 That shewes the frailty of the person, not the unlawfulnesse of the action. 1673 S. Dugard (*title*), Marriages of Cousin Germans, Vindicated from the Censures of Unlawfullnesse and Inexpediency. 1720 Wodrow *Corr.* (1843) II. 522 The treatise I sent you of the Unlawfulness of Limited Episcopacy is answered. a 1779 Warburton *Alliance* ii. Wks. 1788 IV. 190 The unlawfulness of tithes,.. the unlawfulness of oaths. 1824 Mackintosh *Sp. Ho. Comm.* 1 June, Wks. 1846 III. 415 The unlawfulness and nullity of the proceedings. 1874 Motley *Barneveld* II. xviii. 86 Doctors ever wanting to prove the unlawfulnesse of law which interferes with the purposes of a despot.

b. Illegitimacy. (Todd, 1818.)

**Unlaw·learned,** *a.* (Un-1 9.) 1810 Bentham *Offic. Apt. Maximized, Def. Econ.* (1830) 23 To a plain and unlaw-learned understanding, they cannot both be good. **Unlaw·like,** *a.* (Un-1 7 c.) 1649 Milton *Eikon.* vi. 53 A remedy so slender and unlawlike.

**Unlawly,** *adv.*: see Un-1 3.

†**Unlaw·ty.** *Sc. Obs.* [Un-1 12.] Disloyalty, unfaithfulness. 1456 Sir G. Haye *Law Arms* (S.T.S.) 172 Of this wrechit disobeysaunce cummys untreuth and unlautee. a 1568 in *Bannatyne MS.* (Hunterian Cl.) 766/32 Go follow thame, quha list vnlawty leir. **Unlaw·yered,** *a.* (Un-1 9.) 1602 Middleton *Phœnix* iv. i, One quiet, suffering, and unlawyer'd man. **Unlaw·yer-like,** *a.* (Un-1 7 c.) 1874 Lisle Carr *J. Gwynne* I. iii. 84 Nor were these talents much marred by those unlawyer-like attributes. †**Unlay,** *sb. Sc. Obs.* [Un-1 12 + Lay *sb.*] = Unlaw *sb.* 2. 1503 *Sc. Acts, Jas. IV* (1814) II. 242/2 At þat be ane punt of dittay in tyme to cum, and at þe vnlay þerof be x li. *Ibid.*, Item, as anent þe vnlay of þe grene wod.

**Unlay·,** *v.* [Un-2 3.] *trans.* To untwist (a rope) into separate strands.

1726 Shelvocke *Voy. round World* 436 Till we could unlay our best cable to make more. 1748 *Anson's Voy.* ii. ii. 135 We were..obliged to unlay a cable to work into running rigging. 1831 Jane Porter *Sir E. Seaward's Narr.* I. 123, I also took thence a piece of rope, which I unlaid. c 1860 H. Stuart *Seaman's Catech.* 28 Unlay the other two strands.

**Unlayho·ldable,** *a.* (Un-1 7 b.) 1860 W. W. Reade *Liberty Hall* I. xv. 304 The Proctor caught Maidlow..in one of those trivial unlayholdable offences. **Unlea·ched,** *ppl. a.* (Un-1 8.) 1847 Webster s.v., Unleached ashes. 1884 L. F. Allen *New Amer. Farm Bk.* 81 Eight bushels of unleached wood ashes. 1898 *Jrnl. Sch. Geog.* (U.S.) Oct. 288 Unleacht samples of many rocks.

**Unlead,** *dial.*: see Unlede *a.*

**Unlea·d,** *v.* [Un-2 4 + Lead *sb.*] *trans.* To divest or strip of lead.

1591 Percivall *Sp. Dict., Desplomado*, liuely, vnleaded. 1611 Florio, *Spiombare*, to vnleade. a 1661 Fuller *Worthies, Norwich* ii. (1662) 275 A very fair structure, but lately unleaded, and new covered with tyle. 1801 Carter *Cathedral Ch. Durham* 5 The Galilee was unleaded, and its demolition was determined on.

**Unlea·ded,** *ppl. a.* [Un-1 8.]

1. Not weighted, covered, or furnished with lead.

1611 in *Essex Rev.* XV. 47 The church is unleaded and unshingled. 1648 Hexham ii, *Ongeloot*, Vnleaded, or Vnplumbt. 1909 *Westm. Gaz.* 28 Aug. 2/2 The motion of the death-curtain, hanging free and unleaded from its headrope, would be inconceivably graceful.

2. *Printing.* Not spaced with leads; 'solid'.

1902 *Westm. Gaz.* 23 May 7/1 Tucked away in an unleaded telegram..is an item which may possess some significance.

**Unlea·f** *v.* [Un-2 4.] *trans.* = Unleave *v.* 1598 Florio, *Sfogliare*,..to vnleafe. 1611 Cotgr., *Despamper*, to vnleafe, ..pull the leaues off a Vine, &c. 1811 H. G. Knight *Phrosyne* 40 Stern Winter..Unleafs the forest, and unchains the wind. **Unlea·fed,** *ppl. a.* (Un-1 8.) 1848 Lowell *Vision of Sir Launfal* ii. Prelude 7 The chill wind ..carried a shiver..From the unleafed boughs and pastures bare. †**Unlea·gue,** *v. Obs.*—1 (Un-2 3.) c 1645 Howell *Lett.* (1650) II. 107 Monsieur dela Chatre ligu'd you, let him then unligue [F. *desligue*] you. †**Unlea·guer,** *v. Obs.*—1 [Un-2 3.] *trans.* To cause (an army or leader) to abandon an investment. 1592 Greene *Conny Catch.* ii. A 2, Though I cannot as he [*sc.* Scævola]..attempt to vnleager Porsenna: yet [etc.]. **Unlea·kable,** *a.* (Un-1 7 c.) 1902 *C. Baker's Catal. Microscopes*, etc. 34 A Solid [Glass] Trough..practically unleakable.

**Unlea·l,** *a.* Now *arch.* [Un-1 7.] Unfaithful, disloyal, dishonest, false.

a 1300 *Cursor M.* 13173 Wit him-self he wex ful wrath,.. Þat men suld hald him for vn-lele. *Ibid.* 25167 Vr praier es vn-lele And askes gains vr saul hele. c 1375 *Sc. Leg. Saints* vii. (*Jacob*) 456 Sa þat na lele man suld forfare amange vnlele þat wekit ware. 1393 Langl. *P. Pl.* C. xiv. 69 Boþe louye and lene þe leelle and þe vnleelle. *c* 1430 in *Pol., Rel., & L. Poems* (1903) 203 Þou lyuest a letcherouse lijf vnleel. 1456 Sir G. Haye *Law Arms* (S.T.S.) 30 Untrewe and unlele to thair soveraynis lordis. 1528 Lyndesay *Dreme* 313 Sum part thair was of vnleill Lauboraris. *c* 1560 A. Scott *Poems* (S.T.S.) xxiii. 25 Hir fenȝeit wordis fals,..And als the luik vnleill Of hir bricht fair ene twane. 1848 Lytton *Harold* i. i, Words so unleal and foul. *Ibid.* xii. v, I hold it..disgrace to barter words with a knight unleal.

† **Unlea·n,** *a. Obs.*⁻¹ (Un-¹ 7.) *c* 1440 *Pallad. on Husb.* i. 96 But se thyn ayer be feir, and lond vnlene.

**Unlea·red,** *ppl. a. Obs.* exc. *dial.* [OE. *unlǽred* (Un-¹ 8), = ON. *úlærðr* (Icel. *ólærðr*, MSw. *olärdher*, Sw. *olärd*, Da. *ulærd*). Cf. OE. *ungelǽred*, MDu. *ongeleert*, etc.] Unlearned, untaught; ignorant.

*c* 1200 Ormin 17117 Þatt doþ uss tunnderrstanndenn wel Þatt he wass ȝet unnlæredd Off þatt. *a* 1300 *Cursor M.* 13884 Qua herd euer man sua spell, Man vnlerd o boken lare. 1340 Hampole *Pr. C.* 5947 Þam þat er unlered men. 1390 Gower *Conf.* I. 11 Suche as stode of trowthe unliered. *a* 1425 *Cursor M.* 22454 (Trin.), Hidur is good þat þei drawe,.. And here wel þat I shal sey Þat he wende not vnlered awey. 1552 Abp. Hamilton *Catech.* (1884) 26 Thai that ar..unleirit in haly writ. 1876 *Whitby Gloss.* 206 *Unlared*, or *Unleear'd*, unlearned.

**Unlea·rn,** *v.* [Un-² 3. Cf. MDu. *ont-, onleren*, older Fl. *ontleeren*, MLG. and G. *entleren*.]

**1.** *trans.* To discard from knowledge or memory; to give up knowledge of (something).

In very frequent use from *c* 1630.

*c* 1450 tr. *De Imitatione* i. xi. 12 Withstonde þyne inclinacion & unlerne evel custom. 1547 Baldwin *Mor. Philos.* (1551) N iij, The best kynde of learnynge is to vnlearne our euyls. 1575 Vautrollier *Luther on Ep. Gal.* 188 It is to vs no lesse labour to vnlearne and forget the same. 1612 Brinsley *Lud. Lit.* (1627) 9 Those things which are hurtfull,..they must bee taught to vnlearne againe. 1686 W. de Britaine *Hum. Prud.* i. 2 The most necessary learning for mans life, is to unlearn that which is nought and vain. 1779 *Mirror* No. 12, As they have learned many foreign, so have they unlearned some of the..best understood home phrases. 1813 Shelley *Q. Mab* iii. 6 Thou hast given A boon which I will not resign, and taught A lesson not to be unlearned. 1866 Bryce *Holy Rom. Emp.* xviii. 363 The habits of centuries were not to be unlearnt in a few years.

**b.** *absol.*, or const. with inf.

1530 Palsgr. 768/2 It is a payne to lerne thynges, but a man may unlerne by goyng a huntyng. 1584 Lyly *Campaspe* ii. ii, *Alex.* How should one learn to be content? *Diog.* Vnlearn to couet. 1631 P. Fletcher *Piscatory Eclog.* iii. xi, How canst unlearn by learning to forget it? 1649 F. Roberts *Clavis Bibl.* 351 In these I learn to shun sin, I un-learn to blush at repentance for offences. 1799 *Monthly Rev.* XXX. 120 According to an axiom founded on daily experience, to unlearn and forget are very difficult. 1823 *Monthly Mag.* LVI. 125 It is..long since the Romans have unlearned to conquer. 1868 Lowell *Parting of the Ways* 59 That way lies Youth, and Wisdom,..For only by unlearning Wisdom comes.

**2.** To unteach.

1664 Power *Exp. Philos.* Pref. 7 [The microscope] wil ocularly evince and unlearn them their opinions. 1802–12 Bentham *Ration. Judic. Evid.* (1827) V. 495 Legal learning ..can never have unlearnt a man the difference between three and one and a half. 1863 Susan Warner *Old Helmet* v, I must unlearn you a little of your kindness. 1893 *Harper's Mag.* Dec. 61/2 He's jest said what I've been a-learnin' 'im...But he's got to be unlearned.

Hence **Unlea·rning** *vbl. sb.*

1713 Steele *Englishm.* No. 7. 46 Art is only the unlearning of what is unnatural. 1873 E. H. Thompson *Baron de Rendy* ii. 43 A school for the unlearning of every Christian..feeling of compassion.

**Unlearnabi·lity.** (Un-¹ 12.) 1777 H. Walpole *Corr.* (1846) V. 473 The pleasure of correcting my awkwardness and unlearnability. **Unlea·rnable,** *a.* (Un-¹ 7 b.) 1846 Worcester (citing *Ed. Rev.*).

**Unlea·rned,** *ppl. a.* [Un-¹ 8. Cf. Unleared *ppl. a.* and OHG. *ungelirnêt* (MHG. *-lërnet, -lehrnt*, G. *-lernt*).]

**1.** Not possessed of learning; uninstructed; untaught; ignorant.

*c* 1400 Maundev. (1839) xvii. 184 How it semethe to symple men unlerned, that [etc.]. *c* 1420 *Wycliffite Bible* (1850) I. 67/2 Bothe of the lerned man and vnlerned. 14.. *Lat. & Eng. Prov.* (MS. Douce 52) fol. 27 Better is a chylde vnborne þen vnlerned. 1537 in *Bury Wills* (Camden) 131 Because I am rude and vnlernyd, and know not the scriptur. 1582 N. T. (Rhem.) *Luke* x. 21 *margin*, The humble vnlearned Catholike knoweth Christ better than the proud learned Heretike. 1651 Hobbes *Leviath.* ii. xxix. 169 These three opinions..proceeded chiefly from the tongues, and pens of unlearned Divines. 1699 Bentley *Phal.* 331 Andronicus's name was prefix'd to it by a Modern and a very Unlearned Hand. 1765 *Museum Rust.* IV. 450, I will now..give a free translation of it for the sake of your unlearned readers. 1854 Whittier *Maud Muller* 79 She wedded a man unlearned and poor. 1875 Jowett *Plato* (ed. 2) I. 198 But if you were not wise you were unlearned.

**b.** *spec.* (See quots.)

1643 Baker *Chron.* (1653) 236 Another Parliament.., named the unlearned Parliament, either for the unlearnednesse of the persons, or for their malice to learned men. 1878 Stubbs *Const. Hist.* III. xx. 401 The year 1404, when Henry IV stirred up strife by excluding lawyers from his 'unlearned parliament' [at Coventry].

**2.** *absol.* Those who have no learning.

*c* 1500 *Babees Bk.*, etc. (1868) 23/126 In þi dysch sette not þi spone,..os vn-lernyd done. 1549 Olde *Erasm. Par. Ephesians* Prol. to Rdr. C ii, To seke the edification of the playne vnlearned. 1578 Bible (Geneva) Pref. to Christian Reader, I haue so done for the vnlearneds sake. 1656 Stanley *Hist. Philos.* v. 50 He useth variety of names, that his work may not be easily be understood by the unlearned. 1712 Addison *Spect.* No. 457 ⁋ 4 An Account of the Works of the Unlearned. 1746 Francis tr. *Horace, Art of Poetry* 644 With all the Horrours of a desperate Muse The Learned and Unlearned he pursues. 1886 *Fortn. Rev.* Oct. 508 We must acknowledge, too, that experts know better than the unlearned.

**3.** Not skilled or versed *in* something.

1565 Cooper *Thesaurus* s.v. *Rudis*, Vnlearned in the Greeke tongue. *c* 1600 Shaks. *Sonn.* cxxxviii, Some vntuterd youth, Vnlearned in the worlds false subtilties. 1607 — *Timon* iv. iii. 56, I know thee well: But in thy Fortunes am vnlearn'd, and strange. 1725 Pope *Odyss.* ix. 150 Unlearn'd in all th' industrious arts of toil. 1833 Tennyson *To J. S.* v, Alas! In grief I am not all unlearn'd. 1885 'Mrs. Alexander' *At Bay* viii, Unlearned in the world's lore which was so familiar to himself!

**4.** Characterized by want of learning; pertaining to the unlearned class.

1526 Tindale 2 *Tim.* ii. 23 Folisshe and vnlearned questions. 1589 *Marprel. Epit.* D iij b, His booke is a carnall and vnlearned booke. 1604 Herring *Def. Caveat* (title-p.), That unlearned and dangerous opinion. *c* 1657 Cowley *Ode Dr. Harvey* v, A barb'rous Wars unlearned Rage. 1785 Burke *Sp. Nabob Arcot* Wks. IV. 316 The unlearned and vulgar passion of admiration. 1844 Stanley *Arnold* (1858) II. 146 An unlearned familiarity with the Scriptures. 1875 Whitney *Life Lang.* x. 187 The unlearned speech of the lower orders.

**5.** Not acquired by learning. (Cf. Unlearnt.)

1534 Ld. Berners *Gold. Bk. M. Aurel.* (1546) C v, That there shuld be nothyng vnlerned of hym, he aboue all sciences sette his mynd to Cosmography. 1607 Markham *Cavel.* iii. i. 4 My first Arte were better vnlearned then for want of this latter to doe euill by misimployment. 1611 Shaks. *Cymb.* iv. ii. 178 'Tis wonder That an inuisible instinct should frame them To Royalty vnlearn'd, Honor vntaught. 1644 Milton *Educ.* 3 Mispending our prime youth..in learning meere words or such things chiefly, as were better unlearnt.

**Unlea·rnedly,** *adv.* (Un-¹ 11; cf. prec.)

1532 More *Confut. Barnes* viii. Wks. 786/2 He shall speake very vnlernedly. 1578 Lyte *Dodoens* v. lxvi. 631 It is fondly and vnlearnedly named in Englishe, Dittany. 1651 Baxter *Inf. Bapt.* 239 Some..unlearnedly and boldly scold about..unprofitable matters. 1689 W. A. *Herbert's Account Examined* 3 He very unlearnedly clogs the Definition of a Dispensing Power. 1834 Beckford *Italy* II. 226 He..entered minutely and not unlearnedly into the ancient jurisprudence..of his country.

**Unlea·rnedness.** [Un-¹ 12.] The condition of being unlearned; want of learning; ignorance.

1562 Turner *Baths* 1 b, The vnlearnednes..of the Physiciones. 1581 W. Clarke in *Confer.* iv. (1584) Ff j, The errour and vnlearnednesse of your distinction appeareth. 1643 [see Unlearned 1 b]. 1674 W. Allen *Danger Enthus.* 18 Your Leaders manifest a strange degree of Unlearnedness in the things of the Gospel, when [etc.]. 1721 Bailey, *Illiterateness*, Unlearnedness.

**Unlea·rnt,** *ppl. a.* [Un-¹ 8 b.] = Unlearned 5.

1879 Farrar *St. Paul* i. v. I. 97 The inference that the gift of unlearnt languages was designed to help the Apostles in their future preaching.

**Unlea·sed,** *ppl. a.* [Un-¹ 8.] **a.** Not held or let on lease. **b.** Not having a lease.

1716 *Lond. Gaz.* No. 5467/3 Lands unleased. 1801 *Farmer's Mag.* Apr. 143 Landlords..compelling their unleased tenantry to sell below market-price. 1906 *Daily Chron.* 30 Aug. 3/3 The proceeds derived from ordinary Crown lands unsold or unleased.

**Unlea·sh,** *v.* [Un-² 4 b.] *trans.* To free from a leash; to set free in order to pursue or attack. Chiefly *fig.*

1671 Phillips (ed. 3), *To unleash*,..to let go the dogs after the Game. 1821 Shelley *Hellas* 357 Like beasts When earthquake is unleashed. 1854 J. S. C. Abbott *Napoleon* (1855) I. xxvi. 418 The bloodhounds of war were unleashed and England had unleashed them. 1868 Geo. Eliot *Sp. Gipsy* 48 With power to check all rage until it turned To ordered force, unleashed on chosen prey.

**Unlea·st,** *a. rare*⁻¹. (Un-¹ 7.) *c* 1440 *Pallad. on Husb.* i. 487 Another craft vnlest is: Fro floor to floor to chaunge hit ofte, his fest is. †**Unlea·st,** obs. var. *unlest* Unless *adv.* 1574 J. Dee in *Lett. Lit. Men* (Camden) 34 Unleast your honor had putte your helping hand. 1601 Yarrington *Two Lament. Trag.* iii. ii. in Bullen *O. Pl.* IV, I nam'd not God, unleast twere with an othe.

**Unlea·ve,** *v.* [Un-² 4; cf. Unleaf *v.*] *trans.* To strip of leaves. Hence **Unlea·ving** *vbl. sb.*

1589 Puttenham *Eng. Poesie* iii. xxv. (Arb.) 309 The good gardiner..vnleaues his boughes to let in the sunne. 1598 Sylvester *Du Bartas* ii. i. iv. *Handie-crafts* 136 Somtimes they do the far-spread Gourd unleave. 1611 Cotgr., *Effueillement*, an vnleauing. 1648 Hexham ii, *Ontbladeren*, to Vnleave, or, to Take away the Leaves.

**Unlea·ved,** *ppl. a.*¹ [Cf. prec.] Stripped of leaves.

1598 Sylvester *Du Bartas* ii. i. i. *Eden* 122 Amorous Myrtles and immortall Bays Never un-leav'd. 1610 G. Fletcher *Christ's Vict.* ii. lix. Ode 25 See, see the flowers ..How they all unleaved die. 1624 Heywood *Gunaik.* iv. 171 Behold how this lettice now unleaved looketh. 1870 Rossetti *Poems, Ho. Life* v, Nor quite unleaved [is] our songless grove.

**Unlea·ved,** *ppl. a.*² [Un-¹ 8.] Not furnished with leaves.

1501 Douglas *Pal. Hon.* i. iii, Muskane treis.., Combust, barrant, vnblomit and vnleifit. 1770 Langhorne *Plutarch* III. 38 Unleav'd, unhonour'd e'en with bark, See this sad tree, the gibbet of Alcæus!

**Unlea·vened,** *ppl. a.* (Un-¹ 8.)

1530 Tindale *Exod.* xii. 17 See that ye kepe you to vnleuended [*sic*] breed. 1594 Hooker *Eccl. Politie* iv. § 10 The vse of vnleauened bread in that sacrament. 1611 Bible *Exod.* xii. 39 They baked vnleauened cakes of the dough. — *Lev.* ii. 4 Vnleauened wafers. 1702 L'Estrange *Josephus* iii. vi. 64 Twelve Loaves of Unleavened Bread. 1737 Challoner *Cath. Chr. Instr.* (1753) 59 Unleavened Bread is an Emblem or Symbol of Sincerity and Truth. 1822–7 Good *Study Med.* (1829) I. 212 Toasted bread, and unleavened biscuits. 1867 Lady Herbert *Cradle L.* vii. 191 Soft unleavened cakes and some excellent coffee,..completed our repast.

*absol.* *c* 1550 Cheke *Matt.* xxvi. 17 Ye first dai of ye vnlevened cam ye discipils to Jesus.

*fig.* 1611 Bible 1 *Cor.* v. 7 Purge out therefore the olde leauen, that ye may be a new lumpe, as ye are vnleauened. 1814 Byron *Lara* ii. iv, Now rose the unleaven'd hatred of his heart. 1829 Lytton *Disowned* xiv, He is..giving the very goods..to that..starving stripling! No, Warner, no! even this mass is not unleavened.

**Unle·ctured,** *ppl. a.* [Un-¹ 8.] Not lectured to or upon.

1593 G. Harvey *Pierce's Super.* 190 [He] is a prowd man, if he contemne expert artisans,..howsoeuer Vnlectured in Schooles, or Vnlettered in bookes. 1743 Young *Nt. Th.* v. 513 Hast thou ever..study'd the philosophy of tears? (A science, yet, unlectur'd in our schools!)

**Unle·d,** *ppl. a.* [Un-¹ 8 b. Cf. ON. *úleiddr*.]

**1.** Not led; unconducted, unguided.

1615 G. Sandys *Trav.* 66, I haue seene but few go away vnled from the Embassadors table. 1693 Dryden *Ovid's Met.* xiii. *Acis & Gal.* 52 Here on the midst he sate; his Flocks, unled, Their Shepherd follow'd. 1758 *Monthly Rev.* 503 Already reckoning captives yet unled. 1817 Jefferson *Writ.* (1830) IV. 305 The people [were] not only unled by their leaders, but in opposition to them. 1859 Tennyson *Geraint & Enid* 577 His gentle charger following him unled.

**2.** *dial.* Of a crop: Not carried in.

1569 *Richmond Wills* (Surtees) 219 Tathe ledd and unledd.

**3.** *Sc.* Not carried out or prosecuted.

1586 in *Bk. Univ. Kirk Scotl.* (1839) 298 We hold the said proces and sentence as unled, undecydit or pronuncit.

† **Unle·de,** *sb.*¹ *Obs.* [Un-¹ 4 b + Lede *sb.*] A foreign or hostile people.

*c* 1205 Lay. 4982 Heo comen to his neode to driuen vt þa vnleoden. *a* 1300 *Cursor M.* 7641 Wit þat vnled [*v.rr.* unlede, folke] son dauid mete, And wightli wan o þam his dete.

† **Unlede,** *a.* and *sb.*² Forms: 1 unlǽde, 3 vnlede (-ledde), oun-, 4 onlede; 7 unleed, -lead, 9 unlete. [OE. *unlǽd(e* (Un-¹ 7), = Goth. *unlêds* (or *unlêþs*) poor.]

**1.** *adj.* Unhappy, miserable; wicked, evil; dreadful.

*a* 1250 *Owl & Night.* 976 Solde euch mon wonie & grede, Riȝt suich hi weren unlede. *c* 1275 *Sinners Beware* 72 in *O.E. Misc.* 74 To donne he beoþ swete. Þy vs is eþ-gete Helle þat is vnlede. *c* 1315 Shoreham i. 588 Ounde and wreþe and coueytyng, Sleuþe and lestes on-lede. *a* 1400 *St. Alexius* (Trin.) 333 Ofte hy him bete and burste, Þo vnlede fode.

**2.** *sb.* A vile or detestable person or thing.

*c* 1315 Shoreham iv. 235 Þe ferste pryns hys prede, Þat ledeþ þane flok, Þat of alle oþere onlede Hys rote and eke stok. 1677 Nicolson in *Trans. Royal Soc. Lit.* (1870) IX. 321 *Unlead*, outlaw. 1691 Ray *N. C. Words* 138 *Unleed* or *Unlead*,..any crawling venomous creature; as a Toad, etc. It's sometimes ascribed to Man, and there it denotes a sly wicked fellow,..the very pest of Society. 1829 Brockett *N. C. Gloss.* (ed. 2) 315 *Unletes*, displacers or destroyers of the farmer's produce.

† **Unlee·ful,** *a. Obs.* [Un-¹ 7.] Not permissible or allowable; illicit.

*c* 1374 Chaucer *Boeth.* v. pr. iii. (1868) 154 Þe whiche þinge to trowen on god I deme it felonie and vnleueful. *c* 1386 — *Pars. T.* ⁋ 593 The wounde shal nat departe from his hous whil he vseth swich vnleueful [*v.rr.* vnlefful, vnlieful, sweryng. 1449 [see next]. *c* 1491 *Chast. Goddes Chyld.* 25 Her rest was full short by cause it was..unlefull. 1529 More *Dyaloge* i. Wks. 157/2 The thinges nowe forbeden vs, and therfore to vs vnleful. 1547 Boorde *Brev. Health* xxvii. 16 b, Desyre to eate rawe and unlefull thynges, as women with chylde doth. 1567 *Reg. Privy Council Scot.* I. 524 That pretendit and unlefull mariage.

Hence † **Unlee·fulness.** *Obs.*

1382 Wyclif *Wisd.* xiv. 8 The maumet..is cursid,..and he that made it, for he forsothe wroȝte vnleefulnesse. *c* 1449 Pecock *Repr.* ii. i. 136 Ech such doable thing..is in it silf neither leeful neither vnleeful, in eny of the ij. now seid maners of propre taking leefulnes and vnleefulnes. *c* 1475 *Cath. Angl.* 212/1 (A.), To do Vnlefulnesse, *illicebrare*.

† **Unlee·fully,** *adv. Obs.* [Un-¹ 11: cf. prec.] Illicitly; improperly.

*c* 1375 *Sc. Leg. Saints* x. (*Matthew*) 384 How dar þu þane ..fra þi lorde tak hyre to þe, vnlefully to wedyte be? 1386 *Rolls of Parlt.* III. 226/1 Any..wronge suggestion, by which owre lige Lorde hath ybe unleeffullich enfourmed. *c* 1400 *Apol. Loll.* 110 Al þi power of bischopis name þat þei chalang unlefuly to hem wiþ out þe kirk. 1456 Sir G. Haye *Law Arms* (S.T.S.) 288 He suld nocht..unlefully trete him.

† **Unlee·ped,** *ppl. a. Sc. Obs.* [Un-¹ 8 + *leep* to boil slightly.] Uncooked, raw.

*a* 1558 in *Bannatyne MS.* (Hunter. Cl.) 385/4 Ane grit gyre carling..That levit vpoun christiane menis flesche and rewth heidis vnleipit.

† **Unlee·sable,** *a. Obs.* [Un-¹ 7 b.] Incapable of being lost. 1647 Trapp *Comm. Matt.* vii. 26 Saving grace is unleesable, though it may be impaired in the degrees.

† **Unlee·se,** *v. Obs. rare.* [OE. *un-, onliesan* (= MHG. *entlœsen*, MG. *entlôsin*, MLG. *entlosen*, G. *entlösen*): see Un-² 9 and Leese *v.*²] *trans.* To unfasten, undo, open.

1377 Langl. *P. Pl.* B. Prol. 213 Seriauntz..nouȝt for loue of owre lorde vnlese here lippes onis.

**Unlee·some,** *a. Sc.* [Un-¹ 7.] = Unleeful *a.*

*c* 1375 *Sc. Leg. Saints* x. (*Matthew*) 10 Lewy, Þat as a toilare þare wes sate, Vnlessume wynnynge for to get. 1500–20 Dunbar *Poems* xvii. 16 Thir merchantis takis vnlesum win. 1552 Lyndesay *Monarche* 5104 And sum, for thare vnleifsum actis, Ar rent and rewin apone the ractis. **1600** Hamilton in *Cath. Tractates* (S.T.S.) 235 How mony young wemen..hes murtherit the fruict of thair auin wombes, some be vnlisome drinkis. **1864** Latto *Tam. Bodkin* x. 92 The loons that had received the unleisum stoutherie. *Ibid.* xvii. 170 The unleisome possession o' the game.

So **Unlee·somely** *adv.* ? *Obs.*

*c* **1400** *Sc. Trojan War* II. 1103 [To] lat of hyr virgynite The closoures vnlefsomely [L. *illicite*] To be broken. **1528** Lyndesay *Dreme* 230 Vnleifsumlie thay vsit propertie. *a* **1578** Lindesay (Pitscottie) *Chron. Scot.* (S.T.S.) II. 207 Putting hand in the quenis grace vnlesomelie..but athir law or ressoune.

**Unlee·ze,** *v. dial.* [Un-[2] 9 + *leeze* to arrange (threads).] *trans.* To unravel. **1889** H. Johnston *Glenbuckie* iv, The hank she had left me to unleeze was truly a tangled one. **Unle·ft,** *ppl. a.* (Un-[1] 8 b.) *c*1611 Chapman *Iliad* II. 615 Yet were his men unleft Without a chief. **1634** Ford *Perk. Warbeck* v. iii, Your father..Would blush on your behalf, and wish his country Unleft. **1659** *Nicholas Papers* (Camden) IV. 179 All malladies and goutes vnleft behynde at Bathe. **Unle·g,** *v.* (Un-[2] 4.) **1598** Florio, *Sgambare*, to vnleg. **1654** Gayton *Pleas. Notes* III. v. 100 That is to say, with three hard words, un-mule, un-leg and un-able, Alanso Lopez. **Unle·gacied,** *ppl. a.* (Un-[1] 8.) **1556** *Wills & Inv. N. C.* (Surtees, 1835) 149, I will that my said sonne.. shall have..of my goods..on hundreth pounds and the rest vnlegased to be parted betwix barbare and hym. **1846** Worcester (citing *Q. Rev.*). **Unle·gal,** *a.* (Un-[1] 7, 5 b.) **1643** Prynne *Open. Gt. Seal* 29 The unlegall wilfull absence of the..Lord Keeper from the Parliament. *a* **1810** Tannahill *Poems* (1846) 68 Selfish, mean, unlegal deeds. **1899** *Westm. Gaz.* 10 July 3/1 The illegal—or let us say the unlegal—interference of the English Government. **Unle·galized,** *ppl. a.* (Un-[1] 8.) **1830** Bentham *Offic. Apt. Maximized, Further Extr. Const. Codex* (1830) 23 Accustomed, though unlegalized profit in every shape. **1860** Froude *Hist. Eng.* VI. 267 He hated lies—legalized or unlegalized. **Unle·gally,** *adv.* (Un-[1] 11.) **1888** *Pall Mall G.* 3 April 3/1 If such a delicate matter as extradition were left to be dealt with unlegally.

**Unle·gate,** *v.* [Un-[2] 6 b.] *trans.* To deprive of the office of legate.

*a* **1548** Hall *Chron., Hen. VI*, 111 Sone after, the bishop of Rome..vnlegated hym, and set another in his stede. **1651** N. Bacon *Disc. Govt. Eng.* II. xxxi. 150 The Cardinall is Un-Legated, and that Power conferred upon the Arch-Bishop of Canterbury.

†**Unlegated,** *ppl. a. Obs.* [Un-[1] 8.] Not left by will. **1562–3** *N. C. Wills* (Surtees) II. 38 My goodes unlegated I doe give to my brother. **Unle·gged,** *a.* (Un-[1] 9.) **1608** Topsell *Serpents* 609 This monster..nor man nor dragon is.., But man unlegged, and snake unheaded. †**Unle·gible,** *a.* [Un-[1] 7, 5 b.] Illegible. **1611** Speed *Hist. Gt. Brit.* x. i. § 57. 892/2 The letter was..somewhat vnlegible. **1655** Earl Orrery *Parthen.* I. vi. 150 Perceiveing my joy in my Face, it inflam'd his to such a degree, that for a good while his choller was unleagible in any thing else. **1671** Wood *Life* (O.H.S.) II. 226 The base and unlegible hand of the translator. **Unle·gislative,** *a.* (Un-[1] 7.) **1791** Bentham *Panopt.* II. Postscr. 165 More unlegislative minuteness, more unthrifty fixation. †**Unlegi·timate,** *a. Obs.* [Un-[1] 7, 5 b.] Illegitimate. **1655** Earl Orrery *Parthen.* I. vii. 347 Shee persever'd in a Passion which tended to..a more vnlegittimate end. †**Unlegi·timate,** *ppl. a. Sc. Obs.* [Un-[1] 8 b.] Not legitimated. **1516** *Reg. Mag. Sig. Scot.* 23/1 Borne bastard and unlegittimate be ony mariage. †**Unlegi·timate,** *v. Obs.* [Un-[2] 6 a.] *trans.* To make illegitimate. **1606** Marston *Parasit.* II. C 4 b, I will vnlegittimate the issue.

**Unlei·sured,** *a.* (Un-[1] 9.)

*a* **1586** Sidney *Arcadia* II. xxv, But her vnleasured thoughtes ran not ouer the ten first wordes. **1644** Milton *Areop.* (Arb.) 56 Unlesse he carry all his considerat diligence..to the hasty view of an unleasur'd licencer.

Hence **Unlei·suredness.**

**1661** Boyle *Style of Script.* To Rdr., The Unleisurednesse, and Rellish of the Unsetl'dnesse of the Wandering Author.

†**Unle·ke,** *v. Obs.* [Un-[2] 3 + *leke* (cf. *leke*, ME. pa. t. of Louk *v.*[1]).] *trans.* To unlock (a door). *c* **1380** *Sir Ferumbras* 1264 Florippe hure drow to anoþer part, & þar an dore ounlekes þat drow to þe putte ward, & doun in the pyt sche strekes. †**Unle·ngth.** *Obs.*—[1] [Un-[1] 3, 12.] Shortness. *a* **1250** *Owl & Night.* 752 Hwy atwitestu me myne vnstrengþe & myne vngrete & myn vnlengþe. **Unle·nt,** *ppl. a.* (Un-[1] 8 b.) [**1775** Ash.] **1887** *Daily News* 11 June 2/1 Much depends..upon the amount of the unlent surplus of money.

**Unlered:** see Unleared *ppl. a.*

**Unless** (ɒnle·s), *prep. phr.*, *prep.*, *conj.*, and *sb.* Forms: α. 5 **of lasse, oo lesse, o less, oless(e,** *Sc.* **oles,** 9 *Sc.* **aless.** β. 5 **vpon less.** γ. 5 **in lasse, yn las,** 5 **in less** (9 *dial.* **inless),** 6 **inlesse.** δ. 5 **on lasse,** 5–6 **onlesse,** 6 **oon-, oneles, -lez,** 5–7 **onles,** 9 *dial.* **onless.** ε. 5 **vnlasse,** 6–7 **vn-, unlesse,** 6 **vnles,** 6– **unless.** [f. Less *a.* 7, with the preps. *of*, *in*, *upon*, and *on*; the last of these by want of stress has been assimilated in form to the prefix Un-[1]. Cf. Less *conj.*, also Unleast, Unlest.]

†**1.** *prep. phr.* On a less or lower condition, requirement, footing, etc., *than* (what is specified).

With preceding negative, expressed or implied.

*c* **1400** Maundev. (1919) xxi. 122 But þat may not be vpon less þan wee mowe falle toward heuene. *Ibid.* (Roxb.) xxv. 118 [see Less *a.* 7 c]. **1475** *Rolls of Parlt.* VI. 127/1 His Land, which many persones..fere to take.., olesse then they myght be made verrey sure of payment. *a* **1500** in C. Trice-Martin *Chanc. Proc. 15th C.* (1904) 5 Robert wil not suffre hym to be laten to baile on lasse than he will make..a generall acquytaunce.

**2.** Except, if.. not: † **a.** With retention of *than* (cf. prec.), but without a negative. *Obs.*

**1431** *Acts Privy Counc.* IV. 96 It shulde be entendede unto, namely, olesse þan before þ[t] men can se..þ[e] meenes ..of ferþer conduyt of þ[e] werre. *c* **1449** Pecock *Repr.* III. xvi. 386 Alle hise successouris ben..excludid for euer, in lasse thanne the same good be 3ouun a3en. **1467** in *Eng. Gilds* (1870) 408 Vppon peyn of euery man so failynge, vnlesse then he haue a sufficient depute, of xl. *d.* **1530** Tindale *Gen., Prol. Use Script.* A v, Inlesse then we entend to be ydle disputers, and braulers aboute vayne wordes.

† **b.** Followed by *that. Obs.*

**1440** in *Wars Eng. in France* (1864) II. 458 The kyng conceyueth wele that onlesse that it like him so to tendre the said duc he [etc.]. **1470–85** Malory *Arthur* I. x. 47 Onlesse that our kyng haue more chyualry,..he shal be ouercome. **1529** Wolsey in Cavendish *Life* (1825) II. 261 Onles that yow..do helpe & releve me therin. **1534** in Leadam *Star Chamber Cases* (Selden) II. 211 [They] cowde not.. sell so myche..onelez that they wold sell so reasonable a pennyworthe. **1596** Spenser *F. Q.* vi. iii. 39 Ne would I gladly combate with mine host,..Vnlesse that I were thereunto enforst.

**c.** With omission of conjunction before the subordinate clause, and thus passing into *conj.* (Cf. 4.)

**1509** Fisher *Serm.* Wks. (1876) 277 There is no man.. oneles he haue it by reuelacyon that knoweth certaynly [etc.]. **1542** *Lam. & Piteous Treat.* in *Harl. Misc.* (1745) IV. 505/2 It was a verey daungerous and ieoperdous Thinge, ..inlesse they had been..weryd by longe Soiourynge. **1563** *Mirr. Mag., Blacksmith* lxviii, For one [talent] is to much, onles it be well spent. **1607** in *Eng. Gilds* (1870) 442 Margory Davies..wold not remove her habitacion onles she might haue a way..to passe [etc.]. **1662** Stillingfl. *Orig. Sacræ* II. iii. § 5 Will God condemn them for that, which it was impossible they should have, unless God gave it them? **1710** Swift *Jrnl. to Stella* 8 Oct., I was at a loss to-day for a dinner, unless I would have gone a great way. **1752** Young *Brothers* I. i, Dominion, and the princess, both are lost, Unless you gain the king. **1820** Southey *Wesley* II. 211 No person was admitted to this rank, unless he were thought competent by the preachers of the circuit. **1877** Ruskin *Fors Clav.* lxxx. VII. 234, I am never angry with anybody unless they deserve it.

**d.** Followed by a prepositional or participial clause without verb, or by *when*, *where*, etc.

**1548–9** (Mar.) *Bk. Com. Prayer, Offices, Bapt. Priv. Ho.*, [That] the people..defer not the Baptisme of infantes.. onlesse vp on a greate & reasonable cause. **1610** Fletcher *Faithful Sheph.* v. v, [Let] not wine, Unless in sacrifice, or rites divine, Be ever known of Shepherd. **1681** Dryden *Abs. & Achit.* I. 590 Nor ever was he known..[to] Curse, unless against the Government. **1721** Bradley *Philos. Acc. Wks. Nat.* 77 We had no Frost or Snow.., unless in the most Inland Parts. **1749** Fielding *Tom Jones* xvii. ix, Jones passed above twenty-four melancholy hours by himself, unless when relieved by the company of Partridge. **1789** Charlotte Smith *Ethelinde* (1814) II. 147 But I dare not shew them, unless to you. **1818** Scott *Rob Roy* v, A beautiful horse, jet black, unless where he was flecked by spots of.. foam. **1897** Mary Kingsley *W. Africa* 439 They never wear clothes unless compelled to.

**3.** *prep.* **a.** Except, but.

**1531–2** *Act* 23 *Hen. VIII*, c. 1 That no suertye be taken onles suche as maye dyspende..yerly..xxvi.s. viii.d. **1563** Hill *Art Garden.* II. lxiv. (1574) 132 The floures..ought then to be gathered..vnlesse the Lilly..and Rose. **1600** Heywood *If you know not me* Wks. 1874 I. 205 All forbeare this place, vnlesse the Princess. **1683** D. A. *Art Converse* 117 They say nothing unless a meer *yes sir* or *no Madam.* **1709** T. Robinson *Nat. Hist. Westmoreld.* viii. 53 Inconsistent..with the Nature of Lead, Copper, Coal, or any other Mineral, unless Iron. **1796** Morse *Amer. Geog.* II. 33 Unless the Swedish part,..the Laplanders can be said to be under no regular government. **1886** *Pall Mall G.* 4 Aug. 1/2 He did not believe that he would ever obtain anything..unless a species of elevated poor-law system of government.

† **b.** Without; but for. *Obs.*

**1536** *St. Papers Hen. VIII* (1830) I. 469 Soo that, unles the most infinite mercy of God, both bodyes and soules shuld perishe togither. **1796** Mrs. J. West *Gossip's Story* I. 190 You instilled into my infant soul principles, which, unless my own fault, must insure my present and future happiness.

†**4.** *conj.* **a.** Lest. *Obs.*

**1508** Fisher 7 *Penit. Ps.* cii. Wks. (1876) 142, I fere.. oneles I shall fall agayne amonge those theves. **1543** Becon *Invect. agst. Swearing* E iiij b, I feare vnlesse we shall be redy..to runne hedlong into hell fyre. *a* **1592** Greene *Alphonsus* I. i, Presume not, villaine, further for to go, Vnles you do at length the same repent.

† **b.** But that. *Obs.*—[1]

**1608** in *Harl. Misc.* (1744) I. 181 A Flea shall not frisk forth, unless they comment upon her.

**5.** *sb.* An utterance or instance of the word; a reservation, proviso.

**1861** Dickens in *Pall Mall G.* 24 Sept. (1891) 3/2 Let us have no unlesses, sir. **1904** Hichens *Woman with Fan* vii, There's very often an unless hanging about, like a man at a street corner.

**Unle·ssened,** *ppl. a.* (Un-[1] 8.) **1736** Butler *Anal.* I. i. 31 This active power..remains unlessened. **1842** J. B. Fraser *Allee Neemroo* II. 99 His uneasiness remained unlessened and unaltered. **1891** C. M. *J. Mitford's Lett. & Remin.* 163 His love for me remained unlessened.

**Unle·ssoned,** *ppl. a.* (Un-[1] 8.)

*c* **1550** Walker *Dice-Play* D v b, Pety figgers, and vnlessoned laddes. **1596** Shaks. *Merch. V.* III. ii. 161 An vnlessoned girle, vnschool'd, vnpractiz'd. **1807** J. Barlow *Columb.* v. 673 To Fame's hard school the warm disciples came, To learn sage Liberty's unlesson'd lore. **1882** *Century Mag.* XXIV. 658/1 That unlessoned insight which comes of loving them.

† **Unle·st,** obs. var. Unless. (Cf. Unleast.)

**1535** in *Lett. Suppress. Monast.* (Camden) 91 The dean wolde not resign unto hym, unleste he wolde leffe hym other possessions. **1583** Stubbes *Anat. Abus.* II. C 8 b, May subiects..rise against their prince? No, at no hand, vnlest they will purchase to themselues eternall damnation. **1599** Thynne *Animadv.* (1875) 19 Difference of armes semethe a difference of famelyes, vnleste you canne prove that..they altered their armes vppone somme iuste occasione.

**Unle·t,** *ppl. a.* Also 5 **unlate,** 6 **unletton.** (Un-[1] 8 b; cf. Let *ppl. a.*)

**1453** *Paston Lett.* Suppl. (1901) 49, I know not oon rode unlate, but alle ocupyed to your profyghte. **1537** in *Lett. Suppress. Monast.* (Camden) 163 The house..wiche was unlet at the tyme of owre repare thether. **1545** *Act* 37 *Hen. VIII*, c. 12 § 16 Hawles of Craftes.., soo long as they bee keapte unletton. **1769** Gray in *Corr. G. & Nicholls* (1843) 93, I believe all that are unlet will be cheap as the time approaches. **1866** Geo. Eliot *F. Holt* ii, Having three farms unlet. **1885** *Law Times* 28 Mar. 384/2 In the present day, when unlet land is becoming so common.

**Unle·ttable,** *a.* (Un-[1] 7 b.)

In frequent use from *c* 1895.

**1882** *Ch. Times* XX. 21, I fear to find myself with a[n].. unlettable glebe on my hands. **1893** Dk. Argyll *Unseen Found. Soc.* x. 305 Farms which have been unlettable.

†**Unle·tted,** *ppl. a.* [Un-[1] 8. Cf. MLG. *ungeletted*, etc.] Unhindered.

*a* **1500** *Chaucer's Dreme* 1831 A bird song full low and softely,..Unletted of every wight. *a* **1553** Becon *Jewel of Joy* Wks. 1564 II. 35 The holye scripture requireth of us..an vnletted perseueraunce in the vaye of Godlines.

† **Unle·tten,** *ppl. a. Sc. Obs.* [Un-[1] 8 b.] Not let or allowed.

**1574** *Sc. Acts Jas. VI* (1814) III. 87 That all..vagaboundis ..be committit in ward in the commoun presoun;..thair to be kepit vnlettin to libertie,..quhill thay [etc.].

**Unle·ttered,** *a.* [Un-[1] 9. Cf. MDu. *ongeletterd*, Du. *ongeletterd*.]

**1.** Not instructed in letters; not possessed of book-learning.

*c* **1340** Hampole *Prose Tr.* 32 Anoþer mane..unletterede may noght so redyly hafe at his hand Haly Writt. **1387** Trevisa *Higden* (Rolls) VII. 181 A man forsoþe..þat was unlettred, but ful myghty in money. *c* **1440** *Alph. Tales* 468 When þe abbott Pambo was vnletterd, he went vnto a man þat was letterd [etc.]. **1544** Leland *N. Y. Gift* in *Itin.* (1768) I. p. xix, The Italians..counte..al other nations to be barbarus and onletterid saving their owne. **1593** [see Unlectured *ppl. a.*]. **1624** Gataker *Transubst.* 156 As children or unlettered persons, when they looke on bookes, know not the power of the letter. **1642** Milton *Apol. Smect.* 36 Such a lost construction, as no man either letter'd or unletter'd will be able to piece up. **1747** Wesley *Prim. Physick* (1762) p. xxiv, Easy to be applied by plain unlettered Men. **1781** Cowper *Conversat.* 12 As alphabets in ivory employ..the yet unletter'd boy. **1817** Chalmers *Disc. Chr. Revel.* ii. 86 The mind of an ordinary and unlettered peasant. **1867** Augusta Wilson *Vashti* xxv, Sturdy but unlettered mechanics.

*absol.* **1751** Johnson *Rambler* No. 180 ⁋ 2 The unlettered and unenlightened. **1812** G. Chalmers *Dom. Econ. Gt. Brit.* Pref. 14 That the learned are sometimes too confident, and the unlettered always too credulous. **1861** Stanley *East. Ch.* viii. (1869) 273 Sacred pictures..are the Bibles of the unlettered.

**b.** Pertaining to, characterized by, ignorance of letters.

**1588** Shaks. *L. L. L.* iv. ii. 18 After his..vnpolished, vneducated,..or rather, vnlettered..fashion. **1697** Collier *Ess. Mor. Subj.* II. (1703) 99 Books..give a more universal insight into things, than can be learned from unlettered observation. **1763** J. Brown *Poetry & Music* iv. 36 Savages ..in their present unlettered State of Ignorance and Simplicity. **1807** G. Chalmers *Caledonia* I. III. vii. 423 An upright stone still forms the unlettered memorial of his odious end. **1820** Hazlitt *Lect. Dram. Lit.* 186 They were learned men in an unlettered age. *a* **1864** Hawthorne *Amer. Note-bks.* (1879) I. 142 His conversation has much strong, unlettered sense.

**2.** Not expressed in, or marked with, letters.

**1633** P. Fletcher *Poet. Misc., Asclepiads* 1 Unletter'd Word, which never eare could heare. **1782** [T. Maule] *Verbeia* 37 This unlettered tomb is in a mutilated state.

Hence †**Unle·tteredly** *adv.*, **Unle·tteredness.**

*c* **1440** *Promp. Parv.* 366/1 On-letterydly, *illiterate.* **1653** E. Waterhouse *Apol. Learn.* 120 Ignorance and unletteredness ill becomes any man who bears the Image of God. **1890** Bp. Hobhouse *Churchw. Acc.* (Somerset) p. xxiii, The entire unletteredness of the community.

**Unleueful,** variant of Unleeful *a. Obs.*

†**Unle·vable,** *a. Obs.* [Un-[1] 7 b.] Unbelieving, incredulous. **1382** Wyclif *Ecclus.* xvi. 29 Be thou not vnleeuable to the wrd of hym. **14..** *Voc.* in Wr.-Wülcker 589/23 *Incredulus*, unlefable. †**Unle·veful,** *a. Obs.*—[1] [Un-[1] 7: cf. Unbelieffuł *a.* and OE. *ungeléaffull*.] = prec. **1382** Wyclif *Ecclus.* xxiii. 33 In the lawe of the he3est she was vnleeueful.

**Unle·vel,** *a.* (Un-[1] 7; cf. Illevel *a.*)

**1571** Digges *Pantom.* I. xii. D iij b, How vneuen or vnleuell so euer the ground bee. **1644** Quarles *Sheph. Orac.* iii, All things were unlevell, And rude disorder crept into our State. **1683** Moxon *Mech. Exerc., Printing* xxiv. 338 The small un-level lying of every Sheet..makes each Sheet incline to the lowest side of the Heap. **1771** *Ann. Reg., Usef. Projects* 109/2 That unlevel pastures may be ploughed down without any injury. **1817–8** Cobbett *Resid. U. S.* (1822) 286 A place situated..upon high and unlevel lands. **1873** E. Spon *Workshop Receipts* Ser. I. 36/1 Should the cloth have got unlevel.

**Unle·vel,** *v.* [Un-[2] 6 a.] *trans.* To make uneven; to divest of levelness.

*a* **1586** Sidney *Arcadia* III. xi, [The] place..was so plaine, as there was scarcely any bush, or hillock, either to unlevell, or shadowe it. **1624** Quarles *Div. Poems, Job* xix. 10 His Lunatick affections doe vnleuell, What Heauen created by iust Waight and Measure. **1648** Herrick *Hesper., To the Fever* 8 Come thou not neere that Filme so finely spred, Where no one piece is yet unlevelled. **1703** [R. Neve] *City & C. Purchaser* 189 There are as many places that seem to be unlevel'd, as there are level'd. **1834** Southey *Doctor* xlvi. (1862) 109 In 1723 the church floor and church-yard, which had both been unlevelled by Death's levelling course, were levelled anew.

**Unle·velled,** *ppl. a.* [UN-¹ 8.] Not made level; not reduced to a level condition.

**1622** DRAYTON *Poly-olb.* xxiii. 184 Where Cheshire.. with Lancashire doth lie Along th' unlevel'd shores. **1730** TICKELL *Kensington Garden* 30 Where all unlevell'd the gay Garden lies. **1854** DORA GREENWOOD *Haps & Mishaps Tour Eur.* 30 The grandeur of its yet unlevelled walls and towers.

**† Unleventhe,** obs. variant of ELEVENTH *a.*

**13..** *Coer de L.* 2455 The unleventhe day they saylyd in tempest.

**Unle·vied,** *ppl. a.* (UN-¹ 8.)

**1450** *Rolls of Parlt.* V. 211/1 The Subsidie..is yit unlevied and unpaied. **1540** *Act* 32 *Hen. VIII*, c. 5 The residue of the said dett.. remayning unlevied or unreceyvid by the said former execution. **1569** *Lanc. Wills* (Chetham Soc. 1884) 31 Fyve hundrethe marks.. or so muche therof as shalbe then unlevyed. **1634** *Ir. Act* 10 *Chas. I*, Sess. III. c. 7 § 2 [=quot. 1540]. **1864** *Morn. Star* 2 Feb., Arrears of unlevied poor rates.

**Unle·vigated,** *ppl. a.* (UN-¹ 8.) **1768** R. DOSSIE *Elaboratory* 290 The cinnabar should be procured..in an unlevigated state. **† Unle·ving,** *ppl. a. Obs.* [UN-¹ 10.] Unbelieving. *a* **1300** *Cursor M.* 20852 Þe apostlis þat all wide war spred,..til our lagh þe vnleuand led. **1382** WYCLIF *Isaiah* xxi. 1 [He] that vnleeuende [1388 vnfeithful] is, vnfeithfully doth.

**† Unlew·ty.** *Obs.* [UN-¹ 12.] Disloyalty.

*a* **1300** *Cursor M.* 7135 Þat was mikel vnleute, To tell hir husband priuete. **13..** *Gaw. & Gr. Knt.* 2499 Þat he laȝt for his vnleute at þe leudes hondes, for blame. **1456** SIR G. HAYE *Law Arms* (S.T.S.) 25 The thrid part of the sternis was obumbrit with mirknes of unleautee. *a* **1470** HARDING *Chron.* CXIII. xiv, Through theyr vnlewtee [the Scots] Crowned Gilryke a Dane.

**Unli·able,** *a.* (UN-¹ 7 b.)

**1624** QUARLES *Div. Poems, Job* xvi. 32 How can I.., Vnliable to danger, flatter any? **1664** H. MORE *Myst. Iniq.* Pref. 1 *margin*, This Idea..is..unliable to any uncivil construction. **1679** PULLER *Moderat. Ch. Eng.* v. 88 No where judging of them as unliable to error. **1710** NORRIS *Chr. Prud.* vii. 297 Things that..are not so unliable to Disorder and abuse.

**Unli·bbed,** *ppl. a.* (UN-¹ 8.) **1607** TOPSELL *Four-f. Beasts* 324 They vse to geld them in March..: afterward being well nourished, they [*sc.* gelded horses] are no lesse strong..then other vnlibbed. **Unli·beral,** *a. rare*—⁰. (UN-¹ 7.) **1570** LEVINS *Manip.* 15 Vnliberall, *illiberalis.* **1611** FLORIO, *Inliberale*, vnliberall, sparing. **Unli·beralized,** *ppl. a.* (UN-¹ 8 *a* c.) **1793** J. WILLIAMS *Mem. W. Hastings* 40 Are there any so unliberalized as to insist, that..the calumniated should only be allowed a passport to Peace from Death? **Unli·berated,** *ppl. a.* (UN-¹ 8.) **1837** *Penny Cycl.* VIII. 411/1 The removal of pressure upon the nerves, produced by the advancing and unliberated tooth. **1865** *Reader* 14 Oct. 430/2 The irregular weapons of a still unliberated press. **Unlibi·dinous,** *a.* (UN-¹ 7.) **1667** MILTON *P. L.* v. 449 But in those hearts Love unlibidinous reign'd.

**Unli·censed,** *ppl. a.* [UN-¹ 8.]

**1.** Of persons, etc.: **a.** Not authorized by a formal license to carry on some occupation, industry, etc.

**1634** in *10th Rep. Hist. MSS. Commission* App. IV. 428, 100 unlicensed alehowses. **1643** [see 2 a]. **1746** FRANCIS tr. *Horace, Epist.* II. i. 154 A doubtful Drug unlicens'd Doctors fear. **1845** MCCULLOCH *Taxation* II. x, A fine..rigorously exacted from unlicensed dealers. **1855** MACAULAY *Hist. Eng.* xx. IV. 417 With great difficulty and after long search the most important of all the unlicensed presses was discovered.

**b.** Not furnished with authority, sanction, or formal permission to do something.

**1608** SHAKS. *Per.* I. iii. 17 Why, as it were unlicens'd of your loves, He would depart, I'll give some light unto you. **1685** BAXTER *Paraphr. N. T.* To Rdr. A 3 b, The Papists restraint of the Laity unlicensed, from reading it translated in a known Tongue. **1725** POPE *Odyss.* XIII. 175 To warn the thoughtless self-confiding train No more unlicens'd thus to brave the main. **1795** SOUTHEY *Joan of Arc* IV. 414 Did she upon thy parting steps bestow Her free-will blessing, or hast thou set forth..unlicensed and unblest?

**2. a.** Of books, etc.: Published without licence.

**1643** *Order* in *Milton's Areop.* (Arb.) 27 All unlicensed Printing Presses, and all Presses any way imployed in the printing of scandalous or unlicensed Papers. **1644** MILTON *Areop.* (Arb.) 53 All scandalous and unlicenc't books. **1647** (*title*), An Ordinance against unlicenced or scandalous Pamphlets.

**b.** Not authorized or sanctioned.

**1649** JER. TAYLOR *Apol. Liturgy* § 135 Many such cases will occurre in .. unlicenc'd prayers. *a* **1704** T. BROWN *Dial. Dead, Reas. Oaths* Wks. 1720 IV. 184 Is any..of the good People of Doctors Commons [turned] to unlicens'd Marriages? **1728** POPE *Dunciad* IV. 228 For Attic Phrase in Plato let them seek, I poach in Suidas for unlicens'd Greek. **1819** SCOTT *Leg. Montrose* Introd., No less would our sexton.. have held it an unlicensed intrusion. **1856** FROUDE *Hist. Eng.* II. 193 The clergy had promised to abstain..from unlicensed legislation.

**3.** Free from requiring a licence.

**1644** MILTON (*title*), Areopagitica: a Speech..For the Liberty of Vnlicenc'd Printing, To the Parlament of England. **1863** H. COX *Instit.* I. ix. 146 This Act was kept in force..until 1694, when..it expired. The liberty of unlicensed printing dates from that period.

**4.** Unregulated, lawless. *rare*—¹.

**1828** TYTLER *Hist. Scot.* I. 183 This prelate.. with much personal risk, owing to the unlicensed state of the country,..travelled with his suit..as far as Kirkcudbright.

**Unlice·ntious,** *ppl. a.* (UN-¹ 7.) **1768–74** TUCKER *Lt. Nat.* (1834) II. 415 The exercise of sober, unlicentious freedom of thought. **Unli·chened,** *ppl. a.* (UN-¹ 8.) **1843** RUSKIN *Mod. Paint.* I. 239 Unlichened, dead, desolated rock. **Unli·ckable,** *a.* (UN-¹ 7 b.) **1845** D'ISRAELI *Sybil* v. vii, One of the most unlicked and unlickable cubs that ever entered society.

**Unli·cked,** *ppl. a.* [UN-¹ 8. Cf. Du. *ongelikt*, G. *ungeleckt.*]

**1.** Not licked into shape. (See LICK *v.* 4.) Chiefly *fig.*, esp. with *cub* (or *whelp*).

**1593** SHAKS. 3 *Hen. VI*, III. ii. 161 Like to..an vn-lick'd Beare-whelpe, That carryes no impression like the Damme. *c* **1618** MORYSON *Itin.* IV. (1903) 1 Being drawne to the writing hereof..out of a naturall affection to give all the members to this my unlicked whelpe. **1687** DRYDEN *Hind & P.* I. 36 The bloudy Bear, an Independent beast, Unlick'd to form, in groans her hate express'd. **1687** [see CUB *sb.* 3]. **1728** VANBR. & CIB. *Prov. Husb.* II. i, The Son is an unlick'd Whelp, about sixteen. ? **1795** COLERIDGE *After a Walk bef. Supper* 30 A little ape with huge she-bear..: An unlicked mass the one—the other An antic huge. **1845** [see prec.]. **1871** BESANT & RICE *Ready-money Mort.* x, You know, Polly, what an unlicked cub I was when I married you.

**b.** *fig.* Not reduced to form or order; unfinished, unpolished, rude or crude.

**1661** BOYLE *Style of Script.* 185 Confus'd Notions, and Abortive or Unlick'd Conceptions. **1682** DRYDEN *Abs. & Achit.* II. 502 But thou in Clumsy verse, unlickt, unpointed, Hast shamefully defi'd the Lord's Anointed. **1758** WESLEY *Wks.* (1872) II. 457, I rode back..to put the society there (an unlicked mass) into some form. **1773** MME. D'ARBLAY *Early Diary* Oct., I saw..the appearance of unlicked nature in all his motions. **1835** LAMB *Elia* II. Pref., My late friend's writings..are..a sort of unlicked, incondite things.

**2.** Not licked.

**1861** L. L. NOBLE *Icebergs* 296 Poor Pussy,..a creature of backbone and ribs, coated with fur unlicked and scorched. **1895** R. W. CHAMBERS *King in Yellow, Str. Four Winds* i, [The cat's] purple tongue travelled over every unlicked spot ..[of] the saucer.

**Unli·d,** *v.* Also 3 unlide. [UN-² 4. Cf. OE. *unhlidian.*] *trans.* To remove the lid from; to uncover.

*a* **1250** *Ancr. R.* 58 *note* (Trin. MS.), Þe dom is ful grureful & strong o þa þet unliden ham þe put. **1693** R. LYDE *Retaking a Ship* 17, I answered, *alle abau*, for I don't want your help, and then they..unlid the Scuttle and went down. **1821** CLARE *Vill. Minstr.* I. 116 The pitmen often..'neath many a loosen'd block, Unlid coffins in the rock. **1853** C. BRONTË *Villette* xiii, Not a paper but was glanced over, not a little box but was unlidded.

**Unli·dded,** *ppl. a.* [UN-¹ 8.] Not furnished or covered with a lid.

**1819** KEATS *Song Four Faeries* 86 My bare unlidded eyes. **1868** BROWNING *Ring & Bk.* III. 1366 If, with the midday blaze of truth above, The unlidded eye of God awake. **1897** MARY KINGSLEY *W. Africa* 208 These pots..are unglazed, unlidded bowls.

**† Unlie·f,** *a. Obs.* [OE. *unlēof* (UN-¹ 7), = MDu. (Du.) *onlief*, OHG. *unliup, unleub*, MHG. *unliep* (G. *unlieb*), ON. *úljúfr*, Goth. *unliubs.*] Not dear or valued; disliked, distasteful, unpleasant.

*c* **1200** *Trin. Coll. Hom.* 189 Ðe lichame..and þe gost.. fliten and winnen bitwenen hem, þat al þat is on unlef and unqueme, hit is þat oðer iqueme. *c* **1400** *Destr. Troy* 2949 Therfore saintes to seche and to sere halowes,..it ledis vnto laithnes and vnlefe werkes. **1430–40** LYDG. *Bochas* I. i. (1544) 2 Theyr..unware mischeif..It was to them ful uncouth and unlefe. ? *a* **1500** *Chester Pl.* (Shaks. Soc.) I. 42 To all men thou shalbe unleffe,..And over all sette at naughte. **1513** DOUGLAS *Æneid* XII. xiii. 48 Sustenand thus..euery stres, baith lesum and onleif. *a* **1596** SIR T. CHALONER in *Harington's Nugæ Ant.* (1804) II. 379 Nat so unleef, that I shold wysh To be thy Trojan wyfe.

**Unli·felike,** *a.* (UN-¹ 7 c.) **1818** HOGG *Brownie of Bodsbeck* II. iv. 75, I see the chaps are living, an' no that unlife-like, as a body may say. **1881** *Athenæum* 19 Nov. 664/3 The Highland characters of his present story are not unlifelike. **Unli·ftable,** *a.* (UN-¹ 7 b.) [**1775** ASH.] **1818** *Art Preserv. Feet* 93 Facts..not of sufficient importance to form the basis of a huge unliftable quarto. **1854** FERRIER *Inst. Metaph.* 59 Suppose he were to call the latter the unliftable, the imponderable without any qualification. **Unli·fted,** *ppl. a.* (UN-¹ 8.) [**1775** ASH.] **1815** BYRON *Destr. Sennacherib* v, The tents were all silent,..The lances unlifted. **1882** AINGER *Lamb* v. 94 The cloud of domestic anxiety was still unlifted. **Unli·fting,** *ppl. a.* (UN-¹ 10.) **1845** MRS. NORTON *Child of Islands* 131 Veiling dear eyes..With an unlifting veil. **Unli·gable,** *a. rare*—¹. [UN-¹ 7 b.] Incapable of being bound. **1653** R. BAILLIE *Dissuas. Vind.* (1655) 70 Remember what you assert of unligable Proteus.

**Unli·ght,** *a.*¹ [UN-¹ 7 + LIGHT *a.*¹ Cf. ON. *úléttr* (MSw. *olätter*), MHG. *unlîhte.*] Not light (in weight or feeling); heavy.

*c* **1320** *Sir Tristr.* 419 He toke his lod vnliȝt. *Ibid.* 1039 A launce vn-liȝt. *c* **1440** *Ipomydon* 472 He..takith hys leue with hert vnlyght. **1480–1** J. WATTON *Spec. Xristiani* 46 A temple..With walles and pylers here onlyght.

**Unli·ght,** *a.*² *rare*—⁰. [UN-¹ 7 + LIGHT *a.*²] Not bright or clear; dark, obscure. **1570** LEVINS *Manip.* 119 Vnlight, *obscurus.*

**Unli·ght,** *v.* Now *s.w. dial.* [UN-² 9. Cf. dial. *onlight* (1825–).] *intr.* To alight, dismount.

**1623** COCKERAM I, *Degresse*, to vnlight from a Horse. **1796** MRS. M. ROBINSON *Angelina* II. 174 I'm sure you hadn't no companion when you unlighted. **1847** HALLIWELL. **1886–** in Glouc., Som., and Devon glossaries, etc.

**† Unli·ght,** *ppl. a.*¹ *Obs.*—¹ [UN-¹ 8 b + LIGHT *v.*¹ 6.] Not dismounted. *c* **1400** *Destr. Troy* 3446 He raght to the reynes of þe riche qwene,..And led hir vnlight into a large halle. **† Unli·ght,** *ppl. a.*² *Obs.* [UN-¹ 8 b.] = next 1. *a* **1500** *Three 15th Cent. Chron.* (Camden) 104 The torches unlight met hym at the steyre foote,..and so went byfore hym unlyght to the chirche. **1591** SYLVESTER *Du Bartas* I. ii. 670 As lighted Candles doe th' unlight inflame.

**Unli·ghted,** *ppl. a.* [UN-¹ 8.]

**1.** Not lighted; not set on fire; unkindled.

**169.** *Ad Populum Phaleræ* ii, Ask him but whence unlighted Candles came? **1718** PRIOR *Solomon* III. 708 The sacred Wood, which on the Altar lay, Untouch'd, unlighted glows. **1863** THORNBURY *True as Steel* III. 16 The cannonier, rising, unlighted linstock in hand. **1883** D. C. MURRAY *Hearts* xxxiv, With his unlighted pipe between his teeth.

**2.** Not lighted up or illuminated; not furnished with light. Also *fig.*

[**1775** ASH, *Unlighted*,..not directed by light.] **1825** T. HOOK *Sayings* Ser. II. III. 102 The countenance of..Fanny, was the only one unlighted by smiles and happiness. **1855** ARNOLD *Balder Dead* II. 213 Ye..gave me nine unlighted realms to rule. **1886** C. E. PASCOE *London of To-day* (ed. 3) 254 A cell..unlighted except by the door.

**Unli·ghtened,** *ppl. a.* [UN-¹ 8.]

**† 1.** Unenlightened. *Obs.*

**1587** GOLDING *De Mornay* xxii. 389 Princes vnlightened by God, are so desirous of vainglorie. **1627** HAKEWILL *Apol.* 35 Onely this part of [Christendom]..remaines..vnlightned, in the darkenes of ignorance.

**2.** Not lighted up; unbrightened; † unlighted.

**1637–50** ROW *Hist. Kirk* (Maitland Cl.) I. 113 A glorious altar sett vp, with two unlightned candles, and two basins. **1659** W. CHAMBERLAYNE *Pharonnida* III. ii. 19 Whilst she did remain Unlightened with a beam of comfort. **1852** BAILEY *Festus* (ed. 4) 42 Some seem to live, Whose hearts are like those unlightened stars Of the first darkness. **1896** *Westm. Gaz.* 2 May 2/2 Sombre gloom, unlightened save for the red staves of the inverted halberds.

**Unli·ghtsome,** *a.* (UN-¹ 7.)

**1592** R. D. *Hypnerotomachia* 17 This dark vnlightsome place. **1594** CHAPMAN *Shadow of Night* 30 When vnlightsome, vast, and indigest, The formelesse matter of this world did lye. **1667** MILTON *P. L.* VII. 355 Of Celestial Bodies first the Sun A mightie Spheare he fram'd, unlightsom first. **1686** J. S[ERGEANT] *Hist. Monast. Convent.* 167 The place of Election is very unlightsom, as having but a few Lights.

**Unli·gnified,** *ppl. a.* (UN-¹ 8.)

**1875** BENNETT & DYER tr. *Sachs' Bot.* 100 An unlignified gelatinous thickening-mass. **1878** MASTERS *Henfrey's Elem. Bot.* (ed. 3) 414 The cell-walls consist of unlignified cellulose.

**Unli·ke,** *a.* and *sb.* Forms: 3–4 **un-, vnlich,** 4 **-liche** (**-lichy,** 5 **onliche**), **-leche**; 3 **unnlic,** 4 **vnlic, -lijc,** 4–5 **vnlyk,** 5–6 **vnlyke** (6 **-leke**), 3– **unlike.** [ME. *unlīch(e*, *unlīk(e* (UN-¹ 7), corresponding to OE. *ungelic* UNILICHE *a.* Cf. OFris. (NFris.) *unlik*, obs. Du. *onlijk*, MLG. (LG.) *unlīk*, ON. *úlíkr* (Icel. *ólíkur*, MSw. *oliker, olika*, Sw. *olik, olika*, MDa. *ulig, ulige*, Da. and Norw. *ulig*, Norw. *ulik*).]

**1.** Not like or resembling, different from, dissimilar to (some other person or thing).

*c* **1200** ORMIN 16859 Forr all þatt follc let tatt he wass Unnlic all oþerr lede. *a* **1225** *Juliana* 14 Ich am iweddet to an.. þe is unlich him. **1390** GOWER *Conf.* III. 64 He was unlich alle othre there. **1553** ASCHAM *Germany* F 4 He thought it his most honor to be vnlykest such for his gentlenes, which were misliked..for their crueltie. **1596** SHAKS. *Merch. V.* II. ix. 56 How much [thou art] vnlike my hopes and my deseruings! **1634** SIR T. HERBERT *Trav.* 183 [The banana] giues a most delicious..rellish, not much vnlike our choicest Peares. **1676** GLANVILL *Ess.* vi. 30 Those, whose Genius and Ways are so unlike him. **1725** POPE *Odyss.* IX. 221 A form enormous! far unlike the race Of human birth, in stature. **1750** tr. *Leonardus' Mirr. Stones* 112 Some jaspers are not much unlike red porphyry. **1829** JAS. MILL *Hum. Mind* (1869) II. 252 As unlike to any of those..as the sensation of white is unlike the sensations of the seven prismatic colours. **1875** JOWETT *Plato* (ed. 2) I. 401 The philosopher has notions of good and evil unlike those of other men.

**b.** Const. *to*; also (quot. 1873) *from.*

**1340–70** *Alex. & Dind.* 271 Oure lif & oure lawe vnlich is to ȝoure. *c* **1400** *Rom. Rose* 6360 Vnlyk is my word to my dede. *c* **1450** *Myrr. our Ladye* 224 How vnlyke worldely worshyp is vnto gostly ioye. **1531** ELYOT *Gov.* II. xiv, This maner of flatery is mooste unlyke to that whiche is communely used. **1556** OLDE *Antichrist* 116 b, Two heades.., farre unlyke the one to the other. **1670** BAXTER *Cure Ch. Div.* 238 You would shew yourselves much..unliker to Satan the accuser. **1825** SCOTT *Betrothed* xiv, Their very saints are unlike to the saints of any Christian country. **1873** PATER *Stud. Hist. Renaiss.* 80 They were of a spirit as unlike as possible from that of Lorenzo. **1876** GLADSTONE *Glean.* (1879) II. 271 He was very unlike to any other man.

**2.** Not like each other; different, dissimilar.

*c* **1250** *Gen. & Ex.* 1726 Ðoȝ him boren ðes ones bles Vnlike maniȝe and likeles. *c* **1380** *Antechrist* in Todd *Three Treat. Wyclif* (1851) 150 Loke Cristis copborde, and hers; and þei ben ful unlichy. **1565** STAPLETON tr. *Bede's Hist. Ch. Eng.* 25b, The parties there wer farre vnleke of condition. **1605** BACON *Adv. Learn.* II. xxiii. § 29 The unlikest in the worlde; the one being fierce..; the other solemn. **1641** MILTON *Ch. Govt.* I. iv. 13 There can be no possible imitation of Lording over their brethren in regard of their persons altogether unlike. **1704** J. HARRIS *Lex. Techn.* I. s.v., Unlike Quantities and Signs in Algebra. **1807** CRABBE *Par. Reg.* II. 283 How fair these names, how much unlike they look. **1842** FRANCIS *Dict. Arts, Unlike quantities*, in algebra, are such as are expressed by different letters, or different roots or powers of the same letter. **1889** GRETTON *Memory's Harkb.* 125 We may take together two other Judges,..as unlike as the bear and the innate gentleman.

*absol.* **1831** CARLYLE *Sart. Res.* II. v, This approximation of the Like and Unlike. *Ibid.*, In this case of the Like-Unlike.

**b.** *sb. pl.* Dissimilar things or persons.

**1612** W. SCLATER *Sick Souls Salve* 1 He amplifies it in a comparison of unlikes. *a* **1626** — *Comm. Malachy* (1650) 66 It is handled in a plenary comparison of unlikes. **1857** J. PULSFORD *Quiet Hours* 43 Like can reach like, and act upon it, in a way that unlikes cannot.

**3.** † **a.** Differing from others of the kind; incomparable; unusual. *Obs.*

**1390** GOWER *Conf.* II. 275 Bot certes such usure unliche It falleth more unto the riche. **14..** *R. Gloucester's Chron.* (MS. Digby 205) fol. 26 He was in his lyue euer ryȝt ryche Of richesse before al oþer he was vnliche.

**b.** Differing from, dissimilar to, the thing or person in question. Also *absol.*

c 1374 CHAUCER *Boeth.* IV. vi. (1868) 138 Ne it ne is nat an vnlyke miracle to hem þat ne knowen it nat. 1542 UDALL *Erasm. Apoph.* 5 Nor a muche vnlyke aunswere dyd Wylliam, late archebishop of Canterbury, .. gyue vnto me. 1595 DANIEL *Civ. Wars* v. lxxxii, He saw prepard, against his side, Both vnlike fortune, and vnequall force. 1667 MILTON *P. L.* VI. 517 Part hidd'n veins diggd up (nor hath this Earth Entrails unlike) of Mineral and Stone. 1847 HELPS *Friends in C.* Ser. I. I. ix. 166 Not only like likes like, but unlike likes unlike. 1865 SWINBURNE *Atalanta* 620 A god Faultless; whom I that love not, being unlike, Fear, and give honour. 1877 E. R. CONDER *Bas. Faith* ii. 81 Awaiting the presence of unlike atoms to call them forth in turn.

**c.** *sb.* A person differing from another or others.

13.. *Sir Beues* (A.) 1099 Her is..min vnliche, Brademond king, þat is so riche. [Cf. UNILICHE *sb.*] 1875 JOWETT *Plato* (ed. 2) III. 219 The just does not desire more than his like but more than his unlike. 1896 *Pop. Sci. Monthly* Feb. 494 As long as it remains a stranger and an unlike.

**4.** Presenting points of difference or dissimilarity; not uniform or even; unequal.

c 1375 *Cursor M.* 7917 (Fairf.), Þer was wonande þat was vn-like ij men a pouer and a rike. 1387 TREVISA *Higden* (Rolls) VI. 289 Þere was unleche noumbre of array of knyȝtes, for aȝenst an hondred .. come a þowsand. 1535 COVERDALE *Ecclus.* xxvi. 7 Whan an vnlike pare of oxen must drawe together. c 1550 H. LLOYD *Treasury of Health* b 5 If the water do appeare vnlike of substance. 1642 J. EATON *Honey-c. Free Justif.* 261 That unlike likenesse betweene Adam and Christ, which the Apostle speaks of, Rom. 5. 1645 MILTON *Tetrach.* 9 Where the different sexe in most resembling unlikenes, and most unlike resemblance, cannot but please best.

**5.** Unlikely, improbable. Now *dial.* or *arch.*

**a.** With subordinate clause.

c 1400 *Destr. Troy.* 565 The perlouse pointtes þat passe you behoues, Hit is vnlike any lede with his liffe pas. 1400–10 CLANVOWE *Cuckow & Night.* ix, Hit is vnlyk for to be That eny herte shulde slepy be [etc.]. 1535 CROMWELL in Merriman *Life & Lett.* (1902) I. 413 It is not vnlike but that the saide Duke hathe ben deceyued. 1577 HANMER *Anc. Eccl. Hist.* (1663) 235 Neither is it unlike, but that these circumstances might be. 1610 HEALEY *St. Aug. Citie of God, Vives' Comm.* VIII. xi. 317 It is vnlike that so sharpe a wit..found not the difference and multitude of things. 1729 T. INNES *Crit. Essay* (1879) 230 In process of time..it is not unlike there might come..new colonies from Spain. 1795 SOUTHEY *Joan of Arc* III. 401 Whether so [it is] not unlike Heaven might vouchsafe its gracious miracle. a 1905 in *Eng. Dial. Dict.* (Yks., Warw.).

**b.** With inf.

1400–10 [see a]. 1538 HENRY VIII in *Wyatt's Wks.* (1816) II. 498 Unjust..demands, and unlike to proceed out of a willing heart to conclude. 1584 R. SCOT *Discov. Witchcr.* III. xviii. 54 Being through age unlike to live one whole yeare. 1626 in Rushw. *Hist. Coll.* (1659) I. 286 He thought the Match very unlike to be effected. 1655 EARL ORRERY *Parthen.* I. I. 26 This Arabian was not altogether unlike to escape unpunished. 1665 BOYLE *Occas. Refl.* I. iii. 168 Blessings, that I do not so much as know of, and which consequently I am very unlike particularly to acknowledge.

†**c.** Without likelihood *of* something. *Obs.*—[1]

1559 *Mirr. Mag., Fall R. Tresilian* xiv, Thus all went to wracke vnlyke of remedie.

**Unli·ke,** *adv.* Forms: 4–5 vnliche, 4 onlyche; 4–7 vnlike (5 -lyk, 6 -lyke), 7, 9 unlike. [UN-[1] 11 b. Cf. UNILICHE *adv.*]

†**1. a.** Unevenly, unequally; in a higher or lower degree. *Obs.*

a 1300 *Fragm. Seven Sins* 55 in *E.E.P.* (1862) 20 Worldis wel fallip vnliche, and noȝt euch man ilich. 1390 GOWER *Conf.* III. 89 Theologie in such a wise Of hih science and hih aprise Above alle othre stant unlike. c 1425 WYNTOUN *Cron.* VIII. xvi. 2594 Na man..euer couþ tell..A maire commendable memore, As þai did of þis pure kinrik, In þat batall bodin vnlike.

†**b.** Incomparably. *Obs.*

14.. *R. Gloucester's Chron.* (MS. Digby 205) fol. 19 b, Cloten hadde most riȝte to þis kyngeryche But þe oþere were strenger & rycher vnliche [*v.r.* onlyche]. c 1425 *Cursor M.* 5325 (Trin.), Þe kyng lete write lettres ȝare To gider alle..Þe beste in þat londe vnliche.

**2.** †**a.** Differently, diversely. Also const. *to.*

1526 *Pilgr. Perf.* (W. de W. 1531) 5 Whiche the Romayns vsed, but vnlyke to vs. 1552 HULOET, Vnlyke or in a diuers fashyon, *dissimiliter*. 1595 in *Cath. Rec. Soc. Publ.* V. 350 Some tyme yt pleaseth God to reveale his wille..by dreames, as He did to Joseph, Pharo, and others, and here not unlike to His designed martyr.

**b.** In a manner differing from (that of a specified person).

1593 SHAKS. *2 Hen. VI*, I. i. 189 Oft haue I seene the haughty Cardinall..demeane himselfe Vnlike the Ruler of a Common-weale. 1619 SIR A. GORGES tr. *Bacon's De Sap. Vet.* 82 This Loue..directing his pace..by that which it perceaues neerest, not vnlike blind men that goe by feeling. 1634 SIR T. HERBERT *Trav.* 14 A little haire before, bauld else-where, not vnlike occasion. 1818 SCOTT *Br. Lamm.* xxi, The Master has treated me unlike a gentleman. 1841 W. SPALDING *Italy & It. Isl.* II. 387 They stand apart from all the others, because, unlike these, they applied [etc.].

†**3.** Improbably; unlikely. *Obs.*

a 1548 HALL *Chron., Hen. V*, 67 b, Some say that he was therto stirred..by the dolphyn (and not vnlike). 1596 SPENSER *F. Q.* v. v. 38 And, though (vnlike) they should for euer last, Yet in my truthes assurance I rest fixed fast.

†**Unli·ke,** *v.*[1] *Obs. rare.* [UN-[1] 14.] **a.** *intr.* To become displeased. **b.** *trans.* To displease.

c 1275 LAY. 3266 Leir king was wel ipaid and eft onlikede. c 1380 WYCLIF *Sel. Wks.* II. 267 He haþ sorwe of þe synne, bi resoun þat it unlikiþ God.

**Unli·ke,** *v.*[2] *rare.* [UN-[2] 7.] *intr.* To give up liking; to cease to like.

1761 MRS. F. SHERIDAN *Sidney Bidulph* I. 183 My heart is not in a disposition to love... I cannot compel it to like and unlike, and like anew at pleasure.

**Unli·k(e)able,** *a.* (UN-[1] 7 b.) 1841 L. HUNT *Seer* II. (1864) 1 Without trying to render it unlikeable from its inferiority. 1888 *Athenæum* 31 March 396/1 There are touches about her that..make her unlikable.

**Unli·ked,** *ppl. a.* (UN-[1] 8, 8 c.)

1561 B. GOOGE *Palingenius' Zodiac Life* I. A j b, Not worse vnliked now shal I be, yf that thou wylt me blesse. 1620 BP. HALL *Hon. Marr. Clergy* I. xxvii. (1628) 769 That more vnliked epistle which Ignatius wrote to Saint John. 1641 (*title*), An Aprovd Answer to the partiall and unlikt of Lord Digbies Speech to the Bill of Attainder.

**Unli·kelihood.** [UN-[1] 12. Cf. UNLIKELY *a.*, and MDa. *uligelighed.*]

†**1.** Unlikeness, dissimilarity, discrepancy. *Obs.*

1483 CAXTON *Gold. Leg.* 273/1, I fond myself right fer fro the in a Regyon of unlykelyhode [L. *dissimilitudinis*]. 1550 THOMAS *Ital. Dict., Disaguaglianza*, vnseemelinesse, vnlikelyhoode, or the difference that is betwene the comparison of one thyng to an other. 1564 *Brief Exam.* 20 b, Euery man..may see a great vnlikelyhood betwixt those tymes and ours. 1613 PURCHAS *Pilgrimage* (1614) 573 By which likenesse in name great confusion and vnlikelihoods haue happened in Historie.

**2.** The state or fact of being unlikely; improbability.

1548 UDALL, etc. *Erasm. Par. John* xix. 109 So muche vnlikelyhoode was it, that the felowship of punishement should defyle hym. 1598 R. BERNARD tr. *Terence, Andria* II. ii, Hauing gathered by sundrie signes and coniectures the vnlikelihood of the marriage. 1646 EARL MONM. tr. *Biondi's Civil Wars* IX. 199 By the Unlikelyhood and Impossibility that he should escape the hands of a Crafty.. Uncle. 1695 J. EDWARDS *Perfect. Script.* 238 There was no unlikelihood of the thing. 1767 MRS. DELANY *Life & Corr.* Ser. II. (1862) I. 116 Knowing the unlikelihood of your being to return to us. 1794 PALEY *Evid.* II. viii, The extreme unlikelihood that such men should engage in such a measure. 1860 MISS YONGE *Stokesley Secr.* xii, The exceeding unlikelihood of a girl like Elizabeth committing .. a theft. 1877 FREEMAN *Norm. Conq.* I. vi. 462 Statements which have no inherent unlikelihood in them.

**b.** With *a* and pl. An improbable occurrence, fact, statement, etc.

a 1550 LELAND *Itin.* (1769) II. 35 Dyvers Brethren dyed.., and by a great vnlykelihod al the Landes descendid to.. the Yonggest of the Brethren. 1561 DAUS tr. *Bullinger on Apoc.* (1573) 2, I will shew the lykelyhodes and the vnlykelyhodes. 1647 JER. TAYLOR *Lib. Proph.* ii. 41 The rarest mixture..of unlikelihoods that I have observed. 1682 LUTTRELL *Brief Rel.* (1857) I. 188 By the severall contradictions and unlikelyhoods in his evidence. 1738 G. LILLO *Marina* III. ii, What strange unlikelihood assaults my mind! 1814 SOUTHEY *Roderick* XII. 14, I will believe that we have days in store Of hope,..Yea, maugre all unlikelihoods,..of peace. 1862 LEVER *Barrington* xv, He hesitated how to measure an unlikelyhood.

**Unli·keliness.** [UN-[1] 12. Cf. prec. and next.]

†**1.** Unsuitableness. *Obs.*

c 1374 CHAUCER *Troylus* I. 16 For I þat god of loues seruantz serue Ne dar to loue for myn vnliklynesse.

†**2.** Unseemliness, unbecomingness. *Obs.*

1456 SIR G. HAYE *Law Arms* (S.T.S.) 190 Nevertheles and he saw..him mak grete repaire till his hous, and unlyklynes, he mycht mak him..exhortacioun to nocht mak sik unlikly repaire. 1685 H. MORE *Paralip. Prophet.* xxxiv. 306 What unlikeliness or Indecorum is it, that Proclamation be made who he is, that shall..[open] the Book?

†**3.** Dissimilarity, discrepancy. *Obs.*

1561 T. NORTON *Calvin's Inst.* II. 143 It shall be sufficient that we wey the wordes of one of them, to attain the meaning of them both. Albeit, there is some vnlikelinesse betwene them. 1604 T. WRIGHT *Passions* v. iv. 189 Likelinesse or vnlikelinesse are also relatives, and consequently belong to this same predicament. c 1620 BP. HALL *Contempl., N. T.* II. ii, Neither was there more unlikelinesse in their disposition and cariage, than similitude in their function. 1730 BAILEY (fol.), *Dissimilitude*, unlikeliness.

**4.** Unlikelihood, improbability.

1614 RALEIGH *Hist. World* III. vii. § 4. 82 Whether Themistocles perceiued much vnlikelinesse of good successe [etc.]. 1690 LOCKE *Human Understanding* IV. xv. § 2. 332 There being degrees herein, from the very neighbourhood of Certainty and Evidence, quite down to Improbability and Unlikeliness. 1841 GEN. P. THOMPSON *Exerc.* (1842) VI. 160 The unlikeliness that he should get what he asked for. 1881 SAINTSBURY *Dryden* 72 The unlikeliness of his ever having been a very fervent Roundhead.

**Unli·kely,** *a.* (and *sb.*). [UN-[1] 7. Cf. ON. *úlíkligr* (Icel. *ólíklegur*, MSw. *olikliker*, Sw. *oliklig*, MDa. *uligelig*, Norw. *ulikleg*).]

**1.** Not likely to occur or come to pass; improbable in respect of occurrence.

1375 BARBOUR *Bruce* IX. 670 He oft full vnlikly thing Brocht rycht weill to full gud ending. 1488 *Cely Papers* (Camden) 169 They of Bruges sayth all schall be well schorttly but hytt ys onlyckly. 1513 DOUGLAS *Æneid* XI. viii. 119 Tyme..Reducit hes full mony onlikly thyng To bettir fyne than was thair begynning. a 1533 LD. BERNERS *Gold. Bk. M. Aurel.* xxxvi. (1536) R ii, The more yll they vtter, the more vnlykely is the redres therof ageyn. c 1580 *Bugbears* I. ii. 121 Why is it a thing vnpossyble or vnlikelie that sprites wil deall withe gold? 1642 D. ROGERS *Naaman* 200 Thus Papists conceiue it an unlikelyer thing, that [etc.]. 1692 BENTLEY *Boyle Lect.* 218 Which makes it ..more improbable, that they should interfere..even in the last and unlikeliest instance. 1861 PALEY *Æschylus* (ed. 2) *Supplices* 979 *note*, However, κἄωρα is an unlikely crasis.

**b.** Not likely to be true or correct; improbable in respect of fact.

1592 SHAKS. *Ven. & Ad.* 989 The one doth flatter thee in thoughts unlikely, In likely thoughts the other kills thee quickly. 1613 PURCHAS *Pilgrimage* (1614) 595 Josephus and Eusebius thinke them to bee the Israelites, which is vnlikely. 1673 DRYDEN *Marr. à la Mode* III. i, They tell, for news, such unlikely stories! 1712 J. JAMES tr. *Le Blond's Gardening* 141 An Opinion very unlikely, to believe Trees have their Male and Female. 1780 *Mirror* No. 73, If this..be the effect of habit, which is not unlikely. 1871 FREEMAN *Norm. Conq.* IV. xviii. 231 The presence of Matilda..at such a time is in itself unlikely.

**c.** Not likely, in various implications.

1535 COVERDALE *Ecclus.* xi. 6 Many tyrauntes haue bene fayne to syt downe vpon the earth, & ye vnlickly hath worne ye crowne. 1593 *Sidney's Arcadia* IV. ¶ 1 That by unlikeliest meanes greatest matters may come to conclusion. 1622 DONNE *Serm.* 25 A farre vnlikelier sort of people, then any of these. 1656 COWLEY *Davideis* IV. 828 Nor would ill Fate that meant me to surprise, Come cloath'd in so unlikely a Disguise. 1694 ATTERBURY *Serm. Isaiah lx.* 22 14 This..was an Unlikely way of gaining Proselytes. 1749 LAVINGTON *Enthus. Meth. & Papists* II. (1754) 129 He cures Diseases..with unlikely Remedies. 1774 G. WHITE *Selborne* lxi, A succession [of swifts] still haunts the same unlikely roofs. 1847 C. BRONTË *J. Eyre* xxxiv, That a poor lad was come, at that unlikely time, to fetch Mr. Rivers. 1855 A. J. MORRIS *Words for Heart & Life* iii. 52 God is in the habit of employing unlikely instruments. 1898 'MERRIMAN' *Roden's Corner* ii, Cases where brilliant men have failed and unlikely ones have covered themselves with..glory.

*Comb.* 1858 FABER *Spir. Confer.* (1870) 131 Those vices of which the unlikeliest-looking souls are often the likeliest to be guilty.

**d.** *sb.* An unlikely person.

1867 LATHAM *Black & White* 98 He goes round with his.. papers, dealing one to each passenger likely or unlikely (because the unlikelies would be offended if omitted).

**2.** With complement: **a.** With *to* and inf. (active or passive).

1395 PURVEY *Remonstr.* (1851) 84 The noueltees of this Innocent ben vnlicli to be sothe. 1412–20 LYDG. *Chron. Troy* IV. 23 Vnlikly [it was] euere vs to han had victorie. c 1450 *Mirk's Festial* 140 Ierusalem..was þe strengest cyte yn all þe world, and vnlykly forto haue ben wonon. 1611 FLORIO, *Inaccadeuole*, vnlikely to chance or befall. 1658 OSBORNE *Adv. Son* Wks. (1673) 112 The not unlikeliest to know Truth. 1711 STEELE *Spect.* No. 143 ¶ 1 It will be much more unlikely for us to be well-pleased. 1764 *Museum Rust.* IV. 11 Salt-petre Bay, which is not unlikely to have been so denominated from salt-petre there. 1842 LOUDON *Suburban Hort.* 377 They are the most unlikely to become fruit-buds. 1890 'R. BOLDREWOOD' *Col. Reformer* (1891) 216 He was as unlikely as Grahame to take..to the improvement of the common people.

**b.** With *that* and clause.

1412–20 LYDG. *Chron. Troy* IV. 3243 For now, allas! vnlikly is þat we Shal euere wynne..þis cite. 1722 WOLLASTON *Relig. Nat.* v. (1724) 82 Make him understand how unlikely a thing it is, that they should be placed there only to adorn..a canopy over our heads. 1855 *Orr's Circ. Sci., Inorg. Nat.* 226 It is not unlikely that the gas thus formed occupies the place of water. 1884 THOMPSON *Tumours of Bladder* 55 It is not unlikely that some of these may be congenital.

†**3.** Unsuitable, unsuited; not fit or proper. *Obs.*

c 1386 CHAUCER *Merch. T.* 936 That whan I considere youre beautee, And ther with al the vnlikly elde of me, I may nat certes..Forbere to been out of youre compaignye. c 1440 CAPGRAVE *Life St. Kath.* III. 782 His clothis to his woordis arn ful onlykly. 1470–85 MALORY *Arthur* II. viii. 84 Thou art a boystous man and an vnlykely to telle of suche dedes. 1571 *Southampton Court Leet Rec.* (1905) I. 77 Such as arre..unlyklye and unmeete men to serve for that poorpose. 1588 *Nottingham Rec.* LV. 221 Yt ys an onlykelye house for suche one to dwelle there.

**b.** Unseemly, unbecoming; not acceptable or agreeable; objectionable, distasteful. *Obs.* exc. *dial.*

1456 [see UNLIKELINESS 2]. c 1470 HENRY *Wallace* II. 263 On a caar wnlikly thai him cast. a 1586 SIDNEY *Arcadia* II. ii. (1912) 153 For a very unlikely envie she hath stumbled upon, against the Princesses.. beautie. 1590 *Serpent of Devis.* B j/2 The most unlikely person and the most wretch that in any countrye might be found. 1725 RAMSAY *Gentle Sheph.* I. i. 24 Yet I am tall, and as weel built as thee, Nor mair unlikely to a lass's eye. 1889 *N. W. Linc. Gloss.* 586 *Unlikely*, bad, displeasing.

†**c.** Unpromising; poor in quality or condition.

1560 ROLLAND *Seven Sages* 46 This auld tre .. fra the ȝoung takis all substance and air; .. Sa the ȝoung plant is sa vnliklie maid. a 1648 LD. HERBERT *Hen. VIII* (1683) 522 That Forests..should be driven once in the year, and unlikely Tits in them to be killed.

**Unli·kely,** *adv.* [UN-[1] 11: cf. prec. and MSw. *olíklika.*] Improbably.

c 1449 PECOCK *Repr.* III. xiii. 361 The oon bifore seid epistle putt and ascryued vnlikeli to Constantyn. 1641 MILTON *Ch. Govt.* I. vii. 40 [He] may fall not unlikely sometimes..into an uncouth opinion. 1716 POPE *Lett.* (1737) I. 146 The pleasures..must undoubtedly be of a nobler kind, and (not unlikely) may proceed from the discoveries each shall communicate to another, of God and of nature. 1830 SOUTHEY in *Corr. w. C. Bowles* (1881) 199 This provides also (most unlikely) in case of his half-craziness again becoming whole-craziness. 1867 FREEMAN *Norm. Conq.* I. v. 298 The church..may, not unlikely, have been raised.. to commemorate the event.

†**Unli·ken,** *v. Obs.* [UN-[2] 6 a. Cf. MDu. *ontliken.*] *trans.* To dissemble. 1382 WYCLIF *1 Kings* xiv. 5 Whanne she was comen yn, and hadde vnlikned hire self to be that she was. **Unli·kenable,** *a.* (UN-[1] 7 b.) 1845 BAILEY *Festus* (ed. 2) 46 The earth .. Is not so like the unlikenable One As thou.

**Unli·keness.** [UN-[1] 12.]

†**1.** Strangeness. *Obs.*

*c* **1230** *Hali Meid.* 13, I þis world þat is icleopet lond of unlicnesse. *a* **1380** *St. Augustin* 224 in Horstm. *Altengl. Leg.* (1878) 65/2, I fond fro þe þat fer I was, As in a kyngdam of vnlikenes.

**2.** The quality of being unlike; want of likeness or resemblance; dissimilarity.

*c* **1380** WYCLIF *Serm.* Sel. Wks. II. 227 For noo drede licknesse of breþeren causiþ love among hem, and unliknesse is cause of discord. **1398** TREVISA *Barth. De P. R.* II. xii. (1495) c j/1 No violence of tyrannye bendyth theym to oppresse.. the nether angellis. Therfore Denys sayth that they vse theyr lordshypp wyth vnlyknesse of tyrannye. **1533** MORE *Debell. Salem* Wks. 998/2 The causes that he laieth of dyssimilitude & vnlikenes, be twene the witnesses. **1548** UDALL *Erasmus Par. Matt.* v. 37 The unlikenes of manners declareth and argueth a bastarde. **1634** CANNE *Necess. Separ.* (1849) 89 Mark.. what they speak here, touching their likeness and unlikeness with the papists. **1645** MILTON *Tetrach.* 9 Where the different sexe in most resembling unlikenes, and most unlike resemblance cannot but please best. **1709** *Brit. Apollo* II. Supernum. No. 1. 2/1 We meet with some Characters of Unlikeness in this Similitude. **1772** WESLEY *Jrnl.* 11 Feb. (1827) III. 440 For ..unlikeness to all the world beside,..the writer is without a rival! **1846** TRENCH *Mirac.* xxv. (1862) 359 There are.. points of unlikeness in the two miracles. **1853** KINGSLEY *Hypatia* xxi, It was..strange in its utter unlikeness to any teaching..which he had ever heard before. **1875** WHITNEY *Life Lang.* ix. 173 We know of no other way in which this likeness in unlikeness can be brought about.

**b.** With *a* and pl. An instance of dissimilarity or want of resemblance.

**1662** SOUTH *Serm.* (1679) 116 As great an unlikeness, as between St. Pauls a Cathedral, and St. Pauls a Stable. **1667** *Phil. Trans.* II. 611 These two unlikenesses I mention together. **1718** *Freethinker* No. 155 (1733) 240 Such Unlikenesses as, by their Subtility, escape the Observation of Judgments less acute. **1746** W. HORSLEY *Fool* (1748) I. 33 They are the Beau and the Belle; and, if I may be understood in thus speaking, are a similar Unlikeness. **1828** SOUTHEY *Epist. to A. Cunningham* 370, I recognise all these unlikenesses, Spurious abominations though they be. **1879** SIR G. CAMPBELL *Black & White* 22 The likenesses are much more numerous and much more prominent than the unlikenesses.

**3.** A bad or poor likeness.

**1729** T. COOKE *Tales, &c.* 127 His ample Shield..On which th' Unlikeness of the Greek appears. **1843** LONGF. in *Life* (1891) II. 4 In the next number is an *un*-likeness of me,..in a morning-gown.

†**Unli·kening,** *ppl. a. Obs.*⁻¹ [UN-¹ 10.] Differing. *c* **1430** *Pilgr. Lyf Manhode* I. cxxxii. (1869) 70 These ben thinges gretliche unliknynge and discordinge.

**Unli·king,** *vbl. sb.* [UN-¹ 13] Want of liking; dislike; † dissatisfaction.

**1398** TREVISA *Barth. De P. R.* v. xxxvi. (Bodl. MS.), Þe making of he hert..is þe..wel of meuyng and liking [and] of alle vnliking. *c* **1400** *Cato's Morals* in *Cursor M.* App. iv. 242 Quen þou has of þi þing þorou hap vnliking.. behalde þou on oþer men. **1876** MRS. WHITNEY *Sights & Ins.* II. xxiii. 512 A gradual liking that was at first almost unliking. **1886** D. C. MURRAY *First Person Sing.* xxv, Angela had..a genuine unliking for O'Rourke.

†**Unli·king,** *ppl. a. Obs.* [UN-¹ 10.] Unpleasant, disagreeable.

**1393** LANGL. *P. Pl.* C. VIII. 23 Ich hadde leuere..lacke men, and lykne hem in vnlykynge manere, Þan al þat euere Marc made. *a* **1470** H. PARKER *Dives & Pauper* (W. de W. 1496) XII. v. 213/1 Yf one corde..in the harpe be broke,.. all the songe..shall be unlykynge to all that here it. ? *a* **1500** *Chester Pl.* (Shaks. Soc.) I. 83 Lorde, I muste doe thy byddinge, Though yt be to me unlikinge. *c* **1520** SKELTON *Magnyf.* 1958, I am lowsy and vnlykynge and full of scurffe. **1570** LEVINS *Manip.* 137 Vnliking, *displicitus*.

**Unli·mb,** *v.* [UN-² 4.] *trans.* To dismember. **1694** MOTTEUX *Rabelais* IV. liii. 208 Batter 'em, burst 'em, quarter 'em, unlimb 'em,..these wicked Heretics. **1869** J. CONINGTON *Horace, Sat.* (1874) 17 Still The bard remains, unlimb him as you will. **Unli·mber,** *a.* (UN-¹ 7.) *a* **1639** WOTTON *Charac. F. di Medici* in *Reliq.* (1651) 364 To which temper more septentrionall unlimber Nations have not yet bent themselves.

**Unli·mber,** *v.* [UN-² 5.]

**1.** *Mil.* To free (a gun) from the limber, by detaching and withdrawing this, preparatory to bringing the gun into action.

**1802** JAMES *Milit. Dict.* s.v. *Limber*, A two-wheel carriage ..taken off..; which is called unlimbering the guns. **1839** F. A. GRIFFITHS *Artill. Man.* 93 Square can only be formed when..both guns and waggons are unlimbered. **1879** C. R. LOW *Jrnl. General Abbott* ii. 146 Abbott..unlimbered the 24-pounder howitzer.

*fig.* **1864** TREVELYAN *Compet. Wallah* (1866) 272 Then are the 'English name', and the 'development of the resources of India', unlimbered, and trundled out to overawe the.. magistrates.

**b.** *absol.* To perform the operation of detaching and withdrawing the limber.

**1828** SPEARMAN *Brit. Gunner* (ed. 2) 177 Unlimbering, or Coming into Action. **1875** CLERY *Min. Tact.* xi. 136 A H. A. battery..unlimbered and came into action.

*transf.* **1888** *Harper's Mag.* Sept. 555/1 A travelling band which [was]..in the second-class car, and which goodnaturedly unlimbered at the stations.

**2.** To detach and withdraw the front-wheels of (a boat-carriage).

**1853** DOUGLAS *Milit. Bridges* (ed. 3) 92 To launch the bateau, the carriage is placed with the pole towards the river, and unlimbered: by this means an inclined plane is formed.

**Unli·me,** *v.* [UN-² 3. Cf. Flem. *ontlijmen* 'deglutinare' (Kilian), G. *entleimen.*]

†**1.** *trans.* To detach, dissever. *Obs.*⁻¹

**1225** *Ancr. R.* 256 Þet he wot ful wel: & for þi he is umbe ..uorte unlimen ou mid wreððe. [**1648** HEXHAM II, *Ontlijmen*, to Vnglue, or to Vnlime.]

**2.** To free (dressed hides) from lime.

**1885** *Harper's Mag.* Jan. 275/2 This washing in warm water is a preparation for 'drenching', the first process of unliming. **1888** *Pop. Sci. Monthly* Dec. 287 The process of unliming hides and skins.

**Unli·med,** *ppl. a.* [UN-¹ 8. Cf. Du. *ongelijmd*, G. *ungeleimt.*]

**1.** Not smeared or clogged with bird-lime. In quots. *fig.*

**1622** S. WARD *Christ All in All* (1627) 36 Christ, whom hee longed to bee with, and would now with vnlimed and vnentangled wings flye vnto. *a* **1672** STERRY *Freed. Will* (1675) 137 It keeps these wings unlimed..by the filth or guilt of fleshly lusts.

**2.** Not dressed or treated with lime.

**1756** F. HOME *Exper. Bleaching* 215 This makes limed cloth easily distinguishable from unlimed. **1801** *Farmer's Mag.* Nov. 478 As the grain must have lain in the ground for two years, and none was observed in the unlimed part.

**Unli·mitable,** *a.* [UN-¹ 7 b, 5 b.] Incapable of being limited; illimitable.

In frequent use from *c* 1610 to *c* 1650.

**1604** MARSTON *Malcontent* I. vi, O vnlimitable impudencie! **1690** LOCKE *Govt.* I. ii. (1694) 9 An Absolute, Arbitrary, Unlimited, and Unlimitable Power. **1716** M. DAVIES *Athen. Brit.* III. *Diss. Drama* 33 In talking so much..of other People's unlimitable Liberty of Thinking and Worshipping.

**Unli·mited,** *ppl. a.* [UN-¹ 8.]

**1.** Not limited or restricted in amount, extent, or degree: **a.** Of power or authority, a rule, etc.

*c* **1445** PECOCK *Donet* 129 Which gouernaunce in it silf is vnlimited and vnassigned to eny special tyme. *a* **1586** SIDNEY *Arcadia* III. i. (1912) 355 It must be an unlimited Monarchy. *Ibid.* xx. 472, I know thy power is not unlimited. **1644** HUNTON *Vind. Treat. Monarchy* v. 45 That the Power of the Monarch in this Frame is not unlimited. **1690** [see prec.]. **1717** LADY M. W. MONTAGU *Let. to C'tess of Bristol* 1 April, The unlimited power of these fellows. **1777** COOK *Third Voyage* II. xi. (1784) I. 406 The power of the king is unlimited. *a* **1850** CALHOUN *Wks.* (1874) III. 234 Money is not only the sinew of war, but of politics, over which..it exercises almost unlimited control. *Ibid.* VI. 133 A government of unlimited powers.

**b.** In other applications.

*a* **1586** SIDNEY *Arcadia* III. iv. (1912) 371 All such, whom.. youth-like mindes did fill with unlimited desires. **1602** MARSTON *Antonio's Rev.* III. ii, The curse of Heaven raines In plagues unlimited through all his daies. **1647** CLARENDON *Hist. Reb.* I. § 18 The expences of the Court..[were] vast, and unlimited by the old good rules of economy. *a* **1704** T. BROWN *Praise Drunken.* Wks. 1730 I. 35 Their highest excellency consists in having their will unlimited by any superior power. **1782** PRIESTLEY *Corrupt. Chr.* I. II. 158 The absolute and unlimited declarations of the divine mercy. **1846** MRS. MARSH *Father Darcy* II. 149 My confidence in his talents and energy is unlimited. **1878** JEVONS *Prim. Pol. Econ.* 19 We never want an unlimited quantity of anything.

*transf.* **1837** CARLYLE *Fr. Rev.* III. II. vi, So violent..are the Limited Patriots and the Unlimited.

**2.** Not limited in number.

**1665** SIR T. HERBERT *Trav.* (1677) 308 Four Wives the Law tolerates, Concubines are unlimited.

**3.** *Math.* (See quots.)

**1704** J. HARRIS *Lex. Techn.* I. s.v., Unlimited Problem.. is such a Problem in Mathematicks, as is capable of Infinite Solutions. **1843** *Penny Cycl.* XXVI. 31/1 *Unlimited*,..is frequently used by mathematical writers, in the same manner as *Indefinite*, to avoid the entrance of the word *Infinite*. It is also used to describe a problem which may have an infinite number of answers, and which is called an unlimited problem.

**Unli·mitedly,** *adv.* [UN-¹ 11: cf. prec.] Without limitation.

**1611** FLORIO, *Sterminatamente*,..infinitely, vnlimitedly. *a* **1639** W. WHATELEY *Prototypes* II. xxvi. (1640) 81 It is an easie thing for inferiours to obey their Governours..a little too unlimitedly. *a* **1680** CORBET *Non-conf. Plea* (1683) 19 The said promise must be understood either unlimitedly, or with limitation. *a* **1716** BLACKALL *Wks.* (1723) I. 226 If this had been express'd as universally and unlimitedly. **1796** BURNEY *Mem. Metastasio* I. 238 A great..prince, who deigns to be so unlimitedly my protector. **1836** *New Monthly Mag.* XLVIII. 409 His Grace is unlimitedly hospitable. **1891** MEREDITH *One of our Conq.* III. xix. 171 He feels the publishers pouring their gallons through it unlimitedly.

**Unli·mitedness.** [UN-¹ 12.] The fact of being unlimited; absence of limitation.

**1641** FALKLAND in Marriott *Life & Times* (1908) 204 This unlimitednesse and independence is onely in spirituall things. *a* **1664** M. FRANK *Serm.* (1672) 421 The unlimittednesse of His power. **1710** A. B. *Answ. to Argts. in Bp. Oxford's Sp. Resistance* 13 The unlimitedness of our Obedience. **1796** LAMB *Lett.* (1888) I. 41 Omnipresence is an attribute the very essence of which is unlimitedness. **1904** A. C. FRASER *Biog. Philos.* ii. 60 It was impossible to believe either space or time limited: it was equally impossible to understand their unlimitedness.

**Unli·ne,** *v.*¹ [UN-² 4.]

**1.** *trans.* To divest (a garment, etc.) of lining.

**1606** J. DAVIES (Heref.) *Bien Venu* Wks. (Grosart) I. 6/2 Two Kings thus met, make Kingdomes richly thriue, Though it vnlines their Purse with wearing much. **1611** COTGR., *Desdoubler*, to vnlyne; or take the lynings out of a garment.

**2.** *intr.* To separate as a lining.

**1848** LINDLEY *Introd. Bot.* (ed. 4) I. 331 They all pass out of each other (*désemboîtent*); they all unline.

**Unli·ne,** *v.*² (UN-² 4 b + LINE *v.*³)

**1598** MARSTON *Sco. Villanie* I. iv, To morrow doth Luxurio promise me, He will vnline himselfe from bitchery.

**Unli·neal,** *a.* (UN-¹ 7.)

**1593** NASHE *Strange Newes* H 4, The vnlineall vsurper of iudgement from all his true owners. **1605** SHAKS. *Macb.* III. i. 63 They..put a barren Scepter in my Gripe, Thence to be wrencht with an vnlineall Hand. **1832** [R. CATTERMOLE] *Beckett*, etc. 170 The Men of England.. From her last Despot wrung The sceptre,..to grace A wiser nor unlineal race. **1884** *N. & Q.* 6 Oct. 264 The ancient manor house.. has long since passed into unlineal hands.

**Unli·ned,** *ppl. a.*¹ [UN-¹ 8 + LINE *v.*¹] Not furnished with a lining.

In very frequent use from *c* 1890.

**1521** in *Test. Ebor.* (Surtees) VI. 4 My unlynded gowne. *a* **1599** SPENSER *F. Q.* VII. vii. 29 Dight In a thin silken cassock coloured greene, That was vnlyned all. **1630** J. TAYLOR (Water P.) *Trav.* Wks. III. 89/1 The men..are clad in thin buckeram, vnlined. **1655** tr. *Sorel's Com. Hist. Francion* XI. 19 Although it was not unfashionable to have a Cloak unlined as was theirs. **1861** *Eng. Wom. Dom. Mag.* III. 118/2 Stiff muslin petticoats..are very suitable for wearing with..unlined silk dresses. **1878** MARCH. DUFFERIN *Canad. Jrnl.* (1891) 408 Our A.D.C.'s unlined suit of tussore silk.

**Unli·ned,** *ppl. a.*² [UN-¹ 8 + LINE *v.*² Cf. Du. *ongelijnd.*] Not marked with lines.

**1865** MRS. WHITNEY *Gayworthys* I. 6 Round fair face, unlined by any perplexity. **1885** WHITTIER *Pr. Wks.* (1889) II. 316 The faces represented are not so unlined and ruddy.

**Unli·ngering,** *ppl. a.* (UN-¹ 10.) **1849** DE QUINCEY *English Mail Coach* Wks. 1862 IV. 322 By the word 'sudden' [Cæsar] means 'unlingering'. **1887** BOWEN *Æneid* I. 655 Armed with his royal mission the chief unlingering speeds.

**Unli·ning,** *vbl. sb.* [UN-¹ 13.] (See quots.)

**1848** LINDLEY *Introd. Bot.* (ed. 4) I. 332 Here we have a succession of true unlinings; but in Crucifers..the large stamens offer an example of simple unlining in the full meaning of the word, since they present a separation into two parts only. **1862** M. C. COOKE *Man. Bot. Terms* 87 *Unlining*, a separation of parts originally united.

**Unli·nk,** *v.* [UN-² 4 b.]

**1.** *trans.* **a.** To undo the links of (a chain, etc.). Also *refl.*, *fig.*, and in fig. context.

**1600** SHAKS. *A. Y. L.* IV. iii. 112 About his necke A greene and guilded snake had wreath'd it selfe..: but sodainly Seeing Orlando, it vnlink'd it selfe. **1635** QUARLES *Embl.* v. ix. 7, I cannot mount till thou unlink my chaine. *a* **1670** RUST *Disc. Truth* (1682) 185 It will unlink and break that chain and method of Gods Decrees. **1822–56** DE QUINCEY *Confess.* (1862) 154 Those fatally tortuous paths of which the windings can never be unlinked. **1890** TALMAGE *From Manger to Throne* 639 The chain of the most tremendous natural law is unlinked.

**b.** To detach, set free, by undoing or unfastening a link or chain. Also *refl.*, *absol.*, and *fig.*

**1655** R. CRAB in *Harl. Misc.* (1809) IV. 483 Those that will not unlink themselves from the world. *a* **1680** CHARNOCK *Attrib. God* (1834) II. 395 He doth..correct those actions, that unlink the mutual assistance between man and man. **1688** R. HOLME *Armoury* III. xix. (Roxb.) 153/1 March to your horses. Vnlink your horses. Fasten your links. **1796** *Instr. & Reg. Cavalry* (1813) 235 The men move up to their horses, and unlink. *Ibid.*, Unlink Horses! **1802** J. BAILLIE *2nd Pt. Ethwald* IV. iii, (*Stage direction.* The chiefs instantly let go hands...) *Her.* Ha! have I then so suddenly unlink'd you? **1849** H. MAYO *Pop. Superst.* (1851) 79 The attention..is unlinked from the other faculties.

**2.** *intr.* To lose connexion; to part; to become relaxed.

**1641** MILTON *Ch. Govt.* I. v. 15 To make a King a type, we say is an abusive and unskilful speech...Therefore your typical chaine of King and Priest must unlink. **1786** W. GILPIN in *Mrs. Delany's Life & Corr.* (1862) III. 372 We travelled amicably, arm in arm,..we had not one occasion to unlink. **1806** H. SIDDONS *Maid, Wife, & Widow* III. 44 He felt her arms unlink, and saw that a convulsive fit had put an end to all her recollections.

**Unli·nked,** *ppl. a.* [UN-¹ 8.] Not linked, connected, or united.

**1813** SHELLEY *Q. Mab* VI. 170 Whilst, to the eye of shipwrecked mariner,..All seems unlinked contingency and chance. *a* **1859** R. A. VAUGHAN *Mystics* (1860) II. VIII. ii. 37 So his life is a series of starts; his actions..unlinked, unharmonized.

**Unli·quefied,** *ppl. a.* (UN-¹ 8.) **1705** ADDISON *Italy* 237 These huge unwieldy Lumps [of lava]..remain'd in the melted Matter rigid and unliquify'd. **1857** SPENCER *Progress* (1864) 285 Yet the gas remained unliquified!

**Unli·quid,** *a.* [UN-¹ 7.]

**1.** (See LIQUID *a.* 1.)

**1547** BOORDE *Brev. Health* cxcvi. 68 b, Take gargarices lyquide and unliquyde. **1611** COTGR. s.v. *Pot*, Small vessels wherein..liquors, and sometimes vnliquid things, are kept.

**2.** (See LIQUID *a.* 6.)

**1818** COLEBROOKE *Obligations* 195 Though evidently due, it is unliquid, so long as the precise amount of it is unascertained. **1865** CARLYLE *Fredk. Gt.* VI. vi. (1873) II. 188 [She] had left considerable properties;..but all was rather in an unliquid state, not so much as her Will was to be had.

**Unli·quidate,** *a.* [UN-¹ 7.] = next. **1818** COLEBROOKE *Obligations* 194 Unliquidate damages for non-performance of an agreement.

**Unli·quidated,** *ppl. a.* [UN-¹ 8.]

**1.** Not cleared off or paid.

**1765** *Ann. Reg., Chron.* 155/1 They will likewise forfeit all pretensions on their unliquidated papers. **1788** COWPER *Let.* Wks. 1837 XV. 206 The accounts of a large estate unliquidated many years. **1812** G. CHALMERS *Dom. Econ. Gt. Brit.* 180 Every war leaves many unliquidated claims. **1883** *Fortn. Rev.* July 104 There will still remain a considerable debt unliquidated.

**2.** Not made clear or distinct; indefinite.

**1780** BENTHAM *Princ. Legisl.* iii. § 10 The best ideas..of such pains..are altogether unliquidated in point of quality. **1818** — *Ch. Eng., Catech. Exam.* 254 An unliquidated number of instances.

**Unli·quidating,** *ppl. a.* (UN-¹ 10.) **1824** BYRON *Juan* XVI. xcix, The Sinking Fund's unfathomable sea, That most unliquidating liquid, leaves The debt unsunk. **Unli·quored,** *ppl. a.* (UN-¹ 8.) **1642** MILTON *Apol. Smect.* 10, I doubt me whether the very sobernesse of such a one, like an unlicour'd Silenus, were not stark drunk. *a* **1658** CLEVELAND *Inund. Trent* 60 We whose unliquor'd Hides will turn no wet.

†**Unlisible**, *a. Obs.*—1 [UN-1 7.] Unlawful. *c* **1412** HOCCLEVE *De Reg. Princ.* 3357 Hir spiritis benigne.. Thoghten þat craft vnlusty and alenge, And forbaar it; þei knewe it vnlisible [*v. r.* vnlesible]. **Unli·st**, *v.* (UN-2 3.) **1793** PEARCE *Hartford Bridge* II. iii, I told him a bargan was a bargan, and that I defied him to unlist me! **Unli·sted**, *ppl. a.* [UN-1 8.] Not placed on a list. **1644** *God appearing for Parl.* 5 (D.), The names of many are yet unlisted. **1905** *Daily Chron.* 28 Apr. 4/4 Some of the most important securities.. are 'unlisted,' and therefore not dealt in on the Stock Exchange.

**Unli·stened**, *ppl. a.* (UN-1 8, 8 c.)

**1787** BURNS *Death R. Dundas* 31 Hark, injur'd Want recounts th' unlisten'd tale! **1793** WORDSW. *Descr. Sketches* 119 The thicket, where th' unlisten'd stock-dove coos. **1864** PUSEY *Lect. Daniel* iii. 105 Noah was the unlistened-to preacher of righteousness during those 120 years. **1876** MRS. WHITNEY *Sights & Ins.* II. 104 One.. knows by some fine, unlistened sound,.. the nearness of a large body to the touch.

**Unli·stening**, *ppl. a.* (UN-1 10.)

**1736** THOMSON *Liberty* IV. 45 Unlistening, barbarous Force, to whom the sword Is reason, honour, law. **1823** PRAED *Troubadour* I. 215 Brought back from their unlistening sleep. **1839** CARLYLE *Chartism* v, Unlistening multitudes see not but that it is all right. **1897** *Outing* XXX. 450/2 Little Josef talked away to unlistening ears.

**Unli·sty**, *a.* ? *Obs.* [UN-1 7. Cf. OHG. *unlistîg*, *-ik*, and Yorks. dialect *unlisting*.] Indisposed to action; inert; listless.

*c* **1425** *Orolog. Sapient.* i. in *Anglia* X. 334/21 Þe wrecchede sowle sodenlye is chaungete, and is made as seke & vnlistye. *c* **1440** *Promp. Parv.* 366/1 On-lysty, or lystles, *deses.* **1597** *Guistard & Sismond* C 3, He waxed all vnlisty and also somnolent. *a* **1894** in *Northumberland Gloss.* 756 *Unlisty*, listless.

**Unli·t**, *ppl. a.* (UN-1 8 b.) **1852** M. ARNOLD *Youth of Nature* 102 The vastness,.. the gloom Of the unlit gulf of himself. **1855** BROWNING *Statue & Bust* 247 The unlit lamp and the ungirt loin. **Unli·teral**, *a.* (UN-1 7.) **1851** G. S. FABER *Many Mansions* 368 The completely unliteral freedom of the Latin Vulgate. **1857** E. FITZGERALD *Lett.* (1889) I. 249 Not only.. unliteral, but I doubt unoriental, in its form and Expression. **Unli·terally**, *adv.* (UN-1 11.) **1737** *Gentl. Mag.* VII. 13/2 As A.P. has.. unliterally and ungrammatically translated. **Unli·teralness.** (UN-1 12.) **1836** NEWMAN in Liddon *Life Pusey* (1893) I. xvii. 422, I.. do not like diffusive translations; unliteralness is no more diffusive than the contrary.

**Unli·terary**, *a.* (UN-1 7.)

In frequent use from *c* 1880.

**1820** LAMB *Austral. Poetry* Wks. 1908 I. 251 To go and administer tedious justice in inauspicious unliterary Thiefland. **1868** HOOK in Stephens *Life* (1878) II. 482 Here we are very unliterary. **1885** HOWELLS *Silas Lapham* (1891) I. 235 Her talk was very unliterary.

†**Unli·terate**, *a.* [UN-1 7, 5 b.] Illiterate. *a* **1548** HALL *Chron., Hen. IV*, 11 These monasticall persones, lerned and vnliterate. **1688** W. SCOT *Hist. Fam. Scot* p. v, An unliterate Souldier. **Unli·tten**, *ppl. a.* (UN-1 8 b.) **1875** MYERS *Poems* 106 Unlitten dawn of day. **Unli·ttered**, *ppl. a.* (UN-1 8.) **1762** MISS TALBOT *Lett.* (1809) III. 10 Comfort yourself when you sit in your littered room, that.. you can sit in it with an unlittered mind. **1855** SINGLETON *Virgil* I. 159 He.. persevering lies mid flinty stones On an unlittered couch.

†**Unli·ttle**, *a. Obs.* [OE. *unlýtel* (UN-1 7); ON. *úlítill*.] Not little.

*c* **1200** ORMIN 726 Þatt wass till all þe childess kinn Wurrþshipe, & tatt unnlitell. *Ibid.* 16065, I þe ʒife forr þiss mahht Fe mikell & unnlitell.

**Unlitu·rgical**, *a.* (UN-1 7.) **1868** SPROTT *Book Com. Order* p. lxii, Sentiments.. more unliturgical than those of the reformers. **Unli·turgize**, *v.* (UN-2 6 c.) **1659** GAUDEN *Tears Ch.* IV. xxii. 609 These were.. to Directorize, to Unliturgize, to Catechize.. their Brethren.

**Unli·ve**, *v.* [UN-2 3, 4.]

†**1.** *trans.* To deprive of life. *Obs.*

**1593** SHAKS. *Lucr.* 1754 If in the child the father's image lies, Where shall I live now Lucrece is unlived? *c* **1600** CHALKHILL *Thealma & Cl.* 131 Happy had it been, if my stern fate Had.. un-liv'd me then. **1621** QUARLES *Div. Poems, Esther* Introd., These braue Ioynt-tenants that suruiu'd To see a little world of men vnliu'd. **1635** [GLAPTHORNE] *Lady Mother* v. ii. in Bullen *O. Pl.* (1883) II. 188 But.. suppose he did unlive Thurston in faire duell? **1702** *Burlesque Le-strange's Quevedo* 244 A Plot that may himself unlive.

**2.** To reverse, undo, or annul (past life or experience.)

**1614** BP. HALL *Char. Virtues & Vices* I. 249 As if he desired to vnliue his youth. **1661** GLANVILL *Van. Dogm.* 72 We must unlive our former lives. **1688** NORRIS *Love* II. i. 68 To unravel the prejudices of our youth, and.. unlive our former life. *a* **1716** SOUTH *Serm.* (1744) VII. v. 92 Many entertain principles which they defy by their practices, and unlive all that they have believed. **1850** S. DOBELL *Roman* vii, Years are unlived! **1879** *Churchman* I. 16 Not in our power is it to unlive the past.

Hence **Unli·ving** *vbl. sb.*

**1599** NASHE *Lenten Stuffe* K iv b, Nor liuest thou [= a herring] by the vnlyuing or euiscerating of others, as most fishes do.

**Unli·v(e)able**, *a.* [UN-1 7 b.]

**1.** That cannot be lived.

**1869** E. HATCH in *Mem.* (1890) 48 Stoicism did but show them how to live an unliveable life.

**2.** Incapable of being lived in. Also with *in*.

**1898** E. F. BENSON *Money Market* ii, He saw no reason for making his own rooms unlivable-in. **1899** *Contemp. Rev.* Dec. 848 Rural theft makes parts of Sardinia unlivable.

**Unli·ved**, *ppl. a.*1 [UN-2 8.] Deprived of life. **1642** H. MORE *Song of Soul* II. i. I. 15 The hidden might And root of motion, unliv'd, unbeen'd they leave In their vain thoughts. **Unli·ved**, *ppl. a.*2 [UN-1 8.] Not really or fully lived. **1867** J. THOMSON *Two Lovers* (1881) 116 He loathed his unlived life, his unspent force.

**Unli·vely**, *a.* [UN-1 7. Cf. ON. *úlífligr*.]

†**1.** Unliving, lifeless. *Obs.*—1

**1563** MAN *Musculus' Commonpl.* 43 b, What honor is that to God.. to worshippe the dead and unlively shapes as Gods.

**2.** Not lively, animated, or bright; dull.

**1608** WILLET *Hexapla Exod.* 340 Dead and vnliuely colours. **1615** G. SANDYS *Trav.* 114 These [medals] now cut, seeme lame.. and vnliuely counterfets. **1723** GAY in *Lett. C'tess Suffolk* (1824) I. 120 This is no unlively picture of a damsel who might please. **1866** *Athenæum* No. 1999. 235/1 Their hopes are not unlively. **1894** *Daily News* 27 July 5/3 This list was considerably thinned before the long, unlively debate concluded.

Hence **Unli·veliness.**

**1643** MILTON *Divorce* I. 8 All the unlivelines and naturall sloth which is really unfit for conversation.

**Unli·vely**, *adv.* (UN-1 11.) **1641** LD. DIGBY *Parl. Sp.* 9 Feb. 14 As dully, as faintly, as unlively, as in Language these Actions.. have beene expressed.

**Unli·ver**, *v.* ? *Obs.* [UN-2 9 + LIVER *v.*] *trans.* To discharge (a ship or cargo). Also *absol.*

**1637** in Foster *Eng. Factories India* (1912) 10 Haveing unlivered our shipp. **1638** *Ibid.* 54 Begann to unliver. **1805** SIR C. ROBINSON *Admiralty Rep.* VI. 232 That notice was given to the master.., before the whole cargo was unlivered. **Unli·veried**, *ppl. a.* (UN-1 8.) **1823** H. RAVELIN *Lucubrations* 303 A train of liveried and unliveried domestics.

**Unli·very.** *Law.* [Cf. prec. and LIVERY *sb.* 6.] Discharge of a ship or cargo. (Cf. quot. 1867.)

**1805** SIR C. ROBINSON *Admiralty Rep.* VI. 232 A commission of unlivery was taken out by the captor on the same day. **1811** SIR WM. SCOTT *Dodson's Rep.* I. 50 Charges attending the execution of the commission of unlivery and appraisement. **1867** SMYTH *Sailor's Word-bk.* 707 Expenses of unlivery and appraisement are a charge in the first instance against the captors of a prize, to be afterwards apportioned by them ratably against the cargo.

**Unli·ving**, *ppl. a.* [UN-1 10. Cf. OE. *unlifigende* and *unlibbende*, OHG. *unlëbende*, MDu. *onlevende*, MSw. *olivande*.] Not living or alive; lifeless.

**1561** tr. *Calvin's 4 Serm. Idol.* i. B ij b, An vnliuing creature. **1594** SOUTHWELL *M. Magd. Funeral T.* 68 Her heart [seemed but] the cophin of an vnliuing soule. **1611** FLORIO, *Inuiuente*, vnliuing. **1741** in Richardson *Pamela* I. p. xxxvii, Sweet Pamela!.. Thou dear, unliving, yet immortal, Shade! **1809** CAMPBELL *Gert. Wyom.* II. ii, Past those settlers' haunts the eye might roam, Where earth's unliving silence all would seem. **1855** M. ARNOLD *Balder Dead* III. 299 Entreat All living and unliving things to weep For Balder.

**Unloa·d**, *v.* [UN-2 3. Cf. UNLADE *v.*]

**1.** *trans.* To take off, remove (something carried or conveyed); to discharge (a cargo).

**1523** FITZHERB. *Husb.* § 29 Benes.. bounden.. are the more redyer to lode and vnlode. **1600-1** in Willis & Clark *Cambridge* (1886) II. 483 Payd to diuerse labourers for.. vnloadinge great tymber. **1643** BAKER *Chron., Eliz.* 91 The wealth of an East-Indian Caraque was lately unloden. **1722** DE FOE *Plague* (1756) 175 The Man caus'd the Goods to be unloaden and lay'd at the Door. **1817** J. SCOTT *Paris Revisit.* (ed. 4) 31 The canal here.. admitting large vessels to.. unload their cargoes. **1884** *Macm. Mag.* Oct. 426/2 One.. green brig.. was unloading shaddocks from Naxos.

**b.** *fig.* To discharge, give vent to (feelings); to communicate or transfer *to* another.

**1593** SHAKS. 2 *Hen. VI*, I. i. 76 To you Duke Humfrey must vnload his greefe. *a* **1656** HALES *Gold. Rem.* (1688) 159 An Excuse to unlode your faults upon the Devil. **1697** DRYDEN *Æneis* XII. 1165 Reclined upon my breast, thy grief unload. **1775** SMOLLETT *Quixote* II. 296 Now.. you may unrip, and unload, all that lies on your sorrowful heart. **1816** SCOTT *Antiq.* xxii, He unloaded his discontent in such grumblings.

**c.** To discharge or pour (a liquid). *rare.*

**1603** DRAYTON *Bar. Wars* VI. xxiv, When som brook.. By swelling waters.. shouldreth downe his mownd, And from his course dooth quite himselfe vnload. *c* **1630** RISDON *Surv. Devon* § 42 The river Tale.. unloadeth itself into the river Otter. **1891** A. WELCKER *Wild West* 68 He unloaded the other bottle of gin into himself.

**2.** *absol.* To perform the operation of unloading.

**1587** FLEMING *Contn. Holinshed* III. 1544/2 Sheluers.. pulled downe the courts as soone as they came to the place where it was needfull to vnlode. **1614** GORGES *Lucan* VII. 269 Those streames.. spread their springs abrode, And in Timavas flood vnlode. **1635** J. TAYLOR (Water P.) *Very Old Man* B 2, The Harrow, Mattock,.. Goad, And Whip, and how to Load, and to Vnload. **1710** SWIFT *Poems, Atlas* 6 The pedlar overpress'd Unloads upon a stall to rest. **1855** *Poultry Chron.* II. 500/1 One of the company's collecting-carts had just arrived, and was unloading.

*fig.* **1885** HOWELLS *Silas Lapham* (1891) I. 83, I was loaded up with a partner that.. couldn't do anything, and I unloaded; that's all.

**b.** *Naut.* Of vessels: To discharge cargo.

**1799** *Hull Advertiser* 4 May 2/2 The Wasp has come into Leith harbour to unload. **1865** MILTON & W. B. CHEADLE *N.-W. Passage* vi, Whilst it [*sc.* a barge] was unloading.

**3.** *trans.* (and *refl.*). To free, relieve, or divest of a load or burden; to clear of something heavy or bulky.

**1591** H. SMITH *Exam. Vsurie* 3 When hee hath loden himselfe like a cart, he shall be vnloden like a cart againe. **1648** T. GAGE *West Ind.* xvii. 114 The Indians helped one another to unload and load the mule. **1697** DRYDEN *Virg. Georg.* II. 554 Besides thy daily pain T' unload the Branches, or the Leaves to thin. **1751** LABELYE *Westm. Bridge* 81 The Commissioners.. moved the Board.. to unload the said Pier. **1828** STARK *Elem. Nat. Hist.* I. 145 He is trained to lie down when he receives his load and to be unloaded. **1894** S. FISKE *Holiday Stories* (1900) 28 Unload yourself and pull up a chair.

**b.** To relieve by evacuation. Chiefly *Med.*

**1653** J. TAYLOR (Water P.) *Cert. Trav. Uncert. Journ.* 21 If to unload your Bellies, Nature drive ye. **1764** GRAINGER *Sugar Cane* IV. 124 With sempre vive Unload their bowels. **1822** GOOD *Study Med.* III. 437 Brisk purging.. unloads the infarcted viscera. **1875** H. C. WOOD *Therap.* (1879) 441 Tartar emetic is rarely used simply to unload the stomach.

**c.** To relieve (the heart, etc.) by utterance.

**1720** MISS VANHOMRIGH in *Swift's Lett.* (1766) II. 289, I must.. unload my heart, and tell you all its griefs. **1808** SCOTT *Marmion* IV. xviii, By that strong emotion press'd, Which prompts us to unload our breast, Even when discovery's pain. **1816** J. WILSON *City of Plague* I. iii. 40 If thou cam'st hither to unload thy soul, Kneel down.

**d.** To relieve (one) *of* something burdensome.

*a* **1721** SHEFFIELD (Dk. Buckhm.) *Wks.* (1723) II. 207 Antony.. having a secret satisfaction in being unloaded of such a friend; who was.. sometimes troublesome. **1776** *Ann. Reg., Char.* 49/2 When America is better peopled,.. the plains unloaded of their vast forests and cultivated. **1902** *Westm. Gaz.* 15 Oct. 1/2 A very sagacious tendency to unload himself of mansions rather than to take on new ones.

**4.** To discharge the cargo from (a vessel).

**1599** E. WRIGHT *Voy. Earl Cumbld.* 19 in *Cert. Err. Navig.*, Thre of the greatest.. were vnloden of their.. marchandise. **1671** *New Jersey Archives* (1880) I. 64 Wheras a certain Vessell or Ship hath.. bine unloaden & loaden contrary to an Act of Parliament. **1748** *Anson's Voy.* II. v. 173 To assist him in unloading the Sloop. **1836** W. IRVING *Astoria* II. 197 Here it was necessary to unload the canoes. **1885** W. H. WHITE *M. Rutherford's Deliv.* iii, 'Guffy'.. got drunk, unloaded barges [etc.].

**5.** †**a.** To discharge, fire off (artillery, etc.). *Obs.*

**1625** MASSINGER *New Way* v. i, [I can now] Unload my great artillery, and shake.. the walls. **1712** BLACKMORE *Creation* IV. 444 The powder which destructive guns explode, And by its force their hollow wombs unload. **1755** JOHNSON, *Discharge*,.. to unload a gun.

**b.** To withdraw the charge from (a fire-arm, cartridge, etc.).

**1709** STEELE *Tatler* No. 82 ¶ 8 A Pistol which he knew he had unloaded the Night before. **1734** in *10th Rep. Hist. MSS. Comm.* App. I. 192 His instructions.. concerning unloading the Artillery. **1855** KINGSLEY *Westw. Ho!* xxi, 'You took care to flood the powder?' 'Ay, ay, sir, and to unload the ordnance too.'

**6.** *Stock Exchange.* To get rid of, dispose of, sell out (stock, etc.).

**1876** 'E. PINTO' *Ye outside Fools!* 359 Bulls rush in to aid their philanthropic game of *Unloading*, as we term it, their expensive wares. **1893** *Nation* (N.Y.) 21 Sept. 204/2 The American passion for speculation—that is, for getting hold of something to be unloaded rapidly on somebody else. *absol.* **1888** *Daily News* 16 Feb. 6/2 New York,.. 'Bears' selling freely, and 'bulls' unloading, combined to depress values.

Hence **Unloa·der**, one who or that which unloads.

**1611** FLORIO, *Scarcatore*, a discharger, an vnloder. **1880** J. W. HILL *Guide Agric. Implements* 469 An efficient Sack Lifter, Loader, Unloader, and Shooter. **1898** *Allbutt's Syst. Med.* V. 24 As in the case of unloaders of grain-ships.

**Unloa·ded**, *ppl. a.*1 (UN-1 8.)

**1648** HEXHAM II, *Ongeladen*, Vnloaded. **1753** *Stewart's Trial* 273 The unloaded gun. **1800** *Asiat. Ann. Reg., Misc. Tr.* 245/1 Water.. sufficient to give passage to large unloaded boats. **1840** *Civil Eng. & Arch. Jrnl.* III. 89/2 This.. would only be what M. Pambour properly calls the 'unloaded friction'. **1871** 'M. LEGRAND' *Cambr. Freshm.* 181 Shooting with unloaded pistols. **1899** *Allbutt's Syst. Med.* VIII. 11 Holding out the poker or even the unloaded hand at arm's length.

*transf.* **1890** 'R. BOLDREWOOD' *Miner's Right* (1899) 83 You're armed, of course?' I touched my left hip significantly.. 'Too long in the country to travel unloaded.'

**Unloa·ded**, *ppl. a.*2 (f. UNLOAD *v.*) **1807** J. BARLOW *Columb.* IV. 367 As from unloaded waves, the rising sand Swell'd into light. †**Unloa·den**, *ppl. a. Obs.* [UN-1 8 b.] = UNLOADED *ppl. a.*1 **1599** HAKLUYT *Voy.* II. 132 No man wil iudge their fare good, or their bodies vnloden of stripes.

**Unloa·den**, *v. Obs.* exc. *dial.* [UN-2 3.] *trans.* = UNLOAD *v.*

**1567** DRANT *Horace, Ep.* xiii. E iij, If that my booke be burthenouse, shift the of it be tyme, Least thou asslyke vn loden the with greater note of cryme. **1663** BP. PATRICK *Parab. Pilgr.* xxxi, They.. unloadned themselves of the passions which they felt in their hearts.

**Unloa·ding**, *vbl. sb.* [f. UNLOAD *v.*] The action of the verb, in various senses.

*a* **1522** W. LILY *Gram.* (1549) D iij b, Verbes of.. lodyng or vnlodyng, will haue an ablatiue case. **1587** FLEMING *Contn. Holinshed* III. 1544/2 To loose.. the tackle of euerie court immediatlie before the vnloding or sheluing thereof. **1612** in *10th Rep. Hist. MSS. Comm.* App. V. 467 The unlodeing or bringeinge in of any.. merchandize. **1748** *Anson's Voy.* II. xiii. 269 We compleated the unloading of the Carmelo. **1829** LYTTON *Disowned* xvi, The wallet of diurnal anecdote was full, and craved unloading. **1868** GARROD *Mat. Med.* 399 Purgatives.. cause.. an unloading of the large and small intestines.

*attrib.* **1755** MAGENS *Insurances* I. 46 The usual unloading Place on the Weser. **1875** KNIGHT *Dict. Mech.* 2683/1 *Unloading machine*, an apparatus for removing freight from boats, cars, or wagons.

**Unloa·th**, *a.* (UN-1 7.) *a* **1850** ROSSETTI *Dante & Circle* I. (1874) 199 To mine arms I took her tenderly: With no rebuke the beauty laughed unloth. **Unloa·thfulness.** (UN-1 12.) *a* **1470** H. PARKER *Dives & Pauper* (Pynson, 1493) VI. xv, Swete Iesu cryste what is thy gylt That thou thus for me arte spylt, floure of vnlothfulnes? **Unloa·thingly**, *adv.* (UN-1 11.) **1836** E. HOWARD *R. Reefer* xlix, My mind looked not unloathingly on.. suicide. **Unloa·thly**, *adv.* (UN-1 11.) **1844** MRS. BROWNING *Drama of Exile* 2079 Softly and unlothly.. We will draw you soothly Toward the Heavenly people.

**Unloa·thsome,** *a.* (Un-[1] 7.) In quot 1583 misused for 'loathsome' (Un-[1] 15).
c 1440 *Promp. Parv.* 366/1 On-lothesum. 1583 Melbancke *Philotimus* H j, Shee had not neede to sleepe, that wakes a quicke corse, lest her heauie drowsines breede vnlothsome dreames, or sodeyne startinge affright her sleapinge. 1611 Florio, *Inschisoso*, vncoy, vnnice, vnloathsome.

**Unlocali·zable,** *a.* (Un-[1] 7 b.) 1868 Spencer *Princ. Psychol.* (1870) I. 253 Unlocalizable feelings.

**Unlo·calized,** *ppl. a.* (Un-[1] 8.) 1823 Lamb *Elia* ii. *Sydney's Sonn.*, They are not rich in words only, in vague and unlocalised feelings. 1881 Fairbairn *Stud. Life Christ* xii. 211 The incident could find a place in his history only as unlocalized.

**Unlo·cally,** *adv.* (Un-[1] 11.) 1602 Warner *Alb. Eng.* xiii. lxxviii. 321 Superessentiall Being, Selfe-suffising,.. Locall vnlocally each wheare, Super-substantiall.

**Unloca·ted,** *ppl. a.* (Un-[1] 8.) 1776 Jefferson *Writ.* (ed. Ford) II. 80 The idea of Congress selling out unlocated lands has been sometimes dropped. 1828–32 Webster, *Unlocated*, not placed; not fixed in a place. 2. In America, unlocated lands are such new and wild lands as have not been..designated by marks, limits or boundaries. 1876 Bancroft *Hist. U.S.* III. xlviii. 346 The duties on trade and the unlocated lands. 1902 *Academy* 23 Aug. 200/2 He was coo-eeing to some party of unlocated climbers in the cloud-enveloped heights.

**Unlo·ck,** *v.* [Un-[2] 3: cf. Unlouk *v.*]

**1.** *trans.* To undo the lock of (a door, chest, etc.) by turning the key; to make capable of opening by this means. Also in fig. context.
c 1400 *Langland's P. Pl.* B. xii. 112 (Wright), Which is the cofre of Cristes tresor And clerkes kepe the keyes, To unloken it at hir likyng. 14.. *Sir Beues* (M.) 4119, I rede, that ye on-lok the yate. 1426 Lydg. *De Guil. Pilgr.* 23934, I cam after..and she gan vnlokke a chest. 1530 Palsgr. 768/2, I unlocke a dore or cofer. 1560 Daus tr. *Sleidane's Comm.* 327 Yet hath he keyes wherwith to unlock y^e^ same [*sc.* city-gates]. 1612 Donne *Progr. Soule, 2nd Anniv.* 156 Yet Death must usher, and unlocke the doore. 1690 Berlu (*title*), Treasury of Drugs Unlock'd. 1754 Gray *Progr. Poesy* 92 This can unlock the gates of Joy. 1794 Mrs. Radcliffe *Myst. Udolpho* xxvi, That leads to the inner court, which I don't choose to unlock. 1812 Byron *Ch. Har.* i. xviii, The bard..Who to the awe-struck world unlock'd Elysium's gates. 1847 C. Bronte *J. Eyre* xvii, I knelt down at and unlocked a trunk.
*absol.* 1768 Foote *Devil* i. Wks. 1799 III. 247 Unlock, Mrs. Minx! your minion is discovered.

**2.** To set free by undoing a lock; chiefly *fig.*, to allow to flow or come forth; to make open to all.
c 1400 *Gamelyn* 417 He vnlokked gamelyn both hondes and feete. c 1412 Hoccleve *De Reg. Princ.* 1047 Sone, if oght in þin herte elles be loke, Vnlokke it blyue! com of; what seist þou? 1697 Dryden *Virg. Georg.* ii. 245 For thee my tuneful Accents will I raise,..Once more unlock for thee the sacred Spring. 1708 Philips *Cyder* ii. 60 When the kind early Dew Unlocks th' embosom'd Odors. a 1764 Lloyd *Shakespeare* Poet. Wks. 1774 I. 77 Translation has unlock'd the store, And spread abroad the Grecian lore. 1820 Shelley *Prometh. Unb.* iii. i. 74 Let hell unlock Its mounded oceans of tempestuous fire. 1884 *Times* (weekly ed.) 19 Sept. 6/1 Capital, whether public or private, is so very hard to unlock.

**b.** To give or obtain access to; to bring to light; to display.
1593 Shaks. *Lucrece* 16 He the night before..Vnlockt the treasure of his happie state. 1596 — *Merch. V.* ii. ix. 52 Giue me a key for this, And instantly vnlocke my fortunes here. 1649 Jer. Taylor *Gt. Exemp.* ii. xii. 46 Jesus unlock't the secrets of her heart, and let in his grace. 1722 Wollaston *Relig. Nat.* v. 101 The future actions of free agents are at once all unlocked, and exposed to His view. 1809–14 Wordsw. *Excurs.* iv. 570 These hoards of truth you can unlock at will.

**3.** *fig.* To cause to open or unclose.
1531 Tindale *Exp. 1 John* (1537) 5 The doctryne..is the keye, that..locketh and unlocketh the conscience of all synners. 1634 Milton *Comus* 852 She can unlock The clasping charm, and thaw the numming spell. 1662 J. Davies tr. *Olearius' Voy. Ambass.* 214 The small Presents..unlock'd the man's breast, and drew out the whole secret. 1792 Wordsw. *Descrip. Sketches* 627 Mournful measures.. Unlocking bleeding Thought's 'memorial cell'. 1822 Byron *Werner* i. i. 306 Wine he shall have; if that unlock him not, I shall not sleep. 1859 Geo. Eliot *A. Bede* xlv, I know you have a key to unlock hearts.

**b.** To explain, provide a key to (something obscure).
1636 K. Long tr. *Barclay* (title-p.), Argenis, or the Loves of Polyarchus and Argenis,..with a Key Præfixed to vnlock the whole Story. 1690 T. Burnet *Theory Earth* iii. 21 Such a key as this.., that does so easily unlock this hard passage, and makes it intelligible. 1879 S. C. Bartlett *Egypt to Pal.* iii. 51 To unlock and read a tongue of which..not even the nature of the language was known.

**4.** To open, or cause to open, by physical action; to cause to separate or part.
c 1586 C'tess Pembroke *Ps.* (1823) li. vii, Unlock my lipps, shut up with sinnfull shame. 1637 Cowley *Sylva, Verses on Virgin*, The breath gives sparing kisses, nor with powre Unlocks the Virgin bosome of the Flowre. 1694 Salmon *Bate's Dispens.* 269/1 That sulphurous Tincture is better able to unlock, or open the Bodies of the Ingredients. 1707 Mortimer *Husb.* 56 [Clay-lands] hardning with the Sun and Wind, till they are unlocked by industry. 1775 Sheridan *Rivals* iv. ii, Unlock your jaws, sirrah. 1802 J. Baillie *2nd Pt. Ethwald* ii. v, A brawny ruffian, whose firm clenched gripe No struggles can unlock. 1860 Tyndall *Glac.* i. x. 65 The discharge seemed to unlock the clouds above us.

**b.** To undo or unfasten by some mechanical operation, or by force.
1606 Shaks. *Tr. & Cr.* v. vi. 29, I like thy armour well, Ile frush it and vnlocke the riuets all. 1683 Moxon *Mech. Exerc., Printing* xxii. § 16 He must Vn-lock and Loosen the Form. 1704 J. Harris *Lex. Techn.*, *Detents*, in a Clock, are those stops, which..lock and unlock the Clock in striking. 1757 W. Wilkie *Epigon.* ii. 43 The hero..His mail unlock'd; and loos'd the golden chains. 1847 *Infantry Man.* (1854) 109 The sword is..unlocked by the thumb and forefinger. 1892 A. Oldfield *Man. Typog.* viii, Some compositors seem to drive up quoins as if they thought the form would never have to be unlocked again.

**c.** To free from being fixed or immovable.
1735 Arbuthnot *Aliments* 97 The Power of a Lixivium.. to unlock the Salts that are entangled in the viscid Juices. 1798 Wordsw. *Anecd. for Fathers* 53 Then did the boy his tongue unlock. 1819 Scott *Noble Moringer* xxxii, Nor golden meed nor garment gay, unlocks his heavy tongue. 1902 *Brit. Med. Jrnl.* 12 Apr. 879 At first he could unlock the knee easily.

**5.** *intr.* To become unlocked.
1470–85 Malory *Arthur* xi. i. 571 When he came to the chambre..the dores of yron vnlocked and vnbolted. 1748 Richardson *Clarissa* (1811) IV. 396, I heard her lady's door ..unbar, unbolt, unlock, and open. 1804 *Europ. Mag.* XLV. 13/1 They had but just time to make this arrangement, when the door unlocked.

Hence **Unlo·cked** *ppl. a.*[1]; **Unlocker.**
1649 tr. *Warn. Jac. Beem* xxv. 17 Onely the holy spirit is the opener and unlocker. 1890 'R. Boldrewood' *Col. Reformer* (1891) 399 Once more the unlocked earth receives the plough.

**Unlo·cked,** *ppl. a.*[2] [Un-[1] 8, 8 c. Cf. ON. *úlokaðr*.] Not locked (up).
1603 Holland *Plutarch's Mor.* 165 Letting all ly unfortified, unbard, and unlockt. a 1740 Tickell *Fragm. on Hunting* 139 Unlock'd in covers let her freely run To range thy courts. 1813 Scott *Trierm.* iii. xviii, Unbarr'd, unlock'd, unwatch'd, a port Led to the Castle's outer court. 1858 Mrs. Carlyle *Lett.* (1883) II. 366 The only drawer which is unlocked. 1887 S. Cumberland *Queen's Highway*, etc. 63 The unlocked-up land does not appear to tempt the independent purchaser.

**Unlo·cking,** *vbl. sb.* [f. Unlock *v.*] The action of the verb, in various senses.
[1719 Boyer *Dict. Royal* ii, Unlocking, *ouverture*, *l'action d'ouvrir*.] 1825 J. Nicholson *Operat. Mechanic* 509 The scape-wheel teeth..[being] under-cut for the purpose of avoiding friction..and for safe unlocking. 1890 *Retrospect Med.* CII. 128 The sudden unlocking of abnormal metabolic processes.
*attrib.* 1850 Chubb *Locks & Keys* 25 An unlocking notch in the outer edge of the slider. 1884 F. J. Britten *Watch & Clockm.* 276 Unlocking Resistance..[is] the resistance opposed to unlocking..by the draw of the locking faces.

**Unlocomo·tive,** *a.* (Un-[1] 7.) 1828 Scott in Lockhart *Life* (1839) VII. 154, I am getting very unlocomotive. 1863 Ld. Lytton *Ring of Amasis* I. 206 Where these ponderous locomotives of an unlocomotive age used to lurk harnessed.

**Unlo·dge,** *v.* [Un-[2] 5, 7.]

**1.** *trans.* To dislodge; to drive out of a lodging or resting-place.
1560 Whitehorne *Ord. Souldiours* (1588) 36 b, He vnlodgeth thee, and thou arte constrained to issue out of thy fortresse. 1576 Turberv. *Venerie* 37 When the houndes haue unlodged the harte. 1672 T. Venn *Milit. Observ.* 181 The Ensigne hath..a Guard ever about it,..neither is it to be disimbogued, or unlodged, without a special Guard. 1703 S. Parker tr. *Eusebius' Eccl. Hist.* vi. 96 The Gentiles in Alexandria..unlodg'd him from House to House 1796 *Hist. Ned Evans* I. 9 Groping into the kitchen, [he] discovered Molly in her covert, whom he quickly unlodged.

**2.** *intr.* To leave one's lodging.
1560 Whitehorne *Ord. Souldiours* (1588) 36 b, Thou shalt be constrained of some necessitie to vnlodge, and come to fight the field. 1608 D. T[uvill] *Ess. Pol. & Mor.* 19 Beeing constrained one day to vnlodge somwhat in hast, and to leaue a certaine sick friend.

**Unlo·dged,** *ppl. a.* (Un-[1] 8.) 1634 T. Carew *Cœlum Brit.* 10 Now that those heavenly Mansions are to be voyd, you that shall hereafter be found unlodged, will become inexcusable. **Unlo·fty,** *a.* (Un-[1] 7.) 1790 Anna Seward *Lett.* (1811) II. 384 [They] wore their dark hair in reverse curls upon their naturally unlofty foreheads. 1869 *Temple Bar Mag.* July 458 Tennyson's feminine, unlofty way of looking at things. **Unlo·gic.** (Un-[1] 12.) 1843 Carlyle *Past & Pr.* iii. v, The most Conservative English People.. is driven alike by its Logic and its Unlogic..to be wholly a Reforming People.

**Unlo·gical,** *a.* [Un-[1] 7, 5 b.] Illogical.
a 1661 Fuller *Worthies, Kent* ii. (1662) 65 All heartily laughed at his unlogical Reason. 1720–1 *Lett. fr. Mist's Jrnl.* (1722) II. 174 That pert and unlogical Writer. 1748 Richardson *Clarissa* II. 40 An un-learned, un-logical girl. 1829 Scott *Jrnl.* 27 Jan., If [my reflections]..are unlogical. 1867 Atwater *Logic* 189 Unlogical is counterfeit thought.

†**Unlo·ke,** *pa. pple. Obs.*[−1] [Un-[1] 8 b + *loke*, p.p. of Louk *v.*] Unfastened.
c 1400 *Gamelyn* 438 Þou shalt stond vp by the post as þou were hond fast, And I schal leue hem [*sc.* the fetters] vn-loke þat away þou may hem cast.

**Unlo·nged,** *ppl. a.* (Un-[1] 8 c.) 1849 C. Bronte *Shirley* xviii, A gentle human form,..unknown, unloved, but not unlonged-for. **Unloo·k,** *v.* (Un-[2] 3.) 1748 Richardson *Clarissa* V. 135 He..now turn'd his eyes towards me, then from me, as if he would unlook his own looks.

**Unloo·ked,** *ppl. a.* [Un-[1] 8, 8 c.]

**1.** † **a.** Not attended to; neglected. *Obs.*
a 1300 *St. Gregory* 1064 in *Archiv Stud. neu. Spr.* LVII. 70 Ȝe witeþ wel hit may nout longe holye churche vnloked be.

**b.** Not looked *at*, *on*, *to*, etc.; unregarded, unheeded, unexamined.
1563 Nowel *Serm. bef. Queen* (1853) 226 Such errors or heresy ought not..to be unlooked unto. 1581 W. S. *Compend. or Briefe Exam.* 3 Theyr husbandry unlookte to at home. 1615 G. Sandys *Trav.* Ded., Leauing no securitie saue..vnlookt on pouertie. 1654 C. Wase *Gratius' Cyneget.* Pref. 7 The occasion that a polite and classical Poet.. should have been so long unlook'd into,..and unsought for in our Land. 1856 R. A. Vaughan *Mystics* I. 214 The wares lay unlooked at and untouched.

**2.** Not looked *for*; unexpected, unanticipated. (In predicative use sometimes quasi-*adv.*)
1535 Coverdale *Wisd.* xi. 7 Thou gauest vnto thine awne a plenteous water vnloked for. 1544 Betham *Precepts War* ii. xli. K viij b, When they be wythout watch,..then sodaynlye, and vnloked for, rushe vppon them. 1615 G. Sandys *Trav.* 112 The vnlookt-for assault of Achillas. 1672 T. Venn *Milit. Observ.* 192 He shall see them [*sc.* sentinels] changed at due time, and shall now and then visit them unlook'd for. 1725 Pope *Odyss.* xxii. 164 Oh curst event! and oh unlook'd-for aid! 1837 J. D. Lang *New S. Wales* I. p. v, The causes..producing so unlooked-for and so unfortunate a result. 1878 Bosw. Smith *Carthage* 30 Elated by an unlooked-for victory.

† **b.** Without prep., = prec. *Obs.*
1553 T. Wilson *Rhet.* 74 Thei..shal bee able to abashe a righte worthy man,..through the sodein quip & vnloked frumpe geuen. 1594 Shaks. *Rich. III*, i. iii. 214 God, I pray him, That none of you may liue his naturall age, But by some vnlook'd accident cut off. 1618 J. Taylor (Water P.) *Penniless Pilg.* C 2 b, This vnlook'd pleasure, was to me such pleasure, That [etc.].

Hence **Unloo·kedforness.** *rare*[−1].
a 1586 Sidney *Arcadia* iii. xvi, The unlookedfornesse of his comming.

**Unloo·p,** *v.* (Un-[2] 3, 4 b.) 1599 Nashe *Lenten Stuffe* G iij, Which made her at breake of day..to vnloope her luket or casement. 1840 Browning *Sordello* iii. 759 Slouch bonnet, unloop mantle, careless go Alone..Through Venice. **Unloo·ped,** *ppl. a.* (Un-[1] 8.) 1716 Gay *Trivia* i. 197 While you with hat unloop'd, the fury dread Of spouts high streaming. 1850 Allingham *Poems, Pilot's Dau.* ii, [Locks] unbraided, and unloop'd. 1855 Browning *Saul* iii. 4 The tent was unlooped.

**Unloo·sable,** *a.* [Un-[1] 7 b.] Incapable of being loosened.
a 1425 tr. *Arderne's Treat. Fistula* 29 Bounden wiþ tuo knottis or þre vnlouseable. c 1550 Coverdale *Fruitful Lessons* (1593) O iij, [He] dooth..snare himselfe with vnlowsable bands. a 1564 Becon *Art. Chr. Relig.* Wks. 1564 II. 128 The simbole..of that vnloseable bargaine, whiche they call the Communion.

**Unloo·sably,** *adv.* [Un-[1] 11.] † Indissolubly. c 1445 Pecock *Donet* 214 More wo is to me þat þei ben vnlosabli lettid..from þe laboure of meditacioun.

**Unloo·se,** *v.* [Un-[2] 9. Cf. Unleese *v.*]

**1.** *trans.* To relax, slacken the tension or firmness of (some part of the body, one's grasp or hold, etc.).
1362 Langl. *P. Pl.* A. Prol. 87 Seriauns..Not for loue of vr lord vnloseþ heore lippes ones. 1377 *Ibid.* B. xvii. 139 Þe fader was fyrst, as a fyst with o fynger foldynge, Tyl hym loued and lest to vnlosen his fynger. 1545 Raynald *Byrth Mankynde* 89 By that the body is opened, vnlosed, and resolued. 1564 *Child-Marriages* 200 And so, vnlosinge handes, they kissed. 1606 Shaks. *Tr. & Cr.* iii. iii. 223 The weake wanton Cupid Shall from your necke vnloose his amorous fould. 1661 Childrey *Brit. Baconica* 143 The Salmon..takes his tail in his mouth, and with all his force unloosing his circle on a sudden..he mounteth up. 1727 Gay *Begg. Op.* i. xiii, My hand, my heart,..is so riveted to thine that I cannot unloose my hold. 1790 Mrs. A. M. Johnson *Monmouth* III. 152 Her hands were clasped about his neck, which could not be unloosed without the greatest violence. 1834 L. Ritchie *Wand. by Seine* 35 He found it impossible to unloose her arms from his neck. 1853 Miss Yonge *Heir of Redclyffe* xii, Saying 'Good night..,' [she] unloosed her embrace.
*fig.* 1757 Mrs. Griffith *Lett. Henry & Frances* (1767) II. 47 Providence has wisely ordered, that disappointments.. should, by degrees, unloose the hold we take of this dim spot.

**2.** To set free from bonds, harness, etc.; to release from confinement. Also *fig.* and *refl.*
1393 Langl. *P. Pl.* C. ii. 198 Þat is þe lok of loue þat vnloseþ grace [B. i. 200 lateth oute my grace]. a 1400 in *Engl. Studien* XXXII. 19 Þou, lady, vnlose me of þo bondes þat I wrot with myn owyn hondes. 1512 Colet *Serm. Convoc.* C iv b, Vnlouse your selfe frome the worldly bondage. 1593 Shaks. *2 Hen. VI*, v. i. 88 Then Yorke vnloose thy long imprisoned thoughts. 1655 tr. *Sorel's Com. Hist. Francion* iii. 67 After she had unloosed and well washed me. 1664 Jer. Taylor *Dissuas. Popery* i. iii. § 1. 159 You can as well be dispenc'd with for that Perjury as the other; and you cannot be tied so fast, but the Pope can unloose you. a 1711 Ken *Psyche* Poet. Wks. 1721 IV. 299 The Soul.. seem'd from Flesh unloos'd To..spatiate unconfin'd. 1777 Sheridan *Trip Scarb.* v. ii, Unloose my lord there, you scoundrel! 1856 Kane *Arct. Expl.* I. xxiii. 288 They were obliged to unloose the dogs and drive them forward alone. 1872 Holland *Marb. Proph.* 10 [To] unloose a soul from purgatorial bonds.
*absol.* 1851 Ht. Martineau *Hist. Peace* (1858) 144/1 The function of that new spirit was not to bind but to unloose.

**b.** To set free for action; to bring into play.
1735 Thomson *Liberty* ii. 59 When mysterious Superstition came,..Then tyrant Power the righteous scourge unloos'd. 1828 Lytton *Pelham* II. iv, How wonderfully..your city dignities unloose the tongue. 1831 Scott *Cast. Dang.* v, Having unloosed his repartee to this extent.

**3.** To undo, untie, unfasten (a knot, belt, band, bundle, etc.). Also in fig. context.
1526 Tindale *Luke* iii. 16 Whose shue latchet I am nott worthy to vnloose. 1551 T. Wilson *Logike* P v, To confute, is nothyng els but..to vnlose by reason, thynges knit together by craft. 1577 Googe tr. *Heresbach's Husb.* 39 Then the bundels vnloosed and dryed in the Sunne, are beaten with beetelles. 1608 D. Price *Chr. Warre* 1 The Ænigma is disclosed, the knot vnloosed. 1669 Earl Orrery *Parthen.* iii. vii. 200 The Gallies..grappled so strongly, that nothing but Victory was able to unloose them. 1760 Sterne *Tr. Shandy* iii. viii, Dr. Slop must have had three fifths of Job's patience..to have unloosed them [*sc.* knots]. 1765 Blackstone *Comm.* I. 358 To unloose those bands, by which he

is connected to his natural prince. **1821** SCOTT *Kenilw.* xxxviii, There are other means of disengaging such ties, without unloosing the cords of life. **1847** F. W. NEWMAN *Hist. Hebrew Monarchy* viii. 272 To unloose the covering from his loins. **1860** TYNDALL *Glac.* I. xxii. 155, I now unloosed my scrip.

*fig.* **1668** H. MORE *Div. Dial.* I. 93 These Experiments indeed strike very strongly on the..senses, but there is a subtile Reason that presently unlooses all again. **1710** R. WARD *Life H. More* 116 Nothing can unloose the Sophistries of the selfish Animal Life, but [etc.]. **1820** SHELLEY *Prometh. Unb.* II. iii. 96 The Eternal..Must unloose..The snake-like Doom coiled underneath his throne By that alone.

**4.** To detach, so as to get rid of or remove.

*a* **1470** H. PARKER *Dives & Pauper* (W. de W. 1496) vi. Int. 26/1 Unlouse soo thy richesses from the, that [etc.]. **1555** EDEN *Decades W. Ind.* (Arb.) 214 At which tyme they vnlose the stones, & ryse vppe at their pleasure. **1593** SHAKS. *Lucr.* 136 That which they possess They scatter and unloose it from their bond. **1748** HERVEY *Medit.* (ed. 4) I. 214 Those beneficent Hands, which were..stretched out to unloose the heavy Burthens.

**5.** *intr.* To become loose or unfastened. *rare.*

**1594** CAREW *Huarte's Exam. Wits* 321 The creature easily vnlooseth, because the same was moist and watry. **1697** COLLIER *Ess. Mor. Subj.* I. 143 Without this Virtue, the publick Union must unloose.

Hence **Unloo·ser**; **Unloo·sing** *vbl. sb.*

**1860** MISS MULOCK *Domest. Stories* (1862) 152 Thus let us think of thee, O Death; gentle *unlooser of life's burthen. **1611** FLORIO, *Dislegamenti*, *vnloosings, vnbindings. **1831** A. W. FONBLANQUE *Eng. under 7 Administr.* (1837) II. 80 The unloosing of Anti-Christ and Satan. **1866** J. H. NEWMAN *Lett. to Pusey* 37 The knot of Eve's disobedience received its unloosing through the obedience of Mary.

**Unloo·sed,** *ppl. a.*[1] [f. prec.] Made loose, relaxed; let loose.

**1382** WYCLIF *Ecclus.* xxv. 32 Feble hondis and vnloosid knees. **1552** HULOET, Vnlowsed, *discinctus.* **1839** DARWIN *Voy. Nat.* xxi. 603 The strife of the unloosed elements. **1884** *Pall Mall G.* 6 May 1/1 All around him rages the unloosed flood of Moslem fanaticism.

**Unloo·sed,** *ppl. a.*[2] [UN-[1] 8.] Not loosened.

*c* **1430** *York Memo. Bk.* (Surtees, 1912) I. 194 Pro la vaumpedyng xij parium ocrearum lowsed a retro, xiij *d.* ob...Et pro xij paribus unlowsed retro x *d.* ob. **1435** MISYN *Fire of Love* 91 Þe knot vnlousyd of drawynge frenschyp sal comforth heuynes of bodily sondyrynge.

**Unloo·sen,** *v.* [UN-[2] 9.] *trans.* = UNLOOSE *v.*

*c* **1450** *Cov. Myst.* (Shaks. Soc.) 252 There xul ȝe ffyndyn.. An asse tyed... Unlosne þat asse, and brynge it to me. **1586** D. ROWLAND *Lazarillo* II. (1672) M 6, A Cord fastened about my foot, which..was tied to a great Chest..which though I could, I would not unloosen. **1610** MARKHAM *Masterp.* II. xlix. 294 Forget not..to vnloosen the list and to take it away. **1650** EARL MONM. tr. *Senault's Man bec. Guilty* 335 God..would..teach us that accidents might be unloosened from their substance. **1782** V. KNOX *Ess.* ii. I. 11 Fix them [*sc.* religious principles] deeply in your bosom, and let them go with you unloosened and unaltered to the grave. *c* **1845** J. T. GOODSIR in *Ch. Scot. Pulpit* I. 248 Whose power..unloosened the dumb tongue of conscience. **1863** P. BARRY *Dockyard Econ.* 189 Ankle chains..riveted together,..never to be unloosened night nor day.

Hence **Unloo·sening** *vbl. sb.*

**1867** E. S. PURCELL in *Ess. Relig. & Lit.* Ser. II. 476 Everything tends..to the unloosening of all bonds between society and the Church.

**Unloo·sing,** *ppl. a.* (UN-[1] 10.) **1593** Q. ELIZ. *Boeth.* III. met. ii. 46 Nature..strains with vnlousing Knot [L. *irresoluto nexu*] eche thing.

**Unlo·pped,** *ppl. a.* (UN-[1] 8.)

**1573** TUSSER *Husb.* (1878) 78 In lopping,..for feare of mishap, one bough stay vnlopped, to cherish the sap. **1620** BRINSLEY tr. *Virgil* 54 The hills vnlopt lift vp their voices with ioy. **1683** J. REID *Scots Gard.* (1907) 120 Forrest-trees ..with high bodies, and unlopt heads. *a* **1722** LISLE *Husb.* (1757) 359 Those [trees] he had planted with their heads unlopped. **1849** JAMES *Woodman* vii, The dry unlopped shoots, and withered leaves. **1853** M. ARNOLD *Sohrab & Rustum* 409 An unlopp'd trunk it was, and huge.

**Unlo·rd,** *v.* [UN-[2] 6 b.] *trans.* (and *refl.*) To deprive of the rank of lord.

**1572** in Neal *Hist. Purit.* (1732) I. 288 Because..we would have Bishops unlorded. **1648** PRYNNE *Plea for Lords* 1 The treasonable..designe..to..unlord the Lords. **1669** SHADWELL *Royal Shepherdess* III. i, Those wild desires, That made me..then Unlord my Confident. **1714** ATTERBURY in Beeching *Life* ix. (1909) 261 Furnishing the Reverend Bench with such Members as few Churchmen will pity or regret, when they shall be unlorded. **1828** CAROLINE FRY *Scripture Reader's Guide* ii. 20 He would incline to unlord himself again, and return to his companions in the cellar. **1875** TENNYSON *Q. Mary* IV. ii, We had to dis-archbishop and unlord, And make you simple Cranmer once again.

*fig.* **1656** S. WINTER *Serm.* 42 The Papists..make void and unlord the second commandment. **1662** GURNALL *Chr. in Arm.* III. xviii. 171 Ye have made void..the Commandment ..ἠκυρώσατε, you have unlorded it.

Hence **Unlo·rding** *vbl. sb.*

**1649** MILTON *Eikon.* vi. 52 The unlording of Bishops, and expelling them the House.

**Unlo·rded,** *ppl. a.* [UN-[1] 8.]

**1.** Not having the rank of a lord.

**1641** MILTON *Reform.* I. 22 He that will mould a modern Bishop into a primitive, must yeeld him to be elected by the popular voyce, undiocest, unrevenu'd, unlorded. **1808** BENTHAM *Sc. Reform.* 43 For doing Sheriff's work, we should be reduced to men as yet unlorded.

**2.** Not owned by, or subject to, a lord.

**1803** MOORE *To Miss Moore* 54 While Peace..Walks o'er the free unlorded soil.

**Unlo·rdly,** *a.* (UN-[1] 7.)

**1575** CHURCHYARD *Chippes* 40 b, The discourage and infamye of this vnlordly enterpryse. **1626** MIDDLETON *Any-thing for Quiet Life* v. i, The lord Beaufort's most unlordly breach Of promise to him. **1641** MILTON *Reform.* II. 86 The Pastorlike and Apostolick imitation of meeke and unlordly Discipline. **1832** L. HUNT *Gentle Armour* II. 9 A knight unknown, Who..to mortal fight defies Three lordly knights for most unlordly calumnies.

**Unlo·rdly,** *adv.* (UN-[1] 11.)

? *a* **1400** *Morte Arth.* 1267 Saise to syr Lucius, to vn-lordly he wyrkez, Thus letherly agaynes law to lede my pople.

**Unlo·sable,** *a.* (UN-[1] 7 b.)

**1647** TRAPP *Comm. Rev.* iii. 11 Not that crown of eternall life (for that is unlosable). **1662** BOYLE *Examen* ii. 11 For they think Motion..an unlooseable Property, congenit to Matter. **1690** C. NESSE *O. & N. Test.* I. 272 Special saving grace..is certainly unloseable. **1882** *Lit. World* (U.S.A.) 14 Jan. 15 It keeps them clean, smooth, in order,..unlosable.

† **Unlossed,** *ppl. a. Sc. Obs.*[—1] [UN-[1] 8 + LOSS *v.*] Not unloaded; undischarged.

**1580** *Reg. Privy Council Scot.* III. 331 Merchandis that preissis the said schip to transport thair lynt..unloissit furth of the realme.

**Unlo·st,** *ppl. a.* (UN-[1] 8 b.)

**1513** DOUGLAS *Æneid* v. ii. 80 Allace! was it nocht lefull, thow vnlost, The boundis of Itail..to haue socht. **1612** R. DABORNE *Chr. turn'd Turke* 2 Heer's 400 Crowns vnlost yet. **1624** QUARLES *Div. Poems, Job* xvi. 10 It is an influence..vnlost by death. **1746** YOUNG *Nt. Th.* IX. 1071 An Eden, this! a Paradise unlost! **1818** COLEBROOKE *Obligations* 88 An assurance of a ship lost or unlost. **1892** LD. LYTTON *King Poppy* Epil. 57 A few illusions that, unlost, endure.

**Unlo·tted,** *ppl. a.* (UN-[1] 8.) **1758** J. BLAKE *Mar. Syst.* 25 Unless he finds another unlotted man to serve for him.

† **Unlou·k,** *v. Obs.* [OE. *unlúcan, onlúcan* (UN-[2] 3), = WFris. *ont-, ûntluke*, OS. *antlûkan* (MDu. *ontluken*, Du. *ontluiken*, MLG. *entluken*), OHG. *antlûhhan, in(t)luchan* (MHG. *entlûchen*).]

**1.** *trans.* To undo or open (a gate, door, etc.); to unlock.

*c* **1000** *Rule of Chrodegang* x, Þæt he preosta gatu .. alyfedum tidum luce & unluce. *c* **1175** *Lamb. Hom.* 127 Þet is þet loc þe ðe deofel ne con unlucan. *c* **1275** *Pains Hell* 9 in *O. E. Misc.* 147 Hwo haueþ helle dure vnloke Þat þu ert of pyne ibroke. **13..** *Sir Beues* (A.) 3152 Hii vn-lek þe ȝate at þe frome. **1377** LANGL. *P. Pl.* B. XII. 112 Clerkes kepe þe keyes, To vnlouken it at her lykynge. *c* **1420** *Chron. Vilod.* 4510 When all þe ȝates of þe castell weron unloke.

*absol.* **1377** LANGL. *P. Pl.* B. XVIII. 313 Efte þe liȝte bad vnlouke, & Lucifer answered, What lorde artow?

*transf.* **1390** GOWER *Conf.* I. 293 So that his lippes ben unloke And his corage is al tobroke. *c* **1450** *Cov. Myst.* (Shaks. Soc.) 28 Oure fflescly eyn byn al vnlokyn, Nakyd for synne ouresylf we se.

**2.** *fig.* **a.** To unfold, expound, declare.

**13..** *K. Alis.* 69 (Laud MS.), Ac whi ich habbe hem þus vnleke, ȝee shullen me after her speke. *c* **1315** SHOREHAM I. 1504 Nou ich wolle ondo þys eft By þe wey of mystyke; ..Nou lestlich schel ich on-louke þys. **1390** GOWER *Conf.* I. 25 That swevene hath Daniel unloke.

**b.** To evolve or extract.

*c* **1320** *Cast. Love* 77 [Who] con þat muchel of luitel unlouken,..Alle poyntes he fynde may Of vre be-leeue.

**c.** To dissolve, destroy.

**1377** LANGL. *P. Pl.* B. XVIII. 255 But ihesus rise to lyue,.. And conforte al his kynne,..And al þe iuwen ioye vnioignen & vnlouken.

**d.** To set free, make open way for.

**14..** *Langland's P. Pl.* C. II. 198 Þat is þe lok of loue þat vnloseþ [*MS. F.* vnlowketh] grace.

**3.** *intr.* To open; to go asunder.

*c* **1315** SHOREHAM *Poems* v. 178 Ine flom iordanes syche He was ycrystned, þe heuene onleake. *c* **1350** *Lybeaus Disc.* 1816 That deys began to schake,..The rof abone unlek,..As hyt wolde asonder.

**Unlo·vable, unlo·veable,** *a.*[1] (UN-[1] 7 b.)

**1570** LEVINS *Manip.* 4 Vnloueable, *inamicabilis.* **1858** CARLYLE *Fredk. Gt.* IV. viii. I. 465 His masters, though rigorous, were not unlovable to him. **1894** LD. WOLSELEY *Life Marlborough* I. 173 An essentially worldly and vnlovable woman.

† **Unlo·v(e)able,** *a.*[2] *Obs.* [UN-[1] 7 b.] Not to be praised or commended. *c* **1450** HOLLAND *Howlat* 227 The Sparrowe ..Lyand in lichory, laith, vnloveable. *Ibid.* 917 With vnloveable latis nocht till allow.

**Unlo·ve,** *sb.* [UN-[1] 12.] Absence of love.

**1611** FLORIO, *Disamore*, the contrary of loue, vnloue, hate. **1860** PUSEY *Min. Proph.* 541 He now forbids every sort of unlove. **1865** — *Truth Eng. Ch.* 58 Souls purified..from passion..and all unlove. *Ibid.* 65.

**Unlo·ve,** *v.* [UN-[2] 3.] *trans.* To cease to love (a person, etc.).

Sometimes possibly 'not to love': see UN-[1] 14.

*c* **1374** CHAUCER *Troylus* v. 1698, I ne kan..withinne myn herte fynde To vnlouen yow. **1575** PETERSON tr. *Della Casa's Galateo* 8 Ynough to cause men,..if they did loue vs, to vnloue vs againe. **1640** FULLER *Joseph's Coat* 122 How then shall I unlove the world, which hath been my bosome Darling so long? **1712** STEELE *Spect.* No. 310 ⁋ 1 They bid me love him, and I cannot unlove him. **1847** C. BRONTE *J. Eyre* xviii, I have told you..that I had learnt to love Mr. Rochester: I could not unlove him now. **1855** BROWNING *In a Balcony* 582 Remember, I..Would..Do all but just unlove him.

*absol.* **1561** T. HOBY tr. *Castiglione's Courtyer* II. (1577) H iv, More apt to brawling and chyding,..that love and vnlove al at a time. **1635** J. HAYWARD tr. *Biondi's Banish'd Virg.* 10 If we returne not to our former state of freedome, and unlove againe. **1859** MRS. STOWE *Minister's Wooing* xxv, We never know how we love till we try to unlove. **1881** EMMA J. WORBOISE *Sissie* xv, I am sure one cannot unlove, just because one's esteem is lessened!

**Unlo·ved,** *ppl. a.* [UN-[1] 8.]

**1.** Not loved; not held in affection; unrequited with love.

*a* **1395** HYLTON *Scala Perf.* II. xiv. (MS. Bodl. 592), Vnresonabli he werkiþ þt loueþ not þe souereyn good..vnsouȝt & vnloued. **14..** in *Rel. Ant.* I. 71 Wo worth love unlovyd! **1503** HAWES *Examp. Virt.* I. xv, Loue neuer vnloued for that is payne. **1590** SHAKS. *Mids. N.* III. ii. 234 Miserable most, to loue vnlou'd. **1645** MILTON *Tetrach.* 9 A neglected and unlov'd race, the fruits of a delusive marriage. **1671** MRS. BEHN *Forc'd Marriage* v. iii, The embraces of an unlov'd maid. *a* **1718** PARNELL *Hesiod* 253 Here Hesiod lies: ..Unlov'd, unloving, 'twas his fate to bleed. **1821** SHELLEY *To Night* iii, Lingering like an unloved guest. **1891** FARRAR *Darkn. & Dawn* xviii, The void of an unloved heart.

**2.** Not pursued or felt as love.

**1606** SHAKS. *Ant. & Cl.* III. vi. 53 You..haue preuented The ostentation of our loue; which left vnshewne, Is often left vnlou'd.

**Unlo·veliness.** (UN-[1] 12; cf. next.)

*a* **1586** SIDNEY *Arcadia* II. xv, The old man..folowed his suite with..each thing..that might help to countervaile his owne unlovelines. **1628** PRYNNE (*title*), The Vnlouelinesse of Love-Lockes. **1681** FLAVEL *Meth. Grace* xii. 250 [It] excludes all unloveliness and distastefulness from Jesus. **1873** M. ARNOLD *Lit. & Dogma* ix. 298 Pulverising alike the historic churches in their beauty and the dissenting sects in their unloveliness. **1892** *Welsh Rev.* I. 754 This incarnation of ingratitude and unloveliness.

**Unlo·vely,** *a.* [UN-[1] 7.]

**1.** Not evoking feelings of love or affection; unattractive, unpleasant, repellent.

**1377** LANGL. *P. Pl.* B. XII. 244 For þe pekok..is..vnlouelich of ledene. *Ibid.* XV. 114 ȝowre wordes..aren ful vnlouelich. *a* **1586** SIDNEY *Arcadia* III. xii, Both [were] wearie of so unlovely embracements. **1670** BAXTER *Cure Ch. Div.* Pref. II. § 6 They are agreed in the assumption, that their neighbour is unlovely. **1742** YOUNG *Nt. Th.* III. 403 By passionately loving life, we make Lov'd life unlovely. **1817** [W. BELOE] *Sexagenarian* I. 35 This unlovely branch of writing [*sc.* satire]. **1889** *Times* 3 Dec. 9/3 This very unlovely quarrel.

**2.** Unattractive or unpleasing in appearance; unhandsome; ugly.

**1393** LANGL. *P. Pl.* C. XI. 262 Ac let hure be vnloueliche, vnlofsom a bedde [etc.]. *c* **1450** LOVELICH *Merlin* 6447 A ful old man..that onlovely was of face & lere. **1513** DOUGLAS *Æneid* VI. vii. 33 The wofull pule, with wattir wnluffly. **1598** R. HAYDOCKE tr. *Lomazzo* II. 133 A discontented woman..will seeme yl-favored and vnlouely. **1647** TORSHELL *Designe disp. Bible* 7 He that looks upon an unlovely thing, with the eye of love, thinks it lovely. **1734** THOMSON *Liberty* IV. 6 Unlovely forms Of little pomp. **1820** SHELLEY *Sensit. Pl.* II. 42 Gnawing worms, And things of obscene and unlovely forms. **1895** P. HEMINGWAY *Out of Egypt* II. 156 The town of Port Said is unlovely.

† **Unlo·vely,** *adv. Obs.* (UN-[1] 11; cf. prec.)

**1377** LANGL. *P. Pl.* B. v. 363 Is non so hungri hounde.. Durst lape of þe leuynges, so vnlouely þei smauȝte. **14..** *Langland's P. Pl.* C. XI. 271 (Camb. Univ. MS.), Þei lyue here lif vnlouely til deth hem departe. **1613** PURCHAS *Pilgrimage* (1614) 607 The father maketh hatefull loue to the daughter, and the brother is vnlouely louing to the sister.

**Unlo·verlike,** *a.* (UN-[1] 7 c.)

**1797** JANE AUSTEN *Sense & Sens.* xxxix, Shocked at so unlover-like a speech. **1830** MISS MITFORD *Village* Ser. IV. 19 This unlover-like parting occurred..one fine afternoon. **1893** K. SIMPSON *Yorksh. Stories* 278 Oliver had been cold and unloverlike during the last three weeks.

**Unlo·vesome,** *a.* (*adv.*). *Obs.* or *Sc.* (UN-[1] 7.)

**13..** *K. Alis.* 6423 The face of heom is playn, and hard,.. Unlossom is that kynrede. **1393** [see UNLOVELY *a.* 2]. *c* **1420** *Chron. Vilod.* 4333 He was an vnlofsom page. **1513** DOUGLAS *Æneid* VIII. Prol. 119 With a luik vnlufsum he lent me sik wordis. **1721**, **1813–25** in Sc. glossaries, etc. (in forms *unlussum, unlo'e-, unluesome*).

† **b.** As *adv.*

*c* **1480** HENRYSON *Bludy Serk* 61 Vnlusum was his likame dicht, His sark was all bludy.

**Unlo·ving,** *vbl. sb.* (UN-[1] 13.) *a* **1533** LD. BERNERS *Gold. Bk. M. Aurel.* (1546) Nn viij b, The vnlouyng of women, and the vnkyndenesse of men, which are vices committed of malyce.

**Unlo·ving,** *ppl. a.* (UN-[1] 10, 5 d.)

**1529** MORE *Suppl. Souls* Wks. 326/2 In holye scripture ye father is not accompted for vnlouing and cruel, that beateth his childe. **1597** SALUSBURY *Poems* (1914) 75, I loue, inforst by loues vnlouing charmes, My loue is pure. **1645** MILTON *Tetrach.* 4 To lead a wearisom life of unloving and unquiet conversation with one who neither affects nor is affected. *a* **1718** [see UNLOVED 1]. **1757** MRS. GRIFFITH *Lett. Henry & Frances* (1767) III. 38 The cool, unloving stoic Tenets, that..are sure to risk nothing for their Friends. **1840** BROWNING *Sordello* VI. 596 A Power above you still,.. Which thus you can Love, tho' unloving all conceived by man. **1868** MISS YONGE *Cameos* (1877) I. xv. 116 It was an unloving marriage; but he was much respected and beloved.

**Unlo·vingly,** *adv.* (UN-[1] 11; cf. prec.)

**1512** in Ellis *Orig. Lett.* Ser. II. I. 197 Thowȝ..the Kings Grace [be]. unlovingli oon sum partise served. **1583** BABINGTON *Commandm.* (1590) 264 Vnaduisedly, & I feare vnlouingly we speake what wee list. **1866** B. NORTH *Ourselves* 3 If I seem..to speak unlovingly.

**Unlo·vingness.** (UN-[1] 12; cf. prec.)

**1598** FLORIO, *Disamoreuolezza*, vnkindnes, vnlouingness. *a* **1639** W. WHATELEY *Prototypes* I. xix. (1640) 193 A kind of heate and unlovingnesse against the doer of them. *a* **1652** BROME *Eng. Moor* II. iii, Unlovingness of nature, Forgetfulness of blood. **1840** L. HUNT *Seer* I. 83/2 To continue to love every thing which unlovingness has not had a hand in altering. **1868** PUSEY *Serm. Pharisaism* 7 His lack of humility engendered his unlovingness.

**Unloy·al,** *a.* (UN-[1] 7.)

**1594** in *Liturg. Serv. Q. Eliz.* (1847) 661 Her most unloyal, desperate, and rebellious Subjects. **1600** HOLLAND *Livy* IX. xxvi. 332 The Romaines found all unloyall unto them. **1741** S. A. LAVAL *Hist. Reform.* IV. VIII. 992 Any undutiful or unloyal Word.

**Unloy·alty.** (UN-[1] 12.) **1560** DAUS tr. *Sleidane's Comm.* 311 What ende..doe you loke of this obstinacy and vnloy-

-aultie? **Unlu·bricated,** *ppl. a.* (UN-[1] 8). [1775 ASH.] 1879 *Cassell's Techn. Educ.* I. 66 The tallow melted, leaving the rifle unlubricated. **Unlu·cent,** *a.* (UN-[1] 7.) 1819 KEATS *Song Four Fairies* 61 Before the stains Of the mountain soil they take, And thee too unlucent make. 1837 CARLYLE *Fr. Rev.* II. v. iii, A combustion most fierce, but *unlucent.* **Unlu·cid,** *a.* (UN-[1] 7.) 1858 CARLYLE *Fredk. Gt.* VII. ix. II. 287 Rebuke which can still be read in growling, unlucid phraseology.

**Unlu·ck.** (UN-[1] 12. Cf. WFris. *onlok, ûnlok,* MLG. *unlucke,* LG. *unlük,* ON. *úlukka,* etc.; and WANLUCK.)

[The following early instance is of foreign origin:—1556 *Aurelio & Isabell* N 7, The fortune that unto her ennemys makes to seake the onlockes.]

1838 *Cruikshank's Comic Almanack* I. 142 Last Friday was a notable instance of my unluck. 1891 ATKINSON *Moorland Par.* 94 That bad management..might have something to do with the unluck of his stock.

† **Unlu·ckful,** *a. Obs.*—[1] [UN-[1] 7.] Bringing ill-luck. 1542 UDALL *Erasm. Apoph.* 338 Why settest thou thy delite in three the most vnluckeful beastes of y^e worlde?

**Unlu·ckily,** *adv.* [UN-[1] 11. Cf. ON. *úlukkuliga.*]

1. Unfortunately, unhappily.

Usually in parenthetic or loose construction.

1530 PALSGR. 840/1 Onluckely, *de grant malheur.* a 1586 SIDNEY *Arcadia* III. ii, Blind Fortune hating sharpe-sighted inventions, made them unluckily to be killed. 1638 SIR T. HERBERT *Trav.* (ed. 2) 92 Darab..most unluckily denyes, and goes on to levy men to support the rebellion. 1673 [R. LEIGH] *Transp. Reh.* 128 Unluckily..there has happen'd a prodigious conjunction. 1766 GOLDSM. *Vicar* xxviii, Unluckily all our money had been laid out..in provisions. 1825 J. NEAL *Bro. Jonathan* III. 404 Unluckily for him, the order for pursuit was given too early. 1871 FREEMAN *Norm. Conq.* IV. xvii. 74 Of the state of things..we unluckily hear nothing.

b. With verbs of happening, succeeding, etc.

c 1550 *Vertuous Scholehous* H 6 b, Man feareth that it [*sc.* matrimony] myght succede vnluckely. 1592 SHAKS. *Rom. & Jul.* III. iv. 1 Things haue falne out..vnluckily. 1607 — *Timon* III. ii. 51 How vnluckily it hapned, that [etc.]. 1711 SWIFT *Let. to Abp. King* 8 Mar., Nothing could happen so unluckily..as Mr. Harley's death. 1819 SHELLEY *Cenci* V. i. 12 It has turned out unluckily.

† 2. Unsuccessfully, badly. *Obs. rare.*

a 1586 SIDNEY *Arcadia* I. xvi, Urania, whom a rich knight ..had unluckely defended. 1638 JUNIUS *Paint. Ancients* 305 A certain Painter,..who painted cockes most unluckily, gave his boy great charge, to chase the true cockes away from his picture. 1665 BOYLE *Occas. Refl.* IV. xx, Many of those young Ladies..are so unluckily Bred,..that [etc.].

**Unlu·ckiness.** [UN-[1] 12: cf. next.]

1. Want of luck; unlucky character or fortune.

1561 T. HOBY tr. *Castiglione's Courtyer* IV. U vij b, You haue better declared the vnluckinesse of yonge men, then the happynesse of olde menn. 1638 SIR T. HERBERT *Trav.* (ed. 2) 227 Black..they call..a type of hell, and unluckinesse. 1673 KIRKMAN *Unlucky Citizen* A 5 b, Although I had been unlucky, yet I my own self caused that unluckyness. 1734 MRS. DELANY *Life & Corr.* (1861) I. 452 A piece of unluckiness of yours which has disappointed and mortified me. 1835 *Wilson's Tales Borders* I. 65/1 The luckiness or unluckiness of a First Foot. 1897 E. W. B. NICHOLSON *Golspie* 67 A belief in the unluckiness of Friday.

2. Tendency to mischief.

1760–72 H. BROOKE *Fool of Qual.* (1809) I. 163 Ned.. would not willingly have exchanged his unluckiness for the heirship of an estate. *Ibid.* 174 Ned's natural unluckiness.

† **Unlu·ckly,** *a. Obs.* [UN-[1] 7. Cf. Sw. *olycklig,* Da. *ulykkelig,* Norw. *ulukkeleg*; MHG. *unge-,* G. *unglücklich.*] = UNLUCKY *a.*

1585 GREENE *Planetom.* B 1 b, A peeuish Parent, whose celestial (but infortunate) impression ioyned with a perpetuall vnluckly irradiation, breedeth both in mens mindes and bodies..haplesse passions. 1600 HAKLUYT *Voy.* III. 318 The end of their enterprise became vnluckly and vnfortunate. 1678 MOXON *Mech. Exerc.* iv. 73 A negligent or unluckly knock with the Mallet.

**Unlu·cky,** *a.* [UN-[1] 7. Cf. WFris. *on-, ûnlokkich,* MLG. *unluckich.*]

1. Having an unfortunate character or issue; marked by misfortune or failure.

1530 PALSGR. 328/2 Unluckye, *meschant.* a 1548 HALL *Chron., Hen. VI,* 138 b, Accomptyng to hym their euil chaunce & vnluckey fortune. 1563 *Mirr. Mag., Somerset* xxxi, My life I lost in that vnlucky place. 1588 SHAKS. *Tit. A.* II. iii. 251 Brought hither in a most vnluckie houre. 1609 ROWLANDS *Dr. Merrie-man* (1627) C 1 b, One..brake his Arme, And did complaine vnto a Friend Of his vnlucky harme. 1676 HOBBES *Iliad* I. 200 To put an end to this unlucky strife. 1712 ADDISON *Spect.* No. 271 ¶ 4 This unlucky Accident happened to me in a Company of Ladies. 1829 LYTTON *Disowned* 79 It was the unluckiest step we ever made to admit him into the bosom of our family. 1855 MACAULAY *Hist. Eng.* xvi. III. 721 The year which was closing had certainly been unlucky.

2. Boding or involving misfortune; ill-omened, inauspicious.

a 1547 SURREY *Æneid* II. 1026 Th' unlucky figure of Creusaes ghost. 1568 GRAFTON *Chron.* II. 382 The Scottes.. thought John an unluckie name for a King. 1617 MORYSON *Itin.* I. 61 The King and the Queen,..while sometimes they thought Munday, sometimes Friday, to be vnlucky daies, had lost many faire winds. 1686 tr. *Chardin's Trav. Persia* 19 Nor do I know what unlucky star brought him to Constantinople. 1700 ROWE *Amb. Step-Moth.* III. i, Why do you urge my Father's fatal Power To curse you with a sad unlucky Bride. 1843 PRESCOTT *Mexico* (1850) I. 105 On the arrival of the five 'unlucky' days..they abandoned themselves to despair.

3. Having ill-luck; meeting with misfortune or mishap.

1552 HULOET, Vnluckye, to be, or haue yll lucke, *exauspicor.* 1560 DAUS tr. *Sleidane's Comm.* 29 b, You muste haue respecte also that this newe Empire..be not made vnlucky and vnfortunate. 1627 J. TAYLOR (Water P.) *Navy of Land Ships* Wks. (1630) 79/1 Some Ships..are so vnlucky, that they neuer make a good voyage. 1673 *S'too him Bayes* 4 Thou are the unluckyest disputant in the world. 1807 CRABBE *Par. Reg.* I. 705 The unlucky peasant heard the stranger's cry. 1896 HOWELLS *Impressions & Exp.* 239 A pair of grim old ladies, who..lived..aloof from their unluckier sisters.

4. Bringing ill-luck; causing mishap or harm; mischievous, malicious.

a 1586 SIDNEY *Arcadia* I. xi, By an unluckye blow the poore Philoxenus fell dead at his feete. 1598 R. BERNARD tr. *Terence, Phormio* II. ii, Are you vnluckie varlot so ready to doe euerie thing against me? 1712 ADDISON *Spect.* No. 343 ¶ 9 An unlucky Cock-Sparrow that..had before made great depredations upon our Commonwealth. 1727 [DORRINGTON] *Philip Quarll* (1816) 72 These unlucky instruments, which were intended for destruction, shall be employed for..preservation. 1768–74 TUCKER *Lt. Nat.* (1834) I. 571 Schoolmasters may not be displeased at unlucky tricks played by their lads. 1875– in many dialect glossaries (*Eng. Dial. Dict.*).

b. Of a horse: Bad-tempered, vicious.

1707 MORTIMER *Husb.* 151 If he [*sc.* the stallion] be unlucky and mad.

5. Of an unfortunate or regrettable nature; not entitled to commendation.

1628 FELTHAM *Resolves* II. l. 146 In some vnlucky dispositions, there is such an enuious kinde of Pride. 1671 tr. *Charente's Let. Customs Mauritania* 18 There would be much greater [plenty], if it was not for the unlucky custom of those people to bury their Gold. 1746 FRANCIS tr. *Horace, Epist.* I. i. 137 If some unlucky Barber notch my Hair. 1815 SCOTT *Guy M.* i, Mannering resolved..to halt for the night ..unless he could procure a guide to this unlucky village of Kippletringan.

**Unlu·crative,** *a.* (UN-[1] 7.) 1771–2 *Ess. fr. Batchelor* (1773) II. 135 An unlucrative and perillous profession. 1839 CARLYLE *Chartism* viii, The unlucrative fishing of ambergris. † **Unlu·de.** *Obs.*—[1] [UN-[1] 4 b + LUDE[1]. Cf. ON. *úhljóð.*] An unpleasant noise. a 1275 *Prov. Ælfred* 689 in *O. E. Misc.* 138 He wole maken fule luden; he wole grennen, ..and hewere [=ever] faren mid vnluden. **Unlu·ll,** *v.* (UN-[2] 3.) 1743 *Humours of Whist* 40 They love Opera's, say they, because they lull the Passions.., and yet..afterwards they fall to gaming, and very often pay for unlulling them again.

**Unlu·minous,** *a.* (UN-[1] 7.)

1773 *Gentl. Mag.* XLIII. 238 Hell's unluminous domains. 1837 CARLYLE *Fr. Rev.* II. v. iii, A tragical combustion, long smoking and smouldering unluminous. 1872 HOWELLS *Wedd. Journ.* v, The dense unluminous shadows of the moonshine.

† **Unlu·st,** *sb. Obs.* [OE. *unlust* (UN-[1] 12), = MDu. (Du.) *onlust,* MLG. *unlust,* OHG., MHG., G. *unlust* (Sw. *olust*), Goth. *unlustu-s* disinclination, displeasure, dislike. Cf. also ON. *úlyst* (Da. *ulyst*).]

1. Absence of pleasure; distress, weariness.

a 1000 *Sal. & Sat.* 268 (Gr.), Se fuȝel..wylleð hine on ðam wite, wunað unlustum. c 1440 *Jacob's Well* 116 No lyif of sweete deuocyoun ne gostly gladnesse is in ȝou, but dedly heuynes, & angwysch, & vnlust.

2. Want of appetite; nausea.

c 1000 *Sax. Leechd.* II. 158 Læcedomas wiþ unluste & wlætan þe of maȝan cymð. c 1230 *Hali Meid.* 35 Hwat mete se þi mahe hokerliche underfeð; þat is, wið unlust. 1561 HOLLYBUSH *Hom. Apoth.* 22 In all hys meates lette a litle saffron be put:..but it causeth vnluste in the stomacke.

3. Disinclination to be active or bestir oneself; slothfulness, laziness, idleness.

c 1000 ÆLFRIC *Hom.* II. 556 He þolað neadunge þeostra þurh wrace, se þe ær lustlice forbær his unlustes þeostra. c 1200 ORMIN 2623 Forr unnlusst & forrswundennleȝȝc Iss Drihhtin swiþe unncweme. a 1300 *Body & Soul* in *Map's Poems* (Camden) 336 Gloterie and lecherie, prude and wicke coveytise,..And in unlust for to lye. c 1386 CHAUCER *Pars. T.* ¶ 680 He dooth all thyng..with ydelnesse and vnlust. a 1470 H. PARKER *Dives & Pauper* (W. de W. 1496) VII. xxiii. 311/2 Goodes of holy chirche..ben gyuen to helpe of the poore &..not to selle them ayen to ryche men to mayntein them in unlust & in bodely ease.

b. Disinclination (for something). Const. *of, to* (with inf.), *towards.*

1390 GOWER *Conf.* III. 291 For unlust of that aventure Ther was noman which tok tonsure. 1530 TINDALE *Prol. Epist. Romans* A ij b, We fynde in oure silves vnlust and tediousnes to do good. 1535 COVERDALE *Isaiah* xliii. 22 Thou haddest an vnlust towarde me, o Israel.

4. Evil desire or inclination. (UN- 4 b.)

a 1225 *Ancr. R.* 288 (MS. B), Hwon þe heorte draheð to hire unlust [F. *a son mal desir*].

5. Unpleasantness, repulsiveness.

a 1529 SKELTON *El. Rummyng* 148 Theyr tresses untrust, All full of vnlust.

† **Unlu·st,** *v. Obs.* (UN-[2] 6 b.) 1683 *Argt. for Union* 38 It sounded more decently..to pray in the Churches words,.. then to use those of an eminent Dissenter, Lord un-lust us. † **Unlu·sthead.** *Obs.* [UN-[1] 12.] = UNLUST *sb.* 3. 1340 *Ayenb.* 31 Þet uerþe heaued..is onlusthede. *Ibid.* 163 þe zenne of sleawþe and of onlosthede.

† **Unlu·stily,** *adv. Obs.* [UN-[1] 11. Cf. MHG. *unlusticlichen,* MDa. *onlustelijc,* MSw. *olustelika.*] Slothfully, idly; weakly; unwillingly.

c 1360 *Song of Mercy* 143 in *E. E. P.* (1862) 122 Vnlustily vr lyf we lede. a 1470 TIPTOFT *Tulle on Friendsh.* (Caxton, 1481) b iv, That is the cause..that they that be right wys ben moest sory for the thynges whiche be doen unrihtwisly and they that ben stronge for thynges doen unlustely. 1598 FLORIO, *Svogliatamente,*..sadly, vnlustily, without taste.

† **Unlu·stiness.** *Obs.* [UN-[1] 12: see UNLUSTY.]

1. Lack of health and strength; physical weakness or debility. *Obs.*

1486 *Bk. St. Albans, Hawking* b vi b, A medecyne that an hawke shall not lie in mew for unlustynese. 1547 BOORDE *Brev. Health* xlix. 15 [Gaping] doth come of unlustines or els for lake of slepe. 1596 BARROUGH *Meth. Physick* VIII. 470 When..the wearinesse or the vnlustinesse of the sinewes is to bee asswaged. 1620 VENNER *Via Recta* Introd. 4 Vnlustinesse of the limmes.

2. Lack of cheerfulness or readiness; dullness; disinclination.

a 1470 H. PARKER *Dives & Pauper* (W. de W. 1496) I. lix. 101/2 Melodye was ordeyned in holy chirche..to put awaye heuynesse & unlustynesse. 1502 *Ord. Crysten Men* (W. de W. 1506) IV. xxx. 350 By unlustynes in dyffaylynge without desyre to do well. 1583 GOLDING *Calvin on Deut.* x. 54 Wee see what vnlustinesse is in vs when God commaundith vs any thing.

**Unlu·strous,** *a.* (UN-[1] 7.)

1709 ROWE *Shakspere's Cymb.* I. vii. 127 An Eye, Base and unlustrious [*sic*; 1623 illustrious] as the smoaky Light That's fed with stinking Tallow. 1790 ANNA SEWARD *Lett.* (1811) II. 378 How dim and unlustrous is Mr. Merry's muse! 1863 W. LANCASTER *Praeterita* 70 Sweet unlustrous eyes.

**Unlu·sty,** *a. Obs.* exc. *dial.* [UN-[1] 7. Cf. MDu. *onlustich* (Du. *onlustig*), MLG. *unlustich,* MHG. *unlustic* (G. *unlustig*), ON. *úlystugr,* older Da. *ulystig,* MSw. *olustogher* (Sw. *olustig*).]

1. Indisposed to activity or exertion; slothful, lazy; dull, listless. Also const. *to* with inf.

c 1230 *Hali Meid.* 43 And te oðre þat halden ham vnforgult & cleane, beon ase sikere unlustie & wlecche, liueð i godes luue wiðuten euch heate of þe hali gast. a 1240 *Lofsong* in *O.E. Hom.* I. 205 Touel spac and slow to godd, ȝemeleas and unlusti. 1340 *Ayenb.* 170 To þe sleauolle and to þe onlosti þet byeþ slacke to godes service. 1390 GOWER *Conf.* I. 203 Thus his yonge unlusti lif He dryveth forth. c 1450 *Mankind* 538 in *Macro Plays* 20 Thys londe ys so harde, yt makyth wn-lusty & yrke. 1504 C'TESS RICHMOND tr. *De Imitatione* IV. xii. (1893) 276 If thou haue nat that grace whan thou woldest but fele thy selfe drye and vnlusty. 1519 HORMAN *Vulg.* 48 My mynde..when it is cloudy wether.. is vnlusty. 1560 PILKINGTON *Exp. Aggeus* B vi *marg.,* Eate not so that it make ye unlustie to serue God. 1617 HIERON *Wks.* (1620) II. 273 Dauid..went on in a kinde of dull, and heauy, and vnlusty manner with them [*sc.* holy services].

b. *dial.* 'Unwieldy; very fat.'

1881–2 in Cornwall glossaries.

2. Lacking in bodily vigour; deficient in health and strength; weak, feeble.

1400–10 CLANVOWE *Cuckoo & Night.* viii, Thogh I be old and vnlusty. 1577 B. GOOGE *Heresbach's Husb.* 127* The Cowe should..haue but short pasture, and the Bull his belly full: so shall neyther she be too fat, nor he vnlusty. a 1624 BP. SMITH *Serm.* (1632) 249 Infants..borne lame or vnlusty.

b. Of land: Not in good heart.

1573–80 TUSSER *Husb.* (1878) 50 If land be vnlustie, the crop is not great.

3. Having an unattractive or ill-favoured look.

c 1400 *Destr. Troy* 8035 All wan was the weghe.., With lamentacion & langour vnlusty to se. 1430–40 LYDG. *Bochas* I. i. (1554) 2 b, By..great labours, They were unlusty and ugly of their cheres. a 1529 SKELTON *P. Sparowe* 915 His gummes rusty Are full vnlusty.

4. Undesirable, objectionable, unpleasant.

c 1412 HOCCLEVE *De Reg. Princ.* 3356 They often hadde gret cause hem to venge, But hir spiritis..pesible Thoghten þat craft vnlusty and alenge. c 1445 PECOCK *Donet* 24 Forto þus do and procede..wolde be ouer longe and tediose and vnlusty to þe heerers.

**Unlu·te,** *v.* [UN-[2] 4.] *trans.* To remove the lute from (a vessel, etc.).

1661 BOYLE *Sceptical Chym.* I. 68 Upon the unluting the vessels, it infected the Room with a scarce supportable stink. 1662 MERRETT tr. *Neri's Art of Glass* lxxiii, Unlute the Chrysibles. 1758 REID tr. *Macquer's Chym.* I. 226 Let the vessels cool, unlute them. 1839 URE *Dict. Arts* 10 The adopter tube is then unluted, and is slid into its junction pipe. **Unlu·ted,** *ppl. a.* (UN-[1] 8.) 1663 BOYLE *Usef. Exp. Nat. Philos.* II. App. 318 A calcining pot unluted. 1877 TEALE *Dangers to Health* Pl. v, Unluted joints leaking under the floor. **Unluxu·riant,** *a.* (UN-[1] 7.) 1723 *Historical Rev.* VIII. 43 A fruitful, yet unluxuriant and agreeable Imagination. 1805 WORDSW. *Prelude* VIII. 161 The unluxuriant produce of a life Intent on little but substantial needs.

**Unluxu·rious,** *a.* (UN-[1] 7.)

1700 PHILIPS *Pastorals* i. 7 In unluxurious times of yore. 1795 COLERIDGE *Plot Discov.* 50 The enlightened and unluxurious ancients. 1853 MISS YONGE *Heir of Redclyffe* xxiii, Unpretending, unluxurious chairs. 1868 W. R. GREG *Lit. & Soc. Judgm.* 357 A comparatively humble and unluxurious home.

**Unlyca·nthropize,** *v.* (UN-[2] 6 c; cf. LYCANTHROPE.) 1660 HOWELL *Parly of Beasts* 114 She is ready to unlycanthropize you from this Wolfish shape to your former condition. **Unly·rical,** *a.* (UN-[1] 7.) 1833 MILL *Diss. & Disc.* (1859) I. 85 The genius of Wordsworth is essentially unlyrical. **Unly·rically,** *adv.* (UN-[1] 11.) 1891 *Athenæum* 3 Oct. 445/2 The assemblage of trochee words..keeps the rhythm unlyrically staccato.

**Unmaca·damized,** *ppl. a.* (UN-[1] 8.)

1840 HOOD *Kilmansegg, Accident* xvi, So she gathered the awful sense Of the street in its past unmacadamiz'd tense. 1852 SMEDLEY *L. Arundel* xxxii. 238 Flinty hearts, unmacadamised by the smallest grain of pity. 1879 E. WALFORD *Londoniana* I. 40 Along roads rugged, rutty, and un-macadamized.

**Unma·ckly,** *a.* and *adv. north. dial.* [UN-[1] 7, 11: see MACK *a.* and MACKLY *adv.*] Unshapely; ill-favoured(ly).

? a 1600 *Sir Cawline* xxx. (Percy Folio MS.), Vpon his squier [=neck] fiue heads he bare, Vnmackley made was hee. 1811–76 in northern glossaries.

†**Unma·culat,** *ppl. a. Sc. Obs.* [Un-[1] 8 b, 5 b.] Immaculate. **1535** Stewart *Cron. Scot.* (Rolls) II. 158 His awin ladie vnmaculat and clene. **1607** *Melrose Regality Rec.* (1914) 35 The judge..ordanis him to redelyver..the said obligatioun unmaculat, uncuttit. **Unma·d,** *a.* (Un-[1] 7.) **1570** Foxe *A. & M.* (ed. 2) III. 2134/1 Old and yong, blind and lame, madde and vnmadde. **1694** Echard *Plautus* 61 She's th' only unmad Person o' my Family. **Unma·ddened,** *ppl. a.* (Un-[1] 8.) **1797** Coleridge *Osorio* III. i. 22 What sense unmadden'd, might bear up against The rushing of your congregated wings? **1868** E. R. Sill *Poems, Hermitage* xx, Unmaddened by the babble of vain men.

**Unma·de,** *ppl. a.* [Un-[1] 8 b, 5 d.]

**1.** Not (yet) made, in senses of the verb.

*c* **1250** *Gen. & Ex.* 671 Babel, ðat tur, bi-lef un-mad. **1375** Barbour *Bruce* IV. 608 He..thoucht to leif the fyre vnmaid. *c* **1400** *Pilgr. Sowle* (Caxton, 1483) v. i. 74 God..maketh as many werkes as better ben made than vnmade. *c* **1489** Caxton *Sonnes of Aymon* xx. 445 Thys cave sheweth not that it hathe be vnmade this hundred yeres passed. **1526** *Pilgr. Perf.* (W. de W. 1531) 81 Whiche..lefte the lettre .O. that he was in makynge halfe vnmade. **1592** Shaks. *Rom. & Jul.* III. iii. 70 Taking the measure of an vnmade graue. **1623** Sanderson *Serm.* (1632) 151 Lawes..are farre better vnmade, then vnkept. **1680** Sir J. Foulis *Acc. Bk.* (S.H.S.) 165 To [blank] davison for 4 duz[n] unmade pens. **1704** *Lond. Gaz.* No. 3981/4 With new fine Holland Shifts and Hankerchiefs unmade. **1716** *Wodrow Corr.* (1843) II. 132 Whatever of cloth, made or unmade, linen yarn or woollen. **1807** Crabbe *Par. Reg.* III. 180, I die,..My mind unsettled, and my will unmade. **1828** *Lights & Shades* I. 286 A halfclothed mother seated on the corner of an unmade bed. **1885** C. E. Pascoe *Lond. of To-day* 315 The plain unmade satin scarf.

**b.** *spec.* Untrained. (Cf. Made *ppl. a.* 6.)

**1856** H. Dixon *Post & Paddock* i. 4 The largest market in the world for unmade hunters and carriage-horses.

**2.** Existing without having been made; uncreated but existent.

*c* **1350** *Athanasian Creed* in *MS. Bodl. 425* fol. 69 b, Bot on unmade and on mikel is he. **1434** Misyn *Mending Life* 122 O sweit light..þat is my makar vn-made, liȝt þe face ..of my Inward eyn with clernes vn-made. *c* **1449** Pecock *Repr.* II. xvi. 242 Thei..helden that al the bodili heuen..was vnmaad, and was euer withoute bigynnyng of tyme. **1563** Man *Musculus' Commonpl.* 373, I doe fynde generally two Natures, one not made, the other made. Wee call that unmade (*non factam*), which belongeth unto God. **1678** Cudworth *Intell. Syst.* Pref., The Latter asserted an Unmade Mind, whereas the Former Generated all Mind..out of those Qualified Atoms. **1682** Norris *Hierocles* Pref. 23 Unmade, Self-existent, independent Deities. **1720** Waterland *Eight Serm.* 239 If He existed before anything was made, He must..be unmade, and therefore eternal. **1827** Pollok *Course T.* VI. 630 Maker, Upholder, Governor of all! Thyself unmade, ungoverned, unupheld! **1884** *Congregat. Year Bk.* 93 His world is a world without design, atoms are the unmade makers of all things.

**3.** † **a.** *Sc.* (with complement). *Obs.*

**1456** [see Un-[1] 5 d (*b*).] **1596** Dalrymple tr. *Leslie's Hist. Scot.* (S.T.S.) II. 436 Quhat chancet on Pasche day..suld not be vnmaid mentioune of.

**b.** With advs. Not made *out*, *up*, etc.

**1600** Hakluyt *Voy.* III. 87 A Pinnesse..which was caryed in pieces, and vnmade vp. *a* **1631** Donne *Elegy* xv. 97 Countless multitudes Of formlesse curses, projects unmade up. *a* **1680** Butler *Charac.*, *Pedant* (1908) 136 He wears his little Learning, unmade-up, puts it on, before it was half finished. **1707** Mortimer *Husb.* 379 Where the rows and brush lie longer unbound or unmade up. **1833** Lamb *Let. to Cary* in *Final Mem.* viii, I think we scarce left anything unmadeout.

†**Unma·ggled,** *ppl. a. Obs.*[−1] [Un-[1] 8.] Unmangled. *c* **1470** *Gol. & Gaw.* 720 Wes nane forssy on fold, that wes feghtand, Wnmaglit [*edd.* -manglit] and marrit.

**Unma·gic,** *v.* [Un-[2] 6.] *trans.* To disenchant. **1650** H. More *Observ.* in *Enthus. Tri.*, etc. (1656) L 2 b, Poor Galen's Antichrist, though one Purge of his Might so unmagick thee as make thee wise. **Unma·gistrate,** *v.* (Un-[2] 6 b.) **1649** Milton *Tenure Kings* (ed. 2) 55 If this Parlament..might..take all power..out of his hand, which in effect is to unmagistrate him. **Unma·gistrate-like,** *a.* (Un-[1] 7 c.) **1644** Milton *Divorce* (ed. 2) II. xi. 53 What more un-Judge-like, more un-Magistrate-like, and in warre more un-commander-like? **Unmagna·nimous,** *a.* (Un-[1] 7.) **1856** De Quincey *Confess.* Wks. I. 206 *note*, A man so unmagnanimous as Napoleon. **1877** Owen *Wellesley's Desp.* p. xl, The indirect and unmagnanimous revenge ..galled him to the quick.

**Unmagne·tic,** *a.* (Un-[1] 7.)

**1805** *Phil. Trans.* XCV. 283 Such substances as may be sublimed with facility, will gradually quit the oxide,..leaving it unmagnetic, as at first. **1844** Noad *Electricity* (ed. 2) 425 An unmagnetic needle, placed within a close helix, formed by the wire of the circuit. **1860** O. W. Holmes *Prof. Breakf.-t.* i, A new clean unmagnetic word.

**Unmagne·tical,** *a.* [Un-[1] 7.] = prec. **1815** J. Smith *Panorama Sci. & Art* II. 177 If an unmagnetical bar be struck with a hammer. **1832** *Nat. Philos.*, *Magnetism* iv. 34 (L.U.K.), Unmagnetical iron or steel. **Unma·gnetized,** *ppl. a.* (Un-[1] 8.) **1834** Mrs. Somerville *Connex. Phys. Sci.* xxix. (1836) 321 An unmagnetised iron bar. **1873** J. C. Maxwell *Electr. & Magn.* III. vi. II. 76 In the unmagnetized state of ordinary iron. **Unma·gnify,** *v.* (Un-[2] 3.) **1747** E. Poston *Pratler* I. 38 Whenever we think..that we understand the Nature and Ways of God, what do we in Reality, but unmagnify him, or..disrobe him of his Honour and Glory? †**Unma·ht.** *Obs.*[−1] [Un-[1] 12.] One not possessed of any power or means. *a* **1300** *Prov. Hendyng* in *Rel. Ant.* I. 114 Moni mon mid a lutel ahte ȝeveth is dohter an un-mahte, Ant lutel is the bettre. **Unmai·d,** *v.* (Un-[2] 6 b.) **1638** N. Whiting *Albino & Bellama* 3527 Is't not said Spirits have power a damsel to unmaid? †**Unmai·den,** *sb. Obs.*[−1] (Un-[1] 12.) *a* **1380** *Langland's P. Pl.* A. x. 193 (Vernon MS.), Bote Maydens and vn-Maydens clene ow save.

**Unmai·den,** *v.* [Un-[2] 6 b. Cf. Du. *ontmaagden*, G. *entmägden.*] *trans.* To deprive of maidenhood; to deflower.

**1579** Northbrooke *Dicing* 68 b, Through this dauncing many maidens haue beene vnmaidened. **1612** Drayton *Poly-olb.* vii. 47 Least by the Sylvans..She might unmaidned goe unto her soveraigne flood. **1660** J. S. *Andromana* II. v, Sturdy Hercules, When he unmaiden'd fifty in one night. *a* **1693** *Urquhart's Rabelais* III. xii. (1694) 96 He unmaiden'd his Sister Juno. [**1876** *Whitby Gloss.*, *Unmaiden'd*, married.]

*refl.* **1592** Warner *Alb. Eng.* VIII. xli. 179 Think not Lord Cliffords daughter will vn-maiden her for pay.

Hence **Unmai·dening** *vbl. sb.*

*a* **1693** *Urquhart's Rabelais* III. vi 58 The unmaidning or depucelating of a hundred Virgins.

**Unmai·denlike,** *a.* (Un-[1] 7 c.) **1876** Swinburne *Erechtheus* 364 Not moved of mine own will, Unmaidenlike.

**Unmai·denly,** *a.* (Un-[1] 7.)

**1634** Bp. Hall *Contempl.*, *N. T.* IV. iv, [These] wanton gesticulations of a virgin..could be no other than riggish and unmaidenly. **1828** Scott *F. M. Perth* xxv, Such tokens of intimacy..are uncomely and unmaidenly. **1848** Mrs. Gaskell *Mary Barton* xv, The whisperings of her womanly nature..caused her to shrink from any unmaidenly action. **1866** G. Macdonald *Ann. Q. Neighb.* xxxii, At least do not put your character in question by going in this unmaidenly fashion.

Hence **Unmai·denliness.**

**1874** *Fortn. Rev.* Feb. 239 What the poet thinks of the unmaidenliness of Lynette. **1879** Meredith *Egoist* xxi, You, father! you have driven me to unmaidenliness.

**Unmai·l,** *v.* [Un-[2] 4. Cf. MDu. *ontmaelgeren*, *-mailleren.*] *trans.* To break or detach the links of (a mail-coat).

?*a* **1412** Lydg. *Two Merch.* 668 How many a man hath Fortune assayled..Her habiriownys of steel also vnmayled. *c* **1489** Caxton *Sonnes of Aymon* iii. 79 Ye sholde haue seen ..many a goode haubergen vnmayled. **1611** Cotgr., *Desmaillé*, vnmailed; vnlinked; vndone..as a coat of maile.

Hence **Unmai·ling** *vbl. sb.*

**1591** Percivall, *Desmalladura*, vnmailing. **1611** Cotgr., *Desmailleure*, an vnmailing; an vndoing..of maile.

**Unmai·lable,** *a. U.S.* (Un-[1] 7 b.) **1875** *U.S. Official Post Guide* 23 (Flügel), Such matter must be forwarded to the Dead Letters Office, marked as 'unmailable.' **Unmai·led,** *ppl. a.* [Un-[1] 8.] Not covered or protected by mail. **1806** *Ann. Rev.* IV. 562 The brother of Biorn with his mail; Herbert unmailed. **1807** Wordsw. *White Doe* I. 765 With breast unmailed, unweaponed hand. **Unmai·mable,** *a.* (Un-[1] 7 b.) **1565** Golding *Ovid's Met.* XII. (1587) 155 When Ceny had sufficiently giuen Latreus leaue too smyght His flesh which was vnmaymeable.

**Unmai·med,** *ppl. a.* (Un-[1] 8.)

**1470–85** Malory *Arthur* x. lix. 515, I shalle be with yow..yf I be vnslayne or vnmaymed. **1595** Markham *Sir R. Grinvile* clxxi, They..to theyr Generall brought His mangled carkasse, but vnmaimed minde. **1614** T. Godwin *Rom. Antiq.* II. § ii. 5. 40 He was to be..of a life vnspotted, and a body vnmaimed. **1630** Drumm. of Hawth. *Flowres Sion* xxiv. 8 His spight yet so cannot her all throw downe, But that some Statue..Yet lurkes vnmaym'd within her weeping walles. **1715** Pope *Iliad* Pref. E 2, It is the first grand Duty of an Interpreter to give his Author entire and unmaim'd. *c* **1810** J. Baillie *2nd Part Ethwald* I. ii, Standing erect, Unmaim'd and vigorous.

† **Unmai·n.** *Obs.*[−1] [Un-[1] 12. Cf. OHG. *unmagen*, ON. *úmegin*, *úmegn* (Icel. *ómegin*, MSw. *omäghin*, Norw. dial. *umegje*, *umeie*); also OE. *unmægness.*] Want of strength.

**1338** R. Brunne *Chron.* (1810) 55 Þof I had stombled þorgh myn vnmayn, He suld haf..reised me agayn.

**Unmaintai·nable,** *a.* (Un-[1] 7 b.)

**1625** Donne *Serm.* 657 They have bound themselves not to recede from those doctrines, how unmaintenable soever they be in themselves. **1701** Norris *Ideal World* I. vi. 352 The defence of so desperate and unmaintainable a breach. *a* **1832** Bentham *Levelling Syst.* Wks. 1843 I. 362 The good expected..would be altogether unattainable—at least unmaintainable for two instants together. **1853** Grote *Greece* XI. 499 That the festivals..were unmaintainable during such a war. **1883** *Law Times* 22 Dec. 135/1 The society..was..an illegal society..and the action was consequently unmaintainable.

**Unmaintai·ned,** *ppl. a.* (Un-[1] 8.) **1691** Baxter *Nat. Ch.* xv. 72 A Life of unmaintained poverty, and censure. **1885** *Pall Mall G.* 1 July 6/1 Hence we have crime unnoticed, discipline unmaintained. **Unma·kable,** *a.* (Un-[1] 7 b.) **1674** Grew *Disc. Mixture* iii. § 13 No Principle is made by the fire: all Principles being unalterable; and therefore unmakable. **1701** — *Cosm. Sacr.* I. iii. 13.

**Unma·ke,** *v.* [Un-[2] 3. Cf. MDu. (Du.) *ontmaken*, OHG. *in(t)mahhôn* (G. *entmachen*).]

**1.** *trans.* To reverse or undo the making of (some thing or object); to reduce again to an unmade condition.

**1426** Lydg. *De Guil. Pilgr.* 11270 He made [nets], & hem vnmade ageyn. *c* **1430** *Pilgr. Lyf Manhode* I. lxiii. (1869) 38 It is a iewell that was..maad..of my fader with oute smytinge of strok...For noyse and strokes maken it nouht, but tobreken it and vnmaken it. **1641** Milton *Ch. Govt.* vi, So that Prelaty..must be forc't to dissolve and unmake her own pyramidal figure. **1690** T. Burnet *Theory Earth* II. 132 God does not make or unmake things, to try experiments. **1750** Johnson *Rambler* No. 74 ⁋ 11 She compels them to alter their work, then to unmake it. **1857** Emerson *Ode to Beauty* 99 Dread Power!..if God thou be, Unmake me quite, or give thyself to me. **1868** Morris *Earthly Par.* (1870) I. I. 339 And now thou knowest in how short a space The God that made the world can unmake thee.

*absol.* **1426** Lydg. *De Guil. Pilgr.* 11416 And thogh that I make & vnmake, Blame me nat. **1821** Byron *Cain* I. i. 142 But, if he made us—he cannot unmake.

**b.** With immaterial object.

**1377** Langl. *P. Pl.* B. xv. 236 Matrimoigne for monye [they] maken & vnmaken. **1513** Douglas *Æneid* VI. ix. 199 Sum vtheris..That lawis maid and wnmaid, as thaim list. *a* **1536** Tindale in Marbeck *Bk. of Notes* (1581) 746 Who can suffer them.., for their owne profites, to make and vnmake lawes..? **1639** Fuller *Holy War* II. xvii. 67 God will not unmake his miracles by making them common. **1802–12** Bentham *Ration. Judic. Evid.* (1827) V. 266 When a statute..has been unmade by the authority that made it. **1822** Byron *Juan* VI. lx, In perfect innocence she then unmade Her toilet, which cost little. **1860** Gen. P. Thompson *Audi Alt. Part.* III. cxxiv. 77 The study of what has made and unmade military successes.

*absol.* **1604** Shaks. *Oth.* II. iii. 352 His Soule is so enfetter'd to her Loue, That she may make, vnmake, do what she list. **1848** Bailey *Festus* (ed. 3) 17 Then comes the feeling which unmakes, undoes. **1876** Mrs. Whitney *Sights & Ins.* II. 401 Perhaps the very first thing we see that wisdom do, is to unmake and separate, and seem to break and mix yet more.

**2. a.** To deprive of a particular rank or station; to depose.

**1554** Bale *Declar. Bonner's Articles* xix. 68 He is wonte to make kinges, and to vnmake them again at his plesure. **1567** Jewel *Def. Apol.* 418 Saieinge withal, Hee had Power to make Emperours, and to vnmake them. **1651** N. Bacon *Disc. Govt. Eng.* II. xiv. 129 An English King hath power ..to make and unmake Members [of Parliament] as he shal please. **1670** G. H. *Hist. Cardinals* I. III. 70 They made and unmade Popes at their pleasure. **1736** Thomson *Liberty* IV. 879 He mark'd the Barons of excessive sway, At pleasure making and unmaking kings. **1808** Mitford *Hist. Greece* IV. 353 He made and unmade there what kings he pleased. **1894** Ld. Wolseley *Life Marlborough* I. 178 Her authority was such, that she could make and unmake ministers.

**b.** To deprive of a certain character or quality; to alter in nature. Also with compl.

**1616** B. Jonson *Epigr.* lv, At once thou mak'st me happie, and vnmak'st. **1669** Dryden *Tyrannic Love* III. i, You are so pure—That in the act 'twould change the impiety. Heaven would unmake it sin! **1709** *Tatler* No. 66 ⁋ 4 To make our Patient any Thing better, we must unmake him what he is. **1710** Shaftesb. *Charac.* (1711) I. 308 That which we fondly make our Happiness at one time, we may as readily un-make again at another. **1856** Mrs. Browning *Aur. Leigh* IX. 200, I take her as God made her, and as men Must fail to unmake her. **1858** Hawthorne *Fr. & It. Note-bks.* (1871) II. 8 Her modest attitude..is partly what unmakes her as the heathen Goddess, and softens her into woman.

**3.** *fig.* To undo; to ruin or destroy; to bring to nothing.

**1605** Shaks. *Macb.* I. vii. 54 They haue made themselues, and that their fitnesse now Do's vnmake you. **1652** Benlowes *Theoph.* III. lxxxix, Sure, Thou to guilt, Which would unmake thy creatures, wilt Be just. **1674** N. Fairfax *Bulk & Selv.* 189 To mistrust boundless wisdom, to contrive so, that it might have better been contrived, is to unmake its boundlesness. **1867** Felton *Anc. & Mod. Gr.* II. i. 264 If the great powers are going to make a permanent European state out of Turkey, they must unmake the Turk. **1870** Emerson *Soc. & Solit.* vii. 135 The machine unmakes the man.

**4.** To annul a decision of (the mind).

**1897** Mary Kingsley *W. Africa* 4 When you have made up your mind to go to West Africa the very best thing you can do is to get it unmade again.

Hence **Unma·king** *vbl. sb.*

**1591** Percivall, *Deshazimiento*, vndooing, vnmaking. *a* **1676** Hale *Prim. Orig. Man.* III. i. (1677) 254 Though he seems to admit Eternal Vicissitudes of such Making, and Unmaking, and Restitutions of the inferior World. **1867** H. Bushnell *Moral Uses Dark Th.* 285 A general unmaking of the world by transgression. **1871** Smiles *Charac.* xi. 324 A wife may be the making or the unmaking of the best of men.

**Unma·ker.** [Un-[1] 12, or f. prec.] One who unmakes.

*c* **1430** *Pilgr. Lyf Manhode* III. xvii. (1869) 144 This hand is an vnmakere of howses. **1684** Baxter *Par. Congreg.* 40 The Magistrate may command men how to do their office-work, and yet neither be the maker nor unmaker of the office. **1862** Mrs. Crosland *Mrs. Blake* II. 47 That the soldier is rather an 'unmaker' and instrument of destruction than anything else. **1893** W. Watson *Lachrymæ Mus.* 26 Unmaker of all, and renewer, The Lord of Death.

**Unmali·cious,** *a.* (Un-[1] 7.)

**1649** Jer. Taylor *Gt. Exemp.* II. viii. 68 An unconfirmed, unresolved, unmalicious habite. **1663** Cowley *Verses, Ode Cowley's Book* iv, As when a seat in Heaven Is to an unmalicious Sinner given. **1795** T. Wright *Autobiog.* (1864) 17 The sudden little unmalicious quarrel. **1866–7** Carlyle *E. Irving* in *Remin.* (1881) I. 145 A most quizzing, merry, entertaining, guileless, and unmalicious man. **1886** Ruskin *Præterita* I. 382 His subtle,..unmalicious sarcasm.

**Unmali·gnant,** *a.* (Un-[1] 7.) **1841** L. Hunt *Seer* (1864) 47 Nature has a beautiful way of reconciling all necessities that are unmalignant. **Unma·lleabi·lity.** (Un-[1] 12; cf. next.) [**1828–32** Webster.] **1875** Maine *Hist. Inst.* ii. 62 The great unmalleability of all bodies of law. **1887** Ruskin *Præterita* II. i. 13 The density and unmalleability of the world.

**Unma·lleable,** *a.* (Un-[1] 7 b.)

**1609** G. Benson *Serm. 7 Mar.* 55 Be perswaded, let not your hearts be vnmalleable. **1665** J. Spencer *Prodigies* (ed. 2) 341 To grow (like Iron often heated and quench'd) churlish and unmalleable by the hammer of the Divine threatnings. **1779** Johnson *L. P.*, *Dryden* Wks. II. 305 After this he did not often bring upon his anvil such stubborn and unmalleable thoughts. **1795** *Phil. Trans.* LXXXV. 341 Hard unmalleable iron. **1838** Hawthorne *Amer. Note-bks.* (1883) 166 A man of unmalleable habits. **1890** *Spectator* 19 July 79/2 The large masses of rather unmalleable human material which he contrives to collect together.

Hence **Unma·lleableness.**

**1644** R. Chalfont *Serm.* 10 May 8 The hardnesse and unmalleablenesse of heart.

**Unma·ltable,** *a.* (Un-[1] 7 b.) **1778** [W. H. Marshall] *Minutes Agric.*, *Digest* 43 To feed cart-horses on unmaltable barley.

**Unma·lted,** *ppl. a.* (Un-[1] 8.)

**1651** R. Child in *Hartlib's Legacy* (1655) 141 Beer may

be made of Wheat, Barley, Pease, &c. unmalted. 1707 MORTIMER *Husb.* 267 The part of the Corn which it passeth not, will remain unmalted, the rest will be perfect Malt. 1790 LUCKOMBE *Eng. Gazetteer* I. p. xviii, Thirty-four millions of bushels of barley unmalted. 1830 M. DONOVAN *Dom. Econ.* I. 143 The comparative analyses of malted and unmalted barley. 1884 *Law Rep.* 27 Chanc. Div. 497 The gelatinization or conversion of unmalted grain.

**Unma·n**, *sb. rare.* [UN-[1] 12, 4 b. Cf. OE. *unmann*, Du. *onman*, MLG., MHG. *unman.*] **a.** One below the status of a man. **b.** A monster.

*a* 1400 *Minor Poems fr. Vernon MS.* 336/295 Þou seidest I scholde ben holden an vn-mon. *a* 1641 in *Vox Borealis* C 1 b (Old adage), Waters shall waxe, and Woods shall waine, And unman shall be Man, and Man shall be naine. 1879 G. MACDONALD *Sir Gibbie* xxi, He was on the wild hill, with miles on miles of cover! Here the unman could not catch him.

**Unma·n**, *v.* [UN-[2] 6 b. Cf. MDu. (Du.) *ontmannen*, MHG. (G.) *entmannen* ]

**1.** *trans.* To deprive of the attributes of a man; to remove from the category of men.

1598 MARSTON *Sco. Villanie* II. vii. (1599) 204 Why, sower Satyrist, Canst thou vnman him? here I dare insist And soothly say, he is a perfect soule. 1643 TUCKNEY *Balm of G.* 40 It is..the cruell man (saith Solomon) that troubles his owne flesh; nay the Apostle un-manneth him that hates it. 1681 BAXTER *Acc. Sherlocke* vi. 212 Every Humanist that useth..gawdy fashions, is not thereby unchristened, unchurched, or unman'd. 1711 G. HICKES *Two Treat. Chr. Priesth.* (ed. 3) I. p. ccx, We cannot suppose that infinite Goodness would bind us..to such strict unalterable Duties, as unman us in this World. 1751 R. SHIRRA in *Rem.* (1850) 86 The first [Ebion] ungods him; the other [Marcion] unmans him. 1884 BROWNING *Ferishtah, Family* 77, I may put forth angel's plumage, once unmanned, but not before.

**2.** To reduce below the level of man; to degrade, brutalize. Also *refl.*

1637 A. STAFFORD *Vind. Fem. Glory* (1860) p. xxii, Hee that is not tender..unmanneth himselfe, and is but best a Monster..in humane shape. 1660 tr. *Amyraldus' Treat. conc. Relig.* I. vii. 106 They whom barbarisme ha's unman'd in all other things. 1701 W. WOTTON *Hist. Rome* 246 Habits of Vice unman Men's minds.

**3.** To deprive of manly courage or fortitude; to make weak or effeminate.

*c* 1600 CHALKHILL *Thealma & Clearchus* 846 They heard they had unmann'd themselves by ease. 1605 SHAKS. *Macb.* III. iv. 73 What? quite vnmann'd in folly...Fie for shame. *a* 1628 F. GREVIL *Poems, Hum. Learn.* xlii, Engines that did un-man the mindes of men. 1673 HICKERINGILL *Greg. F. Greyb.* 318 Impressions of fear that mollifie and unman vulgar and narrow spirits. 1715 ADDISON *Drummer* III. i, That dear Woman! the sight of her unmans me. 1736 A. HILL *Zara* V. I. 64 Tears!..The first which ever yet unmann'd my Eyes! 1780 *Mirror* No. 90, This blow, for a time, unmanned me quite. 1847 PRESCOTT *Peru* I. 441 For a moment the overwhelming conviction of it unmanned him. 1883 *Manch. Exam.* 24 Nov. 5/1 Thirty or forty years of such treatment is enough to unman any people.

*absol.* 1811 BYRON *Euthanasia* vi, And women's tears, produced at will, Deceive in life, unman in death.

**4.** To divest of the character of a grown man. Also *intr.* (for *refl.*).

1672 PENN *Spir. Truth Vind.* 23 As he is unmanned, that is, again become a little Child. 1889 *Harper's Mag.* Jan. 191/2 But find where children haunt, and there unman, And with them laugh and play.

**5.** To deprive of virility; to emasculate.

1684-9 A. G. in *Plutarch's Morals* (1718) IV. 334 Because the Samians had saved the Children of the Greeks from being unmann'd [*tr.* 1603 from eviration]. 1885 E. CLODD *Myths & Dreams* 36 Gæa..provided Cronus..with an iron sickle, wherewith he unmanned Uranus.

**6.** To denude (a vessel or fleet) of men.

1687 MIÈGE *Gt. Fr. Dict.* II. s.v., To unman a Ship, *desarmer un Vaisseau.* 1696 in *London Gaz.* No. 3250/1 After the Fleet has been Manned, it hath been in a great Measure Unmanned again by Desertion. 1796 NELSON in Nicolas *Disp.* (1846) VII. p. xxxiv, If the Admiral had small Vessels, he could not venture to unman his Fleet.

**7.** *fig.* To deprive (oneself) *of* something.

1694 R. FRANCK *North. Mem.* Ded. p. xv, Let me admonish the more Ingenious Artist to be mindful of Experience, lest peradventure he slide into the slippery Tract of an Author, so unman himself of practical Demonstration.

Hence **Unma·nning** *vbl. sb.* and *ppl. a.*

1610 HEALEY *St. Aug. Citie of God* VII. xxiv. 285 Here they feare not the vn-manning of them-selues. 1624 MIDDLETON *Game at Chess* I. i, I never give absolution To any crime of that unmanning nature. 1831 COLERIDGE *Table-t.* 12 Sept., The most wretched and unmanning reluctance and shrinking from action. 1886 STEVENSON *Dr. Jekyll* 58 A place for sufferings and terrors so unmanning.

**Unma·nacle**, *v.* [UN-[2] 4 b.] *trans.* To free from manacles. Also *fig.*

1582 STANYHURST *Æneis* II. (Arb.) 48 This sayd, my yooncker ..Too stars vp mounting both his hands vnmanacled [L. *exutasvinclis*], aunswer'd. *c* 1629 DONNE *Serm.* (1640) 601 We shall see the Church emancipated, enfranchised, unfettered, unmanacled. 1638 MAYNE *Lucian* (1664) 24 Stretch forth thy right hand: unmanacle him Vulcan, and nail him. 1833 TENNYSON *Two Voices* 236 This anguish fleeting hence, Unmanacled from bonds of sense. 1866 NEALE *Sequences & Hymns* 153 While..they unmanacled cold hands and numbed feet. 1889 G. SMITH *St. Paul at Sea* ii, Caesar and slave alike must be Unmanacled by me.

Hence **Unma·nacling** *vbl. sb.*

1635 A. STAFFORD *Fem. Glory* 208 That Death to the just is no other than..the unmanacling of the Soule.

**Unma·nacled**, *ppl. a.* (UN-[1] 8.)

1726 C. PITT *Vida's Art of Poetry* III. 63 The lurking faults and errors you may see, When the words run unmanacled and free. 1781 COWPER *Table-t.* 589 Language, ..warm As ecstasy, unmanacled by form. 1805 SOUTHEY *Madoc in W.* v. 28 Thus their limbs Unmanacled display'd the truest forms Of strength and beauty. *a* 1849 POE *Loss of Breath* Wks. 1864 IV. 308 His extreme infirmity..had obtained him the privilege of remaining unmanacled.

**Unma·nageable**, *a.* [UN-[1] 7 b.]

**1.** Incapable of being governed or controlled: **a.** Of persons or their disposition.

1632 B. JONSON *Magn. Lady* I. i, My humour being as stubborn as the rest, And as unmanageable. 1665 GLANVILL *Def. Van. Dogm.* p. x, They..are rendred unmanageable by any Authority but that of Absolute Dominion. 1728 MORGAN *Algiers* II. v. 316 That tough, lofty, unmanageable Monarch [*sc.* Henry VIII]. 1791 BENTHAM *Panopt.* I. 39 As to safe custody and good order, four [prisoners] is not such a number as can well be deemed unmanageable. 1804 ABERNETHY *Surg. Obs.* 186 [During] the greater part of the delirium he had been very unmanageable. 1887 *Spectator* 25 June 854/2 The rise of soldiers who might be unmanageable or too successful.

**b.** Of animals. (Also in fig. context.)

1678 MRS. BEHN *Sir P. Fancy* I. i, [The fops] of the Town are the most unmanageable beasts in nature. 1681 R. L'ESTRANGE *Tully's Offices* 45 Horses..grown Fierce, and Unmenageable, by being chaf'd. 1712 WATERLAND *Serm.* Wks. 1823 VIII. 383 When they grow impatient of the curb..they do but show..how much more unruly and unmanageable they had been without it. 1823 SCOTT *Quentin D.* ix, Each fresh gambade of his unmanageable horse. 1855 *Poultry Chron.* II. 611/1 She [*sc.* a hen] was rather conceited, unmanageable, and very touchy about interference. 1878 BOSW. SMITH *Carthage* 314 The elephants..became unmanageable.

**c.** Of things.

1794 PALEY *Evid.* I. II. ii. § 3 Convulsions..are amongst the..most uncertain and unmanageable applications to the human frame. 1898 'MERRIMAN' *Roden's Corner* xxi, When human affairs suddenly appear to become unmanageable.

**2.** Incapable of being properly or conveniently handled or manipulated.

1658 PHILLIPS, *Immanity*,..such a hugenesse as renders a thing unmanageable. 1779 *Phil. Trans.* LXIX. 422 It required an index of an unmanageable length. 1805 in Nicolas *Disp. Nelson* (1846) VII. 166 So that the Ship was entirely unmanageable. 1822 J. FLINT *Lett. Amer.* 75 Travellers..ought not to adopt large boxes, which..are comparatively unmanageable on every occasion. 1885 *Manch. Exam.* 17 Jan. 5/4 A great, awkward, unmanageable goods train.

*transf.* 1827 SCOTT *Two Drovers* i, The hill rung with the discordant attempts of the Saxon upon the unmanageable monosyllable. 1855 *Poultry Chron.* III. 335/1 Irish [oats] are unmanageable and comparatively neglected.

Hence **Unma·nageably** *adv.*

1805 FOSTER *Ess.* (1806) I. 185 If even one of the four [horses] were unmanageably perverse, while the three were obedient. 1860 FROUDE *Hist. Eng.* VI. 329 Meantime, Philip..was becoming unmanageably impatient.

**Unma·nageableness.** (UN-[1] 12, or f. prec.) Also, in recent use, *unmanageability.*

1664 INGELO *Bentiv. & Ur.* VI. 182 The unmanageableness of their Horses. 1701 COLLIER *M. Anton.* (1726) 11 Their unmanageableness ruins their health. 1748 RICHARDSON *Clarissa* VII. 244 Thy servant gives me a dreadful account of thy raving unmanageableness. 1862 A. MEADOWS *Man. Midwifery* 239 Instead of a state of stupor, there is a restless unmanageableness approaching to maniacal excitement. 1877 'H. A. PAGE' *De Quincey* I. 42 Inveterate unmanageableness, under home supervision and French tutors.

**Unma·naged**, *ppl. a.* [UN-[1] 8.]

**1.** Not controlled or regulated.

1603 DRAYTON *Bar. Wars* I. i, A strong nation, whose vnmanag'd might Them from their naturall Soueraigne did diuide. 1646 HAMMOND *Tracts* 22 Mounted on an unmanaged or tender-mouth'd horse. 1673 O. WALKER *Educ.* ii. 22 Indiscreet, impertinent, unmenaged servants. 1746 FRANCIS tr. *Hor., Sat.* II. ii. 11 Pursue the Chace: th' unmanaged Courser rein. 1848 T. AIRD *Christian Bride* III. vi, The abandoned chariots with unmanaged steeds Roll mad about.

**b.** Of language: Unrestrained, outspoken.

1771 BURKE *Corr.* (1844) I. 323 Your lordship's criminal accusations, so heavy in the matter and unmanaged in the epithets. 1791 — *Th. French Aff.* Wks. VII. 63 The Prussian ministers in foreign courts have..talked the most democratick language with regard to France, and in the most unmanaged terms.

†**2.** Unlaboured, uncultivated. *Obs.*[−1]

1634 W. WOOD *New Eng. Prosp.* (1865) 52 The folly..of such as would venture into so rude and unmanaged a countrey, without..much provisions.

**Unma·nful**, *a.* (UN-[1] 7.) 1858 CARLYLE *Fredk. Gt.* III. xix. I. 368 He..suffered a good deal.., not at all in a dishonest or unmanful manner.

**Unma·nfully**, *adv.* (UN-[1] 11.)

*c* 1400 *Destr. Troy* 10426 *heading*, Menon þe Kyng, by Achilles vnmonfully slayn. 1664 ETHEREDGE *Love in Tub* I. ii, Now have I most unmanfully fallen foul upon some Woman. 1670 MILTON *Hist. Eng.* VI. 305 They dy'd not unmanfully,..turning oft upon thir Enemies. 1711 STEELE *Spect.* No. 133 ¶ 2 When a Poor-spirited Creature..bemoaned himself unmanfully, he rebuked him. [1843 CARLYLE *Past & Pr.* III. ii, It was the terror..of doing..unvirtuously, which was their word for *unmanfully.*]

**Unma·ngled**, *ppl. a.* (UN-[1] 8.)

For correct reading in *Gol. & Gaw.* 720, see UNMAGGLED.

1557 CHEKE in T. Hoby *Castiglione's Courtyer* (1561) 235 Our own tung shold be written cleane and pure, vnmixt and vnmangeled with borowing of other tunges. 1587 HOLINSHED *Hist. Eng.* (ed. 2) III. 298/2 From whome Grafton hath deriued his words; sense for sense vnmangled (as he found the same written). 1885 MEREDITH *Diana* i, Let her escape unmangled, it will pass in the record that she did once publicly run.

†**Unma·nhead.** *Obs.* [UN-[1] 12. Cf. OHG. *unmanaheit*, MHG. *unmanheit.*] Unmanliness; unmanly conduct.

*a* 1300 *Cursor M.* 18795 Naman es he dos na man-hede, And of vn-man-hede es it draun, To be again god dede vnknaun. 1387 TREVISA *Higden* (Rolls) V. 227 [The Romans] chargede þe Britouns to leve of unmanhede. *c* 1400 MAUNDEV. (Roxb.) xxxii. 145 It ware grete harme and grete vnmannhede to grefe swilk folk.

†**Unma·nhood.** *Obs.*[−1] (UN-[1] 12.) *c* 1374 CHAUCER *Troylus* I. 824 Sothe hym seyde pandarus, þat for to slen hym self myghte he nat wynne But bothe doon vn-manhode and a synne.

†**Unma·niable**, *a. Obs.*[−1] [UN-[1] 7 b.] Unmanageable. *a* 1618 RALEIGH *Lett.* (1651) 127 The lesser [ship]..is yare, whereas the greater is slow, unmanyable, and ever full of encumber.

**Unma·nifest**, *a.* (UN-[1] 7.)

1535 W. STEWART *Cron. Scot.* (Rolls) III. 555 Trowand sic thing wnmanifest. 1687 STANLEY *Hist. Philos.* (ed. 2) XII. 782/1 It is therefore unmanifest, whether it really hath these qualities. 1760 LAW *Spir. Prayer* II. 49 Nature..is the manifestation of all that in God, which was before unmanifest. 1864 JEAN INGELOW *Poems* 22 Like the dead to sight unmanifest, They are, and they are not.

**Unma·nifested**, *ppl. a.* (UN-[1] 8.)

1683 TRYON *Way to Health* 432 [In] all things and Creatures, in which the divine Principle does predominate, the poysonous wrathful Tree of Life lies hid and unmanifested. 1856 R. A. VAUGHAN *Mystics* II. VIII. viii. 84 The divine One, the unmanifested Subject, seeking an object. 1871 R. H. HUTTON *Theol. Ess.* I. 112 We yet have..an inextinguishable faith in His perfection even as unmanifested.

†**Unma·nkled**, obs. Sc. f. UNMANACLED. 1729 RAMSAY *Sec. Answ. to Somerville* 22 My muse..loves..to frisk.. Unmankl'd, o'er poetic ground.

**Unma·nlike**, *a.* and *adv.* [UN-[1] 7 c, 11 b.]

**1.** Below the level of manly conduct towards others; brutally harsh or cruel; inhuman.

1579 J. STUBBES *Gaping Gulf* E vij, That barbarous vnmanlike, and treasonable victory vpon the noble Admirall. *a* 1586 SIDNEY *Arcadia* I. xii, The unman-like cruelty of mankind. 1633 FORD *'Tis Pity* IV. iii, And wud you..kill her in your rage too? O 'twere most vn-manlike.

**2.** Inappropriate to a man or men.

*a* 1586 SIDNEY *Arcadia* II. xviii, It was the voice of a man, though it were a verie unmanlike voice. 1638 MAYNE *Lucian* (1664) A 4 Rude, un-manlike Raylings; which concluded in a Civil Warre. 1660 T. PIERCE *Inq. Nat. Sin* vi. § 20. 122 As if he were proud of such an unmanlike tergiversation.

**3.** = UNMANLY *a.*

*a* 1586 SIDNEY *Arcadia* II. xviii, Never was there man that could..with a more unmanlike braverie use his tongue to her disgrace. 1619 A. NEWMAN *Pleas. Vis.* (1840) 2 He with vnmanlike Curiousnesse was dect. 1692 WASHINGTON tr. *Milton's Def. Pop.* vii, 'Tis most justly so ordered..that you your self should live in a scandalous most unmanlike slavery at home.

**4.** Unnaturally licentious or debasing.

1752 FIELDING *Amelia* I. iv, Having got possession of a man who was committed for certain unmanlike practices, not fit to be named.

**5.** *adv.* In a manner unlike that of a man.

1611 HEYWOOD *Gold. Age* I. i, Their God-like Issue thrine, Whilst I vn-man-like must destroy my babes. 1881 D. C. MURRAY *Joseph's Coat* xxvii, [He] snuffled unmanlike through his tears.

**Unma·nlily**, *adv.* (UN-[1] 11.) 1795 MARY WOLLSTONECR. *Lett. to Imlay* 10 Feb., Yesterday he very unmanlily exulted over me.

**Unma·nliness.** (UN-[1] 12, or f. next.)

1603 HOLLAND *Plutarch's Mor.* 93 Temperance was thought to be a cloke of effeminate unmanlinesse. 1675 *Charac. Town-Gallant* (Hindley) II. 5 Impudence he calls Boon Assurance, and unmanliness, the Genteel Negligence. 1785 WILKINS *Bhagvat* ii. 28 Yield not thus to unmanliness. 1848 KINGSLEY *Yeast* ii, You and yours make piety a synonym for unmanliness. 1861 MILL *Repr. Govt.* iii. 63 We rightly ascribe this sort of contentment to mere unmanliness and want of spirit.

**Unma·nly**, *a.* [UN-[1] 7. Cf. MDu. *onmanlijc* (Du. *-lijk*), MHG. *unman-, unmenlîch* (G. *unmännlich*), ON. *úmannlig-r* (MSw. *omanliker*).]

**1.** Dishonourable or degrading to a man.

*c* 1475 *Cath. Angl.* 227/2 vn-Manly,..*inhumanus.* 1593 SHAKS. 3 *Hen. VI*, I. i. 186 Be thou a prey vnto the House of Yorke..for this vnmanly deed. 1603 DEKKER *Wonderfull Yeare* Wks. (Grosart) I. 108 Now..thou..basely descendest into bruitish & vnmanly passions. 1697 DRYDEN *Æneis* II. 810 Why this unmanly rage? 1706 S. CLARKE *Attrib.* (ed. 2) 10 All mocking and scoffing at Religion..is the most unmanly and unreasonable thing in the World. 1782 MISS BURNEY *Cecilia* v. vii, [To] be guilty of..unmanly cruelty. 1817 COLERIDGE *Zapolya* II. I. i, Your servants.. Offer'd gross insults, in unmanly sort, To our village maidens. 1855 MACAULAY *Hist. Eng.* xiii. III 310 Hatred, which showed itself by unmanly outrages to defenceless captives.

**2.** Not manly; unbefitting (or unlike) a man in respect of fortitude or energy; weak-tempered, effeminate.

*a* 1547 SURREY *Æneid* IV. 276 That Paris now, with his unmanly sorte, With mitred hats..His rape enjoyth. 1565 COOPER *Thesaurus* s.v. *Infractus*, A softe and vnmanly fourme of speakyng. 1602 SHAKS. *Ham.* I. ii. 94 'Tis vnmanly greefe, It shewes a will most incorrect to Heauen. 1682 FLAVEL *Fear* Ded., An unmanly and unchristian faintness. 1743 FRANCIS tr. *Hor., Odes* V. x. 17 Thy vile, unmanly wailings. 1796 MME. D'ARBLAY *Camilla* IV. 122 An unmanly fop. 1812 BYRON *Ch. Har.* I. xii, Others sate and wept, And to the reckless gales unmanly moaning kept. 1835 THIRLWALL *Greece* I. 339 Unmanly and pernicious luxury.

**Unma·nly**, *adv.* Now *rare.* [UN-[1] 11. Cf. Du. *onmanlijk*, ON. *úmannliga* (MSw. *omanlika*).]

**1.** Dishonourably; treacherously.

*c* 1400 *Destr. Troy* 13785 [A] kyng..By the myrmydons vnmonly murtherit to dethe. *c* 1465 *Eng. Chron.* (Camden, 1856) 50 He was traitorly and vnmanly slayn, and cast in to a pit. 1626 R. PEEKE *Three to One* B 3, Some of our Men were vnfortunately and vnmanly surprised.

**2.** Inhumanely; with unmanly cruelty or unkindness.

*c* **1475** *Cath. Angl.* 227/2 Vn-Manly, *inhumaniter.* **1594** *Selimus* 1513 Shall he thus unmanly be misus'd? **1658** CLEVELAND *Rustic Ramp.* Wks. (1687) 464 A Dominion so unmanly cruel. **1673** HICKERINGILL *Greg. F. Greyb.* 46 If he had not so unmanly..play'd upon the dead. **1717** MRS. CENTLIVRE *Cruel Gift* IV, Unmanly dost thou urge my Father's faults. **1824** T. FENBY *Last Sad Scene* viii, This was all for him who hath, Untimely and unmanly, left me.

**3.** With unmanly weakness.

**1579–80** NORTH *Plutarch* (1595) 908 So he tooke his banishment vnmanly. **1603** HOLLAND *Plutarch's Mor.* 61 We ought not to heare the reprehensions..of Philosophers recklessly.., nor yet unmanly.

**Unma·nned,** *ppl. a.*[1] [UN-[1] 8.]

**1.** Not furnished with men (cf. MAN *v.* 1).

**1544** BETHAM *Precepts War* II. li. L iij, That he leaue not his campe vndefenced and vnmanned. **1592** KYD *Sp. Trag.* IV. iv. 211 Set me with him—Vpon the maine mast of a..ship vnmand. **1670** MILTON *Hist. Eng.* I. 5 Not put to death, but turn'd out to Sea in a Ship unmann'd. **1726** POPE *Iliad* XXII. 469 See, if already their deserted towers Are left unmann'd. **1830** MARRYAT *King's Own* xlvi, One of the unmanned oars. **1844** KINGLAKE *Eothen* vi, Four of the craft..had been left unmanned. **1895** MARG. STOKES *Three Months in France* 230 The phantom ship, sail-less, rudderless, and unmanned.

*fig.* **1602** MARSTON *Antonio's Rev.* I. v, Native heate So prodigally flow'd t' exterior parts, That inner citadell was left unmand. **1675** DRYDEN *Aurengz.* IV. i, To guard that Breach [I] did all my Forces guide And left unmann'd the quiet Senses side.

**2. a.** Devoid of a man; empty.

**1602** WARNER *Alb. Eng.* XII. lxix. 291 At first she feares, but lastly findes the Armor was vn-man'd.

**b.** Unsupported by men; unassisted.

*c* **1620** [FLETCHER & MASS.] *Trag. Barnavelt* IV. i. in Bullen *O. Pl.* (1883) II. 271 Make haste, he is yet unmand: we may come time enough To enter with him. **1642** FULLER *Holy & Prof. St.* Pref. § 5 Nor let it render the modestie of this book suspected, because it presumes to appear in company unmann'd by any Patron.

**c.** Unoccupied by men; unpeopled.

**1680** C. NESSE *Church Hist.* 230 They left it [*sc.* the land] unmann'd thrice in the year. **1764** GOLDSM. *Trav.* 142 Nought remain'd..But towns unmann'd, and lords without a slave.

**3.** Not trained or broken in; *spec.* of a hawk.

**1592** SHAKS. *Rom. & Jul.* III. ii. 14 Come ciuill night,..Hood my vnman'd blood bayting in my Cheekes, With thy Blacke mantle. **1611** COTGR. s.v. *Acheter*, Buy a house made, and a wife vnmand. **1623** J. TAYLOR (Water P.) *Discov. by Sea* Wks. (1630) 28/2 Like a wild Kestrell or vnmand Hawke. *a* **1637** B. JONSON *Sad Sheph.* III. iii, No colt is so unbroken, Or hawk yet half so haggard or unmann'd.

**Unma·nned,** *ppl. a.*[2] [f. UNMAN *v.*] Deprived of courage; made weak or timid.

**1694** F. BRAGGE *Disc. Parables* ix. 317 Imaginary dangers terrifie their unmanned souls.

**Unma·nner,** *v. rare*[−1]. (UN-[2] 6 b.) **1613–8** DANIEL *Coll. Hist. Eng.* Wks. (Grosart) V. 140 Those softnings of Luxury and Idlenesse which vnmanners them.

**Unma·nnered,** *ppl. a.* [UN-[1] 8.]

†**1.** Not duly regulated or moderated. *Obs.*[−1]

**1435** MISYN *Fire of Love* 94 Lufe forsoth of kynsmen, if it be vn-manerd, fleschly affeccione it is cald [= called],..and if it be manerd, kyndely it is calde.

**2.** Of persons: Not possessed of good manners; unmannerly, rude.

**1594** SHAKS. *Rich. III*, I. ii. 39 Vnmanner'd Dogge, Stand'st thou when I commaund. **1610** FLETCHER *Faithf. Sheph.* II. i, I fear I am too much unmanner'd, far too rude. **1693** DRYDEN *Juvenal* VI. 543 No Pray'r can bend her, no Excuse appease. Th' unmanner'd Malefactor is arraign'd. **1745** J. MASON *Self-Knowl.* I. ix, He is not only ignorant and unmanner'd, but unsufferably vain. **1824** SCOTT *St. Ronan's* xxxi, This awkward, ill-dressed, unmannered dowdy. **1879** MEREDITH *Egoist* xix, He knew scholars to be an unmannered species.

*transf.* **1854** S. DOBELL *Balder* i. 5 Thou grim wall, Hemming her in with thine unmannered rock.

**3.** Of conduct: Characterized by want of manners.

**1760–72** H. BROOKE *Fool of Qual.* (1809) IV. 103 He gazed at Louisa with..an unmannered intenseness. **1772** *Ess. fr. Batchelor* (1773) II. 146 His superior abilities..were never exerted with unmannered insolence. **1836** *Lyra Apost.* 27 A ready prey, as though in absent mood They calmly move, nor hear the unmannered mirth. **1871** B. TAYLOR *Faust* (1875) II. III. 176 In most unmannered anger ye Have conjured hither pictures of the shapes of dread.

**4.** Free from artificial manners.

**1813** LAMB *Reynolds* Wks. 1908 I. 190 The plain unmannered old Nobility of the..Plays of Shakspeare.

Hence **Unma·nneredly** *adv.*

**1894** KIPLING in *My First Bk.* 92 All my verses..came without invitation, unmanneredly, in the nature of things.

†**Unma·nneredly,** *a. Obs.* [UN-[1] 7.] Unmannerly. **1792** W. ROBERTS *Looker-On* iv. 30 In flying from two unmanneredly catchpoles, you ran full against me. *Ibid.* xxx. 238 In your unmanneredly haste to interrupt us.

**Unma·nnerliness.** [f. next.] The condition or fact of being unmannerly.

**1580** HOLLYBAND *Treas. Fr. Tong*, *Incivilité*, vnmanerlines, vncurtesie. **1598** HAKLUYT *Voy.* I. 586 Moreouer he noteth much vnmanerlinesse of eating and drinking at bankets. *c* **1629** DONNE *Serm.* Wks. 1839 V. 16 It were unmannerliness to hold you longer in the Entry. **1647** H. MORE *Song of Soul* Ded. A 2 b, What a piece of Unmannerlinesse and Incivility it would be held to seem wiser then them. **1699** LOCKE *Educ.* (ed. 4) 263 A sort of Unmannerliness very apt to grow up with young People. *a* **1782** BP. NEWTON *Wks.* II. 681 The unmannerliness and unruliness of some of his subjects.

**Unma·nnerly,** *a.* [UN-[1] 7. Cf. WFris. *ûn-, onmenearlijk*, MDu. *onmanierlijc*, G. *unmanierlich*; Da. *umanerlig*, Sw. *omanerlig.*]

**1.** Of persons: Devoid of manners; impolite; behaving rudely or discourteously.

**1388** WYCLIF *Rom.* i. 31 Thei ben..vnwise, vnmanerli, withouten loue. **1575** R. B. *Appius & Virg.* in Hazl. *Dodsley* IV. 121 Have ye heard such an unmannerly villain? **1591** SHAKS. *Two Gent.* III. i. 393 An vnmannerly slaue, that will thrust himselfe into secrets. *a* **1616** BEAUM. & FL. *Wit at Sev. Weapons* IV. i, Fall back,..you unmannerly puppy. **1653** R. SANDERS *Physiogn.* 58 A rustick, unmannerly, dull person. **1730** FIELDING *Rape upon Rape* IV. iv, The Fright which that unmannerly Friend of yours occasioned. **1833** HT. MARTINEAU *Brooke Farm* ii. 19 Billy was not fit to go into a gentleman's family, he was so unmannerly. **1885** 'MRS. ALEXANDER' *Valerie's Fate* iv, I fear you must think me very unmannerly, very rude.

*transf.* **1827** POLLOK *Course T.* III. 570 Comets rude, That should unmannerly and lawless drive Athwart the path of Earth.

**2.** Of actions, conduct, speech, etc.: Showing want of manners.

*c* **1425** in *Anglia* VIII. 139 Vnsem and vnmanerly berynge of body. *Ibid.* 194, I wole make an ende of myn vnmanerly wordes. *c* **1510** MORE *Picus* Wks. 15/1 The company of the court..(as it is their vnmanerly maner) descanted therof. **1581** J. BELL *Haddon's Answ. Osor.* 262 b, If there were any reason in all these your unmannerly tauntes. **1617** WOODALL *Surg. Mate* Pref. (1639) B, Comparisons being odious and unmannerly amongst good men. **1699** BENTLEY *Phal.* 122 Breaking his unmannerly Jests upon his own mistakes. **1722** DE FOE *Relig. Courtsh.* I. i. (1840) 29 That's the unmannerliest thing in the World. **1756** WASHINGTON *Let. to Dinwiddie* 24 Nov., I am very sorry any expression in my letter should be deemed unmannerly. **1846** TRENCH *Mirac.* xxx. 425 These ill-timed and unmannerly clamors. **1884** *Manch. Exam.* 27 Nov. 5/2 The opposition to Mr. Caine was singularly unmannerly.

**Unma·nnerly,** *adv.* [UN-[1] 11.]

**1.** In an unmannerly fashion; with lack of good manners; impolitely.

**13..** *Gaw. & Gr. Knt.* 2339 Be not so gryndel; No mon here vn-manerly þe mys-boden habbe[z]. **1460** CAPGRAVE *Chron.* (Rolls) 145 Thei..treted the ladies onmanerly. **1509** BARCLAY *Shyp of Folys* (1570) 192 In praying thou bokest vnmanerly, Spuing vp thy prayers..vndeuoutly. **1594** CAREW *Huarte's Exam. Wits* 210 If..so they should deliuer vs their opinion..we would hold them importunate and vnmannerly brought vp. **1625** K. LONG tr. *Barclay's Argenis* V. xviii. 394 He, out of good manners, came close to him,.. that the King might not be unmannerly left alone in the midst of the roome. **1682** C. IRVINE *Hist. Scot. Nomencl.* Ded. * iij b, They would easily excuse him..that must, with the croud, unmannerly approach your Highness. **1832** J. J. BLUNT *Reform. in Eng.* 209 The Reformers..did not unmannerly reject those Offices of the Church. **1859** TENNYSON *Guinevere* 314 If I seem To vex an ear too sad to listen to me, Unmannerly, with prattling.

†**2.** Improperly, immoderately. *Obs.*[−1]

**1435** MISYN *Fire of Love* 53 Fraward men þer ar, þat þer wyffis for þer bewte vnmanerly lufys.

**Unmanning,** *vbl. sb.* and *ppl. a.*: see UNMAN *v.*

**Unma·nnish,** *a.* (UN-[1] 7.) *a* **1894** STEVENSON *St. Ives* iii, There was something wild and unmannish in his smile.

**Unma·ntle,** *v.* [UN-[2] 4, 7. Cf. Du. *ontmantelen*, G. *entmanteln, -mänteln.*]

**1.** *trans.* To divest of a mantle or covering.

**1598** FLORIO, *Smantellare*, to vnmantle, to vncloke. *c* **1645** HOWELL *Lett.* (1650) I. 26 They unmantled him of a new plush cloke. **1745** H. WALPOLE *Lett.* (1846) II. 86 The newborn babe was shown in a..cradle..under a canopy; the governess advanced to unmantle it. *a* **1800** COWPER *Odyss.* (ed. 2) x. 215 Obedient from the ground, Their folded brows unmantling, all arose, And with admiring eyes..the stag survey'd. **1821** SCOTT *Kenilw.* vii, The Earl..affected to resist when she strove to take his cloak from him. 'Nay,' she said, 'but I will unmantle you'.

*fig.* **1660** C. SOUTHAICK *Fames Genius* (1863) 23 Not to unmantle self and subtilty, But the true Portraicture of honesty.

**b.** *intr.* To take off one's mantle.

**1822** A. CUNNINGHAM *Tradit. Tales* I. 239 Unmantling as she spoke, [she] turned back to the Towers of Haddon the fairest face that ever left them.

**2.** *trans.* To dismantle, unfurnish.

**1828** SCOTT *Tapestried Chamber* ad fin., Lord Woodville [went] to command the Tapestried Chamber to be unmantled, and the door built up.

**Unma·ntled,** *ppl. a.* [UN-[1] 8.] Not mantled or covered.

[**1775** ASH.] **1800** CAMPBELL *Ode to Winter* iii, Shuddering Want's unmantled bed. **1818** BYRON *Ch. Har.* IV. cxlviii, Her unmantled neck, and bosom white and bare.

†**Unma·nuable,** *a. Obs.*[−1] [UN-[1] 7 b.] Unmanageable. **1633** T. JAMES *Voy.* 116 Our sailes froze in lumps to the yards, vnmanuable. **Unmanufa·cturable,** *a.* (UN-[1] 7 b.) **1784** *Phil. Trans.* LXXIV. 468 Whence it should seem, that neither..tend much to render gold unmanufacturable.

**Unmanufa·ctured,** *ppl. a.* (UN-[1] 8.)

[**1775** ASH.] **1796** MORSE *Amer. Geog.* II. 608 Unmanufactured as well as prepared flax. **1841** W. SPALDING *Italy & It. Isl.* III. 385 There are exported, in the unmanufactured state, about 5,508,000 lbs. **1879** *Cassell's Techn. Educ.* II. 114 Unmanufactured cork is admitted into England duty free.

**Unmanumi·tted,** *ppl. a.* (UN-[1] 8.) **1661** HICKERINGILL *Jamaica* 30 The Petticoat Sex (through the rigour of their masters unmanumitted). **1880** MUIRHEAD *Gaius* Dig. 540 Women who had been remancipated.., but were still unmanumitted. **Unmanu·rable,** *a.* [UN-[1] 7 b.] †Uncultivable. **1610** HOLLAND *Camden's Brit.* I. 799 [Land] rough and as it were un-manurable. **1707** SLOANE *Jamaica* I. p. vii, The quantity of Acres are..: Manurable 6,100,000; Unmanurable 100,000.

**Unmanu·red,** *ppl. a.* [UN-[1] 8.]

†**1.** Of land: Uncultivated, untilled. *Obs.*

In frequent use from *c* 1590 to *c* 1640.

**1570** FOXE *A. & M.* (ed. 2) I. 222/2 The prouince lay waste and vnmanured. **1578** LYTE *Dodoens* 257 All rough and unmanured places. **1632** W. LITHGOW *Trav.* III. 85, I could not find a foote of ground vnmanured. *c* **1694** DRYDEN *Let. to J. Dennis* ¶ 4 It looks like a vast tract of land newly discover'd: the soil is wonderfully fruitful, but unmanur'd. **1721** RAMSAY *Prospect of Plenty* 222 To let braid tracts of land lie unmanur'd.

**b.** *fig.* or in fig. contexts.

**1594** *Selimus* 381 It argueth an unmanured wit. *a* **1631** DONNE *Heroical Epist.* 36 Thy body is a naturall Paradise, In whose selfe, unmanur'd, all pleasure lies. **1663** COWLEY *On Orinda's Poems* ii, 'Twere shame. if in thee A Spirit so rich..Should unmanur'd, or barren lye. **1700** T. BROWN *Amusem. Ser. & Com.* 69 Gallantry..which was formerly so well Cultivated,..is at present Desolate, Unmanur'd and Abandoned!

**2.** Not supplied with manure.

[**1828–32** WEBSTER.] **1849** JOHNSTON *Exp. Agric.* 105 The unmanured [crop] might have ripened its seed while the manured was still growing. **1868** *Rep. U.S. Commissioner Agric.* (1869) 419 The average product of unmanured American soil.

**Unma·pped,** *ppl. a.* (UN-[1] 8.)

**1805** *Ann. Rev.* III. 13 Both travellers have..rivers unmapped to navigate. **1857** THOREAU *Maine W.* i. (1869) 87 The country is virtually unmapped. **1876** GEO. ELIOT *Dan. Der.* III. xxiv, There is a great deal of unmapped country within us.

**Unma·rching,** *ppl. a.* (UN-[1] 10.) **1837** CARLYLE *Fr. Rev.* II. v. vii, To all which our poor Legislative, tied up by an unmarching Constitution, can oppose nothing. **Unma·ritime,** *a.* (UN-[1] 7.) **1817** G. S. FABER *Eight Dissert.* (1845) II. 230 The thoroughly unmaritime Empire of Rome.

**Unma·rked,** *ppl. a.* [UN-[1] 8. Cf. ON. *úmarkaðr*; also ON. *úmerktr* (MSw. *omärkter*, Sw. *omärkt*, older Da. *umærket.*)]

**1.** Having received no mark or impress; left without a mark.

**14..** *Sir Beues* (M.) 160/3111 None went vnmarked away, That Beuys hyt wyth Morglay. **1480** *Cely Papers* (Camden) 53, [1093] felles qwherof be iiij[c] xlvj Cottysowlde onmarkyd and the rembnant..be markyd w[t] an O. *a* **1578** LINDESAY *Chron. Scot.* (S.T.S.) II. 320 Nane wald resawe thame [*sc.* pennies] nathir marcat nor onmarcat. **1651** BAXTER *Inf. Bapt.* 199 You may know such a man's Flock of Sheep by the mark; when yet perhaps some may be unmarkt. **1705** *Lond. Gaz.* No. 4104/4 Stoln..,2 Sweet-meat Spoons, forked, unmarked. *c* **1790** IMISON *Sch. Arts* II. 762 That the magnet..may rest with its marked end on the unmarked end of A. **1872** M. S. DE VERE *Americanisms* 211 The name of *Maverick*, used in Texas to designate an unmarked yearling.

*Comb.* **1895** *Daily News* 25 Mar. 8/6 The attempt to unite the unmarked iron firms has not been abandoned.

**b.** Not marked off or out, not distinguished or characterized (*by* something).

**1815** *Monthly Rev.* LXXVI. 455 Virgil's characters are mostly cold, unmarked, and not attaching. **1824** SCOTT *St. Ronan's* xi, Men..whose spirit and courage lie hidden.. under an unmarked or a plain exterior. **1882** FARRAR *Early Chr.* II. 482 Compositions so short..and so unmarked by special features.

**2.** Unnoticed, unobserved.

**1533** MORE *Debell. Salem* Wks. 1026/2 Here was himselfe faine..to begyle the reader vppon the readyng of the place, and make hym passe ouer his faute for the while vnmarked. **1583** BABINGTON *Commandm.* (1590) 251 Sathan breedeth by his vnmarked creeping into our affections a misliking of such a man or woman. **1628** SIR S. D'EWES *Jrnl.* (1783) 42 Hee passed quietlie unmarked..out of the saied hall. **1667** MILTON *P. L.* x. 441 He through the midst unmarkt..past. **1744** AKENSIDE *Pleas. Imag.* II. 184 Oft the hours From morn to eve have stol'n unmark'd away. **1821** SCOTT *Kenilw.* xiii, Like one who has suddenly recognized some mighty hero..in the person of an unknown and unmarked stranger. **1850** TENNYSON *In Mem.* xcviii, Let her great Danube rolling fair Enwind her isles, unmark'd of me.

**Unma·rketable,** *a.* (UN-[1] 7 b.)

Hence, in recent use, *unmarketability, -ableness.*

**1654** in *Manchester Crt. Leet Rec.* (1887) IV. 112 Roger Royle of Eccles for sellinge vnmarkettable Beefe. **1776** *Ann. Reg., Chron.* 139/2 A parcel of hops..badly cured, and, on that account, unmarketable. **1800** G. G. STONESTREET *Portentous Globe* 33 Their trade would be rendered unprofitable—their shares unmarketable. **1861** GEO. ELIOT *Silas M.* iv, His own ill-favoured person, which was unmarketable, escaped without injury. **1885** SIR W. V. FIELD in *Law Times' Rep.* LII. 654/1 So as to render the property unmarketable.

**Unma·rred,** *ppl. a.* (UN-[1] 8.)

*a* **1200** *St. Marher.* 10 Þe edle meiden allunge unmerred wiðuten euereuch weom wende ut of his wombe. **13..** *E. E. Allit. P.* B. 867 Maydenez vnmard for alle men ȝette. [*c* **1470** *Gol. & Gaw.* 720 Wes nane..Wnmaglit and marrit.] **1596** SPENSER *F. Q.* VI. x. 7 His siluer waues did softly tumble downe, Vnmard with ragged mosse or filthy mud. **1744** YOUNG *Nt. Th.* VII. 301 Their good is good entire, unmixt, unmarr'd. **1827** POLLOK *Course T.* VII. 585 Unmarred, unfaded work of Deity. **1851** SIR F. PALGRAVE *Norm. & Eng.* I. 473 The spirit and talent which, unmarred by fate, might [etc.]. **1871** MACDUFF *Mem. Patmos* xix. 263 In the fellowship of unmarred and unbroken communion.

**Unma·rriable,** *a.* (UN-[1] 7 b.)

**1542** UDALL *Erasm. Apoph.* 177 b, Cleopatra..beeyng yet a young damysell vnmariable. **1611** COTGR., *Immariable*, vnmarriable. **1643** MILTON *Divorce* 36 Parted from each other, as two persons unconjunctive, and unmarriable together.

**Unma·rriageable,** *a.* (UN-[1] 7 b.)

[**1775** ASH.] **1787** W. THOMSON tr. *A. Cunningham's Hist. Gt. Brit.* I. 121 Their women are seldom married young; and are indeed long unmarriageable. **1841** EMERSON *Method Nature* (1844) 14 He was hurled into being as..the mediator betwixt two else unmarriageable facts. **1856** S. Dobell *Lyrics War Time, German Legion*, I could kneel down by thee, And o'er thy chill unmarriageable rest Cry [etc.].

**Unma·rried,** *ppl. a.* [Un-[1] 8.]

**1.** Of persons: Not married; unwedded.

**1297** R. Glouc. (Rolls) 737 Þe gode cordeile vnmaried was so. *c* **1400** Maundev. (1839) xix. 209 Wommen that ben unmaryed, thei han Tokenes on hire Hedes. *a* **1450** Lovelich *Grail* lv. 50 Wedded weren..Alle his bretheryn except on.. that tho was vn-maryed. **1491** *Act 7 Hen. VII*, c. 20 § 6 If..Elizabeth dye unmaryed. *a* **1540** Barnes *Wks.* (1573) 364/2 This thing dyd Paphnutius, though that hee hym selfe was vnmaryed. **1591** *Knaresb. Wills* (Surtees) I. 187 All my children bothe maryed and unmaried. **1607–12** Bacon *Ess., Marriage & Single Life* (Arb.) 266 Vnmarryed Men are best Frendes. **1653** H. Cogan *Diod. Sic.* iv. xxii. 152 He lived all his life time unmarried. **1728** Young *Love Fame* vi. 79 Unmarry'd Abra puts on formal airs. **1779** *Mirror* No. 12, The two eldest of my unmarried daughters. **1834** Wellington *Let. to Miss J.* 24 Oct., The Duke is not in the habit of visiting young unmarried ladies. **1875** Ruskin *Fors Clav.* V. lvi. 235 Every unmarried woman should have enough left her by her father to keep herself, and a pet dog.

*transf.* **1611** Shaks. *Wint. T.* iv. iv. 123 Pale Prime-roses, That dye vnmarried, ere they can behold Bright Phœbus in his strength. **1771** *Encycl. Brit.* I. 651/2 [The insect] flies from flower to flower till it arrives at the unmarried female.

**b.** *absol.* and as *sb.*

**1557** N. T. (Geneva) 1 *Cor.* vii. 8, I say vnto the vnmaried, and widowes, it is good [etc.]. **1619** Fletcher *Knt. Malta* v. i, Husband, Wife, There is some holy mystery in those names That sure the unmarried cannot understand. **1728** Eliza Heywood tr. *Mme. de Gomez's Belle A.* (1732) II. 147 Neither did the Night want its Charms both to the married and the unmarried. **1819** *Metropolis* I. 71 We had a very bad turn out of British females, mostly dowagers and elderly unmarrieds. **1871** A. Meadows *Man. Midwifery* (ed. 2) II. 59 In the case of the unmarried, he may..cast a slur upon a spotless character.

**2.** Lived free from marriage.

**1648** Hexham II, *Een eeloosen Staet*, an Unmarried State. **1747** Francis tr. *Horace, Epist.* I. i. 125 How happy then is an unmarried Life! **1755** Johnson, *Celibacy*, single life; unmarried state.

**Unma·rry,** *v.* [Un-[2] 3, 7.]

**1.** *trans.* (and *refl.*). To dissolve the marriage of; to free from the marriage-tie; to divorce.

**1530** Palsgr. 768/2, I can unmary my selfe by ronnyng away. **1588** Parke tr. *Mendoza's Hist. China* 401 He doth vnmarry them, and setteth her at libertie that she may marry with an other. **1637** Shirley *Gamester* I. i, Yes, I did marry you;..I would there were a parson to unmarry us! **1680** Baxter *Answ. Stillingfl.* xii. 20 As he that marrieth Persons may not..unmarry them again, save for Adultery. **1760–72** H. Brooke *Fool of Qual.* (1809) II. 59 If he does not first unmarry himself, I will never see him any more. **1857** Dickens *Dorrit* II. viii, They are fast married, and can't be unmarried. **1881** Besant & Rice *Chapl. of Fleet* II. 177 Nothing can unmarry you now.

*absol.* **1708** O. Dykes *Eng. Prov. & Refl.* 7 In fine, an After-Thought cannot unmarry; it cannot set a broken Leg.

**b.** To put away, to divorce (a wife).

**1645** Milton *Tetrach.* 49 Is it imaginable there should bee among these..a law giving permissions laxative to unmarry a wife and marry a lust? **1797** Mrs. A. M. Bennett *Beggar Girl* (1813) III. 177 Though he did not live with her, he could not unmarry her.

**2.** *intr.* To free oneself from marriage.

**1635** J. Hayward tr. *Biondi's Banish'd Virg.* 172 Having left her father, and unmarried and remarried againe at her pleasure. **1652** J. Wright tr. *Camus' Nat. Paradox* x. 244, I marry without injoying my wife, I unmarry, I marry again. **1769** in *Priv. Lett. Ld. Malmesbury* (1870) I. 172 We are unmarrying among the great; the Duke of Grafton's divorce was finished this morning. **1839** J. Rogers *Antipapopr.* xvi. § 3. 332 Thus people may neither marry nor unmarry without priorly obtaining permission from the priesthood. **1895** *How to get Married* 86 Actors marry and unmarry *ad libitum* in a disgraceful way.

**Unma·rrying,** *ppl. a.* (Un-[1] 10.) **1846** H. G. Robinson *Odes of Horace* II. xv, The unmarrying [L. *cælebs*] plane [will] o'erwhelm Shortly with its growth the elm. **1848** Lady Lyttelton *Corr.* (1912) 385 An unmarrying old young lady. **Unma·rshalled,** *ppl. a.* (Un-[1] 8.) **1767** Lewis *Statius* xii. 906 Ev'ry Plain To Combate sends a rude, unmarshall'd Train. **Unma·rtial,** *a.* (Un-[1] 7.) **1611** Speed *Hist. Gt. Brit.* VI. xxii. § 4. 109 [They] consumed their times in banquetting, and vnmartiall disports. **1797** *Monthly Mag.* III. 306 The effect of the whole is so dry and unmartial as to do little credit to the musical taste of Louis the XVIth. **1880** L. Wallace *Ben-Hur* 520 This most unmartial figure. †**Unma·rtial,** *v. Obs.*—[1] (Un-[2] 6 a.) **1654** Gayton *Pleas. Notes* iv. ii. 180 To unmartiall the whole man, and leave him without steel or iron upon him, is, as if you should pare the nailes of a Lyon. **Unma·rtyr,** *v.* (Un-[2] 6 b.) **1646** Prynne *Canterb. Doome* Ep. Ded. a 2, The setting forth of this History of his Tryall, will soon Un-martyr, Un-saint, Uncrown this Arch-Imposter. **1655** Fuller *Ch. Hist.* II. iv. § 36 Scotus..was made a Martyr after his Death...But since Baronius hath unmartyred him.

**Unma·rtyred,** *ppl. a.* (Un-[1] 8.)

*c* **1580** Munday *View Sundry Examples* (Shaks. Soc.) 88 Beaten..so that from the crown of the hed to the soles of the feet, was left no member unmartired. *a* **1633** W. Austin *Medit.* (1635) 112 They..left not a peece of him unmartyred, till they had killed him. **1908** Rider Haggard *Ghost Kings* i. 7 Should he return..not only unmartyred but a palpable failure..?

**Unma·rvellous,** *a.* (Un-[1] 7.) **1790** Wolcot (P. Pindar) *Ode Jas. Bruce* iv, Thy soul delights in wonder, pomp, and bustle; Mine in th' unmarvellous and placid scene. **1855** Maurice *Learn. & Work.* iv. 107 This Hope..may..shrink into a very obvious, intelligible, unmarvellous quality. †**Unma·sculate,** *v. Obs.*—[1] [Un-[2] 3.] *trans.* To emasculate. **1639** Fuller *Holy War* 255 The sinnes of the South unmasculate Northern bodies.

**Unma·sculine,** *a.* (Un-[1] 7.)

**1649** Milton *Tenure Kings* 5 The unmasculine Rhetorick of any puling Priest or Chaplain. **1829** Lamb *Lett.* (1886) II. 304 My whole heart is faint, and my whole head is sick ..at this damned canting, unmasculine age!

**Unma·sk,** *v.* [Un-[2] 4, 7. Cf. Du. *ont-*, G. *entmasken.*]

**1.** *trans.* To free (the face) from a mask or vizard; to remove a mask or covering from. Also in fig. context.

**1602** Shaks. *Ham.* I. iii. 37 The chariest Maid is Prodigall enough, If she vnmaske her beauty to the Moone. **1626** T. H[awkins] *Caussin's Holy Crt.* 134 An heresy discouered, is a face unmasked, take away the vizard, you disarme her. **1665** Sir T. Herbert *Trav.* (1677) 154 The Bridge..was.. full of Women,..many of which..in a fair deportment unmasqued their faces. **1728** Eliza Heywood tr. *Mme. de Gomez's Belle A.* (1732) II. 24 The Demand I am about to make..is to follow my Example, and immediately be all unmask'd. **1841** Emerson *Lect. on Times* (1844) 72 To-day is a king in disguise...Let us unmask the king as he passes. **1876** J. Saunders *Lion in Path* xxxvii, We must unmask you, pretty Mistress Preston.

*refl.* **1825** Scott *Talism.* x, Putting his hand to his chin, and withdrawing it with the action of one who unmasks himself.

**b.** To remove like a mask.

**1624** G. Raleigh in Farr *Sel. P. Jas. I* (1847) 242 Our tender muse hath labored as she could; Her sable vaile she must of force unmaske.

**2.** *fig.* To divest of a specious appearance or show; to disclose the true character of; to bring into the light; to make plain or obvious.

**1593** Shaks. *Lucr.* 1602 Vnmaske..this moodie heauinesse, And tell thy griefe. **1611** Speed *Theat. Gt. Brit.* I. xlii. 81/2 Since the true God hath vnmasked the errors of those times by the truth of his word. **1646** Gataker *Mistake Removed* 39 Which yet the whole drift of his discours will easily unmaske. **1672** Wilkins *Nat. Relig.* 44 Time..doth by degrees discover & unmask the fallacy of ungrounded perswasions. **1704** Norris *Ideal World* II. iii. 257 Could we but unmask nature, and strip it of all those false ornaments wherewith our prejudiced imagination has clothed it. **1798** *Monthly Mag.* VI. 552 In unmasking the popular heathenism, and in revealing the immortality of the soul. **1844** Thirlwall *Greece* VIII. 241 The accuser..unmasked their conspiracy with Apelles. **1869** Mozley *Univ. Serm.* ii. (1876) 43 That judicial mission which was to unmask false goodness.

**b.** With personal object. Also *refl.*

*a* **1586** Sidney *Arcadia* II. xxiii, Zelmane thought-sicke, unmaskes her selfe. **1640** Sir W. Mure *Counter-Buff* 125 Now thy piece I must anatomize...The frontespiece unmaskes an hypocrite. **1668** Temple *Let. to Ld. Arlington* Wks. 1720 II. 97 They must now suddenly unmask themselves in one way or other, no farther Pretences being left. **1718** *Free-thinker* No. 75. 140 The Person..lives under a perpetual Apprehension of being unmasked. **1797** Mrs. Radcliffe *Italian* ix, 'The hypocrite!' said he to himself ..; 'but I will unmask him'. **1819** Crabbe *T. of Hall* xii. 296 No sooner was it [*sc.* her hand in marriage] ask'd Than she the lovely Jezebel unmask'd. **1872** Morley *Voltaire* i. 4 Christian charity feels constrained to unmask a demon from the depths of the pit.

**3.** *absol.* To take off one's mask. Also in fig. context (quot. 1683).

**1603** Shaks. *Meas. for M.* v. i. 206 My husband bids me, now I will vnmaske, This is that face..Which once [etc.]. **1611** Chapman *May-Day* v. 74 *Quint.* O no, you must not vnmaske. *Innoc.* No, no, Ile kisse her with my maske and all. **1683** Kennett *Erasm. on Folly* 2 At the first sight of me, you all unmasque, and appear in more lively colours. **1728** Fielding *Lov. in Sev. Masques* iv. iii, Unmasque then. If I like your Face no better than your Principles, Madam; I will immediately take my Leave of both. **1756** tr. *Keysler's Trav.* I. 349 A female bed-fellow, who never unmasks till she comes into the bed-chamber. **1818** Lady Morgan *Autobiog.* (1859) 299, I was obliged to unmask from the heat, and soon got a crowd about me.

**b.** *fig.* To display one's true character.

**1622** Bacon *Julius Cæsar* Mor. & Hist. Wks. (Bohn) 502 Though this was ever his scheme, and at last put in execution, yet he did not unmask. **1745** Young *Nt. Th.* VIII. 224 Their treach'rous blessings, at the day of need, Like other faithless friends, unmask, and sting.

**4.** *trans. Mil.* **a.** To reveal the presence of (a gun or battery) by opening fire.

**1747** *Gentl. Mag.* 450 The besieged unmask'd 4 batteries. **1812** *Examiner* 31 Aug. 549/2 He unmasked a battery of forty pieces of cannon. **1884** *Manch. Exam.* 9 Sept. 8/4 The Chinese, unmasking a mountain gun, fired on the Bayard.

**b.** To make patent; to show plainly.

**1816** Sir H. Douglas *Milit. Bridges* iv. 110 The other divisions..hastened their march as soon as the movement was unmasked. **1879** Low *Afghan War* 100 With a view of making the Afghan commandant..unmask his force.

**5.** *intr.* To emerge into view.

**1858** *Merc. Marine Mag.* V. 227 Two Obelisks..on the strand..will..unmask.

Hence **Unma·sking** *ppl. a.*

**1807** J. Barlow *Columb.* VI. 568 Gates guides the onset.. And tells the unmasking batteries when to roar.

**Unma·sked,** *ppl. a.* (Un-[1] 8.)

**1590** Greene *Never too late* (1600) 14 The maids in Rome durst not looke at Venus Temple till they were thirtie, nor went they vnmasked till they were married. **1628** Feltham *Resolves* II. viii. 18 Diseased eyes indure not an vnmasked Sunne. ?**1630** H. R. *Mythomystes*, A 3, To lay downe a naked & vnmasked Trueth. **1679** in *Lond. Gaz.* No. 1406/1 The unmasked Boldness of such as durst openly..assemble themselves together, to Kill..the Primate. **1740** H. Walpole *Corr.* (1820) I. 45, I have found a little unmasqued moment to write to you. **1784** Cowper *Task* II. 695 They..in th' end, disclose a face That would have shock'd credulity herself, Unmask'd. **1811** Scott *Don Roderick* II. xli, He saw her hideous face, and loved the fiend unmask'd. **1855** Pusey *Doctr. Real Presence* 717 An universal suppression of the truths..and the unmasked substitution of falsehood.

**Unma·sker.** [f. Unmask *v.*] One who unmasks.

**1644** Milton *Areop.* 7 The great unmasker of the Trentine Council. **1697** Locke *2nd Vind. Reason. Chr.* 183 The Unmasker smartly convinces me of no small Blunder in these words. **1833** Carlyle *Misc.* (1840) IV. 404 'Far from being modest,' says this Unmasker, 'he brags beyond expression'. **1850** L. Hunt *Autobiog.* v. 98 [They] stood side by side in my imagination as unmaskers of venerable appearance. **1884** *Manch. Exam.* 9 May 5/5 The first unmasker of the forgery.

**Unma·sking,** *vbl. sb.* [f. as prec.] The action of divesting of a mask. Chiefly *fig.*

*a* **1586** Sidney *Arcadia* III. xxiii, Her unmasking of Cecropias fruitlesse sophistrie. **1602** J. H[all] (*title*), The Unmasking of the Politique Atheist. **1641** Milton *Reform.* I. 8 The unmasking of Hypocrites. **1741** Richardson *Pamela* IV. 233 Because of her Freedoms when mask'd; her Unmasking, and her Handkerchief. **1861** Trench *Comm. Ep. Churches Asia* 87 An unmasking of them that said they were Apostles and were not. **1895** *Athenæum* 17 Aug. 218/3 Mr. Meredith's pitiless unmaskings of folly.

**Unma·ssacred,** *ppl. a.* (Un-[1] 8.) **1608–9** Middleton *Widow* III. i, Would you let him 'scape unmassacred? **Unma·ssed,** *ppl. a.* (Un-[2] 6 b, 8.) **1847** *Athenæum* April 393/1 The inside..of the building..is minutely decorated everywhere, but certainly is not dismembered or unmassed anywhere. **Unma·ssy,** *a.* (Un-[1] 7.) **1665** Sir G. Mackenzie *Moral Essay* 52 So unmassie a reputation, that, when it is hammered out [etc.].

**Unma·st,** *v.* [Un-[2] 4. Cf. Du. *ont-*, G. *entmasten.*] *trans.* To divest of a mast.

**1611** Florio, *Disarborare*,..to unmast a ship. **1668** *Lond. Gaz.* No. 238/1 The same Tempest..unmasting several others [*sc.* ships]. **1698** T. Froger *Voy.* 17 We also began to unmast the Fruitful Pink to turn it into a Bomb-Galley.

**Unma·sted,** *ppl. a.* (Un-[1] 8.) [**1775** Ash.] **1804** J. Larwood *Gun Boat* 12 An unruddered, unmasted, unordonanced existence. **Unma·ster,** *v.* (Un-[2] 3.) **1593–4** Sylvester *Profit Imprisonm.* Wks. (Grosart) II. 56/2 Small the honour is to be acknowledg'd King And Monark of the World, one's self un-mastering.

**Unma·sterable,** *a.* (Un-[1] 7 b.)

**1617** Daniel *Coll. Hist. Eng.* (1626) 114 By this violence, thinking to quaile the heart of a most vnmaisterable King. **1625** Jackson *Creed* v. xxxv. § 6 An unexpected instinct or unmasterable impulsion. **1646** Sir T. Browne *Pseud. Ep.* IV. ii. 201 The Faetor whereof may discover it self by sweat .., as being unmasterable by the naturall heat of man.

**Unma·stered,** *ppl. a.* (Un-[1] 8.)

**1561** Norton & Sackv. *Gorboduc* II. ii, Great is the daunger of vnmaistred might. **1593** *Sidney's Arcadia* IV. Wks. 1922 II. 107 The unmastred vertu of Pyrocles. **1602** Shaks. *Ham.* I. iii. 32 If with too credent eare you list his Songs;.. or your chast Treasure open To his vnmastred importunity. **1700** Dryden *Sp. Ajax*, etc. 595 He..cannot his unmaster'd Grief sustain, But yields to Rage. **1793** *Minstrel* II. 194 To appropriate to her own use these evidently unmastered treasures. **1800** Coleridge *Piccolom.* IV. vii, Nature.., like the emancipated force of fire, Unmastered scorches..Their fine-spun webs. **1870** Bryant *Iliad* V. I. 145 Lest, taking flight, they range Unmastered when they hear thy voice no more.

†**Unma·sterly,** *adv. Obs.*—[1] [Un-[1] 11.] Without being supervised. **1684** H. More *Answer* Pref. b 4 b, To act at pleasure, prosperously, freely and unmasterly. **Unma·sticated,** *ppl. a.* (Un-[1] 8.) **1815** J. Smith *Panorama Sci. & Art* II. 643 The unmasticated part contributes nothing to their nourishment. **1896** *Allbutt's Syst. Med.* I. 396 Masses of unmasticated food. †**Unma·tch,** *a.* (Un-[1] 7.) **1570** Levins *Manip.* 38 Vnmatche, *inequalis*.

**Unma·tchable,** *a.* [Un-[1] 7 b.]

**1.** Incapable of being matched or equalled; incomparable, matchless. Also const. *by*.

In very common use from *c* 1590 to *c* 1660.

**1544** Betham *Precepts War* I. lxxxix. E vj, The renoume of that capitayne..is vnmatcheable. **1587** A. Day *Daphnis & Chloe* (1890) 16 Loue, the..Soueraigne of their vnmatchable bewties. **1649** Baxter *Saint's R.* II. v. § 3. 218 Those divine unmatchable Psalms. **1663** *Brit. Spec.* 277 With unmatchable Valor, and Extraordinary Hazard of his Princely Person. *c* **1799** *Villario* III. iii. in *New Brit. Theatre* II. 165 It is the mind that is unmatchable By aught on earth. **1856** Ruskin *Mod. Paint.* IV. v. xvii. § 51 Of such landscape..he has expressed the power in..a central and unmatchable way. **1881** Tennyson *Cup* I. i, The brows and eyes Of Venus: face and form unmatchable!

**b.** Incapable of being compared *to* others.

**1611** Speed *Hist. Gt. Brit.* VI. 45 These Britaines, although ..vnmatchable to them in educated ciuility, yet [etc.].

**c.** To which nothing properly matching can be found. (See Match *v.* 9 b.)

**1809** Sir G. Jackson in *Diaries & Lett.* (1873) I. 3 A scrap of riband..unmatchable in Bath. **1852** Miss Sewell *Experience of Life* xiv. (1858) 95, I was especially directed to match some unmatchable silk.

**2.** Incapable of being matched together.

**1643** Milton *Divorce* 18 He forbids all unmatchable and unmingling natures to consort. **1645** — *Tetrach.* 48 His law tells us he joynes not unmatchable things.

Hence **Unma·tchableness.**

**1627** Bp. Hall *Epist.* IV. ii. 340 In the presumption of his vnmatchablenesse. **1676** *Doctrine of Devils* 182 The Unmatchableness of his Antagonist being considered.

**Unma·tchably,** *adv.* (f. prec., or Un-[1] 11.)

**1603** Ld. Herbert *Corr.* in *Life* (1886) 335 As knowing that his worthy disposition that began it of himself, will continue it as undeservedly as he did unmatchably enter into it. **1609** W. M. *Man in Moon* G 2 b, Seeing therefore it is such an inestimable iewell, how warily are you to keep it?..so vnmatchably allied, how much are you to make of it? **1882** *Harper's Mag.* LXV. 548 The unmatchably pale bright yellow-white of the grain fields.

**Unma·tched,** *ppl. a.* [Un-[1] 8.]

**1.** Not matched or equalled; matchless; unrivalled.

**1581** SIDNEY *Apol. Poetrie* (Arb.) 26 Though we get not so vnmatched a praise as the Etimologie of his names wil grant. **1621** G. SANDYS *Ovid's Met.* VI. (1626) 109 Antigone, who stroue For vnmatcht beautie with the wife of Ioue. **1637** J. RUTTER *1st Pt. Cid* v. iii. 27 It were better that his unmatch'd valour Should get him victory. **1678** DRYDEN *All for Love* IV. i, Your unmatch'd desert. **1780** BURKE *Sp. Bristol* Wks. 1792 II. 313 Refusing to commit this act of unmatched turpitude. **1812** COMBE *Syntax, Picturesque* XXIV. 89 Shakespeare, immortal Bard sublime! Unmatch'd within the realms of time! *a* **1845** HOOD *Lamia* i. 40 Let such an unmatched vision still shine on. **1878** SYMONDS *Sonn. M. Angelo* lix, Nay, nor the unmatched phœnix lives anew, Unless she burn.

*absol.* **1632** R. ALLEN in Lithgow *Trav.* B 3 b, This thy second Pilgrimage of Minde,..in Methode, Phrase, and Stile, May match the most vnmatched in this Ile.

**b.** Const. *by*; *at*, *for*, *in*, or *of*.

**1592** DANIEL *Compl. Rosamond* xxiv, Vnmatch'd by sword, [he] was vanquisht by a glaunce. **1602** WARNER *Alb. Eng.* XII. lxxiii. 304 Fertile grounds, vnmatch't for fruits. **1700** ROWE *Amb. Step-Moth.* II. ii, Long time unmatcht in War the Hero shone. **1789** BURNS *Whistle* iv, Unmatch'd at the bottle, unconquer'd in war. **1810** SCOTT *Lady of L.* I. vii, Two dogs..Unmatch'd for courage. **1868** MORRIS *Earthly Par.* I. II. 629 This is the man, unmatched of heart and limb.

**2.** Not provided with something equal or alike.

**1645** MILTON *Tetrach.* 19 When love findes it self utterly unmatcht, and justly vanishes. **1824** GALT *Rothelan* III. 132 A mean abode,..with old-fashioned unmatched chairs.

Hence **Unma·tchedness.**

*c* **1611** CHAPMAN *Iliad* Pref. A 3 b, His cleare vnmatchednesse in all manner of learning.

† **Unma·tchless,** *a. Obs.*—[1] [UN-[1] 5 a.] Unmatchable, matchless. **1657** F. COCKIN *Div. Blossomes* 49 Those rare unmatchlesse sweets.

**Unmate,** early ME. variant of UNMEET *a.*

**Unma·te,** *v.* (UN-[2] 3.) **1891** C. E. NORTON *Dante's Hell* XXX. 164 The heavy hydropsy which..so unmates the members that the face corresponds not with the belly.

**Unma·ted,** *ppl. a.* (UN-[1] 8.)

**1614** GORGES *Lucan* II. 53 Nothing at all these horrid facts Sylla's vnmated minde distracts. **1633** FORD *'Tis Pity* v. i, Here like a Turtle, (mew'd vp in a Cage,) Vnmated, I conuerse with Ayre and walls. **1850** BLACKIE *Æschylus* II. 236 She in unmated grief to moan Is left alone. **1891** *Anthony's Photogr. Bull.* IV. 380 To immortalize the smiling eyes, which in repose are..unmated.

**Unmate·rial,** *a.* [UN-[1] 7, 5 b.] Immaterial.

**1398** TREVISA *Barth. De P. R.* (1495) II. ii. 27 In somoche he is the more perfyte in contemplacyon of spirytuell and vnmateriall thynges. **1587** GOLDING *De Mornay* xiv. 239 An vnmateriall substance, which hath being of it selfe. **1599** DANIEL *Musoph.* 940 Should we this ornament of glory then, As th' unmaterial fruits of shades, neglect. **1602** WARNER *Alb. Eng.* XIII. lxxix. 326 Vnpassiue, vnmateriall, vncompounded, Infinite. **1883** ROSSETTI in *Athenæum* 15 Dec. 776/2 The scholar who constantly lives an inward and unmaterial life.

**Unmate·rnal,** *a.* (UN-[1] 7.)

**1821** SHELLEY *Epipsych.* 18 Thy panting, wounded breast Stains with dear blood its unmaternal nest! **1885** tr. *A. Monad's Life & Lett.* 17 You only wished to try me, and not seriously to give me such unmaternal advice.

**Unmathema·tical,** *a.* (UN-[1] 7.)

**1720** PRIOR in *Q. Rev.* Jan. (1913) 115 All the cross unmathematical devils upon earth first put it together. **1784** R. BAGE *Barham Downs* I. 230 One unmathematical passion however, Avarice,..had got fast hold of me. **1804–6** SYD. SMITH *Mor. Philos.* (1850) 395 Any immoral, irreligious or unmathematical track of thought.

**Unmathema·tically,** *adv.* (UN-[1] 11.) **1644** in Halliwell *Lett. Sci. Subj.* 80 Mr. Warner's papers..are..most unmathematically divided between the sequestrators and creditors. **Unma·ting,** *ppl. a.* (UN-[1] 10.) **1855** M. ARNOLD *To Marguerite* 32 Or, if not quite alone, yet they Which touch thee are unmating things. **Unmatri·culated,** *ppl. a.* (UN-[1] 8.) **1644** MILTON *Educ.* 2 Instead of beginning with Arts most easie,..they present their young unmatriculated novices at first comming with the most intellective abstractions of Logick and metaphysicks. **1884** *Manch. Exam.* 27 Nov. 5/4 Matriculated and unmatriculated students. **Unmatrimo·nial,** *a.* (UN-[1] 7.) **1572** tr. *Buchanan's Detectioun* F iij b, Within VIII. Dayis, scho finischit that unmatrimoniall Matrimonie. **Unma·tronlike,** *a.* (UN-[1] 7 c.) **1748** RICHARDSON *Clarissa* V. 256 The behaviour of the unmatron-like jilt, whom thou broughtest to betray me. † **Unma·ttered,** *a. Obs.*—[1] [UN-[1] 9.] Immaterial. **1646** J. HALL *Poems* I. 30 Let men desire, like those above Unmatter'd forms, wee'l onely love. **Unmatu·red,** *ppl. a.* (UN-[1] 8.) **1741** W. WHITEHEAD *Danger of Writing Verse* 23 That, unmatur'd by years, My easy numbers pleas'd your partial ears. **1836** F. MAHONY *Rel. Father Prout* (1859) 374 Whatever might have been crude and unmatured in his juvenile lucubrations. † **Unmaw·,** *v. Obs.*—[1] [UN-[2] 3.] *trans.* To empty of knowledge. **1631** MABBE *Celestina* xvii. 175 With my..inticing termes,..I will quite unmaw him, and draw from him all that hee..knowes. † **Unmawe,** *a. Obs. rare.* In 4 **on-, oun-.** [OE. *unmaga* a poor or helpless person.] Helpless. *c* **1380** *Sir Ferumb.* 2658 He hew of heuedes, armes, & haunde of þe Sarasyns þat were on-mawe. *Ibid.* 2766 Hwich þe Sarazyns þat were ounmawe angryde in euery syde. **Unma·ze,** *v.* [UN-[2] 3.] *trans.* To free from amazement or confusion. **1647** R. STAPYLTON *Juvenal* 149 This new man Tully..Set guards, where e're the line of danger ran, Unmaz'd us, and tock pains for all the town.

**Unmea·ning,** *ppl. a.* [UN-[1] 10.]

**1. a.** Of features, etc.: Expressionless, vacant, unintelligent.

**1704** STEELE *Lying Lover* III. i, Poor stupid insipid Lady Fad,..with that unmeaning Face of hers. **1760** DODD *Hymn Good-Nat.* Poems (1767) 3 Daughter of Folly; whose unmeaning front Wears the soft simper of perpetual smiles! **1815** SCOTT *Guy M.* ix, Bertram turned a stupified and unmeaning eye on the messenger. **1836** KINGSLEY *Lett.* (1878) I. 34 The old man spoke in his dreams and muttered with unmeaning visage and fixed eye.

**b.** Of persons: Having no serious aim or purpose.

**1746** ELIZA HEYWOOD *Female Spect.* No. 24 (1748) IV. 305 Being a fool, [she] was thoughtless, giddy, and unmeaning. **1812** MISS MITFORD in L'Estrange *Life* (1870) I. 172 Peace be to them, sweet simpletons! as unmeaning..as their own dinner-bells. **1846** MRS. GORE *Eng. Char.* I. 40 The vapid, unmeaning, unconnected Lady P—.

**2.** Having no meaning or significance; meaningless: **a.** Of actions, conduct, etc.

**1728** ELIZA HEYWOOD tr. *Mme. de Gomez's Belle A.* (1732) II. 228 Turning the Effect of his Admiration into the Appearance of an unmeaning Gallantry. **1776** MICKLE *Camoen's Lusiad* p. lxxvii, Unmeaning slaughter..comprise[s] the whole history of his regency. **1825** T. HOOK *Sayings* Ser. II. III. 320 Full of grimace, affectation, and unmeaning levity. **1869** J. MARTINEAU *Ess.* II. 229 The tendency..is not an unmeaning accident.

**b.** Of words, utterances, etc.

**1709** POPE *Essay on Criticism* 355 At the..only couplet fraught With some unmeaning thing they call a thought. **1727** BOYER *Dict. Royal* II. s.v., Unmeaning Words. **1771** T. PERCIVAL *Ess.* (1777) I. 6 [They] conceal their own ignorance..by unmeaning terms and pompous phrases. **1855** MACAULAY *Hist. Eng.* xv. III. 559 That several neighbouring nations..thought this most unmeaning of all names worth borrowing. **1875** FORTNUM *Maiolica* xi. 109 The unmeaning designs of the oriental porcelain.

*absol.* **1870** DISRAELI *Lothair* lxxvii, I do not believe in the unmeaning.

**3.** Uttering nothing significant.

**1743** W. WHITEHEAD *Ep. Ann Boleyn* 90 Each distant Hint that hung On broken Sounds of an unmeaning Tongue.

**Unmea·ningly,** *adv.* (UN-[1] 11; cf. prec.) **1775** ASH, *Nonsensically*, unmeaningly, foolishly. **1808** *Sketches of Character* (1813) I. 133 Look at the soft soul—how unmeaningly she stares at the Band. **1870** LOWELL *Study Wind., Gt. Publ. Char.*, Those threads of gossamer, the nearest approach to nothing unmeaningly prolonged. **Unmea·ningness.** (UN-[1] 12.) **1796** MME. D'ARBLAY *Camilla* II. 13 She perceived her two little sprigs..under the feet of Indiana, who with apparent unmeaningness..had trampled upon them both. **1825** COLERIDGE *Aids Refl.* 391 The utter emptiness and unmeaningness of the vaunted Mechanico-corpuscular Philosophy. **1864** PUSEY *Lect. Daniel* iv. 189 The unmeaningnesses, which they have brought into the prophecy, cannot be its meaning.

**Unmea·nt,** *ppl. a.* [UN-[1] 8 b.] Not meant or intended.

*a* **1634** CHAPMAN *Revenge for Honour* v. ii, Howere you're pleas'd to mock me..with these impertinent, unmeant discourses, I cannot..give them the least credit. **1697** DRYDEN *Æneis* x. 561 The flying Spear was after Ilus sent, But Rhœtus hapen'd on a Death unmeant. **1738** G. LILLO *Marina* II. i, I who cou'd not bear The unmeant rivalship of sweet Marina. **1820** SHELLEY *Prometh. Unb.* III. iv. 151 That..hollow talk Which makes the heart..question that unmeant hypocrisy. **1891** E. KINGLAKE *Australian at Home* 71 It is the short sighted gentleman..on whom the ball finds its unmeant mark as a rule.

**b.** Const. *by* and with complement.

*c* **1700** CONGREVE *To Cynthia* Wks. 1730 III. 291 Curse on that Word so ready to be spoke, For through my Lips, unmeant by me, it broke. **1745** YOUNG *Nt. Th.* VIII. 682 Can man..strike out A self-wrought happiness unmeant by him Who made us? **1848** BAILEY *Festus* (ed. 3) 211 These mysteries Unmeant by Heaven to be cleared up on earth.

**Unmea·surable,** *a.*, *sb.*, and *adv.* ? *Obs.* [UN-[1] 7 b, 5 b, 12, and 11 b.]

**1.** Incapable of being measured on account of great size, extent, or amount; immense, vast: **a.** Of material things, dimensions, time, etc.

*c* **1386** CHAUCER *Man of Law's T.* 934 O Golias, vnmesurable of lengthe. **1513** DOUGLAS *Æneid* VI. vi. 71 Cerberus, ..Vnmesurable in his cave quhar he lay. *a* **1541** WYATT in *Tottel's Misc.* (Arb.) 70 Lyke vnto these vnmesurable mountaines, So is my painefull life, the burden of yre. **1585** T. WASHINGTON tr. *Nicholay's Voy.* II. iii. 33 The walles..are made of grauen stone..of length and bignesse vnmeasurable. **1610** HEALEY *St. Aug. Citie of God* III. xxxi. 152 A most huge and vnmesurable cloud. **1691** NORRIS *Pract. Disc.* 243 Truth and Falshood..are removed from each other by an unmeasurable distance. **1754** EDWARDS *Freed. Will* IV. viii. 240 Unlimited and Unmeasureable Periods of Time. **1774** J. BRYANT *Mythol.* I. 398 The tower..was of an unmeasurable height.

**b.** Of actions, qualities, feelings, etc.

**1377** LANGL. *P. Pl.* B. xv. 69 (W.), Ye moeven materes unmesurable [*v.rr.* vn-, inmesurables] To tellen of the Trinite. *c* **1450** *Merlin* xx. 329 He..yaf hym soche a stroke with the brasen betell so vn-mesurable, that [etc.]. **1542** BECON *News Heaven* H iij b, Your ioy can not be expressed, your gladnes is vnmeasurable. **1588** in *Harl. Misc.* (1808) I. 143 An unmeasurable deep despair. **1648** SANDERSON *Serm., Ad Aul.* (1681) II. 242 We..shall have an unmeasurable reward..for the good we have done. *a* **1677** BARROW *Serm.* Wks. 1716 I. 345 He did by unmeasurable communications of divine virtue assist his humanity. **17..** WATTS *Hymns*, '*Come, dearest Lord*' ii, The Heighth, and Breadth, and Length, Of thine unmeasurable Grace. **1760–72** H. BROOKE *Fool of Qual.* (1809) II. 120 This..parade of sanctity gave him..unmeasurable credit.

**c.** Used with reference to God.

**1535** COVERDALE *Baruch* iii. 25 Greate is he,..hye and vnmeasurable. **1551** VERON *Godly Saiyngs* E viii, Touchinge his godheade, and vnmeasurable substaunce. **1581** MARBECK *Bk. of Notes* 126 The same one man is locall..as touching his manhood, which is also God unmeasurable from the Father.

**2.** Immoderate, inordinate, unbounded: **a.** Of persons (or other agents).

**1388** WYCLIF *Prov.* xv. 4 The tunge which is vnmesurable, schal defoule the spirit. *c* **1400** *Pilgr. Sowle* (Caxton, 1483) III. ix. 55 These haue ben so vnmesurable in their expensys. *c* **1450** *Mirour Saluacioun* 3936 Nabal..made to hym kyng Dauid his vnmesurable enemy. *c* **1520** BARCLAY *Jugurth* xxvii. 37 b, Their myndes were greatly immoderate and vnmeasurable in their desyre to ouercome thestates. **1597** BRETON *Auspicante Jehoua* Wks. (Grosart) II. 6/2 So great and vnmeasurable a sinner. **1629** J. MAXWELL tr. *Herodian* 155 An vnmeasurable Louer of Money. **1667** SOUTH *Serm.* (1697) 32 He..shall find [sin]..an Unmeasurable Exactor.

**b.** Of desires or the gratification of these.

*c* **1386** CHAUCER *Pars. T.* ⁋ 818 Glotonye is vnmesurable Appetit to ete or to drynke. **1388** WYCLIF *1 Pet.* iv. 3 Whiche walkiden..in myche drinking of wyn, in vnmesurable etyngis and drynkyngis. **1422** YONG tr. *Secreta Secret.* 194 Hit is dedly syn whan that concupiscens is so vnmesurable that [etc.]. **1482** *Monk of Evesham* xxi. (Arb.) 49 Y was..ageyne bonde yn to luste and custome of the same sinne, that was yn mine owne onmeserabulle taking and appetite. **1583** BABINGTON *Commandm.* 176 So euil an example of vnmeasurable sotting in bed. **1594** T. B. *La Primaud. Fr. Acad.* II. 269 Other carnall pleasures.., especially when they are excessiue and vnmeasurable. *a* **1648** LD. HERBERT *Hen. VIII* (1683) 220 His Cardinal['s]..unmeasurable Ambition and Covetousness. **1788** JEFFERSON *Writ.* (1859) II. 371 The unmeasurable ambition of the Emperor.

**c.** In miscellaneous applications.

*c* **1425** in *Anglia* VIII. 139/11 Vnmesurabil laghter or vnsem and vnmanerly berynge of body. **1461** *Rolls of Parlt.* V. 493/2 The inordynat and unmesurable Enditementz and Presentementz..of Felonye. **1535** COVERDALE *Ecclus.* xxxvii. 30 Glotony commeth at the last to an vnmeasurable heate. **1592** TIMME *Ten Eng. Lepers* H 2 Through unmeasurable abstinence, the moysture of the bodie is dried up. **1638** PENKETHMAN *Artach.* K j, Great Tempests, unmeasurable Windes and Raines. **1674** TEMPLE *Let. to Ld. Treas.* Wks. 1720 II. 311 The unmeasurable Burden of their Taxes. **1709** SWIFT *Adv. Relig.* Wks. 1755 II. I. 97 The lustre of that most noble family..which the unmeasurable profusion of ancestors..had too much eclipsed.

**3.** Not admitting of measurement; immensurable.

**1652** *Zeal Examined* Add. § 9. 40 Which rendered the true Church unmeasureable by any outward Formes. **1714** *Barrow's Euclid* Pref. p. ii, Both measurable and unmeasurable Magnitudes.

**b.** *sb.* An immensurable thing.

**1652** BENLOWES *Theoph.* v. lxxxvi, Can measures such Unmeasurables hold? Can time Infinity unfold?

**4.** *adv.* = UNMEASURABLY *adv.*

*c* **1440** *Alph. Tales* 343 When he saw any yong monk lagh vnmesurable. *c* **1445** PECOCK *Donet* 85 God is..vnmesurable greet in goostly greetnes. **1586** T. B. *La Primaud. Fr. Acad.* I. 671 So that great heede is to be taken, that none grow to be unmeasurable great. **1650** BULWER *Anthropomet.* 202 An huge unmeasurable great Ring.

Hence † **Unmea·surableness.** *Obs.*

**1533** FRITH *Book Answ. More's Lett.* H ij, Shewynge the vnmeasurablenes of his Godhead. **1571** GOLDING *Calvin on Ps.* xxxix. 3 To give himself the brydle to anye unmeasurablenesse of greefe. **1634** T. JOHNSON *Parey's Chirurg. Wks.* XXI. i. 776 The unmeasurablenesse of the manifest..qualities whereof they [*sc.* poisons] consist. **1656** JEANES *Fuln. Christ* 204 The unmeasurablenesse of his affection unto us. **1724** WELTON *Chr. Faith & Pract.* 185 His judgments are as the great deep for their obscurity and unmeasurableness.

**Unmea·surably,** *adv.* [UN-[1] 11.]

† **1.** Without measure or moderation; immoderately, unrestrainedly. *Obs.*

*a* **1420** *Wycliffite Bible* Ecclus. xi. 10 *margin*, If thou suest, in sekinge richessis vnmesurably, thou schalt not take. *a* **1450** *Knt. de la Tour* 53 Other that be..enflamed unmesurably like wolues. **1542–5** BRINKLOW *Lament.* 9 b, Ye abvse your riches,..for ye spende vnmeasurably. **1561** HOLLYBUSH *Hom. Apoth.* 40 Eating and drinking vnmeasurably. **1631** ANCHORAN *Comenius' Gate Tongues* 190 To laugh aloud and vnmeasurably. **1679** *Hist. Jetzer* 17 He..frets and fumes unmeasurably. *a* **1693** LUDLOW *Mem.* (1698) II. 624 The Court..grew unmeasurably insolent. **1722** WOLLASTON *Relig. Nat.* v. xviii. (1724) 111 Opposite parties make a merit of blackening their adversaries..undeservedly and unmeasurably.

**2.** To an immeasurable extent or degree; excessively, extremely.

**1513** *Henry V* (1911) 132 Famyne..vnmeasurably raigned amongest them. *c* **1530** LD. BERNERS *Arth. Lyt. Bryt.* (1814) 336 Hys spere..was so long & byg so vnmesurably, y[t] [etc.]. **1624** BP. HALL *Peace Maker* in *Var. Treat.* (1627) 538 Grace sensibly imperfect, sinne vnmeasurably sinfull. *a* **1670** RUST *Disc. Truth* (1682) 180 A Soul unmeasurably breathing after the Embraces of Truth. **1704** NORRIS *Ideal World* II. xii. 510 'Tis not to be imagined..how unmeasurably the powers of that soul must needs be illuminated. *a* **1797** H. WALPOLE *Mem. Geo. II* (1847) I. vi. 186 He was ..unmeasurably obstinate. **1828** LD. GRENVILLE *Sink. Fund* I Unmeasurably more beneficial to mankind, are those qualities. **1866** AIRY *Pop. Astron.* i. 37 That the distance..is unmeasurably small, compared with the distances of the stars.

† **Unmea·surate,** *a. Obs.* [UN-[1] 7.] = UNMEASURED *ppl. a.* (Cf. IMMENSURATE *a.*)

**1557** *Primer, Crede*, Euen as there be not thre vncreat nor thre vnmeasurate, but one vncreat and one vnmeasurate.

**Unmea·sure.** [UN-[1] 12.]

† **1.** Lack of measure; excess. *Obs.*

*a* **1300** *Cursor M.* 15543 Til vnmesur mismai yow noght. *c* **1440** *Jacob's Well* 303 So wast hath manye expensys and costys..in vnmesure & werkys, bareyn wyth-oute fruyte. **1598** FLORIO, *Dismisura*, an vnmeasure, out of measure.

**2.** An improper or illegal measure.

**1820** BENTHAM *Lib. Press* Wks. 1843 II. 283/2 The last, though not the least, of all their fears is—lest un-measures, which..have already been taken..for the extinction of all power of controul [etc.].

**Unmea·sured,** *ppl. a.* [UN-[1] 8.]

**1.** Not limited or known by measurement; immense in size, extent, or amount.

1398 Trevisa *Barth. De P. R.* x. iv. (Bodl. MS.), Fuyre.. is icleped vnmesured, for his vertu..encreseþ wiþoute eende. 1585 T. Washington tr. *Nicholay's Voy.* ii. iii. 33 The stature of a woman..of bignes vnmeasured. *c* 1611 Chapman *Iliad* ii. 78 So from the ships and tents the army's store Troop'd to these princes..along th' unmeasur'd shore. 1646 Crashaw *Sospetto d'Herode* xxii, That the unmeasur'd God so low should sinke, As Pris'ner in a few poore Rags to lye. 1718 Prior *Solomon* i. 640 This ample azure Sky,.. With Stars unnumber'd, and unmeasur'd Light. 1794 R. J. Sulivan *View Nat.* I. 320 Of an unmeasured fluid, we can only reason by conjecture. 1810 Scott *Lady of Lake* ii. xxxi, When..Such startler cast his glance below, And saw unmeasured depth around. 1870 Morris *Earthly Par.* III. iv. 2 Pale stars..make heaven so vast That earth..Seems shrunken 'neath the grey unmeasured height.

*absol.* 1844 Mrs. Browning *Drama of Exile* 1710 As the thunder roars deep in the Unmeasured.

**b.** Of feelings, qualities, etc.

1435 Misyn *Fire of Love* 6 In þe flaume vnmesurde of lufe. *c* 1450 *Mirour Saluacioun* 3008 Gods vnmesured bountee. 1618 in Foster *Eng. Factories Ind.* (1906) I. 22, I have stroven..with their tricks of unmeasured greatenes. 1692 Prior *Ode Imit. Hor.* iii, Distracted Lewis can descry Only a long unmeasur'd Ruin nigh. 1793 Smeaton *Edystone L.* § 179 The unmeasured violence of the sea. 1856 Froude *Hist. Eng.* I. 116 Wolsey..combined practical sagacity with an unmeasured power of hoping. 1864 Skeat *Uhland's Poems* 151 All men are rivals in unmeasured wo.

**2.** Not doled *out* by measure. *rare*—¹.

1667 Milton *P. L.* v. 399 Our Nourisher from whom All perfet good unmeasur'd out, descends.

**3.** Not subjected to measure; not composed of measured syllables.

1715 Pope *Iliad* iv. 298 Unmix'd, unmeasured, are thy goblets crown'd. 1728 Chambers *Cycl.* s.v. *Poetry*, These, in a Discourse that has no poetical Feet or Measures, do yet ..make it a kind of unmeasured Poetry. 1808 L. Murray *Gram.* I. 84 In regard to unmeasured quantities and qualities, the degrees of more and less..may be expressed intelligibly. *a* 1822 Shelley *Def. Poetry, Essays & Lett.* (1840) 9 It is necessary..to determine the distinction between measured and unmeasured language. 1863 Hawthorne *Our Old Home* II. 175 His delightful prose, his unmeasured poetry.

**4.** Immoderate, unrestrained.

1820 Hazlitt *Lect. Dram. Lit.* 106 His pride and unmeasured pretensions. 1839 Hallam *Hist. Lit.* II. 287 The unmeasured eulogies he bestows upon him. 1884 Jebb in *Fortn. Rev.* 1 Apr. 434 The habitual use of unmeasured language [in criticism].

Hence **Unmea·suredly** *adv.*, **-edness.**

1435 Misyn *Fire of Love* 75 No marevayle þof I..vnmesurdnes of þat endles swetnes to ȝow may not opyn. 1602 Marston *Ant. & Mel.* iii. Wks. 1856 I. 43 This vengeance.. will lengthen out My daies unmeasuredly. 1864 G. Gilfillan in *Lett. & Jrnls.* (1892) 373, I intend considering..the energy—the unmeasuredness—of their life.

†**Unmea·surely,** *a.* and *adv. Obs.* (Un-¹ 7, 11.) *a* 1300 *Cursor M.* 27047 Quen þai vn-mesurli ar radd Efter rising to fall egain. 1513 Douglas *Æneid* xii. xii. 33 Twa of sik statur, onmysurly of hycht. **Unmecha·nic,** *a.* (Un-¹ 7.) 1687 *Death's Vision* vii, Magnetic Virtues..Which Unmechanic seem'd and sprung from Laws Of some strange Forreign System. 1789 [see Unmetaphysic *a.*]. 1800 Coleridge in C. K. Paul *W. Godwin* (1876) II. i. 3 His taste acts so as to appear like the unmechanic simplicity of an instinct.

**Unmecha·nical,** *a.* (Un-¹ 7.)

1674 Boyle *Grounds Corpusc. Philos.* 13 The like unmechanical principles and agents. 1693 *Phil. Trans.* XVII. 660 Deep Pools, which could never have been searched by these unmechanical people. 1794 G. Adams *Nat. & Exp. Philos.* III. xxiv. 21 It is absurd in philosophers to use unmechanical principles, where mechanical ones will answer the purpose. 1825 J. Nicholson *Operat. Mechanic* 368 This unmechanical and desultory mode of operation. 1845 Ford *Handbk. Spain* ii. 853 The unmechanical Spaniards still work their mines..as the..Iberians did. 1865 Mrs. Whitney *Gayworthys* xxvii, Unscrupulous, even doubting thoughts, they might be; yet real, unmechanical.

**Unmecha·nically,** *adv.* (Un-¹ 11.) 1833 G. S. Faber *Recapit. Apostasy* 80 It does not therefore follow, that one of the two names is incapable of producing that number, when calculated unmechanically or with wisdom. **Unme·chanize,** *v.* (Un-² 6 c.) 1687 *Death's Vision* ii, When these soft Bellows [*sc.* the lungs] too, Shall all Unmechaniz'd, and all Unactive grow. 1760 Sterne *Tr. Shandy* iv. xix, What one misfortune or disaster in the book of embryotic evils, that could unmechanize thy frame,..has not fallen upon thy head! **Unme·chanized,** *ppl. a.* (Un-¹ 8.) 1802 Paley *Nat. Theol.* ii. § 4 If nothing had been before us but an unorganized, unmechanized substance, without mark or indication of contrivance.

**Unme·ddled,** *ppl. a.* [Un-¹ 8.]

†**1.** Unmixed. *Obs.*

*c* 1380 Wyclif *Sel. Wks.* III. 320 Love of Crist is not, but ȝif it be cleer, unmedlid wiþ errours. *c* 1449 Pecock *Repr.* i. x. 49 Euen as grammer and dyuynyte ben ij. dyuerse ..kunnyngis, and therfore ben vnmedlid. 1555 Watreman *Fardle Facions* ii. iv. I ij, The wisedome, and vnmedled puritie of Language. 1595 Southwell *Poems, 'Times goe by Turnes,'* Unmeddled joyes heere to no man befall.

**2.** Not meddled or interfered *with*. Also without prep.

1535 Coverdale *Judith* xii. 11 That a woman shulde so laugh a man to scorne, that she were come from him vnmedled withall. 1573 *Reg. Privy Council Scot.* III. 292 [The corn] to remane unmedlit or disponit upoun be ony. 1602 Carew *Cornwall* 105 [The flood-gate] is opened and closed for sixe dayes in the whole, continuing..other ten dayes vnmedled withall. 1641 Best *Farm. Bks.* (Surtees) 68 Yow are to lette the water in the tubbe stande all night unmedled with. 1690 W. Walker *Idiomat. Anglo-Lat.* 269 He left it as he found it,—untoucht; unmedled withall. 1884 Sir C. Bowen in *Law Times Rep.* LI. 531/1 To have the enjoyment of his goods and chattels unmeddled with by others. 1898 *Wide World Mag.* Oct. 90/2 This might lie long unmeddled with by the common crowd of the deeps.

**Unme·ddlesome,** *a.* (Un-¹ 7.) 1852 Davies & Vaughan *Republic Plato* viii. 550 He hears the quiet and unmeddlesome called simpletons. 1853 W. Cory *Lett. & Jrnls.* (1897) 59 Goodford is laconic, prudent, unmeddlesome.

**Unme·ddling,** *ppl. a.* (Un-¹ 10.)

1765 Chesterf. *Lett.* (1774) II. 486 She is..a tender mother; and an unmeddling Queen. 1774 'J. Collier' *Mus. Trav.* App. 4 A contented, unmeddling man. 1793 Jefferson *Writ.* (1859) IV. 16 Unmeddling with the affairs of other nations, we [etc.].

Hence **Unme·ddlingly** (Webster, 1847), **-ness.**

*a* 1656 Bp. Hall *Serm.* 1 *Pet.* i. 17 Rem. Wks. (1660) 202 Here must be an ἀπραγμοσύνη, an unmeddlingness with these worldly concernments.

**Unme·diated,** *ppl. a.* (Un-¹ 8.)

1648 Hexham ii, *Ongemiddelt*, Vnmediated. 1850 J. Martineau *Misc.* (1852) 225 This unmediated dualism follows the Evangelical into his theory as to the State of each individual soul before God. 1881 G. Macdonald *Mary Marston* xlviii, In a woman's love there is more of the specially divine element than in a man's—namely, the original, the unmediated.

**Unme·diatized,** *ppl. a.* (Un-¹ 8.) 1839 Lieber *Man. Pol. Ethics* I. 358 Wherever all power that can be obtained, is undivided, unmodified and un-mediatised.

**Unme·dical,** *a.* (Un-¹ 7.)

1809 Malkin *Gil Blas* ix. viii. ⁋ 7 Fancying in his unmedical head that physicians cured fevers. 1840 Dickens *Sk. Loving Couples* 34 The medical gentleman..was observed to laugh and wink, and look as unmedical as might be. 1888 E. W. Benson in *Life Dean Lake* (1901) 293 All his habits are so vigorous and unmedical that he is most difficult, even for doctors.

**Unme·dicative,** *a.* (Un-¹ 7.) 1836 Carlyle in Froude *Life in London* (1884) I. 84 London has been like a course of mercury to body and mind; hard enough, but not unmedicative.

**Unme·dicinable,** *a.* [Un-¹ 7 b, 5 b.]

**1.** Incurable.

1575 Gascoigne *Glasse of Govt.* v. iii, The misgovernment of a mans children..is unto the wysest mynde an unmedicinable wounde. 1624 Heywood *Gunaik.* iii. 160 To give date unto..thy violent and unmedicinable torture.

**b.** Refusing medical treatment.

*c* 1611 Chapman *Iliad* xvi. 24 But these [chiefs]..physicians can recure, Thou yet unmed'cinable still, though thy wound all endure.

**2.** Incapable of effecting a cure.

1606 Chapman *Gent. Usher* iv. ii, Away with this unmedcinable balme Of worded breath. 1614 Latham *Falconry* 116 As it is a thing very medicinable,..being rightly giuen; so also, it is as vnmedicinable and hurtfull if..otherwise vsed.

**Unme·ditated,** *ppl. a.* (Un-¹ 8.)

1624 Heywood *Gunaik.* i. 45 [They] left nothing unmeditated that might stirre up men to the adoration of the divine powers. 1667 Milton *P. L.* v. 149 To praise Thir Maker, in fit strains pronounc't or sung Unmeditated. 1790 Paley *Horæ Paul.* vii. § 5 The intimations upon the subject preserve among themselves..a consistency certainly unmeditated. *a* 1797 H. Walpole *Mem. Geo. II* (1847) I. vi. 174 His wit..was constant and unmeditated.

**Unme·ditative,** *a.* (Un-¹ 7.) 1842 G. S. Faber *Prov. Lett.* (1844) I. 229 This sentence reads well: and, with the unmeditative, will probably tell well. 1866 Carlyle *Remin.* (1881) II. 330 A man..given to meditation, and much contemptuous of the unmeditative world. †**Unmee·dful,** *a. Obs.* (Un-¹ 7.) Undeserving of reward. *c* 1400 *Cursor M.* 28772 (Cott. Galba), Els vnmedeful es þe dede, And makes to þe doer no mede. 1435 Misyn *Fire of Love* 93 Þa trespas fowll þerfore þat say þat all owr dedys inwarde or vtward ar meydfull or vnmedefull. †**Unmee·dy,** *a.* [Un-¹ 7.] Unrewarded. *a* 1300 *Cursor M.* 28772 Elles vnmedi sal it be, Scathel and wrangwise als to þe.

**Unmee·k,** *a.* [Un-¹ 7. Cf. ON. *úmjúk-r.*]

**1.** Not meek or gentle; † unkind, harsh, cruel.

*c* 1200 Ormin 9880 Hæþenndom..Iss harrd & starrc all allse stan, Unnmeoc & all unnmilde. *a* 1300 *Cursor M.* 14616 Wit þaa vn-meke þar was he mett, And son wit þam he was vmsett. ? *a* 1366 Chaucer *Rom. Rose* 590 And she to me was nought vnmeke, Ne of hir answer daungerous. *c* 1374 — *Boeth.* iv. met. vii. (1886) 115 He..as it is sayd hath put an vnmeke lord [as] foddre to his crwel hors. *c* 1449 Pecock *Repr.* i. xvi. 96 The ȝifte which he wol ȝeue into the resoun or vndirstonding of vnmeke men. 1483 *Cath. Angl.* 233/1 Vn Meke, *vbi* felle. 1509 Barclay *Shyp of Folys* 8 Do nat Poetis revyle..all suche as ar vnmeke, Prowde, Couetous? 1595 W. I. *Two Disc. F. Guicciardin* A j b, Old fooles, yong maids,..Daunsing their roundes with Sathans dam vnmeeke. *a* 1653 Binning *Serm.* (1845) 527 An unmeek spirit..troubles itself and annoys others. 1819 Keats *Ode Indolence* iii, The last, whom I love more, the more of blame Is heap'd upon her, maiden most unmeek.

†**2.** Unsupple, stiff. *Obs.*—¹

*a* 1275 *Prov. Ælfred* 538 Elde..makit him wel vnmeke, & binimit him is miȝte.

**Unmee·kened,** *ppl. a.* (Un-¹ 8.) 1612 T. Taylor *Comm. Titus* iii. 2 Rather then by an vnmeekned and vnsubdued stomacke, [to] hurt both themselues and others. **Unmee·kly,** *adv.* (Un-¹ 11. Cf. ON. *úmjúkliga.*) *c* 1380 Wyclif *Sel. Wks.* III. 44 Þat he speke neiþer unmekeli to terre men for to fiȝte, ne [etc.]. *a* 1400 *Cursor M.* 27763 (Cott. Galba), Slewth oft samnes sorow strang, And þat vnmekely lastand lang.

**Unmee·kness.** (Un-¹ 12.)

*c* 1440 *Jacob's Well* 266 Whil vnmekenesse is in þin herte, it faryth as þe see. 1509 Barclay *Shyp of Folys* 198 b, This rauenyng sort..Be theyr vnmekenes the pore oft maketh bare. 1828 E. Irving *Last Days* 255 Unwillingness to obey, or unmeekness or ungentleness in obedience.

**Unmee·t,** *a.* [OE. *unmǽte* (Un-¹ 7 + Meet *a.*). Cf. OHG. *unmâzi* (MHG. *unmâze, unmæze*) and Unimete *a.*]

†**1.** Immoderate or excessive in amount. *Obs.*

*c* 900 tr. *Bæda's Hist.* v. xii. (1890) 422 Ond ealle..mid unmæte eȝe ȝeslæȝene weron & utfluȝon. *c* 1175 *Lamb. Hom.* 103 ȝifernesse..maceð þan men muchele untrumnesse and to deþe bringeð mid unmete drunche. *c* 1200 *Vices & Virtues* 19 Ðar is chiueringe of toðen for ðe unmate chele. *a* 1300 *Cursor M.* 23035 Þat drednes sal be sua vn-mete, Þat it mai all sli plightes bete. *a* 1310 in Wright *Lyric P.* iv. 23 This wilde wille went a-wai, with mone and mournyng muchel un-mete.

† **b.** Excessive in size; immense, huge. *Obs.*

*c* 900 tr. *Bæda's Hist.* v. xiii. (1890) 438 Þa teah he forð boc..unmættre micelnisse. *a* 1300 *Cursor M.* 16566 For to ber it [*sc.* a tree] vte o þe kirk þai fand it ful vn-mete. 13.. *Gaw. & Gr. Knt.* 208 He hade..an ax in his oþer [hand], a hoge & vn-mete. *c* 1350 *Lybeaus Disc.* 1629 Another helm hym was brought, And a schaft unmete. *a* 1400–50 *Alexander* 143 Þen metis he furthe to Messadon full vn-mete gatis. 14.. *Sir Beues* (C.) 2537 Ascopard hys staffe onmeete Smot after hym a strok gret. *c* 1475 *Partenay* 5775 Hys panche as a pipe hug and comerous;..Off hir unmete hugenesse is gret meruaill.

†**2.** Unequal; unevenly matched. *Obs.*

*a* 1300 *Cursor M.* 9362 Als rose and thron ar tua vnmete; And tuix þam fair a-cord es nan. 13.. *E. E. Allit. P.* A. 759 My makelez lambe..Me ches to hys make, al-þaȝ vnmete Sum tyme semed þat assemble. 1390 Gower *Conf.* II. 121 Thou wost nothing of my desese, Hou thou and I be now unmete. *c* 1400 *Destr. Troy* 1324 But vnmete was the Macche at þe mene tyme: The Grekes were grym [etc.]. 1513 Douglas *Æneid* ii. xi. 76 Litle Iulus..With wnmeit paiss his fader fast followand. *a* 1548 Hall *Chron., Hen. V*, 76 b, Their numbre was but small..and far vnmete to compare with halfe the power of his puissaunt armie. 1563 *Mirr. Mag.* Induct. xxviii, We passed on with steppes and pace vnmete. ? *a* 1760 in Child *Ballads* IV. 165/1 Four he killd and five did wound, That was an unmeet marrow!

†**b.** Lacking in equality; inferior. *Obs. rare.*

1390 Gower *Conf.* III. 260 Sche..thoghte hirself unmete And the lest worth of wommen alle. *a* 1547 Surrey in *Tottel's Misc.* (Arb.) 219 He bowed at her feete, In humble wise as who would say I am to farre vnmete.

†**c.** Superior. *Obs. rare.*

1390 Gower *Conf.* I. 163 This Galathee..Above alle othre was unmete Of beaute. *Ibid.* II. 199 The thridde maister scholde mete, Which, as thei seiden, was unmete Above hem alle, and couthe most.

†**d.** As *adv.* Unequally. *Obs.*—¹

1515 *Scottish Field* 188 in *Chetham Misc.* (1856) II, They were numbered nyne hundreth,..And they were x thousand ..upon the other partie; Full unmette were they matched.

†**3.** Not closely united; remote. *Obs.*

1390 Gower *Conf.* I. 316 Fro merci thei ben al unmeete, And thus ben thei the worste of alle Of hem whiche unto wraththe falle. *a* 1500 *Flower & Leaf* 17 As I lay in my bed, sleep ful unmete Was unto me.

**4.** Unfitting, unsuitable, unbecoming, improper. Common *c* 1535–1675, and in 19th cent.

*a* 1529 Skelton *Replyc.* 49 With baudy wordes vnmete Your tonges were to flete. *a* 1602 W. Perkins *Cases Consc.* (1619) 6 Inconuenience is when the thing or action is done in vnmeete circumstances. 1649 Bp. Hall *Cases Consc.* iv. vi. 450 Such a marriage is very unmeet. 1675 Hobbes *Odyss.* 27 While they contending were with words unmeet. 1790 Cowper *Iliad* i. 145 It were much unmeet that I alone.. should want due recompense. 1814 Scott *Lord of Isles* v. vii, With unaccustom'd ears, A language much unmeet he hears. 1850 Neale *Med. Hymns* (1867) 138 It is not for man's devices Here to pry with gaze unmeet. 1885–94 R. Bridges *Eros & Psyche* June xxiv, [There] were noises at the door..Such as..now seem'd most unmeet to be.

**b.** Const. *for*, or *to* with inf. (Cf. next.)

1541 *Act* 33 *Hen. VIII*, c. 21 § 7 Soo allso were it unmete and daungerous to the suretye of our..Kynge..to be construed by any lawe [etc.]. *c* 1555 Harpsfield *Divorce Hen. VIII* (Camden) 97 This kind of reason is..far unmeet for..these learned men. 1583 Stubbes *Anat. Abus.* ii. D 6, It is very vnmeete to feede forren nations, and our owne country famish at home. *a* 1683 Owen *Two Disc. Holy Spirit* (1693) 54 That which some oppose as unmeet for him, and beneath his Glory. *a* 1703 Burkitt *On N. T.* Mark iv. 2 Christ thought..a ship no unmeet place to preach in. 1807 Wordsw. *White Doe* i. 312 Why mention other thoughts unmeet For vision so composed and sweet? 1867 G. Macdonald *Poems* 48 Trailing loose their white attire For the sapphire-floor unmeet. 1868 Morris *Earthly Par.* I. i. 353 He rose and spoke in humble words, unmeet For a great King.

**5.** Unfit or unsuited for some end or purpose; incompetent: **a.** With *for*.

*c* 1522 Skelton *Why nat to Courte* 32 Age is a page For the courte full vnmete. 1577 B. Googe *Heresbach's Husb.* iii. 126 b, The olde that be barraine, or vnmeete for breeding. 1626 Gouge *Serm. Dignity Chivalry* § 2 They were too meane and unmeet persons for a function so high. 1647 N. Bacon *Disc. Govt. Eng.* i. xlvii. 129 The more Baron, the lesse Bishop, and more unmeet for the service of Rome. 1676 Row *Contn. Blair's Autobiog.* xi. (1848) 326 Mr. Blair was now infirm and unmeet for travel. 1855 Tennyson *Maud* i. iv. x, Ah Maud, you milkwhite fawn, you are all unmeet for a wife. 1863 Conington tr. *Hor., Odes* ii. xix. 27 [They] Deem'd thee belike for war's rough game Unmeet.

**b.** With † *to* (prep.), or *to* with inf.

*a* 1513 Fabyan *Chron.* v. cxl. 125 They chase a man of lowe byrth & vnmete to that rome. 1533 Sir T. More *Lett. Impugn. J. Fryth* liv, Fryth is an vnmete mayster to teche vs what we shold praye. 1535 Coverdale *Tit.* i. 16 For so moch as they are..dishobedient, and vnmete to all good workes. 1600 Holland *Livy* 596 They supposed, that they would..bee farre unmeet to contrive a conspiracie. 1642 H. More *Min. Poems* Wks. (Grosart) 177/1 Such surface skill's Unmeet to measure the profounder quill. 1670 Baxter *Cure Ch. Div.* 372 In those cases where violent restraint..is necessary, the Pastor is the unmeetest person to meddle in it. 1808 Scott *Marm.* vi. xiii, To each one whom he lists, howe'er Unmeet to be the owner's peer. 1846 Keble *Lyra Innoc.* 235 Behold me, Lord, a worthless Gibeonite, Unmeet to bear one burthen in thy sight.

**c.** Without const.

1535 Coverdale *Job* xxxvii. 19 Teach vs what we shal saye vnto him, for we are vnmete because of darcknes.

1557 *Act 4 & 5 Phil. & Mary* c. 3 § 1 The same Disability ..notwithstanding, the same unable and unmeet Persons.. have also been released. 1598 GRENEWEY *Tacitus, Ann.* XIII. vi. 187 Neither did that [practice] long continue, because the lot fell oft vpon the vnmeetest. 1706 PRIOR *Ode to Queen* xxxv, That Muse desires.. the lowest Place; Who tho' unmeet, yet touch'd the trembling String. 1825 SCOTT *Betrothed* xii, He were rather an unmeet counsellor in that which we now treat of. 1844 IS. WILLIAMS *Baptistery* III. ii, Then like the Leper stand and pray aloof,—Like the Centurion deem thyself unmeet.

**Unmee·table**, *a.* (UN-¹ 7 b.) 1837 T. HOOK *Jack Brag* i, As light of darkness, fire of water, or any other two unmeetable opposites.

**†Unmee·tly**, *a. Obs. rare.* [UN-¹ 7. Cf. OE. *unmǽtlic*, OHG. (MHG.) *unmâzlich.*]

1. = UNMEET *a.* 1 b.

*a* 1400-50 *Alexander* 321 A mouthe as a mastis hunde, vnmetely to shaw.

2. = UNMEET *a.* 4.

1534 MORE *Treat. Passion* Wks. 1316/1 Peter..thought it in hys mynde vnmetely that hys lorde and mayster shoulde weshe his feete.

**Unmee·tly**, *adv.* [UN-¹ 11. Cf. prec., and ON. *úmátaliga*, OHG. *unmâzlîche* (MHG. *unmæzlîche*).]

†1. Immoderately, excessively. *Obs.*⁻¹

*a* 1300 *Cursor M.* 27763 O suernes cums care to strang And þat vnmetele lastand lang.

2. Unfitly, unbecomingly.

1596 SPENSER *F. Q.* VI. vi. 16 A faire Mayden..Vpon a mangy iade vnmeetely set. 1611 COTGR., *Induëment*, .. vnmeetly, vnfitly. 1826 SCOTT *Woodst.* xxviii, A benevolent smile.. accorded not unmeetly with his glistening eyes. 1864 NEALE *Seatonian Poems* 108 Tell, nor unrashly nor unmeetly, how God came from Teman.

**Unmee·tness.** [f. UNMEET *a.* Cf. OE. *unmǽtness* immenseness.] Unfitness, unsuitableness.

1573 BARET *Alv.* F 796 Unaptnesse or vnmeeteness, .. *ineptia*. 1586 W. WEBB *Eng. Poetrie* (Arb.) 88 In a Satyr greate heede is to be taken .. of the vnmeetenesse or inconuenience of the matter. 1633 BP. HALL *Hard Texts* 228 As there is a disproportion in the legges of a lame man,..so there is much unmeetness in a fooles parable. 1645 MILTON *Tetrach.* 66 A perpetuall unmeetnes and unwillingnesse to all the duties of helpe. *a* 1683 OWEN *True Nat. Gosp. Ch.* (1689) 164 The unmeetness of the People to be lead under this Spiritual Rule. 1827 *Q. Rev.* XXXVI. 36 The unmeetness of the parties being a satisfactory ground of divorce. 1868 WHITTIER *Among the Hills* 312 Love has naught to do With meetness or unmeetness.

**Unme·llow**, *a.* (UN-¹ 7.) 1787 *Generous Attachment* IV. 172 You..shall proclaim the unsavoury news; pert unmellow children shall bear it about. 1863 W. LANCASTER *Praeterita* 44 Gray the mask Of twilight, and the bleak unmellow speed Of blindness on the visage of fresh hills.

**Unme·llowed**, *ppl. a.* (UN-¹ 8.)

1573 GASCOIGNE *Hearbes* Wks. 1907 I. 327 The brall Which raging youth.. Did whilome breede in mine unmellowed brayne. 1591 LYLY *Endym.* III. i, Whose vnmellowed conceits promise rype counsell. 1607 ROWLANDS *Fam. Hist.* 7 In Nature's green unmellowed years Cupid tormenteth Guy. 1743 FRANCIS tr. *Hor., Odes* II. v. 12 The crude, unmellow'd grape. 1781 COWPER *Truth* 492 If the youth, unmellow'd yet by time, Bore on his branch.. Fruits of a blighted size. 1829 LYTTON *Devereux* III. v, These rare scents that make an Araby of this unmellowed clime. 1841 GRESLEY *For. Arden* xv. 167 They drew nearer to the ruins, unmellowed by age.

**Unmelo·dic**, *a.* (UN-¹ 7.) 1849 *Edin. Rev.* July 54 In primitive music we find a preponderance of those ordinary intervals which characterise speech, and which are unmelodic.

**Unmelo·dious**, *a.* (UN-¹ 7.)

1665 SIR T. HERBERT *Trav.* (1677) 173 The unmelodious noise of the braying mules. 1748 THOMSON *Cast. Indol.* II. lxxxi, Of barking dogs the bitter throng Makes them renew their unmelodious moan. 1777 POTTER *Æschylus, Persians* 512 Rude strains, that unmelodious flow. 1808 SCOTT *Marm.* VI. Introd., If unmelodious was the song, It was a hearty note. 1871 DARWIN *Desc. Man* II. xiii. II. 55 Even the unmelodious sparrow has learnt to sing like a linnet.

So **Unmelo·diously** *adv.*, **-ness** (Webster, 1847).

1846 WORCESTER (citing Dr. Allen). 1858 CARLYLE *Fredk. Gt.* v. i. I. 529 An English Parliament jangling and debating unmelodiously. 1867 MORRIS *Jason* IV. 102 Nor toiled the heroes unmelodiously.

**Unme·lodized**, *ppl. a.* (UN-¹ 8.) 1771 LANGHORNE *Fables Flora* xi. 22 Unlike to living sounds it came, Unmix'd, unmelodis'd with breath. **†Unme·lt**, *ppl. a.* [UN-¹ 8 b.] = next. *a* 1642 SUCKLING *Fragm. Aurea* (1646) 29 The other fair hand .. whose perfect white .. shew'd like unmelt snow unto the sight.

**Unme·lted**, *ppl. a.* (UN-¹ 8.)

1549 *Compl. Scot.* vi. 59 The snau..remanis langar onmeltit, be rason that it fallis aye in cald vedthir. 1611 SPEED *Theat. Gt. Brit.* 111/1 The snow..lasteth long vnmelted vnder those..high hils. 1657 G. THORNLEY *Daphnis & Chloe* 114 The snow lay unmelted. 1713 SALMON *Bate's Dispens.* (ed. 4) 438/2 Unmelted Antimony in fine Pouder. 1796 KIRWAN *Elem. Min.* (ed. 2) I. 448 It is found..on gneiss unaltered, on sandstone unmelted. 1833-4 J. PHILLIPS *Geol.* in *Encycl. Metrop.* (1845) VI. 738/1 The houses..which have been enveloped in liquid lava, remained unmelted by it. 1892 M. DODS *Gosp. John* II. xiv. 223 A lens of ice will.. itself unmelted..fire the tinder to which it transmits its rays.

**Unme·lting**, *ppl. a.* (UN-¹ 10.)

1743 FRANCIS tr. *Hor., Odes* II. ix. 5 Nor on Armenia's frozen Plain The loitring Snow unmelting lies. 1798 *Monthly Mag.* V. 208 To yon pale zone Where drifts the unmelting snow. 1896 E. RIDLEY in *Class. Rev.* XI. 271/2 Parched by cruel suns, Or palled by snows unmelting.

**†Unme·mber**, *v.* [UN-² 4.] *trans.* To deprive of membership. Also **Unme·mbering** *vbl. sb.*

*a* 1658 DURHAM *Comm. Revelation* II. iii. (1680) 73 This unmembering or unchurching of a Person. 1683 T. HUNT *Def. Charter Lond.* 41 Every mans particular consent was necessary to make him a member of any society, and so it is to unmember him. 1847 WEBSTER.

**Unme·morable**, *a.* (UN-¹ 7 b, 5 b.)

1598 FLORIO, *Immemorabile*, vnmemorable, not worth the remembrance, forgetfull. 1607 TOPSELL *Four-f. Beasts* 142 Such was the vnmemorable vanity of the Heathens in theyr goddes and sacrifices. 1858 CARLYLE *Fredk. Gt.* v. iii. I. 559 If a few things memorable are to be remembered, millions of things unmemorable must first be..forgotten! 1885 DIXON *Hist. Ch. Eng.* III. 229 A not unmemorable duel.

*absol.* 1879 F. HARRISON *Choice of Bks.* i. (1886) 9 The memoirs of the unmemorable, and lives of those who never really lived at all.

**Unme·moried**, *ppl. a.* (UN-¹ 8.) 1830 JAMES *De L'Orme* xi, The mountains..in the same..forms that they had presented unmemoried centuries ago. 1879 R. BRIDGES *Shorter Poems* II. (1912) 263, Flowers that fade, Within whose magic tents Rich hues have marriage made With sweet unmemoried scents.

**Unme·naced**, *ppl. a.* (UN-¹ 8.)

[1775 ASH.] 1821 BYRON *Sardanap.* I. ii. 640 Here we are still unmenaced. 1837 LYTTON *Athens* I. 212 When Sparta was unmenaced he was lukewarm.

**Unme·ndable**, *a.* (UN-¹ 7 b.)

1584 MELVILLE in *Cal. Sc. Papers* (1913) VII. 175, I assured hym..matters wer able to fall out to her unmendable miscontentement. 1760 MRS. F. SHERIDAN *Sidney Bidulph* lxi. (1796) V. 178 The wheel was unmendable. 1822 T. G. WAINEWRIGHT *Ess. & Crit.* (1880) 281 An unmendable slit. 1855 [J. R. LEIFCHILD] *Cornwall* 76 That vase,..which one puff of wind..would dash down into innumerable and unmendable fragments! 1877 M. ARNOLD *Last Ess.* Pref. p. xii, They dream of patching up things unmendable.

**Unme·nded**, *ppl. a.* (UN-¹ 8.)

[1775 ASH.] 1880 *West Cornwall Gloss.* 62 *Voyder*,..a large basket for holding unmended linen. 1888 MISS BRADDON *Fatal Three* I. iv, The wardrobe-woman left her clothes unmended.

**†Unme·nged**, *ppl. a. Obs.* [UN-¹ 8 + MENG *v.* Cf. OE. *un(ge)menged*, MDu. *on-*, MHG. *ungemenget*, etc., older Da. *umængt.*] Unmixed.

1562 TURNER *Baths* 6 They drink..excessively wyne, and that unmenged.

**Unme·nseful**, *a.* *Sc.* and *dial.* (UN-¹ 7.)

1801 *Marvellous Love-Story* II. 31 Hauld your tongue, ye unmenseful brute! 1818– in dialect glossaries, etc. (Sc., Yks., Lancs., Linc.). 1898 LD. E. HAMILTON *Mawkin* xx. 268 The daft unmensefu' things!

**Unmensken**, *v.*: see UN-² 2.

**Unme·nsurable**, *a.* (UN-¹ 7 b.) 1513 DOUGLAS *Æneid* x. Prol. 93 Consider quhou he [*sc.* God] is onmensurabyll; Him, as he is, to knaw thou art not abyll. 1683 CAVE *Ecclesiastici, Athanasius* 47 This he cryes out upon as..an unmensurable madness. **Unmentionabi·lity.** [UN-¹ 12.] = next b. 1840 *New Monthly Mag.* LX. 373 One whose unmentionabilities are not worth a thought.

**Unme·ntionable**, *a.* and *sb.* (UN-¹ 7 b.)

1837 CARLYLE *Fr. Rev.* I. I. iii, The..whole posthumous hope of Jesuitism now hangs by the apron of this same unmentionable Woman. 1852 MRS. STOWE *Uncle Tom's C.* xiii, Rows of shining tin, suggestive of unmentionable good things to the appetite. 1875 JOWETT *Plato* (ed. 2) V. 422 If any citizen be found guilty of any great or unmentionable wrong.

*absol.* 1848 MRS. CARLYLE in *New Lett. & Mem.* (1903) I. 242 Her tendency towards the unmentionable is too strong for me to stay it.

**b.** *sb. pl.* Trousers. (Cf. INEXPRESSIBLE B. 2.)

1830 in Thornton *Amer. Gloss.* (1912) I. 478 The waist bands of his unmentionables. 1836-7 DICKENS *Sk. Boz, Shabby-Genteel People*, The knees of the unmentionables.. began to get alarmingly white. 1883 S. C. HALL *Retrospect* II. 318 The priest's unmentionables drying on a hedge.

Hence **Unme·ntionableness.** Also **Unme·ntionably** *adv.*

1870 MISS BROUGHTON *Red as Rose* I. 157 At the rate of purity at which we are advancing, 'legs' will soon walk off into the limbo of silence and unmentionableness. 1879 W. COLLINS *Rogue's Life* ii, He asserted, with an unmentionably vulgar oath, his resolution to turn me out of doors.

**Unme·ntioned**, *ppl. a.* (UN-¹ 8, 8 c.)

1545 RAYNALD *Byrth Mankynde* (1552) 5 Muskles of the body left apart and vnmencioned of. 1612 T. WILSON *Chr. Dict.* 146 Melchisedech['s] .. Parents .. be vnmentioned in the holy Story. 1661 BOYLE *Style of Script.* 187 Barabbas his Name is signally Recorded in Scripture, whereas the Penitent Thief is left Unmention'd. 1709 ADDISON *Tatler* No. 102 ¶ 1 There was not a single Accomplishment unmentioned. 1831 SCOTT *Ct. Rob.* viii, And now let this singular person remain for a time unmentioned. 1879 LUBBOCK *Sci. Lect.* vi. 173 Stonehenge .. is unmentioned by any..Roman writer.

**†Unme·nyied**, *ppl. a. Sc. Obs.* [UN-¹ 8: see MANYIE *v.*] Unmaimed. 1500-20 DUNBAR *Poems* ix. 155, I ask thy Passioun in me so to habound, Quhill nocht vnmenȝeit be in me ane member. **Unme·rcantile**, *a.* (UN-¹ 7.) 1783 BURKE *Rep. Aff. India* Wks. XI. 166 The false principles of this unmercantile transaction. 1848 MILL *Pol. Econ.* III. xii. § 3. II. 58 An improvident and unmercantile mode of conducting business.

**Unme·rcenary**, *a.* (UN-¹ 7.)

1643 PRYNNE *Sov. Power Parl.* I. Pref. (ed. 2) A ij b, The cordiallest Endevours of a reall unmercenary Philo-pater. 1692 ATTERBURY *Serm.* (1726) I. 19 Praise is a generous and unmercenary Principle. 1702 S. PARKER tr. *Cicero's De Finibus* II. 135 An Inbred and Unmercenary Goodness of Temper. 1891 MEREDITH *One of our Conq.* xxix, She was all impulse; a shifty piece of unmercenary stratagem occasionally directing it.

Hence **Unme·rcenariness.**

1863 *N. & Q.* 3rd Ser. IV. 301 The genus 'he-flirt,' a race which is unhappily increased by the unmercenariness of mothers and chaperones.

**†Unme·rchandable**, obs. var. of next. 1670 J. SMITH *Eng. Improv. Reviv'd* 264 Vending any unmerchandable Ware..at lower Rates.

**Unme·rchantable**, *a.* (UN-¹ 7 b.)

1602 CAREW *Cornwall* 105 b, They feed on salt vnmarchantable Pilchard. 1722 *Lond. Gaz.* No. 6042/6 Wines..corrupt, or unmerchantable. 1763 *Brit. Mag.* IV. 174 Damaged and unmerchantable wines. 1818 COLEBROOKE *Import Colonial Corn* 9 A permission to dispose of his goods.. before they are..rendered unmerchantable by decay. 1896 *Law Times Rep.* LXXIII. 649/1 So damaged by water as to be unmerchantable as dates.

**Unme·rchantlike**, *a.* (UN-¹ 7 c.) 1622 E. MISSELDEN *Free Trade* 100 The one taketh aduantage of our vnmerchant-like courses.

**†Unme·rciable**, *a.* [UN-¹ 7.] Unmerciful.

1382 WYCLIF *Jer.* l. 42 Cruel thei ben and vnmerciable. *c* 1412 HOCCLEVE *De Reg. Princ.* 3330 Where as our werkes moste ben avowed, The vnmerciable schal be disallowed. 1450 *Rolls of Parlt.* V 212/1 Arraied in fourme of werre, with .. unmerciable forboden wepons. 1509 BARCLAY *Shyp of Folys* 150 Alas mad Fole and man vnmerciable.

**†Unme·rcied**, *a.* [UN-¹ 9.] Merciless. *c* 1600 DRAYTON *Miseries Q. Margaret* xl, The Irish,..with sword and fire, Vnmercied hauocke of the English made.

**Unme·rciful**, *a.* [UN-¹ 7.] Merciless.

1. Of persons: Having or exhibiting no mercy.

1481 CAXTON *Reynard* (Arb.) 37 He was alway to hem vnmercyful. *a* 1548 HALL *Chron., Hen. VI*, 167 b, The vnmercifull pagans and cruel Turkes. 1584 CONSTABLE *Sonn.* VII. vii, Seeke with humble prayer Meanes how to mooue th' unmercifullest fayre. 1631 *High Commission Cases* (Camden) 231 Though he be unmercifull to us olde men, yet we are..mercifull to him. 1667 *Decay Chr. Piety* viii. ¶ 47 There are indeed no such unmerciful exactors as our own lusts. 1711 SWIFT *Jrnl. Stella* 7 June, Why this same Stella is so unmerciful a writer, she has hardly left any room for Dingley. *a* 1770 CHATTERTON *Battle of Hastings* 427 A wight unmercifull. 1825 J. NEAL *Bro. Jonathan* III. 250 Any female..unmerciful to those who had gone astray.

*transf.* *a* 1586 SIDNEY *Arcadia* I. xiii, The unmercifull Sea deprived me of my company.

*absol.* 1795 SOUTHEY *Joan of Arc* I. 445 Will not God In sunder smite the unmerciful, and break The sceptre of the wicked?

2. Of actions, etc.: Devoid of the quality of mercy.

1549 *Compl. Scot.* i. 23 The..distructione of oure nobil barrons..be cruel ande onmercyful slauthyr. 1582 STANYHURST *Æneis* I. (Arb.) 18 Shee bears.. that sept vnmerciful hatred. 1621 J. TAYLOR (Water P.) *Unnat. Father* Wks. (1630) 140/2 Weeping teares of pitilesse pity, and vnmercifull mercy. 1677 WYCHERLEY *Pl. Dealer* IV. i, When a Lover's hopes Are dead,..Life is unmerciful. 1758 JOHNSON *Idler* No. 14 ¶ 10 Some stop might be put to this unmerciful prosecution. 1778 MISS BURNEY *Evelina* lxi, Her unmerciful propensity to satire. 1846 MRS. A. MARSH *Father Darcy* II. x. 170 He had resolved.. upon a course of the most unmerciful policy.

3. Unsparing; excessive in amount, etc.

1706 E. WARD *Wooden World Diss.* (1708) 69 Knock'd down by an unmerciful Bowl of Punch or two. 1710 STEELE *Tatler* No. 207 ¶ 2 There was no enduring that this Fop should outshine us all at this unmerciful Rate. 1811 A. CLARKE *Kneeling* Wks. 1837 XI. 340 In addition to the injury I sustained by his unmerciful prayer, I had the following reproof. 1835 T. MITCHELL *Acharn. of Aristoph.* App. 252 *note*, Explain them he accordingly does at the same unmerciful length as he does every other topic.

Hence **†Unme·rcifulhead.** *Obs.*

*c* 1440 *Jacob's Well* 256 Ryȝtwysnesse may noȝt helpe þe.. in þin vnkyndenesse, in þin vnmercyfulhed.

**Unme·rcifully**, *adv.* [UN-¹ 11.]

1. Without mercy; mercilessly.

1548 ELYOT, *Immisericorditer*, without pitee, vnmercifully. 1596 SPENSER *F. Q.* v. vii. 31 The Amazon..dealt her blowes vnmercifully sore. 1653 H. COGAN tr. *Pinto's Trav.* liii. 209 He caused [them]..to be unmercifully butchered. 1711 STEELE *Spect.* No. 145 ¶ 2 He went on unmercifully to Triumph over my Ignorance. 1766 HAMILTON *Vesuvius* in *Phil. Trans.* LVII. 197, I saw it..unmercifully destroy a poor man's vineyard. 1818 SCOTT *Rob Roy* xxii, The laws concerning debt, in most countries, are..unmercifully severe. 1860 FROUDE *Hist. Eng.* V. 119 A change in the relations between the peasantry and the owners of the soil..was attempted harshly and unmercifully.

2. Unsparingly, excessively. Now *dial.*

1686 F. SPENCE tr. *St. Euvremont's Misc.* Pref. C 3, In a Comedy nothing is so unmercifully insupportable as to.. explicate the Intrigue by a Miracle. 1716 HEARNE *Collect.* (O.H.S.) V. 331 He steals unmercifully, and..without Acknowledgment. 1794 C. PIGOT *Female Jockey Club* 139 If surprised by the sight of a black lobster, she screams unmercifully. 1854 MISS BAKER *Northampt. Gloss.* 369 It's unmercifully bad.

**Unme·rcifulness.** [UN-¹ 12.] The quality of being unmerciful; mercilessness.

1545 ASCHAM *Toxoph.* (Arb.) 81 Made drunke with the frutes of the flesh, as infidelitie,..oppression, vnmercifulnesse. 1565 CECIL *Let.* in Strype *Ann. Ref.* xliv. (1709) 444 To sharpen their tongues against the idols..of..malice, and unmercifulness. 1649 F. ROBERTS *Clavis Bibl.* 423 Babylon being devoted to destruction for her unmercifulnesse to the Jews. 1682 *Sec. Plea Nonconform.* 63 If Justices are not merciful, they have the Countenance of the Law, for Unmercifulness. 1722 WOLLASTON *Relig. Nat.* vi. 141 Injustice, unmercifulness, and cruelty are wrong. 1864 PUSEY *Lect. Daniel* 524 That common sin of conquerors, unmercifulness and oppression.

**†Unme·rciless**, *a.* [UN-¹ 5 a.] Unmerciful.

1545 JOYE *Exp. Dan.* vi. 86 b, Now ye see..their deceites, vnmerciles murther, and ingratitude. 1554 F. YAXLEY in Ellis *Orig. Lett.* Ser. III. III. 313, I was so tormented..in the unmercelesse seas. 1570 GOOGE *Pop. Kingd.* IV. 45 b, Seeking Christ to kill, [Herod] Destroyde the little infants yong, a beast vnmercilesse. 1614 JACKSON *Creed* III. 199 The Egyptians consciousnesse of their vnmercilesse practises against poore Israel.

**†Unme·rcy.** *Obs.* [UN-¹ 12.] Lack of mercy; unmercifulness.

*c* 1380 Wyclif *Wks.* (1880) 72 Wiþ-drawynge goddis word ..for ensaumple of pride, coueitise, wraþþe, vnmercy. *c* 1400 *Found. St. Bartholomew's* (1923) 41 Our synnes askyng the vnmergy of oure Lordys ire. *c* 1407 Lydg. *Reson & Sens.* 6651 Daunger sholde exiled be, Vnmercy also.

**Unme·rged,** *ppl. a.* (Un-[1] 8.) 1818 Cruise *Digest* (ed. 2) II. 481 The estate for life of the joint tenant having the fee, is distinct from, and unmerged in, his greater estate.

**Unme·ritable,** *a.* [Un-[1] 7 b.]

**1.** Unable to claim merit.

1594 Shaks. *Rich. III*, iii. vii. 155 Your loue deserues my thankes, but my desert Vnmeritable, shunnes your high request. 1601 — *Jul. C.* iv. i. 12 This is a slight vnmeritable man, Meet to be sent on Errands. 1797 Ld. Thurlow in *Cowper's Wks.* (1836) III. 212 Cowper's distemper persuades him that he is unmeritable and unacceptable to God. 1884 Child *Ballads* ii. 393/1 An Italian ballad, a slight and unmeritable thing. 1885 Swinburne *Misc.* (1886) 137 He was content to rely on his .. simplicity alone; with a result sometimes merely trivial and unmeritable.

†**2.** Unmerited, undeserved. *Obs.*

1635 J. Hayward tr. *Biondi's Banish'd Virg.* 22 You..are ..come to undoe me with your unmeritable favours. 1666 Earl Orrery in *St. Lett.* (1743) II. 93 Those unmeritable expressions of your grace's kindness.

**Unme·rited,** *ppl. a.* (Un-[1] 8.)

1648 Hexham ii, *Onbedient*, Vndeserved, or Vnmerited. 1667 Milton *P. L.* xii. 278 Favour unmerited by me, who sought Forbidd'n knowledge. 1711 *Spect.* No. 77 ¶ 5 Those Nods of Approbation which I never bestow unmerited. 1740 Richardson *Pamela* (1824) I. 157 This, sir,..is all goodness unmerited on my side. 1808 Wordsw. *White Doe* ii. 525 The excess Of an unmerited distress. 1889 in *Retrospect Med.* CII. 33 Years ago I remember getting a good deal of quite unmerited credit.

Hence **Unme·ritedness.**

1648 Boyle *Seraph. Love* (1659) 70 The freenesse or unmeritednesse of God's love. *a* 1680 Charnock *Attrib. God* (1834) II. 437 The unmeritedness of them doth enhance this.

**Unme·ritedly,** *adv.* (Un-[1] 11. Cf. prec.)

1791 Eliza Clarke *Sword* II. 90 The Regard which you have so unmeritedly shown for me. 1806 Scott *Let.* in *Lockhart* (1837) II. 88 Any prepossession which my literary reputation may, however unmeritedly, have created in my favour. 1840 *New Monthly Mag.* LX. 369 A word thus unmeritedly sent to Coventry.

**Unme·riting,** *ppl. a.* (Un-[1] 10, 5 d.)

Also *absol.*, and with object.

1594 *Zepheria* xix, No no Zepheria, fame is too rich a prize My all vnmeriting lines for to attend on. 1607 Shaks. *Cor.* ii. i. 47 A brace of vnmeriting, proud, violent, testie Magistrates. 1795 *Fate of Sedley* I. 135 Why should we conceal our affections, when they are not improperly placed upon the unmeriting? 1827 Pollok *Course T.* ix. 926 Unmeriting alike reward or blame. 1828 Pusey *Hist. Enq.* I. 83 To charge heresy upon unmeriting and orthodox men.

†**Unme·ritingly,** *adv. Obs.* [Un-[1] 11.] Undeservedly. 1621 Lady M. Wroth *Urania* 399 Bee sure you mistake him not, or vnmeritingly condemne him.

**Unmerito·rious,** *a.* (Un-[1] 7.)

[1775 Ash.] 1855 Faber *Growth in Holiness* xiv. 233 There are a variety of unmeritorious occupations. 1862 Carlyle *Fredk. Gt.* xii. xii. III. 374 You may buy them [*sc.* votes]..by preferments and appointments of the unmeritorious man.

So **Unmerito·riously** *adv.*

1840 De Quincey *Essenes, Suppl. Note* Wks. 1857 VII. 299 Josephus..most unmeritoriously found himself..translated into the meridian sunshine of court favour.

**Unme·rry,** *a.* (OE. *unmyrge*: see Un-[1] 7.)

*a* 1000 *Gloss.* in Wr.-Wülcker 221 *Collidium*, unmyrge pleʒa. *c* 1250 *Owl & Night.* 346 Ne beo þe song ne so murie Þat he ne sal þinche vnmurie If he ilesteþ ouer vnwille. *c* 1384 Chaucer *H. Fame* 74 There slepeth ay this god [*sc.* Sleep] unmerie. *c* 1430 *Syr Gener.* (Roxb.) 9022 To Amanewel that was slaw Into the Citie forto burie, For him was Amalek vnmerie. 1530 Palsgr. 328/2 Unmery, *triste.* 1582 T. Watson *Centurie of Love* lxxxv, Cares rowd with vowes the ship vnmery minde.

**Unme·sh,** *v.* [Un-[2] 4 b.] *trans.* To undo the meshes of; to free from meshes.

*c* 1822 T. L. Beddoes *Poems, Alfarabi* 138 Hands of eternal stone, that would unmesh And fray this starry company of orbs. 1856 Ruskin *Mod. Paint.* III. iv. iv. § 16 They had gone back to their daily work, thinking still their business lay net-wards, unmeshed from the literal rope and drag. 1891 C. E. Norton *Dante's Purgat.* xxi. 136, I see the net which snares you here, and how it is unmeshed.

**Unme·smerized,** *ppl. a.* (Un-[1] 8 a *c.*) 1889 J. M. Robertson *Christ & Krishna* xii. 61 Sufficient to indicate to any student unmesmerised by religion that a nature myth underlies every case.

**Unme·t,** *ppl. a.*[1] (Un-[1] 8 b: cf. Meet *v.*)

1603 B. Jonson *Sejanus* v. i, Winds lose their strength, when they do empty fly, Unmet of woods or buildings. 1641 Earl Monm. tr. *Biondi's Civil Wars* iv. 42 Had Warwick been of this opinion, succour had not come unmet withall. 1798 *Monthly Mag.* V. 367 Back to the desert-air Unmet shall he repair. 1818 Colebrooke *Import. Colonial Corn* 108 Yet are his productions not unthreatened nor unmet by dangerous rivalship. 1868 Morris *Earthly Par.* I. ii. 662 While through this poor land range the heathen men, Unmet of any but my King.

†**Unme·t,** *ppl. a.*[2] *Obs.*[-1] [Un-[1] 8: cf. Mete *v.*[1]] Unmeasured. 1482 in *Charters*, etc. *Edinb.* (1871) 168 Of ilk laid vnmet i obl.

**Unme·talled,** *ppl. a.* (Un-[1] 8.)

1843 in T. J. Dyke *Addr. Public Medicine* (1885) 2 The unmetalled and unchannelled highways and streets. 1862 Patterson *Ess. Hist. & Art* 211 The continuation of this road..is unmetalled. 1897 *Trans. Roy. Hist. Soc.* XI. 72 The balks..seem to be..unmetalled roadways.

**Unmeta·llic,** *a.* (Un-[1] 7.)

1757 tr. *Henckel's Pyritol.* (title-p.), Its Iron, Copper, Unmetallic Earth, Sulphur [etc.]. 1796 Kirwan *Elem. Min.* (ed. 2) I. 487 Metallic substances..held in solution by any unmetallic acid. 1841 Brande *Man. Chem.* 210 Heat is thrown off much more quickly from the unmetallic than from the metallic surface. 1864 Bowen *Logic* vi. 154 All infusible things are unmetallic.

**Unme·tallized,** *ppl. a.* (Un-[1] 8.) 1796 Kirwan *Elem. Min.* (ed. 2) II. 90 Some unmetallic or unmetallized substance. 1805 *Phil. Trans.* XCV. 169 An unmetallized portion of that [ore].

**Unmetamo·rphosed,** *ppl. a.* (Un-[1] 8.)

1600 Tourneur *Transf. Metam.* xvi, If any rest unmetamorphosed. 1787 *Generous Attachment* IV. 35 Many ..affect for a time the rank of Captain, but I continue unmetamorphosed. 1849 Owen *Parthenogenesis* 39 Such unmetamorphosed germ-masses. 1880 Carpenter in *Jrnl. Linn. Soc.* XV. 214 Unmetamorphosed embryonic basals.

**Unmetapho·rical,** *a.* (Un-[1] 7.) 1767 Sterne *Tr. Shandy* ix. xiii, I am got..into a cold unmetaphorical vein of infamous writing. 1831 Carlyle *Sart. Res.* i. xi, An unmetaphorical style you shall in vain seek for. **Unmetaphy·sic,** *a.* [Un-[1] 7.] = next. 1789 H. Walpole *Let. to Mrs. H. More* 4 Nov., My head is as un-mechanic as it is..un-metaphysic, un-commercial.

**Unmetaphy·sical,** *a.* (Un-[1] 7.)

1691 Norris *Pract. Disc.* 301 A notion of God so very natural, that even the Jews as gross and unmetaphysical as they were, could not but imbrace it. 1701 — *Ideal World* i. vi. 323 A blunt unmetaphysical Roman. 1825 Coleridge *Aids Refl.* 252 The unmetaphysical tribes of New Holland. 1871 Fraser *Life Berkeley* ii. 44 The book was too far in advance of an unmetaphysical generation to draw general attention.

**Unme·ted,** *ppl. a.* [Un-[1] 8.] Unmeasured. 1838 Mrs. Browning *Isobel's Child* iii, Its mother's smile, Full of love's unmeted weight. 1853 C. Bronte *Villette* xli, Surely those near me must have felt some little of the anxiety I felt, in degree so unmeted.

†**Unme·th,** *adv.* [Cf. next, and *unimeað* s.v. Un-[1] 3.] Immoderately, extremely.

*a* 1225 *Ancr. R.* 50 Vor aʒein kunde hit is, & unmeð swuc [*v.r.* sullich, selli] wunder, þet te deade totie. *a* 1225 *Juliana* 4 Maximian þe modi keiser..wið unmeð muchel hird & unduhti duheðe.

†**Unme·the,** *sb. Obs.* [OE. *unmǽþ* (Un-[1] 12 + Methe *sb.*).] Immoderation; excess; fault.

*a* 1100 in Assmann *Ags. Hom.* 162 Þa discipulas..wæron on heora modʒeþance swiðlice afyrhte and ʒedrefede, swa hit nan unmæþ næs. *a* 1250 *Owl & Night.* 352 Eurich þing may lesen his godhede Mid vnmeþe and ouerdede. *a* 1300 *Floris & Bl.* (Camb. MS.) 675 Min is þe guld and þe unmeþ, Þat þu for me schalt þolie deþ.

†**Unme·the,** *a. Obs.* [Cf. prec. and Methe *a.*] Unequal; unfair; ungentle.

*c* 1250 *Owl & N.* 1618 (Jesus MS.), Þarfore þe is wel unmeþe, For þhah þu ligge ded & clinge Þi deþ nys nouht to none þinge. *a* 1300 *Cursor M.* 11815 Þat caitif vn-meth and vn-meke Nu bigines he to seke. *c* 1325 *Spec. Gy Warw.* 615 Swich a fiht is vnmeþ, For aʒein þe kinde hit geþ.

**Unmethlich, -ship:** see Un-[1] 3.

**Unmetho·dical,** *a.* (Un-[1] 7.)

1601 Cornwallis *Ess.* ii. l. N n 7, They are unmethodicall, hardly to be caught by one forme, any in truth wil do it. *c* 1720 W. Gibson *Diet Horses* xi. (1731) 165 The..Instructions..are so obscure and un-methodical, that it is not an easy matter to follow them. 1862 Lytton *Str. Story* II. 62 When I saw her..smoothing his papers (in which he was apt to be unmethodical). 1869 Rogers *Smith's Wealth N.* I. Pref. p. xxiv, The resources and defects of vast but unmethodical learning. 1872 Liddon *Elem. Relig.* i. 28 Its form is of necessity unmethodical: it is, if you will, antischolastic.

So **Unmetho·dically** *adv.*

1632 Massinger & Field *Fatal Dowry* iv. i, What fouler obiect in the world, then to see..a hopefull Cheualier vnmethodically appointed in the externall ornaments of nature?

**Unme·thodized,** *ppl. a.* [Un-[1] 8.]

**1.** Not reduced to method.

*a* 1677 J. Harrington *Grounds & Reasons* Wks. (1700) 12 Tho the Understandings of most men seem to agree in som general maxims, but unpolish'd, unnumber'd and unmethodiz'd. 1734 Hervey *Mem. Geo. II* (1848) I. 400 The loose, unmethodized, and often incoherent manner, in which it is put together. 1834 Sir H. Taylor *Artevelde* ii. v. ii, What is earth? A huge congestion of unmethodised matter.

**2.** Not become Methodist.

1751 Lavington *Enthus. Meth. & Papists* iii. (1754) 236 Hence they justly contemn..all the Unmethodized, as of a mean and reprobate Way.

**Unme·thodizing,** *vbl. sb.* (Un-[2] 6 c, 8.) 1818 Coleridge in *Encycl. Metrop.* (1845) I. Introd. 4 To the utter confusion and *unmethodising* of the science of the human mind.

**Unme·trical,** *a.* (Un-[1] 7.)

1791 Boswell *Johnson* Dec. 1784, Discoursing vehemently on the unmetrical effect of such a lapse. 1856 Masson *Ess. Biog. & Crit.* 412 The art of producing, by means of articulate language, metrical or unmetrical, a fictitious concrete. 1885 *Athenæum* 17 Jan. 84/2 A kind of unmetrical narrative so poetic in motive..as [etc.].

**Unmew,** *v.* (Un-[2] 5; cf. Mew *v.*[2]) 1818 Keats *Endym.* i. 132 Let a portion of ethereal dew Fall on my head, and presently unmew My soul. **Unmica·ceous,** *a.* (Un-[1] 7.) 1833-4 *Encycl. Metrop.* (1845) VI. 758/1 A felspathic quartzose rock, of rather dubious character, which may be called..unmicaceous granite. **Unmi·dwifed,** *a.* (Un-[1] 9.) 1747 *Gentl. Mag.* 242 Her uberous store, To these, parturient Earth unmidwif'd yields.

†**Unmi·ght.** *Obs.* [OE. *unmiht, -meht* (Un-[1] 12), = WFris. *on-, ûnmacht*, MDu. (Du.) *onmacht*, MLG. *unmacht* (LG. *unmagt*), OHG. (MHG.) *unmaht* (G. *unmacht*), Goth. *unmaht-s*; cf. also ON. *úmáttr*, MDa. *umagt.*] Want of might or strength; weakness, feebleness.

*c* 897 K. Ælfred *Gregory's Past. C.* xxxii. 208 Ðonne hie onʒietað hiera unbældo & hiera unmihte, hie weorðað oft ormode. *c* 1200 *Vices & Virtues* 129 For þan euel to done nis non strencþe, ac is unmihte. *a* 1290 *Becket* 1408 in *S. Eng. Leg.* I. 146 For mine sunnes and for mine onmiʒte, þat I ne may hire wardi nouʒt. *c* 1330 R. Brunne *Chron. Wace* (Rolls) 15564 An heuinesse, a gret vnmight, On Cadwalyn gan to lepe. *c* 1375 *Sc. Leg. Saints* xxxii. (*Justin*) 205 Þe vnmycht of my compere, Þat to spede had na powere. *c* 1400 *Pilgr. Sowle* (Caxton, 1483) v. xiv. 108 In hym is feblesse and grete vnmyght. 1429 *Rolls of Parlt.* IV. 343 Grete myght on that o syde, and unmyght on that other.

†**Unmi·ghtful,** *a. Obs.* [Un-[1] 7.] **a.** Unable. **b.** Impossible. 1340-70 *Alex. & Dind.* 762 Þei beþ vn-mihtful y-mad, men for to wisse. *c* 1460 *Towneley Myst.* x. 141 No word, lady, that I the bryng, Is vnmyghtfull to heuen kyng. †**Unmi·ght(i)ly,** *advs. Obs.*[-0] [Un-[1] 11.] Weakly, ineffectually. *c* 1440 *Promp. Parv.* 366/1 On-myghtly [*Winch. MS.* on-myhtyly], *inpotenter.* †**Unmi·ghtiness.** *Obs.*[-1] [Un-[1] 12.] Impotence. 14.. in *Anglia* VIII. 124 Dredynge leste þat houge wonderynge of merueylles shulde ..arrecte goddes dedys to vnmyghtynes.

**Unmi·ghty,** *a.* Now *arch.* [OE. *unmihtig* (Un-[1] 7), = OFris. *un-, onmachtich*, WFris. *on-, ûnmachtig*, MDu. *onmachtich* (Du. *-ig*), MLG. *unmechtich*, OHG. *unmahtîg, -îk* (MHG. *unmehtec, -ic*, G. *unmächtich*), Goth. *unmahteig-s*: cf. also ON. *úmáttig-r*, MDa. *umægtug*, early mod. Da. *umægtig.*] Devoid of might or strength; weak, feeble, powerless, impotent.

*c* 888 K. Ælfred *Boeth.* xxix. § 1 Ælc ʒesceadwis man mæʒ witan þæt hi bioð full earme & ful unmihtiʒe. *c* 1200 *Trin. Coll. Hom.* 35 He bicom unmihti & wreche & unhol. *a* 1310 in Wright *Lyric P.* iv. 22 Middel-erd for mon wes mad, un-mihti aren is meste mede. *c* 1374 Chaucer *Boeth.* iv. pr. ii. (1868) 114 Nedes goode folk moten ben myʒty, and shrewes feble and vnmyʒty. 1402 *J. Upland* (Skeat) § 63 He coude not make his rule so good as an-other did his, (..and so were he unmighty and not god). *c* 1450 tr. *De Imitatione* ii. viii. 49 Whan þe grace of god..goþ away, þan shal he be poure & unmiʒty. 1483 Caxton *Gold. Leg.* C ij b, He was..so feble and so unmyghty that hys dysciples susteyned..hym in goyng to chirche. 1545 Raynald *Byrth Mankynde* 79 Yf the matryce be vnmighty and weakened. 1611 Florio, *Impoderoso*, vnmightie, vnpowerfull. 1876 Morris *Sigurd* ii. 97 Myself a little fragment amidst it all I saw,..unmighty as the tempest-driven straw.

*absol.* *c* 1400 *Apol. Loll.* 30 It is necesari to hem to visit þe sek, to pray for þe vnmiʒti. 1549 Allen *Jude's Par. Rev.* 33 Both masters and seruauntes,..hyghe and lowe, myghtie and vnmyghtie. 1587 Golding *De Mornay* Ep. Ded., The welbeloued Sonne of God..must stande for all:.. the mightie for the vnmightie.

**b.** Const. *to*, usually with inf.

*c* 1000 Ælfric *Saints' Lives* x. 257 Hwi come þu mid wæpnum..to anum mædene unmihtiʒum to wiʒe. *a* 1240 *Sawles Warde* in *O. E. Hom.* I. 257 Nu is riht þenne þat we demen us seolf eauer unmihtie to werien ant to witen us ..wið ute godes helpe. *a* 1300 *Cursor M.* 6706 Qua smites vte his thains eie, And mas him vn-mighti for-to seie. *a* 1340 Hampole *Psalter* cvi. 12 Þai ware vnmyghty to stande agayn vicys. 1390 Gower *Conf.* II. 177 Thei withoute lyves chiere Unmyhti ben to se or hiere. 1422 Yong tr. *Secreta Secret.* 235 Who-so hath the paas litill and swyfte, he is suspeccious, of euyl will, on-myghty to werkys.

†**Unmi·ld,** *a. Obs.* [OE. *unmilde* (Un-[1] 7), = MDu. *onmilde* (obs. Du. *onmild*), OHG. *unmilti* (MHG. *unmilte, unmilde*, G. *unmild*), ON. *úmild-r* (MSw. *omilder*, Sw. *omild*, MDa., Da., and Norw. *umild*), Goth. *unmild-s* unkind.]

**1.** Not mild or gentle; harsh, rough, unkind.

*c* 900 tr. *Bæda's Hist.* ii. ii. (1890) 100 Ȝif he þonne is unmilde & oferhyʒdiʒ, þonne is þæt cuð þæt he nis of Gode. *c* 1200 Ormin 9880 Hæþenn lif & hæþenn follkess herrte Iss harrd & starrc all allse stan, Unnmeoc & all unnmilde. *a* 1250 *Owl & Night.* 61 Ich wot þat þu art unmilde Wiþ hom þat ne muʒe from þe schilde. *a* 1290 *Beket* 1460 in *S. Eng. Leg.* I. 148 Ovt of Engelonde he let heom driue:.. muche was he on-milde! *a* 1340 Hampole *Psalter* cxlvi. 6 Synful men þat ere sharpe and vnmyld and contrary. 1398 Trevisa *Barth. De P. R.* xii. x. (Bodl. MS.), Þe crowe..is a iangelingge brid vnmylde [L. *impia*], and greuous to men. 1412-20 Lydg. *Chron. Troy* i. 281 Bolys ful vnmylde, with brasen feet, ramegous and wylde. 1482 *Monk of Evesham* l. (Arb.) 100 Sche was only to her cosynis ryghte gastful and on mylde. 1526 *Pilgr. Perf.* (W. de W. 1531) 113 b, Eschewe the occasyons of testynes or hastynes, and other vnmylde behauour. 1558 Phaer *Æneid* iv. K iij, Some Tigres thee did nurse, and gaue to thee their milke unmild. 1611 Florio, *Immite*, vnmilde, cruel.

**2.** Harsh of taste.

1566 Drant *Horace, Sat.* iii. G j, Eatinge most bitter rootes and leaves, unmilde unto the taste.

Hence †**Unmi·ldness.** *Obs.*

1570 Drant *Two Serm.* I. viij, Mildnes to some is oft tymes vnmildnes and crueltie to many other. 1611 Florio, *Immitezza*, vnmildenesse, cruelty. 1644 Milton *Divorce* (ed. 2) ii. vii. 46 The unmildnesse of Evangelick grace shall turn servant to declare the grace and mildnesse of the rigorous Law.

**Unmi·ldewed,** *ppl. a.* (Un-[1] 8.) [1775 Ash.] *a* 1814 A. Becket *Genii* i. in *New Brit. Theatre* I. 518 Kind Power,..Still give the gold rod of our fields Unmildew'd. **Unmi·litarily,** *adv.* (Un-[1] 11.) *a* 1856 in Strang *Glasgow & Clubs* 585 A prisoner, who most unmilitarily occupied the front of the saddle.

**Unmi·litary,** *a.* [Un-[1] 7.]

**1.** Not in accordance with military practice or conforming to military standards.

1777 W. Dalrymple *Trav. Sp. & Port.* cxliii, The king has a large..army, which had better be reduced, than continue in its present unmilitary state. 1806 *Ann. Rev.* IV. 246 Defence—the very word is unmilitary. 1826 Scott *Woodst.* xii, We must not hazard the whole troops in one sortie—that were unmilitary. 1861 Gen. P. Thompson *Audi Alt. Part.* III. clxxiv. 206 It is simply unmilitary babble, that would talk of the difficulty of doing what is wanted, when once the military superiority is decided.

**2.** Not belonging to, or connected with, the military profession.

1802–12 BENTHAM *Ration. Judic. Evid.* (1827) V. 663 Suppose two persons in office, military and unmilitary. 1883 *American* VI. 233 [This] may be objected to in unmilitary quarters.

**Unmi·lked,** *ppl. a.* (UN-¹ 8.)

1648 HEXHAM II, *Ongemolcken*, Vnmilked. 1725 POPE *Odyss.* IX. 318 The ewes..with distended thighs Unmilked lay bleating. 1891 HARDY *Tess* xxiv, Five unmilked cows chanced to stand apart from the general herd.

**Unmi·lled,** *ppl. a.* (UN-¹ 8.)

1555 *Richmond. Wills* (Surtees) 86 Item ij webbe unmilled...Item xiiij peces of cloth. *c* 1600 *Transcript W. Riding Sessions Rolls* (1888) 160 Duas pecias panni lanei.. vocat. vnmylned Karsey. 1726 LEAKE *Hist. Acc. Eng. Money* 121 A Cutter,..which some have call'd the Unmill'd Guinea. 1783 COOK *First Voy.* III. xiv. III. 766 There are two kinds of coin here, of the same denomination, milled and unmilled.

† **Unmi·nd,** *a. Obs.*—¹ [UN-¹ 7.] Unmindful. *a* 1300 *Cursor M.* 1572 Þai left þe lede of þar lau, Þat es, o settnes and o kind Wit-vtun mensk þai ar [*Gött.* were] vn-mind.

**Unmi·nd,** *v.* [UN-² 3.] *trans.* To reverse the views of. 1859 J. TAYLOR *Logic in Theol.* 239 The attempt to unmind the Christian world at that time was impracticable.

**Unmi·nded,** *ppl. a.* [UN-¹ 8.]

† **1.** Unmentioned; not borne in mind. *Obs.*

*a* 1513 FABYAN *Chron.* I. xxii. 17 This also is vnmynded of wryters..for rudenesse of his dedes, that clerkes lyst nat to spende any tyme in wrytynge of suche dedes. 1590 SPENSER *Muiopot.* Ep. Ded., Which taketh glory..to spend it selfe in honouring you: not so much for your great bounty to my self, which yet may not be vnminded;..as for [etc.].

**2.** Unheeded, unregarded.

1562 J. HEYWOOD *Prov. & Epig.* (1867) 17 Unminded, vnmoned, go make your mone. 1596 SHAKS. 1 *Hen. IV*, IV. iii. 59 When he was..A poore vnminded Out-law, sneaking home. *a* 1625 BEAUM. & FL. *Laws of Candy* v. i, Where was your gratitude, who in your Coffers Hoarded the rustic treasure which was due To my unminded Father? 1667 MILTON *P. L.* X. 332 Hee, after Eve seduc't, unminded slunk Into the Wood fast by. 1710 *Brit. Apollo* No. 61. 3/1 Sable Night unminded past away. 1846 LANDOR *Imag. Conv.* Wks. I. 390/1 Even grandmothers ere now have been unminded by their own grandchildren.

**b.** Left unnoticed, overlooked.

1698 *Christ Exalted* § 99 It is not to be unminded how the Rebuker slides off the three first Conditions.

**Unmi·ndful,** *a.* [UN-¹ 7.] Not mindful; careless, heedless: **a.** Const. *of.*

1382 WYCLIF *Ecclus.* xxxvii. 6 Be thou not vnmyndeful of hym in thi werkis. 1500–20 DUNBAR *Poems* xiii. 47 Religious men..ar vnmyndfull of thair professioun. 1555 EDEN *Decades* (Arb.) 56 Owre predicessoures were not vtterlye vnmyndefull of these benefites. 1631 GOUGE *God's Arrows* II. Ep. Ded., Can I then be unmindfull of her? 1663 BP. PATRICK *Parab. Pilgr.* xxx, When you find them so unmindful of themselves. 1706 E. WARD *Wooden World Diss.* (1708) 16 One so sollicitous about other Men's Healths, cannot be unmindful of his own. 1760–2 GOLDSM. *Cit. W.* lix, Every person was willing to save himself, unmindful of others. 1821 SHELLEY *Epipsych.* 302 At her silver voice came Death and Life, Unmindful each of their accustomed strife. 1874 J. BALDW. BROWN *Higher Life* p. viii, Unmindful of the large blessing which intellectual culture and political activity bring in their train.

**b.** With inf. or clause.

1615 SIR W. MURE *Misc. Poems* xiv. 10 Helping wp treassour wnmyndfull quho lent it. 1652 GAULE *Magastrom.* 323 He caused Cassius Longinus..to be slain; unmindfull that Chærea (the man that did the deed) was so called. 1697 DRYDEN *Virg. Past.* VIII. 125 She seeks the weedy Pools,.. Careless of Night, unmindful to return. *a* 1750 A. HILL *Picture of Love* 173 Unmindful, that of old they veil'd his face.

**c.** Attrib. or without const. *rare.*

1594 SHAKS. *Rich. III*, IV. iv. 446 Dull vnmindfull Villaine, Why stay'st thou here? 1598 FLORIO, *Smemorato*,..a forgetfull, obliuious, or vnmindfull man. 1608 BEAUM. & FL. *Four Plays in One* Wks. 1912 X. 359 Hear me,..And take my wrongs into thy hands, thou justice Done by unmindful man, unmerciful. 1796 SCOTT *Wild Huntsman* xxxix, His courser rooted to the ground, The quickening spur unmindful bears.

Hence **Unmi·ndfulness.**

Also *unmindfully* adv. (1755 Scott, and later Dicts.).

1567 ALLEN *Def. Priesthood* Pref., Loue of sinne,..and vnmyndfulnes of saluation. 1631 MABBE *Celestina* xii. 132 Of my much mindfulnesse for this nights meeting, and your much unmindfulnesse and extreme carelesnesse. *a* 1680 CHARNOCK *Attrib. God* (1834) I. 507 Why should we forget it? yea, what a shame is our unmindfulness of it.

† **Unmi·nding,** *vbl. sb. Obs.* [UN-¹ 13.] The action of forgetting or disregarding.

1382 WYCLIF *Wisd.* xiv. 26 And alle thingus ben mengd togidere,..the vnmynding [L. *immemoratio*] of the goodes of the Lord,..the vnordeynyng of leccherie and of vnclennesse. 1602–9 A. MUNDAY tr. *Palmerin of Eng.* I. (1639) A 5 b, Pleasant passages through the grassy groves, would be an occasion of the vnminding her former fits. *a* 1684 LEIGHTON *Comm. 1 Pet.* v. 8 The fumes..cast us into a deep sleep; a secure unminding of God and of ourselves.

**Unmi·ned,** *ppl. a.* (UN-¹ 8.) *a* 1849 POE *E. B. Browning* Wks. 1865 III. 404 The reader will suffer the most valuable ore to remain unmined to all eternity, before [etc.]. 1895 *Chambers's Jrnl.* XII. 629/1 The coal in the country still unmined. **Unmi·neralized,** *ppl. a.* (UN-¹ 8.) 1843 *Penny Cycl.* XXVII. 112/1 The mineralized hot springs and the unmineralized. **Unmi·nglable,** *a.* (UN-¹ 7 b.) 1661 BOYLE *Scept. Chem.* IV. 231 The Property of Oyle..of being unminglable with the Water. *Ibid.* 257 Divers and unminglable oyles.

**Unmi·ngle,** *v.* (UN-² 3, 7.)

1594 T. B. *La Primaud. Fr. Acad.* II. 155 This facultie of the fantasie changeth and rechangeth, mingleth and vnmingleth, so that it cutteth asunder and seweth vp againe as it listeth. 1626 BACON *Sylva* § 14 It will unmingle the Wine from the Water; the Wine ascending and..the Water descending. 1646 GATAKER *Mistake Removed* 39 To unmingle things that Antichrist hath confounded and put together.

**Unmi·ngled,** *ppl. a.* (UN-¹ 8.)

1548 ELYOT, *Impromiscuus*, vnmyngled, not confuse. 1577 tr. *Bullinger's Decades* IV. i. 559/2 The doctrine of Faith.. ought to bee reteined vnmingled, and vncorrupte in the Churche. 1626 BACON *Sylva* § 396 Springs on the Tops of High-Hills..are most pure and vnmingled. 1665 BOYLE *Refl.* v. vii, Two or three unmingled Liveries, whose single Colours are bright. 1725 POPE *Odyss.* IX. 238 Vessels of unmingled wine. 1746 HERVEY *Medit.* (1748) 38 Where Imagination dreams of unmingled Sweets. 1818 SCOTT *Hrt. Midl.* xix, She looked up with anxious surprise, not unmingled with a cast of horror. 1875 JOWETT *Plato* (ed. 2) III. 252 He to whom is given the cup of unmingled ill.

**Unmi·ngling,** *ppl. a.* (UN-¹ 10.) 1643 [see UNMATCHABLE *a.* 2]. 1855 MILMAN *Lat. Chr.* XIV. iii. VI. 463 Into this separate immaterial and unmingling world.

**Unmi·nished,** *ppl. a.* (UN-¹ 8.)

1533 MORE *Answ. Poysoned Bk.* Wks. 1096/1 By hys ascendyng vp wyth hys body hole and vnminished. 1583 GOLDING *Calvin on Deut.* xxxvi. 215 That he must be so obeyed, as his whole right be reserued to him unminished. 1848 PUSEY *Paroch. Serm.* (1852) I. 121 One Everlasting, Unminished, Unchanging Joy. 1854 S. DOBELL *Balder* xxiii. 102 He walks, Hale and unminished, to and fro. 1870 SWINBURNE *Ess. & Stud.* (1875) 142 For him the sleepless wellsprings of Cephisus are yet unminished and unfrozen.

**Unmi·nister,** *v.* (UN-² 6 b.)

1636 PRYNNE *Unbish. Tim.* (1661) 80 They..Un-church most Protestant Churches in forein parts, and Un-minister their Ministers. 1676 ROW *Contn. Blair's Autobiog.* ix. (1848) 138 They did not unminister him, and therefore did not quarrel his preaching or praying in public.

**Unmi·nistered,** *ppl. a.* and *a.* [UN-¹ 8, 9.]

**1.** Not administered (to a person).

1532 MORE *Confut. Tindale* Wks. 377/1 It were as good to leaue the sacramentes vnministred vnto him as ministred. 1545 COVERDALE *Def. Chr. Man* Wks. (Parker Soc.) II. 473 Therefore must so great a sacrament in no wise be left unministered.

**2.** Destitute of a minister.

1657 W. FENNER *2nd Pt. Christ's Alarm* 97 Any Parish that is unchurched and unministred.

**Unministe·rial,** *ppl. a.* (UN-¹ 7.)

1727 POPE, etc. *Art of Sinking* 118 Used in the praise and dispraise of ministerial and unministerial persons. 1735 HERVEY *Mem. Geo. II* (1848) I. 492 One of the most impolitic unministerial acts I ever knew him guilty of. 1816 COLERIDGE *Lett.* (1895) 660 The plain, unministerial.. spirit of your writings. 1863 EDITH J. MAY *Stronges of Netherstronge* 115 The perplexed minister recollected his office in time to repress a very unministerial reply.

**Unmi·nted,** *ppl. a.* (UN-¹ 8. Cf. Da. *umyntet.*)

1611 SPEED *Hist. Gt. Brit.* IX. xxiv. 164 [She] caused the value of fortie thousand Angels in Bullion, vnminted,..to be sent. 1636 PAGITT *Christianogr.* (ed. 2) II. 40 The Treasury of merits was unminted. 1739 G. OGLE *Gualtherus & Griselda* 87 Virtue, in low, is an unminted Mine. 1845 PETRIE *Round Towers Irel.* 215 The precious metals were used as a circulating medium in large unminted pieces. 1881 DUFFIELD *Don Quixote* II. 402 To rail on the lightness of women,..their unminted promises.

**Unmi·nuted,** *ppl. a.* (UN-¹ 8.) [1775 ASH.] 1778 [W. H. MARSHALL] *Minutes Agric., Observ.* 136 From the above Minutes, as well as from repeated, unminuted Observations, I am clearly of opinion [etc.]. 1824 BENTHAM *Bk. Fallacies* Wks. 1843 II. 465/2 From speeches—spoken and unminuted speeches. **Unmi·racled,** *ppl. a.* (UN-² 6 b, 8.) 1609 F. GREVIL *Mustapha* IV. iv, That our great lord may see Vnmiracled his owne humanitie.

**Unmira·culous,** *a.* (UN-¹ 7.)

1746 YOUNG *Nt. Th.* IX. 1262 Miracles..can not more amaze the mind, Than this, call'd unmiraculous survey. 1858 CARLYLE *Fredk. Gt.* IX. viii. II. 476 The phantom becomes reasonably unmiraculous again. 1882 SEELEY *Nat. Relig.* 254 The unmiraculous part of the Christian tradition.

**Unmi·red,** *ppl. a.* (UN-¹ 8.) *c* 1586 C'TESS PEMBROKE *Ps.* LXIX. vi, Gratious God,..Keepe me safe unsunck, unmyred, Safe from flowing foes retyred. **Unmi·rthful,** *a.* (UN-¹ 7.) 1815 JANE AUSTEN *Emma* xvi, Difficulties.. enough to occupy her in most unmirthful reflections. 1835 LYTTON *Rienzi* I. iv, None saw that the unmirthful flash [of wit] was the token of the coming storm. **Unmi·rthfully,** *adv.* (UN-¹ 11.) 1894 WILKINS & VIVIAN *Green Bay Tree* vii, 'Oh! come now,' exclaimed Coryton, laughing unmirthfully. **Unmi·ry,** *a.* (UN-¹ 7.) 1716 GAY *Trivia* III. 187 There may'st thou pass with safe unmiry feet, Where the rais'd pavement leads athwart the street. **Unmisca·rrying,** *ppl. a.* (UN-¹ 10.) 1657 TRAPP *Comm. Ps.* CXX. 1 The unmiscarrying return of prayer should be carefully observed. **Unmi·schievous,** *a.* (UN-¹ 7.) 1821 LAMB *Elia* I. *Quakers' Meeting*, Nothing-plotting, nought-caballing, unmischievous synod! 1848 R. W. HAMILTON *Sabbath* v. 170 Though overtrading is a solecism, not unmischievous is the unrequired extension of stock. **Unmi·scible,** *a.* (UN-¹ 7.) [1775 ASH.] 1883 R. HALDANE *Workshop Receipts* Ser. II. 441/2 Oil and water are unmiscible.

**Unmisgi·ving,** *ppl. a.* (UN-¹ 10.)

1693 HOWE *Carnality Relig. Contention* Wks. 1724 II. 211 An high and unmisgiving Confidence, and expectation to be saved! 1832 L. HUNT *Poems* Pref. p. xi, A small and unambitious, yet unmisgiving and happy production. 1863 COWDEN CLARKE *Shaks. Char.* i. 6 He has an unmisgiving confidence in his own powers. 1867 LEWES *Hist. Philos.* (ed. 3) II. 24 Discussing, with ardour and unmisgiving ingenuity, topics..necessarily beyond all possible demonstration.

**Unmisgi·vingly,** *adv.* (UN-¹ 11; cf. prec.) 1842 MRS. BROWNING *Bk. Poets* iv. § 6 As it is a fault in the Greek lyrist to leave his buoyancy..too unmisgivingly and entirely for the right reverence of Unity in Beauty. 1861 EARLE *Glouc. Fragm.* 40 Much in the same way as..one..is unhesitatingly and unmisgivingly pronounced 'a saint in glory'. **Unmisgui·ded,** *ppl. a.* (UN-¹ 8.) 1830 W. TAYLOR *Hist. Surv. Germ. Poetry* I. 91 Unmisguided by ecclesiastic missionaries and monastic institutions. **Unmisinte·rpretable,** *a.* (UN-¹ 7 b.) *a* 1631 DONNE *Serm.* 589 This usefull and unmisinterpretable Confession which we speak of.

**Unmi·ssed,** *ppl. a.* (UN-¹ 8.)

*a* 1400 *Relig. Pieces fr. Thornton MS.* (1914) 105/255 Thay menskede the with manhede, with mytir vn-myste. *c* 1520 BARCLAY *Jugurth* (1557) 8 The right kayes..nyghtly were delyuered vnto Hiempsall..soo myght they nat be vnmyssed the space of a nyght. 1621 G. SANDYS *Ovid's Met.* IV. (1626) 68 Then Thisbe..slipping forth, vnmissed of her guard, Comes maskt to Ninus tomb. 1757 GRAY *Let. to Mason* 28 Sept., Why should he not steal away, unmarked and unmissed till the hurry of passions in those.. was a little abated? 1791 COWPER *Iliad* XVI. 652 Thy allies ..Perish, unaided and unmiss'd by thee. 1819 SCOTT *Ivanhoe* vi, Of comfort there was little, and, being unknown, it was unmissed. 1835 *Court Mag.* VI. 59/1 He's only fit for the dunghill, where he would rot among other offal, unmissed.

**Unmi·ssionized,** *ppl. a.* (UN-¹ 8.) 1860 TYLOR *Anahuac* xii. 325 Various tribes of Red Men in Hudson's Bay Territory, as yet unmissionized. **Unmi·st,** *v.* (UN-² 4.) 1611 FLORIO, *Disinebbiare*, to vnmist, to vnfog. 1675 G. R. tr. *Le Grand's Man without Passion* 21 They are not very far distant from the Truth, and by a little light brought in to unmist them, they may easily pass for Articles of our Faith.

**Unmista·kable,** *a.* (UN-¹ 7 b.)

In common use from *c* 1855.

1666 TILLOTSON *Rule of Faith* I. iii. § 9. 31 Unmistakeable, indefectible Oral Tradition. *a* 1834 COLERIDGE *Biogr. Lit.* (1847) I. 305 In Nature..there are unmistakeable foretokens of Evil. 1840 HOOD *Up Rhine* 242 The unmistakeable Roman features of the Centurion. 1860 TYNDALL *Glac.* 390 The veins..cutting each other at an unmistakeable angle.

Hence **Unmista·kableness.**

1866 GROSART in *Lismore Papers* Introd. 13 The frankness and unmistakeableness with which facts are given.

**Unmista·kably,** *adv.* (UN-¹ 11; cf. prec.)

1854 tr. *Hettner's Athens* 51 Architectural fragments, unmistakably of very ancient origin. 1894 SALA *London up to date* xxiii. 347 A cleanly-shaven fellow with..an unmistakably horsey look about the eyes and lips.

**Unmista·ken,** *ppl. a.* (UN-² 8 b.) 1768–74 TUCKER *Lt. Nat.* II. 523 That obedience which is..the genuine product of an unmistaken sanctity. **Unmista·kingly,** *adv.* (UN-¹ 11.) 1870 ROCK *Textile Fabrics* p. xxx, The affection shown by..all our nobility..for cloth of gold in their garments, was unmistakingly set forth in so many of their likenesses. **Unmi·stressed,** *a.* (UN-¹ 9.) 1867 *Chamb. Jrnl.* 21 Dec. 801 The unmistressed labouresses [*sc.* servants] sat in a smaller room. **Unmistru·sted,** *a.* (UN-¹ 8.) 1600 TOURNEUR *Transf. Metam.* xxv, Worlde's trustlesse trust, soule's unmistrusted fall. 1621 LADY M. WROTH *Urania* 393 In stead of loue, to giue me frownes;..and all vnlook'd for, or, vnmistrusted; it wounds my very soule. **Unmistru·stful,** *a.* (UN-¹ 7.) 1768–74 TUCKER *Lt. Nat.* II. 606 A prospect of futurity and unmistrustful hope in the divine goodness.

**Unmistru·sting,** *ppl. a.* (UN-¹ 10.)

*c* 1598 DELONEY *Thomas of Reading* xiv, The vnmistrusting man thinking no euill, went to the doore. 1762 STERNE *Tr. Shandy* VI. xxix, An unmistrusting ignorance of the plies.. of the heart of woman. 1787 BURNS *Highland Tour* Aug. (Friday), Kind openheartedness, mixed with unmistrusting simplicity.

† **Unmithe**: see UN-¹ 3.

**Unmi·tigable,** *a.* (UN-¹ 7 b.)

1610 SHAKS. *Temp.* I. ii. 276 Her most vnmittigable rage. 1628 BP. HALL *Serm. bef. Chas. I*, 100 The desperate man.. pierceth his owne heart with a deepe, irremediable, vnmitigable, killing sorrow. 1646 — *Devout Soul* xii. 42 The unpitiable, interminable, unmitigable tortures of those..neverdying souls. 1805 FOSTER *Ess.* (1806) I. 174 The great Cause..assumed in his administrations an unmitigable urgency. 1862 LYTTON *Str. Story* II. 172 A remembrance of unrelaxed, unmitigable indignation.

**Unmi·tigably,** *adv.* (UN-¹ 11.) 1868 BROWNING *Ring & Bk.* IV. 768 Practising,..Unmitigably from the very first, The finer vengeance.

**Unmi·tigated,** *ppl. a.* [UN-¹ 8.]

**1.** Not softened in respect of severity or intensity.

1599 SHAKS. *Much Ado* IV. i. 308 With publike accusation, ..vnmittigated rancour. 1814 J. AUSTEN *Mansfield Park* ix, The unmitigated glare of day. 1833 L. RITCHIE *Wand. by Loire* 26 [It] is not an unmitigated evil. 1856 KANE *Arct. Expl.* I. xxv. 328 [He] fell sick with the unmitigated fatigue. 1873 SYMONDS *Gk. Poets* v. 129 Supreme art lends solemnity and grandeur to the expression of unmitigated passion.

**2.** Not modified or toned down; absolute.

1840 MILL *Diss. & Disc.* (1859) I. 428 Still more unmitigated savages, the wild Indians. 1849 C. BRONTE *Shirley* vii, Caroline 'was glad to see them' (an unmitigated fib). 1860 *All Year Round* No. 72. 511 In very plain speech, I look on him as an unmitigated humbug. 1871 L. STEPHEN *Playgr. Eur.* iv. 311 A slope of hard, blue, unmitigated ice.

Hence **Unmi·tigatedly** *adv.*

1851 in C. Martyn *W. Phillips* (1890) 242 Of all the institutions of slavery on the face of the earth, there are none so unmitigatedly bad..as [that]..in the United States. 1865 *Ch. Times* 11 Mar. 76/3 The unmitigatedly gloomy manner in which funerals are now conducted. 1884 *Manch. Exam.* 27 Dec. 3/5 Nor is it unmitigatedly depressing, though far from cheerful.

**Unmi·tre,** *v.* (UN-² 4.) 1598 FLORIO, *Dimitriare*, to vnmitre. 1644 MILTON *Areop.* (Arb.) 67 The unmitring of a Bishop. 1675 PENN *Eng. Pres. Interest* 53 [He] hop't.. to inculcate that Doctrine which should un-Mitre the Pope.

**Unmi·tred,** *ppl. a.* (UN-¹ 8.)

1688 R. HOLME *Armory* IV. xi. (Roxb.) 442/2 The Metropolitan..standing vnmittered..saith (the other Bishops standing vnmittered) this prayer. 1848 LYTTON *Harold* II. ii, Nor misdeem me, that I, humble, unmitred priest, should be thus bold. 1856 MASSON *Ess. Biog. & Crit.* 43 Such an archbishop, mitred or unmitred, as England has never seen.

**Unmi·ttened,** *ppl. a.* (UN-¹ 8.) 1853 KANE *Grinnell Exp.* xxxvi. (1856) 325 [It] gave..a warm impression to the unmittened hand.

**Unmi·x,** *v.* (UN-² 3.)

1558 WARDE tr. *Alexis' Secr.* 7 After you haue wel vn-mixed, and purged it from the saied Honnie wyth hote water. **1661** COTTERELL tr. *Calprenède's Cassandra* II. I. (1676) 120 The eye of the mind lost itself in the care of unmixing them. *a* **1693** *Urquhart's Rabelais* III. lii. 421 How would you unmix them?

**Unmi·xable,** *a.* (UN-¹ 7 b.)
**1759** SARAH FIELDING *C'tess of Dellwyn* II. 142 Two things so very unmixable in their Natures as Truth and Falsehood. **1844** W. H. MILL *Serm. Tempt. Christ* Notes 161 Therefore things in themselves unmixable are mingled.

Hence **Unmi·xableness.**
**1881** WHITNEY *Mixt. Lang.* 7 The unmixableness of grammar.

**Unmi·xed,** *ppl. a.* (UN-¹ 8.)
**1526** *Pilgr. Perf.* (W. de W. 1531) 280 b, Myne odour..is as the pure balme vnmixt. **1573** TUSSER *Husb.* (1878) 111 Yet may a good huswife..haue mixt and vnmixt at hir pleasure. **1607** TOPSELL *Four-f. Beasts* 292 The Sarmatican kinde of horsses is..very fit for running, vnmixt, hauing a wel set body. **1667** MILTON *P. L.* VI. 742 Thy Saints unmixt, and from th' impure Farr separate. **1709** PRIOR *Henry & Emma* 172 Great Heav'n, bestow Our Cup of Love unmix'd. **1753** HANWAY *Trav.* I. III. li. 234 If mankind cannot think so abstractedly as a pure effort of unmixed reason implies. **1805** R. W. DICKSON *Pract. Agric.* II. 1124 The Lowland or Fifeshire breed of cattle is rarely met with in an unmixed state. **1889** S. WALPOLE *Life Ld. J. Russell* II. 26 Lord John could not derive unmixed comfort from [such] a victory.

**b.** Const. *with* or †*from.*
**1602** SHAKS. *Ham.* I. v. 104 Thy Commandment all alone shall liue Within the Booke and Volume of my Braine, Vnmixt with baser matter. **1660** SHARROCK *Vegetables* 29 There grew..wild Oates unmixt from any other weeds. **1725** POPE *Odyss.* IV. 767 Joys ever-young, unmix'd with pain or fear. **1816** BYRON *Prisoner Chillon* 185 But these were horrors—this was woe Unmix'd with such. **1861** PALEY *Æschylus* (ed. 2) *Supplices* 1054 *note*, The better part, though not unmixed with evil.

Hence **Unmi·xedness.**
**1612** T. WILSON *Chr. Dict.*, Puritie sig[nifieth] Vnmixednesse with sinne. **1681** DODWELL *Sanchoniathon's Phoenic. Hist.* 87 The particular conveniences they enjoyed, above others, and their unmixedness with the Prophane Vulgar.

**Unmi·xedly,** *adv.* (UN-¹ 11: cf. prec.)
**1642** W. PRICE *Serm.* 1 Our meaning is not that they are unmixtly such, we onely denominate them from their chiefe scope. **1682** INGELO *Bentiv. & Ur.* (ed. 4) I. II. 60 Since nothing is unmixedly pure in this world. **1748** RICHARDSON *Clarissa* (1811) V. ii. 12 How pleasing..to look back upon the happy days I gave her; though mine would doubtless have been more unmixedly so [etc.]. **1833** *Q. Rev.* XLIX. 375 There is nothing..so unmixedly pathetic. **1867** M. ARNOLD *Celtic Lit.* 89 The genius and the literature were purely and unmixedly German.

**Unmoa·n,** *v.* (UN-¹ 14.) **1790** J. WILLIAMS *Shrove Tuesday*, etc. 32 They..pierc'd him as he flew: The Gods unmoan'd him as he bled—Hell yawning gulp'd its due. **Unmoa·ned,** *ppl. a.* (UN-¹ 8.) **1562** [see UNMINDED 2]. **1594** SHAKS. *Rich. III*, II. ii. 64 Our fatherlesse distresse was left vnmoan'd. **1622** WITHER *Philarete* M 4 Yet I..must perish nay-theless,..Vnmoaned I must dye.

† **Unmoar,** obs. var. UNMOOR *v.*
**1750** BLANCKLEY *Nav. Expositor* s.v., When a Ship or Vessel that Rides at two Anchors begins to get them up in order to Sail, she is Unmoaring.

† **Unmo·ble,** *a.* and *sb.* [UN-¹ 7 (5 b), 12. Cf. MDu *onmeubel, -moebel*, etc.] = UNMOVABLE.
**1377** LANGL. *P. Pl.* B. III. 267 Moebles and vnmoebles [*v.r.* vnmebles], and al þat þow myȝte fynde. *c* **1380** WYCLIF *Wks.* (1880) 12 ȝif þei coueiten..þe housis, þat ben goodis vnmeble of here neiȝeboris, as londis or rentis. **1429** *Wills & Inv. N. C.* (Surtees) 80 All remenant and residewe of my goods moblez and vnmoblez. **1456** SIR G. HAYE *Law Arms* (S.T.S.) 261 Gif a man had tane possession of ony gude moble or unmoble. **1594** CAREW *Tasso* (1881) 110 If you also prisonment refuse, And fetters fly, as waight vnmoble fro.
† **Unmo·blety.** *Obs.*—¹ [UN-¹ 12.] = UNMOVABLETY. *a* **1400** *Pauline Ep.* (Powell) Heb. vi. 17 In whiche thyng god wilande to schewe..þe vnmoebilte of his counseil.

**Unmo·cked,** *ppl. a.* (UN-¹ 8.)
**1648** HEXHAM II, *Onbegeckt*, Vnmocked, or not Flouted. **1817** MOORE *Lalla R.*, *Fire-Worshippers* II. 251 Here we may bleed, unmock'd by hymns Of Moslem triumph. **1904** *Westm. Gaz* 2 Apr. 2/2 You'll hear a voice..Aspire a moment, pause, and die—Unmocked of Echo.
**Unmo·ckingly,** *adv.* (UN-¹ 11.) **1872** TENNYSON *Gareth & Lynette* 286 Unmockingly the mocker ending here Turn'd to the right. **Unmo·delled,** *ppl. a.* (UN-¹ 11.) **1875** RUSKIN *Fors Clav.* xlix. V. 4 Not in my model colony only, but as best it can be managed in any unmodelled place or way. **1895** *Westm. Gaz.* 6 Dec. 3/1 The unmodelled homes of the poor.

† **Unmo·derate,** *a. Obs.* [UN-¹ 7, 5 b.] Immoderate.
**1398** TREVISA *Barth. De P. R.* XI. ii. (Bodl. MS.), ȝif þe winde is contrarie and vnmoderat, þanne he bringeþ peril. *Ibid.* XIII. xxvi, Vnmoderat heete greueþ fysche. **1539** ELYOT *Cast. Helthe* 64 If the fluxe be vnmoderate, it engendreth myscheuous diseases. **1584** FENNER *Def. Ministers* (1587) 59 Vnlesse he thinke the..persons..were so vnlearned, vnmoderate, and vngodlie. **1617** MINSHEU, *Un-moderate*,.. immoderate.
† **Unmo·derately,** *adv. Obs.* (UN-¹ 11, 5 b.) **1528** PAYNELL *Salerne's Regim.* Y iv, Wyne vnmoderately taken..febleth the eies and syght. **1548** ELYOT s.v. *Cibus*, To eate vnmoderately. **1647** HEXHAM I, Vnmoderately, *onmatelick.*

**Unmoderly,** obs. Sc. f. UNMOTHERLY *adv.*

**Unmo·dern,** *a.* (UN-¹ 7.)
**1757** MRS. GRIFFITH *Lett. Henry & Frances* (1767) III. 116 Like an unmodern Critic, let me first commend, before I find Fault. **1876** *N. Amer. Rev.* CXXIII. 182 His style is unmodern. **1889** SKRINE *Mem. Thring* 69 His language, so unmodern and so expressive.
**Unmo·dernize,** *v.* (UN-² 6 c *b.*) **1818** KEATS *Lett.* (1848) I. 133, I shall have it bound in Gothique—a nice sombre binding; it will go a little way to unmodernize. **1834** LAMB in *N. & Q.* Ser. VI. IV. 223/1 'Ween', and 'wist',..are antiquated frippery, and unmodernize a poem rather than give it an antique air.

**Unmo·dernized,** *ppl. a.* (UN-¹ 8.)
[**1775** ASH.] *c* **1815** JANE AUSTEN *Persuas.* v, The mansion of the squire,..substantial and unmodernized. **1883** *Harper's Mag.* Mar. 533/2 That, too, had been left unmodernized.
†**Unmo·dest,** *a. Obs.* [UN-¹ 7, 5 b.] Immodest. **1565** COOPER *Thesaurus* s.v. *Immodestus*, A saucie and vnmodest kinde of iestyng. *a* **1586** SIDNEY *Arcadia* II. xxiii, This breaking of my harte..will make you (I hope) think I was not altogether unmodest. **1632** SHERWOOD, Unmodest, *immodeste.* † **Unmo·destly,** *adv.* (UN-¹ 11, 5 b.) **1580** HOLLYBAND *Treas. Fr. Tong*, *Intemperément*, vntemperately, vnmodestly. **1632** SHERWOOD s.v. † **Unmo·desty.** (UN-¹ 12.) **1647** HEXHAM I, Vnmodestie, *ongeschicktheyd.*

**Unmo·difiable,** *a.* (UN-¹ 7 b.)
**1825** COLERIDGE *Lit. Rem.* (1836) II. 353 Reason theoretical and practical,..unapproachable and unmodifiable by the animal basis. **1860** GEO. ELIOT *Mill on Fl.* I. v, Some of her most unmodifiable characters. **1883** F. GALTON *Inq. Hum. Faculty* 156 They remain unmodified and unmodifiable.

Hence **Unmo·difiableness.**
**1876** GEO. ELIOT *Dan. Der.* lviii, A nature not of brutish unmodifiableness.

**Unmo·dified,** *ppl. a.* (UN-¹ 8.)
**1792** BURKE *Let. to Sir H. Langrishe* Wks. VI. 308 An universal unmodified capacity, to which the fanaticks pretend. **1823** H. J. BROOKE *Introd. Crystallogr.* 251 The *o*, by which we have proposed to denote the unmodified angles or edges. **1841** MYERS *Cath. Th.* III. § 30. 106 Our Lord everywhere exhibited a form of Truth unmodified by Individuality. **1871** DARWIN *Desc. Man* II. xiii. II. 67 We have seen that some birds..rattle their unmodified feathers together.

†**Unmo·dish,** *a. Obs.* [UN-¹ 7, 5 b.] Unfashionable.
*c* **1665** C'TESS WARWICK in C. F. Smith *Life*, etc. (1901) 327 To be so unmodish as..to walk in the straight and holy path. **1672** J. PHILLIPS *Montelion's Predict.* 4 To offer more Reasons..would be absurd and unmodish. **1716** LADY M. W. MONTAGU *Toilet* 21 At Chapel..Who..appears at those unmodish Hours But Ancient Matrons? **1728** MORGAN *Algiers* I. Pref. p. i, [I am] so impoliticly unmodish, that I never can speak one thing when I mean another.

**Unmo·dulated,** *ppl. a.* (UN-¹ 8, 5 b.)
**1815** JANE AUSTEN *Emma* iv, The uncouthness of a voice ..wholly unmodulated. **1861** [MRS. A. J. PENNY] *Romance Dull Life* xx. 150 He answered with a short and unmodulated monosyllable. **1866** LIVINGSTONE *Last Jrnls.* (1873) I. xi. 292 A low unmodulated guttural drawl.

**Unmoi·st,** *a.* (UN-¹ 7.)
**1611** FLORIO, *Inhumido*, vnmoist, dry, saplesse. **1708** J. PHILIPS *Cyder* I. 333 With heavy Bulk Volatile Hermes, fluid and unmoist, Mounts on the Wings of Air. *Ibid.* II. 159 The Dew..left unmoist His execrable Glebe. **1825** COLERIDGE *Poet. Wks.* (1912) II. 1111 With unmoist Lip and wreathless Brow I stroll. **1855** SINGLETON *Virgil* II. 287 Jaws, unmoist with blood.
**Unmoi·sted,** *ppl. a.* [UN-¹ 8.] = next. **1492** RYMAN in *Archiv Stud. neu. Spr.* LXXXIX. 185 Beholde, the yerde of Aaron Vnmoysted bare a floure.

**Unmoi·stened,** *ppl. a.* (UN-¹ 8.)
*a* **1625** FLETCHER *Nice Valour* II. i, Mayst thou dye with an unmoist'ned eye. **1708** J. PHILIPS *Cyder* II. 400 The Muses still require Humid Regalement, nor will aught avail Imploring Phœbus, with unmoisten'd Lips. **1735** SOMERVILLE *Chase* I. 176 The drooping Pack..loll their unmoisten'd Tongues. *c* **1830** BRYANT *Murdered Traveller* 28 They..marked his grave with nameless stones, Unmoistened by a tear. **1844** NOAD *Electr.* (ed. 2) 416 If the brass conducting tubes..are grasped..with the unmoistened hands.
†**Unmole·st,** *ppl. a. Obs.* [UN-¹ 8 b.] = next. *c* **1560** A. SCOTT *Poems* (S.T.S.) vi. 6 Thairfoir go,..And lat me leif thus vnmolest. **1773** J. ROSS *Fratricide* III. 1000 (MS.), He sees his Brother's sacrificial fire To Heaven ascending unmolest and bright!

**Unmole·sted,** *ppl. a.* (UN-¹ 8.)
**1531** *Reg. Privy Seal Scot.* II. 134/2 The saidis personis ..to be unattechit,..unmolestit, and untrublit. **1603** KNOLLES *Hist. Turks* (1621) 25 King Baldwin..liued for a season vnmolested by his enemies. **1689** BOYLE *Martyrd. Theodora* xii. 246 The unmolested Exercise of a Religion, that [etc.]. **1740** CIBBER *Apol.* viii. 164 Continuing to act with as little Authority, unmolested. **1772** PRIESTLEY *Inst. Relig.* (1782) II. 26 They..suffered them to live unmolested. **1812** BYRON *Ch. Har.* II. lxxxvi, Where the gray stones and unmolested grass Ages, but not oblivion, feebly brave. **1884** SIR W. B. BRETT in *Law Times Rep.* LI. 530/1 He has a perfect right ..to have his person unmolested by the negligence of another man's servant.

Hence **Unmole·stedly** *adv.*
**1641** LD. DIGBY *Parl. Sp.* 19 Jan. 21 To let them injoy unmolestedly, what belongs unto them. **1665** BOYLE *Occas. Refl.* VI. ix, The Devil sometimes do's unmolestedly suffer us to write well. **1839** LADY LYTTON *Cheveley* viii, They unmolestedly went to..dinners for six months. **1879** FARRAR *St. Paul* II. 510 Teaching the things concerning the Lord Jesus Christ with all confidence unmolestedly.
**Unmole·sting,** *ppl. a.* (UN-¹ 10.) *c* **1792** WOLCOT (P. Pindar) *Old Simon* viii, Sweetly she slept..In good old Simon's unmolesting arms. **1891** *Daily News* 30 Dec. 5/1 Living their quiet useful lives, unmolesting and unmolested.
**Unmo·llified,** *ppl. a.* (UN-¹ 8.) **1628** FELTHAM *Resolves* I. lxxv. 68 So still he rests vnmollified, for all this raine and haile. **1760–72** H. BROOKE *Fool of Qual.* (1809) I. 156 The ..crude element of earth, unmollified by the fluidity of water and light.

**Unmo·lten,** *ppl. a.* [UN-¹ 8 b.] Unmelted.
**1525** in Lindsay *Coinage Scot.* (1845) 232 The gold..beand bocht for vii. Li. the unce unmoltyn. **1555** EDEN *Decades* (Arb.) 164 The snowe lyinge contynually vnmolten. **1613** PURCHAS *Pilgrimage* VI. i. 464 Old Atlas..hath alwayes on his..high toppes vnmolten snow. **1844** MRS. BROWNING *Drama of Exile* 399 The unmolten lightnings vein it motionless.

**Unmo·mentary,** *a.* [UN-¹ 7, 5 b.]
†**1.** Of no moment; unimportant. *Obs.*
**1624** HEYWOOD *Gunaik.* II. 69 Whence soever shee had that name bestowed upon her, it was neither idle nor unmomentarie. **1635** — *Hierarchy* I. 27 Such childish and vnmomentary grounds These Atheists build vpon.
**2.** Not occupying a moment of time. *rare*—¹.
**1635** HEYWOOD *Hierarchy* VII. 439 From heav'n to earth he can descend, and bee Aboue and here in space vnmomentarie.

**Unmome·ntous,** *a.* (UN-¹ 7, 5 b.) **1824** CAMPBELL *Theodric* 168 How our fates from unmomentous things May rise! **1858** CARLYLE *Fredk. Gt.* III. v. I. 229 There is lastly a still more unmomentous Margraf, only son of said Unmomentous and his said Spouse.

**Unmo·narch,** *v.* (UN-² 6 b. Cf. UNKING *v.*)
**1667** KATH. PHILIPS *Poems* 2 As we unmonarch'd were for want of thee. **1681** SIR J. TYRRELL (*title*), Patriarcha non Monarcha. The Patriarch Unmonarch'd..; in which The falseness of those Opinions that would make Monarchy *Jure Divino* are laid open. **1746** W. HORSLEY *Fool* (1748) II. 2 [They] take great Pains to unmonarch me, and constitute themselves in my Stead. **1818** J. HASSELL *Rides & Walks* II. 123 The dignity and sarcasm..so far unmonarched his most Christian majesty, that he burst into a violent fit of passion.

Hence **Unmo·narched** *ppl. a.*
*c* **1844** LOWELL *To the Past* iv, The eternal sorrow In their unmonarched eyes. **1868** HEAVYSEGE *Jezebel* I. 218 Thou didst discrown Thyself. Unmonarched man!
**Unmona·stic,** *a.* (UN-¹ 7.) **1849** I. TAYLOR *Loyola & Jes.* I. vii. 151 Their unmonastic habit..afforded ground enough for such imputations. **1869** TOZER *Highl. Turkey* I. 93 My tumbler..was engraved with most unmonastic Cupids.

**Unmo·neyed,** *ppl. a.* (UN-¹ 8.)
**1677** W. HUGHES *Man of Sin* II. viii. 129 What Rich Bargains of Popish Pardons may be had..both by the Monyed and Unmonyed Chapmen too. **1742** SHENSTONE *Schoolmistr.* xxxiii, Apples with cabbage-net y-cover'd o'er, Galling full sore th' unmoney'd wight, are seen. **1822** *Liberal* I. 210 Their sympathy with the natural unmonied faculties of poets in general. **1868** R. LYTTON *Chron. & Char.* II. 230 This pauper Priest..from thankless doors drave forth The messenger unmonied and amazed.
†**Unmo·nished,** *ppl. a. Obs.* (UN-¹ 8.) **1596** LODGE *Prosopopeia* Wks. (Hunter. Cl.) III. 47 O turn vnto me, whom..no man seeketh vnmonished, and no man findeth vnpurged. **Unmo·nkish,** *a.* (UN-¹ 7.) **1851** CARLYLE *Sterling* I. iv. 45 A singular condition of Schools and High-schools, which have come down..from the monkish ages into this highly unmonkish one. **Unmo·nkly,** *a.* (UN-¹ 7.) **1833** *Fraser's Mag.* VIII. 323 He..shook hands in a cordial and quite unmonkly manner. **Unmonopolized,** *ppl. a.* (UN-¹ 8.) [**1775** ASH.] **1879** H. GEORGE *Progr. & Pov.* III. vi, New countries where land is yet unmonopolized. **1898** *Westm. Gaz.* 21 Jan. 3/2 The profits that would accrue from unmonopolised sale. **Unmono·polizing,** *vbl. sb.* (UN-² 8.) **1641** MILTON *Reform.* II. 85 The unappropriating, and unmonopolizing the rewards of learning and industry, from the greasie clutch of ignorance. **Unmono·polizing,** *ppl. a.* (UN-¹ 10.) **1875** *Encycl. Brit.* I. 216/1 The disinterested and unmonopolising side of æsthetic pleasure. **Unmo·numented,** *ppl. a.* (UN-¹ 8.) **1865** E. BURRITT *Walk to Land's End* 13 [They] lay long in unmonumented..graves.

**Unmoo·r,** *v. Naut.* [UN-² 4 b.]
**1.** *trans.* To free from moorings; *spec.* 'to reduce (a ship) to the state of riding by a single anchor and cable' (Falconer).
**1497** *Naval Acc. Henry VII* (1896) 229 The Remoovyng & Vnmoryng ye said Ship. **1681** *Lond. Gaz.* No. 1663/4 They lye Unmored, and ride single, and intend to Sail this Afternoon. **1704** *Ibid.* No. 3981/3 All the Ships..are unmoor'd, and will sail with the next Opportunity. **1725** POPE *Odyss.* IV. 786 With sails we wing the masts,..Unmoor the fleet, and rush into the sea. **1800** *Hull Pilotage Act* 14 The pilot..shall be paid for unmooring..such ship. **1828** SCOTT *F. M. Perth* xxiv, They seated themselves in the boat and unmoored it from the pier. **1882** 'OUIDA' *Maremma* I. 135 She found her boat safe, and unmoored it and rowed backward.
*transf.* **1866** BRIGHT *Sp.* (1876) 177 They would unmoor the island from its fastenings in the deep.
**2.** *intr.* To cast off moorings. (Cf. UNMOAR.)
**1611** COTGR., *Demarer*, to vnmoore; to loosen a ship thats moored,..and put out to sea. **1693** *Lond. Gaz.* No. 2935/4 Sir Francis Wheeler made the Signal for the Ships to Unmoore. **1745** P. THOMAS *Jrnl. Anson's Voy.* 117 The next Morning we unmoor'd..and at Six weigh'd. **1778** J. ADAMS *Diary* 14 Feb., Wks. 1851 III. 95 At daybreak, orders were given to unmoor. **1840** R. H. DANA *Bef. Mast* xvii. 46 She unmoored and warped down into the bight, from which she got under weigh. **1887** BOWEN *Æneid* III. 639 Fly! and unmoor forthwith from his coasts.

Hence **Unmoo·ring** *vbl. sb.*
**1497** *Naval Acc. Hen. VII* (1896) 252 The vnmoryng of the seid Ship in Portesmouth haven after her comyng owte of Scoteland. **1710** *Lond. Gaz.* No. 4720/3 The Lancaster fired a Gun as a Signal for Unmooring. **1899** F. T. BULLEN *Way Navy* 25, I had..been endeavouring to secure some snap-shots of the fo'castle during the evolution of unmooring.
**Unmoo·red,** *ppl. a.* (UN-¹ 8.) **1683** in *L'pool Munic. Rec.* (1883) I. 308 Noe shipp shall lye upon the strand unmoored. **Unmo·pped,** *ppl. a.* (UN-¹ 8.) [**1775** ASH.] **1848** B. D. WALSH *Aristoph.*, *Clouds* I. i, Dusty, unmopped, reclining at my ease.

**Unmo·ral,** *a.* [UN-¹ 7, 5 b.] Non-moral; not influenced by, or connected with, moral considerations. (Common from *c* 1860.)
**1841** MYERS *Cath. Th.* IV. § 13. 254 The disorganisation and imperfection of the unmoral part of the universe. **1855** [MISS COBBE] *Ess. Intuitive Mor.* 17 These beings are unmoral, and neither virtuous nor vicious. **1871** TYLOR *Prim. Cult.* II. 326 The lower animism is not immoral, it is unmoral.

**Unmora·lity.** (UN-¹ 12, 5 b.)
**1866** LOWELL *Biglow P.* Ser. II. Introd., That half-conscious *un*-morality which I had noticed as the recoil in gross natures from a puritanism that [etc.]. **1879** W. H. MALLOCK

*Is Life Worth Living?* iii. 44 The condition of the completest personal un-morality.

**Unmo·ralize,** *v.* (Un-² 6 c. Cf. Immoralize *v.*) **1640** Bastwick *Ld. Bps.* viii. H 3 They doe unmoralize the 4th Commandement, as concerning the Sabbath day for Christians: they allow profane Sports thereon. **1693** Norris *Pract. Disc.* (1711) III. 109 Contributing..to the unmoralizing and debauching the Age.

**Unmo·ralized,** *ppl. a.* [f. prec., or Un-¹ 8.] Deprived, or devoid, of morality.

**1668** H. More *Div. Dial.* iv. xiv. II. 58 Sensuality..makes holy things..hard and tedious to such unmoralized minds. **1690** J. Norris *Beatitudes* iv. (1694) 106 There being but few so wretchedly wicked and unmoraliz'd as [etc.]. *a* **1866** J. Grote *Exam. Utilit. Phil.* xii. (1870) 185 The difference between the moralized and unmoralized, the better and the worse, human nature. **1886** *New Princeton Rev.* Mar. 180 There are no cabinets of unmoralised or half-moralised conceptions, serving as illustrations of the evolution hypothesis.

**Unmo·ralizing,** *ppl. a.* (Un-¹ 10.) **1889** *Atlantic Monthly* Nov. 701/2 He was primarily the artist, impersonal, unmoralizing. **Unmo·ralness.** (Un-¹ 12.) **1642** D. Rogers *Naaman* 554 Their opinion about the unmoralnesse of the Sabbath.

**Unmo·rdanted,** *ppl. a.* (Un-¹ 8.)

**1838** T. Thomson *Chem. Org. Bodies* 394 When printed on unmordanted cotton and washed..in hot water. **1876** Morris in Mackail *Life* (1899) I. 315 The wool was unmordanted.

† **Unmo·rrised,** *ppl. a.* [Un-¹ 8.] Not prepared for morris-dancing. *a* **1625** Fletcher *Women Pleas'd* iv. i, What a devil ails this fellow..Thus to appear before me too, unmorris'd? **Unmo·rrowing,** *ppl. a.* (Un-¹ 10.) **1855** Bailey *Mystic*, etc. 154 She laid her down, and..slept the long unmorrowing sleep. † **Unmo·rtal,** *a.* (Un-¹ 7, 5 b.) **1538** Elyot, *Immortalis*, vnmortall, that lyueth euer. **1608** Willet *Hexapla Exod.* 75 The soule being unmortall. †**Unmo·rtalize,** *v. Obs.* [Un-² 6 c.] *trans.* To put to death. **1593** Nashe *Christ's T.* 19 b, Man, woman, chylde, he shall vnmortalize and mangle. [**1623** Cockeram ii, *To Kill*,..Vnmortalize, Inage.]

**Unmo·rtared,** *ppl. a.* (Un-¹ 8.)

*a* **1656** Bp. Hall *Christ Mystical* Wks. (1714) ii. 348 Some loose Stones perhaps that lye unmortered upon the Battlements. **1664** Evelyn *Sylva* xxxii. 112 The Haw-thorn well plash'd..is a better..Fence then unmorter'd walls. **1860** Tristram *Gt. Sahara* viii. 124 An empty watercourse, built up of unmortared stone. **1895** *Blackw. Mag.* Nov. 642/1 A carefully mown piece of turf enclosed by an unmortared wall.

**Unmo·rtgage,** *v.* (Un-² 3.) **1637** Heywood *Royall King* iv. iv, Sir, since you did vnmorgage all your meanes, It came into my thoughts.

**Unmo·rtgaged,** *ppl. a.* (Un-¹ 8.)

**1638** Quarles *Hieroglyph.* x. vi, His quick-nos'd armie.. Must now prepare To chase the tim'rous Hare About his yet unmorgag'd grounds. **1676** D'Urfey *Mme. Fickle* v. ii, I have 200*l.* a year, I've my Lands free and unmorgag'd. **1705** Addison *Italy* 210 There is scarce a single Gabel unmortgag'd. **1776** Adam Smith *W. N.* v. iii. (1904) II. 583 The only considerable branch of the public revenue which yet remains unmortgaged. **1828** [G. C. Lewis] tr. *Böckh's Publ. Econ. Athens* II. 247 Cleon..was so deeply involved in debt, that nothing he had was unmortgaged. **1881** *Law Rep. Ch. Div.* XV. 59 The unmortgaged portion [of the estate].

†**Unmorti·ficate,** *ppl. a. Obs.* (Un-¹ 8 b, 5 b.) *c* **1450** tr. *De Imitatione* 126, I desire to cleve to hevenly þinges, but flesshly þinges & unmortificate passions depressen me.

**Unmo·rtified,** *ppl. a.* [Un-¹ 8, 5 b.]

**1.** Not spiritually mortified or subdued: **a.** Of passions, desires, etc.

*c* **1450** tr. *De Imitatione* i. iii. 5 What lettiþ þe more..þan þin unmortified affeccion of herte? **1612** T. Taylor *Comm. Titus* ii. 12 These lusts are fitter for the course of nature vnmortified. **1671** Woodhead *St. Teresa* ii. xii. 101 Their passions are unmortified. *a* **1695** Z. Cradock *Serm. Charity* (1740) 18 His yet unmortified Lusts and Passions. **1748** Hartley *Observ. Man* ii. iv. § 4. 415 He finds many unmortified Desires..in his best Words and Actions. **1857** Susanna Winkworth tr. *Life Tauler* 390 He who wishes to..subdue such an unmortified nature.

**b** Of persons (or the heart).

**1526** *Pilgr. Perf.* (W. de W. 1531) 160 Yᵉ unmortified herte hath not the housholde of yᵉ soule in suche peace. **1641** Milton *Animadv.* 57 Unconfessing and unmortify'd sinners. **1691** Hartcliffe *Virtues* 210 As thou wouldst not demonstrate thy self to be a rash and unmortified Person. **1748** Richardson *Clarissa* (1811) III. xxi. 127 By his soul (the unmortified creature swore,)..he was now in earnest in his good resolutions. *Ibid.* 166 An unmortified libertine. **1894** Hedley *Retreat* xviii. 207 No one can be relaxed, unmortified, and lazy, and at the same time desire to love God with ..a whole heart.

**2.** *Sc. Law.* Not disposed of by mortification.

**1467** *Sc. Acts, Jas. III* (1814) II. 90 Þe soume..to be Raisit of all lordis,..and vþeris quhatsumeuer hafand land vtouth burgh vnmortifijt.

**3.** Not affected by gangrene.

**1732** Monro *Anat.* (ed. 2) 18 An unmortified Part..can have Nerves.., and yet enjoy no Sensation.

Hence **Unmo·rtifiedness.**

**1643** T. Goodwin *Trial Christian's Growth* ii. iii. (1651) 73 This argues much unmortifyednesse, though it run not out into acts. *a* **1677** Manton *Disc. Peace* Wks. 1871 II. 66 The more men increase in grace..the more they know their emptiness, unmortifiedness, and manifold sins. **1727** *Biog. Presbyt.* (1827) I. 338, I have seen some..become fearful Examples of Apostacy, in Covetousness and Unmortifiedness.

**Unmo·rtised,** *ppl. a.*¹ (Un-¹ 8 + Mortised *ppl. a.*) **1678** Moxon *Mech. Exerc.* vi. 103 This Square Peece hath a square wide Mortess in it..to screw against that part of the Wooden Peece un-mortessed at the Top..stiff against the fore-side of the un-mortessed Peece. **Unmo·rtised,** *ppl. a.*² (Un-² 8 + Mortise *v.*¹) **1748** Richardson *Clarissa* (1811) VI. 304 An old broken-bottomed cane couch, unmortised by the failing of one of its worm-eaten legs. **1859** Tennyson *Merlin & V.* 402 The wrist is parted from the hand that waved, The feet unmortised from their ankle-bones Who paced it, ages back. **Unmosa·ic,** *a.* (Un-¹ 7 + Mosaic *a.*²) **1644** Milton *Divorce* (ed. 2) ii. ix. 50 By this reckning Moses should bee most unmosaick, that is, most illegal, not to say most unnaturall. **1868** W. Smith *Book of Moses* p. v, The Separatist Theory..breaks up the whole Pentateuch into un-Mosaic fragments. **Unmossed,** *ppl. a.* (Un-¹ 8.) **1863** Lowell *Memoriae Positum* i. 14 Bleaker than unmossed stone. **Unmo·theaten,** *ppl. a.* (Un-¹ 8 b.) **1574** Hellowes *Gueuara's Fam. Ep.* (1577) 56, I doe craue, from hencefoorth you keepe your letter vnmoatheaten.

**Unmo·thered,** *ppl. a.* [Un-¹ 8 and Un-² 8.]

**1.** Deprived of motherly feelings.

**1607** Tourneur *Rev. Trag.* ii. i, I e'en quake to proceed, my spirit turns edge, I fear me she's unmother'd.

**2.** Deprived or destitute of a mother.

**1847** H. Bushnell *Chr. Nurt.* iii. (1861) 65 The young go forth untended, or unmothered. **1856** Mrs. Browning *Aur. Leigh* i. 95 Nursing me, Unmothered little child of four years old. **1876** Swinburne *Erechtheus* 1057 Thralls of no man's blood, Unchilded and unmothered.

**Unmo·therly,** *a.* (Un-¹ 7.)

Also, in recent use, *unmotherliness.*

**1593** *Sidney's Arcadia* iv. (1629) 413 Well hath my mother reuenged vpon me my vnmotherly hating of thee. **1622** E. Clinton *C'tess Lincoln's Nursery* 13 They argue vnmotherly affection, idlenesse, desire to haue liberty. **1825** Coleridge *Aids Refl.* 357 To asperse my friend's wife for unmotherly conduct in taking an infant six months old to a crowded theatre. **1850** Blackie *Æschylus* I. 120 My mother most unmotherly, her own children With godless hate pursuing.

**Unmo·therly,** *adv.* [Un-¹ 11.] Unkindly.

*c* **1425** Wyntoun *Cron.* ii. viii. 702 Thai at coyme to spy þat lande, þai dressit wnmodyrly; For sum of þaim þai slew richt þar. **1456** Sir G. Haye *Law Arms* (S.T.S.) 30 [They] bitterly and unmoderly will bakbyte behynd bakkis.

**Unmo·tived,** *ppl. a.* (Un-¹ 8.)

**1794** Coleridge *Lett.* (1895) 59 Your gossip with the commanding officer seems so totally useless and unmotived. **1830** W. Taylor *Hist. Surv. Germ. Poetry* I. 286 The sentiments of the personages..[are] often superfluous and unmotived. **1885** *Pall Mall G.* 2 Oct. 5/1 Looking back, we begin to understand actions which seemed dreamily unmotived.

**Unmou·ld,** *v.* [Un-² 3, 5, 7.]

**1.** *trans.* To destroy the mould or form of.

**1611** Cotgr., *Demouler*, to vnmould; breake the mould, ..spoyle the frame, of. **1634** Milton *Comus* 529 His baneful cup..Whose pleasing poison The visage quite transforms of him that drinks,..unmoulding reasons mintage Character'd in the face. [**1745** Warton *Pleas. Melancholy* 89 That charmed cup, which Reason's mintage fair Unmoulds.] **1797** Coleridge *Dungeon* 18 So he lies Circled with evil, till his very soul Unmoulds its essence. **1826** [see Dislimn *v.* 1].

**b.** To take out of a mould.

*c* **1900** *Century Cook Bk.* 493 (Cent. Suppl.), To unmold creams. *Ibid.*, The unmolding of creams requires great care.

**2.** *intr.* or *absol.* To lose form or shape.

**1834** De Quincey *Autob. Sk.* Wks. 1854 II. 223 The restless elements of opinion..mould themselves eternally,..and finally unmould and 'dislimn'.

**Unmou·lded,** *ppl. a.* [Un-¹ 8.] Not moulded or shaped.

**1620** Shelton *Quix.* ii. xlv. 294 Without thee I am dull, vnmolded, and confused. **1636** Pagitt *Christianogr.* (ed. 2) ii. 40 Their Masse was then unmoulded: Transubstantiation unbaked. **1852** Tennyson *Ode Death Wellington* 233 Peace, his triumph will be sung By some yet unmoulded tongue. **1853** Ruskin *Stones Ven.* II. vi. 229 Plain openings in the walls studiously simple, and unmoulded at the sides. **1875** *Carpentry & Join.* 41 A plain unmoulded strip.

**Unmou·ldered,** *ppl. a.* (Un-¹ 8.) [**1775** Ash.] **1843** Poe *Premature Burial* Wks. 1864 I. 327 It was the skeleton of his wife in her yet unmouldered shroud. **Unmou·ldering,** *ppl. a.* (Un-¹ 10.) **1821** Bryant *Ages* xvii, Deeds, engraved On fame's unmouldering pillar. **Unmou·ldy,** *a.* (Un-¹ 7.) **1654** Gayton *Pleas. Notes* i. v. 17 A piece of the Groaning Cake,..which she kept religiously..full forty good yeares unmouldy, and unmouse-eaten. †**Unmou·led,** *ppl. a. Obs.*⁻¹ [Un-¹ 8.] Not grown mouldy. *c* **1450** Capgrave *Life St. Gilbert* 75 Ther was bred kept sextene ȝere aftir his deth, on-corupte, onmouled, whech he blessed. **Unmou·nded,** *ppl. a.* (Un-¹ 8.) *a* **1661** Holyday *Juvenal* vi. (1673) 91 Nor men Fear'd lest their..fruits should be a prey To theives, and gardens all unmounded lay. **1661** Feltham *Resolves* ii. lxv. 326 By Nature, he may be..of a good soyl; yet, if he lyes unmounded, he shall be sure to be alwayes low.

**Unmou·nt,** *v.* [Un-² 5, 8.]

**1.** *trans.* To unfix and take down or remove.

*a* **1680** Butler *Rem.* (1759) I. 23 Others conceiv'd it much more fit T' unmount the Tube, and open it. **1885** C. G. W. Lock *Workshop Receipts* Ser. iv. 397/1 If the print be a mounted one, it is by no means necessary to unmount it previously to treatment.

**2.** To dismount. Also *intr.*

**1787** *Generous Attachment* II. 131, I immediately unmounted, and giving my horse his liberty, wandered about the country. **1892** *Schoolmaster* 26 Mar. 519/2 The German Emperor has had to unmount his high horse, and abandon the..Education Bill.

**Unmou·ntable,** *a.* (Un-¹ 7 b.)

**1549** *Compl. Scot.* xi. 98 That place stude betuix tua strait montanis inhabitabil and onmontabil. **1603** Knolles *Hist. Turks* (1621) 938 Hauing left the fennes of Meotis, and the vnmountable shores of the Blacke sea. *a* **1608** Sir F. Vere *Comm.* (1657) 11 Being reared of a good height with earth, and then with gabions set therevpon of six foot high, made almost unmountable.

**Unmou·nted,** *ppl. a.* [Un-¹ 8.]

**1. a.** Of cannon: Not placed on carriages.

**1627** *Taking St. Esprit* in *Harl. Misc.* (Malh.) III. 550 Twelve pieces unmounted in her hold. **1690** J. Mackenzie *Siege London-Derry* 7/2 [We] found..most of the Guns unmounted for want of Carriages. **1790** Beatson *Nav. & Mil. Mem.* I. 325 In the fort were four guns mounted, and as many unmounted. **1909** G. M. Trevelyan *Garibaldi* 243 The carts that carried the yet unmounted cannon.

**b.** Not fixed up for use or display; not provided with a mount or mounts.

**1888** *Encycl. Dict.* **1890** *Science-Gossip* XXVI. 144/1 Wanted, good unmounted material, also foreign butterflies and shells. **1891** *Anthony's Photogr. Bull.* IV. 235 To use unmounted slides it is necessary to have auxiliary carriers. **1892** *Photogr. Ann.* II. 57 We had also in our album a lot of other unmounted prints.

**2.** Not provided with, or riding on, a horse or horses.

**1592** Nashe *Four Lett. Confut.* H 2, Thy excellent outcast selfe that liu'dst at Cambridge vnmounted. **1630** Capt. Smith *Trav. & Adv.* vi. 10 Captain Smith..was not long unmounted, for there was choice enough of horses. **1688** *Lond. Gaz.* No. 2380/2 A good part of the Cavalry will remain unmounted. **1828** Webster s.v., Unmounted dragoons. **1831** James *Phil. Augustus* III. x, All the most beautiful horses..were led..by the pages and squire, unmounted. **1900** *Westm. Gaz.* 3 Feb. 6/1 The number of mounted and unmounted troops.

**Unmou·rned,** *ppl. a.* (Un-¹ 8.)

**1650** Vaughan *Olor Iscanus, Tristium* iii. iii. 51 Unpittied, and unmourn'd for, my sad head..goes friendless to the dead. **1721** Southerne *Spartan Dame* iv. i, Oh! let me here.. Sink down..Into my grave, unmention'd and unmourn'd. **1813** Byron *Corsair* ii. xiv, Still he goes unmourn'd, returns unsought. *a* **1851** Moir *Poems, Leg. St. Rosalie* v, Down to the dreary caverns of the grave Pass'd,..Unmark'd, unmourn'd, the beauteous and the brave.

**Unmou·se-eaten,** *ppl. a.* (Un-¹ 8 d.) **1654** [see Unmouldy]. **Unmou·thable,** *a.* (Un-¹ 7 b.) **1842** Miall in *Nonconf.* II. 809 A barbarous and unmouthable jargon. **Unmou·thpieced,** *a.* (Un-¹ 9.) **1836–48** B. D. Walsh *Aristoph., Acharnians* ii. vi, Though we've lost all conception Of such matters, and are deaf And un-mouthpieced.

**Unmo·vable,** *a.* and *sb.* [Un-¹ 7 b, 5 b.]

**1.** = Immovable *a.* 1. Now *rare.*

**1382** Wyclif *Exod.* xv. 16 Be thei maad vnmouable as a stoon. *c* **1400** Maundev. (1919) xiii. 67 It is clept the dede see for it..is euere vnmeuable. *c* **1440** *Alphabet of Tales* 447 Hur handis hang vp in þe ayre vnmouable. *a* **1548** Hall *Chron., Edw. IV*, 192 b, He was set in the..stable throne, and vnmoueable chaire, of the croune of his realme. **1594** T. B. *La Primaud. Fr. Acad.* ii. 11 Aristotle also.. sheweth that he knew God vnder the name of the first moouer, who was perpetual and vnmoueable. **1626** Gouge *Serm. Dignity Chivalry* § 15 Like the unmoveable mountaines. *a* **1676** Hale *Prim. Orig. Man.* i. vi. (1677) 123 If we should suppose the Circle *A B C* to move about a fixed unmoveable Center at *D*. **1776** Mickle *Camoens' Lusiad* p. xxxvii, They remained unmoveable on the shore till the fleet..evanished from their sight. **1870** Lowell *Among my Bks.* Ser. i. (1873) 129 Some man whose brain rests on a still more unmovable basis. **1874** W. Humphrey in *Ess. Relig. & Lit.* Ser. iii. 361 The unmoved and unmovable Prime Mover of the ever-moving universe of creatures.

**b.** *sb.* Something immovable.

**1876** Mrs. Whitney *Sights & Ins.* xx, We groped and peered under unmovables and pulled about everything that could be moved.

**2.** = Immovable *a.* 2.

**1388** Wyclif *Heb.* vi. 18 God..puttide betwixe an ooth, that bi twey thingis vnmeuable, bi whiche it is impossible that God lie, we han strengeste solace. *c* **1425** in *Anglia* X. 380/35 Vnmouabil tranquillite and reste of soule. **1502** *Ord. Crysten Men* (W. de W. 1506) i. vii. F i b, Sythen that Iustyce vnmeuable requyreth suche payne. **1599** Sandys *Europæ Spec.* (1632) 111 Having their ground on the unmovable principles of true wisedome and vertue. **1638** Junius *Paint. Ancients* 28 A sad unmoveable countenance. **1650** Baxter *Saints' R.* iii. vii. 383 They that are sure to receive the unmoveable Kingdom must yet serve God with reverence and godly fear. **1691** Norris *Pract. Disc.* 248 This was ever.. an unmoveable Objection.

**b.** = Immovable *a.* 2 b.

**1382** Wyclif *Col.* i. 23 Stable, and vnmouable fro the hope of the gospel. **1445** in *Anglia* XXVIII. 259 Onmevable thou owist not endure, whan benygne preyers be offrid. *a* **1542** Wyatt in *Tottel's Misc.* (Arb.) 70 Wilde beastes in them, fierce loue in me is fed. Vnmoueable am I: and they stedfast. **1570** T. Wilson *Demosth. Orat., Life* 129 Who helde out with a stomacke vpright and vnmoueable, in all the..stormes of fortune. *a* **1624** Bp. M. Smith *Serm.* (1632) 34 Fabricius..remained..vndauntable, and vnmoveable. **1683** Temple *Mem.* Wks. 1720 I. 399 The Prince was unmoveable in the Point of not leaving his Allies. **1748** Richardson *Clarissa* (1811) I. 154 Ungrateful girl, and unmovable as ungrateful! **1856** Miss Warner *Hills Shatemuc* xl, She begged to be allowed to stay..; but Elizabeth was unmoveable.

†**3.** Of property: = Immovable *a.* 3. (Cf. Movable *a.* 4.)

*c* **1375** *Sc. Leg. Saints* xliv. (*Lucy*) 90 Þane sawyt þai..þare gudis unmowable sone. *c* **1449** Pecock *Repr.* i. x. 49 The endewing of preestis bi rentis and bi vnmoueable possessiouns. **1467–8** *Rolls of Parlt.* V. 593/1 The Londes and Tenementes, Goodes and Catalles, meovable and unmeovable. **1535** Coverdale *Judith* viii. 7 Hyr husbande also had lefte her..greate vnmoueable possessions and many catell. **1565** *Wills & Inv. N. C.* (Surtees) 235 Executrix and mynyster of all my goods mewable and vnmewable. *c* **1618** Moryson *Itin.* iv. (1903) 155 In..Italy the father dying intestate, the brothers diuide his mouable and vnmouable goods.

† **b.** *sb. pl.* Immovable goods. *Obs.*

**1536** in *Lett. Suppress. Monast.* (Camden) 146 We..submytt owr selfes and our monasterye, with all the moveables and unmovables therof, unto your majesties accustomede grace. **1562** J. Heywood *Prov. & Epigr.* (1867) 148 Mouables, vnmouables, lande or farme, Thou hast not one grotes woorth, of good or goodnes. *a* **1577** Sir T. Smith *Commw. Eng.* (1609) 121 Touching marriage and the right in moueables and vnmoueables which commeth thereby.

**Unmo·vableness.** (Un-¹ 12, 5 b.)

**1382** Wyclif *Heb.* vi. 17 God willinge for to schewe..the vnmouablenesse, or sadnesse, of his conseil. **1398** Trevisa *Barth. De P. R.* vi. xxiv. (Bodl. MS.), Slepe is a kindelich vnmeuablenes and helpe of þe wittes. **1611** Cotgr.

*Immobilité*, .. firmenesse, assurednesse, unmouablenesse. **1629** H. BURTON *Truth's Triumph* 264 A most stedfast vnmoueablenesse of faith. **1655** EARL ORRERY *Parthen.* II. VI. 550 She..by that Posture, and her unmoveablenesse in it, by degrees took root. **1818** RANKEN *Hist. France* IV. 43 This unmoveablenesse was not the effect of pride. **1885** *In Mem. J. L. Aikman* 38 He was..surefooted with a central unmovableness.

†**Unmo·vablety.** *Obs. rare.* [UN-[1] 12.] Unmovableness. *c* **1374** CHAUCER *Boeth.* IV. pr. vi. (1886) 106 It is constreynyd in to symplicite, þat is to seyn in to vnmoeuablete, and it cesith..to fletyn diuersely. *c* **1400** *Lanfranc's Cirurg.* 140 Vnmouablete of alle þe membris outcept þe lacertis of þe brest.

**Unmo·vably,** *adv.* (UN-[1] 11, 5 b.) *c* **1400** *Found. St. Bartholemew's* (1923) 13 Those thyngis ..[given] to the chirche vnmoueably & stedfastly to beholde. *c* **1440** *Gesta Rom.* lvi. 240 (Harl. MS.), He that..wolle not..leeve synne,..but lithe stille in synnys vnmevabely. *c* **1460** *Oseney Reg.* 161 And þat, as þenne markyng whas i-sette by boundes i-sett.., Surely and vnmevabely hit be keped. **1513** DOUGLAS *Æneid* IV. i. 33 Fix[i]t in my mynd unmovably, That [etc.]. *a* **1555** R. TAYLOR in Coverdale *Lett. Mart.* (1564) 177 But God be praysed,.. I am vnmoueably setled vpon the rocke. *a* **1619** FOTHERBY *Atheom.* I. iv. § 4 (1622) 23 A radicall..conclusion, vnmoueably grounded in the heart of a man. **1683** *Apol. Prot. France* vi. 75 The greatest Protectors of the holy See, to which they have always unmoveably held. **1743** J. ELLIS *Knowl. Div. Th.* 372 So the evil Angels are as unmoveably determined still to adhere to that which is Evil.

**Unmo·ved,** *ppl. a.* [UN-[1] 8, 5 b.]

**1.** Not moved by emotion or excitement; unaffected, undisturbed; collected, calm.

*c* **1375** *Sc. Leg. Saints* xxxvii. (*Vincencius*) 397 His thocht wes vnmowit ay, Sa ferme wes he in cristis fay. **1561** T. NORTON *Calvin's Inst.* I. 2 They which in his absence did stand assured and vnmoued. *a* **1586** SIDNEY *Arcadia* I. i, Holding his head up full of unmoved majestie. **1647** CLARENDON *Hist. Reb.* I. § 44 When he found the Duke unmoved by all the considerations and arguments..he had offered. **1697** DRYDEN *Æneis* v. 526 My soul is still the same, Unmoved with fear, and moved with martial fame. **1720** SWIFT *Fates Clergym.* Wks. 1755 II. II. 26 Only Corusodes was silent and unmoved. **1796** MME. D'ARBLAY *Camilla* IV. 326 Edgar could not hear unmoved the dialogue which ensued. **1830** TENNYSON *Poems* 39 If so be if from doubt at length, Truth may stand forth unmoved of change. **1831** JAMES *Philip Augustus* III. vii, The chilling unmoved glance of her large dark eye. **1885** 'MRS. ALEXANDER' *At Bay* v, The unmoved composure of the practised detectives.

† **b.** Unprovoked. *Obs.*[—1]

**1634** SIR T. HERBERT *Trav.* 212 The Mannatee or Cowfish..is..a gentle fish vnmoued, and some say affects the visage of a man.

**2.** Not moved in position; unstirred; remaining fixed or steady.

*c* **1440** *Promp. Parv.* 366/1 On-mevyd, *immotus.* **1513** DOUGLAS *Æneid* VII. v. 131 His sycht vnmovyt to the erd dyd he prent. **1628** MAY *Virg. Georg.* II. 51 Therefore no windes..orethrow Those Trees; for many yeares unmov'd they grow. **1697** DRYDEN *Virg. Past.* x. 45 Unmoved, and with dejected eyes, he mourned. **1744** BERKELEY *Siris* § 1 The vessel must stand close covered and unmoved three days. *a* **1795** PHILIDOR *Studies of Chess* (1817) 99 An unmoved Rook. **1841** JAMES *Brigand* ix, The heavy vapours hung unmoved around the peaks. **1887** *Field* 15 Oct. 603/2 The unmoved ground..is very dry a few inches from the surface.

**3.** (See MOVE *v.* 5 b.)

**1843** R. J. GRAVES *Syst. Clin. Med.* xiv. 153 He told me he passed the night in great torture, and that the bowels were still unmoved.

Hence **Unmo·vedness.**

**1628** FELTHAM *Resolves* II. xix. 61 They set him almost in the Throne of a Deitie; ascend him to an vnmouednesse. **1687** BOYLE *Martyrd. Theodora* xi. 120 All the unmov'dness of mind, she us'd to be Mistress of.

**Unmo·vedly,** *adv.* (UN-[1] 11; cf. prec.)

**1611** BEAUM. & FL. *Philaster* I. i, If you intreat, I will unmov'dly hear. **1689** POPPLE tr. *Locke's 1st Let. Toleration* 17 Then they can bear most patiently, and unmovedly, the Contagion of Idolatry. **1846** LANDOR *Imag. Conv.* Wks. II. 250/2 Quietly and unmovedly as she was standing. **1883** MYERS *Ess., Mod.* (1885) 44 Through all the perils of the siege they sat unmovedly,..perfecting the new constitution.

**Unmo·ving,** *ppl. a.* [UN-[1] 10.]

**1.** Not moving; devoid of motion.

*c* **1425** WYNTOUN *Cron.* II. xii. 1178 Þan gert he stand Baith sone and mone, still vnmovand As wer þe space all of a day. **1594** *Selimus* 1442 All those moving and unmoving eyes. **1598** FLORIO, *Stella fissa*, a fixed, vnmouing starre. **1610** HEALEY *St. Aug. Citie of God* XIV. ix. 510 The eternall beatitude shall haue both ioye and loue,..firme, and vnmoouing. **1705** CHEYNE *Philos. Princ.* I. (1715) 186 Without this Impulse, they had continued unactive, unmoving Heaps of Matter. **1804** J. GRAHAME *Sabbath* 10 Calmness seems thron'd on yon unmoving cloud. *a* **1834** COLERIDGE *Shaks. Notes* (1849) 35 Succession of time and unmoving eternity. **1900** *Scribner's Mag.* Sept. 289 Everywhere were vast ghostly figures unmoving in the moonlight.

**2.** Unaffecting; stirring no feeling. *rare*[—1].

**1698** NORRIS *Pract. Disc.* IV. 54 How flat and insipid, how dead and unmoving must all Discourse of it be to him!

**Unmo·vingly,** *adv.* (UN-[1] 11.) [1775 ASH.] **1831** JAMES *Phil. Augustus* III. iv, Her eyes were fixed unmovingly on the ground. **Unmow·ed,** *ppl. a.* [UN-[1] 8.] = next. **1763** MILLS *Pract. Husb.* III. 325 [He] ordered a small part of a meadow..to be left unmowed till the seeds were fit for gathering.

**Unmow·n,** *ppl. a.* (UN-[1] 8 b.)

**1549** *Compl. Scot.* vi. 66 Ane onmauen medou. **1557** TUSSER *100 Points Husb.* xcii, Doune with thy hedlondes, ..leaue neuer a dalop, vnmoune or had out. **1616** W. BROWNE *Brit. Past.* II. iii. 1086 As a meade in July, which unmowne Beares in an equall height each bent and stem. **1648** HEXHAM II, *Ongemaeyt*, Vnmowne, or Vnreapt. **1809** BYRON *Bards & Rev.* 636 Let..beer undrawn, and beards unmown, display Your holy reverence for the Sabbath-day. **1820** SHELLEY *Hymn Merc.* xii, Oxen .. pastured in the flowering unmown meadows. **1830** TENNYSON *Arab. Nts.* 29 Deep inlay Of braided blooms unmown.

**Unmu·dded,** *ppl. a.* (UN-[1] 8.) **1780** *Phil. Trans.* LXXI. 450 All the unwashed and unmudded trees that I measured. **1809** W. BLAKE *Descr. Catal.* 1 Clear [water-] colours unmudded by oil. **Unmu·ddied,** *ppl. a.* (UN-[1] 8.) **1654** WHITLOCK *Zootomia* 159 Who I hope in fine, to the unmuddied judgement, it will appeare meant the Literate. **Unmu·ddled,** *ppl. a.* (UN-[1] 8.) **1840** HOWITT *Visits Remark. Places* Ser. I. 233 The Thames, there unmuddled by commerce,..flowing free and pure.

**Unmu·ffle,** *v.* [UN-[2] 4.]

**1.** *trans.* (and *refl.*). To divest of something which muffles or conceals the face.

**1611** COTGR., *Desaffubler*, to vnmuffle, vnhood, vnhoodwinke. **1629** DAVENANT *Albovine* IV. i, Were my lean Iaws unmuffled you should see me mump. *a* **1652** BROME *Queen & Concubine* IV. iv, Take off his false beard;..And let the woman be unmuffled. **1768–74** TUCKER *Lt. Nat.* (1834) I. 442 He muffled up my head all round, as with the hood of a great-coat...In this guise he held me some time...He then unmuffled and let me go. **1838** LYTTON *Alice* VII. iv, The rest..unmuffled themselves of cloaks. **1851** HAWTHORNE *Twice-told T.* II. i. 21 'Villain, unmuffle yourself!' cried he.

*fig.* and in fig. context. **1652** BENLOWES *Theoph.* XI. lxxii, Unmuffle, ye dim clouds, and disinherit From black usurping mists his spirit. **1685** LD. HALIFAX *Char. Trimmer* (1688) 28 'Twill be worth his pains to see if he [*sc.* a papist] can unmuffle himself from the Mask of Infallibility. **1886** W. ALEXANDER *St. Aug. Holiday*, etc. 137 And darkness was unmuffled, and was ripp'd Like crape from heaven's jewell'd hilt.

**b.** To remove the muffling of (a drum).

**1828–32** WEBSTER.

**2.** *intr.* To remove or cast off a muffling.

**1634** MILTON *Comus* 331 Unmuffle ye faint stars, and thou fair Moon,..Stoop thy pale visage through an amber cloud. **1830** tr. *Aristoph., Birds* 941 *Pisthetærus.* What means this? What muffling is this? *Prometheus.* After a while I will unmuffle.

**Unmu·le,** *v.* (UN-[2] 3.) **1654** GAYTON *Pleas. Notes* III. v. 100 With three hard words, [to] un-mule, un-leg, and unable, Alanso Lopez. **Unmu·llioned,** *ppl. a.* (UN-[1] 8.) **1859** JEPHSON *Brittany* II. 15 The large unmullioned windows of the aisles. **Unmu·ltipliable,** *a.* (UN-[1] 7 b.) **1628** JACKSON *Creed* VI. I. iii. § 5 His incomprehensible being, who is..most truly one, because indivisible and unmultipliable.

**Unmu·ltiplied,** *ppl. a.* (UN-[1] 8.)

**1570** BILLINGSLEY *Euclid* 128 b, The one remayning vnmultiplied, and the other being certaine times multiplied, shall be greater then it. **1817** H. T. COLEBROOKE *Algebra*, etc. 211 Now the coefficient of the root is the unmultiplied (or original) coefficient of the square unknown term.

Hence **Unmu·ltipliedly** *adv.*

**1678** CUDWORTH *Intell. Syst.* I. v. 776 It is indivisibly and unmultipliedly and illocally there.

**Unmu·mmied,** *ppl. a.* (UN-[1] 8.) **1822** BYRON *Vis. Judgem.* xi, As the mere million's base unmummied clay. **Unmu·nched,** *ppl. a.* (UN-[1] 8.) **1870** DICKENS *E. Drood* xii, Even Durdles pauses..and looks at him, with an unmunched something in his cheek. **Unmuni·tioned,** *ppl. a.* (UN-[1] 8.) **1626** R. PEEKE *Three to One* C iv b, Cales..was held Poore, Vnmand, and Vnmunitioned.

**Unmu·rdered,** *ppl. a.* (UN-[1] 8.)

**1586** J. MUSH in J. Morris *Troub. Cath. Forefathers* III. (1877) 363 Not one Catholic priest but judged as a traitor or able to escape unmurthered. *a* **1652** BROME *Damoiselle* IV. ii, How know I..that I haue a Son By thee unmurther'd. *a* **1683** OLDHAM *Poems & Transl.* (1684) 47 Poor I am only left unmurder'd yet. **1746** YOUNG *Nt. Th.* IX. 1797 How unlike The lot of man! how few of human race By their own mud unmurder'd!

**Unmu·rmured,** *ppl. a.* (UN-[1] 8.) *a* **1625** FLETCHER *Nice Valour* IV. i, That if my anger chance let fall a stroke,.. Yet it may pass unmurmur'd, undisputed.

**Unmu·rmuring,** *ppl. a.* (UN-[1] 10.)

**1784** R. BAGE *Barham Downs* II. 33 Poverty is the natural parent of..unmurmuring obedience. **1801** SOUTHEY *Thalaba* X. xxvii, I am cut off from all the ties of life, Unmurmuring. **1882** FARRAR *Early Chr.* I. 170 Then come fresh exhortations to unmurmuring hospitality.

**Unmu·rmuringly,** *adv.* (UN-[1] 11.)

**1845** F. E. PAGET *Tales Village Childr.* Ser. II. 142 The thoughts..which best enabled him to submit unmurmuringly. **1861** *Court Life at Naples* II. 119 When we are punished for our sins by pain..it should be borne unmurmuringly.

**Un-Mu·rrayed,** *a.* [UN-[1] 9.] Not described in Murray's Guide. **1873** BROWNING *Red Cott. Nt.-cap* I. 20 Meek, hitherto un-Murrayed bathing-place, Best loved of sea-coast-nook-ful Normandy! **Unmu·scled,** *ppl. a.* (UN-[1] 8.) **1748** RICHARDSON *Clarissa* (1811) VI. 362 Distended their parched mouths!—sunk their unmuscled cheeks!—dropt their under jaws! **Unmu·scular,** *a.* (UN-[1] 7.) **1825** CARLYLE *Schiller* III. 234 [Schiller] was..unmuscular and lean. **1861** READE *Cloister & H.* lii, Shallow women, that have neither read nor suffered, have an unmuscular barbarity of their own. **Unmu·se-like,** *a.* (UN-[1] 7 c.) **1754** A. MURPHY *Gray's Inn Jrnl.* No. 88, An unmuse-like Poem.

**Unmu·sical,** *a.* [UN-[1] 7.]

**1.** Of sounds: Not of a musical nature; unmelodious, harsh.

**1607** SHAKS. *Cor.* IV. v. 64 A name vnmusicall to the Volcians eares. *a* **1637** B. JONSON *Rules Tavern Acad.* ix, Let argument bear no unmusical sound. **1718** LADY M. W. MONTAGU *Let. to C'tess Bristol* 10 Apr., Their pipes..are no unmusical instruments. **1753** CIBBER *Lives Poets* I. 18 His stile..is equally unmusical and obsolete with Chaucer's. **1801** BUSBY *Dict. Mus.*, *Unmusical*, an epithet applied..to whatever is not absolutely harmonious, melodious, or agreeable to a cultivated ear. **1855** *Poultry Chron.* III. 500/2 At this time..its not unmusical cry is heard. **1880** MCCARTHY *Own Times* xlviii. IV. 22 His voice was singularly unmusical and harsh.

**2.** Of persons: Not musically gifted; not appreciative of music. Also *absol.*

**1634** CARTWRIGHT *Ordinary* II. iii, I'll..Give organs to every parish..; And so root out th' unmusical elect. **1861** tr. *Mendelssohn's Lett. Italy* 69 The Papal singers..are almost all unmusical, and do not execute even the most established pieces in tune. **1896** *Westm. Gaz.* 2 June 2/3 The unmusical admired her singing, the musical her acting.

**3.** Not based on musical principles.

**1786** T. TWINING in *Recreat. & Stud.* (1882) 132 All this is unmusical criticism, and goes upon the false notion of the words..being principal.

Hence **Unmu·sicalness.**

Also, in recent use (1890), *unmusicality.*

**1678** CUDWORTH *Intell. Syst.* I. v. 759 Matter..perpetually remains, and all other things whatsoever are but..passions and affections..thereof, as musicalness and unmusicalness.

**Unmu·sically,** *adv.* (UN-[1] 11, 5 b.)

**1609** DEKKER *Gull's Horn-bk.* I, I make a scuruy noise, and..my tunes sound vnmusically. **1631** — *Match me in London* III, The song..did to your eare Vnmusically sound. **1710** NORRIS *Chr. Prud.* vi. 172 Let the Ear be unmusically disposed, the sweetest Sounds..will give it no Entertainment. **1843** CARLYLE *Past & Pr.* III. i, The Honourable Member complains unmusically. **1896** *Advance* (Chicago) 6 Feb. 197/1 The sublime..thoughts which the eloquent preacher has not..unmusically expressed here.

**Unmu·stered,** *ppl. a.* (UN-[1] 8.) **1581** SIDNEY *Apol. Poetrie* (Arb.) 56 Therefore, though Cato misliked his vnmustered person, hee misliked not his worke.

† **Unmu·table,** *a. Obs.* [UN-[1] 7 b, 5 b.] Immutable.

**1414** BRAMPTON *Penit. Ps.* (Percy Soc.) 38 Thou art unmutable be kynd! There is no changyng foundyn in the! **1429** *Pol. Poems* (Rolls) II. 145 Prince excelent, be.. liberal of courage, unmutable. **1491** CAXTON *Vitas Patr.* (W. de W. 1495) II. 272/2 We have one unmutable rule in fastyng. **1548** UDALL *Erasm. Par. Luke* 165 b, Leat that bee dooen, whyche thy wyll beyng vnmutable hath determined. **1550** COVERDALE *Spir. Perle* viii. (1588) 93 His vnmutable truthe, wherby he doth faithfully performe all his promises.

**Unmuta·ted,** *ppl. a.* (UN-[1] 8.) **1888** SWEET *Hist. Eng. Sounds* 129 In other words it..shows the unmutated *eo.*

**Unmu·tilated,** *ppl. a.* (UN-[1] 8.)

[1775 ASH.] **1790** PENNANT *London* 105 The brazier.. buried it unmutilated, and shewed to them some broken pieces of brass in tokens of his obedience. **1825** SCOTT *Betrothed* Concl., It was an unmutilated, unspotted, and beautifully formed hand. **1860** F. MAHONY *Rel. Father Prout* 376 Thy MSS. have come down to us unmutilated by pumice-stone of palimpsestic monk. **1865** F. G. LEE *Direct. Anglic.* 44 As the unmutilated rubric directs.

**Unmu·tual,** *a.* (UN-[1] 7, 5 b.) **1593** *Tell-Troth's N. Y. Gift* A 3, What is the cause of so many housholde breaches ..but vnnaturall disagreementes by vnmutuall contractes?

**Unmu·zzle,** *v.* [UN-[2] 4 b.] *trans.* To free (a dog, etc.) from a muzzle; to remove the muzzle from. Also *fig.*

**1600** SHAKS. *A. Y. L.* I. ii. 74 *Cel.* How proue you that in the great heape of your knowledge? *Ros.* I marry, now unmuzzle your wisedome. **1639** T. DE GRAY *Expert Farrier* 280 Put a muzell upon his mouth..and the next morning unmusell him. **1645** QUARLES *Sol. Recant.* VI. 5 Why Did that corrected Twilight of his eye Vnmussle darknesse, and with morning light Redeeme the day from new baptized night? **1791** BURKE *Let. to Memb. Nat. Assemb.* Wks. VI. 43 The hell-hounds of war, on all sides, will be uncoupled and unmuzzled. **1854** EMERSON *Soc. Aims* Wks. (Bohn) III. 181 Beware of unmuzzling a valetudinarian. **1891** *Daily News* 22 Jan. 3/7 Her dog was muzzled. They unmuzzled him when they got home.

Hence **Unmu·zzling** *vbl. sb.*

**1760–72** H. BROOKE *Fool of Qual.* (1809) III. 37 A licentious unmuzzling from all restraint. **1898** *Daily News* 2 Dec. 5/1 The unmuzzling of London dogs.

**Unmu·zzled,** *ppl. a.* [UN-[1] 8 or f. prec.] Not muzzled; freed from a muzzle.

**1601** SHAKS. *Twel. N.* III. i. 130 Haue you not set mine Honor at the stake, And baited it with all th'vnmuzled thoughts That tyrannous heart can think? **1604** *Nottingham Rec.* IV. 275 Kepyng a banddog vnmusselled. **1669** *N. Riding Rec.* VI. 138 A weaver presented for keeping a mastiff unmusled. **1811** W. R. SPENCER *Poems* 40 When Pestilence was rife, And all her friends unmuzzled rush'd on life. **1891** *Daily News* 22 Jan. 3/7 His dog..was unmuzzled. Plaintiff's dog was also unmuzzled.

**Unmyste·rious,** *a.* (UN-[1] 7.)

**1746** YOUNG *Nt. Th.* IX. 825 Shall God be less miraculous, than what His hand has form'd? Shall mysteries descend From unmysterious? **1846** MRS. GORE *Eng. Char.* Introd., Lord Chancellors have become unmysterious as haberdashers. **1862** SPENCER *First Princ.* I. v. § 28 (1875) 100 The disappearance of those positive dogmas by which the mystery was made unmysterious.

**Unmy·stery,** *v.* (UN-[2] 6 b.) *a* **1661** FULLER *Worthies, Hereford* II. (1662) 40 He hath unmysteried the mysterie of Heraldry. **Unmy·stical,** *a.* (UN-[1] 7.) **1862** MAURICE *Mod. Philos.* ii. § 18. 45 He..is ready to quote..from the most unmystical authors, such as Cicero and Terence. **1899** INGE *Chr. Mysticism* 278 We cannot be surprised that the unmystical Eighteenth Century declared [etc.]. **Unmy·stified,** *ppl. a.* (UN-[1] 8.) **1844** KINGLAKE *Eothen* (1845) 106 A promontory, bare and unmystified by the gloom of surrounding groves.

† **Unna·ck,** *v. Obs.*[—1] [UN-[2] 3 + *nack* NOCK *v.* (?).] *trans.* To disarrange. **1649** G. DANIEL *Trinarch., Rich. II*, cxciv, Soe wee vn-nack the Ballance, where the Spring Beats truly, to enforce another Thing.

**Unnai·l,** *v.* [UN-[2] 3. Cf. MDu. *ontnaghelen* (Du. *-nagelen*), OHG. *innagalen* (G. *entnageln*).]

**1.** *trans.* To undo or unfasten in structure by the extraction or removal of nails.

**1470–85** MALORY *Arthur* II. xviii. 97 Their hawberkes vnnailled that naked they were on euery syde. **1523** LD. BERNERS *Froiss.* I. ccccxii. 718 They made all yᵉ bridge to be vnnayled, redy to be broken downe. **1595** *Caxton's Blanchardyn* B ij, Vnnayling his armor.., he sent him to carry newes of Blanchardines valure. **1704** tr. *I. le Fevre's Memoir* 87 The Almoner..caus'd the Coffin to be unnail'd again. **1884** STEVENSON in *St. James's Gaz.* 10 Apr. (1899) 4/2 If we do possess these opposite gifts, we must unnail the scaffolding.

**2.** To free (artillery) from being spiked.

**1562** WHITEHORNE *Ord. Souldiours* 34 The spediest way to vnnaile them, is firste to charge againe all suche peses of artillerie, with smaller bullettes then their ordinarie.

**3.** To detach or unfasten from something by the removal of nails.

**1598** ROWLANDS *Betraying of Christ* 55 Hands and feet they carefull did vn-naile, Letting the body downe. **1668** EVELYN tr. *Freart's Idea Perf. Paint.* 51 At the foot.. stands the B. Virgin,..whiles Joseph of Arimathea and Nicodemus un-nail our Lord. **1683** MOXON *Mech. Exerc., Printing* xxiv. ⁋ 3 He cannot alter the position of the Rounce without un-nailing and nailing the Girts again. **1797** *Trans. Soc. Arts* XV. 256 This is done by unnailing from the board a part on each side. **1846** LANDOR *Exam. Shaks.* Wks. II. 273/2 Having..unnailed from our chapels, many dozens of decent saints. **1858** GLENNY *Gard. Every-day Bk.* 19/1 We must think it no trouble to unnail even large branches.

*absol.* **1683** MOXON *Mech. Exerc., Printing* xxiv. 278 The Press-man, without nailing or un-nailing, Sets the Rounce to what Position he will.

Hence **Unnai·ling** *vbl. sb.*

**1622** MABBE tr. *Aleman's Guzman d'Alf.* II. 258 Even to the vnnayling from heaven, of the Sunne, and the Moone. **1756** NUGENT *Gr. Tour, France* IV. 99 A picture of the unnailing from the cross,..which is greatly admired.

**Unnai·led,** *ppl. a.* (UN-¹ 8.)

**1625** K. LONG tr. *Barclay's Argenis* I. i. 13 Two plankes artificially closed, but left unnayled. **1748** *Anson's Voy.* II. iii. 143 The scuttle of the fore-castle..happened to be unnailed. *Ibid.*, The unnailed scuttle. **1829** H. HAWTHORN *Visit Babylon* 7 The unnailed branches of the honeysuckle. **1896** *Rural World* 4 Jan. 5/3 Leave the.. nectarine trees unnailed to keep the blossoms as backward as possible.

**† Unnai·t,** *a.* and *adv. Obs.* [UN-¹ 7, 11 b + NAIT *a.* Cf. ON. *úneyt-r* useless, incapable.] Useless, unprofitable, vain.

*a* **1250** *Ancr. R.* 130 Siggeð þet ȝe beoð unnute [*Trin. MS.* unneite] þrelles. *a* **1300** *Cursor M.* 23566 If þai a-noþer heuen wroght, It war vnnait and al for noght. *a* **1340** HAMPOLE *Psalter* xxviii. 7 Þa þat..gas agayn til besynes of þe warld & vnnayte thynge. *c* **1380** WYCLIF *Sel. Wks.* III. 29 Folk þat haþ foule lippis, foulid wiþ vein speche and unnayt. *c* **1400** *Rule St. Benet* (Prose) 9 Wicke þohtis do oway..; and gete yure muþes fra unait wordis.

**b.** As *adv.* Unprofitably, vainly.

*a* **1300** *Cursor M.* 5976 'Do wai,' þai said, 'þou speckes vnnait'.

Hence **† Unnai·tlike** *adv.*, **-ness, -ship.** *Obs.*

*a* **1300** *E. E. Psalter* xxxviii. 15 Vnnaitlike to-droued ilke man is. *Ibid.* xl. 6 Vnnaitnes Spake he, his hert samened to him wicnes. *a* **1300** *Cursor M.* 10135 For-þi rede i þaim þat yee here..And leue your vnnaitschip a quile.

**Unna·ked,** *ppl. a.* (UN-¹ 8.) **1628** *Robin Goodfellow* II. (Percy Soc.) 40 Then..lay I them in the doore, naked or unnaked I care not whether.

**Unna·m(e)able,** *a.* (UN-¹ 7 b.)

In frequent use from *c* 1840.

**1610** HEALY *St. Aug. Citie of God* 354 God is celestiall, ineffable, and un-name-able. **1652** GAULE *Magastrom.* 270 Invisible and unnameable powers and persons. **1824** MISS MITFORD *Village* Ser. I. 234 Oh the saltings, the picklings, ..the unnamed and unnameable confectionery doings over which she presided! **1874** LISLE CARR *J. Gwynne* I. iv. 120 Her lustrous eyes wide distended with unnamable horror.

*absol.* **1818** MILMAN *Samor* XI. 387 Th' Unnameable, he fix'd On his flint pedestal.

Hence **Unnameabi·lity.**

**1862** CARLYLE *Fredk. Gt.* XIV. v. III. 695 The Reich..will go ever deeper into anarchies and unnameabilities.

**Unna·med,** *ppl. a.* [UN-¹ 8. Cf. OFris. *unnamed, onnamd*, MDu. *ongenaemt* (Du. *-naamd*).]

**1.** Not mentioned or specified by name.

**1509** BARCLAY *Ship of Folys* 162 They shall vnnamyd my shyppis haue in cure. **1526** R. WHYTFORD *Martiloge* (1893) 65 A woman vnnamed, with her two chylder twyndles. **1599** DALLAM in *Early Voy. Levant* (Hakl. Soc.) 81, I have not time now to wryte them, but of force muste leave them un-named untill a time of better Leasur. *c* **1620** FLETCHER *False One* II. ii, Cæsar's angry, And our design to please him lost and perish'd; Be glad thou art unnam'd. **1667** MILTON *P. L.* x. 595 Stil at Hels dark threshold to have sate watch, Unnam'd, undreaded. **1728** RAMSAY *Archers diverting themselves* 136 Dear nymphs unnam'd, lay not the blame On us. **1798** S. & HT. LEE *Canterb T.* II. 86 [She] left unnamed, and unprovided for, the young woman she had raised so far above her condition. **1836** [MRS. MAITLAND] *Lett. fr. Madras* (1843) 4 A number of hitherto unnamed gentlemen, who sit down to eat and drink. **1866** MEREDITH *Vittoria* xlv, Throwing the burden..on some unnamed third person.

**2.** Not provided with a name; nameless.

**1611** DONNE *Anat. World* 35 As a child kept from the font, thou unnam'd had'st laid. **1667** MILTON *P. L.* XII. 140 From Hamath Northward to the Desert South (Things by thir names I call, though yet unnam'd). **1848** BAILEY *Festus* (ed. 3) 219 All terms are relative expressing bound, But Deity, interminable being, Hath ever therefore been unnamed. **1868** MORRIS *Earthly Par.* I. I. 338 Robe..Inwrought with flowers of unnamed colours bright. **1876** SMILES *Sc. Natur.* x. 202 Among the plants, were a great number unnamed.

*absol.* **1840** CARLYLE *Heroes* i. ⁋ 13 The Highest Being reveals himself in man. This body, these faculties, this life of ours, is it not all as a vesture for that Unnamed?

**b.** *Unnamed bone*, the innominate bone (INNOMINATE *a.* 3).

**1845** *Encycl. Metrop.* VII. 329/1 [The sides] of the Hipgirdle [are]..formed..by the pair of Unnamed..bones, each consisting..of three pieces whilst the bird is young, but becoming consolidated early. *Ibid.*, Of the Unnamed bone.

**Unna·pkined,** *ppl. a.* (UN-¹ 8.) **1607** BEAUM. & FL. *Woman-Hater* I. iii, An un-napkin'd Lawyers greasie fist.

**Unna·pped,** *ppl. a.* (UN-¹ 8.) **1619** FLETCHER *Knt. Malta* I. i, Did I attempt her with a thread-bare name, un-napt with meritorious actions. **1620** SHELTON *Quix.* II. xxxviii. 248 Countesse Trifaldi.., clad all in finest vn-napped Bayes. **1884** *Imp. Dict.* IV. 509/3 Unnapped cloth.

**† Unna·th,** *v. Obs.*⁻¹ [UN-¹ 3; cf. NATHE.] *trans.* To take the nave or naves off. **1637** N. WHITING *Albino & Bellama* 1304 Methinks I see the sun..Unnath his car, and throw his whipstaff by.

**Unna·tion,** *v.* (UN-² 6 b.) **1646** W. PRICE *Mans Delinquencie* 39 Wee have deserved to be un-nation'd, un-Church'd by a Bill of divorce from heaven.

**Unna·tional,** *a.* (UN-¹ 7.)

**1753** HANWAY *Trav.* I. I. viii. 54 Of the partial and unnational manner in which the trade was managed. **1763** WILKES *Corr.* (1805) I. 227 Three known, hackneyed tools of that very minister, who were..to pursue the same system, the same unnational measures. **1834** G. CROLY *Butler's Anal.* p. xxvi, The rash and unnational peace of Utrecht. **1865** W. G. PALGRAVE *Arabia* II. 366 Their easy-going, unnational, indistinctive character.

**Unna·tive,** *a.* (UN-¹ 7.) **1712** BLACKMORE *Creation* VII. 413 British Gibbons..makes that tree unnative charms assume. **1734** THOMSON *Liberty* I. 336 Against depressing skies,..How could thy spirits hold? where vigour find, Forced fruits to tear from their unnative soil?

**Unna·tive,** *v.* (UN-² 6 b.) **1855** MRS. GASKELL *North & S.* xli, Frederick had written..a pretty vehement letter, containing his renunciation of England as his country; he wished he could unnative himself.

**Unna·tural,** *a.* (*sb.*) [UN-¹ 7, 5 b.]

**1.** Not in accordance or conformity with the physical nature of persons or animals.

*a* **1425** tr. *Arderne's Treat. Fistula*, etc. 60 Also in þe veynez ar gendred vnnaturale humours. *Ibid.* 68 [It] doþ away wicked colour & vnnatural, and it restoreþ natural colour. **1541** R. COPLAND *Guydon's Quest. Chirurg.* B j, He ought to knowe the vnnaturall thynges, that is yᵉ meate, the drynke, &c. **1597** A. M. tr. *Guillemeau's Fr. Chirurg.* 1 b/1 *Physiologia*..wherin is to be..noted on the seaven vnnaturalle thinges. **1614** LATHAM *Falconry* I. xiii. 48 Which is vnnaturall, and therfore must needs be vnwholsome [for the hawk]. **1617** WOODALL *Surg. Mate* Wks. (1639) 301 After extraction of unnaturall things, forced into the wound. **1774** GOLDSM. *Nat. Hist.* (1776) IV. 71 The Black Rat..is.. possessed of all the voracious and unnatural appetites of the former. **1805** *Med. Jrnl.* XIV. 246 The mother..was very solicitous about her on account of this, her unnatural situation, as she always thought it. **1846** MRS. A. MARSH *Father Darcy* II. xi. 179 The tones of their voice sounded..hollow, hoarse, and unnatural. **1890** *Retrospect Med.* CII. 236 The unnatural state occasioned by the presence of sugar.

**2.** Not in accordance or agreement with the usual course of nature. Also *absol.*

*a* **1513** FABYAN *Chron.* ci. (1533) 42/1 Berynge in mynde the vnnaturall deth of her parentes. **1605** SHAKS. *Macb.* II. iv. 10 'Tis vnnaturall, Euen like the deed that's done. **1653** W. RAMESEY *Astrol. Restored* 250 There shall be..unnatural Dews and Rains. **1722** WOLLASTON *Relig. Nat.* i. 13 Nothing can interfere with any proposition that is true, but it must likewise interfere with nature,..and consequently be unnatural, or wrong in nature. **1814** SCOTT *Lord of Isles* v. xv, Faintly the moon's pale beams supply That ruddy light's unnatural dye. **1846** TRENCH *Mirac.* 15 The miracle is not thus unnatural, while the unnatural, the contrary to order, is of itself the ungodly. **1854** KINGSLEY *Misc.* (1859) I. 85 Unnatural weather, so that a fourteen days' voyage takes forty days.

**b.** Abnormal; monstrous.

**1516** *Reg. Privy Seal Scotl.* I. 431/2 The said Johne is be the hand of God dum and defe and unnaturale. **1632** LITHGOW *Trav.* II. 52 Which vnnaturall Childe being brought, I was amazed..to behold the deformity of Nature.

**c.** Devoid of natural qualities or characteristics; artificial.

**1746** FRANCIS tr. *Horace, Epist.* I. x. 28 Among your Columns, rich with various Dyes, Unnatural Woods with aukward Art arise. **1827** STEUART *Planter's G.* (1828) 7 Whatever there was of unnatural or formal,..is now banished from the English garden. **1828** LYTTON *Pelham* III. iii, Hence, you perceive all people timid, stiff, unnatural, and ill at ease.

**3.** At variance with natural feeling or moral standards; excessively cruel or wicked.

**1529** MORE *Suppl. Soulys* Wks. 314/2 In this thei shew their affeccion much more vnnatural & abhominable [etc.]. **1571** *Act* 13 *Eliz.* c. 2 § 1 Moste wycked and unnatural Rebellyon hathe ensued. **1612** DRAYTON *Poly-olb.* xi. 178 The vnnatural'st deed that e're was done by man. **1642** D. ROGERS *Naaman* To Rdr. § 2 Even an unnaturall cruelty. **1732** *Col. Rec. Pennsylv.* III. 497 A final Period was to be putt to all such unnatural Differences. *a* **1800** COWPER *Odyss.* (ed. 2) II. 175 To thrust the mother forth, Who gave me birth.., were a deed Unnat'ral and impossible to me. **1828** SCOTT *Tapestr. Chamb.* ad fin., In yon fatal apartment incest and unnatural murder were committed. **1864** KINGSLEY *Rom. & T.* i. 4 They tar them on to the unnatural fight.

**b.** Of persons: Devoid of natural feeling; acting at variance with the dictates of nature.

**1552** HULOET, Vnnaturall to parentes, *bactri, bactriani.* **1579** GOSSON *Sch. Abuse* (Arb.) 66 Iupiter,..though hee were a cruell tyrant, an vnnaturall childe,..by Poets is made the king of gods. **1611** SHAKS. *Wint. T.* II. iii. 113 A most vnworthy, and vnnaturall Lord Can doe no more. **1685** in P. Wright *New Bk. Martyrs* (1784) 804/1 As vnnatural as children that seek the ruin of their parents. **1819** SCOTT *Ivanhoe* xxix, The messengers of Jehovah's wrath to the unnatural child, who thinks of a stranger's captivity before a parent's. **1836** THIRLWALL *Greece* III. xix. 97 It would be impolitic in the Athenians..to countenance the revolt of an unnatural colony. **1871** JOWETT *Plato* II. 408 Then he is a parricide, and a cruel unnatural son to an aged parent.

**† 4.** Illegitimate; having no natural right or claim. *Obs.*

*c* **1550** BALE *K. Johan* (Camden) 4 *K. J.* They are thy chylderne, thou oughtest to say them good. *Y.* Nay, bastardes they are, unnaturall by the rood. **1570** *Homily agst. Rebellion* ⁋ 1 It may seeme more then maruell, that anye subiectes woulde..holde with vnnaturall forraigne vsurpers.

**5.** At variance with what is natural, usual, or to be expected; unusual, strange.

*a* **1586** SIDNEY *Arcadia* I. i, They ranne unto him, and pulling him backe,..by force stickled that unnatural fray. **1647** CLARENDON *Hist. Reb.* II. § 104 With some cloudiness (which was not unnatural) and trouble in his countenance, he desired his Majesty to give him leave to Travel. **1668** DRYDEN *Dram. Poesy* Ess. (ed. Ker) I. 72 It is unnatural for any one in a gust of passion to speak long together. **1729** BUTLER *Serm.* (1848) 34 Since such an action is utterly disproportionate to the nature of man, it is in the strictest and most proper sense unnatural. **1780** *Mirror* No. 100, An unnatural violence done to the work of his favourite poet. **1849** MACAULAY *Hist. Eng.* v. I. 533 What seemed to his associates to be his unnatural recklessness and audacity. **1850** BAYNES *Analytic* 13 Unnatural, indirect or irregular predication..was..that, to wit, in which the species was predicated of the genus.

**b.** *sb.* An unnatural thing or state.

**1682** SIR T. BROWNE *Chr. Mor.* III. § 20 No practice being able to naturalize such unnaturals or make a man rest content not to be himself.

**Unna·turalism.** (UN-¹ 12.)

**1754** WARBURTON *Bolingbroke's Philos.* ii. 67 Which, however, they were ready to distinguish..from the Unnaturalism (if we may so term it) of ranker Atheism. **1840** T. GORDON tr. *W. Menzel's Ger. Lit.* I. 35 The writings of [our nation]..have a tinge of supernaturalism or unnaturalism; something strange, ghost-like, and ill-suited for this world. **1889** *Harper's Mag.* Nov. 963/1 French naturalism is better at its worst than French unnaturalism at its best.

**Unna·turalist.** *nonce-wd.* [See UNNATURAL *a.* 3 b.] One devoid of natural feeling. **1835** SOUTHEY *Doctor* interchap. xiii, Me, a poor unit of humanity, to be treated like a polypus under the scissors of an experimental naturalist, or unnaturalist.

**Unnatura·lity.** *rare.* [UN-¹ 12.]

**1.** Unnatural feeling or conduct.

*a* **1548** HALL *Chron., Hen. VIII*, 229 b, What vnkyndnes and vnnaturalitie may we impute to you. **1691** Z. HAIG in J. Russell *Haigs* (1881) xi. 324 If I had had any such unnaturality lodged in my breast.

**2.** *Sc.* Imbecility, weak-mindedness.

**1823** GALT *Entail* lii, He has a because o' his ain for keeping his thumb on Watty's unnaturality.

**Unna·turalizable,** *a.* (UN-¹ 7 b.) **1833** LYTTON *Eng. & English* IV. ix. 394 Its minute details of alien and unnaturalizable mythology are carefully preserved.

**Unna·turalize,** *v.* [UN-² 6 c *b.*]

**1.** *trans.* and *refl.* To deprive of natural character; to make unnatural in disposition.

*a* **1613** OVERBURY *A Wife* (1630) M vj, Religion is commonly his pretence of discontent, though he can be of all religions; therefore truely of none. Thus by vnnaturalizing himselfe [etc.]. **1625** LAUD *Serm.* Wks. 1847 I. 69 In all that large discourse..Saint Paul..conceives at full how corruption can unnaturalize nature itself. **1651** JANE *Image Unbr.* 62 Rebellion hath not vnnaturalized them. *a* **1656** HALES *Gold. Rem.* I. (1673) 145 Here he strives, as it were, to unnaturalize himself, and lay by his natural sweetness of disposition. **1894** *Daily News* 5 Oct. 6/5 None the less do they feel the sad influence of the mixed education that has ..unnaturalised them.

**2.** To divest of the status or privileges of a native-born subject.

**1698** J. COLLIER *Immor. Stage* vi. (1730) 157 Any Roman who turn'd Actor was..to be..as it were disincorporated, and unnaturalized. **1754** A. MURPHY *Gray's Inn Jrnl.* No. 84, Mr. Arne..will apply for a private Bill to unnaturalize him, that he may then enjoy the Privileges of an Englishman. **1817** *Parl. Deb.* 1830 This petitioner prayed to be unnaturalized, or to be brought to trial.

**3.** To make unnatural or artificial. Also *absol.*

**1741** RICHARDSON *Pamela* (1824) I. 6 It may disguise the facts,..and unnaturalize the incidents. **1767** *Ann. Reg., Ess.* 196/2 If they should thus endeavour to unnaturalize their singing, they would render it harsh. **1839** DARLEY *Beaum. & Fletcher's Wks.* I. Introd. p. xxv, Our poets.. idealise farther than he; that is, they unnaturalise, often making beautiful chimeras of their virtuous characters.

Hence **Unna·turalizing** *vbl. sb.*

**1647** N. WARD *Simple Cobler* 47 Such usurpations by Rulers, are the unnaturallizings of nature, disfranchisements of Freedome.

**Unna·turalized,** *ppl. a.* (UN-¹ 8.)

**1611** COTGR., *Morte-main*,..the..estate left by..vnnaturalized strangers, and vnaffranchized villaines. **1621** BRATHWAIT *Nat. Embassie* Ded., Nature..thinks she can mend her selfe by being adorned with vnnaturalized ornaments. **1652** EVELYN *St. France* 37 The goods of strangers dying in France, most inhospitably escheat to the King; putting.. no difference between them, and Bastards unnaturalized. **1828–32** WEBSTER, *Unnaturalized*, a.,..not made a citizen by authority. [Freq. in recent use (1914–), of aliens.]

**Unna·turally,** *adv.* [UN-¹ 11.]

**1.** In a manner at variance with normal human nature; with unnatural depravity, wickedness, or want of feeling.

*c* **1485** *Digby Myst.* (1882) IV. 537 Was his..gudnese owt of thy mynd So vn-naturallye? **1540** *Act* 32 *Hen. VIII*, c. 24 § 1 Knightis of Sainct Johnes..have unnaturally..maynteynid the usurped powre..of the Bishop of Rome. **1562** J.

HEYWOOD *Prov. & Epigr.* (1867) 96 Alas mother what is the why, That ye draw from vs vnnaturally? **1610** HOLLAND *Camden's Brit.* 465 The yong man..most vnnaturally waged war against his owne father. **1634** SIR T. HERBERT *Trav.* 30 He..had most vnnaturally..caused his elder Brother..[to] be murdred. **1719** DE FOE *Crusoe* II. (Globe) 361 They had acted..unnaturally by their Countrymen.

**2.** In a manner differing from what is natural or normal; abnormally.

**1611** FLORIO, *Distortione*, a turning awry vnnaturally. **1614** LATHAM *Falconry* I. viii. 31 The fire..pierceth into the bodie, and heateth it most vnnaturallie. **1668** DRYDEN *Dram. Poesy* Ess. (ed. Ker) I. 95 Where you see both the clauses are placed unnaturally, that is, contrary to the common way of speaking. **1721** SOUTHERNE *Fate Capua* IV. i, It was a task unnaturally impos'd. **1848** W. H. KELLY tr. *L. Blanc's Hist. Ten Y.* II. 283 Words of malediction not unnaturally marked his parting adieus. **1878** BRISTOWE *Th. & Pract. Med.* (ed. 2) 850 The former may attain the bulk of a bullock's kidney, and the latter is usually unnaturally small.

**Unna·turalness.** [f. UNNATURAL *a.*]

**1.** Unnatural conduct or disposition.

**1537** CROMWELL in Merriman *Life & Lett.* (1902) II. 86 Promysing hym..forgeuenes..of his most shamefull ingratitude, vnnaturalnes, conspiracie against his honour. **1550** W. LYNNE tr. *Carion's Cron.* 36 Thys cruell dede declareth the vnnaturalnesse of the Barbarous nation. **1643** TRAPP *Comm. Gen.* ix. 25 Their parents also through their unnaturalness are compell'd to curse them. **1689** D. GRANVILLE *Lett.* (Surtees No. 37) 97, I am not..guilty in the lest wise of..injustice and unnaturallness to my fellow-subjects. **1703** QUICK *Dec. Wife's Sister* 26 A Prodigy of Baseness, Unnaturalness and Ungratefulness. **1758** JORTIN *Erasmus* I. 547 Burnet hath retracted his mistake that this Lord..sat in judgment upon his daughter, which would have impeached him of great unnaturalness.

**2.** Unnatural character.

**1605** B. JONSON *Volpone* III. v, That the unnaturalness..of the act..would sure enrage him. **1633** T. JAMES *Voy.* 77 This vnnaturalnesse of the season did torment our men. **1664** INGELO *Bentiv. & Ur.* VI. 349 The Unnaturalness of such Disobedience will appear yet farther. **1859** GEO. ELIOT *A. Bede* xliii, The unnaturalness of her crime. **1865** PUSEY *Truth Eng. Ch.* 12 The unnaturalness and strangeness of the facts. **1884** *Spectator* 4 Oct. 1302/1 The unnaturalness of the situations in which he acts a part.

**3.** Want of natural grace or ease.

? **1803** DOROTHY WORDSWORTH *Recoll. Tour* (1875) 49 The unnaturalness of a modern garden. **1870** LOWELL *Study Wind.* 205 What we call unnaturalness always has its spring in a man's thinking too much about himself. **1876** A. SIDGWICK *Gr. Prose* § 107 He will..be saved from falling into many unnaturalnesses of expression.

**Unna·ture,** *sb.* (UN-[1] 12. Cf. G. *unnatur*, Du. *onnatuur.*)

**1843** CARLYLE *Past & Pr.* III. i. 193 *Un*nature, what we call Chaos, holds nothing in it but vacuities, devouring gulfs. **1858** H. BUSHNELL *Nat. & Supernat.* ii. (1864) 46 So as to be rather unnature, after all, than nature.

**Unna·ture,** *v.* (UN-[2] 6 b. Cf. MDu. *onnaturen.*) Also **Unna·turing** *ppl. a.*

*a* **1586** SIDNEY *Arcadia* III. x, A right heavenly Nature indeed, as it were unnaturing them, doth so bridle them. *a* **1628** F. GREVIL *Inquis. Fame & Hon.* xix, To be nothing to subsistence is A fatall, and unnaturing award. **1640** REYNOLDS *Passions* xv. 141 He can hardly so unnature himselfe, as still to feed on those vanities. **1865** *Reader* 11 March 286/1 Dr. Manning seems to have unnatured himself.

**Unnau·tical,** *a.* (UN-[1] 7.) **1852** MUNDY *Antipodes* (1857) 185 His great rough hands fumbling the small tapes into all sorts of un-nautical knots. **Unnavigabi·lity.** (UN-[1] 12, 5 b; cf. next.) **1835** *Edin. Rev.* LX. 460 We must leave the demonstration of its unnavigability to repose with the..demonstrations of the permeability of the Polar Sea. **1884** LD. HARRIS in *Nat. Rev.* March 125 Frustrated by the unnavigability of its upper waters.

**Unna·vigable,** *a.* [UN-[1] 7 b, 5 b.]

**1.** Incapable of being sailed on or over; not admitting of navigation.

**1579–80** NORTH *Plutarch* (1595) 1 Deepe drye sands without water, full of foule ill fauoured venimous beasts, or much mudde vnnauigable. **1604** E. G[RIMSTONE] *D'Acosta's Hist. Indies* I. xxii. 72 The sea was made unnavigable, through the aboundance of banckes, rockes. **1616** HEALEY *Theophrastus* To the Reader, In Winter, the Seas were lockt vp;..vtterly vnnauigable. **1697** DRYDEN *Æneis* VI. 341 There th' unnavigable Lake extends. **1719** DE FOE *Crusoe* II. (Globe) 595 An unnavigable Ocean, where Ship never sail'd. **1798** S. & HT. LEE *Canterb. T.* II. 440 A river,—wholly unnavigable from its rude course and stony bed. **1836** W. IRVING *Astoria* I. 181 The men returned, therefore, in despair, and declared the river unnavigable. **1898** F. T. BULLEN in *Nat. Rev.* Aug. 856 The unnavigable coast of Palawan.

**b.** *fig.* or in fig. context.

**1656** COWLEY *Pindar. Odes, Praise of P.* i, Pindars unnavigable Song Like a swoln Flood from some steep Mountain pours along. **1688** PRIOR *Ode on Exod. iii. 14* ii, Yet cease to hope thy short-liv'd Bark shall ride Down spreading Fate's unnavigable Tide. **1693** DRYDEN *Juvenal* x. 13 Some who the depths of Eloquence have found, In that unnavigable Stream were Drown'd. **1768–74** TUCKER *Lt. Nat.* (1834) I. 610 Nor would the unnavigable gulph utterly exclude his hopes.

**c.** Adverse to navigation.

*a* **1641** BP. MOUNTAGU *Acts & Mon.* (1642) 253 He puts to Sea..at an unseasonable, and unnavigable time of the yeare.

**2.** Of a vessel: Incapable of being navigated.

**1755** MAGENS *Insurances* II. 139 When a Ship insured is become unnavigable.

**Unna·vigated,** *ppl. a.* (UN-[1] 8.) [**1775** ASH.] **1777** COOK *Voy.* I. Introd. p. xxvi, To traverse a far greater space of sea, till then unnavigated. *a* **1796** ADML. FORBES in Cook *Voy.* (1842) I. p. xix, They have discovered seas unnavigated and unknown before.

† **Unne,** *v. Obs.* Forms: *Inf.* 1 unnan, 3 unnen. *Pres. indic.* 1 ann, onn, 1, 3 an, 3 on (also 3 unne, unnest), *pl.* 1 unnon, 3 unnen (unneð). *Pres. subj.* 1, 3 unne (3 hunne). *Pa. t.* 1, 3 uþe, uðe (3 ouþe); *pl.* 1 uþon, uðon, 3 uðen. *Pa. pple.* 3 i-unnen, unen, unned. Cf. I-UNNE *v.* [OE. *unnan*, = OS. *unnan*, OHG. *unnan, unnen* (MHG. *unnen*), MDu. *onnen*, ON. *unna* (Icel., Norw., Swed. *unna*, Da. *unde*), one of the class of preterite-present verbs. The stem *ann-* is the base of Goth. *anst-s*, OE. *ést* ESTE *sb.*]

**1.** *trans.* To grant, allow, give (freely).

In OE. construed with the genitive.

*Beowulf* 1225 Ic þe an tela sinc₃estreona. *a* **900** *O. E. Chron.* an. 755 (Parker MS.), þa ₃ebead he him hiera a₃enne dom feos & londes, ₃if hie him þæs rices uþon. *c* **1000** *Ags. Ps.* (Thorpe) cxxxi. 4 ₃if ic minum ea₃um unne slæpes. *a* **1122** *O. E. Chron.* an. 1041 (Laud MS.), Eall folc ₃eceas Eadward to cynge..healde þa hwile þe him God unne. *c* **1205** LAY. 14851 Habbe alc god mon his rihte, ₃if godd hit an. *a* **1225** *Ancr. R.* 90 Ase quite ase ₃e beoð..weren alle þe oðre, ure Louerd hit vðe. *c* **1275** *Sinners Beware* 272 in *O. E. Misc.* 81 Loke, seyde god nuþe, Hwat ich for ou ouþe.

**2.** To wish or like (one) to have (something).

*c* **893** K. ÆLFRED *Oros.* III. i. 98 Næs na for þæm þe hie him æni₃ra goda uþen. *c* **1000** *Ags. Psalter* (Thorpe) xxxix. 17 Ondrædon him þa þe me yfeles unnon. *c* **1200** *Trin. Coll. Hom.* 79 Ne wile [he]..naðemore haten him þe..him iuel unnen. *a* **1225** *Leg. Kath.* 2344 Beoð bliðe, ich biseche ow, ₃ef ₃e me blisse unnen. *a* **1310** in Wright *Lyric P.* xi. 40 Ich unne hire wel ant heo me wo; Ycham hire frend ant heo my fo. *c* **1320** *Sir Tristrem* 1928 Meriadok was a man þat tristrem trowed ay; Miche gode he him an.

**3.** To grant, permit, or allow *that.* Also const. with inf.

*Beowulf* 2874 Hwæðre him God uðe,..þæt he hyne sylfne ₃ewræc. *c* **897** K. ÆLFRED *Gregory's Past. C.* 349 Ðæt is ðæt hwa..him unne ðæt he to ryhte ₃ecierre. *c* **950** *Lindisf. Gosp.* Matt., Int. 4 Ic onn [L. *opto*] ðæt in crist ðu ₃etreowfæsti₃. *a* **1200** *Moral Ode* 314 Ac drihte crist..of alle vre gultes unne us come bote. *a* **1225** *Ancr. R.* 380 ₃e nowen nout unnen þet eni vuel word kome of ou. *a* **1250** *Gen. & Ex.* 2249 God hunne him eði modes ben, And sende me min childre agen. **1258** *Charter Hen. III*, We willen and unnen þæt þæt vre rædesmen..habbeþ idon..be stedefæst.

*ellipt.* *a* **1250** *Owl & Night.* 1739 Ich an [*v.r.* vnne] wel, cwað the ni₃tegale.

Hence † **U·nnung** *vbl. sb. Obs.*

*a* **1225** *Ancren R.* 282 Ondes salue, ich seide, þet was feolaulich luue, and god vnnunge: & god wil, þer ase mihte of dede wonteð.

† **Unnea·led,** *ppl. a. Obs.* (UN-[1] 8.)

**1563** HYLL *Art Garden.* (1574) 72 An earthen pot, not glased, or rather vnnealed. **1745** *Phil. Trans.* XLIII. 506 Hollow Balls, made of unnealed glass. **1789** E. DARWIN *Bot. Gard.* I. 203 Thus the slight wound ingraved on glass unneal'd Runs in white lines along the lucid field.

† **Unnea·r,** *prep.* and *adv. Obs.* (UN-[1] 11 b.) **1612** J. DAVIES (Heref.) *Muse's Sacr.* Wks. (Grosart) II. 51/1 Where the Earth was couer'd with her Floud, now Citties stand, vnneere the Oceans Brim. **1648** HEXHAM II, *On-na-by*, vnneere. **Unnea·red,** *ppl. a.* (UN-[1] 8.) **1852** M. ARNOLD *Empedocles on Etna* II. 294 [The stars] renew..Night after night your courses, In echoing unnear'd silence.

**Unnea·t,** *a.* (UN-[1] 7.)

**1648** HEXHAM II, *Ongekuyst*, Vneate, Foule, or Filthy. **1849** D. J. BROWNE *Amer. Poultry Yard* (1855) 71 The white of their plumage is not brilliant, and is sure to be unneat in the places where they are usually kept. **1866** MISS MULOCK *Noble Life* xii, A letter, so unlike Helen's, so unneat, blurred and blotted.

Hence **Unnea·tness.**

**1844** N. PATERSON *Manse Gard.* 91 A great degree of unneatness in the mode of training. *a* **1864** HAWTHORNE *Dr. Grimshawe* vi, The sordidness and unneatness of the apartment.

† **Unneath,** reduced f. UNDERNEATH *prep.*

**1654** VILVAIN *Epit. Ess.* VII. lxx, A noble Pair..ly here unneath one stone. *a* **1718** PARNELL *Fairy Tale* xvi, Where by the back the youth he hung To spraul unneath the roof. *c* **1750** SHENSTONE *Ruin'd Abbey* 174 That their dishonour'd corse..Must sleep with brutes their vassals, on the field Unneath some path. **1847** HALLIWELL, *Unneath*, beneath. *Somerset.*

**Unne·bulous,** *a.* (UN-[1] 7.) **1845** tr. *Humboldt's Cosmos* I. 161 The latter ring..is a mixture of unnebulous stars. † **Unne·cessaire,** *a. Obs.*—[1] [UN-[1] 7.] Unnecessary. *c* **1440** *Pallad. on Husb.* v. 78 Vnnecessaire Is hym to plaunte yf he be wel ysowe.

**Unne·cessarily,** *adv.* [UN-[1] 11.] Without necessity; needlessly.

**1594** HOOKER *Eccl. Pol.* II. iv. § 2, I hope wee shall not seeme altogether vnnecessarily to doubt of the soundnesse of their opinion. **1610** SHAKS. *Temp.* II. i. 260 There be..Lords, that can prate As amply, and vnnecessarily As this Gonzallo. **1691** T. H[ALE] *Acc. New Invent.* 94 Excess of thickness is not only unnecessarily paid for, but it makes the Sheet worse. **1712** *Spect.* No. 283 ¶ 6 Sums which they have spent unnecessarily. **1786** COWPER *Let.* Wks. 1837 XV. 184 Again I remind you, though perhaps unnecessarily, of the two volumes. **1833** T. HOOK *Parson's Dau.* I. viii, You ..unnecessarily agitate yourself. **1879** *Cassell's Techn. Educ.* I. 312/2 Such furniture is unnecessarily heavy and clumsy.

**Unne·cessariness.** (UN-[1] 12.)

**1628** BP. HALL *Old Relig.* 117 An opinion of the vnnecessarinesse of deuotion in these holy businesses. **1685** BOYLE *Enq. Notion Nat.* v. 124 The unnecessariness of such a nature as is pretended. **1720** SIR J. STEWART in *Wodrow Corr.* (1843) II. 489 *note*, The unnecessariness of oaths, as being no security to a government. **1810** COLERIDGE *Lit. Rem.* (1838) III. 337, I should confine my grounds of opposition to the article thus stated to its unnecessariness. **1845** R. BALMER *Lect. & Disc.* II. 307 To demonstrate the unnecessariness of the miraculous gifts of the Spirit.

† **Unnecessa·riously,** *adv. Obs.*—[1] (UN-[1] 11.) **1798** *Lit. Mem. Living Authors* I. 283 The extravagant price at which a Work so unnecessariously sumptuous must be sold.

**Unne·cessary,** *a.* and *sb.* [UN-[1] 7, 12.]

**1.** Not necessary or requisite; needless.

**1548** UDALL, etc. *Erasm. Par. John* xxi. 117 b, This vnnecessarie care that Peter had of another mans death [etc.]. **1596** *Edward III*, III. i. 7 To lay aside vnnecessary soothing. **1623** BINGHAM *Xenophon* 49 To leaue behind vs our vnnecessarie stuffe, and to take with vs only such as..we stand in need of. **1655** EARL ORRERY *Parthen.* I. I. 81 If any thing could make me offended with Artabanes, 'twould be this unnecessary interceding. **1726** SWIFT *Gulliver* II. vii, That a prince..should, from a nice, unnecessary scruple,..let slip an opportunity..that [etc.]. **1791** MRS. RADCLIFFE *Rom. Forest* i, This was a very unnecessary caution to La Motte. **1823** SCOTT *Quentin D.* Introd., Ringing the dinner-bell—a most unnecessary ceremony for assembling three persons. **1898** 'MERRIMAN' *Roden's Corner* iii, A generation..much addicted to unnecessary haste.

**b.** With indefinite subject (*it*, etc.), and usually const. *to* with inf.

**1597** HOOKER *Eccl. Pol.* v. lxviii. § 2 The greatest part of the common multitude..who thinke it either vnmeet or vnnecessary to put them euen man by man. **1612** JAS. I in Ellis *Orig. Lett.* Ser. I. III. 104 To bidde a running man goe faster, quhiche is both unnecessarie and injuriouse. **1757** W. PITT in *10th Rep. Hist. MSS. Comm.* App. I. 214 His Majesty judges it unnecessary to send you particular Orders. **1771** *Junius Lett.* liv. (1788) 300 It is unnecessary to pursue the argument any farther. **1845** MCCULLOCH *Taxation* II. v. 201 This would be inconsistent alike with the objects and limits of this work, and it would, besides, be wholly unnecessary. **1869** TANNER *Clin. Med.* (ed. 2) 10 It is almost unnecessary to say that mediate percussion must be employed.

**c.** *sb. pl.* Unnecessary things.

**1559** AYLMER *Harborowe* P j, Vnfitting superfluitie in apparel, dyet, and other vnnecessaries. **1618** FLETCHER *Loyal Subject* II. v, It contains nothing But rubbish from the other rooms and unnecessaries. **1691** NORRIS *Pract. Disc.* 113 Not to burthen my Discourse or your Patience with Unnecessaries. **1748** RICHARDSON *Clarissa* (1811) IV. 184 Wanting nothing but unnecessaries. **1839** MARRYAT *Diary Amer.* Ser. I. II. 161 Very pretty did its little tiny black feet look, relieved by these expensive unnecessaries. **1881** *Q. Rev.* Jan. 51 Nowhere are the unnecessaries of life..sold at such extravagant prices as in San Francisco.

† **2.** Not requiring much. *Obs.*—[1]

**1605** SHAKS. *Lear* II. iv. 157 Age is unnecessary: on my knees I begge, That you'l vouchsafe me Rayment, Bed, and Food.

**Unnece·ssitated,** *ppl. a.* (UN-[1] 8.)

**1635** JACKSON *Creed* VIII. v. § 5 All other habitual sinnes or vices are not acquired but by many unnecessitated vicious acts. **1650** EARL MONM. tr. *Senault's Man bec. Guilty* 376 To expose himselfe voluntarily to dangers unnecessitated. **1712** BLACKMORE *Creation* VII. 480 From all compulsion free, Unforc'd, and unnecessitated, we Ourselves determine. **1813** SHELLEY *Q. Mab* VI. 172 No atom of this turbulence fulfils A vague and unnecessitated task. **1904** *Brit. Med. Jrnl.* 17 Sept. 692 The category of..unnecessitated motives, which the normal man predicates of part of his mental processes.

**Unnece·ssitating,** *ppl. a.* (UN-[1] 10.) **1738** WARBURTON *Div. Legat.* I. 48 The unnecessitating Command of an intelligent Superior. **Unnece·ssity.** (UN-[1] 12.) **1672** SIR T. BROWNE *Let. Friend* § 9 So that to be carried 'sextâ cervice' to the grave, was but a civil unnecessity.

† **Unnedd,** *ppl. a.*: see UN-[1] 3.

**Unnee·ded,** *ppl. a.* (UN-[1] 8.)

[**1775** ASH.] **1844** R. CHAMBERS *Vestiges Nat. Hist. Creation* 112 Blood circulating in particular vessels,..which are unneeded by mammifers. **1868** E. PEACOCK *Myrc's Instr.* 67 A piece of advice..not entirely unneeded in these days.

**Unnee·dful,** *a.* [UN-[1] 7.]

**1.** Unnecessary; not required.

*c* **1380** WYCLIF *Sel. Wks.* II. 58 So shal cloþis be more unnedeful þan þei weren in staat of innocence. *c* **1450** *Myrr. our Ladye* 227 Her eyne..were neuer lyfte vp to beholde eny vnnedeful thinge. **1543** RECORDE *Arithm.* 119 b, I iudge that good reason, for many are vnnedefull, where one wyll serue. **1597** J. KING *On Jonas* (1618) 281 The matter of all their vowes vnneedefull, in some vnlawfull, in some vnpossible. **1624** CAPT. SMITH *Virginia* I. 2 Which vnneedfull Southerly course..occasioned them..much sicknesse. **1677** *Lond. Gaz.* No. 1170/3 Since your Majesty will see what I write..it is unneedful that I should repeat it. **1768** [W. DONALDSON] *Life Sir B. Sapskull* I. iii. 29 Mere negative qualifications totally unneedful in the education of a polite gentleman. **1905** *Athenæum* 30 Sept. 431/1 The editor has ..also (a rarer thing in editors) refrained from doing what was unneedful.

**2.** Not standing in need *of* something.

**1876** MRS. H. WOOD *Parkwater* (1879) 258 The heart has a language of its own, unneedful of common syllables.

So **Unnee·dfully** *adv.*, unnecessarily.

**1642** MILTON *Apol. Smect.* 2 Yet those I intreat who have found the leasure to reade that name,..unworthily defam'd, would be so good..as to heare the same person not unneedfully defended.

**Unnee·dy,** *a.* (UN-[1] 7.) Also *absol.*

*c* **1440** *Jacob's Well* 108 Whethir þi ney₃boure..be syke or hool, nedy or vnnedy. **1477** RIVERS *Dictes* (1877) 27 b, Som simple folkes yeue to the vnnedy, and refuse hit to thoos that haue nede. **1550** BALDWIN *Mor. Philos.* Q i b, To the vneady a man to make hys dole, Is lyke the ministring of playsters to the whole.

**Unneglе·cted,** *ppl. a.* (UN-[1] 8.) *a* **1652** BROME *Novella* II. ii, My profit in this too is unneglected. **Unne·gligent,** *a.* (UN-[1] 7, 15.) **1597** *Return fr. Parnass.* IV. i. 1250 You are the moste unnegligent Sexton that ever came these forty years. **Unnego·tiable,** *a.* (UN-[1] 7 b.) [**1775** ASH.] **1893** F. F. MOORE *I forbid Banns* xli, Discoveries of an interesting but unnegotiable nature.

**Unnei·ghboured**, *ppl. a.* (UN-[1] 8.) 1657 H. KING *Woes of Esay* 8 Making a dearth Of all inhabitants, until they stand Unneighbour'd, as unblest. 1704 D'URFEY *Night Adventures* 180 Homely, unneighbour'd, and alone. *a* 1800 COWPER *Odyss.* (ed. 2) VI. 9 An unneighbour'd isle, And far from all resort of busy man. 1804 SYMMONS *Milton* (1810) 79 A crowd of beauties, unneighboured by a thought, a line,.. which we can be desirous of changing.

**Unnei·ghbourly**, *a.* (UN-[1] 7.) 1583 BABINGTON *Commandm.* (1590) 372 Haue you not often refused of a meere pinching and an vnneighbourlie mind euen in small matters? 1601 J. WHEELER *Treat. Comm.* 43 The proud, vnneighbourly.. Proscriptions of the Dutchesse of Parma. 1657 PIERCE *Div. Philanthr.* Ded. 1 The late un-Neighbourly usage which I have publickly received. 1705 SIR J. PACKINGTON in Hearne *Collections* (O.H.S.) I. 125 Unneighbourly Proceedings against your own Tenants. 1768–74 TUCKER *Lt. Nat.* (1834) II. 307 These things are unneighbourly or unnatural, if we consider only their present effect upon the party suffering by them. 1807 G. CHALMERS *Caledonia* I. 397 The cause of this unneighbourly irruption into Cumberland. 1895 *Westm. Gaz.* 18 June 5/1 He could not conceive conduct worse and more unneighbourly.

Hence **Unnei·ghbourliness.** 1653 BP. WEBBE *Pract. Quiet.* (1657) 155 Causing barrennesse of all goodnesse where there is that unquiet unneighbourliness. 1865 MEREDITH *R. Fleming* iv, The yeoman's pride struggled.. to vindicate his unneighbourliness.

**Unnei·ghbourly**, *adv.* (UN-[1] 11.) 1549 SIR W. PAGET in Strype *Eccl. Mem.* (1721) II. xix. 156 The French have.. dealt on this side very unfriendly and unneighbourly towards us. 1595 SHAKS. *John* V. ii. 39 Where these two Christian Armies might combine The bloud of malice, in a vaine of league, And not to spend it so vnneighbourly.

†**Unneod, -neomelich**: see UN-[1] 3.

†**Unne·rvate**, *a. Obs.*[—1] [UN-[1] 7.] Nerveless, feeble. 1725 W. BROOME *Notes Pope's Odyss.* II. 107 Scaliger calls them fine and lively in Musæus, but abject, unnervate, and unharmonious in Homer.

**Unne·rve**, *v.* [UN-[2] 3. Cf. Du. *ont-*, G. *entnerven.*]

**1.** *trans.* To destroy the strength of; to render physically weak. Also *fig.*

1621 G. SANDYS *Ovid's Met.* II. (1626) 26 Pale sudden feare vn-nerves his quaking thighs. 1697 ADDISON *Ess. Georgics* ¶ 8 in Dryden's *Virgil*, The Precepts.. are often so minute.. that they weaken and un-nerve his Verse. 1725 POPE *Odyss.* XV. 448 When a length of years unnerves the strong, Apollo comes. 1792 S. ROGERS *Pleas. Mem.* II. 111 The spectre Poverty unnerv'd his frame. 1836 J. GILBERT *Chr. Atonem.* ix. (1852) 271 The sight of mercy so transcendent.. has unnerved the power of determined obduracy. 1850 MERIVALE *Rom. Emp.* xxi. II. 453 This consciousness.. unnerved his arm for the execution of the Herculean task. 1870 BRYANT *Iliad* v. I. 175 The weariness of toil unnerves thy frame.

**2.** To deprive (the mind, etc., or a person) of firmness or courage; to render incapable of acting with ordinary firmness or energy.

1704 *Moderat. Display'd* v, A Modern Coward Principle design'd To stifle Justice, and unnerve the Mind. 1725 POPE *Odyss.* XII. 245 Fear seiz'd the mighty, and unnerv'd the brave. 1780 COWPER *Progr. Err.* 272 'Tis not alone the grape's enticing juice Unnerves the moral pow'rs, and mars their use. 1791 NEWTE *Tour Eng. & Scot.* 57 The horrid and incessant din.. unnerves and overcomes the heart. 1844 TALFOURD *Athenian Captive* I. i, To speak of mortal sickness, and unnerve A soul of noble essence. 1878 BOSW. SMITH *Carthage* 125 The fear which it seems to have inspired completely unnerved the Romans.

Hence **Unne·rving** *ppl. a.* 1722 HAMILTON *Wallace* v. (1816) 73 And sure while Scotia's enemies remain, Unnerving love should ever sue in vain. 1744 P. WHITEHEAD *Gymnasiad* III. 53 He, alas! had felt th' unnerving Blow. 1821 CLARE *Vill. Minstr.* (1823) I. 7 The mystic tribes of night's unnerving breeze. 1894 CROCKETT *Raiders* 354, I had that sense of being hunted, which comes so quickly and is so unnerving.

**Unne·rved**, *ppl. a.* [See prec.] Rendered nerveless or weak; unmanned.

1602 SHAKS. *Ham.* II. ii. 496 With the whiffe and winde of his fell Sword Th' vnnerued Father fals. 1659 W. CHAMBERLAYNE *Pharonnida* III. i. 398 Whilst her brother stands Unnerved with grief. 1718 ROWE tr. *Lucan* 33 Then Sons forsook their Sires un-nerv'd and old. 1781 COWPER *Retirem.* 677 A mind unnerv'd, or indispos'd to bear The weight of subjects worthiest of her care. 1855 MACAULAY *Hist. Eng.* xx. IV. 429 Her recent efforts.. had left her spent and unnerved. 1894 S. FISKE *Holiday Stories* (1900) 83 The situation was becoming terribly strained... Tom had given way under it, and was completely unnerved.

**Unnes**, variant of UNEATHS *adv. Obs.*

**Unne·st**, *v.* (UN-[2] 5. Cf. Du. *ontnesten.*) Chiefly *fig.* (In first quot. *intr.*)

*c* 1374 CHAUCER *Troylus* IV. 305 O soule, lurkynge in þis wo, vnneste; Fle forth out of myn herte. *c* 1532 DU WES *Introd. Fr.* in *Palsgr.* 941 To unneste, *deniser.* *c* 1600 CHALKHILL *Thealma & Cl.* (1683) 120 Alexis rising, thanks his prudent care And as his Father lov'd him; all prepare T'unnest these Pyrates. ? 1658 J. M. in Cleveland *Wks.* (1687) 283 The Presbyterian he did un-nest, With the whole Kennel o' th' two-footed Beast. 1679 J. SOMERVILLE *Mem. Somerville* (1815) I. 222 The queen.. encourages the souldiers ..to unnest from that hold the ancient enemies of ther countrey. 1790 A. WILSON *To J. Kennedy* Poet. Wks. (1846) 16 As.. seeming doubts when told oft take to wing, Permit me here some miseries to unnest, That long have harbour'd in my labouring breast. 1879 H. W. WARREN *Recr. Astron.* iv. 58 The earth on its softly-spinning axle never jars enough to unnest a bird or wake a child.

Hence **Unne·sted** *ppl. a.* 1860 PATMORE *Faithf. for Ever* I. i, No more the unnested blackbird's shriek Startled the light-leaved wood.

**Unne·stle**, *v.* (UN-[2] 3 + NESTLE *v.*[1] Cf. Du. *ontnestelen.*) Chiefly *fig.*

*c* 1430 *Pilgr. Lyf Manhode* II. cix. (1869) 116 He vnnestleth the hye briddes, and overthroweth here feedinges. 1592 BACON *Confer. Pleasure* (1870) 20 Leste anie man should think her intent was to unnestle ill neyghbors. 1658 EVELYN *Fr. Gard.* (1675) 101 There is a Green-Worm which devours the young shoots.., and those are very hard to un-nestle. 1694 MOTTEUX *Rabelais* v. ix. 43 Murther all the Kings.. in the world,.. unnestle the Angels from their Cock-loft.

Hence **Unne·stling** *vbl. sb.* 1653 URQUHART *Rabelais* I. xxiv. 113 Unnestling of sparrowes, taking of quailes, and fishing for frogs.

**Unnet**, var. UNNUT *a. Obs.* **Unnet** (uncompelled): UN-[1] 3. **Unneth(s**, etc., varr. UNEATH(S.

**Unne·tted**, *ppl. a.* (UN-[1] 8.) 1833 TENNYSON *Blackbird* 7 The unnetted black-hearts ripen dark.. against the garden wall. 1860 'OUIDA' *Tricotrin* I. 20 Like the bloom to an unnetted peach.

**Unneu·tral**, *a.* (UN-[1] 7.) 1782 EARL MALMESBURY *Diaries & Corr.* (1844) I. 486 It is in vain to remind her how.. very unneutral her Armed Neutrality is. [Frequent in recent use.]

**Unneu·tralized**, *ppl. a.* (UN-[1] 8.) 1758 *Elaboratory laid Open* 136 A redundant portion of a[n] unneutralized acid. 1771 T. PERCIVAL *Ess.* (1777) I. 31 If they remain unneutralised in the first passages, they will powerfully promote putrefaction. 1848 A. S. TAYLOR *Poisons* 202 The action of sulphuric acid in an unneutralized or imperfectly neutralized condition. 1881 TYNDALL *Ess. Floating Matter* 90 Two [shades] containing strong turnip-infusion and hay-infusion unneutralized.

† **Unne·vened**, *ppl. a. Obs.* [UN-[1] 8. Cf. ON. *unefnd-r*, Da. *unævnt.*] Unnamed. 13.. *E. E. Allit. P.* B. 727 Þat nas neuer þyn note, vnneuened hit worþe, þat art so gaynly a god & of goste mylde! † **Unnew·sed**, *ppl. a. Obs.*[—1] (UN-[1] 8.) 1644 QUARLES *Sheph. Orac.* x, Nuncius never uses To come unnews'd.

**Unni·che**, *v.* (UN-[2] 5.) 1771 *Ess. fr. Batchelor* (1773) I. 30 It is my ambition to un-nich Saint Charles, and place him in his proper rank. **Unni·cher.** (UN-[2] 8.) 1823 D'ISRAELI *Cur. Lit.* Ser. II. I. 344 The learned De Launoi had successfully attacked the legends of saints, and was called the *Denicheur de Saints*—the 'Unnicher of Saints'. **Unni·cked**, *ppl. a.* (UN-[1] 8.) *c* 1480 *Test. Ebor.* (Surtees) III. 253, xij shaffe of clense arros un nykt. *Ibid.*, xxxj shaffe of childre ware, clenst and un nyked. **Unni·ggard**, *a.* (UN-[1] 7.) 1591 SYLVESTER *Du Bartas* I. iv. 375 That sumptuous Canapy, The which th' unniggard hand of Majesty Poudred so thick with Shields so shining cleer. **Unni·ggardly**, *a.* (UN-[1] 7.) 1768–74 TUCKER *Lt. Nat.* (1834) I. 614 Wherein there appears.. no spark of arbitrary or inequitable disposition, but unreserved and unniggardly goodness. **Unni·ght**, *v.* (UN-[2] 3, 7.) 1594 *Zepheria* iv, The summe of life that Chaos did vnnight. 1598 FLORIO, *Disanottare*, to vnnight, to wax day. **Unni·mbed**, *a.* (UN-[1] 9.) 1880 *Smith's Dict. Chr. Antiq.* II. 1400/2 On the tomb.. she is unnimbed, while the Holy Child has the nimbus.

**Unni·mble**, *a.* (UN-[1] 7.) 1566 DRANT *Horace, Med. Morall* A ij, When unnimble age Hath refte them of their warke. 1607 MARKHAM *Cavel.* II. 48 A horse that is slothfull or vnnimble in turning. 1681 RYCAUT tr. *Gracian's Critick* 76 These.. sluggishly moved their unnimble legs. 1703 THORESBY *Let. to Ray* (E.D.S.), *Clunter*, an unnimble stumbler.

Hence **Unni·mbleness.** 1607 MARKHAM *Cavel.* II. 177 Some horses,.. out of vnnimblenesse,.. are.. more apt to turne vpon one hand then vpon another.

**Unni·mbly**, *adv.* (UN-[1] 11; cf. prec.) 1607 MARKHAM *Cavel.* II. 126 Which hee dooing at the first slouenlie, and vnnimbly, you shal.. beat him about the buttocks. 1631 A. TOWNSHEND *Albion's Tri.* B, What mak's me so vnnimbly ryse, That did descend so fleete? 1665 BRATHWAIT *Comment Two Tales* 170 Like another Omphada, she had unnimbly rushed down upon her four Quarters. 1704 *Dict. Rust.* s.v. *Rules buying Horses*, To tread unnimbly, shews a false Pace, that never continues.

† **U·nning**, *vbl. sb. Obs.*[—1] [app. f. UNNE *v.*; but perh. for *inning*, f. ON. *inna* to relate, tell.] Indication, sign.

13.. *E. E. Allit. P.* C. 213 He ossed hym by vnnynges þat þay vnder-nomen, Þat he was flawen fro þe face of frelych dryȝtyn.

**Unni·pped**, *ppl. a.* (UN-[1] 8.) [1775 ASH.] 1855 BROWNING *Lover's Quarrel* xx, Then.. We can stand apart, Heart dispense with heart In the sun, with the flowers unnipped. **Unni·trogenized**, *ppl. a.* (UN-[1] 8 a c.) 1869 TANNER *Clin. Med.* (ed. 2) 149 The nitrogenized and unnitrogenized substances.

**Unnitt**, variant of UNNUT *a. Obs.*

†**Unnobi·lity.** *Obs.*[—1] (UN-[1] 12.) *a* 1400 *Pauline Ep.* (Powell) 2 Cor. vi. 8 In alle þing gife we vsself as goddys mynystris,.. thurgh glorye and vnnobylyte [L. *ignobilitatem*]; thurgh ylle fame and good fame.

**Unno·ble**, *a.* (and *sb.*) Now *rare.* [UN-[1] 7. Cf. IGNOBLE *a.*]

**1.** Not noble or distinguished by rank or birth.

1382 WYCLIF *1 Sam.* ii. 30 Who so euere honourith me, Y shal glorifie hym; forsothe who dispisen me, shulen be vnnoble. — *1 Cor.* iv. 10. 1489 CAXTON *Faytes of A.* I. x. 29 The noble men bare a garment vnlyke to them that were vnnoble. 1545 BRINKLOW *Compl.* 38 b, No noble or vnnoble man shall retayne any of the kyngs subiectys without lauful wagys. 1571 GOLDING *Calvin on Ps.* xlvii. 5 He setting all the world asyde, had adopted to himself a feawe unnoble persons. 1607 COWELL *Interpr.* s.v. *Corruption of blood*, If he were noble, or a gentleman before, he and his children are made vnnoble and vngentle in respect of the father. 1660 WATERHOUSE *Arms & Arm.* 179 They must be contented to stand included under the base and unnoble state of people. 1832 S. AUSTIN tr. *Tour Germ. Prince* III. iv. 80 It is an almost universal weakness of the unnoble in England to parade an acquaintance with the noble. 1855 SINGLETON *Virgil* II. 478 Other unwedded maids In Latium be, and in Laurentine fields, Nor they unnoble in their pedigree.

**b.** *absol.* (chiefly pl.) or as *sb.*

1382 WYCLIF *Isaiah* iii. 5 Ther shal striue the child aȝen the old man, and the vnnoble aȝen the noble. *c* 1400 *Apol. Loll.* 43 Noiþer.. of pore to be maad riche, ne glorioue of þe vnnoble. *a* 1513 FABYAN *Chron.* II. xxxix. 27 Artogayle .. imaginyd causes agayne his nobles to put theym from theyr.. dignyties, and in theyr places to sette & ordeyne vnnoble. 1581 PETTIE tr. *Guazzo's Civ. Conv.* II. (1586) 92 Hee which despiseth the vnnoble, despiseth his first Fathers. 1602 FULBECKE *1st Pt. Parall.* Introd. 3 The noble and vn-noble were put to death. 1688 R. HOLME *Armoury* III. 69/1 It is the Duty of the unnoble to Honor and Salute a Gentleman.

*sb.* 1563 FOXE *A. & M.* 70 b/1 He had followers of his doltish religion, both of the nobles, and vnnobles of Rome.

† **2. a.** Of or pertaining to one who is not of noble birth or rank. *Obs.*

*c* 1520 [see UNNOBLENESS]. 1561 T. HOBY tr. *Castiglione's Courtyer* III. Hh ij b, So glorious a soule, that deserued.. renowme after death, as in lief it dwelled in an vnnoble body. *a* 1586 SIDNEY *Arcadia* II. ii, The perfections are such in the partie I love, as the feeling of them cannot come into any unnoble hart.

† **b.** Of things: Undistinguished, unnoted, common, mean. *Obs.*

1382 WYCLIF *1 Cor.* i. 28 God chees the vnnoble thingis [L. *ignobilia*] and dispisable thingis of the world. 1589 COOPER *Admon.* 199 The.. unnoble things of the worlde .. God hath chosen. 1590 BURROUGH *Meth. Physick* 211 The bloud being driuen backe from the vnnoble members, it rusheth vp to the principal members. 1612 DRAYTON *Poly-olb.* v. 332 Since, holy Dauid's seat; which of especiall grace Doth lend that nobler name, to this vnnobler place. 1631 WIDDOWES *Nat. Philos.* 51 The more un-noble senses are Tasting, and Smelling.

**3.** Not noble in disposition; ignoble, mean, base: **a.** Of persons.

1566 GASCOIGNE, etc. *Jocasta* II. i, So, woulde the Gods, that in this noble realme Shoulde never long unnoble tyrant reigne. 1616 BRETON *Good & Bad* Wks. (Grosart) II. 6/2 An vnnoble man is the griefe of Reason, when the title of honour is put vpon the subiect of disgrace. 1641 EARL CORK *Diary* in *Lismore Papers* Ser. I. (1886) V. 195 Papers concerning the vnnoble Earle of Middlesex.

*transf.* 1607 TOPSELL *Four-f. Beasts* 321 Neither is there any Horsse, swift or slow, noble, or vnnoble, that can be guided without these [reins].

**b.** Of actions, character, etc.

1606 SHAKS. *Ant. & Cl.* III. xi. 50, I haue offended Reputation, A most vnnoble sweruing. 1628 FORD *Lover's Mel.* II. ii, My affections.. are pure, Without all mixture of unnoble thoughts. 1680 *Life Edw. II*, in *Select. Harl. Misc.* (1793) 37 If Lancaster had been of so unnoble a disposition. 1855 SINGLETON *Virgil* I. 152 Him, likewise,.. If now.. he fails, Conceal at home; nor his unnoble eld Forgive.

Hence **Unno·bleness.** *c* 1400 *New Test.* (Paues) 2 Cor. vi. 8 Þoroȝ worschupe & vnnobelnesse, þoroȝ diffamynge & good loos. *c* 1520 BARCLAY *Jugurth* (1557) 75 b, The lownes and vnnoblenes of Marius encreased to hym fauour specially of the commentie which were come of vnnoble bloude, as he was. 1569 J. SANFORD tr. *Agrippa's Van. Artes* 127 b, That they whiche had not slayne some enimie, shoulde go girte with a halter in reproche of vnnoblenes. 1618 FLETCHER *Loyal Subj.* I. iii, You made this Vow, and whose unnobleness, Indeed forgetfulness of good— *Ar.* No more.

**Unno·ble**, *v.* (UN-[2] 6 a.) 1605 HEYWOOD *If you know not me* F 3 b, The treasons of the father being noble, Vnnobles all your children. 1656 JEANES *Mixt. Schol. Div.* 119 A foul incongruity.. is it for us.. to unnoble, and pollute that flesh. † **Unnoblety.** *Obs.*[—1] [UN-[1] 12.] = prec. *a* 1400 *Pauline Ep.* (Powell) 2 Cor. xi. 21 Aftyr þe vnnoblete I seye; as we hadde be syke in þis partye. † **Unno·bley.** *Obs.* [UN-[1] 12.] Low estate. 1382 WYCLIF *1 Cor.* xv. 43 It is sowun in vnnobley, it schal ryse in glorie. — *2 Cor.* vi. 8 By glorie and vnnobley; by yuel fame and good fame.

**Unno·bly**, *adv.* (UN-[1] 11. Cf. IGNOBLY *adv.*) 1618 FLETCHER *Loyal Subj.* v. vi, You do the most unnobly to be angry. *a* 1628 F. GREVIL *Alaham* II. iii, True hearts, to doe vnnobly, haue no spirit. ? 1648 H. KING *Elegy Lucas & Lisle* 314 Which.. Shall.. enhearse this blood unnobly spilt.

**Unno·ck**, *v. rare*[—0]. (UN-[2] 3; cf. NOCK *v.*) 1530 PALSGR. 768/2, I unnocke a shafte, *je descosche*. *Ibid.*, Who hath unnocked my shafte? † **Unno·me**, *pa. pple. Obs.* [UN-[1] 8 b; cf. NIM *v.*] Untaken. 1297 R. GLOUC. (Rolls) 11872 Ȝut he percede þe ost,.. & aliue & vn-nome of scapede among echon. 13.. *Guy Warw.* (A.) 5154 Alle þai ben ded oþer ouer-come: Þer bileued non vn-nome. **Unnoo·ked**, *ppl. a.* [UN-[1] 8.] Having no nooks or corners. 1602 MARSTON *Antonio's Rev.* IV. iii, With innocent upreared armes to Heaven: With my unnookt simplicitie.

**Unno·se**, *v.* (UN-[2] 4.) Hence **Unno·sed** *ppl. a.* 1598 FLORIO, *Snasato*, without a nose, vn-nosed. 1603 — *Montaigne* II. vi. 219 That is now called to vn-nose himselfe. 1620 SHELTON *Quix.* II. xiv. 89 Quoth the vn-nosed Squire. 1738 *Common Sense* II. 106 The persons who remain behind un-nos'd will immediately.. clap on their original Noses. 1742 JARVIS *Quix.* II. I. xiv, 'Indeed am I,' answered the unnosed squire.

**Unno·table**, *a.* and *sb.* (UN-[1] 7 b, 12.) 1528 PAYNELL *Salerne's Regim.* O ij b, Fyshe.. bred in shalowe & vnnotable waters. 1611 FLORIO, *Innotabile*, vnnoteable, not to be noted. 1831 CARLYLE *Sart. Res.* II. v, Nay, who knows.. but Blumine herself might have aforetime noted the so unnotable. 1837 — *Fr. Rev.* II. IV. vi, Unnotable hum of sweet human gossip rises from this Village.

**b.** *sb.* One who is not notable.

1861 H. S. CUNNINGHAM *Wheat & Tares* 324 If you get anybody else better worth having to dinner, I'll come in my sedan.. along with the other unnotables.

**Unno·tched**, *ppl. a.* [UN-[1] 8.]

† **1.** Not cut or trimmed. (Cf. NOTCH *v.* 1, OCHE *v.*) *Obs.*[—1]

1557 *Tottel's Misc.* (Arb.) 159 All ruff of heare, my nayles vnnocht, as to such semeth b st, That wander by theyr wittes.

**2.** Not marked with a notch; unnicked.

[1775 Ash.] 1811 Miss L. Hawkins *C'tess & Gertr.* IV. 5 The un-notched paling, the walls capt with straw and stone. 1844 Noad *Electricity* (ed. 2) 392 Provided the intersecting curves proceeding from A abut upon the notched surface of the knife, and those from B upon the un-notched side. 1883 *Encycl. Brit.* XVI. 648/2 Reptant Azygobranchia with ..the lip of the shell unnotched.

**Unno·ted,** *a.* [Un-[1] 9.] Characterized by absence of musical notes. 1866 Meredith *Vittoria* xxiv, A song of three notes and a sort of unnoted clanging chorus.

**Unno·ted,** *ppl. a.* [Un-[1] 8.]

**1.** Not noticed or observed; unmarked.

1563 Goldinge *Cæsar* III. (1565) 74 b, Bycause the thing was done in y^e^ sight of Cesar and all his army, insomuch that no dede..could escape vnnoted. 1600 *Bodenham's Belvedere* (1875) 59 Gnats are vnnoted where-soe're they flie But Eagles gaz'd vpon with euery eye. *c*1620 Fletcher *False One* I. i, I'le be admitted for a wanton tale To some most private Cabinets, when your Priest-hood..Shall wait without unnoted. 1725 Pope *Odyss.* I. 177 Where the free guest, unnoted, might relate, If haply conscious, of his Father's fate. 1742 Young *Nt. Th.* II. 274 Unnoted, [conscience] notes each moment misapply'd. 1813 Byron *Corsair* I. xvii, Secure, unnoted, Conrad's prow pass'd by. 1894 Mrs. Dyan *Man's Keeping* (1899) 135 Unnoted by him, that vision had faded much of late.

**2.** Not specially noted or observed; undistinguished, obscure.

1592 *Soliman & Pers.* I. ii. 73 Sweet Perseda, vnnoted though I be, Thy beauty yet shall make me knowne ere night. 1621 G. Sandys *Ovid's Met.* IX. (1626) 191 Phæstus ..fostered One, Lydgus, of vn-noted parents bred. 1725 Pope *Odyss.* V. 402 Un-wept, un-noted, and for ever dead! 1789 Burns *Let. to Lady Constable* 16 Dec., Only to add so many units more to the unnoted crowd that followed their leaders. 1860 Ellicott *Life Our Lord* ii. 67 The devout ..Simeon..saw perchance before him no more than two unnoted worshippers. 1883 Myers *Ess., Mod., Mazzini* (1885) 69 It has run its fair course unnoted, and in silence passed away.

† **Unno·teful,** *a. Obs.* [Un-[1] 7.] Unprofitable; useless. *a* 1300 *E. E. Psalter* lii. 4 Alle helded þai, sammen ai Vnnoteful maked ere þai. *a* 1395 Hylton *Scala Perf.* II. xxxvii. (W. de W. 1494), All men are before oure lorde as noughte, & as vnnotefull and nought they are acounted to hym. **Unno·teworthy,** *a.* (Un-[1] 7.) 1881 Saintsbury *Dryden* ii. 24 It is not unnoteworthy that Lady Elizabeth was five and twenty.

**Unno·ticeable,** *a.* (Un-[1] 7 b.)

1775 Adair *Amer. Ind.* 287 They were afraid of being imprisoned,..even for things unnoticeable in the eye of the law. 1810 Wordsw. *Prose Wks.* (1876) II. 304 A light vapour unnoticeable but by a shepherd. 1859 Geo. Eliot *A. Bede* x, A long-neglected and unnoticeable rent in the.. bed-curtain.

Hence **Unno·ticeableness; Unno·ticeably** *adv.*

1883 *Harper's Mag.* Sept. 566/1 Unnoticeableness..is.. the character..of the dwellings. 1885 E. Garrett' *At Any Cost* xv, One seal was broken! So cleanly, too, that she almost thought it might be mended unnoticeably.

**Unno·ticed,** *ppl. a.* (Un-[1] 8.)

In common use from *c* 1750.

1720 Pr. James in *10th Rep. Hist. MSS. Comm.* App. I. 91 To repose yourselves for some time somwhere in France where your usuall prudence will make you unnoticed. 1762 Sterne *Tr. Shandy* VI. v, There are a thousand unnoticed openings,..which [etc.]. 1819 Scott *Leg. Montrose* xix, The strife..had been unnoticed by the stragglers around. 1891 Farrar *Darkn. & Dawn* xxx, It was that little unnoticed impulse of natural kindness..which saved her fortunes.

*absol.* 1841 Carlyle *Heroes* ii. (1904) 77 See, the unnoticed becomes world-notable, the small has grown world-great.

**Unno·ticing,** *ppl. a.* (Un-[1] 5 d, 10.)

(*a*) 1782 Eliz. Blower *Geo. Bateman* II. 42 Unnoticing the looks of surprize. 1796 Mme. D'Arblay *Camilla* III. 78 She was thus employed, unnoticing the passage of time, when Mrs. Arlbery tapped at her door. 1904 Sladen *Lovers Japan* II. ix, They rode..through the delicious avenues of Shiba, unnoticing the temples.

(*b*) 1821 Scott *Pirate* i, He..lived as one of the family, unnoticed and unnoticing. *a* 1873 Lytton *Parisians* x. ii, Lemercier stopped a gentleman who was about to pass him unnoticing.

**Unno·tified,** *ppl. a.* (Un-[1] 8.)

[1775 Ash.] 1802–12 Bentham *Ration. Judic. Evid.* (1827) II. 508 The keeping of the rule of action..in one immense and unorganic mass, undistributed, and consequently unnotified. 1871 *Standard* 27 Jan., It would be hypocrisy..to gloss over this odious outrage of the unnotified bombardment of Paris.

**Unno·tify,** *v.* (Un-[2] 3.) 1757 H. Walpole *Let. to Mann* 3 July, I notified to you the settlement of the ministry, and, contrary to late custom, have not to unnotify it again. **Unno·ting,** *ppl. a.* (Un-[1] 10.) 1868 Morris *Earthly Par.* I. I. 405 Her dizzied eyes..wandered from unnoting face to face. **Unnou·rishable,** *a.* (Un-[1] 7 b.) 1607 Topsell *Four-f. Beasts* 719 Their flesh is not good for meate, but is bitter and vnnourishable. **Unnou·rished,** *ppl. a.* (Un-[1] 8.) *a* 1617 Daniel *To Sir T. Egerton* 96 Having not this skill how to contend, Th' unnourish'd strife would quickly make an end. 1896 *N. Amer. Rev.* CLXIII. 715 As only the unnourished tree can battle.

**Unnou·rishing,** *ppl. a.* (Un-[1] 10.)

1605 Chapman *All Fools* I. i. 185 A gentlewoman: But her unnurishing dowry must be tolde Out of her beauty. 1640 Bp. Reynolds *Passions* xx, The minde being mollified and puffed up with windie and unnourishing comfort. 1826 Lamb *Elia* II. *Pop. Fallacies* xii, The aliment of this poor babe was thin, unnourishing. 1860 Pusey *Min. Proph.* 216 Which..sold to the poor only what, although unnourishing, was wholesome!

**Unnou·rishment.** (Un-[1] 12.) 1662 J. Chandler *Van Helmont's Oriat.* 24 A sickness, which the Rabbins call Binsica: which properly, is an unnourishment, or pining away of the Organ of the phantasie.

† **Unnoy·and, -ing,** *ppl. a. Obs.*^—1^ [Un-[1] 10.] Not causing offence or annoyance; harmless. Also † **Unnoy·andness.** *Obs.*

*a* 1340 Hampole *Psalter* vii. 5 Deme me lord..eftere myn vnnoyandnes abouen me. *Ibid.* xl. 13 Me sothly for vnnoyandes thou vptoke. *a* 1400 *Relig. Pieces fr. Thornton MS.* 61 The noyeand [creatures] þou made vs for to chasty, The vnnoyeand to sustayne vs and fede. *c* 1475 *Cath. Angl.* (MS. A) 256/1 Vn Noying, *innocens* [etc.].

† **Unnoy·ed,** *ppl. a. Obs.*^—1^ [Un-[1] 8.] Not disturbed. *a* 1470 Harding *Chron.* LXXXVII. xii, The Christen faith in thy lande [is] distroyed, That with the peace shuld haue be kept vnnoyed. † **Unnoy·ous,** *a. Obs.*^—0^ [Un-[1] 7.] = Unnoyand *ppl. a.* 1483 *Cath. Angl.* 256/1 Vn Noyous, *innocens*...*innocuus*.

**Unnu·merable,** *a.* [Un-[1] 7 b, 5 b.] Incapable of being numbered; innumerable.

*a* 1340 Hampole *Psalter* xxxviii. 6 How fa my dayes ere here, and how vnnoumberabil in heuen. 1382 Wyclif *Exod.* x. 14 A brennynge wynd reride vp locustes, the whiche.. seeten in alle the coostis of Egipciens vnnoumbrable. *c* 1440 *Gesta Rom.* lvii. 241 (Harl. MS.), Thorow this pryde bethe vnnumberable peple infecte and dede. 1513 Douglas *Æneid* VI. xi. 53 The flude Lethe..About the quhilk peple vnnomerable..fleis fast. 1756 Mrs. Calderwood in *Coltness Collect.* (Maitl. Cl.) 144 The unnumberable wind-milns through Holland. 1774 tr. *Helvetius' Child of Nature* I. 53 Unnumberable are the unfortunate he has relieved. 1852 Bailey *Festus* (ed. 5) 173 With starry globes unnumberable, suns, Planets and moons.

**Unnu·mbered,** *ppl. a.* [Un-[1] 8, 5 b.]

**1.** Not numbered or reckoned up; uncounted.

*c* 1375 *Sc. Leg. Saints* xli. (*Agnes*) 224 Þe gret Ioy in hewine þat he saw, þat vnnovmerit mycht be. 1434 Misyn *Mending of Life* 126 God truly is infinit of gretnes,..of swetnes vn-nowmbyrde. 1480 Caxton *Chron. Eng.* ccxxxii. 249 Ther were take many knyȝtes and squyers and other men that were vnnombred. 1601 Shaks. *Jul. C.* III. i. 63 The Skies are painted with vnnumbred sparkes. 1656 Cowley *Davideis* I. 749 Of Numbers too th' unnumbred wealth he showes. 1725 Pope *Odyss.* II. 212 Unnumber'd Birds glide thro' the aërial way. 1746 Hervey *Medit., Refl. on Flower-Garden* 4 Prodigious Theatre!..Where..Worlds un-numbered roll at large! 1844 Kinglake *Eothen* xi, The fleas of all nations were there:—Asiatic hordes unnumbered. 1891 Farrar *Darkn. & Dawn* lvi, To represent these unnumbered agonies as a festival of expiation.

**2.** Not included in an enumeration; not marked or provided with a number.

*a* 1533 Ld. Berners *Gold. Bk. M. Aurel.* (1546) H vij b, The .ix. Epiphanes of the Egiptiens was vnnoumbred and putte downe. 1654 Ld. Hatton in *Nicholas Papers* (Camden) II. 147, I have received yours (unnumbred) of the 8th of Dec. *a* 1667 [see Unmethodized 1]. 1816 Wilson *City of Plague* II. iii. 94 He for his lust, Unnumber'd lies.

† **Unnu·merable,** *a. Obs.* [Un-[1] 7 b, 5 b.] Innumerable.

*c* 1400 *Brut* 316 Men founden vnnumerable multitudes of hem [*sc.* sparrows] dede in feldes. *c* 1440 *Alph. Tales* 485 He was deseyvid be a fend þat promysid hym to gyff hym ..ane vnnumerable porcion of gude. 1536 in *Songs, Carols*, etc. (E.E.T.S.) 162 At þe Towr..þer was shott vnnumerable many gonnes. 1567 Golding *Ovid's Met.* VIII. (1593) 186 So winding waies Unnumerable Dædalus within his worke convays. 1611 Cotgr., *Innombrable*, innumerable, vnnumerable.

Hence † **Unnu·merableness.** Also † **Unnu·merably** *adv.*

1565 Cooper *Thesaurus, Innumerabilitas*, *vnnumerablenesse: passyng all number. *c* 1440 *Promp. Parv.* 366/1 *Onnumerably, *innumerabiliter*. 1611 Cotgr., *Innumerablement*, innumerably, vnnumerably.

**Unnu·n,** *v.* (Un-[2] 6 b.) 1611 Florio, *Smonacato*, vnmonked, vnnunned, hauing cast of the orders of religion. 1638 N. Whiting *Albino & Bellama* 4217 Albino..to the church did haste T' un-nun Bellama. 1639 Fuller *Holy War* v. vi. 238 Many did quickly unnunne and disfriar themselves. **Unnu·rsed,** *ppl. a.* (Un-[1] 8.) [1775 Ash.] 1875 Ruskin *Fors Clav.* lv. 204 Sternly to forbid cat-nursing, till no child is left unnursed.

**Unnu·rtured,** *ppl. a.* (Un-[1] 8, 5 b.)

*a* 1548 Hall *Chron., Hen. V*, 42 b, The presumptuous saiynges..of the vnnurtered and vnmanerly byshop. 1567 Golding *Ovid's Met.* V. (1593) 126 These unnurtred damsels overcome began to fall a scolding. 1623 Bingham *Xenophon* 40 He esteemed him that was no circumventer, to be vnnurtured and to want education. 1647 Clarendon *Hist. Reb.* VII. § 387 [To] impose upon Men unnurtur'd, and unacquainted with any Knowledge or Science. 1822 Scott *Peveril* xxvii, [I] never saw so unnurtured a cub. 1861 Geo. Eliot *Silas M.* i, Pale-faced weavers, whose unnurtured souls have been..fluttering forsaken in the twilight.

† **Unnu·t, unne·t,** *sb. Obs.* Also 1 unnyt (-nit). [OE. *unnyt* (cf. next and Nut *sb.*[2]), = WFris. *on-, ûnnut*, NFris. *unnatt* useless person, LG. *unnütte* useless thing, MDu. *onnut*, MHG. and G. (now chiefly dial.) *unnutz* damage, loss, harm, ON. *únytja* waste, Sw. *onytta*, Da. *unytte* uselessness.] That which is useless or worthless; idleness, vanity; wrong-doing.

*c* 888 K. Ælfred *Boeth.* xxxv. § 1 Eall þæt yfel & þæt unnet þe he ær on his mode hæfde. *c* 965 *Canons Edgar* § 28 We lærað þæt man æt ciric-wæccan..æniȝ unnit þar ne dreoȝe. *c* 1000 *Ags. Ps.* (Thorpe) xxx. 6 þu hatodest.. þa þe unnyt worhton. *c* 1175 *Lamb. Hom.* 153 Swa deð þe douel ine þe monnes eȝen, if ho boð opene to bihalden idel and unnet. *a* 1225 *Ancr. R.* 352 He isihð & ihereð oðerhwule unnut. *c* 1230 *Hali Meid.* 17 ȝif ȝe þrafter þenne speken tegedere folliche, & talkeð of unnet.

† **Unnu·t, unne·t,** *a. Obs.* Forms: α. 1–2 unnyt, 2–3 unnut. β. 1–4 unnet. γ. 3 unnitt. [OE. *unnyt* (f. *un-* Un-[1] 7 + *nyt* Nut *a.*), = OFris. *un-, onnet*, WFris. *on-, ûnnut, ûnnutte*, NFris. *unnatt*, MDu. *onnutte, onnut* (Du. *onnut*), MLG. *unnutte*, LG. *unnüt*, OHG. *unnuzzi, -nuzze* (MHG. *unnütze, -nutze*, G. *-nütz*), Goth. *unnuts*.] Useless, worthless, unprofitable, vain.

α. *Beowulf* 413 Secgað sæliðend, þæt þes sele stande..idel & unnyt. *c* 1000 *Ags. Gosp.* xxv. 30 Wurpað þone unnyttan þeowan on þa uttran þystru. *c* 1200 *Trin. Coll. Hom.* 129 Al þat folc þat þurh unnutte speche..turneð fro gode. *c* 1250 *Prayer Our Lady* 3 in *O. E. Misc.* 192 Vnnut lif to longe ich lede.

β. *a* 1000 *Boeth. Metr.* x. 17 Is ðæt unnet ȝelp. *a* 1200 *Moral Ode* 5 Vnnet lif ich habbe iled. *a* 1225 *Ancr. R.* 82 Idel is & unnet al þet god ne cumeð of. *c* 1330 *Arth. & Merl.* 1254 (Kölbing), Þis men hadde wonder gret, Him to sle, it were vnnet.

γ. *c* 1200 Ormin 4921 Icc amm an allforrwurrþenn þeoww & all unnitt & idel. *Ibid.* 15127 Acc þatt wass all..Unnitt & idell dede.

**Unnutri·tious,** *a.* (Un-[1] 7, 5 b.) 1846 Worcester (citing *Ed. Rev.*). 1855 Singleton *Virgil* I. 342 An unnutritious food, Berries and stony cornels, boughs purvey. 1861 H. Macmillan *Footn. Page Nat.* 100 Miserable and unnutritious diet. **Unnu·tritive,** *a.* (Un-[1] 7, 5 b.) [1775 Ash.] 1829 Carlyle *Misc.* (1840) II. 50 Germans, who.. have in fact nothing else to live on but that highly unnutritive victual.

**Unoa·th,** *v.* (Un-[2] 3.) 1675 W. Penn *England's Pres. Interest* d 2 b, Q. Elizabeth..calls back Protestancy, ordains a new Oath, to un-Oath Q. Marys Oath.

† **Unobe·dience.** *Obs.* [Un-[1] 12, 5 b.] Disobedience.

*c* 1380 Wyclif *Sel. Wks.* II. 357 Þat were fendis obedience, and unobedience to God. *c* 1440 *Jacob's Well* 71 Þe thrydde cornere of pride..is vnbuxumnes, vnobedyens. *Ibid.* 72. *a* 1470 H. Parker *Dives & Pauper* (W. de W. 1496) x. vi. 247/2 They felle in open unobedyence.

**Unobe·dient,** *ppl. a.* (Un-[1] 7, 5 b.)

1382 Wyclif *Titus* i. 10 Ther ben manye vnobedient, and veyn spekeris. *a* 1425 tr. *Arderne's Treat. Fistula*, etc. 15 Þe pacient is waike of herte or vnobedient for to persew his cure. *c* 1440 *Jacob's Well* 71 Who-so were vnobedyent to his fadyr & modyr. *Ibid.*, It is perylous to be vnobedyent to þi soueraƴn. 1509 Barclay *Shyp of Folys* (1570) 56 O man presumpteous and vnobedient. 1571 Golding *Calvin on Ps.* To Rdr. 7 If they had not bin vtterlye vnobedient too all good counsel. 1614 W. B. *Philosopher's Banquet* (ed. 2) 81 The Wall-nut is vnobedient to Digestion, and much hinders egestion. 1641 Milton *Reform.* II. 50 Pepin, not unobedient to the Popes call,..frees him out of danger. 1801 Southey *Thalaba* VIII. x, But unobedient to that well-known voice, His eye was seeking it.

† **Unobei·sance.** *Obs. rare.* [Un-[1] 12, 5 b.] Disobedience. 1382 Wyclif *Esther* xvi. 24 And so be he don awei, that..[he] be in to euer mor, for exsaumple of dispising and vnobeisaunce. *c* 1420 *Wycliffite Bible* Pref. Ep. (1850) I. 63/2 Redy to vndurȝoke al vnbuxumnesse [*v.r.* vnobeisaunce]. † **Unobei·sant,** *a. Obs.* [Un-[1] 7, 5 b.] Disobedient. 1382 Wyclif *Prov.* xxix. 21 Who delicatli fro childhed nurshith his seruaunt, afterward shal feelen hym vnobeisaunt. *c* 1400 tr. *Secreta Secret., Gov. Lordsh.* 115 He þat hauys gret eghen ys enuyous..., sleuthful, and vnobeyssant. † **Unobei·shing,** *ppl. a. Obs.* [Un-[1] 10.] Disobedient. 1382 Wyclif 1 *Kings* xiii. 26 He..was vnobeshynge to the mouth of God. † **Unobey·,** *v. Obs.*^—1^ [Un-[1] 14.] *intr.* To be disobedient. *c* 1445 Pecock *Donet* 208 O lord,..how myȝt I be so boolde, so vnkinde,..forto vnobeie to þee?

**Unobey·ed,** *ppl. a.* (Un-[1] 8.)

1595 Daniel *Civ. Wars* II. liii, Poorely prouided, poorely followed, Vncourted, vnrespected, vnobayd. 1667 Milton *P. L.* V. 667 He resolv'd..[to] leave Unworshipt, unobey'd the Throne supream. 1772 *Ann. Reg., Hist. Eur.* 61/2 The standing order..had not only been unobeyed, but.. outrageously insulted.

**Unobey·ing,** *ppl. a.* (Un-[1] 10.) 1796 Coleridge *Destiny of Nations* 66 The Laplander beholds the far-off Sun Dart his slant beam on unobeying snows. **Unobje·cted,** *ppl. a.* (Un-[1] 8.) 17.. Atterbury (J.), What will he leave unobjected to Luther, when he makes it his crime that he defied the devil? 1823 Scott *Quentin D.* xxxv, [They] heard from the mouth of Charles of Burgundy, unobjected to by that of Louis,..that [etc.]. **Unobje·ctible,** *a.* [Un-[1] 7.] = next. 1748 Richardson *Clarissa* III. 13 Nor will I ask for your favour, but as upon full proof I shall appear to deserve it: Fortune, alliances unobjectible!

**Unobje·ctionable,** *a.* (Un-[1] 7 b.)

In common use from *c* 1800.

1793 A. Geddes *Addr. to Public* 3 A New Translation, that should be unobjectionable to my brethren of the R. Catholic communion. 1794 Paley *Evid.* III. vi. ¶ 5 There are few cases in which..we cannot suppose something more perfect, and more unobjectionable, than what we see. 1819 G. S. Faber *Dispensations* (1823) II. 152 A safe and unobjectionable medium through which to prove the divine legation of Moses. 1882 Miss Braddon *Mt. Royal* II. iv. 66 His conduct was unobjectionable.

Hence **Unobje·ctionableness; Unobje·ctionably** *adv.*

1828–32 Webster s.v., Unobjectionably. *a* 1849 Poe *E. B. Browning* Wks. 1865 III. 411 The former poem is purely imaginative; the latter is unobjectionably because unobtrusively suggestive of a moral. 1878 W. Walker *Life Bp. Gleig* vii. 299 The Canonical unobjectionableness of the Bishop-elect.

**Unobje·ctive,** *a.* (Un-[1] 7.) 1855 Milman *Lat. Chr.* XIV. x. VI. 613 Allegory in itself is far too unobjective for art. **Unobli·gatory,** *a.* (Un-[1] 7.) 1802–12 Bentham *Ration. Judic. Evid.* (1827) IV. 539 In causes non-criminal, obligatory at one stage, unobligatory at another. 1851 W. R. Greg *Creed Christendom* xiv. 208 If investigation shows the miracles of the Bible to be..unobligatory upon our belief.

**Unobli·ged,** *ppl. a.* [Un-[1] 8.]

**1.** Of persons: Not bound or constrained to do something.

1648 Hexham II, *Ongehouden*, Vnbound, Vnobliged. 1658 Earl Monm. tr. *Paruta's Wars Cyprus* 163 Unobliged thereunto, he had readily assisted, the first year of this war. **1682** SCARLETT *Exchanges* 154 A prudent.. Drawer will judge himself unobliged to make any Bills, but such as make the Value to be received of the Remitter.

**2.** Not made obligatory or necessary.

**1855** FABER *Growth in Holiness* v. 79 Look at the phenomena of the Incarnation, what were they? Helplessness, unnecessary and unobliged suffering.

**Unobli·ging,** *ppl. a.* (UN-[1] 10.) [1847 WEBSTER.] **1891** H. HERMAN *His Angel* 16 An uncivil, unobliging, ugly young brute. **Unobli·gingness.** [UN-[1] 12.] †Absence of obligatoriness. **1646** HAMMOND *Tracts* 63 You see the unobligingnesse of that interdict. **Unobli·terable,** *a.* (UN-[1] 7 b.) **1662** J. CHANDLER *Van Helmont's Oriat.* 263 The unobliterable or undefaceable substance of the soul. **Unobli·teratable,** *a.* (UN-[1] 7 b.) **1865** W. H. GILLESPIE *Argt. Being & Attrib. God* (1906) 253 The relation which does exist, and the existence of which is unobliteratable.

**Unobli·terated,** *ppl. a.* (UN-[1] 8.)

**1644** [H. PARKER] *Jus Populi* 43 Whilst [in the times of Adam] the neare relation of blood was fresh, and unobliterated. **1680** H. DODWELL *Two Lett.* (1691) 68 Those unobliterated impressions of Conscience and Modesty. **1738** G. LILLO *Marina* III. ii, Some traces there.., yet unobliterated, Of my long dead.. Pericles. **1835** LYTTON *Rienzi* x. viii, There was a red stain upon the pavement, unobliterated. **1894** *Daily News* 10 Mar. 3/4 The letter-carrier would either appropriate the stamp.. or he would deliver it unobliterated.

**Unobno·xious,** *a.* [UN-[1] 7, 5 b.]

**1.** Not exposed or liable *to* something. Also *ellipt.*

?**1609** DONNE *Elegy on Lady Marckham* 35 For, graves our trophies are, and both deaths dust. So, unobnoxious now, she hath buried both. **1667** MILTON *P. L.* VI. 404 In fight they stood Unwearied, unobnoxious to be pain'd By wound. **1704** NORRIS *Ideal World* II. iii. 125 But neither the matter, nor yet the form of this division,.. are unobnoxious to just exception. **1809–14** WORDSW. *Excurs.* V. 868 Some, apart, In quarters unobnoxious to such chance. **1862** F. HALL *Hindu Philos. Syst.* 50 The soul is immutable, and unobnoxious to error.

**2.** Not objectionable or offensive.

**1678** *Lively Oracles* vii. § 9 (1684) 308 Surely the meanest unobnoxious laic..might..be trusted with the reading of those sacred books. **1802** H. MARTIN *Helen of Glenross* I. 201 Mr. Mulgrave, unobnoxious to any party, was advised to remain. **1858** *Times* 3 Dec. 8/6 The Roman Catholic priests are lowly, zealous men...We want the same class of men for our unobnoxious Christianity [in China].

**Unobscu·red,** *ppl. a.* (UN-[1] 8.)

**1646** J. HALL *To Stanley* 4 But thou At first appearance dost display A bright and unobscured day. **1667** MILTON *P. L.* II. 265 How oft amidst Thick clouds and dark doth Heav'ns all-ruling Sire Choose to reside, his Glory unobscur'd. **1748** THOMSON *Cast. Indol.* II. lviii, O who can speak the vigorous joys of health! Unclogged the body, unobscured the mind. **1764** *Phil. Trans.* LIV. 146 The unobscured part of the Sun. **1849** HERSCHEL *Outlines of Astronomy* x. 332 The cone of the shadow..permits their occultations to be completely observed both at ingress and egress, unobscured. **1879** *St. George's Hosp. Rep.* IX. 180 Gradual and progressive cough, unobscured by other symptoms.

**Unobse·quious,** *a.* (UN-[1] 7.) [1775 ASH.] **1810** BENTHAM *Packing* (1821) 203 Unobsequious Jurors dropped: or, in the..familiar phrase, cut. **Unobse·quiousness.** (UN-[1] 12, 5 b.) **1661** BOYLE *Style of Script.* 169 Their Succeeders.. are afterwards bold to mis-name all Unobsequiousnesse to their Incogitancy, Presumption. **1810** BENTHAM *Packing* x. § 1 Unobsequiousness found unavoidable by a veteran Advocate.

**Unobse·rvable,** *a.* [UN-[1] 7 b, 5 b.]

**1.** Incapable of being observed; imperceptible, unnoticeable.

**1651** HOBBES *Leviath.* II. xxix. 169 Which accidents.. are not supernaturall, but onely.. unobservable. **1664** BOYLE *Exp. touching Colours* 114 Little and Singly Unobservable Images of the Lucid Body. *a* **1715** SOUTH *Serm.* IV. 163 Such small, such contemptible, and almost unobservable Hints have sometimes unraveled..the deepest-laid Villanies. **1895** BARING-GOULD *Noémi* xiii, He had to beware of putting his hand on fire that was unobservable by daylight.

†**2.** Undeserving of notice or remark. *Obs.*

**1665** J. WEBB *Stone-Heng* (1725) 16 It is not unobservable, that these Stones seem to have been.. more entire, than when Mr. Jones made his Survey. **1675** M. CLIFFORD *Hum. Reason* 40 It is not unobservable, that the Unity of the Church of God is compared [etc.].

**Unobse·rvance.** (UN-[1] 12, 5 b.)

**1654** WHITLOCK *Zootomia* 419 The two first require the more serious inquiry into, for the universality of their Power (and yet generall unobservance of it). **1681** J. KETTLEWELL *Meas. Chr. Obed.* II. iv. 166 The Law..against irreverence, against unobservance, against disobedience. **1788** D. GILSON *Serm. Pract. Subj.* xiii. 381 We are awakened.. to lament our own unobservance and ingratitude. **1844** SOUTHEY *Life A. Bell* I. 182 The various instances of neglect.. on the part of the schoolmaster and ushers, and their unobservance of those rules [etc.]. **1893** F. F. MOORE *Gray Eye or So* I. 180 Nodding himself into a condition of unobservance.

**Unobse·rvant,** *a.* [UN-[1] 7, 5 b.]

†**1.** Unattentive in service. *Obs.*—[0]

**1611** COTGR., *Inofficieux*, vnofficious, vnobseruant, vnseruiceable.

**2.** Not observant; not taking notice.

**1661** GLANVILL *Van. Dogm.* xxiv. 247 The unobservant Multitude may have some general confus'd apprehensions of [etc.]. **1775** ASH, *Disobedient*,.. unobservant of lawful authority. **1782** V. KNOX *Ess.* xc. (1819) II. 173 An unexperienced and unobservant man. **1816** SOUTHEY *Poet's Pilgr.* I. 34 No unobservant travellers they, but well Of what they there had learnt they knew to tell. **1825** SCOTT *Talism.* iv, [This] fear..made her behave with indifference, as if unobservant of his presence. **1888** F. HUME *Mme. Midas* I. v, Vandeloup looked idly at all this beauty with an unobservant eye.

*absol.* **1898** 'MERRIMAN' *Roden's Corner* iv, The unobservant may pass it by without distinguishing it.

Hence **Unobse·rvantly** *adv.*

[1847 WEBSTER.] **1868** MRS. WHITNEY *P. Strong* xvii, I have not read the new style of novel and magazine writing unobservantly.

**Unobse·rved,** *ppl. a.* [UN-[1] 8.] Not observed; unperceived, unnoticed.

**1612** COTTA (*title*), The Unobserved Dangers..of ignorant and unconsiderate Practisers of Physicke in Englande. **1624** MASSINGER *Renegado* v. ii, You shall find, If any look of mine be unobserved, I am not ignorant of a mistress' power. **1673** TEMPLE *Obs. United Prov.* Wks. 1720 I. 46 Most National Customs are the Effect of some unseen, or unobserved natural Causes, or Necessities. **1741** CHESTERF. *Let.* 25 July, This quick and unobserved observation is of infinite advantage in life. **1796** MME. D'ARBLAY *Camilla* III. 322 This was not unobserved by Edgar. **1836** MARRYAT *Midsh. Easy* xxxix, Finding themselves unobserved, ..they dropped gently alongside one of the double-masted latteen vessels. **1864** BOWEN *Logic* x. 343 By detecting hitherto unobserved similarities and conjunctions in time.

**b.** In complementary (quasi-adverbial) const.: Without being observed.

*a* **1616** BEAUM. & FL. *Cust. Country* II. i, He had liv'd unobserv'd By any man of mark. **1671** MILTON *P. R.* IV. 638 Hee unobserv'd Home to his Mothers house private return'd. **1709** STEELE *Tatler* No. 57 Many..live in the constant Practice of baser Methods unobserved. **1796** MME. D'ARBLAY *Camilla* V. 4 He was now waiting but to speak to her unobserved. **1827** FARADAY *Chem. Manip.* xiii. 285 The crucible furnace.. where the heat is not so liable to rise unobserved as in a close furnace. **1891** MARIE A. BROWN tr. *Runeberg's Nadeschda* 35 The gentle maiden had.. stolen unobserved among the group.

**Unobse·rvedly,** *adv.* (UN-[1] 11; cf. prec.)

**1656** EARL ORRERY *Parthen.* III. I. 12 Nicomedes the more unobservedly to gaze on his new Conqueror, had retir'd himself into the throng. **1702** BP. PATRICK *Comm. Judg.* xvi. 1 He went thither secretly and unobservedly, in the dusk of the evening. **1795** *Phil. Trans.* LXXXV. 174 A single instrument, having an excess of light, in which the irradiation may unobservedly extend further than in weaker telescopes. **1861** WRIGHT *Ess. Archæol.* vii. 107 Great numbers of.. tumuli have been destroyed unobservedly in the various processes of agriculture. **1884** *Manch. Exam.* 20 Aug. 5/1 A train came upon him unobservedly, and the poor fellow was literally cut to pieces.

**Unobse·rver.** (UN-[1] 12.) **1713** *Guardian* No. 60, How unheeded must the general character of it be, when given by one of these serene unobservers.

**Unobse·rving,** *ppl. a.* (UN-[1] 10.)

**1690** T. BURNET *Theory Earth* II. 41 Those [prophecies] that concern the end of the world are of this latter sort to unobserving men. **1749** FIELDING *Tom Jones* VIII. xii, There are people who find an inconvenience in this unobserving temper of mankind. **1792** CHARLOTTE SMITH *Desmond* I. 142 An unobserving or disinterested spectator of what was passing. **1815** *Zeluca* III. 106 Wholly unobserving of the earnest conversation of her companions. **1818** SCOTT *Br. Lamm.* xxxii, To an eye so unobserving as that of Bucklaw.

**Uno·bstinate,** *a.* (UN-[1] 7, 5 b.) **1656** [? J. SERGEANT] tr. *T. White's Peripat. Inst.* Auth. Design a 7, This the Order, and Brevity, and the invincible firmnesse, surely of some Consequences will obtain of an unobstinate person. **1665** J. SERGEANT *Sure Footing* 40 As is easy to be evinc't against an unobstinate Adversary. *a* **1859** DE QUINCEY *Posth. Wks.* (1891) I. 63 They were a plastic, yielding, unobstinate race. **Unobstru·ct,** *v.* (UN-[2] 3.) **1659** W. CHAMBERLAYNE *Pharonnida* III. v. 339 Which carelesse pride did unobstruct the way, Through which to liberty love's progress lay.

**Unobstru·cted,** *ppl. a.* (UN-[1] 8.)

**1659** W. CHAMBERLAYNE *Pharonnida* III. iv. 361 Anger, like unobstructed love, breaks forth In flaming haste. *Ibid.* III. v. 516. *a* **1711** KEN *Hymnarium* Poet. Wks. 1721 II. 137 From thence o'er the celestial Vast, Eyes unobstructed cast. **1748** MELMOTH *Fitzosborne Lett.* lxi. (1749) II. 117 Much caution is necessary to give a fine taste its full and unobstructed effect. **1808** MRS. C. KEMBLE *Day after Wedding* 6 You hope to glide along the stream of life, unobstructed by the shoals of misfortune. **1859** PARKINSON *Optics* (1866) 245 The eye having an unobstructed view through the hole.

Hence **Unobstru·ctedly** *adv.*

[1847 WEBSTER.] **1867** H. MACMILLAN in *Macm. Mag.* No. 99. 259/2 The sun to shine down unobstructedly. **1897** *Outing* XXX. 139/2 A huge triangle that led unobstructedly into the wide mouth of this baggy apex.

**Unobstru·ctive,** *a.* (UN-[1] 7.) **1712** BLACKMORE *Creation* II. 307 Why should he halt at either station? why Not forward run in unobstructive sky? **1855** *Poultry Chron.* III. 442/2 The unobstructive nature of the coops to the opportunity of inspection by spectators.

**Unobtai·nable,** *a.* (UN-[1] 7 b, 5 b.)

[1775 ASH.] **1860** FROUDE *Hist. Eng.* V. 129 Her own consent would have been unobtainable. **1876** 'OUIDA' *Winter City* vii, Seeking some unobtainable enamel.

**Unobtai·ned,** *ppl. a.* (UN-[1] 8.) **1594** HOOKER *Eccl. Pol.* I. xi. § 3 As the will doth now worke vpon that obiect by desire, which is as it were a motion towards the end as yet vnobtayned. **1742** YOUNG *Nt. Th.* II. 503 Wisdom,..What is she, but the means of happiness? That unobtain'd, than folly more a fool.

**Unobtru·sive,** *a.* (UN-[1] 7, 5 b.)

In common use from *c* 1800.

**1743** YOUNG *Nt. Th.* IV. 625 Ye Quietists,.. who mildly make An unobtrusive tender of your hearts. **1790** HAN. MORE *Relig. Fash. World* (1791) 131 Those secret habits of self-controul, those interior and unobtrusive virtues. **1828** MACKINTOSH *Char. Canning* Wks. 1846 II. 457 His manner was simple and unobtrusive; his language always quite familiar. **1840** DICKENS *Old C. Shop* xiv, I trace the same current now, flowing through all his quiet and unobtrusive proceedings. **1890** 'L. FALCONER' *Mlle. Ixe* vii, Captain Leslie kept unobtrusive, but attentive watch.

Hence **Unobtru·siveness.**

**1797** JANE AUSTEN *Sense & Sens.* xlvi, She saw only an emotion.. in its unobtrusiveness entitled to praise. **1826** DISRAELI *V. Grey* III. viii, He is an object of observation from his very unobtrusiveness. **1879** *Cassell's Techn. Educ.* II. 152/2 All walls, however decorated,.. must retire even behind the furniture by their unobtrusiveness.

**Unobtru·sively,** *adv.* (UN-[1] 11, 5 b.)

**1796** MME. D'ARBLAY *Camilla* I. 358 The most unobtrusively gay..of almost any young creature I ever beheld. **1852** W. COLLINS *Basil* II. i, He was dressed as unobtrusively as possible, entirely in black. **1884** C. T. SAUNDERS in *Law Times* 25 Oct. 412/2 The abolition of primogeniture was.. unobtrusively proposed.

**Uno·bvious,** *a.* (UN-[1] 7.)

Frequently used by Boyle and Jer. Bentham.

**1643** PRYNNE *Popish R. Favourite* 36 Some more speciall passages in Popish writers,..which because then unobvious and unknown to most, I had an intention to have published. **1661** BOYLE *Style of Script.* 45 Though some unobvious Stars of that bright sphære cannot be discerned without the help of a Telescope. **1676** GLANVILL *Ess.* iii. 44 The knowledge and application of some unobvious and unheeded Properties and Laws of natural things. **1718** *Freethinker* (1733) No. 155. 240 It is able to perceive the unobvious Distinctions between things, which bear a very near Resemblance to one another. **1798** T. GREEN *Diary Lover of Lit.* (1810) 109 Its efficient cause, therefore, must not be sought.. in any unobvious qualities. **1845** MILL *Ess.* II. 183 To trace back this philanthropic movement.. to its small and unobvious beginnings. **1890** *Spectator* 25 Oct., Mr. Orger's amendment..would appear to be as unobvious..as need be.

**Unocca·sional,** *a.* (UN-[1] 7.) **1724** WELTON *Chr. Faith & Pract.* 232 Scripture, the only rule to guide and direct a true unoccasional conscience by. **Unocca·sioned,** *ppl. a.* (UN-[1] 8.) **1586** *Cyuile & Vncyuile Life* (1868) 80 You might haue gathered, that vnoccasioned, or not contryued, no man will resort vnto your Town house. **1747** WARBURTON *Shakespeare's Wks.* VIII. 360 *note*, This observation seems strangely abrupt and unoccasioned. **Uno·ccupancy.** (UN-[1] 12.) **1833** T. HOOK *Parson's Dau.* I. i, The tear-like drippings from its various windows.. during the several years of its unoccupancy.

**Uno·ccupied,** *ppl. a.* [UN-[1] 8.]

**1.** Not occupied or engaged in some work or pursuit; idle.

*c* **1380** WYCLIF *Wks.* (1880) 191 First men ordeyned.. to putte awey ydelnesse & to be not vnoccupied in goode manere for þe tyme. *c* **1440** *Jacob's Well* 231 þou þat syttest stylle here in cherch, vnocupyed & thynkest on þi muk. *c* **1490** CAXTON *Rule St. Benet* 132 Lete theym be assigned to other occupacyons to doo, so that they be neuer vnoccupied in vertu. *c* **1529** CAPON in Ellis *Orig. Lett.* Ser. I. I. 190 So that your workemen shall not be un occupyed for wante of stone. **1555** EDEN *Decades* (Arb.) 137 A valiente mynde can not rest in one place or bee vnoccupyed. **1573** TUSSER *Husb.* (1878) 118 Prouide of thine owne to haue all things at hand, least worke and the workman vnoccupide stand. **1647** HEXHAM I, Vnoccupied, or doing nothing, *onbesich.* **1751** JOHNSON *Rambler* No. 141 ⁋ 2 Acting when his imagination was unoccupied, and his judgment unsettled. **1780** BURKE *Œcon. Reform* Wks. III. 324 The council, or committees of council, were never a moment unoccupied, with affairs of trade. **1827** LYTTON *Falkland* 22, I am unoccupied by a single pursuit. **1898** 'MERRIMAN' *Roden's Corner* xvii, She led a blameless, unoccupied, and apparently purposeless life.

**2.** Not put to use; left unemployed. (In later use only of time.)

**1448–9** METHAM *Amoryus & Cl.* 2210 Tyme on-ocupyid, qwan folk haue lytyl to do. **1486** *Bk. St. Albans* B vj, Tho saame lewnes þou shalt fastyn slackely as a bowstryng vnocupyede. **1523** [COVERDALE] *Old God* (1534) B j, The sword.. beynge through dust & longe beynge unoccupied,.. defiled with ruste. **1561** T. HOBY tr. *Castiglione's Courtyer* IV. (1577) T v, They..fell into decay and loste theyr puissaunce and brightnesse, lyke yron vnoccupied. **1796** MME. D'ARBLAY *Camilla* V. 354 Her time.. hung not upon her unoccupied. **1829** SCOTT *Anne of G.* xxv, As if desirous that the hour should arrive which would put an end to a day unoccupied.

**3.** Of ground, etc.: Not occupied by inhabitants or indwellers; not put to use in this way; not frequented or filled up; empty.

*c* **1425** WYNTOUN *Cron.* IV. xix. 1780 Thare wes vnoccupiit ..A land beȝond ane arme of the se. **1560** BIBLE *Judges* v. 6 The hye wayes were vnoccupied, and the trauelers walked through byways. **1573** TUSSER *Husb.* (1878) 15 No dwellers, what profiteth house for to stand? What goodnes, vnoccupied, bringeth the land? **1691** RAY *Creation* I. (1692) 189 Doubtless, if we shall discover further to the very North-pole, we shall find all that Tract not to be vain, useless, or unoccupied. **1784** COWPER *Task* v. 557 The word That, finding an interminable space Unoccupied, has fill'd the void so well. **1807** *Europ. Mag.* LII. 111/1 This part of Lancashire is.. highly cultivated, not an inch of ground lies waste and unoccupied. **1884** in A. Cawston *Street Improv. London* (1893) 115 There are always a very large number of unoccupied houses even in towns where the building trade is very active.

**b.** Not taken up or appropriated.

**1701** GREW *Cosmol.* II. iii. 43 The Phancy hath full Power to create them in the Sensories themselves, then unoccupy'd by External Impressions. **1830** MISS MITFORD *Village* Ser. IV. 107 She could not have chosen an occupation more completely unoccupied, or more loudly called for. **1832** *Westm. Rev.* Oct. 353 Cadences..highly favourable for leaving the ear unoccupied for any measure which may follow.

**Uno·cular** (yūn-), *a.* [f. L. *ūnocul-us* one-eyed + -AR. Cf. UNIOCULAR *a.*] One-eyed.

**1864** DE MORGAN in Graves *Life Sir W. Hamilton* (1889) III. 613 Accordingly I have always been strictly unocular.

**Unode** (yū·n-). *Geom.* A uniplanar node.

**1869** CAYLEY *Math. Papers* (1893) VI. 362 If there is a unode, then this may be and is taken to be at *D*, and its uniplane may be taken to be $X = 0$. *Ibid.*, There is never, besides the unode, any other node.

†**Uno·dorable**, *a.* [UN-[1] 7 b.] Incapable of being smelled. **1674** GREW *Disc. Mixture* iii. § 17 As in any fixed unodorable or untastable Body. †**Unofea·rned**, *ppl. a. Obs.* [UN-[1] 8 + OF-EARN *v.*] Undeserved. *c* **1200** *Vices & Virtues* 3 Asolkenesse.. me haueð ofte idon eten oðermannes sare swink all un-of-earned. *Ibid.* 51, 59. **Unoffe·ndable**, *a.* (UN-[1] 7 b.) **1839** LADY LYTTON *Cheveley* (ed. 2) II. i. 12 The most obsequious civility and unoffendable good-humour.

**Unoffe·nded**, *ppl. a.* (UN-[1] 8.)

**1481** *Cov. Leet Bk.* 494 That, his highnes vnoffended, we here..may procede amonges our-self to the determinacion therin. **1598** FLORIO, *Inoffeso*, vnoffended, vntoucht, vnwrongd. **1633** BP. HALL *Occas. Medit.* lii. 124 The Bee stings..when she is provoked; these draw blood, unoffended, and sting for their owne pleasure. **1673** [R. LEIGH] *Transp. Reh.* 84 Reverence..might perhaps occasion more sport then a man..could brook unoffended. **1749** JOHNSON *Irene* v. ii, This gen'ral calm Is sure the smile of unoffended heav'n. **1782** V. KNOX *Ess.* c. (1819) II. 218 It is the common people, ..unoffended and unoffending, who chiefly suffer in the evil consequences. **1809** MALKIN *Gil Blas* VII. v. ¶ 4 They, with unoffended nostrils, were engaged in general conversation, though they dined individually.

Hence **Unoffe·ndedly** *adv.*

**1856** RUSKIN *Mod. Paint.* IV. v. xx. § 28 They were both of them..to behold unoffendedly all that was upon the earth.

**Unoffe·nding**, *ppl. a.* (UN-[1] 10, 5 b.)

**1569** *Reg. Privy Council Scot.* I. 668, I..sall keip gude rewle and quietnes unoffending aganis the lawis or makand troubill. *a* **1600** *Grim the Collier of Croydon* (1662) 9 Some will count it Vertue in a woman Still to be bound to unoffending Silence. *a* **1625** BEAUM. & FL. *Laws of Candy* II. i, My prayers pull daily blessings on thy head, My unoffending child. **1703** POPE *Statius' Thebais* I. 771 Yet why must unoffending Argos feel The vengeance due to this unlucky steel? **1796** MME. D'ARBLAY *Camilla* III. 403 How should I rejoice..to rescue this one poor unoffending..animal from such tyranny! **1828** SCOTT *F. M. Perth* xix, Who.. could have thought of harming a creature so simple, and so unoffending? **1876** BANCROFT *Hist. U. S.* II. xxx. 253 The councillors were famed for their unoffending respectability.

†**Unoffe·nsed**, *ppl. a. Obs.*[—1] [UN-[1] 8.] Unoffended. *c* **1440** *Pallad. on Husb.* I. 32 The contrey men colourid wel vchoone, Their wittis cleer and vnoffensid sight.

†**Unoffe·nsive**, *a. Obs.* (UN-[1] 7, 5 b.)

**1612** R. DABORNE *Christian turn'd Turke* 214 [Nature] sent him to the world, All vnoffensiue, vnarm'd. **1642** VICARS *God in Mount* 66 Coming onely in a fair and unoffensive manner. **1674** J. FELL *Hammond* Wks. I. 14 Notwithstanding his unoffensive and cautious return to those ill laid demands. **1768** *Woman of Honor* II. 158 That modest unoffensive turn you gave to your non-acceptance.

So **Unoffe·nsively** *adv.*

**1606** BP. W. BARLOW *Serm.* 21 Sept., Ep. Ded. A j b, Discussing the point sincerely and, I trust, vnoffensiuely.

**Uno·ffered**, *ppl. a.* (UN-[1] 8, 8 c.)

**1526** *Pilgr. Perf.* (W. de W. 1531) 103 Leuynge in hym nothynge vnoffred for vs, but in all partes he suffered payne for our synne. *a* **1586** SIDNEY *Arcadia* III. xxiii, I know too well their cunning (who leave no mony unoffered that may buy mine honour). **1642** CHAS. I *Declar. Intentions Brainford* 7 Unfought with, and unoffered at,..to march away. **1658** *Whole Duty of Man* iii. § 18 Though the gift be already at the Altar, it must rather be left there unoffered, than [etc.]. **1736** WEBSTED *Wks.* (1787) 477 To the end they might do so, no methods were left untried, no motives unoffered. **1747** P. FRANCIS tr. *Horace, Ep.* I. xiii. 4 If he ask'd to read th' unoffer'd Lay. **1848** BUCKLEY *Iliad* 5 Neither on account of a vow unperformed, nor of a hecatomb unoffered.

**Uno·fficed**, *ppl. a.* (UN-[1] 8 or UN-[2] 8.) **1657** BP. H. KING *Elegy* Poems (1664) 3 The now unoffic'd Servants crack their Staves.

**Uno·fficered**, *ppl. a.* (UN-[1] 8.)

**1655** EARL ORRERY *Parthen.* I. VIII. 450 This treachery.. brought a world of confusion in those vn-officer'd Troopes. **1754** P. H. *Hiberniad* iii. 25 Raw, unofficer'd..Militias. **1782** PENNANT *Journ. Chest. to London* 50 A..band of mountaineers, undisciplined, unofficered, and half-armed. **1852** GROTE *Greece* II. lxx. IX. 115 The unofficered Grecian army.

**Uno·fficerlike**, *a.* (UN-[1] 7 c.)

**1803** NELSON in Nicolas *Disp.* (1845) V. 206 Such conduct is highly reprehensible and unofficerlike. **1831** TRELAWNY *Adv. Younger Son* vii, It's unofficer-like to get drunk before sunset. **1871** *Routledge's Ev. Boy's Ann.* Nov. 695 The unofficer-like want of method in these signals.

**Unoffi·cial**, *a.* and *sb.* [UN-[1] 7, 5 b, 12.]

1\. Of things: Not having an official character or stamp.

**1798** *Monthly Rev.* XXVI. 511 Impertinent and unofficial as it seems, it may have been intended to intimate [etc.]. **1866** GEO. ELIOT *F. Holt* Introd. 3 His sheep-dog following with a heedless unofficial air as of a beadle in undress. **1884** HUXLEY in *Life* (1900) II. 80, I wrote to Evans an unofficial letter.

2\. Of persons: Not holding an official position; not acting in an official capacity.

**1829** GEN. P. THOMPSON *Exerc.* (1842) I. 124 Unofficial philosophers must be content to classify appearances as they rise. **1869** J. MARTINEAU *Ess.* II. 97 The theories of these unofficial masters of philosophy.

b\. *sb.* One who is not an official.

**1887** *Pall Mall G.* 29 July 4/1 We have a letter this morning from St. Petersburg, the writer of which is a leader among the 'unofficials'.

**Unoffi·cially**, *adv.* (UN-[1] 11; cf. prec.)

**1830** COBBETT *Hist. Geo. IV*, iii. § 139 He did it unofficially, in letters to Lord Grey. **1860** FROUDE *Hist. Eng.* VI. 275 The two Houses of Parliament were invited to be present unofficially at Whitehall.

**Unoffi·cious**, *a.* (UN-[1] 7, 5 b.)

**1611** FLORIO, *Inficioso*, vnofficious, negligent. **1645** MILTON *Tetrach.* 81 Thus all occasions..are not unofficious to administer somthing which may conduce to explain..the assertion of this book. **1807** *Ann. Rev.* V. 171 The editor.. deserves public thanks for the unostentatious, unofficious propriety, with which his laudable task is performed.

Hence **Unoffi·ciousness.**

**1611** COTGR., *Inofficiosité*, vnofficiousnesse, vnrespectiuenesse, or want of due respect.

†**Unofse·rved**, *ppl. a. Obs.* [UN-[1] 8.] = UNDESERVED *ppl. a.* 1.

*a* **1200** *St. Marher.* 16 Hwet so ich am, þurh godes grace ich hit do ant am wilȝeoue unofservet. *a* **1240** *Lofsong* in *O. E. Hom.* I. 215 Deorwurðe drihten, þu..dest us al þet þu dest þurh þine swete grace al unofserued. **1297** R. GLOUC. (Rolls) 1256 Mi mede þer of is þat he me wole driue of is lond vnofserued iwis.

**Uno·ft**, *adv.* (UN-[1] 11 b; cf. next.) **1864** SIR J. K. JAMES *Tasso* x. xx, Since not Unoft it happens that the wise and strong Carve for themselves the best and happiest lot.

**Uno·ften**, *adv.* [UN-[1] 11 b.] Infrequently; seldom. (Only with negatives.)

**1741** HARRIS *Three Treat.* II. (1765) 194 The Man of Gallantry not unoften has been found to think after the same manner. **1835** LYTTON *Rienzi* I. iii, Nor was it unoften that the mere presence of a noble sufficed to scatter whole crowds. **1864** J. BROWN *Jeems* 15 You get more patient,..and not unoften you come to a stand-still.

**Unoi·l**, *v.* (UN-[2] 3.) **1693** *Dryden's Juvenal* viii. (1697) 205 A tight Maid, e're he for Wine can ask, Guesses his Meaning, and unoils the Flask.

**Unoi·led**, *ppl. a.* (UN-[1] 8.)

**1728** YOUNG *Love Fame* VI. 138 His wounded ears complaints eternal fill, As unoil'd hinges, querelously shrill. *c* **1799** J. FOSTER in *Life & Corr.* (1846) I. 97 The creak of unoiled wheels. **1851** H. D. WOLFF *Pict. Span. Life* 134 The chain again clanks, unoiled hinges creak. **1884** M^c^LAREN *Spinning* (ed. 2) 70 Much dust can be shaken out of the wool when it is unoiled.

**Unoi·ly**, *a.* (UN-[1] 7.) **1674** GREW *Anat. Trunks* II. iv. § 17 A third sort of Gum, is that which is Unoylie. **1682** — *Disc. Mixture* App. § 1 Oyls..easily mingleable with any unoyly Liquor. **Uno·ld**, *a.* (UN-[1] 7.) *c* **1440** *Pallad. on Husb.* IV. 9 The trunkes sadde, in humor that abounde, Vnolde, vnrende. **Uno·ld**, *v.* (UN-[2] 6a.) **1608** SYLVESTER *Du Bartas* II. iv. *Schisme* 697 There ripes the rare cheer-cheek Myrobalan, Minde-gladding Fruit, that can un-old a Man. **Uno·minously**, *adv.* (UN-[1] 11.) **1849** *Brand's Pop. Antiq.* I. 38 The sun would not shine unominously on the day on which the saint was burnt. †**Uno·ning**, *vbl. sb. Obs.* [UN-[2] 3, 8.] Disunion, discord. **1340** *Ayenb.* 65 Þe uerste is strif, þe oþer chidinge,..þe zixte þreapinge, þe zeuende vnonynge. **Uno·ped**, *ppl. a. poet.* [UN-[1] 8.] = UNOPENED *ppl. a.* **1815** SCOTT *Guy M.* xx, The close-press'd leaves unoped for many an age. [Cf. Crabbe *Library* 147.] **Uno·penable**, *a.* (UN-[1] 7 b.) **1832** MISS MITFORD *Village* Ser. v. 36 Trying to lift the lid of the unopenable chest.

**Uno·pened**, *ppl. a.* [UN-[1] 8. Cf. Du. *ongeopened.*]

1\. Not opened; left, or remaining, closed or shut: **a.** Of letters, books, etc.

**1600** E. BLOUNT tr. *Conestaggio* 74 This Letter..remained still with them vnopened. **1700** FARQUHAR *Constant Couple* I. i, Angelica, send it [*sc.* a letter] back unopened! say you? **1711** LADY M. W. MONTAGU *Let. to W. Montagu* 26 Feb., If you write, be not displeased if I send it back unopened. **1766** *Parlt. Deb.* (1813) XVI. 303 [They] went to statute books before unopened,..and there made the amazing, astonishing discovery. **1836** H. COLERIDGE *Northern Worthies* (1852) I. 43 A sealed and unopened epistle. **1865** DICKENS *Mut. Fr.* I. iii, A book..unopened on a shelf. **1888** JACOBI *Printer's Vocab.*, *Unopened edges*, applied to books the edges of which have not been opened.

b\. In other applications.

**1627** MAY *Lucan* III. D 7, Before the yet vnopen'd doore he stay'd. **1742** YOUNG *Nt. Th.* II. 468 Like bales unopen'd to the sun. **1796** WITHERING *Brit. Plants* (ed. 3) III. 689 Unopened flowers nodding. **1843** R. J. GRAVES *Syst. Clin. Med.* ix. 102, I have frequently directed the blister to be left unopened. **1884** in A. Cawston *Street Improv. London* (1893) 117 The consequences of leaving *culs de sac* even of a respectable kind unopened.

2\. Not opened up for use.

**1756** P. BROWNE *Jamaica* 13 Every settler inclined to reserve some unopened land. **1858** LD. ST. LEONARDS *Handy-bk. Prop. Law* xxiii. 179 If you were to sell part of your estate, reserving the unopened mines with a right of entry. **1890** HALLETT *1000 Miles on Elephant* 434 [To] throw open for British commerce the most magnificent, unopened, and available market in the world.

**Uno·pening**, *ppl. a.* (UN-[1] 10.) **1732** POPE *Ep. Bathurst* 194 Benighted wanderers..Curse the sav'd candle, and unop'ning door. **1852** M. ARNOLD *Empedocles* II. 359 Still Thought and Mind Will hurry us..Over the unallied unopening Earth. **Uno·perable**, *a.* (UN-[1] 7 b, 5 b.) **1652** ASHMOLE *Theat. Chem.* Prol. 9 They wrought unoperable Workes. **Uno·perated**, *ppl. a.* (UN-[1] 8.) **1802** *Noble Wanderers* I. 37 Native energy..which, unoperated upon by adversity,..remains an inactive principle in the mind. **Uno·perating**, *ppl. a.* (UN-[1] 10.) **1719** WATERLAND *Vind. Christ's Div.* 158 The perfect Nativity..of the Word: who had been, as it were, quiescent or un-operating from all Eternity, till [etc.]. **1768–74** TUCKER *Lt. Nat.* (1834) I. 507 Neither is it practicable..for us to frame an idea of such unoperating nature.

†**Uno·perative**, *a. Obs.* (UN-[1] 7, 5 b.)

**1641** MILTON *Reform.* II. 48 For if the life of Christ be hid to this world, much more is his Scepter unoperative, but in spirituall things. **1685** SOUTH *Serm.* (1727) I. 389 It..imports no more than an idle unoperative..desire of the end, without any consideration of..the means. **1756** BURKE *Subl. & B.* IV. xxiv, There lie the qualities of beauty either dead or unoperative. **1783** — *Rep. Ind. Com.* Wks. II. 22 By which measure this provision of the Act has proved as unoperative as all the rest. **1818** BENTHAM *Ch. Eng.*, *Catech. Exam.* 248 Mere unoperative existence.

**Unope·rculate**, *a.*, **-ated**, *ppl. a.* (UN-[1] 7, 8, 5 b.) **1847** WEBSTER, *Unoperculated*, having no cover or operculum. **1884** *Imp. Dict.* IV. 510/2 *Unoperculate.* **Unopi·nionated**, *ppl. a.* (UN-[1] 8.) [**1775** ASH.] **1824** MEDWIN *Conversat. Ld. Byron* II. 140 No man was more unopinionated. †**Uno·pportune**, *a. Obs.* (UN-[1] 7, 5 b.) **1787** BENTHAM *Def. Usury* x. 99 The anti-jewish side of it found no unopportune support in a passage of Aristotle. **1802** MRS. J. WEST *Infidel Father* III. 235 Your excusing yourself from that unopportune engagement. †**Uno·pportunely**, *adv. Obs.* (UN-[1] 11, 5 b.) **1657** EARL MONM. tr. *Paruta's Pol. Disc.* 37 They sent their Fleet to regain Sicily; but the counsel was too late and unopportunely taken. **1766** COLMAN & GARRICK *Clandestine Marriage* II. 37, I have broke in upon you a little unopportunely, I believe. **Unoppo·sable**, *a.* (UN-[1] 7 b.) **1667** WATERHOUSE *Fire Lond.* 60 Illiterate men Apostoliz'd and made by him unopposable. **1802–12** BENTHAM *Ration. Judic. Evid.* (1827) IV. 151 The application is either opposable or unopposable.

**Unoppo·sed**, *ppl. a.* (UN-[1] 8.)

**1659** W. CHAMBERLAYNE *Pharon.* v. ii. 345 Impetuous rage, like whirlwinds unopposed. **1672** DRYDEN *Conq. Granada* IV. i, The people, like a headlong torrent goe;..But, unoppos'd, they either loose their force, Or [etc.]. **1780** BURKE *Sp. at Bristol* Wks. III. 415 For what end was that bill to linger beyond the usual period of an unoppos'd measure? **1794** MRS. RADCLIFFE *Myst. Udolpho* xxxviii, His talents for play..were generally successful when unopposed by the tricks of villany. **1841** ELPHINSTONE *Hist. India* I. 507 The Mahometans pursued their success unopposed. **1859** G. WILSON *Mem. E. Forbes* ii. 45 Thus, unopposed but unencouraged, he laboured at Natural History. **1899** MACKAIL *W. Morris* I. 336 An unopposed candidate.

*ellipt.* **1893** *Daily News* 3 May 5/7 The Unopposed Committee of the House of Commons.

**Uno·pposite**, *a.* (UN-[1] 7.) **1802–12** BENTHAM *Ration. Judic. Evid.* (1827) I. 499 In point of affections, let the witness be, with reference to each party, altogether unopposite; ..equally a friend to both.

**Unoppre·ssed**, *ppl. a.* (UN-[1] 8.)

*a* **1572** KNOX *Hist. Ref.* Wks. 1846 I. 357 As alsua the said town mycht..brooke thair ancient lawis and liberteis unoppressed by men of wear. **1659** W. CHAMBERLAYNE *Pharon.* IV. ii. 445 Harmless nature, living unopprest With surfeits. *Ibid.* 453 Fair virgins..unopprest By dark suspicion. **1709** *Brit. Apollo* II. No. 10. 3/2 Your..Spirits, Unopprest, Glide freely on. **1781** COWPER *Table-T.* 272 The soul emancipated, unoppressed,..Learns much.

**Unoppre·ssive**, *a.* (UN-[1] 7, 5 b.)

**1648** W. ASHHURST *Reasons agst. Agreement* 13 They are to have nothing but in a unoppressive way. **1782–3** W. F. MARTYN *Geog. Mag.* I. 355 [The Gentoo laws] are unoppressive. **1790** BURKE *Fr. Rev.* 53 You would have had an unoppressive but a productive revenue. **1874** RUSKIN *Fors Clav.* xl. IV. 78 What was an act of distressing servitude has become an unoppressive act of love.

**Unoppre·ssively**, *adv.* (UN-[1] 11.) **1656** EARL ORRERY *Parthen.* III. III. 152 A negative obedience is the farthest it [*sc.* paternal right] can unoppressively extend it self. **Uno·pulence.** (UN-[1] 12.) **1796** *Monthly Mag.* II. 467 The unopulence of the pastor. **1830** BENTHAM *Offic. Apt. Maximized, Further Extr. Const. Code* 11 But the proposed system—does it not hold up to view unopulence as an efficient cause of aptitude? **Uno·pulent**, *a.* (UN-[1] 7, 5 b.) *a* **1816** BENTHAM *Offic. Apt. Maximized, Introd. View* (1830) 11 Unopulent classes excluded, and thus injured. **1829** *Westm. Rev.* Oct. 472 The poor (i.e. the unopulent, not the absolutely poor). **Unorato·rial**, *a.* (UN-[1] 7.) **1753** N. TORRIANO *Gangr. Sore Throat* Pref., However unoratorial my Expression.

†**Unordai·n**, *a. Obs.*[—1] [f. UN-[1] 7 + *ordeyne* ORDENE *a.*] Not observing order or rule. So †**Unordai·nly** *adv. Obs.*[—1]

*a* **1400** *Pauline Ep.* (Powell) Rom. I. 31 Þei [being]..vnwise, unordeyne [L. *incompositos*], withoute affeccioun. ? *a* **1400** *Spec. Vitæ* (MS. Bodl. 446) fol. 126 b, A man þat wedded es Shuld..no dede vnordeynly wirke Agayne þe sacrament of holy kirke.

**Unordai·n**, *v.* (UN-[2] 3.) *c* **1440** *Wycliffite Bible* (1850) IV. 438 Ne he vnordeynede vs of sum veyn speche feynynge, that vs ouerturne fro the sothfastnesse of the gospel. **1709** J. JOHNSON *Clergym. Vade M.* II. p. lxxi, Tho' Bishops ordain, they cannot unordain.

**Unordai·ned**, *ppl. a.* [UN-[1] 8.]

†1\. Not regulated or controlled. *Obs.*[—1]

*c* **1340** HAMPOLE *Prose Tr.* 13 Þe delyte þat has noghte of vnordaynde styrrynge, and mekely has styrrynge in Criste.

2\. Not ecclesiastically ordained.

**1653** BAXTER *Chr. Concord* 84 They are bound to choose a man unordained to this work. *a* **1691** — in Calamy *Life* vii. (1702) 131 There is a Duty in such a Case of Necessity, even on Persons unordain'd. **1804** *Ann. Rev.* II. 208 The distinction between ordained and unordained preachers. **1865** S. WILBERFORCE in R. G. Wilberforce *Life* (1882) III. 166 Brotherhoods of unordained men not in Holy Orders.

3\. Not appointed or decreed.

**1815** WORDSW. *Ode* 63 Be it not unordained that solemn rites..Shall be performed at pregnant intervals.

**Unordai·ning**, *vbl. sb.* (UN-[1] 13.)

In quot. rendering L. *inordinatio* disorder.

**1382** WYCLIF *Wisd.* xiv. 26 The defouling of soules,..the vnordeynyng of leccherie and of vnclennesse.

**Uno·rder**, *v.* [UN-[2] 3.] *trans.* To recall an order for (something); to countermand.

*c* **1440** *Alph. Tales* 402 He gart take Formosius oute off his grafe & vnordurd all þat he had giffen ordurs to. **1782** MISS BURNEY *Cecilia* VIII. iii, I think I must *unorder* the tea ..if I am to be responsible for any mischief from your drinking it. **1803** NELSON in Nicolas *Disp.* (1845) V. 65 If Lord Keith or any other man is to have her, I must un-order all these things. **1843** F. E. PAGET *Pageant* 94 Mrs. Sawderley was not permitted to unorder her dress.

**Uno·rdered**, *ppl. a.*[1] [UN-[1] 8.]

†1\. Not belonging to a religious order; not properly ordained. *Obs.*

*c* **1386** CHAUCER *Parson's T.* ¶ 85 Thow shalt considere.. wheither thou be..wedded or sengle, ordered or unordred, ..clerk or seculeer. **1588** ALLEN *Admon.* 32 Creatinge..new, hungrie, base, and vnordered Preistes. **1607** T. ROGERS 39

*Art.* (1625) 200 They be vnordered Apostates, pretended, and sacrilegious ministers.

**2.** Not put in order; unarranged.

**1477** NORTON *Ord. Alch.* (MS. Ashm. 1464) Proem, Of all the books vnordered of Alchimy The effectes be heere sett owt orderlie. **1504** ATKYNSON tr. *De Imitatione* III. xliii. 231 God..that lefte nothynge vnordred in all the worlde. **1549** CHEKE *Hurt. Sedit.* (1569) G i b, What is vnordred plentie, but a wastfull spoyle? **1826** MRS. SHELLEY *Last Man* III. 200 The consequence of their journey in their present unordered and chiefless array. **1877** MORLEY *Crit. Misc.* Ser. II. 183 This was not a mere casual reflection..taking a solitary ..position among those various and unordered ideas.

**†3** Not observing due order; disorderly. *Obs.*

**1572** ABP. PARKER *Corr.* (Parker Soc.) 403 [To] inquire of such unordered persons papistically set, not coming to prayers according to the laws. **1582** STANYHURST *Æneis* I. (Arb.) 22 Dare ye..Too raise such raks iaks on seas, and danger vnorderd? **1611** A. STAFFORD *Niobe* 191 To satisfie the vnordred appetites of the body, and vnlawfull desires of the soule.

**4.** Not ordered or commanded.

**1891** *Cent. Dict.* **1906** *Westm. Gaz.* 23 May 4/1 The gay tweeds..remain unordered.

**†Unoˑrdered,** *ppl. a.*[2] *Obs.*[-1] [UN-[2] 6 b.] Disordered. **1621** in Foster *Eng. Factories Ind.* I. (1906) 242 Their shipping rent, battered, and much unordered.

**Unoˑrderly,** *a.* Now *rare.* [UN-[1] 7, 5 b.]

**1.** Not in conformity with good order; irregular in respect of action or conduct.

**1483** *Acta Dom. Audit.* 142*/2 The wrangwis and vnordourly leding of a processe apoune þe said land. **1561** T. NORTON *Calvin's Inst.* I. xi. 26 b, The fountaine of al this whole mischiefe is an vnorderly counterfaiting. **1587** HOLINSHED *Chron.* (ed. 2) III. 1254/1 Although it be somewhat..vnorderlie to treat of vnorderlie officers vnder such an vnorderlie king as Richard the third was. **1601** J. WHEELER *Treat. Comm.* 107 The vnorderlie settinge foorth and publishing of the Emperors Mandate. **1642** *Coll. Rights & Priv. Parl.* 7 How unorderly were it for the satisfying of men, to runne into his displeasure. **1800** COLERIDGE *Piccolom.* IV. vii. 214 The Emperor perpetrated..deeds most unorderly.

**b.** In stronger sense: Disorderly.

**1583** GOLDING *Calvin on Deut.* clxxxv. 1147 Wee see why God hath pronounced that..they be..destitute of vnderstanding when their lyfe is loose and vnorderly. **1626** L. OWEN *Running Register* 16 The Englishmens dissolute liuing, and vnorderly behauiour in the said Seminarie. **1761** *Ann. Reg., Chron.* 235/2 Small parties of the unorderly, undisciplined mob.

**2.** Not observing due order or arrangement; disordered, confused.

**1578** THYNNE in *Animadv.* (1865) p. lix, To desplay my Inwarde mynde, whiche..thus entreth into his vnorderly discourse. **1588** FRAUNCE *Lawiers Log.* I. ii. 7 b, Thereby to giue sentence of methodicall proceeding or vnorderly confusion. **1609** R. BARNERD *Faithf. Sheph.* 83 An vnorderly heaping vp of things together confounds memory. **1656** HOBBES *Liberty, Necess., & Chance* 143 After much unorderly discourse he comes in with This is the doctrine [etc.].

**Unoˑrderly,** *adv.* [UN-[1] 11.]

**1.** Not in good order; not according to a fixed order or arrangement; irregularly.

*c* **1470** HENRY *Wallace* x. 685 Wallace has seyn the Scottis wnordourly Folow the chas. **1547** RECORDE *Judic. Ur.* 9 Nothynge done unorderly cann be well understanded of the reders. **1578** BANISTER *Hist. Man* I. 7 These bones are perforated, here, and there, vnorderly, with a sort of smal holes. **1603** FLORIO *Montaigne* III. viii. 558 Shee seemeth faultie and vnprofitable, being ill placed and vnorderly disposed. **1637–50** ROW *Hist. Kirk* (Wodrow Soc.) 46 Whatever member of the Assemblie does speak unorderlie, and without leave asked..of the Moderator.

**2.** Not in an orderly or well-regulated manner; irregularly, improperly.

**1471** *Act. Audit.* (1839) 16/1 The lordis..deliuers þat þe processis of þe breif of Richt..is vnlachfully and vnorderly procedit. **1559** AYLMER *Harborowe* G 4 b, Paule mente to bridle them..if they had prophecied vnorderly. **1596** *Southampton Court Leet Rec.* (1906) II. 315 So that such disobedient and lawlesse persons may not live so unorderly. **1610** DONNE *Pseudo-martyr* 387 They make Conuenticles against bishopps, and accuse them vnorderly, and against the forme of Canons. *a* **1653** BINNING *Usef. Case Consc.* (1693) 17 Paul would have as much distance kept with a brother walking unorderly, as with a pagan.

**†Unoˑrdinal,** *a. Obs.* [UN-[1] 7.] Not reduced to order; unregulated. *c* **1380** WYCLIF *Serm.* Sel. Wks. I. 2 Þat þere was a myche void place stablid betwene hem, derke and unordynel, þat lettid dampned men to come to hem. *Ibid.* III. 128 Riȝt as pride..is unordynel wille of a monnis owene hyenesse, so envye..is unordynel wille of mon to his neghtbore. **Unoˑrdinarily,** *adv.* (UN-[1] 11; cf. next.) **1574** *Brieff Disc. Troub. Franckford* 79 For that we had proceaded vnordinarilie, that is..contrary to the olde discipline.

**Unoˑrdinary,** *a.* (UN-[1] 7, 5 b.)

**1547** EDW. VI *Jrnl.* in *Lit. Rem.* (Roxb.) II. 213 Order was taken for al his servauntes..and the ordinary and unordinary were appointed. **1574** *Brieff Disc. Troub. Franckford* 79 They made cauillation at the manner off doinge off things as an vnordinary manner. **1610** HEALEY *St. Aug. Citie of God* 646 A proper phrase to the Greeke tongue, but vnordinary in the Latine. **1690** LOCKE *Hum. Und.* III. xi. § 20, I do not know how they can be excused from Murther, who kill monstrous Births (as we call them) because of an unordinary shape. **1730** T. BOSTON *Mem.* App. 45 A man of unordinary application to business. **1909** A. BLACKWOOD *Jimbo* i, A supreme ignorance of unordinary children.

**†Unoˑrdinate,** *a. Obs.* [UN-[1] 7, 5 b.] = INORDINATE *a.* (in various senses).

*c* **1375** in *Rel. Ant.* I. 39 Unordynate love of worldly things. **1398** TREVISA *Barth. De P. R.* v. xxiii. (Bodl. MS.), An vnordinat voice and horrible þat gladeþ not noþer comforteþ. *c* **1425** *St. Mary of Oignies* I. vi. in *Anglia* VIII. 139/10 Ydel worde or vnordynat lokynge or vnhonest hauynge of body. *c* **1491** *Chast. Goddes Chyld.* 22 This feuer tercian comyth somtyme of an unordynate hete. **1561** T. HOBY tr. *Castiglione's Courtyer* II. (1577) I viij, Our Courtier ought not to professe to be a glutton nor a dronkerd, nor riotous & vnordinate in any yll condition. **1591** HARINGTON *Orl. Fur.* VIII. Notes 63 The vncomely and carelesse actes that dishonest or vnordinat loue do prouoke euen the noblest vnto. **1610** S. RID *Martin Mark-all* H i, A iust punishment for their presumptuous and vnordinate proceedings.

**†Unoˑrdinately,** *adv. Obs.* (UN-[1] 11, 5 b.)

*c* **1380** WYCLIF *Sel. Wks.* III. 38 Ech body forȝetiþ him while þer þouȝt is bounden to love ony creature unordynatli. *c* **1425** *St. Mary of Oignies* I. v. in *Anglia* VIII. 138/16 Pronounsynge many wordes vnordynatly. *c* **1440** *Jacob's Well* 161 Whanne a man delyth wyth his wyif vnordynatly & vnkyndely. **1545** RAYNALD *Byrth Mankynde* 137 The sowar maye vnordinatly strewe..the seade on the earth. **1550** T. HOBY *Trav.* (1902) 57 Yf a mann drink unordinatlie of yt, yt makethe him dronke.

**Unoˑrdnanced,** *ppl. a.* (UN-[1] 8.) **1804** LARWOOD *No Gun Boats* 12 Better to give all than suffer their Gun Boats to remain in even an unrudderd, unmasted, unordnanced existence. **Unoˑrganed,** *ppl. a.* [UN-[2] 4, 8 + ORGAN *sb.*[1] 5.] Organically dissolved. **1624** QUARLES *Job* xix. 51 But man (vnorgan'd by the hand of Death) Dyes not, is but transplanted from beneath, Into a fairer soyle. **Unorgaˑnic,** *a.* (UN-[1] 7 and 5 b.) [**1775** ASH.] **1802–12** BENTHAM *Ration. Judic. Evid.* (1827) II. 508 The keeping of the rule of action..in one immense and unorganic mass. **Unoˑrganizable,** *a.* (UN-[1] 7 b, 5 b.) **1868** R. H. QUICK *Ess. Educ. Reform.* viii. 222 To cram the mind with isolated, or as Mr. Spencer calls them, unorganizable facts. **1902** *Encycl. Brit.* (ed. 10) XXXI. 515/2 The floor is covered by dead or dying unorganizable materials, without any layer of regenerative cells.

**Unoˑrganized,** *ppl. a.* [UN-[1] 8, 5 b.]

**1.** Not brought into an organic state.

**1690** LOCKE *Hum. Und.* II. xxx. § 5 An uniform, unorganized body, consisting..all of similar parts. **1746** BERKELEY in Fraser *Life* (1871) viii. 316 To me it seems that stones are vegetables unorganized. **1794** R. J. SULIVAN *View Nat.* I. 467 If we find causes of uncertainty in regard to organized beings, how many more must we find in regard to unorganized beings. **1829** T. CASTLE *Introd. Bot.* 225 That the epidermis is a fine, transparent, unorganized pellicle. **1899** *Allbutt's Syst. Med.* VI. 189 Ordinary unorganised or partly organised polypoid thrombi.

**2.** Not formed into an orderly or regulated whole.

**1836** H. COLERIDGE *North. Worthies* (1852) I. 16 Confiding in the unorganised valour of the English nation..he..opposed a standing army. **1860** FROUDE *Hist. Eng.* V. 213 The sustained fire..threw their dense and unorganized masses into rapid confusion.

Hence **Unoˑrganizedness.**

**1664** H. MORE *Apology* 486 Which makes me..seem to allow of the Unorganizedness of the Æthereal Vehicle of the Soul.

**Unorieˑntal,** *a.* (UN-[1] 7.) **1820** BYRON *Juan* III. xxviii, A most unoriental roar of laughter. **1862** THORNBURY *Turner* I. 194 The Jerusalem is very unoriental.

**Unoriˑginal,** *a.* and *sb.* [UN-[1] 7, 12.]

**1.** Having no origin; uncreated.

**1667** MILTON *P. L.* x. 477 Plung'd in the womb Of unoriginal Night and Chaos wilde.

**2.** Not original; derivative; second-hand.

**1774** GERARD *Ess. Genius* 42 Nothing appears in it uncommon or new; every thing is trite and unoriginal. **1802–12** BENTHAM *Ration. Judic. Evid.* (1827) I. 57 The evidence may be termed unoriginal in so far as the narrating witness..speaks of some other person and not of himself. *a* **1849** POE *Diddling* Wks. 1865 IV. 269 He would return a purse..upon discovering that he had obtained it by an unoriginal diddle. **1897** W. P. KER *Epic & Rom.* 329 The 'Song of Roland' is comparatively late and unoriginal.

**b.** *sb.* One who lacks originality.

**1847** MEDWIN *Life Shelley* II. 203 A cold, selfish, mathematical unoriginal, like Hobbes.

**Unoriginaˑlity.** (UN-[1] 12.)

**1798** LAMB *Let.* in *Final Mem.* iv. 32, I love to anticipate charges of unoriginality. **1802–12** BENTHAM *Ration. Judic. Evid.* (1827) III. 434 The quality of unoriginality seems applicable to an article of evidence in either of two cases. *a* **1849** POE *Longf.*, etc., Wks. 1865 III. 360 Of the unoriginality of the thesis we have already spoken.

**Unoriˑginate,** *a.* and *sb.* [UN-[1] 7, 12, 5 b.] = next.

**1719** J. JACKSON *Let. to Auth. True Doctr. Trinity* 216 Self-existent being the same as unoriginate, is (you think) merely a Negative Character. **1755** AMORY *Mem.* (1769) 183 One spirit possessed of all possible perfections, self-existent, unoriginate, the first cause of the universe. **1855** PUSEY *Doctr. Real Presence* 236 For God is unoriginate, and not generate. **1872** LIDDON *Elem. Relig.* ii. 53 A supreme all-producing Cause, Itself uncaused, unoriginate.

**b.** As *sb.* An unoriginated being.

**1724** WATERLAND *Athan. Creed* 145 That..neither the Son nor Holy Ghost have any share in these Titles or Characters, to make Three Unoriginates. **1875** *Encycl. Brit.* II. 537/2 Arius denied of Christ that He was..part of the Unoriginate.

Hence **Unoriˑginately** *adv.*, **-ness.**

**1720** WATERLAND *Eight Serm.* Pref., It is only saying that he is so emphatically, or unoriginately. **1723** — *Second Vind.* 125 It was to admit of a higher and a lower Sense of the Word God; the higher supposed to have nothing above the other but Self-existence, or Unoriginateness.

**Unoriˑginated,** *ppl. a.* (UN-[1] 8.)

**1696** PAYNE *Let. to Bp. of R—* 15 The Father is the only self-existent, unoriginated Being. **1712** S. CLARKE *Script. Doct. Holy Trinity* II. 243 The Father (or First Person) Alone is Self-existent, Underived, Unoriginated, Independent. **1797** *Encycl. Brit.* (ed. 3) X. 730 Any two unoriginated powers acting upon one another at right angles. **1838** MRS. BROWNING *Measure* i, God, the Creator, with a pulseless hand Of unoriginated power, hath weighed The dust of earth. **1867** H. MACMILLAN *Bible Teach.* i. (1870) 16 The force of gravitation, which is not a mere mechanical agency, unoriginated and uncontrolled.

Hence **Unoriˑginatedness.**

**1862** F. HALL *Hindu Philos. Syst.* 160 The unoriginatedness of souls.

**Unoriginaˑtion.** (UN-[1] 12.) **1755** AMORY *Mem.* (1769) I. 50 [To] worship three distinct conscious beings, of coordinate powers, equal independency and unorigination. **Unoriˑginative,** *a.* (UN-[1] 7.) **1874** SAYCE *Compar. Philol.* iii. 114 Unlike the Aryans they [*sc.* the Etruscans] were unoriginative and receptive.

**†Unoˑrn,** *a. Obs.* [OE. *unorne*, f. *un-* UN-[1] 7 + *orne* unusual, excessive (?).]

**1.** Of persons: Plain (in manners or appearance); humble, simple; mean, wretched.

*c* **1000** *Battle of Maldon* 256 Dunnere þa cwæð,..unorne ceorl ofer eall clypode. *c* **1200** ORMIN 4884 Forr Godess Sune..Warrþ an unnorne & wrecche mann. *a* **1225** *Ancr. R.* 424 Ancre þet naueð nout neih hond hire uode, beoð bisie two wummen,..and þeo beo ful unorne, oðer of feir elde. *a* **1250** *Owl & Night.* 1492 If hire louerd is forwurþe & vnorne at bedde and at borde. *a* **1300** *K. Horn* 330 Ne spek ihc noȝt wiþ horn, Nis he noȝt so unorn; Horn is fairer þane beo he. *c* **1400** *Laud Troy Bk.* 7485 Episcropus that schrewe vnorne Might not his word performe. *a* **1470** H. PARKER *Dives & Pauper* (W. de W. 1496) IV. xxvii. 195/1 Suche ye shall be.., feble, unourne, & loth to the syght.

*transf.* *c* **1412** HOCCLEVE *De Reg. Princ.* 876 Now age vnourne a-wey putteþ fauour, Þat floury youþe in his seson conquerde.

**2.** Of things: Poor or inferior in quality, amount, or appearance.

*c* **1175** *Lamb. Hom.* 85 Þenne he brohte hine uppen his werue, þet is unorne mare, þet bitacned ure unorne fleis. *c* **1200** ORMIN 828, I þe wesste þær he wass Hiss fode wass unnorne. *a* **1225** *Ancr. R.* 108 Uorto leren ancren þet heo ne gruchie neuermore uor none mete, ne uor none drunche, ne beo hit neuer so unorne. *a* **1250** *Owl & Night.* 317 Mi stefne is bold & nouht vnorne. **1398** TREVISA *Barth. De P. R.* v. xiii. (Tollem. MS.), Yf þe nose lakkeþ, all þe toþer del of þe face is þe more unhorne and unsemely.

Hence **†Unoˑrnly** *adv. Obs.*

*c* **1200** ORMIN 3750 Þatt te birrþ aȝȝ..lætenn swiþe unnornelіȝ & litell off þe sellfenn. *Ibid.* 4858. *c* **1300** *Havelok* 1941 Me wore leuere i wore lame, Þanne men dide him ani shame, ..or onne handes leyde, Vn-ornelike.

**Unornameˑntal,** *a.* (UN-[1] 7.)

**1747** G. WEST *Resurrect.* 355 The simple, unaffected, unornamental and unostentatious Manner, in which they deliver Truths so important. **1829** COBBETT *Eng. Gard.* v. § 198 Borage..is by no means unornamental in a flower-garden. **1834** *Gentl. Mag.* CIV. I. 34 Two small arches of massy and unornamental stone-work.

Hence **Unornameˑntally** *adv.*

**1889** *Times* 27 Dec. 11 These cans..are used ingeniously, if unornamentally, as building materials in the repair of roofs.

**Unornameˑnted,** *ppl. a.* (UN-[1] 8.)

**1697** COLLIER *Ess. Mor. Subj.* I. (1703) 236 'Tis more reputable..to prefer a homely, unornamented liberty to a splendid servitude. **1740** CIBBER *Apol.* xiv. 273 Nature, in her plain Dress, and unornamented. **1798** *Brit. Critic* XI. 31 A plain unornamented folio. **1831** JAMES *Phil. Augustus* III. iii, One of those plain and unornamented suits [of armour]. **1878** LECKY *Eng. in 18th C.* II. ix. 532 So in the pulpit they affect the most unornamented simplicity.

**Unoˑrthodox,** *a.* (UN-[1] 7, 5 b.)

**1657** W. RAND tr. *Gassendi's Life Peiresc* I. 127 That he might not any longer persist in an un-orthodox Religion. *a* **1661** HOLYDAY *Juvenal* (1673) 24 There's a parity of reason for these unorthodox philosophers. **1737** *Gentl. Mag.* VII. 15/1 His Doctrine may seem Un-orthodox and Paradoxical to many. **1830** LYELL *Princ. Geol.* I. 48 Buffon was invited by the College..to send in an explanation..of his unorthodox opinions. **1863** MRS. WOOD *Verner's Pride* xlix, If he were a respectable ghost he'd confine himself to the churchyard, and not walk in unorthodox places. **1882** FARRAR *Early Chr.* II. 533 To throw any doubt upon it was to brave the charge of being arrogant or unorthodox.

**Unoˑrthodoxy.** (UN-[1] 12.)

*a* **1704** T. BROWN *Laconics* Wks. 1711 IV. 7 Calvin made Roast-meat of Servetus at Geneva, for his Unorthodoxy. **1860** FROUDE *Hist. Eng.* VI. 130 If they dreaded a Spanish sovereign, they hated unorthodoxy more. **1879** M. PATTISON *Milton* 118 Insinuations of unorthodoxy such as are ever rife in clerical controversy.

**Unorthograˑphically,** *adv.* (UN-[1] 11.) **1687** J. BARNES *Hist. Edw. III*, 568 Whose Names I had rather omit, than set them down, as I find them, unorthographically.

**Unoˑssified,** *ppl. a.* (UN-[1] 8.)

**1726** MONRO *Anat.* 59 The Separation of the unossified Parts. **1778** *Encycl. Brit.* (ed. 2) I. 344/2 A portion of the cranium then [*sc.* in new-born infants] unossified. **1828** RYAN *Man. Midwifery* 12 Owing to its bones being separate and unossified. **1878** A. H. GREEN, etc. *Coal* iv. 122 The occipital condyles appear to have been similarly unossified.

**Unosteˑnsible,** *a.* (UN-[1] 7, 5 b.) [**1775** ASH.] **1851** MERIVALE *Rom. Emp.* xxv. III. 121 The real though unostensible leader of the republic.

**Unostentaˑtious,** *a.* (UN-[1] 7.)

**1747** [see UNORNAMENTAL *a.*]. **1782** V. KNOX *Ess.* iii. (1819) I. 18 They induce idleness..not to neglect the reality as attainable only by a painful and unostentatious application. **1825** SCOTT *Betrothed* xi, Hugo de Lacy was, on most occasions, plain and unostentatious. **1874** GREEN *Short Hist.* vii. § 1 His personal habits were simple and unostentatious.

Hence **Unostentaˑtiousness.** (Worc., 1846, citing Allen.)

**Unostentaˑtiously,** *adv.* (UN-[1] 11; cf. prec.)

**1795** V. KNOX *Chr. Phil.* § 39 I. 281 He is silently and unostentatiously happy. **1844** H. H. WILSON *Brit. India* II. 228 The preparations were conducted as unostentatiously as possible. **1891** DRIVER *Introd. Lit. O. T.* 428 How a religious spirit may be carried unostentatiously into the conduct of daily life.

**†Unoutspeaˑkable,** *a. Obs.* [UN-[1] 7 b.] Unutterable.

**1535** COVERDALE 2 *Cor.* ix. 15 Thanks be vnto God for his vnoutspeakeable gifte. *a* **1564** BECON *Policy War* Wks. 1564 I. 129 What was ye cause of that theyr greuous miserye and vnoutspeakable calamite?

†**Uno·ven,** *v. Obs.* (UN-2 5.) **1611** FLORIO, *Disfornáre*, to vnfurnace, to vnouen. **1653** URQUHART *Rabelais* I. xxii. 95 Gargantua..played..at unoven the iron. **Unover-clou·ded,** *ppl. a.* (UN-1 8.) *a* **1658** LOVELACE *Lucasta Posth.* (1659) 71 I'm un-ore-clowded too! free from the mist! **Unoverco·mable,** *a.* (UN-1 7 b.) *c* **1445** PECOCK *Donet* 160 þat þe peple were..so obstynat and so vnouer-comable and vnaȝendressabli hardid. **1508** DUNBAR *Poems* vii. 44 Welcum thou campioun, in feght vnourcumable.

**Unoverco·me,** *ppl. a.* (UN-1 8 b.)

OE. *unofercumen* occurs as a gloss on L. *indigestus*.

*c* **1375** *Sc. Leg. Saints* xxii. (*Laurence*) 374 Thane decius ..þame commawndit..to dyng hym fast; bot vnourcumyne he can ay last. **1382** WYCLIF *Judith* Prol., The vnouer-comen of alle men she ouercam, and the vnouerpassable she ouerpassede. **1434** MISYN *Mending Life* 123 Truly þen is luf vnouercomyn qwhen with no nodyr desyr it may be ouercomyn. *c* **1520** BARCLAY *Jugurth* (1557) 33 b, Ye vn-ouercome of your ennemies, maisters, and emperours, ouer the most part of the worlde. **1579–80** NORTH *Plutarch* (1676) 507 Though now they lead me bound, yet do I remain free unovercome. *c* **1611** CHAPMAN *Iliad* XVI. 92 O would to Jove..That not..any one of all the Greeks..might live un-overcome.

**Unoverlea·ped,** *ppl. a.* (UN-1 8.) **1849** M. ARNOLD *To Republican Friend, contn.* 7 This Earth, whereon we dream, Is..o'ershadow'd by the high Uno'erleap'd Mountains of Necessity. **Unoverpa·ssable,** *a.* (See UNOVERCOME *ppl. a.*, quot. 1382.) **Unoverta·ken,** *ppl. a.* (UN-1 8 b.) **1629** T. ADAMS *Serm.* Wks. 984 The sunne is vpon his backe, behind him, and his shadow is still vn-ouertaken before him.

**Unoverthrow·n,** *ppl. a.* (UN-1 8 b.)

**1535** STEWART *Cron. Scot.* (Rolls) II. 394 Tha thocht aneuche for to defend thair awin Into sic thrang, and keip thame vnouirthrawin. *a* **1586** SIDNEY *Arcadia* III. xxii, Yet shewed it most the perfection of the beautie, which could remaine unoverthrowne by such enimies. **1621** G. SANDYS *Ovid's Met.* I. (1626) 8 What such a force, vn-ouerthrowne, oppos'd, The higher-swelling Water quite deuoures. **1852** CLOUGH *Poems*, etc. (1869) I. 348 In the prostration to ancient tenets and habits the old character remains upright, unoverthrown and unsubdued.

†**Unovertrow·able**: see OVERTROWABLE *a.*

**Unow·ed,** *ppl. a.* [UN-1 8.] † Unowned.

**1595** SHAKS. *John* IV. iii. 147 And England now is left To tug and scamble, and to part by th' teeth The vn-owed interest of proud swelling State.

**Unow·n,** *v.* [UN-2 3.] *trans.* To disown. *a* **1657** R. LOVEDAY *Let.* (1663) 12 What comes it [to] to lease my self away?..Tis to unown my self, tis to disclaime My will, my head, my hands, all that I am.

**Unow·ned,** *ppl. a.* [UN-1 8.]

**1.** Not possessed as property; destitute of an owner or possessor.

**1611** COTGR., *Vuayves*,..things which bee left, abandoned, escheated, or vnowned. **1635** J. HAYWARD tr. *Biondi's Banish'd Virg.* 57 The Law declareth things unowned to be his that first comes to the enjoying of them. **1681** O. HEYWOOD *Diaries*, etc. (1881) II. 229 They would cry it at the crosse with some other unowned goods. **1829** SOUTHEY *Sir T. More* I. 94 Like the dogs at Lisbon and Constantinople, unowned, unbroken to any useful purpose. **1884** *Pall Mall G.* 12 Jan. 5/1 Unowned wires, he admitted, must be dealt with.

*transf.* **1634** MILTON *Comus* 407 Lest som ill greeting touch attempt the person Of our unowned sister [=350 our lost sister].

**2.** Unacknowledged; unadmitted.

**1715** GAY *Epist. to Earl of Burlington* 40 Here unown'd infants find their daily food; For should the maiden mother nurse her son, 'Twould spoil her match. **1748** RICHARDSON *Clarissa* (1811) II. xliv. 321, I know not my own heart, if I have any of that latent or unowned inclination. **1793** W. ROBERTS *Looker-on* No. 48 (1794) II. 205 An action unowned by the delicacy of its real author. **1865** MISS YONGE *Dove in Eagle's Nest* vii, The poor little unowned bride had more to undergo than her imagination had conceived. **1897** PULLEN-BURRY *Blotted Out* 65 [Her] unowned child..had blossomed into one of the most famous actresses of the day.

**Uno·xidated,** *ppl. a.* (UN-1 8.) **1805** R. W. DICKSON *Pract. Agric.* I. 446 A portion of oil, or of the basis of it in an unoxydated state being diffused through their composition.

**Uno·xidized,** *ppl. a.* (UN-1 8, 5 b.)

Also, in recent use (1894). *unoxidizable*.

**1827** *Edin. Rev.* XLV. 300 Partial productions of these pure unoxydized bases. **1857** MILLER *Elem. Chem., Org.* 22 The amount of unoxidized sulphur in an organic compound.

**Unoxygenated,** *ppl. a.* (UN-1 8.)

**1790** R. KERR tr. *Lavoisier's Elem. Chem.* II. 187 We cannot procure them in their unoxygenated state. **1798** ABERNETHY in *Phil. Trans.* LXXXVIII. 108 Neither could I..so accustom the animal to the circulation of unoxygenated blood, as to lengthen the term of its existence. **1875** tr. *Schmidt's Desc. & Darwinism* (ed. 2) 20 The un-oxygenated constituents of the blood. **1886** HUXLEY in *Life* (1900) II. 148 The sort of uphill exercise which routs out all the un-oxygenated crannies of my organism.

**Unpa·cable,** *a.* (UN-1 7 b.) **1544** BALE *Chron. Sir J. Oldcastle* 15 b, The vnpacable furye of Antichrist thus kyndled agaynst him. **Unpa·ced,** *ppl. a.* (UN-1 8.) [1775 ASH.] **1897** *Daily News* 17 Feb. 11/3 The principal item is a series tandem match, unpaced,..for £100. **Unpa·cifiable,** *a.* (UN-1 7 b.) **1629** T. ADAMS *Serm.* Wks. 804 O the vnpacifiable madnesse, that this worlds musicke puts those into, who will dance after his Pipe. **1702** C. MATHER *Magn. Chr.* IV. x. 217/1 He had an unpacifiable Dissatisfaction at himself.

**Unpaci·fic,** *a.* (UN-1 7.)

**1774** T. TWINING in *Recreat. & Stud.* (1882) 26 The ear left afloat..in the midst of all the flats, and shoals, and breakers..of this unpacific ocean! **1781** WARTON *Hist. Kiddington* 71 Many such works of our disunited and un-pacific ancestors were undoubtedly destroyed..in the early martial ages. **1837** CARLYLE *Fr. Rev.* I. v. vi, The Curé..marches unpacific, at the head of his militant Parish.

†**Unpaci·ficable,** *a. Obs.*−1 (UN-1 7 b.) **1608** TOPSELL *Serpents* 136 The enemy within..sporteth her selfe in the consumption of those vitall parts, which wast and weare away by yeelding to her vnpacificable teeth.

**Unpa·cified,** *ppl. a.* (UN-1 8.)

**1570** LEVINS *Manip.* 50 Vnpacifyed, *impacatus*. *c* **1611** CHAPMAN *Iliad* XVIII. 299 Twelve youths..I'll sacrifice..to thee unpacified. *a* **1680** CHARNOCK *Attrib. God* (1834) I. 283 The approach is to God as gracious, not to God as unpacified.

Hence **Unpa·cifiedly** *adv.*

**1748** RICHARDSON *Clarissa* (1811) V. xli. 373 She was going to speak with an aspect unpacifiedly angry.

**Unpa·ck,** *v.* [UN-2 3, 5. Cf. Du. *ontpakken*.]

**1.** *trans.* To undo or open up (a pack, bale, etc.) and remove or release the contents.

**1472–5** *Rolls of Parlt.* VI. 155/2 Then it be leeffull to the Collectours..to doo unpakke there tho Pakkes and Fardels. **1535** *Act 27 Hen. VIII*, c. 14 § 1 Whiche packes so conveied..to suche portes..to be shipped be never there unpacked. **1611** COTGR., *Desempacquet*, to vnpacke, to vnloose a packe. **1739** J. ELTON in Hanway *Trav.* (1762) I. I. v. 21 The custom-house officers are not to break open and unpack their bales. **1798** S. & HT. LEE *Canterb. T.* II. 478 On the deck sat Lady Emily, unpacking a little basket of fruit. **1838** DICKENS *O. Twist* xxiii, The beadle, stooping to unpack his bundle. **1873** BLACK *Pr. Thule* 34 Go away..and unpack your portmanteau.

*fig.* **1602** SHAKS. *Ham.* II. ii. 614 This is most braue, That I..Must (like a Whore) vnpacke my heart with words. **1874** RUSKIN *Hortus Inclusus* (1887) 15 The difficulty I had in unpacking my mind.

**2.** To take (something) out of a pack or packing.

**1598** HAKLUYT *Voy.* I. 210 That none of our said subiects shall vnlade..nor vnpacke..no kind of wares. **1669** BOYLE *Certain Physiol. Ess.* (ed. 2) *Absol. Rest Bodies* 25 When..he had unpacked them [*sc.* a great parcel of glasses] and rang'd them. **1754** LD. HARDWICKE in Harris *Life* (1847) III. xii. 18 As company is to come soon,..your mother is very busy in unpacking her house [=furniture]. **1810** W. SELWYN *Law Nisi Prius* (ed. 2) II. 1189 Not having any directions from him respecting the goods, [defendant] caused them to be unpacked. **1825** LD. G. CAVENDISH in *Biog. J. Gibson* (1911) 62 It has been unpacked, and placed on a temporary pedestal. **1894** A. ROBERTSON *Nuggets* 38 He unpacked the gold and laid it..on the counter.

*fig.* **1596** NASHE *Saffron Walden* K 4 The strange vn-traffiqu't phrases by him now vented and vnpackt. **1821** LAMB *Elia* I. *Imperfect Sympathies*, He brings his total wealth into company, and gravely unpacks it. **1841** H. MILLER *O. R. Sandst.* vi. 107 The strata..have been un-packed and arranged by the uptilting agent.

**b.** *transf.* To take (a person) out of a conveyance, dress, etc.

**1690** CROWNE *Eng. Frier* III, The elderly Ladies have been unpack'd a good while since. **1837** DICKENS *Pickw.* xxii, A red-haired man..had unpacked himself from a cab at the same moment. **1898** *Westm. Gaz.* 21 May 3/2 My poor child, in what a state of..collapse must you have been when Myrtle unpacked you on your return!

**c.** *refl.* or *pass.* To get one's furniture, luggage, etc., unpacked.

**1791** H. WALPOLE *Let. to Miss Berry* 27 Oct., I..thought it would be very uncomfortable to you, till you had un-packed yourselves, seen some few persons, adjusted your family, etc. **1812** LADY GRANVILLE *Lett.* (1894) I. 40 The Bessboroughs have been unpacked about a couple of hours.

**3.** To remove a pack or load from (a horse, carriage, etc.).

**1570** LEVINS *Manip.* 5 To Unpacke, *esarcinare*. **1598** FLORIO, *Sbastare*, to vnpacke, to vnsaddle a cariers horse. **1835** W. IRVING *Tour Prairies* 27 His first care was to un-pack his horses, and put them in safe quarters. **1853** DOUGLAS *Milit. Bridges* (ed. 3) 66 To unpack the carriage [carrying a pontoon].

**4.** *absol.* To perform the work of unpacking.

**1837** W. IRVING *Capt. Bonneville* II. 22 Two-thirds trap-pers,..and one-third camp-keepers; who cook, pack, and unpack. **1897** MARY KINGSLEY *W. Africa* 626 As her com-mander..asked me on board to lunch, I had to unpack again.

Hence **Unpa·cking** *vbl. sb.*

**1472–5** *Rolls of Parlt.* VI. 155/2 Withoute unpakking or sight of such Clothes. **1797** *Monthly Mag.* III. 261/1, I was present at the unpacking of the machine. **1837** [MRS. MAITLAND] *Lett. fr. Madras* (1843) 97 People never seem to be able to lay their private hands upon them till after they have finished all their unpacking. **1897** MARY KINGSLEY *W. Africa* 272 It was a bundle of bark cloth: I anxiously watched its unpacking.

*attrib.* **1829** in Willis & Clark *Cambridge* (1886) III. 103 Unpacking Rooms connected with the several Museums.

**Unpa·cked,** *ppl. a.*1 [UN-1 8. Cf. MDu. *ongepact*.]

**1.** Not made up in, or put into, a pack.

**1495** *Acc. Ld. High Treas. Scot.* I. 220, xxv sekkis of vnpakkit woll. **1621** in Foster *Eng. Factories Ind.* (1906) I. 270 To imbale four or five fardells yett unpacked. *c* **1887** Miss M. JONES *Games Patience* 40 Any other unpacked card has a chance of being moved, but not so the King.

**2.** Not taken out of a pack or parcel.

*a* **1721** PRIOR *Ess. Opinion* ? 13 Loads of ill Pictures, and worse Books,..lye unpacked and unthought of when they come into the Country.

**Unpa·cked,** *ppl. a.*2 (UN-1 8 + PACKED *ppl. a.*2) **1810** BENTHAM *Packing* (1821) 188 To persuade either a Jury, even though unpacked, or even high-placed Judges.

**Unpa·cker.** [f. UNPACK *v.*] One who unpacks.

**1804** MAR. EDGEWORTH *Ennui* iii, By the awkwardness of the unpacker, the statue's thumb was broken. **1859** F. A. GRIFFITHS *Artill. Man.* (ed. 8) 46 Pole-men, peg-men, and unpackers of tents.

**Unpa·dlocked,** *ppl. a.* (UN-1 or UN-2 8.) **1681** *Penny Post* No. 5, That and the Press being unpadlockt, are two incomparable turns of the Liberty of the Subject! **1846** C. DICKENS *Battle of Life* 60 One of the fire-proof boxes, unpadlocked and opened. **Unpa·gan,** *a.* (UN-1 7.) **1614** SYLVESTER *Bethulia's Rescue* II. 452 The Lord Marshall..Transporteth speedy, neer Bethulia's gate, Th' un-pagan Pagan. **Unpa·ganize,** *v.* (UN-2 6 c *b.*) **1678** CUDWORTH *Intell. Syst.* I. iv. 191 *Contents*, The paganizing of that, which was intended for the unpaganizing of the world. **1801** HEL. M. WILLIAMS *Sk. Fr. Rep.* I. vi. 47 Christianity had long spread its doctrines throughout the Roman empire before the world was quite unpaganized. **Unpa·ged,** *ppl. a.* (UN-1 8.) **1874** BOASE & COURTNEY *Bibl. Cornub.* I. 238/1 Postscript, 6 pages unpaged. **1898** *Sotheby's Sale Catal.* 6 Oct. 41 The rare unpaged leaf 'to the Christen reader'.

**Unpai·d,** *ppl. a.* [UN-1 8.]

**1.** Of persons: To whom payment has not been made; not receiving payment.

**1375** BARBOUR *Bruce* I. 257 Quhethir he his lordis neid suld let, And pay fryst that he awcht,..Or leve onpayit his wyff. **1464** *Paston Lett.* Suppl. (1901) 83, I trow I xall be fayn to contente hem or ellys they xall be unpayyd. **1568** GRAFTON *Chron.* II. 313 A number of the souldyours..whome king Peter promised to pay, came home agayne vnpayde. **1586** SIR A. POULET in Ellis *Orig. Lett.* Ser. I. III. 10 Yf they shall say that they are unpayd of their wages. **1627** DRAYTON *Battle of Agincourt* xliii, The Church to pawne, would see her Challice layde, E'r shee would leaue one Pyoner vnpayde. *a* **1658** LOVELACE *Poems* (1904) 125 Whilst thy unpay'd Musicians, Crickets, sing. **1728** POPE *Dunc.* II. 110 That suit, an unpay'd tailor snatch'd away! **1769** BURKE *Obs. 'Pres. St. Nat.'* 8 If her armies are three years unpaid. **1837** MCCULLOCH *Acc. Brit. Empire* II. 646 The risks arising from the frequent defaults of the unpaid overseers. **1891** *Daily News* 27 June 5/1 Unpaid children..went to their work at six o'clock in the morning.

**b.** With *for*. (Cf. 3.)

**1611** SHAKS. *Cymb.* V. v. 307 Wilt thou vndoo the worth thou art vnpayd for By tasting of our wrath? **1618** J. TAYLOR (Water P.) *Penniless Pilgr.* Wks. (1630) 123 Master Taylor..Vnask'd (vnpaid for) me both lodg'd and fed.

**c.** *The* (*Great*) *Unpaid*, the class of unpaid magistrates or justices.

**1826** *Edin. Rev.* 441 We beg to be acquitted of all intention of affronting, or attacking the Great Unpaid. **1826** *Examiner* 727/2 The miserable canting spirit which actuates the 'Unpaid'.

**2.** Not handed over or given in payment; not discharged or cleared off by payment.

**1387** TREVISA *Higden* (Rolls) IV. 117 Lisia..wente into Pers, ffor þe tribute was unpayde. **1424** *Paston Lett.* I. 16 The fees and the wages of the seid William..unpayed draweth a gret some to hys pouere degree. **1491** *Act 7 Hen. VII*, c. 20 § 5 As often as it shall happen the seid annuall rent..to be behynd and unpayd in part or in all. **1507** *Rec. St. Mary at Hill* 25 Yff it happ ye said yerly ferme of v marke..to be behynd..by a monithe vnpaid. **1547** in Feuillerat *Revels Edward VI* (1914) 26 The sum.., as by the bookes..dothe apere more at large, is vnpayd. **1606** *Arraignm. & Execution Late Traitors* (Hindley II) 7 That his wife might have her jointure.., his sisters their legacies in his hand unpaid. **1661** MORGAN *Sph. Gentry* IV. iii. 41 The party whose portion shall appear to be unpayed. **1764** GOLDSM. *Hist. Eng. in Lett.* (1772) II. 20 Alexander..was indebted to him a large sum, which was still unpaid. **1848** THACKERAY *Van. Fair* lii, A long arrear of unpaid wages. **1878** J. DAVIDSON *Inverurie & Garioch* 349 The fines remaining unpaid.

*fig.* **1421** HOCCLEVE *Min. Poems* 169/817 His brothres reward had nat been vnpayed, Nad promesse of the Emperour him bownde To pardon. **1667** MILTON *P. L.* V. 779 How we may best..Receive him coming to receive from us Knee-tribute yet unpaid. ? **1710** CONGREVE *To Sir G. Kneller*, Fame due to vast desert is kept in store, Un-pay'd, till the deserver is no more. **1791** COWPER *Iliad* I. 112 The seer..spake, Nor vow nor hecatomb unpaid on us He charges.

**b.** Of debts or bills: Undischarged.

**1483** *Act 1 Ric. III*, c. 2 Many worshipful Men..live in great Penury.., their Debts unpaid, and their Children un-preferred. **1492–3** *Rec. St. Mary at Hill* 194 Olde dettes that have be lefte vnpayde by the cherch wardenys. **1681** R. KNOX *Hist. Ceylon* vii. 149 The Interest never runs up higher, tho the Debt lye seven years unpaid. **1754** in *Nairne Peerage Evidence* (1874) 52 A just true and lawful debt wholly resting unpaid. **1781** COWPER *Retirem.* 559 Anticipated rents, and bills unpaid. **1887** GUNTER *Mr. Barnes* xiii. 96 She remembers she has unpaid bills.

**c.** Not rendered or discharged.

**1611** SHAKS. *Cymb.* III. v. 48 She pray'd me to excuse her keeping close, Whereto constrain'd.., She should that dutie leaue vnpaide to you Which dayly she was bound to proffer. **1717** POPE *Elegy Mem. Unfort. Lady* 48 What can atone..Thy fate unpity'd, and thy rites unpaid? **1725** — *Odyss.* XV. 213 With him all night the youthful strangers staid, Nor found the hospitable rites unpay'd.

**3.** Not paid *for*. Also without prep.

**1465** *Paston Lett.* II. 233 [If] the blak hose be payid for, he wyll send the roset un-payd for. **1552** in Feuillerat *Revels Edw. VI* (1914) 124 The like charges of the said lorde..beinge yet behinde and vnpaid for. **1611** SHAKS. *Cymb.* III. iii. 24 Rustling in vnpayd-for Silke. **1653** W. RAMESEY *Astrol. Restored* To Rdr. 11 The Drapers cloth on their back,..and all unpaid for. **1827** POLLOK *Course T.* VIII. 433 A show unpaid for, paying to be seen! **1886** C. E. PASCOE *Lond. of To-day* xliii. (ed. 3) 379 Letters posted unpaid are charged double postage. **1895** LD. FARRER in *Westm. Gaz.* 19 Feb. 2/1, I did not know before I joined the Council how good and how zealous unpaid work can be.

Hence **Unpai·dish** *a.* (from sense 1 c).

**1829** E. ELLIOTT *Village Patriarch* III. ix, Mark his un-paidish sneer, his lordly frown.

**Unpai·n,** *v.* (UN-2 3.) **1545** RAYNALD *Byrth Mankynde* 69 These pylles be of such efficacy and strength, yt it alleuiateth and vnpayneth the byrth.

**Unpai·ned,** *ppl. a.* (UN-1 8.)

*c* **1380** WYCLIF *Sel. Wks.* III. 200 No defoulynge þerof [*sc.* marriage] may askape unpeyned. **1599** B. JONSON *Cynthia's Rev.* V. iii, But there's not one of these who are unpain'd, Or by themsevles unpunished. 1667 Milton *P. L.* vi. 455 Too unequal work we find Against unequal armes to fight in paine, Against unpaind, impassive. *a* 1758 Ramsay *To G. Drummond* xi, And here the Fair may walk unpain'd, Her flowing silks and shoes unstain'd. 1804 *Europ. Mag.* XLV. 61/1 Learning's rever'd abode he leaves With unpain'd soul. 1826 A. A. Watts *First Kiss* 87 A bliss too pure For evil spirits to behold unpained.

**Unpai·nful**, *a.* [Un-1 7.]

†1. Not subject to pain. *Obs.*—1

?*c* 1425 *Lucidarie* (Fr. Schmitt 1909) 21 Aftir his owne kynde, he was unpayneful & undeedly.

2. Not causing or involving pain or discomfort.

1570 Levins *Manip.* 186 Vnpaynful, *immolestus.* 1628 Feltham *Resolves* ii. lxxxii. 236 If we owe a Retribution for vnpainefull Courtesies. 1690 Locke *Hum. Und.* ii. iv. § 4 That being generally call'd..soft, which changes the Situation of its parts upon an easie and unpainful touch. 1713 *Guardian* No. 82, Those who make an honest man a visit.. to make his following year unpainful. 1758 J. S. *Le Dran's Observ. Surg.* (1771) 95 The small Remainder of the Tumour was unpainful. 1823 J. Wilson *Marg. Lyndsay* ix. 67 That unpainful sympathy which is all the poor can afford or expect. 1851 Hawthorne *Twice-told T.* II. vi. 99 A sympathy with the young and gay; an unpainful interest in the business of others.

3. Marked or characterized by absence of pain.

1861 Mrs. Jenkin *Who breaks—pays* II. 261 The first unpainful feeling I have had for three quarters of a year.

**Unpai·ning**, *ppl. a.* (Un-1 10.) 1828 Tennyson *Lover's T.* i. 609 Would I had lain Until..the wild brier had driven Its knotted thorns thro' my unpaining brows.

**Unpai·nt**, *v.* [Un-2 4.]

1. *trans.* To free from paint.

1611 Cotgr., *Defarder*, to vnpaint; to wash, take, or wype off, painting. 1844 *P. Parley's Ann.* V. 265 Nothing now remained but to unpaint the young urchin; and so Sally.. scrubbed till she was tired.

2. To paint out; to obliterate (something painted).

*a* 1717 Parnell *Piety* 53 Unpaint the Love, that hov'ring over Beds, From glitt'ring Pinions guilty Pleasure sheds. 1755 Johnson *Dict.*, *To Dislimn*, to unpaint. 1866 Visct. Strangford *Select.* (1869) II. 320 An unobtrusive little coronet which my wife has had painted..upon the panels of her carriage, and which I defy all the powers on earth.. to induce her to unpaint.

**Unpai·ntable**, *a.* (Un-1 7 b.)

1849 Kingsley *Misc.* (1859) II. 255 Farewell to unpaintable Lynmouth. 1893 *Guardian* 16 Aug. 1291 When he began to try to paint the unpaintable.

Hence **Unpaintabi·lity, -ableness.**

1884 *Athenæum* 16 Aug. 218/1 The artists who complain of the 'unpaintableness' of current attire. 1888 *Pall Mall G.* 4 Oct. 5/2 The unpaintability of Mr. Gladstone.

**Unpai·nted**, *ppl. a.* (Un-1 8.)

1555 Eden *Decades* (Arb.) 106 Rased or vnpaynted tables. 1604 S. Harrison *Archs of Triumph* B j, I would not care if these vnpainted Pictures were more Costly to me, so that [etc.]. 1651 Hobbes *Leviath.* i. x. 45 An unpainted Buckler was a signe of..a common Souldier. 1762 Goldsm. *Cit. W.* xcix, More ugly than an unpainted actress. 1771 R. Cumberland *West Indian* Epil. 24 Unpainted cheeks with blush of health did glow. 1818 Shelley *Let. to Peacock* 8 Nov., Strange-looking unpainted window-shutters. 1855 Dickens *Holly-Tree* i, The rooms..were all of unpainted wood.

**Unpai·red**, *ppl. a.*1 [Un-1 8. Cf. Da. *uparret*, Sw. *oparad*, Du. *ongepaard*, G. *ungepaart.*] Not united or arranged in pairs; not forming one of a pair.

1648 Hexham ii, *Onpaer*, Vn-even, or Vnpaired. 1748 Richardson *Clarissa* IV. 50 All this vast difference in sentiments shews how unpair'd our minds are. 1812 Crabbe *Tales* iv. 5 Others, ill match'd, with minds unpair'd, repent. 1880 Günther *Fishes* 40 The Fins are divided into vertical or unpaired, and into horizontal or paired fins. 1883 Martin & Moale *Vertebr. Dissect.* 133 A single unpaired air sac will be seen just beneath the anterior portion of the sternum.

†**Unpai·red**, *ppl. a.*2 [Un-1 8.] Unimpaired, uninjured. *c* 1400 *Destr. Troy* 13128 But thurgh wilys & wit he wan of his daunger. Vnpairit of his person priuely he stale.

†**Unpai·sed**, *ppl. a. Obs.* [Un-1 8 + Peise *v.*] Not properly weighed or balanced; defective or excessive in weight.

1390 Gower *Conf.* Prol. 64* He that hath his word unpeysed. 1561 Norton & Sackv. *Gorboduc* i. i, Porrex the younger so vnpaised in state, Perhappes in courage will be raised also. 1581 Studley tr. *Seneca, Herc. Œt.* i. 191 b, And coulde I brooke it, Toxeus, to see thy death with woe? That wert vnwaynde in yeares, and eake in pits [? *read* pith; L. *sanguine*] vnpaysde. 1602 Marston *Ant. & Mel.* ii. iii. 1 Seize on reuenge, graspe the sterne bended front Of frowning vengeance, with vnpaized clutch.

**Unpa·laced**, *ppl. a.* (Un-2 8.) 1859 J. S. Mill *Diss. & Disc.* I. 23 Let the State endowments be once withdrawn from the Church of England, her mitred and unpalaced prelates will indulge in no such delusion.

**Unpa·latable**, *a.* [Un-1 7 b, 5 b.]

1. Not agreeable to the palate. Also in fig. context.

1682 Dryden *Medal* 148 The Man..Might laugh again, to see a Jury chaw The prickles of unpalatable Law. 1700 T. Brown *Amusem.* viii. Wks. 1720 III. 76 Our Doctor..cloys his Auditors with that unpalatable Ragoust. 1748 *Anson's Voy.* ii. viii. 218 We found them [*sc.* pearl oysters] extremely tough and unpalatable. 1799 J. Robertson *Agric. Perth* 205 The grass is coarse, unpalatable to cattle. 1846 Soyer *Cookery* 380 It would..cause the fillets to eat tough and altogether unpalatable. 1871 Darwin *Desc. Man* ii. xi. I. 416 It would be highly advantageous to a caterpillar to be.. recognised as unpalatable by all birds.

2. Unpleasant, distasteful, disagreeable.

1711 tr. *Werenfelsius' Disc. Logomachys* 201 These things, my Son, may at first seem, to your Age, unpalatable and hard. 1749 Smollett *Regic.* iv. ii, Candid friendship that disdains to hide Unpalatable truth! 1829 Scott *Anne of G.* xxvii, The Duke's eye lowered gloomily on the deliverer of this unpalatable message. 1849 Macaulay *Hist. Eng.* xx. IV. 467 The King commanded himself sufficiently to return thanks for this unpalatable counsel.

Hence **Unpa·latableness.**

1805 Saunders *Min. Waters* 82 Perhaps the unpalatableness of this drink has caused it to be in worse credit than it deserves.

**Unpa·le**, *v.* [Un-2 4.] *trans.* To strip of pales or palings.

1779 H. Walpole *Let. to Cole* 3 Jan., I hope you have not been untiled or unpaled by the tempest on New-year's morning.

**Unpa·led**, *ppl. a.*1 [Un-1 8.] Not furnished with a paling.

1607 in *Essex Rev.* XV. (1906) 45 The ch[urch]y[ar]d fence ys unpaled on the S. side. 1648 Hexham ii, *Onbetuynt*, Vnhedged, Vnpaled, or Open.

**Unpa·led**, *ppl. a.*2 [Un-1 8.] Not made pale.

1831 James *Phil. Augustus* I. vi, The fire of his eye was unquenched, the rose of his cheek unpaled. 1885 'C. E. Craddock' *Proph. Gt. Smoky Mount.* vii, In a sunshine all unpaled, and against the upper regions of the air, splendidly blue.

**Unpalisa·doed**, *ppl. a.* (Un-1 8.) 1642 *Prince Rupert's Sp. to King* 4 Their graffes or ditches being dry and their vamures unpallisado'd. 1654 Gayton *Pleas. Notes* iii. iv. 91 His mouth was upon the West side like to be unpalisado'd for ever.

**Unpa·lled**, *ppl. a.*1 [Un-1 8.] Not palled or jaded.

*a* 1770 Nugent in Dodsley *Coll. Poems* II. 187 By pain unbitter'd, and unpall'd by fear. 1809 *Edin. Rev.* XV. 111 Where the taste is unpalled by satiety of what is better. 1859 W. H. Gregory *Egypt* II. 130 His appetite..is unpalled as much at the conclusion as at the commencement of the feast.

**Unpa·lled**, *ppl. a.*2 *Cant.* [Un-2 8 + Pal *sb.*1] (See quot.) 1812 J. H. Vaux *Flash Dict.* s.v., A thief whose associates are all apprehended, or taken from him by other means, is said to be *unpalled.* **Unpa·lliable**, *a.* [Un-1 7 b] Incapable of being palliated. 1673 Bp. S. Parker *Reproof Reh. Transp.* 374 A manifest and unpalliable breach..of loyalty.

**Unpa·lliated**, *ppl. a.* (Un-1 8.)

[1775 Ash.] 1798 Southey in Robberds *Mem. W. Taylor* (1843) I. 232 The only person who has ever..advised, and at times reproved, him, in unpalliated terms. 1827 Scott *Napoleon* xlii, There was never a more unpalliated case of ..arbitrary spoliation. 1860 Pusey *Min. Proph.* 255 Jonah leaves his own character unexplained, its severity rebuked by God, unexcused and unpalliated.

**Unpa·lpable**, *a.* Now *rare.* [Un-1 7 b, 5 b.] Impalpable.

1538 Elyot Addit., *Asomatos*, vnpalpable, or that can not be felt. 1576 G. Baker tr. *Gesner's Jewell of Health* 109 b, The same bring to a fine powder in a brasse morter as in a maner unpalpable. 1584 R. Scot *Discov. Witchcr.* iv. ii. (1886) 59 The opinion of them that hold a spirit to be unpalpable. 1611 Cotgr., *Insensible*,..vnpalpable, vnfeelable. 1725 *Fam. Dict.* s.v. *Sallet*, An Ingredient never to be omitted..provided it be not minutely beaten to an almost unpalpable Dust. 1876 Mrs. Whitney *Sights & Ins.* xxvii, We sat in the baptism of the far, unpalpable spray.

**Unpa·lped**, *a.* [Un-1 9.] Not furnished with palps or feelers. 1884 Sedgwick & Heathcote tr. *Claus' Zool.* 470 The unpalped maxilla of the second pair [of mandibles]. **Unpa·lsied**, *ppl. a.* (Un-1 8.) [1775 Ash.] 1798 *Monthly Mag.* V. 367 'No God,' with lips unpalsied they declare. 1850 Tennyson *In Mem.* cxxvii, The love that rose on stronger wings, Unpalsied when he met with Death. **Unpa·mpered**, *ppl. a.* (Un-1 8.) [1775 Ash.] 1794 W. Roberts *Looker-on* No. 90 (1794) III. 448 Unpampered by servile compliance. 1844 Dickens *Mart. Chuz.* xiv, Unspoiled, unpampered in her joys or griefs. **Unpa·nel**, *v.* [Un-2 4.] *trans.* To unsaddle. 1620 Shelton *Quix.* iii. xi. 235 Good betide him that freed vs from the paines of vnpannelling the gray Asse;..yet if hee were here, I would not permit any other to vnpannell him. *a* 1739 Jarvis *Quix.* i. iii. xi, If he were here, I would not consent to his being unpannelled. **Unpa·nelled**, *ppl. a.* (Un-1 8.) 1883 Baring-Gould *John Herring* xxxix, The unpanelled walls were plastered white. **Unpa·nged**, *ppl. a* (Un-1 8.) 1612 *Two Noble K.* i. i, But when could greefe Cull forth, as unpanged judgement can, fit'st time For best solicitation. **Unpa·nniered**, *ppl. a.* (Un-1 8.) 1812 J. Wilson *Isle of Palms*, etc. 354 Th' unpannier'd ass slowly retires From the brown tents. 1869 Browning *Ring & Bk.* ix. 61 Even the poor ass, unpanniered and elate Stands. **Unpa·noplied**, *ppl. a.* (Un-1 8.) 1827 Pollok *Course T.* vii. 422 Innumerous armies rose, unbannered all, Unpanoplied, unpraised. **Unpa·nting**, *ppl. a.* (Un-1 10.) 1721 Southerne *Spartan Dame* iii. ii, I sent this steel with tidings to his heart, Nor parted thence, till..I left the unpanting villain on the earth. **Unpantofle**, *v.* (Un-2 4.) 1643 in *Harl. Misc.* (Malh.) V. 335 They, whose part in a comedy allows them a robe and scepter; who.., as soon as they come to their exit, are un-pantoffled, and return to their own stature.

**Unpa·per**, *v.* [Un-2 4.] *trans.* To remove paper from; *esp.* to strip of a paper covering.

1714 C. Johnson *Country Lasses* ii. ii, The Holland curtains.., up with 'em—unpaper the screens, the sconces, and the andirons. 1769 J. Skeat *Art Cookery* 23 The fat of venison..is apt to waste, so that it is always necessary to paper it;..just before you want to take it up, unpaper it. 1802 H. Martin *Helen of Glenross* I. 54 Dolly employed herself, unpapering and uncovering chairs and carpets. 1828 P. Cunningham *N. S. Wales* (ed. 3) II. 269 A coterie of these nymphs were unpapering their curls.

**Unpa·pered**, *ppl. a.* (Un-1 8.)

[1775 Ash.] 1851 N. Hawthorne in Bridge *Pers. Recollect.* (1893) 125 The boxes..are not all papered, but neither are they all unpapered. 1871 Kingsley *At Last* x, The walls were of cedar and other valuable woods, which good taste left still unpapered.

**Unpa·pering**, *vbl. sb.* (Un-1 13.) 1847 Le Fanu *T. O'Brien* 326 Trimming of ruffles and unpapering of gold lace.

**Unpar**, obs. form of Umpire.

**Unpa·radise**, *v.* [Un-2 5, 6 b.]

1. *trans.* To turn out of, expel from, Paradise. Also *fig.*

1592 Daniel *Compl. Rosamond* 456 Now did I finde my selfe vnparadis'd, From those pure fields. 1605 G. Ellis *Lamentation Lost Sheep* G j b, With shame-sick Adam haue I hid my head, Vnparadiz'd, from my Angell-like state. *c* 1640 Milton *Draft of P. L.* Poet. Wks. (Globe) 12 Adam Unparadized. 1839 F. Barham *Adamus Exul* 47 Widowed, desolate, And quite unparadised in heart. 1846 Lockhart in *Ch. of Scot. Pulpit* II. 156 The old serpent, who deceived and unparadised our first parents. 1858 Caswall *Poems* 170 Archangels guard the gates with flaming swords,..who at an earlier day Did man unparadise.

2. To deprive of the character of Paradise.

1647 Fuller *Wounded Consc.* 28 Thus a wounded conscience is able to unparadise Paradise it selfe. 1742 Young *Nt. Th.* i. 187 That ghastly thought would drink up all your joy, And quite unparadise the realms of light. 1788 V. Knox *Winter Even.* III. vii. vii. 45 This it was which unparadised an Eden. 1827 Montgomery *Pelican Isl.* vi. 254 The serpent.., Whose guile unparadised the world. 1876 C. M. Davies *Unorth. Lond.* 370 Were man to enter Heaven as he now is, it would be unparadised for him at once.

Hence **Unpa·radised** *ppl. a.*

1872 O. W. Holmes *Poet Breakf.-t.* i. 24 Nature is never wholly unkind. Economical as she was in my unparadised Eden,..still the damask roses sweetened the June breezes.

**Unpa·radox**, *v.* (Un-2 3.) 1654 Whitlock *Zootomia* 322 The hardest Task is to perswade the erroneous obstinate ..Woman-Hater, that..any confirmations from History can un-paradox the worth..of that Sex.

**Unpa·ragoned**, *ppl. a.* (Un-1 8.)

1611 Chapman *Widowes T.* iii. i, At hand, sir, with your unparagon'd sister: please you take your chair of honour, sir? 1611 Shaks. *Cymb.* ii. ii. 17 Rubies vnparagon'd. 1640 tr. *Verdere's Rom. of Rom.* iii. xlix. 204 The unparragoned Knight of the Sun. 1824 Miss Mitford *Village* Ser. i. 181 His little dog Viper, unparagoned of terriers. 1874 M. & Fr. Collins *Vill. Comedy* xxii, Even Rough feels poetical as he sees the wondrous towers and spires unparagoned.

†**Unpa·ragonized**, *ppl. a. Obs.*—1 [Un-1 8.] = prec. 1603 Florio *Montaigne* ii. Ded., Give me leave (peerelesse, and in all good gifts vnparagonized Ladies).

†**Unpa·ralable**, obs. var. Unparallelable *a.*

*a* 1639 W. Whateley *Prototypes* i. xi. (1640) 97 Here was an obedience incomparable and unparalable, no man ever did the like except our Lord Jesus Christ.

†**Unpa·railed**, obs. var. Unparalleled *ppl. a.*

1637 A. Stafford *Just Apol.* in *Fem. Glory* (1860) p. xlvi, They are unparall'd Scoldes. 1640 tr. *Verdere's Rom. of Rom.* iii. vi. 20 The two little unparalled Worlds, that so graced her bosome.

**Unpa·rallel**, *a.* [Un-1 7, 5 b.]

1. Not parallel or correspondent.

1652 Th. Pestill in Benlowes *Theoph.* C 1, To That, Unparallel, This comes so neer, That 't is a Glimpse of Heav'n to leade Thee here. 1674 Hickman *Quinquart. Hist.* (ed. 2) 105 In this also the Parallel is unparallel. 1757 Edwards *Orig. Sin* ii. ii. (1807) II. 237 How unlike and unparallel is this? 1826 Lamb *Elia* ii. *Wedding*, Certainly there is a jealousy in unparallel subjects.

†2. = Unparalleled *ppl. a. Obs.*

1665 J. Spencer *Prodigies* (ed. 2) 188 The black and terrible Monitors of that unparallel Destruction which ensued. 1666 J. Smith *Old Age* 115 They had had so many..experiences of his unparallel strength.

Hence **Unpa·rallelness.**

1719 S. Sewall *Diary* 4 Oct., I ride to Byfield Meeting-house; hear Mr. Payson's Son of the Unparallelness of Josiah.

**Unpa·rallelable**, *a.* (Un-1 7 b.)

1640 Bp. Hall *Episc.* iii. ix. 54 The unparallelable glory of this Church, and Nation. 1676 *Doctrine of Devils* 50 His transcendent, unimitable, unparallelable Miracles. 1703 J. Savage *Lett. Antients* cxxi. 303 An Amour, which..I looked upon unparallelable. 1743 J. Glas *Treat. Lord's Supper* ii. Wks. 1761 IV. 38 He expressed his unparallelable good-will to all his elect. 1813 Sir R. Wilson *Priv. Diary* (1861) I. 342 The artillery in unparalleled and unparallelable order. *a* 1843 Southey *Doctor* xxii. (1848) 537 Which cannot with propriety be distinguished by any other name than one derived from its unparalleled and unparallelable author.

**Unpa·ralleled**, *ppl. a.* (Un-1 8, 5 b.)

In very common use from *c* 1610.

1594 Drayton *Leg. Matilda* xvi, The most iudiciall eyes Did giue the gole impartially to me; So did I stand vnparaleld and free. 1608 Machin *Dumbe Knt.* i. i, Dost thou not think, Shee is the mirrour of her beauteous sexe, Unparalleld, and uncompanioned? 1662 Stillingfl. *Orig. Sacr.* iii. i. § 2 Those many unparalleld miracles, which were wrought among them. 1713 Warder *True Amazons* (title-p.), Their..unparallelled Love to their Queen. 1770 *Junius Lett.* xli. (1788) 231 *note*, The..Judge..had the unparalleled impudence to tell [etc.]. 1814 Scott *Diary* 16 Aug. in *Lockhart*, Monuments..otherwise unparalleled in Britain. 1857 Buckle *Civiliz.* I. vii. 354 Progress..made in the face of these unparalleled disasters.

Hence **Unpa·ralleledly** *adv.*, **-edness.**

1667 Waterhouse *Fire Lond.* 5 His intercurrent judgements of Fire between this first and that last president of unparalleledness. 1815 Ann Smith *Diary* in *Life* (1851) 40 The freedom, sovereignty, and unparalleledness of his love. 1854 *Blackw. Mag.* LXXV. 448 It is unparalleledly impudent.

**Unpa·ralyzed**, *ppl. a.* (Un-1 8.) 1846 Worcester (citing Goode). 1889 *Athenæum* 15 June 751/2 An unparalyzed system of misgovernment. 1893 W. R. Gowers *Dis. Nerv. Syst.* (ed. 2) II. 399 The eyelids blink when the finger comes from the unparalysed side. **Unpa·rboiled**, *ppl. a.* (Un-1 8.) 1616 *Rich Cabinet* 56 An vnparboyld pastie of tainted venison. **Unpa·rcelled**, *ppl. a.* (Un-1 8.) [1775 Ash.] 1840 Browning *Sordello* vi. 219 But, portioned duly out, the Future vied Never with the unparcelled Present. 1844 Kinglake *Eothen* xii. 175 You find yourself..proving the mettle of your mare upon the broad and dreary downs, because you feel congenially with the yet unparcelled earth.

**Unpa·rched,** *ppl. a.* (UN-[1] 8.) 1599 THYNNE *Animadv.* (1875) 49 Chaucer of purpose addethe that woorde 'Greene' to explane 'vnseriall', whiche signyfiethe vnsered, vnparched. 1648 HEXHAM II, *Onverdrooght*,.. unpacrhed.

**Unpa·rching,** *ppl. a.* (UN-[1] 10.) 1818 MILMAN *Samor* XI. 237 Th' unconsuming fire Innoxious rang'd th' unparching edifice.

**Unpa·rdon,** *v.* (UN-[2] 3.) 1685 BAXTER *Paraphr. N. T.* Matt. xviii. 34–35 *note*, How God is said..to demand the debt which he had forgiven, and to unpardon it again.

**Unpa·rdonable,** *a.* (*adv.*). (UN-[1] 7 b, 5 b.) 1525 LD. BERNERS *Froiss.* II. cliii. 168 b/2 If they be [broken],..ye ryn in the churches sentence, and to be excommunycate on payne vnpardonable. 1561 T. NORTON *Calvin's Inst.* I. xiii. 36 b, An vnpardonable crime. 1647 CLARENDON *Hist. Reb.* I. § 66 The Earl..thought the very suspecting him to be an injury unpardonable. 1676 GLANVILL *Seasonable Reflect.* 28 We may conclude safely from the Doctrine of the Apostle, that they are incurable and unpardonable. 1712 STEELE *Spect.* No. 312 ¶ 1 The most unpardonable Malefactor in the World. 1827 LYTTON *Pelham* iv, A most unpardonable fault. 1882 MISS BRADDON *Mt. Royal* I. ii. 51 There was nothing unpardonable in Miss Bridgeman's plainness.

**b.** As *adv.* Unpardonably.

1662 HICKERINGILL *Apol. Distressed Innoc.* Wks. 1716 I. 316 He is unpardonable credulous that will lend an Ear to your noise of the Gospel.

**Unpa·rdonableness.** (UN-[1] 12; cf. prec.) 1646 HAMMOND *Tracts* 20 The unpardonablenesse of it is acknowledged. 1677 GILPIN *Demonol.* II. ix. 392 The note of unpardonableness, is indeed affixed to sins under several Denominations. *a* 1714 M. HENRY *Baptism* Wks. 1853 I. 496/2 A mistaken apprehension of the unpardonableness of sin committed after baptism. 1849 RUSKIN *Sev. Lamps* ii. § 1. 28 It would be well if moralists less frequently confused the greatness of a sin with its unpardonableness. 1885 *Athenæum* 26 Dec. 852 The unpardonableness of the offence.

**Unpa·rdonably,** *adv.* (UN-[1] 11, 5 b.) 1645 MILTON *Tetrach.* 12 Those mighty syllables..which take upon them to joyn heavn and hell together unpardnably till death pardon. 1811 MISS L. M. HAWKINS *C'tess & Gertr.* I. 111 We have both deviated most grievously and unpardonably from our duty. 1866 FREEMAN *Hist. Ess.* (1871) 9 English people—more unpardonably still—reject it.

**Unpa·rdoned,** *ppl. a.* (UN-[1] 8.) 1565 ALLEN *Def. Purg.* xvii. 284 There was no sin so smaule vnpardoned, but [etc.]. 1651 BAXTER *Inf. Bapt.* 310 Are you sure so many thousands are all unpardoned? 1692 tr. *B. Jonson's Leges Conviv.* x, Like the old Lapithites, with the goblets to fight, Our own 'mongst offences unpardon'd will rank. 1796 MRS. E. PARSONS *Myst. Warning* ii, [If] informed I was unpardoned, portionless and dependent. 1817 BYRON *Manfred* II. ii, He slew That which he loved,..And died unpardon'd. 1858 FROUDE *Hist. Eng.* IV. 261 The unpardoned..affront which Henry had offered to the Spanish nation.

**Unpa·rdoning,** *ppl. a.* (UN-[1] 10.) 1644 MILTON *Divorce* Introd. A 4 b, His ungirt permissions, his venial and unvenial dispences, wherwith the Law of God pardoning and unpardoning hath bin shamefully branded. 1700 DRYDEN *Pal. & Arc.* II. 344 Curse on th' unpard'ning Prince, whom Tears can draw To no Remorse. 1725 POPE *Odyss.* XX. 351 Whom Pallas with unpard'ning fury fir'd. 1810 *Monthly Mag.* XXIX. 209 A rash, unruly, Unpardoning soul. 1894 *Outing* XXIV. 13/2, 'I have been so hard, so unforgiving, so unpardoning,' she said.

**Unpa·red,** *ppl. a.* [UN-[1] 8.]

**1.** Of fruit: Not having the skin pared off.

*c* 1305 *Pilate* 232 in *E. E. P.* (1862) 117 Þe gayler him tok an appel; he seide hit was vnriȝt Vnpared an appel take, an heȝ man oþer a kniȝt. 14.. *Burlesques* ii. in *Rel. Ant.* I. 83 Adam, Adam, why ete thu the appull unpard? 1530 PALSGR. 652/2 Can you nat eate a peere onpared? 1658 EVELYN *Fr. Gard.* (1675) 190 The fruits being pared or unpared, according to..your curiosity.

**2.** Of nails: Uncut, untrimmed.

1547 BOORDE *Introd. Knowl.* 117 Who shall let me, the deuyls nayles vnpared? 1598 DALLINGTON *Meth. Trav.* X iij, Wearing long vnpared nayles. 1635 QUARLES *Embl.* III. vi. 146 If the peevish Infant fights, and flies, With unpar'd weapons, at his mother's eyes. 1743 FRANCIS tr. *Hor., Epode* v. 60 Her unpar'd Thumbs Canidia gnaws.

**† Unpa·regal, -pe·regal,** *a.* *Obs.* [UN-[1] 7.] Unequal.

*c* 1374 CHAUCER *Boeth.* III. pr. i. (1868) 63 So þat I trowe nat now þat I be vnparygal to the strokes of fortune. 1605 MARSTON *Dutch Courtezan* IV. i, Afore the Lord God, my knaverie growes unperegall; Tis time to take a nap.

**† Unpa·rel,** *v.* *Obs.*[-1] [UN-[2] 4.] *trans.* To divest of apparel. 1603 H. CROSSE *Vertues Commw.* N 1, Perhaps thou wilt say againe, I brought him not to beggery: did I lame him? did I vnparell him?

**Unpa·rented,** *ppl. a.* [UN-[1] 8 and UN-[2] 8.]

**1.** Deprived of the status of a parent.

1650 B. *Discolliminium* 38 Our Politicall Parents..are now unparented or civilly dead.

**2.** Deprived or destitute of a parent or parents.

1668 WILKINS *Real Char.* II. xii. 295 *Orphan* is un-parented. 1885 *American* X. 333 The unparented suggestion that each newcomer should add a stone to the growing pile. 1897 *Fortn. Rev.* 1 Feb. 225 A family of five children, three brothers and two sisters, unparented.

**Un-Pari·sianized,** *ppl. a.* (UN-[1] 8.) 1858 MRS. GORE *Heckington* III. 160 The envy with which the still un-Parisianised Lady Frere surveyed the boudoir furniture.

**Unpa·rliament,** *v.* (UN-[2] 6 b.) 1643 PRYNNE *Sov. Power Parl.* IV. 24 Such a grand difference is there now..between the Irish Rebels,..who may do what they please..; and the English (now un-Parliamented) Parliament. 1648 E. SYMMONS *Vind. Chas. I*, 382 They were once a true Parliament.., but now they swarm so much in evils..that they have plainly un-parliamented themselves.

**Unparliame·ntary,** *a.* (UN-[1] 7.) 1626 JAS. I *Sp.* in *3rd Rep. Hist. MSS. Comm.* 68/1, I am come here to shew you your errors, and, as I may term them, unparliamentary proceedings in this Parliament. 1679 HOBBES *Behemoth* 89 All Unparliamentary raising of Mony upon the Subjects. 1701 SWIFT *Contests Nobles & Comm.* v, That unparliamentary abuse of setting individuals upon their shoulders who were hated by God and man. 1810 *Sporting Mag.* XXXV. 302 The Speaker stated..that..a member had used unparliamentary language. 1876 JEVONS *Logic Prim.* 18 A speech is unparliamentary when it does not agree with the rules of parliamentary debate.

Hence **Unparliame·ntarily** *adv.*, **-ariness.**

1647 CLARENDON *Hist. Reb.* IV. § 81 The Unparliamentariness of their Remonstrance. 1727 BOYER *Dict. Royal* II. s.v., Unparliamentarily. *a* 1797 H. WALPOLE *Mem. Geo. II* (1847) II. ii. 55 The use that had been made of the sacred name of the King, so often and so unparliamentarily.

**Unpa·rrel,** *v.* *Naut.* (UN-[2] 4.) 1627 CAPT. SMITH *Seaman's Gram.* ix. 41 For more haste unparrell the mizen yard and lanch it and the saile ouer her Lee quarter. [1694 MOTTEUX *Rabelais* V. x, We..for more haste unparrell'd the Misen yard, and lanch'd it and the Sail over her Lee-quarter.] 1706 PHILLIPS (ed. Kersey), To *Unparrel* a Yard, (in Sea-Language) is to take off the Frames call'd Parrels, that go round about the Masts.

**† Unpa·rreled,** obs. var. UNPARALLELED *ppl. a.*

1639 W. H. *Zarain Aga* (title-p.), With one Unparreled, Cruell, Furious and Bloudy assault, made by the Turks. 1661 BOYLE *Physiol. Ess.* (1669) 284 Another Author quoted for writing an unparrel'd Story.

**Unpa·rriable,** *a.* (UN-[1] 7 b.) 1813 SCOTT *Let.* in *Lockhart* (1839) IV. 91 A general reluctance to allow that any danger is near, until it is almost unparriable. 1826 *Blackw. Mag.* XIX. 393 How pretty had it been to dally for a few passes, and then, unparryable as the Chevalier St. George, to pierce through heart and back. 1836 in Russell *Mem. Moore* (1856) VIII. 275 A tone of irony.., which..is the most unparryable..weapon ever directed against the [Church's] vitals.

**Unpa·rroted,** *ppl. a.* (UN-[1] 8.) 1817 GODWIN *Mandeville* I. 207 She expressed herself with the greatest ease; her sentiments were unparrotted and unstudied.

**Unparso·nical,** *a.* (UN-[1] 7.) 1858 MOTLEY *Corr.* (1889) I. 232 [Kingsley] seems a good fellow, and entirely unparsonical. 1889 'F. ANSTEY' *Pariah* III. i, A manner which was unparsonical, not to say secular.

**† Unpa·rt,** *v.* *Obs.*[-1] [UN-[2] 9.] *trans.* To take apart. 1536 *MS. Rawl. D.* 780 fol. 73 Not only vpon..framyng of one syde of the same brydge.. butt also aswell in vnpartyng the frame ayen.

**Unpa·rtable,** *a.* (UN-[1] 7 b. Cf. IMPARTIBLE *a.*[1])

*c* 1420 *Wycliffite Bible* Luke, Prol. i, Bi the entringe of the generacioun of vndepartable [*v.r.* unpartable] God. *c* 1555 HARPSFIELD *Divorce Hen. VIII* (Camden) 248 This only consent..is thought to uphold..this unparteable conversation and living together. 1587 GOLDING *De Mornay* XV. 272 That the Soule is a life by it selfe, a life all in one, vnpartable. 1611 COTGR., *Indivisible*,..inseperable, vnpartable.

Hence **Unpa·rtableness.**

1647 HEXHAM I. s.v. 1656 BLOUNT, *Individuality*, inseparableness, unpartableness.

**Unparta·ken,** *ppl. a.* (UN-[1] 8 b.) 1807 ANNA SEWARD *Lett.* (1811) VI. 379 The single solitary Wight, who, in every one of these periodical olios, possesses his separate and unpartaken department.

**Unparta·king,** *ppl. a.* (UN-[1] 10.) 1606 DANIEL *Queen's Arcadia* IV. i, And now hath sorrow no worse plague I see, Then free and vnpartaking companie.

**Unpa·rted,** *ppl. a.* (UN-[1] 8.)

1561 NORTON & SACKV. *Gorboduc* I. ii, When discent on one alone Makes single and vnparted reigne to light. 1587 GOLDING *De Mornay* XV. 280 The one vniuersall capable mind is and worketh whole and vnparted in euery man. 1613 CHAPMAN *Masque Inns Court* Plays 1873 III. 116 Twinns as of one age, so to one desire May both their bloods giue an vnparted fire. 1648 HEXHAM II, *Ongedeelt*, Vnparted, or Vnshared. 1718 PRIOR *Solomon* I. 183 The Object..Becomes mixt Blackness, or unparted Light.

**Unpa·rtial,** *a.* [UN-[1] 7, 5 b.]

**1.** **†a.** Impartial, unbiassed, fair. *Obs.*

Very common from *c* 1590 to *c* 1660.

1579 W. WILKINSON *Confut. Fam. Love* B ij b, Then must the Judge sit vnparciall in judgement place. 1593 *Sidney's Arcadia* V. (1922) 201, I wayed the matter..with most unpartiall and farthest reach of reason. 1637 HEYWOOD *Royall King* 29 Rendring withall a full satisfactory reason to any unpartiall reader, why they are there. *a* 1662 SANDERSON in Walton *Life* (1796) 496 Upon the clear evidence of truth and reason, after a serious and unpartial examination of the grounds.

**b.** Free from inclination or fondness.

1844 THACKERAY *B. Lyndon* xv, The widow was not unpartial to me.

**2.** Unrestricted, ample. *rare*[-1].

1787 BENTHAM *Def. Usury* xiii. 137 On the most unpartial and extensive signification.

Hence **Unpa·rtialness.**

*a* 1639 W. WHATELEY *Prototypes* II. xxxii. (1640) 127 O ignorant..creatures that we be, let us beg more wisdome and unpartialnesse to our selves at Gods hand. 1661 FELTHAM *Resolves* II. xxvii. 237 Even in the unpartialness of War.

**†Unpartia·lity.** *Obs.* (UN-[1] 12, 5 b.) 1579 W. WILKINSON *Confut. Fam. Love* B ij, In vniformenes of hart and vnpartialitye of minde. 1635 HEYWOOD *Hierarchy* IV. 232 Ovid speaking of the unpartialitie of the fatall Sisters.

**† Unpa·rtially,** *adv.* [UN-[1] 11, 5 b.] Impartially. (Common 1610–50.)

1576 W. RAWELY in Gascoigne *Steele Gl.* Wks. 1910 II. 139 This Glasse of Steele unpartially doth shewe Abuses all, to such as in it looke. 1599 SANDYS *Europæ Spec.* (1629) 248 The truth.., which I haue sincerely and unpartially endeavored to deliver. 1655 FULLER *Ch. Hist.* III. i. § 3 About this time Doomes-day-book was made,..unpartially done with rigorous severity. *a* 1662 SANDERSON *Cases Consc.* ix. (1678) 172 Advisedly and unpartially to weigh the benefits.

**†Unpa·rtible,** *a.* *Obs.*[-1] [UN-[1] 7, 5 b.] = UNPARTABLE *a.* *c* 1511 *1st Eng. Bk. Amer.* Introd. (Arb.) 32/1 We beleue in god the father, in god the sonne, and in god the holy gooste. The whyche be vnpartyble and one very god.

**Unparti·cipant,** *a.* (UN-[1] 7.) 1866 CARLYLE *Remin.* I. 282, I strictly unparticipant, sitting silently apart till it was done.

**Unparti·cipate,** *a.* [UN-[1] 7.] Not participant. 1824 J. H. WIFFEN tr. *Tasso's Jerusalem Delivered* II. xii, And what if some be unparticipate In this new crime?

**Unparti·cipated,** *ppl. a.* (UN-[1] 8.)

1678 CUDWORTH *Intell. Syst.* I. iv. 557 In all which several Ranks of Being they supposed One First Universal, and Unparticipated,..and many Particular, or Participated Ones. 1781 COWPER *Friendship* 125 Some..are indeed a bog, that bears Your unparticipated cares Unmov'd and without quaking. *a* 1806 H. K. WHITE *Time* 563 Spirit, rear Thy flag on high!—Invincible, and throned In unparticipated might. 1821 BYRON *Cain* I. i, Creating worlds, to make eternity Less burthensome to His immense existence And unparticipated solitude!

**Unparti·cipating,** *ppl. a.* (UN-[1] 10.) 1795 COLERIDGE *Lett.* (1895) 148 An unparticipating propensity. 1817 — *Biog. Lit.* XV. II. 16 It is throughout as if a superior spirit.. were placing the whole before our view; himself meanwhile unparticipating in the passions. 1831 CARLYLE *Sart. Res.* I. iii, He was a man so still and altogether unparticipating, that to question him..was a thing of more than usual delicacy.

**Unparti·cipative,** *a.* (UN-[1] 7.) 1889 WHITTIER *Pr. Wks.* III. 222 Deep down under the squalid exterior, unparticipative in the..recklessness of the criminal, there is another self.

**Unparti·cular,** *a.* (UN-[1] 7). 1828 L. HUNT *Byron & Contemp.* 93 Written by as unparticular a fellow as one should wish to see with a pair of scissors in his hand.

**Unparti·cularized,** *ppl. a.* (UN-[1] 8.) [1775 ASH.] 1823 BENTHAM *Not Paul* 67 Time as well as place being left thus unparticularized.

**Unparti·cularizing,** *ppl. a.* (UN-[1] 10.) 1835 WILLIS *Pencillings* I. xii. 90 The same lost unexamining, unparticularizing feeling which I cannot overcome in this place.

**†Unpa·rtied,** *ppl. a.* *Obs.*[-1] [UN-[1] 8.] Unassisted, unsupported. 1641 SIR E. DERING *Sp. on Relig.* 63 They..ought not to be bound up unheard, and unpartied.

**†Unpa·rtingly,** *adv.* *Obs.*[-1] [UN-[1] 11.] With close adherence. 1435 MISYN *Fire of Love* 44 Þat, vanite spisyd.., to trewth vnpartyngly we draw.

**Unpartoo·k,** *pa. pple.* (UN-[1] 8 b.) 1836 MRS. BROWNING *Rom. Margret* iv, That dream, by that ladye, Is certes unpartook.

**Unpa·rty.** (UN-[1] 12 b.) 1711 *Peace in Divinity* (title-p.), A Grave Author of Middle and Unparty Principles.

**Unpa·ss,** *v.* (UN-[2] 3.) 1605 DANIEL *Queen's Arcadia* 694 *Clo.* Yes, sure, My promise is already past. *Tec.* And if it be, I trust you are so wise T'vnpasse the same againe for your owne good.

**Unpa·ssable,** *a.* [UN-[1] 7 b, 5 b.]

**1.** = IMPASSABLE *a.* Now *dial.*

Very common in 17th and 18th centuries.

1553 BRENDE *Q. Curtius* 132 In the daye time the countrey is wild and vnpassable, when they can nether finde any tracte nor waye to go in. 1579–80 NORTH *Plutarch* (1595) 314 The riuer..is vnpassable for any shallow it hath. 1649 F. ROBERTS *Clavis Bibl.* 500 Waters..very deep and unpassable. *a* 1698 TEMPLE *Ess. Heroick Virt.* Wks. 1720 I. 196 Vast and unpassable Mountains or Desarts. 1719 DE FOE *Crusoe* I. (Globe) 263 A Grove of Trees,..so thick, that it was unpassable. 1796 J. MOSER *Hermit of Caucasus* I. 192 The caverns were rendered slippery, and nearly unpassable. 1828–32 WEBSTER s.v., Unpassable roads. 1876–88 in Yks. and Somerset glossaries.

**† b.** As *adv.* Impassably. *Obs.*[-1]

1632 LITHGOW *Trav.* IX. 390 The North side..beeing vnpassable steepe.

**2.** Incapable of being transcended or exceeded.

1570 DEE *Math. Pref.* 34 They can not prescribe..certaine vnpassable boundes. 1656 JEANES *Fuln. Christ* 236 The Scotists..say farther, that the degree of Christ's grace was unpassable even by Gods absolute power. *a* 1683 OLDHAM *Wks.* (1686) 109 'Tis I..Who must new Worlds in Vice descry, And fix the pillars of unpassable iniquity.

**3.** Of money: Incapable of being passed or circulated.

1664 in *Aberdeen N. & Q.* (1910) III. 109/2 Ther was some unpassable money in the poors box. 1696 J. CARY *Ess. Coyn* 10 The Trade of England was apparently slackened since the Small Money was made unpassable. 1745 *De Foe's Eng. Tradesm.* (1841) I. xx. 188 A considerable quantity of false and unpassable money. 1828–32 WEBSTER s.v., Unpassable notes or coins.

Hence **Unpa·ssableness.**

1657 R. LIGON *Barbadoes* 75 The unpassableness of the wayes. 1674 EVELYN *Navig. & Comm.* 34 Grave Authors, who speak of the unpassableness of the Ocean. 1691 T. H[ALE] *Acc. New Invent.* 26 Its unpassableness, not to the Water, but to the Worm.

**Unpa·ssageable,** *a.* (UN-[1] 7 b.) 1592 R. D. *Hypnerotomachia* 94 The ruggednesse of the vnpassageable mountaine Caucasus.

**Unpa·ssed, unpa·st,** *ppl. a.* (UN-[1] 8, 5 d.)

1541 *Aberdeen Reg.* XVII. (Jam.), To returne hame on past to the tryst. 1597 MORLEY *Introd. Mus.* To Rdr., Like vnto a great Sea, which the further I entred into, the more I sawe before mee vnpast. 1647 COWLEY *Mistress* 115 Unpast Alps stop mee, but I'le cut through all, And march, the Muses Hanniball. [1775 ASH, *Unpassed, Unpast.*] 1849 ROCK *Ch. of Fathers* III. x. 477 The strong unpassed wall between them and that defenceless town. 1884 *Knowledge* 4 July 6 Barriers as yet unpassed, and probably impassable.

**†Unpa·ssen,** *ppl. a.* *Obs.*[-1] [UN-[1] 8 b.] = prec. 1624 in Capt. Smith *Virginia* Pref. 4 Who loues to liue at home, yet looke abroad, And know both passen and unpassen road.

**† Unpa·ssible,** *a.*[1] *Obs.* [UN-[1] 7.] UNPASSABLE.

1398 TREVISA *Barth. De P. R.* XV. iii. (1495) F iv/2 In many places in yᵉ vttermeste endes [of Assyria] for dystemperate places yᵉ londe is vnpassyble. [1775 ASH.]

**† Unpa·ssible,** *a.*[2] *Obs.* [UN-[1] 7, 5 b.] = IMPASSIBLE *a.*

Freq. as an attribute of the Deity.

*c* 1450 *Mirour Saluacioun* (Roxb.) 140 The gude mens [bodies shall rise] fulle faire with out eend unpassible. 1533 tr. *Erasmus' Com. Crede* 23, I beleue in God the father almyghty vnuysyble and vnpassyble. 1587 GOLDING *De Mornay* iii. 35 First substances, vnchaungeable and vnpassible. 1623 LISLE *Anc. Mon.* (1638) 6 Christs body.. neuer dieth henceforth: but is eternal, and vnpassible.

**Unpa·ssing,** *ppl. a.* (UN-[1] 10, 5 d + PASSING *ppl. a.* 1, 3.)

1592 *Sc. Acts, Jas. VI* (1814) III. 531/1 The haill estaittis ..to remane in this toun vnpassing furth of the samyne. 1887 'H. HALIBURTON' *Scotland's Sake* 219 An unpassing present of passionless repose. 1903 W. SHARP in *Life* (1910) 357 It deals in a new way with a subject of unpassing interest.

**Unpa·ssionate,** *a.* Now *rare.* [UN-¹ 7, 5 b.] Common from *c* 1600 to *c* 1660.

1. Not influenced or swayed by passion or strong feeling; calm, self-possessed: **a.** Of persons, disposition, etc.

1593 *Sidney's Arcadia* (1598) 439 That well appeased gesture, vnpassionate nature bestoweth vpon mankind. 1604 T. WRIGHT *Passions* II. i. 56 That which an vnpassionate mind detested, a passionate soule most effectually pursueth. 1673 CAVE *Prim. Chr.* II. i. 5 We are to be of a meek and unpassionate mind. 1747 CARTE *Hist. Eng.* I. 188 True wisdom .. is ever cool and unpassionate when she takes a resolution. 1852 M. ARNOLD *Summer Night* 80 Ye Heavens, whose pure dark regions .. though so great Are yet untroubled and unpassionate.

**b.** Of actions, feelings, etc.

*a* 1600 HOOKER *Eccl. Pol.* VI. v. § 4 A calm, unpassionate, and just assignation of dreadful punishment. 1610 HEALEY *St. Aug. Citie of God* 532 Gods unpassionate and unaltering anger. 1683 E. HOOKER *Pref. Pordage's Mystic Div.* 48 A prettie and unpassionate replie, that a Steward once made to his angri Lord. 1702 C. MATHER *Magn. Chr.* II. ix. 29/1 He did with a very Unpassionate Aspect and Carriage then say, Friends, I thank you all.

†2. Unprejudiced, impartial. *Obs.*

1602 T. FITZHERBERT *Apol.* 6 But whether it be reason.. I leaue it to the iudgment of any indifferent & vnpassionate man. *a* 1648 DIGBY *Priv. Mem.* (1827) 243, I am sure you will say, who are yet an indifferent and unpassionate judge, that [etc.].

†**Unpa·ssionated,** *ppl. a. Obs.* [UN-¹ 8.] = prec. 1611 FLORIO, *Spassionato*, vnpassionated, sans passion. 1661 GLANVILL *Van. Dogm.* 100 A set of misconceits, which are ..absurd to an unpassionated reason.

**Unpa·ssionately,** *adv.* (UN-¹ 11; cf. UNPASSIONATE *a.*)

1648 *Eikon Bas.* iv. 24 Make us unpassionately to see the light of Reason. 1661 COWLEY *Cromwell* Wks. 1906 II. 366 Truely and unpassionately reflecting upon the advantages of his person. 1707 *Reflex. upon Ridicule* (1717) I. 44 Those who unpassionately hear him, regard his Mystery as importunate Trifles.

**Unpa·ssionateness.** (UN-¹ 12.) 1611 COTGR., *Impassibilité*, ..vnpassionatenesse. 1655 M. CASAUBON *Enthus.* iii. (1656) 159 Stoicks and Cynicks..who..chose to beg, and to be trampled upon.., to make good their profession of unpassionatnesse. 1673 O. WALKER *Educ.* 205 If your election be..made..with indifferency,unpassionateness,and sincerity.

**Unpa·ssioned,** *ppl. a.* [UN-¹ 8.] = UNPASSIONATE *a.*

*a* 1618 J. DAVIES (Heref.) *Witte's Pilgr.* Wks. (Grosart) II. 48/2 O you vnpassiond peacefull Harts That with me liue secure in meane estate. 1678 TEMPLE *Let.* Wks. 1720 II. 515 As unpassioned, and as uninteressed Concernment in the..Service of my Master..as any Man can have. *a* 1764 MRS. CARTER in *Mem.* (1808) II. 103 With calm severity, unpassion'd Age Detects the specious fallacies of Youth.

**Unpa·ssive,** *a.* [UN-¹ 7.] †**a.** = IMPASSIVE *a.* 1. *Obs.* **b.** Active.

1602 WARNER *Alb. Eng.* XIII. lxxix. 326 Sufficeth vs to know he is..vnpassiue, vnmateriall, vncompounded, Infinite. 1768–74 TUCKER *Lt. Nat.* (1834) II. 568 The principal of those [habits] are faith, and hope, and charity,..unpassive compliance, readiness to please, and easiness to be pleased.

**Unpast,** variant of UNPASSED *ppl. a.*

**Unpa·ste,** *v.* (UN-² 3.) 1598 FLORIO, *Spastare*, to vnpaste, to take away the paste or crust of any thing. 1668 R. STEELE *Husbandman's Calling* i. 9 Item, Spent each day..in dressing, painting,..and three hours more at Night in unpasting and undressing again. **Unpa·stor,** *v.* (UN-² 6 b.) 1655 FULLER *Ch. Hist.* VIII. iii. § 12 Preferring rather willingly to un-Pastor..themselves than to retain the place, without the power.

**Unpa·storal,** *a.* (UN-¹ 7.)

1782 WARTON *Rowley Enq.* 95 This very unpathetic and unpastoral idea.., that 'the portcullis of the castle of his heart was fallen'. 1820 SCOTT *Monast.* xxviii, The swain cursed the nymph's bad humour with very unpastoral phrase and emphasis. 1865 RUSKIN *Sesame* 45 The most unpastoral [character] is, instead of feeding, to want to be fed.

**Unpa·sturable,** *a.* (UN-¹ 7 b.) 1796 W. H. MARSHALL *Planting* II. 38 Plantations of Alders should..be confined to swampy, low, unpasturable places.

**Unpa·stured,** *ppl. a.* [UN-¹ 8.]

1. Not led to pasture; unfed.

1548 ELYOT *Impastus*, vnfed, vnpastured, hungry. 1647 HEXHAM I, Vnpastured, *ongeweydt*. *a* 1800 COWPER *Death of Damon* 113 Go, go, my lambs, unpastur'd as ye are. 1821 SHELLEY *Adonais* xxvii, Why didst thou..Dare the unpastured dragon in his den?

2. Not employed for pasture.

1820 SHELLEY *Prometh. Unb.* III. ii. 49 It is the unpastured sea hungering for calm. 1872 BLACKIE *Lays Highl.* 3 Wandering..o'er the wide unpastured sea.

**Unpa·tched,** *ppl. a.* (UN-¹ 8.) [1775 ASH.] 1824 MISS MITFORD *Village* Ser. I. I. 206 The ragged condition of those unpatched shoes. 1875 [see UN-¹ 8].

**Unpa·tented,** *ppl. a.* (UN-¹ 8.)

1719 W. WOOD *Surv. Trade* 160 Any Land..that is unpatented, or not granted to some particular Person. 1809 MALKIN *Gil Blas* VIII. ix. ⁋2 Invested with full powers to make the world his oyster, and leave nothing but the shell to his unpatented competitors. 1879 *Cassell's Techn. Educ.* IV. 33/1 Unpatented Inventions. 1903 *Westm. Gaz.* 27 Aug. 2/2 The various patented and unpatented medicines of the present day.

**Unpa·thed,** *ppl. a.* (UN-¹ 8.)

1611 SHAKS. *Wint. T.* IV. iv. 578 A wild dedication of your selues To vnpath'd Waters, vndream'd Shores. 1628 FELTHAM *Resolves* II. xxxvi. 111 The lonelinesse of vnpathed Desarts. 1671 MARTEN *Voy. Spitzbergen* in *Acc. Sev. Late Voy.* II. (1694) 30 She always keeps her strait way through these unpathed Waves. 1852 *Q. Rev.* Mar. 441 Three galleys.. were sent across these unpathed waters. 1897 BARING-GOULD *Guavas* xiv, He..strode over the unpathed moor.

**Unpathe·tic,** *a.* (UN-¹ 7.)

[1775 ASH.] 1782 [see UNPASTORAL *a.*]. 1818 T. L. PEACOCK *Nightmare Abbey* iv, We are all..puppets of a blind and unpathetic necessity. 1903 *Times Lit. Supp.* 16 Jan. 16/1 The not unpathetic image of a big..ape.

**Unpa·thwayed,** *a.* (UN-¹ 9.) 1805 WORDSW. *Waggoner* VI. 24 While she roves..Along the smooth unpathwayed plain.

†**Unpa·tience.** *Obs.* [UN-¹ 12, 5 b.] Lack of patience; impatience.

1380 *Lay Folks Catech.* (Lamb. MS.) 740 Be grucchyngge and vnpaciens and blasfemynge of god. *c* 1440 *Jacob's Well* 94 Þe sexte fote depe of wose in wretthe is vnpacyence. *Ibid.*, Vnpacyens is full of malyce. 1483 CAXTON *Gold. Leg.* 361 b/2 Neuertheles was neuer sene in her signe of unpacyence but alwey swete wordes. 1549 COVERDALE, etc. *Erasm. Par. Gal.* i. 3 b, Lest any thynke that these my wordes are spoken either of hastynes or of vnpacience. 1643 J. STEER tr. *Exp. Chyrurg.* ix. 43 By reason of the Childs unpatience I could not make the Medicine stay.

†**Unpa·tiency.** *Obs. rare.* [UN-¹ 12, 5 b.] = prec.

1535 COVERDALE *Judith* viii. 24 They that..put them selues forth with vnpaciency and murmurynge agaynst God. 1558 KNOX *First Blast* (Arb.) 14, I might adduce histories, prouing..some for vnpaciencie to haue murthered them selues.

**Unpa·tient,** *a.* Now *dial.* [UN-¹ 7, 5 b.] Impatient.

*c* 1380 WYCLIF *Sel. Wks.* II. 268 Þes þat ben unpacient þat Goddis lawe riȝtid hem. 1387 TREVISA *Higden* (Rolls) II. 167 Ful vnpacient of pees,..and wlatful of sleuþe. *a* 1425 tr. *Arderne's Treat. Fistula*, etc. 22 If ȝe be vnobedient and vnpacient to my commandyngs. *c* 1485 *Digby Myst.* (1882) IV. 948 Nothinge ragid he, ne was vnpaciente. 1560 PILKINGTON *Expos. Aggeus* (1562) 37 The unpacient bearing of [God's scourge]..when it comes. *a* 1586 SIDNEY *Arcadia* I. xii, Though he were very unpatient of long deliberations. 1607 BEAUM. & FL. *Woman-Hater* III. i, *Gond.* Thou hadst better bin a devill. *Orian.* Why my unpatient Lord? 1651 *Fuller's Abel Rediv.*, *Calvin* (1867) I. 321 The commissioners, unpatient of delay, assembled the people together. *a* 1704 T. BROWN *Ess. Women* Wks. 1711 IV. 157, I see..you are unpatient to object against me. 1861 GEO. ELIOT *Silas M.* xiv, The men are..so fiery and unpatient. 1886–96 in Lanc. and Durham glossaries.

†**Unpa·tiently,** *adv. Obs.* [UN-¹ 11, 5 b.] Impatiently.

*c* 1425 *Orolog. Sapient.* i. in *Anglia* X. 335/23 Þat þou take not vnpacientlye þat diuerse graciose visitacione. 1491 CAXTON *Vitas Patr.* (W. de W. 1495) I. cxi. 136/1 The sayd Sirryens..bare full unpacyently that they were brought in bondage. 1548 CRANMER *Catech.* 93 When such yong babes do not lye softly..they crie vnpatientlye. 1576 FLEMING *Panopl. Epist.* 186 It was manifest..that their minds were exceedingly molested, and tooke their repulse very unpatiently. 1610 HEALEY *St. Aug. Citie of God* XIX. iv. 759 Cato ..would not haue done it but that he tooke Cæsar's victory so vnpatiently.

†**Unpa·tientness.** *Obs.* [UN-¹ 12, 5 b.] Impatience.

1548 CRANMER *Catech.* 140 b, Their unpatientnes is encreaced by such aduersitie. 1587 FLEMING *Contn. Holinshed* III. 1391 Parries exclamation of outrage and vnpatientnesse.

**Unpatria·rchal,** *a.* (UN-¹ 7.) 1859 W. H. GREGORY *Egypt* I. 274 Jabbering and mumbling for a full hour in a most ungodlike, unpatriarchal manner. **Unpa·trimonied,** *ppl. a.* (UN-¹ 8.) 1782 ELIZ. BLOWER *Geo. Bateman* I. 100 It is the misfortune of the unpatrimonied, that they can only shew their feelings in words. **Unpa·triot,** *v.* (UN-² 6 b.) 1738 *Common Sense* II. 207, I fairly deliver him up to Freeman and Company to unpatriot and revile as much as they please.

**Unpatrio·tic,** *a.* (UN-¹ 7, 5 b.)

[1775 ASH.] 1828 CARLYLE *Misc.* (1840) I. 362 The French wits of the period were as unpatriotic. 1853 LYTTON *My Novel* XII. xxv, A captain..undertook a long defence of army and navy, from the unpatriotic aspersions of the preceding speakers.

**Unpatrio·tically,** *adv.* (UN-¹ 11.)

1783 EARL MALMESBURY *Diaries & Corr.* II. 34 The clamour, which was very unpatriotically indeed attempted to be raised about it in Parliament. 1850 CARLYLE *Latter-d. Pamph.* i. 23 Of America it would ill beseem any Englishman..to speak unpatriotically, if any of us even felt so. 1861 TROLLOPE *Tales All Countries* vii. 273 Unpatriotically acquiescent as to England's aristocratic propensities.

**Unpa·triotism.** (UN-¹ 12, 5 b.) 1887 *Blackfriars Mag.* Jan. 225 In the desire..lay the germ of unpatriotism, a forgetting that they were Englishmen at all. [Freq. from *c* 1905.] **Unpa·troned,** *ppl. a.* (UN-¹ 8.) 1741 WARBURTON *Div. Legat.* II. Pref. p. xiv, This Disadvantage.. gave his first Volume, unpatroned and unfriended as it was, so very kind a Reception.

**Unpa·tronized,** *ppl. a.* (UN-¹ 8.)

1620 J. BEALE *Ded.* in *Hieron's Serm.*, etc. I. ¶ 2 The author of this present volume..left not only some members of it vnpatroniz'd, but the whole frame without a generall sustainer. 1661 RAWLEY *Resuscitatio* (ed. 2) Ded. a j, This unpatroniz'd Booke. 1751 JOHNSON *Rambler* No. 120 ⁋ 11 Unpatronized and unsupported, he cleared himself by the openness of innocence. 1814 SCOTT *Wav.* ii, The young officer..rose in the army with a rapidity far surpassing the usual pace of unpatronized professional merit. 1865 MILL *Repr. Govt.* vii. 158 Those who are desirous of voting for unpatronized persons of merit.

**Unpa·tterned,** *ppl. a.* [UN-¹ 8.]

1. Unexampled, unequalled. Now *arch.*

1621 FLETCHER *Thierry & Theod.* III. i, To bring forth a second to your self, Was only worthy of my Virgin loss; And should I prize you less, unpattern'd Sir, Then being exemplify'd? 1641 PRYNNE *Dioc. Prel. Tyr.* I. 35 The unpatternd compliency both of the Judges, and Court of Star-Chamber. 1657 BP. H. KING *Poems* (1843) 48 What debt of service I do truly ow To your unpattern'd self. 1899 *Academy* 28 Oct. 479/2 Old Sam Butler, most singular and unpatterned of satirists.

2. Not decorated with a pattern.

1884 *Bazaar* 19 Dec. 658/1 The only rule seems to be that the fabric must be unpatterned.

**Unpau·nch,** *v.* [UN-² 4.] = PAUNCH *v.*¹ 2. 1598 FLORIO, *Sviscerato*, vnbowelled, vnpanched. 1603 — *Montaigne* I. xlviii. 159 To save themselves from the extreamitie of the cold, many advised to kil and vnpanch their horses, and enter into their panches. 1622 MABBE tr. *Aleman's Guzman d'Alf.* I. 39 The old woman was vnpanching the belly of an old rotten sheepe.

**Unpau·perized,** *ppl. a.* (UN-¹ 8.) 1846 WORCESTER (citing *Q. Rev.*). 1896 W. D. HOWELLS *Impressions & Experiences* 135 It could not have been said that she was wholly unpauperised before she took it [*sc.* money].

**Unpau·sing,** *ppl. a.* (UN-¹ 10.)

1837 LYTTON *Athens* II. 371 Restless and unpausing energy. 1857 DUFFERIN *Lett. High Lat.* (ed. 3) 334 Raging and bubbling up.., the unpausing wave sweeps on. 1898 G. WYNDHAM *Poems Shakespeare* 266 The pause in the first line..is heavily pointed to prepare for the unpausing outburst of the last two.

Hence **Unpau·singly** *adv.*

1891 *Athenæum* 4 July 36/2 The brisk and stirring kind [of story] that may be read unpausingly.

**Unpa·ve,** *v.* [UN-² 4.] *trans.* To lift or remove the paving of (a street, etc.).

1598 FLORIO, *Dimattonare*, to vnpaue, to vnbrick. 1623 tr. *Favine's Theat. Hon.* V. i. 44 During that yeare, the Primatiall Church..had the Altars vnpaued..and the Belles vn-hung. 1686 *Lond. Gaz.* No. 2147/2 They have unpaved the Streets. 1769 FALCONER *Dict. Marine* (1780) s.v. *Water-spout*, This whirlwind['s]..general effects on houses were.. forcing up the floors, and unpaving the rooms. 1827 HOOD *Don't you smell fire?* iv, Here's a nice easy bit in the street, That M'Adam has lately unpaved! 1859 SALA *Tw. round Clock* (1861) 28, I might take one house and unroof it, one street and unpave it.

**Unpa·ved,** *ppl. a.* (UN-¹ 8.)

*a* 1533 LD. BERNERS *Gold. Bk. M. Aurel.* (1546) P v, O Rome, I wepe not to see thy streetes vnpaued,..nor that the battylmentes fall downe. 1585 T. WASHINGTON tr. *Nicholay's Voy.* II. xviii. 51 b, A great and large place vnpaued. 1627 HAKEWILL *Apol.* II. vii. 123 The streetes of the citty lying then vnpaued. 1741 tr. *D'Argen's Chinese Lett.* xiii. 82 If most of its Streets were not crooked, narrow, rugged, and generally unpav'd. 1805 *Ann. Rev.* III. 18 In Philadelphia the privies are unpaved. 1833 M. SCOTT *Tom Cringle* xvi, We marched up through a hot, sandy, unpaved street. 1884 *Manch. Exam.* 14 Nov. 5/6 The roads were all unpaved earth roads.

*fig.* 1823 BYRON *Juan* X. ii, The mode In which Sir Isaac Newton could disclose Through the then unpaved stars the turnpike road.

**b.** In allusive use: (cf. STONED *ppl. a.* 4).

1611 SHAKS. *Cymb.* II. iii. 34 It is a voyce in her eares which Horse-haires, and Calues-guts, nor the voyce of vnpaued Eunuch to boot, can neuer amend.

**Unpavi·lioned,** *a.* (UN-¹ 9.)

[1775 ASH.] 1819 SHELLEY *Prometh. Unb.* IV. 184 As the bare, green hill..Laughs with a thousand drops of sunny water To the unpavilioned sky. 1839 G. DARLEY *Nepenthe* I. 5 High on his unpavilioned throne The heaven's hot tyrant sat alone.

**Unpaw·n,** *v.* (UN-² 3.)

1598 FLORIO, *Disimpegnare*, to vnpaune, to redeeme. 1636 DAVENANT *Wits* Wks. (1673) 169 We can't unpawn the Oaths We left at the Bar for the last Reckoning. 1680 *Lond. Gaz.* No. 1496/4 The Murderer..having unpawn'd and changed his Cloaths.

**Unpaw·ned,** *ppl. a.* (UN-¹ 8.)

1638 R. BAILLIE *Lett. & Jrnls.* (1841) I. 58 Would it not grieved them to see the subjects suffer by the relying upon unpauned trust? 1639 MASSINGER *Unnat. Combat* III. i, Tis well I have one [suit] Unpawnd in these dayes. 1728 POPE *Dunc.* I. 116 He roll'd his eyes that witness'd huge dismay, Where yet unpawn'd, much learned lumber lay. 1909 STACPOOLE *Pools of Silence* ii, The cigarettes and the unpawned banjo.

†**Unpay·,** *v.*¹ *Obs.* [UN-¹ 14, 5 d.]

1. *trans.* To displease.

1340 *Ayenb.* 50 Glotounye .. is a vice þet þe dyeuel is moche myde ypayd, and moche onpayþ god.

2. To leave unpaid; not to pay.

1515 *Reg. Privy Seal Scotl.* I. 409/1 At every viage..he frelie and unpaying ony custumez may discharge and charge [etc.]. 1540 *Extr. Aberd. Reg.* (1844) I. 173 To..poind the personis for the rest of the taxt..of thame that hes unpayit the samen. 1697 DE LA PRYME *Diary* 16 Oct., Mr. Elways did ..grant unto his tennants..all their land to be tithe free, which they have unpay'd untill this time.

†**Unpay·,** *v.*² *Obs.*⁻¹ [UN-² 3.] *trans.* To undo, make good.

1597 SHAKS. 2 *Hen. IV*, II. i. 133 Pay her the debt you owe her, and vnpay the villany you haue done her.

**Unpay·able,** *a.* [UN-¹ 7 b, 5 b.]

1. Incapable of being paid: **a.** Of debts, etc.

1463 G. ASHBY *Prisoner's Refl.* 44, I am put to vnpayable det. 1611 COTGR., *Insolvable*, vnpayable, vnlikely to be payed. 1656 EARL ORRERY *Parthen.* III. IV. 269, I finde my scores of gratitude are as unpayable to the Brother, as those of adoration are to the Sister. *a* 1716 SOUTH *Serm.* (1744) X. 295 The debt of a thousand talents due to him from her, yet by reason of this her great poverty..utterly unpayable. 1899 MACKAIL *W. Morris* ii. 27 The price is unpayable.

**b.** Of persons.

1856 LEVER *Martins of Cro' M.* xxxi. 325 Our Club [would] become only an asylum for unpayable tailors. 1868 CARLYLE in *Mrs. C.'s Lett.* (1883) I. 24 A poor creditor, unpayable, overheard Mrs. A. whispering, 'Let us keep' [etc.

2. Incapable of paying; unremunerative.

1880 G. SUTHERLAND *Tales Goldfields* 50 The goldfields

were unpayable. **1896** in Morris *Austral-Eng.* (1898) 487 Unpayable Lines...Of these [railways] 33..do not pay working expenses.

**Unpay·ing**, *ppl. a.* (UN-[1] 10.)
**1682** DRYDEN *Epil. to King & Queen* 26 We've none so great but their unpaying Masters. **1843** SYD. SMITH *Amer. Debts* ii. P 3, I am astonished that the honest States of America do not draw a *cordon sanitaire* round their unpaying brethren. **1894** D. CAMPBELL *Coleridge* vi. 121 Which he spent much of his time inditing in the form of letters to his unpaying correspondents!

**Unpay·ment.** (UN-[1] 12.) *a* **1578** LINDESAY (Pitscottie) *Chron. Scot.* (S.T.S.) I. 351, I know no cause quhairfoir, bot that he discordit witht his persone ffor wnpayment of his teindis.

**Unpea·ce.** Now *arch.* [UN-[1] 12, prob. after *unfrith*. (UN-[1] 3). Cf. MDu. *onpays*, obs. Du. *onpaais*, Flem. *onpeys* (Kilian).] Absence of peace; dissension, strife.
*a* **1300** *Cursor M.* 414 He..sette þam in haly palais, þar neuer mai be of pride unpais. *Ibid.* 13306 To man þai wroght neuer vn-pes. *c* **1380** WYCLIF *Sel. Wks.* I. 250 Men ben now redi to heeren of unpees, batailis, and strives. **1420–22** LYDG. *Thebes* III. 4260 Fell Ethyocles, Rote of vnreste and causer of vnpes. *a* **1470** *Dives & Pauper* (W. de W. 1496) v. xvii. 219/1 He bad them absteyne them from all tokenes of unpacyence, of unpeas, and of crueltee. **1876** MORRIS *Sigurd* II. 89 Where unpeace and troubles and the griefs of the soul abide. **1906** MARY CHOLMONDELEY *Prisoners* vi, There is an unpeace which passes understanding also.

**Unpea·ceable,** *a.* Now *rare.* [UN-[1] 7 b. Cf. UNPEACIBLE *a.*]
**1.** Not disposed to peace; contentious, turbulent.
*c* **1520** M. NISBET *Jas.* iii. 8 Naman may chastice the toung, for it is ane vnpeceabile [*Wyclif* unpesible] euile. **1570** DRANT *Serm.* E vj b, What warres.. hath this foule and vnpeaceable woman brought to passe? **1608** DOD & CLEAVER *Expos. Prov.* ix–x. 86 If our hearts..begin to grow turbulent and unpeaceable. **1682** *Sec. Plea Nonconf.* 66 The Arrians were Calumniators of the Orthodox, and so are the Papists, and unpeaceable Lutherans. **1860** RUSKIN *Unto this Last* i. (1862) 25 An unpeaceable and often irrational person.
**2.** Characterized by want of peace or quiet.
*a* **1548** HALL *Chron., Hen. VI*, 101 The lord Scales and his company,..together in an vnpeaceable fury, set on their enemies. **1635** BRATHWAIT *Arcad. Pr.* 55 We..live both in these factious and unpeaceable times. **1649** MILTON *Eikon.* xviii. 165 Suttle and unpeaceable designes. **1702** ECHARD *Eccl. Hist.* III. vi. 408 His scandalous, irregular and unpeaceable Practices. **1770** LANGHORNE *Plutarch* V. 219 His unpeaceable and unsalutary conduct.
Hence **Unpea·ceableness.** (Common *c* 1655–*c* 1690.)
*c* **1475** *Cath. Angl.* 277/2 Vn Pesseabilnes, *impaciencia*,.. *inquietudo, proteruitas.* **1651** BAXTER *Inf. Bapt.* 246, I would not have unpeaceableness and division to be encouraged. **1690** T. BURNET *Theory Earth* II. 193 The disorders of our passions,..and the unpeaceableness of the world.

**Unpea·ceably,** *adv.* (UN-[1] 11: cf. prec.)
**1651** BAXTER *Inf. Bapt.* 121 The most able may not unpeaceably or intemperately contradict it. **1717** DE FOE *Mem. Ch. Scot.* III. 16 It was alledged by the Persons that were thus taken up,..that they had not acted unpeaceably or undutifully to his Majesty in any Thing.

†**Unpea·ced,** *ppl. a.* *Obs.*[—1] [UN-[2] 8.] Deprived of peace; disquieted. *c* **1450** tr. *De Imitatione* III. xlvii. 117 If þou sette ȝ pes wiþ eny persone for þin owne felyng & lyvinge togidres, þou shalt be unstable & unpesed.

**Unpea·ceful,** *a.* (UN-[1] 7.)
**1611** FLORIO, *Inpacifico*, vnquiet, vnpeacefull. **1645** MILTON *Tetrach.* 80 Man or wife who hates in wedloc, is perpetually unsociable, unpeacefull, or unduteous. **1647** COWLEY *Mistr., Wish* iii, Eas'd of unpeaceful thoughts. **1734** THOMSON *Liberty* IV. 678 Immature, and red with glorious wounds, Unpeaceful death their choice. **1797** LAMB '*Alas! how am I changed*' 54 The not unpeaceful evening of a day Made black by morning storms. **1805** WORDSW. *Prelude* VI. 76 Lofty elms..Bestowed composure on a neighbourhood Unpeaceful in itself. **1831** ARNOLD *Let.* in Stanley *Life* (1858) I. 240 The violence of political quarrels seeming to be something shocking because it was so unpeaceful.

†**Unpea·cible,** *a.* In 4–5 vnpesible, -peisyble, -peysible. [UN-[1] 7.] = UNPEACEABLE *a.*
**1382** WYCLIF *Jas.* iii. 8 The tunge..is an vnquyet, or vnpesible, yuel thing. **1388** — 1 *Thess.* v. 14 Britheren,..repreue ȝe vnpesible men. **1398** TREVISA *Barth. De P. R.* XIII. xxvi. (Tollem. MS.), A criynge see and an unpesible is perilouse. *a* **1400** *New Test.* (Paues) App. i, Jas. iii. 8 Tunge no man may make tame, ful of vnpeisyble yuel. *c* **1430** *Life St. Katherine* (1884) 52 Lest he schold be accused..as wykked and vnpeysible. **1482** *Rolls of Parlt.* VI. 220/2 Many.. been of such evill disposition and unpesible, that the Maier ..may not gyde..the people.
Hence † **Unpea·cibly** *adv.* *Obs.*[—1]
*a* **1400** *Wycliffite Bible* 2 Thess. iii. 11 We han herd summe among ȝou for to wandre inquyet,..or inpesibli [*v.rr.* vnpesiblely, vnpesibly; L. *inquiete*].

**Unpe·ccable,** *a.* [UN-[1] 7 b, 5 b.] Impeccable. **1818** BENTHAM *Ch. Eng.* 333 Still, though never sinning, he was not yet unpeccable.

**Unpeda·ntic,** *a.* (UN-[1] 7.)
**1796** BURNEY *Mem. Metastasio* II. 316 This essay is sufficient to manifest..the solid, unpedantic cultivation of your happy talents. **1829** LYTTON *Devereux* I. iv, He would speak of courts and kings in an easy and unpedantic strain. **1840** MILL *Dissert. & Disc.* (1859) II. 41 [The Americans'] cast of mind is altogether unpedantic and practical.

**Unpe·destal,** *v.* (UN-[2] 5.) Hence **Unpe·destalled** *ppl. a.*
**1821** *Tales Landlord, Witch of Glas Llyn* II. 38 Force me not to unpedestal you from the proud height to which my adoring fancy has raised you. **1839** LADY LYTTON *Cheveley* (ed. 2) I. xii. 278 He did not think..there was any danger of George Sand's un-pedestaling the..Despinasses of the olden time. **1881** T. HARDY *Laodicean* II. iii, His well-curved youthful form looked like an unpedestaled Dionysus.

**Unpe·digreed,** *ppl. a.* (UN-[1] 8.)
**1827** POLLOK *Course T.* VIII. 90 Unscutcheoned all, Uncrowned, unplumed, unhelmed, unpedigreed. **1879** *Cassell's Techn. Educ.* IV. 246/2 The Yorkshire cow, or..unpedigreed shorthorn.

**Unpee·led,** *ppl. a.* (UN-[2] 9.)
In Shaks. *L. L. L.* II. 88 the Quarto has *unpeeled* for *unpeopled* of the Folio.
**1599** A. M. tr. *Gabelhouer's Bk. Physicke* 360/2 Take vnpeeled Barlye,..and Misleden of Abiete,..with his leaues. **1725** *Fam. Dict.* s.v. *Apricock-tree*, Those [apricots] that are over-ripe, whether peeled or unpeeled. **1750** G. HUGHES *Barbados* 182 If this unripe fruit [of the Papaw] when unpeeled is boiled. **1814** SOUTHEY *Roderick* XVIII. 127 He.. held a natural cross Of rudest form, unpeel'd, even as it grew On the near oak that morn. **1887** MOLONEY *Forestry W. Africa* 361 Peeled Colocynth, and Mogador or Unpeeled Colocynth.

**Unpee·rable,** *a.* (UN-[1] 7 b + PEER *v.*[1]) **1604** WEBSTER *Malcontent* III. i, O unpeerable invention! rare!

**Unpee·red,** *ppl. a.* [UN-[1] 8.] Unequalled, unrivalled.
**1602** MARSTON *Antonio's Rev.* I. i, What a toplesse mount Of unpeer'd mischiefe have these hands cast up! **1636** HEYWOOD *Challenge* I. i, Most unpeer'd Lady, that, not for ten Worlds. **1795** MACNEILL *Scotland's Scaith* v. xii, Roslin's banks, unpeered by ony, Save the muses' Hawthornden. **1855** BAILEY *Mystic*, etc. 152 Where's the castle, that on yonder mountain piled Held the prince unpeered in honour?

**Unpe·g,** *v.* (UN-[2] 4 b.)
**1602** SHAKS. *Ham.* III. iv. 193 Vnpegge the Basket on the houses top: Let the Birds flye. **1611** COTGR., *Declaveter*, to vnbolt, vnpinne, vnpeg; loose from. **1863** W. C. BALDWIN *Afr. Hunting* ii. 51 He at length charged against the side of the tent, unpegging two of the ropes.

**Unpe·gged,** *ppl. a.* (UN-[1] 8.) **1697** *View Penal Laws* 253 Neither shall any suffer his swine to run in any such Grounds or Woods unringed or unpegged.

**Unpeisyble**, var. UNPEACIBLE *a.* *Obs.*

**Unpe·n,** *v.* [UN-[2] 5. Cf. OE. *onpennian*, and UNPEND *v.*] *trans.* To let out of, release from, a pen or enclosure.
*a* **1592** GREENE *Jas. IV*, IV. iii, The lamb is vnpent, the fox shal preuaile. **1766** BLACKSTONE *Comm.* II. 395 If one obstructs another's antient windows,..fouls his water, or unpens or lets it out, &c. **1817** J. F. PENNIE *Royal Minstr.* II. 10 Young David from the fold His..playful lambs unpenn'd. **1820** CLARE *Poems* (ed. 3) 127 The shepherd..Unpens and frees the captive sheep.
*fig.* **1818** KEATS *Endym.* III. 2 There are..who unpen Their baaing vanities, to browse away [etc.].

**Unpe·nal,** *a.* (UN-[1] 7.) **1641** CLARENDON *Ess. Divine & Moral* Tracts (1727) 213 It [*sc.* the Law] may render me more potent to do hurt and injury, by making that damage and injury unpenal to me. **Unpe·nanced,** *ppl. a.* (UN-[1] 8.) **1624** MIDDLETON *Game at Chess* III. i, How dares your Pawn unpenanced..Appear in this assembly? **Unpe·ncilled,** *ppl. a.* (UN-[1] 8.) **1628** FELTHAM *Resolves* II. xxiii. 76 There is no disposition, but hath a varnisht vizor, as well as an vnpencill'd face. †**Unpe·nd,** *v.* *Obs.*[—1] [UN-[2] 3.] = UNPEN *v.* **1565** GOLDING *Ovid's Met.* I. 4 b, Poure out your force,..your headdes eche one vnpende, And from your open sprynges your streames with flowyng waters send.

† **Unpe·netrable,** *a.* *Obs.* [UN-[1] 7 b, 5 b.] Impenetrable.
*c* **1400** *Found. St. Bartholomew's* (1923) 17 As yt were with an vnpenytrable scochyn wardid and defendyd. **1581** J. BELL *Haddon's Answ. Osor.* 187 b, God accordyng to his unpenetrable counsell doth determine all thinges. **1630** J. TAYLOR (Water P.) *Pennilesse Pilgr.* Wks. I. 129/2 The Foundation and Walls are vnpenetrable, the Rampiers impregnable. **1652** G. HERBERT *Priest to the Temple* xxxiv. 152 To them an unpenetrable rock, an unaccessible desert.

**Unpe·netrated,** *ppl. a.* (UN-[1] 8.)
[**1775** ASH.] **1781** PENNANT *Hist. Quadrup.* I. 161 In some of those remote parts..unpenetrated yet by Europeans. **1831** CARLYLE *Sart. Res.* II. viii, An American Backwoodsman, who had to fell unpenetrated forests. **1868** MILMAN *St. Paul's* 160 The unpenetrated darkness of futurity.

**Unpe·netrating,** *ppl. a.* (UN-[1] 10.) **1748** RICHARDSON *Clarissa* (1768) I. 217 This, frequently, the unpenetrating world calls Humanity.

**Unpe·nitent,** *a.* ? *Obs.* (UN-[1] 7, 5 b.)
**1546** COVERDALE *Treatise on Lord's Supper* A v b, The vnpenitent herte of the persone whych receyueth it [*sc.* the sacrament]. **1562** PILKINGTON *Expos. Abdyas* 128 It [*sc.* absolution] is no more profitable thanne..the communion is too an hypocrite or unpenitente sinner. **1651** HOBBES *Leviath.* III. xlii. 275 The Apostles had not the Power..to grant it [*sc.* Baptism] to the Un-penitent. **1801** SOUTHEY *Garci Ferrandez* II. iv, Fearless, unpenitent, unblest, Without a prayer they sunk to rest.

**Unpe·nned,** *ppl. a.*[1] [UN-[1] 8.] Unwritten. **1587** TURBERV. *Trag. T.* A iv b, My booke..I send,..Though reason willes it rather left vnpend. **1594** R. WILSON *Coblers Proph.* II. i. 145 Loath was I that vnpend one iote of this should goe. **Unpe·nned,** *ppl. a.*[2] [f. UNPEN *v.*] Let out of a pen. **1596** W. SMITH *Chloris* viii, But I..My vnpend flocke vnto the mountaines led. **Unpe·nnied,** *a.* (UN-[1] 9.) **1822** LAMB *Elia* I. *Praise Chimney-Sweepers*, This is *saloop*—..the delight, and..the envy, of the unpennied sweep. **1848** CLOUGH *Amours de Voy.* I. 132 To introduce at assemblies To the unpennied cadets our cousins with excellent fortunes.

**Unpe·nsioned,** *ppl. a.* (UN-[1] 8.)
**1728** POPE *Dunciad* III. 330 Gay dies unpension'd with a hundred friends. **1732** — *Hor. Sat.* II. i. 116 Could.. I not strip the gilding off a knave, Unplac'd, unpension'd..? **1771** *Ann. Reg., Chron.* 203/1, I come here unplaced, unpensioned, to give my vote voluntarily. **1817** BYRON *Mazeppa* iv, So sung his poets, all but one, Who, being unpension'd, made a satire. **1891** *Daily News* 15 July 3/1 Some of the unpensioned survivors of the Crimean and of the Indian Mutiny campaigns.

**Unpe·nsioning,** *ppl. a.* (UN-[1] 10.) **1853** DICKENS *Bleak Ho.* xl, An ungrateful and unpensioning country.

**Unpe·nt,** *ppl. a.* (UN-[2] 8.)
**1820** SHELLEY *Prometh. Unb.* I. 688 We make there our liquid lair, Voyaging cloudlike and unpent Through the boundless element. **1861** LD. LYTTON & FANE *Tannhäuser* 52 Nor e'er Bade unpent passion wildly start Through the forced portals of thy heart. **1885–94** R. BRIDGES *Eros & Psyche* March xv, The hour When beauty, from its fleshy bud unpent, Flaunts like the corol of a summer flower.

**Unpeo·ple,** *v.* [UN-[2] 4.]
**1.** *trans.* To divest or empty of people; to depopulate.
*a* **1533** LD. BERNERS *Gold. Bk. M. Aurel.* (1546) K vj b, Bycause thou hast vnpeopled the lanes and stretes of workemen and officers, and hast peopled it all about with infinite vacabundes. **1594** KYD *Cornelia* IV. i. 106 [Caesar] hath vnpeopled most part of the earth. **1641** MILTON *Reform.* II. 60 They have unpeopl'd the Kingdome by expulsion of so many thousands. **1685** N. CROUCH *Eng. Emp. Amer.* i. 2 There is no such Torrid Zone where the heat is so noxious as to unpeople any part of the Earth. **1768** STERNE *Sent. Journ., Paris*, Thirty-five years..have unpeopled her dominions of the slaves of love. **1820** BYRON *Mar. Fal.* III. ii. 492 'Tis mine to sound the knell, and strike the blow, Which shall unpeople many palaces. **1865** W. G. PALGRAVE *Arabia* II. 328 Systematic ill government can do more to unpeople a land than..the Black Death.
*transf.* **1712** BLACKMORE *Creation* VII. 40 That costly banquets..May crown thy table,..Ransack the hills,..The lake unpeople, and despoil the flood. **1781** *Westm. Mag.* IX. 263 Now, to unpeople ev'ry brook, The long-neglected mesh repairs.
**b.** *fig.* To divest or strip *of* something.
**1823** CHALMERS *Serm.* I. iv. 114 When the business of devotion is thus unpeopled of all its externals.
**2.** To divest of the status of a people.
**1653** O. SEDGWICK *Doubting Believer* 255 It is an unadvised folly in the suspension of Gods favour, to unsonne our selves, and unpeople our selves.

**Unpeo·pled,** *ppl. a.* [UN-[1] 8.] Not populated; uninhabited; without people.
In some contexts perhaps influenced by UNPEOPLE *v.*
*a* **1586** C'TESS PEMBROKE *Ps.* LXXVIII. xiv, He made them waste their weary yeares Roaming in vain in that unpeopled place. **1627** SPEED *England* xlv. § 7 This Iland so small.. and so vnpeopled and vnprofitable. **1667** MILTON *P. L.* III. 497 The Paradise of Fools, to few unknown Long after, now unpeopl'd, and untrod. **1737** GLOVER *Leonidas* IV. 638 What suff'rings to compensate..for unpeopled realms, And all this waste of nature? **1774** GOLDSM. *Nat. Hist.* VII. 131 The crocodile..found in unpeopled countries. **1816** WILSON *City of Plague* III. i. 122 He loves the silence Of an unpeopled reign. **1839** CARLYLE *Chartism* iv, Ireland will be burnt into a black unpeopled field of ashes. **1887** BOWEN *Æneid* VI. 269 The unpeopled realm of Death.

**Unpe·ppered,** *ppl. a.* (UN-[1] 8.)
**1648** HEXHAM II, *Ongepepert*, Vnpepped, or without pepper. **1814** COLMAN *Vagaries Vind.* (1818) 203 Ye Novel-Readers!—such as relish most Plain Nature's feast, unpepper'd with a Ghost. **1846** LANDOR *Imag. Conv.* Wks. II. 16/1 A plate of unpeppered cucumbers.

**Unpercei·vable,** *a.* [UN-[1] 7 b, 5 b.] Imperceptible.
*a* **1395** HYLTON *Scala Perf.* II. viii. (W. de W. 1494), Thorugh a pryue vnperceyuable worchyng of the holy ghost. *c* **1400** LOVE *Bonavent. Mirr.* (1908) 290 In a moment, that is in an vnperceyuable short tyme. **1603** FLORIO *Montaigne* II. xii. 284 Who knowes not how vnperceivable the neighbourhood betweene folly with the liveliest elevations of a free minde is. **1617** MORYSON *Itin.* III. 45 Their motion, being made in time vnperceiuable by vs. **1709** BERKELEY *Th. Vision* § 72 The particles of the..vapours, which are themselves unperceivable. **1768–74** TUCKER *Lt. Nat.* (1834) I. 619 The chain of causes and effects..divides into so many unperceivable threads. **1801** *Monthly Mag.* XII. 422 One of those French reputations, which, when weighed in the European scale, is almost unperceivable. *a* **1882** T. H. GREEN *Proleg. Ethics* 347 That God is as unimaginable as he is unperceivable.
Hence **Unpercei·vableness.**
**1611** FLORIO, *Impercettibilita*, vnperceiuablenesse.

**Unpercei·vably,** *adv.* [UN-[1] 11, 5 b: cf. prec.] Imperceptibly.
*a* **1395** HYLTON *Scala Perf.* II. viii. (W. de W. 1494), How it is wonderly & vnperceyuably chaunged..vnto the faymes of an angell. **1603** FLORIO *Montaigne* III. iv. 500, I vnperceauable remoued those dolefull humours from hir. **1695** BP. ROCHESTER *Disc. Clergy* 39 With the Scriptures..their Memories will unperceivably be filled. **1713** *Guardian* No. 56, [They] rolled their trains unperceivably beneath their habits.

**Unpercei·ved,** *ppl. a.* [UN-[1] 8.]
**1.** Without being perceived or noticed. Occas. const. *by* or *of*.
*c* **1350** *Will. Palerne* 1676 Þat noþer clerk nor kniȝt..Schal passe vnperceyued & pertiliche of-souȝt. *c* **1400** *Destr. Troy* 8657 Achilles grippit a gret speire,..Vnpersayuit of the prince prikit hym to. **1533** MORE *Apol.* iii. Wks. 848/1 They would ..haue their false folies passe and repasse all vnperceiued. **1593** SHAKS. *Lucrece* 1010 The crow may..unperceiv'd fly with the filth away. **1667** MILTON *P. L.* XI. 224 Hee alone ..took his way, Not unperceav'd of Adam. **1725** POPE *Odyss.* XXII. 194 Behind the felon unperceiv'd they past. **1760–72** H. BROOKE *Fool of Qual.* (1809) III. 17 Unperceived of Harry, he displayed the bills to the company. **1834** *Tait's Mag.* I. 189/2 The intrenchment being cast up unperceived, in the middle of the night. **1875** JOWETT *Plato* (ed. 2) III. 67 Chance words..which fall unperceived on the reader's mind.
**2.** Not perceived; unobserved.
*c* **1500** *Three Kings' Sons* 84 Departid this yonge gentilman..so secretly that he was vnperceyued. **1581** MULCASTER *Positions* xxxiii. 120 Galene also maketh the litle vnperceiued, or for the smallnesse contemned, to be mother of all illes. **1665** BOYLE *Occas. Refl.* IV. ix, Moisture..convey'd but by little and little.., and by unperceivd Passages, and

yet..able to impart Fertility. **1768** BOSWELL *Corsica* p. xii, Even the succession of Chiefs has been unperceived. **1790** COLERIDGE *Progr. Vice* 7 By unperceiv'd degrees she tempts to stray, Till far from Virtue's path she leads the feet away. **1842** Is. WILLIAMS *Baptistery* 43 Time marks not Death with unperceived tread Steal on behind. **1898** LUCY B. WALFORD *Archdeacon* II. ii, St. Andrews was unperceived, and drew back..disconcerted.

Hence **Unpercei·vedly** *adv.*

**1633** T. ADAMS *Exp. 2 Peter* ii. 18 That they may not too unperceivedly catch us, let me a little bare their hooke. **1663** BOYLE *Usef. Exp. Nat. Philos.* II. App. 352 Sometimes in filtration, some of the thinner parts of the oyl have unperceivedly passed through the paper. **1713** DERHAM *Physico-Theol.* III. iv. 78 Descending (though unperceivedly) gently down..to the Sea.

**Unpercei·ving,** *ppl. a.* (UN-[1] 10.) **1723** WATERLAND *Sec. Vindic. Christ's Divinity* xxiii. 448 To make you at length sensible of Two Things, about which you have been hitherto very slow and unperceiving. **1803** *Monthly Mag.* XIV. 490 For an idea to exist in an unperceiving thing is a contradiction. **Unpercei·vingness.** (UN-[1] 12; or f. prec.) **1685** RENWICK *Serm.*, etc. (1776) 144 What unperceivingness of temper is this? †**Unperce·ptable,** *a.* [UN-[1] 7 b.] = next. **1683** MOXON *Mech. Exerc.*, *Printing* xxiv. ¶ 19 The small un-level lying of every Sheet, though unperceptable in a small number of Sheets.

† **Unperce·ptible,** *a. Obs.* [UN-[1] 7, 5 b.] Imperceptible; unperceivable.

**1398** TREVISA *Barth. De P. R.* IX. ii. (Bodl. MS.), Noþing is more vncerteyne þanne tyme, noþing more vnperceptible. **1603** HOLLAND *Plutarch's Mor.* 1086 The diversitie of good things and evill is very small, and unperceptible by the sense. **1653** H. MORE *Antid. Ath.* II. i. § 2 Matter..unperceptible to any of our Senses. **1682** — *Contn. Remark. Stor.* 10 A tugging..for his Sword by an invisible Hand. By which, I suppose, is meant an unperceptible hand.

**Unperce·ptive,** *a.* (UN-[1] 7 b, 5 b.)

**1668** H. MORE *Div. Dial.* II. v. 197 You seem to forget that the strokes of Nature levell not at particulars. For she is an unperceptive Principle. **1691** NORRIS *Pract. Disc.* 171 His Affections..are now become so unperceptive of any thing but the..relishes of the Animal Nature. **1768–74** TUCKER *Lt. Nat.* (1834) I. 298 Those who have asserted that ..a perceptive being may be produced by a combination of unperceptive principles. **1882** *St. James' Gaz.* 30 March 3/2 He cut it out, good man, being unperceptive of the consequences.

**Unpe·rch,** *v.* [UN-[2] 5.] *trans.* To dislodge from a perch. Also *fig.*

**1579** LYLY *Euphues* (Arb.) 114 For honest recreation..vse hunting or haukeing, either rowse the Deere, or vnpearch the Phesant. **1646** CRASHAW *Steps to Temple* 27 Which when I lose, o may at once my Tongue Lose this same busie speaking art Vnpearcht, her vocall Arteries vnstrung. *a* **1659** OSBORNE *Observ. Turks* Wks. (1673) 286 If he but offers to tune his note contrary to the true Dialect of State, he is straight unperched. **1716** M. DAVIES *Athen. Brit.* I. 320 Divines, who never fail to endeavour to unperche that good old Fox's well-meaning Book from its Post and Chain in our Churches. **1734** WATTS *Reliq. Juv.* 287 When..walking through a Grove,..we unperch'd a Squirrel and a Lark. **1846** LANDOR *Exam. Shaks.* Wks. II. 267/2 They never have unperched me from my calling.

Hence **Unpe·rching** *vbl. sb.*

**1589** WARNER *Alb. Eng.* Prose Add. 161 The vnpearching of other, should be fore-preachings to vs.

**Unpe·rched,** *ppl. a.* (UN-[1] 8.) **1732** M. GREEN *The Grotto* 116 Moping like sick linnet..Unperch'd, averse to fly or sing.

**Unperegal,** var. UNPAREGAL *a. Obs.*

**Unpe·rfect,** *a.* Now *rare.* [UN-[1] 7, 5 b.]

**1.** Of persons: Imperfect in respect of nature, conduct, or function.

*a* **1340** HAMPOLE *Ps.* cxxxviii. 15 Thou saghe mercifully my men, that ere vnperfyt. *c* **1380** WYCLIF *Sel. Wks.* II. 45 Þei weren ȝit unperfit, and Petir, after þat Crist was risun.., synnede many weyes. **1402** *Jack Upland* in *Pol. Poems* (Rolls) II. 20 Certes..it seemeth that yee be unperfect. *c* **1449** PECOCK *Repr.* v. xiv. 560 Vnperfit men cumbrid in her freelnes..ouȝten chese ful ofte the..surer good to hem bifore the vnsurer good. **1549** COVERDALE, etc. *Erasm. Par. Heb.* 11 As the vnperfiter priesthood geueth place vnto the perfiter. **1594** CAREW *Huarte's Exam. Wits* xiv. 252 A man vnperfect and void of the gifts of nature. **1617** MORYSON *Itin.* II. 79 The wisest Counsels..are vncertaine, and the wisest men vnperfect. *a* **1628** F. GREVIL *Sidney* (1652) 12 What marvail can it be, if these Iacobs and Esaus strive.. as well before as after they come out of such erring and unperfect wombes? **1766** A. NICOL *Poems* 14 O, Heavens! deliver me..From one that's thriftless, nasty, unperfeit.

**b.** Inexpert, unskilled; not properly trained or practised; not thoroughly up in one's part.

*c* **1440** *Gesta Rom.* xliii. 170 (Harl. MS.), They wer..vnperfite of the crafte, or vncunnynge in the mystery. *c* **1470** HENRY *Wallace* IV. 736 Rycht wnperfyt I am of Venus play. **1545** ASCHAM *Toxoph.* (Arb.) 20, I beyng an vnperfyte shoter. **1577–82** BRETON *Floorish upon Fancie* To Yng. Gentlemen, I was..in a place vnknowne..vnperfect to returne the waye I went. *c* **1600** SHAKS. *Sonn.* xxiii. 1 As an vnperfect actor on the stage, Who with his feare is put besides his part.

**2.** Not brought to perfection or completeness; left unfinished, incomplete, or defective; not full in number, etc.: **a.** Of material things.

**1382** WYCLIF *Ps.* cxxxviii. 16 Myn vnparfit thing seȝen thin eȝen. **1398** TREVISA *Barth. De P. R.* XVII. i. (Bodl. MS.), In some trene þe [humoure] is vnsufficiaunte and vnperfecte. *c* **1449** PECOCK *Repr.* II. ix. 193 The sympler and vnperfiter and lasse representing ymage. **1483** *Act 1 Ric. III*, c. 8 *Preamble*, Wollen clothes..unperfite and deceyvable made. **1535** COVERDALE *Wisd.* iv. 5 The vnparfecte braunches shalbe broken. *a* **1568** ASCHAM *Scholem.* (Arb.) 142 Plautus and Terence, with a litle rude vnperfit pamflet of the elder Cato. **1604** T. WRIGHT *Passions* Ep. Ded., The vncorrected copie..of three..was most vnperfect. **1626** BACON *Sylva* § 546 Mushroomes..are likewise an unperfect Plant. **1683** MOXON *Mech. Exerc.*, *Printing* 8 Some Trades are..sooner sold off, which renders the remainder of the un-sold Exercises unperfect. **1858** H. BUSHNELL *Nat. & Supernat.* xi. (1864) 342 The world..was made, including man, as a thing necessarily unperfect.

**b.** Of qualities, concepts, etc.

*c* **1380** WYCLIF *Wks.* (1880) 302 A fool..bryngiþ in a newe ordre þat is boþe heuy & vnperfiȝt. **1387** TREVISA *Higden* (Rolls) V. 53 He dede oon dede þat semede of unperfiȝt witte. *c* **1475** *Partenay* 5225 The pope assoiled hym ther benyngly, When [he] declared hade hys dedes vnperfight. **1535** COVERDALE *1 Cor.* xiii. 9 Our knowlege is vnparfecte, and our prophecienge is vnparfecte. **1551** T. WILSON *Logike* H iiij, An halfe argument, is an argument vnperfect. **1607** HIERON *Wks.* I. 150 Nurses..doe babble with them in their owne stammering and vnperfite language. **1614** RALEIGH *Hist. World* III. xii. 145 Taking vpon themselues the maintenance of the peace..which Agesilaus..had left vnperfect. **1656** SANDERSON *Serm.* (1689) 537 The sence hangeth unperfect unless we take in the former verse.

† **Unpe·rfect,** *v. Obs.* [UN-[2] 3.] *trans.* To render imperfect.

**1548** GESTE *Pr. Masse* C vii, To renew the sayde sacryfyce is vtterlye to vnperfyt, & disable it quite. *a* **1586** SIDNEY *Arcadia* III. v, The dressing of her haire and apparell..left to a neglected chaunce, which yet coulde no more unperfect her perfections, than a Die..could loose his squarenesse.

**Unpe·rfected,** *ppl. a.* (UN-[1] 8, 5 b.)

*a* **1513** FABYAN *Chron.* VII. 491 By reason of which..trewes the hostes were deseuered, and the ende of yᵉ warre vnparfyted. *c* **1542** SURREY in *Tottel's Misc.* (Arb.) 29 A mark, the which (vnparfited, for time) Some may approche, but neuer none shall hit. **1625** K. LONG tr. *Barclay's Argenis* V. x. 363 The businesse yet stands well; the alliance unperfected; Argenis unmarried. **1657** W. RAND tr. *Gassendi's Life Peiresc* II. 192 He never willingly left anything unperfected. **1716–20** *Lett. fr. Mist's Jrnl.* (1722) I. 308 These.. are but half Gentlemen,..debased, unperfected things. **1864** *Reader* No. 86. 219/2 An unperfected sketch. **1891** FARRAR *Darkn. & Dawn* xli, Shall any germ of good in man's soul perish unperfected?

†**Unperfe·ction.** *Obs.* [UN-[1] 12, 5 b.] Imperfection. *c* **1380** WYCLIF *Sel. Wks.* III. 402 When unperfeccioun is putt upon God. **1388** — *Ecclus.* xxxviii. 31 He schal ȝyue his herte in to the perfourmyng of werkes; and bi his wakyng he schal ourne vnperfeccioun. *c* **1535** NISBET *N. T.* (S.T.S.) III. 344 Christ..now dealis with us daylye, suffering our vnperfectiounn. † **Unperfe·ctive,** *a.* (UN-[1] 7, 5 b.) **1704** NORRIS *Ideal World* II. vi. 320 A pure and unmingled darkness, being..so very unperfective of our natures. *Ibid.* xii. 476 The knowledge of an unperfective object.

† **Unpe·rfectly,** *adv. Obs.* [UN-[1] 11, 5 b.] Imperfectly.

**1398** TREVISA *Barth. De P. R.* VIII. xxix. (Bodl. MS.), Whanne it [*sc.* light] comeþ into fatte mater it is inperfitelich [**1495** vnperfyghtly] ifonge & schedeþ hym þerinne vnperfitelich and semeþ derke withoute. *c* **1449** PECOCK *Repr.* v. xv. 564 It is no nede forto seie ther of eny thing vnperfitli and vnfully and therfore vnsauorili here. **1483** *Act 1 Rich. III*, c. 8 *Preamble*, Wollen Clothes..unperfitly made and deceyvably wrought. **1552** LATIMER *Serm. Lord's Prayer* vi. (1562) 47 b, We beleue vnperfectly, we loue vnperfectly, we suffer vnperfectly..; and so al thinges that we do, ar done imperfectly. **1561** DAUS tr. *Bullinger on Apoc.* 579 Besydes this, we se here vnperfitly. **1639** GENTILIS *Servita's Inquis.* (1655) 20 Yet was it not put to execution according to the Emperours mind, but onely unperfectly.

**Unpe·rfectness.** Now *rare.* [UN-[1] 12, 5 b.] Imperfection.

*α.* *a* **1325** *Prose Ps.* cxxxviii. 15 Þyn eȝen sen myn vnparfitnes. **1387** TREVISA *Higden* (Rolls) I. 5 Art, sciens and lawe al were i-falle,..but þe mercy of God had i-ordyned vs of lettres in remedie of vnparfiȝtnesse of mankynde. *c* **1449** PECOCK *Repr.* III. xi. 349 As he which ofte and miche synned, and as he which knewe his vnperfitnes. *a* **1568** ASCHAM *Scholem.* II. (Arb.) 144 Cicero him selfe doth complaine of this vnperfitnes, but more plainly Quintilian.

*β.* **1543** *Necessary Doctrine* e ii, These workes..for as moch as they be done in the faith of Christe,..theyr vnperfectnes is supplied. **1548** CRANMER *Catech.* 220 b, Althoughe he doth oftentimes ouercome sinne, yet this is a great vnperfectenes, yᵗ he dothe it not willingly. **1625** DONNE *Serm.* 669 If there had not been unbeliefe, weaknesse, unperfectnesse in that Faith. **1661** RUST *Origen's Opin.* 72 Seeing what..was likely to be the lot of some of them from the necessary unperfectness of their Natures. **1900** MARY KINGSLEY *Mem.* in G. H. Kingsley *Sp. & Trav.* vii. 193 In the very unperfectness of that specimen.

**Unperfla·ted,** *ppl. a.* (UN-[1] 8.) **1822–7** GOOD *Study Med.* (1829) II. 203 Confined and unperflated barracks. **Unpe·rforate,** *a.* [UN-[1] 7.] = next. **1713** CHESELDEN *Anat.* (1722) 224 The Edges of this growing together, it continued unperforate.

**Unpe·rforated,** *ppl. a.* (UN-[1] 8, 5 b.)

**1676** H. MORE *Remarks* 153 It will be hard then to find any evasion if the inward Vessel ascend not as it does when the bottom is unperforated. **1726** MONRO *Anat.* 113 The posterior unperforated Part of the Lamella. **1833** J. HOLLAND *Manuf. Metal* II. 196 An unperforated iron plate. **1884** BOWER & SCOTT *De Bary's Phaner.* 328 Very oblique, fibrously thickened (unperforated?) end-surfaces.

**Unperfo·rmable,** *a.* (UN-[1] 7 b, 5 b.) **1674** O. WALKER, etc. *Paraphr. Ep. St. Paul* (1675) 7 An unperformable supposition. **1818** BENTHAM *Ch. Eng.* 238 The unperformable obligation actually taken upon themselves by the Sponsors. † **Unperfo·rmance.** *Obs.* [UN-[1] 12.] Non-performance. **1608** HIERON *Defence* III. 138 Kneeling..is altogether accidentall and uncerteyne, and so, by consequence, liable to an unperformance.

**Unperfo·rmed,** *ppl. a.* (UN-[1] 8.)

**1442** *Rolls of Parlt.* V. 57/2 It may be founden..that parcell therof [*sc.* a will]..remayneth unperfourmede and not executed. **1483** *Ibid.* VI. 261/1 So that the said last Wille..shall reste unperfourmed. **1573** DAUS tr. *Bullinger on Apoc.* 101 b, He shall most fully accomplish such thynges as we see as yet vnperformed. **1591** HARINGTON *Orl. Fur.* XXVI. xxxv. 208/2 Merlin,..by his passing wit, Set here (as yet) their vnperformed deeds. *c* **1611** CHAPMAN *Iliad* I. 59 If unperformed vows He blames in us. **1651** BAXTER *Inf. Bapt.* 308 That condition which is of necessity to the end, though some accidentals be unperformed. **1750** CHESTERF. *Let.* 8 Jan., They have done feats..unperformed by others. **1849** FITZGERALD *Lett.* (1889) I. 197 A large bill for service unperformed. **1870** BRYANT *Iliad* I. II. 41 Yet is the enterprise for which we came still unperformed.

**Unperfo·rming,** *vbl. sb.* (UN-[1] 13.) **1645** MILTON *Tetrach.* 31 No fals dealing, or unperforming should be thrust upon men without redress, if the covnant bee so divine.

**Unperfo·rming,** *ppl. a.* (UN-[1] 10.)

**1670** DRYDEN *Conq. Granada* I. Epil., Yet, though he much has failed, he begs, to-day, You will excuse his unperforming play. **1706** WATTS *Horæ Lyricæ* II. 205 Ye vulgar charms of eyes and ears, Ye unperforming promisers! **1742** MELMOTH *Fitzosborne Lett.* (1749) 153 You..have placed in strong contraste their successful industry, with our unperforming ignorance. **1765** GOLDSM. *Ess.* ii. Wks. (Globe) 288/2 The public has been so often imposed upon by the unperforming promises of others. **1824** LAMB *Elia* II. *Capt. Jackson*, You..reeled under the potency of his unperforming Bacchanalian encouragements.

**Unperfumed,** *ppl. a.* (UN-[1] 8.)

**1706** PHILLIPS (ed. Kersey), *Inodorous*, that is without Scent,..unperfumed. **1784** COWPER *Task* III. 732 Are not wholesome airs, though unperfum'd By roses,..To be prefer'd to smoke? **1860** FARRAR *Orig. Lang.* i. 1 Uttering things simple, and unperfumed.

**Unpe·rilous,** *a.* (UN-[1] 7.)

**1621** in Kempe *Losely MSS.* (1836) 455 [A] not unpleasant waye, though not unperilous. **1628** FELTHAM *Resolves* II. xii. 33 The secure depths, in the most vnperillous Channell. **1805** WORDSW. *Prelude* v. 234 Where had we been..If in the season of unperilous choice..We had been followed! **1847** EMILY BRONTE *Wuthering Heights* xxxiii, Temperate mode of living, and unperilous occupations.

**Unpe·rishable,** *a.* (UN-[1] 7 b, 5 b.)

**1548** UDALL *Erasm. Par. Luke* iii. 33 b, He that hath throughly conceiued the fyer of charitee & loue vnperishable. **1664** INGELO *Bentiv. & Ur.* II. vi. 366 The unperishable nature of the Soul. **1677** YARRANTON *Eng. Improv.* 23 The Moneys will be lent..upon unperishable Commodities. **1712** *Spect.* No. 537 ¶ 7 A contemplation on the unperishable part of his nature. **1793** SMEATON *Edystone L.* § 93 The stone here..was..unperishable by the effects of weather. **1824** GODWIN *Hist. Commw.* I. 425 A king..has an unperishable advantage over a popular assembly. **1858** BIRCH *Anc. Pottery* II. 396 The glyptic and graphic arts only exist in their later forms as exercised on unperishable materials.

Hence **Unpe·rishableness.**

**1648** JENKYN *Blind Guide* 48 This position..of a simple and absolute unperishablenesse. **1768–74** TUCKER *Lt. Nat.* (1834) II. 679 The spirituality and unperishableness of the soul.

**Unpe·rished,** *ppl. a.* (UN-[1] 8.)

*c* **1400** *Destr. Troy* 2460 He cast be course what shuld come after, Shuld neuer purpos vnperisshit be put to a yssu. *c* **1425** WYNTOUN *Cron.* v. xi. 3016 We ask..ȝour help at oure cete And we may als vnperist be. **1531** ELYOT *Gov.* III. vi, He presumed, that faythe beinge obserued unperisshed, shulde please all mighty god aboue all thinges. **1555** EDEN *Decades* (Arb.) 331 Any beastes whose skynnes they desyre to saue vnperysshed. **1624** CAPT. SMITH *Virginia* v. 198 The hull though..in the water, they found vnperished. **1652** T. FROYSELL *Gale Opportunity* 39 The sweet smelling spices of his lovely life..will imbalme him, and keep him unperisht in your thoughts many years. **1720** POPE *Iliad* XXIII. 402 Yon aged trunk.., Or hardy fir, unperish'd with the rains. **1857** RUSKIN *Pol. Econ. Art* 146 You can help some genius yet unperished.

**Unpe·rishing,** *ppl. a.* (UN-[1] 10.)

**1561** T. NORTON *Calvin's Inst.* III. vi. 158 b, Ordeyned to heauenly incorruption and an vnperishing crowne. **1709** SHAFTESB. *Charac.* II. 371 Mighty Being!..Unperishing in Grace, and of undecaying Youth! **1789** COWPER *Annus Memorabilis* 15 Deeds of unperishing renown. *c* **1800** COLERIDGE *On a Cataract* 1 Unperishing youth! Thou leapest from forth The cell of thy hidden nativity. **1852** BILLINGS *Baronial Antiq. Scot.*, *Dunblane* II. 1 The Romans have left unperishing memorials of their far-reaching energy.

**Unpe·riwigged,** *a.* (UN-[1] 9.) **1779** R. GRAVES *Euphrosine* (1783) II. 110 Would'st thou enraptured nature's charm behold,..Un-painted and un-periwig'd survey?

**Unpe·rjured,** *ppl. a.* (UN-[1] 8.)

*a* **1700** DRYDEN (J.), Thou can'st not die unperjur'd, And leave an unaccomplish'd love behind. **1802–12** BENTHAM *Ration. Judic. Evid.* (1827) I. 382 They or he remain unperjured, all the others perjured. **1827** POLLOK *Course T.* v. 523 Days When, on the glittering dews of orient life, Shone sunshine hopes, unfailed, unperjured then.

**Unpe·rmanency.** (UN-[1] 12, 5 b; cf. next.) **1864** R. F. BURTON *Mission to Gelele* II. 197 The unpermanency of the half-breed, and the frequency of sterile marriages amongst mulattos.

**Unpe·rmanent,** *a.* (UN-[1] 7, 5 b.)

**1630** J. TAYLOR (Water P.) *Wks.* II. 160/2 All the world may well be cal'd a Boat, Tost on the troublous waues of discontent, All subject vnto change vnpermanent. **1668** H. MORE *Div. Dial.* IV. xiii. 56 Because it was so short and unpermanent the Prophecy seems to take no express notice of it. **1748** RICHARDSON *Clarissa* III. 362 Who would not, ..to preserve so many essentials, give up so light, so unpermanent a pleasure? **1788** D. GILSON *Serm. Pract. Subj.* i. 9 The splendors he..pursued, have been found both unreal and unpermanent. **1804–9** BLAKE *Select. Milton, Los* 5 Not one moment Of Time is lost, nor one event of Space unpermanent.

**Unpe·rmeable,** *a.* (UN-[1] 7 b, 5 b.) [**1775** ASH.] **1827** MONTGOMERY *Pelican Isl.* III. 159 Where unpermeable foliage made Midnight at noon. **Unpermi·ssible,** *a.* (UN-[1] 7, 5 b.) [**1775** ASH.] **1871** *Athenæum* 14 Jan. 57 The presence of man is held to be unpermissible.

**Unpermi·tted,** *ppl. a.* (UN-[1] 8.)

**1598** SYLVESTER *Du Bartas* II. i. *Eden* 306 Now Heav'ns eternall all-fore-seeing King..Thought good..That he [*sc.* man] should never taste fruits un-permitted. **1777** POTTER *Æschylus, Seven Chiefs* 180 Murd'rous is the rage that fires thee To deeds of death, to unpermitted blood. **1810** H. P. FORSTER *Ess. Princ. Sanskrit Gram.* Introd. p.

xii, My friend,.. I trust, will excuse this unpermitted mention of his name. **1851** CARLYLE *Sterling* I. xv, A rash, false, unwise and unpermitted step.

**Unpermi·xed,** *ppl. a.* (UN-[1] 8.) *c* **1545** G. WISHART *Conf. Faith* in *Misc. Wodrow Soc.* (1844) 14 Christ.. hauynge two natures unpermyxte. **1577** tr. *Bullinger's Decades* 1097/2 Where I haue intreated of one person, and of bothe natures in Christ vnpermixed. **Unpe·rpetrated,** *ppl. a.* (UN-[1] 8.) **1811** LAMB *Trag. Shaks.* Wks. 1908 I. 136 The painful anxiety about the act, the natural longing to prevent it while it yet seems unperpetrated.

**Unperple·x,** *v.* (UN-[2] 3.)
*a* **1631** DONNE *Poems, Extasie* 29 This Extasie doth unperplex (We said) and tell us what we love. **1665** J. SERGEANT *Sure Footing* 205, I believe you are in some wonderment..: I shall endeavour to unperplex you. *a* **1711** KEN *Edmund* Poet. Wks. 1721 II. 238 O Father! you can unperplex my Mind. **1819** KEATS *Lamia* I. 192 Not one hour old, yet of sciential brain To unperplex bliss from its neighbour pain.

**Unperple·xed,** *ppl. a.* [UN-[1] 8.]
**1.** Not puzzled or made uncertain.
**1558** PHAER *Æneid.* VI. Q j b, Proud minds vnperplext Reioysing vile in sinne. *a* **1586** SIDNEY *Arcadia* III. iv, Desiring her (whose thoughts were unperplexed) to use for his sake.. intercession. *a* **1711** KEN *Urania* Poet. Wks. 1721 IV. 452 With Judgment unperplex'd [she] Reviews the Text. **1728** YOUNG *Love Fame* v. 263 Bless'd with health, with business unperplex'd. **1824** CAMPBELL *Theodric* 192 Hers was the brow, in trials unperplexed, That cheered the sad. **1838** MRS. BROWNING *To M. R. Mitford* 10 Thou art unperplext,.. To preach a sermon on so known a text!
**2.** Not involved or intricate.
**1653** WALTON *Angler* i. 31 That good, plain, unperplext Catechism, that is printed with the old service book. *c* **1698** LOCKE *Cond. Und.* § 39 Simple, unperplexed proposition belonging to the matter in hand. **1754** A. MURPHY *Gray's-Inn Jrnl.* No. 104, My Arrangement has been grammatically just, unperplexed and clear. ? **1812** WORDSW. *Water fowl* 13 Progress intricate Yet unperplexed, as if one spirit swayed Their indefatigable flight. **1864** PUSEY *Lect. Daniel* 317 The unperplexed simple pleading.

**Unpe·rsecuted,** *ppl. a.* (UN-[1] 8.) **1642** MILTON *Apol. Smect.* 11 Since I dare not wish to passe this life unpersecuted of slanderous tongues. **Unpe·rsecutive,** *a.* (UN-[1] 7.) **1664** H. MORE *Apology* 540 Whose errours.. are .. themselves of a peaceable and unpersecutive Temper. **Unperseve·rance.** (UN-[1] 12.) *c* **1449** PECOCK *Repr.* II. vii. 177 Vnstable vnconstaunce and variaunce and vnperseueraunce. **Unpe·rsonable,** *a.* (UN-[1] 7 b.) **1632** HOLLAND *Cyrupædia* 46 A man for his body not unpersonable, and in regard of his minde, seeming no ignoble and base pesant.

**Unpe·rsonal,** *a.* and *sb.* [UN-[1] 7, 12, 5 b.]
†**a.** = IMPERSONAL *adj.*, *sb.* 1. **b.** Not personal.
**1530** PALSGR. 83 Of verbes.. some be parsonal, and some be unparsonals. *Ibid.* 614 This verbe.. is ever used as an unparsonal. **1891** *Cent. Dict.*, *Unpersonal*, not personal; not intended to apply to the person addressed, as a remark.

**Unpersona·lity.** (UN-[1] 12.) **1881** S. LANIER *English Novel* (1883) 91 As the third feature of the unpersonality revealed in this play, consider the fact that [etc.]. **Unperso·nified,** *ppl. a.* (UN-[1] 8.) [**1775** ASH.] **1825** COLERIDGE *Aids Refl.* 82 An obscure impersonation of what the Atheist receives unpersonified under the name of Fate or Nature. **Unperspi·cuous,** *a.* (UN-[1] 7, 5 b.) [**1775** ASH.] **1804** RANKEN *Hist. France* III. iv. III. 312 Their unclassical, often barbarous, and unperspicuous Latin. **1834** SOUTHEY in *Corr. w. C. Bowles* (1881) 294 Is not that evidence .. of its exuberant fancy, its richness of diction, unperspicuous as it is. **Unperspi·rable,** *a.* (UN-[1] 7 b.) *a* **1735** ARBUTHNOT (J.), Bile is the most unperspirable of animal fluids. **Unperspi·ring,** *ppl. a.* (UN-[1] 10.) **1881** T. MACLAGAN *Rheumatism* 5 In acute gout the skin is dry and unperspiring.

**Unpersua·dable,** *a.* [UN-[1] 7 b, 5 b.]
†**1.** Not removable by persuasion. *Obs.*—[1]
*a* **1586** SIDNEY *Arcadia* I. xv, Who (finding his sisters unperswadeable melancholy..) had for a time left her court.
**2.** Not susceptible to persuasion; obstinate.
**1611** FLORIO, *Inpersuadibile*, vnperswadable. **1647** TRAPP *Comm. Col.* iii. 6 Unperswadable, unconsellable persons, that regard not good courses. **1668** HOWE *Bless. Righteous* xii. 219 They.. are utterly unperswadable towards God. **1748** RICHARDSON *Clarissa* I. 48 A mind, till now, not thought either unpersuadable or ungenerous! **1817** T. L. PEACOCK *Melincourt* xxi, After a certain period of life.. men in general become perfectly unpersuadable to all practical purposes. **1865** CARLYLE *Fredk. Gt.* XVIII. vii. V. 149 Deploring that sad mistake; but unpersuadable to stand, and try amendment of it.
*absol.* **1685** BAXTER *Paraphr. N. T.* Matt. iii. 12 He will burn the unbelievers and unperswadable as chaff.
Hence **Unpersua·dableness.**
**1615** BYFIELD *Expos. Colos.* iii. 6 They will not be persuaded by the.. servants of God; and so they are children of unpersuadableness. **1685** BAXTER *Paraphr. N. T.* Acts xxi. 14 His resolution and unperswadableness. **1748** RICHARDSON *Clarissa* II. 57 Resentment and unpersuadableness are not natural to you. **1786** A. GIB *Sacr. Contempl.* 306 Children of disobedience, of unpersuadableness.

**Unpersua·ded,** *ppl. a.* (UN-[1] 8.)
**1534** MORE *Comf. agst. Trib.* III. xix. Wks. 1242/1 If you had assented in woordes and in your mynde departed unperswaded. **1570** DEE *Math. Pref.* 10 Who can remaine.. vnpersuaded, to loue.. the excellent Science of Arithmetike? **1709** STANHOPE *Paraphr.* IV. 62 The present stupidity of this unpersuaded Man. **1777** DODD *Let. to Johnson* 23 May in *Boswell*, Not a soul could be left unconvinced and unpersuaded. **1818** SHELLEY *Rosal. & Helen* 648 His very gestures touched to tears The unpersuaded tyrant, never So moved before. **1882** FARRAR *Early Chr.* I. 540 Myriads of Jewish Christians remained secretly unpersuaded.
Hence **Unpersua·dedness.**
**1617** AINSWORTH *Annot. Ps.* lviii. 5 The serpent Python.. noteth .. the unperswadednes which this Psalm showeth to be naturally in that beast.

†**Unpersua·sibleness, -sua·sion.** *Obs.* (UN-[1] 12.) *a* **1684** LEIGHTON *Com. 1 Pet.* ii. 7 The word here us'd for disobedience, signifies properly unpersuasion: .. We are Children of disobedience, or unpersuasibleness.

**Unpersua·sive,** *a.* (UN-[1] 7.)
**1748** RICHARDSON *Clarissa* (1811) V. 207, I traversed the room, and bit my unpersuasive lips.. for vexation. **1783** BLAIR *Lect.* II. 122 That argumentative manner, bordering on the dry and unpersuasive, which is.. the character of English Sermons. **1847** F. W. NEWMAN *Hist. Hebrew Mon.* ix. 328 In his own town of Anathoth,.. his [*sc.* Jeremiah's] extreme youth would make him unpersuasive to his neighbours. **1905** HOLMAN-HUNT *Pre-Raphaelitism* II. 419 Actuality, without which all painting is characterless and unpersuasive.
Hence **Unpersua·sively** *adv.*
**1855** PUSEY *Doctr. Real Presence* 347 So not unpersuasively might it be said on this passage. **1865** GROSART *Lambs all Safe* 106, I have indeed written poorly and vnpersuasively.

†**Unpertai·ning,** *ppl. a. Obs.*—[1] (UN-[1] 10.) *c* **1449** PECOCK *Repr.* v. xiii. 552 Vsis and expendingis vnperteynyng to tho religiouns and to her persoones.

†**Unpe·rtinent,** *a. Obs.* (UN-[1] 7, 5 b.)
*c* **1380** WYCLIF *Sel. Wks.* II. 388 In general crede ben conteyned many treuþis þat us nediþ not to dispute, but bileve hem as unpertinent. *c* **1400** *Apol. Loll.* 72 To warn men to fle in weddingis couetous lustis, and pride, and swilk oþer vices vnpertinent to þe mariage. *c* **1445** PECOCK *Donet* 206 Maters vnpertinent to þe maters of þi preising and preiyng. **1579** FULKE *Heskins' Parl.* 439 This controuersie .. is vnpertinent to this cause. **1598** FLORIO, *Inpertinente*, vnpertinent, not fit, not belonging.
Hence †**Unpe·rtinently** *adv. Obs.*—[1]
*c* **1449** PECOCK *Repr.* IV. iv. 441 Ellis this clausul.. hadde be seid vnpertynently and vnhangingli fro the materis of the clausulis folewing.

**Unpertu·rbed,** *ppl. a.* (UN-[1] 8.)
**1420–22** LYDG. *Thebes* II. 1714 That he.. Myght allone regnen in quiete;.. Vnperturbed of Polymyte his brother. **1611** COTGR., *Impassible*,.. vnpassionate, vnperturbed. **1671** R. MACWARD *True Non-conf.* 389 What in the ordinary and unperturbed condition of things would be accounted.. an usurpation. **1674** BOYLE *Excell. Theol.* II. iii. 150 The great plenty of unperturbed light that is reflected from snow. **1823** SCOTT *Quentin D.* xxvi, The King,.. unperturbed by the.. violent gestures of the Duke. **1876** GEO. ELIOT *Dan. Der.* vi, His own love seemed a guarantee of hers, since it was one with the unperturbed delight in her image.
Hence **Unpertu·rbedness.**
**1676** HALE *Contempl.* II. (1677) 149 Nothing so much gratifies an ill Tongue, as when it finds an angry hearer: nor nothing so much disappoints and vexeth it as Calmness and Unperturbedness. **1867** LEGGE *Confucius* 265 A calm unperturbedness may be attained.

**Unperu·sed,** *ppl. a.* (UN-[1] 8.) **1553** in Strype *Eccl. Mem.* (1721) III. App. iii. 6 His letters, which.. we have sent you here unperused by us. **1605** BACON *Adv. Learn.* II. xxiii. § 6 He burned Sertorius papers unperused. **Unperva·ded,** *ppl. a.* (UN-[1] 8.) [**1775** ASH.] **1852** H. ROGERS *Ecl. Faith* 388 That the Old Testament is unpervaded by any distinct traces of expectations of a future life. **Unperve·rse,** *a.* (UN-[1] 7.) **1868** BROWNING *Ring & Bk.* VII. 545 Either you have prayed him unperverse, Or I have talked him back into his wits. **Unperve·rt,** *v.* (UN-[2] 3.) **1655** FULLER *Ch. Hist.* x. iv. § 64 His wife could never be unperverted again, but perished in her Judaism. **1768** STERNE *Sent. Journ., Paris*, I declare I had the credit all over Paris of unperverting Madame de V***.

**Unperve·rted,** *ppl. a.* (UN-[1] 8.)
**1653** W. RAMESEY *Astrol. Restored* 203 So long as God upholdeth the order and course of Nature unperverted. **1674** COKE & DAVIS *England's Independency* (title-p.), Those who are yet unperverted to the Court or Church of Rome. **1782** J. SCOTT *Poet. Wks.* 4 Pleasing vestiges.. Of unperverted Nature's golden reign. **1838** KEBLE *Serm.* ix. (1848) 238 What unperverted conscience can fail to see the offence? **1871** FRASER *Life of Berkeley* ix. 352 He was unperverted by controversial theology.

**Unpe·stered,** *ppl. a.* (UN-[1] 8.)
**1588** T. P. tr. *Orders Span. Fleet* in *Harl. Misc.* (1744) I. 114 That all soldiers have their room clean, and unpestered of chests, and other things. **1598** BARRET *Theor. Warres* 103 It is a place of armes, and it is to bee left free and vnpestered for onely the battell when it is to be set. **1824** MACTAGGART *Gallovid. Encycl.* (1876) 233 Unpestered, sequestered, Deep hidden I remain.

**Unpeti·tioned,** *ppl. a.* (UN-[1] 8.) **1675** CROWNE *Calisto* IV, Thou hast pleas'd me so, My favors unpetition'd I'll bestow. **Unpe·trified,** *ppl. a.* (UN-[1] 8.) **1646** SIR T. BROWNE *Pseud. Ep.* II. v. 91 All Corall is not hard, and in many concreted plants some parts remaine unpetrified. **1735** THOMSON *Liberty* III. 208 Their generous hearts, Unpetrify'd by Self, so naked lay.. that [etc.]. **Unpe·trify,** *v.* (UN-[2] 3.) **1815** *Hist. J. Decastro* iv. 22 This unpetrified the waiter, who seized a poker to drive her out of the house. **1838** ROBERTSON *Let.* in Brooke *Life* (1865) I. 40 We all agreed that the distance of eighteen miles had a marvellous effect in unpetrifying us.

**Unpe·tticoated,** *ppl. a.* (UN-[1] 8.)
**1846** *Browning Lett.* (1899) II. 321 Flush [the dog] hates all unpetticoated people. **1848** A. HERBERT in Todd *Irish Nennius* Notes p. lvii, The unpetticoated government of their Milesian wives.

†**Unpeysible**: see UNPEACIBLE *a. Obs.*

**Unphilanthro·pic,** *a.* (UN-[1] 7.) **1831** CARLYLE *Sart. Res.* II. iv, I have heard affirmed.. by not unphilanthropic persons, that [etc.]. **Unphilo·sopher.** (UN-[1] 12.) **1829** CARLYLE *Misc.* (1840) II. 219 The English Unphilosopher believes it without demonstration. **Unphiloso·phic,** *a.* (UN-[1] 7.) **1776** *Phil. Trans.* LXXXV. 189 Those censures, which unphilosophic severity may throw on him. **1834** DE QUINCEY *Autob. Sk.* Wks. 1853 I. 349 It would be unphilosophic to say, that [etc.].

**Unphiloso·phical,** *a.* (UN-[1] 7.)
**1649** MILTON *Eikon.* vi. 57 Straining her wise dictates to un-philosophicall purposes. **1656** COWLEY *Davideis* I. Note x, One of the most unphilosophical opinions in all Aristotle. **1696** J. EDWARDS *Exist. & Provid. God* I. 31 This is unphilosophical, and therefore we may justly look upon the argument drawn from it as so too. **1771** *Encycl. Brit.* I. 652/1 The very supposition.. must be unphilosophical, whimsical, and absurd. **1847** HELPS *Friends in C.* I. i. 5 A man more fierce and unphilosophical in the pursuit of it I never saw. **1862** GOULBURN *Educ. World* 30 Surely this statement is both unphilosophical and unscriptural.
*absol.* **1877** LAING *Bacon's Philos. Exam.* 15 The minds of the unphilosophical.
Hence **Unphiloso·phicalness.**
**1687** NORRIS *Coll. Misc.* (1699) 169 The unphilosophicalness of this their Hypothesis.

**Unphiloso·phically,** *adv.* (UN-[1] 11.)
**1674** R. GODFREY *Inj. & Ab. Physic* 179, I should not easily have believed that any Physician had been.. so unphilosophically bred, as to ascribe the cure of Diseases to the Devil. **1705** CLARKE *Unch. Obligat. Nat. Relig.* (1716) 278 These latter indeed, explained themselves very weakly and unphilosophically. **1778** *Phil. Trans.* LXVIII. 814 An experiment thus loosely and unphilosophically made. **1830** MACKINTOSH *Eth. Philos.* Wks. 1846 I. 203 Believing unphilosophically, as well as dangerously, that there can be any measure.. so useful [etc.]. **1854** JAMES *Ticonderoga* III. 43 Sometimes.. Woodchuck would talk, neither unphilosophically, nor unlearnedly,.. upon a life to come.

**Unphilo·sophize,** *v.* (UN-[2] 3.) **1713** POPE *Let. to Caryll* 14 Aug., Our passions, our interests, flow in upon us, and unphilosophise us into mere mortals. **Unphilo·sophized,** *ppl. a.* (UN-[1] 8.) **1828–32** WEBSTER s.v., Unphilosophized revelation. **1900** F. H. STODDARD *Evol. Eng. Novel* 156 The honest, unbiassed, unphilosophized portrayal of life-conditions. **Unphlebo·tomized,** *ppl. a.* (UN-[1] 8.) [**1775** ASH.] **1791** [see UNPILLED *ppl. a.*[2]].

**Unphone·tic,** *a.* (UN-[1] 7.)
**1857** LD. CAMPBELL *Chief Justices* III. xlviii. 153 A word of two syllables without any unphonetic consonants. **1879** *Encycl. Brit.* IX. 634/2 French orthography is now quite as traditional and unphonetic as English. **1888** [see next].
Hence **Unphone·ticness.**
**1888** SWEET *Hist. Eng. Sounds* 68 Unphoneticness is mainly the result of the retention of originally phonetic spellings after they have become unphonetic through sound-change.

**Unphra·sed,** *ppl. a.* (UN-[1] 8.)
**1663** SIR G. MACKENZIE *Religious Stoic* 145 He furnish'd only to the other Prophets the mater and subject unphrased. **1891** MEREDITH *One of our Conq.* xxxiii, That was the thought, unrevolved, unphrased, all but unconscious.

**Unphy·sical,** *a.* (UN-[1] 7.)
**1593** NASHE *Christ's T.* V iij b, In another corner, enhabiteth a Phisition and a Coniuerer, who.. can coniure vp an vnphisicall drabbe at all times. **1763** *Museum Rust.* I. 364 It will not contribute to the encrease.. of the root, in the unphysical or over heavy manner in which I have seen it done. **1874** TYNDALL *Fragm. Sci.* (1879) II. ix. 151 His notions of motion were entirely unphysical. **1885** *Century Mag.* XXIX. 953 Probably no unphysical argument addressed to genuine dynamiters would be likely to have any powerful effect.
So **Unphy·sically** *adv.*
**1782** ELIZ. BLOWER *Geo. Bateman* I. 230, I cannot believe you would act so unphysically as to walk out clad so loosely.

**Unphy·sicked,** *ppl. a.* (UN-[1] 8.)
*a* **1596** *Sir T. More* III. ii. 233 This is noe age for poets..; And, as great subiects of ther pen decay, Even so vnphisickt they doe melt away. **1641** HOWELL *Poem Royal* (1650) I 3, Free limbs, unphysic'd health, due appetite, Which no sauce else but Hunger may excite. **1691** COTTON in *Aubrey's Lett.*, etc. (1813) i. 20, I enjoy at present so firm and an unphysick'd health, that I hope to do somewhat before I die.

**Unphysiolo·gical,** *a.* (UN-[1] 7.) [**1775** ASH.] **1859** AGASSIZ *Ess. Classification* 288 An entirely unphysiological principle. **1898** P. MANSON *Trop. Diseases* xii. 202 Impaired by disease, or by trying unphysiological conditions.

**Unpi·ck,** *v.* Also 4–5 -pike, -pyke. [UN-[2] 9.]
†**1.** *trans.* To pick (a lock); to undo (a door) in this way. Also *fig. Obs.*
**1377** LANGL. *P. Pl.* B. XIII. 368 Atte laste I stale it, Or pryuiliche his purse shoke, vnpiked his lokkes. **1390** GOWER *Conf.* II. 347 Ek fulofte he goth a nyht.. And with his craft the dore unpiketh. *c* **1412** HOCCLEVE *De Reg. Princ.* 1103 (MS. Reg. 17, D v 1), He dremethe theves come in, And on his coffres knokke,.. And some of hem unpyke withe a sotelle gynne. **1433** LYDG. *St. Edmund* III. 1201 Another [thief] besy.. To vnpyke lokys. *a* **1661** FULLER *Worthies, Kent* II. (1662) 76 Cunning his hands, who could unpick the Cabinets in the Popes Conclave.
**2.** To undo the sewing of (a garment, etc.); to take out (stitches). Also in fig. context.
[**1775** ASH.] **1809** MALKIN *Gil Blas* x. x. ¶ 14, I unpicked his pillow, where I found.. fifty crowns. **1842** MRS. BROWNING *Grk. Chr. Poets* iii. Wks. (1904) 612 Was it not enough.. that he was turned once, like her own cast imperial mantle, .. but that he must be unpicked again by Eudocia..? **1856** MISS YONGE *Daisy Chain* I. vii, Ethel sat down.. and began to assist in unpicking the merino.
*absol.* **1890** *N. & Q.* 5 July 12/2 While we boys 'unpicked', the bigger girls would sew the patchwork covers.

**Unpi·ckable,** *a.* (UN-[1] 7 b.)
**1612** BEAUM. & FL. *Coxcomb* II. ii, Not a door open now, but double barr'd;.. and their locks unpickable. **1862** *Catal. Internat. Exhib.* II. No. 5993, The so-called 'unpickable' locks. **1869** MRS. WHITNEY *We Girls* xii, She put her principles into her unpickable pocket.

**Unpi·cked,** *ppl. a.* [UN-[1] 8.]
**1.** Not picked out or selected; not freed from what is of inferior quality.
**1587** PALFREYMAN *Baldwin's Mor. Philos.* To Rdr. (1600) B ij b, Some curious or scornfull person finding it vnpicked, emptie, barren of eloquence. **1641** MILTON *Prel. Episc.* 3 Whatsoever time, or the heedless hand of blind chance, hath drawne down.. in her huge dragnet, whether Fish, or Seaweed, Shells, or Shrubbs, unpickt, unchosen. **1765** *Museum*

*Rust.* IV. 384 A small sample of each kind of seed, certified ..to have been taken indifferently and unpicked out of the gross quantity gathered. **1830** M. DONOVAN *Dom. Econ.* I. 277 An inferior quality of wine will be afforded by unpicked clusters. **1887** in Moloney *Forestry W. Africa* 135 In a rough state unpicked, but simply roughly..sifted, it sells for £45 to £60 per ton.

**2.** Not gathered or culled.

**1597** SHAKS. 2 *Hen. IV*, II. iv. 397 Now comes in the sweetest Morsell of the night, and wee must hence, and leaue it vnpickt. **1612** PARKES *Curtain-Drawer* 4 Then Tobacco was an Indian, vnpickt and vnpiped, now made the common Iuy-bush of luxury.

**3.** Not unfastened or opened; not rifled or robbed. Also in fig. context.

**1598** GREENE *Jas. IV*, I. ii, I cannot abide..a fat capon vncaru'd, a full purse vnpickt. *a* **1704** T. BROWN *Laconics* Wks. 1711 IV. 2 How is it possible..for a Woman to keep her Cabinet unpick'd, when every Rascal has got a Key to 't?

**†4.** Without incision. *Obs.*—1

**1605** J. MOSAN *Wirtzung's Gen. Pract. Phys.* 420 Bathing in sweet water is very profitable. So are also boxing cups set vnpickt vpon the sides, whereby to extract all windinesse.

**Unpi·cket,** *v.* (UN-2 3.) **1839** ALISON *Hist. Eur.* VII. lii. 191 Before..the horses in many places [could be] unpicketted, the British dragoons were upon them. **Unpi·ck-eted,** *ppl. a.* (UN-1 8.) **1860** TRISTRAM *Gt. Sahara* xvi. 270 A large courtyard, where picketed horses, unpicketed mules,..jostled in hopeless confusion. **Unpi·ckled,** *ppl. a.* (UN-1 8.) **1620** VENNER *Via Recta* viii. 132 The greene.. Cucumbers preserued in a pickle..are much better then those that are eaten..vnpickled. **1757** W. THOMPSON *R. N. Advoc.* 9 Pickled, unpickled, and undrained Casks rolled away together.

**Unpicto·rial,** *a.* (UN-1 7.)

**1860** I. TAYLOR *Spir. Heb. Poetry* (1873) 80 Giving to the aerial aspect of Palestine that clear, sharp, and unpictorial visibility which is now its characteristic. **1884** *19th Cent.* May 813 The idea..was of the most unpictorial kind.

Hence **Unpicto·rially** *adv.*

*a* **1864** HAWTHORNE *Amer. Note-bks.* (1879) II. 168 He dresses very..unpictorially. **1887** HISSEY *Holiday on Road* 308 Outlined unpictorially sharp against the sky.

**Unpicturabi·lity.** (UN-1 12.) **1887** DUKE OF ARGYLL in *Mem.* (1906) II. 525 The multiplicity of motions..resulting, to my mind, in the same 'unpicturability'.

**Unpi·cturable,** *a.* (UN-1 7 b.)

**1837–8** SIR W. HAMILTON *Lect.* (1859) I. xxxv. 312 Objects so different as the images of sense and the unpicturable notions of intelligence. **1888** J. MARTINEAU *Stud. Relig.* II. 337 By a mixture of the two, an insertion of unpicturable power between the successive picturable things.

**Unpi·ctured,** *ppl. a.* (UN-1 8.) [**1775** ASH.] **1875** BROWNING *Aristoph. Apol.* 83 The hero of each painted monster—so Suggesting the unpictured perfect shape.

**Unpicture·sque,** *a.* (UN-1 7.)

**1791** W. GILPIN *Forest Scenery* I. 54 The walnut is not an unpicturesque tree. **1821** CRAIG *Lect. Drawing*, etc. v. 301 It might be supposed that stone lying in regular layers, would be unpicturesque. **1870** LOWELL *Among my Bks.* Ser. I. (1873) 229 Looked at on the outside, New England history is dry and unpicturesque.

Hence **Unpicture·squely** *adv.*, **-ness.**

**1840** POE *Domain Arnheim* Wks. 1864 I. 394 Our disorder may seem order—our unpicturesqueness picturesque. **1876** 'ANNIE THOMAS' *Blotted out* viii, My hair has been unpicturesquely out of order.

**Unpie·ced,** *ppl. a.* (UN-2 8, 3.) **1483** CAXTON *Gold. Leg.* 231 b/2 His vestement..he ware..so long that it was broken & unpeced.

**Unpie·rceable,** *a.* (UN-1 7 b.)

**1600** FAIRFAX *Tasso* XX. lxvi, Is he then vnpearceable.. That neither force nor foe he needes regard? **1611** COTGR., *Impenetrable*,..vnpierceable. **1801** SOUTHEY *Thalaba* II. viii, O'er the two remaining lives A cloud unpierceable had risen. **1849** MANGAN *Poems* (1903) 76 Conal's unpierceable shirt of mail.

**Unpie·rced,** *ppl. a.* (UN-1 8.)

**1593** B. BARNES *Poems* (Grosart) 95 Thine hart of Adamant, which none can wound: Thine eye of Adamant, vnperced found. **1607** CHAPMAN *Bussy d'Ambois* v. ii, Counsels (as your entrails) Should be unpierc'd and sound kept. **1633** P. FLETCHER *Purple Isl.* VI. xxix, Such is this famous Prince, such his unpierced beam. **1744** THOMSON *Autumn* 852 Where, unpierc'd by Frost, the Cavern sweats. **1759** *Phil. Trans.* LI. 377 The leaves on each side of the foil were pierced, while the foil itself remained unpierced. **1862** LYTTON *Str. Story* II. 192 My dark guess into the Shadowland unpierced by Philosophy. **1864** J. H. FOLEY in Willis & Clark *Cambridge* (1886) III. 223 An arch, unpierced,.. making..a shallow recess.

**Unpie·rcing,** *ppl. a.* (UN-1 10.) **1768–74** TUCKER *Lt. Nat.* (1834) I. 512 Our unpiercing optics reaching a very little way into the chain of events around us. **Unpi·ety.** *Obs.*—1 [UN-1 12, 5 b.] Impiety. **1675** BAXTER *Cath. Theol.* II. 192 Some [children] the Parents apostatizing educate in Heresie or unpiety themselves. **Unpi·gmented,** *ppl. a.* (UN-1 8.) **1887** LUBBOCK in *Linn. Soc. Jrnl., Zool.* XX. 124 It is, however, easy to imagine that in unpigmented animals.. the light might act directly on the nervous system. **1898** P. MANSON *Trop. Diseases* ii. 49 The earlier unpigmented phase [of the malaria parasite]. **†Unpi·ked,** *ppl. a.* *Obs.* [UN-1 8: see PICKED *ppl. a.* 2.] Untrimmed. **1542** UDALL *Erasm. Apoph.* 80 b, He brought theim foorth vnkembed, and vnpiked,..bare foote and bare-leggued.

**Unpi·le,** *v.* [UN-2 3, 5.] *trans.* To demolish (a pile or heap); to remove from a pile. Also *absol.*

**1611** COTGR., *Desamasser*, to vnheape, vnpile. **1792** *Comm. Jrnl.* XLVII. 363/1 The Expence of piling, unpiling, &c. &c. as is practised in His Majesty's Yards. **1847** *Infantry Man.* (1854) 27 *Unpile Arms.* At the word Unpile, the whole advance their right feet. **1871** MISS YONGE *Cameos* II. 281 The English began to unpile the fearful heaps of dead.

**Unpi·lfered,** *ppl. a.* (UN-1 8.) [**1775** ASH.] **1844** LOWELL *Prometheus* 298 That spirit which doth ever brood..on the unpilfered nest Of man's deep heart. **Unpi·llaged,** *ppl. a.* (UN-1 8.) **1753** GLOVER *Boadicia* I. i, Did not Prasutagus.. On your insatiate emperor bestow Half of his rich possessions, vainly deeming, The rest might pass unpillag'd to his children? **Unpi·llared,** *ppl. a.* [UN-1 8 and UN-2 8.] Not furnished with, deprived of, pillars. **1706** WATTS *Horæ Lyricæ* I. 77 Thou bulky globe,..That hangs unpillar'd in an empty space! **1728** POPE *Dunc.* III. 107 See, the Cirque falls, th' unpillar'd Temple nods.

**† Unpi·lled,** *ppl. a.*1 *Obs.* [UN-1 8 + PILL *v.*1]

**1.** Unpeeled.

**1538** *Inv. W. Gebon of Sutterton, Linc.* (MS.), Hempe vnpillid and flaxe vnswyngled. **1562** PHAER *Æneid* C c iv, An vnshapen bunchy speare with barke unpilde. **1639** T. DE GRAY *Expert Farrier* 232 Beate the garlicke unpilled in a stone morter.

**2.** Not robbed or plundered.

**1577** DEE *General & Rare Mem.* 4 Their Marchantlike Ships ..may, in our Seas.., pas quietly vnpilled, vnspoyled, and vntaken by Pyrates. **1580** *Reg. Privy Council Scot.* III. 308 The remanent guidis..left unpilleit within the samin schip.

**Unpi·lled,** *ppl. a.*2 (UN-1 8 + PILL *v.*2) **1791** HUDDESFORD *Salmag.* 140 No Doctor feed, no regimen advised, Unpill'd, unpoultic'd, unphlebotomiz'd!

**Unpi·llowed,** *ppl. a.* (UN-1 8.)

**1634** MILTON *Comus* 355 Perhaps..'gainst the rugged bark of som broad Elm [she] Leans her unpillow'd head. **1652** BENLOWES *Theoph.* XII. lxxii, We there, on grassy tufted tapestries..Leaning unpillow'd heads, view Nature's ants and bees. **1868** GEO. ELIOT *Span. Gipsy* 177 In carved dark-oaken chair, unpillowed, sleeps..a small man.

**Unpi·loted,** *ppl. a.* (UN-1 8.)

[**1775** ASH.] **1794** COLERIDGE *Lett.* (1895) 122 Launching our frail and unpiloted bark on a rough sea of anxieties. **1820** SHELLEY *Witch Atl.* lxiii, We, the weak mariners of that wide lake,..Our course unpiloted and starless make O'er its wide surface. **1853** C. BRONTE *Villette* xxxv, You see me void of affection and religion,..unpiloted by principle or faith.

**Unpi·n,** *v.* [UN-2 3, 4.]

**1.** *trans.* To withdraw the pin or bolt of (a door); to unbolt.

**13..** *Coer de L.* 4212 On schal dwelle the clos withinne, The gate to unschette and unpynne, And stylly to unschette the lok. **1377** LANGL. *P. Pl.* B. XI. 108 Þe porter vnpynned þe ȝate. *Ibid.* XX. 328. *c* **1400** *Beryn* 484 'Away, dogg, with evil deth,' quod he, þat was within, And made hym al redy, the dorr to vnpyn. *a* **1547** SURREY *Æneid* II. 328 Sinon ..Let fourth the Grekes enclosed in the womb, The closures eke of pine by stealth vnpind. **1596** DRAYTON *Legends* iv. 825 Peace, the good Porter, readie still at hand It doth unpin. **1753** SMOLLETT *Ct. Fathom* xxix, The quaker..unpinned the other coach-door..and trundled himself into the mud. **1826** SCOTT *Woodst.* xiii, Joan unpinned the door, to demand who was without.

*absol.* **1377** LANGL. *P. Pl.* B. XVIII. 261 Prynces of þis place, vnpynneth & vnlouketh!

**2.** To remove pins or pegs from; to unfasten or detach in this way. Also *fig.*

**1611** COTGR., *Declaveter*, to vnboult, vnpinne, vnpeg; loose from. **1633** G. HERBERT *Temple, Constancie* i, Whom neither force nor fawning can Unpinne, or wrench from giving all their due. **1673** R. HEAD *Canting Acad.* 76 Unpinning a wheel [he] took it off. *a* **1699** J. BEAUMONT *Psyche* XVI. xvii, Unclasp my Joints; unlace my nerves; and try My finest tenderest membranes to unpin. **1701** WARWICK *Mem. Reign Chas. I*, 6 They have in a great measure unpinned the firmness of the government. **1825** J. NICHOLSON *Operat. Mechanic* 500 When the upper part of the frame..is unpinned and removed.

*transf.* **1674** GREW *Anat. Plants* (1682) 228 [The atoms of] any fixed unodorable, or untastable Body..being not able to make any Smell or Taste, unless they were first dissolved; that is to say, unpin'd one from another.

**3.** To undo the dress of (a woman) by the removal of pins. Also *absol.*

**1604** SHAKS. *Oth.* IV. iii. 35 *Æmilia.* Shall I go fetch your Night-gowne? *Desdemona.* No, vn-pin me here. *c* **1680** *Roxb. Ball.* (1891) VII. 459 Prithee begin; don't delay, but unpin. **1745** FIELDING *Tom Jones* XIII. iii, Mrs. Etoff, who had the honour to pin and unpin the Lady Bellaston. **1815** *Hist. J. Decastro* III. 331 Come and unpin me, O my dearest husband!

*fig.* **1641** MILTON *Animadv.* 9 The peremptory Analysis.. will be so hardy as once more to unpinne your spruce fastidious oratory, to rumple her laces [etc.].

**4.** To remove a pin or pins from (an article of dress, etc.); to detach by removing or releasing a pin or pins. Also in fig. context.

**1605** ERONDELLE *Fr. Gard.* O 8 b, Go to, take of my cloathes vnpinne that, vntie this. **1630** I. CRAVEN *God's Tribunall* 33 A day..when all maskes shall be vnpinned, and all disguises taken off. **1662** GURNALL *Chr. in Arm.* III. xxx. 256 Unpinne this story, take off that gaudy phrase, and nothing is left in the discourse. **1709** STEELE *Tatler* No. 36 ¶ 3 She..began to unpin her hood. **1740** RICHARDSON *Pamela* II. 21 He began to unpin my Handkerchief. **1769** LADY MARY COKE *Jrnl.* 8 Feb. (1892) III. 19 My Maids had pin'd up the train of my Sack to my back, and had forgot to unpin it. **1849** C. BRONTE *Shirley* xxv, Who gave you this little brooch? Let me unpin it and look at it. **1860** EMILY EDEN *Semi-attached Couple* vi, Sarah unpinned a gigantic bunch of camellias. **1887** FENN *Master of Cerem.* i, Unpinning a piece of paper that guarded the gay silks and wools

**b.** *intr.* To become unpinned.

**1716** LADY MONTAGU *Town Ecl., Tuesday* 74 Reaching the kettle made her gown unpin.

**Unpi·nched,** *ppl. a.* (UN-1 8.) **1648** HEXHAM, *Onvernepen*, ..vnpinched. **1854** MRS. CARLYLE in Froude *Life in London* (1884) II. 164 Habits of *unpinched* housekeeping. **Unpinda·rical,** *a.* (UN-1 7.) **1729** YOUNG *Merchant* Pref., Nothing is so unpindarical as following Pindar on the foot.

**† Unpi·ned,** *ppl. a.* *Obs.* [UN-1 8.] Unpained; unpunished.

*c* **1200** *Trin. Coll. Hom.* 69 Þenche we ure giltes er þe dom cume,..þat god ne finde þanne on us no gilt unpined. *c* **1200** ORMIN 1367 Cristess Goddcunndnesse wass All cwicc & all unnpinedd. *c* **1290** *St. Edmund Conf.* 184 in *S. Eng. Leg.* I. 436 He nolde þat no lime un-pined scholde beo.

**Unpi·nion,** *v.* [UN-2 4.] *trans.* To deprive of pinions. **1593** NASHE *Christ's T.* G j, My wings her..disobedience hath now cleane vnpinioned and broken. **1691** NORRIS *Pract. Disc.* 170 The Soul..is not only broken and wounded in her Wings, but utterly unpinioned, she has dropt her Feathers. **Unpi·nioned,** *ppl. a.*1 [UN-1 8.] Not furnished with pinions. **1615** BRATHWAIT *Strappado* (1878) 26 Vnpiniond Muses (such as nere could flie) Further than vnplum'd birds now presse as high As Eagles.

**Unpi·nioned,** *ppl. a.*2 [UN-1 8.]

**1.** Not having the pinions cut.

**1622** F. MARKHAM *Bk. War* V. x. 199 His power must be ..vnrestrained, that flying with vnpinion'd wings it may seeme to be hid within the Skie of the greatest Actions.

**2.** Not bound or tied.

**1775** ADAIR *Amer. Ind.* 394 When they were taking him unpinioned..to the place of torture.

**Unpi·nked,** *ppl. a.* (UN-1 8.) **1596** SHAKS. *Tam. Shr.* IV. i. 136 Gabrels pumpes were all vnpinkt i' th heele.

**Unpi·nned,** *ppl. a.* [UN-1 8.] Not fastened with a pin or pins.

**1390** GOWER *Conf.* I. 293 He berth evere his mowth unpinned, So that his lippes ben unloke. **1568** *Depositions* XVI, 11 May (MS. Cant. Cath. Lib.), The said wif with her peticote vnpynned. **1655** tr. *Sorel's Com. Hist. Francion* VI. 18 Her waiting Gentlewoman had..her Gorget unpinned.

**Unpi·ped,** *ppl. a.* [UN-1 8.] Not put into a pipe. **1612** [see UNPICKED *ppl. a.* 2]. **Unpi·rated,** *ppl. a.* (UN-1 8.) **1840** DE QUINCEY *Style* I. (1860) 194 We have lying before us..the unpirated edition of Hartknoch. **Unpi·tched,** *ppl. a.* [UN-1 8.] Not smeared or dirtied with pitch. **1634** SIR T. HERBERT *Trav.* 105 In this Riuer are some long, deepe prams, sowed together with hempe and cord (but vnpitcht or calkt). **1648** HEXHAM II, *Onbepeckt*, Vnpitcht, or Vndefiled with pitch.

**† Unpi·teous,** *a.* *Obs.* [UN-1 8, 5 b.]

**1.** Impious, wicked. Also *absol.*

*c* **1374** CHAUCER *Boeth.* I. met. i. (1868) 4 But now..myn vnpitouse [*Camb. MS.* vnpietous] lijf [L. *impia vita*] draweþ along vnagreable dwellynges in me. **1382** WYCLIF *Prov.* xxviii. 1 The vnpitouse [L. *impius*] fleeth, no man pursuende. *c* **1400** *Apol. Loll.* 61 ȝe schal not..tak to hond to sey fals witnes for þe vnpitous.

**2.** Pitiless, unmerciful.

**1390** GOWER *Conf.* III. 206 As the rages of the See Ben unpitous in the tempeste. *c* **1412** HOCCLEVE *De Reg. Princ.* 3371 It is ful hard To lakke mercy and ben vnpitous. **1447** BOKENHAM *Seyntys* (Roxb.) 15 Have mercy lord jhesu up on me And lese not my soule with unpetous men. *a* **1586** SIDNEY *Ps.* (1823) XL. vi, Lett them with shame be cloied,.. Who so unpittious be. **1612** T. JAMES *Corrupt. Script.* III. 8 Whilst the vnpitious man defouleth a rightfuller than himselfe. **1725** POPE *Odyss.* XX. 253 The tyrant, not the father of the skies! Unpiteous of the race thy will began.

**Unpi·teously,** *adv.* [UN-1 11.]

**†1.** Impiously, wickedly. *Obs.*

**1382** WYCLIF *Prov.* xii. 2 Who forsothe trostith in his thoȝtis, vnpitously [L. *impie*] doth. — 2 *Pet.* ii. 6 Puttinge ensaumple of hem that weren to doynge yuel, or vnpitously.

**2.** Pitilessly; unmercifully.

**1390** GOWER *Conf.* (1901) II. 470 He yit nevere unpitously Ayein the liges of his lond..Thurgh cruelte vengaunce soghte. **1502** *Ord. Crysten Men* (W. de W. 1506) II. xvii. 130 Ye darte yt the deuyll casteth subtylly, & ryght unpytuously. **1513** BRADSHAW *St. Werburge* I. 3465 Whiche danes..Punysshed vnpiteously all this region With a wofull plage of great crudelite. *a* **1856** SIR W. HAMILTON (Imp. Dict.), Oxford..so unpiteously cramming her alumni with the shells alone.

**† Unpi·teousness.** *Obs.* [UN-1 12.]

**1.** Impiety, wickedness.

**1382** WYCLIF *Lev.* xix. 7 If eny..etith of it, he shal be cursid, and gilti of vnpitowsnes [L. *impietatis*]. — *Ps.* v. 11 After the multitude of the vnpitousnessis [*v.r.* vnpiteousnessis; L. *impietatum*] of hem, put hem awei.

**2.** Pitilessness; unmercifulness.

*c* **1380** WYCLIF *Sel. Wks.* III. 474 Leste Crist dampne ȝowe for traytouris and monquellers..for ȝoure unpityuousnes. **1447** BOKENHAM *Seyntys* (Roxb.) 108 O unpetousnesse, o unryhtful Domys, and o pervers entent.

So **† Unpiteousty**, impiety. *Obs.*—1

**1382** WYCLIF *Ecclus.* xlvi. 23 He..enhauncede his vois..to don awey the vnpitouste [L. *impietatem*] of the folc.

**Unpi·tiable,** *a.* (UN-1 7 b.)

**1646** BP. HALL *Devout Soul* xii. 42 The unpitiable, interminable, unmitigable tortures of those..never-dying souls. **1748** RICHARDSON *Clarissa* (1811) VII. 34 Such as sad accident, or unpitiable presumption, threw in their way. **1844** in *Life A. Fonblanque* (1874) 259 An elderly gentleman with the military mania is as unpitiable a case as one of the same years in the measles. **1873** GEO. ELIOT in Cross *Life* (1885) III. 193, I..am at that unpitiable stage of illness which is counterbalanced by extra petting.

**Unpi·tiably,** *adv.* (UN-1 11, 5 b.) **1821** SCOTT *Le Sage* Biogr. Mem. (1834) I. 419 Carambola is employed in reading to slumber the Member of the Council.., who unpitiably awakens at every instant when his reader stops.

**Unpi·tied,** *ppl. a.* (UN-1 8.)

*a* **1586** SIDNEY *Arcadia* II. xxix, With unpittyed teares idly protesting, he had rather die. **1601** *2nd Pt. Ret. fr. Parnass.* Prol. 85 To you we seeke to shew a schollers state, His scorned fortunes, his vnpittyed fate. **1693** G. STEPNEY in *Dryden's Juvenal* VIII. (1697) 197 Think what Rewards upon the Good attend, And how those fall unpitied who offend. **1735** BERKELEY *Querist* § 335 Whether there be a more wretched, and..a more unpitied case, than for men to make precedents for their own undoing? **1781** COWPER *Retirem.* 512 The unpitied victim of ill-judg'd expence. **1819** CRABBE *T. of Hall* XII. 305 While all beheld her just, unpitied pain, Grown in neglect! **1891** FARRAR *Darkn. & Dawn* xxxi, A herd of wretches clothed in rags, ill-fed, untended, unpitied.

So **Unpi·tiedly** *adv.*

**1628** FELTHAM *Resolves* II. 296, I beg no more, then may keepe mee vncontemnedly, and vnpittiedly-honest.

**Unpi·tiful,** *a.* [UN-¹ 7.] Pitiless.
c 1449 PECOCK *Repr.* v. vi. 516 Vnpiteful questmongers and forsworen iurers. c 1510 BARCLAY *Mirr. Gd. Manners* (1570) D. vj, Unpitifull art thou and cruell tormentour Which thine owne proper minde thus drownest in errour. a 1563 BALE in Marbeck *Bk. of Notes* (1581) 753 The vnpitifull murderers are also the same bloudthirstie Prelates. 1651 tr. *De-las-Coveras' Don Fenise* 27 The unpitifull hardnesse of these rockes where I was abandoned. 1658–9 *Burton's Diary* (1828) III. 479 Where they have power, they are the unpitifullest people in the world.

**Unpi·tifully,** *adv.* [UN-¹ 11.] Pitilessly.
1598 SHAKS. *Merry W.* IV. ii. 215 He beate him most vnpittifully, me thought. 1709 MRS. MANLEY *Secret Mem.* (1720) III. 217 Never were Barbarian Pirates..so unpittifully insulted.

**Unpi·tifulness.** [UN-¹ 12.] Absence of pity.
1526 *Pilgr. Perf.* (W. de W. 1531) 90 b, Periury, vnquyetnes, obduracion or vnpitefulnes. a 1586 SIDNEY *Arcadia* III. xviii, The unpitifulnes of his owne neere-threatning death. 1679 G.R. tr. *Boaystuau's Theat. World* II. 332 [The] unpitifulness of one violent Creature against another.

**Unpitous, -ness, -ty**: see UNPITEOUS *a.*, etc.

† **Unpi·ty.** *Obs.* [UN-¹ 12.]
**1.** Impiety, wickedness.
a 1340 HAMPOLE *Psalter* lxxii. 6 Hilde þai er in wickidnes & in þaire impite [*v.r.* vnpete]. c 1400 *Apol. Loll.* 62 Wam þu fynd wickid þu schall condempne of vnpite.
**2.** Lack of pity.
1447 BOKENHAM *Seyntys* (Roxb.) 72 O cruel tyraunth ful of unpyte. 1491 CAXTON *Vitas Patr.* (W. de W. 1495) I. cxlv. 155/2 Of leesynges, of couetise,..of unpyte, of euyll mynde. 1653 H. WHISTLER *Upshot Inf. Baptisme* Pref., For preservation of..freedom of holy Right herein, against Advances of Opposit unpitty.

**Unpi·tying,** *ppl. a.* (UN-¹ 10.)
1605 DRAYTON *Heroical Ep., Matilda to K. John* 12 As though thy hard vnpittying hand had sent me Some new deuised torture to torment me. 1646 CRASHAW *Carmen Deo Nostro, Weeper* xxvii, So sigh tormented sweets, opprest With proud unpittying fires. 1777 POTTER *Æschylus, Prom. Bd.* 10 Yet upbraid not My ruder and unpitying ruthlessness. 1796 MRS. M. ROBINSON *Angelina* I. 59 Instances.. where the purest sentiments have been contaminated..by sordid and unpitying parents! 1846 MRS. A. MARSH *Father Darcy* II. i. 25 The proud, haughty, unpitying expression to be read there. 1870 L'ESTRANGE *Miss Mitford* I. vi. 173 All these evils fall with an unpitying hand on the devoted heads of their correspondents.

**Unpi·tyingly,** *adv.* (UN-¹ 11.)
1741 RICHARDSON *Pamela* IV. 422 [She] listens eagerly to Stories told to the Disadvantage of Individuals of her own Sex: Will unpityingly propagate such Stories. 1817 LADY MORGAN *France* I. (1818) I. 9 The smallest infringement of the dreadful code was unpityingly punished. 1895 *Forum* (U.S.) Oct. 210 The effects..would operate in a socialistic state even more rigidly, more unpityingly and more openly than they do now.

† **Unpi·zzled,** *a. Obs. rare.* (UN-² 5.)
1535 LYNDESAY *Satyre* 2765 Bot thay, lyke rams, rudlie in thair rage, Vnpysalt, rinnis amang the sillie ȝowis. 1552 — *Monarche* 4707.

† **Unpla·cable,** *a. Obs.* (UN-¹ 7 b, 5 b.)
1553 BALE *Vocacyon* 48 b, A perpetuall and vnplacable enemye. 1594 ? GREENE *Selimus* Prologue 10 You shall behold him character in blood The image of an unplacable King. a 1619 FOTHERBY *Atheom.* I. xiii. § 3 (1622) 141 An vnplacable hatred. 1676 BP. N. FRENCH *Vnkinde Desertor* Pref., A hard-harted man, and our vnplacable enemy.

**Unpla·ce,** *v.* Now *rare.* [UN-² 5.] *trans.* To displace. Hence **Unpla·cing** *vbl. sb.*
1554 in Gairdner *Hist. Eng. Ch. 16th c.* (1903) xvii. 349 The unplacing of so many godly laws set forth touching the true religion of Christ. 1597 BRETON *Arb. Amorous Deuices* Wks. (Grosart) I. 5/2 If God for goods shalbe vnplac'd. 1623 COCKERAM, *Dislocate*, to vnplace. 1876 R. A. ARNOLD in *Contemp. Rev.* June 31 No writhing..can unplace them.

**Unpla·ced,** *ppl. a.* [UN-¹ 8.]
**1.** Not assigned to, or set in, a definite place.
1512 *Northumbld. Househ. Bk.* (1770) 423 The Steward and Chaplaine must sit down in the Hall, and call unto them the Gentlemen if there be any unplaced above. 1591 SYLVESTER *Du Bartas* I. i. 529 Th' unplac'd Climates of that deep disorder. 1610 HOLLAND *Camden's Brit.* I. 77 Augustus gift unplaced lay, none would it undertake. 1849 G. R. GLIDDON *Otia Ægyptiaca* 39 My own List of Unplaced Kings..who preceded the XVIIIth. Dynasty. 1861 HULME tr. *Moquin-Tandon* I. v. 34 Languages either unplaced or Indo-European (so called).
**b.** *Racing.* (See PLACE *v.* 5 d.)
1881 *Racing Analysis* I. 366 Aeronaut..also ran unplaced at 135 and 196. 1883 *Sat. Rev.* 24 Nov. 665/2 Last year,.. Hackness started first favourite for the Liverpool Cup, and was unplaced.
**2.** Not appointed to a place or office.
1558 in Strype *Ann. Ref.* (1709) I. App. iv. 4 All such as governed..and now remain unplaced and uncalled to Credit. 1575 GASCOIGNE *Glasse of Govt.* I. ii, It is not like that he should have returned from thence unplaced. 1732, 1771 [see UNPENSIONED]. 1823 J. WILSON *Marg. Lyndsay* xliii. 345 Young preachers, yet unplaced. 1849 MACAULAY *Hist. Eng.* ii. I. 241 The other fifteen were to be unplaced noblemen and gentlemen of ample fortune.

**Unpla·cid,** *a.* (UN-¹ 7.) 1848 J. H. NEWMAN *Loss & Gain* III. vi. 335 His face had that worn, or, rather, unplacid appearance, which [etc.].

**Unpla·gued,** *ppl. a.* (UN-¹ 8.)
1550 CROWLEY *Last Trumpet* 50 Then thincke Gods iustyce could not leaue The[e] unplaged. 1560 BECON *New Catech.* Wks. 1564 I. 542 He shal not escape vnplaged, neither in this world nor in the world to come. 1592 SHAKS. *Rom. & Jul.* I. v. 19 Ladies that haue their toes Vnplagu'd with Cornes. 1833 DE QUINCEY *Rev. Greece* Wks. 1859 XI. 143 The inestimable advantage of being unplagued with a Turkish population.

**Unplai·n,** *a.* (UN-¹ 7.)
1390 GOWER *Conf.* I. 77 Who that is to trowthe unplein. 1500–20 DUNBAR *Poems* lxvi. 11 The figurit speiche, with faceis tua, The plesand toungis, with hartis unplane. c 1530 L. COX *Rhet.* (1899) 86 It was a great folye to put in tho wordes which made a playne mater to be vnplaine. 1538 ELYOT, *Salebrosus*, vnplayne, where a manne can not goo, excepte he do leape.
Hence **Unplai·nness.**
1619 SIR J. SEMPILL *Sacrilege Handled* 56 Paul then is wrong quarrelled for his vnplainenesse.

**Unplai·n,** *v.* (UN-² 3). 1611 FLORIO, *Dispianáre*, to vnplaine. 1638 N. WHITING *Albino & Bellama* 720 Though earldoms court her, her disdains Nonsuits their service, and her brow unplains. †**Unplai·ned,** *ppl. a.*¹ *Obs. rare.* [UN-¹ 8 + PLAIN *v.*] Unlamented. 1591 SPENSER *Daphn.* 79 That thou are bent To die alone, vnpitied, vnplained. **Unplai·ned,** *ppl. a.*² [UN-¹ 8; cf. PLAIN *a.*¹] Not made plain. 1598 BARRET *Theor. Warres* IV. i. 98 They will breake and disaray,..when they come to any straight or vnplained way.

**Unplai·t,** *v.* (UN-² 3.)
c 1374 CHAUCER *Boeth.* II. pr. viii. (1868) 61 It is a wondyr þat I desyre to telle, and forthi vnnethe may I vnpleyten [L. *explicare*] my sentense with wordes. c 1586 C'TESS PEMBROKE *Ps.* CIV. vii, Oile, whose juyce unplaites the folded brow. 1638 N. WHITING *Albino & B.* 76 Dull-aged Saturne..his waightie head did bow, And with a smile unplaited every frowne. 1865 *Cornh. Mag.* Oct. 487 She unplaited her hair and threw it back..over her shoulders. 1867 MISS BOWDEN *Fathers of Desert* 160 Paul unplaited all the fifteen ells, and then plaited them together again.
Hence **Unplai·ting** *vbl. sb.*
1611 COTGR., *Desplissure*, an vnfoulding, vnplaiting. 1902 BARNES GRUNDY *Thames Camp* iv, This seemed a sensible idea, but why the unplaiting of her hair?

**Unplai·ted,** *ppl. a.* (UN-¹ 8.)
1659 W. CHAMBERLAYNE *Pharonnida* IV. I. 229 Where her richest ornament (Although with art unpleited) Nature in A lovely landscape wore. 1702 ADDISON *Dial. Medals* ii. (1726) 36 Rude from her forehead fell th' unplaited hair. 1877 DE COSSON *Cradle of Blue Nile* II. 73 Their hair, which they wear unplaited, is short and woolly.

**Unpla·n,** *v.* (UN-² 3.) 1819 BUSBY *Hist. Music* II. 490 The drama,..first planned, and partly written, by..Dr. Kenrick, and then..un-planned, and re-written, by Rolt.

**Unpla·ned,** *ppl. a.* (UN-¹ 8.)
[1775 ASH.] 1810 CRABBE *Borough* xviii. 362 That floor, once oak, now pieced with fir unplaned. 1879 MISS BIRD *Rocky Mount.* 43 Two unplaned wooden shelves.

**Unpla·nished,** *ppl. a.* (UN-¹ 8.) 1683 MOXON *Mech. Exerc., Printing* ii. ¶ 2 Brass well Planish't will be stiffer.. at half the thickness than unplanish't Brass will at the whole.

**Unpla·nk,** *v.* (UN-² 4.)
1654 GAYTON *Pleas. Notes* III. xii. 74 Having no notice the place was unplankt and laid open. c 1660 J. GWYNNE *Milit. Mem.* (1822) 33 One man might..cut down an arch of the bridge, or unplank it, and so make it inaccessible. 1834 J. S. MACAULAY *Field Fortif.* 246 While the repair of the third bay was in progress, the remaining bay was partly unplanked.

**Unpla·nked,** *ppl. a.* (UN-¹ 8.) 1648 HEXHAM II, *Ongeberdert*, vnboarded, or vnplanckt. 1855 KINGSLEY *Westw. Ho!* xx, The upper-deck beams were left open and unplanked.

**Unpla·nt,** *v.* (UN-² 3, 4. Cf. Du. *ontplanten.*)
1569 HAWKINS *3rd Voy.* (1878) 77 The vice Roy..sent.. commandement to vnplant all things suspicious. 1575 *Veron's Dict. Lat.-Eng.* (1584), *Explanto*, to vnplant, or pull vp. 1624 CAPT. SMITH *Virginia* IV. 163 Being enioyned by our Commission not to vnplant nor wrong the Saluages. a 1658 LOVELACE *Poems* (1904) 155 He..Unplanted had this Plantane plant.

**Unpla·ntable,** *a.* (UN-¹ 7 b.) 1683 *Pres. St. Jamaica* 2 It's imagined, if this Island were divided into eight parts,.. [three parts are] Barren or unplantable. 1788 CLARKSON *Impol. Slave Tr.* 110 The rocky, unplantable parts.

**Unpla·nted,** *ppl. a.* [UN-¹ 8. Cf. ON. *úplantaðr.*]
**1.** Not set in the ground; growing without having been planted. Also *fig.*
In first quot. rendering L. **implantatus*, a misreading of *implanatus* 'deceived'.
1382 WYCLIF *Ecclus.* xxxiv. 11 Who is vnplauntid, shal abound shreudenesse. 1600 SURFLET *Countrie Farme* 735 No more..can the vine well..endure after it is cut to be long kept vnplanted. 1639 WALLER *Battle Summer Isl.* I. 5 Figs there unplanted through the fields do grow. a 1750 A. HILL *Happy Man* 5 Unplanted groves rise round his shelter'd seat.
**2. a.** Of countries, etc.: Not occupied or colonized; not developed by cultivation.
1612 CAPT. SMITH *Proc. Virginia* 104 But God that would not it [*sc.* Virginia] should be unplanted, sent Sir Thomas Gates..to preserue us. 1660 F. BROOKE tr. *Le Blanc's Trav.* 354 The countrey remaining unplanted by any forrainers. 1719 DE FOE *Crusoe* II. (Globe) 436 To be lock'd up in an unplanted Island. 1807 J. BARLOW *Columb.* IV. 572 The future sires of our unplanted states.
**b.** Of ground: Not set with plants. Also *fig.*
? a 1800 PITT in *Nat. Rev.* (1892) XIX. 298, I..left for thee my downy bed, Unplanted yet with thorns. 1805 *Monthly Mag.* XX. 110 [Land] unsown, unplanted, untilled.
**3.** Not put in position.
1615 G. SANDYS *Trav.* 38 At the East end..lies a number of great Ordnance vnplanted.
**4.** *Sc.* Not provided with a minister.
a 1651 CALDERWOOD *Hist. Kirk* (1843) II. 186 It was ordeaned..that Mr. George Hay..preache in the unplanted kirks of Carrick.

**Unpla·nt-like,** *a.* (UN-¹ 7 c.) 1837 *Edwards' Bot. Register* XXIII. pl. 1942 That there must be something of an animal nature infused into this most unplant-like production. **Unpla·ster,** *v.* (UN-² 3.) 1598 FLORIO, *Sgommare*, to vngum, to vnplaister. 1671 TRENCHFIELD *Cap Gray Hairs* (1688) 38 As if you had undertaken the publick unplaistering of a painted Face.

**Unpla·stered,** *ppl. a.* (UN-¹ 8.)
1648 HEXHAM II, *Ongemortert*, Vnplaistered. 1669 WOODHEAD *St. Teresa* II. viii. 77 The Portall..being ill floored, and the Walls unplaistered. 1804 SOUTHEY *Let. to Coleridge* 11 June, And so unplastered it [*sc.* a room] is likely to remain another winter. 1886 W. J. TUCKER *E. Europe* 411 Its dark-grey unplastered walls.

**Unpla·stic,** *a.* (UN-¹ 7, 5 b.) 1787 *Generous Attachment* IV. 231 Those [articles] which the subtle Mr. Archer..endeavoured to hammer out of the unplastic disposition of the relentless Sir James. 1883 C. C. PERKINS *Italian Sculpture* III. i. 244 Statues of Apollo, Mercury, Minerva and Peace.. thoroughly unplastic in action and conception. 1894 *Illustr. Lond. News* 24 Mar. 364/3 The idea of harsh unplastic feeling. **Unpla·t,** *v.* (UN-² 3.) 1591 PERCIVALL *Sp. Dict.*, *Destravar*, to vnplat, to vndoo. 1607 MARKHAM *Cavel.* VI. vi. 36 Then you shall vnplat both his maine and taile. **Unplato·nically,** *adv.* (UN-¹ 11.) 1668 H. MORE *Div. Dial.* I. 288 That also, O Sophron, is very perversly and un-Platonically done of Cuphophron. †**Unplau·sable,** *a. Obs.* [UN-¹ 7 b. Cf. next.] Unpraiseworthy. 1670 G. H. *Hist. Cardinals* III. III. 326 No body will rob himself..of his hopes ..for an unplausable person.

**Unplau·sible,** *a.* (UN-¹ 7, 5 b.)
1575 FENTON *Gold. Epist.* (1582) 232 It shall not be..the more vnplausible to the reader. 1604 BACON *Apol.* Wks. 1879 I. 436 This proceeding..was a thing towards the people very unplausible. a 1677 BARROW *Serm.* Wks. 1687 III. xlv. 531 We never..should..embrace his institution, consisting of such unplausible Propositions, and precepts. 1757 HUME *Hist. Eng.* II. 198 He must have had some reasons, and perhaps not unplausible ones, for this affirmation. 1860 MILL *Lett.* (1910) I. 236 Nothing can be at first sight more entirely unplausible than his theory. 1891 F. W. NEWMAN *Early Hist. Cdl. Newman* 47 Your assumption is to me arbitrary and unplausible.

**Unplau·sibly,** *adv.* (UN-¹ 11, 5 b. Cf. prec.)
1733 W. CRAWFORD *Infidelity* (1836) 217 Some may allege, and not unplausibly, that [etc.]. 1795 BURKE *Regic. Peace* iv. Wks. IX. 56 Men would reason not unplausibly, that it would be better [etc.]. 1820 COLERIDGE *Lit. Rem.* (1839) IV. 138 Others, again, and not unplausibly, contend [etc.]. 1862 M. HOPKINS *Hawaii* 85 Cook's two ships..appeared to them, not unplausibly, islands, the masts being trees.

†**Unplau·sive,** *a. Obs.* (UN-¹ 7.) 1606 SHAKS. *Tr. & Cr.* III. iii. 43 'Tis like heele question me, Why such vnplausiue eyes are bent? why turn'd on him?

**Unplay·able,** *a.* [UN-¹ 7 b.] Incapable of being played.
1833 LYTTON *Godolphin* xxxv, Having an unplayable hand and a bad partner. 1839 DARLEY *Introd. Beaum. & Fl.'s Wks.* p. xxvii, These..form the real attraction of their 'plays,' altogether unplayable now. 1881 *Sat. Rev.* 2 July 14/1 The two slow bowlers seemed quite unplayable. 1884 *Lillywhite's Cricket Comp.* 39 The wicket was unplayable. 1902 CORNISH *Naturalist Thames* 33 After that, I must trust to the strength of the gut, for the fish would be unplayable.

**Unplay·ed,** *ppl. a.* (UN-¹ 8.)
[1775 ASH.] 1850 BOHN *Hand-bk. of Games* (1867) 161 The highest card unplayed of a suit. 1875 J. BISHOP *Otto's Violin* iv. 47 *note*, An unplayed violin does not improve.

**Unplea·dable,** *a.* [UN-¹ 7 b, 5 b.]
† **1.** Improper for legal pleadings. *Obs.*⁻¹
1569 J. SANFORD tr. *Agrippa's Van. Artes* 85 b, The yeere diuided in XII monethes with the varietie of pleadable and unpleadable dayes.
**2.** Incapable of being pleaded or urged.
a 1716 SOUTH *Serm.* (1744) VII. 202 All ignorance, that is merely negative.., is utterly inconsistent with [this], and makes [it] absolutely unpleadable. 1869 BROWNING *Ring & Bk.* IX. 1443 A flight..unpleadable in court!

**Unplea·ded,** *ppl. a.* (UN-¹ 8.) 1682 OTWAY *Venice Preserved* IV. 55 Doom'd to die! condemn'd unheard! unpleaded!

**Unplea·sable,** *a.* (UN-¹ 7 b.)
1561 T. NORTON *Calvin's Inst.* IV. xx. 170 Let parentes shew themselues so hard and vnpleasable to their children,.. that [etc.]. 1604 T. WRIGHT *Passions* I. viii. 31 To pleasure the unpleasable appetites, and lusts of the flesh. 1786 BURGOYNE *Heiress* II. ii, What a change have I made to please my unpleasable daughter!

**Unplea·sant,** *a.* [UN-¹ 7.]
**1.** Not pleasant, displeasing: **a.** To the senses.
1538 ELYOT, *Rancidus*,..vnsauery, or vnpleasaunt. 1551 TURNER *Herbal* I. 109 The colour is vnpleasanter and blacker. 1575 GASGOIGNE *Making of Verse* § 5 Wordes of many syllables do cloye a verse and make it unpleasant. 1585 T. WASHINGTON tr. *Nicholay's Voy.* III. i. 69 b, An euill fauoured and vnpleasant harmonie. 1611 FLORIO, *Inameno*, vnpleasant to the view. 1667 DRYDEN *Dram. Poesy* Ess. (ed. Ker) I. 69 Does not the eye pass from an unpleasant object to a pleasant in a much shorter time than is required to this? 1725 DE FOE *Voy. round World* (1840) 253 Innumerable rills..falling from the cliffs, making a barbarous and unpleasant sound. 1796 MME. D'ARBLAY *Camilla* IV. 223 The aspect of Mrs. Mittin..was..unpleasant to him. 1879 LUBBOCK *Sci. Lect.* ii. 32 Flies prefer unpleasant smells, such as those of decaying meat. 1892 *Photogr. Ann.* II. 103 A dilute solution..changes the colour of the image to a not unpleasant brown.
*Comb.* 1869 TOZER *Highl. Turkey* II. 109 A most unpleasant-looking piece of water, marshy and full of reeds.
**b.** To the mind or feelings.
1535 COVERDALE *Ecclus.* xxii. 6 Euen so is the..doctryne of wyszdome euer vnpleasaunt vnto fooles. a 1568 ASCHAM *Scholem.* II. (Arb.) 132 Preceptes in all Authors..without applying vnto them the Imitation of examples, be..barrayn, vnfruitfull and vnpleasant. 1596 SHAKS. *Merch. V.* III. ii. 254 The vnpleasant'st words That euer blotted paper. a 1679 HOBBES *Rhet.* I. xi. (1681) 28 Unpleasant are those things, which proceed from Necessity, as Cares, Study, Contentions. c 1721 MRQ. TULLIBARDINE in *10th Rep. Hist. MSS. Comm.* App. I. 126 Tho' your Majesty permitts me to wryte even on ane unpleasant subject. 1762 GOLDSM. *Nash* 200 That a man of pleasure leads the most unpleasant life in the world. 1839 THIRLWALL *Greece* III. xxvi. 419 To execute a commission which would require them to deliver many un-

pleasant truths. **1875** JOWETT *Plato* (ed. 2) I. 466 All of us ..had an unpleasant feeling at hearing them say this.

**2.** Unentertaining, unfacetious.

**1712** *Spect.* No. 408 ⁋ 4 It would be no unpleasant Notion, to consider the several Species of Brutes, into which we may imagine that Tyrants..might be changed. **1768** *Junius Lett.* (1850) II. 220 In his assertions..there is something really not unpleasant...It puts me in mind of the consulship which Caligula intended for his horse.

**3.** Unamiable.

**1654** [see UNPLEASING *ppl. a.* b].

Hence **Unplea·santish** *a.*

**1827** HOOD *Parthian Glance* 28, I can't but..pronounce 'Heads or tails' with a child, an unpleasantish game. **1844** — *Etching Moralised* 229 'Tis a rather unpleasantish job.

**Unplea·santly,** *adv.* (UN-[1] 11.)

**1549** COVERDALE, etc. *Erasm. Par. Rom.* 34 Let him, that hath, gyue hym some thyng, not louryngly and vnpleasantly, ..but euen as one that rekeneth al he hath commen. **1551** BP. GARDINER *Explic., Christes Presence* 70 b, If fleshe did appeare, we should be vnpleasauntly disposed to the communion of it. **1677** GREW *Anat. Fruits* iv. § 6 A White Corin, without taking off the Skin, sheweth not unpleasantly how the Seeds are fastned. **1718** DIGBY in Pope *Wks.* (1751) VIII. 34 We don't live unpleasantly in primitive simplicity and good-humour. **1818** BYRON *Juan* I. ccxx, You've pass'd your youth not so unpleasantly. **1861** GEO. ELIOT *Silas M.* iv, The lane was becoming unpleasantly slippery.

*Comb.* **1804** WOLCOT (P. Pindar) *Gt. Cry* To Pitt, Machinery which has contracted a most unpleasantly-looking rust.

**Unplea·santness.** [UN-[1] 12.] The quality of being unpleasant. (Also with *a* and pl.)

**1548** ELYOT, *Iniucunditas*, vnpleasauntnesse. **1594** O. B. *Quest. Profit. Concern.* K 3 b, I stand in very little neede..to haue these vnpleasantnesses renued or made lasting vnto me. **1596** BARROUGH *Meth. Physick* VIII. 461 So great inconuenience and vnpleasauntnesse of tast. **1603** HOLLAND *Plutarch's Mor.* 1156 The Mathematical rudiments which children be taught, at the beginning trouble them..; but this unpleasantnesse continueth not alwaies with them. **1635** J. SWAN *Spec. M.* vi. § 2 (1643) 201 Sea-water..by passing through divers windings..of the earth, is deprived of all unpleasantnesse. *a* **1665** GOODWIN *Filled with the Spirit* (1670) 394 Which would occasion a great disparagement and unpleasantness in the World. **1808** L. MURRAY *Eng. Gram.* I. 455 Here there is some degree of harshness and unpleasantness [in the rhythm]. **1830** WORDSW. in C. Wordsw. *Mem.* (1851) II. 226 Another unpleasantness arose from the same cause. **1852** DICKENS *Bleak Ho.* xlv, I have made some advances out of pocket to accommodate these unpleasantnesses.

**Unplea·santry.** [UN-[1] 12.] Unpleasantness.

**1830** 'JON BEE' in *Wks. S. Foote* IV. p. xli, It would have been well..if this were all the unpleasantry to which he subjected himself. **1844** ALB. SMITH *Adv. Mr. Ledbury* xvi, Had he allowed himself to be depressed by every unpleasantry, he would have had a sad time of it. **1847** DE QUINCEY in *Tait's Mag.* XIV. 520 Without any 'unpleasantries' occurring. *Ibid.* Note, 'Unpleasantries'..is a new word, launched a very few years back in some commercial towns. **1883** BURTON & CAMERON *Gold Coast* I. i. 16 A very low barometer, which suggested unpleasantries.

**Unplea·sed,** *ppl. a.* [UN-[1] 8.]

**1.** Not pleased; displeased. Now *rare.*

*c* **1450** tr. *De Imitatione* III. xxv. 96 As ofte tymes as I fele me unplesid & greved. **1520** CAXTON *Chron. Eng.* IV. 33/1 It was no meruayle all though the prynce was vnpleased. **1593** SHAKS. *Rich. II,* III. iii. 193 Me rather had, my Heart might feele your Loue, Then my vnpleas'd Eye see your Courtesie. **1613** CHAPMAN *Rev. Bussy d'Ambois* III. F 3 b, Hee that vnpleas'd to hold his place, will range. **1692** WASHINGTON tr. *Milton's Def. Pop.* ii. Wks. 1851 VIII. 65 God..was extreamly unpleas'd with them for asking a King. **1733** HERVEY *Mem. Geo.* (1848) I. 198 A sort of unpleased smile. **1762** COWPER *Miss Macartney* 64 The phlegm of sullen elves, Who..Extend no care beyond themselves, Unpleasing and unpleas'd. **1831** WORDSW. *Avon* 14 Never.. may the good Shrink from thy name, pure Rill, with unpleased ears. **1901** CLIVE HOLLAND *Mousmé* 204 Glances of frank admiration which Lou looked not unpleased to see.

†**2.** Unpaid. *Obs.*[−1]

**1604** MIDDLETON *Father Hubburd's T.* F 3, I am not worth ..three farthings: beside my Lodging vnpleasde.

**Unplea·sing,** *ppl. a.* [UN-[1] 10, 5 b.] Not pleasing; displeasing, unpleasant: **a.** To the senses.

*c* **1480** HENRYSON *Test. Cres.* 338, I mak Thy voice sa cleir, vnplesand, hoir, and hace. **1595** SHAKS. *John* III. i. 45 If thou..wert grim, Vgly,..Full of vnpleasing blots and sightlesse staines. **1617** WOODALL *Surg. Mate* (1639) 344 It hath an unpleasing taste. **1670** BAXTER *Cure Church-Div.* 169 Some of them will not take such unpleasing medicines. **1770** SIR J. REYNOLDS *Disc.* iii. (1778) 83 [Such] a figure..may still have a certain union of the various parts, which may contribute to make them on the whole, not unpleasing. **1797** DALLAWAY *Constantinople* v. 86 A man of rank, remarkably unpleasing in his countenance and figure. **1817** STEPHENS in Shaw *Gen. Zool.* X. II. 476 Each leap being accompanied by a note that is far from unpleasing. **1867** LADY HERBERT *Cradle L.* i. 15 Instruments which sounded unpleasing to English ears.

**b.** To the mind or feelings.

**1533** BELLENDEN *Livy* IV. ii. (S.T.S.) II. 57 ȝe wald defend sic thingis vnder colour of ȝoure rigorus & vnplesand lawis. **1588** SHAKS. *L. L. L.* v. ii. 912 Cuckow, Cuckow: O word of feare, Vnpleasing to a married eare. **1605** *Gunpowder Plot* in *Harl. Misc.* (Malh.) III. 5, I thought it would not be unpleasing unto thee to join them together in the press. **1654** GATAKER *Disc. Apol.* 43 These Digressions ..will not be unpleasing to a Reader of no over-rigid and unpleasant Disposition. **1735** JOHNSON *Lobo's Abyssinia, Descr.* xv. 140 To put the unpleasing Remembrance of our past Labours out of our Minds. **1818** SCOTT *Br. Lamm.* ix, The first thing which recalled him to those unpleasing circumstances. **1885** *Manch. Exam.* 6 July 4/6 The appointment in itself must be unpleasing to the English Government.

**Unplea·singly,** *adv.* (UN-[1] 11.)

**1597** MORLEY *Introd. Mus.* 82, I thinke it goeth but vnpleasinglie to the eare. **1623** BINGHAM *Xenophon* 27 Young man you looke like a Philosopher, and speake not vnpleasingly. **1633** BP. HALL *Occas. Medit.* 319 This flowre is but unpleasingly fulsome for sent. **1852** MUNDY *Antipodes* III. viii. 251 The Van Diemonians, as they unpleasingly call themselves. **1862** CALVERLEY *Verses & Transl.* (ed. 2) 36 A happy child,..Not unpleasingly apparelled In a tightish suit of blue.

**Unplea·singness.** (UN-[1] 12.)

**1611** COTGR., *Mauplaisance*, vnpleasantnesse, vnpleasingnesse. **1652** HEYLYN *Cosmogr.* I. 123 The misery and unpleasingness of his present condition. **1673** O. WALKER *Educ.* 228 A corrective to the harshness and unpleasingness of the other. **1727** BAILEY (vol. II) s.v. *Unpleasantness.*

†**Unplea·sive,** *a. Obs.*[−1] (UN-[1] 7.) **1644** BP. HALL *Rem. Wks.* (1660) 108 Grief is never but an unpleasive passion; the rest have some life and contentment in them.

**Unplea·surable,** *a.* (UN-[1] 7 b.)

**1768–74** TUCKER *Lt. Nat.* (1834) I. 373 Many of our waking hours pass irksome and insipid, unprofitable to others, and unpleasurable to ourselves. **1796** CHARLOTTE SMITH *Marchmont* IV. 183 Unpleasurable sensations. **1860** RUSKIN *Mod. Paint.* V. IX. xi. § 22 Let no technical labour be wasted on things useless or unpleasurable. **1879** MRS. A. W. HUNT *Basildon* II. xvi. 288 The visit, though a melancholy one, would not be wholly unpleasurable to him!

**Unplea·surably,** *adv.* (UN-[1] 11.) **1826–7** DE QUINCEY *Lessing* Wks. 1859 XIII. 300 The comic interest..would at once disarm the inherent meanness in the subject, of all power to affect us unpleasurably. **Unplea·sure.** (UN-[1] 12.) **1814** COLERIDGE *Lett.* (1895) 639, I don't like to use any words that might give you *un*pleasure. **1839** J. HODGSON in Raine *Mem.* (1858) II. 411 Walked about half a mile with great unpleasure. **Unplea·t,** *v.* (UN-[2] 3.) **1614** J. DAVIES (Heref.) *Eclogue* 17 Droope not for that (man) but vnpleate thy browes. **1648** HEXHAM II, *Het haer ontvlechten,* to unpleat or untie ones Haire.

**Unplea·ted,** *ppl. a.* (UN-[1] 8.)

**1612** W. PARKES *Curtaine-Dr.* (1876) 54 Let not the seruant with vnpleated browes and presented innocency abuse the trust committed to his charge. **1648** HEXHAM II, *Ongeploýt,* Vnfoulded, or Vnpleated. **1889** *Daily News* 22 Oct. 6/1 These are necessarily in unpleated material, in order to give firmness to the whole.

**Unple·dged,** *ppl. a.* (UN-[1] 8.)

**1605** CHAPMAN *All Fools* v. ii. 68 *Val.* Ile be their pledge. *For.* Not yet Valerio; This hee must drinke unpledgd. **1630** J. TAYLOR (Water P.) *Thiefe* Wks. II. 123/1 If a Drunkard be vnpledgd a kan. **1741–2** GRAY *Agrippina* 21 They are aware Of th' unpledg'd bowl. **1823** S. ROGERS *Italy* 160 For deeds of violence..came the unpledged bowl, The stab of the stiletto. **1834** MOORE *Mem.* (1856) VII. 24 Sir Robert Peel..is unpledged to any one for his next turn at the Charter House.

**Unple·nished,** *ppl. a.* Chiefly *Sc.* (UN-[1] 8.)

**1535** *Sc. Acts, Jas. V* (1814) II. 346/2 Ane grete part of þe Realme .. hes bene þir mony ȝeris .. vnplenissit. **1535** STEWART *Cron. Scot.* (Rolls) II. 532 Mony sted wnpleneist lyand waist. **1857** J. HAMILTON *Lessons fr. Gt. Biog.* 290 In a lonely unplenished room.

**Unple·t,** *ppl. a. Sc.* [UN-[1] 8 b.] Unplaited. *c* **1425** WYNTOUN *Cron.* II. i. 49 The tane half of hir haire vnplet. †**Unpley·ed,** *ppl. a. Sc. Obs.*[−1] [UN-[1] 8.] Not assailed at law. **1445** *Sc. Acts, Jas. II* (1814) II. 33/2 All & sindri landis..as his fadir broukit þaim vndemandit and unpleyit of ony man befor ony Juge.

**Unpli·able,** *a.* [UN-[1] 7 b, 5 b.]

**1.** Unyielding, obstinate, stubborn.

*c* **1400** *Wycliffite Bible* Heb. x. 23 We..holde the confessioun of oure hope vnbowynge [*v.r.* vnpliable; L. *indeclinabilem*]. **1603** HOLLAND *Plutarch's Mor.* 687 Their stiffenesse and unpliable disposition, the roughnesse also of their skinne, argueth their dry nature. **1627** I. BARGRAVE *Serm.* 4 Wee are all as oxen unpliable to the yoake. **1652** URQUHART *Jewel* 250 Such..sinners as should prove unpliable to the stamp of his wholesome admonitions. **1774** REID *Aristotle's Logic* IV. § 3 It is somewhat unpliable to rules. **1885** S. COX *Expositions* I. 101 He saw a new heaven and a new earth,..free from all that renders it hostile or unpliable to the spirit of man.

**2.** Unbending, inelastic, stiff. Also *fig.*

**1622** F. MARKHAM *Bk. War* I. x. 38 Buckram..is too stiffe and unplyable. **1747** COOKE in Hanway *Trav.* IV. lvi. (1762) I. 260 The paper was very hard and unpliable. **1759** *Phil. Trans.* LI. 290 [Wires] so unpliable and brittle, as to be rendered quite useless. **1773** JOHNSON 8 Oct. in Boswell *Tour Hebrides,* She had no notion of a joke,..had a mighty unpliable understanding. **1806** FORSYTH *Beauties Scotl.* IV. 31 The spruce..has unpliable branches. **1825** SCOTT *Betrothed* iii, A broad countenance, with heavy and unpliable features.

Hence **Unpli·ableness.**

**1635** BRATHWAIT *Arcad. Pr.* 99, I feele very usually such a stiffnesse, or unpliablenesse in my selfe. *c* **1720** GIBSON *Diet Horses* i. (1731) 11 From an Unpliableness or Straitness of the Ligaments. **1754** HUME *Hist. England* I. 158 That the commons,..by their unpliableness and independance, were insensibly changing. **1787** BEST *Angling* (ed. 2) 9 The line by reason of their unpliableness must be much endangered.

**Unpli·ancy.** (UN-[1] 12; cf. next.)

**1737** BRACKEN *Farriery Impr.* (1757) II. 106 The Stiffness and Unpliancy of our Limbs. **1831** CARLYLE *Misc. Ess., Schiller,* In all other provinces exhibiting a certain inaptitude, an elephantine unpliancy. **1842** PRICHARD *Nat. Hist. Man* 494 The aboriginal American is at once in the incapacity of infancy and unpliancy of old age.

**Unpli·ant,** *a.* [UN-[1] 7.]

**1.** Not bending readily or easily; stiff.

**1624** WOTTON *Archit.* 89 The Chissell..being so hard an Instrument, and working vpon so vnpliant stuffe. **1720** WELTON *Suffer. Son of God* II. xvii. 465 Like Iron, which is..unpliant, when it is not throughly softened by the Forge. **1735** SOMERVILLE *Chase* III. 120 His stiff unpliant Limbs Rooted in Earth, unmov'd..he stands. **1791** COWPER *Odyss.* XXI. 208 Thou wast not born to bend The unpliant bow, or to direct the shaft. **1825** GOOD *Study Med.* (ed. 2) IV. 330 We..render the dejected muscles torpid and unpliant. **1855** MILMAN *Lat. Chr.* XIV. x. VI. 610 The beautiful but too regular face, or the hard, but not entirely unpliant form.

**2.** Unyielding, obstinate, stubborn.

**1659** EVELYN *Char. Eng.* 40 Ill Courtiers, unplyant, morose, and of vulgar address. **1674** *Govt. Tongue* 178 Men are.. prone in all companies to arraign such an unpliant Person, as if he were an enemy to mankind. **1710** *Tatler* No. 214 ⁋ 1 These are Persons of a stubborn, unpliant Morality. **1768–74** TUCKER *Lt. Nat.* (1834) II. 591 The love of rectitude becomes a preciseness and rigidity unpliant to the common occasions of life. **1821** JOANNA BAILLIE *Metr. Leg., Lady G. B.* li, The dull unpliant dame refused. **1822** GOOD *Study Med.* IV. 195 *Parodynia Implastica.* Unpliant Labour.

**3.** Not easily adapted or managed.

**1717** ADDISON *Ovid's Met.* III. Notes, The short speeches ..which make the Latin very natural, cannot appear so well in our language, which is more stubborn and unpliant. **1751** JOHNSON *Rambler* No. 173 ⁋ 12 By him who..enters late into the gay world with an unpliant attention and established habits.

**Unpli·antly,** *adv.* (UN-[1] 11.) [JOHNSON s.v. *Rigidly.*]

**Unpli·ght,** *sb. Obs.* or *dial.* [UN-[1] 4 b.] Evil plight; danger, risk.

Cf. mod. Whitby dial. *unplight*, a state of disorder.

*c* **1330** *Assump. Virg.* (B.M. MS.) 194 ȝif I any þinge haue mys wrouȝt,..I it wole amende with my myȝt, That my soule haue no vnplyȝt.

†**Unpli·ght, unpli·te,** *v. Obs.* [UN-[2] 3: see PLIGHT *v.*[2]] *trans.* To unfold; *fig.* to evolve.

*c* **1374** CHAUCER *Boeth.* v. met. iv. (1868) 167 Yif þe þriuyng soule ne vnplitiþ no þing, þat is to sein ne doþ no þing by hys propre moeuynges. *c* **1430** *Pilgr. Lyf Manhode* III. lvi. (1869) 164 The Scripture j vndide, and vnplytede it, and redde it. **1511** *Guylforde's Pilgr.* (Camden) 50 Ther was delyuerd to hym y^e^ booke of Isaie y^e^ prophete, and as he vnplight the booke he founde the place [etc.].

†**Unpli·table,** *a. Obs.*[−1] (UN-[1] 7 b + *plite* PLIGHT *v.*[2]; intended to render L. *inexplicābilis.*) *c* **1420** *Chaucer's Boeth.* I. pr. iv. (1876) 9 Whan..ther was estabelissed.. greuos and vnplitable [*v.r.* inplitable] coempcion. **Unplo·tted,** *ppl. a.* (UN-[1] 8.) **1598** J. DICKENSON *Greene in Conc.* (1878) 123 Leauing no deuice vnplotted, no deceipt vnpractised to make gratious her gracelesse selfe.

**Unplou·ghed,** *ppl. a.* [UN-[1] 8, 8 c. Cf. Du. *ongeploegd*, MLG. *ungeploget*, MSw. *oplögdher* (Sw. *oplöjd*), Da. *upløjet*, Norw. *upløgd.*]

**1.** Not turned up by the plough. Also with *up.*

**1580** LUPTON *Sivqila* 25 What is it to sowe seede uppon the grasse or greene swarde, unplowed or undigged? **1613** W. BROWNE *Brit. Past.* I. ii. 328 Like to that smell, which oft our sense descries Within a field which long unplowed lyes. **1649** LOVELACE *The Scrutinie* iii, Like skilfull Minerallists that sound For Treasure in un-plow'd-up ground. **1765** A. DICKSON *Treat. Agric.* (ed. 2) 42 Allow two fields to lie unplowed;..they will produce very different plants. **1832** *Scoreby Farm Rep.* 4 in *Husb.* III. (L.U.K.), The ridge freshly turned up then covers the unploughed ground. **1891** MALDEN *Tillage* 106 To throw the split-furrows on to the unploughed land.

*transf.* **1839** HALLAM *Hist. Lit.* II. 287 The daring adventurer that violates their unploughed waters. **1859** MAURY *Phys. Geog.* ii. 38 This unploughed sea would be an oft-used thoroughfare. **1864** BRYANT *New & Old* 21 Brows unploughed by care.

**2.** Of books: Not trimmed with the plough.

**1886** *W. George's Catal.* No. 129. 1 Cloth and boarded books are always edges unplowed (if so issued.)

**Unplou·ghing,** *vbl. sb.* (UN-[2] 8, 3.) **1740** TULL *Horse-hoeing Husb.* (1822) xiii. 166 The second is a sort of unploughing, for it turns the turf the same side uppermost as before it was ploughed at all.

**Unplu·cked,** *ppl. a.* (UN-[1] 8, 8 c. Cf. Du. *ongeplukt*, older Da. *uplukket*, Sw. *oplockad.*)

**1568** SKEYNE *Pest* (1860) 8 The third part of the people.. war not left vnplukit away, be sic ane..manslayar. **1610** G. FLETCHER *Christ's Tri.* I. lviii, And you sweete flow'rs,.. Your selues vnpluckt would to his funerals hie. **1659** W. CHAMBERLAYNE *Pharonnida* I. iii. 75 His hands bereft His hoary head of all that time had left Unplucked before. **1819** CRABBE *T. of Hall* VIII. 860 The green cold moss above it grown, Unpluck'd of all but maiden hand. **1878** BROWNING *Poets Croisic* vii, Unplucked grace Of soul, ungathered beauty. **1889** CLARK RUSSELL *Marooned* vi. (1890) 27 The bird came to the table.. somewhat prickly with unplucked quills.

**Unplu·g,** *v.* (UN-[2] 4.)

[**1775** ASH.] **1840** R. H. DANA *Bef. Mast* xxx, By unplugging the holes, we let the soap-suds off the decks. **1876** PREECE & SIVEWRIGHT *Telegraphy* 270 The whole of the resistance in each arm..should be unplugged.

**Unplu·mb,** *a.* (UN-[1] 7.) **1828** CARLYLE in Froude *Life* (1882) II. 27 She watches over her joiners..with an eye like any hawk's, from which nothing crooked, unplumb or otherwise irregular can hide itself. **Unplu·mb,** *v.* [UN-[2] 4.] *trans.* To take out of lead coffins. **1796** BURKE *Let. to Noble Lord* Wks. VIII. 6 They unplumb the dead for bullets to assassinate the living. [**1845** FORD *Handbk. Spain* I. III. 389 Nor have the dead been unplumbed to furnish missiles of death against the living.]

**Unplu·mbed,** *ppl. a.* [UN-[1] 8.] Unsounded, unfathomed.

**1623** W. C[RASHAW] *Fatal Vesper* B 4 b, The height whereof mans vnderstanding cannot aspire vnto, nor the vnplummeld [*sic*] depth thereof sinke vnto. *c* **1852** M. ARNOLD *Isolation* iv, The unplumb'd, salt, estranging sea. **1892** STEVENSON *Across the Plains* 216 Justice is not done to..the unplumbed childishness of man's imagination.

**Unplu·me,** *v.* [UN-[2] 4. Cf. Du. *ontpluimen.*]

**1.** *trans.* To strip of plumes or feathers. Also in fig. context.

**1587** GREENE *Carde of Fancie* (1593) I 3 b, He would vnplume thee of all his feathers, that like Æsops Crow thou mightest receiue the reward of thy rashnesse. **1608** L. Machin *Dumbe Knt.* I, Envies sword, Which like a rasor shall unplume thy crest. **1673** *Lady's Call.* I. i. § 28 Should we have the like distinction observed, I fear many of our gaiest birds would be unplumed. **1744** H. Brooke *Love & Van.* 95 She..Exalts the meek..; Of Pride unplumes the lofty crest. **1804** Charlotte Smith *Conversations*, etc. II. 202 The nest is robbed, and she a second time unplumes herself for the accommodation of her young. **1841** Lady F. Hastings *Poems* 212 When Time's allotted course is done, His wings unplumed, his hour-glass run.

**2.** *fig.* To deprive of distinction, prestige, etc.

**1626** T. H[awkins] *Caussin's Holy Crt.* 82 Ladyes of court vnplume him, other women..filch from him. **1641** J. Shute *Sarah & Hagar* (1649) 55 God can soon unplume us, and take away that which swelleth us so. **1725** Pope *Odyss.* xix. 104 Her lov'd Lord [may] unplume thy tow'ring pride. **1744** E. Moore *Fables* xiv. 301 The partner of thy scorn'd embrace, Shall play the wanton in thy face, Each spark unplume thy little pride.

Hence **Unplu·ming** *vbl. sb.*

**1592** Nashe *P. Pennilesse* E 2 b, We delight..in the vnpluming of pullerie, and quartering of Calues and Oxen.

**Unplu·med,** *a.* [Un-1 8. Cf. Du. *ongepluimd.*] Not furnished with plumes or feathers.

[**1598** Florio, *Spennato*, vnfeathered vnplumed.] **1601** Holland *Pliny* I. 338 They will..kill young pigeons whiles they be calow and unplumed. **1638** Davenant *Madagascar* 3 Their Arrowes were unplum'd, Their Bowes unstrung. **1777** Potter *Æschylus, Agamemnon* 217 Like vulturs, which, their unplumed offspring lost, Whirl many a rapid flight. **1804** *Europ. Mag.* XLV. 413/2 Whether it was..plain or coloured, plumed or unplumed, covered or uncovered. **1871** H. King *Ovid's Met.* vi. 946 Not with their birth Those pinions came;..young Calaïs And Zethes grew unplumed.

*fig.* **1818** Milman *Samor* vii. 267 Had it seem'd love, her very pride had quell'd The unplum'd phantasy.

**Unplummed,** obs. var. Unplumbed *ppl. a.*

**Unplu·ndered,** *ppl. a.* (Un-1 8. Cf. Du. *ongeplunderd*, Sw. *oplundrad.*)

**1655** Fuller *Ch. Hist.* ix. v. § 9, I count it a blessing that providence hath preserved such a treasure unplundred. **1855** Singleton *Virgil* II. 460 Then I..The pitiable corse, and arms Unplundered, to the sepulchre will bear. **1865** J. Cameron *Malayan India* 263 To waste your time cutting the throat of a dead man while his house is yet unplundered.

**Unplu·nge,** *v.* (Un-2 3.) *a* **1645** Heywood *Fort. by Land & Sea* III. iii, Any meanes that can unplunge me from this gulf of trouble.

**Unply·,** *v.* [Un-2 3.] *trans.* To unfold, unfurl.

*c* **1330** *Arth. & Merl.* 5063 (Kölbing), Þese Sarrazins þo gun vnplie Her baners & after heiȝe. **13..** *K. Alis.* 3000 (Laud MS.), A clerk gan þe lettre vnplye. **1830** James *De L'Orme* xxviii, A pistole for every fold he unplied in the rich white silk.

**Unpo·cket,** *v.* (Un-2 5.)

**1611** Florio, *Sgaglioffare*,..to vnpouch or vnpocket. **1844** Tupper *Heart* xi. 104 Mutual participation in profit and loss:..the bookseller pocketing the first, and the author unpocketing the second. **1894** A. Morrison *Mean Streets* 136 Sam unpocketed a greasy paper.

Hence **Unpo·cketed** *ppl. a.*

**1797** Mrs. M. Robinson *Walsingham* I. 102 A thousand times..did my eyes glance..at my unpocketed guinea.

**Unpoe·tic,** *a.* (Un-1 7. Cf. next.)

? **1619** Corbet *Death Q. Anne* Poems (1672) 126 Do not..for an Epithite that fails, Bite off your Unpoetick Nails. **1786** Miss Seward in *Mrs. Delany's Life & Corr.* (1862) III. 395, I have seen nothing of him since he sunk into his very unpoetic union. **1812** J. Wilson *Isle of Palms*, etc. 371 Light Fauns, That the good owner's unpoetic soul Could not.. Imagine. **1863** 'Ouida' *Held in Bondage* vi, There is something unpoetic, and coarse,..about blood and bruises.

*Comb.* **1865** G. Macdonald *A. Forbes* xxxix, The most unpoetic-looking Mr. Cupples.

**Unpoe·tical,** *a.* (Un-1 7. Cf. prec.)

*a* **1746** Holdsworth *Remarks Virgil* (1768) 270 Ruæus's interpreting..is very unpoetical. **1776** Mickle *Camoens' Lusiad* Introd. 149 A loose unpoetical paraphrase of the Lusiad. **1812** *Examiner* 4 May 284/1 The unpoetical lucubrations of Lord Coke. **1861** Paley *Æschylus* (ed. 2) *Persians* 547 The superlative is here tame and unpoetical.

**Unpoe·tically,** *adv.* (Un-1 11.)

**1697** Dryden *Virgil* Notes 633 How unpoetically and baldly had this been translated: Thou shalt Marcellus be! **1756** J. Warton *Ess. Pope* I. 7 How coldly and unpoetically Pope has copied the subsequent appeal to the nymphs. **1786** Mrs. Delany *Life & Corr.* (1862) II. 358 My poor muse has been asleep these thirty years, during which time I have been very unpoetically..employed!

**Unpo·etized,** *ppl. a.* (Un-1 8.) **1831** Scott *Jrnl.* 26 Nov., I got home about midnight; but remain unpoetised and unspeeched. **Unpoi·nded,** *ppl. a.* (Un-1 8.) **1533** *Extr. Aberd. Reg.* (1844) I. 149 Gif he thollis ony bestis to cum in the kyrkyerd frathinfurtht vnpundyt. **1539** *Reg. Privy Seal Scot.* II. 472/2 The said Johnne to be..unpowndit and untrublit for ony actioun civile bigane.

**Unpoi·nted,** *ppl. a.* [Un-1 8.]

†**1.** Not furnished with tagged points or laces. *Obs.*

**1574** Hellowes tr. *Gueuara's Fam. Ep.* (1577) 254 His shirt ragged, his doublet lose and vnpoynted.

**2. a.** Not punctuated.

**1593** Marlowe *Edw. II*, v. iv, But read it thus, and thats an other sence:..Vnpointed as it is, thus shall it goe. **1641** Prynne *Antip.* 267 This ambiguous sentence unpointed, they take for a sufficient warrant, and most pittifully murthered the innocent King. **1655** Fuller *Ch. Hist.* III. 107 He returned unto them a Ridling Answere, altogether unpointed.

**b.** Not provided with vowel-points or similar marks.

**1640** Sir E. Dering *Carmelite* (1641) 30 Three words in Greek, whereof one was unpointed. **1659** Bp. Walton *Consid. Considered* 278 There is no such uncertainty in the Text unpointed, as is pretended by them. **1778** Bp. Lowth *Transl. Isaiah* Notes 236 It is upon a rasure in a third; and left unpointed at first, as suspected, in a fourth. **1845** *Proc. Philol. Soc.* II. 172 An *i*, written in certain cases, but more generally in unpointed texts only perceptible in the pronunciation. **1877** Caird *Philos. Kant* 203 Like the reader of unpointed Hebrew, who supplies for himself the vowels.

**3.** Not furnished with a point; lacking point or finish.

**1632** B. Jonson *Magn. Lady* IV. iii, *Pro.* Which, ending here, would have shown dull, flat, and unpointed; without any shape or sharpness. **1681** Dryden *Abs. & Achit.* II. 502 But thou in Clumsy verse, unlickt, unpointed, Hast Shamefully defi'd the Lord's Anointed. **1887** Bowen *Æneid* VI. 760 [He] leans on a lance unpointed and bright.

**4.** Not pointed *at.*

*a* **1555** J. Philpot *Apol.* (1559) A 5 b, That the simple people maye beware of their Pharisaical venome,..suffre them not to passe by you vnpointed at. **1642** Howell *For. Trav.* (Arb.) 13 Yet one's..personall conversation will still find out something new and unpointed at by any other.

**Unpoi·nting,** *vbl. sb.* [Un-1 13.] Omission of punctuation. **1612** T. James *Corrupt. Script.* v. 10 The transposition..of words, or vnpointing of Books,..doe so farre alter the sense, and obscure the Author. **Unpoi·nting,** *ppl. a.* (Un-1 10.) **1814** *Monthly Mag.* XXXVII. 240 She too stands mute, th' unpointing fingers fall.

**Unpoi·se,** *v.* (Un-2 3.)

**1700** S. Parker *Six Phil. Essays* 50 Instead of poizing, I look upon such a mass as rather fitted to unpoize and break the mystick Chains upon which the body of the earth hangs. **1800** Coleridge *Tri. Loyalty* 372 The violent pull.. Unpois'd me and I fell. **1824** Syd. Smith *Wks.* (1859) II. 185/2 The balance of Justice is unpoised.

**Unpoi·sed,** *ppl. a.* [Un-1 8.] Unbalanced.

*c* **1600** W. Fowler *Wks.* (S.T.S.) I. 260, Vnpoized hambers strikes vntimely howers. **1735** Thomson *Liberty* II. 150 Oft on the brink Of ruin..Totter'd the rash Democracy; unpois'd. **1827** Hood *Mids. Fairies* lxi, Languid fish, unpois'd, grow sick and yearn. **1903** W. H. Hudson *Rousseau* 7 The restless, flighty, unpoised Jean Jacques.

**Unpoi·son,** *v.* (Un-2 6 b.)

**1598** Florio, *Suelenire*, .. to vnpoison, to vnrankle. *c* **1620** in Farr *S. P. Jas.* (1848) 99 When sin befriends us, 'tis that we should dread The mighty one, that sin unpoisoned hath. **1644** G. Plattes in *Hartlib's Legacy* (1655) 174 Their minds are so poysoned, that there is no other way to unpoyson them, but to win their belief. *c* **1685** South *Serm.* (1717) V. 43 Such a Course could not, but in a short time, have Unpoisoned their perverted Minds. **1868** Browning *Ring & Bk.* v. 1038, I was shaken wide awake, Doctored and drenched, somewhat unpoisoned so. **1896** in *Westm. Gaz.* 17 Sept. 5/1 His mind has been poisoned and 'unpoisoned', and he is now..open to receive information.

**Unpoi·sonable,** *a.* (Un-1 7 b.) **1628** Feltham *Resolves* II. lxxix. 226 It fell out to be part of Mithridates misery, that hee had made himselfe vnpoisonable.

**Unpoi·soned,** *ppl. a.* (Un-1 8.)

[**1775** Ash.] **1821** Lamb *Elia* I. *Old Benchers I. T.*, So may the sparrows..unpoisoned hop about your walks! **1859** R. F. Burton *Centr. Afr.* in *Jrnl. Geog. Soc.* XXIX. 197 Bows and arrows, the latter unpoisoned, but..cruelly barbed.

**Unpoi·sonous,** *a.* (Un-1 7.) *a* **1843** *Encycl. Metrop.* (1845) VII. 306/2 The Unpoisonous,..the Fang-less Poisonous, and..the Fanged Poisonous Snakes. **Unpo·lar,** *a.* (Un-1 7.) **1856** Tyndall *Fragm. Sci.* (1879) I. 374 A simple unpolar force.

**Unpo·larized,** *ppl. a.* (Un-1 8.)

**1827–8** Herschel in *Encycl. Metrop.* (1845) IV. 524 The unpolarized portion [of light] will continue to be half transmitted. **1856** Scoffern in *Orr's Circ. Sci., Pract. Chem.* 96 Whether the..rays be polarized or unpolarized. **1871** B. Stewart *Heat* (ed. 2) § 179 If the vibrations have no reference to any particular plane, then the wave is unpolarized.

**Unpoli·ced,** *ppl. a.* (Un-1 8.) [**1775** Ash.] *a* **1797** H. Walpole *Mem. Geo. III* (1845) III. vii. 220 In a vast capital,—free, ungoverned, unpoliced, and indifferent to everything but its pleasures and factions!

**Unpo·licied,** *ppl. a.* (Un-1 8.)

**1606** Shaks. *Ant. & Cl.* v. ii. 311 Oh could'st thou speake, That I might heare thee call great Cæsar, Asse, vnpolicied. **1654** Whitlock *Zootomia* 448 The unpolicied Schollar. **1738** Warburton *Div. Legat.* I. 75 [Modern savages] being yet unpolicied, and in a State of Nature.

**Unpo·lish,** *v.* (Un-2 3.)

*a* **1697** Aubrey *Lives* (1898) I. 216 Denham was unpolished with the small pox: otherwise a fine complexion. **1748** Richardson *Clarissa* (1768) V. 261 How anger unpolishes the most polite! **1823** Moore *Mem.* (1853) IV. 69 His chimney pieces, by Bartollini, spoiled from over-polish; hopes to be able to un-polish them again.

**Unpo·lishable,** *a.* (Un-1 7 b.)

**1687** J. Reynolds *Death's Vis.* Pref. (1713) 3 'Tis true such Matter is Restive, Refractory and Unpolishable Enough. *a* **1797** H. Walpole *Mem. Geo. II* (1822) I. 170 The duke's outside was unpolished, his inside unpolishable. **1836** Landor *Pericles & Asp.* Wks. 1846 II. 416 A coarse grained, unpolishable people. **1863** Hawthorne *Old Home* (1879) 344 The unpolishable ruggedness of the native character.

**Unpo·lished,** *ppl. a.* [Un-1 8, 5 b.]

**1.** Not made smooth or bright by polishing.

**1382** Wyclif *Deut.* xxvii. 6 An auter..of stonus vnfourmed and vnpolishid. *c* **1475** *Cath. Angl.* 293/1 (A.), Vn Pulysched .., *jmpolitus.* **1552** Huloet, Vnpollished, and not perfitly wrought, *raudus.* **1605** Bacon *Adv. Learn.* II. xvii. § 13 The better sort of Rules haue beene not vnfitly compared to glasses of steele vnpullished. **1662** J. Bargrave *Pope Alex. VII* (1867) 122 Another thin piece of jasper stone, unpollished. **1751** Johnson *Rambler* No. 166 ¶ 3 Fortitude, and probity,..are cast aside like unpolished gems. **1815** J. Smith *Panorama Sci. & Art* I. 5 If the tool be unpolished. **1874** J. Geikie *Gt. Ice Age* vi. 73 Rough, unpolished angular fragments that have tumbled..from cliffs.

*transf.* **1635** Swan *Spec. M.* iii. § 2 (1643) 48 Both of them [*sc.* the heavens] remained as it were unpolished or unfinished untill the fourth day.

**2.** Inelegant or rude in respect of style, language, etc.; not carefully finished.

*c* **1489** Skelton *Death Earl Northumbld.* 127 My wordes vnpullysht be, nakide and playne. **1575** Laneham *Let.* (1871) 15 The thing which heer I report in vnpolisht proez. **1585** Daniel *Paulus Iouius* Pref., Wks. (Grosart) IV. 4 In like maner..haue I aduentured to place these my vnpolished labors on the Piller of your worthines. **1635** in *Verney Mem.* (1907) I. 99 Not daring to present any unpolished lines to such a judicious reader. **1673** *Phil. Trans.* VIII. 5178 Of which many pregnant Instances..are registred in these un-polish't Volumes. *a* **1704** T. Brown *Satire Ancients* Wks. 1720 I. 26 To hear..Horace [called] an Author unpolished, languid, and without force. **1781** Harris *Philol. Enq.* III. xi. 468 At a time when the Languages of England and France were barbarous and unpolished. **1839** Hallam *Hist. Lit.* I. v. § 16 Budæus..is hard and unpolished. **1891** Farrar *Darkn. & Dawn* xxii, It cannot be Chrysippus; the Greek is too modern, and too unpolished.

**3.** Left rude or imperfect.

**1596** *Edward III*, I. i. 76 His lame vnpolisht shifts are come to light. **1647** Clarendon *Contempl. Ps.* Tracts (1727) 527 To reduce our unpolished speculations and conceptions into a prompt and ready practice.

**4.** Not refined in manners or ways of living; marked or characterized by lack of culture.

**1593** Shaks. *2 Hen. VI*, III. ii. 271 The Commons, rude vnpolisht Hindes. **1647** Clarendon *Hist. Reb.* I. § 4 The spirit of Craft and Subtilty in some, and the Unpolished Integrity of others. **1672** Dryden *Def. Epilogue* ¶ 28 They were unlucky to have been bred in an unpolished age. **1703** J. Savage *Lett. Antients* xxxvii. 99, I have had an unpolish'd Education..in Barbarous Nations. **1776** Gibbon *Decl. & F.* ix. (1788) I. 277 The unpolished wives of the barbarians. *c* **1815** Jane Austen *Persuas.* ix, Their parents' inferior, retired, and unpolished way of living. **1853** Lynch *Self-Improv.* v. 112 An unpolished man need not be an ill-mannered one.

Hence **Unpo·lishedness.**

**1647** Clarendon *Hist. Reb.* VII. § 279 That roughness and unpolishedness of his nature. **1652** J. Wright tr. *Camus' Nat. Paradox* v. 90 Those hearts, which may bee said to bee of Iron for their rude unpolishedness.

**Unpoli·te,** *a.* [Un-1 8, 5 b.]

†**1.** Unpolished; unrefined. *Obs. rare.*

**1646** G. Daniel *Poems* Wks. (Grosart) I. 94 What but vnpolite fformes, and ffancies raw, Can such a time produce? **1726** Waldron *Descr. Isle of Man* (1744) 93 However unpolite and savage..the Natives of Man may be. **1727** Swift *Further Acc. E. Curll* ¶ 1 A faithful, though unpolite historian of Grubstreet.

**2.** Lacking in politeness; impolite: **a.** Of actions, conduct, etc.

**1709** *Tatler* No. 140 ¶ 8 [He calls] my cousin Jenny Distaff, Madam Distaff; which..is very unpolite. **1753** Richardson *Grandison* (1781) I. xxiii. 164 His unpolite behaviour to the dear creature. **1838** Dickens *O. Twist* ix, As an apology to the company for his unpolite behaviour.

**b.** Of persons.

**1712** *Spect.* No. 506 ¶ 4 The Spirit of Love..is very often.. lost, by some little Accidents which the Careless and Unpolite never attend to. **1747** Richardson *Clarissa* (1811) I. 205 An unpolite and disobliging brother. **1802–12** Bentham *Ration. Judic. Evid.* (1827) IV. 417 He will not be so unpolite..as to suffer this..suspicion to pass the bounds of his own lips. **1871** Smiles *Charac.* ix. 238 The unpolite impulsive man will..rather lose his friend than his joke.

†**3.** Unfashionable, inelegant. *Obs.*

**1740** Cibber *Apol.* I. 11 In these unpolite Amusements he has laugh'd like a Rake. **1741** Watts *Improv. Mind* I. xvii, How ever they may be now fancied to sound unpolite or unfashionable. **1753** *Songs Costume* (Percy Soc.) 234 Next a coat of embroidery from foreigners come; 'Twou'd be quite unpolite to have one wrought at home.

**Unpoli·tely,** *adv.* (Un-1 11, 5 b; cf. prec.)

**1748** Richardson *Clarissa* (1811) II. 72, I acted very unpolitely. **1857** Dickens *Little Dorrit* II. xxiii, Arthur asked his pardon, if he had stared at him unpolitely.

**Unpoli·teness.** [Un-1 12, 5 b.]

†**1.** Lack of culture or refinement. *Obs.*

**1702** Echard *Eccl. Hist.* 20 People of great Courage.. and of no less Plainess and Unpoliteness. **1728** Morgan *Algiers* I. iii. 49 A People so prone to Unpoliteness as were the natural Africans.

**2.** Want of politeness.

**1707** *Refl. upon Ridicule* (1717) I. 28 Unpoliteness is a Vice that gives the World a Right to complain of us. **1748** Richardson *Clarissa* (1811) III. 187, I have just carried unpoliteness far enough to make her afraid of me. **1858** Carlyle in Froude *Life in London* (1884) II. 197 The shocking unpoliteness of breaking an express promise. **1880** *Athenæum* 5 June 725 Their own unpoliteness and ill temper.

†**3.** Inelegance. *Obs.*

**1725** Blackwall *Sacr. Class.* (1727) I. 80 Sad outcries are made of the unpoliteness of the style.

**Unpo·litic,** *a.* [Un-1 7, 5 b.] Impolitic.

*a* **1548** Hall *Chron.*, *Hen. V*, 65 He imagined that all mischiefes..whiche chaunced in the common wealth should bee imputed and assigned to his vnpolitike doyng. **1591** G. Fletcher *Russe Commw.* (Hakl. Soc.) 44 It might seeme.. to bee no bad nor unpollitique way for conteyning of so large a commonwealth. **1647** Clarendon *Hist. Reb.* I. § 150 The Circumstances and Proceedings..were very Unpolitick, and even Destructive to the Services intended. **1664** H. More *Myst. Iniq.* vi. 17 It had been the most unpolitick action..to offer them any strange God to worship. **1721** Amherst *Terræ Fil.* No. 45 (1726) 240 In this odd, unpolitic manner, did I conduct myself. **1747** Carte *Hist. Eng.* I. 268 The great slaughter..put their affairs into a condition, which rendered it very unpolitick to provoke new enemies.

**Unpoli·tical,** *a.* (Un-1 7, 5 b.)

**1643** Caryl *Sacr. Covt.* 22 Some have thought it unpoliticall to set a foote this Covenant. **1778** W. H. Mar-

SHALL *Minutes Agric., Digest* 37 Feeding Farming-servants at their master's expence is unpolitical. **1792** A. YOUNG *Trav. France* 564 A proof that the measures of the National Assembly have been ill-judged, ill-advised, and unpolitical. **1894** *Thinker* VI. 63 This condition of things authorizes the political nations .. to answer the call of the unpolitical populations for aid.

† **Unpo·liticly,** *adv.* [UN-¹ 11, 5 b.] Impoliticly.

**1589** WARNER *Alb. Eng.* II. 160 A sport [*sc.* riding on horse-back] lately vsed of our English youthes, but now .. vnpollitickly .. discontinued. *a* **1677** BARROW *Serm.* (1686) I. 407 We .. deal as unpoliticly, as the members of the body should act unnaturally, in subtracting mutual assistance. **1748** RICHARDSON *Clarissa* II. 64 Mr. Solmes .. had told Her, that .. I acted very unpoliticly.

†**Unpo·liticness.** *Obs.* [UN-¹ 12, 5 b.] Impoliticness. **1664** H. MORE *Apology* 532 It would lose the appellation of Veracity, and deserve the style of Unpolitickness. **Unpo·llarded,** *ppl. a.* (UN-¹ 8.) **1830** J. G. STRUTT *Sylva Brit.* 16 The Beggar's Oak is a fine sample of the real Park Oak, unpruned, unpollarded. **1891** E. R. PENNELL *Stream Pleas.* 124 The cut, with its unpollarded willows, .. was like a bit of a French canal.

**Unpo·lled,** *ppl. a.* [UN-¹ 8.]

**1.** Uncut, unshorn.

**1647** HEXHAM I, Vnpowled, *ongeschoren.* **1727** BAILEY (vol. II), *Unpolled,* the hair being uncut.

†**2.** Untold, uncounted. *Obs.*

**1647** FANSHAW *Poems* 299 Though richer then unpoll'd Arabian wealth, and Indian Gold.

**3.** Not brought to, or recorded at, the poll; not having voted at an election.

**1818** TODD, *Unpolled,* not registered as a voter. **1824** HOOK *Sayings & Doings* I. 134 There were upwards of a thousand freeholders unpolled. **1837** DICKENS *Pickw.* xiii, Fourteen unpolled electors. **1893** *Westm. Gaz.* 1 Jan. 6/1 There has always in this constituency been a wide margin of unpolled voters.

† **Unpo·llushed,** *ppl. a. Obs.*⁻¹ [Irreg. f. OF. *impollus, -ue.*] Unpolluted. *c* **1489** CAXTON *Blanchardyn* v. 23 That by vyolent opressyon that traytour .. shall enioye youre yoguthe vnpolusshed. **Unpollu·table,** *a.* (UN-¹ 7.) **1711** G. HICKES *Two Treat. Chr. Priesth.* (1847) II. 77 After it is consecrated .. it becomes .. an unpollutable altar.

**Unpollu·ted,** *ppl. a.* (UN-¹ 8, 5 b.)

**1602** SHAKS. *Ham.* v. i. 262 From her faire and vnpolluted flesh, May Violets spring. **1653** W. RAMESEY *Astrol. Restored* Ep. Ded. 2 Among the .. graver sort of people in all Ages, this Science (being unpolluted and unsophisticated) hath been still had in most high esteem. **1732** BERKELEY *Alciphr.* III. § 1 Honour is a noble unpolluted source of virtue. **1771** SMOLLETT *Humph. Cl.* (1815) 262 A man must tread with great circumspection to get safe housed with unpolluted shoes. **1812** J. WILSON *Isle of Palms* I. 21 A woman's unpolluted soul! **1865** DICKENS *Mut. Fr.* III. viii, The young river .. unpolluted by the defilements that lie in wait for it on its course.

**Unpollu·ting,** *ppl. a.* (UN-¹ 10.) **1817** SHELLEY *Rev. Islam* IX. xviii, The shafts of falsehood unpolluting flew. **Unpo·llux,** *v.* [UN-² 6 b.] *fig.* To castrate. **1654** GAYTON *Pleas. Notes* III. vii, The story of the Castor [= beaver] unpolluxing himselfe is very well applyed. **Unpo·mpous,** *a.* (UN-¹ 7.) **1656** W. DU GARD tr. *Comenius' Gate Lat. Unl.* 297 Jesus of Nazareth (rejected by the Jews for his unpompous life).

**Unpo·pe,** *v.* (UN-² 6 b.)

**1563** FOXE *A. & M.* 13/1 Benedictus vnderstanding them to be set against him .. vnpoped him self. **1655** FULLER *Ch. Hist.* XI. v. § 74 Rome will never so farr un-Pope it self, as to part with her pretended Supremacy. **1677** W. HUGHES *Man of Sin* II. xii. 212 They took the boldness to un-pope four of their Infallibilities. **1868** BROWNING *Ring & Bk.* x. 73 He is unpoped, and all he did I damn. **1880** — *Pietro* 403 We're Pope—once Pope, you can't unpope us!

**Unpo·pular,** *a.* [UN-¹ 7, 5 b.] Not possessed of popular favour.

**1647** CLARENDON *Hist. Reb.* I. § 8 That Meeting being, upon very unpopular .. reasons, immediately Dissolved. **1652** *Nicholas Papers* (Camden) 295 Those who put his Majesty on such unpopular and unpleasing things. **1731** CHESTERF. *Let.* 16 Jan. in *10th Rep. Hist. MSS. Comm.* App. I. 245 The disagreeable and unpopular situation we are at present in. **1855** MACAULAY *Hist. Eng.* xviii. IV. 163 James was unpopular because he was a Papist. **1863** H. COX *Instit.* III. iii. 628 An unpopular government.

**Unpopula·rity.** [UN-¹ 12; cf. prec.] The quality or fact of being unpopular.

**1735** LD. LYTTELTON *Lett. Persian* (ed. 3) I. 214 You are afraid of the Unpopularity of the Sound. **1781** JOHNSON *L. P., Dryden* Wks. 1787 II. 412 The original impropriety, and the subsequent unpopularity of the subject. **1810** COLERIDGE *Friend* 355 The last War .. had yet causes of unpopularity peculiar to itself. **1878** LECKY *Eng. in 18th C.* I. iii. 432 The Government was now too weak to bear the strain of additional unpopularity.

**Unpo·pularize,** *v.* [UN-² 6 c.] *trans.* To make unpopular.

**1831** *Examiner* 185/1 The Citizen King is completely unpopularized. **1884** *Nonconf. & Indep.* 24 July 723/3 Spontaneous emigration .. unpopularised a noble cause.

**Unpo·pulate,** *v.* [UN-² 4.] *trans.* To depopulate.

**1658** COKAINE *Trappolin* IV. ii, It is a frequent thing .. To have the Plague .. rage and even unpopulate places. **1880** *Cornh. Mag.* Dec. 673 The growth of manufactures .. had been unpopulating the country to swell the towns.

**Unpo·pulated,** *ppl. a.* (UN-¹ 8.) **1885** *Manch. Exam.* 4 Apr. 4/6 The march of the European invader into the unpopulated regions.

**Unpo·pulous,** *a.* (UN-¹ 7.)

[**1775** ASH.] **1827** SCOTT *Chron. Canongate* iv, Some sequestered and unpopulous district. **1887** *Field* 24 Dec. 975/2 In so remote and unpopulous a part of the country. **Unpo·pulousness.** (UN-¹ 12: cf. prec.) **1599** SANDYS *Europæ Spec.* (1632) 208 The unpopulousnesse .. makes that no one Country is defence for it selfe. **Unpo·rous,** *a.* (UN-¹ 7, 5 b.) **1822–7** GOOD *Study Med.* (1829) IV. 25 We behold the etherial fluids .. transmitted .. by substances still more solid and unporous. **1841** *Florist's Jrnl.* (1846) II. 121 Whenever we find the soil close and unporous.

† **Unpo·rtable,** *a. Obs.* [UN-¹ 7 b, 5 b.]

**1.** Too burdensome or grievous to be borne; unbearable, intolerable.

**1382** WYCLIF *Matt.* xxiii. 4 Greuouse chargis, and vnportable, or that mown nat be born. **1424** *Paston Lett.* I. 17 To here grete and unportable drede .. in here spirites. *c* **1470** G. ASHBY *Active Policy* 172 Ther hath be in late daies .. To myche folk unportable punicion. **1526** *Pilgr. Perf.* (W. de W. 1531) 299 b, All the great & unportable paynes whiche it was thy blessed wyll to suffre. **1540** in Ellis *Orig. Lett.* Ser. III. III. 273 That I may be delyvered from the cure, and to me the unportable burden in governance of this House. **1611** SPEED *Hist. Gt. Brit.* IX. viii. 491 These important and vnportable matters did no whit moue him.

**2.** Extremely large.

**1536–7** *Act Hen. VIII,* in Bolton *Stat. Irel.* (1621) 178 Whose Majestie .. hath with the expence of an vnportable summe of his own treasure, defended vs.

**3.** Too heavy to carry.

*a* **1618** RALEIGH *Invent. Shipping* 9 Had their Cables of Iron chains held any great length, they had been unportable. **1728** E. SMITH *Compl. Housew.* Pref., [It] would fill an unportable volume. **1782** W. F. MARTYN *Geog. Mag.* II. 78 Which pieces are so large and unportable, that .. a cart or wheel-barrow is necessary.

**Unporte·ntous,** *a.* (UN-¹ 7.) **1813** T. BUSBY *Lucretius* II. VI. 538 Clouds unportentous of the future storm. **Unpo·rtioned,** *ppl. a.* (UN-¹ 8.) **1744** YOUNG *Nt. Th.* VII. 1167 'Has virtue charms?'—I grant her heavenly fair; But if unportion'd; all will int'rest wed. **1747** FRANCIS tr. *Horace, Ep.* I. xvii. 69 My Sister lies unportion'd on my Hands. **1828–32** WEBSTER s.v., An unportioned daughter. **Unportma·nteaued,** *ppl. a.* (UN-¹ 9.) **1819** WHEWELL in Todhunter *Acc. Writ.* (1876) II. 33 We .. wended our way dolorous and discontented, .. untravelled and unportmanteaued. **Unpo·rtraited,** *ppl. a.* (UN-¹ 8.) **1611** GUILLIM *Heraldry* II. i. 39 Leigh reckoneth such vnportraicted bearing to bee good. **Unportray·able,** *a.* (UN-¹ 7 b.) **1873** M. COLLINS *Squire Silchester* II. xi. 131 A mighty dusky unportrayable figure, stalking over the furrows. † **Unpo·rtunate,** *a. Obs.* [UN-¹ 7, 5 b.] Importunate. *a* **1533** LD. BERNERS *Gold. Bk. M. Aurel.* (1536) p. iii, Amonge so many vnportunate wyndes and vnstable waters ther is great necessitee of good ores. **1603** HOLLAND *Plutarch's Mor.* 57 For they .. are troublesome and unportunate hearers. **Unpo·rtuous,** *a. rare*⁻¹. [UN-¹ 7 + L. *portus* harbour. Cf. L. *importuōsus.*] Harbourless. **1797** BURKE *Regic. Peace* iii. ⁋ 25 Had the West of Ireland been an unportuous coast, the French naval power would have been undone.

† **Unposse·ss,** *v. Obs. rare.* [UN-² 3.] *trans.* To dispossess.

*c* **1449** PECOCK *Repr.* III. xvi. 380 Preestis .. mowen iustli be vnpossessyd (that is to seie, mowen iustli be putt out of possessioun of the same godis). *a* **1542** WYATT in *Tottel's Misc.* (Arb.) 84 The holde that is geuen ouer, I vnpossest, so hangeth in balance Of warre.

**Unposse·ssed,** *ppl. a.* [UN-¹ 8.]

**1.** Not possessed or owned; unoccupied.

**1594** DANIEL *Compl. of Rosamond* ciii, Seeing how many seeke to vndermine The treasury that's vnpossest of any. **1603** KNOLLES *Hist. Turks* (1621) 105 The riuer was yet vnpossessed by the enemie. **1664** H. POWER *Exp. Philos.* 92 If you let in the outward ayr into the cavity unpossessed by the mercury. **1725** DE FOE *Voy. round World* (1840) 281 If he leaves the country unpossessed, he leaves it free for any other nation to come in. **1748** *Anson's Voy.* I. vi. 64 [Patagonia] is unpossessed by the Spaniards. **1833** WORDSW. *Itin. Poems, Iona* 12 A grace by thee unsought and unpossest.

†**2.** Not preoccupied; unprejudiced. *Obs.*

*a* **1586** SIDNEY *Arcadia* III. xv, When a while that instrument had made a brave proclamation to all unpossessed mindes of attention. **1665** J. SPENCER *Vulg. Proph.* 61 All the Heralds of Heaven had the badg of some divine Signs, whereby unpossest minds might easily distinguish them from Impostors. **1685** TEMPLE *Ess., Gardening* (1690) 11 The want of Demonstration or Satisfaction, to any thinking and unpossessed Man.

**3.** Not having possession *of* something.

**1795** V. KNOX *Chr. Philos.* § 22 *note,* The mind, unpossessed of virtue. **1840** GEN. P. THOMPSON *Exerc.* (1842) V. 69 A witness .. absolutely unpossessed of all idea of obligation to speak the truth. **1899** F. T. BULLEN *Way Navy* 25 Many of them quite unpossessed of any knowledge of our most thrilling episode.

Hence **Unposse·ssedness.**

**1819** COLERIDGE in *Lit. Rem.* (1836) II. 239 How truly Shakspearian is the opening of Macbeth's character given in the unpossessedness of Banquo's mind.

**Unposse·ssing,** *ppl. a.* (UN-¹ 10, 5 d.)

**1605** SHAKS. *Lear* II. i. 69 Thou vnpossessing Bastard, dost thou thinke [etc.]. **1757** MRS. GRIFFITH *Lett. Henry & Frances* (1767) II. 191 With a taste and relish for them all, yet unpossessing any of them.

**Unpossibi·lity.** (UN-¹ 12, 5 b; cf. next.)

**1621** AINSWORTH *Annot. Pentat., Exod.* xix. 8 The unpossibility of the Law, which is weake through the flesh. **1623** COCKERAM II, Vnpossibilitie of beleefe, *Incredulitie.* *a* **1849** POE *King Pest* Wks. 1865 II. 372 It would be a matter of utter unpossibility. **1866** FLORENCE MARRYAT *For Ever & Ever* II. 194 Why, it would be an unpossibility, Sir.

**Unpo·ssible,** *a.* Now only *dial.* [UN-¹ 7, 5 b.] Impossible. (Very common *c* 1400–1660.)

**1362** LANGL. *P. Pl.* A. XI. 225 Poul prouiþ it is vnpossible riche men in heuene. *c* **1400** *Lanfranc's Cirurg.* 153 Þer is no þing vnpossible to stalworþe nature. **1453** in *Wars Eng. in France* (1864) II. 488 It is unpossible unto us so sone to purvey for the saide socours. **1471** FORTESCUE *Wks.* (1869) 535 The forsayd minor is now clerely proved unpossible. **1523** LD. BERNERS tr. *Froiss.* I. cxlv. 173 The frenchemen coude natte passe no way, without they wolde haue gone through the marshes, the whiche was vnpossyble. **1570** T. WILSON *Demosth. Orat., Life* 127 Vnpossible it is for anye one to deceyue him. **1610** FLETCHER *Faithful Shepherdess* II. i, Whose grief .. to anothers eye May seem unpossible of remedy. **1697** BURGHOPE *Disc. Relig. Assemb.* 169 There's nothing requir'd of us .. which is unpossible. **1773** GOLDSM. *Stoops to Conq.* II. i, By the laws, your worship, that's parfectly unpossible. **1825** BROCKETT *N. C. Words, Unpossible,* for impossible. The word is frequent with the vulgar in the North. **1844–** in Sc. and dialect use (*Eng. Dial. Dict.*). **1866** FLO. MARRYAT *For Ever & Ever* II. 194 That is an unpossible thing, Sir.

*absol.* **1581** MULCASTER *Positions* iv. 17 Nothing giuen to the vnpossible, where possibilitie must take place.

Hence † **Unpo·ssibleness;** † **Unpo·ssibly** *adv.*

**1561** T. HOBY tr. *Castiglione's Courtyer* IV. Ss ii, The vnpossiblenes of yᵉ matter. **1658** OSBORNE *Adv. Son* Wks. (1673) 175 Therefore not unpossibly the cause why the Devil was so earnest .. to make them commit it [*sc.* a sin]. **1659** — *Misc. Ess. Paradoxes* 176, I confesse the Party may not unpossibly be very Rich.

**Unpo·sted,** *ppl. a.* (UN-¹ 8.) [**1775** ASH.] **1860** W. H. RUSSELL *Diary India* I. 4 A few younger men, unposted, who expected to be attached to Queen's regiments. **Unpostpo·nable,** *a.* (UN-¹ 7 b.) **1854** J. WILSON *Let.* in *Mem.* (1859) 304 Whatever was not altogether imperative and unpostponable. **1890** GUNTER *Miss Nobody* xvii, Important and unpostponable business. **Unpo·t,** *v.* (UN-² 5.) **1754** JUSTICE *Scots Gard. Director* 127 As for the small Plants .., I do not choose to unpot them until Michaelmas.

**Unpo·table,** *a.* [UN-¹ 7 b, 5 b.] Undrinkable. **1848** S. WELLS WILLIAMS *Mid. Kingd.* I. 14 The water .. is brackish and unpotable. **1902** *Act 2 Edw. VII,* c. 7 § 8 The applicant .. will .. render the spirits unpotable .. during use. **Unpou·lticed,** *ppl. a.* (UN-¹ 8.) [**1775** ASH.] **1791** [see UNPILLED *ppl. a.*²].

**Unpo·wdered,** *ppl. a.* [UN-¹ 8.]

**1.** Not sprinkled with salt.

*c* **1440** *Promp. Parv.* 366/2 On-powderyd, on-saltyd, *insalitus.* ? **1619** HIERON *Wks.* II. 484 As an vnpowdered masse of flesh .. is enough to poyson with the stench. *Ibid.* 492 Those particulars .. will, like so many vnpowdered morsels mixed in with others, make the whole lump to become vnsauory.

**2.** Not whitened with hair-powder.

**1751** JOHNSON *Rambler* No. 109 ⁋ 6 My hair unpowdered, and my hat uncocked. **1847** LYTTON *Lucretia* I. i, The dark hair which he wore unpowdered. **1898** R. S. HICHENS *Londoners* vii, Various footmen, powdered and unpowdered.

**Unpow·er,** *sb. Obs.* exc. *dial.* [UN-¹ 12. Cf. NON-POWER.] Want of power; inability; weakness; helplessness.

*c* **1380** WYCLIF *Serm.* Sel. Wks. I. 371 Þis drede haþ no peyne, but unpower for to synne. **1402** *Jack Upland* in *Pol. Poems* (Rolls) II. 36 Then puttest thou on Christ .. unkunning, unpower, and evill will. *c* **1440** *Gesta Rom.* lii. 233 Þerfor do not aftir the worlde, ne abide not age, vnpower, or blyndnesse. *a* **1470** H. PARKER *Dives & Pauper* (W. de W. 1496) II. xiv. G iiij b, Yf it be soo that þᵗ othe be made .. the man that he made it to can not .. vnbynde hym from that othe .. but nede or unpower excuse hym. **1847–** in south-western dial. glossaries.

†**Unpow·er,** *v. Obs.* [UN-² 4.] *trans.* To deprive of power. **1643** W. GREENHILL *Axe at Root* 8 Now the Lord did .. un-church them, un-power them, un-saint them. **1657** REEVE *God's Plea* 287 Why are they ministers, if they unpower, cassate their own function?

**Unpow·erful,** *a. rare.* (UN-¹ 7.)

**1611** FLORIO, *Impoderoso,* vnmightie, vnpowerfull. **1656** COWLEY *Davideis* I. 48 He .. envy'd him a Kings unpowerful Hate. **1777** J. RICHARDSON *Dissert. East. Nations* 21 A distinct body of harmless and unpowerful people.

Hence **Unpow·erfulness.**

**1625** DARCIE *Ann.* a 4 It lies meerely in their owne vnpowerfulnesse, that they doe not ouerthrow his .. Empire.

†**Unpra·ctic,** *a. Obs.* [UN-¹ 7.] Not practical. **1659** W. CHAMBERLAYNE *Pharonnida* IV. ii. 551 A speedy, though unpractic sympathy.

**Unpra·cticable,** *a.* [UN-¹ 7 b, 5 b.] Impracticable. (Common 1650–1700.)

**1647** CLARENDON *Hist. Reb.* III. § 176 Such Objections .. as rendered it [*sc.* the proposition] Ridiculous and Unpracticable. **1673** *Remarques Humours Town* 52 They have made Love .. unpracticable to the World. **1692** BENTLEY *Boyle Lect.* 16 Such unpracticable conditions as these. **1702** *Eng. Theophrast.* 135 Many things that seem'd unpracticable to their Thoughts.

Hence **Unpra·cticableness.**

**1667** OWEN *Indulg. & Tolerat. Consid.* 30 The unpracticableness of such an Indulgence. **1680** H. DODWELL *Two Lett.* (1691) 180 That unpracticableness wherewith they are changed. **1894** *N. W. Congregationalist* (U.S.) 5 Jan., There is a certain amount of unpracticableness about this.

**Unpra·ctical,** *a.* (UN-¹ 7, 5 b.)

**1637** BP. REYNOLDS *Serm.* (1638) 26 To foment their jealousies and censures .. by novell, speceious, and unpracticall Curiosities. **1668** HALE *Pref. to Rolle's Abridgm.* 5 Some of their Laws grew .. obsolete, some unpractical, some obscure. **1849** C. BRONTE *Shirley* vii, Caroline was feeling .. what an unpractical life she led. **1890** R. 'BOLDREWOOD' *Col. Reformer* (1891) 152 An unpractical, unsuccessful enthusiast.

Hence **Unpractica·lity; Unpra·ctically** *adv.*; **Unpra·cticalness.**

**1875** HOWELLS *Foregone Concl.* (1882) 313 That poor fellow with his whole stock of helplessness, dreamery and *unpracticality. **1880** *Athenæum* 18 Dec. 812/3 The delightful unpracticality of good Mrs. Brooke. **1881** *Trans. Obstet. Soc. Lond.* XXII. 5 Where we cannot foresee any immediate effect on practice, that is, so far as we can see, *unpractically. **1880** VERNON LEE *Stud. Italy* II. iii. 49 To this charming *unpracticalness .. must be added the fact that [etc.].

† **Unpra·ctisable,** *a.* (UN-¹ 7 b, 5 b; cf. PRACTISABLE *a.*) **1594** in Halliwell *Lett. Sci. Subjects* (1841) 36 Converted to

sundrie other uses..which have hetherto byn supposed to be unpracytzable. **1644** G. PLATTES in *Hartlib's Legacy* (1655) 295 It is neither unpossible, strange, nor unpracticeable. **Unpra·ctise**, *v.* (UN-² 3.) **1727** *Art of Speaking in Publick* v. (ed. 2) 67 If you find it comes only from an ill Habit you have got,..you ought to take up a resolution of unpractising it.

**Unpra·ctised**, *ppl. a.* [UN-¹ 8.]

**1.** Not familiarized or skilled by practice; inexperienced, inexpert.

**1551** ROBINSON tr. *More's Utopia* I. (1895) 49 Your newe made and vnpractysed soldiours. **1562** A. BROOKE *Romeus & Jul.* 1416 A wise mans wit vnpractised doth stand him in no steede. **1606** SHAKS. *Tr. & Cr.* I. i. 12 But I am..skillesse as vnpractis'd Infancie. **1672** MARVELL *Reh. Transp.* I. 207 To harden their unpractis'd modesty. **1748** *Anson's Voy.* III. viii. 380 Of so little consequence are the most destructive arms in untutored and unpractised hands. **1805** WORDSW. *Prelude* v. 589 In his youth..in that raw unpractised time. **1849** MACAULAY *Hist. Eng.* vi. II. 143 The most unpractised eye at once perceived that they were taller..than their successors. **1890** *Retrospect Med.* CII. 109 The unpractised operator is far less likely to do harm with the forceps than with version.

**b.** Const. *in.*

**1665** BOYLE *Occas. Refl.* III. xx. 131 These are..altogether unpractis'd in that Civility. **1687** DRYDEN *Hind & P.* III. 614 The latter brood, who just began to fly, Sick-feathered and unpractis'd in the sky. **1759** HUME *Hist. England* I. 96 Albany..was totally..unpractised in their language. **1844** UPTON *Physioglyphics* Pref. p. ii, A person unpractised in authorship. **1900** *Longm. Mag.* Mar. 466 Supposing that I speak to anyone who is unpractised in the art.

**2.** Not practised; unemployed, untried.

**1540** *Commemoration of Inestimable Graces of God* B ij, The old prouerbe..is not lefte vnpractised by the sayde Antichrist. *c* **1584** *An Abstract, Certaine Acts Parl.* (title-p.), Certaine Canons, Constitutions, and Synodals prouinciall..for the most part heretofore vnknowen and vnpracticed. **1611** BEAUM. & FL. *Maid's Trag.* II. i, I..must try Some yet unpractis'd way to grieve and die. **1686** *Col. Rec. Pennsylv.* I. 184 An unsafe and hetherto unpractised way in procedure. **1753** HANWAY *Trav.* XIV. x. (1762) II. 382 No barbarities were left unpractised. **1848** AKERMAN *Introd. Study Anc. & Mod. Coins* v. 90 This description of artifice seems to have been..unpractised among the Romans.

†**b.** Untraversed, unfamiliar. *Obs.*

**1621** G. SANDYS *Ovid's Met.* I. (1626) 4 Ships..Then plow'd th' vnpractiz'd bosom of the Flood. **1778** BP. LOWTH *Transl. Isaiah* Notes 187 A journey..through desert and unpracticed countries.

Hence **Unpra·ctisedness.**

**1628** EARLE *Microcosm.* (Arb.) 61 He ascribes all honestie to an vnpractis'dnesse in the World. **1672** FLAMSTEED in Rigaud *Corr. Sci. Men* (1841) II. 130 My unpractisedness in such observations at the first essays.

**Unpragma·tical**, *a.* (UN-¹ 7.) **1673** CAVE *Prim. Chr.* II. i. 6 Whoever would govern his life aright must be modest and unpragmatical.

**Unprai·sable**, *a.* [UN-¹ 7 b.]

**1.** That cannot be praised.

**1483** *Cath. Angl.* 290/1 Vn Praysabylle, *illaudabilis.* **1892** A. LANG *Lett. Dead Authors* 178 Thou splendid warrior with the world at odds, Unpraised, unpraisable, beyond thy merit.

†**2.** Incapable of being appraised or valued; above valuation. *Obs.*

**1526** *Pilgr. Perf.* (W. de W. 1531) 173 b, Thou shalt haue inestimable or vnpraysable rychesse. **1598** STOW *Surv.* 325 Vessels of gold, and siluer vnpraiseable, and many pretious stones.

**Unprai·se**, *v.* [UN-² 3.] *trans.* To dispraise.

*c* **1375** *Cursor M.* 27585 (Fairf.), We agh ilkman our-self vpraise & in our hert vs vnpraise [*Cott.* dispraise]. *a* **1500** *Praise of Women* in *Rel. Ant.* I. 275 To onpreyse womene, yt were a shame. **1728** YOUNG *Love Fame* VII. 45 Cannot thrice ten hundred years unpraise The boist'rous boy, and blast his guilty bays? **1729** SAVAGE *Wanderer* I. 345 Shou'd some nobler Bard their Worth unpraise, Deserting Morals, that adorn his Lays.

**Unprai·sed**, *ppl. a.* (UN-¹ 8.)

**1390** GOWER *Conf.* I. 229 If reson be wel peised, Ther mai no vertu ben unpreised. **1422** YONG tr. *Secreta Secret.* 130 Of the dyuersyte..of maneris wych ben praside and vnprayside. **1570** LEVINS *Manip.* 50 Vnpraysed, *illaudatus.* **1590** SPENSER *F. Q.* II. x. 5 The land..was saluage wildernesse, Vnpeopled, vnmanurd, vnprou'd, vnpraysd. **1634** MILTON *Comus* 723 Th' all-giver would be unthank't, would be unprais'd. **1700** DRYDEN *Cymon & Iph.* 469 Unprais'd by me, tho' Heav'n sometime may bless An impious Act with undeserv'd Success. **1784** COWPER *Task* v. 539 There is yet a liberty,..by senators unprais'd. **1827** POLLOK *Course T.* VII. 422 Innumerous armies rose, unbannered all, Unpanoplied, unpraised. **1856** R. A. VAUGHAN *Mystics* IX. iii. II. 151 How many women..are far surpassing St. Theresa in their self-sacrifice and patience, unseen and unpraised of men. **1892** [see UNPRAISABLE 1].

**Unprai·seful**, *a.* (UN-¹ 7.) **1868** LYNCH *Rivulet* CLII. ii, Not..with unpraiseful prayer We live below.

**Unprai·seworthy**, *a.* (UN-¹ 7.)

**1589** FLEMING *Virg. Georg.* IV. 59 Th' other king ill-fauoured is,..And vnpraiseworthy drags his large brode belly all along. **1876** LOWELL *Among my Bks.* Ser. II. 45 We do not mean to say that this minute exegesis is useless or unpraiseworthy.

**Unpray·**, *v.* (UN-² 3.)

**1611** COTGR., *Desprier*, to vnpray,..recall prayers. **1662** GURNALL *Chr. in Arm.* III. xiii. 102, I pray'd with so little faith, that I..unprayed my own prayer. **1676** HALE *Contempl.* I. 128 The freeness and purity of his obedience..made him, as it were, un-pray what he had before prayed. **1842** FABER *Styrian Lake*, etc. 289 And he unprayed his curse, his passion sunk. **1862** CHR. G. ROSSETTI *Poems* (1904) 235/1 My sins unpray My prayer.

**Unpray·able**, *a.* [UN-¹ 7 b.] †Inexorable. **1382** WYCLIF *Lam.* iii. 42 Wee wickeli diden, and to wrathe terreden; therfore thou art vnpreiable [L. *inexorabilis*].

**Unpray·ed**, *ppl. a.* [UN-¹ 8.]

**1.** Of persons: **a.** Not entreated or besought; unasked; uninvited. Also with *to.*

*c* **1374** CHAUCER *Troylus* IV. 513 Syn þat thow slest so fele ..Ayeins hir wil vnpreyed day and nyghte, Do me..this seruyse. *c* **1400** LOVE *Bonavent. Mirr.* (1908) 116 In that oure lord mekely vnpreide wente bodily to hele the sike seruaunt. *c* **1440** *Gesta Rom.* lxv. 290 (Add. MS.), The lyon, the Ape, and the Serpent, yelded hym mede, because he drew hem out of the pitte vnpraied. **1536** in *10th Rep. Hist. MSS. Comm.* App. V. 407 Whatsoever man..goeth in to anny such housse..unpraied or bidden. **1600** FAIRFAX *Tasso* XVI. xlv, To my sutors old what I denaid, That gaue I thee.. vnpraid. **1681** H. MORE in *Glanvill's Sadducismus* I. Postscr. 51 The holy Angels..which..reinforce the prayers of good and holy men..unprayed to themselves. **1849** M. ARNOLD *Fragm. of 'Antigone'* 5 Who, weighing that life well Fortune presents unpray'd, Declines her ministry.

†**b.** Not moved by prayer. *Obs.*⁻¹

**1567** DRANT *Horace, Ep.* A iiij, If thou wouldest set Achilles oute,.. Let him be swift, chafing, vnprayed, inflamde to vengaunce sone.

**2.** Not prayed *for*; without being prayed *for*.

**1533** MORE *Apol.* xxviii. Wks. 894/1 Yf they leue nothing vnpraied for that mai perteine to the pacificacion of this diuision. **1703** DE FOE *More Reform.* 50 What Capital offence Could bar thee from the Priests Benevolence, That they..should..let thee live unbless'd, unprayed for Die.

**Unprea·ch**, *v.* (UN-² 3.)

**1692** BP. STRATFORD *Charge, 5 May* 22 Can they think, that he does in good earnest believe what he preaches, when he unpreaches the same again in his life? **1701** DE FOE *Trueborn Eng.* II. 256 The Clergy..Unpreach'd their Non-resisting Cant, and Pray'd To Heaven for Help. **1855** KINGSLEY *Westw. Ho!* xviii, To show the white feather in the hour of need, is to unpreach in one minute all that he had been preaching his life long.

**Unprea·ched**, *ppl. a.* (UN-¹ 8.) [**1775** ASH.] **1843** CARLYLE *Past & Pr.* III. xii, This unpreached, inarticulate,.. forever-enduring Gospel.

**Unprea·ching**, *ppl. a.* [UN-¹ 10.]

**1.** Omitting or neglecting to preach; characterized by absence of preaching.

**1549** LATIMER *6th Serm. bef. Edw. VI* (Arb.) 167 The deuill ..hath set vppe a state of vnpreachynge prelacye in this Realme...He hath made vnpreachynge prelates. **1585** ABP. SANDYS *Serm.* iii. 60 Woe therefore to the idle and Idol pastor, to the dumme dogge, to the vnpreaching minister! **1630** J. TAYLOR (Water P.) *Sculler* Wks. III. 20/1 Who dares say that like a drone or moath, Like an vnpreaching Priest he liues by Sloath? **1660** PRYNNE *Unbish. Tim.* (ed. 2) 95 Idle, proud, ambicious, unpreaching Prelates. **1732** NEAL *Hist. Purit.* I. 372 There are severe expressions against the unpreaching clergy. **1828** J. T. RUTT *Burton's Diary* III. 203 Praising that Bishop at the expense of unpreaching prelates. **1850** MARSDEN *Early Purit.* iv. 124 Her successor on the throne..discouraged preaching...We became an unpreaching church.

†**2.** *spec.* Not undertaking the duty of preaching; merely reading the services of the Church. *Obs.*

**1574** WHITGIFT *Def. Answ.* 482 Bycause a chylde may reade the booke, dothe it therefore mainteyne an vnpreaching ministerie? **1588** J. UDALL *Demonstr. Discipline* (Arb.) 38 If vnpreaching ministers cannot be made without the manifest breach of the commaundement of God. **1597** HOOKER *Eccl. Pol.* v. xxxii. § 3 That..we..maintaine an vnpreaching ministerie, is neither aduisedly nor truly spoken. **1642** FULLER *Holy & Prof. St.* v. xi. 402 Sacraments received from ignorant and unpreaching Ministers. **1710** H. BEDFORD *Vind. Ch. Eng.* 161 There were several unpreaching Ministers, whose..Business it was to read the publick Prayers.

**Unpreca·rious**, *a.* (UN-¹ 7.)

**1712** BLACKMORE *Creation* II. 532 The Stars..grace the high expansion, bright By their own beams, and unprecarious light. **1745** YOUNG *Nt. Th.* VIII. 968 Bliss there is none, but unprecarious bliss. **1843** TIZARD *Brewing* 5 Even were brewing as simple and unprecarious as some are willing to imagine.

**Unprecau·tioned**, *ppl. a.* (UN-¹ 8.) **1694** FRANCK *Northern Mem.* 128 Because unprecautioned how to distinguish the Elements,..she frequently encounters the boiling Water.

**Unprece·ded**, *ppl. a.* (UN-¹ 8.)

**1846** WORCESTER (citing J. Johnson). **1884** *Law Times* 6 Sept. 320/2 Hostile acts unpreceded by declaration of war.

**Unprecede·ntal**, *a.* [UN-¹ 7.] = next. **1768** CAPT. COOK in *Roy. Soc. Archives, Lett.* (1908) 18 This, I believe to be the reason for the unpresidental reception we met with here.

**Unpre·cedented**, *ppl. a.* (UN-¹ 8.)

In frequent use from *c* 1760.

*a.* **1623** in Rushw. *Hist. Coll.* (1659) I. 101 To forbid the Judges against their Oathes..is a thing unpresidented in this Kingdom. **1650** WELDON *Crt. Jas. I*, 37 Which was a strange Judgement, and unpresidented. **1707** HEARNE *Collect.* II. 24 Yᵉ Delegates..declar'd the Dʳˢ sentence pronounc'd against him by himself, as Assessor, to be unjust and unpresidented.

*β.* **1716** ADDISON *Freeholder* No. 16 ¶ 5 Nor did the Legislature do any thing in this that was unprecedented. **1743** BULKELEY & CUMMINS *Voy. S. Seas* p. xiv, An audacious and unprecedented Action. **1837** HT. MARTINEAU *Soc. Amer.* II. 147 Some startling circumstance..which I was assured was unprecedented. **1874** GREEN *Short Hist.* viii. § 3. 487 A speech of unprecedented boldness.

Hence **Unpre·cedentedly** *adv.*, **-ness.**

**1678** MARVELL *Growth Popery* 46 There was but one Reason given herein for declining the granting Money, and that is the Unpresidentedness. **1826** T. TOOKE *Currency* 56 The late disastrous, and unprecedentedly numerous failures. **1884** *Manch. Exam.* 27 Nov. 5/4 The number of students attending was no doubt unprecedentedly great.

**Unprecede·ntial**, *a.* [UN-¹ 7.] = prec.

*a* **1700** EVELYN *Diary* 19 July 1641, It was condemned as unprecedential, and not justifiable. **1846** WORCESTER (citing *Ec. Rev.*).

**Unpre·cedently**, *adv.* (UN-¹ 11.) **1748** RICHARDSON *Clarissa* I. 242 The imaginary prerogative he was so unprecedently fond of asserting. **Unpreci·pitable**, *a.* (UN-¹ 7 b.) **1782** *Phil. Trans.* LXXIII. 76 Now this compound of calx of silver, and silver in its metallic form, may well be unprecipitable by iron.

**Unpreci·pitated**, *ppl. a.* (UN-¹ 8.)

**1663** BOYLE *Usef. Exp. Nat. Philos.* II. App. 314 The aqua fortis preserving none [of the silver] unprecipitated. **1698** COLLIER *Immor. Stage* i. 28 His Incidents are often surprising, and his Plots unprecipitated. **1850** L. HUNT *Autobiog.* viii. (1860) 150 The horse suddenly came to a stand,.. and I was agreeably surprised to find myself..unprecipitated over his head.

**Unpreci·se**, *a.* (UN-¹ 7, 5 b.)

[**1775** ASH.] **1782** WARTON *Rowley Enq.* 47 Chatterton gave a vague unprecise explanation. **1820** *Monthly Rev.* XCI. 219 The antiquated and unprecise division of emotions into sublime and beautiful. **1858** CARLYLE *Fredk. Gt.* VIII. iv. II. 322 Here is the unprecise but indubitable fact.

**Unpreci·sely**, *adv.* (UN-¹ 11; cf. prec.) **1869** ROSSETTI *Mem. Shelley* p. xcix, Lord Eldon either spoke loosely or was reported unprecisely. **Unpreclu·dible**, *a.* (UN-¹ 7.) **1825** COLERIDGE *Lett., Conv.*, etc. (1836) II. 187 Demands on such quantity of time, as bodily pain and disqualification, with unprecludible interruption, have enabled me to make use of. **Unpre·dicable**, *a.* (UN-¹ 7 b, 5 b.) **1865** MASSON *Rec. Brit. Philos.* 392 Under the name of Faith..Hamilton affirmed..much which he declared to be utterly unpredicable in the name of Reason. **Unpredi·ct**, *v.* (UN-² 7.) **1671** MILTON *P. R.* III. 395 Means I must use thou say'st, prediction else Will unpredict and fail me of the Throne.

**Unpredi·ctable**, *a.* (UN-¹ 7 b.)

In frequent use from *c* 1880.

**1857** M. PATTISON *Ess.* (1889) II. 405 The constant tendency of discovery [is] to reduce to order classes of facts, once thought irregular and unpredictable. **1874** J. SULLY *Sensation & Intuition* 113 The many chances of some unpredictable accident.

**Unpre·faced**, *ppl. a.* (UN-¹ 8.) [**1775** ASH.] **1801** BLOOMFIELD *Rural T.* (1802) 51 [He] straight began..Th' unpreface'd History of his latter years. **1859** HOOKER in Darwin *Life & Lett.* (1887) II. 242 The three volumes, unprefaced by this, would have choked any Naturalist.

**Unprefe·rred**, *ppl. a.* [UN-¹ 8.]

†**1.** Not advanced or promoted.

**1483** *Act 1 Rich. III*, c. 2 § 1 Mony worshipfull men..were compelled..to lyff in greate penurie.., their dettes unpaied and their childeryn unpreferred. **1564** HAWARD *Eutropius* X. 123 He..would not see them vnpreferred to honoures. **1572** *Wills & Inv. N. C.* (Surtees, 1835) 370, I will yᵗ Alice my wyf & ..my doughters being vnmarried & vnpreferred shall haue their full portions of my goods. **1607** DEKKER *Northward-Hoe* IV. Wks. 1873 III. 45 A poore vnpreferd scholler. **1655** FULLER *Ch. Hist.* IX. vi. § 36 Of which order fourteen only could be found..which were unmarried, unpreferred to cures. **1697** COLLIER *Ess. Mor. Subj.* I. 25 There is no such way to make a Scholar, as to keep him under while he is young, or unpreferred.

**2.** Not regarded with preference.

**1884** *Imperial Dict.* s.v.

†**Unpre·gnable**, *a.* [UN-¹ 7 b, 5 b.] Impregnable.

*a.* **1386** *Rolls of Parlt.* III. 225/1 The Mairaltee,..were it never so unprenable. **1481** CAXTON *Godfrey* cxxxii. 196 A dongeon..upon an hylle.., whiche the turkes holde so strongly that it is unprenable. **1560** DAUS *Sleidane's Comm.* 211 The Castell..which for the situation was vnprennable.

*β.* **1545** ELYOT, *Inexpugnabilis*, vnpreignable. **1561** DAUS tr. *Bullinger on Apoc.* 536 Therefore was there neuer any thing..so mightie or vnpregnable, whiche the inuincible power of God can not bring to naught. **1572** TWYNE *Dionysius' Surv. World* E ivb, Semiramis..enuironed it wᵗ an vnpregnable wal. **1632** SHERWOOD s.v.

**Unpre·gnant**, *a.* (UN-¹ 7.)

**1602** SHAKS. *Ham.* II. ii. 594 Yet I..peake Like Iohn a-dreames, vnpregnant of my cause, And can say nothing. **1603** — *Meas. for M.* IV. iv. 23 This deede vnshapes me quite, makes me vnpregnant And dull to all proceedings. **1868** *Lond. Rev.* 8 Aug. 166/2 His work has never been unpregnant in illustration of his mind. **1878** *N. Amer. Rev.* CXXVI. 48 No such interest can arise when the misfortune is unpregnant.

**Unpreju·dged**, *ppl. a.* (UN-¹ 8.) [**1775** ASH.] **1888** *Times* 31 Aug. 3/1 The question of sovereignty remained unprejudged.

†**Unpreju·dicate**, *a. Obs.* [UN-¹ 7, 5 b.] Unprejudiced. (Common in 17th c.)

**1609** *Hoby's Let. to T. H.* Printer to Rdr. 115 For the better satisfaction of the vnpreiudicate Reader. **1650** H. MORE *Observ.* in *Enthus. Tri.*, etc. (1656) 78 His humility and purity of mind and unprejudicate reason. **1679** J. GOODMAN *Penit. Pard.* I. i. 11 Discourses..plain and intelligible to such unprejudicate minds.

Hence **Unpreju·dicately** *adv.*, **-ness.**

*a* **1662** SANDERSON *Cases Consc.* iii. (1678) 74 Doubts and difficulties meet to be..unprejudicately weighed against those other probabilities. **1668** H. MORE *Div. Dial.* II. 416 All the difficulty is to get to that state of Unprejudicateness. **1683** E. HOOKER *Pref. Pordage's Mystic Div., Postscr.* 111 Shold you pleace to lai the..Ear of conscientious unpræjudicateness as close to the voice of these Mysteries as I did.

†**Unpreju·dicated**, *ppl. a.* [UN-¹ 8.] = prec. **1633** PRYNNE *Histrio-m.* 2nd Ep. Ded., Imploring..your unprejudicated affections too. **1644** JESSOP *Angel of Eph.* 63 Let the impartiall and unprejudicated Reader peruse his words. **1660** STILLINGFL. *Iren.* II. vi. § 9 That evidence..which will command assent from an unprejudicated mind. †**Unpreju·dicating**, *ppl. a.* (UN-¹ 10.) **1602** CAREW *Cornwall* 69 Who (as I conceive) looked heerinto with an indifferent and unprejudicating eye. **Unpre·judice.** (UN-¹ 12, 5 b.) *c* **1800** COLERIDGE in *Sotheby's Sale Catalogue* 20 Nov. (1899) 16 Religious Musings, which you will read with a Poets eye, with the same unprejudices. **1871** LOWELL *Study Wind.* 92 Carlyle..has now been so long before the world that we may feel toward him something of the unprejudice of posterity.

**Unpre·judiced**, *ppl. a.* [UN-¹ 8.]

**1.** Not affected prejudicially.

**1613** HEYWOOD 2 *Edward IV*, M 4 b, On whom I vow, Leauing King Lewis vnprejudizde in peace, To spend the whole measure of my kindled rage.

**2.** Free from prejudice: **a.** Of persons, the mind, eye, etc.

**1637–50** ROW *Hist. Kirk* (Wodrow Soc.) 437 Let the unprejudiced reader judge whither [etc.]. **1678** CUDWORTH *Intell. Syst.* 728 To the full Conviction of all Minds Unprejudiced, and Unprepossessed with false Principles. **1710** STEELE *Spect.* No. 4 ¶ 5, I have the high Satisfaction of beholding all Nature with an unprejudiced Eye. **1794** R. J. SULIVAN *View Nat.* II. 72 It is clear to unprejudiced reason, that experiments in philosophy should unremittingly be made. **1842** BORROW *Bible in Spain* xlix, Surely it is not the part of unprejudiced people to disparage that of which they are ignorant. **1885** J. PAYN *Talk of Town* II. 259 William Henry's affidavit will acquit you of all blame in this matter in the eyes of unprejudiced persons.

*absol.* **1739** GORDON (*title*), An Appeal to the Unprejudiced Concerning the present Discontents Occasioned by the late Convention with Spain. **1755** T. EDWARDS *New Transl. Psalms* 19 These few instances may be sufficient to convince the unprejudiced, that [etc.].

**b.** Of opinions, inquiries, etc.

*a* **1670** SOUTH *Serm.* (1715) IV. 291 Some such Principle of Reason..universally granted by the unprejudiced Apprehensions of Mankind. **1709** ADDISON *Tatler* No. 101 ¶ 2 To consider Things in so unprejudiced a manner, that [etc.]. **1770** A. YOUNG *Six Months' Tour North* (1771) I. Pref. p. xiii, I was forced to make more than one honest farmer half drunk, before I could get sober, unprejudiced intelligence. **1809** *Med. Jrnl.* XXI. 307 An unprejudiced perusal of these cases. **1839** DE LA BECHE *Rep. Geol. Cornw.*, etc. iv. 101 Fair and unprejudiced discussion. **1856** OLMSTED *Slave States* 702 Reliable and unprejudiced information.

Hence **Unpreˈjudicedly** *adv.*, **-ness.**

**1674** BOYLE *Excell. Theol.* II. v. 230 By having the reasons it presents perspicuously proposed, and *unprejudicedly entertained. **1685** H. MORE *Paralip. Prophet.* li. 476 Whoever reads considerately and unprejudicedly the 23. Chapter, ..cannot but be fully assured. **1889** *Amer. Naturalist* Oct. 897 Let us consider this evidence as unprejudicedly..as we can. **1672** H. MORE *Brief Reply* Pref. a ij, My impartialness and *unprejudicedness. **1704** CLARKE *Attrib.* (1706) 10 Hearing the Reason of the Case with Patience and Unprejudicedness.

**Unprejudiˈciable,** *a.* (UN-[1] 7 b.) **1673** O. WALKER *Educ.* 37 In denying all, or most of his desires, though the things be reasonable, or unprejudiciable. **Unprejudiˈcial,** *a.* (UN-[1] 7.) **1641** *Vind. Smectymnuus* ix. 104 Not only unprejudicial to the honour of Episcopacy, but behoveful to the Church. **1657** J. SERGEANT *Schism Dispach't* 156 A bare word, capable of a different (and so unprejudicial) signification. **Unprejudiˈcialness.** (UN-[1] 12.) **1642** J. GOODWIN *Anti-Cavalierism* 10 The unprejudicialnesse or inoffensivenesse of it to Sauls kingly Throane and dignity. **Unpreˈlate,** *v.* (UN-[2] 6 b.) *a* **1670** HACKET *Abp. Williams* II. (1693) 120 The Archbishop thought not himself absolute, till this man was unprelated. **Unprelaˈtic,** *a.* [UN-[1] 7.] = next. **1880** F. G. LEE *Ch. under Q. Eliz.* I. 215 In a fierce dispute..the language uttered and written was both unprelatic and violent.

**Unprelaˈtical,** *a.* (UN-[1] 7.)

**1647** CLARENDON *Hist. Reb.* III. § 198 The archbishop of York,..by such Unprelatical, Ignominious Arguments, in plain terms advised him..to pass that Act. *a* **1661** FULLER *Worthies, Leicester.* II. (1662) 129 Some highly commended the Zeal of the Bishop,..whilest others condemned this in him, as an unprelatical act. **1857** TROLLOPE *Barchester T.* v, A new sofa had been introduced,..most unprelatical and almost irreligious. **1858** BUSHNELL *Nat. & Supernat.* x. (1864) 329 Vindicator of..a free unprelatical religion.

**Unpremeˈditable,** *a.* (UN-[1] 7 b.) **1768** STERNE *Sent. Journ., Fragment*, A capfull of wind..comes against you ..with such unpremeditable puffs.

**Unpremeˈditate,** *ppl. a.* Now *arch.* [UN-[1] 8 b, 5 b.] = next.

**1551** ROBINSON *More's Utopia* (1895) 2 As his talke cold not be fine and eloquent,..but sodein and vnpremeditate. **1600** TATE in Gutch *Coll. Cur.* I. 7 Either unpremeditate, and in hot blood, or else upon..grounded malice. **1651** *Life Father Sarpi* 174 His answers how unpremeditate soever. **1702** *Toleration* 10 There is something more excellent that men may hope by unpremeditate Prayer. **1825** SOUTHEY *Tale Paraguay* III. xxxvi, The voice..Is one which ..Utters all unpremeditate, at will, A modulated sequence.

**Unpremeˈditated,** *ppl. a.* (UN-[1] 8)

**1591** SHAKS. 1 *Hen. VI*, I. ii. 88 Aske me what question thou canst possible, And I will answer vnpremeditated. **1619** A. NEWMAN *Pleas. Vis.* 2 His vnpremeditated words. **1699** BENTLEY *Phal.* 237 Both Comedies and Tragedies for some time were unpremeditated and extemporal. **1768–74** TUCKER *Lt. Nat.* (1834) II. 444 Those unpremeditated addresses to Heaven called ejaculations. **1814** SCOTT *Wav.* xxvi, The hint..respecting Flora was not unpremeditated. **1878** STUBBS *Const. Hist.* xviii. III. 9 The scene in Westminster Hall..was no unpremeditated pageant.

Hence **Unpremeˈditatedness.**

**1802–12** BENTHAM *Ration. Judic. Evid.* (1827) I. 295 There is no such absolute incompatibility..between recollectedness and unpremeditatedness. **1883** H. DRUMMOND *Nat. Law in Spir. W.* 280 The suddenness and unpremeditatedness of Prayer.

**Unpremeˈditatedly,** *adv.* (UN-[1] 11.)

**1776** G. SEMPLE *Building in Water* 4 The cost did not exceed..100 guineas, as I had unpremeditatedly mentioned to Mr. Prior. **1826** DISRAELI *V. Grey* II. i, He could unpremeditatedly clothe his conceptions in language characteristic of the style of any particular author. **1884** *Contemp. Rev.* Feb. 250 There is not one of his writings which does not do for us..as it were by the way and unpremeditatedly, what [etc.].

†**Unpremeˈditately,** *adv. Obs.* [UN-[1] 12; cf. UNPREMEDITATE *ppl. a.*] = prec.

**1671** F. PHILIPS *Reg. Necess.* Ep. Ded., Answers not seldom suddainly and unpremeditately given. **1685** BOYLE *Of High Veneration* 1 Divines..who..talk of Him and his Attributes as freely and as unpremeditately, as..of a Geometrical Figure. *a* **1721** in W. Ayre *Life Pope* (1745) I. 140, I, who always speak unpremeditately.

**Unpremeditaˈtion.** (UN-[1] 12, 5 b.)

**1807** *Ann. Rev.* V. 237 It has the vivacity of unpremeditation. **1884** W. BESANT *Dorothy Forster* xxxvi, Asking each other..what means this naked plea of unpremeditation.

†**Unpreoˈccupated,** *ppl. a.* (UN-[1] 8.) **1666** J. SERGEANT *Let. Thanks* 26 To all unprejudic't and unpreoccupated Understandings.

**Unpreoˈccupied,** *ppl. a.* (UN-[1] 8.)

Frequent in recent use (1896–).

[**1775** ASH.] **1827** COLERIDGE *Lit. Rem.* (1839) IV. 408 Every reader whose imagination supplies an unpreoccupied, unrefracting medium to the Apostolic assertion. **1886** B. HARTE *Snowbound* 193 Lee, the only unpreoccupied..spirit in the party.

†**Unpreˈparate,** *ppl. a. Obs.*[−1] [UN-[1] 8 b.] Unprepared. **1576** TURBERV. *Venerie* 224 Let the scamony be unpreparate, the which you shall mingle amongst all those iuyces.

**Unpreparaˈtion.** *rare.* [UN-[1] 12, 5 b.] Unpreparedness.

**1627** BP. HALL *Holy Observ.* § 77 Our cowardlinesse, our vnpreparation, is his aduantage. **1646** — *Balm Gil.* 330 Thy unpreparation shall make him dreadfull. **1883** *Standard* 9 Jan. 2 The state of unpreparation may be imagined.

**Unprepaˈre,** *v. rare.* [UN-[2] 3 or UN-[1] 14.]

**1.** *trans.* To undo the preparation of.

**1598** FLORIO, *Sparecchiare*, to vngarnish, to vnprepare, to vndecke.

**2.** To make unprepared; to unfit.

**1645** MILTON *Tetrach.* 36 Nothing more unhallows a man, more unprepares him to the service of God in any duty. **1788** WESLEY *Wks.* (1872) VII. 154 No business..can hinder any man..unless it be such as unprepares him for heaven. **1852** LEVER *M. Tiernay* iii, The gloom of the place..equally unprepared me for what was to come.

**Unprepaˈred,** *ppl. a.* [UN-[1] 8.]

**1.** Of persons: Not in a state of preparation; not ready (for defence, reply, etc.).

**1549** CHEKE *Hurt Sedit.* (1569) G ij b, Although ye thinke your selues able to match with a fewe vnprepared Gentlemen, and put them from their houses. **1555** EDEN *Decades* (Arb.) 79 Where so euer they fownde any of owre men vnprepared, they slewe them. ?**1606** DANIEL *Funeral Poem Earl Devon.* Wks. (1623) 11 He brauely came to disappoint his foe, And many times surpris'd him vnprepared. **1667** MILTON *P. L.* VIII. 197 What is more,..renders us in things that most concerne Unpractis'd, unprepar'd, and still to seek. **1695** TRYON *Dreams* i. 3 Such discourses seem very ..extravagant to their unprepared Apprehensions. **1760** GOLDSM. *Cit. W.* iv, We were overtaken by a heavy shower of rain. I was unprepared; but they..had large coats. **1818** BYRON *Ch. Har.* IV. cxxvii, Lest the truth should shine Too brightly on the unprepared mind. **1849** MACAULAY *Hist. Eng.* v. I. 662 Cornish was arrested..and was brought altogether unprepared to the bar of the Old Bailey. **1889** GRETTON *Memory's Harkb.* 165 His Lordship requested one of the clergymen..to preach the sermon. Naturally they one and all declined, as unprepared.

*absol.* *a* **1643** S. GODOLPHIN *Quatrains* ii. 11 The unprepar'd this grace do find, Ye cool and do refresh the mind.

**b.** Const. *for*, or *to* with inf.

**1549** CHEKE *Hurt Sedit.* (1569) F ij, Exeter..being..vnfurnished, vnprepared, for so long a siege. **1678** *Proph. & Predict. Jas. Usher* (Hindley, III) 11 Look that you be not found unprepared for it. **1722** HAMILTON *Wallace* VIII. (1816) 135 Wallace..Surpris'd the English, unprepar'd for fight. **1794** S. WILLIAMS *Hist. Vermont* 174 That they might not be wholly unprepared to begin their course. **1819** SCOTT *Leg. Montrose* xvii, Being taken by surprise, they were totally unprepared for resistance. **1865** DICKENS *Mut. Fr.* I. xv, I am rather unprepared to see you.

**c.** *spec.* Not prepared for death.

**1594** SHAKS. *Rich. III*, III. ii. 65 'Tis a vile thing to dye, ..When men are vnprepar'd. *c* **1600** CHALKHILL *Thealma & Cl.* 1215 Death at no time finds goodness unprepared. **1611** BEAUM. & FL. *Maid's Trag.* v. i, Stir not; if thou dost, I'le take thee unprepar'd, thy fears upon thee, That make thy sins look double. **1665** BOYLE *Occas. Refl.* II. xi, Upon a Death Bed,..that very Thought might justly prove Dismal to an unprepar'd Man. **1796** SOUTHEY *Joan of Arc* x. (1853) 124 Hurried the confessor To shrive them, lest with unprepared souls They to their death might go. **1846** MRS. A. MARSH *Father Darcy* II. xii. 215 The slaughter of hundreds..of human beings totally unprepared.

*transf.* **1897** B. CAMM *Benedict. Mart. in Eng.* i. 31 Carried off by sudden and unprepared death before the priest could be summoned.

†**2.** Const. *of.* Not provided with. *Obs.*[−1]

**1732** J. LOUTHIAN *Form of Process* (1752) 45 If the Prisoner, through Ignorance, come unprepared of Lawyers.

**3.** Not made ready; left, introduced, taken, etc., without special preparation.

**1595** SHAKS. *John* II. i. 560 This vnlook'd for vnprepared pompe. *a* **1751** BOLINGBROKE *Study Hist.* ii. (1752) I. 41 The events we are witnesses of..appear to us very often original, unprepared, single, and un-relative. **1796** MME. D'ARBLAY *Camilla* V. 397 Her sight, thus unprepared,..might be too affecting for his weak frame. **1838** G. F. GRAHAM *Mus. Comp.* 23/2 Monteverde began to introduce unprepared sevenths and ninths. **1858** GREENER *Gunnery* 376 An ordinary unprepared gun, taken from a number promiscuously. **1874** PUSEY *Lent. Serm.* 8 We take refuge in the thought, that these were not sudden unprepared apostasies.

**Unprepaˈredly,** *adv.* (UN-[1] 11; cf. prec.)

**1606** BP. HALL *Medit. & Vows* I. lvi. 63 If hee die suddainly, yet hee dies not vnpreparedly. **1684** J. GOODMAN *Old Relig.* II. vi. 319 It seems far the more pardonable to come, though somewhat unpreparedly, than not to come because of unpreparedness. **1780** S. J. PRATT *Emma Corbett* (ed. 4) I. 194 She hath an affecting trick of..shedding tears, which burst upon her so unpreparedly, that [etc.]. **1825** J. NEAL *Bro. Jonathan* II. 134 We are like the young waterfowl,..launched upon their natural..element, unpreparedly. **1857** GEN. P. THOMPSON *Audi Alt.* I. xxxiv. 131 There is such a thing as going into danger with a full knowledge of where the danger lies, and there is doing it blindly and unpreparedly.

**Unprepaˈredness.** (UN-[1] 12.)

**1627** in Foster *Eng. Factories India* (1909) III. 169 Any advantage possible to bee taken (by theire unpreparednes). **1640** HABINGTON *Edw. IV*, 77 There could bee no excuse but in the unpreparednesse of his mind. **1684** [see prec.]. *a* **1716** BLACKALL *Wks.* (1723) I. 250 Our Unpreparedness for the Duty will not excuse the Omission of it. **1748** RICHARDSON *Clarissa* VII. 416 They had, for..his unpreparedness for it [*sc.* his fate], but too much grounds for apprehension with regard to his future happiness. **1824** BENTHAM *Bk. Fallacies* Wks. 1843 II. 411/1 Supposing the unpreparedness real, the reasonable and practical inference is—say nothing. **1873** SPENCER *Stud. Sociol.* ix. (1877) 213 The French..suffered catastrophes from this and other kinds of unpreparedness.

**Unprepoˈnderating,** *ppl. a.* (UN-[1] 10.) **1818** RANKEN *Hist. France* v. i. V. 204 Henry..proposed to throw his weight into the unpreponderating scale.

**Unprepossеˈssed,** *ppl. a.* (UN-[1] 8.)

**1648** BOYLE *Seraph. Love* (1659) 15 That with compos'd and unprepossessed thoughts you may judge of the Object, I propose to you. **1659** SOUTH *Serm.* (1679) 72 The Unprepossessed on the one hand, and the well disposed on the other. **1705** STANHOPE *Paraph.* I. 39 The Miracle upon Lazarus..which put the unprepossessed Multitudes upon celebrating the Glories of this Mighty Prophet. **1768** STERNE *Sent. Journ.* (1775) I. 67 Being pretty much unprepossessed, there must have been grounds for what struck me the moment I cast my eyes over the parterre. **1818** FOSTER *Ess.* (1844) I. 468 A mind of..strong intelligence.., entirely unprepossessed with any theory or system.

Hence **Unpreposseˈssedly** *adv.*

**1748** RICHARDSON *Clarissa* III. 211 Had she been left unprepossessedly to herself, she would have shewn favour to me.

**Unpreposseˈssing,** *ppl. a.* (UN-[1] 10.)

**1816** TUCKEY *Narr. Exped. R. Zaire* iii. (1818) 108 The faces..were by no means unprepossessing. **1869** TOZER *Highl. Turkey* I. 154 The marsh used to bear the unprepossessing name of Borboros, or 'Mud'. **1889** W. S. GILBERT *Gondoliers* II. 39 It's extraordinary what unprepossessing people one can love if one gives one's mind to it.

**Unprepoˈsterous,** *a.* (UN-[1] 7.) *a* **1618** SYLVESTER *Elegiac Epistle* 79 That Hand alone,..Un-partiall ever, Unpreposterous; How ever Other it may seem to us. **Unpresaˈgeful,** *a.* (UN-[1] 7.) **1882** SWINBURNE *Tristram of Lyonesse*, etc. 144 Unwittingly, with unpresageful eyes. **Unpreˈsbyterated,** *ppl. a.* (UN-[1] 8.) **1650** JEANES *Want of Ch. Govt.* (title-p.), Whether or no the Sacrament of the Lord's Supper may..be lawfully administered in an unPresbyterated Church, that is, a Church destitute of Ruling Elders. **1656** G. COLLIER *Ans. 15 Quest.* 10 While this church is unpresbyterated.

**Unpreˈscient,** *a.* (UN-[1] 7.)

**1866** LYTTON *Lost Tales Miletus, Secret Way* 15 Having heard all with not unprescient fears. **1874** LEWES *Probl. Life & Mind* I. 229 A blind impulse unprescient of means and end.

**Unprescriˈbed,** *ppl. a.* (UN-[1] 8.)

**1642** BP. HALL *Let. from Tower* 4, I have grated upon no mans conscience by the pressure..of the late Oath, or any unprescribed Ceremonie. **1690** C. NESSE *O. & N. Test.* I. 72 He left nothing unprescribed, that..mans foolish brain might find no room to foist anything into his service. **1768** R. WOOD *Ess. Genius Homer* (1775) 170 A certain proportion of voluntary attention in one sex, and of unprescribed reserve in the other.

**Unpreseˈntable,** *a.* (UN-[1] 7 b.)

**1828** *Q. Rev.* XXXVIII. 204 Another worse evil, the name of which, in his days, was not unpresentable, 'in prose or rhyme'. **1857** J. G. WOOD *Objects Sea Shore* 55 A pair of snowy white trowsers were covered with the sable fluid, and rendered entirely unpresentable. **1876** T. HARDY *Ethelberta* xlviii, She still felt so distressed and unpresentable that she resolved not to allow Lord Mountclere to see her.

Hence **Unpresentabiˈlity, -ableness.**

**1862** ROSSETTI in *Fraser's Mag.* July 73 For years past it has..candidly admitted its own unpresentableness. **1882** 'SARAH TYTLER' *Bride's Pass* ii, His unpresentability when fresh from some of his functions. **1886** RUSKIN *Præterita* I. x. 330 My own shyness and unpresentableness were farther stiffened..by a patriotic and Protestant conceit.

**Unpreseˈnted,** *ppl. a.* (UN-[1] 8.)

(*a*) **1523** in W. H. Turner *Select. Rec. Oxford* (1880) 42 All the trespassors..have byn permitted to passe unpresented. **1548** in Strype *Eccl. Mem.* (1721) II. App. Q. 57 We also.. advertise you, that for no Favour ye go about to excuse or leave unpresented, those that..have offended. **1620** QUARLES *Div. Poems, Feast for Worms* IX. ix, No crime unsifted, no sinne unpresented, Can lurke unseene. **1732** J. LOUTHIAN *Form of Process* (1752) 185 You shall present no Person for Hatred, Malice, or Ill-will; nor leave any thing unpresented for Fear, Favour or Affection.

(*b*) **1657** BAYNES in *Burton's Diary* (1828) II. 278 There are many things yet unpresented in the Petition. *c* **1732** in A. Thomson *T. Boston of Ettrick* (1895) 251 [He] was.. scrupulous of anything new or unpresented, until he was thoroughly satisfied of its necessity. **1895** PETRIE *Egypt. Tales* Ser. I. Introd. 1 It is strange that..the oldest literature ..should yet have remained unpresented to English readers.

(*c*) **1864** G. A. SALA in *Daily Tel.* 25 Feb., I went back to New York unavoidably unpresented [to the President]. **1897** W. C. HAZLITT *4 Generations* II. 221 The Queen and the Court,..their almost affecting solicitude for the health even of the Unpresented.

**Unpreseˈrvable,** *a.* (UN-[1] 7 b.) **1841** E. FORBES in Geikie *Mem.* x. (1861) 277, I am..drawing all the unpreservable animals..that fall in my way. **Unpreserˈved,** *ppl. a.* (UN-[1] 8.) **1648** HEXHAM II, *Onbehoedt*, Vnpreserved, or Vnsaved. [**1775** ASH.] **1859** ATKINSON *Walks & Talks* 380 As good a day's fly-fishing as in almost any unpreserved stream in the kingdom.

**Unpreˈssed,** *ppl. a.* [UN-[1] 8.]

**1.** Not pressed or squeezed; not subjected to pressure.

**1552** *Acc. Ld. High Treas. Scot.* X. 123 Thre elnis, thre quarteris, unprest blak. **1606** SHAKS. *Ant. & Cl.* III. xiii. 106 Haue I my pillow left vnprest in Rome,..to be abus'd By one that lookes on Feeders? **1615** G. SANDYS *Trav.* 65 A beastly kind of vnpressed cheese. **1718** PRIOR *Solomon* I. 346 Unpress'd their Vintage, and untill'd their Ground. **1794** MRS. RADCLIFFE *Myst. Udolpho* i, The forest-walk, where flowers unprest, Bow not their tall heads. **1812** CARY *Dante, Purg.* VI. 90 What boots it, that thy reins Justinian's hand Refitted, if thy saddle be unpressed? **1879** E. ARNOLD *Lt. Asia* IV. 90 On our bed there lay An unpressed pillow.

**b.** Not obtained by pressing.

**1630** QUARLES *Div. Poems* 309 Our tender Vine Should cheare thy palate with her unprest wine. **1708** J. PHILIPS *Cyder* I. 414 Snails, that creep O'er the ripe Fruitage,..and unprest Cyder drink. **1802** LAMB *J. Woodvil* III, Because your poet-born hath an internal wine,..unpressed in mortal wine-presses.

**2.** Not pressed into service; unconstrained.

**1603** J. DAVIES *Microcosmos* Wks. (Grosart) I. 58/2 Our Kings might warre with Tenants of their owne, Who would vnprest haue yet bin prest for shame To follow their Liege-land-lords. **1871** H. KING *Ovid's Met.* XIII. 43 The first to arms who sprang Unpressed, by no informer dragged to war.

†**Unpre·st**, *a. Obs.* [UN-[1] 7.] Not ready, willing, or well-disposed. **13..** *St. Erkenwolde* 285 Nas I a paynym vnpreste þat neuer thi plite knewe? **1568** T. HOWELL *Newe Sonets* (1879) 131 When Pen is vnprest, And witte wanteth conning thervnto adrest. **Unpresu·med,** *ppl. a.* (UN-[1] 8.) **1741** RICHARDSON *Pamela* I. p. xx, It adorn'd her with such unpresum'd Increase of Loveliness.

**Unpresu·ming,** *ppl. a.* (UN-[1] 10.)

**1770** AKENSIDE *Pleas. Imag.* IV. 16 An unpresuming guest. **1779** MOORE *View of Soc. France*, etc. I. 28 Unpresuming in argument, and..as well bred as those who have no other pretension. **1793** V. KNOX *Lett. to Yng. Nobleman* Wks. 1824 V. 91 To the entire exclusion of modest unpresuming men. **1830** W. L. BOWLES *Ken* I. p. xviii, The descendant of the great though unpresuming Locke. **1866** LIDDON *Bampton Lect.* i. (1875) 7 The most unpresuming of the titles of the Messiah.

Hence **Unpresu·mingness.**

*a* **1859** DE QUINCEY in H. A. Page *Life* (1877) II. xix. 199 Two sound qualities are at the root of these unpleasant phenomena—modesty or unpresumingness in the first place.

**Unpresu·mptuous,** *a.* (UN-[1] 7.)

**1704** ARWAKER *Embassy Heaven* xi, Henceforth, I'll urge my unpresumptuous Prayer. **1784** COWPER *Task* v. 746 A propriety that none can feel, But who..Can lift to heaven an unpresumptuous eye. ?**1813** LAMB *Christ's Hospital* Wks. 1908 I. 182 The common mass of that unpresumptuous assemblage of boys. **1822** WORDSW. *Eccles. Sonn., Concl.* 3 The Word..with unpresumptuous faith explored.

**Unpresu·mptuously,** *adv.* (UN-[1] 11.) **1846** WORCESTER (citing Thacher). **1850** W. ANDERSON *Regener.* 262 Such a state of mind..is sometimes..attained to unpresumptuously and legitimately. **Unprete·nded,** *ppl. a.* (UN-[1] 8.) **1611** FLORIO, *Impretenso*, vnpretended. **1649** JER. TAYLOR *Gt. Exemp.* Disc. xx. § 21 It is to be supposed he hath no great account to make for unpretended injuries.

**Unprete·nding,** *ppl. a.* (UN-[1] 10.)

**1697** COLLIER *Ess. Mor. Subj.* I. 101 Ought they not to be somewhat Frugal, and Unpretending in their Appearance? **1730** POPE *Let.* in Johnson *L. P., Fenton*, Feeling himself honest, true, & unpretending to more than was his own. **1795–6** WORDSW. *Borderers* II. 933 The unpretending ground we mortals tread. **1827** SCOTT *Chron. Canongate* Introd., Mere dignity of mind and rectitude of principle, assisted by unpretending good sense and temper. **1859** J. LANG *Wand. India* 7 She..has brought up a large family in the most respectable and unpretending style. **1885** 'MRS. ALEXANDER' *At Bay* i, Charmed with the unpretending refinement of her surroundings. **1891** FARRAR *Darkn. & Dawn* xliv, His house..was so unpretending as to excite the wonder of those who saw it.

**Unprete·ndingly,** *adv.* [UN-[1] 11; cf. prec.]

**1.** Without pretence; genuinely.

**1828** MOORE in *Mem.* V. 264 It is impossible for a royal personage to be more naturally and unpretendingly unaffected.

**2.** Without pretension; unassumingly.

**1855** CDL. WISEMAN *Fabiola* 359 Miriam would follow up, humbly and unpretendingly,..the instructions given by the holy Dionysius. **1859** W. COLLINS *Q. of Hearts* I. iv. 99 These narratives were written plainly and unpretendingly.

**Unprete·ndingness.** [UN-[1] 12.] Absence of pretension; unassumingness.

**1727** BOYER *Dict. Royal* II, Unpretendingness, *modestie.* **1768** *Woman of Honor* III. 254 There was in her..so sweet an unpretendingness..as astonished and captivated me. **1832** S. AUSTIN tr. *Tour Germ. Prince* III. xi. 315 She is goodness, cordiality, and unpretendingness itself. **1863** COWDEN CLARKE *Shaks. Char.* xvii. 427 One of the most agreeable [scenes] in the whole play, by reason of its familiar domestic unpretendingness.

**Unprete·ntious,** *a.* (UN-[1] 7.)

**1859** E. FITZGERALD in Shorter *Borrow & His Circle* (1913) 359 They are all perfectly quiet, sensible, and unpretentious girls. **1874** MICKLETHWAITE *Mod. Par. Churches* 175 Unpretentious village towers. **1887** *Spectator* 26 Mar. 422/2 The story is quite simple and unpretentious.

Hence **Unprete·ntiously** *adv.*, **-ness.**

**1863** GEO. ELIOT *Romola* ix, He wore that fortune..easily and unpretentiously. **1867** *Sat. Rev.* 17 Aug. 228/1 Its entire unpretentiousness of style..and unimaginative narrative.

**Unpre·ttiness.** (UN-[1] 12; cf. next.) **1675** S. SEWALL *Diary* 29 Apr., My Father..goes to live there, notwithstanding the littleness and unpretines of the house. **1753** RICHARDSON *Grandison* (1781) III. vii. 49 She says, it is not pretty in a young Lady to sigh: But where is the unprettiness of it?

**Unpre·tty,** *a.* (UN-[1] 7.)

**1782** MME. D'ARBLAY *Let.* 15 Oct., His English is blundering, but not unpretty. **1828** MISS MITFORD *Village* Ser. III. 40 Too refined for the youths of her own station, and too unpretty to attract those above her. **1856** SUSAN WARNER *Hills of Shatemuc* xxviii. 308 [She] shewed the white ivory between her not unpretty parted [lips].

**Unprevai·ling,** *ppl. a.* [UN-[1] 10.]

**1.** Ineffective, unsuccessful.

**1602** SHAKS. *Ham.* I. ii. 107 *King.* We pray you throw to earth This vnpreuayling woe, and thinke of vs As of a Father. **1693** LOCKE *Educ.* § 78 If she had left off sooner..she had spoil'd the Child for ever, and, by her unprevailing Blows, only confirm'd her Refractoriness. **1716–20** *Lett. fr. Mist's Jrnl.* (1722) I. 292 Beauty draws but by a Hair, and that's but weak and unprevailing. *a* **1806** HORSLEY *Serm.* xxvii. (1816) II. 344 The bare unprevailing wish that we were what we necessarily understand we ought to be. **1813** SHELLEY *Q. Mab* VII. 248 The unprevailing malice of my Foe.

**b.** Quasi-*adv.* Ineffectively, vainly.

**1632** LITHGOW *Trav.* VII. 326 We were..assayled by the Cursares..; yet vnpreuailing, for we were well prouided with good Munition. **1817** SHELLEY *Rev. Islam* I. xiv, Wile baffled wile, and strength encountered strength, Thus long, but unprevailing.

**2.** Not prevalent or usual.

**1859** MILL *Liberty* 97 It is only desired to restrain the employment of them against the prevailing opinion: against the unprevailing they may..be used without general disapproval.

**Unpre·valent,** *a.* (UN-[1] 7.) **1690** BOYLE *Christian Virtuoso* Pref. A 1, The formerly unprevalent Desires of those that would have it appear in Public. **1880** RAMSAY in *Daily News* 26 Aug. 5/7 In 1855 the old idea was still not unprevalent. †**Unpreva·ricate,** *a. Obs. rare.* (UN-[1] 7.) Not perverted. **1652** CHARLETON *Darkn. Atheism Dispelled* 27 To that unprevaricate judgment, that shall maturely perpend the contents. **Unpreva·ricating,** *ppl. a.* (UN-[1] 10.) **1792** V. KNOX *Serm.* viii. 186 The unprevaricating dictates of a clear conscience.

**Unpreve·ntable,** *a.* (UN-[1] 7, 5 b.)

**1616** *Rich Cabinet* 31 A cuckold is an vnpreuentable destiny. *a* **1670** HACKET *Abp. Williams* I. (1693) 21 Nineteen Parts of a great Incorporation should be Condemn'd, for the Frowardness, and that unpreventable by all the Power we had of the twentieth Part. **1787** BENTHAM *Def. Usury* iii. 29 There are so many unpreventable ways of letting it run out at the bung-hole. **1816** — *Offic. Apt. Maximized, Extr. Const. Code* (1830) 55 Of this repugnance ..the existence is unpreventable. **1895** *Voice* (N.Y.) 5 Sept. 1/2 One of those terrible, unforeseen, and apparently unpreventable accidents.

Hence **Unpreve·ntableness.**

**1884** *Mind* July 342 The element of unpreventableness or inescapableness.

**Unpreve·ntably,** *adv.* (UN-[1] 11.) *a* **1639** W. WHATELEY *Prototypes* I. xxi. (1640) 260 Though death should present itselfe to you naked,..and that in shew unpreventably. **1816** BENTHAM *Chrestom.* Wks. 1843 VIII. 82 Constantly and unpreventably it actually is so.

**Unpreve·nted,** *ppl. a.* (UN-[1] 8.)

**1585** GREENE *Planetomachia* H 4, Hee that seeketh to haue his purpose vnpreuented. **1602** CAMPION *Art Eng. Poesie* iv. 10 The more secure, the more the stroke we feele Of vnpreuented harms. **1667** MILTON *P. L.* III. 231 Shall grace not find means, that..Comes unprevented, unimplor'd, unsought? **1735** THOMSON *Liberty* III. 499 The meanly-patient death, That waits a tyrant's unprevented stroke.

**Unpreve·ntible,** *a.* (UN-[1] 7.)

**1676** *Doctrine of Devils* 120 This seems unpreventible where this Doctrine is entertained. **1885** DUCANE *Punishm. Crime* 124 The evils of the hulk system were..unpreventible.

**Unpreve·ntive,** *a.* (UN-[1] 7.) **1667** WATERHOUSE *Fire Lond.* 96 So dangerous a thing is that, which the consequence calls unpreventive wisdom. **Unpri·ceable,** *a.* [UN-[1] 7.] Inestimable. *a* **1641** BP. MOUNTAGU *Acts & Mon.* (1642) 39 This unpriceable benefit conferred upon man.

**Unpri·ced,** *ppl. a.* [UN-[1] 8.]

**1.** Beyond price; priceless.

**1857** WHITTIER *Last Walk in Autumn* xvi, He, who to the lettered wealth Of ages adds the lore unpriced. **1858** NEALE *Bernard de M.* 27 Thine ageless walls are bonded With amethyst unpriced.

**2.** Not having the price affixed.

**1888** *Athenæum* 15 Sept. 355/3 The books offered for sale are unpriced.

**Unpri·cked,** *ppl. a.* [UN-[1] 8.]

**1.** Not marked with pricks or dots; † *spec.* (of a Hebrew text), unpointed.

**1588** J. MELLIS *Briefe Instr.* F iij b, Diuers parcels more may remaine vnpricked in the Leager, which ought not to bee put in the Iournall. **1690** C. NESSE *O. & N. Test.* I. 426 The Septuagint, who in their unprick'd Bibles did read [etc.]. **1695** J. EDWARDS *Perfect. Script.* III. 493 These Interpreters in their unpricked Bibles mistook [the Hebrew text].

**2.** Not subjected to pricking; unpunctured.

**1611** COTGR. s.v. *Plumer*, To pill, or vnhuske, a chestnut..which..few can doe easily, or with vnprickt fingers. **1882** J. PARKER *Apost. Life* I. 74 If your heart be left unpricked, ..the word has been in vain.

†**3.** Not turned sour. *Obs.*

*c* **1645** HOWELL *Lett.* (1650) I. 58, I have sent you a Runlet of it..: and, if it com safe and unprick'd, I pray bestow som Bottles upon the Lady (you know).

**Unpri·ckled,** *ppl. a.* (UN-[1] 8.) *a* **1711** KEN *Hymnotheo* Wks. 1721 III. 318 Sweet Rosebuds on unprickel'd Bushes blew. **1728** CHAMBERS *Cycl.* s.v. *Fish*, The Smooth, or unprickled Hound-Fish. **Unpri·ckly,** *a.* (UN-[1] 7.) **1660** *Catal. Plant. Cantab.* Index 23 Unprickly Sowthistle, *Sonchus lævis.* **1758** *Phil. Trans.* L. 513 Smooth or unprickly Sowthistle. **Unpri·ded,** *ppl. a.* (UN-[2] 8, 6 b.) **1628** FELTHAM *Resolves* II. xxxiii. 104 Pittifull! that we should rather mischiefe our selves, then be content to be vnprided. **Unprie·d,** *ppl. a.* (UN-[1] 8 c.) **1757** *Hist. 2 Mod. Advent.* II. 191, I left no Corner unpryed into, to find out a Lady to my Taste.

**Unprie·st,** *v.* [UN-[2] 6 b, 4. Cf. Du. *ontpriesteren.*]

**1.** *trans.* To deprive (a person) of the character or office of priest.

**1550** BALE *Eng. Votaries* II. 63 b, If he were a secular prest, or one vnprested by them, he shuld clerely lose his benefyce. **1581** J. BELL *Haddon's Answ. Osor.* 285 One Stephen was made Pope, who..doth first vnpriest, and afterwardes newpriest agayne all such as Const. before him had priested. **1641** R. BROOKE *Eng. Episc.* 74, I finde..some others unpriested by Councells because ordained by Presbyters alone. **1691** GRASCOMBE *Reply Vind. Disc.* 11 To take away our Orders, and Unpriest and Unbishop us. **1713** CALAMY *Life Baxter* (ed. 2) xvii. 466 No Secular Power could Unbishop and Unpriest, or disable them. A Clergy-man's Authority (said they) is from God. **1839** J. ROGERS *Antipopopr.* xvii. § 2. 340 Thousands of men may have..brought disorder and nullity into the kirk, unpriesting the priesthood. **1868** BROWNING *Ring & Bk.* VI. 1870 Unpriest me,..Remove me from the midst, no longer priest.

**2.** To deprive, or make free, of priests.

**1844** MOZLEY *Ess.* (1878) II. 33 This ideal of a Church of course utterly unpriested it, and a priest, accordingly, Arnold could not tolerate.

**Unprie·sted,** *ppl. a.* [UN-[1] 8.] Not furnished with a priest.

**1548** GESTE *Pr. Masse* E iii b, Paul spoke the selue same wordes vnto the vnprested Corinthians. **1596** BELL *Surv. Popery* III. x. 406 S. Paul..did communicate the vnpriested Corinthians vnder both kinds. **1858** ALLINGHAM *50 Mod. Poems* (1865) 46 Though living unpriested and dying unshriven.

**Unprie·stly,** *a.* (UN-[1] 7.)

**1537** LATIMER *Serm. & Rem.* (Parker Soc.) 390 That unpriestly priest, whose damsel was brought to bed alate. **1546** BALE *Eng. Votaries* I. 66 Kynge Edgare..rebuked the prestes..for..their vnpriestlye aparellynges. **1611** SPEED *Hist. Gt. Brit.* IX. viii. 1 The two vnjust Intruders on the Crowne;..the one by vnprincely forces, the other by vnpriestly fraud. **1790** PENNANT *London* 19 The people, enraged at his unpriestly conduct, would have torn him to pieces. **1837** J. H. NEWMAN *Proph. Office Ch.* 403 The Asmonæans, who, besides their unpriestly character, were many of them stained with crimes.

**Unprie·stly,** *adv.* (UN-[1] 11.) **1554** BONNER *Articles* A iij, Whether they..vse common games or playes, or behaue themselfes otherwyse vnpriestly and vnsemely. **Unpri·me,** *a.* (UN-[1] 7.) **1879** *Encycl. Brit.* IX. 839/1 Unprime fur seals part with their overhair very reluctantly. **Unpri·med,** *ppl. a.* (UN-[1] 8.) [**1775** ASH.] **1862** THORNBURY *Turner* I. 265 Turner had the greatest horror of the picture being lined, having commenced it with sized colours on unprimed cloth. **1881** LE CONTE *Sight* 234 The position[s]..shown by the unprimed and the primed vinculum respectively.

**Unpri·mitive,** *a.* (UN-[1] 7, 5 b.)

**1708** COLLIER *Eccl. Hist.* v. 481 [To] acquiesce under so unprimitive, and uncatholick a Practice. **1746** J. CHAPMAN *Popery* 2 The unscriptural, unprimitive Crudities of the Romish Principles. **1899** FILLEUL (*title*), A Sacerdotal Ministry in the Christian Church: Unscriptural, Unprimitive, and High Treason against Christ.

**Unpri·nce,** *v.* (UN-[2] 6 b.)

**1602** CHETTLE *Hoffman* II. (1631) C 4, You were better vnknighted then vnprinced. *a* **1661** FULLER *Worthies, Warwick* III. (1662) 121 Queen Mary..would not Unprince herself to Obey his Holiness.

**Unpri·ncelike,** *a.* and *adv.* (UN-[1] 7 c, 11 b.)

**1579** J. STUBBES *Gaping Gulf* F 4 b, This vnmanlike, vnprincelike, secrete,..french kind of woeng [= wooing]. **1611** SPEED *Hist. Gt. Brit.* VII. xli. § 2. 347 With shamelesse and vnprincelike lust, hee abused a Lady of great estate. **1639** FULLER *Holy War* I. xv. 23 Alexius..most unprincelike brake his word.

**Unpri·nceliness.** (UN-[1] 12; cf. next.) **1860** FORSTER *Gr. Remonstr.* 97 Never was Kirk so rebellious, in flaming up..against the sovereign's unprinceliness and ungodliness.

**Unpri·ncely,** *a.* (UN-[1] 7.)

**1536** Q. ANNE BOLEYN *Lett.* (1714) 38 Your unprincely and cruel usage of me. **1593** *Sidney's Arcadia* v. (1922) II. 201 Constant suffering, that your unprincely dealing hath purchased unto you. **1611** [see UNPRIESTLY *a.*]. **1613** SHERLEY *Trav. Persia* 29 As farre from..vanity as from all vnprincely signes, or acts. **1649** MILTON *Eikon.* ix. 78 Not forgetting the unprincely usage, and..the abolishing of Parlaments. **1748** RICHARDSON *Clarissa* (1811) II. 12 Nor would the unprincely wretch marry her till [etc.]. **1821** JOANNA BAILLIE *Metr. Leg., Wallace* lxix, A base unprincely compact. **1881** TENNYSON *Cup* I. i, Some unprincely violence to a woman.

**Unpri·ncely,** *adv.* (UN-[1] 11.) *a* **1548** HALL *Chron. Hen. IV*, 7 b, He most tirannously and vnprincely said that [etc.]. **1611** SPEED *Hist. Gt. Brit.* IX. viii. 486/1 If Princes can bee thus vnprincely degenerous. **Unpri·ncess,** *v.* (UN-[2] 6 b.) **1663** R. STAPYLTON *Slighted Maid* II. 22, I have Unlorded my self and Unprincess'd thee, Granchild Fritilla. **Unpri·ncipal,** *a.* (UN-[1] 7.) **1541** R. COPLAND *Guydon's Quest. Chirurg.* c ij, Howe many pryncypal membres be there, and howe many vnpryncypal? **Unpri·nciple,** *v.* (UN-[2] 6 b.) **1713** *Gentl. Instructed* II. 108 The Press has not only effeminated the Mind, but Unprincipl'd the Understanding. **1760–72** H. BROOKE *Fool of Qual.* (1809) I. 87 When I behold so many scoundrels..I reflect, that they have been principled, or rather unprincipled, by such tutors as Mr. Vindex.

**Unpri·ncipled,** *ppl. a.* [UN-[1] 8.]

**1.** Not instructed or grounded *in* something.

**1634** MILTON *Comus* 367, I do not think my sister so to seek, Or so unprincipl'd in vertues book. **1644** — *Educ.* 3 Others betake them to State affairs, with souls so unprincipl'd in vertue, and true generous breeding, that [etc.].

**2.** Of persons, etc.: Not possessed of fixed, sound, or honourable principles of conduct.

**1644** MILTON *Judgm. Bucer* 26 God..will also give them..to inform themselvs rightly in the midst of an unprincipl'd age. **1681** FLAVEL *Meth. Grace* v. 102 An unprincipled professor must be squeezed by some weight of affliction, ere he will yield one tear. **1771** GOLDSM. *Hist. Eng.* I. 353 Every office..was bestowed on these unprincipled strangers. **1796** MME. D'ARBLAY *Camilla* V. 506 [It] opened to his unprincipled mind a scheme yet more flagitious. **1849** MACAULAY *Hist. Eng.* vi. II. 113 Several men not less unprincipled than Sunderland. **1878** E. JENKINS *Haverholme* 30 A couple of unprincipled rascals.

*absol.* **1834** *Tait's Mag.* May 222/2 These clamours of the wealthy, the timid, or the unprincipled.

**3.** Based upon, exhibiting, want of principle.

**1782** V. Knox *Ess.* cxx. (1819) II. 9 There are, indeed, many who are esteemed good sort of persons, but whose goodness is unprincipled. **1797** Burke *Regic. Peace* ii. ⁋ 22 Whilst the monarchies subsisted, this unprincipled cession was what the influence of the elder branch..never dared to attempt on the younger. **1841** Thackeray *Gt. Hoggarty Diam.* vii, I thought this rather cruel and unprincipled conduct. **1871** Freeman *Hist. Ess.* Ser. i. xi. 331 The ambition of Philip the Good was quite..unprincipled.

Hence **Unpri·ncipledness.**

*a* **1812** Buckminster *Serm.* (1827) 362 Their strange union ..of exquisite sensibility and practical unprincipledness. **1865** *Pall Mall G.* 12 Dec. 2 A settled unprincipledness has been eating its way into the public opinion of Europe.

**Unpri·nt,** *v.* (Un-2 3.) **1842** S. R. Maitland *Notes* ii. 81 Whatever he may say now, he cannot unprint his Vindication of Fox.

**Unpri·ntable,** *a.* and *sb.* [Un-1 7 b, 12.]

**1.** *adj.* Not fit to be printed. (Common *c* 1893–.)

**1871** *St. Paul's Mag.* Aug. 457 Articles that were utterly unprintable. **1898** *Punch* 9 July 10/1 What the groom says is unprintable!

**2.** *sb. pl.* Trousers; = Unmentionable *sb.*

**1860** W. W. Reade *Liberty Hall* I. iii. 32 Arrayed in black coat, tie, studs, waistcoat, unprintables.

**Unpri·nted,** *ppl. a.* (Un-1 8.)

**1532** More *Confut. Tyndale* Wks. 627/2 When he cometh to my seconde boke, [he] goeth fro the first Chapiter to the third, as though the prynter had left the second vnprinted. **1551** Recorde *Pathw. Knowl.* ii. Pref., The other bookes, whiche now are lefte vnprinted. **1609** Boys *Expos. Princ. Script.* 93 This may teach..all superiours who prescribe lawes vnto other, to become first an vnprinted law themselues. *a* **1683** Oldham *Wks.* (1686) 112 Wit should be open, ..Not lurk in sly unprinted privacy. **1729** T. Innes *Crit. Essay* (1879) 117 The most ancient now extant even of the unprinted Irish historians. **1796** Lamb *Let. to Coleridge* in *Final Mem.* ii. 211 You have scarce enough unprinted to make a second volume with Lloyd. **1860** Tyndall *Glac.* ii. xiv. 299 The paper..might have remained unprinted, had not another publication..called it forth. **1884** A. R. Pennington *Wiclif* viii. 247 He expresses himself still more strongly in his unprinted writings.

**Unpri·son,** *v.* [Un-2 5.] *trans.* To free from prison.

**1390** Gower *Conf.* III. 202 Therbellis king of Bulgarie.. Justinian hath unprisoned. **1598** Florio, *Discarcerare*, to vnprison. **1633** Heywood *Eng. Trav.* iv. H 3, Now is the Goale deliuerie; Through this backe gate Shift for your selues, I heere vnprison all. **1635** *To C'tess Huntington* Donne's Wks. 1912 I. 418 Fire rose, and each from other but unty'd, Themselves unprison'd were and purify'd. **1827** Montgomery *Pelican Isl.* i. 119 Then the wind Unprisoned, blew its trumpet loud.

**Unpri·sonable,** *a.* (Un-1 7 b.) **1878** M. & F. Collins *Vill. Comedy* I. xx. 269 The agile and unprisonable spirit of man. **Unpri·soned,** *ppl. a.*[1] [Un-1 8.] Not put in prison. *a* **1844** Campbell *Napoleon & Sailor* 10 They suffer'd him ..Unprison'd on the shore to roam. **Unpri·soned,** *ppl. a.*[2] [Un-2 8 or f. Unprison *v.*] Released from prison. **1840** Dickens *Old C. Shop* lii, Perhaps not one of the unprisoned souls had been able [etc.]. **†Unpriva·tion.** *Obs.*-1 [Un-1 12.] Continuance (of existence). *a* **1628** F. Grevil *Cælica*, '*Down in the Depth*' iii, With glory scourging all the Sp'rits infernall, And vncreated hell with vnpriuation.

**Unpri·vileged,** *ppl. a.* (Un-1 8.)

**1590** Swinburne *Testaments* 112 Such disposition..maie be lawfullie and properlie said to be a testament, whether the same be..priuiledged or vnpriuiledged. **1592** Warner *Alb. Eng.* vii. xxxiv. 149 But of vnpriuiledged bloud yet had he store to spill. **1702** Rowe *Tamerl.* i. i. 100 The Boast and Master-piece of the great Maker, That wears in vain th' Impression of his Image Unprivileged from thee. **1791** Mackintosh *Vind. Gallicæ* 255 They are a small body, united to the mass.., and returning to it, undistinguished and unprivileged, the majority of their children. **1818** Hallam *Mid. Ages* (1819) I. 443 The arrangement..had still left several kinds of artisans unincorporated, and consequently unprivileged. **1881** L. Wallace *Ben-Hur* vi. ii, To dwell with none but lepers; to be utterly unprivileged.

**Unpri·zable,** *a.* [Un-1 7 b.]

**1.** Not to be prized; of little worth.

**1601** Shaks. *Twel. N.* v. i. 58 A bawbling Vessell was he Captaine of, For shallow draught and bulke vnprizable.

**†2.** Beyond all price; inestimable. *Obs.*

**1604** T. Wright *Passions* v. iv. 246 Some gifts are..so vnprizable, that a man is never able perfitly to recompence them. **1616** Breton *Good & Bad* Wks. (Grosart) 12/2 A Quiet Woman is..a iewell vnprizeable and a ioy vnspeakable. **1634** W. Tirwhyt tr. *Balzac's Lett.* (vol. I) 258 She is rich, but my liberty is unprizeable.

**Unpri·zed,** *ppl. a.* [Un-1 8.]

**†1.** Unpriced; of which the price has not been fixed. *Obs.*

**1445** *Extr. Aberdeen Reg.* (1844) I. 14 That thai sell na flesche vnprisit,..vnder the payne of tynsal of the flesche.

**2.** Not prized or valued.

*c* **1600** Donne *Elegy* iii. 6 Women are like the Arts, forc'd unto none, Open to all searchers, unpriz'd, if unknowne. **1615** G. Wither *Fidelia* 707 Though my faith must now despised be, Vnpriz'd, vnualued at the lowest rate. **1648** Hexham ii, *Ongelovet*, Vnprised, or Vnrated. **1821** Wordsw. *Italian Itinerant* 82 Seemingly a Thing despised; Even by the sun and air unprized.

**†3.** ? Priceless. *Obs.* (Probably = prec.)

**1605** Shaks. *Lear* i. i. 262 Not all the Dukes of watrish Burgundy Can buy this vnpriz'd precious Maid of me.

**†Unproa·chable,** *a.* *Obs.*-1 [Un-1 7 b, 5 b.] Unapproachable. **1544** Betham *Precepts War* i. cxvii. F viij, The vnprocheable humanitie of Cesar.

**† Unpro·bable,** *a.* *Obs.* [Un-1 7 b, 5 b.] **a.** Incapable of proof. **b.** Improbable, unlikely.

**1532** More *Confut. Tyndale* Wks. 429/1 When Tyndall hath proued by thys vnprobable case, that women may consecrate the body of Christ. **1588** Fraunce *Lawiers Log.* Ded. ¶ 3 The unprobable assertion comprized in your last two Epithetes. **1602** T. Fitzherbert *Apol.* 4 The one [point], no doubt in their owne opinions vncertayne, and in ours altogeather vnprobable, if not vnpossible. **1652** Gaule *Magastrom.* 108 Is not, then, the latter..supposition still more unprobable? **1684** Boyle *Porousn. Anim. & Solid Bod.* vi. 104, I thought it not very unprobable that the great heat ..might cleave..some of the Crystalline Fragments.

**† Unpro·bably,** *adv.* [Un-1 11, 5 b.]

**1.** Without good reason.

**1613** Purchas *Pilgrimage* (1614) 62 The Iew not vnprobably thinketh that mixtures..were forbidden. **1721** Strype *Eccl. Mem.* I. i. 373 Being able to diminish, by the authority of wise and knowing men, things unjustly and unprobably crept in.

**2.** Without probability; improbably.

**1606** *Choice, Chance*, etc. (1881) 53 Pardon me..if I speak vnprobably and Let me say what I think.

**Unpro·bated,** *ppl. a.* (Un-1 8.) **1570** Levins *Manip.* 50 Vnprobated, *improbatus*.

**Unpro·bed,** *ppl. a.* (Un-1 8.)

[**1775** Ash.] **1827** Pollok *Course T.* vi. 148 The frothy orator..leaving still the heart unprobed. **1866** C. J. Vaughan *Plain Words* xi. 211 He knows the misery..of having any unprobed, unexplored secrets between the heart and its God. **1879** Browning *Ivan Ivanovitch* 31 Each village death-begirt By wall and wall of pine—unprobed undreamed abyss.

**Unproblema·tic,** *a.* (Un-1 7.) **1683** E. Hooker *Pref. Pordage's Mystic Div.* 107 It beeing altogether unproblematic and without the less'st shadow of scrupl. **Unproblema·tical,** *a.* (Un-1 7.) **1799** E. Du Bois *Piece Family Biog.* I. 65 Which he [neglected]..for this plain and unproblematical reason. **Unpro·cessed,** *ppl. a.* (Un-1 8.) **1539** *Reg. Privy Seal Scot.* II. 472/2 The said Johnne to be ..unprocessit, unpoyndit, and untrublit for ony actioun civile bigane.

**Unproclai·med,** *ppl. a.* (Un-1 8.)

**1648** Hexham ii, *Onverkondight*, vnproclamed. **1667** Milton *P. L.* xi. 220 Against the Syrian King, who,..Assassin-like had levied Warr, Warr unproclam'd. **1795–1802** Wordsw. *Excurs.* i. 94 Else surely this Man had not left His graces unrevealed and unproclaimed. **1844** De Quincey *Greece under Rom.* Wks. 1858 VIII. 335 Armistices.., truces, or unproclaimed suspensions of war. **1878** B. Taylor *Deukalion* iii. ii, The..Heir Who, unproclaimed, awaits his lordship.

**Unpro·creant,** *a.* (Un-1 7.) **1870** Lowell *Among my Bks.* Ser. i. (1873) 190 A knowledge..which comes of mere learning is sapless and unprocreant. **Unpro·create(d,** *ppl. a.* (Un-1 8.) **1630** Drumm. of Hawth. *Flowres of Sion, Hymne of Fairest Faire* 126 O most holie One, Vnprocreat'd [*ed.* 1711 unprocreate] Father, euer-procreat'd Sonne.

**Unprocu·rable,** *a.* (Un-1 7 b.)

**1607** Hieron *Wks.* I. 351 The dignity of this estate..was vnprocurable, saue only by this infinit price. **1654** Boyle in T. Birch *Life* B.'s Wks. 1772 I. p. liv, A barbarous country, where..chemical instruments were..unprocurable. **1864** Carlyle *Fredk. Gt.* xvii. v. IV. 568 Draught-cattle seem absolutely unprocurable. **1875** Jowett *Plato* (ed. 2) III. 29 Not of an Eleusinian pig, but of some unprocurable animal.

**Unprocu·red,** *ppl. a.* (Un-1 8.)

**1534** More *Comf. agst. Trib.* ii. Wks. 1177/2 [To] fall in the dyspleasure of God, or leaue Goddes pleasure vnprocured. *a* **1600** Hooker *Serm. Pride* ⁋ 10, I bless thee..for thy goodness,..not in regard of my merits,..but of thy mere unprocured benignity. **1655** Jer. Taylor *Unum Necess.* vii. § 3. 464 The meer ineffective, unprocured desirings or lustings after evil things.

**Unprocu·ring,** *vbl. sb.* (Un-1 13.) **1622** Mabbe tr. *Aleman's Guzman d'Alf.* i. 135 A man ought to venture his life, for the keeping of a friend,..for the vn-procuring of an enemie. **Unprodu·ceable,** *a.* (Un-1 7 b.) **1802–12** Bentham *Ration. Judic. Evid.* (1827) II. 497 While the witnesses are alive and produceable,..when they are dead, or otherwise unproduceable. **1834** De Quincey *Autob. Sk.* Wks. 1854 II. 313 Everybody agrees in our days to think this accomplishment..unproduceable, unless existing in an exquisite state of culture. **Unprodu·ceably,** *adv.* (Un-1 11.) **1865** Miss Yonge *Clever Woman* II. 206 To have an unproduceably eccentric melancholy bride.

**Unprodu·ced,** *ppl. a.* [Un-1 8, 5 b.]

**1.** Not brought into existence; uncreated.

**1674** Boyle *Ground's Corpusc. Philos.* 9 For their sakes that would have matter to be unproduced. **1712** Blackmore *Creation* p. iv, Those who believe an innate Idea of a Divine Being, unproduced by any Operation of the Mind. **1768–74** Tucker *Lt. Nat.* (1834) I. 499 The rules of justice are apprehended immutable and unproduced, because you cannot draw them directly from any object before you.

**2.** Not extended or lengthened.

**1768** *Phil. Trans.* LX. 250 A new equation, all whose roots shall fall upon the line OT unproduced. **1882** Minchin *Unipl. Kinemat.* 83 Supposing that the lines..intersect each other at a point, *O*, in their unproduced lengths.

Hence **Unprodu·cedness.**

**1862** F. Hall *Hindu Philos. Syst.* 37 Unproducedness thereby does not belong to them.

**Unprodu·ctive,** *a.* [Un-1 7.]

**1.** Not productive: **a.** Const. *of.*

**1756** Burke *Subl. & B.* i. xix, The use of the passions.. cannot be..unproductive to ourselves of that noble..union of science and admiration. **1768–74** Tucker *Lt. Nat.* (1834) II. 130 The enjoyment distilling from this source is sure and sincere,..and unproductive of future inconvenience. **1828** Hawthorne *Fanshawe* iii, A few months passed..unproductive of events that [etc.]. **1839** Carlyle *Chartism* x, Most paralytic, uninstructive: unproductive of any comfort to one!

**b.** Without const., or in attributive use.

**1784** Cowper *Task* ii. 124 The gloomy scenes Where beauty oft and letter'd worth consume Life in the unproductive shades of death. **1791** Newte *Tour Eng. & Scot.* 383 Shall ..the poor..[be doomed] to unproductive labour, in order to gratify barbarian ignorance and pride? **1815** Scott *Guy M.* xv, Sampson picked up some other scholars..whose lessons were proportionally unproductive. **1849** Cobden *Speeches* 4 Unproductive services like your fighting establishments..in a time of peace. **1870** Burton *Hist. Scot.* lxxii. VII. 73 The king..does not see the use of their attempting to hold a meeting—in Scotland it would be dangerous, in England unproductive.

**2.** Not materially productive; not yielding crops, minerals, etc.

**1766** *Parl. Deb.* (1813) XVI. 303/1 The harvest had failed, and was unproductive. **1796** Withering *Brit. Plants* (ed. 3) II. 389 A female plant..produced small unproductive seeds. **1855** *Orr's Circ. Sci., Inorg. Nat.* 222 Unproductive portions of the fields. **1877** Raymond *Statist. Mines & M.* 192 They are unproductive as yet in minerals.

Hence **Unprodu·ctively** *adv.*, **-ness.**

*c* **1815** Jane Austen *Persuas.* xx, The anxious interval wore away *unproductively. **1813** Sir H. Davy *Agric. Chem.* 177 Any particular ingredient which is the cause of their *unproductiveness. **1869** Tozer *Highl. Turkey* II. 343 The unhealthiness and unproductiveness of marshes.

**Unproducti·vity.** (Un-1 12.) **1888** *19th Cent.* June 836 The unproductivity of the soil. **Unprofa·nable,** *a.* (Un-1 7 b.) *a* **1641** Bp. Mountagu *Acts & Mon.* (1642) 178 Nor did the Romanes..hold any thing so sacred, sanctified and unprophanable, as Sibyll's Oracles. **1869** Mrs. Whitney *We Girls* xii, The sanctity..would be as unprofanable as ever. **Unprofa·ne,** *a.* (Un-1 7.) **1576** Fleming *Panopl. Epist.* 196 Passing..through Ægypt, there to conferre with the unprophane priestes, and learned Astronomers. **1646** Mayne *Serm. Unity* 58 How seemingly holy,..how unprofane soever his Behaviour be.

**Unprofa·ned,** *ppl. a.* (Un-1 8.)

**1650** R. Stapylton *Strada's Low C. Wars* v. 125 The greatest wonder was..that..a few men..should before midnight, when they began but in the evening, have nothing at all left entire or unprofaned. **1659** Gauden *Tears Ch.* iii. iv. 274 They easily preserved the doctrine of Christian Religion uncorrupted, the Mysteries unprophaned. **1774** Beattie *Minstrel* ii. xliv, May your influence unprofaned To god-like worth the generous bosom raise! **1818** Byron *Ch. Har.* iv. lxvi, Surely that stream was unprofaned by slaughters. **1894** Blackmore *Perlycross* 435 Resting placidly, unprofaned, untouched.

**Unprofe·ssed,** *ppl. a.* (Un-1 8.)

*c* **1430** *Paston Lett.* I. 30 The poure hous of Bromholm.., in wheche arn divers vertuous yongge men, monkes clad and unprofessyd. *a* **1450** in Myrc *Par. Pr.* (1902) 61 Alle þat leyne hand on preste or clerke..off religione professed or vnprofessud. **1808** Scott *Marm.* ii. v, Sister Clare,..As yet a novice unprofess'd. **1809–14** Wordsw. *Excurs.* vii. 309 Whose mind could..beguile A solitude, unchosen, unprofessed.

**Unprofe·ssing,** *ppl. a.* (Un-1 10.) **1748** Richardson *Clarissa* (1811) V. 158 The unprofessing Mrs. Moore.

**Unprofe·ssional,** *a.* and *sb.* [Un-1 7, 12.]

**1806** *Med. Jrnl.* XV. 299 The solution unfortunately having become a very common medicine with unprofessional people. **1847** De Quincey *Span. Mil. Nun* Wks. 1853 III. 59 No authority could overrule the concurrent testimony of all symptoms, and of all unprofessional opinions. **1895** *Westm. Gaz.* 31 July 8/1 As a wicket-keeper he has had no unprofessional superior. **1899** *Ibid.* 17 June 3/2 He had not intended any disrespect to the Court, or to do anything unprofessional.

*sb.* **1863** Reade *Hard Cash* II. 244 The unexpected turn the evidence had taken..cleared Mr. Hardie with the unprofessionals.

**Unprofe·ssionally,** *adv.* (Un-1 11.) **1840** Willis *Loiterings* III. 75 Your physician and dentist are distinguished persons, who meet you in Society, and call on you unprofessionally.

**Unprofi·ciency.** [Un-1 12, 5 b.] † Lack of moral or spiritual progress.

**1625** Bp. Hall *Contempl., O. T.* iv. iii. Wks. 870 As on the contrary, carelesnesse caries vs to a meere vnproficiency vnder the best meanes of God. **1665** Boyle *Occas. Refl.* iv. ix. 59 'Tis no mean sign of Proficiency in Piety, to be apt to deplore ones unproficiency. **1691** Norris *Pract. Disc.* Pref. 4 The unproficiency of the World under such extraordinary Advantages.

**Unprofi·cient,** *a.* and *sb.* (Un-1 7, 12.)

*a* **1653** Binning *Serm.* (1735) 464/2 This makes us such Unproficients in Mortification, so that scarce any Sin is killed.

**Unpro·fit.** (Un-1 12. Cf. MDu. *onprofijt*, MLG. *unprofit.*)

**1382** Wyclif *Heb.* vii. 18 Forsoth reprouyng of the maundement bifore goynge is maad, for the vnsadnesse and vnprofyt of it. *a* **1420** *Wycliffite Bible* Eccl. i. 1 *marg.*, Kunnyng getun bi mannus weye is vnprofit and diseseful. *c* **1430** *Pilgr. Lyf Manhode* i. iii. (1869) 58 Who so hath on this garnement he dooth his profyt, with that that oothere doon here vnprofyt and here harm. **1483** *Cath. Angl.* 292/1 Vn Profett,..*incomoditas*. **1598** Florio, *Disutile*,..vnprofit. **1840** Browning *Sordello* v. 327 Through his youth's daybreak of unprofit, quite To his noon's labour.

**†Unpro·fit,** *v.* *Obs.* (Un-2 3.) **14..** *Latin-Ang. Voc.* (MS. Harl. 2257), *Incommodo*, vnproffite. **1541** R. Copland *Galyen's Terap.* 2 C iv, A clere and notable vntemperatnes, ..which is the greatest cause..that maye vnproffyte and anoye in the vlceres.

**Unpro·fitable,** *a.* (Un-1 7 b, 5 b.)

*a* **1325** *Prose Psalter* xiii. 4 Alle boweden, to-gider hij ben vnprofitable. **1390** Gower *Conf.* I. 263 Envie..is..to mankinde unprofitable. *c* **1412** Hoccleve *De Reg. Princ.* 2268 Swiche an eschaunge [is] but vnprofitable. *c* **1435** *Chron. London* (Kingsford, 1905) 42 Demyng hym sylff..vtterly vnprofitable to the Rewle and good gouernaunces off the Rewme. **1526** Tindale *Heb.* xiii. 17 That is an vnproffitable thynge for you. **1577** Googe tr. *Heresbach's Husb.* 139 So that the Master be not deceiued with an olde unproffitable flocke. **1630** Capt. Smith *Trav. & Adv.* xv. 27 Any beast unprofitable for service they kill. **1654** S. Clarke *Eccl. Hist.* (ed. 2) i. 25 Such men as labor for shortlived honour are but like froth, which though it be uppermost, yet is unprofitablest. **1735** Johnson *Lobo's Abyssinia, Voy.* i. 7 To expose ourselves..to a Death almost certain and unprofitable. 1826 F. Reynolds *Life & Times* II. 377 This arduous, unprofitable, and ungracious office. 1878 Lecky *Eng. in 18th C.* II. vii. 302 Prizes offered .. for reclaiming unprofitable bogs.

*absol.* 1838 *Penny Cycl.* XI. 345/2 To distinguish good from evil,..the profitable from the unprofitable.

†**b.** As *adv.* Unprofitably. *Obs.*$^{-1}$

c 1425 *Orolog. Sapient.* v. in *Anglia* X. 360/12 Þat I hadde so vnprofitabil spendid þe tyme.

**Unpro·fitableness.** (Un-$^1$ 12, 5 b; cf. prec.) 1526 Tindale *Heb.* vii. 18 The commaundment .. is disanulled, be cause of his weaknes and vnproffitablenes. 1641 Prynne *2nd Pt. Antip.* (title-p.), Touching the..unprofitablenesse, and mischievousnesse of Lordly Prelates, both to King, State, Church. 1673 *Lady's Call.* ii. ii. § 54 Servants, whose unprofitableness usually increases together with their number. 1765 *Museum Rust.* IV. 269 The unprofitableness arising from their keeping men and horses for that work alone. 1837 Hallam *Hist. Lit.* i. vi. § 30 Their yellow leaves, their thousand folio pages, do not more repel us than the unprofitableness of their substance. 1875 Manning *Mission H. Ghost* iv. 116 Learn, then,..your unprofitableness before Him.

**Unpro·fitably,** *adv.* (Un-$^1$ 11.) 1395 Purvey *Remonstr.* (1851) 25 The comoun puple is.. vnprofitabli ocupied. c 1425 *Eng. Conq. Ireland* 142 Such that .. al thynge vnprofytably wasteden, to harme of peesmen. 1508 Fisher *Wks.* (1876) 75 Euery worde spoken vnproufytably and in vayne. 1561 T. Norton *Calvin's Inst.* iv. xx. 162 b, This is not vnprofitablye appointed by the prouidence of God. 1611 B. Jonson *Catiline* i. i, I should not now vnprofitably spend my selfe in words. a 1677 Barrow *Serm.* Wks. 1687 I. xxxi. 451 To prevent this being necessarily and unprofitably deprived of our goods. 1737 Glover *Leonidas* iv. 237 Unprofitably wasting precious hours In vain discussion. 1819 Shelley *Cenci* ii. ii. 140 Thus unprofitably I clasp the phantom of unfelt delights. 1856 De Quincey *Confess.* Wks. I. 135 Impressing ..a new movement upon dialogues that loitered painfully, or see-sawed unprofitably.

**Unpro·fited,** *ppl. a.* (Un-$^1$ 8, 8 c.) 1601 Shaks. *Twel. N.* i. iv. 22 Be clamorous, and leape all ciuill bounds, Rather then make vnprofited returne. 1796 Coleridge *Destiny of Nations* 381 Why, uninjured and unprofited, Should multitudes against their brethren rush? 1813 T. Busby *Lucretius* II. vi. Comm. p. xxii, Never to permit a circumstance of importance..to pass unprofited of, as a moral lesson. 1820 W. Jay *Prayers* 296 How unprofited have we been under the richest means of religious prosperity.

**Unpro·fiting,** *vbl. sb.* (Un-$^1$ 13.) 1867 H. Bushnell *Mor. Uses Dark Th.* (1869) 268 The key we start upon there is lower, by the whole unprofiting of a misspent life.

**Unpro·fiting,** *ppl. a.* (Un-$^1$ 10.) 1616 B. Jonson *Epigr.* i. xc, The vnprofiting foole, Vnworthy such a mistris. 1693 Fleetwood *Serm.* 18 Another sort of unprofiting Hearers, are represented..by the Seed that fell among the Thorns. 1880 *Victorian Rev.* I. 602 Finding themselves in a hopeless and unprofiting minority.

**Unprofou·nd,** *a.* (Un-$^1$ 7.) a 1859 De Quincey *Posth. Wks.* (1891) I. 26 The joy of an infant, or joy-generation, without significance to an unprofound and common mind.

**Unprofu·se,** *a.* (Un-$^1$ 7.) 1727 Thomson *To Mem. Newton* 68 O unprofuse magnificence divine!

**Unprogre·ssive,** *a.* (Un-$^1$ 7, 5 b.) [1775 Ash.] 1851 H. W. Torrens *Jrnl. Asiat. Soc. Bengal* 40 Such a description of unprogressive civilization. 1869 Tozer *Highl. Turkey* I. 141 Their mode of life..left them ..uninstructed and unprogressive. 1886 Tennyson *Locksley Hall 60 Years After* 153 Cries of unprogressive dotage ere the dotard fall asleep!

Hence **Unprogre·ssively** *adv.*, **-ness.** 1800 Coleridge in C. K. Paul *Godwin* (1876) II. 13 Life is too melancholy a thing for men in general for the doctrine of unprogressiveness to remain popular. 1869 Farrar *Fam. Speech* iv. (1870) 159 Tribes..in every stage of nomad unprogressiveness or squalid savagery. 1881 *Echo* 28 June 3/6 The Bulgarians of the Principality would be only too content to live quietly, stolidly, and unprogressively.

**Unprohi·bited,** *ppl. a.* (Un-$^1$ 8.) 1641 Milton *Animadv.* 51 Lest his conversation unprohibited, or unbranded, might breath a pestilentiall murrein into the other sheepe. 1679 C. Nesse *Antid. agst. Popery* 21 To abstain from unprohibited ceremonies as well as from unprohibited meats.

**Unproje·cted,** *ppl. a.* (Un-$^1$ 8.) 1653 Cromwell *Sp.* in *Harl. Misc.* (1810) VI. 63 Your call ..is of God, and it hath been unprojected, unthought of by you and us. a 1715 South *Serm.* IV. 367 Heresies .. have been often taken up at first by meer Accident, or upon some slight, trivial, unprojected Occasion. 1806 Foster *Ess.* (1844) I. 9 Some great, and as yet .. unprojected, plan for the relief of their pressing physical wants.

**Unproje·cting,** *ppl. a.* (Un-$^1$ 10.) 1647 Clarendon *Contempl. Ps.* Tracts (1727) 387 He is quiet and unprojecting, and even unconcerned to help himself. 1787 Bentham *Def. Usury* xiii. 179 Birmingham and Sheffield are pitched upon by you as examples, the one of a projecting town, the other of an unprojecting one.

**Unproli·fic,** *a.* (Un-$^1$ 7, 5 b.) a 1676 Hale *Prim. Orig. Man.* ii. ix. (1677) 210 Inundation .. drowns oftentimes many sorts of Insects, and renders their..Eggs unprolifick. 1724 Gay *Captives* Epil., [The dame] brings her unprolifick Spouse a Son. 1784 Cowper *Task* vi. 138 Th' icy touch Of unprolific winter. 1854 *Poultry Chron.* I. 62/2 Frequently a great part of the eggs are unprolific. 1869 Dunkin *Midn. Sky* 60 An unprolific part of Draco below Polaris.

**Unpro·mise,** *v.* (Un-$^2$ 3.) 1598 Florio, *Spromettere*, .. to vnpromise, to breake promise. 1605 Chapman *All Fools* ii. i. 70 Promises are no fetters; with that tongue Thy promise past, unpromise it againe. 1672 Ravenscroft *Cit. turned Gentl.* iv. i. 64 *Luc.* But you have promis'd I should be his Wife. *Jord.* If I promised you, I unpromise you.

**Unpro·mised,** *ppl. a.* (Un-$^1$ 8.) 1596 Spenser *F. Q.* v. 49 Say, and do all, that may thereto preuaile; Leaue nought vnpromist, that may him perswade. a 1689 Mrs. Behn *Fair Jilt* in *Novels* (1905) 102 He is unenjoyed, unpromised; and so am I.

**Unpro·mising,** *ppl. a.* [Un-$^1$ 10.]

**1.** Not affording promise of excellence or success. 1663 J. Spencer *Prodigies* 81 God often accomplisheth his biggest ends by means unpromiseing. 1721 *Lond. Gaz.* No. 5999/1 The Vintage Season,..though very backward and unpromising.., has..begun. 1786 tr. *Beckford's Vathek* 187 The Caliph, to whom these complaints were but unpromising auguries. 1827 Scott *Surg. Dau.* i, So you will often find.., under an unpromising and blunt exterior, professional skill and enthusiasm. 1871 Freeman *Norm. Conq.* IV. xix. 418 Hermann .. began vigorously to build a church in the unpromising spot.

†**2.** Unprepossessing. *Obs.* 1632 Massinger & Field *Fatal Dowry* iv. i, *Liladam.* What d'ee take me for? *Pontalier.* A long thing with a most vnpromising face. 1669 Clarendon *Ess.* Tracts (1727) 101 The beauty of the mind doth frequently reconcile..all men to the most unpromising countenances.

Hence **Unpro·misingness.** 1655 Earl Orrery *Parthen.* i. ii. 135, I doe now in some sort rejoyce at the unpromisingnesse of my Condition. 1727 Bailey (vol. II), *Inauspiciousness*, unpromisingness.

**Unpro·misingly,** *adv.* (Un-$^1$ 11; cf. prec.) 1848 Dickens *Dombey* xiii, Looking over his white cravat, as unpromisingly as Mr. Dombey himself could have looked. **Unpromo·table,** *a.* (Un-$^1$ 7 b.) 1836 Carlyle *Corr. w. Emerson* (1883) I. 103, I suppose there is no more unpromotable, unappointable man now living in England than I. **Unpromo·ted,** *ppl. a.* (Un-$^1$ 8.) [1775 Ash.] 1801 W. Taylor in Robberds *Mem.* (1843) I. 381 You must turn over the *Critical* to us unpromoted politicians.

**Unpro·mpted,** *ppl. a.* (Un-$^1$ 8.) 1659 W. Chamberlayne *Pharon.* iv. iv. 32 To ask The way; for more his youth's unprompted fear Expects not there. c 1700 Congreve *To Cynthia* Wks. 1730 III. 291 And my tongue talks, unprompted by my heart. 1761 Glover *Medea* iv. i, Jason would have come Uncall'd, unprompted, but by love alone. 1810 Crabbe *Borough* x. 100 Then may you call in aid the moderate glass, But let it slowly and unprompted pass. 1860 Tyndall *Glac.* i. 169 A respect for him, which this unprompted idea of his augmented.

**Unpro·mptly,** *adv.* (Un-$^1$ 11.) 1837 Carlyle *Fr. Rev.* ii. ii. vi, The Mutineer deputies vanish, not unpromptly.

**Unpromu·lgated,** *ppl. a.* (Un-$^1$ 8.) [1775 Ash.] 1802-12 Bentham *Ration. Judic. Evid.* (1827) II. 474 Every law unpromulgated is, moreover, an Act of tyranny. 1836 J. Gilbert *Chr. Atonem.* ix. 387 The unpromulgated law of nature.

**Unpromu·lged,** *ppl. a.* (Un-$^1$ 8.) [1775 Ash.] 1832 Austin *Outl. Lect. Jurispr.* p. viii, Unwritten law, or unpromulged law, is law which flows immediately from some subordinate source. **Unpro·ne,** *a.* (Un-$^1$ 7.) 1611 *Coryat's Crudities* e i, Vlysses had a wife to lust vnprone. 1883 Wright *Scientific Dogmatism* 9 The vain deceit which Philosophy was not unprone to keep company with. **Unpronou·nce,** *v.* (Un-$^2$ 3.) 1745 *Matrimony, pro & con.* 3 Could his loath'd Fair-One unpronounce 'I will', Not Worlds shou'd buy him to a Thing so ill.

**Unpronou·nceable,** *a.* (Un-$^1$ 7 b.) 1831 Scott *Ct. Rob.* ii, Foreigners bearing unpronounceable names. 1863 Miss Braddon *Aurora Floyd* xviii, Hock, the name of which was in fourteen unpronounceable syllables. 1889 Doyle *Micah Clarke* xviii, A score of unpronounceable fights in the Styrian Alps.

**Unpronou·nced,** *ppl. a.* [Un-$^1$ 8.]

**1.** Unuttered, unspoken. [1586 in *Bk. Univ. Kirk Scotl.* (1839) 298 We hold the said proces and sentence as unled, undecydit or pronuncit.] 1611 Cotgr. s.v. *Cet*, Those [words] which begin .. with *H* vnpronounced. 1628 Milton *Vac. Exerc.* 4 Hail native Language, that..mad'st imperfect words with childish tripps, Half unpronounc't, slide through my infant-lipps. 1796 Mme. D'Arblay *Camilla* V. 35 He wanted her to seize his meaning unpronounced.

**2.** Not prominent or distinct. 1863 Dana *Man. Geol.* 748 Although the grand systems in Zoology are unpronounced, there are still faint indications of them generally observable.

**Unpro·p,** *v.* (Un-$^2$ 4.) 1611 Cotgr., *Destamper*, to vnprop; to take the tressles from. 1676 Hobbes *Iliad* ii. 137 [They] strait unpropt their Ships. 1717 *Entertainer* No. 5. 29 Nor can they be assured their own Minions .. may not more unprop the Throne, than guard it. 1897 P. Warung *Tales Old Régime* 114 ''Ardy, jest unprop West!' Hardy obeyed, and lifted the cadaver to the centre of the chamber.

**Unpropense,** *a.* [Un-$^1$ 7.] Unbiassed. 1640-1 Ld. Digby *Parl. Sp.* 9 Feb. 17 To preserve an equall and unpropense judgment.

**Unpro·per,** *a.* Now *rare.* [Un-$^1$ 7, 5 b.]

†**1.** = Improper *a.* 1. *Obs.* c 1380 Wyclif *Sel. Wks.* II. 269 We seen now bi a myror, in fer siȝt, and unpropre, but we shulen se after in blis þe firste trouþe face to face. 14.. *Voc.* in Wr.-Wülcker 589 *Impropriam*, unpropre. 1594 Blundevil *Exerc.* i. xxii. (1597) 23 b, The vnproper [compound musical proportion] is, when to 3 numbers giuen, 2 other seuerall numbers are ioyned [etc.]. a 1619 Fotherby *Atheom.* i. i. § 5 (1622) 8 So that Demonstrations are here vnproper and vnprofitable. 1661 Campion *Counterpoint* ii. 122 The last close being to be made in the greater or sharp third, is unproper.

†**b.** *spec.* Of language. *Obs.* c 1449 Pecock *Repr.* i. v. 27 Bi vnpropre maner of speche and bi figure. *Ibid.*, In this present purpos of grounding and of the vnpropir speking vsid ther upon. 1550 Veron *Godly Saiyngs* B iv b, An abused and an vnpropre speache. a 1568 Ascham *Scholem.* ii. (Arb.) 87 To traine his Scholler to a iudgement, in cutting out..ouer old and vnproper wordes. 1607 Markham *Cavel.* ii. xix. 203 Speaking of these loftie ayres, hee calles them Cariering horses; an epithiton most vnproper.

**2.** = Improper *a.* 2. Now *dial.* 1581 Mulcaster *Positions* xxxix. 221 Ignorance .. will cause them selues to be their owne Gnatoes, a most vnproper part, to be seene vpon a stage, when [etc.]. 1605 Camden *Rem.* 14 It will not be vnproper I hope to this purpose if I note out of the epistles of..Busbequius. a 1659 Osborne *Piso & Vindex* Wks. (1673) 373 An endeavour no less indecent for here in Honour, than unproper for a Tyrant. 1678 Moxon *Mech. Exerc.* vi. 101 The use of which .. is unproper for me to meddle with in this Place. 1773 Johnson (ed. 4), *Unproper*,..unfit, not right. 1869- in various dialect glossaries, etc.

**3.** = Improper *a.* 3. *rare.* 1868 Mrs. Whitney *P. Strong* ix, As foolish and happy and unproper as one pleases.

†**4.** = Improper *a.* 4. *Obs.* 1604 Shaks. *Oth.* iv. i. 69 Millions .. nightly lye in those vnproper beds, Which they dare sweare peculiar.

†**Unpro·perly,** *adv. Obs.* [Un-$^1$ 11, 5 b.] Improperly. (Freq. c 1560–c 1650.)

**a.** In respect of the use of words. c 1340 Hampole *Pr. Consc.* 8129 Ffor if endlesnes any end moght hald, þan war it endlesnes unproperly cald. 1398 Trevisa *Barth. De P. R.* v. xxxii. (Bodl. MS.), It is vnpropirliche seide þat oþer bestes haue backes. a 1425 tr. *Arderne's Treat. Fistula*, etc. 55 Þai ar called emeroydez, bot neþerlez vnproperly. a 1470 H. Parker *Dives & Pauper* (W. de W. 1496) i. xiii. 45/2 They take that Dulia full largely, and full unproprely. 1553 T. Wilson *Rhet.* 93 Long talke, and small matter, are spoken vnproperly, for we cannot measure either talke or matter by length or breadth. 1579 Fulke *Heskins' Parl.* 100 This worde sacrifice, is either taken properly, or vnproperly, and figuratiuely. 1636 M. Walbancke in *Ann. Dubrensia* (1877) 3 You to whom I may not unpropperly give the denomination of an Hero. 1678 Moxon *Mech. Exerc.* v. 95 They..say..'Lay a kerf in that piece of Stuff'; and sometimes, (but most unproperly,) 'Cut, or Slit that piece of Stuff'.

**b.** In other contexts. 1561 T. Norton *Calvin's Inst.* ii. 153 Those thinges yt were done in his nature of man, are vnproperly, & yet not without reason, geuen to hys Godhed. 1577 tr. *Bullinger's Decades* 463 Iustification is somtimes somewhat vnproperly attributed to workes. 1613 Purchas *Pilgrimage* i. viii. 41 A part of the hill Taurus (unproperly ascribed to Caucasus). 1683 Moxon *Mech. Exerc., Printing* ii. ¶ 2 They commonly, but unproperly, imploy Joyners to make them.

†**Unpro·perness.** *Obs.* [Un-$^1$ 12, 5 b.] Lack of propriety or appropriateness. 1561 T. Norton *Calvin's Inst.* iv. xix. 148 b, So that a godly sense be kept, although there be some vnproprenesse in the speaking. 1581 Pettie tr. *Guazzo's Civ. Conv.* i. (1586) 23 b, You shall offende Boccace, rather with the vnpropernesse, then with the vnusualnesse of words. 1652 Sparke *Prim. Devot.* 217 Their insufficiency..and unproperness for such imployment. 1692 Tryon *Gd. House-w.* i. (ed. 2) 8 The unproperness and contrariety of these Prescriptions to the end intended.

**Unpro·pertied,** *ppl. a.* (Un-$^1$ 8.) 1793 Anna Seward *Lett.* (1811) III. 217 The protecting influence of represented property, extending to the unpropertied. 1794 *Ibid.* 369 The ignorant and unpropertied mass of people. 1886 W. Graham *Soc. Problem* 335 Since under it there is no safety for the unpropertied man. [Freq. in recent use.]

**Unpro·phesiable,** *a.* (Un-$^1$ 7 b.) 1883 Lowell *Rich. III*, Latest Lit. Ess. (1891) 122 Like those pulses of pale flame with which the sky throbs at unprophesiable intervals.

**Unprophe·tic,** *a.* (Un-$^1$ 7.) 1725 Pope *Odyss.* xxii. 13 Wretch that he was, of unprophetic soul! 1728 Savage *Bastard* 47 Thus unprophetic, lately misinspir'd, I sung. 1821 Shelley *Ginevra* 124 Unprophetic of the coming hours, The matin winds..awaken The earth. 1843 Carlyle *Past & Pr.* ii. viii, Alas, ye *un*prophetic..! 1886 Tennyson *Opening Indian & Col. Exh.* iii, Unprophetic rulers they.

**Unprophe·tical,** *a.* (Un-$^1$ 7.) 1743 Ellis *Knowl. Div. Things* 254 How unprophetical would it be, to say they should some time know what they already knew? **Unprophe·tically,** *adv.* (Un-$^1$ 11.) 1861 T. Wright in *Pol. Poems* II. p. xxvii, Elmham warns the king (not unprophetically) of the..uncertain character of human life. †**Unpropi·ce,** *a. Obs.*$^{-1}$ [Un-$^1$ 7.] Unpropitious. a 1529 Skelton *Bk. 3 Fooles* Wks. 1843 I. 200 Shee is so debylyte, colde, vnpropyce, vnnaturall, and vndyscurrente. **Unpropi·tiable,** *a.* (Un-$^1$ 7 b.) [1775 Ash.] 1891 *Academy* 28 Mar. 296/1 That unpropitiable avenger who waits on secular misconduct.

**Unpropi·tious,** *a.* (Un-$^1$ 7.) 1699 Pomfret *To Another Friend* 12 Beneath the pond'rous Weight Of angry Stars, and unpropitious Fate. 1702 Addison *Dial. Medals* ii. (1726) 65 Ye sue the unpropitious maid in vain. 1776 Mickle *Camoen's Lusiad* Introd. 149 In the unpropitious age of a Cromwell. 1847 Helps *Friends in C.* I. 39 The whole life appears to be shut up in the one unpropitious affection. 1875 Jowett *Plato* (ed. 2) III. 425 Sleep and exercise are unpropitious to learning.

Hence **Unpropi·tiousness.** 1844 W. H. Smyth *Cycle Celestial Obj.* II. 6 Had this been done, every notion of stellar unpropitiousness and malevolence must have vanished.

**Unpropi·tiously,** *adv.* (Un-$^1$ 11.) 1602 Marston *Ant. & Mel.* ii, My legge is not altogether unpropitiously shap't. There's a word: unpropitiously? I thinke I shall speake unpropitiously as well as any courtier in Italy. **Unpropo·rtion.** [Un-$^1$ 12, 5 b.] Disproportion. 1844 Kinglake *Eothen* xvii. 265 You stare at the wide unproportion between this slender Company, and the boundless plains of sand.

†**Unpropo·rtionable,** *a. Obs.* [Un-$^1$ 7 b, 5 b.] Disproportionate. Also const. *to*, or (rarely) *with.* (Common in 17th c.) 1586 T. B. *La Primaud. Fr. Acad.* i. 672 Too much increase and unproportionable growth..procureth the change and ruine of commonwealthes. 1613 Purchas *Pilgrimage* (1614) 39 The roofe is not to be thought vnproportionable. 1650 Fuller *Pisgah* v. xi. 163 To give a thing and take a thing is unproportionable with his [*sc.* God's] proceedings. 1697 C. Leslie *Snake in Grass* (ed. 2) Advert., The Preface was an Eye-Sore, because of its Length, unproportionable to the Book. 1704 N. N. tr. *Boccalini's Advts. from Parnass.* III. 255 Some of her limbs swell to an unproportionable

Bulk. **1766** *Compl. Farmer* s.v. *Surveying*, If you protract .., you will put your closes into unproportionable shapes.

Hence † **Unpropo·rtionableness.** *Obs.*

**1653** GAUDEN *Hierasp.* 74 This unproportionableness of the Creators dealing with man. **1659** — *Tears Ch.* 586 The unproportionableness of any other Church-government than a right Episcopacy to the temper of England.

† **Unpropo·rtionably,** *adv. Obs.* [UN-¹ 11; cf. prec.] Disproportionately.

**1558–9** ABP. PARKER *Corr.* (Parker Soc.) 62 And now for the upholding of two or three years more of life, to heap unproportionably, I count it madness. **1594** R. ASHLEY tr. *Loys le Roy* 2 Being duely tempered for generation, and vnproportionably distempered for corruption. **1626** BACON *Sylva* § 360 A Chameleon is a Creature about the Bignesse of an Ordinary Lizard: His Head vnproportionably bigge. **1641** J. JACKSON *True Evang. T.* III. 166 The Gospell too bids us 'not bee unequally yoaked,' but what is it to be unproportionably yoaked, if this bee not? **1790** *Phil. Trans.* LXXX. 355 Though nature..may permit a particular species of animal to become so unproportionably numerous. **1819** W. S. ROSE *Lett. fr. N. Italy* II. 172 There is, perhaps, no offence which is so unproportionably punished.

**Unpropo·rtional,** *a.* (UN-¹ 7.) **1714** DERHAM *Prelim. Disc. to Astro-Theol.* (1726) p. xiii, Which are Motions [of the moon, etc.] so unproportional,..that [they] are sufficient to subvert the whole Hypothesis. **Unproportiona·lity.** (UN-¹ 12.) **1818** BENTHAM *Ch. Eng., Catech. Exam.* 273 Uncertainty, unproportionality, abstractiveness.., and degradingness. **Unpropo·rtionally,** *adv.* (UN-¹ 11.) **1820** HOGG *Tales & Sk.* (1836) II. 204 The next three volumes were..unproportionally thick.

**Unpropo·rtionate,** *a.* Now *rare.* [UN-¹ 7, 5 b.] Disproportionate, unproportioned.

**1581** MULCASTER *Positions* xxx. 109 The whole bodie..is anoyed with vnproportionate heat. **1601** DANIEL *Civ. Wars* VI. xxviii, No swelling member, vnproportionate, Growne out of forme. **1651** H. MORE *Second Lash* in *Enthus. Tri.*, etc. (1656) 184 Where is my Fancie distorted, unproportionate, unproper? **1679** J. GOODMAN *Penit. Pard.* III. v. 336 That the powers and objects are mis-matched and unproportionate to each other. **1897** *Advance* (Chicago) 21 Jan. 77 Unsound, unproportionate teachings.

So **Unpropo·rtionately** *adv.*, **-ness.**

**1495** *Trevisa's Barth. De P. R.* VII. xx. p iij b/2 A man is byrefte..of his syght somtyme..for vnproporcyonat[n]es of the blacke of the eye to yᵉ spyryte of syghte. **1897** *Trans. Amer. Pediatric Soc.* IX. 22 The paralysis..progressing by degrees and sometimes unproportionately.

**Unpropo·rtioned,** *ppl. a.* (UN-¹ 8, 5 b.)

*c* **1586** C'TESS PEMBROKE *Ps.* CXXXV. vii, What unproportion'd odds To thee, these idolls gold and silver beare? **1595** DANIEL *Civ. Wars* II. xix, Huge vnproportion'd mountaines. **1602** SHAKS. *Ham.* I. iii. 60 Giue thy thoughts no tongue, Nor any vnproportion'd thought his Act. **1650** BULWER *Anthropomet.* 186 Crook-back't men..are justly accounted unproportioned. **1712** ATTERBURY *Serm.* (1737) IV. 216 Such a mock worship,..how unproportioned it is to the Divine Nature. **1799** J. ROBERTSON *Agric. Perth* 231 A multitude of soldiers, unproportioned to the extent or fertility of Scotland. **1828** TENNYSON *Lover's Tale* I. 187 That porch, So unproportion'd to the dwelling-place.

**Unpropo·sed,** *ppl. a.* (UN-¹ 8.) *a* **1700** DRYDEN (J.), The means are unpropos'd. **1884** *Imp. Dict.* IV. 513 The motion or candidate is as yet unproposed.

**Unpro·pped,** *ppl. a.* (UN-¹ 8.)

**1616** W. BROWNE *Brit. Past.* II. v. 342, I have beheld A widow vine stand, in a naked field,..Unpropt, unsuccoured, by stake or tree. **1675** OTWAY *Alcibiades* v. i, When success me to my wishes calls, I'll shake him off, and then unpropt he falls. **1700** DRYDEN *Meleager & Atalanta* 132 The Nerves no more sustain The Bulk; the Bulk unprop'd, falls headlong on the Plain. **1802–12** BENTHAM *Ration. Judic. Evid.* (1827) I. 396 The ceremony of an oath in its pure state, unpropped by that support. **1827** POLLOK *Course T.* II. 740 He..tried to stand Alone, unpropped, to be obliged to none.

**Unproscri·bable,** *a.* (UN-¹ 7 b.) **1817** LADY MORGAN *France* III. (1818) I. 310 The unproscribable influence of fashion and beauty. **Unproscri·bed,** *ppl. a.* (UN-¹ 8.) [**1775** ASH.] **1840** TYTLER *Hist. Scot.* (1864) III. 294 Not a baron who espoused the cause of the queen would have been left unproscribed.

**Unpro·secuted,** *ppl. a.* (UN-¹ 8.

**1655** MOUFET & BENNET *Health's Improv.* xvi. 139 Tasting of every..part of mans body, not leaving the nails unprosecuted. **1665** BOYLE *Occas. Refl.* v. vi. 164 To make him leave his Endeavours unprosecuted. **1802–12** BENTHAM *Ration. Judic. Evid.* (1827) V. 97 The example is bad, when a man supposed to be guilty is seen to remain unprosecuted.

**Unpro·selyte,** *v.* (UN-² 3.) **1655** FULLER *Ch. Hist.* x. iv. § 8. 63 It happily unproselyted some inclinable to his Opinions. **Unproso·dian,** *a.* (UN-¹ 7.) **1836** MOORE *Mem.* (1856) VII. 160 Such an unprosodian school as Dublin College then was. **Unprospe·cted,** *ppl. a.* (UN-¹ 8.) **1882** *U.S. Rep. Prec. Met.* 79 An unprospected part of the channel. **Unpro·sperable,** *a.* (UN-¹ 7.) **1690** C. NESSE *O. & N. Test.* I. 298 Solitariness..is an unprofitable and unprosperable thing. **Unprospe·rity.** (UN-¹ 12, 5 b.) *a* **1628** F. GREVIL *Sidney* (1652) 33 [He] left the success to his will, that governs the blinde prosperities and unprosperities of Chance. *Ibid.* 173 A perspective into vice, and the unprosperities of it. *a* **1843** SOUTHEY *Doctor* cxcvii. (1848) 525 The thriftless man..finds some satisfaction in imputing his unprosperity to the Stars. † **Unpro·sperly,** *adv. Obs.*⁻¹ [UN-¹ 11.] Unprosperously. **1608** P. GOLDING *Sleidane's Epit. Frossard* 62 The matter had falne out so vnprosperly before.

**Unpro·sperous,** *a.* (UN-¹ 7, 5 b.)

*a* **1578** LINDESAY (Pitscottie) *Chron. Scot.* (S.T.S.) I. 257 The king heirand of his vnprosperous iournay. ? **1586** HOOKER *Answ. Travers' Supplic.* § 5 Which vnprosperous beginning of a thing..did..disgrace that order in their conceit. **1631** GOUGE *God's Arrows* III. § 57. 289 No marvell therefore that the warre..was unprosperous. **1665** BOYLE *Occas. Refl.* VI. i, Endeavours, which..are oft-times so unprosperous. **1776** ADAM SMITH *W. N.* I. x. II. (1869) I. 139 That unprosperous race of men, commonly called men of letters. **1861** M. ARNOLD *Pop. Educ. France* 185 Not that primary instruction is unprosperous in the Canton of Vaud. **1884** PEARSON in *Law Rep.* 26 Chanc. Div. 676 The tenant for life received nothing from the unprosperous year, 1881.

**Unpro·sperously,** *adv.* (UN-¹ 11; cf. prec.)

**1630** *Camden's Hist. Eliz.* II. 117 Two famous Pilots.. sought as vnprosperously to discouer a neere way to East-India. **1650** JER. TAYLOR *Holy Living* ii. § 6. 153 When a Prince fights justly, and yet unprosperously. **1663** BOYLE *Usef. Exp. Nat. Philos.* II. i. 10 It is possible to be safely made, though many..have but unprosperously attempted it. **1848** THACKERAY *Van. Fair* lvii, Her life, begun not unprosperously, had come down to..a long ignoble bondage. **1876** MISS YONGE *Womankind* xxxii, Love affairs come early and unprosperously.

**Unpro·sperousness.** (UN-¹ 12.)

*a* **1660** HAMMOND *Serm.* Wks. 1683 IV. 492 The unprosperousness of the arm of flesh. **1698** FRYER *Acc. E. India & P.* 88 The True Cause of the Unprosperousness of the Ancient Undertakers. **1741** RICHARDSON *Pamela* III. 117 After a Series of Unprosperousness in all they undertook.

**Unpro·stitute,** *ppl. a.* (UN-¹ 8 b; cf. next.) **1606** BIRNIE *Kirk-buriall* (1833) 28 Under these three conditions (to wit, of amplitude, ornacy, and vnprostitude [*sic*] chastity to any other vse). **1681** *Whole Duty Nations* 24 Retaining their Honour untouch'd,..and presenting to the Honour of Christianity a Supremacy unprostitute.

**Unpro·stituted,** *ppl. a.* (UN-¹ 8.)

**1721** AMHERST *Terræ Fil.* No. 41 (1726) 213 Some future unprostituted, ungarbled history of a rebellion. **1753** *Gray's Inn Jrnl.* No. 29 (1756) I. 190 That unprostituted, dignified Independence, which will always do Honour to the Man. **1785** *Rolliad, Prob. Odes* xix. 96 With unprostituted pen, ..unmov'd by gain, I'll call thee..' most chaste of men'.

**Unprote·cted,** *ppl. a.* (UN-¹ 8.)

*a* **1593** MARLOWE *Ovid's Elegies* II. ii. 12 Nor is her husband wise, what needes defence When vn-protected ther is no expence? **1597** HOOKER *Eccl. Pol.* v. i. § 4 Such euils..as men either destitute of grace diuine may commit, or vnprotected from aboue, indure. **1748** RICHARDSON *Clarissa* VII. 97 A defenceless unprotected woman. **1791** MRS. RADCLIFFE *Rom. Forest* iv, The idea of leaving his family unprotected. **1844** NOAD *Electricity* (ed. 2) 429 It is necessary to observe..that the lamps were unprotected. **1879** LUBBOCK *Sci. Lect.* ii. 41 It might be an advantage to a flower which was quite unprotected, to open early for the bees.

Hence **Unprote·ctedly** *adv.*, **-ness.**

**1823** *Blackw. Mag.* XIV. 461 Seeing their friends massacred unprotectedly all round them. **1824** MISS MITFORD *Village* Ser. I. 13 His unprotectedness, his utter defencelessness. **1895** MEREDITH *Amazing Marriage* xlvi, Lady Arpington's mention of Henrietta's unprotectedness.

**Unpro·testant,** *a.* (UN-¹ 7.)

**1841** WISEMAN *Remarks Lett. fr. Palmer* 53 How moderate, how un-Protestant, is the language of St. Epiphanius! **1881** W. R. SMITH *Old Test. in Jew. Ch.* i. 7 This point of view is, however, thoroughly unprotestant.

**Unpro·testantize,** *v.* (UN-² 6 c.)

**1833** R. H. FROUDE *Rem.* (1838) I. 332, I wish you could get to know something of S. and W., and un-—ise, un-Protestantise, un-Miltonise them. **1842** G. S. FABER *Prov. Lett.* (1844) II. 291 We must unprotestantise the National Church. **1895** *Bulwark* Sept. 98/1 Mr. Gladstone and Lord Salisbury ..have vied with each other in unprotestantising the Church of England.

Hence **Unpro·testantizing** *vbl. sb.* and *ppl. a.*

**1841** *British Critic* July 45 The unprotestantizing..of the national Church. **1847** H. MILLER *First Impr. Eng.* xiii. 244 The unprotestantizing leaven introduced into the mass of the English Establishment.

**Unpro·testantlike,** *a.* (UN-¹ 7 c.) **1641** MILTON *Anim-adv.* 35 Not caring otherwise to answer this un-Protestant-like Objection. **Unprotru·ded,** *ppl. a.* (UN-¹ 8.) [**1775** ASH.] **1777** PENNANT *Brit. Zool.* (ed. 4) IV. 9 Doctor Baster ..counted 12,444 eggs under the tail, besides those that remained in the body unprotruded. **1812** *Examiner* 24 Aug. 541/2 You left scarcely one of his faults unprotruded on inspection. **Unprotru·sive,** *a.* (UN-¹ 7.) **1825** COLERIDGE *Aids Refl.* 148 *note*, The unprotrusive and unindicated Convolutes of the Brain.

**Unprou·d,** *a.* (UN-¹ 7.)

**1570** LEVINS *Manip.* 217 Vnproude, *inglorius.* **1666** J. SERGEANT *Let. Thanks* 20 'Tis your weak and unproud conjecture. **1820** L. HUNT *Indicator* No. 16 (1822) I. 123 They spoke to me more familiarly than usual, and yet somehow or other, didn't seem so kind nor so *un*-proud. **1900** *Academy* 28 July 75 He is not unconscious nor unproud of this freedom.

**Unpro·vable,** *a.* [UN-¹ 7 b.]

**1.** Incapable of being proved.

*c* **1425** WYNTOUN *Cron.* IX. xix. 2042 Eftyr þat he had beyn ..in exile Be fenȝheid fals suspicion, And all wnprowabil be resson. **1553** GRIMALDE *Cicero's Offices* II. (1556) 65 So we, dissenting from them, do saie again some thinges be prouable, some vnprouable. **1609** BP. HALL *Dissuas. Poperie* 35 A Religion, that depends wholly vpon nice and poore vncertainties, and vnproueable supposals. **1677** GILPIN *Demonol.* II. vii. 325 Though Satan's injections of Nonelection be altogether unproveable. **1825** BENTHAM *Offic. Apt. Maximized, Indic.* (1830) 79 By an unpunishable and unprovable, though solemn act of insincerity. **1883** MYERS *Ess., Mod., Mazzini* (1885) 60 Unprovable speculations about the firmament.

† **2.** Incapable of succeeding. *Obs.*⁻¹

**1653** BLITHE *Eng. Improver Impr.* xxiv. 156 Avoid the getting of Eaten, Bitten, Rough, and Brushy, all being unproveable sets.

Hence **Unprovabi·lity, -ableness.**

*a* **1881** BARRATT *Phys. Metempiric* (1883) 23 The unproveability of the hypothesis. **1883** *Contemp. Rev.* Nov. 697 There is always a great deal of vagueness, and..of unprovableness, in charges of immorality against a whole race.

† **Unpro·ve,** *v. Obs.* [UN-² 3, 7. Cf. MDu. *ontproeven.*]

**1.** *trans.* To disprove; to deny or reject.

**13..** *Gosp. Nicod.* 591 His folk vnproues him king, And kingdom claymes he. *c* **1440** *Promp. Parv.* 366/2 Onprevyn, or imprevyn,..*improbo.* *c* **1449** PECOCK *Repr.* I. xviii. 104 Thei schulen suffice forto vnproue this iiijᵉ opinioun here, as thei vnproven the ijᵉ opinioun there.

**2.** *intr.* To disapprove.

**1528** GARDINER in Pocock *Rec. Reform.* (1870) I. 104 His holiness,..neither approving ne unproving, said, he had sent it to the cardinal.

Hence † **Unpro·ving** *vbl. sb. Obs.*

*c* **1449** PECOCK *Repr.* IV. iii. 430 Thus miche is ynowȝ for vnprouyng of the seid skile.

**Unpro·ved,** *ppl. a.* [UN-¹ 8.]

† **1.** Not put to proof or trial; untried. *Obs.*

*c* **1440** *Pallad. on Husb.* I. 236 Preue eek thonpreued greyne afore eschaunge. *c* **1445** PECOCK *Donet* 7 Y wote weel þat ..scant ynouȝ oon leef schulde stonde vnprovid or colowrabily vnrebukid. **1550** BALDWIN *Mor. Philos.* K. iiij, Proue not thy frende wyth dammage, nor vse thou hym vnproued. **1561** B. GOOGE *Palingenius' Zodiac Life* I. A ij b, Willing to trede vnproued pathes that haue not yet ben gon. **1590** SPENSER *F. Q.* I. vii. 47 For to find a fresh vnproued knight.

**2.** Not demonstrated to be true or genuine.

**1532** MORE *Confut. Tindale* Wks. 609/2 Both is his purpose on his part vnproued, & the contrarye to hym proued. **1533** FRITH *Answ. More* G 8, His mastership hathe lefte one thinge vnproued. **1628** DONNE *Serm.* (1640) 291 The proofe lies on their side; and it rests yet unproved. **1693** DRYDEN *Juvenal* VI. 313 Prov'd, or unprov'd, the Crime, the Villain dies. **1843** J. H. NEWMAN *Miracles* 63 A fact is not disproved, because the testimony is..insufficient, it is only unproved. **1866** GEO. ELIOT *F. Holt* xvii, The essence of bribery is that it should be legally proved; there is not such a thing..as unproved bribery. **1874** MAHAFFY *Social Life Greece* 335 However unproved or doubtful this ancient creed.

Hence **Unpro·vedness.**

*a* **1400–50** *Alexander* 1019 For barnes in þar bignes it baldis þam mekill, Oft with vnprouednes in presse to pas out of lyfe.

**Unpro·ven,** *ppl. a.* [UN-¹ 8 b.] = prec. 2.

**1853** *Westm. Rev.* April 475 We do not expect the preacher to prove anything before unproven. **1875** JOWETT *Plato* (ed. 2) III. 149 Plato does not like to make an assertion which is unproven.

**Unprovi·de,** *v.* (UN-² 3. Cf. DISPROVIDE *v.*)

**1530** PALSGR. 768/2, I unprovyde, *Je despouruoys.* **1604** SHAKS. *Oth.* IV. i. 218 Ile not expostulate with her; least her body and beautie vnprouide my mind againe. **1793** A. MURPHY *Tacitus* I. 339 Increasing honours, he had no doubt, would unprovide his mind, and..produce the genuine features of his character.

**Unprovi·ded,** *ppl. a.* [UN-¹ 8, 5 b.]

**1.** Not furnished, supplied, or equipped (with something): **a.** Const. *of* (now *rare* or *Obs.*) or *with.*

**1523** LD. BERNERS *Froiss.* I. cccxxi. 498 The countre was voyde, and vnprouyded of men of warre. **1579** SPENSER *Sheph. Cal.* May 114 The shepheards God so wel them guided, That of nought they were vnprouided. **1600** SURFLET *Countrie Farme* I. xvi. 105 The countrie farme being for the most part vnprouided of the benefits and easements of water. **1673** [R. LEIGH] *Transp. Reh.* 45 It being a thing wholly unlikely that the wise Astragon should be unprovided of such excellent authors. **1720** SWIFT *Fates of Clergymen* Wks. 1755 II. II. 22 Courts are seldom unprovided of persons under this character. **1735** BERKELEY in Fraser *Life* (1871) vii. 241 Those places where they are unprovided with churches. **1785** T. BALGUY *Disc.* 174 Men, whose understandings are..unprovided of the principles of knowledge. **1844** KINGLAKE *Eothen* viii, Assailants..unprovided with regular means of attack. **1875** JOWETT *Plato* (ed. 2) III. 102 The actual drone is unprovided by nature with a sting.

**b.** Without const. Also *for* (a person, etc.).

(*a*) *a* **1586** SIDNEY *Arcadia* II. xii, And whose good haps do leave him unprovided, Condoling cause of friendship he will borrow. **1603** G. POWEL *Papist's Reas. for Toleration* 127 Whereby they haue left the Ministrie so marveilously vnprouided and so beggerly. **1627** CAPT. SMITH *Seaman's Gram.* xii. 56 Neither should her Gunroome be vnprouided: not manned like a Merchant-man. **1760–72** H. BROOKE *Fool of Qual.* (1809) III. 78 Since you will go, you must not go unprovided. **1818** SCOTT *Br. Lamm.* xxv, We are totally and literally unprovided [*sc.* with provisions]. **1833** MACAULAY *Ess., War Succession in Spain* ¶ 12 The arsenals were deserted. The magazines were unprovided.

(*b*) **1530** PALSGR. 768/2 He shalbe hertely welcome, but I am yet unprovyded for him. **1603** BRETON *Mad World* Wks. (Grosart) II. 10/1 He..led me into his house, the doore open, as unfearefull of theeves, as vnprovided for strangers. **1725** DE FOE *Voy. round World* (1840) 333 As for going by water, that they were unprovided for.

**c.** Not provided for. (Cf. 4.)

**1640** HABINGTON *Edw. IV*, 33 The inconvenience of raising a widow to his bed, who could bring nothing with her but her poverty, and an unprovided issue. **1892** CHILD *Ballads* IV. 391/2 The bower of an unprovided seamstress.

**2.** Not in a state of preparation or readiness; unprepared (to resist attack, make reply, etc.).

**1525** LD. BERNERS *Froiss.* II. xxxiii. 41/2 So that whan oure enemyes come, let them nat fynde vs vnprouided. **1578** *Chr. Prayers* in *Priv. Prayers* (1851) 447 Take me not unawares and unprovided to thy judgment-seat. **1599** SHAKS. *Hen. V*, IV. i. 183 If they dye vnprouided. **1615** BRATHWAIT *Strappado*, etc. (1878) 334 Alas, faire queene, why should you thus assault the vnprouided fortresse of mine hart? **1647** COTTERELL *Davila's Hist. France* I. 43 The armed men..appearing on a sudden.., the King being found unprovided, and the Court disarmed. **1722** DE FOE *Plague* (1756) 140 The unprovided Condition that..the People were in at the first coming of the Calamity. **1805** SOUTHEY *Madoc in Azt.* II. 231 So saying, I left The astonish'd men, whose unprovided minds Fail'd them. **1819** SHELLEY *Cenci* III. i. 377 You are unprovided where to fly, How to excuse or to conceal.

**3.** Against which provision has not (or cannot) be made; unforeseen.

**1514** BARCLAY *Cyt. & Uplondyshm.* (Percy Soc.) 9 Nought is more noysom..Than sodayne tempeste, and unprovyded colde. **1536** *Goodly Primer, Litany* R iv b, Sodeyn & vnprouided dethe. 1627 C. Mageoghagan tr. *Ann. Clonmacnois* 75 The Emperor dyed of a sudaine and unprovided death. 1660 *Trial Regic.* 20 You must give your direct Answer, Guilty, or Not guilty. You cannot say, it is sudden, or unprovided. You spend time in vain. 1739 in *Cath. Rec. Soc. Publ.* VIII. 263 Her Death,..by the holy life she led, was not unprovided. 1817 F. Lewis in *Parl. Debates* 1361 Very heavy expenses..under the head called 'unprovided services,' which ought to comprise nothing except what could not possibly be foreseen. 1841 Alison *Hist. Eur.* IX. lxxii. 702 The unprovided expenditure of the year.

**4.** Not provided *for*. (Cf. 1 c.)

1575 Gascoigne *Glasse of Govt.* II. v, If ever I live to enherit Phylocalus, then Eccho shall not be unprovided for. 1647 Clarendon *Hist. Reb.* I. § 5 The necessary Subsistence of the household was unprovided for. 1676 Temple *Let. to Sir J. Williamson* Wks. 1720 II. 413 They cannot, upon that Pretence, be pressed to Things..wholly unprovided for by the very Letter of the Treaty. 1794 S. Williams *Vermont* 239 Many officers..were then unprovided for. 1839 *John Bull* 15 Sept., The income upon which he and the unprovided for members of his family exist. 1897 *Outing* XXX. 376/2 Unprovided-for tasks are best decided by drawing lots.

**5.** Not furnished, supplied, or made ready.

1621 Fletcher *Isl. Princess* I. ad fin., That's all That's unprovided,..The rest wee'l councel as we goe. 1726 Leoni *Alberti's Archit.* I. 21 b, You will have occasion for a great number of things.., and..if but one is unprovided, it may stop or spoil the whole Work.

Hence **Unprovi·dedly** *adv.*, **-ness.**

1567 *Reg. Privy Council Scot.* I. 522 He mycht *unprovidittie oppres..that innocent infant. 1652 Urquhart *Jewel* 112 Another young Lady..so unprovidedly was surprised. *a* 1652 Brome *Covent Garden Weeded* II. ii, My unsettlednesse and *unprovidednesse..may well excuse us all. 1861 [Mrs. A. J. Penny] *Romance Dull Life* xl. 296 From the fear of unprovidedness during her stay in this great house.

**Unpro·videnced,** *ppl. a.* (Un-1 8.) *a* 1661 Fuller *Worthies* I. (1662) 57 If those must be accounted unfortunate (which I in the true meaning of the word must interpret unprovidenced) who swim not in equal Plenty with others.

**† Unpro·vident,** *a. Obs.* [Un-1 7, 5 b.] Improvident; incautious.

1572 Buchanan *Detection of Mary* (1727) 71 Ane Hous.. prouydit for ane ȝoung Gentilman unprouydent be ȝouth. *c* 1600 Shaks. *Sonn.* x, Deny that thou bear'st loue to any, Who for thy selfe art so vnprouident. 1619 J. King *Serm.*, etc. 39 Hath it made you proud,..and improvident, and unprovident against your enemies? 1658 J. Webb *Cleopatra* VIII. II. 55 Must the unfortunate Alcamenes be ignorant, whence this unprovident ruine comes?

**Unprovide·ntial,** *a.* (Un-1 7, 5 b.) 1813 T. Busby *Lucretius* II. VI. Comm. p. x, Lucretius, reasoning from the unprovidential casualities of thunder, denies that it springs from the hand of Jupiter. 1837 Lytton *Athens* I. 21 [He] reclaimed his barbarous subjects from a wandering and unprovidential life. **† Unpro·vidently,** *adv. Obs.* (Un-1 11, 5 b.) 1611 Florio, *Improuidamente*, vnprouidently. 1805 Forsyth *Beauties Scotl.* III. 354 Forests.. unprovidently and wastefully destroyed. **Unpro·ving,** *ppl. a.* (Un-1 10.) 1640 Bp. Hall *Episc.* III. § 2 Since this one litigious, and unproving text is the onely place in the whole New Testament, that can beare any pretence for the lay-Presbytery. 1641 — *Def. Humble Remonstr.* 118 Your unproving illustrations, and unregardable testimonies.

**† Unprovi·sed,** *ppl. a. Sc. Obs.* [Un-1 8, 5 b.] Unforeseen; unconsidered.

*c* 1480 Henryson *Fables, Fox & Wolf* 162 This suddand deith and vnprouysit end Of this fals Tod. 1533 Bellenden *Livy* I. ii. (S.T.S.) I. 19 He wald nocht opin ane haisty and vnprovisit mater.

Hence **† Unprovi·sedly** *adv. Obs.*

1513 Douglas *Æneid* VI. iii. 28 With his bois trump as he Went vnprowysitlie blawand by the se. 1567 *Sc. Acts, Jas. VI* (1814) III. 27/2 Proceding to ane pretendit mariage with him suddandlie, and vnprouisitlie thairefter.

**Unprovi·sion.** (Un-1 12, 5 b.) *a* 1638 Mede *Wks.* (1672) 231 Whatsoever..among the Beasts of the field..is.., by unprovision, of all others the most wretched and miserable. **Unprovi·sioned,** *ppl. a.* (Un-1 8.) 1796 Coleridge *Lett.* (1895) 189, I shall be again afloat on the wide sea, unpiloted and unprovisioned. 1827 Pollok *Course T.* II. 242 Choosing, thus unshipped, Uncompassed, unprovisioned,..To swim a sea of breadth immeasurable. **Unprovo·kable,** *a.* (Un-1 7 b.) 1803 Bentham *Mem. & Corr.* Wks. 1843 X. 403 Better ..would it be if your..principals were as placable, or rather as unprovokable.

**Unprovo·cative,** *a.* (Un-1 7.)

Frequent in recent use.

1821 Lamb *Elia* I. *Grace before Meat*, At a poor man's table, or at the simple and unprovocative repast of children. 1893 *Scribner's Mag.* June 747/2 As he placidly walked along, unprovocative of even passing curiosity.

**Unprovo·ke,** *v.* (Un-2 3.) 1605 Shaks. *Macb.* II. iii. 32 Lecherie, Sir, it prouokes, and vnprouokes: it prouokes the desire, but it takes away the performance.

**Unprovo·ked,** *ppl. a.* (Un-1 8.)

1585 Abp. Sandys *Serm.* xv. 264 The voluntarie and vnprouoked operation of the spirite. 1641 Bp. Hall *Answ. Vind. Smectymnuus* To Rdr. A 3, When..the Smectymnuans,..unprovoked, unthought of,..flye in my face, as men wrongfully accused. 1712 Steele *Spect.* No. 427 ¶ 2 This Heroine had..out-done the whole Sisterhood of Gossips, in ..unprovoked Malice. 1759 Sterne *Tr. Shandy* II. xii, These unprovoked strokes at my uncle Toby's [hobby-horse]. 1819 Scott *Ivanhoe* xli, To discover..who have been my unprovoked enemies. 1849 C. Bronte *Shirley* xxiii, In answer to unprovoked insult.

Hence **Unprovo·kedly** *adv.*, **-ness.**

1663 Boyle *Usef. Exp. Nat. Philos.* I. v. 95 Galen..somewhere *unprovokedly and causelessly enough derides Moses. 1781 T. Davies *Mem. Garrick* (ed. 3) I. 23 He was rudely and unprovokedly attacked by a boisterous man. 1864 Carlyle *Fredk. Gt.* XVI. xii. IV. 455 His conduct..has nothing of bad, at least of unprovokedly bad. 1856 Faber *Creator & Creature* II. i, God's..tenderness,..His extraordinary *unprovokedness.

**Unprovo·king,** *ppl. a.* (Un-1 10.) 1710 Fleetwood *Serm.* 7 To..dash against the Stones the innocent and unprovoking Children. 1759 Sterne *Tr. Shandy* II. xii, But to hurt a brother..so unprovoking,—and so unresenting;—'tis base. 1821 Cobbett *Rur. Rides* (1885) I. 38 It is no very unprovoking reflection.

**† Unpru·dence.** [Un-1 12, 5 b.] Imprudence.

1382 Wyclif *Prov.* xiv. 8 The vnprudence of foolis [is] erring. 1533 Bellenden *Livy* II. xvi. (S.T.S.) I. 193, I drede þat sum thing be done by vnprudence or folie of my pepill. 1652 Gaule *Magastrom.* 239 Whether you shall become poor by..luxuriousnesse, unprudence.

**† Unpru·dent,** *a. Obs.* [Un-1 7, 5 b.] Imprudent; unwise.

1382 Wyclif *Mark* vii. 18 So and ȝe ben vnprudent, or vnwyse. 1395 Purvey *Remonstr.* (1851) 119 In this vnprudent geuinge [of the Sacrament]. 1412–20 Lydg. *Chron. Troy* I. 3650 For to provide þei ben graceles, Ful vnprudent and wilful rekeles. 1611 Speed *Hist. Gt. Brit.* IX. xi. 555/2 Peirs,..to establish his interest in the vnprudent Prince,.. filled the Court with buffons.

**Unprude·ntial,** *a.* (Un-1 7, 5 b.)

1650 Milton *Eikon.* (ed. 2) xxviii. 224 [This] were the most unwise and unprudential act as to civil goverment. 1685 D. Granville *Lett.* (Surtees, No. 37) 198, I thought it not unprudentiall so to do. *a* 1832 Bentham *Deontol.* (1834) II. 101 Of evil contingent on prudential or unprudential conduct.

**† Unpru·dently,** *adv. Obs.*-1 (Un-1 11, 5 b; cf. Unprudent.) 1412–20 Lydg. *Chron. Troy* II. 1474, I wondre gretly ..What auenture..Vnprudently meveth now þi kyng Vn-to me to make swiche a sonde. **Unpru·ned,** *ppl. a.*1 [Un-1 8 + Prune *v.*1] Not smoothed with the beak. 1820 Keats *Eve St. Agnes* xxxvii, A dove..with sick unpruned wing.

**Unpru·ned,** *ppl. a.*2 [Un-1 8 + Prune *v.*2] Not trimmed by cutting or lopping.

1593 Shaks. *Rich. II*, III. iv. 45 Her Fruit-trees all vnpruin'd, her Hedges ruin'd. 1621 Burton *Anat. Mel.* III. iii. I. ii. 673 If they [*sc.* women] be not curbed in time, as an vnproyned tree. 1649 Ogilby tr. *Virg., Bucol.* ii. (1684) 12 On th' Elm my unprun'd Vines neglected are. 1743 Francis tr. *Hor., Epodes* xvi. 52 Where..Vines unprun'd their blushing Clusters yield. 1801 Southey *Thalaba* XII. xviii, The unpruned taper flares a longer flame. 1863 Hawthorne *Our Old Home* II. 24 The hedges grow in unpruned luxuriance. 1882 *Garden* 21 Jan. 49/3 An idea prevails that birds are not so likely to spoil an unpruned tree.

**b.** In fig. uses.

1588 Shaks. *L.L.L.* IV. ii. 18 After his..vnpolished, vneducated, vnpruned, vntrained..fashion. 1619 Middleton *Love & Antiq.* B 3, A Common-wealth That is vndrest, vnpruin'd, wilde in her health. 1628 Feltham *Resolves* II. xxviii. 89 No man ha's preheminence, but wishes to preserue it in vnpruned state. 1814 *Monthly Rev.* LXXIV. 308 Addison lives, but not undecaying, nor unpruned. 1878 *Masque Poets* 181 They let their unpruned fancies roll Round some old theme like hop-vines round a pole.

**Unpry·ing,** *ppl. a.* (Un-1 10.) 1771 Mrs. Griffith *Hist. Lady Barton* II. 269 He..should wait upon him at..a respectful and unprying distance. 1803 *Forest of Hohenelbe* II. 215 The unprying few that composed her humble circle. **Unpsycholo·gical,** *a.* (Un-1 7.) 1885 *Athenæum* 8 Aug. 170/2 Hence the first main division into unpsychological and psychological ethical theories. **Unpu·blic,** *a.* (Un-1 7.) 1643 W. Greenhill *Axe at Root* A iv, Wee hope your spirits are all unselvished, that none are now unpublique. 1650 Jer. Taylor *Holy Living* ii. § 3. 90 Virgins must be retired and unpublick.

**Unpu·blishable,** *a.* (Un-1 7 b.)

1815 Coleridge *Lett.* (1895) 644 Making a MS. collection of all my poems—publishable and unpublishable. 1842 Lytton *Zanoni* I. i, His unpublished—his unpublishable and imperishable opera of the 'Siren'. 1891 Smiles *J. Murray* I. 441 Irving says..that Moore showed him the Byron recollections, and that they were quite unpublishable.

Hence **Unpu·blishably** *adv.*

1860 De Morgan in *Macm. Mag.* I. 223 Their ways of conducting themselves were unpublishably singular.

**Unpu·blished,** *ppl. a.* [Un-1 8.]

**1.** Not made generally known or accessible, esp. in print.

1607 Markham *Cavel.* (title-p.), The discovery of the subtill trade..of horse-coursers:..Secrets before vnpublished. 1684 T. Burnet *Theory Earth* I. 261 The ancient glosses and catenæ upon Scripture..are many of them either lost or unpublisht. 1731 *Hist. Litteraria* III. 259 Authors.. whose Writings still remain unpublished in the Libraries of Rome, Venice, and Paris. 1828 P. Buchan (*title*), Ancient Ballads and Songs of the North of Scotland hitherto unpublished. 1862 *Numism. Chron.* II. 104 Unpublished Greek Imperial Coins.

**2.** Not divulged or disclosed.

1605 Shaks. *Lear* IV. iv. 16 All blest Secrets, All you vnpublish'd Vertues of the earth Spring with my teares. *a* 1850 Bryant *The Past* 30 Labours of good to man, Unpublished charity, unbroken faith. 1886 Mrs. Hungerford *Mental Struggle* vii, 'Nobody can help me,' declares the as yet unpublished sinner.

**Unpu·cker,** *v.* (Un-2 3.) [1775 Ash.] 1831 Carlyle *Sart. Res.* I. iii, Let but Teufelsdröckh open his mouth, Heuschrecke's also unpuckered itself into a free doorway. 1862 — *Fredk. Gt.* XII. xi. III. 360 Belleisle..unpuckers his stern brow again. **Unpu·ckered,** *ppl. a.* (Un-1 8.) [1775 Ash.] *c* 1830 *Encycl. Brit.* (ed. 7) III. 38/1 Ruminants, in which the cæcum is moderate in size and unpuckered. 1862 *Catal. Internat. Exhib., Brit.* II. No. 2747, A plain unpuckered surface. **Unpu·ddled,** *ppl. a.* (Un-1 8.) *a* 1618 Sylvester *Maidens Blush* 1437 When the Ægyptians could no more perceive Nile's over-floud, nor any mud to leave; But pure, unpuddled on the sand to slide. 1842 *Civil Eng. & Arch. Jrnl.* V. 128/1 The whole surface of the hill is to be left unpuddled. **Unpu·ff,** *v.* (Un-2 3.) 1591 Sylvester *Du Bartas* I. iv. 526 We might unpuff our Heart, and bend our Knee. 1598 Florio, *Disenfiare*, to vnswel, to vnpuffe, to alay, to asswage. **Unpu·ffed,** *ppl. a.* (Un-1 8.) 1608 Sylvester II. iv. IV. *Decay* 452 Pure in Religion, Wise in Counselling,..Un-puft in Sun-shine, un-appall'd in Storms. **† Unpu·issant,** *a. Obs.*-1 [Un-1 7, 5 b.] = Impuissant *a.* ? *c* 1597 Bacon *Let.* in *Resuscitatio* II. (1657) 91 A Letter, carrying so empty an offer of so unpuissant a service.

**Unpu·lled,** *ppl. a.* (Un-1 8, 8 c.)

*c* 1440 *Pallad. on Husb.* XII. 230 Ek plauntis fair excuse To stonde vnpuld, that they be not to seke. *c* 1450 *Two Cookery Bks.* 99 Cast x. or xij. oynons hole vnpullud, and lete hem seth togidre. *c* 1536 Bellenden *Chron. Scot.* (1821) I. p. ix, The lillyis, and the violet, Unpullit, sone ar with the wind ouirset. 1551 Cranmer *Answ. Cra ty & Sophist. Cavillation* To Rdr. A iij b, What auaileth it..so long as ii. chief rootes remayne vnpulled vp? 1608 H. Clapham *Errour Left Hand* 72 Some doubts, which yet (as stumps) remaine behind vnpulled vp. 1641 Earl Monm. tr. *Biondi's Civil Wars* II. 95 If some few [houses] remained un-pulled down. 1694 Dryden *Love Triumph.* III. i, 'Tis indeed a Fruit; Seen and desir'd of all, while yet unpull'd. 1765 *Museum Rust.* V. 120 Ground as much over-run with seagrims as any part else of the pasture which had been unpulled! 1895 *Westm. Gaz.* 15 June 3/2 The greatest of devils must be in that carriage [= a cable-tram], making it crawl along unpulled, unpushed.

**Unpu·lleyed,** *ppl. a.* (Un-1 8.) 1839 Landor *Andrea of Hungary* 16 But intellect.., unpullied and adrift, Burns its dull heart away in smouldering scorn. **Unpu·lped,** *ppl. a.* (Un-1 8.) 1806 A. Hunter *Culina* (ed. 3) 59 Some part of the vegetables may be left unpulped. **Unpu·lverize,** *v.* (Un-2 6 c.) 1733 Tull *Horse-Hoeing Husb.* xxv. 417 Crushing has such a contrary Effect from squeezing, that if this Roller should be us'd when the Land is moist, it would be very pernicious, by unpulverizing it. **Unpu·lverized,** *ppl. a.* (Un-1 8.) [1775 Ash.] 1839 *Mag. Dom. Econ.* IV. 214 A lump of unpulverised magnesia. 1883 *Daily News* 30 July 4/8 If he took French leave and went off..leaving.. the Government undetected, the Opposition unpulverised. **Unpu·mpable,** *a.* (Un-1 7 b.) 1831 Disraeli *Young Duke* III. xiii, Arundel Dacre was proverbially unpumpable.

**Unpu·mped,** *ppl. a.* (Un-1 8, 8 c.)

1633 T. James *Voy.* 98 The Ship to be left vnpumpt. 1669 Boyle *Contin. New Exp.* xliv. 154 Air that yet remain'd unpump'd out. 1873 Ruskin *Fors Clav.* xxxiii. 17 A real pump in a pump room,..instead of the unpumped Tweed.

**Unpu·nctated,** *ppl. a.* (Un-1 8.) 1870 H. A. Nicholson *Man. Zool.* I. 247 *Spiriferidæ*...Shell punctated or unpunctated. **Unpuncti·lious,** *a.* (Un-1 7.) 1753 Richardson *Grandison* (1781) III. xxiii. 237 Lovers, said she, are the weakest people in the world; and people of punctilio the most *un*-punctilious.

**Unpu·nctual,** *a.* (Un-1 7.)

1740 Pope *Let. to Swift* Wks. 1751 IX. 333, I am a very unpunctual correspondent, tho' no unpunctual agent or friend. 1828 Lytton *Pelham* II. xii, Very young men are seldom unpunctual at dinner. 1841 Lady Lyttelton *Corr.* (1912) xii. 316 They are immensely unpunctual, and make the poor Queen wait for dinner. 1884 *Expositor* June 467, I am not unpunctual, as you know.

**Unpunctua·lity.** (Un-1 12, 5 b; cf. prec.)

1828–32 Webster. 1841 Emerson *Ess.* Ser. I. vii. 230 The discomfort of unpunctuality..is of no nation. 1868 Stanley *Westm. Abbey* ii. 71 He came to the Abbey with an ostentatious unpunctuality.

**Unpu·nctuated,** *ppl. a.* (Un-1 8.)

1866 Mrs. Stowe *Lit. Foxes* 46 That little unpunctuated scrap of life's poetry. 1890 'R. Boldrewood' *Col. Reformer* (1891) 261 His usual slow, unpunctuated direction of speech.

**Unpu·nctuating,** *ppl. a.* (Un-1 10.) 1866 De Morgan *Budget of Paradoxes* (1872) 139 Of this unpunctuating paradoxer I shall give an account in his own way. **Unpu·ncturable,** *a.* (Un-1 7 b.) 1891 *Daily News* 28 Nov. 6/1 An 'unpuncturable' tyre,..so constructed that the pressure of the air closes up holes. 1901 G. Paston *Little Mem. 18th Cent.* 201 An equally unpuncturable power of self-delusion.

**Unpu·nishable,** *a.* (Un-1 7 b.)

1531 *Dial. on Laws Eng.* II. 4 b, He is vnpunysshable of waste by the lawe. 1584 R. Scot *Discov. Witchcr.* III. viii. (1886) 40 An impossible purpose is unpunishable. 1648 Fairfax, etc. *Remonstr.* 49 While your own proceedings admit themselves unpunishable. 1682 Evats tr. *Grotius* (title-p.), In the Third [Book] is declared, What in War is Lawful, that is Unpunishable. *a* 1700 Dryden tr. *Ovid's Art of Love* 38 Th' unpunishable Pleasures of the Kind. *a* 1797 H. Walpole *Geo. II* (1847) I. ii. 334 It is the cause of sovereigns that their crimes should be unpunishable. 1802–12 Bentham *Ration. Judic. Evid.* (1827) I. 354 Mendacity ..remains altogether unpunishable. 1837 Carlyle *Fr. Rev.* I. v. i, Inertia alone is at once unpunishable and unconquerable.

Hence **Unpu·nishably** *adv.*

1649 Milton *Eikon.* xxviii. 230 It were yet absurd to think that the Anointment of God should..give them privilege, who punish others, to sin themselves unpunishably. 1829 Bentham *Justice & Cod. Petit.* 27 The now written, and above described unpunishably mendacious, pleadings.

**Unpu·nished,** *ppl. a.* (Un-1 8.)

*a* 1340 Hampole *Psalter* xxxiii. 16 He þat does ill, wen he not to be vnpunyst. 1387 Trevisa *Higden* (Rolls) VII. 185 Whos see after his deth none myȝte oppresse slepyng unpunsched. *c* 1440 *Alph. Tales* 276 So he had levur lefe þe blame vnpunysshid. 1484 Caxton *Fables of Æsop* VI. xv. N viij b, Men ought not to leue hym vnpunysshed. 1512 *Helyas* in Thoms *Prose Rom.* (1828) III. 75 A good dede is never unrewarded nor an evyll unpunisshed. 1573 L. Lloyd *Marrow of Hist.* (1653) 136 They suffered theft to be unpunished. 1613 J. Taylor (Water P.) *Waterm. Suit* Wks. (1630) 174/1 Few or none escapes vnpunished if their faults be knowne. 1651 Hobbes *Leviath.* II. xxx. 183 Crimes.. which unpunished, seem Authorised. 1712 Blackmore *Creation* VII. 71 His sword unpunish'd criminals defy. 1766 Gibbon *Decl. & F.* vi. (1782) I. 163 The crime went not unpunished. 1827 Pollok *Course T.* II. 553 An individual sovereignty, that none Created might, unpunished, bind or touch. 1875 Jowett *Plato* (ed. 2) I. 319 The impious..ought not to go unpunished.

Hence **Unpu·nishedly** *adv.*

1561 T. Norton *Calvin's Inst.* Pref. A iiij b, They doe so ..licentiously as vnpunishedly fome agaynst vs. 1611 Florio, *Impunitamente*, vnpunishedly.

**Unpu·nishing,** *vbl. sb.* (Un-1 13.) *a* 1340 Hampole *Ps.* xciii. 11 þai hete til þaim selfe vnpunyssynge of syn. *a* 1662 Heylin *Laud* (1668) 354 The unpunishing of the first Tumult. **Unpu·nishing,** *ppl. a.* (Un-1 10.) 1644 Milton *Divorce* ii. iii. 41 Nay this is.. to incarnat sin into the unpunishing and well pleas'd will of God. **Unpu·nishingly,** *adv.* [Un-1 11.] †With impunity. 1499 *Promp. Parv.* (Pynson), Onponysshingly, *impunite*. **†Unpu·nishment.** *Obs.*−1 (Un-1 12.) *a* 1555 Philpot *Exam. & Writ.* (Parker Soc.) 335 Yet eftsoons they be so hauwtiff with power, riches and unpunishment. 1648 Hexham ii, *Ongestraftheydt*, Vnpunishment, or Impunity.

**Unpu·rchas(e)able,** *a.* (Un-1 7 b.)

1611 Florio, *Inacquisteuole*, vnpurchasable. 1792 W. Roberts *Looker-on* No. 18 (1794) I. 238 The unpurchasable beauties and chaste decorations of rural scenery. *a* 1834 Coleridge *Lit. Rem.* (1839) IV. 170 To others, they are not only not easy and cheap, but unpurchaseable and impossible too. 1880 McCarthy *Own Times* IV. 215 The country gentleman, whose own vote.. was unpurchasable by any money bribe.

**Unpu·rchased,** *ppl. a.* (Un-1 8.)

1545 *Test. Ebor.* (Surtees) VI. 236 Where as I covenante withe hym.. to leave hym lande in yerlie value xls.. and have unpurchased xxs value of it. ? 1608 *J. Reynard's Deliv.* in *Harl. Misc.* (1808) I. 187 Nor [is] any treasure of the earth.. left unpurchased. 1665 Boyle *Occas. Refl.* iv. iii, As she is rich in Natures bounty, [she] appear'd .. satisfy'd with the unpurchas'd Treasures she possesses. 1736 Thomson *Liberty* v. 613 Justice, like the liberal light of Heaven, Unpurchas'd shines on all. 1781 Cowper *Hope* 343 But oh the strife,..and debate, The tidings of unpurchased heaven create! 1831 Scott *Ct. Rob.* xxviii, Let him keep unpurchased the crown, for which he has paid.. a price which it is not worth. 1893 F. Adams *New Egypt* 75 The poor unpurchased and, so far, unpolluted free-lance.

**†Unpu·re,** *a.* *Obs.* [Un-1 7, 5 b. Cf. MDu. *onpuur*, MLG. *unpûr*, MSw. *opur*.]

1. Morally impure.

*a* 1375 *Lay Folks Mass Bk.* App. iv. 226 Of sunnes we beþ vnpure. 1393 Langl. *P. Pl.* C. i. 116 (Ilchester MS.), For þay were prestes vnpure. *c* 1450 tr. *De Imitatione* iii. xxxvi. 106 Hov vnpure all oure werkes are we weyle not. 1509 Barclay *Shyp of Folys* 258 b, Nought chaste thou techyst, but thynge vnpure and vyle. 1550 Bale *Eng. Votaries* ii. F iij, Thus was the churche fylled wyth vnpure ministers. 1604 T. Wright *Passions* v. 237, I hope such vnpure minds will amend their impure errours. 1624 Donne *Devot.* 210 Of so vnpure constitutions, as that we can present no obiect but sin. 1742 in Wesley *Jrnl.* (1749) 41 Dost thou believe, thy heart must be thus unpure?

2. Not physically pure or clean.

*a* 1500 *Ratis Raving* i. 156 Quhilk is stinkand aire vnpure. 1548 *Act 2 & 3 Edw. VI*, c. 10 § 1 Malte unpure and unseasonable. 1576 Newton *Lemnie's Complex.* 9 b, When the humours be not sufficiently..concocted and attenuate, vnpure Spirites proceede out of them. 1651 Wittie *Primrose's Pop. Err.* iv. iii. 213 The mixture of pure, and unpure, that is to say, of different parts in..the same mixt body.

3. Not genuine or true.

1590 Burrough *Meth. Physick* 246 If one feuer do exceede the other, then it is called an vnpure hemitrice.

Hence † **Unpu·rely** *adv.*, **-ness.** *Obs.*

1550 Bale *Eng. Votaries* ii. A ij b They.. teache the veryte of God *vnpurely. 1548 Udall *Erasm. Par. Luke* ii. 20 b, For what point of *vnpurenes coulde suche a woman haue in bearyng childe, as..had conceiued by the onely power and vertue of God. 1573 T. Cartwright *Replye to Answ. Whitgift* 13 Christe..shall couer all oure vnpurenesse and not impute it vnto vs.

**†Unpu·red,** *ppl. a.* *Obs.* [Un-1 8.] Unpurified. 1398 Trevisa *Barth. De P. R.* xvii. i. (Bodl. MS.), Þerin þe fedinge pured is itempred fro þe vnpured, as it is in þe guttes of a beeste. *c* 1400 Maundev. (1919) 200 Þei fynen the pured gold & casten awey the vnpured. 1579 Langham *Gard. Health* 519 Put them in dishes with vnpured hony. **Unpu·rgeable,** *a.* (Un-1 7 b.) 1876 Swinburne *Erechtheus* 299 A stain of blood unpurgeable with tears.

**Unpu·rged,** *ppl. a.* [Un-1 8.]

1. Not cleansed or freed from baser elements or admixture.

1555 Eden *Decades* (Arb.) 268 Ginger Mechino.. is sould vnclensed or vnpurged. 1601 Shaks. *Jul. C.* ii. i. 266 The Rhewmy, and vnpurged Ayre. *a* 1661 Holyday *Persius* (1673) 306 This from th' unpurged earth made us desire To strain out veins of gold by purging fire. 1667 Milton *P. L.* v. 419 Whence in her visage round those spots, unpurg'd Vapours not yet into her substance turn'd. 1788 V. Knox *Winter Even.* II. iv. x. 61 Instruments sweeter than the unpurged ear ever heard. 1874 Farrar *Christ* I. 118 Which to the dull unpurged ear was but inarticulate thunder.

2. Not freed or cleared from wrong-doing, accusation, etc.

1530 Rastell *New Bk. Purgatory* iii. viii. f 4 b, That the soule vnpurged maye do some meane & lowe seruyce to god in heuen. 1586 J. Hooker *Hist. Irel.* in *Holinshed* II. 70/1 The prisoner deceased in the castell, and because he stood vnpurged, long he laie vnburied. 1642 Milton *Apol. Smect.* 11 So long as I should suffer my honest estimation to lye unpurg'd from these insolent suspicions. 1653 Jer. Taylor *Serm. for Year* i. xix. 250 Hell is wide open..to euery unpurged person. 1738 Wesley *Ps.* vi. iii, Who dies unpurg'd for ever dies.

3. Not removed or cleared away.

*a* 1617 Hieron *Wks.* (1620) II. 415 That there is some secret euill in vs, which is vnpurged and vnreformed. 1682 Flavel *Fear* 39 The unpurged relicts of unbelief. 1835 T. Mitchell *Acharn. of Aristoph.* 874 A man who had yet the unpurged pollution of a mother's blood upon him. 1884 *Chr. Commw.* 14 Feb. 415/2 The Church,..corrupted by the unpurged influences of the great Apostacy.

**Unpu·rified,** *ppl. a.* (Un-1 8.)

1574 T. Cartwright *Full Declar.* a 2 b, That vnreuenged, and vnpurified shedinge off giltlesse bloud. 1617 Moryson *Itin.* i. 10 Vnpurified siluer as it comes from the Mines. 1667 *Decay Chr. Piety* ii. 37 Our sinful Nation..is indeed now come out [of the furnace], but so unpurified, that [etc.]. *a* 1779 Warburton *Div. Leg.* vi. Notes, Wks. 1788 III. 576 This active Watchman of the Church militant will let nothing escape him,..nor leave any thing unpurified that has once passed through my hands. 1791 Cowper *Yardley Oak* 12 The conscience, yet Unpurified by an authentic act Of amnesty. 1832 G. R. Porter *Porcelain & Gl.* 275 The presence of iron in the unpurified sea-sand and ashes of which it is composed.

**Unpu·rifying,** *ppl. a.* (Un-1 10.) 1862 'Shirley' (J. Skelton) *Nugæ Crit.* vii. 319 The discipline which teaches humility is not unpurifying.

**Unpu·rposed,** *ppl. a.* (Un-1 8.)

1570 Dee *Math. Pref.* 15 Of second vnpurposed frute,.. arrising by Geometrie. 1606 Shaks. *Ant. & Cl.* iv. xiv. 84 Do it at once, Or thy precedent Seruices are all But accidents vnpurpos'd. 1645 Milton *Tetrach.* 32 The restorement of a freeborn man from an unpurpos'd, and unworthy bondage to a rightfull liberty. 1827 Pollok *Course T.* v. 362 The lonely bard.., when forth he walked, Unpurposed. 1885 W. J. Sendall *Calverley's Rem.* 53 The work which he has left behind him.. is, as to much of it, unpurposed and fragmentary.

**†Unpu·rposedly,** *adv.* *Obs.*−1 [Un-1 11; cf. prec.] Not purposely. *a* 1639 W. Whateley *Prototypes* i. xix. (1640) 185 Had they unpurposedly fallen to wanton embraces. **Unpu·rpose-like,** *a.* (Un-1 7 c.) [1825 Jam.] 1856 Lever *Martins of Cro' M.* 22 The unpurpose-like vacuity, the intense vulgarity of his Oughterard friends.

**Unpu·rse,** *v.* [Un-2 5, 4, 3.]

1. *trans.* To take (money) out of a purse; to disburse.

1390 Gower *Conf.* II. 146 The time is ofte cursed, That evere was the gold unpursed, The which was leid upon the bok. 1570 Levins *Manip.* 191 To vnburse and vnpurse, *expendere, insumere*. 1580 Hollyband *Treas. Fr. Tong*, *Grand d'esboursement d'argent*, a great vnpursing of mony. 1611 Tourneur *Ath. Trag.* v. i. (Stage direct.), Unpurses the gold.

2. To rob of one's purse.

1827 Pollok *Course T.* viii. 382 The uncivil robber, who unpursed The traveller on the highway.

3. To relax from a pursed state. Also *intr.*

1871 Browning *Pr. Hohenst.* 45 Now I permit your plump lips to unpurse. *c* 1880 R. Bridges in A. D. Coleridge *Eton in Forties* (1896) 174 Unpursed his mouth, empty his mighty chest, His run is o'er.

**Unpursu·ed,** *ppl. a.* (Un-1 8.)

1469 *Sc. Acts, Jas. III* (1814) II. 95/1 Þe obligatione..sall prescrife & be of nain avail þe said fourtj ȝeris beand ronnyng & vnpersewit be þe law. 1531 *Reg. Privy Seal Scot.* II. 134/2 The saidis personis.. to be.. unaccusit, unfollowit, unpersewit,..for quhatsumever actioun or cryme. 1667 Milton *P. L.* vi. 1 All night the dreadless Angel unpursu'd Through Heav'ns wide Champain held his way. 1675 Hobbes *Odyssey* (1677) 189 To the ship we unpursued pass. 1782 J. Scott *Poet. Wks.* 235 Pale fear, who unpursued still flies. 1810 Scott *Lady of L.* ii. xxvi, This youth..Guided my steps not unpursued. 1861 Clara F. Bromley *Woman's Wand. West. World* 168 They made a precipitate..retreat, but were unpursued.

**Unpurvey·ed,** *ppl. a.* [Un-1 8.]

†1. Of persons: Unprovided, unfurnished, unsupplied (with something): **a.** Const. *of*.

*a* 1300 *Cursor M.* 5444 'Now leue sun ioseph,' he said, 'O þe es [= am] i noght vnpuruaid'. *c* 1375 *Lay Folks Mass Bk.* 424 (Royal MS.), If þou of ane be vn-puruayde. 1471 *Paston Lett.* III. 4 It is soo that my brother is on purveyed off monye. *a* 1548 Hall *Chron., Edw. IV*, 197 You may thinke that kyng Edward was not..so vnpurueyed of counsail, to forsake thys beneficiall alliaunce. 1596 Spenser *F. Q.* vii. vi. 14 All the heauenly crew Of happy wights, now vnpurvaide of light, Were much afraid.

†**b.** Without const. Also = not provided for.

1491 Caxton *Vitas Patr.* (W. de W. 1495) i. cxlii. 153 b/1 That yf I wexed an almes gyuer, god sholde neuer leue me unpurueyed. *a* 1500 *Assemb. Ladies* 382 Than we began to dresse us in our gyse, That folk shuld see we were nat unpurvayd. 1509 Barclay *Shyp of Folys* 50 For one small faute..out is he cast bare and vnpuruayde. *c* 1530 *Court of Love* 561 And ye that ben unpurveyed, praye her eke Comfort you soon.

†2. Unprepared; not in readiness (to resist attack, etc.). *Obs.*

1387 Trevisa *Higden* (Rolls) VII. 111 In þe nyȝt.. Englische men..disperbled and chased þe enemyes unpurveied. *c* 1425 *Orolog. Sapient.* v. in *Anglia* X. 359/7 Take me not so vnpurveyed fro þis liȝte of life. *a* 1450 *Knt. de la Tour* (1906) 146 The .v. maidenes that were folys, that slepte and were vnpurueyed. *a* 1548 Hall *Chron., Hen. VIII*, 32 It was forsene that the kyng nor his people should be taken vnpuruyed. 1586 Day *Eng. Secretorie* ii. 114 It seemeth a matter incident to his accompt..that..he be not vnpurueyed in his owne person.

†3. Unforeseen; unexpected(ly). *Obs.*

*c* 1374 Chaucer *Boeth.* ii. pr. i. (1868) 30 Til þat she confounde wiþ vnsuffreable sorwe hem þat she haþ left in despeir vnpurueyed [L. *insperata*]. *c* 1425 Wyntoun *Cron.* ii. xvi. 1531 He slew of þaim a gret party As he come on vnpurva'd, Vnwarnyst wer þai. 1456 Sir G. Hay *Gov. Princes* Wks. (S.T.S.) II. 112 Rycht sa of ane unkynde ȝere .. men may better purvay na it war unknawin na unpurvayde of before. 1483 Caxton *Gold. Leg.* 359 b/2 As they fled they..mette the holy body sodenly unpoureyed.

4. Of things: Not furnished beforehand.

*a* 1548 Hall *Chron., Edw. IV*, 243 He.. left nothyng apperteignyng to the warre, vnpurueyed or vnlooked for.

**Unpu·shed,** *ppl. a.* (Un-1 8.) [1775 Ash.] 1895 [see Unpulled].

**Unput,** *ppl. a.* (Un-1 8, 8 c.)

Chiefly with advs. and preps.

*c* 1470 Henry *Wallace* vi. 624 Dede corssys that lay wnputt in graiff. 1491 *Sc. Acts, Jas. IV* (1814) II. 225/1 The tennentis..sall remane vnput furth or removit. 1509 Hawes *Past. Pleas.* xxix. (Percy Soc.) 143 Towarde Rome a great circuite aboute, There was no fyre that was un-put-out. 1565 in Hay Fleming *Reform. Scot.* (1910) 611 Certane tymmer and glas unput in the memoriall. 1600 Surflet *Countrie Farme* i. iii. 4 One tyle in the roofe..being left vnrepaired and vnput in againe, causeth others also to fall. 1665 Sir T. Herbert *Trav.* (1677) 56 This holy Fire.. continued un-put out for many Generations. 1732 J. Louthian *Form of Process* 267 Which Act as yet remains unput to due Execution anent the forenamed Persons. 1843 Mrs. Browning *Lett. R. H. Horne* (1877) I. 65 She has.. a natural exaltation, perfectly unaffected and un-put-on. 1897 Flandrau *Harvard Episodes* 37 Bradley suddenly answered the unput questions by suggesting ways and means.

**Unpu·trefied,** *ppl. a.* (Un-1 8.)

1579 W. Fulke *Heskins' Parl.* 353 It was kept many yeres..vnputrified. 1626 Bacon *Sylva* § 341 So wee see that Meat and Drinke will last longer, Vnputrified, or Unsowred, in Winter, than in Summer. 1663 Boyle *Usef. Exp. Nat. Philos.* ii. i. 25 An embrio..preserved unputrified for several years. 1735 Arbuthnot *Aliments* 180 No Animal unputrify'd, being burnt, yields any alkaline Salt. 1799 Kirwan *Geol. Ess.* 60 The rhinoceros was found intire and unputrified. 1843 Carlyle *Past & Pr.* iii. x, All human things do require ..to have some Soul in them,..were it only to keep the Body unputrefied.

**Unpu·trid,** *a.* (Un-1 7, 5 b.) 1657 B. W. tr. *Bauderon's Expert Phisic.* 72 An unputrid Synochus hath no small Analogy with an Ephemera. **Unpythago·rically,** *adv.* (Un-1 11.) *a* 1687 H. More *Conject. Cabbal.* (1713) 133 By all which terms is meant nothing else but Cybele or Vesta, but how Unpythagorically, any one may discern.

**†Unquae·rable,** *a.* *Obs.*−1 [Un-1 7 b + Quære *v.*] Indubitable, certain. 1657 J. Watts *Vind. Ch. Eng.* 58 An unquestionable and unquaerable Rule. **Unqua·ffed,** *ppl. a.* (Un-1 8.) [1775 Ash.] 1812 Byron '*If sometimes*' iii, If not the goblet pass unquaff'd, It is not drain'd to banish care.

**Unquai·led,** *ppl. a.* (Un-1 8.)

1583 Golding *Calvin on Deut.* cxcix. 1237 Let vs..praye him to giue vs power to holde out vnquailed. 1613 W. Browne *Brit. Past.* i. iv, So Griefe..In longest iourneys hath the strongest strength, And is at hand suppress, unquail'd at length. 1839 Coleridge *Constit. Ch. & State* (ed. 2) 145 The lion-hearted Luther with unquailed spirit.

**Unquai·ling,** *ppl. a.* (Un-1 10.)

1836 Whittier *Mem. T. Shipley* 49 The unquailing eye of innocence. 1853 Rock *Ch. of Fathers* III. ix. 217 His heart was unquailing when he met his foemen. 1884 R. W. Church *Bacon* i. 25 Elizabeth's..unquailing spirit at the time of the Spanish invasion.

Hence **Unquai·lingly** *adv.*

1845 [Jane Robinson] *Whitehall* lxviii, [He] fixed his eyes steadily and unquailingly upon him.

**Unquai·nt,** *a.* [Un-1 7.] †Uncunning, ignorant. *a* 1340 Hampole *Psalter* ciii. 26 Waytynges of þaim..occupyes vnquaynte men anence þaire saule. *Ibid.* cxl. 4 It is þe manere of vnquaynt men..to excuse þaim wiþ falshede. **†Unquai·nted,** *ppl. a.* *Obs.*−1 [Un-1 8.] Unfamiliar. 1587 W. Fowler *Wks.* (S.T.S.) I. 26, I who was not muche acquent with such vnquented sight. **Unqua·kerish,** *a.* (Un-1 7.) 1822 Lamb *Lett.* (1900) III. 80 It is a visiting, unquiet, unquakerish season. **Unqua·kerlike,** *a.* (Un-1 7 c.) 1852 Savage *R. Medlicott* i. iii, A fair..girl, with a most unquakerlike expression of mirth in her eye. **Unqua·kerly,** *a.* (Un-1 7.) 1846 B. Barton *Select.* (1849) 41 The bell, with the somewhat unquakerly inscription of 'Mr. Barton's bell'. **Unqua·king,** *ppl. a.* (Un-1 10.) 1816 Wilson *City of Plague* ii. iii. 99 That awful happiness That walks unquaking through the shades of death. 1881 Ruskin *Bible Amiens* iv. § 10 On the unquaking and fruitful earth.

**Unqua·lifiable,** *a.* (Un-1 7 b.)

With recent quots. cf. mod.F. *inqualifiable*.

*a* 1734 North *Lives* (1742) 271 He would not put the Seals to any Commissions to Persons unqualifiable. 1871 *Union Rev.* 78 This unqualifiable proceeding. 1899 *Westm. Gaz.* 28 June 2/1 The march played over and over..with quite unqualifiable iteration.

**Unqualifica·tion.** (Un-1 12.) 1657 W. Morice *Coena quasi Κοινὴ* xvi. 261 Qualifications (I should think them rather unqualifications). 1708 Hearne *Collect.* (O.H.S.) II. 106 He..express't his unqualification for ye Place.

**Unqua·lified,** *ppl. a.* [Un-1 8.]

1. Not qualified or fitted; not having the necessary qualifications.

1556 Lauder *Tractate* 364 Quhow God sall ȝow correct, Geue ȝe vnqualifeit hirds Elect. 1631 *Star Chamb. Cases* (Camden) 73 Allen, being a Vicar in Sudbury and beneficed and unqualifyed, accepted of another living. 1673 *S'too him Bayes* 22 The bishop would not have unqualify'd people read the scriptures. 1780 Harris *Philol. Enq.* i. iv. (1781) 27 As Translators are infinite, and many of them (to borrow a phrase from Sportsmen) unqualified Persons. 1836 Jas. Grant *Random Recoll. Ho. Lords* ix. 192 He was always the unqualified denouncer of State prosecutions of the press. 1891 E. Kinglake *Australian at Home* 46 It is no use sueing a quack...Why did you employ him? You know he is unqualified.

**b.** Const. *for*, or *to* with inf.

1667 *Decay Chr. Piety* xix. 409 Till he have thus denudated himself..he is utterly unqualified for these Agones. 1689 S. Johnson *Remarks Sherlock's Bk.* 41 A Person may be unqualified by Law, to execute a Commission. 1736 Butler *Anal.* i. v. 113 Capable of naturally becoming qualified for States of life, for which they were once wholly unqualified. 1781 Gibbon *Decl. & F.* xviii. (1787) II. 109 Dominions which they were unqualified to govern. 1847 Harris *Life Ld. Hardwicke* I. 504 A minister..unqualified for his situation.

2. Not endowed with specific qualities.

1678 Cudworth *Intell. Syst.* 220 If he neither derived them from..unqualified Matter,..nor yet from..an irrational and maleficent soul.

3. Not modified, limited, or restricted.

1796 Mme. D'Arblay *Camilla* I. 76 [He] could scarce refrain from a smile at this unqualified opening. 1857 Prescott *Philip II*, i. (1857) 145 His ardour did not precipitate him into any unqualified declaration of his passion. 1878 Bosw. Smith *Carthage* 7 The unsparing and unqualified denunciations of Tyre and Sidon..in Joel and Amos.

**Unqua·lifiedly**, *adv.* [UN-[1] 11.] Without qualification.

**1862** R. H. PATTERSON *Ess. Hist. & Art* 107 M. Guizot.. inculcates much too unqualifiedly the preservation of repose in statuary. **1873** MORLEY *Rousseau* II. 178 An exercise of sovereignty which might be atheistic, mahometan, or anything else unqualifiedly monstrous.

**Unqua·lifiedness.** (UN-[1] 12.)

**1666** BOYLE *Hydrostatical Paradoxes* Pref. A 7 b, The unqualifiedness of most Readers, to examine Mathematical things. **1674** A. G. *Quest. Oath Allegiance* To Rdr. p. iii, My own unqualifiedness extreamly discourag'd me from doing it. **1720** S. PARKER *Biblioth. Bibl.* 65 The inadvertency and unqualifiedness of Copyers.

**Unqua·lify**, *v.* [UN-[2] 3.] *trans.* To make unqualified; to disqualify. (Common *c* 1675–1750.)

**1655** SPURSTOWE *Wels of Salvation* 164 Earthly things defile the heart with..corrupt affections, which do unqualifie it for the reception of..precious promises. **1694** S. JOHNSON *Notes Past. Let. Bp. Burnet* I. 73 The Duke of York had unqualified himself for that High Office. **1709** ADDISON *Tatler* No. 103 ¶ 16 These particularities..in dress and behaviour..oftentimes..unqualify them from doing any Good in the World. **1794** MRS. A. M. BENNETT *Ellen* III. 72 His ill health..unqualified him to be a public [tutor]. **1836** T. ERSKINE *Baxter's Saint's R.* Pref. p. xxxiv, [To] unqualify the mind for present exertion. **1853** C. H. SPURGEON in *Daily News* 2 Feb. (1892) 6/1 If you think my years would unqualify me for your pulpit.

Hence **Unqua·lifying** *ppl. a.*

**1737** *Common Sense* I. 30 The most unqualifying Circumstances for any Employment, where Bribery and Corruption can possibly enter.

**Unqua·lifyingly**, *adv.* (UN-[1] 11.) **1841** S. WARREN *Ten Thou.* v. i, Unqualifyingly submitting to every one of the requisitions. **Unqua·litied**, *ppl. a.* (UN-[2] 8.) **1606** SHAKS. *Ant. & Cl.* III. xi. 44 Madam, speake to him, Hee's vnqualited with very shame. **Unqua·lity-like**, *a.* (UN-[1] 7 c.) **1784** R. BAGE *Barham Downs* I. 100 An unaccountable unquality-like fit of the spleen. **Unqua·ntified**, *ppl. a.* (UN-[1] 8.) **1864** BOWEN *Logic* vi. 162 The same naked or unquantified Subject and Predicate. **1865** MILL *Exam. Hamilton* xxii. 443 Forms..in which unquantified conclusions can be drawn from unquantified premises. **Unqua·rrellable**, *a.* (UN-[1] 7 b.) **1646** SIR T. BROWNE *Pseud. Ep.* VI. x. 323 There arising unto examination no such satisfactory and unquarrellable reasons. **1698** in Sir H. Dalrymple *Decisions* (1792) 1 It necessarily followed, that the sentence should be final, and unquarrellable. **Unqua·rrelled**, *ppl. a.* (UN-[1] 8.) **1606** in De Foe *Hist. Ch. Scot.* II. Add. (1717) 224 By a just Sentence of a lawful Judge, standing unquarrelled and unreduc'd. **Unqua·rrelsome**, *a.* (UN-[1] 7.) **1836** SIR H. TAYLOR *Statesman* xv. 101 A statesman should be..the most unquarrelsome of men. **Unqua·rried**, *ppl. a.* (UN-[1] 8.) **1788** D. GILSON *Serm.* 19 The fragment of an useful Column, has more honour than the whole unquarried rock. **1901** *Daily News* 21 Feb. 6/3 It was the work of a poetic pioneer in the unquarried rocks of daily life. **Unqua·rtered**, *ppl. a.* (UN-[1] 8.) [1775 ASH.] **1887** BOWEN *Æneid* VI. 253 He..Flings on the flames whole bodies of bulls unquartered to blaze. **Unqua·shed**, *ppl. a.* (UN-[1] 8.) **1647** N. BACON *Disc. Govt. Eng.* I. xlviii. 131 Preserving the particular subservient jurisdictions of the kingdome, intire and unquashed.

**Unquee·n**, *v.* [UN-[2] 6 b, 4.]

**1.** *trans.* To deprive of, depose from, the rank or position of queen.

**1579** J. STUBBES *Gaping Gulf* D ij, Is it not more then probable..that the next prince..wyl drawe it [*sc.* England] also..under the law Salique, and so quite vnqueen the desolate sister? **1613** SHAKS. *Hen. VIII*, IV. ii. 171 Embalme me, Then lay me forth (although vnqueen'd) yet like A Queene. **1673** *Season. Disc. Maintain. Establ. Relig.* 9 Nor was she unqueen'd enough by all this. **1821** *To the King* 9 We must un-queen your wife, because she is immoral. **1833** H. COLERIDGE *Poems* I. 38 Old times unqueen thee, and old loves endear thee. **1873** *Athenæum* 22 Feb. 240/2 The divorce which was to unqueen Catherine of Arragon.

**2.** To remove the queen from (a hive).

**1884** *Bee-keeping* 23 Unqueen your diseased stock, cutting out all queen-cells ten days after.

Hence **Unquee·ned** *ppl. a.*

**1820** SCOTT *Abbot* xxiii, Go thou..and render the usual service of the meal to this unqueened Queen. **1826** SOUTHEY *Vind. Eccl. Angl.* 388 The un-queened, un-sexed, un-Lutheranized, Christina.

**Unquee·nlike**, *a.* (UN-[1] 7 c.) *a* **1683** OLDHAM *Wks.* (1686) 13 Unqueenlike pity marr'd her Royal Pow'r.

**Unquee·nly**, *a.* (UN-[1] 7.)

**1865** SWINBURNE *Chastelard* IV. i. 164 Methinks I am growing unqueenly. **1884** *Truth* 13 Mar. 383/1 Her..modest bearing and unqueenly ways.

**Unque·lled**, *ppl. a.* (UN-[1] 8. Cf. MDu. *ongequelt*, ON. *úkvaldr*.)

? *a* **1400** *Morte Arth.* 3811 Qwhylles he es qwykke and in qwerte unquellyde with handis. **1605** SYLVESTER *Du Bartas* II. iii. *Law* 1307 Thou shalt dye quiet, thou shalt live unquell'd. **1654** FANSHAWE *Love for Love's Sake*, That so famous Queen For unquell'd valour. **1727** THOMSON *Summer* 509 Thy Meadows..rise unquell'd Against the Mower's Sythe. *a* **1800** COWPER *Iliad* (ed. 2) v. 121 Diomede unquell'd By that keen shaft, retreated. **1813** BYRON *Giaour* xxxii, A spirit yet unquell'd and high.

† **Unque·me**, *a. Obs.* [OE. *uncwéme* (UN-[1] 7): cf. *uniqueme* (UN-[1] 3), MSw. *oqväm*, MDa. *ukvem*.]

**1.** Displeasing.

*c* **1000** *Vercelli MS.* fol. 79 a, For þære [unsibbe] bið sio ure onsæзdnes Gode uncweme. *c* **1200** *Trin. Coll. Hom.* 9 Ure lif we leded richtliche toзenes ure louerd.., зif we forberð al þat þat him is unqueme. *c* **1200** ORMIN 4629 All þatt follзheþþ unnclænleззc All iss Drihhtin unncweme.

**2.** Unfit, unsuitable; awkward.

*a* **1300** *Cursor M.* 12411 Þis tre..Þat first vnquemest was to see Nu es it quem als it mai be. **1611** COTGR., *Maladroict*, vnwieldie, aukward, vnwheeme.

**3.** Uncomfortable, uneasy.

*a* **1300** *Cursor M.* 22597 Þe self angels sal quake vnqueme For dute of him þat all sal deme.

So † **Unque·mable**, *a.*, **-ably** *adv.*, **Unque·mefully** *adv.*, **Unque·mely** [cf. MSw. *oqvämelika*] *adv.* Also **Unque·me** *v.* [UN-[2] 3], to trouble, unsettle. *Obs.*

*a* **1300** *Cursor M.* 3566 Þe heued biginnes for to scak, His hend vnquemli for to quak. *Ibid.* 22551 Vnquemfulli þan sal þai quak, Þat all þe erth it sal toscak. *c* **1400** *Destr. Troy* 2693 Þou qwene, þat vnqwemyt has on sum qwaint wise, The angur thee is, Ecuba, entrond on honde! *Ibid.* 13681 Þen fortune his fall felli aspies, Vnqwemys his qwate, & þe qwele turnys. *c* **1440** *Promp. Parv.* 366/2 On-qwemable, *inplacabilis. Ibid.*, On-qwemably, *inplacabiliter.*

**Unque·nchable**, *a.* [UN-[1] 7 b, 5 b.] Incapable of being quenched; inextinguishable: **a.** Of fire. (Also *fig.*)

**1382** WYCLIF *Matt.* iii. 12 Chaffis he shal brenne with fyr unquenchable. *c* **1450** tr. *De Imitatione* III. lxiii. 147 Þei þat..brennen in an unquenchable fire of charite. **1535** COVERDALE *Luke* iii. 17 He..shal burne the chaffe with vnquencheable fyre. **1565** CALFHILL *Answ. Martiall's Treat. Cross* To Rdr. 2 To burne in hell wyth flames vnquenchable. **1627** HAKEWILL *Apol.* IV. xiv. § 4. 462 That [fire] burneth eternally without feeding, and is vnquenchable. **1652** VAUGHAN *Mount of Olives* Wks. 1914 I. 169 Those furious and unquenchable burnings of hell (which the Scripture calls the lake of fire, &c.). **1741-2** GRAY *Agrippina* 128 The spark Unquenchable, that glows within their breasts. **1791** COWPER *Iliad* XVII. 107 Fierce as Vulcan's fire Unquenchable. **1811** LAMB *Genius of Hogarth* Wks. 1908 I. 106 Her unquenchable spark is not utterly out. **1825** MACAULAY *Ess., Milton* ¶ 50 Those mighty principles..have kindled an unquenchable fire in the hearts of the oppressed. **1870** BRYANT *Iliad* XVI. II. 119 The eager enemy hurled the blazing brands.., and wrapped the stern in flames Unquenchable.

**b.** Of thirst, hunger, or greed.

**1567** JEWEL *Reply Harding* 735 The Pope..beinge diseased ..with an vnquencheable thirst of monie. **1577** HOLINSHED *Hist. Scot.* I. 62/2 Hee was giuen to suche vnquenchable couetyse that nothing mighte suffice hym. *a* **1619** FOTHERBY *Atheom.* II. ii. § 5. 204 Thus vnquenchable is the thirst of ambition. **1723** DE FOE *Col. Jack* (1840) 186 By these things he raised an unquenchable thirst in me. **1795** SOUTHEY *Maid of Orleans* II. 71 Often impatiently to quench their thirst Unquenchable, large draughts of molten gold They drink insatiate. **1857** ROBERTSON *Serm.* Ser. III. xix. 273 The more unquenchable his hunger for the high and the good, the sooner will he find that out. **1901** TROWBRIDGE *Lett. Mother to Eliz.* x. 51 Her thirst for information is apparently unquenchable.

**c.** In other contexts. (Common in recent use.)

*a* **1586** SIDNEY *Defence of Earl of Leicester* Wks. 1923 III. 65 An evident proof of an unquencheable malice. **1671** MILTON *Samson* 1422 The people on thir Holy-days Impetuous, insolent, unquenchable. **1805** WORDSW. *Prelude* I. 184 Firm devotion, zeal unquenchable. **1859** MILL *Liberty* iv. 164 Polygamy..seems to excite unquenchable animosity when practised by persons who speak English. **1883** *Harper's Mag.* Apr. 696/2 There is just the same unquenchable interest here.

Hence **Unque·nchableness.**

**1627** H. BURTON *Baiting Pope's Bull* 63 Wee pray God, that wee neuer come to feele the fierie vnquenchablenesse of it. **1629** in Hakewill *Apol.* (1630) Advts. Yy 4 b, Visiting him [*sc.* a bled man] I was amazed to see the vnquenchableness of this fire.

**Unque·nchably**, *adv.* (UN-[1] 11.)

**1652** GAULE *Magastrom.* 288 He..hath brought..his bookes to be burnt (by which himselfe might have burned unquenchably). *a* **1711** KEN *Hymn.* Poet. Wks. 1721 II. 104 In pure Love Jesus on the Cross expir'd, That Sinners might unquenchably be fir'd. **1805** SCOTT *Last Minstrel* II. xvii, That lamp shall burn unquenchably, Until the eternal doom shall be. **1856** MRS. BROWNING *Aur. Leigh* III. 86 All true poets laugh unquenchably Like Shakespeare and the gods.

**Unque·nched**, *ppl. a.* [UN-[1] 8.]

**1.** Unextinguished; unsuppressed: **a.** Of fire or light. Also *fig.*

*c* **1200** ORMIN 10491 Inntill þatt fir þatt bærnenn shall A butenn ende unncwennkedd. ? *a* **1400** *MS. Cantab. Ff.* ii. 38 fol. 26 (Halliw.) I lycken the worlde to fyre un-queynte. **1596** SPENSER *F. Q.* IV. v. 4 Vulcan..This pretious ornament.. wrought in Lemno with vnquenched fire. *a* **1626** BACON *Prayer* Wks. 1879 I. 340 My heart..hath been an unquenched coal upon thine altar. **1703** ROWE *Fair Penit.* II. D 4, If any Spark from Heav'n remain unquench'd Within her Breast. **1764** GOLDSM. *Trav.* 222 Their level life is but a smouldering fire, Unquench'd by want. **1812** BYRON *Ch. Har.* II. lxxv, Who but would deem their bosoms burn'd anew With thy unquenched beam, lost Liberty! **1836** *Lyra Apost.* (1849) 180 On high th'unquenched stars Blaze. **1882** FARRAR *Early Chr.* I. 286 Even amid the moral aberrations of heathenism it was granted to some..to keep that light unquenched.

**b.** Of feelings, qualities, etc.

**1590** MARLOWE *2nd Pt. Tamburl.* v. iii, His teare-thyrsty and vnquenched hate. **1593** *Sidney's Arcadia* III. (1598) 367 Being depriued of her vnquenched desire. *a* **1625** FLETCHER *Woman's Prize* IV. iv, My unquench'd charity shall tell you thus much, (Though you deserve it well) you shall not beg. **1762** FALCONER *Shipwr.* III. 168 On the youthful mind th' impression cast Of ancient glory..; There all unquench'd by cruel fortune's ire, It glows. **1797** COLERIDGE *Osorio* v. 100 The Tyger, that with unquench'd cruelty, Still thirsts for blood. **1817** BYRON *Lament of Tasso* v, All unquench'd is still my better part. **1890** 'R. BOLDREWOOD' *Col. Reformer* (1891) 116 The ardour of his unquenched philanthropy.

† **2.** Of lime: Unslaked. *Obs.*

*c* **1500** *Melusine* 142 Barels full of vnquynched lyme. *c* **1550** H. LLOYD *Treas. Health* U j b, Make an oyntment..of Aloes and vnquenchyd lime wyth comon oyle. **1608** TOPSELL *Serpents* 43 Vnquenched Lyme, mixeth with Honnie and oyle. **1660** SHARROCK *Vegetables* 129, I..sometimes have added unquenched lime into the infusions.

† **Unque·rt**, *sb. Obs.* [UN-[1] + QUERT, QUART *sb.*[1]] Disquiet, annoyance, trouble, hurt.

*a* **1300** *Cursor M.* 1788 Þe leon suam beside þe hert, Til oþer did na beist vn-quert. *a* **1300** *E. E. Psalter* xxx. 15 To forgetelnes for vnquert Am I giuen. *a* **1400** *Minor Poems fr. Vernon MS.* I. 250/1121 Þis fals folk of Religioun..ben as riche in vnquerte As þeos oþure. *c* **1400** *Beryn* 2057 The man þat wrouзt me this vnquert. *c* **1475** *Golagros & Gaw.* 675 Than thair hors with thair hochis sic harmis couth hint, As crasit in vnquart quakand thai stand.

† **Unque·rt**, *a. Obs.* [UN-[1] + QUERT *a.*]

**1.** Disquieted, distressed.

*a* **1300** *E. E. Psalter* x. 2 Þair bowe..þai schot to make un-quert, In mirkenes rightwise of herte.

**2.** Unquiet, troublesome, wicked.

**13..** in Herrig *Archiv Stud. Neu. Spr.* LXXXI. 310/95 Þis Pharesens weore vnquert, Þey knewe not heor owne hert. *c* **1425** *Cast. Persev.* 3354 in *Macro Plays* 177 Þe Jeves þat were vnquert dressyd þee drynke. *c* **1470** HARDING *Chron.* CCX. ii, This wormes mete, this caryon full vnquerte, That some tyme thought in worlde it had no pere.

**Unque·stionable**, *a.* and *sb.* [UN-[1] 7 b, 12.]

**1.** Having an assured character or position; unexceptionable.

**1603** DANIEL *Def. Rhime* G 3, The Generall Custome, and vse of Ryme..hauing beene so long..held vnquestionable. **1648** WILKINS *Math. Magic* I. xviii. 131 Attested by the experience of divers unquestionable witnesses. *a* **1687** PETTY *Pol. Arith.* i. (1690) 29 For what summ the Keepers of the Bank are unquestionable Security. **1796** MORSE *Amer. Geog.* II. 91 [It] would be incredible, were it not attested by the most unquestionable authors. **1828** LYTTON *Pelham* I. xvii, The rope was of the most unquestionable thickness. **1846** MRS. A. MARSH *Father Darcy* II. xiv. 237 His ability is great, his principles unquestionable.

**2.** Incapable of being doubted or disputed; indisputable, indubitable, certain.

**1631** GOUGE *God's Arrows* III. § 93. 353 The Crowne..by just and unquestionable title descended on her. **1695** J. EDWARDS *Perfect. Script.* 349 The learned professor..renders it unquestionable that Moses..was the author. **1709** BERKELEY *Th. Vision* § 150 The contrary being held an unquestionable truth. **1782** MARTYN *Geog. Mag.* I. 225 Authentic facts, and unquestionable evidence. **1850** HT. MARTINEAU *Hist. Peace* v. iii. (1877) III. 226 The evil was unquestionable. **1879** S. C. BARTLETT *Egypt to Pal.* xxi. 453 This is one of the unquestionable antiquities, the fountain of Elisha.

**b.** *sb.* An unquestionable fact or truth.

**1661** GLANVILL *Van. Dogm.* 231 The love of God and our neighbour, those Evangelical unquestionables. **1898** *Westm. Gaz.* 1 Feb. 1/3 One of the unquestionables is, that the German Government cannot dare to challenge the hostility of Russia.

**3. a.** Not submitting to question; impatient.

**1600** SHAKS. *A. Y. L.* III. ii. 393 *Orl.* What were his markes? *Ros.* A leane cheeke, which you haue not:..an vnquestionable spirit, which you haue not.

**b.** Not liable to question.

**1649** MILTON *Tenure Kings* 19 What hath a native King to plead,..why he..should think to scape unquestionable, as a thing divine?

Hence **Unquestionabi·lity, -ableness.**

**1727** BAILEY (vol. II), *Indisputableness*, unquestionableness. **1843** CARLYLE *Past & Pr.* II. vi, Our Religion is..a great heaven-high Unquestionability. **1873** HAMERTON *Intell. Life* III. viii. 112 The modern linguist can never fence himself behind that stately unquestionableness which shields the Classical scholar.

**Unque·stionably**, *a.* [UN-[1] 11, 5 b.] Without or beyond question; indisputably, indubitably.

Chiefly in loose construction, qualifying the clause or sentence, as in (*a*).

(*a*) **1644** VICARS *God in Mount* 167 Such a Magistrate unquestionably is this present Lord Major. **1661** COWLEY *Cromwell* Wks. (1906) 365 It was bold unquestionably for a man..so outragiously to murder his Master. **1756** *Keysler's Trav.* I. 18 Europe is unquestionably not a little indebted to him. **1800** *Asiat. Ann. Reg., Char.* 7/2 Unquestionably a person of great prudence. **1884** F. TEMPLE *Relat. Relig. & Sci.* viii. 228 Newton's investigations were unquestionably pursued..in reliance on the truth of the uniformity of nature.

(*b*) **1655** FULLER *Ch. Hist.* XI. ii. § 100 Wherein they conceived themselves to be before unquestionably estated. **1678** CUDWORTH *Intell. Syst.* 360 It might be made unquestionably evident. **1736** BUTLER *Anal.* I. vii, How unquestionably little..the pleasures and profits of it are at the best. **1740** CIBBER *Apol.* 318 Whose Repentance I have been unquestionably inform'd, appear'd [etc.]. **1846** HUXLEY in *Life* (1900) I. 28 It is an unquestionably dull day. **1894** ILLINGWORTH *Personality* iii. 60 Man finds the world outside him to be intensely, unquestionably real.

† **Unque·stionate**, *ppl. a. Obs.* [UN-[1] 8 b.] = next. **1423** JAS. I *Kingis Q.* cxxv, The maister portare, callit pacience, ..frely let vs in, vnquestionate.

**Unque·stioned**, *ppl. a.* [UN-[1] 8.]

**1.** Of persons: Not subjected to questioning; uninterrogated.

**1601** SHAKS. *All's Well* II. i. 211 More should I question thee..From whence thou cam'st, how tended on, but rest Vnquestion'd welcome. **1655** *Nicholas Papers* (Camden) II. 295 It lookes straingly that he passeth to and fro with that liberty he doth vnquestioned. **1742** RICHARDSON *Pamela* IV. 144, I could wish..that, even in Jest, my Mamma's Daughter might pass unquestioned. **1810** SCOTT *Lady of L.* I. xxix, That fellest foe might join the feast, And from his deadliest foeman's door Unquestioned turn. **1868** MORRIS *Earthly Par., Atl. Race* 45 Wherethrough, unquestioned of his race or name, He entered.

*absol.* **1898** B. GREGORY *Side Lights Confl. Meth.* 525 Permitting the great Questioner to be the great Unquestioned.

**2.** Not inquired into; unexamined.

**1603** SHAKS. *Meas. for M.* I. i. 56 Our haste from hence is of so quicke condition, That it..leaues vnquestion'd Matters of needfull value.

**3.** Not called in question; undisputed.

*c* **1622** ROWLEY, etc. *Birth of Merlin* I. i. 6 His safety being unquestion'd. **1653** W. RAMESEY *Astrol. Restored* 3

The case [is]..clear and unquestioned amongst rational men. **1712** ADDISON *Spect.* No. 469 ¶ 5 The stated and unquestioned Fee of his Office. **1781** COWPER *Expost.* 645 To praise him is to serve him, and fulfil.. his unquestion'd will. **1809** CRABBE *Tales* ix. 62 He must be one with manners like her own, His life unquestion'd, his opinions known. **1885** *Manch. Exam.* 4 Feb. 4/7 She has put forward her largest claims, and..they pass unquestioned.

**b.** Quasi-*adv.* Without question.

**1734** THOMSON *Liberty* IV. 862 On Aid, unquestion'd, liberal Aid was given.

Hence **Unque·stionedly** *adv.*

**1644** DIGBY *Nat. Bodies* xxxiii. § 5. 287 The memory, till then, keepeth quietly and vnquestionedly for the true obiect, what either the thought or chance..had patched up.

**Unque·stioning,** *ppl. a.* (UN-[1] 10.)

Both adj. and adv. (see next) are common from *c* 1860.

**1828-32** WEBSTER (citing J. M. Mason). **1846** MRS. A. MARSH *Father Darcy* II. xxi. 356 Unquestioning obedience to the authority of his superiors. **1861** GEO. ELIOT *Silas M.* ii, The unquestioning activity of a spinning insect. **1875** E. WHITE *Life in Christ* IV. xxvii. 470 Schools which have.. accepted with unquestioning faith, the everlasting duration of the soul.

Hence **Unque·stioningly** *adv.*, **-ness.**

**1857** SUSANNA WINKWORTH tr. *Life Tauler* 90 Inclined to follow..blindly and unquestioningly their spiritual masters. **1876** MRS. WHITNEY *Sights & Ins.* III. 98 His eyes were as steadfast as hers; but they had not her unquestioningness.

**Unqui·bbled,** *ppl. a.* (UN-[1] 8.) **1860** PRIOR *Anc. Danish Ball.* II. 266 He sware a clear unquibbled oath.

**Unqui·ck,** *a. rare.* [UN-[1] 7. Cf. MDa. and Norw. *ukvik*.]

**1.** Lifeless, dead.

*c* **1449** PECOCK *Repr.* II. ix. 193 Ech lyuyng man is verier.. ymage of Crist..than is eny vnquyk stok or stoon. *Ibid.*, The making..of suche vnquyke gay ymagis.

**2.** Not lively or active.

*c* **1445** PECOCK *Donet* 208 þat þou be not in eny of hem [*sc.* matters] to sluggy, vnquyke and heuy. *a* **1560** PHAER *Æneid.* IX. (1562) Ee iij b, We wear our lyues in spending stele,..nor age vnquick enfebleth ought our mynds.

**Unqui·ck,** *v.* [UN-[2] + QUICK *v.*[1]] *intr.* To lose vivacity. **1595** DANIEL *Civ. Wars* III. lxii, His sences droope, his steedy eye[s] vnquicke, And much he ayles.

**Unqui·ckened,** *ppl. a.* (UN-[1] 8.)

**1610** HEALEY *St. Aug. Citie of God* 489 Bodyes that haue a liuing soule (though as yet vnquickned by the spirit). **1639** BP. REYNOLDS *Lord's Supper* xvii, A bodily and unquickned service. **1712** BLACKMORE *Creation* VI. 290 Which numerous, but unquicken'd progeny,..inwrapt within each other lie. **1755** H. WALPOLE *Lett.* (1846) III. 125 You may imagine our land-spirit will not be unquickened neither. **1868** BOYD *Less. Middle Age* 382 Shakspere..probably wrote, with pulse unquickened, the wildest bursts of Othello. **1876** MISS YONGE *Womankind* xi. 83 It is constant use of the powers that is needed, not only dead acquirement unquickened by exertion.

**Unquie·scent,** *a.* (UN-[1] 7.) **1859** F. MAHONY *Rel. Father Prout* 385 The human breast..Throbs thus unawed, Untamed and unquiescent.

**Unqui·et,** *sb.* [UN-[1] 12, 5 b.] Absence or want of quiet; disquiet, disturbance.

**1551** in Froude *Hist. Eng.* (1860) V. 328 Occasions of disorder and unquiet in the realm. **1592** KYD *Sp. Trag.* III. xv. 23 Nor dies Reuenge, although he sleepe awhile; For in vnquiet quietnes is faind. **1613** SHERLEY *Trav. Persia* 106 [It] did aggrauate both the griefe of my minde and unquiet of my bodie. **1668** PEPYS *Diary* 10 Jan., The unquiet which her ripping up of old faults will give me. **1746** ELIZA HEYWOOD *Female Spect.* No. 23 (1748) IV. 258 The cause of his own unquiet, and that of one so dear to him. **1862** 'SHIRLEY' (J. Skelton) *Nugæ Crit.* i. 48 The unquiet and unrest of the day are gradually subdued as the evening descends. **1887** *Spectator* 1 Oct. 1300 The unquiet of the sea.

**Unqui·et,** *a.* [UN-[1] 7, 5 b.]

**1.** Marked by unrest, disturbance, or disorder.

**1523** [COVERDALE] *Old God & New* (1534) Aj, In this so vnquiet & troblous estate of comen weales. *a* **1548** HALL *Chron., Hen. IV*, 32 b, The end of the vnquiet tyme of kyng Henry the fourth. **1634** SIR T. HERBERT *Trav.* 68 Their vnquiet Country,..lying twixt two great Kings, is a prey many times to the Turke or Persian. **1674** *Essex Papers* (Camden) I. 191, I have..written at large..concerning y[e] unquiet motions which have of late bin in this Citty. **1743** *Johnson's Debates* (1787) II. 340 Measures which could produce no other effect than that of making their reign unquiet. **1796** MRS. M. ROBINSON *Angelina* III. 36 That I should not fear to sleep alone in the very apartments which were supposed to be unquiet. **1826** MISS MITFORD *Village* Ser. II. 126 Some relics of those picturesque but unquiet days. **1849** MACAULAY *Hist. Eng.* ii. I. 253 Temple himself, as was his wont in unquiet times, retired to his garden.

**2.** Not disposed to be quiet or inactive; restless, active, stirring (esp. so as to cause trouble).

**1526** *Pilgr. Perf.* (W. de W. 1531) 2 b, This worlde..is and euer shall be vnquiet. **1560** DAUS tr. *Sleidane's Comm.* 442 Vnquiet and troublesome persons. *a* **1648** LD. HERBERT *Hen. VIII* (1683) 327 The more unquiet sort being..worn out and spent, the rest..came to a composition with the Emperor. **1697** WALSH *Dryden's Virg. Past.* Pref. ¶ 1 We.. can scarcely pass..a whole Day not ruffled by some unquiet Passion. **1701** SWIFT *Contests Nobles & Comm.* iv, Those hot, unquiet spirits, who disturb assemblies. **1719** — *Abstr. Hist. Eng.* Wks. 1841 I. 545 Those perpetual troubles and vexations given to his kingdom by that unquiet people. **1849** MACAULAY *Hist. Eng.* vii. II. 253 The daring, unquiet, and vindictive seaman now sate in the councils. **1871** SMILES *Charac.* vii. 202 France has been the unquiet spirit among the nations of Europe.

**b.** In a state of physical unrest or commotion. Also in fig. context.

**1535** COVERDALE 2 *Esdras* xvi. 12 Y[e] see aryseth up.., and the floudes of it are vnquyete. **1627** J. TAYLOR (Water P.) *Navy of Land Ships* Wks. (1630) 87/1 The tossing of the billow, and vnquiet surges of the sea. **1644** MILTON *Educ.* 2 To be tost and turmoild..in fadomles and unquiet deeps of controversie. **1707** MORTIMER *Husb.* 598 In case the Liquor [*sc.* cider in a cask] be unquiet. **1793** SMEATON *Edystone L.* § 293 They found the sea so unquiet about the rocks, that [etc.]. **1853** KANE *Grinnell Exp.* xlix. (1856) 466 On every side..are the unquiet grinding floes. **1863** CONINGTON *Hor., Odes* IV. xii. 1 The gales of Thrace, that hush the unquiet Sea.

**c.** Not still or silent.

**1655** STANLEY *Hist. Philos.* III. 45, I sent away the women lest they should be so unquiet.

**3.** Uneasy, perturbed, anxious: **a.** Of persons, the mind, look, etc.

**1535** COVERDALE *Ps.* xli. 5 O my soule,..why art thou so vnquiete within me? **1582** N. LICHEFIELD tr. *Castanheda's Conq. E. Ind.* I. ix. 25 Being unquiet and greatly greeued at their falshood. *a* **1628** SIR J. BEAUMONT *Bosw. Field*, etc. (1629) 71 Whose counsels make men draw unquiet breath. *c* **1698** LOCKE *Cond. Underst.* § 6 (1754) 28 The mind.. hastens to some hypothesis to bottom it on; till then it is unquiet and unsettled. **1719** DE FOE *Crusoe* I. (Globe) 187, I slept unquiet. **1740** RICHARDSON *Pamela* II. 185 As the Hours grew on..my silly Heart was the unquieter. **1760-72** H. BROOKE *Fool of Qual.* II. 73 A countenance visibly unquiet and confused. **1831** JAMES *Phil. Augustus* I. viii, Walking up and down the hall, with an unquiet and somewhat irritated air. **1871** PALGRAVE *Lyr. Poems* 98 On the eve of the marriage morrow The bride is unquiet by night.

**b.** Of states or conditions.

**1576** FLEMING *Panopl. Epist.* 199 The vnquiet estate of a tyrant. **1613** PURCHAS *Pilgrimage* (1614) 610 Guagida betwixt two stooles had vnquiet sitting, paying tribute [etc.]. **1665** BOYLE *Occas. Refl.* v. viii, The unquiet Pleasure that the sight of the Stars gives to this Child. **1679** *Establ. Test* 18 That insecurity..makes..their dayes unquiet. **1772** W. BUCHAN *Dom. Med.* 574 His sleep is unquiet with frightful dreams. **1802** WORDSW. *Excurs.* I. 873 Nine long years, She lingered in unquiet widowhood. **1844** LYTTON in *Life & Lett.* (1883) I. 115, I cried myself into an unquiet doze.

**Unqui·et,** *v.* [UN-[2] 3. Cf. INQUIET *v.*] *trans.* To disturb the quiet of; to disquiet.

Common *c* 1525–*c* 1625; also occurring in recent use.

**1382** WYCLIF *Acts* xv. 19 For which thing I deme hem..for to be not vnquyetid, or disesid. **1407** *Exam. Wm. of Thorpe* (MS. Rawl. C. 208) fol. 21, My conscience schulde euer be herwiþ ouer mesure vnquyetid. **1526** *Pilgr. Perf.* (W. de W. 1531) 15 b, These irefull thoughtes..neuer ceaseth to vnquiet and trouble the same. **1540** *Act* 32 *Hen. VIII*, c. 38 § 1 The usurped power of the Bishop of Rome, hathe ..unquietid..the subjectis of the same. **1576** LAMBARDE *Peramb. Kent* 322 They gaue him both othes and hostages to depart the Realme, and neuer after to vnquiet it. **1602** WARNER *Alb. Eng.* XII. lxxiii. 304 Thus erring Rome ..will our christian World vnqueate. **1648** GAGE *West Ind.* xii. 80 Who thought it safer sleeping in a whole skinne, then to be unquieted by fighting.

Hence **Unqui·eted** *ppl. a.*, **Unqui·eting** *vbl. sb.*

**1538** in *Lett. Illustrious Ladies* (1846) III. 39, I was then half unquieted..all day. *a* **1548** HALL *Chron., Hen. IV*, 20 To the great displeasure and long vnquieting of kyng Henry and his partakers. **1562** T. WILSON *Rhet.* (ed. 2) 72 b, The gentleman..departed with an vnquieted minde.

† **Unquieta·tion.** *Sc. Obs.* (UN-[1] 12, 5 b.) **1604** *Extr. Aberd. Reg.* (1848) II. 253 Na vtheris..sall trubill this burgh, or mak ony vnquietatioun or perturbatioun in the same.

**Unqui·etly,** *adv.* [UN-[1] 11, 5 b.] Without being or keeping quiet; restlessly; *esp.* with disquiet or discomfort (of body or mind); uneasily.

*c* **1510** BARCLAY *Mirr. Gd. Manners* (1570) G iij, Least his giftes..augment envy And cause him liue after much more vnquietly. **1565** COOPER *Thesaurus* s.v. *Inconstanter*, To be alway mouyng vnconstantly and vnquietly. **1592** CHETTLE *Kind-harts Dr.* (1841) 33 My quiet ghost (vnquietly disturbed). **1605** SHAKS. *Lear* III. i. 2 *Kent.* Who's there besides foule weather? *Gen.* One minded like the weather, most vnquietly. **1640** BP. HALL *Chr. Moder.* I. xi. 109 When he was asked, what man lived most unquietly. **1671** SALMON *Syn. Med.* I. xxxviii. 86 They sleep little, and that unquietly. **1715** J. CHAPPELOW *Rt. way Rich* (1717) 79 The one bears the Trouble very unquietly. **1797** COLERIDGE *Christabel* I. 323 If she move unquietly [in sleep]. **1800** *Med. Jrnl.* III. 520 He slept very unquietly, and the pain..extended up towards his shoulders. **1881** *Atlantic Monthly* XLIX. 51 Nell started, as from a dream, and then laughed slightly, but unquietly.

**Unqui·etness.** [UN-[1] 12, 5 b.]

**1.** A source of trouble or disquiet.

**1514** BARCLAY *Egloges* II. (1570) B i b, When thou wouldest slepe..,Then is their musike to thee vnquietnes. **1585** ABP. SANDYS *Serm.* 340 Some are troubled with one vnquietnes, and som with another. **1654** R. BAKER tr. *Balzac's Lett.* (vol. II) 13 If he have no other unquietness but what he is like to have from me.

**2.** An unquiet condition or state of things; a state of trouble or discord.

**1523** [COVERDALE] *Old God & New* (1534) A j, In this greate unquietnes of comen weales. **1560** DAUS tr. *Sleidane's Comm.* 216 The state of the prouince..tendeth to greate vnquyetnes. **1603** in *Buccleuch MSS.* (Hist. MSS. Comm.) I. 48 Tumultuous behaviour..whereby great unquietness did grow. **1674** *Essex Papers* (Camden) 262, I hope there will be nothing to disturbe y[e] peace, or bring any unquietnesse here. **1860** BP. S. WILBERFORCE *Addr. Cand. Ordination* 217 This evil of unquietness, religious strife, and discord.

**3.** The condition or fact of being restless or turbulent in conduct.

**1526** *Pilgr. Perf.* (W. de W. 1531) 90 b, Treason, fraude,.. periury, vnquyetnes, obduracion,..with suche other. **1555** EDEN *Decades* (Arb.) 53 Isopes frogges to whom for theyr vnquietnesse Iupiter sent a hearon. **1647** N. BACON *Disc. Govt. Eng.* I. lvi. 160 The unquietnesse of some of the English brought the King to some thoughts of arbitrary rule. **1681** H. NEVILE *Plato Rediv.* 19 He cannot be denyed to be a great motive of the Peoples unquietness. **1724** WELTON *Chr. Faith & Pract.* 188 Men's unquietness and wavering in their principles. **1829** LYTTON *Disowned* 116 The unquietness and agitation of man's character.

**b.** Physical restlessness.

**1670** EVELYN *Sylva* (ed. 2) 24 Stubbed Oak is the fittest Timber for the Case of a Sider-Mill..as best enduring the unquietnesse of a ponderous Rolling-stone. **1856** MISS YONGE *Daisy Chain* I. i, An unquietness at the ends of her shoes, betraying the restlessness of the digits therein contained.

**4.** The condition of being disquieted or disturbed.

**1548** ELYOT, *Inquies*,..care, vnquietnesse,..lacke of reste. **1553** BRENDE *Q. Curtius* VI. 110 b, With a bashed countenaunce (wel declaring the vnquietnes of his minde). **1589** COOPER *Admon.* 243 To the great hindrance..& vnquietnes of the church of God. **1638** R. BAKER tr. *Balzac's Lett.* III. 19 My unquietnesse would have continued still, if you had not taken the paines to calme it. **1649** T. FORD *Lusus Fort.* 93 Seeking rest in it's unquietnesse, but finding none. **1683** *Apol. Prot. France* vi. 93 Her great unquietness of Spirit. **1702** ECHARD *Eccl. Hist.* III. viii. 469 Being overprest with a Load of Grief and Guilt, he resolv'd to put an End to his Unquietness. *a* **1806** H. K. WHITE *Time* 628 Time..Will waft him to repose ..Far from the unquietness of life. **1855** KINGSLEY *Misc.* (1859) I. 54 The Queen's continual unquietness will grow to contentment.

† **Unqui·etous,** *a. Obs.* [UN-[1] 7.] Unquiet. **1553** BALE *Vocacyon* 37 The vnquietouse harte of the Captaine. **1641** *Cheke's Hurt Sedition* To Rdr. b, An unquietous kind of men. **Unqui·etude.** (UN-[1] 12, 5 b.) *a* **1639** WOTTON in *Reliq.* (1651) 318 That a rod or barre of iron..will bewray a kind of unquietude and discontentment till it attain the former position. **Unqui·lleted,** *ppl. a.* (UN-[1] 8.) **1885** A. N. PALMER *Anc. Tenures in Marches N. Wales* 27 All the unquilleted fields that lie within the quilleted area. **Unqui·lt,** *v.* (UN-[2] 4.) **1611** FLORIO, *Discoltrare*, to vnquilt, to vnhill. **1634** MILTON *Comus* 614 Correction (Birch), He with his bare Wand can unquilt thy Joynts, And crumble every Sinew.

† **Unqui·t,** *ppl. a. Obs.* [UN-[1] 8 b, c.]

**1.** Unrequited; not repaid.

*a* **1300** *Cursor M.* 21431 Þe dai es gan, þe dett vn-quitte, Þe bodi most beleue for it. *c* **1412** HOCCLEVE *De Reg. Princ.* 4177 Seruice vnquyt and murdre.. Bifore al-mighty god auxen vengeaunce. *c* **1450** *Cov. Myst.* (Shaks. Soc.) 308 That rebuke that he gaf me xal not be unqwyt. **1500-20** DUNBAR *Poems* xv. 41 Suppois the servand be lang vnquit, The lord sumtyme rewaird will it. *Ibid.* xlvii. 67 Vnquyt I do no thing. *a* **1542** WYATT in *Tottel's Misc.* (Arb.) 64 Thinke not alone vnder the sunne Vnquit to cause thy louers plaine.

**2.** Not quitted or left.

**1603** B. JONSON *Sejanus* V. v, We must pray you hold your Guards Vnquit, when Morning comes.

† **Unqui·te,** *ppl. a. Obs. rare.* [UN-[1] 8 b, c.] **a.** Unrequited. **b.** Unredeemed. *c* **1450** *Mirk's Festial* 89 Þus þer schall no good dede be vnquyte. **1496** *Reg. Cupar Abbey* I. 251 That the saidis landis remayne with us and our successouris wnquite-owt be the lard of Burlie. **Unqui·tted,** *ppl. a.* (UN-[1] 8; cf. UNQUIT *ppl. a.* 2.) **1713** C'TESS WINCHELSEA *Misc. Poems* 243 Some rough Blast too far above conveighs, Or to unquitted Earth confines your weak Essays.

**Unqui·vering,** *ppl. a.* (UN-[1] 10.)

*a* **1811** J. GRAHAME *Sabbath Walks* (1827) 81 The breast And wing unquivering of the wheeling lark. **1844** LD. HOUGHTON *Mem. Many Scenes* 195 He who..with unquivering heart and hand can meet Ever distress. **1864** SALA in *Daily Tel.* 14 Dec., The same Indian.., with unquivering lip and unfaltering eye.

**Unqui·zzable,** *a.* (UN-[1] 7 b.) **1829** MARRYAT *F. Mildmay* xv, Each was dressed out in..most exact and unquizzable uniform.

† **Unquod,** obs. variant of UNKED *a.*

*a* **1470** HARDING *Chron.* To Rdr., It wer an vnquod thyng, if we..chaunge, that old menne haue write. **1548** UDALL *Erasm. Par. Luke* i. 22 He..declared at large the cause of y[t] his vnquod & straunge greting.

**Unquo·table,** *a.* (UN-[1] 7 b.)

Hence, in recent use, *unquotability*.

*a* **1843** SOUTHEY *Doctor* ccxlii. (1848) 663 An epigram.. unquotable at length. **1862** J. H. BURTON *Bk. Hunter* 114 Words..unquotable in this nineteenth century.

**Unquo·ted,** *ppl. a.* (UN-[1] 8.)

[**1775** ASH.] **1825** *Q. Rev.* XXXIII. 85 It is not easy to conceive that they could have existed as Scripture, unquoted, till the close of the fifth century. **1892** LE GALLIENNE *Retrosp. Rev.* (1896) I. 133 Not forgetting the unquoted 'Eve of St. Mark'.

**Unquoth,** obs. or dial. var. UNCOUTH *a.*

**1567** DRANT *Horace, Ep.* II. ii. H iv, Thou must abandon vnquoth words. **1583** STUBBES *Anat. Abus.* II. H 5 b, These names..are so vnquoth and strange to my eares, that [etc.]. **1615** W. HULL *Mirr. Maiestie* 113 An vnquoth sight and nouelty was..seene in heauen. **1684** MERITON *Yorksh. Dial.* 64 An unquoth Dog hes monny barkers at. **1873** *Swaledale Gloss.* 27.

† **Unra·ced,** *ppl. a.*[1] *Obs.* [UN-[1] 8 + RACE *v.*[4]] Not torn up. *c* **1374** CHAUCER *Boeth.* IV. pr. i. (1868) 110 Yif þe þinges þat I haue concluded a litel here byforne ben kept hoole & vnraced [*ed.* 1560 vnaraced; L. *inconvulsa*]. † **Unra·ced,** *ppl. a.*[2] *Obs.* [UN-[1] 8 + RACE *v.*[3]] Unrazed. *c* **1611** CHAPMAN *Iliad* XII. 5 Nor could the brode dike of the Greeks, nor that strong wall they made To guard their fleete, be long vnrac't.

**Unra·cked,** *ppl. a.*[1] [UN-[1] 8; cf. RACK *v.*[5]] Not drawn from the lees.

**1602** WARNER *Alb. Eng.* XIII. lxxvii. 319 Euen horror would from Tyrants, shame from harlots flow vnrack't. **1626** BACON *Sylva* § 306 Pour the lees of the racked vessel into the unracked vessel.

**Unra·cked,** *ppl. a.*[2] [UN-[1] 8; cf. RACK *v.*[3]]

**1.** Not exhausted by exactions.

**1659** W. CHAMBERLAYNE *Pharon.* IV. ii. 440 Each in his own unracked inheritance Where born expired.

**2.** Not stretched or strained.

**1887** BROWNING *Parleyings, C. Avison* ix, Because he.. spread out phrase unracked By modulations fit to make each hair Stiffen upon his wig.

**Unra·cy,** *a.* (UN-[1] 7.) *a* **1859** DE QUINCEY *Posth. Wks.* (1893) II. 151 Christianity in a soil so shallow and unracy as the Græco-Latin, could not [etc.]. **Unrai·led,** *ppl. a.*

Un-1 8.) [1775 Ash.] 1900 J. P. Struthers in *Life* (1918) 267 He went down the little unrailed stair. **Unrai·ny,** *a.* (Un-1 7.) 1865 W. G. Palgrave *Arabia* I. 354 In this unrainy climate the roads are very seldom paved.

**Unrai·sed,** *ppl. a.* [Un-1 8.] Not raised, in various senses of the verb.

1523 Ld. Berners *Froiss.* I. cccxxxviii. 529 So yt by their neglygence the Siege shulde nat be vnreysed. 1599 Shaks. *Hen. V,* Prol. 9 The flat vnraysed Spirits, that hath dar'd, On this vnworthy Scaffold, to bring forth So great an Obiect. 1694 Dryden *To Sir G. Kneller* 55 Flat Faces,..Such as in Bantam's Embassy were seen, Unrais'd, unrounded. 1697 D. F. *Char. Dr. S. Annesley* 6 When Griefs come threatning on, or Comfort flows, He was undepress'd by these, unrais'd by those. 1809–14 Wordsw. *Excurs.* iv. 959 Go, demand Of mighty Nature, if 'twas ever meant That we should pry far off, yet be unraised. 1817 Coleridge *Biog. Lit.* II. 132 The poem..is for the greater part written in language, as unraised and naked as any perhaps in the two volumes. 1873 Herschel *Pop. Lect.* i. § 7. 6 The raised portion still stands up above the unraised.

**Unra·ke,** *v.* [Un-2 3 + Rake *v.*1 5.] *trans.* To uncover or expose by raking. Also *absol.*

?*a* 1400 *MS. Cantab. Ff.* i. 6, fol. 12 (Halliw.), Eke as charbokylle casteth ryght bemys, With rody lighte, as cole that is unrake. 1611 Speed *Hist. Gt. Brit.* ix. xiii. 598 This againe vnraked the burning coales of enuie..against the said Lord Duke. 1655 Vaughan *Silex Scint.* 60 When thou unrak'st thy fire, those sparks will bring New flames. *Ibid.*, When thy Nap's over, stir thy fire, unrake In that dead age. 1861 L. L. Noble *Icebergs* 91 At every dip of the oars it was like unraking the sparkling embers.

**Unra·ked,** *ppl. a.* (Un-1 8. Cf. MDa. *uraget*, MSw. *orakadher.*)

1598 Shaks. *Merry W.* v. v. 48 Where fires thou find'st vnrak'd, and hearths vnswept, There pinch [etc.]. 1659 Milton *Hirelings* 128 [The] Lord of all things..doubtles will command the people to make good his promises of maintenance more honorably unask'd, unrak'd for. 1683 J. Reid *Scots Gard'ner* (1907) 38 Delve and mix [manure] together, to lye all winter un-raked. 1828–32 Webster s.v., Land unraked. 1854 Whittier *Maud Muller* 64 Till the rain on the unraked clover fell.

**Unra·llied,** *ppl. a.* (Un-1 8.) *c* 1644 W. Chamberlayne *Pharon.* ii. iii. 255 Death..in's march prevents The unition of unrallied regiments. 1662 Hickeringill *Apol. Distr. Innoc.* Wks. 1716 I. 273 Pompey blasphemously rav'd after his fatal and unrallied Pharsalian defeat. *a* 1835 Hogg *Dream Confirmed* in *C. L.* (1896) IV. 34/2 His ideas were as yet unrallied. **Unra·ncid,** *a.* (Un-1 7.) 1884 McLaren *Spinning* 46 [In] the power of remaining fresh and unrancid ..olive [oil] is pre-eminent. 1888 J. Ellis *New Christianity* x. 231 Unrancid oil. **Unra·nged,** *ppl. a.*1 (Un-1 8; cf. Range *v.*1) 1633 Ford *'Tis Pity* i. i, Thou has mov'd a Majesty above, With thy unranged (almost) blasphemy. 1851 C. L. Smith tr. *Tasso* ix. xxii, The Soldan rushes on, the foremost he, Upon the guards' unranged and startled pow'r. †**Unra·nged,** *ppl. a.*2 *Obs.* (Un-1 8; cf. Range *v.*2) 1611 Cotgr., *Pain de balle,* vnranged bread; or, a course bread wherein there is much chaffe. 1694 Motteux *Urquhart's Rabelais* Pref. p. lxxx, That course, unraung'd Bread, or some of the great brown Houshold Loaf was good enough for such Shepherds.

**Unra·nk,** *v.* [Un-2 3.] *trans.* To throw out of rank.

1611 Cotgr., *Desarrengement*, an vnranking, disordering, disarraying. *Ibid.*, *Desfiler*,..to vnranke, disorder; put off a file. 1640 tr. *Verdere's Rom. of Rom.* iii. xli. 182 [They] charged the Christians through and through, till they scarce left a ranke [not] unranked.

**Unra·nsacked,** *ppl. a.* (Un-1 8. Cf. ON. *úrannsakaðr*, MSw. *oransakadher.*)

1529 More *Dyaloge* ii. Wks. 187/1, I will for none hast leue any corner of the matter unransaked, as far as we can any doubte find therin. 1555 Watreman *Fardle Facions* ii. viii. 178 Leauing no element vnransaked to get a gowbin for their glotenous gorge. 1603 Knolles *Hist. Turks* (1621) 651 His soldiers..left neither house nor corner thereof unransacked. 1785 Cowper *Let. to Newton* Wks. 1837 XV. 177, I shall not leave my books unransacked. 1845 [Jane Robinson] *Whitehall* xiv, Such carcasses as he imagined were yet unransacked. 1895 R. Ellis in *Class. Rev.* Feb. 41/2 A still unransacked mine of quite new materials.

**Unra·nsomed,** *ppl. a.* (Un-1 8.)

1554 in *10th Rep. Hist. MSS. Comm.* App. V. 415 If the said silver platte be..unranesomid or redemid of the owners. 1599 Sandys *Europæ Spec.* (1605) X 4 b, They are charitable among them selves, leaving no poore vnrelieved, no prisoner vnransomed. *a* 1625 Fletcher *Hum. Lieut.* ii. iv, 1 *Gent.* Do you grieve, we are come off? *Dem.* Unransom'd, was it? 2 *Gent.* It was, Sir. 1669 Earl Orrery *Parthen.* iii. vi. 96 Giving me an unransomed Liberty. 1791 Cowper *Iliad* xxiv. 151 The Gods..say..that he still detains Amid his fleet..Unransom'd Hector. 1813 Scott *Rokeby* iv. vi, Safe and unransom'd [he] sent them home. 1877–9 Ruskin *St. Mark's Rest* vii. § 80 The Norman chief sent them home unransomed.

**Unra·ptured,** *ppl. a.* (Un-1 8.) 1742 Young *Nt. Th.* iv. 261 Such contemplations..should mount The mind still higher; nor ever glance on man, Unraptured, uninflamed. 1746 Warton *Ode to Fancy* 114 Teach him to scorn with frigid art Feebly to touch th' unraptur'd heart. 1819 Campbell *To Rainbow* 36 Nor ever shall the Muse's eye Unraptured greet thy beam. **Unra·refied,** *ppl. a.* (Un-1 8.) 1660 Boyle *New Exp. Phys. Mech.* xviii. 134 If that whole space had been full of unrarified Air. **Unra·sh,** *a.* (Un-1 7.) 1669 Clarendon *Ess.* Tracts (1727) 120 The temperate unrash and dispassionate man,..by being unmoved himself, discerns all advantages whilst he gives none.

**Unra·table,** *a.* (Un-1 7 b.)

1629 *Leather* 7 For common vse..vnratable value, and vnmatchable goodnesse. 1766 Burrow *Rep.* II. 1060 It would be most unreasonable that this Property which was always rateable before, should..be rendered unrateable. 1856 Olmsted *Slave States* 560, I found that, more than any people I had ever seen, they were unrateable by dress, taste, forms, and expenditures.

**Unra·ted,** *ppl. a.* (Un-1 8.)

1648 Hexham ii, *Ongelovet*, Vnprised, or Vnrated. 1703 *Act* 2–3 *Anne* c. 18 § 15 The Values of any vnrated Goods imported. 1704 *Ibid.* c. 4 § 8 Unrated Drugs..which are imported within the Days and Times last mentioned. 1772 *Ann. Reg., Chron.* 146/1 Duties due on certain unrated goods. 1896 *Daily News* 23 Apr. 5/5 The burdens upon rated and unrated property.

**Unra·tified,** *ppl. a.* (Un-1 8.)

1611 Speed *Hist. Gt. Brit.* ix. viii. 500 Some therefore haue imagined, that such Instruments might happily then be mentioned and drawne, and yet die vnratified, though the copies stand recorded. 1652 Row *Let.* in *Hist. Kirk* (Wodrow Soc.) 538 Our Commissione of the Generall Assemblie..excommunicating most precious men transgressing unratified Acts. 1856 Froude *Hist. Eng.* II. 194 The parliament reviewed the Annates Act, which had been left unratified. 1887 *Pall Mall G.* 27 June 1/1 The Egyptian Convention is still unratified.

†**Unra·tionable,** *a. Obs.*—1 [Un-1 7 b, 5 b.] Irrational. *a* 1500 in *Ratis Raving*, etc. 6 Sic folkes suld erar be callyt bestes vnracionable, than man rasonable. **Unra·vaged,** *ppl. a.* (Un-1 8.) [1775 Ash.] 1796 Burke *Let. to Noble Lord* Wks. VIII. 21 These obscene harpies..leave nothing unrent, unrifled, unravaged. 1888 *St. James's Gaz.* 11 Feb. 7/1 Few collections..can be more interesting, than underground and unravaged Cyprus.

**Unra·vel,** *v.* [Un-2 3. Cf. Du. *ontrafelen*, † *ontravelen.*]

**1.** *trans.* To take out of a ravelled, tangled, or intertwined condition; to disentangle; also, to pull down, to undo (a woven fabric).

Freq. in fig. context: see quots. under (*a*).

(*a*) 1603 Dekker *Wonderfull Yeare* Wks. (Grosart) I. 131 She..vnraueld the bottome of her frailetie at length. 1639 Fuller *Holy War* iv. i. 166 Frederick..unravelled the fair web of John Brens victory, even to the very hemme thereof. 1709 Swift *Tritical Ess.* Wks. 1755 II. i. 144 We shall be forced to..unravel in the night what we spun in the day. 1792 Burke *Corr.* (1844) IV. 3 The web has been too long weaving to be unravelled in an instant. 1856 Kingsley in *N. Brit. Rev.* XXVI. 78 To unravel patiently the tangled web of good and evil. 1878 Browning *La Saisiaz* 81, I, link by link, unravelled any tangle of the chain.

(*b*) 1688 Boyle *Final Causes Nat. Things* iv. 172 Those curious oval prisons in which they [*sc.* silkworms] enclose themselves, and which are unraveled into silk. 1727 [Dorrington] *Philip Quarll* (1816) 54 He was obliged to unravel the sail. 1768–74 Tucker *Lt. Nat.* (1834) I. 352 As often happens in trying to unravel an entangled thread, while they loosen the knot in one place they draw it tighter in another. 1871 A. Meadows *Man. Midwifery* (ed. 2) 46 So intimate is the union in later months, that it is impossible to unravel the meshes. 1883 Martin & Moale *Vertebr. Dissect.* 143 Unravel the small intestine, cutting it away from the mesentery.

*transf.* 1860 Tyndall *Glac.* ii. i. 227 By prisms we can unravel the white light into pure red, orange, yellow [etc.].

†**2.** *fig.* To reverse, undo, annul. *Obs.*

1644–7 Cleveland *Char. Lond. Diurn.* 2 It differs..as a black Witch doth from a white one, whose office is to unravell her inchantments. 1667 Dryden & Davenant *Tempest* iv. iv, All my designs Are ruin'd and unravell'd by this blow. 1673 *Lady's Call.* i. iv. § 10, I wish they would.. unravel that injurious mirth by a penitential sadness. 1710 Palmer *Proverbs* 382 One season let slip, breaks the series of our conduct, unravels the order of life. 1762 H. Walpole *Vertue's Anecd. Paint.* (1765) I. 57 Though at last He wofully unravelled most of the pursuits of his early age. 1766 Blackstone *Comm.* II. 248 After the land had descended to his issue, they would not unravel the matter again, and suffer his estate to be shaken.

**3.** To free from intricacy or obscurity; to make plain or obvious; to reveal or disclose.

1660 Jer. Taylor *Ductor* i. iv. rule ii. § 22 A religion that would..unravel all the intrigues of hearts. 1674 Jeake *Arith.* (1696) 529 Simple Disjunct Proportions have at large ..been unravelled in the foregoing Part. 1709 Steele *Tatler* No. 178 ¶ 1 With these..Passages..[he] was breaking his Brains Day and Night to..unravel their Sense. 1789 Belsham *Ess.* II. xxxii. 207 Without attempting to unravel all the intricacies of scholastic theology. 1827 Lytton *Falkland* i. 23, I unravelled the intricacies which knit servility with arrogance. 1862 Burton *Bk. Hunter* 377 To unravel the mystery of these primitive sculptures. 1884 A. R. Pennington *Wiclif* vi. 188 Unravelling difficult questions of theology.

*refl.* 1791 Paine *Rights of Man* 108 In a few days..the plot unravelled itself. 1863 Stanley *Jew. Ch.* i. xiii. 295 As the story unravels itself.

**4.** *intr.* To come undone; to become unknit or disentangled. Freq. *fig.*

1650 T. Vaughan *Anthroposophia* 55 When the Harmony is broken..., the vitall Twist..Disbands and unravells. 1656 T. Watson *One Thing Necessary* 53 Our life doth unravell apace. 1664 H. More *Myst. Iniq.* 566 As if to leave the Church of Rome were at last to unravel into a mere canting Paganism. 1744 Young *Nt. Th.* vi. 158 In an eternity, what scenes shall strike!..What webs of wonder shall unravel, there! 1768–74 Tucker *Lt. Nat.* (1834) I. 489 My vehicle did not begin to unravel like a torn stocking. 1815 J. Smith *Panorama Sci. & Art* II. 533 The stuff..increases in thickness..., and will not unravel when it is cut. 1820 Shelley *Prometh. Unb.* ii. i. 23 As the burning threads Of woven cloud unravel in pale air.

Hence **Unra·velled** *ppl. a.*

1659 W. Chamberlayne *Pharon.* iv. v. 193 Whose serious souls are busied to compose Unravelled thoughts into a method. *a* 1720 J. Hughes *Ode to Creator* ix, Proceed my muse! Time's wasting thread pursue, And see at last the unravel'd clue. 1762 Falconer *Shipwr.* iii. 41 'Tis mine the unravell'd prospect to display. 1814 Byron *Lara* i. xvi, Vain thought! that hour of ne'er unravell'd gloom Came not again. 1859 Sala *Tw. round Clock* (1861) 168 The genuine Skye [terrier],..like an unravelled ball of worsted.

**Unra·vellable,** *a.* (Un-1 7 b.) 1846 Worcester (citing *Phil. Mag.*). 1881 Duffield *Don Quixote* I. p. xlvi, The putative Shelton renders an obvious printer's error.., and so makes unravellable nonsense of a phrase. 1885 H. O. Forbes *Wand. E. Archip.* 308 The unravellable matted wisp.

**Unra·veller.** [f. prec.] One who unravels.

*a* 1704 T. Brown *Wks.* (1715) III. 263 Mythologists are indeed..mighty Unravellers of the Fables of the old Ethnicks. 1764 P. Hiffernan *Earl of Warwick* i. i, Time.., th' unraveller of all The great events which actuate this world. 1814 Miss Mitford in L'Estrange *Life* (1870) I. 189 An unraveller of state cyphers. 1889 *Athenæum* 20 Apr. 502/1 The 'improved' telephone is..dragged in to serve the purposes of fiction as an unraveller of crime.

**Unra·velling,** *vbl. sb.* [f. as prec.] The action of disentangling, etc.

1607 Dekker *Knt.'s Conjur.* (1842) 32 When..the bottome of my patrimony came within 200 pound of vnraueling. 1668 Dryden *Dram. Poesy* Ess. (Ker) I. 45 The Catastrophe, which..the French [call] *le denouement*, and we the discovery or unravelling of the plot. 1713 *Guardian* No. 36, Are not..all their pompous distinctions only so many unravellings of double meanings? 1742 West *Let.* in *Gray's Poems* (1775) 142 No unravelling of your web, dear Sir! only pursue it a little further. 1801 S. & Ht. Lee *Canterb. T.* IV. 455 A mystery, the unravelling of which..engaged all my attention. 1868 Tyndall *Fragm. Sci.* (1871) 102 The mental exercise..involved in the unravelling of a language.

**Unra·velling,** *ppl. a.* [f. Unravel *v.* 4.] Becoming unwound. 1827 Montgomery *Pelican Island* iii. 77 The unravelling clew not for a moment lost Hold of the silent hand that drew it out.

**Unra·velment.** [f. Unravel *v.*] The process of unravelling.

1776 Mickle *Camoens' Lusiad* Introd. 131 Collateral Episodes..assist..to facilitate and produce the Unravelment, or Catastrophe. 1779 Hamilton *Wks.* (1886) VII. 586 The unravelment of the plot. 1835 *Court Mag.* VI. 244/1, I felt it as the unravelment of fate. 1880 Burton *Reign Q. Anne* II. 319 His tedious work with the unravelment of all these difficulties.

**Unra·vished,** *ppl. a.* (Un-1 8.)

(*a*) 1622 Wither *Philarete* G iv, I would not permit an eare To attend vnrauisht heere.

(*b*) 1628 Feltham *Resolves* ii. xxxvii. 114 Had not Dinah had so good a one [*sc.* face], she had come home vnrauished. 1717 Pope *Iliad* ix. 480 My beauteous captives thither I'll convey, And all the rest of my unravish'd prey. 1820 Keats *Ode Grecian Urn* i, Thou still unravish'd bride of quietness!

**Unra·vishing,** *ppl. a.* (Un-1 10.) 1781 Warton *Hist. Eng. Poetry* III. 171 The more sober and unravishing ecstasies.

**Unray·,** *v.*1 Now *dial.* [Un-2 4.] *trans.* and *refl.* To divest of clothes; to undress, strip.

1485 *Rutland Papers* (Camden) 16 The King shalbe vnraied and vnclothed by his Chamberlayn. 1510 *Bonavent. Mirr.* (Pynson) xiv. E iv b, Now take we here gode hede howe that high lorde of mageste unrayeth hym and doeth of his clothes. *c* 1550 Cheke *Matt.* xxvii. 28 Vnraieng of him, [they] put on him a scarlet mantil. 1599 Hakluyt *Voy.* II. ii. 57 One of the Spaniards vnraied himselfe, and lept into the water. 1611 Cotgr., *Desabiller*, to vncloath, vndresse, vnray. 1825– in s.w. dialect glossaries.

*absol.* 1867 W. F. Rock *Jim an' Nell* lxxix, Zum..chap 'll help thee to unray.

**Unray·,** *v.*2 (Un-2 4; cf. Ray *sb.*1) 1824 J. Telfer *Border Ball.* 133 The letters shone With such effulgence, that they half-unray'd Some minor names. †**Unray·ed,** *ppl. a.*1 *Sc. Obs.* [Un-1 8.] = Unarrayed *ppl. a.* 2. *c* 1425 Wyntoun *Cron.* iii. ii. 322 (Cott.), Þai..set þar wachis for to se Qwhen wnrayid al was he. **Unray·ed,** *ppl. a.*2 (Un-1 + Rayed *ppl. a.*1) 1830 Tennyson *Arab. Nts.* 91 Dark-blue the deep sphere overhead, Distinct with vivid stars unrayed [1842 inlaid], Grew darker. **Unra·zed,** *ppl. a.* (Un-1 8.) 1586 J. Mush in J. Morris *Troub. Cath. Forefathers* iii. (1877) 363 Not one Religious house standeth, not one altar unrased and undefiled. 1610 Holland *Camden's Brit.* ii. 101 They left scarce one village..unrased and unrifled. 1674–5 A. Capel in *Essex's Lett.* 3 Feb. (1770) 38 It will be a precedent very dangerous to the government here, that.. these very things [ordered to be erased] in after times shall appear unrazed.

**Unra·zored,** *ppl. a.* [Un-1 8.] Unshaven.

1634 Milton *Comus* 290 As smooth as Hebe's their unrazor'd lips. 1774 *Westm. Mag.* II. 9 Apollo, the unrazored Macaroni God. 1845 Ld. Campbell *Chancellors* xlv. II. 153 By his flowing locks and unrazored lip [he] had captivated her affections. 1902 Snaith *Wayfarers* xx, My unrazored chin passed without comment.

**Unrea·chable,** *a.* (Un-1 7 b.)

Freq. from *c* 1865. Also, in recent use, *unrea·chableness.*

1593 *Sidney's Arcadia* v. (1622) 456 As their course neuer alters, so is there nothing done by the vnreachable ruler of them, but hath an euerlasting reason for it. 1802 Southey in Robberds Mem. (1843) I. 436, I would not remove to an unreachable distance from Herefordshire. 1846 Ruskin *Mod. Paint.* II. iii. i. v. § 13 The apparent, though unreachable, nearness and promise of them.

Hence **Unrea·chably** *adv.*

1881 Palgrave *Vis. Eng.* 247 The..brimming jars In fiendish mock borne past their dungeon bars, Upheld unreachably high.

**Unrea·ched,** *ppl. a.* (Un-1 8.)

*c* 1611 Chapman *Iliad* xxi. 251 As he would try If all the Gods inhabiting the broad unreached sky Could daunt his spirit. 1679 Dryden & Mulgrave *Ess. Sat.* 279 Now labour ..to climb That lofty hill, unreach'd by former time. 1713 C'tess Winchelsea *Misc. Poems* 113 Between which two Extreams true Pleasure lies, O'er-run by Fools, unreach'd at by the Wise. 1818 Byron *Ch. Har.* iv. cxxii, The unreach'd Paradise of our despair. 1878 Whittier *Seeking of Waterfall* 100 Evermore the end shall tell The unreached ideal guided well.

**Unrea·d,** *v.* (Un-2 3.)

1533 More *Debell. Salem* Wks. 1025/1 Can I both gather vp al hys bookes & go hyde theim, & also make them that haue red them goe vnreade them againe, or forget what they haue redde? 1797 *Monthly Rev.* XXIII. 511 Can his countrymen unread Freret, Boulanger, and Voltaire, or unlearn the sophisms which they have impressed?

**Unrea·d,** *ppl. a.* [UN-1 8 b.]

**1.** Not read; unperused.

**1456** SIR G. HAYE *Law Arms* (S.T.S.) 63 [He] held the letter in his hand unred. *a* **1553** UDALL *Roister D.* III. ii, Ye a woman? and your letter so long vnredde. **1596** SPENSER *F. Q.* IV. xii. 2 Then blame me not, if I haue err'd in count Of Gods, of Nymphs, of riuers yet vnred. **1693** *Dryden's Juvenal* VII. (1697) 173 His Muse had starv'd, had not a Piece unread, And by a Player bought, supply'd her Bread. **1728** POPE *Dunciad* III. 103 Her grey-hair'd Synods damning books unread. **1796** MME. D'ARBLAY *Camilla* II. 389 She therefore determined that..she would..deliver the unread letter to Sir Hugh. **1838** LYTTON *Leila* I. ii, An open manuscript..lay unread before the Moor. **1879** FROUDE *Cæsar* xxvii. 469 He burnt unread the correspondence of Pompey and Scipio.

**2.** Not instructed by reading. Also *absol.*

**1606** SHAKS. *Tr. & Cr.* I. iii. 24 The Wise and Foole, the Artist and vn-read,..seeme all affin'd, and kin. **1687** DRYDEN *Hind & P.* III. 409 And last, uncertain whose the narrower span, The clown unread, and half-read gentleman. *a* **1743** SAVAGE *To John Powell* 47 To unread Squires, illiterately gay; Among the learn'd, as learned full as they. **1811** BYRON *Hints fr. Hor.* 237 Unread,..Fool'd, pillag'd, dunn'd, he wastes his term away. **1865** *St. James's Mag.* Oct. 354 The Great Unread. **1884** *Graphic* 4 Oct. 358/1 The Khedive himself is far from unlearned and unread.

**b.** Const. *in* (a matter or subject).

**1602** WARNER *Alb. Eng.* IX. lii. 234 Such as be vnreade In that sweete Promise. **1790** BURKE *Fr. Rev.* 185 Not being wholly unread in the authors. **1816** COLERIDGE *Lay Serm.* 314 A fact that none but the unread in history will deny. **1865** MEREDITH *R. Fleming* viii, Algernon was unread in the hearts of women.

**Unrea·dable,** *a.* [UN-1 7 b.]

**1.** Too dull or distasteful to read.

**1802–12** BENTHAM *Ration. Judic. Evid.* Wks. 1843 VI. 441 Take up a history of an old French lawsuit, the evidence is absolutely unreadable. **1837** HALLAM *Hist. Lit.* I. iv. § 70 Making the entire work unreadable by the most patient..of mankind. **1867** DARWIN in F. Darwin *Life & Lett.* (1887) III. 96 After the horrid, tedious, dull work of my present huge, and I fear unreadable, book.

**2.** Illegible through careless or indistinct writing.

**1830** MISS MITFORD *Village* Ser. IV. 182 Oh such letters! ..and in such a hand! so pretty and so unreadable! **1861** WYNTER *Soc. Bees* 13 An immense number of letters..with directions perfectly unreadable to ordinary persons.

*transf.* **1839** CARLYLE *Chartism* iii, The emblem of darkness, of unreadable confusion.

**3.** Inaccessible to any reader.

**1852** C. B. MANSFIELD *Paraguay*, etc. (1856) 66 Whether I go down by steamer to Monte Video..or whether I go into the interior of San Paulo..is at present written in the Unreadable Book.

Hence **Unreadabi·lity, Unrea·dableness.**

**1856** VAUGHAN *Mystics* II. VIII. vii. 74 Reason will not attempt to rescue him from condign sentence of unreadableness. **1870** LOWELL *Among my Bks.* Ser. I. (1873) 338 Klopstock himself is..an immortality of unreadableness. *a* **1871** DE MORGAN *Budget Parad.* (1872) 123 It is a climax of unsaleability, unreadability, and inutility.

**Unrea·dily,** *adv.* (UN-1 11.)

**1599** HAKLUYT *Voy.* II. I. 117 Men being first inforced to write their actes..in barkes of trees, or otherwise perchance as vnreadily. **1755** JOHNSON, *Awkwardly*, clumsily; unreadily; inelegantly. **1804** MITFORD *Inquiry* 75 Instruments like the harpsichord,..incapable or unreadily capable of variety in loudness. **1871** PROCTOR *Light Science* 138 It is astonishing how unreadily two sea-currents exchange their temperatures.

**Unrea·diness.** (UN-1 12; cf. UNREADY *a.*1)

**1526** *Pilgr. Perf.* (W. de W. 1531) 131 We shold expell all slouth & vnredynes in doynge our dutye to god. *a* **1548** HALL *Chron., Hen. VI*, 154 The Frenchemen hauing perfyte vnderstanding of the infirmitie and vnreadinesse..of Englande. **1611** SPEED *Hist. Gt. Brit.* VII. xliv. § 39. 366 Accusing him with sloath and vnreadinesse of Armes. **1665** BOYLE *Occas. Refl.* To Sophronia, My Unreadiness to Publish these very long neglected Papers. *a* **1761** LAW *Comf. Weary Pilgr.* (1809) 26 Every unreadiness to do good ..makes us schismaticks. **1861** HUGHES *Tom Brown at Oxf.* ii, He couldn't realise the fact of his unreadiness in a boat. **1887** *Spectator* 5 Nov. 1494 Our unreadiness as to a sufficient supply of arms.

**Unrea·ding,** *ppl. a.* (UN-1 10.)

**1829** *Edin. Rev.* L. 183 There is but one chance of making this unreading cast readers. **1852** H. ROGERS *Ess.* (1874) I. vii. 348 The unreading 'philosophers who avoided books'. **1879** F. HARRISON *Choice of Bks.* iv. (1886) 81 The idle and unreading world.

**Unrea·dy,** *a.*1 [UN-1 7.]

**1.** Not in a state of readiness or preparation: **a.** Without const.

*c* **1340** HAMPOLE *Pr. Consc.* 1990 If a man þat unredy es, Be tane with dede in his wykednes. **1382** WYCLIF *2 Cor.* ix. 4 Lest when Macedonyes schulen come with me, and schulen fynde ȝou vnredy, we schamen [etc.]. *c* **1450** tr. *De Imitatione* I. xxiii. 31 Lyue so þat deþe finde þe neuer unredy. *c* **1560** *Jack Juggler* B ii b, And as you see for the most part our witts be best When wee be takyne most vnrediest. **1570** FOXE *A. & M.* (ed. 2) 69/2 Some other there were vnready and not so well prepared. **1603** J. DAVIES (Heref.) *Microcosmos* Wks. (Grosart) I. 56/2 Our force lies most dispersed at the Plow, Vnready, rude, and oft rebellious too. **1671** CLARENDON *Hist. Reb.* IX. § 30 Fairfax was..not in readiness to march; yet reported to be much more unready than he was. **1790** A. WILSON *Death* Poet. Wks. (1846) 64 And, if unready, we are caught by Death, He throws us howling to the gulph beneath. **1855** MACAULAY *Hist. Eng.* xix. IV. 268 His enemies, while still unready, learned with dismay that he had taken the field in person.

*absol.* **1838** G. JOHNSTON *Brit. Zoophytes* 102 Should the prey prove too tough, woe! to the unready!

**b.** Const. *to* with inf.

*a* **1300** *Cursor M.* 25478 Vnworthi am i..And al vnredi for to rise On domesdai be-for iustise. **1510–20** *Everyman* in Hazl. *Dodsley* I. 104 Full unready I am such reckoning to give. **1590** SPENSER *F. Q.* I. v. 45 False Duessa..found the Faery knight Departed thence, albe his woundes wide Not throughly heald, vnreadie were to ride. **1615** W. LAWSON *Country Housew. Gard.* (1626) 29 Want of strength may make them vnready to receiue sap. **1707** S. SEWALL *Diary* 15 Dec., I express'd my self unready to vote for it. **1871** R. H. HUTTON *Ess.* v. I. 125 If it be a righteous life and will ..that stirs human nature thus deeply, and finds us..unready to adapt ourselves to it.

**c.** Const. *for*, † *of*, or *with*.

**1617** WOODALL *Surgeon's Mate* (1639) 191 He is an unworthy Chirurgion, which is at any time unready with such needfull instruments. **1702** ROWE *Tamerl.* I. i, Secure of Peace and for Defence unready. **1737** WHISTON *Josephus, Antiq.* v. iii. § 2 The Israelites grew so indolent, and unready of taking pains. *a* **1865** KEBLE *Lett.* (1870) 165 Very unready with any plan for meeting it. **1865** RUSKIN *Arrows of Chace* (1880) II. 72, I am not usually unready for a controversy.

**2.** Not prepared or made ready.

*c* **1380** WYCLIF *Sel. Wks.* II. 40 Þerfore make þi tresoure in God, for..þis tresoure mai not perishe, to be unredi whanne þou hast nede. *a* **1500** *Ratis Raving* I. 1003 It is wnreddy payment That þow has fristit out or lent. **1542** UDALL *Erasm. Apoph.* 187 It is an eivill man of warre that wil have his weapen unreadie when he should occupie it. *a* **1548** HALL *Chron., Edw. V*, 12 b, And so all thyng was vnredy, when this message came. **1632** HOLLAND *Cyrupædia* 125 When he vieweth your forces, he will thinke his owne to be yet unready. **1721** STRYPE *Eccl. Mem.* II. xx. 405 The money was unready when Cæsar had present need thereof.

† **b.** *Sc.* Not easy or plain. *Obs.*

**1535** STEWART *Cron. Scot.* (Rolls) I. 440 Nocht ane..wist weill quhair away for till wend, The gait wes sa vnreddy and miskend.

**3.** Undressed; in deshabille. *Obs.* or *dial.*

In common use from *c* 1595 to 1640.

**1591** SHAKS. *1 Hen. VI*, II. i. 39 [*stage-dir.*] The French leape ore the walles in their shirts. Enter..Bastard, Alanson, Reignier, halfe ready, and halfe vnready. *Alan.* How now my Lords? what all vnreadie so? **1625** in Ellis *Orig. Lett.* Ser. I. III. 198 The Queene,..though she were unready,.. hasted down a pair of stairs to meet him. **1678** *Yng. Man's Call.* 364 She desired to go..to dress her head, which by the violence of the wind was made all unready. **1823–** in Suffolk and Lincoln glossaries.

**4.** Not quick or prompt; hesitating, slow; † not responding readily to command.

**1594** T. BEDINGFIELD tr. *Machiavelli's Florentine Hist.* VI. (1595) 149 These newes grieued the Earle exceedingly, bicause he thought his army not fully paid, would be vnreadie. **1607–12** BACON *Ess., Youth & Age* (Arb.) 260 Like an vnready horse that will neither stopp nor tourne. **1672** SIR T. BROWNE *Let. Friend* § 22 To become more narrow-minded..and tenacious, unready to part with anything. **1708** ROWE *Royal Convert* I, There needs no more; For I would spare thee the unready tale. **1824** MISS MITFORD *Village* Ser. I. 124 So alive and eloquent in conversation, that I feel more than ever puzzled and unready. **1855** MRS. GASKELL *North & S.* vii, 'Mr. Thornton, I believe!' said Margaret, after a half-instant's pause, during which his unready words would not come. **1857** in Mrs. Gaskell *C. Bronte* (ed. 3) II. 138 She had become unready, nervous, excitable, and either incapable of speech, or talked vapidly.

*Comb.* **1670** COTTON *Espernon* II. 409 One of the most unwieldy, and unready footed Animals, that is to say, a Mule.

Hence † **Unrea·dy** *v. trans.*, to undress. *Obs.*—1

**1593** *Sidney's Arcadia* III. (1598) 365 After his wife was departed to her fained repose, as long as hee remayned with his daughter, to giue his wife time of vnreadying her selfe.

**Unrea·dy,** *a.*2 [Later form of UNREDY *a.*, after prec. Cf. UNREDE b.] = REDELESS *a.* (but usually regarded as = prec. 1 or 4).

Only as an epithet of Ethelred II (died 1016): cf. Polydore Vergil *Angl. Hist.* (1534) VII. 124 'qui pigritia omnia faciebat'.

**1580** STOW *Chron.* 134 Etheldrede, commonly called Unready. **1643** BAKER *Chron.* (1653) 18 Ethelred,..by reason of his backwardnesse in Action, was commonly called the Unready. **1655** FULLER *Ch. Hist.* II. 136. **1867** FREEMAN *Norm. Conq.* I. 286 A prince, who..has received no nobler historical surname than that of the Unready. *Ibid.* 327 The Unready King showed occasional glimpses of vigour.

**Unre·al,** *a.* (UN-1 7.)

**1605** SHAKS. *Macb.* III. iv. 107 Hence horrible shadow, Vnreall mock'ry hence. **1645** MILTON *Tetrach.* 60 Only for the fals keeping of a most unreal nullity, a mariage that hath no affinity with Gods intention. **1667** — *P. L.* x. 471 Th' unreal, vast, unbounded deep Of horrible confusion. **1711** STEELE *Spect.* No. 53 ¶ 3 You should..teach the Men not to be any longer dazzled by false Charms and unreal Beauty. **1746** FRANCIS tr. *Horace, Epist.* II. i. 289 He gives a desperate Trial of his Art,..Who with unreal Terrours fills my Breast. **1810** SOUTHEY *Kehama* IV. iv, Musing so long he lay, that all things seem Unreal to his sense, even like a dream. **1842** MANNING *Serm.* x. (1848) 139 Surrounding ourselves with an unreal world of hopes, and fears. **1871** LOWELL *Study Windows* 153 Those who have most loudly advertised their passion for seclusion..have been mostly sentimentalists, unreal men.

*spec.* **1838** G. F. GRAHAM *Mus. Comp.* 17/2 What are called passing notes, or unreal notes, and which are said not to form any real part of the melody or the harmony. **1883** A. SIDGWICK *Fallacies* 42 The distinction between *Real* and what may be called *Unreal. Ibid.*, The name 'Unreal' as here applied to propositions, is somewhat wider than what is usually meant by 'verbal'.

**Unre·alism.** (UN-1 12.) **1859** *Sat. Rev.* 29 Jan. 118/2 The ideal unrealism of statesmanship which invented Mr. Gladstone's mission. **1875** LOWELL in *N. Amer. Rev.* CXX. 387 It is only a world of unrealism. **Unreali·stic,** *a.* (UN-1 7.) **1865** KINGSLEY *Lett.* (1878) II. 215 The very unrealistic turn of mind which I have in common with this generation.

**Unrea·lity.** (UN-1 12.)

**1751** WARBURTON *Pope's Wks.* III. 42 They conclude in the most extravagant and senseless inferences; such as the unreality of matter; the reality of space. **1798** LAMB *Ros. Gray* xi, Past associations revived with the music—blended with a sense of unreality. **1850** CARLYLE *Latter-d. Pamph.* vi. 8 Unreality is death, to Parliaments and to all things. **1880** E. WHITE *Cert. Relig.* 45 They are seen in a glory mist which throws a certain unreality over their outlines.

**b.** With *an* and pl.

**1817** SOUTHEY *Fragm. Th. on Son's Death* Wks. (1909) 741/1 They are not, though, Mere unrealities. **1843** CARLYLE *Past & Pr.* IV. i, The unrealities, beaten into dust, flew gradually off. **1863** E. V. NEALE *Anal. Th. & Nat.* 31 If time is not to become an unreality to us.

**Unre·alizable,** *a.* [UN-1 7 b, 5 b.] Incapable of being realized, in various senses.

**1840** CARLYLE *Heroes* iv. (1841) 247 We may rejoice that he could not realise it; that it remained, after two centuries of effort, unrealisable. **1860** J. YOUNG *Prov. Reason* 81 Power which is truly infinite, must be for ever..unrealizable in its utmost extent. **1883** *St. James's Gaz.* 1 Dec. 7/2 The great financial establishments..are believed to be still overloaded with unrealizable stock.

**Unre·alize,** *v.* [UN-2 3.] *trans.* To make unreal; to deprive of reality.

**1804** SOUTHEY *Let.* in *Life* (1850) II. 259 The least breath stirring would have shaken the whole vision, and at once unrealised it. **1854** H. MILLER *Sch. & Schm.* xv. 331 The painted canvass, and the..too palpable acting, served but to unrealize what I saw, and to remind me that I was merely in a theatre. **1875** LOWELL *Spenser* Prose Wks. 1890 IV. 337 His fancy, habitually moving about in worlds not realized, unrealizes everything at a touch.

Hence **Unre·alizer**; **Unre·alizing** *ppl. a.*

**1814** SOUTHEY *Roderick* x. 60 The flame..cast upon the leaves A floating, grey, unrealizing gleam. **1845** MOZLEY *Ess.* (1878) II. 127 How little do we feel the past! On flows Time, the great unrealiser. *a* **1859** DE QUINCEY *Posth. Wks.* (1893) II. 204 This postulate of fiction..would have operated with an unrealizing effect upon all that followed.

**Unre·alized,** *ppl. a.* (UN-1 8.)

[**1775** ASH.] **1803** *Man in Moon* (1804) 82 What real good are we to expect from this new scheme to which we so foolishly attach unrealized riches. **1852** H. ROGERS *Ecl. Faith* 290 There is such a thing in the human mind as unrealised truth, both intellectual and spiritual. **1876** MRS. WHITNEY *Sights & Ins.* xxx, Behind us a southwest wind was driving the mists, all unrealized by us, from off the mountain faces.

**Unre·ally,** *adv.* (UN-1 11.) **1855** PUSEY *Doctr. Real Presence* Note E. 69 Some distinct case..in which proper terms..are, without any hint or notice, to be understood unreally. **Unrea·lmed,** *ppl. a.* (UN-2 8, 4 + REALM.) **1845** BAILEY *Festus* (ed. 2) 386 That unrealmed tyrant drew his mortal dart And drave it through himself. **Unre·alness.** (UN-1 12; cf. UNREAL *a.*) **1834** LYTTON *Pilgr. Rhine* v, The unrealness of literary fame.

**Unrea·ped,** *ppl. a.* (UN-1 8.)

**1577** HELLOWES *Gueuara's Chron.* 143 Losse of their corne, both reapt and vnreapt. *a* **1625** BEAUM. & FL. *Cust. Country* IV. i, My first love here begun, rests here unreapt yet. **1670** MILTON *Hist. Eng.* II. 39 In that place which only they had left unreap'd of all thir Harvest. **1737** GLOVER *Leonidas* IV. 370 There the corn Bent by its golden burthen sheds unreap'd Its plenteous seed. **1795** SOUTHEY *Joan of Arc* III. 7 The autumnal rains had beaten to the earth The unreap'd harvest. **1817** KIRBY & SP. *Entomol.* II. 480 Those moths ..betake themselves to the yet unreaped fields. **1834** M. SCOTT *Cruise Midge* (1859) 289 Half of my beard has been left unreaped by that villanous razor of Brail's.

**Unrea·son,** *sb.* [UN-1 12.]

† **1.** Unreasonable action or intention; injustice, impropriety. *Obs.*

*a* **1300** *Cursor M.* 3747 He has me don oft vn-resun And no[w] me reft mi benisun. **13..** *Metr. Hom.* (Vern. MS.) in *Archiv Neu. Spr.* LVII. 303 Wiþ muchel wrong and vnresoun Dost þow me þis tresoun. *c* **1400** *Pilgr. Sowle* IV. ix. (Caxton) 62 It semeth me vnreson..that he that nought ne oweth shal payen for the dettour hym seluen. *c* **1500** *Priests of Peblis* 141 And that ȝe think vnressoun or wrang, Wee al and sundrie sings the samin sang. **1597** SKENE *De Verb. Sign.* s.v. *Tort*, Tort, et non reason, vn-reason, wrang, and vnlaw. **1609** [see UNLAW *sb.* 1].

† **2.** *Abbot* (*of*) *Unreason*, a mock personage elected as the leading character in certain popular revellings formerly in Scottish use. *Obs.*

**1496** *Acc. Ld. High Treas. Scot.* I. 270 To Gilberte Brade, ..for spilling of his hous in Striuiling be the Abbot of Vnresoun, x.li. **1555** *Sc. Acts Parlt., Mary* (1814) II. 500/1 It is..ordanit that in all tymes cumming na maner of persoun be chosin, Robert Hude nor Lytill Johne, Abbot of vnressoun, Quenis of Maij nor vtherwyse. *a* **1572** KNOX *Hist. Ref.* Wks. 1846 I. 40 The same Frear maid ane uther sermoun of the Abbote Unreassone, unto whome..he compared the prelattis of that age. [**1820** SCOTT *Abbot* xiv, and note.]

**3.** Absence of reason; indisposition or inability to act or think rationally or reasonably. (Common from *c* 1850.)

**1827** CARLYLE *Misc.* (1840) I. 47 Other forms of Unreason have taken its place. **1847** HELPS *Friends in C.* I. vii. 115 Many a woman is brought up in unreason and self-will from these causes that he has given. **1861** M. ARNOLD *Pop. Educ. France* 174 A system which, to the loud blasts of unreason and intolerance, sends forth no certain counterblast. **1883** PATTISON *Mem.* (1885) 2 All my energy was directed..to free myself from the bondage of unreason.

**b.** That which is contrary to, or devoid of, reason.

**1847** HELPS *Friends in C.* I. vii. 114 Women may talk the greatest unreason out of doors, and nobody kindly informs them that it is unreason. **1865** J. GROTE *Explor. Philos.* I. 210 That unreason or nonsense which it is the business of the higher part to convert into knowledge.

**Unrea·son,** *v.* [UN-2 4, 3.]

**1.** *trans.* (and *refl.*). To deprive of reason.

*a* **1676** HALE *Prim. Orig. Man.* (1677) 343 We shall have such Solutions as must make us first unreason and unman our selves, before we can subscribe to them. **1755** SMOLLETT *Quix.* I. i. I. 2 The unreasonable usage..so unreasons my reason, that I have reason to complain of your beauty. **1829** T. HOOK *Bank to Barnes* 40 Were I to tease on, It would nearly unreason your reason.

**2.** To disprove, refute.

**1661** R. L'ESTRANGE *State Divinity* 25 Their Reasons I have un-Reason'd already. *a* **1716** SOUTH *Serm.* (1744) XI. 257 However a man may for a while..seem to himself to unreason the equity of God's proceedings; yet [etc.].

**Unrea·sonabi·lity.** (UN-[1] 12; cf. next.) **14..** in *E. E. P.* (1862) 143 Arystotelle..sayethe that euery man nedethe To be ware of the vnresonabylite That comethe of the sensualite.

**Unrea·sonable,** *a.* (*adv.*). [UN-[1] 7 b.]

**1.** Not endowed with reason; irrational.

*c* **1340** HAMPOLE *Pr. Consc.* 599 He..fares als an unresonabel beste, þat his awen wille folowes. **1382** WYCLIF 2 *Peter* ii. 12 Thes sotheli [ben] as vnresonable beestes. *c* **1400** *Destr. Troy* 4428 A Roid beste vnreasonable. *c* **1450** *Myrr. our Ladye* 287 But vnresonable creatures..prayse god, in that they do as god hathe..ordeyned them to do. **1509** BARCLAY *Shyp of Folys* 119 Other creatures that ar vnresonable Goeth on all foure. **1569** J. SANFORD tr. *Agrippa's Van. Artes* 69 b, All the Pagans..doo affirme..that reasonable soules goo into unreasonable bodies. **1615** W. BEDWELL *Moham. Impost.* II. § 89 We shall leade our life..as beasts and vnreasonable creatures do. **1655** MOUFET & BENNET *Health's Improv.* 265 Nay, go to your Raven and Stag, those longest livers of all the unreasonable breathers. **1675** BROOKS *Gold. Key* 231 All the creatures, both reasonable and unreasonable, do in some sort set forth the praises of Christ. **1795** SOUTHEY *Soldier's Fun.* 35 Whilst his fellow-man..Must as the unreasonable beast drag on A life of labour. **1861** READE *Cloister & H.* lxxiii, There were buffaloes, lizards,..leopards; any unreasonable beast but the right one.

*transf.* **1592** SHAKS. *Rom. & Jul.* III. iii. 111 Thy wild acts denote The vnreasonable Furie of a beast.

**2.** Not acting in accordance with reason or good sense; not reasonable in conduct, demands, expectations, etc.

*c* **1375** *Cursor M.* 6614 (Fairf.), Quen þai þis sagh, qua soþ wil say, þa vnresonable folk þuȝt na play. *c* **1400** *Comm. Luke* i. 22 (MS. Bodl. 143), þe puple of iewes semeþ lyk to doumb sacarie, whiche puple is so vnresonable þat it may not ȝyue resoun of his dedis. **1483** CAXTON *G. de la Toure* vi b, This newe kynge..was to them full hard and felon, & also to al his comyns he was vnresonable. **1496** *Act* 12 *Hen. VII*, c. vii, Divers unresonable and detestable persones..wilfully committe murdre. *a* **1548** HALL *Chron., Hen. VI*, 126 Least thei beyng nedy and innocente people, should be..turmented with the vnreasonable men of warre. **1596** SHAKS. *Merch. V.* v. i. 203 What man is there so much vnreasonable, If you had pleas'd to haue defended it With any termes of Zeale. **1669** STURMY *Mariner's Mag.* I. i. 3 [This] will give the most reasonable men satisfaction; for the unreasonable, I care not a fig for them. *c* **1670** HOBBES *Dial. Com. Laws* (1681) 10 When the greatest part of Men are so unreasonable as they are. **1740** LD. HARRINGTON in *10th Rep. Hist. MSS. Comm.* App. I. 275, I hope therefore that I shall not be thought unreasonable in preferring this Petition to the King. **1829** SCOTT *Anne of G.* xxxiv, He was capricious, unreasonable, peremptory, and inconsistent. **1876** MOZLEY *Univ. Serm.* x. (ed. 2) 205 They are not so unreasonable as to expect that they can like persons without knowing them.

**3.** Not in accordance with reason; not based upon sound reason or good sense.

*a* **1340** HAMPOLE *Psalter* lxxvii. 76 Nurishynge of vnresonabill thoghtis. **1377** LANGL. *P. Pl.* B. VI. 153 For it is an vnresonable Religioun þat hath riȝte nouȝte of certeyne. *c* **1450** *Cov. Myst.* (Shaks. Soc.) 221 O, holy prophete! graunt me mercy! Of my synnys unresonable. **1533** MORE *Debell. Salem* Wks. 983/1 To shew that the same spiritual law, which this man would proue vnreasonable, is not in dede proued vnreasonable. **1560** DAUS tr. *Sleidane's Comm.* 226 b, Neyther that he enforce them to any vnreasonable condicyon or vnworthye for them. **1660** *Trial Regic.* 54, I do hold the Prisoner's Plea vain, and unreasonable. **1688** BUNYAN *Jerus. Sinner Saved* (1886) 50 It would be the unreasonablest thing in the world to render hatred for love. **1711** ADDISON *Spect.* No. 164 ⁋ 1 He contracted an unreasonable Aversion towards his Son. **1760** STERNE *Tr. Shandy* III. xxxi, I think it a very unreasonable demand. **1849** MACAULAY *Hist. Eng.* vi. II. 159 The panic was not unreasonable. **1885** 'MRS. ALEXANDER' *At Bay* iv, A vague, unreasonable anxiety about Elsie haunted him.

† **b.** Inequitable, unfair; unjustifiable. *Obs.*

? *a* **1400** *Morte Arth.* 3453, I rede thow rekkyne and reherse un-resonable dedis. **1525** LD. BERNERS *Froiss.* II. cxc. [clxxxvi.] 582 We haue to laye to his charge dyuers artycles vnresonable whiche requyre iudgement of punisyon. **1651** HOBBES *Leviath.* II. xxvi. 140 That..which thou thinkest unreasonable to be done by another to thy selfe.

**4.** Going beyond what is reasonable or equitable; excessive in amount or degree.

*c* **1380** WYCLIF *Wks.* (1880) 233 Lordis many tymes don wrongis to pore men by..vnresonable mercymentis & vnresonable taxis. *c* **1450** *Mirk's Festial* 101 Pharao..oppressyth the pepull of Israell wyth bondage and wyth vnresynabull werkes. *c* **1460** FORTESCUE *Abs. & Lim. Mon.* xiv. (1885) 144 Yff this ordre be kept,..suytours..shall [not] be importunite or brocage optayne any vnresonable desires. **1542** BRINKLOW *Compl.* xxiv. (1874) 73 But the forkyd persecutors haue vnreasonable riches..in their handys. **1583** STUBBES *Anat. Abus.* II. C 8, Is not this too vnreasonable, to take a crowne..for writing six or seuen lines? **1617** MORYSON *Itin.* I. 220 No Christian may enter this place..except he will giue an vnreasonable reward. **1680** PRIDEAUX *Lett.* (Camden) 79 Ye unreasonable prices set upon Bibles. **1725** DE FOE *Voy. round World* (1840) 195 Almost any reasonable quantity might have been sold there; but the truth is, we had an unreasonable quantity. **1796** MME. D'ARBLAY *Camilla* III. 416 She could never again consent to interfere in his unreasonable requests. **1855** MACAULAY *Hist. Eng.* xix. IV. 373 He had to wait a most unreasonable time for a judgment. **1893** *Law Times* XCIV. 600/2 The [income] tax falls with..undue severity upon one class, and with unreasonable lightness upon others.

† **b.** As *adv.* Excessively, extremely. *Obs.*

**1581** PETTIE *Guazzo's Civ. Conv.* II. (1586) 115 There are some, who coueting to be counted unreasonable honest, frowne [etc.]. **1583** STUBBES *Anat. Abus.* II. F 3, Thus..they make shooes vnreasonable deere.

**Unrea·sonableness.** [UN-[1] 12.]

**1.** The quality (in things or actions) of being unreasonable or at variance with reason.

**1532** *Dial. on Laws Eng.* (ed. 2) II. xlviii. 122 It were a greate vnreasonablenes in the lawe if it shulde prohibit hym [etc.]. **1560** DAUS tr. *Sleidane's Comm.* 305 Considering the vnreasonablenes of the thing. **1645** VANE *Lost Sheepe* 24 The vnreasonablenesse of this assertion. **1691** RAY *Creation* I. (1692) 18 The folly and unreasonableness of this..ungrounded Figment. **1748** *Anson's Voy.* III. ix. 388 The Commodore urging the unreasonableness of this procedure, from the inability of the forts to have done otherwise. **1778** MISS BURNEY *Evelina* xlvi, The folly and unreasonableness of this speech. **1830** GEN. P. THOMPSON *Exerc.* (1842) I. 248 There are depths of unreasonableness, which surpass all human folly. **1886** *Law Times Rep.* LIII. 660/1 The agreement is invalidated by the unreasonableness of the restriction.

† **b.** Unfairness, injustice. *Obs.*

*a* **1533** LD. BERNERS *Huon* xviii. 48 Ye..haue well herde the grete vnresonablenes that the kynge do too one of oure peres. *Ibid.*, The place wher as suche extorsyon and vnresonableness is vsed.

**c.** Immoderateness; excessiveness.

**1665** SIR T. HERBERT *Trav.* (1677) 282 The Ambassadour..acquainted his Master with the unreasonableness of the Turks demands. **1797** MRS. RADCLIFFE *Ital.* xxxi, The unreasonableness of her claims was forgotten.

**2.** The quality (in persons) of being unreasonable in action, demands, etc.

**1542** UDALL *Erasm. Apoph.* 184 Here maye a manne doubte whether of these twoo thynges he ought rather to maruaill at, the kynges liberalitee in geuyng, orels the vnreasonablenes of the philosophier, in askyng. **1598** R. BERNARD tr. *Terence, Andria* v. i, You would (now at last) giue ouer to cumber me with your vnreasonablenesse. **1703** MRS. CENTLIVRE *Beau's Duel* v. i, Did ever man of your hairs ask such questions? I vow I blush at your unreasonableness. **1736** BUTLER *Anal.* I. vi. 156 This is vanity, conceit and unreasonableness. **1855** MACAULAY *Hist. Eng.* xv. III. 595 The difficulties by which the government was beset on all sides, the malignity of its enemies, the unreasonableness of its friends. **1879** L. STEPHEN *Hours in Library* Ser. III. 322 The grand unreasonableness of the average Englishman.

† **3.** Lack of reason; irrationality. *Obs.*

**1598** FLORIO, *Irationalita*, vnreasonableness, brutishnes. **1647** H. MORE *Song of Soul* I. ii. 88 But what with judgement doth them both compare? Is't reason or unreasonableness, I pray.

**Unrea·sonably,** *a.* [UN-[1] 11.]

**1.** In a manner at variance with reason; without due observance of reason or good judgement.

*c* **1380** WYCLIF *Wks.* (1880) 12 ȝif þei coueiten vnresonabiliche þe housis..of here neiȝeboris. *c* **1450** *Myrr. our Ladye* 109 By whyche..thow shuldest hate no creature vnreasonabely. **1535** COVERDALE 2 *Macc.* xiv. 23 Nicanor, whyle he abode at Ierusalem, ordred himself not vnreasonably. **1561** T. NORTON *Calvin's Inst.* I. 10 To passe ouer all the rest, which are much more vnreasonably foolish, Plato himself..vainly erreth in his round globe. **1641** R. BROOKE *Eng. Episc.* I. v. 27 Else Reason doth unreasonably determine me not to Marry. **1670** CLARENDON *Contempl. Ps.* Tracts (1727) 757 They only consider..how unreasonably men deal with them. **1729** LAW *Serious C.* x. 143 Do but suppose a man acting unreasonably. **1823** SCOTT *Quentin D.* xxiii, Said Quentin, not unreasonably offended at the turn thus given to his gallantry. **1881** BENHAM in *Macm. Mag.* XLV. 115/1 The Essay..was, not unreasonably, regarded as the most objectionable in tone.

**2.** To an unreasonable extent; excessively, immoderately.

*a* **1450** *Knt. de la Tour* (1906) 53 There be..other that be lykerous of moche mete and drinke, takyng unresonably therof. **1470–85** MALORY *Arthur* VII. i. 213, I am come hyder to praye you..to gyue me thre yeftes and they shalle not be vnresonably asked. **1512** *Act* 4 *Hen. VIII*, c. 6 § 2 If..the same Collectours..unresonably delay or tary the said Marchauntes. **1568** GRAFTON *Chron.* II. 402 When they..would ryde, they found horses vnreasonably deare. **1607** SHAKS. *Cor.* I. iii. 84 Fye, you confine your selfe most vnreasonably. **1697** WALSH *Life V.* ⁋ 20 in Dryden *Virgil*, Venus grows..unreasonably confident. **1723** ATTERBURY *Serm.* (1726) I. ix. 314 To grant that to others, which we our selves perhaps..might be willing enough, unreasonably willing, to obtain from them. **1782** *Phil. Trans.* LXX. 352 Under all these disadvantages in the machine (if not unreasonably ill made) the rod *ef* will ascend to *d*. **1840** ALISON *Hist. Eur.* lii. VII. 109 A nation..unreasonably jealous of its military expenditure. **1884** *Law Rep.* 25 Ch. Div. 492 To discourage unreasonably early marriages.

† **Unrea·sonal,** *a. Obs.*[−1] (UN-[1] 7.) **1653** E. CHISENHALE *Cath. Hist.* 129 Therefore for the Doctor, to deny us to be a Church,..seems to me strange and unreasonall.

**Unrea·soned,** *ppl. a.* [UN-[1] 8.]

**1.** Not gifted with reason; devoid of reason.

**1582** STANYHURST *Æneid* IV. (Arb.) 115 Might not I my lief tyme..Spend lyk an vnreasoned wild beaste? **1805** EUGENIA DI ACTON *Nuns of Desert* II. 230 A wretch..so totally un-reasoned as to say [etc.].

**2.** Not evolved or developed by reasoning.

**1790** BURKE *Fr. Rev.* 286 The citizens are interested from old prejudices and unreasoned habits. **1854** FERRIER *Inst. Metaph.* Introd. 3 An unreasoned philosophy, even though true, carries no guarantee of its truth. **1880** *Fraser's Mag.* May 658 Our unreasoned confidence that every vision of truth is in itself a glorious..vision.

**Unrea·soning,** *vbl. sb.* (UN-[1] 13.) *a* **1871** DE MORGAN *Budget Parad.* (1872) 317 He is..the ablest head at unreasoning,..of all who have tried in our day to attach their names to an error. **1889** 'MARK TWAIN' *Yankee at Crt. K. Arthur* xiii, It was the stubborn unreasoning of the time.

**Unrea·soning,** *ppl. a.* (UN-[1] 10.)

(*a*) **1751** G. WEST *Education* lxii, The unreasoning vulgar willingly obey. **1800** COLERIDGE *Piccolom.* IV. vii, I cannot traffic in the trade of words With that unreasoning sex. **1865** PUSEY *Truth Eng. Ch.* 13 The authors..were mostly unsystematic, disjointed, unreasoning. **1883** *19th Cent.* May 773 That somewhat unreasoning personage who is called the British Public.

(*b*) **1812** L. HUNT in *Examiner* 11 May 289/2 The caprices of an unreasoning resentment. **1855** MILMAN *Lat. Chr.* XIV. i. VI. 357 An unthinking and unreasoning impulse of the inward being. **1878** E. WHITE *Life in Christ* (ed. 3) IV. xxvi. 437 There is no influence to which men yield so easily as to unreasoning fear.

Hence **Unrea·soningly** *adv.*

**1848** MRS. GASKELL *Mary Barton* xxxii, Job Legh pressed out of court, and Jem followed unreasoningly. **1885** *N. Amer. Rev.* March 194 Most fathers, schoolmen, and divines..have done so most unanimously and most unreasoningly.

**Unrea·sty,** *a.* (UN-[1] 7.) **1853** G. J. CAYLEY *Las Alforjas* II. 88 The first unreesty sample [of ham] we have met with since Seville. **Unrea·ve,** *v.* Now *dial.* [UN-[2] 3 + REAVE *v.*[3]] *trans.* To unravel. **1593** BILSON *Govt. Christ's Ch.* p. v, The warpe and webbe of the laie Presbyterie..hath so enfolded some mens wits, that they cannot vnreaue their cogitations from admiring their newe founde Consistories. **1594** SPENSER *Amoretti* xxiii, Penelope..Deuiz'd a Web..in which the worke that she all day did make, the same at night she did againe vnreaue. **1898** R. BLAKEBOROUGH *Wit*, etc. *N. Riding Yorks* 466 *Unreave*, to unwind. † **Unrea·ved,** *ppl. a. Obs.*[−1] [UN-[1] 8 + dial. *reave* to strip (a roof or house).] Not stripped of its roof. **1646** BP. HALL *Balm of Gilead* i. § 9 Couldst thou think that a Cottage, not too strongly built, and standing so bleak in the very mouth of the Windes, could..hold tight, and unreaved?

**Unreba·ted,** *ppl. a.* [UN-[1] 8.]

† **1.** Unblunted; undulled. *Obs.*

**1579–80** NORTH *Plutarch* (1595) 241 He shewed the people the cruell fight of fensers at vnrebated swords. **1630** J. TAYLOR (Water P.) *Heauens Blessing* Wks. III. 118/2 Saint George (being armed at all points but especially) with an vnrebated courage. **1681** J. SCOTT *Chr. Life* iii. § i. 74 They are full of sharp and unrebated Desires. **1745** WESLEY *Wks.* (1872) VIII. 195 Those dogs of hell are let loose to prey upon your soul, with their whole unrebated strength.

**2.** Not subject to rebate or deduction.

**1894** *Q. Rev.* Jan. 208 Thus the unrebated income-tax becomes..a special tax on labour.

**Unre·bel,** *v.* (UN-[2] 6 b.) **1642** HOWELL *Twelve Treat.* (1661) 24 The Treatie began, which the Scot wold not conform himself to do, unless he were first unrebell'd and made Rectus in Curia. **Unrebe·llious,** *a.* (UN-[1] 7.) **1570** LEVINS *Manip.* 226 Vnrebelliouse, *impertinax*. **1879** MORLEY *Burke* 205 A composed spirit.., an unrebellious temper.

**Unrebu·keable,** *a.* (UN-[1] 7 b.)

**1530** TINDALE *Prol. Philippians* Wks. (1572) 52/1 He him selfe had liued in such false righteousnes, and holinesse Vnrebukeable. **1537** BIBLE 1 *Tim.* vi. 14 That thou..be without spotte & vnrebukeable. *c* **1585** [R. BROWNE] *Answ. Cartwright* 80 There were those that..were vnrebukeable. **1619** W. SCLATER *Exp.* 1 *Thess.* 173 Plinie to Traian giues testimonie of Christians inoffensiue life; except in matter of their Superstition (as he calls it) they were vnrebukeable. **1650** S. CLARKE *Eccl. Hist.* 465 Justitiaries, and such as were unrebukeable in their lives. **1868** LYNCH *Rivulet* CLXI. iv, Not unrebukable am I, Not spotless Thy command have kept.

Hence **Unrebu·keably** *adv.*

*a* **1639** HARSNET *Repent.* (1640) 182 Paul..lived before his Conversion as unrebukeably as any civill person doth.

**Unrebu·ked,** *ppl. a.* (UN-[1] 8.)

*c* **1445** PECOCK *Donet* 7 Scant ynouȝ oon leef schulde stonde vnprovid or colowrabily vnrebukid. **1547** BECON in *Certain Hom.* P iv b, He would rather suffer death..then to suffer whordom to be vnrebuked, euen in a King. **1697** C. LESLIE *Snake in Grass* (ed. 2) 107 Tho' they have let no suppos'd contempt of their own Books go unrebuked. **1857** SUSANNA WINKWORTH tr. *Life Tauler* xvi. 306 When one finds this evil inclination in a man,..and he remains unrebuked, all this is the world. **1870** MORRIS *Earthly Par.* II. III. 401 All unrebuked he let her soft eyes claim Kindness from his.

**Unrebu·ttable,** *a.* (UN-[1] 7 b, 5 b.) **1869** JAMES in *Law Rep.* 7 Equity 537 The strong and unrebuttable presumption.

**Unrebu·tted,** *ppl. a.* [UN-[1] 8.]

† **1.** Not repulsed or driven back. *Obs.*

*c* **1470** HENRY *Wallace* III. 131 Vnraboytyt [**1570** unrebutit] the Sothroun was in wer. **1513** DOUGLAS *Æneid* IX. xiii. 48 That onrebutit knycht Endlang the wallys put thame to the flycht.

**2.** Not disproved or refuted.

**1884** *Law Times Rep.* L. 215/2 The evidence is clear and unrebutted that [etc.].

**Unreca·llable,** *a.* (UN-[1] 7 b.)

**1611** COTGR., *Irrevocable*, irreuocable, vnrecallable. **1628** FELTHAM *Resolves* II. lxxxix. 257 That which is done, is vnrecallable. **1798** SOUTHEY *Wife of Fergus* 39 The unrecallable vow That made me his.

**Unreca·lled,** *ppl. a.* (UN-[1] 8.)

**1601** R. CHESTER *Love's Mart., K. Arthur* (1878) 43 Merlin..told him vnrecalled Time did stay [=await], To haste him from his pleasure thence away. *a* **1648** LD. HERBERT *Occas. Poems, To his Watch*, The doom of fate, whose unrecall'd decree You date, bring, execute. **1679** T. JENISON in R. Jenison *Popish Plot* 18 As long as your Oath stands unrecalled. **1742** YOUNG *Nt. Th.* II. 260 While she seems, nodding o'er her charge, to..give us up to licence, unrecall'd, Unmarkt. **1883** LD. MONCREIFF *Law Rep.* 9 App. Cases 317/2 While [the conveyance]..remained unrecalled it was absolute.

**Unreca·lling,** *ppl. a.* (UN-[1] 10.) **1593** SHAKS. *Lucr.* 993 And euer let his vnrecalling crime Haue time to waile th' abusing of his time. **Unreca·nted,** *ppl. a.* (UN-[1] 8.) [**1775** ASH.] **1826** *Q. Rev.* XXXIII. 356 After living in the unrecanted profession of The Confession of Faith. **Unrece·ding,** *ppl. a.* (UN-[1] 10.) **1810** JANE PORTER *Scottish Chiefs* xxxviii, Why, then, this unreceding determination to invade us? 1881 *Scribner's Mag.* XXII. 810 A steady and unreceding advance. **Unreceiˑpted**, *ppl. a.* (UN-[1] 8.) 1881 *Cambridge Trifles* 3 Files of bills, receipted or unreceipted.

**Unreceiˑvable**, *a.* [UN-[1] 7 b.]

1. Incapable of being received.

1611 COTGR., *Inadmissible*, vnadmittable, vnreceiuable, vnacceptable. 1802–12 BENTHAM *Ration. Judic. Evid.* (1827) V. 132 There is a receipt..whereby any man..may render his testimony unreceivable. 1877 M. ARNOLD *Last Ess. on Ch.* p. xxx, Those who had thrown it aside because what was presented to them under its name was so unreceivable.

†2. Unfit to receive one. *Obs.*—[1]

1634 HERBERT *Trav.* 118 If that Kingdome haue a purgatory, so a conspiracie of..scalding sand, the burning Sun, and vnreceiueable Cottages, can make one.

**Unreceiˑved**, *ppl. a.* (UN-[1] 8.)

1540 *Act 32 Hen. VIII*, c. 5 The residue of the said dett.. remayning unlevied or unreceyvid by the said former execution. 1597 HOOKER *Eccl. Pol.* v. lvii. § 5 Where the signes..of his grace are not either through contempt vnreceiued, or receiued with contempt. 1651 G. W. tr. *Cowel's Inst.* 66 It is much questioned whether Tenant for life..hath any right..to profits and fruits unreceived. 1725 BERKELEY *Lett.* Wks. 1871 IV. 112 Stock, and dividends unreceived make up the sum. 1748 RICHARDSON *Clarissa* (1811) V. xx. 235 Miss Howe's answer to my last unreceived. 1825 COLERIDGE *Aids Refl.* 196 The right though unreceived Owner of the House.

**Unreceiˑving**, *ppl. a.* (UN-[1] 10.) 1566 in *Three 15th Cent. Chron.* (Camden) 138 To quyat ye matter ye churche dores wer fayn to be closyd, and ye paryschyns to departe unreseyvynge for that day. **Unreceˑptant**, *a.* (UN-[1] 7.) 1851 RUSKIN *Mod. Paint.* I. II. v. i. § 5 To maintain themselves obstinately unreceptant of the good.

**Unreceˑptive**, *a.* (UN-[1] 7, 5 b.)

1778 HARTLEY *Pref. to Swedenborg's Heav. & Hell* p. xlviii, The self-hardened..render themselves unreceptive of mercy. 1865 M. PATTISON *Ess.* (1889) I. 349 To sharpen the attention of a defiant and unreceptive mind such as Wolf. 1877 H. A. PAGE *De Quincey* II. xix. 147 That wholly unreceptive..mood which cannot even temporarily condescend to sympathy.

**Unreceptiˑvity**. (UN-[1] 12, 5 b.) 1849 ALFORD *Gk. Test.* I. 524 Instances of unreceptivity of spiritual meaning. **Unreciˑprocal**, *a.* (UN-[1] 7, 5 b.) [1775 ASH.] 1841 J. J. SYLVESTER in *Lond.*, etc. *Phil. Mag.* XVIII. 138 The unreciprocal implication of systems of equations. **Unreciˑprocated**, *ppl. a.* (UN-[1] 8.) 1860 PATMORE *Faithful for Ever* 100 This poor, complaining wraith Of unreciprocated faith. 1887 RIDER HAGGARD *Jess* iv, Nor was the liking unreciprocated.

**Unreciˑted**, *ppl. a.* (UN-[1] 8.)

1587 CHURCHYARD *Worth. Wales* (1876) 10 An act so noble ..shall not passe my pen vnresited. 1662 BOYLE *Examen* vi. 72, I have left un-recited several..undesired Expressions. 1760–72 H. BROOKE *Fool of Qual.* (1809) III. 126 Did you.. meet with any adventure..yet unrecited?

**Unreˑcked**, *ppl. a.* (UN-[1] 8.) 1808 SCOTT *Marm.* I. xvii, Unmark'd, at least unreck'd, the taunt. 1862 ELLICOT *Destiny of Creature* i. (1865) 5 These animals..die unrecked of and unheeded. **Unreˑcking**, *ppl. a.* (UN-[1] 10.) 1868 GEO. ELIOT *Sp. Gipsy* 290 Unrecking of time-woven subtleties. 1873 MRS. WHITNEY *Other Girls* xxx, An utterance of hard unrecking distinctness. **Unreˑckingness**. (UN-[1] 12.) 1873 MRS. WHITNEY *Other Girls* xxx, The hard unreckingness was only the reflex of a tenderness quick, not dead. **Unreˑckon**, *v.* (UN-[2] 3.) 1561 EDEN *Art Navig.* II. vi, The dayes of the Moone beynge knowen, then unrekenyng or disrekenynge backwarde, we shall knowe the daye. 1598 FLORIO, *Discontare*, to vnreckon, to abate in reckoning.

**Unreˑckonable**, *a.* (UN-[1] 7 b.)

1851 HAWTHORNE *Ho. Seven Gables* iv, An uncle..might ..make her the ultimate heiress of his unreckonable riches. 1880 A. RALEIGH *Way to City* 267 It is even more so by unreckonable degrees.

**Unreˑckoned**, *ppl. a.* (UN-[1] 8, 8 c. Cf. MDu. *ongerekent* (Du. *ongerekend*), MHG. *ungerechent* (G. *ungerechnet*), ON. *úreiknaðr*, Sw. *oräknad*, Da. *uregnet*.)

c 1340 HAMPOLE *Pr. Consc.* 2462 Na syn þan unrekend sal be. c 1450 *Cov. Myst.* (Shaks. Soc.) 166 Suche a carpynge is unknowe, Onrekenyd in my regne. 1464 *Mann. & Househ. Exp.* (Roxb.) 161 Afftyr the same rekenynge Keverstonys men..askyd more wiche was onrekenyd as thei seyd, vj. s. viij. d. 1551 BP. GARDINER *On Sacram.* 75 The foure substaunces, whiche this auctor..numbreth of Christ, might haue bene left vnrekened by tale. 1599 DANIEL *Musoph.* (1601) A iiij, Who doth touch the tenour of that vaine, Is held but vain; and his vnreckned pen The title but of Leuitie doth gaine. 1628 GAULE *Pract. The.* (1629) 100 These were his Names, Many and Great; yet is Jesvs (the Name aboue all names) vnreckoned. 1690 DRYDEN *Don Sebastian* III. i, Add that falshood To a long Bill that yet remains unreckon'd. 1875 LOWELL *Under Old Elm* 135 The casual gleanings of unreckoned years. 1879 BARING-GOULD *Germany* II. 283 The theory may be wrong,..the calculation put out by unreckoned elements.

b. With *for*.

1680 C. NESSE *Ch. Hist.* 452 God left not his cruelty long unreckon'd for. 1894 MRS. DYAN *Man's Keeping* (1899) 47 This unreckoned-for encounter..was a bitter pang.

**Unreclaiˑmable**, *a.* [UN-[1] 7 b, 5 b.]

1. Incapable of being reclaimed or reformed; incorrigible: **a.** Of actions, qualities, etc.

1577 tr. *Bullinger's Decades* 438/1 The Iewes..for their vnreclaymeable affiaunce in the lawe are vtterly reiected. 1607 TOPSELL *Four-f. Beasts* 305 He..faleth into some furious and vnreclaimable euill qualities. 1652 SCLATER *Civ. Magistracy* (1653) 8, Men, who are full of savage and unreclaimable desires.

b. Of persons. Also const. *from*.

a 1656 BP. HALL *Serm. 2 Pet.* i. 10 Wks. 1863 V. 681 That dreadful place of torment, which is the unavoidable portion of careless and unreclaimable sinners. 1680 C. NESSE *Ch. Hist.* 195 He finds her unreclaimable from her idols. a 1716 BLACKALL *Wks.* (1723) I. 258 He is not unreconcileable to us until we become unreclaimable. 1717 FLEETWOOD *Burdett's Let.* 11 'Tis the Proceeding of the..tenderest Fathers ..with their Sons, when so enormously ungracious, wicked, and unreclaimable.

*absol.* 1685 J. SCOTT *Chr. Life* II. iv. § 1 To pour out the Vials of his Wrath upon the obstinate and unreclaimable.

†2. Untameable, uncontrollable. *Obs.*

1609 HOLLAND *Amm. Marcell.* 401 This kind of men so quicke and nimble, so untamed and unreclaimable. 1611 COTGR., *Bœuf bran*,..a kind of wild Oxe..vnreclaimable, and onely good for the shambles.

3. Not liable to be claimed back.

1777 POTTER *Æschylus, Supplicants* 107 That we might be permitted here to dwell Free, unreclaimable, inviolate.

Hence **Unreclaiˑmably** *adv.*

1645 BP. HALL *Peace Maker* vii. 57 Those..who doe pertinaciously, and unreclaimably maintaine Doctrines destructive to the foundation of Christian Religion. 1652 HEYLYN *Cosmogr.* III. 106 Unreclamably addicted to their antient Judaism.

**Unreclaiˑmed**, *ppl. a.* [UN-[1] 8, 5 b.]

1. †a. Not summoned to return. *Obs.*—[1]

c 1470 HARDING *Chron.* CXXII. ii, He then his lawe and peace alwaye proclaymed..And so held on to London vnreclaymed.

b. Not demanded back.

1748 EARL NUGENT *To Mankind* xviii, Wise nature mocks th' wrangling herd; For unreclaim'd, and untransfer'd, Her pow'rs and rights remain.

2. Not reclaimed from error or wrong-doing; not reduced to order or good ways; unreformed.

1602 SHAKS. *Ham.* II. i. 34 The flash and out-breake of a fiery minde, A sauagenes in vnreclaimed bloud of generall assault. 1611 SPEED *Theat. Gt. Brit.* IV. i. 138/1 Their manners vnreclaimed, and barbarisme.., doe witnesse no such ciuilitie sowen, to bee in that plot. 1757 W. WILKIE *Epigon.* IX. 281 Yet, unreclaim'd, from such atrocious deeds, To more and worse your desp'rate rage proceeds. 1827 POLLOK *Course T.* II. 483 In tormenting, pained; Unawed by wrath, by mercy unreclaimed. 1830 MACKINTOSH *Progr. Eth. Philos.* Wks. 1846 I. 256 They retain whatever was admirable in their unreclaimed state.

3. Untamed; unsubdued.

1618 LATHAM *Falconry* Contents, Of the Ostringer, and.. Goshawke compared with other Fowles of the ayre, as they are vnreclaimed and wilde. 1631 CHAPMAN *Cæsar & Pompey* Plays 1873 III. 193 *Antony*: [of Cato]. Vnreclaimed man! 1693 DRYDEN *Ovid's Met.* XIII. *Acis* 81 Bullocks, unreclaim'd to bear the Yoke.

4. Uncultivated, wild.

1781 COWPER *Expost.* 468 This island, spot of unreclaim'd rude earth. 1832 *Planting* 23 (L.U.K.), [Such] unreclaimed lands..can seldom be prepared as above. 1856 OLMSTED *Slave States* 157 Land of this description..in its unreclaimed state.

Hence **Unreclaiˑmedness**.

1611 COTGR., *Sauvageté*, sauagenesse, wildnesse, unreclaimednesse. 1646 S. BOLTON *Arraignm. Err.* 28 Unreclaimednesse under any sin whatever will bring in errour.

**Unreclaiˑming**, *ppl. a.* (UN-[1] 10.) 1820 SHELLEY *Prometh. Unb.* III. iv. 187 Love Dragged to his altars..And slain amid men's unreclaiming tears. **Unrecliˑning**, *ppl. a.* (UN-[1] 10.) 1777 POTTER *Æschylus, Prom. Bd.* 7 Therefore the joyless station of this rock Unsleeping, unreclining, shalt thou keep.

**Unrecogniˑtion**. (UN-[1] 12, 5 b.)

1869 MRS. WHITNEY *Hitherto* ix, Everybody who has a goading ambition has knowledge..of a cold exasperating unrecognition. 1875 HOWELLS *Foregone Concl.* (1882) 299 She kept her eyes upon him with a dreamy unrecognition.

**Unreˑcognizable**, *a.* (UN-[1] 7 b, 5 b.)

1817 COLERIDGE *Biog. Lit.* II. 83 When a number of successive lines can be rendered..unrecognizable as verse,.. by simply transcribing them as prose. 1847 LD. LINDSAY *Chr. Art* I. p. cxlii, He returned so disfigured.., that he was unrecognisable save by his voice.

Hence **Unrecognizableness**; **-ably** *adv.*

1879 STEVENSON *Trav. Cevennes* 49 The mist had almost unrecognisably exaggerated their forms. 1883 H. DRUMMOND *Nat. Law in Spir. W.* 303 One of the most recognisable characteristics of life is its unrecognisableness.

**Unreˑcognized**, *ppl. a.* (UN-[1] 8.)

[1775 ASH.] 1813 SHELLEY *Q. Mab* VI. 189 Not a thought, .. Nor the events enchaining every will,..pass Unrecognized, or unforeseen by thee. 1861 [MRS. A. J. PENNY] *Romance Dull Life* xxxvii. 265 She felt she was still in unrecognised disgrace.

**Unreˑcognizing**, *ppl. a.* (UN-[1] 10.)

a 1814 *Witness* III. iii. in *New Brit. Theatre* I. 35 A kinsman proudly rich, Whose haughty and unrecognizing eye Had never glanc'd on him. 1858 SEARS *Athan.* II. x. 233 He walked to Emmaus with the two unrecognizing disciples. 1890 'R. BOLDREWOOD' *Miner's Right* xxxviii, He gazed for one moment at me with strange, unrecognising air.

Hence **Unreˑcognizingly** *adv.*

1891 COTES *2 Girls on Barge* 76 The Essingtons had passed us, unrecognisingly.

**Unrecolleˑcted**, *ppl. a.* (UN-[1] 8.)

(*a*) 1733 WATTS *Philos. Ess.* (1734) 127 Our unrecollected and useless Dreams. 1802–12 BENTHAM *Ration. Judic. Evid.* (1827) I. 276 Unrecollected, when occasion comes for recollecting it, it will be tantamount to silence.

(*b*) 1850 J. H. NEWMAN *Diffic. Anglic.* 235 Such a soul, so selfish, so unrecollected.

**Unrecommeˑndable**, *a.* (UN-[1] 7 b.) 1830 MISS MITFORD *Village* Ser. IV. 237, I should have objected to it..as being utterly unrecommendable by one rational person to another.

**Unrecommeˑnded**, *ppl. a.* (UN-[1] 8.)

c 1550 CHEKE *Let.* in *Athenæum* 28 Aug. (1909) 237/2, I would rather that you would, unproved and unrecommended, do well. 1704 *Moderat. Displ.* v, A Notion undefin'd in Vertues Schools, Unrecommended by her sacred Rules. 1792 A. YOUNG *Trav. France* 190 Unknown and unrecommended at Nice, I expected nothing but what could be shot flying in any town.

**Unreˑcompensable**, *a.* [UN-[1] 7 b, 5 b.]

† Incapable of being remedied.

1526 *Pilgr. Perf.* (W. de W. 1531) 203 b, Surely this offence is..of man vnrecompensable. 1560 BECON *New Catech.* Wks. 1564 I. 304 Whiche miserye and wretchednesse was so greate and vnrecompensable, that from it.. no creature..coulde delyuer me. 1587 FLEMING *Contn. Holinshed* III. 1329/1 The heinous and vnrecompensable defamation of the course of iustice.

**Unreˑcompensed**, *ppl. a.* (UN-[1] 8.)

1469 *Paston Lett.* II. 379 Yif ye any thyng doo..to the pleasir of my Lordes, it will neither be unremembrid ne unrecompensid. 1555 EDEN *Decades* (Arb.) 310 He shall returne..not vnrecompensed with iust rewards. 1581 A. HALL *Iliad* I. 5 Thinkst thou it fit I leaue the maide, and emptie go my wayes Vnrecompenste. 1621 FLETCHER *Wild Goose Chace* IV. iii, Heaven will not see so true a love unrecompenc'd. a 1763 SHENSTONE *Ess.* Wks. 1777 II. 29 To retire at last unrecompensed..was beyond all power of resolution. 1822 LAMB *Elia* I. *Bachelor's Compl.*, The display of married happiness..is throughout pure, unrecompensed, unqualified insult. 1840–1 WORDSW. *Mem. Tour Italy* iii. 10 Yet not unrecompensed are they who learn [etc.].

†**Unrecoˑmptless**, *a.* [UN-[1] 7, 15.] Incapable of being related or reckoned. 1593 LODGE *Misc. Pieces* (Hunter. Cl.) 14 Fvll fraught with vnrecomptles sweete Of your faire face that stole mine eie.

**Unreˑconcilable**, *a.* Now *rare*. (UN-[1] 7 b, 5 b.)

1577 tr. *Bullinger's Decades* IV. ii. 574/1 That vnreconcileable and harde hart. 1618 *Fenton's Guicciard.* (ed. 3) 344 The Pope shewing signes of a person vnreconcileable against Alphonso. 1646 HAMMOND *Tracts* 25 Whether it be reconcileable or unreconcileable with a good conscience. 1685 BAXTER *Paraphr. N. T.* 2 Tim. iii. 3 Men that will not live in peace, but are unreconcileable. a 1716 [see UNRECLAIMABLE *a.* 1 b]. 1896 *Advance* (Chicago) 2 Apr. 475/2 Teachings..absolutely unreconcilable with the teachings of the New Testament.

Hence **Unreconcilableness**; **-ably** *adv.*

1650 *Vind. Hammond's Addr.* iii. § 7 The *unreconcileablenesse of those two opinions (the one with the other). c 1620 BP. HALL *Contempl.*, *O. T.* XV. vii, How much lesse shall the God of mercies bee *unreconcileably displeased with his owne. 1653 H. MORE *Antid. Ath.* I. ii. (1655) 6 The minde of man..will fully and unreconcileably disagree.

**Unreˑconciled**, *ppl. a.* (UN-[1] 8, 5 b.)

c 1450 *Myrr. our Ladye* 152 Wretched were that persone that..wolde be vnreconcyled and dysceuered from that holy vnyte. 1513 BRADSHAW *St. Werburge* I. 872 Dredynge sore the iustyce of god almyght For his fathers demerytes vnreconsyled On hym to fall. 1564 DORMAN *Proofe Cert. Art. Relig.* 33 b, He..was forced to leaue the two places at a iarre vnreconciled. 1604 SHAKS. *Oth.* v. ii. 27 Any Crime Vnreconcil'd as yet to Heauen, and Grace. 1671 MRS. BEHN *Forc'd Marr.* I. ii, As those unreconciled to Heaven Would bear the pangs of death. 1711 G. HICKES *Two Treat. Chr. Priesth.* (1847) II. 48 The offering of unreconciled Christians. 1769 BURKE *Obs.* '*Late St. Nat.*' 90 The unreconciled principles of the original discord of parties. 1817 SHELLEY *Rev. Islam* I. xxvii, He changed from starry shape..To a dire Snake, with man and beast unreconciled. 1873 SYMONDS *Grk. Poets* xii. 420 Yet the spirit and the flesh still remained in unreconciled antagonism.

† **Unreconciˑliable**, *a. Obs.* [UN-[1] 7 b, 5 b.] Unreconcilable.

1589 T. WHITE *Serm. Paules Crosse* 47 Deuiding his [*sc.* Christ's] Bodie by vnreconciliable hatred among our selues. 1606 SHAKS. *Ant. & Cl.* v. i. 47 Let me lament..that our Starres Vnreconciliable, should diuide our equalnesse to this. 1628 tr. *Mathieu's Powerf. Favorite* 87 From this instant their mindes became vnreconciliable.

†**Unreconciliate**, *ppl. a. Sc. Obs.*—[1] [UN-[1] 8 b.] Unreconciled. 1588 *Reg. Privy Council Scot.* IV. 283 Sa lang as the said deidlie feid..standis unreconsiliat. **Unreconnoiˑtred**, *ppl. a.* (UN-[1] 8.) 1899 *Westm. Gaz.* 13 Dec. 5/1 Country unreconnoitred is unknown in a military sense.

**Unreconstruˑcted**, *ppl. a.* (UN-[1] 8; cf. RECONSTRUCTION 1 b.)

1869 *Nation* 25 March 221/2 Butler's Committee on Reconstruction reported in favor of extending..the time during which an 'unreconstructed' Southerner may retain his Government employment. 1877 LONGF. in *Life* (1891) III. 277 A letter from Mr. —, of Washington, a fierce and 'unreconstructed' rebel.

**Unrecoˑrdable**, *a.* (UN-[1] 7 b, 5 b.) 1874 M. COLLINS *Transmigr.* III. xviii. 271 That delicious unrecordable nonsense which some people fancy can only be talked once in a life-time.

**Unrecoˑrded**, *ppl. a.* (UN-[1] 8.)

1585 ABP. SANDYS *Serm.* 287 Had Salomon neuer beene, or had his fall been vnrecorded. 1662 STILLINGFL. *Orig. Sacræ* II. i. § 2 Supposing that God had left the matters of Divine revelation unrecorded at all. 1671 MILTON *P. R.* I. 16 Deeds..in secret done, And unrecorded left through many an Age. 1725 POPE *Odyss.* IV. 276 Antilochus, a name Not unrecorded in the rolls of fame. 1847 KEBLE *Serm.* Pref. p. lxviii, The more established theory of silent unrecorded Tradition. 1881 P. BROOKS *Candle of Lord* 133 A thousand unrecorded patriots helped to make Washington.

**Unrecoˑrding**, *ppl. a.* (UN-[1] 10.) 1849 TENNYSON '*You might have won the Poet's name*' 7 A life that moves to gracious ends Thro' troops of unrecording friends. †**Unrecouˑnselled**, *ppl. a. Sc. Obs.* [UN-[1] 8.] Unreconciled. 1533 BELLENDEN *Livy* III. xix. (S.T.S.) II. 26 He declarit him Inemye and as ȝit vnreconsellit to þis man. 1565 *Reg. Privy Council Scot.* I. 407 The said unrecounsalit bluid and inymitie. **Unrecouˑnted**, *ppl. a.* (UN-[1] 8.) 1613 SHAKS. *Hen. VIII*, III. ii. 48 Marry this is yet but yong, and may be left To some eares vnrecounted.

**Unrecoˑverable**, *a.* [UN-[1] 7 b, 5 b.]

†1. That cannot be recovered; completely lost.

14.. *Brut* 319 ȝet thilk Northren wynd..lost good wiþoute nombre vnrecouerable. 1448 *Extr. Aberd. Reg.* (1844) I. 401 Al sumes..bath recouerable and unrecouerable. a 1500

*Chaucer's Dreme* 1753 This hasty farme had bene a feast, And now is unrecoverable. *a* 1586 SIDNEY *Arcadia* I. v, To lament the losse of such a jewell, so much the more, as that skilful men in that arte assured it was unrecoverable. 1617 MORYSON *Itin.* I. 278 The vnrecouerable losse of time. 1650 BAXTER *Saints' R.* III. ii. 281 Oh my unconceiveable unrecoverable loss!

**2.** From which no recovery is possible; past remedy or cure.

1561 DAUS tr. *Bullinger on Apoc.* 533 The most certaine, vnrecouerable, and most weightie destruction of Rome. 1584 R. SCOT *Discov. Witchcr.* XIII. xxxiv. (1886) 287 To make an unrecoverable wound in your bellie. 1608 MACHIN *Dumbe Knt.* III, I doe not think this ill Is yet so big as unrecoverable. 1644 VICARS *God in Mount* 1 An unrecoverable cursed estate of damnation. 1888 *Amer. Jrnl. Psychol.* Feb. 333 Loss of memory is so commonly associated with unrecoverable cases.

† **Unreco·verably,** *adv.* *Obs.* [UN-¹ 7 b, 5 b.] Irrecoverably.

*c* 1445 PECOCK *Donet* (1921) 160 ȝitt if þei be not vnrecouerabli [unre]dressable, þouȝ to so redresse happily longiþ sum labour. 1578 WALSINGHAM in Nicolas *Life & T. Sir C. Hatton* (1847) 60 We shall estrange Scotland from us unrecoverably. 1628 T. SPENCER *Logick* 125 Thereby we finde, that this condition befalls them secretly, certainly, vnrecoverably. *a* 1652 BROME *Damoiselle* III. ii, [He is] most unrecoverably mad! 1690 BAXTER *Kingd. Christ* iv. (1691) 49 They are unrecoverably Extinct.

**Unreco·vered,** *ppl. a.*¹ [UN-¹ 8.]

**1.** From which no recovery is or has been made.

*c* 1611 CHAPMAN *Iliad* IX. 247 Consider these affairs in time,..And have the grace to turn from Greece fate's unrecover'd hour. 1612 DRAYTON *Poly-olb.* II. 74 Too late (alas) we find The softness of thy sword..To be the onely cause of vnrecouer'd spoile. 1630 J. TAYLOR (Water P.) *Siege Jerus.* Wks. 12 Then fell they to an vnrecouered wane.

**2.** Not recovered or regained.

*a* 1692 POLLEXFEN *Disc. Trade* (1697) 4 The other half Million..we may be sure they did not give, or left unrecovered, but took it from us. 1855 M. ARNOLD *Balder Dead* III. 235 They bind us..To leave for ever Balder in the grave, An unrecover'd prisoner. 1897 *Daily News* 21 Jan. 6 A telegram..states that the body of Fowler is unrecovered.

**3.** Not having recovered (*from* something).

1737 PARNELL *Poems* 94 Lychenor following with a downward Blow, Reach'd in the Lake his unrecover'd Foe. 1860 FROUDE *Hist. Eng.* VI. 235 With a stomach unrecovered from the sea..he sate down..to a public English supper. 1880 EMMA MARSHALL *Troubl. Times* IV. 288 Being yet on my bed, unrecovered of that fore-mentioned illness.

† **Unreco·vered,** *ppl. a.*² *Obs.* [UN-¹ 8.] Not covered up, obvious. 1577 tr. *Bullinger's Decades* IV. i. 534/2 The vnfigured and vnrecouered promises..in the Psalmes.

**Unre·creating,** *ppl. a.* (UN-¹ 10.) *a* 1861 T. WINTHROP *Life in Open Air* xii. (1863) 90 A feeble, restless, unrecreating slumber. **Unrecrui·table,** *a.* (UN-¹ 7 b. Cf. UNRECRUITIBLE *a.*) [1775 ASH.] 1884 *Imp. Dict.* IV. 514/2 Unrecruitable health, strength, &c.

**Unrecrui·ted,** *ppl. a.* (UN-¹ 8.)

1649 J. ARNWAY *Tablet* 33 To avoide the next storme which His unrecruited Armie might not encounter. *a* 1661 FULLER *Worthies, Cheshire* I. (1662) 187 Had the Royalists pursued this Single Enemy, (as yet unrecruited with additional strength,) they had finally worsted him. 1712 BLACKMORE *Creation* V. 240 By unrecruited waste..His glorious stock long since had been consum'd. 1859 *Macm. Mag.* IV. 47 Lest the ranks of the ministry should be unrecruited by candidates from this first class of intelligence. 1891 E. KINGLAKE *Australians at Home* 107 The ranks of larrikins do not go unrecruited from among the sons of the more respectable poor.

† **Unrecrui·tible,** *a.* *Obs.* [UN-¹ 7.] Incapable of getting recruits. 1644 MILTON *Educ.* 7 Their empty and unrecrutible [*ed.* 1738 unrecruitable] Colonells of twenty men in a company. **Unre·ctifiable,** *a.* (UN-¹ 7 b.) *a* 1678 STANLEY *Hist. Philos.* (1687) IX. 541/2 Such a person must be unlearned, and unrectifiable.

**Unre·ctified,** *ppl. a.* [UN-¹ 8.]

**1.** Not corrected or amended.

1638 RIDER *Horace, Odes* III. xiv, You youths,..Forbeare all languages unrectifi'd. 1662 HIBBERT *Body Divinity* I. 306 Many things were left unrectified, which..they did not see. 1686 JEFFREYS in Howell *State Trials* (1811) XI. 591/2 That one mistake in point of law might not go unrectified. 1837 WORDSW. *Mem. Tour Italy* i. 329 Diligence uninspired, Unrectified, unguided..By godlike insight. 1895 W. H. HUDSON *Spencer's Philos.* 171 The unrectified egotistic emotions of the dweller in cave and wilderness.

**2.** Not purified or refined.

1663 BOYLE *Usef. Exp. Nat. Philos.* II. ii. 36 Unrectified spirit of man's blood. 1694 SALMON *Bate's Dispens.* 144/1 The Oil..stinks so abominably, that it is scarce possible to be used alone, especially unrectified. 1766 *Compl. Farmer* s.v. *Purging*, Unrectified oil of amber. 1840 HOOD *Kilmansegg, Misery* ix, Drops of unrectified spirit distill'd From the limbeck of Pride and Vanity.

**Unrecu·mbent,** *a.* (UN-¹ 7.) 1784 COWPER *Task* V. 29 The cattle..seem half petrified to sleep In unrecumbent sadness. † **Unrecu·perable,** *a.* *Obs.*—¹ [UN-¹ 7 b, 5 b.] = UNRECOVERABLE *a.* 2. 1430-40 LYDG. *Bochas* I. xxv. (1494) f ij/1 For comfortles and vnrecuparable [1558 unrecurable] Are thilke hepyd sorowes. *c* 1535 ELYOT *Let.* in *Gov.* (1883) p. cxvi, To my importable charges and unrecuperable decay of my lyving.

† **Unrecu·rable,** *a.* *Obs.* [UN-¹ 7 b, 5 b.] = UNRECOVERABLE *a.*

*c* 1450 *Cov. Myst.* (Shaks. Soc.) 313 Thus oure lawys dystroyd myth be, And to us alle unrecurabyl! 1465 *Paston Let.* II. 182 A newe mater a newe cost and many smale growe to a gret summe, and summe mater onrecurabyll. 1546 BALE *Eng. Votaries* I. 77 b, An unrecurable dyshonoure it were unto yow. 1597 G. HARVEY *Trimming Nashe* Wks. (Grosart) III. 24 If this remedie helpe not, surely thou art vnrecurable.

† **Unrecu·red,** *ppl. a.* *Obs.* [UN-¹ 8, 5 b.] Not alleviated or remedied. 1430-40 LYDGATE *Bochas* I. x. (1494) d j b/1 My sorowes let se If any sorowe or myscheef vnrecuryd May counturpeyce to that I haue enduryd. † **Unrecu·ring,** *ppl. a.* *Obs.*—¹ [UN-¹ 10.] Not admitting of recovery. 1588 SHAKS. *Tit. A.* III. i. 90, I found her..Seeking to hide herselfe as doth the Deare That hath receiude some vnrecuring wound. **Unre·d,** *a.* *rare*—¹. (UN-¹ 7.) *a* 1300 *Cursor M.* 24471 Þi face es wan as ros vnrede.

† **Unre·de.** *Obs.* [OE. *unrǣd* (f. *un-* UN-¹ 4 a, b + *rǣd* REDE *sb.*¹), = OFris. *unrêd*, WFris. *on-, ûnrie(d)*, MDu. *onract* (Du. *-raad*), OHG. (MHG.) *unrât* (G. *unrath*), ON. *úráð* (MSw. *oradh*, Sw. *oråd*, MDa. *urad*, Da. and Norw. *uraad*).] Lack of counsel or wisdom; evil counsel; folly.

*c* 893 K. ÆLFRED *Oros.* IV. xii. 210 Scipia..self sæde..þæt hit wære se mæsta unræd & se mæsta ȝedwola. *c* 1100 *O. E. Chron.* (MS. D) an. 1048, Ac hit þuhte unræd eallum folce. *c* 1205 LAY. 8011 Wale, wale, vnræd [*c* 1275 onread], mani cniht þu makest dæd. *c* 1250 *Gen. & Ex.* 1906, xii. ȝer or ysaac was dead Iacobes sunes deden un-red. *c* 1275 *Sinners Beware* 303 in *O. E. Misc.* 82 He gredeþ þanne heye, Þe wrecches and þe vnsleye, Þat luuede þe vnredes.

**b.** As the epithet given to King Ethelred II: see UNREADY *a.*²

*c* 1210 *Leges Edw.* in Lambarde *Archaionomia* fol. 138 b, Ældredus unrade,..Edmundus yrenside. ?*c* 1275 *Livere de Reis de Engletere* (Rolls) 96 Cesti Eilred aucone genz apelent Eilred Unred; e assez propement.

**Unrede,** variant of UNRIDE *a.*

**Unredee·mable,** *a.* (UN-¹ 7 b, 5 b.)

1584 *Reg. Privy Council Scot.* III. 672 Heretabill tennendreis unredimabill. 1593 *Sidney's Arcadia* III. (1598) 363 Zelmanes graue [shall] become her mariage bed,..before I will leaue a marke in my selfe of an vnredeemeable trespasse. 1611 COTGR., *Irrachetable*, vnredeemable; not to bee bought ..at any price. 1813 L. HUNT in *Examiner* 11 Jan. 17/2 Men, who..would have left us, unredeemed and unredeemable, the habitual slaves of every species of despotism. 1856 RUSKIN *Mod. Paint.* III. IV. xv. § 9 This absence of colour from rocks..was in their eyes an unredeemable defect.

**Unredee·med,** *ppl. a.* [UN-¹ 8.]

†**1.** Unretrieved, unremedied. *Obs.*—¹

1526 *Pilgr. Perf.* (1531) 264 b, That no circumstance sholde be lefte vnredemed that myght let thy saluacyon.

**2.** Not spiritually redeemed; unsaved.

1548 GESTE *Pr. Masse* I viij b, Ther shuld be made..prayer for the dead to..release them wyth al (as otherwyse vnredemed and payned). 1662 JER. TAYLOR *Three Serm.* (1663) 82 The state of a carnal, unredeemed, unregenerate person. 1760 LAW *Spir. Prayer* I. 76 Our redemption is this new birth; if this is not done,..we are still unredeemed. 1850 HAWTHORNE *Scarlet L.* xviii, Breathing the wild, free atmosphere of an unredeemed, unchristianized, lawless region. *absol.* 1827 POLLOK *Course T.* VIII. 796 He stood With eye, of all the unredeemed, most sad.

**3.** Not recovered, ransomed, or released, by purchase or otherwise. (In quot. 1896 = IRREDEEMED.)

1554 [see UNRANSOMED]. 1572 N. ROSCARROCKE *Prelim. Verses* in Bossewell *Armorie*, Caparisons ther fixed hang, ..With armors fully furnished, and gauntlets vnredeemd. 1648 HEXHAM II, *Ongelost*, Vnredeemed, or Vnreleased. 1845 MCCULLOCH *Taxation* I. i. 59 *note*, The land-tax redeemed amounts to 737,285*l.* a-year, and the unredeemed to 1,069,904*l.* a-year. 1856 KINGSLEY *Misc.* (1859) II. 3 [Lands] yet unredeemed from the wild beast and the wild hunter. 1896 *Daily News* 16 Oct. 5/3 The most elaborate [wreath] being sent by the other 'unredeemed' Italian city of Trieste.

**b.** *spec.* Not recovered from pawn.

1859 SALA *Tw. round Clock* (1861) 180 The articles sold.. are all pawnbrokers' pledges unredeemed. 1881 E. F. POYNTER *Among the Hills* II. 30 Teapot and candlesticks both had..been pledged and unredeemed.

**4.** Not remedied or relieved (*by* some good quality or feature); unmitigated; absolutely bad.

1805 W. ROSCOE *Leo X*, II. 22 A man so totally unredeemed by a single virtue. 1843 CARLYLE *Past & Pr.* III. xii, The unredeemed ugliness is that of a slothful People. 1862 'SHIRLEY' (J. Skelton) *Nugæ Crit.* vi. 320 The villain of the piece, who is..an unredeemed and impossible blackguard. 1896 H. G. WELLS *Wheels of Chance* viii, He was not an unredeemed rough taking advantage of a mistake.

**5.** Not performed or realized.

1812 L. HUNT in *Examiner* 7 Dec. 770/2 Your promise has remained unredeemed. 1862 GOULBURN *Pers. Relig.* II. ix, The great gulf of unredeemed possibilities.

Hence **Unredee·medly** *adv.*

1885 *Athenæum* 28 Feb. 276/3 If she had..one touch of refinement,..instead of being unredeemedly vulgar.

† **Unre·dely,** *adv.* *Obs.*—¹ [UN-¹ 11; cf. next and OE. *unrǣdlīce*, ON. *úráðliga*.] Without restraint.

*c* 1200 *Trin. Coll. Hom.* 173 He bit here unbette sennes.. bigraden hem shameliche, and biten hem unradeliche.

† **Unre·dily,** *adv.* *Obs.* [UN-¹ 11, or f. UNREDY *a.* Cf. prec.] Without counsel or consideration; imprudently, unwisely, inadvisedly.

1398 TREVISA *Barth. De P. R.* XVII. lv. (Tollem. MS.), Auctoures meneþ þat yt is a ful violent herbe, and schall be take redily and warly; for he greueþ and soone sleþ, yf it is unredily [L. *indiscrete*] take to any person. *c* 1445 PECOCK *Donet* 142 Þerfore hem silf in þo mater þei blamenden so rudely and so vnredily. *c* 1449 — *Repr.* II. xx. 274 Al this vndirstonde not y of the Bible aloon, as summen ouer vnredili ..vndirstonden.

† **Unredou·bting,** *ppl. a.* *Obs.* [UN-¹ 10.] Not anticipative; unapprehensive. 1665 J. SERGEANT *Sure Footing* 49 That the Rule of Faith must be apt to justify unreflecting and unredoubting persons..is found most exactly in Tradition. **Unredre·ssable,** *a.* (UN-¹ 7 b, 5 b.) 1607 S. COLLINS *Serm.* (1608) 81 If it had come any later, the euill had beene almost vnredressable. 1665 J. SERGEANT *Sure Footing* 41 That Principle which is the necessary Parent of such ruinous and unredressable disorders. 1716 M. DAVIES *Athen. Brit.* I. Pref. 55 He thereupon grew unredressable and irreconcilable with the whole order.

**Unredre·ssed,** *ppl. a.* (UN-¹ 8, 8 c.)

1563 *Reg. Privy Council Scot.* I. 244 All attemptatis committit upoun the subjectis of Scotland and unredressit for. 1590 SPENSER *F. Q.* IV. viii. 41 That vnto death had doen him vnredrest, Had not the noble Prince his readie stroke represt. 1617 CAMPION *Third Bk. of Ayres* xvii. 11 So may I dye vnredrest, Ere my long loue be possest. 1639 FULLER *Holy War* II. xxv. 76 Wearied with delayes, [he] returned back with his grievances unredressed. 1721 AMHERST *Terræ Fil.* No. 6 (1726) 30 The king's friends remain still unredress'd, and the king's honour unrepair'd to this day. 1806 *Ann. Rev.* IV. 886 An important public paper..which makes many allegations of grievance, still true, and still unredressed. 1877 MRS. OLIPHANT *Makers Flor.* ix. 230 Wickedness unwarned and wrong unredressed.

**Unredu·ceable,** *a.* (UN-¹ 7 b.) 1851 RUSKIN *Stones Ven.* I. p. x, I determined to separate the text and the unreduceable plates.

**Unredu·ced,** *ppl. a.* [UN-¹ 8.]

† **1.** *Sc.* Not annulled or repealed. *Obs.*

1572-3 *Reg. Privy Council Scot.* II. 185 The saidis first charter and confirmatioun following thairupoun standing unreducit. 1606 [see UNQUARRELLED]. *a* 1639 SPOTTISWOOD *Hist. Ch. Scot.* VI. (1655) 307 The sentence of forfeiture.. stood unreduced.

**2.** Unsubdued; not taken by force.

1689 *Apol. Fail. Walker's Acc.* 20 Whether some Men are not satisfy'd..Ireland be entirely lost,..and remain unreduc'd for some years, rather than Dissenters be employ'd in retrieving it. 1884 *Leeds Merc.* (Weekly Suppl.) 15 Nov. 6/2 Stirling Castle, the chief place of strength.., still remained unreduced.

**3.** *Med.* Not restored to a normal state.

1749 T. GATAKER *Le Dran's Operat. Surg.* 101 When an intestine is gangrened and remains unreduced. 1782 MONRO *Anat.* 39 The annihilation..of the head of a bone.., after an unreduced fracture. 1837 QUAIN *Elem. Anat.* (ed. 4) 57 Those cases of unreduced dislocations where the tendons slide over bones. 1857 T. WATSON *Lect. Physic* (ed. 4) I. 35 The dislocation remaining unreduced.

**4.** Not dissolved or comminuted.

1782 *Phil. Trans.* LXXIII. 63 Dr. Priestley having..dissolved mercury in the nitrous acid,..constantly found a considerable proportion of it unreduced. 1815 J. SMITH *Panorama Sci. & Art* II. 609 Those [lands] which contain a large proportion of unreduced vegetable matter. 1880 J. DUNBAR *Pract. Papermaker* 24 The rags must..be..drawn out into fibre without having the smallest particle of rag unreduced to half-stuff.

**5.** Not brought down to simple terms; not applied *to* some use.

1798 HUTTON *Course Math.* I. 251 The rule may be applied at once to an unreduced equation. 1827 POLLOK *Course T.* VIII. 213 The bigot theologian, in minute Distinctions skilled, and doctrines unreduced To practice.

**6.** Unlessened, undiminished.

1830 BENTHAM *Offic. Apt. Maximized, Further Extr. Const. Code* 15 The emptional mode; according to which, mention is made of the greatest sum he will give for it, if unreduced. 1885 in *Longm. Mag.* Mar. (1900) 434 To enable them to maintain their existence, with unreduced vitality, against the severities of the climate.

**Unredu·cible,** *a.* [UN-¹ 7, 5 b.] Irreducible.

1643 MILTON *Divorce* 44 By Laws commanding over the unreducible antipathies of nature. 1736 *Phil. Trans.* XXXIX. 333 This Rupture was..fixed and unreducible. 1768 *Woman of Honor* II. 159 Those have laughed at it in theory on judging it unreducible to practice. 1858 H. BUSHNELL *Nat. & Supernat.* xii. (1862) 276 There is nothing eccentric that..will not fall into the general aim of the plan..; no fantastic matter that is unreducible. 1861 SIR W. FAIRBAIRN *Iron* 14 An invention..to smelt otherwise useless and unreducible ores.

Hence **Unredu·cibleness.**

1694 SOUTH *Serm.* (1698) III. 271 Their Strangeness and Unreducibleness to the common Methods and observations of Nature.

† **Unredu·ct,** *ppl. a.* *Obs.*—¹ [UN-¹ 8 b.] Unreduced. 1608 MIDDLETON *Fam. Love* III. i, Thought vnreduct to Art, Is but an Embrion in the truest sence.

† **Unre·dy,** *a.* *Obs.* [UN-¹ 7. Cf. UNREADY *a.*²] Not well advised; incautious, rash, foolish.

1387 TREVISA *Higden* (Rolls) II. 91 Eyþer manere symmynge is as vnredy as oþer. 1393 LANGL. *P. Pl.* C. XIII. 216 An vnredy reue þi residue shal spene..in a myntewhile. *c* 1449 PECOCK *Repr.* Prol. 3 Ech such vnrgroundid and vnredy and ouer hasti..blamer.

**Unre,e·dified,** *ppl. a.* (UN-¹ 8.)

1519 in *Somerset. & Dorset. N. & Q.* (1893) III. 244 Every half yere that the said scolehouse shall be unbuylded or unreedefyed. 1534 *Act 26 Hen. VIII*, c. 8 § 1 By reason of whiche burninge..many voide groundes..[are] remayninge now at this daye unreedyfied. 1541 *Act 32 Hen. VIII*, c. 19 § 1 Houses of habitation..whiche nowe are fallen downe decayed and at this tyme remayne unreedified.

**Unree·l,** *v.* [UN-² 3.]

**1.** *trans.* To unwind from a reel or skein.

Chiefly *fig.* Quot. 1605 is echoed by several later writers, as in quot. 1652.

1567 GOLDING *Ovid's Met.* X. 122, I Beseech yee of Eurydicee vnreele the destinye. 1598 FLORIO, *Sgominare*,..to vnreele yarne. 1605 SYLVESTER *Du Bartas* II. iii. III. *Law* 1377 Un-winde the bottom of old Times again, Of Ages past un-reel the snarled skain. 1606 J. RAYNOLDS *Dolarney's Prim.* (1880) 77 Ye fates vnreele my lou's sad destinie. 1652 BENLOWES *Theoph.* XII. lxxxvi, Unwinde Times ball again, Unreel through ages its snarl'd skain. 1889 *Engineer* 15 Nov. 413 A measured mile course was laid off by unreeling from an anchored stake buoy one mile of fine wire.

**2.** *intr.* To become unwound.

1886 *Tribune Bk. Sports* 163 (Cent.), The line will unreel faster than it is needed. 1899 *Westm. Gaz.* 13 Jan. 2/1 They shall mark the Empire's line unreel From Cairo to the Cape.

**Unree·lable,** *a.* (UN-¹ 7 b.)

1611 COTGR., *Indevidable*, vnwindable, vnreelable. 1863 *All Year Round* 11 July 467/2 That the moth, in escaping from the cocoon,..cuts it, and renders it unreelable. **1887** *Encycl. Brit.* XXII. 62/2 Unreelable cocoons, *i.e.*, those which are pierced, torn, or cut.

**Unreeˑve,** *v.* [UN-[2] 3.] *trans.* To withdraw (a rope, etc.) from being reeved.

**1600** in Hakluyt *Voy.* III. 847 Wee vnriued our sheates, tackes, halliers, and other ropes. *c* **1625** *Nomencl. Navalis* (Harl. MS.) s.v. *Reeve*, When wee would haue that Roape pulled out of the Block, &c. wee say vnreeue that Roape, or the Brases, Lifts, Sheats, &c.are vnreeued. **1692** *Capt. Smith's Seaman's Gram.* I. 81 To pull a Rope out of a Block is called unreeving the Rope. **1730** CAPT. W. WRIGLESWORTH *MS. Log-bk. of the 'Lyell'* 1 Aug., Yesterday afternoon unreeved the runing Rigging. **1745** P. THOMAS *Jrnl. Anson's Voy.* 148 We unreev'd [*sc.* the rope]..And reev'd a new one. **1804** *Naval Chron.* XII. 480 The chain-pumps were unrove, and leathered afresh. **1840** R. H. DANA *Bef. Mast* v, We..sent down the royal yards, and unrove the gear. **1883** *Man. Seamanship for Boys* 59 Jib or flying-jib stays can be unrove,..and then rove through the lacing.

*refl.* **1847** KIPPING *Sailmaking* 49 By the loosening of which they unreeve themselves.

**b.** *fig.* (See quots.)

**1840** R. H. DANA *Bef. Mast* xxix, Cockroaches, fleas and other vermin..must have unrove their life-lines before the hatches were opened. **1867** SMYTH *Sailor's Word-bk.* 707 *Unrove his life-line*, departed this life.

Hence **Unreeˑved** *ppl. a.*[1], **Unreeˑving** *vbl. sb.*

**1730** CAPT. W. WRIGGLESWORTH *MS. Log-bk. of the 'Lyell'* 14 Aug., All our unreev'd Rigging is a shore. [**1775** ASH, *Unreeving*.] **1892** KIPLING *Life's Handicap* 182 The reeving and unreeving of the bed-tapes.

**Unreeˑved,** *ppl. a.*[2] (UN-[1] 8.) **1793** SMEATON *Edystone L.* Expl. Plate 18 The greater sheaves, before left unreeved.

†**Unrefeˑllable,** *a.* (UN-[1] 7 b.) **1593** BILSON *Govt. Christ's Ch.* 258 Which to all..is an argument vnrefellable. **1622** F. MARKHAM *Bk. War* III. ix. 116 Doubtlesse I could hold.. almost an unrefellable disputation therein. **Unrefeˑrring,** *ppl. a.* (UN-[1] 10.) **1655** FULLER *Ch. Hist.* III. ix. § 5 He.. began the innocent Order of the Garter, unreferring to any of his former atchievements. **1824** MISS L. M. HAWKINS *Mem.*, etc. I. 207 There is about them..so unreferring a recoil into themselves, that [etc.]. **Unrefiˑne,** *v.* (UN-[2] 3.) **1792** W. ROBERTS *Looker-on* No. 27 (1794) I. 392 How I wish you could a little unrefine yourself. **1869** H. BUSHNELL *Wom. S.* v. 101 Where away goes the refinement of the polls, when the polls have unrefined the refiner?

**Unrefiˑned,** *ppl. a.* [UN-[1] 8.]

**1.** Not refined in manners, feelings, or speech.

**1595** W. CLERKE *Polimanteia*, etc. R iij, With Chausers praise, with Lydgate,..and suchlike, whose vnrefined tongues ..wrote simplie and purelie as the times weare. **1704** SWIFT *T. Tub.* ix, The Vulgar dictates of unrefined Reason. **1756** BURKE *Vind. Nat. Soc.* Wks. I. 61 In these early and unrefined ages. **1807** G. CHALMERS *Caledonia* I. II. vi. 309 In this unrefined state, the Scoto-Irish long continued. **1861** WHYTE MELVILLE *Market Harb.* 60 A confirmed bachelor, ..somewhat rough and unpolished and unrefined.

**2.** Not freed from gross or inferior matter.

*c* **1610** *Rates of Marchandizes* F 1 b, Camphire refined the pound. Camphire vnrefined. **1611** COTGR., *Borras Pierreux*, vnrefined Borax, as it comes out of the rocke, or mine. **1659** W. CHAMBERLAYNE *Pharon.* I. v. 65 Like gold yet unrefined. **1703** DAMPIER *Voy.* III. 55 Which makes it whiter and finer than our Muscovada, as we call our unrefin'd Sugar. **1791** NEWTE *Tour Eng. & Scot.* 108 Rocksalt in the raw and unrefined state. **1868** G. DUFF *Pol. Surv.* 190 Brazil sends us..raw cotton and unrefined sugar. **1900** *Jrnl. Soc. Dyers* xvi. 10 Unrefined natural indigo.

Hence **Unrefiˑnedness.**

**1607** WALKINGTON *Opt. Glass* 18 The vnrefinednesse of the spirits doe seeme to affect the soule.

**Unrefiˑnement.** (UN-[1] 12.) **1886** LINSKILL *Haven under Hill* i, Nor did [her speech]..strike you with any jarring sense of unrefinement. **Unrefiˑning,** *ppl. a.* (UN-[1] 10.) **1759** FRANKLIN *Ess.* Wks. 1840 III. 370 A plain, unrefining reader would think that..the issue could not but be happy.

**Unrefleˑcted,** *ppl. a.* [UN-[1] 8, 8 c.]

**1.** Not reflected *on* or *upon*; not thought over.

**1670** CLARENDON *Contempl. Ps.* Tracts (1727) 372, I suffered those papers..to lie neglected and unreflected upon, during ..my too great prosperity. **1720-1** *Lett. fr. Mist's Jrnl.* (1722) II. 71 That..their every Action..should pass uncensured and unreflected on. **1755** CHESTERF. in *World* No. 112. 66 All these unreflected and unexamined opinions of our cobler.

**2.** Not returned by reflection.

[**1775** ASH.] **1810** SCOTT *Lady of L.* v. x, The sun's last glance was glinted back,..The next, all unreflected, shone On bracken green. **1869** TYNDALL in *Fortn. Rev.* 1 Feb. 245 In two directions we should have the solar light reflected; in two others unreflected.

**Unrefleˑcting,** *ppl. a.* (UN-[1] 10.)

**1665** J. SERGEANT *Sure Footing* 49 Unreflecting and unredoubting persons. **1704** J. TRAPP *Abra-Mulé* II. i. 498 Ill Success Renders a Sultan odious in the Eyes Of th' unreflecting Vulgar. **1769** *Junius Lett.* iii. (1788) 44, I place them to the account of an honest, unreflecting indignation. **1848** R. I. WILBERFORCE *Doctr. Incarnation* v. 128 The unreflecting simplicity of that early faith. **1891** MEREDITH *One of our Conq.* xxviii, She did not reflect;..she was unreflecting, feeling only a beyond and hidden.

*absol.* **1748** RICHARDSON *Clarissa* II. 281 The censures of the busy and the unreflecting.

Hence **Unrefleˑctingly** *adv.*, **-ness.**

**1816** COLERIDGE *Lay Serm.* (Bohn) 308 The habitual unreflectingness, which..may be susceptible of more or less palliation. **1866** GEO. ELIOT *F. Holt* v, Quite unreflectingly, he drew forth a pair of spectacles.

**Unrefleˑctive,** *a.* (UN-[1] 7, 5 b.)

Also, in recent use, *unreflectively*.

**1854** FARADAY *Exp. Res.* (1859) 466 The observant, but unreflective infant. **1874** SAYCE *Princ. Compar. Philol.* iii. 95 The unreflective fetichism of the savage.

**Unrefoˑrmable,** *a.* [UN-[1] 7 b, 5 b.]

**1.** Incapable of being reformed or amended.

**1583** GOLDING *Calvin on Deut.* cxvi. 711 They continued stubborne and vnreformable still. *a* **1600** HOOKER *Eccl. Pol.* VII. v. § 8 The proud, tyrannical, and unreformable dealings of her bishops. **1624** BP. HALL *True Peace Maker* Wks. (1625) 542 The vnreformable drunkard. **1648** OWEN *Righteous Zeal Encouraged* (1649) 14 To swim against the streame of an unreformable multitude. **1791** COWPER *Corresp.* (1824) II. 274 Endeavouring to reform the unreformable great. **1848** PHILLIMORE *Introd. Stud. Rom. Law* 319 If I may coin a word to express an evil it is so hard to describe, the unreformable Court of Chancery.

**2.** Incapable of being re-cast or altered.

**1624** BEDELL *Lett.* i. 43 You had that same one onely immoueable and vnreformable rule of faith..recited in your hearing. **1649** *Bounds Publ. Obed.* 47 Unalterable and unreformable as a divine text. **1837** J. H. NEWMAN *Proph. Office Ch.* 267 This rule..is sole, unalterable, unreformable.

**Unreformaˑtion.** (UN-[1] 12.) *a* **1656** BP. HALL *Wks.* (1863) V. 632 Yea, have not too many amongst us added to their unreformation an impudence in sinning?

**Unrefoˑrmed,** *ppl. a.* [UN-[1] 8, 5 b.]

**1.** Of faults, etc.: Not amended or made good.

**1528** CROMWELL in Merriman *Life & Lett.* (1902) I. 318, I trust that no defaulte..is lefte vnrefourmed. **1542** HEN. VIII *Declar.* A iv b, The kyng of Scottis dedes..could not.. be passed ouer vnreformed. **1653** JER. TAYLOR *Serm. for Year* I. xii. 161 Every vicious habit, or unreformed sin. **1679** MOXON *Mech. Exerc.* viii. 145 Upon penalty..for every default Ten Shillings, and Ten Shillings every week it continues unreformed. **1694** S. BETHAL *Providences of God* 94 There being no such Traitors to the Strength of a Land.. as are unreformed Provocations.

**2.** Not reformed or made better; unimproved:

**a.** Of persons, the heart, etc.

**1583** GOLDING *Calvin on Deut.* xxvii. 223 If wee..in the meane while leaue our heartes vnreformed. **1644** HAMMOND *Of Conscience* 44 Never to lye downe..unhumbled unreformed in any such sinne. **1671** MILTON *P. R.* III. 429 Who freed,..Unhumbl'd, unrepentant, unreform'd, Headlong would follow. **1717** DE FOE *Mem. Ch. Scot.* II. 27 The Church formally absolv'd him, and yet secretly believed him to be unreformed. **18..** MOORE (*title*), Musings of an Unreformed Peer. **1872** GEO. ELIOT *Middlem.* lxi, The unreformed provincial mind distrusted London.

**b.** Of practices, institutions, etc.

**1614** *Act 12 Jas. I*, in Bolton *Stat. Irel.* (1621) 425 Your gracious disposition..towards the settling of this unreformed kingdom. **1792** BURKE *Let. to Dundas* Wks. 1812 V. 199 It is better to allow the evil, in order to correct it, than..to leave it under an illegal, and therefore an unreformed existence. **1840** ARNOLD in *Life* (1844) II. 189 If a system goes on long unreformed, it is not then reformed, but destroyed. **1849** MILL *Diss. & Disc.* (1859) II. 352 The majority of even the unreformed House of Commons. **1898** *Westm. Gaz.* 1 Mar. 2/1 Then I would rather that the Church should remain unreformed.

**3.** Not affected by the Reformation.

**1788** BURKE *Sp. agst. W. Hastings* Wks. XIV. 20 [You] have seen in the unreformed countries of Europe churches filled with persons, who take sanctuary in them. **1892** MAYOR *Ep. James* p. xviii, The churches of Western Christendom, reformed and unreformed.

Hence **Unrefoˑrmedness.**

**1607** HIERON *Wks.* I. 248 Denouncing the heauy vengeance of God vpon vnreformednesse. **1655** S. ASHE *Funeral Serm. Gataker* 13 During the time of his impenitency and unreformednesse. **1677** I. MATHER *Preval. Prayer* (1864) 244 That which aggravateth our Unreformedness, is, that in the Time of our Trouble [etc.]. **1888** *Contemp. Rev.* Sept. 345 One who, in that day of its unreformedness, did not regard the constitution of the Royal Academy as absolutely perfect.

**Unrefraˑcted,** *ppl. a.* (UN-[1] 8, 5 b.)

*a* **1676** HALE *Prim. Orig. Man.* (1677) 303 To distribute this Light..which unrefracted might have been too..violent to the other parts of Nature. **1728** CHAMBERS *Cycl.* s.v. *Refraction*, The perpendicular Ray..will pass unrefracted to K. **1796** COLERIDGE *Destiny of Nations* 463 Whether thy Love with unrefracted ray Beam on the Prophet's purged eye. **1862** R. H. PATTERSON *Ess. Hist. & Art* 83 The purity and brilliance of unrefracted light.

**Unrefraˑcting,** *ppl. a.* (UN-[1] 10.) **1827** COLERIDGE *Lit. Rem.* (1839) IV. 408 An unpreoccupied, unrefracting medium. **1863** J. C. MORISON *St. Bernard* III. v. 369 Looking through the pure unrefracting ether as we do at the stars. **Unrefraiˑnable,** *a.* (UN-[1] 7 b.) **1828** E. IRVING *Last Days* 174 A wild, inconstant, unrefrained and unrefrainable disposition. **Unrefraiˑned,** *ppl. a.* (UN-[1] 8.) *c* **1550** ROLLAND *Crt. Venus* I. 825 With cruell mind thair vnrefrenit In this degre [he] Rehersit wordis iniurious. **1593** *Sidney's Arcadia* III. (1598) 354 Delay, the racke of vnrefrain'd desire. **1648** HEXHAM II, s.v. *Ontoomigh*. **1828** [see prec.].

**Unrefreˑshed,** *ppl. a.* (UN-[1] 8.)

**1736** ARBUTHNOT *Rules Diet* 384 Unrefresh'd by Sleep. **1769** FALCONER *Dict. Marine* (1780) s.v. *Water-spout*, A tract of land..unrefreshed by the wind. **1791** COWPER *Odyss.* IV. 955 Unrefresh'd with either food or wine. **1797** COLERIDGE *Remorse* I. ii, I am old and heartless!..Hectic and unrefreshed with rest. **1881** CHR. ROSSETTI *Later Life* 4 So unrefreshed by foregone weariness.

**Unrefreˑshful,** *a.* (UN-[1] 7.) **1819** SCOTT *Leg. Montrose* xvi, The viands..were..unrefreshful to my body. **1858** FARRAR *Eric* 361 Even his sleep seemed unrefreshful when the waking brought no change in his condition.

**Unrefreˑshing,** *ppl. a.* (UN-[1] 10.)

**1814** SCOTT *Wav.* xxxvii, His slumbers were broken and unrefreshing. **1870** MISS BRIDGMAN *R. Lynne* II. v. 115 He fell into a troubled and unrefreshing sleep.

**Unrefreˑshingly,** *adv.* (UN-[1] 11; cf. prec.) **1889** *Scribner's Mag.* Aug. 164/2 It was unrefreshingly hot, and just about slack water after ebbing at all. **Unreˑft,** *ppl. a.* [UN-[1] 8 b.] Undespoiled. **1535** STEWART *Cron. Scot.* (Rolls) I. 291 His dochteris tua..In tutorie to Cesar that he left, Into thair rycht for to kepe thame vnreft. **Unrefuˑlgent,** *a.* (UN-[1] 7.) **1879** STEVENSON *Edinburgh* 32 The unrefulgent sun going down. **Unrefuˑnding,** *ppl. a.* (UN-[1] 10.) [**1727** BOYER *Dict. Royal* II, Unrefunding, *qui ne rend jamais*.] **1744** YOUNG *Nt. Th.* VII. 831 Whose horrid universal shall descend..On that enormous, unrefunding tomb, How just this verse!

**Unrefuˑsable,** *a.* (UN-[1] 7 b, 5 b.)

**1691** SEWEL, *Onontzeggelyk*, Vnrefusable, that which will take no denial. **1704** NORRIS *Ideal World* II. i. 37 Upon this fair and unrefusable supposition. **1843** CARLYLE *Past & Pr.* III. xii, The most unrefusable demand! **1865** MRS. WHITNEY *Gayworthys* xxvi, Skylie..said this with her most unrefusable expression.

Hence **Unrefuˑsably** *adv.*

**1710** NORRIS *Chr. Prud.* iii. 131 Happiness abstractly considered, which is necessarily and unrefusably lovely.

**Unrefuˑsed,** *ppl. a.* (UN-[1] 8.) **1548** in *Compl. Scotl.* (1872) 242 Because nothyng should be left..of your part vnrefused. **1648** HEXHAM II, s.v. *Ongeweygert*.

**Unrefuˑsing,** *ppl. a.* (UN-[1] 10.)

*a* **1586** SIDNEY *Arcadia* III. x, Thinking..that beauty, carefully set forth, wold soone prove a signe of an unrefusing harborough. **1621** LADY M. WROTH *Urania* 374 What power had those instruments sweete speach, more sweete and vnrefusing conuersation ouer my heart? **1728** THOMSON *Spring* 38 There, unrefusing to the harness'd yoke They lend their Shoulder.

**Unrefuˑtable,** *a.* Now *rare.* (UN-[1] 7 b, 5 b.)

**1594** NASHE *Christ's T.* (ed. 2) To Rdr., Henceforth..for an vnrefutable principle I will hold it. **1629** MASSINGER *Picture* IV. ii, As I must grant, It being vnrefutable in reason. **1859** HERSCHEL *Pop. Lect. Sci.* iii. § 54 (1866) 140 That positive and unrefutable demonstration.

**Unrefuˑted,** *ppl. a.* (UN-[1] 8.)

**1589** GREENE *Menaphon* (Arb.) 38 In nature this is an vnrefuted principle, that [etc.]. **1846** LEWES *Hist. Philos.* IV. 85 So long must Berkeley remain unrefuted by any theory of perception. **1875** JOWETT *Plato* (ed. 2) III. 507 This argument of ours remains unrefuted.

**Unregaiˑnable,** *a.* (UN-[1] 7 b.) **1649** J. H. *Motion to Parl. Adv. Learn.* 22 The time is unregainable. **1866** CARLYLE *Remin.* (1881) I. 281 The wild struggles..towards the unattainable, the unregainable.

**Unreˑgal,** *a.* (UN-[1] 7.)

**1611** SPEED *Hist. Gt. Brit.* IX. vi. 35 King Henry..seeing no issue of his long disquietnesse, and vnregall vsages. **1846** WORCESTER (citing *Ed. Rev.*). **1880** F. G. LEE *Ch. under Q. Eliz.* II. 240 With unregal meanness, she sent Lord Hunsdon..to 'draw him out' as regards religion. **1894** *Persian Pict.* 114 We stopped before an unregal gateway.

**Unregaˑrd,** *sb.* (UN-[1] 12.) *a* **1656** BP. HALL *Rem. Wks.* (1660) 256 When he saw a woman bowing her self forward too low in her devotion, [the cynic] could chide her for her unregard to those deities, which beheld her on all sides. **1876** *Gd. Words* 687 Worth yet shall..Outlive the death of unregard.

†**Unregaˑrd,** *v. Obs.* [UN-[2] 3.] *trans.* To disregard.

**1545** RAYNALD *Byrth Mankynde* Prol. C iv, Sholde men.. denye or vnregard the blessyd sacrament? **1600** ROWLANDS *Lett. Humours Blood* 4 Carelesse of wronges, and vnregarding right. **1627** BP. HALL *Passion Serm.* 431 Not onely [hast thou]..smitten me, vnregarded me, but, as it were, forgotten—yea, forsaken—me.

†**Unregaˑrdable,** *a. Obs.* [UN-[1] 7 b.] Not deserving regard or consideration. **1614** RALEIGH *Hist. World* VIII. vi. 618 Neither is it vnregardable, that the Tyrants..were not all of them good men of warre. **1641** BP. HALL *Def. Humble Remonstr.* 118 Away then with those your unproving illustrations, and unregardable testimonies. **Unregaˑrdant,** *a.* (UN-[1] 7.) **1814** SOUTHEY *Roderick* x. 69 With fix'd eyes intent Yet unregardant of the countenance Whereon they dwelt.

**Unregaˑrded,** *ppl. a.* (UN-[1] 8.)

**1561** T. NORTON *Calvin's Inst.* I. Pref., Beyng in dede but one man alone, and vnregarded, but out of whoes mouthe came truthe. **1614** RALEIGH *Hist. World* III. (title-p.), When Israel was..an unregarded Nation. **1670** R. COKE *Disc. Trade* 62 A poor and unregarded Village. **1726** POPE *Odyss.* XVII. 612 Time steals away with unregarded wing. **1767** WILKES *Corr.* (1805) III. 100 That so many other publications..., full of the most deadly venom, should pass totally unregarded. **1813** BYRON *Corsair* II. v, Each bears a prize of unregarded charms. **1883** RUSKIN *Fors Clav.* xc. 172 In the dormitory..on an unregarded shutter.. she cuts her notch.

**b.** Const. *by* or †*of*.

**1571** GOLDING *Calvin on Ps.* xli. 18 We surmise him to be unregarded of God. **1612** W. PARKES *Curtaine-Dr.* (1876) 17 The lawes of nature,..vassayled, obliterate and vnregarded by him. **1728** R. MORRIS *Ess. Anc. Archit.* 13 Architecture is so unregarded by our modern Builders. **1805** WORDSW. *Prelude* XIII. 278 God..loveth us, When we are unregarded by the world. **1884** tr. *Lotze's Metaph.* 464 Many external stimuli, therefore, are unregarded by us.

Hence **Unregaˑrdedly** *adv.*

**1685** BOYLE *Salubr. Air* 12 Bodies..wont to be unregardedly compris'd under the confus'd name of Earths.

**Unregaˑrdful,** *a.* (UN-[1] 7.)

**1598** FLORIO, *Inconsiderato*, rash, vnregardfull, inconsiderate. **1812** J. HENRY *Camp. agst. Quebec* 183 Unregardful of the dogs, we awaited the management of the flight. **1853** RUSKIN *Stones Ven.* II. vi. 184 This is design unregardful of facts. **1879** FARRAR *St. Paul* I. 338 The sea which four times wrecked him with its unregardful storms.

**Unregaˑrding,** *ppl. a.* (UN-[1] 10.)

*c* **1585** T. PROCTOR *Triumph of Truth* (1866) 5 Who vnregarding of him self, forgets his Parents cares. **1593** *Sidney's Arcadia* III. (1922) II. 52 The debate betwixt Basilius shinnes and the unregarding fourmes. **1660** JER. TAYLOR *Ductor* III. v. rule 8 § 29 Their not complying..is only then a sin when it is done with unregarding circumstances. **1720** POPE *Iliad* XX. 202 The lion,..viewing first his foes with scornful eyes,..Stalks careless on, with unregarding pride. **1732** J. WHALEY *Poems* 27 Unregarding of his useful Pains, The surly Carter wounds his [*sc.* a horse's] stretching Veins. **1851** KINGSLEY *Yeast* xvii, His employer ..walked before him silent and unregarding.

**Unregeˑneracy.** (UN-[1] 12, 5 b; cf. next.)

**1622** W. WHATELY *Gods Husb.* II. 118 A man in his vtter vnregeneracy is dead in sinne. **1688** J. BUNYAN *Jerus. Sinner Saved* (1886) 49 Paul was the most outrageous of all the apostles, in the time of his unregeneracy. **1818** G. S.

Faber *Horæ Mosaicæ* II. 293 He derives no benefit from the external sign, remaining still..in a state of unregeneracy. **1870** *Athenæum* 19 Nov. 652 Ned went to Astley's in the blackest state of unregeneracy.

**Unrege·nerate,** *a.* and *sb.* (Un-[1] 7, 12, and 5 b.)

**1612** T. Taylor *Comm. Titus* i. 12 What properties haue vnregenerate men, which are not more beseeming..beasts than men? **1651** Baxter *Inf. Bapt.* 225 No man hath any sign given him..by which to judge of the unregenerate Elect. *a* **1740** Waterland *Inquiry Communion* Wks. 1823 IX. 483 In or by their natural, unregenerate state. **1795** Coleridge *Eolian Harp* 55 These shapings of the unregenerate mind. **1839** Hallam *Hist. Lit.* III. ii. § 31 The human virtues..of unregenerate men. **1876** Canon Mozley *Univ. Serm.* xiii. (1877) 237 Instances of what unregenerate human nature can attain to.

*absol.* **1655** Jer. Taylor *Unum Necess.* vii. § 2. 460 As in the unregenerate there might be some good.

*fig.* **1876** Geo. Eliot *Dan. Der.* xxxvii, I was unregenerate then [in matters of art].

**b.** *sb.* An unregenerate person.

*c* **1625** Bp. Hall *St. Paul's Combat* Wks. 1634 II. 441 Those carelesse unregenerates. **1627** — *Salomon's Song Paraphr.* ii. 251 All the assemblies of aliens and unregenerates.

**Unrege·nerate,** *v.* (Un-[2] 3.) **1861** Ld. Lytton & Fane *Tannhäuser* 9 Suffered for a space..To range the wide world, and assay their powers To unregenerate redeem'd mankind.

**Unrege·nerated,** *ppl. a.* (Un-[1] 8.)

**1579** W. Wilkinson *Confut. Fam. Love* B iij b, They are vnilluminated, vnregenerated. *a* **1791** V. Knox *Serm.* (1792) iii. 49 Man in his corrupt and unregenerated state. **1826** Scott *Woodst.* xiv, I..have fought prizes when I was unregenerated.

Hence **Unrege·neratedness.**

**1664** H. More *Myst. Iniq.* Pref. 5 In a state of Unregeneratedness, and utterly devoid of the Life of God.

**Unrege·nerating,** *ppl. a.* (Un-[1] 10.) **1657** Reeve *God's Plea* 145 Were ever so many Pulpits despised? were there ever so many unregenerating sermons?

**Unregenera·tion.** (Un-[1] 12, 5 b.)

**1625** Pemble *Justification* v. ii. 176 All men..which are in state of infidelity and vnregeneration. **1662** Hibbert *Body Divinity* I. 119 Conforming us to the nature of the devil; pleading mans unregeneration. *a* **1812** H. Martyn *20 Serm.* (1822) 224 The wickedness and unregeneration of his heart. **1870** Miss Bridgman *R. Lynne* II. xiii. 270 Cheerfulness of disposition she considered a..sign of unregeneration.

**Unre·gimented,** *ppl. a.* (Un-[1] 8.)

**1684** *List Military* Title-page, A general and compleat List Military..(Excepting the Un-Regimented Companies). *a* **1725** Ld. Whitworth *Acc. Russia* (1758) 102 Unregimented Soldiers and free companies in the lesser garrisons of Ingria. **1850** Carlyle *Latter-d. Pamphl.* i. 45 These outcast soldiers of his, unregimented roving banditti.

**Unre·gistered,** *ppl. a.* [Un-[1] 8.]

**1.** Not entered in a register; unrecorded.

**1604** E. G[rimstone] *D'Acosta's Hist. Indies* iv. iv. 216 That which came for Merchants and private men being registred, and much that came vnregistred. **1606** Shaks. *Ant. & Cl.* III. xiii. 119 Besides what hotter houres Vnregistred in vulgar Fame, you haue Luxuriously pickt out. **1679** C. Nesse *Antichrist* 235 By those few [witnesses] we may conjecture many more..lay hid unregistred. **1716** *Lond. Gaz.* No. 5467/1 The unregistered [part of the effects] is valued at half as much more. **1826** Kirby & Sp. *Entomol.* IV. 440 Its animal productions shall no longer remain unregistered and undescribed. **1871** *Leisure Hour* 9 Sept. 576/1 Unregistered letters and book packets.

**2.** Not made to register or correspond.

**1816** Singer *Hist. Cards* 133 It is printed upon vellum.., and the right margin is quite as irregular or unregistered as in the Dutch Speculum.

**Unregre·tful,** *a.* (Un-[1] 7.) **1873** T. W. Higginson *Oldport Days* vii. 196 [She] grew up into a well-behaved mediocrity, unregretful of the show-tent. **Unregre·tfully,** *adv.* (Un-[1] 11.) **1862** 'Shirley' (J. Skelton) *Nugæ Crit.* xi. 453, I remember, not unregretfully, the simple rustic procession. **Unregre·tfulness.** (Un-[1] 12.) **1876** L. Tollemache in *Fortn. Rev.* Jan. 117 To this unregretfulness..they owed much of [their] lighthearted joyousness. **Unregre·ttable,** *a.* (Un-[1] 7 b.) **1768** *Woman of Honor* II. 120 A very unregrettable sacrifice of..an object of vanity.

**Unregre·tted,** *ppl. a.* (Un-[1] 8.)

**1676** Row *Contin. Blair's Autobiog.* xii. (1848) 453 He died unregretted by good men. **1781** Cowper *Retirem.* 167 A few.., unregretted, are soon snatch'd away From scenes of sorrow. **1782** V. Knox *Ess.* clxviii, Those [works] of the frothy declaimer are daily dropping unregretted into the gulph of oblivion. **1843** Ruskin *Mod. Paint.* I. II. III. i. § 3 All has passed unregretted as unseen. **1891** Meredith *One of our Conq.* xxv, Since she had taken a step..unregretted, if fatal.

**Unregre·tting,** *ppl. a.* (Un-[1] 10.) **1800** P. L. Courtier *Pleas. Solitude* III. 39 We,..unregretting, other joys resign.

**Unre·gular,** *a.* Chiefly *dial.* (Un-[1] 7, 5 b.)

**1609** Douland *Ornithoparcus' Microl.* 29 It hath his Finall regular place in *Dsolre*, or his vnregular in *alamire*. **1828**- in dialect glossaries, etc. **1884** 'Mark Twain' *Huck. Finn* xxviii, It's so kind of strange and unregular, I never see nothing like it.

**Unre·gulated,** *ppl. a.* (Un-[1] 8, 5 b.)

**1721** Amherst *Terræ Fil.* No. 1 (1726) 5 The universities, ..in their present unregulated state. **1791** Boswell *Johnson* an. 1744 ¶ 1 He undoubtedly had a warm and vigorous, though unregulated mind. **1808** Scott in *Lockhart* I. i. 35 These studies were totally unregulated. **1871** B. Taylor *Faust* (1875) I. Notes 282 An indolent unregulated habit of life.

**Unrehea·rsable,** *a.* (Un-[1] 7 b.) **1513** Douglas *Æneis* XI. vi. 72 Of ws hail the remanis Bene punyst sore with onrehersabill panis.

**Unrehea·rsed,** *ppl. a.* [Un-[1] 8.]

**1.** Not related or mentioned; untold.

**1472** *Cov. Leet Bk.* 378 All thees moo, whoos names be vndrewreton besyde many moo vnrehersyd. **1562** T. Wilson *Rhet.* (ed. 2) 76 b, The holie mother Church willeth me to leaue nothing vnrehearsed. **1613** Shirley *Trav. Persia* 92 A discourse proued true..by many examples which he would leaue unrehearsed. **1629** Sir W. Mure *True Crucifixe* 670 Expos'd to paine, to horrors vnrehearsed. *a* **1800** Cowper *Odyss.* (ed. 2) xiv. 236, I could exhaust..the circling year Complete, my woes rehearsing, and at last Leave unrehearsed large portion of the toil. **1827** Pollok *Course T.* x. 32 New scenes of bliss..unrehearsed by mortal tongue.

**2.** Not previously practised.

**1845** E. Holmes *Mozart* 289 The unrehearsed overture was then commenced. **1875** C. L. Kenney *Mem. Balfe* 44 An alarm of fire through some unrehearsed effect in the incantation scene.

†**Unrei·gn,** *v. Obs.*[−1] [Un-[1] 14.] *intr.* To fail to reign. **1434** Misyn *Mending Life* 122 As qwo say: syn in vs may vnrene [L. *non regnare*], bot it may not vnbe.

**Unrei·n,** *v.* (Un-[2] 4 b.)

**1603** Daniel *Paneg. Congrat.* lix, An imperiall lust, that being vnrain'd, Will hardly be resisted any where. **1694** Addison *Eng. Poets* Wks. 1721 I. 41 How negligently graceful he unreins His verse, and writes in loose familiar strains! **1702** De Foe *Reform. Manners* I. 15 Tell us why he..Unreins no Vengeance, lets no Thunders fly, When Villains prosper. **1707** Tickell *Oxford* 273 Codrington and Steele, their verse unrein, And form an easy, unaffected strain. **1851** *Bentley's Misc.* Aug. 147 If a soldier's life..can atone for the sad consequences of unreining an ungovernable temper.

**Unrei·ned,** *ppl. a.* (Un-[1] 8.)

**1609** Daniel *Civ. Wars* vi. vi, Whil'st this wilde vnrained multitude..Ransacke the Cittie. **1628** Feltham *Resolves* II. viii. 18 When the Minde is madded with vn-reined passions. **1667** Milton *P. L.* vii. 17 Least from this flying Steed unrein'd,..Dismounted, on th' Aleian Field I fall. **1751** J. Brown *Shaftesb. Charac.* 312 The delirious flights of an unreined imagination. **1825** Longf. *Burial of Minnisink* vii, Leading the war-horse of their chief..Uncurbed, unreined, and riderless. **1850** Blackie *Æschylus* II. 10 We cannot but condemn the spirit of unreined independence. **1851** C. L. Smith tr. *Tasso* vi. xvii, Unreined By aught of fear, thy message here expound.

**Unreje·cted,** *ppl. a.* (Un-[1] 8.) **1757** Dyer *Fleece* II. 81 There the tender eye May view..the lame, employ'd, And unrejected age. **1778** Chatham in *Ann. Reg., Chron.* App. 247/2 His conversations..are..to my feeling too offensive to be continued, or unrejected. **Unrejoi·ced,** *ppl. a.* (Un-[1] 8.) **1814** Byron *Lara* I. vii, Not unrejoiced to see him once again, Warm was his welcome. **1816** Wordsw. *Morning Gen. Thanksgiving* i, Thou, impartial Sun,..Not unrejoiced I see thee climb the sky.

**Unrejoi·cing,** *ppl. a.* (Un-[1] 10.)

**1726** Thomson *Winter* (ed. 2) 267 In Russia's..Moors, Where Winter keeps his unrejoicing Court. **1745** Warton *Pleas. Mel.* 230 Amid Siberia's unrejoicing wilds. *a* **1814** *Hortensia* II. iii. in *New Brit. Theatre* IV. 161 Within the castle walls, Let not one un-rejoicing soul be found. **1876** Ruskin *Fors Clav.* lxxii. 388 The unrejoicing manner of travel adopted by the..modern tourist.

†**Unre·ke,** *v. Obs.* [Un-[2] 3 + Reke *v.*[3]] *trans.* To uncover, display.

**1412-20** Lydg. *Chron. Troy* I. 2196 Whan þat Loue of manhod wolde speke, Þe wode fire out of his brest to vnreke, ..Cometh Schame anoon, & outterly seith nay. *c* **1421** Hoccleve *Min. Poems* 117/197 Lo, frinde, nowe haue I myne entent vnreke of my longe tale.

†**Unre·ken,** *a. Obs.* [Un-[1] 7.] **a.** Unready, awkward. **b.** Uneasy; unpleasant; rough.

*c* **1250** *Gen. & Ex.* 2817 Louerd, ic am wanmol, vn-reken Of wurdes. *a* **1310** in Wright *Lyric P.* xxxvi. 100 Al unreken is my ro, Loverd Crist, whet shal y say? **13..** *Cursor M.* 24847 (Gött.), Þaim bleu mani vnrekind [*Cott.* brem, *Edinb.* bremli] blast, Þair mast raf.

Hence †**Unre·kenly** *adv. Obs.*

*a* **1300** *Cursor M.* 15786 Wit maces and wit neues smert vn-rekenli on him [þai] ran.

**Unrela·psing,** *ppl. a.* (Un-[1] 10.) **1740** Cheyne *Regimen* 27 To..establish in perpetual and unrelapsing Order and Purity, free and lapsed intelligent Beings. **Unrela·table,** *a.* (Un-[1] 7 b.) **1621** Lady M. Wroth *Urania* 276 The vnrelatable exquisitenesse of his youth.

**Unrela·ted,** *ppl. a.* [Un-[1] 8, 5 b.]

**1.** Not connected by blood; not akin.

*a* **1661** Fuller *Worthies, London* II. (1662) 207 But let others unrelated unto him write his Character. *a* **1677** Barrow *Serm.* (1686) III. 36 'Tis not the example..of a stranger, of one indifferent, or unrelated to us. **1706** De Foe *Jure Div.* x. 219 Of foreign Breed, of unrelated Race,..A spurious Birth of interming'd Blood. *a* **1752** Warburton *Serm.* Wks. 1788 V. 79 They..despised the rest of the sons of Adam, who ..were deemed to be naturally unrelated to them. **1875** Maine *Hist. Inst.* iii. 65 The tribesmen of an alien and unrelated tribe. **1882** Farrar *Early Chr.* II. 218 Seven emperors..for the most part entirely unrelated to one another.

**2.** Not standing in relationship or connexion.

**1668** H. More *Div. Dial.* I. xxxv. 156 If they were so unrelated indeed in the..apprehension of them,..then I confess the Inference might be sound. **1701** Norris *Ideal World* I. ii. 92 For things to be only conditionally related.. is really to be unrelated to, and separated from one another. **1785** Burke *Corr.* (1844) III. 42 Detached and unrelated offences. **1817** R. Jameson *Cuvier's Ess. Theory Earth* (ed. 3) p. vii, Petrifactions are no longer viewed..as things isolated and unrelated to the rocks. **1860** Tyndall *Glac.* I. i. 6 A theory..which..apparently referred a great number of unrelated phenomena to a common cause.

**3.** Not recounted or told.

**1764** *Museum Rust.* IV. 32 Some peculiar circumstance in the soil,..or..some unrelated circumstance in the culture. **1796** Mme. D'Arblay *Camilla* x. xiii, A reciprocal confidence that left nothing untold, not an action unrelated.

Hence **Unrela·tedness.**

**1854** Sylvester *Coll. Math. Papers* (1908) II. 32 The number of singularities (including absolute unrelatedness and entire coincidence within the purview of the term).

**Unrela·ting,** *ppl. a.* (Un-[1] 10.) **1697** Norris *Treat. Sev. Subj.* (1698) 240, I would fain know, whether any of these Misconducts of Life be..more unrelating to our grand Concern [etc.]. **Unrela·tional,** *a.* (Un-[1] 7.) **1865** H. Bushnell *Vicar. Sacr.* III. v, A state unrelational with God. **1869** H. Spencer *Princ. Psychol.* (1872) I. 181 The extremely unrelational states of different orders.

**Unre·lative,** *a.* (Un-[1] 7, 5 b.)

*a* **1751** Bolingbroke *Study Hist.* ii. (1752) I. 41 The events ..appear to us very often..single, and un-relative, if I may use such an expression for want of a better in English. **1757** Chesterf. *Lett.* (1774) II. 371 *A propos*, (an expression which is commonly used to introduce whatever is unrelative to it). **1776** Burney *Hist. Mus.* I. 62 If the mutations were too sudden and unrelative. **1819** Busby *Hist. Music* II. 122 The sudden and unrelative modulation from F to E♭.

**Unre·latively,** *adv.* (Un-[1] 11, 5 b.) *a* **1751** Bolingbroke *Study Hist.* ii. (1752) I. 46 They saw the measures they took singly, and unrelatively, or relatively alone to some immediate object. **Unrela·xable,** *a.* (Un-[1] 7 b.) **1860** Ruskin *Mod. Paint.* V. 36 These pre-Raphaelite laws..are unrelaxed yet, and unrelaxable for ever.

**Unrela·xed,** *ppl. a.* (Un-[1] 8.)

**1508** *Reg. Privy Seal Scot.* I. 258/1 Throw the said Androis being..our souerane lordis rebell and at his horne unrelaxit thairfra. **1569** *Reg. Privy Council Scot.* I. 687 [He was] put to the horne,..quhairat he hes remanit lyke as he dois yit continewallie sensyne unrelaxit. **1589** *Ibid.* IV. 358. **1737** Glover *Leonidas* VIII. 611 The hosts Maintain in strong and unrelax'd array The conflict undecided. **1766** in Hansard *Parl. Debates* (1813) XVI. 286 To maintain, unrelaxed and unenervated, the fundamentals of the constitution. **1810** Southey *Kehama* II. xiii, At the length he raised His brow yet unrelax'd. **1825** Scott *Betrothed* ix, One wide-spread scene of..unrelaxed pursuit. **1862** Lytton *Str. Story* II. 172 Unrelaxed, unmitigable indignation.

**Unrela·xing,** *ppl. a.* (Un-[1] 10.)

**1781** J. Moore *View Soc. It.* xlvi. II. 4 A man of unrelaxing wisdom. **1796** Burke *Letter to Noble Lord* Wks. VIII. 40 To support with unrelaxing vigilance every right,..every franchise, in this my adopted..country. **1801** Southey *Thalaba* x. 233 His unrelaxing brow. **1822** Keble *Serm.* i. (1848) 5 The most blameless and unrelaxing diligence. **1890** 'R. Boldrewood' *Col. Reformer* (1891) 75 The unrelaxing grip of the law.

Hence **Unrela·xingly** *adv.*

[**1847** Webster.] **1858** *Westm. Rev.* Oct. 310 He is unrelaxingly wedded to the conception of the Empire as it was.

**Unrelea·sed,** *ppl. a.* (Un-[1] 8.)

*c* **1400** *Rom. Rose* 2729 In sorwe and thought..Ayee vnrelesed woo to make, Whether..they slepe or wake. **1619** in Foster *Eng. Factories India* (1906) I. 80 The fruicts..you may..perceave by your goods detencion these six months in customehouse, and yett unreleaced. **1679** Oldham *Sat. Jesuits* iii. (1681) 55 Souls in Purgatory unreleast.

**Unrele·ntable,** *a.* [Un-[1] 7 b.] Incapable of relenting or giving way. **1611** Cotgr., *Inflexible*,..vnrelentable, hardhearted. **1716** M. Davies *Athen. Brit.* I. 113 The Popish Clergy..render their respective Countries..Reformation-proof and Unrelentable to any redress. **Unrele·ntance.** (Un-[1] 12.) **1637** Jackson *Serm. Lk.* xiii. 5, 61 This unrelentance presupposeth some other fouler sin then rebellion. **Unrele·nted,** *ppl. a.* [Un-[1] 8.] Unrelaxed. **1676** *Life Father Paul Sarpi* in *Brent's Counc. Trent* 90 This unrelented way of reading and writing..is a kind of intemperance. **1846** Worcester (citing Scott). **1876** *Whitby Gloss.* 206 *Ungeen*,..unthawed or unrelented.

**Unrele·nting,** *ppl. a.* [Un-[1] 10, 5 b.]

**1.** Not softening or yielding; *esp.* not giving way to feelings of kindness or compassion.

(*a*) **1588** Shaks. *Tit. A.* II. iii. 141 Be your hart to them, As vnrelenting flint to drops of raine. **1621** G. Sandys *Ovid's Met.* v. (1626) 93 The blade from vnrelenting stone rebounds. **1749** Smollett *Regicide* IV. ix, Him hath the unrelenting dagger torn From my parental arms. **1870** Bryant *Iliad* v. I. 148 The unrelenting edge Cleft at its root the tongue.

(*b*) **1590** Marlowe *2nd Pt. Tamburl.* v. iii, If the vnrelenting eares Of death and hell be shut against my praiers. **1593** Shaks. *3 Hen. VI*, II. i. 58 The irefull Arme Of vn-relenting Clifford. **1634** Cowley *Elegy R. Clerke* 27 Who hath such hard, such unrelenting Eyes, As would not weep when so much Vertue dyes? **1717** Pope *Iliad* xi. 178 These words.. The youth address'd to unrelenting ears. **1774** *Monthly Misc.* June 309 Thy [*sc.* Death's] unrelenting hand..snatch'd Chaucer from our arms. **1813** Byron *Br. Abydos* II. xxvii, Woe to thee, rash and unrelenting chief! **1844** H. H. Wilson *Brit. India* I. 257 To save him from falling alive into the power of his unrelenting foes. **1853** Miss Yonge *Heir of Redclyffe* xxxii, I don't think you can be very unrelenting when you see..how altered he is.

(*c*) **1608** *Yorksh. Trag.* x. 7 In the handes of vnrelenting lawes. **1647** Stanley *Poems, Despair*, I will no more Vainly implore The unrelenting Destinies. **1697** Dryden *Æneis* VI. 763 These are the realms of unrelenting Fate. **1809-11** Combe *Syntax* xv. 26 The car Of furious, unrelenting War Leaves the dire track of streaming gore. **1813** Lamb *Recoll. Christ's Hosp.* Wks. 1908 I. 186 The heavy unrelenting arm of this temporal power.

**b.** Not slackening or relaxing in respect of severity, harshness, or determination.

(*a*) **1609** Daniel *Civ. Wars* IV. lxxxiii, [His] vnrelenting paines do neuer cease. **1656** Cowley *Pindar. Odes* I. vi, Unrelenting torments prove The heavy Necessary effects of Voluntary Faults. **1743** Francis tr. *Hor., Epodes* xvii. 44 You glow with unrelenting Fire, Till by the rapid Heat calcin'd, Vagrant I drive before the Wind. **1795** Burns '*Now Spring has clad*' 15 Love, wi' unrelenting beam, Has scorch'd my fountains dry. **1816** Shelley *Let.* in *Sothern's Catal.* No. 12 (1899) 51 Precipitous mountains, the abodes of unrelenting frost. **1844** H. H. Wilson *Brit. India* III. 377 The unrelenting pressure of the revenue system.

(*b*) **1614** Jackson *Creed* III. xiii. § 12 Vnrelenting perseuerance in traiterous plots. **1689** Cotton *Poems Sev. Occas.* 648 Bow-men of unrelenting Minds, Whose Shafts are Feathered with the Winds. **1715** Atterb. *Serm.* (1734) I. 119 An Act..of deliberate and unrelenting Malice. **1788** Gibbon *Decl. & F.* xlii. IV. 245 The slaughter still raged with unrelenting fury. **1821** Lamb *Elia* I. *Old Benchers In. T.*, The long-resolved..puttings off of unrelenting bachelorhood.

1855 Macaulay *Hist. Eng.* xiii. III. 316 With unwearied, unscrupulous and unrelenting ambition.

**2.** Not slackening or slowing down.

1817 Scott *Harold* v. x, With unrelenting pace, From grave to cradle [he] ran the evil race.

Hence **Unrele·ntingly** *adv.*, **Unrele·ntingness.**

1637 Jackson *Serm. Lk. xiii. 5*, 61 It is one thing to be rebellious, another to bee *unrelentingly rebellious. 1777 Potter *Æschylus, Furies* 409 Cloath'd in terrors we appear, Unrelentingly severe. 1812 L. Hunt in *Examiner* 4 May 275/1 [He] is..unrelentingly orthodox. 1869 Tozer *Highl. Turkey* II. 49 The Albanian soldiery..unrelentingly pursued their object. 1727 Bailey (vol. II), *Impenitentness*,..*unrelentingness. 1834 De Quincey *Autob. Sk.* Wks. 1853 I. 359 Such in its unrelentingness was the persecution. 1861 Geo. Eliot *Silas M.* viii, He had constantly suffered annoyance from witnessing his father's sudden fits of unrelentingness.

†**Unrele·ntless,** *a. Obs.* [Un-[1] 5 a.] Relentless. 1606 Marston *Parasit.* iv. G 4, Thinke how vnrelentles you were to her but supposed fault. **Unrele·ntor.** [Un-[1] 12.] One who is relentless. 1818 Keats *Endym.* iv. 600 He'll be shent, Pale unrelentor, When he shall hear the wedding lutes a playing. †**Unre·levant,** *a. Obs.*[−1] [Un-[1] 7, 5 b.] Irrelevant. 1650 in Davidson *Inverurie & Earld. Garioch* (1878) 313 The excuses always be[ing] found unrelevant.

**Unreliabi·lity.** (Un-[1] 12.)

1860 Worcester (citing *N. B. Rev.*). 1867 H. Bushnell *Moral Uses Dark Th.* (1869) 393 There must be surprises, incalculable somersets, infinite unreliabilities,..else [etc.]. 1883 *Harper's Mag.* Mar. 496/1 The unreliability of epitaphs ..is proverbial.

**Unreli·able,** *a.* (Un-[1] 7 b.)

In common use from *c* 1860.

1840 De Quincey in *Blackw. Mag.* XLVIII. 516 Alcibiades ..was too unsteady, and (according to Mr. Coleridge's coinage) 'unreliable'. 1859 Maury *Phys. Geog.* xiv. 232 Wind and weather in this part..are very unreliable and changeable. 1874 W. R. Greg *Rocks Ahead* 63 This calculation is..not only unreliable, but purely deceptive.

Hence **Unreli·ableness.**

1862 F. Hall *Hindu Philos. Syst.* 86 They are involved in the suspicion of unreliableness. 1872 Spurgeon *Treas. Dav.* Ps. lxxiii. 4 The unreliableness of mere feelings shown.

**Unrelie·vable,** *a.* (Un-[1] 7 b, 5 b.)

*a* 1586 Sidney *Arcadia* i. x, My ruin being but by one unrelieveable. 1648 Boyle *Seraph. Love* v. (1659) 39 No degree of Distress is unrelievable by his power. 1676 Temple *Let.* Wks. 1720 II. 420 Finding the Swedes weak, divided, and unrelieveable by France. 1820 Bentham *Mem.* Wks. 1843 X. 517 Communicate not to a friend..vexations of yours unrelievable by him. 1898 *Daily News* 29 July 2/6 No operative procedure should be suggested..until the case had been..found to be unrelievable by other means.

Hence **Unrelie·vableness.**

1654 'Palæmon' *Friendship* 12 The unrelievablenesse of our bad condition.

**Unrelie·ved,** *ppl. a.* [Un-[1] 8.]

**1.** Not freed from some obligation.

1533 Bellenden *Livy* v. xii. (S.T.S.) II. 189 The senate.. wald nocht suffir him to be..vnrelevit of þe vote be him made to apollo.

**2.** Not provided with relief; not aided or assisted.

1599 [see Unransomed]. 1609 Drayton *Leg. T. Cromwell* 23 It better should him please, Farre out of sight to perish here vnknowne, Then vnrelieu'd be pitied of his owne. 1656 Cowley *Davideis* iv. 446 If unrelieved seven days by Israels aid, This bargain for ore-rated Life is made. 1694 F. Bragge *Disc. Parables* vii. 269 The thefts..of such, whose unrelieved poverty forced to be thus wicked. 1719 J. Roberts *Spinster* 335 To leave the afflictions..of their..fellow-creatures neglected and unrelieved. 1757 W. Wilkie *Epigoniad* ii. 49 Has..unreliev'd the stranger left my door? 1857 Ruskin *Pol. Econ. Art* 25 That none of their distresses should be unrelieved. 1885 C. E. Pascoe *Lond. of To-day* xxxii. 283 Many sufferers..are altogether unrelieved for want of funds.

**3.** Not freed from depressing or monotonous character; not diversified or varied (*by* something).

1764 Gibbon *Misc. Wks.* (1814) IV. 397 Torments the more horrible in his..solitary state, unrelieved by the hope of glory. 1828 *Q. Rev.* XXXVIII. 219 An unrelieved series of miseries and crimes. 1857 Robertson *Serm.* Ser. iii. vii. 112 Sacrifice alone, bare and unrelieved, is..dead. 1882 Floyer *Unexpl. Baluchistan* 248 An oval lake of rough boulders, quite flat, and unrelieved by tree or shrub.

Hence **Unrelie·vedly** *adv.*

1876 Meredith *Beauch. Career* xv, The poor are everlastingly, unrelievedly, in the abysses of the great sea. 1899 Mackail *Life Morris* II. 41 Modern glass, some of it unpainted, the rest..unrelievedly hideous.

**Unreli·gioned,** *ppl. a.* (Un-[2] 8.) 1674 Penn *Chr.-Quaker* i. xxv. 126 Thus is this Man Unravel'd, Unreligion'd, Unbottom'd as to his former State. †**Unreligio·sity.** *Obs.*[−1] [Un-[1] 12, 5 b.] Irreligiosity. 1382 Wyclif 1 *Esdras* i. 42 Of his vnclennesse and unreligiosite [1388 vnreligioustee; Vulg. *irreligiositas*], it is writen in the boc.

**Unreli·gious,** *a.* [Un-[1] 7, 5 b.]

**1.** Irreligious.

1382 Wyclif 1 *Esdras* i. 24 Who so euere weren vnreligious aȝen the Lord. *c* 1450 tr. *De Imitatione* i. xxiv. 34 Þan shal ..euery vnreligious man sorowe. *c* 1500 *Melusine* xlii. 314 The monkes.., whiche were of euyl, inordinate, & vnrelygious lyuyng. 1548 Udall, etc. *Erasm. Par. John* xi. 74 Nothyng is more vnreligyouse than Jewish religion, whiche consisteth in visible thinges. 1577 Fulke *Answ. True Christian* 11 These vnreligious and vngodly opinions of God. 1606 Dekker *Double PP* Wks. (Grosart) II. 163 Hee dare presse To th' Eaves of Bishops Pallaces: Where, harsh and vn-religious notes Hee singes against their Reuerend Coates. 1814 Wordsw. *Excurs.* iv. 607 If unreligious, let him be at once, Among ten thousand innocents, enrolled A pupil.

**2.** Non-religious; not connected with religion.

1855 Milman *Lat. Chr.* xiv. v. VI. 508 The popular poetry ..became profane, unreligious, at length in some parts irreligious. 1871 R. H. Hutton *Ess.* I. 88 The difficulties involved in the conception of Creation being, however, totally unreligious. 1898 *Educat Rev.* XV. 392 In the general movement.., education has become quite unreligious.

Hence **Unreli·giously** *adv.*, **Unreli·giousness.**

*c* 1535 in Ellis *Orig. Lett.* Ser. iii. II. 363 Whom, after myn opynyon, war better to be at large and dymyssed from ther bondage then so vnrelygiously to remayne ayenst ther conscyens. 1579 Fulke *Heskins' Parl.* 30 Although there be great rashnesse in some, and vnreligiousnesse in more. 1847 Emerson *Poems, Blight* 38 We invade them impiously for gain; We devastate them unreligiously.

**Unreli·nquishably,** *adv.* (Un-[1] 11.) 1643 Milton *Divorce* 28 To clogge a rational creature to his endles sorrow unrelinquishably.

**Unreli·nquished,** *ppl. a.* (Un-[1] 8.)

[1775 Ash.] 1781 Cowper *Conversat.* 673 While at heart sin unrelinquish'd lies. 1806 Foster *Ess.* (1844) I. 16 Their ..unrepented and unrelinquished sins. 1881 Mrs. Oliphant *H. Joscelyn* II. 304 That familiar unrelinquished name.

**Unre·lishable,** *a.* (Un-[1] 7 b, 5 b.) 1606 G. W[oodcocke] *Hist. Ivstine* Pref., A tun of Wine, which..is made vnrellishable by being mingled with some other compound. 1727 Bailey (vol. II), *Disgustful*, unrelishable.

**Unre·lished,** *ppl. a.* (Un-[1] 8.)

1593 Drayton *Ecl.* ii. 10 My Rymes seeme harsh to thy vnrelish'd taste. 1863 Mrs. Whitney *Faith Gartney's Girlh.* vii, Sleepless nights,..and forgotten, or unrelished meals.

**Unre·lishing,** *ppl. a.* (Un-[1] 10.) 1611 Florio, *Insulso*, vnsauorie.., vnrelishing, tastelesse. 1633 T. Adams *Exp. 2 Peter* i. 2 Idle, profane, and unrelishing compliments. 1676 Glanvill *Seasonable Reflect.* 147 All things [in the other world]..are uneasie and unrelishing at the best. †**Unre·lishness.** *Obs.*[−1] [Un-[1] 12.] Lack of relish. 1615 A. Niccholes *Marr. & Wiving* vii. (1620) 19 The vnrealishnesse of that which is lawful, desire of that which is restrained.

**Unrelu·ctant,** *a.* (Un-[1] 7, 5 b.)

1737 Glover *Leonidas* i. 233 Death, receive My unreluctant hand, and lead me on. 1774 *Trinket* 188 The consent is..granted with an unreluctant frankness. 1820 Shelley *Ode Lib.* xi, The eager hours and unreluctant years. 1854 Milman *Lat. Chr.* iii. iii. I. 316 An orthodox Empire would not repose in unreluctant submission under an Arian.

**Unrelu·ctantly,** *adv.* (Un-[1] 11.)

1655 Earl Orrery *Parthen.* ii. iii. 271 The Armenians have vnreluctantly submitted to that Government. 1768–74 Tucker *Lt. Nat.* (1834) II. 289 It will sometimes carry them through self-denials unreluctantly upon proper occasions. 1799 Han. More *Fem. Educ.* (ed. 4) I. p. xiv, Unreluctantly yielding themselves to be carried down the tide of popular practices. 1849 C. Bronte *Shirley* xxix, She resigns herself to me unreluctantly. 1874 H. Rogers *Orig. Bible* ii. 60 They unreluctantly received such as spontaneously sought their communion.

**Unremai·ning,** *ppl. a.* (Un-[1] 10.) 1817 Shelley *Rev. Islam* i. i, Like a brief dream of unremaining glory. 1818 — *Rosal. & Helen* 997 My dream of unremaining gladness.

**Unrema·rkable,** *a.* [Un-[1] 7 b, 5 b.]

**1.** Unworthy of remark or note.

1611 Cotgr., *Irremarquable*, vnremarkable,..no way to be noted. 1632 G. Sandys *Ovid's Met.* xi. Notes 397 Nor is this vnremarkable,..that the Kings-fisher being dead and hung vp by the Neb, turnes alwaies her belly to the wind. 1643 Sir T. Browne *Relig. Med.* 55 It is not unremarkable what Philo first observed, That [etc.].

†**b.** Incapable of being observed. *Obs.*[−1]

1644 Digby *Nat. Bodies* v. § 2. 34 Our vnderstanding to make a compleate notion, must adde something else to this fleeting and vnremarkable superficies that may bring it vnto our acquaintance.

**2.** Not notable or striking.

1850 Kingsley *A. Locke* xxvii, As we may see by the histories of every remarkable, and many an unremarkable, man. 1853 G. J. Cayley *Las Alforjas* I. 155 We..saw Arahal, an unremarkable white town, on a slight eminence. 1879 *St. George's Hosp. Rep.* IX. 520 An unremarkable sprinkling of other workers.

**Unrema·rked,** *ppl. a.* (Un-[1] 8, 8 c.)

[1775 Ash.] 1793 *Minstrel* III. 159 The extreme attention of Edward to her daughter, was not unremarked by Jaqueline. 1830 Herschel *Study Nat. Phil.* 348 It cannot be supposed, that all the indications of nature continually passed unremarked. 1871 Fraser *Life of Berkeley* x. 382 Some hitherto unremarked phases of the Berkleian conception.

(*b*) 1856 Craik *English of Shaks.* Pref., Not leaving any passage unremarked upon which seemed..obscure.

†**Unreme·diable,** *a. Obs.* Also 5 *Sc.* vnremedable, 6 onremedabil. [Un-[1] 7 b, 5 b.] Irremediable.

1382 Wyclif *Tobit* x. 4 Thanne wepte his modir with vnremediable teris. *c* 1480 Henryson *Want of Wyse Men* 63 (Bann. MS.), Sic sturtfull stering in to godis neis it stinkis; Bot he haif rew, all is vnremedable. 1549 *Compl. Scot.* 1 Ther cruel inuasions aperis to be onremedabil. *a* 1586 Sidney *Arcadia* ii. x. (1912) 213 An unremediable mischiefe already committed. 1645 Bp. Hall *Remedy Discontents* 125 The miseries of an unremediable disappointment. 1695 S. Lobb *Let. Dr. Bates* 21 An antecedent desert of hell, and a sinfulness so deserving (tho' not by an unremediable guilt).

**Unre·medied,** *ppl. a.* (Un-[1] 8.)

Also in 16th c. *unreme·died*, Sc. *unreme·dit.*

1563 *Reg. Privy Council Scot.* I. 250 Salang as this inobedience is unremedit. 1595 Spenser *Clorinda* 8 The authors.. And workers of my vnremedied wo. 1644 Milton *Divorce* (ed. 2) A 3 b, The unremedied loneliness of this remedy. 1768 Blackstone *Comm.* III. 385 Should [these defects]..continue unremedied and unsupplied. 1791 Cowper *Odyss.* ii. 272 Waste will continue and disorder foul Unremedied. 1864 Pusey *Lect. Daniel* 523 *note*, God is often said to 'awake' for His people, when He notices that which He had before left unremedied.

**Unreme·mber,** *v.* [Un-[1] 14.] *trans.* To fail (or omit) to remember. 1484 in *Lett. Rich. III & Hen. VII* (Rolls) I. 78 Whiche [fidelity] we shalle not unremembre. 1616 W. Haig in J. Russell *Haigs* vii. (1881) 159 Unremembering so kendspeckle a thing wherein they were put.

**Unreme·mberable,** *a.* (Un-[1] 7 b, 5 b.)

1803 *Ann. Rev.* I. 68 The topography of a country wherein every place has an unrememberable name. 1858 Carlyle *Fredk. Gt.* ii. iii. I. 89 The smallest flint-spark, in a world all black and unrememberable, will be welcome. 1887 Saintsbury *Hist. Elizab. Lit.* viii. 292 Vast heaps of things altogether unrememberable.

**Unreme·mbered,** *ppl. a.* [Un-[1] 8.]

**1.** Not borne in mind; allowed to drop out of mind; forgot.

With early examples cf. Unremember *v.*

*c* 1400 *Found. St. Bartholomew's* xii. 17 Innumerable were schewid tokynnys of myracles, but..they be almoyste vnremembred. 1422 Yong tr. *Secreta Secret.* 203 For als moche as good newe ensamples sholde not ben vnremembrid for lerynge of tho that arne to come. 1584 Hutton *Let.* in Campbell *Chancellors* (1856) II. 273 Towards yourself leave not the causes of my presumptions unremembered. 1607 Hieron *Wks.* I. 260 This feare causeth them..to be vnwilling to let any of it [*sc.* comfort of the Scriptures] fall to the ground vnremembred. 1641 Milton *Reform.* ii. 69 Nor must their sincere..proceeding hitherto, be unremember'd. 1734 A. Hill *On Death Dennis* 9 The furious petulence, the jealous start,..Veil'd in thy grave shall unremember'd lie. 1798 Wordsw. *Tintern Abbey* 31 Feelings too Of unremembered pleasure. 1816 Southey *Lay of Laureate* lxxvi, Where in elder time Earth's unremember'd conquerors held the sway. 1853 G. Johnston *Nat. Hist. E. Borders* I. 29 A skirmish of unremembered date.

†**b.** (Left) unrecorded or unmentioned. *Obs.*

*c* 1477 Caxton *Jason* 52 Hit is not to be vnremembrid that thenuie of..Peleus grewe so terribly that he..coude haue no reste. *a* 1513 Fabyan *Chron.* i. i, Whiche if any suche wonder had ben there wroughte, shuld nat haue ben vnremembred [by] the wryters. 1570 Foxe *A. & M.* (ed. 2) 19/2 Which doubtles shoulde not haue bene vnremembered, if he had bene then in Rome. 1603 G. Owen *Pembrokeshire* (1892) 219 For the better memorye of these..members, not to suffer them vnremembered in this my Discripcion of their Country. *c* 1650 P. Smith *Life Willet* in Fuller *Abel Red.* (1651) 565, I thought good..to adde some remarkable things then unremembred or undiscovered.

†**2.** Of persons: Unmindful, forgetful. *Obs.*

1467 *Paston Lett.* II. 306 He thynkyth indoubted that William Worcetre shuld not be unremembred of this. *a* 1528 Bp. R. Fox in Ellis *Orig. Lett.* Ser. ii. II. 6, I am not unremembred of my deutye towardes the Kyng. 1536 E. Lee *Ibid.* Ser. iii. II. 326, I trust your Highnes is not unremembred, that [etc.].

**Unreme·mbering,** *ppl. a.* (Un-[1] 10.)

1540 *Sc. Acts Parlt., Jas. V* (1814) II. 363/2 That he will nocht be vnremembrand and vngrate for þe gude..seruice done to him. 1697 Dryden *Æneis* vi. 1020 That, unrememb'ring of its former Pain, The Soul may suffer mortal Flesh again. 1882 J. Hawthorne *Fort. Fool* i. xvii, It would become human like ourselves, and lose its thoughtless and unremembering happiness.

**Unreme·mbrance.** (Un-[1] 12.) *c* 1449 Pecock *Repr.* iv. ix. 474 The vnknowing and the vnremembraunce of these thre..notabilitees. 1725 Watts *Logic* i. iv. § 2 There are some Words which are negative in their original Language, but seem positive to an Englishman,..as..*Amnesty*, an Unremembrance or general Pardon. **Unremi·nded,** *ppl. a.* (Un-[1] 8.) [1775 Ash.] 1881 M. C. Hay *Missing* II. 214, I never could allow him to be unreminded that [etc.]. †**Unremi·ssible,** *a. Obs.* (Un-[1] 7, 5 b.) 1593 Nashe *Christ's T.* 30 There is the Tabernacle of the Lord,..there if we shold drawe our blades, it were abhomination vnremissible. 1603 Florio *Montaigne* iii. v. 511 It is a capitall crime, and vnremissible offence.

**Unremi·tted,** *ppl. a.* [Un-[1] 8.]

**1.** Not pardoned or cancelled.

1646 Hammond *Tracts* 27 Sin unretracted..doth certainly stand upon the sinners score unremitted.

**2.** Not allowed to slacken or fall off; maintained at the same pitch or force; continuous.

Very common from *c* 1760.

1722–7 Boyer *Dict. Royal* ii, Unremitted, (incessant), *continuel.* 1744 Akenside *Pleas. Imag.* i. 430 Against the ..stubborn hill To urge bold Virtue's unremitted nerve. 1781 C. Johnston *Hist. J. Juniper* I. 13 Her endeavours ..had been unremitted. 1820 Scott *Monast.* xi, Assiduity and unremitted attention. 1842 H. Rogers *Introd. Burke's Wks.* I. 26 The fatigues of such years of unremitted toil.

**3.** Of persons: Unremitting.

1796 Morse *Amer. Geog.* I. 329 Several men of abilities.. were unremitted in their endeavours. 1833 Sir W. Hamilton *Discuss.* (1853) 588 The pastor..ought to be..unremitted in his superintendence of the masters.

Hence **Unremi·ttedly** *adv.*

1786 tr. *Beckford's Vathek* 22 His wives..unremittedly supplied him with water. 1792 in J. Morse *Amer. Geog.* (1796) I. 510 Through which aperture the water unremittedly drops. 1889 *Engineer* 10 May 408 An advantage which Swansea has been striving for unremittedly, and will gain this autumn.

**Unremi·ttent,** *a.* (Un-[1] 7.) 1871 Palgrave *Lyr. Poems* 28 The lark scattering in the crystal morn His unremittent gush of silver rain. 1895 *Athenæum* 16 Feb. 224/2 An atmosphere of unremittent work. **Unremi·ttently,** *adv.* (Un-[1] 11.) 1895 *Athenæum* 26 Oct. 576/3 Mr. Manns has laboured..unremittently in the interests of native art.

**Unremi·tting,** *ppl. a.* [Un-[1] 10.] Never relaxing or slackening; continuing with the same force; incessant: **a.** Of activity, etc.

1728 Thomson *Spring* 700 Inspiring God! who boundless Spirit all, And unremitting Energy,..agitates the Whole. 1768 Boswell *Corsica* ii. (ed. 2) 79 With unremitting constancy [he] endeavoured to restore the liberties of his country. 1819 Busby *Hist. Music* II. 256 We find in the music a continued and unremitting echo to the sense of the language. 1833 T. Hook *Parson's Dau.* i. i, [They] lived in the most unremitting hostility towards each other. 1871 Macduff *Mem. Patmos* v. 56 Engaged in unremitting toil.

**b.** Of persons. Also quasi-*adv.*

1736 Thomson *Liberty* iv. 711 Fleet on fleet Of barbarous pirates unremitting tore The miserable coast. 1796 Mme. D'Arblay *Camilla* IV. 238 [She] was..unremitting in boasting how well she had..kept them in order. 1817 J. Scott *Paris Revisit.* (ed. 4) 359 He..was unremitting in his exertions. 1876 Bancroft *Hist. U.S.* I. xiii. 420 He was unremitting in argument and entreaty to prevent the taking of their lives.

Hence **Unremi·ttingness.**

1812 Shelley *Proposals* Pr. Wks. 1888 I. 283 Considering the unremittingness of its pressure. 1865 M. Arnold *Ess. in Crit.* vi. (1875) 243 The very intensity and unremittingness of its appeal.

**Unremi·ttingly,** *adv.* [Un-1 11.] Without remission; incessantly, continually.

1796 Mme. D'Arblay *Camilla* IV. 184, I watched her unremittingly. 1824 Dibdin *Libr. Comp.* 608 Having secretly and unremittingly formed his style. 1878 A. H. Markham *Gt. Frozen Sea* i. 6 Officers and men were unremittingly engaged in the various duties.

**Unremo·nstrant,** *a.* (Un-1 7.) 1865 Meredith *R. Fleming* xxxix, As mute and unremonstrant as a fallen tree. **Unremo·nstrated,** *ppl. a.* (Un-1 8 c.) 1818 Bentham *Ch. Eng. Catech. Exam.* 151 Such connivance should be left unremonstrated against. 1860 Dickens *Lett.* (1880) III. 193 You are..far too able a man to be left unremonstrated with by an admiring reader.

**Unremo·rseful,** *a.* (Un-1 7.)

c 1611 Chapman *Iliad* ix. 597 O unremorseful man!..thee a..cruel spirit the Gods for plague have given. 1616 R. Niccols *Sir T. Overbury's Vis.* B 1 b, Vnremorsefull fate Did worke the falls of those two Princes dead. *Ibid.* C 2, Monsters..vnremorsefull of my forepast woes. 1855 Lynch *Rivulet* lxxviii. v, By unremorseful joys, O, woo Our hearts to holy efforts still. 1876 Stedman *Victorian Poets* 316 Sebald and Ottima have murdered the latter's aged husband, and are unremorseful in their guilty love.

**Unremo·rsefully,** *adv.* (Un-1 11.) 1846 Hawthorne *Old Manse* ii. 31 Thus making his own actual serpent..the type of each man's..unquiet conscience, and striking his sting so unremorsefully into the sorest spot. **†Unremo·rseless,** *a. Obs.*-1 [Un-1 5 a.] Remorseless. 1634 Cowley *Elegy R. Clerke* 10 His mellifluous breath Could not at all charme unremorselesse Death. **Unremo·te,** *a.* (Un-1 7.) 1837 Whittock *Bk. Trades* (1842) 239 (*Fruiterer*) The 'unremote' period when many of our most familiar garden products were introduced.

**Unremo·vable,** *a.* [Un-1 7 b, 5 b.]

**†1.** Incapable of being moved; immovable; steady, firm, constant. *Obs.*

a 1500 in *Ratis Raving*, etc. 11 The erde remanis euermare vnremouable. 1579 Fulke *Heskins' Parl.* 476 It still remaineth vnremouable, that a signe and the thing signified, be distinct things. c 1595 Capt. Wyatt *Dudley's Voy.* (Hakl. Soc.) 25 Caryinge soe great a majestie in his march with such unremovable resolucions in his proceedings. a 1642 Bedell *Erasmus* in Fuller *Abel Rediv.* (1867) I. 91 He was of an unremoveable constancy. 1670 Walton *Lives, Wotton* 72, I..contracted with him an unremovable affection.

**2.** = Irremovable *a.* 1. Now *rare.*

a 1586 Sidney *Arcadia* i. v, He manifested himself an unremoveable suiter to her daughter. 1614 Bp. Hall *Contempl., O.T.* viii. v, Their neernesse of abode was an unremoveable barre of peace. a 1680 Corbet *Non-conf. Plea* (1683) 25 Unnecessary terms, that are unlawful to them by unremovable doubts of conscience. a 1740 Waterland *Sec. Def.* Wks. 1823 III. 70 This..left the charge fixed and unremovable upon the Pagans. 1752 Carte *Hist. Eng.* III. 27 The lord Areskine, his constant and unremoveable guardian. 1802 *Sk. Paris* II. xlvii. 123 The pretended unremoveable rights.

Hence **Unremo·vableness.**

1611 Cotgr., *Constance*,..vnremoueablenesse. 1634 Bp. Hall *Contempl., Resurrection* 276 They brag of the surenesse of the place, and unremoveablenesse of that load.

**Unremo·vably,** *adv.* [Un-1 11, 5 b: cf. prec.] Irremovably.

1604 Sir T. Coningsby in 14*th Rep. Hist. MSS. Comm.* App. II. 2 Yours unremovably, yf you remoufe him not. 1617 Hieron *Wks.* 1620 II. 236 That wee may bee so settled in a right way.., as that we may..goe on sincerely, and vnremouably to the end. 1646 Hammond *Tracts* 102 So heavy an arreare of sinne lying unremovably upon every ones score.

**Unremo·ved,** *ppl. a.* [Un-1 8, 5 b.]

**1.** Not removed or done away with.

1455 *Rolls of Parlt.* V. 330/1 Whiche doubte..unremoved, is not unlike to set..division. 1674 R. Godfrey *Inj. & Ab. Physic* 4 So long as the spurious Ferment in both Stomach and Blood is unremoved. 1680 C. Nesse *Church Hist.* 363 This rubb and remora is still unremoved. 1812 Crabbe *Tales* iii. 290 Gwyn something felt..was wrong; He wish'd to know, for he believed the thing, If unremoved, would other evil bring. 1860 Westcott *Introd. Study Gosp.* iii. 153 Their external disinclination for literature was unremoved.. by their special work. 1901 *N. Amer. Rev.* Feb. 236 The unremoved deteriorating influences.

**b.** Not removed or shifted in place.

a 1450 in *MS. Rawl. D.* 251 fol. 86, Let it ly iij dayes onremevyd. c 1490 *Paston Lett.* III. 338 Ye must send me wryghtyng..hough longe..[the plaster] shold abyd on hys kne unremevyd. 1563 Hyll *Art Garden.* (1574) 117 If they [*sc.* rape] growe to thicke, then remoue..them,..whereby the other vnremoued may growe the bigger in the roote. 1613 W. Browne *Brit. Past.* i. iv. 529 As yonder mill..Yet by the head-strong torrent from his beame Is unremov'd. 1632 Lithgow *Trav.* i. 31 [They] placed it in a high broad way, where it standeth vnremoued to this day. 1707 Mortimer *Husb.* 472 Being sown very thin..where they may stand unremoved in the Ground for two Years. 1784 *Phil. Trans.* LXXIV. 428 They continued unremoved in their several places. 1837 Carlyle *Fr. Rev.* ii. vi. viii, A hundred and eighty bodies of Swiss lie piled there; naked, unremoved till the second day. 1889 21*st Rep. Dep. Keeper Irel.* 16 Other testamentary Records, unremoved to this Department.

**c.** Fixed in place; firmly stationed.

1551 Recorde *Pathw. Knowl.* i. xlii, Then sette I one foote of the compas vnremoued in B. 1591 Harington *Orl. Fur.* ix. lxix, So great a sound, As seemed..to remove the unremoved ground. 1667 Milton *P. L.* iv. 987 Satan.. dilated stood, Like Teneriff or Atlas unremov'd. 1820 Shelley *Prometh. Unb.* iv. 380 Making shiver Thought's stagnant chaos, unremoved for ever. 1873 Symonds *Grk. Poets* x. 325 The mountain stands for ever unremoved.

**†2.** Firm, steadfast, constant. *Obs.*

1589 *Rare Tri. Love & Fort.* ii. M 4, The unremoved love I beare my lady. 1606 G. Woodcock *Hist. Ivstine* xv. 64 With an vnremooued courage, neither arrogant in happinesse, nor altred in distresse. 1627 Drayton *Elegies, To Lady I. S.* 85 Your noble heart..With vnremoued constancie is still The same it was. 1655 Earl Orrery *Parthen.* ii. viii. 816 An unremoved resolve of sharing in his despair.

**Unremu·nerated,** *ppl. a.* (Un-1 8.) [1775 Ash.] (Freq. in recent use.) **Unremu·nerating,** *ppl. a.* (Un-1 10.) 1855 [J. R. Leifchild] *Cornwall* 247 If a mine..just meets its working expenses at a low and unremunerating standard.

**Unremu·nerative,** *a.* (Un-1 7.)

Hence, in recent use, *unremuneratively, -ness.*

1854 *Poultry Chron.* I. 26/2 Evidence that the raising of poultry was by no means the unremunerative folly idlers supposed it to be. 1869 Tozer *Highl. Turkey* II. 120 A girl is considered an expense and unremunerative.

**†Unrena·vigable,** *a. Obs.* (Un-1 7 b.) 1661 J. Boys *Æneas* vi. 17 How gladly would they..see blest light again? Fates thwart: an unrenavigable sound..doth them surround.

**† Unre·nde(d,** obs. varr. Unrent *ppl. a.*

c 1440 *Pallad. on Husb.* iv. 9 The trunkes sadde, in humor that abounde, Vnolde, vnrende. 1646 J. Gregory *Notes & Obs.* 117 The suspension of these waters..I no more marvaile at then that the thicke Clouds..should hang in the Aire unrended under them.

**Unre·nderable,** *a.* (Un-1 7 b, 5 b.) 1860 Ruskin *Mod. Paint.* V. vi. x. § 8 The best beauty of flowers being wholly inimitable, and their sweetest service unrenderable by art. 1889 *Athenæum* 10 Aug. 187/3 A rendering of Sappho's unrenderable 'Ode to Aphrodite'.

**Unre·ndered,** *ppl. a.* (Un-1 8.)

[1775 Ash.] 1851 Mayhew *Lond. Labour* I. 199 Cakes, made of flour and 'unrendered' (unmelted) lard. 1865 Grosart *Palmer's Mem.* Introd. 15 The suggestive and invaluable treatise of M. Rémusat still lies unrendered.

**Unrenew·able,** *a.* (Un-1 7 b, 5 b.) 1548 Geste *Pr. Masse* B ij, Christes body (whose creatyon is vnrenuable).

**Unrenew·ed,** *ppl. a.* (Un-1 8.)

1579 W. Wilkinson *Confut. Fam. Love* B iij b, They are ..vnrenewed, vngodded, vnsent. 1678 R. Barclay *Apol. Quakers* (1703) 363 Acting in their own natural and unrenewed Wills. 1683 J. Corbet *Free Actions* ii. xvi. 24 Whatsoever an unrenewed person doth, hath necessarily.. a disconformity to Gods Law. 1764 J. Witherspoon *Pract. Treat. Regeneration* ii. § 2 All unrenewed persons..place their supreme happiness in something that is not God. 1828–32 Webster s.v., The lease is unrenewed. 1865 Gladstone *Farewell Addr. Edinb. Univ.* 61 The spirit of the unrenewed world. a 1866 D. Duncan *Disc.* (1867) vii. 144 Prayer is not an exercise congenial to the unrenewed soul.

**Unrenou·nceable,** *a.* (Un-1 7 b.) 1851 [see next]. **Unrenou·nced,** *ppl. a.* (Un-1 8.) 1775 Ash.] 1851 Mrs. Browning *Casa Guidi Wind.* ii. 117 The people rose up in the dust.., and shouted..'Live the People,' who remained and must, The unrenounced and unrenounceable. **Unre·novated,** *ppl. a.* (Un-1 8.) [1775 Ash.] 1856 Ruskin *Mod. Paint.* IV. v. xiv. § 25 Age after age may only prolong the unrenovated ruin.

**Unrenow·ned,** *ppl. a.* Also 6 -nowmed. (Un-1 8. Cf. Irrenowmed.)

1570 Levins *Manip.* 50 Vnrenowned, *incelebris.* 1594 Marlowe & Nashe *Dido* iv. iii, The dreames..that did beset my bed,..Commaunds me leaue these vnrenowmed reames. 1827 Pollok *Course T.* ix. 479 Nor unrenowned among the most renowned..stood the bard. a 1851 Moir *Sonn.* i, Nor unrenowned, as, with an ampler tide, Thou windest through the glens of Woodhouselee.

**Unre·nt,** *a.* (Un-1 7.)

1596 Spenser *F. Q.* vi. vi. 40 Were not, that the Prince did him appeaze, He had not left one limbe of him vnrent. 1727 Pope, etc. *Art of Sinking* 102 Distended with the waters in 'em pent, The clouds hang deep in air, but hang unrent. 1796 Burke *Let. Noble Lord* Wks. VIII. 21 These obscene harpies..leave nothing unrent, unrifled. 1816 Byron *Siege of Cor.* xxxiii, The hills that shake, although unrent. 1858 Carlyle *Fredk. Gt.* v. v. I. 577 Daily had some loop fallen,.. but daily was he there to pick it up again, and keep the web unrent. 1879 R. T. Smith *Basil Gt.* ix. 113 The garment without seam..preserved unrent even by the soldiers.

**Unre·ntable,** *a.* (Un-1 7 b.) 1826 Galt *Last of Lairds* v. 40 An untenanted and unrentable portion of the Laird's domain.

**Unrepai·d,** *ppl. a.* (Un-1 8.)

1655 Earl Orrery *Parthen.* i. viii. 456 To leave so liberall a guift vnrepay'd. 1697 Creech in *Dryden's Juvenal* xiii. xvii. 334 Thy Loss continues, unrepaid by Pain. 1738 Wesley *Hymn, To Thee, O Father of Mankind* iii, Nor shall their Love be unrepaid. 1750 Johnson *Rambler* No. 54 ⁋ 10 We recollect..a thousand favours unrepaid. 1826 Scott *Woodst.* xxviii, That my affection was not unrepaid. 1890 'R. Boldrewood' *Col. Reformer* (1891) 316 The very substantial aid in cash..still unrepaid.

**Unrepai·r.** [Un-1 12, 5 b.] Lack of repair; disrepair, irrepair.

1873 in *Daily News* 5 Mar. 2/4 He might send them to sea in a condition of unrepair, both as to equipment and hull. 1886 *American* XIII. 57 Everywhere the combined efforts of ill-construction and unrepair are visible.

**Unrepai·rable,** *a.* (Un-1 7 b, 5 b.)

1611 Cotgr., *Irrecuperable*, vnrecouerable, vnrepairable. 1617 Moryson *Itin.* ii. 192 The losse of them would be for many yeeres vnrepairable. 1680 Rushw. *Hist. Coll.* II. 301 These great Abuses are..increased to the publick Nuissance, and likely to..become unrepairable.

**Unrepai·red,** *ppl. a.*1 [Un-1 8.] Not repaired.

1523 Ld. Berners *Froiss.* I. ccccxxxiv. (1812) 762 Whan the frenche kynge went oute of that countrey it was vnrepayred,..for all was brent and beaten downe. c 1550 W. Clopton in Halliwell *Shaks.* (1887) II. 171 Bentlye hath lefte the said mannour place in great ruyne, and unrepayryd. 1617 Campion *3rd Bk. Ayres* ix. 11 Great sorrows vnrepayred Admit no meane in mourning. a 1637 B. Jonson *Underwoods, Execration Vulcan* 196 Paul's steeple.., though a divine Loss, remains yet as unrepair'd as mine. 1693 Tate *Dryden's Juvenal* xv. 5 Where, Thebes, thy Hundred Gates lie unrepair'd. 1721 [see Unredressed]. 1805 Southey *Madoc* i. xii. 32 As the floods of spring had broken down Their barrier, so its breaches unrepair'd Were left. 1837 Carlyle *Fr. Rev.* ii. v. v, Robbers scour the Highways, which wear down unrepaired.

**Unrepai·red,** *ppl. a.*2 [Un-1 8 c.] Not resorted *to.* 1615 T. Adams *Lycanthropy* 33 The Temples unrepaired and unrepaired to—neyther adorned nor frequented. **†Unre·parable,** *a. Obs.* (Un-1 7 b, 5 b.) 1611 Speed *Hist. Gt. Brit.* ix. viii. § 55. 503/1 His French affaires had sustained vnreparable impeachments. 1645 Milton *Tetrach.* 90 We grant divorce..not for lesse then many tedious and unreparable yeares of desertion. **Unrepa·rtable,** *a.* (Un-1 7 b.) 1592 R. D. *Hypnerotomachia* 8 b, Compassed with fowlded haires of vnrepartable curiousnes.

**Unrepa·ssable,** *a.* (Un-1 7 b, 5 b.)

1600 J. Pory tr. *Leo's Africa* Introd. 35 A report, that the streights of Magellan were unrepassable. 1611 Cotgr., *Irrepassable*, vnrepassable, ouer which no returne can be made. 1734 Watts *Reliq. Juv.* 110 Narrow Limits indeed! and when once pass'd, they are unrepassable. 1794 H. Boyd *Ind. Observer* No. 49 ⁋ 3 The eternal shore of the unrepassable river.

**Unrepay·able,** *a.* (Un-1 7 b.) 1881 Shairp *Aspects of Poetry* 312 A debt still unrepaid, perhaps now unrepayable. **Unrepay·ing,** *ppl. a.* (Un-1 10.) 1866 *Chamb. Jrnl.* Dec. 785 Another almost as unrepaying a branch of literary labour. 1868 R. L. Poole in *Contemp. Rev.* Jan. 112 As we study the dry and unrepaying pages of the Ritual.

**Unrepea·lable,** *a.* (Un-1 7 b, 5 b.)

1601 Dent *Pathw. Heaven* 376 His decree is vnrepealeable. 1656 Jeanes *Fuln. Christ* 180 An irreversible, and unrepealable promise of an omnipotent God. a 1711 Ken *Hymns Evang.* Poet. Wks. 1721 I. 151 Unrepealable and dreadful Doom. 1730 Waterland *Suppl. to Nat. Chr. Sacr.* iii. 21 That Love of God,..which is unrepealable, abiding for ever. 1784 Cowper *Task* v. 610 Unrepealable enduring death. 1803 Jane Porter *Thaddeus* xv, These words fell like an unrepealable sentence on the heart of Thaddeus. 1860 Lowell *Election in Nov.* Prose Wks. 1890 V. 38 Truth is the unrepealable thing.

Hence **Unrepealabi·lity, -ableness.**

1651 W. Durham *Maran-atha* (1652) 24 The un-repealablenesse of this judgment, it can never be revers'd. 1820–30 Coleridge in *Lit. Rem.* (1838) III. 25 The unrepealability of their decisions.

**Unrepea·led,** *ppl. a.* (Un-1 8.)

1479 in *Eng. Gilds* (1870) 417, I shall..meyntene all laudable ordinauncez..vnreuokid and vnrepelid. 1603 Holland *Plutarch's Mor.* 1126 Say a man did abolish lawes, and yet withall leave behind unrepealed and uncondemned the doctrines and books of Parmenides. 1649 Milton *Tenure Kings* 13 Which Edict of his remaines yet unrepeald in the Code of Justinian. 1712 Blackmore *Creation* i. 626 Could they [*sc.* moist elements] dispense to lie below the land, With nature's law, and unrepeal'd command. 1771 *Junius Lett.* xlviii. (1788) 264 The resolutions..stand upon your Journals, uncontroverted and unrepealed. 1819 G. S Faber *Dispensations* (1823) I. 180 That the original sentence continued wholly unaltered and unrepealed. 1891 Farrar *Darkn. & Dawn* xlii, An unrepealed decree of the senate.

**Unrepea·table,** *a.* [Un-1 7 b, 5 b.]

**1.** Too coarse to be re-uttered.

1843 Mozley *Ess.* (1878) I. 84 The most disgusting and unrepeatable indecencies went on. 1859 W. H. Gregory *Egypt* II. 47 Droll but somewhat unrepeatable anecdotes. 1887 *Punch* 19 Mar. 136/2 An account of his most infamous exploits in unrepeatable language.

**2.** Incapable of being done or made again.

1880 Littledale *Plain Reas.* lxxv. 157 The..unrepeatable privilege and glory of being the first to unlock the doors of the kingdom. 1901 G. H. Howison *Limits of Evol.* 362 The absolutely singular and unrepeatable personality of each soul.

**Unrepea·ted,** *ppl. a.* [Un-1 8.]

**1.** Not re-uttered or recounted.

a 1586 Sidney *Arcadia* ii. xxix, To leave that unrepeated, which I finde my daughters have told you. 1649 Milton *Eikon.* Pref. B ij, The further mention of his deeds..perhaps for the present age might have slept with him unrepeated. a 1839 Praed *Poems* (1864) I. 236 Believe not that those uttered words In the far winds have fleeted..Uncherished, unrepeated.

**2.** Not renewed.

1786 *Francis the Philanthropist* II. 3 'If you are serious in your bets..I'll hold ye both, gentlemen.'..The bets were unrepeated. 1811 Scott *Don Roderick* ii. xix, First shrill'd an unrepeated female shriek!

**Unrepe·llable,** *a.* (Un-1 7 b.) 1665 J. Gadbury *London's Deliv. Predicted* i. 3 Which.., by an (almost) uncontrolable and unrepellable siccity, dries up and destroys the Natural Powers.

**Unrepe·lled,** *ppl. a.* (Un-1 8.)

[1775 Ash.] 1795 Coleridge *Plot Discov.* 27 Dreadful encroachments yet unrepelled. 1818 Shelley *Rosal. & Helen* 205 They sate With linked hands, for unrepelled Had Helen taken Rosalind's. 1850 Browning *Christmas Eve* xxi, I caught At the flying Robe, and unrepelled Was lapped again in its folds.

**Unrepe·nt,** *v.* (Un-2 7.) 1833 Carlyle *Ct. Cagliostro* Misc. Ess. 1872 V. 123 He..wanders necessitous hither and thither; repents, unrepents; knows not what to do. **Unrepe·ntable,** *a.* (Un-1 7 b, 5 b.) 1827 Pollok *Course T.* x. 421 Unrepented deeds, Now unrepentable for evermore.

**Unrepe·ntance.** (Un-1 12, 5 b.)

c 1410 *Wycliffite Bible* 1 John v. 7 *marg.*, Fynal unrepentaunce, bi which a man dieth in deedly synne. 1563 *Form Common Prayer* B iv, Thy pacyence beynge..ouercome at the laste, wyth oure obstynate vnrepentaunce. 1579 W. Fulke *Heskins' Parl.* 482 With vnreuerence and vnrepentance, they presume against..so high a mysterie. 1623 Bp. Hall *Contempl., O.T.* xix. x, Hee might have averted it by his prayers: their unrepentance disabled him. 1661 COWLEY *Cromwell* Ess., etc. (1906) 372 Though the outward unrepentance of his death afford but small materials for the work of Charity. 1690 H. WHARTON *Serm.* (1700) 383 Man continuing in a state of unrepentance. 1860 BP. S. WILBERFORCE *Addr. Cand. Ordination* 45 To all..who do not, by actual unrepentance and unbelief, bar His gracious working. 1882 BESANT *All Sorts* II. 275 My brother is hardened in his unrepentance.

**Unrepe·ntant,** *a.* (UN-[1] 7, 5 b.) *c* 1380 WYCLIF *Sel. Wks.* III. 108 Þurghe his wyckede and unrepentant herte. 1395 PURVEY *Remonstr.* (1851) 119 The curat shulde remove hem fro Goddis boord, if he parceyuith hem vnrepentaunt. *c* 1440 *Jacob's Well* 9 In þis cursyng, who-so deye vnrepentaunt, schal haue a dredeful ende! 1548 CRANMER *Catech.* 222 b, Unrepentaunte synners and vnbelevers. 1588 *Marprel. Epist.* (Arb.) 45 The soule of the vnrepentant papist. 1631 *High Commission Cases* (Camden) 213 The body of the unrepentant sinner. 1671 MILTON *P. R.* III. 429 Should I of these the liberty regard, Who,..unrepentant, unreform'd, Headlong would follow. 1813 SCOTT *Rokeby* III. xiv, Among the feasters waited near Sorrow, and unrepentant Fear. 1856 FROUDE *Hist. Eng.* I. 358 The two offenders were hopelessly unrepentant. 1869 MOZLEY *Univ. Serm.* ii. (1877) 34 False goodness is..an unrepentant type of evil.

*absol.* 1581 A. GOLDING *Test. 12 Patriarchs* 59 The Lorde, who either taketh away his benefites from the wicked,..or els reserueth them in the vnrepentant, to their endlesse punishment. 1617 J. BARBIER *Janua Ling.* 4 The sinnes of the vnrepentant.

Hence **Unrepe·ntantly** *adv.*, **-ness.**

*c* 1440 *Promp. Parv.* 366/2 *On-repentawntly, *inpenitenter*. 1647 TRAPP *Comm. Matt.* xxvi. 75 Stephen Gardiner..both stinkingly and unrepentantly died. 1859 *Lyndesay's Wks.* 440 *marg.*, Princes that, unrepentantly, live amiss. 1561 DAUS tr. *Bullinger on Apoc.* (1573) 126 b, The *vnrepentauntnesse and lasciuiousnes of them. 1571 GOLDING *Calvin on Ps.* lxix. 29 This is the last curse..that foloweth the unrepentantnesse, of which he spake.

**Unrepe·nted,** *ppl. a.* (UN-[1] 8, 5 c.) [*a* 1500 in *Ratis Raving*, etc. 3 The synis that he has done, wnconfessyt of or rapentyt.] 1649 OGILBY tr. *Virgil's Æneis* VI. (1684) 255 Crimes at their last Hour unrepented were. 1659 GAUDEN *Slight Healers* (1660) 45 What peace can there be or true healing, while..the deepest wounds..are unpunished and unrepented? 1729 LAW *Serious C.* xxiii. 460 The guilt of unrepented sins. 1795 SOUTHEY *Joan of Arc* IX. 38 Sent before the Eternal Judge, With all their unrepented crimes upon them. 1806 [see UNRELINQUISHED]. 1830 G. S. FABER *Diffic. Romanism* (ed. 2) I. v. 168 An act of unrepented idolatry. 1867 H. MACMILLAN *Bible Teach.* xii. 243 Humbling discoveries..of secret, unsuspected, unrepented sins.

**b.** With *of* († *on*, † *for*).

1597 HOOKER *Eccl. Pol.* v. lxxii. § 13 Heapes of grieuous transgressions..vnrepented of. 1629 RUTHERFORD *Let. to Lady Kenmure* 15 Jan., Fear of God's anger for old, unrepented-of sins. 1645 E. CALAMY *Indictm. Eng.* 23 This sin alone unrepented on will shut a man out of heaven. 1646 FULLER *Wounded Consc.* xvi. (1647) 122 Some unrepented-for sinne. *a* 1716 BLACKALL *Wks.* (1723) I. 77 His known, allow'd, unrepented-of Breach of that one Law. 1824 MISS L. M. HAWKINS *Annaline* III. 209 Where sin unrepented of cannot enter. 1889 M. HOUSTON *Sylvanus Redivivus* 164 The burden of unrepented-of sins.

**Unrepe·nting,** *ppl. a.* (UN-[1] 10.) *a* 1586 SIDNEY *Arcadia* III. xiv, Wicked woman,..whose unrepenting harte can find no way to amend treason, but by treason. 1655 JER. TAYLOR *Unum Necess.* v. § 3. 245 Unrepenting or habitual sinners. 1678 CUDWORTH *Intell. Syst.* 156 It goes on in one Constant, Unrepenting Tenor, from Generation to Generation. 1700 DRYDEN *Theod. & Hon.* 168 In unrepenting Sin she dy'd. 1730 A. PETRIE *Rules Good Deportm. Ch. Officers* 127 To their last Hour of unrepenting Death. 1790 GIBBON *Misc. Wks.* (1814) III. 396 The unrepenting tyrant had accomplished the measure of his sins. 1827 POLLOK *Course T.* VI. 496 The sword of Justice, red With..unrepenting wrath. 1839 HALLAM *Hist. Lit.* III. ii. § 25 A Jesuit wrote a book to prove that unrepenting Protestants could not be saved.

Hence **Unrepe·ntingly** *adv.*, **-ness.**

1615 HIERON *Wks.* I. 606 Such is the stablenesse of His counsell,..the vnrepentingnesse of His conferring sauing grace. 1789 CHARLOTTE SMITH *Ethelinde* (1814) V. 333 Though he now unrepentingly was gone where all his crimes were registered.

**Unrepi·ned,** *ppl. a.* (UN-[1] 8, 8 c.) 1626 BP. HALL *Contempl.*, *O. T.* XXI. iii, To continue those [taxes] he found unrepined at.

**Unrepi·ning,** *ppl. a.* (UN-[1] 10.) 1637 BP. HALL *Rem. Prophaneness* II. § 11 (1662) 80 What unrepining subjection to the rod? 1654 *Nicholas Papers* (Camden) II. 118 That I may be able to keepe him in the present free and unrepyning humor. 1739 GLOVER *Hosier's Ghost* 65 Unrepining at thy glory, Thy successful arms we hail. 1815 SCOTT *Guy M.* xxix, She would sit up..to nurse me with the most unrepining patience. 1850 MRS. JAMESON *Leg. Monast. Ord.* 402 She endured all unrepining.

Hence **Unrepi·ningly** *adv.*

1626 WOTTON *Let.* in *Rem.* (1651) 507 His indisputable will must be done, and unrepiningly received by his own Creatures. 1748 RICHARDSON *Clarissa* II. 237 [As] the will of Providence..leads, let me patiently and unrepiningly follow. 1876 BANCROFT *Hist. U.S.* I. ix. 277 He unrepiningly went to meet impoverishment..for the welfare of Massachusetts.

**Unrepla·ceable,** *a.* (UN-[1] 7 b, 5 b.) 1801 SOUTHEY *Lett.* (1856) I. 153 Humphry Davy is an unreplaceable companion. 1856 RUSKIN *Mod. Paint.* IV. v. xx. § 41 The head of the Lake of Geneva being..unreplaceable if destroyed. 1894 *Blackw. Mag.* Oct. 463 He was, like Napoleon, unreplaceable.

**Unrepla·ced,** *ppl. a.* (UN-[1] 8.) 1883 LD. LYTTON *Life & Lett. Lytton* II. 36 There is a charm in sympathetic female companionship unapproached, and unreplaced, by any friendship.

**Unreple·nished,** *ppl. a.* (UN-[1] 8.) 1562 BACON in D'Ewes *Jrnl.* (1682) 60/1 Few came to Service, and the Church so [was] unreplenished. 1614 GORGES *Lucan* VII. 280 The townes are vnreplenished. The champian vninhabited. 1660 BOYLE *New Exp. Phys. Mech.* xvii. 126 Some Air..kept the Mercury out of the unreplenish'd space. 1817 SHELLEY *Pr. Athan.* I. 59 Though his life..Was failing like an unreplenished stream. 1854 J. S. C. ABBOTT *Napoleon* (1855) I. 478 Gradually the unreplenished piles burnt out.

† **Unrepli·able,** *a. Obs.* [UN-[1] 7 b, 5 b.] Unanswerable.

1653 R. BAILLIE *Dissuas. Vind.* (1655) 1 Arguments of no lesse than steel, and that unsheathed and shining, evident and unrepliable. 1663 GRIFFITH *Serm. Four Admirable Beasts* 23 His wise, unreprovable and unrepliable answers. 1716 M. DAVIES *Athen. Brit.* II. To Rdr. 41 The unreplyable A[rch]b[ishop] Tenison's Tract of Idolatry.

† **Unrepli·ably,** *adv. Obs.* (UN-[1] 11.) 1648 N. HOMES in J. Cotton *Congregat. Ch. Cleared* A 2, You will meet with..divers precious Saints..evidently and unrepliablely vindicated. 1715 M. DAVIES *Athen. Brit.* I. Pref. 34 Topicks..answer'd unrepliably innumerable times. **Unrepli·ed,** *ppl. a.* (UN-[1] 8, 8 c.) 1825 SCOTT *Talism.* vii, The Scottish barons..were not men to bear his scorn unobserved or unreplied to. 1856 LEVER *Martins of Cro' M.* xviii, Three [letters] of hers had been left unreplied to! **Unreply·ing,** *ppl. a.* (UN-[1] 10.) 1791 COWPER *Iliad* v. 817 He spake; but Hector unreplying pass'd Impetuous. 1812 CARY *Dante, Parad.* I. 126 Oft-times, but ill accords the form To the design of art, through sluggishness Of unreplying matter. 1892 *Pall Mall G.* 16 Apr. 7/1 The voiceless lips of the unreplying dead.

**Unrepo·rtable,** *a.* (UN-[1] 7 b, 5 b.) 1611 SPEED *Hist. Gt. Brit.* IX. viii. § 37 Which brought..his Kingdome to vn-reportable calamities. 1871 L. STEPHEN *Playgr. Europe* iii. 124 A volley of unreportable language from the Chamouni guides. 1883 *Harper's Mag.* Jan. 208/1 Stirring stories some of them, but as unreportable as the..metaphors in which they were portrayed.

**Unrepo·rted,** *ppl. a.* (UN-[1] 8.) 1622 MALYNES *Anc. Law-Merch.* 284 This finesse of Siluer hid and vnreported in the bullion. 1808 MITFORD *Hist. Greece* III. 65 On some turn in the popular mind,..unreported by antient writers, they were imprisoned. 1850 THACKERAY *Pendennis* lxii, In consequence of that unreported conversation. 1884 *Marshall's Tennis Cuts* 21 Some unreported club or local handicap.

**Unrepo·sed,** *ppl. a.* (UN-[1] 8.) 1827 POLLOK *Course T.* VII. 581 Great Ocean! strongest of creation's sons, unreposed, untired. **Unrepo·seful,** *a.* (UN-[1] 7.) 1883 *Fortn. Rev.* July 118 The passions, and the foible of that unreposeful time. **Unrepo·sing,** *ppl. a.* (UN-[1] 10.) 1817 SHELLEY *Rev. Islam* II. i, The murmur of the unreposing brooks. 1862 MILMAN *Mem. Macaulay* 19 The ballad['s]..whole excellence is in..unreposing, unflagging, vigorous, stirring life. **Unreprehe·nded,** *ppl. a.* (UN-[1] 8.) *a* 1614 DONNE Βιαθανατος (1644) 195 Some of the Patriarches lived unreprehended in Polygamie. 1739 R. BULL tr. *Dedekindus' Grobianus* 40 Unreprehended there, supine, you lie. **Unrepresе·ntable,** *a.* (UN-[1] 7 b, 5 b.) 1840 *Penny Cycl.* XVI. 20/2 Unrepresentable by any kind of musical instrument at present known. 1850 H. BUSHNELL *God in Christ* 156 The Unapproachable, and, as far as all measures of..conception are concerned, the Unrepresentable God. **Unreprese·ntative,** *a.* (UN-[1] 7.) 1832 A. W. FONBLANQUE *Eng. under 7 Administr.* (1837) II. 236 An unrepresentative House of Representation. 1884 *Pall Mall G.* 18 July 10/2 An irresponsible and unrepresentative House of Lords.

**Unreprese·nted,** *ppl. a.* [UN-[1] 8.]

**1.** Not represented by a member of a legislative body.

1681 *Jedburgh Town Council Records* 29 Sept. (MS.), That the Burgh may not be unrepresented by Magistrates, Councillors and others. *c* 1778 *Conquerors* 13 No subjects can be tax'd unrepresented. 1787 HAWKINS *Life Johnson* 502 The far greater number of the subjects of England..are unrepresented in parliament. 1849 MACAULAY *Hist. Eng.* i. I. 135 Very few unrepresented towns had yet grown into importance. 1884 *Manch. Exam.* 10 Sept. 5/3 The county..would [not] be indifferent to the claims of the unrepresented two millions.

**2.** Not represented by an instance, individual, etc.

1854 *Poultry Chron.* I. 350/2, 13 classes..were entirely unrepresented in the entries! 1885 *Mag. of Art* June 350 The exhibition at the Grosvenor Gallery, with Mr. Whistler at Suffolk Street, Mr. Burne Jones unrepresented,..is [etc.].

**3.** Not yet produced upon the stage.

1888 *Daily Telegr.* 13 Feb. (Encycl. Dict.), A single performance of hitherto unrepresented works.

†**Unrepre·ssable,** *a. Obs.* [UN-[1] 7 b.] Irrepressible. 1607 MARKHAM *Cavel.* II. 95 Diuers horses..bee so vnrepressable in the violence of their furies, that [etc.].

**Unrepre·ssed,** *ppl. a.* (UN-[1] 8.) 1583 GOLDING *Calvin on Deut.* xxxv. 211 His bearing with such blasphemie so as it hath full scope vnrepressed. 1803 EUGENIA DE ACTON *Ess.* I. 82 The fervour of a youthful mind,..if unrepressed by the precepts of..prudence. 1830 TENNYSON *Arab. Nts.* 74 Life, anguish, death, immortal love, Ceasing not, mingled, unrepress'd. 1861 TRENCH *Comm. Ep. Churches Asia* 50 Every disorder..which has remained unrepressed.

**Unrepre·ssible,** *a.* [UN-[1] 7, 5 b.] Irrepressible. 1804 EUGENIA DE ACTON *Tale without Title* II. 158. 1846 WORCESTER (citing Dr. Barton).

**Unreprie·vable,** *a.* (UN-[1] 7 b.) 1593 NASHE *Christ's T.* 36 b, The best remedy of thyne vnreprieuable peruerse destiny was death. 1595 SHAKS. *John* v. vii. 48 There the poyson Is, as a fiend, confin'd to tyrannize, On vnreprеeuable condemned blood. *a* 1625 FLETCHER *Elder Brother* II. i, Thou unreprieveable Dunce! ..dost thou tell me I should?

Hence **Unreprie·vably** *adv.*

1594 NASHE *Unfort. Trav.* Ded., Vnrepriuebly perisheth that booke whatsoeuer to wast paper, which [etc.]. 1596 — *Saffron Walden* F ij, His bedred stuffe..else would haue laine vnrepriuably spittled at the Chandlers.

**Unreprie·ved,** *ppl. a.* (UN-[1] 8.) 1667 MILTON *P. L.* II. 185 There to converse with everlasting groans, Unrespited, unpitied, unrepreevd. 1735 SOMERVILLE *Chace* III. 213 But unrepriev'd he [*sc.* a captive fox] dies. 1820 SHELLEY *Prometh. Unb.* I. 423 The slow years Which thou must spend in torture, unreprieved.

**Unrepri·nted,** *ppl. a.* (UN-[1] 8.) [1775 ASH.] 1872 W. MINTO *Eng. Lit.* I. i. 82 One of his unreprinted papers. 1885 *Athenæum* 5 Sept. 305/3 It was ..intended to confine it to unreprinted pieces.

† **Unreproa·chable,** *a. Obs.* (UN-[1] 7 b, 5 b.) 1603 HOLLAND *Plutarch's Mor.* 244 The purenesse of our life and innocencie unreprochable. 1625 DONNE *Serm.* (1626) 40 These bills must be well testified, with vnreproachable witnesses. *a* 1711 KEN *Hymn.* Poet. Wks. 1721 II. 143 Whether God hears the Pray'rs of Saints or not,..God unreproachable remains. 1737 WHISTON *Josephus, Hist.* I. ix. § 4 An unreproachable witness. 1768 BLACKSTONE *Comm.* III. xxii. 347 Where the defendant bore a fair and unreproachable character.

**Unreproa·ched,** *ppl. a.* (UN-[1] 8.) 1648 *Eikon Bas.* viii. 49 Sir John Hotham unreproached, unthreatned, uncursed by any language or secret imprecation of Mine. 1753 FOOTE *Englishm. in Paris* II, Full fifteen years, in wedlock's sacred bands, have I liv'd unreproach'd. *a* 1812 BUCKMINSTER *Serm.* (1827) 262 He passed through the world unreproached. He now sees, that his innocence.. was unreproached, because unknown or despised.

**Unreproa·chful,** *a.* (UN-[1] 7.) *c* 1720 GAY in *Pope's Wks., Addits.* (1776) I. 99 Friendly Congreve, unreproachful man! 1837 LYTTON *Athens* II. 574 An anxious, earnest unreproachful devotion of conjugal love. 1838 MRS. BROWNING *Seraphim* II. 362 With these forgiving hands upraising Their unreproachful wounds. 1869 LYTTON *Orval* 56 Nay, not till..all the love I render back With unreproachful tears.

**Unreproa·chfully,** *adv.* (UN-[1] 11.) 1671 CLARENDON *Hist. Reb.* x. § 171 He could never have been rid of him again so unreproachfully, as by his changing his own countenance.

**Unreproa·ching,** *ppl. a.* (UN-[1] 10.) 1742 RICHARDSON *Pamela* xx. (1785) III. 103 Nay, [she would have] reproach'd you more, by her unreproaching obligingness. 1766 GOLDSM. *Vicar W.* xxii, That books were sweet unreproaching companions to the miserable. 1858 FARRAR *Eric* 15 An unreproaching conscience. 1876 GEO. ELIOT *Dan. Der.* lxiv, The unreproaching voice of birds.

Hence **Unreproa·chingly** *adv.*

1753 RICHARDSON *Grandison* (1781) V. xli. 257 How unreproachingly may we call each other by that sacred name!

**Unreprodu·cible,** *a.* (UN-[1] 7, 5 b.) 1880 GOLDW. SMITH *Cowper* vi. 92 It belongs to an unreproducible past. 1893 *Nation* (N. Y.) 18 May 371/1 Desperate efforts to reproduce the unreproducible. 1899 KIPLING *Stalky* 225 An unreproducible sniff..rounded the retort. [Freq. in recent use.]

**Unrepro·vable,** *a.* Now *rare.* [UN-[1] 7 b, 5 b.] Irreprovable, irreproachable. (Common *c* 1550–1680.)

1382 WYCLIF *Tobit* x. 13 Monestende hir..to gouerne the hous, to ȝiue hirself vnreprefable. *c* 1385 CHAUCER *L. G. W.* 691 *Cleopatra*, Vnreprouable on to myn wyfhod ay, The same wolde I fele, lyf or deth. *a* 1548 HALL *Chron.*, *Hen. VIII*, 227 In life and conuersacion vnreprouable. 1581 J. BELL *Haddon's Answ. Osor.* 76 b, Whose wordes and deedes we may accoumpt without exception unreproveable. 1615 G. SANDYS *Trav.* 135 She was..of life vnreproueable. 1635 PAGITT *Christianogr.* I. i. 4 Historiographers, and other unreproveable Authors. 1712 STEELE *Spect.* No. 302 ⁋ 14 Ye guardian Angels,..lead her gently hence innocent and unreprovable to a better Place. 1791 COWPER *Iliad* IX. 650 Thy wrath was unreproveable and just. 1851 RUSKIN *Stones Ven.* I. xxvii. § 17 His work is absolutely unreproveable.

Hence **Unrepro·vableness, -ably** *adv.*

1634 SANDERSON *Serm., Ad Mag.* iii. (1681) II. 286 See to it..that you walk orderly and unreproveably your selves. 1680 W. CLAGETT *Disc., Answ.* 24 The unreproveableness of the Spiritual man in assenting to the mysteries of the Gospel.

**Unrepro·ved,** *ppl. a.* (UN-[1] 8.) *a* 1400–50 *Alexander* 3092 For-þi ȝour werke ay be witt ȝe wirke vnreproued [*v.r.* vnreprefytt]. *c* 1400 *Found. St. Bartholomew's* (1923) 13 He..yn his techynge vnrepreuyd was fownde. 1420–2 LYDG. *Thebes* 4152 That we bygan we knyghtly han achieuyd Vpon our foon, with worship vnrepreuyd. 1578 WHETSTONE *Promos & Cass.* II. III. i, God graunt I scape this blacke day unrepprev'd. 1590 SPENSER *F. Q.* II. vii. 16 The antique world..with glad thankes, and vnreproued truth, The gifts of soueraigne bountie did embrace. 1615 G. SANDYS *Trav.* 14 Yet haue the Christians their Churches, and vnreproued exercise of religion. 1667 MILTON *P. L.* IV. 493 With eyes Of conjugal attraction unreprov'd. 1703 DE FOE *More Reform.* 8 Let them expose thy Errors to the Town, Thou shalt go unreprov'd, 'till they repent. 1760–72 H. BROOKE *Fool of Qual.* (1809) III. 18 Man..riots at large and unreproved. 1820 SCOTT *Monast.* iv, The servants mingled,..unreproved and with freedom, in whatever conversation was going forward. 1861 LD. ACTON in Gasquet *Ld. A. & Circle* (1906) 165 Newman's view of the Council of Trent should not go unreproved.

**Unrepro·ving,** *ppl. a.* (UN-[1] 10.) 1748 THOMSON *Cast. Indol.* I. xxviii, Here dwells kind ease, and unreproving joy. *a* 1850 MRS. BROWNING *Woman's Shortcomings* ii, She..Hears bold words, unreproving. **Unrepu·blican,** *a.* (UN-[1] 7.) 1878 *N. Amer. Rev.* CXXVI. 13 Erasmus's description of what he calls the unrepublican bird [*sc.* the eagle]. 1885 *Atlantic Monthly* April 450 The importation of uneducated, un-American, un-republican workmen. † **Unrepu·gnable,** *a. Obs.* (UN-[1] 7 b, 5 b.) *c* 1440 *Gesta Rom.* xxvii. 102 (Harl. MS.), Thow most sey iij. trewe poyntes, þat shul be vnrepugnable. 1611 SPEED *Hist. Gt. Brit.* VIII. ii. § 11. 389/1 So mighty and almost vnrepugnable an enemie.

**Unrepu·gnant,** *a.* (UN-[1] 7.) 1594 HOOKER *Eccl. Pol.* III. ix. § 1 When [Scripture gives] Positiue [laws], which way to make Lawes vnrepugnant vnto them. 1642 CHAS. I *Answ. to Bristol & Dorset* 3 Severall and farre different conceptions; yet none unrepugnant to reason. 1823 SCOTT *Quentin D.* xviii, The unrepugnant acquiescence of Hayraddin in their change of route.

**Unrepu·lsable,** *a.* (Un-[1] 7 b.) **1814** Jane Austen *Mansf. Park* xxxiv, Fanny..was trying..to repulse Mr. Crawford, and avoid both his looks and inquiries; and he, unrepulsable, was persisting in both. **Unrepu·lsing,** *ppl. a.* (Un-[1] 10.) **1748** Richardson *Clarissa* (1811) IV. 254, I kissed her unrepulsing hand. **Unrepu·lsive,** *a.* (Un-[1] 7.) **1835** Willis *Pencillings* I. iii. 26 We sat down once more to clean cloths and unrepulsive food.

**Unre·putable,** *a.* (Un-[1] 7 b, 5 b.)
**1698** Collier *Immor. Stage* vi. 240 The Athenians.. thought a Comedy so unreputable a Performance, that [etc.]. **1703** J. Savage *Lett. Antients* cxiii. 277 It is..unreputable to change ones Friends often. **1724** *Briton* No. 26 (1724) 115 Let Fools..of unreputable Praise be proud.

**Unrepu·ted,** *ppl. a.* (Un-[1] 8.) **1596** *Edward III*, ii. i. 436 An vnreputed mote, flying in the Sunne, Presents a greater substaunce then it is. **Unreque·st,** *v.* (Un-[2] 3.) **1552** Hooper *Let.* Wks. (Parker Soc.) p. xx, When that I perceived my request for jurisdiction made before unto you, upon further deliberation I thought it good to unrequest that again.

**Unreque·sted,** *ppl. a.* (Un-[1] 8.)
**1576** R. Peterson *G. della Casa's Galateo* 60 To offer aduyse vnrequested. **1587** Golding *De Mornay* xxxiv. 634 How vnindifferent are these people, which will needes both beleeue and be beleeued of all men without witnesse and vnrequested [F. *sans enqueste*]. **1609** W. M. *Man in Moon* G 4 b, How hee would..proffer, vnrequested, many seruile ceremonies. **1641** Earl Monm. tr. *Biondi's Civil Warres* v. 93 Though unrequested on Henries behalfe, the soveraigntie of France was demanded on Charles. **1709** Mrs. Centlivre *Gamester* iv, Valere has..exposed my unrequested bounty. *a* **1768** Secker *Serm.* (1771) V. vii. 136 Without this no Person would have..more Assistance in Distress from his Neighbour, than..unrequested Goodness [would] incline him to bestow.

**Unrequi·red,** *ppl. a.* [Un-[1] 8.]
**1.** Of persons: Not requested or asked; without being asked.
**1412–20** Lydg. *Chron. Troy* i. 2405 But more frely, with herte ful entere, Liste vnrequered on my wo to rewe. **1514** Barclay *Cyt. & Uplondyshman* (Percy Soc.) 13 And unrequyred presentynge them, sayde she, O Lorde, these also my veray chyldren be! **1561** T. Hoby tr. *Castiglione's Courtyer* ii. (1577) H vj b, They..that rashly before a greate man enter into talk vnrequired. **1594** T. Bedingfield tr. *Machiavelli's Florentine Hist.* (1595) 172 Many times also vnrequired he did lend to those Gentlemen. **1634** Bp. Hall *Contempl., N. T.* iv. xxxii. 266 So free, that he shall willingly undergoe it, when it is laid upon him; not so free as that he shall lay it upon himselfe, unrequired. **1748** Richardson *Clarissa* (1811) III. 13 How artfully does he (unrequired) promise to observe the conditions?
**2.** Of things: Unasked for, unsought; not demanded or called for.
*c* **1510** Barclay *Mirr. Gd. Manners* (1570) G v, Desire thou none office nor cure...If it unrequired be geuen vnto thee,..do not the same despise. **1559** in Tytler *Hist. Scot.* (1864) III. 396 As I have found this your good mind unrequired,..I am bold to desire you..to continue in the same. **1687** Boyle *Martyrd. Theodora* x. 179 A young Lady, in whose Sex, Courage is..an unrequired, if not an altogether improper, Vertue. **1818** Scott *Rob Roy* xxxix, His unrequired presence prevented me from speaking freely to Syddall.
**3.** Not requisite; unnecessary.
**1847** C. Bronte *J. Eyre* xxxv, He would make me sensible that it was a superfluity, unrequired by him. **1849** Eastwick *Dry Leaves* 163 The caution was unrequired.

**Unre·quisite,** *a.* (Un-[1] 7, 5 b.)
**1594** Hooker *Eccl. Pol.* iii. xi. § 16 Much may be requisite which the scripture teacheth not, and much which it hath taught, become vnrequisite. **1603** J. Davies (Heref.) *Microcosmos* Wks. (Grosart) I. 31/2 Too full Of fearefull thoughts, and cares vnrequisit. **1621** in Foster *Eng. Factories Ind.* I. (1906) 270 It is nott unrequizite that some Englishman accompany the goods. **1817** Keatinge *Trav.* I. 278 Without allowing the meats to cool by unrequisite delay.

**Unrequi·table,** *a.* (Un-[1] 7 b, 5 b.)
**1584** W. Warner *Syrinx* (1597) O j, Vnrequitable are the duties, wherein we are..indebted to our Mothers. **1617** Donne *Serm.* Wks. 1839 VI. 3 There are persons which are unrequitable, though they be believed to loue. **1646** Sir T. Browne *Pseud. Ep.* v. xxi. 269 An unrequitable evil may ensue. **1683** Kennett *Erasm. on Folly* 17 An unrequitable obligation.

**Unrequi·tal.** (Un-[1] 12, 5 b.)
**1865** Mrs. Whitney *Gayworthys* xxx, Old love sleeps, if it do not die. It has..its pains and its unrequital. **1867** *Spectator* 6 Apr. 386 Glorious in their unrequital.

**Unrequi·ted,** *ppl. a.* (Un-[1] 8.)
*a* **1542** Wyatt in *Tottel's Misc.* (Arb.) 53 Complaint for true loue vnrequited. **1622** J. Hagthorpe in Farr *S. P. Jas. I* (1848) 347 If from a friend some trifle we receiue,..We think ourselues ungratefull if we leaue These vnrequited. **1634** Bp. Hall *Contempl., N. T.* iv. iii, Who can ever say, Lord, this favour I did to the least of thine, unrequited? **1741–2** Gray *Agrippina* 76 Benefits, too great To be repaid, Sit heavy on the soul, As unrequited wrongs. **1793** J. Tweddell *Rem.* (1815) 48 Productive..of unrequited bloodshed. **1814** Wordsw. *Excurs.* vi. 109 Being crazed in brain By unrequited love. **1857** J. H. Newman *Serm. Var. Occas.* xii. 261 The times of patience,..of humble, unrequited service. **1893** [see Unrequiter].
Hence **Unrequi·tedly** *adv.*, **Unrequi·tedness.**
**1648** Boyle *Seraph. Love* xiv. (1659) 94 So far from enabling us by them, to Requite his Love,..it encreases the Unrequitednesse of it. **1867** Miss Broughton *Not wisely but too well* I. 108 Falling in love violently, and as it now appeared unrequitedly, with a man her superior in station.
**Unrequi·tement.** (Un-[1] 12.) **1890** Talmage *Manger to Throne* 425 In wrath at this unrequitement of the mercy.. shown him. **Unrequi·ter.** (Un-[1] 12.) **1893** A. Kenealy *Molly & Man-of-War* 94 The story of an unrequited love, and a sight of the photograph of the unrequiter. **Unresci·nded,** *ppl. a.* (Un-[1] 8.) **1716** in *Records of Stitchill* (S.H.S.) 173 So long as this Act stands unrescinded. **Unre·scued,** *ppl. a.* (Un-[1] 8.) [**1775** Ash.] **1846** Worcester (citing *Ec. Rev.*). †**Unrese·mblable,** *a.* (Un-[1] 7 b.) **1678** Cudworth *Intell. Syst.* i. iv. 189 Thereby debasing both themselves and God, not glorifying Him according to His spiritual and unresembleable nature. †**Unrese·mblant,** *a.* [Un-[1] 7.] Dissimilar. **1653** F. G. tr. *Scuderi's Artamenes* (1655) IV. vii. iii. 191 One and the same Passion produced in them effects very unresemblant.

**Unrese·mbling,** *ppl. a.* (Un-[1] 10, 5 d.)
**1598** Florio, *Dissimile*,..vnlike, vnresembling. **1655** Earl Orrery *Parthen.* i. viii. 383 He had once seene some features not vnresembling his. **1683** Dryden *Ded. to Plutarch's Lives* 26 Malice will make a picture more unresembling than ignorance. **1702** S. Parker tr. *Cicero's De Finibus* iv. 262 Some of your Unresembling Similitudes! **1799** Lamb *Let. to Southey* 2 March, Following, at unresembling distance, Sterne, and greater Cervantes.
Hence **Unrese·mblingly** *adv.*
**1662** Ormonde in Carte *Life* (1735) III. 23, I have the honour, how unworthily and how unresemblingly soever, to represent the Majesty of my Great Master. **1665** Boyle *Occas. Refl.* i. i. 162 Not unresemblingly deals God with us.

**Unrese·nted,** *ppl. a.* (Un-[1] 8.)
**1705** Vanburgh *Mistake* iii. i, You must not think so daring an affront to my family can go long unresented. **1711** Addison *Spect.* No. 99 ¶ 7 One may tell another he..Drinks, Blasphemes, and it may pass unresented. **1748** Richardson *Clarissa* VII. 47 It is still a worse imputation, that she should pass over so mortal an injury unresented. **1811** Miss L. M. Hawkins *C'tess & Gertr.* 239 He had suffered to pass, unnoticed and unresented, her former ill-humor. **1886** A. Weir *Hist. Basis Mod. Europe* iii. 115 To suffer unresented the contemptuous demeanour of his unprofitable superiors.

**Unrese·ntful,** *a.* (Un-[1] 7.)
**1773** Melmoth tr. *Cato* (1777) I. 252 The same philosophers, who contended for this innoxious and unresentful character of the Deity. **1805** Wordsw. *Prelude* v. 414 A race of real children;..Not unresentful where self-justified. **1862** 'Shirley' (J. Skelton) *Nugæ Crit.* x. 441 He bore the pang..with proud confidence and unresentful regret.
Hence **Unrese·ntfully** *adv.*, **-fulness.**
**1862** Lowell *Biglow P.* Ser. ii. Poet. Wks. (1912) 320 Good-nature..becomes a positive crime when it leads us to look unresentfully on peculation. **1899** G. Tyrrell in Petre *Life* (1912) II. 16 Abounding in sympathy, unresentfulness,.. loyalty, fidelity.

**Unrese·nting,** *ppl. a.* (Un-[1] 10.)
**1716** Collier tr. *Gregory of Nazianzus* 57 'Twas this [patience] which made..Stephen unresenting when ston'd 'to death'. **1759** Sterne *Tr. Shandy* ii. xii, But to hurt a brother of such gentle manners,—..so unresenting;—'tis base. **1810** Coleridge *Friend* 358 To remain in nominal Peace and unresenting Passiveness with an insolent neighbour. **1861** Geo. Eliot *Silas M.* iii, Godfrey..left the room, followed humbly by the unresenting Snuff.

**Unrese·rve.** [Un-[1] 12.] Absence of reserve; frankness.
**1751** J. Duncombe in *Richardson's Corr.* (1804) II. 273 He has rather more openness and unreserve than his brother. **1777** Wraxall *Court of Berlin* (1799) I. 92, I was as much penetrated with her condescension and unreserve, as I was charmed by her..love of knowledge. **1826** Disraeli *Viv. Grey* v. xi, 'May I really speak with freedom?'..'With the most perfect unreserve and confidence,' answered Vivian. **1862** Lytton *Str. Story* I. 80 You have done well to confide in me with so generous an unreserve.

**Unrese·rved,** *ppl. a.* [Un-[1] 8.]
**1.** Unrestricted, unlimited, absolute.
**1539** Hen. VIII in *Wyatt's Wks.* (1816) II. 498 He will send to my Lady Regent..full and unreserved power..to..conclude the same upon reasonable conditions. *a* **1729** Rogers *19 Serm.* (1735) 311 An entire unreserved Obedience to his Commands. **1768–74** Tucker *Lt. Nat.* (1834) II. 422 We may have an unreserved trust in His mercy. **1771** *Junius Lett.* lix. (1788) 321 A determination so entire and unreserved. **1818** Scott *Hrt. Midl.* xiv, A friend,..whose attachment deserved her full and unreserved confidence. **1858** Froude *Hist. Eng.* III. 260 Her name is mentioned ..with unreserved respect.
**2.** Free from reserve; frank, open.
**1713** Pope *Lett.* (1735) I. 199 That we have lived many Years together in an unreserved Conversation. **1751** Earl Orrery *Remarks Swift* ii. 15 Her manners were humane, polite, easy, and unreserved. **1827** R. Peel *Let. to Croker* 3 Oct., In consequence of unreserved communications with you, you were in possession of my opinions. **1884** *American* VIII. 277 Mr. Bright was more unreserved in his language. *absol.* **1756** Cowper *Wks.* (1837) XV. 278 The character of the open and unreserved, who thinks it a breach of friendship to conceal any thing from his intimates.

**Unrese·rvedly,** *adv.* [Un-[1] 11.]
**1.** Without reservation or limitation; absolutely.
**1651** Baxter *Inf. Bapt.* 224 The entrance into Covenant, and acceptation of the terms of it (though not sincerely and unreservedly). **1687** Boyle *Martyrd. Theodora* xi. 201, I should have been very much, if not unreservedly, guided by your wishes. **1768–74** Tucker *Lt. Nat.* (1834) II. 399 We may trust unreservedly to the words..of the perfect wise man. **1823** Scott *Quentin D.* xxvi, My own person I have this morning placed unreservedly in your power. **1850** Thackeray *Pendennis* ii, Everything was left unreservedly to her, except in case of a second marriage.
**2.** Without reserve; openly, frankly.
**1718** Addison *Let. to Swift* 20 Mar., To tell you unreservedly, I have been unwilling [etc.]. **1747** Richardson *Clarissa* (1811) I. 48 This I may the more unreservedly say to you. **1817** Ponsonby in *Parl. Deb.* 286/2 When the bill came before them, he should state his sentiments unreservedly. **1867** Mrs. H. Wood *Orville College* xxiii, Full of her griefs and grievances, she spoke out unreservedly.

**Unrese·rvedness.** [Un-[1] 12.] The quality of being unreserved.
**1648** Boyle *Seraph. Love* (1659) 23 The tendernesse and unreserv'dnesse of his Love. **1713** Pope *Lett.* (1735) I. 203 I am conscious I write with more unreservedness than ever Man wrote, or perhaps talk'd to another. **1742** Richardson *Pamela* IV. 226 An Unreservedness of Air and Behaviour, that I had not before seen so becoming. **1821** in Picton *L'pool Munic. Rec.* (1886) II. 391, I will do so with all unreservedness, but I hope with all due civility. **1844** Stanley *Arnold* I. Pref. p. viii, The familiarity and unreservedness of epistolary intercourse. **1882** *Macm. Mag.* XLV. 304 The freedom..of his speech, its buoyancy and unreservedness.

†**Unre·sident,** *sb. Obs.*[−1] [Un-[1] 12.] = Non-resident *sb.* 2. **1683** *Col. Rec. Pennsylv.* I. 65 Publique houses to credit no Vnresident for above 20ˢ. †**Unre·sident,** *a. Obs.*[−1] (Un-[1] 7.) **1574** *Reg. Privy Council Scot.* II. 352 Nor yit ar the unresident personnis admoneist.

**Unresi·gned,** *ppl. a.* (Un-[1] 8.)
*a* **1641** D. Baker *Holy Practises* (1657) 11 Contrarie to the proprietarious or vnresigned will of our corrupt nature. **1893** F. Adams *New Egypt* 170 Petulant and unresigned with his own, but..submissive to dictation when it came.

†**Unresi·stable,** *a. Obs.* [Un-[1] 7 b, 5 b.] Irresistible. (Common *c* 1590–1660.)
**1581** Sidney *Apol. Poetrie* (Arb.) 67 Many of such writings, as come vnder the banner of vnresistable loue. **1610** B. Jonson *Alch.* iii. iv, He will winne you By vnresistable lucke.. Inough to buy a baronie. **1614** Lithgow *Trav.* E 1 b, It pleased him..to send downe an vnresistable tempest. **1672** Temple *Ess., Govt.* (1680) 88 The unresistable force and conquests of some Nations over others.
**Unresi·stably,** *adv.* (Un-[1] 11, 5 b.) *a* **1591** H. Smith *Six Serm.* (1612) A 4 b, Till..Gods iust iudgements [came] as the whirle-winde suddenly, vnresistably. †**Unresi·stance.** *Obs.* (Un-[1] 12, 5 b.) **1644** Hunton *Vind. Treat. Monarchy* iv. 27 Being authoritative, they authorize the Instrument, and give him an unresistance. *a* **1656** Bp. Hall *Soliloquies* § 66 How do they [*sc.* dumb creatures] bear our stripes with a trembling unresistance? **Unresi·stant,** *a.* (Un-[1] 7.) **1830** Mangan *Poems* (1903) 283 The blast.., soon a tempest,..Will swoop down on its unresistant prey. **1884** *Cent. Mag.* XXIX. 7 He draws her, unresistant, to him.

**Unresi·sted,** *ppl. a.* [Un-[1] 8, 5 b.]
**1.** Not resisted; not meeting with resistance; † irresistible.
**1526** *Pilgr. Perf.* (W. de W. 1531) 66 b, Leest perauenture other heryinge theyr infamy vnresysted, despyse theyr holy prechynge. *c* **1586** C'tess Pembroke *Psalm* lxxi. ii, Show thy unresisted power, Working now thy wonted will. **1593** Shaks. *Lucr.* 282 As corne ore-growne by weedes: so heedfull feare Is almost choakt by unresisted lust. *a* **1614** Donne *Βιαθανατος* (1644) 128 That for the spirituall good of another, a man should expose his own life, is an unresisted doctrine. **1651** Baxter *Inf. Bapt.* Apol. 19 Our God..rather then Schism shall go unresisted, will [etc.]. **1705** Addison *The Campaign* 197 To Donavert, with unresisted force, The gay victorious army bends its course. **1789** Mrs. Piozzi *Journ. France* II. 370 Black heaths,..over which the unresisted wind sweeps. **1855** Macaulay *Hist. Eng.* xviii. IV. 119 The white flag, which..had ranged the Channel unresisted. **1881** Meredith *Tragic Com.* i, An unresisted lady-killer is probably less aware that [etc.].
† **2.** Uninterrupted. *Obs.*[−1]
**1603** Florio *Montaigne* iii. iii. 498 It hath three baye-windowes, of a farre-extending, ritch and vnresisted prospect.
Hence **Unresi·stedly** *adv.*
**1673** Boyle *Ess. Effic. Effluviums* vi. 33 These pass unresistedly thorow the pores of all solid Bodies, and even Glass it self. **1845** E. Warburton *Crescent & Cross* I. 351 The influence of that discipline..was now sending them unresistedly to encounter..privation in the depths of Africa. **1889** Welch *Text Bk. Naval Archit.* iii. 50 The purely hypothetical case of a vessel rolling unresistedly in still water.

**Unresi·stible,** *a.* Now *rare.* [Un-[1] 7, 5 b.] Irresistible.
**1608** *Great Frost* in *Arber's Garner* I. 90 The swift, violent, and unresistible land currents. *a* **1631** Donne *80 Serm.* (1640) 358 Which reproofe is an uncontrollable sense, and an unresistible remorse. *Ibid.* 384. **1653** Holcroft tr. *Procopius, Vandal Wars* ii. 38 To think the enemy unresistible because of his victory. **1760** Sterne *Tr. Shandy* iii. xxxviii, A mighty and unresistible call within me. **1891** Farrar *Darkn. & Dawn* lxvi, The Church..'by the unresistible might of weakness shook the world'.
Hence **Unresi·stibleness, -ibly** *adv.*
**1644** Hunton *Vind. Treat. Monarchy* v. 45 He is like to goe alone in this wild untroden path of defending an unresistiblenesse on such supposals. **1685** Baxter *Paraphr. N. T.* Jas. i. 13 God..tempteth no man to it (much less forceth them to it, or unresistibly..makes them sin).

**Unresi·sting,** *ppl. a.* (Un-[1] 10.)
**1625** K. Long tr. *Barclay's Argenis* ii. xi. 98 The River.. gently mingled itselfe with the unresisting Sea. **1653** Jer. Taylor *Serm. for Year* I. xx. 270 The bondage of conquered, wounded, unresisting people. **1691** Norris *Pract. Disc.* 329 As a Stone..[falling] through an unresisting Medium. **1744** Thomson *Spring* 440 To the Shore You gayly drag your unresisting Prize. **1786** tr. *Beckford's Vathek* 116 That unresisting languor, so frequently fatal to the female heart. **1855** Macaulay *Hist. Eng.* xiii. III. 282 The Jacobites, silent and unresisting, became prisoners. **1874** J. Geikie *Gt. Ice Age* xxi. 270 The rocky crust of the earth must needs have been as unresisting as putty.
Hence **Unresi·stingly** *adv.*, **-ness.**
**1797** Mrs. Radcliffe *Italian* vi, Ellena followed unresistingly up a path. **1844** Kinglake *Eothen* xxvi, They..unresistingly left their property to the hands of the spoilers. **1883** *Knowledge* 20 July 34/2 Groaningly it may be, but still unresistingly. **1900** Mrs. H. Ward *Eleanor* vi, Her attitude by its sad unresistingness appealed to Lucy.

†**Unre·snably,** *adv. Obs.* [Un-[1] 11 + Renably *adv.*] Unreasonably. **1461** *Paston Lett.* (1904) IV. 16 An evyll rewlyd felawschep..ferd ryth fowle with the Undyr Scheryfe, and onresnably as I herd sey.

**Unre·solute,** *a.* (Un-[1] 7, 5 b.)
**1579** Fenton *Guicciard.* 36 Mens witts wandring, and their mindes vnresolute. **1581** E. Campion in *Confer.* iii. (1584) O j, I am not vnresolute. **1600** Holland *Livy* i. xiv. 11 Whilest the Cavallirie stood unresolute as it were, in a mammering whither to flie or fight. *a* **1628** F. Grevil *Alaham* ii. iv. Chorus ii, Those Scenes still tedious are, those Acts too long, Where thy unresolute Images be strong.

**Unreso·lvable,** *a.* (Un-1 7 b, 5 b.)
**1611** Florio, *Irresolubile,* vnresolueable. **1624** Wotton *Elem. Archit.* 18 The Triangle which hath the fewest sides and corners, is..vnresoluable into any other regular Forme then it selfe. **1694** South *Serm.* (1698) III. 306 Men of Parts.., after all their Study,..are forced to give them over as Things Unresolveable. **1744** Young *Nt. Th.* vii. 606 Call; and with endless questions be distrest, All unresolve-able, if earth is All. **1850** McCosh *Div. Govt.* (1852) 260 Others..have distinctly recognised the importance of the will as an unresolvable and independent faculty. **1870** Ruskin *Lect. Art* (1875) 181 Your telescope..reveals nebula beyond nebula, far and farther,..unresolvable. **1874** Willshire *Anc. Prints* ii. 12 Various examples which..link the time of surety to that of *unresolvable* doubt.

**Unreso·lve,** *sb.* (Un-1 12, 5 b.) **1679** Mrs. Behn *Feign'd Curtizan* III. i, Come, lay by all sullen unresolves! **1895** *Outing* XXVI. 345/1 Her heart was torn, her mind a chaos of unresolve.

**Unreso·lve,** *v.* (Un-2 3, 7.)
**1675** Howe *Living Temple* 109 That the same thing is not ..resolved and unresolved a thousand times in a day. **1707** *Reflex. upon Ridicule* 331 Adriastus resolves and unresolves in the same Moment. **1746** W. Horsley *Fool* (1748) I. 188 He..consider'd, resolv'd, and unresolv'd, all in the same Moment. **1805–6** Cary *Dante, Inf.* ii. 39 As one who unresolves What he hath late resolved.

**Unreso·lved,** *ppl. a.* [Un-1 8, 5 b.]
**1.** Of questions, etc.: Undetermined, undecided, unsolved.
**1577** Holinshed *Chron.* II. 445/2 For to confesse..myne ignorance, or rather vnresolued doubt herein, I can not satisfie my selfe with any thing that I haue red. **1621** *First Bk. Discipl.* 10 Because..Articles thereanent remaine yet unresolved, and referred to further conference. **1652** Heylyn *Cosmogr.* I. 152 It is unresolved who this Samothes was. **1692** Ray *Disc.* III. ix. (1693) 348 So I leave this Question unresolved. **1754** Edwards *Freed. Will* II. iv. 48 [He] leaves all the Difficulty unresolved and the Question unanswered. **1856** Froude *Hist. Eng.* I. 101 Doubt on such a subject once mooted might not be left unresolved. **1856** *Orr's Circ. Sci., Pract. Chem.* 327 The reason of this is an unresolved enigma.

**2. a.** Uncertain or undetermined how to act; irresolute. Also *transf.* (quot. 1611).
**1594** Shaks. *Rich. III,* IV. iv. 436 To our Shores Throng many doubtfull hollow-hearted friends, Vnarm'd, and vnresolu'd to beat them backe. **1611** Tourneur *Ath. Trag.* II. i, With A kinde of unresolu'd unwilling pace. **1653** H. Cogan tr. *Pinto's Trav.* xvi. 52 Being unresolved what course to take. **1691** Norris *Pract. Disc.* 151 To be Doubtful and Unresolved in a business of such vast moment. **1725** De Foe *Voy. round World* (1840) 67 A crew of unresolved divided rogues. **1777** Robertson *Hist. Amer.* vi. (1778) II. 236 He ..was still unresolved, when the violence of the viceroy.. moved him to quit his residence. **1821** Scott *Pirate* xxxiv, Several were unresolved upon engaging in a..conflict.
*absol.* *a* **1659** Osborne *Wks.* (1673) 675 Nor did the readiness of the Scots to arm portend less in the ears of the unresolved, than a possibility of Conquest.

**b.** Uncertain in opinion; undecided.
**1597** Hooker *Eccl. Pol.* v. lxii. § 18 S. Augustines doubtfulnes..should not be mentioned by them which presume to define peremptorily of that wherein he was content to professe himselfe vnresolued. **1649** F. Roberts *Clavis Bibl.* 259 Authors seem much unresolved herein. **1673** [R. Leigh] *Transp. Reh.* 142 The way is so difficult and my guides unresolv'd. **1707** *Curios. in Husb. & Gard.* 235 Boyle..is very much unresolved, and knows not what to think of these ..Vegetations. **1784** Cowper *Task* vi. 160 Unresolv'd Which hue she most approv'd. **1864** F. W. Robinson *Mattie, a Stray* III. 220 She [was] unresolved as to what was best and just—for others, as well as for herself!

† **c.** Const. *of.* *Obs.*
**1655** Fuller *Ch. Hist.* II. vi. § 32 Either displeased at the Collect read,..or unresolved of the Efficacy of the Gold pendent about the Patients Neck. **1697** Dryden *Æneis* IX. 1078 So Turnus..unresolved of flight, Moves tardy back.

† **3.** Not formed of set purpose. *Obs.*—1
**1649** Jer. Taylor *Gt. Exemp.* II. viii. 68 If the backsliding be but the interruption of the first sanctity by a single act, or an unconfirmed, unresolved, unmalicious habite.

**4.** Not broken up or dissolved.
(*a*) *c* **1801** Busby *Dict. Music* s.v. *Canon,* There are various kinds of canons: as the..resolved, the unresolved, the finite, and the infinite canon. **1837** [Mrs. Maitland] *Lett. fr. Madras* (1843) 56 Imagine a succession of unresolved discords, selected at random. **1869** Ouseley *Counterp.* xvi. 127 The unprepared and unresolved sevenths..produced by its inversion.
(*b*) **1843** R. J. Graves *Syst. Clin. Med.* xxi. 252 The hepatisation [of the lung] remains unresolved. **1850** Nichol *Archit. Heav.* 54 The cluster in Hercules..never appeared devoid of unresolved light about its central regions. **1898** *Allbutt's Syst. Med.* V. 894 Fibroid disease of the lung.. secondary to pleuritic effusion or unresolved pneumonia, &c.

Hence **Unreso·lvedly** *adv.*
**1621** Lady M. Wroth *Urania* 182, I gaue my answers vnresoluedly.

**Unreso·lvedness.** [f. prec.] Irresolution.
**1628** Le Grys tr. *Barclay's Argenis* 274 This vnresoluednesse of minde. **1642** H. More *Min. Poems* Wks. (Grosart) 174/1 Grave matrons will wax wanton and betray Their unresolv'dnesse in their wonted grace. **1694** Kettlewell *Comp. Penitent* 131 Remove from me perplexing doubts, and unresolvedness about my Duty. **1734** J. Edwards *Serm.* Wks. 1811 VII. 415 Many grow old, in an unresolvedness whether to embrace Christianity or not. **1888** *Pall Mall G.* 24 Feb., The apparent unresolvedness..of many of the English electors.

**Unreso·lving,** *ppl. a.* (Un-1 10.) **1697** Congreve *Mourn. Bride* I. vi, In long suspense she stands, Shifting the prize in unresolving hands. **1737** *Gentl. Mag.* VII. 120/1 Behold! sweet ruin! the unhappy scene, Now on my pen I unresolving lean. **Unresou·nded,** *ppl. a.* (Un-1 8.) **1755** Young *Centaur* vi, Is it not also far too much for human gratitude to leave unproclaimed, unresounded, unadored? **Unresou·nding,** *ppl. a.* (Un-1 10.) **1841** Mangan *Poems* (1903) 293 Forth flow the moments,..And, as their unresounding stream Departs away [etc.]. **1854** Faber *Growth in Holiness* xiii. 223 The shore of that unresounding sea.

† **Unrespe·ct,** *sb. Obs.* [Un-1 12.] Lack of respect; disrespect.
? **1615** Sylvester *Tobacco Battered* 822 Those, that on Earth will still..Offend their Friends, with a Most vn-Respect. *a* **1656** Bp. Hall *Rem. Wks.* (1660) 251 A palpable unrespect to the blessed Angels of God.

**Unrespe·ct,** *ppl. a.* [Un-1 8 b.] Unregarded. **1854** S. Dobell *Balder* i. 4 As one Who in a temple passes unrespect Between the kneeling suppliant and the saint.

**Unrespe·ctable,** *a.* (Un-1 7 b, 5 b.)
**1765** Langhorne in *Collins' Wks.* 164 The small Marino, which however unrespectable with regard to power or extent of territory, has, at least [etc.]. **1789** J. White *Earl Strongbow* II. 94 The unrespectable pride of being descended from some ancient..ruffian. **1802** Mrs. J. West *Infidel Father* I. 41 With some pretty appellative..it did not look unrespectable at the bottom of a letter. **1850** Kingsley *A. Locke* xx. 151 Let those of the respectable press who are without sin, cast the first stone at the unrespectable. **1889** J. J. Thomas *Froudacity* 187 The handful of malcontents whose unrespectable grievance he holds up to public sympathy.

**Unrespe·cted,** *ppl. a.* [Un-1 8.]
† **1.** Unregarded, unnoticed. *Obs.*
*a* **1586** Sidney *Arcadia* III. xxviii, The last grone of his brother was the onely answere he could get to his unrespected eloquence. **1596** B. Griffin *Fidessa* xxxvii, Whil'st I..doe sit in heauie plight, Wayling alone my unrespected loue. *a* **1628** F. Grevil *5 Years K. James* (1643) 42 There being none to looke after him, it would passe unregarded, or unrespected. **1634** Sir T. Herbert *Trav.* 149 Women..wrap themselues in a large receiuing sheet;..they passe and repasse vnknowne and vnrespected.

**2.** Not held in respect or regard.
**1595** Daniel *Civ. Wars* II. xx, Which wounds with griefe poore vnrespected zeale. **1610** Healey *St. Aug. Citie of God* XVI. i. 572 Through the second inundation of impiety.. Gods religion lay wholy vnrespected. **1647** Trapp *Comm. 1 John* iii. 1 Princes unknown are unrespected. **1735** Pope *Ep. Lady* 125 From loveless youth to unrespected age, No Passion gratify'd except her Rage. **1784** Cowper *Task* I. 747 Till sabbath rites Have dwindled into unrespected forms. **1829** Scott *Anne of G.* xxxiv, I am, as you say, an unrespected exile. **1865** W. G. Palgrave *Arabia* II. 66 A retreat..where he led a tranquil nor unrespected life.

† **3.** Not carefully considered. *Obs.*
**1601** *Pasquil & Kath.* IV. 128 The man is such a man, That he is matchlesse! Oh, I shall prophane His name with vnrespected vtterance.

**Unrespe·ctful,** *a.* [Un-1 7, 5 b.] Lacking in respect; disrespectful.
**1611** Cotgr., *Inofficieux,* vnofficious,.. vnrespectfull, vnkind. **1621** Bp. Mountagu *Diatribæ* 284 As vnrespectfull, vndutifull and sawcy a censure as the former. **1872** J. L. Sanford *Estimates Eng. Kings* 383 The unrespectful and invidious patronage of relatives.

**Unrespe·ctfully,** *adv.* (Un-1 11; cf. prec.) *a* **1648** Ld. Herbert *Hen. VIII* (1683) 99 He..behaved himself so unrespectfully to the Cardinal, that he was cast into Prison. **1709** Strype *Ann. Ref.* lii. 528 How odly and unrespectfully he was used by some of his Bristol ill-willers. **Unrespe·cting,** *ppl. a.* (Un-1 10, 5 b.) **1592** Daniel *Delia* xlix, Celestiall fires, and vnrespecting powers! That deigne not view the glory of your might. **1868** Milman *St. Paul's* 377 Their tombs were respected until the unrespecting fire.

**Unrespe·ctive,** *a.* [Un-1 7, 5 b.]
† **1.** Inattentive, heedless. *Obs.*
**1594** Daniel *Cleopatra* III. i, When dissolute impiety possest Th' vnrespectiue mindes of such a people. **1594** Shaks. *Rich. III,* IV. ii. 29, I will conuerse with..vnrespectiue Boyes: none are for me, That looke into me with considerate eyes. **1633** Bp. Hall *Hard Texts, O. T.* 239 A true hearted loving neighbour is better than an overlie and unrespective brother. [**1822** Scott *Nigel* Introd. Ep., Bargaining for the objects of my curiosity with an unrespective shop-lad.]

**2.** Making no distinction; undiscriminating.
**1606** Shaks. *Tr. & Cr.* II. ii. 71 Nor the remainder Viands We do not throw in vnrespectiue siue. **1648** Bp. Hall *Select Th.* xxxiv. 102 To cast the envy of their condemnation meerly upon the absolute will of an unrespective power. *a* **1656** Hales *Gold. Rem.* III. (1673) 53 These general and unrespective judgments of God, by famine, or sword, or the like. **1850** S. Dobell *Roman* i, She was not born To..bear Rude licence of the unrespective waves. **1866** J. B. Rose tr. *Virg. Ecl. & Georg.* 107 But onward, onward,.. Doth unrespective Time..in silence move.

† **3.** Disrespectful, rude. *Obs.*
**1611** Cotgr., *Irrespectueux,* vnrespectiue, inofficious, rude. *a* **1624** Bp. M. Smith *Serm.* (1632) 23 Nothing [is] more vncertain then the minds of the multitude..: humorous, clamorous, vnrespective. *a* **1643** J. Shute *Judgem. & Mercy* (1645) 197 So in David towards Saul;..not one unrespective word comes from him.

† **4.** Not deserving of respect. *Obs.*—1
**1626** Donne *Serm.* 825 Which to lesse reverend and unrespective Persons we should be lesse willing to do.

Hence **Unrespe·ctively** *adv.*, **-ness.**
**1611** Speed *Hist. Gt. Brit.* IX. xxiii. § 112 This great victory made the English..carelesse,..and the Forts thereabout ..were *vnrespectiuelie regarded. **1633** Bp. Hall *Hard Texts, N. T.* 152 Were he so..I would haue forborne to speake unreverently and unrespectively to him. **1656** Trapp *Comm. Heb.* vii. 23 All our learning also is soon refuted with one black Theta, which..snappeth us unrespectively without distinction. **1611** Cotgr., *Inofficiosité,* vnofficiousnesse, *vnrespectiuenesse, or want of due respect. *a* **1628** F. Grevil *Sidney* vi. (1652) 75 Finding unrespectiveness in himself..not respected by this Princely Spirit.

† **Unrespe·ctless,** *a. Obs.*—1 [Un-1 5 a.] Unrespective. **1614** Rowlands *Fooles Bolt* E 3 b, Can I regard this vnrespectlesse dealing, If one be longing sicke, is this call'd healing?

**Unrespirable,** *a.* (Un-1 7 b, 5 b.)
**1807** Aikin *Dict. Chem.* II. 94/2 Foul or unrespirable air. **1836** Brande *Chem.* 392 Ammonia is..acrid, and of course unrespirable. **1839** Ure *Dict. Arts* 991 The pit..is rendered unsafe..by the unrespirable gases.

**Unre·spited,** *ppl. a.* (Un-1 8.)
**1593** Nashe *Christ's Teares* 30 The Marble flore of it they made slippery, with theyr vnrespited..blood-shed. **1667** Milton *P. L.* II. 187 There to converse with everlasting groans, Unrespited. **1708** J. Philips *Cyder* II. 618 Horror thus, And wild Uproar, and Desolation, reign'd Unrespited.

**Unrespo·nding,** *ppl. a.* (Un-1 10.) **1858** Lytton *What will He do?* I. xiv, He pressed Lionel's unresponding hand.

**Unrespo·nsable,** *a.* (Un-1 7 b, 5 b; cf. Unresponsible *a.*) *a* **1661** Fuller *Worthies, Essex* I. (1662) 346 Of whom when still alive, he justly..demanded reparations, though since his unresponsable memory can make us no satisfaction.

† **Unrespo·nsal,** *a. Obs. rare.* [Un-1 7, 5 b.]
**1.** = Unresponsible 1.
**1579** *Sc. Acts, Jas. VI* (1814) III. 145/2 In calss the committar of þe wrang be vnresponsall, he sall for the first falt be put in þe stokkis. **1579** *Reg. Privy Council Scot.* III. 231 Williame Forbes,..a brokin and unresponsall man.
**2.** = Unresponsible 2.
*a* **1670** Hacket *Abp. Williams* I. (1692) 106 A Tithe or a Crop of Hay or Corn, which are ready to be carried away by force, by unresponsal Men.

**Unrespo·nsible,** *a.* [Un-1 7, 5 b.]
† **1.** Lacking substance or standing. *Obs.*
**1634** *Jedburgh Town Council Records* 28 Nov. (MS.), That no person..set any of their houses or buiths to unresponsible persons. **1710** *Ess. Hist. Last Ministry* 67 The losses sustain'd by employing Unresponsible Persons in the Collection of Taxes.

**2.** Irresponsible.
**1653** [implied in *unresponsibleness*; see below]. **1786** Burke *Charges agst. W. Hastings* v. ix, Thereby..changing him from a minister of the Company..to a dependant upon an unresponsible power. **1797** Gillies *Aristotle's Ethics & Pol.* II. 59 *note,* A power unbalanced and unresponsible, and therefore..not made for man. **1802–12** Bentham *Ration. Judic. Evid.* (1827) II. 333 Because the judges are unexperienced, uninformed, numerous, unresponsible. **1852** Grote *Greece* II. lxxxi. X. 610 Vesting in Dionysius a single-handed power..above the laws—unlimited and unresponsible.

Hence **Unrespo·nsibleness.**
**1653** Gauden *Hierasp.* 439 That unresponsiblenesse to any other;..that independence or absolute liberty in their will.

**Unrespo·nsive,** *a.* [Un-1 7, 5 b.]
**1.** Unable to reply.
**1668** Wilkins *Real Char.* 341 To render a man Vnresponsive, is to Confound, Poze, Puzzle, Non-plus.

**2.** Not responsive; irresponsive.
[**1775** Ash.] **1816** Scott *Old Mort.* xxxviii, The hand.. turned cold within her grasp, and lay..unresponsive to her caresses. **1871** Macduff *Mem. Patmos* xviii. 242 All now dull, pulseless, unresponsive as the insensate stone. **1886** Hall Caine *Son of Hagar* I. iv, Hugh took the proffered hand with unresponsive coldness.

Hence **Unrespo·nsively** *adv.*, **-ness.**
**1881** E. F. Poynter *Among the Hills* II. 114 She divined the blank unresponsiveness with which her questions would be met. **1898** 'Merriman' *Roden's Corner* xxv. 266 Dorothy saw this in a glance, and her own face hardened unresponsively.

**Unre·st,** *sb.* [Un-1 4, 12. Cf. WFris. *on-, ûnrêst,* MLG., MHG. *unreste*; MDu. *onraste* (Du. *onrast*), MLG., MHG. *unraste* (G. *unrast*); MDu. *onruste* (Du. *onrust*), MLG. *unruste* (LG. *unrust, unrüst, unrost*), and Wanrest.] Absence of rest; disturbance, turmoil, trouble.
*a* **1340** Hampole *Psalter* lxxxiv. 8 Þe vnrest of þis life. *Ibid.* cxviii. 165 Charite puttis away..vnrest of thoght. *c* **1374** Chaucer *Troylus* IV. 879 That cause is of þis sorwe and þis vnreste. **14..** *Rule Syon Monast.* liii. in *Collect. Topogr.* (1834) I. 31 In the dortour..none schal..make any noise of unreste, aboute makyng of ther beddes. *c* **1440** *Gesta Rom.* xlvii. 196 (Harl. MS.), Wher so euer..eny discorde or vnrest was regnynge. *a* **1513** Fabyan *Chron.* VII. 417 Which tourned hym to great dishonoure and his lordes to great vnrest. **1559** *Mirr. Mag.* (1563) V iv, Furth streamde the teares, recordes of his vnrest. **1638** W. Sclater *Serm. Experimentall* 50 A sweet soliloquie of David with his soul, checking it..for the disquiet, and unrest it passionately had plunged it self into. **1685** Dryden tr. *Lucretius* III. 273 If the foolish race of man..Cou'd find as well the cause of this unrest, And all this burden lodg'd within the breast. **1815** Byron *Parisina* v, And mutters she in her unrest A name. **1849** Robertson *Serm.* Ser. I. i. (1866) 10 The unrest and the agony that lie hid in the heart of man. **1873** Symonds *Grk. Poets* i. 18 To the anarchy and unrest of transition succeeds the demand for constitutional order.

**b.** In pl. Somewhat *rare.*
**1477** Earl Rivers (Caxton) *Dictes* (1877) 17 Of thought cometh the wakyngis and vnrestis. **1513** Douglas *Æneid* XIII. ii. 74 Be all wais noysum and onrestis, And all that horribill was. *c* **1611** Chapman *Iliad* VIII. 405 Both Goddesses..contriving still afflicted Troy's unrests. **1628** Wither *Brit. Rememb.* VI. 1957 Nor, thereby, many other mens unrests Occasion they alone.

† **Unre·st,** *v. Obs.* [Un-2 3.] *trans.* To disturb, trouble.
**1382** Wyclif *1 Sam.* xxvi. 14 Who art thou that criest, and vnrestist the kyng? *c* **1430** *Life St. Kath.* (1884) 49 A Cyte..whom noon aduersite troubleth..ne noon heuynesse vnresteth. *c* **1440** *Pallad. on Husb.* VI. 174 Good is hem to sle, For they the swarm vnrestith.

**Unre·stable,** *a.* (Un-1 7 b.) **1662** J. Chandler *Van Helmont's Oriat.* 74 This therefore is the unrestable appointment of the water, that by proceeding continually upwards and downwards, it [etc.].

**Unre·sted,** *ppl. a.*[1] [UN-[1] 8.] **a.** Not laid to rest. **b.** Not refreshed by rest.

**a.** 1607 CHAPMAN *Bussy d'Ambois* v. iv. 154 My unrested soul. 1612 — *Rev. Bussy d'Ambois* IV. v. 82 Th' unrested spirit of your slaughter'd brother. **b.** [1775 ASH.] 1846 WORCESTER (citing Erving). Also in recent use (1908).

**Unre·sted,** *ppl. a.*[2] [UN-[2] 8, 5.] Thrown out of the rest. 1760–1 SMOLLETT *Launcelot Greaves* xix, Sir Launcelot, perceiving his rival's spear unrested, had just time to throw up the point of his own.

**Unre·stful,** *a.* [UN-[1] 7. App. not in use between 16th and 19th century: cf. RESTFUL *a.*]

**1.** Restless, stirring, unquiet. (Freq. *c* 1875–.)

1382 WYCLIF *Baruch* iv. 15 A folc vnsaciable, or vnrestful, and of an other tunge. *c* 1400 *Apol. Loll.* 104 þei are..vnschamful to axe,..vnrestful tul þei talk, vnkynd wan þei han tane. *a* 1420 *Wycliffite Bible* Prov. vii. 13 *marg.*, With wowing cheer; that is, vnresteful, and with out schame. *c* 1475 *Cath. Angl.* (A.) 305/1 Vn Restfulle, *inquietus.* 1533 MORE *Debell. Salem* Wks. 961/2 That good peacible folke..should not for suche inquiete & vnrestfull wretches without some ruffle liue in peace long. 1553 *Primer* in *Lit. & Doc. Edw. VI* (1844) 474 We are..besieged of cruel and unrestful enemies. 1565 ABP. PARKER *Corr.* (Parker Soc.) 237 The talk..is much increased, and unrestful they be, and I alone they say am in fault. 1837 CARLYLE *Fr. Rev.* II. v. ix, So wags..this unrestful World, day after day. 1891 *Spectator* 7 Mar. 340/1 This unrestful and fussy energy.

†**2.** Disturbed, troubled. *Obs.*

*a* 1395 HYLTON *Scala Perf.* II. xxvii. (W. de W. 1494), It bereth downe the thoughte; and makyth it vnrestfull. 1435 MISYN *Fire of Love* II. vi. 82 Lorde, þou art my takar, þat malicius prikkyngis of my fraward enmys me make not vnrestfull.

**3.** Marked by absence of rest or quiet.

14.. *Rule Syon Monast.* liii. in *Collect. Topogr.* (1834) I. 31 Suche as gretly rowte or make any unrestful noyse in ther sleppe..schal be purveyd a nother place, wher they may slepe withoute unrestyng of other. *c* 1445 PECOCK *Donet* 94 þouȝ al þis lijf be..laboriose, vnrestful. 1542 UDALL *Erasm. Apoph.* 242 The bedde of a persone beeyng in greate debte is an unrestefull thyng. 1548 BODRUGAN *Epit. King's Title* (1873) 254 What properties procedeth of warre, but outragious costes,..consumyng anger, vnrestfull quietness. 1600 *Look About You* i. A 2, If drousie age keepe not thy stiffened ioyntes On thy vnrestfull bed. 1884 *Pall Mall G.* 9 Dec. 11/2 There is on every face a craving, unrestful expression.

Hence **Unre·stfully** *adv.*

1483 *Cath. Angl.* 305/1 Vn Restfully, *jnquiete, jnoportune.*

**Unre·stfulness.** (UN-[1] 12; cf. prec.)

1382 WYCLIF *Luke* xi. 8 If he schal contynue knockynge,.. for his vnrestefulnesse he schal rise, and ȝyue to hym. *c* 1450 tr. *De Imitatione* III. xxxiii. 102 Of inordinate loue.. growiþ all unrestfulnes of herte. 1491 CAXTON *Vitas Patr.* (W. de W. 1495) II. 234 b/2 The holy fader..axed hym, yf ..he sholde praye god for hym; that he wolde releue hym from this unrestfulnesse. *c* 1557 ABP. PARKER *Ps.* lv. 157, I would me flitche..to wildernes: More there to dwell, than here wyth such in such unrestfulnes. 1579 E. K. *Gloss. to Spenser's Sheph. Cal.* March (Emblem), Loue..vexeth the body..with vnrestfulnesse all night.

**Unre·sting,** *vbl. sb.* ? *Obs.* [f. UNREST *v.*, or UN-[2] 8.] The depriving of rest.

14.. [see UNRESTFUL *a.* 3]. 1615 T. ADAMS *Blacke Devill* 9 Well; gone he is out of this Man; and we must therein consider..1. His vnroosting. 2. His vnresting. [Hence in 1670 EACHARD *Cont. Clergy* 68.]

**Unre·sting,** *ppl. a.* (UN-[1] 10.)

1582 STANYHURST *Æneis* IV. (Arb.) 114 The poore vnresting Dido could catch no such happye Season too be quiet. 1604 A. SCOLOKER *Daiphantus* F 4 The wandring soule Seeking for rest in his vnresting spirit. *a* 1652 BROME *Eng. Moor* IV. iv, What is she? I am fear-struck Tis some unresting shadow. 1748 THOMSON *Cast. Indol.* II. lxxxi, But ay the ruthless driver goads them on,..Ne ever find they rest from their unresting fone. 1812 BYRON *Ch. Har* I. lxxxiii, Life-abhorring gloom Wrote on his faded brow curst Cain's unresting doom. 1856 H. DIXON *Post & Paddock* x. 168 Those ballads, which they sing with such unresting diligence. 1870 M. D. CONWAY *Earthw. Pilgr.* xxi. 256 This unresting life of the enquiring soul.

Hence **Unre·stingly** *adv.*; **Unre·stingness.**

1831 CARLYLE *Sartor Res.* I. x, The silent Arachnes that weave unrestingly in our imagination. 1839 DE QUINCEY *Roman Meals* Wks. (1854) III. 269 *note*, The German imagination has been most struck by the duration of the man's life,..the English, by the unrestingness.., his incapacity of repose.

**Unre·stless,** *a.* (UN-[1] 5 a.) 1513 DOUGLAS *Æneid* IV. x. 13 The onrestles fey spreit..Of this wnhappy Phenician Dido. 1894 in Heslop *Northumberland Gloss.* s.v. †**Unre·stily,** *adv. Obs.*—[1] [UN-[1] 11.] Not restfully. 1561 HOLLYBUSH *Hom. Apoth.* 6 b, If one slepeth vnrestly, let him eat lettice.

**Unresto·red,** *ppl. a.* (UN-[1] 8.)

*c* 1445 PECOCK *Donet* 87 His ordinaunce þat man.. schulde be restorid into saluacioun, þouȝ aungel..was left vnrestorid. 1473 *Acta Auditorum* (1839) 25/2 To restore again the samyn [cattle] in sa fer as is vnrestorit. 1500–20 DUNBAR *Poems* xxi. 64 O! quha sall weild the wrang possessioun,..Quhilk vnrestorit helpis no confessioun? *c* 1586 C'TESS PEMBROKE *Ps.* CXL. iv, Flames shall fling them low, Ay unrestor'd to drown in deepest woe. 1606 SHAKS. *Ant. & Cl.* III. vi. 27 Then does he say, he lent me Some shipping vnrestor'd. *a* 1649 DRUMM. OF HAWTH. *Hist. Jas. V*, Wks. (1711) 81 Whose Father was banished for Treason..and died un-restored. 1742 YOUNG *Nt. Th.* II. 643 If unrestor'd by this, despair your cure. 1818 BYRON *Ch. Har.* IV. xi, The Bucentaur lies rotting unrestored. 1860 PUSEY *Min. Proph.* 596 The Jews He brought back, Edom He left unrestored. 1899 C. K. PAUL *Memories* 129 The old unrestored choir of St. Paul's Cathedral.

**Unresto·ring,** *ppl. a.* (UN-[1] 10.) 1811 W. TAYLOR in Robberds *Mem.* (1843) II. 333 The corse, the spectre, the veiling pall, the unrestoring tomb. 1823 LAMB *Elia* II. *Old Margate Hoy*, Ships, and sumless treasures swallowed up in the unrestoring depths.

**Unrestrai·nable,** *a.* (UN-[1] 7 b, 5 b.)

1430–40 LYDG. *Bochas* III. xx. (1561) 86/1 Their colorike fumes, yᵉ fury vnrestraynable. 1608 BP. J. KING *Serm. 5 Nov.* 34 In the timely execution of your Lawes, and.. coercion of their vnrestrainable audaciousnesse. 1609 HOLLAND *Amm. Marcell.* 187 Like as out of a drie wood the sparkes.., with an unrestrainable course, reach to the daunger of countrey townes. *a* 1711 KEN *Edmund* Poet. Wks. 1721 II. 111 Wonder not that a Virgin makes this Court, Of Love the unrestrainable Effort. 1815 ABERNETHY *Surg. Obs.* (ed. 2) 125 *note*, An unrestrainable hæmorrhagic tendency. 1863 MOUAT *Andaman Islanders* 227 An unrestrainable fit of laughter.

Hence **Unrestrai·nably** *adv.*

1615 SANDYS *Trav.* 148 A Iew..did poison his sonne, whom he knew to be vnrestrainably lasciuious. 1849 RUSKIN *Seven Lamps* i. § 12. 23 There is occasionally a burst upwards and blossoming unrestrainably to the sky.

**Unrestrai·ned,** *ppl. a.* [UN-[1] 8.]

**1.** Not kept in check or under control; allowed free course or vent.

*a* 1600 HOOKER *Remedie agst. Sorrow* (1612) 3 Naturall compassion..caused them..to poure forth vnrestrained teares. 1712 BERKELEY *Pass. Obed.* Wks. 1871 III. 131 So unrestrained [are] the passions of men. 1796 MME. D'ARBLAY *Camilla* V. 516 Her tears now flowed fast from unrestrained delight. 1828 LYTTON *Pelham* II. xxv, They all rose in a mirth sufficiently unrestrained to be any thing but patrician. 1879 MCCARTHY *Own Times* II. xxiii. 172 He was attacked with all the bitterness of a..very unrestrained animosity.

**b.** Not restricted or limited.

1622 [see UNPINIONED[2].] 1647 CLARENDON *Hist. Reb.* II. § 41 There being..an unrestrained Intercourse between the King's Camp and Edenborough. 1670 — *Ess.* Tracts (1727) 184 The spacious fields of their unlimited and unrestrained contemplation. 1776 ADAM SMITH *W. N.* v. i. I. ii. (1904) II. 414 The emulation which an unrestrained competition never fails to excite. 1806 SURR *Winter in London* III. 219 The unrestrained intermixture of ranks..is a remarkable trait of your national manners. 1856 KANE *Arct. Expl.* I. xxviii. 364 The men..had frequent and unrestrained intercourse with them. 1899 *Allbutt's Syst. Med.* VII. 376 The 'unantagonised' or 'unrestrained' influence exerted by the cerebellum.

**c.** Not limited in application.

1827 JARMAN *Powell's Devises* II. 117 They admitted that the general words, if unrestrained, would carry the reversion.

**2.** Not subjected (or subject) to restraint in respect of action or conduct.

*a* 1586 SIDNEY *Arcadia* II. xxix, Zelmanes..unrestrained parts, the minde & eie, had their free course to the delicate Philoclea. 1593 SHAKS. *Rich. II*, v. iii. 7 There.. he dayly doth frequent, With vnrestrained loose Companions. 1628 T. SPENCER *Logick* 34 The vnrestrained, and free choyse of the will. 1691 HARTCLIFFE *Virtues* 68 He that is guilty of the Excess, is said to be..unrestrained and let loose to all Debauchery. 1751 EARL ORRERY *Remarks Swift* (1752) 67 With heads and hearts elated by affluence, and unrestrained by foresight or discretion. 1760–72 H. BROOKE *Fool of Qual.* (1809) III. 122 What will not power effect, when unrestrained by conscience? 1825 SCOTT *Betrothed* ii, The revellers were unrestrained by the stricter rules of good-breeding. 1864 TREVELYAN *Compet. Wallah* (1866) 349 The free and unrestrained life of an English lady. 1890 *Retrospect Med.* CII. 351 He walks about the room,..and in many respects is unrestrained in his movements.

*absol.* 1770 GLOVER *Leonidas* (ed. 5) IV. 713 The unrestrain'd and free Will fly from danger.

**b.** In appositive use: Without restraint; unrestrainedly.

1596 *Edward III*, III. ii. 52 Slaughter and mischiefe walke within your streets, And, vnrestrained, make hauock as they passe. 1812 BYRON *Ch. Har.* I. lxxxix, While o'er the parent clime prowls Murder unrestrain'd. 1848 THACKERAY *Van. Fair* xxxv, The girls indulged unrestrained in their grief. 1867 E. F. BOWDEN *Fathers of Desert* 374 Vice stalks abroad unrestrained.

**3.** Free from restraint of manner; easy, natural.

1856 FROUDE *Hist. Eng.* I. ii. 159 His letters..are simple, easy, and unrestrained. 1876 T. HARDY *Ethelberta* xliii, Whose manner..had little in common with Sol's warm and unrestrained bearing.

Hence **Unrestrai·nedness.**

[1775 ASH.] 1889 *Pop. Sci. Monthly* July 296 No men on earth ever have had liberty in the sense of unrestrainedness of action.

**Unrestrai·nedly,** *adv.* [UN-[1] 11.] Without restraint.

1655 EARL ORRERY *Parthen.* II. III. 287 Shee shedd hirs [*sc.* tears] the more vnrestrain'dly. *Ibid.* II. VII. 653 Surena permitted Parthenissa unrestrainedly to visit him. 1852 THACKERAY *Esmond* I. ix, He..yawned unrestrainedly. 1862 H. AÏDE *Carr of Carrlyon* II. 57 She and her child wept unrestrainedly. 1876 MISS YONGE *Womankind* v. 32 She will see enough of them unrestrainedly to understand their dispositions.

**Unrestrai·nt.** (UN-[1] 12.)

1804 *Ann. Rev.* II. 235 The spirit of antijacobinism was as yet so strongly bent on the restoration of royal unrestraint. 1867 MILL *Subj. Women* (1869) 66 His conduct.. in the unrestraint of home. 1885 *Encycl. Brit.* XVIII. 146/1 A simple and fine and light stroke,..and unrestraint in the flow of writing.

**Unrestri·cted,** *ppl. a.* (UN-[1] 8.)

1766 SMOLLETT *Trav.* xvii, His military power and unrestricted authority. 1785 H. WALPOLE *Mod. Gardening* Wks. 1798 II. 537 They extended their branches unrestricted. 1807 WORDSW. *White Doe* IV. 60 Happy as others of her kind, That..Range unrestricted as the wind. 1854 RÖHNER *Mus. Composition* III. 197 Unrestricted Canon is founded upon a melodic subject which [etc.]. 1884 *Contemp. Rev.* Oct. 525 The unrestricted intermeddling of the State.

Hence **Unrestri·ctedly** *adv.*; **-stri·ctedness.**

1844 W. H. MAXWELL *Wand. Highl.* I. 195 To him, every discovery..is unrestrictedly unfolded. 1846 G. S. FABER *Lett. Tractar. Secess.* 42 The unrestrictedness of his own liberty and power. 1861 WHYTE MELVILLE *Good for Nothing* I. 293 A process..that the weaker sex seldom leave unrestrictedly to their servants.

**Unrestri·ctive,** *a.* (UN-[1] 7, 5 b.) 1817 H. T. COLEBROOKE *Algebra*, etc. 329 The foregoing rule..is unrestrictive. 1863 COWDEN CLARKE *Shaks. Char.* xx. 504 Temperament, unrestrictive teaching, and a desire to amend.

**Unre·sty,** *a. Obs.* exc. *Sc. dial.* [UN-[1] 4, 7. Cf. WFris. *on-*, *ûnrestich*, MDu. *onrustich* (Du. *onrustig*), MLG. *unrust-*, *unrostich.*] Unquiet; full of unrest.

*a* 1340 HAMPOLE *Psalter* cxl. 10 Kepe me fra lettyngis of vnristy men. *c* 1374 CHAUCER *Troylus* v. 1355, I dar not pleyne more, But humbely..Yow wryte ich myne vnresty sorwes sore. *c* 1412 HOCCLEVE *De Reg. Princ.* 116 Boote fonde I non In myn vnresty bed lenger to lye. ? *a* 1500 *Lydgate's Ballad* in Thynne *Chaucer* (1530) 374/2 Unto vnresty bothe rest and remedye Fruteful to al tho that in her assye. 1606 S. GARDINER *Bk. Angling* 137 Worldly cares maketh a man very vnrestie with himself.

**Unresu·ltive,** *a.* (UN-[1] 7.) 1833 MRS. BROWNING *Prometh. Bound* 451, I discern An empty wish,—and unresultive work. **Unretai·ned,** *ppl. a.* (UN-[1] 8.) [1775 ASH.] 1822 COLERIDGE *Lett.* (1895) 720 The taste for unconnected, and for that reason unretained single thoughts. **Unreta·liated,** *ppl. a.* (UN-[1] 8.) 1683 TRYON *Way to Health* 630 Men ..turn the natural use of things into Wantonness, which cannot pass unretaliated. 1805 FOSTER *Ess.* (1806) I. 62 The overawed timidity and unretaliated injuries of the unfortunate beings within his power. 1831 SCOTT *Cast. Dang.* xix, Obliged to submit to national insults, unretaliated and unrevenged.

**Unreta·rded,** *ppl. a.* (UN-[1] 8.)

1615 T. ADAMS *Lycanthropy* 7 What Paul speakes of his unretarded execution of Christs message. 1636 B. JONSON *Discov.* Wks. (Rtldg.) 747/1 Which they will utter unretarded without any shamefastness. 1793 V. KNOX *Let. to Yng. Nobleman* Wks. 1824 V. 109 Then go on in your virtuous progress, unretarded by those..who laugh at your virtuous solicitude. 1820 E. KEAN in *9th Rep. Hist. MSS. Comm.* App. 488/2 Friends such as will come uninvited, [and] go unretarded.

**Unre·tched,** *ppl. a. rare*—[1]. [UN-[1] 8 c.] Not stretched out. 1674 N. FAIRFAX *Bulk & Selv.* 33 When our Author tells us..of a *now* longer than Ages, and a being unretcht out.

**Unrete·ntive,** *a.* (UN-[1] 7, 5 b.)

1748 CHESTERF. *Lett.* (1774) I. 336 Discovering to them such an unretentive weakness as must convince them that you will tell it to twenty others. 1782 BAKER *Biog. Dramatica* I. 238/2 So unretentive was his memory. 1825 COLERIDGE *Aids Refl.* 363 You are not so unretentive a Scholar as to have forgotten the *pateris et auro* of your Virgil. 1851 [J. B. HUME] *Poems Early Years* 165 What further may have chanc'd my sleepy brain, In unretentive dulness, noted not.

**Unre·tinued,** *ppl. a.* (UN-[1] 8.) 1855 SINGLETON *Virgil* I. 378 To be left Forlorn unto herself she seemeth, aye, Unretinued. **Unreti·red,** *ppl. a.* (UN-[1] 8.) 1648 HEXHAM II, *Ongeweken*, Vnretyred, or Vnretreated. 1766 W. GORDON *Gen. Counting-ho.* 36 Bills unretired at the dates they are payable. **Unreto·rted,** *ppl. a.* (UN-[1] 8.) 1618 *Barnevelt's Apol.* Ded. A 4 Else I shrewdly feare, lest many..fall away to that side, where we are assaulted with vnretorted weapons. **Unretou·ched,** *ppl. a.* (UN-[1] 8.) 1880 SWINBURNE *Stud. Shakes.* 218 Possibly we have a survival of some lines' length, not unretouched by Fletcher. **Unretra·ctable,** *a.* (UN-[1] 7 b.) 1627 JACKSON *Creed* VI. x. § 1 That God..did set the course of nature a-going with an irresistible and unretractable swinge. 1900 OMOND *Romantic Triumph* 276 An unretractable gift to France.

**Unretra·cted,** *ppl. a.* (UN-[1] 8.)

1646 HAMMOND *Tracts* 27 Any such act of sin unretracted by repentance. 1697 COLLIER *Ess. Mor. Subj.* II. 66 Malevolence shewn..in a single Outrage unretracted. 1739 *Wks. Learned* I. 73 Content to leave the Calumnies of Fatalism and Spinozism unretracted. 1834 MACKINTOSH *Revolution of 1688* ix. 257 To consider the silence of the King as a virtual assent to their unretracted condition. 1855 MILMAN *Lat. Chr.* XIV. iv. VI. 502 The monkish Latin satire maintained its unretracted protest against the Church.

**Unretrea·ting,** *ppl. a.* (UN-[1] 10.) 1791 COWPER *Iliad* v. 590 The powers of Troy..the Grecians dense Expected, unretreating, void of fear. 1858 J. ROBERTSON *Poems* 78 As light is mixed in the unretreating air. †**Unretrie·vable,** *a. Obs.* (UN-[1] 7 b, 5 b.) 1705 STANHOPE *Paraphr.* I. 241 The unretrievable Misery of those who will not suffer themselves to be rescued from Destruction. **Unretrie·vingly,** *adv.* (UN-[1] 11.) 1844 MRS. BROWNING *Cry of Children* 145 They..Are worn as if with age, yet unretrievingly The harvest of its memories cannot reap. **Unre·trograde,** *a.* (UN-[1] 7.) 1817 MALTHUS *Popul.* (ed. 5) II. 231 A regular and unretrograde increase. **Unre·tted,** *ppl. a.* (UN-[1] 8.) 1839 URE *Dict. Arts* 490 Unretted flax. 1856 *Farmer's Mag.* Nov. 379 Either green or unretted straw.

**Unretu·rnable,** *a.* [UN- 7 b, 5 b.]

†**1.** Admitting of no return. *Obs.*

Chiefly as a rendering of L. *irremeabilis.*

1513 DOUGLAS *Æneid* VI. i. 60 The naimcouth hous, that Laborinthus hait, Full of wrinkillit vnreturnable dissait. *Ibid.* vii. 4 The fludis bank.., Quhais passage is vnreturnable went. 1611 COTGR., *Irremeable*, vnreturnable, or, from which one cannot goe backe. 1648 HEXHAM II, *Onwederkeerlick*, vnreturnable [Kil. *irremeabilis*].

**2.** Incapable of being returned.

1740 RICHARDSON *Pamela* (1741) II. 343, I am even oppress'd with unreturnable Obligations. 1788 MRS. HUGHES *Henry & Isabella* III. 151 The unexpected, and as he esteemed it, unreturnable proof of friendship he had given him. 1795 *Jemima* II. 195 Having such unreturnable benefits to thank him for. 1884 *Marshall's Tennis Cuts* 114 He can..place it in the opposite corner at such a pace that the stroke is practically unreturnable.

Hence **Unretu·rnably** *adv.*

1513 DOUGLAS *Æneid* v. x. 81 Laborynthus..a thousand slychtis wrocht, For to dissave all wncouth tharin brocht, To wavir and er thar wnreturnably. 1788 MRS. HUGHES *Henry & Isabella* II. 72 Where there is a certain equality..

of advantages, so as to leave neither parties unreturnably obliged to the other.

**Unretu·rned,** *ppl. a.* [Un-1 8.]

1. Not having returned or come back.

1589 *Reg. Privy Council Scot.* IV. 428 The Chancellair.. being yit unreturned oute of Lauder. 1600 Fairfax *Tasso* xv. xxvi, They whom storme hath forced that way sence, Are drowned all, or vnreturn'd from thence. 1802 *Noble Wanderers* I. 131 Selisme was still unreturned :—..my suspicions gained strength. 1885 W. Watson *Sonn., Soudanese* 13 Thousands that weep their warriors unreturn'd.

2. That is not reciprocated or responded to.

a 1643 S. Godolphin *Constancy* i, Love unreturn'd, howe'er the flame Seem great and pure, may [etc.]. 1710 Addison *Tatler* No. 250 ¶ 10 Supercilious Looks, unreturned Smil s. 1766 Goldsm. *Hermit* xvii, Dost thou..grieve for friendship unreturned? 1820 Scott *Monast.* xx, I..will brook no insult unreturned. 1896 *McClure's Mag.* VI. 492 The proud and unreturned gaze of the dead who have died in their glory.

**Unretu·rning,** *ppl. a.* (Un-1 10.)

a 1628 F. Grevil *Sidney* (1652) 159 Yet these unreturning steps seemed well worth the observing. 1816 Byron *Ch. Har.* iii. xxvii, And Ardennes..Grieving..Over the unreturning brave. 1856 Whittier *Panorama* 507 Ghosts of unreturning sails. 1897 *Outing* XXIX. 440/2 We grew weary of waiting for the unreturning hounds.

Unretu·rningly, *adv.* (Un-1 11; cf. prec.) 1818 Shelley *Rosal. & Helen* 668 Like a vile weed Which the sea casts unreturningly. 1845–6 Trench *Huls. Lect.* Ser. ii. ii. 175 That sepulchre, to which it had seen its sons..unreturningly descend. Unrevea·lable, *a.* (Un-1 7 b, 5 b.) 1611 Cotgr., *Irreveland*, vnreuealable, not to be reuealed. ? 1826 Coleridge *Ne Plus Ultra* 11 The Dragon foul and fell—The unrevealable, And hidden one. 1846 G. Moore *Power of Soul* (ed. 2) 9 These proposers of an unrevealable divinity.

**Unrevea·led,** *ppl. a.* (Un-1 8, 5 b.)

1529 More *Dyaloge* i. Wks. 167/2 If there were any thing ..that in the church sometyme was doubted and reputed for vnreueled and vnknowen. 1543–4 *Act* 35 *Hen. VIII*, c. 5 § 1 Untrue accusacions..kept secret unreveled. 1592 Kyd *Sp. Trag.* iii. ii. 9 If this incomparable murder..Shall vnreueald and vnreuenged passe. 1651 Hobbes *Leviath.* iii. xl. 250 The effect..of the unrevealed will, and of the power of God. 1697 Dryden *Æneis* vi. 374 Ye realms, yet unreveal'd to human sight. 1732 Berkeley *Alciphr.* v. § 27 Religion of any kind, either revealed or unrevealed. 1798 Lamb *R. Gray* iv, The secret, unrevealed, hung upon his conscience. 1850 Tennyson *In Mem.* xxxi, The rest remaineth unreveal'd; He told it not. 1875 Manning *Mission H. Ghost* i. 9 God in His unrevealed mercies will [etc.].

**Unrevea·ling,** *ppl. a.* (Un-1 10, 5 d.)

1628 Feltham *Resolves* ii. xxiv. 79 The Physician that hath a Soueraigne Receit, and dyeth vnreuealing it, robbes the world of many blessings. 1835 Lytton *Rienzi* ii. iii, The greater barons..preserved a strict and unrevealing silence. 1899 G. Matheson *Stud. Portr. Christ* xv. 182 We have all our unrevealing moments—our moments when the spring of life seems dry.

**Unreve·nged,** *ppl. a.* (Un-1 8.)

1533 Bellenden *Livy* iv. xv. (S.T.S.) II. 105 Than tempaneus..drew þame all togidder.., nocht vnrevengit of his Inemyis. 1553 Eden *Treat. New Ind.* (Arb.) 39 Hauinge thus sustayned so greuous iniuries vnreuenged. 1621 Brathwait *Nat. Embassie* (1877) 27 Her husbands death,..effected, but not vnreuenged. 1669 Shadwell *Royal Shepherdess* ii, *Neander.* O Madam! your eyes will revenge your quarrels. *Evadne.* Or they must be unreveng'd, for you. 1726 Pope *Odyss.* xvi. 277 With such a foe th' unequal fight to try, Were by false courage unreveng'd to die. 1796 *Monthly Mag.* II. 449 Ampanani never bled unrevenged. 1821 Shelley *Hellas* 1021 Keep holy This jubilee of unrevenged blood!

Unreve·ngeful, *a.* (Un-1 7.) 1660 *Nicholas Papers* (Camden) IV. 220 The Kinge of Englands..unreuengefull disposition. a 1670 Hacket *Abp. Williams* i. (1693) 191 He was un-revengeful,..and no longer displeased with those he overcame. Unreve·ngefulness. (Un-1 12.) a 1586 Sidney *Arcadia* ii. ix, A Tyrant also, not thorow..unrevengefulnes,..but..of a wanton crueltie. Unreve·nging, *ppl. a.* (Un-1 10.) a 1593 Marlowe & Nashe *Dido* iv. i, Curse that vnreuenging Ioue, Whose flintie darts slept in Typhous den. 1711 Pope *Lett.* (1735) I. 169 The unrevenging Spirit of primitive Christianity. Unreve·ngingly, *adv.* (Un-1 11.) 1650 B. *Discolliminium* 15 A King.. that..Reign'd justly, peaceably, and un-revengingly after. Unre·venue, *v.* (Un-2 4.) 1673 Bp. S. Parker *Reproof Reh. Transp.* 142 They had unrevenued the Clergy. Unre·venued, *ppl. a.* (Un-1 8.) 1641 Milton *Reform.* i. 22 He that will mould a modern Bishop into a primitive, must yeeld him to be..undiocest, unrevenu'd, unlorded.

**Unre·verence,** *sb.* [Un-1 12, 5 b.]

†1. Lack of reverence; irreverence. *Obs.*

1388 Wyclif *Ecclus.* xxv. 29 The ire and vnreuerence of a womman is grete schenschipe. 1422 Yong tr. *Secreta Secret.* 135 Wreth engendryth vnreuerence, Vnreuerence engendryth enemyte. 1491 Caxton *Vitas Patr.* (W. de W. 1495) v. xiv. 343 b/2 Defaultes commysed in the unreuerence of god. 1526 *Pilgr. Perf.* (W. de W. 1531) 237 That is the moost vnreuerence that may be done to god. 1597 Beard *Theatre God's Judgem.* (1612) 317 The disobedience, vnreuerence, & contempt of children towards their parents. 1649 W. Sclater *Comm. Malachy* (1650) 27 Unreverence more displeaseth, than outward observance can please. 1684 Baxter *Answ. Theol. Dial.* 16 Praying with the Hatt on, is..a sign of unreverence.

2. Used as the negative of Reverence *sb.* 6.

1823 W. H. Lyttleton in *Corr. Lady Lyttleton* (1912) 248 The sooner I see your Un-Reverence a-shooting the better I shall be pleased.

Unre·verence, *v.* [Un-2 3.] *trans.* To treat irreverently. 1553 Bale *Vocacyon* 11 This write I, not in vnreuerencinge the sacrament, but [etc.]. 1642 Fuller *Holy & Prof. St.* iii. xxiv. 222 S. Paul thought their materiall Church..abused and unreverenced, by their lay meetings of Love-feasts therein. Unre·verenced, *ppl. a.* (Un-1 8.) a 1470 H. Parker *Dives & Pauper* (1496) 35/2 Oftentyme that crosse that the preest holdeth..is full unreuerenced. 1603 Knolles *Hist. Turks* (1621) 101 The sepulchre of our blessed Sauiour..not vnreuerenced by the Turkes themselues. 1881 H. James *Portr. Lady* lii, She saw..the dry, staring fact that she had been a dull un-reverenced tool. † Unre·verency. (Un-1 12.) c 1680 *Roxb. Ball.* (1874) II. 195, I must not come in place where their friends merry be, Lest I should my son disgrace with my unreverency.

**Unre·verend,** *a.* [Un-1 7, 5 b.]

†1. Irreverent. *Obs.* (Common c 1580–1660.)

1562 in Strype *Ann. Ref.* xxviii. (1709) 295 All unreverend speaking of God's holy predestination. 1584 R. Dudley *Lett.* 161 Inveying against their souerain with..vnreuerend tearmes, and insolent controlmentes. 1591 Shaks. *Two Gent.* ii. vi. 14 Fie, fie, vnreuerend tongue, to call her bad. 1613 Dekker *Four Birdes Noah's Arke* Wks. (Grosart) V. 20 Cleanse my heart..from all foule, loose and vnreuerend languages. 1659 W. Chamberlayne *Pharon.* iv. i. 257 That it might unreverend gazers tell It once was sacred. 1820 Lamb *Elia* i. *Oxford in Vac.*, They rather hold such curiosities to be impertinent—unreverend.

2. Unworthy of reverence.

[1828–32 Webster.] 1874 J. Thomson *City Dreadf. Nt.* xviii. iv, Long grey unreverend locks befouled with mire. 1876 Geo. Eliot *Dan. Der.* lxii, The presence of this unreverend father..affected Mirah with..shame and grief.

Hence † **Unre·verendly** *adv.*, irreverently. *Obs.*

1603 Knolles *Hist. Turks* (1621) 352 Thou hast vnreuerendly spoken. 1663 Boyle *Usef. Exp. Nat. Philos.* ii. iv. 118 He..was wont..(unreverendly enough) to compare our Physitians to Bishops. 1673 *S'too him Bayes* 24 Whose person you shall not find me speak so unreverendly of.

**Unre·verent,** *a.* Now *rare.* [Un-1 7, 5 b.]

1. Irreverent: a. Of actions, conduct, etc.

In frequent use from c 1550 to c 1640.

1388 Wyclif *Ecclus.* xxiii. 17 Thi mouth be not customable to vnreuerent speche. 1532 More *Confut. Tindale* Wks. 622/1 Such euyl fashion of vnreuerent railing vpon great personages. 1583 Babington *Commandm.* (1590) 220 If we be parentes, and greeued with vnreuerent regarde in our children of vs. 1608 Willet *Hexapla Exod.* 62 The Corinthians were chastised..for vnreuerent receiuing of the Lords supper. a 1661 Fuller *Worthies, Yorks.* iii. (1662) 206 Greatly guilty in his ill language, which to any Author was uncivil, to a Bishop unreverent. 1858 H. Bushnell *Nat. & Supernat.* x. (1864) 313 That unreverent feeble laxity, that lets the errors be as good as the truths.

b. Of persons.

1526 *Pilgr. Perf.* (W. de W. 1531) 85 b, Se thou be not vnreuerent or stately of behauour to thy company. 1552 in *Vicary's Anat.* (1888) App. xvi. 313 A swearer, or an vnreuerent vser of his mouth. 1612 T. Taylor *Comm. Titus* ii. 12 They durst not shewe themselues..so vnreuerent and retchles in hearing, as most men doe. 1675 Baxter *Cath. Theol.* i. i. 9 We must be very fearful and not unreverent and rash, in ascribing such a..lusus of notions to God.

*transf.* c 1590 *Sir T. More* ii. iv. 134 Your vnreuerent knees, Make them your feet to kneele to be forgyuen! 1593 Shaks. *Rich. II*, ii. i. 123 Wert thou not Brother to great Edwards sonne, This tongue..Should run thy head from thy vnreuerent shoulders.

†2. = Unreverend *a.* 2. *Obs.*—1

1576 Lambarde *Peramb. Kent* 256 Erasmus opinion and judgment touching such vnreuerent Reliques. 1659 W. Chamberlayne *Pharon.* iii. iv. 356 Their rage Neglected youth slights like unreverent age.

Hence † **Unre·verentness**, irreverence. *Obs.*

1579 Northbrooke *Dicing* 32 [They] that do vse and handle vpon scaffolds Gods diuine mysteries with such vnreuerentnes. 1636 Henshaw *Horæ Succ.* 294 That unreverentnesse..which they durst not use to this or that Mr Gentleman, they use to God.

† **Unre·verently,** *adv. Obs.* [Un-1 11, 5 b.] Irreverently; without reverence. (Common c 1510–1660.)

c 1386 Chaucer *Pars. T.* ¶ 582 Whan they treten vnreuerently the sacrement of the Auter. 1421 Hoccleve *Jereslaus' Wife* 218 He answerde and spak vnreuerently. c 1449 Pecock *Repr.* v. xv. 563 The ixe principal gouernaunce for which summe of the lay peple vnwijsly and vnreuerentli blamen the clergie. 1543 Grafton *Contn. Harding* 460 His corps was brought vnreuerently from the toure..vnto Poules. 1576 Fleming *Panopl. Epist.* 80 That is supposed a loose kinde of writing, to talke of any man vnreuerently. 1638 Bp. Mountagu *Art. Enq. Visit.* A 4 b, Hath any of your parish unreverently used your Minister? a 1677 Manton *Serm. Ps. cxix*, cxxxi. Wks. 1725 I. 605/1 Will not God be as severe to me, if I behave my self unreverently?

Unreve·rsable, *a.* (Un-1 7 b, 5 b.) 1802–12 Bentham *Ration. Judic. Evid.* (1827) I. 141 The decision remaining unreversed, and, but for legislative authority, unreversable.

**Unreve·rsed,** *ppl. a.* (Un-1 8.)

1591 Shaks. *Two Gent.* iii. i. 223 The doome (Which vnreuerst stands in effectuall force). 1648 Prynne *Plea for the Lords* 63 His sentence..remaines..unreversed. 1657 *Decree Excheq., Hatfield Chase* 7 While the said Decree stands in force, and unreversed. 1802–12 [see prec.]. 1855 Macaulay *Hist. Eng.* xiii. III. 271 A legal sentence, passed in due form, and still unreversed. 1878 Abney *Treat. Photogr.* xxxiv. 278 It is possible to obtain an unreversed impression of the thermal spectrum.

† Unreve·ssed, -ve·sted, *pa. pple. Obs.* (Un-2 4, 8.) c 1450 *Chron. London* (Kingsford, 1905) 131 Whan the byshope hadde don the masse and whas unrevessed. 1483 Caxton *G. de la Tour* c vij b, When he had songen and was vnreuested it was not knowen where he bicam.

**Unreview·ed,** *ppl. a.* (Un-1 8.)

[1775 Ash.] 1819 Busby *Hist. Music* II. 255 There are particular..reasons why his Te Deum should not pass unreviewed. 1837 Carlyle *Fr. Rev.* i. vi. iii, After long unreviewed centuries.

Unrevi·led, *ppl. a.* (Un-1 8.) 1470 Hardyng *Chron.* Pref. p. x, As lyon fell he putte hym forth in prese, The werre maynteynde and kepte hym vnrevylde.

**Unrevi·sed,** *ppl. a.* (Un-1 8.)

[1775 Ash.] 1845 *Syd. Smith's Wks.* (1859) II. 333/1 The following unrevised fragment. 1847 Stanley *Arnold* Suppl. 22 The unblotted, unrevised manuscript. 1897 Goldw. Smith *Guesses Riddle Exist.* 83 Readers of the Bible who continue to use the unrevised version.

Unrevi·vable, *a.* (Un-1 7 b.) 1802–12 Bentham *Ration. Judic. Evid.* (1827) V. 171 When I say unrevivable, I mean by common law.

**Unrevi·ved,** *ppl. a.* (Un-1 8.)

1631 Weever *Anc. Funeral Mon.* 417 Old, moth-eaten, vnreuiued penall Lawes. 1680 H. More *Apocal. Apoc.* xi. 106 That..they may not seem to prophesie and be dead at the same time, nor lye too long unburied or unrevived. 1877 Conder *Basis Faith* ii. 75 Those memories of the past, unrevived for years.

† **Unre·vocable,** *a. Obs.* (Un-1 7 b, 5 b.)

1535 Stewart *Cron. Scot.* (Rolls) II. 581 Vnreuocabill, withoutin fraude or gyle, At thair plesour sic peax for to compyle. 1589 Greene *Menaphon* (Arb.) 43 The heauens.. sent vnreuocable Fates to depriue me of her life. 1608 L. Machin *Dumbe Knight* iii, My vow..is like fate still unrevocable. 1616 B. Parsons *Mag. Charter* 2 By an unrevocable patent.

Unre·vocably, *adv.* (Un-1 11.) 1472 in Ramsay *Bamff Charters* (1915) 29 Assignit hym unrevocably to the said annualerent of sex markis.

**Unrevo·ked,** *ppl. a.* [Un-1 8.]

1. Not revoked, recalled, or annulled.

1479 [see Unrepealed]. 1570 Levins *Manip.* 50 Vnreuoked, *irreuocabilis.* 1667 Milton *P. L.* v. 602 Hear all ye Angels,..Hear my Decree, which unrevok't shall stand. 1740 Cibber *Apol.* (1756) I. 310 This unrevoked order of silence. 1790 Cowper *Mother's Pict.* 112 Time, unrevok'd, has run His wonted course. 1835 *Court Mag.* VI. 35/1 The morrow arrived, and the Sultan's command remained unrevoked. 1858 Ld. St. Leonards *Handy-bk. Prop. Law* xx. 157 The general gift in your will to your child..will belong to him if you leave it unrevoked.

†2. Not called back. *Obs.*—1

1654 Gayton *Pleas. Notes* ii. vi. 59 As she unrevoked ran Shee thought each tree to be a man.

Unrevolu·tionized, *ppl. a.* (Un-1 8.) 1804 Larwood *No Gun Boats* 39 The old Lillies of unrevolutionized France. Unrevo·lved, *ppl. a.* (Un-1 8.) [1775 Ash.] 1891 Meredith *One of our Conq.* xxxiii, That was the thought, unrevolved, unphrased, all but unconscious, in Nesta. Unrevo·lving, *ppl. a.* (Un-1 10.) 1843 Carlyle *Past & Pr.* iii. xi, Of an idle unrevolving man the kindest Destiny..can bake and knead nothing other than a botch. Unrewa·rdable, *a.* (Un-1 7 b.) c 1445 Pecock *Donet* 94 Not wiþstonding synne is..vncleene, vnrewardable, punyschable.

**Unrewa·rded,** *ppl. a.* [Un-1 8.]

1. Not rewarded; unrequited.

c 1412 Hoccleve *De Reg. Princ.* 2890 No goode dede vnrewardid is, or quytte. c 1440 *Alph. Tales* lxxxi. 64 God will hafe no gude dede vnrewardid. 1512 *Helyas* in Thoms *Prose Rom.* (1828) III. 75 A good dede is never unrewarded ne an evyll unpunisshed. 1576 Abp. Sandys *Serm.* (1585) 171 Their seruice was vnrewarded, because it was vncontinued. 1628 R. H. *J. Owen's Epigr.* i. 7 Verses giuen for a Newyeeres-gift, vnrewarded. 1656 Sir E. Nicholas in *N. Papers* (Camden) III. 270 None can..imagine that so glorious an act can possibly be unrewarded. 1712 Blackmore *Creation* vii. 74 While Heaven's adorers..Their unrewarded innocence maintain. 1779 *Mirror* No. 35, My obsequious services in the drawing-room passed unrewarded. 1821 Byron *Sardanap.* iii. i. 357 Slain! unrewarded!..that's hard, poor slave. 1863 Mouat *Andaman Islanders* 153 Our persevering search, and our repeated use of the line, were unrewarded with the success we desired.

2. Unpunished.

1621 J. Taylor (Water P.) *Unnat. Father* Wks. (1630) 140/1 God did neuer suffer Murder to goe vnrewarded. 1907 *Verney Mem.* II. 128 Wickedness does not go for ever unrewarded.

Unrewa·rdedly, *adv.* (Un-1 11.) 1888 *Scribner's Mag.* Dec. 757/1 He had transfused two months of her life with such a delicate sweetness, so unrewardedly. Unrewa·rding, *vbl. sb.* (Un-1 13.) a 1586 Sidney *Arcadia* iii. xiv, It was the unrewarding, & not the evil employing her service, which grieved her.

**Unrewa·rding,** *ppl. a.* (Un-1 10.)

1653 Jer. Taylor *Serm. for Year* i. xix. 255 He findes it an unrewarding interest, to walk seven dayes..only to see a place from whence he must come back in an hour. 1854 Lever *Dodd Family Abroad* lxx. 592 [It] is a very unrewarding process. 1882 Myers *Renewal of Youth* 120 [To] come bootless back from the unrewarding quest.

**Unrheto·rical,** *a.* (Un-1 7, 5 b.)

[1775 Ash.] 1822 De Quincey *Confess.* 78 The literal and unrhetorical use of the word *myriad.* 1859 G. Wilson *Mem. E. Forbes* ii. 68 The style..is strikingly unrhetorical. 1875 E. White *Life in Christ* iv. xxiv. 405 Certain unrhetorical explicit statements of doctrine.

**Unrhy·med,** *ppl. a.* (Un-1 8; cf. Unrimed.)

1828 Carlyle *Misc.* (1857) I. 219 The grand unrhymed Romance of his earthly existence. 1848 Longf. *Secret of Sea* iv, With a soft, monotonous cadence, Flow its unrhymed lyric lines.

**Unrhy·thmic,** *a.* (Un-1 7.)

1884 *Athenæum* 2 Aug. 142/2 No unrhythmic verse was ever yet remembered beyond the generation that produced it.

**Unrhy·thmical,** *a.* (Un-1 7.)

Also, in recent use (1904), *unrhythmically.*

1777 Richardson *Persian & Arab. Dict.* 1935 Discordant, unrhythmical, wretchedly composed verse or prose. 1840 De Quincey *Style* Wks. 1859 XI. 167 Excess of awkwardness, or of inelegance, or of unrhythmical cadence. 1871 *Edin. Rev.* Apr. 432 His lines are never unrhythmical.

**Unri·bbed,** *ppl. a.* (Un-1 8.)

[1775 Ash.] 1834 K. H. Digby *Mores Cath.* v. viii. 288 See, then to what a distance your unribbed bark is driven. 1851 Ruskin *Stones Ven.* I. xxix. § 3 When the vaulting is unribbed, as in plain waggon vaults.

Unri·ch, *a.* (Un-1 7.) 1875 Morris *Æneid* xii. 519 By fruitful fishy Lerna's flood was once his life and gain, And unrich house. † Unri·d, *ppl. a.*1 [Un-1 8.] Unridden. 1640 H. Mill *Night's Search* i. 194 Give me a jade unrid, that's plump and fat.

**Unri·d,** *ppl. a.*2 *Sc.* and *dial.* [Un-1 8 b. Cf. ON. *úrudd-r* (Norw. *urudd, urydd,* Sw. *orödd,* Da. *uryddet*) uncleared.] Not put in order.

1637 RUTHERFORD *Lett.* (1664) 132 So marches lie still unrid & counts uncleared betwixt us. 1824 [CARR] *Craven Dialect* 5 Awr house is vara unrid and grimy. 1856 CARLYLE *Lett.* (1904) II. 179 [More of] my Book..lies in heaps ahead of me, in the unrid state.

**Unri·dden,** *ppl. a.* (UN-1 8 b.)

(*a*) 1574 *Richmond. Wills* (Surtees) 248 Horses at Burghe. Ridden horsses and mares, xv...Stages and fillies unreden, xij. 1607 MARKHAM *Cavel.* IV. 5 Foales, vnridden horses, or horses that are of any..sobrietie in iourneying. 1831 JAMES *Phil. Augustus* III. v, Horses..which have stood there unridden for months. 1857 DUFFERIN *Lett. High Lat.* (ed. 2) 83 Having caught, saddled and bridled the three unridden ponies.

(*b*) 1615 *Extr. Aberd. Reg.* (1848) II. 323 Leaving the saidis merches unridden.

**Unri·ddle,** *sb. rare*[−1]. [UN-2; cf. next.] A solution of a riddle. 1756 *Connoisseur* No. 107 ⁋ 7 Reading over the Riddles, and Unriddles, the Questions, and the Answers.

**Unri·ddle,** *v.* [UN-2 3. Cf. G. *enträtseln.*] *trans.* To solve, explain (a mystery, etc.). (Cf. RIDDLE *v.*1 2.)

*a* 1586 SIDNEY *Arcadia* III. vii, But nowe Amphialus helped to unriddle his doubts; for he [etc.]. 1634 PEACHAM *Compl. Gent.* xii. 111, I will give you..examples of these, with which..you may easily unriddle the rest. 1648 PRYNNE *Plea for Lords* 63 Let him..unriddle and assoyle..his owne Dilemma. 1714 ADDISON *Spect.* No. 567 ⁋ 7 If any sagacious Person can fairly unriddle it, I will print his Explanation. 1785 REID *Intell. Powers* IV. ii. 371 Take this description altogether, and it would require an Œdipus to unriddle it. 1820 KEATS *Hyperion* II. 150 No, no-where can [I] unriddle.. why ye..Should cower beneath..untremendous might. 1858 MERIVALE *Rom. Emp.* liii. VI. 218 To unriddle some of the perplexing questions. 1885 MISS BRADDON *Wyllard's Weird* I. 194 If we can unriddle the railway mystery, all may yet come right.

*refl.* 1653 R. C[ODRINGTON] *Lloyd's Marrow of Hist.* 1 This at first may seem a paradox; but upon a deliberate consideration it will easily unriddle itself.

*absol.* *a* 1642 SUCKLING *Goblins* I. i, Pray, unriddle. 1710 PARNELL *Hermit* 207 Confess th' Almighty just, And where you can't unriddle, learn to trust. 1768 H. WALPOLE *Myst. Mother* IV. vi, Unriddle, priest. My soul is too impatient To wait [etc.].

Hence **Unri·ddling** *vbl. sb.*

*a* 1680 BUTLER *Char. Religion* Wks. (1908) 306 They..are wonderfull acute at unriddling of Mysteries. 1821 BYRON *Juan* III. xxviii, The cause being past his guessing or unriddling.

**Unri·ddleable,** *a.* (UN-1 7 b.)

1647 EVELYN *Let.* in *Diary*, etc. (1852) III. 6 Things were never more unriddleable than at this instant of time. *a* 1675 LIGHTFOOT *Serm.* Wks. 1684 II. 1246 These difficulties..in Scripture..are not unriddleable riddles, and tyring-irons never to be untied, but [etc.].

**Unri·ddled,** *ppl. a.* [UN-1 8.] Unsolved. 1823 BYRON *Juan* XI. iii, This unriddled wonder, The World.

**Unri·ddler.** [f. UNRIDDLE *v.*] One who, or that which, solves or explains.

1657 TRAPP *Comm. Job* xxxvi. 22 A Teacher of perplexed things, an unriddler of Riddles. 1663 BOYLE *Usef. Exp. Nat. Philos.* I. iii. 64 If our posterity be not much happier unriddlers then..we have been. 1824 SCOTT *St. Ronan's* iii, He was also a deviser of charades and an unriddler of riddles. 1871 EARLE *Philol. Eng. Tongue* 365 That frequent unriddler of philological problems, the Hebrew language.

†**Unri·de,** *a. Obs.* Also 3 vnrude, 5 -ruyde; 4–5 vn-, 6 unryde, 4 oun-, 5 onride, vnrid; 4 vnrede. [OE. *ungerýde* (ME. *unirude* UN-1 3) rough, violent, f. *gerýde* (once), ? smooth, pleasant; of obscure origin. Cf. UNRUDE *a.*1]

**1.** Severe; causing much suffering.

*c* 1200 ORMIN 4779 All þiss wass utenn wiþþ unnhal Þurrh swiþe unnride unnhæle. *Ibid.* 4784 Her wass unnseoll þe unnride inoh Till an mann forr to dreȝhenn. *c* 1300 *Havelok* 1981 He haues a wunde in the side, With a gleyue, ful unride,.. And he haues on þoru his þe, Þe vnrideste þat men may se. *c* 1380 *Sir Ferumb.* 747 Wel neȝ ys guttes þat swerd him ran, & made hym a wounde ounride. *a* 1400 *St. Alexius* (Laud 108) 542 Al þat folk þat stod be-syde Þat say þe sorwe so vnruyde, Þey wepe ful tendreliche. *c* 1460 *Towneley Myst.* III. 40 Man..was put out, in that tyde, In wo & wandreth for to be, in paynes full vnrid To knawe.

**2.** Of large size; of great size and strength; so large as to be cumbersome or unwieldy.

*c* 1220 *Bestiary* 646 Ðanne cumeð ðis elp unride. *a* 1240 *Sawles Warde* in *O. E. Hom.* I. 249 Euch an [*sc.* devil] bereð..an unrude raketehe gleowinde of fure. *c* 1300 *Havelok* 1795 Þe barre..was unride, and gret ynow. *c* 1380 *Sir Ferumb.* 3691 Þe dent of þat sper oun-ryde. *a* 1400 *Sir Per.* 1160 To morne..salle we togedir playe With wapyns unryde. ? *a* 1600 *Merline* 1501 (Percy Folio), His tayle was great.. his bodye was unryde with-all.

**b.** Large in number; numerous.

*c* 1300 *Havelok* 2947 [All] it sawe..Hwou he it bar with mikel pride For his barnage þat was vnride. *c* 1330 *King of Tars* 142 The soudan gederet an ost unryde.

**c.** Large in extent. *rare*[−1].

13.. *Metr. Hom.* (MS. Ashm. 42) fol. 136, An vnridde spase es now Makid betwix vs and ȝow Þat none of vs maie come ȝou nere Ne none of ȝou maie come here.

**3.** Rough; violent.

*a* 1300 *Cursor M.* 24845 Þe wind ras gains þam vnride. 1338 R. BRUNNE *Chron.* (1810) 174 Þe noyse was vnride, it lasted alle day. *c* 1350 *Ipomedon* 6492 Is knyght non, That darre fyght wyth hym alonne, So is the fende vnryde. *a* 1400–50 *Alexander* 737 Reviles he þis oþire renke with vnrid [*v.r.* vnrode] speche. *c* 1470 *Golagros & Gaw.* 630 [He] raught to the renk ane rout wes vnryde.

**Unri·d(e)able,** *a.* (UN-1 7 b.)

Common in recent use. Hence *unrid(e)abi·lity.*

1831 *Daily News* 5 Jan. 6/5 Over a fine open country, till the land became almost unrideable. 1883 C. HOWARD *Roads Eng. & Wales* (ed. 3) 94 Steep unrideable ascents and descents.

**Unri·deably,** *adv.* (UN-1 11. Cf. prec.) 1851 KINGSLEY *Yeast* i, Lancelot had bought him..for half his value, as unrideably vicious, when he had killed a groom.

†**Unri·dely,** *adv. Obs.* Forms: (see quots.). [OE. *ungerýdelice* (rare), f. *ungerýde*: see UNRIDE *a.*] Violently, roughly, harshly.

*c* 1200 ORMIN 15567 *note*, And oferrwarrp þær i þe flor Unnriddliȝ þeȝȝre bordess. *a* 1225 *Juliana* 54 [Juliana] reat him mitte raketehe unrudeliche swiðe. *a* 1300 *Cursor M.* 24391 It raght mi hert al thoru þe rote, Vnrideli on me rane. 13.. *Gaw. & Gr. Knt.* 1432 Þer as þe rogh rocher vn-rydely was fallen. *a* 1400–50 *Alexander* 566 Þen rekils it vnruydly & raynes doune stanys. *Ibid.* 638 If any of his feris Raged with him vnridly. *c* 1400 *Song Roland* 990 He rent hym vnredly euyn to the sadill.

**Unri·dge,** *v.* (UN-2 4.) 1647 TRAPP *Comm. Rev.* i. 16 The word..slits open, and as it were, unridgeth the conscience.

**Unridi·culous,** *a.* (UN-1 7.) 1646 SIR T. BROWNE *Pseud. Ep.* VII. xvi. 372 If an indifferent and unridiculous object could draw his habituall austerenesse unto a smile.

**Unri·fe,** *a.* (UN-1 7.) 1599 T. M[OUFET] *Silkwormes* 4 His brother Linus first began The Flaxmans craft (a secret then vnrife).

**Unri·fled,** *ppl. a.*1 (UN-1 8 + RIFLE *v.*1)

1603 KNOLLES *Hist. Turks* (1621) 83 Nothing..left vnpolluted and defaced, no place vnsought, no corner vnrifled. 1653 JER. TAYLOR *Serm. for Year* I. xix. 246 The estate.. remains unrifled, and descends upon the heir. 1743 FRANCIS tr. *Hor., Odes* III. xxiv. 1 Though of th' unrifled Gold possest Of gorgeous Ind. 1835 *Court Mag.* VI. 205 Sing Birds!.. Give thanks in song for your unrifled nest! 1864 I. TAYLOR *Words & Places* 171 The hope of capturing the rich and unrifled prize.

*fig.* 1637 HEYWOOD *Royall Kings* Prol., No History We have left unrifled.

**Unri·fled,** *ppl. a.*2 (UN-1 8 + RIFLE *v.*3)

1860 *All Year Round* No. 73. 546 The shot of the ordinary unrifled service gun is round.

**Unri·g,** *v.* [UN-2 4.]

**1.** *trans.* To divest (a ship) of its rigging (both standing and running).

1579–80 NORTH *Plutarch* (1595) 541 He vnrigged and bestowed his ships in docks. 1615 *Britain's Buss* in Arber *Garner* III. 632 That the other two weeks be also spent.. in unrigging and laying up the Buss. 1667 *Lond. Gaz.* No. 169/4 They were constrained to Unrigg her, and to take down her Topmast. 1720 DE FOE *Capt. Singleton* xiv. (1840) 240 We unrigged our top-masts. 1768 *Ann. Reg., Chron.* 106/1 Some sailors began to unrig the ships. 1806 A. DUNCAN *Nelson* 124 A broadside..nearly unrigged the Foudroyant. 1820 SCORESBY *Acc. Arct. Reg.* II. 451 It would be necessary first to discharge the cargo, and to unrig the ship.

**b.** *absol.* To remove or take down rigging.

*a* 1647 PETT in *Archaeologia* (1796) XII. 227 Friday the 16th, we unrigged, and shot the bridge. 1799 NELSON in Nicolas *Disp.* (1845) III. 238 Malta then was half-starving, and the Ships had unrigged. 1897 tr. *Nansen's Farthest North* II. vii. 327 We..rigged up mast and sail. But..we were soon obliged to unrig, and take to paddling.

**c.** In pres. pple. = Being unrigged.

1673 *Lond. Gaz.* No. 773/4 The other, mounted with 24 Guns, is now unrigging. 1810 *Naval Chron.* XXIII. 121 A small frigate unrigging.

**d.** *trans.* (See quot.)

1769 FALCONER *Dict. Marine* (1780), *Dégarnir le cabestan*, to unrig the Capstern, by taking off the voyol, and unshipping the bars.

**2.** *transf.* To strip of clothes; to undress.

1591 LYLY *Endym.* III. iii, Vnrigge mee. Hey ho! 1693 *Dryden's Juvenal* xiv. (1697) 367 The Shrine was..lin'd with a strong Guard of Souldiers, who had an Eye to their God ..lest he should be stoln, or unrigg'd. 1723 *Pres. St. Russia* I. 162 The French Gentlewoman,..whom they had almost unrigged, withal telling the Men that they had stript first. 1793 WOLCOT (P. Pindar) *Ep. to the Pope* 132 Out with her ear-rings and the Dame unrig. 1820 SCOTT *Monast.* xvi, He secured my spare doublet..—I was enforced to beat a retreat before I was altogether unrigged. 1880– in Shropshire and Yks. use (*Eng. Dial. Dict.*).

*absol.* 1693 CONGREVE *Old Bach.* v. i, *Bell.* I wou'd unrig. *Setter.* I attend you, Sir. 1865 MRS. WHITNEY *Gayworthys* v, Gabriel..fibbed again when he said he 'didn't feel much like rigging up for a party;' which had been true but for the last five minutes since he unrigged.

**b.** To unharness.

1690 *Lond. Gaz.* No. 2552/3 The Sailors went ashore and unrigged his Horse. 1881 DUFFIELD *Don Quixote* II. 575 The express command of his master that..Rozinante should not be unrigged.

**Unri·gged,** *ppl. a.* [f. prec., or UN-1 8.] **a.** Divested of rigging. **b.** Not furnished with rigging.

*a* 1593 MARLOWE *Edw. II*, II. ii, While in the harbor ride thy ships vnrigd. — *Dido* III. i, Yet..are my ships vnrigd, My Sailes all rent. 1623 in Foster *Eng. Factories Ind.* II. (1908) 215 The carricke..nowe lyeth alltogeather unrigged. 1695 *Lond. Gaz.* No. 3088/3 The Ships that lay hard by unrigg'd. 1748 *Anson's Voy.* III. iv. 330 Our shrowds were loose, and our top-masts unrigged. 1799 *Hull Advertiser* 30 Mar. 1/4 She being totally unrigged, struck. 1830 *Encycl. Brit.* (ed. 7) II. 633/2 An unrigged boat. 1834 MARRYAT *P. Simple* II. 281 Our guns became..hot from quick firing. ..By this time we were almost..unrigged.

**Unri·ght,** *sb. Obs.* exc. *arch.* [OE. *unriht* (f. *un-* UN-1 12 + *riht* RIGHT *sb.*1), = OFris. *on-*, *unriucht* (WFris. *on-*, *ûnrjucht*, NFris. *ünrocht*), MDu. (Du.) *onrecht*, OS. *unreht* (MLG., LG. *unrecht*, LG. *-regt*), OHG. (MHG.) *unreht* (G. *unrecht*), Norw. *urett*, (M)Da. *uret*, (M)Sw. *orätt.*]

**1.** Wrong, wrong-doing, iniquity.

*Beowulf* 1264 Siþðan goldsele Grendel warode, unriht æfnde. *a* 1122 *O. E. Chron.* (Laud MS.) an. 1100, He on middewardan his unrihte butan behreowsunge..ȝewat. *c* 1205 LAY. 6553 Vnriht him wes leof, and rihtwisnesse him wes lað. *c* 1330 R. BRUNNE *Chron. Wace* (Rolls) 11513 Com, & amende þyn vnright, þat þou so slowe ffrolle oure knyght. *c* 1380 WYCLIF *Sel. Wks.* II. 91 Þis is a trewe man, and unriȝt is not in him. *c* 1449 PECOCK *Repr.* v. iii. 498 The oon [god] is maker of riȝt and of good thingis, and the other is maker of vnriȝt and of badde thingis. *a* 1547 SURREY in *Early XVI Cent. Lyrics* xlv. 46 Prowd people that drede no fall, clothed with falshed and vnright. 1578 PROCTOR *Gorgeous Gallery Inventions* B ij, Well mayst thou wayle thy want of troth; & rue thy great vnright. 1610 H. BROUGHTON *Job* xxvii. 4 My lippes shall not speak the vnright. [1876 FREEMAN *Norm. Conq.* V. xxiv. 394 It was because they still spake of right that right in the end outlived unright.]

**b.** In the phr. *to do* (or *work*) *unright.*

*c* 888 K. ÆLFRED *Boeth.* xxxviii. § 3 Forþamðe ðu ær cwæde ðæt he unriht dyde þæt he lete unwitnod ða yflan. *c* 1000 ÆLFRIC *Deut.* xxxi. 29 Þonne ȝe unriht wirceað beforan drihtene. *a* 1300 *Cursor M.* 24158 Ye Iuus,..Vn-reufulli yee wirc vnright. 13.. *Ibid.* 5084 (Gött.), I am a-knau i did vnriht. *c* 1412 HOCCLEVE *De Reg. Princ.* 5040 [God] may done non vnright. 1535 COVERDALE *Zeph.* iii. 5 But the iust Lorde that doth no vnright, was amonge them. *a* 1547 SURREY in *Early XVI Cent. Lyrics* xlv. 16 All such as wourke vnright. 1607 J. DAVIES *Summa Totalis* G 2, With neither Will, nor Pow'r to do vnright.

**2.** Unfairness, injustice (done or suffered).

*c* 888 K. ÆLFRED *Boeth.* xxxix. § 9 Hwylc unriht mæȝ beon mare þonne ȝeþafiȝe [etc.]. *c* 1020 *Ags. Laws* (Thorpe) I. 388 We nellað ȝeþafian þæt unriht. *c* 1175 *Lamb. Hom.* 115 He scal wissian mid wisdome his folke and unriht aleggen. 1297 R. GLOUC. (Rolls) 8625 More vnriȝt þan he dede ne miȝte nomon ise. *c* 1325 *Spec. Gy Warw.* 613 To suffre wrong and vnriht For þe loue of god almiht. *c* 1400 *Beryn* 557 That were grete vnryȝte, To aventur oppon a man þat with hym did nat fiȝte. 1456 *Cov. Leet Bk.* 290 Boldly to fight, Yf any man of curage wold bid you vnright. 1530 TINDALE *Pract. Prelates* A v b, There was neuer creature that sofred so greate vnright so pacyentlye..as he. 1581 A. HALL *Iliad* IX. 162 Suffice it him he hath me wrongde, and that his own vnright Doth hel him like a man forlorne.

**b.** In phr. *to do one unright*, or variations of this.

*c* 1200 *Vices & Virtues* 113 Nis him idon non unriht. *c* 1250 *Gen. & Ex.* 1276 Ðor ben he boren feren pliȝt, ðat here neiðer sal don oðer un-riȝt. 13.. *K. Alis.* 7491 (Laud MS.), And amendyng I bidde þee to Of vnriȝth þat is me do. 1340 *Ayenb.* 221 Hi ssolle loki hare bodi þe on to þe opre..treweliche wyþ-oute do onriȝt þe on to þe oþren. *c* 1402 LYDG. *Compl. Bl. Knt.* 334 Notwithstonding his manhood..Love unto him did ful greet unright. 1532 TINDALE *Expos. Matt.* (1550) F vij b, Be patient..., what soeuer vnright be done the. 1599 DANIEL *Lett. Octauia to M. Antonius* xxii, Is it, that loue doth take no true delight In what it hath,..Which drawes you on to doe vs this vnright?

**3.** *With* (also *on*) *unright*, wrongfully, unjustly.

*Beowulf* 2739 Ic..ne sohte searoniðas, ne me swor fela aða on unriht. ? *a* 900 K. ÆLFRED *Laws* § 1 Ne wilna þu þines nehstan ierfes mid unryhte. *c* 1205 LAY. 7374 Þu ahtest me to ȝulden ȝauel of þine londe, And þu hit halst on unriht. 1297 R. GLOUC. (Rolls) 4040 He nom it verst mid vnriȝt, & broȝte þat lond in wo. 13.. *E. E. Allit. P.* B. 1142 He loses hit ille, As hit were rafte wyth vnryȝt & robbed wyth þewes. *a* 1425 *Cursor M.* 19012 (Trin.), Þat ihesus..ȝe duce on rode wiþ vnriȝt. 1563 FOXE *A. & M.* 564/1 To discerne in what wise ther iudgement passed, whether with right or vnright.

**4.** An instance of wrong or wrong-doing; a wrong or unjust act.

*c* 888 K. ÆLFRED *Boeth.* xvi. § 4 Betwuh þyllecum unrihtum wæs him [*sc.* Nero]..underþeod eall þes middanȝeard. *a* 1122 *O. E. Chron.* (Laud MS.) an. 1086, Maniȝe oðre unriht hi dydan, þe sindon earfeþe to areccenne. *c* 1200 *Vices & Virtues* 79 Ða ðat he hadde mid maniȝe unrihtes biȝeten. *a* 1300 *Cursor M.* 11812 Þis herods..vn-rightes biginnes to ripe! *c* 1380 *Sir Ferumb.* 1031 Þe Sarasyns.. schullaþ abigge þys ounriȝt. *c* 1400 tr. *Secreta Secret., Gov. Lordsh.* 59 Draw to þe þe good wylles of þy subgitz, and putte away þaire vnryghtys and wronges. ? *a* 1500 *Chester Pl.* III. 142, 40 dayes and 40 nightes Rayne shall fall for ther vnrightes. 1528 LYNDESAY *Dreme* 262 Partycipant thay wer of thare vnrychtis.

**Unri·ght,** *a.* [OE. *unriht* (f. *un-* UN-1 7 + *riht* RIGHT *a.*), = OFris. *on-*, *unriucht* (WFris. *on-*, *ûnrjucht*, NFris. *ünrocht*), MDu. and obs. Du. *onrecht*, OS. *unreht* (MLG. and LG. *unrecht*, LG. *-regt*), OHG. (MHG.) *unreht* (G. *unrecht*), ON. *úréttr* (Norw. *urett*, Da. *uret*, MSw. *orätter*, Sw. *orätt*).]

**1.** Not right, just, or equitable; improper, unfair, wrong. Now *Sc.* or *arch.* (common in 16th c.).

*c* 888 K. ÆLFRED *Boeth.* xxxviii. § 3 Ic..wundrie forhwy swa rihtwis dema æniȝe unrihte ȝife wille forȝifan. *c* 1000 *Ags. Ps.* (Thorpe) cxviii. 104 Ic me betst onceneow, þæt ic unrihte weȝas ealle of-eode. *c* 1200 *Vices & Virtues* 121 Unriht domesmann. 1297 R. GLOUC. (Rolls) 8726 He let grede þoru al þe lond þe vnriȝte lawes vndo. *c* 1375 *Cursor M.* 26711 (Fairf.) He salle..on domisday haue wreyers harde, þat is to say..þe werlde, þe deuil, his didis vnriȝt. *c* 1449 PECOCK *Repr.* III. xx. 415 Open it is..thilk deede or gouernaunce in him silf is vnriȝt and wrong. 1532 MORE *Confut. Tindale* Wks. 545/2 [To] walke in the commaundementes of life, & do nothing that is vnright. 1603 J. DAVIES (Heref.) *Microcosmos* 157 These senseless spunges of Improbity Are full of pleasure, but it is vnright. 1627 BP. HALL *Dauids Ps. Metaphr.* i, The man vnright, As chaffe.., With euery blast Is cast on hie. 1856 W. H. GILLESPIE *Truth Evang. Hist.* vii. 129 Such un-right and self-inconsistent deprivation. 1880 G. MACDONALD *Diary Old Soul* 16 Feb., If I should slow diverge..Into some thought, feeling, or dream unright.

*absol.* 1610 H. BROUGHTON *Job* xxix. 17, I brake the tuskes of the vnright.

†**2.** Incorrect; inexact. *Obs. rare.*

1562 TURNER *Herbal* II. 32 Amatus gyueth an vnryght duche name vnto Sion when he calleth it bauchbungen. 1591 WOTTON in *Reliq.* (1685) 641, I..alleg'd further, that the Copy was unright. 1605 VERSTEGAN *Dec. Intell.* i. 17 So many haue aleaged so many vnright and vnlykely causes thereof.

†**Unri·ght,** *adv. Obs.* [OE. *unrihte* (f. *un-* UN-[1] 11 b + *rihte* RIGHT *adv.*), = MDu. *onrechte* (Du. *onrecht*), OS. and OHG. *unrehto* (MHG. *unrehte*, G. *unrecht*), Da. *uret*, Sw. *orätt*.] Improperly; not in the right way; wrongly.

*Beowulf* 3059 Þa wæs ȝesyne þæt se sið ne ðah þam ðe unrihte inne ȝehydde wræte under wealle. *a* **1000** *Ags. Ps.* (Thorpe) cxviii. 78 Beon þa oferhydeȝan ealle ȝescende, þe me unrihte ahwær gretan. *c* **1374** CHAUCER *Troylus* v. 661 Hym thought..þat þe sonne wente his course vnright. *a* **1400** *Northern Passion* 1624 Þai lukyd tyll hys fete full bryght; Sone þai sayd þai lay vnryght [*v.r.* noghte aryghte]. *c* **1480** HENRYSON *Test. Cres.* 205 As King Royall he raid vpon his Chair, The quhilk Phaeton gydit sum tyme vnricht. **1513** DOUGLAS *Æneid* XIII. Prol. 138 Gyf thou hes afore tyme gayn onrycht, Followand sa lang Virgill, a gentile clerk. ? **1555** COVERDALE tr. *Bk. Death* vii. 24 Therefore wryteth gregory not vnright whan he saith [etc.]. **1603** J. DAVIES (Heref.) *Microcosmos* 167 See how blinde a Guide Is lothsome Lust, that leades men so vnright.

† **Unri·ght,** *v.*[1] *Obs. rare.* [f. UNRIGHT *sb.* or *a.* Cf. MDu. *onrechten*, MHG. *unrechten*, to do injustice, treat unjustly.] *trans.* To wrong, injure.

**1390** GOWER *Conf.* I. 176, I wolde swiche tales sprede..That I scholde al his love unrihte. *Ibid.* II. 355 That he thurgh eny sleihte myhte Hire lusti maidenhod unrihte. **1647** in Rushworth *Hist. Coll.* IV. (1701) I. 555 Rather than they will be unrighted in the matter of their Honesty and Integrity,.. they will lose all.

†**Unri·ght,** *v.*[2] [UN-[2] 4. Cf. OFris. *on(t)riuhta*, MDu. *ontrechten* (Du. *-richten*), MLG. *entrihten*, OHG. *intrihtan* (MHG. *entrechten*, G. *-richten*).] *trans.* To deprive of rights.

*c* **1449** PECOCK *Repr.* III. xvi. 386 This man mai not iustli be vnriȝtid and vnpossessid, that is to seie, be putt out of riȝt and out of possessioun of the seid..good.

Unri·ghted, *ppl. a.* [UN-[1] 8.] Not righted. [**1775** ASH.] **1883** F. M. PEARD *Contrad.* II. 269 If the wrong were unrighted,..then—what would become of her?

**Unri·ghteous,** *a.* Forms: (see RIGHTEOUS *a.*). [OE. *unrihtwís* (UN-[1] 7 + RIGHTEOUS). Cf. ON. *úréttvís* (MDa. *uretvis*, Sw. *orättvis*).]

**1.** Not righteous or upright; unjust, wicked: **a.** Of persons.

*c* **888** ÆLFRED *Boeth.* xxxvii. § 1 Geher nu an spell be..þam unrihtwisum cyningum. *c* **1000** *Ags. Gosp.* Luke xvi. 10 Se þe ys on lytlum unrihtwis, se ys eac on maran unrihtwis. *c* **1175** *Lamb. Hom.* 115 Þe nihȝeðe unþeau is þet þe king beo unrihtwis. *c* **1200** *Trin. Coll. Hom.* 19 Alle þe unrihtwise men..hersumieð þe deuel. *c* **1380** WYCLIF *Sel. Wks.* III. 19 Alle unriȝtwise men þat serven to him [*sc.* the devil] as hise trewe knyȝtis. **14..** *Tundale's Vis.* 274 Þou art not lele iustise, Þou art fals and unryghtwyse. **1474** CAXTON *Chesse* 28 Cambyses..had an vnrightwis juge. **1526** TINDALE *Heb.* vi. 10 God is not vnrighteous that he shulde forget youre worke. **1572** R. T. *Discourse* 48 The Sadduces..were most vnrightuous. **1651** HOBBES *Leviathan* III. xlii. 306 There being nothing in mens Manners that makes them righteous, or unrighteous. **1712** M. HENRY *Expos., Isaiah* lv. 7 Here's a Call..to the Wicked, and the Unrighteous Man. ? **1791** BENTHAM *Draught Code* Wks. 1843 IV. 316 An unrighteous judge, or rather a judge who would otherwise be unrighteous. **1871** JOWETT *Plato* I. 158 Many men are utterly unrighteous, unholy, intemperate.

*absol. c* **825** *Vesp. Psalter* v. 6 Ne ðorhwuniað ða unrehtwisan biforan eȝum ðinum. *c* **1200** *Vices & Virtues* 83 Ic wile tache ðo unrihtwisen ðine weiȝes. *a* **1400** *New Test.* (Paues) App., 1 Pet. iii. 18 For onys Crist was for oure synnes deed, þe riȝtwyse for the vnriȝtwise. **1623** R. CARPENTER *Conscionable Christian* 14 What then shall the vnrighteous be able to say..for themselues? **1712** M. HENRY *Expos., Isaiah* lv. 7 The Unrighteous that live in the neglect of plain Duties. **1835** *Wilson's Tales Borders* I. 58/1 The innocent have been left to perish amang the unrighteous.

**b.** Of actions, etc.

**971** *Blickl. Hom.* 33 Se awyrȝda gast is heafod ealra unrihtwisra dæda. *c* **1250** *Gen. & Ex.* 2014 His wif wurð wilde, and nam in ðoȝt vn-riȝt-wis luue. *a* **1300** *Cursor M.* 29507 O thrijn wijs Mai cursing be tald onrightwijs. *c* **1400** *Destr. Troy* 3539 The rape vnrightwis of his Riche qwene. **1481** CAXTON *Reynard* xlii. (Percy Soc.) 160 Somme helpe them forth in theyr vnryghtwys dedes. **1535** COVERDALE 2 *Macc.* iv. 35 The vnrightuous death of so godly a man. **1590** SPENSER *F. Q.* II. x. 60 Octauius here lept into his roome, And it vsurped by vnrighteous doome. **1667** MILTON *P. L.* III. 292 Thir own both righteous and unrighteous deeds. **1725** POPE *Odyss.* IX. 630 Angry Neptune heard th' unrighteous prayer. **1846** MRS. A. MARSH *Father Darcy* II. xxi. 365 Those who have dared to prostitute holy things to unrighteous purposes. **1863** 'OUIDA' *Held in Bondage* i. I. 17 He was..full of most unrighteous oaths.

† **c.** Incorrect, false. *Obs.*[−1]

**1507** *Extr. Aberd. Reg.* (1844) I. 437 That the mettis and mesouris be assait,..and quhar thai be fundin unrichtuus be distroit.

**2.** Not rightly due or deserved.

**1855** SINGLETON *Virgil* II. 100 Anchises' offspring..from his soul Compassionated their unrighteous lot.

Hence **Unri·ghteous** *v.*, to make unrighteous.

**1593** NASHE *Christ's T.* K ij b, Thou that ere this hast disparradiz'd our first Parent Adam, and vnrighteouzd the very Angels.

**Unri·ghteously,** *adv.* [OE. *unrihtwíslíce* (UN-[1] 11 + RIGHTEOUSLY *adv.*). Cf. ON. *úréttvísliga* (MDa. *uretvislige*, MSw. *orätvislika*).] In an unrighteous manner; unjustly, wrongfully.

*c* **897** K. ÆLFRED *Gregory's Past. C.* liv. 425 Ic cwæð to ðæm unryhtwisum, ne do ȝe unryhtwislice. *a* **1200** in Kemble *Cod. Dipl.* IV. 24 Butan he toforan ðam deaðe..sebete ðæt he unrihtwislice forȝette. *a* **1300** *Cursor M.* 18274 Qui gaf þou rede þis ilk iesu to crucifi, Wit-vten skil, vn-rightwisli? **1382** WYCLIF *Wisdom* xii. 13 For not vnriȝtwisly thou demest dom. *c* **1425** AUDELAY *XI Pains Hell* 333 What chamful end þay haue þat leuyn here vnryȝtwysly. **1509** BARCLAY *Shyp of Folys* (1570) 29 Remember Richarde ..In Englande reigning vnrightwisely a while. **1559** *Mirr. Mag.* 43 Was never prince that other dyd oppresse Unrighteously, but died in distresse. **1611** BEAUM. & FL. *Philaster* II. i, Who unrighteously Holds wealth or state from others, shall be curst. **1687** DRYDEN *Hind & P.* III. 1077 Their Foes a deadly Shibboleth devise: By which unrighteously it was decreed [etc.]. *a* **1768** SECKER *Serm.* (1770) V. 422 Whether they do not..persecute most unrighteously..both Christian Faith, and natural piety. **1807** FOSTER *Ess.* (1844) I. 21 They have sometimes been most unrighteously accused. **1847** PRESCOTT *Peru* III. vii. I. 428 The distribution of spoil so unrighteously acquired.

**Unri·ghteousness.** [f. UNRIGHTEOUS *a.*] The quality of being unrighteous; an instance of this, an unrighteous action.

*c* **825** *Vesp. Psalter* v. 7 Ðu fedest..alle ða ðe wircað unrehtwisnisse. *c* **1055** *Byrhtferth's Handboc* in *Anglia* VIII. 332 Iniquitas on lyden on englisc ys ȝecweden unrihtwisnys. *c* **1200** *Vices & Virtues* 37 Ðurh his unrihtwisnesse he bringþ his saule in to helle pine. *a* **1300** *E. E. Psalter* xxxvi. 7 In man..Unrightwisnes þat es doand. *c* **1380** WYCLIF *Wks.* (1880) 240 A grete vnriȝtwisnesse regneþ among lordis whanne þei wolen not distroie pride. **1422** YONG tr. *Secreta Secret.* 132 Vnryghtuossnes disherityth kynges and Pryncis. **1535** COVERDALE 2 *Esdras* vii. 35 The righteousnesses shall watch, and the vnrighteousnesses shall beare no rule. **1590** BABINGTON *Expos. Commandm.* 70, I am not worthie to beholde the height of Heauen, for the multitude of my vnrighteousnesse. **1611** BIBLE *Rom.* i. 18 The wrath of God is reueiled from heauen against all..vnrighteousnesse of men. *a* **1677** BARROW *Serm.* Wks. (1686) II. v. 80 The inherent unrighteousness consequent upon Adam's sin. ? *a* **1758** WITHERSPOON *Ess.* Sel. Wks. 1804 I. 36 He is a God..with whom unrighteousness can have no communion. **1833** S. HOOLE *Discourses* xv. 200 The unrighteousness of living to himself alone. **1871** JOWETT *Plato* II. 330 If only he can..be pure from evil or unrighteousness.

**Unri·ghtful,** *a.* Now *rare.* [UN-[1] 7.] Unrighteous, unjust, wrong.

*a* **1325** *Prose Psalter* c. 3 Y ne sett nouȝt to-fore myn eȝen þyng vnryȝtful. **1393** LANGL. *P. Pl.* C. XI. 215 A rybaud þei engendrede and a gome vnryghtful. *c* **1440** *Jacob's Well* 285 An Heremyte ȝaf hym to ydell & vnryȝtefull thouȝtys,.. for hym thouȝte þat god was vnryȝtfull. **1482** *Monk of Evesham* (Arb.) 85 The onrightful scheding of mennys blode. **1545** BALE *Myst. Iniq.* 15 Pylate the vnryghtfull iudge. *a* **1586** SIDNEY *Astr. & Stella* Sonn. v. x, A rightfull prince by unrightfull deeds a tyrant groweth. **1606** G. W[OODCOCKE] *Hist. Ivstine* XXII. 84 Obiecting vnto them sometime their vnrightfull entrapping of Hanno. **1664** MORE *Myst. Iniq.* iv. 11 Malicious or inconsiderate spirits, that.. pass unrightfull censures upon what is at least allowable. **1880** MCCARTHY *Own Times* IV. 336 The unrightful things that were sometimes done.

**Unri·ghtfully,** *adv.* Now *rare.* [UN-[1] 11.] Without right; unjustifiably, unfairly, wrongly.

*a* **1325** *Prose Psalter* cv. 6 We han wroȝt vnryȝtfullich. *c* **1374** CHAUCER *Boeth.* I. met. v. (1868) 23 Anoienge folk treden..vnryȝtfully in þe nekkes of holy men. **1433** *Rolls of Parlt.* IV. 455/1 Whan they been often tymes unrightfully empeched. **1470–85** MALORY *Arthur* VIII. ii. 276 That is vnryghtfully asked, said kyng Melyodas. **1513** BRADSHAW *St. Werburge* I. 336 A kynge..In batayle slayne vnryghtfully, now a martyr gloryous. *c* **1557** ABP. PARKER *Ps.* xxxvi. 99 The wordes of hys mouth be unrightfully wayed. **1793** JEFFERSON *Writ.* (1859) IV. 61 Between restraining it ourselves, and permitting her enemies to restrain it unrightfully, is no difference. **1866** HOWELLS *Venet. Life* iv. 53 A great humbug and unrightfully in the guide-books.

**Unri·ghtfulness.** Now *rare.* [f. UNRIGHTFUL *a.*] The quality of being unrightful.

*a* **1250** *Owl & Night.* 1742 Ic nolde þat vnrihtfulnesse Me at þen ende ouercome. *a* **1325** *Prose Psalter* vii. 15 Lo, þe sinner doþ vnryȝt-fulnesse. **1382** WYCLIF *John* vii. 18 This is sothfast, and vnriȝtfulnesse is not in him. ? *c* **1450** in Roy *Rede me*, etc. (Arb.) 183 The wrathe of god is shewyd..vpon cruelnes and vnryghtfulnes of these men. *a* **1470** H. PARKER *Dives & Pauper* (W. de W. 1496) II. xvii. 128/1 Periury is cause..of all unrightfulnesse. **1821** JEFFERSON *Autobiog.* Writ. 1892 I. 62 The unrightfulness and inefficacy of the punishment of crimes by death.

†**Unri·ghtly,** *a. Obs.*[−1] [UN-[1] 7. Cf. next and OE. *unrihtlic*.] Wrong, erroneous.

**1422** YONG tr. *Secreta Secret.* 161 Verite caste doune, whan any vnryghtly thynge is preferrid to trouthe.

**Unri·ghtly,** *adv.* Now *rare.* [OE. *unrihtlíce* (UN-[1] 11 + RIGHTLY *adv.*), = MDu. *onrechtelike* (obs. Du. *-lijk*), MLG. *unrechteliken*, OHG. *unrehtlîhho* (MHG. *unrehtlîche*, etc.), ON. *úréttliga* (MDa. and Da. *urettelig*, MSw. *orätlika*).] Not rightfully; unfairly, wrongly.

*a* **900** *O. E. Martyrol.* 18 May 84 Fram þæm mannum..þa he ær unrihtlice ofsloh on þyssum life. *c* **1000** *Rule St. Benet* (1888) 104 Unrihtlice he ne ȝedihte [nan þing]. *c* **1425** *Eng. Conq. Ireland* 128 To setten yn har londes, Thay that wyth streynth & vnryghtly weren out i-dryue. **1544** BALE *Chron. Sir J. Oldcastell* 55 b, Not all vnryghtlye ded saynct Augustyn speake yt. **1583** tr. *Maison Neuve's Gerileon* I. 29 b, Thereby to burden you with the fault, wherein not vnrightly you are culpable. **1643** PRYNNE *Sov. Power Parl.* III. 108 If any inferiour Officers..unrightly governe the people, they may lawfully be resisted by them. **1878** *Prodigal Son* IV. in Simpson *Sch. Shaks.* 110 We are such honest folk that we covet nothing unrightly.

†**Unri·ghtness.** *Obs.* [UN-[1] 12.] Unfairness. *c* **1445** PECOCK *Donet* 134 Þei ben..forbodis of oure vniustnesse, of oure vnriȝtnes anentis oure neiȝboris. †**Unri·ghty,** *a. Obs.*[−1] [UN-[1] 7 + RIGHT *a.* Cf. Du. *onrechtich* (Du. *-ig*), MLG. *unrichtich*, OHG. *unrihtig* (G. *unrichtig*), etc.] Devoid of right condition. *c* **1315** SHOREHAM I. 1075 Þou wreþest god almyȝty, To holy cherche on-bouxam þart, Makest þy selue on-ryȝty. **Unri·med,** *ppl. a.* [UN-[1] 8 a.] = UNRHYMED *ppl. a.* **1774** [W. MITFORD] *Ess. Harmony Lang.* 142 Rimed verse..is far inferior to unrimed. **1886** SKEAT *Wars Alex.* p. xx, Any other unrimed alliterative poem. **Unri·mple,** *v.* (UN-[2] 4. Cf. Du. *ontrimpelen.*) **1800** *Monthly Mag.* X. 318 Fresh blossoms of diction [would] unrimple their roseate petals. **Unri·mpled,** *ppl. a.* (UN-[1] 8.) [**1775** ASH.] *a* **1839** GALT *Demon Destiny* III. (1840) 21 The placid waters..Were all unrimpled by the gentle air.

**Unri·nd,** *v.* Also 6 vnrine. [UN-[2] 4. Cf. G. *entrinden.*] *trans.* To strip of rind or bark. Hence **Unri·nded** *ppl. a.*[1]

**1382** WYCLIF *Gen.* xxx. 37 Jacob takynge green popil ȝerdis..a parti vnryendide hem. **1598** FLORIO, *Sbucciare*,.. to pare..or vnbarke or vnrinde trees. **1611** COTGR., *Escorcée*, ..the pilled, or vnrinded part of a Plant. **1648** HEXHAM II, *Ontschoeyen*, to Pill or Vnrinde a tree.

**b.** *fig.* To undress.

**1872** T. HARDY *Under Greenw. Tree* IV. ii, I've been forced to go upstairs and unrind myself.

† **Unri·nded,** *ppl. a.*[2] *Sc. Obs.* [UN-[1] 8 + RIND *v.*[2]] Unrendered; not melted down.

**1581** *Burgh Rec. Edinb.* (1882) IV. 217 The talloun bocht be him als weill ryndet and vnryndet. **1702** in W. R. Mackintosh *Glimpses of Kirkwall* (1887) 42 That none of the flesshers exact any more than twentie pennies Scots for the merk of unrynded tallow.

**Unri·nged,** *ppl. a.* [UN-[1] 8. Cf. MDu. *ongeringet*, older Da. *uringet.*] Of swine: Not furnished with a nose-ring. (Cf. UNRUNG *ppl. a.*[2])

**1510** *Burgh Rec. Prestwick* (Maitl. Club) 42 For þe wrangwis worttyne of þar swyne, & wnryngyt. **1576** GASCOIGNE *Steele Gl.* (Arb.) 70 Like rude vnringed swine. **1624** in H. Maclean *Watermillock Reg.* (1908) 157 Sub poena for every swine so unringed iiij[d]. **1664** BUTLER *Hud.* II. II. 310 Is't fit [it] should..Be forc'd t' impeach a broken hedge, And Pigs unring'd. **1733** in Climenson *Hist. Shiplake* (1894) 307 No person..shall suffer his hogs to go unringed.

**Unri·nsed,** *ppl. a.* (UN-[1] 8.)

**1661** FELTHAM *Resolves* (ed. 8) II. i. 174 Loose and unrins'd expressions are the..spurcitious exhalations of a corrupted mind. **1847** LANDOR *Hellenics, Thrasymedes & E.* 6 Ye shall not..taste From unrinsed barrel the diluted wine. **1860** FLOR. NIGHTINGALE *Nursing* i. 14, I have actually seen..the utensils..put back, unrinsed, under the bed.

**Unri·oted,** *ppl. a.* (UN-[1] 8.) **1627** MAY *Lucan* IX. 235 A chast vnriotted house, and neuer stain'd With her Lords fortune.

**Unri·p,** *v.* [UN-[2] 9 + RIP *v.*[2]]

**1.** *trans.* To strip (a house or roof) of tiles, slates, etc. (Cf. RIP *v.*[2] 2 c.) Now *dial.*

*a* **1513** FABYAN *Chron.* VII. 414 [They] vnryppyd the howse in dyuers places that the rayne..myght entre. **1543** in Parker *Dom. Archit.* (1859) III. 61 Serching, vnryppyng, new tylyng and poyntyng ouer the west syde of the Quenes pallet chambre. **1887** PARISH & SHAW *Kentish Gloss.* 129 To unrip the roof of a stable or outbuilding, is to take off the tiles, slates, &c.

**2.** To lay open, slit up, or detach, by ripping.

Stigmatized in 1708 as 'a barbarous, improper word' (*British Apollo* No. 75, 2/1; cf. quot. 1880). In 19th c. somewhat rare in literary use; but freq. in dialect.

**1534** [see b]. **1594** SHAKS. *Rich. III*, I. iv. 212 [Thou] Did'st breake that Vow, and with thy treacherous blade, Vnrip'st the Bowels of thy Sou'raignes Sonne. **1601** B. JONSON *Poetaster* III. iv, You should ha' seene me vnrip their noses now, and haue sent 'hem to the next barbers, to stitching. **1661** WALTON *Angler* I. v. (ed. 3) 122 We heard as high a contention amongst the beggers, Whether it was easiest to rip a cloak, or to unrip a cloak? **1700** SWIFT *Poems, Mrs. Harris' Petition* 11 My smock was unript, And, instead of putting it [= a purse] into my pocket, down it slipt. **1743** FIELDING *J. Wild* IV. ix, He unript the lining of his waistcoat and pulled forth several jewels. **1837** MARRYAT *Dog Fiend* xi, They..proceeded to unrip them [*sc.* bags]. **1863** MISS BRADDON *Aurora Floyd* xxi, He took his clasp-knife..[and] carefully unripped a part of one of the seams in the waistcoat. **1880** *Plain Hints Needlework* 106 To say un-rip, as is often heard, is at least manifestly wrong, to describe the act of tearing open.

**b.** In fig. contexts.

**1534** R. WHITINTON *Cicero* I. G vij, Amytes and loue that lesse delyte vs..wyse men iudge rather to become vs by lytell and by lytell to vnrippe them than sodaynly to cutte them awaye. **1586** HOOKER *Disc. Justification* § 5, I cannot stand now to vnrip this building, and to sift it piece by piece. **1611** BEAUM. & FL. *Philaster* I. i, Though thy breath doth strike me dead..I have unript my breast. *a* **1652** A. WILSON *Inconstant Ladie* IV. iii, Thy lookes are full of honestie; I dare Vnrip my breast to thee. **1697** COLLIER *Ess. Mor. Subj.* II. 67 As Cato well observes, though in the Phrase of a Taylor, Friendship ought not to be Vnrip'd, but Vnstitch'd.

*refl.* **1614** J. COOKE *Greene's Tu Quoque* E 1, Had'st thou not vnrip't thy selfe to me, I should neuer haue knowne thee.

† **c.** To break (a seal); to open (a sealed document). *Obs.*

**1583** GREENE *Mamillia* 26 b, His daughter..receiuing the Letter, could scarcely stay to vnrip the seale, while she came in her closet. **1633** FORD *'Tis Pity* V. I 2, *Friar.* Looke there, 'tis writt to thee. (Gives the letter.) *Gio.* From whom? *Friar.* Vnrip the seales and see. **1634** HEYWOOD *Maidenh. well lost* I. 47 b, His seal'd Commission He had vnript.

† **3.** *fig.* **a.** To rip up, bring to light or notice, expose to view. *Obs.*

**1577** SIR W. DRURY in Grosart *Spenser's Wks.* I. 66, I would not seem to unrip old matters. **1591** *Troub. Raigne K. John* i. 88 Before I once open my mouth to vnrippe the shameful slaunder of my parents. **1615** BRATHWAIT *Strappado* 211 For many Errors and fowle crimes I knowe.. Which I'le in part vnrip, and so make cleare. **1633** FORD *'Tis Pity* III. F 3 b, You haue vnript a soule, so foule and guilty,..I maruaile how The earth hath borne you vp.

† **b.** To unfold, disclose, reveal, make known.

**1579–80** NORTH *Plutarch* (1595) 832 When he beganne to vnrip his whole intents and practises..he..offended the Senate. **1598** MARSTON *Pygmal., Sat.* ii. 143 Delphick

Apollo, ayde me to vnrip These intricate deepe Oracles of wit. 1615 BRATHWAIT *Strappado*, etc. (1878) 253 Her blush, her smile, her biting of her lip, did all the secrets of her hart vnrippe. 1755 SMOLLETT *Quix.* II. 296 You may unrip, and unload, all that lies upon your sorrowful heart.

†**c.** To undo, annul. *Obs.*

1622 BACON *Hen. VII*, 176 Hee could not now with his Honour so vnrippe, and (in a sort) put a Lye vpon all that hee had said and done before.

Hence **Unri·pped** *ppl. a.*; **Unri·pping** *vbl. sb.*

1641 MILTON *Animadv.* 8 Such an unripping, such an Anatomie of the shiest, and tenderest particular truths. 1707 MORTIMER *Husb.* 144 Let down the Bag by unripping of the Hoop. 1850 THACKERAY *Pendennis* xi, Milly..took an unripped satin garment off the only vacant seat.

**Unri·pe,** *a.* [OE. *unripe* (f. *un-* UN-1 7 + *ripe* RIPE *a.*), = WFris. *on-, ûnryp*, NFris. *ünrip(þ*, MDu. (Du.) *onrijp*, OHG. *unrîfi* (MHG. *unrîf*, G. *unreif*).]

†**1.** Of death: Untimely, premature. *Obs.*

*c* 1000 ÆLFRIC *Gloss.* in Wr.-Wülcker 149 *Immatura* [*mors*], unripe dea?. 1548 UDALL *Erasmus Par. Luke* vii. 69 b, The unripe death of the young strieplyng. *a* 1586 SIDNEY *Arcadia* II. vi, Dorilaus, whose unripe death doth yet..draw teares from vertuous eyes. 1633 P. FLETCHER (*title*), Elisa, or An Elegie upon the Unripe Decease of Sr Antonie Irby.

**2.** Immature; not arrived at full development.

*a* 1340 HAMPOLE *Psalter* cxviii. 147, I ran in barnhede, þat is vnrype til perfeccioun. 1548 UDALL *Erasm. Par. Luke* 141 b, That same stemme of the Judaicall figtree brought foorth..vnsauourie, & vnripe people. 1620 *Southampton Court Leet Rec.* (1907) III. 582 The teaching of a Stranger ..vnripe of yeres. *a* 1639 WALLER *Battle Summer-Isl.* I. 59 So in this northern tract our hoarser throats Utter unripe and ill-constrained notes. 1659 W. CHAMBERLAYNE *Pharon.* II. iii. 612 Yet Justice slumbers I' the prosecution of his unripe fate. 1700 DRYDEN *Sigism. & Guisc.* 254 Resolv'd his unripe Vengeance to defer, The Royal Spy..Sought not the Garden. 1704 J. TRAPP *Abra-Mulé* I. i. 33 Thy tender Innocence, and unripe Beauty. 1819 SHELLEY *Peter Bell 3rd* Prol. 15 The First Peter—he who was Like the shadow in the glass Of the second, yet unripe. 1847 EMERSON *Each & All* 38 Beauty is unripe childhood's cheat. 1891 *Spectator* 28 Feb., To try unripe and ill-conceived schemes for improving their condition.

**b.** Of years or age.

1568 GRAFTON *Chron.* II. 120 The election beyng vnfree, and the yeres vnripe, eche of them almost of necessitie must hate the other. 1596 SPENSER *F. Q.* VI. ii. 9, I whose vnryper yeares are yet vnfit For thing of weight. 1633 P. FLETCHER *Purple Isl.* Ep. Ded., These raw Essayes of my very unripe yeares. 1659 W. CHAMBERLAYNE *Pharon.* IV. v. 235 The old Experienced courtiers kneel; by which ..those of unriper age [etc.]. 1800 WORDSW. *Brothers* 297 The boy..of unripe years, a stripling only. 1814 CARY *Dante, Parad.* XVII. 77 His unripe age Yet holds him from observance.

**3.** Of fruit, etc.: Not matured by growth.

*a* 1250 *Owl & Night.* 320 Mi stefne is bold.. & þin is iliche one pype Of one smale weode vnripe. 1382 WYCLIF *Rev.* vi. 13 As a fijge tree sendith his vnripe fyges. 1535 COVERDALE *Wisd.* x. 7 The vnripe and vntymely frutes that growe vpon the trees. 1555 EDEN *Decades* (Arb.) 67 While they be soure and vnripe, they are white. 1614 R. TAILOR *Hog hath lost Pearl* II, Unripe fruit will ask more shaking before they fall than those that are. 1732 ARBUTHNOT *Rules of Diet* in *Aliments*, etc. I. 247 Unripe, they are sour, and rather astringent. 1798 COLERIDGE *Fears in Solitude* 9 Fresh and delicate As vernal corn-field, or the unripe flax. 1849 CLARIDGE *Cold Water Cure* 112 To eat plentifully of common unripe plums. 1882 *Garden* 4 Feb. 72/3 Unripe wood is liable to get injured by frosts.

*transf.* *a* 1425 tr. *Arderne's Treat. Fistula*, etc. 93 Rude [roset] is made of vnripe oile and of rosez. 1693 SIR T. BLOUNT *Nat. Hist.* 250 Erastus affirms..that..there hath been Unripe and Unconcocted Silver found in Mines. 1751 WARBURTON *Pope's Wks.* IV. 128 *note*, The image is taken from half-formed unripe lightning, which streams along the sky. 1799 KIRWAN *Geol. Ess.* 279 No. 10. Red and yellow, unripe pouzzolana. *Ibid.*, Unripe black pumice. 1884 J. PHIN *Dict. Apiculture* 73 Unripe Honey.—Honey from which the water has not been sufficiently evaporated.

**Unri·ped,** *ppl. a.* [UN-1 8.] Unripened. 1423 JAS. I *Kingis Q.* xiv, Thou ȝouth, of nature Indegest, Vnrypit fruyte with windis variable. **Unri·pely,** *adv.* (UN-1 11.) 1597 MIDDLETON *Wisd. Solomon* ii. 3 Unripely withering in a flowery prime. 1755 JOHNSON, *Crudely*,..unripely; without due preparation.

**Unri·pened,** *ppl. a.* (UN-1 8.)

1588 KYD *Househ. Philos.* Wks. (1901) 244 Mellons..that ..taste like Goords and Cowgomers which also hang vpon the earth vnripened. 1589 [? LYLY] *Pappe w. Hatchet* D iij b, Vnripened youthes, whose wisedomes are yet in the blade. 1611 SPEED *Hist. Gt. Brit.* IX. xii. § 63. 682/2 They would not haue found that euer this Iland brought forth a Prince of such excellency at so vnripened yeares. 1675 HAN. WOOLLEY *Gentlew. Comp.* 181 Take of unripened Galls one dram. 1720 POPE *Iliad* XXIII. 671 The errors of unripen'd age. 1768–74 TUCKER *Lt. Nat.* (1834) II. 228 To..wade through the mud of indolence, with the slender staff of unripened reason. 1831 SCOTT *Ct. Rob.* ix, The vehemence of their own appetite for raw fruits and unripened wines. 1895 *Cent. Mag.* Aug. 542/2 All the unripened nymphs that played at hide-and-seek among the maples.

**Unri·peness.** (UN-1 12.)

*a* 1340 HAMPOLE *Psalter* cxviii. 147, I bifore come in vnrypnes and i cried. 1548 ELYOT, *Immaturitas*, vnrypenesse, to muche haste in doyng a thynge before the tyme. 1593 *Sidney's Arcadia* v. (1922) II. 199 The unripenesse of theyr age. 1625 BACON *Ess., Delays* (Arb.) 525 The Ripenesse, or Vnripenesse, of the Occasion (as we said) must euer be well weighed. 1678 MARVELL *Growth Popery* 42 In this state of uncertainty and unripeness, the House Adjourned. 1783 *Phil. Trans.* LXXIII. 244 The unripeness of the barley. 1844 PRICE in Stanley *Arnold* I. iv. 196 The unripeness of England for a free and unfettered discussion. 1886 C. SCOTT *Sheep-farming* 46 Let the same conditions or unripeness be present in any kind of roots, and their effects will be much the same.

**Unri·pening,** *ppl. a.* (UN-1 10.) 1864 SWINBURNE *Atalanta* 531 Death Crushes with sterile feet the unripening ear.

**Unripped, -ripping**: see UNRIP *v.*

**Unri·ppled,** *ppl. a.* (UN-1 8.)

[1775 ASH.] 1816 BYRON *Siege Cor.* xix, The sea..was unrippled as glass may be. 1882 FARRAR *Early Chr.* I. 248 The unity so secured is but the stagnancy of the unrippled water. 1883 *Congregationalist* Nov. 902 The secret of our unrippled intercourse is that we have always acted on the principle of non-intrusion.

**Unri·pplingly,** *adv.* (UN-1 11.) *a* 1861 T. WINTHROP *Life in Open Air* viii. (1863) 63 Its current, unripplingly smooth,..bore on our bark.

**Unri·sen,** *ppl. a.* (UN-1 8 b.)

[1775 ASH.] *a* 1806 H. K. WHITE *To Morning* ii, The lark..soars till the unrisen sun Gleams on her speckled breast. 1879 MISS BIRD *Lady's Life in Rocky Mount.* 139 The moon, as yet unrisen here.

**Unri·tual,** *a.* (UN-1 7.) 1791 ANNA SEWARD *Lett.* (1811) III. 80 The quiet dispassionate simplicity of unritual devotion. **Unrituali·stic,** *a.* (UN-1 7.) 1876 ALEXANDER *Bampton Lect.* (1877) 6 A religion, tolerant, unritualistic, and unsectarian. **Unri·valable,** *a.* (UN-1 7 b.) 1834 SOUTHEY *Doctor* I. 34 The present unique, unrivalled, and unrivalable production.

**Unri·valled,** *ppl. a.* (UN-1 8.)

1591 SHAKS. *Two Gent.* v. iv. 144, I heere..Plead a new state in thy vn-riual'd merit, To which I thus subscribe. 1667 MILTON *P. L.* III. 68 Uninterrupted joy, unrivald love In blissful solitude. 1693 DRYDEN *Juvenal* x. 492 But your Endymion,..Unrivall'd, shall a Beauteous Dame enjoy. 1708 J. PHILIPS *Cyder* II. 7 Thou view'st..what Unrival'd Authors by their Presence made For ever venerable. 1771 *Junius' Lett.* lxvii. (1772) II. 305 *note*, In the memoirs of private treachery they stand first and unrivalled. 1849 MACAULAY *Hist. Eng.* iv. I. 445 Unrivalled powers of argument and eloquence. 1877 MRS. OLIPHANT *Makers Flor.* xv. 369 [He] had shown himself unrivalled and above all competitors.

†**Unri·ve,** *v. Obs.* [UN-2 9 + RIVE *v.*1] *trans.* To tear apart; to open up.

1592 WYRLEY *Armorie, Capitall de Buz* 109 Such one as ..troubles makes him faster for to twind Fast gaged band of loue, and scorns to liue More rather then the same he will vnriue. 1652 BENLOWES *Theoph.* VI. xciv, Thus, they ..Into each others knowledge dive; And, by consent, thoughts, else inscrutable, unrive.

**Unrive,** obs. var. of UNREEVE *v.*

**Unri·ven,** *ppl. a.* (UN-1 8 b. Cf. MSw. *orivin*, Sw. *orifen*.)

*c* 1400 *Sege Jerus.* 607 ȝit wer þe Romayns as rest, as þey fram Rome come, Ronnen ouer [*v.r.* vnrevyn] eche a renk, & noȝt a ryng brosten. 1817 MOORE *Lalla R., Veiled Prophet* III. 219 The last sole stubborn fragment, left unriv'n, Of the proud host that late stood fronting Heav'n. 1845 HIRST *Com. Mammoth*, etc. 25 Mocking, as he rushed on unriven, The innocuous bolts of mighty heaven.

**Unri·vet,** *v.* [UN-2 3.]

**1.** *trans.* To undo, unfasten, or detach, by the removal of rivets.

1591 HARINGTON *Orl. Fur.* XLV. lxxii, No more the damsels force did now preuayle To pierce a plate, or to vnriuet nayle. 1627 DRAYTON *Agincourt* 46 Their Curates are vnriuetted with blowes. 1631 *Celestina* XVIII. 181 Who hewes, and unriviteth the finest maile but it [*sc.* the sword]? 1755 T. H. CROKER *Orl. Fur.* XXXI. xxi, While from their shields immense the sides they tear, Armour unrivetted, and mail unbound. 1758 GOLDSM. *Mem. Protestant* (1895) II. 83 At nine o'Clock..our Chains were again unrivetted. 1863 CONINGTON *Hor., Odes* III. v. 18 Should aught but death the prisoner's chain Unrivet. 1885 *Law Rep.* 15 Q.B.D. 360 The belts..could be removed from the shafting altogether by being unrivetted or unlaced.

**2.** *fig.* To undo, loosen, relax, detach, etc.

1620–51 I. JONES *Stone-Heng* (1725) 13 He..sought to be ..revenged on the British Nobility, who had wholly unrivetted his Designs. 1665 BRATHWAIT *Comment Two Tales* (1901) 78 Some..unriveted the very Secrets of their own Brests, and told him what they most desired. 1706 BAYNARD in Floyer *Hot & Cold Bath.* II. 199 Nothing is harder than to unrivet a wrong Notion. 1803 SCOTT *Let.* in *Lockhart* (1837) I. xi. 378 We sincerely hope Mrs. Ellis and you will unrivet yourselves from your forest. 1853 MISS E. S. SHEPPARD *Ch. Auchester* III. 158 Before I had spoken or even unriveted my gaze.

Hence **Unri·vetting** *vbl. sb.*

1611 COTGR., *Desrivement*, an vnriuetting. *a* 1662 HEYLYN *Laud* (1668) 370 By which he screwed himself so far into his Majesties good opinion, that whosoever undertook the unrivetting of him, made him faster in it. 1885 W. MORRIS in Mackail *Life* (1899) II. 134 Only the complete unriveting of the chain will really free us.

†**Unro.** *Obs.* (See also UNRUFE.) [UN-1 4, 12. Cf. ON. *úró* (Norw., MDa., and Da. *uro*, MSw. and Sw. *oro*), NFris. (Sylt) *unruu*, MLG. *unro(u)we*, MHG. *unruowe, unruo* (G. *unruhe*).] Unrest, disquiet.

*a* 1300 *Cursor M.* 7438 Ai quen he [*sc.* Saul] was trauaild mast Thoru a wreche vn-roful gast, And he [*sc.* David] bigan to gleu or sing, Of his vn-ro he tok lething. *Ibid.* 28250 In kyrk i wroght oft syth vn-ro Quen goddis seruis was to do. 13.. *Metr. Hom.* in *Archiv Stud. neu. Spr.* LVII. 250/2 Wiþ pyne and vnreste and vn-Ro. *a* 1400 *Sir Perc.* 362 Thou wirkeste thiselfe mekille unroo.

Hence †**Unro·ful** *a.* (See prec., quot. *a* 1300.)

†**Unroa·st,** obs. variant of next.

1665 PEPYS *Diary* 21 Dec., A good chine of beef..; but, being all frost-bitten, was most of it unroast.

**Unroa·sted,** *ppl. a.* (UN-1 8.)

1377 LANGL. *P. Pl.* B. v. 612 Tho Adam and Eue eten apples vnrosted. 1600 HAKLUYT *Voy.* III. 511 The worst in the ship thought scorne..of sodden lambe, which they disdained to eate vnrosted. 1622 FLETCHER *Sea-Voy.* III. i, Why should we consume thus, and starve,..And she live there that bred all our miseries, Unrosted, or unsod? 1751 J. HILL *Hist. Plants* 281 A decoction of the raw or unroasted seeds is a powerful diuretic. 1839 URE *Dict. Arts* 693, 19 hundred weight of limestone are employed; constituting nearly 1 of limestone for 3 of unroasted ore. 1882 *U.S. Rep. Prec. Met.* 600 Two parcels of pyrites of 20 tons each—one roasted, the other unroasted.

**Unro·bbed,** *ppl. a.* (UN-1 8.)

1393 LANGL. *P. Pl.* C. XIV. 1 He may walke vnrobbed Among pilours in pees yf pacience hym folwe. *c* 1450 *Mirk's Festial* 39 A man myght goo wher he wold vnrobbed, wyth his good yn hys hond. *c* 1530 LD. BERNERS *Arth. Lyt. Bryt.* (1814) 318 They leue no house vnrobbed. 1599 HAKLUYT *Voy.* II. I. 238 Although you haue set so many eyes to looke there for your benefit, that you escape vnrobbed of the slaues. 1660 EVELYN *The Late News* 2 Those ready Jewels of honour (the only Treasure he is, or can be unrob'd of). 1794 H. WALPOLE in Miss Berry *Jrnls.*, etc. (1865) I. 436 At night I went to Lady Onslow's,..and came back unrobbed. 1891 *Pall Mall G.* 24 Dec. 2/3 An amateur bushranger..'stuck up' a coach, which, however, got away unrobbed.

**Unro·be,** *v.* [UN-2 4.] To divest of a robe or robes: **a.** *trans.* or *refl.* Also const. *of.*

1598 FLORIO, *Spogliare*,..to disaray, to vnrobe. 1687 in *Magd. Coll. & Jas. II* (O.H.S.) 25 Several went into the outward Chapel to unrobe themselves. 1711 G. HICKES *Two Treat. Chr. Priesth.* (1847) II. 290 He robed and unrobed himself in his throne. 1797 COLERIDGE *Christabel* I. xxvi, But now unrobe yourself; for I Must pray, ere yet in bed I lie. 1838 ELIZA COOK *Love's First Dream* iii, It fades..; Leaving the spirit, unrobed of light, In darkness and tears behind. 1850 R. G. CUMMING *Hunter's Life S. Afr.* xii. I. 263, I considered myself..fortunate in having secured so noble a specimen of the lion,..and I at once set men to work to unrobe him. 1874 SPURGEON *Treas. Dav.* lxxxii. 7 How quickly death unrobes the great!

**b.** *absol.* (for *refl.*).

1743 YOUNG *Nt. Th.* IV. 44 When, on their exit, souls are bid unrobe,..And drop this mask of flesh behind the scene. 1766 ENTICK *London* IV. 117 There is no vestry room for the minister to robe and unrobe. 1837 McCULLOCH *Acc. Brit. Empire* II. 240 The Lords also adjourn..to unrobe. 1855 MACAULAY *Hist. Eng.* XV. III. 574 The King..unrobed, took his seat,..and listened..to the debate.

Hence **Unro·bing** *ppl. a.*

1810 MONTGOMERY *West Indies*, etc. 157 Still the unrobing spirit cast Diviner glories to the last.

**Unro·bed,** *ppl. a.* (UN-1 8.)

[1775 ASH.] 1861 H. MACMILLAN *Footnotes fr. Page Nat.* 189 Unrobed prophets that see no sad visions themselves. 1899 *Westm. Gaz.* 8 May 5/1 The two Archbishops entered unrobed.

**Unrobu·st,** *a.* (UN-1 7.) [1775 ASH.] 1891 HANNAH LYNCH *G. Meredith* 36 Deeming our taste questionable and unrobust.

**Unro·cked,** *ppl. a.* (UN-1 8.)

With the Sc. quots. in (*a*) cf. ROCKED *ppl. a.* 1, quot. *a* 1500, and ROCK *v.*1 1, quot. 1796.

(*a*) *c* 1480 HENRYSON *Fables, Fox, Wolf & Husb.* 116 Schir, be the Rude, vnroikkit now ȝe raif. 1530 LYNDESAY *Test. Papyngo* 969 Thow rauis vnrockit,..So to reproue ryches or propertie. *a* 1583 POLWART *Flyting w. Montgomerie* 802 (Tullib. MS.), Proud slaif, ȝe raif vnrokkit.

(*b*) 1648 HEXHAM II, *Ongewieght*, vnrocked. [1775 ASH.] 1892 *Daily News* 4 Feb. 5/8 The absolute stillness of her tall masts, unrocked by any motion of the sea.

**Unro·ll,** *v.* [UN-2 3, 5, 7. Cf. Du. *ont-*, G. *entrollen*.]

**1.** *trans.* To open out from a rolled-up state; to uncoil.

1412–20 LYDG. *Chron. Troy* III. 171 Ful knyȝtly þei han take her weye..with baneris..displaied, And her penouns vnrollid eueryehon. 1523 LD. BERNERS *Froiss.* I. ccxli. 145/1 [He] rested on the felde, and caused his banerr to be vnrolled. 1611 COTGR., *Desrouler*, to vnroule, vnfould, lay open. *a* 1700 EVELYN *Diary* 15 Jan. 1645, On which lay the 5 Bookes of Moses, and the Commandments a little unrowled. 1769 MRS. RAFFALD *Eng. Housekpr.* (1778) 89 Then unroll the cloth, and roll it tight again. 1786 ABERCROMBIE *Gard. Assist.* 267 Turf..when to be laid, unrolled, joining..close edge to edge. 1828 DUPPA *Trav. Italy*, etc. 98 In this Museum [at Naples] is carried on the operation of unrolling the ancient papyri. 1873 J. RICHARDS *Wood-working Factories* 122 By unrolling the blade on the floor, it can be tested as to straightness.

*refl.* 1815 SCOTT *Guy M.* xxxviii, Rolling up..the long lash of his horsewhip, and then by a jerk causing it to unroll itself into the middle of the floor. 1855 KINGSLEY *Westw. Ho!* xvii, Till not..an armadillo [dare] unroll himself.

**b.** In fig. contexts.

1678 DRYDEN *All for Love* V. i, Time has unrowl'd her Glories to the last, And now clos'd up the Volume. 1750 GRAY *Elegy* 50 But Knowledge to their eyes her ample page ..did ne'er unroll. 1757 — *Bard* 106 But oh! what solemn scenes on Snowdon's height Descending slow their glitt'ring skirts unroll? 1818 BYRON *Ch. Har.* IV. clvii, Until thy mind..unroll In mighty graduations, part by part, The glory. 1866 LE FANU *All in Dark* xiii, One could see..that she was reading to herself the romance that was unrolled within her pretty girlish head. 1876–89 R. BRIDGES *Growth of Love* xlvii, The busy mind Will in one woeful moment more upwind Than lifelong years unroll of bitter or black.

**c.** To extend, spread out; to disperse.

1813 SCOTT *Trierm.* III. xii, And still..Were..bastions dimly seen, And Gothic battlements between Their gloomy length unroll'd. 1817 SHELLEY *Rev. Islam* I. xxxviii, Wisdom had unrolled The clouds which hide the gulf of mortal woe. 1831 SCOTT *Cast. Dang.* iii, The mist had settled upon the hills, and unrolled itself upon brook, glade, and tarn.

**d.** *fig.* To develop or expand fully.

1854 EMERSON *Lett. & Soc. Aims, Eloquence*, Jenny Lind ..complained of concert-rooms and town-halls, that they did not give her room enough to unroll her voice. *a* **1871** GROTE *Eth. Fragm.* iv. (1876) 92 That all these elements are really present, is shewn most incontestably when the sentiment comes to be deliberately unrolled.

**2.** *intr.* To become unrolled. Also *fig.*

**1588** SHAKS. *Tit. A.* II. iii. 35 Euen as an Adder when she doth vnrowle To do some fatall execution. ?**1797** BLAKE *Four Zoas* IX. 20 The Books of Urizen unroll with dreadful noise! **1807** J. BARLOW *Columb.* II. 132 The venturous soul Bids greater powers and bolder thoughts unrol. **1816** J. WILSON *Misc. Poems* 194 As the clouds of the morning unroll. **1827** FARADAY *Chem. Manip.* xx. 532 To fold..this projecting part down, in such a manner as to..prevent the slip from unrolling.

†**3.** *trans.* To remove from a roll or list. *Obs.*—[1]

**1611** SHAKS. *Wint. T.* IV. iii. 130 If I make not this Cheat bring out another,..let me be vnrold, and my name put in the booke of Vertue.

Hence **Unro·lled** *ppl. a.*[1]; **Unro·ller**; **Unro·lling** *vbl. sb.* and *ppl. a.*[1]

**1805** LUCCOCK *Nat. Wool* 113 When we find a line of sand strewed along the *unrolled fleece. **1890** *Retrospect Med.* CII. 27 Passing the unrolled end [of the bandage] over the shoulder and down the back. **1843** *For. Q. Rev.* II. 364 A pale-faced *unroller of dusty records. **1648** HEXHAM II, *Een Ontrollinge*, an *Vnroling, or an Vnfolding. **1856** STANLEY *Sinai & Pal.* i. 3 There is..no unrolling of a great drama, no beginning, middle and end of a moral progress. **1870** BURTON *Hist. Scot.* lxi. VI. 93 The unrolling of secrets. **1699** C. HOPKINS *Crt. Prosp., Peace* iii, *Unrowling Waves steal softly to the Shore. *a* **1850** BRYANT *To a Cloud* 9, I would I were with thee..To rest on thy unrolling skirts.

**Unro·lled,** *ppl. a.*[2] [UN-[1] 8. Cf. G. *ungerollt*.] Not rolled; not subjected to rolling.

**1573** TUSSER *Husb.* (1878) 100 See when ye rowle it, the weather be drie, or else it were better vnrowled to lie. **1600** [see STONE *sb.* 16 c]. **1640** HOWELL *Dodona's Gr.* 114 Hee.. left no stone unrolld to bring this mighty worke to passe. **1839** DE LA BECHE *Rep. Geol. Cornwall*, etc. viii. 241 The prevalence of unrolled chalk flints above the green sand. **1851** *Quart. Jrnl. Geol. Soc.* VII. 359 The local and unrolled character of such surface-accumulations.

**Unro·lling,** *ppl. a.*[2] (UN-[1] 10.)

**1647** CLARENDON *Contempl. Ps.* Tracts (1727) 503 With downcast looks, and unrowling or fixt eyes.

**Unro·llment.** *rare*—[1]. [UNROLL *v.*] The action of unrolling. **1878** G. D. BOARDMAN *Creative Week* 124 You cannot unroll what was not inrolled...And yet these Gentlemen.. confound *Unrollment* with transmutation.

**Un-Ro·man,** *a.* (UN-[1] 7.)

**1682** *Whitelocke's Mem.* Pref., A more degenerate un-Roman generation. **1843** DENNIS *Cities & Cem. Etruria* iv. I. 97 Its mode of construction is decidedly un-Roman. **1864** PUSEY *Lect. Daniel* v. 284 The un-Roman retreat of Cestius Gallus.

**Unro·manized,** *ppl. a.* (UN-[1] 8 a *c.*)

**1771** WHITAKER *Hist. Manchester* I. 312 Before the third century the fruit appears to have..stocked the..unromanized regions of Shetland with large plantations of the trees. **1847** WEBSTER, *Unromanized*,..not subjected to the principles or usages of the Roman Catholic Church. **1855** MILMAN *Lat. Chr.* XIV. vii. VI. 530 The kindred language enabled them to communicate..with the un-Romanised races. **1861** CRAIK *Hist. Lit.* I. 36 Evidence of the comparatively unromanized condition of the Early English church.

**Unroma·ntic,** *a.* (UN-[1] 7.)

**1731** SWIFT *Let. to Gay & Duchess of Queensberry* 28 Aug., I own it is a base, unromantick spirit in me. **1824** MISS L. M. HAWKINS *Annaline* I. 41 If I were a young man, I should not like such an unromantic proceeding. **1850** THACKERAY *Pendennis* lxxi, This unromantic conclusion to a rather sentimental scene.

**Unroma·ntical,** *a.* (UN-[1] 7.) **1850** THACKERAY *Pendennis* xlvii, Mr. Pen was blushing whilst he made this reply to his unromantical friend. **Unroma·ntically,** *adv.* (UN-[1] 11.) **1846** WORCESTER (citing Allen). **1884** W. BLACK in *Athenæum* 11 Oct. 463/1 Her unromantically long spinsterhood. **Unroma·nticized,** *ppl. a.* (UN-[1] 8 a *c.*) **1855** MILMAN *Lat. Chr.* XIV. vi. VI. 525 Toulouse owns only her own unidealised, unromanticised Counts.

**Unroo·f,** *v.* (UN-[2] 4.)

**1598** FLORIO, *Disculminare*,..to vnroofe, or vntile a house. **1607** SHAKS. *Cor.* I. i. 222 Sdeath, The rabble should haue first vnroof't the City Ere so preuayl'd with me. **1779** HERVEY *Nav. Hist.* II. 457 Three hundred houses were unroofed by it. **1844** KINGLAKE *Eothen* viii, They actually unroofed a great part of the building. **1868** FREEMAN *Norm. Conq.* viii. II. 288 Houses were unroofed, and the timbers were thrown into the fosse.

*transf.* **1804** COLLINS *Scripscrap* 59 Time had unroof'd all the thatch from his pate. **1862** JAS. GRANT *Capt. of Guard* xii, Servers, pages, and pantrymen..unroofed the huge pasties of pigeons and venison.

Hence **Unroo·fed** *ppl. a.*[1], stripped of the roof, made roofless; **Unroo·fing** *vbl. sb.*

*a* **1550** LELAND *Itin.* (1768) II. 68 At the which tyme al the Chirch..lay to wast, and was *onrofid. **1779** *Phil. Trans.* LXX. 68 The sight of this town, unroofed, half buried under black scoriæ and ashes. **1814** SCOTT *Wav.* lxiii, Unroofed cottages, trees felled for palisades, and bridges destroyed. **1876** BRYANT *Flood of Years* 79 Temples stand Unroofed, forsaken by the worshippers. **1831** JAMES *Phil. Augustus* I. xv, The *unroofing of the hovels.

**Unroo·fed,** *ppl. a.*[2] [UN-[1] 8.] Not furnished with a roof; not roofed in.

[**1775** ASH.] **1805** EUGENIA DE ACTON *Nuns of Desert* II. 203 Miss Blenheim..had repaired to the un-roofed temple. **1851** RUSKIN *Stones Ven.* I. xiv. § 18 Walls surrounding unroofed courts.

*transf. a* **1854** H. REED *Lect. Eng. Lit.* ii. (1855) 83 The rude places of the open and unroofed world.

**Unroo·st,** *v.* [UN-[2] 5 and 7.]

**1.** *trans.* To dislodge from a roost or perch. Also *fig.*, to dislodge or force out of a place, to drive out or away.

**1598** FLORIO, *Disnidare*, to vnroost, to vn-nest. **1611** SHAKS. *Wint. T.* II. iii. 74 Thou dotard, thou art woman-tyr'd: vnroosted By thy dame Partlet heere. **1647** TRAPP *Comm. Rev.* xiv. 20 The Pope being driven from Rome, shall flie and sit, till Christ shall unroost him. **1682** BUNYAN *Holy War* 236 He also saw..how he was unroosted and made to quit the Castle. **1780** JOHNSON *Let. to Mrs. Thrale* 12 June, Though I am sorry that you should be so outrageously unroosted, I think that Bath has had you long enough. **1834** M. SCOTT *Cruise Midge* II. 12 Shoving the blade to the drowning man, with some danger of being unroosted myself in the attempt.

**2.** *intr.* To leave a roost; *fig.* to rise from bed.

**1614** J. COOKE *Greene's Tu Quoque* L 3, [It is] time to goe to Church, and not a man vnroosted. **1821** CLARE *Vill. Minstr.* II. 24 The crows, unroosting as he comes in sight.

Hence **Unroo·sted** *ppl. a.*; **Unroo·sting** *vbl. sb.*

**1615** [see UNRESTING *vbl. sb.*]. **1691** DRYDEN *K. Arthur* IV. i, The pass is free; The unroosted fiends have quitted this abode.

**Unroo·t,** *v.* [UN-[2] 4 b and 7.]

**1.** *trans.* To tear, pluck, or dig up by the roots. Also in fig. context and *transf.*

**1570** LEVINS *Manip.* 178 To vnroote, *eradicare.* **1593** G. HARVEY *New Letter* B 3, Riotous Vanitie was wont to roote so deeply, that it could hardly be vnrooted. **1601** SHAKS. *All's Well* v. i. 6 Be bold you do so grow in my requitall, As nothing can vnroote you. **1635** SHIRLEY *Coronat.* IV, His love was firm to you, and cannot be Unrooted with one storme. **1687** DRYDEN *Song St. Cecilia's Day* vii, Trees unrooted left their Place. **1740** PITT *Æneid* VI. 9 To feed the fires, [some] unroot the standing woods. **1774** GOLDSM. *Nat. Hist.* I. 133 There are sometimes whole plains unrooted from the main lands, by floods and tempests. **1852** TH. ROSS tr. *Humboldt's Trav.* I. iii. 130 The causes that unroot these weeds at depths where..the sea is but slightly agitated.

**b.** *fig.* To eradicate, clear away, remove or detach altogether. Also **Unroo·ting** *vbl. sb.*

*c* **1449** PECOCK *Repr.* I. ii. 8 Forto meete aȝens the firste bifore spoken opinioun, and forto vnroote and updrawe it. *Ibid.*, This vnrooting of the first opinioun. **1574** HELLOWES *Gueuara's Fam. Ep.* (1577) 181 Vices be so euill to be vnrooted where they once take place. **1603** G. OWEN *Pembrokeshire* iii. (1892) 36 The Conqueror..purposed to haue vnrooted the Saxon or Englishe tongue out of England. *Ibid.* iv. 38 He gaue diuerse of them theire ancient landes to hold of him, and did not vtterlye vnroote them. **1738** WARBURTON *Div. Legat.* I. 277 They unrooted and destroyed all that good to Society. **1856** DICKENS *Lett.* (1880) I. 419 My present idea, if nothing should arise to unroot me sooner, is to stay here until the middle of May.

**2.** *intr.* To lose root-hold; to withdraw the root from the soil.

*a* **1616** BEAUM. & FL. *Bonduca* III. i, Make their strengths totter, and their topless fortunes Unroot and reel to ruine. *c* **1800** W. BLAKE *Four Zoas, Last Judgem.* 39 The trees unroot; The rocks groan horrible and run about.

**Unroo·ted,** *ppl. a.*[1] [UN-[1] 8 c + ROOT *v.*[1] 6.] Not rooted *out.*

**1550** BALE *Image both Churches* xiv. II. N j, Nothinge shalbe vnrooted out that the heauenly father hath not planted. **1567** *Satir. Poems Reform.* vi. 108 Leif nathing that belangis to the Paip Unrutit out as it had neuer bene. **1649** MILTON *Eikon.* xvii. 155 So long as they remain'd in any of his three Kingdoms unrooted out. **1661** ARNWAY *Tablet* (ed. 3) 154 Can you imagine..The rooters up of Religion and Monarchy can be unrooted out; seeing the Loppers of the branches brak their neckes? **1859** SALA *Twice round Clock* 384 Gambling dens in Leicesterian slums, yet unrooted out by lynx-eyed policemen.

**Unroo·ted,** *ppl. a.*[2] [UN-[1] 8.] Not furnished with roots.

**1648** HEXHAM II, *Ongewortelt*, Vnrooted. **1650** BAXTER *Saints' R.* IV. 588 What makes..the green blade of unrooted faith, to wither before the heat of persecution? **1849** *Sk. Nat. Hist., Mammalia* IV. 172 The molar teeth..are cylindrical, unrooted. **1893** *Barrows' Parl. Relig.* II. 1542 Hinduism is not the idolatry and unrooted polytheism of savages.

**Unro·pe,** *v.* [UN-[2] 4 b.] *trans.* To detach by undoing a rope.

**1883** *Philadelphia Times* 30 July (Cent.), The horse was unroped from the wagon and turned loose. **1883** *Pall Mall G.* 1 Sept. 4/1 They unroped themselves, and sent three of their four guides to see what was the matter.

**Unro·ped,** *ppl. a.* (UN-[1] 8.) **1881** BLACKMORE *Christowell* ii, An avalanche of pots from the unroped crate fell..upon him. **Unro·sined,** *ppl. a.* (UN-[1] 8.) **1714** E. WARD *Field-Spy* 9 Where dejected Scrapers us'd to..Thrash their smooth Cats-guts with unrozen'd Bows.

**Unro·tted,** *ppl. a.* (UN-[1] 8.)

*c* **1440** *Pallad. on Husb.* x. 201 And thenne vnroted wol the grape abide. **1844** H. STEPHENS *Bk. Farm* II. 488 The unrotted stubble..may form obstacles under..the plough. **1876** ROCK *Text. Fabr.* i. 2 The few unrotted shreds still cleaving to its bones.

**Unro·tten,** *a.* (UN-[1] 7.)

**1574** R. SCOT *Hop Garden* 33 Rather vse no dung than vnrotten dunge about the dressing of your Hoppes. **1683** J. REID *Scots Gard'ner* II. ii, Let not the root of any tree stand on..unrotten-manure. **1742** YOUNG *Nt. Th.* II. 564 Since friends grow not thick on ev'ry bough, Nor ev'ry friend unrotten at the core. **1763** MILLS *Pract. Husb.* II. 20 The yet un-rotten straw might be apt to clog the shares of the drill.

**Unrou·ged,** *ppl. a.* (UN-[1] 8.) **1837** CARLYLE *Fr. Rev.* III. II. vii, Further aloft reigns Mère Duchesse with her unrouged Amazons. **1887** RUSKIN *Præterita* II. 39 Unveneered, unrouged, and well finished things.

**Unrou·gh,** *a.* [UN-[1] 7; cf. OE. *unrūh*.] Not rough; *spec.* not rough-chinned; unbearded.

*c* **1440** *Pallad. on Husb.* VII. 186 And thus the kinges [of bees] may be fonde:..in colour shynyng pure, And smothe, vnrough. **1605** SHAKS. *Macb.* v. ii. 10 There is Seywards Sonne, And many vnruffe youths, that euen now Protest their first of Manhood.

**Unrou·ghened,** *ppl. a.* (UN-[1] 8.) [**1775** ASH.] **1865** CARLYLE *Fredk. Gt.* XIX. vi. V. 572 Cavalry, unroughened, make sad sliding.

**Unrou·nd,** *a.* (UN-[1] 7. Cf. WFris. *on-, ûnroun*, Du. *onrond*.)

**1588** LUCAR tr. *Tartaglia's Colloq. Shooting* App. 24 To make round pellettes of unround yron pellettes by two waves. **1676** NEWTON in Rigaud *Corr. Sci. Men* (1841) II. 383 This [image]..will be..not much unround, unless the angles be very unequal. **1877** E. SANG (*title*), The Toothing of Unround Discs, which are intended to Roll upon each other.

**Unrou·nd,** *v.* (UN-[2] 6 a.)

Now *spec.* in phonetics: cf. ROUND *v.* 1 c. Also *Unrou·nding* vbl. sb.

**1611** COTGR., *Desrondir*, to vnround, vnbow, vncompasse. **1648** HEXHAM II, *Ontronden*, to vnround, or take away the roundnesse of any thing. **1874** H. SWEET in *Trans. Philol. Soc.* 471 Rounded front vowels are often unrounded. *Ibid.* 475 Rounding of back [vowels]; unrounding of front. **1877** — *Handbk. Phonetics* 25 This vowel..is best obtained by unrounding (u).

**Unrou·nded,** *ppl. a.* (UN-[1] 8.)

**1519** HORMAN *Vulg.* 112 b, Rounded heare becometh men: and vnrounded women. *a* **1631** DONNE *Elegies* xi. 33 Unfil'd pistolets..Which, negligently left unrounded, looke Like many angled figures, in the booke Of some great Conjurer. **1694** DRYDEN *To Sir G. Kneller* 55 Flat Faces, such as wou'd disgrace a Skreen,..Unrais'd, unrounded. **1815** J. SMITH *Panorama Sci. & Art* I. 388 Three teeth rounded from point to point;..three full teeth, unrounded. **1852** LYELL *Man. Elem. Geol.* vii. (ed. 4) 82 Similar unrounded nodules of flint. **1877** SWEET *Handbk. Phonetics* 17 The narrow back unrounded vowels.

†**Unrou·nged,** *ppl. a.* *Sc. Obs.* [UN-[1] 8 + ROUNGE *v.*[2]] Unclipped. **15..** *Aberd. Reg.* (Jam.), The baillyeis chargit him to take the Inglis grot vnrovngit for thre sous in pament.

**Unrou·sable,** *a.* (UN-[1] 7 b.) **1894** MRS. DYAN *Man's Keeping* xvi, Urquhart submitted to all [this]..with unrousable apathy.

**Unrou·sed,** *ppl. a.* (UN-[1] 8.)

[**1775** ASH.] **1802** COLERIDGE *Dejection* 4 This night, so tranquil now, will not go hence Unrous'd by winds. **1834** *Tait's Mag.* I. 540/2 In that visionary world, Unroused by Pleasure's fierce extreme. **1882** FLOYER *Unexpl. Baluchistan* 214 Totally unroused reasoning powers.

**Unrou·ted,** *ppl. a.* (UN-[1] 8.) **1622** FLETCHER *Prophetess* IV. v, Of all the Persian Forces, one strong Squadron..Stands firm, and yet unrouted. **1888** *Leisure Hour* Sept. 594/1 The ladies..did not leave him with so much as an unrouted doubt on this point.

**Unrove,** var. of UNRUFE *Sc. Obs.*

**Unrow·,** *v.* (UN-[1] 14, or UN-[2] 3.) **1897** F. T. BULLEN *Cruise 'Cachalot'* xiv, My gloomy cogitations were abruptly terminated by the order to 'unrow'—we were alongside.

†**Unrow·ed,** *ppl. a.* *Obs.* [UN-[1] 8 + ROW *v.*[7]] Not having the nap raised.

**1487** *Act 3 Hen. VII*, c. xi. § 1 The seid Clothes..arne.. conveyed out of this realme, unroweed and unshorne. **1535, 1541, 1643** [see UNBARBED 1].

**Unroy·al,** *a.* [UN-[1] 7.]

**1.** Unbefitting or inappropriate to a king or queen.

*a* **1586** SIDNEY *Arcadia* II. ix, He..sent them with unroyall reproches to Musidorus. *a* **1680** CHARNOCK *Attrib. God* (1834) I. 71 A Roman king, who counted it the most unroyal thing to be religious. **1780** W. BECKFORD *Italy* (1834) I. 62, I scolded in an unroyal style. **1842** FR. A. KEMBLE *Rec. Later Life* (1882) II. 239 The unroyal indignity of being waited upon after her guests. **1880** F. G. LEE *Ch. under Q. Eliz.* II. 155 With unroyal discourtesy and unwomanly harshness.

**b.** Not associated with royal authority.

**1867** BAGEHOT *Eng. Constitution* 99 The unroyal species of cabinet government.

**2.** Not of royal rank or birth.

*a* **1618** J. DAVIES *Witte's Pilgr.* Wks. (Grosart) II. 35/2 Then, Rimes how ere vnroiall run you on, You may, in time, perhaps come neer that Crowne. **1814** MOORE *Mem.* (1852) II. 21 A certain *un*-royal person in Derbyshire. **1861** TROLLOPE *Framley P.* III. 230 That none of the blood royal shall raise to royal honours those of the subjects who are by birth un-royal.

Hence **Unroy·ally** *adv.* Also **Unroy·alist.**

**1777** POTTER *Æschylus, Choephoræ* 345 My royal father, who unroyally Wast murder'd! **1788** MME. D'ARBLAY *Diary* 11 Feb., He is so privileged a favourite with all the Royal Family, that he utters all his flights to them almost as easily as to unroyalists. **1829** MOORE *Mem.* (1854) VI. 38 Not quite liking to refuse him, as being always so unroyally good-humoured and good-natured.

**Unru·bbed,** *ppl. a.* (UN-[1] 8.)

*c* **1380** WYCLIF *Sel. Wks.* III. 231 As a horce unrubbed, þat haves a sore back, wynses when..rubbed on his rugge. **1648** HEXHAM II, *Onbestreken*, Vnrubbed, or Vnsmeared. **1847** GEO. ELIOT in Cross *Life* (1885) I. 161 You are a bright golden sovereign to me, with edges all unrubbed. **1877** MEREDITH *Lett.* (1912) I. 282, I am consequently dull, unrubbed, no reflector.

**Unru·bbish,** *v.* (UN-[2] 4.) **1645** MILTON *Colast.* 26 This under-work of scowring and unrubbishing the low and sordid ignorance of such a presumptuous lozel. **Unru·brical,** *a.* (UN-[1] 7.) **1843** LD. COLERIDGE in *Life & Lett.* (1904) I. 115 Commencing the service..with..a hymn is unrubrical, uncatholick. **Unru·ddered,** *ppl. a.* (UN-[1] 8 or UN-[2] 8.) -**ing,** *vbl. sb.* (UN-[2] 8.) **1804** LARWOOD *No Gun Boats* 12 Better to give all than suffer their Gun Boats to remain in even an unruddered, unmasted, unordonanced existence. *Ibid.* 15 The inutility of dismasting, unruddering, or scuttling.

†**Unru·de,** *a.*[1] *Obs.* [var. of UNRIDE *a.*, but prob. associated with RUDE *a.*]

**1.** Violent, rough, dreadful.

*c* **1400** *Laud Troy Bk.* 17162 Ther were ȝit..of sqwyers gret multitude, And ȝaff thanne strokes wel vnrude. **1513** DOUGLAS *Æneid* VI. ii. 114 The laithlie flude Cochitus, with his drery bosum vnrude. *Ibid.* v. 3 Hellis flude of Acheron; With holl bisme, and hiduus swelth wnrude. **1825** JAMIESON s.v., This term is still used in Ayrs[hire], and expl. 'Base, vile, diabolical; detestable;' as, 'unrude bleeries,' abominable falsehoods.

**2.** Rude, unmannerly, uncouth.

1561–2 W. Fullwood in *Ballads*, etc. (Percy Soc.) 57 For you may see he is in deed An unrude simple man. 1599 B. Jonson *Ev. Man out of Hum.* iv. i, The good Gentleman vouchsaft to make him his companion, .. and now see how the vnrude Rascall back-bites him! 1616 — *Masque of Christmas* 116 They have need o' mending: unrude people they are, your Courtiers. *a* 1630 J. Taylor (Water P.) *Wit & Mirth* cii, Truly, said the fellow [*sc.* a countryman], I am no schollar, I am altogether vnrude, and very ingrum.

Hence † **Unru·deness**, rudeness. *Obs.*—1

1561–2 W. Fullwood in *Ballads*, etc. (Percy Soc.) 57 A Supplication to Eldertonne for Leache's Unlewdnes, Desiring him to pardone his manifest unrudenes.

**Unru·de**, *a.*2 [Un-1 7.] Not rude; mannerly. 1648 Herrick *Hesper.*, *Panegerick to Pemberton* 31 Manners knowes distance, and a man unrude Wo'd soon recoile, and not intrude His Stomach to a second Meale. † **Unrue·fully**, *adv.* *Obs.* [Un-1 11.] Unmercifully, pitilessly. *a* 1300 *Cursor M.* 24023 Vn-reufulli þai can him raipe. *Ibid.* 24158 Vn-reufulli [*Edin.* vnrewfullik] yee wirc vnright.

† **Unrufe** (also unrove), Sc. var. Unro *Obs.*

*c* 1470 *Gol. & Gaw.* 499 May nane do thame na deir... Yit sal I mak thame vnrufe. *c* 1550 *Clariodus* (Maitl. Cl.) 44 ȝit glaidlie for his saik I sould ȝow love, That this regioun hes brocht from sik unrove. *c* 1550 Rolland *Crt. Venus* ii. 446 Quhy sufferis thow ane creature mortall, For none defalt to incur sic vnrufe?

**Unru·ffable**, *a.* (Un-1 7 b.) 1837 Dickens *Pickw.* xxxiii, Sam..obeyed all his master's behests with..unruffable composure. **Unru·ffed**, *a.* (Un-1 9.) 1872 Coues *N. Amer. Birds* 133 Bill moderate, unruffed, but with a little tuft of feathers at the base of the rictus.

**Unru·ffle**, *v.* [Un-2 7 and 3.]

**1.** *intr.* To become smooth or tranquil.

1697 Dryden *Æneis* i. 212 Where e're he guides His finny Coursers,..The Waves unruffle, and the Sea subsides. 1871 [see Unruffling *ppl. a.*2].

**2.** *trans.* To restore from a ruffled state.

1827 Lamb *Wife's Trial* Wks. 1908 II. 805 A witch .. can by a backward charm Unruffle the foul storm she has just been raising. 1833 Lady Granville *Lett.* (1894) II. 148 This does not seem to unruffle Dolly's plumes.

**Unru·ffled**, *ppl. a.* [Un-1 8.]

**1. a.** Not affected by any violent feeling; not agitated or disturbed; calm, unmoved.

1659 W. Chamberlayne *Pharonnida* Ded., I have, with an unruffled confidence, given these papers a capacity of being publicly viewed. 1712 Addison *Spect.* No. 381 ¶ 4 His Temper is even and unruffled. 1751 Smollett *Per. Pic.* xcv, 'Why shouldn't I lend a hand?'..(answered the unruffled Pipes). 1754 *Connoisseur* No. 4 ¶ 9 Whose conversation flows with one even tenor, undisturb'd by sentiment, and unruffled by passion. 1829 Lytton *Devereux* ii. ii, The most unruffled composure. 1874 Green *Short Hist.* vii. § 3. 369 Her mind was unruffled by the spiritual problems which were vexing the minds around her.

**b.** Not excited by drinking.

1709 Steele *Tatler* No. 27 ¶ 2 When he is himself, and unruffled with Intemperance. 1748 *Anson's Voy.* iii. vii. 363 Perceiving that after they had dispatched four or five bottles.., the Mandarine still continued unruffled.

**2.** Not physically ruffled or made rough: **a.** Of water, etc. Also in fig. context.

1713 Addison *Cato* i. iv, Calm and unruffled as a summer-sea. 1757 W. Wilkie *Epigon.* v. 135 A lake..Whose surface smooth, unruffled by the breeze, The hills inverted shows. 1814 Wordsw. *Excurs.* ii. 365 Days unruffled by the gale Of public news or private. 1824 Miss L. M. Hawkins *Annaline* II. 229 Crags mantled in unruffled snow. 1883 Tyndall in *Knowledge* 3 Aug. 73/2 Between the ferry and this bridge, the river Niagara flows unruffled.

**b.** Of feathers, leaves, the forehead, etc.

1816 Wilson *City of Plague* ii. iv. 106 Like an angel With hair unruffled in its radiance. 1821 Scott *Kenilw.* v, Now for..an open and unruffled brow! 1854 *Poultry Chron.* I. 328/2 A pen of birds .. unruffled in their plumage. *a* 1878 Sir G. Scott *Lect. Archit.* (1879) I. 320 Here the Byzantinesque foliage is nearly all of the plain unruffled form.

**3.** Not furnished with ruffles.

*c* 1825 Ld. Cockburn *Mem.* i. (1856) 13 A shirt fastened at the neck by a black ribbon, and except on dress days unruffled.

Hence **Unru·ffledness.**

1858 Hawthorne *Fr. & It. Note-bks.* (1881) II. 177 His propriety, his cleanliness and unruffledness. 1880 Ruskin *Hortus Inclusus* (1887) 77 The perfect cleanliness and unruffledness of white cap [in Chartres] is always a marvel.

**Unru·ffling**, *ppl. a.*1 [Un-1 10.] Not ruffling; not becoming ruffled.

1762 Falconer *Shipwr.* ii. 307 Th' involving clue, Swell'd by the wind, aloft unruffling flew. 1797 Southey *Donica* 19 The powerless storm unruffling swept Across the calm dead lake.

**Unru·ffling**, *ppl. a.*2 [f. Unruffle *v.*] Becoming unruffled.

1871 Tennyson *Last Tourn.* 368 As, when a gust hath blown, Unruffling waters re-collect the shape Of one that in them sees himself.

**Unru·inable**, *a.* (Un-1 7 b.)

*a* 1693 *Urquhart's Rabelais* iii. viii. (1708) I. 353 Nature, having a fervent desire .. to eternize, and continue them .. unruinable. 1706 Watts *Horæ Lyricæ* II. 163 The spirit.. flies upward, an undoubted guest Of the third heaven, th' unruinable sky. *a* 1740 — *Remnants of Time* ix. Wks. 1753 IV. 612 May the unruinable world be but my portion.

† **Unru·inated**, *ppl. a. Obs.* [Un-1 8.] = next.

1566–7 *Reg. Privy Council Scot.* I. 498 Of the haill ludgeing walles .. thair is na thing left unruinated and doung in drosse. 1610 Bp. Hall *Apol. Brownists* § 30. 74 These you will proue vnruinated Towers of that Babell. 1658 Bromhall *Treat. Specters* ii. 175 They should leave nothing unruinated and not pull'd down.

**Unru·ined**, *ppl. a.* (Un-1 8.)

1610 J. Healey *St. Aug. Citie of God* 4 So long the City should continue unruined. *a* 1649 Drumm. of Hawth. *Hist. Jas. III*, Wks. (1711) 58 He sent to all such of his Friends, whom his Disasters had left unruined, to take Arms for the King. 1820 Bentham *Liberty of Press* Wks. 1843 II. 283/1 Under whom it has hitherto been my good hap to live unhanged, .. unbanished and unruined. 1853 Ruskin *Stones Ven.* II. vii. § 46. 268 He can still see the strong sweep of the unruined traceries drawn on the deep serenity of the starry sky.

**Unru·lable**, *a.* (Un-1 7 b.)

1680 H. Dodwell *Two Lett.* (1691) 68 Preventing the occasion or increase of passion, which will be also so much easier if it be taken before it grow unrulable. 1716 M. Davies *Athen. Brit.* II. 289 Rendring a Country-property..untainable as well as unrulable even by an Hereditary Pretender. 1881 in J. Hatton *New Ceylon* vii. 185 People.. found to be unruleable by other nations.

**Unru·lableness.** *rare.*—1 (Un-1 12. Cf. prec.) *c* 1445 Pecock *Donet* 94 Þouȝ al þis lijf be foule..for wijldenes and vnreuleablenes, in tyme of ȝongþe.

**Unru·le.** [Un-1 12.] Absence of rule or government.

1422 Yong tr. *Secreta Secret.* 136 Whyle he regnyd in this vnrule.., into the land of Irlande he arryuete. *c* 1425 Wyntoun *Cron.* v. xii. 3724 (Wemyss MS.), Forthy it nedis þat ressoune Thyne vnreullis habandoun.

1818 Scott *Rob Roy* xxii, Now let's hear .. how, in the name of unrule, they got here at this time o' night. 1861 *Sat. Rev.* II. 670 A very few years more of republican unrule.

**Unru·led**, *ppl. a.* [Un-1 8.]

**1.** Not ruled or governed; ungoverned, disorderly.

*c* 1375 *Sc. Leg. Saints* xxx. (*Theodera*) 107 Certis, vnreulyt ware my wil gyf for þe my-self I suld spil. *a* 1395 Hylton *Scala Perf.* iii. i. (W. de W. 1494), For charyte vnruled tourneth somtyme in to vyce. *c* 1425 Wyntoun *Cron.* v. xiii. 4717 (Cott. MS.), Our Lady..repruffit hym fast Off his wnrewllit wilfulnes. *a* 1513 Fabyan *Chron.* vii. 530 Theyse vnrulyd Company gatheryd vnto them great multytude of the commons. 1538 Starkey *England* ii. ii. 180 Man ys then myserabul .. when reson ys ouer-run and vnrulyd affectys gouerne and reyne in hys ordur of lyfe. 1596 Spenser *St. Irel.* Wks. (Globe) 617/1 The realme was left, like a shipp in a storme,..unruled, and undirected of any. 1615 Chapman *Odyss.* iv. 925 But their unrul'd acts show their minds' estate. 1655 Gentilis *Servita's Inquis.* xxxi. 136 Because the desire of gain is so unruled, that .. it doth induce men to commit things against honesty. 1813 Hogg *Queen's Wake* Concl. xvii, To end this strife, unruled and vain, Let all the three be called again. 1897 *Westm. Gaz.* 29 Mar. 3/1 The same strong and unruled passions.

† **2.** Not decided or decreed. *Obs.*—1

1456 *Paston Lett.* I. 387 The atteynte abidith unreuled til the next terme.

† **3.** Irregular. *Obs.*—1

1551 Recorde *Pathw. Knowl.* i. Defin., They haue no syde equall to an other.., neither keepe they any rate in their corners, and therefore are they counted vnruled formes.

**4.** Not having ruled lines.

1888 E. M. Gallaudet *Life T. H. Gallaudet* 23 It is written on unruled paper.

Hence **Unru·ledly** *adv.* *rare.*

1580 Hollyband *Treas. Fr. Tong*, *Desreiglëement*, vnruledly. 1587 [see Unrulily *adv.* 2, quot. 1561].

**Unru·leful**, *a.* *Sc.* and *dial.* (Un-1 7.)

1438 *Sc. Acts, Jas. II* (1814) II. 32/2 Quhare þar is ony rebellys or vnrewlful men within ony castellys or fortalicis resett or haldyn. 1678 in Wodrow *Hist. Suff. Ch. Scot.* (1722) I. App. 191 Spilling the Country by unreasonable and unruleful men. 1898 in *Eng. Dial. Dict.* s.v.

† **Unru·lely**, obs. variant of Unruly *a.*

*a* 1581 in Marbeck *Bk. of Notes* 540 If our passions be so vnrulely,..then doth impatiencie ouer master vs. 1653 Holcroft *Procopius, Goth. Wars* iv. 153 He took order .. to be rid of his unrulely Lombards, who were infinitely disorderly.

† **Unru·lily**, *adv.* *Obs.* [f. Unruly *a.*]

**1.** Immoderately.

*c* 1445 Pecock *Donet* 98 Liȝtnessis,..whanne þei ben vnmesurably and vnreulili aȝens doom of resoun. *c* 1456 — *Bk. Faith* (1909) 109 Manye of the lay peple whiche.. attenden over unreulili to the Bible.

**2.** In an unruly or disorderly manner.

1549 Cheke *Hurt Sedit.* (1569) D ij, Ye..vnrulilye haue ruled, where ye listed to commaund. 1561 T. Norton *Calvin's Inst.* ii. ii. 11 b, Wylde horses whyche..dooe range vnrulyly [1587 vnruledly] and wythout measure. 1571 Golding *Calvin on Ps.* lvi. 8 The ungodly have unrulily roysted without let. 1690 C. Nesse *O. & N. Test.* I. 312 Evil concupiscence..groweth unrulily headstrong.

† **Unru·liment.** *Obs.*—1 [-ment.] = next. 1596 Spenser *F. Q.* iv. ix. 23 They breaking forth with rude vnruliment, From all foure parts of heauen doe rage full sore.

**Unru·liness.** [f. next.] The quality of being unruly. (Of persons, animals, etc.)

1547 *Act 1 Edw. VI*, c. 12 § 1 The Insolency and Unruliness of Men. 1577 B. Googe *Heresbach's Husb.* iii. 150 You must keepe the Boare from them; for with his vnrulinesse, he maketh them to cast. 1577 tr. *Bullinger's Decades* 301/1 Therein doth patience make proofe of it self,..that it neuer breaketh forthe to immoderate vnrulynesse. 1638 Rawley tr. *Bacon's Life & Death* 210 For the Quieting of the vnruliness of the spirits. 1684 J. S. *Profit & Pleas. United* 14 For the better preservation of your Cattle, both from sickness and hurt, which may happen through their unruliness. 1695 J. Edwards *Perfect. Script.* 440 Excellent caveats..touching..unruliness of the tongue. 1704 *Dict. Rust.* s.v. *Mare*, His own unruliness being so great, the Cure [of the colt] may be very difficult. 1768–74 Tucker *Lt. Nat.* (1834) II. 356 We ascribe the..unruliness of inordinate desires..to the fatal effects of original sin. 1805 Wordsw. *Prelude* vi. 392 Some vapoured in the unruliness of joy. 1858 Froude *Hist. Eng.* IV. xix. 110 The governments affected to regret the unruliness of their subjects.

**Unru·ly**, *a.* (and *sb.*). Forms: 5–6 vnruely, 6–7 vnrulye, -lie, 6– unruly; 5 onreuli, vnrewely, 6 vnrewly. [Un-1 7 + Ruly *a.*2]

**1.** Not amenable to rule or discipline; ungovernable; disorderly, turbulent: **a.** Of persons.

1400 R. de Grey in Ellis *Orig. Lett.* Ser. ii. I. 4 Hitt woll be an unruely Cuntrie within short tyme. 1422 Yong tr. *Secreta Secret.* 160 When they were full woxen, prowte, onreuli, fiers, and presumpteous. *a* 1533 Ld. Berners *Gold. Bk. M. Aurel.* (1559) U ij, Sith the worlde is so chaungeable, and the people so vnruly. 1592 Greene *Disput.* 20 Ouer kind fathers make vnruly daughters. 1665 Boyle *Occas. Refl., Disc.* § iv. i. 53 That he should of all others prove the most unruly, who alone has been endowed with Reason to rule himself withall. *a* 1715 Burnet *Own Time* i. iv. (1897) I. 108 The dispersing of that little unruly army. 1781 Cowper *Tiroc.* 262, I blame not those who..O'erwatch the num'rous and unruly clan. 1855 Macaulay *Hist. Eng.* xvi. III. 685 William had found it no easy matter to decide what course should be taken with that capricious and unruly body. 1896 W. K. Leask *H. Miller* 29 He seems rather to have become an unruly lad.

*sb.* and *absol.* 1611 Speed *Hist. Gt. Brit.* ix. xxii. § 31. 807/1 These vnrulies presently chose him for their ringleader. 1684 Bunyan *Pilgr.* ii. (1900) 265 All things must be managed here to..the warning of the Unruly. 1782 Priestley *Inst. Relig.* (ed. 2) I. p. xli, We cannot possibly warn all the unruly.

*transf.* 1667 Dryden *Ind. Emperor* iv. iv, Th' unruly Sword will no distinction make. 1888 Barrie *When a Man's Single* xii, She softly pushed the invalid's unruly hair off his brow.

**b.** Of animals. Also in fig. context.

1565 Cooper *Thesaurus* s.v. *Bos*, Restie or vnrulie oxen. 1577 Googe *Heresbach's Husb.* 141 b, To keepe the weaker [sheep]..from the strong and vnruly. *Ibid.* 145 The horned, by reason of theyr weapons, are hurtful, and vnruely. 1627 J. Taylor (Water P.) *Navy of Land Ships* Wks. (1630) 91/1 A ship is an vnruly beast. 1682 Sheffield (Dk. Buckhm.) *Ess. Poetry* 8 The Muses most unruly Horse. 1768–74 [see Unshaken 2]. *a* 1821 V. Knox *Serm.* Wks. 1824 VI. 196 Like the spirited and unruly steed.

**c.** Of the heart, tongue, passions, etc.

1526 Tyndale *Jas.* iii. 8 The tonge can no man tame. Yt is an vnruely evyll full off deedly poyson. 1598 Barret *Theor. Warres* i. ii. 11 A generous minde, not subiect vnto passions and vnrulie fits. 1612 T. Taylor *Comm. Titus* i. 6 An vnruly heart will breake out one time or other. *a* 1674 Clarendon *Surv. Leviath.* (1676) 239 When his unruly invention suggests to him an addition to the Text. 1712 Pope *Spect.* No. 408 ¶ 7 Young Men whose Passions are not a little unruly. 1729 Butler *Serm.* Wks. 1874 II. 40 To imagine he keeps that unruly faculty [*sc.* the tongue] in due subjection. 1800 Colquhoun *Comm. Thames* viii. 262 It is impracticable to control their unruly passions. 1846 Keble *Lyra Innoc.* (ed. 3) 293 Nor time nor tune are there, Yet sounds the unruly joy.

**d.** Characterized by disorder or disquiet.

1439 *Cases bef. King's Council* (Selden) 105 Wawton..seid ..it is the unruliest session that I haue euer sey in Bedford. 1582 Stanyhurst *Æneis* i. (Arb.) 21 These vnrulye reuels ..thee sea king Neptun awaked. 1805 Wordsw. *Prelude* i. 136 The Poet, gentle creature as he is, Hath, like the Lover, his unruly times.

† **2.** Of things: Unmanageable. *Obs.*

1577 Googe *Heresbach's Husb.* iii. 158 When they sitte, with theyr vnruly spurres they breake theyr egges. 1598 Florio *Dict.* To Rdr. 9 A more vnruly..vessell then the biggest hulke on Thames. 1633 Herbert *Temple, Ch. Porch* xli, Wit's an unruly engine, wildly striking Sometimes a friend, sometimes the engineer. 1681 R. Knox *Hist. Ceylon* 9 These Ploughs..if heavier..would sink and be unruly in the mud.

† **3.** Violent; incurable. *Obs.*

1596 Spenser *F. Q.* vi. vi. 5 Their wounds..had festred priuily, And ranckling inward with vnruly stounds, The inner parts now gan to putrify. 1606 G. Woodcocke *Lives Emperors in Hist. Ivstine* K k 6 Dying of an vnruly disease.

**4.** Stormy, tempestuous; impetuous.

1593 Shaks. *Lucrece* 869 Unruly blasts wait on the tender spring; Unwholesome weeds take root. 1605 — *Macb.* ii. iii. 59 The Night ha's been vnruly; Where we lay, our Chimneys were blowne downe. 1647 Clarendon *Hist. Reb.* v. § 449 The standard itself was blown down..by a very strong and unruly wind. 1697 Dryden *Virg. Georg.* iii. 396 He makes his way o'er Mountains, and contemns Unruly Torrents, and unfoorded Streams.

**Unru·minated**, *ppl. a.* (Un-1 8.) 1735 Bolingbroke *Study Hist.* (1752) I. 4 Those who..store their minds with crude un-ruminated facts and sentences.

**Unru·mmaged**, *ppl. a.* (Un-1 8.)

†**a.** 1591 Raleigh *Last Fight Revenge* cij, The ships growne foule, vnroomaged, and scarcely able to beare anie saile for want of balast.

**b.** 1775 Ash s.v., Unrummaged. 1910 *Athenæum* 29 Jan. 117/3 No relevant archives have remained unrummaged.

**Unru·mple**, *v.* (Un-2 3.) 1694 Addison *Virg. Georg.* iv. Wks. 1721 I. 22 Daffadils, that late from earth's slow womb Unrumple their swoln buds. 1728 Gardiner tr. *Rapin Of Gardens* (ed. 3) 36 Wide o'er the Garden now she sheds Perfumes, Unrumples her swol'n Buds, and gayly blooms.

**Unru·mpled**, *ppl. a.* (Un-1 8.)

1641 W. Cartwright *Siege* ii. ii, We cannot keep a pleat unrumpled..for them. 1692 Wood *Life* (O.H.S.) IV. 25, I shall put it into the hands of Dr Levet that he might convey it to you..unrumpled. 1776 Mrs. Delany *Life & Corr.* Ser. ii. (1862) II. 218, I leave the rest of her unpacking to your delicate fingers. I hope to hear she arrives unrumpled—feathers and all. 1821 Scott *Kenilw.* iv, You must..wear ..your falling band unrumpled and well starched. 1865 Mrs. Whitney *Gayworthys* xxiii, Her bright hair was put back over her ears, not quite unrumpled.

**Unru·n**, *ppl. a.* [Un-1 8 b.] Not past or completed.

1474 *Acta Dom. Audit.* (1839) 37/1 Þe tak of þe said landis..for sa mony termes now to cum as was vnrunnyn of þe xix ȝeris. 1591 *Knaresb. Wills* (Surtees) I. 176 The reste of the yeares I have to come unron.

**Unru·ng,** *ppl. a.*[1] [UN-[1] 8 b + RING *v.*[2]] Not sounded by ringing.

**1422–61** in *Cal. Proc. in Chanc. Q. Eliz.* (1827) I. Introd. 20 It wer better bell unrogne at þe sauntes tyme þan þe messe unsogne. **1742** BLAIR *Grave* 53 The Great Bell has toll'd, unrung, untouch'd.

**Unru·ng,** *ppl. a.*[2] [UN-[1] 8 b + RING *v.*[1]] = UNRINGED *ppl. a.*

**1548** *Fen Laws* in Thompson *Hist. Boston* (1856) 643 No swine were to be put in the fens unrung. **1654** in Picton *L'pool Munic. Rec.* (1883) I. 191 Swyne that shalbee found unrung. **1707** MORTIMER *Husb.* 530 He let his Hogs go into his Orchard unrung. **1727** E. LAURENCE *Duty of Steward* 125 Paying Ten shillings for each Hog suffer'd to be unrung or unyoked. **1885** W. RYE *Hist. Norfolk* 114 Men were often prosecuted for..keeping unrung pigs, or savage dogs.

**Unru·nkled,** *ppl. a. Sc.* (UN-[1] 8.) **1721** RAMSAY *Keitha* 43 Her..brow, smooth as th' unrunkled deep.

**Unru·ptured,** *ppl. a.* (UN-[1] 8.)

[**1775** ASH.] **1862** A. MEADOWS *Man. Midwifery* VI. i. 211 Even if the membranes are unruptured, we shall generally be able to feel a small coil. **1875** BROWNING *Aristoph. Apol.* 118 Odusseus..Holding as surely on to Herakles, Who touched Zeus, link and link, the unruptured chain!

**Unru·sted,** *ppl. a.* (UN-[1] 8.)

*a* **1653** BINNING *Serm.* (1845) 257 Take heed to walk suitably and preserve your seal of adoption unblotted, unrusted. **1797** COLERIDGE *Osorio* IV. iii, The point Is bright, unrusted with the villain's blood! **1851** MRS. BROWNING *Casa Guidi Wind.* I. 1086 Bring thoughts and words, Unrusted by a tear of yesterday's. **1868** *Lond. Rev.* 19 Dec. 670/2 The book.. has the quality of gold, and will keep unrusted for an age.

**Unru·stling,** *ppl. a.* (UN-[1] 10.) **1749** COLLINS *Superst. Highlands* vi, For watchful, lurking, 'mid the unrustling reed, At those mirk hours the wily monster lies.

**Unru·th.** Now *arch.* (UN-[1] 12.)

*c* **1440** *Jacob's Well* 294 To haue..vnrewthe of hem þat arn in peyne. **1888** W. MORRIS *Dream of J. Ball* iv. 32 All this hast thou lost for..a little winking of the eyes amidst murder and wrong and unruth. **1899** W. S. BLUNT *Satan Absolved* 18 Thy Will found counterpart Only in Man's un-Will, Thy Truth in his un-Truth,..Ruth in his un-Ruth.

**Unru·thfully,** *adv.* [UN-[1] 11.] = UNRUEFULLY *adv.* *c* **1375** *Cursor M.* 24023 (Fairf.), Vnreuþfulli þai con him raipe. *Ibid.* 24158 Vn-reuþfulli ȝe wirk vn-riȝt.

**Uns,** obs. Sc. form of OUNCE *sb.*[1]

**Unsabba·tical,** *a.* (UN-[1] 7.) **1882** 'EDNA LYALL' *Donovan* x, A most unsabbatical..shooting-jacket. **1896** *Daily News* 6 April 2/3 For an altogether unsabbatical outburst of levity. **Unsa·bred,** *ppl. a.* (UN-[1] 8.) **1820** BENTHAM *Liberty of Press* Wks. 1843 II. 283/1 Under whom it has..been my good hap to live unhanged, unsabred, unimprisoned.

**Unsacerdo·tal,** *a.* (UN-[1] 7.)

**1847** MAURICE *Relig. World* I. iii. 71 Such an utterly unsacerdotal people as the Mahometans. **1860** *All Year Round* No. 44. 412 Popes who have scandalised mankind by their unsacerdotal vices.

**Unsacerdo·tally,** *adv.* (UN-[1] 11.) **1834** H. O'BRIEN *Round Towers Irel.* 502 They then very unsacerdotally make a serpent bite him.

**Unsa·ck,** *v.* [UN-[2] 5.] *trans.* To take out of a sack. Also *fig.*

**14..** *Voc.* in Wr.-Wülcker 581 *Exsacco*, to vnsacke. **1598** FLORIO, *Dissaccare*, to vnsacke, to emptie out of a sacke. **1846** LANDOR *Imag. Conv.* Wks. II. 81/2 The state is founded on follies, the Church on sins. Come then, unsack them.

**Unsa·cked,** *ppl. a.* [UN-[1] 8.] Not plundered.

**1590** MARLOWE *2nd Pt. Tamburlane* IV. iii. 59 This same Boy..must..Rifle the kingdomes I shall leaue vnsackt. **1595** DANIEL *Civ. Wars* v. lxxxvi, From yonder turrets yet vnsackt, Your valiant fellowes stand your worth to see. **1791** COWPER *Iliad* XII. 14 The city yet Of royal Priam was unsack'd. *c* **1813** SOUTHEY *At Santarem* 4 Loth to leave Rich Lisbon yet unsack'd, he kept his ground.

**Unsa·crament,** *v.* (UN-[2] 6 b.) **1642** T. FULLER *Holy & Prof. St.* v. xi. 402 Whereas the profanenesse of a bad man administring it, doth unsacrament baptisme itself. **Unsacrame·ntally,** *adv.* (UN-[1] 11.) **1840** G. S. FABER *Christ's Disc. Capernaum* 62 Under the phraseology of Eating the Flesh and Drinking the Blood of Christ, the same vital doctrine..is successively propounded.., first unsacramentally, next sacramentally. †**Unsa·cred,** *ppl. a.*[1] *Obs.* [UN-[1] 8.] Unconsecrated. **1382** WYCLIF in Knighton *Chron.* (Rolls) II. 161 Þe Sacrament of the Autere white and ronde and like tyl oure brede or ost unsacrede. **1387** TREVISA *Higden* (Rolls) VII. 263 Thomas wolde ȝit nouȝt assent, but..wente his wey unsacred. *c* **1440** *Alph. Tales* 112 Þai cownceld þe preste to feche ane hoste þat was vnsacred & giff hym. **Unsa·cred,** *ppl. a.*[2] [UN-[2] 8.] Deprived of sacred character. **1652** HOWELL *Giraffi's Rev. Naples* II. 35 A Jesuite was also beheaded, but he was unsacred and degraded first of his function.

**Unsa·cred,** *a.* [UN-[1] 7 and 5 b.] Not sacred; profane.

**1608** SYLVESTER *Du Bartas* II. iv. III. *Schisme* 188 Th' unsacred Altar sudden slent in twain. *a* **1641** BP. MOUNTAGU *Acts & Mon.* (1642) 204 No person, uncleane, common, unsacred, must approach unto Gods altar. *c* **1712** W. KING *Case Consc.* Wks. 1776 III. 249 If from a place unsacred you should take A sacred thing,..Or an unsacred thing from sacred place. **1755** LAVINGTON *Moravians Compared* 113 The Valentinians' unsacred Sacraments, and profane Initiations. **1872** SWINBURNE *Under Microscope* 28 The unsacred secrets of no Eleusinian initiation.

**Unsa·credly,** *adv.* (UN-[1] 11.) **1852** S. R. MAITLAND *8 Ess.* 37 No doubt Orpheus sung *Ho perso il caro ben*, and the chorus followed him..naturally, and *un*sacredly, and operatically.

**Unsacrifi·ceable,** *a.* (UN-[1] 7 b, 5 b.)

**1580** W. FULKE *Stapleton Confut.* II. iv. 82 That great and vnsacrificable sacrifice (as I may call it). **1618** AINSWORTH *Annot. Lev.* vii. 18 The Greek translateth it sundry wayes, a thing polluted, unsacrificeable, and profane. [**1650** TRAPP *Comm. Lev.* vii. 18 Kept beyond the time; and so uneatable, unsacrificeable.]

**Unsa·crificed,** *ppl. a.* (UN-[1] 8.)

[**1775** ASH.] **1849** ROCK *Ch. of Fathers* I. ii. I. 91 The bread which is unsacrificed is then changed into what is sacrificed. **1855** PUSEY *Doctr. Real Presence* 483 In Thy Temple, where thou art sacrificed unsacrificed.

†**Unsa·d,** *a. Obs.* [UN-[1] 7. Cf. OE. *unsæd* unsated (= obs. Du. *onzat*).]

**1.** Not firm or steadfast; unreliable.

**1382** WYCLIF *Rom.* xv. 1 The feblenesse of syke men, or vnsadde in feith. *c* **1386** CHAUCER *Clerk's T.* 995 O stormy peple vnsad and euere vntrewe. *c* **1412** HOCCLEVE *De Reg. Princ.* 705 O lord! þis world vnstabyl is, & vnsad. **1455** *Rolls of Parlt.* V. 341/2 Blynded with unsad trust and promysse of mariage. **1495** *Cov. Leet Bk.* 564 Þe vnsadde demeasnyng & dealyng þat he hath be of in tymes past.

**2.** Not firm, hard, or solid.

**1398** TREVISA *Barth. De P. R.* VI. v. (Tollem. MS.), The childes flesche, þat is newe bore, is tendir, nesche, quauy and unsad. *c* **1440** *Promp. Parv.* 491/2 Thoke, as onsadde fysche, *humorosus*.

**3.** Free from sadness.

*a* **1450** *Le Morte Arth.* 1508 Off sorow were they neuyr vnsad, Myght they neyther drynke ne ete.

Hence † **Unsa·dness.** *Obs.*

**1382** WYCLIF *Heb.* vii. 18 Reprouyng of the maundement bifore goynge is maad, for the vnsadnesse and vnprofyt of it. **1398** TREVISA *Barth. De P. R.* XVII. cl. (Bodl. MS.), Þere it is iseide þat..it happiþ & comeþ of vnfastenes & vnsadnes of þe tre.

**Unsa·d,** *v.* (UN-[2] 6 a.) **1640** QUARLES *Sighes* xvii, We'l change our Scene, & we'l unsad our Stile; We'l teach your sighes to sing. **Unsa·dden,** *v.* (UN-[2] 6 a.) **1654** WHITLOCK *Zootomia* 483 It unsaddens the melancholy, quickens the dull, awaketh the drowsie. **1748** RICHARDSON *Clarissa* (1811) IV. 355 The unsaddened heart..will not now, I hope, give the sable turn to every address of the man she dislikes not. *Ibid.* V. 224 [He] began to untwist and unsadden his features. **Unsa·ddened,** *ppl. a.* (UN-[1] 8.) ? *c* **1840** MRS. BROWNING *Paraphr. Homer, Hector & A.* 2 The nurse..Bore on her bosom the unsaddened child.

**Unsa·ddle,** *v.* [UN-[2] 4, 5. Cf. older Du. and Flem. *ontsadelen* (Du. *ontzadelen*), OHG. *intsatalôn* (MHG. *entsatelen*, G. *entsatteln*).

**1.** *trans.* To remove the saddle from (a horse, etc.). Also *absol.*

**1382** WYCLIF *Gen.* xxiv. 32 He ladde hym into the hows of herbergrye and unsadelynge dischargide the camelis. *c* **1440** *Promp. Parv.* 367/1 Onsadelyn hors,..*desterno*. **1560** BIBLE (Geneva) *Gen.* xxiv. 32 He vnsadeled the camels and broght lytter & prouander. **1609** ARMIN *Ital. Taylor* B 3 b, When you shall see The bargaine full assignd, Vnsaddle me, and leaue me sold. **1716** B. CHURCH *Hist. Philip's War* (1865) I. 43 The Horses that he and his company came on standing at the door (for they had not been unsaddled). **1798** *Hull Advertiser* 8 Sept. 1/4 After a march of ninety miles, without unsaddling our horses. **1837** W. IRVING *Capt. Bonneville* II. 263 Their horses, too, were unsaddled, and turned loose to graze. **1890** 'R. BOLDREWOOD' *Col. Reformer* (1891) 185 His attendants proceeded to unsaddle the whole troop.

**2.** To dislodge from a saddle. Also *fig.*

*a* **1470** H. PARKER *Dives & Pauper* (Pynson, 1493) x. v, Therfore..kepe you wele in the sadyl of pacience, & let no angre,..no tribulacion, no seknesse unsadle you of pacience. **1564** BULLEYN *Dial. agst. Pest.* 42 b, Helpe me, my horse starteth, and had like to haue..vnsadled me. **1623** DONNE *Serm.* 176 A froward and peremptory Refuter unsaddles me at first. *a* **1700** EVELYN *Diary* 22 March 1649, Another ..whose ambition..is resolved to neglect no tentative.. that may unsaddle the General, and fairly hold him the stirrup. **1821** HUISH *Life Geo. III*, I. 10/1 Magnus..engaged Otho personally, and unsaddled him. **1860** ADLER *Prov. Poet.* xviii. 404, I expect to unsaddle many a knight on the fair centre of the bridge.

**3.** To free from spectacles.

**1753** SMOLLETT *Ct. Fathom* xl, The prince unsaddled his nose, and..our hero was introduced in form.

Hence **Unsa·ddling** *vbl. sb.* Also *attrib.*

[**1775** ASH.] **1855** KINGSLEY *Westw. Ho!* ii, Sir Richard Grenvile's house is like a very tavern, with eating and drinking, and unsaddling. **1892** *Star* 15 June 4/2 The small unsaddling paddock.

**Unsa·ddled,** *ppl. a.* [UN-[1] 8. Cf. OE. *unsadelod*, *ungesadelod*, MDu. *ongesadelt* (Du. *ongezadeld*), G. *ungesattelt*; NFris. *unsadeld*, Da. *usadlet*, Sw. *osadlad*.] Not saddled. Also *transf.* (cf. prec. 3).

**1623** FLETCHER & ROWLEY *Maid in Mill* IV. ii, If thy spectacles be not easie, Keep thy nose unsadl'd, and ope thine ears. **1817** *Blackw. Mag.* I. 57/1 There were at her wedding fifty saddled asses, and unsaddled asses without number. **1892** *Daily News* 28 Sept. 3/5 Each mounted soldier leading an unsaddled charger.

**Unsadness:** see UNSAD *a.*

**Unsa·fe,** *a.* [UN-[1] 7.]

**1.** Not enjoying safety; exposed to danger or risk.

**1605** SHAKS. *Macb.* III. ii. 32 Vnsafe the while, that wee must laue Our Honors in these flattering streames. *a* **1618** RALEIGH *Rem.* (1664) 151 People that were..un-safe, or unsure for their lives. **1676** HALE *Contempl.* I. 277 Which makes the man's estate unquiet and unsafe, because he hath many competitors. **1892** TENNYSON *Foresters* IV. i, I have let them know Their lives unsafe in..our woods.

**2.** Of actions, etc.: Involving, or not free from, danger or risk.

**1597** HOOKER *Eccl. Pol.* v. xlii. § 2 Yet others should be taught how unsafe it was to continue his friends. **1604** SHAKS. *Oth.* v. i. 43 Let's think't vnsafe To come into the cry. **1611** — *Wint. T.* II. ii. 30 These dangerous, vnsafe Lunes i' th' King. **1662** J. DAVIES tr. *Olearius' Voy. Ambass.* 84 This great number of slaves make it unsafe to walk the streets..unarm'd. **1722** WODROW *Corr.* (1843) II. 665 Our Assembly..declared the unsafe tendency of several propositions advanced by them. **1798** S. & HT. LEE *Canterb. T.* II. 168 [He] thought its appearance so unsafe, that..he chose to mount a horse. **1836** THIRLWALL *Greece* xxii. III. 259 A small number whom it appeared unsafe to trust. **1864** E. A. PARKES *Pract. Hygiene* 427 Rain water may be unsafe, if the tanks are not clean.

**b.** Of ways or places: Dangerous from natural or other causes.

**1621** in Foster *Eng. Factories Ind.* (1906) I. 274 The tyme of winter had made the wayes unsafe. **1650** in *Verney Memoirs* (1907) I. 464 The wayes are everywhere unsafe for travell. **1686** HORNECK *Crucif. Jesus* xxii. 661 Where the roads are unsafe, there men carry swords. **1748** *Anson's Voy.* III. ii. 315 Full of sharp-pointed coral rocks, which.. renders it a very unsafe place to lie at. **1781** COWPER *Heroism* 33 Oh, bliss precarious, and unsafe retreats! **1830** WORDSW. *Russian Fugitive* II. ii, And midway in the unsafe morass, A single Island rose Of firm dry ground. **1891** FARRAR *Darkn. & Dawn* xx, While Nero..made the streets..unsafe with riot and assault.

**3.** Not to be trusted to; unreliable.

**1601** SHAKS. *Twel. N.* III. iv. 88 No obstacle, no incredulous or vnsafe circumstance,..can come betweene me, and the full prospect of my hopes. **1615** G. SANDYS *Trav.* 92 A number of wracks..did miserably testifie the unsafe protection of that harbour. **1660** JER. TAYLOR *Ductor* II. iii. rule 14 § 2 The topick of traditions..was..false in many things, and therefore unsafe in all questions. **1815** J. SMITH *Panorama Sci. & Art* II. 635 Land..on which it is deemed unsafe to sow grain, on account of the worm. **1863** *Smith's Dict. Bible* II. s.v. *Phut*, Such mere similarity of sound is a most unsafe guide. **1894** A. ROBERTSON *Nuggets* 34 We say 'As unsafe as a bank', after what has occurred in Melbourne.

**Unsa·fely,** *adv.* [UN-[1] 11.] In an unsafe manner; without safety or surety.

**1621** G. SANDYS *Ovid's Met.* x. (1626) 209 Valour vnsafelie copes with valiant foes. **1692** DRYDEN *Eleonora* 368 Take it,..before my rage Unsafely just, break loose on this bad Age. **1774** BEATTIE *Minstr.* II. xl, Even there, if left without a guide, The young adventurer unsafely plays. **1870** PROCTOR *Other Worlds* ii. 45 It may not unsafely be asserted, that.. those elements..exist in..every single star.

**Unsa·feness.** [UN-[1] 12.] The quality of being unsafe.

**1673** *S'too him Bayes* 89 As for the unsafeness of it, if uncontroulable libertie prove safe, all's well. **1678** CUDWORTH *Intell. Syst.* I. v. 794 Unevenness and Unsafeness of.. [Plotinus's] Temper. **1884** *Law Times* 22 Nov. 64/1 The unsafeness and impropriety of the manner of removal.

**Unsa·fety.** [UN-[1] 12, 5 b.] Absence or want of safety.

**1596** BACON *Max. Com. Law* Ep. Ded. (1630) A 4, The great hollownesse and vnsafety in assurances of lands. **1614** — *Charge touching Duels* 9 It may cause suddaine stormes in Court, to the disturbance of his Majestie, and vnsaftie of his person. *a* **1684** LEIGHTON *Com.* 1 *Pet.* iii. 15 Perceiving the unsafety and vanity of these..external things. **1844** J. WATSON in Churton *Mem.* (1861) II. 222 The unsafety of determining authorships by internal evidence. **1872** HOWELLS *Wedding Journ.* ix, The unsafety of all bridges of that design.

**Unsa·ge,** *a.* (UN-[1] 7.) **1584** HUDSON *Du Bartas' Judith* v. 305 And, with their wicked hands, and words vnsage, They did our sacred messengers outrage. **Unsa·gely,** *adv.* (UN-[1] 11.) **1801** MOORE *Morality* 71 The plain good man.. Pursues his course, unsagely blest, His tutor whispering in his breast.

**Unsai·d,** *ppl. a.* [OE. *unsǽd* (UN-[1] 8 b), = NFris. *unsad*, MDu. *ongeseit*, Du. *ongezegd*, MLG. *ungesegget*, *-gesecht*, MHG. *ungesaget*, *-geseit* (G. *ungesagt*), ON. *úsagðr* (Sw. *osagd*, (M)Da. *usagt*, Norw. *usagd*).] Not said or uttered.

*c* **1000** ÆLFRIC *Hom.* II. 466 Eac þæs dæges godspel is swiðe earfoðe læwedum mannum to understandenne..; ac we hit lætað unsæd. *c* **1375** *Sc. Leg. Saints* xxx. (*Theodera*) 234 Theodera þane cane hyr pray þat scho wald tel hyr..& lef vnsad til hyr richt nocht. *c* **1425** *Cast. Persev.* 693 in *Macro Plays* 98 Þer-fore I am mad massenger..þorwe all þe world..vnsayd sawys for to seye. *c* **1440** *Alph. Tales* 324, I hafe lefte þe laste colett vnsaid. *c* **1450** *Merlin* x. 143 Merlyn..tolde hym alle these thynges, that nought be lefte vn-seide. **1532** MORE *Confut. Tindale* Wks. 345/2 He held ..that al diuine seruice may be left vnsaied without ani sinne. **1593** *Sidney's Arcadia* v. (1922) II. 192 Leaving nothing unsaide which a filthy minde can imagine. **1609** DONNE *Elegie Mrs. Boulstred* 1 Death I recant, and say, unsaid by mee What ere hath slip'd, that might diminish thee. **1699** BENTLEY *Phal.* 46 This was..a thing unsaid before. **1730** SWIFT *Poems, Traulus* II. 20 He..Talks whate'er comes in his head; Wishes it were all unsaid. **1805** SCOTT *Last Minstrel* v. xxvii, Half his tale he left unsaid. **1848** THACKERAY *Van. Fair* lxvi, You leave me under the weight of an accusation which, after all, is unsaid. **1889** WALPOLE *Life Ld. J. Russell* II. 266 Forced, therefore, to leave unsaid the words..necessary for his own defence.

**Unsai·lable,** *a.* (UN-[1] 7 b.)

**1570** LEVINS *Manip.* 4/15 Vnsaylable, *innauigabilis.* **1587** GOLDING *De Mornay* vii. 102 Ye shall make the Sea for the most part vnsayleable. **1627** MAY *Lucan* V. H 8 b, Cæsar.. findes The sea vnsaileable for dangerous windes.

**Unsai·led,** *ppl. a.* (UN-[1] 8, 8 c.)

*a* **1572** KNOX *Hist. Ref.* Wks. 1846 I. 293 To bring this head to pass,..the Quein Regent left no point of the compas unsailled. **1807** J. BARLOW *Columb.* I. 457 There spreads, belike, that other unsail'd main I sought so long. **1866** SWINBURNE *Poems & Ball., Lament.* 86 Lo, what hath he seen or known Of..the wave Unbeholden, unsailed-on? **1870** MORRIS *Earthly Par.* II. III. 272 'Twixt inaccessible cliffs and unsailed sea.

**Unsai·lorlike,** *a.* (UN-[1] 7 c.)

**1841** THACKERAY *Yellowplush Papers* Wks. 1898 III. 375 Nothing can be more unsailorlike than his namby-pamby starlit descriptions. **1865** J. CAMERON *Malayan India* 41 The unsightly and unsailorlike aspect of the craft.

**Unsai·lorly,** *a.* (UN-[1] 7.) **1883** STEVENSON *Treas. Isl.* II. ix, I think his conduct unsailorly.

**Unsai·ned,** *ppl. a.* Now *arch.* [UN-[1] 8. Cf. OE. *ungesénod*, MDu. *ongesegent* (Du. *ongezegend*),

MLG. *ungesegnet*, MHG. *ungesëgenet*, *-ent* (G. *ungesegnet*).] Unblessed; *esp.* not formally blessed or protected by a blessing.

*a* 1275 *Ancr. R.* 312 [A] wardein, þet wit & wereð us euer wið þe unseiene [*Cotton MS.* unseinede] gostes. 1513 *Acc. Ld. High Treas. Scot.* IV. 417 To Thomas Drummond, alias Thom Unsanit,..vij li. 1691 R. Kirk *Secret Commw.* i. (1815) 10 Those who are unseened or unsanctified (called Fey). 1881 W. Gregor *Folk-Lore N.-E. Scotl.* xi. 62 To carry off unsained and unchurched mothers.

**Unsai·nt,** *v.* [Un-² 6 b.] *trans.* To deprive of saintly character or status.

1572 R. T. *Discourse* 29 Thomas Becket, whom King Henry dyd vnsainte, and disgrade. 1594 *Zepheria* xiv, No neuer shall that face..Emblemisht be, defaced or unsaynted, Till death shall blot it. 1612 T. James *Corrupt. Scripture* iv. 51 The Master of the sacred Palace hath vnsainted him. 1655 Gurnall *Chr. in Arm.* i. 114 Satan's scope in accusing the Christian,..is to unsaint him, and perswade him he is but an hypocrite. 1701 Howe *Some Consid. Pref. Enquiry* 29 Power..to saint themselves, and unsaint all other men, at their own pleasure. 1766 Entick *London* IV. 123 That saint's bones being..burnt, and unsainted, by the powers in being. 1834 Southey *Doctor* liv. (1848) 122 Most assuredly they ought to be unsainted! 1870 *Temple-Bar Mag.* XXIX. 186 Young women..mutter in tender tremulous voices, which..might unsaint an anchorite.

Hence **Unsai·nted** *ppl. a.*[1]

1851 Morier *Adv. Hajji Baba* II. vi. 172, I marvelled how of a sudden I had become such an unsainted lion.

**Unsai·nted,** *ppl. a.*[2] [Un-¹ 8.] Unsanctified; not canonized.

*a* 1642 Suckling *Acc. Relig.* Ep., Wks. (1648) 100 The Fathers of the Church..had slept now un-Sainted in their Graves,..benighted with Oblivion. 1647 Wharton *Bellum Hybern.* 1 As Iohn Booker prognosticated in his un-sainted state-lying-Kalender. 1768 [W. Donaldson] *Life Sir B. Sapskull* I. vii. 90 St. Austin,..Chrysostom, and many other sainted and unsainted fathers. 1862 E. Arnold *Hymn of Priestess of Diana* iii, O ear, that hears no word..unfit! O breast, which thought unsainted never felt! 1895 *Outing* April 6/1 Shame! shame! upon those unsainted ones!

**Unsai·nt-like,** *a.* (Un-¹ 7 c.) 1681 J. Scott *Chr. Life* iii. 225 Our wicked and unsaint-like Lives. 1891 *Pall Mall G.* 19 March 3/3 The saint's [*i. e.* John Wesley] very unsaint-like love affairs.

**Unsai·ntly,** *a.* (Un-¹ 7.)

Also, in recent use (1887-), *unsaintliness*.

1659 Gauden *Tears Ch.* ii. xix. 209 What (I pray) can be more unsaintly, than to..delight and glory..in most unjust and uncharitable actions? 1809 Foster *Ess.* (1844) I. 272 There is something unsaintly spread over the character. 1837 Gen. P. Thompson *Exerc.* (1842) IV. 301 Bring up the most unsaintly cases you can find. 1899 B. Harraden *Fowler* i. ix, A most unsaintly-looking pair of shoes.

†**Unsa·ked,** *a. Obs.* [Un-¹ 9 + Saked *a.*] Innocent.

*a* 1300 *Cursor M.* 572 Alle virtus has saul i-wis, Þat vte o sin vnsaked is. *Ibid.* 17336, I am vn-saked of his blod.

**Unsa·laried,** *ppl. a.* (Un-¹ 8.)

1836 Disraeli *Runnymede Lett.* (1885) 185 Happy England, whose fortunes are supervised by such an unsalaried steward! 1866 *Ch. Times* 1 Sept. 277/3 The cost..has been borne..chiefly by its founder, the unsalaried secretary. 1898 *Dict. Nat. Biog.* LVI. 247/1 A comfortable though unsalaried post as tutor.

**Unsa·leable,** *a.* and *sb.* (Un-¹ 7 b, 12.)

1565 Cooper *Thesaurus* s. v. *Merx*, Vnsalehable ware. 1644 Milton *Areop.* (Arb.) 60 Sermons..vented in such numbers,..as have now wellnigh made all other books unsalable. 1692 Ray *On Creation* (ed. 2) Advt., By publishing a Second Edition of a Book, with large Additions, to render the former worthless and unsalable. 1762 Sterne *Tr. Shandy* vi. xxxiii, An unsaleable piece of cambrick. 1798 *Hull Advertiser* 23 June 4/4 Middling and ordinary qualities are quite unsaleable. 1817 Coleridge *Biogr. Lit.* I. 178 The unsaleable nature of my writings. 1860 Ruskin *Unto this Last* (1862) 112 A horse is useless, and therefore unsaleable, if no one can ride.

*sb.* 1811 Byron *Hints from Hor.* 657 'Scott's thirty thousand copies sold,' which must sadly discomfit poor Southey's unsaleables. 1843 E. FitzGerald *Lett.* (1889) I. 116 A desperate collection of pictures..: among them old unsaleables by Maclise.

Hence **Unsaleabi·lity; -ableness.**

1872 De Morgan *Budget of Paradoxes* 123 A climax of *unsaleability, unreadability, and inutility. 1775 Ash, *Unsaleableness. 1903 *Saturday Rev.* 10 Jan. 43/1 The unsaleableness of landscape.

**Unsa·lt,** *a.* (Un-¹ 7. Cf. OE. *unsealt*, Du. *onzout*, ON. *úsaltr*, Icel. *ósaltur*, older Sw. *osalt*.)

1435 Misyn *Fire of Love* 89 Þis warld..has also salt vnsalt, sauyr vnsauyrd. 1598 Florio, *Fresco*, fresh, new, vnsalt.

**Unsa·lt,** *v.* (Un-² 6 and 7. Cf. Du. *ontzouten*, G. *entsalzen*.) 1547 *Bk. of Marchantes* c ij, Of suche wares their store houses are ful, and these be called, store hous masses, or salted masses. That god..ryght soone vnsalte and water it. 1611 Cotgr., *Dessaler*, to vnsalt; make fresh; become fresh. **Unsa·ltatory,** *a.* (Un-¹ 7.) 1846 Ford *Gatherings from Spain* xxiii. 334 Our immelodious labourers and unsaltatory operatives.

**Unsa·lted,** *ppl. a.* (Un-¹ 8. Cf. NFris. *unsalted*, (M)Sw. *osaltad*, (M)Da. *usaltet*.)

*c* 1440 *Promp. Parv.* 366/2 On-powderyd, on-saltyd, *insalitus*. 1541 R. Copland *Guydon's Quest. Chirurg.* Q i, A maturatife made with butter wel wasshed and vnsalted. 1579 Langham *Gard. Health* 473 Pease.., whether they be gray or white vnsalted. 1600 Surflet *Countrie Farme* v. xvi. 682 Sprinkled with neats blood mingled with oile oliue vnsalted. 1725 *Fam. Dict.* s.v. *Poupelin*, Good melted and unsalted Butter. 1731 Arbuthnot *Aliments* (1735) 187 The Cure of this Distemper lies in a Diet of fresh unsalted things. 1820 Scoresby *Acc. Arctic Reg.* I. 342 Unsalted mutton and beef. 1860 O. W. Holmes *Elsie V.* vii, Villages lying along the unsalted streams.

**b.** *fig.* (See quots.)

1602 Marston *Antonio's Rev.* iv. ii, Your unsalted fresh foole is your onely man. 1619 Hieron *Wks.* II. 489 It is impossible for a man of an vnsalted heart, so to counterfait the language of Canaan. 1649 Milton *Eikon.* xiv. 139 Compiler of that unsalted and Simonical praier annex'd. 1879 Atcherley *Trip Boërland* 208 'Unsalted' horses, *i. e.* those which have not passed through the ordeal [of the disease].

**Unsalu·brious,** *a.* (Un-¹ 7, 5 b.) 1781 J. Moore *View Soc. It.* II. 97 Descending from that town..we traversed an unsalubrious plain to Sermonetta. **Unsalu·brity.** (Un-¹ 7, 5 b.) 1694 Falle *Jersey* ii. 78 The Unsalubrity of any Country arising chiefly from a low Ground, and a stagnating Air and Water.

**Unsa·lutary,** *a.* (Un-¹ 7 and 5 b.)

1770 Langhorne *Plutarch* V. 219 His unpeaceable and unsalutary conduct. 1778 *Eng. Gazetteer* (ed. 2) s.v. *Norfolk*, The air..is aguish, and otherwise unsalutary. 1840 Forster *Treat. Pop. Progr. Eng. Hist.* p. xlviii, It is fearful, but not unsalutary, to cast a parting glance at it. 1846 Landor *Imag. Conv.* Wks. I. 544/2 It is just..to shake a salutary fear into..stupid despots, when they shake an unsalutary one into thousands.

**Unsalu·ted,** *ppl a.* (Un-¹ 8.)

1542 Becon *Pathw. Prayer* xxxvi. O vii, He that leaueth God vnsaluted with his prayers at these thre tymes. *a* 1586 Sidney *Arcadia* iii. ii, My sleepes were inquired after, and my wakings never unsaluted. 1607 Shaks. *Cor.* v. iii. 50 You Gods, I pray, And the most noble Mother of the world Leaue vnsaluted. 1694 tr. *Milton's Lett. State* 260 We have given him in Command, not to pass by your Lordships Unsaluted in our Name. 1795 [see next]. 1805 Wordsw. *Prelude* iv. 47 The rooms, the court, the garden were not left Long unsaluted. 1821 Scott *Pirate* xxiii, He suffered them to go away unsaluted.

**Unsalu·ting,** *ppl. a.* (Un-¹ 10.) 1795 Coleridge *Lett.* (1895) 144, I met you in Redcliff, and, unsaluted and unsaluting, passed by the man to whom [etc.].

**Unsa·lvable,** *a.* (Un-¹ 7 b and 5 b.)

1624 T. Scott *Vox Pop.* ii. 14 He found the rootes of eithers discontent so deepe, and the sore so vnsalueable, that hee gaue it ouer. 1638 Chillingw. *Relig. Prot.* i. v. § 60 The words by you cited, and charged with unsalvable contradiction. 1659 Fuller *App. Inj. Innoc.* ii. 102 Else we were all..in an unsalvable condition. 1895 Salmond *Chr. Doctr. Immort.* vi. iv. 668 Neither to make the heathen unconditionally unsalvable, nor to represent salvation as possible apart from Christ.

Hence **Unsalvabi·lity, -ableness.**

1684 H. More *Answer* xiv. 105 Touching the Idolatrousness of the Church of Rome, and the Unsalvableness of those in her Communion. 1891 *Wesleyan Method. Mag.* June 465/1 The unsalvability of any heathen.

**Unsa·lvatory,** *a.* (Un-¹ 7.) 1850 Carlyle *Latter-d. Pamph.* iii. 6 Dalai-Lama pills, manufactured let not refined lips hint how, and quite *un*salvatory to mankind.

**Unsa·lved,** *ppl. a.* (Un-¹ 8. Cf. MHG. *ungesalbet*, G. *ungesalbt*, Du. *ongezalfd*.)

*a* 1240 *Ureisun* in *O. E. Hom.* I. 202 Hwoa þerf beon unsalued þet haueð se mihti salue. 1641 Milton *Prel. Episc.* 23 Nor caring how slightly they put off the verdit of holy Text unsalv'd. 1837 Youatt *Sheep* xvii. 549 The *laid* wool ..was..lower in price than the white or unsalved wool.

†**Unsa·me,** *v. Obs.* [Un-² 6 + Same *a.*] *trans.* To alter, change. 1632 Quarles *Div. Fancies* ii. xxxiii, What secret mischiefe can Vn-same thy peace? 'Twas not the selfe same Man. †**Unsa·men,** *adv. Obs.* [Un-¹ 11 b.] Not in union or harmony. *a* 1400–50 *Alexander* 605 With grete glesenand eȝen grymly he lokis, Þat were..sett vn-samen of serelypy hewys.

**Unsa·mpled,** *ppl. a.* [Un-¹ 8.]

†**1.** Unexampled. *Obs.*

*a* 1638 Mede *Wks.* (1672) 220 The unsampled irregularity of our whole nature. 1675 Alsop *Anti-sozzo* 312 The Burning of Rome and his unsampled Butcheries.

**2.** Untried; not experienced.

1890 *Pall Mall G.* 28 Aug. 1/2 It is the unknown and the unsampled that bewilders us.

**Unsanctifica·tion.** (Un-¹ 12, Un-² 8.)

*a* 1684 Leighton *Comm.* 1 *Pet.* i. 2 (1693) 28 From present unsanctification, a Man cannot inferre that he is not Elected. 1804 *Europ. Mag.* XLV. 96/2 Whether this tavern had, from the time of its unsanctification, been always kept by Quakers, cannot now be ascertained.

**Unsa·nctified,** *ppl. a.* (Un-¹ 8.)

1570 *Homilies* ii. *Agst. Rebellion* iii. (1859) 570 Rebels.. leave the Sabbath day of the Lord unsanctified. 1602 Shaks. *Ham.* v. i. 252 She should in ground vnsanctified haue lodg'd. 1650 Bulwer *Anthropomet.* 199 In the Indies, among barbarous and unsanctified Nations. 1747 Doddridge *Col. Gardiner* 28 A Heart as yet quite unsanctified. 1796 Mme. D'Arblay *Camilla* V. 430 My own prayers may be too unsanctified to be heard. 1827 Pollok *Course T.* x. 306 The others..stand unsanctified, unpardoned, sad. 1855 Milman *Lat. Chr.* xiv. viii. VI. 578 To the Ecclesiastic belonged the chancel, not to be entered by unsanctified feet.

Hence **Unsa·nctifiedly** *adv.*, **-ness.**

1634 Ld. Warriston *Diary* (S.H.S.) 226, I most confesse ..the unsanctifiednes of my affections. 1650 Hubbert *Pill Formality* 183 Thou livest..unholily, and unsanctifiedly.

**Unsa·nctify,** *v.* (Un-² 6 c.)

1594 *Zepheria* xxv, Let not disdayne thy soule vnsanctifie. 1633 Prynne *Histrio-m.* 668 If therefore Stage-playes unsanctifie or pollute the one,..needes must they defile the other too. 1693 Shadwell *Volunteers* iv, *Lettice.* You may see the most unhallow'd sight. *Hackwell.* Will it not unsanctifiy my eyes? 1831 Wordsw. *Yarrow Revisited* 91 Nor deem that localised Romance..Unsanctifies our tears. 1862 Burton *Bk. Hunter* iv. 323 To imagine any process by which they could be unsanctified.

Hence **Unsa·nctifying** *ppl. a.*

*a* 1859 Macaulay *Hist. Eng.* xxiv. (1861) V. 193 The sanctity of their profession has an unsanctifying influence on them.

**Unsanctimo·nious,** *a.* (Un-¹ 7.) *a* 1797 H. Walpole *Geo. II* (1847) III. vi. 158 A woman of so unsanctimonious a character. **Unsa·nction,** *v.* (Un-² 4.) 1854 Patmore *Angel in Ho.*, *Betrothal* 160 Love blabb'd of is a great decline; A careless word unsanctions sense.

**Unsa·nctioned,** *ppl. a.* (Un-¹ 8.)

1784 Cowper *Task* ii. 524 Their [*sc.* sages'] rules of life Defective and unsanctioned. 1833 J. H. Newman *Arians* i. iii. 64 From a fear of using unsanctioned language on a sacred subject. 1866 C. J. Vaughan *Plain Words* vi. 92 'Society'..is a thing not unnoticed, not unsanctioned by Him who made us.

**Unsa·nctity.** (Un-¹ 12.) *a* 1639 W. Whateley *Prototypes* ii. xxvi. (1640) 81 Those rules..doe discover rather the unsanctity of love in other respects, than the excesse. 1838 S. Bellamy *Betrayal* 85 From whose Unsanctity incense doth ev'n recoil. †**Unsa·nctuary.** (Un-¹ 12.) ? 1615 Sylvester *Tobacco Battered* 709 In som Play-house, or some Ordinary, Or in som piece of som Vn-sanctuary.

**Unsa·ndalled,** *ppl. a.* (Un-¹ 8.)

1772 Mason *Eng. Garden* i. 16 Many a glade..where if Art E'er dar'd to tread, 'twas with unsandal'd foot. 1820 Shelley *Prometh. Unb.* iii. i. 15 As ice wounds unsandalled feet. 1887 Bowen *Æneid* iv. 518 One foot all unsandalled, her robe ungirdled, she stands.

**Unsa·nded,** *ppl. a.* (Un-¹ 8.) 1843 *Farmer's Mag.* Jan. 29/2 The unsanded spot is visible to this day.., being almost bare of grass.

**Unsa·ne,** *a.* [Un-¹ 7, 5 b.]

†**1.** Unsound, unhealthy. *Obs.*

*c* 1690 tr. *Plutarch's Mor.* (1718) IV. 177 A Man begotten by an unsane Body, does not therefore deserve Punishment.

**2.** Lacking sanity. *rare.*

1867 H. Bushnell *Moral Uses Dark Th.* 267 It results.. not that we are insane, but short of perfect sanity, practically unsane.

**Unsa·nguine,** *a.* (Un-¹ 7.)

1728 Young *Ocean* lxxi, Prophetic schemes, And golden dreams, May I, unsanguin, cast away! 1862 [Eliz. Johnston] *Gifts & Graces* xxiv. 238 To one of her unsanguine disposition such cheerfulness was very admirable. 1883 Lytton *Life & Lett. Ld. L.* II. 25 The unsanguine nature of his disposition.

Hence **Unsa·nguineness.**

1841 Lady Lyttelton in *Corr.* (1912) 309 This, however, is ..only my usual unsanguineness.

**Unsa·nitary,** *a.* (Un-¹ 7 and 5 b.)

1871 Geo. Eliot *Middlemarch* xxiii, In any grim street of that unsanitary period. 1883 *Century Mag.* XXVI. 77 Unsanitary dwellings.

**Unsa·nitated,** *ppl. a.* (Un-¹ 8.) 1888 *Daily Tel.* 5 Mar. (Encycl. Dict.), Unsanitated workrooms, or..sweating dens. **Unsapo·nifiable,** *a.* (Un-¹ 7 b.) 1885 W. L. Carpenter *Soap & Candles* 91 Estimation of Unsaponifiable Oils in Fats. **Unsapo·nified,** *ppl. a.* (Un-¹ 8.) 1839 Ure *Dict. Arts* 729 The unsaponified fat of the coccus insect. †**Unsa·pory,** *a. Obs.* [Un-¹ 7 and 5 b + Sapor.] Unsavoury. 1638 Sir T. Herbert *Trav.* (ed. 2) 13 A meale..unsapory and offensive. *Ibid.* 241 The cheese is..of an unsaporie taste. **Unsa·pped,** *ppl. a.* (Un-¹ 8.) 1768 Sterne *Sent. Journ.*, *Act of Charity*, Two upright vestal sisters, unsapp'd by caresses. 1896 *Amer. Ann. Deaf* Feb. 106 Sound and vigorous in body, unsapped in vitality. **Unsa·ppy,** *a.* (Un-¹ 7. Cf. OE. *unsæpig*.) *a* 1722 Lisle *Husb.* (1757) 248 A small, thin, unsappy leaf. **Unsarra'd,** dial. var. Unserved *ppl. a.* **Unsa·shed,** *ppl. a.* (Un-¹ 8.) [1775 Ash.] 1841 Dickens *Barn. Rudge* xli, A gleam of sun shining through the unsashed window. **Unsa·table,** *a.* [Un-¹ 7 b.] Insatiable. 1850 Browning *Easter Day* xxvi, His saints..knew He would not disallow Their spirit's hunger, ..Unsated,—not unsatable.

**Unsa·ted,** *ppl. a.* (Un-¹ 8.)

1693 Dryden *Juvenal* vi. 185 Tir'd with the Toyl, unsated with the Sin. 1744 Young *Nt. Th.* vi. 69 Long life might lapse, age unperceiv'd come on; And find the soul unsated with her theme. 1798 Ferriar *Illustr Sterne*, etc. i. 6 His imagination..unsated by a long acquaintance with literary folly. 1834 Lytton *Pompeii* iii. x, Now contracting, now lengthening, its folds, in pain and unsated anger. 1879 Farrar *St. Paul* I. 177 To the High Priest therefore he went, unsated by all his previous cruelties.

Hence **Unsa·tedness.**

1845 Bailey *Festus* (ed. 2) 258 Contrasting the pure joys of earlier years With the unsatedness of current sin.

**Unsa·tiable,** *a.* Now *rare.* [Un-¹ 7 b and 5 b.] Of persons, desires, etc.: Insatiable. (Common *c* 1540–*c* 1675.)

(*a*) 1382 Wyclif *Baruch* iv. 15 He brouȝte vpon hem..a folc vnsaciable. *c* 1440 *Alph. Tales* 523 With mony we sall fyll þine vnsaciable harte. 1500–20 Dunbar *Poems* xvii. 38 Sum wald tak all this warldis breid,..Throw hairt vnsatiable. *a* 1540 Barnes *Wks.* (1573) 342/1 Beecause you bee..vnsaciable belly Gods. 1631 Gouge *God's Arrowes* iii. § 70. 311 To them that are unsatiable in sin. 1684 Burnet tr. *More's Utopia* 21 When any unsatiable Wretch..resolves to inclose many thousand Acres of Ground.

(*b*) *c* 1440 J. Shirley *Dethe K. James* 28 All mene saye that the unsacionable [*sic*] covetise was the..cause of the Kynges dethe. *a* 1513 Fabyan *Chron.* vii. ccxxiv. 251 The vnsaceable couetous [*sic*] of Ranulph. 1535 Coverdale *Judith* Contents ii, The vnsaciable desyre that Nabuchodonosor had to raigne. 1579 W. Wilkinson *Confut. Fam. Love* To Rdr. p. iv b, Vnsatiable greadines. 1643 Sir T. Browne *Relig. Med.* i. § 47 That essence, whose infinite goodnesse is able to terminate the desires of it selfe, and the unsatiable wishes of ours. 1692 N. Mather *Pref. Owen's Disc. Holy Sp.* (1693) A 3 b, An unsatiable Desire to do Service to Christ. 1810 *Monthly Mag.* XXIX. 321 His hate [is] unsatiable, where he mistrusts.

(*c*) 1528 Roy *Rede me* (Arb.) 102 They are the divels fornace, Oven infernall vnsaciable. 1691 tr. *Emilianne's Frauds Rom. Monks* (ed. 3) 375 An unsatiable Gulf which swallows all, and gives up nothing again.

**Unsa·tiableness.** Now *rare.* [Un-¹ 12 and 5 b.] Insatiability.

1539 Elyot *Cast. Helthe* (1541) 28 To content the unsaciablenes of wanton appetites. 1547 Recorde *Judic. Ur.* 1 Unsaciablenes is never satisfied. 1656 Earl Monm. tr. *Boccalini's Advts. fr. Parnass.* 437 To satisfie the ravenous and dog-like unsatiableness of such a company of starvelings. *a* 1699 J. Beaumont *Psyche* xvi. ccxxx, O pardon my Unsatiableness, Since Thou thy self alone art cause of it. 1823 BENTHAM *Not Paul* 282 The unsatiableness of Paul's ambition.

† **Unsa·tiably,** *adv. Obs.* (UN-[1] 11 and 5 b.) 1540–1 ELYOT *Image Gov.* 154 b, They vnsaciably fedde therewith theym selues. 1583 GOLDING *Calvin on Deut.* xlix. 291 To haue crammed and glutted themselues after that fashion vnsatiably. 1615 J. STEPHENS *Satyr. Ess.* II. ii. 236 The steame of a roasted ioynt attracts his nostrils vnsatiably. *a* 1665 J. GOODWIN *Filled w. the Spirit* xix. (1670) 540 By following Lusts and Pleasures unsatiably.

**Unsa·tiate,** *a.* (UN-[1] 7 and 5 b.)

Frequent *c* 1540–1650; now *rare*.

1528 ROY *Rede me* (Arb.) 78 The dayly cravynge..Of the vnsaciate fryer beggers. 1594 SHAKS. *Rich. III*, III. v. 87 (Q.), When that my mother went with child Of that vnsatiate Edward. 1614 RALEIGH *Hist. World* III. 51 The unsatiate desire of man to obtaine more and more thereof. 1681 DRYDEN *Abs. & Achit.* I. 987 But save me most from my Petitioners, Unsatiate as the barren Womb or Grave. 1876 MORRIS *Sigurd* III. 183 Their eyes are all unsatiate of gazing on his face.

**Unsa·tiated,** *ppl. a.* (UN-[1] 8 and 5 b.) 1701 NORRIS *Ideal World* I. viii. 436 To behold the bright Sun of truth with an unwearied, as well as unsatiated eye. 1745 H. WALPOLE *Lett.* (1846) II. 90 The Prince of Wales has had unsatiated curiosity about him. 1812 J. HENRY *Camp. agst. Quebec* 48 Though we gorged the stomach, the appetite was unsatiated. 1880 NICHOL *Life Byron* 143 The feeling of affronted or unsatiated pride.

*absol.* 1890 SARAH J. DUNCAN *Soc. Depart.* 364 [We] looked at them with all the pleasure of the uncritical and the unsatiated.

**Unsa·tiating,** *ppl. a.* (UN-[1] 10.) 1768 TUCKER *Lt. Nat.* (1834) II. 312 He might have excited sensations..permanent, unfading, and unsatiating. 1786 tr. *Beckford's Vathek* 3 The Eternal or unsatiating Banquet. **Unsa·ting,** *ppl. a.* (UN-[1] 10.) 1818 KEATS *Endym.* I. 816 So delicious is the unsating food. 1863 GILCHRIST *Life Blake* I. 73 There is something unsating about them, a perfume as of a growing violet. **Unsa·tire,** *v.* (UN-[2] 6 b.) 1638 N. WHITING *Albino & Bellama* To Ld. Lovelace 16 Some worthy peer, Whose very name unsatire can a jeer. **Unsati·rical,** *a.* (UN-[1] 7.) 1592 G. HARVEY *Four Lett.* iii. 44 Those vnsatyricall Satyres, which M. Spencer long since embraced with an ouerlouing Sonnet.

**Unsatisfa·ction.** [UN-[1] 12 and 5 b.]

**1.** Absence of satisfaction.

1643 DIGBY *Observ. Relig. Med.* (1644) 36 Nor have [I] any unsatisfaction in believing there are Spirits. 1675 T. PLUME *Life Hacket* in Hacket *Cent. Serm.* p. xliii, He thought the permission of conventicles did shew great irresolution and unsatisfaction in the truth. 1865 MRS. WHITNEY *Gayworthys* xxx, An earnestness that searched through all things even to unsatisfaction and scepticism. 1880 CARPENTER in *Mod. Review* I. 49 The unsatisfaction (if I may revive an obsolete word) of resting in any inherent 'potency' of Matter as the *ultima ratio* of the existing Kosmos.

†**2.** Unsatisfactoriness. *Obs.*

1645 BP. HALL *Remedy Discontents* 94 The mean valuation of all these earthly things, for their transitorinesse, unsatisfaction, danger. 1668 R. STEELE *Husbandman's Calling* vi. § 5 Thence he learns the unsatisfaction of the creature and that God and Heaven are the only rest of the soul.

**Unsatisfa·ctorily,** *adv.* (UN-[1] 11 and 5 b.) 1657 F. ROBERTS in Spurgeon *Treas. Dav.* III. 239 Augustine also expounds the words much to the same effect, but altogether as unsatisfactorily. 1685 BAXTER *Paraphr. N. T.* A 3, Many..are too large and costly for this use: some..are unsatisfactorily brief. *c* 1714 POPE *Let.* Wks. 1751 VII. 138 To shew you how very unsatisfactorily you write,..you've never told me how you do. 1794 R. J. SULIVAN *View Nat.* IV. 11 Materialism, as I have repeatedly said, and I hope not unsatisfactorily proved, is [etc.]. 1838 JAMES *Louis XIV*, III. 50 Completing that which had been thus imperfectly and unsatisfactorily begun. 1884 *Law Rep.* 12 Q. B. D. 583 The scope and effect of an Act so unsatisfactorily framed.

**Unsatisfa·ctoriness.** (UN-[1] 12.) 1643 PRYNNE *Sov. Power Parl.* I. (ed. 2) Pref. A 2 The insufficiency and unsatisfactorinesse of all late Printed Pleas. 1679 J. GOODMAN *Penit. Pard.* I. iv. 113 The emptiness and unsatisfactoriness of all the Incomes of sin. 1807 G. CHALMERS *Caledonia* I. II. vi. 275 The unsatisfactoriness of the one, and the silence of the other, lead us to suppose [etc.]. 1876 LOWELL *Among my Bks.* Ser. II. 116 The unsatisfactoriness of science leads Faust to seek repose in worldly pleasure.

**Unsatisfa·ctory,** *a.* (UN-[1] 7.) 1637–50 ROW *Hist. Kirk* (Wodrow Soc.) 65 This ansuer wes judged..unsatisfactorie. 1652 BENLOWES *Theoph.* Pref., All external splendours being unsatisfactory. 1714 R. FIDDES *Pract. Disc.* II. 212 The very enjoyments of life..are..in themselves unsatisfactory. 1777 J. RICHARDSON *Dissert. East. Nations* 9 [It] opens a wide field for unsatisfactory enquiry. 1818 COBBETT *Pol. Reg.* XXXIII. 692 To assert without stating particulars, would be unsatisfactory. 1843 BETHUNE *Sc. Fireside Stor.* 88 As his visit proved unsatisfactory, he determined to make his stay short. 1890 *Retrospect Med.* CII. 17 The treatment of this dangerous complication is most unsatisfactory.

**Unsa·tisfiable,** *a.* [UN-[1] 7 b.]

**1.** Incapable of being satisfied.

1539 TAVERNER *Gard. Wysd.* II. 26 Onles thou haddest bene an euell man & with money unsatisfyable. 1593 G. HARVEY *Pierce's Super.* To Friends, Aduisedly weigh.. the impossible satisfaction of vnsatisfiable expectation. 1648 GAGE *West Ind.* 76 An unsatisfiable minde and greedy covetousnesse. 1680 C. NESSE *Church Hist.* 60 Their envy and ambition are restless and unsatisfiable. 1802 PALEY *Nat. Theol.* xxvi. Wks. (1834) 545/1 Well-directed tastes and desires, compared with the dominion of..unsatisfied, and unsatisfiable passions. 1896 DK. ARGYLL *Philos. Belief* 544 The unsatisfied, and apparently unsatisfiable, desires of men.

†**2.** For which no satisfaction can be made. *Obs.*

1593 G. HARVEY *New. Let.* B 3 b, The more notorious the offence, and the more vnsatisfiable the Iniurie was. 1648 SYMMONS *Vind. Chas. I*, 166 Until we have quite destroyed him, whom we hate,..for those unsatisfiable wrongs, which ourselves have done him.

Hence **Unsa·tisfiableness, -ably** *adv.*

1647 TRAPP *Comm. 1 John* ii. 17 There is a curse of *unsatisfiablenesse lies upon the creature. 1664 INGELO *Bentiv. & Ur.* VI. 350 [Appetites which] do gall the Soul by a ravenous unsatisfiableness. 1652 N. CULVERWEL *Lt. Nature* II. 70 The Hart pants *unsatisfiably after the water-brooks.

**Unsa·tisfied,** *ppl. a.* [UN-[1] 8 and 5 b.]

**1.** Not satisfied in respect of something desired; not having obtained all that, or as much as, is wished for: **a.** Predicatively, also const. *with*, † *of*.

*c* 1430 LYDG. *Min. Poems* (Percy Soc.) 31 Thou tolde me, frende,..That thou kneuhest one..Unsatisfied a day in tymes twelfe. *a* 1586 SIDNEY *Arcadia* III. xviii. (1912) 457 So the more they strake, the more unsatisfied they were with striking. 1592 SHAKS. *Rom. & Jul.* II. ii. 125 *Rom.* O wilt thou leaue me so vnsatisfied? *Iuli.* What satisfaction can'st thou haue to night? 1597 HOOKER *Eccl. Pol.* V. lx. § 7 That the Church..should repell them and see them dye vnsatisfied of these their Ghostly Desires. 1613 SHAKS. *Hen. VIII*, IV. ii. 55 Though he were vnsatisfied in getting, ..yet in bestowing..He was most Princely. 1685 DRYDEN *Lucretius* III. 155 Unsatisfy'd with all that Nature brings; Loathing the present, liking absent things. 1758–63 GIBBON *Misc. Wks.* (1814) III. 41 His ambition was yet unsatisfied. 1808 MITFORD *Hist. Greece* IV. 457 They were unsatisfied with the composition of the appointed embassy. 1866 GEO. ELIOT *F. Holt* i, To feel a woman's hunger of the heart for ever unsatisfied. 1897 MARY KINGSLEY *W. Africa* 52 A warning to others of the dangers of being unsatisfied.

**b.** Attributively.

1611 SHAKS. *Cymb.* I. vi. 49 The Cloyed will: That satiate yet vnsatisfi'd desire. 1665 MANLEY *Grotius' Low C. Wars* 279 Casting their unsatisfied eyes upon his countenance, they gratefully reverenced that tender Age. *a* 1704 T. BROWN *Sat. agst. Woman* Wks. 1730 I. 57 Raging with unsatisfy'd desire. 1757 FOOTE *Author* I, You know the unsatisfied mind of man, no sooner is one object possessed, but another starts up. 1849 GROTE *Greece* II. lxxii. [?] VI. 355 Bitter and as yet unsatisfied hatred against Platæa. 1871 MORLEY *Carlyle* in *Crit. Misc.* Ser. I. (1878) 168 The deep unrest of unsatisfied souls.

**2.** Not satisfied in respect of information or knowledge; doubtful, dubious.

1575 CHURCHYARD *Chippes* 38 b, At whoes elloquence the heerars rather stoede astonyed than vnsatysfyed in any poynt or parssell. 1602 SHAKS. *Ham.* V. ii. 351 Report me and my causes right To the vnsatisfied. 1646 SIR T. BROWNE *Pseud. Ep.* 187 In submission to future information, we are unsatisfied unto great dubitation. 1655 FULLER *Ch. Hist.* IX. ii. § 25 Others were unsatisfied in the Authenticalness of the instrument, who never did..see the original. 1736 BUTLER *Anal.* II. viii. 384 It will yet leave the mind in a very unsatisfied state.

† **b.** Not certain *of* something. *Obs.*

1665 MANLEY *Grotius' Low C. Wars* 593 They mistrusted their Borders, and were unsatisfied of their more inward Garrisons.

**3.** Not satisfied with some circumstance, result, etc.; dissatisfied, displeased.

Common in latter half of the 17th cent.; now *rare*.

*a* 1648 LD. HERBERT *Hen. VIII* (1683) 526 Both Princes remained unsatisfied of the others actions. 1652 J. WRIGHT tr. *Camus' Nat. Paradox* x. 253 Miestas [was] very unsatisfied with his Son's deportments. 1669 TEMPLE *Let. to Trevor* Wks. 1720 II. 202 He seemed a good deal unsatisfied that the Spanish Ambassador had received the Advice from England. 1731 *Gentl. Mag.* I. 436 Fortune..declar'd that whoever was unsatisfied with their Lot should complain to her. 1795 V. KNOX *Chr. Phil.* vi. I. 57 When he is observed, he is ashamed; and when he has done, he is unsatisfied. 1883 *American* VI. 250 Mr. Freeman is..unsatisfied with the review.

† **b.** Not satisfied by being paid. *Obs.*

1654 WHITLOCK *Zootomia* 130 The short, and long is now no sight so unpleasant as their unsatisfied Doctor. 1796 MME. D'ARBLAY *Camilla* IX. viii. V. 174 If they [*sc.* gamesters] were left unsatisfied, the credit of the young man would fall a sacrifice of their ill treatment.

**4.** Not settled by payment, etc.

1588 SHAKS. *L. L. L.* II. i. 139 If then..your father will restore But that one halfe which is vnsatisfied, We will giue vp our right in Aquitaine. 1632 in *10th Rep. Hist. MSS. Comm.* App. V. 483 Howe the same debt was paid..and what is yet behinde and unsatisfied. 1682 SCARLETT *Exchanges* 114 Upon pain of forfeiture of twenty five Guilders, and the Bill to be accounted unsatisfied. 1763 *Act 4 Geo. III*, c. i. 29 The Monies so remaining unsatisfied, or not discharged. 1879 F. HITCHMAN *Publ. Life Beaconsfield* I. 182 He was deeply in debt, and had a number of unsatisfied judgments out against him.

Hence **Unsa·tisfiedly** *adv.*

1661 BOYLE *Style of Script.* 172 Some of them,..after having Unsatisfiedly Travell'd thorough all sorts of Human Volumes, have Rested..only in these Divine Ones.

**Unsa·tisfiedness.** [UN-[1] 12.] The condition of being unsatisfied. (Freq. in 17th cent.)

1646 LD. DIGBY in Carte *Ormonde* (1735) III. 476 Rather out of an unsatisfiedness of his safety..than [etc.]. 1653 GAUDEN *Hierasp.* 74 Whence that unsatisfiedness, which carries the soul of man..to this height of coveting after a blessed eternity. 1741 RICHARDSON *Pamela* II. 387, I may ..rejoice in that happy State, where is..no Unsatisfiedness. 1860 PUSEY *Min. Proph.* 13 The soul..seeks to distract herself from her unrest and unsatisfiedness. 1886 LINSKILL *Haven under Hill* xxii, He had seen her loneliness, her soul's dimness and unsatisfiedness.

†**Unsa·tisfy,** *v. Obs.* (UN-[2] 3.) 1652 SHIRLEY *Doubtful Heir* Ded., I have presumed thus rather to let you know I can still honour you than unsatisfy myself by neglecting the first opportunity of presenting my service.

**Unsa·tisfying,** *ppl. a.* (UN-[1] 10.) 1656 JEANES *Fuln. Christ* 234 Not resting therefore in this unsatisfying answere, we will in the next place shew [etc.]. 1665 BOYLE *Occas. Refl.* IV. xiii, Parting with unsatisfying Trifles. 1760–2 GOLDSM. *Cit. W.* xxxvii, In this also..enthusiastic confidence or unsatisfying doubts terminate all our inquiries. 1813 SHELLEY *Q. Mab* IV. 248 Days of unsatisfying listlessness. 1837 LYTTON *Athens* I. 469 With this unsatisfying reply the messenger returned. 1879 MᶜCARTHY *Own Times* xxviii. II. 351 The political results of the war were to many minds equally unsatisfying.

Hence **Unsa·tisfyingness.**

1650 TRAPP *Comm. Gen.* xxv. 29 The curse of unsatisfyingness that lies upon them [*sc.* carnal pleasures]. 1883 H. DRUMMOND *Nat. Law in Spir. W.* 363 Its vagueness to the mere intellect,..its satisfying unsatisfyingness, its vast atmosphere.

**Unsa·tisfyingly,** *adv.* (UN-[1] 11.) 1653 JER. TAYLOR *Serm. for Year* iii. 41 They speak variously, and uncertainly, and unsatisfyingly. **Unsa·turable,** *a.* (UN-[1] 7 b and 5 b.) 1535 STEWART *Cron. Scot.* (Rolls) II. 426 Sleipand in sleuth, ..Vnsaturabill als of gulositie. 1816–30 BENTHAM *Offic. Apt. Maximized, Extr. Const. Code* 16 The perpetual saturation of appetites essentially unsaturable.

**Unsa·turated,** *ppl. a.* (UN-[1] 8.) 1758 REID tr. *Macquer's Chym.* I. 395 That portion of the Acid which remains unsaturated will dissolve the Mercury. 1791 *Phil. Trans.* LXXXI. 219 Any surplus of..air would only have remained unsaturated. 1832 *Nat. Philos., Electr.* II. § 53 (L.U.K.), Its unsaturated matter would have exerted an attractive force on the fluid. 1879 ROOD *Chromatics* xviii. 307 He must mainly use the pale unsaturated colours of nature.

**Unsatura·tion.** (UN-[1] 12.) 1885 REMSEN *Org. Chem.* 209 The condition of unsaturation is met with among carbon compounds in several forms.

**Unsau,** variant of ONSAW *Obs.*

†**Unsau·ght,** *sb. Obs.* [Late OE. *unseht* (f. *un-* UN-[1] 12 + *seht* SAUGHT *sb.*), **unsaht*, = ON. and Icel. *úsátt*, *ósátt*, *úsætt*, MSw. *osät*, MDa. *usæt*.] Discord, dissension; hostile speech.

*a* 1122 *O. E. Chron.* (Laud MS.) an. 1052, Hi macodon mæst þet unseht betweonan Godwine eorle & þam cynge. *c* 1205 LAY. 11456 Wulleð Romleode cumen to þissere þeode, ..& maken vnsæhte. *a* 1300 *Cursor M.* 28198 Wit flitt, wit brixil,..Myn euen-cristen haue i hurt, And oft vn-saght o him i said. 1710 RUDDIMAN *Gloss.* s.v. *Saucht*, *To live in unsaucht*, i.e. trouble. 1808 JAMIESON.

†**Unsau·ght,** *a. Obs.* [Late OE. *unseht* (f. *un-* UN-[1] 7 + *seht* SAUGHT *a.*), **unsaht* = ON. and Icel. *úsáttr*, MSw. *osatt*, *osätt*, MDa. *usaat* in sense 1.]

**1.** At variance or enmity; hostile.

*c* 1100 *O. E. Chron.* (MS. D.) an. 1067, Eadric cild & þa Bryttas wurdon unsehte. *c* 1205 LAY. 3930 Þas breþren weren swa wode..Þat al heo weren vn-sahte. 1303 R. BRUNNE *Handl. Synne* 482 With holy chyrche þey ben vnsaght. *c* 1350 *Lybeaus Disc.* 1421 For þey were unsauȝte [*v.r.* vnsyȝt] And eiþer oþres fo. 13.. *St. Erkenwald* 8 In Hengyst dawes þat þe Saxones vnsaȝt hadene sende hyder. ? *a* 1400 *Morte Arth.* 1306 That here are semblede in sale, vn-sawghte mott ȝe worthe! *c* 1475 *Golagros & Gaw.* 456 Than thai schupe for to assege segis vnsaught.

**2.** Dissatisfied, displeased.

? *a* 1300 *Salomon & Sat.* (1848) 275 Hit is mony gedelyng when me him ȝeueþ a lutel þyng, waxen wol vnsaþt. *a* 1310 in Wright *Lyric P.* xii. 42 Ant swore somme unsaht, That hem wes werk by-taht, longe er hit were lyht. 1390 GOWER *Conf.* III. 153 Of thilke folk that were unsauhte Toward here king for his pilage. *c* 1400 *Destr. Troy* 5057 Yf we be cause of þi kene yre, And þou vnsaght of þi sight sothely of vs two.

**3.** Not at ease; embarrassed; troubled, distressed.

*a* 1375 *Joseph Arim.* 64 Þe kyng..wolde haue red of his folk,..& þei forsaken hit han, & he vnsauht sittes. *a* 1400 *Sir Perc.* 2152 Thenne was scho unsaughte. Scho gret and cried in hir mone. *a* 1450 *Le Morte Arth.* 3189 The kynge gan lowde crye and calle, As marred man of wytte vnsaught. 1513 DOUGLAS *Æneid* XII. v. 201 This Chorineus als so fast Ruschit on his fa, thus fyrefangit and onsaucht.

Hence †**Unsau·ghtly** *adv.*; †**Unsau·ghtness.**

*a* 1000 in *Vercelli MS.* fol. 80 b, Þurh þæt þonne ariseð unsehtnesse betweoh twam cyningum & twam ȝebroðrum. *c* 1200 ORMIN 7187 Alle þa þatt lufenn toþþ & woh & unnsahhtnesse. ? *a* 1400 *Morte Arth.* 1501 Vnsaughtely he saide hyme þese sittande wordez. *Ibid.* 1847 Vnsaughtyly þey sette thane appone oure sere knyghttez.

**Unsa·veable,** *a.* (UN-[1] 7 b.) 1647 TRAPP *Marrow Gd. Authors* in *Comm. Ep.* 613 One that is unsaveable, or one that is undone by himself. 1874 M. ARNOLD in *Contemp. Rev.* Oct. 816 All the devices to save those unsaveable things, the Bible-miracles.

**Unsa·ved,** *ppl. a.* (UN-[1] 8.) 1648 HEXHAM II, *Onbehoedt*, vnpreserved, or vnsaved. [1775 ASH.] 1818 BENTHAM *Ch. Eng.*, *Catech. Exam.* 437 Why are these [souls] to be left unsaved..? 1838 S. BELLAMY *The Betrayal* 168 And there did answer these, unseen, but loud,..th' unsaved Of earth. 1866 B. NORTH *Ourselves* 36 A man..when he says he does not know the Lord..confesses that he is unsaved.

**Unsa·ving,** *ppl. a.* (UN-[1] 10.) 1628 FELTHAM *Resolves* II. lxiii. 179 If hee takes policie, that is both endlesse and vncertaine:..What to day is good, is to morrow vnsaving. 1714 POPE *Lett.* (1737) VI. 46, I would no more make a judgment of an author's genius from a damning critick, than I would of a man's religion from an unsaving zealot.

†**Unsa·vour,** *v.* [UN-[1] 14.] *intr.* To have no savour or agreeableness. *a* 1547 SURREY *Poems, Eccl.* iv. 58 In boost of outwarde works he taketh no delight, Nor wast of wourds; suche sacryfice unsauereth in his sight.

**Unsa·voured,** *ppl. a.* (UN-[1] 8.) 1435 [see UNSALT *a.*]. 1562 J. HEYWOOD *Prov. & Epigr.* (1867) 139 As yl is this othing: Ill sauerd sumthing, as vnsauerd nothyng. 1580 HOLLYBAND *Treas. Fr. Tong* s.v. *Goguelu*, A nice one, an vnsauoured one, a proud foole.

1897 *Allbutt's Syst. Med.* II. 880 Of what possible service are..blows unfelt, salts and feathers unsavoured?

Hence **Unsa·vouredly** *adv.*

1603 Florio *Montaigne* I. xxv. 84 He that meanes to speake vnsavouredly.

† **Unsa·vourest**, obs. superl. of Unsavoury *a.*

1599 Sandys *Europæ Spec.* (1605) Y 1 b, All which [*sc.* idols] are the vnsavorest dregs to the Iew in the world.

**Unsa·vourily**, *adv.* [Un-[1] 11.]

† **1. a.** So as to savour ill. **b.** Without savour; insipidly. *Obs.*

14.. *Langland's P. Pl.* C. xvi. 49 (MS. Laud 656), Here sauce was ouersoured & vnsauerilich ygrounde. *c* 1440 *Promp. Parv.* 367/1 Onsaveryly, *insipide.* *c* 1449 Pecock *Repr.* v. xv. 564 It is no nede forto seie ther of eny thing vnperfitli..and therfore vnsauorili here.

**2.** In an unpleasant or disagreeable manner.

1611 Cotgr., *Mausadement*, harshly, vnsauorily. 1641 Milton *Animadv.* 60 So often and so unsavourily has it been repeated, that the Reader may well cry, Downe with it. 1647 Trapp *Marrow Gd. Authors* in *Comm. Ep.* 646 Yea many times most unseasonably and unsavourily..they fell into those absurd disputes. 1899 *Westm. Gaz.* 21 Mar. 2/1 Tenanted by myriads of penguins, which nest unsavourily on the steep slopes.

**Unsa·vouriness.** [Un-[1] 12.]

† **1.** Want of savouriness; insipidity. *Obs.*

1398 *Trevisa's Barth. De P. R.* xix. lii. (1495) kk iiij, The nynthe sauour hyght werysshenesse & vnsaueryness. 1548 Elyot, *Insulsitas*,.. foolysshenesse, vnsauourynesse, lacke of grace. 1721 Bailey, *Insipidity*, Unsavouriness, Flatness.

**2.** The quality of being unsavoury or disagreeable.

1557 in Hakluyt *Voy.* (1598) I. 296 Any anoyance, stinke, or other vnsauorinesse..in the shippe. 1571 Golding *Calvin on Ps.* xxxiii. 7 It is an unsaverines not worthy the disproving. 1617 Woodall *Surg. Mate* (1639) 356 If any person, for the unsavourinesse of a medicine, will refuse helpe [etc.]. 1646 Sir T. Browne *Pseud. Ep.* iv. x. 202 If we concede a nationall unsavourinesse in any people, yet shall we finde the Iewes lesse subject hereto then any. 1654 T. Gouge *Chr. Directions* xx. 173 The unsavouriness of thy words and speeches. 1727 A. Hamilton *New Acc. E. Ind.* I. iii. 44 The Sea affords Variety of Fish, but not savoury. I believe their unsavouriness proceeds from the extreme Saltness of the Sea-water. 1765 Sterne *Tr. Shandy* vii. xxxii, In the little peevish contentions of nature betwixt hunger and unsavouriness. 1864 R. Kerr *Gentlem. House* 291 Flies..follow their noses, and their presence..is but an index of unsavouriness. 1884 *Manch. Exam.* 23 Sept. 5/2 Mudbanks .. in their unsightliness and unsavouriness when exposed.

† **Unsa·vourly**, *adv. Obs.* [Un-[1] 11.] = Unsavourily *adv.*

1377 Langl. *P. Pl.* B. xiii. 43 Her sauce was ouer soure & vnsauourely grounde. *a* 1395 Hylton *Scala Perf.* ii. xxxii. (W. de W. 1494), This seeth the soule..not..nakydly and vnsauourly as doth a clerke that seeth hym by his clergye onely. 1540–54 Croke *13 Ps.* (Percy Soc.) 20 My fode doeth taste vnsavourly. 1592 Greene *Groat's W. Wit* (1617) 8 Our fathers Precepts..were most vnsauerly to one of your yeeres applyed. 1660 Hickeringill *Jamaica* 38 Without it other things seem to want their taste, or relish out unsavourly.

† **Unsa·vourness**, obs. var. Unsavouriness.

1422 Yong tr. *Secreta Secret.* 98 Saltnesse, & vnctuosite, Egrenesse & vnsauournesse.

**Unsa·voury**, *a.* [Un-[1] 7.]

† **1.** Having no savour; not attractive to the taste; tasteless, insipid. *Obs.*

*a* 1225 *Ancr. R.* 262 Loke nu hwo grucche..of mistrum, oðer leane mel of unsauure metes, of poure pitaunce? 1377 Langl. *P. Pl.* B. xv. 425 Fresshe flesshe other fisshe whan it salt failleth, It is vnsauory. *c* 1400 Love *Bonavent. Mirr.* (1908) 108 Til thoruȝ his mercy..the vnsauery water and colde of aduersitie..be torned in to wyne and conforte. 1477 Norton *Ord. Alch.* v. in Ashm. (1652) 74 Also is Weerish tast called Unsavoury. 1576 Newton *Lemnie's Complex.* I. 87 Choler is bitter: .. Phlegme, vnsavery as water. 1601 Bp. W. Barlow *Defence* 89 The white of an egge, without salt, is flash, and vnsavery, sayth Job. 1610 Bp. Carleton *Jurisd.* 261 The Pope would hereby prooue vnsauery salt good for nothing but to be troden vnderfoot of men. 1652 Gaule *Magastrom.* 284 Crying out ..tread me under feet, as unsavory salt. 1784 Cowper *Task* i. 125 Hard fare! but such as boyish appetite Disdains not; nor the palate, undeprav'd By culinary arts, unsav'ry deems.

*transf.* 13.. *E. E. Allit. P.* B. 822 Þis vn-sauere hyne Louez no salt in her sauce. 1548 Udall *Erasm. Par. Luke* xix. 141 b, That same stemme of the Judaicall figtree brought foorth..vnsauourie, & vnripe people. 1585 Greene *Planetomachia* F 4 b, Phlegme..doulce, vnsauory & natural.

**b.** *fig.*

*c* 1449 Pecock *Repr.* i. xvi. 89 If such maner of arguyng.. schulde be sett in sermonyng, the sermon schulde be ful vnsauory. *c* 1450 tr. *De Imitatione* ii. viii. 48 Hov dry & hov harde þou art wiþoute ihesu! hov unsauory, hov veyne, if þou coueite eny þinge wiþoute ihesu! 1534 More *Treat. Passion* Wks. 1291/1 The context of the story shuld..seme very farre vnsauery, by reason of the often interposicion of the iniciall letters. 1540 Morysine *Vives' Introd. Wysd.* G ij, Bodely workes be unsavery, excepte they have sauce from the hart. 1603 Holland *Plutarch's Mor.* 1188 Some ..will say, that the oracles..be none of his [*sc.* Apollo's], because they are but rudely made and unsavery. 1634 Milton *Comus* 742 The good thereof Consists in mutual and partak'n bliss, Unsavoury in th' injoyment of it self.

† **c.** *Bot.* (See quots.) *Obs.*

1548 Turner *Names Herbes* (E.D.S.) 77 Symphytum petreum..; this herbe..maye be called in english vnsauery Margerum. 1597 Gerarde *Herbal* ii. 948 *Abrotanum Inodorum*, Vnsauorie Sothernwood, .. growes flat vpon the grounde with broade leaues. 1660 *Catal. Plant. Cantab. Index* 6 Unsavoury field Cranes-bill, *cicutæ folio inodorum.* 1728 Bradley *Dict. Bot.*, *Thymum Inodorum*, Unsavory Thyme.

**2. a.** Unpleasant or disagreeable to the taste.

*c* 1380 Wyclif *Serm.* Sel. Wks. II. 46 For scheep ben goode for to ete, and getis fleish is unsavery. *c* 1400 *Pilgr. Sowle* (Caxton, 1483) iv. ii. 58 These fowle buskes and wylde myght nought fructyfyen no.. lusty fruyte, but bytter and vnsauoury. 1555 Eden *Decades* (Arb.) 222 The flesshe of this beaste is fylthy and vnsauery. 1577 B. Googe *Heresbach's Husb.* ii. 86 b, The geathered Olyue, if it lye to long in heapes, putrifieth by reason of heate, and makes vnsauery oyle. 1617 Woodall *Surg. Mate* (1639) 356 An approoved good Medicine, and not much unsavovry to bee taken. 1667 Milton *P. L.* v. 401 Unsavourie food perhaps To spiritual Natures. 1812 J. Henry *Camp. agst. Quebec* 97 Towards March they become unsavoury, but in no way tainted. 1856 Kane *Arct. Expl.* II. iii. 42 As unsavory a dose of flax-seed and quinine as was ever honored by the name of beer.

**b.** Disagreeable or offensive to the sense of smell, or to refined feelings.

1539 Elyot *Cast. Helthe* 55 These excrementes be none other, but matter superfluouse and vnsauery. 1582 Stanyhurst *Æneis* iii. (Arb.) 78 Thee victals..They do leaue haulf mangled with sent vnsauerye bepoudred. 1591 Unton *Corr.* (Roxb.) 199 In his sicknes none could endure to be with him, he was so unsavorie. *a* 1656 Bp. Hall *Rem. Wks.* (1660) 108 Those..which scent an unsavory breath turne their heads aside. 1684 *Contempl. St. Man* ii. vi. (1699) 196 Unsavoury Smells, so proper unto Prisons. 1725 Pope *Odyss.* iv. 598 Unsavoury stench of oil. 1784 Cowper *Task* iv. 196 The smoke of lamps, The pent-up breath of an unsav'ry throng. 1825 Waterton *Wand. S. Amer.* ii. 103 An unsavoury little beast, called bug.

*fig.* 1547 J. Harrison *Exhort. Scottes* 213, I will stirre that vnsauery sinke of treson and trecherie.

*Prov.* 1546 J. Heywood *Prov.* (1867) 30 Great bost and small roste, Maketh vnsauery mouthes.

**3.** Unpleasant, disagreeable, distasteful.

*c* 1380 Wyclif *Wks.* (1880) 177 Þei sclaundren goddis lawe ..& maken it vnsavory to worldly men. *c* 1386 Chaucer *Pars. T.* ¶ 510 Thurgh which bitternesse euery good dede of his neighebor semeth to hym bitter and vnsauory. *c* 1440 *Gesta Rom.* xxiii. 80 This is an vnsavery question; this rebavde we saw never before. *c* 1456 Pecock *Bk. of Faith* (1909) 116 Oold custom..wole make that these bokis at first schulen be unsavery. 1573 Tusser *Husb.* (1878) 17 To keepe no more but needfullie, and count excesse vnsauerie. 1591 Savile *Tacitus, Hist.* iii. xxvi. 130 All that tended to safety was vnsauory. 1637 Gillespie *Eng. Pop. Cerem.* iv. viii. 37 This..will be very unsavory language, to many Arminianized Conformitans. 1657 Sparrow *Bk. Com. Prayer* 256 Suppose some Preachers should be so careful, as not to vent any thing unsavoury. 1845 James *Arrah Neil* v, You came hither upon an unsavoury errand.

† **b.** Ill-natured. *Obs.*[—1]

1568 T. Howell *Arb. Amitie* (1879) 45 Then pleasant speech suppresse, and faine a sowre unsauerie looke.

**4.** Objectionable on moral grounds; having an unpleasant or disagreeable character or association.

**a.** Of persons.

1401 *Pol. Poems* (Rolls) II. 52 For Sathanas by ȝour sawes is sent into soulis, that ben ful unsavery. *c* 1450 tr. *De Imitatione* i. xxiv. 33 O þou most wrecchid and unsauory synner, what shalt þou answere god? 1552 Huloet, Vnsauery queane, *blittea meretrix.* 1605 Camden *Rem.* 219 That they be the salt of the earth, and if the salt once appall, the world must needes waxe vnsauerie. 1849 James *Woodman* vi, They are very unsavoury fellows.

**b.** Of things, language, etc.

1536 Elyot in Croft *E.'s Gov.* (1883) I. p. cxxvi, Unsavery gloses and commentes. 1550 Bale *Eng. Votaries* ii. iii, Professinge the vnsauery vse of Sarum. 1586 W. Webbe *Eng. Poetrie* (Arb.) 54 The motion of some vnsauery loue, such as in the sixt Eglogue he seemeth to deale withall. 1615 Day *Festivals* Ep. Ded., The Unsavorie Pamphlets.. that have passed the Presse as well as Sermons. 1657 Trapp *Comm. Ezra* vi. 11 Those..who turne it into a.. pest-house of noysome lusts by their unsavoury speeches. 1723 Wodrow *Corr.* (1843) III. 26, I heard some account of his unsavoury carriage when a student.., and that he was stopped in his licentiatory trials for some immorality. 1882 *Athenæum* 23 Dec. 842/3 A number of grim anecdotes and unsavoury details. 1894 Sir E. Sullivan *Woman* 44 There are many unsavoury laws in our code.

**Unsaw·ed**, *ppl. a.* [Un-[1] 8.] Not saw-edged. Also = next (Ash, 1775).

1786 Abercrombie *Gard. Assist.*, *Arr.* 42 Mock privet,.. Oval unsawed leaved. 1799 *View Agric. Lincoln.* 128 An unsawed sharp reaping hook.

**Unsaw·n**, *ppl. a.* (Un-[1] 8 b.)

1572 *Wills & Inv. N. C.* (Surtees) I. 349 Wood tymber for buylding, bords sawen and vnsawen. 1678 Moxon *Mech. Exerc.* v. 95 When he draws back his Saw, the Work-man bears it lightly off the unsawn Stuff. 1865 Cameron *Malayan India* 31 Huge rafts of unsawn newly-cut timber.

**Un-Sa·xon**, *a.* (Un-[1] 7.) 1848 Lytton *Harold* iv. iii, A lover of things un-Saxon. 1877 Tennyson *Harold* ii. ii, When that un-Saxon blast..drave and crack'd His boat on Ponthieu beach. 1885 Sweet *O. E. Texts* 177 Both texts show several un-Saxon forms.

**Unsay·**, *v.* [Un-[2] 3, 7. Cf. OE. *ontsecgan* (once), to renounce, abjure, OHG. *antsagên*, MHG. (G.) *entsagen*, MDu. (Du.) *ontzeggen*.]

† **1.** *trans.* To deny. *Obs.*

*c* 1460 *Oseney Reg.* 167 Fore þ[e] saide Richard..may not vnsay but þat þ[e] saide Hugh of Tywe yafe..the foresaide tenement.

**2.** To withdraw, retract, or revoke (something said or written).

1483 *Vulgaria abs Terentio* 29 J say & vnsay itt. 1557 N. T. (Genev.) *Acts* xi. 18 *note*, That they were not ashamed to vnsay that wherof they had vniustely blamed Peter. 1571 Golding *Calvin on Ps.* lxxiii. 1 They openly unsaid that which they had sayd afore. 1613 T. Milles tr. *Mexia's Treas. Anc. & Mod. T.* II. 964/2 So shall you be sure, neuer to vnsay your owne words. 1687 *Reflect. on Hind & Panther* 21 He has Face enough to say or unsay any thing. 1741 Richardson *Pamela* III. 322 The less you said against her, the less you'd have to unsay. 1819 Shelley *Cenci* iv. i. 137 For thine own sake unsay those dreadful words. 1884 W. C. Smith *Kildrostan* 53 Yet you can speak thus calmly of unsaying All we have said.

*transf.* 1745 Akenside *Odes Sev. Subjects, On Love* x, Even now, While thus I preach the Stoic strain, Unless I shun Olympia's view, An hour unsays it all again.

**b.** *intr.* (Freq. in 17th cent.)

1575–85 Abp. Sandys *Serm.* vii. 111 That it is good Christendome to lie, sweare, and forsweare, to say and vnsay to any. 1646 Evance *Noble Order* 3 How can God be said to Say and unsay? 1692 Washington tr. *Milton's Def. Pop.* ii. 43 Who would trust him..that in things of so great concern says and unsays without any consideration? 1878 Spurgeon *Treas. Dav.* Ps. cxvi. 11 It is so much easier to say than to unsay.

Hence **Unsay·ing** *vbl. sb.*; **Unsay·er.**

1583 Golding *Calvin on Deut.* clxxxix. 1177 Hee is no vnsaier as mortall men bee. 1647 Hexham i. s.v., An Vnsaying of that which one hath spoken or written. 1669 Stillingfl. *Serm.* x. (1673) 190 As though the unsaying what we had done..were abundant compensation..for the affronts. 1710 Steele *Tatler* No. 178 ¶ 2 A most happy art in saying and unsaying. 1856 R. A. Vaughan *Mystics* xiii. i. II. 301 Such saying and unsaying is not convenient merely,..but in the highest degree artistic.

† **Unsay·ed**, *ppl. a. Sc. Obs.* [Un-[1] 8 + Say *v.*[2]] Untried. *a* 1598 Ferguson *Scot. Prov.* (1667) 7 All things are good unseyed.

**Unsca·bbard**, *v.* (Un-[2] 5.)

1611 Florio, *Sfoderare*, to vn-sheathe, to vn-scabbard. 1813 Scott *Rokeby* ii. xxi, A warlike form..steps 'twixt Wilfrid and his foe; Nor then unscabbarded his brand. 1848 Steinmetz *Hist. Jesuits* I. 130 The fiend of religious persecution unscabbarded the sword.

**Unsca·bbarded**, *ppl. a.* (Un-[1] 8, or f. prec.)

1562 in Strype *Stow's Surv.* (1720) II. 307/1 No Man shall go in the Streets..with Bow bent,..nor with Sword unscabber'd. 1804 Larwood *No Gun Boats* 37 The unscabbarded sword of the bombastic Invader.

**Unsca·lable**, *a.* (Un-[1] 7 b and 5 b.)

1579–80 North *Plutarch* (1595) 1083 After he had measured the height of the wall, he reported that the place was not vnscalable. 1611 Shaks. *Cymb.* iii. i. 20 Your Isle, which stands As Neptunes Parke, ribb'd, and pal'd in With Oakes vnskaleable. 1652 Heylyn *Cosmogr.* iii. 222 High and unscalable walls. 1751 R. Paltock *P. Wilkins* I. 91, I saw no Entrance into the Island,..nor any thing but the same unscalable Rock. 1818 Keats *Endym.* iii. 23 There are throned seats unscalable But by a patient wing. 1850 Lynch *Theoph. Trinal* xi. 211 The frowning unscalable rocks of worldly custom.

**Unsca·lded**, *ppl. a.* (Un-[1] 8.) 1615 J. Stephens *Satyr. Ess.* (ed. 2) vi. 189 That mountebank preparing oyle which kept his hands vnscalded.

**Unsca·le**, *v.*[1] [Un-[2] 4, 4 b + Scale *sb.*[2]]

**1.** *trans.* To clean (fish, etc.) from scales.

*a* 1510 Stanbridge *Vulgaria* (W. de W.) A vj b, *Desquamo*, [I] vnscale fysshe. 1598 Florio, *Scagliare*, to skale or vnskale fish. 1655 Moufet & Bennet *Health's Improv.* 168 [Shrimps] are unscaled, to vent the windiness which is in them, being sodden with their scales. 1719 *Glossogr. Angl. Nova*, Disquamation, is an unscaling a Fish, or the like.

**2.** *fig.* To free (the eyes or sight) from scales.

1635 Quarles *Embl.* iii. Prol. 44 Grones fresht with vowes, and vowes made salt with teares, Vnscale his eyes. 1644 Milton *Areop.* (Arb.) 72 Methinks I see her as an Eagle.. purging and unscaling her long abused sight at the fountain it self of heav'nly radiance. 1827 Pollok *Course T.* i. 3 Thou who of old The prophet's eye unscaled. 1867 H. Macmillan *Bible Teach.* xiii. 265 The Spirit unscales our eyes, and unveils Christ before us.

**Unsca·le**, *v.*[2] [Un-[2] 7 + Scale *v.*[3]] *intr.* To climb down again. *c* 1470 Harding *Chron.* ccxviii. i, They shot their gonnes, and with their ladders scaled, But nought auailed, thei were so wel of bet, When they our hoste sawe anone they vnscaled.

**Unsca·led**, *a.* [Un-[1] 9 + Scale *sb.*[2]] Not furnished with scales; smooth-skinned.

1562 Bulleyn *Bulwarke, Bk. Simples* 78 b, Vnscaled Fyshes, as Eeles, Tenches. 1647 Hexham i, Vnscaled, *ongeschubt.*

**Unsca·led**, *ppl. a.*[1] [Un-[1] 8 + Scale *v.*[2]] Not having the scales removed.

1585 Holinshed *Chron.* II. *Hist. Scot.* 128/2 Now had the king appointed for euerie one of their chambers one man apparelled in garments pretilie deuised and made of fish skins vnscaled [L. *haud desquammatis*].

**Unsca·led**, *ppl. a.*[2] [Un-[1] 8 or Un-[2] 8 + Scale *sb.*[2]] Not darkened by scales; free or freed from scales.

1827 Pollok *Course T.* vii. 527 Messengers Of peace,.. whose eye, unscaled, Saw up the path of immortality. 1844 Is. Williams *Baptistery* xxiv. 251 We learn to look with your unscaled eyes On all things here we prize.

**Unsca·led**, *ppl. a.*[3] [Un-[1] 8 + Scale *v.*[3]] Unascended.

1812 J. Wilson *Isle of Palms*, etc. 373 The cliffs, In unscaled majesty, must frown no more. 1860 Tyndall *Glac.* i. ii. 21 The Weisshorn, then..unscaled. 1886 *Pall Mall G.* 6 Aug. 5/2 Vast glaciers and unscaled snowfields.

**Unsca·lped**, *ppl. a.* (Un-[1] 8.)

[1775 Ash.] 1814 Southey *Lett.* (1856) II. 388 Philip had waylaid and murdered a party of these Indians, and left them unscalped. 1884 Nourse *Early Rec. Lancaster, Mass.* 229 Women and children, scalped or unscalped, were paid for at half price.

**Unsca·ly**, *a.* (Un-[1] 7.) 1715 Gay *Trivia* ii. 416 The jointed lobster and unscaly soale. **Unsca·ndalize**, *v.* (Un-[2] 6 c.) 1781 Charl. Burney in *Early Diary F. Burney* (1889) II. 294, I said a great deal to her to *un*scandalize her, but I don't know whether I did at last. **Unsca·ndalized**, *ppl. a.* (Un-[1] 8.) 1618 T. Gainsforde *Hist. P. Warbeck* 78 [He] may sit downe with a safe conscience, but not vnscandalized or maligned of some of his owne rancke. **Unsca·ndalous**, *a.* (Un-[1] 7.) 1614 R. Harris *Samuel's Funerall* (1618) To Rdr., He much respected .. euery learned and vnscandalous Preacher. *a* **1628** F. GREVIL *Sidney* (1652) 3 This representing of..actions of men unfeigned and unscandalous Images.

**Unsca·nnable,** *a.* (UN-[1] 7 b.)
**1815** W. TAYLOR in Robberds *Mem.* (1843) II. 458 The lines..are unscannable. **1856** BADHAM in *Cambr. Ess.* 291 Hopeless nonsense and unscannable verse. **1876** M. COLLINS *Fr. Midn. to Midn.* II. ii. 223 Analytic unscannable blank verse.

**Unsca·nned,** *ppl. a.* (UN-[1] 8.)
**1577** HOLINSHED *Chron.* II. *Descr. Irel.* 5, I woulde haue beene easily perswaded..to rest as a lukewarme Neuter in omitting the one and the other vnskande. **1595** DANIEL *Civ. Wars* I. xciii, What he had in hand Left it [*sc.* the vision] to his diuerted thoughts vnskand. **1607** SHAKS. *Cor.* III. i. 313 This Tiger-footed-rage, when it shall find The harme of vnskan'd swiftnesse. **1652** BENLOWES *Theoph.* VII. lxxxvi, O Light unscann'd! Of wisdom every glance Beams only from Thy countenance. **1813** SHELLEY *Q. Mab* III. 15 Turn thee, surpassing Spirit! Much yet remains unscanned. **1842** J. B. FRASER *Allee Neemroo* II. 283 Furtive sidelong glances ..which left nothing unobserved or unscanned. **1872** CALVERLEY *Fly Leaves, Motherhood* 92 Where the sunbeams fall Unscanned upon the broken wall.

**Unsca·nted,** *ppl. a.* (UN-[1] 8.) **1599** DANIEL *Musoph.* 846 Maiestie..with her full face,..with all her raies, Vnscanted of her parts, vnshadowed In any darkened poynt.

† **Unsca·pable,** *a. Obs.* [UN-[1] 7 b.] Unescapable.
**1382** WYCLIF *Wisd.* xvii. 16 Vnscapable, or that myȝt not be fled, nede he suffrede. *c* **1449** PECOCK *Repr.* v. vi. 514 The synne is as it were vnscapeable and vnavoidable of him. *c* **1455** — *Folewer* 95 Þis vnscapable peruertid doom. **1554** KNOX *Faythf. Admon.* G 5 To instructe vs that lyuelye fayth..is able to carye vs thorowe such parelles as be unscapable to nature.

Hence † **Unsca·pably** *adv. Obs.*
*c* **1449** PECOCK *Repr.* III. v. 308 If eny man be in contrarie wise vndisposid vnscapabili. *Ibid.* v. vi. 516. *c* **1455** — *Folewer* 95 Þe doom of resoun is derkid ful oft..vnscapabli bi passions of þe louȝer wittis.

**Unsca·red,** *ppl. a.* (UN-[1] 8.)
**1742** R. BLAIR *Grave* 247 The high-fed worm..Riots unscared. **1784** COWPER *Task* IV. 561 Then sleep was..unscar'd By drunken howlings. **1842** J. WILSON *Chr. North* I. 46 Birds..sung their best, unscared on hedge, bush, and tree. **1878** B. TAYLOR *Deukalion* IV. iv. 159 These simple lives may own contentment now unscared.

**Unsca·rfed,** *ppl. a.* (UN-[1] 8; cf. SCARF *v.*[1]) **1634** SIR T. HAWKINS tr. *Caussin's Holy Court* III. 58 The great God.. was vnscarfed in the crib..in such sort, that you need lift vp but simple clothes to know him. **Unsca·rified,** *ppl. a.* (UN-[1] 8.) [1775 ASH.] *a* **1834** COLERIDGE *Lit. Rem.* (1836) II. 239 An unsullied, unscarified mirror!

**Unsca·rred,** *ppl. a.* (UN-[1] 8.)
**1594** SHAKS. *Rich. III*, IV. iv. 209 So she may liue vnscarr'd of bleeding slaughter. **1598** B. JONSON *Ev. Man in Hum.* I. iv, Is't like, that factious beauty will preserue The soueraigne state of chastitie vnscard? **1607** SHAKS. *Timon* IV. iii. 161 The vnscarr'd Braggerts of the Warre. **1817** BYRON *Mazeppa* xvii, Flanks unscarr'd by spur or rod. **1856** MISS MULOCK *Noble Life* xiv, A battle from which no woman ever comes out unwounded or unscarred. **1884** *Harper's Mag.* Mar. 524/2 Solid and defiant as it looks, the sea has not left it unscarred.

**Unsca·thed,** *ppl. a.* (UN-[1] 8. Cf. ON. and Icel. *ú-*, *óskaðaðr*, MSw. *oskadhad*, Sw. *oskadad.*)
Before 19th cent. *Sc.* and somewhat rare.
*c* **1375** *Sc. Leg. Saints* vii. (*James min.*) 608 Þat I and þai ..In gud fath sal vnschait be. **1425** *Sc. Acts Parlt., Jas. I* (1814) II. 11/2 Quhil it be knawin..at þe cuntre be vnscaithit of þaim. **1461** *Extr. Aberd. Reg.* (1844) I. 22 That man.. sal..kepe the toun vnscathit..of all dettis and chargis acht be hym. **1567–8** *Reg. Privy Council Scot.* I. 613 To be unharmit, unskaythit, or unmolestit be ony of the liegis. **1787** BURNS *Tam Samson's Elegie* xvii, Unskaith'd by Death's gleg gullie, Tam Samson's livin! **1827** LYTTON *Falkland* 25, I passed through the ordeal unshrinking, yet not unscathed. *a* **1862** BUCKLE *Misc. Wks.* (1872) I. 103 That intellect which had conducted them unscathed through such..dangers. **1882** A. W. WARD *Dickens* i. 9 Whatever his experiences of this kind may have been, he passed unscathed through them.

† **Unsca·thely,** *a. Obs.*—[1] [UN-[1] 7. Cf. ON. *úskaðligr* (MSw. *oskadheliker*).] Harmless. **13..** *St. Erkenwald* 278 Þe skilfulle & þe vnskathely skelton ay to me. **Unsca·thing,** *pres. pple.* [UN-[1] 5d.] Unharming. **1437** *Dunfermline Reg.* (Bann. Cl.) 285 Þai sel kepe þe wateris lauchfully vnskathand vthir. **Unsca·ttered,** *ppl. a.* (UN-[1] 8.) **1531** ELYOT *Gov.* I. ii, Whiche..was wonderfully pacified, and the armie unscatered, by the maiestie of Agamemnon. **1814** WORDSW. *Excurs.* IV. 453 The cawing rooks, and seamews from afar, Hovering..By the rough wind unscattered. † **Unscau·berked,** *ppl. a. Obs.*—[1] [UN-[1] 8.] Unscabbarded. *c* **1430** *Pilgr. Lyf Manhode* I. cxxv. (1869) 66 That oother..hadde his swerd vnshethed and vnscauberked. **Unsca·vengered,** *ppl. a.* (UN-[1] 8.) **1846** DICKENS *Pict. Italy* Lyons, etc., The undrained, unscavengered qualities of a foreign town. **Unsce·nt,** *v.* (UN-[2] 4.) **1632** QUARLES *Div. Fancies* IV. xxxi, Weeds that fall Into thy Garden, . Whose loathsom smel unscent thy sweeter Flow'rs. **Unsce·nted,** *ppl. a.* (UN-[1] 8.) [1775 ASH.] **1784** COWPER *Task* I. 416 Who..Renounce the odours of the open field For the unscented fictions of the loom. **Unsce·ptical,** *a.* (UN-[1] 7.) **1851** MRS. BROWNING *Casa Guidi Wind.* II. 92 Forgive, that I forgot the mind which runs Through absolute races, too unsceptical!

**Unsce·ptre,** *v.* (UN-[2] 4. Cf. Du. *ontsc(h)epteren*, G. *entsceptern*, *-zeptern.*)
**1594** *Zepheria* xxxviii, Needes must I wish..That thou vnsceptred be of natures royaltie. **1628** QUARLES *Argalus & P.* I. Wks. (Grosart) III. 247/1 If he had, with his victorious hand, Unsceptred halfe the Princes in the land. **1642** T. CASE *God's Rising* (1644) 8 The Enemies of Gods truth and people would..not unscepter him only, but un-essence him.

**Unsce·ptred,** *ppl. a.* [UN-[1] 8 and UN-[2] 8.] Having no sceptre; deprived of a sceptre.
**1752** YOUNG *Brothers* I. i, How say'st, unsceptred boaster! This to me! **1798** *Anti-Jacobin* No. 24, So..the unscepter'd Lear Heav'd the loud sigh. **1820** KEATS *Hyperion* I. 19 Upon the sodden ground His old right hand lay..dead, Unsceptred. **1854** J. D. BURNS *Vis. Proph.* 20 The idols fall unsceptred from their thrones.

**Unsche·duled,** *ppl. a.* (UN-[1] 8.) **1889** *Daily News* 24 July 3/1 Consumers [of electric light] in the unscheduled districts. **Unscho·lar,** *sb.* (UN-[1] 12.) **1545** ASCHAM *Toxoph.* (Arb.) 38, I tell you plainlye, scholer or vnscholer, ..I wolde thinke it were my dutie..to set forwarde that thing. **Unscho·lar,** *v.* (UN-[2] 6 b.) **1823** CHALMERS *Serm.* I. 351 You cannot unscholar demagogues down to the level of an untaught multitude.

**Unscho·larlike,** *a.* (UN-[1] 7 c.)
**1616** CHAMPNEY *Voc. Bps.* 70 Hence likewise is solved that vnscholerlike question. **1716** M. DAVIES *Athen. Brit.* III. 24 Dissenting Sermons,..full of such Unscholar-like Vulgarities. **1760** STERNE *Tr. Shandy* III. xxxvi, 'Tis just as discreditable and unscholar-like a question, Sir. **1834** *Gentl. Mag.* CIV. I. 10 The Duke of Bedford he represented as coarse and unscholarlike. **1881** *Athenæum* 30 July 140/2 The execution of the work can only be described as essentially unscholarlike.

**Unscho·larly,** *a.* (UN-[1] 7.)
**1784** SIR W. JONES *Gods of Greece* Wks. 1799 I. 269 The confusion of analogy in the names of the planets is inelegant, unscholarly, and unphilosophical. **1879** MISS YONGE *Cameos* IV. xviii. 206 The unscholarly way in which the debate had been conducted. **1884** *Athenæum* 16 Feb. 215/3 Strype.. states that the custom of ordaining unscholarly candidates speedily passed away.

**Unschola·stic,** *a.* (UN-[1] 7.)
**1690** LOCKE *Hum. Und.* III. x. 242 It was to the unscholastick Statesman, that the Governments of the World owed their..Liberties. **1701** NORRIS *Ideal World* II. xii. 441 Which way of speaking is also not altogether unscholastick. **1826** J. GILCHRIST *Lect.* 63 The understanding of every commonsense, unscholastic inquirer. **1843** BETHUNE *Sc. Fireside Stor.* 120 This piece of ethical philosophy..is perhaps new to the schoolmen, though by no means new to their unscholastic brethren.

**Unschoo·l,** *v.* (UN-[2] 3.)
**1820** MILMAN *Fall Jerusalem* 10 We must unschool our royal pupil, And cast him back to the common herd of men. **1862** LOWELL *Biglow P.* Ser. II. ii. P 3 [I] have heard those talk of England, who..could not unschool their lips from calling her the Mother-Country. **1862** LYTTON *Str. Story* II. 159 If I unschool myself to believe that in what I have just experienced there is no mental illusion.

**Unschoo·led,** *ppl. a.* and *a.* [UN-[1] 8, 9.]
**1.** Uneducated, untaught.
**1594** HOOKER *Eccl. Pol.* IV. xiv. § 2 They were..poore, simple, vnschooled altogether and vnlettered men. **1615** SYLVESTER *Job Triumphant* Proem 54 Mine un-schooled and unskilfull Muse. **1762** FALCONER *Shipwr.* I. 184 In art unschool'd, each veteran rule he prized. **1865** GROTE *Plato* I. vi. 222 He especially warns Dionysius against talking about these matters to unschooled men. **1873** BLACKIE *Lett. to Wife* (1909) 222 The vulgar unschooled mind.
**b.** *spec.* Not educated at school; not made to attend school. Also *absol.*
**1841** EMERSON *Ess., History* ad fin., The Indian, the child, and unschooled farmer's boy. **1847** *Eng. Rev.* No. II. 18 There were only 21,609 children unschooled. **1898** *Daily News* 14 Oct. 4/7 It is the unschooled that make the gaolbirds.
**2.** Untrained, undisciplined.
**1589** NASHE *Anat. Absurditie* Ep., From such entercourse of excuse, let my vnschooled indignities conuert them selues to your courtesie. **1602** SHAKS. *Ham.* I. ii. 97 It shewes..a Minde impatient, An Vnderstanding simple, and vnschool'd. **1811** MISS L. M. HAWKINS *C'tess & Gertr.* I. 69 Any power, that her..experience might give her over the errors of so unschooled a husband. **1838** PRESCOTT *Ferd. & Is.* x. II. 8 A panic-struck mob, unschooled by discipline or experience. **1871** MISS BRADDON *Lovels of Arden* iii. 41 A generous and somewhat lofty nature, perhaps, but unschooled and unchastened as yet.
**b.** Not affected or made artificial by education; natural, spontaneous.
**1815** MOORE *Epil. to Lady Dacre's Ina* 43 When lovely Woman, all unschool'd and wild, Blush'd without art. **1873** M. ARNOLD *Lit. & Dogma* iii. 100 The artless, unschooled perception of a child. **1883** R. BRIDGES *Prometheus* 648 The unschooled promptings of his best desire.
**3.** Not provided with a school.
**1872** M. COLLINS *Princess Clarice* II. ii. 28 A dingy village, undrained and unschooled.

**Unsci·ence.** (UN-[1] 12 and 5 b.)
*c* **1374** CHAUCER *Boeth.* v. pr. iii. (1868) 156 It nys nat oonly vnscience, but it is deceiuable oppinioun..fer fro þe soþe of science. **1603** FLORIO *Montaigne* III. xii. 629 Purposely I treate of nothing, but of nothing; nor of any one science, but of vnscience. **1878** PUSEY (*title*), Un-science, not Science, Adverse to Faith. A Sermon preached before the University of Oxford. **1896** *Trans. Victoria Inst.* XXVIII. 200 This Method..has been influential both in the science and the unscience of all time.

**Unsci·enced,** *a.* (UN-[1] 9.) **1891** *Harper's Mag.* July 316/1 What a work like Mr. James's..does for the unscienced reader is [etc.].

**Unscienti·fic,** *a.* (UN-[1] 7.) Also *absol.*
[1775 ASH.] **1813** F. S. N. DOUGLAS *Ess. Greeks* ii. 85 The admiration, with which the beautiful Caryatides.. inspire the most unscientific. **1827** FARADAY *Chem. Manip.* vii. 204 This distinction is known to be very unscientific, but it is convenient in operations. **1877** *N. & Q.* 22 Dec. 498/1 In this matter of Latin pronunciation old fogies like myself are..on the side..of the unscientific.

**Unscienti·fically,** *adv.* (UN-[1] 11.)
[1775 ASH.] **1794** HUTTON *Philos. Light*, etc. 107 A principle perhaps no less unscientifically conceived;..that of reflected heat. **1858** GREENER *Gunnery* 278 Unscientifically formed projectiles. **1886** *Contemp. Rev.* Jan. 11 To talk then, in.. [nature's] name, of the rights of conscience,..is to talk unscientifically.

**Unsci·ntillating,** *ppl. a.* (UN-[1] 10.) **1807** J. BARLOW *Columb.* v. 676 Prometheus like, to snatch a beam of day And homeward bear the unscintillating ray.

**Unsci·ssored,** *ppl. a.* (UN-[1] 8.)
**1608** SHAKS. *Per.* III. iii. 29 (Q.[1]), Till she be married, madam,..Vnsistered [*read* Vnsissered]..shall this hair of mine remain. *c* **1631** T. CAREW *Elegy Death Donne* 5 The uncisor'd Churchman. *a* **1639** — *Poems, To my Friend G. N.* 64 Nor, on a Marble Tun, his face besmear'd With grapes, is curl'd uncizard Bacchus rear'd.

**Unsco·ffed,** *ppl. a.* (UN-[1] 8.) **1622** WITHER *Philarete* B 4 b, What hopes haue I to passe vnscoft I pray..? **Unsco·lded,** *ppl. a.* (UN-[1] 8.) [1775 ASH.] **1855** E. FORBES *Lit. Papers* vi. 176 We like this book too well to permit us to pass over a fault unscolded. † **Unsco·mfited,** *ppl. a. Obs.* [UN-[1] 8.] Unconquered. *c* **1400** *Found. St. Bartholomew's* 23 The vertu in her conceyuyd of vnskunfitid feith. *Ibid.* 34 The coronacioun of the most vnskunfitid kynge of Englonde, Henry the secunde. **Unsco·nced,** *ppl. a.* (UN-[1] 8 + SCONCE *sb.*[4] or *v.*[2]) **1735** SAVAGE *Progr. Divine* 17 Him, quite unsconc'd, the butt'ry book shall own.

**Unsco·rched,** *ppl. a.* (UN-[1] 8.)
**1601** SHAKS. *Jul. C.* I. iii. 18 His Hand, Not sensible of fire, remain'd vnscorch'd. **1612** WARNER *Alb. Eng.* XI. lxvii. 285 Thogh thou could'st buzze about the flame, & keepe vnskorcht thy wings. **1651** STANLEY *Poems, Love Deposed* iv, We..unscorch'd may Like atoms play, And wanton in the sunshine of your eyes. **1816** SCOTT *Antiq.* xviii, The moss and wild flowers were unscorched. **1843** PRESCOTT *Mexico* II. iv. I. 247 From all these fiery trials..he came out unscorched. **1856** FROUDE *Hist. Eng.* ix. II. 345 If he threw them [*sc.* toads] into the fire, they hopped back to him unscorched.

**Unsco·re,** *v.* (UN-[2] 3. Cf. SCORE *v.* 6.)
**1621** BP. MOUNTAGU *Diatribæ* 184 Goe and unskore your margine with those many quotations,..ranged wel-nigh from the top to the bottome of that page.

**Unsco·red,** *ppl. a.* (UN-[1] 8.)
**1596** NASHE *Saffron Walden* T ij b, He hath..not left anie..Almain scribe..vncompared or vnscoard. **1818** BUSBY *Gram. Mus.* 491 He..should ascertain his powers of invention, in unscored Composition. **1894** *Westm. Gaz.* 7 Mar. 2/1 He will leave no point unscored in favour of the people.

**Unsco·rned,** *ppl. a.* (UN-[1] 8.)
*a* **1425** tr. *Arderne's Treat. Fistula*, etc. 4 He that skorneþ other men shal not go away vnskorned. **1622** WITHER *Philarete* M 4, I..yet, vnscorned, serue a gentle Nymph. **1721** YOUNG *Revenge* I. i, Africk I quell'd, in hope by that to purchase Your leave to sigh unscorn'd. **1828** WORDSW. *Power of Sound* 51 Unscorned [be] the peasant's whistling breath.

**Unsco·rnful,** *a.* (UN-[1] 7.) **1858** TENNYSON in Ld. Tennyson *Memoir* (1897) I. 427 He is such a good fellow, so unscornful and genial. **Unsco·rnfully,** *adv.* (UN-[1] 11.) **1844** tr. *Mem. Babylonian Princess* II. 307 Hanging his majestic head, and unscornfully pacing to and fro in his narrow cage. **Unsco·rnfulness.** (UN-[1] 12.) **1840** L. HUNT *Leg. Florence* II. i, Your look, madam, is wondrous logical;.. and cramm'd with scorn, from pure unscornfulness. **Unsco·tch,** *v.* (UN-[2] 3.) **1839** F. A. GRIFFITHS *Artill. Man.* 191 Unsling gun and carriage. Limber up. Hold on. Unscotch the wheels. **Unsco·tted,** *ppl. a. local.* [UN-[1] 8 + SCOT *sb.*[2] 3.] Not subject to a 'scot' or tax. **1865** *Level of Hatfield Chase* (Notice of Annual Meeting) 18 Oct., The Owners of Unscotted Lands affected by 'The Level of Hatfield Chase Act, 1862.' **Unsco·ttified,** *ppl. a.* (UN-[2] 8.) **1773** JOHNSON 1 May in *Boswell*, You are the most unscottified of your countrymen. **1858** E. B. RAMSAY *Remin.* (ed. 2) v. 39 Numerous examples..might be taken from the works of Robert Burns..which lose their charm altogether when *unscottified*. **Un-Sco·ttish,** *a.* (UN-[1] 7.) **1825** *Monthly Rev.* CVI. 14 The Un-Scotish name of Griffiths.

**Unscou·red,** *ppl. a.* (UN-[1] 8. Cf. Sw. *oskurad.*)
*c* **1460** *Stans Puer ad Mensam* 58 in *Babees Bk.* 30 Brynge no knyves vnskoured to the table. **1567** DRANT *Horace, Ep.* iii. c vj, Thy witte is not of meanest sorte; it doth not lye vnskowrde. **1592–3** *Act* 35 *Eliz.* c. 10 § 1 Beinge rawe unscowred..as yt cometh from the Weavers Beame. **1603** SHAKS. *Meas. for M.* I. iii. 171 Like vn-scowr'd Armor. **1630** J. TAYLOR (Water P.) *Jacke-a-Lent* Wks. I. 115 Making the band of vnscowred Halberdiers retire. **1702** *Guide for Constables* 141 He that scours not his ditches..shall forfeit 12 pence for every rod so left unscoured. **1830** CARLYLE *Misc.* (1840) II. 345 Her kettles hung unscoured on the wall. **1894** *Outing* XXIV. 229/1 A handful of unscoured worms.

**Unscou·rged,** *ppl. a.* (UN-[1] 8.)
*c* **1412** HOCCLEVE *De Reg. Princ.* 1257 They þat swymmen in richesse..Vnscourgid ay of any aduersitee. **1648** HEXHAM II, *Ongegeesselt*, Vnwhipped, or Vnscourged. **1825** CAMPBELL *Hallowed Ground* 5 Man..Erect and free, Unscourged by superstition's rod.

**Unscra·ped,** *ppl. a.* (UN-[1] 8. Cf. ON. *úskrapaðr*, (M)Sw. *oskrapad*, MDa. *uskrabet.*)
**1725** RAMSAY *Gentle Sheph.* IV. i, With vile, unscrapit tongue. **1881** *Cheq. Career* 323 They threw it [*sc.* a dead iguana] on the coals, unscraped and uncleaned. **1887** MOLONEY *Forestry W. Africa* 427 The coated or unscraped sort is similarly prepared, excepting that the rhizomes are unscraped; this is sometimes called Black Ginger.

† **Unscra·pen,** *ppl. a. Obs.*—[1] [UN-[1] 8 b.] = prec. **1599** GARNET *Let. to Parsons* May (Stonyhurst MSS.), I was willing to let it go naturally, that you may rather mend it, if it be necessary, or deliver it unscrapen.

**Unscra·tched,** *ppl. a.* (UN-[1] 8.)
**1595** SHAKS. *John* II. i. 225 To saue vnscratch'd your Citties threatned cheekes. *a* **1667** JER. TAYLOR *Lib. Proph.* (1817) 394 They are his image undefiled, unscratched, unbroken by any act or consent of their own. **1853** DICKENS *Bleak Ho.* lxiii, You must make up your mind to remain unscratched [*sc.* out of a will].

**Unscraw·led,** *ppl. a.* (UN-[1] 8.) **1612** BRINSLEY *Lud. Lit.* 39 That the schollars keep their copies and books fair, vnblotted and vnscrauled.

**Unscree·n,** *v.* (UN-[2] 5.)
**1628** WITHER *Brit. Remembr.* v. N xi b, Secrets to unskreene, That cannot by our mortall eyes be seene. **1635** QUARLES *Embl.* III. vii. 28 Unskreen those Heav'nly lamps, or tell me why Thou shad'st thy face. **1654** GAYTON *Pleas.*

*Notes* IV. viii. 223 But he bustling still to unscreen her fully, she then shreekt out.

**Unscree·ned,** (*ppl.*) *a.* [Un-1 8, 9.]

**1.** Not protected or covered with a screen.

1648 Boyle *Seraph. Love* xxvi. (1659) 167 Their being expos'd (unskreen'd) to the Sun's refulgent beams. 1783 R. Graves *Euphrosyne* II. 113 Yet in those eyes we see.. (More bright un-screen'd) the pow'r..To make new conquests. 1801 *Monthly Mag.* XII. 224 If I sit unscreened, with my back to the fire. 1859 Geo. Eliot *A. Bede* liv, The little, grey, desolate-looking hamlet, unscreened by sheltering trees. 1891 *Nature* 20 Aug., Similar actions on cometary matter, unscreened as it is by an absorptive atmosphere.

**2.** Not passed through a screen; unsifted.

1851 Laxton *Builder's Price Bk.* 132 Gravel unscreened, 5s. od. Per cubic yard. 1888 *Encycl. Dict.* s.v., Unscreened coal. 1900 *Daily News* 21 May 2/1 Unscreened town's refuse.

**Unscrew·**, *v.* [Un-2 3 and 7. Cf. WFris. *ont-, ûntskroeve, -je*, Du. *ontschroeven.*]

**1.** *trans.* To slacken or detach by turning a screw (either separate or forming part of the thing turned).

1651 Davenant *Gondibert* I. vi. xiii, His Hilts round Pommel he did then unskrew. 1669 Sturmy *Mariner's Mag.* v. i. 2 You may unscrew the perpendicular from the sight. 1683 Moxon *Mech. Exerc., Printing* xxii. ¶ 4 He must unskrew the Skrew of his Composing-stick. 1722 De Foe *Plague* (1754) 71 They found Ways to unscrew the Locks. 1739 Labelye *Piers Westm. Bridge* 24 They were secured by proper Iron-work; which being unskrew'd, would permit the Sides to part asunder. 1815 J. Smith *Panorama Sci. & Art* II. 24 Shut the stop-cock, and unscrew the syringe. 1848 Dickens *Dombey* xlix, He..unscrewed his hook, screwed his fork into its place, and did the honours of the table. 1900 Hasluck *Model Engin. Handybk.* 118 This rod ..can be lengthened..by unscrewing one of the joints.

**b.** To remove the stopper from (a flask) by unscrewing.

1653 Urquhart *Rabelais* I. xxiv. 114 He unscrewed his borracho (which was a great Dutch leathern bottle).

**c.** *intr.* To undergo, or admit of, being unscrewed.

1822 T. Mitchell *Aristoph.* II. 225 Like the tones of a lyre, When the pins and pegs are unscrewing. 1874 H. H. Cole *Catal. Ind. Art S. Kens. Mus.* 166 Amulet Case...It unscrews at one end. 1888 Rutley *Rock-Forming Min.* 21 Fitted on a separate stand the foot of which unscrews.

**2.** *fig.* (In various applications.)

1605 B. Jonson *Volpone* v. vii, To the Court..will I; and if't be possible, Vn-screw my Aduocate, vpon new hopes. ? *a* 1616 Fletcher, etc. *Q. Corinth.* III, I should curse my fortune..to be made the ginne To unscrew a Mothers love unto her Son. 1627 N. Burley in Capt. Smith *Seaman's Gram.* a ij, What long trauels..Haue made thee know, thou ..do'st vnscrew To those that want like knowledge. 1664 H. More *Myst. Iniq.* 295 The Thirteenth Chapter would not fail to unscrue the meaning with the considerate and intelligent. 1761 Churchill *Rosciad* 468 Courtiers will, like reasonable creatures, Suspend vain Fashion, and unscrew their features.

**Unscrew·ed,** *ppl. a.* [Un-1 8.] Not furnished with a screw. 1887 D. A. Low *Machine Draw.* 18 If the countersunk head be lengthened so as to take up the whole of the unscrewed part of the bolt. **Unscri·bbled,** *ppl. a.* (Un-1 8.) 1628 Earle *Microcosm., Child* (Arb.) 21 His Soule is yet a white paper vnscribled with obseruations of the world. †**Unscri·ed,** *ppl. a. Obs.*$^{-1}$ [Un-1 8.] Undescried. 1560 Rolland *Seven Sages* 86 Thay..Wan to the Gold..and vnscryit come away. †**Unscri·p,** *v.* (Un-2 4.) *c* 1430 *Pilgr. Lyf Manhode* II. xii. (1869) 79 A cherl..wole bineme hem her burdouns and vnscrippe hem of here scrippes.

**Unscri·ptural,** *a.* (Un-1 7.)

1653 Gauden *Hierasp.* 14 How unscriptural..do they seem to many..Christians? 1683 E. Hooker *Pref. Pordage's Mystic Div.* 71 Unwritten Traditions, inhumane inventions, unscriptural institutions. 1719 Waterland *Eight Serm. Div. Christ* iii. 103 That is as manifestly unscriptural, false, and groundless, as either Socinian or Arian. 1782 Priestley *Corrupt. Chr.* II. vii. 104 Wickliffe..saw nothing unscriptural in extreme unction. 1825 Coleridge *Aids Reflect.* 311 The View or Scheme..I believe to be altogether unscriptural. 1849 Macaulay *Hist. Eng.* vi. II. 112 Prelacy was abhorred..both as an unscriptural and as a foreign institution.

Hence **Unscri·pturally** *adv.*, **-alness.**

1677 W. Hughes *Man of Sin* III. ii. 27 Besides the unscripturalness of such visits. 1824 D. Russell *Covenants* (1843) 182 Some have spoken very..unscripturally of the good works and holy tempers of believers. 1868 Miall *Congregationalism in Yorks.* 15 Cartwright had openly proclaimed..the unscripturalness of the Anglican hierarchy.

**Unscriptura·lity.** (Un-1 12.) 1733 *Revolution Politicks* vi. 18 The Unscripturality and Irregularity of the Doctrine. 1827 G. S. Faber *Sacr. Calend. Prophecy* (1844) II. 19 The flagrant unscripturalities of that notoriously apostatising period. **Unscri·pture,** *sb.* [Un-1 12 b.] *attrib.* Unscriptural 1697 G. Keith *2nd Narr. Proc. Turner's Hall* 9 They that find..Fault with unscripture Language. **Unscri·pture,** *v.* (Un-2 4.) 1690 Stillingfl. *Charge* 11 Sept. 6 They who go about to Unbishop Timothy and Titus, may as well Unscripture the Epistles, that were written to them. †**Unscri·pturely,** *a. Obs.*$^{-1}$ [Un-1 7.] Unscriptural. 1549 Latimer *2nd Serm. bef. Edw. VI*, To Rdr. (Arb.) 48 This maintenance of so many vnscripterlye opinions. **Unscru·bbed,** *ppl. a.* (Un-1 8.) [1775 Ash.] *c* 1900– in periodical use. **Unscru·ple,** *v.* (Un-2 4.) 1647 M. Hudson *Div. Right Govt.* II. ii. 75 To unscruple all vocabular doubts and difficulties, let us but look into the fourteenth Ch. of Gen. **Unscru·pled,** *a.* (Un-1 9.) Unscrupulous. 1813 Scott *Rokeby* vi. vii, In their favour oft we see Unscrupled, useful men like thee. **Unscru·pled,** *ppl. a.* (Un-1 8; cf. Scruple *v.* 4.) 1665 Boyle *Occas. Refl.* vi. iii. 195 Either the same [practice], or little better, may be found unscrupled at among our selves. **Unscrupulo·sity.** (Un-1 12; cf. next.) 1847 Harris *Life Ld. Hardwicke* III. 270 The unscrupulosity with which he ever gratified his passion. 1879 Geo. Eliot *Theo. Such* xi. 191 The dirty work of unscrupulosity.

**Unscru·pulous,** *a.* (Un-1 7.)

1803 Godwin *Chaucer* xli. II. 265 A person..boundless in ambition, and unscrupulous in his choice of means for gratifying it. 1829 Scott *Anne of G.* xix, The priest took instant and unscrupulous possession of his seat of honour. 1875 Jowett *Plato* II. 222 The worse he is the more unscrupulous he will be.

Hence **Unscru·pulously** *adv.*, **-ness.**

1808 Mitford *Hist. Greece* IV. 356 Their unscrupulousness in using the arbitrary powers of democratical government. 1833 J. H. Newman *Arians* iv. § ii. 315 This mere handful of divines unscrupulously pressing forward into the highest ecclesiastical stations. 1879 Farrar *St. Paul* xxxviii. II. 248 The unscrupulousness of a worldly ecclesiasticism. 1884 Church *Bacon* iii. 61 Lawyers..who unscrupulously pushed their way to preferment.

†**Unscru·table,** *a. Obs.* (Un-1 7 b, 5 b.) 1562 Cooper *Answ. Priv. Masse* 96 b, Is it not merueilous,..and to oure iudgement vnscrutable, that [etc.]? [1775 Ash.] **Unscru·tableness.** (Un-1 12; cf. prec.) 1657 J. Sergeant *Schism Dispatch't* 449 The profound unscrutableness of those mysteries.

**Unscru·tinized,** *ppl. a.* (Un-1 8.)

1728 Morgan *Hist. Algiers* I. v. 167 Their Consciences he leaves wholly unscrutinized. 1795 Bentham *Protest agst. Law Taxes* 52 His unscrutinized notion of its supposed tendency to check litigation. 1802–12 — *Ration. Judic. Evid.* (1827) I. 478 Scrutinized or unscrutinized, evidence may speak. 1852 J. H. Newman *Scope Univ. Educ.* 60 Every received but unscrutinized assertion.

**Unscru·tinizing,** *ppl. a.* (Un-1 10.)

1802–12 Bentham *Ration. Judic. Evid.* (1827) I. 123 Unreflecting and unscrutinizing caprice. 1872 Morley *Voltaire* i. 9 Unscrutinising acquiescence in half-thoughts and faint guesses.

**Unscru·tinizingly,** *adv.* (Un-1 11; cf. prec.) 1891 Han. Lynch *G. Meredith* 136 He adores her unscrutinizingly. **Unscu·lptured,** *ppl. a.* (Un-1 8.) [1775 Ash.] 1816 Shelley *Mont Blanc* 27 The aethereal waterfall, whose veil Robes some unsculptured image. 1891 *Cent. Dict.*, *Unsculptured*,..in *zoology*, smooth; without elevated or impressed marks on the surface. **Unscu·mmed,** *ppl. a.* (Un-1 8. Cf. Sw. *oskummad.*) *c* 1440 *Pallad. on Husb* VIII. 128 A sester of vnscomed hony. 1562 *Apol. Priv. Masse* (1850) 40 If the servant would leave the pot unscummed. **Unscu·re,** *v. s. dial.* [Un-2 3. Cf Isle of Wight *skure* to secure.] *trans.* To untie, undo. 1749 Mrs. Robert Goadby *Carew* v. 51 They were now all employed in unscuring the Children from his Back [Cf. *Ibid.* 49 It was quickly resolved to tie two to his Back.] **Unscu·tcheoned,** *ppl. a.* (Un-1 8.) 1827 Pollok *Course T.* VIII. 89 No King, no subject was; unscutcheoned all, Uncrowned, unplumed. **Unscy·thed,** *ppl. a.* (Un-1 8.) *a* 1818 in Scott *Hrt. Midl.* i, Skiddaw hears afar The rattling of the unscythed car.

**Unsea·l,** *v.* [Un-2 3, 4. Cf. MDu. *ontsegelen*, (Du. *-zegelen*), OHG. *intsigilan* (MHG. *entsigelen*, G. *-siegeln*).]

**1.** *trans.* To remove a seal from, to break the seal of (a letter, etc.).

*c* 1425 *Seven Sag.* (P.) 1054 His emys bokes he vnselde. *c* 1425 Audelay *XI Pains Hell* 179 Þe angel..lad him to þe blak pit þo, With vij. selys was selid treuly...Anon he vnselid þe pit þore. 1596 Shaks. *Merch. V.* v. i. 275, I haue better newes in store for you Then you expect: vnseale this letter soone. 1666 in *10th Rep. Hist. MSS. Comm.* App. V. 23 He..resolved to unseale the bags. 1693 Dryden *Persius* vi. 37 Nor yet [will I] unseal the Dregs of Wine that stink Of Cask. 1746 Francis tr. *Horace, Epist.* I. vii. 12 The long Lawyer's Plea unseals our Wills. 1791 Cowper *Odyss.* III. 495 Charging high the cup With wine of richest sort, which she.. First broach'd, unsealing the delicious juice. 1818 Coleridge in *Encycl. Metrop.* (1845) I. Introd. 33 Henceforward the book is unsealed for him; the depth is opened. 1851 Longf. *Gold. Leg.* I. *Court-yard*, Then was the family tomb unsealed. 1884 *Cassell's Fam. Mag.* Mar. 203/1 The oven is then unsealed, and the coke withdrawn.

*fig.* 1830 Mrs. Hemans *Songs Affec., Spirit's Return* i, This long-shut heart for thee shall be unseal'd.

**2.** *fig.* **a.** To free from some constraining influence; to allow free action to.

1589 Greene *Menaphon* (Arb.) 59 She ought to shut vp her dores, and solemnize continuall night, till her husband, her sunne, making a happie return, vnsealeth her silence. 1652 Benlowes *Theoph.* I. lxxxviii, Renew my heart, direct my tongue, unseal My hand. 1826 Mrs. Hemans *Forest Sanctuary* II. xxx, When stars..are shining, How their soft glance unseals each thought of thee! 1847 Emerson *Compensation* ii, And why when mirth unseals all tongues Should mine alone be dumb?

**b.** To free from the condition (or necessity) of remaining closed. (Cf. Seal *v.*1 6 b.)

With reference to the eyes (*b*) probably in part replacing Unseel *v.*

(*a*) *a* 1586 Sidney *Arcadia* I. ii, I pray you (said Musidorus, then first unsealing his long silent lips) what countries be these? 1621 Quarles *Div. Poems, Esther* iii, Memucan.. Vnseal'd his serious lips, and thus bespake. 1815 Scott *Guy M.* xli, Speaking as if his utmost efforts were unable to unseal his lips beyond the width of a quarter of an inch. 1852 Merivale *Rom. Emp.* (ed. 2) iii. I. 129 Cicero's mouth was unsealed. 1884 *Manch. Exam.* 24 Nov. 5/2 Gladstone ..is therefore extremely anxious that his lips should..be unsealed.

(*b*) 1652 Benlowes *Theoph.* XI. xxx, Still to have toting waits unseal thine eyes. 1700 Dryden *Ovid's Met., Ceyx & Alcyone* 303 The God disturb'd with this new Glare of Light .., unseal'd his Sight. 1725 Pope *Odyss.* xv. 8 In sleep profound the Son of Nestor lies; Not thine, Ulysses! Care unseal'd his eyes. 1855 Singleton *Virgil* I. 364 Others 'neath rueful Tartarus he sends; Grants slumbers, and withdraws [them], and the eyes At death unseals. 1863 Cowden Clarke *Shaks. Char.* xiii. 333 The discovery of that patron's baseness..acts like a talisman to unseal his eyes.

**3.** To disclose, reveal.

1640 Fletcher, etc. *Coronation* II. i, If this preserve thee not, I must unseal Another mistery. 1871 B. Taylor *Faust* (1875) II. II. iii. 147 He the future hath unsealed.

Hence **Unsea·ler**; **Unsea·ling** *vbl. sb.*

1683 Jane Lead *Revelation* (title-p.), An Essay towards the Unsealing, Opening and Discovering The Seven Seals. 1844 Lowell *Leg. Brittany* II. xxii, Remembering when he stood Not fallen yet, the unsealer of her heart. 1895 W. Watson *Hymn to Sea* i, While, with throes, with raptures, with loosing of bonds, with unsealings,—Youth .. wakes like a wondering rose.

**Unsea·lable,** *a.* [Un-1 7 b.] Incapable of being sealed. 1831 E. Irving *Expos. Rev.* I. 91 The apocalypse is..an unsealed and unsealable book.

**Unsea·led,** *ppl. a.*1 [Un-1 8. Cf. MDu. *ongesegelt*, Du. *ongezegeld*, G. *ungesiegelt.*]

**1.** Not stamped or marked with a seal.

1377 Langl. *P. Pl.* B. XIV. 292 Wynneth he nauȝt with weghtes fals ne with vnseled mesures. 1492 *Extr. Aberd. Reg.* (1844) I. 419 Conuikit..for the wrangwiss haldin of a wrang pek of less mesour, and unselit. 1550 *Southampton Court Leet Rec.* (1905) I. 9 We present that [they]..sell beere and wyne by vnlawful and vnsealled measures contrary to the statute. 1629 *Leather* 15 The Market is full of excellent Leather;..all this in the Morning lyes vnsealed. 1660 in J. Davidson *Inverurie*, etc. (1878) 361 Giv onie person have ane unseilit stoup they sall braik the same.

*fig.* 1680 C. Nesse *Church Hist.* 447 They could never kill the souls of any of Gods sealed ones, as they did of the unsealed.

**2.** Not having a seal imposed or attached; not closed by means of a seal.

*c* 1430 *Pilgr. Lyf Manhode* I. xxxvi. (1869) 22 He þat holt his swerd naked, and þe keyes vnbownde, naked and vnseeled. 1523 Ld. Berners *Froiss.* I. ccccxxv. 301/2 So he toke the letters vnsealed, and retourne in to Englande agayne. 1646 *Bury Wills* (Camden) 192 All my bookes, papers, and parchments vnsealed. 1665 Boyle *Exp. & Obs. Conc. Cold* Pref. c 6, Judging it fit to make further Trial, with an unseal'd Weather-glass. 1726 Berkeley in Fraser *Life* Wks. 1871 IV. 140 In case it be a bond in form, or..a promissory note unsealed. 1793 T. Twining in *Recreat. & Stud.* (1882) 184 Sending the parcel unsealed that you might have read..the MS. 1848 W. H. Kelly tr. *L. Blanc's Hist. Ten Y.* II. 89 This letter..was..delivered, unsealed, to M. de Montalivet.

*fig.* *a* 1649 Crashaw *Carmen Deo Nostro, Hymn St. Thomas* 54 When this dry soul those eyes shall see, And drink the unseal'd sourse of thee. 1820 Shelley *Prometh. Unb.* IV. 115 The murmurings Of the unsealed springs. 1831 [see prec.].

*transf.* 1868 *Rep. U. S. Commissioner Agric.* (1869) 278 Moisture, emanating in part from unsealed honey,..becomes condensed in the hive from external cold.

**3.** *fig.* Not formally confirmed or ratified.

1601 Shaks. *All's Well* IV. ii. 30 Therefore your oathes Are words and poore conditions, but vnseal'd. 1665 J. Spencer *Vulg. Proph.* 87 That very many of these Modern Prophecies have been very punctually accomplish'd, though unseal'd by any divine Sign attending the delivery of them. 1831 James *Phil. Augustus* II. iii, My fate is yet an unsealed one.

**Unsea·led,** *ppl. a.*2 [Un-1 8 + Seel *v.*2 Cf. Unseal *v.* 2 b *b.*] Not closed.

1800 Coleridge *Piccolom.* I. xi, The unsealed eye Of Jupiter's glad children born in lustre.

**Unsea·m,** *v.* [Un-2 4.] *trans.* To undo the seam or seams of (a garment, etc.). Also *fig.*, to rip up.

1592 Greene *Groat's W. Wit* (1617) 28 In a thread-bare cloake,..his hose vnseamed. 1605 Shaks *Macb.* I. ii. 22 Till he vnseam'd him from the Naue to th' Chops, And fix'd his Head vpon our Battlements. 1608 Beaum. & Fl. *Four Plays in One* I. iii, Nor a vein runs here From head to foot, but Sophocles would unseame, and..shoot his scornfull blood Into their eyes. 1631 in *Verney Mem.* (1907) I. 131 Our barke..had her bottome strucken out and was unseamed. 1812 Byron *Ch. Har.* I. lxxvii, One gallant steed is stretch'd a mangled corse; Another, hideous sight! unseam'd appears. 1824 in *Spirit Pub. Jrnls.* (1825) 194 Giving Mr. Trotter a thump on the eye, and unseaming his shirt from top to bottom! 1848 T. Aird *Chr. Bride* I. xiii, The monster's.. tusks backward glance To gather fury for his onset dread, To unseam her lovely limb.

**Unsea·manlike,** *a.* (Un-1 7 c.) 1726 Shelvocke *Voy. round World* 7 His unseamanlike behaviour in the late storm. 1865 *Sat. Rev.* 2 Sept. 301/2 The idea of a French Sailor as a weedy, unseamanlike kind of 'loafer'.

**Unsea·med,** *ppl. a.* [Un-1 8. Cf. Du. *ongezoomd*, MLG. and MHG. *ungesûmet*, G. *ungesäumt*, Sw. *osömmad.*] Having no seam.

1592 Sylvester *Tri. Faith* II. xlix, The Schismatiks.. renting Christ's unseamed coat in twain. 1635 F. White *Sabbath* 310 The unseamed coat of Christ.

**Unsea·rchable,** *a.* and *sb.* [Un-1 7 b, 12, and 5 b.]

**1.** That cannot be searched into, so as to be ascertained or exactly estimated; inscrutable.

1382 Wyclif *Rom.* xi. 33 Hou incomprehensyble ben his domes, and his weyis vnserchable. *c* 1400 *Found. St. Bartholomew's* 43 God, that makith grete and vnsercheable thyngis with-owte numbre. 1549 Latimer *3rd Serm. bef. Edw. VI* (Arb.) 100 Mans hart is vnserchable. 1584 B. R. tr. *Herodotus* II. 77 They fell..to discourse..of Nilus, the head whereof was vnsearchable, and not to be knowne. 1622 Peacham *Compl. Gent.* viii. 69 To consider how Nature .., by an vnsearchable and stupendious worke, sheweth vs [etc.]. 1667 Milton *P. L.* VIII. 10 To relate Things else by me unsearchable, now heard With wonder. 1703 Rowe *Ulysses* IV. i, 'Tis all the mighty working of the gods, Unsearchable and dark to human Eyes. 1759 Johnson *Rasselas* xi, The unsearchable will of the Supreme Being. 1809–14 Wordsw. *Excurs.* III. 112 Lost in unsearchable eternity. 1835 Thirlwall *Greece* I. vi. 193 As his might is irresistible, so is his wisdom unsearchable. 1876 R. Bridges *Sonn.* viii, The unsearchable and secret aims Of nature.

**b.** *sb.* An unsearchable thing.

1725 Watts *Logick* I. vi. § 1 It is a vast Hindrance..if we spend too much of our Time and Pains among Infinites and

Unsearchables. **1741** — *Improv. Mind* I. xviii, To busy yourselves..amongst unsearchables.

**2.** That cannot be sought for.

**1878** B. TAYLOR *Pr. Deukalion* III. v. 128 A something lost, Because vnsought, perchance unsearchable, Assails my sight.

Hence **Unsea·rchableness, -ably** *adv.*

**1611** FLORIO, *Inscrutabilita*, *vnsearchableness. *a* **1653** BINNING *Serm.* (1845) 38 God's unsearchableness, God's unchangeableness. **1683** BURNET tr. *More's Utopia* 197 Unless, according to the unsearchableness of his Mind, he is pleased with a variety of Religions. **1856** RUSKIN *Mod. Painters* IV. v. v. § 21 In an Italian twilight.. there is still unsearchableness, but an unsearchableness without cloud or concealment. **1873** SYMONDS *Grk. Poets* ix. 290 The unsearchableness of God's dealings. **1706** STEVENS *Span. Dict.* I, *Inscrutablemente*, inscrutably, *unsearchably. **1746** HERVEY *Refl. Flower Garden* 21 The various Expedients which Providence, unsearchably wise, uses. **1847** DE QUINCEY *Sp. Mil. Nun* Wks. 1862 III. 98 A female..who..perished by a fate so unsearchably mysterious.

**Unsea·rched,** *ppl. a.* [UN-[1] 8, 8 c.]

**1.** Not searched; unexamined, uninvestigated: **a.** In predicative use, after *leave, go, pass*, etc.

**1526** *Pilgr. Perf.* (W. de W. 1531) 131 b, It shall leaue no corner of our soules..vnserched. *a* **1548** HALL *Chron., Edw. V*, 7 Watchyng, that no person..should passe vnserched. **1621** FLETCHER *Thierry & Theod.* v. i, Since you have your tricks..we will not leave a wrinkle of you unsearcht. **1691** T. H[ALE] *Acc. New Invent.* 12 Suffering a Ship..to lye.. in Harbour unsearched. **1765** WILKES *Corr.* (1805) II. 138 The two trunks..were suffered to go out of Rome unsearched. **1832** G. DOWNES *Lett. Cont. Countries* I. 399 The custom-house officers..letting all ours [*sc.* luggage] pass unsearched. **1865** DICKENS *Mut. Fr.* III. vi, The chimney was not left unsearched.

**b.** In attributive use.

**1568** *Jacob & Esau* I. iii. B j, Whatsoeuer mysterie the Lorde therein ment, Must be referred to his vnserched iudgement. **1615** CHAPMAN *Odyss.* xxiv. 640 Pallas spake To Ioue..And askt of him, what his vnsearched mind Held vndiscouer'd. *a* **1649** CRASHAW *Carmen Deo Nostro, To C'tess Denbigh* 36 The self-shutt cabinet of an unsearcht soul. **1753** *Chambers' Cycl.* Suppl. s.v. *Fossile Shells*, Other yet unknown or unsearched seas and shores. **1821** BYRON *Heaven & Earth* iii. 912 The ocean..grasps each drowning hill, Nor leaves an unsearch'd cave. **1879** FARRAR *St. Paul* xxxi. II. 24 That unsearched borderland which lies between the natural and the supernatural.

**2.** Not searched *for*.

**1730** A. GORDON *Maffei's Amphith.* p. x, All which..have been unsearch'd for, and unknown.

**Unsea·rching,** *ppl. a.* (UN-[1] 10.) **1599** DANIEL *Musoph.* (1602) C iij b, Then would they only labour to extend Their now vnsearching spirits beyond these bounds Of others powres, wherein they must be pend. **1828–32** WEBSTER (citing J. Q. Adams).

**Unsea·red,** *ppl. a.* [UN-[1] 8.]

**1.** Not made sear; unwithered.

**1599** THYNNE *Animadv.* (1875) 48 That is, (as some do expounde this worde vnseriall,) vnsered, vnsinged, vnwithered. **1829** J. L. KNAPP *Jrnl. Nat.* 102 Preserving..a portion of its foliage unseared by frosts. *a* **1847** ELIZA COOK *Like the Evergreen* iii, It remaineth unseared in the deluge of light.

*fig.* **1827** POLLOK *Course T.* III. 153 The stripling youth of plump, unseared hope. **1863** W. LANCASTER *Prætérita* 37 We'll keep a merry heart up still, Unsered, fresh, young, and callow.

**2.** Not made hard or callous.

**1860** TRENCH *Serm. Westm. Abbey* vi. 59 Many things which he would have shrunk back from at first, while his conscience was yet unseared.

†**Unsea·son,** *sb. Obs.*[−1] [UN-[1] 12.] *In unseason*, out of season.

*a* **1400–50** *Alexander* 4439 ȝoure sowping in vnseson, ȝoure surfete of drinkis.

**Unsea·son,** *v.* [UN-[2] 4.] *trans.* To deprive of seasoning or relish. In quots. *fig.*

**1590** SPENSER *F. Q., To Sir W. Raleigh*, Why doe I send this rusticke Madrigale, That may thy tunefull eare vnseason quite? ?*a* **1600** *Nobody & Someb.* in Simpson *Sch. Shaks.* (1878) I. 310 The remembrance that I was a king, Unseasons the content of povertie. **1728** THEOBALD *Double Falshood* I. ii, What Fortune soever my Going shall encounter, cannot be good Fortune; What I part withal unseasons any other Goodness.

**Unsea·sonable,** *a.* [UN-[1] 7 b.]

**1.** Not suited to, not in accordance with, the time or occasion; untimely, inopportune.

*c* **1448** *Ten Commandments of Love* in *Stow's Chaucer* (1561) 342 b, Take measure in langage,..For mesure.. Thynges vnseasonable setteth in season. **1591** *Acts Privy Council* (1900) XXI. 123 The unordinate and unseasonable taking of the same [spawn] by the common fishers. **1607–12** BACON *Ess., Dispatch* (Arb.) 248/1 To chuse tyme is to save tyme, and an vnseasonable mocion is but beating the ayre. **1667** MILTON *P. L.* VIII. 201 Whence haply mention may arise Of somthing not unseasonable to ask. **1718** *Free-thinker* No. 7. 42 A Notion prevails..that Marriage in Lent, is at least unseasonable. **1752** JOHNSON *Rambler* No. 207 ⁋ 9 Unseasonable importunity of discontent. **1817** JAS. MILL *Brit. India* II. v. v. 522 The English fleet.. dispersed by the weather, incurred considerable danger of a very unseasonable rencounter. **1839** W. C. TAYLOR *Anc. Hist.* xvii. § 2 (ed. 2) 501 This rash conspiracy induced Galba to sully the commencement of his reign by unseasonable severities. **1844** H. H. WILSON *Brit. India* II. 497 The omission to inspect the accounts was unseasonable and injudicious.

*transf.* **1722** STEELE *Consc. Lovers* III. i, The familiar, learned, unseasonable Puppy!

**b.** Of time: Not suitable for the action specified or implied.

Freq. (with *hour*) implying an unusual time of the night.

**1595** SHAKS. *John* IV. ii. 20 This acte..Being vrged at a time vnseasonable. **1621** in Foster *Eng. Factories Ind.* I. (1906) 261 The said ship..at last at unseasonable time made tryall to com for Petapolie. **1674** *Jackson's Recant.* B 1, To let them out at unseasonable hours, and stay up for them, till it be early. **1715** DE FOE *Fam. Instruct.* I. iii. (1841) I. 62 Who knows but God may bless instruction, though begun at an unseasonable time. **1759** FRANKLIN *Ess.* Wks. 1840 III. 218 Neither did they conceive the time to be unseasonable for an application to the crown. **1800** MRS. HERVEY *Mourtray Fam.* II. 176 If I presume to intrude upon you at an unseasonable hour. **1838** LYTTON *Leila* I. vi, The alarm it might occasion..if he endeavoured at so unseasonable an hour, to force an entrance.

**c.** As *adv.* Unseasonably; out of season.

*a* **1634** CHAPMAN *Bussy d'Ambois* III. (1641) 42 How most unseasonable thou playest the Cucko, In this thy fall of friendship. **1680** R. L'ESTRANGE tr. *Erasmus' Colloquies* 174 This came very Unseasonable; Or if there had been any Errour, it might have been dissembled.

**2.** Of fish, etc.: Not in season.

*c* **1450** *Cal. Letter-bks. London, D.* (1902) IV. 198 Ye shalle not suffre no fysshe corrupt ne unsesynable to be solde. **1477** [see VICTUAL *sb.* 1 γ]. **1488–9** *Act 4 Hen. VII*, c. 21 Aswell grete fisshes unsesonable as the seid frie. **1533–4** *Act 25 Hen. VIII*, c. 7 Kyllyng of salmons when they be unsesonable and not holsome for manns body. **1563** in *Liturg. Serv. Q. Eliz.* (1847) 488 The same poor which either lack food, or else that which they have is unseasonable and cause of sickness. **1653** WALTON *Angler* vi. 133 The old Salmon..grow sick in fresh waters, and by degrees unseasonable. **1677** *Quarter Sess. Rec.* (N. Riding Rec. Soc.) VII. 6 A Startforth yeoman for catching ten unseasonable fish called scurfes. **1842** *Act 5–6 Vict.* c. 106 § 74 If any Person shall..have in his Possession any..unclean or unseasonable Salmon or Trout.

†**b.** Not properly matured; unseasoned. *Obs.*[−1]

**1515** *Nottingham Rec.* III. 344 We present Ser John Bagula for makyng on seysnabulle tyle. **1548** *Act 2 & 3 Edw. VI*, c. 10 § 1 Sondrie persons..made myche Malte unpure and unseasonable.

**3.** Of weather: Not appropriate to the season of the year; *esp.* stormy, tempestuous. Also of days, seasons, etc., marked by such weather.

*a* **1513** FABYAN *Chron.* VII. 433 Great scarcete of corne and frute..by meane of vnsesonable wederynge. **1593** SHAKS. *Rich. II*, III. ii. 106 An vnseasonable stormie day. **1602** in Moryson *Itin.* (1617) II. 261 Their Haruest was so vnseasonable, and their Corne was so destroied by the weather, as numbers of subiects will vndoubtedly die of famine. **1610** HOLLAND *Camden's Brit.* 466 By reason of vnseasonable weather the corne..was choked and blasted in the eare. **1645** BOATE *Ireland's Nat. Hist.* xxi. (1652) 166 The ripeness of the fruits..is greatly retarded by the abundance of unseasonable rain. **1696** RAY in *Lett. Lit. Men* (Camden) 203 Heer hath been a very unseasonable Summer, for the most part very cold and wet. **1707** MORTIMER *Husb.* 212 A cold, dry, unseasonable Spring. **1820** SHELLEY *Prometh. Unb.* II. iv. 52 The unseasonable seasons drove With alternating shafts of frost and fire, Their..pale tribes to mountain caves. **1854** *Poultry Chron.* I. 578/1 Notwithstanding the cold, dark, unseasonable day. **1879** S. C. BARTLETT *Egypt to Pal.* xx. 442 Plucking lilies of the field from beneath the unseasonable snow.

**Unsea·sonableness.** [f. prec.] The quality or fact of being unseasonable: **a.** Of weather.

**1523** FITZHERB. *Husb.* § 14 The vnseasonablenes of the wether. **1577** B. GOOGE *Heresbach's Husb.* I. 2 b, Yf either the vnseasonablenesse of the weather, or sicknesse cause me to keepe my bed. **1600** SURFLET *Country Farme* V. x. 674 The Oxen..better indure the vnseasonablenes of times, and ..draw a deeper draught. **1695** LUTTRELL *Brief Rel.* (1857) III. 515 The lords justices, considering the unseasonablenesse of the weather, have..prohibited the exportation of corn. **1796** *Phil. Trans.* LXXXVI. 280 During last January, nothing was more common than to hear expressions of the unseasonableness of the weather.

**b.** Of time.

**1548** UDALL *Erasm. Par. Luke* iv. 49 b, He neuer did so muche as laie for his excuse the importunitee or vnseasonablenesse of tyme. **1628** in Rushw. *Hist. Coll.* (1659) I. 582 Our next Argument is drawn..from the unseasonableness of the time. **1656** EARL MONM. tr. *Boccalini's Pol. Touchstone* (1674) 273 About one a clock at night, forty Carts..were seen to enter the Royal Palace..: and because of the unseasonableness of the time..inquiry was made [etc.]. **1694** *Phil. Trans.* XVIII. 45 They were generally taken notice of,.. because of the unseasonableness of the time for Grashoppers. *a* **1748** WATTS *Disc. Educ. Childr.* ix. (1795) 177 The unseasonableness of the midnight hour [for dancing].

**c.** Of actions, etc.

**1610** HEALEY *Theophrastus* (1616) 49 Vnseasonnablenesse is a troublesome..assaulting of those with whom we haue to doe. **1693** *Mem. Ct. Teckely* III. 28 The unseasonableness of the ill Policy of the Turks. **1741** RICHARDSON *Pamela* IV. 387 Forgive, dearest Sir, the Unseasonableness of your very impertinent..Pamela. **1799** HAN. MORE *Fem. Educ.* (ed. 4) I. 14 A sneer, not at the truth of religion, ..but at its gravity, its unseasonableness. **1815** JANE AUSTEN *Emma* I, The suddenness and ..the unseasonableness with which the affair burst out. **1884** *Manch. Exam.* 1 July 3/1 The unseasonableness of the proposed discussion.

**Unsea·sonably,** *adv.* [UN-[1] 11.] In an unseasonable manner; at an unfitting time; out of season.

**1588** LAMBARDE *Eiren.* IV. xix. 603 It wil fall out unseasonablie. **1589** WARNER *Alb. Eng.* Prose Add. 164 Whilest he vnseasonably amongst blowes, deliuered vnregarded perswasions of Peace. **1610** HEALEY *Theophrastus* (1616) 12 A Pratler or Babler..vnseasonably setting vpon any stranger. **1687** WOOD *Life* (O.H.S.) III. 233 That night there should have been an illumination in the quadrangle, but by the folly of the proctor it was unseasonably done the night before. **1719** DE FOE *Crusoe* II. (Globe) 332, I unhappily and unseasonably disturb'd him. **1780** *Mirror* No. 72, The thoughts of futurity..may surely sometimes, not unseasonably, press upon our imagination. **1819** SHELLEY *Cenci* IV. iv. 2 Lady, my duty to his Holiness Be my excuse that thus unseasonably I break upon your rest. **1868** *Rep. U.S. Commissioner Agric.* (1869) 21 Unseasonably cool and..wet weather set in, followed by early frosts.

**Unsea·soned,** *ppl. a.* [UN-[1] 8.]

**1.** Not made palatable by seasoning.

**1582** STANYHURST *Æneis* IV. (Arb.) 108 Caucasus haggish Bred the, with a tigers soure milck vnseasoned. **1601** *Song of Mary* D j b, If it may be, let this vnseasoned cup Of sorrow passe. **1611** FLORIO, *Incondite uiuande*, vnseasoned meates.

**b.** Not appreciative of dainties.

**1598** MARSTON *Sco. Villanie* 169 For whose vnseasoned palate I wrote the first Satyre, in some places too obscure.

**2.** Not matured by growth or time. Also in fig. context.

**1601** B. JONSON *Poetaster* V. iii, We haue no vacant eare, now, to receiue The vnseason'd fruits of his officious tongue. **1641** BEST *Farm. Bks.* (Surtees) 32 The best stricles..are made of froughy, unseasoned oake. **1683** MOXON *Mech. Exerc., Printing* iii, If they be made of unseason'd Stuff,.. as the Stuff dries it shrinks. **1832** *Planting* 74 (L.U.K.), Comparative trials of seasoned and unseasoned wood in the same building. **1833** LOUDON *Encycl. Archit.* § 243 Unseasoned timber, or other materials.

**b.** Not habituated by time or experience.

**1601** SHAKS. *All's Well* I. i. 80 'Tis an vnseason'd Courtier, good my Lord, Aduise him. **1608** DAY *Law Trickes* III. ii, These words..Are but like Ignes Fatui, to delude Greene and vnseason'd wits. **1614** LATHAM *Falconry* I. ix. 33 These hawkes being vnseasoned in their bodies. **1638** SHIRLEY *Mart. Soldier* I. ii, Your unseason'd valour Had thrice ingag'd our fortunes and our men Beyond recovery. **1730** *2nd Contin. Baker's Chron.* 531/2 The unseason'd Orkney Men immediately yielded themselves. **1770** PITTMAN *European Settlem. Mississ.* p. viii, The twenty-first regiment.. being..unseasoned to such a climate, suffered almost as much. **1840** E. E. NAPIER *Scenes & Sports For. Lands* II. App. 243 The exposure of his unseasoned person alternately to night damps and the burning rays of the sun. **1857** DICKENS *Dorrit* I. xxxii, The depressed unseasoned prisoner.

†**3.** Unseasonable. *Obs.*

**1589** COOPER *Admon.* 21 Their virulent and unseasoned speeches. **1597** SHAKS. *2 Hen. IV*, III. i. 105 These vnseason'd howres perforce must adde Vnto your Sicknesse. **1598** — *Merry W.* II. ii. 174 The which hath something embolдned me to this vnseason'd intrusion. **1615** BRATHWAIT *Strappado*, etc. (1878) 282 Each..tun'd their odes with that vnseasoned time. **1796** MME. D'ARBLAY *Camilla* I. 202 Camilla looked hastily away, and her whole set, abashed by so unseasoned an inquiry, cast down their eyes.

†**4.** Rendered unhealthy. *Obs.*[−1]

**1638** SIR T. HERBERT *Trav.* (ed. 2) 213 A great and lovely Citie,..over-topt by no hill, unseasoned by no marishes.

**Unsea·soning,** *ppl. a.* (UN-[1] 10.) *a* **1617** HIERON *Wks.* (1619) II. 474 This miserie of hauing none among them but an vnseasoning and vnsufficient minister.

**Unsea·t,** *v.* [UN-[2] 5.]

**1.** *trans.* To dislodge from a seat (*esp.* on horseback).

**1596** SPENSER *F. Q.* IV. x. 10 Whom boldly I encountred.. And by good fortune shortly him vnseated. **1784** COWPER *Task* VI. 553 His horse..Rush'd to the cliff, and..stood. At once the shock unseated him. **1835** W. IRVING *Tour Prairies* 177 Beatte was nearly unseated from his saddle. **1845** J. COULTER *Adv. in Pacific* xvi. 247 The boat plunged down..with so violent a shock, that nearly all were unseated. **1895** SCULLY *Kafir Stories* 170 My horse..wheeled sharply to the right, completely unseating me.

*transf.* **1609** HOLLAND *Amm. Marcell.* 84 But Constantine ..displaced and unseated this huge masse. **1839** MARRYAT *Phant. Ship* ii, The probing of the wound would half unseat my reason. **1891** *Cent. Dict.* s.v., To unseat a boiler; to unseat a valve.

**2.** To dislodge from some place or position; to deprive of rank or office.

**1611** SPEED *Hist. Gt. Brit.* Summary, In Germany by intrusion they vnseated the Sueuians. **1661** J. DAVIES *Civ. Warres* 371 [They] resolved next morning to unseat the Parliament once more. **1826** HOOD *Recipe for Civiliz.* 89 Whereas a cook would soon unseat him [*sc.* Apis], And make his own churchwardens eat him. **1870** EMERSON *Soc. & Solit.* iv. 67 A greater power of carrying the thing loftily, and with perfect assurance,..might..unseat any sovereign, and abrogate any constitution in Europe and America. **1878** TAYLOR *Deukalion* III. vi. 135 The Gods of races I unseat, as Time or Tyranny of old Unseated them.

**b.** *spec.* To deprive of, or depose from, a seat in Parliament or other representative body.

**1834** *Tait's Mag.* I. 541/1 Had one third of the exceptions held good, it was clear the Governor must be unseated. **1882** SERGT. BALLANTINE *Exper.* xxx. 294 The first case..was speedily disposed of by unseating the member.

**Unsea·ted,** *ppl. a.* [UN-[1] 8.]

†**1.** *U.S.* Of land: Unsettled, unoccupied. *Obs.*

**1662** *Laws of Virginia* lxxii. 43 [It] must in a short time leave the greatest part of the Countrey, unseated and unpeopled. **1689** *Col. Rec. Pennsylv.* I. 318 Where land is unseated. **1724** *Acts Assembly Pennsylv.* (1762) I. 102 Exempting..all unsettled Tracts or Parcels of Land, That is to say, such Tracts of Land as..are unseated. **1800** *Farmer's Reg.* 29 March (Thornton), The owners of unseated lands in Westmoreland. **1877** BURROUGHS *Taxation* 208.

**2.** Not seated; not provided with a seat.

[**1775** ASH.] **1883** D. C. MURRAY *Hearts* ix, She was still unseated, and he approached her.

**Unseaulich**: see UNSEWLY *a.*

**Unsea·worthiness.** (UN-[1] 12. Cf. next.)

**1824** *Cowen's Rep.* (N. Y. State Supreme Crt.) 106 Every vessel has a point of time at which it..arrives at a situation of unseaworthiness. **1832** MᶜCULLOCH *Dict. Commerce* 648 Unseaworthiness may be caused in various ways, such as want of repair, want of stores [etc.]. **1875** *Economist* 27 Feb. 246/1 Ought not the underwriters to have been able to plead 'unseaworthiness'?

**Unsea·worthy,** *a.* (UN-[1] 7.)

**1820** TOMLINS *Law Dict.* (ed. 3) I. s.v. *Insurance*, A ship..

sailed on her voyage in an unseaworthy state. **1857** Dickens *Dorrit* II. xxvi, Drowning men clinging to unseaworthy spars. **1896** 'H. S. Merriman' *Sowers* xxxiv, A sailor never believes that his own ship is unseaworthy.

† **Unse·cond,** *v. Obs.*—1 (Un-1 14.) **1616** J. Lane *Contn. Sqr.'s T.* x. 59 Wear't not as good to have betraid oure lord, as to vnsecond him, as twice wee did?

**Unse·conded,** *ppl. a.* [Un-1 8.]

**1.** Not backed up or supported.

**1597** Shaks. 2 *Hen. IV*, II. iii. 34 O Miracle of Men! Him did you leaue (Second to none) vn-seconded by you. **1608** [Tofte] *Ariosto's Sat.* III. (1611) 33 So that in rank of fauour, I alone Stood still vnseconded of any one. **1691** T. H[ale] *Acc. New Invent.* 9 Nor lay this long unseconded by concurrent Advices from Portsmouth. **1734** Thomson *Liberty* I. 166 Unseconded by art, the spinning race..idly toil. **1778** Hamilton *Wks.* (1886) VII. 558 He attempted, single and unseconded, to possess himself of one of the enemy's field-pieces. **1809–14** Wordsw. *Excurs.* VI. 221 He..Urged unremittingly the stubborn work, Unseconded, uncountenanced. **1884** *Law Times* 8 Nov. 27/2 [A] result..obtained by his own unseconded efforts.

**b.** *spec.* (See Second *v.*1 3.)

**1816** *Monthly Mag.* XLI. 144 Applause revives. All cry, To France, To France! And Westmoreland unseconded remained. **1865** *Reader* 27 May 594/3 His proposal was unseconded, and fell to the ground.

†**2.** Unparalleled, unique. *Obs.*—1

**1646** Sir T. Browne *Pseud. Ep.* III. vii. 120 Even as in the body of man from putred humours..there have succeeded strange and unseconded shapes of wormes.

**Unse·crecy.** *rare*—1 (Un-1 12.) **159.** H. Walpole in *Cath. Rec. Soc. Publ.* V. 225 By some mens unsecrecy, which I will not name, my iourney is much known.

**Unse·cret,** *a.* (Un-1 7.)

*a* **1586** Sidney *Arcadia* III. xviii, Which hopes, Hate (as unsecrete as Love) could not conceale. **1606** Shaks. *Tr. & Cr.* III. ii. 133 Who shall be true to vs When we are so vnsecret to our selues? **1614** Raleigh *Hist. World* IV. iv. § 8. 251 Hee was driuen by necessitie to trust many, of whom he stumbled vpon some, that were vnsecret. **1655** Earl of Norwich in *Nicholas P.* (Camden) II. 259 For what I heare of my being thought vnsecret (a hard censure after fifty yeares seruice in your Royall Family).

**Unse·cret,** *v.* [Un-2 4.] *trans.* To disclose.

**1607–12** Bacon *Ess., Counsel* (Arb.) 318 But lett Princes beware that the vnsecreting of theire affaires come not from themselves. **1654** Whitlock *Zootomia* 447 Things nere done hee'l sweare; All he unsecrets: such black Sheep beware. **1659** Fuller *App. Inj. Innoc.* III. 17 They say, It is..another thing, to look on Gods Secrets, in some sort unsecreted. **1666** Bp. S. Parker *Free & Impart. Censure* 65 The Intrinsick Essence of any one Being is no more explain'd & unsecreted after all their Labour, then it was afore.

**Unsecre·ted,** *ppl. a.* (Un-1 8.) **1750** G. Hughes *Barbados* 246 The more gross returns back unsecreted to the radical Vessels. **Unse·cretness.** (Un-1 12.) **1526** *Pilgr. Perf.* (W. de W. 1531) 110 Vnkyndnesse, Vntrustynesse or vnsecretnesse, Discorde or contencyon.

**Unsecta·rian,** *a.* and *sb.* (Un-1 7 and 12.)

*adj.* **1847** Webster (citing Buckham). **1854** *Edin. Rev.* Oct. 413 Their devotion to the one God and his Prophet [is] unsectarian in its character. **1887** Ruskin *Præterita* II. 195 A standard of the purest unsectarian Christianity.

*sb.* **1888** *Pall Mall G.* 20 Nov. 4/1 In Sheffield the victory was with the Unsectarians, in Manchester it was with the Sectarians.

**Unsecta·rianism.** (Un-1 12; cf. prec.) **1866** *Spectator* 1 Dec. 1325 Making such a fuss about unsectarianism in religion. **Unsecta·rianize,** *v.* (Un-2 6 c *b.*) **1836** Mill *Diss. & Disc.* (1859) I. 200 The very first step..should be to unsectarianize them [*sc.* the Universities] wholly.

**Unse·cular,** *a.* (Un-1 7.)

**1846** Worcester (citing *Ec. Rev.*). **1849** A. Baker in J. Aiton *Domest. Econ.* (1857) 33* All will agree..that they [*sc.* buildings] should have..a humble unsecular air. **1859** Dickens, etc. *Haunted House* vi, We were every Sunday advertising the establishment in an unsecular way.

**Unse·cularize,** *v.* (Un-2 6 c *b.*)

**1816** A. Knox *Rem.* (1844) I. 66 The humbled and unsecularized priesthood of the English Church. **1842** Pusey *Crisis Eng. Ch.* 127 Our Church has been in part un-Catholicized by those who helped..to unsecularize her. **1897** W. C. Hazlitt *Ourselves* 60 The clergy..more or less unsecularise them [*sc.* women].

† **Unsecu·re,** *a. Obs.* (Un-1 7 and 5 b.)

**1636** [Denham] *Destr. Troy* (1656) 2 Now but an unsecure and open Bay. **1685** Ld. Perth in *Lond. Gaz.* No. 2031/7 They render us unquiet and unsecure at home. **1700** Blackmore *Job* 67 He in his prosperous state is unsecure. **1726** Leoni *Alberti's Archit.* II. 100/1 It may be unsecure against sudden incursions of enemies. **1729** T. Innes *Crit. Ess.* (1879) 184 Looking on their religion as unsecure as long as the queen's authority was acknowledged.

**b.** Const *of*, or *to* with inf.

? *a* **1685** Roscommon *Virgil's Sixth Ecl.* Poems (1749) 77 None who under that protection came Was ever ill receiv'd, or unsecure of fame. **1693** Fleetwood *Serm.* 13 Depending ..on Accidents in Nature, which are varying every Day, uncertain, unsecure to be relied upon.

**Unsecu·red,** *ppl. a.* (Un-1 8.)

**1780** Burke *Œcon. Reform* Wks. 1906 II. 319 A supply of unsecured money..wholly at the discretion of ministers. **1821** Scott *Kenilw.* xli, He left, therefore, the Countess's door unsecured on the outside. **1866** *Sat. Rev.* 22 Sept. 361/1 All corn, therefore, unsecured, cut or uncut, is considerably discoloured. **1882** De Windt *Equator* 86 Their jet-black hair was unsecured and allowed to fall in profusion down their backs.

† **Unsecu·rity.** *Obs.*—1 (Un-1 12 and 5 b.) **1591** Coningsby *Jrnl. Siege Rouen* in *Camden Misc.* I. 64 Lytle provision commeth to our markett, what for the unsecurytie of the passage for pore men. **Unseda·te,** *a.* (Un-1 7.) **1823** Hone *Anc. Mysteries* 262 Their obsolete costume and hobbling walk are sport for the unsedate. **Unse·dentary,** *a.* (Un-1 7.) **1814** Wordsw. *Excurs.* VII. 193 Meanwhile the unsedentary Master's hand Was busier with his task.

**Unsedu·ce,** *v.* (Un-2 3.) **1664** N. Ingelo *Bentiv. & Ur.* Index, *Misoplanus*, one that hates Cheaters, takes pains to discover their Frauds and to unseduce the deceiv'd.

**Unsedu·ced,** *ppl. a.* (Un-1 8 and 5 c.)

**1565** [see Un-1 5 c]. **1611** Shaks. *Cymb.* I. iv. 173 If shee remaine vnseduc'd..you shall answer me with your Sword. **1667** Milton *P. L.* v. 896 Unshak'n, unseduc'd, unterrifi'd His Loyaltie he kept. **1721** Southerne *Spartan Dame* II. i, Among so many false one man yet true, Unshaken, unseduced. **1751** Smollett *Per. Pic.* lxxxi, He remained unshaken, unseduced, preserving his attachment for me. **1830** Mackintosh *Progr. Eth. Philos.* (1862) 200 Having been unseduced by the temptations either of scepticism, or of useless idealism. **1866** Felton *Anc. & Mod. Gr.* I. xi. 195 Still unseduced, unstained by vice.

**Unsedu·cible,** *a.* (Un-1 7.) **1869** *Lyndesay's Wks.* 436 *marg.*, A judge, come from afar, unwavering, unseducible.

**Unsee·,** *v. rare.* [Un-1 14 and Un-2 3.] *trans.* To avoid seeing; to leave, or make, unseen.

*a* **1395** Hylton *Scala Perf.* II. xl. (W. de W. 1494), Whan he sheweth him the soule may not vnsee hym, for he is lyghte. **1865** J. Grote *Explor. Philos.* I. 243 We cannot unsee the prospect before us. **1871** Kingsley *At Last* xvii, At last we had seen it; and we could not unsee it.

**Unsee·able,** *a.* [Un-1 7 b.] Invisible.

*a* **1400** in *Hampole's Wks.* (1895) I. 124 Our blyssed vnseable god may be perseyued alanle be inly vnderstandyng. *Ibid.* 165 It is..nerhand vnpossibull to a fleshle saule..for to ryse in knawyng of vnseabull þ[i]nges. ? **1531** Tindale *Exp. 1st Ep. John* Wks. (1572) 427/2 Of the very Sacrament it selfe we know no other thyng then that we come thether to see an vnseable miracle. **1548** Geste *Pr. Masse* C ii, That the substance of ye bred, whiche is vnseable, shuld be worshipped. **1719** De Foe *Vis. Angelic World* 44 To see things unseeable, as St. Paul heard things unutterable. **1880** *Boston Jrnl. Chem.* Dec. 134/2 It is assumed that spirit is unseeable.

Hence † **Unsee·ably** *adv. Obs.*

*a* **1395** Hylton *Scala Perf.* II. xi. (MS. Bodl. 592), Þee fforȝifnesse of synne is doon ghostli and vnseabli þoruȝ grace of þe hooligoost. *Ibid.* II. xxx, He was vnseabli felid in þe myȝtes of her soulis.

**Unsee·ded,** *a.* [Un-1 9.] Not having or bearing seed. **1884–** *Imp. Dict.*, etc. **Unsee·ded,** *ppl. a.* [Un-1 8.] Unsown. [**1775** Ash.] **1791** Cowper *Odyss.* IX. 140 The unseeded and unfurrow'd soil..food for blatant goats supplies. **1828–32** Webster, *Unseeded*,..not sown. (Local.) *N. England.* **Unsee·ing,** *vbl. sb.* (Un-1 13.) **1860** Ruskin *Mod. Paint.* V. VIII. i. § 14. 164 False seeing is unseeing,—on the negative side of blindness.

**Unsee·ing,** *ppl. a.* [Un-1 10, 5 d. Cf. OE. *ungesëonde* not yet seeing, MHG. *unsëhende* (G. *unsehend*) in sense 2.]

†**1.** Unseen, invisible. *Obs.*

*a* **1300** *Cursor M.* 25010 Wit þis word 'heuen' þou vnderstand Al gastli thing and vnseand.

**2.** Not seeing; lacking sight.

Freq. in recent use, esp. with *eyes*.

**1591** Shaks. *Two Gent.* IV. iv. 209 Else by Ioue, I vow, I should haue scratch'd out your vnseeing eyes. *c* **1600** — *Sonn.* xliii, How would thy shadowes forme, forme happy show,.. When to vn-seeing eyes thy shade shines so? **1795** Southey *Joan of Arc* IV. 66 With a full eye, that of the circling throng And of the visible world unseeing, seem'd Fix'd upon objects seen by none beside. **1819** *Monthly Mag.* XLVIII. 33 As one who, sever'd from the maid he loves, Rolls an unseeing eye on all beside. *a* **1830** Ld. Cockburn *Mem.* (1856) 17 But the garden!..unseen and unseeing, it was a world of its own. **1873** Miss Braddon *Lucius Davoren* I. 57 He looked at his friend's face with blank unseeing eyes. **1888** D. C. Murray *Weaker Vessel* ii, After an apparently unseeing glance at one of its pages.

**3.** With object: Without seeing.

**1632** Lithgow *Trav.* x. 445, I haue gone eighteene leagues, ..vnseeing house or Village. **1798** Southey *Joan of Arc* (ed. 2) I. I. 124, I sat in silence,..unheeding and unseeing all Around me.

Hence **Unsee·ingly** *adv.*

**1893** Marie Corelli *Barabbas* xxxiii, Barabbas went out, wandering almost unseeingly in the open street.

**Unsee·king,** *ppl. a.* (Un-1 5 d, 10.)

**1583** *Reg. Privy Council Scot.* III. 586 Quhairintill his Hienes hes occupeit himself..unseiking the hurt and ruyne of quhatsumevir his subjectis. **1799** Coleridge *Lett.* (1895) 272 He might as well have been in England as at Goslar, in the situation which he chose and with his unseeking manners. **1878** Mrs. Stowe *Poganuc P.* xxiii. 207 Love faithful, devoted, unseeking of self, and asking only to bless.

† **Unsee·l,** *v. Obs.* [Un-2 3.]

**1.** *trans.* To unsew (the eyes of a hawk, etc.); *fig.*, to open, unclose.

**1530** Palsgr. 766/2, I unceyle a haukes eyes, or other byrdes, I cut the stytches that closed his eyes togyther. *a* **1587** Q. Eliz. in Puttenham *Eng. Poesie* III. xx. (Arb.) 255 Then dazeld eyes with pride, which great ambition blinds, Shalbe vnseeld by worthy wights. **1612** J. Davies (Heref.) *Muse's Sacr.* Wks. (Grosart) II. 37/1 Vnseele mine Eyes, that long thy Light to see. **1652** Benlowes *Theoph.* XI. xxx, Still to have toting waits unseel thine eyes In bed, at board.

**2.** To unsew or uncover the eyes of (a hawk, etc.). Also *fig.*

**1530** Palsgr. 766/2 Unceyle your pigyon and..he wyll go from your hauke. **1575** Turberv. *Falconrie* 91 Watche hir all that nighte that you unseale hir. **1612** Warner *Alb. Eng.* XIII. lxxvi. 315 This Athiest and that Epicure grant thou whom they offend That I vnceele, and of my Verse thy Glory be the end. **1618** Latham *Falconry* xxvii. 124 Let them haue the rest [*sc.* doves] giuen vnseild with some few feathers drawne from them. **1686** Blome *Gentl. Recr.* II. 36 In the Evening by Candle-light unseal her, giving her something to tyre upon. **1728** Chambers *Cycl.* s.v. *Falcon*, Give her a bit or two upon the Lure, and unseel her.

† **Unseeled,** obs. var. Unceiled *ppl. a.*

**1594** Nashe *Unfort. Trav.* I iij, Whiles I, thorough a crannie of my vpper chamber vnseeled, had beheld all this sad spectacle.

† **Unsee·liness.** *Obs.* [Un-1 12. Cf. OE. *ungesǽlignes*.] Unhappiness.

*a* **1300** *E. E. Psalter* xiii. 7 Forbreking and vnselines ai [are] In waies of þaim. *c* **1374** Chaucer *Boeth.* IV. pr. v. (1868) 131 Þus see I wel..what blisfulnesse or ellys what vnselinesse is establissed in þe desertys of goode men and of shrewes.

† **Unsee·ly,** *a. Obs.* [OE. *unsǽlig* (*un-* Un-1 7 + *sǽlig* Seely *a.*), = WFris. *on-*, *ûnsillich*, NFris. *unsaleg*, MDu. *onsâlich* (Du. *onzalig*), MLG. *unsalich*, OHG. *unsâlig* (MHG. *unsælich*, *unsælic*, *-ec*, G. *unselig*).]

**1.** Of persons: **a.** Unfortunate, unhappy, miserable, wretched; deserving pity.

*a* **900** *Juliana* 450 Ic þec halsiȝe..þæt þu miltsiȝe me.. þæt [ic] unsælig eall ne forweorþe. *a* **1023** Wulfstan *Hom.* (1883) 52 Deofol..ȝedeð swa þurh þæt, þæt unsælig man wisdomes ne ȝymeð. *c* **1200** Ormin 4812 Unnseliȝ mann Amm icc onn eorþe wurrþenn. *c* **1275** *xi Pains Hell* 7 in *O. E. Misc.* 147 Vnselv gost hwat dostu here? *c* **1374** Chaucer *Boeth.* IV. pr. iv. (1868) 124 ȝit mot it nedes be þat shrewes ben more wrecches and vnsely. **1388** Wyclif *Rom.* vii. 24 Y am an vnceli man; who schal delyuer me fro the bodi of this synne? **14..** *Seven Points Wisd.* iii. (MS. Douce 114) fol. 108 Loo I vnselye..sowht abowte to gete me a wyfe. **1513** Douglas *Æneid* I. xi. 36 The fey wnsely Dido, For the mischeif to cum predestinate, Mycht not refrene. *Ibid.* V. viii. 86 Vnsilly wycht! quhow did thi mynd invaid Sic gret wodnes? *a* **1555** Philpot tr. *Curio* Exam. & Writ. (Parker Soc.) 418 Barbarous words by the which unto unsely [L. *incautis*] and foolish folk they avaunt themselves to be marvelled at.

**b.** Bringing misfortune on oneself or others; unlucky; evil-doing, wicked.

*a* **900** *Andreas* 561 Þæt..Iudea cynn wið Godes bearne ahof hearmcwide, hæleð unsæliȝe. *a* **1200** *St. Marher.* 16 Sathanas the unseli, the..of parais lihte so lahe. *c* **1205** Lay. 2531 Bi hire he hæfde twein sunen ah beine heo weoren unseli. *a* **1300** *Cursor M.* 1223 Vnseli caym..Wit god and man þan was..hated. **1340–70** *Alex. & Dind.* 987 We ben of-set wiþ no sinne for vnsely godus. *c* **1400** Love *Bonavent. Mirr.* (1908) 225 How paciently..he resceyuede that false feyned clippynge and traitoures cusse of that vnsely disciple. **1412–20** Lydg. *Chron. Troy* II. 4233 Vnhappy woman, causere of oure peyne, Hard & vnsely.

**c.** Of animals: Mischievous, harmful.

**13..** *Gaw. & Gr. Knt.* 1562 Þe lorde..Swez his vncely swyn, þat swyngez bi þe bonkkez, & bote þe best of his brachez þe bakkez in sunder. **1804** R. Couper *Poetry* II. 84 My bacon ham..Th' unseely tyke has ta'en.

**2.** Of things, conditions, etc.: Causing or involving, accompanied by, misfortune or unhappiness.

*a* **900** *Genesis* 637 Sum hire æt heortan læȝ æppel unsælȝa. **13..** *Metr. Hom.* (MS. Ashm. 42) fol. 148 b, To þat ilk vnceli lande þare he bees bonden fote and hand Full hard wiþ þe deuils band. **13..** *Cursor M.* 15842 (Gött.), 'Ha men,' he said, 'quat ȝe er of ane vnseli toght'. *c* **1374** Chaucer *Boeth.* II. pr. iv. (1868) 39 þe most vnsely kynde of contrariouse fortune. **1412–20** Lydg. *Chron. Troy* II. 3249 A! Priam kyng! vncely is þi chance! *a* **1450** *Northern Passion* (D.) 2024 We han pleyd vnseli plawis. **1513** Douglas *Æneid* IV. Prol. 230 Lo! with quhat thocht, quhat bitternes and pane Luif vnseilly breidis in euery wycht! *a* **1828** *Young Allan* i. in *Buchan's Ball.* (1875) II. 11 There fell a-rousing them amang, On an unseally time.

†**Unsee·m,** *a. Obs.*—1 (Un-1 7 + Seem *a.*) = Unseemly *a.* 1. *c* **1425** in *Anglia* VIII. 139/11 Vnmesurabill laghter or vnsem and vnmanerly berynge of body. **Unsee·ming,** *pres. pple.* [Un-1 13.] Not seeming or appearing. **1588** Shaks. *L. L. L.* II. i. 156 You..wrong the reputation of your name, In so vnseeming to confesse receyt Of that which hath so faithfully beene paid.

† **Unsee·ming,** *ppl. a. Obs.* [Un-1 10, 5 d.] Unbecoming, unseemly; = Unbeseeming *a.* 2.

*a* **1340** Hampole *Psalter* lxxii. 15 Lo þis misemand [*v.r.* vnsemand] þing folous. **1382** Wyclif *Prov.* xxvi. 7 So vnsemende thing is in the mouth of foolis a parable. **1535** Stewart *Cron. Scot.* (Rolls) III. 146 But quhois counsall nother prince nor king Ma gif consent to sic wnsemand thing. **1549** Coverdale, etc. *Erasm. Par. Rom.* 33 Cutte out of thy mynde superfluous and vnsemyng desyres. **1662** Baxter *Saints' R.* III. xi. 473 Unsavoury, harsh, and unseeming [*ed.* 1650 unseemly] language.

**b.** In predicative use, sometimes with dependent clause.

*c* **1400** *Destr. Troy* 3891 He spake neuer dispituosly,..Ne sagh, þat was vnsemond, slipped hym fro. *c* **1400** *Laud Troy Bk.* 10029 Hit is foly and vnsemyng A man to leue on fals dremyng. *c* **1460** G. Ashby *Dicta Philos.* 967 On erthe ther is no thing so vnsemyng As a kynge to be in predacion. **1549** Coverdale, etc. *Erasm. Par. Rom.* 27 Vnseamyng is it for loue of suche a meane, to dispise the ende. **1550** Bale *Eng. Votaries* II. 29 Remembrynge..that nothynge was more vnsemynge, than an olde dottynge fole..so to rage.

**c.** Const. *for* or *to*.

**1382** Wyclif *Prov.* xxvi. 1 What maner snoȝ in somer,.. so vnsemende is to the fool glorie. *c* **1400** *Destr. Troy* 1846 Þat hynd..þat ye kepe in youre company..As subiecte vnto syn, vnsemyng for you. **1536** Bellenden *Cron. Scot.* (1821) I. 64 With thir, and siclike inhumane cruelteis, unsemand to ane prince. **1592** Wyrley *Armorie* 20 As these things are vnseeming for him to weare.

**d.** With direct object.

**1592** Golding *De Mornay* (ed. 2) i. 12 He is tempted of his lustes, a thing altogether vnseeming the Godhead. **1620** Mason *Newfoundland* 5 Fishing is a beastly trade and unseeming a Gentleman. **1648** Gage *West Ind.* 44 The beds only were unseeming this great state, very poor. **1701** *Stanley's Hist. Philos.* (ed. 3) 100, I think it most unseeming a Philosopher to sell his advice.

Hence † **Unsee·mingness.** *Obs.*

**1540** Wyatt in Flügel *Neuengl. Lesebuch* I. 348 Here I allegid the vnsemingnes to gyve credence to his word.

**Unsee·mingly,** *adv. rare.* [Un-1 11; cf. prec.] Unbecomingly.

**1619** A. Newman *Pleas. Vis.* (1840) 13 Euen some of.. tender age Vnseemingly can vaunt how they will..carouse. **1656** *Eirenikon* 28 Love.. Unseemingly doth not itself behave. **1897** *Westm. Gaz.* 23 Dec. 2/3 That ophthalmia is unseemingly rife still is proved by [etc.].

† **Unsee·mlily,** *adv. Obs.* [Un-1 11.] = Unseemly *adv.*

**1483** *Cath. Angl.* 329/2 Vn Semelily, *jndecenter, jnconuenienter.* **a 1661** Holyday *Juvenal* (1673) 177 Such [gifts] as thou..dost unseemlily receive at the same times.

**Unsee·mliness.** [f. next, or Un-1 12.]

**1.** The quality of being unseemly in respect of action, conduct, etc.

**c 1380** Wyclif *Sel. Wks.* III. 43 Unsemelynes schulde not be in Cristes Chirche. **1549** Udall, etc. *Erasm. Par.* 2 *Thess.* iii. 11 b, Getting their liuyng with their owne handes, rather than to be greuouse vnto other with shamles crauinges & vnsemelines. **1577** tr. *Bullinger's Decades* 510/2 What vnseemelinesse soeuer is committed against God and his Church. **1678** Wanley *Wond. Lit. World* v. i. § 82. 466/2 The Emperour did expostulate the unseemliness of the deed with him. **1829** Lytton *Devereux* I. xiii, I saw the unseemliness of fighting with my preceptor, and a priest. **1871** Jowett *Plato* IV. 170 His virtue being such, that he never ..fell into any great unseemliness.

**2.** The quality of being unseemly in appearance; uncomeliness.

**1597** A. M. tr. *Guillemeau's Fr. Chirurg.* 23/1 The cleavinge in the lippes is such an vnseemlines and deformitye. **1603** G. Owen *Pembrokeshire* (1892) 44 Parchinge of the sunne, and starveinge with cold is a cheefe cause of the vnseemelynes of the comon people of the countrey. **1846** Landor *Imag. Conv.* Wks. I. 195 *Johnson.* It makes an unseemly appearance in the type. *Tooke.* The unseemliness is not equal to the absurdity.

**Unsee·mly,** *a.* (and *sb.*). [Un-1 7. Cf. ON. *úsǽmilig-r* (Icel. *ósæmilegur,* Da. *usømmelig,* Norw. *usømeleg,* etc.).]

**1.** Unbecoming, unfitting; indecent.

**a 1310** in Wright *Lyric P.* viii. 31 Ofte in song y have hem set, that is unsemly ther hit syt. **1338** R. Brunne *Chron.* (1810) 171 Þei did a foule trespas, it was vnsemly þing. **a 1400-50** *Alexander* 29 For soth it is vnseemly slike sawis of a prynce. **c 1440** *Promp. Parv.* 367/1 On-semely, *indecens, inconveniens.* **1542** Hen. VIII *Declar. Scots* A iv, With that vnsemely dissimulation, we were not a lytell moued. **1597** Hooker *Eccl. Pol.* v. xlviii. § 4 Things in themselues vnholie or vnseemly we may not aske. **1645** Ussher *Body Div.* 218 That no unseemely behaviour proceed from us. **1692** E. Walker tr. *Epictetus' Mor.* l, Nor would they anything unseemly say. **1738** Waterland *Chr. Sacr. Expl.* Appendix i. 6 An unseemly Reflection upon.. The Sacrifices of God. **1791** Cowper *Odyss.* xvii. 243 A squalid beggar..in unseemly garb attir'd. **1824** Dibdin *Libr. Comp.* 616 Shall..all editions be passed over in a sort of unseemly silence? **1855** Macaulay *Hist. Eng.* xvii. IV. 39 The news..threw him into a passion..which hurried him into many foolish and unseemly actions. **1871** Freeman *Norm. Conq.* xviii. IV. 155 To offer to William..an insult as unseemly as it was senseless.

*absol.* **1880** *Sat. Rev.* 7 Aug. 162/2 Partaking not a little of the unwise as well as of the unseemly.

**b.** Const. *for* († *of, to*) and with inf.

**a 1300** *Body & Soul* in *Map's Poems* (Camden) 335 Thouȝ art unsemly for to se, uncomli for to cussen suwete. **c 1375** *Sc. Leg. Saints* xxi. (*Clement*) 659 Sayand, vnsemly ware to se cristine man begare to be. **c 1445** Pecock *Donet* 139 Ful vnseemely and vntreuli it is to seie þat [etc.]. **1551** Recorde *Pathw. to Knowl.* i. Def., It shall not be vnsemely to call all suche shapes, formes and figures [etc.]. **1581** Mulcaster *Positions* ii. 5 It is a thing not vnseemely for me to deale in. **1583** Stubbes *Anat. Abus.* i. P vij, How vnhonest soeuer, or vnseemly of christian eares his argument be. **a 1598** Rollock 1 *Thess.* (1606) 183 Any thing, that is vnsetting, or vnseemlie to this Christian calling. **1667** Milton *P. L.* x. 155 Unseemly to bear rule, which was thy part.., had'st thou known thy self aright. **1843** Lytton *Last Bar.* viii. vii, Unseemly it may be for one of your quality..to quit this place with me.

**c.** *sb.* An unseemly thing.

**1654** Whitlock *Zootomia* Pref. A 7 The Candid Interpreter of modest Endeavours, not Exacter of Impossibles, or unseemlies.

**2.** Uncomely, unhandsome.

**c 1340** Hampole *Pr. Consc.* 5023 Þair bodys sal alle unsemely be, And foul, and ugly, opon to se. **1390** Gower *Conf.* I. 96 Which of alle kinde Of wommen is thunsemlieste. **1393** Langl. *P. Pl.* C. ii. 55 The dupe dale and durke vnsemely to see to. **c 1400** *Pilgr. Sowle* (Caxton) iv. xxxviii. (1859) 63 He found..an old vnsemely one. I ne can nought calle hyr lady. **a 1513** Fabyan *Chron.* vi. cxciv. 198 The Erle..prayed his wyfe..yt she wold..make herselfe as fowle and as vnsemely as she coude. **1581** Pettie *Guazzo's Civ. Conv.* ii. (1586) 114 A man of vnseemelie personage. **1683** Moxon *Mech. Exerc., Printing* xvii. ¶ 2 Their Faces stand closer or wider assunder, which is unseemly, when the Letter comes to be Printed. **1684** J. S. *Profit & Pleas. United* 138 If you buy your Bees, Observe they be..Smooth and Shining; Rejecting the Rough and unsemly Ones. **1838** *Civil Eng. & Arch. Jrnl.* I. 394/2 Making the vessel frightfully crank and most unseemly to look at. **1843** James *Forest Days* ii, In other respects he was not an unseemly man. **1870** Dickens *E. Drood* i, He lies, dressed, across a large unseemly bed.

**Unsee·mly,** *adv.* [Un-1 11. Cf. ON. *úsǽmiliga* (Icel. *ósæm-*).] In an unseemly or unbecoming manner.

**c 1375** *Cursor M.* 24504 (Fairf.), On him mi heued I shoke & saide, vn-semeli, leue sone, artow graide! **? a 1400** *Morte Arth.* 1044 The syghte had he rechide, How vn-semly that sott satt sowpande hym one. **c 1449** Pecock *Repr.* ii. x. 207 Ellis it wolde folewe that ther yn thei diden vnaccordingli and vnsemeli. **1591** Drayton *Harmonie of Ch., Song of Annah* 8 Nor yet vnseemly speak such things, so proud and arrogant. **1610** Holland *Camden's Brit.* 297 English women..rode very unseemely astride, like as men doe. **a 1641** Bp. Mountagu *Acts & Mon.* (1642) 293 In which action hee..demeaned himself..unseemly for a King. **1725** Pope *Odyss.* i. 292 Yon' jovial Troop..Unseemly flown with insolence and wine. **1871** B. Taylor *Faust* (1875) I. xii. 143 Ah, thought I, in my conduct has he read it,—Something immodest or unseemly free?

**Unsee·n,** *ppl. a.* and *sb.* [Un-1 8 b, 12. Cf. OE. *ungesewen,* MDu. *ongesien* (Du. *ongezien*), OHG. *ungesëhan* (MHG. *ungesëhen,* G. *-gesehen*), NFris. *unseen;* ON. and Icel. *úsénn, ósénn.*]

**1.** Not seen; not apprehended by sight; unperceived, invisible.

*α.* **a 1225** *Leg. Kath.* 1784 For he halt in his hond..alle ischepene þing, sehene & unsehene. **a 1225** *Ancr. R.* 312 Þet wit & wereð us euer wið þe unseiene [*v.r.* unsehene] gostes. **c 1375** *Cursor M.* 566 (Fairf.), Saule..has vnderstandynge clene of þinge sayde and vnseyne. **1390** Gower *Conf.* II. 247 If a man wol ben unsein, Withinne his hond hold clos the Ston, And he mai invisible gon. **c 1440** *Jacob's Well* 263 No counseyl may be hyd in þe vnseyn & vnknowyn.

*β.* **a 1300** *Cursor M.* 566 Saul..has als vnderstanding clene O thing it seis and of vnsene. **1387-8** T. Usk *Test Love* i. Prol. (Skeat) l. 57 Wherthrough..arn the unsene privitees of god made to us sightful and knowing. **c 1470** Henry *Wallace* x. 626 Off the out watch thus chapyt thai wnseyn. **1500-20** Dunbar *Poems* lxxxv. 39 Haile, schene, vnseyne with carnale eyne! **1590** Spenser *F.Q.* ii. i. 1 Himselfe he frees by secret meanes vnseene. **1644** Digby *Nat. Bodies* xix. § 8 When by meanes of an vnseene haire, they [*sc.* jugglers] draw light bodies to them. **1681** Cotton *Wond. Peak* 59 When a..Ship..Suddenly strikes upon some unseen Rock. **1750** Gray *Elegy* 55 Full many a flower is born to blush unseen. **1798** S. & Ht. Lee *Canterb. T.* II. 27 [He] saw her there, and was not himself unseen. **1855** Tennyson *Maud* i. iv. v, Do we move ourselves, or are moved by an unseen hand..? **1867** H. Macmillan *Bible Teach.* Pref. p. xii, The work of the world is carried on by the unseen force of steam.

*absol.* **1829** Carlyle *Misc.* (1840) II. 226 The veil and mysterious Garment of the Unseen. **1841** Myers *Cath. Th.* iii. xxxiv. 125 Concerning the Unseen..no device..can preclude the possibility of Doubt.

**b.** Const. *of* (= by). Also *absol.*

**a 1586** Sidney *De Mornay* Wks. 1923 III. 305 Looke up to that same only King..Who,..unseene of any mortall wight, Beholdeth all things. **1623** Bp. Hall *Contempl., O.T.* xviii. iv, What an idleness it is for foolish hypocrites to hope they can dance in a net, unseen of heaven! **c 1800** R. Cumberland *John De Lancaster* (1809) II. 161 Davis.. had entered the room, unseen of young Owen. **1802** J. Baillie *1st Pt. Ethwald* iv. iii, Through the dank and through the dry, Through th' unseen of mortal eye.

**2.** Not seen previously or hitherto; *esp.* † unfamiliar, strange, unknown.

**a 1200** *St. Marher.* 10 Þa seh ha hwer set an unsehen unwiht,..blaccre þen euer eni blamon. **a 1300** *Cursor M.* 5946 Þe frosse deid all vp be-dene, Þe hepes o þam war gret vnsene Þat men gadird on þe grund. *Ibid.* 9091 Þat scrift was soruful and vn-sene,..þat salamon yod vnder. **a 1400-50** *Alexander* 2536 Be þis ser Philip son..of feȝtand folk Had semblid ane vnsene sowme. **1435** Misyn *Fire of Love* 69 Bot in treuth in me is cunne an vnsein Ioy. **1549** Coverdale, etc. *Erasm. Par. Rom.* 25 If it be an vnsene and a hiddeous presumpcion, that the clay should with the potter pratle. **1592** R. D. *Hypnerotomachia* 55 A Diamond..of a huge and unseene bignes. **1604** E. G[rimstone] *D'Acosta's Hist. Indies* vii. xxiii. 565 A bird as bigge as a Crane,..but of a strange and vnseene form. **1667** Milton *P. L.* xii. 361 A Starr Unseen before in Heav'n. **1725** Berkeley *Proposal,* etc. Wks. 1871 III. 230 Unseen countries and after ages may feel the effects of his bounty.

**b.** Of passages for translation: Not previously read. Hence as *sb.*, an unprepared passage.

**1879** C. S. Jerram *Anglice Reddenda* Pref., An exercise book in 'unseen', that is, unprepared translations. **1882** *Athenæum* 30 Dec. 897/2 A proposal..to substitute 'unseens' for 'set books' in..examinations. **1892** J. Edgar (*title*), Latin Unseens. *Ibid.* 23 A specimen unseen from Livy. **1897** E. S. Smith (*title*), Greek Unseens in Prose and Verse.

† **3.** Unskilled, inexperienced. *Obs.*

**1606** Holland *Sueton.* 254 Neither was he unseene in Musick. **1653** W. Ramesey *Astrol. Restored* 279 Somewhat difficult to those who are as yet altogether unseen therein. **1682** T. Flatman *Heraclitus Ridens* No. 63 (1713) II. 142 For any Man now to wonder at it, would but shew him very much unseen in the English History.

† **Unsee·nly,** *adv. Obs.*—1 [Un-1 11; cf. *unseȝenlike* s.v. Un-1 3.] Invisibly. **1398** Trevisa *Barth. De P. R.* viii. xxviii. (Bodl. MS.), Þe vertu of liȝt worcheþ vnseynlich [L. *invisibiliter*] feling and meuynge in beestes.

**Unse·gmented,** *ppl. a.* (Un-1 8.)

**1848** *Proc. Berw. Nat. Club* II. 297 Body ovate, ventricose, ..even and unsegmented. **1875** Huxley & Martin *Elem. Biol.* 206 Its posterior unsegmented part..nearly as long as the segmented part.

**Unsei·zable,** *a.* (Un-1 7 b.)

**1862** R. H. Patterson *Ess. Hist. & Art* 44 Beauty,.. beaming forth like an essence, felt but unseizable, in the wide sunny landscape. **1885** Meredith *Diana* xiii, She swam above them in a cocoon of her spinning, sylphidine, unseizable.

† **Unsei·ze,** *v. Obs.* [Un-2 3.]

**1.** *trans.* To detach from something held or that holds; *spec.* in hawking.

**1575** Turberv. *Faulconrie* 95 When she hath fedde, take it from hir and vnseaze hir. **1622** Mabbe tr. *Aleman's Guzman d'Alf.* i. To Vulgar, Who is hee that can be so happy as to..unseaze himselfe from thy griping talons? **1635** Quarles *Embl.* i. xii. 1 Be thy lips skrew'd so fast To th' earth's full breast? For shame, for shame unseise thee. *Ibid.* 3 Unseise thy lips. **1728** Chambers *Cycl.* s.v. *Falcon,* To which if she come well..and hastly seize it, let her cast two or three bits thereon. That done, unseize, take her off the Lure.

**2.** To let go, take one's hands off.

**1663** Tuke *Adv. 5 Hours* i. 8 He, at the stroke, unseas'd me, and gave back.

**Unsei·zed,** *ppl. a.* (Un-1 8.)

**a 1400-50** *Alexander* 5334, I sall surely þe saue vnsesid of þe berbrens. **1681** Dryden *Abs. & Achit.* i. 258 If unseiz'd, she glides away like wind; And leaves repenting Folly far behind. **a 1700** Evelyn *Diary* 6 Sept. 1666, Watching at all places contiguous to unseised houses. **1818** Keats *Endym.* ii. 464 He was..content to see An unseiz'd heaven dying at his feet. **1895** *Nat. Counc. Congregat. Ch.* (U. S.) 177 The unseized opportunities of this..mission field.

† **Unsel,** *a.* and *sb. Sc.* and *north. Obs.* Also 6 vnsall, -sale, -sell, 7 ouncel. [var. of Unsele *a.*]

**1.** *adj.* Unlucky, wretched; wicked.

**c 1375** *Sc. Leg. Saints* xv. 40 Gais furth, I send ȝou, I ȝou tel, as lammys amang wolfis vnsel. **1500-20** Dunbar *Poems* xiv. 79 Off Sathanis senȝie syne sic ane vnsall menȝie ..was nevir hard nor sene. **a 1583** Montgomerie *Flyting* 87 (Tullib. MS.), Arpit angrie Ettercoip, and auld vnsell aip. **a 1614** J. Melvill *Diary* (Wodrow Soc.) 49, I haiff dreamed an unsell dream.

**b.** As *adv.* Wickedly, vilely.

**a 1583** Polwart *Flyting w. Montgomerie* 622 (Tullib. MS.), He was ane fals schismatik, notorlie namit; Baith hurdome, & homeceid, vnsell he vsit.

**2.** *sb.* A vile or worthless person; a wretch.

*Kittie unsel* (Sc.): see Kitty1 1.

**155.** Lyndesay *Play* 2038 (Bann. MS.), Quhat sayis thow, cairle, art thow Gud Counsale? Swyth, pass the hence, vnhappy vnsale. **a 1583** Montgomerie *Flyting* 282 There ane elf on ane ape ane vnsell begat. **1677** Nicolson in *Trans. Royal Soc. Lit.* IX. 321 *Unsell,* wretched fellow. **1691** Ray *N. Co. Words* (ed. 2) 150 *Unsel,* Nomen..opprobriosum. **1825** Jamieson s.v., In Dumfries-shire, *Scoury unsell* is a contemptuous designation applied to a child, by one who is in bad humour. **1894** *Northumb. Gloss.* 757.

**b.** The Evil One. *rare.*

**c 1669** Garbutt *One Come from Dead* (1675) 27 He is right the Devils Child, the Ouncels Elfe. *Ibid.* 26.

† **Unse·lde,** *adv. Obs.* [OE. *unseldan* (*un-* Un-1 11 b + *seldan:* see Seld *adv.*), = Du. *onzelden,* G. *unselten,* ON. *úsjaldan.*] = next.

Only in phr. with *oft:* cf. ON. *oft úsjaldan.*

**a 950** *Laws Edw. & Guthrum* Prol. in Thorpe *Ags. Laws* I. 166 Þa witan eac..oft & unseldan þæt seolfe ȝeniwodon. **c 967** *Canons of Edgar* ibid. II. 278 Mislice men agyltað oft & unseldon þurh deofles scyfe. **c 1320** *Sir Tristr.* 2313 Oft and vnselde Of triamour tok he pray.

**Unse·ldom,** *adv.* [Un-1 11 b. Cf. prec.] *Not unseldom* (misused for), not rarely, not infrequently.

Du. *niet onzelden* is similarly used.

**1658** W. Burton *Itin. Anton.* 204 It is a thing not unseldome seen. **1686** Parr *Life of Usher* 83 Gaming..too often administred to Passion,..and not unseldom to Duelling. **a 1836** Mrs. Sherwood *Nun* ii, They not unseldom spent the afternoon under the cedar-trees. **1860** Trench *Deficiencies Eng. Dict.* 64 Johnson..quotes, not altogether unseldom .., Hacket's Life of Archbp. Williams. **1882** *Athenæum* 23 Sept. 401/2 A style which was generally diffuse, and not unseldom obscure.

† **Unse·le,** *sb. Obs.* Forms: 1 unsæl, 2–3 un-, vnsel, 4–5 vnsell, -sele; 4 vncel(e, 5 vnceyll(e. [OE. *unsǽl* (*un-* Un-1 12 + *sǽl* Sele *sb.*) = ON. and Icel. *úsæla, ósæla* unhappiness.]

**1.** Unhappiness, misery; misfortune, ill-luck.

**a 1023** Wulfstan *Hom.* (1883) 236 Þa deoflu..wæron on miclum unsælum, and þa englas wæron on swiðe micelre blisse. **c 1205** Lay. 30541 Unsel him wes on mode. **a 1250** *Owl & Night.* 1263 Ich wolde þer hi wel vnderstonde scholde þat sum vnsel heom is ihende. **c 1275** *xi Pains Hell* 90 in *O. E. Misc.* 149 Snaken..dreyeþ heom in-to a wel þer heo þolyeþ al vn-sel. **1338** R. Brunne *Chron.* (1810) 278 Þe Scottis I telle for sottis, & wrecchis vnwar, Unsele dyntis to dele þam drouh to Dunbar. **13..** *Guy Warw.* (A.) 1267 Of an vnsele y may ȝou telle, & ȝe wil a stounde duelle. **a 1400** *Hymns Virgin* (1867) 106 Þat þou..help to sauen hem from vncele, So þat heore soules beo not schent. **c 1400** *Laud Troy Bk.* 5985 Ector thanne with mochel vnsele Graunted his askyng. **c 1460** *Towneley Myst.* xii. 3 Here is mekyll vnceyll, and long has it last.

**b.** Unseemly matter. *rare*—1.

**a 1400** *Minor Poems fr. Vernon MS.* 503/377 Bi heore onswere þei wuste ful wel þat þei hedde spoken muchel vncel.

**2.** An improper time.

**c 1200** *Trin. Coll. Hom.* 13 Ȝef man haueð to done mid his rihte spuse on unsele oðer an untime þan man faste sal.

† **Unse·le,** *a. Obs.* [OE. *unsǽle* (Un-1 7), = ON. and Icel. *ú-, ósæll* (Sw. *osäll,* Da. *ussel*), unhappy, wretched, Goth. *unsēls* evil, wicked. Cf. Sele *sb.*]

**a.** Unlucky, bad. **b.** Unfortunate, wretched.

**c 1050** *Voc.* in Wr.-Wülcker 421 *Inprobus,* unsæle, ȝemah. **a 1200** *Moral Ode* 199 Nere namon elles ded ne sec ne nan unsele. **c 1275** Lay. 23868 Þe king was onseale þat he euere þoht wiþ Arthur to fihte. **c 1300** *Prov. Hendyng* in *Rel. Ant.* I. 113 Holde ich no mon for vnsele Oþer whyle þah he fele Sum þyng þat him smerte. **13..** *Cursor M.* 6149 (Gött.), Þaim he did þair asking haue, For to reue þat folk vn-sele.

Hence † **Unse·l(e)ly** *adv. Obs.*—1

**c 1275** Lay. 7022 Suþþen was his sone king, þat onselliche lifuede.

**Unsele·ct,** *a.* (Un-1 7.)

**1826** Miss Mitford *Village* Ser. ii. 256 A prodigious bundle of autographs, particularly unselect. **1867** P. Fitzgerald *75 Brooke St.* ii. xiii, Select, even in their unselect way. **1882** *Athenæum* 2 Sept. 299/1 The modern Jew as he lives and moves among the unselect.

**Unsele·cting,** *ppl. a.* (Un-1 10.) [**1828-32** Webster.] **1895** *Daily News* 11 June 4/7 Realists try to look at life with the unselecting eyes of the camera.

**Unse·lf,** *sb.* (Un-1 12.)

**1822** Coleridge *Lett., Convers.,* etc. II. 116 There was neither self nor unself in the flash..of pleasurable sensation. **1893** J. Pulsford *Loyalty to Christ* II. 367 Let us examine ..whether His spirit of unself, or the spirit of self and of the world, be the more in us.

**Unse·lf**, *v.* (Un-[2] 6 b, 8.) Also **Unse·lfed** *ppl. a.*, **Unse·lfing** *vbl. sb.*

**1654** Whitlock *Zootomia* 265 Canst thou afford lying, Dissembling,..and servile unselfing thy free born Minde, or Body? **1668** H. More *Div. Dial.* II. 28 God himself, who is that pure, free, and perfectly-unselfed Love. **1765** J. Brown *Chr. Jrnl.* 286 O to be unearthed, unselfed, that I may be like him! **1806** Surr *Winter in Lond.* III. 121, I cannot unself or unsex myself sufficiently to write in the narrative form; it must be I—I—I, and all about me—me—me. **1856** Faber *Creator & Creature* (1886) 55 Holiness is an unselfing of ourselves. **1868** Browning *Ring & Bk.* vii. 707 The grotesque intrigue To make me and my friend unself ourselves. **1890** J. Pulsford *Loyalty to Christ* I. 39 His unutterable sympathy..and His utterly unselfed character.

**Unselfcha·nging** *ppl. a.*, **-deli·cious** *a.*, † **-i·nterested** *ppl. a.*, **-know·ing** *ppl. a.*, **-like** *a.*, **-ness**, **-reflecting**, **-va·luing** *ppl. adjs.*, **-wi·lledness.** (Un-[1] 7, 7 b, 8, 10, 12; cf. Self 1 e, 1 f.)

**1591** Sylvester *Du Bartas* i. ii. 212 The World's owne Matter is the waxen Lump, which, *un-self-changing, takes all kind of stamp. *Ibid.* iii. 1057 Such were not yerst Cincinnatus, Fabricius, Serranus, Curius, who *vn-self-delicious,.. With ploughs triumphant plough'd the Roman lands. **1664** H. More *Exp. 7 Epist.* viii. 134 Thou art a lover of unity, *un-self-interessed, a foe to no body. **1685** — *Paralip. Prophet.* l. 465 That full, free, and absolute unself-interested Good. **1649** Milton *Eikon.* ix. 78 He twitts them with his Acts of grace; proud, and *unself-knowing words in the mouth of any King. **1598** Sylvester *Du Bartas* ii. ii. iv. *Columnes* 195 All Solids else (cast in the Aire) reflect *Unself-like-forms: but in a Globe each tract seems still the same. **1886** G. Macdonald *What's Mine's Mine* xx, He would have attracted attention anywhere, if only from his look of quiet *unselfness. **1668** H. More *Div. Dial.* II. 69 Like an *un-self-reflecting and an *un-self-valuing childe. **1684** — *Answer* 242 The Wheels and living Creatures being ..acted by the spirit, does not signifie an Earthly state in them, but..an *Unselfwilledness.

**Unselfco·nscious**, *a.* (Un-[1] 7.)

**1866** G. Macdonald *Ann. Q. Neighb.* xxviii, Instances of quiet unselfconscious faith. **1884** Ruskin *Fors Clav.* xcvi. 286 One who has in some signal..unself-conscious way done her duty. **1899** S. Brooke *Eng. Lit.* 146 This poem..belongs to the joyous, unself-conscious time.

So **Unselfco·nsciousness.**

Also, in recent use (1903–), *unselfconsciously*.

**1838** J. Sterling *Ess.*, etc. (1848) I. 199 One other great form of poetry..in which self-consciousness projects itself into external figures, and appears as unself-consciousness. **1894** Lucy H. M. Soulsby *Home Rule* 32 It may be urged that theatricals teach unself-consciousness, but this form of unself-consciousness is worth very little.

**Unse·lfish**, *a.* (Un-[1] 7. Cf. Da. *uselvisk*, Sw. *osjälfvisk.*)

**1698** J. Norris *Pract. Disc.* IV. 289 That Noble and Generous, disinterested and unselvish Kind of Love. **1714** H. Grove *Spectator* No. 588 ⁋ 2 Notwithstanding which, the Inclination is nevertheless unselfish. **1834** T. Keble in *Tracts for Times* No. 43. 14 St. Paul, that most heroic, and (if there were such a word,) that most *unselfish* of men. **1851** Longf. *Gold. Leg.* Epil. 10 Rise up..And scatter with unselfish hands Thy freshness on the barren sands. **1880** McCarthy *Own Times* xl. III. 224 One of the most unselfish men that ever lived.

Hence **Unse·lfishly** *adv.*, **Unse·lfishness.**

**1812** Coleridge *Lit. Rem.* (1836) I. 351 The unselfishness of self-love in the hopes and fears of religion. **1850** Lynch *Theoph. Trinal* v. 77 A most womanly unselfishness. **1862** Shirley (J. Skelton) *Nugæ Crit.* v. 218 A cause, whose success demanded perfect union and unselfishness. *Ibid.* x. 435 Steady, sagacious, moderate, never unselfishly imprudent. **1863** 'Ouida' *Held in Bondage* I. 185 None will ever love you more unselfishly than I.

**Unse·lfished**, *ppl. a.* [Un-[2] 8.] Deprived of selfish qualities; rendered unselfish. **1643** W. Greenhill *Axe at Root* A iv, The Axe is at the root of our Tree, we hope your spirits are all unselvished, that none are now unpublique.

†**Unse·lfly**, *adv.* (Un-[1] 11.) **1605** Sylvester *Du Bartas* ii. iii. iii. *Law* 253 All Beings Be not (or else un-selfly be) But, from my Being, all their Being gather. **Unse·lling**, *ppl. a.* (Un-[1] 10; cf. Selling *ppl. a.* 1.) *a* **1704** T. Brown *Dial. Dead* Wks. 1711 IV. 98 As a Bookseller hates an unselling Author. **1720** *Humourist* 124 As you may see in certain unselling Dialogues of the Art of Poetry.

† **Unse·lth.** *Obs.* [OE. *unsǽlþ* (*un-* Un-[1] 12; also *ungesǽlþ*, see Un-[1] 3), = OHG. *unsâlida*, *unsâlda*, *unsâltha* (MHG. *unsælde*, MLG. *unsâlde*, etc.).] Unhappiness, infelicity, misery.

*c* **888** K. Ælfred *Boeth.* x, Þæt is seo mæste unsælð on þys andweardan life. *c* **1000** *Ags. Ps.* (Thorpe) xiii. 7 Hie wilniað ealle mægne oþera manna unsælþa. *a* **1200** *Moral Ode* 374 Nis þer sorewe ne sor, ne neure nan vn-sealþe. *c* **1250** *Gen. & Ex.* 3026 Ðo wex vn-selðe on hem wel hard. *c* **1315** Shoreham I. 823 Na more ne greueþ..Þaȝ eny best deuoured hyt, Oþer eny oþer onselþe. *c* **1425** *Eng. Conq. Ireland* 50 Euery selth hath wnselth at þe end.

**Unsembly**, obs. var. Unseemly *a.*

† **Unse·minared**, *ppl. a.* *Obs.*—[1] [Un-[2] 8.] Deprived of virility. **1606** Shaks. *Ant. & Cl.* i. v. 11 Tis well for thee, That being vnseminar'd, thy freer thoughts May not flye forth of Egypt.

† **Unse·ne**, *a.* *Obs. rare.* [Un-[1] 7 + Sene *a.* Cf. OE. *ungesėne* and ON. *úsýnn.*] Invisible; not obvious.

*c* **1200** *Trin. Coll. Hom.* 47 On ure helendes lichame wiðuten sene, þe holie saule wiðinne unsene. *c* **1250** *Gen. & Ex.* 2878 Ic..swanc and michel sorwe dreȝ; ȝet ist vnsene hu ic it bi-teȝ?

†**Unse·nsably**, *adv.* [Un-[1] 11.] = Unsensibly *adv.* 1. *a* **1395** Hylton *Scala Perf.* ii. xxiv. (MS. Bodl. 592), Not in bodili liknesse but vnsensabli bi preuie hid presence of his goostli myȝt. †**Unse·nsate**, *a.* *Obs.*—[1] [Un-[1] 7, 5 b.] Insensate. **1561** Eden *Arte Nauig.* Pref., Yf they be lyuely members and not wythered or otherwyse vnsensate by reason of dead fleshe.

**Unsensa·tional**, *a.* (Un-[1] 7.)

Also, in recent use, *unsensationalism*, *-ally* adv.

**1865** *Pall Mall G.* 8 Aug. 11 The name of a French novel, quiet and unsensational. **1881** 'Rita' *My Lady Coquette* xxii, Altogether life is very drowsy and unsensational.

**Unse·nse**, *v.* [Un-[2] 6 b.] *trans.* To deprive of sense; *esp.* to render insensible.

**1611** Florio, *Disensato*, sencelesse, vnsensed, out of reason. **1793** *Minstrel* I. 185, I was a little unsensed by my sudden souse into the stream. *a* **1809** T. Paine *Farmer's Dog* Poems (1834) 163 And get such mischief by the hit As should unsense him of his wit. **1851** Borrow *Lavengro* I. 331 One blow given with the proper play of his athletic arm, will unsense a giant. **1895** *Educat. Rev.* Sept. 158 The mind has been unsensed or dematerialized.

**Unse·nsed**, *ppl. a.* (Un-[1] 8.)

**1667** Jer. Taylor *Dissuas. Popery* ii. i. § 2. 75 They tell you the Scripture is but a dead letter, Unsensed Characters, words without sense, or unsensed. **1675** R. Fleming *Short Acc. Doctr. Rom. Ch.* 6 They have no..authentick record to prove their Religion, but what is a Mass of dead unsensed Characters. **1734** Waterland *Imp. Doct. Holy Trinity* i. 18 We do not mean unsensed Characters, or empty Sounds. **1876** Mrs. Whitney *Sights & Ins.* vi, They were like apparitions shining out of the unsensed. **1897** F. Thompson *New Poems* 22 The incredible excess of unsensed sweet, And mystic wall of strange felicity.

† **Unsensibi·lity.** (Un-[1] 12, 5 b. Cf. next.)

**1551** Robinson tr. *More's Utopia* ii. (1895) 204 For to be wythowte greyffe, not hauinge health, that they call vnsensybylyte and not pleasure. *a* **1650** May *Satyr. Puppy* (1657) 13 A passionate Man is..nor Man nor Beast: for he wants the sence of the one, and in some kinde the vnsensibilitie of the other.

**Unse·nsible**, *a.* *Obs.* exc. *dial.* or as *nonce-wd.* [Un-[1] 7, 5 b.]

**1.** = Insensible *a.* 1.

*c* **1380** Wyclif *Serm.* Sel. Wks. II. 55 It was bigynnyng of tyme unsensible to mannis witt. *Ibid.* 148 Þei trowen to sensible wordis, and oþer signes þat men maken, but unsensible wordis of Goddis Sone..þei trowen litil or nouȝt. *c* **1400** *Apol. Loll.* 100 To a-wowe is, a resonable creature to obey him to his souereyn, to kep sum hard þing þat is sensible, or vns[en]sible. **1534** More *Treat. Passion* Wks. 1335/2 Vnder anye of the twoo outwarde sensible Sacramentes..the whole inwarde vnsensyble Sacramente..is.. fullye conteyned. **1581** E. Campion in *Confer.* iii. (1584) Q j b, That you say vnsensible, it is true, if you meane the spirituall grace, which is not subiect to sense. **1587** Golding *De Mornay* xv. 285 To extend reason from..things sensible to things vnsensible,..from bodily to spirituall. **1656** M. Casaubon *Enthus.* To Rdr., Neither do I think so meanly of any truth, that can be reduced to any reality, whether sensible or unsensible.

**b.** = Insensible *a.* 1 b.

**1545** Raynald *Byrth Mankynde* Y vj, The blud the whiche daylye and hourely, by vnsensyble swettinge euaporatith. *a* **1586** Sidney *Arcadia* i. xiii, It being set upon such an unsensible rising of the ground, as you are come to a prety height before almost you perceive that you ascend. **1614** Brerewood *Lang. & Relig.* 12 For which reason, the corruption of speech growing upon them, by little and little, the change hath been unsensible. **1633** Prynne *Histrio-m.* 957 No man becomes extreamely vitious on a sudden, but by unsensible gradations.

**c.** Imperceptible by reason of minuteness.

**1551** Recorde *Pathw. Knowl.* i. Def., A Poynt..is named of Geometricians that small and vnsensible shape, whiche hath in it no partes. **1571** Digges *Pantom.* i. xv. E ij, The angle..groweth so acute, and vnsensible, that great errour ensueth the least mistakyng. **1602** Fulbecke *Pandectes* 9 The present time is so small and unsensible, that it is almost of no continuance.

**2.** = Insensible *a.* 2.

**1555** Eden *Decades* (Arb.) 53 If the greefes of them bee to thee vnsensible by reason of thy..longe sickenes.

**3.** = Insensible *a.* 3 a.

*c* **1532** Tindale *Answ. More* Wks. (1572) 279/1 [Christ] dyed not to purchase such honour vnto vnsensible thinges, that [etc.]. *c* **1555** Harpsfield *Divorce Hen. VIII* (Camden) 252 Unless he be as unsensible as a man that will put and hold his finger in the hot fire and say the fire burneth not. **1583** Melbancke *Philotimus* S ij, The two vnsensible pictures. **1611** Cotgr., *Cal*, a thicke, and vnsensible skin, or brawnie hardnesse of skin. **1627** *Lisander & Cal.* i. 11 The secret places of Calista's affection, which were not marble, nor of any unsensible matter. **1677** W. Hubbard *Narrative* Postscr. 10 This unsensible and hardhearted Monster answered, he liked it very well.

**b.** = Insensible *a.* 3 b, 3 c.

**1568** Turner *Herbal* iii. 50 Rasis in his Simples writeth that the Methel maketh num or vnsensible. *a* **1616** Beaum. & Fl. *Wit without M.* ii. iv, Your Land has lain long bedrid, and unsensible. **1632** J. Hayward tr. *Biondi's Eromena* 191 Her often swounding kept her alive by making her become unsensible of the sharpenesse of the paine which shee felt. **1669** Worlidge *Syst. Agric.* 160 When the doors are shut..they [*sc.* bees] are dark, and unsensible of so small a heat. **1891** in G. L. Gower *Surrey Words* (1893) 44, I was unsensible for loss of blood.

**4.** = Insensible *a.* 4 a.

(*a*) **1610** Heywood *Gold. Age* iv. i, Vnsensible of loue, or amorous pitty. **1621** G. Sandys *Ovid's Met.* viii. (1626) 167 They the time beguile with speech: Vnsensible of stay. **1692** South *Serm.* (1697) I. 498, I mean not, that he is unsensible of the good it self, but that..he is wholly unsensible ..of the Benignity of him that does it. *a* **1804** in Miss Betham *Biog. Dict. Celebrated Women* 452 She thought herself..too unsensible of our Lord's love to her.

(*b*) **1663** Gerbier *Counsel* a ij, It would doubtlesse make me pass for uncensible, how your Majesty..inherited that same clemency. **1664** Ingelo *Bentiv. & Ur.* v. 39 One not altogether unsensible that he hath over-charg'd his Vocation with burthensome Cares. **1719** W. Wood *Surv. Trade* 224, I am not unsensible, how very disadvantagious it is for us [etc.]. **1735** J. Price *Stone-Br. Thames* 16, I am not unsensible that it may be suggested [etc.].

**b.** = Insensible *a.* 4 b.

**1619** J. King *Serm.* 2, I thinke there is none so unsensible that is not moved hereat. **1650** O. Sedgwick *Christ the Life* 26 Dull and unsensible men; of such did one long since complain, That [etc.]. **1676** Etheredge *Man of Mode* ii. i, *Town.* Methinks you speak very feelingly, Brother. *Old Bell.* I am but Five and Fifty, Sister, you know, an Age not altogether unsensible! *a* **1699** J. Kirkton *Hist. Ch. Scot.* (1817) 65 Many a sober man was tempted to exceed, lest he should be condemned as unnatural, disloyal, unsensible.

**5.** = Insensible *a.* 5.

**1560** Pilkington *Expos. Aggeus* Dd ij, Lyke vnreasonable beastes and vnsensyble. **1565** Stapleton *Fortr. Faith* 136* What is now more reuiled of vnsensible protestants then the shauen crowne of reuerent priesthood? *a* **1586** Sidney *Arcadia* i. iv, He found some of his aunswers..not unsensible. **1814** [Mary Brunton] *Discipline* xxii. III. 26 The poor lad was not so unsensible, but he knew to do his bidding. **1861** Geo. Eliot *Silas M.* xiv, When the drink's out of 'em, they aren't unsensible.

**6.** Not showing good or sound sense.

*a* **1586** Sidney *Arcadia* iii. xix, For nothing can be more unsensible, then to thinke what one doth, & to forget the end why it is done. **1858** Bagehot *Lit. Stud.* (1879) II. 154 The strongest *un*sensible feeling in Scott was perhaps his Jacobitism.

† **Unse·nsibleness.** *Obs.* [Un-[1] 12 and 5 b. Cf. prec.] Insensibility.

*a* **1568** Coverdale *Bk. Death* xxxvii. (1579) 171 That is a very blockish vnsensiblenesse of wilde madde barbarous people. **1571** Golding *Calvin on Ps.* xxviii. 5 Through stubbornesse [they] harden themselues vntoo vnsensiblenesse. **1603** Florio *Montaigne* ii. xii, I commend not that vnsensiblenesse, which is neither possible nor to be desired. **1676** I. Mather *K. Philip's War* (1862) 94 Our great unsensibleness of the Displeasure of the Lord, in suffering these abominations to be perpetuated. **1730** Bailey (fol.), *Indolency*, unsensibleness of Pain or Grief.

† **Unse·nsibly**, *adv.* *Obs.* [Un-[1] 11, 5 b.]

**1.** = Insensibly *adv.* 1.

**1627** Abp. Abbot in Rushw. *Hist. Coll.* (1659) I. 444 So being unsensibly hatched, it came flying into the World. **1679** C. Nesse *Antichrist* 213 It stole into the world..unsensibly, and at unawares.

**b.** Unknowingly, unconsciously.

**1658** J. Jones *Ovid's Ibis* 127 Though unsensibly she shed bitter tears for her transgression.

**2.** = Insensibly *adv.* 2.

**1565** Jewel *Reply Harding* 217 That after so many wordes ..ye shoulde be founde so nakedly, and so vnsensibly to deceiue the people. **1596** Spenser *State Irel.* Wks. (Globe) 622/2 The later [statute]..is soe unsensibly contryved that it scarce carryeth any reason in it.

†**Unse·nsical**, *a.* *Obs.*—[1] [Un-[1] 7.] Nonsensical. **1692** S. Johnson *Argument* 18 His Unsensical Apothegm, 'No Bishop, no King'.

**Unse·nsitive**, *ppl. a.* (Un-[1] 7 and 5 b.)

Also, in recent use (1895–), *unsensitiveness*.

**1610** Healey *St. Aug. Citie of God* 283 One [soul] liuing in all bodies vnsensitiue, onely hauing life. **1816** *Monthly Mag.* XLI. 209 But figures never affect the feelings; numerical calculations go on in an unsensitive part of the mind. **1838** Mill *Diss. & Disc.* (1859) I. 323 In a world which, for any but the unsensitive, is not a place of contentment. **1881** P. Brooks *Candle of Lord* 273 Some knowledge which the life in its best health was too hard and unsensitive to take.

**Unse·nsitized**, *ppl. a.* (Un-[1] 8 a *c.*) **1889** *Anthony's Photogr. Bull.* II. 53 An unsensitized piece..will soon cause discoloration on any sensitized paper placed against it. †**Unse·nsive**, *a.* *Obs.*—[1] [Un-[1] 7.] Not perceptible by the senses. **1616** J. Lane *Contn. Sqr.'s T.* x. 284 Feare bears it knowne, thoughe (ofte) no man knoes how, Yea ofte b' vnsensive meanes (as clerkes avowe). **Unse·nsual**, *a.* (Un-[1] 7.) **1850** Lynch *Theoph. Trinal* v. 76 Wisdom hath a pure unsensual love. **1866** *Sat. Rev.* 3 Mar. 255/2 It is true, that..Plato dwells prominently on the anti-sensual, or at least on the unsensual, side of love.

**Unse·nsualize**, *v.* (Un-[2] 6 c.)

**1792** W. Roberts *Looker-on* No. 29 (1794) I. 410 Love is so unsensualized and sublimed above passion, that it has forgotten its old retreats. **1796** Coleridge *Destiny of Nations* 80 For Fancy is the power That first unsensualises the dark mind, Giving it new delights. *a* **1849** H. Coleridge *Ess.* (1851) II. 147 Certain divines who thought to unsensualize mankind by making the body as disgusting as possible. **1889** *Spectator* 7 Sept., An almost Pharisaic observance of the rites and ceremonies which unsensualised them.

**Unse·nsuous**, *a.* (Un-[1] 7.) **1850** Mrs. Browning *Sonn.*, *H. S. Boyd* 12 Till Sensuous and Unsensuous seemed one thing, Viewed from one level. **1856** R. A. Vaughan *Mystics* I. 270 The higher calm of unsensuous, imageless contemplation.

**Unse·nt**, *ppl. a.* Also 8 *Sc.* unsenn. [Un-[1] 8 b and 8 c. Cf. ON. *úsent* (Da. *usendt*).]

**1.** Not sent for, unsummoned. (Cf. b.)

*c* **1530** *Crt. of Love* 174 Of your free will ye should have come unsent. **1717** Ramsay *Elegy Lucky Wood* ii, Death, wha came unsenn To Lucky Wood.

**b.** With *for* expressed.

**1501** *Plumpton Corr.* (Camden) 157 If I wold come up unsent for. **1598** Dallington *Meth. Trav.* X 3 b, They take one of a suddaine, comming vnlooked for and vnsent for. *a* **1641** Bp. Mountagu *Acts & Mon.* (1642) 298 Herod, unsent for, went to visit him. **1673** Wycherley *Gentl. Dancing-Master* v, We Fiddlers, Sir, often come unsent for. **1717** De Foe *Mem. Ch. Scot.* ii. 36 But Mr. Andrew Melvin..went unsent for. **1753** Richardson *Grandison* (1781) IV. xiv. 104 That no third person, unsent for, can be welcome.

**2.** Not sent or dispatched.

In recent use esp. of letters or telegrams.

*c* **1550** Crowley *Inform. & Petit.* iv b, The same Spirite..

wytnesseth wyth my conscience that I renne not vnsent. *c* **1586** SIDNEY *Arcadia* I. vi, He armed himselfe, and those few of his servants he had left unsent. **1608** DOD & CLEAVER *Expos. Prov. xi–xii.* 122 That we goe not unsent. **1647** JER. TAYLOR *Lib. Proph.* vi. 124 More able men may be unsent then sent. **1841** *Fraser's Mag.* Jan. 111/2 Ye came na here unsent, and ye maun perform your errand. **1855** KINGSLEY *Westw. Ho!* xxvii, Her strange affection for the English was not unsent by Heaven.

**b.** With advs. or preps.

**1549** PAGET in Froude *Hist. Eng.* (1860) V. 182 Send for all the council that be remaining unsent abroad. **1606** BP. HALL *Heaven upon Earth* xiii. Wks. (1625) 83 Thy heauenly Physician,..vnsent to, sends thee..a soueraigne remedie. **1656** in Picton *L'pool Munic. Rec.* (1883) I. 176 Whylst they stay at home unsent away.

**Unse·ntenced,** *ppl. a.* (UN-[1] 8.)

**1526** *Customs of Pale* in *Archæol.* (1893) LIII. 373 The king's iudicate officers..shall..suffer no accion to departe unsentenced before them. **1612** *Two Noble K.* v. i. 163, I could doombe neither; that which perish'd should Goe too't unsentenc'd. **1661** HEYLIN *Hist. Ref.* Q. Mary (1670) 6 The King..privately marryeth her within few days after his return, the divorce being yet unsentenced betwixt him and the Queen. **1822** BEDDOES *Brides' Trag.* IV. ii, Some vengeance will fall on us in the night If he remain unsentenced. **1862** SHIRLEY (J. Skelton) *Nugæ Crit.* 140 To leave them rather unsentenced and in hope to the mercy.. which alone can fully extenuate..their guilt. **1896** *Harper's Mag.* April 672/2 The secular judge..forgot his duty, and Joan went to her death unsentenced.

**Unsente·ntious,** *a.* [**1775** ASH.] **1846** WORCESTER (citing *Qu. Rev.*).

**Unse·ntient,** *ppl. a.* (UN-[1] 7 and 5 b.)

**1768–74** TUCKER *Lt. Nat.* (1834) I. 315 We may admit a sentient composed of unsentient parts. *Ibid.* 583 An eternal First Cause, whether intelligent, or unsentient. **1835** J. YOUNG *Lect. Intell. Philos.* xlviii. 485 There could be no sensation in an unsentient being. **1864** BOWEN *Logic* xiii. 422 Only in the sentient mind, and not in the unsentient matter of the body.

**Unsentime·ntal,** *a.* (UN-[1] 7.)

**1810** SCOTT in *Lockhart* (1839) III. 228 The despair.. gave me a most unsentimental horror for sentimental letters. **1853** C. BRONTE *Villette* xxi, Never man had a more unsentimental mother than mine. **1898** HADDON *Stud. Man* xiv. 409 An unsentimental survival of this pretty custom.

Hence **Unsentimenta·lity**; **-me·ntalize** *v.*; **-me·ntally** *adv.*

**1824** HOOK *Sayings & Doings* III. 168 Gaieties..calculated ..to enliven and unsentimentalize the mind. *Ibid.* Ser. II. I. 28 The impropriety and unsentimentality of her behaviour. *Ibid.* xiv. III. 300 She was..most unsentimentally employed in swallowing a very hearty supper. **1837** LEWIS *Lett.* (1870) 84 For the sake of..unsentimentalizing the cause of the Catholic clergy. **1847** L. HUNT *Men, Women, & B.* II. ii. 25 The unsentimentalizing effects of the gallantry of the court of Charles II.

**Unse·ntinelled,** *ppl. a.* (UN-[1] 8.) **1817** *Edin. Rev.* XXVIII. 87 The old castle..was ungarrisoned and unsentinelled. **1859** *All Year Round* No. 36. 219 A huge gateway, not unsentinelled.

†**Unse·parable,** *a. Obs.* (UN-[1] 7 b and 5 b.)

**1398** TREVISA *Barth. de P. R.* XVI. v. (Bodl. MS.), þe onynge is vnseperable so þat þei mowe not afterward be parted atwynne. **1532** MORE *Confut. Tindale* Wks. 495/1 Was himself..companion to saynt Poule, & that so continuall and so vnseparable, yt..he neuer departed from him? **1561** T. HOBY tr. *Castiglione's Courtyer* IV. Xx iij b, This is the beawtye vnseperable from the high bountye. **1587** GOLDING *De Mornay* v. 67 Fire..hath in it both heate and brightnesse vnseparable. **1645** MILTON *Divorce* (ed. 3) I. i. 7 The first institution will be objected to have ordain'd marriage unseperable. **1697** JEREMY COLLIER *Ess. Mor. Subj.* I. 5 Self-love..is an unseparable Passion of humane nature. **1737** *Gentl. Mag.* VII. 14/2 Placed between two Words joyned together in unseparable Concord.

Hence **Unse·parableness.**

**1587** FENNER *Def. Ministers* 116 Hee maketh the case of both alike in regarde of the propertie and vnseparablenes of the bande.

†**Unse·parably,** *adv. Obs.* (UN-[1] 11 and 5 b.)

**1532** MORE *Confut. Tindale* Wks. 514/2 And with them the godhead vnseperably ioyned. **1586** W. WEBBE *Eng. Poetrie* (Arb.) 80 Thys verse is alwayes vnseperably adioyned vnto the Hexameter. **1622** CALLIS *Stat. Sewers* (1647) 14 A pretty difference, where the act to be done is unseparably tied to ones person, and where not. **1698** S. CLARKE *Script. Justif.* iv. 18 That Pardon is unseparably join'd with Justification.

† **Unse·parate,** *ppl. a. Obs.* (UN-[1] 8 b, 5 b; cf. next.) Hence †**Unse·parateness.** *Obs.*—[1]

**1553** *Short Catech.* in *Liturgies*, etc. (Parker Soc.) 513 True faith and works *unseparate. **1563** FOXE *A. & M.* 540 As heat followeth euer with the fire vnseparate there from. **1591** JAS. I *Lepanto, Chorus Angel.* 11 Our onlie one vnseparate, And yet in persons three. **1668** H. MORE *Div. Dial.* I. 121 Then Rest and Unseparateness of parts are all one,..and *Unseparateness and Union all one.

**Unse·parated,** *ppl. a.* (UN-[1] 8.)

**1545** COVERDALE *Def. Certain Chr. Man* E iiij b, Therfore will we discerne these thre thinges,..but so that they remayne vnseparated. **1577** tr. *Bullinger's Decades* III. vi. 373/1 He being one and the same Christ vnseperated. **1620** QUARLES *Medit.* i, Three speciall Attributes of God .., all Vnseparated From Gods pure Essence. *a* **1671** LD. FAIRFAX *Mem.* (1699) 99 The two Houses of Parliament.., so great an Authority which was then unseparated from the Royal interest. **1725** POPE *Odyss.* x. 585 To whom Persephone, entire and whole, Gave to retain th' unseparated soul. **1860** FARRAR *Orig. Lang.* ii. 44 The field and the snow were unseparated. **1893** TUCKEY *Amphioxus* 104 The unseparated mesoblast fold.

†**Unse·parately,** *adv. Obs. rare.* [UN-[1] 11, 5 b.] Inseparably. **1580** HOLLYBAND *Treas. Fr. Tong, Indissolublement*, vnseparately. **1593** NASHE *Christ's T.* A ij, She thought the Lord vnseparately tyde to his Temple. **Unse·ptate,** *a. Bot.* (UN-[1] 7.) **1900** JACKSON *Gloss. Bot. Terms* 283 *Unseptate*,..applied to a plant which has not partitioning divisions. **Unse·ptated,** *a. Bot.* (UN-[1] 8 a *b.*) **1899** J. R. GREEN *Soluble Ferments* xx. 325 A fungus which developes a much-branched unseptated mycelium. **Unse·pulchre,** *v.* (UN-[2] 5.) **1856** in *Oxford Ess.* 217 As his ploughshare that unsepulchred the 'empty helmets and the mighty bones' of the buried foemen.

**Unse·pulchred,** *ppl. a.* (UN-[1] 8.)

*c* **1611** CHAPMAN *Iliad* XXII. 306 Dead, vndeplor'd, Vnsepulcherd; he lies at fleete. **1624** QUARLES *Sion's Elegies* ii. 21 Unsepulchred my murthred people lye. **1795** SOUTHEY *Joan of Arc* IX. 42 For hills of human slain, unsepulchred, Steam pestilence. **1816** BYRON *Ch. Har.* III. lxiii, The Stygian coast Unsepulchred they roam'd, and shriek'd each wandering ghost. **1862** GRATTAN *Beaten Paths* I. 142 To discover the unsepulchred, uncoffined, and uncereclothed tailor, standing stiff against the chapel wall.

**Unse·pultured,** *ppl. a.* (UN-[1] 8.) [**1847** WEBSTER.] **1862** R. H. PATTERSON *Ess. Hist. & Art* 269 Some unsepultured one, who had departed to join the troop of shivering ghosts. **1897** GOMME *C. Macfarlane's Camp of Refuge* Introd. p. lxv, The cause that so many men were slaughtered and lay unsepultured. †**Unseque·ster,** *v. Obs.* (UN-[2] 3.) **1664** KATH. PHILIPS *Poems* 146 By a flame from thy blest Genius lent..Unsequester our Fancies, and create A Worth that may upon thy Glories wait. **Unseque·stered,** *ppl. a.* (UN-[1] 8.) **1654** WHITLOCK *Zootomia* 149 Which if impartially compared,..our Librarys might be repreived, and our Colledges unsequestred. **1655** FULLER *Ch. Hist.* XI. iii. § 6 His unsequestred Spirit so supported him, that [etc.]. **Unsere·ne,** *a.* (UN-[1] 7.) **1664** INGELO *Bentiv. & Ur.* v. 124 How unserene are all the Joyes..upon Earth! **1829** LAMB in *The Gem* 26 The sad orbs..blinded through unserene drops for her dead lord.

**Unse·rious,** *a.* (UN-[1] 7.)

**1655** EARL ORRERY *Parthen.* II. v. 493 To speake any thing unserious. **1673** FLAVEL *Saint Indeed* 199 Frothy, vain and unserious persons. **1755** WESLEY *Wks.* (1872) II. 326 Any one who behaved in a light or unserious manner. **1860** HAWTHORNE *Fr. & It. Note-bks.* (1871) II. 357 A plaything, a trifle, an unserious affair.

Hence **Unse·riousness.**

**1680** H. DODWELL *Two Lett.* (1691) To Rdr. §9 The lives and unseriousness of some of our conformable Clergy.

**Unse·rrated,** *ppl. a.* (UN-[1] 8.) **1840** *Cuvier's Anim. Kingd.* 79 The edge of the long inferior incisors is unserrated.

**Unse·rved,** *ppl. a.* [UN-[1] 8.]

**1.** Not served or furnished with something; not attended to.

*c* **1350** *Leg. Rood* (1871) 85 Sen sekenes es sent to þe þir men sall noght vnserued be, þai sall haue nayles or þai ga. **1433** *Rolls of Parlt.* IV. 439/1 Yf I should paye hem, youre Household, Chambre and Warderope..shuld be unservid and unpaide. **1542** UDALL *Erasm. Apoph.* 302 Onely Phocion was remainyng unserved by reason that the poison had been all consumed by the others. *a* **1585** MONTGOMERIE *Cherry & Slae* 1083 Who came uncald, unserv'd shuld sit. *a* **1600** DELONEY *Jack of Newberie* iv, Well, looke there be not one hog vnserued. **1624** *Essex his Ghost* 16 His people I hope will turne your golden..Coates into Coates of Male, ..rather then your Soueraigne..shall bee vnserued. **1786** R. HEATHCOTE *Sylva* (1788) 256 His boy therefore sent away unserved a customer. **1804** R. ANDERSON *Cumbld. Ball.* 79 The witch weyfe begg'd in our back seyde, But went unsarra'd away. **1832** HT. MARTINEAU *Each & All* iii. 33 Conscience awakes..to the cry of unserved humanity. **1899** *Daily News* 3 Nov. 7/6 Several of their unserved guns were shelled vigorously.

**b.** *spec.* Not attended to by a priest or incumbent. (See SERVE *v.* 14.)

The app. early instance in Wyclif's *De Ecclesia* is prob. an error for 'unlerned', the reading of MS. Bodl. 788.

**1562** in Strype *Ann. Ref.* (1709) I. xxxi. 312 So that the people be not unserved or defrauded of a reasonable minister. **1587** HOLINSHED *Chron.* (ed. 2) III. 1142/1 Where through died manie..priests, so that a great number of parishes were vnserued. **1643** BAKER *Chron., Q. Mary* 106 This yeer.. was great mortality, and specially of Priests, so as many Churches were unserved. **1765** BLACKSTONE *Comm.* I. 466 It permits an infant to present a clerk..rather than..suffer the church to be unserved till he comes of age.

**2.** Not worshipped, regarded, or observed.

**1387** TREVISA *Higden* (Rolls) II. 85 Þese feyned goddes.. beeþ i-served in Chestre..Þan is Pluto not vnserued, god of helle. **1390** GOWER *Conf.* I. 355 The cherche is brent, the priest is slain,..The lawe is lore and god unserved. *c* **1450** *Mirk's Festial* 267 Mony seyntys-dayes we leuen yn þe ȝere vnseruet; for þay ben so many þat we may not serue hom all. **1532** MORE *Confut. Tindale* Wks. 495/2 Nor saint Paule..meaneth not yet they shall leaue the sacramentes vnserued which God hath taught.

**3.** *Law.* **a.** Of writs, summonses, etc.: Not served upon a person.

**1465** *Paston Lett.* II. 201 The shyrf sayd playnly that he.. derst not serve it [*sc.* a writ],..and so it ys yet unservyd. **1476** *Acta Auditorum* (1839) 49/2 Þe persons of þe inqueste allegeit before þe lordis þat þe said breve wes vnseruit. **1908** *Daily Chron.* 10 Jan. 3/5 The constabulary were withdrawn, and the processes remained unserved.

† **b.** *Sc.* Not returned as heir. *Obs.*

**1490** *Acta Dom. Conc.* (1839) 125/2 Patrik and William.. sall nocht fortify þe partij þat beis one seruit be that inquest.

**4.** Not served up.

**1871** RUSKIN *Fors Clav.* iii, The waiter then and there packed his knapsack and departed,..leaving my dinner unserved.

**5.** With *for*: For which service has not been done.

**1555** *Inv. Ch. Goods* (Surtees) 157, xij li bequeithed..to the finding of a prieste there for iij yeares.., whereof remayned unserved for at the tyme.., xiijs. iiijd.

†**Unse·rviable,** *a. Obs.*—[1] [UN-[1] 7 b.] Unserviceable. **1544** BETHAM *Precepts War* I. xcii. E vj b, They [*sc.* gunners] be vnseruyable, and can do no good. †**Unse·rvice.** *Obs.* (UN-[1] 4 b, 12.) **1611** FLORIO, *Disseruitu*, vnseruice, disseruice. **1624** MASSINGER *Parl. Love* I. v, Where you tax us for unservice, lady, I never knew a soldier yet that could Arrive into your favour.

**Unse·rviceable,** *a.* [UN-[1] 7 b and 5 b.]

**1.** Of things: Not capable of being employed for their proper purpose.

**1535** *Wardr. Kath. Arragon* 33 in *Camden Misc.* III, The thurde [chair] is broken and unservesable. **1590** SPENSER *F. Q.* I. xi. 25 The beast..his late wounded wing vnseruiceable found. **1600** in *St. Papers, Dom.* (1869) 437 The others [= signets] having become unserviceable from long use. **1663** BOYLE *Usef. Exp. Nat. Philos.* II. App. 328 Besides a not despicable quantity of terrestrial and unserviceable matter. **1690** LOCKE *Hum. Und.* III. iii. § 17 The supposition ..is so..unserviceable to any part of our knowledge. **1713** BERKELEY *Guard.* No. 35, His intellectuals, I observed, were grown unserviceable by too little use. **1737** tr. *Le Comte's Mem. & Remarks China* Pref., They might not be unserviceable to those who might..take up such a design. **1801** *Farmer's Mag.* Aug. 339 The horse I hire..may be in any degree serviceable or unserviceable. **1830** H. N. COLERIDGE *Grk. Poets* 1 A perusal of these Introductions may not be unserviceable to many well educated readers. **1857** DICKENS *Dorrit* I. xxxii, What with her flapping cap, and..her unserviceable eye.

**b.** *spec.* Of ships, guns, etc.

**1610** HOLLAND *Camden's Brit.* 35 The ships..so shaken with the tempest, that they became altogether unserviceable. **1618** in *Essex Rev.* (1908) XVII. 102 The moderne use doth altogether exclude the caliver as unservicable. **1707** *Lond. Gaz.* No. 4362/2, 10 Ships were destroyed.., and several others rendred wholly unserviceable. **1748** *Anson's Voy.* II. iv. 165 Three four pounders, which were altogether unserviceable. **1811** *Regul. & Orders Army* 91 The disposal of Unserviceable Arms. **1865** CAMERON *Malayan India* 246 It is not that the forts are ungarrisoned,..but that they are unserviceable. **1876** VOYLE & STEVENSON *Milit. Dict.* 446/2 *Unserviceable*, the term is applied..to all stores which are no longer of use, being either obsolete or worn out.

**2.** Of persons: Unable to be of service; not rendering service or help; useless.

**1598** HAKLUYT *Voy.* I. 240 You haue too much liuing, and are vnseruiceable to your prince, lesse will serue you. **1614** W. B. *Philosophers Banquet* (ed. 2) 121 One that would be vnseruiceable to him, and vnprofitable to the Commonwealth. **1655** *Nicholas Papers* (Camden) II. 217, I did long since tell you that poore man would be made onseruiceable to you. **1856** KANE *Arct. Expl.* II. i. 13 Our sick are about the same;..McGary and Riley unserviceable. **1865** DICKENS *Mut. Fr.* III. ii, I am an unserviceable friend of hers.

**b.** *spec.* Not capable of rendering military (or naval) service.

**1596** SPENSER *State Irel.* Wks. (Globe) 653/2 The rebells.. will turne away all theyr rascall people, whom they thinke unserviceable. **1601** SHAKS. *All's Well* IV. iii. 152 Fiue or sixe thousand, but very weake and vnseruiceable: the troopes are all scattered. **1681** LUTTRELL *Brief Rel.* (1857) I. 151 Poor souldiers rendred unserviceable by age, wounds, &c. **1786** BURKE *Art. agst. W. Hastings* Wks. 1842 II. 191 The country troops..would be ill-disciplined and unserviceable, if not worse. **1834** MARRYAT *P. Simple* I. 124 Some of them were retained, but most of them sent on shore as unserviceable. **1881** JOWETT *Thucyd.* I. 146 The Plataeans had already conveyed to Athens their wives,..with the rest of their unserviceable population.

*transf.* **1867** SMYTH *Sailor's Word-bk.* 707 *Unserviceable ticket*; this is made out in the same manner, and requires the same notations, as a sick-ticket.

**3.** Marked by disinclination to be of service.

**1614** RALEIGH *Hist. World* v. vi. 657 Such men of note.. as had any way discouered an vnseruiceable disposition towards the Romans.

**4.** Prejudicial, disadvantageous.

**1698** NORRIS *Pract. Disc.* IV. 386 To reform his Temper, which I'm afraid is more unserviceable to Religion than any Hypothesis of mine can be.

Hence **Unserviceabi·lity.**

**1884** *Cyclists' Tour. Cl. Gaz.* Nov. 335/1 The unserviceability of the new substitute.

**Unse·rviceableness.** (UN-[1] 12; cf. prec.)

**1611** COTGR., *Inutilité*,..vnseruiceablenesse. **1640** SANDERSON *Serm.* (1681) II. 173 The unserviceableness of any thing to edification. **1683** PEPYS *Diary at Tangier* in *Life*, etc. (1841) I. 452 The unserviceableness of the Mole by reason of those winds. *a* **1832** BENTHAM *Draught of Code* Wks. 1843 IV. 399 How many bad and unserviceable ones have, by this very unserviceableness, become popular! **1864** MISS YONGE *Trial* II. 20 The unserviceableness of his maimed arm.

**Unse·rviceably,** *adv.* (UN-[1] 11.)

**1611** COTGR., *Inutilement*,..vnseruiceably. **1661** BEVERIDGE *Priv. Th.* (1709) 156 What is the reason, I have hitherto liv'd so unserviceably to God? **1695** WOODWARD *Nat. Hist. Earth* I. 48 It..does not enlarge the Dimensions of the Globe, or..lye idly and unserviceably there.

**Unse·rvicelike,** *a.* (UN-[1] 7 c.) **1614** ANDREWES *Serm. on Easter Day* 39 They see how vnseruicelike our seruice is.

**Unse·rvile,** *a.* (UN-[1] 7.)

**1701** COLLIER *M. Aurel.* IV. xlix. 61 Does the present Accident hinder your being Honest..and Unservile? **1773** MRS. GRANT *Lett. fr. Mount.* (1807) I. ii. 19 We are charmed with..unservile courtesy in the lower class. **1847** CARLYLE in Froude *Life in Lond.* (1884) I. 409 Reporters to the daily papers, whose industry is the humblest of all real or unservile kinds in literature. **1866** ELIZA METEYARD *Wedgwood* II. 273 Wedgwood's exquisite yet unservile copies of antique art.

**Unse·t,** *v.* [UN-[2] 3, 7. Cf. OE. *unsettan* (once), to take down.]

**1.** *trans.* To put out of place or position; to undo the setting of.

**1602** MARSTON *Ant. & Mel.* III. Wks. 1856 I. 37 O, you spoyle my ruffe, unset my haire. **1611** COTGR., *Desplanter*, ..to vnplant, vnset, remoue. **1761** GRAY *Lett.* (1900) II. 204 The man was sent for: he unset it; it was a paste not worth 40 shillings. **1775** MRS. DELANY in *Life & Corr.* Ser. II. (1862) II. 105 There is some hazard in unsetting enamel for fear of chipping the edges. **1836** MARRYAT *Midsh. Easy* xxxii, How could he put the young men to fresh tortures by removing splints and unsetting limbs? **1884** *Law Times* 1 Nov. 8/1 On the morning in question Dawson had unset the gun.

**2.** *intr.* To get out of place or position.

**1703** THORESBY *Let. to Ray, Spelk*, a wooden splinter tied on, to keep a broken bone from bending or unsetting again.

**Unse·t,** *ppl. a.* [UN-[1] 8 b, 8 c. Cf. Du. *ongezet* in sense 1.]

†**1.** Of time or place: Not previously appointed or arranged. *Obs.*

Chiefly in phr. *at unset steven*: see STEVEN *sb.*[2] 2.

*c* **1386** [see STEVEN *sb.*[2] 2]. **1430–40** LYDG. *Bochas* II. xxi. (1494) h iiij/1 At the vnset houre their falsnesse he wyll quyte. **1476** *Paston Lett.* III. 162 The Duke toke grete corage to goo..to conquer them, butt the[y] berded hym att an onsett place. **1543–***a* **1600** [see STEVEN *sb.*[2] 2]. *a* **1600** MONTGOMERIE *Misc. Poems* v. 47 For man may meit at unset stevin, Thoght montanis nevir meitis.

†**b.** Of events: Not predetermined; unfixed, uncertain. *Obs.*

**1550** BALDWIN *Mor. Philos.* P vi, But yf that the chaunce of thynges be vnset, It is folly to feare that we knowe we maye let. **1559** *Mirr. Mag., O. Glendour* xxvii, Of thinges to cum the haps be so vnset That none but fooles may warrant of them make.

†**2.** Not seated at table. *Obs.*[—1]

*c* **1475** *Rauf Coilȝear* 148 'Gang begin the buird,' said the Coilȝear. 'That war vnsemand, forsuith, and thy self vnset.'

**3.** Not assigned or allocated (*to* one); unlet.

**1480** *Acta Dom. Conc.* (1839) 70/2 Land..haldin of our souuerain lorde and fre vnset for termes or for male. **1523** *Lincoln Wills* (L. Rec. Soc.) V. 120, I will that..all myne inward stuf that was myne owne unset to my wyf remayne to..my daughters. **1580–1** *Reg. Privy Council Scot.* III. 358 To warrand the same unsett, sauld, assignit, or disponit to utheris. **1736** in Picton *L'pool Munic. Rec.* (1886) II. 165 There are some few back seats yet unsett. **1825–9** MRS. SHERWOOD *Lady of Manor* I. viii. 334 During the absence of Lord T—, the family-mansion had remained untenanted, the houses of servants and dependents unset.

**4.** With advs. Not set *down*, *forth*, *out*, *up*, etc.

*c* **1445** PECOCK *Donet* 138 Þese ij..forbodis of avoutrye.., whi ben not þei stillid and vnset forþ expressely? **1530** PALSGR. Introd. p. v, I have..assayde..that there shulde fewe wordes..worde for worde be unsetforthe. **1547** *Act* 1 *Edw. VI*, c. 6 § 1 The same poore persons..be now unoccupied and unset aworke. **1594** HOOKER *Eccl. Pol.* III. xi. § 8 They vrge that God left nothing in his word vndescribed, ..nothing vnset-downe. **1629** HOBBES *Thucyd.* 75 The Athenians..recriminated the Megareans, for hauing tilled holy ground, and vnset-out with bounds. **1639** *Knaresb. Wills* (Surtees) II. 168 One new stand bed unsett upp.

**5.** †**a.** *Unset leek*, a (young) leek not transplanted. *Obs.*

**1530** PALSGR. 249/2 Onsetleke, *porret*. **1563** HYLL *Art Garden.* (1593) 128 If you desire only to haue vnset Leekes. **1601** HOLLAND *Pliny* II. 424 Ashes for to be drunke with the juice of unset leeks in cold water. **1611** COTGR., *Porrette*, Maidens Leeke, bladed Leeke, vnset Leeke.

**b.** Not planted.

**1573** TUSSER *Husb.* (1878) 75 Set..yoong bay and his berie. Or set their stone, vnset leaue out none. **1577** HARRISON *England* III. viii. (1878) II. 57 Notwithstanding that they haue remained there vnset by the space of fortie dais and more: yet some [saffron heads]..haue brought foorth two or three floures a peece. **1597** GERARDE *Herbal* I. i. 2 Common Medow grasse groweth of it selfe, vnset or vnsowen, euery where. **1653** BLITHE *Eng. Improver Impr.* 169 Shouldst thou be occasioned..to keep thy sets longer unset, be thou sure thou get their Roots into the ground.

**c.** Not furnished with plants.

*c* **1600** SHAKS. *Sonn.* xvi, Many maiden gardens yet vnset, With vertuous wish would beare your liuing flowers.

**6.** Not placed in a setting; unmounted.

**1561** T. HOBY tr. *Castiglione's Courtyer* II. R i b, A iewell that vnsett seemeth faire. *c* **1592** BACON *Conf. Pleasure* (1870) 15 If these rich peeces be so faire vnsett, what are they sett? **1684** *Lond. Gaz.* No. 1906/4 An Emerald unset, ..having a narrow Bizel. **1702** *Ibid.* No. 3811/4 Lost.., a large Diamond-drop,..unset. **1884** *West. Daily Press* 20 June 7/5 Necklets of unset amethysts,..and other stones. **1891** *Science-Gossip* XXVII. 36/1 Lack of uniformity in unset specimens.

**7.** Not composed or arranged.

**1631** BRATHWAIT *Whimzies, Traveller* 93 Not an irregular haire about him, nor an unset looke to attend him, nor an uncomposed cringe to accoutre him. **1821** LAMB *Elia* I. *Ears*, Those unconnected, unset sounds are nothing to the measured malice of music.

**8.** Not surgically set.

*a* **1661** FULLER *Worthies, General* I. (1662) 6 An unset bone is better then a bone..ill set.

**9.** Of the sun: Not gone beneath the horizon.

**1860** W. W. READE *Liberty Hall* I. ix. 158 Though very pretty she was only a moon with the sun unset, for [etc.].

†**Unse·te,** *a.* Also unseete. *Obs.* [UN-[1] 7. Cf. SETE *a.* and UNSETY *a.*]

**1.** Unbecoming, improper; bad.

*a* **1310** in Wright *Lyric P.* viii. 31 For-thi on molde y waxe mot, that y sawes have seid un-sete. *Ibid.* xv. 49 Gabbes, les, ant luthere lore, sunnes bueth un-sete. *c* **1325** *Body & Soul* in *Map's Poems* (Camden) 342 A! thou foule flesch, unseete, Ful of falsnesse.

**2.** Unpleasant; painful.

*a* **1310** in Wright *Lyric P.* iv. 23 That i telle a povre play, that furst is feir ant seththe un-sete. *c* **1320** *Sir Tristr.* 1238 His bon brast vnder skinne, His sorwe was vnsete.

**3.** Unwholesome. (Cf. UNSETY *a.*)

**13..** in *Archiv Stud. neu. Spr.* LXXXI. 319 Þe watures bitter and vnseete were ymad boþe gode and swete. **1387** TREVISA *Higden* IV. 11 His frendes trowede þat unsete mete þat he hadde i-ete at soper was cause of his siknesse.

**4.** Of persons: Ill-disposed · dissatisfied or discontented.

*a* **1310** in Wright *Lyric P.* xii. 43 This mon that Matheu ȝef A peny that wes so bref; this frely folk unsete, ȝet he ȝyrnden more.

**Unsett,** var. of UMSET *v. Obs.*

**Unse·tting,** *ppl. a.* [UN-[1] 10.]

†**1.** Unbecoming, unfitting. *Obs.*

**1567** DRANT *Horace, Ep.* B ij, I will tell them..what doth becom, and what unsetting is. *a* **1598** ROLLOCK 1 *Thess.* (1606) 183 Any thing that is vnsetting, or vnseemlie to this Christian calling.

**2.** Not going beneath the horizon.

**1607** *Merry Devil Edmonton* III. ii. 101 Thou bright vnsetting star..! **1819** CRABBE *T. of Hall* xix. 543 Some spoke of wonders they before had seen, When on their travels..: How they beheld for months th' unsetting sun. **1844** LOWELL *Prometheus* 230, I Shall be a power and a memory,..a light Unsetting as the pole-star. **1869** MCLAREN *Serm.* Ser. II. viii. 132 The full light of the unsetting Sun.

*fig.* **1838** MRS. BROWNING *An Island* xxvii, The undim Unsetting Godlight.

**Unse·ttle,** *v.* [UN-[2] 3 and 7.]

**1.** *trans.* To undo from a fixed position; to unfix, unfasten, loosen.

**1598** FLORIO, *Discasciare*,..to make loose the teeth, to dismount artillerie, to vnsettle anything. [**1755** JOHNSON, *To Unsettle*, v. a., to move from a place.] **1818** KEATS *Endymion* IV. 414 He..strives in vain to unsettle and wield A Jovian thunderbolt.

**2.** To force out of a settled condition; to deprive of fixity or quiet: **a.** a state of things, institutions, etc.

**1651** HOBBES *Leviath.* II. xxvii. 154 Such as..take upon them..to unsettle the Lawes with their publique discourse. **1679** ALSOP *Melius Inq.* I. i. 91 To set Religion upon its proper Basis, and unsettle it from the feeble foundations upon which former Ages had erected it! *a* **1700** EVELYN *Diary* 21 April, 1695, Never were so many private Bills pass'd for unsettling estates. **1704** ATTERBURY *On* 1 *Tim.* ii. 7 Those Mighty Events, that fix, or unsettle the Peace of the World. **1803** WORDSW. '*England! the time is come*' 4 Old things have been unsettled. **1849** MACAULAY *Hist. Eng.* i. I. 71 This theory, though intended to strengthen the foundations of government, altogether unsettles them. **1884** *Leeds Merc.* 15 Nov. 6/4 Such a struggle..must unsettle all the institutions of the country.

**b.** beliefs, thoughts, the mind, etc.

**1644** MILTON *Divorce* (ed. 2) I. viii. 19 They should but seek..to unsettle our constancie with timorous and softning suggestions. **1662** STILLINGFL. *Orig. Sacr.* III. i. § 2 When men bent their wits to unsettle the Beleef of such things as tended to Religion. **1671** in *Verney Mem.* (1907) II. 354 My thoughts are unsettled. **1759** SARAH FIELDING *C'tess of Dellwyn* II. 261 His Father had unsettled his Resolution. **1794** MRS. RADCLIFFE *Myst. Udolpho* xlvii, The long struggle which Agnes suffered..at length unsettled her reason. **1816** SCOTT *Bl. Dwarf* xviii, The shock was even sufficient to unsettle his wits. **1839** DICKENS *Nickleby* iv, None of those ill-judged comings home twice a year that unsettle children's minds so. **1885** *Spectator* 25 July 971/2 That his mind had been unsettled by his peril.

**c.** persons (in respect of beliefs, etc.).

**1833** COLERIDGE *Table Talk* (1884) 225 What is the spirit which seems to move and unsettle every other man..at this time? **1851** HELPS *Comp. Solit.* xii. 236 Provided they do not, as they would say, unsettle their neighbours. **1880** R. G. WHITE *Every-Day Eng.* 140 A phonetic printing of those two words would unsettle all these people.

**3.** *intr.* To become unsettled.

**1605** SHAKS. *Lear* III. iv. 167 His wits begin t' vnsettle. **1624** SANDERSON *Serm.* I. 102 The house cannot but unsettle apace, and without speedy repairs fall to the ground. **1543** MILTON *Divorce* 8 Their wild affections unsetling at will have been as so many divorces to teach them experience. *a* **1859** DE QUINCEY *Posth. Wks.* (1891) I. 14 He gazes, and slowly under the blazing scenery of his brain the scenery of his eye unsettles.

**4.** *trans.* To clear of settlers.

**1895** *Advance* (Chicago) 11 Apr. 991/1 Probably no [other] section of our country has ever been un-settled so rapidly.

Hence **Unse·ttling** *vbl. sb.* and *ppl. a.*

Also, in recent use (1901), *unsettler.*

**1665** BOYLE *Occas. Refl.* I. vii, Troublesome and unsettling Employments. **1775** ASH, *Disconcerting*, p. a.,.. unsettling, discomposing. **1828** MISS MITFORD *Village* Ser. III. 70 The unsettling, and the journey, and the settling again,..fairly killed her. **1866** *Cornh. Mag.* XIII. 437 Christianity..must have raised among the believers in the Law very unsettling questions much akin to these. **1894** H. GARDENER *Unoff. Patriot* 10 The unsettling times which brought Methodism..into the ranks of established things.

**Unse·ttleable,** *a.* (UN-[1] 7 b.) **1864** CARLYLE *Fredk. Gt.* XVI. iii. IV. 276 All details being, in the interim, either got settled, or got flung into corners as unsettleable.

**Unse·ttled,** *ppl. a.* [UN-[1] 8, or f. UNSETTLE *v.*]

**1.** Not peaceful, tranquil, or orderly; disturbed; not (yet) quietly or firmly established.

**1591** SYLVESTER *Du Bartas* I. ii. 424 Of winged Clouds the wide inconstant House, Th' unsettled Kingdome of swift Æolus. **1659** *Nicholas Papers* (Camden) IV. 265 The new and unsettled Government in England. **1697** DRYDEN *Æneis* I. 791 My cruel fate, And doubts attending an unsettled state, Force me to guard my coast from foreign foes. **1759** STERNE *Tr. Shandy* I. xi, But the two extremes are more common, and in a greater degree in this unsettled island. **1800** MRS. HERVEY *Mourtray Fam.* I. 41 The hurry and unsettled state which..had attended their first arrival in the country. **1826** SCOTT *Woodst.* v, The times were dangerous and unsettled. **1876** BANCROFT *Hist. U.S.* I. vi. 171 A report of a committee concerning the unsettled government of Virginia.

**b.** Of weather, etc.: Changeable, variable.

**1707** MORTIMER *Husb.* 587 If unsettled or moist Weather happen at the time of its working. **1773** COOK *Voy.* (1777) I. 59 The wind continued unsettled. **1803** MARY CHARLTON *Wife & Mistress* IV. 114 His health, which was yet very unsettled. **1879** FROUDE *Cæsar* xvi. 255 The weather was too unsettled for his fleet..to join him.

*Comb.* **1788** J. WHITE *Jrnl. Voy. N.S. Wales* (1790) 105 Strong breezes, with unsettled-looking weather.

**c.** That has not yet settled down; still in a state of flux or motion.

**1691** J. HARRINGTON *Introd.* in *Wood's Ath. Oxon.* II. a i b, The Graces of Measure and numbers..are not to be expected in a rude and unsettled Language. **1845** J. PHILLIPS *Geol.* in *Encycl. Metrop.* VI. 552/1 [Remains of plants] might be long suspended in the unsettled water, and be transported along with the finer matter. **1894** MRS. DYAN *Man's Keeping* (1899) 100 The dust flying in unsettled clouds about him.

**2.** Not settled in a particular place or position.

**1594** HOOKER *Eccl. Pol.* II. vi. § 3 To set himselfe in an house of cedar trees, and to behold the arke of the Lord's couenant vnsetled. **1729** T. INNES *Crit. Ess.* (1879) 284 The Francs..appear in history as a people unsettled, roving up and down. **1761** CHURCHILL *Rosciad* 988 Next follows Sheridan—a doubtful name, As yet unsettled in the rank of Fame. **1782** MARTYN *Geog. Mag.* I. iii. I. 205 A considerable encampment of these unsettled Arabs. **1807** J. BARLOW *Columb.* II. 212 These tribes have forester'd the fruitful zone, Their seats unsettled, and their name unknown. **1863** BOYD *Graver Th. Country Parson* vii. 106 They were a race of hunters; unsettled, cruel and deceitful. **1896** *Harper's Mag.* XXIII. 26/1, I am a single woman, unsettled as yet.

**b.** *Path.* Not confined to a definite part or spot.

**1793** ABERNETHY *Surg. Ess.* 18 He was..teized with unsettled rheumatic pains. **1819** LADY MORGAN *Autobiog.* (1859) 267 A severe illness, arising..from unsettled gout.

**3.** Not settled or staid in character; of a restless or turbulent disposition.

**1594** *Selimus* 823 Resolue to venture it, Fortune doth fauour euery bold assay, And t'were a trick of an vnsetled wit Because [etc.]. **1595** SHAKS. *John* II. i. 66 All th' vnsetled humors of the Land, Rash, inconsiderate, fiery voluntaries. **1607** *Puritan* I. iv. 31 Many desprate, vnsetled souldiours. **1675** HAN. WOOLLEY *Gentlewom. Comp.* 38 These unstaid dimensions argue unsetled dispositions. **1803** *Censor* 1 July 84, I am sorry you seem so unsettled; I now..advise you to settle in service. **1837** HT. MARTINEAU *Soc. Amer.* II. 63 Young people, who might be 'unsettled;' that is, not sufficiently subservient. *Ibid.* III. 136 Too many of them are unsettled, reckless, slovenly.

**b.** Marked by absence of regularity, uniformity, staidness, or tranquillity.

*c* **1714** POPE *Lett.* (1735) I. 150 What is commonly called an unsettled Life (and what you with too much unjust Severity call a Vagabond Life). **1787** BURNS *Let. to Jas. Smith* 11 June, Should I stay, in an unsettled state, at home, I would only dissipate my little fortune. **1824** MISS L. M. HAWKINS *Annaline* I. 307 High compassion called forth at her unsettled and forlorn condition. **1825** LAMB *Mr. Liston* Wks. 1908 I. 315 The orthography varying, according to the unsettled usage of the times. **1830** *Forrester* II. 270, I have already told you..of the unsettled life I led, after the loss of my mother.

**c.** Unsteady; unquiet.

**1794** MRS. RADCLIFFE *Myst. Udolpho* xxviii, She..then viewed the face with a long unsettled gaze. **1810** SOUTHEY *Kehama* xv. xii, How often did she..from unsettled slumber start, and hear The Winds that moan above!

**4.** Undetermined, unresolved.

**1593** MARLOWE *Lucan* I. 264 Now light had quite dissolu'd the mysty night, And Cæsars mind vnsettled musing stood. **1600** HAKLUYT *Voy.* III. 667 The Spaniard is not so simple, vnsetled & vncertaine in his determinations, as..to make our papers his Bulwarks. **1618** GAINSFORD *Hist. P. Warbeck* P 27 Such humility..won the hearts of many as yet unsettled unto him. **1671** MILTON *P. R.* IV. 326 Uncertain and unsettl'd [he] still remains, Deep verst in books and shallow in himself. *a* **1768** SECKER *Serm.* (1770) IV. 2 What the prophet Elijah said to the Israelites belongs equally to all of this unsettled Character: How long halt ye between two Opinions? **1823** MRS. HEMANS *Siege of Valencia* v, Ere yet th' unsettled heart hath closed its long Impatient conflicts. **1897** MARY KINGSLEY *W. Africa* 360 The chiefs came in an unsettled state of mind, and showed at first much opposition to the conclusion of a treaty.

**5.** Of the mind: Unbalanced, disturbed.

**1611** SHAKS. *Temp.* v. i. 59 A solemne Ayre, and the best comforter To an vnsetled fancie. **1693** *Dryden's Juvenal* xiv. (1697) 353 It shews a manifest unsetled Brain. **1751** JOHNSON *Rambler* No. 141 P 2 A combination of circumstances acting when his imagination was unoccupied, and his judgment unsettled. **1779** *Mirror* No. 17, Such violent procedure might have effects too dreadful upon a brain which..is already much unsettled. **1807** CRABBE *Par. Reg.* III. 180 Accounts perplex'd,..My mind unsettled, and my will unmade. **1825** SCOTT *Betrothed* xxvii, Is his brain unsettled,..or is there some dreadful mystery in these broken words?

**b.** Of persons: Mentally affected.

**1611** SHAKS. *Wint. T.* I. ii. 325 Do'st thinke I am so muddy, so vnsetled, To appoint my selfe in this vexation? **1768** STERNE *Sent. Journ., Maria*, She said, she was unsettl'd much at that time. **1823** S. ROGERS *Italy, Foscari* 121 Unnerved, and now unsettled in his mind. **1879** *Cassell's Techn. Educ.* IV. 107/1 A failure so annoyed him, that he became unsettled,..and at length died by his own hand.

**6. a.** Not assigned by will.

**1671** SHADWELL *Humourists* III, Your Estate, by being unsettled, may come to be divided among the Lawyers, after I have killed you. **1800** MRS. HERVEY *Mourtray Fam.* II. 232 You shall not..command a sixpence of my fortune, which I shall keep unsettled, as a check upon you.

**b.** Undischarged, unpaid.

**1811** *Regul. & Orders Army* 214 The Nature of the Claims of any Man which remain unsettled. **1816** 'QUIZ' *Grand Master* II. 53 Here parcels of unsettl'd bills.

**c.** Not determined or fixed; not freed from doubt or uncertainty; undecided.

**1844** J. S. MILL (*title*), Essays on Some Unsettled Questions of Political Economy. **1857** RUSKIN *Pol. Econ. Art* ii. § 65, I haven't made up my mind about the number yet, and there are several other points in the system yet unsettled. 1884 *Imp. Dict.* s.v., An unsettled dispute.

7. Not occupied by settlers.

1724 [see Unseated *ppl. a.* 1]. 1788 *Encycl. Brit.* (ed. 3) I. 617/2 This immense extent of unappropriated western territory, or vacant unsettled land. 1859 Cornwallis *Panorama New World* I. 154 Those occupying runs in the then 'unsettled' districts. 1869 Froude *Short Stud., Educ.* (1871) 328 A new and unsettled country.

Hence **Unse·ttledly** *adv.*

1599 Jas. I *Basilikon Doron* (1603) 115 Neither looking sillely, like a stupide pedant, nor unsettledly. 1651 Culpepper *Astrol. Judgem. Dis.* Ep. A 3 b, That so you may..not float unsettledly upon the waves of Errour. 1685 *Case of Doubting Conscience* 4 The Ballance no longer hangs in *aequilibrio*, or moves unsetledly this way or that. 1725 N. Bailey *Erasm. Colloq.* (1878) I. 72 Whenever any one that is your Superior speaks to you,..look neither..saucily, malapertly, nor unsettledly. 1824 Scott *Redgauntlet* ch. vii, If I thought you were unfortunate in former undertakings,..which might cause you to live unsettledly.

**Unse·ttledness.** [f. prec.] The quality or condition of being unsettled.

1619 Ld. Herbert *Corr.* in *Life* (1886) 346 And for their unsettledness, it is such as..they know not whom to trust. 1682 Flavell *Fear* 81 The unsetledness and distraction of our own thoughts. 1748 Hartley *Observ. Man* I. iv. § 6. 495 Sceptical Unsettledness and fool-hardy Impiety. 1799 J. Robertson *Agric. Perth* 427 The present unsettledness in the value of grain. 1832 *Examiner* 436/1 A sense of unsettledness pervades everything. 1873 Morley *Rousseau* II. 209 If the former is not acquired.., a man grows up with a drifting unsettledness of will.

**Unse·ttlement.** [f. Unsettle *v.*, or Un-¹ 12.]

1. The act or process of unsettling.

1648 Fairfax, etc., *Remonstr.* 8 To entertain motions tending to the unsettlement of what you had resolved. 1691 T. H[ale] *Acc. New Invent.* p. iv, Whoever attempts the settlement of any Question, which would be the unsettlement of any mens Interest [etc.]. 1844 Ld. Brougham *A. Lunel* III. xiv. 106 The universal unsettlement of all received ideas, and ancient opinions. 1862 Trollope *N. Amer.* I. 221 Delay in travelling..causes the unsettlement of a settled purpose.

2. Unsettled state or condition.

1650 Baxter *Saints' R.* iv. i. § 4 They have..lived in much trouble and unsettlement, and have just overcome them. 1655 *Nicholas Papers* (Camden) II. 281 The yet great vnsetlement in England. 1681 *Treat. E. India Trade* 10 Our Neighbours are not now at leasure..to make their Advantage of our Unsettlement, during the Transition from one Stock to another. 1867 H. W. Wilberforce in *Ess. Relig. & Lit.* II. 342 A general spirit of unsettlement and presumption. 1875 E. White *Life in Christ* xxviii. v. 492 A not uncommon feeling is that..'the faith' is of such a quality that reasoning upon it..is likely to lead to unsettlement.

**Unse·ttling,** *vbl. sb.* and *ppl. a.*: see Unsettle *v.*

† **Unse·ty,** *a. Obs.*⁻⁰ = Unsete *a.* 3. c 1440 *Promp. Parv.* 367/1 On-sety, *idem quod* on-holsum, *supra.* [*Ibid.* 365/2 On-holsum, *insalubris.*] † **Unse·ven,** *v. Obs.*⁻¹ [Un-² 6 a.] *trans.* To reduce from seven in number. 1655 Fuller *Ch. Hist.* xi. 137 He much decryed the necessity thereof, (though not so far as to un-seven the Sacraments of the Church of Rome). † **Unse·ver,** *v. Obs.*⁻¹ (Un-² 7.) 1609 Heywood *Brit. Troy.* v. cx, Both his lips unsever, His head bends backe, legs stride. **Unse·verable,** *a.* (Un-¹ 7 b, 5 b.) 1579 Tomson *Calvin's Serm. Tim.* 234/2 Hee sheweth the thinges whiche are alwayes ioyned with faith, and are as it were vnseuerable. 1644 Digby *Nat. Soul* xi. § 5. 438 They..yet were vnseuerable from one an other, as being compartes of the same substance. **Unse·verably,** *adv.* (Un-¹ 11, 5 b.) c 1425 in *Anglia* VIII. 153 Wheþere for þee, þat as vnseuerably was ioyned to god [etc.]. 1548 Geste *Pr. Masse* C iij b, Only soch a presence of christes body in the bread wherwyth they both shuld be unseuerably personed. 1561 T. Norton *Calvin's Inst.* ii. 81 By whose knittyng together they might perfectly and vnseuerably cleaue vnto God. **Unseve·re,** *a.* (Un-¹ 7.) 1646 Codrington *Life or Death Essex* 11 If any unseverer houres of leisure offered themselves in his study. 1651 Jer. Taylor *Serm. for Year* II. xxii. 284 Angry against servants for..easing their labours with a lesse prudent and unsevere refreshment.

**Unse·vered,** *ppl. a.* (Un-¹ 8.)

1453 *Rolls of Parlt.* V. 231/2 The said..Archers shall be..kept hole, undepartid, undevided and unsevered. 1513 Douglas *Æneis* ix. viii. 133 Sa lang as thir sammyn vnsyuerit war. 1607 Shaks. *Cor.* iii. ii. 42, I haue heard you say, Honor and Policy, like vnseuer'd Friends, I' th' Warre do grow together. 1657 H. King *Departure* 28 'Tis only the Triumphant Church where we Shall in unsever'd neighbourhood agree. 1712 Blackmore *Creation* i. 645 The unsever'd parts the greatest pressure bear. a 1800 Cowper *Odyss.* (ed. 2) xiv. 530 He..honouring Ulysses most, On Him the long unsever'd chine bestow'd. 1849 M. Arnold *Strayed Reveller, Sonnet* 5 One lesson..Of Toil unsever'd from Tranquillity. 1885 *Manch. Exam.* 2 Feb. 6/2 How long this tie would remain unsevered..is open to doubt.

Hence **Unse·veredly** *adv. rare*⁻¹.

1661 Boyle *Style of Script.* 209 The..Scripture was so Unsever'dly his Study.

**Unsew,** *v.* [Un-² 3.]

1. *trans.* To undo the sewing of (a garment, etc.); to remove the stitches from.

1362 Langl. *P. Pl.* A. v. 48 Heo wolde vn-souwen hire smok and setten þer an here. 1382 Wyclif *Lev.* xiii. 45 He shal haue his clothis vnsewyd [L. *dissuta*], the heed nakid, the mouth couered with the cloothe. 1491 Caxton *Vitas Patr.* (W. de W. 1495) i. xxxix. 54/1 He commaunded hym to doo thynges agaynst reason, as..to unsowe his gowne, and after to sowe it agayne. 1552 Huloet, Vnsow,.. *resuo.* 1611 Cotgr., *Descoudre*, to vnsowe, vndoe stitches. 1712 tr. *De Marolles' Mem.* 104 A pair of Old-Shoes unsew'd on both Sides. 1728 Chambers *Cycl.* s.v. *Marroquin*, The Skins..are taken out, drain'd on a Rack, unsewed, the Sumac taken out [etc.]. 1809 Malkin *Gil Blas* x. x. ¶ 14, I often observed the old man at work upon his pillow, unsewing and sewing it up again. 1848 Thackeray *Van. Fair* xxxiv, When she unsewed herself, and let out of her dress all those..valuables which she had secreted in the wadding.

*fig.* 1340 *Ayenb.* 184 Salomon þus zayþ: 'þer no guod red ne ys, þet uolk to-ualþ and is al enzauwed. 1620 Shelton *Quix.* ii. lx. 411 Sancho was amazed, and purposed not to vnsow his lips, as long as he was in that company. 1661 Feltham *Resolves* ii. xliii. 268 Even in those [friendships] that have been ill contracted, Cato's advice is good, They are rather to be unsewed then cut. 1853 Reade *Chr. Johnstone* 181 Time was to be given him to unsew a connection which he could not cut asunder.

2. To unwrap, uncover, set free, by the removal of stitches.

1390 Gower *Conf.* III. 315 Thei founde A bodi ded, which was bewounde In cloth of gold..Unsowed was the bodi sone. 1692 O. Walker *Grk. & Rom. Hist.* 270 Bacchus being born in Arabia, or rather unsowed from the Thigh of his Mother Semele. 1740 Richardson *Pamela* (1824) I. 113 So I took off my undercoat, and..unsewed them [*sc.* papers] from it.

Hence **Unsew·er**; **Unsew·ing** *vbl. sb.*

1611 Cotgr. s.vv. *Descouseur, Descousure.*

**Unsew·ed,** *ppl. a.* (Un-¹ 8, 8 c.)

Also with advs., as *together, up.*

a 1225 *Ancr. R.* 344 Cloðes unseouwed bireined oðer unwaschen. c 1325 *Pilate* 169 in *E. E. P.* (1862) 115 Oure louerdes curtel he dude on..þat vnsued was of þred. 1535 Coverdale *John* xix. 23 The cote..was vnsowed from the aboue, wrought thorow and thorow. 1550 Bale *Image Both Ch.* ii. Pref. A iiij b, An heape of barbarous tearmes and vnsowed togither sentences. 1596 Spenser *F. Q.* vi. iv. 14 But the bare ground..Must be their bed, their pillow was vnsowed. 1603 J. Davies (Heref.) *Extasie* Wks. (Grosart) I. 90/2 On either side from her Armes to her Wast, It was vnsow'd, and made with Buttons fast. 1765 Sterne *Tr. Shandy* viii. i, If slits in petticoats are unsewed up.

**Unsew·ered,** *ppl. a.* (Un-¹ 8.)

1844 R. H. Horne *New Spirit of Age* I. 113 The unsewered, undrained, and uncleansed localities. 1864 R. A. Arnold *Cotton Fam.* 440 The unsewered towns of the south. 1885 *Atlantic Monthly* Apr. 467/1 Roadways, ungraded, unsewered, and unpaved.

† **Unsew·ly,** *a. Obs.* Also 3 unseaulich. [Un-¹ 7, with obscure second element.] Uncomely.

a 1225 *Ancr. R.* 10 Ich am blac & tauh hwit, heo seið, unseaulich wiðuten, & shene wiðinnen. c 1450 *Mirk's Festial* 81 In lykenes of a ʒong chyld wyth long herus, and hory, and vnsewly [*Douce MS.* vnsemely].

**Unsew·n,** *ppl. a.* [Un-¹ 8 b.] = Unsewed *ppl. a.*

1648 Hexham ii, *Ongenaeyt*, Vnsowne, or not Sowne on. 1869 *Athenæum* 25 Sept. 396 Why, we ask, do they [German publishers] send out books unsewn?

**Unse·x,** *v.* [Un-² 6 b.] *trans.* To deprive or divest of sex, or of the typical qualities of one or other (*esp.* the female) sex.

1605 Shaks. *Macb.* i. v. 42 Come you Spirits, That tend on mortall thoughts, vnsex me here. 1793 Murphy *Tacitus* I. 73 If a woman can thus unsex herself at the head of the eagles. 1844 Mrs. Browning *To G. Sand* 13 Beat purer, heart,..Till God unsex thee on the heavenly shore. 1852 Smedley *L. Arundel* xxxviii. 289 A foreign education, than which we know not a better receipt for unsexing the minds of the daughters of Albion.

Hence **Unse·xing** *vbl. sb.* and *ppl. a.*

[1775 Ash.] 1812 *Examiner* 11 May 302/2 Her unsexing ambition. 1851 *Illustr. Lond. News* 27 Sept. 395/2 In reply to the objection of unsexing.

**Unse·xed,** *ppl. a.* (Un-¹ 8, or f. Unsex *v.*)

1797 Mathias *Purs. Lit.* iv. Adv. p. ii, Our unsexed female writers now instruct or confuse us and themselves in the labyrinth of politics. 1827 Scott *Surg. Dau.* xi, I doubt the propriety of your being under the charge of this unsexed woman. 1860 O. W. Holmes *Elsie V.* xvi, To think that a woman is never to be a woman again, whatever she may come to as an unsexed angel. 1876 T. Hardy *Ethelberta* viii, To have an unsexed judgment is as precious as to be an unsexed being is deplorable.

**Unse·xual,** *a.* (Un-¹ 7.)

Also, in recent use (1905), *unsexually.*

1819 Shelley *Peter Bell 3rd* vi. xix, Turned to a formal puritan, A solemn and unsexual man. 1834 De Quincey *Autob. Sk.* Wks. 1853 I. 353 An air of something unsexual, mannish, and..ludicrous. 1875 Whitney *Life Lang.* x. 207 The world of untraceably sexual or of unsexual objects.

**Unsha·ckle,** *v.* [Un-² 4 b. Cf. Du. *ontschakelen.*]

1. *trans.* To free from a shackle or fetter. Also *fig.*

1611 Cotgr., *Destraver*, to vnshackle, vngyue. 1650 *Gentilis Considerations* 129 But to doe it [*sc.* overcome his enemy] when he is shackled and bound, without unshackling or unbinding is very much. 1699 South *Serm.* (1715) IV. 518 Unshackle his Nature, and turn his Desires loose, and then you shall see what he will choose. 1827 Pollok *Course T.* vii. 464 The patriot bands that..unshackled nations. 1828–32 Webster s.v., To unshackle the hands.

b. To untie, detach.

1694 Echard *Plautus* 195 Only t'unshackle your rope, that hangs at your heels.

2. *Naut.* To remove a shackle from (a chain, etc.).

1840 R. H. Dana *Bef. Mast* vii, We hove in upon our chain, and after stoppering and unshackling it again and again,..we at length tipped our anchor. 1899 F. V. Kirby *Sport E. C. Africa* ix. 97 Unshackling the anchor, I put the shackle in my pocket.

**Unsha·ckled,** *ppl. a.* [Un-¹ 8.]

1. Not shackled or fettered. Also *transf.*

[1775 Ash.] 1816 Byron *Parisina* xvii, These hands are chain'd, but let me die At least with an unshackled eye. 1821 Scott *Pirate* xli, Cleveland and Bunce..were permitted to walk unshackled.

2. Not restricted or impeded *by* something.

1776 Burney *Hist. Mus.* I. p. xiii, Freedom of thought, unshackled by the trammels of authority. 1782 Miss Burney *Cecilia* iii. ii, Surrounded as you are by the opulent and the splendid, unshackled by dependance. 1853 Huxley in *Life & Lett.* (1900) I. 115 To be unshackled by anything that may prevent you taking the highest places. 1884 *Law Times* 17 May 42/2 The discretion of the court was unshackled by any obligation of hearing evidence.

b. Unrestricted, unimpeded, unhampered, free.

1796 Mme. D'Arblay *Camilla* III. 21, I can desire no one to abstain from pursuing the dictates of their own sense of honour. I leave you, therefore, unshackled. 1820 Byron *Mar. Fal.* iii. ii. 534 Ages of prosperity and freedom To this unshackled city. 1850 Grote *Greece* ii. lxvii. VIII. 450 The full and unshackled force of comedy.

**Unsha·de,** *v.* (Un-² 4 b.)

1611 Cotgr., *Desumbrer*, to vnshade, or depriue of shadow. 1625 Quarles *Sion's Sonn.* ii. 1 Vnshade thy Face, cast backe those golden Locks. 1633 P. Fletcher *Purple Isl.* xii. li, Ah now unshade thy face, uncloud thy sight.

**Unsha·ded,** *ppl. a.* [Un-¹ 8.]

1. a. Not darkened or obscured by shade; not covered by a shade or blind.

a 1668 Davenant *To Queen* Wks. (1673) 218 Faire as unshaded Light; or as the Day In its first birth. 1792 Wordsw. *Descr. Sk.* 101 There, all unshaded, blazing forests throw Rich golden verdure on the lake below. 1843 *Florist's Jrnl.* (1846) IV. 78 A small uncovered and unshaded bed of prepared earth. 1880 Miss Bird *Japan* II. 187 Buildings..with..unshaded windows.

b. Not provided with shade; fully exposed to light (or heat).

1802 H. Martin *Helen of Glenross* III. 166 No nankeen monkey figures then frisked round a muslin-dressed dabbish, unshaded mamma. 1837 Ht. Martineau *Soc. Amer.* II. 49 We passed an unshaded meadow, where the grass had caught fire.

2. 'Not having shades in coloring' (Webster, 1828); not modified or toned down.

1823 Mrs. Hemans *Vespers Palermo* ii. i, A very boy, on whose unshaded cheek The spring-time glow is lingering. 1893 W. H. Hudson *Patagonia* 158 Nothing here surprised me more than the song of the British wren—a current of sharp high unshaded notes.

3. Not marked with shading lines.

1868 Lyell *Princ. Geol.* (ed. 10) II. 348 The annexed map, all the lands which are shaded belonging to the Australian and those which are unshaded to the Indian region. 1880 C. R. Markham *Peruv. Bark* 325 The identical plant figured in Plate X..(the unshaded branch with capsules).

**Unsha·dow,** *v.* [Un-² 4 b.] *trans.* To free from shadow; *fig.* to disclose, reveal.

In quot. 1599 = Shadow *v.* 7; perh. an error.

1550 Thomas *Ital. Dict.*, *Sgombrare*, to vnshadowe or leaue voide. 1595 R. Barnfield *Cynthia* To Rdrs. (Arb.) 44, I will vnshaddow my conceit: being nothing else, but an imitation of Virgill. 1599 R. Linche *Anc. Fiction* I iv, This picture of Honor..was oftentimes set forth with two wings on the shoulders thereof, intending & vnshadowing thereby, that honour and glorie doe as it were lend wings vnto men of vertue and merit. 1818 Byron *Let. to Moore* 2 June, The dawn gleams over the Grand Canal, and unshadows the Rialto. 1821 Southey *Vis. Judgem.* i. 51 To thy mortal sight shall the Grave unshadow its secrets.

**Unsha·dowable,** *a.* (Un-¹ 7 b.) 1640 Bp. Reynolds *Passions* xxxiii. 402 There are indeed some Attributes of God..absolutely inimitable, and unshadowable by any excellency in mans soule. 1885 Tennyson *Anc. Sage* 238 The gain of such large life as match'd with ours Were Sun to spark—unshadowable in words.

**Unsha·dowed,** *ppl. a.* [Un-¹ 8.] Not covered or darkened by shadow.

1593 B. Barnes *Poems* (Grosart) 10 Whose shadow trembling on her louely face He left vnshadow'd. 1599 Daniel *Musophilus* 846 Maiestie..Shining with all her beames, with all her raies,..vnshadowed In any darkened point. 1682 Wheler *Journ. Greece* iii. 268 Nothing but a Rock..unshadowed by Trees. 1823 Mrs. Hemans *Vespers Palermo* iii. i, The skies themselves..Unshadow'd by a cloud. 1855 [Miss Cobbe] *Ess. Intuitive Morals* 111 The true splendour of the Sun..in a heaven of unshadowed light. 1870 Morris *Earthly Par.* III. iv. 53 In the unshadowed noontide light.

*fig.* 1649 Quarles *Virgin Widow* v. i, Thou before whose open eye All unshadow'd secrets lye. 1661 Glanvill *Van. Dogm.* 238 He alone sees all things with an unshadowed comprehensive Vision, who eminently is All. 1828 Ld. Grenville *Sinking Fund* 85 The bare and unshadowed outline of the view..of these interesting topics. 1891 Farrar *Darkn. & Dawn* xxxv, A beauty as yet unshadowed by evil secrets and base desires.

**Unsha·fted,** *a.* (Un-¹ 9.) 1883 R. Bridges *Prometheus* 798 The white unshafted darts of day.

**Unsha·keable,** *a.* (Un-¹ 7 b.)

1611 Cotgr., *Inescroulable*, vnshakeable. 1621 S. Ward *Happiness of Practice* 16 The wise, that build on the Rocke of Doing, vnshakeable. a 1715 South *Serm.* IV. viii. 328 A Bottom so firm and sure for Christianity to rest upon, that it cannot be placed upon a surer and more unshakable. 1866 Hare *Guesses* 106 There is still one rock indeed, stout and bold and unshakable as can be desired. 1890 *Times* 6 Feb. 5/1 He is Stambouloff's brother-in-law, and consequently unshakeable in his post.

b. Of belief, conviction, etc.

a 1677 Barrow *Serm.* Wks. 1687 I. 471 To express..his unshakeable Faith in God..under so fierce a trial. 1711 in 10th *Rep. Hist. MSS. Comm.* App. V. 188 This fundation of unshakeable patience. 1805 Southey *Madoc* ii. xxvii. 377 With..unshakeable resolve My soul maintains its purpose. 1891 Farrar *Darkn. & Dawn* xviii, To these good Christians that doctrine was an unshakeable conviction.

Hence **Unsha·keably** *adv.*

1864 Hawthorne *S. Felton* (1872) 167 Desire nothing too fervently, not even life; yet keep thy hold upon it..unshakably.

† **Unsha·ked,** obs. variant of next.

a 1586 Sidney *Arcadia* iii. xii, The horses with smooth running, their staves with unshaked motion, obediently performed their cholericke commandements. 1593 *Sidney's*

Arcadia IV. (1922) II. 107 An unshaked magnanimity. 1601 SHAKS. Jul. C. III. i. 70, I do know but One That vnassayleable holds on his Ranke, Vnshak'd of Motion. 1611 — Cymb. II. i. 68 Keepe vnshak'd That Temple thy faire mind. 1642 H. MORE Song of Soul II. iii. IV. xiv, Wherein we stedfast stand, unshak'd, unmov'd.

**Unsha·ken,** *ppl. a.* [UN-1 8 b and 8 c.]

1. Not shaken or agitated.

c1460 [see UN-1 5 c]. 1602 SHAKS. Ham. III. ii. 201 Which now like Fruite vnripe stickes on the Tree, But fall vnshaken, when they mellow bee. 1712 BLACKMORE Creation I. 343 These strong, unshaken mounds, resist the shocks Of tides. 1762 FALCONER Shipwr. II. 314 [The canvas] lies at length unshaken by the wind. 1798 W. L. BOWLES Poems, St. Michael's Mt. 75 Firm as stands the rock's unshaken base.

2. Not moved from a firm position or state; unweakened; steadfast, steady.

1548 UDALL, etc. Erasm. Par. John i. 12 Able to stand stable and vnshaken against al temptacions of the deiuill. 1613 SHAKS. Hen. VIII, III. ii. 199 My Duty..Should the approach of this wilde Riuer breake, And stand vnshaken yours. 1659 W. CHAMBERLAYNE Pharon. I. iii. 384 With such unshaken confidence as we Pray on the expanded wings of faith. 1711 STEELE Spect. No. 75 ¶ 7 A firm and unshaken Expectation of another Life. 1768–74 TUCKER Lt. Nat. (1834) II. 361 He will never get an unshaken seat in the saddle, who never rides an unruly horse. 1823 SCOTT Quentin D. xxii, The Bishop cast a melancholy but unshaken look upon the grisly satellite. 1848 MRS. JAMESON Sacr. & Leg. Art II. 188 Her unshaken constancy. 1883 A. ROBERTS O. T. Revis. ii. 29 The tradition..remains unshaken.

3. Not shivered or cracked. *rare.*

1573 TUSSER Husb. (1878) 42 Now sawe out thy timber.. to haue it vnshaken, and ready to sale. 1828 Craven Gloss. Unshacken, not cracked.

4. Not shaken out; unscattered.

1765 Museum Rust. IV. 134, I found a considerable quantity of the nameless grass, the seed unshaken.

Hence **Unsha·kenly** *adv.*

1882 MISS C. F. WOOLSON Anne 384 Feeling drearily, unshakenly sure.

†**Unsha·kened,** *ppl. a. Obs.*-1 (UN-1 8.) 1659 FULLER App. Inj. Innoc. I. 49* My words stand an un-shakened truth. **Unsha·king,** *ppl. a.* (UN-1 10.) 1818 MILMAN Samor VII. 956 A soft step approach'd Light as the wren along the unshaking spray. **Unsha·kingly,** *adv.* (UN-1 11.) 1846 WORCESTER (citing Qu. Rev.). **Un-Shakspe·rian,** *a.* (UN-1 7.) a1834 COLERIDGE Lit. Rem. (1836) II. 115 One of the most un-Shakespearian speeches in all the genuine works of our poet. 1875 DOWDEN Shakspere 55 Even if it were a work of Shakspere, we should still call it un-Shaksperian.

†**Unsha·le,** *v. Obs.* [UN-2 5.]

1. *trans.* **a.** *fig.* To disclose, reveal, expound.

c1576 THYNNE Animadv., etc. (1875) 108 To vnshale this dowte, and laye abrode this clowdye hidden speache. 1606 MARSTON Parasit. IV. G 2, I wil not vnshale the rest before it be ripe. 1611 in Coryat Crudities l 2 marg., Those courteous Dames called cortesans (as M. Thomas himselfe hath elegantly vnshaled the word vnto vs). a1652 BROME Novella II. i, Nic. I could unshale a plot. Pi. Ny noble Nicolo out with't I say.

**b.** To strip.

1604 MARSTON Malcontent I. iii. B 2 b, Pietro. Speake: vnshale him quick. Mal. With most tumbler-like nimblenes.

2. To unhusk.

1611 COTGR., Goussepiller,..to vnshale, or take pulse out of the swads. 1681 R. KNOX Hist. Ceylon 11 They unshale their Rice from its outward husk by beating it in a mortar.

**Unsha·led,** *ppl. a.* [UN-1 8.] Not taken out of the pod or husk. a1661 HOLYDAY Juvenal (1673) 43 With whose vineger And unshal'd bean d'ye swell? 1733 TULL Horse-Hoeing Husb. xiii. 159 Beans..so large as to fill the Bushel almost as full when shal'd as unshal'd.

**Unsha·med,** *ppl. a.* [UN-1 8. Cf. MHG. *ungeschamt, -schemt,* MDa. *uskæmmet.*] **a.** Not put to shame. **b.** Unashamed.

1382 WYCLIF 2 Tim. ii. 15 To ȝyue thi self prouable, or able, werk man to God, vnschamyd, or worthi not for to be schamed. 1450 Rolls of Parlt. V. 176/2 If it ever shall like our Lord, that I dey otherwise than in my bedde, my blode unshamed. a1470 HARDING Chron. CXX. xiv, Thus by witte she kept her selfe vnshamed. 1562 LEGH Armory (1597) 62 To keepe his cote armour vnshamed in tryall. 1700 DRYDEN Pal. & Arc. III. 741 Unsham'd, though foil'd, he does the best he can. 1725 C. PITT Vida's Art of Poetry ii. 76 Th' immortal Virgil..Shines out unsham'd, and tow'rs above the rest. 1838 MRS. BROWNING Seraphim I. 289 Are ye unshamed that ye cannot dim Your alien brightness to be liker Him? 1897 H. N. HOWARD Footsteps Proserpine 97 Afraid to die, This other love thou wouldst unshamed deny?

**Unsha·mefaced,** *a.* (UN-1 9 b.)

1533 FRITH Mirror A vii b, They..with vnshamefaced beggynge, polle them so nye, that in a maner they leue nothinge behinde. 1545 JOYE Exp. Dan. 145 The vnshamefaced arrogant boldenes and serpentine fraudes of anticryste. 1603 HOLLAND Plut. Mor. 23 This so bolde and unshamefaced queane. 1647 LILLY Christian Astrology cviii. 540 Cruel men,..bloody minded, unshameface't, sumtuous.

Hence **Unsha·mefacedness.**

1596 LADY BACON Let. in Birch Mem. (1754) II. 218 Both unchast and impudent, with as it were an incorrigible unshamefacedness. 1611 COTGR., Impudence, impudence,.. vnshamefac'dness. 1632 HOLLAND Cyrupædia 4 It seemeth, that unthankefulnesse is accompanied especially with unshamefacedness.

†**Unsha·mefast,** *a. Obs.* [UN-1 7.] Immodest: **a.** Of persons, the mind, heart, etc.

a1100 Voc. in Wr.-Wülcker 337 Impudens, unsceamfæst. c1380 WYCLIF Sel. Wks. III. 469 Suche a bischop is raþer an unschamefast dogge þen a bischop. 1382 — Dan. viii. 23 There shal ryse a kyng vnshamfast in face. a1470 TIPTOFT Orat. G. Flamineus (Caxton, 1481) f iv/2 Peradventure thou hast be prodigal unto wantone & unshamefast creatures. 1535 COVERDALE Ecclus. xxiii. 6 An vnshamefast and obstinate mynde. 1592 GREENE Disput., etc. 26 Take heede of her that hath an vnshamefast eye. 1608 WILLET Hexapla Exod. 128 An hard heart..vnshamefast in euill things.

**b.** Of conduct, actions, etc.

c1400 Found. St. Bartholomew's (1923) 49 He was nat forȝeitfull of the vnshamefaste boldnes wher that euer the mayde he sawh aloyne. 1407 Exam. Wm. of Thorpe Prol. (MS. Rawl. C 208), Þoruȝ her olde & her newe vnschamefast synnes. 1436 Rolls of Parlt. IV. 501/2 Ye grete dredeles and unshamefast Perjurie, that orriblely contynueth. a1533 LD. BERNERS Gold. Bk. M. Aurel. (1546) Nn j b, Thy shame is so shamefull, and thy malyce so unshamefast, that I can not answere the. 1586 FERNE Blaz. Gentrie 63 This law.. would peradventure call some backe from vnshamefast lasciuiousnes.

†**Unsha·mefastly,** *adv. Obs.* [UN-1 11. Cf. prec.] Immodestly.

1382 WYCLIF Pref. Ep. St. Jerome i, More wilnyng other mennus thingis shamfastli to lernen, than his owne vnshamfastli to prece forth. c1440 Promp. Parv. 367/1 Onschamefastly, inpudenter. 1561 T. HOBY tr. Castiglione's Courtyer Zz 2 Not to loue promotions so,..nor vnshamefastlye to begg any office. 1580 T. LUPTON Sivqila 63, I am sure a greate sorte woulde not..so vnshamefastly, and so commonly vse that filthy vice. 1632 SHERWOOD, Unshamefastly, eshontément.

†**Unsha·mefastness.** *Obs.* (UN-1 12.) Common c1540–1590.

?a1400 Wycliffite Bible Job xv. 27 (MS. Bodl. 277), Outward fatnesse, that is vnschamefastnesse, hangith doun of his sidis. a1470 TIPTOFT Orat. G. Flamineus (Caxton, 1481) f iv b/1 Supposest thou with thy..unshamefastnes to get that worshipful fame which they gate? 1520 Calisto & Melib. A iij b, Theyre enbawmyng & theyre vnshamfastnes. 1549 CHALONER Erasm. on Folly R j b, Whiche their sayd iugglyng they conueigh yet by so happie an vnshamefastnesse, as..Ciuilians haue cause..to enuie. 1608 WILLET Hexapla Exod. 403 Contrarie hereunto are immodestie and vnshamefastnes. 1653 W. RAMESEY Astrol. Restored 73 This is the face of boldness,..unshamefastness, resoluteness and confidence.

†**Unsha·meful,** *a.* [UN-1 7.] Shameless.

c1400 Apol. Loll. 104 Þei are..vnschamful to axe, bolde to denay. c1430 Life St. Kath. (1884) 45 O thou most vnschameful dogge! 1561 T. HOBY tr. Castiglione's Courtyer IV. Qq iii b, [It] maketh them desperate for ye wronges & vnshameful dealing that they receiue. 1566 PAINTER Pal. Pleas. I. 192 b, Reforme thy unshamefull and disordinate appetites. 1648 HEXHAM II, [Onschamel], Vnshamefull, Impudent, or Brazen fact.

†**Unsha·mefully,** *adv. Obs.* [UN-1 11.] Shamelessly.

c1375 Sc. Leg. Saints xxxii. (Justin) 387 The feynde.. becuth vnschamefully to diffule hyre thru lychery. c1400 Found. St. Bartholomew's 48 It is no prudent mannys dede ..suche a conseyuyd desire yn herte so vnshamfully to vttyr. c1430 Wycliffite Bible (1850) I. 61/2 To prece forth his owne [studies] vnshamefully. 1561 T. HOBY tr. Castiglione's Courtyer Yy iv, Not to praise himself vnshamefully and out of reason. 1648 HEXHAM II, Onbeschaemdelick, vnshamefully, or impudently. a1660 Contemp. Hist. Irel. (Ir. Archæol. Soc.) II. 26, I will..prove you to be a lyer, in what you unshamfully formerly asserted.

†**Unsha·mefulness.** *Obs.* [UN-1 12.] Shamelessness.

c950 Lindisf. Gosp. Mark vii. 21 From innueard..ofcymeð unrehtwisnise, esuicnis, unsceomfulnise. 1357 Lay Folks Catech. 468 Of this syn [sc. pride] comes..Despite, and ypocrisie, and unshamefulnesse. c1440 Jacob's Well 77 Þe seuenthe cornere of wose in pride is vnschamfulnes. 1534 BARNES Suppl. Hen. VIII, E 2, But oh lorde God, what an vnshamefulnes is this? thus to delude with wordes all the hole worlde? 1648 HEXHAM II, Onbeschaemtheyt, Vnshamefulnesse.

†**Unsha·meless(ness.** *Obs.* (UN-1 5 a.) 1555 H. PENDILTON in Bonner Homilies 41* The vnshameles breakynge of the deade mennes testamentes. 1565 COOPER Thesaurus, Impudentia, impudencie; vnshamelesnesse. †**Unsha·mely,** *adv. Obs.*-1 [UN-1 11. Cf. OE. *unsceamlíce.*] Shamelessly. c1375 Sc. Leg. Saints xv. (Barnabas) 162 Ethnykis, þat oysit sa nakit one-schamely to ga. †**Unsha·mous,** *a. Obs.*-1 [UN-1 7.] Shameless. a1500 in Asloan MS. fol. 274 Of thare syn sum schrewis are vnschamous.

**Unsha·pe,** *v.* [UN-2 3, 4. Cf. MHG. *entschepfen.*] *trans.* To deform; to destroy. Also *fig.*

a1400 New Test. (Paues) App. 219 Vnschapynge þer body wiþ newe manere of degyse. 1603 SHAKS. Meas. for M. IV. iv. 23 This deede vnshapes me quite. 1857 DE QUINCEY Whiggism Wks. VI. 77 The sandy columns of the Great Desert, which the caprices of the wind build up and scatter, shape and unshape, within..a minute.

**Unshape,** obs. var. UNSHAPEN *a.*

**Unsha·peable,** *a.* [UN-1 7 b.] Having no definite shape; shapeless.

Also *unshapable* (Worcester, 1846, citing Good).

1630 R. Johnson's Kingd. & Commw. 115 The unshapeable and rough Mountaine Grampius. 1846 LOUISA S. COSTELLO Tour Venice 369 Like the back of some huge antediluvian monster, unshapeable and mysterious.

**Unsha·ped,** *ppl. a.* [UN-1 8. Cf. ON. *úskapaðr,* Sw. *oskapad,* Da. *uskabt.*] Not reduced or moulded into shape; imperfectly formed; left rude or rough. Freq. *fig.*

1572 BOSSEWELL Armorie 11 A sleue, vnshaped, and vnsowed. 1602 SHAKS. Ham. IV. v. 8 Her speech is nothing, Yet the vnshaped vse of it doth moue The hearers to Collection. c1680 P. AYRES Embl. Love (1906) 355 See how the bear industriously does frame, And bring in time to form, her unshaped young. 1730 BAILEY (fol.), Mola Carnea.. is a spungy unshaped Substance, without Bones or Bowels. 1798 WORDSW. P. Bell 296 All the unshaped half-human thoughts Which solitary Nature feeds. 1841 BROWNING Pippa Passes II. Poems (1905) 179/1 Shall to produce form out of unshaped stuff Be Art? 1860 HAWTHORNE Marb. Faun ii, He spoke..with the Tuscan rusticity of accent, and an unshaped sort of utterance.

Hence **Unsha·pedness.**

1587 GOLDING De Mornay x. 166 A certeine vnshapednesse, which is the cause of all mishapennesse.

†**Unsha·peful,** *a. Obs.*-1 (UN-1 7.) 1598 CHAPMAN Hero & Leander III. 298 Her right hand leand on her hart-bowing knee, Wrapt in vnshapefull foulds. †**Unsha·pefulness.** *Obs.*-1 [UN-1 12.] Shapelessness. 1535 Trevisa's Barth. De P. R. XIII. xxii. 181/1 It was called Abyssus, for vnshapfulnesse: for it was dystynguyed with no fourme nor shape. †**Unsha·peless,** *a. Obs.*-1 (UN-1 5 a.) 1640 J. GOWER Ovid's Festiv. I. 4 A rude unshapelesse load.

**Unsha·peliness.** (UN-1 12; cf. next.)

1741 RICHARDSON Pamela I. p. xxvi, What, in the Name of Unshapeliness, cou'd he find to complain of, in a beautiful Girl of Sixteen. a1834 COLERIDGE Constit. Ch. & State (1839) 118 note, Gold or silver ingots,..their unshapeliness and want of the mint impression. 1871 ALABASTER Wheel of Law 252 Its unshapeliness has not prevented Buddhists from claiming it as made by the foot of Buddha.

**Unsha·pely,** *a.* (UN-1 7. Cf. ON. *úskapligr* (Sw. *oskaplig,* Norw. *uskapleg*) misshapen, etc.)

c1200 Trin. Coll. Hom. 163 Ðe meshakele [is] of medeme fustane,..ðe corporeals sole, and unshapliche. 13.. Guy Warw. (A.) 7160 His bodi..is michel,..Fram þe nouel vpward vnschepliche. ?a1400 Morte Arth. 1099 Schouellefotede was that schalke With schankez unschaply. c1485 Digby Myst. (1882) III. 1158 On-shaply þou art to see! 1589 PUTTENHAM Eng. Poesie (Arb.) 89 Our auncient rymers.. many times made their meetres..of such vnshapely wordes as would allow no conuenient Cesure. 1615 CROOKE Body of Man 113 It is an vnshapely body, very loose, all glandulous. 1645 BOATE Ireland's Nat. Hist. (1652) 64 Things like Boats, but very unshapely, being nothing but square peeces of timber made hollow. 1752 HUME Ess. on Original Contract II. xii. (1777) I. 471 The people being commonly very rude builders,..it is natural to imagine, that their workmanship must be a little unshapely. 1802 PLAYFAIR Illustr. Hutton. Th. 114 An immense mass of solid rock, naked and unshapely. 1874 J. FISKE Cosmic Philos. I. ii. I. 26 An apparently-solid edifice, which fell into unshapely ruin at the first rude blast of criticism.

**Unsha·pen,** *a.* [UN-1 8 b. Cf. OE. *unsceapen, ungesceapen,* MDu. *ongescapen* (Du. *-schapen*), MLG. *ungeschapen,* OHG. *-scaffan* (MHG. and G. *-schaffen*).] = UNSHAPED *ppl. a.*

13.. Cursor M. 367 (Gött.), Þe mater of foure elementis, Þat ȝeit was þan of forme vnschapin. c1350 Athanasian Creed in MS. Bodl. 425 fol. 69 b, Vnshapen fadir unshapen son is, Vnshapen heli gost in blis. 1387 TREVISA Higden (Rolls) II. 163 Al þe longage of þe Norþhumbres..is..scharp, slitting, and frotynge and vnschape [L. incondita]. a1560 PHAER Æneid IX. (1562) Ff i b, An vnshapen bunchy speare ..Sir Pandare whirling threw. 1594 SHAKS. Rich. III, I. ii. 251 (Q 1), Will she yet debase her eyes..On me that halt, and am vnshapen thus. 1646 SIR T. BROWNE Pseud. Ep. III. vi. 116 A Bear brings forth her young informous and unshapen. 1695 J. EDWARDS Perfect. Script. 322 This unshapen mass without form and void. 1728 R. MORRIS Ess. Anc. Archit. 42 Columns were originally made of unshapen Trees. 1747 CARTE Hist. Eng. I. 44 A rough unshapen stone, of an enormous size. a1814 Mermaid I. ii. in New Brit. Theatre II. 478 They ran to mock her hump'd unshapen form. 1872 MORLEY Voltaire 9 Pale unshapen embryos of social sympathy.

Hence **Unsha·penness.**

1398 TREVISA Barth. De P. R. XIII. xxii. (Tollem. MS.), It was clepid abbissus for unschapnesse,..for it was distinged with no forme noþer schappe. 1648 HEXHAM II, Ongeschapenheydt, Vncreatednesse, or Vnshapennesse.

**Unsha·red,** *ppl. a.* [UN-1 8.] Not shared with, or by, another or others.

c1616 W. BASSE Shakespeare Poet. Wks. (1893) 116 Thy unmolested peace, vnshared Caue, Possesse as Lord, not Tenant, of thy Graue. 1667 MILTON P. L. IX. 880 For bliss, as thou hast part, to me is bliss, Tedious, unshar'd with thee. a1774 W. WHITEHEAD Enthusiast xii, Each bliss unshar'd is unenjoy'd. 1809–14 WORDSW. Excurs. IX. 587 Merely from a wish To impart a joy, imperfect while unshared. 1886 GURNEY, etc. Phantasms of Living I. 458 Both sensory and non-sensory hallucinations are idiosyncratic and unshared.

Hence **Unsha·redness.**

1896 G. MATHESON Lady Ecclesia vii. 57 It was not the fault of my new faith, but of its unsharedness.

**Unsha·rp,** *a.* (UN-1 7. Cf. OE. *unscearp,* Du. *onscherp*). 1611 FLORIO, Inaspro, vnsowre, sweet, vnsharpe. 1889 Anthony's Photogr. Bull. II. 204 People often call unsharp, fuzzy pictures 'artistic'. **Unsha·rpened,** *ppl. a.* (UN-1 8.) 1620 E. BLOUNT Horæ Subs. 385 The place where our thoughts cannot be perturbed, nor our sences vnsharpened. 1813 SCOTT Rokeby I. v, Though no human ear, Unsharpen'd by revenge and fear, Could e'er distinguish horse's clank.

**Unshathiness, -shathy:** see UN-1 3.

**Unsha·ttered,** *ppl. a.* (UN-1 8.)

1634 BP. HALL Serm. Wks. II. 427 Where brasse meets with clay, how can that brittle stuffe escape unshattered? 1657 THORNLEY tr. Longus' Daphnis & Chloe 191 How intire and unshatter'd their horns. 1809 COLERIDGE Friend 123 Their own good health and unshattered nerves. 1870 WILBERFORCE Heroes Hebrew Hist. 175 His casting down ..left their rising spirit unshattered.

**Unsha·veable,** *a.* (UN-1 7 b.) 1809 Q. Rev. I. 214 A harrie, or [one] of any other unshaveable cast.

**Unsha·ved,** *ppl. a.* (UN-1 8; cf. next.)

1648 HEXHAM II, Onbeschoren, Vnshorne, or Vnshaved. 1862 Lond. Rev. 30 Aug. 192 The sturdy philosophy of the unshaved Warrington. 1900 G. SWIFT Somerley 66, I found Dobson unshaved and in the tattered remnants of a dress-suit.

**Unsha·ven,** *ppl. a.* [UN-1 8 b. Cf. prec. and MDu. *ongescaven.*]

1. Not shaved.

1382 WYCLIF 2 Sam. xix. 24 The feet vnwasshen, and the beerd vnshauen. c1450 Mirk's Festial 125 Þis man..abode half schauen and half vnschauen tyll þe Monday aftyr. 1532 MORE Confut. Tindale Wks. 430/2 Though beefore those ceremonyes vsed, priestes myghte consecrate vnshauen &

vnannoynted,..yet nowe can there none dooe so, syth there is no priest made vnshauen and vnannoynted. **1646** Sir T. Browne *Pseud. Ep.* v. 269 The indicidious and unshaven locks of Apollo. **1759** Sterne *Tr. Shandy* ii. iv, My uncle began..to dismiss his barber unshaven. **1838** Dickens *O. Twist* xxi, The unwashed, unshaven, squalid, and dirty figures. **1863** Miss Braddon *Aurora Floyd* xxii, His unshaven chin, dark with the blue bristles of his budding beard. **1870** Black *Kilmeny* iii, He went about in a frightfully unshaven and ragged condition.

**2.** Not smoothed or planed.

*a* **1547** Surrey *Æneid* iv. 527 Their oares..from wood they bring, And mastes vnshaue, for hast to take their flight.

Hence **Unsha·venness.**

**1667** Waterhouse *Fire Lond.* 62 What avails Sampson's strength, if God give a key to the secret of it which resides in its unshavenness.

**Unshaw·l,** *v.* (Un-[2] 7 and 4.)

**1817** Lady Morgan *France* ii. (1818) I. 238 While I was unshawling, I caught the first stanzas of the following song. **1828** Miss Mitford *Village* Ser. iii. 62 [She] sate down on her dear sofa, and was forthwith unclogged, unshawled and unbonneted. **1849** C. Bronte *Shirley* vii, And now Caroline had to help them to unshawl.

**Unshea·f,** *v.* (Un-[1] 3.) *a* **1722** Lisle *Husb.* (1757) 182 [He] unsheafed some of his wheat to dry it. **†Unshea·f,** obs. var. Unsheathe *v.* **1658** tr. *Bergerac's Satyr. Char.* xvi. 67 I'le not unsheafe, to drive your enemy by death far from you.

**Unshea·red,** *ppl. a.* [Un-[1] 8.] = Unshorn.

**1707** Mortimer *Husb.* 481 The part [of the rose-tree] unsheared will spend that Strength and Sap. **1788** tr. *Chenier's St. Morocco*, etc. I. 283 Their household furniture consists in a mat, two sheep-skins, unsheard, to sit upon [etc.]. **1826** Hood *Stag-eyed Lady* 27 A trail Of bristly hair—that, honour'd and unshear'd, Grew downward.

**Unshea·the,** *v.* [Un-[2] 4, 5.]

**1.** *trans.* To dislodge.

*c* **1374** Chaucer *Troylus* iv. 776 Than shal no mete or drynk come in me, Til I my soule out of my breste vnsheþe. **1593** Shaks. *Lucr.* 1724 She sheathed in her harmless breast A harmful knife, that thence her soul unsheathed.

**2.** To draw (a weapon) out of the sheath or scabbard. *To unsheathe the sword*, to begin hostilities or slaughter. (Cf. Sheathe *v.* 2.)

*a* **1542** Wyatt *Ps.* xxxvii. 41 They have unsheathed eke their bloudye brands. *a* **1547** Surrey *Æneis* iv. 774 Aeneas ..his glistering sword unshethes,..[and] the cabels cut in twaine. **1600** *1st Pt. Sir J. Oldcastle* v. x. 78 Wherefore were your sharpe edgde kniues vnsheathde? **1649** Milton *Eikon.* ix. 78 Never was King less in danger of any violence from his Subjects, till he unsheath'd his Sword against them. **1683** Waller *Invasion of Turks* 60 Unsheathing the destructive sword. **1807** J. Barlow *Columb.* vi. 686 Are these..the swords Thy hand unsheath'd and gave the savage hordes? **1884** A. R. Pennington *Wiclif* v. 176 The sword of the persecutor would be unsheathed against him.

*fig.* and *transf.* **1692** A. Pitcairne *Babell* 287 He did his trustie tongue unsheath...It was a blade that he could trust. **1774** Goldsm. *Nat. Hist.* VII. 335 Nature has furnished her [*sc.* the grasshopper] with an instrument at her tail,.. which she can sheathe and unsheathe at pleasure. **1810** Southey *Kehama* xvi. xiv, The Beast.., His mouth half-open, and his teeth unsheath'd. **1855** Kingsley *Westw. Ho!* xxvii, A tame leopard, whose claws might be unsheathed ..at any moment.

**3.** To take out of, strip of, a sheath or covering. Also *fig.* and *refl.*

**1638** N. Whiting *Albino & Bellama* 2275 At time of rest her body she unsheathed, And housed within the linen walls her limbs. **1664** H. Power *Exp. Philos.* i. 30 If you unsheath her body, and take off her spotted short crustaceous wings. **1875** Sears *Serm. & Songs* 6 When our spiritual senses are first unsheathed. **1893** J. Pulsford *Loyalty to Christ* II. 225 Sing for joy;..and others will be moved to unsheathe themselves of their wintry earthliness.

**4.** *intr.* 'To come out from a sheath' (*Cent. Dict.*).

Hence **Unshea·thing** *vbl. sb.*

**1611** Cotgr., *Desgaine*, an vnsheathing..of a weapon. **1823** Lamb *Elia* ii. *Old Margate Hoy*, Whistling to the sheathing and unsheathing of their cutlasses. **1871** Macduff *Mem. Patmos* 152 The unsheathings of that terrible sword.

**Unshea·thed,** *ppl. a.* [f. prec. or Un-[1] 8.]

**1.** Of a weapon: Drawn from the sheath; not covered by a sheath.

*c* **1430** *Pilgr. Lyf Manhode* i. xxxv. (1869) 22 It is bettere the swerd be shethed than vnshethed. *a* **1593** Marlowe *Ovid's Eleg.* ii. ii. 64 My hands an vnsheath'd shyning weapon haue not. **1611** Cotgr. s.v. *Blanc*, A naked or vnsheathed..sword. **1638** Suckling *Aglaura* iii. i, Blesse me, what means this unsheath'd minister of death [= a sword]? **1700** Dryden *Pal. & Arc.* ii. 253 He..with his Sword unsheath'd..Commands both Combatants to cease their Strife. **1814** Scott *Lord of Isles* ii. xxiii, Do dirks unsheathed suit bridal cheer? **1842** Borrow *Bible in Spain* x, He held his unsheathed knife in his hand.

*fig.* **1830** Mrs. Hemans *Songs Affec., Spirit's Return*, Yet something..as that unsheathed spirit-glance I met, Made my soul faint.

**2.** Not protected by a sheath or sheathing; uncovered, exposed.

**1691** T. H[ale] *Acc. New Invent.* 9 Any unsheathed or Wood-sheathed Ships. *Ibid.* 24 Not only in sheathed Ships ..but unsheathed too. **1790** Beatson *Nav. & Mil. Mem.* I. 126 An unsheathed fire ship..was left to act as an advice-boat. **1884** Bower & Scott *De Bary's Phaner.* 393 The delicate unsheathed parts of the vascular bundles.

**Unshe·d,** *ppl. a.* [Un-[1] 8 b.]

**1.** Not shed or poured out.

*c* **1450** *Mirk's Festial* 242 Forto haue savytte gyltles blode vnsched on boþe parties. **1667** Milton *P. L.* xii. 176 To blood unshed the Rivers must be turnd. **1768–74** Tucker *Lt. Nat.* (1834) II. 43 He..can make the same mass of blood exist at once unshed in the wafer, and shed in the cup. **1816** Byron *Dream* v, An unquiet drooping of the eye, As if its lid were charged with unshed tears. **1880** Miss Braddon *Just as I am* v, Dulcie's eyelids were heavy with unshed tears

**2.** Unparted.

**1596** Spenser *F. Q.* iv. vii. 40 His faire lockes..He let to grow..Vncomb'd, vncurl'd, and carelesly vnshed.

**†Unshee·n,** *a. Obs.*[-1] (Un-[1] 7.) *a* **1400** *Sir Degrev.* 1656 Some lorkus undur tres In slowes unshene. **Unshee·t,** *v.* (Un-[2] 4.) *a* **1814** *Sorceress* iii. i. in *New Brit. Theatre* III. 20, I saw Th' accursed robbers..With hideous burglary unsheet a corpse. **1888** Jacobi *Printers' Vocab.*, *Unsheet*, to withdraw the interleaving sheets between printed work which have been placed there to prevent set-off. **Unshee·ted,** *a.* (Un-[1] 9.) [**1775** Ash.] **1816** J. Wilson *City of Plague* i. iv. 52 Down the drunken wretch doth lie Unsheeted in the cemetery. *Ibid.* 53 The bodies Of the unsheeted dead.

**Unshe·ll,** *v.* [Un-[2] 5. Cf. Du. *ontschillen*, *-schellen.*] *trans.* To extract from, to strip of, the shell. (Chiefly *fig.*)

**1599** Nashe *Lenten Stuffe* D iij, Of him and none but him, ..that euer Yarmouth vnshelled or ingendred. **1611** Cotgr., *Challer*,..to shale, or vnshell, Nuts, &c. **1642** Fuller *Holy & Prof. St.* ii. x. 90 Our Perkins brought the schools into the Pulpit, and unshelling their controversies out of their hard school-terms, made thereof..wholsome meat for his people. **1652** Benlowes *Theoph.* vi. xvii, Thou, Love,.. did'st unshell My Spirit (fledg'd with Grace) from that dis-order'd cell. **1761** Murphy *Citizen* ii, Sir! Turn out pray, turn out—you won't—Then I'll unshell you. **1819** Scott *Leg. Montrose* v, By this time he was unshelled, and stood before the fire. **1892** *Sat. Rev.* 17 Dec. 719/1 You have got but to unhusk and unshell it, and there it is.

Hence **Unshe·lled** *ppl. a.*[1]; **Unshe·lling** *vbl. sb.*

*a* **1668** Lassels *Voy. Italy* (1698) II. 277 Whose ingenious book gives light to many books by the unshelling of a world of ancient customs. **1799** Sheridan *Pizarro* iv. i, O'er her unshelled brood the murmuring ring-dove sits not more gently.

**Unshe·lled,** *ppl. a.*[2] [Un-[1] 8. Cf. NFris. *unskelled*, MDu. *ongescelt* (Du. *ongescheld*), MHG. *ungeschelt* (G. *ungeschält*).] Not taken out of the shell. Also (of husks), unremoved.

**1594** Nashe *Terrors of Night* G iij b, Their naturall vnshelled shining mother pearle proportions might be more imprintingly apprehended. **1647** Wither (*title*), Amygdala Britannica, Almonds for Parrets. A Dish of Stone-Fruit, partly shel'd and partly unshel'd. **1769** *Phil. Trans.* LIX. 382 Ten gallons of the pease, with the husks unshelled. **1802** *Naval Chron.* VIII. 28 Sweet almonds, unshelled.

**Unshe·lterable,** *a.* (Un-[1] 7 b.) **1841** Lytton *Nt. & Morn.* ii. x, As if to protect him even from the wrath of the unshelterable flame.

**Unshe·ltered,** *ppl. a.* (Un-[1] 8.)

**1599** Daniel *Musoph.* Wks. (1602) C i b, For this it practises to dissipate Th' vnsheltred troupes. **1665** Boyle *Occas. Refl.* iv. xx, Shunning all beaten Paths, and unshelter'd Grounds. **1667** *Decay Chr. Piety* vi. 143 [To] leave him unsheltred to that scorching wrath of God. **1726** Leoni *Alberti's Archit.* I. 28 An open place, unshelter'd either by Woods or Hills. **1760–72** H. Brooke *Fool of Qual.* (1809) II. 133, I did not dare to leave my child alone and unsheltered. **1815** Kirby & Sp. *Entomol.* iv. I. 85 We should soon be..unsheltered, except by caves. **1855** [J. R. Leifchild] *Cornwall* 64 A bleak and unsheltered country.

**Unshe·ltering,** *ppl. a.* (Un-[1] 10.)

**1614** R. Tailor *Hog hath lost Pearl* i. i, Whilst dear Carracus Wanders..through th' unshelt'ring field, Seeking me. **1766** Goldsm. *Vicar* xxiii, My son, observe this bed of straw, and unsheltering roof. **1892** *Pall Mall G.* 2 Dec. 2/2 Mr. Mitchell still roams the unsheltering streets.

**Unshe·lve,** *v.* (Un-[2] 5.) *a* **1819** *Edin. Rev.* (Seager), To unshelve books. **1876** *Nature* 13 Jan. 206/2 He is not likely to unshelve works of travel of a past generation. **†Unshe·nd,** obs. var. Unshent. *c* **1440** *Pallad. on Husb.* xii. 610 Al yeer Thy duc attende,..or laste Vnshende. **†Unshe·nding,** *ppl. a. Obs.*[-1] [Un-[1] 10.] Not harming or injuring. *c* **1450** *Mirour Saluacioun* (Roxb.) 162 So was crist borne of the thy maydenhode vnsheendyng.

**Unshe·nt,** *ppl. a.* Now *arch.* [Un-[1] 8 b. Cf. OE. *unscended*, MDu. *ongescendet*, *-scent*, *-scant* (obs. Du. *ongeschent*, Du. *ongeschend*), OHG. *ungeschendet* (MHG. *ungescant*), etc.] Uninjured, unharmed, unspoiled, etc.

**1303** R. Brunne *Handl. Synne* 2733 Vndyrstand..þat.. wrong Iugement Shul neuer more be vnshent. *a* **1400** *Minor Poems fr. Vernon MS.* 680/6 Þer nis no mon fer ne nere þat may him-seluen saue vn-schent, But he þat casteþ ..To kepe wel Cristes Comaundement. *a* **1400–50** *Alexander* 2143 If at ȝe shap ȝow to shount vnschent of oure handis. *c* **1460** *Towneley Myst.* xv. 3 If thou wyll saue thy self vnshent. **1597** Bp. Hall *Sat.* iv. i, Ho! all ye Females that would liue vnshent. **1628** Wither *Brit. Rememb.* i. 975 In hope their number keep them shall unshent. **1653** J. Taylor (Water P.) *Cert. Trav. Uncert. Journ.* 20 Time never was, nor n'ere I thinke shall be, That Truth (unshent) might speake, in all things free. **1817** Keats *Sleep & Poetry* 379 The patient weeds, that now unshent by foam Feel all about their undulating home. **1868** Browning *Ring & Bk.* iii. 1409 Let the priest retire, unshent, unshamed, Unpunished. **1898** T. Hardy *Wessex Poems* 62 Like one of those the Furnace held unshent.

**Unshe·pherded,** *ppl. a.* (Un-[1] 8.) **1850** Blackie *Æschylus* I. 194 Depart, ye sheep unshepherded. **1880** *Blackw. Mag.* Mar. 283 A strange flock, evidently unshepherded. **Unshe·riff,** *v.* (Un-[2] 6 b.) *a* **1661** Fuller *Worthies, Kent* ii. (1662) 95 But he was soon un-Sheriffed by the Kings death, and another of more true Integrity substituted in his room. **Unshew·ed,** *ppl. a.* [Un-[1] 8.] Unshown. *c* **1386** Chaucer *Par. T.* ⁋ 909 Right so fareth synne þat longe tyme is in a man vnshewed. **1559** W. Bercher *Nobil. Women* Pref. (Roxb.) 90 That no parte shoulde be vnshewed vnto me, a gentleman..wolde nedes haue me with hym in to the contreye. **Unshew·ing,** *ppl. a.* [Un-[1] 10.] † Secret. **1598** R. Markham in *Harington's Nugæ Ant.* (1804) I. 242 When a man hath so manie shewing friendes, and so manie unshewing enemies.

**Unshie·lded,** *ppl. a.* (Un-[1] 8.)

**1700** Dryden *Ovid's Met.* xii. 135 Th' inviolable Body stood sincere; Though Cygnus..scornful offer'd his unshielded Side. *c* **1790** A. Wilson *Poems, Tears of Britain*, Soon will the tempest..This unshielded bosom most fatally wound. **1817** Scott *Harold* iii. viii, Unshielded, mail-less, on he goes Singly against a host of foes. **1883** *Hardwick's Photogr. Chem.* 290 Exposing a small slip of the sensitive paper, unshielded, to the sun's rays.

**Unshi·ftable,** *a.* [Un-[1] 7 b.]

**†1.** Incapable of helping oneself. *Obs.*

**1622** S. Ward *Life of Faith in Death* 118 These fooles.. neuer thinke of the euill day, and when away they see they must goe, how vnshyftable are they! **1633** T. Adams *Exp. 2 Peter* ii. 9 How unshiftable otherwise shall we be in that houre, how unable to answer at the day of Iudgement!

**2.** Incapable of being shifted; immovable.

**1890** W. J. Gordon *Foundry* 36 Secured so as to be unshiftable in a sea-way.

**Unshi·fted,** *ppl. a.* (Un-[1] 8.)

**1643** Greaves *Morbus Epidemicus* 9 Filth, and nastinesse in Diet,..unshifted apparrell, &c. **1674** N. Fairfax *Bulk & Selv.* 182 It never shall be, or at least never was it body unshifted. **1863** Hawthorne *Our Old Home* (1879) 268 Wearing the unbrushed coat, unshifted linen, and unwashed faces of yesterday.

**Unshi·ftiness.** (Un-[1] 12.) **1870** *Sat. Rev.* 23 April 538/2 A molluscous man, too, suddenly ejected from his long-accustomed groove,..presents just as wretched a picture of helplessness and unshiftiness. **Unshi·fting,** *ppl. a.* (Un-[1] 10.) **1811** Wordsw. *To Beaumont* 18 An unshifting weather-cock. **1817** Chalmers in *Edin. Rev.* Mar. 15 A small and unshifting population. **Unshi·fty,** *a.* (Un-[1] 7. Cf. Unshiftiness.) **1570** Levins *Manip.* 111 Vnshifty, *improuidus*. **Unshi·mmering,** *ppl. a.* (Un-[1] 10.) **1868** Geo. Eliot *Span. Gipsy* 50 All thought-teaching form Utters itself in firm unshimmering hues. **Unshi·ngled,** *ppl. a.* (Un-[1] 8.) **1611** in *Essex Rev.* XV. 47 The church is unleaded and unshingled. *c* **1805** A. Wilson *Foresters*, The owner, indolent and poor, His house unshingled and without a door. **Unshi·ning,** *ppl. a.* (Un-[1] 10.) **1682** Creech *Lucretius* v. 158 Else the Sun hath secret stores of Heat, Dark and unshining stores, but vastly great. **1867** E. F. Burr *Ecce Cœlum* iii. 63 [The earth] seemed..so different from them [*sc.* the heavenly bodies], so unshining.

**Unshi·p,** *v.* [Un-[2] 5, 4, 7. Cf. Du. *ontschepen*, G. *entschiffen.*]

**1.** *trans.* To take out of, remove or discharge from, a ship; to put on shore (or into a boat, etc.) from a vessel.

*a* **1450** *Contn. Brut* 542 He..saylet toward Normaundy, and londit at Hogges,..and vnshippit his pepill. **1497** *Naval Acc. Hen. VII* (1896) 324 Ladders for to Shep men and vnship men with. **1523** Ld. Berners *Froiss.* I. ccxviii. 113 b/2 The kynge of Ciper..arriued at Douer,..and refresshed hym tyll all his cariage was vnshipped. **1568** Grafton *Chron.* II. 210 They vnshipped their horse and harneys, not knowing in what part of England they were. **1624** Capt. Smith *Virginia* v. 174 They vnshipped all their goods..into their Boats. **1641** W. Hakewil *Libertie of Subject* 102 Impositions are not paid upon the buying and selling of Merchandize, but when they are to ship or unship. **1719** De Foe *Crusoe* ii. (Globe) 426 In the Voyage..he had had the Misfortune to be five Times shipp'd and unshipp'd. **1726** Swift *Gulliver* ii. i, We unshipped our goods. **1837** Ht. Martineau *Soc. Amer.* II. 6 All hands were busy in unshipping the cargo, to lighten the vessel. **1885** *Act* 48–49 *Vic.* c. 41 § 17 Any harbour..at which vessels can..ship or unship goods or passengers.

*refl.* *a* **1604** Hanmer *Chron. Irel.* (1809) 253 They forthwith landed, and unshipped themselves.

**b.** To deprive of, dismiss from, a ship.

**1829** Marryat *F. Mildmay* xxi, I should have unshipped him next cruise.

**2.** *Naut.* To detach or remove (esp. a mast, rudder, or oar) from a fixed place or position.

**1598** Hakluyt *Voy.* I. 235 We were not able to beare in, but by violence were constrained to take the sea agayne, our Pinnesse being vnshipt. **1769** Falconer *Dict. Marine* (1776), *Dégarnir le cabestan*, to unrig the capstern, by taking off the voyol, and unshipping the bars. **1773** Cook *S. Voy.* (1777) ii. ii. I. 205 He..dived under the boat, and..unshipped the rudder. **1806** Pike *SourcesIssiss.* (1810) 102 Obliged to unship our mast to prevent its rolling overboard. **1865** Dickens *Mut. Fr.* i. i, The speaker at the same time unshipping his scull on that side. **1874** Bedford *Sailor's Pocket Bk.* viii. 241 So that..the apparatus..may..be..unshipped and re-shipped again at pleasure.

*fig.* **1816** *Sporting Mag.* XLVII. 277 Crocken..beat a Knightsbridge wheelwright..by unshipping his jaw in the fourth round.

**b.** In general use.

**1793** Smeaton *Edystone L.* § 140 Unshipping the tackle belonging to the lantern. **1832** *Lincoln Herald* 13 Jan. 2 John Page saw Clarke unship the flag on the top of the governor's house. **1839** F. A. Griffiths *Artill. Man.* 87 No 1 unships the handspike. **1882** Sala *Amer. Revis.* (1885) 384 Tell the porter not to unship the little one-legged flap table..fixed to the wall of the car.

**3.** *intr.* **a.** To admit of being detached or removed.

**1834** Marryat *P. Simple* II. 30 Six large pieces of iron, ..with a gimblet at one end of each, and a square at the other, which fitted to a handle which unshipped. **1844** Stephens *Bk. Farm* III. 1169 The top-sides..are fitted to ship and unship as occasion may require. **1862** *Catal. Internat. Exhib., Brit.* II. No. 2256, The upper ladders unship by means of shifting levers.

**b.** To become detached.

**1867** Smyth *Sailor's Word-bk.* 161 *Capstan-bar Pins*, pins inserted through their ends to prevent their unshipping. **1883** *Pall Mall G.* 13 Mar. 10/2 The boat's rudder unshipped and caused the boat to capsize.

**4.** To undergo unloading from a vessel.

**1860** Dickens *Christmas Stories, Message fr. Sea* i, Such other cargo as was..unshipping at the pier.

**5.** *trans.* **a.** Of a horse: To unseat, throw (the rider).

**1831** Scott *Let.* in *Westm. Gaz.* 14 June (1904) 12/2 My forester walks by his [*sc.* the pony's] head for fear a start or sudden stumble should unship me altogether. **1853** R. S. Surtees *Sponge's Sp. Tour* lxvii, One [horse] has still his muzzle on, lest he should unship his rider and eat him.

**b.** To unbalance, upset.

**1827** Chalmers in Hanna *Life* (1851) III. 163, I really fear lest his [*sc.* Irving's] prophecies may unship him altogether.

Hence **Unshi·pped** *ppl. a.*, **Unshi·pping** *vbl. sb.*

**1868** Morris *Earthly Par.* (1870) II. III. 389 A ring of Icelanders, who sat Upon the bales of *unshipped goods. **1497** *Naval Acc. Hen. VII* (1896) 327 Ladders for shippyng & *vnshippyng of men. **1709** *Act* 8 *Anne* c. 7 § 17 The Persons..to whose Hands the same shall knowingly come, after the unshipping thereof. **1803** *Act* 43 *Geo. III*, c. 132 § 28 To prevent the fraudulent unshipping or re-landing of Goods.

**Unshi·plike,** *a.* (Un-[1] 7 c.) **1842** Dickens *Amer. Notes* (1868) 46 A sullen, cumbrous, ungraceful, unshiplike leviathan. **1859** — *Lett.* (1880) II. 101, I thought her [*sc.* the Great Eastern] the ugliest and most unshiplike thing these eyes ever beheld. **Unshi·pment.** (f. Unship *v.*) **1846** Worcester (citing *Penny Mag.*). **1879** Miss Braddon *Vixen* III. 273 Mr. Vawdrey..came round to assist in the unshipment of Violet's belongings.

**Unshi·pped,** *a.* [Un-[1] 9.] Not provided with a ship.

**1720** De Foe *Capt. Singleton* v. (1840) 82 We were..all upon a level, as to our travelling, being unshipped. **1725** — *Voy. round World* (1840) 200 We should be like a company of freebooters loose and unshipped. **1827** Pollok *Course T.* II. 241 Choosing, thus unshipped, Uncompassed, unprovisioned,..To swim a sea of breadth immeasurable.

**Unshi·pshape,** *a.* (Un-[1] 7.) **1883** *Harper's Mag.* Jan. 198/2 Never was seen so unshipshape and disreputable a locomotive as that on duty here. **Unshi·pwrecked,** *ppl. a.* (Un-[1] 8.) *c* **1637** H. King *The Sovereign* 14 That golden constellation..guides the seaman..Safe and unshipwrack'd through the troubled streams. **Unshi·vered,** *ppl. a.* (Un-[1] 8.) **1597** Bp. Hall *Sat.* v. iii, Theirs, like anuilles, bore the hammers head, Our glasse can neuer touch vnshiuered. ? **1827** Mrs. Hemans *Last Constantine* x, So may thy helmet tower Unshiver'd through the storm. **Unshi·vering,** *ppl. a.* (Un-[1] 10.) **1818** Milman *Samor* VIII. 555 On Went Samor with unshivering naked foot.

**Unsho·cked,** *ppl. a.* (Un-[1] 8.)

**1712** Tickell in *Spect.* No. 532, Thy spotless Thoughts unshock'd the Priest may hear. **1774** Foote *Cozeners* II, You must have the heart of a tiger, to stand unshocked at such a horrible scene. **1816** Byron *Prisoner of Chillon* vi, The very rock hath rock'd, And I have felt it shake, unshock'd. **1891** H. Herman *His Angel* 57 Though her seasoned ear..remained unshocked by an occasional outburst.

**Unsho·d,** *ppl. a.* [Un-[1] 8 b, or f. Unshoe *v.* Cf. Unshoed *ppl. a.* and Sw. *oskodd.*]

**1.** Of persons, or the feet: Having a shoe or shoes not put on, or taken off; not wearing shoes, barefooted.

*c* **897** K. Ælfred *Gregory's Past. C.* v. 45 Đonne bið us suiðe fracoðlice oðer fot unscod. *c* **1000** Ælfric *Deut.* xxv. 10 Nemne hine ælc man on Israhela folce unsceoda. *a* **1300** *Cursor M.* 15099 Tuelue or ma o men vnscod þan has he wit him broght. **1382** Wyclif *Isaiah* xx. 3 As wente.. Isaie nakid and vnshod. *Ibid.* 4. **1596** Spenser *F.Q.* II. xi. 23 There follow'd fast at hand two wicked Hags,..Their feet vnshod, their bodies wrapt in rags. **1627** Drayton *Battle of Agincourt* 26 Vnshod, and without stockings are the best. **1693** tr. *Emilianne's Hist. Monast. Ord.* 156 The Order of the Unshod Carmelites. **1728** Pope *Dunc.* III. 114 Men bearded, bald,..shod, unshod. **1781** Cowper *Ep. Prot. Lady* 16 With unshod feet they yet securely tread. **1849** C. Bronte *Shirley* xxxiii, He left his shoes on the mat; mounted the stairs unshod. **1870** Rossetti *Burden Nineveh* ix, Any god Before whose feet men knelt unshod.

*absol.* **1382** Wyclif *Deut.* xxv. 10 The hows of the vnshod. **1847** F. Prandi tr. *Cantù's Ref. Europe* I. 212 The Order of the Unshod.

*transf.* **1535** Coverdale *Deut.* xxv. 10 And his name shalbe called in Israel, the vnshodd house.

**2.** Of horses: Having cast a shoe or shoes; not furnished with shoes.

**1523** Ld. Berners *Froiss.* I. xviii. 9/2 Most part of their horses [were] hurt on their back, nor they had nat wherwith to shoo them, that were vnshodde. **1530** Palsgr. 768/2 Your horse is unshod of bothe his hynder fete. **1610** Holland *Camden's Brit.* 529 They use their Horses unshod. **1680** *Lond. Gaz.* No. 1569/4 One dark bay Nag,..lately rowelled, and trots all, and unshod. **1839** Darwin *Voy. Nat.* x. 225 [It] would soon disable an unshod horse from taking part in the chase.

**3.** Not protected by an iron rim, toe-piece, etc.

**1497** *Naval Acc. Hen. VII* (1896) 87 A pair wheles vnshodd. **1557** in Raine *Richmond. Wills* (1853) 101 One yron bound wayne and ij. unshode cowpes. **1601** in Moryson *Itin.* II. (1617) 204 Ten Culuerings..mounted vpon vnshod wheeles. **1660** *Act* 12 *Chas. II*, c. 4 *Rates*, Shovells, unshod, the dozen, iijs. iiijd. **1869** A. Hume *Brit. Antiq.* 27 The unshod wooden wheels of timber carriages.

**Unsho·dden,** *ppl. a.* (Un-[1] 8 b.) **1836** F. Mahony *Rel. Father Prout* 176 It is far from my purpose..to tread on such solemn ground save with..feet duly unshodden. **1838** Lytton *Calderon* iv, To place our unshodden feet upon the necks of kings.

**Unshoe·,** *v.* [Un-[2] 4. Cf. OE. *an-, on-, unscógian*, MDu. *ontscoeyen, -scoen* (Du. *-schoeien*), MLG. *entschoien*, OHG. *in(t)scuohôn* (MHG. *entschuohen*, G. *-schuhen*).] *trans.* To remove a shoe or shoes from; to strip or deprive of shoes.

**1481** Caxton *Reynard* xix. (Arb.) 45 Whan Isegrym was vnshoed, Tho muste..his wyf lye doun in the grasse [etc]. **1530** Palsgr. 768/2, I unshoo a horse, *je deferre.* **1591** Sylvester *Du Bartas* I. iii. 767 O Moon-wort! tell us where thou hid'st the Smith, Hammer, and Pincers, thou unshoo'st them with? **1628** tr. *Mathieu's Powerfull Fav.* 1 They are unshod of their high shooes that eleuated them aboue others. **1653** Culpepper *Eng. Phys. Enlarged* (1656) 163 Moon-wort is an herb which they say wil..unshoo such Horses as tread upon it. **1677** Gilpin *Demonol.* I. xiii. 102 They were told.. that this did unshoo their Foot, and afflicted them with Thirst and Want. **1827** Hone *Every-day Bk.* II. 197 They were to unshoe themselves. **1868** Holme Lee *B. Godfrey* xliii, Joan unshod her feet.

*transf.* **1852** Burn *Naval & Mil. Techn. Dict.* II. 302/1 To Unshoe a wheel, *ôter la bande, les bandes de roue.*

**b.** *Unshoe-the-horse*, the plant moonwort. ? *Obs.*

**1635** Swan *Spec. M.* vi. § 4 (1644) 251 The Italians call it Vnshoe-the-horse; because if they tread upon it, they lose their shoes. **1653** Culpepper *Eng. Phys. Enlarged* (1656) 163 Country people that I know, cal it Unshoo the Horse. **1878** Dickinson *Cumbld. Gloss.* 85 *Unshoe the horse*, I have heard the *Botrychium Lunaria* plant so called.

Hence **Unshoe·ing** *vbl. sb.*

**1580** Hollyband *Treas. Fr. Tong*, *Dechaussement*, an vnshoing. **1653** Urquhart *Rabelais* I. xxii. 95 Gargantua.. played..at [the game] the unshoing of the Asse.

**Unshoe·d,** *ppl. a.* [Un-[1] 8, or f. Unshoe *v.* Cf. MDu. *ongescoeit, -scoet* (Du. *-schoied*, † *-schoed*), MLG. *ungeschoiet*, MHG. *-schuohet* (G. *-schuht*), ON. *úskúaðr* (Da. *uskoet*).] = Unshod *ppl. a.* Also *transf.*

**1388** Wyclif *Isaiah* xx. 3 As my seruaunt Ysaie ȝede nakid and vnshood. *c* **1440** *Pallad. on Husb.* I. 860 A menstruate vngird womman, vnshood, Vntressed. **1479** *Cely Papers* (Camden) 19 To bye for me a carthe at Caleys..unschude the wyllys [= wheels]. **1530** Tindale *Deut.* xxv. 10 His name shalbe called in Israel, the vnshoed housse. *a* **1564** Becon *Wks.* Pref. c iij b, The shooe, that is moulde with thee, is the shooe of him that is vnshoed. **1865** H. H. Dixon *Field & Fern, South* 34 There are ponies, too,..fat and unshoed.

† **Unshoo·k,** obs. var. Unshaken *ppl. a.*

**1633** Ford *Broken H.* v. ii, Stretch out Thine arm with vigour, and unshook virtue. *a* **1644** Quarles *Sol. Recant.* IX. ii. 42 They gain the Port..With Ribs unshook. **1736** Thomson *Liberty* IV. 430 On the groaning mast With unshook knee to know their giddy way.

**Unsho·p,** *v.* [Un-[2] 5.] (See quot.) **1839** F. Lieber *Pol. Ethics* II. iv. § 38. 349 High rewards were paid for discovering any disobedience, or even for 'unshopping,' that is, throwing out of employment, highly skillful hands. **Unsho·red,** *a.* [Un-[1] 9.] Shoreless. **1881** Masson *De Quincey* 63 Unshored astronomical abysses.

**Unsho·rn,** *ppl. a.* [Un-[1] 8 b. Cf. OE. *unscoren*, MDu. *ongescoren* (Du. *-schoren*), OHG. *ungescoran* (MHG. *ungeschorn*, G. *-schoren*), ON. *úskorinn* (Sw. *oskuren*, Da. *uskaaren*).]

**1.** Not shorn, cut, or cropped: **a.** Of cloth.

**1464** *Rolls of Parlt.* V. 564/2 [No person shall buy] eny Wolles than unshorn, or take promesse of bargayn of eny Wolles than unshoren. **1486** *Bk. St. Albans* b v, A dagon or pece of Rough blanket vnshoron. **1535**- [see Unbarbed 1]. **1597** Shaks. *Lover's Compl.* 94 His phenix downe began but to appeare Like vnshorne veluet. **1675** Hobbes *Odyssey* (1677) 232 He wore a purple vest, Unshorn, and lin'd. **1700** Dryden *Flower & Leaf* 266 White Velvet, but unshorn, for Cloaks they wore. **1716** Gay *Trivia* I. 47 True Witney broad-cloth, with its shag unshorn.

**b.** Of persons or animals, hair, etc.

*c* **1449** Pecock *Repr.* I. xx. 118 The heer of wommennys heed vnschorn. **1565** Cooper *Thesaurus* s.v. *Intonsus*, Sheepe vnshorne. **1577** B. Googe *Heresbach's Husb.* 138 Bye not your Sheepe but washed and vnshorne. **1596** W. Smith *Chloris* xlviii, Those curled locks which thou wast wont to twist, Vnkempt, vnshorne, and out of order beene. **1628** Milton *Vac. Exerc.* 37 Listening to what unshorn Apollo sings. **1693** Dryden tr. *Ovid's Met.* I. 766 As the Locks of Phœbus are unshorn. **1820** Keats *Eve St. Agnes* viii, All amort, Save to St. Agnes and her lambs unshorn. **1848** Thackeray *Van. Fair* xxxix, The caresses of the old gentleman, unshorn and perfumed with tobacco.

**c.** Of corn, fields, etc.

**1573** Tusser *Husb.* (1878) 105 Some mowe vp their hedlonds and plots among corne, and driuen to leaue nothing, vnmowne, or vnshorne. **1601** Campion *Wks.* (1909) 21 A Meadow yet vnshorne. **1631** Quarles *Samson* Wks. (Grosart) II. 155/2 His rip'ned Corne; Whereof, some part ..stood unshorne. **1697** Dryden *Virg. Past.* v. 98 The mountain-tops unshorn, the rocks, rejoice. **1757** Akenside *Pleas. Imag.* I. 316 The pathless woods unshorn That wave o'er huge Olympus. **1810** Scott *Lady of L.* I. xxvi, Of mountain fir, with bark unshorn. *a* **1850** Bryant *Prairies* 2 These are..The unshorn fields, boundless and beautiful. **1873** Symonds *Grk. Poets* vii. 222 This garland..Of wilding flowers plucked from an unshorn meadow.

**2.** *fig.* Not reduced or diminished; not deprived *of* something.

**1818** Byron *Ch. Har.* IV. lxxii, An Iris sits..and..bears serene Its brilliant hues with all their beams unshorn. **1818** Keats '*There is a charm*' 12 One who was great through mortal days, and died of fame unshorn. **1821–2** Shelley *Chas. I*, II. 142 To his God Alone he must deliver up his trust, Unshorn of its permitted attributes.

**Unsho·rtened,** *ppl. a.* (Un-[1] 8.)

**1744** Young *Nt. Th.* VI. 542 Unshortened by progression infinite! Futurity for ever future! **1805** *Ann. Rev.* III. 244 Every tax should..leave unshortened to speculation his casting-net, and to industry his oar. **1855** *Poultry Chron.* III. 496/1 The buds..may be left unshortened until the end of September. **1878** Ruskin *Notes* 77 His full, final, unshortened strength is in these [drawings].

**Unsho·t,** *ppl. a.* [Un-[1] 8 b.]

**1. a.** Not fired or let off.

**1544** *Exped. Scotl.* in *Fragm. Sc. Hist.* (1798) 14 The Scottes fledde from theyr ordinaunces, leuyng them vnshot. **1645** Waller *Night Piece* 32 He..With Cupid's pointed Arrows plays; They, with a touch, they are so keen, Wound us unshot, and She unseen. **1899** J. Milne *Romance of Pro-Consul* vi. 52 For his own gun, he snatched an unshot one which the man was struggling to release from its cover.

**b.** Not struck by a shot; not shot *at.*

[**1755** Johnson.] **1897** *Outing* XXIX. 368/1 The deer left suddenly and unshot. *Ibid.*, We found them easily,..and as before they whirled away unshot at to the cover.

**2.** Of grain: Not come into ear; not sprouted.

**1854** H. Miller *Sch. & Schm.* xxv. 527 Fields..waving with the yet unshot corn. **1893** *Times* 8 June 12/4 Barley and oats had been lying in the soil for a long time unshot.

**3.** Not shot out or deposited.

**1882** *Pall Mall G.* 7 Oct. 1 France is full of the unshot, unburned rubbish of her last financial orgie.

**Unsho·t,** *v.* (Un-[2] 5.) **1805** James *Milit. Dict.* (ed. 2), *To unshot a gun*, to take the ball out of a piece of ordnance.

**Unsho·tted,** *ppl. a.* [Un-[1] 9.] Not loaded with shot.

**1802** *Naval Chron.* VII. 18 The Phœnix fired a gun..unshotted. **1856** Froude *Hist. Eng.* vii. II. 229 Mere idle sounds, like the bellow of unshotted cannon.

**Unshou·lder,** *v.* [Un-[2] 4.]

**1.** *trans.* (See quot.) *rare*—°.

**1598** Florio, *Spallare*, to vnshoulder, to put ones shoulders out of ioint.

**2.** To remove from the shoulder.

**1625** Markham *Souldiers Accid.* 11 The two Rankes next it must vnshoulder their Musquets. **1650** R. Elton *Military Art* (1659) 192 Unshoulder your Musket and poyse. **1859** R. F. Burton in *Jrnl. Geog. Soc.* XXIX. 414 At a short distance they halt, unshoulder their burdens. **1882** Elwes tr. *Fr. Benguella to Yacca* I. xii. 346 The goods all unshouldered and dispersed.

**Unshou·ldered,** *a.* (Un-[1] 9.) **1790** Speechly *Culture Vine* 6 The berries of this species..compose long unshouldered bunches. **Unshou·t,** *v.* (Un-[2] 3.) **1607** Shaks. *Cor.* v. v. 4 Vnshoot the noise that banish'd Martius; Repeale him, with the welcome of his Mother. **Unsho·vel,** *v.* [Un-[2] 4 b.] *trans.* To uncover by removing a shovel-hat. **1836** T. Hook *G. Gurney* III. 228 'Sir,' said my clerical friend, unshovelling his head, 'I am extremely glad to see you'. **Unsho·velled,** *ppl. a.* (Un-[1] 8.) [**1775** Ash.] **1828** *Craven Gloss.*, *Unshooled*, not shovelled, uncleansed. **1855** Whitman *Song of Myself* xxii, Sea of the brine of life and of unshovell'd, yet always-ready graves.

**Unshow·ered,** *ppl. a.* [Un-[1] 8.] Not moistened by showers.

**1629** Milton *Hymn Nativ.* xxiv, Nor is Osiris seen.. Trampling the unshowr'd Grasse with lowings loud. **1873** Symonds *Grk. Poets* vii. 196 Bringing Oedipus to die among the unshowered meadows of those Dread Ladies.

**Unshow·n,** *ppl. a.* (Un-[1] 8 b.)

**1606** Shaks. *Ant. & Cl.* III. vi. 52 You..haue preuented The ostentation of our loue; which left vnshewne, Is often left vnlou'd. **1614** Sylvester *Bethulia's Rescue* IV. 45 Though, as unknown, to pass unshown shee ween, Her Odors made her smelt, her Jewels seen. **1648** Hexham II, *Ongetoont*, Vnshowne, or Vndemonstrated. **1832** L. Hunt *Gentle Armour* ii. 16 The stranger, with his face unshewn, Rides in. **1865** M. Arnold *Ess. Crit.* 286 Marcus Aurelius saw it [Christianity] with its future yet unshown.

**Unshow·y,** *a.* (Un-[1] 7.) **1838** Lytton *Alice* III. vi, There was another, equally hard-favoured and unshowy,.. and that virtue was Justice.

**Unshri·ne,** *v.* [Un-[2] 5.] *trans.* To remove from, cast out of, a shrine. Also *fig.*

**1599** *Life Sir T. More* in Wordsw. *Eccl. Biog.* (1853) II. 181 We have of late unshrined him [*sc.* Thomas of Canterbury]. **1609** Holland *Amm. Marcell.* 230 The image of Apollo Chomeus being displaced, unshrined, and brought to Rome. **1652** Benlowes *Theoph.* VII. xvii, Could'st thou .., from each golden cell, unshrine Those beams. **1807** J. Barlow *Columb.* IX. 612 Descartes..Unshrines old errors and propounds his own. **1827** Carlyle *Germ. Rom.* I. 5 Musäus grasped his satirical hammer; and with lusty strokes, defaced and unshrined the false divinity.

**Unshri·ned,** *ppl. a.* [Un-[1] 8.] Not enshrined; unburied.

**1297** R. Glouc. (Rolls) 10661 Sein tomas body..adde ileye an erþe vnssrined vifti ȝer. **1614** Gorges *Lucan* VI. 242 If that she..doe finde A carkasse on the ground vn-shrinde. **1846** Worcester (citing Southey).

**Unshri·nement.** (f. Unshrine *v.*) **1891** *Athenæum* 21 March 382/3 Of the disposal of St. Thomas's skeleton at the unshrinement there are two stories.

**Unshri·nkable,** *a.* (Un-[1] 7 b.)

**1885** *Army & Navy Co-op. Soc. Price List* July 1300 Flannels..Unshrinkable so-called. **1897** *Voice* (N.Y.) 1 Apr. 3/4 The Methodist vote is one of the unshrinkable assets of that party.

**Unshri·nking,** *ppl. a.* [Un-[1] 10.] Not shrinking or drawing back; unyielding, firm.

**1605** Shaks. *Macb.* v. viii. 42 The which no sooner had his Prowesse confirm'd In the vnshrinking station where he fought, But like a man he dy'de. **1706** Watts *Horæ Lyr.* II. (1743) 169 He that unshrinking and without a Groan, Bears the first Wound. **1799** Sheridan *Pizarro* IV. ii, Thy unshrinking ears may at last be feasted with the music of my cries. **1845** M. Pattison *Ess.* (1889) I. 15 A union of prudence, tact, firmness, and unshrinking principle. **1878** B. Taylor *Deukalion* I. iv. 34 The firm-set lips, And level glance of thine unshrinking eyes.

Hence **Unshri·nkingly** *adv.*

**1826** Mrs. Hemans *Forest Sanctuary* I. xlv, There was one, with whom..Thou might'st perchance, unshrinkingly have died. **1857** Susanna Winkworth tr. *Life Tauler* 135 They ..unshrinkingly declared their adherence to all that they had hitherto taught.

**Unshri·ved,** variant of next.

[**1775** Ash.] **1812** J. Wilson *Isle of Palms*, etc. 258 Had unshrieved guilt for one moment been there, His heart had turn'd to stone! **1819** Shelley *Cenci* IV. i. 89 As she shall die unshrived and unforgiven. **1820** Scott *Monast.* xxiii.

**Unshri·ven,** *ppl. a.* (Un-[1] 8 b.)

*a* **1225** *Ancr. R.* 314 Me telleð..of on oðer mon þet..deide unschriuen þerof. *a* **1300** *Cursor M.* 23122 Vn-scriuen war þai at þair end, Bot deied in dedli sin. *c* **1395** *Plowman's Tale* III. vii, Though all her paryshe dye vnshriue. *c* **1440** *Jacob's*

*Well* 181 For on dedly synne vnschreuyn, þou schalt be dampnyd. *c* 1450 *Mirk's Festial* 100 He may do..mony venyall synnys vnshryuen. 1813 Hogg *Queen's Wake* 287 Sires, in dread of sins unshriven. 1850 S. Dobell *Roman* i. 9 Thoughts, which..would have gone..down to hell, unblest, unshriven. 1858 [see Unpriested].

**Unshrou·d,** *v.*[1] [Un-[2] 5, 3.]

**1.** *trans.* To strip of a shroud; *fig.* to uncover, lay bare, expose. Also **Unshrou·ding** *vbl. sb.*

1594 Southwell *M. Magd. Funeral Teares* 27 b, Yea, would he haue bin so venturous, as to haue stayed the vnshrowding of the corse? 1633 P. Fletcher *Purple Isl.* xii. xxv, At length the piercing Sunne his team unshrouds, And with his arrows th' idle fogge doth chase. 1653 A. Wilson *Inconstant Ladie* v. iii, Vnshroud thyselfe thou night-rauen. *a* 1773 Fergusson *Poems* (1879) 177 Turn, fair Amanda! cheer your swain, Unshroud him from his veil of woe. 1791 E. Darwin *Bot. Gard.* ii. 133 Now the broad Sun his golden orb unshrouds. 1821 Scott *Kenilw.* viii, Unshrouding the dark lantern, which had hitherto only emitted an indistinct glimmer. 1824 Campbell *Dream* 26 Methought I beheld two hands a space Slow unshroud a spectre's face.

**2.** To open out.

1846 *New Monthly Mag.* Dec. 488 Without..unshrouding the folds of my mantle, I stalked towards the sofa.

**Unshrou·d,** *v.*[2] [Un-[2] 4.] *trans.* To strip (a vessel) of shrouds or ropes.

1584 Hudson *Judith* ii. (1608) 36 The quiet see..growes .., And lastly beates the banks, and ships vnshrouds.

**Unshrou·ded,** *ppl. a.* [Un-[1] 8.] Not wrapped in, or covered with, a shroud. Also *fig.*

1410 Healey *St. Aug. Citie of God* 384 So be thy face unshrouded And thy pure hornes unclouded! 1742 Blair *Grave* 152 There's not a Dungeon-Slave, that's bury'd In the High-way, unshrouded and uncoffin'd, But..sleeps as sound as He. 1799 Sheridan *Pizarro* iii. ii, He will..open ..his unshrouded eyes, and bless me with his last look. 1823 Praed *Troubadour* i. 516 They walked upon the earth, Unshrouded, in a ghastly mirth. 1855 Singleton *Virgil* II. 266 Had Cytherea not a token deigned From the unshrouded Sky.

**Unshru·bbed,** *a.* (Un-[1] 9.) 1610 Shaks. *Temp.* iv. i. 81 Who..with each end of thy blew bowe do'st crowne My boskie acres, and my vnshrubd downe. **Unshru·nken,** *ppl. a.* (Un-[1] 8 b.) 1862 Lytton *Str. Story* II. 39 With enough of vigour for years to come..in the unshrunken muscle of his limbs. 1897 *Allbutt's Syst. Med.* IV. 475 When the skin is cut into..it remains unshrunken. **Unshu·ffled,** *ppl. a.* (Un-[1] 8.) [1775 Ash.] 1901 *Munsey's Mag.* XXIV. 871/2 Playing with unshuffled cards.

**Unshu·nnable,** *a.* (Un-[1] 7 b.)

1604 Shaks. *Oth.* iii. iii. 275 'Tis destiny vnshunnable, like death. 1839 F. Barham tr. *Grotius' Adamus Exul* v. 47 Deadly rage, And the black hurricane of thick despair Urge on the unshunnable doom. 1890 Furness *Variorum Shaks.* VIII. Pref. p. vii, It makes no difference whether the unshunnable outcry is in French, or German, or English.

**Unshu·nned,** *ppl. a.* (Un-[1] 8.) 1603 Shaks. *Meas. for M.* iii. ii. 63 An vnshun'd consequence, it must be so. 1648 Hexham ii, *Ongemijdt*, Vnshunned, or Vn-avoided. **Unshu·nning,** *ppl. a.* (Un-[1] 10.) †Unavoidable. 1593 Q. Eliz. *Boeth.* v. pr. i. 50 Order it self that goes on with an vnshonning [L. *inevitabili*] turne. **Unshu·nted,** *ppl. a.* (Un-[1] 8.) 1873 F. Jenkin *Electr. & Magn.* xvi. § 3 The sensibility..of the unshunted galvanometer.

**Unshu·t,** *v.* [Un-[2] 3, 7. Cf. OE. *unscyttan.*]

**1.** *trans.* To open or unlock (a door, etc.); †to undo (a lock). Now *rare.*

13.. *Coer de L.* 4212 On schal dwelle the clos withinne, The gate to unschette and unpynne, And stylly to unschette the lok. *c* 1315 Shoreham i. 2228 Nou, lord, þat coudest maky open þet no man coude ounschette. 1370–80 *Visions of St. Paul* 198 in *O. E. Misc.* 228 He opened þe Mouþ of þat put, Hit stonk foule wʒon hit was vn-schut. *c* 1412 Hoccleve *De Reg. Princ.* 679 My purs I wole vnschete. 1470–85 Malory *Arthur* xi. iii. 574 Anone as he had vnshet the wyndowe. *c* 1475 *Mankind* 52 in *Macro Plays* 3 On-schett yowur lokke, & take an halpenye. 1530 Palsgr. 768/2, I unshote, I open, *je defferme*. *Ibid.*, Unshote the doore. [Cf. 285/2 Unshittyng, *deffermure.*] 1611 Cotgr., *Deffermer*, to open; to vnshut, or vndoe a thing shut. 1873 Browning *Red Cott. Nt.-cap* 274 Compare such paragon With any scarabæus of the brood That..keeps wing in wingcase;.. the couple yonder..never bade unshut from sheath the gauze.

*absol.* *c* 1430 Lydg. *Min. Poems* 52 Off Abyssi this Aungel bar the keyes, Callid *Clauis Dauid* to shettyn and vnshette.

*fig.* *c* 1412 Hoccleve *De Reg. Princ.* 1573 Thre causes ben, whiche I þe wole vnschette And open a-non, whi þou schalt with hire dele. 1513 Douglas *Æneid* xii. Prol. 121 Gymp gerraflouris thar royn levys vnschet. 1589 Fleming *Virg. Georg.* ii. 24, I enter..on things of old and ancient praise,.. being bold t'vnshut or open holie springs.

**b.** *intr.* To become open.

1390 Gower *Conf.* II. 102 Ther is no dore, which mai charke, Wherof an yhe scholde unschette. *a* 1400 *Stockholm Med. MS.* ii. 390 in *Anglia* XVIII. 317 Ley hem on neuer so strong a lok, It schal onschetyn & onstrok. 1649 G. Daniel *Trinarch., Hen. V*, cxxix, Wee..need not feare an Asse's Load Of Solar Earth, can force the Gates vnshutt.

**2.** *dial.* To unharness (a horse).

1817 in Burne *Folk-Lore* (1883) 611 His team's unshut, his whip's laid up. 1841 Hartshorne *Salop. Ant.* Gloss., *Unshut*, to unlink, or ungear horses. 1879 *Shropshire Word-bk.* 310.

**Unshu·t,** *ppl. a.* [f. prec. or Un-[1] 8 b.]

**1.** Opened, unclosed; not closed or shut.

*c* 1384 Chaucer *H. Fame* iii. 1953 And be day..Been al the dores opened wide And be nyght echon vnshet. 1426 Lydg. *De Guil. Pilgr.* 23403 The gate..Of the castel stood vnshet. 1491 Caxton *Vitas Patr.* (W. de W. 1495) ii. 259/2 An hous the whiche byfore outwarde is moche ornate..but behynde all unshytte &..ruynous. ? 1606 Rowlands *Terrible Battell* (Hunterian Cl.) 36 From eare to eare thou hast a mouth vnshut. 1691 E. Taylor *Behmen's Theos. Philos.* 331 Whereby we ascend into his Arms, the unshut Light-World. 1849 M. Arnold *Forsaken Merman* 44 Where great whales come sailing by, Sail and sail, with unshut eye. *a* 1851 Moir *Poems, Tombless Man* iii, And, in the midst,.. An unshut gateway.

**2.** Not shut *up.*

1610 Bp. Hall *Apol. agst. Brownists* lv. 134 The plague.. of sinne vnshut vp and vncouered.

**Unshu·tter,** *v.* (Un-[2] 4.)

1861 Hughes *Tom Brown at Oxf.* xvii, He unshuttered the little lattice window of the room on the ground-floor. [Also in recent use (1901–).]

**Unshu·ttered,** *ppl. a.* (Un-[1] 8.)

1845 James *Arrah Neil* II. iii. 39 From an open door, or unshuttered window, the lights..served also for the benefit of the passenger. 1883 'Ouida' *Wanda* I. 58 She seated herself here by the unshuttered casement.

**Unshy·,** *a.* (Un-[1] 7.) 1748 Richardson *Clarissa* II. 45 It would be doing Mr. Solmes a spight, to wish him such a shy, un-shy girl. 1841 Lady Lyttelton *Let.* 29 July, I was thinking how totally unshy I was! **Unshy·ly,** *adv.* (Un-[1] 11.) 1814 Lady Lyttelton *Let.* 12 Sept., Pretty [German school-] girls of all ages answering very unshyly.

**Unsib,** *sb.*: see Un-[1] 3 (s.v. *unisibbe*).

**†Unsi·b,** *a. Obs.* [Un-[1] 7. Cf. OE. *ungesib*, OHG. *unsibbi, -sippi* (MHG. *unsippe*), Goth. *unsibjis.*] Not related, not of kin. In quots. *absol.*

*c* 1200 Ormin 2474 And ȝhot [= she it] forrhall wiþþ alle menn Wiþþ sibbe & wiþþ unnsibbe. 1303 R. Brunne *Handl. Synne* 1198 To holy land, ȝyf þou haue hyt hette; Syb, ne vnsyb, may hyt lette.

**Unsi·ck,** *a.* (Un-[1] 7. Cf. older Du. *onziek*, ON. *úsjúkr*, MSw. *osiuker*, MDa. *usjug.*)

*a* 1500 *Chaucer's Dreme* 1205 And I..Up rose..Hole and vnsicke, right wele at ease. *c* 1540 Copland *Hye Way to Spyttel Ho.* 198 Bedrid folke, and suche as can not crave,.. But not every unseke stoborne knave. 1594 Daniel *Cleopatra* K 4 b, What comforts vnsicke Eloquence can sound, And yet all fayles vs in the poynt of trying.

**Unsi·cker,** *a. Obs.* exc. *Sc.* [Un-[1] 7. Cf. NFris. *unseker*, MDu. *onseker* (Du. *onzeker*), MLG. *unseker*, OHG. *unsichûre* (MHG. and G. *unsicher*), MDa. *usekker*, Da. *usikker*, Sw. *osäker.*] Uncertain; unsafe; insecure.

*a* 1225 *Ancr. R.* 144 Deað þet we beoð siker of & unsiker hwonne. *c* 1325 *Metr. Hom.* 83 Gode ensaumpil may thai lere, Unsikir of thaim self to be. *c* 1330 R. Brunne *Chron. Wace* (Rolls) 9636 Bot þer hap was al vnsyker; For synne of Octa..Dide al his felawes & hym be lorn. 1387 Trevisa *Higden* (Rolls) VIII. 327 Þe buldyng uppon..unsikergrounde bygynneþ to slyde. *c* 1412 Hoccleve *De Reg. Princ.* 41 Thus vnsikir of my smal lyfloode. 1470–85 Malory *Arthur* xvii. xxiii. 724 Galahad prayed yow to remembre of this vnsyker world. 1533 Bellenden *Livy* iv. v. (S.T.S.) II. 66 He had levir returne to rome with sikkir victorie þan vnsikkir pece of wolchis. *a* 1578 Lindesay (Pitscottie) *Chron. Scot.* (S.T.S.) I. 33 It was wnsickir to comit his lyfe and honoure in the binding wp of bandis witht the Earle of Douglas. 1796 Burns *To Colonel de Peyster* iii, Dame Life,..Oh! flickering, feeble, and unsicker I've found her still. 1819 W. Tennant *Papistry Storm'd* (1827) 5 Thou.. flaff't thy wings, and in a crack Flew frae th' unsicker stance!

Hence **Unsi·ckerness**, uncertainty. Also **Unsi·ckerly**, unsafely, insecurely.

*c* 1340 Hampole *Pr. Consc.* 9049 Alle þe sykernes þat had Ennoc and Ely..War noght bot als unsykernes. 1387 Trevisa *Higden* (Rolls) III. 287 Þou schalt have..unsikernes..of þy children ende. ? *a* 1400 *Morte Arth.* 966 Thow saynned the vnsekyrly to seke to these mountez. *c* 1440 *Jacob's Well* 221 A-forn me I se vnsykernes to wyth-stonde feendys þat temptyn me. *a* 1568 in *Bannatyne MS.* (Hunterian Cl.) 201/55 With wrechitnes wofull away thow wendis; The deid certane, the hour vnsickirnes.

**Unsi·ckled,** *ppl. a.* (Un-[1] 8.) 1820 Shelley *Let. Mar. Gisborne* 278 The surface of the unsickled corn Trembles not in the slumbering air. **Unsie·ge,** *v.* (Un-[2] 4 b.) 1592 Sylvester *Tri. Faith* iii. xi, Hee..Whom Heav'nly arms, from Assur did unsiege; The most religious, matchlesse Ezechias. 1594 *Zepheria* xxv, Let not disdayne thy soule vnsanctifie,..Vnsieging where it seekes to fortifie With deadly frownes the canons of the brow.

**Unsi·fted,** *ppl. a.* [Un-[1] 8. Cf. Du. *ongezift.*]

**1.** Not passed through a sieve; unstrained.

1589 Cogan *Haven Health* (ed. 2) iv. 25 When meale wholly vnsifted..is made into Bread. 1628 May *Virg. Georg.* i. 5 The ground one yeare at rest; forget not than.. to hearten it againe..with unsifted ashes. 1784 Cowper *Task* vi. 108 Swallowing..The total grist unsifted, husks and all. 1870 Tyndall *Fragm. Sci.* (1871) 138 Pure unsifted solar light is white.

**2.** Unexamined, unscrutinized.

1620 Quarles *Div. Poems, Feast for Wormes* ix. ix, No crime unsifted, no sinne unpresented, Can lurke unseene. 1826 Southey *Lett.* (1856) IV. 38 There must be abundant matter of unsifted information in our public collections. 1858 Gladstone *Homer* I. 219 A poet who, as to facts, was at the mercy of unsifted information. 1882 Pusey *Paroch. & Cathedr. Serm.* i. 3 The unsifted, unexamined conscience of a sinner.

**3.** Untried, inexperienced.

1602 Shaks. *Ham.* i. iii. 102 You speake like a greene Girle, Vnsifted in such perillous Circumstance.

**Unsi·ghed,** *ppl. a.* (Un-[1] 8, 8 c.)

1814 Wordsw. *Laodamia* 100 The past unsighed for, and the future sure. 1898 R. W. Seton Watson *Scotland for Ever* 38 Queen Elizabeth..sank, unsighed for, to a gilded grave.

**Unsi·ghing,** *ppl. a.* (Un-[1] 10.) *a* 1743 Ld. Hervey *Epist.* i. 65 The change I cou'd unsighing see. 1822 Byron *Juan* viii. lxvii, The solitudes Of this unsighing people of the woods. 1838 Mrs. Browning *Vanities* v, Those ye love are not unsighing.

**Unsi·ght,** *sb.* [Un-[1] 12.] Lack of sight or seeing.

*c* 1412 Hoccleve *De Reg. Princ.* 5002 The ymages..Maken folke þenke on god..Whan þe ymages þei be-holden & seen; Were oft vnsyte [*v.r.* vnsight] of hem causith restreyntes Of þoughtes gode. 1898 Hardy *Wessex Poems* 163 In vain do I urge my unsight To conceive my lost prize.

**Unsi·ght,** *v.* [Un-[2] 6 b.]

**1.** *trans.* To deprive of sight. *rare.*

1615 Chapman *Odyss.* ix. 595 Their full bags so sore, With being vnemptied; but their shepheard more, With being vnsighted. 1638 N. Whiting *Il Insonio Insonnadado* 468 His armed brow fell down; and lighting right His antlers did the marching god unsight.

**2.** In *pa. ppl.* Of a coursing dog: Deprived of a sight of the hare.

1825 *Sporting Mag.* XVI. 268/2 If one or both dogs be unsighted, owing to the hare running through bushes or a live hedge,..the course shall be deemed to end there. 1876 *Coursing Calendar* 124 Miss Alice on a strong inside led Handicraft, who threw her head up as though unsighted.

**†Unsi·ght,** *ppl. a.*[1] *Obs.* [? var. of Unsighted *ppl. a.* 1.] Only in phr. *unsight, unseen*, without inspection or examination.

? 1622 Middleton & Rowley *Old Law* iii. i, Take that at hazard, sir...Unsight, unseen, I take 3. to one. 1632 Brome *North. Lasse* ii. i, I would I had his Neece unsight and unseen I faith for her monies sake. 1710 Palmer *Proverbs* 352 A generous mind..gives unsight and unseen, and trusts the Divine Goodness for the return. 1764 Chesterf. *Lett.* (1774) II. 479 He tells you true as to Comtesse Cosel's diamonds, which certainly nobody will buy here unsight unseen, as they call it. 1790 Cowper *Private Corr.* (1824) II. 217 My very best compliments attend Mrs. Hill, whom I love, unsight unseen, as they say. 1810 *Splendid Follies* I. 167 So you don't dance with me?.. Bernard, I find, is to enjoy that felicity, unsight unseen.

**Unsi·ght,** *ppl. a.*[2] [Un-[1] 8 b.] Unsighed for. *a* 1618 Sylvester *Elegiac Epistle* 8 What Sea..Could..drown a Sidney's Name..so quickly,..So vn-bewayled, so vn-sigh't, vnsung? **Unsi·ghtable,** *a.* (Un-[1] 7 b.) *a* 1420 *Wycliffite Bible* 1 Tim. i. 17 To the kyng of worldis, vndeedly and invisyble [*MS. Magd. Coll. Cambr.* vnsiʒtable]. 1893 Leveson-Gower *Surrey Words* 44 Trees..very unsightable from anywhere.

**Unsi·ghted,** *ppl. a.* [Un-[1] 8.]

**1.** Unexamined; unperceived, unseen.

1584 *Reg. Privy Council Scot.* III. 687 To subscrive.. letters presentit be thame,..unsichtit first and fund ressounable be the officiaris of his estait. *a* 1642 Suckling '*When, Dearest*' i, Beauties that from worth arise, Are like the grace of Dieties, Still present with us, though unsighted. 1898 Meredith *Poems, Day Dau. Hades* ix, Sights that made the unsighted appear.

**2.** Not furnished with a sight.

1891 *Cent. Dict.* s.v., An unsighted gun.

**†Unsi·ghtful,** *a.*, **-fully,** *adv. Obs.*[—1] [Un-[1] 7, 11.] Invisible; invisibly. *c* 1375 *Sc. Leg. Saints* l. (*Catharine*) 369 A god..wnsichtfull and sichtfull bedene. *Ibid.* xxxvi. (*John Baptist*) 331 Þat quha hofine is..resawis þan þe haly gaste vnsichtfully. **†Unsi·ghtily,** *adv. Obs.*[—0] [Un-[1] 11.] Invisibly. *c* 1440 *Promp. Parv.* 367/1 On-syghtyly, *invisibiliter.*

**Unsi·ghtliness.** (Un-[1] 12; cf. next.)

1611 Florio, *Sparutezza*,..vnhandsomnesse, ill-fauoredness, vnsightliness. 1647 Trapp *Comm. Matt.* xiii. 54 The unsightlinesse of his person. 1648 Milton *Observ. Peace Ormond* Wks. 1851 IV. 559 The unsightlinesse of such a Ceremony. 1676 Wiseman *Surgery* i. xiv. 66 If the unsightliness and pain be in the Legs. 1845 Ford *Handbk. Spain* 122 Time has healed the wounds of our ecclesiastical ruins, but in Spain they remain in all the unsightliness of recent onslaught. 1874 Micklethwaite *Mod. Par. Churches* 35 The argument from their unsightliness is of no value.

**Unsi·ghtly,** *a.* [Un-[1] 7. Cf. MDu. *onsicht(e)lijc, -lic* (Du. † *onzichtelijk*), invisible, ugly, MLG. *unsichtlik*, MHG. *unsihtlîh, -lich* invisible.] Unpleasing to the eye; unhandsome, ugly.

In first quot. perhaps = 'unable to see'.

*a* 1425 *Cursor M.* 6706 (Trin.), Who so smiteþ out his þralles eʒe And makeþ him vnsiʒtiliʒe [*Gött.* vnsihti for to sie; *Cott.* vn-mighti for-to seie]. 1548 Udall *Erasm. Par. Luke* xviii. 139 Beeyng a slouenly felowe and vnsightly in his geare. 1594 T. B. *La Primaud. Fr. Acad.* ii. 59 The face woulde bee euill fauoured and vnsightly, if it were hairy. 1634 Milton *Comus* 629 A small unsightly root, But of divine effect. 1673 [R. Leigh] *Transp. Reh.* 82 They..betray their breeding by..an unsightly bow. 1757 W. Wilkie *Epigon.* vi. 162 Now the place Unsightly shrubs o'erspread. 1784 Cowper *Task* ii. 588 There..it compresses hard The..most unsightly bones. 1855 Prescott *Philip II*, i. iii. I. 34 The unsightly trophies of the heads and limbs of numerous victims. 1892 Stevenson *Across the Plains* vi, You can never have dwelt in a country more unsightly than that part of Caithness.

**b.** Applied to immaterial things.

1605 Shaks. *Lear* ii. iv. 159 Good Sir, no more: these are vnsightly trickes. 1644 Milton *Areop.* (Arb.) 76 Truth,.. whose first appearance to our eyes..is more unsightly and unplausible than many errors. 1787 Cowper *Poet's N. Year's Gift* 8 To wish thee fairer is no need,..or more freed From temper-flaws unsightly. 1810 Wordsw. *Ess. Epitaphs* P 6 The unsightly manner in which our monuments are crowded together.

**†Unsi·ghtly,** *adv. Obs.*[—1] [Un-[1] 11.] In an unsightly manner.

1726 Leoni *Alberti's Archit.* I. 5/1 No Building..can be placed more unsightly or inconveniently, than in a Valley.

**†Unsi·ghty,** *a. Obs.* [Un-[1] 7. Cf. MDu. *onsichtich* (obs. Du. *onzichtig*), MLG. *unsichtich*, MHG. *unsihtic, -ec* (older G. *unsichtig*) invisible.] **a.** Unsightly. **b.** Invisible.

13.. *Cursor M.* 6706 (Gött.), Qua-so smytes vte his thrales eye, And mas him vnsihti for to sie. *c* 1440 *Promp. Parv.* 367/1 On-syghty, *invisibilis.*

**Unsi·gnable,** *a.* (Un-[1] 7 b.) 1802 Canning *Let.* in *Diaries Ld. Malmesbury* (1844) IV. 96, I commit the paper to your discretion. If signable people should fall in your way, or if unsignable,..use it. **Unsi·gnalized,** *ppl. a.* (UN-[1] 8 a *c.*) [1775 ASH.] **1810** COLERIDGE *Friend* 314 A newly-invested Knight appearing with his blank unsignalized Shield. **Unsi·gnalled,** *ppl. a.* (UN-[1] 8.) **1868** GEO. ELIOT *Sp. Gipsy* 81 In haste He rushed unsignalled through the corridor. **1874** BLACKIE *Self-Cult.* 40 An unsignalled railway train. **Unsi·gnatured,** *ppl. a.* (UN-[1] 8.) **1807** BRYDGES *Censura Lit.* III. 342 Such notes..as appear unsignatured at the bottom of the page. **1877** BLACKIE *Wise Men* 338 Blind inorganic hinderment, mere man Unsignatured, uncharactered.

**Unsi·gned,** *ppl. a.* (UN-[1] 8.)
**1598** CHAPMAN *Hero & Leander* III. 148 She..Tolde him how poore was substance without rites, Like bils vnsignd. **1694** *Lond. Gaz.* No. 3017/4 All such Adventurers that took out any Tickets..(either signed or unsigned). **1740** *Col. Rec. Pennsylv.* IV. 417 Bills..unsign'd by either [the Governor or the Secretary]. **1753** *Scots Mag.* Jan. 47/2 Three unsigned letters were..put into the post-office. **1812** COMBE *Syntax, Picturesque* xxv, On the wing there upwards sprung A flight of Dockets, who were join'd By dire Certificates unsign'd. **1885** 'MRS. ALEXANDER' *At Bay* viii, These lines were unsigned, and might be meant for any one, as there was no address.

**Unsi·gneted,** *ppl. a.* (UN-[1] 8.) **1585** *Reg. Privy Council Scot.* IV. 15 Be vertew of the saidis letters purchest be him unsignetit. †**Unsigni·ficancy.** *Obs.* [UN-[1] 12, 5 b. Cf. next.] Insignificance. **1659** HEYLIN *Animadv.* in Fuller *App. Inj. Innoc.* (1840) 501 But we shall see..that the activity of the next Convocation will make amends for the silence and unsignificancy of this. **1685** in *15th Rep. Hist. MSS. Comm.* App. VIII. 133 The unsignificancie of the militia.

†**Unsigni·ficant,** *a. Obs.* [UN-[1] 7 and 5 b. Cf. UNSIGNIFYING.] Not significant, unmeaning; insignificant. (Freq. *c* 1635–*c* 1665.)
**1603** HOLLAND *Plutarch's Mor.* 643 Yet will they..participate with them in a kinde of voice, not altogether inarticulate and unsignificant. **1630** *R. Johnson's Kingd. & Commw.* 82 The Duke..is but a voice unsignificant; for the Senate carrieth the sword. **1673** R. ALLESTREE *Ladies Calling* I. 123 She..is like..to give but an unsignificant attendance at it.

Hence †**Unsigni·ficantly** *adv. Obs.*
**1644** MILTON *Areop.* (Arb.) 74 The Temple of Janus..might now not unsignificantly be set open. *a* **1662** HEYLIN *Laud* (1668) 5 Which words had been impertinently, and unsignificantly used.

**Unsigni·ficative,** *a.* (UN-[1] 7, 5 b.) **1664** H. MORE *Myst. Iniq.* 227 They are not unsignificative of that Wisdom that is said to be more quick and moving then any motion. **Unsi·gnified,** *ppl. a.* (UN-[1] 8.) [1775 ASH.] **1809** BUCKMINSTER in *Biogr. Mem.* (1831) 17 As to the..most important charge in the review, that of unsignified alterations.

**Unsi·gnifying,** *ppl. a.* (UN-[1] 10.)
**1665** J. SERGEANT *Sure Footing* Ep. Ded., They carry the war out of the bounds of Science..and transfer it to a kind of Spatium Imaginarium of Fancy and unsignifying sounds. *a* **1680** GLANVILL in *Disc.*, etc. (1681) 407 Such a Faith as this is that which St. James writes so earnestly against, as dead, and unsignifying (of it self alone) to the purpose of Justification. **1727** DE FOE *Syst. Magic* I. iii. (1840) 65 Muttering over them some unsignifying significations. **1884** *Encycl. Brit.* XVII. 86/1 A tune is named generally after some place, as 'York',..or by some other unsignifying word.

†**Unsile,** *v. Sc.* [UN-[2] 3 + SILE *v.*[3]] = UNSEEL *v.*
**1628** SIR W. MURE *Spirit. Hymn* 229 He doth vnsyle the eyes alone Of soules sincere. **1629** — *True Crucifixe* 32 The Serpent offring..to vnsile his sight.

**Unsi·lenceable,** *a.* (UN-[1] 7 b.)
**1678** *Lively Oracles* iii. § 70. 279 How sadly will conscience then revenge all its stifled admonitions by an unsilenceable clamor. **1875** M. ARNOLD *God & Bible* iii. 131 The great, standing, unsilenceable, unshaken witness. **1884** *Harper's Mag.* Mar. 524/2 The winds moaned with unsilenceable grief.

**Unsi·lenced,** *ppl. a.* (UN-[1] 8.)
**1615** CHAPMAN *Odyss.* Ep. Ded. xlvi, Singing their praises in unsilenced story. **1828** MISS MITFORD *Village* Ser. III. 294 One, however, of his adversaries..still remained unsilenced. **1865** MRS. WHITNEY *Gayworthys* xix, This unsilenced haunting 'If' of fruitless regret.

**Unsi·lent,** *a.* [UN-[1] 7.] ?Causing a noise, notorious. **1597** Q. ELIZ. in Nichols *Progr.* (1805) III. B 7, More at this time we will not write of this unsilent subjecte. **Unsili·cified,** *ppl. a.* (UN-[1] 8.) **1877** HUXLEY *Anat. Inv. Anim.* iii. 117 Silicious spicula, the majority of which..contain a fine central canal filled with an unsilicified substance.

**Unsilly,** variant of UNSEELY *a. Obs.*

**Unsi·lvered,** *ppl. a.* (UN-[1] 8.)
**1772** *Phil. Trans.* LXII. 100 The back-horizon-glass was silvered,..the upper part being left unsilvered. *a* **1853** PEREIRA *Polarized Light* (1854) 113 This combination of Fresnel's rhomb and an unsilvered glass. **1895** *Outing* XXVI. 397/1 The mirror..has a small unsilvered spot in the centre.

**Unsi·milar,** *a.* (UN-[1] 7.)
Rarely used without preceding negative.
**1768** TUCKER *Lt. of Nat.* (1834) I. 274 It is not unsimilar to a declaration of St. Paul's. **1804** EUGENIA DE ACTON *Tale without Title* II. 161 This speech, which..was seriously made upon an occasion not unsimilar, raised a laugh. **1863** MRS. OLIPHANT *Salem Chapel* ii, They..[were] much of an age, and not unsimilar in worldly means.

**Unsi·mple,** *a.* (UN-[1] 7. Cf. MDu. *onsimpel.*)
**1541** COPLAND *Galyen's Terap.* A ij b, For to a symple dysease a symple healynge is due, and to a composed dysease a healynge vnsymple. *a* **1750** A. HILL *Wks.* (1753) II. 274 Every thing is..unsimple, that has foreign and unnatural annexions. **1797** LAMB *Let. to Coleridge* 13 Feb., I wonder you do not perceave..something unsimple and artificial in the expression, 'voiced a sad tale'. **1862** H. AÏDÉ *Carr of Carrl.* II. 230 The very unsimple manners of the English lady (they could hardly be called affected, they were so much a part of herself).

**Unsimpli·city.** (UN-[1] 12.) **1855** KINGSLEY *Westw. Ho!* iv, In his simple unsimplicity, and cunning foolishness. **Unsi·mulated,** *ppl. a.* (UN-[1] 8.) **1840** DE QUINCEY *Style* Wks. 1858 XI. 171 Ebullitions of absolute unsimulated feeling. **1894** A. K. H. BOYD *St. Andrews* 126 To which the driver replied, with unsimulated heartiness.

**Unsi·n,** *v.* [UN-[2] 4 b, 6 b.]
**1.** *trans.* To annul (a sin) by subsequent action.
**1628** FELTHAM *Resolves* II. lxxxix. 257 When a sinne is past, griefe may lessen it, but not vnsinne it. **1670** CLARENDON *Contempl. Ps.* Tracts (1727) 593 They who..observe the other injunction of the prophet..have unsinned their former sins. **1705** J. DUNTON *Life & Errors* 405, I can't Un-Sin the Errours of my past Life. **1868** BROWNING *Ring & Bk.* IV. 285 The proper process of unsinning sin Is to begin well-doing somehow else.
**2.** To free (a person) from being a sinner.
*c* **1629** DONNE *Serm.* (1640) 645 *Expeccabis*; and if in our language, that were a word in use, it might be translated, 'Thou shalt un-sin me', that is, look upon me as a man that had never sinned.
**3.** To maintain or prove to be no sin; to divest of the character of a sin.
**1682** SOUTHERNE *Loyal Brother* v. i, Gifted Rogues, That ..zealously, upon a fit of Conscience, Sin or Unsin Rebellion to the Croud. *a* **1715** SOUTH *Serm.* IV. 123 He who defends it [*sc.* a sin], utterly denies its Guilt, and (as I may so speak) absolutely unsins it.

**Unsince·re,** *a.* [UN-[1] 7 and 5 b.]
**1.** = INSINCERE *a.* 1: **a.** Of actions, etc.
**1577** tr. *Bullinger's Decades* 566/1 The consideration of the vnsincere feare of God. **1646** HAMMOND *Death-bed Repent.* 62 Sure there is such a thing as unsincere resolution. **1683** TEMPLE *Mem.* Wks. 1720 I. 410 To act an unsincere Part either in Friendship or in Love. **1718** *Freethinker* No. 83, An affected, unsincere Humility towards God.
**b.** Of persons. Also *absol.*
**1617** HIERON *Wks.* 1620 II. 155 Judas [was] an apostle, yet what careth God for him, being vnsincere? **1664** H. MORE *Myst. Iniq.* xxii. 85, I cannot pronounce any thing in the behalf of the unsincere, but that Hell it self is their portion. **1700** CONGREVE *Way of World* I. C 1 b, What, I warrant he's unsincere, or 'tis some such Trifle. *c* **1742** SHENSTONE *Song, 'On ev'ry tree'* v, My friends..Might well demand one tender tear; For when was Damon unsincere?
†**2.** = INSINCERE *a.* 2. *Obs.*
**1664** BOYLE *Exper. touching Colours* 197 The Light of a Candle..made unsincere, and..Ting'd with a Yellow Colour. **1666** DRYDEN *Ann. Mirab.* ccix, But ah! how unsincere are all our Joys! **1725** POPE *Odyssey* IV. 1060 O why, Penelope, this causeless fear, To render sleep's soft blessings unsincere?
Hence **Unsince·reness.**
**1683** TEMPLE *Mem.* Wks. 1720 I. 435 When the Dutch should grow more impatient of the Slowness or Unsincereness of their Allies Proceedings in the General Treaty.

**Unsince·rely,** *adv.* (UN-[1] 11, 5 b.) *c* **1555** HARPSFIELD *Divorce Hen. VIII* (Camden) 65 The adversaries, that..have so unfaithfully and unsincerely demeaned themselves. **1684** *Pennsylv. Arch.* I. 91 As unsincerely all along as I have been dealt with.

†**Unsince·rity.** *Obs.* [UN-[1] 12 and 5 b.]
**1.** Impurity; admixture. Cf. INSINCERITY 1.
**1668** BOYLE *Physiol. Ess.* 108 A Spirit of Sea-Salt may without any unsincerity be so prepar'd, as to dissolve the body of crude Gold.
**2.** Lack of sincerity; = INSINCERITY 2.
**1646** HAMMOND *Tracts* 42 An argument of the unsincerity of that contrition. **1692** NORRIS *Two Treat. Div. Light* I. 67 See the Inconsistency and Unsincerity of this Writer! **1707** *Reflex. upon Ridicule* (1717) II. 189 All this opens a prospect to the Bottom of their Hearts, and manifests their Unsincerity.

**Unsi·new,** *v.* [UN-[2] 6 b and 4.]
**1.** *trans.* To weaken the sinews of; to render weak or feeble; to enervate.
**1598** FLORIO, *Sneruare*, to vnsinew, to weaken ones bodie. **1639** FULLER *Holy War* v. xv. 255 It is not so much the climate, as bad and unwholesome diet,..which unsineweth those Northern nations when they come into the South. **1645** WITHER *Vox Pacif.* 119 This imprudencie will..Your bones unsinnew, and your joynts untie. **1693** DRYDEN *Persius* VI. 89 Now Toys and Trifles from their Athens come, And Dates and Pepper have unsinnew'd Rome. **1845** *Blackw. Mag.* LVII. 781 Death unsinews the hand that held her against the world.
**b.** *fig.* To weaken, enfeeble.
**1599** DANIEL *Musoph.* Wks. (1602) B iiij b, This skill.. Vnsinewes all your powres, vnmans you quite. **1609** G. BENSON *Serm. 7 May* 57 The want of this knowledge vnsinewes the powers of a man. **1697** DRYDEN *Æneis* Ded. ¶ 84 The affected purity of the French has unsinnewed their heroic verse. **1744** AKENSIDE *Epistle to Curio* 160 What spells unsinew'd thy determin'd soul? **1866** LYTTON *Lost Tales Miletus, Secret Way* 16 The hold Of a strong phantasy, which, night and day,..unsinews life.
**2.** (See quot.)
**1753** *Chambers' Cycl.* Suppl. s.v. *Sinew*, To unsinew a horse,..is to cut the two tendons on the side of the head, about five inches under the eyes.

**Unsi·newed,** *ppl. a.* [f. prec. or UN-[1] 8.] Not furnished with sinews; not sinewy or strong; weakened in sinews, enfeebled.
**1541** R. COPLAND *Guydon's Form.* S iij, The seconde intencyon is accomplysshed by hote yron in vnsynewed places..and by corosyues, in meane places. **1615** DANIEL *Hymen's Tri.* II. i, Those vnsinewed amorous heardsmen. **1678** DRYDEN *All for Love* I. i, Can any Roman see and know him now,..Unbent, unsinew'd, made a woman's toy? **1863** W. LANCASTER *Præterita* 116 Old brand, art shamed with my unsinew'd gripe? **1872** R. W. BUCHANAN *St. Abe* II. v, As each Saint sank unsinew'd, In his arm-chair he continued: 'Goodman Jones' [etc.].
**b.** *fig.* (Cf. prec. 1 b.)
**1602** SHAKS. *Ham.* IV. vii. 10 O for two speciall Reasons, Which may to you (perhaps) seeme much vnsinnowed, And yet to me they are strong. **1643** *Lanc. Tracts Civil War* (Chetham Soc.) 169 From him I must expect an unsinewed and faithles agreement. **1683** DRYDEN (& SOAME) tr. *Boileau's Art Poetry* III. 189 Without these Ornaments before our Eyes, Th' unsinew'd Poem languishes. **1746** FRANCIS tr. *Horace, Sat.* II. i. 3 My Lines are weak, unsinew'd, others say.

**Unsi·newy,** *a.* (UN-[1] 7 and 5 b.)
**1622** J. HAYWARD *David's Tears* To Rdr. A 8 Some other form-lesse vnsinewie writings. **1641** EARL MONM. tr. *Biondi's Civil Wars* Ep. Ded., I doe not praise the soft unsinnowy goodnesse of Henry the sixth. *a* **1658** CLEVELAND *Poems, Agst. Ale* iv, May Bards that drink thee, write a small, Unsubstanc'd Line pedantical, Unsinewy, ænigmatical.

**Unsi·nful,** *a.* (UN-[1] 7.)
**1598** FLORIO, *Impeccabile*, that cannot sin,..vnsinfull. **1681** BAXTER *Answ. Dodwell* iii. 22 They may command any unsinful thing, and excommunicate him that doth not obey. **1767** COWPER *Lett.* (1863) 94 They who are his servants here, shall pay him an unsinful obedience for ever. **1893** A. WHYTE *Bunyan Char.* Ser. I. i. 6 Our Lord made His own unselfish and unsinful will to bow to silence and to praise before the holy will of His Father.
Hence **Unsi·nfulness.**
**1598** FLORIO, *Impeccabilita*, vnsinfulnes, puritie. **1681** BAXTER *Answ. Dodwell* iii. 22 One that knoweth the unsinfulness of all things in the world that are such.

**Unsi·nfully,** *adv.* (UN-[1] 11. Cf. prec.)
*c* **1400** *Apol. Loll.* 15 No creature mai do iustli,..perfitly, vnsinfully,..ani þing, not but if God wirk þat þing bi him. **1627** SANDERSON *Serm.* I. 265 He did it unwittingly, and therefore..unsinfully, as to that species of sin. **1862** T. A. TROLLOPE *Marietta* I. ii. 30 No usance could be unsinfully received.

**Unsi·ng,** *v.* (UN-[2] 3.) **1701** DE FOE *True born Eng.* II. 242 They soon their New Deliverer Despise;..Unsing their Thanks, and pull their Trophies down. **1876** H. GARDNER *Sunflowers, Rose Garden* 21 A thought once thought is never unthought, Or a melody sung unsung! **Unsi·ngable,** *a.* (UN-[1] 7 b.) **1882** *Athenæum* 4 Feb. 153/2 The lyrics throughout the volume are as unlike songs—as 'unsingable' and unlyrical—as ever.

**Unsi·nged,** *ppl. a.* [UN-[1] 8. Cf. Du. *ongezengd.*] Not singed; untouched by fire.
**1599** [see UNSEARED]. **1646** SIR T. BROWNE *Pseud. Ep.* VII. x. 358 He was cast into a Cauldron of burning oyle, and came out againe unsinged. **1697** DRYDEN *Æneis* XI. 1158 By thee protected, with our naked soles, Through flames unsinged we march. **1737** EARL ORRERY *Let. to Swift* 15 Mar., Let the thunder burst where it will, so that you are safe, and unsinged. **1755** DODDRIDGE '*Let Jacob*' iv, Then let the fires their rage display,..Unburnt, unsinged, He leads them through. **1834** T. MOORE in Walpole *Life Ld. J. Russell* (1889) I. 203 You at least come safe and unsinged out of the furnace. *a* **1850** BRYANT *Medit. Rhode Isl. Coal* 54 That men might to thy inner caves retire, And there, unsinged, abide the day of fire.

**Unsi·ngled,** *ppl. a.* (UN-[1] 8.) **1697** DRYDEN *Æneis* IV. 221 The Stags, a trembling Train In Herds unsingl'd, scour the dusty Plain. **Unsi·ngleness.** (UN-[1] 12.) *a* **1658** DURHAM *Comm. Rev.* (1660) 189 Sinfull defects, and unsinglenesse and want of zeal.

**Unsinkabi·lity.** (UN-[1] 12. Cf. next.)
**1865** *Times* 11 Mar. 8/6 He, too, puts speed first of all.., and armour-plating or 'unsinkability' nowhere. **1891** *Naut. Mag.* Mar. 236 The unsinkability of cargo-carrying vessels.

**Unsi·nkable,** *a.* (UN-[1] 7 b.)
Also, in recent use (1912), *unsinkableness.*
**1655** MRQ. WORCESTER *Cent. Inv.* Index p. ij, An unsinkable Ship. **1861** *Times* 10 July, Unsinkable Iron Ships. **1883** *Fisheries Exhib. Catal.* 62 Unsinkable Suits for Fishermen.

**Unsi·nking,** *ppl. a.* (UN-[1] 10.)
Also, in recent use (1920), *unsinkingly.*
**1705** ADDISON *Italy* 191 All the dewy Strand Lyes cover'd with a smooth, unsinking Sand. **1816** J. WILSON *City of Plague* I. iii. 38 Let me walk the waves of this wild world Through faith unsinking. **1821** BYRON *Cain* III. i. 529 Oh! thou..whose unsinking Blood darkens earth and heaven! **1823** MRS. HEMANS *Siege Valencia* ii. 429 Enough of woe.. For man to bear, unsinking.

**Unsi·nnable,** *a.* (UN-[1] 7 b.) **1570** FOXE *A. & M.* (ed. 2) 2059/2 By that power or authority he is not become vnsinneable. **1612** R. SHELDON *Serm. St. Martin's* 57 It was impeccable, vnsinneable, and not capable of any the lest spot of sinne. **Unsi·nning,** *vbl. sb.* (See UNSIN *v.* 2.) *c* **1629** DONNE *Serm.* (1640) 645 It is only this expeccation, this unsinning, this taking away of sins formerly committed, that restores me. **1681** J. SCOTT *Chr. Life* I. iv. 471 Till by an actual unsinning and Revocation of the Facts, we have totally cross'd and discharged them.

**Unsi·nning,** *ppl. a.* (UN-[1] 10.)
*c* **1375** *Sc. Leg. Saints* xvi. (*Magdalene*) 34 Mare Ioy is With angelis..Of a synful, pennance dowand, Þane nyne & nynte vnsynnand. **1642** MILTON *Apol. Smect.* 23 To expell quite the unsinning predominance of his anger. *a* **1680** CHARNOCK *Attrib. God* (1834) II. 652 Above the unsinning angels, and perfectly renewed spirits in glory. **1705** STANHOPE *Paraphr.* II. 392 That First Covenant..promised Immortality to unsinning Obedience. **1760–72** H. BROOKE *Fool of Qual.* (1809) III. 31 In compassion to Adam, and.. to his yet unsinning progeny. **1837** LYTTON *Athens* II. 567 Great Jove! a grateful spectacle—if thus May it be said unsinning. **1872** BUSHNELL *Serm. Living Subjects* 419 He chooses this most passive, most unsinning, unoffending creature.

**Unsi·phon,** *v.* [UN-[2] 5, 7.] *trans.* To deprive of the function of a siphon. Hence **Unsi·phoned** *ppl. a.*
**1878** J. A. RUSSELL *Sanitary Houses* 19 Traps may be unsiphoned by a body of water coming down the soil pipe,.. making suction behind it. **1884** E. F. WILLOUGHBY *Hygiene* v. 194 This simple..preventative of unsyphoning is..little appreciated. **1894** *Times* 20 Feb. 3/6 The unsyphoned traps ..of the waterclosets.

**Unsi·ster,** *v.* (UN-[2] 6 b.) **1875** TENNYSON *Q. Mary* I. i, There will be plenty to sunder and unsister them again. **Unsi·stered,** *ppl. a.* (UN-[1] 8.) **1738** G. LILLO *Marina* II. i, I vow'd..That all unsister'd shou'd this heir of mine

Remain till she were marry'd. **1860** O. W. Holmes *Prof. Breakf.-t.* x, A lonely and unsistered creature. **Unsi·sterliness.** (Un-1 12.) **1748** Richardson *Clarissa* I. 296 Don't let me be surprized at your seeming unsisterliness. **1879** Stevenson *Edinburgh* iv. 16 Never did four walls look down upon an uglier spectacle than these sisters rivalling in unsisterliness.

**Unsi·sterly,** *a.* (Un-1 7. Cf. Du. *onzusterlijk*, Sw. *osysterlig*.)

**1747** Richardson *Clarissa* (1811) I. 96 Your Bell's unsisterly behaviour. *c* **1815** Jane Austen *Persuas.* vi, Mary was not so repulsive and unsisterly as Elizabeth. **1860** W. S. Hayward *Beautiful Demon* 103 You wrong me, Regina. It is cruel, it is unsisterly of you.

† **Unsi·sting,** *ppl. a.* (Of doubtful meaning.) **1603** Shaks. *Meas. for M.* iv. ii. 92 That spirit's possest with hast, That wounds th' vnsisting [*Fol. 4* insisting] Posterne with these strokes. **Unsi·tten,** *ppl. a.* (Un-1 8 b. Cf. Sit *v.* 31 b.) **1611** A. Standish *Commons Compl.* 20 If they finde any [wild ducks'] egges therein that be vnsitten.

† **Unsi·tting,** *ppl. a. Obs.* [Un-1 10.] Unbecoming, unfitting. (Common *c* 1390–1550.)

Freq. in later eds. misread or misprinted as *unfitting*: cf. the note to Unfitting.

*c* **1390** Chaucer *Troylus* ii. 307 Were it þyng þat me þoughte vnsittynge To yow nold I no suche tales brynge. **1390** Gower *Conf.* III. 143 It were an unsittende thing. *c* **1412** Hoccleve *De Reg. Princ.* 2361 Þat vn-to hygh degre, Vnsittynge is to swere in any wise. **1456** T. Beckington *Corr.* (Rolls) II. 144 The unsittyng, unleful, and unlawful quarell. **1533** More *Apol.* xii. Wks. 872/1 The priestes agaynste laye people..haue vsed..to speake vnsyttyng woordes. **1567** Turberv. *Epit.*, etc. 91 Vlysses wiues renowne Unsitting is for hir whose loue endureth but a stowne. **1585** Holinshed *Descr. Scotl.* Ded., It is much vnsitting for him that professeth Diuinitie, to applie his time any otherwise.

Hence † **Unsi·ttingly** *adv. Obs.*

*c* **1412** Hoccleve *De Reg. Princ.* 2349 As he þat custumably Clappith and ianglith..Moot othir while speke vnsittyngly. *Ibid.* 3639 Fresche apparaile and herte leccherous Unsittynly ben in a Prince ioynt. **1476** *Paston Lett.* III. 153 It was nott thowght..that I dalt onkyndly or onsyttyngly, but that I was moor onresonably dalte with.

**Unsi·zeable,** *a.* [Un-1 7 b.]

† **1.** Unequal in size; not of the proper or exact size. *Obs.*

**1653** Blithe *Eng. Improver Impr.* 197 Make your Horses and Oxen as equall as you can possibly; if they be unsizeable, your highest draw up your lowest, and your lowest draw down the highest. **1678** Moxon *Mech. Exerc.* v. 78 [Do not let] the edge of your Hatchet cut too deep into the stuff, lest you..spoil your stuff by making it unsizeable. **1704** *Lond. Gaz.* No. 3888/3 The 35 Tun of unsizeable and crackt Brass Ordance. **1716** B. Church *Hist. Philip's War* (1867) ii. 26 Bullets..so unsizeable that some of them were forc'd to make slugs while they were ingag'd.

**2.** Of excessive size; too large or bulky. *Obs.*

**1698** Fryer *Acc. E. India & P.* 9 An unsizeable Sword to their Backs. *Ibid.* 162, I was made at by an unsizable Snake. **1710** *Tatler* No. 241 ᴾ 3, I am not without hopes, that by this method I shall bring some unsizable friends of mine into shape and breadth. **1736** T. Prince *Chron. Hist. New Eng.* I. 250 If I now proceed to the End of this Second Section, it will make the First Volume too unsizeable. *fig.* **1755** Pitt in *Anecd.* (1810) I. xii. 202 This unsizable project, impracticable and desperate as it is,..will..bring bankruptcy upon Great Britain. **1759** Franklin *Ess.* Wks. 1840 III. 529 And who or what are these proprietaries? In the province, unsizable subjects and unsufficient lords.

**3.** Not grown to a proper size; immature.

**1746** R. Griffiths *Ess. Conservacy Thames* 52 [They] annually destroy infinite Numbers of unsizeable Smelts. **1759** *Act* 33 *Geo. II*, c. 27 § 13 Any Spawn, Fry, or Brood of Fish, or any unsizeable Fish, or any Fish out of Season. **1833** J. Cornish in *Rep. Sel. Comm. Brit. Channel Fisheries* 148 Millions of young and unsizeable fish. **1887** *Field* 24 Dec. 953/2 The keepers are..instructed to..prosecute the possessors of unsizeable pike.

Hence **Unsi·zeableness.**

**1746** *Lond. Mag.* 324 Diversity of Weapons.., Unsizeableness of the Men, and Want of..Discipline in their Officers.

**Unsi·zed,** *ppl. a.*1 [Un-1 8 + Size *v.*1]

† **1.** = Unassized. *Obs.*—1

**1613** *Southampton Court Leet Rec.* (1907) iii. 469 Having made view of vnsissed bread in the markett [and] findinge.. howshold Loaves of no assize.

**2.** Not made of an exact size or fit; not formed or sorted into sizes.

**1700** Congreve *Way of World* iv. I 3, I must have been let out and piec'd in the sides like an unsiz'd Camlet. **1857** *Local Act* 20 & 21 *Vict.* c. 141 Sched. (C), Slates..Unsized Rag, Half Rag, Queen or sized Rag. **1877** Raymond *Statist. Mines & Mining* 426 Several tests made in concentrating unsized ore.

**Unsi·zed,** *ppl. a.*2 [Un-1 8 + Size *v.*2] Not treated with size.

**1794** Kirwan *Elem. Min.* (ed. 2) I. 461 Filtres formed of unsized paper. **1827** Faraday *Chem. Manip.* ix. 235 The thinner varieties of unsized paper, or white blotting-paper. **1888** Jacobi *Printers' Vocab.*, *Unsized paper*, paper made entirely without size, and consequently very absorbent and adapted for plate printing.

**Unske·tchable,** *a.* (Un-1 7 b.) **1851** Curtis *Nile Notes* 123 Sundry veiled spectres were sketching the unsketchable.

**Unski·lful,** *a.* [Un-1 7.]

† **1.** Unreasonable. *Obs.*

*c* **1370** *Lay Folks' Catech.* (L.) 1342 Glotony..is an vnskylful lykyng or loue in tast or tastynge of mete or drynke. **1377** Langl. *P. Pl.* B. xiii. 277 Of vnboxome speche,..of scoffyng and of vnskilful berynge. *c* **1400** *Pilgr. Sowle* (Caxton) i. xxx. (1859) 34 They shold serue theyr creatour.. with resonable werkes doyng, and vnskyful werkes forbering. *c* **1491** *Chast. Goddes Chyld.* (Caxton) 25 Her rest was full short by cause it was unskillfull and also unlefull.

† **b.** Undiscerning; unwise, foolish. *Obs. rare.*

*c* **1374** Chaucer *Troylus* i. 790, I may not endure þat þow dwelle In so vnskilful [*v.r.* onskylful] an opynyoun. *c* **1449** Pecock *Repr.* iii. xix. 413 But that this seiyng is vnskilful may be schewid thus. **1568** Grafton *Chron.* II. 30 Robert Losaunge that..by the gift of a thousand pound to the King, was made Bishop of Thetforde, repented him after, and bewayled that vnskilfull deede.

† **2. a.** Ignorant of propriety. *Obs.*—1

*c* **1475** *Rauf Coilȝear* 159 Schir, thow art vnskilfull,..Thow byrd to haue nurtour aneuch, and thow hes nane.

† **b.** Ignorant *of* something. Also with inf. or dependent clause. *Obs.*

*a* **1547** Surrey *Æneis* ii. 493 Striken with dred, vnskilfull of the place. **1573** Tusser *Husb.* (1878) 106 Ill huswife vnskilful to make hir owne chees. **1600** Holland *Livy* xxii. xxxi. 451 They fell unadvisedly into an ambush, and being unskilfull of the countrie,..they were soon enclosed among many. **1667** Milton *P. L.* xi. 32 Unskilful with what words to pray, let mee Interpret for him.

**3.** Lacking in skill; inexpert.

**1565** Golding *Cæsar* 32 The whyche pollicie, though it hadde taken place agaynst sauage and vnskylfull people, yet was not Ariouistus so folysh to loke that it should preuaile against oure army too. **1573** Tusser *Husb.* (1878) 15 The father an vnthrift, what hope to the sonne? The ruler vnskilfull, how quickly vndonne? **1617** Moryson *Itin.* ii. 49 At his first entering the gouernment, when he was yet vnskilfull in the affaires of that State. **1639** in *Verney Mem.* (1907) I. 183 Ther was never soe Rawe, soe unskilfull and soe unwilling an Army brought to fight. **1709** Berkeley *Th. Vision* § 12 Those unskilful in optics. **1765** *Museum Rust.* IV. 460 This operation is nice, and may provedangerous in unskilful hands. **1840** Thackeray *Shabby-genteel Story* vi, He was not unskilful at this kind of exercise. **1867** M. E. G. Duff in *N. Brit. Rev.* XLVII. 484 The attempts of the foreign evangelizers may often be unskilful enough. *absol.* **1565** Cooper *Thesaurus*, *Imperitum vulgus*, the ignorant, rude, or vnskilfull. *c* **1580** [see Void *v.* 11]. **1612** B. Jonson *Alch.* To Rdr., It is onely the disease of the vnskilfull to thinke rude things greater then polish'd. **1726** Leoni *Alberti's Archit.* III. 12 b, It hardly happens..that what delights the Judges, shou'd at the same time strike the Unskilful. **1762** Falconer *Shipwr.* ii. 251 The gallant boatswain..Prompt to direct the unskilful still appears. *transf.* **1687** P. Ayres *To Dryden* 15 Could my unskilful pen augment his fame.

**b.** Displaying lack of skill; clumsy.

*a* **1586** Sidney *Arcadia* i. ix, No more..then..the diligent Pilot in a daungerous tempest doth attend the unskilful words of a passinger. **1614** Latham *Falconry* ii. vii. 94 Such Hawkes haue beene euelly ordered, and continued in vncleane and vnskilfull keeping. **1651** Hobbes *Leviath.* iii. xxxii. 195 When it seemeth so, the fault is either in our unskilfull Interpretation, or erroneous Ratiocination. **1737** Glover *Leonidas* iii. 250 Assyria's sons Their brazen helms display, th' unskilful work Of rude Barbarians. **1798** Lamb *R. Gray* xiii, His wounds by unskilful treatment had been brought to a dangerous crisis. **1831** James *Phil. Augustus* I. vii, De Coucy..took the instrument, over the strings of which he threw his hand, in a bold but not unskilful manner.

**Unski·lfully,** *adv.* [Un-1 11.]

† **1.** Unreasonably; without good reason; to an unreasonable extent. *Obs.*

**1338** R. Brunne *Chron.* (1810) 152 Þe kyng..said he was redy, Þe testament to fulfille of kyng William, & þat his men fulle ille vnskilfully nam. **1387** Trevisa *Higden* (Rolls) IV. 433 ȝif it is good to lyve, it is sacrelegy to forsake it unskilfulliche. *c* **1400** Love *Bonavent. Mirr.* (1908) 147 We haue ensaumple that we schulle not lette to do gode werkes for occasioun of sclaundre vnskilfully taken of othere. *a* **1470** H. Parker *Dives & Pauper* (W. de W. 1496) iv. xxv. 192/2 We sholde loue all men..with drede to offende them unskylfully.

† **2.** Without discernment; foolishly; ignorantly.

**1340–70** *Alex. & Dind.* 871 For almus-dede do ȝe non as ȝe demen alle, But skarsete & skaþe vn-skilfully fonden. **1390** Gower *Conf.* III. 251 Tarquinus made unskilfully A werre..Ayein a toun with walles stronge. *c* **1460** G. Ashby *Dicta Philos.* 1211 He wol..euery thinge determen wilfully, Ayenste Reason, & eke vnskilfully. **1565** Cooper *Thesaurus* s v. *Inscienter*, Thei sayde he did vnskilfully. **1603** Shaks. *Meas. for M.* iii. ii. 156 Therefore you speake vnskilfully: or, if your knowledge bee more, it is much darkned in your malice.

**3.** In an unskilful manner; inexpertly.

**1565** Cooper *Thesaurus*, *Imperite*, vnexpertly, vnskilfully, vnlearnedly. **1664** H. More *Myst. Iniq.* 496 Upon which Grotius doth freely and not unskilfully comment after this manner. **1685** Boyle *Enq. Notion Nat.* vii. 266 To clear all those unskilfully framed axioms and phrases, I found to be so intricate a task [etc.]. **1735** Johnson *Lobo's Abyssinia, Voy.* v. 29 One [of the muskets] being unskillfully charged too high, flew out of the Soldier's Hand. **1768–74** Tucker *Lt. of Nat.* (1834) II. 381 That it is highly blasphemous..to imagine that God should have contrived His order of second causes so unskilfully. **1848** Miss Mitford in L'Estrange *Life* (1870) III. xii. 213 The story is very unskilfully told, with an entire want of dramatic power. **1885** *Law Times Rep.* LIII. 325/2 The defendant..negligently and unskilfully navigated..the said vessel.

**Unski·lfulness.** [Un-1 12.] The quality of being unskilful; inexpertness, † ignorance.

*c* **1410** *Lanterne Lizt* 115 God forbediþ þe vnleful takyng of oþir mennes goodis & so..refreyneþ þe vnskilfulnes of mannes dede. **1544** Betham *Precepts* i. ccii, Theyr vnskylfulnesse is the great destruction of the whole hoste, when they knowe not howe for to kepe theyr arraye. **1576** Fleming *Panopl. Epist.* ¶ iiij, In consideration of the gatherers vnskilfulnesse. **1613** Purchas *Pilgrimage* (1614) 399 They double their numbers at foure, as we doe at ten, through vnskilfulnesse in numbring. **1691** Hartcliffe *Virtues* 231 Hence we are obliged not to impose upon any Man's ignorance or unskilfulness. **1748** *Anson's Voyage* ii. x. 242 The indolence and unskilfulness of the Spanish sailors. **1776** Gibbon *Decl. & F.* vi. (1782) I. 193 The siege..was protracted to the tenth year..by the unskilfulness of the besiegers. **1828** Lytton *Pelham* III. xi, Tyrrell, who believed he should readily recruit himself by my unskilfulness in the game, fell easily into the snare. **1869** Dk. Argyle *Primeval Man* iii. 100 This..may be due to the unskilfulness of early art.

**Unski·ll.** [Un-1 12 and 4 b. Cf. ON. and Icel. *úskil*, *óskil* (Norw. dial. *uskil*, etc., MSw. *oskiäl*, etc., Sw. *oskäl*, MDa. *uskæl*, Da. *uskel*, in sense 1 or 1 b).]

† **1.** Improper or foolish conduct; folly; wrongdoing; wrong. *Obs.*

*c* **1175** *Lamb. Hom.* 65 Lauerd forȝef us ure unskile, and alswa we alle oðre wile. *c* **1275** *XI Pains Hell* 58 in *O. E. Misc.* 148 [He] þat..nolde leten his fleysses wil, Ac folewede al þat wes vnskil. *c* **1300** *Cursor M.* 201 How Iuus wit þer gret vnschill Wend his vprisyng to dill. **1303** R. Brunne *Handl. Synne* 8798 ȝyf þou dedyst euer þat vnlawe,..þou hast synned yn moche vnskyl. *c* **1420** *Sir Amadace* (Camden) lxvii, I wille do the no vnskille, Thou schalt dele hit atte thi wille, The godus that here now is. *a* **1500** *Ratis Raving* i. 1033 Bot alway serf hyme elyk,..Bot gif he do the al wnskill.

† **b.** Want of reason; unreasonableness. *Obs.*

*c* **1380** Wyclif *Sel. Wks.* II. 415 If we taken hede to þingis þat touchen þis staat, we moun fynde fulli unskil in ech of hem. *a* **1500** *Ratis Raving* i. 1269 It louis weill to leif be wyll, And callis resone oft vnskill.

† **2.** *With unskill*: **a.** Wrongly, wrongfully, improperly. (Also with *at*.) *Obs.*

*c* **1200** Ormin 427 Swa we don itt wiþþ unnskill þatt itt maȝȝ anngrenn oþre. *c* **1250** *Gen. & Ex.* 3506 Ne slo ðu noȝt wið hond ne wil, Ne rend, ne beat noȝt wið vn-skil. *c* **1330** R. Brunne *Chron. Wace* (Rolls) 12643 ȝif y ha lore hit at vnskyle, Y schal hit wynne eft when God wyle. *c* **1330** *King of Tars* 712 So long i wis hit is agon, I have ilived in prison of ston, With wrong and muchel unskille.

† **b.** Unreasonably, excessively. (Also with *till*, *to*.) *Obs.*

*c* **1220** *Bestiary* 433 He bit us don ure bukes wille, eten and drinken wið unskil. *a* **1300** *Cursor M.* 26991 Hop es god at hald wit houe, Bot til [*Fairf.* to] vnskil noght worth a gloue. **13..** *Guy Warw.* 514 After þe hete me comeþ a chele, Þat me greueþ wiþ vn-skele.

**3.** Lack of skill; inexpertness; † ignorance (*of* something). Now *arch.*

**1565** Martial in Harding *Answ. to M. Ivelle's Challenge* A 3 b, Where the faultes of the printers be infinite for the vnskill of the language. **1576** Lambarde *Peramb. Kent* 293 I..doe preferre plaine vnskill and ignorance, before vaine lying and presumptuous arrogance. **1598** Sylvester *Du Bartas* ii. i. i. *Eden* 276 That even light Pirrhon's wavering fantasies Reave him the skill his un-skill to agnize. **1611** Florio, *Inarte*, vnartnesse, ignorance, vnskill. **1905** J. Brierley *Eternal Relig.* 100 Hence more and more the idea will prevail that ignorance, unskill in things,..is in itself a kind of lower morality.

**Unski·lled,** *ppl. a.* [Un-1 8.]

**1.** Not skilled or expert *in* something; ignorant *of*; untrained or unable *to.*

**1581** T. Howell *Deuises* H iv, Thus harte to faine vnskilde, in being whole is broke. **1612** Drayton *Poly-olb.* iv. 174 In fing'ring some unskill'd, but only us'd to sing Unto the other's harp. **1693** Dryden *Persius* iii. 63 Down goes the Wretch at once, unskill'd to swim. **1717** Pope *Iliad* ix. 568 Thy youth as then in sage debates unskill'd. **1725** — *Odyss.* iv. 1021 Thus he [spoke], unskill'd of what the Fates provide! **1791** Cowper *Iliad* v. 77 Unskill'd to spell aright The oracles predictive of the woe. **1823** Mrs. Hemans *Vespers of Palermo* iii. v, If in this unskill'd, you stand alone Amidst our court of pleasure. **1863** H. Cox *Instit.* i. viii. 123 The members of the committee are usually unskilled in the rules of evidence.

**b.** Without const.

**1693** Prior *To C'tess of Exeter* 3 Unskill'd and young, yet something still I writ, Of Ca'ndish Beauty join'd to Cecil's Wit. *a* **1749** A. Hill *Epilogue* 20 The world's wide stage..Sees some act nobly, others play unskill'd. **1818** Shelley *Rosal. & Helen* 1066 An unskilled hand..had the marble warmed With that pathetic life. **1856** Kane *Arct. Expl.* II. 94 Butter..melted from salt beef;..the unskilled might call it tallow. **1871** Jowett *Plato* I. 154 None of us unskilled individuals can..become physicians.

**c.** *spec.* Not skilled in some handicraft; devoid of technical training.

**1851** Mayhew *London Labour* II. 323/1 With unskilled labourers it is otherwise. **1856** Froude *Hist. Eng.* I. 4 Any able-bodied unskilled labourer earns as soon as he has arrived at man's estate.

**2.** Not involving or requiring skill; displaying lack of skill.

**1833** Ht. Martineau *Tale of Tyne* i. 8 All works of tillage have been mixed up together under the name of unskilled labour. **1849** G. Ticknor *Span. Lit.* I. 109 If their unskilled verses were preserved at all. **1869** Froude *Short Stud.* (1871) 337 Take the lowest and most unskilled labour of all, that of the peasant in the field.

†**Unski·lly,** *adv.* [Un-1 11.] Unskilfully. **1648** Hexham ii, *Hoetelen*, to doe a thing unskilly,..to Bungle. **1658** tr. *Ussher's Ann.* 142 Which Artemon the Engineer, Ephorus the Historian doth unskilly confound with Artemon Periphresus.

† **Unski·lwise,** *a. Obs.* [Un-1 7.]

**1.** Irrational; not endowed with reason.

*c* **1340** Hampole *Pr. Consc.* 166 Þat man þat..lyves als an unscylwys best, Þat nother has skil, witt, ne mynde. ? *a* **1375** *Relig. Pieces fr. Thornton MS.* 63 For þou..gafe hym lordechipe and powere Abowen all oþer vnskillwise creatures sere.

**2.** Unreasonable, excessive.

*a* **1340** Hampole *Psalter* lxxxv. 10, I..ioy in þe wihouten vnscilwis sikirnes. *a* **1350** *St. Barthol.* 367 in Horstm. *Altengl. Leg.* (1881) 123 Þai gaf him many unskilwis scorn. **1357** *Lay Folks Catech.* (T.) 493 Glotony..is ane unskilwise likyng, or loue, In taste, or in takyng of mete and of drynk.

So † **Unski·lwisely** *adv. Obs.*

*a* **1300** *Cursor M.* 19149 Es it..resun þat we Calanged for ur gode dede be? Vn-skilwisli þan can yee blam. *a* **1340** HAMPOLE *Psalter* xxxv. 7 Men, þat lifis rightwisly, and..ill men, þat lifis vnscilwisly.

**Unski·mmed,** *ppl. a.* (UN-1 8.)

**1634** T. JOHNSON *Parey's Chirurg. Wks.* xxiv. vi. 891 A certaine thinne skinne..like unto that..over vnscimmed milke. **1687** MONTAGUE & PRIOR *Hind & P. Transv.* 12 He..could not on a sudden Knead up with unskim'd Milk this Reas'ning Pudding. *a* **1722** LISLE *Husb.* (1757) 275 They wean them with unskimmed cow's-milk. **1858** FLINT *Milch Cows* 309 Sweet milk cheese is made of the unskimmed milk. **1894** *Westm. Gaz.* 20 April 8/1 The milk..is very often skimmed, and the skimmed milk mixed with unskimmed.

**Unski·n,** *v.* [UN-2 4.] *trans.* To divest of skin; to flay. Also *fig.*

**1598** FLORIO, *Discotennare*, to flea, to vnskin. *a* **1652** BROME *New Acad.* IV. ii, I'le..not only unmask, but unskin her face too. **1655** MOUFET & BENNET *Health's Improv.* xxx. 278 Flaying and unskinning themselves as it were of reasons robe.

**Unski·nned,** *ppl. a.*1 [UN-2 8, or f. prec.] Stripped of the skin.

**1607** MARKHAM *Cavel.* VII. 63 Then casting that powder vpon any vnskinde part, it will presently bring on the skinne againe. **1790** J. WILLIAMS *Shrove Tues.* 24 Deal out contumely with dread.., Nor make that ulcerous that's scarce unskinn'd.

**Unski·nned,** *ppl. a.*2 [UN-1 8.] Not having the skin taken off.

[**1775** ASH.] **1882** J. F. S. GORDON *Prov. Moray* I. 36 Unskinned peas boiled into a soup were also a favourite dish. **1899** *Daily News* 7 June 8/3 They threw the unskinned animal on the embers.

**Unski·rmished,** *ppl. a.* (UN-2 8 c.) **1627** DRAYTON *Agincourt* 24 And more then this, his Iourneyes to foreslowe He scarce one day vnskirmish'd with doth goe. **Unski·rted,** *ppl. a.* (UN-1 8.) [**1775** ASH.] **1886** *Col. & Ind. Exhib., Catal. Exhibits N.S. Wales* (ed. 2) 93 Wool,..Six unskirted fleeces off prize ewes.

**Unsla·ck,** *a.* (UN-1 7. Cf. OE. *unsleac, unslæc.*) **1622** WITHER *Philarete* O 7 b, Thy ioynts are yet nimble, thy sinnewes vnslacke.

**Unsla·cked,** *ppl. a.* [UN-1 8.]

**1.** Unslackened, unrelaxed.

**1593** NASHE *Christ's T.* 24 b, God is mooued and mollified ..with often, and vnslacked intercessions. **1848** AIRD *Herod. & Azala* I. i, Still their [*sc.* lions'] fronts were racked With lust of blood, their forms were still unslacked.

**2.** Of lime: (see SLACKED *ppl. a.* 2).

**1656** EARL MONM. tr. *Boccalini's Advts. fr. Parnass.* I. xxi. (1674) 22 Tyrannies are laid with..the unslackt Lime of..injustice. **1703** MOXON *Mech. Exerc.* 286 Unslackt or Quick Lime. **1760** BROWN *Compl. Farmer* II. 17 Unslacked lime beat to powder. **1808** *Phil. Trans.* XCVIII. 346 They ..were in the highly caustic or unslacked state. *c* **1860** H. STUART *Seaman's Catech.* 63 Neither should unslacked lime..be allowed below.

**3.** Of thirst, etc.: Not slacked.

**1798** COLERIDGE *Anc. Mar.* III. iv, With throat unslack'd (**1805** unslaked), with black lips bak'd Ne could we laugh, ne wail.

**Unsla·ckened,** *ppl. a.* (UN-1 8.)

**1770** GLOVER *Leonidas* (ed. 5) VI. 418 They well may keep the field, Who with unslaken'd [**1772** unslacken'd] nerves endur'd that day. **1844** MRS. BROWNING *Sonn., Patience* 7 Ocean girds Unslackened the dry land. **1870** *Daily News* 23 Apr., He drove down a narrow road..followed by the waggon and horses with unslackened speed. **1890** 'R. BOLDREWOOD' *Miner's Right* xlii, Still the quartz-crushing machine..went thundering on..unchecked, unslackened.

**Unsla·ckening,** *ppl. a.* (UN-1 10.)

**1768–74** TUCKER *Lt. Nat.* (1834) I. 628 To turn his steps into the way that..unslackening prudence would have led. **1793** W. ROBERTS *Looker-on* No. 85 (1794) III. 371 After an unslackening course of..fasting, mortification, and watchfulness. **1836** KEBLE in *Lyra Apost.* (1849) 18 Faster each hour, on Time's unslackening gale, The dreaming world drives on. **1848** MILL *Pol. Econ.* I. xi. § 1 There is no obstacle to an increase of production..of unslackening rapidity.

**Unslai·n,** *ppl. a.* [UN-1 8 b. Cf. ON. and Icel. *úsleginn* in sense 2, MSw. *oslaghin* in sense 1, Sw. *oslagen* in sense 3.]

**1.** Not put to death; not killed.

*c* **1250** *Gen. & Ex.* 1332 Ðo wurð abraham friȝti faȝen, for ysaac bi-leaf un-slaȝen. **13..** *Gaw. & Gr. Knt.* 1858 Myȝ[t] he haf slypped to be vn-slayn, þe sleȝt were noble. *c* **1400** *Laud Troy Bk.* 18250 Prest, ne clerk,..Leffte the Gregais non vn-sclayn. **1470–85** MALORY *Arthur* x. lix. 515, I shalle be with yow by that day yf I be vnslayne or vnmaymed. *a* **1533** LD. BERNERS *Gold. Bk. M. Aurel.* ii. (1535) 101 b, They leaue no cattayle vnslayne, no gardeyne vnrobbed. **1555** PHAER *Æneid* III. (1558) F iiij, Saue of Troy this last remayne, The leauinges of Achilles wyld and Grekes abiectes onslayne. **1633** T. STAFFORD *Pac. Hib.* I. ix. (1821) 117 The rest which were unslaine, returned into the Castle. *a* **1661** HOLYDAY *Juvenal* (1673) 187 To Ceres's son-in-law few kings descend Unslain. **1715** TICKELL *Iliad* I. 112 Nor does the god complain Of vows withheld or hecatombs unslain. *fig.* *c* **1412** HOCCLEVE *De Reg. Princ.* 1972 O deth!..his hy vertu astertith Vnslayn fro þe. **1674** R. GODFREY *Inj. & Ab. Physic* 8 Spurious Mercurial [remedies], and ill-made Antimonial ones, that..have the Mercury unslain. **1779** COWPER *Olney Hymns* lvii, One sin, unslain, within my breast, Would make that heav'n as dark as hell.

†**2.** Uncut, unmown. *Obs.*

*c* **1440** *Pallad. on Husb.* I. 239 Lupyne and ficchis slayn.. are as dongyng, londis boote. And let hem drie vnslayn, and vp they drinke The londis iuce.

†**Unslake,** obs. var. UNSLAKED *ppl. a.*

**1660** SHARROCK *Vegetables* 19 Unto the ashes of every hill [*sc.* heap] you must put a peck of unslake Lime.

**Unsla·k(e)able,** *a.* (UN-1 7 b.) **1820** C. R. MATURIN *Melmoth* xxviii. IV. 262 An unslakeable appetite for the restored splendours of her former state. **1872** C. KING *Mountain. Sierra Nev.* i. 21 In a few miles, the unslakable desert has drunk it dry.

**Unsla·ked,** *ppl. a.* [UN-1 8.]

**1.** Of lime: Unslacked.

**1598** FLORIO, *Calce vergine*, vnslaked lyme. **1651** FRENCH *Distill.* I. 4 Take unslaked Lime, and Linseed Oil, mix them well together. **1669** STURMY *Mariner's Mag.* v. xii. 67 Plaster ..four parts, of Unslak'd Lime one part. **1816** SCOTT *Old Mort.* xxi, Would ye build a wall with unslaked mortar? **1837** J. T. SMITH *Vicat's Mortars* 79 Those hydraulic mixtures, which are used unslaked, and ground previous to mixture. **1889** *Science-Gossip* XXV. 151/1 The leaves are.. chewed with a little unslaked lime.

**2.** Unrelaxed.

*c* **1625** FLETCHER *Chances* II. ii, A likely man, a man Made up like Hercules, unslak'd with service.

**3.** Of thirst, etc. (See SLAKE *v.*1 10.)

**1692** DRYDEN *Don Sebastian* III. i, Her desires new rouz'd, And yet unslak'd, will kindle in her fancy. **1805** [see UNSLACKED 3]. **1818** BYRON *Ch. Har.* IV. cxxvi, We gasp away ..; unfound the boon, unslaked the thirst. **1874** FARRAR *Christ* 36 Stung by remorse, yet still unslaked with murder.

**Unsla·ndered,** *ppl. a.* (UN-1 8.) **1621** SANDERSON *Serm.* I. 24 If seldom truth scape unslandered, marvel not: the reasons are evident. **1648** HEXHAM II, *Ongelastert*, Vnslaundered, or Vncalumniated.

**Unsla·te,** *v.* (UN-2 4.) Also *fig.*

**1598** FLORIO, *Scoppare*, to vntile, to vnslate. **1637** SALTONSTALL *Eusebius' Constantine* 70 Some of the Chappels by his command were unslated. **1648** HERRICK *Hesper.*, *To the Detracter*, A fellon take it, or some Whit-flaw come For to unslate, or to untile that thumb! **1795** COLERIDGE *Lines at Shurton Bars* 39 Where stands one solitary pile Unslated by the blast. **1872** BRIERLEY *Cotters of Mossburn* xxiii, He's gone clean off his head. Unslated.

**Unslau·ghtered,** *ppl. a.* (UN-1 8.)

**1719** YOUNG *Par. Job* 230 Hov'ring o'er Th' unslaughter'd host, [the eagle] enjoys the promis'd gore. *a* **1800** COWPER *Odyss.* (ed. 2) XI. 463 The woful end Of other Grecians,.. Who 'scap'd, indeed, unslaughter'd from the field of Ilium. **1827** SOUTHEY *Hist. Penins. War* II. 553 The few mules and horses which remained unslaughtered. **1870** *Eng. Gilds* 354 *margin*, Having..goats, sheep, or swine, and selling them unslaughtered.

**Unsla·ve,** *v.* (UN-2 4 b. Cf. Du. *ontslaven.*)

*a* **1618** SYLVESTER *Maiden's Blush* 1641 I'll give you all the golden good I have,..your Brother to un-slave. **1633** P. FLETCHER *Poet. Misc., A vow* 25 Thou freest Servant, from this yoke unslave me. **1719** D'URFEY *Pills* VI. 210 Suppose a Man does all he can, To unslave himself from a scolding Wife. **1729** SWIFT *Let.* 31 Oct., L— C—, who doth his duty of a good governor in unslaving this kingdom as much as he can.

†**Unslaw(e,** obs. varr. UNSLAIN *ppl. a.*

*a* **1400** in *Eng. Gilds* (1870) 354 þulke, þat..byggeth get, shep, swyn, & a-ȝen selleþ vn-shlawe [*sic*]. *c* **1430** *Syr Gener.* (Roxb.) 8159 Thei that gate in, and wer vnslaw, The gates thei shet.

†**Unslea·kable,** *a.* *Obs.*−1 [UN-1 7 b.] Unquenchable. *c* **1400** *Apol. Loll.* 75, I schal brenne þe chaffe wiþ fire vnslekable.

†**Unslea·ked,** *ppl. a.* *Obs.* [UN-1 8.] = next.

**1525** *Grete Herbal* cxix. (1529) H j, Lyme, whan it is vnsleked. **1594** PLAT *Jewell-ho.* 55 Fill a sheepes gut with smal vnsleakt limestones. **1615** G. SANDYS *Trav.* 69 A composition of Rusma..and vnsleakt lime.

**Unsle·cked,** *ppl. a.* [UN-1 8. Cf. MSw. *osläkt*, Sw. *osläckt.*] = UNSLACKED *ppl. a.* 2.

Frequent *c* 1570–*c* 1600.

*c* **1386** CHAUCER *Can. Yeom. Prol. & T.* 806 Vnslekked lym, Chalk, and gleyre of an ey. **1563** T. GALE *Antidot.* II. 53 Take vnslecked Lime, and quench it in water. **1607** TOPSELL *Four-f. Beasts* 365 Take..so much vnslect lime as will make that hony thicke like paast.

**Unslee·k,** *a.* (UN-1 7.) **1859** TENNYSON *Elaine* 811 Then she that saw him lying unsleek, unshorn,..Utter'd a little tender dolorous cry. **Unslee·p,** *v.* (UN-2 3.) **1555** *Inst. Gentleman* *iii b, Slepe once passed cannot be vnslept againe. †**Unslee·piness.** *Obs.* [UN-1 12.] Sleeplessness. **1540** R. JONAS *Byrth Mankynde* 70 b, Agaynste vnslepynesse, that is, when the chylde..wanteth his due and naturall reste. †**Unslee·ping,** *vbl. sb.* *Obs.* [UN-1 13.] Lack of sleep. *a* **1425** tr. *Arderne's Treat. Fistula*, etc. 56 Brennyng with greuous prikkyng, and smertyng, and vnslepyng. *Ibid.* 72 If þat þe thenasmon last long, it bringeþ to..vnslepyng and feblenes of vertu.

**Unslee·ping,** *ppl. a.* (UN-1 10.)

**1667** MILTON *P. L.* v. 644 The unsleeping eyes of God. **1744** THOMSON *Autumn* 415 She sits Conceal'd, with folded Ears; unsleeping Eyes. **1777** POTTER *Æschylus, Prom. Bd.* 7 The joyless station of this rock Unsleeping, unreclining, shalt thou keep. **1805** SOUTHEY *Madoc in Wales* III. 195 The unsleeping eye Of justice. **1863** LD. LYTTON *Ring Amasis* II. 293 Dear heart! Again you have passed a whole night long unsleeping.

*fig.* *a* **1613** OVERBURY *A Wife*, etc. (1614) H 2, Policie is the vnsleeping night of reason. **1796** COLERIDGE *Destiny of Nations* 106 Whose unheard name..Unsleeping Silence guards. **1802–12** BENTHAM *Ration. Judic. Evid.* (1827) I. 428 Unerring and unsleeping steadiness. **1841** ELPHINSTONE *Hist. Ind.* II. 520 The unsleeping suspicions of Aurangzíb were stirred up.

Hence **Unslee·pingly** *adv.*

**1877** *Daily News* 16 Jan. 4/5 Our pressure must be friendly, but very firm and unsleepingly watchful.

**Unslee·ve,** *v.* (UN-2 4 b, 5.) **1598** FLORIO, *Dimanicare*, to vnhandle, to vnhaft, to vnsleeue. *Ibid.*, *Smanicare*, to unsleaue. *a* **1814** *Gonzanga* IV. vii. in *New Brit. Theatre* III. 143 Unsleave thy arm, that I may kiss a mark, stamped there indelible by nature's finger.

**Unsle·pt,** *ppl. a.* [UN-1 8 b, c.]

**1.** Not having slept.

*a* **1500** *Chaucer's Dreme* 1836 An aged knight..With visage ..pale, as man longe unslept. **1500–20** DUNBAR *Poems* lxxviii. 9 The sentence lay full evill till find, Vnsleipit in my heid behind. **1876** J. GRANT *One of the '600'* i. 10 My poor mother, pale, anxious, and unslept,..stole softly into my room. **1894** FROUDE *Life & Lett. Erasmus* 230, I hurry on board unsupped and unslept.

**2.** Not slept *in*; not slept *off*.

**1821** BYRON *Sardanap.* I. ii, Is this moment A fitting one for the resumption of Thy yet unslept-off revels? **1864** MISS YONGE *Trial* I. 289 She had..found..never before, Mr. Ward's bed unslept in. **1880** MRS. PARR *Adam & Eve* xxxv. 476 The untasted food, the unslept-in bed.

†**Unsli·ckt,** var. UNSLEAKED or UNSLECKED *ppl. adjs.*

**1573** *Arte of Limning* C iv, Vnslickt lyme. Poulder of white bones. **1605** TIMME *Quersit.* III. 180 Take unslickt lime: let it lye in spring water.

**Unsli·ding,** *ppl. a.* (UN-1 10.) **1806** O. GREGORY *Treat. Mechanics* I. 101 Let E be the unsliding body, which acts in the direction EK.

**Unsli·ng,** *v.* [UN-2 3, 4 b.] *trans.* To detach from a sling; to free from being slung or suspended.

(*a*) **1630** CAPT. J. SMITH *True Trav.* xx. 40 Many of them were got to the top to unsling the maine saile. **1783** in *Naval Chron.* (1802) VIII. 364 [We] unslung our lower yards. **1815** BURNEY *Falconer's Marine Dict.* 603/2 *To unsling* is to take off the slings from boats, butts, buoys, yards, etc. **1839** F. A. GRIFFITHS *Artill. Man.* 187, [No.] 7..slings, and unslings the gun, and lashes it to the pry pole.

(*b*) **1688** HOLME *Armoury* III. xix. (Roxb.) 153/1 Vnsling your musket. **1798** *Naval Chron.* XXV. 200 An Arab.. unslung his carbine. **1818** SCOTT *Rob Roy* xxx, He..commanded his soldiers to unsling their firelocks. **1838** JAMES *Robber* iii, Lord Harold unslung his sword, and gave it to one of the servants. **1865** VISCT. MILTON & W. B. CHEADLE *N.-W. Passage by Land* vii. 101 He unslings his pack, and sets to work to construct a..wooden trap.

**Unsli·p,** *v.* [UN-2 3, 4 b.]

**1.** *trans.* To let slip, set free.

**1611** FLORIO, *Sguinzagliare*, to vncouple, to vnslip, to let goe as Spaniels. **1801** SURR *Splendid Misery* III. 215 'Tis not the sudden impulse of a fleeting passion that has unslipped from caution's trammel a rebellious tongue. **1846** WHITTIER *To Southern Statesman* 6 When thy eager hand With game afoot, unslipped the hungry pack To hunt down Freedom in her chosen land.

**2.** To slip back.

**1892** ZANGWILL *Bow Mystery* 125 [He] went downstairs, [and] unslipped the bolt of the big lock.

**Unsli·pping,** *ppl. a.* (UN-1 10.)

**1606** SHAKS. *Ant. & Cl.* II. ii. 129 To hold you in perpetuall amitie, To make you Brothers, and to knit your hearts With an vn-slipping knot. **1822** AINSLIE *Land of Burns* 71 The unslipping bauns o' matrimony.

†**Unsli·ssed,** *ppl. a.* *Obs.* [UN-1 8, after obs. Du. *ongeslist.*] Unslacked. **1597** A. M. tr. *Guillemeau's Fr. Chirurg.* 26 b/2 Like vnslissed lime. **1599** [see SLISS *v.*]. **Unsli·t,** *ppl. a.* (UN-1 8 b.) **1679** MOXON *Mech. Exerc.* ix. 164 Bauk, a peece of Fir unslit, from four to ten Inches square. **Unslo·ckenable,** *a.* *Sc.* [UN-1 7 b.] Unquenchable. *c* **1520** M. NISBET *Luke* iii. 17 The caffis he sal birne with fire vnsloknabile. **1856** H. S. RIDDELL *Matt.* iii. 12 He will burn up the caff wi' unslockenable fire.

**Unslo·ckened,** *ppl. a.* *north.* and *Sc.* [UN-1 8.] Unextinguished.

**1434** MISYN *Mending Life* 126 O mery lufe, stronge, rauischand, byrnand,..vnslokynd, þat all my saull brynge to þi seruis. **1435** — *Fire of Love* 97 þis lufe to fyre vnslokynd I lykyn. **1596** DALRYMPLE tr. *Leslie's Hist. Scot.* (S.T.S.) II. 164 Not willing to leiue ane spunk vnsloknet, [he] receiuet in fauour the Erle of Angus. **1896** CROCKETT *Grey Man* xxxiii, There burned a still and unslockened fire in her eye.

**Unslo·ken,** *ppl. a.* *rare*−1. [Cf. prec.] = UNSLAKED *ppl. a.* 3. **1871** SWINBURNE *Songs bef. Sunrise, Tenebræ* 23 A slow song beaten and broken, As it were from the dust and the dead, As of spirits athirst unsloken.

**Unslo·t,** *v.* *north.* and *Sc.* [UN-2 3.] *trans.* To unfasten (a door).

**1819** W. TENNANT *Papistry Storm'd* (1827) 46 Thus said, Don Andrew..Unslot his yett, and out gaed whiddin'. **1855** [ROBINSON] *Whitby Gloss.* s.v., To *Unslot* or *Unsteck*, to unlatch, to open.

**Unslo·thful,** *a.* (UN-1 7.) **1648** HEXHAM II, *Ontraegh*, vnslothfull, vigilent. **1887** E. JOHNSON *Antiq. Mater.* 251 Your unslothful love unto the glory of God. **Unslo·thfulness.** (UN-1 12.) **1700** RAY *Persuas. Holy Life* Add., Unslothfulness in Labour, if I may make such a Word, is the means to preserve health.

†**Unslow·,** *a.* *Obs.* [OE. *unsláw* (UN-1 7).] Not slow; active, quick, swift.

In *Beowulf* 2564 the emendation *unslaw* has been suggested for the MS. reading *unglaw*.

*c* **1000** ÆLFRIC *Saints' Lives* xxv. 375 Hi sloȝon þa togædere unslawe mid wæpnum. *a* **1023** WULFSTAN *Hom.* x. (1883) 72 Se ðe wære full slaw, weorðe se unslaw to cyrican. **1382** WYCLIF *Prov.* vi. 11 If forsothe vnsloȝ thou shul be, shal come as a welle thi rip. *c* **1400** *Destr. Troy* 908 The dragon ..gird him agayne with a grym noyse: Mony slecynges vnslogh throughe hys slote yode. **1483** *Cath. Angl.* 343/2 Vn Slawe, *vbi* wyghte.

**Unslui·ce,** *v.* [UN-1 4 b, 5.]

**1.** *trans.* To let out as from a sluice; to allow to flow.

**1611** FLORIO, *Schiuso*,..vnshut, vnlockt, vnsclused. **1648** HERRICK *Hesper.*, *Sailing fr. Julia*, Forbeare (In my short absence) to unsluce a teare. *a* **1711** KEN *Hymns Evang.* Poet. Wks. 1721 I. 237 Unsluce his Blood, till now undrein'd. **1787** *Generous Attachment* I. 167 Enough to unsluice the water from any female eye. **1826** J. MONTGOMERY *Chron. Angels* Wks. 1841 IV. 309 Angels, with healing virtue in their wings,..unsluice earth's bosom-springs.

**2.** To furnish with an outlet.

**1652** BENLOWES *Theoph.* III. xcv, Here did she seal her lips, unsluice her eyes To flowing rhet'ric. **1700** DRYDEN *Ovid's Met., Mel. & Atalanta* 365 Now lofty Calidon in Ruines lies; All Ages, all Degrees unsluice their Eyes. **1721** YOUNG *Revenge* II. ad fin., I must unsluice my overburthen'd heart And let it flow.

**Unslu·mbering,** *ppl. a.* (UN-[1] 10.) 1718 G. SEWELL *Proclam. Cupid* 17 High God,..Who pierces Nature with unslumb'ring Eyes. 1787 *Generous Attachment* IV. 184 So many hours..devoted to unslumbering nights. 1841 JAMES *Brigand* xxix, There will be an unslumbering eye upon you which you cannot escape. 1862 TYNDALL *Mountaineer.* xii. 95 We wound along the meadows, by the slumbering houses, and the unslumbering river. 1887 BOWEN *Æneid* IV. 199 A hundred altars, on each an unslumbering fire.

*absol.* 1831 CARLYLE *Sart. Res.* I. viii, But Him, the Unslumbering,..we see not.

**Unslu·mbrous,** *a.* (UN-[1] 7.) 1818 KEATS *Endym.* I. 912 How dark the dreadful leisure Of weary days, made deeper exquisite, By a fore-knowledge of unslumbrous night!

† **Unsly·,** *a.* (*adv.*). *Obs.* [UN-[1] 7, 11 b. Cf. ON. *úslœg-r* not sly or cunning.]

**1.** Of persons: Unskilful, unwise, foolish, careless. *c* 1275 *Sinners Beware* 302 in *O.E. Misc.* 82 He gredeþ þanne heye, þe wrecches and þe vnsleye, þat luuede þe vnredes. *a* 1300 *Cursor M.* 21631 Mani o trouth es sua vn-slei, þai tru noght bot þat þai se wit ei. *c* 1340 HAMPOLE *Pr. Consc.* 1938 Þarfor me thynk he es unsleghe þat mas hym noght here redy to deghe. 1382 WYCLIF *Prov.* xxiii. 28 She waiteth in the weie, as a thef; and whom vnsleiȝ [1388 vnwar] she seeth, she shal slen. *c* 1425 *Cast. Persev.* 2781 In all hys werkis he is vnslye; mekyl of hys lyf he hath myspent. *c* 1450 *Mirk's Festial* 6 Vnsley old man, goo heþen! for I se apon þe mony meruayles.

**2.** Unskilfully made or done; awkward. *a* 1300 *Cursor M.* 1684 Þou lok þi werk be noght vnslei. 13.. *Northern Passion* 1356 (Camb. MS. Gg. I. 1), Als þei droth [= drew] þe tre on heie, þe werk waxed so vnsleie. *a* 1585 POLWART *Flyting w. Montgomerie* 159 To answere thee In sermon short I am content; And sayes thy similitudes vnslie Are na wayes verie pertinent.

**b.** As *adv.* Unskilfully, awkwardly. *a* 1400 *Northern Passion* 144/217 (Camb. MS. Gg. 5. 31), Þe tre..was wroght so vnslegh þat it was schortir þan þe make Be four fute.

† **Unsly·ly,** *adv. Obs.*—[1] [UN-[1] 11. Cf. prec.] Unskilfully, clumsily. ?*a* 1400 *Morte Arth.* 979 He slewe hir un-slely, and slitt hir to þe navylle.

**Unsma·rt,** *a.* (UN-[1] 7.) *c* 1480 HENRYSON *Fables, Prol.* 23 Ane Bow that is ay bent Worthis vnsmart and dullis on the string. *a* 1817 JANE AUSTEN *Watsons* (1879) 330 The convenient though very un-smart family equipage. 1861 G. F. BERKELEY *Eng. Sportsman* i. 13 To tell an American..that you guess 'he's pitching it in considerable smart', and departing from unsmart fact, is no insult whatever.

Hence **Unsma·rtness.** 1802 MISS BERRY *Jrnl.* (1865) II. 147 A general unsmartness of appearance pervaded them all.

**Unsmea·red,** *ppl. a.* (UN-[1] 8.) 1648 HEXHAM II, *Onbestrecken*, vnrubbed, or vnsmeared. 1805 FORSYTH *Beauties Scotl.* II. 179 Some farmers keep a few sheep perfectly unsmeared for domestic uses. 1825 R. WILSON *Hist. Hawick* xxvi. 267 Wool..of the white or unsmeared sorts. **Unsme·lled, unsme·lt,** *ppl. a.* (UN-[1] 8, 8 b.) [1775 ASH.] 1812 *Monthly Mag.* XXXIV. 15 Odors may exhale unsmelt. 1856 G. WILSON *Gateways Knowl.* 83 Unsmelled or odourless incense. **Unsme·lling,** *ppl. a.* (UN-[1] 10.) *c* 1440 *Pallad. on Husb.* IX. 71 The marl hath veynys [of water] thynne, vnsmellyng best [L. *nec optimi saporis*]. 1674 N. FAIRFAX *Bulk & Selv.* 47 All tastless, nothing relishing; all unsmelling, nothing scented. **Unsme·lted,** *ppl. a.* (UN-[1] 8.) 1824 MACTAGGART *Gallovid. Encycl.* (1876) 470 While earth Unsmelted will around her axle fly. 1887 *Daily News* 11 July 3/6 Black or unsmelted tin.

**Unsmethe**: see UN-[1] 3.

**Unsmi·led,** *ppl. a.* (UN-[1] 8 a, c.) 1841 LADY F. HASTINGS *Poems* 26 They pass'd me ever—all unsmiled on—by. 1860 S. DOBELL in *Macm. Mag.* Aug. 328 In that pure face where woe grown bright Seems rapture chastened to the mild And equal light of smiles unsmiled. 1867 JEAN INGELOW *Story of Doom* v. 161 Pale she was As lily yet unsmiled on by the sun.

**Unsmi·ling,** *ppl. a.* (UN-[1] 10.) 1826 MISS MITFORD *Village* Ser. II. II. 129 Her fixed, settled, unsmiling silence hung over the banquet like a cloud. 1847 C. BRONTË *J. Eyre* xxxi, An unsmiling..gaze it was. 1873 DIXON *Two Queens* XIX. v. IV. 26 Charles, with meek, unsmiling face, knelt in his chapel.

Hence **Unsmi·lingly** *adv.*, **Unsmi·lingness.** 1873 MISS BROUGHTON *Nancy* II. 65 The utter unsmilingness of his expression. 1879 HOWELLS *L. Aroostook* xxvi, 'Is it something disagreeable?' asked Stainford lightly. 'It's right,' assured Lydia, unsmilingly.

**Unsmi·rched,** *ppl. a.* (UN-[1] 8.) 1602 SHAKS. *Ham.* IV. v. 119 The chaste vnsmirched brow Of my true Mother. 1784 COWPER *Task* III. 73 Matrons.. of character unsmirch'd, And chaste themselves. 1813 *Examiner* 1 Feb. 73/2 He courts the applause of unsmirched artificers. 1884 *Fortn. Rev.* Mar. 321 [His] innocence is unsmirched by any electioneering experience.

**Unsmi·rking,** *ppl. a.* (UN-[1] 10.) 1750 CHESTERF. *Lett.* 18 Jan., An open, cheerful, but unsmirking countenance.

**Unsmi·tten,** *ppl. a.* (UN-[1] 8 b.) 13.. *E. E. Allit. P.* B. 732 Nay for fyfty..I schal for-gyue alle þe gylt..& let hem smolt al unsmyten smoþely atonez. *c* 1425 in *Anglia* VIII. 177 She myghte byholde þe compas of þe material sunne wiþ þe sighte of hir eyen vnsmyten ageyn. *c* 1430 *Wycliffite Bible* Gen. xxxii. 8 (MS. Bodl. 277), Þe ooþir cumpanye whiche is left vnsmyten schal be saued. 1435 MISYN *Fire of Love* 34 With mynde vnsmytyn to heuyns þe self itt raises & stirris to lufe. 1648 HEXHAM II, *Ongesmeten*, vnsmitten, or vnstricken. 1743 YOUNG *Nt. Th.* IV. 158 Too long I set at nought the swarm Of friendly warnings, which around me flew; And smil'd, unsmitten. 1805 WORDSW. *Prelude* VI. 50 Four years and thirty..Have I been now a sojourner on earth, By sorrow not unsmitten. 1868 MILMAN *St. Paul's* 41 The godless John alone remained unsmitten, untouched.

**Unsmo·kable,** *a.* (UN-[1] 7 b.) 1892 *Nation* (N.Y.) 15 Sept. 201/3 Cigars..to the cultivated taste unsmokable.

**Unsmo·ked,** *ppl. a.* [UN-[1] 8.]

**1.** Not exposed to smoke. 1648 HEXHAM II, *Onberoockt*, Vnsmoaked. 1828–32 WEBSTER, *Unsmoked*,..not dried in smoke. 1890 *Spectator* 31 May, Men and women who consciously exult in the fresh air, the unsmoked sky. 1894 *Daily News* 1 Mar. 5/3 Unsmoked bacon of a particular cut.

**2.** Not consumed by smoking. 1731 SWIFT *Cassinus & P.* 24 His ancient pipe in sable dy'd, And half unsmok'd, lay by his side. 1827 DE QUINCEY *Last Days of Kant* Wks. 1854 III. 121 He smoked a pipe of tobacco..so rapidly, that a pile of reliques partially a-glow remained unsmoked. 1894 H. NISBET *Bush Girl's Rom.* 20 Turning abruptly..and flinging away his unsmoked cigar.

**Unsmo·kified,** *ppl. a.* (UN-[1] 8.) *a* 1693 *Urquhart's Rabelais* III. xxxvii. 311 Having ravined his..Loaf, whereof no Morsel had been unsmoakified. **Unsmo·king,** *ppl. a.* (UN-[1] 10.) 1559 MORWYNG *Evonym.* 298 Tiles made of red earth..must be..set on fire with unsmoking coles. **Unsmo·ky,** *a.* (UN-[1] 7.) 1675 HAN. WOOLLEY *Gentlew. Comp.* 122 Then broil it..over a temperate and unsmoaky fire.

**Unsmoo·th,** *a.* [UN-[1] 7. Cf. OE. *unsmóðe* (usually *unsméðe*).] Not smooth; rough. 1597 A. M. tr. *Guillemeau's Fr. Chirurg.* 9/2 A suture is vnsmothe and rugged. 1621 FLETCHER *Thierry & Theod.* III. i, Can there be any way unsmooth, has end So fair? 1638 MAYNE *Lucian* (1664) 356 May my limbes be for ever rough, and my chinne unsmooth. 1667 MILTON *P. L.* IV. 631 Those dropping Gumms, That lie bestrowne unsightly and unsmooth, Ask riddance. 1786 BURNS *Lament* v, Alas! Life's path may be unsmooth! 1856 MRS. BROWNING *Aur. Leigh* VI. 165 A peasant's brow, Unsmooth, ignoble, save to me and God.

**b.** Of sounds, speech, etc. 1610 G. FLETCHER *Christ's Vict.* xliii, How may weake mortall ever hope to file His unsmooth tongue, and his deprostrate stile? 1642 FULLER *Holy & Prof. St.* II. viii. 79 Yet his own Poems are harsh, and unsmooth. 1812 COLERIDGE in *Lit. Rem.* (1836) I. 366 Its unsmooth mixture of the vocal and the organic..of language. 1846 MANGAN *Poems* (1903) 41 The things I sing of in verse unsmooth.

**c.** Of manners or conduct. 1648 HERRICK *Hesper., Hymn to Graces*, Give me..Sweetnesse to allay my sowre And unsmooth behaviour. 1782 V. KNOX *Ess.* clxv. II. 328 A-propose, pray do you reconcile your unsmooth address to those rules of decorum?

Hence **Unsmoo·thness.** 1597 A. M. tr. *Guillemeau's Fr. Chirurg.* 9/2 We perceave noe vnsmoothnes; than [= but] all even and smothe.

**Unsmoo·th,** *v.* [UN-[2] 6 a.] *trans.* To deprive of smoothness; to ruffle. 1621 G. SANDYS *Ovid's Met.* IX. (1626) 181 Yet Iupiters last words Vnsmooth her forehead with obseru'd distaste. 1654 W. MONTAGU *Dev. Ess.* II. viii. 155 Her forehead not unsmooth'd by any wrinkle. 1805 *Miniature* No. 33 (1806) II. 166 Wine..which causes..the reverend churchman to unsmooth his episcopal sanctity. 1849 M. ARNOLD *New Sirens* 123 Storms unsmooth'd your folded valleys.

**Unsmoo·thed,** *ppl. a.* [UN-[1] 8.] Not made smooth; left rough, uneven, etc. 1614 WITHER *Sat. to King* 30 Let it not therefore now be deemed strange, My vnsmooth'd lines their rudenesse do not change. 1648 HEXHAM II, *Ongevlackt*, vnplained, or vnsmoothed. 1841 LYTTON *Nt. & Morn.* I. i, The clothes.. were thrown carelessly about, unsmoothed, and unbrushed. 1866 G. STEPHENS *Runic Mon.* I. 225 A tolerably even slab, ..unsmoothed except by the hand of nature.

**Unsmo·te,** *ppl. a.* [UN-[1] 8 b.] Unsmitten. 1815 L. HUNT *Feast Poets* 147 Ye shall try..how well ye can bear What Dryden has witness'd, unsmote with despair. 1815 BYRON *Destr. Sennacherib* vi, The might of the Gentile, unsmote by the sword.

**Unsmo·therable,** *a.* (UN-[1] 7 b.) *c* 1624 DONNE *Serm.* Wks. 1839 V. 304 That unsmotherable, that unquenchable spirit of adoption. 1766 J. ADAMS *Diary* 13 Jan., The unsmotherable pride of his own heart. 1837 DICKENS *Pickw.* xxviii, To the unsmotherable delight of all the porters.

**Unsmo·thered,** *ppl. a.* (UN-[1] 8.) [1775 ASH.] 1840 MANGAN *Poems* (1903) 136 The startled soul, upbounding from the mire Of earthliness,..Unsmothered by the lethargy of years. 1893 SIR W. M. CONWAY *Guide E. Pennine Alps* p. viii, I made way willingly..and, as was intended, overheard the unsmothered remark.

**Unsmu·tched,** *ppl. a.* (UN-[1] 8.) [1775 ASH.] 1809 MALKIN *Gil Blas* II. iv. ⁋ 12 Purer than unsmutched snow. 1879 TOURGEE *Fool's Err.* viii. 37 [The estate] came into his hands a new toy, unsmutched by any suspicion that [etc.].

**Unsmu·tty,** *a.* (UN-[1] 7.) 1698 COLLIER *Immor. Stage* i. 54 The Expression of his Theodore was altogether unsmutty. 1764 *Museum Rust.* II. 225 If smutty seed be worse than unsmutty.

**Unsna·ffled,** *ppl. a.* (UN-[1] 8 a.) [1775 ASH.] 1846 LANDOR *Exam. Shaks.* Wks. II. 280/2 There is not one of them that doth not sweat at some secret sin committed, or some inclination toward it unsnaffled. **Unsna·ky,** *a.* (UN-[1] 7.) 1851 DE QUINCEY *Pope* Wks. 1858 IX. 26 [He] might, with advantage, have amputated this unsnaky chapter on snakes.

**Unsna·p,** *v.* [UN-[2] 3 and 7.]

**1.** *trans.* To reverse or undo the action of snapping; to release or detach by undoing a snap or catch. 1862 DICKENS *Somebody's Luggage* ii, As if nothing should ever tempt her to unsnap that snap [of the fingers]. 1901 *Munsey's Mag.* XXV. 736/2 The colt..was led in, the tie strap was unsnapped from his halter, and he was allowed [etc.]. 1904 A. L. ARTUS *Mere English* 62 At dusk of the day we unsnapped our teeth, And spewed him out.

**2.** *intr.* To give way with a snap. 1866 MEREDITH *Vittoria* vii, After he had drawn the seal ..over the lamp, the green wax bubbled and unsnapped.

**Unsna·pped,** *ppl. a.* (UN-[1] 8.) [1775 ASH.] 1864 SKEAT *Uhland's Poems* 282 Round his limbs..Clings, unsnapped, the fetters' might. 1891 C. DAWSON *Avonmore* 162 Each harp has yet an unsnapped string That waits the touch of God. **Unsna·re,** *v.* (UN-[2] 4 b.) 1550 THOMAS *Ital. Dict., Dislacciare*, to vnsnare. 1611 COTGR., *Desreté*, vnsnared,.. deliuered out of a net. [In modern dicts.]

**Unsna·rl,** *v.* [UN-[2] 3 and 7.] *trans.* To disentangle. 1555 WATREMAN *Fardle Facions* I. i. 27 Some fel into errours whereout they could neuer unsnarle themselues. 1633 P. FLETCHER *Purple Isl.* I. lvii, For ever had this Isle in that foul ditch..strai'd,..Had not the King..Unsnarl'd that chain. *a* 1699 T. BEAUMONT *Psyche* III. cxc, How Shall I unsnarle my Promise, and contrive That..the Saint may live! 1879 P. BROOKES *Influence of Jesus* iv. 160 Material fact and impalpable vision shoot through each other and cannot be unsnarled. 1893 KATE D. WIGGIN *Cathedr. Courtship* 53 It is Salemina who always unsnarls the weekly bill.

*intr.* 1876 MRS. WHITNEY *Sights & Ins.* xxiii, Things do cool down. And snarls unsnarl just by putting quietly away.

Hence **Unsna·rling** *vbl. sb.* 1640 FULLER *Joseph's Coat* 189 Ones Excellency may consist in the unsnarling of a knowne controversie.

**Unsnea·ped,** *ppl. a.* [UN-[1] 8.] Unchecked. 1647 H. MORE *Song of Soul* III. ii. 2 When centrall life its outgone energie Doth spreaden forth, unsneep'd by foe-man keen. **Unsne·ck,** *v. north.* and *Sc.* [UN-[2] 3.] *trans.* To unlatch. 1785 W. HUTTON *Bran New Wark* (E.D.S.) 199 The girl unsneck'd the raddle heck. 1806 JAMIESON *Pop. Ball.* II. 339 She drew the bar, unsneck'd the door. 1825– in northern dial. glossaries, etc. **Unsne·cked,** *ppl. a. north.* and *Sc.* [UN-[1] 8.] Unlatched; off the latch. 1796 R. GALL *Tint Quey* 67 [To] gang an' leave the door unsnecket. 1824 CARR *Craven Gloss., Unsnecked*, unlatched. **Unsne·d,** *ppl. a. Sc.* [UN-[1] 8 b.] Uncut. 1513 DOUGLAS *Æneid* IX. xi. 44 Onsned branchis wavand heyr and thayr. 1887 *Suppl. Jamieson* 180 In the West of S. some thirty years ago a common street cry was, 'Birk besoms; heather besoms; sned an' onsned!'

**Unsnu·bbable,** *a.* (UN-[1] 7 b.) Also, in recent use (1898), *unsnubbableness.* 1847 BP. W. How in *Mem.* (1898) 31 It is a most unsnubbable cat. 1898 C'TESS VON ARNIM *Eliz. & Germ. Gard.* 93 You can't snub that sort of people; they're unsnubbable.

**Unsnu·ffed,** *ppl. a.* (UN-[1] 8.) [1775 ASH] 1825 LD. COCKBURN *Mem.* ii. (1856) 124 The smoky unsnuffed candles in greasy tin candlesticks. 1837 CARLYLE *Fr. Rev.* I. v. v, This latter, as nocturnal Vice-President,..sits sleepless, with lights unsnuffed. 1879 W. COLLINS *Rogue's Life* xiii, With one long unsnuffed candle lighting us smokily.

**Unsoa·ked,** *ppl. a.* (UN-[1] 8) 1570 LEVINS *Manip.* 50 Vnsoked, *insopitus.* [1775 ASH.] **Unsoa·ped,** *ppl. a.* (UN-[1] 8.) [1775 ASH.] 1837 DICKENS *Pickw.* xxiv, The unsoaped of Ipswich brought up the rear. 1859 GEO. ELIOT *A. Bede* ii, Bessy belonged unquestionably to that unsoaped, lazy class of feminine characters.

**Unso·ber,** *a.* [UN-[1] 7. Cf. MDu. *onsober.*]

†**1.** Uncontrolled, immoderate. *Obs.* *c* 1400 *Destr. Troy* 3800 Dyamede..was..Vnsober with seruaundes,..Dredfull in dole for dissait þat he vsit. *Ibid.* 12507 The sea was vnsober, sondrit the nauy. 1535 JOYE *Apol. Tindale* (title-p.), To..defende himself ageinst so many sclaunderouse lyes fayned vpon him in Tindals vncharitable and vnsober Pystle. 1589 FLEMING *Virg. Georg.* II. 35 Ne hath he seene (hard) yron lawes nor pleadinges at the bar Vnsober, mad, and quarellous. 1648 HERRICK *Hesper., To J. Wingfield*, For ordaining, that thy words not swell To any one unsober syllable. *a* 1680 BUTLER *Char., Mel. Man*, He..takes Pleasure in nothing but his own un-sober Sadness.

**2.** Unregulated in conduct; not staid or grave. 1542 UDALL *Erasm. Apoph.* 134 A young strepleyng must remedylesse from excessive and unsober revellyng come home lesse honest. 1550 BALE *Eng. Votaries* II. 88 Her eyes, her talke, her pase, all were vnsober, wylde, and wanton. 1637 R. CLERKE *Serm.* 485, I censure it [*sc.* drinking of healths] not simply, but for some unsober Ceremonies, that become not Christians. 1682 *Gov. Pennsyl.* 10 All that.. are not convicted of Ill Fame, or unsober and dishonest Conversation. 1730 A. PETRIE *Rules Good Deportm. Ch.-Officers* 121 [Deacons] must not be Drunkards, nor Unsober, nor Covetous. 1812 W. TENNANT *Anster F.* II. xiii, Th' unsober spirit of the fiddle. 1829 LANDOR *Imag. Conv.* II. 309 She is verily an unsober jade, who in her gravest humour will lead thee into quarrels, and in her gayest will pick thy pocket.

**3.** Affected by, addicted to, drinking. 1611 FLORIO *Insobrio*, vnsober, drunken. 1846 LANDOR *Imag. Conv.* Wks. II. 193/1 We must do all we have to do, while the nation is feasting and unsober. 1852 MUNDY *Antipodes* I. 164 The loss or destruction of these fragile liabilities in the hands of rough, careless, and unsober characters.

Hence **Unso·berness.** 1548 ELYOT, *Immodestia*, malapertnesse,..vnsobrenesse. 1681 KETTLEWELL *Chr. Obed.* V. ii. 605 Several instances of unsoberness, when there is no scandal to our Brethren joined with them.

**Unso·ber,** *v.* [UN-[2] 6 a.] *trans.* To make unstaid. 1856 FABER *Creator & Creature* III. i. (1858) 334 While we grow in merits we are getting hugely into debt to the greatness.. of God's mercies, and this at times unsobers us.

**Unso·berly,** *adv.* [UN-[1] 11.] Without sobriety or restraint; immoderately. *c* 1400 *Destr. Troy* 2506 Lest it tyde after, þat ye be drepit with dole,..Your sones vnsoberly slayne in the place. *Ibid.* 12494 Sodonly the softe winde vnsoberly blew. 1547 *Homilies* I. *Contention* I. Sij b, So vnsoberly to reason and dispute, that..they fal to chiding and contencion. 1551 CRANMER *Answ. Cavillation* 8 Which counsell if you had..folowed, you wolde not haue doone so vnsobrely in manny thynges, as you haue doone.

**Unsobri·ety.** (UN-[1] 12 and 5 b.) 1669 R. FLEMING *Fulfill. Script.* (1726) 155, I think without any challenge of unsobriety such a remark very suitable.

**Unsociabi·lity.** (UN-[1] 12, 5 b. Cf. next.) **1758** WARBURTON *Div. Legat.* Pref., Wks. 1788 II. 326 A Principle which subverted the whole system of their religion, namely, the unsociability of the Christian faith. *a* **1797** BURKE *Regic. Peace* i. Wks. 1802 IV. 445 The systematick unsociability of this new-invented species of republick. **1837** LYTTON *E. Maltrav.* I. v, He..had his fits of unsociability. **1885** C. E. PASCOE *London of To-day* xiii. 125 The Richmond Club members invited guests to their dinner-table, and thus escaped the charge of unsociability.

**Unso·ciable,** *a.* [UN-[1] 7 b and 5 b.]

**1.** Not sociable or companionable; not readily or pleasantly associating with others.

**1600** HOLLAND *Livy* 292 The Tyburts..had in times past joined armes with the Frenchmen, a savage and unsociable nation. **1646** H. LAWRENCE *Comm. Angells* 188 Men were so form'd for Communion, as no doctrine can be avowed for good, which renders them unsociable. **1703** *Rules Civility* 274 [Baseness] rather makes them to be accounted base, vindictive, savage, and unsociable. **1841** DICKENS *Barn. Rudge* i, He looked unsociable enough. **1871** JOWETT *Plato* II. 319 Whether a man is righteous and gentle, or rude and unsociable. **1899** W. T. GREENE *Cage-Birds* 32 At other times..he is unsociable with his kind.

**b.** Of disposition, conduct, etc.

**1630** J. TAYLOR (Water P.) *Water-Cormorant* Wks. III. 1 His best seruice is harsh and vnsociable. **1688** SAVILE *Lady's New-Years Gift* 13 The Sullen are apt to place a great part of their Religion in Dejected and Ill-humour'd Looks, putting on an unsociable Face. **1710** *Tatler* No. 149 ⁋ 5 A severe, distant, and unsociable temper. **1802** MAR. EDGEWORTH *Moral T., Forester* vii, Surprised at his unsociable silence. **1861** PALEY *Æschylus* (ed. 2) *Agam.* 314/2 You would..reproach them for their unsociable behaviour.

**2.** Not readily or naturally going together; incompatible, incongruous.

**1611** SPEED *Hist. Gt. Brit.* 779/1 This Ecclesiasticke text is handled elsewhere, and seemeth vnsociable to our begunne Subiect **1697** COLLIER *Ess. Mor. Subj.* I. 26 If Sense and Learning are such unsociable imperious things. **1779** JOHNSON *L. P., Cowley* ad fin., A boundless verse, a headlong verse,..seem to comprise very incongruous and unsociable ideas. **1827** POLLOK *Course T.* V. 558 Combining things Unseemly, things unsociable in nature, In most absurd communion.

**b.** Incapable of, averse to, uniting.

**1676** BOYLE in *Phil. Trans.* II. 785 The Vial..contain'd two unsociable Liquors. **1678** NEWTON *Let.* Boyle's Wks. 1772 I. p. cxiv, There is a certain secret principle in nature, by which liquors are sociable to some things, and unsociable to others.

**3.** Devoid of, interfering with, social intercourse.

**1638** SIR T. HERBERT *Trav.* (ed. 2) 164 An old rotten weather-beaten Inn..placed in part of an unsociable desart. **1642** HOWELL *For. Trav.* (Arb.) 45 Many Colonies..which lye squandered up and down in disadvantagious unsociable distances. **1861** LD. LYTTON & FANE *Tannhäuser* 105 As one..Sunder'd by savage seas unsociable From kin and country.

Hence **Unso·ciableness; Unso·ciably** *adv.*

**1611** FLORIO, *Insociabilità*, *vnsociablenesse. **1644** PRYNNE *Ch. Govt.* xii. 7 An extraordinary strangnes, unsociablenesse, and coldnesse of brotherly affection. **1871** SMILES *Charac.* ix. 258 The comparative unsociableness of the Englishman. **1665** BRATHWAIT *Comm. Two Tales* 2 None should be so *unsociably retired, as to ingross his Conceits to himself. **1787** J. WHITE *Voy. N. S. Wales* (1790) 58 The pavement..is so very unsociably narrow, that two persons cannot walk with convenience together.

**Unso·cial,** *a.* [UN-[1] 7 and 5 b.] Not social; not inclined for, adapted to, or fond of society: **a.** Of persons (or animals).

**1731** A. HILL *Adv. Poets* Ep. p. vii, Even Tartary, uncultivated, and unsocial, as she is, has given the World a Tamerlane. **1758** L. TEMPLE *Sketches* (ed. 2) 67 To be perpetually wise, is forbidding, unsocial, and something that does not become human Nature. **1817** KIRBY & SP. *Entomol.* xvi. II. 12 Neither of these motives can operate in causing unsocial insects to congregate. **1889** GRETTON *Memory's Harkb.* 298 My unsocial neighbour startled me..by gravely propounding that he [*sc.* Scott] was not a Christian.

*transf.* **1781** COWPER *Charity* 126 To give the pole the produce of the sun, And knit th' unsocial climates into one.

**b.** Of habits, conditions, etc.

**1734** A. HILL *On Death of Dennis* 1 Adieu! unsocial excellence! at last Thy foes are vanquish'd. **1744** HARRIS *Three Treat.* (1765) 152 A solitary, unsocial State, can never supply tolerably the common Necessaries of Life. **1791** BOSWELL *Johnson* 25 June 1763, The mode of dining..at such houses in London, is..particularly unsocial. **1826** LAMB *Elia* II. *Pop. Fallacies* xv, What savage unsocial nights must our ancestors have spent..! **1884** *Century Mag.* XXVIII. 620 The unsocial effect of the drinking habit.

**c.** Of disposition, temper, etc.

**1739** GLOVER *London* 212 Benignant peace With hospitality begin to sooth Unsocial rapine, and the thirst of blood. **1775** SHERIDAN *Rivals* v. i, Perhaps the recollection of a deed my conscience cannot justify may haunt me in such gloomy and unsocial fits, that [etc.]. **1816** *Remarks Eng. Mann.* 3 Our unsocial turn he ascribes to 'that independence Britons prize too high'. **1837** HALLAM *Hist. Lit.* I. ii. § 15 The man himself was of too unsocial and forbidding a temper to conciliate them. **1885** *Manch. Exam.* 12 Feb. 4/7 The unsocial selfishness which excluded the toiling populations from their national health-giving scenes.

Hence **Unso·cialism.**

**1849** HANNA *Mem. Chalmers* II. 422 Behind all his assumed unsocialism there lay a true warm heart.

**Unsocia·lity.** (UN-[1] 12. Cf. prec.)

**1852** LEVER *M. Tierney* xlv, All his habits were temperate, even to the extent of unsociality. **1873** MORLEY *Rousseau* I. 278 The bitter, irritable, and suspicious form which this unsociality now first assumed.

**Unso·cially,** *adv.* (UN-[1] 11.) **1656** J. SERJEANT in *Blount's Gloss.* A 8, Nay homebred heads unsocially did strive T'estrange themselves. **†Unso·ciated,** *ppl. a.* (UN-[1] 8.) **1706** WATTS *Horæ Lyr.* II. 230 O happy pair! Envy'd by yet unsociated souls Who seek their faithful twins!

**Unso·cket,** *v.* (UN-[2] 5.)

*a* **1711** KEN *Hymns Evang.* Poet. Wks. 1721 I. 161 It racks his Joints, unsockets all his Bones. *a* **1745** SWIFT *Right of Prec.* Wks. 1841 II. 75/1 Not to oblige him [*sc.* an old parson] uncover in the cold, and unsocket his head with both hands. **1881** TENNYSON *Cup* II. ii. 159 Great Goddess, whose storm-voice Unsockets the strong oak.

**Unso·d,** *ppl. a.* [UN-[1] 8 b.] = next.

*a* **1250** *Owl & Night.* 1007 Hi eteþ fys & fleys vnsode, Suych wolues hit hadde tobroude. **1562** WHITEHORNE *Ord. Souldiours* xxxiv. 43 Addinge to the sayde mixture that is vnsod..haulfe a parte of baye salte. **1577** B. GOOGE *Heresbach's Husb.* I. 31 b, A bushell of sodden meate, made of three quarters wet and vnsodde. **1622** FLETCHER *Sea-Voy.* III. i, Why should we consume thus,..And she live there that bred all our miseries, Unrosted, or unsod? *a* **1634** CHAPMAN *Alphonsus* III. i. 142 A schinken of good raw bacon, And that's a common meat with us, unsod.

**Unso·dden,** *ppl. a.* [OE. *unsoden* (UN-[1] 8 b), = MDu. *ongesoden* (Du. *-zoden*), OHG. *unca-, unkisotan* (MHG. *ungesoten*, G. *ungesotten*), MSw. *osudhin*, MDa. *usaaden*, Da. *usoden* in sense 1.]

**1.** Unboiled, uncooked.

*c* **1000** *Sax. Leechd.* II. 38 Sceapes hohscancan unsodenne tobrec, ȝedo þæt mearh on þa eaȝan. **1511** FABYAN *Will* in *Chron.* (1815) p. v, If my said monethes mynde fall in Lent, or upon a fysshe day, than I will that the said .xxiiij. peces of fleshe be altered unto saltfyche or stokfyshe, unwatered and unsodeyn. **1571** GOLDING *Calvin on Ps.* lviii. 10 Like unsodden flesh, and such as hathe scarce yit felt the first warmth of the fyre. **1608** WILLET *Hexapla Exod.* 247 The manna..was raw and vnsodden.

**2.** Not sodden or soaked. Also *fig.*

**1818** SHELLEY *Eugan. Hills* 295 The plains that silent lie Underneath; the leaves unsodden. **1859** MEREDITH *R. Feverel* xxii, A non-dancing, stout-dining congregation, in the midst of which a gay young guardsman..would not have obtruded his unsodden spirit.

**†Unso·ft,** *a. Obs.* [UN-[1] 7. Cf. MDu. *onsoft, -saft(e, sacht(e*, etc. (Du. *onzacht*), MLG. *unsacht*, OHG. (MHG.) *unsamft* (G. *unsanft*).] Not soft; hard, severe.

*c* **1275** *Serving Christ* 25 in *O. E. Misc.* 91 Þer is þe sunfulle vnsofte to beon. *c* **1386** CHAUCER *Merch. T.* 1824 He kisseth hire ful ofte With thikke brustles of his berd vnsofte. **1390** GOWER *Conf.* I. 283 Mi wofull herte is so tobete, That all my wittes ben unsofte And I am wroth. **1430-40** LYDG. *Bochas* v. vii. (1494) r j b/2 And Affricans felt full vnsoft Whan she to theym list be contrarye. *c* **1470** HENRY *Wallace* x. 332 Quham euir he hyt, thair sawchnyng was wnsoft. **1513** DOUGLAS *Æneid* II. ii. 96 The north wynd onsoft Held thaim abak.

**†Unso·ft,** *adv. Obs.* [OE. *unsófte* (f. *un-* UN-[1] 11 b + *sófte* SOFT *adv.*), = WFris. *on-, ûnseaft, -sêft, -sacht*, MDu. *onsacht(e, -socht(e*, etc. (Du. *onzacht*), MLG. *unsachte*, OHG. *unsamfto* (MHG. *unsanfte*, G. *unsanft*).] Not softly; severely.

*a* **900** *Guthlac* 858 (Gr.), Hu he monȝe..ȝehælde..þe hine unsofte adle ȝebundne..ȝesohtun. *c* **1000** *Sax. Leechd.* II. 260 Hwær mon unsofte ȝetilað on forewearde þa adle. *?a* **1400** LYDG. *Chorle & Birde* (Roxb.) 10 And who desireth to clymbe hygh a lofte Be sodeyn turne falleth ofte unsofte. **1430-40** — *Bochas* VI. (1494) t ii b/1 Another honde griped full vnsofte Which cast another in greate aduersite. **1509** HAWES *Past. Pleas.* XXXII. (Percy Soc.) 159 In holly bushes they did hange aloft, Theyr hedes downeward for to fall unsofte. **1579** SPENSER *Sheph. Cal.* July 12 This reede is ryfe, that oftentime Great clymbers fall vnsoft.

**Unso·ftened,** *ppl. a.* (UN-[1] 8.)

**1645** HAMMOND *Death-bed Repent.* 29 When the hard heart is unsoftned, unhumbled. **1715** ATTERBURY *Serm.* (1734) III. 121 Impatient of Delay, and unsoftned by all these Applications. **1789** T. TWINING *Aristotle's Treat. Poetry* 352 The unsoftened and unflattered character of Achilles. **1802** *Noble Wanderers* II. 143 The multitude of his sins were unsoftened by a single charity. **1855** [J. R. LEIFCHILD] *Cornwall* 76 The same primitive rock..is still durable and unsoftened. **1857** N. HAWTHORNE *Eng. Note-Bks.* (1870) II. 291 Scenery..with very hard outlines, which are unsoftened..by any foliage.

**Unso·ftening,** *ppl. a.* (UN-[1] 10.) **1857** DICKENS *Dorrit* II. xxx, She.., with an unsoftening face, looked at the worked letters within. **1873** PATER *Stud. Hist. Renaiss.* 74 This last passion would be the most unsoftening..of all. **†Unsoi·lable,** *a. Obs.* [UN-[1] 7 b + SOIL *v.*[2] 4.] Unanswerable, irrefutable. *c* **1449** PECOCK *Repr.* II. v. 162 An other vnsoilable proof for this..principal conclusioun is sett bifore. **†Unsoi·lably,** *adv. Obs.* [UN-[1] 11; cf. prec.] Indisputably. *c* **1445** PECOCK *Donet* 141 As it is bifore sufficientli and vnsoilably provid. **†Unsoi·led,** *ppl. a.*[1] *Obs.*[—1] [UN-[1] 8 + SOIL *v.*[2] 3.] Unsolved, unanswered. **1533** MORE *Answ. Poysoned Bk.* Wks. 1061/2 That question Christ left vnsoyled. **†Unsoi·led,** *ppl. a.*[2] *Obs.* [UN-[1] 8 + SOIL *sb.*[3] 8 or *v.*[3]] Not covered or treated with manure. **1616** MARKHAM *Cheap Husb.* (ed. 2) 46 You shall remoue her into the best grasse you haue, which is fresh and unsoiled.

**Unsoi·led,** *ppl. a.*[3] [UN-[1] 8.] Not soiled or dirtied. Also in fig. context.

*c* **1592** MARLOWE *Jew of Malta* II. 419 *Lod.* This is thy Diamond, tell me, shall I haue it? *Bar.* Win it, and weare it, it is yet vnsoyl'd. **1649** LOVELACE *Poems* 131 Which..Lookes..Like Gold in Canvas, or with dirt Unsoyled Ermins close begirt. **1686** DRYDEN *To Mem. Mrs. Anne Killigrew* iv, Her Arethusian Stream remains unsoil'd..and undefil'd. **1784** COWPER *Task* IV. 212 Time, as he passes us, has a dove's wing, Unsoil'd and swift. **1818** SCOTT *Hrt. Midl.* iii, A white handkerchief was thrust into the muzzle of the piece, and returned unsoiled or blackened. **1867** MORRIS *Jason* II. 71 With unsoiled feet scarce touching the wet way.

*fig.* **1603** SHAKS. *Meas. for M.* II. iv. 155 My vnsoild name, th' austerenesse of my life,..Will..your accusation ouerweigh. **1699** LD. TARBUT in *Pepys' Diary*, etc. (1870) 691 That common opinion that young infants (unsoiled with many objects) do see apparitions which are not seen by those of older years. **1704** D'URFEY *Abrad. & Panthea* I. 9 Yet shall her honour be unsoil'd and clear. **1815** CHALMERS *Let.* in Hanna *Life* (1850) II. 29 An unsoiled gracefulness and brilliancy of character. **1848** JAMES *Sir T. Broughton* I. 159 Her spirit [was] unsoiled by the world.

**Unsoi·ling,** *vbl. sb.* (UN-[2] 4.) **1895** *Funk's Stand. Dict.*, *Unsoiling*, the act or process of removing soil, as for working a bed of brick-clay. **Unso·laced,** *ppl. a.* (UN-[1] 8.) [**1775** ASH.] **1796** COLERIDGE *Ode to Departing Year* v, By the Earth's unsolaced groaning, Seize thy terrors, Arm of might! **1862** [ELIZ. JOHNSTON] *Gifts & Graces* xxii. 215 Unsolaced by ministering hands of loved ones.

**Unso·ld,** *ppl. a.* [UN-[1] 8 b. Cf. MSw. *osalder*, Sw. *osåld*.] Not disposed of by sale.

**1362** LANGL. *P. Pl.* A. v. 122 Bote nedde þe grace of gyle i-gon a-mong my ware, Hit hedde ben vn-sold þis seuen ȝer. **1388** WYCLIF *Acts* v. 4 Whethir it vnseld was not thin; and whanne it was seld, it was in thi power? **1489** *Paston Lett.* III. 354 If Bayard be onsolde, I pray yow late hym be made fatte. *a* **1513** FABYAN *Chron.* (1811) 594 All suche marchaundyse, beyng than vnsolde, to be forfayted vnto the kyng. **1583** MELBANCKE *Philotimus* R iv b, Pertinax..did rather leaue his wood vnsould, then abate one blancke of his price. **1620** in Foster *Eng. Factories Ind.* I. (1906) 207 The last yers corrall is unsould. **1683** MOXON *Mech. Exerc., Printing* 8 Some Trades are..sooner sold off, which renders the remainder of the un-sold Exercises unperfect. **1725** DE FOE *Voy. round World* (1840) 246, I always reserved a small quantity of all goods unsold. **1809** PINKNEY *Trav. France* 57 When the property of the emigrants is unsold. **1878** JEVONS *Prim. Pol. Econ.* 100 She begins to fear that she may have to carry her butter back unsold.

**Unso·lder,** *v.* [UN-[2] 3. Cf. Flem. *ontsoudeeren* (Kilian).] *trans.* To undo the soldering of. Also *fig.*, to dissolve.

**1538** ELYOT, *Replumbo*, to vnsowlder. **1611** COTGR., *Dessoulder*, to vnsolder, loose, dissolue. **1633** T. ADAMS *Exp. 2 Peter* ii. 5 Who feares..that his marrying a wife should unsoulder his conjunction with Christ? **1813** *Examiner* 12 Apr. 237/2 The leaden coffin being unsoldered, a body appeared. **1842** TENNYSON *Morte d'Arth.* 14 The sequel of to-day unsolders all The goodliest fellowship of famous knights Whereof this world holds record. **1889** *Anthony's Photogr. Bull.* II. 171 The weak point of the lamp..is the danger of unsoldering its parts by this down rush of the flame.

**Unso·ldered,** *ppl. a.* [UN-[1] 8.] Not fixed or closed with solder. Also *fig.*

**1641** J. TAYLOR (Water P.) *Reply* (title p.), A Rusty, Rayling,..Lying Libell,..lately written by an impudent unsoder'd Ironmonger. **1876** PREECE & SIVEWRIGHT *Telegraphy* 303 The soldering iron, and fire-pot,..are more or less cumbersome, and lead to unsoldered joints remaining in the wire. **1891** CLARK RUSSELL *Curatica* 104 If he is a plumber, he will not leave your pipes unsoldered.

**Unso·ldier,** *v.* [UN-[2] 6 b and 4.] *trans.* To divest of the character of a soldier or soldiers.

**1611** FLORIO, *Dissoldato*, vnsoldiered. **1776** S. J. PRATT *Pupil of Pleas.* II. 53 A tender woman will..unsoldier the boldest of us. **1780** — *Emma Corbett* (ed. 4) II. 67 Death sometimes comes at the bottom of the account to unsoldier a man. **1791** MACKINTOSH *Vind. Gallicæ* 286 Two grand operations conduct to it—arming the people, and unsoldiering the army.

**Unso·ldiered,** *ppl. a.* [f. prec. or UN-[1] 8.] Free from, not attended by, soldiers. Also as *adv.*, in an unsoldierly manner.

**1609** HEYWOOD *Brit. Troy* XV. xi, The people yssue free, Th' unsouldierd fields and deserts plaine to see. **1618** FLETCHER *Loyal Subj.* I. i, This young Prince..drew 'em up..so poorly, So raggedly and loosely, so unsouldier'd, The good Duke blush'd. **1834** DISRAELI *Rev. Epick* 35 Behold With eager homage..This mystical Omnipotence who breathes Unsoldiered edicts to a martial world.

**Unso·ldierlike,** *a.* (UN-[1] 7 c.)

**1590** SIR J. SMYTH *Disc. Weapons* Ded. 3 Their infinite vnsoldiorlike proceedings and disorders. **1600** DYMMOK *Ireland* (1843) 41 That advantage which was geven them by this unsoldior lyke encampinge. **1652** J. WRIGHT tr. *Camus' Nat. Paradox* III. 50 The unsoldier-like countenance of Iphigenes. **1721** DE FOE *Mem. Cavalier* (1840) 291 This was the most unsoldier-like action. **1777** ROBERTSON *Hist. Amer.* II. 80 From their unsoldier-like impatience..their general permitted them to retire. **1810** SYD. SMITH *Wks.* (1859) I. 193/1 Those allowances have been abused in the meanest..and most unsoldier-like manner. **1861** G. MUSGRAVE *By-Roads* 300 An abnormal and most unsoldierlike condition of things, which involved all the elements of weakness, incompetency, and defeat.

**Unso·ldierly,** *a.* (UN-[1] 7.)

**1598** BARRET *Theor. Warres* II. i. 29 [An] vnsoldiarly trick of a training captaine. **1644** PRYNNE & WALKER *Fiennes' Trial* 33 The most absurd, irrational, if not unsoldierly distinction, that ever was heard of in the world. **1693** RYMER *Short View of Tragedy* 134 The General..should..have turn'd his Eyes away from so unsouldierly an Execution. **1721** DE FOE *Mem. Cavalier* (1840) 299 Avoiding..the putting any unsoldierly extremities upon us. **1863** KINGLAKE *Crimea* II. 356 This movement..was scarcely wrong or unsoldierly. **1895** *Eclectic Mag.* Mar. 294 The unsoldierly appearance of a dandified subaltern.

**†Unso·ldiery,** *a. Obs.* [UN-[1] 7.] = prec. **1598** BARRET *Theor. Warres* II. i. 22 That the souldiers take not example from him of vnsoldiarie negligence. **1648** (*title*), An Elegie on the Most Barbarous, Vnparallel'd, Vnsouldiery Murder, committed at Colchester upon..Sir Charles Lucas and Sir George Lisle. **Unso·le,** *v.* (UN-[2] 4. Cf. Du. *ontzolen.*) **1598** FLORIO, *Dissolare*,..to part as the shoe from the sole, to vnsole. **1611** COTGR., *Dissemeler*, to vnsole, or pull the soles off a shoe. **1805** J. BOARDMAN *Dict. Veterinary Art* s.v. *Sole*, A horse that has been unsoled..will recover in a month's time.

**Unso·lemn,** *a.* [UN-[1] 7.]

**†1.** Uncelebrated. *Obs.*

*c* **1374** CHAUCER *Boeth.* I. pr. iii. (1868) 11 Of wyche folk þe renoun is neyþer ouer oolde ne vnsolempne [L. *incelebris*].

**2.** Not solemn; lacking in formal gravity.
*c* 1555 HARPSFIELD *Divorce Hen. VIII* (Camden) 124 The power..of that kind of vowe is stronger than in..a single unsolempe vow. 1660 JER. TAYLOR *Ductor* I. ii. rule 8 § 30 Conscience can oblige a Judge to an unsolemn absolution. 1825 R. P. WARD *Tremaine* II. 106 The not unsolemn rhythm of the regular trot of the horses. 1885 *Law Rep.* 14 Q.B.D. 702 A thing..which by the rules of the House is disorderly and unsolemn.

**b.** *Law.* Of a will: Informal.
1590 SWINBURNE *Testaments* 18 Vnsolemne testamentes are so tearmed, whereas the solemnities of the Ciuil law.. are omitted. *a* 1661 HOLYDAY *Juvenal* (1673) 50 Our lawiers therefore now call those ancient ones 'solemn testaments', as the latter sort unsolemn. 1726 AYLIFFE *Parergon* 527 Such a perfect Will may either be a solemn or unsolemn will. 1774 S. HALLIFAX *Rom. Law* 34 The Privilege of Unsolemn Testaments granted to Soldiers. 1844 H. TENNANT *Notary's Man.* ii. 32 The word 'Codicillus' or Codicil ..denotes any unsolemn last will, in which no heir is named.

Hence **Unso·lemnly** *adv.*
1821 J. HODGSON in J. Raine *Mem.* (1857) I. 367 He read the prayers very unsolemnly.

**Unso·lemnized,** *ppl. a.* (UN-[1] 8.) 1603 TAMWORTH in E. Lodge *Illustr.* (1791) III. 229 He is enfermed by deathenesse [*sic*]; and that made him unsolempnized at the coronacion. **Unsoli·citated,** *ppl. a.* (UN-[1] 8.) 1807 COGAN in *Treat. on Passions*, etc. (1813) II. 470 The thoughts which suggest themselves to the mind, not only unsolicitated, but completely unexpected.

**Unsoli·cited,** *ppl. a.* [UN-[1] 8.]
**1.** Of persons: Not approached with solicitation; unasked.
1588 SHAKS. *Tit. A.* IV. iii. 60 Of my word, I haue written to effect, Ther's not a God left vnsollicited. 1613 — *Hen. VIII*, II. iv. 219, I then..got your leaue To make this present Summons vnsolicited. 1680 C. NESSE *Church Hist.* 365 The devil..steps in..though unsolicited by those conspirators. 1756 *Connoisseur* No. 116 ⁋ 2 The graduate in medicine, finding himself unsolicited for prescription or advice. 1813 COLERIDGE *Lett.* (1895) 604 A number of unsolicited, unknown yet predetermined plauditors in the theatre. 1851 HUXLEY in *Life & Lett.* (1900) I. 90 He had previously been civil enough to sign my certificate...unsolicited. 1883 MEREDITH *Melampus* x, Not unsolicited,..the pendulous flower of the plants of sloth..answered question and squeeze.

**b.** *spec.* Not asked in marriage.
1750 JOHNSON *Rambler* No. 73 ⁋ 2 My aunts, being..neither young nor beautiful,..were suffered to live unsolicited.

**2.** Not asked for; given or done voluntarily.
1689 SAVILE *Let. to Dissenter* 30/2 Thanks must be voluntary, not only unconstrained, but unsollicited. 1782 MISS BURNEY *Cecilia* II. v, [He called] to bring her..fresh and unsolicited intelligence. 1818 SCOTT *Br. Lamm.* xxv, I am obliged to your lordship for your unsolicited intercession. 1847 HARRIS *Ld. Hardwick* III. 107 This appointment was entirely the unsolicited act of His Majesty.

**3.** Not affected or influenced.
1857 MILLER *Elem. Chem., Org.* 184 If thus, whilst unsolicited by any extraneous chemical forces, its molecular arrangement is so readily altered.

Hence **Unsoli·citedly** *adv.*
1815 W. H. IRELAND *Scribbleomania* 285 He..refused the first ecclesiastic dignities, which were unsolicitedly pressed upon him.

**Unsoli·citous,** *a.* (UN-[1] 7.)
(*a*) 1668 CLARENDON *Vind.* Tracts (1727) 66 Which refusal, and many others, shew how unsollicitous I have always been in the way of getting. 1768–74 TUCKER *Lt. Nat.* (1834) II. 453, I could easily conceal this slip of memory, ..but I choose to let it stand, agreeably with the character of the Searches, unsolicitous to hide their defects. 1778 SIR J. REYNOLDS *Disc.* (1779) 21 That natural energy of men engaged in real action, unsolicitous of grace. 1817 BENTHAM *Parl. Reform* Introd. 110, I have not been unsolicitous in my endeavours to collect it. 1884 *19th Cent.* Feb. 198 Yet St. Matthew is admitted..to be unsolicitous as to order of time. 1891 MISS DOWIE *Girl in Karp.* 259 With the fortune that attends the unsolicitous.
(*b*) 1758 JOHNSON *Idler* No. 9 ⁋ 3 How many unsolicitous hours should I bask away, warmed in bed.., could I..tumble from thence in a moment.

Hence **Unsoli·citousness.**
*a* 1683 OWEN *Gospel Grounds* Wks. 1851 V. 449 An unsolicitousness about present affairs and future events.

**Unso·lid,** *a.* [UN-[1] 7, 5 b. Cf. G. *unsolid.*]
**1.** Not materially solid.
1611 COTGR., *Insolide*, vnsolide, vnsound. 1615 CHAPMAN *Odyss.* XI. 60, I..would not suffer any one to dip Within our offring, his vnsolide lip, Before Tiresias. 1646 MAYNE *Serm. Unity* 38 A thin, unsolid, brittle, painted blast of wind. 1690 LOCKE *Hum. Und.* II. iv. § 5 The continuity of unsolid, inseparable, and immoveable Parts. 1733 WATTS *Philos. Ess.* v. i. (1734) 116 'Tis not solid Extension, for that is Body or Matter...'Tis not empty or unsolid Extension, for that is pure Space. 1768–74 TUCKER *Lt. Nat.* (1834) I. 298 Nor is it conceivable that any assortment of unsolid.. parts should form a solid..body. 1829 J. PHILLIPS *Geol. Yorks.* 73 These unsolid materials fall and waste away into slopes. 1896 *Daily News* 22 Jan. 5 German manufacturers are advised..to forsake the making of unsolid or ugly furniture.
*fig.* 1845 MILL *Diss. & Disc.* (1859) II. 256 The breaking up of the great unsolid structure which Charlemagne had raised.

**2** *fig.* Having no substance or sound basis.
1593 in *Maitl. Club Misc.* (1840) I. 58 The presbiterie debarris Connald Strutheris for his vnsolid speichis..fra the communioune at this present seasoun. 1639 W. SCLATER *Worthy Commun.* 37 Its cleare, that this Consubstantiation of the Lutherans is unsolid. 1642 MILTON *Apol. Smect.* 45 Unsolid and corrupted judgements both in doctrine and life. 1730 THOMSON *Winter* 753 Whither now are fled.. those unsolid hopes Of happiness? 1792 G. WAKEFIELD *Mem.* (1804) I. 115 The generality of them [*sc.* criticisms] are triviall or unsolid. 1854 H. MILLER *Sch. & Schm.* 204 To separate the solid from the unsolid thinking contained in my abstract. 1873 M. ARNOLD *Lit. & Dogma* p. xxiv, To what is unsolid in the New Testament he applies a negative criticism ably enough.

**3.** Lacking solid worth or merit.
1731 A. HILL *Advice to Poets* 193 But ah! far short the unsolid tinklers rise, Nor soar, but flutter, in the muse's skies.

Hence **Unso·lidly** *adv.*; **Unso·lidness.**
1611 COTGR., *Insolidement*, vnsoundly, vnsolidely. *a* 1684 LEIGHTON *Comm. 1 Peter* ii. (1693) 261 Consider this as our happiness, and the unsolidness of other comforts, and priviledges. 1755 JOHNSON, *Loosely*,..unsolidly; meanly; without dignity.

**Unsoli·dity.** (UN-[1] 12, 5 b; cf. prec.) 1736 BAILEY (fol.) Addit., *Unsolidity*, unsolidness, unsoundness. 1802–12 BENTHAM *Ration. Judic. Evid.* (1827) V. 22 Wearing on the face of it a proof of its own injustice, a proof of the unsolidity of the ground. 1889 *Atlantic* May 655/2 The pen that has indulged itself to an extent disproportionate.. to the apparent unsolidity of its topic. **Unso·lomonize,** *v.* (UN-[2] 6 c.) 1755 J. SHEBBEARE *Lydia* (1769) I. 60 We should then..squeeze him to a confession of the truth, or unsolomonise him by superior wisdom. †**Unsolubi·lity.** *Obs.*[—1] (UN-[1] 12, 5 b.) 1789 J. KEIR *Dict. Chem.* 29/2 The absolute unsolubility of bismuth.

†**Unso·luble,** *a. Obs.* [UN-[1] 7, 5 b.] Insoluble; *fig.* unanswerable, irrefutable.
1559 AYLMER *Harborowe* K 3 b, I do not vrge this, as an vnsoluble reason. 1587 GOLDING *De Mornay* x. 170 Let us conclude..by vnsoluble reasons..that God..did in deede create the World of nothing. 1756 F. HOME *Exper. Bleaching* 279 By the..influence of the air, it [*sc.* lime] becomes an unsoluble earth.

**Unsolute,** app. an error for *unsolide* UNSOLID *a.* 1611 SPEED *Th. Gt. Britain* I. xxxiii. 63/1 The Aire vpon the East and South part is both thicke and foggie, by reason of the Fennes and vnsolute grounds.

**Unso·lvable,** *a.* [UN-[1] 7 b and 5 b.]
†**1.** Insolvent. *Obs.*[—1]
1656 COWLEY *Misc.* Pref. ⁋ 5, I have the real excuse of the honestest sort of Bankrupts, which is, to have been made Unsolvable..by some notorious accidents and publike disasters.

**2.** Insoluble.
[1775 ASH.] 1821 J. Q. ADAMS *Report Weights & Meas.* 79 The problem, hitherto unsolvable to man, of squaring the circle. 1865 *Reader* 4 Feb. 130/1 He alone has produced paintings, before which we stand..as though they were unsolvable enigmas. 1894 S. FISKE *Holiday Stories* (1900) 155 Who had assumed the name..and hidden the receipt in our butler's pantry were unsolvable mysteries.
*absol.* 1894 H. GARDENER *Unoff. Patriot* 6 Human longing to solve the unsolvable.

Hence **Unso·lvableness.**
1884 *Nonconf. & Indep.* 10 Jan. 30/1 The question is depressing to the spirits in its very unsolvableness.

†**Unso·lve,** *v. Obs.* [UN-[2] 9.] *trans.* To solve.
1631 QUARLES *Samson* xii. 16 Perchance, my Fancy would have bin so kinde, T' unsolve the doubts of my perplexed minde. 1639 G. DANIEL *Ecclus.* Induct. 75 Ah! deare, I faint: can only this vnsolve The sentences which wisedome doth involve?

**Unso·lved,** *ppl. a.* (UN-[1] 8.)
1665 SIR R. HOWARD *Four New Plays* Pref. A 4, If this were let pass, the Argument is yet unsolv'd in it self. 1697 DRYDEN *Æneis* Ded. ⁋ 70 As Virgil propounds a riddle, which he leaves unsolved. 1741 WATTS *Improv. Mind* I. i. (1786) 17 Those knots and perplexities which have hitherto been unsolved. 1827 POLLOK *Course T.* v. 62 Vain question this,..and worthy to be left Unsolved. 1886 F. M. CRAWFORD *Tale Lonely Parish* v, He nevertheless represented in the minds of all an unsolved enigma.

†**Unso·lvible,** *a. Obs.* [UN-[1] 7.] = UNSOLVABLE *a.* 2. 1664 H. MORE *Exp. 7 Epist.* x. 164 If unsolvible otherwise, there is still the more assurance of undeniable Demonstration. †**Unso·me,** *a. Obs.* [UN-[1] 7. Cf. *unisome* (UN-[1] 3).] At variance; hostile. *c* 1205 LAY. 3931 Al heo weren vn-sahte & a heo weren vn-some. 13.. *R. Gloucester's Chron.* (Rolls) App. G. 134 Hit bifel þat time.. For defaute of weyes muche folc was vnsome.

**Unso·n,** *v.* [UN-[2] 6 b.] *trans.* To deprive of the character or status of a son.
1652 BP. HALL *Rem. Wks.* (1660) 144 He may so sin as to be frowned on,..not so as to be unsonned, or dis-herited. 1653 O. SEDGWICK *Doubting Believer* 255 It is an unadvised folly in the suspension of Gods favour, to unsonne our selves, and unpeople our selves. 1752 YOUNG *Brothers* III. i, Thy heart, how dead to ev'ry call of nature! Unson'd! unbrother'd! nay, unhumaniz'd! 1882 G. MACDONALD *Weighed & Wanting* III. 165 The father came back..determined..that his son, having unsonned himself, should nomore be treated as a son.

**Unso·nlike,** *a.* and *adv.* (UN-[1] 7 c, 11 b.)
1657 OWEN *Communion*, etc. III. v. 300 A Spirit of bondage ..casting them into an unsonlike frame of Spirit. 1687 R. L'ESTRANGE *Answ. Diss.* 41 Not among the Persecutors of the Dissenters; which he (most Un-son-like) Reflects upon in this Clause. 1690 C. NESSE *O. & N. Test.* I. 314 Their irreverent and unson-like repartee. 1879 CHR. G. ROSSETTI *Seek & Find* 315 An vnsonlike, unsympathetic, grudging spirit.

**Unsono·rous,** *a.* (UN-[1] 7, 5 b.) 1720–1 *Lett. Mist's Jrnl.* (1722) I. 62 Words harsh, and altogether unsonorous, and..incongruous in meaning. 1821 *Monthly Mag.* LI. 12 The harsh and unsonorous letters j and s.

**Unso·nsy,** *a. Sc.* and *north.* [UN-[1] 7.]
**1.** Luckless, unlucky, ill-omened, uncanny.
1560 ROLLAND *Seven Sages* 47 The Mairch [= marrow] heirof I sall declair, The quhilk pertenis to ȝour vnsonsie Air. *Ibid.* 82 That verry sarie weill sic ane vnsonsie Sanct. 1683 G. M[ERITON] *Yorks. Dial.* (1684) 71 You are unsawncy, I think by my life. 1728 RAMSAY *Anacreontic on Love* 32 He leugh, and with unsonsy jest, Cry'd,..Did not my arrow flie right smart? 1771 FOOTE *Maid of B.* II, My father was so unsaunzy as to gang out with Charley in the forty-five. 1814 SCOTT *Wav.* lxvii, At these unsonsy hours the glen has a bad name. 1897 W. BEATTY *Secretar* xiv. 105 As unsonsy a place as I could have chanced on.

**2.** Unhandsome, plain.
1894 CROCKETT *Raiders* xxi, I'm nane so unsonsy yet, though I be auld eneuch to be the laddie's mither.

†**Unsoo·t,** *a. Obs.* [UN-[1] 7.] = UNSWEET *a.*
1420–2 LYDG. *Thebes* I. 574 Al be that some founde ful vnsoote Rather a pley of werre than of pees. 1430–40 — *Bochas* I. iv. 1628 This flood..Causid also scarsete off vetaile, That many a man felte ful vnsoote. 1579 SPENSER *Sheph. Cal.* Dec. 118 And I..Sike follies nowe haue gathered as too ripe, And cast hem out, as rotten and vnsoote.

**Unsoo·thed,** *ppl. a.* (UN-[1] 8.)
1648 HEXHAM II, *Ongevleyt*, Vnflattered, or Vnsoothed. 1814 BYRON *Lara* II. viii, Cheerful was his gate; For thence the wretched ne'er unsoothed withdrew. 1853 RUSKIN *Stones Ven.* II. iii. § 10 The irritated pride of the antagonists remained unsoothed by the love-feast of St. Stephen's day.

**Unsoo·thfast,** *a.* [UN-[1] 7. Cf. OE. *unsóþfæst.*] Not truthful or true. *a* 1300 *Cursor M.* 26874 ȝof his scrift vnsothfast be, It sal him serue o thinges thre. 1570 LEVINS *Manip.* 36 Vnsoothfast, *infidelis.*

**Unsophi·stical,** *a.* [UN-[1] 7.]
†**1.** Unsophisticated. *Obs.*[—1]
1741 *Compl. Fam.-Piece* I. i. 58 Take red and unsophistical Oil of Petre.

**2.** Not sophistical.
[1775 ASH.] 1836 LANDOR *Peric. & Asp.* xcv, Certainly these words are very unsophistical. 1886 J. PULSFORD *Infold. & Unfold. Div. Genius* 13 With childlike unsophistical affections, let us love 'the Maker of Heaven and earth'.

Hence **Unsophi·stically** *adv.*
1794 R. J. SULIVAN *View Nat.* II. 309 If..men would allow themselves the free exercise of their reason.. when unsophistically established.

**Unsophi·sticate,** *ppl. a.* (UN-[1] 8 b. Cf. next.)
1607 MARKHAM *Cavel.* VI. Ded., Yet when I shall be tride, I hope I shall proue vnsophisticat. 1659 T. PECKE *Parnassi Puerp.* 172 Few English men dare purchase an Estate; Unless your Wisdom's unsophisticate The Title vouch. 1688 NORRIS *Lett.* 165 The unsophisticate and genuine relish of the Soul. 1760 WESLEY *Prim. Physick* Pref. ⁋ 3 Medicines ..good in their Kind; pure, genuine, unsophisticate. 1781 COWPER *Conversat.* 451 Nature, unsophisticate by man, Starts not aside from her Creator's plan. 1867 LOWELL *Fitz Adam's Story* 605 Men unsophisticate, rude-nerved as bears.

**Unsophi·sticated,** *ppl. a.* [UN-[1] 8.]
**1.** Unmixed, unadulterated.
1630 J. TAYLOR (Water P.) *Begger* Wks. I. 98/1 Vnsophisticated drinke, That neuer makes men stagger. 1664 BOYLE *Exp. touching Colours* 141 Take Blew, but Unsophisticated, Vitriol. 1706 E. WARD *Wooden World Diss.* (1708) 17 He never wants for two Sorts of Liquors, the Good and the Bad;..and that to be sure unsophisticated with the other. 1861 in *Daily Chron.* 12 Sept., An infusion made from the unsophisticated [tea-] leaves. 1894 *Cosmopolitan* XVII. 128 Pure air and a sky unsophisticated with the lights and smokes of civilization.

**2.** Not tampered with, altered, or falsified; uncorrupted, genuine.
1664 H. MORE *Myst. Iniq.* 438 They shall use the Sword of the Spirit,..which is unsophisticated Reason and Scripture. 1690 D. GRANVILLE *Lett.* (Surtees) 234 This low ebb of pure unsophisticated devotion. 1790 BURKE *Fr. Rev.* 128 We preserve the whole of our feelings still native and entire, unsophisticated by pedantry and infidelity. 1843 [MRS. MAITLAND] *Lett. fr. Madras* p. v, To give the correspondence in its genuine unsophisticated state. 1897 MARY KINGSLEY *W. Africa* 380 It was difficult to tell..which was the bottom of the canoe and which was the unsophisticated log.

**3.** Not sophisticated in habits, manners, or mind; natural, ingenuous, inexperienced.
1665 BOYLE *Occas. Refl.* IV. iii. 16 If some Ladies..were bound to change Dresses with this unsophisticated and unadorn'd Maid. 1668 H. MORE *Div. Dial.* II. 362 They shall be..untainted and unsophisticated by the unwholesome Converse of men. 1814 JANE AUSTEN *Mansf. Park* xxiv, Her young, unsophisticated mind. 1854 THACKERAY *Newcomes* II. 118 What an unsophisticated little country creature you are! 1873 TRISTRAM *Moab* xiii. 234 Trotter..drew out the unsophisticated fish as fast as he could bait his hook.

Hence **Unsophi·sticatedness.**
1858 ABP. BENSON in *Life* (1899) I. 139 Some..footmen.. took away my umbrella, but amazed my unsophisticatedness in making me keep my hat on my head. 1866 ALGER *Solit. Nat. & Man* IV. 336 To appreciate natural unsophisticatedness more highly, and conventionality more lowly.

**Unsophistica·tion.** (UN-[1] 12.)
1825 T. HOOK *Sayings* Ser. II. II. 356 Affecting delight.. at their unsophistication and curiosity. 1846 MRS. GORE *Eng. Char.* (1852) 29 The unsophistication which exposes the less wary classes..to be quacked to death by plausible doctors. 1887 T. HARDY *Woodlanders* III. 99 A proposal due rather to his unsophistication than to his prudence.

†**Unso·pited,** *ppl. a. Sc. Obs.* [UN-[1] 8.] Not put to rest. 1734 KEITH *Hist. Ch. & St. Scot.* 186 To beget and maintain Friendship..after so late and as yet unsopited Jars. **Unso·rdid,** *a.* (UN-[1] 7, 5 b.) 1857 SMILES *Stephenson* xxxiv. 464 Though a thrifty and frugal man, [he] was essentially unsordid. **Unso·re,** *a.* (UN-[1] 7. Cf. OE. *unsár*, ON. *úsárr*, MSw. *osar*, MDa. *usaar.*) 1500–20 DUNBAR *Poems* lxxxiii. 23 Thane had my dyt beine all in duill,..Quhair now I sing with heart onsair. **Unso·rrowed,** *ppl. a.* (UN-[1] 8.) 1597 HOOKER *Eccl. Pol.* v. lxxii. § 13 What heapes of grieuous transgressions haue we committed,..and yet cleane passe them ouer vnsorrowed for, and vnrepented of. 1619 FLETCHER *M. Thomas* II. iv, *Val.* What shall I do? *Cel.* Dye like a fool unsorrow'd, A bankrupt fool, that flings away his Treasure. **Unso·rtable,** *a.* (UN-[1] 7 b.) 1716 M. DAVIES *Athen. Brit.* II. 289 An Arian, Papist and Jacobit, dealing in their respective unsortable patch-work, make up to themselves unseizable Chymera's.

**Unso·rted,** *ppl. a.* [UN-[1] 8.]
**1.** Not arranged or put in order.
1533 MORE *Apol.* xlvii. Wks. 921/2 Good Tomme Truthe.. bringeth neuer a wytnesse with hym, and all hys euydence vnsorted. 1741 WATTS *Improv. Mind* xx. (1786) 408 Their

ideas..will lie in the brain unsorted, and thrown together without order. **1861** Wynter *Soc. Bees* 22 The last letters.. are, of course, vnsorted, and have to go through that process as the train proceeds. **1895** *Educat. Rev.* Nov. 352 A new science has been developed out of what were unsorted and uninterpreted fragments.

† **2.** Unfitted, unsuitable. *Obs.*—1

**1596** Shaks. *1 Hen. IV*, ii. iii. 13 The purpose you undertake is dangerous, the Friends you haue named vncertaine, the Time it selfe vnsorted.

**Unsou·ght,** *ppl. a.* [Un-1 8 b, c. Cf. MDu. *ongesocht* (Du. *ongezocht*), MHG. *ungesuochet* (G. *ungesucht*), Da. *usøgt*, Sw. *osökt*.]

**1.** Not searched out or sought after; not sought or asked for.

*a* **1225** *Ancr. R.* 324 A wummon þet haueð forloren hire nelde..secheð hine anonriht,..and God forloren uor sunne schal liggen unsouht fulle seoue dawes. **1374** Chaucer *Troylus* i. 809 Vnknowe vnkyst and lost þat is vn-sought. *a* **1395** Hylton *Scala Perf.* ii. xiv. (W. de W. 1494), Vnresonably he werkith þat leuith the souereyn gode..vnsought and vnloued. *a* **1470** Gregory *Chron.* in *Hist. Coll. Cit. Lond.* (Camden) 192 They lefte noo thynge unsoffethe, and they serchyd all that nyght. *a* **1548** Hall *Chron., Hen. VI*, 103 A thyng discended from heauen, of theim vnsought, vnimagined and not deuised. **1576** Gascoigne *Kenelworth Castle* Wks. 1910 II. 92 Nothing shall rest unsought, That may bring pleasure to your mind. **1634** Milton *Comus* 732 The Sea o'refraught would swell, and th' unsought diamonds Would so emblaze the forhead of the Deep,..that [etc.]. **1688** T. Flatman *Lines to Abp. Sancroft* 1 When I Your unsought Glories view'd,..some great thing to Write I meant. *c* **1708** Fenton *First Fit of Gout* 19 Whence comes this unsought honour unto me? **1751** Warburton *Pope's Wks.* IX. 247 To the issue of that unasked and unsought compliment these words allude. **1837** Lockhart *Scott* IV. i. 13 This novel seems to me to possess..a kind of simple unsought charm. **1856** Kane *Arct. Expl.* II. iii. 44 How often relief has come at the moment of extremity, in forms strangely unsought.

**b.** Not obtained by search or effort. Freq. in loose const.: Without being sought for; without search.

*c* **1350** *Ipomadon* 6519 Nowe I se vnsoughte, My travayle hedyr is all in vayne! *c* **1368** Chaucer *Compl. Pite* 104 What maner thinge may encrese my wo That haue I redy vnsoghte euyr where. *c* **1400** *Ywaine & Gaw.* 798 Bot the knight thar fand thai noght; Than was thar mekil sorow unsoght. *c* **1460** *Towneley Myst.* iii. 97 In erth I se right noght Bot syn that is vnsoght. ? *a* **1500** *Chester Pl.* (Shaks. Soc.) 206 Endles paine muste I have unsoughte To my rewarde. **1596** Spenser *F. Q.* vi. iv. 28 Oftimes..sorrowes of the mynd Find remedie vnsought, which seeking cannot fynd. **1601** Shaks. *Twel. N.* iii. i. 168 Loue sought, is good: but giuen vnsought, is better. **1671** Milton *P. R.* ii. 59 Thus they out of their plaints new hope resume To find whom at the first they found unsought. **1725** Ramsay *Gentl. Sheph.* iii. ii, That's kind unsought. **1784** Cowper *Task* iii. 288 What pearl is it..which the poor..Seek and obtain, and often find unsought? **1817** Scott *Harold* Introd. 55 Oft at such season, too, will rhymes unsought Arrange themselves in some romantic lay. **1855** *Poultry Chron.* III. 338/2 The greatest gain will often, unsought and unwished, attend the first-class.

**c.** With advs., esp. *for*.

**1611** Florio, *Inesplorato*, unsought out. **1622** Wither *Philarete* M 3 b, Those sad Straines..Which you composd, when greatest discontent Vnsought-for helpe to your Inuention lent. **1650** Cromwell *Let.* 12 Sept. (Carlyle), Which we earnestly desire may not be laid aside unsought after. **1727** [Dorrington] *P. Quarll* (1816) 26, I had him..by mere accident, unexpected, and unsought for. **1816** Wilson *City of Plague* iii. ii. 137 Unsought-for bliss Coming..from all the points of heaven. **1863** H. Cox *Instit.* i. x. 249 This arrangement..at least was unsought for by him.

**2.** † **a.** Unassailed. *Obs. rare.*

*a* **1300** *Cursor M.* 2440 He lued hir wil mare þan are, For wirscipp þat sco did him win, And sco vnsoght saccles o sin. *c* **1400** *Sowdone Bab.* 2081 Ye bene biseged in this toure... Charles wole not leve you vnsought.

**b.** Unasked; without being requested.

*a* **1500** *Chaucer's Dreme* in *C's Wks.* (1598) 359/1 So verily, ech thing vnsought, He said as he had knowne my thought. **1613** Hieron *Bridegroome* 18 Christ leadeth his Church with benefits, and that vnsought to. *a* **1704** T. Brown *Sat. Quack* Wks. 1720 I. 71 Death, tho' unsought, waits on thy murd'ring Quill. **1873** Symonds *Grk. Poets* xi. 392 Then on my lyre, unasked, unsought, there flew A grasshopper. **1878** B. Taylor *Deukalion* i. vi. 49 Ere ye approach me, I shine unsought.

**3.** Unexamined, unexplored.

*c* **1375** *Cursor M.* 26637 (Fairf.), Hit faris of shrift as dos of wound þat lange vnsoȝt is to þe grounde. **1400** tr. *Secreta Secret., Gov. Lordsh.* 48, I haue noght left vnsoght no stede no temple whare Philosophers vsyd to wryte. **1426** Lydg. *De Guil. Pilgr.* 4450 And ther ys no corner vnsouht, But that I go to euery place. **1590** Shaks. *Com. Err.* i. i. 136 Loth to leaue vnsought Or that, or any place that harbours men. **1600** Fairfax *Tasso* xv. xxvii, So that this mighty sea is yet unsought, Where thousand isles and kingdoms lie unknown. **1625** Quarles *Sion's Sonn.* xv. 6 Thus..no place I left unsought, No eare vnask'd.

**4.** Not resorted to; untried.

**1582** Stanyhurst *Æneis* iv. (Arb.) 109 No meane vnattempted, ne vnsoght..leauing. **1626** Chas. I in *Buccleuch MSS.* (Hist. MSS. Comm.) I. 264 We..have left no means unsought that might truly enable us to these great works. **1708** Rowe *Royal Convert* iii. i, Is there a Remedy in human Wisdom, My Mind has left unsought, to help this Evil?

**Unsou·l,** *v.* [Un-2 6 b and 4. Cf. Du. *ontzielen*, G. *entseelen*.]

**1.** *trans.* To deprive of spirit or courage.

*a* **1634** Chapman *Rev. for Honour* i. i. 204 For shame, sir! ..Your sad appearance, should they thus behold you, Would half unsoul your army. **1641** Shirley *Cardinal* ii. i, Such Another were enough to unsoul an Army; Ignobly talk of patience till they drink And reel to death?

**2.** To deprive of soul; to make soulless. Also const. *of*.

**1652** Benlowes *Theoph.* i. xxi, Such are their ranting catches, to unsoul And out-law man. **1654** Cokaine *Dianea* iv. 336 But Cruelty..spoiles, unbowels, unsoules the world. *a* **1743** Ozell tr. *Brantome's Sp. Rhodom.* (1744) 123 Heaps of Bodies they had un-soul'd and deprived of vital air. **1805** Wordsw. *Prelude* xii. 83 Even so could I unsoul As readily by syllogistic words Those mysteries of being. **1858** J. Culross *Lazarus Revived* 46 There is a way of making truth plain and comprehensible by unsouling it of all that is ..most precious in it.

**3.** To deprive of the essential qualities of a soul.

**1653** H. More *Antid. Ath.* Wks. (1712) 13 You may as soon unsoul the Soul. *a* **1680** Charnock *Attrib. God* (1834) I. 88 [When] we seem to deny the being of God,..we seem also to unsoul our souls.

**Unsou·led,** *ppl. a.* [f. prec. or Un-1 8. Cf. G. *entseelt*; also MHG. *ungesêlt* (obs. G. *ungeseelt*), G. *unbeseelt*.] **a.** Deprived of soul. **b.** Not endowed with soul.

**1596** Spenser *F. Q.* vii. vii. 46 Death..[is not] ought to see, but like a shade to weene, Vnbodied, vnsoul'd, vnheard, vnseene. **1620** Shelton *Quix.* i. iv. v. 336, I know not what vnsouled folke they be, and so without conscience. **1633** Ford *Love's Sacr.* i. ii, Thus, bodies walke vnsold. **1722** Hamilton *Wallace* v. (1816) 67 The chief retires,..While twenty foes unsoul'd, adorn the fatal scene. *a* **1750** A. Hill *Ronald & Dorna* v, Trembling, I wait, unsoul'd, till you inspire. **1800** Coleridge *Piccolom.* i. iv. 127 The painful toil..Left me a heart unsoul'd and solitary. **1840** Mangan *Poems* (1903) 136 To be The world's applauded and degraded martyr, Unsouled, enthralled. **1885–94** R. Bridges *Eros & Psyche* Mar. xii, Her fair Hellenic empire..For which she had..left her wanton images unsoul'd In Babylon and Zidon.

**Unsou·lish,** *a.* (Un-1 7.) **1890** J. Pulsford *Loyalty to Christ* I. 226 He felt for the moment that he was living a miserably thin, formal, unsoulish life.

† **Unsou·nd,** *sb. Obs.* [Un-1 12. Cf. MHG. *ungesunt* (obs. G. *ungesund*) in sense 1.]

**1.** Physical unsoundness; malady or sickness; a wound or sore.

*c* **1205** Lay. 29315 Þe king him gon crepen an heonden and a futen, swulc he mid unsunde al uorwunded weore. *a* **1300** *Marina* 207 in Horstm. *Altengl. Leg.* (1878) 173 Þer heo lay mid vnsounde Fourteniht faste ybounde. *c* **1315** Shoreham i. 82 Water wassheþ þe felthe a-wey, Þer me wesscheþ by liste þe on-sounde.

**2.** Harm, distress, annoyance.

**13..** *E. E. Allit. P.* C. 58 Did not Ionas in Iude such Iape sum-whyle, To sette hym to sewrte, vnsounde he hym feches? *Ibid.* 527 He þat is to rakel to renden his cloþez, Mot efte sitte with more vn-sounde to sewe hem togeder. *c* **1470** *Golagros & Gaw.* 590 Was neuer sa vnsound set to my hert.

**Unsou·nd,** *a.* [Un-1 7. Cf. NFris. *ünsün* (*-sünj*), MLG. *unsund* (hence Sw. *osund*, Da. *usund*); also MDu. *ongesont* (Du. *ongezond*), MLG. *ungesund*, MHG. *ungesunt* (G. *ungesund*).]

**1.** Of persons, etc.: Not physically sound; unhealthy, diseased; † suffering from wounds or injuries.

*c* **1320** *Sir Tristr.* 1175 Men wounded him and band Vnsounde. *Ibid.* 3342. *c* **1330** *King of Tars* 522 Summe heore scolles icleved, With serwe thei weore unsounde. *c* **1400** *Destr. Troy* 1255 Þai hurlet hym fro horse fete, & of hond toke, Set hym in his sadill þof he vnsound were. *a* **1450** *Le Morte Arth.* 2165 Oute of the felde was he drayne, For he was seke and sore vn-sounde. *c* **1470** Henry *Wallace* viii. 787 The wery ost..Wysche woundis with wyn, off thaim that was wnsound. **1513** Douglas *Æneid* iv. i. 1 The Queyn, with havy thochtis onsound, In euery vane nurisis the greyn wound. **1601** B. Jonson *Poetaster* iii. v, Enuy..Shall find me solid, and her teeth vnsound. **1667** *Decay Chr. Piety* viii. 211 And like an unsound limb, the healing of one Sore is the breaking out of another. **1722** De Foe *Plague* (1896) 57 It brought abundance of unsound people to the markets. **1787** 'G. Gambado' *Acad. Horsemen* (1809) 47 It seems as if one might work a lame horse thus, and keep his unsound leg quiet. **1824** Byron *Def. Transf.* i. i. 564 Merrily! merrily! never unsound, Shall our bonny black horses skim over the ground! **1879** Harlan *Eyesight* vi. 80 An eye with a high degree of short-sight is almost always an unsound one.

**b.** *transf.* Of wounds, ailments, etc.

*c* **1400** *Destr. Troy* 495 Medea the mylde..Wox pale for pyne..With a Sykyng vnsounde, þat sonet to hir hert. **1596** Spenser *F. Q.* vi. iv. 16 But that same Ladies hurts no herbe he found Which could redresse, for it was inwardly vnsound. **1613** Heywood *Brazen Age* H 2 b, I did neglect the smart: At length it rankled and it grew vnsound. **1813** J. Thomson *Lect. Inflam.* 425 The unsound appearances of the granulations show to what a stand the animal powers are put on such occasions.

† **c.** Quasi-*adv.*, in the phrase *to sigh unsound*.

? *a* **1400** *Morte Arth.* 3290 Ofte he syghede vn-sownde, and said theis wordes. *a* **1440** *Sir Degrev.* 316 The eorl hovede and beheld..How they fayre in the feld, And syght unsound. *c* **1470** *Gol. & Gaw.* 638 For pure sorow of that sight thai sighit vnsound.

**d.** Of substances, plants, fruits, etc.: Not in sound or good condition.

**1617** Moryson *Itin.* iii. 273 Officers..who ouersee the shambles, that no vnsound meate be sold. **1707** Mortimer *Husb.* 167 Some Lands will make unsound Cheese, notwithstanding all the Care the good Housewife can take. **1815** A. T. Thomson *Lond. Disp.* 402 In some places the grapes are..picked from the stalks, and freed from all the unsound ones with great care. **1855** *Poultry Chron.* III. 546/1 Shake the earth from the roots, cut off any unsound parts.

**2.** Morally corrupt or vitiated; wicked, evil.

**13..** *E. E. Allit. P.* B. 575 Þe venym & þe vylanye & þe vycios fylþe, Þat by-sulpez mannez saule in vnsounde hert. ? *a* **1400** *Morte Arth.* 3942 [He] ses theme alle in a soppe..With the Sarazenes vn-sownde enserclede a-bowte. **1597** Hooker *Eccl. Pol.* v. iv. § 1 That wherein vnsounder times haue done amisse, the better ages ensuing must rectifie, as they may. **1601** Weever *Mirr. Mart.* A 7 b, Seeking how she might the more inhaunce me, Though lewd my hauiour was, vnsound my carriage. **1811** Lamb *Hogarth* Wks. 1908 I. 107 That he..took a pleasure in exposing the unsound and rotten parts of human nature. *a* **1862** Buckle *Civiliz.* (1869) III. iii. 130 If the people are unsound,..the nation perishes.

**b.** Not sincere or true.

**1714** Gay *Sheph. Week* iv. 104 Boobyclod soon drops upon the ground, A certain token that his love's unsound.

**3.** Unwholesome, unhealthy.

**1598** Florio, *Insanare*,..to make vnsound, or vnholsome. **1660** F. Brooke tr. *Le Blanc's Trav.* 385 The Mine of Porto ..is..of little benefit for want of workmen, by reason of the unsound ayre. **1707** Mortimer *Husb.* 179 In unsound Pasture they reckon it the best for Lambs to run with the Ewes. *c* **1830** *Glouc. Farm Rep.* 18 (L.U.K.), In summer they depasture on the unsound grass land.

**4.** Not mentally sound or normal; not sane.

*a* **1547** Surrey *Æneis* ii. 308 But we goe on, vnsound of memorie. *Ibid.* iv. 11 When all unsound, her sister of like minde Thus spake she to. **1642** tr. *Perkins' Prof. Bk.* iv. 131 If a man of unsound memory..exchange the same land with a stranger. **1693** *Humours Town* 32 A debilitated Body, and unsound Mind. **1746** Francis tr. *Hor., Sat.* ii. iii. 400 His Master sure..Must have confess'd the Slave unsound of Brain. **1818** Cruise *Digest* (ed. 2) V. 538 Finding that Nicholas Hume..was not an idiot or person of unsound mind. **1898** *Daily News* 9 Nov. 4/5 The jury found..that he was occasionally unsound in mind.

**5.** Not soundly based in reasoning or fact.

**1595** Spenser *Epithal.* 237 Modesty, That suffers not one looke to glaunce awry, Which may let in a little thought vnsownd. **1631** Gouge *God's Arrows* 210 The ground of the objection is unsound. **1641** Milton *Ch. Govt.* ii. 6 Therfore it is unsound to say that God [etc.]. **1746** Dunkin tr. *Horace, Epist.* i. ii. 22 When doating Monarchs urge Unsound Resolves, their Subjects feel the Scourge. **1818** Byron *Ch. Har.* iv. vii, Waking Reason deems Such overweening phantasies unsound. **1849** Macaulay *Hist. Eng.* x. II. 614 Their old theory, sound or unsound, was at least complete and coherent. **1873** M. Arnold *Lit. & Dogma* vi. 180 When they air their unsound criticism in public.

**b.** Of persons in respect of opinion or belief.

**1597** Hooker *Eccl. Pol.* v. lii. § 4 So Eutyches, of sound beliefe.., became vnsound by denying the difference. *a* **1658** Durham *Comm. Rev.* (1660) 187 If an unsound hypocriticall man may be sent Minister of Christ? **1680** C. Nesse *Church-Hist.* 196 God tenderly covers Asa's frailty,..which he would not do for unsound Jehu. **1891** Ld. Acton in *Westm. Gaz.* 10 Oct. (1906) 2/3 St. John, I have even heard, was unsound about Old Testament dates and authorships.

**6.** Lacking in solidity or firmness.

**1590** Spenser *F. Q.* ii. xi. 20 Of such subtile substance and vnsound, That like a ghost he seem'd, whose graue-clothes were vnbound. **1760** Beattie *The Hares* 170 Some new phenomenon..Which..From its proud summit to the ground Proves the whole edifice unsound. **1800** Southey *St. Gualberto* viii, The pile was ruinous, the base unsound. **1844** *Act* 7 & 8 *Vict.* c. 84 § 46 If an unsound Party Wall..be pulled down and rebuilt. **1856** Kane *Arct. Expl.* I. 126 The ice is too unsound for us to attempt to ride with a large team.

**7.** Of sleep: Broken or disturbed.

**1584** C. Robinson, etc. *Handf. Pleas. Delights* (Arb.) 44 My sleepe vnsound hath dreadfull dreams.

**Unsou·nd,** *adv.* [Un-1 11 b.] Not soundly. **1595** Daniel *Civil Wars* iii. lxii, The now sad king..still muses, sleepes vnsound.

† **Unsou·nd,** *v. Obs.* [Un-2 6 b.] **a.** *trans.* To tear or rend. **b.** To make unsound. *c* **1450** *Mirour Saluacioun* (Roxb.) 97 Jacob sonnes thaire brothere cote with thaire handis vnsoundid. **1560** W. Baldwin *Funeralles K. Edw. Sixt* A iv b, When thou hast his.. person found, I will thou shalt his helthy body vnsound.

† **Unsou·ndable,** *a.*1 *Obs.*—1 [Un-1 7 b.] Not sounding well; improper. *c* **1440** *Alph. Tales* 408 It wer ane vnsondabyll thyng to do, if it sulde be he lefte & I taryd with þe.

**Unsou·ndable,** *a.*2 [Un-1 7 b, 5 b.] Incapable of being sounded; unfathomable.

**1627** Jackson *Creed* vi. v. § 1 Some Schoole-braines have beene so puzled in passing this unsoundable gulfe, as to suspect [etc.]. **1660** F. Brooke tr. *Le Blanc's Trav.* 216 The so famous Nile..sallying, as some say, out of an unsoundable lake. *a* **1684** Leighton *Comm. 1 Pet.* ii. (1693) 295 The thoughts of God are..deep, and unsoundable by us. **1843** Carlyle *Past & Pr.* iii. xi, There shall be a depth of Silence in thee..; a Silence unsoundable. **1884** *Graphic* 4 Oct. 358/2 His eyes will be large, black, with long lashes and unsoundable. **1897** Baring-Gould *Guavas* vii, One track..betwixt unsoundable bogs.

† **Unsou·nded,** *ppl. a.*1 *Obs.*—1 [Un-1 8: cf. Sound *v.*3] Not healed. **1420–2** Lydg. *Thebes* ii. 2438 Wherto shuld I write..of the sorowe that Polymytes Mad in hym-silf to sen hym so forwounded, His greuous hurtes, his soorys, ek vnsounded.

**Unsou·nded,** *ppl. a.*2 Also 6 unsounde. [Un-1 8.] Not sounded, uttered, or pronounced; not made to sound.

**1530** Palsgr. Introd. 16 No vowell is left unsounded..in a frenche worde. *c* **1532** Du Wes *Introd. Fr.* in *Palsgr.* 899 If the next worde..be a consonant, than shall the said *s* remayne unsounde. **1807** J. Barlow *Columb.* v. 766 Every honest Muse with horror flings The name unsounded from her sacred strings. **1865** *Trans. Philol. Soc.* 15 The unsounded syllable of the third person plural of the French verb. **1884** H. R. Haweis *Musical Life* 119, I keep my Strad. in a cabinet behind glass. There he rests unsounded and unstrung.

**Unsou·nded,** *ppl. a.*3 [Un-1 8.]

**1.** Not sounded or plummeted; unfathomed.

**1591** Shaks. *Two Gent.* iii. ii. 81 Orpheus Lute,..Whose golden touch could..Make Tygers tame, and huge Leuiathans Forsake vnsounded deepes, to dance on Sands. **1616** W. Browne *Brit. Past.* ii. i. 130 The tyde..whereon his carre should sweepe, Deckt with the riches of th' unsounded deepe. **1651** T. STANLEY *Poems, Venus Vigils* 77 Piercing through the unsounded sea. **1861** L. L. NOBLE *Icebergs* 243 Where with the surf around its shoulders..it stood far up from the unsounded valleys of ocean.

**b.** *fig.* or in fig. contexts.

**1593** SHAKS. 2 *Hen. VI*, III. i. 57 Glouster is a man Vnsounded yet, and full of deepe deceit. **1607** CHAPMAN *Bussy D'Ambois* III. F 1, O the vnsounded Sea of womens bloods, That when tis calmest, is most dangerous. **1634** JACKSON *Creed* VII. xix. § 6, I would request every ingenuous sober reader..not adventure to saile in a narrow..and unsounded sea only with the help of a generall carde. *a* **1750** A. HILL *The Muse to the Writer* xxxiii, This is a subject, that, outstretching thought, Through depths unsounded, wit's long plummet draws. **1826** MRS. HEMANS *Forest Sanctuary* lxxi, Th' unsounded gulfs of human woe! **1876** SWINBURNE *Erechtheus* 939 Mine unknown children of unsounded years. **1878** EMERSON in *N. Amer. Rev.* CXXVI. 409 To good men, as we call good men, this doctrine of Trust is an unsounded secret.

**2.** Unprobed, unexamined.

*c* **1620** ROBINSON *Mary Magd.* 534 Vaine woman!..shall thy heart vnsounded, still remaine vnsound?

**Unsou·ndly,** *adv.* [UN-[1] 11.]

†**1.** So as to do hurt or harm; injuriously. *Obs.*

**13..** *E. E. Allit. P.* B. 201 Ne neuer so sodenly soȝt [God] vn-soundely to weng, As for fylþe of þe flesch þat foles han vsed. **13..** *Gaw. & Gr. Knt.* 1438 Þenne þay beten on þe buskez, & bede hym vp ryse, & he vnsoundyly out soȝt seggez ouer-þwert.

**2.** In an unsound or unsolid manner.

**1594** HOOKER *Eccl. Pol.* Pref. viii. § 1 All such partes of the word of God..no lesse unsoundly taught and interpreted by all authorized English pastors, then by antichrists factors themselues. **1611** COTGR., *Insolidement*, vnsoundly, vnsolidely,..feebly. **1668** H. MORE *Div. Dial.* II. v. 195 If it were notable to bear such small Fillips, it would be a sign that things hung very crazily and unsoundly together. **1828–32** WEBSTER s.v., He sleeps unsoundly. **1851** MANSEL *Proleg. Log.* i. 2 That it is possible to transgress those [mental] laws, or to think unsoundly.

**Unsou·ndness.** [UN-[1] 12.]

**1.** The quality of being physically or materially unsound. Also *fig.*

**1599** SANDYS *Europæ Spec.* (1605) V 2 b, The bond of common feare, is the strongest indeed of all other,..and the daunger once past falles in sunder of his owne vnsoundnesse. **1614** LATHAM *Falconry* II. i. 79 When through our disorder..we haue wrought their [*sc.* hawks'] vnsoundnes, we forget to looke backe. **1763** MILLS *Pract. Husb.* III. 449 If these [livers] were livid or corrupted, they offered others, as the unsoundness of the first might be owing to some casual distemper. **1820** STARKIE *Rep. Cases N. P.* II. 81 If a horse be affected by any malady which renders him less serviceable for a permanency, I have no doubt that it is an unsoundness. **1860** TYNDALL *Glac.* II. xix. 333 The unsoundness of ice at and near its melting point. **1880** *Encycl. Brit.* XII. 189/2 A pimple on the body where the saddle would cover it is an unsoundness in a hunter while it lasts. *Ibid.*, A temporary cough is also an unsoundness.

**b.** Unwholesomeness.

**1660** F. BROOKE tr. *Le Blanc's Trav.* 370 A Colony..displanted for the unsoundnesse of the ayre.

**2.** The quality of being unsound in belief, opinion, principles, etc.

**1597** HOOKER *Eccl. Pol.* V. lxii. § 6 By reason of vnsoundnes in the highest articles of Christian faith. **1641** MILTON *Animadv.* 20 They need not carry such an unworthy suspicion over the Preachers of Gods word, as to tutor their unsoundnesse with the Abcie of a Liturgy. **1680** S. MATHER *Iren.* 3 Fundamental unsoundness and Corruption of Judgment. **1769** J. GILL *Body Pract. Divinity* II. ii. 302 They..agree to differ..and not charge one another with unsoundness and heterodoxy. **1794** G. ADAMS *Nat. & Exp. Philos.* II. xvii. 259 It was not uncommon formerly to suspect every one who professed to pursue the light of nature, of unsoundness of principles. **1841** [MRS. MOZLEY] *Lost Brooch* II. 71 Every sermon of his betrays his unsoundness. **1877** *Smith & Wace's Dict. Chr. Biog.* I. 11/2 The breach was widened by mutual accusations of unsoundness in the faith.

**b.** Of doctrine, principles, etc.

**1586** HOOKER *Answ. Travers* § 6 Any thing that shalbe spoken concerning the vnsoundnes of my Doctrine. **1607** *Stat.* in *Hist. Wakefield Gram. Sch.* (1892) 61 The unsoundnes of his or theire religion. **1712** ADDISON *Spect.* No. 507 ¶ 6 The Unsoundness of this Principle..is..universally acknowledged. **1844** H. H. WILSON *Brit. India* I. 551 The unsoundness of the conclusion..might inspire a reasonable distrust of the correctness of the persuasions. **1881** WESTCOTT & HORT *Grk. Test.* Introd. § 93 The presumed unsoundness of the text.

**3.** The quality of being mentally unsound.

**1825** MACAULAY *Ess., Milton* ¶ 14 Perhaps no person can be a poet..without a certain unsoundness of mind. **1856** J. W. H. WILLIAMS (*title*), On Unsoundness of Mind, in its medical and legal considerations. **1884** *Law Rep.* 27 Ch. Div. 119 The soundness or unsoundness of mind of the alleged lunatic.

†**Unsou·ndy,** *a. Obs.*—[1] Irreg. var. UNSOUND *a.*

*a* **1529** SKELTON *E. Rummyng* 35 Her eyen gowndy Are full vnsoundy, For they are blered.

**Unsouped,** obs. variant of UNSUPPED.

**Unsou·r,** *a.* (UN-[1] 7. Cf. OE. *unsúr*, ON. *úsúrr*.)

**1611** FLORIO, *Inaspro*, vnsowre, sweet. **17..** RAMSAY *To D. M'Ewen* ii, Health, T' enjoy ilk hour a saul unsow'r.

**Unsou·red,** *ppl. a.* (UN-[1] 8. Cf. NFris. *unsürred*, MSw. *osyrdh* (Sw. *osyrad*), older Da. *usuret* (Da. *usyret*); Du. *ongezuurd*, MHG. *ungesiuret* (G. *ungesäuert*) chiefly of bread, = unleavened.)

**1626** BACON *Sylva* § 341 Wee see that Meat and Drinke will last longer, Vnputrified, or Vnsowred, in Winter, than in Summer. **1685** DRYDEN *Horace* I. ix. 26 Secure those golden early joyes, That Youth unsowr'd with sorrow bears. *c* **1791** BURNS *To Mr. Maxwell* i, Health, ay unsour'd by care or grief. **1853** C. BRONTE in Mrs. Gaskell *Life* (1858) 471 A serene spirit and an unsoured disposition!

**Unsow·ed,** *ppl. a.* [UN-[1] 8. Cf. MDu. *ongesaeit* (Du. *ongezaaid*), G. *ungesäet*, Da. *usaaet*, Sw. *osådd*.] = next.

**1648** HEXHAM II, *Onbezaeyt landt*, an vnsowed land, or a Fallowe field. **1791** COWPER *Odyss.* IX. 125 Earth unsow'd, untill'd, brings forth for them All fruits, wheat, barley, and the vinous grape.

**Unsow·n,** *ppl. a.* Also 4 unsowe, -sawe. [UN-[1] 8 b. Cf. OE. *unsáwen* (of land), ON. *úsáinn*, and prec.]

**1.** Of seed: Not sown; left without being sown. Also of vegetation: Growing without having been sown.

*c* **1374** CHAUCER *Former Age* 10 Corn vp-sprong vnsowe of mannes hond. ? **15..** in Thynne *Animadv.*, etc. (1875) 88 Wher the seyd of god is vnsawn. **1539–40** *N. C. Wills* (Surtees) 169 All my corne sowen and unsowen. **1573** TUSSER *Husb.* (1878) 85 Sowe lintels ye may, and peason gray. Keepe white vnsowne, till more be knowne. **1626** BACON *Sylva* § 546 Mushromes..come vp so hastily; As in a Night; And yet they are Vnsowne. **1693** DRYDEN *Ovid's Met.* I. 138 The Flow'rs un-sown, in Fields and Meadows reign'd. **1883** R. W. DIXON *Mano* I. iv. 10 The crops remained unsown this year.

**2.** Of land: Not supplied with seed.

*c* **1400** *Gamelyn* 83 He þought on his landes þat lay vnsawe. *a* **1513** FABYAN *Chron.* IV. lxxv. 53 The grounde was vntylled and vnsowen, Wherof ensued great scarsytie. **1539** *Act* 31 *Hen. VIII*, c. 5 Duryng all suche time as the same landes shalbe and remayne vnsowen. **1600** SURFLET *Countrie Farme* I. xxiv. 147 The trampling which they keepe about trees, medowes, and vnsowne places. **1626** BACON *Sylva* § 482 If the Ground lie fallow, and vnsowne. **1725** POPE *Odyssey* IX. 143 Nor knows the soil to feed the fleecy care,.. But uninhabited, untill'd, unsown It lies. **1730** LYTTELTON *Epist. to Pope* 28 Unhappy Italy!..Her cities [are] desert and her fields unsown. **1842** TENNYSON *Dora* 71 Dora..went her way Across the wheat, and sat upon a mound That was unsown.

**Unspa·n,** *v. rare.* (UN-[2] 3 + SPAN *v.*[2] Cf. OE. *un-*, *onspannan*, Du. *ontspannen*.)

**1648** HEXHAM II, *Outspannen*,..to Vnspan, or to Vnyoake. *Ibid.*, *Een Outspanninge*,..an Vnbending, or an Vnspanning. **1659** W. CHAMBERLAYNE *Pharon.* III. v. 92 The grave sad man, Whose counsel could conspiracies unspan When ready to give fire.

**Unspa·ned,** *ppl. a. Sc.* [UN-[1] 8.] Unweaned. **1500–20** DUNBAR *Poems* lxxv. 36 My clype, my vnspaynit gyane With moderis milk ȝit in ȝour mychane. †**Unspa·ng,** *v. Obs.* [UN-[2] 4 b.] *trans.* To detach (horses) from a cart. **1580** HOLLYBAND *Treas. Fr. Tong*, *Desteler les chevaux*, to lose horses, or vnspang them from the carte. **1611** COTGR. s.v. *Desteler*. **Unspa·ngled,** *ppl. a.* (UN-[1] 8.) **1628** QUARLES *Argalus & P.* I. Wks. (Grosart) III. 251/1 Whenas the universall shade Of the unspangled heaven..had made An utter darknesse.

**Unspa·r,** *v.* [UN-[2] 3. Cf. Du. *ontsperren*, OHG. *intsperran*, *-en* (MHG. *ent-*, *ensperren*).] *trans.* To unbar (a door, etc.); to open.

*c* **1200** ORMIN 12158 Cristess þohht wass sperrd swa wel.. Þatt naness kinness sinnfull lusst Ne mihhte itt nære unnsperrenn. *a* **1225** *Ancr. R.* 70 Heo schal habben leaue to openen [*MS. B.* unsperren] hire þurl enes oðer twies. **1393** LANGL. *P. Pl.* C. XXI. 89 The blood sprang doun by þe sper, and vnsperrede þe knyghtes eyen. *Ibid.* 272 A spirit ..bit vnsperre þe ȝates. *a* **1542** WYATT in *Tottel's Misc.* (Arb.) 225 Lyke as the birde within the cage enclosed, The dore vnsparred, her foe the hawke without. **1599** T. M[OUFET] *Silkwormes* 12 How feately then vnsparred she the doore. **1611** COTGR., *Desverouiller vn huis*, to..vnsparre a doore. **1808** SCOTT *Marm.* I. iv, Forty yeomen.. The lofty palisade unsparr'd And let the drawbridge fall. **Unspa·rable,** *a.* (UN-[1] 7 b.) *c* **1449** PECOCK *Repr.* V. vii. 519 Sithen it is profitable..and vnsparable that such a meyr and such a bischop shulden be in tyme comyng.

**Unspa·red,** *ppl. a.* [UN-[1] 8. Cf. MDu. *ongespaert* (Du. *ongespaard*), MLG. *ungesparet*, MHG. (and G.) *ungespart*; ON. *úsparðr* (Sw. *ospard*, Da. *usparet*, dial. *uspard*).]

**1.** Not spared or reserved. † Also in loose const., without sparing, unsparingly.

**13..** *St. Erkenwolde* 335 in Horstm. *Altengl. Leg.* (1881) 273 With vnsparid murthe. **1535** STEWART *Cron. Scot.* (Rolls) I. 504 Euerilk man, baith ill and gude vnspaird, As he had wrocht, sall get ane just rewaird. **1667** MILTON *P. L.* X. 606 Thou therefore..whatever thing The Sithe of Time mowes down, devour unspar'd. **1881** RUSKIN *Love's Meinie* iii. § 87 Unspared labour, and attentive skill.

†**2.** Indispensable. *Obs.*—[1]

**1614** T. ADAMS *Physicke fr. Heaven* Wks. (1629) 291 No Physitian then cures of himselfe; no more then the hand feedes the mouth;..though the Physitian and the hand be vnspared instruments to their seuerall purposes.

†**Unspa·rely,** *adv. Obs.* [UN-[1] 11. Cf. ON. *úsparliga* (MSw. *osparlika*).] Unsparingly.

*a* **1225** *Juliana* 59 Heo as þe deouel spurede ham to donne, dude hit unsparliche. **13..** *Gaw. & Gr. Knt.* 979 Chefly þay asken Spycez, þat vn-sparely men speded hom to bryng. ? *a* **1400** *Morte Arth.* 235 Thane spyces vn-sparyly þay spendyde there-aftyre. *Ibid.* 3160 Thus they..Spendis vnsparely, þat sparede was lange.

**Unspa·ring,** *ppl. a.* [UN-[1] 10.]

**1.** Showing no forbearance or mercy.

*a* **1586** SIDNEY *Arcadia* III. vii, The pittilesse launce.. (angry with being broken)..full of unsparing splinters, lighted upon that face. **1599** DANIEL *Musoph.* 323 No, no, vnsparing Time will prowdly send A warrant unto Wrath. **1649** MILTON *Eikon.* Pref. C, The unsparing Sword of Justice. **1770** GLOVER *Leonidas* (ed. 5) VI. 166 Unsparing Mars Heap'd carnage round thee. **1781** COWPER *Lett.* 2 Apr., Men of a rough and unsparing address. **1818** MITFORD *Hist. Greece* V. 155 Unsparing of himself, he seems however to have been strongly disposed to be considerate of others. **1844** KINGLAKE *Eothen* viii, Cool, decisive in manner, unsparing of enemies. **1869** TOZER *Highl. Turkey* II. 244 His unsparing, merciless character,..never diverted from its fell purpose.

**2.** Not niggardly; liberal, lavish.

**1667** MILTON *P. L.* V. 344 Fruit of all kindes..She gathers, ..and on the board Heaps with unsparing hand. **1736** THOMSON *Liberty* V. 584 Unsparing love Their endless treasure, and their deeds their praise. **1781** COWPER *Expost.* 677 Gratitude and temp'rance in our use Of what he gives, unsparing and profuse. **1819** SHELLEY *Cyclops* 167 See, here are sheep,..Here are unsparing cheeses of pressed milk. **1856** *N. Brit. Rev.* XXVI. 23 The four or five ideas..are.. turned over and over again with so unsparing a profuseness, that [etc.].

Hence **Unspa·ringness.**

**1818** MITFORD *Hist. Greece* V. 426 His extraordinary.. successes, but especially his profuse unsparingness of himself,..had [etc.].

**Unspa·ringly,** *adv.* (UN-[1] 11. Cf. prec.)

*a* **1500** *Bernardus de cura rei fam.* (1870) 2 Þe man þat spendis Vnsparandly mar þan his rent extendis. *a* **1631** DONNE *Lament. Jeremy* II. ii, The Lord unsparingly hath swallowed All Jacobs dwellings. **1805** SOUTHEY in Robberds *Mem. W. Taylor* (1843) II. 85, I am squeezing out the whey, and shall cut out unsparingly. **1849** MACAULAY *Hist. Eng.* I. I. 98 On the chief ministers..the vengeance of the nation was unsparingly wreaked.

**Unspa·rkling,** *ppl. a.* (UN-[1] 8.) [**1775** ASH.] **1816** WILSON *Misc. Poems* 293 Unsparkling eyes where smiles appear More mournful far than many a tear. **1895** W. M. ROSSETTI *D. G. Rossetti* I. 171 Tall, finely formed, with.. greenish-blue unsparkling eyes. †**Unspa·rpled,** *ppl. a. Sc.* [UN-[1] 8.] Undivided. **1508** *Reg. Privy Seal Scotl.* I. 253/1 For keping of his heretage..unsparpalit and unanalyt in favouris of his sone. **Unspa·tial,** *a.* (UN-[1] 7.) **1865** J. GROTE *Moral Ideals* (1876) 370 Concurrently..there is going on thought in our spiritual, unspatial, being. **1884** tr. *Lotze's Metaph.* 185 Every real Thing..would have to be itself infinitely divisible into unspatial multiplicities.

**Unspaw·ned,** *ppl. a.* (UN-[1] 8.)

[**1775** ASH.] **1814** *Monthly Mag.* XXXVII. 335 She instant resolv'd such a gala to give, As thro' ages unspawn'd should continue to live. **1847** STODDART *Angler's Comp.* 214 The female parr..retaining..the unspawned ova. **1884** *St. James' Gaz.* 11 Jan. 4 The death of..many unspawned fish.

**Unspea·k,** *v.* (UN-[2] 3.) **1605** SHAKS. *Macb.* IV. iii. 123 Euen now I put my selfe to thy Direction, and Vnspeake mine owne detraction. **1615** G. WITHER *Fidelia* 1222, I will vnspeake againe what is mis-spoken. **Unspeak·abi·lity.** (UN-[1] 12. Cf. next.) **1845** CARLYLE *Cromwell* (1871) II. 93 No modern reader can conceive the..unspeakability of this fact.

**Unspea·kable,** *a.*, *sb.*, and *adv.* [UN-[1] 7 b and 5 b.]

**1.** Incapable of being expressed in words; inexpressible, indescribable, ineffable.

*a* **1400** *Hampole's Wks.* (1895) I. 199 Þe vnspekeabill & þe vnmesurabill charite, bothe of þe ffadire and of þe sone. *a* **1425** tr. *Arderne's Treat. Fistula*, etc. 37 It may neuer be cured..but if it plese god..for to help wiþ his vnspekeable vertu. *c* **1445** PECOCK *Donet* 84 A þing..fer aboue alle creaturis speche vnspekable. **1534** MORE *Treat. Passion* Wks. 1346/1 It is chaunged by an vnspeakeable woorking, although it seme bread to vs that be weake. *a* **1586** SIDNEY *Arcadia* I. i, The flocke of unspeakeable vertues laid up.. in that best builded folde. **1615** W. LAWSON *Country Housew. Gard.* (1626) 6 It is vnspeakable, what fatnesse is brought to low grounds by Inundations of waters. **1675** TRAHERNE *Chr. Ethics* 204 Those bodies are superadded, certainly for unspeakable and most glorious ends. **1754** *Connoisseur* No. 6 ¶ 4, I had the unspeakable mortification to see my favours sometimes not inserted. **1841** W. SPALDING *Italy & It. Isl.* II. 57 The laws and the system of society conspired together to work unspeakable evils. **1871** MORLEY *Carlyle* in *Crit. Misc.* Ser. I. 216 He had the unspeakable advantage of being..respectable.

*absol.* **1831** CARLYLE *Sart. Res.* II. ix, In what words.. [can we] speak even afar-off of the unspeakable?

**b.** *spec.* Indescribably or inexpressibly bad or objectionable.

Freq. of the Turk, after quot. 1876. Also *absol.*

**1831** CARLYLE in *Westm. Rev.* July 6 How they sailed.. into Paynim land; fought with that unspeakable Turk, King Machabol. **1843** — *Past & Pr.* I. iii, How ye came among us, in your cruel armed blindness, ye unspeakable County Yeomanry! **1876** — *Let.* in *Mem.* (1881) II. 311 The unspeakable Turk should be immediately struck out of the question, and the country left to honest European guidance. **1896** *Advance* (Chicago) 30 Jan. 153/1 We were..even more guilty than the Unspeakable himself. **1902** CROSLAND (*title*), The Unspeakable Scot.

**c.** *sb.* An ineffable being.

**1843** CARLYLE *Past & Pr.* III. xv, Through all thy.. melancholy Business and Cant, there does shine the presence of a Primeval Unspeakable.

**2.** Incapable of being spoken or uttered; that may not be spoken.

**1568** H. B. tr. *P. Martyr, Ep. Rom.* 224 They are called vnspeakeable sighes, for that we speake not expressedlye what the spirite asketh. **1611** BIBLE 2 *Cor.* xii. 4 He.. heard vnspeakeable wordes, which it is not lawfull for a man to vtter. **1770** GLOVER *Leonidas* (ed. 5) x. 574 Leonidas, whose looks Declar'd unspeakable applause.

**3.** *U.S.* Unwilling or unable to speak.

**1888** *Advance* (Chicago) 29 Nov., The distinguished but unspeakable witness. **1890** LOWELL *Lett.* (1894) II. 465 My dog..looks up at me as who should say, 'You are become unspeakable as one of us, poor old fellow!'

**4.** *adv.* Unspeakably, indescribably.

**1635** PAGITT *Christianogr.* 34 Beyond the Land of Cathaie, which they prayse to be civill, and unspeakable rich. **1657** BAXTER *Call to Unconverted* (1660) 59 How certainly and unspeakable happy you may be if you will.

Hence **Unspea·kableness.**

*a* **1586** SIDNEY *Arcadia* I. xi, The unspeakeablenes of his griefe. **1657** J. Smith *Myst. Rhet.* 54 That we may rather conceive the unspeakablenesse then the untruth of the relation. **1691** Bunyan (*title*), The Greatness of the Soul, and unspeakableness of the loss thereof.

**Unspea·kably,** *adv.* [f. prec.] Unutterably, indescribably.

**1526** *Pilgr. Perf.* (W. de W. 1531) 154 The clere syght of fayth..gyueth more ioye vnspekably to the contemplatyue seruauntes of god, than [etc.]. **1597** Hooker *Eccl. Pol.* v. liv. § 8 God hath in Christ vnspeakablie glorified the nobler ..part of our nature. **1647** H. More *Song of Soul* Notes 358 Some inhabit God himself, who is unspeakably infinite. **1681** Flavel *Meth. Grace* x. 224 It is unspeakably delightful. **1705** *Phil. Trans.* XXV. 1910 A Confluence..of unspeakably small Salt Particles. **1754** Edwards *Freed. Will* iv. v. 226 Man is..unspeakably different from a meer Machine. **1842** Dickens *Amer. Notes* (1850) 150/1 The effect is said to be unspeakably absurd. **1871** Le Fanu *Rose & Key* II. 298 It was unspeakably provoking.

**Unspea·king,** *vbl. sb.* (Un-1 13.) **1860** Ruskin *Mod. Paint.* V. 164 False speaking [is] unspeaking,—on the negative side of silence.

**Unspea·king,** *ppl. a.* [Un-1 10. Cf. OE. *unsprecende*, OFris. *unsprekand*, MDu. *onsprekende* (obs. Du. *onsprekend*), OHG. *unsprëchente* (MHG. *unsprëchende*) in sense 2 (chiefly of children).]

†1. Unspeakable, ineffable. *Obs.*—1

**1340** *Ayenb.* 266 Ich yzez þe ilke onspekynde an[d] ontodelinde mageste of þe holy trinyte.

2. Not speaking; unable to speak. Also *fig.*

**1382** Wyclif *Job* xxxviii. 9 With clothis of vnspekende childhed. — *Ps.* viii. 3 Of the mouth of vnspekende childer.. thou performedist preising. **1611** Shaks. *Cymb.* v. v. 178 His description Prou'd vs vnspeaking sottes. **1796** Eliza Hamilton *Lett. Hindoo Rajah* (1811) II. 81 All was placid uniformity, and unspeaking regularity of feature. **1811** Shelley *Mother & Son* iii, The proofs of an unspeaking sorrow dwelt Within her ghastly hollowness of eye.

**†Unspea·r,** *v.*1 *Obs.* [Un-2 4 + Spear *v.*1] *trans.* To unbar; to open.

*c* **1250** *Gen. & Ex.* 25 Quhu lucifer..held hem sperd in helles male til god..unspered al ðe fendes sped. **1377** Langl. *P. Pl.* B. xviii. 259, I here..How a spirit speketh to helle & bit vnspere þe ȝatis. *c* **1400** *Laud Troy Bk.* 1039 When it was with-inne ther lippes, Faste to-gedur hit hem grippes, That thei myȝt not her mouth vn-spere. *c* **1430** Lydg. *Min. Poems* (Percy Soc.) 54 Late at eve thou wolt unspere the gate. *c* **1450** Capgrave *Life St. Aug.* 20 Poncian vnsperd þe bok and say wel þat it was a bok longing to cristen feith.

**Unspear,** *v.*2 [Un-2 4 b + Spear *v.*2] *trans.* To free from being transfixed **1859** Geo. Eliot *Adam Bede* xxxii, Mrs. Poyser,..unspearing her knitting, began to knit again with her usual rapidity.

**Unspe·cialized,** *ppl. a.* (Un-1 8.)

**1874** E. D. Cope *Orig. Fittest* xviii. (1887) 398 The Doctrine of the Unspecialized. **1886** G. Allen *Maimie's Sake* xv, A vague flood of unspecialized emotion. **1902** S. & B. Webb *Hist. Trade Unionism* (ed. 5) Introd. p. x, The general mass of unskilled and unspecialised labour.

**Unspe·cie.** (Un-1 12 b.) **1711** *Lond. Gaz.* No. 4822/4, 13 unspecie Exchequer Bills, of 100 *l.* each. *Ibid.* No. 4825.

**Unspeci·fic,** *a.* (Un-1 7.)

**1807** W. Coxe *Hist. House of Austria* II. 713 It is no wonder so unspecific a declaration..should not be followed by any important consequence. **1822–7** Good *Study Med.* (1829) III. 417 An incidental and unspecific irritation of the prepuce. **1884** *Solicitors' Jrnl.* 8 Nov. 26/2 A contract for the sale of unspecific goods.

**†Unspeci·ficate,** *a.* and *sb.* *Obs.* [Un-1 7, 12.]

1. *adj.* (See quot.)

**1674** *Phil. Trans.* IX. 70 This Aerial Salt,..whilst in the Air, is altogether un-specificate, I mean, freed from all Union with..any Seminal principle.

2. *spec.* Unsexed. Also as *sb.*

**1734** *Prompter* 19 Nov. 2/1 It is a Prodigy to see an Actor, General, Plastick, and unspecificate. *Ibid.* 4 Dec. 2/1 One of these Vocal Unspecificates.

**†Unspeci·ficated,** *ppl. a.* *Obs.* [Un-1 8.] = prec. 1.

**1651** French *Distill.* v. 162 Whether this *primum ens salium* be so unspecificated.., or no, it matters not much. **1675** E. W[ilson] *Spadacrene Dunelm.* 65 There are unspecificated acids in the humours of our Body.

**Unspe·cified,** *ppl. a.* (Un-1 8.)

**1624** Heywood *Gunaik.* ix. 427, I desire to leave nothing unspecified, or not remembered in this worke. *a* **1661** Fuller *Worthies, London* ii. (1662) 204 The laxity of so populous a place leaving them as unspecified as it found them. **1883** *Specif. Alnwick & Cornhill Railway* 14 Facilitating the construction of any unspecified works.

**Unspe·cked,** *ppl. a.* (Un-1 8.)

[**1775** Ash.] **1781** Cowper *Truth* 281 A demeanour holy and unspecked. **1868** Geo. Eliot *Sp. Gipsy* 234 Gazing from his narrow shoal of sand On the unspecked round of blue and blue.

**Unspe·ckled,** *ppl. a.* (Un-1 8.) **1570** Levins *Manip.* 50 Vnspeckled, *immaculatus.* [**1775** Ash.] **1887** Morris *Odyss.* x. 525 A sheep of black unspeckled, of all thy flock most fair. **†Unspe·ctable,** *a.* *Obs.* [Un-1 7 b, 5 b.] Incapable of being regarded. **1502** Atkynson tr. *De Imitatione* iii. iii. (1893) 197 The vnspectable & inestymable Ioy in heuen. **1526** *Pilgr. Perf.* (W. de W. 1531) 16 We be not worthy to come to that vnspectable glory.

**Unspe·ctacled,** (*ppl.*) *a.* (Un-1 8, 9.)

**1791** Huddesford *Salmag.* 140 Why did your will the Pylian chief decree Three centuries unspectacled to see. **1824** Scott *St. Ronan's* xiv, Many a nose, spectacled and unspectacled, was popped out of the adjoining windows. **1893** *Atlantic Monthly* Feb. 146/2 She pored over them with unspectacled eyes.

**Unspe·culating,** *ppl. a.* (Un-1 10.) **1828** Pusey *Hist. Enq.* i. 109 A recurrence to practical and unspeculating Christianity.

**Unspe·culative,** *a.* (Un-1 7.)

**1659** *Gentl. Calling* 40 Their whole time..to be taken up in other unspeculative Exercises. **1674** *Govt. Tongue* 160 Some unspeculative men may not have the skill to examine their assertions. **1874** J. Donaldson *Apost. Fathers* 51 This unspeculative character of the apostolic teaching. **1891** T. Hardy *Tess* xii, She obeyed the signal to wait for him with unspeculative repose.

**Unspe·d,** *ppl. a.* [Un-1 8 b.] a. Not having succeeded in an errand or effort. b. Not accomplished or discharged; not brought to a successful result or issue.

*a* **1300** *Cursor M.* 17596 For-þi þaa Iuus war full medd, Þair sandes come again vn-spedd. **1390** Gower *Conf.* III. 293 So was he come ayein unsped. *c* **1450** *Myrr. our Ladye* 82 That prayer..is neuer lefte vnspedde. *a* **1533** Ld. Berners *Gold. Bk. M. Aurel.* xxxviii. (1536) 67 b, Nor for all the affaires of his house, he wolde not leaue one of thempire vnsped. *a* **1568** in *Bannatyne MS.* (Hunter. Cl.) 617/8 Onsped speche bettir vnspokin be. **1624** Quarles *Job* xiii. xxiv, To Athens, gown'd, he goes, and..Returnes unsped. **1717** Garth *Ovid's Met.* xiv. (1732) 477 Thus Diomedes Venulus withdraws; Unsped the Service of the common Cause. **1895** R. Bridges *Ode to Music* iv. iii, When the winds fatigued..Have left the drooping banks unsped.

**Unspee·chful,** *a.* (Un-1 7.) **1853** Faber *All for Jesus* (1854) 365 Lighting up their land of pain and unspeechful expectation.

**†Unspee·d.** *Obs.* [OE. *unspéd* (Un-1 12), = WFris. *on-*, *ûnspoed*, MDu. *onspoet* (Du. *onspoed*), OS. *unspôd* (MLG. *unspôt*), OHG. *unspuot*, *-spuet*, chiefly in sense 2. Cf. Wanspeed.]

1. Poverty. (OE. only.)

*c* **950** *Lindisf. Gosp.* Mark xii. 44 Ðios..of unspoed hire alle ða ðe hæfde sende. *c* **1000** *Ags. Ps.* (Spelman) lxxxvii. 9 Eaȝan mine sarȝodon for unspeda [L. *inopia*].

2. Lack of good speed or success; misfortune, detriment, harm.

*a* **1300** *Cursor M.* 10468 If þou mai na barns brede, Quam wites þou þin aune vnspede? *Ibid.* 15420 Bot to þaim þat þe cheping did, it fel to mikel vnspede. **14..** *Northern Passion* (MS. I.) 1214 Ȝet þei maden at vnspede in his riht hand to halde a rede. *c* **1440** *Lay Folks Mass Bk.* (MS. C.) 88 To þe priest herken þan Hys office.., And answere þereto.., Or on a boke þy-selfe it rede, I wate þerfore nane unspede.

3. Unprofitable labour.

*a* **1300** *Cursor M.* 4230 Bot al his quainning for to rede Or for to spek, it war vn-spede.

**†Unspee·dful,** *a.* *Obs.* [Un-1 7.] Unprofitable; of no avail.

*a* **1340** Hampole *Psalter* cxxviii. 4 When þei..seme vnspedful in all þat þei did here. *c* **1374** Chaucer *Boeth.* v. pr. vi. (1868) 178 Prayeres, þat ne mowen nat ben vnspedful..whan þei ben ryȝtful. *c* **1440** *Jacob's Well* 184 Ȝif þis handyl be wrong, it is vnspedefull to werke wyth. **1482** *Monk of Evesham* (Arb.) 29 Thy contynual prayer..may not be onspedeful before the presens and goodnes of god. **1570** Levins *Manip.* 186 Vnspeedful, *inexpeditus.*

**Unspee·dy,** *a.* [OE. *unspédig* (Un-1 7), = MDu. *onspoedich* (Du. *-spoedig*), OHG. *unspuotîg.* Cf. Wanspeedy *a.*]

†1. Poor, indigent. (OE. only.) *Obs.*

*c* **893** K. Ælfred *Oros.* i. i. § 23 Þa ricostan men drincað myran meolc, & þa unspediȝan & þa þeowan drincað medo. *c* **1000** Ælfric *Hom.* I. 578 He ȝeendebyrde þone unspediȝan fiscere ætforan ðam rican casere.

†b. Of land: Barren, unproductive. *Obs.*—1

*a* **1000** *Genesis* 962 Ȝesæton þa æfter synne sorȝfulre land, eard & eðyl unspediȝran.

†2. Unprofitable; unsuccessful.

*a* **1300** *E. E. Psalter* lxxxviii. 34 Ne wemme mi witeworde, and þat forthga Of mi lippes, vnspedy noght make þa. *a* **1340** Hampole *Psalter* xvi. 14 Make þaim vnspedy and kast þaim down. *c* **1449** Pecock *Repr.* i. xvi. 89 The werk ther of schulde be the vnsauerer and the vnspedier.

3. Slow, sluggish. *rare.*

**1615** G. Sandys *Trav.* 117 The water..passing along with a mute and vnspeedy current.

**Unspee·red,** *ppl. a.* Latterly *Sc.* [Un-1 8.] Unasked; without inquiry. Also with *at.*

**13..** *Gaw. & Gr. Knt.* 918 Wich spede is in speche, vnspurd may we lerne. *a* **1568** in *Bannatyne MS.* (Hunter. Club) 641/44 Than suld I..cum to yow, I ken the gait onsperd. **1599** Jas. I Βασιλ. Δωρον Ep. Ded., It will not come vncalled, neither speake vnspeered at.

**Unspe·ll,** *v.* [Un-2 3.]

1. *trans.* To undo or dissolve (a spell).

**1611** Cotgr., *Descharmer*, to vncharme, vnspell, frustrate a charme. **1671** Tuke *Adv. 5 Hours* v. (ed. 3) 94 *Her.* Sure w'are enchanted, and all we see's illusion. *Cam.* Allow me, Henrique, to unspel these Charms.

2. To free from a spell.

**1635** Quarles *Embl.* iv. xv, Ah, if my voyce could, Orpheus-like, unspell My poore Eurydice, my soul, from hell. **1681** Dryden (Tate) *Abs. & Achit.* ii. 117 Such Practices as These, too gross to lye Long unobserv'd,..The more judicious Israelites Unspell'd, Though still the Charm the giddy Rabble held. **1777** Johnson *Let. to Mrs. Thrale* 6 Oct., I am glad Master unspelled you, and run you all on rocks. **1890** *Handbk. Folklore* (ed. Gomme) 132 A prince is transformed into a loathsome beast;..he is unspelled and they marry.

†3. To decipher, read. *Obs.*—1

**1665** Sergeant in Digby *Nat. Bodies* *4 Even that great Soule, which fathomes th' Universe, Unspells the Heaven's broad volume.

4. (See quot.)

**1846** *Printing Apparatus for Amateurs* 34 In the process of distributing [the type] the word is unspelt, beginning with the first letter of the word.

Hence **Unspe·lling** *vbl. sb.* Also *attrib.*

**1897** A. Nutt in K. Meyer *Voy. Bran* II. 16 Manawyddan obtains..the unspelling of the land. **1902** — *Leg. Holy Grail* 52 The unspelling theme. *Ibid.* 53 In Crestien..it is subordinated to the unspelling quest.

**Unspe·llable,** *a.* (Un-1 7 b.)

**1852** Mundy *Antipodes* II. 97 Unspellable intonations ..supply the place of the letters. **1872** 'Mark Twain' *Roughing it* xxiv, A Spanish saddle,..furnished with the ungainly sole-leather covering with the unspellable name.

**Unspe·lled,** *ppl. a.* [Un-1 8.] Not put under a spell.

**1684** Tate *Medea to Jason* 12 No doubt but he.., with the fierce Bulls, unspell'd had fought. **1806** M. A. Shee *Rhymes Art* 27 While yet unspell'd, unplighted you remain, Pause, ere you join the art-enamour'd train.

**Unspe·lt,** *ppl. a.* (Un-1 8 b.) **1892** Meredith *Sage Enamoured* i, Her eyes were the sweet world desired of souls, With something of a wavering line unspelt. **†Unspen,** *v.* *Obs.*—1 [Un-2 3 + Spen *v.*] *trans.* To release. *a* **1225** *Ancr. R.* 158 Seint Johan baptiste..ine his iborenesse unspende [*v.r.* unspennede] his feder tunge into prophecie.

**Unspe·ndable,** *a.* (Un-1 7 b.) **1876** Mrs. Whitney *Sights & Ins.* III. xiv. 263 Every day a large piece of unspendable delight in the anticipation,..to last us [etc.].

**† Unspe·nded,** obs. var. Unspent *ppl. a.*

*c* **1440** *York Myst.* xxv. 450 Haue [= half] my gud I haue vnspendid Poure folke to geue it till. **1533** Bellenden *Livy* iii. xxv. (S.T.S.) II. 48 He was fer rvn in ȝeris, and few dayis vnspendit of his live. **1564** *Wills & Inv. N. C* (Surtees, 1835) I. 225 So mutch hay vnspended as is valud to ijs.

**Unspe·nt,** *ppl. a.* [Un-1 8 b.]

1. Not expended: not employed or used.

**1466** *Mann. & Househ. Exp.* (Roxb.) 326 He ad of myn onspente in is and, vj.s. viij.d. **1483** in *Somerset Med. Wills* (1901) 239 As moch as than shal..remayne unspent of the seid xij torches. **1550** Crowley *Last Trump* 269 If ought remayne vnspent Upon thyne owne necessity. **1632** Lithgow *Trav.* vii. 313 The French men had only left unspent..three-score and nine Chickens of Gold. **1674** Hobbes *Odyssey* (ed. 2) 9 We had Wine enough as yet unspent. **1745** in Picton *L'pool Munic. Rec.* (1886) II. 110 A proportionable part of what remains unspent. **1895** *Westm. Gaz.* 24 May 5/2 The revolver..contained one spent and five unspent cartridges. **1899** *Parlt. Debates* LXVII. 554/2 What [he].. pressed was the use of the unspent balance for that purpose.

2. Unexhausted; not used up.

*c* **1611** Chapman *Iliad* xiv. 344 For fervour of his unspent strength. **1663** Dryden *Ep. to Charleton* 36 Whose Fame.. Flies like the nimble journeys of the Light; And is, like that, unspent too in its flight. **1732** Pope *Ess. Man* i. 274 All are but parts of one stupendous whole,..That..extends thro' all extent, Spreads undivided, operates unspent. **1770** Glover *Leonidas* (ed. 5) xii. 355 He impell'd His spear. The point with violence unspent..reach'd the Persian's throat. **1799** Cowper *Castaway* 39 So long he, with unspent pow'r, His destiny repell'd. **1857** Emerson *Poems*, '*Give all to Love*' ii, High and more high It dives into noon, With wing unspent.

**Unsphe·re,** *v.* [Un-2 5.] *trans.* To remove (a star, etc.) from its sphere. Also in fig. context.

**1611** Shaks. *Wint. T.* i. ii. 48 Though you would seek t'vnsphere the Stars with Oaths. **1643** Howell *Parab. reflect. Times* 5 Touching the malignant Planets..I put them over to you, that..they may be unspher'd or extinguished. **1796** C. Anstey *Pleaders' Guide* (1803) 124 Th' adventrous Engineer Who swore he would the Earth unsphere,..Give him but where to set his foot. **1820** Milman *Fall Jerus.* 117 If ye have seen the moon unsphered, And the stars fall. **1857** P. Freeman *Princ. Div. Serv.* II. 57 Thus too did it supply..a new centre or centres for the gravitation of its mighty forces..in lieu of that which had been, so to speak, unsphered.

*fig.* **1632** Milton *Penseroso* 88 Where I may..unsphear The spirit of Plato. **1806** H. K. White *Fragments* vi, Mine ear Longs for some air of peace,..That may the spirit from its cell unsphere. **1882** J. Brown *Horæ Subs.* 3rd Ser. 4 Many have been the attempts to unsphere the spirit of a joke and make it tell its secret.

Hence **Unsphe·red** *ppl. a.*

**1598** Chapman *Hero & Leander* iii. 186 Thou..That..with the wings Of thy vnspheared flame visitst the springs Of spirits immortall. **1833** H. Coleridge *Poems* I. 41 Like a spectre of an age departed, Or unsphered Angel woefully astray—She glides along. **1849** M. Arnold *New Sirens* 251 The sunk eyes, the wailing tone, Of unspher'd, discrowned creatures.

**Unspi·able,** *a.* (Un-1 7 b.) **1615** Sylvester *Job Triumph.* i. 367 Him would I seek..Whose works are great,.. Unspiable, Unspeakable by Man. **Unspi·ced,** *ppl. a.* (Un-1 8.) **1655** Moufet & Bennet *Health's Improv.* vi. 48 A great difference..betwixt fri'd meats and bak't meats, spiced and unspiced, salt and fresh. **1899** *Westm. Gaz.* 11 Aug. 8/1 There are English firms which export the genuine unspiced article in tins.

**Unspie·d,** *ppl. a.* (Un-1 8.)

**14..** *Chaucer's Troylus* iv. 1457 (Harl. MS.), It is ful hard to halten vnspied Bifor a crepul. *a* **1542** Wyatt '*Take heed by time*' v, To love unspied is but a hap; Therefore, take heed! **1561** Norton & Sackv. *Gorboduc* i. ii. 317 Traiterous corrupters of their pliant youthe Shall have unspied a muche more free accesse. **1624** Quarles *Sion's Elegies* i xxii, Thinke you to flourish euer? and (vnspide) To shoot the flowers of your fruitlesse pride. **1667** Milton *P. L.* iv. 529 I must walk round This Garden, and no corner leave unspi'd. *a* **1740** Tickell *Misc., Fatal Curiosity* 5, I..went prepared to pry,..Resolv'd to find some fault before unspy'd. **1798** in A. D. Coleridge *Eton in Fourties* (1896) 14 When waving fresh each woolly wing, That..serv'd..to hold unknown, unspied, A loaf or pudding in.

**Unspi·ke,** *v.* [Un-2 3, 4 b.]

1. *trans.* To extract a spike from (a cannon).

**1680** *Exact Jrnl. Siege Tangier* 6 The Moors took our Guns.., and unspik'd them, & clear'd them. **1842** R. Burn *Naval & Mil. Dict.* (1852) 118/2 *Désenclouer*, to unspike a piece of ordnance. *c* **1860** H. Stuart *Seaman's Catech.* 14 Suppose your gun is spiked.., how will you unspike it?

2. To release by the removal of a spike.

**1846** *Edin. Rev.* Oct. 504 In this case the iron bar [*sc.* rail], worn thin and unspiked, gets detached from the plank.

**Unspi·ked,** *ppl. a.* (Un-1 8.) [**1775** Ash.] **1902** *Daily Chron.* 16 July 8/6 Six [rail-] chairs..had been left unspiked.

1904 *Westm. Gaz.* 8 Sept. 7/1 They..[captured 97] cannon, mostly unspiked. **Unspi·llable,** *a.* (Un-[1] 7 b.) 1885 *Chamb. Jrnl.* 560 Our readers will be acquainted with the unspillable ink-bottle.

**Unspi·lled, -spi·lt,** *ppl. a.* (Un-[1] 8, 8 b. Cf. MDa. and Da. *uspildt.*)

1573 Tusser *Husb.* (1878) 35 Then haue of thine owne, without lending vnspilt, what followeth needfull, here learne if thou wilt. 1641 in Rushw. *Hist. Coll.* (1692) I. 217 The very Blood that runs unspilt in our Veins. 1643 Denham *Cooper's H* (1668) 7 That bloud, which thou and thy great Grandsire shed,..Had been unspilt. 1837 Dickens *Pickw.* v, The first care of the two unspilt friends was to extricate their unfortunate companions from their bed of quickset. 1877 Browning *La Saisiaz* 369 Only grant my soul may carry high through death her cup unspilled.

**Unspi·n,** *v.* (Un-[2] 3. Cf. Du. *ontspinnen.*)

a 1585 in Holinshed *Chron.* II. 416/1 Oh cruel fates! the which so soone, his vitall thred vnsponne. 1638 Mayne *Lucian* (1664) 304 Is't not in your power to change, and unspinne their decrees? 1638 N. Whiting *Albino & Bellama* 1176 My teeming fancy strives..to..make those garden-minutes see the sun Entombed in darkness, and the earth unspun Ere they expire. a 1703 J. Pomfret *Last Epiphany* vi, Whilst backward all the Threads shall haste to be unspun. 1845 Mozley *Ess.* (1878) II. 102 The web was respun, that it might be unspun again.

**Unspi·rit,** *v.* [Un-[2] 4.] *trans.* To deprive of spirit.

1607 B. Jonson *Volpone* iii. v, I am unmask'd, unspirited, undone. 1647 Trapp *Marrow Gd. Authors* in *Comm. Ep.* 604 We may not neglect the body,..maserate and unspirit our selves overmuch. 1687 Norris *Coll. Misc.* (1699) 367 Nor did I ever think that it could be in the Power of any Temporal loss, so much to discompose and unspirit my Soul.

**Unspi·rited,** *ppl. a.* [Un-[1] 8.] Destitute of spirit; spiritless.

1621 Fletcher *Thierry & Theod.* ii. i, A poor, cold, unspirited, unmanner'd..fool. 1649 Arnway *Tablet* 74 Leave no stone unmoov'd, to cousen an unspirited (and so apt to be unchristen'd) Nation into the way..of the Alcoran. 1751 Smollett *Per. Pick.* lxxxv, The new productions of the stage,..generally unspirited and insipid.

Hence **Unspi·ritedness.**

1669 Owen *Exp. Ps. cxxx,* 15 Vnspiritedness and disability unto Duty, in doing or suffering.

**Unspi·ritual,** *a.* (Un-[1] 7.)

1643 Milton *Divorce* 3, I see it the hope of good men, that those irregular and unspirituall Courts have spun their utmost date in this Land. 1679 Puller *Moder. Ch. Eng.* 494 These Divisions (the Character of a Carnal and Unspiritual Temper)..dishonour the Protestant Cause. 1818 Byron *Ch. Har.* iv. cxxv, Circumstance, that unspiritual god and miscreator. 1872 Liddon *Elem. Relig.* v. 175 Prayer ceases to be itself, by degenerating..into a mechanical and unspiritual routine.

Hence **Unspi·ritually** *adv.*; **-ness.**

1642 D. Rogers *Naaman* 476 Through that unspiritualnesse of our heart. 1669 Owen *Expos. Ps. cxxx,* 352 The more spiritual any man is, the more he sees of his unspiritualness in his spiritual Duties. 1863 H. Allon *Mem. J. Sherman* Coll. Life i. 53 Unspiritualness had generated scepticism. 1871 Tylor *Prim. Cult.* II. 325 Those..may say..that I have written..unspiritually of spiritual things.

**Unspiritua·lity.** (Un-[1] 12, or f. prec.) 1842 Sara Coleridge in Coleridge *Aids Refl.* App. C. (1843) II. 384 Calvin..missed this truth..neither from natural inability, nor from unspirituality, nor from a tendency to rationalism, but [etc.]. 1863 Grosart *Small Sins* 27 Despondent..through..coldness, deadness, unrealness, unspirituality.

**Unspi·ritualize,** *v.* [Un-[2] 6 c.] *trans.* To divest of spiritual qualities.

a 1716 South *Serm.* (1727) VI. 243 Enjoyments..such as..will by Degrees certainly indispose, and unspiritualize the Mind. 1846 Hawthorne *Old Manse* ii. 115 Those evil habits..which unspiritualize man's nature. 1851 Ruskin *Mod. Paint.* II. iii. ii. v. § 17, I recollect no single instance of a naked angel that does not look..unspiritualized. 1881 H. Drummond *Ideal Life* (1897) 133 God would never unspiritualise three-fourths of man's active life by work, if work were work, and nothing more.

**Unspi·ritualized,** *ppl. a.* [Un-[1] 8.] Not made spiritual. 1816 Coleridge *Lay Serm.* (1839) 291 The idolism of the unspiritualized understanding. 1878 T. Sinclair *Mount* v. 10- The unspiritualised 'man of land,' when left to his instincts, is sufficiently marked in history the slave-maker of his fellows.

**Unspi·t,** *v.* [Un-[2] 4 b.] *trans.* To remove from a spit.

1574 T. Newton *Health Mag.* I iij b, Rosted fleshe is then best to be vnspitted and taken from the broche. 1611 Cotgr., *Desembrocher,* to vnspit; pull off the broach. 1648 Hexham, *Ontspeten,* to Vnspit, or to Vnbroach a peece of meate. 1798 in *Spirit Public Jrnls.* (1799) II. 290 The pigs and geese were all unspitted. 1820 T. Mitchell *Aristoph.* I. 116 The science which he displays in boiling, roasting, spitting, and unspitting.

**Unsplee·ned,** *ppl. a.* (Un-[1] 8.) 1633 Ford *'Tis Pity* i. ii, Yet the villanie of words..may be such, As would make any vnspleen'd Doue, Chollerick. †**Unsplee·ted,** *ppl. a.* (Un-[1] 8. Cf. Spleet *v.*[1]) 1609 C. Butler *Fem. Mon.* F 8 Lay the vnspleeted hiue along hard by. **Unsple·ndid,** *a.* (Un-[1] 7.) 1809 Syd. Smith *Serm.* II. 307 In the tumult of life the man, who can please for the passing hour, is..greater than him who has difficult, and unsplendid virtues. **Unspli·nt,** *v.* (Un-[2] 4 b.) 1615 Markham *Country Contentm.* i. i. 24 Let it so rest nine daies at least, before you vnsplint it.

**Unspli·t,** *ppl. a.* (Un-[1] 8 b. Cf. Du. *ongesplit.* MSw *osplitad,* older Da. *usplit.*)

1656 Earl Monm. tr. *Boccalini's Advts. fr. Parnass.* 262 To repair those his Gallies, which were yet unsplit. 1802-12 Bentham *Ration. Judic. Evid.* (1827) II. 194 The man is split into two persons..: or, he remaining unsplit, an ideal person is fabricated to speak of the real one. 1875 Bennett & Dyer tr. *Sachs' Bot.* 72 The originally unsplit fragments of cell-wall.

†**Unspoi·l,** *v.*[1] *Obs.* [Un-[2] 9.] *trans.* To despoil. a 1400 *Sir Perc.* 742 Now es Percyvelle lyghte To unspoyle the rede knyghte. **Unspoi·l,** *v.*[2] [Un-[2] 3.] *trans.* To restore from being spoiled. 1778 Miss Burney *Evelina* xxxiv, And what good will that do now?—that won't unspoil all my clothes. 1834 Mar. Edgeworth *Helen* xliii, 'I am quite spoiled, I believe,' said Helen; 'you must unspoil me'.

**Unspoi·lable,** *a.* (Un-[1] 7 b.)

1836 E. Howard *R. Reefer* lv, He contrived..to spoil our almost unspoilable meals. 1888 Marzials *Life V. Hugo* 204 One trusts that Master Georges and Miss Jeanne were unspoilable.

Hence **Unspoi·lableness.**

1881 *Daily News* 1 Oct. (Encycl. Dict.), A prevalent style of furniture and decoration should have this character of what may be called unspoilableness.

**Unspoi·led,** *ppl. a.* [Un-[1] 8.]

**1.** Not despoiled or plundered; not taken as plunder.

c 1500 *Melusine* xxxvi. 256 None passed by the said Fortresse vnspoyled. 1513 *Life Hen. V* (1911) 34 All Churches..shoulde be kepte inviolat, vnspoyled and vnharmed. 1577 Dee *General & Rare Mem.* 4 Their Marchantlike Ships..may..pas quietly vnpilled, vnspoyled, and vntaken by Pyrates. 1603 Knolles *Hist. Turks* (1621) 268 The Bassa..began..with fire and sword to wast that part of the countrey which yet remained vnspoiled. 1697 Dryden *Æneis* xi. 890 Unspoil'd shall be her Arms, and unprofan'd Her holy Limbs with any Human Hand. 1802 J. Baillie *2nd Pt. Ethwald* i. ii, A land of peace! Where yellow fields unspoil'd..smile gladly. 1870 Bryant *Iliad* v. I. 177 He left the corpse of Periphas unspoiled where he had fallen.

**2.** Not spoiled or deteriorated.

1732 Pope *Ep. Bathurst* 226 O teach us, Bathurst! yet unspoil'd by wealth! That secret rare. 1746 Collins *Ode to Pity* iv, He sung the female heart, With youth's soft notes unspoil'd by art. 1821 V. Knox *Grammar Schools* 117 An unspoiled boy,..possessing talent and sensibility. 1860 H. Marryat *Resid. Jutland* I. xiv. 209 The Castle of Rosenborg..is a fine specimen of the period, and is unspoiled by modern improvements. 1888 Child *Ballads* III. 1/1 This precious specimen..of the unspoiled traditional ballad.

**Unspoi·lt,** *ppl. a.* [Un-[1] 8 b.] = prec. 2.

1796 Mme. D'Arblay *Camilla* III. 180 An original feeling, unspoilt by the apathy of satiety. *Ibid.* IV. 353 Having brought with her whatever was unspoilt of her Tunbridge apparel. 1884 *World* 20 Aug. 20/1 An unspoilt English girl.

**Unspo·ke,** arch. variant of next.

1605 Shaks. *Lear* i. i. 239 A tardinesse in nature, Which often leaues the history vnspoke That it intends to do.

**Unspo·ken,** *ppl. a.* [Un-[1] 8 b, 8 c, 5 d. Cf. (M)Du. *ongesproken,* MLG. *ungesproken,* MHG. *ungesprochen.*]

**1.** Not spoken *of.* † Also with *to.*

1375 Barbour *Bruce* xv. 268 Till king Robert will we gang, That we haf left vnspokyn of lang. c 1530 L. Cox *Rheth.* (1899) 62, I can nat let passe his diuine wysdome vnspoken of. 1588 Kyd *Househ. Philos.* Wks. (1901) 284 Albeit somethings vnspoken of might be reuiued and produced. 1607 S. Collins *Serm.* (1608) 35, I am faine to passe by some things of moment, vnspoken-to here. 1634 Sir T. Herbert *Trav.* 147 The [Persian] women as vnseene may passe vnspoken of.

**2.** Not spoken, unsaid, unuttered; not expressed in speech.

c 1449 Pecock *Repr.* iii. xiv. 373 The oon premisse is expressid.., and the other premysse is stille vnspokun for schortnes. 1461 *Paston Lett.* II. 76 Desyreng the said schref if ony thyng of the Kyngs comaunded were be hynd unspoken by hym self that [etc.]. 1548 W. Patten *Exped. Scotl.* L v, Causes..that..ar better vnspoken then vttred. 1577 Grange *Golden Aphrod.* K iij, No doubte but I.I. wished his wordes vnspoken. 1611 Shaks. *Cymb.* v. v. 139 Thou'lt torture me to leaue vnspoken, that Which to be spoke, wou'd torture thee. 1640 Quarles *Enchyrid.* iii. xxxii, A word unspoken is like the Sword in thy Scabberd, thine. 1773 Goldsm. *1st Epil. to 'Stoops to Conq.',* And that our friendship may remain unbroken, What if we leave the Epilogue unspoken? 1818 Coleridge in *Encycl. Metrop.* I. Introd. 13 The unspoken alphabet of nature. 1862 Shirley (J. Skelton) *Nugæ Crit.* v. 210 Rigorous edicts..which punished the unspoken thought as well as the visible act.

**3.** Not spoken *to;* unaddressed.

1616 Hieron *Wks.* II. 23, I shall also teach that which shall be for the best behoofe of euery one in this assembly, that so none may goe away vnspoken to. 1721 Kelly *Scot. Prov.* 249 When People out of Bashfulness leave..a Person unspoken to. 1855 Trollope *Warden* vi, She had sat the whole evening through.., not speaking, and unspoken to.

**4.** *Sc.* Without having spoken. *rare*$^{-1}$.

1597 in *Spalding Cl. Misc.* (1841) I. 91 Jonet Wischert..commandit..Katherine Ewyn to ryss airlie befoir the sone, on betechit hir self to God, and on spokin.

**b.** (See quot.)

1825 Jamieson, *Unspoken water,* water..brought..to the house of a sick person, without the bearer's speaking either in going or returning.

**Unspo·ngy,** *a.* (Un-[1] 7.) a 1774 Goldsm. *Surv. Exp. Philos.* (1776) I. 366 When an unspongy or solid body sinks in a vessel of water.

**Unsponta·neous,** *a.* (Un-[1] 7.)

1791 Cowper *Odyssey* xx. 419 Wide they stretch'd Their jaws with unspontaneous laughter loud. 1885 *Wesleyan Method. Mag.* Dec. 955/2 Cases of unspontaneous Scripture-study. 1896 *Westm. Gaz.* 15 Dec. 2/1 His acting..is so mechanical,..so painfully unspontaneous.

**Unsponta·neously,** *adv.* (Un-[1] 11.) 1640 Reynolds *Treat. Passions* xlii. 545 Whereby the Will of man is..inforced or unspontaneously determined to the producing of such Effects. **Unspo·rted,** *ppl. a.* [Un-[1] 8 + Sport *v.* ii b.] Open. 1871 'M. Legrand' *Cambr. Freshm.* xi. 200 Come on, Golightly, your door is unsported. **Unspo·rtful,** *a.* (Un-[1] 7.) 1837 Carlyle *Fr. Rev.* ii. iv. iv, 'A Republic!' said the Seagreen, with one of his dry, husky, *un*sportful laughs, 'what is that?'

**Unspo·rting,** *ppl. a.* (Un-[1] 10.)

1859 W. H. Gregory *Egypt* II. 388 Then we beat the bed of the river, but in a most unsporting manner. 1894 *19th Cent.* July 130 A most pernicious and unsporting custom.

**Unspo·rtsmanlike,** *a., adv.* (Un-[1] 7 c, 11 b.)

1754 *Connoisseur* No. 31 ⁋ 12 It is unsportsman-like to admit dunghill cocks into the Pit. 1789 Wolcot (P. Pindar) *Subj. for Painters* Wks. 1816 II. 34 On which he..cry'd, 'See, ho!' Then jump'd (unsportsman like) upon his hare. 1803 in *Spirit Pub. Jrnls.* VII. 298 We stayed till it was dark, that we might not be seen returning in such an unsportsmanlike manner. 1845 Ford *Handbk. Spain* 107 They use nets, spears, night lines, and every unsportsmanlike abomination. 1873 G. C. Davies *Mount. & Mere* ii. 8 It was all very well once in a way, but too unsportsmanlike to be repeated often.

**Unspo·rtsmanly,** *a.* and *adv.* (Un-[1] 7, 11.) 1778 [W. H. Marshall] *Minutes Agric.* 9 Sept. 1776, To behave in this churlish, unsportsmanly manner! *Ibid.,* I will not suffer any man to trample unsportsmanly upon me with impunity. **Unspo·t,** *v.* (Un-[2] 4.) 1598 Florio, *Dimacchiare,* to vnspot, to take away spots. a 1711 Ken *Hymnotheo* Poet. Wks. 1721 III. 115 It seem'd an easier labour at first Sight, T' unspot Leopards, or wash Ethiops white. **Unspo·ttable,** *a.* (Un-[1] 7 b.) a 1711 Ken *Christophil* Poet. Wks. 1721 II. 516 Robes unspottable and bright.

**Unspo·tted,** *ppl. a.* [Un-[1] 8.]

**1.** Not marked with spots; free from any spot or stain.

1382 Wyclif 1 *Pet.* i. 19 Bi the precious blood of the lomb vndefoulid and vnspottid. 1446 Lydg. *Nightingale Poems* i. 185 The lombe vnspotted, the grounde of Innocence. ?1567 Stowe in *Three 15th C. Chron.* (Camden) 143 About that tyme [1567] were many congregations of the Anabaptysts in London, who cawlyd themselvs Puritans or Unspottyd Lambs of the Lord. 1626 Bosworth *Arcadius & Sepha* ii. 219 The tables did unspotted carpets hold Of Tyrian dyes. 1643 (*title*), The Parliaments Unspotted-Bitch: in answer to Prince Roberts Dog. 1709 Addison *Tatler* No. 97 ⁋ 2 Her beauty was natural and easy, her Person clean and unspotted. 1743 Francis tr. *Hor., Odes* ii. v. 24 Like the Moon's unspotted Light, O'er the Waves. 1804 Shaw *Gen. Zool.* V. 73 Unspotted Salmon, *Salmo Immaculatus*...Salmon with unspotted body. 1835 J. Duncan *Beetles* (Nat. Libr.) 220 The head, thorax, and scutellum are velvet black, and unspotted. 1870 Hooker *Stud. Flora* 353 Leaves lanceolate acute unspotted.

**2.** Not morally stained; unblemished, pure: **a.** Of persons, the mind, etc.

c 1400 *Found. St. Bartholomew's* (1923) 48 She..myghtly troid them vndir foit, vnspottid euermore abidyng. c 1450 *Myrr. our Ladye* 140 Sonne of the clene and vnspotted vyrgyn. 1526 Tindale *Jas.* i. 27 To kepe hym silfe vnspotted from the worlde. 1576 Gascoigne *Kenelw. Castle* Wks. 1910 II. 108 The stately tower of your unspotted myndes. 1629 Prynne *Anti-Armin.* 84 Being thus rescued from the power of sinne, may they keepe themselues vnspotted from it. 1709 Addison *Tatler* No. 75 ⁋ 4 My Sister Jenny..is as unspotted a Spinster as any in Great Britain. 1743 Francis tr. *Hor., Odes* i. xxiv. 9 Modesty, unspotted Maid, And Truth in artless Guise array'd. 1812 Crabbe *Tales* vi. 346 A heart unspotted, and a life unblamed. 1863 Conington *Horace, Odes* i. x. 17 Thou lay'st unspotted souls to rest.

**b.** Of character, qualities, etc.

1455 *Rolls of Parlt.* V. 280/2 Alwey kepyng oure trouthe to his said Highnesse unspotted and unbrused. a 1568 Ascham *Scholem.* ii. (Arb.) 87 The vnspotted proprietie of the Latin tong,. whan it was..at the hiest pitch of all perfitenesse. 1579 Spenser *Two Commend. Lett.* i. ad fin., The..inuiolable Memorie of our vnspotted friendshippe. 1638 M. Griffith in Hearne *Collect.* (O.H.S.) I. 160 Christendome cannot shew in one person..a more Angelical Life, unspotted of ye Worlde & the Flesh. 1665 Bunyan *Holy Citie* 73 The twelve Apostles, in their own pure, primitive, and unspotted Doctrine. 1712 Steele *Spect.* No. 276 ⁋ 2, I am a Woman of an unspotted Reputation. 1772 Priestley *Inst. Relig.* (1782) II. 132 A being of unspotted purity. 1841 Browning *Pippa Passes* ii. 136 Never to overtake the rest of me, All that, unspotted, reaches up to you.

Hence **Unspo·ttedly** *adv.*; **Unspo·ttedness.**

1598 Florio, *Puramente,* purely, cleanlie, *vnspottedlie. 1602 F. Hering *Anat.* 6 He may religiously, vnspottedly, and charily, preserue the precious health and life of man. 1598 Florio, *Purità,* puritie, clenlines, neatenes, *vnspottednes. 1624 Donne *Devotions,* etc. (ed. 2) 303 Doeth the Son dwell bodily in this flesh, that thou shouldst looke for an unspottedness here? 1682 Ingelo *Bentiv. & Ur.* (ed. 4) iv. 156 The unspottedness of our Virgin-life. 1706 tr. *Liger's Compl. Florist* 273 A violation of the candor and unspottedness of her Manners. 1828 T. Brown *Serm.* 86 Valens spared Paulinus out of respect to the unspottedness of his life.

**Unspou·sed,** *ppl. a.* (Un-[1] 8.) 1587 Fleming *Contn. Holinshed* III. 1299 Unspoused Pallas present is, O Phebus bright retire. **Unspou·selike,** *a.* (Un-[1] 7 c.) 1611 Speed *Hist. Gt. Brit.* viii. vi. 401/2 All which vnprincelie and vn-Spouslike vsage..was, because shee onely should not liue in comfort.

†**Unspray·ed,** *ppl. a.*[1] *Obs.* [Un-[1] 8 + Spray *sb.*[1]] Not furnished with sprays or branches. 1486 *Bk. St. Albans, Her.* a j b, Adam the begynnyng of man kynde was as a stokke vnsprayde and vnfloreshed. **Unspray·ed,** *ppl. a.*[2] [Un-[1] 8 + Spray *v.*[4]] Not sprayed with a chemical. 1894 *Times* 19 Nov. 4/4 Neither Puritan nor The Bruce yielded any diseased tubers on the unsprayed portions of the crop.

**Unsprea·d,** *ppl. a.* Also 7 unspreaden. [Un-[1] 8 b.] Not spread (out).

1589 Fleming *Virg. Georg.* iii. 44 Lodging all night long he lies..Vpon a couch vnmade (vnspread). 1642 H. More *Song of Soul* ii. iii. 21 Remember that some things unspreaden be, How shall it find them out? 1644 G. Plattes in *Hartlib's Legacy* (1655) 188 Where dung hath. layen unspread for a moneth or six weeks. 1776 C. Keith *Farmer's Ha'* lxi, The dishes set on unspread table. 1827 Pollok *Course T.* vi. 633 Bounding immensity, unspread, unbound! 1838 Mrs. Browning *Young Queen* 1 The shroud is yet unspread. **1844** — *Confessions* iii, Unquickened, unspread My fire dropt down.

**Unsprea·d,** *v.* (UN-[2] 3.) **1661** K. W. *Conf. Charac.* (1860) 69 He's so used to spread cloaths, that he's ne're well but when he's unspreading of aprons.  **† Unspri·ghty,** *a. Obs.*—[1] [UN-[1] 7.] Not sprightly or lively. **1607** MARKHAM *Cavel.* VIII. 14 Anie of these constant and vnsprity carriages are signes of dulnes.

**Unspri·ng,** *v.* [UN-[2] 7, 4 b. Cf. OE. *onspringan*, OS. *antspringan*, Du. *ontspringen*, OHG. *intspringan* (MHG., G. *entspringen*).]

† **1.** *intr.* To burst open. *Obs.*—[1]

**13..** *K. Alis.* (W.) 2902 Mury hit is in sonne-risyng! The rose openith and unspryng [*Laud MS.* wile vpspringe].

**2.** *trans.* To release or detach by pressing a spring.

**1802** JAMES *Milit. Dict.*, *To unspring*, a word of command formerly used in the exercise of cavalry. *Ibid.*, Unspring your carbine. **1833** *Reg. Instr. Cavalry* I. 96 'Unspring' by disengaging the swivel from the carbine. **1859** F. A. GRIFFITHS *Artill. Man.* (ed. 8) 48 Unspring arms.

**Unspri·nging,** *ppl. a.* (UN-[1] 10.) **1821** MILMAN *Judicum Regale* 140 The red havoc of unspringing fire.  **Unspri·ngy,** *a.* (UN-[1] 7.) **1672** *Phil. Trans.* VII. 5167 An Un-springy Fluid (which presseth but as a Weight not as a Spring).

**Unspri·nkled,** *ppl. a.* [UN-[1] 8.] Not sprinkled with water, etc.; *spec.* not baptized by sprinkling.

**1648** HEXHAM II, *Ongewatert*, vnwatered, or vnsprinckled. **1735** SAVAGE *Progr. Divine* Wks. 1775 II. 112 Let babes of poverty convulsive lie; No bottle waits, tho' babes unsprinkl'd die. **1802–12** BENTHAM *Ration. Judic. Evid.* (1827) II. 659 If the child remains unsprinkled,..no registration is to take place. **1843** TIZARD *Brewing* 62 Unsprinkled malt.

**Unspru·ng,** *ppl. a.* [UN-[1] 8 b.] Not having sprung up or sprouted.

**1600** FAIRFAX *Tasso* I. xlix, His hopes Vnsprong, his cares were fit to mowe. **1684** J. S. *Profit & Pleas. United* 106 To prevent the Crows or daws falling on the Corne unsprung.

† **Unspu·lyied,** *ppl. a. Sc. Obs.* [UN-[1] 8.] = UNSPOILED *ppl. a.* 1.

**1513** DOUGLAS *Æneid* XI. xi. 134 My self..the reuthfull corps..sall cary away, Onspulȝeit of hir armour or array. **1559** *Extr. Aberd. Reg.* (1844) I. 316 The sklayttis, tymmir, and stanis..that are in place onspoulȝet. *a* **1578** LINDESAY (Pitscottie) *Chron. Scot.* (S.T.S.) II. 285 That nane mycht travell onspuilȝeit on bayth the sydes. *a* **1670** SPALDING *Troub. Chas. I* (1850) I. 157 To saif..his houssis on spolȝeit, and his freindis and seruandis on plunderit.

**Unspu·n,** *ppl. a.* (UN-[1] 8 b. Cf. OHG. *ungispunnan* (MHG. *ungespunnen*, G. *-sponnen*), ON. *úspunninn* (older Da. *uspunden*, Sw. *ospunnen*).)

**1545** *Rates of Custom* a vi, Cotton vnsponne..xxvi. s. viii. d. **1565** COOPER *Thesaurus*, *Linum infectum*, flaxe vnspunne. **1571** *Wills & Inv. N. C.* (Surtees, 1835) 352, I haiue in the howse spunn and vnsponne vj ston of lynt. **1586** in Kyd *Wks.* (1901) 340 Her thred still holds, thine perisht though vnspun. **1827** FARADAY *Chem. Manip.* ii. 49 A filament of unspun silk.

**Unspurd,** obs. var. UNSPEERED *ppl. a.*

† **Unspu·rn,** *v. Obs.*—[1] [UN-[2] 9.] *trans.* To force open. *a* **1300** *K. Horn* 1074 (Camb. MS.), Horn gan to þe ȝate turne, And þat wiket vnspurne [*v.r.* op spurne].

**Unspu·rred,** (*ppl.*) *a.* [UN-[1] 8, 9.]

**1.** Not urged on by a spur. Also *fig.*

*a* **1635** CORBET *Iter Bor.* Poems (1647) 12 His Mare went truer then his Chronicle; And..unspurr'd, unbeaten, Brought us sixe miles. **1865** MEREDITH *R. Fleming* xviii, The replenished glass enabled Stephen to add the picturesque bits of the affray, unspurred by a surrounding eagerness of his listeners. **1886** *Pall Mall G.* 31 July 2/2 Not altogether unspurred by hints from home.

**2.** Not furnished with a spur.

**1852** C. W. HOSKYNS *Talpa* xvi. 133 Grazing Mr. Greening's unspurred foot with the point of the leader's stretcher.

**Unsqua·ndered,** *ppl. a.* (UN-[1] 8.)

[**1775** ASH.] **1799** J. ROBERTSON *Agric. Perth* 416 The public have a right to any effects he left unsquandered away. **1812** CRABBE *Tales* xx. 175 His pension, with what sums remain Due or unsquander'd.

† **Unsquare,** obs. f. ANSWER *v.*

*c* **1420** *Avow. Arth.* xix, The tother vnsquarut him withskille.

**Unsqua·re,** *v.* [UN-[2] 3, 6 b, 7.] **a.** *trans.* To divest of squareness; to undo the squaring of. **b.** *intr.* To lose squareness of form or structure.

**1611** FLORIO, *Disquatrare*, to vnsquare. **1790** *Trans. Soc. Arts* VIII. 168 [The loom] is not liable to unsquare; and yet..may be more easily removed than the old loom. **1872** DE MORGAN *Budget of Paradoxes* 470 Montucla charges Cluvier with unsquaring the parabola, which Archimedes had squared as tight as a glove.

**Unsqua·red,** *ppl. a.* [UN-[1] 8.] Not made square; not reduced to a square form or section.

**1549** COVERDALE, etc. *Erasm. Par. 1 Cor.* viii. 23 b, An idole..hathe no more Godhead in it, than an other vnsquared piece of tymber. **1598** GRENEWEY *Tacitus, Germanie* ii. (1622) 262 They..vse to all buildings vnsquared and vnwrought timber. **1633** T. ADAMS *Exp. 2 Peter* ii. 5 An unsquared stone..must not be put into the building of Christ. **1664** EVELYN *Sylva* xxix. 90 Such Trees as one would leave round, and unsquar'd. **1798** HUTTON *Course Math.* II. 95 To find the Solidity of Round or Unsquared Timber. **1883** STEVENSON *Treas. Isl.* IV. xix, The log-house was made of unsquared trunks of pine.

*fig.* **1592** KYD *Sp. Trag.* III. xi. 23 The more he growes in stature.., The more vnsquard, vnbeuelled he appeares. **1606** SHAKS. *Tr. & Cr.* I. iii. 159 With tearmes vnsquar'd, Which from the tongue of roaring Typhon dropt, Would seeme Hyperboles. **1607** MARSTON *What you will* Induct., Were I to passe Through publick verdit, I should feare my forme, Least ought I offerd were vnsquard or warp'd.

**Unsque·amish,** *a.* (UN-[1] 7.) **1893** *Athenæum* 4 Feb. 157/3 This pushing, unsqueamish age.

**Unsquee·zed,** *ppl. a.* (UN-[1] 8.)

**1683** MOXON *Mech. Exerc.*, *Printing* xi. ¶ 1 The natural Spring that all these Joynts have, when they are unsqueez'd. **1736** THOMSON *Liberty* v. 198 Rich, as unsqueez'd favourite, to them, Is he who can his Virtue boast alone! **1757** GARRICK *Lilliput* Prol. 8 Gently you'll ride, as in a Fairy Dream, Your Hoops unsqueez'd. **1824** MACTAGGART *Gallovid. Encycl.* (1876) 29 The primrose..and the crawtae grow unsqueez'd and unlooked at.

**Unsqui·re,** *v.* (UN-[2] 6 b.) **1721** SWIFT *Let. to King at Arms* Wks. 1841 II. 70/2 If this should be the test of squirehood, it will go hard with a great number of my fraternity,..who must all be unsquired because a greyhound will not be allowed to keep us company.  † **Unsqui·ssed,** *ppl. a. Obs.*—[0] [UN-[1] 8.] Unsqueezed. **1648** HEXHAM II, *Ongepijnden honigh*, Vnpressed, or Vnsquissed hony.

**Unstabi·lity.** Now *rare*. (UN-[1] 12, 5 b.)

*a* **1470** *Dives & Pauper* (W. de W. 1496) VI. x. 247/2 Eue synned more by freelte and unstabylyte..than by shrewdenes. **1572** *Wills & Inv. N. C.* (Surtees, 1835) 386 Perceivynge..the vnstabilitie and soden changes of the worlde, ..and the vncertentye of deathe. **1603** KNOLLES *Hist. Turks* (1621) 50 The head was forthwith strucke off from this miserable carkasse (the mirrour of honours vnstabilitie). **1646** P. BULKELEY *Gospel Covt.* v. 363 When you see uncertainty and unstability of all things. **1886** *Science* 5 Nov. 401/2 The unstability of such an association is..beginning to be understood.

**Unsta·ble,** *a.* [UN-[1] 7, 5 b. Cf. obs. Du. *onstabel*, MHG. *unstabel*.]

**1.** Not remaining steadily in the same place; apt to move or be moved about.

*a* **1225** *Ancr. R.* 122 Ne scheaweð heo þet heo is dust, & vnstable þinc, þet mid a lutel wind of a word is anon to blowen. *a* **1340** HAMPOLE *Ps.* x. 1 If i doe i sall be like a sparou, þat is, vnstabile and lyght. **1388** WYCLIF *Gen.* iv. 14 Y schal be vnstable of dwellyng and fleynge aboute in erthe. **1483** *Cath. Angl.* 357/2 Vn Stabylle, *argus, vagus.* **1597** R. TOFTE, etc. *Laura* I. xviii, If Sea no other thing doth shew to bee Than most vnstable waters mooning oft. **1634** SIR T. HERBERT *Trav.* 91 Sands..in great drifts..so light and vnstable, that the high wayes are neuer certaine. **1653** W. RAMESEY *Astrol. Restored* 179 Aries,..though it be a sign fiery, yet is it moveable and unstable.

**b.** Not steady in position; readily swaying or shaking; liable to swing or fall.

**1390** GOWER *Conf.* I. 200 Now herke how thilke unstable whel, Which evere torneth, wente aboute. **1393** LANGL. *P. Pl.* C. XI. 37 Stonde he neuere so styfliche þorgh steryng of the bote, He bendeþ and boweþ, þe body is vnstable. *c* **1480** HENRYSON *Fables, Cock & Fox* 199 Thy strenth is nocht, thy stule standis vnstabill. *a* **1542** WYATT in *Tottel's Misc.* (Arb.) 38 So foloweth me remembrance of that face: That with my teary eyn, swolne, and vnstable, My desteny to beholde her doth me lead. **1567** *Gude & Godlie B.* (S.T.S.) 106 As quheill vnstabill and caffe befoir the wind. **1600** FAIRFAX *Tasso* XIX. xiii, When the still windes stirre not th' vnstable maine. **1736** THOMSON *Liberty* IV. 302 On each hand Amazing seen amid unstable waves, The splendid palace shines. **1760** GOLDSM. *Cit. W.* ii, A strange people..who have founded an empire on this unstable element [*sc.* the ocean]. **1857** BUCKLE *Civiliz.* vii. 347 The sailor is naturally more superstitious than the soldier, because he has to deal with a more unstable element. **1873** MAXWELL *Electr. & Magn.* I. 141 The body therefore is unstable even when constrained to move parallel to itself, *à fortiori* it is unstable when altogether free.

**c.** Of movement: Unsteady; irregular.

**1549** *Compl. Scot.* vi. 54 It makkis ane onstabil reuolution in thre hundretht xlviij dais. **1819** SCOTT *Ivanhoe* xlii, Down he came, with an unstable step and a strong flavour of wine.

**d.** *Mech.* Of equilibrium (q. v.).

**1839** G. BIRD *Nat. Philos.* 31 The body will be in a state of unstable equilibrium. **1860** *All Year Round* No. 69. 450 An acrobat balances a ladder on his shoulder; on the ladder, perhaps will mount a child...The whole are in unstable equilibrium.

**2.** Not stable in purpose; vacillating, fickle, changeable.

*c* **1290** *S. Eng. Leg.* I. 319/685 Wrathþe he berth luytel ȝwyle:..Glad and bliþe, and onstable of þat he hath to done. **1297** R. GLOUC. 10507 He made of þe olde lawes is chartre atte laste,..& aselede is vaste inou, Ac suþþe as vnstable man wiþ sede & wiþ drou. *c* **1305** *Pilate* 183 in *E. E. P.* (1862) 116 Alle þat ihurde þis cas Wondrede moche of þemperour, þat he vnstable was. *c* **1380** WYCLIF *Sel. Wks.* II. 10 ϸis Emperour..was unstable as watir. *c* **1400** *Destr. Troy* 8057 Hit is a propertie apreuit..To all wemen..To be vnstable & not stidfast. *c* **1450** tr. *De Imitatione* III. l. 121 Euery man is a lyer, sike, unstable, and slydyng. *c* **1485** *Digby Myst.* (1882) III. 588 Woman, why art þou so onstabyll?..why art þou a-ȝens god so veryabyll? **1509–10** *Act 1 Hen. VIII*, c. 11 Many lyght and unstable Persons. *a* **1548** HALL *Chron., Hen. V*, 38 The Cambers, otherwise called the vnstable Welshemen. **1607** SHAKS. *Cor.* III. i. 148 It must omit Reall Necessities, and giue way the while To vnstable Slightnesse. **1653** MILTON *Ps.* v. 25 In his faltring mouth unstable No word is firm. **1661** SOUTH *Serm.* (1715) III. 192 Such Pretenders may beguile Factious and Unstable Minds. **1791** WOLCOT (P. Pindar) *Lousiad* III. ix, [A deed] Which Cain perform'd, in godliness unstable. **1855** MACAULAY *Hist. Eng.* xv. III. 613 His nature, lamentably unstable, was not ignoble. **1891** FARRAR *Darkn. & Dawn* xxv, Onesimus was too unstable to withstand the combined temptations by which he was surrounded.

*absol.* **1582** N. T. (Rhem.) 2 *Pet.* iii. 16 Certaine things hard to be vnderstoode, which the vnlearned and vnstable depraue. **1630** H. LYNDE (*title*), Via Devia: The By-Way: Mis-leading the weake and vnstable into dangerous paths of Error. **1650** BAXTER *Saints' R.* III. xi. § 18. 497 Drawing off the unstable from the doctrine and way of life.

**3.** Not fixed in character or condition; exposed to vicissitude or chance; apt to change or alter; variable.

*c* **1340** HAMPOLE *Pr. Consc.* 1420 Þe worlde is swa unstable, Alle þat men sese þar-in es chaungeable. *c* **1375** *Lay Folks Mass-Bk.* (MS. B.) 390 Þo weders grete & vnstable, Lord make gode. **1387** TREVISA *Higden* (Rolls) I. 139 Hap was vnstable and vnstedefast; ones wiþ þat oon side, and eft wiþ þat oþer. *c* **1412** HOCCLEVE *De Reg. Princ.* 705 O lord! þis world vnstabyl is. *c* **1450** tr. *De Imitatione* III. lxiv. 149, I finde all vnferme & vnstable, what euere I beholde oute of þe. **1513** DOUGLAS *Æneid* XI. viii. 118 The variant chance Of our onstabill lyfe. *a* **1542** WYATT in *Tottel's Misc.* (Arb.) 35 Vnstable dreame,..Be stedfast ones, or els at least be true. *a* **1642** KYNASTON *Leoline & Sydanis* 141 O wretched state unstable Of mortal men! **1657** in *Verney Mem.* (1907) 560 These giddy and unstable times. **1768** BOSWELL *Corsica* ii. 73 The Genoese..were..in an unstable, and perilous condition. **1796** MME. D'ARBLAY *Camilla* III. 75 We must allow to our unstable virtues all the encouragement that can prop them. *Ibid.* V. 540 The perpetual vicissitudes of our unstable condition. **1829** HOOD *Eugene Aram* 46 Or is it some historic page Of kings and crowns unstable? **1863** H. COX *Instit.* III. iii. 628 That all oligarchies and democracies are unstable. **1884** CHURCH *Bacon* ix. 223 English seemed to him too homely to express the hopes of the world, too unstable to be trusted with them.

**b.** *spec.* in *Chem.*

**1849** D. CAMPBELL *Inorg. Chem.* 216 Its [*sc.* suboxide of copper] salts are very unstable. **1857** MILLER *Elem. Chem.*, *Org.* 59 Grape sugar forms definite but unstable combinations with the alkaline bases. **1890** *Retrospect Med.* CII. 2 The chloral hydrate is, comparatively, an unstable compound.

**4.** Not firm or solid; insecure.

**1565** JEWEL *Repl. Harding* (title-p.), The Weake and vnstable Groundes of the Romaine Religion. **1613** PURCHAS *Pilgrimage* (1614) 597 The Earth was couered with sand, which yeelded an vnstable footing.

**Unsta·ble,** *v.* [UN-[2] 5.] † *trans.* To free *of*. **1612** T. ADAMS *Gallant's Burden* 32 If our harts be vnstabled of these beastiall lusts.  **Unsta·bled,** *ppl. a.*[1] [UN-[1] 8.] Not established or made stable. **1622** *Babington's Wks.* 9 Complaints of wauering weakenesse and vnstabled [*ed.* 1596 vnstayned (*read* vnstayed)] mutability..brought against vs. **1681** RYCAUT tr. *Gracian's Critick* 120 A tottering Cottage, founded on an unstabled Sand.  **Unsta·bled,** *ppl. a.*[2] [UN-[1] 8.] Not put into a stable. **1853** C. BRONTË *Villette* xxxix, Behold the branchless tree, the unstabled Rosinante!

**Unsta·bleness.** [f. UNSTABLE *a.*] The condition of being unstable; instability: **a.** Of persons, the mind, etc.

*c* **1380** WYCLIF *Sel. Wks.* II. 58 Medling of freris cloþis telliþ unstablenesse [in virtue] of þes ordris. **1387** TREVISA *Higden* II. 175 Þe vnstabilnesse of þouȝtes schal be bytokened by many manere dyuersite of cloþinge. *c* **1425** *Eng. Conq. Irel.* 136 Thegh thay, throgh kynd falsnesse & vnstablenesse that yn ham ys, lytyl tel of othes. **1539** ELYOT *Cast. Helthe* 75 Unstablenesse of wytte and slipper remembraunce. **1590** GREENWOOD *Answ. Gifford* 13 Your vnstablenes in denying and affirming with one breath. **1646** P. BULKELEY *Gospel Covt.* v. 368 By reason of our unstablenesse of spirit, we are apt to make many a breach. **1676** HALE *Contempl.* II. 49 Unstableness, Vanity, Love of Pleasures, Easiness to be corrupted in Youth. **1815** W. H. IRELAND *Scribbleomania* 124 His natural unstableness debars him from adopting any fixed mode of action.

**b.** Of conditions, life, etc.

*c* **1340** HAMPOLE *Pr. Consc.* 353 Þe unstabelnes of þis werld. *c* **1374** CHAUCER *Boeth.* II. pr. iv. (1868) 43 Þe vnstablenesse of fortune. *c* **1430** LYDG. *Compl. Bl. Knt.* 457 Thy stormy wilful variaunce I-meynt with chaunge and gret vnstablenesse. *c* **1440** *Gesta Rom.* lxxxix. 411 A woman..that sawe..the synnes, and the vnstablenesse, that was in the worlde. *a* **1589** PALFREYMAN *Baldwin's Mor. Philos.* (1600) 52 O world thou hast so many countenaunces in thy vanitie, that thou leadest all wandering in vnstablenesse. **1601** SIR W. CORNWALLIS *Ess.* II. xxxvi, The frailty and vnstablenes of wealth. **1670** in Somers *Tracts* I. 27 To shew unto those insolent Commanders of the Army, the Unstableness of their Condition. **1807** G. CHALMERS *Caledonia* I. III. vii. 421 A weaker prince would have lost his crown, considering its unstableness.

**Unsta·bly,** *adv.* [UN-[1] 11. Cf. prec.] In an unstable manner; unsteadily.

*a* **1380** *Eufrosyne* 390 in Horstm. *Altengl. Leg.* (1878) 178 I stunte, I stonde, vnstabli I stalke. **14..** *Wyclif's De Ecclesia* (1851) p. xiii, But her þenken trewe men þat þe fend failiþ her, & goiþ vnstably [*v.r.* unstable] bi two weies. *c* **1440** *Promp. Parv.* 367/2 Onstabylly, *instabiliter.* **1502** ATKYNSON tr. *De Imitatione* III. xix. 212 He standeth casually and vnstably that castith nat all his busynes in the. **1611** COTGR., *Instablement*, vnstably, vnsteadily. **1654** ELLISTONE & SPARROW tr. *Boehme's Myst. Magnum* lxxvi. 579 As Adam suddenly and unstablely therein, departed from his Glory. **1830** PUSEY *Hist. Enq.* II. 109 Others, who are unstably 'halting between the two opinions'. **1879** THOMSON & TAIT *Nat. Phil.* I. I. § 351 A particle placed on the inner circle..would move perpetually in that circle, but unstably.

**Unsta·ck,** *v.* [UN-[2] 3.] *trans.* To remove, take down, from being stacked or piled up.

**1859** R. F. BURTON *Centr. Afr.* in *Jrnl. Geog. Soc.* XXIX. 414 The porters..unstack the loads propped against the trees. **1863** W. THORNBURY *True as Steel* III. 39 The enemy..already were beating the alarm, unstacking their weapons, and gathering outside their tents. **1888** *Pall Mall G.* 18 Feb. 6/2 In unstacking some timber..the men came across a newly-made sparrow's nest.

**Unsta·cked,** *ppl. a.* (UN-[1] 8.) [**1775** ASH.] **1846** WORC. (citing More). **1884** *Spectator* 4 Oct. 1326/1 She has left some wood unstacked at home.  **Unsta·gnant,** *a.* (UN-[1] 7.) **1822–7** GOOD *Study Med.* (1829) III. 45 A pure and unstagnant air.  **Unsta·gy,** *a.* (UN-[1] 7.) **1882** *Macm. Mag.* XLVI. 332/2 A room altogether natural and unstagey. [Freq. in recent use.]

**Unstai·d,** *a.* Also 6–7 unstaied, -stayed, etc. [UN-[1] 7.]

**1.** Of persons: Not staid or regulated in deportment or conduct.

*c* **1550** CHEKE *Matt.* xxiii. 25 Thei be called in greek ἀκρατεῖς,..which we mai cal rightli vnstaid. **1621** BURTON *Anat. Mel.* III. ii. II. iii. 567 When they are so new fangled,

so vnstaide, so prodigious in their attires. **1636** HEYWOOD *Love's Mistr.* v. L 4, Now Psiche, you must see your sisters judg'd, Vnstaid Petrea, and unkind Astioche.
*transf.* **1591** SHAKS. *Two Gent.* II. vii. 60 How will the world repute me For vndertaking so vnstaid a iourney?

† **b.** Of a hawk: Not properly trained. *Obs.*—[1]
**1614** LATHAM *Falconry* I. v. 21 With the first of these three orders, I haue reclaimed an outragious vnstaied hawke.

**2.** Of the mind, etc.: Not subjected to restraint or control; unrestrained, unregulated.
(*a*) **1579** E. K. *Ded. to Spenser's Sheph. Cal.* § 5 His vnstayed yougth had long wandred in the common Labyrinth of Loue. **1593** SHAKS. *Rich. II*, II. i. 2 Will the King come, that I may breath my last In wholsome counsell to his vnstaid youth? **1603** KNOLLES *Hist. Turks* (1621) 158 All those vaine delights which vnstaied youth most desireth.
(*b*) **1587** HOLINSHED *Chron.* III. 488/1 To lash out whatsoeuer his vnstaied mind affoorded. **1605** ROWLANDS *Hell's Broke Loose* (Hunterian Club) 23 The easier to beguile The simple sort, which haue vnstayed mindes. *a* **1678** H. SCOUGAL *Disc. Imp. Subj.* (1735) 136 Our blood is hot, and our spirits unstayed and giddy. **1685** BAXTER *Paraphr. N. T.* 1 Tim. iii. 11 Women..in danger..of unstayed Levity. **1812** CARY *Dante, Purg.* x. 112 O poor and wretched ones! That ..lean your trust Upon unstaid perverseness. **1832** L. HUNT *Sir R. Esher* i. 38 Unripe and unstaid thoughts, the vanities of youth. **1840** LOWELL *The Moon* 5 My soul was like the sea,..Moaning in vague immensity,..Unrestful and unstaid.
(*c*) **1592** LYLY *Gallathea* III. i, I feele my thoughts vnknit, mine eyes vnstaied. **1638** BRATHWAIT *Spirit. Spicery*, etc. 398 Those poore objects wherewith my unstayed eyes were fed.
(*d*) **1590** SPENSER *Muiopot.* 161 To the gay gardins his vnstaid desire Him wholly caried, to refresh his sprights. **1612** DRAYTON *Poly-olb.* xi. 348 Ethelbald..by the wise reproofe of godly Bishops brought From those vnstay'd delights by which his youth was caught.

**3.** Not settled or stable in opinion or resolve; not clearly determined or decided.
**1561** T. NORTON *Calvin's Inst.* I. 5 That vnstayed and wandring opinion of the maiestie of God. **1603** HARSNET *Pop. Impost.* 121 If they had brought the old renowmed Reliques from Rome, some unstayed body would haue made question whether they had been Saints bones indeed. **1613** BP. HALL *Serm.* v. 93 A private man unsettled in opinion, is..troublesome and useless: but a public person unstayed is dangerous. **1631** WEEVER *Anc. Funeral Mon.* 515 King Henry,..vnstayed in religious resolutions, did cut them off vpon false suggestions. *a* **1750** A. HILL *Muse to Writer* viii, While roving thus, uncenter'd and unstaid, I lik'd by turns, and did by turns refuse.

**4.** Liable to change or alter; uncertain.
**1586** DAY *Eng. Secretary* I. (1595) 116 Is there anie thing on earth so assured, that by vnstaied incertaintie is not continuallie guided? **1628** FELTHAM *Resolves* II. xlvi. 135 Change is the great Lord of the World; Time is his Agent, that brings in all things to suffer his vnstaid Dominion. **1642** H. MORE *Song of Soul* III. iii. 15 They frisque about in circulings unstay'd.

Hence **Unstai·dly** *adv.*
**1556** GRIMALDE *Cicero's Offices* III. 123 Nothing..vniustly, nothing wantonly, nothing vnstayedly is meete to be done. **1571** GOLDING *Calvin on Ps.* xxxvii. 9 If were were not shifted hither and thither unstayedly. **1611** COTGR., *Incontinemment*,..disorderedly, vnstayedly, immoderately.

**Unstai·dness.** [f. prec.]
**1.** Absence of staidness in conduct or opinion.
*c* **1550** CHEKE *Matt.* xxiii. 25 For ie clense y^e^ outward part of y^e^ cup..but y^e^ insijd is ful of robri and vnstaidnes. **1583** GOLDING *Calvin on Deut.* xxxviii. 227 That we must not defile our selues with any vnchastitie or vnstayednesse. **1650** HOLYDAY *Persius' Sat.* v. 41 Nothing hinders thee.. But Luxurie. That doth seduce thy weake Unstayednesse. **1675** BARCLAY *Apol. Quakers* xi. § 8. 358 The unstayedness of their Minds. **1828** E. IRVING *Last Days* 326 The former [trait] expressing haste, precipitancy, and unstayedness.

†**2.** Physical unsteadiness. *Obs.*
*a* **1586** SIDNEY *Arcadia* I. ix, With a kind of shaking unstayednes over all his body. **1607** MARKHAM *Cavel.* VII. 59 When..the orifice by the vnstaidnes of the Farriers hand, is made too great.

**Unstai·n,** *v.* [UN-[2] 3.] *trans.* To free from stain or stains.
**1639** N. WHITING *Albino & Bellama*, etc. H 10, What other errours thou findest, let thy pen amend, excusing the presse, and un-staining the Authour. **1639** FULLER *Holy War* II. ix. 55 They sought to unstain their credits by going again. **1687** J. REYNOLDS *Death's Vis.* vii, How Blooming Trees ..Unstain Dy'd Cloaths, and call their Atoms forth.

**Unstai·nable,** *a.* (UN-[1] 7 b.)
**1584** LODGE *Hist. Forbonius & Prisc.* (Shaks. Soc.) 96 Alas, unfortunate Ægyptian! whose faithful affections are so immutable, as thy naturall colour is unstainable. **1864** CARLYLE *Fredk. Gt.* XVII. i. IV. 502 The unstainable fidelity of Weingarten Senior. **1878** GROSART *H. More's Poems* Mem. Introd. p. xxii/1 A pure white life unstained and unstainable as the light.

**Unstai·ned,** *ppl. a.* [UN-[1] 8.]
**1.** Not stained or (dis)coloured; spotless, clean, pure.
**1555** in Feuillerat *Revels Q. Mary* (1914) 182 The same white cloth of sylver vnstayned. **1597** SHAKS. 2 *Hen. IV*, v. ii. 114 Th' vnstained Sword that you haue vs'd to beare. **1629** MILTON *Hymn Nativ.* iv, The hooked Chariot stood Unstain'd with hostile blood. **1736** THOMSON *Liberty* v. 556 Languedocian skies, That, unstain'd ether all, diffusive smile. **1807** CRABBE *Par. Reg.* I. 24 By sighs unruffled or unstain'd by tears. **1860** TYNDALL *Glac.* I. xiv. 97 The unstained blue of heaven. **1899** *Allbutt's Syst. Med.* VIII. 903 An unstained or faintly stained zone..across the bacillus.

**2.** Not morally stained or sullied; unblemished, untarnished.
**1573** DAUS tr. *Bullinger on Apoc.* (ed. 2) 84 The Byshops began to defile the Lordes supper and other vnstained doctrines of fayth. *a* **1586** SIDNEY *Arcadia* II. x, Any sparkes of unstained duety lefte in them towardes me. **1624** QUARLES *Job* xv. 19 Preserue he then, vnstained in his brest, A milke-white Conscience. **1689** D. GRANVILLE *Lett.* (Surtees) 81 The consideration whereof hath..kept me untainted and unstained. **1744** THOMSON *Spring* 761 The towering Seat.. of his Empire; which, in Peace, Unstain'd he holds. **1746** FRANCIS tr. *Horace, Epist.* II. ii. 196 A Person, who maintain'd A due Decorum, and a Life unstain'd. **1813** SHELLEY *Q. Mab* VII. 236 No year of my eventful being Has passed unstained by crime and misery. **1863** MRS. H. WOOD *Verner's Pride* xviii, He was proud of his independence, his unstained name.

Hence **Unstai·nedness.**
**1685** H. MORE *Paralip. Prophet.* 327 Sacerdotal,..because of the unstainedness of their condition as to Externals. **1727** BAILEY (vol. II), *Pureness*,..Unspottedness, Unstainedness.

**Unsta·led,** *ppl. a.* (UN-[1] 8.) **1883** LD. R. GOWER *Reminisc.* I. i. 5 A source of intense pleasure, ever fresh and unstaled. **Unsta·lked,** *a.* (UN-[1] 9.) **1875** HUXLEY & MARTIN *Elem. Biol.* 93 Free swimming unstalked bells. **1884** ELLACOMBE *Plant-Lore Shaks.* 115 Female blossoms ..completely sessile or unstalked. **Unsta·lled,** *ppl. a.* (UN-[1] 8.) [**1775** ASH.] **1829** LYTTON *Devereux* IV. i, My horse stood unstalled at the gate.

**Unsta·mped,** *ppl. a.* [UN-[1] 8. Cf. MDa. *ustampet.*]
**1.** Not crushed by stamping.
**1594** PLAT *Jewell-ho.* II. 46 Malaghie reasons..either stampt or unstampt. **1595** R. SOUTHWELL *Mæoniæ, Christ's Bloody Sweat* 3 Sweete oliue, grape of blisse,..vnstampt, vntoucht of presse. **1648** HEXHAM II, *Ongestooten Peper*, Vnstamped Pepper.

**2.** Not marked by stamping; not stamped with a device or official mark: **a.** Of metals.
**1622** *Strange Accid.* in *Harl. Misc.* (1808) I. 26/2 Silver of three sorts, all unstamped. *a* **1643** GODOLPHIN *Sonn. fr. Harl. MS.* 25 Like unstamped gold I weigh each grate. **1767** *Curiosities of London* 71 Putting in the unstamped piece with his forefinger and thumb. **1801** *Farmer's Mag.* 196 A bit of unstamped bullion. **1853** TRENCH *Proverbs* 15 The same advantage..which..has the recognised coin of the realm over the rude unstamped ore.

**b.** Of paper or publications.
**1809** R. LANGFORD *Introd. Trade* 13 Country Bankers can..issue bills of exchange on unstamped paper. **1855** *Instructions to Postmasters* June, Unstamped Publications ..can be forwarded..under the regulations of the Book Post. **1861** *Sat. Rev.* 23 Nov. 532 So all the benefits of a free press, unstamped, unexcised, may be altogether thrown away.

**3.** Not having a stamp affixed.
**1892** 'H. S. MERRIMAN' *Slave of Lamp* xxi, Posting an unstamped letter addressed to England.

**Unsta·nchable,** *a.* [UN-[1] 7 b.]
**1.** Incapable of being stopped or ended.
*c* **1374** CHAUCER *Boeth.* II. pr. vii. (1868) 58 By þe regard of eternite, þat is vnstauncheable [L. *inexhausta*] and infinit. **1430–40** LYDG. *Bochas* VIII. xvi. (1558) 12 With heed enclyned no word he spake again, Fyll in wepinge, with subbyng vnstaunchable. **1571** GOLDING *Calvin on Ps.* xxiii. 6 Gods goodnesse is unstaunchable. **1670** SWAN *Spec. M.* 440 The wounds of the Hæmorrhois procure unstanchable bleeding. **1837** CARLYLE *Necklace, Misc. Ess.* (1840) V. 104 He burst into unstanchable blubbering of tears. **1880** SWINBURNE *Stud. Shaks.* (ed. 2) i. 51 That perpetual source of debate unstanchable and inexhaustible dispute.

**2.** Unquenchable, insatiable.
**1426** LYDG. *De Guil. Pilgr.* 13053 Evere ther glotons appetyt Ys so ful off ffals delyt, So gredy and so vnstaunchable. *c* **1430** *Pilgr. Lyf Manhode* III. xiv. (1869) 142 Vnstaunchable is my wille;..my affeccioun may haue no fulfillinge. **1440** J. SHIRLEY *Dethe K. James* (1818) 25 Considerying his unstaunchable covetise. **1590** *Serpent of Deris.* A iij b/2 His greedy unstancheable thirste of covetousnes. **1625** JACKSON *Creed* v. xxxii. § 3. 307 The flames of..ill-kindled loue..hath caused his stonie heart to boyle over with vnstaunchable bloudie malice.

**Unsta·nched,** *ppl. a.* [UN-[1] 8.]
**1. a.** Not satisfied; unsated.
*c* **1374** CHAUCER *Boeth.* II. pr. vi. (1868) 54 Rycchesse may nat restreyne auarice vnstaunched. **1591** LYLY *Endym.* II. ii, I will..teare the flesh with my teeth, so mortall is my hate, and so eger my unstaunched stomacke. **1596** SHAKS. 3 *Hen. VI*, II. vi. 83 Stifle the Villaine, whose vnstanched thirst Yorke, and yong Rutland could not satisfie. **1613** HEYWOOD *Silver Age* III. i, His maw Vnstaunch't, He still the thicke Nemean groues doth stray.

**b.** Unrestrained; not stopped.
**1621** *N. Riding Rec.* (1894) 34 Being unstaunchte they [*sc.* deer] raunge over all the adjacent fieldes. **1826** SCOTT *Woodst.* xiv, I conjure thee by the unstanch'd wound. **1850** BLACKIE *Æschylus* II. 263 Fresh and unstaunched woes.

**2.** Not made staunch or water-tight.
**1607** J. CARPENTER *Plaine Mans Plough* 220 Slugging on the waves of this ocean with an unstancht ship. **1760–72** H. BROOKE *Fool of Qual.* (1809) II. 126 The elements..came pouring from unstanched roofs.
*fig.* **1610** SHAKS. *Temp.* I. i. 51 Though the Ship were.. as leaky as an vnstanched wench.

†**Unsta·nged,** *ppl. a.* *Obs.*—[1] [UN-[1] 8.] Not stung. **13..** *Metr. Hom.* (MS. Ashm. 42) fol. 126 b, Nedders vnstangid sall þai bere; Poysonouse drink sall þaim noȝt dere.

**Unsta·rch,** *v.* [UN-[2] 4.] *trans.* To free from stiffness.
**1600** B. JONSON *Cynthia's Rev.* III. ii, [He] dares not smile Beyond a point, for fear t'unstarch his look. **1641** J. TRAPP *Theol. Theol.* iv. 174 [Paul] unstarcht the Oratours speech (as one phrases it) afore Felix. **1683** KENNETT *Erasm. on Folly* 32 He cannot unstarch his gravity.

Hence **Unsta·rching** *vbl. sb.*
**1647** TRAPP *Comm.* 1 *Cor.* i. 17 Witness his [*i.e.* Paul's] artificiall unstarching of the Oratours speech, *Act.* 26.

**Unsta·rched,** *ppl. a.* [UN-[1] 8.] Not starched; *fig.* free from stiffness.
[**1775** ASH.] **1827** *Archæologia* XXI. 254 An unstarched or unplaited pocket. **1861** T. A. TROLLOPE *La Beata* I. vi. 124 The unstarched ease of her own undisguised character. **1894** MRS. DYAN *Man's Keeping* II. 137 You look..as limp as an unstarched collar.

**Unsta·rred,** *ppl. a.* [UN-[1] 8.] Not marked with a star or asterisk; not decorated with a star. Also *fig.*
[**1775** ASH.] *a* **1849** J. C. MANGAN *Poems* (1859) 65 Perfect bliss, unstarred with woe. **1854** S. DOBELL *Balder* iii. 12 The keeper of the palace-gate.., although he come In fashion as a commoner, unstarred, Lets the prince pass. **1890** HESSELS *Latin-A. S. Glossary* p. xli, I trust that..no A.S. words [are] left unstarred.

**Unsta·rted,** *ppl. a.* [UN-[1] 8.]
**1.** Unstartled.
**1659** W. CHAMBERLAYNE *Pharonnida* I. IV. 215 Sound sleeps, unstarted innocence, Softn'd their Beds.

**2.** Not started or begun.
[**1775** ASH.] **1898** *Daily News* 14 Nov. 5/1 Three blocks are now approaching completion,..and only two remain unstarted.

**Unsta·rting,** *ppl. a.* (UN-[1] 10.) **1748** RICHARDSON *Clarissa* (1811) VI. 118 Unbroken, unstarting slumbers.

**Unsta·rtled,** *ppl. a.* (UN-[1] 8.)
**1659** W. CHAMBERLAYNE *Pharonnida* I. I. 96 Desp'rate men, Unstartled with those dangers. *Ibid.* III. v. 474 Unstartl'd at The Rivers depth. **1796** COLERIDGE *Destiny of Nations* 346 The plough-man..Turned up fresh sculls unstartled. **1823** MRS. HEMANS *Siege of Valencia* i, Train'd to hear The trumpet's blast unstartled. **1833** M. SCOTT *Tom Cringle* xix, [The snake], the only unstartled thing in the neighbourhood, continued steadily..on its course.

**Unsta·rtling,** *ppl. a.* (UN-[1] 10.) **1729** SAVAGE *Wanderer* II. 230 Calm thoughts the deed revolve, And now, unstartling, fix the dire resolve. **1891** J. C. ATKINSON *Moorland Par.* 38, I have been accustomed to regard the sheep as a quiet unimpressive sort of creature, with unstartling habits.

**Unsta·te,** *v.* [UN-[2] 6 b.]
**1.** *trans.* To deprive of state, rank, or estate.
*c* **1586** C'TESS PEMBROKE *Ps.* LXXXIX. xiv, Takes he his weapon? thou the edge rebatest.. Would march with kingly pomp? thou him unstatest. **1605** SHAKS. *Lear* I. ii. 108, I would vnstate my selfe, to be in a due resolution. **1611** SPEED *Hist. Gt. Brit.* IX. viii. 490/2 [They] proceeded to vnstate him of that goodliest portion of France. **1624** F. WHITE *Repl. Fisher* 572 The Romane Pope hath a direct power to depose and vnstate them [*sc.* kings]. **1879** J. TODHUNTER *Alcestis* 30 Alack! the best of us May Zeus unstate.

**2.** To deprive of the character of a state.
**1647** WARD *Simp. Cobler* 22 States are unstated, Rulers growne Over-rulers..Churches decayed.

**Unsta·ted,** *ppl. a.* [UN-[1] 8.] Not stated or declared.
[**1775** ASH.] **1864** PUSEY *Lect. Daniel* i. 14 Daniel..left unstated the grounds of his non-participation in their steadfastness. **1900** *Westm. Gaz.* 19 June 9/3 The assertions he makes, and especially the points he leaves unstated.

**Unsta·tely,** *a.* (UN-[1] 7.) **1860** RUSKIN *Mod. Painters* V. 296 Within certain black and unstately iron railings.

**Unsta·tesmanlike,** *a.* (UN-[1] 7 c.)
**1796** LD. SHEFFIELD in *Ld. Auckland's Corr.* (1862) III. 357 The miserable unstatesmanlike mode of taxation which has prevailed. **1837** LYTTON *Athens* I. 456 A daring, but no unstatesmanlike stroke of policy. **1880** MCCARTHY *Own Times* IV. 397 Mr. Gladstone's sudden resolve was openly condemned as petulant and unstatesmanlike.

Hence **Unsta·tesmanlikely** *adv.*
**1846** MRS. GORE *Eng. Char.* I. 326 There are moments.. when the strongest ministerial mind becomes unstatesmanlikely enfeebled.

**Unstathelfast,** *a.*: see UN-[1] 3.

**Unsta·tion,** *v.* (UN-[2] 3.) **1840** BROWNING *Sordello* v. 603 The men and women stationed hitherto Will I unstation. **Unsta·tionary,** *a.* (UN-[1] 7.) **1832** WHEWELL in *Life* (1881) 149, I shall be very unstationary (if there be such a word) for the next three weeks. **Unsta·tioned,** *a.* (UN-[1] 9.) **1760** C. JOHNSTON *Chrysal* I. 23 Though I could give their ships information how to avoid our squadrons, yet they fell into the hands of unstationed privateers. **Unstati·stic,** *a.* (UN-[1] 7.) **1839** CARLYLE *Chartism* iv. (1858) 21 So much can observation altogether unstatistic..ascertain for itself. **Unstati·stical,** *a.* (UN-[1] 7.) **1868** VISCT. STRANGFORD *Select.* (1869) II. 304 That unstatistical city [Constantinople].

**Unsta·tutable,** *a.* [UN-[1] 7 b.] Not in accordance with, contrary to, a statute or statutes.
**1634** LAUD *Wks.* (1857) VI. 388 That they use not long, undecent hair,..nor any other like unstatutable novelty. **1691** *Case of Exeter Coll.* 22 These severe and unstatutable proceedings. **1723** SWIFT *Argts. agst. Power Bps.* Wks. 1841 II. 218/2 In the present bishop of Meath's case that plea did not avail, although the lease were notoriously unstatutable. **1794** BURKE *Corr.* IV. 237 A deputation to remonstrate against an unstatutable arrangement proposed for the succession to the provostship. **1851** J. B. MOZLEY *Lett.* 208 The President has summarily squashed the whole scheme, on the ground of being unstatutable.

Hence **Unsta·tutably** *adv.*
**1688** in *Magd. Coll. & Jas. II* (O.H.S.) 224 The one being unstatutably admitted. **1721** N. AMHERST *Terræ Fil.* No. 27 (1726) 147 That he governs his college arbitrarily, unjustly, and unstatutably. **1876** *Encycl. Brit.* V. 228/2 The establishment of 'vicars', or, as they are now more usually but unstatutably called, 'minor canons'.

**Unstau·nch,** *a.* Also unstanch. [UN-[1] 7.] Not sound, firm, watertight, etc.
**1606** WARNER *Alb. Eng.* XVI. ci. 400 Who can lesse than smile that sees vnstanch and riueld faces, To shelter coylie vnderneath Fannes. *a* **1674** MILTON *Hist. Mosc.* v. Wks. 1851 VIII. 505 The Ships being unstaunch,..sunk by the way. **1896** E. A. KING *Ital. Highways* 223 Not one [column] has proved unstanch through..the storms of these long.. centuries.

**Unstaunchable, -ed,**: see UNSTANCHABLE, etc.

**Unsta·ved,** *ppl. a.* [UN-[1] 8.] Not furnished with staves **1481–90** *Howard Househ. Bks.* (Roxb.) 333 My Lord paied to J. Gravele uppon vj. bylles staved, and v. unstaved, iij. s. iiij. d. **Unstay·able,** *a.* (UN-[1] 7 b.) **1633** T. ADAMS

*Exp.* 2 *Peter* ii. 2 There is..in these a desperate and unstayable precipitation.

**Unstay·ed,** *ppl. a.*[1] [UN-[1] 8 + STAY *v.*[1]] Not stayed or stopped; unhindered, unimpeded.

**1600** FAIRFAX *Tasso* XX. xciii. 382 A thunderbolt he was.. that..of his comming swift, and flight vnstaid, Eternall signes in hardest rockes hath wrought. **1638** JUNIUS *Paint. Ancients* 314 His vast and unstayed understanding. **1820** PRAED *Poems* (1864) II. 40 Unchecked, unstayed, he hurries on. **1851** MRS. BROWNING *Casa Guidi Wind.* I. 730 To strike electric influence through a race, Unstayed by city-wall and barbican.

**Unstay·ed,** *ppl. a.*[2] [UN-[1] 8 + STAY *v.*[2]] Unsupported, † unstable.

**1594** T. B. *La Primaud. Fr. Acad.* II. 184 For one kinde thereof [*sc.* consent] is firme and stedfast, and another weake and vnstayed. **1596** SPENSER *F. Q.* VI. i. 20 He..layd On hideous strokes..That oft he made him stagger as vnstayd. *a* **1649** DRUMM. OF HAWTH. *Poems* Wks. (1711) 55 Some young Phaeton, Whose skilless and unstayed Hand May prove the Ruin of the Land. **1881** CHR. ROSSETTI *Pageant*, etc., *Late Life* iii, Bear Thou in mind..our feebleness unstayed Except Thou stay us.

**Unstay·ed,** *ppl. a.*[3] [UN-[1] 8 + STAY *sb.*[2] 3.] Not furnished with, or confined by, stays.

**1820** PRAED *Bachelor* 97 My waist, unvexed, unstayed, By fetters of the tailor's trade. **1894** *Idler* Sept. 140 In hygienic clothing, A waist and heels deep-loathing, Thy unstayed figure freely flounders.

**Unstayed,** obs. var. UNSTAID *a.*

**Unstay·edness.** [f. UNSTAYED *ppl. a.*[2]] Lack of support. **1874** PUSEY *Lent. Sermons* 326 He clad Himself with our fear, that He might array our unstayedness with the solidity of His virtue.

**Unstay·ing,** *ppl. a.* [UN-[1] 10.] Not stopping or pausing.

**1616** W. BROWNE *Brit. Past.* II. iv. ad fin., I feare,..Ere I have ended my sad history, Unstaying Time may bring on his last houre. **1682** OTWAY *Venice Preserved* IV. i, If I not revenge, With..unstaying fury, Thy sufferings. **1845** E. JONES *Studies* (1879) 186 Laughing maids, unstaying,.. O'er the lights shall dart. **1883** B. SMITH *Life Ld. Lawrence* II. 449 His unstaying and pitiless advance across the wilds of Central Asia.

**Unstea·dfast,** *a.* [UN-[1] 8 and 5 b. Cf. ON. *ústaðfast-r* (older Da. *ustadfæst*).]

**1.** Of persons, the mind, etc.: Not steadfast in conduct or opinion; inconstant, fickle.

*a* **1200** *Moral Ode* 241 in *O. E. Hom.* I. 175 Þo boð þa þe weren her a þanke unstedefeste. *c* **1200** *Trin. Coll. Hom.* 61 We turnen ofte to him and fro him, for we beð unstedefaste. *a* **1300** *Cursor M.* 6516 Þi folk..has don a suik; Sin þat þou com fra þam last, Þou sal þam find ful vn-stedfast. **1340–70** *Alex. & Dind.* 944 Huo wolde wene þat a weih woxen on elde Were wist for vnstedefast of word or of dede? *c* **1450** *Mankind* 207 in *Macro Plays* 8, I am onstedfast in lywynge; my name ys 'Mankynde'. **1502** ATKYNSON tr. *De Imitatione* III. xxii. 214, I am ryghte feble and vnstedfaste. **1568** GRAFTON *Chron.* II. 193 This king was..vnstedfast of maners and disposed to lightnesse. **1601** CAMPION *Bk. Ayres* xiv. 4 My heart..is dismaid by thee, Who art so cruell and vnsteadfast growne. **1647** H. MORE *Song of Soul*, etc. 319 When my weakened soul Unstedfast, into this Outworld doth reel. *a* **1850** ROSSETTI *Dante & Circle* I. (1874) 123 He answers Dante, confessing his unsteadfast heart. **1850–1** LONGF. *Gold. Leg.* ii. *Village Church*, Pardon in me The oscillation of a mind Unsteadfast.

*absol.* **1825** COLERIDGE *Aids Refl.* 379 In the perfect foreknowledge that they would confirm the disbelieving, alienate the unsteadfast.

**2.** Not remaining in the same state; liable to change or alteration: **a.** Of the world, life, etc.

*c* **1200** *Moral Ode* 320 in *O. E. Hom.* II. 229 We wilnieð after wereldes wele þe longe ne mai ilaste, And legeð mast al ure swinc on þing unstedefaste. **1456** SIR G. HAYE *Law Arms* (S.T.S.) 33 Be caus of this divisioun, all the warld is in a wylde thocht, unstedefast. **1475** *Bk. Noblesse* (Roxb.) 3 Thoroughe sodein and variable chaunces of unstedfast fortune. *a* **1500** in *Ratis Raving*, etc. 22 Leid thi lyf with thaim that the louis for the day of the vnstedfast lyf. **1574** HYLL *Conject. Weather* i, Then shall follow an unstedfast Winter. **1591** SPENSER *Daphn.* 518 For all mens states alike vnstedfast be. **1600** TOURNEUR *Transf. Metam.* iv, Subiect unto th' unstedfast moone's controle.

**b.** Of persons, qualities, etc.

**1483** CAXTON *Gold. Leg.* 388 b/2 Whome ought I better to chese of thyse two, or the kyng puyssaunt pardurable..or one seek unstedfast. **1513** MORE *Rich. III* (1883) 6 With large giftes he get hym unstedfaste frendeshippe. **1535** COVERDALE *Prov.* v. 6 She regardeth not the path of life, so vnstedfast are hir wayes, that thou canst not knowe them. **1600** HOLLAND *Livy* 671 The assured loialtie of the captaines..was but vaine, fickle, and unsteadfast.

**3.** Not firmly established or fixed; readily moving or changing place; not firm or steady.

**13..** *Propr. Sanct.* 158 in *Archiv Stud. neu. Spr.* LXXXI. 93 He made Nettes to beo cast In to þe se vnstudefast. **1398** TREVISA *Barth. De P. R.* XII. xxxii. (Bodl. MS.), Þe pecock haþ an vnstedefaste and an yuel schape heede. **1563** *Mirr. Mag.*, *Induct.* xxxiii, Her iyes vnstedfast rolling here and there. **1596** SHAKS. *1 Hen. IV*, I. iii. 193 As full of perill..As to o're-walke a Current, roaring loud, On the vnstedfast footing of a Speare. **1657** AUSTEN *Fruit Trees* II. 28 The farther off the Branches are from the Roote, the more loose, and unsteadfast they are. **1793** WORDSW. *Descr. Sk.* 252 Bare steeps, where Desolation stalks, afraid, Unsteadfast, by a blasted yew upstay'd. **1864** DORA GREENHILL *Lyra Myst.*, *Soul Garden.* xii, These Lilies..That quiver with unsteadfast light.

*fig.* **1817** JAS. MILL *Brit. India* II. v. vii. 621 The unsteadfast basis on which the power of the leaders at Poonah was placed.

Hence **Unstea·dfastly** *adv.*

**1559** GUEST *Let. to Cecil* in Strype *Ann. Ref.* (1709) I. App. xiv. 38, I have neither ungodly allowed anything against the Scripture, neither unstedfastly done anything contrary to my writing. **1611** COTGR., *Inconstamment*,.. vnstedfastly, mutably, wauueringly.

**Unstea·dfastness.** [f. prec.] The quality of being unsteadfast: **a.** Of persons or conduct.

*a* **1300** *Cursor M.* 27793 O suernes cums..vnstedfastnes, o will wandring. **1384** CHAUCER *L. G. W.* Prol. 526 A ful gret neglygence Was it to the to write onstedefast-nesse Of women. *c* **1440** *Promp. Parv.* 367/2 Onstedefastnesse, *instabilitas.* *a* **1500** *Chaucer's Dream* 200 Wherefore I doubt .. Her variance and vnsteadfastnes. *a* **1548** HALL *Chron.*, *Hen. VIII*, 144 b, Then was rehersed to the Frenchemen their doublenes [and] their vnstedfastnes. **1649** BP. REYNOLDS *Hosea* ii. 91 The falsenesse and unstedfastnesse of our Hearts. **1694** KETTLEWELL *Comp. Persecuted* 58 Let not any other Persons unsteadfastness in thy ways..cause me to waver. *a* **1850** ROSSETTI *Dante & Circle* I. (1874) 99 Many times I cursed the unsteadfastness of my eyes. **1860** PUSEY *Min. Proph.* 90 God, in answer, promises to heal.. their fickleness and unsteadfastness.

**b.** Of life, fortune, etc.

**1508** *Dunbar's Poems* (S.T.S.) 321/19 Sen in this warld thare is no sekernes,..I tak my leve at all unstedfastnes. **1561** BECON *Sick Man's Salve* (1572) 5 O the vnstedfastnesse of mans life! **1585** T. WASHINGTON tr. *Nicholay's Voy.* IV. xxix. 150 b, By chaunge of time and vnstedfastnesse of fortune this so flourishing a citie is brought to..ruine.

**Unstea·died,** *ppl. a.* (UN-[1] 8.) **1809–14** WORDSW. *Excurs.* VII. 115 A Priest he was by function; but..By books unsteadied, by his pastoral care Too little checked. **1865** *Sat. Rev.* 19 Aug. 240/1 It is not the drunkenness of the unsteadied hand, the rolling gait, and stammering tongue.

**Unstea·dily,** *adv.* [UN-[1] 11. Cf. UNSTEADY *a.*] In an unsteady manner.

**1556** J. HEYWOOD *Spider & Flie* Bb iij b, To se these flies now: so vnstedily stagger, So late so redie. **1690** LOCKE *Hum. Und.* III. x. § 31 He that uses his Words loosly and unsteadily, will either be not minded, or not understood. *c* **1700** CONGREVE *Ovid's Art of Love* Wks. 1773 III. 276 This way and that unsteadily they rove, And, never fix'd, are fugitives in Love. **1738** BOLINGBROKE *Idea Patriot King* (1749) 71 Considering how unsteadily and unsystematically even the best of men are apt often to proceed. **1817** COLERIDGE *Lay Serm.*, '*Blessed are ye*' 37 The cup of sorrow overflows by being held unsteadily. **1847** DE QUINCEY *Sp. Mil. Nun* Wks. 1853 III. 60 As idle as the flapping sail that fills unsteadily with the breeze upon a stranded ship. **1897** MRS. E. L. VOYNICH *Gadfly* I. vii, The man approached unsteadily along the water side.

**Unstea·diness.** [f. next.] The quality of being unsteady.

**1611** COTGR., *Volubilité*,..vnsteadinesse, or an inconstant mouing. **1646** H. LAWRENCE *Comm. Angels* 120 The cause of loosenes, and laxenesse, and unsteddines in our course. **1698** FRYER *Acc. E. India & P.* 2 The unsteadiness of the Weather. **1722** WOLLASTON *Relig. Nat.* v. (1724) 85 If things are now and then mis-shaped, this infers no unsteadiness or mistake in nature. **1796** MME. D'ARBLAY *Camilla* v. 7 The unsteadiness of the boat. **1808** MITFORD *Hist. Greece* III. 88 The gross evils inherent in the Athenian constitution; its irremediable unsteadiness, its gross tyranny. **1869** TANNER *Clin. Med.* (ed. 2) 289 The insidious form begins by numbness,..unsteadiness on the legs,..till the loss of power is complete. **1875** *Economist* 16 Jan. 68/1 The unsteadiness of the [stock-] markets.

**Unstea·dy,** *a.* [UN-[1] 7. Cf. OFris. *un-, onstedich*, MLG. *unstedich*, MHG. *unstætec* (G. *unstätig*); MDu. *onstadich*, LG. *unstadig*; etc.]

**1.** Not steady in position; not firm or secure; not held or kept steady.

**1598** FLORIO, *Insollare*, to make loose or vnsteadie. **1601** HOLLAND *Pliny* II. 440 Some there bee, who..advise their patients to wash their unsteedie teeth with the said infusion. **1622** MABBE tr. *Aleman's Guzman d'Alf.* I. 258 Walking to and fro on the vnsteddy legges of Dis-rest. **1703** DE FOE *Hymn to the Pillory* viii, The Statesmen..Who guide us with unsteady hand. **1743** R. BLAIR *Grave* 205 The busto moulders, and the deep-cut marble, Unsteady to the steel, gives up its charge. **1800** COLERIDGE *Christabel* II. 590 Christabel in dizzy trance Stumbling on the unsteady ground. **1815** SCOTT *Guy M.* li, He glanced at some passages of the letters with an unsteady eye and an agitated mind. **1867** MORRIS *Jason* VI. 238 On their quest [they]..began to plough The unsteady plain.

*transf.* **1885** 'MRS. ALEXANDER' *At Bay* v, Her voice was unsteady, and Glynn noticed that she was trembling.

**2.** Not steady or constant in respect of conduct or purpose; fluctuating, fickle, wavering.

**1598** DALLINGTON *Meth. Trav.* X 2 b, Men of light and vnsteadie braines, haue commonly sudden and sharpe conceites. **16..** MIDDLETON, etc. *Old Law* v. i, Our unsteady fancies Would question whether we yet lived or no. **1647** CLARENDON *Hist. Reb.* I. § 49 So fluctuating and unsteady a testimony is the Applause of Popular Councils. **1677** YARRANTON *Eng. Improv.* a 3 b, I could not imagine which way what I lay down in my Book..should in this unsteady Age ever come to be put into Practice. **1712** BERKELEY *Pass. Obed.* Wks. 1871 III. 121 The violent humours and unsteady opposite wills of a multitude of savages. *a* **1770** JORTIN *Serm.* (1774) III. 16 The tyranny of evil habits, and the easy descent from an unsteddy virtue to those habits. **1819** KEATS *Otho* I. i, You have intrigued with these unsteady times To admiration. **1849** FROUDE *Nemesis of Faith* 136 Unsteady minds began to grow uneasy. **1871** B. TAYLOR *Faust* II. I. v. 6 Let naught howe'er it sound make thee unsteady.

*absol.* **1828** MOIR *Mansie Wauch* Prelim., The unsteady may take a hint concerning what it is possible for one of..a stout heart to go through with. **1872** [see UNSTEADY *v.*]

**3.** Marked or characterized by absence of steadiness or regularity; not regular, even, or uniform.

**1690** LOCKE *Hum. Und.* II. xiv. § 22 If the Motion of the Sun were as unequal as that of a Ship driven by unsteady Winds. **1759** STERNE *Tr. Shandy* II. ii, The unsteady uses of words, which have perplexed the clearest and most exalted understandings. **1798** SOUTHEY *Henry the Hermit* 58 The lamp that stream'd a long unsteady light. ? **1821** BRYANT *Winter Piece* 4 When the unsteady pulse Beat with strange flutterings. **1862** A. MEADOWS *Man. Midwifery* 186 Unsteady gait; when the woman walks the chest is held back. **1884** *Truth* 13 Mar. 372 The badness of the road is aggravated by unsteady driving, and a defective type of rolling stock.

**Unstea·dy,** *v.* [UN-[2] 6 a.] *trans.* To deprive of steadiness; to render unsteady.

**1532** W. WALTER *Guystarde & S.* A ij, The wretched lyfe of osyosyte..Unstedyeth the wyt. **1646** H. LAWRENCE *Comm. Angels* 122 How doth hee unsteddy our steps, and intimidate us, by putting scruples in our wayes. **1748** RICHARDSON *Clarissa* VII. xliv. 176 Unless the shock..(by unsteadying my hand) shall divert my aim from his head. **1812** *Examiner* 24 Aug. 540/1 Shot, shells, grape,..could not unsteady the step..of the..infantry. **1872** H. BUSHNELL *Serm. Living Subj.* 245 Waiting always on the unsteady, unsteadies even the sense of principle. **1883** STEVENSON *Treas. Isl.* ii, I was quite unsteadied by all that had fallen out.

Hence **Unstea·dying** *ppl. a.*

**1865** MASSON *Rec. Brit. Philos.* 174 A point whence the appearance of an unusual amount of unsteadying thought may be dated.

**Unsteek,** *v.* Now *dial.* [UN-[2] 3.] *trans.* To undo, unfasten, open. Also *fig.*

*c* **1250** *Hymn* in *Trin. Coll. Hom.* App. 258 He mai binde & to breke...He mai luke & unsteke michte of al þinge. *c* **1250** *Gen. & Ex.* 2828 Aaron..can wel speken; ðu salt him meten and vnsteken Him bodeword min. *a* **1300** in Horstmann *Altengl. Leg.* (1875) 26 He getþ þe Dore to vnsteke. **1390** GOWER *Conf.* II. 128 Thus whanne he hath his cofre loken, It schal noght after ben unstoken. *c* **1400** *Laud Troy Bk.* 8239 Many a coffre was vnstoken, To drawe out robes that were y-loken. **1855, 1868** in Yks. glossaries (*unsteck*).

**b.** In *pa. pple.* not clearly distinguishable from 'not closed, left open' (UN-[1] 8). Cf. UNSTOKEN.

**13..** *Sir Beues* (A.) 1663 Þe chaumber dore a fond vnsteke. *c* **1350** *Lybeaus Disc.* 1450 At a posterne unsteke Lybeauus gan out-breke. *c* **1470** HENRY *Wallace* IX. 1655 Gat nane, bot ane, with lyff out off that sted, For that the ȝet so lang wnstekit was.

**Unstee·l,** *v.* (UN-[2] 6 b.) **1748** RICHARDSON *Clarissa* V. 215 Why then should this enervating pity unsteel my foolish heart? **1851** C. L. SMITH tr. *Tasso* III. xxv, Her strokes on one descend Already trembling, suppliant and unsteeled.

**Unstee·led,** *ppl. a.* (UN-[1] 8.) **1744** W. WHITEHEAD *Atys & Adrastus* 409 Why was I singl'd to perform the Part, Unsteel'd my Heart, unpetrified my Heart? **1760–72** H. BROOKE *Fool of Qual.* (1809) III. 75 My conscience was yet unsteeled. **1899** R. BRIDGES *Pater Filio* 2 Sense with keenest edge unused, Yet unsteel'd by scathing fire.

**Unstee·p,** *v.* (UN-[2] 3 + STEEP *v.*[1])

**1598** FLORIO, *Dimollare*, to vnsteepe. **1633** P. FLETCHER *Purple Isl.* VI. xvii, Anon the rattling hail On earth poures down his shot..; His powder spent, the Sunne puts off his vail, And fair his flaming beauties now unsteeps.

**Unstee·ped,** *ppl. a.* (UN-[1] 8.)

**1626** BACON *Sylva* § 402 Next the wheat simple of itself, unsteeped and unwatered. *Ibid.*, There was also other wheat sown unsteeped. **1766** *Compl. Farmer* s.v. *Seed*, The ground had been prepared exactly in the same manner for the steeped and the un-steeped grain. **1853** *Nicholson's Operat. Mechanic* (ed. 4) 407 For the purpose of discharging the colour out of the unsteeped flax or hemp.

**Unstee·red,** *ppl. a.* (UN-[1] 8. Cf. MSw. *ostyrad*, Sw. *ostyrd.*) **1729** SAVAGE *Wanderer* III. (1761) 49 Like a frail Bark thy weaken'd Mind is tost, Unsteer'd, unbalanc'd, 'till its Wealth is lost. **1886** *Pall Mall G.* 23 Feb. 4/2 The unsteered, storm-driven voyage of the crazy craft.

**Unste·mmed,** *ppl. a.*[1] [UN-[1] 8 + STEM *v.*[2] Cf. MDu. *ongestemt.*] Not stemmed or stopped. **1732** BERKELEY *Serm. to S.P.G.* 25 This unstemmed Torrent of Profaneness.

**Unste·mmed,** *ppl. a.*[2] [UN-[1] 8 + STEM *v.*[4] 3 a.] Not having the stalk and midrib removed. **1883** J. R. DODGE *Manuf. Tobacco* iii. 24 The law established the rate at 5 cents per pound for unstemmed smoking, with 2 cents for stemmed. **1894** *Times* 16 Aug. 6/5 (U.S. tariff), Wrapped tobacco, unstemmed. **Unste·nched,** *a.* (UN-[1] 9.) **1822** COBBETT *Rur. Rides* (1885) I. 103 It is one of those pretty, clean, unstenched, unconfined places that [etc.]. **†Unste·nted,** *ppl. a. Sc. Obs.* [UN-[1] 8 + STENT *v.*[2]] Not assessed. **1605** *Extr. Aberd. Reg.* (1848) II. 272 To disburding thame of the taxatioun of fyue hundreth pundis,.. quhilk sowme of fywe hundreth pundis lyis yit vnstentit.

**Unste·p,** *v.* (UN-[2] 5, 7 + STEP *v.* II, 7.)

**1853** READE *Christie Johnstone* xiii. 202 Flucker..unstepped his mast in two fathom water. **1883** *Man. Seamanship for Boys* 243 If there is anything wrong at the mast-head,..unstep the mast and rectify it. **1883** *Pall Mall G.* 9 May 2/1 The novelty consists in the mast being made to unstep in rough weather.

**Unste·rcorated,** *ppl. a.* (UN-[1] 8.) **1821** SCOTT *Pirate* iv, A man's mind always grovelling in mould, stercorated or unstercorated.

**† Unste·rn,** *a. Obs.* Also 4 **vnsterne, -sterin, -sturen.** [App. an alteration of *austern* AUSTERE *a.*, by association with STERN *a.*] Severe, stern.

*a* **1300** *Cursor M.* 464 Bot he was merred of hys mint, Fulson he fand vnsterne stint. *Ibid.* 3461 Þair strut it was vn-stern stith. *Ibid.* 24540 (Edinb.).

**† Unste·rnly,** *adv. Obs.* Also 4 **vnsturne-, vnsturen-, vnsterly.** [f. prec + -LY.[2]] Severely, sternly; grimly.

*a* **1300** *Cursor M.* 7450 O bodi gret, o granis lang, Vnsternli [*Gött.* vnsterly] semed he be strang. *Ibid.* 16031 Þai stert þam forth vnsterli [*Gött.* vnsternli], Wit a ful bald bere.

**Unsti·ck,** *v.* (UN-[2] 3.) **1706** STEVENS, *Desempegar*,..to unstick, unglew. **1748** RICHARDSON *Clarissa* VII. 125 The other [foot] riveted to its native earth, bemired..beyond the possibility of unsticking itself.

**Unsti·ffen,** *v.* (UN-[2] 6.)

**1611** FLORIO, *Distirizzare*, to vnstiffen, to vnbenum. **1855** MRS. GASKELL *North & S.* xxvi, Then her rigid face unstiffened from its gray frostbound expression. **1894** A. ROBERTSON *Nuggets*, etc. 20 The prospect of a fee unstiffened his rheumatic joints.

**Unsti·ffened,** *ppl. a.* (Un-1 8.) 1648 Hexham II, *Ongestijft*, Vnstifned, or Loose. 1889 Swinburne *Study B. Jonson* 96 The poem..would be worthy of very high praise if the texture..were unstiffened and undisfigured by..awkward inversions. 1893 *Daily News* 17 Apr. 6/3 Some..have determined to abide by the unstiffened dresses of last year. **Unsti·ffening,** *vbl. sb.* (Un-1 13.) 1832 Coleridge *Lett.* (1895) 761 A sort of unstiffening of my long dormant joints and muscles.

**Unsti·fled,** *ppl. a.* (Un-1 8.)
1742 Young *Nt. Th.* II. 121 Art, brainless art! our furious charioteer (For nature's voice unstifled would recal) Drives headlong. 1842 Browning *Christina* iv, Just this or that poor impulse Which for once had play unstifled, Seems the sole work of a life-time. 1863 *Pilgr. over Prairies* I. 156 A profusion of nut-brown hair..fell unstifled by cap, untortured by steel or curl paper.

**Unsti·gmatized,** *ppl. a.* (Un-1 8 a *c.*)
[1775 Ash.] 1778 [W. H. Marshall] *Minutes Agric., Digest* 6 Should this Impostor be suffered to stroll abroad unstigmatized. 1806–7 J. Beresford *Miseries Hum. Life* VII. lxxi, Who..manage their inuendos so adroitly, that you are obliged to let them pass unstigmatized. 1814 Wordsw. *Excurs.* VII. 798 Nor left unstigmatized those fatal fields On which the sons of mighty Germany Were taught a base submission.

**Unsti·ll,** *a.* (Un-1 7. Cf. OE. *unstille*, OHG. *unstilli*, MLG. *unstil*, obs. Du. *onstil.*)
[1648 Hexham II, *Onstil*, Vnstill, or Disquiet.] 1743 C. Wesley in *Jrnl.* (1805) I. 247 Some very unstill sisters, who always..tried who could cry loudest. 1823 E. Moor *Suffolk Words* 184 A maid undressing an unstil child. 1903 Kipling in *Windsor Mag.* Sept. 363/1 She never kept still. She kept very unstill.

Hence **Unsti·llness.** (In quots. after OE. *unstillnes, -nys.*)
1846 Thorpe tr. *Ælfric's Hom.* II. 375 He..tries these five senses, who through curiosity and unstillness wastes them uselessly. 1875 *Anderida* I. vii. 121 When some..attendants discovered the unstillness to Osgod's companions.

**Unsti·lled,** *ppl. a.* (Un-1 8. Cf. Sw. *ostillad.*)
1648 Hexham II, *Ongestilt*, Vnstilled, or Vn-appeased. 1817 Coleridge *Biog. Lit.* ix. I. 140 Unstilled yearning, and an original ebulliency of spirit. 1874 Pusey *Lent. Serm.* 43 To hear the cries of their unstilled hunger.

**Unsti·mulated,** *ppl. a.* (Un-1 8.)
[1775 Ash.] *a* 1800 Cowper *Iliad* (ed. 2) XXIII. 469 He..wept to see..his own Unstimulated coursers thrown behind. 1825 Scott *Talism.* xxii, The future..glittered with such hues, as..his unstimulated imagination had not been able to produce. 1882 Vines tr. *Sachs' Bot.* 893 The elasticity of the stimulated and of the unstimulated filament is the same.

**Unsti·mulating,** *ppl. a.* (Un-1 10.)
[1828–32 Webster.] 1844 J. Epps *Dom. Homœop.* 147 Plain, nutritious, unstimulating food. 1899 Fr. H. Burnett *De Willoughby Claim* xiii, A lifetime of narrow, unstimulating years.

**Unsti·ng,** *v.* [Un-2 4.] *trans.* To deprive of a sting.
1612 J. Davies (Heref.) *Muse's Sacr.* Wks. (Grosart) II. 79/1 God unstings such angry Waspes and Bees. 1656 Trapp *Comm. 1 Cor.* xv. 56 Christ having unstinged death, and as it were disarmed it. 1692 South *Serm.* (1697) II. 564 He has disarmed his Afflictions, unstung his Miseries. 1827 Pollok *Course T.* II. 341 For temporal death, although unstinged, remained. 1850 R. Simpson *Mem. Worth* vi. 83 [Death] was unstinged when it encountered him.

Hence **Unsti·nged** *ppl. a.* (Cf. Unstung 2.)
1782 J. Brown *Nat. & Rev. Relig.* III. ii, An unstinged and sweetened death.

**Unsti·nted,** *ppl. a.* (Un-1 8: see Stint *v.*)
1480 *Cov. Leet Bk.* 438 þe seid Maire & Recordor mayntey the..Frankleyns of þe Forreins..contynually to go vnstynted, and the Comons of the Cite be stynted, no man to passe his rate. 1599 Sandys *Europæ Spec.* (1632) 41 To all such..as should oppose against his Soveraigntie and unstinted power. 1622 Callis *Stat. Sewers* (1647) 24 A general Law unstinted and unbounded. *a* 1711 Ken *Hymn Festiv.* Poet. Wks. 1721 I. 410 Saints..crop unstinted Shares In the twelve pleasant Fruits it bears. 1740 Somerville *Hobbinolia* III. 29 With unstinted Joy His Heart o'erflows. 1811 Scott *Don Roderick* I. ix, Lands, where the near Sun Gives with unstinted boon ethereal flame. 1877 'H. A. Page' *De Quincey* II. xvi. 20 His unstinted, if not reckless liberality.

Hence **Unsti·ntedly** *adv.*
1849 Rock *Ch. of Fathers* I. i. 8 Both these prelates borrowed unstintedly from the book of St. Osmund. 1883 *Standard* 13 April 6/4 General Angus .. condemns the management unstintedly.

**Unsti·nting,** *ppl. a.* [Un-1 10.]
†1. Unceasing. *Obs.*—1
*c* 1380 Wyclif *Sel. Wks.* III. 52 Alle angels.., and alle powers in þis world,..crien bi vois and unstyntinge to þee.

2. Ungrudging, lavish.
1845 Herschel *Ess.* (1857) 644 The spirit in which the demands of science have been met..has been..munificent and unstinting. 1883 W. E. Norris *No New Thing* xi, With so unstinting a hand had he ministered to the necessities of the poor.

Hence **Unsti·ntingly** *adv.*
1857 Ruskin *Pol. Econ. Art* 200 All of these should be completely and unstintingly given. 1885 Agnes Clerke *Pop. Hist. Astron.* 147 He poured his earnings unstintingly into his crucibles.

**Unsti·rrable,** *a.* (Un-1 7 b.) *a* 1340 Hampole *Psalter*, etc. (1884) 506 Made be þai vnstirabil as a stane til þat þi folke pass.

**Unsti·rred,** *ppl. a.* (Un-1 8.)
*a.* 13.. *E. E. Allit. P.* B. 706 At a stylle stollen steuen, vnstered wyth syȝt, Luf lowe hem bytwene lasched so hote. *c* 1375 *Sc. Leg. Saints* xliv. (*Lucy*) 255 Vnsterit scho stud stil as a crag. 1513 Douglas *Æneid* VII. xi. 53 Vnsterit lang tyme and vnmovit, Itale Now birnis into fury bellicale. 1535 Stewart *Cron. Scot.* (Rolls) III. 61 Neuir ane ox wes ȝokkit into bow, Bot lay full still into thair stall vnsteird.

*β.* *a* 1340 Hampole *Psalter* xxv. 12 Mi fote..departid not fro þi ryȝtwysnes bot stod vnstird ogeyne alle sclaunders. 1470–1 *Rolls of Parlt.* VI. 233/1 Uncompelled, unstirred or undesired soo to doo. 1551 Recorde *Pathw. Knowl.* I. xiv, Set the one foote of the same compasse vnsturred, in the eande of the other line. 1589 Fleming *Virg. Georg.* II. 28 Vnstird it doth remaine, And conquereth..by lasting many yeares. 1624 Gataker *Transubst.* 55 The selfe same body..sitting there still unstirred and untouched. 1628 Feltham *Resolves* 221 Like the Wind..It disperses Exhalations from the muddy Earth, which would, vnstirr'd, infect it. 1699 Bentley *Phal.* 506 It was immortal Vellum..that could last for ten Ages, though untouch'd and unstirr'd. 1830 Mrs. Hemans *Lady of Provence* 11 Many a Chatillon.., Unstirr'd by the ringing trumpet's breath, His shroud of armour wore. 1843 Ruskin *Mod. Paint.* I. II. v. iii. § 27 Glassy pools, upon which the drinking cattle cast an unstirred image. 1882 'Ouida' *Maremma* I. 192 The ilex leaves..drooping above their heads, unstirred by any breeze.

**Unsti·rring,** *ppl. a.* (Un-1 5 d, 10.)
1. Not causing to stir or give way. *rare.*—1
*c* 1375 *Sc. Leg. Saints* vii. (*Jas. minor*) 785 Al vnsteryinge þe stekyne Of þe presone & þe selynge.

2. Not stirring or moving; inactive.
*a* 1684 Leighton *Comm. 1 Peter* iv. (1849) II. 323 A slothful, unstirring life, will make a sickly, unhealthy life. 1818 Milman *Samor* III. 210 The dead unstirring ocean bears them on. *a* 1851 Moir *Night-Hawk* i, The midnight moon Looks sombred o'er the forest depths, that sleep Unstirring.

**Unsti·tch,** *v.* [Un-2 3.] *trans.* To remove stitches from; to detach or separate in this way.
1538 Elyot, *Resuo*,..to vnstytche. 1639 T. de Gray *Expert Farrier* 331 Stop both your horse eares;..stitch them up, and..[later] unstitch them. 1648 Hexham II, *Ontnaeyt*, vnsowne, or vnstitcht. 1688 R. L'Estrange *Tully's Offices* 79 As Wise men say of..Ill Grounded Friendships; 'tis better to unstich than to tear them all to pieces on a suddain. *a* 1774 Goldsm. tr. *Scarron's Com. Romance* (1775) II. 25 When he scuffled with anybody,..he ever tore or unstitched the cloaths of his adversary. 1860 *Ure's Dict. Arts* (ed. 5) I. 547 After washing, the pieces [of calico] are unstitched, and put in the hydro-extractor.

**Unsti·tched,** *ppl. a.* [Un-1 8.] Not stitched; unsewed.
1599 A. M. tr. *Gabelhouer's Bk. Physicke* 304/1 Nether doth the sinewe water so greate harme in an vnstitched wounde as it doth in a stitched. 1856 Geo. Eliot *Ess.* (1884) 86 To the typical German..it is indifferent..whether or not his book have every other leaf unstitched.

**†Unsti·the,** *a. Obs.*—1 [Un-1 7.] Not strong; feeble, weak. *c* 1400 *Destr. Troy* 117 Till it fell hym by fortune, faintyng of elde, Unstithe for to stire, or stightill the Realme.

**Unsto·ck,** *v.* [Un-2 5 and 4.]
1. *trans.* a. To remove (a ship) from the stocks.
*a* 1547 Surrey *Æneis* IV. 524 Where the Troyans fast Fell to their worke, from the shore to unstock High rigged ships.

b. To dismount (a gun).
1598 Florio, *Scalcagnare*,..to vnstock, or dismount any kinde of great ordinance or artillerie.

c. To remove the stock from (a gun, etc.).
1706 Phillips (ed. Kersey), *To Unstock a Gun*, is to take off its Stock. 1726 Shelvocke *Voy. round World* 70 After we had got well to sea, we unstock'd our anchors and brought them aft. 1849 W. S. Mayo *Kaloolah* viii, Unstocking my rifle-barrel.

2. To deprive of stock.
1647 Digges *Unlawf. Taking Armes* 169 The husbandmans store being consumed, the pastures unstocked,..we shall be devoured by famine. 1667 Waterhouse *Fire Lond.* 169 Turned out of their callings, and unstocked by the loss of that ruffle.

3. To empty of occupants.
1655 G. S. in Hartlib *Ref. Commonw. Bees* 28, I am confident, had I continued my digestions any considerable time, I had soon unstock[ed] nigh a dozen of Hives. 1865 W. G. Palgrave *Arabia* II. 328 The conflict of the Roses did not unstock the England of a few years later.

**Unsto·cked,** *ppl. a.* [Un-1 8.]
1. Not furnished with a stock.
1388 in Nicolas *Hist. Royal Navy* (1847) II. 475 La hulk ..ove lapparaill..v. ankres dont un de eux est unstokked. 1497 *Naval Acc. Hen. VII* (1896) 290 Serpentynes..stokked cxvj, vnstokked xxv. 1513 N. West in Ellis *Orig. Lett.* Ser. I. I. 70 A greate piece of ordenaunce of iij. yerds longe and mor, unstocked. 1599 Hakluyt *Voy.* II. II. 107 We had nowe but two ankers left vs, which were vnstocked and in hold. 1681 *Cal. Treas. Bks., 1681–5*, 4 The value of 200 barrels of guns or muskets unstocked. 1805 W. Hunter in *Naval Chron.* XIII. 8 Our anchors being unstocked, as is the custom in Indiamen,..we found great difficulty in ..steadying them, in order to get the anchors in the stocks.

2. Not provided with a stock of goods.
1633 D. R[ogers] *Treatise Sacr.* i. 161 A poore unstockt man is easily perceived in his wares, the small store and choice therof.

3. Not stocked with animals, etc.
1697 Walsh *Life V.* ℙ 7 in Dryden *Virgil*, Wars had laid Italy almost waste; the Ground was Uncultivated and Unstock'd. 1750 T. Carte *Hist. Eng.* II. 719 The lands lay uncultivated and the farms unstocked, by reason of..continual depredations. *a* 1787 G. White *Selborne* vii, This chase remains un-stocked to this day. 1794 R. J. Sulivan *View Nat.* I. 24 One bold and inartificial whole, unstocked with animation.

4. (See Stock *sb.*1 44.)
1825 T. Hook *Sayings* Ser. II. II. 94 While sleepy lacqueys, their hose ungartered, and themselves unstocked, are crawling down the second staircase to breakfast.

**Unsto·ckinged,** *ppl. a.* (Un-1 8.)
[1775 Ash.] 1812 W. Tennant *Anster F.* II. xxvii, Her roguish boys with bare unstocking'd feet. 1845 Talfourd *Vac. Rambles* I. 232 They were clad in brown serge, unstockinged.

**†Unsto·ic,** *v. Obs.*—1 (Un-2 6 b.) 1735 Swift *Let.* in Maggs *Cat.* No. 445 (1923) 238, I long apprehended you would have the power to corrupt me. I shall therefore unstoick myself to attend you. **Unsto·ken,** *ppl. a. Obs.* or *dial.* [Cf. Unsteek *v.* b.] Opened; not closed or shut. 1421 Hoccleve *Min. Poems* 151/333 On a nyght..Left was the Erles Chambre dore vnstoken. 1828 Carr *Craven Gloss.*, *Unstoken*, unshut. **Unsto·len,** *ppl. a.* (Un-1 8 b. Cf. MDu. *ongestolen.*) 1533 J. Heywood *Johan & Tib* (Brandl) 246 Yet it may lye safe ynough vnstolen. 1837 Carlyle *Misc. Ess.* (1840) V. 19 The world would let us keep it unstolen for Fourteen whole years.

**Unsto·ne,** *v.* [Un-2 3 and 4.]
1. *trans.* To convert from a stony state.
1594 Carew *Tasso* (1881) 49 But let his hand that hardest harts gently Doth pierce, them both vnstone and mollifie. *Ibid.* 92 This fained sorrow drew from many a freake True teares, and harts vnstoand most hardened.

2. To castrate.
1611 Cotgr., *Escouiller*, to geld, lib, vnstone, cut away the stones of. *a* 1693 *Urquhart's Rabelais* III. xxxi. 255 He had unstoned Friar Caulderiel.

**†Unsto·nied,** *ppl. a. Obs.*—1 [Un-1 8.] Unastonished. *c* 1475 *Golagros & Gaw.* 642 Thair wes na staluart vnstonait, so sterne wes the stound! **Unsto·niness.** (Un-1 12. Cf. next.) 1661 J. Childrey *Brit. Baconica* 49 The unstoniness of the Country. **Unsto·ny,** *a.* (Un-1 7.) 1611 Florio, *Insassoso*, vnstonie, without stones. 1675 Evelyn *Terra* (1676) 132 The dust of unstony high-wayes, where the drift of Cattel, and much passage is.

**Unstoo·ping,** *ppl. a.* (Un-1 10.)
1593 Shaks. *Rich. II*, I. i. 121 The vn-stooping firmenesse of my vpright soule. 1816 Byron *Ch. Har.* III. xlvii, As stands a lofty mind, Worn, but unstooping to the baser crowd. 1818 Milman *Samor* II. 272 The crash Of branches rent by his unstooping helm. 1869 Ruskin *Q. of Air* (1874) 17 She wears the crested and unstooping helmet.

**Unsto·p,** *v.* [Un-2 3 and 7. Cf. (M)Du. *ontstoppen.*]
1. *trans.* To free from being stopped up or closed.
(*a*) 1398 Trevisa *Barth. De P. R.* XVII. xiii. (Bodl. MS.), Comyn merche vnstoppeþ and openeþ þe splene and brekeþ þe stone. *c* 1489 Caxton *Sonnes of Aymon* xii. 306 He..vnbounde hym and vnstopped his eyen. *c* 1561 Veron *Free-will* 57 b, Except the Lorde did..unstop their eares, and cleare the eyes of theyr myndes. 1584 Cogan *Haven Health* ix. 31 It maketh ..the bellie laxatiue,..and vnstoppeth the veines. 1611 Bible *Isaiah* xxxv. 5 Then..the eares of the deafe shalbe vnstopped. 1637 N. Whiting *Albino & Bellama* 1963 Who will not..Galen try, To weaken humours, and unstop the pores? 1700 Motteux *Quix.* (1733) II. 186 The first thing we did was to unty the Hands of Zoraida's Father, and to unstop his Mouth. 1809 Malkin *Gil Blas* VII. vii. ℙ 9 My heart was softened, and my ears unstopped. 1871 Spurgeon *Treas. Dav.* Ps. li. 15 He..fears to speak till the Lord unstops his shame-silenced mouth.
(*b*) 1530 Palsgr. 768/2 Unstoppe nat the bottell tyll we shall drinke on it. 1584 B. R. tr. *Herodotus* II. 102 Priuily vnstopping one or two of hys bottles, the wyne flowed out. 1604 E. G[rimstone] *D'Acosta's Hist. Indies* IV. xii. 241 When the melting is finished, they vnstoppe the pottes and draw forth the mettall. 1645–50 Boate *Ireland's Nat. Hist.* xvii. § 7 (1652) 138 The Iron it self descendeth to the lowest part of the furnace, called the Hearth; the which being filled,..they unstop the Hearth, and open the mouth thereof. 1660 Boyle *New Exp. Phys. Mech.* i. 21 To unstop the Valve to let out any Air. 1742 *Lond. & Country Brew.* I. (ed. 4) 73 In the Spring you must unstop your Vent-hole, and thereby see whether your Drink doth ferment or not. 1758 Reid tr. *Macquer's Chym.* I. 265 Unstop all the registers of the reverberatory. 1823 J. Badcock *Dom. Amusem.* 45 If the bottle be stopped, the colour will presently disappear; but when it is unstopped, the colour soon returns again. 1854 *Hull Improv. Act* 32 [To] make, rebuild, clear out, unstop, or in anywise alter any sewer. 1866 Furnivall *Bk. Quinte Essence* 4 *marg.*, After many days unstop your distiller.
*transf.* 1664 Boyle *Exper. Colours* 35 Such White Fumes I have seen afforded by unstopping a Liquor.

b. *intr.* To become opened.
*c* 1440 *Ipomydon* 1261 Ipomydon was sore travailed...Hys arme vnstoppid; þe blode gan falle.

2. To pull or draw out (an organ-stop).
1855 Browning *Master Hugues* 139 Say the word, straight I unstop the Full-Organ, Blare out the mode Palestrina.

3. (See Stop *v.* 28.)
1840 R. H. Dana *Bef. Mast* xxv, They were heave-ho-ing, stopping and unstopping, pawling, catting, and fishing for three hours.

Hence **Unsto·pping** *vbl. sb.*
1611 Cotgr., *Desbouchement*, an vnstopping. 1660 Boyle *New Exp. Phys. Mech.* xxxvii. 314 Upon the unstopping of the Glass. 1676 More *Remarks* 83 Upon the unstopping of the lower end, all the water..will run down.

**Unsto·ppable,** *a.* (Un-1 7 b.)
1836 T. Hook *G. Gurney* v, 'And,' said I, 'you carried home your spoils'. 'Not I,' exclaimed my unstoppable companion. 1895 W. Platt *Women* 15 A cattle-train—a blind, rolling, unstoppable force.

**Unsto·pped,** *ppl. a.* [Un-1 8. Cf. Sw. *ostoppad* in sense 2.]
1. Not stopped up or closed.
1398 Trevisa *Barth. De P. R.* VII. x. (Bodl. MS.), Þe weies of þe brayne be vnstopped of þat humoure. *c* 1440 *Jacob's Well* 216 ȝif ȝoure pyt in his entrees be stylle opyn & vnstoppyd. 1513 Sir E. Howard in Ellis *Orig. Lett.* Ser. III. I. 149 He hath bored an C agore hoolis in her and left unstopte, that the water cam in. 1599 T. M[oufet] *Silkwormes* 58 If also carelesnesse haue left a rift, or chincke vnstopped in thine aged wall. *a* 1608 Dee *Relat. Spir.* I. (1659) 419 The hole which was not greater then the thickness of a brick unstopped. 1683 Boyle in *Phil. Trans.* XVII. 636, I have kept the Bottle of prepar'd Water..in the same unstopt Vessel. 1758 *Ann. Reg., Chron.* 96/2 Suffocated..by the steam of 40 buts of unstopped beer. 1825 J. Nicholson *Operat. Mechanic* 719 Gilding the unstopped parts with the proper amalgam. 1887 *Field* 24 Dec. 952/2 Our fox ran within short distance of main earths in a wholly unstopped country.

† 2. Unstuffed. *Obs.*—1
1434 *E. E. Wills* (1882) 102, iij quisshonus of the same colour vn-stopped.

3. Not stopped or hindered.
1621 G. SANDYS *Ovid's Met.* III. (1626) 60 So haue I seene an unstopt torrent glide With quiet waters. *Ibid.* XV. 319 He might, vnstopt, haue entred without feare: But I withstood. 1796 *Ann. Reg.* 168 Let the frequent wain, unstopp'd by rains, Clear the dry hayfield of its dusky piles! 1803 *Edwin* I. x. 152 That Edwin is no more, the voice of rumour, unstopped by opposition, has long declared. 1816 J. SCOTT *Paris Revisit.* (ed. 3) 20 We passed on with our trunks unopened and unstopped.

4. *Phonetics.* (See STOPPED *ppl. a.* 7.)
1874 H. SWEET in *Trans. Philol. Soc.* 471 Relaxation: a) stopped consonants to unstopped:..b) unstopped to diphthongal vowel. 1877 — *Handbk. Phonetics* 78, 79.

5. *spec.* Of verse-lines: Not ending with a stop.
1874 FURNIVALL in *Trans. New Shaks. Soc.* I. 73 Shakspere's often use of the unstopt line.

**Unsto·pper,** *v.* (UN-2 3, 4.)
1839 F. A. GRIFFITHS *Artill. Man.* 185 [He] runs the carriage up and back, assists to hold on the fall, stoppers and unstoppers it. 1860 *Family Economist* 7 Jan. 15/1 Unstoppering.—This operation is..likely to be required.., for the stoppers of decanters, smelling-bottles, &c...frequently become fixed. 1879 *Man. Artill. Exerc.* 473 Stopper and shift the fall. Unstopper.

**Unsto·ppered,** *ppl. a.* (UN-1 8.) 1861 WYNTER *Soc. Bees* 455 An unstoppered bottle of ipecachuana. **Unsto·pple,** *v.* (UN-2 3, 4.) 1611 COTGR., *Destoupé*, vnstopped, vnstoppelled. *a* 1693 *Urquhart's Rabelais* III. Prol. 6 There did he..unbung it,..unstopple it [F. *destouppoit*].

**Unsto·re,** *v.* [UN-2 4 and 5.]
1. *trans.* To deprive of stock.
1618 BRETON *Court. & Countryman* A 4 b, Your state is weakened and your Land wasted, your woods vntimberd, your Pastures vnstored.

2. To take out of store.
1883 *Daily News* 18 Sept. 3/3 Until the furniture and other articles..stored hastily..have been unstored and examined.

**Unsto·red,** *ppl. a.* [UN-1 8.]
1. Not supplied with a store or stores; unfurnished. Const. *of*, *with*.
1603 KNOLLES *Hist. Turks* (1621) 1209 The fields at length lay now untilled, the pastures unstored. 1636 PAGITT *Christianogr.* (ed. 2) III. 92 Neither was our Countrey unstored of reliques. 1807 J. BARLOW *Columb.* IX. 92 And mark thy native orb!..Tho' still unstored with light her silver horn. 1854 LEVER *Dodd Family Abroad* lxxiii. 611 My ungifted and unstored intellect.

2. Not stored up; unhoarded.
*a* 1770 AKENSIDE *Inscriptions*, '*Ye powers unseen*' 27 Nor shall a passion move Across my bosom unobserv'd, unstor'd By faithful memory.

**Unsto·ried,** *ppl. a.* (UN-1 8.)
[1775 ASH.] 1880 *Contemp. Rev.* Mar. 425 He laid his 'Prentice-hand upon the fair Unstoried smoothness of the column. 1890 'R. BOLDREWOOD' *Col. Reformer* (1891) 224 Farewell they of the unstoried herd!

**Unsto·rmed,** *ppl. a.* (UN-1 8.) 1695 ADDISON *To Somers* Wks. 1721 I. 7 To you the Hero of my verse reveals His great Designs,..determining the doom Of Towns Unstorm'd, and Battels yet to come. **Unsto·rmy,** *a.* (UN-1 7.) 1823 BYRON *Age of Bronze* ii, A calm, unstormy wave, Which oversweeps the world. **Unstou·t,** *a.* (UN-1 7.) 1545 ASCHAM *Toxoph.* I. (Arb.) 75 Make moche of those shaftes of youres, for they knowe neyther stoute nor vnstoute. 1746 D. GRAHAM *Writings* (1883) I. 107 Long to resist they seem'd unstout. **Unsto·ved,** *ppl. a.* (UN-1 8.) [1775 ASH.] 1863 *Act* 26 *Vict.* c. 22 Refined Sugar unstoved, pounded, crushed, or broken.

**Unstow·,** *v.* [UN-2 3.] *trans.* To take out of stowage; to clear (a hold, etc.) of the articles stowed in it.
1726 SHELVOCKE *Voy. round World* 75 Half the hold must have been unstow'd to get at them. 1745 P. THOMAS *Jrnl. Anson's Voy.* 106 We..unstow'd the Anchor, to be in Readiness. 1800 COLQUHOUN *Comm. Thames* ii. 59 The Lumpers unstowed the casks in the hold. 1856 KANE *Arct. Expl.* I. x. 105 We have to unstow the hold, and deposit its contents in the store-house. 1891 *Labour Commission* Gloss., *Unstowing* or *Breaking out*, the act of conveying the goods packed in a ship from the place occupied whilst travelling to the square immediately under the hatchway.
*fig.* 1748 SMOLLETT *Rod. Rand.* xli, When they found my hold unstowed, they went all hands to shooling and begging.

**Unstow·ed,** *ppl. a.* [UN-1 8.] Not stowed. [1775 ASH.] 1884 *Imp. Dict.* IV. 519/3 Unstowed cargo or cables.

**Unstrai·ght,** *a.* (UN-1 7.)
1650 J. NICOLL *Diary* (Bann. Cl.) 39 The unstraght Royall airmy, or these quha foght for the King. 1671 [R. MACWARD] *True Non-conf.* 122 The Church-policie..only holdeth out indirect, unstraight and ambiguous rules, applicable to any forme. 1860 H. MARRYAT *Resid. Jutland* I. 8 On the opposite side..rise the tall unstraight church spires.

**Unstrai·ghtened,** *ppl. a. rare*—0. (UN-1 8.) [1775 ASH.] 1846 WORCESTER (citing Taylor). **Unstraight-fo·rward,** *a.* (UN-1 7.) 1887 A. C. YATE *Eng. & Russia* 443 Blame attaches solely to the Liberal Government then in power, for its tortuous and unstraightforward policy. **Unstrai·ghtness.** (UN-1 12.) *a* 1693 *Urquhart's Rabelais* III. xliv. 363 The unstreightness is so irregular, or the Corruption so evident.

**Unstrai·n,** *v.* [UN-2 3.] *trans.* To free from strain; to relax. Chiefly *fig.*
1616 B. JONSON *Masques, Love freed fr. Ignorance*, 'Lesse they could the knot vn-straine Of a riddle, which she put. 1650 FULLER *Pisgah* II. xi. 236 Since which time the Levites had unstrained their credit by their exemplary zeale against the Idolaters. 1843 E. JONES *Sens. & Event* 120 Omnipotent sleep shall thy life unstrain. 1883 R. HALDANE *Workshop Receipts* Ser. II. 125/1 To clean morocco leather, strain well over a board;..when done, unstrain the leather, and dry.

†**Unstrai·nable,** *a. Sc. Obs.* [UN-1 7 b + STRAIN *v.*2] Not distrainable. 1609 SKENE *Reg. Maj.* Table 62 The Lord of ane vnstrenzeabill tenement, may saise the samine in his awin hands, for the arrierages, and byrunne fermes.

**Unstrai·ned,** *ppl. a.* [UN-1 8, 8 c.]
1. Not subjected to straining or stretching; free from strain. Also *fig.*
13.. *E. E. Allit. P.* A. 248 Pensyf, payred, I am for-payned, & þou in a lyf of lykyng lyȝte In paradys erde, of stryf vnstrayned. 1612 DRAYTON *Poly-olb.* ix. 418 Taking a milk-white Bull, vnstrained with the yoke. 1690 CHILD *Disc. Trade* viii. 132 The Dutch..would buy our unstrained Cloth, and carry it into Holland, and there strain it. 1882 MINCHIN *Unipl. Kinemat.* 126 The ratio of the strained to the unstrained area. 1894 *Westm. Gaz.* 1 June 1/1 Their loyalty to the Cabinet would be unstrained by the work and worry of an Autumn Session.
*transf.* 1659 W. CHAMBERLAYNE *Pharonnida* V. II. 158 That usurped diadem; which he..beheld without His unstrained reach.

b. With *for*: Not strained after.
1748 RICHARDSON *Clarissa* (1811) VI. 177 The blush..was a deep-dyed crimson, unstrained for.

2. Not forced or produced by effort.
1580 STANYHURST *Æneis*, etc. (Arb.) 152 Heere percase carpers wyl twight his iollitye youthful. Strong reason vnstrayned that weake obiection aunswers. 1627 HAKEWILL *Apology Power & Providence of God* I. ii. 13 Which [Greek word] by an easie and vnstrained derivation, implies the breath of God. *a* 1639 T. CAREW *Poems* (1651) 130 The true brood of Actors, that alone keep naturall unstrain'd Action in her throne. 1776 MICKLE *Camoens' Lusiad* Introd. 140 The most natural unstrained harmony, is the just characteristic of the style of Camoens. 1802 LAMB *G. F. Cook* Wks. 1908 I. 47 This quality of unstrained mirth ..is a prime feature in his character. 1871 MRS. WHITNEY *Real Folks* xii, The pure, clear spaces where such things seemed to be fit and unstrained. 1898 *Contemp. Rev.* Aug. 188 Honours, like the gentle rain from heaven, fell upon him unstrained.

3. Not passed through a strainer; not cleared or purified by straining.
1828–32 WEBSTER s.v., Unstrained oil. 1853 ROYLE *Mat. Med.* (ed. 2) 477 Press out the juice, and evaporate it, unstrained, to a proper consistence.

**Unstrai·tened,** *ppl. a.* (UN-1 8.) 1665 GLANVILL *Scepsis Sci.* (ed. 2) i. 2 All those enoblements that were suitable to the measures of an unstraightned Goodness. [1755 JOHNSON, *Unstraitened*, not contracted.] 1855 SINGLETON *Virgil* II. 473 On their fainty shoulders bear they off Their bows unstraitened. **Unstra·nge,** *a.* (UN-1 7.) *c* 1391 CHAUCER *Astrol.* II. § 17 To knowe the verrey degree of any maner sterre straunge or vnstraunge after his longitude. **Unstra·ngulable,** *a.* (UN-1 7 b.) 1824 LAMB *Lett.* (1886) II. 190 Are we unstrangulable, I ask you?

**Unstra·p,** *v.* (UN-2 4 b.)
1828 SPEARMAN *Brit. Gunner* (ed. 2) 178, [No.] 2 unstraps the rammer-head,..and [no.] 4 unstraps the sponge. 1836 DICKENS *Sk. Boz, Gt. Winglebury Duel*, Up started the ostlers,..unstrapping, and unchaining, and unbuckling. 1862 *Cornhill Mag.* V. 34, I had a large cape folded up with my *valise*; so unstrapping this [etc.].
Hence **Unstra·pping** *vbl. sb.*
1851 *Household Words* IV. 299/2 She..busies herself with the unstrapping of my knapsack.

**Unstrate·gic,** *a.* (UN-1 7.) 1831 CARLYLE *Sart. Res.* III. iii, The most undiplomatic and unstrategic of these [men].

**Unstra·tified,** *ppl. a.* (UN-1 8.)
[1775 ASH.] 1802 PLAYFAIR *Illustr. Hutton. Th.* 57 The unstratified minerals exist..in veins intersecting the stratified. 1873 DAWSON *Earth & Man* xi. 269 Boulder clay..is usually destitute of any lamination or subordinate stratification; whence it is often called Unstratified Drift.

**Unstrea·ked,** *ppl. a.* (UN-1 8.) [1775 ASH.] 1861 WHYTE MELVILLE *Good for Nothing* I. 101 Her black hair was as yet unstreaked with a line of grey. 1871 GEO. ELIOT *Middlem.* xxxvi, Mrs. Viney's openness and simplicity were quite unstreaked with suspicion.

† **Unstre·nge,** *v. Obs. rare.* [UN-2 6 a, 7 + *strenge* STRENGH *v.*] **a.** *trans.* To unstrengthen. **b.** *intr.* To lose strength.
*a* 1225 *Leg. Kath.* 1269 Is nu se storliche unstrenget ower strengðe..swa þet [etc.]? *a* 1225 *Juliana* 44 Heo unstrengeð þerwið ant we strengeð on ham.

† **Unstre·ngth,** *sb. Obs.* [UN-1 12.] Lack of strength; weakness, feebleness.
*c* 1200 ORMIN 16915 Þatt follc þatt..nohht ne darr ȝet stiȝhenn upp To follȝhenn heȝhe mahhtess..Forr hiss flæshess unnstrenncþe. *a* 1225 *Ancr. R.* 232 We iknowen ure owune feblesce & ure owune muchele unstrencðe. *a* 1250 *Owl & Night.* 751 Hwy atwitestu me myne vnstrengþe? 1382 WYCLIF 2 *Macc.* iii. 24 Alle that weren hardye for to obeye to hym..weren togidre turnyd in to vnbyndynge, or vnstrengthe, and inward dreed.

†**Unstre·ngth,** *v. Obs.* [UN-2 6 b.] *trans.* To weaken, enfeeble. *a* 1225 *Ancr. R.* 138 Þis fette kelf haueð þe ueondes strencðe to unstrencðen, & forte makien buwen touward sunne. *Ibid.* 274 Heo unstrencðeð þe unwhit [*v.r.* unwicht] & deð him suluen o fluhte anonrihte.

**Unstre·ngthen,** *v.* [UN-2 6.] *trans.* To deprive of strength; to weaken.
1598 FLORIO, *Sgagliardare*,..to enfeeble, to vnstrengthen. 1604 MARSTON *Malcontent* II. iii. D j, If griefe that..Beduls the eye, vnstrengthens all the blood, Chance to remooue me to another world. 1890 TALMAGE *From Manger to Throne* 244 Enervated by his long fasting, and doubly unstrengthened by a sudden relaxation.
Hence **Unstre·ngthening** *vbl. sb.*
1623 SIR J. ELIOT in J. Forster *Life* (1864) I. 166 Reason affected not the cries..of the people, nor policy the unstrengthening of the state.

**Unstre·ngthened,** *ppl. a.* (UN-1 8.)
1597 HOOKER *Eccl. Pol.* V. viii. § 4 Surely the Church..is neither of capacity..so weak, nor so unstrengthened, I know, with authority from above. 1806–20 WORDSW. *Resting-place* 3 If we advance unstrengthened by repose. 1836 *Going to Service* xviii. 233 The thin places left unstrengthened, and broken loops untaken up.

**Unstre·ssed,** *ppl. a.* (UN-1 8.) 1883 H. SWEET in *Trans. Philol. Soc.* 212 Not only in most unstrest syllabls of polysyllabic words, but also in the unstrest monosyllabic words. **Unstre·ssedness.** (UN-1 12. Cf. prec.) 1894 F. J. CURTIS *Rimes Clariodus* 48 In its unstressedness it was not long *ē*.

**Unstre·tch,** *v.* [UN-2 3, 7.] *trans.* and *intr.* To relax, slacken.
1611 COTGR., *Destendre*, to vnbend, slacken, vnstretch. 1825 J. NICHOLSON *Operat. Mechanic* 752 The mechanism by which the strings of a violin are stretched or unstretched. 1888 *Philos. Mag.* Feb. 109 An annealed iron wire which is being heated when..it is stretched by a slight weight.. suddenly unstretches.
Hence **Unstre·tching** *vbl. sb.*
1611 COTGR., *Destenture*, an vnbending, vnstretching, slackening. 1844 *Civil Eng. & Arch. Jrnl.* VII. 365 The consequent stretching and unstretching [of the rope].

**Unstre·tched,** *ppl. a.* (UN-1 8, 8 c.) 1648 HEXHAM II, *Ongereckt*, Vnstretched,..or Vnextended. 1678 CUDWORTH *Intell. Syst.* 781 A Substance whose Duration is Vnextended or Vnstretched out in Time. **Unstrew·ed,** *ppl. a.* (UN-1 8.) [1775 ASH.] 1791 COWPER *Iliad* VIII. 569 On the river's brink..space he found unstrew'd With carcases. *Ibid.* X. 235 A vacant space..Unstrew'd with bodies of the slain. **Unstri·ated,** *ppl. a.* (UN-1 8.) 1877 HUXLEY *Anat. Inv. Anim.* viii. 480 Bundles of muscular fibres, usually unstriated. 1895 *Naturalist* 339 Numerous small unstriated pebbles.

**Unstri·cken,** *ppl. a.* (UN-1 8 b.)
1548 ELYOT, *Impercussus*, vnstryken. [Also in Baret, Florio, and Hexham.] 1848 T. AIRD *Nebuchadnezzar* I. ii, He..lies through night unstricken by the winds. 1863 KINGLAKE *Crimea* (ed. 4) II. vi. 137 Those who remained unstricken [by cholera].

**Unstri·dden,** *ppl. a.* (UN-1 8 b.) 1570 LEVINS *Manip.* 61 Vnstriden horse, *incons*[*c*]*ensus*. **Unstri·de,** *v.* (UN-2 3.) 1635 QUARLES *Embl.* III. ii. 21 If the fool unstride His prauncing Stallion, thou mayst up and ride. **Unstridulo·sity.** (UN-1 12.) 1871 BROWNING *Pr. Hohenst.* 1363 Dumb menace in that mouth, Malice in that unstridulosity!

**Unstri·ke,** *v.* [UN-2 9.] (See quot. 1678.)
1614 LATHAM *Falconry* I. iii. 10 Then vnstrike her hood, and lure her..with a bitte or two of meate. [1678 PHILLIPS (ed. 4), *To Unstrike the hood*, in Faulconry, to draw the strings that it may be in a readiness to pull off.] 1852 R. F. BURTON *Falconry Valley Indus* iii. 26 After slipping the knot that held the jesses to the leash, I gently 'unstruck' my Shikrah's hood, [and] pulled it off.

**Unstri·king,** *vbl. sb.* (UN-2 3, 8.) 1567 *S. P. Dom. Eliz.* XLIV. 17 (P.R.O.), The vnstrikinge shavinge Blackinge newe nailinge bucklinge and letheringe of..decaied Corselettes..sore cankared and Rustie. **Unstri·king,** *ppl. a.* (UN-1 10.) 1768–74 TUCKER *Lt. Nat.* (1834) II. 36 The mental eye..will see it obscure, unstriking, and no better than common objects. 1880 'MARK TWAIN' *Tramp Abroad* II. 223 A monotonous variety of unstriking dishes.

**Unstri·ng,** *v.* [UN-2 4 and 4 b.]
1. *trans.* To relax or remove the string(s) of (a lyre, bow, etc.).
(*a*) 1611 FLORIO, *Discordare*,..to vnstring, to vntune. 1621 BURTON *Anat. Mel.* I. ii. iii. xv, A musitian will string and vnstring his lute. 1725 POPE *Odyssey* VIII. 107 His golden lyre Demodocus unstrung. *a* 1774 W. WHITEHEAD *Enthusiast* xv, Enthusiast, go, unstring thy lyre; In vain thou sing'st. 1869 SPURGEON *Treas. Dav.* Ps. xxi. 1 Our weakness unstrings our harps, but his strength tunes them anew.
(*b*) 1707 E. SMITH *Phædra & Hippolitus* II. 24 His idle Horn on fragrant Mirtles hung, His Arrows scatter'd, and his Bow unstrung. 1833 J. RENNIE *Alph. Angling* 52 Let us suppose that a bow..be bent and unstrung in the water. 1856 'STONEHENGE' *Brit. Rural Sports* 507/1 To Unstring the Bow. [Directions follow.]

b. To undo the strings of (a purse). Also *absol.*
1681 *Swearing Master* 1 Come Wil, unstring, and pay your Groat. 1685 *Roxb. Ball.* (1888) IV. 285 Now unstring your purse, and be kind to the poor. 1771 COLMAN *Prose Sev. Occas.* (1787) III. 188 To swathe and dress it [he] first unstrings his purse. 1861 GEO. ELIOT *Silas M.* ix, My father wasn't quite so ready to unstring as some other fathers I know of. 1884 *Manch. Exam.* 11 June 5/1 They would have to unstring the national purse, and find the money.

2. To detach from a string. Also *fig.*
1697 DRYDEN *Virg. Past.* VI. 29 For want of better Bands His Garland they unstring, and bind his Hands. 1763 GIBBON *Misc. Wks.* (1814) V. 387 Unstringing the beads from the rosary of antiquity. 1850 R. G. CUMMING *Hunter's Life S. Africa* xvi. I. 367 Having unstrung the dice,..they rattle them between their hands, and drop them on the ground.

b. To detach from union; to separate, sever.
1674 N. FAIRFAX *Bulk & Selv.* 46 So do but unstring my soul and body,..the thing is gone.

3. To render lax or weak; to disorder (the nerves, etc.).
1700 DRYDEN *Ovid's Met.* XII. 748 Light was the Wound; but in the Sinew hung The Point: and his disabled Wing unstrung. 1768–74 TUCKER *Lt. Nat.* (1834) II. 273 Terror and trepidation would unstring our nerves. *Ibid.* 498 So far as to unstring the very sinews of government. 1800 S. & HT. LEE *Canterb. T.* IV. 51 The very apprehension..might unstring her nerves. 1817 SHELLEY *Rev. Islam* XI. xx, That voice unstrung his sinews, and he threw His dagger on the ground. 1845 M. PATTISON *Ess.* (1889) I. 26 His conscience must have been unstrung by the..engagement he had made.

b. To unnerve, upset (a person).
1897 Miss F. F. MONTRÉSOR *At Cross Roads* ii, I could not live with so much sympathy, it would unstring me.
Hence **Unstri·nging** *vbl. sb.* and *ppl. a.*
1824 LADY GRANVILLE *Lett.* (1894) I. 256 The fatigue and worry..have been very unstringing. 1833 HT. MARTINEAU *Cinnamon & Pearls* ii. 28 It gave more time for the unstringing of his nerves.

**Unstri·nged,** *ppl. a.* [UN-1 8.] Not furnished with a string or strings; not arranged on a string. Also *transf.*, not accompanied by music.

1593 SHAKS. *Rich. II*, I. iii. 162 An vnstringed Vyall, or a Harpe. 1599 NASHE *Lenten Stuffe* D iij b, Or thou wilt commend thy muse to sempiternity, and haue images.. erected to her after the vnstringed silent interment and obsequies. 1655 SPURSTOWE *Wels Salvation* 73 Like loose and unstringed pearles.

**Unstri·p**, *v.* Now *dial.* and *rare.* [UN-[2] 9.] *trans.* To strip.

1596 WARNER *Alb. Eng.* XII. lxxvii. 313 The Oste and Ostlers..Came in, where he, almost vnstript, but wholly skar'de, did stand. 1637 R. ASHLEY tr. *Malvezzi's David Persecuted* 250 Any, to whom he may unstrip himselfe, and discover the secrets of his heart. 1654 GAYTON *Pleas. Notes* IV. xxiv. 281 The Villaine..charg'd Leandra to unstrip her. 1691 T. H[ALE] *Acc. New Invent.* 27 The..continuance of these Ships..in their sheathing, without their being in all that time unstripp'd, for the necessary searching of their bottoms. 1764 GOLDSM. *Hist. Eng. in Lett.* (1772) II. 182 Pretended patriotism unstripped of its mask. 1823 E. MOOR *Suffolk Words* 460. 1905 in *Eng. Dial. Dict.*

**Unstri·ped**, *ppl. a.* (UN-[1] 8.)

*a* 1841 *Encycl. Metrop.* (1845) VII. 493 The unstriped variety of muscular fibre. 1859 *Todd's Cycl. Anat.* V. 262/1 In man and mammalia the tracheal muscles belong to the unstriped variety. 1882 *Garden* 28 Jan. 69/2 The unstriped form produces seed readily in cultivation.

**Unstri·pped**, *ppl. a.* [UN-[1] 8.] Not stripped; not removed by stripping.

1676 HOBBES *Iliad* 158 Upon the field unstript they left these two. 1822 J. H. ALLAN *Bridal of Caolchairn* 278 An unsafe footway formed of the trunk of trees..unstripped of their bark, and destitute of either plank or rail. 1822 COBBETT *Rur. Rides* (1830) 19 Here are farmers unable to pay men for working for them...There lie the hop-poles unstripped. 1888 *Field* 7 Jan. 27/1 Those growers whose crop [of tobacco] is still unstripped from stalks.

**Unstri·ving**, *ppl. a.* (UN-[1] 10.) 1868 W. R. GREG *Lit. & Soc. Judgm.* 62 Unambitious and unstriving,..he finds that everything conspires to teach him the same lesson.

**Unstro·ng**, *a. Obs.* or *dial.* [OE. *unstrang*, f. *un-* UN-[1] 7 + *strang* STRONG *a.*] Not strong; feeble, weak. Also *absol.*

*a* 900 *O. E. Martyrol.* 13 Aug. 146 His þrowung wæs þe lengre..þy þe hyra handa wæron unstrange hine to acwellanne. *c* 960 *Rule St. Benedict* (1885) lxiv. 121 Þæt þa strangan furðor wilnien, and þa unstrangan..heora þeowdom ne forfleon. *c* 1200 ORMIN 7911 Maȝȝdenn child iss all unnstrang Affterr wifmanne kinde. *a* 1250 *Owl & Night.* 561 Þu art lutel and vnstrong. 13.. *R. Gloucester's Chron.* (Rolls) App. G. 49 Her was hunger & hete; wo was þe vnstronge. 1382 WYCLIF 1 *Cor.* xi. 30 Therfore among ȝou manye syke, and vnstronge, or feble. 1398 TREVISA *Barth. De P. R.* XVIII. xiii. (Bodl. MS.), Breste plates and oþer armure bi þe whiche vnstronge places of mannes bodie beþ warded. *c* 1440 *Pallad. on Husb.* I. 1110 The chaumburs in the bathis may be wrought..other weyis fele..al though they be vnstrenger [*v.r.* unstronger]. 1868 ATKINSON *Cleveland Gloss.* 551 He's varrey unstrong, puir chap.

**Unstru·ck**, *ppl. a.* (UN-[1] 8 b, 8 c.)

1615 J. TAYLOR (Water P.) *Faire & fowle Weather* B 3, As a measure fild with Oates or Rye Vnstrooke and heap'd, doth lye confusedly. 1705 J. PHILLIPS *Blenheim* 40 Over dank, and dry, They journey..unstruck with Horror at the sight Of Alpine Ridges bleak. 1728 YOUNG *Ocean* lv, Who can gaze On restless seas, Unstruck with life's more restless state? 1790 BEATSON *Nav. & Mil. Mem.* I. 251 General Hawley..sent orders to set fire to the tents, which were still unstruck in the camp. 1838 J. HILDYARD in *Life & Lett. S. Butler* (1896) II. 311 Could I bring my unstruck-off sheets with me, and insert the few remarks..in them? 1897 *Westm. Gaz.* 29 July 7/2 She had seen 'unstruck' matches lying on the shop floor.

**Unstru·cken**, *ppl. a.* (UN-[1] 8 b.) *c* 1620 FLETCHER *False One* II. i, If this inhumane stroak be yet unstrucken. **Unstru·ggling**, *ppl. a.* (UN-[1] 10.) 1822 MILMAN *Martyr of Antioch* 65 Bounteous God! That..leaves you..To feed unstruggling the fierce beast of rapine..! 1868 GEO. ELIOT *Sp. Gipsy* 241, I should..rest for ever from the thought of bliss, And wear my weight of life's great chain unstruggling.

**Unstru·ng**, *ppl. a.* [f. UNSTRING *v.*, or UN-[1] 8 b.]

**1.** Having the string(s) relaxed or removed: **a.** Of a harp, etc.

1598 FLORIO, *Scordato*,..put out of tune, vnstrung. 1633 [? F. DAVISON] *Ps. 137* iii, Our mute harpes, untun'd, unstrung, Up wee hung On greene willowes. 1694 PRIOR *Hymn to Sun* viii, 'Till Nature's Musick lyes unstrung. 1738 WESLEY *Ps.* CXXXVII. ii, Our Harps..We cast aside, untun'd, unstrung. 1820 BYRON *Juan* v. xxxvi. (MS.), As silent as an unstrung drum. 1821 SHELLEY *Adonais* xxxvi, The song, Whose master's hand is cold, whose silver lyre unstrung. 1871 MACDUFF *Mem. Patmos* 333 The unstrung tuneless harp.

*transf.* 1613 CAMPION *Descr. Lords Maske* Wks. (1909) 99 The good old Sage is silenc't, her free tongue That made such melodie, is now vnstrung. 1646 CRASHAW *Steps Temple, Ps. 137* 21 O may at once my tongue Lose this same busie speaking art, Unpearch't, her vocall Arteries unstrung. 1784 COWPER *Task* II. 728 His voice, unstrung, Grew tremulous, and mov'd derision more Than rev'rence.

**b.** Of a bow. Also = not strung.

1744 W. WHITEHEAD *Atys & Adrastus* 259 Behind him hung His rat'ling Quiver, and his Bow unstrung. 1797 *Encycl. Brit.* (ed. 3) II. 209/2 Now the long-bow (when unstrung) may be most conveniently covered. 1831 JAMES *Phil. Augustus* I. iv, His features..had expanded like an unstrung bow. 1856 FITZGERALD *Salámán* (1879) 69 Salámán Call'd for an unstrung Bow—himself the cord Fitted unhelpt.

**2.** Weakened, relaxed; unnerved.

1692 DRYDEN *Don Sebastian* v. iii, These Sinews are not yet so much unstrung, To fail me. 1746 HERVEY *Medit. Among Tombs* 57 The Nervous Arm is unstrung; the brawny Sinews are relaxed. 1794 R. J. SULIVAN *View Nat.* II. 49 In the Sirocco wind at Naples,..the whole system is unstrung, and the nerves seem to lose..their tension. 1847 C. BRONTË *J. Eyre* xxix, It gave new tone to my unstrung nerves. 1866 LE FANU *All in Dark* v, Their entertainer remained behind unstrung and melancholic.

**Unstu·bbling**, *vbl. sb.* (UN-[2] 9.) 1778 [W. H. MARSHALL] *Minutes Agric., Digest* 85 General reflections on Unstubbling. **Unstu·ccoed**, *ppl. a.* (UN-[1] 8.) 1882 *Cent. Mag.* XXIII. 645 The houses are built in long low lines of gray, unstuccoed adobe.

**Unstu·died**, *ppl. a.* [UN-[1] 8.]

**1.** Not meditated on; neglected as a subject of study or thought.

*c* 1380 WYCLIF *Wks.* (1880) 192 Þus bi þis nouelrie of song is goddis lawe vnstudied & not kepte. ? 1608 *Reynard's Deliv. fr. Turks* in *Harl. Misc.* (1744) I. 183 There is.. no language, be it never so barbarous, or hard to learn, left unstudied. 1614 in Overbury *A Wife*, etc. A 4 b, For that word, 'A goodly woman,' Prints it selfe in such a letter That it leaues vnstudied no man.

**2.** Not having studied; unversed (*in* something).

1642 MILTON *Apol. Smect.* 15, I..was not unstudied in those authors which are most commended. 1650 BAXTER *Saints' R.* I. vii. 104 Men voyd of Learning, and strength of parts, unstudied and untaught. 1685 E. BOHUN *Life Jewell* in *Apol.* 30 That Learned Prelate..was not so unstudied in the nature of Councils, as [etc.]. 1817 COLERIDGE *Lay Serm.* 77 The strict, but unstudied and uninquiring, Religionists of every denomination. 1846 HAWTHORNE *Mosses* 85 The young stranger..was not unstudied in the great poem of his country.

†**b.** Not spent in or devoted to study. *Obs.*[-1]

1645 MILTON *Tetrach.* Int. A 3 b, To cloak the defects of their unstudied yeers.

**3.** Not elaborated by study or care; not laboured or artificial.

1657 H. KING *Poems* 122 They bring Course and unstudy'd stuffs for offering. 1674 HICKMAN *Quinquart. Hist.* (ed. 2) Ep. A 3 Had I thought so unstudied a scrible meet to be exposed to publick view. 1697 DRYDEN *Virg. Georg.* Ded., A clearness of Notion, express'd in ready and unstudied Words. 1730 THOMSON *Winter* 468 With sense refin'd,..Unstudy'd wit, and humour ever gay. 1798 S. & HT. LEE *Canterb. T.* II. 57 This scheme was not quite so unstudied as it appeared. 1817 W. GODWIN *Mandeville* I. 207 She expressed herself with the greatest ease, her sentiments were unparrotted and unstudied. 1856 *N. Brit. Rev.* XXVI. 233 He had a homely,—apparently unstudied mode of expression. 1884 CHURCH *Bacon* ix. 220 Easy and unstudied as his writing seems.

**Unstu·dious**, *a.* (UN-[1] 7.) Also *absol.*

1663 BOYLE *Usef. Exp. Nat. Philos.* I. 9 To live ignorant or unstudious of the laws and constitutions of that great Commonwealth. 1841 MYERS *Cath. Th.* III. § 17. 64 The boundary line between them is really more indistinct than the unstudious would suppose. 1859 HELPS *Friends in C.* Ser. II. I. 228 Besides, how encrusted their names are with the curses of unstudious boys.

**Unstuff**, *v.* [UN-[2] 3, 4.]

**1.** *trans.* To empty (*of* people).

*c* 1450 *Merlin* xx. 358 Moo [men] he myght haue hadde yef he wolde, but he seide he wolde not lete the reame be vnstuffed of peple.

**2.** To free from being stuffed.

1611 COTGR., *Desestouffer*, to emptie, euacuate, vnstuffe. 1675 HAN. WOOLLEY *Gentlew. Comp.* 163 Saffron is a great Cordial, and unstuffs the pipes of the Lungs. 1852 *Meanderings of Mem.* I. 56 The brain [it] will scavage and the breast unstuff.

**Unstu·ffed**, *ppl. a.* [UN-[1] 8.] Not stuffed; †unfurnished.

1480 *Wardr. Acc. Edw. IV*, (1830) 131 Pilowe beres off fustian unstuffed, iiij. 1573 *Arte of Limming* A iij, A litle borde..couered with a calues skin raysed or vnderstuffed with wolle or floxe or else vnstuffed. 1592 SHAKS. *Rom. & Jul.* II. iii. 37 Where vnbrused youth with vnstuft braine Doth couch his lims, there golden sleepe doth raigne. 1647 H. MORE *Song of Soul* II. To Rdr., If any space be left out unstuffd with Atoms.

**Unstu·mbled**, *ppl. a.* (UN-[1] 8.) 1399 LANGL. *Rich. Redeles* II. 82 Ho so had kunnynge and conscience bothe, To stonde vnstombled and stronge in his wittis.

**Unstu·ng**, *ppl. a.*[1] [UN-[1] 8 b.] Not stung.

1615 GODDARD *Neaste of Waspes* F iij, Why howe nowe Waspes, are you returnd agen? I knowe vnstung remaines a worlde of men And therefore once more out. 1807 CRABBE *Birth of Flattery* 147 Such was the fiend, and so secure of prey, That only Misery pass'd unstung away. 1816 KIRBY & SP. *Entomol.* xx. II. 203 Some of them flew after me; I escaped however unstung. 1864 'ANNIE THOMAS' *D. Donne* III. 135 He knew too that the Bishop knew it also, and was unstung by the knowledge.

**Unstu·ng**, *ppl. a.*[2] [f. UNSTING *v.*] Having the sting removed; deprived of the sting.

1671 JANEWAY (*title*), Death Unstung; A Sermon [on Rev. xiv. 13] at the funeral of T. Mowsley. 1687 RENWICK *Serm.*, etc. (1776) 333 To the believing soul death is unstung.

**Unstu·nned**, *ppl. a.* (UN-[1] 8.) [1775 ASH.] 1797 COLERIDGE *Osorio* III. i. 11 What ear unstun'd..might bear up against The rushing of your congregated wings? †**Unstu·rted**, *ppl. a. Sc.* [UN-[1] 8.] Undisturbed. 1535 STEWART *Cron. Scot.* (Rolls) III. 265 To the thrid day the parteis baith did ly Into thair tentis wnsturtit richt still. **Unsty·**, *v.* (UN-[2] 5.) 1614 MARKHAM *Cheap Husb.* I. i. 90 The orderliest feeding of Swine is..in the Morning earely when you vnstie them [etc.]. **Unsty·lish**, *a.* (UN-[1] 7.) 1863 MRS. WHITNEY *F. Gartney's Girlh.* vi, Her respectable but somewhat unstylish figure and dress.

**Unsubdu·able**, *a.* (UN-[1] 7 b and 5 b.)

1611 COTGR., *Invincible*,..vnsubduable, vnconquerable. 1622 W. WHATELY *God's Husb.* II. 108 The most mischievous, ..and but by his strength vnsubduable corruptions of their nature. 1810 SOUTHEY *Kehama* XVIII. v, Her Father's eye.. spake..Stern patience unsubduable by pain. 1840 CARLYLE *Heroes* iv. (1858) 291 Unsubduable granite, piercing far and wide into the Heavens! 1878 P. BAYNE *Purit. Rev.* xi. 499 An unsubduable capacity to make the best of things.

**Unsubdue·d**, *ppl. a.* (UN-[1] 8.)

1590 SPENSER *F. Q.* III. iii. 38 T'afflict the other Saxons vnsubdewd. *a* 1628 F. GREVIL *Sidney* (1652) 99 The yet unsubdued Princes of Germany. *c* 1630 SANDERSON *Serm.* II. 312 There may lurk in our hearts some secret noysome lust undiscovered, and so unsubdued. 1712 BLACKMORE *Creation* IV. 9 If dread of death still unsubdued remains. 1794 S. WILLIAMS *Vermont* 170 His passions unsubdued, undisciplined. 1831 JAMES *Phil. Augustus* II. iv, The still unsubdued terror of the bishop. 1863 CONINGTON *Horace, Odes* IV. xiv. 8 They know thee now, thy strength in war, Those unsubdued Vindelici.

*absol.* 1835 MILMAN *Nala & Damayanti* 32 In his wicked thought the dastard—her yet powerless to subdue, On the unsubdued stood gazing.

Hence **Unsubdue·dness.**

*a* 1665 GOODWIN *Filled w. the Spirit* vi. (1670) 141 Weakness in Faith,..unsubduedness of the Flesh. *a* 1732 T. BOSTON *Crook in Lot* (1805) 165 Unsubduedness of spirit. 1839 PUSEY in Liddon *Life* (1893) II. 142 Vanity, unsubduedness, self in some form, has been the source of all heresy. 1878 ABP. BENSON *Let.* in *Life* (1901) 176 It is, I am afraid, interior unsubduedness.

**Unsu·bject**, *a.* (UN-[1] 7.)

1382 WYCLIF *Heb.* ii. 8 In that thing that he sugetide alle thingis to him, he lefte no thing vnsuget [*v.r.* vnsugetted] to him. 1583 GOLDING *Calvin on Deut.* xlviii. 281 Not any of vs..can excuse himselfe to bee vnsubiect to such naughtinesse. 1597 HOOKER *Eccl. Pol.* V. lxx. § 4. 294 Aboue the highest mooueable sphere there is nothing which feeleth alteration,..but all things immutable, vnsubiect to passion. 1652 BENLOWES *Theoph.* V. lxiii. 75 'Tis but a Creature, though its Essence be To change unsubject. 1672 PENN *Spir. Truth Vind.* 36 Perhaps he hath followed an Erronious Judgment, or Unsubject Affection. 1754 MISS BOOTHBY in *Life Johnson* (1805) 75 Thus is whirled about this little machine [= Miss Boothby], which..contains a mind unsubject to rotation. 1788 D. GILSON *Serm. Pract. Subj.* xiii. 368 Were the residence of man unsubject to mutation. 1842 TENNYSON *Will Waterproof* 86 My head, Which bears a season'd brain about, Unsubject to confusion. 1881 CLELAND *Evol., Express. & Sens.* p. x, No doubt spirit seems a vague and intangible entity because unsubject to those methods.

**Unsubject**, *v.* (UN-[2] 6 b.) 1647 DIGGES *Unlawf. Taking Arms* 114 Women cannot unmarry, nor the people unsubject themselves. **Unsubje·ctable**, *a.* (UN-[1] 7 b.) 1829 BENTHAM *Corr.* Wks. 1843 XI. 29 Statements unsubjected and unsubjectable to the test of cross-examination.

**Unsubje·cted**, *ppl. a.* (UN-[1] 8.)

138. [see UNSUBJECT *a.*]. 1513 DOUGLAS *Æneid* VII. vii. 67 All cuntre wnsubiekyt wnder our wand. 1693 *Mem. Ct. Teckely* III. 83 There remain'd nothing but Mongats unsubjected to the Emperor. 1697 C. LESLIE *Snake in Grass* (ed. 2) 252 This shews them..the utter Inconsistency of that Principle (to use their own Word) of an *Un-subjected* Light within, to all Rule, Order, or Good Government. 1758 AKENSIDE *Ode to Gentlemen Eng.* x, Shall war's heroic arts no more engage The unbought hand, the unsubjected mind? 1800 COLERIDGE *Piccolom.* I. xii, A new army Unsubjected to my control. 1823 SCOTT *Quentin D.* i, Wild beasts.. who, if unsubjected by his arts, would..have torn him [*sc.* the keeper] to pieces. 1829 SOUTHEY *Sir T. More* I. 269 The unsubjected natives..recovered the greater part of their country.

Hence **Unsubje·ctedness.**

1682 PENN *Salut. Faithf. Friends* 5 Such as these,..by a loose Conversation, or Highmindedness and Unsubjectedness cause grief.

**Unsubje·ction.** (UN-[1] 12 and 5 b.) *a* 1653 BINNING *Sinner's Sanct.* xx. Wks. (1735) 271 His Unsubjection and unsubmissive Disposition towards the good Pleasure of the Lord. 1658 MANTON *Exp. Jude* iv. 227 Which argueth much unsubjection of heart to Christ. **Unsu·bjectlike**, *a.* and *adv.* (UN-[1] 7 c, 11 b.) 1590 *Acts Privy Counc.* (1899) XIX. 406 Lady Broome lyveth soe disorderly and unsubjectlyke. 1606 BP. J. KING *Serm.* Sept. 21 A forrest of the most..vnchristian, vnsubject-like practises, that ever were heard of. **Unsu·bjugate**, *v.* (UN-[2] 3.) 1834 SIR H. TAYLOR *Artevelde* II. v. ii, Those powers by this nocturnal inroad wild Surprised..., vainly I essayed To rally and unsubjugate. **Unsu·bjugated**, *ppl. a.* (UN-[1] 8.) [1775 ASH.] 1837 LYTTON *Athens* I. 416 Babylon alone remained unsubjugated by the Mede. **Unsubli·mable**, *a.* (UN-[1] 7 b.) 1753 *Chambers' Cycl.* Suppl. s.v. *Sublimable*, Those things, which render unsublimable bodies sublimable. 1803 *Phil. Trans.* XCIII. 26 The apparent sublimation of the common flowers of zinc at the instant of their production, though totally unsublimable afterwards.

**Unsubli·med**, *ppl. a.* (UN-[1] 8.)

1694 SALMON *Bate's Dispens.* 416/2 Some prepare it..with the crude Sulphur and unsublimed Salt. *Ibid.* 610/1 The unsublimed Sal-Armoniack. 1771 *Phil. Trans.* LXI. 125 Any solution or combination of tin, unsublimed or undistilled. 1814 SCOTT *Wav.* xxiii, A simple and unsublimed taste now, like my own, would perfer a jet d'eau at Versailles to this cascade.

**Unsubme·rged**, *ppl. a.* (UN-[1] 8.) 1883 *Century Mag.* XXVII. 188 Only a thin scattered fringe of bluffs was unsubmerged. **Unsubme·rsible**, *a.* (UN-[1] 7, 5 b.) 1891 W. K. BROOKS *Oyster* 58 Two beautiful unsubmersible claires [= oyster-tanks].

**Unsubmi·ssion.** (UN-[1] 12.)

1845 JANE ROBINSON *Whitehall* II. 252 After this evidence of unsubmission, he was detained..a close prisoner. 1865 PUSEY *Eirenicon* 15 A spiritual disease, which is part of man's unsubmission to his God.

**Unsubmi·ssive**, *a.* (UN-[1] 7 and 5 b.)

*a* 1653 [see UNSUBJECTION]. *a* 1716 SOUTH *Serm.* (1744) X. v. 154 A stubborn unsubmissive frame of spirit in men. 1849 EASTWICK *Dry Leaves* 55 [He] would hardly brook a band of unsubmissive strangers so near his own throne. 1868 LYNCH *Rivulet* CXXV. ii, The lord of quarrel..And unsubmissive will.

Hence **Unsubmi·ssiveness.**

Also *unsubmissively* adv. (Webster, 1847).

1868 PUSEY *Serm. Pharisaism* 7 Heresy, unbelief, misbelief, unsubmissiveness,..spring from pride.

**Unsubmi·tting**, *ppl. a.* (UN-[1] 10.)

1730 THOMSON *Autumn* 840 A generous race Of unsubmitting spirit. **1783** W. F. MARTYN *Geog. Mag.* II. 366 Those unsubmitting heroes. *a* **1796** BURNS '*All devil as I am*' 8 The honest man.., Whose unsubmitting heart was all his crime. *a* **1835** MRS. HEMANS *Abencerrage* III. viii, Heroic spirits, unsubmitting yet. *Ibid.* xviii, A sterner tone of unsubmitting thought.

† **Unsubo·rdinate,** *a. Obs.* (UN-[1] 7 and 5 b.) **1641** MILTON *Reform.* II. 66 A certaine unquestionable Patriarchat, independent and unsubordinate to the Crowne. **1678** CUDWORTH *Intell. Syst.* f 2 b, An Absolute, Independent, and Un-subordinate Co-equality. **1709** SHAFTESB. *Charac.* (1711) II. 335 Perpetual Strifes..shew either no Controul, or several uncontroul'd and unsubordinate Powers in Nature.

**Unsubo·rdinated,** *ppl. a.* (UN-[1] 8.) **1658** BP. REYNOLDS *Lord's Supper* xii. Wks. 600 There was no Schism in the Body, no part unsubordinated, or unjoynted from the rest. † **Unsubo·rdinately,** *adv. Obs.* (UN-[1] 11, 5 b. Cf. UN-SUBORDINATE *a.*) **1634** BP. REYNOLDS *Shieldes of Earth* (1636) 19 This belongeth only unto Princes (and that independently, and unsubordinately to any higher power or person, save God). † **Unsubordina·tion.** *Obs.* (UN-[1] 12, 5 b.) **1656** JEANES *Mixt. Schol. Div.* 43 This is a sufficient argument, that in the manner of the soules being there is an unsubordination unto all second causes.

**Unsubo·rned,** *ppl. a.* (UN-[1] 8.) **1656** OSBORNE *Observ. Turks* 3 Such marks of Worship.. as he was pleased to impresse upon their yet unsuborned imaginations. **1689** HICKERINGILL *Ceremony-Monger* Concl. ii, The Legislative Power (unsuborn'd by Priest-craft). **1754** HUME *Hist. Eng.* I. 467 The very pulpits were bedewed with unsuborned tears. **1797** BURKE *Regic. Peace* iii. 30 Such a tone..is the true, unsuborned, unsophisticated language of genuine natural feeling.

† **Un-sub-presbytery.** *Obs.* (UN-[1] 12.) **1659** GAUDEN *Tears Ch.* 449 Factions, confusions are the genuine fruites of an un-sub-Presbytery.

**Unsubscri·bed,** *ppl. a.* (UN-[1] 8, 8 c.) **1571** BP. LESLEY in Bercher *Nobility Women* (Roxb.) 26 Those Letters..were unsubscribid. **1639** FULLER *Holy War* III. viii. 122 A concealed Christian,..with letters unsubscribed with any name, gave them..intelligence. **1682** SCARLETT *Exchanges* 358 Bills unsubscribed are like Bonds without Seals, and are not obligatory at all. **1754** RICHARDSON *Grandison* V. 326 A call for supper makes me leave my paper unsubscribed. **1791** COWPER *Let. to W. Bagot* 21 Sept., He had sold..a hundred of the unsubscribed-for copies.

**Unsubscri·bing,** *ppl. a.* (UN-[1] 10.) **1790** COWPER *Let. to J. Hill* 17 Sept., The sum subscribed..will defray the expense of printing; which is as much as, in these unsubscribing days, I had any reason to promise myself. **1837** *Westm. Rev.* July 73 As far as the unsubscribing public were concerned. **1851** H. D. WOLFF *Madrilenia* 50 Three rows of benches, where the bourgeoisie and unsubscribing portion of the aristocracy can take places. **Unsubse·rvient,** *a.* (UN-[1] 8.) **1656** BRAMHALL *Replic.* ii. 84 These observations..are so innocent, so indifferent, and so unsubserviant to either party, that I hoped they might pass without any censure. **Unsubsi·ded,** *ppl. a.* (UN-[1] 8.) **1804** EUGENIA DE ACTON *Tale without Title* III. 192 Their joy was mixed with a still unsubsided surprise. **1815** SCOTT *Guy M.* xxxix, The froth of the last draught of twopenny yet unsubsided on his upper lip.

**Unsu·bsidized,** *ppl. a.* (UN-[1] 8.) **1756** *World* No. 204 ⁋ 2 Certain unsubsidized pamphleteers. **1807** SYD. SMITH *Lett. Catholics* iv, The winds, those ancient and unsubsidised allies of England. **1875** *N. Amer. Rev.* CXX. 125 The criticism and denunciation of the unsubsidized press.

**Unsubsi·stence.** (UN-[1] 12, 5 b.) **1642** D. ROGERS *Naaman* 180 From the old yrkesomenesse, vanity, bondage and unsubsistence. **Unsu·bstanced,** *ppl. a.* (UN-[1] 8.) *a* **1658** [see UNSINEWY]. **1838** S. BELLAMY *Betrayal* 162 A vasty world of form Unsubstanc'd.

**Unsubsta·ntial,** *a.* [UN-[1] 7 and 5 b.]

**1.** Having no real basis or foundation in fact.

*c* **1455** PECOCK *Folewer* 114 þe dyuersite..was not but in wordis oonli and in fame of þe peple wiþout þe trouþ, which ful oft is founde ful vntrewe, vnsubstancial and perilose. **1715** ROWE *Lady Jane Gray* IV. 48 The vain Dream Of Empire, and a Crown,..With all those unsubstantial empty Forms. **1776** GIBBON *Decl. & F.* xiii. I. 399 These deep but unsubstantial meditations. **1810** SOUTHEY *Kehama* VII. xi, Nor build on unsubstantial hope thy trust. **1833–4** J. PHILLIPS *Geol.* in *Encycl. Metrop.* (1845) VI. 688/2 Every new, fanciful, and unsubstantial theory. **1883** SIR H. COTTON in *Law Rep.* 11 Q. B. Div. 532 If the counter-claim is frivolous and unsubstantial.

**2.** Having no bodily or material substance.

**1592** SHAKS. *Rom. & Jul.* V. iii. 103 Shall I beleeue that vnsubstantiall death is amorous? **1605** — *Lear* IV. i. 7 Welcome then, Thou vnsubstantiall ayre that I embrace. **1671** MILTON *P. R.* IV. 399 Darkness..brought in lowring night Her shadowy off-spring, unsubstantial both. **1742** YOUNG *Nt. Th.* IX. 118 What lengths of far-fam'd ages.. roll along In unsubstantial images of air! **1794** G. ADAMS *Nat. & Exp. Philos.* III. xxix. 198 Time and space, which in themselves are unsubstantial, inanimate, and destitute of intelligence. **1827** POLLOK *Course T.* III. 412 Of all the phantoms,.. Most unsubstantial, unessential shade, Was earthly Fame. **1871** L. STEPHEN *Playgr. Eur.* ii. 82 Hill and plain, apparently unsubstantial as a mountain mist. **1885** R. BRIDGES *Eros & Psyche* I. vi, To man's purer unsubstantial part The brightness of her presence was addressed.

**b.** Lacking in substance or solidity. Also *Comb.*

**1617** HIERON *Wks.* II. xxvi. 363 If you shall pill it [*sc.* a rush], what is vnder it but a kind of spongious, vnsubstantiall substance? **1773** *Cook's Voy.* III. xi. III. 690 They taste not unlike a green cocoa-nut, and, like them, probably they yield a nutriment that is watry and unsubstantial. **1825** J. NEAL *Bro. Jonathan* II. 195 Wasted away, in her unsubstantial proportions. **1842** DICKENS *Amer. Notes* (1850) 18/1 The suburbs are..even more unsubstantial-looking than the city. **1848** MILL *Pol. Econ.* I. xi. § 3. 203 We can scarcely conceive more unsubstantial or temporary fabrics.

Hence **Unsubsta·ntialness.**

**1860** PUSEY *Min. Proph.* 465 The unsubstantialness of it all, the unsubstantiality of his lies.

**Unsubstantia·lity.** [f. prec.] The quality of being unsubstantial; insubstantiality.

**1838** A. CLISSOLD *Pract. Nature* 182 If we allow this doctrine of unsubstantiality to prevail. **1847** C. BRONTË *J. Eyre* xxiv, Something of unsubstantiality and uncertainty had beset my hopes. **1860** [see prec.]. **1883** *Fortn. Rev.* Apr. 565, I have no consciousness of what happened, after this feeling of unsubstantiality came upon me.

**Unsubsta·ntialize,** *v.* (UN-[2] 6 c.) **1809–14** WORDSW. *Excurs.* IX. 66 While the gross and visible frame of things.. seems All unsubstantialized. **1894** S. BROOKE *Tennyson* v. 148 The sudden unsubstantialising of the outward world.. was Wordsworth's frequent feeling. **Unsubsta·ntially,** *adv.* (UN-[1] 11.) **1529** *Act 21 Hen. VIII,* c. 16 § 1 Wares whiche they untruely, subtely, unsubstauncially, and dysceytfully have made. [**1847** WEBSTER.] **Unsubsta·ntiate,** *a.* (UN-[1] 7, 5 b.) **1890** *Cath. News* 3 May 4/3 A second glance ..is enough to expose the unsubstantiate fraud.

**Unsubsta·ntiate,** *v.* [UN-[1] 6.] *trans.* To divest of substance; to render unsubstantial.

**1799** COLERIDGE *Lett.* (1895) 284 Death!—that..so unsubstantiates the living things that one has grasped. **1819** CHALMERS *Congregat. Serm.* (1836) I. 345 You unsubstantiate all the solemnity of his proclaimed sayings. **1881** FRASER *Berkeley* 91 The premises that unsubstantiate matter, they would argue, unsubstantiate everything.

**Unsubsta·ntiated,** *ppl. a.* (UN-[1] 8.)

[**1775** ASH.] **1837** HT. MARTINEAU *Soc. Amer.* II. 139 An unsubstantiated rumour of his having been seen conversing with slaves. **1856** FROUDE *Hist. Eng.* II. 46 Wolsey..set aside these unsubstantiated rumours.

**Unsubstantia·tion.** (UN-[1] 12.) **1881** FRASER *Berkeley* 201 [Berkeley] would probably have been satisfied with this acknowledgment, as a sufficient unsubstantiation of matter. **Unsu·btle,** *a.* (UN-[1] 7.) *a* **1500** *Ratis Raving* I. 877 For sen [? *read* few] vnsubtill that are fals Eschapis vnhyngyt be the hals.

**Unsubve·rted,** *ppl. a.* (UN-[1] 8.)

[**1775** ASH.] **1809–14** WORDSW. *Excurs.* III. 149 Pyramid Of Egypt, unsubverted, undissolved. **1835** KIRBY *Hab. & Inst. Anim.* I. v. 186 The reefs of coral that were left unsubverted. **1872** BRIERLEY *Cotters of Mossburn* xxiv. 245 Invested with much of the feeling and understanding of unsubverted human nature.

**Unsuccee·dable,** *a.* (UN-[1] 7 b.) **1646** SIR T. BROWNE *Pseud. Ep.* I. ii. 6 Whereof had he remained assured, he had continued silent, nor would his discretion attempt so unsucceedable a temptation. **Unsuccee·ded,** *ppl. a.* (UN-[1] 8.) **1667** MILTON *P. L.* V. 821 To binde with Laws the free, And equal over equals to let Reigne, One over all with unsucceeded power. **1831** T. HOPE *Ess. Origin Man* III. 229 To many a man the storms of the day remain unsucceeded by a serene sunset. **Unsuccee·ding,** *ppl. a.* (UN-[1] 10.) **1639** FULLER *Holy War* IV. xxix. 220 None will willingly father unsucceeding villany. **1661** BOYLE *Certain Physiol. Ess.* (1669) 75 The Second Essay Of Un-succeeding Experiments.

**Unsucce·ss.** [UN-[1] 12 and 5 b.] Lack of success, failure; an instance of this.

*a* **1586** SIDNEY *Arcadia* II. viii, He deemed his unsuccesse [**1590** unsuccessings] proceeded of their unwillingnes to have him prosper. **1655** *Nicholas Papers* (Camden) II. 292 The late busines, whose vnsuccess, as hee thought, wolde prooue of aduantage to Cromwell. **1710** STRYPE *Life & Acts of E. Grindal* vii. 70 These Unsuccesses were justly looked upon to proceed from the punishing Hand of Heaven. **1797** J. PINKERTON *Hist. Scotland* I. 86 Fortune preserved his government from any signal unsuccess. **1837** MISS MITFORD *Country Stories* (1850) 129 Chilled by so much unsuccess, the ardour of my pursuit began to abate. **1883** SWINBURNE *Misc.* (1886) 128 The definitions he gives us of his object and the tests which these offer of his success and unsuccess.

**Unsucce·ssful,** *a.* [UN-[1] 7 and 5 b.] Not attended by, not meeting or attaining, success.

**a.** Of actions, endeavours, etc.

**1617** MORYSON *Itin.* II. 48 Griefe of vnsuccessefull loue. **1651** BAXTER *Infant Baptism* 161 They are cited by Conradus Bergius in his most excellent Pacificatory (though hitherto much unsuccessfull) Treatise. **1685** DRYDEN *Sylvæ* Pref. ⁋ 6 These..deserve the pains I have taken with them, which I hope have not been unsuccessful, or unworthy of my author. **1744** BERKELEY *Siris* § 6 Which trials I never knew unsuccessful. **1809** COLERIDGE *Friend* 37 An unsuccessful attempt to deceive him. **1837** LOCKHART *Scott* II. xii. 407 Mr. Southey's application was unsuccessful. **1863** W. C. BALDWIN *Afr. Hunting* vii. 300, I have shot nothing; two hard unsuccessful days.

**b.** Of persons.

**1659** W. CHAMBERLAYNE *Pharon.* II. i. 309 The unsuccessful rebel thus secured By speedy flight. **1714** ADDISON *Spect.* No. 592 ⁋ 1 Which, as I am informed, are the Plays of many unsuccessful Poets artificially cut and shreaded for that Use. **1790** BEATSON *Nav. & Mil. Mem.* I. 100 To be unsuccessful or unfortunate, is generally to be criminal in the opinion of mankind. **1828** LYTTON *Pelham* II. x, My unsuccessful opponent..preferred a petition against me, for what he called undue means. **1890** 'R. BOLDREWOOD' *Col. Reformer* (1891) 152 If a man doesn't make money..he is regarded only as an unpractical, unsuccessful enthusiast.

*absol.* **1750** JOHNSON *Rambler* No. 87 ⁋ 9 The unsuccessful vent their discontent upon those that excel them. **1898** 'H. S. MERRIMAN' *Roden's Corner* iv, So many sail to those distant havens of the unsuccessful.

**Unsucce·ssfully,** *adv.* [UN-[1] 11. Cf. prec.] Without success.

**1649** J. H. *Motion to Parl. Adv. Learn.* 35 Propensions.. which if disobeyed succeeded untowardly and unsuccessfully. **1664** DRYDEN *Rival Ladies* Ep. Ded. ⁋ 2 Fortune.., with which wisdom does often unsuccessfully struggle in the world. *a* **1674** MILTON *Free Commw.* Wks. 1851 V. 425 Nor was the heroic Cause unsuccessfully defended to all Christendom, against the Tongue of a famous and thought invincible Adversary. *a* **1721** SHEFFIELD (Dk. Buckhm.) *Wks.* (1753) II. 177 Several letters shew his punctual performance of it, tho' unsuccessfully. **1819** SCOTT *Ivanhoe* xxv, Has your suit, then, been unsuccessfully paid to the Saxon heiress? **1873** PROCTOR *Expanse Heav.* 287 Our short-lived race..has..not unsuccessfully carried out the daring scheme [etc.].

**Unsucce·ssfulness.** (UN-[1] 12 and 5 b.) *c* **1630** SANDERSON *Serm.* (1681) 307 The weakness, frailty, and unsuccessfulness of mens devices. **1687** BOYLE *Martyrd. Theodora* ix. 171 The unsuccessfulness he had hitherto met with in his attempt. **1742** *Johnson's Debates* (1787) II. 107 The unsuccessfulness of their endeavours. **1761** STERNE *Tr. Shandy* IV. vi, When recollecting the unsuccessfulness of his first effort in that attitude. **1837** CARLYLE *Fr. Rev.* III. IV. vi, Custine was..found guilty..of one thing, unsuccessfulness.

† **Unsucce·ssible,** *a. Obs.*—[1] [UN-[1] 7.] Not admitting of succession. **1579** FULKE *Refut. Rastel* 736 So great blasphemie, as none can lightly be greater,..because it taketh away the eternall and vnsuccessible priesthood of Christ.

† **Unsucce·ssing,** *vbl. sb.* (See UNSUCCESS, quot. *a.* 1586.)

**Unsucce·ssive,** *a.* [UN-[1] 7 and 5 b.]

† **1.** Unsuccessful. *Obs.*—[1]

**1617** WOODALL *Surg. Mate* Pref. (1639) B 6 b, To keepe a Iournall in writing..as well of the unsuccessive applications, as of the successive.

**2.** Not exhibiting succession.

**1646** SIR T. BROWNE *Pseud. Ep.* 345 Although we be measured by the Zone of time,..yet can we not thus..summe up the unsuccessive and stable duration of God. *a* **1676** HALE *Prim. Orig. Man.* I. iii. 90 Such parts of the visible Universe as are incorruptible, unalterable, and unsuccessive. **1737** A. BAXTER *Enq. Nat. Human Soul* 375 If this necessary Being hath no change or succession in his nature, his existence must of course be unsuccessive. **1811** A. M[c]LEAN *Comm. Heb.* Wks. 1847 II. 281 He hath an unsuccessive priesthood, which passeth not from him to any other.

Hence **Unsucce·ssively** *adv.*, † unsuccessfully.

**1707** *Lond. Gaz.* No. 4333/4 The Union with Scotland,.. so often..unsuccessively attempted,..is the Joy..of all Your ..Subjects.

**Unsucce·ssiveness.** (UN-[1] 12. Cf. prec.) **1737** A. BAXTER *Enq. Nature Human Soul* 375 On the other hand, it is, I think, scarce intelligible, to apply this successiveness or unsuccessiveness (so to speak) to time itself, or to eternity, abstractedly taken. **Unsu·ccourable,** *a.* (UN-[1] 7 b.) **1593** *Sidney's Arcadia* (1598) IV. 414 That in the ende some one or other might hap to do an vnsuccourable mischiefe. **1599** SANDYS *Europæ Spec.* (1605) Z 4 An vnexplicable & vnsuccorable calamitie. **1611** FLORIO, *Insoccorenole*, vnsuccourable.

**Unsu·ccoured,** *ppl. a.* (UN-[1] 8.)

**1422** YONG tr. *Secreta Secret.* 183 He shal be vnsocowrid whan he moste nede hath. **1596** SPENSER *F. Q.* IV. viii. 51 Him wretched thrall vnto his dongeon [he] brought, Where he remaines, of all vnsuccour'd and vnsought. **1616** W. BROWNE *Brit. Past.* II. v. 342, I have beheld A widow vine stand..Unpropt, unsuccoured, by stake or tree. **1660** *Gentl. Calling* v. 78 The many unsuccour'd extremities of the Poor. **1807** J. BARLOW *Columb.* VII. 225 He..Hems on all sides the long unsuccour'd place. **1864** *Realm* 17 Feb. 5 Is Germany to leave her kindred unsuccoured, because they cannot be counted by millions?

**Unsuccu·mbing,** *ppl. a.* (UN-[1] 10.) *a* **1833** MRS. BROWNING *Tempest* ad fin., High-seeming Death, I..have hope.. of showing to thy face An unsuccumbing spirit. **Unsu·cked,** *ppl. a.* (UN-[1] 8.) *a* **1652** BROME *City Wit* IV. i, Were't not a sin to let such a foole passe unsuckt? **1667** MILTON *P. L.* IX. 583 The Teats Of Ewe or Goat dropping with Milk at Eevn, Unsuckt of Lamb or Kid.

**Unsue·d,** *ppl. a.* (UN-[1] 8, 8 c.)

**1594** W. WEST *2nd Pt. Symboleographia, Chancerie* § 139 It can not be intended, that..he would have left the elder bond and debt, being of a greater summe, unsued for. **1616** T. ADAMS *Soules Sicknesse* 27 Gilianus..rewarded deserts vnsued to. **1629** MASSINGER *Picture* I. i, I will not leave a saint unsued to For your protection. **1842** WORDSW. *Poems* p. x, Such is the grace Which, though unsued for, fails not to descend With heavenly inspiration.

† **Unsufferabi·lity.** [UN-[1] 12.] Incapacity of suffering. *c* **1425** *St. Mary of Oignies* I. v. 38 in *Anglia* VIII. 137 She lafte þe manhede of Criste, and helde vp hir mynde to þe godhede & mageste, þat she myghte fynde comforte in his vnsufferabilite.

**Unsu·fferable,** *a.* and *adv.* Now *rare* or *Obs.* [UN-[1] 7 b, 11 b, 5 b.]

**1.** Incapable of being suffered with patience or equanimity; not to be tolerated or endured; going beyond all natural limits: **a.** Of injuries, wrongs, etc.

*a* **1325** *MS. Rawl. B.520* fol. 31 b, We undoinde so muche unsufferable luere of oure poeple..stabblissez ant ordeinez [etc.]. *c* **1440** *Promp. Parv.* 367/2 On-sufferabyl, or ontollerable, *intollerabilis, insufferabilis.* *c* **1449** PECOCK *Repr.* III. xvii. 395 Ellis vnsufferable myscheuys of hasty domes wolde ofte falle. **1533** BELLENDEN *Livy* I. xviii. (S.T.S.) I. 100 þe baterent and vnsufferabil tyrannye of kingis. **1597** HOOKER *Eccl. Pol.* V. xxx. § 3 We know no reason wherefore any man should yet imagine it an vnsufferable euill. **1621** in Foster *Eng. Factories Ind.* (1906) I. 301 To call them to accompt..for these unsufferable wrongs. **1660** JER. TAYLOR *Ductor* I. ii. rule 8 § 30 The injustice may be frequent and unsufferable. **1725** POPE *Odyssey* II. 69 Unsufferable wrong Cries to the Gods, and vengeance sleeps too long. **1763** LD. HALIFAX in *10th Rep. Hist. MSS. Comm.* App. I. 361 The Outrages..are most abominable and unsufferable.

**b.** Of actions, conduct, qualities, etc.

**1548** GESTE *Pr. Masse* D ij, What an vnsufferable mockedge is this..of God. **1582–3** *Reg. Privy Council Scot.* III. 541 A power strange and unsufferabill to be in the persoun of ony inferior subject. **1608** MACHIN *Dumb Knt.* V. I 3, Thine adulterat..lust, Shamefull and grosse and most vnsufferable. **1651** BIGGS *New Disp.* ⁋ 250 Unsufferable fallacies..are couched under these four. **1711** STEELE *Spect.* No. 38 ⁋ 10 The unsufferable Affectation you are guilty of in all you say and do. **1720** SWIFT *Let. to Yng. Clergyman* Wks. 1755 II. II. 12 The common unsufferable cant of taking all occasions to disparage the heathen philosophers. *a* **1774** GOLDSM. tr. *Scarron's Com. Romance* (1775) I. 27 Upon these vast accomplishments, he had built an unsufferable degree of pride.

c. Of persons. Also *absol.*
1382 WYCLIF 2 *Macc.* viii. 5 Machabeus..was maad vnsuffreable to heithen men; forsothe the wrath of the Lord is conuertid in to mercye. c1450 HOLLAND *Houlate* 926 Thir birdis ilkane Besocht Natur to cess that vnsufferable. c1470 HENRY *Wallace* I. 267 Unsouerable ar thir pepille of Ingland. 1586 T. B. *La Primaud. Fr. Acad.* I. 112 The more that an ignorant man is lift up unto some excellencie of dignitie.., the more unsufferable he is. 1619 A. NEWMAN *Pleas. Vis.* (1840) 49 All know (vnsufferable Man) they [*sc.* women] are..beyond compare. 1678 MRS. BEHN *Sir P. Fancy* I. i, The pertest unsufferable fool he ever saw.

2. Too distressing, severe, or painful to be borne; going beyond the limits of physical endurance: a. Of outward things.
a1340 HAMPOLE *Psalter* cxlvii. 6 As wha say, vnsufferabil ware þat kald, if he lesid it noght. 1382 WYCLIF *Num.* xi. 10 Thanne Moyses herde the puple wepynge bi meynees,.. and to Moyses it was seen a thing vnsufferable [L. *intolerandam*]. 1395 PURVEY *Remonstr.* (1851) 22 Thei wolen putten to a man confessid to hem, greuouse chargis and vnsuffrable. 1544 BETHAM *Precepts Warr* I. cxxiii. G ij b, They were ashamed, that they dydde not abyde suche lyke labours, yea and moche more vnsufferable. 1562 TURNER *Baths* 8 An unsufferable raynye, windye, or colde weather. 1613 PURCHAS *Pilgrimage* (1614) 720 The high ridges..are vnsufferable for cold. 1658 T. WALL *Charact. Enemies Ch.* 53 [To] lie under the..dreadful apprehensions, or unsufferable strokes of divine wrath. 1729 SAVAGE *Wanderer* II. 50 Like noon-tide summer-suns the rays appear, Unsuff'rable, magnificent and near! 1742 *Lond. & Country Brew.* III. (1743) 202 An unsufferable, ill palated oily Juice, that will spoil all the Liquor. 1869 SPURGEON *Treas. David* Ps. xviii. 6 The king heard it in his palace of light unsufferable.

b. Of pain, grief, fear, etc.
c1374 CHAUCER *Boeth.* III. pr. vii. 79 Grete sekenesse and ..grete sorwes vnsuffrable. 1388 WYCLIF *Judith* xiv. 17 Vnsuffrable drede and tremblyng felde doun on hem. a1425 tr. *Arderne's Treat. Fistula*, etc. 40 Þe pacient feleþ as it war vnsufferable ychyng. c1425 *St. Christina* xvi. in *Anglia* VIII. 125 She was stired of god vnto an vnsufferabil þriste. c1445 PECOCK *Donet* 71 For eesing of his vnsuffrable fleischli freelte. a1589 PALFREYMAN *Baldwin's Mor. Philos.* (1600) 140 b, Conscience..worketh..vnsufferable torments,..to the condempnation of the vngodly. 1595 CLERKE *Polimanteia* S j b, To my vnsufferable and vnpitied griefe. 1639 S. DU VERGER tr. *Camus' Admir. Events* 301 A torture unsufferable unto this young gentlewoman. 1700 BLACKMORE *Job* 138 My fullness gives unsufferable pain. 1722 DE FOE *Hist. Plague* (1754) 261 The unsufferable Torment of the Swellings.

†3. Incapable of self-restraint. *Obs.*$^{-1}$
1387 TREVISA *Higden* (Rolls) V. 61 Þis was a swiþe evel man,..and he was unsuffrable of leccherie [L. *libidinis impatientissimus*].

†4. Not involving suffering. *Obs.*$^{-1}$
1548 GESTE *Pr. Masse* C vj, They greuously erre, who hold opinion y$^t$ our faultes ar pardoned through theyr vnsufferable & vnbloudy sacrificing of christes bodi.

†5. Incompatible. *Obs.*$^{-1}$
a1586 SIDNEY *Arcadia* III. x, Eternity, and Chaunce are things unsufferable together.

†6. As *adv.* = UNSUFFERABLY *adv.* 1. *Obs.*
c1420 *Prose Life Alex.* 76 Than commanded Alexander þat þay schuld make many fyres. For it began for to be vnsufferable calde. 1683 MOXON *Mech. Exerc., Printing* xi. ¶23 Sometimes the Inck proves so unsufferable Pale, that [etc.].

Hence **Unsu·fferableness.**
1611 FLORIO, *Inpatibilità*, vnsufferablenesse. 1677 HORNECK *Gt. Law Consid.* iv. 175 His passions..represent to his mind..the unsufferableness of the disgrace. 1679 KID in Hickes *Spirit of Popery* (1680) 2 There is something in a Christians condition, that can never put him without the reach of unsufferableness.

**Unsu·fferably,** *adv.* [UN-$^1$ 11 and 5 b.]
1. Intolerably; unendurably.
c1440 *Promp. Parv.* 367/2 On-sufferably.., *intollerabiliter.* 1644 PRYNNE & WALKER *Fiennes's Trial* App. 20 Captain Bagnall..was baffled unsufferably by the Defendant..before the Councell. 1661 PEPYS *Diary* 31 May, [His mother] being so unsufferably foolish and simple. 1702 ECHARD *Eccl. Hist.* I. vi. 138 Finding his Soul unsufferably oppress'd. 1727 DE FOE *Hist. Appar.* iv. (1840) 28 Saturn and Jupiter are uncomfortably dark, unsufferably cold.

†2. Without suffering. *Obs.*$^{-1}$
1548 GESTE *Pr. Masse* C vj b, We ar already redemed..by y$^e$ ones offering of christ neuer to be reuyued eyther sufferablye or vnsufferably, bloudely or vnbloudely.

†**Unsu·fferance.** *Obs.* [UN-$^1$ 12.]
1. Impatience.
a1400 *Spec. Vitæ* (MS. Bodl. 2685) fol. 79 Þe syns of þe hert bene þese:..vnconable gladnes, Vnsuffrance & werldly drerines.
2. Impassiveness.
1611 FLORIO, *Inpassibilita*, vnsufferance. 1625 GILL *Sacr. Philos.* IV. 32 That Stoicall vnsufferance of His mind, which Clemens Alex[andrinus]..thought not to bee subject either to joy or sorrow.

**Unsu·ffered,** *ppl. a.* [UN-$^1$ 8.]
1. Not suffered; unendured.
1549 COVERDALE, etc. *Erasm. Par.* 2 *Cor.* 52 b, For your welth I leaue nothyng vndone and vnsuffered. [1775 ASH.]
†2. Unsufferable. *Obs.*
c1611 CHAPMAN *Iliad* III. 6 Eschuing the vnsufferd stormes, shot from the winters starre. *Ibid.* VIII. 198 O Father Ioue, hath euer yet thy most unsuffred hand Afflicted, with such spoile of soules, the king of any land? *Ibid.* XI. 530, XIX. 357.

†**Unsu·ffering,** *vbl. sb. Obs.*$^{-1}$ [UN-$^1$ 13.] Impossibility of enduring. 1382 WYCLIF 2 *Macc.* ix. 10 No man miȝte beere hym, for vnsuffryng [L. *intolerantiam*] of stynke.

**Unsu·ffering,** *ppl. a.* [UN-$^1$ 10, 5 d.]
1. Not permitting or enduring. *rare.*
1568 *Reg. Privy Council Scot.* I. 626 Unsufferand the said Johnne..to be supportit..be the said hous. 1570 LEVINS *Manip.* 137 Vnsuffering, *impatiens.*
2. Not undergoing suffering.
1717 ATTERBURY *Serm.* (1737) III. 153 Can a man so treated ..be said to be in an unsuffering state? 1736 THOMSON *Hymn Seasons* 75 For the Great Shepherd reigns; And His unsuffering kingdom yet will come. 1838 H. BLUNT *Sev. Ch. Asia* 24 To an extent, to which the fairest mansion of the unsuffering Christian is utterly a stranger.

**Unsuffi·ced,** *ppl. a.* (UN-$^1$ 8.)
1586 L. LLOID *Pilgr. Princes* 13 Yet vnsufficed here with hee slue the Queenes owne sonne. a1644 QUARLES *Sol. Recant.* vi. 3 Who multiply their loynes and years, yet have Souls unsuffic'd with good. c1850 NEALE *Hymns East. Ch.* (1866) 103 Hell fire fierce and unsufficed.

†**Unsuffi·cience.** *Obs.* (UN-$^1$ 12, 5 b.) 1445 in *Wars Eng. in France* (1861) I. 467 Letters..deliverede for paiement into the Staple, and for unsufficience..refusede. c1455 PECOCK *Folewer* 123 Vnsufficience of kunnyng longyng to eny effect. †**Unsuffi·cienced,** *ppl. a.* (UN-$^2$ 4, 8.) *Obs.* a1661 FULLER *Life Smith* (1675) b 2, Allowing dispensation to such who were unsufficienced by weaknesse.

†**Unsuffi·ciency.** *Obs.* (UN-$^1$ 12 and 5 b.)
1580 HOLLYBAND *Treas. Fr. Tong, Incompetence*, not meete or fitte for, vnsufficiencie. 1594 HOOKER *Eccl. Pol.* II. viii. § 3 The vnsufficiencie of the light of Nature. 1597 *Ibid.* v. lxxxi. § 14 There are Ciuill as well as Ecclesiasticall Vnsufficiencies, Non-residences, and Pluralities. 1625 T. GODWIN *Moses & Aaron* IV. i. 172 The Arabians perceiuing the vnsufficiency of their knowne gods, dedicated their altars, *Ignoto Deo.* 1661 K. W. *Conf. Charac.*, [*Empirick*] (1860) 65 The weakness and unsufficiency of other doctors.

†**Unsuffi·cient,** *a. Obs.* [UN-$^1$ 7 and 5 b.]
1. = INSUFFICIENT *a.* 1.
1395 PURVEY *Remonstr.* (1851) 82 It is not declarid..that the clerk was vnsufficient, neither vnable. c1445 PECOCK *Donet* 145 And þanne, wherto schulde þe sufficient be lefte, and þe vnsufficient be taken,..in a purpos so necessarye? c1450 *Myrr. our Ladye* 137 We oughte to knowe oure selfe vnsuffycyente & therfore pray for helpe. a1513 FABYAN *Chron.* VI. cxlix. 136 Consyderynge the vnablenesse of Hilderich the kynge, that he was vnsufficient to rule so great a charge. 1535 COVERDALE *Bible* Prol. ¶7 As for the commendacyon of Gods holy scripture..I am farre vnsufficient therto. a1617 HIERON *Wks.* (1619) II. 474 This miserie of hauing none among them but an vnseasoning and vnsufficient minister. 1646 SIR T. BROWNE *Pseud. Ep.* I. iii. 9 Being unprovided, or unsufficient for higher speculations.
2. = INSUFFICIENT *a.* 2.
1398 TREVISA *Barth. De P. R.* XVII. i. (Bodl. MS.) fol. 185 b, Also in some trene þe [humoure] is vnsufficiaunte and vnperfecte. 1482 *Monk of Evesham* (Arb.) 109 Wat sum euer may be seyde of hyt by mannys mowthe, ful lytyl hyt ys, and onsufficient to expresse the ioy of myne herte. 1551 ROBINSON tr. *More's Utopia* I. (1895) 96 He perceiued the same stocke of money to be to litel, and vnsufficient. 1597 HOOKER *Eccl. Pol.* v. lx. § 7 When vnder vnsufficient pretences wee defraude them of such ordinarie outward helpes as wee should exhibit. 1625 GILL *Sacr. Philos.* Pref., You say that reason is an unsufficient meane, and unable to bring us to the knowledge of those things. 1656 JEANES *Mixt. Schol. Div.* 5 Our Saviour's discourse sheweth, that these were weak and unsufficient grounds.

Hence †**Unsuffi·ciently** *adv.*; **-ness.** *Obs.*
1398 TREVISA *Barth. De P. R.* VII. xxxi. (Bodl. MS.), Whanne þe lunges beþ igreued with..bocches..he serueþ þe hert *vnsufficiantlich of aier. c1440 *Alph. Tales* 143 One of þe cardynals when he hard þis, began to gruche agayn þe pope, & said he demyd vnsufficientlie. c1455 PECOCK *Folewer* 204 Ellis y wolde graunte þat y vnsufficientli nombrid þe poyntis of goddis lawe in þe..tablis. a1600 HOOKER *Eccl. Pol.* VI. vi. § 13 Absolving of unsufficiently disposed penitents. 1685 PETTY *Will* p. v, The admeasurement of the lands..was most unsufficiently and absurdly managed. 1533 *Reg. Mag. Sig. Scot.* 286/2 Sua that oure soverane lord and his liegis be nocht begylit tharewith anent the *unsufficientnes of the samyn.

†**Unsu·ffisance.** *Obs.* [UN-$^1$ 12, 5 b.] = INSUFFISANCE. c1400 *Pilgr. Sowle* (Caxton) I. xviii. 19 Yf I personelly shold not be herde..for myn vnsuffysaunce. †**Unsu·ffisant,** *sb. Obs.* [Cf. next.] Insufficiency. 1387 TREVISA *Higden* (Rolls) VII. 381 It is seide þat kyng William..wolde have depreved hym for unsufficiant [*v.r.* unsuffysant; L. *insufficientiam*] of lettrure. 1425 *Rolls of Parlt.* IV. 267 Ye grete unabilte and unsuffisante, that the same Wauter felte in hymself. †**Unsu·ffisant,** *a. Obs.* [UN-$^1$ 7, 5 b.] = INSUFFISANT *a.* c1400 *26 Pol. Poems* 136 Though I be, lorde, vnsuffisaunte, Any helpe to gete of the, Yet..*Parce michi, domine!* 1423 *Rolls of Parlt.* IV. 255 Thoo werkes of Brouderie there founden unsuffisant. c1440 *Pallad. on Husb.* I. 196 Olyuys grete out of that lond wol reke With drasty, wattry fruyt..Unsuffisaunt the costis forto acquyte.
**Unsu·ffocate,** *v.* (UN-$^2$ 3.) 1818 BYRON *Juan* I. cxxx, Like the apparatus Of the Humane Society's beginning, By which men are unsuffocated gratis. **Unsu·ffocative,** *a.* (UN-$^1$ 7.) 1822 GOOD *Study Med.* I. 536 When this difficulty [of breathing] is moderate and unsuffocative.

**Unsu·gared,** *ppl. a.* (UN-$^1$ 8.)
1592 NASHE *Four Lett. Confut.* E iij, Your vnsugred pilles ..would not haue beene so harsh in the swallowing. 1626 BACON *Sylva* § 883 Trie it with Sugar put into Water, formerly Sugred; And into other Water Vnsugred. 1871 *Daily News* 11 Feb., They may hereafter have an unsugared pill to swallow.

**Unsugge·stive,** *a.* (UN-$^1$ 7).
1797 LAMB *Let. to Coleridge* 10 Jan., My eyes are heavy and sleepy, and my brain unsuggestive. 1866 MARK LEMON *F. Lyle* II. 198 A single cup and saucer,..a diminutive teapot!—so unsuggestive of the pleasant gossip with which 'taking tea' is generally associated. 1900 *Daily News* 23 Feb. 5/1 The design was unsuggestive of date.
Hence **Unsugge·stiveness.**
1858 *Househ. Words* XIX. 181/2 An expression of countenance which..was a combination of aggression and pronounced patience, with a dogged unsuggestiveness.

†**Unsu·ing,** *vbl. sb. Obs.*$^{-1}$ [UN-$^1$ 13.] Lack of agreement. c1425 *Saints' Lives* in *Anglia* VIII. 195/35 Vnsuynge of englyshe, as vmwhile soþeren, oþere-while norþen.

†**Unsui·t,** *a. Obs.*$^{-1}$ [UN-$^1$ 7. Unfitting. 1704 J. BLAIR in W. S. Perry *Hist. Coll. Amer. Col. Ch.* (1870) I. 135 Aspersed with the most unsuitest imputations as if I had been raising sedition or rebellion.

**Unsui·t,** *v.* [UN-$^1$ 14.]
1. *trans.* To be at variance with.
1635 QUARLES *Embl.* IV. xv. 241 The sprightly Twang of the melodious Lute Agrees not with my voice; and both unsuit My untun'd fortunes.
2. To render unsuitable.
1869 *Pall Mall G.* 8 July 3/2 The health of the former cripple unsuiting her for convent life. 1902 *Daily Chron.* 8 Dec. 8/5 Their training..completely unsuits them for the proper performance of the duties.

**Unsuitabi·lity.** (UN-$^1$ 12, 5 b. Cf. next.)
1814 MRS. J. WEST *Alicia de Lacy* III. 220 The unsuitability of her white glittering dress for such a purpose. 1866 DICKENS *Lett.* (1880) II. 249 A limited reference to its unsuitability to these pages [of *All the Year Round*]. 1880 A. R. WALLACE *Isl. Life* 102 Anomalies of distribution other than such as may be connected with unsuitability of climate.

**Unsui·table,** *a.* (UN-$^1$ 7 b and 5 b.)
1597 HOOKER *Eccl. Pol.* v. xxxviii. § 3 Wanton, or light or vnsuteable harmonie, such as only pleaseth the eare. 1601 SHAKS. *All's Well* I. i. 170 Virginitie like an olde Courtier, weares her cap out of fashion, richly suted, but vnsuteable. 1665 BOYLE *Occas. Refl.* I. iii, I make him but very unsuitable Returns for the Blessings..I have receiv'd. 1671 MILTON *P. R.* III. 132 Hard recompence, unsutable return For so much good, so much beneficence. 1831 JAMES *Phil. Augustus* II. iv, At so unsuitable an hour. 1869 TOZER *Highl. Turkey* II. 346 The expression..would hardly appear unsuitable. 1890 'R. BOLDREWOOD' *Col. Reformer* (1891) 216 He thought..him not wholly unsuitable as a companion.
b. Const. *to* or *for*.
a1586 SIDNEY *Arcadia* III. xxiii, An unkinde answere,.. but not unsutable to the rest of your behaviour. 1601 SHAKS. *Twel. N.* II. v. 222 Hee will smile vpon her, which will now be so vnsuteable to her disposition,..that [etc.]. 1651 HOBBES *Leviath.* III. xlii. 293 Their ordinary maintenance was not unsuitable to their employment. 1768–74 TUCKER *Lt. Nat.* (1834) II. 547 If our devotion be overstrained it becomes unsuitable for practice. 1780 *Mirror* No. 94, A train of thinking..neither unpleasing nor unsuitable to the character of a rational being. a1834 COLERIDGE *Lit. Rem.* (1838) III. 382 Never did so wise a man adopt means so unsuitable to his end. 1879 HARLAN *Eyesight* ix. 131 Ground-glass globes are condemned..as unsuitable for school purposes.

**Unsui·tableness.** (UN-$^1$ 12.)
a1586 SIDNEY *Arcadia* III. vii, The unsutablenes of a weake broken voice to high brave wordes. 1644 MILTON *Areop.* (Arb.) 73 To suppresse opinions for the newnes, or the unsutablenes to a customary acceptance. a1697 SOUTH *Serm.* (1715) II. 167 The real Unsuitableness, that every thing sinful, or dishonest, bears to the Nature of Man. 1754 EDWARDS *Freed. Will* IV. viii. 239 The Unsuitableness of such a Necessity to the Liberty..of the divine Being. 1845 LD. CAMPBELL *Chancellors* lxxxiii. (1857) IV. 135 From the unsuitableness of his manner and style he is not..entertaining. 1886 *Law Times* LXXXII. 173/2 Those who allege my unsuitableness for the high position I now hold.

**Unsui·tably,** *adv.* (UN-$^1$ 11.)
1624 GATAKER *Transubst.* 198 Their religion indeed being ..patched together out of olde condemned heresies and unsutably composed. a1715 SOUTH *Serm.* IV. 110 That natural..Sensibility of Mind, which renders them apprehensive of any Thing done unsuitably to their Nature. 1774 WARTON *Hist. Eng. Poetry* I. 396 The modern monuments unsuitably placed in Westminster-abbey. 1859 *Habits of Gd. Society* iii. 143 He has never attempted to dress..unsuitably to his station. 1898 *Westm. Gaz.* 27 Aug. 2/1 When a girl marries unsuitably.

**Unsui·ted,** *ppl. a.* [UN-$^1$ 8, 8 d.]
†1. Not sued *for*. *Obs. rare*$^{-1}$.
1599 *Extr. Aberd. Reg.* (1848) II. 189 Sindrie our subjectis ..sustening gryt loss..in thair persones and gudes, be the piracie of Ingland, quhilkis..hes lyin ouer vnsuted for.
2. Not suited or adapted; unfitted, unfit.
1598 *Sidney's Astr. & Stella* li, My heart..is euen irkt that so sweet Comedie, By such vnsuted speech should hindred be. 1657 AUSTEN *Fruit Trees* II. 74 Therefore are his waies often so unsuted to the apprehensions of men. 1677 GILPIN *Demonol.* III. ix. 55 A work..such as had neither bee unsuited to the power of Christ, nor unlawful in it self. 1819 SCOTT *Ivanhoe* xliv, Like a garment unsuited to the climate in which I seek to dwell. 1847 SMEATON *Builder's Man.* 142 It is unsuited for the purpose to which it is applied. 1861 BUCKLE *Civiliz.* II. i. 136 The municipal privileges..being unsuited to the habits of the people.
b. Not accommodated or supplied.
1796 BURKE *Let. Noble Lord* Wks. VIII. 59 So that no constitution-fancier may go unsuited from his shop.

**Unsui·ting,** *ppl. a.* (UN-$^1$ 10.)
1596 HARINGTON *Metam. Ajax* I 2 b, Yet I will end with this good counsell, not vnsuting to the text I haue thus long talked of. 1604 SHAKS. *Oth.* IV. i. 78 (Q. 1), A passion most vnsuting such a man. 1639 FULLER *Holy War* v. xix. 261 The armie will be very heterogeneous, patched up of different people unsuiting in their manners. 1685 DRYDEN *Lucretius* III. 161 Leave those joys, unsuiting to thy age, To a fresh Comer. 1852 M. ARNOLD *Human Life* 16 Winds from our side the unsuiting consort rive.

**Unsu·llen,** *a.* (UN-$^1$ 7.) 1605 MARSTON *Dutch Courtezan* II. i, What harty gratefulnes, Unsulleine silence, unaffected modesty. **Unsu·lliable,** *a.* (UN-$^1$ 7 b.) 1766 J. MACGOWAN *Death* (1814) 560 Blessed afflictions, which..have fitted me for those unsulliable mansions of uninterrupted felicity! 1881 *Contemp. Rev.* Apr. 568 One block of long white light unsullyable Glows in deep azure.

**Unsu·llied,** *ppl. a.* (UN-$^1$ 8.)
1588 SHAKS. *L. L. L.* v. ii. 352 By my maiden honor, yet as pure As the vnsullied Lilly. 1621 G. SANDYS *Ovid's Met.* III. (1626) 56 The linked Deities their Graces fix! Where Roses with vnsullied Lillyes mix! 1717 LADY M. W. MONTAGU *Let. to C'tess of Mar* 18 April, That lovely bloom of complexion, unsullied by art. 1755 J. G. COOPER *Tomb Shaks.* 26 Here

Fancy sat, (her dewy fingers cold Decking with flow'rets fresh th' unsullied sod). **1828** LYTTON *Pelham* I. xiv, Gloves of most unsullied doeskin. **1863** M. J. BERKELEY *Brit. Mosses* i. 3 Stems..of a clear unsullied green.

**b.** In fig. use.

**1659** W. CHAMBERLAYNE *Pharon.* Ded., My more youthful labours..passed the public view unsullied by the cloudy aspect of the most critic spectator. **1665** MANLEY *Grotius' Low C. Wars* 113 His Mind, that never was greedy after Wealth, and, in that respect, unsullied and upright. **1743** FRANCIS tr. *Hor., Odes* IV. v. 29 Nobly conscious of unsullied Fame. **1774** W. WHITEHEAD *Plays & Poems* II. 171 The pure unsullied thoughts, and sallies of our souls. **1849** MACAULAY *Hist. Eng.* II. 247 In the midst of a corrupt court he had kept his personal integrity unsullied. **1879** FARRAR *St. Paul* I. 256 The unsullied sanctity of Jehovah's Temple.

Hence **Unsu·lliedness.**

**1863** MRS. WHITNEY *F. Gartney's Girlh.* xx, Her sweet look and fair unsulliedness of attire. **1865** W. H. GILLESPIE *Arg. Being & Attrib. God* IV. ii. (1871) 142 Holiness is moral stainlessness, spotlessness, unsulliedness.

**Unsu·lphurated,** *ppl. a.* (UN-[1] 8 a *b.*) **1825** J. NICHOLSON *Operat. Mechanic* 768 About as much [gold] as was reserved unsulphurated from the mass. **Unsulphu·reous,** *a.* (UN-[1] 7.) **1781** *Encycl. Brit.* (ed. 2) VII. 4932/1 To separate Mercury out of an unsulphureous Ore by Distillation. **Unsu·lphurized,** *ppl. a.* (UN-[1] 8 a *c.*) **1846** *Mechanic's Mag.* 4 July 2/2 Gutta percha either sulphurised or unsulphurised. **Unsu·ltry,** *a.* (UN-[1] 7.) **1826** J. WILSON *Noctes Ambr.* (1855) I. 170 On a chosen day of cloudless sunshine, yet unsultry air. **Unsummable,** *a.* (UN-[1] 7 b.) **1667** WATERHOUSE *Fire Lond.* 112 A Mart of Trade and a Mine of Wealth,[of] which the inexhaustion of this last twenty-six years by Sums unsummable,..would be incredible.

**Unsu·mmed,** *ppl. a.* [UN-[1] 8.]

**1.** Not summed up; uncounted.

*a* **1400–50** *Alexander* 1991 For as þis sede þat I send vnsoumed [*v.r.* vnsowmyd] is euer, So ben we..vnnowmyrd. **1579** *Richmond. Wills* (Surtees) XXVI. 286 Some of these gold and mony above writen. By those unsomed iij c. ij*li.* vjs. viij*d.* **1649** G. DANIEL *Trinarch., Hen. IV*, cclxiv, The wise Man has an vnsumm'd Librarye; Himselfe and Man, and Bookes, are all his Bookes. **1772** MASON *Eng. Garden* I. 18 Egregious madness; yet pursu'd With pains unwearied, with expense unsumm'd. **1791** COWPER *Iliad* II. 568 So the Grecians swarm'd An unsumm'd multitude o'er all the plain. **1857** H. MILLER *Test. Rocks* vi. 239 Armed with the experience in evil of unsummed ages. **1869** McLAREN *Serm.* Ser. II. xi. 194 After unsummed eternities of advance.

†**2.** (See quot. and cf. SUMMED 1.) *Obs. rare.*

**1615** LATHAM *Falconry* ¶ 3 b, Vnsumm'd is when a Hawkes feathers are not come forth, or els not com'd home to their full length.

**Unsu·mmered,** *a.* (UN-[1] 9.) **1879** TENNYSON *Pref. Poem to Brother's Sonn.* III. Poems (1894) 574/1 And, now to these unsummer'd skies The summer bird is still. **Unsu·mmer-like, -ly,** *adjs.* (UN-[1] 7, 7 c.) **1863** *Chamb. Jrnl.* Oct. 655/1 The unsummerly summer of eighteen sixty-nine. **1880** *Cassell's Mag.* 440 Another unsummer-like fashion. **1883** MISS BROUGHTON *Belinda* IV. ii, A chill and unsummerlike night.

**Unsu·mmoned,** *ppl. a.* (UN-[1] 8.)

**1474** *Acta Audit.* (1839) 35/2 Henry..protestit þat þe decrete..suld turne him to na preiudice becauss he was vnsummond. **1480** *Acta Dom. Conc.* (1839) 55/2 The lordis..ordanis him to hafe lettres to summond his prufis þat Is vnsummond gife he ony has. **1633** P. FLETCHER *Purple Isl.* v. xli, The lazie sense still sleeps, unsummon'd with his drum. **1673** DRYDEN *Marr. à la Mode* IV. v, Like an unsummon'd guest. **1763** MALLET *Elvira* III. iii, She [is]..unsummon'd too To this high task. *a* **1800** COWPER *Odyss.* (ed. 2) XXII. 551 Then bid Penelope with her attendants down, Nor leave unsummon'd one of all the train. **1839** MRS. JAMESON *Visits & Sk.* II. 74 Those whom the rules of etiquette allowed to approach unsummoned and pay their respects. **1860** FORSTER *Gr. Remonstr.* 31 An unsummoned tenant..could not take his place in the Council.

**Unsu·mmoning,** *vbl. sb.* (UN-[2] 3, 8.) **1632** in Nichols *Hist. Leics.* (1804) IV. 386 Paid apparitor for summoning and unsummoning. **Unsu·mptuary,** *a.* (UN-[1] 7.) **1720–1** *Lett. fr. Mist's Jrnl.* (1722) I. 83 Should rigid unsumptuary Laws pass the House [etc.].

**Unsu·ndered,** *ppl. a.* [UN-[1] 8. Cf. MDu. *ongesondert*, MLG., MHG. *ungesundert* (G. *ungesondert*).] Not parted or separated.

**1594** NASHE *Unfort. Trav.* H ij b, Those siluer pipes,..by many edged vnsundred writhings.., strayed from bough to bough. **1609** HEYWOOD *Brit. Troy* v. xxiv, The stout Centaures came..They seemd at first halfe horse halfe man unsundred. [Also in Minsheu, Sherwood, and Hexham, s.v.]

†**Unsu·nderly,** *adv. Obs.* [UN-[1] 11.] Inseparably. *c* **1440** *Gesta Rom.* xliv. 174 Late vs in this wordle be so vnsundirlye couplid to the holye trenitee, that [etc.].

**Unsu·ng,** *ppl. a.* [UN-[1] 8 b. Cf. MHG. and G. *ungesungen*, Sw. *osjungen*.]

**1.** Not sung; not uttered by singing.

**1422–61** in *Cal. Proc. in Chanc. Q. Eliz.* (1827) I. Introd. 20 It wer better bell unrogne at þe sauntes tyme þan þe messe unsogne. **1539** *Abst. Protocols Town Clerks Glasgow* (1897) IV. 118 Geif it faillies to be left on-sung thre nychtis togidder. **1613** W. BROWNE *Brit. Past.* I. i. 8 Drawne by time..To sing those layes as yet unsung of any. **1843** CARLYLE *Past & Pr.* III. v, Thy Epic, unsung in words, is written in huge characters on the face of this Planet. **1860** FABER *Bethlehem* 100 Numberless unlanguaged and unsung Magnificats. **1889** STEVENSON *South Seas* III. vi. (1900) 265 [They] gave up the unsung remainder of their ballet.

**2.** Not celebrated in or by song.

**1667** MILTON *P. L.* VII. 253 Thus was the first Day..: Nor past uncelebrated, nor unsung By the Celestial Quires. **1697** DRYDEN *Æneis* VII. 1014 Nor Œbalus, shalt thou be left unsung. **1701** ADDISON *Let. from Italy* 14 Here..not a mountain rears its head unsung. **1743** YOUNG *Nt. Th.* IV. 533 Why doubt we, then, the glorious truth to sing, Tho' yet unsung, as deem'd, perhaps, too bold? **1805** [see UNHONOURED]. **1828** CARLYLE *Misc.* (1840) I. 343 A thousand battle-fields remain unsung. **1875** F. I. SCUDAMORE *Day-Dreams* 10 It is one of the unsung beauties of the earth.

**Unsu·nk,** *ppl. a.* (UN-[1] 8 b.)

*a* **1300** *Cursor M.* 2847 Es noþer leued, ne tre, ne gress, Ne nathing of þat land vn-sonken [*v.rr.* vn-sunkyn, vnsunke]. *c* **1586** C'TESS PEMBROKE *Ps.* LXIX. vi, Keepe me safe unsunck, unmyred. **1611** SPEED *Hist. Gt. Brit.* IX. xii. § 56 Not halfe of their Shippes escaped vntaken or vnsuncke. *a* **1687** H. MORE *Conject. Cabbal.* (1713) 77 The Angels and the Souls of Men unsunk into generation. [*Ibid.* All Souls as they descend εἰς γένεσιν.] *c* **1740** A. HILL *To Author of 'Pamela'* 28 What..Though taste like thine each void of time can fill, Unsunk by spleen. **1824** BYRON *Juan* XVI. xcix, The Sinking Fund's unfathomable sea..leaves The debt unsunk, yet sinks all it receives. **1837** CARLYLE *Fr. Rev.* I. II. iv, Nimble old man, who..in the worst confusion will emerge, cork-like, unsunk.

**Unsu·nned,** *ppl. a.* [UN-[1] 8.]

**1.** Not penetrated or reached by sunlight; not exposed or accessible to the sun.

**1607** TOURNEUR *Rev. Trag.* III. F 1, [I] did wish his impudent grace To meete her here in this vn-sunned-lodge. **1634** MILTON *Comus* 398 The unsun'd heaps Of Misers treasure. **1652** BENLOWES *Theoph.* X. lxxvi, Why start'st? Unlock thy unsunn'd hoard. **1759** MASON *Caractacus* 22 The unsunn'd silver of the mine. **1797** COLERIDGE *Lime-tree Bower* 14 That branchless ash, Unsunn'd and damp. **1806** R. MANT *Poems, Country Gent.* I. 32 Where..horror shaggs the unsunn'd precipice. **1860** FLOR. NIGHTINGALE *Nursing* ix. 49 The unsunned sides of narrow streets. **1885** JEAN INGELOW *Sleep of Sigismund* xxxviii, With name unsaid and fame unsunned He walks that was King Sigismund.

**b.** *fig.* Not made patent or public.

**1809–14** WORDSW. *Excurs.* VII. 281 With his cheerful throng Of open projects, and his inward hoard Of unsunned griefs. **1821** J. HODGSON in J. Raine *Mem.* (1857) I. 347 He has promised to communicate to our Society some very curious and unsunned letters of Lord Dacre's. **1862** *Athenæum* 30 Aug. 278 The unsunned historical treasures in the possession of the London Corporation.

**2.** Not touched or affected by the light or heat of the sun. Also *fig.*

**1611** SHAKS. *Cymb.* II. v. 13, I thought her As Chaste, as vn-Sunn'd Snow. **1795** SOUTHEY *Vis. Maid of Orleans* I. 311 As white as unsunn'd snow, Or as the spotless lily of the vale. **1820** *Ellen Fitzarthur* 54 Crystal drops of unsunned dew. **1843** F. E. PAGET *Warden of Berkingholt* 119 The unsunned purity..of the Master of Berkingholt Union.

**b.** Not coloured or tanned by the sun.

**1821** CRAIG *Lect. Drawing*, etc. vi. 344 The dark, yet clear, complexion of the Italians, which would ill suit on unsunned English faces. **1835** WILLIS *Pencillings* II. xlix. 80 They venture to drop their jealous veils and ramble about in their unsunned beauty. **1882** *Century Mag.* XXV. 103 A lady..[with] pure, unsunned complexion.

*fig.* **1830** TENNYSON *Confess. Sensit. Mind* 140 In my morn of youth, The unsunn'd freshness of my strength.

**3.** Not lighted up by the sun. Also *fig.*

**1840** LADY C. BURY *Hist. of Flirt* xvi, Her still countenance unsunned by a smile. *a* **1864** HAWTHORNE *Amer. Note-Bks.* (1879) I. 36 All the near landscape lay unsunned. **1874** FARRAR *Christ* II. lix. 350 The unsunned outer darkness of miserable self-condemnation.

**Unsu·nny,** *a.* (UN-[1] 7.) **1859** TENNYSON *Pelleas & Ettarre* 176 We marvel at thee much, O damsel, wearing this unsunny face To him who won thee glory. **1860** FABER *Bethlehem* ii. (1865) 87 The warm air of the noon has heated the unsunny forest. †**Un-su·n-seen,** *ppl. a.* (UN-[1] 8 d.) **1654** BLOUNT *Acad. Eloq.* 48 An un-Sun-seen cave. †**Un-su·nshine,** *v.* (UN-[2] 6 b.) **1659** FULLER *App. Inj. Innoc.* III. 31 Military preparations..must needs give our Nation great troubles, and (for the time) un-Sunshine England.

†**Unsu·perable,** *a. Obs.* (UN-[1] 7 b and 5 b.)

**1526** *Pilgr. Perf.* (W. de W. 1531) 241 The vnsuperable loue & goodnes of god. **1617** MINSHEU s.v. (hence in Sherwood). **1644** DIGBY *Nat. Bodies* I. § 4. 3 It..is the occasion of exceeding great errours, and entangleth one in vnsuperable difficulties. **1777** POTTER *Æschylus, Agamemnon* 293 To wear The form of friendship, and with circling wiles Inclose him in th' unsuperable net.

**Unsupe·rfluous,** *a.* (UN-[1] 7.)

**1571** GOLDING *Calvin on Ps.* lxii. 11 How unsuperfluous this warning is, wee learne by daylye experience. **1634** MILTON *Comus* 773 Natures full blessings would be well dispenc't In unsuperfluous eeven proportion. **1832** L. HUNT *Poems* 197 Swans..which..glide With unsuperfluous lift of their proud wings. **1842** J. WILSON *Chr. North* (1857) I. 145 Not scanty but unsuperfluous fare is theirs.

**Unsuperscri·bed,** *ppl. a.* (UN-[1] 8.) *a* **1711** KEN *Sion* Poet. Wks. 1721 IV. 390 A silken Cord around his Neck was hung, At which unsuperscrib'd a Letter hung. **1748** RICHARDSON *Clarissa* I. 163 [A] letter..from my mother, unsealed, and unsuperscribed also. **Unsuperse·ded,** *ppl. a.* (UN-[1] 8.) [**1775** ASH.] **1857** TOULMIN SMITH *Parish* 133 The anomalies that have hence arisen leave the action of the Parish unsuperseded. **1890** 'R. BOLDREWOOD' *Col. Reformer* (1891) 162 That much-abused but as yet unsuperseded garb. **Unsupersti·tious,** *a.* (UN-[1] 7.) **1652** SPARKE *Prim. Devot.* (1660) 469 This kinde of Sortilegium was usual with Antiquity, such an undeceitful, and unsuperstitious Lottery. **1863** *Blackw. Mag.* Sept. 291 If we consult history in an unprejudiced, unsuperstitious spirit. **Unsupervi·sed,** *ppl. a.* (UN-[1] 8.) **1899** *Educat. Rev.* Dec. 470 He is, unsupervised, irresponsible. [Common in recent use.]

**Unsu·pped,** *ppl. a.* [UN-[1] 8.] Without having supped; supperless.

**1382** WYCLIF *Dan.* vi. 18 The kyng..slepte vnsoupid [L. *incœnatus*], and metis be not brouȝt to byfore hym. **1483** *Cath. Angl.* 350/1 Vn Sowped, *jncenatus.* **1508** KENNEDIE *Flyting w. Dunbar* 382 Sic reule gerris the..sitt vnsoupit oft beȝond the sey. *c* **1563** *Jack Jugler* in *Four Old Plays* (1848) 43, I wolde gladly byne vnsupped, soo you had your fyll. **1609** BIBLE (Douay) *Dan.* vi. 18 The king went to his house, and slept unsupped. **1894** [see UNSLEPT 1].

**Unsuppla·nted,** *ppl. a.* (UN-[1] 8.) **1708** J. PHILIPS *Cyder* II. 384 Gladsome they quaff,..[and] well bedew'd repair Each to his Home with unsupplanted Feet. **Unsu·pple,** *a.* (UN-[1] 7.) **1621** G. SANDYS *Ovid's Met.* II. (1626) 43 Againe shee struggl'd to baue stood on end: But, those vnsupple sinewes would not bend. **Unsu·ppled,** *ppl. a.* (UN-[1] 8.) **1761** EARL PEMBROKE *Milit. Equitation* (1762) 8 A raw, unsuppled, and unprepared lad, who is put at once upon a rough horse.

**Unsuppli·able,** *a.* (UN-[1] 7 b.)

**1638** CHILLINGW. *Relig. Prot.* I. ii. § 67. 77 The unsuppliable defect of any necessary Antecedent. **1793** HOLCROFT tr. *Lavater's Physiog.* vi. 42 Are they not equally indispensable, equally unsuppliable? **1802–12** BENTHAM *Ration. Judic. Evid.* (1827) III. 413 Why admit it, under the danger of incorrigible incorrectness and unsupplyable incompleteness?

**Unsu·pplicated,** *ppl. a.* (UN-[1] 8.) **1634** BP. HALL *Contempl., N. T.* IV. xii, Saul himself would..offer a burnt-offering to the Lord, rather than the Philistines should fight with him unsupplicated.

**Unsupplie·d,** *ppl. a.* [UN-[1] 8, 8 c.]

**1.** Not supplied or provided with something.

**1599** Q. ELIZ. in Moryson *Itin.* (1617) II. 56 Therefore we command you, not onely to raise no more [men], when these shall be decaied, but to keepe them vnsupplied [*sc.* with money] that are already. **1618** HALES *Let. fr. Synod of Dort* Gold. Rem. (1673) 23 When the Church was unsupplied, either by the death, or absence, or sickness of their Pastor. **1709** STRYPE *Ann. Ref.* vii. 106 Forced to keep them [*sc.* divines] in the Church, lest otherwise it should be wholly unsupplied. **1712** STEELE *Spect.* No. 294 ¶ 1 Every Man who..is unmindful of the unsupplied Distress of other Men. **1784** COWPER *Task* V. 31 The cattle..wait Their wonted fodder; not like hung'ring man, Fretful if unsupply'd.

**b.** Const. *with* (also † *by, of*).

**1616** HIERON *Wks.* II. 37 They..shall not be left vnsupplyed of earthly things. **1652** DAVENANT *Verses to Author* in Benlowes *Theoph.*, Her Pow'r,..which unsupply'd By what wise Art would carefully provide, Is but love's lightning. **1740** JOHNSON *Blake* Wks. 1787 IV. 360 The town was..unsupplied with almost every thing necessary for supporting a siege. **1844** STOCQUELER *Handbk. Brit. India* 254 Its principal defect, as a place besieged, would consist in its being..unsupplied with drinkable water.

**2.** Not met or satisfied; not made up or replaced.

**1616** BRETON *Good & Bad* 2 A Worthy King:..his bosome must not be searched, his will not disobeyed, his wants not unsupplied, nor his place vnregarded. **1700** DRYDEN *Sigism. & Guiscard.* 38 But, prodigal in ev'ry other Grant, Her Sire left unsupply'd her only Want. **1768** BLACKSTONE *Comm.* III. 385 These defects,..should they, after all, continue unremedied and unsupplied, still [etc.]. **1788** V. KNOX *Winter Even.* lii. (1790) I. 453 Nor is the loss of a Goldsmith's..sentimental strain unsupplied by a Cowper.

**3.** Not provided or furnished.

**1808** G. EDWARDS *Pract. Plan* iv. 59 In fine, nothing need be left unsupplied in any respect.

**Unsuppo·rtable,** *a.* [UN-[1] 7 b and 5 b.]

**1.** Too objectionable or annoying to be endured with equanimity or patience.

**1586** SIDNEY *Let. to Walsingham* 14 Aug., We are now four monethes behynd [with pay], a thing unsupportable in this place. **1654** *Nicholas Papers* (Camden) II. 91 Indeed D. Gloucesters carriage to all persons is unsupportable. **1679** SOUTH *Serm.* (1697) I. 130 A disgrace put upon a man in company is unsupportable. **1710** ADDISON *Tatler* No. 221 ¶ 4 A passionate Woman..is one of the most unsupportable Creatures in the World. **1792** BURKE *Let. to Langrishe* Wks. 1842 I. 558 The unsupportable mortification of asking his neighbours..for their votes.

**b.** Too oppressive or distressing to be endured; unendurable, intolerable.

**1602** SIR R. WILBRAHAM *Jrnl.* (1902) 50 Tyme and treasure, the wast wherof is unsupportable. **1644** MILTON *Divorce* (ed. 2) A 3 b, As well may he..redeem himself from unsupportable disturbance, to honest peace. **1750** G. HUGHES *Barbados* 17 This hardship is not so unsupportable to them. **1788** CLARA REEVE *Exiles* II. 215 This thought was unsupportable; it led to despair. **1801** CHARLOTTE SMITH *Lett. Solit. Wand.* II. 243 The most unsupportable of all her distresses. **1832** BREWSTER *Nat. Magic* xii. 309 A heat..unsupportable by the spectators. **1885** FARGUS *Slings & Arrows* 140 Had he by word or gesture shown that the constant presence of the man who had done his best to kill him was unsupportable.

**2.** That cannot be supported by physical strength.

**1688** HOLME *Armoury* III. 312/2 Goalers..when they meet with sturdy and unruly Prisoners, to Lock and Chain them to some strong Post, or unsupportable Block.

**3.** Not admitting of support or defence; indefensible.

**1710** SIR J. ST. LEGER *Managers Pro & Con.* 21 To support that unsupportable Sense of the Homilies, the Doctor produces the concurrent Opinions of many Learned Fathers. **1777** *Burke's Corr.* (1844) II. 191 The unsupportable claim of this country to the right of taxing America without reserve.

Hence **Unsuppo·rtableness; -ably** *adv.*

**1664** H. MORE *Myst. Iniq.* Pref. 4 To be affected, nay deeply and unsupportably afflicted. **1672** WILKINS *Nat. Relig.* II. vii. 386 'Tis the unsupportableness of this, that many times doth cause men..to chuse..death rather than life. *a* **1697** SOUTH *Serm.* (1715) II. 177 His Conscience..assures him, that he shall be infinitely, unsupportably miserable, if he does it.

**Unsuppo·rted,** *ppl. a.* [UN-[1] 8.]

**1.** Not supported by aid or assent; not backed up or corroborated.

**1420–2** LYDG. *Siege Thebes* III. 2985 Farwel wisdam..For lakke only of supportacioun. For vnsupported..Amphiorax sighen gan ful sore. **1609** DANIEL *Civ. Wars* III. lxxix, He ..will not avouch thy fact, But let the weight of thine owne infamie Fall on thee, vnsupported, and vnbackt. **1646** SIR T. BROWNE *Pseud. Ep.* Pref., To despaire the favourable looke of learning upon our single and unsupported endeavours. **1753** *Stewart's Trial* 270 Deposing to a long romantic story, in which he is altogether unsupported. **1798** S. & HT. LEE *Canterb. T.* II. 393 An idle..unsupported assertion. **1812** WELLINGTON in Gurw. *Desp.* (1837) IX.

349 Leaving behind them unprotected and unsupported the guns of Captain M'Donald's troop. **1854** GREENWOOD *Haps & Mishaps* 54 Yet thus far have I taken not one lonely and unsupported step.

**b.** Const. *by*.

**1694** ATTERBURY *Serm.* (1726) I. iii. 103 How utterly unsupported either by the Secular Arm, or Secular Wisdom! **1752** JOHNSON *Rambler* No. 194 ¶ 12 What can be expected from reason unsupported by fashion, splendour, or authority? **1831** T. HOPE *Ess. Orig. Man* II. 235 This doctrine is..too unsupported by anything we see, to have had many adherents. **1897** MARY KINGSLEY *W. Africa* 618 This statement is utterly unsupported by facts.

†**c.** Not bold or confident. *Obs.*

**1697** COLLIER *Ess. Mor. Subj.* I. 210 Whereas a diffident and unsupported Behaviour in a Clergyman, is often supposed to proceed from ignoble Qualities.

**2.** Not physically supported or sustained.

**1635** PERSON *Varieties* I. 33 The false-Prophet Mahomet, his Chest of Iron,..doth hang miraculously unsupported of any thing. **1681** STAIR *Instit.* II. xxvi. 97 Whether Convalescence can be proven otherways, then by going unsupported to Kirk and Mercat, I have seen no decision. **1707** MORTIMER *Husb.* 106 [Peas] run upon the ground unsupported with sticks. **1813** SCOTT *Rokeby* II. xiv, Now, like the wild-goat, must he dare An unsupported leap in air. **1862** ANSTED *Channel Isl.* II. xi. 288 The falling in of the unsupported roof.

*fig.* **1667** MILTON *P. L.* IX. 432 Her self, though fairest unsupported Flour, From her best prop so farr, and storm so nigh. **1776** GIBBON *Decl. & F.* I. 328 On the slightest touch, the unsupported fabric of their pride and power fell to the ground.

Hence **Unsuppo·rtedly** *adv.*; **-ness.**

**1825** *Q. Rev.* XXXII. 286 Mr. Bowles tells us (as insidiously, and as unsupportedly as usual) Pope was much more explicit. **1890** J. H. STIRLING *Philos. & Theol.* xvi. 307 Contingency in the sense of unsupportedness, the powerlessness of things in themselves.

**Unsuppo·rting,** *ppl. a.* (UN-[1] 10.) **1595** DANIEL *Civ. Wars* V. cv, For loosing war abroad, at home lost peace; Being with our vnsupporting selues close pent. **1653** TAYLOR *Serm. for Year* I. xiii. 165 People whose arme is all flesh, whose foot is all leather, and an unsupporting skin.

**Unsuppo·sable,** *a.* (UN-[1] 7 b and 5 b.) **1650** FULLER *Pisgah* 373 Such sacriledge being unsupposable in that age. **1701** BEVERLEY *Apoc. Quest.* 44 It is utterly Unsupposeable, That All the little Turns of History..should have Place in it. **1814** SCOTT *Wav.* lvii, Were such an unsupposable case to happen.

**Unsuppo·sed,** *ppl. a.* [UN-[1] 8.]

†**1.** As *adv.* Unexpectedly. *Obs.*—[1]

*c* **1425** *St. Christina* xxiv. in *Anglia* VIII. 128/34 Sodeynly and vnsupposid alle hir body was taken of spirite, & turnyd in to a whirlynge about.

**2.** Not supposed or imagined.

[**1775** ASH.] **1821** COLERIDGE *Lett., Convers.*, etc. II. 38 If that judgment were given avowedly, on the mere unbelieved possibility, on an unsupposed supposition of the worst.

**Unsuppre·ssable,** *a.* (UN-[1] 7 b.) **1781** MOORE *View Soc. & Mann. Italy* I. 220 How many of our acquaintance..have we seen doing painful penance at the Hay-market; and, in the midst of unsuppressable yawnings, calling out, Charming! exquisite! bravissimo, etc.

**Unsuppre·ssed,** *ppl. a.* (UN-[1] 8.) **1621** G. SANDYS *Ovid's Met.* X. (1626) 212 Their feet, unwet, the sea might well haue borne: Or vnsuppressed stalks of standing corne. **1649** MILTON *Eikon.* xxvi. 208 Driv'n away by unsuppressed Tumults. *a* **1691** BP. BARLOW *Rem.* (1693) 277 The unsuppressed Abby Lands are a fourth of the whole. **1809–14** WORDSW. *Excurs.* V. 118 Simple manners, feelings unsuppress And undisguised. **1855** MILMAN *Lat. Chr.* XIV. vii. VI. 557 The secret influence of these teachers, unsuppressed by years of persecution. **1881** MISS BRADDON *Asphodel* II. 145 That suppressed gout..was only another name for unsuppressed ill-temper.

**Unsuppre·ssible,** *a.* (UN-[1] 7, 5 b.) **1669** EARL ORRERY *Parthen.* III. VI. 184 If some unsuppressible groan force it selfe from me. **Unsu·ppurative,** *a.* (UN-[1] 7.) **1822** GOOD *Study Med.* II. 271 A multitude of tumours or tubercles of different degrees of inflammation, some suppurative, some unsuppurative. **Unsurcha·rge,** *v.* (UN-[2] 3.) **1642** FULLER *Holy & Prof. St.* II. xxii. 144 Our Herald knows also to cure the surfet of Coats, and unsurcharge them, and how to wash out stained colours.

**Unsure** (vnʃūə·ɹ), *a.* [UN-[1] 7.]

**1.** Not safe against attack or mishap; liable to danger or risk; exposed to hazard or peril; insecure.

*a* **1400–50** *Alexander* 2136 Bot, for þe cite was vnsure, þe seggis within Miȝt noȝt þe braidis a-bide of bernes enarmed. *c* **1520** in *Yorks. Archæol. Jrnl.* (1892) XII. 208 Who that puttith his trust in them I call hym most unsure. *a* **1542** WYATT *Poems* (1913) I. 350 There is a rok..of suche nature, That drawithe the yron from the woode, And leveth the ship unsure. **1586** J. HOOKER *Hist. Irel.* in *Holinshed* II. 73/2 In Wales..he found his defense so weake, and vnsure, that [etc.]. **1600** HOLLAND *Livy* IX. 345 [They] had seene by experience..how unsure a cittie they inhabited and not unpregnable. **1649** G. DANIEL *Trinarch., Hen. IV*, cclii, Hee knew his Claime, and how vnsure he sate Midst many enimies.

**b.** Not affording or conducive to safety; lacking in security; unsafe, liable to yield or give way.

**1426** LYDG. *De Guil. Pilgr.* 13355 Placys that be most perryllous,..Most dredful and most vnsure, Ther I logge, off nature. *c* **1530** MORE *Answ. Frith* Wks. 842/2 If ye will..deale surely for youre self, ye should rather leaue your vnsure waye whiche ye belieue, and come..to beleue as we doe. *a* **1547** SURREY *Æneid* II. 31 Now but a bay, and rode vnsure for ship. **1588** *Reg. Privy Council Scot.* IV. 299 Throw the multitude of deidlie feidis and unsure passage. **1609** HOLLAND *Amm. Marcell.* 201 Neither is it possible..to set firme footing upon the ground, so unsure it is and slipperie. *a* **1661** HOLYDAY *Juvenal* (1673) 232 The ship..made but of unsure or dangerous planks. **1727** P. WALKER *Biogr. Presbyt.* (1827) I. 225 A very loose unsure Foundation. **1774** BURKE *Sp. Amer. Tax.* Wks. II. 420 It was indeed a very curious show, but utterly unsafe to touch, and unsure to stand on. **1830** CUNNINGHAM *Brit. Paint.* II. 200 It seems they make unsure work at that church. **1866** G. MACDONALD *Ann. Q. Neighb.* vi, Down the oak staircase..[I] came very deliberately, feeling the unsure contact of sole and wax.

**2.** Marked or characterized by uncertainty or unsteadfastness; dependent on chance or accident; liable to fail; uncertain, precarious.

*c* **1412** HOCCLEVE *De Reg. Princ.* 16 Bysily in my mynde I gan revolue The welthe onsure of everye creature. *c* **1430** LYDG. *Min. Poems* (Percy Soc.) 197 The world unsuyr, fortune transmutable. *c* **1449** PECOCK *Repr.* V. xiv. 560 Vnperfit men..ouȝten chese ful ofte the sikerer and surer good to hem bifore the vnsurer good. **1509** BARCLAY *Shyp Folys* 17 b, He that is symple, and on the grounde doth lye, ..Is surer by moche than he that lyeth on hye: Nowe vp, nowe downe vnsure as a Balaunce. **1559** *Mirr. Mag.* B j, Ryches and promocion be vaine thynges and vnsure. **1584** C. ROBINSON, etc. *Handf. Pleas. Delights* D 3 b, Svch bitter fruit thy loue doth yeelde,..such hope vnsure. **1614** T. ADAMS *White Devil* 37 Their dwelling, like Cains, [is] very vnsure. **1629** MAXWELL tr. *Herodian* 108 Holding it a sufficient guerdon of an vnsure Soueraignty. **1641** BAKER *Chron., Edw. VI*, 82 King Edward supposing his state to be most safe when indeed it was most unsure. **1711** POPE *Temple Fame* 508 Unsure the tenure, but how vast the fine! **1755** J. DUNCOMBE in *Connoisseur* No. 50. 296 Whose houses are as unsure a possession, as if they were built with cards. **1848** T. AIRD *Chr. Bride* II. xvi, Old dragon Erc must we secure;..our scheme were else unsure. **1873** M. ARNOLD *Lit. & Dogma* 138 The moral is, what an unsure stay, then, must miracles be!

**3. a.** Of persons, etc.: Not to be trusted or relied upon; unreliable, untrustworthy.

*c* **1445** PECOCK *Donet* 208 þou schalt considre..how brotyl, vnsure a wrecche þou art. *a* **1470** HARDING *Chron.* Ded. v, That people..Hath..been so vntowarde, So vnstedfast, inconstaunte, and vnsure, That [etc.]. *Ibid.* XXXIX. viii, [Catellus] Tenne yere reigned,..And dyed so vnder his vnsure deité. *a* **1589** PALFREYMAN *Baldwin's Mor. Philos.* (1600) 70 Hee is..deceiptfull, of his promise vnsure. **1610** HEALEY *St. Aug. Citie of God* (1620) 409 The senses are weake, dull and vnsure teachers. **1635** HEYWOOD *Hierarchy* VI. 331 Than th' Heart of man..There's nothing more inconstant and vnsure. **1653** HOLCROFT *Procopius, Goth. Wars* IV. 145 If we prove unsure to them, we shall not be trusty to you. **1790** BURKE *Fr. Rev.* 94 They are always bad citizens, and perfectly unsure connexions. **1807** COLERIDGE *Lett.* (1895) 513 Which *sures* are such very unsure folks that [etc.]. **1867** SWINBURNE *Songs bef. Sunrise* (1871) 58 Though she slay them, yet shall they trust in her, For unsure there is nought nor unjust in her. **1888** STEVENSON *Black Arrow* 21 Keep an eye on Sir Daniel; he is unsure.

†**b.** Weak, feeble. *Obs. rare*—[1].

**1432–50** tr. *Higden* (Rolls) VI. 51 Grawntynge to theyme a lytelle wyne..thro the whiche the unsure flesche [L. *caro infirma*] scholde be noryschede.

**4.** Subject to doubt or uncertainty; not fixed, sure, or certain; doubtful.

*c* **1445** PECOCK *Donet* 107 If in dyuynite were no strenger groundis..dyuynite were a symple and an vnsure faculte. **1534** MORE *Treat. Passion* Wks. 1279/2 Sure sory looking, for the vnsure time of deathe. *a* **1586** SIDNEY *Arcadia* I. iv, A thing no more unpleasant, then unsure, for the preserving of vertue. **1595** DANIEL *Civ. Wars* II. iv, That, in the smoake of innouations strange Builde huge vncertaine plots of vnsure pride. **1612** R. CARPENTER *Soule's Sent.* 90 The speedy approach of death, sure in the end, vnsure in the time. **1646** SIR T. BROWNE *Pseud. Ep.* II. vi. 100 It will be unsure to rely on any preservative. **1691** *Weesils* ii. 10 Conquest unsure made you refuse before. **1849** CUPPLES *Green Hand* xiv, In the unsure dusky sight I had of it, certainly, it [*sc.* a landmark] wore somewhat of that look.

**5.** Of persons, etc.: Lacking certainty, assurance, or confidence; not sure, assured, or certainly knowing; uncertain. Const. *of, for, to,* or with clause.

*c* **1400** *Destr. Troy* 11540 And now is nedfull for noye..All my gold for to geue,..Kepid in hurd, holdyn full long; ..And I vnsure of my-self, my sorow is the more. **1412–20** LYDG. *Chron. Troy* IV. 2144 She wolde for no þing be vnsure Of puruyaunce, nor with-oute stoor. *a* **1461** *Pol. Poems* (Rolls) II. 241 Ful unsewyr atte the laste may he be To sette hys herte in swyche abundaunce. *a* **1500** *Chaucer's Dreme* 1732 Wild beastes..ran as of their lives unsure. **1534** MORE *Comf. agst. Trib.* I. vi. (1573) 14 b, So blind is our mortalitie..., so vnsure also what maner mind we wil haue to morow. **1564** FECKENHAM *Let. to Cecil* in Strype *Ann. Ref.* xlv. (1709) 460 Being always after unsure, how, or by what means, he might be..knit thereunto again. **1579** FENTON *Guicciard.* I. 15 He is..of nothing more vnsure then to find remedy in his perils. **1595** DANIEL *Civ. Wars* II. xlvii, And here my sou'raigne to make longer stay T' attend for what you are vnsure will fall May slippe th' occasion and incense their will. *a* **1618** RALEIGH *Observ.* (1651) 56 Numbers of people that were..thrust out of their habitations, or unsafe, or unsure for their lives. **1628** BP. HALL *Old Relig.* 147 That God euer heares vs, wee are as sure, as wee are vnsure to be heard of Saints. **1679** in Wodrow *Hist. Suff. Ch. Scotl.* (1722) II. App. xviii. 18 Not finding it fit to unhinge himself of the one Party, while he was yet unsure of the other. *a* **1850** ROSSETTI *Dante & Circle* (1874) 49 Thus, being all unsure which path to take. **1855** SIR J. PAGET in *Mem. & Lett.* (1901) 209, I am unsure whether I can ever again have time. **1884** A. VAMBÉRY *Life & Advent.* vii. (1889) 71 Unsure of my discovery, I did not address him.

**b.** Without const.

*a* **1500** *Chaucer's Dreme* 894 Thus was I in a joyous dout, Sure and unsurest of that rout. *a* **1536** TINDALE in Marbeck *Bk. of Notes* (1581) 366 For then shall the conscience be vnsure, doubting [etc.]. *a* **1555** LATIMER *Let.* in Foxe *A. & M.* (1563) 1327/1 If they saye they bee vnsure, when shall you bee sure that hathe so doubtefull teachers and vnsure? **1624** HEYWOOD *Gunaik.* IV. 193 A man within himselfe unsure. **1896** MRS. CAFFYN *Quaker Grandmother* 155 His mother looked as meek and unsure as a grocer's widow.

**6.** Marked or characterized by lack of sureness, assurance, or certainty.

**1633** P. FLETCHER *Purple Isl.* VIII. xiii, With him went Doubt, stagg'ring with steps unsure, That every way, and neither way enclin'd. **1829** CUNNINGHAM *Brit. Paint.* I. 207 His touch was unsure and he painted somewhat coarsely. **1867** M. ARNOLD *New Poems* 132 Light ignorance, and hurrying, unsure thoughts. **1883** R. W. DIXON *Mano* II. i. 66 Never would he..His friend forsake, or make his faith unsure.

**Unsu·red,** *ppl. a.* (UN-[1] 8.) **1595** SHAKS. *John* II. i. 471 For by this knot, thou shalt so surely tye Thy now vnsur'd assurance to the Crowne, That [etc.].

**Unsu·rely,** *adv. rare.* [UN-[1] 11.] Uncertainly; insecurely.

**1595** DANIEL *Civ. Wars* II. cxix, The vanity of greatness he had tride, And how vnsurely standes the foote of pride. **1645** HAMMOND *View Infallib.* 38 Scripture when surely sensed..is a different medium from the same Scripture sensed unsurely.

**Unsu·reness.** [UN-[1] 12.]

**1.** Uncertainty; insecurity.

**1430–40** LYDG. *Bochas* I. i. (1494) A vi b/1 Where they stode first in sykernesse Of ioye..Oute of their rest they fyll in vnsurenesse In sorowe and sighynge. *c* **1440** *Eng. Conq. Ireland* 51 And euery Surnesse hath vnsurnes at the ende. **1530** PALSGR. 285/2 Unsurenesse, *deseurete*. **1565** COOPER *Thesaurus* s.v. *Infirmitas*, What vnsurenes doe you see in the mariage hetherto? **1573** *Satir. Poems Reform.* I. 275 The greit frailtie and vnsureness of all strenthis eirthly. **1611** SPEED *Hist. Gt. Brit.* VI. xxii. 226 The state of man..doth shew..with what vnsurenesse the seat of maiesty is possest. **1863** HOLME LEE *A. Warleigh* III. 133 Her hints to Rachel..touching the unsureness of the future.

†**2.** Unsteadiness, fickleness. *Obs.*—[1]

*a* **1470** TIPTOFT *Tulle on Friendsh.* (Caxton, 1481) C ij, There ben two thynges, which prove in many men lightnesse and unsurenesse.

†**Unsu·rety.** *Obs.* [UN-[1] 12.] Insecurity, uncertainty.

*c* **1460** FORTESCUE *Abs. & Lim. Mon.* v. (1885) 119 What dishonour is this, and abatynge of the glorie of a kynge. But yet it is most to his vnsuyrte. **1483** *Act 1 Rich. III*, c. 1 § 1 By privey and unknowen feoffementes greate unsuertie..and grevous vexacions daily growen among the King's Subgiettis. **1534** MORE *Comf. agst. Trib.* III. Wks. 1219/1 Of the vnsuretye of landes and possessions. **1563** *Mirr. Mag.* (ed. 2) S j, To shewe thereby the vnsuerty in this life, Marke wel my fal. **1609** J. DAVIES (Heref.) *Humours Heaven* I. lxxiii, Where's vnsuretie, feare must needs be there. **1625** R. HORN *Shield of Righteous* 86 Earthly Princes are subject to..great vnsuretie of life and estate.

**Unsu·rfeiting,** *ppl. a.* (UN-[1] 10.) **1653** GAUDEN *Hierasp.* 70 To follow him with all obediential love;..unsatiably satisfied with his unsurfetting-sweetness. **1772** JAS. USHER *Clio* (ed. 3) 140 The engaging image..of easy unsurfeiting joys. **Unsu·rgical,** *a.* (UN-[1] 7.) **1807** S. COOPER *First Lines Surg.* 201 To increase these evils by rough handling of the part is..unsurgical. **1884** C. B. KELSEY *Dis. Rectum & A.* xi. 297 The operation is rough, uncertain, and unsurgical. **1897** *Allbutt's Syst. Med.* II. 1057 The harpoon designed..for this purpose produces an unsurgical wound. **Unsu·rging,** *ppl. a.* (UN-[1] 10.) **1619** DRAYTON *Poems, Matilda* 344 As a Ship, that in a quiet Calme Flotes vp and downe on the vnsurging Seas. **Unsurmi·sed,** *ppl. a.* (UN-[1] 8.) [**1775** ASH.] **1818** KEATS *Isabella* xliii, She had devised..How her short absence might be unsurmised. **1885** *Encycl. Brit.* XVIII. 681/2 Michelangelo..was opening men's eyes..to possibilities of achievement as yet unsurmised.

**Unsurmou·ntable,** *a.* [UN-[1] 7 b and 5 b.]

**1.** Incapable of being surpassed or exceeded. *rare.*

**1611** COTGR., *Insurmontable*, vnsurmountable, vnexceedable. **1745** YOUNG *Nt. Th.* VIII. 328 That unsurmountable extreme of guilt!

**2.** Incapable of being surmounted or overcome; insurmountable: **a.** Of difficulties, etc. (Common in 18th c.)

**1701** *Lond. Gaz.* No. 3713/1 We passed the Mountains..Which were thought unsurmountable. **1757** FOOTE *Author* I. Wks. 1799 I. 141 The obscurity..of your birth, will prove an unsurmountable bar. **1788** *Trifler* No. 11. 134 The Prolixity of six and thirty Stanzas in a Pastoral Tale, proves an unsurmountable Exception. **1911** RIKER *Henry Fox* II. 126 The obstacle was not unsurmountable.

**b.** Of feelings.

*c* **1740** MRS DELANY *Life & Corr.* (1861) I. 29 The courtship..was awkward to Gromio (who saw too well my unsurmountable dislike). **1771** GOLDSM. *Hist. Eng.* II. 85 An unsurmountable aversion to the English government. **1791** BURKE *Let. to Memb. Nat. Assemb.* 50 If disgust, if unsurmountable nausea, drive them away from such spectacles,..I cannot blame them.

**3.** Inextinguishable, unquenchable.

**1725** *Fam. Dict.* s.v. *Fever*, It causes a violent Heat and unsurmountable Thirst.

Hence **Unsurmou·ntableness.**

**1894** *Thinker* VI. 76 Superstitious faith in nature's unsurmountableness.

**Unsurmou·nted,** *ppl. a.* (UN-[1] 8.) [**1775** ASH.] **1787** T. MONRO, etc. *Olla Podrida* No. 25 ¶ 1 Difficulties unsurmounted in biography.

**Unsurpa·ssable,** *a.* (UN-[1] 7 b and 5 b.) **1611** COTGR., *Insurmontable*,..vnsurpassable, vnvanquishable. **1799** W. TAYLOR in Robberds *Mem.* (1843) I. 243 The descriptive parts of this idyll are capital—are unsurpassable. **1837** CARLYLE *Fr. Rev.* I. III. iii, For freshness of style,..that opening Harangue of his was unsurpassable. **1876** *Contemp. Rev.* June 36 A sea-board..capable of producing..fruits, in quantities unsurpassable.

Hence **Unsurpa·ssably** *adv.*

**1859** RUSKIN *Two Paths* App. I. 254 Entirely, admirably, unsurpassably right, under the conditions. **1872** *Carlyle's Schiller* Wks. 1899 XXV. 226 Dannecker..has unsurpassably cut this head in marble for us.

**Unsurpa·ssed,** *ppl. a.* (Un-1 8.)
[1775 Ash.] 1818 Byron *Ch. Har.* iv. xxxix, Oh, victor unsurpass'd in modern song! 1840 Thackeray *Barber Cox* Nov., A speech..unsurpassed for eloquence. 1882 *Nature* XXV. 429 On such a topic he is entitled to speak with at least an unsurpassed authority.

**Unsurpri·sed,** *ppl. a.* (Un-1 8.)
1591 Florio *2nd Fruites* 77 A pawn that could passe the pikes of seuen places vnsurprised. 1593 Marlowe *Edw. II*, ii. v, Though deuorsed from king Edwards eyes, Yet liueth Pierce of Gaueston vnsurprizd. 1629 H. Burton *Truth's Triumph* 250 They may be certain of keeping their weak fort of vncertainty vnsurprised. 1655 Fuller *Wounded Consc.*, etc. (1867) 314 Nor was there any Herb or Flower in the whole Garden left unsurprised with fear. 1841 Emerson *Eng. Traits* xiv. *Literature*, The unique fact in literary history, the unsurprised reception of Shakespeare. 1876 T. Hardy *Ethelberta* xxxv, She..gave him an unsurprised gesture of recognition. 1882 Chr. Rossetti *Resurgam* Poems (1904) 412 Strenuous thro' day and unsurprised by night He runs a race with Time and wins the race.

**Unsurpri·sing,** *ppl. a.* (Un-1 10.)
1671 Woodhead *St. Teresa* i. Pref. 34 Purity from committing any, foreknown, and unsurprising, venial sin. 1688 in Ellis *Orig. Lett.* Ser. i. III. 351 It was no unsurprising spectacle. 1740 Cibber *Apol.* 69 Without this..the Performance will come out..somewhere defectively, unsurprizing to the Hearer.

**Unsurre·ndered,** *ppl. a.* (Un-1 8.)
[1775 Ash.] *a* 1800 Cowper *Iliad* (ed. 2) vii. 376 Helen is mine, an unsurrender'd prize For ever. 1827 Jarman *Powell's Devises* II. 123 None of this reasoning is now applicable to a devise of unsurrendered copyholds. 1848 J. Martineau in *Life* (1902) I. 185 Military parties were told off to..search every house for the unsurrendered arms. *a* 1850 J. C. Calhoun *Wks.* (1863) I. 147 It must..remain unsurrendered and unimpaired in the people of the several States.

Unsurre·ndering, *ppl. a.* (Un-1 10.) 1840 Carlyle *Heroes* iii. ⁋ 13 The face of one wholly in protest, and life-long unsurrendering battle, against the world.

**Unsurrou·nded,** *ppl. a.* (Un-1 8.)
[1775 Ash.] 1813 T. Busby *Lucretius* I. i. Comm. p. xxix, We cannot imagine an unsurrounded convex. 1859 Cornwallis *Panorama New World* I. 242 There she lay,..unsurrounded by the comforts that were most needful. 1863 Tyndall *Heat* ix. 283 The lamp is naked, unsurrounded by its camera.

Unsurvey·able, *a.* (Un-1 7 b.) 1833 Carlyle *Misc.* (1840) IV. 256 Every Man..reaches downwards and upwards unsurveyable, fading into the regions of Immensity and of Eternity. 1847 Hare *Guesses* (ed. 3) 383 The field of operation is so vast and unsurveyable.

**Unsurvey·ed,** *ppl. a.* (Un-1 8.)
1546 in *Vict. Co. Hist., Warwick.* II. (1908) 303/1 Divers Chantries unsurveyed and no rentalls thereof delyvered. 1758 Johnson *Idler* No. 3 ⁋ 3 My predecessors..had the whole field of life before them, untrodden and unsurveyed. 1843 *Penny Cycl.* XXV. 241/2 In 1833..more than three-fifths of the island [was] unappropriated and unsurveyed. 1879 Miss Bird *Lady's Life in Rocky Mount.* 120 Such as it is, Estes Park is mine. It is unsurveyed, 'no man's land'.

Unsusceptibi·lity. (Un-1 12, 5 b. Cf. next.) [1775 Ash.] 1805 *Monthly Mag.* XX. 231 Proofs of the permanency of the state of Unsusceptibility of the Small Pox. 1850 Robertson *Serm.* Ser. iii. ix. (1857) 133 That which ought to be men's shame becomes their boast—unsusceptibility of any fresh emotion.

**Unsusce·ptible,** *a.* [Un-1 7 and 5 b.]
†1. Unable to receive and retain. *Obs.*—1
1692 Dryden *Cleomenes* iv. 43 Some Men are made of such a leaky Mould, That their fill'd Vessels can no fortune hold: ..Of that unsusceptible Make am I.

2. Not susceptible *of* some operation, influence, etc.; = Insusceptible *a.* a.
(*a*) 1731 Swift *Strephon & Chloe* 86 While she a Goddess dy'd in Grain Was unsusceptible of Stain. 1799 Kirwan *Geol. Ess.* 5 What then should render these facts and the circumstances attending them unsusceptible of testimony? 1816 Bentham *Chrestom.* 99 Although not perhaps completely susceptible, it is however not altogether unsusceptible, of a remedy. 1868 M. Pattison *Academ. Org.* iv. 69 Statements..entirely unsusceptible of proof. 1890 *Retrospect Med.* CII. 237 Cases where the sugar..is unsusceptible of entire removal from the system by dietetic treatment alone.
(*b*) 1751 Johnson *Rambler* No. 153 ⁋ 16 An old friend, who professed himself unsusceptible of any impressions from prosperity or misfortune. 1784 *Cook's 3rd Voy.* iv. ii. II. 310 They are certainly not wholly unsusceptible of the tender passions. 1814 Southey *Let. to J. King* 27 Feb., My skin ..may very possibly be unsusceptible of this particular irritation. 1849 Macaulay *Hist. Eng.* ix. II. 519 His serene intellect, singularly unsusceptible of enthusiasm, and singularly averse to extremes.

b. Const. *to*. = Insusceptible *a.* b.
1872 Sanford *Estimates Eng. Kings* 400 They rendered him comparatively unsusceptible to the feelings of resentment and implacability.

3. Not readily liable to impressions; = Insusceptible *a.* c.
1779 *Mirror* No. 14, Men unfeeling and unsusceptible, commonly beat the beaten track with activity and resolution. 1860 Froude *Hist. Eng.* VI. 92 She was unsusceptible; she had no experience in love. 1893 F. F. Moore *I Forbid Banns* xxvii, Surely the ivory—that most unsusceptible of materials—was warm from her hand.

Unsusce·ptive, *a.* (Un-1 7 and 5 b.) 1825 Good *Study Med.* (ed. 2) II. 373 The habit, or idiosyncracy of most anatomists fortunately renders them altogether unsusceptive of its impression.

†**Unsuspe·ct,** (*ppl.*) *a.* *Obs.* Chiefly *Sc.* [Un-1 7, 8 b, and 5 b.] Not subject to suspicion.
*c* 1380 Wyclif *Sel. Wks.* II. 107 Þe dedis þat Crist dide, ben unsuspect evydence þat Crist is boþe God and man. 1388 — *Ecclus.* xxv. 9, I magnefiede nyne thingis vnsuspect of the herte. 1409 in *Exch. Rolls Scotl.* IV. p. ccxi, Askand thaim to be submitted to thaim and to their counselis unsuspect apon sic complaintis. *c* 1480 Henryson *Fables, Wolf & Lamb* 74, I oblis me rycht heir, That I sall byde ane vnsuspect Assyis. 1512 *Reg. Privy Seal Scotl.* I. 369/2 Befor the lordis of counsale or utheris unsuspect jugis. 1583 *Leg. Bp. St Androis* 139 Grit oethes he sweirs,..And bad thame hald him vnsuspect. 1606 Sylvester *Du Bartas* ii. iv. i. *Tropheis* 1055 David's foule defect Was yet un-seen, uncensur'd, un-suspect. 1665 Glanvill *Def. Van. Dogm.* 83 Though his writings were never so unsuspect and certain in the main. 1678 Sir G. Mackenzie *Crim. Laws Scot.* i. xxvi. § 6 (1699) 134 Proved by most unsuspect Witnesses.

Unsuspe·ctable, *a.* (Un-1 7 b.) 1660 H. More *Myst. Godl.* vii. x. 323 That vigorous passion and elevation of spirit, and yet all so unsuspectable of any humane artifice. 1748 Richardson *Clarissa* III. 108 Shall the man be guilty, yet expect the woman to be guiltless, and even unsuspectable? Unsuspe·ctably, *adv.* (Un-1 11. Cf. prec.) 1748 Richardson *Clarissa* III. 30 Grief so unsuspectably sincere.

**Unsuspe·cted,** *ppl. a.* [Un-1 8 and 5 b.]
1. Without being suspected.
*c* 1530 More *Answ. Frith* Wks. 833/1 Our english heretikes..might there imprynt theyr heresies amonge other matters, & so sende them hither vnsuspected. 1660 *Nicholas Papers* (Camden) IV. 251 To haue occasion therby to act unsuspected something..contrary vnto his professions. 1725 De Foe *Voy. round World* (1840) 97 The governor putting so much confidence in us, that we might go on shore in the very fort unsuspected. 1798 S. & Ht. Lee *Canterb. T.* II. 123 [He was] enabled, unsuspected, to trace..the emotions of the heart he best loved. 1813 Coleridge *Remorse* ii. i. 57 But I had traced her, stolen unnotic'd on them, And unsuspected..heard the whole.

2. Not regarded with suspicion; not considered to be suspicious or doubtful.
*a* 1586 Sidney *Arcadia* i. xiv, Hoping that (going for a woman) my lookes would passe, either unmarked, or unsuspected. 1594 Shaks. *Rich. III*, iii. v. 23 That ignoble Traytor, The dangerous and vnsuspected Hastings. 1603 Knolles *Hist. Turks* (1621) 147 For his too profuse bountie he could not be vnsuspected of his brother. 1670 Clarendon *Hist. Reb.* xii. § 129 Those principal heads of the Clans who ..were of known, or unsuspected Affection to the King. 1747 J. Lind *Lett. Navy* (1757) I. 16 The courage of our common seamen is hitherto generally unsuspected. 1760 *Ann. Reg., Hist.* 39/2 They will find, both in his fortune and his virtue, abundant matter for just and unsuspected panegyric. 1827 Scott *Chron. Canongate* vi, Well judging that he would observe more wholesome caution if he conceived his character unsuspected, than if he were detected. 1855 Macaulay *Hist. Eng.* xviii. IV. 234 Russell, as far as can now be discovered, was still unsuspected.
*absol.* 1800 *Asiat. Ann. Reg., Proc. E. Ind. Ho.* 115 It was not justice to confound the unsuspected with the suspected.

b. Const. *to* with inf., or *of*.
1647 Clarendon *Hist. Reb.* i. § 202 Those Infusions proceeded from those unsuspected to have any inclinations to Change. 1800 *Asiat. Ann. Reg., Proc. E. Ind. Ho.* 137/2 The director..was quite unsuspected of being concerned in the sale of it.

3. Not suspected to exist, or to bear a certain character; not thought of.
1620 J. Taylor (Water P.) *Jack a Lent* B 3 b, Some againe..doe scout into..diuers secret vnsuspected places. 1654 Fuller *Two Serm.* 23 Many a close, secret and unsuspected Christian. 1693 Congreve in *Dryden's Juvenal* xi. (1697) 284 This Day..thou shalt perceive Whether, my self I keep those Rules I give, Or else, an unsuspected Glutton live. 1759 Sterne *Tr. Shandy* ii. xvii, An unsuspected fissure in thy master's pocket. 1784 Cowper *Task* vi. 545 A storm was near, An unsuspected storm. 1810 Scott *Lady of L.* i. xxv, The mountain-maiden show'd A clambering unsuspected road. 1874 J. Geikie *Gt. Ice Age* iii. 26 It..opens up new channels of discovery which otherwise might have remained unsuspected and unknown.

Hence **Unsuspe·ctedness.**
1655 Fuller *Ch. Hist.* x. ii. § 27 They hoped..(by the strangenesse of the act, and unsuspectednesse of the actors) to amuze all men. 1802–12 Bentham *Ration. Judic. Evid.* (1827) II. 433 The popularity, the unsuspectedness, is not purchased, but at the expense of appropriate experience.

**Unsuspe·ctedly,** *adv.* [Un-1 11.]
1. Without being suspected.
1645 W. Jenkyn *Stil-Destroyer* 44 Poyson is..given.. under the notion of good food.., and so it is taken unsuspectedly. 1663 Boyle *Usef. Exp. Nat. Philos.* ii. 267 The subtle murtherers do as unsuspectedly as fatally, execute their malice or revenge. 1695 D. Turner *Apol. Chyrurg.* 24 That he the more unsuspectedly may carry on his Cheats. 1720 Mrs. Manley *Power of Love* 156 Caton understood no Geography but what had been taught her.. in the Country of Love, whence Fauxgarde might unsuspectedly betray her to his wish. 1808 Han. More *Cœlebs* xiii. I. 172 Till he has unsuspectedly landed his opponent in the pure ethics of the gospel.

b. Beyond suspicion; evidently.
1748 Richardson *Clarissa* (1811) III. 2 Grief so unsuspectedly sincere, for an escape so critical.

2. Unsuspectingly.
1826 P. Pounden *France & Italy* 177 The Jews.. unsuspectedly bear in their hands the prophetic records.

Unsuspe·ctful, *a.* [Un-1 7.] Unsuspicious. 1781 Gibbon *Decl. & F.* xxxiii. (1787) III. 334 The credulous and unsuspectful count had armed the province. Unsuspe·ctfulness. (Un-1 12. Cf. prec.) 1852 Lever *M. Tiernay* xlii, 'What a glorious gift is unsuspectfulness,' said he, feelingly. Unsuspe·ctible, *a.* (Un-1 7.) 1802–12 Bentham *Ration. Judic. Evid.* (1827) II. 105 Of all conceivable sources the most trustworthy and unsuspectible.

**Unsuspe·cting,** *ppl. a.* [Un-1 10, 5 d.] Not suspecting; not harbouring any suspicion.
1595 Daniel *Civil Wars* iv. lxxiii, He such deepe aduise applide..To circumuent an vnsuspecting wight, Before he could discerne of their despight. 1703 Rowe *Fair Penit.* ii. ii. 594 My unsuspecting, valiant, honest Friend. 1703 — *Ulysses* i. i, Temper..open as the Day and unsuspecting. 1776 Gibbon *Decl. & F.* xii. I. 339 They..indulged their appetite for revenge and plunder, by frequent descents on the unsuspecting shores of Asia, Greece, and Africa. 1864 Pusey *Lect. Daniel* iii. 160 [His] simple unsuspecting trust ..in the Romans. 1891 Farrar *Darkn. & Dawn* xxxiii, He..ventured to make her an unsuspecting agent in his little plot.

b. Const. *of*, or with direct object.
1654 R. Codrington tr. *Iustine* xiii. 221 The Traytors.. unsuspecting their advance..were assaulted themselves. 1725 Pope *Odyssey* ix. 522 He felt their fleeces..and let them safely go, All unsuspecting of their freight below. 1758 Goldsm. *Mem. Protestant* (1895) II. 108, I had the Pleasure of seeing them, unsuspecting my Design, and greedily catching at the seeming Victory. 1838 Foster *Ess.* (1844) I. 565 To take this step..unsuspecting of the advantage that would be taken of a needy youth. 1885 Fargus *Slings & Arrows* 114 The moment when, utterly unsuspecting of our contiguity, Eustace Grant would find himself confronted by me.

Hence **Unsuspe·ctingness.**
1883 H. James *Portraits of Places* xii. 253 Her quiet-eyed unsuspectingness only makes her the more a part of his delicate entertainment.

**Unsuspe·ctingly,** *adv.* [Un-1 11.] Without suspicion.
1656 Jer. Taylor *Deus Justif.* Pref. 3 It became almost a shame to examine what the world believed so unsuspectingly. 1787 A. Hilditch *Rosa* II. 44 He waited patiently and unsuspectingly her return. 1798 *Lit. Mem. Living Authors* II. 162 Those talents which he had unsuspectingly cultivated in the groves of the academy. 1818 Lady Morgan *Autobiog.* (1859) 94 One of those charming *causeries* with the general, to which he unsuspectingly lent himself. 1883 D. C. Murray *Hearts* viii, For a moment she felt as a swimmer feels when he floats unsuspectingly into a sudden, powerful eddy.

**Unsuspe·nded,** *ppl. a.* (Un-1 8.)
1701 Norris *Ideal World* i. ii. 111 If an ideal proposition be an actual unsuspended truth. 1792 Wordsw. *Descr. Sk.* 39 While unsuspended wheels the village dance. 1891 T. Hardy *Tess* xxxvi, His thought had been unsuspended; he was becoming ill with thinking.

**Unsuspi·cion.** [Un-1 12.] Lack of suspicion or suspiciousness.
1792 W. Roberts *Looker-on* No. 10 (1794) I. 134 In such a case..the vanquished has nothing to shame him, unless truth and unsuspicion can do it. *a* 1849 H. Coleridge *Ess.* (1851) I. 315 A calm unsuspicion, a grave taking of the matter for granted. 1876 'Annie Thomas' *Blotted out* xxv, I fear that Sydney, in his unsuspicion, will be readily won.

**Unsuspi·cious,** *a.* (Un-1 7).
1595 Daniel *Civil Wars* iv. xxxv, But vnsuspicious magnanimitie Shames such effects of feare, and force to show. 1671 Milton *Samson* 1635 His guide..unsuspicious led him. 1727 Thomson *Britannia* 110 Like brothers live, in amity combin'd, And unsuspicious faith. 1777 Robertson *Hist. Amer.* iii. I. 211 The unsuspicious confidence of a man conscious of no crime. 1825 Scott *Talism.* xx, The unsuspicious object of the dark treachery. 1871 B. Taylor *Faust* (1872) II. iii. 165 This place all unsuspicious I forsook For Cytheræa's fane.

b. Const. *of* or with clause.
1589 Warner *Alb. Eng.* 158 Her Sister,..simply unsuspitious of the sequell, prouided..a pyle of dry Faggots. 1796 Mme. D'Arblay *Camilla* III. 279 Unsuspicious of his remarks..[she] was gay. *Ibid.* V. 7 Edgar [was] not wholly unsuspicious such an accident might happen. 1825 Scott *Betrothed* iii, He was not unsuspicious, though altogether fearless, of the result.

Hence **Unsuspi·ciously** *adv.*; **Unsuspi·ciousness.**
*a* 1812 Buckminster *Serm.* (1827) 94 Epistles..*unsuspiciously authentic. 1854 Thackeray *Newcomes* i, Little lambkin was lying unsuspiciously at the side of the wolf. 1809 Mar. Edgeworth *Manœuvring* iv, A fluent panegyric upon the hereditary *unsuspiciousness of his temper. *a* 1834 Coleridge *Lit. Rem.* (1836) II. 267 Her absolute unsuspiciousness, and holy entireness of love.

**Unsustai·nable,** *a.* (Un-1 7 b.)
*a* 1677 Barrow *Serm.* Wks. 1687 I. 255 A weapon..whose impression is altogether inevitable and unsustainable. 1716 M. Davies *Athen. Brit.* III. 61 [To] revive an unsustainable Cause, so often sunk, and so often irretrievably baffled. 1740 *Phil. Trans.* XLI. 414 This Notion is certainly as unsustainable as the First. 1857 Toulmin Smith *Parish* 297 It was unanimously held that these pleas were unsustainable. 1885 Sir J. Bacon in *Law Times' Rep.* LII. 210/2 The application is wholly unsustainable.

**Unsustai·ned,** *ppl. a.* [Un-1 8.]
1. Not materially sustained or supported.
1630 Drumm. of Hawth. *Flowers Sion, Hymn Passion* 9 Seeing..How vnsustain'd the Earth still steadfast stands. 1667 Milton *P. L.* ix. 430 Each Flour..whose head..Hung drooping unsustained. 1725 Pope *Odyssey* xii. 517 All unsustain'd between the wave and sky, Beneath my feet the whirling billows fly.

2. Not supported by assistance, etc.
1697 Dryden *Æneis* xi. 1238 The Volscians quit the Field; And, unsustain'd, the Chiefs of Turnus yield. 1719 Young *Par. Job* 236 Hale are their young, from human frailties freed; Walk unsustain'd, and unassisted feed. 1809–14 Wordsw. *Excurs.* vi. 767 With a sigh She spake, yet, I believe, not unsustained By faith in glory [etc.]. 1856 Kane *Arct. Expl.* II. xii. 129 A penalty is denounced against..the accuser for his unsustained prosecution. 1876 Bancroft *Hist. U.S.* I. i. 17 Unsustained by Cartier, Roberval accomplished no more than a verification of previous discoveries.

3. Not maintained at a uniform level of excellence; flagging in interest.
1817 Coleridge *Biog. Lit.* xiv. II. 9 An unsustained composition, from which the reader collects rapidly the general result unattracted by the component parts.

**Unsustai·ning,** *ppl. a.* (Un-1 10.)
1818 Shelley *Julian* 538 One unsustaining reed. 1820 — *Sensit. Pl.* 78 The light winds which from unsustaining

wings Shed the music of many murmurings. 1880 Miss Bird *Japan* II. 267 Rice and eggs were..unsustaining food.

† **Unswac**, *a.*: see Swac *a.*

**Unswa·ddle**, *v.* [Un-² 4.] *trans.* To free from, take out of, swaddling bands or clothes.

1580 North *Plutarch* (1595) 382 His wife did vnswadell the young boy to wash and shift him. 1633 B. Jonson *Tale Tub* I. iv, Puppy ha' scarce unswadled my legges yet. 1662 Greenhalgh in Ellis *Orig. Lett.* Ser. II. IV. 16 When they had brought it to the altar, four or five were busied in uncovering and unswaddling the roll. 1853 G. J. Cayley *Las Alforjas* I. 184 Standing at the foot of the mattress, we fell back like tragic heroes, so as not to unswaddle our feet in lying down.

*fig.* 1600 Nashe *Summer's Last Will* Prol., Their censures we wey not, whose sences are not yet vnswadled. 1631 Fuller *David's Punishm.* vii, As when a tender rose begins to blow, Yet scarce unswaddled is.

**Unswa·llowed**, *ppl. a.* (Un-¹ 8, 8 c.)

13.. *E. E. Allit. P.* B. 1253 Alle þat swypped vnswolȝed of þe sworde kene, Þay wer..broþely broȝt to babyloyn. 1663 Waterhouse *Fortescutus Illustr.* 398 Thinking his unswallowed-down carcase happiness..enough for him. 1760 H. Brooke *Fool of Qual.* (1809) I. 70 The guests..sat some time with open mouth, and unswallowed victuals. 1837 Carlyle *Fr. Rev.* II. III. iv, A man may moderate its paroxysms,..and keep himself unswallowed on the top of it [*sc.* a 'whirlpool of Babylonish confusions']. 1859 Tennyson *Geraint & Enid* 1479 The brawny spearman let his cheek Bulge with the unswallow'd piece, and turning, stared.

**Unswa·n**, *v.* (Un-² 6 b.) 1864 Browning *Worst of it* 6 Not you, the pride Of the day, my swan, that a first fleck's fall On her wonder of white, must unswan, undo! **Unswa·n-like**, *a.* (Un-¹ 7 c.) 1837 Dickens *Pickw.* xxx, Mr. Winkle..was being assisted over the ice by Mr. Weller, in a very singular and un-swan-like manner.

**Unswar(e**, obs. ff. Answer *sb.* and *v.*

**Unswa·thable**, *a.* (Un-¹ 7 b.) 1846 Landor *Imag. Conv.* Wks. I. 78/1 There not being bone nor muscle nor blood enough.., he collapses into unswathable flabbiness.

**Unswa·the**, *v.* [Un-² 4.] *trans.* To free from swathings; to unswaddle.

*a* 1400 *Octovian* 302 Her chylderen sche douȝte þer to baþe; Sche sat adoun hem to vnswade. 1598 Florio, *Sfasciare*, to vnswathe, to vnbind. 1604 Drayton *Moses Map Miracle* 13 This most sweete princesse..Soone on her knee vnswathes it as her owne. 1711 Addison *Spect.* No. 90 ¶ 7 About Nine a Clock..an old Woman came to unswathe me. 1788 Mrs. Hughes *Henry & Isabella* I. 115 Sir George ..insisted upon the nurse's immediately unpinning and unswathing him. *a* 1822 Shelley *Fragm. Unf. Drama* 207 Spring indeed Came to unswathe her infants. 1837 P. Keith *Bot. Lex.* s.v. *Bulb*, An Egyptian mummy that was lately unswathed in this country. 1896 *Allbutt's Syst. Med.* I. 419 At the end of every three hours the child is unswathed.

*fig.* 1593 Nashe *Christ's T.* I j b, I will vnswathe thy breast with my sharpe knyfe. 1827 Coleridge *Lit. Rem.* (1839) IV. 319 Spinoza himself describes his own philosophy as in substance the same with that of..the Cabalists—only unswathed from the Biblical dress. 1833 Tennyson in Ld. Tennyson *Mem.* (1897) I. 115 The clouds unswathe them from the height. 1873 H. Rogers *Orig. Bible* i. 42 How came any of them to unswathe themselves from all these lifelong notions.

**Unsway·able**, *a.* (Un-¹ 7 b.) 1607 Shaks. *Cor.* v. vi. 26 To this end, He bow'd his Nature, neuer knowne before, But to be rough, vnswayable, and free.

**Unsway·ed**, *ppl. a.* [Un-¹ 8.]

1. Unwielded; uncontrolled.

1594 Shaks. *Rich. III*, IV. iv. 470 Is the Chayre emptie? is the Sword vnsway'd? Is the King dead? *c* 1600 — *Sonn.* cxli, Nor my fiue sences can Disuade one foolish heart from seruing thee, Who leaues vnswai'd the likenesse of a man, Thy proud hearts slaue..to be.

2. Uninfluenced, unaffected.

1615 Sandys *Trav.* III. 154, I will declare what I haue obserued, vnswayed with either of their vices. 1652 Benlowes *Theoph.* II. li, Make haste Lest you into despair be cast: The Judge unsway'd. 1718 J. Hughes *Patriot* 14 Where's the patriot, by these virtues known, Unsway'd by others' passions, or his own? 1808 Wellington in Gurw. *Desp.* (1835) IV. 249 It was my opinion (unswayed, I trust, by any unworthy motives) that [etc.]. 1847 Harris *Life Ld. Hardwicke* II. 327 Perseverance in the strict line of honesty and duty, unswayed by any considerations of this nature.

3. Unmoved, unstirred.

1851 Hawthorne *Snow Image*, etc. (1883) 200 The drops of rain that came down in monotonous succession, unswayed by a breath of wind.

Hence **Unsway·edness**.

*a* 1656 Hales *Gold. Rem.* I. (1673) 246 That constancy and unswayedness in our lives and actions.

**Unswea·r**, *v.* [Un-² 3, 7. Cf. OFris. *unswera*, *und-*, *untswera*, MDu. *ontsweren* (Du. *ontzweren*), MLG. *entsweren*, MHG. *untswern*.] *trans.* To retract (something sworn or asserted).

1595 Shaks. *John* III. i. 245 [To] Vn-sweare faith sworne. 1596 *Edward III*, II. i. 326 Thinkst that thou canst unswere thy oth againe? *c* 1640 J. Smyth *Lives Berkeleys* (1883) I. 94 The kinge repents and purposeth to undoe and vnsweare what to his Barons hee had done. 1690 Dryden *Amphitryon* IV. i, Think what thou wert, and who cou'd swear too much? Think what thou art, and that unswears it all. 1706 De Foe *Jure Div.* IV. 79 Their vow'd Allegiance early they withheld,..And unswore all Allegiance to his Line. 1829 Landor *Imag. Conv.* II. 447 What you propose to swear to-morrow you will unswear the day after. 1874 Swinburne *Bothwell* II. xvii, He..shall oversay the word he said In your own ear, or else unswear it.

*absol.* 1591 Spenser *M. Hubberd* 1058 Who would not oft sweare, And oft vnsweare, a Diademe to beare? 1681 Hickeringill *Sin Man-catching* Wks. 1716 I. 175 False Witnesses, whose Tongues can swear and unswear. *a* 1734 North *Lives* (1826) I. 88 Her adversary defamed her for swearing and unswearing. 1872 Tennyson *Last Tourn.* 637 Unsay it, unswear!

Hence **Unswea·ring** *vbl. sb.*

[1775 Ash.] 1822 Shelley *Chas. I*, II. 321 Thou wilt preside Over a knot of censurers, To the unswearing of thy best resolves.

**Unswea·t**, *v.* (Un-² 3.) 1644 Milton *Educ.* 7 The interim of unsweating themselves..may..be taken up in recreating and composing their travail'd spirits. **Unswea·ted**, *ppl. a.* (Un-¹ 8.) 1774 W. Mason *Heroic Postcript to Chambers* 12 Each glittering orb the sacred features bore Of George.. Unfil'd, unsweated, all of sterling weight. 1891 *Daily News* 5 Oct. 2/3 Matches, the produce of unsweated match makers. **Unswea·ting**, *ppl. a.* (Un-¹ 10.) 1693 Dryden *Juvenal* III. 178 In Frost and Snow, if you complain of Heat, They rub th' unsweating Brow, and swear they sweat. **Unswee·pable**, *a.* (Un-¹ 7 b.) 1866 Ruskin *Crown Wild Olive* (1873) 4 The little piece of dead ground within..was thus left, unsweepable by any ordinary methods. **Unswee·r**, *a. Sc. rare.* [Un-¹ 7.] Not lazy or unwilling; not heavy or sad. *a* 1500 *Ratis Raving* I. 1012 Be lel,.. Honest, wnswere, & answer fare. *Ibid.* 1264 This eild is thowles and wnswere, And ȝarnis play, and al blycht chere.

**Unswee·t**, *a.* [OE. *unswéte* (Un-¹ 7), = WFris. *on-*, *ûnswiet*, OS. *unswôti*, MLG. *unsote*, MDu. *onsoete* (Du. *onzoet*), OHG. *unsuozi* (MHG. *unsüeze*, G. *unsüss*). Cf. Unsoot *a.*]

1. Unpleasant, disagreeable, distasteful.

*c* 890 Wærferth tr. *Gregory's Dial.* IV. xxxvii. 318 Þæt.. of þære ea wære reocende se mist..unswetes stences. *c* 1000 *Saxon Leechd.* II. 48/14 Þonne ne biþ he to unswete to ȝestincanne. *c* 1320 *Sir Tristr.* 968 Tristrem, y telle it þe, A þing, is me vnswete. *c* 1384 Chaucer *H. Fame* I. 72 A floode of helle vnswete. 1412–20 Lydg. *Chron. Troy* II. 895 Þe meschef of her vnhappy fyne, And how Fortune was to hem vnswete— Al þis was tolde..of þe poete. *Ibid.* III. 3928, I hope..so mortally to greue Þe Grekis alle,..Þat þei & þou shul fele ful vnswete. 1509 Fisher *Wks.* I. 279 Worldly pleasures were to hym vnswete. 1590 Spenser *F. Q.* II. vii. 14 The troublous stormes, that tosse The priuate state, and make the life vnsweet. 1603 J. Davies (Heref.) *Microcosmos* Wks. (Grosart) I. 34 Wakfull thoughts..That make their sleepes vnsweet, and yet as short. 1633 T. Adams *Exp. 2 Peter* ii. 8 Yet how unsweet were our sacrifice, the bran and dregs of our dotage. 1848 L. Hunt *Jar Honey* i. 7 Provided the result..be not un-sweet to the reader. 1876 Meredith *Beauch. Career* III. i. 2 Certain terms in the letters.., unsweet to ladies, began to trouble his mind.

b. Of a person. *rare.*

? *a* 1600 in *Percy Folio* (1867) I. 114 Alle the contraye had wonder greatt Fro whens she com, that foule vnswete; They sawe neuer of so fowlle a thyng.

2. Not sweet or pleasant to the taste.

*c* 1440 *Pallad. on Husb.* IX. 72 Slak sonde [yields water] lymous and lene, vnswete & depe. 1530 Palsgr. 328/2 Unswete, *mal sauouré*. 1547 *Homilies* I. *Falling fr. God* II. ¶ 3 We..bring forth wild grapes, that is to say, sour works, unsweet, unsavoury, and unfruitful. *a* 1643 J. Shute *Judgem. & Mercy* (1645) 201 God will poure him out of his mouth as a man doth that that is unsavory and unsweet that troubles his tongue. 1661 Lovell *Hist. Anim. & Min.* 202 But the flesh is soft, unsweet, ferine, mucous.

3. Not smelling sweetly.

1605 Breton *Olde Man's Lesson* Wks. (Grosart) II. 17/1 Which is the sweetest Beast in the world? A Ciuit Cat. And which is the moste vnsweet? A dogge when he hath eaten carrion. 1607 Topsell *Four-f. Beasts* 110 Tame Conies which are kept in a close and vnsweet ayre. 1825 *Q. Rev.* XXXI. 381 Edinburgh has been (to use a gentle term) unsweet in former times. 1860 Thackeray in *Cornh. Mag.* II. 635 The canals not unsweet, and busy and picturesque with old-world life. 1879 *Pall Mall Budget* 17 Oct. 12 That damp, chill, and unsweet little cluster of rooms.

*fig.* 1811 Lamb *Hogarth* Wks. 1908 I. 107 That his imagination was naturally unsweet, and that he delighted in raking into every species of moral filth.

4. Unpleasant to the ear.

1579 G. Harvey *Commend. Let.* in *Spenser's Wks.* (1912) 641/1 The sweetest Farewell..that so vnsweete a Tong, and so sowre a paire of Lippes can affoorde. *a* 1586 Sidney *Astr. & Stella* lxxxiv, My Muse, to some eares not vnsweet, Tempers her words [etc.]. 1589 Fleming *Virg. Georg.* To Rdr., How vnsweete a sound so euer they seeme to make in the eare. *a* 1616 B. Jonson *Epigr.*, *On Famous Voy.* Wks. 817 When the noise doth beate Vpon your eares, of discords so vn-sweet. 1875 Clodd *Childh. Relig.* i. 2 If you wish to open..your ears to the sounds that give forth no unsweet notes. 1894 Mrs. H. Ward *Marcella* I. 312 A little laugh, which..was not unsweet.

5. Not sweetly attractive.

1866 Miss Mulock *Noble Life* xiv, Nor was her face unsweet; but it bore tokens of what she had gone through.

Hence **Unswee·tly** *adv.*; **Unswee·tness**.

1596 Barrough *Meth. Physick* (ed. 3) 425 Which deceit.. you may easilie find out by the vnsweetnes of smelling. 1842 Mrs. Browning *Grk. Chr. Poets* i. ¶ 1 The voice..sang not unsweetly, if more faintly than before.

**Unswee·ten**, *v.* (Un-² 6 a.) 1611 Florio, *Disadolcire*, to vnsweeten. *a* 1634 Chapman & Shirley *Chabot* v. iii. 14 Were all my joys essential, and so mighty As the affected world believes I taste, This object were enough to unsweeten all. **Unswee·tened**, *ppl. a.* (Un-¹ 8.) [1775 Ash.] 1817 Peacock *Melincourt* I. 53 Sir Telegraph poured some cream into his unsweetened tea. 1844 Mrs. Browning *Dead Rose* ii, The breeze..,—If breathing now,—unsweetened would forgo thee. 1880 *Act* 43 & 44 *Vict.* c. 24 § 123 Unsweetened foreign spirits.

**Unswe·ll**, *v.* [Un-² 7.] *intr.* To recover from a swollen state.

*c* 1374 Chaucer *Troylus* IV. 1146 Ebben gan þe welle Of here teris, and þe herte vnswelle. *Ibid.* v. 214 But þo bygan a lytel his herte vnswelle, Thorugh teris, which þat gonnen vp to welle. 1530 Palsgr. 328/2 Unswolne, *desgourdy*. 1580 Hollyband *Treas. Fr. Tong*, *Se desenfler*, to vnswel, to asswage. 1658 A. Fox *Würtz' Surg.* II. xxviii. 195 When the Fracture is opened the Member unswels, if the matter runs out. 1663 Boyle *Usef. Exp. Nat. Philos.* II. v. xi. 229 Her whole hand, which was before tumid, unswelled again. 1753 N. Torriano *Gangr. Sore Throat* 26 On Friday Morning..the Throat appeared unswelled, and there was a greater Freedom in swallowing. 1778 Earl Pembroke *Milit. Equitation* (ed. 3) 117, I have seen by repeated experiments legs swell, and unswell, by leaving litter, or taking it away.

**Unswe·pt**, *ppl. a.* (Un-¹ 8 b.)

1597 Middleton *Wisd. Solomon* xii. 3 A house-room long unswept will gather dust. 1607 Shaks. *Cor.* II. iii. 126 The Dust on antique Time would lye vnswept. 1678 R. L'Estrange *Seneca's Morals, Of Anger* vii. II. 73 A spot upon a Dish.., or an unswept Hearth. 1683 Dryden *Life Plutarch* in *P.'s Lives* (1700) I. 24 To these he added a curious collection.., that he might leave nothing unswept behind him. 1760 Sterne *Tr. Shandy* III. xix, His head [was] like a smoke-jack;—the funnel unswept, and the ideas whirling round and round about in it. 1821 Lamb *Wks.* (1908) I. 511 The intolerable crash of the unswept cinder, betwixt your foot and the marble. 1852 James *Pequinillo* II. 63, I have left nothing unswept for want of a broom.

*transf.* 1851 Carlyle in Froude *Life* (1884) II. 84 The town had a dirty unswept look still.

**Unswere**, obs. f. Answer *v.*

**Unswe·rved**, *ppl. a.* (Un-¹ 8, 8 c.) 1849 M. Arnold *Fragm. of 'Antigone'* i, Justice not infring'd, Makes his own welfare his unswerv'd-from law. 1869 Lowell *Under the Willows* 295 Simple souls Unswerved by culture from their native bent.

**Unswe·rving**, *ppl. a.* [Un-¹ 10.] Not turning aside; steady, constant.

1694 Kettlewell *Comp. Penitent* 136 Keep up clear knowledge and unswerving righteousness in my Soul. 1797 Coleridge *Osorio* v. i. 9 She moved steadily on Unswerving from the path of her resolve. 1810 *Monthly Mag.* XXIX. 211 That unswerving loyalty To thee. 1858 *Househ. Words* XIX. 165/1 The same unswerving face at the wheel. 1878 Bosw. Smith *Carthage* 317 But Fortune..was unswerving in her devotion to the son.

**Unswe·rvingly**, *adv.* (Un-¹ 11. Cf. prec.)

1805 in A. Duncan *Nelson* (1806) 339 The unswervingly patriotic Nelson. 1834 L. Ritchie *Wand. by Seine* 65 The Seine..flows calmly and unswervingly on. 1896 Tout *Edw. I*, iv. 81 Henry Lacy..remained unswervingly faithful to Edward.

**Unswi·lled**, *ppl. a.* (Un-¹ 8.) 1545 Milton *Colast.* 25 His farewell..is to be a concluding taste to his jabberment in law, the flashiest and the fustiest that ever corrupted in such an unswill'd hogshead. **Unswi·ng**, *v.* (Un-² 3.) 1835 James *Gipsy* ii, The pot was unswung from the cross-bars that sustained it. 1856 J. Strang *Glasgow & Clubs* 395 To unswing a golden fleece was a common trick. **Unswi·ngled**, *ppl. a.* (Un-¹ 8.) 1538 *Inv. W. Gebon of Sutterton, Linc.* (MS.), Hempe vnpillid and flaxe vnswyngled. **Unswo·llen**, *ppl. a.* (Un-¹ 8 b.) 1648 Hexham II, *Ongeswollen*, vnswollen, or vnpuffed. 1812 Colman *Br. Grins, Reckoning w. Time* x, My lank purse unswoln by fees. † **Unswo·re**, *ppl. a.* [Un-¹ 8 b.] ? = next. *a* 1400 *Gloss* in *Rel. Ant.* I. 7 *Jusjurandum*, a othe unswore.

**Unswo·rn**, *ppl. a.* [Un-¹ 8 b. Cf. MHG. *ungesworn*, MSw. *os(v)orin*, Sw. *osvuren*, MDa. *us(v)oren*, not having sworn.]

1. Of persons: Not subjected to, or bound by, an oath.

1529 More *Dialoge* Wks. 133/2 For none of them can tel what was said to an other, & yet they be vnsworne also. 1533 — *Debell. Salem* Wks. 973/1 Yet are there many that dare secretely detecte,..and wyll not vncalled and vnsworen, tel no tale at all. 1581 Lambarde *Eiren.* I. x. (1588) 58 Albeit that it be the first Oath that I find to have bene ministred to Iustices of the Peace, yet I thinke they were neither unsworne before, nor at any time after. 1602 Segar *Hon. Mil. & Civ.* I. v. 7 That no Citizen unsworne, should remaine out of Italie more then three yeares. 1678 Dryden *All for Love* v. i, Is there one God unsworn to my Destruction? 1701 Prideaux *Direct. Ch.-wardens* 11 Whatever they do.., while unsworn, is all to their own wrong. 1710 J. Chamberlayne *St. Gt. Brit.* I. II. xv. 128 There are in this Court Three Officers unsworn. 1852 *Fraser's Mag.* March 246/1 He may consequently be supposed, to use the language of the law, 'to stand unindifferent as he stands unsworn'. 1884 Church *Bacon* iii. 75 An unsworn and unpaid member of the Learned Counsel.

2. Not confirmed by, or sworn as, an oath.

*a* 1623 Swinburne *Spousals* (1686) 11 Of Spousals, some be sworn and some unsworn; that is to say, some Spousals be confirmed by an Oath and some contracted without an Oath. *a* 1800 Cowper *Odyssey* (ed. 2) x. 419 When, therefore, nought of all her solemn oath Unsworn remain'd, I climb'd her stately bed. 1843 *Act* 6–7 *Vict.* c. 22 (title), The Admission, in certain Cases, of unsworn Testimony in Civil and Criminal Proceedings. 1887 *Pall Mall G.* 9 July 9/2 Granting summonses..on unsworn information.

**Unsyght, -syker**, var. Unsaught *a.*, Unsicker.

**Unsylla·bic**, *a.* (Un-¹ 7.) 1864 Jean Ingelow *Poems* 69 What work so high as mine,..Nature's..unsyllabic voices to combine.

**Unsy·llabled**, *ppl. a.* [Un-¹ 8.] Not formed into, not expressed in, syllables.

1594 Southwell *M. Magd. Funeral Teares* 69 b, The heart pressing out the vnsillabled breath at once. 1594 *Zepheria* xl, If She shall attend what fortunes sequeld The *naufrage* of my poore afflicted barke, Then tell, but tell in words unsillabled. 1832 Motherwell *Jeanie Morrison* ix, When freely gushed all feelings forth, Unsyllabled—unsung. 1843 Carlyle *Past & Pr.* II. xvii, With gaspings, gesturings, with unsyllabled cries. 1873 Mrs. Whitney *Other Girls* xxxiii, She was..trying to put something clearly into syllables that said itself, unsyllabled, to her.

**Unsyllogi·stical**, *a.* (Un-¹ 7.) 1638 Chillingw. *Relig. Prot.* vi. § 14. 334 To the first proposition of this unsyllogisticall syllogisme, I answer [etc.]. **Unsymbo·lic**, *a.* (Un-¹ 7.) 1871 Earle *Phil. Eng. Tongue* 211 Infantine speech is unsymbolic. 1878 H. G. Guinness *End of Age* 130 The Apocalypse..translated into unsymbolic language. **Unsymbo·licalness.** (Un-¹ 12. Cf. prec.) 1681 H. More *Exp. Dan.* v. 149 Which Writing..is called Scripture, and for its plainness and unsymbolicalness, as I may so speak,.. the Scripture of Truth. **Unsy·mbolized**, *ppl. a.* (Un-¹ 8 a c.) [1775 Ash.] 1881 H. Sweet in *Trans. Philol. Soc.*

196 Bell's providing a sign..for the very rare (ꝛv), while leaving the frequently occurring (sj), (ʃj), (ʒv), (ʒv), unsymbolized.

**Unsymme·trical,** *a.* (Un-¹ 7.)

**1755** Johnson, *Disproportionate*, unsymmetrical. **1816** R. Jameson *Char. Min.* (ed. 2) 207 A Crystal is said to be.. Unsymmetrical, when two ranges of facets situated one above another, on each extremity, exhibit a want of symmetry. **1830** Lindley *Nat. Syst. Bot.* 141 An imbricated calyx with.. unsymmetrical flowers, definite pendulous ovules. **1893** Tucky *Amphioxus* 119 This is an unsymmetrical movement of the mesoblastic somites.

Hence **Unsymme·trically** *adv.*

**1755** Johnson, *Disproportionately*, unsuitably, unsymmetrically. **1839–47** *Todd's Cycl. Anat.* III. 603/1 These ganglia are disposed unsymmetrically throughout the body. **1879** Spencer *Data of Ethics* i. § 1. 4 The unsymmetrically-pierced disk of an eccentric.

**Unsy·mmetrized,** *ppl. a.* (Un-¹ 8 a *c.*) **1825** Lamb *Last Ess. Elia, Wedding*, Visitors huddled up in corners; chairs unsymmetrised; candles disposed by chance. **Unsy·mmetry.** (Un-¹ 12.) **1867** Spencer *Principles of Biol.* II. 129 Each member of a plant will display..unsymmetry or asymmetry where there is partial or entire departure from a balance of surrounding actions. **1867** J. M. Wilson in Farrar *Ess. Lib. Educ.* 274 The pelargonium, and its more visible unsymmetry.

**Unsympathe·tic,** *a.* (Un-¹ 7.)

**1823** Byron *Island* iv. xiii, But calm and careless heaved the wave below, Eternal with unsympathetic flow. **1857** Mrs. Gaskell *C. Bronte* II. 327 The critical, unsympathetic public. **1867** H. Macmillan *Bible Teach.* ii. 36 We are not left in the power of blind unsympathetic nature.

Hence **Unsympathe·tically** *adv.*

**1861** Dickens *Gt. Expect.* vii, The ridgy effect of a wedding-ring, passing unsympathetically over the human countenance.

**Unsympathizabi·lity.** (Un-¹ 12.) **1818** Coleridge in *Lit. Rem.* (1836) I. 144 A craving for sympathy in exact proportion to the oddity and unsympathizability of what he proposes. **Unsy·mpathized,** *ppl. a.* (Un-¹ 8 a *c*, 8 c.) **1818** Mrs. Shelley *Frankenst.* xv, Finding myself unsympathized with, [I] wished to tear up the trees.

**Unsy·mpathizing,** *ppl. a.* (Un-¹ 10.)

**1735–6** Savage *Volunteer Laureat* iv. 7, I, jocund Spring, unsympathizing, see. **1768–74** Tucker *Lt. Nat.* (1834) II. 628 When they come out into the world they..become partial, overbearing, and unsympathizing. **1828** Lytton *Pelham* II. xix, The same stern, cold, unsympathising reserve, which made him..an object of universal conversation and dislike. **1882** Farrar *Early Chr.* I. 89 Jews..by whom the name and work of the Apostle of the Gentiles were regarded..with unsympathising coldness.

Hence **Unsy·mpathizingly** *adv.*

**1856** R. A. Vaughan *Mystics* i. ii. I. 16 Unless, indeed, the enquiry were conducted unsympathizingly.

**Unsy·mpathy.** (Un-¹ 12.) **1856** Bp. Wilberforce in *Life* (1881) II. 305 How true the unsympathy as well as the sympathy of nature. **1871** Palgrave *Lyrical Poems* 19 The mountains in their gray unsympathy..Mock'd her. **Unsynta·ctical,** *a.* (Un-¹ 7), **-ally,** *adv.* (Un-¹ 11.) **1865** Farrar *Chap. Lang.* 93 The fact..shows that their unsyntactical character is merely an accident of language. **1879** — *St. Paul* II. 258 This general exhortation is then carried into details, unsystematically indeed, and even unsyntactically, but [etc.].

**Unsystema·tic,** *a.* (Un-¹ 7.)

**1770** Burke *Pres. Discont.* 71 His single, unsupported, desultory, unsystematic endeavours. **1780** — *Œcon. Reform.* Wks. III. 285 A blind unsystematick observance of every trifle. **1836** J. Gilbert *Chr. Atonem.* ii. 45 The Bible..is, in general, an unsystematic, miscellaneous communication. **1862** 'Shirley' (J. Skelton) *Nugæ Crit.* x. 430 We miss the spontaneous and unsystematic music..of the true ballad. **1875** B. W. Richardson *Dis. Mod. Life* 11 The naming of these groups..has been unsystematic and fanciful.

**Unsystema·tical,** *a.* (Un-¹ 7.)

**1780** Burke *Œcon. Reform.* Wks. III. 235 Thus, between the resistance of power, and the unsystematical process of popularity, the undertaker and the undertaking are both exposed. **1791** Paine *Rights of Man* 58 A wild unsystematical display of paradoxical rhapsodies. *a* **1812** Buckminster *Serm.* (1827) 208 The occasional, and unsystematical addresses of your mioisters.

**Unsystema·tically,** *adv.* (Un-¹ 11. Cf. prec. and Unsystematic *a.*)

**1738** [see Unsteadily]. **1865** *Trans. Philol. Soc.* 15 One is systematically and the other unsystematically wrong. **1879** [see Unsyntactically *adv.*].

**Unsy·stematizable,** *a.* (Un-¹ 7 b.) **1799** Southey in *Sir H. Davy's Rem.* (1858) 42 The unconnected and unsystematizable fables of Hindoo absurdity. **1858** H. Bushnell *Nat. & Supernat.* ii. (1864) 41 Some desultory, unsystematizable action.

**Unsy·stematized,** *ppl. a.* (Un-¹ 8.)

[**1847** Webster.] **1849** *Edin. Rev.* April 290 Fragments of uncertain, inaccurate, ill-remembered, unsystematised information. **1863** *Austin's Jurispr.* III. 277 The bulk and uncognoscibility of unsystematized law. **1870** *Athenæum* 17 Sept. 359/3 The last stage of what we may term unsystematized volunteer aid in a campaign.

**Unt**: see Unct *v. Obs.* (to anoint).

†**Unta·che,** *v. Obs.* [Un-² 9 + Tache *v.*² 1.] *trans.* To carve (a beaver or curlew).

14.. in *Porkington MS. 10* fol. 188 A Bytter vntachyd. **1486** *Bk. St. Albans* F vij b, A Bevure untachid. **1508** *Bk. of Kerving* (W. de W.) A j b, Vntache that curlewe. [Hence in later lists.]

**Unta·ck,** *v.* [Un-² 3 + Tack *v.*¹]

**1.** *trans.* To take apart, break up.

**1641** Milton *Reform.* ii. 54 The little adoe, which me thinks I find in untacking these pleasant Sophismes. *a* **1715** Burnet *Own Time* vii. (1734) II. 401 If they [*sc.* the Lords] should untack the Bill, and separate one from the other. [Cf. Tack *v.*¹ 5.]

**b.** To detach (*from* something); to set free.

**1667** Marvell *Instr. Dutch Wars* Poems (1870) 153 Ruyter forthwith a squadron doth untack. *a* **1677** Barrow *Serm.* (1683) II. 49 It alone can untack our minds and affections from this world. **1741** Richardson *Pamela* II. 21 Besides, I must all undress me in a manner to untack [the papers].

**2.** To detach by the withdrawal of tacks. Also *absol.*

**1693** Evelyn *De la Quint. Compl. Gard.* II. 41 We must never begin to Prune an Espalier..until it be quite untack'd. **1707** Mortimer *Husb.* 138 When the Blanket..is full, they untack it and carry it away, and empty it. **1718** J. Laurence *Fruit-Gard. Kalendar* 43 To Exercise his Knife..in correcting the great Disorders of his..Peach-trees; first untacking them from the Wall.

**Unta·ckle,** *v.* [Un-² 4, 4 b. Cf. Du. *onttakelen.*]

**1.** *trans.* To strip (a vessel) of tackle. Hence *untackled* ppl. a.

**1552** Huloet, Vntakle a shyppe, *exarmare nauem.* **1598** Grenewey *Tacitus, Ann.* ii. v. 40 At length the sea growing lower, and the wind more fauourable, the lame and vntackled shippes..returned. **1626** Laud *Fast Serm.* 15 That no Tempest may vntackle them,..or hewe down their Masts. **1656** Davenant *Siege of Rhodes* i, I'le to our Gallies haste, Untackle ev'ry Mast.

**2.** To unharness (a horse).

**1573** Tusser *Husb.* (1878) 62 But vse to vntackle them once in a day. **1885** *Even. News* 25 July 2/6, I then untackled the horse from the car.

**3.** To free from tackling or fastenings.

**1905** 'Q' (Quiller Couch) *Shining Ferry* iv, Groping for the rod, [she] drew the float ashore and untackled it.

**Unta·ctful,** *a.* (Un-¹ 7.)

**1860** E. Eden *Semi-attached Couple* xx. I. 181 When her vanity was in a state of mortification, she became unusually untactful. **1900** *Daily News* 20 Oct. 3/1 The untactful conduct of a few of his friends.

**Unta·gged,** *ppl. a.* [Un-¹ 8.] Not furnished with a tag or tags.

**1557** North *Gueuara's Diall Pr.* iv. viii. (1568) 129 The courtier..that is content to tye his hose with vntagged poynts. *a* **1625** Fletcher *Woman's Prize* iv. iii, And your Money..if I forfeit, Make me a Jack o' Lent, and break my shins For untag'd Points and Compters. **1705** E. Ward *Hud. Rediv.* ii. 27 Or else those Points we shew our Art in Must often go untag'd. **1714** *Welsh Monster* 26 Tag'd or untag'd, his biting Satyrs..Were spun..exquisitly fine.

**Untai·led,** *ppl. a.*¹ [Un-¹ 8 and Un-² 8.] **a.** Not furnished with a tail. **b.** Deprived of a tail.

**1611** Florio, *Discodato*, vntailed, curtailed. **1648** Hexham ii, *Ongestaert*, Vntailed, or a Horses taile cutt off as our English horses are. **1807** in *Spirit Pub. Jrnls.* XI. 79 He acknowledged that the os coccygis in untailed animals was indeed no tail. **1836** Fonblanque *Eng. under 7 Administr.* (1837) III. 285 The old story of the untail'd fox's quarrel with tails.

†**Untai·led,** *ppl. a.*² *Obs. rare.* Also *Sc.* wntaillȝied. [Un-¹ 8.] Unentailed.

**1461** *Paston Lett.* II. 80 Bothe the forseyd manerys were ontayled. *a* **1578** Lindesay (Pitscottie) *Chron. Scot.* (S.T.S.) I. 47 The landis that was wntaillȝied.

**Untai·lorly,** *a.* (Un-¹ 7.) **1775** S. J. Pratt *Liberal Opin.* (1783) III. 82 That you may be permitted to go by so genteel and untaylorly a conveyance to the place of execution. **Untai·nt,** *v.* (Un-² 6 b.) **1855** Bailey *Mystic*, etc. 80 That heart-soothing herb..Held to untaint from sin the savage soul. †**Untai·nt,** *ppl. a.* [Un-¹ 8 b.] Untainted. **1638** W. Lisle *Heliodorus* ix. 159 Let him passe Along with them, to keepe vntaint the Lasse.

**Untai·ntable,** *a.* (Un-¹ 7 b.)

*a* **1610** Healey *Epictetus, Life* (1616) A 5, His life was spotlesse and vntaintable. *a* **1670** Hacket *Cent. Serm.* (1675) 238 His integrity was untaintable. **1895** *Cent. Mag.* July 339 One like himself should praise him! Soul of grace, untaintable white brightness!

**Untai·nted,** *ppl. a.* [Un-¹ 8.]

†**1.** Not attainted. *Obs.*⁻¹

**1594** Shaks. *Rich. III*, iii. vi. 9 And yet within these fiue houres Hastings liu'd, Vntainted, vnexamin'd, free, at libertie.

**b.** Not dishonoured. *rare*⁻¹.

**1627** Drayton *Agincourt* ccxlvi, Now Excester with his vntaynted Reare Came on, which long had labour'd to come in.

**2.** Not affected by any physical taint.

*c* **1600** Shaks. *Sonn.* xix, Him in thy course vntainted doe allow, For beauties patterne to succeding men. **1651** Vaughan *Benefit by Enemies* Wks. 1914 I. 99 Vultures..flock to them, but passe by the sound and untainted bodies. **1725** Bolingbroke *Let. to Swift* 24 July, But the attainder is kept.. prudently in force, lest..his bad leaven should sour that sweet, untainted mass. **1760–72** H. Brooke *Fool of Qual.* (1809) IV. 127 Her..flesh remained..pure and untainted. **1810** Southey *Kehama* x. iv, The stream..delights to lie..at rest Beneath the untainted sky. **1861** Ld. Lytton & Fane *Tannhaüser* 8 Till came the crack of that tremendous Doom..and on the lurid world Let in effulgence of untainted light.

**3.** Of qualities, etc.: Unsullied, unblemished, perfectly pure.

**1590** Greene *Never too late* (1600) 41 Isabel, whose beauty is deuine,..whose constancy vntainted. **1625** B. Jonson *Staple of N.* ii. iv, A Gentleman..Of an vntainted credit. **1673** Temple *Obs. United Prov.* Wks. 1720 I. 53 A Man of.. deep Understanding, with untainted Integrity. **1750** Collins *Superstit. Highlands* i, Let us wish him..joy untainted, with his destined bride. **1786** Mme. D'Arblay *Diary* 28 Nov., There was an evidence of her untainted worth in her very countenance. **1809–14** Wordsw. *Excurs.* viii. 241 Where is ..The character of peace,..And honest dealing, and untainted speech? **1831** Scott *Ct. Rob.* x, The knight passed on, not unmoved with wonder, though untainted by fear. **1879** R. K. Douglas *Confucianism* iv. 93 No virtue can remain untainted without learning.

**4.** Of persons, etc.: Free from moral taint.

*c* **1590** *Sir T. More* iv. v. 103 Liuing thus vntainted, you are well. **1593** Shaks. *2 Hen. VI*, iii. ii. 232 What stronger Brest-plate then a heart vntainted? **1651** W. Durham *Maran-atha* (1652) 24 The Judge of Israel..is..untainted in point of Judicature. **1689** D. Granville *Lett.* (Surtees) 81 The consideration whereof hath..kept me untainted and unstained. **1709** Addison *Tatler* No. 75 ¶ 9 From such an untainted Couple, we can hope to have our Family rise to its ancient Splendour of Face. **1763** Churchill *Poems* I. 86, I her snares defy, And look on riches with untainted eye. **1814** Byron *Lara* i. xxiii, He will not that untainted line belie. **1815** Scott *Guy M.* xvi, Persons..untainted perhaps in morals, and fair in character. **1890** J. Pulsford *Loyalty to Christ* I. 170 Very few ever come forth untainted, from scenes and circumstances of temptation.

**b.** Const. *by*, *with*, or † *of*.

**1612** T. Taylor *Comm. Titus* i. 6 The goodnes of God in keeping them altogether..vnreprooueable, that is vntainted of greiuous crimes. **1649** *Alcoran* p. iv, To keep thy selfe untainted of their follies. **1710** Addison *Spect.* No. 9 ¶ 3 This Sir-name of King, which..declared the Owners of it to be altogether untainted with Republican..Principles. **1757** Foote *Author* ii. (1777) 10/2 If George remains as untainted by affluence, as he has been untempted by distress. **1802** G. Canning *Poet. Wks.* (1827) 36 A statesman..By power uncorrupted, untainted by gold. **1850** Kingsley *A. Locke* ii, He alone was untainted with the sin around him.

Hence **Untai·ntedly** *adv.*, **Untai·ntedness.**

**1611** Cotgr., *Pudiquement*, chastly, purely, vntaintedly, modestly. **1640** Bp. Hall *Rem. Wks.* (1660) 37 The light hath a quality..Of purity and untaintedness in respect of any mixture of corruption. **1686** tr. *Chardin's Trav. Persia* 30 A Person untaintedly faithful to the Grand Vizier. **1817** Chalmers *Astron. Disc.* iv. 139 The untaintedness of his glory.

**Untai·nting,** *ppl. a.* (Un-¹ 10.) **1813** Shelley *Q. Mab* iv. 132 The untainting light of day. **Unta·k(e)able,** *a.* (Un-¹ 7 b.) **1652** Earl Monm. tr. *Bentivoglio's Hist. Relat.* 11 A place which is thought almost untakable. **1882** Paxton Hood *Cromwell* iii. 65 Nutt..was an untakable man, and he had several pirate ships.

**Unta·ken,** *ppl. a.*¹ Also 4 untak(e, 5–6 *Sc.* untane, 5 wntayne, etc. [Un-¹ 8 b, c, and 5 c. Cf. ON. *útekinn*, MSw. *otakin.*]

**1.** Not taken by force; not made prisoner; uncaptured.

*c* **1350** *Will. Palerne* 1280 Riȝt fewe went a-wey vn-woundet or take. *c* **1400** *Song of Roland* 89 He left vntak the toun, and to his tent ridis. *c* **1470** Henry *Wallace* v. 853 Lest he in strenth wntayne, This haill kynryk he wyll wyn. **1523** Ld. Berners *Froiss.* I. xciii. 115 Sir Robert Dartoyes was sore hurte, and scapedde hardely vntaken. **1577** Dee *General & Rare Mem.* 4 Their Marchantlike Ships..may.. pas quietly vnpilled, vnspoyled, and vntaken by Pyrates. **1610** Holland *Camden's Brit.* 499 Albeit the foulers doe.. catch great store of young water-foule, yet..abundance.. remaineth untaken. **1697** Dryden *Æneis* x. 1173 Untouch'd thy Arms, untaken be thy Sword. **1722** De Foe *Col. Jack* (1840) 188 The most prosperous untaken thief. **1768–74** Tucker *Lt. Nat.* (1834) II. 562 A wise general will ..leave no little stronghold untaken behind him. **1847** Mrs. A. Kerr tr. *Ranke's Hist. Servia* 317 Whilst that [fort] remained untaken. **1870** Morris *Earthly Par.* III. iv. 108 That he..scarce had trod Untaken on its floor.

**2.** Not taken, in other senses of the verb. Also const. *from.*

**1456** Sir G. Haye *Law Arms* (S.T.S.) 204 He levis it [*sc.* the consecrated wafer] untane for despising of the sacrament. **1474** *Cov. Leet Bk.* 410 In case the oportunite of this tyme shuld nowe..be vntaken or sett a-part. **1543–4** *Act 35 Hen. VIII*, c. 6 § 3 The Jurie is like to remayne untaken for defaulte of Jurors. **1586** T. B. *La Primaud. Fr. Acad.* i. 159 It is expedient sometime to leave untaken that which a man may lawfully take. **1600** Surflet *Countrie Farme* ii. lxv. 412 The honie..which is left vntaken from them. **1613** Sherley *Trav. Persia* 4, I left no paines untaken to accelerat it [*sc.* a journey]. **1735** Bolingbroke *Study Hist.* i. (1752) 7 That they might leave no liberty untaken. **1880** 'Ouida' *Moths* xvii, Resolute to leave no pains untaken.

**b.** With advs., as *away*, *down*, *off*, *up.*

**1483** *Acta Audit.* in *Acta Dom. Conc.* II. Introd. 120 The malis and fermes..to be untakin up be ony party. **1526** Tindale *2 Cor.* iii. 14 Vntill this daye remayneth the same coverynge vntaken awaye. **1539–40** Coverdale in Money *Parish Goods Berks.* (1879) p. vi, All the beams..remain still untaken down. **1562** Turner *Herbal* ii. 33 If they [*sc.* lentils] be sodden with theyr shilles vntaken of. **1610** J. Dove *Advt. Seminaries* 3 That veile..untill this time hath continued untaken away. **1683** J. Reid *Scots Gard'ner* (1907) 77 Bark..untaken off at the upper end. **1701** *Col. Rec. Pennsylv.* II. 43 All other lands that are mine untaken up. **1822** A. Cunningham *Tradit. T.* (1887) 136 My supper shall be the untaken-down spirit. **1836** [see Unstrengthened].

**c.** With other constructions.

**1583** A. Melvill in *J. Melvill's Autob. & Diary* (Wodrow Soc.) 155 Na obstinat Papist..hes it sufferit lang to converse amangs us, untean ordour withe. **1647** Clarendon *Hist. Reb.* iii. § 105 The King and Queen sate untaken notice of. **1904** E. Nesbit *Phœnix & Carpet* vii. 127 The four children found themselves at Waterloo Station quite untaken-care-of.

**Unta·ken,** *ppl. a.*² (Un-² 3, 8.) **1893** Baring-Gould *Cheap Jack Zita* II. 150 Whether taken and confiscated I cannot say..But I have paid ten pounds to have it untaken and set at liberty. **Unta·king,** *vbl. sb.* (Un-² 3, 8.) **1656** O. Sedgwick *Humble Sinner Resolved* vi. § 5. 47 If I take a servant, I take him so, that..I can put him off againe; but if I take a wife, there can be no untaking on my part.

**Unta·king,** *ppl. a.* [Un-¹ 10, 5 d.] **a.** *Sc.* Without taking. **b.** Not receptive; not attractive.

**1587** *Reg. Privy Council Scot.* IV. 168 Giff the Quene of England culd not persave hir awin securitie untaking his Majesteis moderis lyff. **1683** Moxon *Mech. Exerc., Printing* 377 When the Balls do not Take, the Un-taking part of the Balls that touches the Form will be left White. **1885** O. Crawfurd *Woman's Reput.* i, She has a harsh voice or an untaking manner.

**Untalelich**: see Un-¹ 3.

**Unta·lented,** *ppl. a.* (Un-¹ 8.)

**1753** Richardson *Grandison* (1754) VI. i. 6 This is the sort of stuff you must be satisfied with from a poor untalented girl. **1815** *Zeluca* III. 141 The means the untalented have of filling up their time. 1831 CARLYLE *Sart. Res.* II. viii, Your numerous talented men, and your innumerable untalented men.

**Unta·lkative,** *a.* (UN-[1] 7.) 1739 J. SPENCE in *Academy* 20 Feb. (1875) 191/3 He's..untalkative, tolerably read and a great dealer in Relicks. 1866 *Standard* 29 June 5/3 Government is extremely untalkative, while the..telegraph communication with..Germany is almost completely interrupted. **Unta·lked,** *ppl. a.* (UN-[1] 8 c.) 1592 SHAKS. *Rom. & Jul.* III. ii. 7 That run-awayes eyes may wincke, and Romeo Leape to these armes, vntalkt of and vnseene. 1669 DRYDEN *Tyrannic Love* III. i, Th' unknown, untalk'd of man is only blest. **Unta·ll,** *a.* (UN-[1] 7. Cf. TALL *a.* 1 c.) *c* 1395 *Plowman's Tale* I. iii, The other side ben poore and pale,..And seeme caitives sore a-cale..; Who toteth on hem, they ben untall.

**Unta·me,** *a.* [UN-[1] 7. Cf. Du. *ontam*, OHG. (MHG.) *unzam* (G. *unzahm*), MDa. *utam*, (M)Sw. *otam*.] Not tame or gentle; wild.

1382 WYCLIF *Ecclus.* xxx. 8 The vntame hors shal scapen hard. 1390 GOWER *Conf.* I. 287 Whanne al his resoun was untame. 14.. *Voc.* in Wr.-Wülcker 589 *Indomitus*, vntame, wylde. 1555 EDEN *Decades* (Arb.) 376 If the vntame brayne of Wyndam had..gyuen eare to the counsayle. 1584 R. SCOT *Discov. Witchcr.* XII. xv. 204 How untame by nature these vipers..are. 1609 BP. HALL *David's Ps. Metaphr.* viii, Thou hast..stretcht thy raigne Vnto the heards, and beasts vntame. 1655 W. HAMMOND *Death* 54 The whole world obeys Creation's law; only untame man strays.

Hence **Unta·meness.**

1727 BAILEY (vol. II), *Ungentleness*, Untameness, Rudeness. 1871 KINGSLEY *At Last* xvii, In curious contrast to the natural tameness of the Kinkajou was the natural untameness of a beautiful little Night-Monkey.

**Unta·me,** *v.* (UN-[2] 3.) 1646 SHIRLEY *Upon Death of C. Dalby* Wks. 1833 VI. 449 Nor did his courage know to make a pause, When honour call'd so loud, and such a cause As would untame a hermit.

**Unta·m(e)able,** *a.* (UN-[1] 7 b.)

(*a*) 1576 FLEMING tr. *Caius' Dogs* D 2, Be the bull neuer so monsterous,..neuer so vntameable. 1577 HELLOWES *Gueuara's Chron.* 58 The Parthians were a people so vntameable to be subdued, that [etc.]. 1607 TOPSELL *Four-f. Beasts* 112 The Indian little Pig-Cony..is..more tractable in hand; howbeit vntamable. 1692 DRYDEN *Don Sebastian* I. i, Still untameable! In what a ruine has thy head-strong Pride..plung'd thy People. 1764 HARMER *Observ.* viii. § 11. 326 The Arabs have been always looked upon as an untameable people. 1774 GOLDSM. *Nat. Hist.* III. 343 This animal..[is] more savage and untameable than any other quadrupede. 1818 MILMAN *Samor* VII. 172, I know thee now, majestic Rebel! thee The untraceable, untameable! 1833 J. RENNIE *Alph. Angling* 25 The pike is held to be a more wild, untameable fish than the carp. 1870 N. F. HELE *Aldeburgh* vii. 77 They [*sc.* short-horned owls] are very untameable. 1890 *Spectator* 11 Jan., Cruel and untameable though they [*sc.* the Masai] seem.

*fig.* 1836 F. MAHONY *Rel. Father Prout* 274 A genuine poet..enjoys the mental chase in proportion to the wild and untameable nature of the game.

(*b*) 1567 R. MULCASTER *Fortescue's De Laud. Leg.* 92 The lustes of the fleash are wanton, & almoste vntamable. 1571 GOLDING *Calvin on Ps.* ix. 21 He subdeweth their untamable wilfulnesse by force. *a* 1677 BARROW *Serm.* Wks. 1687 I. 33 His own unsatiable desires,..and untameable passions, will disquiet him. 1742 YOUNG *Nt. Th.* v. 262 A Pomp untameable of Weed prevails. 1768–74 TUCKER *Lt. Nat.* (1834) II. 380 This vigour and untamable violence of the sensitive faculties. 1818 SHELLEY *Let.* Pr. Wks. 1888 II. 224 The untameable profusion and loveliness of nature. 1860 HAWTHORNE *Marb. Faun* xviii, It was a delight to behold this untamable water.

Hence **Unta·m(e)ably** *adv.*

1807 *Trans. Linn. Soc.* (1808) IX. 177 In a state of confinement, they appear to be untameably savage.

**Unta·m(e)ableness.** (UN-[1] 12, or f. prec.)

1662 T. BROOKS *Crown & Glory of Christianity* 404 The Greeks call it an Adamant from its untameableness. 1790 BEWICK *Hist. Quadrup.* 144 The Rhinoceros..possesses all the properties ascribed to that animal,—rage, untameableness,..and immense strength. 1837 CARLYLE *Misc.*, *Diamond Necklace* xiv, Her grand quality is rather to be reckoned negative: the 'untameableness' as of a fly. 1865 M. ARNOLD *Ess. Crit.* 179 By his intensity, by his untamableness,..[Heine] is Hebrew.

**Unta·med,** *ppl. a.* [UN-[1] 8. Cf. ON. *útamdr*, Sw. *otamd*, Norw. *utamd*; also OHG. *ungizamot*, MHG. *ungezamt*, and UNTEMED *ppl. a.*] Not tamed (in various senses); wild; unsubdued.

(*a*) *a* 1340 HAMPOLE *Psalter* xxiv. 11 He leris..sothfastnes thurgh þe whilke he is vntamed. 1382 WYCLIF *Jer.* xxxi. 18 Y am lerned as a ȝungling vntamed. 1495 GLANVIL *Barth. De P. R.* XVIII. lxviii. 831 Suche asses be grete..and vntamyd. 1535 COVERDALE *Ecclus.* xxx. 8 An vntamed horse wylbe harde. 1596 SPENSER *F. Q.* V. i. 2 Bacchus, that with furious might All th' East, before vntam'd, did ouerronne. 1623 BINGHAM *Xenophon* p. ii, Of vntamed beasts, the most were wilde Asses. 1659 CHAMBERLAYNE *Pharon.* IV. iii. 248 Base Amarus,..more beastly rude Than untamed Indians. 1718 PRIOR *Solomon* I. 199 Untam'd and fierce the Tiger still remains. 1762 FALCONER *Shipwr.* II. 518 Like some strong watch-tower nodding o'er the deep,..Untamed he stood. 1817 MOORE *Lalla R.*, *Veiled Prophet* III. 226 He..there, untam'd, the approaching conq'ror waits. 1868 *Rep. U. S. Commissioner Agric.* (1869) 254 A door for the inroads of untamed swine.

(*b*) 1585 ABP. SANDYS *Serm.* xii. 205 Which thing rightly..weied, would bridle these vntamed affections of ours. 1600 *1st Pt. Sir J. Oldcastle* v. viii. 8 There dwell vntamed thoughts that hardly stoupe To such abasement. 1653 W. RAMESEY *Astrol. Restored* To Rdr. 11 His wilde untamed accustomary life. 1746 FRANCIS tr. *Horace, Art of Poetry* 177 With untam'd Fury let Medea glow. 1781 GIBBON *Decl. & F.* xxvii. (1787) III. 38 Their native fierceness was yet untamed. 1840 DICKENS *Old C. Shop* xlv, Monsters, whose like they almost seemed to be in their wildness and their untamed air. 1859 F. MAHONY *Rel. Father Prout* 385 The human breast..Throbs thus unawed, Untamed and unquiescent.

(*c*) 1600 SURFLET *Countrie Farme* III. xlix. 539 The perries which are pressed out of wilde peares, and all such as are vnhusbanded, vntamed. 1623 J. TAYLOR (Water P.) *Discov. by Sea* A 8 b, The windes and seas continued still their course,..vntam'd [seemed] their force. 1743 FRANCIS tr. *Hor.*, *Odes* IV. xiv. 23 The Winds arise And work the Seas untam'd. *c* 1790 COLERIDGE *Death Chatterton* 159 Where Susquehannah pours his untamed stream. 1818 MILMAN *Samor* VIII. 130 The strong freedom of thy untam'd locks. 1841 CARLYLE *Heroes* i. (1904) 33 The untamed Forests and dark brute Powers of Nature. 1865 F. PARKMAN *Pioneers of France in New World* (1876) p. x, An untamed continent; vast wastes of forest verdure.

Hence **Unta·medly** *adv.*, **Unta·medness.**

1592 LYLY *Gallathea* II. v, Curse..the vntamednes of thy affections. 1612 AINSWORTH *Annot. Ps.* xl. 2 The untamednesse of the tongue. 1653 BLITHE *Eng. Improver Impr.* xxviii. 196 If the horse be kindly used, and taken of his untamedness by degrees,..he is made a horse for ever. 1706 STEVENS *Span. Dict.* I, *Seneramente*,..wildly, untam'dly, outrageously. 1727 BAILEY (vol. II), *Wildness*, Untamedness, Furiousness.

† **Unta·meful,** *a.* *Obs.*[−1] [UN-[1] 7.] Untameable. 1607 TOPSELL *Four-f. Beasts* 745 Their Epithites..are most cleare demonstrations of their disposition; as sowre,..vnhonest, vntameful, harmeful.

**Unta·mpered,** *ppl. a.* (UN-[1] 8, 8 c.)

1682 *Lenten Prol.* 52 If it dare speak th' untamper'd Nations sence. 1827 POLLOK *Course T.* VIII. 25 The true untampered witness of the heart. 1856 AYTOUN *Bothwell* II. xviii, The juice Of the untampered vine. 1858 FROUDE *Hist. Eng.* IV. 290 The Bible, as edited by Cranmer, was left untampered with.

**Unta·ngible,** *a.* (UN-[1] 7, 5 b.) [1775 ASH.] 1816–30 BENTHAM *Offic. Apt. Maximized*, *Extr. Const. Code* 6 The special good will,..tangible or untangible, naturally flowing from these sentiments. 1818 T. L. PEACOCK *Nightmare Abbey* xii, No, sir, genuine untangible ghosts.

**Unta·ngle,** *v.* [UN-[2] 3 and 7.]

**1.** *trans.* To free from a tangled state.

1550 THOMAS *Ital. Dict.*, *Disbrigare*, to vntangle any thyng encombred, tangled, or carefull. 1573 TUSSER *Husb.* (1878) 135 See then..ech pole ye out get. Which being vntangled aboue in the tops, Go carrie to such as are plucking of hops. 1592 SHAKS. *Rom. & Jul.* I. iv. 91 This is that very Mab that..bakes the Elf-locks in foule sluttish haires, which once vntangled, much misfortune bodes. *c* 1696 PRIOR *Love Disarmed* 35 Untangle but this cruel Chain, And freely let Me fly again. 1871 B. TAYLOR *Faust* (1875) II. 31 Useless webs she long untangled, Dragging them to air and light.

*intr.* *a* 1668 LASSELS *Voy. Italy* (1670) II. 415 Sometimes meeting too thick in the arches of the wooden bridge,..they..are stopt for an hour together without being able to untangle.

**b.** In fig. uses. Also *refl.*

1601 SHAKS. *Twel. N.* II. ii. 41 O time, thou must vntangle this, not I. *a* 1625 FLETCHER *Fair Maid Inn* II. i, My care now Must be to untangle this division, That our most equal flames may be united. 1677 WYCHERLEY *Pl. Dealer* v. iii, He's the best in England at untangling a flourish, Madam. 1702 VANBRUGH *False Friend* III. iii, If Leonora's innocent, she may untangle all. 1883 D. C. MURRAY *Hearts* xx, The letter went unwritten. She would leave it to events to untangle themselves. 1894 *Advance* (Chicago) 19 Apr., They must untangle their own fate.

**2.** To set free, to release, from entanglement.

1576 TURBERV. *Venerie* 36 Vntangle him out of the net or stall and let him go. 1588 DEE in Ellis *Lett. Eminent Lit. Men* (Camden) 46 [We will] endeuour our selues..diligently to ryd and vntangle our selues from hence. 1648 FANSHAWE *Il Pastor Fido* 89 Come, fumbler, let me see; I can my self untangle without thee. 1652 J. WRIGHT tr. *Camus' Nat. Paradox* v. 900 Like..Fowlers, who glad to see the innocent Creatures fall into their Gins, instead of untangling them doe ingage them further in their Snares. 1898 HOWELLS *Open-eyed Conspir.* 173 The young..have not had our experience in getting untangled, and think they are never going to get out alive.

**Unta·ngled,** *ppl. a.* [UN-[1] 8.] Free from entanglement. 1539 TAVERNER *Erasm. Prov.* (1545) 27 Meanyng that it is excedyng harde for sucn as flowe in worldly goodes to haue a mynde vntangled with the same. 1598 FLORIO, *Sciolto*, loose, free,..vnsnared,..vntide, vntangled.

**Unta·nned,** *ppl. a.* [UN-[1] 8. Cf. Du. *ongetand.*] Not subjected to tanning.

1535 *Act 27 Hen. VIII*, c. 14 § 5 Any manner of Lether tanned or untanned. 1555 EDEN *Decades* (Arb.) 361 Sackes made of raw or vntande hydes. 1639 T. DE GRAY *Expert Farrier* 320 Take the shreds of white leather untanned. 1683 MOXON *Mech. Exerc.*, *Printing* 386 Sheep Skins untan'd, used for Ball Leathers. 1709 LITTLEBURY *Herodotus* II. 194 A small Buckler compos'd of untann'd Hides. 1821 CAMPBELL *Song of Hybrias* 2 A right good shield of hides untanned. 1844 H. STEPHENS *Bk. Farm* II. 400 Untanned sheep-skin is employed to sew on the capes of the collars. 1883 BURTON & CAMERON *Gold Coast* I. 137 Long leather gaiters..and untanned shoes.

**Unta·p,** *v.* (UN-[2] 9, 7.) 1622 MABBE tr. *Aleman's Guzman d'Alf.* II. 229 If I should suffer her still to vntap my vessel, she would suck me dry at last. 1689 N. LEE *Princ. Cleve* II. iii, Does not your Politician,..after all his Plotting, Drudging and Sweating at Lying, retire to some little Punk and untap at Night? **Unta·pered,** *ppl. a.* (UN-[1] 8.) [1775 ASH.] 1851 RUSKIN *Stones Ven.* I. viii. § 9 The Egyptian shaft is often untapered, like the Northern. **Unta·pestried,** *ppl. a.* (UN-[1] 8.) 1849 JAMES *Woodman* ii, The fourth side of the room was untapestried. 1851 SIR F. PALGRAVE *Norm. & Eng.* I. 206 It was an untapestried Hall; the bowing walls freshly built with untempered mortar.

† **Unta·pis,** *v.* *Obs.* [UN-[2] 7 + TAPIS *v.*[1]] *intr.* To come out of cover or hiding.

1602 *2nd Pt. Return Parnass.* II. v. 830 At the vnkennelling, vntapezing, or earthing of the Fox. 1634 MASSINGER *Very Woman* III. v, Now I'll untappice. (Comes forward with the bottle.)

**Unta·pped,** *ppl. a.* (UN-[1] 8. Cf. Da. *utappet.*) In frequent use (esp. fig.) from *c* 1890.

[1775 ASH.] 1779 WARNER in Jesse *Selwyn* (1844) IV. 254 An untapped barrel of ale. 1863 BATES *Nat. Amazons* I. 143 Untapped [india-rubber] trees still growing in the wilds. 1889 C. EDWARDES *Sardinia* 164 What a fund of mirth..lay untapped within him!

**Unta·rnishable,** *a.* (UN-[1] 7 b.) 1888 *Microcosm* (N. Y.) Dec. 1 The same..untarnishable metal [*sc.* aluminium] wrought into every variety of cooking utensils.

**Unta·rnished,** *ppl. a.* (UN-[1] 8.)

1732 GREEN *Grotto* 185 Come, nymph,..With charms untarnish'd, innocence Display, and Eden shall commence. 1798 S. & HT. LEE *Canterb. T.* II. 386 The yet untarnished bridal vestments she..saw packed. 1818 MILMAN *Samor* VII. 386 Yon flag..shook Untarnish'd in the sun its blazon broad. 1859 TENNYSON *Enid* 501 If I fall her name will yet remain Untarnish'd. 1876 E. JENKINS *Blot on Queen's Head* 14 Its glorious and wondrous colours remained fresh and untarnished.

† **Unta·rpage.** *Obs.*[−1] [UN-[2] 5. Cf. UNTAPIS *v.*] An instance of unharbouring an animal. *c* 1700 *Fox-chace* 88 in *Roxb. Ballads* (1871) I. 363 Then to Skipland Wood he goes,..An untarpage there we had, Which made our Huntsmen full glad.

**Unta·rred,** *ppl. a.* [UN-[1] 8. Cf. Sw. *otjärad*, Du. *ongeteerd.*] Not smeared, etc., with tar.

1579 W. WILKINSON *Confut. Fam. Love* 24 Least that M. Rogers should scape vntarred with their opprobrious Eloquence. *c* 1610 *Rates of Marchandizes* E 3 b, Cordage Tard or vntard the hundred waight. 1769 FALCONER *Dict. Marine* (1780), *Cordage blanc*, White, or untarred cordage. *a* 1844 CAMPBELL *Napoleon & Brit. Sailor* 35 A wherry..Untarr'd, uncompass'd, and unkeel'd. 1875 KNIGHT *Dict. Mech.* 2773/2 An untarred cord or rope.

**Unta·rried,** *ppl. a.* (UN-[1] 8.) 1438 in *Wars Eng. in France* (1864) II. 438 We have disposed oure cousin..to passe in al haste, for whoos passage untaried we pray you that ye doo to hym your devoir. **Unta·rtarized,** *ppl. a.* (UN-[1] 8 a *c.*) 1737 BAILEY (vol. II) Add., *Untartarized* (in Chymistry) not mixed with tartar. **Unta·sked,** *ppl. a.* (UN-[1] 8.) [1775 ASH.] 1802 WORDSW. *Excurs.* I. 384 To pass the remnant of his days, untasked With needless services. 1850 DICKENS *D. Copperfield* iv, Miss Murdstone never could endure to see me untasked. **Unta·ste,** *v.* (UN-[2] 4.) 1609 DANIEL *Civ. Wars* VIII. lxxxiii, Whil'st he himself, deceiu'd, suffers with them: And could not..Vntaste them of this violent disgust. **Unta·steable,** *a.* (UN-[1] 7 b, 5 b.) 1656 BLOUNT, *Ingustable*,..untasteable. 1674 GREW *Disc. Mixture* iii. § 16 In any fixed unodorable, or untasteable Body.

**Unta·sted,** *ppl. a.* (UN-[1] 8.)

1538 ELYOT, *Illibatus*, vntouched, vntasted. 1593 *Extr. Aberd. Reg.* (1848) II. 89 The aill being untaistit nor yit price maid thairupoun. 1665 BOYLE *Occas. Refl.* IV. v, [He] pour'd it untasted on the Ground. 1725 POPE *Odyss.* XXII. 100 Th' untasted viands, and the jovial bowl. 1802 MAR. EDGEWORTH *Moral T.* II. 11 With a yet untasted pinch of Snuff between her fingers. 1823 SCOTT *Quentin D.* vii, The old Lord..placed the untasted wine-cup before him. 1849 MACAULAY *Hist. Eng.* vi. II. 71 The dishes were removed untasted from the table.

**b.** In fig. uses.

1606 SHAKS. *Tr. & Cr.* II. iii. 130 All his vertues,..like faire Fruit in an vnholesome dish, Are like to rot vntasted. 1692 DRYDEN *Don Sebastian* II. i, A new Scene of yet untasted Joys. 1742 R. BLAIR *Grave* 76, Bursts of sorrow gush from either eye, Fast falling down her now untasted cheek. 1818 [S. WESTON] *La Scava*, etc. 44 A garbled essay of his abilities, for the most part misunderstood and untasted. *a* 1865 MRS. GASKELL *Wives & Dau.* (1866) I. 67 The squire withdrew into his study to read the untasted newspapers.

**Unta·steful,** *a.* (UN-[1] 7.) 1618 WITHER *Juvenilia*, *Abuses Stript* II. i, He marres the bounty of his loving feast By his ill chusing some untastefull guest. 1884 A. VAMBÉRY *Life & Adv.* vii. 60 My patient and untasteful occupation. **Unta·stefully,** *adv.* (UN-[1] 11.) 1828–32 WEBSTER (citing *Br. Rev.*). 1863 *Pilgr. over Prairies* II. 157 A tunic..profusely and untastefully ornamented with red beads. **Unta·sting,** *ppl. a.* (UN-[1] 10.) 1707 E. SMITH *Phædra & H.* III. 31 Cydonian Oyl, Whose balmy Juice glides o'er th' untasting Tongue. **Unta·sty,** *a.* (UN-[1] 7.) 1566 DRANT *Horace*, *Sat.* III. G j b, If one..drincke nothing but vinaiger, untastie and unfyne. *a* 1733 LD. BINNING *Lady's Complaint* v. in Maidment *Ball.* (1844) 62 But camblet's an untasty thing. **Unta·ttered,** *ppl. a.* (UN-[1] 8.) [1775 ASH.] 1856 N. HAWTHORNE *Eng. Note-bks.* (1879) I. 363 Banners..so untattered, that I think they must be modern. **Untattoo·ed,** *ppl. a.* (UN-[1] 8.) 1884 G. TURNER *Samoa* vii. 89 Variegated..with neat regular stripes of the untattooed skin.

**Untau·ght,** *ppl. a.* [UN-[1] 8 b.]

**1.** Not enlightened or trained by teaching; uninstructed, ignorant.

*c* 1340 HAMPOLE *Pr. Consc.* 5873 Maysters [shall give account] of þair disciples..Þat þai lete be unthewed, and untaght ga. 1382 WYCLIF *Ecclus.* viii. 5 Comune thou not to a man vntaȝt. *c* 1460 *Play Sacram.* 558 [636] Syr, thu art ontawght to come in thus henly [*sic*]. 1567 DRANT *Horace*, *Ep.* I. i. G vj, The greater companye, in vertue few, and base, Vntaught blockheads, braineles. 1596 SHAKS. *1 Hen. IV*, I. iii. 43 He call'd them vntaught Knaues, Vnmannerly. 1602 *2nd Pt. Return Parnass.* v. i. 1986 With vntaught hand, and with vntuned hart. 1649 DAVENANT *Love & Hon.* III. ii. 3 Fit only to perswade the easinesse Of untaught babes. 1709 STEELE *Tatler* No. 167 ¶ 1 The rude and untaught Multitude. 1784 COWPER *Task* II. 359 He teaches those to read, whom schools dismiss'd, And colleges, untaught. 1847 C. BRONTË *J. Eyre* xxxii, Wholly untaught, with faculties quite torpid, they seemed to me hopelessly dull. 1882 BESANT *All Sorts* xxviii, The crude theories of untaught, if generous, youth.

*absol.* 1382 WYCLIF *1 Chron.* xxv. 8 Thei leyden lottis by their whilis euenly,..the tauȝt and vntauȝt to gyder. 1728 CHAMBERS *Cycl.* s.v. *Substantive*, The Taught have the Advantage of the Untaught. *a* 1832 CRABBE *Posth. Tales* II. 169 He knew not how For the untaught and ill-taught to allow. *Prov.* *c* 1530 in *Songs, Carols*, etc. (E. E. T. S.) 129 Better it is to be wnborne than wntawght. 1557 F. S[EAGER] *School Virtue* C iij, The common prouerbe remember ye oughte, 'Better vnfedde then vn-taughte'.

**b.** Const. with inf., *in*, or objective complement.

**1581** Howell *Devises* M ij, Like a childe agayne, vntaught the sleightes of dayntie mindes. *a* **1593** Marlowe *Hero & Leander* I. 392 Her mind pure, and her toong vntaught to glose. **1642** H. More *Song of Soul* II. III. iii. 42 Untought In subtilties they shew themselves in jangling stout. **1683** Dryden *Ovid's Ep., Helen to Paris* 139 My hand is yet untaught to write to Men. **1762** Sir W. Jones *Arcadia* Poems, etc. (1772) 135 Daphne, yet untaught in am'rous lore, Felt..pains unknown before. **1784** Cowper *Tiroc.* 379 Untaught The knowledge of the world, and dull of thought! **1794** Wordsw. *Guilt & Sorrow* xxxiii, We gazed with terror on their gloomy sleep, Untaught that soon such anguish must ensue. **1827** Keble *Chr. Y., Convers. St. Paul* vi, His strain'd eye..Still gazing, though untaught to bear Th' insufferable light.

**c.** Of animals, etc.

**1697** Dryden *Æneis* VI. 348 Four sable bullocks, in the yoke untaught. **1725** Pope *Odyss.* VII. 153 The balmy spirit of the western gale Eternal breathes on fruits untaught to fail. **1743** Francis tr. *Hor., Epodes* xvi. 57 Where Goats untaught forsake the flowery Vale. **1817** Byron *Mazeppa* ix, A noble steed,..Wild as the wild deer, and untaught. **1863** Conington *Horace, Odes* III. iii. 14 For this..tigers drew Thy glorious car, untaught to slave In harness.

**2.** Not imparted or acquired by teaching; hence, natural, spontaneous.

*c* **1445** Pecock *Donet* 6 Bettir it is..þan forto leve alle suche þingis vnwritun and vntauȝt. *c* **1449** — *Repr.* I. xx. 127 This other maner of..witnessing bi Holi Scripture, which is left here vnseid and vntauȝt. **1533** More *Answ. Supper of Lord* I. xvii. Wks. 1064/1 Leauing that vntaught til yͤ time of his maundy supper. *a* **1586** Sidney *Arcadia* III. xxiv, Delivering from his hart two or three (untaught) sighes. **1611** Shaks. *Cymb.* IV. ii. 178 'Tis wonder That an inuisible instinct should frame them To Royalty vnlearn'd, Honor vntaught. **1656** Cowley *Davideis* I. 821 Flocks of Birds..Teaching their Maker in their untaught lays. **1712** Steele *Spect.* No. 276 ⁋ 3, I have a natural Voice, and a pretty untaught Step in Dancing. **1742** Gray *Spring* 7 The untaught harmony of spring. **1836** Cdl. Wiseman *Lect. Cath. Ch.* (1847) 3 Many doctrines untaught by Him. **1865** Tylor *Early Hist. Man.* ii. 19 The untaught signs made by born deaf-mutes.

Hence **Untau·ghtness.**

**1840** S. Clark in *Mem. Jrnls. & Lett.* (1878) 131, I have to suffer from my untaughtness.

**Untaw·ed,** *ppl. a.* (Un-[1] 8 + Taw *v.*[1] 2.)

**1545** *Rates of Customs* b iv, Graye vntawed the timber, iiis. iiiid. *Ibid.* b vii, Lettuis vntawed the timber, iis. vid. **1617** *Bk. Rates Marchandise* G 2, Furres:..Budge, blacke vntawed. **1642** *Ibid.* D 2 b, Letwis..Vntawed. **1662** *Stat. Irel.* (1786) II. 406 Furs:..Calabar, untawed the timber, containing forty skins, 6s. 8d.

**Unta·x,** *v.* [Un-[2] 4 b.] *trans.* To exempt from a tax; to remove a tax from.

*c* **1831** E. Elliott *Corn-Law-Rhymes* (1833) 102 Who will untax our bread? **1834** Ht. Martineau *Moral* III. 119 To untax the prime necessary of life.

**Unta·xable,** *a.* [Un-[1] 7 b and 5 b.]

†**1.** That cannot be taxed or charged with wrong-doing. Also const. *of*. *Obs.*

*a* **1610** Healey *Cebes* (1616) 137 Behold there a faire and florishing matrone, enthroned in state,..yet vntaxable of profuseness. **1624** Bp. Mountagu *Gagg* 130 It is not said, that They kept the commandements of God...But they walked in them..untaxable, unblameable. *a* **1688** W. Clagett *17 Serm.* (1699) 289 His untaxable justice in bringing upon them that punishment.

**2.** Not liable to taxation.

**1648** Hexham II, *Onschatbaer*, Vntaxable, or Free and Franck. **1818** Bentham *Ch. Eng.* p. x, The Lower House was indeed untaxable. But the Upper House..taxed themselves.

**Unta·xed,** *ppl. a.* [Un-[1] 8. Cf. G. *untaxirt*, older Da. *utaxeret* in sense 2.]

†**1.** Unassailed; unchallenged. *Obs.*

*c* **1460** *Oseney Reg.* 17 Ordeynyng þat all maner possessions ..sure to yow..vntaxid abyde. **1605** Bacon *Adv. Learn.* I. vii. § 7 In common speech (which leaves no virtue untaxed) he was called..a divider of cummin seed. **1645** G. Daniel *Poems* Wks. (Grosart) II. 101 May not I,..To my best Child, Vtter a Truth vntax'd? *a* **1691** Boyle *Hist. Air* (1692) 76 A mistake that must not pass untaxed amongst learned men.

**2.** Not required to pay taxes.

**1464–5** in *Acta Parlt. Scotl.* (1875) XII. 31/2 Any personis ..within þe boundis of thare office vntaxt. **1746** Warton *Progr. Discontent* 119, I..din'd untax'd, untroubled, under The portrait of our pious founder. **1776** Adam Smith *W. N.* v. ii. (1904) II. 513 Those who exercise the untaxed employments. **1826** Lamb *Wks.* (1908) I. 389 The Beadle..looks like a whole parish, full, important—but untaxed. **1835** Lytton *Rienzi* IX. iv, To live unbutchered by the Barons, and untaxed by their governors.

**Unta·xing,** *ppl. a.* (Un-[1] 5 d.) **1851** Lytton *Not so bad* 134 A College; Where teacher and student alike the subscriber, Untaxing the Patron,..The State,..Or the briber.

**Unte:** see Unct *v. Obs.* (to anoint).

**Untea·ch,** *v.* [Un-[2] 3.]

**1.** *trans.* To cause (a person) to forget or discard previous knowledge. Occas. const. *to* with inf.

**1532** Tindale *Expos. Matt. v–vii*, 36 b, Thou hast vntaught hir to feare God. **1650** Baxter *Saints' R.* III. 535 We have a double task; first to unteach them, and then to teach them better. **1802–12** Bentham *Ration. Judic. Evid.* (1827) I. 8 The peasant wants only to be taught, the lawyer to be untaught. **1833** *Q. Rev.* XLIX. 72 Much of their time was employed in *un*teaching them to read. **1845** Keble in A. Mozley *Lett. Newman* (1891) II. 473 You have taught me so, and I scarce think you can unteach me. **1870** Emerson *Soc. & Solit.* vii. 135 Every new step in improving the engine restricts one more art of the engineer,—unteaches him.

**b.** With double object. (Also in passive.)

**1620** Sir T. Matthew tr. *St. Augustine's Confessions* III. xii. 121 To teach me that which was good, and to vnteach me that which was otherwise. **1661** Boyle *Style of Script.* 148 The Complaint was ordinary, That the Reading of the Bible untaught them the Purity of the Roman Language. **1732** Berkeley *Alciphr.* v. § 24 Gentlemen are untaught by the world what they have been taught at the college. **1743** Francis tr. *Hor., Odes* II. ii. 19 But Virtue can the Croud unteach Their false, mistaken Forms of Speech. **1814** Byron *Lara* I. iv, His faults..Might be untaught him by his varied lot.

**2.** *absol.* To undo previous knowledge or teaching.

**1531** Elyot *Gov.* I. xv, It is difficulte to put out of the mynde that whiche is ones settilled,..and verily moche more to unteache than to teache. **1573** Tusser *Husb.* (1878) 63 To teach and vnteach in a schoole is vnmeete. *a* **1589** Palfreyman *Baldwin's Mor. Philos.* (1600) 74 The..burthen beeing..verily much more to vnteach then to teach. **1839** Bailey *Festus* 317 Once—teach and unteach—nay, to use more arts Than would outdo the Devil of his throne.

**3.** To remove from the mind (something known or taught) by different teaching.

**1562** Turner *Herbal* II. 57, I will be content..to vntech my error, whiche I haue taught before. **1633** T. Adams *Exp. 2 Peter* II. 12 That the holy Ghost should sit in the Chaire, to crosse and vnteach their principles. **1643** Sir T. Browne *Relig. Med.* II. § 8 Wee doe but learne to day, what our better advanced judgements will unteach to morrow. **1709** O. Dykes *Eng. Prov.* (ed. 2) 92 Over-grown Habits may be untaught by diligent Care. **1801** *Monthly Mag.* XII. 590 Must not the Anti-gallicans seek fresh sophists to unteach all their lessons of the last decennium? **1857** Ellis & Blackburn *Rep. Cases Q. Bench* VII. 190 Reasons..instilled into her in the process of unteaching those prayers.

Hence **Untea·ching** *vbl. sb.*

**1876** W. Cory *Lett. & Jrnls.* (1897) 414 The inevitable *un*teaching of young men, the purging from delusion.

**Untea·chable,** *a.* [Un-[1] 7 b.]

**1.** Incapable of being instructed.

*c* **1475** *Cath. Angl.* 378/2 (A.), Vn Techeabylle, *indocibilis.* **1580** Hollyband, *Indocile*, vntractable, vnteachable. **1594** T. B. *La Primaud. Fr. Acad.* II. 188 The ignorant person that knoweth not himselfe..is as vnteachable a beast as can be. **1645** Milton *Tetrach.* 42 Our Saviour at no time exprest any great desire to teach the obstinate and unteachable Pharises. **1707** *Reflex. upon Ridicule* 387 They are more unteachable, more heady, more interested. **1797** Coleridge *Osorio* IV. iv. 182 And so the babe grew up..A pretty boy, but most unteachable. **1871** Meredith *H. Richmond* xlvii, I chafed at his unteachable spirit.

*absol.* and as *sb.* **1819** Shelley *Cyclops* 492 Let us with some comic spell Teach the yet unteachable. **1850** Carlyle *Latter-day Pamph.* ii. 14 If I had schoolmasters,..do you imagine I would set them on teaching a set of unteachables..?

**2.** Incapable of being imparted by teaching.

*a* **1667** Petty in Sprat *Hist. R. Soc.* 306 This being infinite and almost unteachable by words. **1813** Scott *Rokeby* I. xxvi, His was minstrel's skill, he caught The art unteachable, untaught. **1860** Emerson *Cond. Life* v. (1861) 116 We are continually surprised with graces..not only unteachable, but undescribable. **1867** Lewes *Hist. Philos.* (ed. 3) I. 215 Opinions..which in other dialogues Socrates is made to exhibit as untaught, perhaps unteachable.

Hence **Untea·chableness.**

**1607** Hieron *Wks.* I. 462 Doe not ignorant persons continue in blindnes and vnteachablenes? **1702** Penn *Fruits Solit.* II. § 243 The worst part of this Vanity is its Unteachableness. **1850** L. Hunt *Autobiog.* II. 79 When kings themselves tried hard to make honest men republicans by their apparent unteachableness.

**Untea·ching,** *ppl. a.* (Un-[1] 10.)

**1587** Fenner *Def. Ministers* 137 The Senate of teaching and vnteaching Elders. **1610** Bp. Hall *Apol. Brownists* xxvii. 70 What Congregation of Christendome..affoorded you the necessary patterne of an vnteaching Pastor, or an vnfeeding Teacher? **1642** Milton *Apol. Smect.* 56 The Prelats..after their preferment most usually change the teaching labour of the word, into the unteaching ease of Lordship over consciences, and purses.

**Untea·m,** *v.* [Un-[2] 4 b.] *trans.* To unyoke.

**1548** Elyot, *Interiungo*, to vnteeme the horses, that they maie reste. **1592** Warner *Alb. Eng.* VIII. xlii. 158 Our Cattell vnto stronger draughts we..would vnteame. **1667** Jer. Taylor *Gt. Exemp.* (ed. 4) II. 310 Since Justice and Authority laid by the Rods and Axes as soon as the Sun unteamed his chariot. **1675** Cotton *Scoffer Scoft* 81 Let the Hours unteam thy Horses.

*absol.* **1662** J. Davies tr. *Olearius' Voy. Ambass.* 413 The Muscovian Ambassador having cudgell'd one of the Waggoners, all the rest would unteam and return homewards.

**Untea·rable,** *a.* (Un-[1] 7 b.)

**1648** Hexham II, *Onverscheurlick*, Vntearable. **1859** F. Francis *Newton Dogvane* iv, The pudding appeared,..an indigestible mass, composed of untearable steak. **1900** Pollok & Thom *Sports Burma* 252 Shooting-suits..of some strong untearable material.

**Untea·sed,** *ppl. a.* (Un-[1] 8.) [**1775** Ash.] **1843** E. Jones *Sens. & Event* 71 These multitudinous varying boughs, Unteased with leaves slept still. **Untea·seled,** *ppl. a.* (Un-[1] 8.) [**1775** Ash.] **1877** C. Geikie *Christ* II. 38 A piece of raw unteazled cloth.

**Unte·chnical,** *a.* (Un-[1] 7.)

**1845** *Encycl. Metrop.* II. 751/1 These authorities are of two kinds, untechnical and technical. **1860** Geo. Eliot *Mill on Fl.* III. vii, Tom's untechnical mind. **1882** Farrar *Early Chr.* I. 149 The word occurs but once in his letter, and that in its purely general and untechnical signification.

**Unte·chnically,** *adv.* (Un-[1] 11. Cf. prec.) **1818** Cruise *Digest* (ed. 2) IV. 381 The intention of the parties, however untechnically expressed. **Unte·dded,** *ppl. a.* (Un-[1] 8 + Ted *v.*[1]) *c* **1380** Wyclif *Sel. Wks.* II. 301 Þes lumpis failen here, as mowen gras þat were untedded. **Untee·m,** *v.* [Un-[2] 3 + Teem *v.*[1]] *trans.* To unburden, discharge. **1635** [Glapthorne] *Lady Mother* III. i, Lest the full clouds..unteeme their big wombl laps And raise a sudden deluge. **1683** in J. Russell *Haigs* (1881) 314 It seems to me that Europe is unteaming herself to plant these Western parts of the world. **Untee·med,** *ppl. a. dial.* [Un-[1] 8 + Teem *v.*[2]] Unemptied. **1641** H. Best *Farm. Bks.* (Surtees) 53 Wee sette (att night) the..two last waines to the mowe brest, and leave them unteamed till the morninge. **Untei·nded,** *ppl. a. Sc.* [Un-[1] 8.] Untithed. **1527** *Burgh Rec. Prestwick* (Maitl. Club) 52 For the wrangus takin in of peis onteendyt. **1663** *Min. Baron Court of Stitchill* (S.H.S.) 25 For hydeing and conceiling of his cornes in the yaird unteynded. †**Untei·nted,** *ppl. a. Obs.* [Un-[1] 8. Cf. F. *teinté.*] Untinted, uncoloured. **1745** *Phil. Trans.* XLIII. 525 [He] produced several Samples of the Apples; an unteinted Russetting; a Russetting changed in Complexion. †**Unte·ld,** *v. Obs.*[−1] [Un-[2] 4 + Teld *sb.* b.] *trans.* To clear of tents or awnings. *a* **1400** *Morte Arth.* 737 Qwen all was schyppede that scholde, they schounte no lengere, Bot vntelde [*MS.* ventelde] them tyte. †**Unte·ll,** *v. Obs.* (Un-[2] 3.) ? **1603** Heywood *Woman killed w. Kindness* (1617) G 2, That time could turne vp his swift sandy glasse, To vntell the dayes, and to redeeme these houres.

**Unte·llable,** *a.* [Un-[1] 7 b, 5 b.] Unspeakable, unutterable; indescribable.

In earlier use somewhat rare. Freq. from *c* 1880. The absence of evidence from 16th to 19th c. is remarkable.

**1382** Wyclif *Ecclus.* xxxvi. 16 Fulfil Syon with thin vntellable vertues, and thi puple with thi glorie. *c* **1410** *Lantern Liȝt* 136 Feer intollerable, drede vntellable. *c* **1425** *St. Eliz. of Spalbeck* in *Anglia* VIII. 113 With sobbynges & weymentynges vntelabil. *c* **1440** *Promp. Parv.* 367/2 Ontelleable, *inenarrabilis.* **1513** Douglas *Æneid* I. xii. 6 Thi desyir, lady, is Renewing of ontellable sorow. **1552** Abp. Hamilton *Catech.* (1884) 16 The glore of the saule quhilk is untelabil.

**1830** Mrs. Opie in Brightwell *Mem.* (1854) 246 It fills me with untellable wonder and admiration of him. **1865** Trench *Gustavus Adolphus* ii. 76 Which, though not absolutely untellable, had yet better remain untold. **1886** Ruskin *Præterita* I. 422 The joy of approved love, and the untellable, incalculable motive of its sympathy.

Hence **Unte·llably** *adv.*

*c* **1425** *St. Eliz. of Spalbeck* in *Anglia* VIII. 109/21 Whanne þese and oþere lyke are doon often and vntellably. **1513** Douglas *Æneid* VIII. ix. 38 The fader than..full tenderly Apone him hingis, wepand ontellably. **1889** *Missionary Herald* Feb. 50 [The character of the people] is terribly bad, ..untellably bloodthirsty, cruel, and lascivious.

**Unte·lling,** *ppl. a. north.* and *Sc.* [Un-[1] 10.]

†**1.** Innumerable, countless. *Obs.*

*a* **1300** *Cursor M.* 2107 Inde, and pers, and arabi,..And mani oþer vntelland contre. *Ibid.* 6441 Þis ilk folk was vntelland, þat moyses had vnder hand. **1816** G. Muir *Clydesdale Minstrelsy* 7 The royal banner that has splendid flown Its annual course for ages past untellin'. **1825** Jamieson, *Untelling*, adj.,..denoting what cannot be counted. Roxb.

**2.** = Untellable *a.*

**1823** Hogg *Shepherd's Cal.* i, It was untelling what land that man possessed. **1885** [J. Tod] *More Bits fr. Blinkbonny* i, It was untellin' what Tibbie did for poor Mrs. Gemmell.

†**Unte·med,** *ppl. a. Obs.* [OE. *untemed* (Un-[1] 8), = MLG. *untem(m)et*, MDa. *utæm(me)t*, Da. *utæmmet*. Cf. OE. *ungetemed*, MDu. *ongetemmet*, *-temt* (Du. *ongetemd*), MLG. *ungetemet*, G. *ungezähmt.*] Untamed.

*a* **1000** *Gloss.* in Wr.-Wülcker 226 *Edomitus* [sic], untemed, wilde. *a* **1100** *Cambridge Ps.* xxxii. 17 Leas *vel* untemed hors. **1388** Wyclif *Ecclus.* xxx. 8 An hors vntemyd..schal ascape hard. **1398** Trevisa *Barth. De P. R.* XVIII. lxxvii. (Bodl. MS.), Onager is a wilde asse..and suche asses been grete..& vntemed. *c* **1420** *Prose Life Alex.* 8 A prynce of Macedoyne broghte þe kyng a horse vn-temed, a grete and a faire.

**Unte·mper,** *v.* (Un-[2] 3.) **1685** Cotton tr. *Montaigne* I. 233 Examples have demonstrated to us that..the study of sciences does more soften and untemper the courages of men than any way fortifie and incite them. **1758** Reid tr. *Macquer's Chem.* I. 65 By the same operation Steel may be untempered. †**Unte·mperable,** *a.* (Un-[1] 7 b, 5 b.) = Intemperable *a.* **1571** tr. *Buchanan's Detect. Mary* (1572) H iij, A woman..in..corrupt affectiounis vnbridelit, vntemperable by her estayt, raging by hyr power.

†**Unte·mperance.** *Obs.* (Un-[1] 12 and 5 b.)

**1541** R. Copland *Galyen's Terap.* 2 A. iv, The fyrste maner [of ulcers] haboundeth by the vntemperaunce of the flesshe subiecte. **1587** Fleming *Contn. Holinshed* III. 1268 The successors may be taught by their predecessors,..sobrietie by their vntemperance. **1614** Gorges *Lucan* IV. 124 The hazards that ensue,..From the vncertaine motions grew, When then the aires vntemperance drew.

†**Unte·mperant,** *a.*: see Untemperate *a.* 2 (quot. 1388).

†**Unte·mperate,** *a. Obs.* [Un-[1] 7, 5 b.]

**1. a.** Of weather, etc.: = Intemperate *a.* 1.

**1525** Ld. Berners *Froiss.* II. cxxiv. 353 In Castyle there is no thynge but harde rockes and Mountaynes,..and an vntemperate ayre. *a* **1548** Hall *Chron., Hen. VI*, 137 Of these vntemperate stormes rose suche a scacety, that wheat was sold at iii.s. iiii.d. the busshell. **1614** *Archdeaconry of Essex* (MS.) *Minutes* fol. 101 [The weather] was wett and vntemperate.

**b.** Distempered, disordered. *rare*[−1].

**1539** Elyot *Cast. Helthe* (1541) 17 b, [To] the bodyes untemperate, suche meates or drynkes are to be gyven, which be in power contrary to the distemperance.

**2.** = Intemperate *a.* 2.

**1388** Wyclif *Ecclus.* xxxi. 23 Colre..and gnawyng to an vndiscreet either vntemperat [*C. C. Coll. Camb. MS.* vntemperaunt] man. **1561** T. Norton *Calvin's Inst.* I. xiii. 43 b, [They] that do delite in an vntemperate desyre of speculacion. **1589** Cooper *Admon.* 2 A lamentable state of time it is, wherin such vntemperat boldenes is permitted. **1607** Markham *Cavel.* II. 101 If the Ryder haue an vntemperate hand, which euer pulleth..vpon the horses mouth. *a* **1633** Cary *Edw. II* (1680) 16 The King, by his untemperate and undiscreet actions, had lost the hearts of his People.

**3.** = Intemperate *a.* 3.

*a* 1589 Palfreyman *Baldwin's Mor. Philos.* (1600) 116 Youth vntemperate, and full of carnall affections, quickly turneth the bodye into age. 1592 Nashe *P. Penilesse* G ij b, Vntemperate venerie, and that hatefull sinne of selfe-loue. 1613 Shirley *Trav. Persia* 55 Hee that can restraine himselfe from being transported by vntemperate appetites. 1625 Shirley *Love Tricks* ii. ii, I would not leaue Rufaldo for a world Of rash, vntemperate youth.

Hence † **Unte·mperately** *adv. Obs.*

1398 Trevisa *Barth. De P. R.* xvii. clxxxviii. (Bodl. MS.), Wyne drinkinge vntemperatlych is to man kinde..venym. 1548 Udall, etc. *Erasm. Par. John* ii. 14 b, When their geastes..haue their mouthes out of taste, & powre in drinke vntemperately. 1560 Daus tr. *Sleidane's Comm.* 237 b, They hearde also howe vntemperately the Freers that were collocutours handled the matter. 1602 Segar *Hon., Mil. & Civ.* iv. i. 209 He that immoderately and vntemperately pampereth his own body.

† **Unte·mperateness.** *Obs.* [Un-1 12, 5 b.]

**1.** Distempered physical condition.

1398 Trevisa *Barth. De P. R.* xvii. ii. (Bodl. MS.), þe temporat place bringeþ oute of vntemporatenes and makeþ it gode to ete. 1541 R. Copland *Galyen's Terap.* C iv, Some dysease of the lyuer, or the weykenes of the party greued, the which is none other thynge but a clere and notable vntemperatnes. 1580 Blundeville *Horsemanship* iv. 36 b, To learne at the Physicians handes, which..as touching the weakenesse of the Liuer, proceeding of the vntemperatenesse thereof, will bid you to heale euerie such vntemperatenesse by his contrarie. 1597 A. M. *Guillemeau's Fr. Chirurg.* 35 b/1 The glowinge Cautery..amendeth the vntemperatnes of that parte. 1621 Burton *Anat. Mel.* i. ii. v. iii, An innate burning vntemperatnesse, turning blood and choler into melancholy.

**2.** = Intemperateness 1.

1577 tr. *Bullinger's Decades* 238/2 A dwelling place conueniently situated against the vntemperatenesse of the ayre. 1594 R. Ashley tr. *Loys le Roy* 26 The vntemperatenes of Winter, and Sommer. *a* 1656 Ussher *Ann.* (1658) 723 The work..being hindred by no untemperatenesse of the weather. 1665 Manley *Grotius' Low C. Wars* 405 Many of his men, ..by the untemperateness of the Air,..dyed. 1758 J. S. *Le Dran's Observ. Surg.* (1771) Dict., *Intemperies*, an Unseasonableness, Untemperateness.

**3.** = Intemperateness 2.

1578 Timme *Calvin on Gen.* 213 By reason of vntemperatnesse they doe degenerate from their nature. 1599 Minsheu *Span. Gram.* To Students, Vntemperatenes, Vnshamefastnes, Vnfaithfulnes, and Vnthankefulnes. 1637 Saltonstall *Eusebius' Constantine* 137 Untemperatenesse of life, covetousnesse, murder.

†**Unte·mperature.** *Obs.*[−1] [Un-1 12, 5 b.] Distempered state. *a* 1604 Hanmer *Chron. Irel.* (1809) 396 [After the] Earthquake..there followed..a continuall untemperature of the ayre, with a filthy skurfe.

**Unte·mpered,** *ppl. a.* [Un-1 8. Cf. MDu. *ongetempert*, Du. *ongetemperd*, MHG. *ungetempert*.]

**1.** Unregulated; not moderated or controlled.

1377 Langl. *P. Pl.* B. ix. 102 Wolde neuere þe faithful fader his fithel were vntempred. *a* 1547 Surrey *Eccl.* v. 52 What lyef leede testeye men that consume their dayes In inwarde freets, untempred hates. 1561 Norton & Sackv. *Gorboduc* iii. i, Your eldest sonne, misledd By traitours framde of young vntempered wittes Assembleth force against your yonger sonne. 1631 A. Wilson *Swisser* iii. ii, I wilbee your Stickler, You too vntemper'd Vermin! 1808 Wm. Mitford *Hist. Greece* I. 584 Every untempered government must be jealous. *Ibid.* III. 72 The spirit of party will pervade a state with..untempered and..lasting violence.

**b.** Unmodified, unqualified. Freq. const. *by*.

1768–74 Tucker *Lt. Nat.* (1834) II. 603 The utmost rigour of legal justice untempered by equity. 1794 S. Williams *Vermont* 203 The spirit of monarchy, untempered by representation. 1847 H. Rogers *Ess.* (1860) I. 240 His eyes ache with that too untempered brilliance. 1868 Freeman *Norm. Conq.* x. II. 481 Rigid justice, untempered by mercy.

**2.** Of lime or mortar: Not properly mixed and prepared. Also in fig. context.

*c* 1440 *Pallad. on Husb.* iii. 395 Vntempred lime yf with the graffes be Putte in the plages. 1535 Coverdale *Ezek.* xiii. 11 Ye wall, that ye haue dawbed with vntempered morter. 1637 Gillespie *Eng. Pop. Cerem.* iii. i. 7 He laboureth to plaister over his Superstition with the vntempered morter of this quidditative distinction. 1661 Cowley *Cromwell* Wks. 1906 II. 362 That none of these untempered Mortars can hold out against the next blast of Wind. 1755 Young *Centaur* v. 311 This castle was built out of the various ruins of many demolish'd forts of infidelity,..and cemented with untemper'd mortar. 1826 Southey *Vind. Eccl. Angl.* 44, I have not been labouring in the quarries for thirty years, that I should build with untempered mortar. 1896 A. D. Coleridge *Eton in Forties* 8 His gloves..[being] bedaubed..with untempered mortar.

*transf.* 1781 Cowper *Hope* 627 To storm the citadels they build in air, And smite th' untemper'd wall, 'tis death to spare.

**b.** Not properly digested or concocted.

1822 Good *Study Med.* II. 757 The untempered fluid contained in the tubercles. *Ibid.* IV. 695 A defective secretion of the rete mucosum, which..seems to be..untempered or imperfectly elaborated.

**c.** Unhardened.

1820 Good *Syst. Nosology* 427 Bones untempered in their substance, and incapable of affording their proper support. 1825 J. Nicholson *Operat. Mechanic* 322 A screw of untempered steel. 1839 Noad *Electricity* 239 A disc of untempered steel.

**Unte·mpering,** *ppl. a.* (Un-1 10.) 1599 Shaks. *Hen. V*, v. ii. 241 My blood begins to flatter me, that thou doo'st [love me], notwithstanding the poore and vntempering effect of my Visage. **Unte·mpested,** *a.* (Un-1 9.) 1846 Worcester (citing Millman). 1890 'R. Boldrewood' *Col. Reformer* (1891) 244 The serene untempested heavens of the isles of the blest. **Untempe·stuous,** *a.* (Un-1 7, 5 c.) 1864 Swinburne *Atalanta* 400 Like kindled lights in untempestuous heaven. **Unte·mpled,** *a.* (Un-1 9.) 1850 S. Dobell *Roman* v. 61 A bare Untempled spot, unblest, unconsecrate. 1855 Bailey *Mystic* 16 He, the untempled God, above man's thought. **Unte·mporary,** *a.* (Un-1 7.) 1784 R. Bage *Barham Downs* I. 235 Oh, for the actual, undisturbed, untemporary enjoyment of two such friends! **Unte·mptable,** *a.* (Un-1 7 b.) 1819 *Monthly Mag.* XLVIII. 306 With this second marriage, the untemptable Adam is extremely delighted. 1837 Sir F. Palgrave *Merch. & Friar* iv. 243 They wish to earn the character of the most untemptable and rigid justice.

**Unte·mpted,** *ppl. a.* [Un-1 8.]

**1.** Not tempted; unassailed by temptation.

1607 Beaum. & Fl. *Woman-Hater* iv. i, Can you imagine A Maid, whose beauty could not suffer her To live thus long untempted? 1652 Bp. Hall *Invis. World* iii. xii, Those objects of dread, and horror,..not so confined to their hell, as to leave us untempted. 1716 Gay *Trivia* ii. 287 Careful observers,..Untempted,..contemn the jugler's feats, Pass by the Meuse, nor try the thimble's cheats. 1757 [see Untainted *ppl. a.* 4 b]. 1809–14 Wordsw. *Excurs.* viii. 259 Those..yet untempted to forsake The simple occupations of their sires. 1865 Grosart *Mem. H. Palmer* 44 The issue of profound meditation,..not untempted of doubt. 1890 'R. Boldrewood' *Col. Reformer* (1891) 366 An unworn, untempted nature.

**b.** Not due to or resulting from temptation or enticement.

1744 Akenside *Ep. Curio* 67 Yet must you one untempted vileness own. 1753 Fielding *Eliz. Canning* Wks. 1903 XI. 39 A pitch of wanton and untempted inhumanity, beyond all possibility of belief. 1871 Ruskin *Fors Clav.* vii. 23 There is no physical crime..so without parallel in its untempted guilt, as the making of war machinery.

**2.** Unattempted, untried. *rare*[−1].

1744 Akenside *Pleas. Imag.* i. 573 Let the breath of thy extended praise Inspire my kindling bosom to the height Of this untempted theme.

†**Unte·mpter.** *Obs. rare.* (Un-1 12.) 1382 Wyclif *Jas.* i. 13 Sotheli God is vntempter [L. *intentator*] of yuel thingis, forsothe he temptith no man. **Unte·mptible,** *a.*, **-ibly,** *adv.* (Un-1 7, 11.) 1828 E. Irving *Serm.* I. p. lxvii, Infallibility and holiness untemptible..in that which heretofore had been human, fallible and temptible flesh. 1858 Bushnell *New Life* xiii, Absolute purity is untemptible, as in God. *Ibid.*, God..is untemptible. *Ibid.*, He can make us untemptibly pure.

**Unte·mpting,** *ppl. a.* (Un-1 10.)

1824 Lytton in *Life & Lett.* (1883) I. 294 The poor animal ..bent his head languidly over the untempting food. 1859 F. E. Paget *Curate Cumberworth* 353 A schoolboy repugnance to go back to my smoky lodgings, and Mrs. Ferrall's untempting fare.

Hence **Unte·mptingly** *adv.*

[1847 Webster.] *a* 1856 H. Miller *Rambles Geologist* (1858) 357 The day was still unfavorable, and the [geological] sections seemed untemptingly indifferent.

**Unte·mptingness.** (Un-1 12. Cf. prec.) 1646 Hammond *Sinnes* 12 The naturall intrinsecall untemptingnesse of that sinne. **Unte·msed,** *ppl. a.* [Un-1 8.] Unsifted. 1641 Best *Farm. Bks.* (Surtees) 105 Wee have received a pecke and a halfe more of tempsed meale from the one, than wee have had of the other, of untempsed meale.

**Untenabi·lity.** (Un-1 12, 5 c. Cf. next.)

1644 Prynne & Walker *Fiennes' Trial* 76 The weaknesse and untenability of it was no ground of its surrender. 1841 Herschel *Ess.* (1857) 188 The complete untenability of a simple aqueous doctrine. 1884 *Law Times* 1 Nov. 7/1 The untenability of the modern American contention.

**Unte·nable,** *a.* [Un-1 7 b and 5 b.]

**1.** Incapable of being held against attack.

1647 Clarendon *Hist. Reb.* viii. § 60 Having lain so long with such a strength before so vile and untenable a place, without reducing it. *a* 1671 Ld. Fairfax *Mem.* (1699) 9 In a council of war the Town was judged untenable. 1769 Robertson *Chas. V*, iv. Wks. 1813 V. 418 That ill-provided and untenable fort. 1796 *Campaigns 1793–4*, I. i. ix. 91 The post..was abandoned as untenable. 1844 H. H. Wilson *Brit. India* II. 54 Measures were taken to render the position of the besiegers untenable. 1879 *Cassell's Techn. Educ.* I. 287 The fire of the Prussian artillery rendered the interior of the works..untenable.

**b.** *fig.* (Cf. sense 2.)

1692 Dryden *Juvenal* (1697) p. lii, Casaubon..thinks it time to abandon a Post that was untenable. He acknowledges that Persius is obscure in some places. 1765 Sterne *Tr. Shandy* viii. xxxiv, If there was any one post more untenable than the rest, he would be sure to throw himself into it. 1807 *Med. Jrnl.* XVII. 534 An impartial retrospect ..will..convince Mr. Dawson, that he has occupied untenable ground. 1880 McCarthy *Own Times* lxiii. IV. 429 He withdrew from what he felt to be an untenable position.

**c.** Incapable of being occupied or retained.

1699 Boyer *Dict. Royal* s.v., His new Lodgings were made in a Moment as untenable as the others. 1721 Amherst *Terræ Fil.* No. 40 (1726) 211 Not content with..college-offices, they have lately found out a method of augmenting them with good livings, which, according to statutes and prescription, are untenable together. 1860 *Merc. Marine Mag.* VII. 291 A ship could lay there in safety when Table bay would be untenable. 1883 Stevenson *Silverado Sq.* 5 The site has proved untenable.

**2.** Incapable of being maintained or supported.

1650 Fuller *Pisgah* ii. xiii. 268 A Tenet unteinable with truth. 1664 H. More *Apol.* 507, I am..far from rejecting or condemning the Opinion of the Schools from being altogether untenable. 1724 Waterland *Farther Vindic. Christ's Divin.* Introd., Their main Scheme appearing so gross, and so untenable, that they..are..ashamed to own it. 1835 Thirlwall *Greece* iii. I. 78 A not untenable hypothesis. 1886 *Law Rep.* 31 Chanc. Div. 365 The claim is of the most untenable description.

Hence **Unte·nableness.**

1833 G. S. Faber *Recapit. Apostasy* 40 The untenableness of the various names..crudely propounded by the wantonness of expositorial licence. 1846 Lewes *Hist. Philos.* IV. 95 The untenableness of the theory of innate ideas.

**Unte·nant,** *v.* [Un-2 4, 5.]

**1.** *trans.* To dislodge from a dwelling.

1614 T. Adams *Devils Banquet* 104 Hee gets possession of their affections, whence all the power of man cannot vntenant him.

**2.** To deprive of a tenant or tenants.

1640 Shirley *St. Patrick for Irel.* i. i, You know I can Untenant hell, dispeople the wide air. 1796 Coleridge *Destiny of Nations* 35 All Those blind Omniscients, those Almighty Slaves Untenanting creation of its God. 1799 *Monthly Rev.* XXVIII. 528 It is only wonderful that the official cadastres should not wholly have untenanted the soil. 1832 R. Chambers *Eminent Scotsmen* I. 46 The Reformation untenanted its walls. 1846 M'Gee *Irish Writers* 30 Dempster..began to untenant every niche in the national temple of Ireland. 1861 Ld. Lytton & Fane *Tannhäuser* 67, I, whose heart of all that lived in it He hath untenanted.

**3.** To depart from, to quit.

1795 Coleridge *Lines at Shurton Bars* iv, Untenanting its beauteous clay My Sara's soul has wing'd its way.

**Unte·nantable,** *a.* (Un-1 7 b.)

*a* 1661 Fuller *Worthies, Essex* i. (1662) 347 Winchester Castle was..ordered to be made Untenable; but the over-officious malice of such who executed the Order (wilfully mistaking the word) made it Untenantable. 1772 *Ann. Reg., Chron.* 141/1, 400 houses..destroyed, or rendered untenantable. 1774 *Phil. Trans.* LXV. 274 They may so abound with fleas as to become untenantable. 1833 Whewell *Astron.* vii. 64 The apparently frozen and untenantable regions in the neighbourhood of the pole. 1862 Galton *Vac. Tour.* 208 Beds untenantable, charges unconscionable, is the state of things now as then.

**Unte·nanted,** *ppl. a.* [Un-1 8.] Not occupied by a tenant or tenants.

1673 Temple *Ess. Irel.* Wks. 1720 I. 117 The Country seems to be full stock'd, no Ground that I hear of being untenanted. 1677 Yarranton *Eng. Improv.* 16 There needed not one House to stand empty and untenanted. 1741 Richardson *Pamela* II. 203 A pretty little Farm and House, untenanted. 1808 Scott *Marm.* ii. Introd., All silent now —for now are still Thy bowers, untenanted Bowhill. 1887 *Spectator* 22 Oct. 1413 There are not now so many untenanted spaces on the globe suitable for human habitation.

*fig.* 1830 Carlyle *Misc.* (1872) III. 53 In that hour thou wilt look back on thy untenanted life.

**Unte·nded,** *ppl. a.* [Un-1 8.]

1598 Florio, *Incustodito*, not kept, not looked vnto, vntended. 1732 Lyttelton *Progr. Love* i. 17 His flock.. untended lay, To ev'ry savage a defenceless prey. 1736 Thomson *Liberty* v. 10 Let Asia's woods, Untended, yield the vegetable fleece. 1794 Wordsw. *Guilt & Sorrow* lxiii, Nor shall she perish there, untended and alone! 1807 J. Barlow *Columb.* vi. 160 He comes..untended by his usual train. 1854 H. Miller *Sch. & Schm.* xi, The hedges [were] gapped by the almost untended cattle. 1861 *Peaks, Passes & Glac.* Ser. ii. I. 163 The same fitful glare from the pine-log fire, as the untended embers crumble together!

**Unte·nder,** *a.* [Un-1 7.]

**1.** Not tender in dealing with others; ungentle, unkind. Also const. *of*.

1605 Shaks. *Lear* i. i. 108 So young, and so vntender? 1611 — *Cymb.* iii. iv. 12 Why tender'st thou that Paper to me, with A looke vntender? *c* 1678 J. B. in *Spirit of Popery* (1680) 75 Is it reasonable..to be thus tender of a few men, and untender of the grand Concerns of..our Master? ?*c* 1710 Congreve *Lament. Helen over Hector* 9 In all which time ..Not one untender Word or look of Scorn, Which I too often have from others born. 1774 Beattie *Minstrel* ii. xxxi, Let untender thoughts afar be driven. 1825 Lamb *Elia* ii. *Wedding*, Is there not something untender..in the hurry which a beloved child is sometimes in to tear herself from the paternal stock. 1898 G. W. E. Russell *Collect. & Recoll.* ii. 14 In those untender days he was considered too delicate to remain at a Public School.

†**2.** Not having a tender conscience; lacking in religious susceptibility. Also *transf. Obs.*

*a* 1658 Durham *Comm. Rev.* (1660) 187 We will find, that many who have been untender, have had hand at this work. 1680 in *Proc. Soc. Antiq. Scot.* XLV. 235 This wofull dreadfull defection in these two emenent men is to be lamented. ..Among them Mr. Castairs elder is the most unsound and untender. 1730 T. Boston *Mem.* (1899) 37 He, being both a weak and untender man, was unacceptable to the parish. *Ibid.* 136 The untender carriage of some ministers in Nithsdale. 1765 J. Brown *Chr. Jrnl.* 262 Untender professors loudly bawl against the sins of others. *a* 1812 Maclean *Disc.* Wks. 1848 VI. 195 By an untender walk guilt has accumulated upon the conscience.

**3.** Not immature.

1879 Bain *Educ. as Science* xii. 416 The effect produced on tender years will be submerged in the un-tender years that follow.

Hence **Unte·nderness.**

*a* 1658 Durham *Comm. Rev.* (1660) 181 There was much.. unwatchfulness and untenderness in both these respects before God. 1680 in *Proc. Soc. Antiq. Scot.* XLV. 248 An untenderness and sinfull love of life. 1724 E. Erskine *Serm.* Wks. (1791) 122 If through untenderness ye provoke him to withdraw. 1883 *Century Mag.* 55 This education..he had never got.—Hence his untenderness.

**Unte·ndered,** *ppl. a.* [Un-1 8.] Not offered. 1607 Middleton *Michaelmas Term* iii. iv. 45 Is not the day past, the money untendered? 1611 Shaks. *Cymb.* iii. i. 10 Cassibulan.. granted Rome a Tribute, Yeerely three thousand pounds; which (by thee) lately Is left vntender'd.

**Unte·nderly,** *adv.* (Un-1 11.)

?*a* 1400 *Morte Arth.* 1144 Vn-tenderly fro þe toppe þai tiltine to-gederz. *c* 1425 Wyntoun *Cron.* vii. ii. 128 (Cott. MS.), He sende þaim in to Normondy, Þar tretyt þai war wntendyrly. 1651 Warriston *Diary* (S.H.S.) II. 143, I heard of Suynton's..leaving of all family exercises..and walking untenderly on the Lords Day. *a* 1658 Durham *Comm. Rev.* (1660) 188 A Minister..prone to foster their securitie, or rifle their wounds untenderly. 1780 S. J. Pratt *Emma Corbett* (ed. 4) III. 154, I have too much contributed to her happiness for her to treat me untenderly. 1856 Mrs. Browning *Aur. Leigh* ii. 823 If I spoke untenderly This morning,..pardon it. 1868 Browning *Ring & Bk.* vi. 196 The snow-white soul that angels fear to take Untenderly.

**Unte·nible,** *a.* [Un-$^1$ 7.] Untenable. 1783 Hailes *Antiq. Chr. Ch.* 135 A conclusion most illogical and untenible. †**Unte·nnanted,** *ppl. a. Obs.*$^{-1}$ [Un-$^1$ 8.] Not furnished with a tenon. 1678 Moxon *Mech. Exerc.* v. 84 Make also a Tennant on each un-Tennanted end of the Stiles. **Unte·nt,** *v.* (Un-$^2$ 4, 4 b.) 1606 Shaks. *Tr. & Cr.* ii. iii. 178 Why, will he not vpon our faire request, Vntent his person, and share the ayre with vs? 1611 Florio, *Stendare*, to remooue the tents of a camp, to vntent. **Untenta·culated,** *ppl. a.* (Un-$^1$ 8.) *a* 1830 McCulloch *Attributes* (1843) III. 394 The untentaculated Medusæ.

**Unte·nted,** *ppl. a.*$^1$ [Un-$^1$ 8 + Tent *v.*$^4$] Unprobed, undressed.

1605 Shaks. *Lear* i. iv. 322 Th' vntented woundings of a Father's curse Pierce euerie sense about thee. 1822 Milman *Martyr of Antioch* 65 With open and untented wounds. 1828 Scott *Aunt Margaret's Mirror* ad fin., The wounds of an untented conscience.

†**Unte·nted,** *ppl. a.*$^2$ *Obs.* [Un-$^1$ 8 + Tent *v.*$^2$] Not tempted. 1725 in Peterkin *Ork. & Zetl.* (1822) I. 223 The straight pathes of virtue and untented honesty.

**Unte·nted,** *ppl. a.*$^3$ *Sc.* or *arch.* [Un-$^1$ 8 + Tent *v.*$^1$] Unheeded, unregarded.

1791 J. Learmont *Poems* 61 The least untentit, lowse spoke word, Gars them draw the duellin' sword. *c* 1800 R. Gill *Elegy Pudding Lizzie* xiii, While busy time still jogged on, Unmark'd, untented. 1867 Morris *Jason* x. 300 Great herds of deer and neat,..Seeming all wild.., For quite untented here and there they ran.

**Unte·nted,** *ppl. a.*$^4$ [Un-$^1$ 8 + Tented *ppl. a.*] Not furnished with a tent or tents. 1891 *Cent. Dict.* s.v., An untented army;..an untented field.

**Unte·nty,** *a. Sc.* [Un-$^1$ 7.] Careless, heedless. 1819 Scott *Leg. Montrose* x, What is to become of me, if Gustavus.. should be lamed among their untenty hands! 1893 Stevenson *Catriona* vii, I would never be so untenty as to commit myself. †**Unte·rmed,** *ppl. a.* [Un-$^1$ 8.] Unbounded, unlimited. *c* 1586 C'tess Pembroke *Ps.* cv. ii, He eternally that treaty mindeth, Which him to us untearmed ages bindeth. 1633 Ford *Love's Sacr.* iii. iii, Thy reward..Shall be our speciall thanks, and loue vn-term'd. †**Unte·rminable,** *a. Obs.* (Un-$^1$ 7 b, 5 b.) *a* 1677 Manton *Serm. Ps. cxix.* (1725) 436/2 Eternal Duration implies an immutable and unterminable abode in Being. **Unte·rminably,** *adv.* (Un-$^1$ 11, 5 b.) 1631 R. Skene in A. Craig *Pilgr. & Hermit* 3 For the singular and ever bound duetie, wherevnto..I ever acknowledge my selfe to be vnterminably tied, to loue, serue, and honour, You and Yours. **Unte·rminated,** *ppl. a.* (Un-$^1$ 8.) [1775 Ash.] 1853 Kane *Grinnell Exp.* xxvii. (1856) 225 The broad, unterminated expanse of ice. 1891 E. T. Dixon *Found. Geom.* 33 Any unterminated straight line. **Unte·rminating,** *ppl. a.* (Un-$^1$ 10.) 1821 Scott *Biogr. Mem.* (1834) I. 368 The unterminating succession of misfortunes. **Unte·rraced,** *ppl. a.* (Un-$^1$ 8.) [1775 Ash.] 1879 Stevenson *Trav. Cevennes* 166 The ground, where it was unterraced, was usually too steep. †**Unte·rred,** *ppl. a. Obs.*$^{-1}$ [Un-$^1$ 8.] Uninterred. 1633 Marmion *Fine Companion* i. i, Those That lye unterr'd, wanting their funerall rites. **Unterre·strial,** *a.* (Un-$^1$ 7.) 1746 Young *Nt. Th.* ix. 1752 The natives of this world sublime, Of this so foreign, un-terrestrial sphere. 1813 Shelley *Q. Mab* vii. 175 No pain assailed His unterrestrial sense. **Unte·rrifiable,** *a.* (Un-$^1$ 7 b.) 1875 Helps *Soc. Press.* xxiii. 352 There remain no unterrifiable witnesses but children.

**Unterri·fic,** *a.* (Un-$^1$ 7.)

1788 H. Downman *Infancy* vi. 637 The stream Of lightning,..safe convey'd, In unterrific silence, to the ground. 1831 Carlyle *Sart. Res.* ii. iii, Not unterrific was the aspect; but we looked on it like brave youths. 1887 Ruskin *Præterita* II. 393 A majestic, but unterrific fortalice of cliff.

**Unte·rrified,** *ppl. a.* (Un-$^1$ 8.)

Also *U.S.* 'derisively applied to the Democratic party': 1832–63 in Thornton *Amer. Gloss.* s.v.

1609 Daniel *Civ. Wars* vi. lxxviii, Yet standes he stiffe, vndash't, vnterrifi'd. 1670 Flatman *Death of Albemarle* v, Ever unterrified his valour stood Like some tall rock amidst a sea of blood. 1753 Smollett *Ct. Fathom* xli, The chevalier, unterrified by this dreadful salutation, desired he would accompany him to a more convenient place. 1764 *Ann. Reg., Chron.* 87/1 The robin..comes in..unterrified by the number of persons. 1821 Shelley *Adonais* iv, He went, unterrified, Into the gulf of death. 1856 Olmsted *Slave States* 178 The attempt to suppress discussion has given every advantage to the unterrified partisans on both sides.

**Unte·rrifying,** *ppl. a.* (Un-$^1$ 10.)

1691 Norris *Pract. Disc.* 149 What a mild and unterrifying thing is Death to such a Man as this! 1821 Lamb *Elia* i. *Chapter on Ears*, The genuine unterrifying aspects of my pleasant-countenanced host and hostess. 1877 Swinburne *C. Brontë* 79 Lips already whitened..by the present shadow of unterrifying death.

†**Unte·state,** *a.* [Un-$^1$ 7, 5 b.] Intestate.

*c* 1440 *Jacob's Well* 20 Þe godys of here tenauntys þat dyen vntestate. 1559 *Richmond. Wills* (Surtees) 138 Not willinge to dye untestate,..I provide..this my last will. 1591 Savile *Tacitus, Hist.* ii. 89 If they dyed vntestate the ordinary course of the law..was obserued. 1600 Rowlands *Lett. Humours Blood* iv. 65 It was his fathers lucke of late to die Untestate. 1617 Minsheu. (Hence in Hexham.)

**Unte·sted,** *ppl. a.* [Un-$^1$ 8.]

†**1.** Intestate. *Obs.* (Cf. prec.)

1570 Foxe *A. & M.* (ed. 2) I. 409/1 The courte [of Rome]..aspired how to vsurpe the goods of them that die vntested. 1586 Spenser *Will* Wks. 1882 I. p. xvii, Suche as dye untestyd. 1608 in *T. Pont's Acc. Cunningham* (Maitl. Cl.) 183 Johne Blair..deceist vntestit in the moneth of Januar, 1604 zeiris.

**2.** Not tested or proved.

[1775 Ash.] 1828–32 Webster (citing *Adams' Lect.*). 1881 Fitch *Lect. Teach.* 179 To leave him unquestioned and untested. 1884 Church *Bacon* viii. 197 His whole doctrine of 'Forms'..is an example of loose and slovenly use of unexamined and untested ideas.

**Unte·sticled,** *ppl. a.* (Un-$^2$ 8, 4.) 1668 Wilkins *Real Char.* 291 So *Ox* is untesticled or gelt Bull. †**Unte·tche,** *Obs.*$^{-1}$ [Un-$^1$ 4 b + *tetche* Tache *sb.*$^1$] Wrongful act; fault. *c* 1350 *Will. Palerne* 509 His maners were so menskful, a-mende hem miȝt none, & seþþe forsoþe til þis time non vntetche he ne wrouȝt. **Unte·ther,** *v.* (Un-$^2$ 4 b.) [1775 Ash.] 1888 W. G. Black *Heligoland* 9 The herd-girl who comes to untether the patient sheep. **Unte·thered,** *ppl. a.* (Un-$^1$ 8.) [1775 Ash.] 1826 W. A. Miles *D. Barrow* 5 [These evidences, etc.] give a free untethered flight to the imagination. 1907 *Daily Chron.* 6 June 5/5 Old untethered horses and donkeys..browsing on the slopes. **Untew·ed,** *ppl. a.* [Un-$^1$ 8 + Tew *v.*$^1$] Untrimmed. 1591 Lyly *Endym.* ii. ii, That..cruell enemie that beareth rough and vntewed lockes vpon his bodie.

**Untha·ck,** *v.* [Un-$^2$ 4.] = Unthatch *v.*

*c* 1400 *Pepysian Gospel Harmony* 22 Hij cloumben on þat hous and vnþakkeden it.

†**Unthank,** *sb. Obs.* [OE. *unþanc* masc. (f. *un-* Un-$^1$ 12 + *þanc* Thank *sb.*), = OFris. *unthonk* (WFris. *ontank*, NFris. *untoonk*), MDu. *ondanc* (Du. *ondank*), MLG. *undank*, OHG. *undanch*, *unthank* (MHG. *undanc*, G. *undank*) ingratitude, displeasure, etc.; ON. *úþökk* fem., a reproach, censure, etc. (MSw. *othak*, Sw. *otack*, MDa. and Da. *utak* ingratitude, etc.).]

**I. 1.** Absence of gratitude or good-will; unfavourable thought or feeling; ill-will, disfavour; displeasure expressed in actions or words.

*c* 893 K. Ælfred *Oros.* iv. x. § 11 Þa wæs Hannibale æfter hiera hæðeniscum ȝewunan þæt andwyrde swiþe lað, & him unþanc sæde þæs andwyrdes. *a* 1000 *Sal. & Sat* 98 Ðonne hiene on unðanc..R. ieorrenga ȝeseceð. *c* 1205 Lay. 22370 Mid Arðure he win dronc; Þat him wes mucheles unðonc. 13.. *E. E. Allit. P.* C. 55 Þenne þrat moste I þole, & vnþonk to mede. *c* 1380 Wyclif *Sel. Wks.* I. 256 And in travaile aboute þese goodis..stondiþ al þe mede in þis liif, and al unþank of peyne of helle. *c* 1386 Chaucer *Reeve's T.* 161 Vnthank come on his hand that boond hym so. 1435 Misyn *Fire of Love* 92 Frenschyp..has also a grete likynge with it knytt in qwhilk it adyls no meyde ne vnþanke. 1483 *Cath. Angl.* 381/2 Vn Thanke, *demericio*. 1557 *Tottel's Misc.* (Arb.) 203 Vnthanke to our desert be geuen, Which merite not a heauens gift to kepe.

**b.** In the phrase *to have unthank*.

*c* 1325 in Wright *Pol. Songs* (Camden) 327 But unthank have the bishop that lat hit so go. 13.. *E. E. Allit. P.* B. 183 For þeft, & for þrepyng, vnþonk may mon haue. *c* 1380 *Sir Ferumb.* 3061 'Wel depardieux,' quaþ þis barouns, 'ounþank habbe þat spare'.

**2.** An act or circumstance causing displeasure or annoyance; an offence or injury.

*c* 897 K. Ælfred *Gregory's Past. C.* xlix. 379 And ða forðyðe he forwandode ðæt he swa ne dyde, ða aȝeaf he hit [*sc.* ðæt feoh] to unðances. *c* 1000 *Apollonius of Tyre* 26 Cweðe ȝe þæt ic..eow dide æfre ænigne unþanc? *c* 1050 *O. E. Chron.* (MS. C) an. 1049, Eac fela oðra unþanca þe he him dyde. *c* 1205 Lay. 11769 Þe eorl Caredoc..ȝet hit mai ilimpe; hit is þe an vnðonke. *a* 1225 *Ancr. R.* 202 Uor lure of eie worldliche þinge, oðer of freond, oðer uor eni unðonc. 13.. *Guy of Warw.* 5311 His brond..brac vnto his hond. 'Allas,' quaþ Gij, 'þis vnþang! Were no may y me nouȝt lang'.

**II.** In uses denoting disinclination, reluctance, or involuntariness.

**3.** In genitive, used adverbially, = Unwillingly; compulsorily; against a person's wish or will; without one's consent; also, involuntarily.

The genitive is similarly used in OFris., MDu., OHG., etc.

*c* 960 *Laws Edgar* in Thorpe *Laws* I. 264 Niman [hi] unþances þone teoðan dæl to þam mynstre. ? 1066 *O.E. Chron.* (MS. C) an. 1066, Tostiȝ..nam of þam butse karlon sume mid him, sume þances, sume unþances. *c* 1175 *Lamb. Hom.* 17 Gif þu agultest wið þine efen-nexta unðonkes, bet hit þin þonkes hu se þu miht wið him. *a* 1300 *Cursor M.* 27192 [It] sceus quat nede Was man at drau him to þis dede,.. Quar vnthankes [*Fairf.* queþer vnþankis] or wit will, And quatkin strengh him draf þer-till.

**b.** More freq. with poss. adj. (or sb. in poss. case).

*c* 893 K. Ælfred *Oros.* ii. ii. § 1 Hi swaþeah heora unðances mid swicdome hie beȝeaton. *c* 1100 *O.E. Chron.* (MS. D) an. 905, Þa ȝerad Æþelwold æðeling..þone ham æt Winburnan & æt Tweoxnam þæs cynges unþances. *c* 1200 Ormin 7194 Miccle bettre iss to þe mann..To don all hiss unnþannkess god Þan ifell hise þannkess. *c* 1205 Lay. 4502 Brennes.. hauede heo biwedded, & ihaued heo to bedde, al hire vnðonkes. *a* 1240 *Sawles Warde* in *O. E. Hom.* I. 247 Strengðe stont nest hire, þat ȝef ei wule in, warschipes vn þonkes, warni strengðe fore, þat is hire suster, ant heo hit ut warpe. *c* 1330 R. Brunne *Chron. Wace* (Rolls) 14172 Wyþ hym to fighte leuere he wylde Þan, his vnþankes, to þem ȝelde. 13.. *Coer de L.* 2208 Natheles many he cleaved, And their unthanks ther bylived. *c* 1450 *St. Cuthbert* (Surtees) 201 Þis virgyne þus hir vnthankes fyled perceyued þat sho was with chiled. *a* 1470 Harding *Chron.* l. iv, Kyng Edward with longshankes Brought it awaye again, the Scottes vnthankes. *Ibid.* lxviii. ii, Vpon the north sea bankes, He faught with theim in battaill their vnthankes.

**c.** Without inflection in absolute use.

*a* 1225 *Juliana* 36 He schal unþonc in his teð cuðen þe þat tu wilnest. [Cf. Tooth *sb.* 5.] *c* 1230 *Hali Meid.* 47 Þurh þis weorre, he ȝarkeð þe, unþonc hise [*v.r.* in his] teð, þe blisse..of cristes icorene. *c* 1330 R. Brunne *Chron. Wace* (Rolls) 6093 Walwes þey tok, al his vnthank, & leddym to Atyngal. 1338 — *Chron.* (1810) 241 Þe Walsch com þam ageyn, did our men alle arere, Þat turnyng þer vnthank, as heuy was þe charge, Vnder þam alle sank.

**4.** *At one's unthanks*, against one's will.

*a* 1400–50 *Alexander* 4698 Forþi enhabete ȝe in angwysch at ȝoure vnthankis. *c* 1420 *Anturs of Arth.* 424 (Th.), Or he weldene my landes, at myne vn-thankes. By alle þe welthe of this werlde, he salle þame neuer welde.

**Untha·nk,** *v.* [Un-$^2$ 3.] *trans.* To unsay or recall one's thanks to. 1640 Shirley *Love's Cruelty* iii. iii, *Duke.* We are not pleasd, she should depart. *Seb.* Then I'le vnthanke your Goodnesse.

**Untha·nked,** *ppl. a.* (Un-$^1$ 8.)

1562 Legh *Armory* Pref., Suche they are, as be gone from the world, of whome I am sure to be vnthanked. 1634 Milton *Comus* 723 If all the world Should in a pet of temperance feed on Pulse,..Th' all-giver would be unthank't, would be unprais'd. 1666 Dryden *Ann. Mirab.* cxcii, Their batter'd Admiral too soon withdrew, Unthank'd by ours for his unfinish'd Fight. 1700 — *Pal. & Arc.* i. 388 Unwelcom Freedom and unthank'd Reprieve. 1814 Coleridge *Lett.* (1895) 630 Unthanked, and left worse than defenceless, by the friends of the Government. 1897 H. N. Howard *Footsteps Proserpine* 95 Though unthanked he fall Midway.., His soul shall mount to Heav'n.

**Untha·nkful,** *a.* [Un-$^1$ 7. Cf. OE. *unþancful*, OHG. *undancfol*.]

**1.** Not earning thanks or gratitude; unacceptable, unappreciated, thankless; disagreeable.

*c* 1400 *Apol. Loll.* 45 What þing þat þu werkyst is vnþankful to þe Holi Goost. 1533 Bellenden *Livy* i. x. (S.T.S.) I. 56 Baith þe pepil[s]..beheld þis vnthankful sicht. *Ibid.* I. 60. 1598 Sylvester *Du Bartas* ii. i. iii. *Furies* 626 Those that (broken with unthankfull toyl) Seek others' Health. 1623 J. Taylor (Water P.) *Discov. by Sea* B 7, Which make themselues sicke with drinking such vnthankfull healths. 1759 Goldsm. *Bee* No. 8 ¶ 14 It is, therefore, one of the most unthankful offices in the world. 1815 Coleridge *Lett.* (1895) 642 To be a prophet is..an unthankful office. 1855 *Poultry Chron.* III. 363 It must be an unthankful task for judges to award prizes to inferior birds.

†**b.** Inadequate, insufficient. *Obs.*$^{-1}$

1491 *Reg. Aberdon.* (Maitl. Cl.) I. 328 Gyf it beis fundin onthankful payment be þe said Jhone to þe said vicar.

**2.** Not rendering thanks; not feeling or exhibiting gratitude.

1499 *Contempl. Sinners* Prol. A v b, Vnthankfull mannes myndes. 1526 Tindale *2 Tim.* iii. 2 Men shalbe..vnthankfull, vnholy, churlisshe. 1565 Cooper *Thesaurus*, *Animus ingratus*, an vnthankfull harte. 1602 *2nd Pt. Return fr. Parnass.* iii. ii. 1199 An vnthankefull Viper that will sting the man that reuiued him. 1647 N. Bacon *Disc. Govt. Eng.* i. lvii. 168 These concurring with unnaturall troubles from most unthankfull sonnes. 1702 *Eng. Theophrastus* 91 He that in silence suppresses a favour received is an unthankful Fellow. 1722 De Foe *Relig. Courtsh.* i. ii. (1840) 77, I do not think you will ever be unthankful. 1768 Ross *Helenore* 60 I'm seeking after twa unthankfu' men. 1805 Wordsw. *Prelude* vii. 543 Could a youth..Sit, see, and hear, unthankful, uninspired?

*absol.* 1535 Coverdale *Luke* vi. 35 The Hyest..is kynde, euen to the vnthankfull. 1893 J. Pulsford *Loyalty to Christ* II. 367 The Good Shepherd giveth Himself to the unthankful and the evil.

*transf.* 1614 B. Jonson *Barth. Fair* iii. i, The husbandman ought not, for one unthankful year, to forsake the plough. 1615 Brathwait *Strappado*, etc. (1878) 326 But time vnthankfull time, too soone forgot the Gem she had. 1665 Boyle *Occas. Refl.* v. vii, The Thorns and Thistles that are the unthankful Earths wonted productions.

**b.** Const. *for* or †*of* (a thing), *to* (a person).

*c* 1500 Kennedie *Passion of Christ* 373 As seik vnthankfull to þe medicinar. 1542 Brinklow *Compl.* iii. 16, I pray God, that we be not vnthanckful for that delyuerance. 1580 J. Hay in *Cath. Tract.* (S.T.S.) 33 That I swild nocht appear to be onthankfwll of the said benefeit. 1610 Donne *Pseudo-martyr* 289 When Otho..became vnthankfull to the Pope. 1711 Steele *Spect.* No. 82 ¶ 5 Your Ingratitude..shall not make me unthankful for the Good you have done me. 1729 Law *Serious C.* xi. 171 Quarrelsome with others, and unthankful to God. 1855 Singleton *Virgil* II. 394 He looks back, Unconscious of events, and for escape Unthankful.

**3.** Characterized by ingratitude.

1614 Bp. Hall *Contempl., O. T.* v. vi. 107 If yee had said, Choose vs another gouernour, it had been a wicked and vnthankfull motion. 1643 *Secrets Discovered* (title-p.), Their perfidious, deceitful, and unthankful proceedings against the welfare of this Kingdom. 1665 Boyle *Occas. Refl.*, etc. (1848) 54 It were..unthankful towards the Father of Lights, not to make use of the great Light we receive..by the Moon. 1721 Kelly *Scot. Prov.* 188 When they whom we have supported make unhandsome, and unthankful Returns.

**Untha·nkfully,** *adv.* [Un-$^1$ 11.] Ungratefully.

*a* 1470 Harding *Chron.* cxxxiii. i, He awnswered hym full vnthankefully. 1531 Elyot *Gov.* iii. ii, The riches that he hym selfe gaue hym, whiche the other unthankefully dothe attribute to his owne fortune. 1577 tr. *Bullinger's Decades* 285/2 Such as do vnthankfully abuse the benefites..of their good God. *c* 1620 Moryson *Itin.* iv. v. iii. (1903) 475 This all experienced strangers doe confesse, but they vnthanckfully misconceaue the cause. 1697 *Verdicts conc. Virgil & Homer* v. 21 If these shipwrackt Banditti came sneakingly to Carthage, they go from it as unthankfully. 1814 Wordsw. *Excursion* iv. 479 You judge unthankfully; distempered nerves Infect the thoughts. 1848 Dickens *Dombey* xlvii, A stubborn disposition..unthankfully indulged in.

**Untha·nkfulness.** [Un-$^1$ 12.] Ingratitude.

Very frequent from *c* 1550 to *c* 1650.

*c* 1500 in *Asloan MS.* (S.T.S.) II. 220 Vnthankfulness of man thrillit his [*sc.* Christ's] hart. 1553 T. Wilson *Rhet.* 102 b, Suche should suffer death as felons, whiche were found faultie with vnthankfulnesse. 1617 Moryson *Itin.* ii. 89 Without great vnthankefulnesse..he could not have beene questioned upon this weake ground. *a* 1665 J. Goodwin *Filled w. the Spirit* ii. (1670) 28 The Spirits withdrawing of himself from men..proportionably to mens unthankfulnes, neglect, and opposition to him. 1728 Young *Love Fame* v. 173 When surfeit or unthankfulness destroys ..our solid joys. 1803 Malthus *Popul.* iv. ix. 563 If the proposed relief be given, it is of course received with unthankfulness. 1850 Lynch *Theoph. Trinal* viii. 145 For pride will in thy doings lurk, And in thine heart unthankfulness.

**Untha·tch,** *v.* [Un-$^2$ 4. Cf. OE. *unþeccan* and Unthack *v.*] *trans.* To strip of thatch.

1699–1700 *Laws Nevis* xxx. § 4 (1740) 25 That the Constables..may the better know what Houses to unthatch. 1771 *Ann. Reg., Chron.* 104/1 Many peasants were under the necessity of unthatching their houses to maintain their cattle. **1894** *Daily News* 23 May 6/5 They think the landlords are wrong to unthatch a tenant's house.

**Untha·tched,** *ppl. a.* [Un-[1] 8.] Not covered with thatch.

**1570** Levins *Manip.* 50 Vnthatched, *intectus.* **1629** [see Untrellised]. **1633** Hall *Occas. Medit.* 279 An old unthached Cottage. **1664** Ingelo *Bentiv. & Ur.* v. 33 Streight Cottages, unthatch'd above, full of Smoak and Rain within. *a* **1860** Alb. Smith *Med. Student* (1861) 58 An unthatched cottage on a common. **1897** *Daily News* 1 Oct. 2/6 The storm was accompanied by drenching rain, and..a large number of unthatched corn stacks were completely saturated.

**Unthaw·,** *v.* Now *dial.* [Un-[2] 9 and 7.] *trans.* and *intr.* To thaw. Also *fig.*

**1598** Florio, *Disquagliato*, melted, vnthawed, liquified. **1633** T. James *Voy.* 77 In the woods, wee found the Snow partly wasted away...The ponds were almost vnthawd: but the sea..[was] all firme frozen. **1699** T. Brown *Gent. Holland* Wks. 1711 IV. 316 The Men..are cold to such a degree, that neither Love nor Wine can unthaw them. **1764** J. G. Cooper *Power Harmony* i, The flood of life, Loos'd at its source.., Flows like some frozen silver stream unthaw'd, At a warm Zephyr of the genial Spring. **1847–** in southern dial. glossaries. **1895** *Times* 23 Jan. 9/3 Harcourt..would not or could not unthaw.

**Unthaw·ed,** *ppl. a.* [Un-[1] 8.] Not thawed; remaining frozen.

**1611** Florio, *Indileguato*, vnthawed, vnuanished. **1657** H. King '*Tell me, you stars*' 10 Or give her my flame to melt that snow Which yet unthaw'd does on her bosom grow. **1665–6** *Phil. Trans.* I. 260 Solid Ice, that continued a considerable while unthaw'd. **1734** Pope *Hor. Sat.* ii. ii. 14 Your wine lock'd up, your Butler stroll'd abroad, Or fish deny'd (the river yet unthaw'd). **1774** *Phil. Trans.* LXV. 122 Whilst that [snow]..continues so many hours unthawed. **1825** Hook *Sayings & Doings* II. 283 His maiden aunt, whose heart had remained unthawed for upwards of sixty winters. **1856** Mrs. Browning *Aur. Leigh* vii. 243 [She bore] A babe upon her breast,..Unseasonable outcast on such snow Unthawed to this time.

**Unthea·tric,** *a.* (Un-[1] 7.) **1858** Lytton *What will He do* i. ix, The cobbler yielded to the impulse of an untheatric man. **Unthea·trical,** *a.* (Un-[1] 7.) **1745** Ayre *Mem. Pope* I. 92 His Opera called Rosamond..did not succeed on the Stage, being wholly un-theatrical. **1898** *Westm. Gaz.* 12 Dec. 2/1 The piece..is remarkably untheatrical in style. †**Unthee·,** *v. Obs.* [Un-[1] 14 + Thee *v.*[1]] *intr.* To fail to thrive; to be unsuccessful. *c* **1470** Ashby *Active Policy* 330 Who that is withoute..pite,..he shall vnthe. — *Dicta Philos.* 784 So shal he thriue or vnthe. **Unthema·tic,** *a.* (Un-[1] 7.) **1888** Kennedy *Revised Lat. Primer* 94 Personal Endings in Unthematic and Thematic Verbs.

†**Unthe·nde,** *a. Obs.* [ME. *unthēnde*, f. Un-[1] 10 + *thēnde*, pres. pple. of Thee *v.*[1]]

**1.** Not in good condition; bad or poor in quality or kind.

**1377** Langl. *P. Pl.* B. v. 177, I ete there vnthende fisshe and fieble ale drynke. *a* **1400** *Partonope* 6660 He was so megere and so vnthende,..So hugely wasted a-wey is he. **1447** Bokenham *Seyntys* (Roxb.) 27 My penne also..ful ny is waxyn unthende. *a* **1470** H. Parker *Dives & Pauper* (W. de W. 1496) i. iv. 35/2 Oftentyme that crosse that the preest holdeth in his honde is full unreuerenced & unthende.

**b.** Unwholesome.

*c* **1425** *Cast. Persev.* 2262 in *Macro Plays* 145 Þi metis & drynkys arn vnthende, whanne þei are out of mesure take.

**2.** Unthriving; unprosperous.

*c* **1400** *Pety Job* 654 in 26 *Pol. Poems* 142 The worldes wyles ryght nat me payes, For they ben false and full vnthende. *c* **1412** Hoccleve *De Reg. Princ.* 2464 Rightwisnesse..out of this ile Purposeth fully for to fare & wende, So is our reule vnthrifty & vnthende. *c* **1425** *Cast. Persev.* 510 in *Macro Plays* 92 Who-so wyl alwey foly fle, In þis werld schal ben vnthende.

**b.** Weak, feeble.

*c* **1425** *Cast. Persev.* 287 in *Macro Plays* 85 Nakyd I am, as ȝe may se. a! Lord God in trinite! Whow Mankende is vnthende! *c* **1440** *Promp. Parv.* 367/2 On-thende, *invalidus.*

Hence †**Unthe·ndely** *adv. Obs.*

*c* **1440** *Promp. Parv.* 367/2 On-thendly, *invalide.*

**Untheolo·gical,** *a.* (Un-[1] 7.)

**1641** Milton *Animadv.* 16 This untheologicall Remonstrant. *a* **1656** Bp. Hall *Let.* in *Rem. Wks.* (1660) 300 To argue from Scripture negatively in things of this nature is somewhat untheological. **1865** *Reader* 14 Oct. 420/2 The untheological or secularist philologist. **1893** Liddon, etc. *Life Pusey* I. 365 The dull untheological temper of the time.

**Untheore·tic,** *a.* (Un-[1] 7). **1809** Coleridge *Friend* 87 Did those, who opposed the theories of Innovators, conduct their untheoretic Opposition..to a happier Result? **1863** Geo. Eliot *Romola* iii. vi, The untheoretic virtues of her godfather. **Untheore·tical,** *a.* (Un-[1] 7.) **1797** *Monthly Mag.* III. 227 The bass..is no where untheoretical. **Unthe·orizing,** *ppl. a.* (Un-[1] 10.) **1820** Lamb *Elia* i. *Two Races of Men*, I would put it to the most untheorizing reader..whether [etc.]. **1856** Ruskin *Mod. Paint.* IV. v. App. ii, I..set myself..to see the Alps in a simple, thoughtless, and untheorizing manner.

†**Unthew·.** *Obs.* [OE. *unþēaw*: see Un-[1] 4 b and Thew *sb.*[1]] A bad habit or custom; a vice.

*c* **897** K. Ælfred *Gregory's Past. C.* 23 Feorðe [ðara dæla] is hu he his aȝene unðeawas onȝietan wille. *c* **1175** *Lamb. Hom.* 107 Twelf unþeawes beoð on þissere weorlde to hermen alle monnen. *a* **1200** *Moral Ode* 346 Þat buð ða þe heom sculdeð ȝeorne wid elche un-ðeawe. *a* **1250** *Owl & Night.* 194 He is of worde swyþe gleu, And him is loþ eurich vnþeu. **1303** R. Brunne *Handl. Synne* 4850 A chylde þat wyþ vnþewys wexyþ wylde, Þat wyl boþe myssey and do. **13..** *E. E. Allit. P.* B. 190 Man may mysse þe myrþe, þat much is to prayse, For such vnþewez as þise & þole much payne. *a* **1400** *Relig. Pieces fr. Thornton MS.* 54 Þe conscience, þat chases owte alle vnthewes, and calles in alle gud vertus.

†**Unthew·ed,** *ppl. a. Obs.* [Un-[1] 8.]

**1.** Ill-mannered; unruly, wanton.

*c* **1200** Ormin 2186 Forr son se maȝȝdenn wurrþeþþ bald, Ȝho wurþeþþ sone unnþæwedd. *Ibid.* 6371. *c* **1250** *Ten Abuses* 9 in *O. E. Misc.* 185 Child un-þeaud [*v.r.* vnþewed]. *c* **1325** *Metr. Hom.* 112 That ilke childe Was sa unthewed and sa wilde, That alle the schathe that he moht do, He did. *c* **1340** Hampole *Pr. Consc.* 5873 Maysters of þair disciples alswa, Þat þai lete be unthewed, and untaght ga, And chastid þam noght. **1390** Gower *Conf.* I. 144 Thus is schewed What is to ben of Pride unthewed.

**2.** Unrefined, coarse.

*c* **1250** *Gen. & Ex.* 2555 Summe he deden in vn-ðewed swinc,..Muc and fen ut of burȝes beren.

†**Unthew·ful,** *a. Obs.* [Un-[1] 7.] Unmannerly; unseemly.

*c* **1050** *Voc.* in Wr.-Wülcker 425 *Indisciplinatorum*, unþeawfulra. *a* **1200** Ormin 2191 Full wel birrþ ure maȝȝdenn ben Forrshamedd, ȝiff mann brinngeþ Biforenn hire unnþæwfull word. *c* **1320** in Wright *Pol. Songs* (Camden) 159 Suche chaffare y chepe at the chapitre, That maketh moni thryve-mon un-theufol to be.

**Unthi·ck,** *a.* (Un-[1] 7. Cf. ON. *úþykkr.*) **1587** W. Fowler *Wks.* (S.T.S.) I. 65/196 The passage owt and going furthe wes high and rair vnthik. **Unthi·ckened,** *ppl. a.* (Un-[1] 8.) [**1775** Ash.] **1870** Rolleston *Anim. Life* 119 The thickened glandular three-fourths of these segments are separated off from the ventrally placed and unthickened fourth. **1884** Bower & Scott *De Bary's Phaner.* 160 The unthickened portion of the membrane. **Unthie·vish,** *a.* (Un-[1] 7.) **1858** Gen. P. Thompson *Audi Alt.* II. lxxxi. 39 The unthievish portion of mankind. **Unthi·mble,** *v. Cant.* [Un-[2] 4.] *trans.* (See quot.) **1812** J. H. Vaux *Flash Dict.* s.v., To *unthimble* a man, is to rob, or otherwise deprive him of his watch.

**Unthi·nk,** *v.* [Un-[2] 3.] *trans.* To remove from thought; to annul or reverse by a mental effort. Also *absol.*

*c* **1600** Chalkhill *Thealma & Cl.* 537 Still the king burns, and still his working brain Plots and displots, thinks and unthinks again. **1613** Shaks. *Hen. VIII*, ii. iv. 104, I do beseech You (gracious Madam) to vnthinke your speaking, And to say so no more. **1640** C. Harvey *Confusion* i, One while I think, and then I am in pain To think how to unthink that thought again. **1675** J. Howe *Living Temple* i. iii. 109 That the same thing is not thought and unthought, resolved and unresolved a thousand times in a day. **1709** O. Dykes *Eng. Prov. & Refl.* (ed. 2) 6 There's no unthinking a Misfortune, after it has befallen us for want of Precaution or Foresight. **1811** *Henry & Isabella* I. 6 They knew not how to think, and unthink so often that this world is, and is not a good place. **1818** Cobbett *Pol. Reg.* XXXIII. 527 To imagine that gags..will induce the people to unthink their present thoughts and unfeel their present feelings! **1849** *D'Israeli's Cur. Lit.* II. 428 Bayle stands among those masters of the human intellect who taught us to think, and also to unthink! **1894** Illingworth *Personality* iv. 91 There is no question of the inevitableness of this conclusion; we cannot avoid it, we cannot unthink it.

**Unthinkabi·lity.** (Un-[1] 12. Cf. next.) **1865** Mill *Exam. Hamilton* 134 An endeavour to think what cannot be thought..is the test by which we ascertain its unthinkability. **1897** F. H. Balfour *Unthinkables* 11 This involves unthinkabilities just as unthinkable as either of the other two.

**Unthi·nkable,** *a.* and *sb.* [Un-[1] 7 b.]

**1.** Too great, numerous, etc., to be conceived or apprehended by thought; unimaginable.

*c* **1430** *Life St. Kath.* (1884) 48 Þey sawe al þe prison ful of vnthencable and vnspecable swetnesse of sauour. *a* **1450** *Myrr. our Ladye* 183 Wherfore the nombre of crownes is to be beleued vnthyncable. **1526** *Pilgr. Perf.* (W. de W. 1531) 28 b, He hath gyuen..treasour spirituall whiche be in valour vnthynkable. **1623** Lisle *Ælfric on O. & N. Test.* p. xxiv, The losse whereof is vnspeakable, vnthinkable, vnsufferable misery. **1674** N. Fairfax *Bulk & Selv.* 193 The unthinkable care and forecast in all its evennesses and entwinings. **1879** M. Pattison *Milton* 112 The bathos is unthinkable. **1897** *Westm. Gaz.* 6 July 2/1 You wander.. in cool glades of unthinkable beauty.

**2.** Incapable of being framed or grasped by thought; incogitable.

*c* **1445** Pecock *Donet* 84 A þing fer aboue alle creaturis þouȝt vnþenkable. *c* **1530** tr. *Erasmus' Serm. Ch. Jesus* (1901) 7 Jesus, whiche by an vnspeakable, nay, with an vnthynkable reason, is borne God of God. **1830** W. Taylor *Hist. Surv. Germ. Poetry* I. 453 Separate from her To live is quite unthinkable—is death. **1884** H. Spencer in *Contemp. Rev.* July 33 From whatever point of view we consider it, Bentham's proposition proves to be unthinkable.

*absol.* and *sb.* **1871** Jowett *Plato* III. 134 The negative of measure or limit; the unthinkable, the unknowable; of which nothing can be affirmed. **1897** F H. Balfour (*title*), Unthinkables.

Hence **Unthi·nkably** *adv.*

**1526** *Pilgr. Perf.* (W. de W. 1531) 244 b, The paynes y[t] he suffred..excedeth vnthynkably all the paynes that ony creature myght suffre. **1895** *Young England* XVI. 30/1 Our hearths are warmed by the stored-up sunshine of unthinkably distant ages.

**Unthi·nker.** (Un-[1] 12.) **1837** Carlyle *Fr. Rev.* i. iv. i, Thinkers and unthinkers..are spontaneously at their post.

**Unthi·nking,** *ppl. a.* [Un-[1] 10.]

**1.** Not exercising the faculty of thought; thoughtless; unreflecting, undiscriminating.

**1676** Glanvill *Ess. Philos. & Relig.* i. 29 The shallow, unthinking Vulgar, are sure of all things. **1683** D. A. *Art Converse* 14 Women are generally an unthinking sort of Creatures. **1748** Smollett *R. Random* vii, I was no longer a pert unthinking coxcomb. **1780** *Mirror* No. 72, The effect of scenes like that I have described, on minds neither frigid nor unthinking. **1849** Macaulay *Hist. Eng.* iii. I. 393 Even the unthinking King showed some signs of concern. **1868** Morris *Earthly Par.* I. i. 311 Then swelled his vain unthinking heart with pride.

*absol.* **1697** C. Leslie *Snake in Grass* (ed. 2) p. ii, Atheism takes none But the Un-thinking and Debauch'd. **1769** Robertson *Chas. V*, ii. Wks. 1813 V. 238 Even the most unthinking were shocked. **1873** Proctor *Expanse Heav.* 298 That steadfastness which, to the unthinking, would have had no significance.

**2.** Characterized by absence of thought.

**1688** R. Pepys *Let.* in *S. Pepys' Life* (1841) II. 127 The unthinking conduct of a violent passion. **1693** T. Creech in *Dryden's Juvenal* xiii. (1697) 324 All laugh to find Unthinking Plainness so o'er-spread thy Mind. **1709** Addison *Tatler* No. 75 ¶ 8 You see a deep Attention and a certain unthinking Sharpness in every Countenance. **1796** Mme. D'Arblay *Camilla* I. 25 Even in the unthinking period of earliest youth. **1832** Lytton *Eugene A.* i. xi, When I see the unthinking and lavish idolatry you manifest. **1873** Black *Pr. Thule* xiv, She walked on, in a blind and unthinking fashion.

**3.** Not possessing the faculty of thought.

*a* **1688** Cudworth *Immut. Mor.* (1731) 299 If all Being.. may..arise out of the dark Womb of unthinking Matter. **1710** Berkeley *Princ. Hum. Knowl.* § 10 They who assert that figure, motion,..do exist without the mind in unthinking substances. **1794** R. J. Sulivan *View Nat.* IV. 8, I can never conceive, that a capacity of thinking can be the effect of the combination and motion of unthinking elements.

**Unthi·nkingly,** *adv.* [Un-[1] 11.] Without thought; unreflectingly.

**1717** Mrs. Centlivre *Cruel Gift* iv, Cardono's Love unthinkingly obey'd me. **1768–74** Tucker *Lt. Nat.* (1834) II. 27 Yet are we still liable unthinkingly to fall into little artifices for working upon the divine affections. **1829** Arnold in Stanley *Life* (1844) I. 235 The part which you object to, was not put in unthinkingly. **1884** J. Gilmour *Mongols* 222 These phrases are often uttered unthinkingly.

**Unthi·nkingness.** (Un-[1] 12.)

*a* **1695** Ld. Halifax *Char. Chas. II* (1750) 4 In this kind of Indifference or Unthinkingness,..I will suppose he might pass some considerable part of his Youth. **1744** *Lond. Mag.* 27 Men begin to be convinced that Indolence and Unthinkingness, are the greatest Blessings upon Earth. **1796** Mme. D'Arblay *Camilla* I. 229 [He will] never go astray again, in wicked unthinkingness of this great mercy. **1857** Bagehot *Biog. Stud.* 53 The unfeeling unthinkingness of our Home administration. *a* **1866** J. Grote *Exam. Utilit. Phil.* xviii. (1870) 297 To make a state of unthinkingness desirable for the human mind.

**Unthi·nned,** *ppl. a.* (Un-[1] 8.) **1648** Hexham, *Ongedunt*, Vnthinned. **1816** Byron *Siege Cor.* xxix, Fast they fill The ranks unthinn'd, though slaughter'd still. **1848** Aird *Frank Sylvan* ii, With ear Patient attend his [*sc.* the gardener's] manifold complaints Of birds unthinned. †**Unthi·rlable,** *a. north. Obs.* (Un-[1] 7 b.) **1483** *Cath. Angl.* 383 Vn Thyrleabylle, *inpenetrabilis.* †**Unthi·rled,** *ppl. a.*[1] *north. Obs.* [Un-[1] 8.] Unpierced, unopened. **1435** Misyn *Fire of Love* 74 To qwhome herefore so sal be opynd þe wyndow vnþirlyd of all. †**Unthi·rled,** *ppl. a.*[2] *Sc. Obs.* [Un-[1] 8.] Unsubjugated. **1533** Bellenden *Livy* iii. xxv. (S.T.S.) II. 48 Sa lang as Coriolos stude fre and vnthirlit to romanis. **1536** — *Cron. Scot.* (1821) I. 148 We, as maist vailyeant pupil,..hes kepit us evir unthirllit to Romane dominion. **Unthi·rsty,** *a.* (Un-[1] 7.) [**1775** Ash.] **1882** J. Parker *Apost. Life* I. 74 To the unthirsty man the Bible spring is without attraction. †**Untho·leful,** *a. Obs.*—[1] [Un-[1] 7.] Intolerable. *a* **1425** tr. *Arderne's Treat. Fistula*, etc. 39 Som hauyng a ful gret brennyng..and vntholeful smertyng.

†**Untho·lemood,** *a.* and *sb. Obs.* [Un-[1] 7, 12. Cf. next and ON. *úþolinmóðr* a., *-móði* sb.]

**1.** *adj.* Impatient.

*c* **1200** *Vices & Virtues* 13 Ac ȝif..godd me wolde swingen mid ani swinge,..ic was ðar aȝean unþolemod.

**2.** *sb.* Impatience.

*a* **1400** *Spec. Vitæ* (MS. Bodl. 1885) 139 b, Vnboxsomnesse and vntholemode, Grucchyng also and drerynesse.

†**Untho·lemoodness.** *Obs.* [OE. *unþolemódness* (Un-[1] 12). Cf. prec.] Impatience.

*c* **1000** *Confess. Peccat.* (Toller), Þurh unðolemodnesse. *c* **1200** *Vices & Virtues* 13 *Inpaciencia* hatte an oðer senne, þat is, unþolemodnesse. *a* **1340** Hampole *Psalter* i. 1 Whaim ..na tribulacioun bryngs in till gruchynge or vntholemodnes. *a* **1400** *Spec. Vitæ* (MS. Bodl. 1885) fol. 140 Vntholmodnesse wrong wol lere A man þat wil noȝt bledly here [etc.]. *a* **1400** in *Hampole's Wks.* (1896) II. 289 Vntholemodnes oure soueraines to. *a* **1500** in *Ratis Raving*, etc. 4 The þrid temptacioune is in-paciens or vntholemudnes.

†**Untho·ling,** *ppl. a. Obs.* [Un-[1] 10. Cf. ON. *úþolandi*, MSw. *otholande*, in sense 1.]

**1.** Intolerable.

*a* **1300** *Cursor M.* 25892 Þe paine of hell, How hard it es, and vntholand. *a* **1300** *E. E. Psalter* cxxiii. 4 (E.), Þurgh hap hade ouerfaren owr saule water vnþoland [*v.r.* vntholandlik]. **1340** *Ayenb.* 265 Þer me geþ uram chele in to greate hete of uere, and buoþe onþolyinde.

**2.** Impatient.

*a* **1300** *Cursor M.* 28208 Ic ha ben wrath and vn-tholand Quen i was bunden in godds band.

**Untho·ng,** *v.* (Un-[2] 3, 4 b.) **1829** Landor *Imag. Conv.* II. 308, I would..unthong the drenching-horn from my stable-door. **1843** E. Jones *Sens. & Event* 4 His muscles glisteningly unthonged As burst each ringing peal [of laughter]. **Untho·rned,** *a.* (Un-[1] 9.) **1803** Moore *Ep. to Miss Moore* 6 When every night my weary head Sunk on its own unthorned bed. **Untho·rny,** *a.* (Un-[1] 7.) **1646** Sir T. Browne *Pseud. Ep.* i. v. 18 It were some extenuation of the curse, if.. there still remained a Paradise or unthorny place of knowledge. **Untho·rough,** *a.* (Un-[1] 7.) **1868** W. R. Greg *Lit. & Soc. Judgm.* 277 Some singular inconsistencies, which..showed how imperfect and unthorough was his political philosophy. **1891** Atkinson *Moorland Par.* 142 Knowing..how utterly unscientific and unthorough all such investigations then were. **Untho·roughfaresome,** *a.*, **-ness,** *sb.* (**1868** Trench *Engl. Past & Pres.* 74.) = Unthroughfareness, -some. **Unthou·ght,** *sb.* (Un-[1] 12.) **1866** Mrs. Whitney *L. Goldthwaite* xii, Something different in thought and purpose from the apparent unthought about her. **1892** P. W. Clayden *Eng. under Coalition* xv. 315 To show to which side the charge of credulity, of rashness and of unthought belonged.

**Unthou·ght,** *ppl. a.* [UN-¹ 8 b, 8 c. Cf. MHG. *ungedaht* (G. *ungedacht*), Du. *ongedacht.*]

**1.** Not thought of, unexpected.

*a* 1548 HALL *Chron., Hen. VI*, 110 b, While kyng Charles did politiquely consider..what a sodain and vnthought chaunce of a smal thyng, might do in a battaill. 1653 J. TAYLOR (Water P.) *Cert. Trav. Uncert. Journ.* 16 Undeserv'd, unlook'd for, and unthought From them my purse and person both were fraught. 1738 G. LILLO *Marina* II. i, The hot salt tears this unthought loss drew from me. 1745 YOUNG *Nt. Th.* VIII. 114 As they spin our hours On Fortune's wheel, where accident unthought Oft, in a moment, snaps life's strongest thread. 1903 KIPLING *5 Nations, Wage-Slaves* 61 They that have wrought the end unthought Be neither saint nor sage.

**b.** With *on, of.* (Cf. THINK *v.*² 5 c, 7 b.)

1538 ELYOT, *Inopinatus*, vnthought on or vnloked for. *a* 1586 SIDNEY *Arcadia* I. iv, It may be, his pen with more leasure doth polish the rudenesse of an unthought-on songe. 1596 SHAKS. I *Hen. IV*, III. ii. 141 The day..That..This gallant Hotspur..And your vnthought-of Harry chance to meet. 1621 LADY M. WROTH *Urania* 451 One night he came vnlook'd for to our house, but not vnthought on by me. 1666 BOYLE *Orig. Forms & Qual.* 418 By a way unthought on (that I know of) by any Body. 1676 HALE *Contempl.* I. 52 A little..accident..may put a period to all those pleasures..in an unthought of moment. 1713 BERKELEY *Hylas & Phil.* III. Wks. 1871 I. 356 What security can I have ..that no unthought-of objection or difficulty will occur hereafter? 1748 RICHARDSON *Clarissa* (1811) III. xxxvi. 216 Consequences, unthought of by you or me. 1860 FROUDE *Hist. Eng.* V. 490 A return to communion with the See of Rome was unthought of. 1890 'R. BOLDREWOOD' *Col. Reformer* (1891) 449 This distant, long-dry, unthought-of reservoir.

†**2.** (With complement or *ellipt.*) Not regarded in a certain (specified or implied) way. *Unthought long*, without feeling time long. *Obs.*

1595 SPENSER *Epithal.* 378 Thou likewise didst loue, though now vnthought. *a* 1637 B. JONSON *Underwoods, Eupheme* ix. 44 As spirits had stolne her spirit in a kisse,.. And left her lovely body unthought dead! *a* 1806 in R. Jamieson *Pop. Ballads* I. 94 He harpit to the king, To haud him unthought lang.

**3.** Unimagined; not devised in thought.

1639 COKAINE *Masque* Dram. Wks. (1874) 10 Forsake the woods, fond Satyr, and but try The unthought difference 'twixt them and us! 1672 MARVELL *Reh. Transp.* II. (1674) 46, I wish it unsaid as it was unthought. 1743 YOUNG *Nt. Th.* V. 147 Each salutation may slide in a sin Unthought before. 1815 MILMAN *Fazio* 67 Is't to be mad..To speak with..continuous flow, Yet know not how the unthought words start from me? 1850 THACKERAY *Pendennis* lxxii, If you knew..how I lie awake and think of those hard sentences,..and wish them unspoken, unthought!

†**4.** Unheeded, disregarded. *Obs.*

1640 YORKE *Union Hon.* 185 [He] returned from his unthought banishment, [and] tooke King Richard prisoner.

†**5.** Unpremeditated. *Obs.*

1648 *Pol. Ballads* (1860) I. 74 With speech unthought, quick revelation,..See a new Teacher of the Town.

**Unthou·ghted,** *ppl. a.* [UN-¹ 8.] Not contemplated; not formed in thought.

1598 ROWLANDS *Betraying of Christ* (Hunterian Cl.) 9 What furies guided this misguided swarme? To bend their force against vnthoughted harme. 1860 O. W. HOLMES *Elsie V.* xiv, There are states of mind..which remain not only unworded, but unthoughted, if such a word may be coined for our special need.

**Unthou·ghtful,** *a.* [UN-¹ 7.]

**1.** Not taking thought, unmindful or regardless, *of* something.

1456 SIR G. HAYE *Govt. Princes* Wks. (S.T.S.) II. 141 Wyne..makis man to be unthochtfull of his honour. 1702 C. MATHER *Magn. Chr.* IV. x. 220/2 He was not unthoughtful of the Time when publick Ones [*sc.* sermons] might be expected from him. 1728 R. MORRIS *Ess. Anc. Archit.* 106 How unthoughtful of the Affair in hand? 1887 R. F. BURTON *Arab. Nts.* (abr. ed.) III. 71 We have foes who are not unthoughtful of us.

**2.** Unthinking, thoughtless.

*a* 1533 LD. BERNERS *Gold. Bk. M. Aurel.* xxxvii. (1536) 67 They as vnthoughtfull,..leaue the iust trauayle, and take vniust idelnes. *a* 1667 COWLEY *Ess. in Verse & Prose, Solitude* iv, Here let me, careless and unthoughtful lying, Hear the soft winds above me flying. 1698 NORRIS *Pract. Disc.* IV. 62 People..that have..a lazy, unthoughtful, listless, yawning way of talking of Religion. 1715 JANE BARKER *Exilius* I. 72 The vulgar Part of the Africans are extremely unthoughtful and unpolished. *a* 1834 COLERIDGE *Lit. Rem.* (1836) II. 10 Without which poetry becomes..evaporated into a hazy, unthoughtful, day-dreaming. 1895 C. SCOTT *Apple Orchards* 131 The reckless, unthoughtful, but ill-directed youth of to-day.

Hence **Unthou·ghtfully** *adv.*; **Unthou·ghtfulness.**

1661 J. FELL *Hammond* 205 During the current of that Tyranny,..he kept a constant equable serenity and unthoughtfulness in outward accidents. 1701 NORRIS *Ideal World* I. vi. 322 Never was any question..more ignorantly and unthoughtfully moved. 1709 MRS. MANLEY *Secret Mem.* (1736) IV. 185 Should he begin by this unthoughtfulness of enterprize, it would render him..formidable. 1884 E. W. BENSON in *Life* (1899) II. 29 A ceaseless reproach to the unthoughtfulness of this busy existence.

**Unthra·ll,** *v.* [UN-² 4 b.] *trans.* To emancipate, set free.

*c* 1586 C'TESS PEMBROKE *Ps.* CXVIII. v, God answere gave me when I called, And me inlarging, me unthralled. 1650 H. B. *To Vaughan* in Vaughan *Anima Magica*, But who from envies sordid mire Is washt,..a light shall see, (Unthral'd from errors Sophistry). 1652 HOWELL *Giraffi's Rev. Naples* II. 28 Thou chopst his neck, who thy head did unthral.

**Unthra·lled,** *ppl. a.* (UN-¹ 8.) [1775 ASH.] 1865 W. G. PALGRAVE *Arabia* I. 136 A sort of chivalresque knight-errants and representatives of unthralled freedom.

**Unthra·shed, -thre·shed,** *ppl. a.* [UN-¹ 8. Cf. Sw. *otröskad.*]

**1.** Of corn, etc.: Not thrashed.

α. 1561 *Wills & Inv. N.C.* (Surtees, 1835) 193, xx threives of wheat unthresshed. 1573 TUSSER *Husb.* (1878) 56 Such wheat..vnthreshed till March in the sheafe let it lie. 1660 in *Sadler St. Papers* (1809) III. 360 Barley, threshed and unthreshed. 1766 *Compl. Farmer* s.v. *Harvest*, Wheat keeps better when stacked in the ear unthreshed. 1798 *Hull Advertiser* 24 Mar. 2/3 Insurance upon..outhouses, and upon unthreshed stock therein. 1885 *Athenæum* 5 Sept. 298/1 A wooden stage on which unthreshed corn is placed. 1891 T. HARDY *Tess* xlviii, The unthreshed sheaves remaining untouched.

β. 1702 *Guide for Constables* 136 Carts carrying..corn unthrashed. 1799 J. ROBERTSON *Agric. Perth* 323 Others throw hay or unthrashed corn in handfuls upon the snow to feed them. 1844 H. STEPHENS *Bk. Farm* II. 286 The unthrashed corn..is delivered into the machine.

*fig.* 1853 RUSKIN *Stones Ven.* III. ii. § 27 It is to be remembered, that knowledge in this form may be kept..in such unthreshed disorder that it is of no use.

**2.** Unbeaten, unflogged.

1892 *Daily News* 5 Oct. 3/1 A couple of youths..tore the lower part of it, but they ran off unthrashed.

†**Unthra·shen,** *ppl. a. Obs. Sc.* and *north.* [UN-¹ 8 b. Cf. MHG. (G.) *ungedroschen.*] = prec. 1.

1482 *Acta Auditorum* (1839) 109/1, xij thrafe vnthreschin corne. 1537 *Stanlowe Cell Inv.* (P.R.O.), vj thrayf of vnthrashen Barlycorne. 1578 *Reg. Privy Council Scot.* II. 680 The said unthreschin corne. 1601 in *T. Pont's Acc. Cunningham* (Maitl. Cl.) 180 Ane mow of vnthressin beir. 1629 *Orkney Witch Trial* in *County Folk-Lore* III. (1903) 77 Ye said ye may give me ane lock..out of the cassie under the unthreachin corne.

**Unthrea·d,** *v.* (UN-² 3.)

Chiefly in figurative uses.

1595 SHAKS. *John* V. iv. 11 Vnthred the rude eye of Rebellion, And welcome home againe discarded faith. 1634 MILTON *Comus* 616 He with his bare wand can unthred thy joynts, And crumble all thy sinews. 1699 BOYER *Royal Dict.* I, *Desenfiler*, to unthread a Needle. 1801 LAMB *Lett.* (1900) II. 40 Who can disentangle and unthread the rich texture of Nature and Poetry,..without spoiling both lace and coat? 1818 KEATS *Isabella* xxxvii, The while it did unthread the horrid woof Of the late darken'd time. 1847 DE QUINCEY *Sp. Mil. Nun* Wks. 1854 III. 43 Under Kate's guidance..they soon unthreaded the labyrinth of rocks. 1865 MISS BRADDON *Doctor's Wife* x. 93 Threading and unthreading her needle very often.

**Unthrea·ded,** *ppl. a.* (UN-¹ 8.) [1775 ASH.] 1895 K. GRAHAME *Golden Age* 109 A signal for retreat..into unthreaded copses.

**Unthrea·tened,** *ppl. a.* (UN-¹ 8.)

1647 CLARENDON *Hist. Reb.* II. § 86 The Arch Bishop.. lodged..in Whitehall; which place was likewise not unthreatned in their seditious meetings. 1648 [see UNREPROACHED]. 1813 WORDSW. '*Stay, bold Adventurer*' 25 All around Had darkness fallen—unthreatened, unproclaimed. 1818 COLEBROOKE *Import Colonial Corn* 108 Yet are his productions not unthreatened..by dangerous rivalship of less skilful..artists.

**Unthri·d(den,** *ppl. adjs.* [UN-¹ 8 b + THREAD *v.* 4.] Unthreaded. 1843 E. JONES *Sensation & Event* 125 He stands again before the unthridden gloom. 1866 MRS. WHITNEY *Gayworthys* iv, Piny forests, untouched, unthrid.

**Unthri·ft,** *sb.* (and *a.*). [UN-¹ 4 a, 12. Cf. WANTHRIFT.]

†**1.** A malpractice; a defect or fault in conduct.

1303 R. BRUNNE *Handl. Synne* 12339 Þer ys an vnþryfte Þat doþ moche skaþe yn shryfte. *c* 1430 *Pilgr. Lyf Manhode* II. cxxii. (1869) 121 Þis mantelle..was maad for to..mantelle with my defautes, and consele myne vnthriftes.

**2.** Want of thrift or economy; neglect of thriving or doing well; † dissolute conduct, loose behaviour, impropriety.

13.. *E. E. Allit. P.* B. 516 Hit is sothe, þat alle mannez wyttez To vn-þryfte arn alle þrawen with þoȝt of her herttez. *c* 1374 CHAUCER *Troylus* IV. 431 To don his wo to falle, He rought nought what vnthrift þat he seyde. *c* 1400 *Pilgr. Sowle* (Caxton, 1483) III. viii. 55 These ben the children of tristesse,..ful of ydelnes and al maner vnthrifte. *a* 1475 G. ASHBY *Dicta Philos.* 469 That the myddyl of your liffe be not spent In ydelnesse, ne in vnthrifte myswent. 1483 *Cath. Angl.* 385/2 Wn Thryfte, *deuigencia.*

1721 KELLY *Sc. Proverbs* 250 Many one blames their Wife, for their own unthrift. 1830 CARLYLE *Misc.* (1840) II. 320 The Hof public openly finding her guilty of Unthrift. 1860 *All Year Round* No. 53. 62 No idleness was allowed in her house; no unthrift, no useless dawdlings. 1887 *American* XIV. 23 Both fell an easy prey to every adverse circumstance which poverty and unthrift can offer.

**3.** An unthrifty († unthriving), shiftless, or dissolute person; a spendthrift, prodigal.

Freq. *c* 1520–1690. Occas. *to play the unthrift.*

*c* 1330 R. BRUNNE *Chron. Wace* (Rolls) 7231 Go we now, & sle þat vnþrift. *c* 1375 *Sc. Leg. Saints* xl. (*Ninian*) 661 Þai..tretyt weile þat vnthrifte, til eld had it brocht fra schrifte. 1491 CAXTON *Vitas Patr.* (W. de W. 1495) I. cxl. 152 b/2 At theyr metynge togyder this Unthryft gaaf hym a buffeth. 1509 BARCLAY *Shyp of Folys* 142 b, A folysshe man rurall If he a churle, a fole and vnthrift be, The more he loketh to come to hye degree. 1556 *Chron. Grey Friars* (Camden) 73 Vacobondes that wold not labor, but play the unthryftes. *a* 1602 W. PERKINS *Cases Consc.* (1619) 74 The young vnthrift in the Gospell, called the Prodigall child. 1639 FULLER *Holy War* 124 If he played the unthrift with this golden occasion. 1693 DRYDEN *Persius* iv. 237 Shall I ..My Friends disgrace, And be the first lewd Unthrift of my Race? 1765 BLACKSTONE *Comm.* I. 295 When a man on an inquest of idiocy hath been returned an unthrift and not an idiot, no farther proceedings have been had. 1821 SCOTT *Kenilw.* xxxi, The Earl of Oxford, a young unthrift, whom Foster had more than once accommodated with loans. 1862 SIR H. CAIRNS in *Times* 2 Jan., The Roman law made no distinction between unthrifts and idiots.

*fig.* 1571 E. WOLLAY *Pl. Pathway* 14 Wee know what thanckes wee owe to God for all his giftes; Yet contrary we showe to him ourselves unthriftes. 1654 GATAKER *Disc. Apol.* 18 As we count him a bad Husband, that foloweth game on the Market-day, so may we as wel count him a spiritual unthrift, that spends the Sabbath in that sort.

†**b.** One who is prodigal *of* something. *Obs.*

1640 QUARLES *Enchyrid.* I. xciii, Fury..being an unthrift of its owne strength. *a* 1659 in *Bann. Club Misc.* (1827) 324, I do confess thou 'rt sweet, yet find Thee such an unthrift of thy sweets. 1666 SPURSTOW *Spir. Chym.* lix. 175 The most of men are such unthrifts of time.

**4.** *attrib.* or as *adj.* Prodigal, spendthrift.

*a* 1562 G. CAVENDISH *Wolsey* (1893) 45 Thow hast allwayes byn a prowd, presumpcious, disdaynfull, and a very onthryft waster. 1592 NASHE *P. Penilesse* A ij b, Sir Rowland Russet-coat..hath much adoo..to keepe his vnthrift elbowes in reparations. 1596 SHAKS. *Merch. V.* v. i. 16 In such a night Did Iessica steale from the wealthy Iewe, And with an Vnthrift Loue did runne from Venice. 1650 VAUGHAN *Silex Scint., Regeneration* vi, The unthrift Sunne shot vitall gold A thousand peeces. 1865 A. CARY *Ballads*, etc. 66 When I met a man, unthrift and lorn. 1869 LOWELL *Cathedral* 142 This unthrift housekeeping that will not brook A dish warmed-over at the feast of life.

Hence **Unthri·ft-like** *a.* or *adv.*

1603 HEYWOOD *Wom. Kilied w. Kindn.* (1617) D 4 b, Now Nichlas you want money; And vnthrift-like would eate into your wages.

†**Unthr·iftfully,** *adv. Obs.* (UN-¹ 11.) 1549 CHEKE *Hurt Sedit.* (1569) G i b, That such plentie of vittayle, as was aboundauntly in euery quarter,..is nowe all wastfully and vnthriftfully spent. †**Unthri·ftihead.** *Obs.* [UN-¹ 12.] Thriftlessness. 1590 SPENSER *F. Q.* II. xii. 18 The quicksand of Vnthriftyhed. *Ibid.* III. xii. 25 Emongst them was sterne Strife,..Vnquiet Care, and fond Vnthriftihead.

**Unthri·ftily,** *adv.* [UN-¹ 11.] In an unthrifty manner; prodigally; † dissolutely.

13.. *E. E. Allit. P.* B. 267 Þay..controeued agayn kynde contrare werkez, & vsed hem vn-þryftyly vchon on oþer. *c* 1386 CHAUCER *Can. Yeom. Prol. & T.* 893 If a man wole aske hem pryuely, Why they been clothed so vnthriftily. 1493 *Festivall* 53/2 Truly to laboure & not to slombre & slepe slewffully & vnthryftely. 1509 BARCLAY *Shyp of Folys* b ij b, Some thynkinge them self moch wyse & commendable Thoughe al theyr dayes they lyue vnthryftely. 1571 GOLDING *Calvin on Ps.* xxxvi. 8 The ungodly ronne ryot unthriftely in their oune wickednes. 1605 WILLET *Hexapla Gen.* 436 All such as spend their time vnthriftily. 1697 COLLIER *Ess. Mor. Subj.* II. Pref., Our Attainments cannot be over-large; and yet we manage a narrow Fortune, very Vnthriftily. 1909 FIRTH *Last Years Protectorate* I. 8 The government had not managed the treasury unthriftily.

**Unthri·ftiness.** [UN-¹ 12.]

**1.** The quality of being unthrifty; thriftlessness, prodigality, wastefulness; † dissoluteness.

*c* 1430 *How the Good Wyf* 154 in *Babees Bk.* (1868) 43 Pride, reste, & ydilnes, makiþ on-þriftines. *a* 1475 G. ASHBY *Dicta Philos.* 116 Wele manered people bene of goode lif,..Euel named bene often in striff, And men fle theim for thair vnthriftynesse. 1509 BARCLAY *Shyp of Folys* 141 b, Sawynge in hym sede of moche vnthryftynes And than to spoyle hym; and leue hym pore and bare. *a* 1548 HALL *Chron., Hen. VIII*, 149 b, Some fell to drinkyng,..and stealyng of Dere in Parkes, and other unthriftines. 1609 DEKKER *Gull's Horn-bk.* 35 You are to cherish the vnthriftinesse of such yong tame pigions, if you be a right gentleman. 1642 FULLER *Holy & Prof. St.* I. xiv. 46 Neither wasting his paternall estate by his unthriftinesse, nor marring it by parcelling his ancient mannours..among his younger children. 1688 R. HOLME *Armoury* III. 266/2 Unthriftiness, Slothfulness, Carelessness, and Rashness in Business. 1710, 1802–74 in Sc. glossaries (defining *Wanthrift*).

†**2.** Lack of thriving in growth. *Obs. rare.*

1707 MORTIMER *Husb.* 394 When any of its Roots happen to perish,..the unthriftiness of its Branches will quickly discover it. *Ibid.* 418 The grubbing up of Woods and Trees may be needful upon the account of their Unthriftiness.

**Unthri·fty,** *a.* [UN-¹ 7. Cf. WANTHRIFTY *a.*]

**1.** Producing or bringing about no advantage, profit, or gain; tending to, resulting in, or marked by thriftlessness, waste, or extravagance; unprofitable, wasteful; harmful.

*c* 1374 CHAUCER *Troylus* IV. 1530, I-wys my dere herte trewe We may wel stele a-way as ye deuyse And fynde swyche vnthryfty weyes newe. *c* 1412 HOCCLEVE *De Reg. Princ.* 2464 Rightwisnesse..out of this ile Purposeth fully for to fare & wende, So is our reule vnthrifty & vnthende. *c* 1470 ASHBY *Active Policy* 681, I mene nat for vnthrifty Cowardise, whiche is in al Realmes abhominable. 1513 DOUGLAS *Æneid* IX. x. 25 Quhat onthrifty God in sic foly Hes ȝou bywavyt heyr till Italy? 1529 *Supplic. to King* (E.E.T.S.) 40 Common players at all vnthryftye games. 1579 NORTHBROOKE *Dicing* 60 b, Venerous people haue all their whole pleasance, Their vice to nourishe by this vnthriftie daunce. 1590 SPENSER *F. Q.* I. iv. 35 Full many mischiefes follow cruell Wrath;..Vnmanly murder, and vnthrifty scath. 1627 SIR R. COTTON in Rushw. *Hist. Coll.* (1659) I. 471 The spending of much Munition, Victuals and Money,..is counted an unthrifty error. 1647 CLARENDON *Hist. Reb.* I. § 147 The Subject might be taught how unthrifty a thing it was, by too strict a detaining of what was His, to put the King as strictly to enquire what was his Own. 1652 BENLOWES *Theoph.* III. lxvii, Unthrifty death has spread where thriving peace did range. 1697 DRYDEN *Virg. Georg.* I. 226 Tough Thistles..kill'd the Corn, And an unthrifty Crop of Weeds was born. 1776 ADAM SMITH *W. N.* v. ii. II. 473 They are all more or less unthrifty taxes that increase the revenue of the sovereign..at the expence of the capital of the people. 1809 MALKIN *Gil Blas* IX. vi. ¶ 3 The commerce of the eyes being so unthrifty, I had recourse to different agents. 1819 SCOTT *Leg. Montrose* ii, Having by unthrifty courses reduced a fair patrimony to a nonentity. 1869 FREEMAN *Norm. Conq.* III. xii. 101 The rebuilding..

had been possibly interrupted during the unthrifty reign of Malger.

†**b.** Of language: Unprofitable, idle. *Obs.*

*c* **1440** *Alph. Tales* 215 Oft sithes, with þer vnthrifti langguage, hym at had rewle of þaim þai provoked..to be angrie. **1467** *Mann. & Househ. Exp.* (Roxb.) 172, I wolde avysse ȝowe to sese..of ȝower onthreffety langwage.

**2.** Not thriving or flourishing; lacking vigour or promise in growth. (Cf. THRIFTLESS *a.* 1.)

*c* **1440** *Promp. Parv.* 367/2 Onthryfty, *idem quod* onthende [*Ibid.*, Onthende, *invalidus*]. **1484** CAXTON *Fables of Æsop* III. iii, Thynke now, how thow arte lene and vnthryfty. **1486** *Bk. St. Albans* b vij b, Euell meetis to make her vnthrefti. **1674** N. FAIRFAX *Bulk & Selv.* Ep. Ded., Such an underly Shrub in Knowledge, and unthrifty Sucker in Philosophy as I am. **1709** *Phil. Trans.* XXVI. 450 The Cow was very unthrifty, for which they gave her Cow Physick. **1796** C. MARSHALL *Gardening* xii. (1813) 145 Consider the soil about an unthrifty tree. **1831** YOUATT *Horse* viii. 122 The horse will lose flesh;..his coat will be unthrifty, and readily come off. **1846** LANDOR *Imag. Conv.* Wks. II. 224/1 That..we should think it expedient to plant unthrifty thorns over bitter wells of blood.

*transf.* **1812** *Examiner* 11 May 292/1 Poor, ill-cultivated.. soils, the early appearance of which was unthrifty, show.. very thin.

**b.** Characterized by absence of well-being; indicative of unprosperousness.

*c* **1400** *Three Kings Cologne* 24 Þer was nothyng left bote.. a litel cave vndir erþe and a litil vnthrifti hows tofore þe cave. *c* **1425** *MS. Sloane 73* fol. 201 Whanne þi bagge chaungiþ clene out of þe rede colour..in to a manere of an vnþryfty wan colour. *a* **1450** *Knt. de la Tour* 9 Atte the yongest doughtres hous it was turned up-so-doun, and alle unthrifti. *c* **1529** LATIMER in Foxe *A. & M.* (1563) 1298/2 Whiche vnthriftye state that wee be borne vnto, is come vnto vs for oure owne desertes.

**3.** Loose or lax in respect of conduct, morals, or virtue; unchaste, wanton, profligate.

**1388** *Pol. Poems* (Rolls) I. 272 Goddes dere halydayys ar noght, non observantur honeste; For onthryfty pley ys worght. *a* **1450** *Knt. de la Tour* 30 The good women..that hathe not take the state of the unthrifti women that bene euelle women of her body. *c* **1485** *Digby Myst.* (1882) II. 558 Non shall in heuyn posses that be so vnthryfty. **1523** LD. BERNERS *Froiss.* I. ccclxxxvi. 660 Suche rybaudes and vnthriftye people, as desyred nothynge but yuell and noyse. **1530** in W. H. Turner *Select. Rec. Oxford* (1880) 80 Certen onthryfty persons brekyng of the Kyngs pesse. *a* **1571** JEWEL *On Thess.* (1583) 219 Withdrawe thy selfe from the companie, of such vnthriftie, and light, and suspected persons.

*transf. c* **1400** *Pilgr. Sowle* (Caxton, 1483) II. lvii. 55 Thou madest me to lede a ful vnthryfty lyf. **1476** *Stonor Papers* (Camden) II. 7 Comaunde me to the Cloke [= clock], and pray hym to amend his unthryffte maners: ffor he strykes euer in vndew tyme. **1535–6** *Act 27 Hen. VIII*, c. 28 ¶ 1 Reformacion of suche unthrifty carnall and abhomynable lyvyng.

**4.** Not thrifty, economical, or frugal; careless or improvident of one's means or substance; wasteful, extravagant, prodigal. (Cf. THRIFTLESS *a.* 3.)

**1532** HERVET *Xenophon's Househ.* 59 The grounde doth best examyne, which be good, and whiche be vnthryfty husbandes. **1551** ROBINSON tr. *More's Utopia* II. (Arb.) 87 The vnthrifty heire suffereth ye houses that his father buylded..to fall in decay. **1596** BACON *Max. & Use Com. Law* II. (1635) 49 Or to be in hazard of undoing his house by unthrifty posterity. **1639** J. TAYLOR (Water P.) *Part this Summers Trav.* 18 Such an unthrifty Rascall as thou will never be worth such a halter, it cost me two pence. **1662** HIBBERT *Body Divinity* I. 197 The wormes shall have his carkass, and unthrifty heires his estate. **1684** J. GOODMAN *Old Relig.* 336 A querulous, uneasy, lean, hungry and unthrifty sort of people. **1780** S. J. PRATT *Emma Corbett* (ed. 4) II. 108, I am one of those whom the world calls an unthrifty fellow. **1849** HAWTHORNE *Twice-told T.* 213 Next comes a sledge, laden with wood for some unthrifty housekeeper. **1904** *Verney Mem.* II. 215 Before the wine arrives, this unthrifty host discovers that he does not require it.

*fig. c* **1600** SHAKS. *Sonn.* iv, Vnthrifty louelinesse why dost thou spend, Vpon thy selfe thy beauties legacy? **1659** O. WALKER *Oratory* 109 This ingrafting..parenthesis, if it argues a good wit, it shews a weak and unthrifty Orator. **1682** MRS. BEHN *False Count* II. i, Should we be unthrifty in our loves, And for one moment's joy give all away? **1703** ROWE *Fair Penit.* II. i, Oh wherefore did I play th' unthrifty Fool, And wasting all on others, leave myself Without one thought of Joy to give me comfort?

*absol.* **1876** BANCROFT *Hist. U. S.* II. xlii. 567 To insure an estate even to the sons of the unthrifty.

**b.** Prodigal or lavish *of* something; unsparing.

**1620** DONNE *Serm.* (1640) 418 God is content to be told, that he is unthrifty, and prodigall of his servants lives. **1670** COTTON *Espernon* II. vi. 289 He was not altogether so unthrifty of his own Interest. **1713** BLACKMORE *Creation* V. 243 Of light unthrifty, and profuse of day, The ruin'd globe has spent his latest ray.

**Unthri·lled**, *ppl. a.* (UN-¹ 8.) [**1775** ASH.] *a* **1861** MRS. BROWNING *Ragged Schools London* xxii, Calm, unthrilled in Our heart's pulses.

† **Unthri·ve**, *v. Obs.* [UN-² 7.]

**1.** *intr.* To fail to thrive; to be unprosperous.

*c* **1380** WYCLIF *Sel. Wks.* II. 411 In Cristis tyme and long aftir þroof þe Chirche,..but siþ it haþ unþrivun. **1390** GOWER *Conf.* II. 211 For that a man scholde al unthryve Ther oghte no wisman coveite. **1426** LYDG. *De Guil. Pilgr.* 23767 God wil,..to chastice hem, his hond with-drawe, suffre her goodes to vnthryve. **1465** *Paston Lett.* II. 237 Upon trust of Calles promise, we may soon onthryve. **1477** NORTON *Ord. Alch.* Proem, in Ashm. (1652) 7 Whereby they were pore and made to unthrife. **1618** LITHGOW *Pilgrim's Farew.* E 1, If hee vnthrives, hee hates anothers weele. *a* **1706** EVELYN *Sylva* II. viii. (1776) 419 Shade and dripping..are certainly causes of their [*sc.* trees'] unthriving till removed.

**2.** *trans.* To make unprosperous.

*a* **1550** *Image Hypoc.* II. 345 in Skelton *Wks.* (1843) II. 427/1 His expectatyves Many a man vnthrives.

**Unthri·ven**, *ppl. a.* Now *Sc.* (UN-¹ 8 b. Cf. WANTHRIVEN.) **1680** W. ALLEN *Peace & Unity* 136 Such as were but Babes still, and unthriven in the Life and Spirit of Christianity. **1825** JAMIESON, *Crile*,..a child or beast that is unthriven. **1875** W. ALEXANDER *Ain Folk* 187 Willikie had assumed an unthriven look.

**Unthri·ving**, *ppl. a.* [UN-¹ 10.]

†**1.** Not doing well; lacking merit or excellence; unworthy. *Obs.*

*c* **1325** *Metr. Hom.* 130 Als did unthriuand [*v.r.* unthrewand] Giezye, That wex unhale thoru his gilrye. **13..** *Gaw. & Gr. Knt.* 1499 Good is your speche, Bot þrete is vn-þryuande in þede þer I lende. *c* **1400** *Destr. Troy* 4893 And we.. Answarth hym..with angur & skorne, With thretyng vnthriuand. *c* **1460** *Wisdom* 784 in *Macro Plays* 784 Here was a meny on-thryvande.

**2.** Not growing vigorously or thriving; not prospering or flourishing.

**1600** SURFLET *Countrie Farme* III. xlvi. 517 After you haue thus cut it you may take the vnthriuing grafts [etc.]. **1628** QUARLES *Argalus & P.* III. Wks. (Grosart) III. 276/2 My quill would wast Th' unthriving stock of my bespoken time. **1673** *Lady's Call.* II. ii. § 49 They will often find temtation enough here to discard their honesty, as the most unthriving trade. **1793** *Residence in France* (1797) I. 121 An unthriving tree of liberty, which seems to wither under the baneful influence of the *bonnet rouge.* **1848** AIRD *Mother's Blessing* II. ii, Filling up With stakes the gaps of the unthriving hedges. **1875** W. ALEXANDER *Ain Folk* 59 The poor wan bairnie..looked even more shrivelled and unthriving than before.

**3.** Bringing no gain or profit; unprosperous.

**1617** BP. HALL *Quo Vadis?* § 5 Whiles in the meane season, their vnthriuing intermission is assailed with a thousand suggestions. *a* **1656** in *Raleigh's Remains* 110 It is now more than a seasonable time to alter the course of so unthriving a husbandry. **1624** HEYWOOD *Gunaik.* IX. 442 Hee was compelled..to prostitute his owne bodye to unnaturall lusts, for bruitish and unthriving gaine. *a* **1722** LISLE *Husb.* (1757) 107 The vetches continued in an unthriving way till the first of February. **1723** MRS. HOWARD in *Lett. C'tess Suffolk* (1824) I. 111 Sincerity is so very unthriving, that I can never give consent that you should practise it.

Hence **Unthri·vingly** *adv.*, **Unthri·vingness.**

**13..** *E. E. Allit. P.* B. 135 A þral þryȝt in þe þrong vnþryuandely cloþed. **1387** TREVISA *Higden* (Rolls) IV. 397 Þe childe was i-bore to fore his tyme, and þerfore it was so unþryvyngeliche and so evel i-schape. **1704** *Dict. Rust.* s.v. *Enclosures*, The unthrivingness of Trees.

**Unthro·ne**, *v.* [UN-² 4. Cf. Du. *onttronen*, G. *entthronen.*] *trans.* To dethrone.

**1611** COTGR., *Desthroner*, to disthronize, or vnthrone. **1637** EARL MONM. tr. *Malvezzi's Romulus & Tarquin* 9 Amulius is not content to have unthron'd his brother. **1658** W. CHAMBERLAYNE *Loves Vict.* I. 13 Do not..Unthrone thy soul with this unmanly passion. **1665** DRYDEN *Indian Queen* V. i, Think, what pride, unthroned, must undergo. **1721** SOUTHERNE *Spartan Dame* III. i, She means to bring her Father in again, And to unthrone her Husband. **1838** TUPPER *Proverb. Philos.* 167 The shock that splitteth the globe, shall not unthrone thy self-possession. **1883** WHITELAW *Sophocles, Oedipus King* 386 Creon..Seeks to unthrone me, springing unawares.

Hence **Unthro·ning** *vbl. sb.* (also *attrib.*).

**1653** W. RAMESEY *Astrol. Restored* 324 An un-throning of some King. **1661** J. DAVIES *Civil Warres* 216 They resolved to send him four (as one called them) un-throning bills.

**Unthro·nged**, *ppl. a.* (UN-¹ 8.) **1648** HEXHAM II, *Ongedrongen sitten*, to Sitt unpressed or unthronged. [**1775** ASH. **1847** WEBSTER.] † **Unthrou·ghfareness.** [UN-¹ 12.] Impenetrability. **1674** N. FAIRFAX *Bulk & Selv.* 112 The soul not agreeing with body, so much as in that one belonger of unthroughfareness. † **Unthrou·ghfaresome**, *a.* [UN-¹ 7.] Impenetrable. **1674** N. FAIRFAX *Bulk & Selv.* 138 Body being a stour unweildsom thing, or at least a boaky unthroughfaresom thing.

**Unthrow·n**, *ppl. a.* (UN-¹ 8 b, 8 c.)

*a* **1547** SURREY *Æneis* II. 605 No stone vnthrown, nor yet no dart vncast. **1642** T. WILSON *Jerichoes Down-fall* (1643) 86 Wherefore downe must the house, leave not one stone upon another unthrowne downe. **1651–7** T. BARKER *Art of Angling* (1820) 6 If any of the Line falleth into the water before the Flie, it is better unthrown then thrown. *a* **1716** SOUTH *Serm.* (1842) III. 522 As long as the old ferment remains unthrown out, a man cannot be safe.

**Unthru·st**, *ppl. a.* (UN-¹ 8 b.) [**1775** ASH.] **1842** MRS. BROWNING *Grk. Chr. Poets* iv. Wks. (1904) 623 Objurgation vain To soulless nature, powerless to contain One ill unthrust upon it! **Unthu·mbed**, *ppl. a.* (UN-¹ 8.) [**1775** ASH.] **1797** COLERIDGE *Lett.* (1895) 7 His various works, uncut, unthumbed, have been preserved free from all pollution. **1846** MRS. GORE *Eng. Char.* (1852) 99 In his time, newspapers..were unthumbed in the pantry.

**Unthwa·rted**, *ppl. a.* (UN-¹ 8.)

[**1775** ASH.] **1805** WORDSW. *Prelude* IX. 523, I with him believed..that we should see the earth Unthwarted in her wish. **1853** WHITTIER *Trust* 18 Resting..upon His will Who moves to His great ends unthwarted by the ill. **1872** RUSKIN *Fors Clav.* xvi. 12 Such as the unthwarted sun in his season brings.

† **Unthwyuond**, *pres. pple. Obs.* (Origin and meaning obscure; the alliteration requires *tw.*)

*c* **1400** *Destr. Troy* 6360 The xij [= twelfth] vnthwyuond, þat twyet not in fight, Was..mightful Henex. *Ibid.* 6378 With xxij [= two and twenty] vnthwyuond twyet to filde.

**Unti·cketed**, *ppl. a.* (UN-¹ 8.) [**1775** ASH.] **1865** TYLOR *Early Hist. Man.* viii. 203 An unticketed collection. **1899** *Westm. Gaz.* 20 Apr. 7/1 The unticketed crowd..was..perfect in its quiet behaviour. **Unti·ckled**, *ppl. a.* (UN-¹ 8.) **1736** CHESTERFIELD *Fogg's Jrnl.* No. 377 ¶ 5 There is not an ear in the whole country untickled.

**Unti·dily**, *adv.* (UN-¹ 11.)

*c* **1440** *Promp. Parv.* 367/2 On-tydely. **1530** PALSGR. 472/2, I bungyll, or do a thyng untydyly, or lyke an yvell workeman. [**1775** ASH.] **1825** JAMIESON s.v., She was very untidily dressed. **1847** C. BRONTË *J. Eyre* viii, Untidily folded articles pinned to her shoulder. **1885** *Manch. Exam.* 12 Jan. 6/3 The table over which the remains of a fish dinner were untidily scattered.

**Unti·dy**, *a.* [ME. *untīdi* (UN-¹ 7), = WFris. *on-*, *ûntidich*, MDu. *ontidich* (Du. *ontijdig*), MLG. *untidich*, OHG. *unzītich* (MHG. *unzitec*, *-zitic*, G. *unzeitig*), MSw. *otidig*, (M)Da., Norw. *utidig* untimely, unseasonable, unfavourable, etc.]

†**1.** Untimely, unseasonable; unsuitable, unseemly.

*a* **1225** *Leg. Kath.* 2400 Aflei from ham al uuel, Weorre & weane baðe, & untidi wederes! **1377** LANGL. *P. Pl.* B. xx. 118 With his vntydy tales he tened ful ofte Conscience and his compaignye. **1393** *Ibid.* C. x. 262 The tarre is vntydy þat to þyne sheep by-longeþ. *c* **1440** *Promp. Parv.* 367/2 On-tydy, *intemptatus* (P. *intemperatus*). **1661** J. ARNWAY *Tablet* 91 Hitherto ye are come by an untidy Parliament, wherein..many..made grievous..shiprack of the Faith.

**2.** Of poor, mean, or uncared-for appearance; not kept in good order; not neat or orderly.

For the break in the evidence (as in the *adv.* above), cf. the history of TIDY *a.* (esp. sense 4).

*c* **1350** *Will. Palerne* 1455 Sche schal..haue mo solempne cites and semliche casteles, þan ȝe treuly han smale tounes or vntydi houses. *a* **1529** SKELTON *E. Rummyng* 151 Theyr lockes about theyr face, Theyr tresses vntrust,..Full vntydy tegges, Lyke rotten egges. **1545** BALE *Image Both Ch.* I. ix. (1550) Ki, Bishoppes, preestes, monkes,..were poore, abiecte, and vntydye. **1570** FOXE *A. & M.* (ed. 2) I. 116 Therfore this vntydie ground of ours, bringeth forth so many weedes.

[**1775** ASH.] **1824** CARR *Craven Gloss.* 119 *Unheppen*,.. indecent, untidy. *a* **1825** FORBY *Voc. E. Anglia*, *Untidy*, unclean; sluttish. **1855** *Poultry Chron.* II. 541 The untidy one [*sc.* bee-keeper] permits cobwebs to occupy the corners of the bee-shed. **1884** F. M. CRAWFORD *Rom. Singer* I. 4 There can be nothing so untidy about a house as children and chickens.

Hence **Unti·diness.**

[**1775** ASH.] **1845** E. B. BARRETT *Lett. Browning* (1899) I. 115, I rather like blots than otherwise—being a sort of patronsaint of all manner of untidyness. **1875** W. S. HAYWARD *Love agst. World* 13, I must be in a dreadful state of untidyness.

**Unti·dy**, *v.* [UN-² 3, or f. UNTIDY *a.*] *trans.* To make untidy.

**1891** R. DOWLING *Isle of Surrey* 112 He was busy tidying, or rather untidying, his room all one day. **1893** BARING-GOULD *Cheap Jack Zita* I. 192 The wildness of her appearance thus untidied by the wind.

**Untie·**, *v.* [OE. *untīgan* (UN-² 3, 7).]

**1.** *trans.* To release, set free, detach, by undoing a cord or similar fastening.

*c* **1000** *Ags. Gosp.* Matt. xxi. 2 Þonne sona finde ȝyt ane assene ȝetiȝȝede..: untiȝeað hiȝ, and lædað to me. *Ibid.* Mark xi. 5 Hwæt do ȝyt þone folan untiȝende? **13..** *K. Alis.* 784 (Laud MS.), He it [*sc.* Bucephalus] vntyed & lete gon. **1388** WYCLIF *Mark* xi. 5 Thei..founden a colt tied bifore the ȝate,..and thei vntieden hym. **1530** PALSGR. 768/2, I untey, ..*je deslie.* Untey my hosen. **1581** A. HALL *Iliad* VIII. 147 His goodly steedes the Marine god..vnties. *c* **1586** C'TESS PEMBROKE *Ps.* XCI. ii, From snare..He shall thee sure unty. **1639** T. DE GRAY *Expert Farrier* 236 Untye him, and give him meat. **1659** HAMMOND *On Ps.* lx. 6 As when the master reaches out his shooe to his meanest servant, to be untyed and taken off by him. **1719** DE FOE *Crusoe* II. (Globe) 494 They said,..if they untied her [*sc.* a cow], they should see which Way she went. **1725** POPE *Odyss.* IX. 208, I climbed my vessel's lofty side; My train obeyed me, and the ship unty'd. **1794** WORDSW. *Guilt & Sorrow* lxiv, They..busily ..untie Her garments. **1847** EMERSON *Daemonic Love* 148 Therefore comes an hour from Jove Which his ruthless will defies, And the dogs of Fate unties.

*absol.* **1638** JUNIUS *Paint. Ancients* 193 The unlearned.. use to think it a matter of greater strength..to teare asunder, than to unty.

**b.** To free from a confining or encircling cord, bond, etc.

*c* **1450** *Cov. Myst.* (1922) 224 Goo forthe,..and lazare ȝe vntey, And all his bondys losyth hem asundyr. *a* **1533** LD. BERNERS *Huon* ci. 333 Huon came to yᵉ fote of yᵉ ladder, where as he founde Gerames as then not vntyed. **1596** SHAKS. *Tam. Shr.* II. i. 21, I prethee sister Kate, vntie my hands. **1683** MOXON *Mech. Exerc., Printing* xxii. ¶ 7 He unties all the Pages of that Quarter. **1747** MRS. GLASSE *Cookery* ii. 38 Untye your Cucumbers, but take care the Meat don't come out. **1781** COWPER *Charity* 471 With slow deliberation he unties His glitt'ring purse. **1819** SHELLEY *Peter Bell 3rd* VI. vii, All these Reviews the Devil made Up in a parcel... Peter..Untied them—read them. **1891** FARRAR *Darkn. & Dawn* lv, The executioner has untied your hands.

**c.** In various fig. uses.

**13..** *Cast. Love* (H.) 1603 Hevyn and erthe shull byn aleyde, And the foure elementes shull be unteyede. **1390** GOWER *Conf.* III. 21 If thou be forto wyte In eny point..Wherof thi wittes ben unteid. **1565** COOPER, *Linguam resoluere*,.. to vntie his tongue. **1586** DAY *Eng. Secretary* I. (1625) 87 Before this time the like breach..was neuer seene betweene vs: but what (mischiefe) shal I now terme it..that..hath in this vilde sort, giuen meanes to vntie vs. **1605** SHAKS. *Macb.* IV. i. 52 Though you vntye the Windes, and let them fight Against the Churches. *a* **1654** SELDEN *Table-T.* (Arb.) 66, I cannot bind my self, for I may untie my self again. **1655** EARL ORRERY *Parthen.* I. VI. 131, I will vntye my Soule from that Cley which invirons it. *a* **1845** WORDSW. *Eccl. Sonn.*, *Crusaders* 10 When Heaven unties Her innost,.. tenderest harmonies. **1847** DISRAELI *Tancred* IV. iv, We shall be at Hebron before they untie their eyelids.

**2.** To undo, unfasten (a cord, knot, etc.); also *transf.* to relax (a hold).

**1590** SPENSER *F. Q.* I. xi. 42 He forst him to vnty One of his grasping feete. **1602** *2nd Pt. Return Parnass.* III. iv. 1378 If he will not vnty the purse stringes of his liberality. **1639** J. TAYLOR *Summers Trav.* (Hindley, III) 17 You might have untied it [*sc.* a halter], that it might have serv'd another time. *a* **1718** PRIOR *Love Disarmed* 39 The Chain I'll in

Return unty; And freely Thou again shalt fly. **1791** Cowper *Odyssey* VIII. 339 A snare Of bands indissoluble, by no art To be untied. **1858** Trollope *Dr. Thorne* iii, The old squire of Greshamsbury, whose shoe ribbons Dr. Fillgrave would not have objected to untie. **1885** 'Mrs. Alexander' *Valerie's Fate* i, She untied and removed her veil.

*fig.* **1581** G. Elliot in Arber *Garner* VIII. 208 Even then (by God's great goodness..) all their..devilish devices and practises were so broken and untied in me that [etc.].

**b.** *fig.* To solve or clear away (a difficulty). Freq. with *knot* in fig. sense (cf. Knot *sb.*[1] 10).

(*a*) *a* **1586** Sidney *Arcadia* II. xiii, The love of him commaundid him to preserve his life: which knot might well be cut, but untied it could not be. **1601** Shaks. *Twel. N.* II. ii. 42 O time, thou must vntangle this, not I; It is too hard a knot for me t'vnty. **1643** R. Baker *Chron., Stephen* 65 A Gordian knot, which no Writer helpes me to unty. **1732** Berkeley *Alciphr.* VI. § 32 He will endeavour to untie knots as well as tie them. **1746** Francis tr. *Hor., Sat.* II. v. 56, I know the Doubles of the mazy Laws, Unty their Knots, and plead with vast Applause. **1761** Sterne *Tr. Shandy* IV. vii, That is cutting the knot, said my father, instead of untying it. **1818** Cobbett *Pol. Reg.* XXXIII. 714 We cannot cut the knot: we must, therefore, take time to untie it. **1889** S. Walpole *Life Ld. J. Russell* II. 374 The new King tried to cut instead of untying the Gordian knot.

(*b*) **1611** Shaks. *Cymb.* v. iv. 149 'Tis still a Dreame..Or senselesse speaking, or a speaking such As sense cannot vntye. **1649** Davenant *Love & Hon.* IV. iv. 80 We must to Delphos sure t'untie these doubts..with an oracle. **1654** Jer. Taylor *Real Pres.* 65 The whole party wanders in eternal intricacies, and inextricable riddles; which..themselves cannot untie.

**c.** *fig.* To dissolve (a bond, esp. of union).

(*a*) **1634** B. Jonson *Love's Welcome* Wks. (1641) 282 A true-love Knot will hardly be unti'd. **1651** Hobbes *Leviath.* IV. xlvii. 385 First, the Power of the Popes was dissolved... And so was untyed the first knot. **1671** R. MacWard *True Non-conf.* 166 Unless the error be of greater importance,..it ought not to unty the bond of the unity of the Catholick Church. **1784** Cowper *Task* II. 685 Profusion..unties the knot Of union. **1805** Scott *Last Minstrel* VI. ii, Land of my sires! what mortal hand Can e'er untie the filial band, That knits me to thy rugged strand! **1895** *Daily News* 15 Nov. 7/3 If a husband got tired of his wife,..the State winked at a collusive suit by which the knot was untied.

(*b*) **1606** Shaks. *Tr. & Cr.* II. iii. 111 The amitie that wisedome knits, not folly may easily vntie. **1610** — *Temp.* v. i. 253 Come hither Spirit, Set Caliban and his companions free: Vntye the Spell. *a* **1683** Sidney *Disc. Govt.* iii. § 15 (1698) 316 But if these obligations were untied, we may easily guess [etc.].

**3.** *intr.* To become loosened or untied.

**1590** *Tarlton's Newes Purgat.* 30 He threwe his armes about him with such violence, that his wide sleeue vntyed. **1651** Jer. Taylor *Serm. for Year* II. v. 59 Then their resolution unties like the cords of vanity or the gossamere against the violence of the Northen winde. *Ibid.* II. xxiii. 290 Their promises are but fair language,..and disband and unty like the air that beat upon their teeth, when [etc.].

Hence **Untie·d** *ppl. a.*[1]

**1565** Cooper s.v. *Recinctus, Zona recincta,* a girdle vntied. **1619** Fletcher *Knt. Malta* v. i, I am..a vessel crack'd, A Zone unti'd. **1891** T. Hardy *Tess* xlvii, She..had to supply the man with untied sheaves.

**Untie·d,** *ppl. a.*[2] [Un-[1] 8.]

**1.** Not tied, in various senses.

*c* **1374** Chaucer *Troylus* II. 752, I am myn owene woman wel at ese,..Right yong and stond vntyd in lusty lese. **1390** Gower *Conf.* I. 307 Suche adaies be now fele..That lete here tunges gon unteid. *Ibid.* II. 117 Mi sorwe is everemore unteid, And secheth overal my veines. **1398** Trevisa *Barth. De P. R.* v. xxiii. (Bodl. MS.), Þat partie of þe tunge þat is ny3e þe pipe of þe lunges is vntied. **1509** Hawes *Past. Pleas.* XVIII. (Percy Soc.) 86 Myne owne I am, what that I lyste to do I stand untyed. *a* **1529** Skelton *Agst. Venemous Tongues* 4, I care muche the lesse what euer they say, For tunges vntayde be rennyng astray. **1617** Daniel *Coll. Hist. Eng.* 114 There were Excesses to many committed in a time so vntied as this was. **1651** Hobbes *Leviath.* II. xviii. 89 The untyed hands of that Man..that hath the Soveraignty. **1725** Pope *Odyss.* IX. 158 A port there is, inclos'd on either side, Where ships may rest, unanchored, and unty'd. *c* **1730** Ramsay *Bonny Tweedside* iv, Unty'd to a man..We never can thrive. **1888** *Stamford Mercury* 27 Apr., An untied beerhouse, cottages and land.

**2.** Wrongly used for 'unloosed'.

**1608** Shaks. *Per.* IV. ii. 160 If fires be hot, knives sharp, or waters deep, Untied I still my virgin knot will keep.

†**Unti·ffed,** *ppl. a.* [Un-[1] 8: see Tiff *v.*[1]] Unadorned.

*a* **1225** *Ancr. R.* 420 To Godes eien heo is lufsumere, þet is, uor þe luue of him, untiffed wiðuten.

†**Unti·ght,** *sb. Obs.*[—1] [Un-[1] 12 + Tight *sb.*[1] Cf. Du. *ontucht*, OHG., MHG. *unzuht* (G. *unzucht*).] An immoral act or practice.

*a* **1300** *Body & Soul* in *Map's Poems* (Camden) 336 3wanne thou3 me tau3tist on unti3th, an me gan ther offe mone. [*Ibid.* 341 (Vernon MS.), Whon I dude an untiht.]

**Unti·ght,** *a.* (Un-[1] 7.)

**1622** F. Markham *Bk. War* I. vi. 21 However crazie or untight my pore Vessell may be, it must stil put forth into the Sea. **1622** Malynes *Anc. Law-Merch.* 142 If the overloope of the Ship be vntyth, or the Pumpe be faultie. **1815** W. Finlayson *Scot. Rhymes* 27 Like some poor bodie, in his mind untight. **1823** P. Nicholson *Pract. Build.* 336 When lime has been long kept in..untight casks.

**Unti·ghten,** *v.* (Un-[2] 3.) [1775 Ash.] **1836** Browning *Porphyria's Lover* 46, I untightened next the tress About her neck.

**Until** (ʌnti·l), *prep.* and *conj.* Forms: α. 3 *Orm.* unntill, 4–7 vn-, 4–9 untill (7 untell), 4, 6 vn-, 5–6 untyll (5 unetyll); 4–5 vn-, 5 (9 *arch.*) untille, 5 un-, vntylle (yn-); 4–7 vntil, 5–6 vntyl, 4– until. β. 4 (9 *dial.*) ontil, *Sc.* 5 ontyll, onetil, 5–6 ontill. [ME. (originally northern) *untill*, f. ON. *und* (retained only in *unz*, *undz* = *und es*), = Goth. *und* (and *untē*), OS. *und* (usually *unt*), OFris. *und* (*ont*), up to, as far as + *till* Till *prep.* and *conj.*] **A.** *prep.*

In poetry occasionally put after the sb. (or pron.).

**I.** Local (and derived senses), dative, etc. Latterly *Sc.* and *north.*

**1.** To, unto (denoting motion to and reaching a person or place); = Till *prep.* 1.

*c* **1200** Ormin 1399 Forr whatt te33 fellenn sone dun Off heoffne unntill helle. *a* **1300** *Cursor M.* 5123 Þan he went vntil his in. *c* **1330** R. Brunne *Chron. Wace* (Rolls) 13086 Wiþ hym vntil wode þey fled. *c* **1380** *Sir Ferumb.* 2311 Þe Amerel vn-til a wyndow ran. *a* **1450** *Le Morte Arth.* 3858 Streyght vnto hys bed he yode, And clepyd the bysshope hym vntylle. **1478** *Eng. Misc.* (Surtees Soc. 85) 37 Unto all theis untill whome this presentes shal com. **1526** Tindale *Matt.* iv. 3 Then came vntyll hym the tempter. **1561** *Godly Q. Hester* (1873) 12 Then shall I brynge her the kynge untyll. **1590** Spenser *F. Q.* I. xi. 4 He rousd himselfe full blith, and hastned them vntill. ? *a* **1800** *Jock o' the Side* xiii. in Scott *Min.*, When they cam the gate until. **1824** J. Telfer *Border Ball.* 43 It dirlit upthrow the twinklinge holes, The second lifte untille.

**b.** Up to (a point or limit); as far as; so as to reach; = Till *prep.* 1 b.

*c* **1330** R. Brunne *Chron. Wace* (Rolls) 10554 Fro þe Weste or Est vntil Moungow He was told of non honour. **1338** — *Chron.* (1810) 42 Þe folk vntille Humber to Suane gan þei loute. *c* **1440** *York Myst.* xxxvii. 52, I prechid in Neptalym, þat lande, And Zabulon even vn-till ende. **1535** Coverdale *Judg.* xx. 1 Then wente the children of Israel out and gathered a congregacion,..from Dan vntill Bersaba. **1552** *Bk. Com. Prayer, Communion*, Upon the holy dayes..shalbe sayde al that is appoynted.., vntyl the ende of the Homelie. **1599** Hakluyt *Voy.* II. I. 211 Staires of yron ascending vp vntill the midst of the pillers. **1616** J. Lane *Contn. Sqr.'s T.* xi. 311 A woman..Which att her necke, vntill her dugges dependinge, Wore the ritch rubie. *a* **1765** *Ld. Thomas & Fair A.* xxviii. in Child *Ball.*, Lord Thomas..strake the dagger untill his heart.

**c.** In contact with; against.

*c* **1440** *Pallad. on Husb.* III. 1138 Sarmentes..Vntil a reed for turnyng bounden fast. **1785** R. Forbes *Ulysses* 38 He shook the blade, an'..Set the heft to the ground, The nib until his breast. *a* **1803** *Cruel Mother* iii. in Child *Ball.* I. 221/1 She's set her back untill an oak. *Ibid.* iv.

**2.** To, towards; unto; = Till *prep.* 2.

*a* **1300** *Cursor M.* 23286 Þai..Ne wald noght here bot þair delices, Þat drogh þam vntil oþer vices. **1303** R. Brunne *Handl. Synne* 6484 Þogh now we 3aue alle þy gode vntyl pore mannes fode. **1338** — *Chron.* (1810) 237 3it auanced he þat file vntille a faire þing. *c* **1440** *Pallad. on Husb.* I. 448 Mynge hit yurne Tyl euery part vntyl on body turne. *c* **1535** Fisher *Wks.* II. (E.E.T.S.) 429 Howe terribly shall he lay this vntyll our charge, whan we shal be called vntyll a rekenynge for this matter! **1566** Sternhold & H. *Ps.* cxxxix. 6 It is so hye that I the same Can not attayne vntill. **1587** M. Grove *Pelops & Hipp.* (1878) 77 Perchance yᵉ gods haue you preseru'd vntil some better end. *c* **1675** in *Shirburn Ball.* (1907) 171 Good or euill, which his minde was bent vntill. *c* **1800** in Chambers *Pop. Poems Scotl.* (1862) 64 Ge—en—tlemen o' the Jury, Ye'll answer until a' your names. **1814** Scott *Wav.* x, The Laird..had devoted his leisure *untill* tillage and agriculture.

†**b.** *Like until*, like; resembling. *Obs. rare.*

*c* **1375** *Leg. Rood* (1871) 123 It was like untill a heuyn. *c* **1400** Maundev. (Roxb.) vii. 26 Þe fruyt..es lyke vntill hostez.

**3.** Indicating the person towards whom an action, feeling, statement, etc., is directed. Freq. after verbs of telling, teaching, calling, doing, giving, making, listening, etc. = Till *prep.* 3.

*a* **1300** *Cursor M.* 1069 Vntil his broþer nith he bare. **1357** *Lay Folks' Catech.* (T.) 56 Seuen dedis of merci until oure euen-cristen. **1377** Langl. *P. Pl.* B. Prol. 227 Tauerners vn-til hem tolde þe same. *c* **1400** *Rule St. Benet* (Verse) 378 Al þat scho sal tech oþer vntill. **1417** *York Memo. Bk.* (Surtees) I. 183 He that es noght obeiant untill sercheours and till his crafte. *c* **1450** Lovelich *Grail* lvi. 77 What is that the vntylle? **1470–85** Malory *Arthur* XVIII. xv. 752 She cryed on loude vntyl hym. *a* **1500** *Coventry Corpus Chr. Pl.* 966 The furst byddyng, Wyche Moses dyd rede vs vntill. **1521** Fisher *Serm. agst. Luther* iv. D v, He shal be a comforter vntyl vs. **1565** J. Hall *Crt. Virtue* 31 The rounde earth he hath forth lente The sonnes of mortall men vntyll. **1567** *Gude & Godlie B.* (S.T.S.) 82 Than 3e present ane peirles sing, Of lyfe serene, the warld vntill. *a* **1780** *Archie o' Cawfield* xxxv. in Child *Ball.*, The lieutenant Until a bonny lad said..'Who is the man..?' *Ibid.* xxxvi.

†**4.** Up to (a given number); amounting or extending to. *Obs. rare.*

*c* **1400** Maundev. (Roxb.) xxii. 102 Diuerse bestez, as marmusetes, apes and oþer many vntil iiiᵐ or iiiiᵐ. **1539** Bible (Great) *Matt.* xviii. 22 Lorde howe oft shall I forgeue my brother..: Tyll seuen tymes? Iesus sayeth vnto him: I saye not vnto the vntill seuen tymes: but seuenty times seuen tymes. **1582** N.T. (Rhem.) *Luke* ii. 37 And she was a widow vntil eightie and foure yeres.

**II.** With reference to time.

**5.** Onward till (a time specified or indicated); up to the time of (an action, occurrence, etc.); = Till *prep.* 5.

*a* **1300** *Cursor M.* 1424 Stil ai stod þai wandes thre Fra adam tim until noe. *c* **1340** Hampole *Pr. Consc.* 555 Þe wilk reches fra þe bygynnyng Of mans lyfe un-til þe endyng. *a* **1352** Minot *Poems* (ed. Hall) iii. 39 All þat land vntill þis day Fars þe better for þat iornay. *c* **1420** *Anturs of Arth.* (T.) 702 Þay made hyme..a knyghte of þe tabylle rownde, Vn-tille his lyues ende. *a* **1466** *Paston Lett.* Suppl. (1901) 105, I pray zow that hyt may be repytyd un tyll the tyme that I speke with zow. **1539** Bible (Great) *Luke* xvi. 16 The lawe and the Prophetes raygned vntyll Iohn. **1554** in Feuillerat *Revels Q. Mary* (1914) 154 From the laste daye of Maye..vntill the vjᵗ daye of June. **1592** *Arden of Feversham* III. vi. 36, I doo but slip it vntil better time. **1652** J. Wright tr. *Camus' Nat. Paradox* x. 229 Intreating him to stay there untill further intelligence from him. *a* **1682** Sir T. Browne *Tracts* (1683) 138 With little action with foreign Nations untill the union of the Heptarchy under Egbert. **1721** Mortimer *Husb.* (ed. 2) II. 133 [To] hang them up until the end of February. **1754** in *Nairne Peerage Evid.* (1874) 55 Taking upon himself the stile or title of lord Nairn..until pay[men]t. **1853** Thackeray *Eng. Hum.* i. 10 He waits and waits until nightfall. **1889** *Science-Gossip* XXV. 255/2 Brooks's comet..may be visible..until the end of the year.

**b.** With (usu. after) a negative, = Till *prep.* 5 b.

**1543** *Star Chamber Cases* (Selden) II. 267 Straungers..will not vtter their wares..vntill the Faire. **1590** Shaks. *Mids. N.* II. ii. 117 Things growing are not ripe vntill their season. **1628** tr. *Mathieu's Powerfull Favorite* 103 Tiberius ceased not vntill such time as the Senate did content him. **1671** tr. *Frejus' Voy. Mauritania* 21 Although this be a countrey where, untill this very day, we see no man so venterous as to hazard himself, but by Hostages. **1764** H. Walpole *Otranto* v, Until this hour I never set eyes on this damsel. **1872** J. L. Sanford *Estimates Eng. Kings, Chas. I*, 333 He did not become a person of real importance..until the death of his elder brother. **1893** W. O. Morris *Napoleon* (1894) 158 Nelson had not left Europe until the second week of May.

**c.** Followed by an adv. (or advb. phrase) of time. = Till *prep.* 5 c.

**1338** R. Brunne *Chron.* (1810) 58 Godwyn..fro London went away, He stode vntille no more, defaute he mad þat day. **1538** Elyot, *Etiamnum*, vntyll than. **1539** Bible (Great) *Num.* xiv. 19 As thou hast forgeuen this people from Egipte euen vntyll now. **1582** N. T. (Rhem.) *Matt.* xi. 12 From the dayes of Iohn the Baptist vntil novv. *a* **1631** Donne *Paradoxes* (1652) 81 A vertue which,..untill then, is kept with a modest chastity. **1648** Hexham II, *Tot wanneer?* Untill when? **1721** in *Cath. Rec. Soc. Publ.* VIII. 301 From the end of Compline untill after Prime the next day. **1764** H. Walpole *Otranto* v, It was not until after frequent discourses with Isabella..that he was persuaded. **1826** *Art Brewing* (ed. 2) 126 [It] has, until lately, been a question among chemists. **1838** *Encycl. Metrop.* (1845) XXV. 175/2 The results..cannot be appreciated until after the lapse of years. **1849** Rock *Ch. of Fathers* I. v. 385 Until late in the thirteenth century. **1873** F. Hall *Mod. Eng.* p. xv, Until four years ago.

**6.** Before (a specified time).

**1887** Lady Brassey *Last Voy.* 201 Having quite abandoned all hope of our appearing until the morning.

**B.** *conj.* (See Till *conj.*)

Not common during 18th c.; in freq. use from *c* 1820.

**a.** Up to the time that; till the point or degree when; = Till *conj.* 1. Also with *that*.

*c* **1300** *Harrowing of Hell* (Auch.) 29 [They were in woe] Vntil Crist loked þaim vnto. **1338** R. Brunne *Chron.* (1810) 56 Þei..duelled þer for drede, Untille þe kyng turned, & his wrath ouer 3ede. *c* **1440** *Pallad. on Husb.* I. 619 The cok..his briddis hateth Vntil the crest uppon theire hedis growe. **1526** Tindale *Luke* xxiv. 49 Tary ye in..Jerusalem vntill ye be endewed with power. **1556** Lauder *Tractate* 481 The Maledictione of the pure Sall on 3ow and 3our seid Indure, Vntyll that 3e be rutit oute. **1580** in *10th Rep. Hist. MSS. Comm.* App. IV. 426 [The jury] shall contynue together..untill they be fullie agreed upon their verdicte. **1602** *Ld. Cromwell* IV. v. 39 Now get you in, vntill I call for you. **1684** Bunyan *Pilgr.* II. (1900) 228 He..did them all abuse; Until that I..arose. **1729** T. Innes *Crit. Essay* (1879) 267 In the meantime, until exact copies be published,..variations and alterations..may be shown [etc.]. **1764** H. Walpole *Otranto* v, Manfred..pushed on the feast until it waxed late. **1802** *Lochmaben Harper* xvi. in Scott *Min.*, The fiend dought they do but listen him to, Until that the day began to daw. **1870** M. Arnold *St. Paul & Prot.* 9 Man is altogether passive in this call, until the Holy Spirit enables him to answer it.

*ellipt.* **1596** Shaks. *Merch. V.* III. ii. 149 As doubtfull whether what I see be true, Vntill confirm'd, sign'd, ratified by you. **1855** *Poultry Chron.* III. 296/2 After this, until feathered, they should be fed on rich food.

**b.** With negative (expressed or implied) in the principal clause, = Till *conj.* 1 b. Also with *that*.

*a* **1300** *E. E. Psalter* xciii. 15 For lauerd sal noght his folke schouue awai,..Vntil þat rightwisenes Be turned in dome. *c* **1340** Hampole *Pr. Consc.* 3213 Na man may..Out of þat hard payn þam wyn, Until þe fire haf wasted þair bandes of syn. *Ibid.* 3271 Til þat sight þai may never wyn, Until þai be clensed þar of al syn. *c* **1477** *Stonor Papers* (Camden) II. 29 Fore we may nat go yn-tylle 3e comme. **1535** Coverdale *Job* xiv. 12 But when man slepeth, he ryseth not agayne, vntill the heauen perish. **1590** Shaks. *Com. Err.* v. i. 115, I will fall prostrate at his feete, And neuer rise vntill my teares..Haue won his grace to come in person hither. **1662** Dryden *To Ld. Chancellor* 32 In open Prospect nothing bounds our Eye Until the Earth seems join'd unto the Sky. **1692** E. Walker tr. *Epictetus' Mor., On Enchiridion*, That Truth they could not find Until the Morning-Star..form'd the Gospel Day. **1766** Smollett *Trav.* iv, It will not freeze at all, until it has deposited all its salt. **1798** Wordsw. *Peter Bell* Prol. 4 Through the clouds I'll never float Until I have a little Boat. **1868** Morris *Earthly Par.* I. 187 No man living should see this Until that thou..Hast given it to the seneschal. **1893** *Spectator* 22 July 101 The answer..will probably not be published until these pages are in our readers' hands.

*ellipt.* **1895** C. J. Cornish *Wild England of to-day* 248 Often they will..not move until almost trodden on.

**c.** In similar sense without a negative: Before the time that; before. Cf. Till *conj.* 1 c.

**1601** J. Weever *Mirr. Martyrs* A 3 b, One tale is good vntill another's told. **1621** Elsing *Debates Ho. Lords* (Camden) 51 He refused to yield..untell the fees..were payed him. *c* **1645** Howell *Lett.* (1655) II. 70 'Tis held a great part of incivility for maidens to drink wine untill they are married. **1841** J. R. Hope-Scott in R. Ornsby *Mem.* (1884) I. 305 There will probably be an interval of six months, at least, until they can meet. **1852** Rock *Ch. of Fathers*

III. 76 The unfitness of man's soul to go to heaven until cleansed from every smallest speck of sin.

**d.** = TILL *conj.* 1 d.

1609 HOLLAND *Amm. Marcell.* 417 Mallobantes .. was much troubled, thinking it long untill he might advance his standerd against the enemie. 1611 R. FENTON *Treat. Usury* 97 The time is not long, vntill thou must trust him with a far greater matter. 1804 LADY HUNTER in *Jrnl. Sir M. Hunter* (1894) 202 We had not sat long until one roll of the ship brought such a sea on deck as [etc.].

**e.** So long or so far that; = TILL *conj.* 1 e.

*c* 1440 *Pallad. on Husb.* III. 1143 In water first this opium relent, Of sape vntil hit ha similitude. 1535 COVERDALE *Jer.* xliv. 27 All the men of Iuda..shal perish with the swearde,..vntill they be vtterly destroyed. 1567 JEWEL *Def. Apol.* VI. vii. 625 They eate, vntil they be faine to perbreake. 1598 *Epulario* K iij, Heat it vntill the Cheese curd. 1652 CULPEPPER *Eng. Physic.* 5 If the decoction stand..for two or three dayes untill the yellow colour be changed black. 1748 *Anson's Voy.* I. viii. 82 We were obliged to bear away until they had made all fast. 1764 H. WALPOLE *Otranto* v, A silly wench, who has heard stories of apparitions until she believes them. 1836 THIRLWALL *Greece* III. 247 The flames were spread by the wind, until almost the whole island was left bare. 1901 *Scribner's Mag.* XXIX. 511/2 It was comparatively easy to repeat the drawing until the whole design was accurately copied.

*ellipt.* 1827 FARADAY *Chem. Manip.* xviii. 476 A mixture made by rubbing down very poor cheese with water.., until of the consistency of cream.

†**f.** *So long* (...) *until*, = TILL *conj.* 1 f. *Obs.*

1470–85 MALORY *Arthur* VII. xxxi. 263 So this syr Gareth rode soo longe in that forest vntyl the nyghte came. 1565 COOPER *Thesaurus* s.v. *Eatenus*, Thou shouldest so longe beare vntill he had..neglected those lawes. 1595 in *Cath. Rec. Soc. Publ.* V. 346 The Universitie of Oxford, where he continwed so longe untill he was thought fitt for the degree of Bacheler of Artes. 1597 BEARD *Theatre God's Judgem.* (1612) 129 Eating grasse like oxen, even so long untill his haire was growne stiffe. 1651 WITTIE tr. *Primrose's Pop. Err.* 226 Wee must persist so long in the use of remedies, untill..we perceive [etc.].

**Until(l**, erron. varr. (now dial.) of INTIL *prep.*

*a* 1300 *Cursor M.* 2501 Þai fled and fell vntill a sogh. *c* 1375 *Ibid.* 2692 (Fairf.), Our lorde went vp vn-til [*Cott.* in-til] his blis. 1858 in *N. W. Linc. Gloss.* (1877) 264 Chuck some more stoäns until her [*sc.* a cart].

**Unti·le**, *v.* [UN-[2] 4.] *trans.* To strip (a roof, etc.) of tiles. (Common *c* 1590–1760.)

*c* 1400 *Destr. Troy* 9114 The taburnacle titly vntild was aboue. 1468–9 *Paston Lett.* Suppl. (1901) 123 Ye shall have doubyll cost for to untylle your howsys ayen. 1536 *MS. Rawl. D. 780* fol. 94 b, Rypyng and vntyllyng the Rouffes. 1589 *Whip for Ape* A iij, Cathedrall Churches he would faine vntile. 1604 T. WRIGHT *Passions* v. § 3. 182 Pull down this rafter, cut that beame, vntile the house. 1633 HEYWOOD *Eng. Trav.* I. ii, Rough tempests rise, Vntile the roofe, which..Left vnrepaired, the stormy showres beat in. 1690 LUTTRELL *Brief Rel.* (1857) II. 5 [The wind] untiled the tops of most houses more or lesse. 1713 *Lond. Gaz.* No. 5103/2 The Houses have been .. Untiled .. by the Wind. 1774 G. WHITE *Selborne* lxi, I untiled the eaves of a house where many pairs build.

*fig.* 1648 HERRICK *Hesper., To the Detractor* 4 A fellon take it, or some Whit-flaw come For to unslate, or to untile that thumb! 1699 T. BROWN *Sev. New Coll.* 60 What, is your House until'd already, and is it come to a Rupture between you?

**Unti·led**, *ppl. a.* [UN-[1] 8.] Not covered with tiles.

1377 LANGL. *P. Pl.* B. XIV. 252 Had þei no þyng but of pore men her houses were vntyled! 1600 BRETON *Pasquil's Passe* Wks. (Grosart) I. 8/1 From dwelling in a house that is vntilde..good Lord deliuer me. 1649 J. H. *Motion to Parl. Adv. Learn.* 20 Our houses were..untiled and obvious to..injuries of the weather. *a* 1721 PRIOR *Down-Hall* xxxvii, A low ruin'd white Shed..Untyl'd and unglaz'd.

**Unti·ll**, *v.* (UN-[2] 3.) 1733 TULL *Horse-Hoeing Husb.* vi. 52 It rather Untills the Land, and Anticipates the subsiding of the Ground.

**Unti·llable**, *a.* (UN-[1] 7 b.)

1714 *Welsh Monster* 26 In a wild Corner of the World,.. Worthless, untillable, and barren. 1791 COWPER *Iliad* I. 398 On the shore..Of the untillable and barren deep. 1812 BRACKENRIDGE *Views Louisiana* (1814) 27 An extensive region of open plains and meadows, interspersed with bare untillable hills. 1889 *Times* 20 Apr. 5/1 A considerable portion of the district being untillable.

**Unti·lled**, *ppl. a.* (UN-[1] 8.)

1297 R. GLOUC. (Rolls) 7667 Muche lond þer is As al wast & vntuled [*v.rr.* vntyled, -teled]. 1377 LANGL. *P. Pl.* B. XV. 451 Heth and vntiled erthe. 1382 WYCLIF *Ezek.* xxxvi. 36, I the Lord haue..plantid vntilied [1388 vntilid] thingus. 1445 in *Anglia* XXVIII. 277 Londys which were vntilied. 1469 *Paston Lett.* Suppl. (1901) 128 Thei byd them lete there land lye on tilled. 1538 STARKEY *England* 12 The erth..els schold haue leyne..rude and vntylled. 1598 SYLVESTER *Du Bartas* II. i. *Eden* 598 There lives the Sea-Oak in a little shell; There growes untill'd the ruddy Cochenel. 1638 JUNIUS *Paint. Ancients* 245 An unbroken or untilled ground. ?1674 TRAHERNE *Poems Felicity* (1910) 86 A Globe of Gold must Barren be, Untill'd & Useless. 1766 *Compl. Farmer* s.v. *Hoeing*, The tilled earth receives an advantage from these dews, which the untilled does not. 1819 SHELLEY *England* 7 A people starved and stabbed in the untilled field. 1874 STUBBS *Const. Hist.* I. ii. 19 The wide forests and untilled plains are common property.

*fig.* 1592 R. D. *Hypnerotomachia* 95 Fearing to offend hir ..with my rude and vntilled toong. 1651 JER. TAYLOR *Holy Dying* ii. § 4 His beastly nature, and desart and untilled manners. 1803 WORDSW. *Poems Nat. Indep.* I. xx. 6 Men unto whom..minds not stinted or untilled are given.

†**Unti·lthed**, *ppl. a. Obs. rare.* [UN-[1] 8.] = prec. 1495 GLANVIL. *Barth. De P. R.* XIV. xlviii. F i b/2 That londe þat is tilthyd hyghte Ager and þat londe that is vntylthyd [*Bodl. MS.* vntilied] highte Rus. †**Unti·lward**, *prep. Obs.*—[1] [f. UNTIL *prep.* + -WARD. Cf. TILWARD.] Toward. *a* 1300 *Cursor M.* 15739 Iesus went him forþerward..Vntilward a littel yard O cedron ouer þe strand.

**Unti·mbered**, *ppl. a.*[1] [UN-[1] 8.]

**1.** Not furnished with timbers; frail.

1606 SHAKS. *Tr. & Cr.* I. iii. 43 Where's then the sawcy Boate, Whose weake vntimber'd sides but euen now Coriual'd Greatnesse? 1814 SIR R. WILSON *Priv. Diary* (1861) II. 371 The vessel of state is yet too weak and untimbered to buffet the waves.

**2.** Unprovided with timber; not wooded.

1808 PIKE *Sources Mississ.* II. App. (1810) 8 The vast tract of untimbered country..between the..Missouri, Mississippi, and the western Ocean. 1828–32 WEBSTER s.v., Untimbered land.

**Unti·mbered**, *ppl. a.*[2] [UN-[2] 4, 8.] Stripped of timber; deforested.

1618 BRETON *Court. & Countryman* A 4 b, Your state is weakened and your Land wasted, your Woods vntimberd, your Pastures vnstored.

†**Unti·me**, *sb. Obs.* [OE. *untíma* (UN-[1] 12, 4 b), = ON. and Icel. *útími*, *ótími* (MSw., Norw. dial. *otime*).]

**1.** *In* (earlier *on*) *untime*, at an unsuitable, improper, or wrong time. Also in pl.

Cf. ON. *í útíma*, MSw. *i otima*, *i otimom*, in same sense.

*c* 897 K. ÆLFRED *Gregory's Past. C.* xxi. 153 Swa se læce, ðonne he on untiman lacnað wunde, hio wyrmseð & rotað. *c* 1000 ÆLFRIC *Saints' Lives* xii. 76 Ælc þæra manna þe yt oððe drincð on untiman on þam halȝan lenctene. *c* 1200 *Trin. Coll. Hom.* 207 He habbe ofte agilt on golliche dedes, on untime oðer on unluuede stede. *a* 1225 *Ancr. R.* 344 Of vres misseide wiðuten ȝeme of heorte oðer in untime. 1303 R. BRUNNE *Handl. Synne* 2962 Ȝyf þou þys foly haunte.. Yn vntyme,.. For soþe þou synnest þer dedly. *c* 1386 CHAUCER *Pars. P.* ¶ 1051 A man shal nat ete in vntyme, ne sitte the lenger at his table to ete for he fasteth. *c* 1440 *Jacob's Well* 105 To pleyin at þe tablys,..& at swyche oþere vayn pleyis, in vntyme & out of mesure. 1486 *Bk. St. Albans, Hawking* c vii b, A lombe that was borne in vntime. *a* 1500 in *Ratis Raving*, etc. 18 Oft fore thocht of his riches he walkis in wntymis.

**b.** *Untimes* (gen. sing.), untimely, untimeous.

*a* 1300 *Cursor M.* 27799 O suernes cums..Vntimes spech or to be still. *c* 1470 HENRY *Wallace* IX. 1630 This hour.. thow mycht haiff beyn away; Wntymys thow art, for it is scantly day.

**2. a.** A bad time, inclement season. (OE. only.)

*a* 1023 WULFSTAN *Hom.* 297 Ic asende ofer eower land ælcne untiman, þæt bið eȝeslice great haȝol..and unasecgendlice þunras. *c* 1130 *O. E. Chron.* an. 1124, Ðes ilces ȝeares wæron fæla untime on Englelande, on corne & on ealle westme.

**b.** An unsuitable time for action.

14.. *Northern Passion* (MS. I) 601 Thys is vn tyme of þe nyghte, In thys tharkenesse to preue ȝoure myghte.

†**Unti·me**, *a. Obs.* [OE. *untíme* (UN- 4 b).] Untimely; ill-timed.

*c* 1000 ÆLFRIC *Saints' Lives* xii. 74 Se dysiȝa dranc butan bletsunge.. He his feorh forlet and ȝebohte swa ðone untiman drenc. *c* 1200 *Trin. Coll. Hom.* 13 Continencia:..Ðat feorðe is, þat man þe spuse haueð, his golliche deden wið-teo, swo hit be untime. 1338 R. BRUNNE *Chron.* (1810) 227 Whan he com to London Tiþing com him vntime, Sir Lowys dede he fond. 1414 *26 Polit. Poems* 56 Slouþe vn-tyme eft mon swete When it is hot, and gloweþ as glede.

†**Unti·meable**, *a. Obs.*—[0] [UN-[1] 7 b.] Untimely. 1570 LEVINS *Manip.* 4 Vntymeable, *intempestiuus*. **Unti·med**, *ppl. a.* (UN-[1] 8.) [1775 ASH, *Untimed*, not timed, not regulated as to time.] 1888 MEREDITH *Poems* (1898) II. 168 With thee, O fount of the Untimed! to lead. †**Unti·meless**, *a. Obs.* [UN-[1] 5 a.] Untimely. 1602 CHETTLE *Hoffman* v. (1631) I 2, In memory of his vntimelesse fall.

**Unti·meliness.** [f. next.] The quality of being untimely.

1580 HOLLYBAND *Treas. Fr. Tong*, *Importunité*, vntimelinesse. 1656 JER. TAYLOR *Let. to Bp. Rochester* 87 The solemnities..and untimeliness of temporal death. 1670 G. H. *Hist. Cardinals* II. II. 169 Had not the untimeliness of his death prevented it. 1846 TRENCH *Mirac.* xxxi. 438 Putting out of sight the untimeliness of those leaves and of that pretence of fruit. 1850 L. HUNT *Autobiog.* II. xi. 54 The latter calamity, by a most unfortunate climax of untimeliness, took place a little before his enemy's reverses.

**Unti·mely**, *a.* [UN-[1] 7. Cf. MDa. *utimelig* of weather, etc.]

**1.** Coming before the proper or natural time; premature: **a.** Of fruit. Also, not fully or properly ripened; immature.

1535 COVERDALE *Isaiah* xxviii. 4 It shal happen vnto him, as to an vntymely frute before the haruest come. 1561 DAUS tr. *Bullinger on Apoc.* 209 That y[e] vntimely figges fal downe in great plentie. 1568 BIBLE (Bishops') *Rev.* vi. 13 Euen as a figge tree casteth her vntimely figges. 1644 MILTON *Educ.* 2 These are not matters to be wrung from poor striplings, like ..the plucking of untimely fruit. 1825 A. L. BARBAULD '*Praise to God*' vi, Should the fig-tree's blasted shoot Drop her green untimely fruit.

**b.** Of birth(s).

1538 ELYOT, *Abortus*, an vntymely byrthe. 1634 T. JOHNSON tr. *Parey's Chirurg. Wks.* XXIV. xxx. 921 The causes of abortion or untimely birth, whereof the child is called an abortive, are many. 1710 BERKELEY *Princ. Hum. Knowl.* § 151 Monsters, untimely births, fruits blasted in the blossom. 1755 JOHNSON, *Abortment*, an untimely birth.

**c.** Of death, fate, etc.

1548 ELYOT, *Praematura mors*, vntymely death. 1596 DRAYTON *Leg. Matilda* 648 Some say, the King repentant for this Deed,..Offered His Teares on my vntimely Graue. 1599 B. JONSON *Cynthia's Rev.* I. i, Th' untimely fate of that too beauteous boy. 1651 HOBBES *Leviath.* II. xxix. 167 The bodies of children, gotten by diseased parents, are subject.. to untimely death. 1709 ADDISON *Tatler* No. 154 ¶ 5 Souls of Infants..snatched away by untimely Ends. 1776 GIBBON *Decl. & F.* xii. I. 322 A life of pleasure or virtue,..of indolence or glory, alike led to an untimely grave. 1819 SCOTT *Ivanhoe* xlii, Their guide pointed with solemn air to the untimely bier of Athelstane. 1847 PRESCOTT *Peru* I. 452 Heaven..bringing them all to an untimely and miserable end.

**d.** In other contexts.

1565 COOPER *Thesaurus* s.v. *Praecox*, Vntimely laughter & that happeneth very soone, as before the childe is fortie dayes olde. *c* 1586 C'TESS PEMBROKE *Ps.* LVIII. iv, O let their brood..of springing thornes Be by untymely rooting overthrowne. 1634 SIR T. HERBERT *Trav.* 157 Few of them attending patiently the death of their Predecessours, but by impious meanes labour their vntimely establishment. 1746 BERKELEY *Sec. Let. Tar-water* § 9 Unhappy drinkers ..bringing on the untimely symptoms of old age.

**e.** Perishing before due time. *rare*—[1].

1605 SYLVESTER *Du Bartas* II. iii. *Law* 667 Som, thrill'd with..shafts, through hundred holes Shall ghastly gasp-out our untimely soules.

**2.** Unseasonable (in respect of the time of year).

**a.** Of frost, blight, etc.

1576 GASCOIGNE *Steele Gl.* 455 So those imps..Are..nipt, with such untimely frosts. 1591 SPENSER *Daphn.* 238 O that so faire a flower so soone should fade, And through vntimely tempest fall away. 1730 THOMSON *Spring* 115 If brush'd from Russian wilds a cutting gale Rise not, and.. breathe Untimely frost. 1751 W. WHITEHEAD *Hymn to Nymph* 46 Life's latter fruits..at last fall off Shook by no boist'rous, or untimely blasts. 1797 GODWIN *Enquirer* I. v. 35 [It] may..suffer an untimely blight. 1847 LONGF. *Ev.* I. ii. 98 The harvests in England By untimely rains or untimelier heat have been blighted. 1853 C. BRONTE *Villette* xxxii, I have read of those who sowed in tears, and whose harvest.. perished by untimely blight.

**b.** In other contexts.

1593 DRAYTON *Shepherd's Garl.* iv. 33 O dismall day,.. O stormy winter,..O most vntimely and eclipsed morrow. 1627 ABP. ABBOT in Rushw. *Hist. Coll.* (1659) I. 448 It is an unseasonable time to brew now, and as untimely to cut Wood. 1712 *Spect.* No. 404 ¶ 3 By the Assistance of Art and an hot Bed, we may possibly extort an unwilling Plant, or an untimely Sallad. 1879 STEVENSON *Trav. Cevennes* 40 They were cutting aftermath,..which gave the neighbourhood..an untimely smell of hay.

**3.** Unseasonable, ill-timed, inopportune.

1581 J. FIELDE (*title*), A Caveat for Parsons Hovvlet, concerning his vntimely flighte, and scriching in the cleare day lighte of the Gospell. 1590 SPENSER *F. Q.* II. x. 68 So vntimely breach The Prince him selfe halfe seemeth to offend. 1607–12 BACON *Ess., Of Empire* (Arb.) 298 The vnequall and vntimely interchaunge of pressing power. 1617 WOODALL *Surg. Mate* (1639) 3 Many dangers attending the unskilfull or untimely use thereof. 1665 BOYLE *Occas. Refl.*, etc. (1848) 68 Men's overeager and untimely pursuits of several desirable things. 1756 C. LUCAS *Ess. Waters* III. 240 [It is] wise and just in general; but often..untimely; that is, too late. 1796 MME. D'ARBLAY *Camilla* II. 370 [She] felt so much hurt by this untimely sight, that..she bent her eyes another way. 1830 PRAED *Poems* (1865) I. 234 All untimely question Ruffles the temper. 1867 FREEMAN *Norm. Conq.* I. v. 328 The cause of all this untimely activity.

**b.** Of hours: Unusually late (or early).

1827 SCOTT *Highl. Widow* v. ad fin., There are many who are still unwilling, at untimely hours, to pass the oak-tree.

**Unti·mely**, *adv.* [UN-[1] 11. Cf. MSw. *otimelika* in sense 1.]

**1.** At an unsuitable or improper time; unseasonably, inopportunely.

Not in common use before the end of the 16th cent.

*c* 1200 *Trin. Coll. Hom.* 11 Swilche oðre [sins]..alse ben oueretes and untimeliche eten alehuse. 1382 WYCLIF *Ps.* civ. 28 He sente dercnessis, and made derc; and vntymely he fullfilde not [L. *non exacerbavit*] his woordis.

1596 SPENSER *F. Q.* v. v. 29 Now is the time, that I vntimely must Thereof make tryall, in my greatest need. 1596 *Edward III*, III. i. 184 Thus my tale is donne: We haue vntimly lost, and they haue woone. 1618 ROWLANDS *Night Raven* (1620) D 2 b, I behold abuses..By such as doe vntimely haunt the street. 1667 KATH. PHILIPS *Poems* 111 He only dies untimely who dies late. 1702 ROWE *Tamerl.* III. ii, If I not press untimely on his leisure, You would [etc.]. 1743 W. WHITEHEAD *Ann Boleyn to Hen. VIII*, 74, I fell untimely, and lament my Fall. 1828 SCOTT *F. M. Perth* xxii, To avenge the deed expelling Thee untimely from thy dwelling. 1882–3 *Schaff's Encycl. Relig. Knowl.* II. 851/2 The moment for this controversy was very untimely chosen by the Pope.

**2.** Before the proper or natural time; prematurely.

*a* 1586 SIDNEY *Arcadia* III. x, O sweet youth,..how untimely subject it is to devotion? 1611 GUILLIM *Heraldry* II. iv. 46, I haue inserted the same (although vntimely) in this place, which otherwise I would haue reserued to some other. 1660 *Trial Regic.* 36 When that Blessed King was untimely taken away. 1721 POPE *Ep. to Earl Oxford* 2 'Till Death untimely stopp'd his tuneful tongue. 1766 *Museum Rust.* VI. 74 Trees..untimely taken off, before they arrive at any valuable maturity. 1833 HT. MARTINEAU *Loom & Lugger* I. ii. 17 Legs bowed from having been made untimely to bear the weight of the swollen body. 1857 PUSEY *Real Presence* i. 64 Melanchthon..prolonged the conference, only lest he should seem to break it off untimely.

**Unti·meous**, *a.* Chiefly *Sc.* Forms: 5 wn-, 6–7 vn-, untymous, 6 untimus, 7–8 untimous; 6 untymeus, 7 -tymeous, 9 -timeous. [Alteration of earlier *untimes*, *untymys* (see UNTIME *sb.* 1 b), by assimilation to adjs. in -(E)OUS. For this change of ending cf. UNDEEMOUS *a.*]

**1.** Unseasonable; = UNTIMELY *a.* 2, 3.

*a* 1500 *Ratis Raving* 95 Tak not delyt in morne slepinge, Wntymous eting na drynkynge. *a* 1584 MONTGOMERIE *Cherrie & Slae* 397 Vntymous spurring spillis the steid. 1586 *Reg. Privy Council Scot.* IV. 74 The inoportune and untymous sutes of divers personis. 1640 R. BAILLIE *Canterb. Self-convict.* Pref., We could not but leave..to you..the legacie of an untimous repentance. 1670 RAY *Prov.* 280 Of untymous persons:..He is as welcome as snaw in harvest.

1823 SCOTT *Quentin D.* xvi, It required all the authority.. which Quentin could exert over him, to restrain his irreverent and untimeous jocularity. 1883 *Contemp. Rev.* Oct. 612 You do not find yourself oppressed by untimeous volunteered順 franknesses.

**b.** Of times (esp. of the night).

1728 RAMSAY *Monk & Miller's Wife* 60 Wha's that gi'es fowk a fright At sic untimous time of night? 1836 M. SCOTT *Cruise Midge* I. 349 Wha makes such an indecent uproar.. at such an untimeous season? 1837 BARHAM *Ingol. Leg.* Ser. I. *Grey Dolphin*, To inquire who sought admittance at that untimeous hour. 1894 CROCKETT *Raiders* iii, It was this which had raised me at such untimeous hours.

**2.** Premature; = UNTIMELY *a.* 1.

1536 BELLENDEN *Cron. Scot.* (1821) II. 408 He..was prevenit be untimus deith. 1603 JAS. I. Βασιλ. δωρον To Rdr. A 8 b, So as this their great concurrence in curiositie..hath inforced the vn-timous divulgating of this booke. 1634 CANNE *Necess. Separ.* 88 If his death was vntimous, it was rather for his secret intentions crossing his fathers courses. 1646 R. BAILLIE *Anabaptism* (1647) 66 The change..ere long..brought upon him an untimous and cruell death. 1828 MOIR *Mansie Wauch* xiii, I believe he came to some untimeous end.

**Unti·meously,** *adv.* Chiefly *Sc.* [UN-[1] 11, or f. prec.] = UNTIMELY *adv.*

1513 DOUGLAS *Æneid* VI. vii. 11 3oung babbeis..From the sweit lyf twynnit vntymusly. 1533 BELLENDEN *Livy* II. xv. (S.T.S.) I. 188 The romanis..had bene vntymuslie invadit be þe wolchis. *a* 1578 LINDESAY (Pitscottie) *Chron. Scot.* (S.T.S.) I. 56 Scho pairtit wntymouslie witht ane deid bairne. 1640 BAILLIE *Lett.* (1841) I. 262 The cold[ness] of the good old Generall..did shortlie cast water on this spunk, beginning most untymouslie to reek. *a* 1670 SPALDING *Troub. Chas. I* (1851) II. 273 This commvnion wes thocht to be vntymouslie givin heir. 1821 SCOTT *Kenilw.* xv, It must be some perilous cause puts her Grace in motion thus untimeously. 1851 BORROW *Lavengro* lxxi, My husband..came to his death untimeously. 1894 HALL CAINE *Manxman* I. x, Dreaming that the poor lad has come to his end untimeously.

†**Unti·ming,** *ppl. a. Obs.*—[1] [UN-[1] 10.] Careless, regardless. *c* 1350 *Commem. Dead* 20 in Horstm. *Altengl. Leg.* (1881) 146 If þe preste, þat schryues þe, Vn-timand or so rekles be þat he gif þe noght penance right [etc.]. **Unti·morous,** *a.* (UN-[1] 7.) *a* 1548 HALL *Chron., Edw. IV*, 196 b, A man of suche haute corage,..and vntimerous audacite,.. as fewe or none was sene in hys tyme. *Ibid., Rich. III*, 56 b, Let us..set on our enemies like vntimerous Tigers. **Unti·nct,** *ppl. a.* [UN-[1] 8 b.] Untinged. 1642 H. MORE *Song of Soul* II. 68 A reall infinite matter, distinct And yet proceeding from the Deitie, Although with different form as then untinct.

**Unti·nctured,** *ppl. a.* [UN-[1] 8.]

**1.** *fig.* Untinged, uncoloured, unaffected. Const. *by* or *with*.

1760–2 GOLDSM. *Cit. W.* lxvi, Simple gratitude, untinctured with love. 1769 E. BANCROFT *Guiana* 329 They are not untinctured with vanity. 1774 GOLDSM. *Nat. Hist.* II. 397 [Zebras] caught sufficiently young, so as to be untinctured by their original state of wildness. 1801 *Lusignan* I. 113 A degree of awe..not untinctured with [fear]. 1866 *Q. Rev.* Apr. 327 Oracles of the common law, but untinctured by scholarship. 1874 H. ROGERS *Orig. Bible* i. 43 Virtue..untinctured with..austerity.

**2.** In literal use; *spec.* in *Her.*

1880 WARREN *Book-plates* ii. 10 The arms are..at that period untinctured.

**Unti·ne,** *v. Obs.* exc. *dial.* Forms: 1 untynan, 2 untinen, 3 untunen (ontune), 5 vntynde, 9 *dial.* untine. [OE. *untȳnan* (var. of *an-, ontȳnan*), f. *un-* UN-[2] 3 + *tȳnan* TINE *v.*[1], = OHG. *antzûnen, inzûnen* (G. *entzäunen*).]

**1.** *trans.* To open.

*c* 950 *Lindisf. Gosp.* Matt. ii. 11 [Hia] untyndon striona hiora. *Ibid.* ix. 30 Untynde weron ego hiora. *c* 1000 ÆLFRIC *Gen.* xli. 56 Iosep untynde ealle þa bernu. *c* 1200 *Trin. Coll. Hom.* 115 Openeð ʒiure gaten, and ech gate untineð ʒiu seluen to-ʒenes þe king of blisse. *c* 1205 LAY. 9781 Amarʒen þa hit dæi wes duren heo vntunden. *Ibid.* 18949 Nis nan cniht..þe..þe ʒeten mihten un-tunen [*v.r.* ontune]. 1888 DONALDSON *Takin' th' New Year in* 8 (E.D.D.), Hoo told me hoo'd untined th' door.

**2.** To separate, sever.

*c* 1495 *Epitaffe*, etc. in *Skelton's Wks.* (1843) II. 392 Howe durst thou [*sc.* Death] his flessh and spyryte vntynde?

†**Unti·ng,** *v. Obs.*—[1] [UN-[2] 4 b. Cf. TINGER[2] and s.w. dial. *ting* to bind, fasten together.] *trans.* To loosen (a cart-body) so as to prepare it for tipping. So †**Unti·nger.** *Obs. rare.*

1587 FLEMING *Contn. Holinshed* III. 1544/2 There attended ..eight men called vntingers, to loose and vndoo the tackle of euerie court immediatlie before the vnloding or sheluing thereof [at Dover harbour]. *Ibid.* 1545/1 When the first court came nigh to the place where he should vnlode, one vntinged it, and the driuer proceeded with his court..into the ouze or water.

**Unti·nged** (-ti·ndʒd), *ppl. a.* (UN-[1] 8.)

1664 BOYLE *Exp. Hist. Colours* III. 191 In a Darken'd Room..where it may appear what Beams [of light] are Unting'd. 1732 SWIFT *Let. to Gay* 10 July, Pope has the same defect..: neither is my lord Bolingbroke untinged with it. 1744 W. WHITEHEAD *Atys & Adrastus* 283 The foaming Boar['s]..horny Sides repel Unting'd the plumy Shaft, and blunted Steel. ? 1813 LAMB *Christ's Hosp.* Wks. 1908 I. 180 This religious character in him is not always untinged with superstition. 1817 COLERIDGE *Lay Serm.* p. xxiii, Not a ray of light could enter, untinged by the medium through which it passed. 1882 FLOYER *Unexpl. Baluchistan* 61 Copper gives green, and the untinged limestone snowy white.

**Unti·nned,** *ppl. a.* (UN-[1] 8.)

[1775 ASH.] 1825 J. NICHOLSON *Operat. Mechanic* 400 A little sea-water is..put into..an untinned copper kettle. 1859 F. S. COOPER *Ironmongers' Catal.* 88 Saucepans..Tinned,.. Untinned. 1898 *Daily News* 6 Sept. 4/6 Frequent detections of unsound food, tinned and untinned.

**Unti·nt,** *ppl. a. Sc.* [UN-[1] 8 b.] Not lost. 1513 DOUGLAS *Æneid* I. x. 43 The auld Troiane geir..fra the storme of see is left ontynt. **Unti·nted,** *ppl. a.* (UN-[1] 8.) 1849 C. BRONTË *Shirley* xxix, There she is, a lily of the valley, untinted, needing no tint. 1866 R. M. FERGUSON *Electr.* 29 The space included between those two lines..is left untinted. **Unti·pped,** *ppl. a.*[1] [UN-[1] 8 + TIPPED *ppl. a.*[1]] Not furnished with a tip. 1679 *Lond. Gaz.* No. 1373/4 A Case of seven Tip Razors,..with eight other Razors, &c. some Tipt, some Untipt. 1775 ASH, *Untipped,.. Untipt.* **Unti·pped,** *ppl. a.*[2] [UN-[1] 8 + TIP *v.*[4]] Not presented with a gratuity. 1860 W. W. READE *Liberty Hall* I. xi. 203 The untipped ostler scowling from the yard. **Untirabi·lity.** (UN-[1] 12. Cf. next.) 1855 *Household Words* X. 31/2 Hence..a rapidity of hæmatosis, which explains the untirability of the wings of birds.

**Unti·rable,** *a.* Also untireable. (UN-[1] 7 b.)

1607 TOPSELL *Four-f. Beasts* 31 They are..of hardest hoofe, a leane body, but of a generous and vntierable stomack. 1607 SHAKS. *Timon* I. i. 11 A most incomparable man, breath'd as it were, To an vntyreable and continuate goodnesse. 1836 T. ALLSOP *Lett. & Recol. Coleridge* II. 226 The sympathy and untireable kindness of my revered friend. 1846 MRS. GORE *Eng. Char.* (1852) 38 The Chaperon has, constitutionally, an untirable voracity. 1875 M. COLLINS *Sweet & Twenty* II. xix, It might have gone on for ever, if everyone had been as untireable as Charlie Hawker.

† **Unti·re,** *v.*[1] *Obs.* [UN-[2] 4.] *trans.* To undress. Also *refl.* and *fig.*

1597 BEARD *Theatre God's Judgements* 342 Who being suspected, was in the presence of many vntired, and found to be a man. 1613 PURCHAS *Pilgrimage* (1614) 536 Then doe they vntire themselues, and..eate the cheere in the Platters. 1651 *Life Diazius* in Fuller *Abel Rediv.* 143 Diazius in his youthfull dayes had cloath'd His heart with Popery...When he was inspir'd By Heaven, he searcht for truth, and soon untyr'd Himselfe.

**Unti·re,** *v.*[2] [UN-[2] 3.] *trans.* To free from being tired; to rest.

In quot. 1845 after Sp. *descansar* (as in quot. 1853).

1677 *Phil. Trans.* XII. 919 A way of untiring a Soldier after a long march, *viz.* by making a Decoction of Mugwort, and washing the feet therewith. 1845 FORD *Handbk. Spain* I. 162 Let [him] remember..to invite his friend to walk in and untire himself. 1853 G. J. CAYLEY *Las Alforjas* I. 170 He..pressed us to bait our horses and *descansar* (untire) ourselves at his farm.

**Unti·red,** *ppl. a.* [UN-[1] 8.] Not tired or exhausted; unwearied.

1594 SHAKS. *Rich. III*, IV. ii. 44 Hath he so long held out with me, vntyr'd, And stops he now for breath? 1616 W. BROWNE *Brit. Past.* II. i. 10 The great effects of vntirde industry. *a* 1660 *Contemp. Hist. Irel.* (Ir. Archæol. Soc.) II. 21 Greate is the preparation, by thunderinge proclamations and untyred poastes to and fro. 1753 HANWAY *Trav.* III. xxxviii. (1762) I. 175 With..untired attention he applied himself to business. 1799 WORDSW. *Influence Nat. Obj.* 32 Exulting like an untired horse That cares not for his home. 1839 T. MITCHELL *Frogs of Aristoph.* 651 *note*, The canary, with its untired throat and labyrinth of sounds. 1889 A. LANG *Lett. Lit.* iii. (ed. 2) 37 The poor have..in him an untired advocate and friend.

**b.** Const. *by, with*, and † *of*.

1600 FAIRFAX *Tasso* I. lii, Vnfear'd in fight, vntir'd with hurt or wound. 1624 HEYWOOD *Gunaik.* v. 226 Most patient of labour, untyred with travell. 1698 ATTERBURY *Serm.* (1734) IV. 235 When the Mind is fresh and vigorous, untired with the Business of the Day. 1802 H. MARTIN *Helen of Glenross* III. 139, I am still untired of sight or visits. 1813 BYRON *Corsair* I. xii, Unmoved by absence,..And yet..untired by time. 1839 ARNOLD in Stanley *Life* (1844) II. 175, I was so perfectly untired by my past work.

Hence **Unti·redly** *adv.*

1855 FABER *Growth in Holiness* xxvi. 481 Fervour..thus immediately and untiredly..works at present duties.

**Unti·ring,** *ppl. a.* (UN-[1] 10.)

Common from *c* 1850.

1822 B. W. PROCTER *Girl of Provence* xxiv, The untiring seasons bring, for aye, To night rich slumber, and fresh life to day. 1859 JEPHSON *Brittany* xix. 312 The passengers were chiefly English, those untiring travellers. 1871 WHYTE MELVILLE *Sarchedon* I. 20 Yet a few more furlongs of those smooth untiring strides.

Hence **Unti·ringly** *adv.*

[1847 WEBSTER.] 1860 RUSKIN *Unto this Last* iv. § 82 No scene is continually and untiringly loved, but one rich by joyful human labour.

**Un-Ti·taned,** *a.* [UN-[1] 9.] Sunless. 1635 QUARLES *Embl.* II. i. 3 Thy Torch will burn more clear In night's un-Titan'd Hemisphere. **Untitheabi·lity.** (UN-[1] 12. Cf. next.) 1885 A. N. PALMER *Anc. Tenures Marches N. Wales* 28 The untitheability of the common fields of Erbistock. **Unti·theable,** *a.* (UN-[1] 7 b.) 1775 *Ann. Reg., Chron.* 133/2 This gentleman..filed a bill for..the tythe of lands before held untytheable. 1885 A. N. PALMER *Anc. Tenures Marches N. Wales* 28 The existing untitheable tract of arable and hay land.

**Unti·thed,** *ppl. a.* [UN-[1] 8. Cf. OE. *untéoðod*, and UNTEINDED *ppl. a.*]

**1.** On which no tithe is levied.

1621 BP. MOUNTAGU *Diatribæ* 540, I will complaine vpon thee vnto the Prytanes, because thou detainest..to thine owne vse, the consecrated inwards..that belong vnto the gods, vntithed. 1801 HELEN M. WILLIAMS *Sk. Fr. Rep.* I. vi. 57 The lavish produce of the earth unfeudalized, and untythed. 1845 MCCULLOCH *Taxation* II. iv. 176 It then encourages cultivation as much on the untithed as it discourages it on the tithed lands. 1871 LONGF. *Div. Trag.* II. i. 35 In thy court-yard grows the untithed rue.

**2.** Not receiving tithes.

1827 POLLOK *Course T.* VIII. 81 Not from him Could be distinguished then the priest untithed.

**Unti·tle,** *v.* (UN-[2] 4.) 1824 HOOK *Sayings* II. 48 His Lordship untitled himself with the greatest safety.

**Unti·tled,** *ppl. a.*[1] [UN-[1] 8.]

**1.** Having no title or right (to rule).

1605 SHAKS. *Macb.* IV. iii. 104 O Nation miserable! With an vntitled Tyrant, bloody Sceptred.

**2.** Unnamed, undesignated.

1612 W. PARKES *Curtaine-Dr.* (1876) 11 When these things were thus vnknowne, and vntitled, a good and happy world was I then.

**3.** Not distinguished by a title.

1798 S. & HT. LEE *Canterb. T.* II. 425 There, untitled and unknown, may we fix our home. 1825 J. NEAL *Bro. Jonathan* I. 71 What have we to do with the blazonry of an old people any more than..he, the untitled Adam? 1856 EMERSON *Eng. Traits, Aristocr.*, An untitled nobility possess all the power without the inconveniences that belong to rank. 1870 BURTON *Hist. Scot.* lvi. V. 400 They have precedence over the untitled clergy.

*absol.* 1859 *Habits of Gd. Society* 26 My Lady A—..can scarcely appreciate the wide diffusion of wit and intellegence among the untitled.

**Unti·tled,** *ppl. a.*[2] [UN-[2] 8. Cf. UNTITLE *v.*] Deprived of the title of.

1596 SPENSER *F. Q.* v. ix. 42 But false Duessa, now vntitled Queene, Was brought to her sad doome.

**Unti·ttering,** *ppl. a.* (UN-[1] 10.) 1749 in A. Dobson *Fielding* (1883) 137 Girls of an untittering Disposition. **Untittleta·ttling,** *ppl. a.* (UN-[1] 10.) 1779 H. WALPOLE in Tovey *Gray's Lett.* (1900) II. 92 There is not so untittletattling a village as Twickenham in the island. † **Unti·tuled,** *ppl. a. Obs.*—[1] [UN-[1] 8.] = UNTITLED *ppl. a.*[1] 2. 1610 HEALEY *St. Aug. Citie of God* XVII. xiv. 640 Hee made all the 150, entitling them sometimes with other names,..and leauing some others vntituled at all.

**Unto** (*v*·ntu), *prep.* and *conj.* Forms: *α.* 4– unto (5 untoo), 4–7 vnto (5 *north.* vntew), 5, 6 *Sc.* wnto. *β.* 5–6, 7 *Sc.*, 9 *dial.* onto (5 onne-to, *Sc.* one-to). [f. on the analogy of UNTIL *prep.*, by substitution of To *prep.* in place of the northern equivalent *til* TILL *prep.* Cf. the independent OS. *untō.*]

Since the end of the 17th c. less frequent, and employed chiefly in poetry, or in formal, dignified, or archaic style, or after Biblical use. Very rare in standard writers of the 18th c., and hence noted by Johnson as 'now obsolete'.

**A.** *prep.* (Ordinarily governing a sb. or pron.)

In poetry often placed after the sb. or pronoun.

**I.** Indicating spatial or local relationship.

**1.** Expressing or denoting motion directed towards and reaching (a place, point, or goal); = To *prep.* 1.

*a* 1300 *Cursor M.* 17547 Helias..Was taken up als vnto heuen. *c* 1300 *Havelok* 2399 Cum nu swiþe un-to him. 1338 R. BRUNNE *Chron.* (1810) 104 Vnto þe se side chaced þei Sir Lowys. 1387 TREVISA *Higden* (Rolls) II. 123 And the seete of Welles was chaungede vn to Bathe. *c* 1420 *Anturs of Arth.* (T.) 111 Vn-to þat gryseIy gaste Sir Gaweayne es gane. *c* 1440 *Alph. Tales* 215 He tuke bread & keste vnto it [*sc.* a swine]. *c* 1475 *Rauf Coilȝear* 5 Thay past vnto Paris. 1526 *Pilgr. Perf.* (W. de W. 1531) 4 Theyr iourney out of Egypte vnto the countre of Jerusalem. *a* 1548 HALL *Chron., Hen. VIII*, 85 He called unto him a servaunt of the kynges. 1587 HOLINSHED *Chron.* (ed. 2) III. 1187/1 The campe remooued from Linton brigs vnto salt Preston. 1590 SHAKS. *Mids. N.* III. ii. 310, I told him of your stealth vnto this wood. 1633 G. HERBERT *Temple, The Bag* iv, He did repair unto an inne. 1654 H. DUNSTER in Quincy *Hist. Harvard Univ.* (1840) I. 19 The place unto which I go, is unknown to me. 17.. *Jock o' the Side* xiii. in Caw *Poet. Museum*, When they cam the gates unto. 1768 ROSS *Helenore* 83 We came unto a gentle place. 1801 WORDSW. *Prioress' T.* 52 A little scholar..Who day by day unto this school hath gone. 1866 EMERSON *Daemonic & Celest. Love* 48 So shall the lights ye pour amain Go.. Through from the empyrean walls Unto the same again. 1887 MORRIS *Odyssey* I. 90 Then speed we..Hermes the Flitter, to go Unto the isle Ogygia.

**b.** In various fig. uses. (Cf. To *prep.* 1 b.)

*c* 1440 *Alph. Tales* 218 With þatt sho come agayn vnto hur selfe, & thankid God. *Ibid.* 448 When he come vnto his spyrittis agayn. 1526 TINDALE *Heb.* vii. 19 By which hope we drawe nye vnto god. 1535 COVERDALE *Psalm* xxiii. 4 Which lifteth not vp his mynde vnto vanite. 1538 STARKEY *England* 21 Though..I dowtyd no thyng of thys mater, that you so ernystely moue me vnto. 1568 GRAFTON *Chron.* II. 263 They put all their goodes vnto the Englishmens pleasures. 1600 HOLLAND *Livy* 1123 In this last speech he came neere unto the LL. of the Senat, and touched them to the quick. 1606 G. WOODCOCK *Hist. Ivstine* v. 27 It was secretly come vnto their eare, that [etc.]. 1639 LD. DIGBY *Lett. conc. Relig.* (1651) iv. 87 It is a farre more evident impossibility, then what you drive unto. 1683 *Pennsylv. Archives* I. 60, I cannot but believe y[t] you will take my great Wrong..unto your serious consideration. 1801 WORDSW. *Troilus* 63 In that very place My Lady first me took unto her grace. 1838 MRS. BROWNING *The Sleep* i, Of all the thoughts of God that are Borne inward unto souls afar.

**c.** With ellipsis of verb of motion. (Cf. To *prep.* 1 c.)

*a* 1593 MARLOWE & NASHE *Dido* II. i, Let vs vnto our ships, ..why stay we here? 1596 SHAKS. *Tam. Shr.* II. i. 316, I will vnto Venice To buy apparell. 1768 ROSS '*To the Begging*' iv, I'll then unto the cobler, An' cause him sole my shoon.

**2.** In the direction of; directed towards; = To *prep.* 2.

*a* 1300 *Cursor M.* 10479 Sco lift hir hend vn-to þe lift, And þus to prai sco gaf a scift. 1338 R. BRUNNE *Chron.* (1810) 217 Unto þe kinges partie Edward turned tite. 1390 GOWER *Conf.* I. 8 Unto him which the heved is The membres buxom scholden bowe. *Ibid.* 45 Whanne I..caste up many a pitous lok Unto the hevene. 1535 COVERDALE *Gen.* xiv. 22, I lift vp my honde vnto the Lorde. *Ibid.* xlix. 8 Thy fathers children shall stoupe vnto the. ? *a* 1600 '*Gentle heardsman*' i. in *Percy Folio* (1868) III. 526 Vnto the towne of Walsingham which is the right and ready way? 1611 [see LIFT *v.* 5]. 1796 BURNS '*When Januar' wind*' iii, I bow'd fu' low unto this maid. 1858 WHITTIER *Cable Hymn* i, Lean down unto the white-lipped sea The voice of God to hear!

*fig.* **1535** COVERDALE *Prov.* ii. 18 Hir house is enclyned vnto death, and hir pathes vnto hell. — *Dan.* ix. 3, I turned me vnto God..for to praye. **1826** SCOTT *Woodst.* i, There is no light in England that shall come nigh unto it.

**b.** At. (Esp. after *look*, †*smell*. Cf. To *prep.* 2 b.)

*a* **1300**– [see LOOK *v.* 23]. *a* **1400** *New Test.* (Paues) Acts iii. 4 Peter wiþ Ioon bihelde vnto hym. *c* **1430** *Pol., Rel. & L. Poems* (1903) 180 A semeli man to ben a king, A graciouse face to loken vnto. **1535** COVERDALE *Bel. & Dr.* 18 The kinge loked vnto ye altare. **1579** TOMSON *Calvin's Serm. Tim.* 222/2 Ministers..must marke why this office is given them;..it is not because a few should be sene vnto [= looked up to]. **1594** HOOKER *Eccl. Pol.* II. v. § 7 God made flowers sweet and beautiful, that being seen and smelt unto they might so delight. **1670** J. SMITH *Eng. Improv. Reviv'd* 213 The Root smelled vnto is good for the same purpose. **1848** AIRD *Chr Bride* II. vii, Majestic men who looked unto the skies.

**c.** In (a specified course or direction, *lit.* or *fig.*). Cf. To *prep.* 2 c, e.

*a* **1300** *Cursor M.* 2117 Þis land lies mast vnto þe south. *Ibid.* 2120 Þe thrid part..lies mast vnto þe west. *c* **1386** CHAUCER *Miller's T.* 386 [To break] an hole an heigh vp on the gable Vnto the gardynward. *c* **1400** *Melayne* 135 He sawe a bryghtenes of a beme Vp vn-to heuenwarde glyde. **1549** COVERDALE, etc. *Erasm. Par. Rom.* Prol. + v, Such a newe herte and lusty corage vnto the lawe warde, canste thou neuer come by.

†**d.** Indicating a means of access. (OE. *tō* and *intō*.) *Obs.*—1

**1535** COVERDALE 2 *Kings* iv. 5 She wente, and shut the dore vnto her with hir sonnes.

**3.** Indicating the limit or dimension of a movement, extension, or continuance in space: As far as; even to; not short of; = To *prep.* 3.

Occas. correlative to *from* (the remoter of two limits).

*a* **1300** *Cursor M.* 24346 Quen we na hele moght se on him, Fra hefd vnto his fote. *a* **1325** *Prose Psalter* cvi. 3 Fram þe rysyng of þe sunne vnto þe goynge adoune. *c* **1330** R. BRUNNE *Chron. Wace* (Rolls) 181 Mayster Wace..rymed [his romance]..vnto þe Cadwaladres. *c* **1400** *Destr. Troy* 95 All the ferlies þat fell vnto the ferre ende. *c* **1470** *Gol. & Gaw.* 1313 All thi braid landis, Or all the renttis fra thyne vnto Ronsiwall. *c* **1500** *Melusine* xxxvii. 297 He..sawe melusyne within the bathe vnto her nauell. **1535** COVERDALE *Exod.* xxxviii. 4 A brasen gredyron of net worke rounde aboute, from vnder vp vnto the myddest of the altare. **1548–9** (Mar.) *Bk. Com. Prayer, Communion of Sick*, With the firste parte of the exhortacion and all other thynges unto the Psalme. **1597** LYLY *Wom. in Moon* I. i, The rundle of this Massiue earth, From vtmost face vnto the Centers point. **1768** ROSS *Helenore* 31 Ye see her rigs run just unto our ain. *a* **1774** GOLDSM. *Hist. Greece* I. 223 A strong haven, with walls reaching unto the city. **1801** WORDSW. *Prioress' T.* 198 My throat is cut unto the bone. **1812** CARY *Dante, Parad.* xxii. 149 This petty area..from the havens stretched unto the hills.

**b.** In figurative uses.

**1508** DUNBAR *Ballad Ld. Stewart* 5 Onto the sterris vpheyt is thyne honour. **1535** COVERDALE *Ps.* xxxv. 5 Thy mercy (O Lorde) reacheth vnto the heauen. **1591** DRAYTON *Harmonie of Church, Song Jonah* 2 My voice I did extend Unto the Lord. **1609** BP. HALL *David's Psalms Metaphr.* viii, Thou hast..stretcht his raigne Vnto the heards, and beasts vntame.

**4.** Upon (and in contact with); on, against; = To *prep.* 5 a.

*a* **1300** *E. E. Psalter* cxvii. 26 Settes miri daie in thickenesse, Vnto horn þat of weued esse. *c* **1386** CHAUCER *Wife's T.* 973 She leyde hir mouth vn-to the water doun. *c* **1440** *Alph. Tales* 368 Þe ymage..fell down vnto þe hard erth. **1480** *Cov. Leet Bk.* 447 The pepull..carryen their Donge,..& leyen hit vnto the walles & yate. **1535** COVERDALE *Exod.* xxii. 8 He hath not put his hande vnto his neghbours good. **1550** T. LEVER *Serm.* (Arb.) 135 Beware therefore that ye staye not your selfe vnto a bryttell staffe. **1559** Q. ELIZ. in Strype *Ann. Ref.* (1709) I. II. App. x. 440 We have but a weake staff to leane unto. **1602** MARSTON *Antonio's Rev.* IV. iii, Thou bur, that only sticks Unto the nappe of greatnesse. **1607**, **1624** [see LEAN *v.* 2, 2 c]. **1768** ROSS *Helenore* 21 She..lean'd her head unto the kindly tree. **1836** R. ALLAN *Evening Hours* 98 The hope thus to press thee Unto my fond bosom.

*fig.* *c* **1386**, *c* **1400** [see STAND *v.* 76 f, g].

**b.** In contiguity or proximity to; in front of; by, close beside. Cf. To *prep.* 5 b.

**1590** SHAKS. *Com. Err.* I. ii. 91 Wilt thou flout me thus vnto my face? **1606** — *Ant. & Cl.* IV. xiv. 29 What thou would'st do Is done vnto thy hand. **1677** W. HUGHES *Man of Sin* III. iii. 79 Which..plainly gives them the lye unto their Teeths.

**5.** Expressing relative location (esp. with *nigh* or *near*).

**1526** TINDALE *Mark* v. 21 Iesus..was nye vnto the see. **1558** *Child. Marr.* 145 Nether in his house.., nether within iiij myle compas vnto the same Citie. **1600** J. PORY tr. *Leo's Africa* III. 171 Neere vnto the said plaine are diuers woods. *Ibid.* v. 262 The citie of Tunis..hath no mountaines nigh vnto it. **1768** ROSS *Helenore* 89 They began to speer Gin they were unto Flaviana near.

*fig.* **1526** TINDALE *Heb.* vi. 8 But that grounde..is reproved, and is nye vnto cursynge. **1539** BIBLE (Great) *Lev.* xxv. 49 Any that is nye of kynne vnto hym. **1548** UDALL, etc. *Erasm. Par. Matt.* xii. 75 b, He is moste nere and moste dere vnto me. **1785** BURNS *Letter to J. Goudie*, Auld Orthodoxy [is]..Nigh unto death. **1870** MORRIS *Earthly Par.* III. 390 Death had need be near Unto such men.

**II.** Indicating a temporal relationship.

**6.** Until (a final limit in time); till as late as; = To *prep.* 6 and 6 c.

*a* **1300** *Cursor M.* 24739 All mi liue vn-to min end, In hir loueword þof i moght spend. *a* **1325** *Prose Psalter* lxxxix. 15 Lord, be þou turned vnto nov. *Ibid.* cxii. 2 Be þe name of our Lord blisced, nou of þis & vnto heuen. **1382** WYCLIF *Ps.* cxii. 2 Be the name of the Lord blissid; fro this now and vnto the world. *c* **1386** CHAUCER *Man of Law's T.* 765 Kepeth this child .. vn to myn hoom comynge. *c* **1440** *Alph. Tales* 439 Þer devotelie he servid our Ladie vnto his lyfis ende. **1480** *Cov. Leet Bk.* 436 Certain Common pastures belongyng to the seid Cite vnto nowe. **1484** CAXTON *Fables of Alfonce* ix, The wulf..hyd hym self nyghe them vnto the nyght. **1523** LD. BERNERS *Froiss.* I. lxvii. 89 The bysshoppe..toke hym as his lorde, vnto suche season as somme other shulde come. **1539** BIBLE (Great) *Rom.* v. 13 For euen vnto the lawe was synne in the worlde. **1582** N. T. (Rhem.) *Luke* xvi. 16 The law and the prophets, vnto Iohn. **1613** *Acts Privy Council* 4 Yow shall..keepe the same unto suche tyme as..publicacion shall [be] moved thereof. **1691** in E. Walker *Epictetus* (1692) A 1 b, All good and perfect Gifts..Which Mortals have from th' Womb unto the Tomb. **1801** WORDSW. *Troilus* 56 She..there so graciously did me behold, That hers unto the death my heart I hold. **1896** 'IAN MACLAREN' *K. Carnegie* 356 Doctor Manley..praises Kate unto this day.

**7.** After a negative, = UNTIL *prep.* 5 b.

*c* **1400** *Brut* 322 The clergye..wolde not graunte hit vnto Ester next comyng. **1450–80** tr. *Secreta Secret.* lviii. 34 Shewe not thi thought vnto tyme thou performe thi wille. **1485** CAXTON *Paris & V.* (1868) 11 Never I shal have playsyr ne Ioye unto the tyme that I knowe. **1515** in Leadam *Star Chamber Cases* (Selden) II. 88 He neuer vnto this last yere knew eny man occupye a nothur mans Craft without Interrupcion. **1559** W. CUNNINGHAM *Cosmogr. Glasse* 105 Before the sonne be vnder th' Earth, which is not vnto .6. of the clocke.

**III.** Expressing the relation of aim, design, destination, result, consequent status or condition.

**8.** In order to begin, perform, accomplish, or obtain. Cf. To *prep.* 8 b.

*a* **1300** *E. E. Psalter* ciii. 24 Oute sal man ga vnto his werke. **1303** R. BRUNNE *Handl. Synne* 9098 Vn-to þe karolle asswyþe he ȝede. *c* **1400** *Destr. Troy* 10734 The sun in his sercle set vnto rest. *c* **1440** *Alph. Tales* 424 In þe mornyng he went vnto his prayers. **1470–85** MALORY *Arthur* VII. xxvi. 271 Many bold knyghtes wente vnto mete. **1587** TURBERV. *Trag. T.* (1837) 134 The Lady, somewhat hungrie, fell unto the Cates. **1596** R. L[INCHE] *Diella*, etc. D 7, They all sat downe vnto a soone-made feast. **1768** ROSS *Helenore* 68 Unto their supper they right yaply fa'.

**b.** With a view to; for the purpose of; for. Cf. To *prep.* 8.

*c* **1440** *Pallad. on Husb.* III. 1166 This wyne al medicine is take vnto. **1486** *Naval Acc. Hen. VII* (1896) 10 Diuers cabilles of hym bought vnto the Kyngs use. **1487** in Nichols *Illustr. Manners & Exp.* (1797) 83 For hokes and hengles unto the skolehouse dore,..and for nailes to the same dore, 4½*d.* **1539** CRANMER *Let.* in *Misc. Writ.* (Parker Soc.) 396, I pray you that the same may be delivered unto the said Whitchurche unto printing. **1549** THOMAS *Hist. Italye* (1561) 74 b, Vpon a very smal warnyng they [*sc.* galleys] may be furnyshed out vnto the sea. **1582** N. T. (Rhem.) *Mark* i. 4 Preaching the baptisme of penance vnto remission of sinnes. **1592** WARNER *Alb. Eng.* VIII. xlii. 158 Our Cattell vnto stronger draughts we..would vnteame.

**9.** Indicating a condition, state, or situation, conferred or imposed upon a person. Cf. To *prep.* 9.

*a* **1300** *E. E. Psalter* xviii. 16 Mi helper ai he isse, And mi bier vn-to blisse. *c* **1400** *Destr. Troy* 1418 Wemyn & wale children vnto wo put. *a* **1425** tr. *Arderne's Treat. Fistula* 34 Vnto a loueable ende wiþ goddes help aboute half a ȝere I cured hym. *c* **1440** *York Myst.* xxxvii. 319 Vnto my dome I schall þame drawe, And juge þame worse þanne any Jewe. *c* **1529** LATIMER in Foxe *A. & M.* (1563) 1298/2 Which vnthriftye state that wee be borne vnto. **1548** in Starkey *England* (1878) p. xciii, If vnto Office they after bee electe. **1591** DRAYTON *Prayer of Mardocheus* iv, To destroy and bring us unto nought. **1603** KNOLLES *Hist. Turks* (1621) 1119 Some [traitors] they roasted, and some they put vnto the Tenalia. **1648** WILKINS *Math. Magic* I. xi. 75 That slavery, which those..Nations were subjected unto. **1710** BLACKWELL *Schema Sacrum* v. 103 The Decree of Divine Reprobation..necessarily inferred Man's Fall, Sin and Damnation violenting him (as it were) unto the same. **1807** WORDSW. '*Nuns fret not*' 8 The prison, unto which we doom Ourselves.

**10.** Indicating result, effect, or consequence: So as to result in, bring about, cause, or produce; = To *prep.* 10.

*a* **1300** *Cursor M.* 24746 Þof mans wijt be neuer sa strait, Sco mai well bring it vnto nait. **1430–40** LYDG. *Bochas* II. 2812 Senacherib..Leffte his siege & took hym onto flyht. *c* **1440** *Alph. Tales* 440 He was ferd at þai or þer fadurs shulde desyre hym to be maryd or to fall vnto syn. **1526** TINDALE 1 *Cor.* xv. 34, I speake this vnto youre rebuke. **1591** DRAYTON *Harmonie of Church* x, They..by their sin provoke Him unto ire. **1601** BRETON *Longing Blessed Heart* xxii, Th' Artificer..bringes his hand vnto his heads deuise, Longes till he see, what it will come vnto. **1660** *Nicholas Papers* (Camden) IV. 250 The unexpected..admitting to audience and afterwards vnto treatie of the Portugal ambassador.

**11.** Indicating a resultant condition, status, or capacity: In or into the character, nature, or quality of; = To *prep.* 11, 11 b.

**13..** *E. E. Allit. P.* A. 772 Quat-kyn þyng may be þat lambe, Þat þe wolde wedde vnto hys vyf? **1390** GOWER *Conf.* I. 114 This lord a worthi ladi hadde Unto his wif. *c* **1400** *Rule St. Benet* (Verse) 1374 If þat þe priores wor dede, Þo same..Wold ches me vnto priores. **1470–85** MALORY *Arthur* I. vii. 43 We wille haue Arthur vnto our kyng. **1556** *Chron. Gr. Friars* (Camden) 28 The gray freeres chaungyd their habbetts from London rossette unto whytt gray. **1590** SHAKS. *Mids. N.* I. i. 207 (Q.), Hee hath turnd a heauen vnto a hell! **1599** DRAYTON *Idea* xlvi, I meruaile not thou feelst not my delight..Whose stomack vnto gaule hath turn'd thy foode. **1609** BIBLE (Douay) 2 *Kings* xxi. 14 And they shal be unto waste, and unto spoile to al their adversaries. **1749** C. WESLEY *Hymns* I. 57 Turn unto Flesh my Heart of Stone.

**12.** Indicating the object of desire, right, or claim. Cf. To *prep.* 12, 12 b.

**1338** R. BRUNNE *Chron.* (1810) 57 He þat had gode right vnto þe regalte. **1530** PALSGR. 538/1 By what meanes is he entyteled unto these landes. **1535** COVERDALE *Ps.* cxviii. 20 The very feruent desyre that I haue allwaye vnto thy iudgmentes. **1593** NASHE *Christ's T.* 29 b, There is no better clayme vnto wealth. **1738** in *Nairne Peerage Evid.* (1874) 42 Such personal estate as he..shall become..intitled unto.

**IV.** Followed by an expression denoting or indicating a limit in extent, number, amount, or degree.

**13. a.** Up to as many, as much, or as often as. Cf. To *prep.* 13.

*a* **1300** *Cursor M.* 12648 Ai to iesu was cummen neir Vn-to þe eild of thritte yeir. *a* **1325** *Prose Psalter* lii. 4 Þer nys non þat doþ god, þer nys non vn-to on. *c* **1400** *Brut* 295 Shippez & barges were take, vnto þe noumbre of .CC. & xxx. *c* **1500** *Melusine* xxiii. 156 There nys thing .. that I shuld reffuse you vnto myn owne deth. **1526** TINDALE *Mark* vi. 23, I will geve it the, even vnto the one halfe of my kyngdom. **1530** in Leadam *Star Chamber Cases* (Selden) II. 46 It was..unknowne what the charges..would drawe vnto. **1596** SHAKS. 1 *Hen. IV*, IV. i. 129 What may the Kings whole Battaile reach vnto? *Vernon.* To thirty thousand. **1610** HEALEY *St. Aug. Citie of God* XIX. i. 752 Thus doth the number arise vnto twelve. **1663** BP. PATRICK *Parab. Pilgr.* xiv, There cannot be so much interruption given to them, as the scratch of a pin among us amounts unto. **1812** CARY *Dante, Parad.* xxiii. 57 Not..Unto the thousandth parcel of the truth, My song might shadow forth that saintly smile. **1895** PETRIE *Egypt. Tales* Ser. I. 70 He came again unto him, even unto six times. **1896** 'IAN MACLAREN' *K. Carnegie* 328 There is nothing unto life itself I would not give for your good.

**b.** Down to (an ultimate grade, point, or number).

*a* **1325** *Prose Psalter* cxxxiv. 8 Þe which..smote þe first borne of Egipt fram man vnto beste. **1515** *St. Papers Hen. VIII*, II. 11 The King..dyd conqyure all the lande, unto lytyll. **1535** COVERDALE *Exod.* xxii. 4 Yf ye theft be founde by him alyue (from the oxe vnto the Asse or shepe). **1592** SHAKS. *Rom. & Jul.* I. iii. 11 Faith I can tell her age vnto an houre. *a* **1623** FLETCHER *Love's Cure* v. iii, No Town in Spain, from our Metropolis Unto the rudest hovel. **1646** SIR T. BROWNE *Pseud. Ep.* 274 The whole world perished unto eight persons before the floud.

**c.** So as to be equivalent or equal to. Cf. To *prep.* 14.

**1568** GRAFTON *Chron.* II. 308 Three Millions of Scutes of Gold,..the which do come unto sterlyng money, fyve hundreth thousand pound. **1660** WILLSFORD *Scales Commerce* I. 108 How much comes 10d. a day unto by the year?

**14.** To such an extent or degree, so far, as to cause; so much as to bring about or result in; = To *prep.* 14 b.

**1382** WYCLIF 2 *Kings* xx. 1 In tho dayes sijknede Ezechias vnto [1388 til to] the deeth. *a* **1425** tr. *Arderne's Treat. Fistula*, etc. 73 Be þai brissed and boiled in watre vnto mene þikkenez. *c* **1425** *St. Christina* xvi. in *Anglia* VIII. 125 She was stired of god vnto an vnsufferabil þriste. *c* **1440** *Alph. Tales* 154 Þe Emperour tuke it vnto so grete wrath, þat he garte smyte of his head. *Ibid.* 408 He fell into a dispayre, vnto so mekull þat he myght not liff with-owten venyall syn. **1542–5** BRINKLOW *Lament.* 3 To persecute vnto dethe all and euery godly person. **1571** GOLDING *Calvin on Ps.* xxviii. 5 Through stubbornnesse [they] harden themselues vntoo vnsensiblenesse. **1611** COTGR., *Esgoüer*,..to eat vnto sacietie. **1640** BP. REYNOLDS *Passions* XV. 141 Those vanities what hee seeth doe provoke others unto loathing. **1652** SCLATER *Civ. Magistracy* (1653) Ep. Ded., His Singular Contentation accompanyed with Temperance unto Admiration. **1812** CARY *Dante, Purg.* xxiv. 22 That face beyond him, pierced Unto a leaner fineness than the church. **1896** 'IAN MACLAREN' *K. Carnegie* 153 [The] fields, now yellow unto harvest, shone in the moonlight.

**V.** Expressing addition or accumulation, attachment, appurtenance, or possession.

**15. a.** Denoting attachment, union, adherence, or kinship to a person. Cf. To *prep.* 16.

**1338** R. BRUNNE *Chron.* (1810) 65 Felawes vnto þefes, to robbours of ilk cuntre. *Ibid.* 90 With scrite vnto William Sir Dunkan him bond. **1423** JAS. I *Kingis Q.* cxxxiii, Lat wisedom ay vnto thy will be Iunyt. *c* **1440** *Alph. Tales* 219 [She] wold not be wed vnto a wurthi man þat wold hafe had hur. **1470–85** MALORY *Arthur* x. liii. 501 A ful noble Knyghte nyghe kynne vnto sire Launcelot. **1535** COVERDALE *Gen.* ii. 24 For this cause shal a man..cleue vnto his wife. **1544** in Leadam *Star Chamber Cases* (Selden) II. 279 Factoures vnto one Jacob vanganspole merchaunt of Andwerpe. **1591** DRAYTON *Harmonie of Church, Song Sol.* vii. 25, I am unto my Love a faithful friendly fere. **1601** *Important Consid. Priests* 21 Some of his own subiects were ..drawne, rather to adhere vnto them then to himselfe. **1649** LOVELACE *Lucasta, Paradox* iv, The God that constant keepes Unto his Dieties. *a* **1658** *Ibid., Sanazar* 190, I was ally'd dear Uncle unto thee In blood, but thou alas not unto me.

**b.** Denoting fastening, securing, or junction to something.

**1470–85** MALORY *Arthur* VIII. xxxiv. 326 He loked vpon bothe his handes that were fast bounden vnto two knyghtes. **1535** COVERDALE *Gen.* xlix. 11 He shall bynde his foale vnto the vyne. **1585** T. WASHINGTON tr. *Nicholay's Voy.* II. 47 Two sides are washed by the sea, and the thyrd ioyneth vnto the firme land. **1646** SIR T. BROWNE *Pseud. Ep.* 239 The use of the Navell is to continue the infant unto the Mother. **1662** DRYDEN *To Ld. Chancellor* 32 Nothing bounds our Eye Until the Earth seems join'd unto the Sky. *a* **1881** ROSSETTI *House of Life* i, Still some golden hair Unto his shoulder clinging, since the last Embrace.

**16.** Denoting appurtenance or possession. Freq. after verbs, as *appertain, behove, belong, long, pertain*, q.v. Cf. To *prep.* 17, 17 b.

**1390** GOWER *Conf.* I. 6 The vice Which longeth unto this office. **1445** in *Anglia* XXVIII. 273 He þat knowith the fadirlaw vnto themperours sone. *a* **1450** *Knt. de la Tour* cxvii. 159 Suche an instrument as longithe vnto a mynstralle. **1513** BRADSHAW *St. Werburge* I. 452 Elflede .. Doughter vnto Oswy. **1568** Grafton *Chron.* I. 144 He was Cosyn germaine unto him on the fathers syde. **1594** Drayton *Sonn.* viii, Vnto the World, to Learning, and to Heauen, Three nines there are, to euerie one a nine. **1634** Bp. Reynolds *Shieldes of Earth* (1636) 19 This belongeth only unto Princes. **1682** Sir T. Browne *Chr. Mor.* III. § 8 So may'st thou be..a Father unto thy contemporaries. **1768** Ross *Helenore* 60 Ye maun, I ween, unto the kards belang. **1845** Bailey *Festus* (ed. 2) 194 From this highest orb, the crown of space And footstool unto Heaven.

**17.** By way of increase to; in addition to; with, besides; = To *prep.* 15.

**1526** Tindale *Acts* ii. 41 The same daye there were added vnto them aboute a thre thousande soules. **1535** Coverdale *Ecclus.* xviii. 6 There maye nothinge be taken from them, nothinge maye be put vnto them. **1595** Shaks. *John* IV. iii. 46 This is the very top, The heighth, the Crest: or Crest vnto the Crest Of murthers Armes. **1600** — *A. Y. L.* I. ii. 250, I should haue giuen him teares vnto entreaties. **1642** Denham *Sophy* II. i. 18 Wisedome he ha's, and to his wisedome courage; Temper to that, and unto all, successe. **1660** Sharrock *Vegetables* 19 Unto the ashes of every hill [*sc.* heap] you must put a peck of unslake lime. **1896** 'Ian Maclaren' *K. Carnegie* 329 You have many friends, and may God add unto them good men and faithful.

**VI.** Expressing comparison or correspondence, relation to a standard, etc.

**18.** After words denoting correspondence, agreement, comparison, proportion, etc. = To *prep.* 21.

See also Like *a.* 1, Resemble *v.*[1] 2, 6, Resembling 1 b.

*c* **1325** *Metr. Hom.* 37 For mani man mai bisend be Unto the rede, als thinc me. *c* **1386** Chaucer *Prol.* 243 Vn to swich a worthy man as he Acorded nat..To haue with sike lazars Aqueyntance. **1423** Jas. I *Kingis Q.* clv, The pantere, like vnto the smaragdyne. *c* **1460** *Towneley Myst.* iii. 506 Like vnto the turtill. **1553** Eden *Treat. New Ind.* (Arb.) 5 Which..he thought to be muche inferiour vnto his. **1591** Drayton *Harmonie of Church, Song Sol.* ii. 6 No more the sons unto my Love may ought compared be. **1611** Cotgr. s.v. *Deschargé*, [A colour] neere vnto a light blew, or of a light blew; light. **1634** T. Johnson *Parey's Chirurg.* Wks. XXIV. vi. 891 A certaine thinne skinne..like unto that..over vnscimmed milke. **1644** Digby *Two Treat.* II. (1645) 67 When a thing is identifyed unto the soule [etc.]. **1809–14** Wordsw. *Excurs.* IX. 56 A throne that may be likened unto his. **1875** Jowett *Plato* (ed. 2) III. 30 The second principle is like unto it.

**19.** With regard to; in respect of; as to, concerning; = To *prep.* 22.

*c* **1400** *Cursor M.* 25119 (Cott. Galba), Seuin askinges er þarin to rede..both vnto lifing here a space, and whare oure sawl more mister hase. **1502** *Ord. Crysten Men* (W. de W. 1506) I. iii. C iii, And this is vnto the sygnyfycacyon of the salte. **1520** *Chron. Calais* (Camden) 92 And as unto ladies ther were..the duches of Norfolk, with her iij doughters. **1591** *Wills & Inv. N. C.* (Surtees, 1860) 199 For engrossing his will, twice vnto paipar, after vnto parchment *xlxs.* **1611** Bible *Rom.* vi. 11 Likewise reckon yee also your selues to be dead indeed vnto sinne. **1641** J. Jackson *True Evang. T.* I. 3 A Commentator unto the Text askes the question. **1669** N. Morton *New Eng. Memorial* (1910) 46 They also brought a full intelligence in reference unto the particulars. **1729** Law *Serious C.* x. 147 We are to live wholly unto God. **1778** Ross *Helenore* 22, I ken nought unto his dispraise. **1885–94** R. Bridges *Eros & Psyche* Jan. xxi, Shut thy soft ear unto his clamour thin.

**20.** In comparison or as compared with; in relation to; = To *prep.* 18.

*c* **1400** *Rom. Rose* 5600 [He] never shal make his richesse Asseth unto his gredinesse. *a* **1500** in *Ratis Raving*, etc. 4 Al his seknes [is] lytill, in comparesone one-to the luf at god schawyt till ws. **1539** Bible (Great) *Matt.* vi. 34 Sufficient vnto the daye, is the trauayle therof. *a* **1566** R. Edwards *Damon & Pithias* (1571) H ij b, But now I see there is no garde vnto a faithfull friend. **1682** Sir T. Browne *Chr. Mor.* III. § 8 So may'st thou be coetaneous unto thy elders. **1768** Ross *Helenore* 93 But a' their cushel-mushel was but jest, Unto the coal that brunt in Lindy's breast. **1842** Tennyson *Locksley Hall* 152 All thy passions, match'd with mine, Are as moonlight unto sunlight. — *Talk. Oak* 107 As cowslip unto oxlip is, So seems she to the boy. **1854–5** Longf. *Hiawatha's Wooing* 1 As unto the bow the cord is, So unto the man is woman.

**21.** In accordance, agreement, or correspondence with; according to; after; = To *prep.* 20.

*c* **1420** *Contn. Brut* 340 So oure Kyng..graunted hem trewes certyn yeres vnto her axyng. **1430–40** Lydg. *Bochas* I. 492 Whan he us made onto his liknesse, He putte vs bothe into Paradis. **1515** *Festivall* (W. de W.) 117 We praye you of a place to bury his body unto his worshypp. **1596** Spenser *State Irel.* Wks. (Globe) 613/2 Lawes ought to be fashioned unto the manners..of the people to whom they are ment. ? *a* **1600** in *Percy Folio* (1867) I. 63 Shooes of gold the porter had on, And all his other rayment was vnto the same. **1602** Shaks. *Ham.* I. iii. 23 Therefore must his choyce be circumscrib'd Vnto the voyce and yeelding of that Body, Whereof he is the Head. **1710** Blackwell *Schema Sacrum* viii. 151 Disposing of Angels..suitably unto the Tenor of their own Actings. **1803–6** Wordsw. *Ode Intim. Immort.* 96 And this hath now his heart, And unto this he frames his song. **1842** Tennyson *Ld. of Burleigh* 80 A trouble..perplex'd her ..With the burthen of an honour Unto which she was not born. **1870** Morris *Earthly Par.* III. 418 Meanwhile to Kiarton,..Unto all seeming, life went merrily.

**b.** As far as; to the extent of. Cf. To *prep.* 20 b.

**1502** *Ord. Crysten Men* (W. de W. 1506) II. ix. I viii, To socour our neyghbour in kepynge hym vnto our power in place and in tyme that he..falle not. **1642** tr. *Perkins' Prof. Bk.* III. § 205. 92 Unto divers respects a man shall take by a liverie of seisin which he made in his owne right.

**VII.** Expressing relations in which the idea of course or direction tends to blend with the dative use.

**22.** After words denoting attention, care, trust, etc.; = To *prep.* 24.

Freq. after verbs, as *apply, attend, betake, hearken, intend, listen, look*: see these words.

*a* **1300** *Cursor M.* 255 To laud and Inglis man i spell.. Sumquat vnto þat thing to tent. *c* **1386** Chaucer *Sqr.'s T.* 67 Vn to my firste I wole haue my recours. *c* **1440** *Alph. Tales* 446 He fell vnto his prayers. **1455** *Paston Lett.* I. 326 Not to plese to geve trust or confidence unto the sinistrez ..rapportes of our sayd ennemyes. *c* **1477** Caxton *Jason* 20 My herte Iugeth that ye shall haue grete Regard vnto my good wil. **1535** Coverdale *Ps.* xvi. 1 Herken vnto my prayer. **1585** T. Washington tr. *Nicholay's Voy.* I. xviii. 21 The castle..hath been so ill looked vnto..it is againe fallen into the hands of the Barbaries. **1613** Jackson *Creed* I. § iv. i. 219 Whose beleefe vnto diuine Oracles hath beene confirmed. **1642** *Remonstr. Ch. Irel.* 5 He wanted powder, having no more..than his Bandeleers to trust unto. **1656** Earl Monm. tr. *Boccalini's Advts. fr. Parnass.* I. xlvii. 95 Flocks..grow lean..through the meer carelesness of him that looks unto them. **1710** Blackwell *Schema Sacrum* v. 104 It was..Man alone, voluntarily hearkening unto Satan. **1812** Cary *Dante, Parad.* v. 119 Say on; and trust As unto gods.

**23.** Against, in respect of opposition or hostility. Cf. To *prep.* 25 b.

*a* **1300** *E. E. Psalter* liii. 5 Torne iuels vnto mi faas. *a* **1400** *New Test.* (Paues) Acts iv. 1 As þei stoden..þer kome fallande vnto hem prestes..ande Saduceys. **1412–20** Lydg. *Chron. Troy* IV. 2452 Archilogus A mortal cours ran vn-to Brumvs. **1439** *Rolls of Parlt.* V. 17/2 Phelip..hath contynuelly..made werre unto the seide John. *a* **1450** *Knt. de la Tour* 120 So it befell he had do a forfeit vnto the kinge Dauid. **1585** T. Washington tr. *Nicholay's Voy.* I. xvii. 19 b, [They]dyd daily make warre vnto his highnesse. **1591** Shaks. *1 Hen. VI*, IV. i. 73 Then gather strength, and march vnto him straight.

**24.** Indicating the person addressed, etc.; = To *prep.* 26. Usu. after verbs, as *cry, say, speak, tell.*

*a* **1300** *E. E. Psalter* xxvi. 6 (E.), I sall synge and salm sai Un-to Loverd. *Ibid.* xc. 15 He cried vnto me witerli. **1338** R. Brunne *Chron.* (1810) 99 Lowys wrote his letter vnto þe kyng Henry. **1390** Gower *Conf.* I. 282 To speak a goodli word unto me. *c* **1440** *Alph. Tales* 122 Þis suster said vnto hur brother. *c* **1450** Capgrave *Life St. Aug.* 5 The book of Seynt Augustin..on-to his sistir, a widow. **1477** *Stonor Papers* (Camden) II. 28, I spake vnto my lady.., and she wold scarsely oppyn hir mouthe vnto me. **1511** in W. H. Turner *Select. Rec. Oxford* (1880) 2 The mayer answered aȝen onto the forsayd John. **1535** Coverdale *Deut.* xxxii. 46 Ye wordes, which I testifye vnto you this daye. **1569** *Southampton Crt. Leet Rec.* (1905) I. 56 Be yt comaunded vnto all those..that they make chimnes. **1610** J. Healey *St. Aug. Citie of God* XVII. v. 628 These words of the Prophet vnto Heli. **1643** Caryl *Expos. Job* I. 635 Would you know what the visiting of God is? It is praying unto him. **1710** Blackwell *Schema Sacrum* vi. 112 Some special One of their Number intimateth the great News unto the Shepherds. **1768** Ross *Helenore* 101 The squire well saw't, an' unto Lindy says [etc.]. **1844** Whittier *Texas* 32 Let the North unto the South Speak the word befitting both. **1896** 'Ian Maclaren' *K. Carnegie* 328 John,..is this all you have in your heart to say unto me?

**b.** To or for the worship of; in honour, adoration, or salutation of; = To *prep.* 26 b.

*a* **1300** *E. E. Psalter* lxv. 15 Offrand meryhed, gode þat be, Sal I offre unto þe. *a* **1400** *New Test.* (Paues) Acts xxi. 25 Demande þat þei abstene hem fro þinge þat es sacrified vnto idoles. **1430–40** Lydg. *Bochas* VIII. 552 Egipciens dide.. Ther sacrefises & rihtes..Vnto Isis. *c* **1440** *Pallad. on Husb.* I. 1178 Laude, ymne,..& songe vnto The flour of Iesse spronge in Bethleem. **1526** Tindale *Acts* xvii. 23, I founde an aultre wher in was written: vnto the vnknowen god. **1598** Lodge *Looking-Gl. Lond. & Eng.* H 2 b, Villaines, why skinck you not vnto this fellow? **1599** Shaks. *Much Ado* v. iii. 22 Now vnto thy bones good night. **1615** W. Bedwell *Arab. Trudg.* L 1, *Abu' lkibla*, was an idoll..which..the Arabians did..offer sacrifice vnto. **1842** Macaulay *L. Regillus* ii, Unto the Great Twin Brethren We keep this solemn feast. **1882** Bible (R. V.) *Exod.* xxxii. 8 They have made them a molten calf,..and have sacrificed unto it.

**25.** Expressing or denoting response, responsive action, or reaction. = To *prep.* 27, 27 b.

Freq. with *assent, consent, obey*, etc. (q.v.).

*c* **1440** *Alph. Tales* 448 He wolde not consent vnto hur to ly by hur. **1502** *Ord. Crysten Men* (W. de W. 1506) I. ii. 12 Whan Adam & eue..dysobeyed unto God. **1518** in Leadam *Star Chamber Cases* (Selden) II. 148 The said bille is vncerteyn and insufficient to be aunswerd vnto. **1576** Gascoigne *Steel Glas* (Arb.) 59 To yeld good smacke vnto their daintie tongues. **1597** Hooker *Eccl. Pol.* v. lxii. § 13 Nature as much as is possible inclineth vnto validities and preseruations. **1612** Drayton *Poly-olb.* iv. 175 Some..only us'd to sing Unto the other's harp. **1710** Blackwell *Schema Sacrum* vii. 140 To say Amen, unto Isaiahs Description of our Lord. **1768** Ross *Helenore* 88 Afore mishap had forc'd him to comply Unto a match. **1881** N. T. (Revised) *Luke* xiv. 6 They could not answer again unto these things.

**VIII.** Supplying the place of, assuming or taking over the functions of, the dative.

**26.** Denoting the recipient of a gift or the like, or the person affected by an event, etc. = To *prep.* 29.

*a* **1300** *E. E. Psalter* ciii. 22 Lyoun whelpes..seke fra god mete vnto þa. *c* **1380** *Antecrist* in Todd *3 Treat. Wyclif* 134 Þei putten grete penaunce unto men, þere Cristis charge is liȝt. **1426** in *Surtees Misc.* (1890) 10 Þe charge..þat is put vnto me. *c* **1440** *Alphabet of Tales* 207 He putt þaim [*sc.* his goods] vnto þe bisshopp. *c* **1470** Henry *Wallace* I. 447 Syluir and gold he gert on to him geyff. **1532** Hervet *Xenoph. Househ.* 32 b, As for suche thynges,..we deliuered them vnto a woman. **1581** in *Lanc. & Cheshire Wills* (1893) 3 I geue and bequeath vnto Richard..tenne shepe. **1610** Holland *Camden's Brit.* I. 726 Deliuering vnto him a verge of gold. **1678** Bunyan *Pilgr.* I. 168 This could not but be a great grief unto him. **1695** in *Jrnl. Friends' Hist. Soc.* Oct. (1915) 173 She hath borne unto mee three sonnes. *c* **1708** Fenton *First Fit of Gout* 19 Whence comes this unsought honour unto me? **1768** Ross *Helenore* 9 Nory..a glack of bread an' cheese..unto Lindy gees. **1814** Cary *Dante, Inf.* xxiii. 5 He told What fate unto the mouse and frog befel. **1829** in *Nairne Peerage Evid.* (1874) 76 We are graciously pleased to give and allow unto Caroline baroness Nairn an annuity. *a* **1865** Emerson *Woodnotes* II. 342 Unto every race and age He emptieth the beverage.

**b.** Indicating the recipient of an impression, the holder of an opinion or the like; used esp. after verbs, as *appear, seem*, †*think*, etc. Cf. To *prep.* 29 b.

*a* **1470** Harding *Chron.* (MS. Lansd.) Pref. vi, If it lyke vn to ȝour owne avyse..To Comforte now..ȝour pore subgite. **1526** Tindale *Luke* xxiv. 11 Their wordes semed vnto them fayned thinges. **1599** Shaks. *Much Ado* III. v. 55, I am now in great haste, as may appeare vnto you. **1611** Speed *Hist. Gt. Brit.* IX. xviii. § 29 It was thought vnto the Protector, and vnto the whole Councell, that [etc.]. *a* **1613** Bacon *Case Post-nati Scot.* Wks. 1826 V. 116 For it seemeth admirable unto me, to consider [etc.]. **1710** Blackwell *Schema Sacrum* viii. 147 One Attribute seemeth more Dear unto him than another.

**27.** For the advantage, benefit, convenience, use, or disposal of; for. Cf. To *prep.* 30.

*a* **1300** *E. E. Psalter* lxx. 8 In þe ai alle mi singinge. Made am i als fortakeninge Vnto mani. *a* **1400** *New Test.* (Paues) Acts ii. 41 Ande þat day weren wonnen vnto God ande turned abowte þreo þowsande. **1539** Bible (Great) *Gen.* iii. 21 Unto the same Adam also and to his wife dyd the Lorde God make lethren garmentes. **1591** Drayton *Harmonie of Church, Song Sol.* v. 15 Then opened I the door unto my Love at last. **1613** Heywood *Silver Age* I. i. B 3, Expose thy selfe Vnto that monstrous beast of Cicily, Cal'd the Chimera. **1664** Butler *Hud.* II. i. 616 By which Astrologers..can tell What strange Events they do foreshow Unto her Under-world below. *a* **1678** H. Scougal *Disc. Imp. Subj.* (1735) 179 A happiness we can never secure unto our selves. **1702** C. Mather *Magn. Chr.* III. 178 An opportunity..to Vindicate another great Man, unto the Churches of our Lord Jesus Christ. *a* **1714** in Ledwich *Antiq. Sarisb.* 6 Therein you may find many an excellent Lore That unto your Wives you may teach. *a* **1784** *Hobie Noble* i. in Child *Ball.*, For in it there was baith meat and drink, And corn unto our geldings gay. **1816** Wordsw. *Ode, 1814*, 51 Those palms and amaranthine wreaths Unto their martyred Countrymen decreed. **1891** *Cornh. Mag.* Dec. 664 He took unto himself a village maid, and settled in Lyndhurst.

**b.** Indicating the person or thing towards which an action, feeling, etc., is directed; = To *prep.* 30 b.

Freq. with *beholden*, †*holden* (Hold *v.* 10 b), *recommend*, etc.

*a* **1300** *E. E. Psalter* xviii. 13 And fra outen..Forbere vnto þi hine ai. **13..** *Cursor M.* 1069 (Gött.), Vnto his broþer ire he bare. *a* **1400** *New Test.* (Paues) Acts xxvi. 27 Ande þo kenge Agrippa trowes vnto þo prophetes. *c* **1440** *Alph. Tales* 103 He askid hym whi he wuld not ryse vnto hym. *c* **1465** *Stonor Papers* (Camden) I. 70 Y werr be-hold unto yow. **1508** Kennedie *Flyting w. Dunbar* 482 Lat newir this synfull sot Do schame..vnto your nacion! **1555** in *Rep. Hist. MSS. Comm.* Var. Coll. IV. (1907) 283 The leke paines..shall ronne and be unto all those free Burgesses. **1587** in *Cath. Rec. Soc. Publ.* V. 137 Goolde..referred me over unto Mr. Baylye to be payed upon youre head. **1623** in *Eng. Hist. Rev.* July (1919) 408 Delivered to St. Raby.. as a present..without any fees or charge unto him. **1654–66** Earl Orrery *Parthen.* (1676) 378 More from a desire of being alone, than from any aversion she seem'd to have unto it. **1710** Blackwell *Schema Sacrum* vii. 130 Our Lord.. having all their Iniquities..imputed unto him. **1763** C. Smart *Song to David* lxxiv, Sweeter [is]..The glory of thy gratitude, Respired unto the Lord. **1796** Mme. D'Arblay *Camilla* IV. 169 The Lord be good unto me! **1803** C. K. Sharpe *Lett.* (1888) I. 165 If Jane hath done this fault, woe be unto her! **1887** E. Johnson *Antiq. Mater.* 251 Your unslothful love unto the glory of God.

**28.** Denoting the relation of an adj. (or derived sb. or adv.) to a sb. indicating a person or thing to which its application is directed or restricted. = To *prep.* 33.

Used in construction with many adjs.; cf. To *prep.* 33, and see Merciful *a.*, Open *a.* 15, Subject *a.*, True *a.* 1 c, Unkindfully *a.*, Untolerable *a.*, etc.

**1390** Gower *Conf.* II. 285 Hast thou be scars or large of yifte Unto thi love? *c* **1407** Lydg. *Reson & Sens.* 948 The which..wern..vn-to manne ryght vayllable. *c* **1450** *Crt. of Love* 14, I can-not write Unto the princes..No termes digne unto her excellence. **1485** *Digby Myst.* III. 8, I am soveren of al soverens subjugal On-to myn empere. **1526** Tindale *Acts* xxvi. 19, I was not disobedient vnto the hevenly vysion. **1593** in J. Morris *Troub. Cath. Forefathers* Ser. III. (1877) 124 Yet their life-labour is..costly unto us. **1639** S. Du Verger tr. *Camus' Admir. Events* 301 A torture unsufferable unto this young gentlewoman. **1669** Owen *Exp. Ps. cxxx*, 15 Vnspiritedness and disability unto Duty, in doing or suffering. *a* **1687** Petty *Pol. Arith.* (1690) 72 It will be dangerous unto England, that Ireland should be in the Hands of any other Nation. **1795–6** Wordsw. *Borderers* 2168, I (so filled With horror is this world) am unto thee The thing most precious that it now contains. **1801** — *Troilus & Cresida* 83 So cruel do not be Unto the blood of Troy,.. As Juno was unto the Theban blood.

**b.** After *known, unknown*, †*uncouth*, †*unwist*, †*unwitting*, etc.; = To *prep.* 33 b.

In later use (esp. in or after Biblical usage) with *known*.

*a* **1400** *New Test.* (Paues) Acts xix. 17 Þis was made knowne vnto alle þe Iewes. **1423** Jas. I *Kingis Q.* lxiii, Quhen sall ȝour merci rew vpon ȝour man, Quhois seruice is ȝit vncouth vnto ȝow? **14..** Hoccleve *Minor P.* 231/418 How [we] thidir come, vn-to vs vnwist. *c* **1440** *Generydes* 3396 Vppe they rose,..And chaungyd horses onto them bothe vnknowyng. **1514** Barclay *Cyt. & Uplondyshman* (Percy Soc.) 32 Seth God wyll be unknowen unto us. **1556** *Chron. Grey Friars* (Camden) 17 The othe that he made un to the kynge of Ynglonde unwyttynge unto the pope. **1605** Shaks. *Lear* I. iv. 224 By making this well knowne vnto you. **1795–6** Wordsw. *Borderers* 628 If compassion..Be known unto you. **1843** — *G. Darling* 7 One..Known unto few but prized as far as known.

**IX.** †29. = *To* with the infinitive. *Obs.*

c 1352 MINOT *Poems* (ed. Hall) v. 25 King Edward vnto sail was ful sune dight. a 1400 *Northern Passion* 461 (Camb. MS. Gg 5. 31), Þare come downe a aungell..Vnto comforthe ihesu well still. ?1481 *Cely Papers* (Camden) 203 Any thing that I cane do unto ples ye.

**B.** *conj.* †**a.** = UNTIL *conj.* a. Also (*a*) with *that.*

(*a*) a 1300 *E. E. Psalter* xciii. 15 (H.), For Laverd sal noght his folke schonne awai, Ne his heritage for-lete never a dai; Unto þat rihtnes be turned in dome with quert. a 1425 tr. *Arderne's Treat. Fistula*, etc. 61 Þe pacient ow to abide still in þe watre, vnto þat þe blode..chaunge into fairer colour. c 1475 *Partenay* 4132 In thys place abide vnto that ye see Ho bering hym best and ho better haue. 1556 *Chron. Gr. Friars* (Camden) 19 A gret multytude.. there abode seven dayes contynually unto that the kynge.. came..toward Grenewich.

(*b*) 1303 R. BRUNNE *Handl. Synne* 9055 Þys songe sunge þey yn þe chercheȝerd..Vn-to þe matynes were alle done. c 1381 CHAUCER *Parl. Foules* 647 Almyghty queen vnto this ȝer be gon I axe respit. 1411 *E. E. Wills* (1882) 20 Also y wille..þat lucie my wyf have gouernauns þer-of.. vn-to þe forseyd william be of age xviij. ȝhere. c 1489 CAXTON *Sonnes of Aymon* ix. 223 They wente to bed, & slepte vnto the daye appered. 1526 *Pilgr. Perf.* (W. de W. 1531) 2 b, It is & euer shall be vnquiet, vnto I come to the. 1549 *Wills & Inv. N. C.* (Surtees, 1860) 132, I give vnto my wife my house vnto my boy be of xxiiij yeirs of age. 1572 MASCALL *Plant. & Graff.* (1592) 52 The which may also keepe vnto the new come againe.

†**b.** = UNTIL *conj.* b. Also with *that. Obs.*

1303 R. BRUNNE *Handl. Synne* 5994 Here synne shal noþer be forȝyuen ne slakyn Vn-to þey ȝelde þat þey haue takyn. c 1400 *Northern Passion* (H.) 958 Þe men þan letted for no thing Vnto þai come to herod. c 1425 in *Anglia* VIII. 139/46 She..hadde no reste in spirite, vnto she hadde made a-seth. c 1457 *Stonor Papers* (Camden) I. 53, I can..not gefe hym no comfort onto that I have wurd fro yowr maistership. 1502 *Ord. Crysten Men* (W. de W. 1506) I. ii, None were baptysed vnto that y[e] he were suffycyentlye cathecysed. 1535 BP. TUNSTALL in Strype *Eccl. Mem.* (1721) I. App. lix. 147 The commissioners..occupied the said auditors so long, that unto they were dispatched we could not have them [etc.]. 1573 J. TYRIE *Refutation* Pref. 6 Wnto he proue that he defendes that same caus,..he will neuer caus me to beleue nor graunt that [etc.].

†**c.** So that at length; = UNTIL *conj.* e. *Obs.*

a 1395 HYLTON *Scala Perf.* I. xci. (W. de W. 1494), My dere chyldern whyche I bere..vnto cryste be ayenshapen in you. c 1400 tr. *Secreta Secret., Gov. Lordsh.* 84 Alle þes þinges shal be vpon þe fyr all a nyght and a day, vnto all þayre stryngh be out passyd. c 1425 tr. *Arderne's Treat. Fistula*, etc. 73 Boile it agayne vnto it be ane vnement haldyng fast ynoȝ. 1502 ATKYNSON tr. *De Imitatione* III. xii. (1893) 207 This sensuall appetite is to be subdued..vnto it haue lerned to be content with fewe thynges. 1541 R. COPLAND *Guydon's Quest. Chirurg.* Q j b, Apply vpon it a maturatife..vnto the scar be fallen.

†**d.** = UNTIL *conj.* d. *Obs.*

1490 *Plumpton Corr.* (Camden) 100, I thinke long unto I here word from you.

**Untoa·sted,** *ppl. a.* (UN-[1] 8.)

1769 MRS. RAFFALD *Eng. Housekpr.* (1778) 361 Lay untoasted sippets round the inside of the dish. 1865 DICKENS *Mut. Fr.* I. vii, Mr. Venus dives, and produces another muffin, yet untoasted.

**Unto·chered,** *ppl. a.* Chiefly *Sc.* (UN-[1] 8.)

1823 BYRON *Juan* XI. xlix. *note*, The '*untochered*' but 'pretty virginities'..of the *then* day. 1850 A. M'GILVRAY *Poems* 65 His sons..marry poor Untochered lasses. 1866 FREEMAN *Hist. Ess.* i. (1871) 12 Whom his father had left unmarried and untochered.

†**Unto-come,** *v. Obs.*[−1] [f. UNTO + COME *v.* Cf. TO-COME *v.*] *intr.* To arrive, come to a place.

c 1440 *Alph. Tales* 102 On a tyme Petur & Clemett vnto-come þer þis Matidiana begid hur meatt.

†**Untofore,** *prep. Obs.*[−1] [f. UNTO, after TOFORE *prep.*] = TOFORE *prep.* 1 c.

c 1430 LYDG. *Min. Poems* (Percy Soc.) 86 Theyr labour.. They..remembred by writyng ful notable, Unto-fore God a thyng ful commendable.

**Unto·ggle,** *v.* (UN-[2] 4 c.) 1859 F. A. GRIFFITHS *Artill. Man.* (ed. 8) 213, [Nos.] 5 and 6..shift side-tackles, untoggle breeching, and span it when the gun is in. 1883 *Man. Seamanship for Boys* 129 The first reef-beckets must be untoggled when taking in the third reef.

**Untoi·led,** *ppl. a.* [UN-[1] 8, 8 c.]

†**1.** Untilled, uncultivated. *Obs.*

1578 LYTE *Dodoens* I. ii. 4 The common wormwood groweth naturally in..dry, rude, and untoyled places. 1601 HOLLAND *Pliny* II. 224 It commeth up..in untoiled and neglected places, and namely, common high waies. a 1633 G. HERBERT tr. *Cornarus on Temp.* (1634) 40 The reducing of many rude and untoiled places..to cultivation. 1683 J. REID *Scots Gard'ner* (1907) 80 Trenching doth well prepare..untoil'd ground.

**2.** Not subjected to, or overcome by, toil.

1598 SYLVESTER *Du Bartas* II. ii. *Babylon* 262 Un-toyld, un-tutor'd, sucking tender food, We learn'd a language all men understood. 1649 G. DANIEL *Trinarch., Hen. V*, ccli, A Iollitie Sprung from vntoyled Limbes. 1744 ELIZA HEYWOOD *Female Spect.* No. 9 (1748) II. 143 He who preserves it [*sc.* hope]..is untoiled with disappointment, and never loses the prospect of his wish.

**3.** Not toiled *for*; got without toil.

1651 H. VAUGHAN *Olor Iscanus, To best Couple* 20 Like the dayes Warmth may all your Comforts be, Untoil'd for, and Serene as he.

**Untoi·leted,** *ppl. a.* (UN-[1] 8.) 1819 MOORE *Mem.* (1853) II. 325 Obliged to fly from bed and home, unshaved, untoileted.

**Untoi·ling,** *pr. pple.* and *ppl. a.* (UN-[1] 10.)

1748 THOMSON *Cast. Indol.* I. xxxvi, It is of vanities most vain, To toil for what you here untoiling may obtain. 1821 BYRON *Cain* II. ii, It is not with the earth..I feel at war, but that I may not profit By what it bears of beautiful, untoiling. 1839 CARLYLE *Chartism* vii, The Toiling Classes of mankind declare..to the Untoiling, that they will be governed.

**Unto·ld,** *ppl. a.* [OE. *unteald* (UN-[1] 8 b), = MDu. *ongetellet, -telt* (Du. *ongeteld*), MLG. *ungetelt* (LG. *-tald*), MHG. *ungezalt, -zelt* (G. *ungezahlt, -zählt*), ON. *útalíðr, útaldr*, (M)Da. *utalt.*]

†**1. a.** Not counted or reckoned; not counted out or paid. *Obs.*

c 1000 *Sax. Leechd.*, etc. III. 264 Be ðam dæȝe spræc se wisa Augustinus,..ȝyf he byð forlæten unteald, þær rihte awent eall ðæs ȝeares ymbryn þwyres. c 1386 CHAUCER *Miller's T.* 594 Certes were it gold Or in a poke nobles all vntold, Thou sholdest have. a 1400 *Octouian* 821 He tok the floryns all vntold. 14.. *Tundale's Vis.* 64 He went.. To a mon to ascon his pay For thre horsis that he had sold For the whych the pennys wer untold. c 1600 SHAKS. *Sonn.* cxxxvi, Among a number one is reckon'd none. Then in the number let me passe vntold.

†**b.** Not enumerated or reckoned up; unspecified. *Obs.*

a 1300 *Cursor M.* 18549 Þaa Iuus sau þis ilk man do signes sere—Þe blind to se, þe dumb at here,..And oþer takens fele vn-teld. c 1340 HAMPOLE *Pr. Consc.* 7447 Wha couth þan telle..Alle þe syns..And leve nane untald, gret ne smale, Þe whilk a man has here fallen in. c 1425 *Cursor M.* 23139 (Trin.), In pride & triccherY..And in vntolde synnes fele. a 1450 *Le Morte Arth.* 3239 Forthe went they..To syr mordred and hys lordis,..And an C knyghtis all vn-tolde. 1607 TOURNEUR *Rev. Trag.* II. i, Fair trees..Are cut to maintain head-tires—much untold—All thrives but chastity, she lies a cold.

**2.** Uncounted, unreckoned, because of amount or numbers; immense, vast.

*Untold gold* (= any amount of gold), prob. originally in sense 1 a (= not carefully or exactly counted).

a 1400-50 *Alexander* 2677 Þare fand he tresour vntald. c 1440 *Gesta Rom.* viii. 22 Þe kyngdom of hevene, in þe which is tresour vntold. 1672 W. WALKER *Parœm.* 24 You may trust him in the dark; with untold gold. 1754 *Connoisseur* No. 18 ⁋ 3 He..boasts that you may safely trust him with untold gold. 1782 COWPER *Alex. Selkirk* 25 Religion! what treasure untold Resides in that heavenly word! 1849 GROTE *Greece* II. liv. VI. 605 The untold number of these barbarians was reported as overwhelming. 1853 J. H. NEWMAN *Hist. Sk.* (1873) I. I. ii. 83 All the untold riches of his treasury.

**b.** With plural sbs.: In large numbers; numberless, countless.

?a 1500 *Peblis to the Play* 46 The bagpyp blew, and thai out threw out of the townis vntald. 1659 W. CHAMBERLAYNE *Pharon.* I. III. 4 A fruitful pasture..Where in untold droves did feed His bellowing herds. 1819 SHELLEY *Mask of Anarchy* lxxii, Ye who suffer woes untold. 1868 HELPS *Realmah* viii. I. 280 Untold ages have passed since the day when [etc.]. 1874 GEIKIE *Gt. Ice Age* xxvii. 376 The genial climate..lasted for untold centuries.

**c.** With abstract sbs. Unmeasured, unlimited.

In early ME. *unitald fultum* occurs (*Cott. Hom.* 233).

1781 COWPER *Table-t.* 330 Incomparable gem! thy worth untold. 1825 J. NEAL *Bro. Jonathan* I. 60 His mouth was agitated..with untold sorrow. 1868 MORRIS *Earthly Par.* I. 147 He seemed to see the ancient sage Shrivelled yet more with untold age. 1875 T. W. HIGGINSON *Hist. U. S.* xxi. 212 It had also cost the Americans untold suffering.

**3.** Not related or recounted.

c 1386 CHAUCER *Pars. T.* ⁋ 1010 Lat no blotte be bihynde, lat no synne been vntoold as fer as thow hast remembraunce. c 1400 *Destr. Troy* 563 The truthe of the tale [is] vntold to your ere. a 1450 *Knt. de la Tour* (1868) 12 Whanne a man is shreue, he shulde leue no thinge vntolde. 1533 MORE *Debell. Salem* Wks. 1009/1, I haue..proued afore that he must mene so: or elles must haue left his tale vntold. 1565 STAPLETON tr. *Staphylus' Apol.* 175 b, Rather then to suffer a..heresy vncomptrolled, or the truthe vntolde. 1623 MIDDLETON & ROWLEY *Sp. Gipsy* I. v, The cause..shall be to all the world untold. a 1645 MILTON *Arcades* 41 Where ye may more neer behold What shallow-searching Fame hath left untold. 1700 DRYDEN *Pref. to Fables* ⁋ 13 Such tales shall be left untold by me. 1796 MME. D'ARBLAY *Camilla* x. xiii, A reciprocal confidence that left nothing untold, not an action unrelated. 1827 MRS. HEMANS *Last Constantine* xxv, In their mien..Things by the brave untold may fearfully be read! 1875 J. P. HOPPS *Princ. Relig.* xvii. 53 Until a thought or a disclosure is comprehended, it is as though it were untold—it is not revealed.

**4.** Not informed (of a fact).

1590 SPENSER *F. Q.* I. iii. 38 For the old man well knew he, though vntold, In..magicke to haue wondrous might.

†**Unto·lerable,** *a. Obs.* (UN-[1] 7 b and 5 b.)

1382 WYCLIF *Judith* xiv. 17 Vntolerable drede and trembling fel vp on hem. 1422 YONGE tr. *Secreta Secret.* 182 He was..a crowel Tyraunt ontollerabill. c 1440 *Alph. Tales* 147 The bitter payn of hell..is vntollerable vnto me. 1535 COVERDALE *Bible* Ded., The vntollerable iniuries..done vnto God. 1597 MORLEY *Introd. Mus.* 154 Which is a thing vntolerable except [etc.]. 1612 T. TAYLOR *Comm. Titus* iii. 1 Those in authority, who may..returne our frowardnes with vntolerable displeasure.

**Unto·lled,** *ppl. a.* (UN-[1] 8 + TOLL *v.*[2]) 1592 GREENE *Conny Catch.* II. 5 That no man may buy a horse vntould, nor the toule be taken without lawful witnesses. [See TOLL *v.*[2] 3.] 1775 ASH, *Untolled*, not tolled; not diminished by the toll.

**Unto·mb,** *v.* [UN-[2] 5.] *trans.* To disentomb. Also *fig.*

1594 *Zepheria* i, All in the humble accent of my Muse, ..My grieues I here vntoombe. Sweete, them peruse. 1614 GORGES *Lucan* VI. 243 The babe within the mothers wombe With gashing wound she will vntombe. 1646 SIR T. BROWNE *Pseud. Ep.* VII. xviii. 382 The wonderfull corps of Antæus untombed a thousand years after his death by Sertorius. 1712 T. STAVELEY *Hist. Churches* 271 Being advised once to untomb the bones of an enemy. 1840 THACKERAY *Paris Sk.-bk.* (ed. 2) II. 229 The fair Rachel has been trying to revive this *genre* and to untomb Racine.

**Unto·mbed,** *ppl. a.* [UN-[1] 8.] Not provided with, or placed in, a tomb. Also *transf.*

1560 J. HEYWOOD *Thyestes* D i, That whiche the worste was wont to be, were heere a wisshed thyng, That them theyr father sawe vntombde [L. *insepultos*]. 1582 STANYHURST *Æneis* I. (Arb.) 29 But loa, the proper image of corps vntumbed apeered In dreame too Dido. 1818 MILMAN *Samor* IV. 510 The burial on cold battle field, unhymn'd, Unmourn'd, untomb'd. *Ibid.* XII. 234 Th' untomb'd slumbers of far battle vales. 1835 TALFOURD *Ion* IV. i, Spirits that have left..their plague-tormented flesh To rot untomb'd.

**Unto·ne,** *v.* [UN-[2] 6 b.] *trans.* To deprive of tone. Hence **Unto·ned** *ppl. a.*[1]

1803 C. W. ETHELSTON *Suicide* 9 Is there a hope that o'er this unton'd frame Awakened Health her wonted glow shall spread? 1847 H. BUSHNELL *Chr. Nurt.* II. ii. (1861) 266 Nothing..untones more completely the divine affinities of the childish nature.

**Unto·ned,** *ppl. a.*[2] (UN-[1] 8 + TONED *ppl. a.*)

1807 J. BARLOW *Columb.* IX. 104 But frail at first his frame, with nerves ill strung, Unform'd his footsteps, long untoned his tongue. 1896 A. H. KEANE *Ethnol.* xii. 326 A distinctly polysyllabic group of untoned languages. 1897 *Daily News* 12 Jan. 6/5 Its dominant black and blue, its almost strident red, its untoned white.

**Unto·ngue,** *v.* [UN-[2] 4. Cf. older Du. *onttongen.*] *trans.* To deprive of (the use of) the tongue; to render speechless.

1598 FLORIO, *Dislinguare*, to vntoong. c 1600 CHALKHILL *Thealma & Cl.* 3136 Speak he could not,..they had him quite untongued. 1628 FELTHAM *Resolves* II. lix. 170 It hath vntongued some on the sudden; and from some hath snatcht their naturall abilities. 1655 FULLER *Ch. Hist.* XI. 218 Such ..condemn him in keeping such a Diary about him in so dangerous days. Especially he ought to untongue it from talking to his prejudice.

**Unto·ngued,** *ppl. a.* [UN-[1] 8.] Destitute of a tongue; tongueless.

a 1600 M. COSOWARTH *Ps. xxx.* in Farr *S. P. Eliz.* (1845) II. 407 The mute and the untongued dust. 1623 MIDDLETON & ROWLEY *Sp. Gipsy* I. iii, If every orator of folly plead In silence, like this untongu'd piece of violence. 1648 HEXHAM II, *Ontongigh*,..Vntongued, or without a tongue. 1891 C. DAWSON *Avonmore* 28 Untongued voices whispered.. comfort to the troubled breast.

**Unto·ngue-tied,** *ppl. a.* (UN-[1] 8 d.) 1640 BROME *Sparagus Gard.* II. iv, Ide give another hundred Peeces now..that I might be untongue ty'd, And triumph o're my adversary.

**Unto·nsed,** *ppl. a.* [UN-[1] 8.] Unlopped. 1819 J. HODSON in J. Raine *Mem.* (1857) I. 231 The abundance of untonsed trees..give a richness..to all the suburban villages.

**Unto·nsured,** *ppl. a.* (UN-[1] 8.) 1855 MILMAN *Lat. Chr.* VI. 359 Schools of medicine..freely admitted unsonsured.. students. 1863 GEO. ELIOT *Romola* III. xxiii, There came the train of untonsured secular priests.

**Untoo·led,** *ppl. a.* (UN-[1] 8.) 1862 BURTON *Bk. Hunter* 381 Whatever sort of work..went on around these untooled fragments of the living rock.

**Untoo·mly,** *adv.* [UN-[1] 11.] Hastily; hurriedly. c 1400 *Destr. Troy* 1822 Antenor vntomly turnet his way Withoutyn lowtyng.

**Untoo·th,** *v.* (UN-[2] 4. Cf. Du. *onttanden*, G. *entzahnen.*) 1791 COWPER *Odyssey* xviii. 37 As men untooth a pig pilf'ring the corn. 1820 *Blackw. Mag.* VII. 678 We called to untooth them your friend the gay dentist.

**Untoo·thed,** (*ppl.*) *a.* [UN-[1] 9, UN-[2] 8. Cf. G. *ungezähnt.*] Not having, deprived of, teeth.

1513 MORE *Rich. III* (1883) 6 Hee came into the worlde with the feete forwarde,..and (as the fame runneth) also not vntothed. 1550 THOMAS *Ital. Dict.*, *Isdentato*, vntoothed, or without teethe. 1603 S. HARSNET *Pop. Impost.* 136 An olde weather-beaten Croane,..hollow eyed, vntoothed. 1611 FLORIO, *Disdentato*, vntoothed, toothlesse.

**Untoo·thsome,** *a.* [UN-[1] 7.]

**1.** *fig.* Unpalatable, disagreeable.

1548 UDALL *Erasm. Par. Luke* Pref. vi, Suche thynges as these, so ferre contrarie to all mennes..thynkyng, and thynges so vntouthsome for menne to be fond on. 1583 BABINGTON *Commandm.* (1590) 354 Vntoothsome is that trueth euer, that treadeth downe my liking. 1632 SHIRLEY *Hyde Park* II. iv, You shall not ask me..How old I am—a question most untoothsome. a 1680 CHARNOCK *Attrib. God* (1834) II. 89 Their doctrine was..untoothsome to the world.

**2.** Unpleasant or unattractive to the taste.

1576 R. PETERSON *G. della Casa's Galateo* 99 The selly sickman, to whom al cates neuer so..sweete, seeme vntoothsome. 1601 HOLLAND *Pliny* I. 407 Their grapes..be very harsh and in tast untoothsome. 1630 J. TAYLOR (Water P.) *Wks.* I. 60/1 The drugs, the drenches, and vntoothsome drinks. 1655 MOUFET & BENNET *Health's Improv.* 245 Nay ..,is it not unwholesom, heavy and untoothsom without Salt?

*Comb.* 1900 *Morning Post* 3 March 5/7 A sparse, dried, untoothsome-looking herbage, which man and beast accepted as fodder.

Hence **Untoo·thsomeness.**

1623 BP. HALL *Contempl., O. T.* XIX. x, The asse was (besides the untoothsomnesse) an impure creature.

**Unto·p,** *v.* [UN-[2] 4. Cf. TOP *v.*[1]] *trans.* To deprive of a top. Also *fig.*

1598 FLORIO, *Disculminare*, to vntop, to vnroofe, or vntile a house. 1630 J. TAYLOR (Water P.) *Bk. Martyrs* Wks. III. 141/1 So our Eliza stoutly did begin Untopping and beheading Romish sin. [1775 ASH.]

**Unto·pped,** *ppl. a.* [UN-[1] 8.] Not deprived of the top. 1864 R. L. DE COIN *Cotton & Tobacco* 273 You will leave [tobacco] plants untopped enough to produce all the seeds you may want.

**Untorme·nted,** *ppl. a.* (UN-[1] 8.)

c 1374 CHAUCER *Troylus* I. 1004 Troylus..wex of his wo as who seyth vntormentid But hotter weex his loue. 1668 [see UNTORTURED]. 1744 YOUNG *Nt. Th.* VII. 774 Was it then.. Too much for chaos to permit my mass A longer stay with essences unwrought, Unfashion'd, untormented into man? 1868 MORRIS *Earthly Par.* I. I. 393 If thou couldst forget, And live unholpen, lonely, loveless yet, But untormented. 1869 RUSKIN *Q. of Air* iii. § 145 With perfect, untormented serenity of ease.

**Unto·rn**, *ppl. a.* [UN-1 8 b.]

**1.** Not torn or lacerated.

*c* **1547** GARDINER in Foxe *A. & M.* (1563) 751 We shoulde not..mangle them or cut them, but suffer them to stand vntorne. **1599** T. M[OUFET] *Silkwormes* 18 They..Leaue yet no leaues vntorne that may be seene. **1621** G. SANDYS *Ovid's Met.* I. (1626) 3 The yet-free Earth..(Vntorne with ploughs). **1649** F. ROBERTS *Clavis Bibl.* 513 Preserving them un-torn in the Lyons Den. **1791** COWPER *Iliad* XXIV. 26 Apollo, with compassion touch'd Ev'n of the lifeless Hector,..preserved him, although dragg'd, untorn. **1855** BROWNING *Saul* v, Our sheep..are white and untorn by the bushes. **1890** *Retrospect Med.* CII. 249 The..tissue is usually torn through in front,..but remains untorn behind.

**2.** Not taken away by force.

*c* **1691** SOUTH *Serm.* (1717) V. 443 As long as that small remainder of Land, belonging to the Church, shall continue yet untorn from her.

**Unto·rrefied**, *ppl. a.* (UN-1 8.) **1829** TOGNO & DURAND *Mat. Med.* 190 The untorrefied coffee seems to possess very energetic tonic properties. **Unto·rture**, *v.* (UN-2 4 b.) **1650** FULLER *Pisgah* 58 To rectify his mistake, and to untorture him from the apprehension of his son's supposed death. **Unto·rtured**, *ppl. a.* (UN-1 8.) **1648** HEXHAM II, *Ongepijnt*, Vnpained,..Vntortered, or Vntormented. **1813** SCOTT *Rokeby* VI. xiii, Thy racks could give thee but to know The proofs, which I, untortured, show. †**Untosmi·tten**, *ppl. a. Obs.* (UN-1 8 b.) **1382** WYCLIF *Rom.* Prol., The Tessalonycensis..kepten the feith of treuthe, vntosmyten. **Unto·ssed**, *ppl. a.* (UN-1 8.) **1611** FLORIO, *Inagitato*, vnmooued, vntossed. **1819** BYRON *Juan* II. clxxxi, The sands untumbled, the blue waves untost. **Unto·ttering**, *ppl. a.* (UN-1 10.) **1637** C. DOW *Answ. to H. Burton* 203 The onely way to have constant and untottering comfort. **1671** CLARENDON *Dial.* Tracts (1727) 324 That they may keep the ship steady and untottering in that troublesome and unruly sea.

**Untou·chable**, *a.* [UN-1 7 b.]

**1.** Incapable of being touched; immaterial.

**1567** JEWELL *Def. Apol.* 239 Theophylacte saithe, The Body of Christe is Eaten; but the Godheade is not Eaten: bicause it is vntoucheable, and vncomprehensible vnto our senses. **1611** COTGR., *Immateriel*,..impalpable, vntouchable. *absol.* **1833** S. AUSTIN *Char. Goethe* I. 185 Differentializing the Unchangeable and Untouchable.

**b.** Beyond the reach of touch.

**1622** G. G. *Creat. Praysing God* 33 The vntouchable height of his [*sc.* God's] glory. **1886** J. PARKER *Apost. Life* II. 169 With the heavens above it, hell below it, an untouchable horizon round about it. **1890** HALL CAINE *Bondman* III. i, Seas beneath of an untouchable depth.

**c.** *fig.* Unapproachable, unrivalled.

**1867** E. YATES *Forlorn Hope* xv, A worthy woman, untouchable in Mangnall, devoted to the backboard. **1884** — *Recoll.* I. 189 In his day untouchable as a romantic actor.

**2.** Exempt from touch; that one may not touch.

**1607** S. COLLINS *Serm.* (1608) 46 Euery mans conscience is as free and as vntouchable as anothers before God, one price was paid for all. **1647** TRAPP *Comm. Jas.* iii. 7 Sons of Belial, untamable, untractable, untouchable. **1661** FELTHAM *Resolves* II. lxvi. 327 Were not their Persons Sacred, that is, by the Laws of God and Man, untouchable as to prejudice. **1737** *Gentl. Mag.* VII. 35/1 Her Majesty's Foot hitch'd in the Stirrup, and the Horse dragg'd her along.., but the untouchable Foot retain'd the grave Spaniards from intermedling in so delicate an Affair. **1879** J. HINGSTON *Austral. Abroad* ix. 101 The graves..are held as sacred and untouchable by the present owners.

**b.** *spec.* That cannot legally be interfered with or made use of.

**1734** SWIFT in Mrs. Delany *Life & Corr.* (1861) I. 524, I hope the young lady has an untouchable settlement. **1815** *Zeluca* I. 263 Your own untouchable property. **1874** W. R. GREG *Rocks Ahead* 45 Declaring this peasant's farm inalienable,..untouchable for any debt.

**3.** Too bad or unpleasant to touch.

Also, in recent use, as *sb.*: a Hindoo outcast.

**1873** MRS. WHITNEY *Other Girls* x, Fried potatoes, or whatever else was economical and untouchable.

**Untou·ched**, *ppl. a.* [UN-1 8.]

**I. 1.** Not touched with the hand (finger, foot, etc.): not handled or treated by hand, etc.

**1382** WYCLIF 2 *Kings* xxiii. 18 The citeȝeens..vntouchid laften the boonys of hym. *c* **1440** *Pallad. on Husb.* VI. 4 Now euery grayne almeest hath floures swete; Vntouched now the tilman let hem growe. **1502** ATKYNSON tr. *De Imitatione* I. xiii. (1893) 162 A bell untouchyd is not perfytely knowen whether it be hole..or dyscrased. *a* **1586** SIDNEY *Arcadia* III. xvi, I pray you..to let my maides take my body untouched by you. **1673** [R. LEIGH] *Transp. Reh.* 43 Romances are thumb'd more than..Gondibert is Dogs-ear'd, while the Rabbies are untoucht. **1697** DRYDEN *Æneis* X. 1173 Untouched thy arms, untaken be thy sword. **1725** POPE *Odyssey* II. 396 Untouch'd and sacred may these vessels stand Till great Ulysses views his native land. **1801** SCOTT *Glenfinlas* xxxviii, Untouch'd, the harp began to ring. **1816** J. WILSON *City of Plague* I. ii. 26 Buy poison, and 'twill lie for years untouch'd Beneath thy pillow. **1877** HUXLEY *Physiogr.* p. viii, The manuscript remained untouched until last year.

**b.** Not touched by another body, etc.; † *spec.* (quot. 1730), unmagnetized.

*a* **1595** SOUTHWELL *Mæoniæ, Christ's Bloody Sweat* 3 Fat soile, full spring, sweete oliue, grape of blisse, Vntil'd, vndrawne, vnstampt, vntoucht of presse. **1730** *Phil. Trans.* XXXVI. 295 Of Touched Iron or Steel (or of Untouched, so long as it remains in a Posture which gives it Polarity). **1736** THOMSON *Liberty* IV. 416 Even yet untouch'd by daring keel, be theirs The vast Pacific.

**c.** Not approached, crossed, or traversed.

**1628** MAY *Virg. Georg.* III. 75 Let us follow the Woods, and Lands Vntouch'd. **1729** T. INNES *Crit. Essay* I. 28 The northern wall..was of no use at all to keep off the enemies, who leaving it untouch'd, passed easily over the narrow Friths. **1882** H. S. HOLLAND *Logic & Life* 50 We are carried forward to explore new regions of our souls as yet untouched and untrodden.

**2.** Not affected physically, esp. in an injurious manner; not damaged, harmed, or meddled with; unhurt, uninjured; intact. Const. *by*, † *of*.

*c* **1400** *Found. St. Bartholomew's* 62 Of an howse vntouchid yn myddyl of the fyer. *c* **1440** *Jacob's Well* 183 His suster ..be þe vertu of schryfte, was vntowchyd of þe fyir. **1526** *Pilgr. Perf.* (W. de W. 1531) 136 b, Whiche came out safe & vntouched of ye fyre. **1571** GOLDING *Calvin on Ps.* xvi. 10 No one [of the faithful] becommeth partaker of incorruptible lyfe, untowched of rotting. **1603** KNOLLES *Hist. Turks* (1621) 101 The Sultan..polluted the sepulchre of our blessed Sauiour,..of all nations vntouched & reuerenced. **1666** BOYLE *Orig. Forms & Qual.* 112 The Rudiments of the Chick..is nourish'd..onely by the White of the Egg...In effect you may see the Chick furnish'd not onely with all the necessary, but divers other parts,..whilst the Yolk seems yet as it were untouch'd. **1690** DRYDEN *Don Sebastian* v. ii, Untouch'd, and Seal'd, as when intrusted with me, Such I restore it [*sc.* a paper]. **1736** THOMSON *Liberty* II. 246 Then stood untouch'd the solid base Of Liberty, the Liberty of Mind. **1749** JOHNSON *Van. Hum. Wishes* 35 Untouch'd his Cottage, and his Slumbers sound, Tho' Confiscation's Vulturs clang around. **1820** SHELLEY *Hope, Fear, & Doubt* 9 Nor did I hope to pass Untouched by suffering, through the rugged glen. **1856** KANE *Arct. Expl.* I. 317 We landed at the point where we left our life-boat a year ago, and to our great joy found it untouched! **1890** OMAN *Hist. Greece* 303 The plague had left the rest of Greece almost untouched.

†**b.** Not having had sexual connexions; immaculate, chaste, undefiled. *Obs.*

*c* **1400** *Found. St. Bartholomew's* 49 She skapid vntowchid. *c* **1450** *Myrr. our Ladye* 171 O vntouwched mother of the kynge of peace. *Ibid.* 296 Yet that maydes wombe is alway vntowched. **1577** tr. *Bullinger's Decades* 62/2 The vntouched Virgine Marie. **1621** LADY M. WROTH *Urania* 343 Shee loues the Prince of Iambolly much better then the King;.. yet on my conscience shee is vntouched, and iust to her Husband. *a* **1649** DRUMM. OF HAWTH. *Hist. Jas. II*, Wks. (1711) 31 The earl..sought..to have her in marriage, alledging her untouched of his brother. **1683** DRYDEN tr. *Ovid, Helen to Paris* 30 Rude force might some unwilling Kisses gain, But that was all he ever could obtain...Untouch'd the Youth restor'd me to my friends.

**c.** Not used at all, left intact; *esp.* not partaken of, untasted.

**1538** ELYOT, *Illibatus*, vntouched, vntasted. **1577** B. GOOGE *Heresbach's Husb.* 36 Lupines,..for the bitternesse thereof whyle it is greene, they [*sc.* cattle] leaue vntouched. *a* **1589** MASCALL *Govt. Cattle* (1596) 69 Cattell..leaue many tufts of grasse here and there vntouched. **1610** HOLLAND *Camden's Brit.* I. 303 Choosing rather..to send away whole dishes vntouched, than other commers vnbidden to call for more viands. **1666** EARL ORRERY *St. Lett.* (1742) 184 The 10,000 *l.* stock..I humbly beg your grace will keep..untouched to answer a dead lift with. **1679** PEPYS *Mem. Royal Navy* (1906) 5 A further Reserve [of Supplies] remain'd untoucht in Magazine. **1725** POPE *Odyssey* X. 447 Untouch'd before thee stand the cates divine. **1798** J. NAISMITH *Agric. Clydesdale* 93 The pastures are allowed to grow untouched, from..May to..August. *a* **1828** *Arab. Nts.* (1853) 328 A great quantity of provisions left untouched. **1839** THACKERAY *Fatal Boots* Dec., That famous rum-punch..which she and my sisters left untouched. **1863** MISS BRADDON *Aurora Floyd* ii, He had sent his dinner away untouched.

**3.** Not worked upon or at; not touched or treated by way of improvement, alteration, operation, etc.

**1726** LEONI *Alberti's Archit.* I. 39/1, I am..for preserving the old Structures untoucht. **1736** T. PRINCE *N. Eng. Chronol.* II. ii. 231 The General Frame of Diocesan Episcopacy had no doubt remain'd untouched. **1815** J. SMITH *Panorama Sci. & Art* II. 778 In engraving upon copper, every part which is to be white must be left untouched. **1833–4** *Encycl. Metrop.* (1845) VI. 706/1 The mighty forests of America, untouched by human industry. **1862** *Catal. Internat. Exhib., Brit.* II. No. 3168, Untouched and coloured photographs. **1884** THOMPSON *Tumours of Bladder* 41 [He] found a large tumour, which, after consultation, was left untouched.

**II. 4.** Not dealt with in discourse, etc.; not treated, written about, or spoken of; unmentioned. Also with *upon*.

*c* **1380** WYCLIF *Sel. Wks.* III. 362 Þus no þing untouchid in þis lawe shulde be dun or axid to do. **1382** — *Joshua* viii. 35 No thing..that Moyses comaundide, he left vntowchyd; but alle thingis he openyde [1388 declaride] before al the multitude. **1532** MORE *Confut. Tindale* Wks. 609/2 Wherein whoso consider what I haue aunswered hym, shal..perceiue that it had been better for him to haue lefte that matter vntouched. **1594** SHAKS. *Rich. III*, III. vii. 19, I..left nothing ..Vntoucht, or sleightly handled in discourse. **1667** BOYLE *Orig. Forms & Qual.* (ed. 2) 293 The nature of our present discourse forbids me to leave it altogether untouch'd. **1697** [C. LESLIE] *Snake in Grass* (ed. 2) 307 In his Answer..he passes this Section of their Diabolical Possessions, wholly untouch'd. **1793** WORDSW. *Descrip. Sketches* Ded. ¶ 4, I might have inscribed to you a description of some of the features...But the Alpine steeps of the Conway..remain yet untouched. **1841** SPALDING *Italy & It. Isl.* I. 150 The earliest progress of Grecian art..must here be left untouched. **1866** G. STEPHENS *Runic Mon.* I. p. vi, The comparatively few hitherto almost untoucht and unredd older or Old-Northern Runic pieces. **1900** *Handbk. Austral. Assoc., Melbourne* 74 The aquatic worms are an untouched group.

(*b*) **1746** ELIZA HEYWOOD *Female Spect.* No. 24 (1748) IV. 319 They will needs have us take up the pen again, and promise to furnish us with a variety of topics yet untouched upon. **1856** CARLYLE *Lett. Emerson* (1883) II. 258, I must end, in mid-course; so much still untouched upon.

**5.** Not affected, modified, or influenced, esp. in a prejudicial or adverse manner.

*a* **1586** SIDNEY *Def. Earl Leicester* Wks. 1923 III. 67 If awncient undouted and untouched nobility bee worthi to match with the most noble hows that can bee. **1593** *Sidney's Arcadia* V. (1622) 475 How can any lawes..be obserued, if the law-giuers, and law-rulers bee not held in an vntouched admiration? **1696** PRIOR *Presented to King* 32 Be William's Life untouch'd, as is his Fame. **1699** BENTLEY *Phal.* 232 In the third Verse..Mr. Stanley corrected it..,as appears by his Translation, utile; the other word he leaves untouch'd. **1732** BERKELEY *Alciphr.* I. § 9, I will shew you..That whatever was sound and good we leave untouched, and encourage it to grow in the Mind of Man. **1761** STERNE *Tr. Shandy* IV. xxix, In the case cited,..where *patriae* is put for *patris*, *filia* for *filii*, and so on—as it is a fault only in the declension, and the roots of the words continue untouched. *a* **1763** W. KING *Anecd.* (1818) 163 Clodia..was descended from an old Patrician family...Her behaviour was modest, and her reputation untouched. **1894** H. DRUMMOND *Ascent Man* 182 [In North Queensland you] will find the child of Nature still untouched, and neither by intercourse nor imitation removed by one degree from the lowest savage state.

**b.** Not affected or prejudiced in mind or feeling; not biassed or moved by excitement or emotion; unmoved, undisturbed, calm.

**1616** T. ADAMS *Div. Herball* 89 Some Sage, honest policie; ..such as may stand with an vntouched conscience. **1697** VANBRUGH *Æsop* I. i, Is it possible any thing that I am Father of, can be untouch'd with so much Merit? **1709** STEELE & SWIFT *Tatler* No. 71 ¶ 4 If a Man could be untouched at so warm an Accusation. **1748** RICHARDSON *Clarissa* VII. i. 3 The roughest and most untouched creature that ever enter'd a sick man's chamber. **1768–74** TUCKER *Lt. Nat.* (1834) II. 678 Every one proceeding by a softness and milkiness of temper, untouched by injuries, unmoved at offences. **1805** WORDSW. *Prelude* v. 182 Think not that I could pass along untouched By these remembrances. **1838** LYTTON *Alice* I. x, Her heart is as yet untouched;—if she can love you, may you deserve her affection. **1876** MISS BRADDON *J. Haggard's Dau.* II. 60 The young people were ..untouched by the blighting influence of this aggrieved spinster.

**6.** Not equalled in respect of excellence or high character; unexampled, unparalleled.

**1736** THOMSON *Liberty* II. 194 Greece in their view, and glory yet untouch'd, Their steady column..held its way Triumphant. **1878** GROSART *H. More's Poems* p. xxxiii, I have been struck with the untouched perfection of all that arrests you in reading.

**7.** Not entered upon; not begun.

**1876** *Coursing Cal.* 21 The day finished at dusk, with only twenty-seven trials, leaving the all-aged stake untouched.

**Untou·ching**, *ppl. a.* [UN-1 5 d, 10.]

**1.** Not touching (something).

**1602** W. BASSE *Three Past. Elegies* i. (1893) 46 My flocks ..saw their maisters eie Perus'd in things vntutching their estate. **1632** LITHGOW *Trav.* VII. 327 Their flight will bee the length of a Cables Rope, vntouching Water. **1846** MANGAN *Poems* (1903) 6 Untouching the earth I then sped forth To Inver-lough.

**b.** Not having contact.

*a* **1811** J. GRAHAME *Poems* (1827) 88 Like that untouching cincture which enzones The globe of Saturn.

**2.** Having no effect upon the feelings; unaffecting.

**1745** ELIZA HEYWOOD *Female Spect.* No. 10. II. 204 All the Protestations they made..were..unfelt by themselves, and equally untouching to those they were address'd.

**Untou·chingly**, *adv.* (UN-1 11. Cf. prec. 2.) **1861** MISS YONGE *Young Stepmother* iii. 26 Albinia had been strongly interested by the touching facts, so untouchingly narrated.

**Unto·ward**, *a.* [UN-1 7.]

†**1.** Not having or showing inclination, disposition, or readiness *to* or *for* something; disinclined.

**1526** *Pilgr. Perf.* (W. de W. 1531) 42 b, Syth of our selfe we be insufficient & all vntowarde to all goostly thynges. **1575** VAUTROLLIER *Luther on Ep. Gal.* 252 If Satan did not vexe vs inwardly with spirituall tentations,..we should become vtterly careles, negligent, and vntoward to all good workes. **1594** CAREW *Huarte's Exam. Wits* i. (1596) 5 Those who are vntoward for one science, are very apt to another. **1628** WITHER *Brit. Rememb.* Pref. 713 Yea, so untoward was I to conforme My Will,..That [etc.]. **1665** MANLEY *Grotius' Low C. Wars* 73 The Captains were yet not skilled in managing their Men, and the Men were untoward to be commanded.

†**b.** Showing lack of proficiency or aptitude; inept, slow. *Obs. rare.*

**1557** NORTH *Gueuara's Diall Pr.* Prol. A ij, Greate travayle taketh a scole maister in teaching an untowarde scholler. **1592** NASHE *Four Lett. Confut.* F 4 Lamentable, that an indifferent vntoward ciuill Lawyer..should be no more set by but..thrust aside.

**2.** Of persons (or animals), their disposition, etc.: Difficult to manage, restrain, or control; intractable, unruly, perverse.

In frequent use from *c* 1580 to *c* 1700.

**1526** TINDALE *Acts* ii. 40 Save youre selves from this vntowarde generacion. **1548** UDALL, etc. *Erasm. Par. Luke* i. 16 b, If the same commyng of ye Lorde shoulde fynde the hertes of men stoubthfully sluggyng, & vtterly vntowarde. **1587** *Norton's Calvin's Inst.* III. xxiv. 326 b, The vnchangeable decree of God concerning the destruction of the wicked is the ground of their vntoward disposition. **1624** GATAKER *Good Wife* 3 It is no small vexation for a man to find vntoward and vnfaithful cariage toward him in those..that feed at his boord. *a* **1654** — *Antid. Errour* (1670) 54 The verie prohibitions..of the Law..ar to mans untoward spirit, but as water to qick lime. **1656** EARL MONM. tr. *Boccalini's Pol. Touchstone* (1674) 257 The very untoward Spanish Mules, who are so..given to lay about them with their heels. **1714** GAY *Sheph. Week* v. 53 Th' untoward creatures to the stye I drove. **1771** MACKENZIE *Man Feel.* vii, The young man was so untoward in his disposition. **1789** BELSHAM *Ess.* I. iii. 55 This..answer..mollified the untoward and uncourtly disposition of the House. **1814** JANE AUSTEN *Mansf. Park* ii, A most untoward gravity of deportment. **1817** BYRON *Mazeppa* viii, The devil!—I'm loth to do him wrong, It might be some untoward saint. **1865** M. ARNOLD *Ess. Crit.* ix. (1875) 379 The untoward generation of metaphysical Article-makers.

*transf.* **1809** W. IRVING *Knickerb.* I. i, The untoward planet pertinaciously continued her course, notwithstanding that she had..a whole university of learned professors opposed to her conduct.

**b.** Of things: Difficult to manipulate, work, deal with, or perform; stubborn, stiff.

**1566** DRANT *Sat.* I. x. E vj, Why maye not we inquyre..if the matter to vntoward, hath made his style to harde. **1601** B. JONSON *Poetaster* I. i, Nay looke, what a rascally vntoward thing this poetrie is. **1620** SANDERSON *Serm.* (1632) 101 God..out of mankinde, as out of an vntoward lumpe of clay,..maketh vp vessels for the vse of his Sanctuary. **1664** BUTLER *Hud.* II. II. 293 A Vow Which afterward he found untoward, And stubborn to be kept. **1693** CONGREVE *Old Bach.* III. viii, Pish! This is the untowardest lock [of hair]. **1799** J. ROBERTSON *Agric. Perth* 278 A piece of untoward ground..cannot be improved with equal success in any other way. **1831** CARLYLE in Froude *Life* (1882) II. 203 A noisy, untoward lodging-house. **1833–5** J. H. NEWMAN *Hist. Sk.* Ser. III. (1873) 49 Basil had to deal on all hands with most untoward materials. **1875** TAIT & STEWART *Unseen Universe* ii. (1878) 81 There is a periodicity even in such untoward phenomena.

† **c.** Awkward, clumsy; ungainly, ungraceful.

**1590** SPENSER *F. Q.* I. viii. 31 But very vncouth sight was to behold, How he did fashion his vntoward pace. **1592** LYLY *Gallathea* II. i, I neither like my gate, nor my garments; the one vntoward, the other vnfit. **1628** FORD *Lover's Mel.* v. i, I am..so poor and feeble, That my untoward joints can scarcely creep Unto the grave. **1632** LITHGOW *Trav.* x. 433 Their..Ploughes..are onely fastned with Straw..to their bare Rumps, marching..three or foure in a Ranke, and as many men hanging by the ends of that vntoward Labour. **1658** A. FOX *Würtz' Surg.* II. xviii. 125, I will write now of Knees that are much pained..and grow untoward and unshaped. **1762** H. WALPOLE *Vertue's Anecd. Paint.* (1765) III. 65 His drawing even of the neck and shoulders..[was] incorrect and untoward. *a* **1791** SIR J. REYNOLDS in Boswell *Johnson* an. 1739, Accompanying his thoughts with certain untoward actions [*ante* 'improperly called convulsions'].

**3.** Characterized or attended by misfortune, calamity, vexation, or annoyance; unlucky, unfortunate, ill-starred: **a.** Of conditions, times, etc.

**1570** T. WILSON tr. *Demosth. Orat.* vii. 95 Thorowe the Lacedemonians vntowarde lucke. **1603** HOLLAND *Plutarch's Mor.* 238 The diseases, the debts, the hard usage of men to their owne wives, and the untoward life betweene them. **1782** WOLCOT (P. Pindar) *Lyric Odes* vii, The courtly Abington's untoward Star Wanted her reputation much to mar. **1805–6** WORDSW. *Char. Happy Warrior* 68 Who, with a toward or untoward lot,..Plays, in the many games of life, that one [etc.]. **1868** ROGERS *Pol. Econ.* ii. (1876) 103 A man..should have a..reserve from which he can draw when the times are untoward. **1878** STUBBS *Const. Hist.* III. xviii. 88 No untoward omen..threw a shadow over the second epoch of the war. **1898** 'H. S. MERRIMAN' *Roden's Corner* xxx, Percy ..looked back later to this as one of his most untoward hours.

**b.** Of occurrences, enterprises, etc.

Esp. with *accident*, *circumstance*, *event*, and in very frequent use from *c* 1800.

**1632** LITHGOW *Trav.* x. 482 When Charles the fift returned from that vntoward voyage of Algier. **1638** SIR T. HERBERT *Trav.* (ed. 2) 92 The report of this vntoward massacre is soone knowne. **1647** CLARENDON *Hist. Reb.* III. §1 An untoward, and in truth an unheard of accident, which brake many of the King's measures. **1760** STERNE *Tr. Shandy* III. xxiv, The foulmouth'd trumpet of Fame carried it from ear to ear,..with this untoward circumstance along with it. **1798** W. HUTTON *Autobiog.* 115 An untoward trade is a dreadful sink for money. **1814** JANE AUSTEN *Mansf. Park* i, She could hardly have made a more untoward choice. **1833** HT. MARTINEAU *Berkeley* I. ii, There were no untoward delays. **1893** LIDDON *Life Pusey* I. viii. 176 He felt anxious as to the untoward influence..of these books.

*absol.* **1887** RUSKIN *Præterita* II. 120 Every soul of us has to do its fight with the Untoward, and for itself discover the Unseen.

**4.** Unfavourable or adverse to progress; unpropitious, unprosperous.

**1621** in Foster *Eng. Factories Ind.* (1906) I. 283 The wayes soe untoward that in the best season..they are unpassable for carts. **1662** J. DAVIES tr. *Olearius' Voy. Ambass.* 391 Bridges, raised very high,..so untoward to pass over, that they put a man into a fright. **1725** *Portland Papers* (Hist. MSS. Comm.) VI. 120 We came down by a very steep, untoward descent. **1731** CAPT. W. WRIGLESWORTH *MS. Log-bk. of the 'Lyell'* 4 Mar., Wee have had a very untoward ugly Sea all these 24 Hours. **1791** SMEATON *Edystone L.* 145 The weather being untoward, the short sea..occasioned ..a motion of the yawls. **1833** HT. MARTINEAU *Three Ages* II. 35 The present had been an untoward season, as regarded the nation's prosperity. **1849** GROTE *Hist. Greece* II. xliv. V. 381 An untoward storm drove the vessel to the island. **1886** C. SCOTT *Sheep-farming* 83 In untoward seasons..the lambs often do not exceed 100 per cent. of the ewes.

**5. a.** At variance with good conduct or propriety; indecorous, unseemly, improper; foolish.

**1628–9** DIGBY *Voy. Medit.* (Camden) 57 Because idlenesse should not fixe their mindes vpon any vntoward fansies. **1658** T. WHITE in Spurgeon *Treas. Dav.* Ps. lxxiii. 17 They came to a very wicked man's house, where they had very untoward entertainment. **1695** WOODWARD *Nat. Hist. Earth* III. (1723) 179 Some Men there are who have made a very untoward Use of this. **1709** STRYPE *Ann. Ref.* I. i. 44 The popish priests..took frequent occasion..to speak very untoward words against the Queen. **1802** WORDSW. *Resolution & Indep.* 53 When I with these untoward thoughts had striven.

† **b.** Marked by lack of reason or fitness. *Obs.*

**1682** H. MORE *Annot. Glanvill's Lux O.* 95 If you paraphrase (*me*) thus, My Hypostasis consisting of my Humane and Divine Nature, it will be as untoward sence. **1701** NORRIS *Ideal World* I. v. 225 It seems..untoward, to inquire whether a thing be,..before we know what it is we inquire about. **1733** BERKELEY *Th. Vision Vind.* § 6 Such is the ill effect of untoward defences and explanations of our faith.

† **6.** Of taste: Disagreeable; unpleasant. *Obs.*[−1]

**1662** J. DAVIES tr. *Mandelslo's Trav.* 245 It had so untoward a taste, that the Sea-men would not take it for their..drink.

†**Unto·ward**, *prep. Obs.* [f. UNTO *prep.* + -WARD. Cf. UNTILWARD.] Toward; in the direction of. **1390** GOWER *Conf.* II. 20 Whanne I am mi ladi fro And thenke untoward hire drawe. *Ibid.* 215 Nevere for no worldes good Min herte untoward hire stod. *Ibid.* III. 127.

**Unto·wardliness.** (UN-1 12. Cf. next.)

**1598** BARCKLEY *Felic. Man* v. 427 The fathers felicitie is deminished by the childrens vntowardlinesse. **1603** FLORIO *Montaigne* I. xxv. 86 Who..could..winke at..my vntowardlinesse, and such other faults that were in mee. **1707** *Pennsylv. Hist. Soc. Mem.* X. 235 The more privileges the more presumption and untowardliness.

**Unto·wardly**, *a.* Now *rare.* [UN-1 7.]

**1.** Unbecoming, improper.

**1483** *Cov. Leet Bk.* 511 Not beyng content with such answer [he] desired a copy of þat Evidence,..&..other vntowardly wordes there vttered. **1598** GRENEWEY *Tacitus, Ann.* I. ii. 3 Little doubt but Augustus, complaining of the yong mans vntowardly behauior, caused his exile to be confirmed. **1693** LOCKE *Educ.* 70 [Children] frequently learn from unbred or debauched Servants..untowardly Tricks and Vices.

**b.** Froward, perverse, ill-disposed.

**1561** T. HOBY tr. *Castiglione's Courtyer* IV. Z z iii, Not to be haughtie, enuious,..contentious nor vntowardlye. **1598** BARCKLEY *Felic. Man* v. 427 If they [*sc.* children] prooue vntowardly and giuen to lewdnesse, what greater griefe can happen to a man? *a* **1678** H. SCOUGAL *Disc. Imp. Subj.* (1735) 193 Sad and heavy looks, morose and untowardly deportment. **1712** STEELE *Spect.* No. 442 ¶ 3 The Serene or Cloudy, Jovial or Melancholy, Untowardly or Easy [Temper]. **1791** WASHINGTON *Let. Writ.* 1892 XII. 85 If you are disobliging, self-willed, and untowardly, it is hardly to be expected that they will engage themselves in unpleasant disputes with you. **1887** *S. Cheshire Gloss.* 320 Ay, he's..an unto'artly yowth, is Joe.

**2.** Awkward, clumsy.

**1611** COTGR., *Faire le pied de veau*, to make an vntowardlie, or clownish leg; or, to vse a foolish lifting vp of the leg in dauncing, &c. *a* **1642** SIR W. MONSON *Naval Tracts* II. (1704) 270/1 They went the most untowardly way I ever saw. **1668** ETHEREDGE *She wou'd if she cou'd* III. ii, Well, thou hast seduc'd me; But I shall look so untowardly.

**3.** Ill-suiting; adverse; unfavourable.

**1756** C. LUCAS *Ess. Waters* II. 257, I have observed at Spa..one most untowardly effect. **1856** CARLYLE *Let.* 22 Feb. (Encycl. Dict.), Travelling is at all times very untowardly to me. **1864** — *Fredk. Gt.* XV. iii. IV. 32 The Expedition does not improve in promise;..the march one of the most untowardly.

**Unto·wardly**, *adv.* [UN-1 11.]

**1.** Unskilfully, awkwardly, clumsily, badly.

**1550** BALE *Apol.* 146 b, That rawe and ragged clause whych ye haue vntowardly torne out of hys xxi. homely. **1561** T. NORTON *Calvin's Inst.* III. 159 No man shal go so vntowardly, but he shal euery day get some ground, though it be but litle. **1576** R. PETERSON *G. della Casa's Galateo* 105 Their cloathes doe sit vppon them so vntowardly. **1642** FULLER *Holy & Prof. St.* IV. ix. 281 Generally the most dexterous in spiritual matters are left-handed in temporall businesse, and go but untowardly about them. **1667** DRYDEN *Sir Martin Mar-all* v. i, He played well, and yet methinks he held his lute not untowardly. **1697** DAMPIER *Voy.* I. 190 They rig their Ships but untowardly,..and are as meanly furnished with Warlike Provisions. **1762** STERNE *Tr. Shandy* VI. xxxiii, A large uneven thread..running along the whole length of the web, and so untowardly, you cannot so much as cut out..a fillet. **1764** HARMER *Observ.* ix. 23 There is no scripture from whence he attempts to deduce it, as he doth the time of the latter rain, though very untowardly.

**b.** Unsuitably (for use).

**1686** PLOT *Staffordsh.* 352 If there be any such land that lyes so untowardly.

**2.** Unluckily; unpropitiously; with likelihood or suggestion of misfortune or mishap.

**1568** GRAFTON *Chron.* II. 262 As he lept out of his ship,..he fell so vntowardly, that the blood brast out of his nose. **1571** GOLDING *Calvin on Ps.* ii. 8 Least this Prophecie should bee spoken in vayne, yea and untowardly concerning the largenesse of dominion. **1599** SHAKS. *Much Ado* III. ii. 134 O day vntowardly turned! **1603** HOLLAND *Plutarch's Mor.* 108 Which as many as use, worke their own..destruction, dauncing..a daunce untowardly about a pits brinke. **1699** BENTLEY *Phal.* Introd. 2 Mr. B. here seems to enter upon his work a little untowardly and ominously.

**b.** Unsuccessfully; unfortunately.

**1649** J. H. *Motion to Parl. Adv. Learn.* 35 There were some propensions and aversions,..which if disobeyed succeeded untowardly and unsuccessfully. **1679** *Hist. Jetzer* 26 The Prior swore things went very untowardly against them. *a* **1722** LISLE *Husb.* (1752) 180 Such barley..will come away very untowardly in the malting. **1815** JANE AUSTEN *Emma* xxxvi, If things are going untowardly one month, they are sure to mend the next. **1889** GRETTON *Memory's Harkb.* 269 On his death-bed he..sent urgently for the clergyman, who untowardly happened to be from home.

**3.** Rudely, roughly; frowardly.

**1682** BUNYAN *Holy War* 223, I charge you, therefore,..that you carry it not ruggedly, or untowardly to my Captains, or their men. **1693** SOUTHERNE *Maid's Last Prayer* II. ii, Give me thy Hand dear Bully; Faith, I'm sorry you provok'd me to use you so untowardly. **1868–9** BROWNING *Ring & Bk.* IX. 259 Let the heifer bear the yoke!..What if..all untowardly she pursue her way With groan and grunt?

**Unto·wardness.** [UN-1 12.]

**1.** Disinclination to be accommodating or pleasant; perversity, obstinacy.

**1481** *Cov. Leet Bk.* 500 We fynde them therunto in no wyse towardly disposed,..which their vntowardnesse sowneth not to oure pleasure. **1538–9** HENRY VIII in *Wyatt's Wks.* (1816) II. 501 Continuing our good mind and affection to join with him (his said untowardness and coldness in that behalf notwithstanding.) **1569** in Bolton *Stat. Irel.* (1621) 339 Which is occasioned by the sluggardy, idlenesse and vntowardnes of the Marchants. **1607** HIERON *Wks.* I. 129 Gods first work in them is..to remooue their naturall vntowardnesse, and to make their hearts more..pliable vnto good. **1658** *Whole Duty Man* 120 Complaint not of the hardness of the duty, but of the untowardness of thy own heart. **1723** *Pres. St. Russia* I. 16 The Untowardness of these People made me astonished. **1765** MRS. MACAULEY *Hist. Eng.* II. 232 Finding him not at so entire leisure to discipline their untowardness as in time of peace. **1873** HAMERTON *Intell. Life* II. ii. 54 Our untowardness was a hopeful sign.

**b.** Const. *to* (esp. with inf.).

*c* **1547** LATIMER in Foxe *A. & M.* (1563) 1352/1 So should I haue bene without this inwarde sorrow of my harte, to see suche vntowardnes of you bothe to godlines. **1557** EARL WESTMORLD. in Lodge *Illustr. Brit. Hist.* (1791) I. 287, I ame sory to see suche an untowardnes to serve in the Bushopriche men as ys now. **1579** J. STUBBES *Gaping Gulf* E j b, If ther be..a generall vntowardnes to desire that state of lyfe.

† **2.** Lack of good progress or promise, *esp.* in respect of physical condition. *Obs.*

**1538** AUDLEY in *St. Papers Henry VIII*, I. 588 Besechyng you to travayle therin [*sc.* the suit] and to advertise me..of the towardnes or ontowardnes therof. **1555** WATREMAN *Fardle Facions* II. viii. 184 Yf thei spie vntowardnes in the infante, deformitie, or lacke of lymmes, [they] commaunde it to be slayne. **1601** HOLLAND *Pliny* I. 359 Even in trees as well as in other living creatures, there is a certaine infelicitie, which may be well tearmed, A dwarfish untowardnesse.

† **3.** Lack of aptitude; awkwardness. *Obs.*

**1598** FLORIO, *Inettudine*, vnaptnesse, vntowardnesse, grossenes. **1604** T. WRIGHT *Passions* v. iii. 176 Some..eloquent [men],..for lack of action or rather vntowardnesse,..were accounted infants. **1622** F. MARKHAM *Bk. War* v. ii. 168 There will be such disparity and untowardnesse in his actions, that all his labour will be to little or no purpose.

**4.** Unpropitiousness; adverseness.

**1778** [W. H. MARSHALL] *Minutes Agric., Observ.* 101 The untowardness of circumstances prevented any Experiment ..from being made. **1803–5** WORDSW. *Rob Roy's Grave* 62 Through untowardness of fate..He came an age too late. **1847** HELPS *Friends in C.* I. iii. 44 The untowardness of things present, the miseries of the past. **1871** MORLEY *Vauvenargues* in *Crit. Misc.* 7 His nature had such.. quality that the perpetual untowardness of circumstances left no evil print upon him.

† **Unto·wards**, *a. Obs.* [Cf. TOWARDS *prep.* and *adv.*] = UNTOWARD *a.* 1 and 2.

**1525** in Ellis *Orig. Lett.* Ser. III. I. 360 Ther is no wise man but wool thinke..that it apperith, seing they be thus vntowards, that they be lincked together, for commonlye they aggreid in oon aunswer. **1548** UDALL, etc. *Erasm. Par. John* 40 The lustes of this worlde maketh many one vntowardes to bee taughte.

† **Untow·e(n**, *ppl. a. Obs.* Forms: (see quots.). [OE. *ungetogen* (UN-1 8 b), = OHG. *ungizogan*, *unkazogan*, etc. (MHG. and G. *ungezogen*, obs. G. *unzogen*), MLG. *un(ge)togen* uneducated, undisciplined, ill-bred, etc., MSw. *otughin* improper, disreputable, etc. Cf. WANTON *a.*] Untaught, untrained; unmannered, wanton.

*c* **1000** ÆLFRIC *Hom.* I. 576 Fisceras and unȝetoȝene menn ȝeceas Drihten him to leorning-cnihtum. *a* **1225** *Ancr. R.* 102 Eni totilde ancre..þet bekeð euer utward ase untowe brid ine cage. *Ibid.* 372 So tendre of þe bodie þet hit iwurðe untowen. *a* **1240** *Sawles Warde* in *O. E. Hom.* I. 245 For alle hit beoð untohene ant rechelese hinen. *Ibid.* 267 To..leaden him..nawt efter wil, þe untohe lefdi,..ah efter þat wit wule, þat is husebonde. *a* **1310** in Wright *Lyric P.* viii. 32 Thah told beon tales untoun in toun. **13..** *Metr. Hom.* in *Archiv Stud. neu. Spr.* LVII. 252/1 þis ilke childe was so vntoun and so wylde. *c* **1425** in *Anglia* VIII. 145 Wiþ hir vntoune & lacches songes [she] kyndeliþ þe fyre of lecchery.

Hence † **Untow·e(n)ly** *adv.*, wantonly; **Untow·e(n)ship**, wantonness. *Obs.*

*a* **1225** *Ancr. R.* 170 Schomeleas is þe mon oðer þeo wummon þet deð eni untoweschipe, oðer seið, biuoren ancren. *a* **1230** *Hali Meid.* 22 ȝef ȝe þenne hondlið ow in ei stude untuliche [*v.r.* untoheliche]. *a* **1240** *Sawles Warde* in *O. E. Hom.* I. 247 Nis hare nan þe ne feareð ofte untoheliche ant gulteð ilome. *c* **1450** *Cursor M.* 10135 (Laud MS.), I rede of hem ye here That may you help in your mystere And leve your vntounship a-while.

**Unto·wn**, *v.* (UN-2 6 b.) **1783** WOLCOT (P. Pindar) *Odes R. A.'s* VI. i, Find me in Sodom out..Ten gentlemen, the place shan't be *untown'd.*

**Untra·ce**, *v.* [UN-2 4 b.] *trans.* To free (horses) from the traces.

**1604** MIDDLETON *Father Hubburd's T.* B 1, The fiery Horses of the Sun Were from their golden-flaming Car vntrac'de. **1819** W. S. ROSE *Lett. N. Italy* I. 87 We again put to the horses, necessarily untraced during the preceding operation.

**Untra·ceable**, *a.* (UN-1 7 b.)

**1661** BOYLE *Style of Script.* 20 Who can alone..fathom the depths of Satan, and track him through all his windings and (otherwise untraceable) Labyrinths. *a* **1684** LEIGHTON *Comm.* 1 *Pet.* i. (1693) 199 If the wayes of Gods universall providence be untraceable. **1758** *Monthly Rev.* 507 A proper and salutary quantity of this untraceable fluid. **1782–3** W. F. MARTYN *Geog. Mag.* I. 335 The untraceable way by which Divine Wisdom issues from the infinite ocean of God. **1807** *Med. Jrnl.* XVII. 293 The..hooping-cough..was untraceable to any apparent source. **1883** J. PARKER *Apost. Life* II. 167 Physical circumstances..operate in a subtle and often untraceable manner upon our..spiritual constitution.

*absol.* **1818** MILMAN *Samor* VII. 172, I know thee now, majestic Rebel! thee The untraceable, untameable!

Hence **Untra·ceableness**; **Untra·ceably** *adv.*

**1856** RUSKIN *Mod. Paint.* III. IV. xvii. § 4 This comparative Dimness and Untraceableness of the thoughts which are the sources of our admiration. **1875** WHITNEY *Life Lang.* x. 207 The world of untraceably sexual or of unsexual objects.

**Untra·ced**, *ppl. a.* (UN-1 8.)

**1641** G. SANDYS *Paraphr. Song Sol.* III. i, No Angle my unwearyed Feet Vntraced left. **1643** DENHAM *Cooper's H.* 11 Through untrac'd ways, and aery paths I flye. **1713** C'TESS WINCHELSEA *Misc. Poems* 63 More wakeful Trundle

..Follows the scent untrac'd by nobler Hounds. **1809–14** Wordsw. *Excurs.* vi. 662 There are..good reasons why we should not leave Wholly untraced a more forbidding way. **1826** Milman *Anne Boleyn* 51 That vast body That shall bespread the world, uncheck'd, untrac'd—Like God's own presence. **1900** *Daily News* 20 Sept. 5/3 It is needless for me to say that a number of these [removals] remain untraced.

**Untra·cked,** (*ppl.*) *a.* Also 6–7 untract. [Un-1 8 and 9. The spelling *untract* is due to Tract *sb.*3 8–11 and *v.*2 4–5. Cf. Untracted.]

**1.** Through which no way has been found or made; not furnished with a track or path.

α. **1603** Knolles *Hist. Turks* (1621) 309 The rest..hauing on horsebacke all alone by vncouth and vntract waies, trauailed three dayes without meat. **1684** Otway *Atheist* iii. 32 Drawn by wing'd Horses through the untract Air. **1706** Rowe *Ulysses* iii. 40 So the Eagle..beholds his hardy youthful Offspring Forsake the Nest, to try his tender Pinions, In the wide untract Air.

β. **1612** Bp. Hall *Contempl.* iv. 353 That they might not erre in that sandy and untracked wildernesse. **1659** T. Pecke *Parnassi Puerp.* 172 The untrack'd path to Bliss. **1750** Carte *Hist. Eng.* II. 391 After a long day's march through untracked ways. **1812** A. Plumtre *Lichtenstein's S. Africa* I. 350 The road was untracked and fatiguing. **1830** *New Monthly Mag.* Hist. Reg., Jan. 8/1 Regions yet untracked by any Europeans. **1894** *Outing* XXIII. 347/2 A long, dark object lying..on the untracked snow beneath the trees.

**2.** Not tracked or traced; not followed up.

**1680** Otway *Orphan* iii. 504 At midnight thus the us'rer steals untract [1735 untrack'd] To make a visit to his hoarded gold. **1872** Ruskin *Fors Clav.* xiv. 12 Just persons..untracked by the hounds of war. **1890** 'R. Boldrewood' *Miner's Right* (1899) 146/2 A reflection of the deed still untracked and unavenged.

**Untractabi·lity.** (Un-1 12. Cf. next.) **1791** Burke *Th. French Aff.* Wks. VII. 58 His untractability to these leaders ..alone prevented that part of the arrangement.

**Untra·ctable,** *a.* Now *rare.* [Un-1 7 b, 5 b.]

**1.** = Intractable *a.* 1. (Common *c* 1550–1800.)

**1538** Elyot, *Insanus*, madde, peuyshe,..vntractable. **1548** Udall, etc. *Erasm. Par. Matt.* xviii. 75 Yf he be so vntractable that he wyll not be moued neyther wyth shame, nor wyth feare of iudgemente. **1586** T. B. *La Primaud. Fr. Acad.* i. 320 His horses..are become resty, furious, and untractable. *a* **1619** Fotherby *Atheom.* i. xii. § 4 (1622) 130 Pharaoh..was as stiffe, and as vntractable, as a rocke. **1670** Cotton *Espernon* ii. viii. 409 Birds..of those kinds which with us are the most wild, and untractable. **1714** R. Fiddes *Pract. Disc.* ii. 300 Persons of a base and untractable temper. **1777** Robertson *Hist. Amer.* v. II. 78 The untractable arrogance of Narvaez. **1818** [see Untameable *a.*]. **1824** Miss L. M. Hawkins *Annaline* III. 32 His followers..[were] more furious and untractable from the dreadful excesses they had committed.

**2.** = Intractable *a.* 2.

**1601** Holland *Pliny* II. 118 Other hearbs, hideous to the eye, and untractable in hand. *c* **1630** Risdon *Surv. Devon* (1810) 5 Hills are untractable to tillage. **1667** Milton *P. L.* x. 476 But I Toild out my uncouth passage, forc't to ride Th' untractable Abysse. **1743** W. Emerson *Fluxions* 85 If you have an untractable Fluxion that will answer to none of the Forms. **1823** Scott *Quentin D.* xxiv, He..wrung bitterly the hands, which his mail-gloves rendered untractable. **1837** Whewell *Hist. Ind. Sci.* II. 177 There was room, among these hitherto untractable irregularities, for the additional results of the theory.

Hence **Untra·ctableness.**

**1599** Sandys *Europæ Spec.* (1605) T 3, The vntractablenesse of Papacy to it. *a* **1600** Hooker *Serm. on Pride* i. § 9 Disobedience of children, stubbornes of servants, vntractablenesse in them, who..should..bee also subiect. **1690** Locke *Hum. Und.* iv. xx. § 5 In the Dulness or Untractableness of those Faculties for want of Use. **1752** H. Walpole *Lett.* (1846) II. 432 Will they ever expect a peaceable prelate, if untractableness is thus punished? **1817** Jas. Mill *Brit. India* II. iv. ii. 70 The untractableness of his own disposition.

**Untracta·rian,** *a.* (Un-1 7.) **1846** Caroline Fox *Jrnls.* (1882) II. 64 His untractarian and unsectarian convictions, and his broad charity.

† **Untra·cted,** *ppl. a. Obs. rare.* [Un-1 8.] = Untracked *ppl. a.* 1.

**1610** Healey *St. Aug. Citie of God* xviii. i. 654 My way lying through deserts, and vntracted woods. **1649** Ogilby tr. *Virgil, Georgics* iii. 42 Meane while let us seek Groves.. and search untracted woods. **1680** *Tides* (MS. Bodl. Add. A. 202) 14 By what tædious, crooked, and untracted Journeys through that world of variety itt passes.

†**Untra·ctible,** *a. Obs.* [Un-1 7.] = Untractable *a.* 1. **1670** G. H. tr. *Hist. Cardinals* iii. i. 226 Who were 18 in number, all obstinate and untractible. †**Untra·ctibleness.** *Obs.* (Un-1 12. Cf. prec.) **1676** Hubbard *Happiness of a People* 23 When that Generation..manifested such untractibleness and impatience.

**Untra·ded,** (*ppl.*) *a.* [Un-1 8 and 9.]

†**1. a.** Unskilled, inexperienced, unfamiliar. *Obs.*

**1542** Udall *Erasm. Apoph.* 172 No manne beeyng untraded in philosophie is an apte..persone to bee a kyng. **1548** — *Erasm. Par. Luke* i. 7 A people not vtterly vntraded or vnentred in his discipline. **1570** Levins *Manip.* 50 Vntraded, *insolens.*

† **b.** Not customary; unhackneyed. *Obs.*

**1606** Shaks. *Tr. & Cr.* iv. v. 178 By Mars his gauntlet thanks, Mocke not, that I affect th' vntraded Oath.

† **2.** Not frequented, *spec.* for trade. *Obs.*

**1600** Hakluyt *Voy.* III. 682 Our English that to steale the first blessing of an vntraded place, will perhaps secretly hasten thither. **1603** H. Crosse *Vertues Commw.* (1878) 44 Two waies are proposed,..the first is combersome, intricate, vntraded, ouergrowne.

**Untra·desmanlike,** *a.* (Un-1 7 c.) **1863** *Sat. Rev.* XV. 175/1 If any manufacturer did more than this, he would certainly be behaving in a very untradesmanlike manner.

**Untra·ding,** *ppl. a.* (Un-1 10.) **1691** Locke *Lower. Interest* (1696) 60 Men..leave Estates to their Children in Land, as..not so liable to Casualties as Money, in untrading or unskilful Hands. **1828–32** Webster s.v., An untrading country or city.

**Untra·fficked,** *ppl. a.* (Un-1 8.) **1596** Nashe *Saffron-Walden* K iv, When I record (as I doo often) strange vntraffiqu't phrases, by him new vented and vnpackt, as of *incendarie* for fire.

**Untra·gic(al,** *adjs.* (Un-1 7.) **1837** Carlyle *Fr. Rev.* i. v. vi, The nodus of a drama, not untragical, crowding towards solution. *Ibid.* ii. v. xii, Emblems not a few..of the tragic and the untragic sort.

**Untrai·nable,** *a.* (Un-1 7 b.) **1864** Eliz. Murray *E. Norman* I. 276 She was as untrained as a young savage, and apparently untrainable.

**Untrai·ned,** *ppl. a.* [Un-1 8.]

Hence, in recent use, *untrainedness.*

**1.** Not trained by instruction or experience.

**1548** Udall *Erasm. Par. Luke* xxiv. 180 b, Yet these shadowes of thynges visible wer geuen for a tyme to the grosse and vntrained people. **1591** Shaks. 1 *Hen. VI,* i. ii. 73, I am by birth a Shepheards Daughter. My wit vntrayn'd in any kind of Art. **1633** G. Herbert *Temple, Content* ii, Gad not abroad at ev'ry quest and call Of an untrained hope or passion. **1642** Milton *Apol. Smect.* 55, I cannot say that I am utterly untrain'd in those rules. **1805** Wordsw. *Prelude* x. 197 Men who, to business of the world untrained, Lived in the shade. **1823** Scott *Quentin D.* xv, The low size, and wild, shaggy, untrained state of the animal. **1834** Newman *Par. Serm.* (1837) I. xxii. 325 Nothing is done effectually through untrained human nature. **1864** [see prec.].

**2.** *spec.* Not trained in military exercises.

**1591** Smith *Instr. Military* (1595) Ep. Ded. 8 That the people of kingdomes..should bee disarmed, vntrayned, and vnexercised, for feare of reuoltes. **1608** tr. *J. de Gheyn's Exercise of Arms* 1 b, To instruct the vntrained souldiers. **1667** Milton *P. L.* xii. 222 For life To noble and ignoble is more sweet Untraind in Armes. **1726** Pope *Odyssey* xix. 212 Untrained to martial toil I lived inglorious in my native isle. **1770** Glover *Leonidas* (ed. 5) vii. 510 The unabating fortitude of Greece Maintains her line, th' untrain'd Barbarians charge In savage fury.

**3.** Not trained in figure.

**1871** *Figure Training* 17 The untrained form of the dairy-maid.

† **Untrai·st,** *a. Sc. Obs.* [Un-1 7.] Unreliable. Also † **Untrai·sted** *ppl. a.*, unexpected, unlooked for; † **Untrai·stful** *a.*, unbelieving; † **Untrai·sty** *a.*, untrustworthy.

**1456** Sir G. Haye *Law Arms* (S.T.S.) 170 Peple..flowand and *untraist in all thair dedis. **1530** Lyndesay *Test. Papyngo* 367 Sen ilke court bene vntraist and transitorie, Cheangyng als oft as woddercok in wynd. **1533** Bellenden *Livy* iii. ix. (S.T.S.) II. 304 Na thing mycht happin less [*sic*] *vntrastit nor less belevit þan þe samyn. *c* **1375** *Sc. Leg. Saints* viii. (*Philip*) 93 *Vntrastefull folk of þat land fore gret invy tuk hym & band. **1567** *Gude & Godlie B.* (S.T.S.) 214 Traist the *vntraistie quha that will.

**Untrai·tored,** *ppl. a.* (Un-1 8.) **1840** Clough *Dipsychus* ii. viii. 23 Yet I could deem it better too to starve And die untraitored.

**Untra·mmelled,** *ppl. a.* (Un-1 8.)

In common use from *c* 1850.

[**1775** Ash.] **1795** R. Anderson *Life Johnson* 201 He.. has adopted all the good sense of Aristotle, untrammelled by his forms. **1867** Lewes *Hist. Philos.* (ed. 3) I. 1 Through the history of thought, how difficult it has been to keep the scientific attitude untrammelled. **1888** Oman *Hist. Greece* xvi. (1901) 161 No previous constitution..had given the.. citizens such untrammelled power to sway the state.

**Untra·mpled,** *ppl. a.* (Un-1 8.)

**1648** Hexham ii, *Ongetreden*, Vntrodden, or Vntrampled. **1817** Moore *Lalla R., Fire-Worshippers* 320 To die upon that Mount of Flame—..Before her last untrampled Shrine! **1861** Gladstone *Iliad* i. 329 They reluctant paced the margin of the free untrampled main. **1900** S. Phillips *Paolo & Fr.* i. 4 Still have we foes untrampled, wavering friends.

**Untra·nquil,** *a.* (Un-1 7.)

**1817** Keats *Sleep & Poetry* 263 Nought more untranquil than the grassy slopes Between two hills. **1850** J. H. Newman *Diffic. Anglic.* 76 Fanatical doctrine and untranquil devotion. **1869** Tyndall *Notes Lect. Light* § 188 A tranquil pellucid portion..and a turbid or untranquil portion.

**Untra·nquillize,** *v.* (Un-1 6 c.) **1874** M. Collins *Transmigr.* II. viii. 153 Why should mere physical ideas trouble and untranquillize the brain? **Untra·nquillized,** *ppl. a.* (Un-1 8 a c.) **1846** Worcester (citing Goode). **1857** De Quincey *Whiggism* Wks. VI. 145 Unwilling to leave us with..the agitations of sympathy in the reader as yet untranquillised. **Untransa·cted,** *ppl. a.* (Un-1 8.) *c* **1825** Hogg *Tales & Sk.* (1837) V. 146 Business that..must remain untransacted. **Untransce·nded,** *ppl. a.* (Un-1 8.) **1846** Mangan *Poems* (1903) 39, I also found..Fasting as Christ hath recommended, And noble councillors untranscended. **1852** Bailey *Festus* (ed. 5) 171 A spirit..Who..sojourns In untranscended light. **Untranscende·ntal,** *a.* (Un-1 7.) **1865** Mrs. Whitney *Gayworthys* xxi, I think Wealthy felt it so, in her untranscendental way. **Untranscri·bable,** *a.* (Un-1 7 b.) **1874** in *Folklore* (1919) XXX. 149 An untranscribable baboon song. **1883** [see Un-1 7 b].

**Untra·nsferable,** *a.* (Un-1 7 b and 5 b.)

**1649** Howell *Pre-em. Parlt.* 6 Though the Soverainty remaine still entire, and untransferable in the person of the Prince. **1794** Coleridge *Lett.* (1895) 71 The Demetrius is dry, and utterly untransferable to modern use. **1858** J. Martineau *Stud. Christianity* 80 The personal character and untransferable nature of Sin. **1881** P. Brooks *Candle of Lord* 326 The habits are rigid, uniform and untransferable.

**Untransfe·rrable,** *a.* (Un-1 7 b.) **1826** C. Anderson *Gen. Dom. Constitution* 378 That department of parental training, which is at once unpurchaseable and untransferable. **Untransfe·rred,** *ppl. a.* (Un-1 8.) **1748** Earl Nugent *To Mankind* xviii, For unreclaim'd, and untransfer'd, Her pow'rs and rights remain.

**Untransfo·rmable,** *a.* (Un-1 7 b, 5 b.)

**1570** Dee *Math. Pref.* 2 The generall Formes..are constant, vnchaungeable, vntransformable. **1851** Sylvester *Coll. Math. Papers* (1904) I. 230 All the distinct systems of ..conjugate forms that have been, and will be given, are mutually untransformable.

**Untransfo·rmed,** *ppl. a.* (Un-1 8.)

[**1775** Ash.] **1890** *Restrospect Med.* CII. 218 It..leaves masses of starchy food untransformed in the stomach. [Freq. from *c* 1900.]

**Untransgre·ssed,** *ppl. a.* (Un-1 8.) **1621** Quarles *Div. Poems, Esther* iii, Let him proclayme (which vntransgressed be) His royall Edict. *a* **1866** J. Grote *Exam. Utilit. Phil.* i. (1870) 23 A general and untransgressed rule. †**Untra·nsible,** *a. Obs.*—1 [ad. L. *intransibilis*: see Un-1 7, 5 b.] That cannot be crossed. **1644** Digby *Nat. Soul* x. § 7. 428 There is..no vntransible gappe, or Chaos to seuer them. **Untra·nsitory,** *a.* (Un-1 7.) **1632** Quarles *Div. Fancies* iii. xlv, That Time untransitory. **1644** — *Sheph. Orac.* v, Whose Kingdome's endlesse and untransitory. **Untranslatabi·lity.** (Un-1 12. Cf. next.) **1860** G. P. Marsh *Lect. Eng. Lang.* xxvii. 611 Of this untranslatability of single words..German offers us many examples.

**Untransla·table,** *a.* (Un-1 7 b, 5 b.)

Very common from the beginning of the 19th c.

**1655** Fuller *Ch. Hist.* v. v. § 36 Some few [words] untranslatable, without losse of life or lustre. **1694** *Gracian's Courtier's Oracle* A 3 b, The French Author..counts him unintelligible, and by consequence untranslatable. **1742** Gray *Lett.* II. 28 Pray put me the following lines into the tongue of our modern Dramatics:..To me they appear untranslatable. **1811** Coleridge *Table-t.* (1835) II. 353 The excellence of verse, he said, was to be untranslatable into any other words. **1880** T. Hodgkin *Italy & Inv.* i. ii. I. 193 The untranslateable grandeur of Claudian's epithet.

Hence **Untransla·tableness; -la·tably** *adv.*

**1817** Coleridge *Biogr. Lit.* II. 160 The infallible test of a blameless style; namely, its untranslatableness in words of the same language without injury to the meaning. **1855** Smedley *Occult Sciences* 250 Concerning dreams—*ut de accentibus somni*—as he untranslatably styles them. **1889** *Athenæum* 16 Nov. 671/1 The ugly proceedings untranslatably known as *brique.*

**Untransla·ted,** *ppl. a.* [Un-1 8.]

**1.** Not turned into another language.

**1530** Palsgr. 34 [Those writers] have left none auctours written in the latyn tonge untranslated. **1540** Morysine *Vives' Introd. Wysd.* A 5, No one boke untranslated..hath halfe soo many holsome documentes as this hathe. **1651** Hobbes *Leviath.* iii. xxxviii. 244 Which ought not to have been left untranslated..in the Latine. **1768** Tucker *Lt. Nat.* II. iii. xxx. 458 The term translated Everlasting, ought to be preserved untranslated, as a kind of technical term. *a* **1778** Pegge *Anonym.* (1809) 472 We have in English now, several untranslated French words. **1852** Lewis *Meth. Obs. & Reason. in Pol.* I. 105 Others may resort to periphrasis, or may use the original word untranslated. **1883** A. Roberts *O. T. Revis.* iv. 83 'Bethel' is rendered..'the house of God', but should have been left untranslated.

**2.** Not transferred to another sphere.

**1746** Young *Nt. Th.* ix. 1753 This world sublime,..Where mortal, untranslated, never stray'd. **1878** B. Harte *Man on Beach* 58 Of course, he will be there to see his untranslated Goddess.

**Untransmigrated,** *ppl. a.* (Un-1 8.) **1821** Scott *Kenilw.* xxii, Thus, Alasco will leave your pewter artillery untransmigrated. **Untransmi·ssible,** *a.* (Un-1 7, 5 b.) **1590** Swinburne *Testaments* 173 Because the testator maie if he will, make that transmissible, which otherwise is vntransmissible. **1882–3** *Schaff's Encycl. Relig. Knowl.* I. 472 The apostolic office was..unique and untransmissible. **Untransmi·tted,** *ppl. a.* (Un-1 8.) [**1775** Ash.] **1802–12** Bentham *Ration. Judic. Evid.* (1827) III. 447 The nature of original untransmitted evidence. **1820** Shelley *Prometh. Unb.* iii. iii. 171 Those Who bear the untransmitted torch of hope Into the grave. **Untransmu·table,** *a.* (Un-1 7 b, 5 b.) **1611** Florio, *Intrasmutabile*, vntransmutable. **1682** H. More *Annot. Glanvill's Lux O.* 52 Spirits specifically different, are untransmutable one into another. *a* **1776** Hume *Ess.* (1777) II. 351 Each character..appears to me, in practice, pretty durable and untransmutable. **Untransmu·ted,** *ppl. a.* (Un-1 8.) **1666** Boyle *Orig. Formes & Qual.* 409 The untransmuted Rain water. **1805** Wordsw. *Prelude* vi. 464 The untransmuted shapes of many worlds. †**Untransparable,** *a. Obs.*—1 [Un-1 7 b.] = next. *a* **1618** Raleigh *Rem.* (1644) 210 The unjust Magistrate that fancieth to himselfe a solid and untransparable body of Gold, every ordinary wit can vitrifie, and make transparent.

**Untranspa·rent,** *a.* [Un-1 7 and 5 b.] Not transparent; opaque.

**1591** Sylvester *Du Bartas* i. i. 290 Suppose an Earth.. without Hill or Plaine, A Heav'n un-hanged, un-turning, un-transparent. **1675** Evelyn *Terra* (1676) 33 An impalpable whitish Sand, untransparent. **1754** *Phil. Trans.* XLVIII. 659 The matter appeared of a dark blackish colour, untransparent. **1862** Tyndall *Mountaineer.* v. 38 The water [resolves itself] to transparent vapour, and the vapour to untransparent cloud. **1888** O. Crawfurd *Sylvia Arden* 361 So dark and untransparent was the flood water.

**Untranspa·ssable,** *a.* (Un-1 7 b.) **1594** Daniel *Cleopatra* N 8, Are these the bounds y' haue giuen Th' vntranspassable barres, That limit pride so short..? **Untranspla·nted,** *ppl. a.* (Un-1 8.) [**1775** Ash.] **1832** *Planting* 3 (L.U.K.), Equal, if not superior to untransplanted seedlings. **Untranspo·rtable,** *a.* (Un-1 7 b.) **1611** Florio, *Intransporteuole*, vntransportable. **1838** Emerson *Addr., Lit. Ethics*, Truth is..so untransportable and unbarrelable a commodity.

**Untranspo·rted,** *ppl. a.* [Un-1 8.]

**1.** Not conveyed or carried.

**1549** *Acc. Ld. High Treas. Scot.* IX. 357 Chargeing him to keip Schir Robert Bowis, Inglisman, untransporttit hame in his awin cuntre.

**2.** Not carried away by feeling.

**1641** Earl Monm. tr. *Biondi's Civil Wars* ii. 72 Hee received all these injuries not onely untransported, but with a setled judgement. **1701** Collier *M. Aurel.* p. xxiii, He ..was Religious without Affectation, untransported and free from Eagerness upon all occasion. **1768–74** Tucker *Lt. Nat.* (1834) II. 586 To preserve an even steady temper,.. untransported by allurements.

**Untranspo·sed,** *ppl. a.* (Un-[1] 8.) **1751** Johnson *Rambler* No. 86 ¶ 10 To preserve the series of sounds untransposed in a long composition, is..very difficult. **1810** Bentham *Offic. Apt. Maximized, Def. Econ.* (1830) 21 The thread of his argument is delivered unbroken, and the parts of it untransposed.

**Untransubsta·ntiated,** *ppl. a.* (Un-[1] 8.)
**1672** H. More *Brief Reply* 325 The said Individual matter untransubstantiated and remaining Bread still. **1830** G. S. Faber *Diffic. Romanism* (ed. 2) 143 The unconsecrated, and therefore (in latin phrase) the untransubstantiated, bread and wine. **1854** Milman *Lat. Chr.* iii. vii. I. 467 The Redeemer's spiritual presence, yet undefined and untransubstantiated.

†**Untransu·med,** *ppl. a. Obs.*[-1] (Un-[1] 8. Cf. Transume *v.* 1.) **1526** *Sc. Acts, Jas. V* (1814) II. 313 Þe sall bring þe writingis laitlie maid be our souerane lorde..vntransumyt auctentily. **Untra·pped,** *ppl. a.* (Un-[1] 8.) **1648** Hexham ii, *Onbeklickt*,..Vnsurprised, or Vntrapt. *Ibid.*, *Onbetrapt*, Vntrapped, or Vnsnared. [1775 Ash.]

**Untra·pped,** *a.* [Un-[1] 9.] Of a sink or drain: Not fitted with a trap.
**1860** Flor. Nightingale *Nursing* 15 An untrapped sink may..spread fever..among the inmates of a palace. **1877** Teale *Dangers to Health* 7 A rain water tank, which had an untrapped overflow into the drain. **1884** *19th Cent.* May 847 Untrapped drains.

**Untra·vellable,** *a.* (Un-[1] 7 b.) **1652** Heylyn *Cosmogr.* iii. 113 Full of untravellable Desarts. **1846** *Chr. Watchman* Sept., Fearful precipices and rocky passes..abound in this almost untravellable district.

**Untra·velled,** *ppl. a.* [Un-[1] 8.]
**1.** That has not travelled.
**1585** T. Washington tr. *Nicholay's Voy.* Ep. Ded., They are among men vntrauelled as Hesperus among the smaller starres. **1611** Beaum. & Fl. *Philaster* i. i, If they should, I say, they were never abroad:..it writes them directly untravel'd. **1667** Sprat *Hist. R. Soc.* 73 Untravell'd Gentlemen,..and Generals, that had scarce ever before seen a Battel. **1712** Addison *Spect.* No. 407 ¶ 1 That an untravelled Englishman cannot relish all the Beauties of Italian Pictures. **1812** Scott *Let.* in *Lockhart* (1837) III. 19 Sophia and Walter hold their heads very high among their untravelled companions. *a* **1862** Buckle *Misc. Wks.* (1872) I. 524 We rarely find an untravelled man who is not full of prejudice.
*transf.* and *fig.* **1606** *Sir G. Goosecappe* i. ii. B i, *Fo.* Why this is the vntrauaild rudnes of our grose Englesh ladies now. **1764** Goldsm. *Traveller* 8 Where'er I roam,..My heart untravell'd fondly turns to thee. **1805** *Ann. Rev.* III. 199 The author is apparently untravelled in continental literature. **1861** Geo. Eliot *Silas M.* i, To their untravelled thought a state of wandering was a conception as dim as the winter life of the swallows.
**2.** Not travelled over or through.
**1661** Feltham *Resolves* ii. xlix. 281 He..that is illiterate, and unactively lives hamletted in some untravail'd village. *a* **1720** J. Hughes *Ode to Creator* 35 Beyond the untravell'd limits of the sky. **1762** Falconer *Shipwr.* 335 Pilots, tutor'd to divine Th' untravel'd course by geometric line. **1809–14** Wordsw. *Excurs.* vi. 455 To the deep shade of those untravelled Wilds. **1864** R. S. Hawker *Quest Sangraal* 41 Neither landmarks, nor fences, bounded..the bold, free, and untravelled Cornish domain.
*fig.* **1646** Sir T. Browne *Pseud. Ep.* To Rdr. A 5, Wee.. are oft-times faine to wander in America and untravelled parts of truth. **1672** Lloyd *F. S. on Bp. Wilkins* 27 He shewed it in whatsoever Argument he undertook; sometimes beating out new untravel'd ways, sometimes repairing those that had been beaten already.

**Untra·versable,** *a.* (Un-[1] 7 b, 5 b.)
**1856** Ruskin *Mod. Paint.* III. 200 The endless undulation of the untraversable hills. **1890** *Spectator* 3 May, The Southern desert..is practically untraversable and uninhabitable.

**Untra·versed,** *ppl. a.* (Un-[1] 8.)
[1775 Ash.] **1807** J. Barlow *Columb.* i. 57, I..Tamed all the dangers of untraversed waves. *Ibid.* ix. 37 To thee is given To..inquire of heaven, To mark untraversed ages. **1843** Ruskin *Mod. Paint.* I. ii. iv. iv. § 6 Few, if any, of the rocks of nature are untraversed by delicate and slender fissures. **1876** A. S. Murray *Mythol.* iii. 37 A personification of the untraversed regions of the sea.

**Untrea·d,** *v.* [Un-[2] 3.] *trans.* To retrace.
**1592** Shaks. *Ven. & Ad.* 908 She treads the path that she untreads again. **1596** — *Merch. V.* ii. vi. 10. **1615** G. Sandys *Trav.* 169 Vntreading a good part of the fore-said alley, we entered the Ile. *a* **1659** Osborne *Ess.* iii. 36 Who onely knew the Way to untread the Maze, in which Man had lost Himself. **1710** Norris *Chr. Prud.* viii. 398 He has made abundance of false steps..which..he would willingly untread. **1837** De Quincey *Revolt of Tartars* Wks. 1854 IV. 153 The question was formally debated..whether, even at this point, they should untread their steps.

**Untrea·dable,** *a.* (Un-[1] 7 b.) **1857** Livingstone *Trav.* xxiii. 461 Impassable forests and untreadable bogs.

**Untrea·sure,** *v.* [Un-[1] 4, 3.] *trans.* To rob, or empty, of a treasure. Also const. *of.*
**1600** Shaks. *A. Y. L.* ii. ii. 7 In the morning early, They found the bed vntreasur'd of their Mistris. **1819** Moore *Mem.* (1853) III. 64 Niches untreasured of their busts, and rooms depopulated of their statues. *a* **1859** J. Mitford (Webster), The quaintness with which he untreasured, as by rote, the stores of his memory.

**Untrea·table,** *a.* [Un-[1] 7 b, 5 b.]
†**1.** Intractable; incapable of being treated or dealt with; unmanageable. *Obs.*
*c* **1374** Chaucer *Boeth.* ii. pr. viii. (1868) 61 For-as-mochel as thow shalt nat wenen..þat I bere vntretable batayle ayenis fortune. **1430–40** Lydg. *Bochas* i. xv. 5638 For Narcisus was nat merciable Toward Echcho,..But in his port was founden ontretable. *c* **1450** Burgh *Secrees* 2196 Yif he be wood and vntretable, He may..thy Reem destroye. **1509** Barclay *Shyp of Folys* 68 If that deth vntretable Arrest the with his mace. **1571** Golding *Calvin on Ps.* ii. 9 The greater part avanceth itselfe against him with untreatable feercenesse. **1604–5** in *Trans. Roy. Hist. Soc.* Ser. iv. IV. 137 Parishioners doe fynde mutch faulte with his untreatable reading in the tyme of public prayer. **1675** G. R. tr. *Le Grand's Man without Passion* 137 Anger that wild and untreatable Passion. *a* **1745** Swift *Serm.* Wks. 1765 XVI. 31 [It] caused many of them..to be..supercilious and untreatable.
**2.** Not admitting of medical treatment.
**1865** *Q. Rev.* July 33 Untreatable by any known remedy, this malady would seem now to have nearly worn itself out.
Hence **Untrea·tableness.**
**1693** C. Mather *Wonders Invisible World* Def. A 2, The unaccountable Frowardness, Asperity, Untreatableness, and Inconsistency of many persons.

**Untrea·ted,** *ppl. a.* (Un-[1] 8 and 8 c.)
*c* **1456** Pecock *Bk. of Faith* (1909) 120 The articlis which ben spokun in the Represser, and left there untretid. **1665** Boyle *Occas. Refl.* a 6 b, Themes..untreated of by others. **1666** — *Orig. Forms & Qual.* B 2 b, He has left most of the other Qualities Untreated of. **1883** *Pall Mall G.* 10 Nov. 4/1 The untreated sewage of London. **1890** *Retrospect Med.* CII. 292 The risk of leaving untreated a clot [etc.].

†**Untree·,** *v.* (Un-[2] 4.) **1611** Florio, *Disarborare*, to vntree, to cut downe trees. **1624** *Trag. Nero* iii. (1633) D 4, The shores And hollow caves of forrests now untreed. **Untre·llised,** *ppl. a.* (Un-[1] 8.) **1629** Gaule *Holy Madn.* 340 He keepes an open House: but..it is the Roofe vnthatcht, or Windowes vntrellessed; for the Doore is neuer vnbolted.

**Untre·mbling,** *ppl. a.* (Un-[1] 10.)
**1570** Levins *Manip.* 137 Vntrembling, *intrepidus.* **1708** J. Philips *Cyder* i. 109 Nor untrembling can'st thou see, How from a scraggy rock..hardy men..Cut samphire. **1742** Blair *Grave* 386 Then might the Debauchee Untrembling mouth the Heav'ns. **1846** Keble *Lyra Innoc.* 179 Not to the quick untrembling gaze..Loves He to say, Go higher. **1881** A. Austin in *Macm. Mag.* XLIII. 403 The roll of that untrembling diapason that makes all things tremble.
Hence **Untre·mblingly** *adv.*
*a* **1832** Bentham *Deontol.* (1832) II. 12 Stand up untremblingly, then, and avow that [etc.].

**Untreme·ndous,** *a.* (Un-[1] 7.) **1820** Keats *Hyperion* ii. 155 Why ye, Divinities,..Should cower beneath what, in comparison, Is untremendous might.

**Untre·mulous,** *a.* (Un-[1] 7.)
**1826** Mrs. Hemans *Forest Sanctuary* i. lxx, I heard a sweet ..strain Piercing the flames, untremulous and clear. **1832** Miss Mitford *Village* V. 348 Thy cheek unflush'd; Thy lip untremulous. **1853** C. Bronte *Villette* xxi, Here was the seal..deftly dropped by untremulous fingers.

**Untre·nched,** *ppl. a.* [Un-[1] 8 and 8 c.] **a.** Not entrenched. **b.** Not trenched by digging. **c.** Not encroached *upon.*
[1775 Ash.] **1807** J. Barlow *Columb.* v. 759 Untrench'd before the town, they dare oppose Their fielded cohorts to the forted foes. **1849** Johnston *Exp. Agric.* 101 Whether oats are after lea trenched or untrenched, or after turnips. **1887** Browning *Parleyings, G. de Lairesse* xi, Yonder space extends Untrenched upon by any vagrant tree.

†**Untre·nd,** *v. Obs.*[-1] [Un-[2] 3.] *trans.* To unroll. *a* **1272** *Luue Ron* 195 in *O. E. Misc.* 99 Þis rym..ich þe sende open and wiþ-vte sel; Bidde ic þat þu hit vntrende. **Untre·nded, †-trend,** *ppl. a.* (Un-[1] 8: see Trend *v.* 2 b.) *c* **1395** *Plowman's Tale* ii. 594 He culleth the sheep as doth the cook; Of hem they taken the woll untrend. **1805** Luccock *Nat. Wool* 301 That the quality of the untrended wool is not so good as the other. **Untre·spassed,** *ppl. a.* (Un-[1] 8.) **1854** S. Dobell *Balder* iii. 14 The untrespassed rest Of immemorial pastures. **Untre·spassing,** *ppl. a.* (Un-[1] 10.) **1642** Milton *Apol. Smect.* 22 Others were sent.. as it were at large, in the midst of an untrespassing honesty. **Untre·ss,** *v.* (Un-[2] 4 b.) **1587** A. Day *Daphnis & Chloe* (1890) 18 Chloe..vntressed quickly her golden wirie lockes.

**Untre·ssed,** *ppl. a.* [Un-[1] 8.] Not arranged in tresses; loose, dishevelled.
*c* **1381** Chaucer *Parl. Foules* 268 Her gylt heares with a gold threde Ybounde were, vntressyd [*Camb. Univ. MS.* vntrussede] as she lay. *c* **1386** — *Knt.'s T.* 1431 Hir brighte heer was kempd vntressed [*MSS. Camb. & Lansd.* vntrussed] al. **1412–20** Lydg. *Chron. Troy* iii. 4124 Vntressid hir her abrod gan sprede, Like to gold wyr, for-rent & al to-torn. *c* **1440** *Pallad. on Husb.* i. 861 A..womman, vnshood, Vntressed, al aboute to goon is good. **1582** Stanyhurst *Aeneis* i. (Arb.) 33 Troy dames..with locks vntressed al hanging. **1621** G. Sandys *Ovid's Met.* vii. (1626) 131 Her haire Vntrest, her garments loose. *a* **1849** H. Coleridge *Poems* (1851) II. 387 She..with her untress'd hair Still wiped the feet.

†**Untre·st.** [Un-[1] 12.] Mistrust. *c* **1400** *Lanfranc's Cirurg.* 17 Greet drede, ouþir vttereste [*read* vntreste; *v.r.* vntryst] of heelþe of his wounde. *c* **1450** *Mirour Saluacioun* (Roxb.) 132 Be vntrest and incredulitee he dos some grete disese. **Untri·able,** *a.* (Un-[1] 7 b.) **1612** S. Sturtevant *Metallica* 78 An vntryable inuention is a new proiect or discouery, whose worth and goodnesse requireth no tryals.

† **Untri·al,** *a. Obs.* [Of obscure origin.] *Gentleman untrial*: (see quot. 1486).
**1486** *Bk. St. Albans, Heraldry* B ii b, Ther be ij dyuerse Gentylmen made of gromys that be nott gentilmen of cotearmure nother of blode. Oon is calde in armys a gentylman vntriall, that is to say made vp emong religyous men as priorys, Abbottis, or Byschoppis. **1562** Legh *Armorie* 27 b, The eight is called a gentleman vntrial, and such is he, as being brought vp in an Abbey, or with a bishop [etc.]. **1600** W. Watson *Decacordon* (1602) 257 This vntriall gentleman was one of that nobleman father Parsons spies. *Ibid.* 270 Our Frankelings, Gentlemen vntriall, or substantiall Yeomen.

**Untri·butary,** *a.* (Un-[1] 7.) [1775 Ash.] **1796** Coleridge *Watchman* 27 April, The probable Loss and Gain of unprotected and untributary Independence. †**Untri·ck,** *a. Obs.*[-0] (Un-[1] 7. Cf. Trick *a.* 2.) **1570** Levins *Manip.* 121 Vntricke, *inconcinnus.*

**Untrie·d,** *ppl. a.* [Un-[1] 8.]
**1.** Not tried, proved, or tested.
**1526** *Pilgr. Perf.* (W. de W. 1531) 132 That no worde passe out vntryed & nothynge entre vnexamyned. *a* **1586** Sidney *Arcadia* i. iii, Her skin like burnisht gold, her hands like silver ure untryde. **1591** Spenser *F. Q.* i. iii. 34 Loth was that other..To taste th' vntryed dint of deadly steele. **1647** Cowley *Mistr., Encrease* iii, So the new-made, and untride Spheres above, Took their first turn from th' hand of Jove. **1697** Dryden *Virg. Georg.* iv. 781 Four fair Heifars yet in Yoke untry'd. **1739** Labelye *Piers Westm. Bridge* 28 Not to leave one single square Foot in the whole Surface of the Foundation untried. **1783** Crabbe *Village* ii. 146 When smit with Glory's charms, The untried youth first quits a father's arms. **1833** Ht. Martineau *Cinnamon & Pearls* v. 95 Can anything equal the presumption of human decisions on untried matters! **1871** Dixon *Tower* III. i. 1 A man of untried power.
*absol.* **1839** Carlyle *Chartism* ix, The New, Untried ascertains how it will fit itself into the arrangements of the Old. **1887** Meredith *Ballads & P.* 112 She marched toward the gloomy gate Of earth's Untried.
**2.** Not tried by a judge.
*a* **1618** Sylvester *Job* iv. 12 Against Job began his wrath to flame,..And..his Foe-friends, for so strict Condemning Job, untry'd and unconvict. **1784** Cowper *Task* v. 398 Condemn'd untried, Cruelly spar'd, and hopeless of escape! **1824** S. Smith *Wks.* (1859) II. 32 Cruel Treatment of Untried Prisoners. **1842** Dickens *Amer. Notes* v, The best Jail for untried offenders in the world.

**Untri·fling,** *a.* (Un-[1] 10.) *a* **1743** Savage *Epitaph Young Lady* 7 Modest knowledge, fair untrifling youth. **Untri·g,** *a. Sc.* [Un-[1] 7.] Not neat or trim. **1821** Galt *Ann. Parish* xvii. 160 His wife kept an untrig house. **1850** McGilvray *Poems* 197 She is so big, and so untrig.

**Untri·lled,** *ppl. a.* (Un-[1] 8.)
**1869** Ellis *E. E. Pron.* ii. 603/1 The peculiar English untrilled *r*. **1874** Sweet in *Trans. Philol. Soc.* 471 Untrilled consonants.

**Untri·lling,** *vbl. sb.* (Un-[2] 3, 8.) **1874** Sweet in *Trans. Philol. Soc.* 471 Untrilling [is] a common phenomenon in.. English, in which the trilled *r* is quite lost. **Untri·m,** *a.* (Un-[1] 7.) **1570** Levins *Manip.* 131 Vntrym, *inconcinnus.* **1898** N. Munro *J. Splendid* xv, His hair was untrim.

**Untri·m,** *v.* [Un-[2] 3.]
**1.** *trans.* To deprive of trimness or elegance; to strip of ornament.
*c* **1600** Shaks. *Sonn.* xviii, Euery faire from faire some-time declines, By chance, or natures changing course vntrim'd. **1611** J. Davies (Heref.) *Sco. Folly* cxcvii, Their hairlesse scalpes..Barely affirme they were vntrimm'd by trulls. **1832** Hood *Ode to J. Hume* 40 Don't trim though, but untrim their [*sc.* soldiers'] jackets.
**2.** To unbalance.
**1884** Harrop *Bolingbroke* i. 21 The success of the French King's intrigues at Madrid had threatened..to untrim the balance of power.

**Untri·mmable,** *a.* (Un-[1] 7 b.) **1863** Hawthorne *Our Old Home* (1879) 361 Shovelling the untrimmed and untrimmable ideas out of his mind.

**Untri·mmed,** *ppl. a.* [Un-[1] 8.]
**1.** Not put in good order or condition; not carefully or neatly arranged or attired.
In quot. 1595 the word has been variously explained, and may be formed on Untrim *v.*
**1532** Hervet *Xenophon's Househ.* 18 b, The horse beareth hym..that wyll se the grounde be nat let alone vntylled and vntrymmed. **1540** Hyrde tr. *Vives' Instr. Chr. Wom.* (1541) I ii, A mayde nat pyked, and fayre, and wanton..: but sad, pale, and vntrimmed. **1592** R. W[ilmot] *Tancred & Gism.* v. ii, So let thy tresses..Vntrimmed hang about thy bared necke. **1595** Shaks. *John* iii. i. 209 The deuill tempts thee heere, In likenesse of a new vntrimmed Bride. **1648** J. Quarles *Fons Lachrym.* 71 Man's like a house..; If we survay The inward rooms, there we may find enough Of untrim'd natures sluttish houshold-stuff. **1813** Scott *Rokeby* i. xxxii, Yon untrimm'd lamp, whose yellow gleam Is mingling with the cold moonbeam. **1817** Byron *Beppo* xlvi. *note*, Without the sex, our sonnets Would seem unfinish'd, like their untrimm'd bonnets.
**2.** Not made trim by cutting, pruning, or otherwise reducing to shape.
**1625** K. Long tr. *Barclay's Argenis* v. xi. 367 The pleasing young Groves..with their deepe silence and untrimmed simplicity. **1633** Ford *Love's Sacrifice* v. i, A crooked leg, a scambling foot,..or such an untrimm'd beard As yours. **1687** *Lond. Gaz.* No. 2307/4 The said Nag is..rough Coated and untrim'd. **1808** Scott *Marm.* iii. Introd., Prune the vine, But..leave untrimm'd the eglantine. **1848** Akerman *Introd. Study Coins* iv. 56 A grim bearded untrimmed head. **1892** Oldfield *Man. Typog.* v, A demy 8vo. page measures, untrimmed, about $8\frac{3}{8}'' \times 5\frac{1}{2}''$.
*fig.* **1849** M. Arnold *New Sirens* 138 Germs, your untrimm'd passion overgrew. **1863** [see Untrimmable *a.*].
**3.** Not properly balanced.
*a* **1732** Gay *Fables* (1738) II. v. 44 The boat untrimm'd admits the tide.
Hence **Untri·mmedness.**
**1883** H. James *Portr. Places* viii. 167 [The old castle's] quiet rustiness and untrimmedness only help it to be familiar.

**Untri·pe,** *v.* (Un-[2] 4.) **1611** Cotgr., *Estripé*, vntriped, vnbowelled, with his..bowels about his heeles. **1653** Urquhart *Rabelais* i. xliii. 190 The broile and defeat, wherein Tripet was untriped [F. *estripé*]. **1808** E. S. Barrett *Miss-led General* 69 We must either embowel them, or they will untripe us.

† **Untrist,** *sb. Obs.* [Un-[1] 12 + Trist *sb.*[1]] Distrust. Also †**Untri·st** *a.* [Un-[1] 7 + Trist *a.*[1]], unfaithful; unbelieving. †**Untri·sted** *ppl. a.* [Un-[1] 8 + Trist *v.*], unhoped for. †**Untri·sty** *a.* [Un-[1] 7], faithless; unreliable.
**1390** Gower *Conf.* II. 151 Jelousie of his *untrist Makth that full many an harm arist. *c* **1400** *Comm. Luke* i. 19 (MS. Bodl. 143), In beyng doumb he suffriþ þe peyne of vntrist disseruyd. *c* **1374** Chaucer *Troylus* iii. 839 Whi hastow mad Troylus to me *vntriste? *c* **1460** *Towneley Myst.* xxvii. 210 Me thynk you all vntrist to trow,..All that the prophetys told to you before, it is no trane. **1387** Trevisa *Higden* (Rolls) VII. 115 A Goddes man seide..þat þere was to comen and *untristed [L. *insperatum*] a lordschipe fro Fraunce. *Ibid.* III. 265 Þe firste tweie artes beeþ untrusty [*Cotton MS.* *vntrysti.] *c* **1400** *Destr. Troy* 11973 Þan happit hom to mete The traytor with tene, vntristy Eneas. *c* **1460** *Promp. Parv.* (Winch. MS.), On-trysty, *idem quod* on thende.

**Untri·te**, *a.* (Un-[1] 7.) **1781** T. Twining in *Recreat. & Stud.* (1882) 110 There is very little pleasing or untrite in his melody or harmony. **Untri·umphable**, *a.* (Un-[1] 7 b.) **1663** Butler *Hud.* i. ii. 502 This blood..Which now y' are bent to throw away In vain, untriumphable fray. **1768** *Woman of Honor* I. 161. **Untriu·mphant**, *a.* (Un-[1] 7.) **1659** Gauden *Serm.*, etc. (1660) 72 A civil intestine War, where victory itself is sad and untriumphant. **1858** Carlyle *Fredk. Gt.* ix. xi. II. 536 The French Ambassador..did much intriguing,..first in a signally triumphant way, and then in a signally untriumphant. **Untri·umphed**, *ppl. a.* (Un-[1] 8.) **1627** May *Lucan* viii. O 6, I..Suffer'd you only, when I conquer'd all, To goe vntriumph'd.

**Untro·d**, *ppl. a.* [Un-[1] 8 b, 8 c. Cf. older Da. *utraadd*, Sw. *otrådd*.] = next.

**1593** Marlowe *Lucan* i. 567 Clashing of armes was heard in vntrod woods. **1601** Shaks. *Jul. C.* iii. i. 136 Mark Antony ..will follow..Thorough the hazards of this vntrod State, With all true Faith. **1633** Ford *Broken H.* iii. v, That remedy Must be a winding-sheet,..And some vntrod-on corner in the earth. **1667** Milton *P. L.* iii. 497 The Paradise of Fools,..now unpeopl'd, and untrod. **1737** Glover *Leonidas* ii. 151 The secret paths, Which..through the forests wind, Untrod by human feet. **1771** *Hunter's Georgian Ess.* II. 10 Sheep..are never found in countries untrod by man. **1864** J. Brown *Minchmoor* 6 We..looked down its grassy and untrod avenue to the pallid, forlorn mansion. **1879** Browning *Halbert & Hob* 49 Untrod Leave this last step we reach.

**Untro·dden**, *ppl. a.* [Un-[1] 8 b.] Not trodden or stepped on; untraversed. Also in fig. context.

*a* **1300** *E. E. Psalter* xvii. 31 Mi God un-filed [L. *inpolluta*; *E.*, *H.* un-troden] es his wai. **1535** Coverdale *Ps.* cvi[i]. 4 They wente astraye..in an vntroden waye. **1593** *Sidney's Arcadia* iv. (1922) II. 119 Vagabonding in those untroden places. **1606** Marston *Parasitaster* iv. G 4, Vntrodden snow is not so spotless. **1656** Cowley *Davideis* i. 28 Guid my bold steps..In these untrodden paths to Sacred Fame. **1735** Berkeley *Querist* § 418 So many roads untrodden, fields untilled, houses desolate. **1760–2** Goldsm. *Cit. W.* lxxxvii, Those untrodden forests..which formerly covered the face of the country. **1826** Mrs. Hemans *Forest Sanctuary* i. xiii, The red grapes untrodden strew'd the ground. **1849** Grote *Greece* ii. xxxviii. V. 57 A wild, woody, and untrodden country.

Hence **Untro·ddenness.**

**1644** Digby *Nat. Bodies* xxiii. § 1. 203 The ruggednesse, and vntrodenesse of the pathes we haue walked in. **1681** R. Fleming *Fulfilling Script.* ii. Pref. (1726) 249 The untroddenness of this path, the weight..of the truths, with some study..to believe what I wrote.

**Untro·lled**, *ppl. a.* (Un-[1] 8 + Troll *v.* 2.) **1693** S. Harvey *Juvenal* ix. 12 Hard Fate! untroll'd is now the Charming Dye. **Untro·phied**, *a.* (Un-[1] 9.) **1756** W. Whitehead *Elegy* iv. 61 O why, Britannia, why untrophied pass The patriot deeds thy godlike Sons display? *a* **1861** T. Winthrop *Life in Open Air* x. (1863) 81, I entered skulkingly, as a gameless hunter may, and hid my untrophied head beneath a mound of ancient hay.

†**Untro·th.** *Obs.* [Un-[1] 12. Cf. Troth *sb.*, Untruth, and Wantroth.]

**1.** Unfaithfulness, treachery; = Untruth 1. (Common *c* 1385–*c* 1450.)

*c* **1374** Chaucer *Troylus* v. 1448 He þought ay wel he hadde his lady lorn, And þat Ioues..Hym shewed hadde in sleep þe signyfyaunce Of hire vntroþe. *c* **1384** — *H. Fame* i. 384 But weleaway the harme the routhe That hath betyd for suche vntrouthe. *c* **1425** *Eng. Conq. Irel.* 8 Bot Robert ..for no t[h]ynge wold do thynge wher-of he myght be afterward i-wyted of wntrowth. **1483** Caxton *G. de la Tour* E viii b, He slewe his broder Amon that suche desloyalte and untrouth had done to his Suster. **1523** Ld. Berners *Froiss.* I. ccxxxi. 313 The kyng..pituously complayned hym of yᵉ untrouthe of his men, shewyng howe they had all forsaken him. *a* **1548** Hall *Chron., Hen. VI*, 154 b, The capitaines perceyuing their vntrought & trayterous demeanour, retrayted themselves into the Castell or Palaice, where.. they sore molested and vexed the vntrew citizens. **1606** G. W[oodcocke] *Hist. Ivstine* xi. 45 Which deed..might rather be imputed to the oresight of light credit, then to any vntroth or infidelity.

**b.** Wickedness, mischief. *rare.*

**1470–85** Malory *Arthur* xvii. viii. 702 Thenne dyd they grete vntrouthe; they slewe clerkes and preestes. **1484** Caxton *Fables of Æsop* i. iv, The euylle hongry peple..by theyr grete vntrouthe and malyce robben..the poure folke.

**2.** Unbelief; = Untruth 2.

*c* **1380** Wyclif *Sel. Wks.* II. 204 Þe fadir..seide, Sire, Y bileve; helpe myn untrouþe. *a* **1395** Hylton *Scala Perf.* ii. vi. (Bodl. MS.), Þei schulden streiȝt flee to heuene,..hadde þei do neuer so myche synne bifore in time of her vntrouþe. *c* **1400** *Apol. Loll.* 28 Crist..miȝt not do ani vertu þer, for þe vntrouþ.

**3.** Falsehood; = Untruth 3.

*c* **1386** Chaucer *Man of Law's T.* 687 This false knyght was slayn for his vntrouthe. *c* **1449** Pecock *Repr.* ii. xv. 234 Thei worschipiden God bi ydolatrie, and therfore by vntrouthe. *a* **1592** Greene *Alphonsus* ii. ii, If you find my words to be vntroth, Then let me die to recompence the wrong.

**b.** = Untruth 3 b.

**1581** T. Howell *Deuises* I ij, A false vntroth to me the same doth seeme. **1598** R. Bernard tr. *Terence, Phormio* ii. ii, If then I had spoken an vntroath. **1623** Fletcher & Rowley *Maid in Mill* iv. i, There will be a yard of dissimulation At least (City measure) and cut upon an untroth or two.

†**4.** A company (of summoners). *Obs.*—⁰

**1486** *Bk. St. Albans* f vi b, An vntrouth of sompneris.

†**Untro·thful**, *a. Obs.*—¹ [Un-[1] 7.] Unbelieving. *a* **1400** *New Test.* (Paues) Acts xiv. 2 Þo Iewes þat wore vntrowþeful stired persecucyone. **Untrou·ble**, *v.* (Un-[2] 4 b.) *a* **1684** Leighton *Comm. 1 Pet.* v. (1849) II. 468 Art thou troubled with fears, enemies, and snares? untrouble thyself of that, for He is with thee.

**Untrou·bled**, *ppl. a.* [Un-[1] 8.]

**1.** Not subjected to trouble or disquiet.

**1484** *Acta Auditorum* (1839) *146/2 Þe said venerable fader ..salbe vntrublit for þat some. **1531** *Reg. Privy Seal Scot.* II. 134/2 The saidis personis..to be..unmolestit, and untrublit, for quhatsumever actioun or cryme. **1590** Spenser *F. Q.* i. i. 33 Vntroubled night they say giues counsell best. *Ibid.* ii. vii. 15 With how small allowaunce Vntroubled Nature doth her selfe suffise. *a* **1625** Fletcher *Love's Pilgrimage* iv. ii, Make your spirit an untroubled way To pass to what it ought. **1648** Boyle *Seraphick Love* (1659) 14 A sight, whose glory made them look on fading Beauties, with..untroubled eyes. **1671** Milton *P. R.* iv. 401 Our Saviour meek and with untroubl'd mind..betook him to his rest. **1743** Francis tr. *Hor., Odes* ii. x. 17 He who enjoys th' untroubled Breast, Of Virtue's awful Lore possest. **1816** Wilson *Misc. Poems* 268 Thou with that untroubled voice. **1846** Mrs. A. Marsh *Father Darcy* II. ii. 62 The priest preserved all the usual untroubled gravity and dignity of his demeanour. **1890** 'R. Boldrewood' *Col. Reformer* (1891) 246 Untroubled by care or consuming anxiety.

**2.** Not rendered turbid. Also *fig.*

*c* **1614** Sir W. Mure *Dido & Æneas* ii. 776 Whose vertew's streame vntrubled still runnes pure. **1662** Charleton *Myst. Vintners* (1675) 191 The equal distribution of the Spirits of the liquor, which always rendreth bodies clear and untroubled. **1810** Southey *Kehama* x. iv, The stream..there delights to lie, Untroubled and at rest Beneath the untainted sky. **182.** Mrs. Hemans *Evening Prayer* iv, Fresh within your breasts th' untroubled springs Of hope make melody.

Hence **Untrou·bledness.**

*a* **1660** Hammond *Wks.* (1683) IV. 479 He hath..robb'd.. the Sceptick of his indifference and untroubledness.

**Untrou·blesome**, *a.* (Un-[1] 7.)

**1757** Mrs. Griffith *Lett. Henry & Frances* (1767) IV. 208 My Companion is a chearful, civil, untroublesome Person. **1848** Mill *Pol. Econ.* v. vii. § 3. II. 436 The progress of industry is gradually affording other modes of investment almost as safe and untroublesome. **1894** *Blackw. Mag.* Mar. 393 Things which make cricket easy and untroublesome.

Hence **Untrou·blesomeness.**

**1874** Micklethwaite *Mod. Par. Churches* xxiv. 185 Above all, its [*sc.* gas's] exceeding untroublesomeness.

†**Untrow·**, *v. Obs.* [Un-[1] 14.]

**1.** *intr.* To lack faith.

*c* **1200** *Trin. Coll. Hom.* 197 On alle þese limpes ne untrowede neure Iob to-ȝenes ure drihten.

**2.** *trans.* To have no belief in; to disbelieve.

*c* **1380** Wyclif *Sel. Wks.* II. 400 But who shulde untrowe Petris sentence? **1387** Trevisa *Higden* (Rolls) I. 17 Wondres beþ not al to be vntrowed [L. *discredenda*]. *a* **1395** Hylton *Scala Perf.* ii. xxxii. (Bodl. MS.), He seeþ it so sooþfastli þoruȝ grace þat he may not vntrowe it.

†**Untrow·able**, *a. Obs.* [Un-[1] 7 b.] Unbelievable, incredible.

**1382** Wyclif *Judg.* xx. 5 My wijf traueylynge with vntrowable woodnes of lust. — *Esther* ii. 15 She was ful semeli, and with vntrouable fairnesse. *c* **1475** *Cath. Angl.* 394/1 (A.), Vn Trowabylle, *incredibilis, incredulus.* **1533** Bellenden *Livy* iv. xiv. (S.T.S.) II. 99 Þe samyn is na les difficill..þan vntrowabil. **1552** Lyndesay *Monarche* 2760 Nynus..rasit vp one gret arme.., Quhose nummer bene.. vntrowabyll.

**Untrow·ed**, *ppl. a. Obs.* exc. *arch.* [Un-[1] 8.] Unbelieved, uncredited.

**1432** *Rolls of Parlt.* IV. 405/2 For..unreasonable excesse of suche lyes, or sum other untrowed meschevyng. **1434** Misyn *Mending Life* 126 More tollerabyll it wer to þe a vntrowyd greife to suffyr þen ons syn deedly. *a* **1583** Montgomerie *Flyting* 372 (Tullib. MS.), Vntrowit be thy tounge, ȝit tratling all tymes. *a* **1657** Sir W. Mure *Sonn.*, *Vile Priest* 11 Quhose..tounge vntrou'd Hath oft intrappit many a wanton wench.

†**Untrow·ful**, *a. Obs.* [Un-[1] 7.] Unbelieving. *c* **1375** *Sc. Leg. Saints* v. (*John*) 360 Sancte Iohne tuk of þan his kirtill, and to þe vntreufull gawe it till. *Ibid.* xiii. (*Mark*) 35. *c* **1380** Wyclif *Sel. Wks.* II. 204 O kynrede untroweful, how longe shal I be wiþ ȝou! †**Untrow·ing**, *ppl. a. Obs.* [Un-[1] 10.] Faithless. *c* **1320** *Sir Tristr.* 1731 Her wening was al wouȝ Vntroweand til hem to. †**Untrowness**: see Untrueness. **Untru·ced**, *a.* (Un-[1] 9.) *c* **1613** Middleton *No Wit like Woman's* ii. i, All those four Maintain a natural opposition And untruc'd war the one against the other. **Untru·ckling**, *ppl. a.* (Un-[1] 10.) **1850** Mrs. Browning *Prometh. Bound* 89 But revile not me For the firm will and the untruckling hate.

**Untrue·**, *a.* and *adv.* [OE. *untréowe*, *ungetréow(e*, etc. (Un-[1] 7, 11 b), = NFris. *untraw*, WFris. *on-*, *ûntrou*, MDu. *on(ge)trouwe* (Du. *ongetrouw*, usu. *ontrouw*), MLG. *un(ge)truwe*, OHG. *un(gi)triuwi*, *-gitrûwi*, *-getreowe* (MHG. *un(ge)triuwe*, G. *un(ge)treu*), ON. *útryggr* (MSw. *otrygger*), (M)Da. *utryg*), Goth. *untriggws*.]

**A.** *adj.* **1.** Of persons, etc.: Unfaithful, faithless.

*c* **1040** *Laws Cnut* in *Liebermann* i. 330 Ʒyf hwylc man sy swa untrywe ðam hundrede. *c* **1290** *St. Edmund* 100 in *S. Eng. Leg.* I. 434 Ich wot wel, ȝuyt men miȝhten finde.. Summan..untreowore to is wiue. *c* **1300** *K. Horn* 645 Þe kyng rod on hontynge,..ant Fykenyld bi is syde, Þat fals wes ant vntrewe. *a* **1340** Hampole *Psalter* xxx. 9 To..haf ill susspeccioun of a trew frend, or goed of an vntrew. **1390** Gower *Conf.* I. 21 The world as of his propre kynde Was evere untrewe. **14..** Hoccleve *Of Pride* (MS. Laud Misc. 735) fol. 69, Fy vp on tonges vntrew, They displeasaunce in lordis courtes brew. **1446** Lydg. *Two Nightingale Poems* ii. 17 To take vengeaunce On false lovers whiche that bien vntriewe. *c* **1489** Caxton *Sonnes of Aymon* xii. 285 Yᵉ gretest traytour & the vntruest kyng of the worlde. *a* **1547** Surrey in *Tottel's Misc.* (Arb.) 219 For my vaunt I dare well say my blood is not vntrue. *a* **1548** [see Untroth 1]. **1611** Shaks. *Cymb.* i. v. 86 When to my good Lord I proue vntrue, Ile choake my selfe. **1700** Dryden *Flower & Leaf* 564 The Men inglorious Knights, the Ladies all untrue. **1738** Wesley *Ps.* v. iii, The Hearts unkind and Hearts untrue Are both abhor'd by Thee. **1802** Leyden *Mermaid* vi, Know that thy favourite fair is dead, Or proves to thee and love untrue. **1818** Wordsw. '*Not seldom*' 6 The smoothest seas will sometimes prove, To the confiding Bark, untrue. **1879** Froude *Cæsar* xx. 341 He had refused to believe that Labienus could be untrue to him.

*absol.* *a* **1400** *Pauline Ep.* (Powell) Titus i. 15 To þe fuylyd ..and to þe vntrewe no thyng is clene. **1866** Morris *Ayenb.* 270 *margin*, The untrue, the evil, thieves, &c., are dark.

**2.** Contrary to fact; false; erroneous.

**13..** *E. E. Allit. P.* A. 897 Neuer lesyng ne tale vn-trwe, Ne towched her tonge for no dysstresse. *c* **1370** *Hymns Virg.* (1867) 108 And ȝif þei talke of tales vn-trewe, þou torn hem out of þat entent. *c* **1400** *Cursor M.* 28012 (Cott. Galba), Ʒe traist ouer mekill in thing vntrew. **1446** Lydg. *Two Nightingale Poems* ii. 80 Feynt and vntriew thyne exposicioun. **1531** *Pilgr. Perf.* (W. de W.) 187 b, Sooner shall heuen and erth be dissolued, than one..lettre of yᵉ lawe of god sholde be vnfulfylled or founde vntrue. **1577** B. Googe *Heresbach's Husb.* i. 43 Others thinke it an assured remedie..; but Columella thinkes it vntrue. **1612** Sir J. Digbye *Let.* in *10th Rep. Hist. MSS. Comm.* App. I. 609 But for myne owne parte, I holde this like the reste, to bee alltogeather untrue. **1644** Milton *Areop.* 38 When God shakes a Kingdome..'tis not untrue that many..false teachers are then busiest in seducing. **1765** *Museum Rust.* IV. 400, I do not apprehend that it any ways tends to prove my assertion untrue. **1802–12** Bentham *Ration. Judic. Evid.* (1827) III. 360 The motives by which a man may be urged to give credit to untrue facts. **1875** Jowett *Plato* (ed. 2) IV. 156 There is nothing true which is not from some point of view untrue.

*absol.* **1807** Wordsw. *White Doe* 836 Less would not..be due To us, who war against the Untrue. **1882** *N. & Q.* 6th Ser. VI. 429/2 Belief in the untrue. **1891** *Science-Gossip* XXVII. 1/1 It has all the fascination of the untrue for the popular taste.

**3.** Dishonest; unfair, unjust; wrong.

**1393** Langl. *P. Pl.* C. i. 98 And boxes ben broght forþ.. To vnder-take þe tol of vntrewe sacrifice. **1399** — *Rich. Redeles* i. 11 By drede, or be dyntis or domes vntrewe. **1444** *Rolls of Parlt.* V. 105/2 Be cause it was of untrue makyng, and untru stuff, no man sette therby. **1495** *Act 11 Hen. VII*, c. 24 § 1 Every untrue verdite herafter geven. **1542–3** *Act* 34–35 *Hen. VIII*, c. 20 Untrue and fained recoveries to be had against them. *Ibid.*, To thentent by fraude, covyne, and untrue meanes..to bynde and defeate theyre heyres. **1596** Dalrymple tr. *Leslie's Hist. Scot.* (S.T.S.) I. 199 To..craue the succour..of God and man against the Romane vntrue tyrannie. **1622** in Foster *Eng. Factories Ind.* (1908) II. 44 Wee shall fynde it deficulte to.. cleare their demaunds, which what they are or howe untrewe wee are not justly posest. **1865** Pusey *Truth Eng. Ch.* 5 Nothing..so dispels untrue prejudice as personal intercourse.

**4.** Not straight or direct; inexact; not agreeing with a standard.

*c* **1220** *Bestiary* 77 in *O. E. Misc.* 3 Ðer he wurdeþ heil & sund,..Ne were his bec untrewe. *Ibid.* 111 His muð is ȝet untrewe. **1503–4** *Act 19 Hen. VI*, c. 6 § 1 Deceivable and untrewe Beames and Scales. *a* **1513** Fabyan *Chron.* ccxxvi. (1516) 147 b/1 This Henry chastysed the olde vntrewe mesure, and made a yerde of the length of his owne Arme. **1780** Cowper *Progr. Error* 571 None sends his arrow to the mark in view, Whose hand is feeble, or his aim untrue. **1844** H. Stephens *Bk. Farm* III. 891 Thereby producing wool of unequal size, and therefore untrue. **1867** A. Barry *Sir C. Barry* ii. 57 The perspective gives an untrue figure.

**b.** Improper, imperfect.

**1541** R. Copland *Guydon's Quest. Chirurg.* C i, There is ii. maners of consolydacyon, one is trewe,..and yᵉ other is vntrue consolydacyon. **1884** tr. *Lotze's Metaph.* i. 23 One of the oldest thoughts in Philosophy is that of the opposition between true being and untrue being.

**B.** *adv.* = Untruly *adv.*

*a* **1310** in Wright *Lyric P.* xlii. 114 Whose loveth untrewe, his herte is selde seete. *c* **1386** Chaucer *Prol.* 735 Or ellis he moot telle his tale vntrewe Or feyne thyng or fynde wordes newe. *c* **1600** Shaks. *Sonn.* lxxii, Least your true loue may seeme falce in this, That you for loue speake well of me vntrue. **1622** J. Taylor (Water P.) *Merry-Fery-Wherry Voy.* Wks. (1630) 13/1 Some fooles would say I flatter'd, spake vntrue.

†**Untrue·ful**, *a. Obs. rare.* [Un-[1] 7.] Untruthful, false. *c* **1380** Wyclif *Serm.* Sel. Wks. I. 137 Wole þou not be untrewful but trewe in bileve. **1491** Caxton *Vitas Patr.* (W. de W. 1495) i. lxxviii. 120/1 Orygenes by his false doctryne hadd gyuen many untruefull techynges contrary to the holy scrypture.

**Untrue·ness.** [Un-[1] 12. Cf. OE. *ungetréowness*.] **a.** Unfaithfulness. **b.** Absence of trueness or truth; falsity, inexactness.

*a* **1200** *Moral Ode* 265 (Lamb. MS.), Þa þe untrownesse [*v.r.* untrewnesse] duden þon þe ho sculden bon holde. **1727** Bailey (vol. II), *Falsness*, falshood, untrueness. **1862** F. Hall *Hindu Philos. Syst.* 161 This untrueness does not belong to the universe,..for the causes of that universe..are free from all defect. **1886** Huxley in *Fortn. Rev.* Dec. 789 If there be gradations in untrueness.

**Untru·ism.** [f. Untrue *a.*, after Truism.]

**1.** An untruth.

**1845** *Q. Rev.* LXXV. 115 This continual repetition of amiable untruisms. **1857** Trollope *Barchester T.* vi, No one but a preaching clergyman can revel in platitudes, truisms, and untruisms; and yet receive..the same respectful demeanour.

**2.** That which is untrue.

**1868** Visct. Strangford *Select.* (1869) I. 188 This tiresome literary trick of making an appeal..to the genius of Untruism.

**Untru·ly**, *adv.* [OE. *untréowlice* (Un-[1] 11), = MDu. *ontrouwelike* (obs. Du. *ontrouwelijk*), MHG. *untriuwelîche*, ON. *útrúliga* (MSw. *otrolika*, older Da. *utrolig*).]

†**1.** Unfaithfully, dishonestly; guilefully, treacherously. *Obs.*

c893 K. ÆLFRED *Oros.* IV. v. § 5 Agothocles ȝedyde untreowlice wið hiene. 1303 R. BRUNNE *Handl. Synne* 1834 She..here wedlak Ful falsly an on-truly brak. 1340 *Ayenb.* 44 Huanne me heþ riȝtuolle wyȝtes and riȝtuolle mesures and zelleþ ontreweliche. c1400 *Destr. Troy* 12074 Achilles ..with treson in þe temple vntruly was slayn. 1444 *Rolls of Parlt.* V. 105/2 The Slayes and Yern therto belangyng, untruly were..wrought. 1495 *Act 11 Hen. VII*, c. 24 § 1 Jurrours untruly gevyng ther verdite. 1532–3 *Act 24 Hen. VIII*, c. 1 § 1 Great multitude of Hydes..is vntruely insufficiently and deceyvably tanned. a1548 HALL *Chron., Hen. V*, 78 b, Ye..ought to haue kept your faith and promise, whiche you haue vntruly and vnhonestly broken.

**2.** Incorrectly, falsely.

c1380 WYCLIF *Wks.* (1880) 430 For þanne..goddis lawe shulde be vntreweliere knowun boþe bi clerkis & bi comyns. c1394 *P. Pl. Crede* 312 Þere we lengeden full longe..For-to all þis freren folke weren founded in townes, And tauȝten vntrulie. 1425 *Paston Lett.* I. 19 Johne Wortes, that..affermith hym untrewely to be my cousyn. c1449 PECOCK *Repr.* Prol. 4 Whiche summe of the comoun peple vnwijsly and vntreuli iugen and condempnen to be yuele. ?a1533 FRITH *Another Bk. agst. Rastell* C viij b, Now are we come to the fourth erroure where Rastel vntrulye reporteth on me [etc.]. 1579 FULKE *Heskins' Parl.* 438 He would get credite to that whiche is vntruely ascribed to Saint Iames. 1625 DONNE *Serm.* (1640) 26 It is..dangerously said,..that it is not absurd to say..that God does sometimes speake untruly. 1839 HALLAM *Hist. Lit.* II. cvi. § 8 It was said foolishly..of Shakspeare, and we may be sure untruly, that he never blotted a line. 1864 PUSEY *Lect. Daniel* 122 They allege, even untruly, that he copied the prayer of Nehemiah.

**3.** Inexactly; not in a true course.

1844 MARDON *Billiards* 107, I cannot recollect a single instance of the balls having run untruly.

† **Untrum**, *v.*: see UN-¹ 14.

† **Untru·m**, *a.* *Obs.* Also 4 ontrom. [OE., f. *un-* UN-¹ 7 + *trum* strong.] **a.** Weak, ailing, ill.

c825 *Vesp. Ps.* civ. 37 [God] utalaedde hie in seolfre & golde & ne wes in cyn heara untrum. c900 tr. *Baeda's Hist.* IV. xxiv. 346 Wæs þær in neaweste untrumra monna hus. 971 *Blickl. Hom.* 217 Þa wearð he untrum on feforadle. a1200 *St. Marher.* 22 Þa..tuhen alle to hire bodi þe untrume weren, and hefden hare heale.

**b.** Diffident, hesitating.

c1315 SHOREHAM *Poems* I. 595 Þanne auȝte we wel aryȝt to be To fange hym on-tromme.

† **Untru·mness.** *Obs.* [OE., f. prec. Cf. UN-¹ 12.] Weakness, infirmity; ill-health.

c897 K. ÆLFRED *Gregory's Past. C.* liv. 423 Forðæm wæs sanctus Paulus ȝecostod mid his modes untrumnesse. c1000 *Ags. Gosp.* Matt. viii. 17 He onfeng ure untrumnessa. a1122 *O. E. Chron.* (Laud MS.) an. 1043, Be þes cynges ȝelæfan..for his mycelre untrumnysse. c1200 ORMIN 5379 Forr to takenn hæle att himm Off iwhillc unntrummnesse. *Ibid.* 18329 Icc amm i me sellfenn wac & full off unntrummnesse.

**Untru·mpeted**, *ppl. a.* (UN-¹ 8.) [1775 ASH.] 1861 READE *Cloister & Hearth* i, The strange history of a pair, who lived untrumpeted, and died unsung. 1864 E. SARGENT *Peculiar* III. 298 The important and hazardous though untrumpeted labours of a scout. **Untru·nked**, *ppl. a.* (UN-² 5, 8.) 1582 STANYHURST *Æneid* II. (Arb.) 63 At leingth with rounsefal, from stock vntruncked, yt harssheth.

**Untru·ss**, *v.* [UN-² 4 b.]

**1.** *trans.* To free from a pack or burden. *rare.*

1390 GOWER *Conf.* II. 294 With this worde his Asse anon He let untrusse. c1430 *Pilgr. Lyf Manhode* II. xlvii. (1869) 94 Whan vntrussed thus j was, j was rauished in to the ayr an hygh. c1530 LD. BERNERS *Arth. Lyt. Bryt.* (1814) 484 There he saw the goodly yong squyers vntrussing of their somers & cariages. 1598 FLORIO, *Sfardellare*,..to vntrusse, or disburthen.

**2.** To unfasten or undo (a pack, etc.); to remove or free from some fastening.

c1400 *Pilgr. Sowle* (Caxton, 1483) II. xlv. 51 He vntrussed my fardel, and soone was I taught that sooth was that he seyde. 1570 GOOGE *Pop. Kingd.* IV. 56 The Pedler doth his packe vntrusse, the Host his pots doth fill. 1600 in Swayne *Sarum Churchw. Acc.* (1896) 148 Laborer to vntrusse the bels, 6d. 1777 SHERIDAN *Trip Scarb.* v. ii, Now ..that I am untrussed [=set free], give me leave to thank thee for the very extraordinary reception I have met with.

**b.** *fig.* To put off, discard.

1608 CHAPMAN *Byron's Consp.* III. iii, Be free, all worthy spirits, And stretch yourselves for greatness.., Untruss your slaveries.

**3.** To undo, unfasten (a 'point' of a garment). In later use chiefly allusively (see quot. 1721). *Obs.* exc. *Hist.*

1577 HOLINSHED *Hist. Eng.* I. 8/2 He was slain..by one of his own soldiors, as he was about to vntrusse his pointes. 1614 SYLVESTER *Bethulia's Rescue* II. 78 For..while hee plyes T' untrusse his Points, [he] them (fumbling) faster tyes. 1622 MABBE tr. *Aleman's Guzman d'Alf.* II. 356 One of the Souldiers was going to vntrusse a point. 1721 BAILEY, *To untruss a Point*, i.e. to unbutton one's Breeches in order to ease his Body. 1727 SOMERVILLE *Fables, Welshman & Fly*, A noisy fly..perch'd upon his worship's crown;..his skin he tore, And stuff'd himself with human gore. At last, in manners to excel, Untruss'd a point, some authors tell. 1739 [see POINT *sb.*¹ B. 5]. 1796 *Grose's Dict. Vulgar T.* s.v. 1837 BARHAM *Ingol. Leg.* I. *Grey Dolphin*, The Clerk of Chatham was untrussing his points preparatory to seeking his truckle-bed.

**b.** In fig. contexts.

1591 LYLY *Endym.* III. iii, Loue..kept such a tumbling in his bodie, that he was glad to vntrusse the poynts of his hart. 1622 DEKKER *Virg. Martir* II. i, Vntrusse the Codpeece point of our reward. 1891 MEREDITH *One of our Conq.* xiii, Lawyers can be brought to untruss a point over a cup of claret.

**c.** *absol.* To unfasten one's points; to undo one's dress (*spec.* one's lower garments).

1592 NASHE *P. Penilesse* D iv b, Off with thy gowne and vntrusse, for I meane to lash thee mightily. 1604 E. GRIMSTONE *Siege Ostend* 67 Making a shewe as if hee went to vntrusse. 1648 HERRICK *Hesper.*, *Upon Pagget*, Untrusse, his Master bade him; and that word Made him take up his shirt. a1683 OLDHAM *Rem.* (1684) 123, I must beg my Reader's Distance: as if I were going to Untruss. 1705 HICKERINGILL *Priest-cr.* II. vi. 57 To do which Business, they untrussed, and stript themselves. 1837 BARHAM *Ingol. Leg.* I. *Leech* (1905) 84 Now strip thee, Master Marsh, and that quickly: untruss, I say!

*transf.* 1649 W. M. *Wandering Jew* 19 His breeches if hee takes wide strides, will untrusse of themselves.

**4.** To undo or unfasten the garments of (a person); to assist in undressing. Also *refl.*

a1625 FLETCHER *Elder Brother* IV. iv, Well done, give me my night-cap. So. Quick, quick, untruss me. 1786 tr. *Beckford's Vathek* 99 [He] had untrussed himself to eat with greater advantage. 1809 MALKIN *Gil Blas* x. ix. ¶ 11 They also undressed Beatrice and Scipio, who..gravely allowed themselves to be untrussed. 1861 READE *Cloister & H.* lv, Soon he bade me untruss him, for he felt sadly.

† **5.** *fig.* **a.** To expose, disclose, reveal. *Obs.*

1600 ROWLANDS *Lett. Humours Blood* iv. 63 Who nominates his Bread and Cheese a name, (That doth vntrusse the nature of the same). 1601 B. JONSON *Poetaster* v. iii, Our Muse is in mind for th'vntrussing a poet. 1651 CLEVELAND *Poems* 20 Yet here's not all, I cannot half untruss &c. it's so abominous.

† **b.** To take apart, dissect, disintegrate. *Obs.*

a1618 J. DAVIES (Heref.) *Witte's Pilgr.* Wks. (Grosart) II. 37/1 Then, to vntrusse him..Whose Muse hath power to vntrusse what not? Was a vaine cast. 1645 MILTON *Colast.* 16 But hee goes on to untruss my Arguments, imagining them his Maisters points. 1651 CLEVELAND *Poems* 20 Scatter th' accumulative King; untruss That five-fold fiend.

**Untru·ssed**, *ppl. a.* [UN-¹ 8, or f. prec.]

† **1.** Unburdened. *Obs.*⁻¹

a1225 *Ancr. R.* 350 Þeo men þet..goð untrussed lihte ase pilegrimes touward heouene.

† **2.** Untressed; loose. *Obs.*

c1400 [see UNTRESSED *ppl. a.*]. 1494 *Lydgate's Bochas* VI. Prol. 32 Hir here vntrussyd [*MSS.* vntressid, -ed] harde sharpe and horryble. a1529 SKELTON *E. Rummyng* 147 Theyr lockes about theyr face, Theyr tresses vntrust. 1587 TURBERV. *Trag. T.* (1837) 30 Untrust her haire hoong rounde about her head. 1600 FAIRFAX *Tasso* XVIII. xxvii. 320 The Dryads..Whose armes, halfe naked; lockes vntrussed bee.

**3.** Having the garments unfastened or undone.

1544 PHAER *Regim. Lyfe* (1553) I iiij, Ye ought..to lette your backe be vntrussed in the sommer. 1596 LODGE *Wits Misery* (Hunter. Cl.) IV. 69 His common course is to go alwaies vntrust, except when his shirt is a washing. 1607, 1647 [see UNGARTERED 1]. 1652 BENLOWES *Theoph.* XI. iv, All his clothes so loosely spread, He's so untrust, as if it were not long to bed. 1822 SCOTT *Nigel* v, Three or four pages in the royal livery, but untrussed, unbuttoned. 1829 *Q. Rev.* XXXIX. 106 The poor boy who..has stood untrussed and trembling before him.

† **b.** Of points: Unfastened. *Obs.*

1589 GREENE *Span. Masquerado* Wks. (Grosart) V. 244 His cappe pulde ouer his eies, and his pointes vntrust. 1616 R. C. *Times' Whistle* v. 2135 Old Monsier Grey-beard with your poynts vntrust.

**4.** Not trussed for cooking.

1846 SOYER *Cookery* 217 Have four spering chickens untrussed.

**Untru·sser.** [f. UNTRUSS *v.* 5.] †A severe critic. 1599 B. JONSON *Ev. Man out of Hum.* II. i. E iij b, Welcome gentlemen: and how doest thou, thou Grand Scourge, or Second Vntrusse [*sic*] of the time? 1601 — *Poetaster* v. iii, Ambitiously affecting the title of the vntrussers, or whippers of the age. *Ibid.* To Rdr. 141 *Pol.* Will you not answere then the libells? *Avt.* No. *Pol.* Nor the vntrussers?

**Untru·ssing**, *vbl. sb.* [f. UNTRUSS *v.*] The action of the vb., chiefly in fig. senses.

1597 *Return fr. Parnass.* II. i. 762 One that will give his scholler leave to prove as verie a dunce as his father and nere commaunde the untrussinge of his points. 1601 B. JONSON *Poetaster* IV. vii, Come, wee'll goe see how forward our iourney-man is toward the vntrussing of him. 1602 DEKKER (*title*), Satiro-Mastix, or, the Untrussing of the Humorous Poet. 1603 SHAKS. *Meas. for M.* III. ii. 190 Marrie this Claudio is condemned for vntrussing.

**Untru·st**, *sb.* [UN-¹ 12. Cf. WANTRUST.]

**1.** Unbelief, distrust. Now *rare.*

a1225 *Ancr. R.* 332 Þeos two unðeawes, untrust and ouertrust, beoð þes deofles tristren. 1382 WYCLIF *Rom.* iv. 20 In the byheeste of God he doutide not with vntrust. 1390 GOWER *Conf.* II. 147 This fievere of Jelousie Somdel..groweth of sotie, Of love, and somdiel of untrust. 1421–2 HOCCLEVE *Dialog* 336 Frendshipes lawe nat worth wer a myte, If þat vntrust vn-to it wer annexid; Vntrust hath many a wight ful sore vexid. c1450 *Cov. Myst.* (Shaks. Soc.) 153 Alas!..For my grett dowth and fals beleve,.. My fals vntrost hath wrought myscheve! 1581 HOWELL *Devises* M j, Condemde thou art for thine vntruste. 1890 J. PULSFORD *Loyalty to Christ* I. 152 We should linger over the words 'Our Father', till nothing of doubt, or untrust, remains.

† **2.** Untrustworthiness. *Obs.*

1430–40 LYDG. *Bochas* Prologue 429 To shewe thuntrust off al worldli thyng. 1563 *Mirr. Mag.* X ii, Of my death let..princes wete The worldes vntrust, that they thereby be taught. 1579 HAKE *Newes out of Powles* (1872) H iij, Suche is the vntruste that is in man, moe men can speake plausibly in time of good happe,..then [etc.].

† **Untru·st**, *v.* *Obs.*⁻¹ [UN-¹ 14.] *intr.* To have no confidence; to be in despair.

a1225 *Ancr. R.* 332 Dred wiðuten hope makeð mon untrusten, and hope wiðute dred makeð ouertrusten.

**Untru·stable**, *a.* (UN-¹ 7 b.) 1863 KINGSLEY *Water-Bab.* iii. 118 Dennis will look up at you with his..good-natured untrustable Irish grey eye.

**Untru·sted**, *ppl. a.* (UN-¹ 8.)

1552 HULOET, Vntrusted, *perfidus.* a1586 SIDNEY *Arcadia* III. xix, I could wish my faith untried, and my counsell untrusted. c1710 CONGREVE *Of Pleasing* 13 The untrusted wretch to secresy pretends, Whispering his nothing round to all as friends. a1750 A. HILL *Picture of Love* 41 Curb your untrusted hearts while yet they're free. 1796 MME. D'ARBLAY *Camilla* IV. 389 Even her beloved sister..is untrusted.

**Untru·stful**, *a.* (UN-¹ 7.) 1569 PRESTON *Cambyses* C j b, Untrustfull traitor and corrupt Judge, how likest thou this complaint? 1829 SCOTT *Anne of G.* xxviii, The untried and untrustful services of those, whom we have only known as ..malignant neighbours.

† **Untru·stiness.** *Obs.* [f. UNTRUSTY *a.*] Unfaithfulness. (Common c 1545–1625.)

1526 *Pilgr. Perf.* (W. de W. 1531) 110 These be yᵉ vices, ..Sleyghtnesse or deceyte,..Vntrustynesse or Vnsecretnesse. a1548 HALL *Chron., Edw. IV*, 232 Such is the end of vntrustynes & promisbrekyng. 1614 R. HARRIS *Samuels Funerall* (1618) 16 Ah our idlenesse and vntrustines! and all. 1685 BAXTER *Paraphr. N. T.* Rom. iii. 4 All [shall] be silenced that dare accuse him of untrustiness or lying.

† **Untru·sting**, *vbl. sb.* (UN-¹ 13.) c1440 *Jacob's Well* 294 Þe synnes of þe herte arn þise:..vntrustynge, wrong wenyng, foly loue [etc.]. **Untru·sting**, *ppl. a.* (UN-¹ 10.) 1861 [H. S. CUNNINGHAM] *Wheat & Tares* 364 She had been suspicious, untrusting, ungenerous. †**Untru·stly**, *adv.* *Obs.*⁻⁰ [UN-¹ 11.] Unfaithfully, unreliably. c1440 *Promp. Parv.* 368/1 On-trostly (*P.* ontruly, or ontrustly, *infideliter, insecure*).

**Untru·stworthiness.** (UN-¹ 12. Cf. next.) 1808 BENTHAM *Sc. Reform* 91 The mass of evidence,..the comparative untrustworthiness of which is thus recognised. 1867 FREEMAN *Norm. Conq.* I. ii. 10 To show the untrustworthiness of the traditional account.

**Untru·stworthy**, *a.* (UN-¹ 7.)

1846 WORCESTER (citing *Ec. Rev.*). 1853 RUSKIN *Stones Ven.* III. ii. § 20 Knowledge is not only very often unnecessary, but it is often untrustworthy. 1878 BOSW. SMITH *Carthage* 314 The Gauls, untrustworthy as ever—except when led by Hannibal—were drawn up on a hill to the left.

**Untru·sty**, *a.* [UN-¹ 7.]

**1.** Untrustworthy, not to be trusted (to), unreliable: **a.** Of things.

1387 TREVISA *Higden* (Rolls) III. 265 Þe firste tweie artes beeþ untrusty [*L. erroneæ*]. 1430–40 LYDG. *Bochas* I. 3026 So variable she [*sc.* Fortune] is in hir delites, Hir wheel vntrusti & frowardli meuyng. 1593 T. LODGE *Phillis* H 3 b, Tongue vntrustie, subtil sighted, Wanton will, with change delighted. 1609 HOLLAND *Amm. Marcell.* 67 The residue ..abandoning the Islands as an untrustie place of defence. 1639 FULLER *Holy War* II. xvii. 67 Relying on their own strength, which never is more untrusty then when most trusted. 1677 GILPIN *Demonol.* 58 Others..make them the Effects of our untrusty and deceitful Senses. 1842 MANNING *Serm.* xvii. (1848) 253 It is a dubious and untrusty faith,.. which is reconcileable with an ambitious life. 1870 MORRIS *Earthly Par.* III. IV. 8 To bid them come aboard, and take such rest As they might have of the untrusty sea.

**b.** Of persons.

1430–40 LYDG. *Bochas* VIII. xxv. 3000 His cosyn Modred, vntrusti & vnstable. c1440 *Promp. Parv.* 148/1 False, and vntrosty, *perfidus.* a1513 FABYAN *Chron.* (1516) 20 b/1 Edricus was..vntrusty and false of thought and promyse. 1542 UDALL *Erasm. Apoph.* 294 To mistruste an untrustie persone, is a poincte of wysedome. 1597 J. PAYNE *Royal Exch.* 14 The vntrustie that borrow moche, and repay.. little. 1642 D. ROGERS *Naaman* 435 Faithfull in the cheefe treasure, and yet untrusty in the smaller. 1691 E. TAYLOR *Behmen's Theos. Philos.* 421 In Adam all Men became untrusty. 1846 W. CROSS *Disruption* xxix, The untrusty domineering laun'-steward. 1876 MORRIS *Sigurd* IV. 327 She dwells with a folk untrusty and a king that knows not ruth.

†**2.** Unfaithful *to* another. *Obs.*

1553 GRIMALDE *Cicero's Offices* III. (1556) 142 How manye mo, thinke ye, were vntrue, and vntrusty to that king. 1575 GASCOIGNE *Glasse of Govt.* I. v, I was never yet untrusty to any of you both. 1612 T. TAYLOR *Comm. Titus* ii. 10 A strong theefe is he, that is vntrusty to him that trusteth him.

**Untru·th.** [OE. *untrēowþ*, *untriewþ* (UN-¹ 12). Cf. ON. *útrygð*, also UNTROTH, WANTRUTH.]

**1.** Unfaithfulness; lack of fidelity, loyalty, or honesty. Now *arch.* and *rare.*

c893 K. ÆLFRED *Oros.* III. xi. § 5 He..him wende from Antigones hamfærelte micelra untreowða. *Ibid.* IV. v. § 5. a1122 *O. E. Chron.* (Laud MS.) an. 1086, Þa Dænescan.. wurdon awende to þære meste untriwðe. 1340 *Ayenb.* 17 Þe uerste boȝ of prede þet is ontreuþe. 1400 tr. *Secreta Secret., Gov. Lordsh.* 62 Hold trewly þy fayth hyght, ffor euer moor to all vntreuthe folwys euyl ende. c1489 CAXTON *Sonnes of Aymon* xvi. 387 Be my suretees, I praye you,..Ye knowe that I dyde never vntrewth. 1559 *Mirr. Mag.* C ij, I through flattery abused his wanton youth, And his fonde trust augmented my vntruth. 1593 SHAKS. *Rich. II*, II. ii. 101, I would to heauen (So my vntruth had not prouok'd him to it) The King had cut off my head.

1859 TENNYSON *Elaine* 126 He never spake word of reproach to me, He never had a glimpse of mine untruth. — *Guinevere* 537 Too wholly true to dream untruth in thee.

† **2.** Unbelief; lack of faith. *Obs.*

c1380 WYCLIF *Serm.* Sel. Wks. I. 45 He shal reprove þe worlde of þe synne of untreuþe. *Ibid.* II. 20 Crist woundride of his kyn, for þe untreuþe þat þei hadden.

**3.** Falsehood, falsity.

1439 *Cases bef. King's Council* (Selden) 105 To sey the playn trouth and nouȝt to melle it with eny ontrouth. 1482 in *Surtees Misc.* (1890) 40 To put down all falsett and untrewit. 1559 BP. SCOT in Strype *Ann. Ref.* (1709) I. App. x. 32 Bringinge..others from the truthe unto untruthe. 1577–82 BRETON *Toyes Idle Head* Wks. (Grosart) I. 27/2 Such youthes there are..As with vntrueth their Ladies fancies feede. 1587 GOLDING *De Mornay* Pref., But yet cannot any vntruth preuayle..against truth...For vntruth is contrary to nature. 1632 LITHGOW *Trav.* I. 2 This stinging censure of absurd vntrueth. 1748 RICHARDSON *Clarissa* III. 299 For his boldness in hoping to make me..testify to his great untruth. 1843 CARLYLE *Past & Pr.* III. i, A poor braggart; fast hastening to be a falsity and speaker of the Untruth.

1873 SPENCER *Stud. Sociol.* xi. (1877) 265 Everyone discovers the untruth of this assumption.

**b.** A falsehood; a false or incorrect statement.

*c* 1449 PECOCK *Repr.* III. xvii. 396 It is open that tho ij opinious, conclusiouns, and holdingis..ben errouris and vntreuthis. 1565 JEWEL *Reply Harding* 554 Therefore M. Harding concludeth this mater with twoo vntruethes bothe togeather. 1585 in *Cath. Rec. Soc. Publ.* V. 109 He saythe it is a great untruthe and cannot be prooved. 1634 SIR T. HERBERT *Trav.* 2 All Trauellers are subject to imputations of vntruths. 1651 HOBBES *Leviath.* I. viii. 36 So singular a truth (as they think it, though it be many times an untruth they light on). *a* 1716 BLACKALL *Wks.* (1723) I. 23 A very strange Paradox, or rather a most palpable Untruth. 1756 *Gentl. Mag.* XXVI. 144 The author of three letters..is taken into custody for the virulent abuse, and notorious untruths they contain. 1819 SCOTT *Leg. Montrose* ii, I would be loath to reply to you with an untruth. 1863 P. BARRY *Dockyard Econ.* 215 He..asserts either an impudent or an ignorant untruth.

*Comb.* 1799 SOUTHEY *Devil's Walk* liii, He is an untruth-telling whoreson.

**4.** Inexactness.

1869 RANKINE *Machine & Hand-tools* Pl. H 9, The washers have sufficient play..to allow them to accommodate themselves to any untruth..on the surface of the nut.

Hence **Untru·ther**, one who utters untruths.

1889 JEROME *Three Men in Boat* vii, 'You are an untruther,' I replied, getting roused.

**Untru·thful**, *a.* [UN-[1] 7. Cf. UNTROTHFUL.]

†**1.** Unbelieving, infidel. *Obs.*

*c* 1375 *Sc. Leg. Saints* xxvii. (*Machor*) 846 Dewenik can to catnes pas, to folk þat þan wntreuthtfull was. 1456 SIR G. HAYE *Law Arms* (S.T.S.) 108 The traytouris untreuthfull sais that the grete Cane is lord of all the warld.

**2.** Not truthful; untrue.

[1847 WEBSTER.] 1854 PATMORE *Angel in Ho.* I. viii. 5 The candid skies At our untruthful strangeness laugh'd. 1871 JOWETT *Plato* II. 20 As men become better such theories appear more and more untruthful to them.

Hence **Untru·thfully** *adv.*, **Untru·thfulness.**

[1847 WEBSTER, *Untruthfully.] 1879 *Temple Bar Mag.* Sept. 45, 'I am sorry', says Tremaine, untruthfully. 1830 CARLYLE *Misc. Ess.* (1872) III. 53 But it always is our duty ..not to avoid unweddedness by *untruthfulness. 1863 MANSEL *Lett., Lect.*, etc. (1873) 239 The glaring untruthfulness and incongruity of the story.

**Untu·ck**, *v.* [UN-[2] 3.] *trans.* To undo or free from being tucked up.

1611 COTGR., *Destrousser*, to vntrusse, vntucke. 1765 STERNE *Tr. Shandy* VIII. ix, When Bridget untucked the feet of the bed. 1857 J. G. WOOD *Com. Obj. Seashore* 67 In due time it untucks itself, and tosses away the indigestible portions of its food. 1882 *Blackw. Mag.* July 15/1 With a dignified gesture he untucked his legs from under him.

**Untu·cked**, *ppl. a.* [UN-[1] 8 + TUCK *v.*[1]] **a.** Of cloth: Not stretched or tentered. **b.** Not tucked up; loose.

1467 *Rolls of Parlt.* V. 621 To bie rawe Clothes, untoked and unfulled. 1592–3 *Act* 35 *Eliz.* c. 10 § 1 Eyche Kersey ..beinge rawe, unscowred, untucked, and unwett. 1597 SHAKS. *Lover's Compl.* 31 Her haire nor loose nor ti'd in formall plat,..For some vntuck'd, descended her sheu'd hat. 1797 *Monthly Mag.* III. 536 Another, ungirded, or untucked, called *Orthostades*, or streight robes.

**Untu·ckered**, *a.* (UN-[1] 9.) 1713 ADDISON *Guardian* No. 109 ¶ 5 One of those Untuckered Ladies whom you were so sharp upon on Monday was sennight. *Ibid.* No. 140 ¶ 1 The attacks he has made on the untuckered stays and short petticoat. **Untu·fted**, *ppl. a.* (UN-[1] 8, 9.) 1872 COUES *N. Amer. Birds* 206 Very small; head untufted.

**Untu·mbled**, *ppl. a.* (UN-[1] 8.)

1675 WYCHERLEY *Country Wife* v. 91 Women of quality, like the richest Stuffs, lie untumbled and unask'd for. 1781 *Gentl. Mag.* LI. 616 The ocean [was] left in an easy untumbled bed. 1819 BYRON *Juan* II. clxxxi, The sands untumbled, the blue waves untost.

**Untumu·ltuated**, *ppl. a.* (UN-[1] 8.) 1659 GAUDEN *Tears Ch.* 107 They were left to their free votes and untumultuated suffrages.

**Untumu·ltuous**, *a.* (UN-[1] 7.)

1741 LADY HARTFORD *Lett.* (1805) III. 193 Necessitated to see nothing but what offers itself to me in the most easy and untumultuous manner. 1786 *Francis the Philanthropist* I. 23 Tasting the untumultuous enjoyments of rational society. ?1818 KEATS *Ep. to Reynolds* 91 An untumultuous fringe of silver foam. 1897 F. THOMPSON *New Poems* 16 In skies that no man sees to move Lurk untumultuous vortices of power.

**Untu·nable**, *a.* [UN-[1] 7 b.]

**1.** Not tuneful; unmelodious, inharmonious, harsh-sounding.

1545 ELYOT, *Absonus voce*, he that hath an vntunable voyce. 1569 SANFORD *Agrippa* 185 b, The vnpleasaunte and vntunable roringe of Asses. 1595 SPENSER *Col. Clout* 374 Or be the shepheards which do serue her laesie,..Or be their pipes vntunable and craesie. 1655 tr. *Sorel's Com. Hist. Francion* IV. 11 The most untunable musick in the world. 1688 in Wood *Life* (O.H.S.) III. 274 A boy..with a cat under his coat..made her make..an untunable noise. 1748 MELMOTH *Fitzosborne Lett.* lix. (1749) II. 100 [It] might probably give musick to those lines in Horace, which now seem so untuneable. 1796 BURNEY *Mem. Metastasio* III. 307 Constructed in measures wholly untuneable. 1841 D'ISRAELI *Amen. Lit.* I. 100 The Normans could not endure the Saxons' untunable consonants. 1887 W. G. PALGRAVE *Ulysses* 34 The four church bells..have been ringing a very hospitable, though untuneable, peal.

**b.** *fig.* or in fig. context.

1591 SHAKS. *Two Gent.* III. i. 208 In dumbe silence will I bury mine [*sc.* news], For they are harsh, vn-tuneable, and bad. 1599 SANDYS *Europæ Spec.* (1605) B 2 b, I will not heere warble long vpon this vntuneable harsh string. 1610 P. HOLLAND *Camden's Brit.* I. 8 It is wholly patched up of untuneable discords and jarring absurdities. 1645 [see UNATONABLE 1]. 1661 J. STEPHENS *Procurations* 129 That which..in him..seemeth..untunable and out of square and friendly compasse.

**2.** Incapable of being tuned.

1801 BUSBY *Dict. Mus.* s.v.

**3.** Not appreciative of music.

1851 KEBLE *Occas. Papers & Rev.* (1877) 251 The colours are spread before the blind; the music falls on untunable ears.

Hence **Untu·nableness.**

1611 COTGR., *Desaccord*, a jarre, discord, untuneablenesse. 1659 H. MORE *Immort. Soul* III. ix. 420 The tenderer Ear cannot but feel..some harshness and untunableness or other, in the best consorts of Musical Instruments and Voices. 1691 NORRIS *Pract. Disc.* 217 As the untunableness of one or two Instruments dis-recommends the whole Musical Consort. 1756 J. WARTON *Ess. on Pope* I. ii. 65 The harshness and untuneableness of modern languages. 1832 *Westm. Rev.* Oct. 357 An age which finds beauties in untuneableness, and believes exact intonation would be an evil and a loss.

**Untu·nably**, *adv.* [UN-[1] 11.] Unmelodiously, inharmoniously.

1504 in *Archiv Stud. neu. Spr.* CXX. 423 A harpe gewythe sownd as yt ys set: The harper may wreste vntvnably. 1564 J. RASTELL *Confut. Jewell's Serm.* 111 b, This would sound ..vntuneablie. 1610 HOLLAND *Camden's Brit.* I. 131 A Poet ..sung not untunably in this maner. 1653 H. COGAN tr. *Pinto's Trav.* lxxiii. 301 They fell to playing on divers instruments,..though very barbarously and untunably.

†**Untu·ne**, *sb. Obs.*[−1] [UN-[1] 12.] The state of being out of sorts. 1603 FLORIO *Montaigne* III. xiii. 646 Men..much troubled and vexed with their bellies untune and disorder.

**Untu·ne**, *v.* [UN-[2] 4.]

**1.** *trans.* To put out of tune; to render inharmonious. Freq. in fig. context.

1598 FLORIO, *Distonare*, to vntune. 1602 *2nd Pt. Return Parnass.* v. i. 1996 The cold of wo hath quite vntun'd my voyce. 1643 HERLE *Answ. Ferne* 15 There would be a discontinuity in the whole, enough to..untune the Organ of the Creation. 1711 ADDISON *Spect.* No. 135 ¶ 9 We have drawn two Words into one, which has likewise very much untuned our Language. 1743 in *Mem. Eliz. Carter* (1808) II. 55 When..The last dread thunders..Untune the concord of the spheres. 1807 J. BARLOW *Columb.* VIII. 45 The drum's rude clang, the war wolf's hideous howl,..Untuned the harp for all but misery's pains. 1856 C. READE *Never too late* III. 106 The quail['s]..Crake!—crake!—crake! untuning the night. 1876 SWINBURNE *Erechtheus* 1741 Never tear Shall stain for shame nor groan untune the song.

*refl.* *a* 1661 HOLYDAY *Juvenal* (1673) To Rdr., Certainly I believe he [*sc.* Horace] injuriously untun'd himself in his fall from the ode to the satyre.

**b.** *fig.* To disorder; to discompose; to render unapt or averse *to* (something).

1638 N. WHITING *Albino & Bellama* 343 Madam, what passion does untune your mind? *a* 1657 R. LOVEDAY *Lett.* (1659) 199 The continuance of my trouble..does often untune and discompose my soul. 1697 DRYDEN *Virg. Past.* IX. 71 Cares and Time Change all things, and untune my Soul to Rhyme. 1753 HOGARTH *Anal. Beauty* xiv. 119 Do we not see in most collections that much time disunites, untunes, blackens, and by degrees destroys even the best preserved pictures. 1798 BLOOMFIELD *Farmer's Boy, Autumn* 228 Disappointed hope untunes the Soul. 1822 SCOTT *Halidon Hill* II. ii, *Gordon.* If music touch thee— *Swinton.* It did, before disasters had untuned me. 1860 EMERSON *Cond. Life* vii. 232 Despair is no muse, and untunes the active powers.

**2.** *intr.* To go out of tune. *rare*[−0].

1598 FLORIO, *Discordare*, to disagree, to vntune, to contend, to iarre.

†**3.** *absol.* ? To relax, unbend. *Obs.*

1609 *Everie Wom. in her Humor* A 2 b, Come thou hast bene a sinner: vnloade, discharge, vntune, confesse, is venus dominatrix? art not in loue?

**Untu·ned**, *ppl. a.* [UN-[1] 8, or f. UNTUNE *v.*]

**1.** Not tuned; not made tuneful or melodious; also, rendered untuneful.

1592 DANIEL *Delia* xxi, Vexing with vntun'd moane her dainty eares. 1594 SHAKS. *Rich. II*, I. iii. 134 Rouz'd vp with boystrous vntun'd drummes. 1612 CHAPMAN *Rev. Bussy d'Ambois* I. i, The cities' bells Jangling together in untun'd confusion. 1630 DRAYTON *David & Goliah* 294 The harmony of the vntuned'st string Torments the spirit which so torments the King. 1702 POPE *Sappho* 229 Untun'd my lute, and silent is my lyre. 1733 *Satirist* 9 For Sat'rists write in so untun'd a Strain, Thy claim no Title to th' harmonious Train. 1773 J. HERRIES *Elem. Speech* 53 A string in an instrument broken or untuned.

*transf.* 1590 SHAKS. *Com. Err.* v. i. 310 That heere my onely sonne Knowes not my feeble key of vntun'd cares. *c* 1626 BOSWORTH *To Fairest Lady* 5 O that it might have been While she had liv'd, and had my verses seen, Before sad cries deaf'd my untuned ears. 1684 EARL ROSCOM. *Ess. Transl. Verse* 337, I lose my Patience, when, with Sawcy Pride, By untun'd Ears I hear His Numbers try'd.

**b.** Not furnished with a tune.

1853 READE *Chr. Johnstone* 69 The Newhaven men..are agreed that this song lifts them through more work than untuned fishermen can manage.

**2.** *fig.* Not brought into, put out of, a state of harmony or concord; disordered.

1602 *2nd Pt. Ret. fr. Parnass.* v. i. 1986 With vntaught hand, and with vntuned hart. 1648 J. BEAUMONT *Psyche* XVII. v, At the first,..when in th' untuned Deep Each Thing was wroth and snarled with his brother. 1687 *Death's Vision* v, The Intellective, Vital Flame..Is Thoughtless struck, and Dies By the Untun'd Contexture of the Unthinking Frame! 1794 GODWIN *Caleb Williams* 65 Mr. Tyrrel would have gone also; his mind was untuned. 1805 WORDSW. *Prelude* IV. 145 For cold and raw the air was, and untuned. 1834 MACAULAY *Ess. Pitt* ¶ 27 When his mind was untuned.

**Untu·neful**, *a.* (UN-[1] 7.)

1709 *Brit. Apollo* No. 9. 3/2 My Voice is so Hoarse and Untuneful. 1760 STERNE *Tr. Shandy* IV. *Slawkenb. T.*, Harsh and untuneful are the notes of love, Unless my Julia strikes the key. 1803 *Monthly Mag.* XVI. 25 He had a voice rough and untuneful. 1830 TENNYSON *The Owl* II. 6 Her voice untuneful grown, Wears all day a fainter tone. 1890 *Pall Mall G.* 24 June 2/3 Liszt's ambitious but untuneful..Symphony.

Hence **Untu·nefully** *adv.*, **Untu·nefulness.**

1881 *Athenæum* 25 June 840/2 So does he demonstrate Byron's innate untunefulness. 1884 *Manch. Exam.* 19 Feb. 5/2 A cold which causes a man to sing untunefully.

**Untu·rbaned**, *a.* (UN-[1] 9.) 1801 SOUTHEY *Thalaba* II. xxvii, Unturban'd and unsandal'd there, Abdaldar stood before the Flame. 1887 W. G. PALGRAVE *Ulysses* 14 Visited by turbaned and unturbaned pilgrims. **Untu·rbid**, *a.* (UN-[1] 7.) 1820 SCOTT *Monast.* ii, The little brook..danced carelessly on from stream to pool, light and unturbid. **Untu·rf**, *v.* (UN-[2] 4.) 1890 *Nature* 27 Nov. 80/1 A wild hill-top..had been unturfed, the turves and gorse being piled in heaps. **Untu·rn**, *v.* (UN-[2] 3, 7.) 1816 KEATS *Sonn. when L. Hunt left Prison*, Think you he naught but prison walls did see, Till, so unwilling, thou unturn'dst the key? 1825 J. NICHOLSON *Operat. Mechanic* 320 Then, unturning the finger-screw,..I released the screw from the wheel. *Ibid.* 322 Screws..which are prevented from unturning by tightening the finger-nuts. **Untu·rnable**, *a.* (UN-[1] 7 b.) 1847 TENNYSON *Princ.* II. 186 That iron will, That axelike edge unturnable. 1891 H. HERMAN *His Angel* 14 Honesty, sterling and unturnable, was emblazoned there.

**Untu·rned**, *ppl. a.* [UN-[1] 8.]

**1.** Not turned over, round, away, etc.

*c* 1550 [see STONE *sb.* 16 c]. 1575 *Gamm. Gurton* I. iv. 12 So see in all the heaps of dust thou leave no straw vnturned. 1665 R. OLIVER in Earl Orrery *St. Lett.* (1742) 120, I will leave no stone unturned, till I find out the root, from whence those wicked branches grow. 1670 [see STONE *sb.* 16 c]. 1760 LAW *Spir. Prayer* II. 79 Whilst man stood in his first perfection, unturned from God. 1814 *Monthly Mag.* XXXVIII. 438 Oft I took, and oft return'd This key, and left the lock unturn'd. 1822 BYRON *Vis. Judgem.* lxvii, Behold a candidate with unturn'd coat! 1904 E. RICKERT *Reaper* 303 He wanted to see how much ground was unturned.

**2.** Not shaped by turning.

1816 J. SMITH *Panorama Sci. & Art* I. 61 The part thus left unturned may be cut off either in the lathe or afterwards. 1875 *Carpentry & Join.* 88 The head..of the bed..may be made of unturned posts.

**Untu·rning**, *ppl. a.* [UN-[1] 10.]

**1.** Not turning round; not revolving.

1591 [see UNTRANSPARENT *a.*].

**2.** Not turning back or aside; continuing in a straight course; undeviating.

1593 Q. ELIZ. *Boeth.* IV. pr. vi. 93 Yf the euerlasting purenes of Godes mynde doth prescribe an vnturning order of causes. *c* 1611 CHAPMAN *Iliad* XV. 254 The clamorous fray Calls out a lion,..and his abhorred view Turns headlong in unturning flight (though vent'rous) all the crew. 1862 T. A. TROLLOPE *Marietta* iv, The long unturning path.

**Untu·sked**, *a.* (UN-[1] 9.) 1859 *All Year Round* No. 32. 129 The untusked elephants of Ceylon have 'tushes'. **Untu·telar**, *a.* (UN-[1] 7.) 1667 WATERHOUSE *Fire Lond.* 2 Men may see the dreadful effects of providence, untutelar to their acquisitions.

**Untu·tored**, *ppl. a.* [UN-[1] 8.]

**1.** Uneducated, untaught; simple, unsophisticated; † rude, boorish: **a.** Of persons.

1593 SHAKS. 3 *Hen. VI*, v. v. 32 Vntutor'd Lad, thou art too malapert. 1598 SYLVESTER *Du Bartas* II. ii. *Babylon* 262 Un-toyld, un-tutord,..We learn'd a language all men understood. 1618 FLETCHER *Loyal Subj.* IV. iii, We are two simple maids, untutor'd here Sir. 1663 J. SPENCER *Prodigies* 15 Those Secretaries of Nature..fell under the hatred of the untutor'd rabble. 1725 POPE *Odyss.* I. 491 What God to your untutor'd youth affords This headlong torrent of amazing words? 1780 BENTHAM *Princ. Legisl.* xviii. § 17 *note*, It is not for this that the untutored many could have originally submitted themselves to the dominion of the few. 1809–14 WORDSW. *Excurs.* v. 840 The untutored bird may..so construct..her nest..That the thorns wound her not. 1858 MERIVALE *Rom. Emp.* lii. VI. 66 [These] women..were exceptions to the mass of the untutored matrons of Rome. 1878 H. S. PALMER *Sinai* iv. 75 The superstitious and untutored inhabitants of the Desert.

**b.** Of the mind, intellect, etc.

1597 *Pilgr. to Parnassus* I. 9 Urge mee to advise youre younge untutord thoughts. 1619 A. NEWMAN *Pleas. Vis.* (1840) 7 Vaine will vntam'd, vntutored, Left Reasons rule. 1693 PRIOR *To Dr. Sherlock* 29 Thy even Thoughts with so much Plainness flow; Their Sense untutor'd Infancy may know. 1732 POPE *Ess. Man* I. 99 The poor Indian! whose untutor'd mind Sees God in clouds, or hears him in the wind. 1784 COWPER *Task* II. 570 A relaxation of religion's hold Upon the roving and untutor'd heart Soon follows. 1837 DISRAELI *Venetia* III. vii, Her unsophisticated and untutored spirit. 1867 PEARSON *Hist. Eng.* I. 15 Their wants were still undeveloped, their taste untutored.

**c.** Of instruments (esp. pen or pencil).

1611 RICH *Honest. Age* (Percy Soc.) 7, I come not to implore a Lawrell Crowne, Wherewith to decke my rude untutred quill. 1623 J. TAYLOR (Water P.) *Discov. by Sea* C 2 b, What my vntutor'd Pen cannot sufficiently commend, I am forced with silence to ouerpasse. 1706 E. WARD *Wooden World Diss.* (1708) A 6 b, This rough Draught of my untutor'd Pencil. 1748 *Anson's Voy.* III. viii. 380 Of so little consequence are the most destructive arms in untutored and unpractised hands. 1865 F. PARKMAN *Champlain* iv. (1875) 240 A scene oddly portrayed by the untutored pencil of Champlain.

**d.** Of places or conditions.

1751 W. WHITEHEAD *Hymn to Nymph* 312 Ev'n then, the scene We now behold to such perfection wrought, Charm'd with untutor'd wildness. 1760 W. SMITH *Disc. Public Occas.* (1762) 119 The Propagation of Christ's religion through the untutored parts of the earth. 1796 MME. D'ARBLAY *Camilla* V. 204 The children of untutored nature. 1809 WORDSW. *Poems Nat. Indep. & Liberty* II. xiii, Is it among rude, untutored Dales..only, that the heart is true? 1887 *Cornh. Mag.* Jan. 39 A camping-out expedition in the untutored woodlands.

**2.** Not produced or formed as the result of education or training; not improved by instruction.

1593 SHAKS. *Lucr.* Ded., The worth of my vntutord Lines. 1644 MILTON *Educ.* 2 Besides the ill habit which they get of wretched barbarizing..with their untutor'd Anglicisms. 1744 AKENSIDE *Pleas. Imag.* I. 422 The gracious Power Who first awakened my untutored song. 1768 BOSWELL *Corsica* iii. (ed. 2) 196 Those heroes whose untutored patriotism had shone with such lustre. 1788 GIBBON *Decl. & F.* xliv. IV. 334 The laws of marriage,..the authority of parents,..are ascribed to the untutored wisdom of Romulus. 1810 CRABBE *Borough* i. 122 We prune our hedges, prime our slender trees, And nothing looks untutor'd and at ease. 1859 JEPHSON *Brittany* v. 61 The rough untutored vocal expression of worship offered by a whole congregation. 1873 SYMONDS *Grk. Poets* viii. 251 The peculiar glories of Aristophanes style are its untutored beauties.

**3.** Not subject to a tutor or tutors.

1641 MILTON *Reform.* II. 72 Where under a free, and untutor'd Monarch, the..most prudent men..have in their power the supreame..determination of highest Affaires.

† **Untwi·ght,** *pa. pple. Obs.* [UN-[1] 8 b. Phaer also uses *twight* for 'touched'.] Untouched: intact.

1558 PHAER *Æneid* I. B j, For her to him her father gaue a virgyn yet ontwight. *Ibid.* II. C iv b, Whiles yet hys kingdom stood ontwight.

† **Untwi·nd,** *v. Obs. rare.* [UN-[2] 3.] = next. Hence **Untwi·nding** *vbl. sb.*

*c* 1460 *Promp. Parv.* (Winch.) 323 On-wyyndyn or ontwyndyn, *destorqueo.* *a* 1542 WYATT *Penit. Ps.* xxxvii. 104 All wicked folk reversed shall untwind. 1592 WYRLEY *Armorie* 34 Their linked chaines do binde Bigge ships so fast, they cannot soone vntwinde. 1597 SHAKS. 2 *Hen. IV*, II. iv. 213 Why then let..gaping Wounds vntwin'd the Sisters three. 1608 MACHIN *Dumb Knt.* II. D 2 b, Euen with ease, and gentle tangled knots, Thou shalt vntwind thy clew of miseries. 1642 R. CARPENTER *Experience* III. v. 47 The untwinding of my heart from all idle affection to these low base things of earth.

**Untwi·ne,** *v.* [UN-[2] 3. Cf. WFris. *ont-, untwine*, Du. *onttwijnen.*]

**1.** *trans.* To untwist; to undo by untwisting or disentangling. Freq. in fig. context.

*c* 1407 LYDG. *Reson & Sens.* 1252 To shewen..How the threde shal be vntwyned Of hir lyf. 1447 BOKENHAM *Seyntys* (Roxb.) 43 Or than deth the threed untwyne Of oure fatal web. 1551 T. WILSON *Logike* B ij b, Knitting together true Argumentes, and vntwining all knotty Subtiltees. 1577 HOLINSHED *Chron.* I. *Hist. Irel.* 14/1 This knotte (saith our Authour) might be vntwyned with more facilitie thus. 1601 CAMPION *Bk. of Ayres* II. ix. 6 The sprites..Affect for pastime to vntwine her tressed haire. *a* 1656 HALES *Gold. Rem.* III. (1673) 24 Idleness, Fulness, and Lust, they are a three-fold cord, twisted by the devil, and hardly untwined and severed by any man. *a* 1687 WALLER *Thyrsis, Galatea* 41 Since the Sisters did so soon untwine So fair a thread, I'll strive to piece the line. 1789 BURNS '*O Poortith cauld*' i, O why should Fate sic pleasure have, Life's dearest bands untwining? 1813 SCOTT *Rokeby* III. xxii, On his sad brow nor mirth nor wine Could e'er one wrinkled knot untwine. 1847 J. MARTINEAU *Chr. Life* 347 Philosophy..endeavours to untwine the finished web of thought.

**b.** *fig.* To dissolve, undo, destroy.

13.. *E. E. Allit. P.* B. 757 'What for twenty,' quoth þe tolke, 'vntwynez þou hem þenne?' *a* 1470 HARDING *Chron.* LXXIII. v, With hoost full great of Britons..On Douglas water the Saxons he did vntwine. 1523 SKELTON *Garl. Laurel* 1445 This goodly flowre with stormis was vntwynde. *a* 1529 — *P. Sparowe* 282 O cat..,The fynde was in thy mynde Whan thou my byrde untwynde. 1560 DAUS tr. *Sleidane's Comm.* 274 b, So did also the frendshyp..not a litle greue you and full ofte haue assayed that the same might be vntwyned. 1594 CAREW *Huarte's Exam. Wits* 322 At the instant when he beginneth to be shaped, he likewise beginneth to be vntwined. 1625 QUARLES *Sion's Sonn.* ix. 1 The world cannot vntwine The joyfull vnion of His heart, and Mine. 1718 POPE *Iliad* XVI. 950 There ends thy glory! there the fates untwine The last, black remnant of so bright a line.

**2.** To detach, remove, release, extract, by untwisting. Also *fig.*

*a* 1568 ASCHAM *Scholem.* I. (Arb.) 75 Whom all the Siren songes of Italie could neuer vntwyne from the maste of Gods word. 1582 STANYHURST *Æneis* IV. (Arb.) 108 When death hath vntwined my soule from carcas his holding. 1600 FAIRFAX *Tasso* XX. cxxx, His strong arme..She would haue thrust away, loos'd, and vntwin'd. 1611 SHAKS. *Cymb.* IV. ii. 59 Let the stinking-Elder (Greefe) vntwine His perishing roote with the encreasing Vine. 1799 SHERIDAN *Pizarro* I. i, He sued to..untwine the sword from my determined grasp. 1841 BROWNING *Pippa* Introd. 199 Untwine me from the mass Of deeds which make up life. 1846 LANDOR *Imag. Conv.* Wks. II. 46/2 Some privy councillor..come to untwine and wheedle your secrets out of you.

**3.** *intr.* To become untwisted or undone.

1592 *Arden of Feversham* IV. iv. 80 What, so familiare?..Vntwyne those armes. *Ales.* I, with a sugred kisse let them vntwine. 1644 MILTON *Divorce* (ed. 2) vi. 14 For strait..his silk'n breades untwine, and slip their knots. 1871 B. TAYLOR *Faust* II. III. 266 Soon shall, I fear me, The sweet bond untwine!

Hence **Untwi·ning** *vbl. sb.*

1577 HOLINSHED *Chron.* I. *Hist. Irel.* 1 b, And that our Irishe hystorie..yeeldeth al these commodities, I trust the indifferent reader, vpon the vntwyning thereof, will not denie. 1626 BACON *Sylva* § 494 Which is caused by the untwining of the Beard by the Moisture. 1664 POWER *Exp. Philos.* III. 177 Our thread by often untwining broke it self.

**Untwi·neable,** *a.* (UN-[1] 7 b.) 1609 J. MELTON *Sixefold Politician* v. 73 That damnable and vntwineable traine and owsell of perdition. 1617 J. MOORE *Mappe Mans Mort.* III. viii. 234 The most strong and untwineable cable. **Untwi·ned,** *ppl. a.* (UN-[1] 8, or f. UNTWINE *v.*) 1649 LOVELACE *Lucasta, A Forsaken Lady* v, Must we..Be dragg'd on still By the weake Cordage of your untwin'd will? **Untwi·nkling,** *ppl. a.* (UN-[1] 10.) 1880 AGNES GIBERNE *Sun, Moon & Stars* 175 A brilliant untwinkling star-like form.

† **Untwi·nned,** *ppl. a.*[1] *Obs.*[−1] [UN-[1] 8.] Unparted, undivided. *c* 1450 *Mirour Saluacioun* (Roxb.) 1 Ye blyssed Trinitee In o substaunce vntwynned. **Untwi·nned,** *ppl. a.*[2] [UN-[1] 8.] *Cryst.* Not furnished with a twin. 1879 RUTLEY *Stud. Rocks* x. 97 Untwinned crystals [of albite] are rare. 1888 — *Rock-forming Min.* 227. **Untwi·rl,** *v.* (UN-[2] 3.) *a* 1703 WALLIS in Greenwood *Eng. Gram.* (1711) 283 Untwirling the twine that intwisteth between. **Untwi·st,** *sb.* [UN-[2] 3, 8.] A reversive twist. 1889 *Telegr. Jrnl.* 26 April 467/2 Each coil of the cable..as it comes out receives a twist in the opposite direction, or 'untwist'.

**Untwi·st,** *v.* [UN-[2] 3 and 7.]

**1.** *trans.* To restore from a twisted state; to untwine. Also in fig. context.

1538 ELYOT, *Retexo*, to vntwyste. 1587 GREENE *Penelope's Web* Wks. (Grosart) V. 151 A shift to make her work endlesse, by vntwisting as much in the night as she woue in the day. *c* 1590 L. BRYSKETT *Mourning Muse* 148 Which made them eftsoones feare the daies of Pirrha shold..their fatall threds vntwist. 1626 JACKSON *Creed* VIII. x. § 1 The Sonne of God..began to untwist that triple cord, wherewith our first parents..were bound by Satan. 1632 MILTON *L'Allegro* 143 Untwisting all the chains that ty The hidden soul of harmony. 1700 DRYDEN *Ovid, Pythagorean Philos.* 381 Restless they soon untwist the Web they spun. 1731 SWIFT *Nymph going to Bed* 19 She..Untwists a wire, and from her gums A set of teeth completely comes. 1760 R. BROWN *Compl. Farmer* II. 68 Hempen ropes cut small and untwisted, are beneficial [as manure] for lands. 1823 J. BADCOCK *Dom. Amusem.* 54 Hop plants, growing round a pole ..; if you untwist any, and confine them in the contrary direction, they die. *a* 1834 COLERIDGE *Friend* (1837) III. 213 Cutting the knot which it cannot untwist. 1860 GEO. ELIOT *Mill on Fl.* III. vi, Bob had drawn out..[and began] to untwist his canvas bag.

*transf.* 1834 COLERIDGE *Table-t.* (1835) II. 295 A serpent ..makes a fulcrum of its own body, and seems for ever twisting and untwisting its own strength.

**b.** *fig.* and in fig. context. To dissolve, break up, decompose.

1611 SPEED *Hist. Gt. Brit* VIII. vii. § 39. 408 The English supposing the Normans to have fled,..began in eager pursuit carelesly to vntwist and display their ranckes. 1640 SIR J. WRAY *Speech* in Rushworth *Hist. Coll.* (1692) I. 40 The Divisions of Great Britain have half untwisted our Long Union. *a* 1644 QUARLES *Hieroglyphikes* I. 21 Whose errour-chacing beams..untwist The clouds of ignorance. 1653 JER. TAYLOR *Serm. Year* I. xiii. 168 The faith of very many men, seems a duty so weak.., is so often untwisted by violence, or ravel'd and intangled in weak discourses. 1727 THOMSON *To Mem. Newton* 98 Ev'n light itself..Shone undiscover'd, till his brighter mind Untwisted all the shining robe of day. 1751 WARBURTON *Pope's Wks.* I. 105 *note*, The prismatic glass..untwisting, by its obliquities, those threads of light. 1896 A. AUSTIN *England's Darling* I. i, The outlandish dogs..Untwisting what he bound, and to their will Enserfing all.

† **2.** To disentangle by explanation or exposition; to expound, make plain. *Obs.*

1577 tr. *Bullinger's Decades* 5/2 This is the brief summe of the holy fathers tradition, whiche it is best to vntwist more largely. 1606 SYLVESTER *Du Bartas* II. iv. *Magnif.* 1314 Hee..at pleasure frees Such doubts, as..might have taskt, t'untwist, The Brachman, Druide, and Gymnosophist. *a* 1625 FLETCHER *Woman Pleas'd* v. i, Tis a Witch sure, And by her means he came to untwist this Riddle. 1660 JER. TAYLOR *Worthy Commun.* Introd. 8 The Holy Communion..is too much untwisted and nicely handled by the writings of the Doctors. 1773 TOPLADY in Boswell *Johnson* 7 May, You have untwisted this difficult subject with great dexterity.

**3.** To loosen, detach, or set free, by untwining. Also *fig.*

1637 S. MARMION *Cupid & Psyche* I. iii. 394 He took her wrist, And wrung it hard, and did her hands untwist. 1638 SIR T. HERBERT *Trav.* (ed. 2) 167 A raging storme..separated us; insomuch as we had hardly recovered our companies, had not the..jingling of the Cammells bells revoked, yea untwisted us out of these Caspian or Zagrian straits. *a* 1652 J. SMITH *Sel. Disc.* iv. 86 Our souls,..untwisting themselves from all corporeal complications. 1692 DRYDEN *Don Sebastian* III. i, *Alm.* How can we better dye than close embrac'd, Sucking each others Souls while we expire?..*Emp.* No I'll untwist you: I have occasion for your stay on Earth.

**4.** *intr.* To pass out of a twisted condition; to become untwined.

1589 PUTTENHAM *Eng. Poesie* III. xviii. 156, I will well that ye wist, The thred is spon, that neuer shall vntwist. *a* 1703 WALLIS in Greenwood *Eng. Gram.* (1711) 282 If one of the twines of the twist do untwist, The twine that untwisteth, untwisteth the twist. 1728 CHAMBERS *Cycl.* s.v. *Hygrometer*, The Cord or Gut twisting and untwisting.. will indicate the Change of Moisture. 1786 BONNYCASTLE *Astronomy* xi. 184 As the thread untwists, the globe..will turn round its axis. 1825 J. NICHOLSON *Operat. Mechanic* 435 Either of the two palls *x* and *y* may..prevent the strands from untwisting. 1897 GRANT ALLEN *Type-writer Girl* i, There..you shall see spring buds untwisting.

*fig.* 1653 JER. TAYLOR *Serm. for Year* I. ii. 22 His purposes untwist as easily as the rude conjuncture of uncombining cables. 1670 EACHARD *Cont. Clergy* 67 Sometimes the words naturally fall asunder;..sometimes they untwist.

Hence **Untwi·st** *ppl. a.*, = UNTWISTED *ppl. a.*[2]

1607 MARSTON *What you will* II. i, My spirit is untwist; My heart is raveld out in discontents. 1647 N. WARD *Simple Cobler* 30 When States dishelv'd [= dishevelled] are, and lawes untwist, Wise men keep their tongues. 1651 JER. TAYLOR *Serm. for Year* II. xv. 190 By little and little our strongest resolutions be untwist, and crack in sunder.

**Untwi·stable,** *a.* (UN-[1] 7 b.) 1816 *Monthly Mag.* XLII. 521 The origin of the profoundest impressions, and the most untwistable associations. 1879 THOMSON & TAIT *Nat. Phil.* I. I. § 109 A perfectly flexible, untwistable cord.

**Untwi·sted,** *ppl. a.*[1] [UN-[1] 8.] Not twisted or twined.

1575 TURBERV. *Faulconrie* 97 Threade it with untwisted threade. 1825 J. NEAL *Bro. Jonathan* III. 323 Have you forgotten..how you broke away from us like the Philistine from the untwisted flax? 1865 TYLOR *Early Hist. Man.* vii. 188 The warp consists of strands of un-twisted fibre. 1866 R. M. FERGUSON *Electr.* 21 A magnetic bar, suspended by.. a few untwisted filaments of cocoon silk.

**Untwi·sted,** *ppl. a.*[2] [f. UNTWIST *v.*] Taken out of a twisted state.

1611 FLORIO, *Sfilaccio*, okame of vntwisted ropes. 1629 FORD *Lover's Melancholy* IV. 59 If the Fates Haue spun my thred and my spent clue of life Be now vntwisted. ? 1738 WARBURTON *Div. Legat.* II. App. (R.), The solar light is not less real in the rainbow where it's rays become thus untwisted. 1848 BUCKLEY *Iliad* 26 The ropes have become untwisted.

*fig.* *a* 1700 B. E. *Dict. Cant. Crew*, *Untwisted*, Undone, Ruin'd. 1756 *Monitor* No. 35. I. 329 Mrs. Bull..cries out, ..Lord, Doctor! we are all untwisted, all undone. 1785 GROSE *Dict. Vulgar T.* s.v.

**Untwi·sting,** *vbl. sb.* [f. UNTWIST *v.*] The action or result of taking out of twist; also *pl.*, untwisted fibres or threads.

1591 PERCIVALL, *Deshiladura*, vntwisting. 1611 FLORIO, *Sfiaccij*, vntwistings, rauelings, lint for Chirurgions. 1651 BAXTER *Inf. Bapt.* 92 There should be no difficulty in the untwisting of all this which Mr. T. hath so ravelled. 1728 CHAMBERS *Cycl.* s.v. *Hygrometer*, This alternate Twisting and Untwisting in a Cord. 1875 R. F. MARTIN tr. *Havrez' Winding Mach.* 27 Without any untwisting of the eight strands.

**Untwi·tted,** *ppl. a.* (UN-[1] 8.) 1651 H. VAUGHAN *Of the Benefit by our Enemies* ad fin., Neither must wee leave them untwitted with that [saying] of Solon. † **Untwi·tten,** *ppl. a. Obs.*[−1] (Meaning obscure.) 1613 R. C. *Times' Whistle* (1871) 132 When every gull may see his booke's vntwitten, And Epigrams as bad as e're were written.

**Unty·ing,** *vbl. sb.* [f. UNTIE *v.*] The action of the vb.

1597 A.M. tr. *Guillemeau's Fr. Chirurg.* 45 b/2 Concerninge the vntyinge [of a bandage]. *a* 1637 B. JONSON *Horace's Art Poetrie* 274 Nor must the fable..have a god come in; except a knot Worth his untying happen there. 1644 HUNTON *Vind. Treat. Monarchy* vii. 55 The non observance of it by the King did not amount to an untying of the bond of subjection in the people. 1668 DRYDEN *Ess.* (ed. Ker) I. 86 For the contrivance of the plot, 'tis..withal easy; for the ..untying of it, 'tis so admirable, that [etc.]. *a* 1844 CAMPBELL *Song*, '*How delicious*' i, When two mutual hearts are sighing For the knot there's no untying. 1891 T. HARDY *Tess* xlvii, Tess..was one of those who best combined strength with quickness in untying.

**Unty·pical,** *a.* (UN-[1] 7.) 1848 MOZLEY *Ess.* (1878) I. 345 It is not untypical of Luther's temper. 1884 *Harper's Mag.* Apr. 771/2 An instance, not untypical of London. † **Unty3tel,** *adv. Obs.*[−1] (Obscure; perh. an error for *unsty3tel*: see STIGHTLE *v.*) 13.. *Gaw. & Gr. Knt.* 1114 Þay dronken & daylyeden, & dalten vnty3tel.

† **Unu·lcerate,** *ppl. a. Obs.* (UN-[1] 8 b.) 1590 BARROUGH *Meth. Physick* v. xxvi. (1596) 356 Of an vnulcerate cancre, there often proceedeth an vlcerate tumor. 1634 *Lowe's Chirurg.* (ed. 3) IV. xvi. 115 The unulcerate [cancer], is called the hidden Cancer. **Unu·lcerated,** *ppl. a.* (UN-[1] 8.) [1775 ASH.] 1879 *St. George's Hosp. Rep.* IX. 431 The ileum presented several as yet unulcerated swellings. **Unu·llaged,** *ppl. a.* (UN-[1] 8.) 1646 in Picton *L'pool Munic. Rec.* (1883) I. 180, 65 tunnes of un-ulleged Wynes. **Un-u·ltra,** *a.* (UN-[1] 7.) 1817 LADY GRANVILLE *Lett.* (1894) I. 97 He says these unultra men have neither the *petit maître* or grand polished manner of *vieille cour* Frenchmen.

**Ununderstandable,** *a.* (UN-[1] 7 b.)

*a* 1631 DONNE *Serm.* i. (1634) 8 Let him have known..ununderstandable things, unrevealed decrees of God. *a* 1843 SOUTHEY *Common-pl. Bk.* Ser. II. (1849) 251 The vile and ununderstandable Machabeo he ranks with Homer and Virgil! 1872 BRIERLEY *Cotters of Mossburn* xxiv. 252 There is something very 'ununderstandable' going on between Luke Brundrett and Miss Louisa Gerrard. 1891 H. HERMAN *His Angel* 46 He stammered a few un-understandable words.

**Ununderstanding,** *ppl. a.* (UN-[1] 10, 5 b.)

1611 FLORIO, *Ininteligente*, vnunderstanding. *a* 1658 LOVELACE *Lucasta, Peinture*, Let's walk hand in hand, And smile at this un-understanding land. 1862 MRS. N. CROSLAND *Mrs. Blake* II. 219, I know that the most crystalline phrases ..have been dragged through the mud of common un-'understanding' usage. 1891 H. HERMAN *His Angel* 77 The thoughtless ununderstanding girl was gone, and a blushing..woman stood there in her stead.

**Ununderstoo·d,** *ppl. a.* (UN-[1] 8 b.)

1639 FULLER *Holy War* IV. v. 174 With us they consent in ..the overplus of Merits, Services ununderstood, Indulgences. 1655 — *Ch. Hist.* IX. i. § 50 English being..in the most Parishes of Wales utterly un-understood. 1860 PUSEY *Min. Proph.* 537 The deep saying, ununderstood even by Joseph and Mary. 1880 BARING-GOULD *Mehalah* vii, Some such vague sea of ununderstood, unestimated elements.

**Unu·nified,** *ppl. a.* (UN-[1] 8.) 1862 H. SPENCER *First Princ.* § 37 Knowledge of the lowest kind is ununified.

**Ununiform** (vnyū·nifǫɹm), *a.* (UN-[1] 7.)

1659 ALLESTREE *Gentl. Calling* v. § 25. 85 Nor will they be so Ununiform, as not to have their Drink bear a full proportion with their Meat. 1697 COLLIER *Ess. Mor. Subj.* I. 101 How patched and ununiform does it..make the Figure of some Families? 1749 HURD *Hor. Ars Poet.* 54 Let the manners be uniform, or, if ununiform, yet consistently so, or uniformly ununiform. 1842 GWILT *Archit.* Gloss. s.v. *Casting*, The ununiform texture of the material.

**Unu·niformed,** *a.* (UN-[1] 9.) 1867 MOTLEY *Corr.* (1887) II. 263, I, of course, was ununiformed, having left my official finery at Vienna. 1898 D. C. MURRAY *Tales* 140 Uniformed and ununiformed men were chaffing each other. **Ununifo·rmity.** (UN-[1] 12.) 1749 HURD *Hor. Ars Poet.* 54 Here is a manifest ununiformity. 1803 *Monthly Mag.* XV. 3 We now reserve only enough of the diphthongal spelling to add to the un-uniformity of our very anomalous language. **Unu·niformly,** *adv.* (UN-[1] 11.) 1656 [? J. SERGEANT] tr. *T. White's Peripat. Inst.* 171 It must alwayes be mov'd ununiformly. 1891 C. CHAPMAN *Preorganic Evol.* 166 Any one familiar with the action of physical laws in masses of matter *un*uniformly composed and related *un*symmetrically to 'forces external to it'. **Unu·niformness.** (UN-[1] 12. Cf. UNUNIFORM *a.*) **1716** S. CLARKE *Several Lett.* 41 The different Attributes of which One Uniform Being are not a Variety of Parts, or an un-Uniformness (if I may so speak) of the Necessity by which it exists; but [etc.]. **Ununi·table,** *a.* (UN-[1] 7 b.) **1678** CUDWORTH *Intell. Syst.* 564 Minds or Intellects..who also are absolutely Ununitable to any Bodies. **1881** P. BROOKS *Candle of Lord* 183 To us they seem to stand opposite, even against each other, ununited, ununitable. **Ununi·tableness.** (UN-[1] 12.) **1664** H. MORE *Myst. Iniq.* 336 The Ununitableness of the Kings of the Age into one Head. †**Ununi·te,** *v. Obs.* [UN-[1] 14.] *trans.* To abstain from uniting. **1596** R. L[INCHE] *Diella*, etc. F 1 b, You ruthlesse Fates.., Why ioy you so in vnuniting vs?

**Ununited** (vnyunəi·tėd), *ppl. a.* (UN-[1] 8.)

**1587** GOLDING *De Mornay* ii. 19 In vnvnited diuersitie wee finde waste. **1626** SIR D. DIGGES *Sp.* in Rushw. *Hist. Coll.* (1659) I. 302 Scotland..ununited, Ireland not setled in peace. **1678** CUDWORTH *Intell. Syst.* 795 In the World to come, they should..continue Pure Souls, Ununited to any Body. **1736** BUTLER *Anal.* I. iii. 59 Ten Men united, might be able to accomplish, what ten thousand..wholly ununited, could not. **1738** WARBURTON *Div. Legat.* I. 251 Unsupported by, and ununited with the State. **1852** M. ARNOLD *Tristr. & Iseult* II. 89 But, since living we were ununited, Go not far.. from my grave. **1872** ERICHSEN *Surg.* (ed. 6) I. 301 Ununited Fractures and False Joints.

**Ununive·rsitied,** *ppl. a.* (UN-[2] 4 and 8.) **1655** FULLER *Hist. Camb.* 14 On the Kings letters Patents Northampton was un-universitied, the Scholars therein returning to the place from whence they came.

**Unupbrai·ded,** *ppl. a.* (UN-[1] 8.)

**1682** MRS. BEHN *City-Heiress* II. ii, Knowest thou not he has abus'd my fame, And does he think to pass thus unupbraided? **1683** — *Ovid's Ep. Oenone to Paris* 239 Then unupbraided with my wrongs thou'dst been. **1746** YOUNG *Nt. Th.* IX. 695 Nor stands thy wrath depriv'd of its reproof, Or un-upbraided by this radiant choir. **1864** SWINBURNE *Atalanta* 1668 Each unupbraided, each without rebuke Convicted.

**Unupbrai·ding,** *ppl. a.* (UN-[1] 10.)

**1780** *Mirror* No. 109, The quiet and unupbraiding sorrows of Louisa. **1816** L. RICHMOND *Let.* in Grimshawe *Mem.* (1828) 362 Your affectionate unupbraiding, and liberal conduct. **1831** W. SEWELL *Clergym. Recreat.* (1835) 89 Friends whom we lov'd in anguish hide Their unupbraiding look.

**Unupbrai·dingly,** *adv.* (UN-[1] 11.) *a* **1711** KEN *Hymns Evang.* Poet. Wks. 1721 I. 96 A Conscience unupbraidingly sincere. **Unuphe·ld,** *ppl. a.* (UN-[1] 8 b.) **1827** POLLOK *Course T.* VI. 630 God of truth!..Thyself unmade, ungoverned, unupheld! **1850** NICHOL *Archit. Heav.* 241 Shall aught that it contains be unupheld by the same preserving law? **Unuplifted,** *ppl. a.* (UN-[1] 8.) **1802** WORDSW. *Excurs.* II. 575 Resting on its lid In silent grief their unuplifted heads. **1833** — '*Most sweet it is*' i With unuplifted eyes To pace the ground. **1891** J. L. ALLEN *Sister Dolorosa* x, She passed him with unuplifted eyes. **Unu·pright,** *a.* (UN-[1] 7.) **1585** *Reg. Privy Council Scot.* III. 758 Throw sik craftie and unupricht dealing. [**1775** ASH.] **Unu·prightness.** (UN-[1] 12.) *a* **1680** T. GOODWIN *Work Holy Ghost* III. v, That sense of his sin and own Un-uprightness. **Unurba·ne,** *a.* (UN-[1] 7.) **1759** STERNE *Tr. Shandy* II. ii, So, Sir Critic, I could have replied; but I scorn it. 'Tis language unurbane. †**Unu·rred,** *a. Obs.*[-1] [UN-[1] 9 + *ure* EURE *sb.*] Unfortunate, unhappy. *c* **1510** *Songs* (MS. Royal, App. 58) in *Anglia* XII. 266 But kepe hyt styll yn remembrance With my vnvrid desteny.

† **Unu·red,** *ppl. a. Obs.* [UN-[1] 8 + URE *v.*] Unaccustomed, unused.

**1567** DRANT *Hor., Sat.* I. x, A Greek poeme I dreamed to indite, (A Romaine I disioynde by sea, vnured so to write). **1610** *Histrio-m.* II. 241 This toung's unur'd to carpe or contrary.

**Unu·rged,** *ppl. a.* [UN-[1] 8.]

**1.** Not urged or incited to some course of action.

**1590** SHAKS. *Com. Err.* II. ii. 115 The time was once, when thou vn-vrg'd wouldst vow, That neuer words were musicke to thine eare. **1628** FELTHAM *Resolves* I. xxxv. 33 If hee reueales ought vn-vrged, my aduice is..free. **1648** HERRICK *Hesper., Twelfe Night* iii, Let not a man then be seen here, Who unurg'd will not drinke. **1838** FR. A. KEMBLE *Rec. Later Life* I. 187 [The] teeming soil produced, unurged, the means of life. **1868** GEO. ELIOT *Sp. Gipsy* 243 You..are brave, unurged by aught Save the sweet overflow of your good will.

**2.** Not thrust or pressed upon one.

**1594** KYD *Cornelia* IV. i. 160 Shall we then..Submit vs to vnurged slauerie? **1595** SHAKS. *John* v. ii. 10 Albeit we sweare..an vn-urg'd Faith, To your proceedings. *a* **1614** DONNE Βιαθανατος (1644) 37 Augustine, Anselm, and Hierome, betray themselves by unurged confessions. *a* **1689** MRS. BEHN *Fair Jilt* (1887) 33 She leaves nothing unurged that might debauch and invite him. **1728** ELIZA HEYWOOD tr. *Mme. de Gomez's Belle A.* (1732) II. 128 Being one day alone with his Son, he..left unurg'd those Arguments which he had prepar'd in his Mind.

**Unu·rn,** *v.* (UN-[2] 5.) **1837** A. TENNENT *Vis. Glencoe* 48 Foul human relics grisly shown,..From the dark grave unurn'd. **Unu·rned,** *ppl. a.* (UN-[1] 8.) **1830** MANGAN *Poems* (1903) 284 What time my unurned Ashes lie trodden in the churchyard dell. **1834** LD. HOUGHTON *Mem. Tour in Greece* 95 Let him not be deeply mourned, As dead inglorious, or cast out unurned.

**Unu·sable,** *a.* (UN-[1] 7 b.) **1825** SYD. SMITH *Wks.* (1850) 418 All seems doubly dear in proportion as it is antiquated, worthless, and unusable. **1884** *Eng. Illustr. Mag.* May 494 [The cave] is now inaccessible and unusable. †**Unu·sage.** *Obs.*[-1] (UN-[1] 12.) *c* **1374** CHAUCER *Boeth.* II. pr. vii. (1868) 57 What for difficulte of weyes and..what for defaute of vnusage [and] entercomunynge of marchaundise [L. *commercii insolentia*]. **Unu·se.** (UN-[1] 12.) **1611** FLORIO, *Indisusanza*, vnuse, disuse. **1835** *Wilson's Tales Borders* I. 289 Allowing..the heel o' a kebbuck to gaun to unuse [= waste]. **1861** DUTTON COOK *P. Foster's Dau.* III. 126 He spoke with that heavy breathing and unuse of the nose peculiar to Jews.

**Unused** (vnyū·zd), *ppl. a.* [UN-[1] 8.]

**1.** Unaccustomed (esp. *to* something, or with inf.).

**1297** R. GLOUC. (Rolls) 4367 Vor þer ȝe abbeþ nou vif ȝer of batayle vn-vsed be. *c* **1449** PECOCK *Repr.* IV. iii. 431 Suche persoones as ben vnkunnyng and vnvsid in vertues. **1538** ELYOT, *Inceduus*, vnvsed to be cutte. *a* **1586** SIDNEY *Arcadia* III. xxvi, So that, unused to a way of courtesie,..he hastily went away. **1604** SHAKS. *Oth.* v. ii. 349 One, whose subdu'd Eyes, Albeit vn-vsed to the melting moode, Drops teares. **1697** DRYDEN *Æneis* x. 815 Æneas couch'd his Spear, Unus'd to Threats, and more unus'd to Fear. **1741–2** GRAY *Agrippina* 17 A thousand haughty hearts, unus'd to shake When a boy frowns. **1796** MME. D'ARBLAY *Camilla* V. 436 [She was] unused to transact any sort of business for herself. **1827** FARADAY *Chem. Manip.* ix. 235 The student who is unused to the examination of papers. **1868** MORRIS *Earthly Par.* I. I. 411 Her gaoler's torches filled with light The dreary place, blinding her unused eyes. **1870** *Ibid.* III. IV. 362 He..felt the golden circle of the crown..upon his unused head.

*transf.* **1617** CAMPION *Third Bk. of Ayres* xxviii. 8 Hils [would prove] too high for my vnused pace.

**2.** Not made use of; unemployed.

**1398** TREVISA *Barth. De P. R.* VI. xxix. (Bodl. MS.), Yren ..rosteþ if it is to longe vnne vsed. *c* **1480** HENRYSON *Fables, Fox, Wolf & H.* ii, The oxin wes vnwsit, ȝoung and licht. **1546** *Sc. Acts, Mary* (1814) II. 472 Þe said remissioune blank & obligatioune..one vsit. **1590** SPENSER *F. Q.* I. viii. 30 A bounch of keyes.., The which vnused rust did ouergrow. **1604** SHAKS. *Ham.* IV. iv. 39 (Q. 2), Sure, he..gaue vs not That capabilitie..To fust in vs vnvsd. **1819** SHELLEY *Cenci* V. iii. 125 Some dull old thing, Some outworn and unused monotony. **1860** FORSTER *Gr. Remonstr.* 37 A maxim not unused by even Norman kings. **1887** *Spectator* 22 Oct. 1415 One of the churches..is unused, being considered dangerous.

**3.** Not in use; unusual; unwonted. Now *arch.*

**1513** DOUGLAS *Æneid* VI. i. 33 By a quent vnvsit [L. *insuetum*] way to knaw, Towart the frosty poil artik he flaw. **1568** GRAFTON *Chron.* II. 390 Inuentyng flatteryng wordes and vnused termes. **1570** T. NORTON tr. *Nowel's Catech.* 32 b, Neither is it vnused among men,..to be suretie..for an other. **1637** G. DANIEL *Genius of Isle* 417 My frozen witts,.. Enlivened by a Splendor far more great, Have vnus'd Raptures. **1671** R. MACWARD *True Non-conf.* 127 Yet I wish you had..forborn the hard and unused expression of an Inward Crown. **1835** BROWNING *Paracelsus* I. 767 In unused conjuncture, When sickness breaks the body. **1867** MORRIS *Jason* VI. 497 Strange dainty things they ate, Of unused savour.

Hence **Unu·sedness.**

**1593** *Sidney's Arcadia* (1598) v. 466 Comparing the vnusednesse of this act with the vnripenesse of their age. **1865** MRS. WHITNEY *Gayworthys* i. (1879) 10 That air of unusedness which a black silk dress..may keep.

**Unuseful** (vnyū·sfŭl), *a.* [UN-[1] 7.] Unprofitable, useless. (Very common in 17th c.)

In later use chiefly with negatives.

**1598** DALLINGTON *Meth. Trav.* V j, Bowling, carding, dicing, and other vnlawful and vnuseful games. **1624** HEYWOOD *Gunaik.* v. 219 Gold and silver they despise,..esteeming it rather an unusefull burden than a profitable merchandize. **1675** GREW *Nature of Mixture* 6 Which Definition..is both Vnintelligible, and Vnuseful. **1726** LEONI *Alberti's Archit.* I. 57 b, A new, and not unuseful Invention. **1788** PRIESTLEY *Lect. Hist.* I. iii. 32 It is no unuseful sentiment that we collect from reading [etc.]. **1817–8** COBBETT *Resid. U. S.* (1822) 216 This may be no unuseful hint for the English Boroughmongers. **1827** J. MONTGOMERY *Pelican Isl.* II. 160 Still-life was theirs, well pleasing to themselves, Nor yet unuseful.

**b.** Const. *to*; also *for, towards.*

**1625** K. LONG tr. *Barclay's Argenis* II. xx. 133 The streamers unusefull to the sailes, and onely hanging for bravery. **1653** H. MORE *Antid. Ath.* II. x. § 3 Birds that will flutter with their wings when..as yet [they are] utterly unuseful for flying. **1733** W. CRAWFORD *Infidelity* xvi, The Law of Nature..became unuseful to the End it was made for. **1756** BURKE *Subl. & B.* IV. i, Something not unuseful towards a distinct knowledge of our passions. **1793** *Residence in France* (1797) II. 10 My ideas..may not be unuseful to.. my countrymen.

**Unu·sefully,** *adv.* [UN-[1] 11. Cf. prec.] Uselessly, unprofitably.

**1626** LD. CONWAY in Rushw. *Hist. Coll.* (1659) I. 231 Whereas divers jealousies have been raised in the House, that the Moneys have been expended unusefully. *a* **1680** GLANVILL *Sadducismus* (1681) I. 180 Such as will not unusefully nor unseasonably conclude this First Part. **1747** *Phil. Trans.* XLIV. 588, I thought it might not unusefully be joined with Alum. **1799** E. DU BOIS *Piece Family Biog.* I. 111 He is not unusefully occupied. **1885** *Manch. Exam.* 12 Jan. 5/1 Prudent men..might discharge such functions not unusefully.

**Unu·sefulness.** [UN-[1] 12.] Uselessness.

**1694** R. BURTHOGGE *Reason* ix. 268 His notion of a Person, the unusefulness of it to the salving of the Holy Trinity shewed. *c* **1850** JAS. SKINNER in *Life* (1883) 120 The notion of —'s usefulness to the Church and of —'s so-called unusefulness is a purely human..notion. **1886** *N. Amer. Rev.* Sept. 304 Frivolous unusefulness, or passion for diversion and excitement.

**Unu·shered,** *ppl. a.* (UN-[1] 8 c.) **1659** W. CHAMBERLAYNE *Pharon.* Introd. A 5 Wonder not, that I appear un-usher'd in with a Train of Encomiums. **1865** W. G. PALGRAVE *Arabia* II. 28 Death unushered in by any direct morbid change. †**Unu·sing,** *vbl. sb. Obs.* (UN-[1] 13.) *c* **1550** CHEKE *Matt.* xxv. 26 Neglecting and vnusing of his commandmentes. **1598** FLORIO, *Disusanza*, disuse, an vnusing. †**Unu·sing,** *ppl. a. Obs.*[-1] [UN-[1] 10.] Not usually resorting. **1605** DANIEL *Philotas* 267 My brother..I left behinde, lest the conspirators Seeing him here vnusing to this place,..might shift away.

**Unu·sual,** *a.* [UN-[1] 7 and 5 b.] Not usual; uncommon; exceptional.

In common use from *c* 1630.

**1582** STANYHURST *Æneis* II. (Arb.) 60 Priamus..On rusty shoulders sloa clapt his vnusual armoure. **1596** SHAKS. *Tam. Shr.* III. ii. 98 Some Commet, or vnusuall prodigie. **1628** WITHER *Brit. Rememb.* 284 God will..Put some vnusuall Plague in execution. **1682** LISTER *Godartius Of Insects* 28 This is a Rare and unusuall Catterpillar. **1724** SWIFT *Drapier's Lett.* iv, A new governor, coming at an unusual time, must portend some unusual business. **1773** *Life N. Frowde* 56, I returned to my Book.., in a Situation quite unusual to what I had ever before experienced. **1821** SCOTT *Kenilw.* xli, Varney received his profligate servant with a rebuke of unusual bitterness. **1877** HUXLEY *Physiogr.* 196 A cloud of unusual size and shape was seen hanging over the mountain.

Hence **Unusua·lity.**

**1799** W. TAYLOR in Robberds *Mem.* (1843) I. 259 They have ..an unusuality which startles. **1807** SOUTHEY *Let. to J. May* 27 Jan., From its unusuality it would have a better chance of being read. *a* **1849** POE *Marginalia* lvi, It is to be said of Sallust..that his obscurity, his unusuality of expression,..bore the impress of his genius.

**Unu·sually,** *adv.* [UN-[1] 11.] In an unusual manner; to an unusual extent; uncommonly, exceptionally.

**1615** CROOKE *Body of Man* 263 If her monthly courses do stop vnvsually. **1620** T. GRANGER *Div. Logike* 246 More obscurely, and vnusually when the negatiue particle is set before the coniunction discretiue. **1796** MME. D'ARBLAY *Camilla* I. 355 Camilla, unusually thoughtful, walked alone into the garden. **1818** SCOTT *Hrt. Midl.* x, She was unusually cross and fretful. **1871** LE FANU *Rose & Key* II. 123 Very unusually for him, he was first to speak.

**Unu·sualness.** [UN-[1] 12.] The quality of being unusual or exceptional.

**1579** W. WILKINSON *Confut. Fam. Love* To Rdr., The vnusualnesse of their Methode. **1626** C. POTTER tr. *Sarpi's Hist. Quarrels* 399 Beleeuing it an indignity (besides the vnusualnesse of the matter) which would diminish his Reputation. **1668** WILKINS *Real Char.* 9 Varying the way of pronunciation, according to the unusualness and difficulty of several sounds to several Countries. **1718** *Entertainer* No. 43. 306 Some Persons..wondered at the Unusualness of his Running in that Place. *a* **1754** CARTE *Hist. Eng.* (1755) IV. 402 The unusualness of the thing served to countenance the unreasonable outcries. **1836** M. SCOTT *Cruise Midge* I. 120 Totally unconscious of the unusualness of their costume. **1876** GEO. ELIOT *Dan. Der.* iv, The answer may seem to be..in..a certain unusualness about her, a decision of will.

† **Unu·suring,** *ppl. a.* (UN-[1] 10.) **1622** MIDDLETON *Hon. & Virt.* in Bullen *O. Pl.* VII. 361 All the wealth Which thou with an unusuring hand hath got.

† **Unu·tile,** *a. Obs.* Also *Sc.* 5 wnwtyle, 6 onutil. [UN-[1] 5 b.] Useless; = INUTILE *a.*

*c* **1425** WYNTOUN *Cron.* II. viii. 700 (Cott. MS.), Þai þat duelt in to þat ile Wnhonest was and wnwtyle. **1541** R. COPLAND *Galyen's Terap.* B iv, But after yᵗ the present dysease is all togyther knowen, than the cause prymytyfe is totally vnutyle. **1549** *Compl. Scot.* 28 The file..is vorne ande cassin auaye as ane thing onutil to serue to do ony gude verk.

**Unu·tilized,** *ppl. a.* (UN-[1] 8, 5 b.) **1868** W. R. GREG *Lit. & Soc. Judgm.* 466 It is too probable that the negro race..is doomed..to pass away neglected and unutilized. **Unutterabi·lity.** (UN-[1] 12. Cf. next.) **1837** CARLYLE *Fr. Rev.* II. I. iii, They come; with hot unutterabilities in their heart.

**Unu·tterable,** *a.* and *sb.* [UN-[1] 7 b, 5 b.]

**A.** *adj.* **1.** Transcending utterance; inexpressible, ineffable; = UNSPEAKABLE *a.* 1.

*a* **1586** SIDNEY *De Mornay* (1587) 33 The vnvtterable cause which Plato teacheth vs vnder two names. **1621** FLETCHER *Thierry & Theod.* II. i, He is, Sir, The most unutterable coward that e'er nature Blest with hard shoulders. **1652** BENLOWES *Theoph.* v. lxxviii, That most unutterable blaze Of Heav'n's all-luminating rays. **1746** HERVEY *Refl. Flower Garden* 115 One transient Glimpse of those unutterable Beatitudes would captivate our souls. **1771** BEATTIE *Minstrel* I. xliv, Hags, that suckle an infernal brood, And ply in caves th' unutterable trade. **1806** J. BERESFORD *Miseries Human Life* IV. xxxii, A barrow of cat's meat, the unutterable contents of which employ your eyes and nose. **1831** JAMES *Phil. Augustus* I. vi, The unutterable multitude of weathercocks, with which every pinnacle of the castle was adorned. **1873** PROCTOR *Expanse Heav.* 304 By unutterable pace the light swept to them.

*absol.* **1896** *Edin. Rev.* Oct. 302 The vision of the utterable passes into the vision of the unutterable.

**b.** Of sorrow, anger, or other emotion.

**1658** T. WALL *Charact. Enemies Ch.* 9 The carnal delights which he has promised you will turn to unutterable dolours of soul. **1697** CONGREVE *Mourn. Bride* IV. vii, What means these Tears, but Grief unutterable? **1707** E. SMITH *Phædra & Hipp.* IV. 50 How it wounds my Soul! To think of your unutterable Sorrows! **1766** GOLDSM. *Vicar* xxix, Our bliss shall be unutterable. **1832** COLERIDGE *Lett.* (1895) 762 Yours, with unutterable and unuttered love and regard. **1880** 'OUIDA' *Moths* II. vi. 185 She turned her face with unutterable scorn..on it.

**c.** In the phr. *unutterable things.*

*a* **1711** KEN *Psyche* Poet. Wks. 1721 IV. 299 Bless'd Paul.. was..heav'nly things unutterable taught. [Cf. 2 Cor. xii. 4.] **1727** THOMSON *Summer* 848 They..talked the flowing Heart, Or sigh'd and look'd unutterable Things! **1791** W. MAXWELL in Boswell *Johnson* (1831) I. 381 Jacob Behmen, whom Law alleged..to have seen *unutterable things.* **1818** BYRON *Juan* I. xc, Juan wander'd by the glassy brooks, Thinking unutterable things. **1873** BLACK *Pr. Thule* ii, Sheila..rarely speaks, but looks unutterable things with her soft..eyes.

**2. a.** That may not be uttered or spoken.

**1656** COWLEY *Davideis* IV. 260 Witness th' unutterable Name, there's nought Of private ends into this question brought. **1708** WATTS *Horæ Lyricæ* (1727) 161 My Tongue ..with a noble Aim Attempts th' unutterable Name, But faints. **1883** WHITELAW *Sophocles, Ajax* 773 Dread words, unutterable, back he flung.

**b.** Incapable of being uttered; unpronounceable.

**1852** *Jrnl. Ethnol. Soc.* (1854) III. 271 The peculiarly harsh, deep-toned guttural, unknown and unutterable to the European. **1867** WHITNEY *Lang.* iii. 95 Sounds..in the alphabet of one tongue which are unutterable by the speakers of another.

**B.** *sb.* **1.** An unutterable thing.

**1788** J. NEWTON in W. Roberts *H. More* (1835) II. 126 The

Apostle Paul..was rapt into the third heavens, saw invisibles, and heard unutterables. **1797** MRS. A. M. BENNETT *Beggar Girl* II. 51 Rosa did not faint or betray any of the unutterables some of our young readers may expect.

**2.** *pl.* Trousers. (Cf. UNMENTIONABLE *sb.*)

**1843** MRS. ROMER *Rhone, Darro*, etc. I. 322 His..short unutterables, garnished down the seams with silver buttons. **1860** *Slang Dict.* 242.

Hence **Unu·tterableness.**

**1681** H. MORE *Exp. Dan.* iii. 75 The ineffableness and unutterableness of the admirable union..of the Humane nature with the Divine. **1890** J. PULSFORD *Loyalty to Christ* I. 162 With what unutterableness of meaning, we breathe the prayer!

**Unu·tterably,** *adv.* [f. prec.] Inexpressibly, indescribably; unspeakably.

**1746** HERVEY *Refl. Flower Garden* 111 At that awful, that unutterably important Juncture. **1801** COLERIDGE *Lett.* (1895) 352, I need not observe..how unutterably silly and contemptible these opinions would be. **1866** MRS. WHITNEY *Leslie Goldthwaite* xi, I'll..thank you unutterably, if you'll only let me have my way in this. **1885** 'MRS. ALEXANDER' *At Bay* viii, The sweet eyes were unutterably sad.

**Unu·ttered,** *ppl. a.* [UN-[1] 8.]

**1.** Not given out in trade. *rare.*

**1463** *Cases bef. King's Council* (Selden) 111 Fer which cause the seid wolles ben yet as by youre seid suppliaunt unuttred. **1618** GAINSFORD *Glory Eng.* I. ix. 77 That the countrey commodities might be vnuttered.

**2.** Not uttered or expressed.

**1651** J. READING *Guide Holy City* 347 Hee cannot know the unuttered secrets of the heart. **1696** TATE & BRADY *Ps.* cxxxix. 4 Thou know'st..My yet un-utter'd Words intent. *a* **1771** GRAY *Dante* 5 Anguish, that unutter'd wrings My inmost Heart. **1798** SOUTHEY *St. Patrick's Purgatory* xxvi, How should he pass that molten flood?..A Fiend, as in a dream, 'Thus!' answer'd the unutter'd thought. **1844** A. B. WELBY *Poems* (1867) 72 As..meeting glances tell The unuttered tale of love. **1883** J. PARKER *Tyne Ch.* 277 Self-control..begins upon the subtle and un-uttered thought.

*absol.* **1843** CARLYLE *Past & Pr.* III. v, The cloudy-browed..Practicality..has in him what transcends all logic-utterance: a Congruity with the Unuttered.

**Unuxo·rial,** *a.* (UN-[1] 7.) **1877** BLACKMORE *Cripps* xxi, Unconjugal, perhaps, is what I mean; unuxorial, or what it may be.

**Unva·ccinated,** *ppl. a.* (UN-[1] 8.) **1871** *Daily News* 28 Jan., We need..somebody to look after unvaccinated children. **1883** LYON PLAYFAIR in *Scotsman* 25 June 7/7 In this way nearly half..of the unvaccinated die. **Unva·cillating,** *ppl. a.* (UN-[1] 10.) **1821** SCOTT *Kenilw.* xvii, Like one..whose only safety consists in moving onwards, by firm and unvacillating steps. **1825** BEDDOES *Let.* in *Poems* (1851) 166 In the unvacillating soar of song. **†Unva·dable,** *a. Obs.*[-0] (UN-[1] 7 b. See VADE *v.*) **1611** COTGR., *Immarcessible*, incorruptible, vnuadeable, vnwitherable.

**Unvail,** obs. f. UNVEIL *v.*

**† Unvai·lable,** *a. Obs.* Also 5 *Sc.* **wnwalable,** 6 **vnuaylable,** etc. [UN-[1] 7 b.] Of no avail; unavailing; useless.

*a* **1500** in *Ratis Raving*, etc. 24 Al that is bot vanite and lycht, transitoure blythnes, wnwalable. **1502** ATKYNSON tr. *De Imitatione* III. l. (1893) 236 Mannes helpe is but vayne & vnuaylable in such nedis. **1612** T. TAYLOR *Comm. Titus* iii. 5 Without which..it would be vnuailable to regeneration. **1679** C. NESSE *Antichrist* 228 Julian the 2d. who threw Peters keys into Tyber as unvaileable.

**Unvai·n,** *a.* (UN-[1] 7.) **1863** COWDEN CLARKE *Shaks. Char.* xvi. 396 Her habit of speech is perceptibly un-vain. **1897** *Harper's Mag.* Apr. 748 A tyrant may be unvain. **Unvaletu·dinary,** *a.* (UN-[1] 7, 5 b.) **1650** BULWER *Anthropomet.* i. 11 This ought not to be accounted among the non-natural or unvaletudinary figures. **†Unva·lid,** *a. Obs.* (UN-[1] 7, 5 b.) **1658** W. BURTON *Itin. Anton.* 172 Where I found not sufficient proof for what I met with,..I rejected it as unvalid. *a* **1660** *Contemp. Hist. Irel.* (Ir. Archæol. Soc.) I. 133 Why did you..embrace such a groundlesse and unvalid a peace?

**Unva·luable,** *a.* [UN-[1] 7 b, 5 b.]

**†1.** Of inestimable value; = INVALUABLE *a.* 1. *Obs.* (Common in 17th c.)

**1569** T. NORTON *Warning agst. Papists* A ij, Thinke vpon the..miseries that we all shalbe like to susteine by losse of her vnualuable presence. **1591** HORSEY *Trav.* (Hakl. Soc.) 160 The riches..caried owt of these citties..was unvaluable. *a* **1616** BEAUM. & FL. *Lit. Fr. Lawyer* III. i, That Jewel, Because it had no flaw, you held unvaluable. **1691** W. NICHOLLS *Answ. Naked Gospel* 21 When he hath sent his only begotten Son..to purchase our Redemption by such an unvaluable price. **1691** RAY *Creation* II. (1692) 4 The use of our Hand, that unvaluable Instrument. **1712** *Lond. Gaz.* No. 5037/6 The Blessings of Peace are unvaluable.

**†b.** Incalculable; = INVALUABLE *a.* 1 b. *Obs.*

**1638** ROUS *Heav. Acad.* 132 It is an unvaluable losse, that men doe so much divide the outward Teacher from the inward. *a* **1661** FULLER *Worthies, Yorks.* III. (1662) 225 Debasing the Forraign estimation of our Cloth to the unvaluable damage of our Nation. *a* **1683** OLDHAM *Rem.* Wks. (1686) 6 Her Dowry..Which..we never gain But with unvaluable Cost.

**2.** Of no value, worthless; = INVALUABLE *a.* 2. Now *rare.*

**1615** T. ADAMS *England's Sickness* 57 If nature..deny health, how vnualuable are their riches. *a* **1674** CLARENDON *Surv. Leviath.* (1676) 55 To render those precious words unvaluable and of no signification. **1728** R. MORRIS *Ess. Anc. Archit.* 89 The unvaluable Deformities of Singleness and Novelty. **1766** *Museum Rust.* VI. 15, I think the burnet so unvaluable, as to design to root it out of my ground. **1860** RUSKIN *Unto this Last* (1862) 118 In proportion as it leads away from life it is unvaluable or malignant.

Hence **Unva·luableness.**

**1665** DK. ORMONDE in Earl Orrery *St. Lett.* (1742) 133 The cry was so great, upon the unvaluableness of the clothes given to the soldiery, that [etc.].

**†Unva·lue,** *v. Obs.*[-1] [UN-[2] 6 b.] *trans.* To deprive of value. **1550** BALE *Eng. Votaries* II. 33 Peruersely alleging Malachyes prophecye, as though [it]..in hys mouthe myght vnualue or dysable their masses.

**Unva·lued,** *ppl. a.* [UN-[1] 8, 5 b.]

**1.** Not estimated or fixed in value; extremely great or valuable. Now *rare.*

**1586** MARLOWE *1st Pt. Tamburl.* I. ii, Whatsoeuer you esteeme of this successe, and losse vnvallued, Both may inuest you Empresse of the East. **1594** SPENSER *Amoretti* lxxvii, There in a siluer dish did ly twoo golden apples of vnualewd price. **1607** MIDDLETON *Fam. Lov.* I. ii, Art or nature never yet could set A valued price to her unvalued worth. **1638** ALEYN *Hen. VII*, 73 He..drew him clad In furniture of an unvalued worth. **1662** H. HIBBERT *Body of Divinity* II. 30 The saving benefits of his unvalued passion. **1713** JOHNSON *Guard.* No. 4 ₱ 3, I have been so happy in my searches..that I have found unvalued repositories of learning. **1736** THOMSON *Liberty* V. 503 The kind Art, that, of unvalu'd price, The fam'd and only picture, easy, gives. **1820** SHELLEY *Arethusa* 60 Through the weltering floods, Over heaps of unvalued stones [= jewels].

**b.** Not subjected to formal valuation.

**1807** *Ann. Rev.* V. 176 If real property, instead of passing entire and unvalued to the heir at law, were put up to the highest bidder.

**2.** Not regarded as of value.

**1602** SHAKS. *Ham.* I. iii. 19 Hee may not, as vnuallued persons doe, Carue for himselfe. **1615** G. WITHER *Fidelia* 707 Though my faith must now despised be, Vnpriz'd, vnualued at the lowest rate. **1670** CLARENDON *Contempl. Ps.* Tracts (1727) 740 The inestimable, tho' unvalued benefit of health, we seldom thank God for. **1823** MRS. HEMANS *Siege Valencia* viii, I have cast Thy life's fair honour, in my wild despair, As an unvalued gem upon the waves. **1852** MRS. STOWE *Uncle Tom's C.* xxxv, A hard-tempered sire, on whom that gentle woman had wasted a world of unvalued love. **1870** LOWELL *Among my Bks.* Ser. I. (1873) 203 Recalling and confirming our own unvalued sensations and perceptions.

**Unva·mped,** *ppl. a.* (UN-[1] 8.) **1638** FORD *Lady's Trial* I. i, The newest news, unvampt. [**1775** ASH.] **1880** *E. Cornwall Gloss.* 105 *Unvamped*, not added to or embellished.

**Unva·nquishable,** *a.* Also 4 **unuenkus-,** 5 *Sc.* **unvencusable.** [UN-[1] 7 b.] Incapable of being vanquished or overcome.

**1382** WYCLIF *Wisd.* v. 20 He shal take the sheeld vnuenkusable. **1456** SIR G. HAYE *Bk. Knychthede* vii. (S.T.S.) 56 Man has..stark curage unvencusable. **1561** T. N[ORTON] tr. *Calvin's Inst.* III. xxi. 239 The vpholdyng stay of sounde affiance..to make vs vnuanquishable among so many dangers. **1613** JACKSON *Creed* I. xxv. § 3 Ouid faines Nisus his vnuanquishable fortune, to haue been seated in one haire. **1657** EARL MONM. tr. *Paruta's Pol. Disc.* 162 He waged War with people..who were till then thought unvanquishable. **1728** ELIZA HEYWOOD tr. *Mme. de Gomez's Belle A.* (1732) II. 76 Able to make some little Incroachments on that Liberty which seem'd unvanquishable. **1813** SHELLEY *Q. Mab* III. 120 Toil and unvanquishable penury. **1865** DICKENS *Mut. Fr.* I. ii, He is only stunned by the unvanquishable difficulty of his existence.

**Unva·nquished,** *ppl. a.* Also 4 **vnuenkushid,** 5 **vnuenquiste,** 6 *Sc.* **unvencust, wnwencust,** etc. [UN-[1] 8.] Not vanquished or overcome; unsubdued.

**1382** WYCLIF *Ecclus.* xviii. 1 God alone..dwelleth vnuenkushid king withoute ende. ? *a* **1400** *Morte Arth.* 2049 The vassalage of Viterbe to daye schalle be reuengede! Vnuenquiste for þis place voyde schalle I neuer! *c* **1510** MORE *Picus* Wks. 23 Enforce thy self..to stande, Unvainquished against the deuils might. **1548** UDALL, etc. *Erasm. Par. John* xvi. 97 b, Ye shalbe through my spirite strong and vnuanquished. **1614** GORGES *Lucan* VI. 221 Deare mates we yet vnuanquisht stand. **1697** DRYDEN *Æneis* IV. 290 Unvanquished Scylla now alone remains. **1770** GLOVER *Leonidas* (ed. 5) II. 49 The gods conceal, how long our strength May stand unvanquish'd. **1820** SHELLEY *Prometh. Unb.* I. 315 'Tis but some passing spasm, The Titan is unvanquished still. **1883** J. PARKER *Apost. Life* II. 279 Such an unvanquished devil mocks the impotent exorcist.

**Unva·ntaged,** *ppl. a.* (UN-[1] 8.) **1791** COWPER *Iliad* XI. 868 Yet, even thus, unvantag'd and on foot, Superiour honours I that day acquir'd To theirs who rode.

**Unva·riable,** *a.* Now *rare.* (UN-[1] 7 b and 5 b.)

*c* **1425** *St. Mary of Oignies* II. vii. in *Anglia* VIII. 169/40 Þe most souerayn sympyl and vnvaryabil mageste. *c* **1440** *Pallad. on Husb.* I. 354 Grauellis dolue in iij naturis vary: In red, & hoor, & blak vnvariable. *a* **1586** SPENSER *De Mornay* (1587) i. 5 Wee must imagine..of all these so constant diuersities, one (vnuariable) alwaies like it selfe. **1624** WOTTON *Elem. Archit.* 8 A steadie and vnuariable light. **1697** COLLIER *Ess. Mor. Subj.* II. 189 It becomes the Greatness of the Deity, to work by the most comprehensive, unvariable Methods. **1738** WARBURTON *Div. Legat.* II. 213 In the fullest and most unvariable Manner. **1759** JOHNSON *Rasselas* xlviii, She..would gladly be fixed in some unvariable state. **1896** W. M. THOMSON *Leaders of Chr. & Anti-Chr.* Th. 7 To impose a fixed and unvariable creed is to build prison walls round the soul.

Hence **Unva·riableness; Unva·riably** *adv.*

**1611** FLORIO, *Inuariabilità*, vnuariablenesse. **1644** FEATLY *Roma Ruens* 7 The immutability of our faith, or unvariablenesse of the doctrine..of the church. **1734** KAMES *Decis. Crt. Sess.* (1799) 13 The real right..continues unvariably the same till the last farthing be recovered.

**Unva·riant,** *a.* [UN-[1] 7, 5 b.] Unchanging. **1582** STANYHURST *Æneis* IV. (Arb.) 111 His mynd vnuariant [L. *immota*] doth stand, tears vaynelye doe gutter.

**Unva·ried,** *ppl. a.* (UN-[1] 8 and 5 b.)

**1570** LEVINS *Manip.* 51 Vnuaried, *inuariatus.* **1690** LOCKE *Hum. Und.* II. xiv. § 13. 87 Whether he can keep one unvaried single Idea in his Mind without any other. **1748** *Anson's Voy.* III. iii. 328 The equable and unvaried character which he had hitherto preserved. **1791** NEWTE *Tour Eng. & Scot.* 2 The unvaried and uninteresting voids of life. **1840** THIRLWALL *Greece* lvii. VII. 241 He seasoned the plain unvaried meal by his cheerful..conversation. **1879** G. ALLEN *Colour Sense* iv. 38 The unvaried panorama of green overhead and brown beneath.

Hence **Unva·riedly** *adv.*

**1780** M. MADAN *Thelyphthora* II. 242 The word..which we have as uniformly and unvariedly translated *adultery.*

**Unva·riegated,** *ppl. a.* (UN-[1] 8.) *a* **1763** SHENSTONE *Ess. Men* Wks. 1768 II. 130 Large, unvariegated, simple objects have the best pretensions to sublimity. **1846** WORCESTER (citing *Edin. Rev.*).

**Unva·rnished,** *ppl. a.* [UN-[1] 8.]

**1.** *fig.* Of statements, etc.: Not embellished or rendered specious; plain, direct.

**1604** SHAKS. *Oth.* I. iii. 90, I will a round vn-varnish'd Tale deliuer, Of my whole course of Loue. **1780** BURKE *Sp. at Bristol* Wks. III. 367 This is a true, unvarnished, undisguised state of the affair. **1790** WOLCOT (P. Pindar) *Adv. Future Laureat* II. i, Were I monarch of this mighty isle! By verse unvarnish'd should my merits smile. **1806** SURR *Winter in Lond.* II. 238 State to this company, without exaggeration, and without palliation, your own unvarnished story! **1883** MISS M. BETHAM-EDWARDS *Disarmed* xxxi, Valerian..had set out with the intention of adhering to the unvarnished truth, but finally ended in romancing.

**b.** Of persons, etc.: Unsophisticated, unpolished; plain and simple.

**1827** POLLOK *Course T.* VIII. 107 A congregation..Of unappendaged and unvarnished men; Of plain, unceremonious human beings. **1831** [MARY BERRY] *Soc. Life Eng. & France* 192 Strong appeals to all the unvarnished feelings of human nature. **1864** MRS. H. WOOD *Verner's Pride* xli, Lady Verner liked Lord Garle..ten times better than she liked unvarnished Jan.

**2.** Not covered with, or as with, varnish.

**1758** REID tr. *Macquer's Chym.* I. 372 Into an unvarnished earthen dish put the quantity of Tin you intend to calcine. **1784** COWPER *Task* VI. 174 The deep dark green of whose unvarnish'd leaf..illumines more The bright profusion of her scatter'd stars. **1875** SIR T. SEATON *Fret-Cutting* 33 The mortification of ultimately finding some place left unvarnished or unfinished.

Hence **Unva·rnishedly** *adv.*

**1824** HOGG *Tales & Sk.* V. 68, I had kept by the naked truth too unvarnishedly.

**Unva·rying,** *ppl. a.* (UN-[1] 10.)

**1690** LOCKE *Hum. Und.* II. xiv. § 18 We cannot keep by us any standing unvarying measure of Duration. **1757** AKENSIDE *Pleas. Imag.* III. 418 With contempt I gazed On that tame garb, and those unvarying paths. *a* **1763** SHENSTONE *Elegies* iii. 52 The generous rustics mourn'd the friendly swain, But Pow'r and Wealth's unvarying cheek was dry! **1803** MATHIAS *Purs. Lit.* (ed. 12) 320 *note*, At the general..Boarding houses, the expences of which are liberal, unvarying, and regulated. **1825** SOUTHEY *Tale of Paraguay* IV. xxx, All was verdant there throughout the unvarying year. **1897** MARY KINGSLEY *W. Africa* 96 Apparently endless walls of mangrove, unvarying in colour, unvarying in form, unvarying in height.

Hence **Unva·ryingly** *adv.*; **Unva·ryingness.**

**1814** SHELLEY *Ess. & Lett.* (1887) 151 Mediocrity alone seems unvaryingly to escape rebuke. **1851** SPENCER *Soc. Stat.* 40 An unvaryingness which renders the eclipse of a hundred years hence predicable to a moment! **1861** GEO. ELIOT *Silas M.* xvii, His..more wavering nature, too averse to facing difficulty to be unvaryingly simple and truthful.

**Unva·scular,** *a.* (UN-[1] 7.) **1846** OWEN *Comp. Anat. Invert.* 224 In the Diodon the dental plates consist wholly of hard or unvascular dentine. **Unvau·lted,** *ppl. a.* (UN-[1] 8.) **1589** IVE *Fortific.* 25 As for the passage from one flanke vnto another, that may bee left vnuaulted. **1777** T. WARTON *Ode Vale-Royal Abbey* 51 Beneath yon tower's unvaulted gate, Forlorn she sits. **Unvau·lting,** *ppl. a.* (UN-[1] 10.) **1797** MATHIAS *Purs. Lit.* IV. 338 Yet with unvaulting sober wishes blest, Ambition fled with envy from my breast.

**Unvei·l,** *v.* [UN-[2] 4 and 4 b.]

**1.** *trans.* To free (the eyes, etc.) from a veil so as to give clearer sight. Also in fig. context.

**1599** *Warn. Faire Wom.* II. 872 Now she unvailes their sight, and lets them see The horror of their foule immanity. **1650** HUBBERT *Pill Formality* 109 Hereby the understanding is unvailed. **1678** BUTLER *Hud.* III. II. 1085 Truth no more unvail'd your Eyes, Than Maggots are convinc'd to Flies.

**2.** To disclose, display, allow to appear, by removing a veil or covering.

**1657** THORNLEY tr. *Longus' Daphnis & Chloe* 43 Daphnis..could not be merry, because he had seen..her beauty which before was not unvailed. **1692** DRYDEN *Don Sebastian* I. i, Unveil the Woman; I wou'd view the Face That warm'd our Mufti's Zeal. **1754** GRAY *Progr. Poesy* 86 What time..To him the mighty Mother did unveil Her awful face. **1797** MRS. RADCLIFFE *Italian* xxvii, I claim the privilege..awarded me, and bid you unveil your countenance. **1817** SHELLEY *Rev. Islam* I. xx, She unveiled her bosom. **1820** — *Witch Atlas* Ded. vi, If you unveil my Witch, no priest nor primate Can shrive you of that sin.

*fig.* **1667** MILTON *P. L.* IV. 608 Till the Moon Rising in clouded Majestie, at length Apparent Queen unvaild her peerless light. **1725** POPE *Odyssey* VI. 36 When the gay morn unveils her smiling ray. **1747** HERVEY *Contempl. Night* (1748) II. 81 She unveils her peerless Light, and becomes 'the Beauty of Heaven'.

**b.** *absol.* and *refl.* Also *fig.*

**1770** GLOVER *Leonidas* (ed. 5) X. 170 She unveils, Then with a voice, a countenance compos'd, Go, Medon [etc.]. **1819** SCOTT *Ivanhoe* xxxvii, The Grand Master commanded Rebecca to unveil herself. **1862** J. H. NEWMAN *Two Worlds* i, Unveil, O Lord, and on us shine In glory and in grace.

**c.** *spec.* To remove the covering from (a statue, etc.) so as to display it for the first time in public.

**1865** *Punch* 23 Sept. 17 Paulina (Britannia) unveils the Statue. **1884** *American* VII. 218 The statue..was unveiled recently at Utrecht.

**3.** *fig.* To uncover, disclose, display, reveal.

**1606** SHAKS. *Tr. & Cr.* III. iii. 200 The prouidence..Keepes place with thought; and almost like the gods, Doe thoughts vnuaile in their dumbe cradles. 1638 Chillingw. *Relig. Prot.* i. Ded. § 3 The lustre of this blessed Doctrine I have here endeavoured to uncloud and unveile. 1700 Dryden tr. *Ovid, Pythagorean Philos.* 212 For I will..Dark Oracles unveil, and open all the Skies. 1796 Kirwan *Elem. Min.* (ed. 2) I. p. ix, Hitherto its treasures have been unveiled only to my eyes. 1860 Pusey *Min. Proph.* 421 Man veils foul deeds under fair words; God, in His word, unveils the foulness. 1885 Mrs. Alexander *At Bay* viii, What secrets would that meeting unveil?

**b.** To display to the sight; to make visible.

1656 Cowley *Davideis* iv. 804 When the new Ebb of Night Did the moist world unvail to humane sight. 1740 Dyer *Ruins Rome* 36 While the vine-mantled brows The pendent goats unveil. 1791 Mrs. Radcliffe *Rom. Forest* ii, Unveiling the whole face of Nature. 1821 Shelley *Hellas* 624 The splendour of the moon, When as the wandering clouds unveiled or hid Her boundless light. 1872 Jenkinson *Guide Eng. Lakes* (1879) 115 The summit is gained, and an exquisite prospect is unveiled.

**4.** *intr.* To become free from a veil or covering.

1655 H. Vaughan *Silex Scint.* i. 73 When first thy Eies unveil, give thy Soul leave To do the like. 1849 Longf. *Lighthouse* vii, Eager faces, as the light unveils, Gaze at the tower.

Hence **Unveiˑler**; **Unveiˑling** *vbl. sb.* and *ppl. a.*

1674 Boyle *Excell. Theol.* i. i. 44 Much better encomiasts of the Divine mysteries..than *unveilers. 1611 Florio, *Disuelamento*, an *vnualing. 1768–74 Tucker *Lt. Nat.* (1834) II. 421 Lest they should esteem the very unveiling of mystery indiscreet. 1854 Gosse (*title*), The Aquarium; an Unveiling of the Wonders of the Deep Sea. 1885 *Harper's Mag.* March 644/2 The unveiling of Fielding's bust at Taunton. 1802 J. Baillie *1st Pt. Ethwald* i. ii, Th' *unveiling moon Which calls the advent'rer forth.

**Unveiˑled,** *ppl. a.* [Un-¹ 8, or f. Unveil *v.*] Not covered with, free or freed from, a veil.

1606 N. B[axter] *Sydney's Ourania* E 3 b, Leauing faire Tellus with vnuailed face, Drie and vnmantled. 1659 W. Chamberlayne *Pharon.* ii. ii. 236 The unveiled face of War Looks big with horror. *Ibid.* iii. v. 336 He dares Affront unveiled report. 1717 Lady M. W. Montagu *Let. to Pope* 1 April, Their wives and daughters..go unveiled. 1801 Southey *Thalaba* vi. xxviii, Unveil'd women bade the advancing youth Come merry-make with them! 1825 Scott *Talism.* vi, Richard's unveiled contempt for his brother sovereigns. 1890 J. Pulsford *Loyalty to Christ* I. 213 His higher and unveiled teaching belongs only to His disciples.

Hence **Unveiˑledly** *adv.*; **Unveiˑledness.**

1661 Boyle *Physiol. Ess.* (1669) 37 Not yet knowing..what use you will make of what has been unveiledly communicated to you. 1902 R. C. Moberly *Christ our Life* xxi. 178 This unveiledness of face; this reflecting, as a mirror, of the being of God.

**Unveiˑned,** (*ppl.*) *a.* (Un-¹ 8, 9.) 1826 Miss Mitford *Village* II. 173 The flowers unveined and colourless. 1869 Ruskin *Q. of Air* § 82 Under gray sky, unveined by vermilion or by gold. **Unveˑlvetly,** *adv.* (Un-¹ 11.) 1663 Waterhouse *Fortescutus Illustr.* 424, The hard hand of power unvelvetly lined. **Unveˑndable,** *a.* (Un-¹ 7 b.) 1753 Hanway *Trav.* iii. xlvii. (1762) I. 217 They were utterly unvendable. 1893 *Daily News* 15 June 5/2 These..precious but entirely unvendable books.

**Unveˑndible,** *a.* (Un-¹ 7, 5 b. Cf. prec.)

1642 *Compl. Ho. Commons* 7 That unvendible commodity of Ship-mony. 1747 W. Horsley *Fool* (1748) II. 274 It is best to lay them [*sc.* taxes] on Things unvendible. 1841 D'Israeli *Amen. Lit.* III. 95 Nearly a third of Pope's original subscription edition..[was] left unvendible. 1859 Masson *Brit. Novelists* 81 To..carry off that otherwise unvendible work.

Hence **Unveˑndibleness.**

1618 in Foster *Eng. Factories Ind.* (1906) I. 42 The unvendiblenesse of the rest [of the goods].

**Unveneeˑred,** *ppl. a.* (Un-¹ 8.) [1775 Ash.] 1887 Ruskin *Præterita* II. 39, I had my father's love..of unveneered, unrouged, and well finished things.

**Unveˑnerable,** *a.* (Un-¹ 7 b.)

1611 Shaks. *Wint. T.* ii. iii. 77 For euer Vnvenerable be thy hands, if thou Tak'st vp the Princesse. 1616 Champney *Voc. Bps.* 224 A Bishop howsoeuer vnuenerable he be,..so long as he is a Bishop,..suffereth not the losse of his Pastorall vocation. 1836 J. H. Newman in *Lyra Apost.* 127 O aged blind Unvenerable! 1867 Swinburne *Ess. & Stud.* (1875) 148 So excellent and noble a thing that even error cannot make it unvenerable.

**Unveˑnged,** *ppl. a. Obs.* exc. *arch.* (Un-¹ 8.)

1382 Wyclif *Job* xxiv. 12 The liues of woundid men..God suffreth not vnuengid [L. *inultum*] to gon awey. *a* 1470 H. Parker *Dives & Pauper* (W. de W. 1496) vi. xiii. 253/1 The..pryde of araye that is now used in this londe..wyll not be unenged. 1855 Singleton *Virgil* I. 159 Moaning ..for the loves Which he, unvenged, hath lost.

**Unveˑnial,** *a.* (Un-¹ 7.) 1589 Nashe *Almond for Parrat* B ij b, He wil be-pistle thee so peuishly, with allegations of vnuenidall [*sic*] sinnes. 1644 Milton *Divorce* (ed. 2) Pref. A 4 b, His venial and unvenial dispences. **Unveˑnom,** *v.* [Un-² 4.] *trans.* To deprive of venom. 1611 Florio, *Disuiperato*, vnuipered, vnuenomed. 1675 Allestree *Art Contentm.* xi. 206 He may..unvenem all those calamities which are to others the gall of Asps. **Unveˑnomed,** *ppl. a.* [Un-¹ 8.] Without being envenomed. 1597 Bp. Hall *Sat.* Postscr., If thou maist spit vpon a toade unvenomed, why maist thou not speake of a vice without danger? **Unveˑnomous,** *a.* (Un-¹ 7.) 1659 Gauden *Tears Ch.* 297 Their errour is not solitary, nor the sting of their schisme either soft, or blunt, or unvenomous. 1774 Goldsm. *Nat. Hist.* VII. 100 The toad..is an harmless, defenceless creature, torpid and unvenomous. **Unveˑntable,** *a.* (Un-¹ 7 b + Vent *v.*²) 1633 T. Adams *Exp. 2 Peter* ii. 4 But O..the unventable sorrow of the goates on his left!

**Unveˑnted,** (*ppl.*) *a.* [Un-¹ 8, 9.] Not provided with a vent or outlet; not allowed to issue.

*c* 1618 Fletcher *Mad Lover* ii. i, Things like our selves, as sensual, vain, unvented Bubbles, and breaths of air. 1624 Quarles *Job Militant* xvi. 26 I'me full, and I must speake, Or, like vnuented vessels, I must breake. 1630–40 — *Funeral Elegies* xviii, The false teare, that's forc'd, or slides by Art,..Or dares (unvented) come to composition. 1866 Geo. Eliot *F. Holt* xi, The company..perhaps felt the more, as they seated themselves with an expectation unvented by utterance.

**Unveˑntilated,** *ppl. a.* [Un-¹ 8.]

**1.** Not purified (as) by, not provided with means of, ventilation.

1712 Blackmore *Creation* ii. 706 For, should the air unventilated stand, The idle deep, corrupted, would contain Blue deaths. 1743 S. Hales *Ventilators* 144 Ventilated and unventilated Hops. 1849 in Huxley *Life & Lett.* (1900) I. 50 The lower and main decks are utterly unventilated. 1877 Teale *Dangers to Health* 14 Unventilated water closets.

**2.** Not ventilated or discussed.

1872 Latham. Also in recent use (1916).

**Unveˑntured,** *ppl. a.* (Un-¹ 8 and 8 c.)

1605 Sylvester *Du Bartas* ii. iii. *Vocation* 631 Our way to vertue lyes so..plain, With pain-lesse Honour and unvent'red Gain. ? 1608 *Reynard's Deliv. fr. Turks* in *Harl. Misc.* (1744) I. 183 There is no Coast..left unsought,..no People, never so wild, left unventured upon. 1854 S. Dobell *Balder* xxiii. 117 Nor less above yon midway crag the calm Unventured summit.

**Unveˑnturous,** *a.* (Un-¹ 7.) 1865 Lowell *Ode Harvard Commem.* 14 The common grave Of the unventurous throng. **Unveˑnued,** *ppl. a.* [Un-¹ 8. Cf. Venue 2.] † Not hit or wounded in fencing. 1581 Pettie tr. *Guazzo's Civ. Conv.* iii. (1586) 135 b, They ly so open that they are soone venued ..: and if they do chaunce to scape vnuenued or vnhurt, yet they leaue the world in doubt of their honestie.

**Unveraˑcious,** *a.* (Un-¹ 7 and 5 b.)

Hence, in recent use (1922), *unveraciously*.

1845 Mrs. Carlyle *Lett.* (1883) I. 301 A quick tact for detecting everything unveracious. 1894 Jeaffreson *Bk. Recoll.* II. xvii. 33 The unveracious man left the drawing-room, which he never again entered.

**Unveraˑcity.** (Un-¹ 12 and 5 b.) 1839 Carlyle *Chartism* v, What is injustice? Another name for disorder, for unveracity, unreality. 1843 — *Past & Pr.* iii. i, Such superincumbent weight of Unveracities. 1870 Ruskin *Lect. Art* (1875) 96 They will never permit themselves in uselessness or in unveracity.

**Unveˑrdant,** *a.* (Un-¹ 7.)

1646 G. Daniel *Poems* Wks. (Grosart) I. 120 The Earth vnverdant may goe seeke Her Flowers in Winter. ? *c* 1710 Congreve *Ovid's Art of Love* iii. Wks. 1730 III. 308 Ungraceful 'tis to see..A Leaf-less Tree, or an unverdant Mead. 1859 W. H. Gregory *Egypt* I. 20 The parched, baked, and unverdant clay that had replaced the greensward of Western city parks.

**Unveˑrifiable,** *a.* (Un-¹ 7 b.) 1861 Maine *Anc. Law* v. 114 A non-historic, unverifiable, condition of the race. 1876 Spencer *Princ. Sociol.* Pref., Many facts from other sources had to be sought out and incorporated; and..I left them in an unverifiable state.

**Unveˑrified,** *ppl. a.* (Un-¹ 8.)

[1775 Ash.] 1816 J. Gilchrist *Philos. Etym.* p. iii, There is not one of them which he has been obliged to abandon.. as contradicted or unverified by experimental evidence. 1867 Spencer *First Princ.* (ed. 2) ii. iii. 159 The looking-glass.. proves how deceptive is sight when unverified by touch. 1887 *Spectator* 24 Sept. 1273 The array of loose statements and unverified conjectures.

**Unveˑritable,** *a.* (Un-¹ 7 b.)

1589 Puttenham *Eng. Poesie* i. xii. (Arb.) 42 They could not..vse in their lauds any maner of grosse adulation or vnueritable report. 1646 Sir T. Browne *Pseud. Ep.* vii. x. 359 All these [beliefs] proceeded upon unveritable grounds. **Unveˑrity.** (Un-¹ 12.) 1572 Forrest *Theophilus* in *Anglia* VII. 81 To tell fable of unveryte. 1574 *Life 70th Abp. Canterb.* Pref. E 3 b, Lest..the sowishe papiste.. gredily swallow uppe this litle vomited gobbett of written vnverities.

**Unveˑrsed,** *ppl. a.*¹ [Un-¹ 8.] Inexperienced.

1675 *Camden's Hist. Eliz.* iii. 328 A young man raw and unversed in military matters. 1712 Blackmore *Creation* i. 437 The bright Natives of th' unlabour'd Field, Unverst in Spinning, and in Looms unskill'd. 1779 J. Moore *View Soc. Fr.* (1789) I. iv. 27 A stranger..unversed in their language. 1808 Mitford *Hist. Greece* IV. 232 A collegue.. unversed in military command. 1885 R. Buchanan *Annan Water* xxiv, He was unversed in the ways and the by-ways of the great city.

**Unveˑrsed,** *ppl. a.*² [Un-¹ 8.] Not versified; not expressed in verse. 1648 Hexham ii, *Ongerijmt*, Vnversed, or without Rhime. 1891 *Cent. Dict.* s.v., Thoughts unversed. **Unveˑrsified,** *ppl. a.* (Un-¹ 8.) [1775 Ash.] 1846 Worcester (citing Scott). † **Unveˑrty,** *a. Sc. Obs.*⁻¹ [Un-¹ 7.] Imprudent. 1456 Sir G. Haye *Law Arms* (S.T.S.) 236 Nocht that ony ambassadouris war sa unverty, na sa folily avisit. **Unveˑssel,** *v.* (Un-² 5.) 1633 Ford *Love's Sacr.* v. iv. L 2 b, So; I grow sweetly empty; all the pipes Of life vn-vessel life. 1656 Trapp *Comm.* (ed. 2) *Acts* xv. 24 The word signifies unvesselling them, unpacking them, .. scattering them.

**Unveˑst,** *v.* [Un-² 4.]

**1.** *trans.* To divest, strip.

1609 Bible (Douay) *Lev.* vi. 11 He..shal be unvested of his former vestments. 1610 Guillim *Heraldry* iii. vii. 106 This being mortified and vnuested of the verdour which sometimes it had.

**2.** *refl.* and *absol.* To divest (oneself) of ecclesiastical vestments.

1740 Challoner *Gard. Soul* (1801) 87 The priest returns.. to the sacristy and unvests himself. *c* 1771 in E. H. Burton *Life Challoner* (1909) I. ix. 140 The Bishop having unvested, remained kneeling. 1853 Dale tr. *Baldeschi's Ceremonial* 15 They assist the sacred Ministers to unvest.

**Unveˑstal,** *a.* (Un-¹ 7.) 1757 Mrs. Griffith *Lett. Henry & Frances* (1767) IV. 4 Our Vestal..has lately..had a Flame lighted up in her Breast, but of a most unvestal Kind. **Unvexaˑtious,** *a.* (Un-¹ 7.) 1802–12 Bentham *Ration. Judic. Evid.* (1827) II. 373 The collection of.. evidence in a mode thus comparatively undilatory, unexpensive, unvexatious.

**Unveˑxed,** *ppl. a.* (Un-¹ 8.)

1456 Sir G. Hay *Gov. Princes* Wks. (S.T.S.) II. 125 The mannis persone restis..in the nycht, and the membris and the wit ar bathe unvexit. 1485 *Acta Dom. Conc.* (1839) *94/1 To be..Joisit be him vnvext be þaim bot as law will. 1508 *Reg. Privy Seal Scotl.* I. 234/2 To..defend [them].. unvexit and undistroublit. 1595 Shaks. *John* ii. i. 253 With a blessed and vn-vext retyre,..We will beare home that lustie blood againe. 1611 Donne *Anat. World* 363 In whom all white, and red, and blew (Beauties ingredients) voluntary grew, As in an unvext Paradise. 1697 Dryden *Virg. Georg.* ii. 659 Unvex'd with Quarrels, undisturb'd with Noise. 1791 Huddesford *Salmag.* 105 Unvex'd by the cares that ambition and state has. 1809 Malkin *Gil Blas* viii. ii. ¶ 9 Which put forth shoots like a plantation in a fat and unvexed soil. 1864 Tennyson *En. Arden* 526 Unvext She slipt across the summer of the world. 1869 Lowell *Ode to Happiness* 71 These in unvexed dependence lie, Each 'neath his strip of household sky.

**Unviˑcar,** *v.* (Un-² 6 b.) *c* 1561 Underhill *Autobiog.* (Camden Soc.) 157 Yff I hadde your auctoryte I wolde be so bolde to unvycker hym. † **Unviˑciate,** *ppl. a. Sc. Obs.*⁻¹ (Un-¹ 8 b.) 1593 *Sc. Acts, Jas. VI* (1816) IV. 25/2 Sa mony of the rentis & fruittis thairof as ar presentlie frie and vnviciat. **Unviˑcious,** *a.* (Un-¹ 7.) 1456 Sir G. Hay *Gov. Princes* Wks. (S.T.S.) II. 136 Gude quhete brede and gude lycht flesche and gude unvicious wynis. † **Unviˑct,** *a.*, **Unviˑcted,** *ppl. a. Obs.* [Un-¹ 7, 8, 5 b.] = Invict *a.* 1560 Phaer *Æneid* ix. (1562) E e ij, Depe mourning maks them slack, vnuicted strengthes begin to pal. *Ibid.* x. Gg ij, That shield which..the fyry-puissant god vnuict, gaue thee with golden grates. † **Unvicˑtable,** *a. Obs.*⁻¹ [Un-¹ 7.] Invincible. 1533 Bellenden *Livy* ii. xxi. (S.T.S.) I. 217 The fabis [= Fabii]..belewit þir vnvictable [*v.r.* invincibill; L. *invicta*] armoure and wappinnys mycht nother be winccust nor ȝit resistit.

**Unvictoˑrious,** *a.* (Un-¹ 7.)

1611 Florio, *Inuittorioso*, vnuictorious. 1853 Carlyle in Froude *Life* (1884) II. 135, I am a most unvictorious man surely. 1892 Rider Haggard *Nada* xxi, Never before for many years had a Zulu impi returned unvictorious.

**Unviˑctualled,** *ppl. a.* (Un-¹ 8.)

1484 *Cov. Leet Bk.* 519 Wherthorough..straungers resortyng to þe seid Cite..were vnvittailled. 1549 Cheke *Hurt Sedit.* (1569) F ij, Exeter..being in the middest of Rebelles, vnuittailed, vnfurnished, vnprepared, for so long a siege. 1598 Sylvester *Du Bartas* ii. ii. *Babylon* 351 Jayes, that in their wyerie gail Can ask for victuals, and unvictual'd rail. 1648 Hexham ii, *Ongespijst*, Vnvictualled.

**Unviewˑed,** *ppl. a.* (Un-¹ 8.)

1570 Levins *Manip.* 51 Vnuewed, *inæstimatus*. 1608 Sylvester *Du Bartas* ii. iv. *Schism* 971 Another cals on Heav'n's un-viewed Lights. 1641 Peacham *Worth of a Penny* 27 Our Ladies..will..shiver in the hardest frost, rather than they will suffer their bare necks and breasts to passe your eyes unviewed. 1712 Blackmore *Creation* vi. 475 From thee, Democritus, it lay conceal'd,..'Twas by the Coan's piercing eye unview'd. 1810 Crabbe *Borough* i. 164 But who to thee (A wonder yet unview'd) shall paint the sea?

**Unviˑgilant,** *a.* (Un-¹ 7, 5 b.) 1611 Florio, *Inuigilante*, vnuigilant, vnwatchful. 1648 Hexham ii, *Onwacker*, Vnwakened, or Vnvigilent. 1891 Atkinson *Moorland Par.* 324 A wild wary bird..so dazed..by hunger and cold as to become dulled, muffled, unvigilant. **Unviˑgorously,** *adv.* (Un-¹ 11.) 1641 Milton *Ch. Govt.* i. v. 25 Many other courses he tries,..but so unvigorously, that I do not feare his winning of many to his cause. † **Unviˑnceable,** *a. Obs.*⁻¹ [Un-¹ 7 b.] = next. *a* 1567 *Dunbar's Lament for Makaris* 25 (Bann. MS.), That strang, vnvynsable tirrand.

† **Unviˑncible,** *a. Obs.* (Un-¹ 7 and 5 b.)

1554 *Dial. on Laws Eng.* i. xvi. 28 b, Though ignorance vnuincible of a statute excuse the party against God. *a* 1557 Mrs. M. Basset tr. *More's Treat. Passion* M.'s Wks. 1392/2 To sende hym..a myghtye stronge vnuyncible armie of Aungels from heauen. 1594 Carew *Huarte's Exam. Wits* xiii. 205 Imagination..deuiseth the engins..wherby vnuincible fortresses are won. *a* 1612 H. Broughton *Wks.* (1662) III. 713 The assertion..is by an unvincible consequent denied by the Geneveans. 1658 J. Webb *Cleopatra* viii. iii. 69 Fanc[y]ing her Troops unvincible had this great person fought at their head.

Hence † **Unviˑncibleness**; † **Unviˑncibly** *adv.*

1581 Fulke in *Confer.* iii. (1584) U iiij b, Though the communion vnder both kindes bee proued vnuincibly by that testimonie. 1611 Florio, *Inuincibilita*, vnuinciblenesse.

**Unviˑndicated,** *ppl. a.* (Un-¹ 8.) 1654 Gayton *Pleas. Notes* iii. v. 97 Whom those Inchanters, Moors, and Witches..had coffin'd up unvindicated untill this present houre. 1879 Chr. Rossetti *Seek & F.* 220 His [*sc.* Christ's] royalty, scoffed at by malice, remained unvindicated. **Unvindiˑctive,** *a.* (Un-¹ 7.) [1775 Ash.] 1857 J. W. Donaldson *Chr. Orthod.* 333 With an unvindictive selection of epithets. 1883 Croft *Elyot's Governour* II. 650/2 Anecdote of [Emperor Augustus], illustrating his unvindictive nature. **Unviˑntaged,** *ppl. a.* (Un-¹ 8.) 1869 Blackmore *Lorna D.* xxxiii, That eternal morning, when crag and chasm shall be no more, neither hill and valley, nor great unvintaged ocean.

† **Unviˑolable,** *a. Obs.* (Un-¹ 7 b, 5 b.)

1565 Cooper *Thesaurus*, *Inuiolabilis*,..vnuiolable. 1583 Golding *Calvin on Deut.* iii. 14 This order..ought to be vnuiolable. 1596 Sir H. Knyvett *Def. Realme* Ded. (1906) 9 The fountaine of unviolable faith. 1624 Capt. Smith *Virginia* iv. 144 Such a firme peace, as most men there thought sure and vnuiolable. 1656 Earl Monm. tr. *Boccalini's Advts. fr. Parnass.* ii. lxi. (1674) 213 Religion, Faith, and unviolable Friendship. 1718 Rowe tr. *Lucan* 255 Who views the Gorgons with intrepid Eyes, And your unviolable Flood defies?

Hence † **Unviˑolably** *adv. Obs.*

1534 tr. *Lyndwode's Const. Provinc.* 3 b, We charge & commaunde the constitucions..to be vnuiolably obserued & kept. 1647 Hexham i, Vnviolablely, *onverderffelicken*.

† **Unviˑolate,** *ppl. a. Obs.* [Un-¹ 8 b, 5 b. Cf. next.] = Inviolate *a.*

*a* 1548 Hall *Chron., Hen. V*, 39 To thentent that this league and amitee should be kept unviolate. 1570 T. Norton tr. *Nowel's Catech.* 11 Any other matter of great importance, wherein we are..to mainteine vnuiolate the honor of God. *a* **1589** Palfreyman *Baldwin's Mor. Philos.* (1600) 127 b, Common lawes..ought to bee..kept vnuiolate. **1681** *Whole Duty Nations* 24 The retaining their Honour untouch'd, in spite of any creature.

**Unvi·olated,** *ppl. a.* (Un-1 8, 5 b.)

**1555** Eden *Decades* (Arb.) 342 The nation..dooth not longe keepe the condicions of peace vnuiolated. **1590** Shaks. *Com. Err.* iii. i. 88 Th' vnuiolated honor of your wife. **1639** Fuller *Holy War* ii. vi. 51 His tombe is unviolated at this day. **1671** Milton *Samson* 1144 The pledge of my unviolated vow. **1727** Thomson *Britannia* 134 Unviolated, him the virgin sings. **1786** Burke *Art. agst. W. Hastings* Wks. 1842 II. 215 A treaty of peace.., unviolated on his part. **1861** Wynter *Soc. Bees* 20 The letter..reaches the person to whom it is directed, apparently unviolated. **1891** Meredith *One of our Conq.* xxv, Not until we are driven back upon an unviolated Nature, do we call to the intellect to think radically.

**Unvi·olenced,** *ppl. a.* (Un-1 8.) *a* **1711** Ken *Hymns Evang.* Poet. Wks. 1721 I. 146 He ever lives unviolenc'd by ill, Who to his God devoted, has no will. — *Hymnarium* Ibid. II. 142 How God..Governs unviolenc'd Contingency.

**Unvi·rgin,** *v.* (Un-2 6 b.) **1638** N. Whiting *Albino & Bellama* 2593 It seems some roister bold Them to unvirgin cunningly did lurk. **Unvi·rginal,** *a.* (Un-1 7.) **1546** Bale *Eng. Votaries* i. 29 b, If their unvirginall vowes had not bene, lytle should the worlde haue neded thys lecherous learnynge. **Unvi·rgined,** *ppl. a.* (Un-2 6 b, 8.) **1602** Warner *Alb. Eng.* x. lix. 258 Her now vn-virgin'd Eyes did shame to view the common Light. **1638** Mayne *Lucian* (1664) 167 The other tooke his bride, led her into his chamber, and a while after brought her forth unvirgin'd. **Unvi·rginlike,** *a.* (Un-1 7 c.) **1671** H. M. tr. *Erasm. Colloq.* 361, I am much afraid, lest some unvirginlike thing was committed that night. **Unvi·rile,** *a.* (Un-1 7, 5 b.) **1884** H. S. Wilson *Stud. Hist.*, etc. 122 James..was unstable, pedantic, undignified, and unvirile. **†Unvi·rtuate,** *v. Obs.*-1 [Un-2 6 c.] *trans.* To render ineffective. **1611** Speed *Hist. Gt. Brit.* ix. xxiv. § 125 Neither continuance of time, nor subtilty of ayre could checke or vn-vertuate the strength [of the poison]. **Unvi·rtue.** (Un-1 12.) **1869** W. M. Rossetti in *Q. Eliz. Academy*, etc. ii. 108 Every Un-virtue has Both her service and her council. **1869** Ruskin *Q. of Air* § 141 Evil by outlawry and unvirtue.

**Unvi·rtuous,** *a.* (Un-1 7.)

**1432** *Paston Lett.* I. 32 The whiche lak or defaulte mighte be caused by ungodely or unvertuous men. *c* **1456** Pecock *Bk. of Faith* (1909) 149 Forto so bileeve withoute evydence is unresonable, and therfore unvertuose. *a* **1548** Hall *Chron., Hen. IV*, 19 He beyng netteled with these vncurteous ye vnuertuous prickes..serched out the authours. **1586** Ferne *Blaz. Gentrie* 16 The coate-armours, and nobilities of the vaine and vnvertuous Gentlemen. **1645** Milton *Tetrach.* 54 An opinion both ungodly, unpolitic, unvertuous, and void of all honesty and civil sense. **1741** Richardson *Pamela* III. 44 It must be a very unvirtuous Man, that can form any other Ideas..than those of..Pity for you. **1867** *Month* VI. 17 An unvirtuous Priest..ruins many souls in these days. **1886** A. Weir *Hist. Basis Mod. Europe* ii. 37 He was [deeply] involved in the unvirtuous statecraft of his time.

Hence **Unvi·rtuously** *adv.*; **Unvi·rtuousness.** *a* **1500** *Bernardus de cura rei fam.* (E.E.T.S.) 10/245 Wyrk thow oder wnwerteusly or vele. **1520** *Caxton's Chron. Eng.* iv. 32 b/2 Many tymes he regned vnuertuously that is a kynge borne. **1682** N. Ingelo *Bentiv. & Ur.* iv. (ed. 4) 115 Love less, and you will love better and longer. You love Arete unvertuously. **1843** Carlyle *Past & Pr.* iii. ii, It was the terror..of doing unworthily, doing unvirtuously, which was their word for un*man*fully. **1865** W. H. Gillespie *Argt. Being & Attrib.* iii. iii. § 6 The same sort of thing holds with regard to..unvirtuousness.

**†Unvi·sed,** *ppl. a. Obs.* [Un-1 8.] **a.** Unintended. **b.** Unadvised.

*a* **1300** *Cursor M.* 28569 Drunkennes if it vnvisd be. **1609** R. G. *Good speed to Virginia* C 4 b, They holde it an vnuised course to set the same attempt on foote againe.

Hence **†Unvi·sedly** *adv.*, imprudently. *Obs.* *c* **1470** Henry *Wallace* xi. 231 A lord off court..Wnwisytly sperd, with outyn prouisioun; 'Wallace, dar ye go fecht on our lioun?'

**†Unvi·sible,** *a. Obs.* (Un-1 7 and 5 b.)

**1388** Wyclif *Tobit* xii. 19 Y vse vnuysible meete. *c* **1402** Lydg. *Compl. Bl. Knt.* 623 When Vulcanus..with a cheyne vnvisible yow bounde. **1483** Caxton *Cato* c j b, The whyche hath myght..vpon alle thynges vysyble and vnuysyble. **1558** Bp. Watson *Sev. Sacram.* vii. 36 Christ geueth vnto vs his vnuisible graces, in sensible sacramentes. **1593** *Pass. Morrice* F ij b, I would I..went not so vnuisible. [Also Hexham and Ash s.v.]

Hence **† Unvi·sibleness**; **† Unvi·sibly** *adv.* *c* **1380** Wyclif *Sel. Wks.* III. 522 It is nedeful þat it be understonden *unvesibily. **1647** Hexham i, Vnvisible, or unvisibly. **1721** Strype *Eccl. Mem.* III. 279 You..adore the same flesh in substance, altho' unvisibly [*orig.* invisible] in the sacrament, which we al shal se in the latter day visible. **1611** Florio, *Inuisibilita*, *vnuisiblenesse.

**Unvi·sionary,** *a.* (Un-1 7.) **1794** R. J. Sulivan *View Nat.* II. 167 Whatever turns the mind intensely upon unvisionary contemplation. **1870** Ruskin *Lect. Art* (1875) 48 A measured..observance of the quite unvisionary facts of the surrounding world.

**Unvi·sitable,** *a.* [Un-1 7 b.]

**1. a.** Unable to visit. **b.** Unfit to be visited.

**1638** Wotton in *Reliq.* (1672) 570 The B. of Lincoln being in an unvisitable case himself. **1832** Miss Mitford *Village* V. 38 A series of bachelor lords, whose female companions have been thoroughly unvisitable.

**2.** Not suitable for visiting.

**1749** Fielding *Tom Jones* xiii. iii, The next morning..she huddled on her clothes, and at a very unfashionable, unseasonable, unvisitable hour, went to Lady Bellaston.

**Unvi·sited,** *ppl. a.* [Un-1 8.] Not visited, in various senses.

(*a*) **1549** Latimer *Ploughers* (Arb.) 31 He goeth on visitacion daylye. He leaueth no place of hys cure vnuisited. **1600** Hakluyt *Voy.* III. 171 There remayned some farre remote Countries vnvisited by them. **1693** S. Hervey *Juvenal* ix. 13 The Play-House and the Parks unvisited must lie. **1799** Wordsw. *Nutting* 17, I came to one dear nook Unvisited. **1853** Kane *Grinnell Exp.* xxiv. (1856) 197 Another opportunity of seeing the unvisited shores of Wellington Sound.

(*b*) *a* **1586** Sidney *Arcadia* iii. xxvi, Giving order to his brother to keepe the prisoners safe, and unvisited. **1588** Shaks. *L. L. L.* v. ii. 358 You haue liued in desolation heere, Vnseene, vnuisited. **1612** in *Buccleuch MSS.* (Hist. MSS. Comm.) I. 126, I resolved to leave him unvisited until I should receive answer. **1734** Mrs. Delany *Life & Corr.* (1861) I. v. 447 She must live unvisited by me till I know where to find her. **1831** Carlyle *Sart. Res.* ii. v, Thus was the young man..not unvisited by hosts of true Sky-born. **1868** Pusey *Lent. Serm.* viii. (1883) 165 While His members are..sick and by us unvisited.

(*c*) **1667** Milton *P. L.* ii. 398 In some milde Zone [we may] Dwell not unvisited of Heav'ns fair Light. **1760–72** H. Brooke *Fool of Qual.* (1809) II. 158 Abandoned by God, and unvisited by his gracious motions in the heart. *c* **1815** Jane Austen *Persuas.* viii, The utter impossibility..that he could be unvisited by remembrance. **1831** Carlyle in Froude *Life* (1882) II. 189 The day [being] unvisited by any adventure except a little message from Mrs. Austin. **1870** Bryant *Iliad* ix. I. 281 So have I Had many a night unvisited by sleep.

**Unvi·sor,** *v.* [Un-2 4. Cf. Unvizard *v.*] *trans.* To strip of a visor; to unmask.

**1572** Buchanan *Detect. Mary* (1727) 28 This..Strangeris Hap was to spill the Play, and unvisor all the Disguising. **1602** Warner *Alb. Eng.* x. lviii. 255 The Barricados Feast, when Guise vn-vizard was. **1630** J. Taylor (Water P.) *Vertue of Tayle* Wks. ii. 126 Whilst I vnmaske, vnvisor, or vnveile The vertues of a Taylor and a Tayle.

**Unvi·sored,** *ppl. a.* [Un-1 8.] Not wearing a visor; not masked. **1827** Pollok *Course T.* viii. 24 On their grim features, now The plain unvisored index of the soul,..No smile of hope..was seen. **1881** *Daily News* 8 Apr. 5/3 Unvisored foes in open fray he'll meet.

**Unvi·tal,** *a.* (Un-1 7.)

**1661** Rust *Origen's Opin.* 79 The matter she [*sc.* the soul] is then surrounded with being all of that unvital temper. **1837** Whewell *Hist. Induct. Sci.* III. 129 Lavoisier showed that the atmospheric air..[contains] an *unvital* air, which he thence called *azot*. **1854** E. G. Holland *Mem. J. Badger* x. 171 Some dry and unvital difference in theological belief. **1865** M. Arnold *Ess. Crit.* i. 23 A sphere..perfectly unvital, a sphere in which spiritual progression is impossible.

Hence **Unvi·talness.**

**1661** Rust *Origen's Opin.* 69 Purged from all material unvitalness or mortality.

**Unvi·talized,** *ppl. a.* (Un-1 8.) **1874** Lewes *Probl. Life & Mind* I. 116 The inorganic, unvitalised material becoming there transformed into organisable, vitalised material.

**Unvi·tiated,** *ppl. a.* (Un-1 8.)

**1632** B. Jonson *Magn. Lady* iv. viii, Render then Your Neice a Virgin and unvitiated, And make all plaine and perfect (as it was). **1779** Forrest *Voy. N. Guinea* 297 The poor Papua people..follow nature unvitiated, and sing most melodiously. **1797** B. S. Barton *New Views* p. xv, The traditions of a people cannot be preserved long in a pure, unvitiated stream. **1838** Lytton *Alice* ii. i, Her unvitiated and guileless taste had a logic of its own. **1864** Disraeli in *Daily Tel.* 22 Sept., To breathe and enjoy pure and unvitiated air.

**Unvitrescibi·lity,** (Un-1 12), **Unvitre·scible,** *a.* (Un-1 7.) **1782** Wedgwood in *Phil. Trans.* LXXII. 309 A clay sufficiently apyrous or unvitrescible. **1786** — *Ibid.* LXXVI. 401, I..found it to answer my wishes completely..in..increasing its unvitrescibility.

**Unvitrifi·able,** *a.* (Un-1 7 b, 5 b.)

**1758** Reid tr. *Macquer's Chem.* I. 7 A species of Earth absolutely unvitrifiable in its nature. **1778** Pryce *Min. Cornub.* 253 The micose clay..is known to be absolutely unvitrifiable. **1879** *Cassell's Techn. Educ.* II. 338/2 The alkali ..facilitates the vitrification of the earthy particles, which separately are unvitrifiable.

**Unvi·trified,** *ppl. a.* (Un-1 8.)

[**1775** Ash.] **1779** *Encycl. Brit.* (ed. 2) IV. 2674/1 Another sort of glass,..[having] some unvitrified particles in its substance. **1839** Ure *Dict. Arts* 1160 The superficial film of colours will remain unvitrified. **1888** *Encycl. Brit.* XXIV. 264/1 The vitrified walls are supported by masses of unvitrified stone.

**Unvi·triolized,** *ppl. a.* (Un-1 8.) **1757** tr. *J. F. Henckel's Pyritologia* 298 That sort..yet remaining unvitriolized as the other [*sc.* white pyrites].

**Unvi·zard,** *v.* [Un-2 4.] *trans.* = Unvisor *v.*

**1620** E. Blount *Horæ Subs.* 490 Whereas they that are more cunning in their trade, are hardly visible, if not vnvizarded, which is my now endeuour to doe. **1642** *Remonstr. Ch. Ireland* 6 But others more fully unvizard themselves, professing, That they would have a King of their owne. **1655** Earl Orrery *Parthen.* ii. v. 469 Merinzor..began lately so much to unvizard his designes, that [etc.].

Hence **Unvi·zarding** *vbl. sb.*

*a* **1628** F. Grevil *Life Sidney* (1652) 113 The unvizarding of this masked triplicity.

**Unvi·zarded,** *ppl. a.* [Un-1 8.] = Unvisored *ppl. a.* **1612** N. Field *Woman a Weathercock* v. ii. Stage direct., Enter Scudmore unvizarded. **Unvo·cable,** *a.* [Un-1 7.] Incapable of utterance. **1826** Galt *Last of Lairds* xiii. 118 The same genial power..prompteth unvocable as well as intelligent nature to..rejoice in the spring.

**Unvo·cal,** *a.* (Un-1 7.)

**1773** J. Herries *Elem. Sp.* 58 The simple elements of speech [include] some vocal, some unvocal, some open, some shut. **1858** Carlyle *Fredk. Gt.* iv. ii. I. 393 He is a man to keep the world's tongue wagging,..though himself of very unvocal nature. **1885** *Athenæum* 17 Jan. 94/3 The composer indulges in unvocal intervals and harsh progressions.

**Unvo·calized,** *ppl. a.* (Un-1 8.) **1878** Bristowe *Th. & Pract. Med.* 477 The result is that unvocalised air escapes through the chink.

**Unvoi·ce,** *v.* [Un-2 4.] *trans.* To deprive of voice; *spec.* in *Phonetics*, to utter with 'breath' in place of 'voice'.

**1637** N. Whiting *Albino & B.* 402 As though an Incubus..Enclaspt their bosomes, and un-voyc'd their tongues. *Ibid.* 702. **1879** Sweet *Coll. Papers* (1913) 456 In Russian, as in French, a high final vowel is often unvoiced after a breath stop. **1888** — *Eng. Sounds* 19 Liquids and nasals are not often unvoiced.

Hence **Unvoi·cing** *vbl. sb.*

**1887** Skeat *Eng. Etym.* Ser. i. 392 Unvoicing of voiced consonants. **1888** Sweet *Eng. Sounds* 198 This unvoicing of weak stops.

**Unvoi·ced,** (*ppl.*) *a.* (Un-1 8, 9. Cf. Voice *v.* 5, 7 b.) **1859** Emerson *Art & Criticism* Wks. 1903 XII. 298 A book holding so many memorable and heroic facts,..things unvoiced before. **1874** Holland *Mistr. Manse* i. 10 That word, ineffable to man,..Remains unvoiced since time began. **1881** W. E. Dickson *Pract. Organ-building* ix. 119 A wooden pipe, similarly put together but unvoiced. **Unvoi·ceful,** *a.* (Un-1 7.) **1872** Howells *Wedd. Journ.* ix, The unvoiceful stir of the new week had begun again. **Unvoi·dable,** *a.* [Un-1 7 b + Void *v.* 3.] Irreversible. **1725** Bailey *Erasm. Colloq.* (1877) 173 He will from on high pronounce that unvoidable sentence. **†Unvoi·ded,** *ppl. a. Obs.* [Un-1 8.] = Unavoided *ppl. a.* 2 a. **1612** R. Daborne *Chr. turn'd Turke* 228 How idle then were he Should striue to crosse vnuoided desteny? **Unvo·latile,** *a.* (Un-1 7, 5 b.) **1823** Lady Granville *Lett.* (1894) I. 228 A straight Dutch road, broad and unvolatile as the natives. **Unvo·latilize,** *v.* (Un-2 6 c.) **1875** Browning *Aristoph. Apol.* 201 Who would imprison, unvolatilize A violet's perfume. **Unvo·latilized,** *ppl. a.* (Un-1 8.) **1807** Aikin *Dict. Chem. & Min.* I. 37/2 The ashes being the fixed or unvolatilized part of the plant. **†Unvo·latized,** *ppl. a. Obs.* (Un-1 8.) **1669** W. Simpson *Hydrol. Chym.* 347 Deprav'd matter..unvolatiz'd by the ferment.

**Unvo·luntary,** *a.* ? *Obs.* (Un-1 7, 5 b.)

**1570** Levins *Manip.* 107 Vnvoluntarie, *inuitus*. **1632** tr. *Bruel's Praxis Med.* 66 An vnuoluntary motion in the part which vsually did moue of its owne accord. *a* **1676** Hale *Prim. Orig. Man.* i. i. (1677) 30 They are not acts that are imperate by the Will, but they are in a manner natural and unvoluntary. **1706** E. Ward *Wooden World Diss.* (1708) 21 'Tis unvoluntary, to be sure, if he spill of the one or the other. **1725** *Fam. Dict., Diabetes*,..an unvoluntary Discharge of Urine. **1834** *Tait's Mag.* I. 10/1 The unvoluntary listener to his grey-haired father's earnest prayers.

**Unvolu·ptuous,** *a.* (Un-1 7.) **1871** Geo. Eliot *Middlem.* xxiii, He had written stanzas as pastoral and unvoluptuous as his flute-playing.

**Unvo·te,** *v.* [Un-2 3 and 7.]

**1.** To reverse or annul by revoting.

*trans.* **1647** in *7th Rep. Hist. MSS. Comm.* App. 456/2 They were forced to unvote what they had passed the day before. **1708** *Deplorable State of New Eng.* 35 The Business was so managed..that altho'..one Day it was Voted, That the Fort should be Attack'd, it was by'nd by, Unvoted again.

*intr.* **1647** R. Kentish *Serm. to Comm.* (1648) 12 They..will vote and un-vote, as the times turn. **1653** *Pol. Ballads* (1860) I. 108 They voted, unvoted, as fancy did guide.

**2.** *trans.* To deprive by a vote. Const. *of*.

**1658** J. Harrington *Prerog. Pop. Govt.* i. vii. 35 If they unchirotonized or unvoted God of the Kingdome.

Hence **Unvo·ting** *vbl. sb.*

**1642** Howell *Twelve Treat.* (1661) 40 A Bill for the unvoting, and utter exclusion of the Spirituall Lords from the Parliament. **1643** Prynne *Sov. Power Parl.* iv. 24 His Majesties..unvoting of their Votes in Parliament.

**Unvo·ting,** *ppl. a.* (Un-1 10.) **1839** Carlyle *Chartism* ix, Shall we blame the unvoting disappointed millions..?

**Unvou·ched,** *ppl. a.* [Un-1 8, 8 c.] Not guaranteed by evidence; not vouched *for*.

**1775** L. Shaw *Hist. Moray* 134 This wholly unvouched account. **1783** Hailes *Antiq. Chr. Ch.* iii. 56 This hypothesis, fanciful at the best and unvouched. **1858** Froude *Hist. Eng.* IV. 496 [A legend] unvouched for, unalluded to by any contemporary authority. **1878** J. Davidson *Inverurie* vii. 244 A picture..which, if unvouched, would now surpass belief.

**Unvouchsa·fed,** *ppl. a.* (Un-1 8.) **1661** Boyle *Style of Script.* 246 God has Veyl'd in an Obscure..Stone an Attractivenesse (Unvouchsaf'd to Diamonds and Ruby's). ? **1810** Wordsw. *Maternal Grief* 19 Beams of that celestial light To all the Little-ones on sinful earth Not unvouchsafed.

**Unvow·ed,** *ppl. a.* [Un-1 8.] Not bound by a vow; not rendered on account of a vow.

**1570** Levins *Manip.* 51 Vnuowed, *inuotiuus*. *a* **1600** Hooker *Eccl. Pol.* vii. xxiii. § 4 They had the free and unvowed oblations of men. **1615** G. Sandys *Trav.* 229 If vnuowed to another Order,..he vowes in this order. **1856** Mrs. Browning *Aur. Leigh* vi. 57 Some equal poise of sex, some unvowed love Inviolate. **1878** *Masque Poets* 151 She sat apart In widowed saintliness, an unvowed nun.

**Unvo·welled,** (*ppl.*) *a.* (Un-1 8, 9. Cf. Vowel *v.* 3.) **1624** Skinner in *Ussher's Lett.* (1686) 357, I note..That Moses left unvowelled Copies to the Tribes, save one which had both Accents and Vowels to the custody of the Priests. **1894** W. Wright in *Bibl. Soc. Rec.* (N.Y.) Aug., A set of plates of the unvowelled Bible.

**Unvoy·ageable,** *a.* (Un-1 7 b.)

**1667** Milton *P. L.* x. 366 This unvoyageable Gulf obscure. **1809–14** Wordsw. *Excurs.* v. 342 Here standing, with the unvoyageable sky..Stretched overhead. **1853** Ruskin *Stones Ven.* II. 10 The lifeless, impassable, unvoyageable plain.

**Unvoy·aged,** *ppl. a.* (Un-1 8.) **1816** J. Wilson *City of Plague* iii. iii, A kingdom Lying unknown amid unvoyaged seas. **1856** Ruskin *Mod. Paint.* III. iv. xiv. § 8 The flowing flame of some calm unvoyaged river. **Unvu·lcanized,** *ppl. a.* (Un-1 8.) **1884** Knight *Dict. Mech.* Suppl. 916/2 A material..made of unvulcanized rubber and other substances.

**Unvu·lgar,** *a.* [Un-1 7 and 5 b.]

**†1.** Uncommon, unusual; above the common, refined, rare. *Obs.*

**1598** Sylvester *Du Bartas* ii. i. 40 O! furnish me with an un-vulgar stile. **1615** J. Stephens *Satyr. Ess.* I. xv. 192 In his behauiour hee would seeme French, Italian, Spanish, or any thing, so he may seeme vnvulgar. **1654** Gayton *Pleas. Notes* IV. v. 199 There were no living..with us, unlesse something new and unvulgar be in our houses. **1713** Berkeley *Hylas & Phil.* Pref., When they have taken a circuit through so many refined and unvulgar notions. **1736** Welsted *Wks.* (1787) 427 Philosophers..too unvulgar to relish any Divinity that is not Pagan.

**2.** Free from vulgarity.

**1819** L. Hunt *Indicator* No. 3 (1822) I. 19 The whole story is..unvulgar and..sweetly serious. **1839** J. H. Frere *Aristoph. Knights* p. iv, That admirable and most unvulgar exhibition of vulgar life, the Pickwick Papers.

**Unvu·lgarize,** *v.* (Un-² 6 c.) **1811** Lamb *Hogarth* Wks. 1908 I. 95 The quantity of thought..would alone unvulgarize every subject which he might choose. **1881** *Mag. Art* IV. 290/2 It might..have..made the entire aspect of English home-life delightful, unvulgarising a domestic nation. **Unvu·lgarized,** *ppl. a.* (Un-¹ 8.) **1858** *Nat. Rev.* Oct. 352 The grace and depth of unvulgarised emotions. **Unvu·lgarly,** *adv.* [Un-¹ 11.] †Uncommonly, remarkably. **1602** Marston *Antonio's Rev.* III. iv, I haue taken a murre, which makes my nose run most patheticallie, and vnvulgarlie. **†Unvu·lnerable,** *a. Obs.* (Un-¹ 7 b, 5 b.) **1607** Shaks. *Cor.* v. iii. 72 The God of Souldiers..informe Thy thoughts with Noblenesse, that thou mayst proue To shame vnvulnerable. **1666** *Third Advice to Painter* 20 Leave then (said he) th'unvulnerable Keele. **†Unvu·lnered,** *ppl. a. Obs.*⁻¹ [Un-¹ 8, 5 b. Cf. Vulnerate *v.*] Unwounded. **1613** Heywood *Silver Age* III. i, This Lyons case shall on our shoulders hang, Wee'l arme our body with th' vnvulner'd skin.

**Unwa·dded,** *ppl. a.* (Un-¹ 8.) [**1775** Ash.] **1835** Dickens *Sk. Boz, Scenes* xi, Can our friend in the military uniform ever..descend to the comparatively un-wadded costume of every-day life? **Unwa·fered,** *ppl. a.* (Un-¹ 8.) **1844** Stocqueler *Handbk. Brit. India* 218 Scraps of paper..unwafered or unsealed. **†Unwa·fted,** *ppl. a. Sc.* [Un-¹ 8.] = Unweft *ppl. a.* **1662** *Stirling Burgh Rec.* I. 239 Ilk weaver is to leave the bounds of a large inch at the end of each pair [of plaids] unwafted.

**Unwa·ged,** *ppl. a.* [Un-¹ 8.] †Not recompensed with wages; unpaid.

**1538** Latimer *Serm. & Rem.* (Parker Soc.) 397 His highness should..remember them with some piece of some broken abbey..; for, as I hear, the vicars and other ministers sing and say unwaged. *c* **1550** *Dice Play* (Percy Soc.) 11 With less relief of victuals than had the worst unwaged adventurer here. **1563** *Mirr. Mag.* M iij, Now all stormy gales Of..rancor vtterly are swaged, And we our owne to lyve or dye vnwaged.

**Unwa·gged,** *ppl. a.* (Un-¹ 8.) **1788** Hurdis *Village Curate* (1797) 94 The silent pointer.. Now motionless.. stands, one foot lift up, His nostril wide-distended, and his tail Unwag d. **Unwai·led,** *ppl. a.* (Un-¹ 8.) **1802** J. Baillie *2nd Pt. Ethwald* v. ii, Where dying warriors groan unheard, and things Horrid to nature are as though they were not, Unwail'd, unheeded. **†Unwai·ndandly,** *adv. Sc. Obs.* [Un-¹ 10, 11.] Unsparingly. *c* **1425** Wyntoun *Cron.* VI. xv. 1526 Quhen þat he..spilt gret blude vnwayndandly [*v.r.* vnwanandly]. **Unwai·nscot(t)ed,** *ppl. a.* (Un-¹ 9.) **1709** *Phil. Trans.* XXVI. 481 The Top or Cieling of an Unwainscotted Church. **Unwai·ted,** *ppl. a.* (Un-¹ 8 c.) **1592** Timme *Ten Eng. Lepers* E 4 b, Pride..disdaineth to go alone, unwaited upon. *c* **1618** Fletcher *Mad Lover* II. i, To wander up and down unwaited on..Is for a Sowter's Soul, not an old Souldiers. **1648** Hexham II, *Onverbeydt*, Un-attended, Un-expected, or Vnwaited for.

**Unwa·ked,** *ppl. a.* (Un-¹ 8.)

**1390** Gower *Conf.* III. 258 Sche unwaked Abedde lay, but what sche mette God wot. *a* **1720** J. Hughes *Barn-elms* 4 Smooth was the Thames, his waters sleeping lay, Unwak'd by winds. **1824** Praed *Troubadour* III. 192 You might think the instrument Unwaked by any touch replied To all its master said or sighed.

**Unwa·kened,** *ppl. a.* (Un-¹ 8.)

**1621** G. Sandys *Ovid's Met.* XII. (1626) 245 Vnwakened with the tumult of this fray, Dissolu'd in death-like sleepe, Aphidus lay. **1667** Milton *P. L.* v. 9 So much the more His wonder was to find unwak'nd Eve With Tresses discompos'd. **1835** Campbell *Dead Eagle* 14 Whilst yet the unwakened world was dark below.

**Unwa·kening,** *ppl. a.* (Un-¹ 10.) **1818** Milman *Samor* XI. 882 Some knelt before their cold deaf Gods, some scoff'd ..Their stony and unwakening thunders. **1821** Byron *Sardanap.* IV. i, The realm Of thy stern, silent, and unwakening twin [*sc.* Death]. **Unwa·king,** *ppl. a.* (Un-¹ 10.) **1818** Milman *Samor* IV. 23 Within the grave She slept unwaking.

**Unwa·lkable,** *a.* [Un-¹ 7 b.] **a.** Unfit for walking in. **b.** Unable to walk.

**1813** Mme. D'Arblay *Diary* (1846) VII. 7 How teased I am ..by this eternal unwalkable weather! **1831** Howitt *Seasons* 273 Even the unwalkable infant sits propt with sheaves.

**Unwa·lked,** *ppl. a.*¹ [Un-¹ 8.] Unfulled.

**1488** *Acta Dom. Concil.* (1839) 95/2 A wob of tanny claith, ..delivierit..to þe said Robert in vnwawkit claith. **1570** *Wills & Inv. N. C.* (Surtees) 348, xiiij yards of vnwaukid caresey and xvj yards of playne whit vnwaukid. **1583** *Durham Wills & Invent.* (Surtees) 78 In unwalked cloth, xiij yeirds of white cearsey [etc.]. **1601** in *T. Pont's Acc. Cunningham* (Maitl. Cl.) 179 Fyve pair of vnwalkit blankettis.

**Unwa·lked,** *ppl. a.*² [Un-¹ 8.] **a.** Not made to walk. **b.** Not traversed by walking.

**1607** Topsell *Four-f. Beasts* 400 Let him rest vnwalked, for feare of loosening his hooues. **1648** Hexham II, *Onbewandelt*, Vnwalked, not Haunted, or Vnfrequented.

**Unwa·lking,** *ppl. a.* (Un-¹ 10.) **1789** H. Walpole *Let. to Conway* 5 Sept., I am so unwalking, that prospects are more agreeable to me when..I look at them through a window.

**Unwa·ll,** *v.* [Un-² 4. Cf. Du. *ontwallen.*] *trans.* To deprive of, to free from, a wall or walls; to demolish (a wall).

**1598** Florio, *Smurare*, to vnwall, to raze..any walles. **1641** Trappe *Theol. Theol.* i. 26 *margin*, Christ shall unwall (or cast down the wals) of all the children of Seth. **1663** Davenant *Siege Rhodes* Wks. (1672) 8 It were more honour, Sultan, to assail A publick Strength..Then to unwall this private Tenement. **1686** J. S[ergeant] *Hist. Monast. Convent.* 176 The Masons unwalled and unclosed the Conclave.

**Unwa·lled,** (*ppl.*) *a.* [Un-¹ 8 and 9.] Not furnished with, or defended by, a wall.

*c* **1440** *Jacob's Well* 114 Slowthe makyth þe as a cyte vnwallyd. **1542** Elyot s.v. *Arabia*, The townes ar vnwalled, bycause the people doo alwaye lyue in peace. **1577** Harrison *England* II. xiii. (1877) I. 255 The citie..laie then vnwalled. **1589** Bigges *Sum. Drake's W. Ind. Voy.* 31 There was onely so much of this straight vnwalled, as might serue for the issuing of the horsemen. **1638** Sir T. Herbert *Trav.* (ed. 2) 336 China has no fewer than..2000 wall'd Townes; 4000 unwalled. **1690** C. Nesse *O. & N. Test.* I. 14 The soul now dwells in an unwalled, unfortifyed city. **1760–2** Goldsm. *Cit. W.* cxxii, An unwalled town, called Islington. **1807** J. Barlow *Columb.* x. 540 Cities unwalled stand sparkling to the sun. **1860** O. W. Holmes *Elsie V.* xviii, The round unwalled horizon of the open sea.

**Unwa·llet,** *v.* (Un-² 5.) *a* **1739** Jarvis *Quix.* II. IV. xiv, The lacquey laughed, unsheathed his calabash, and unwalleted his cheese. **†Unwa·llowable,** *a.* (see Unwelewable *a.*). **Unwa·llowed,** *ppl. a. Sc.* [Un-¹ 8.] Unfaded. *c* **1425** Wyntoun *Cron.* IV. Prol. 7 A garland.. Grene suld lestand be lang quhile, Vnwallowit [*v.r.* vnwalewit] throu ony interwall Off tyme, bot ay in vertu haill.

**Unwa·ndered,** *ppl. a.* [Un-¹ 8. Cf. MDu. *ongewandert*, G. *ungewandert*; older Da. *uvandret*, Sw. *ovandrad.*] **a.** Untraversed. **b.** Of persons: Untravelled.

**1654** E. Johnson *Wonder-wkg. Provid.* 35 Pilots, missing ofttimes of their skill on those unwandered Coasts. **1799** W. Taylor in Robberds *Mem.* (1843) I. 279 In Wales I am unwandered, and should like to go some summer's day. **1868** Browning *Ring & Bk.* I. 751 My soul..in its pilgrimage O'er old unwandered waste ways of the world.

**Unwa·ndering,** *ppl. a.* (Un-¹ 10.)

*a* **1568** Coverdale *Fruitful Less. Passion* (1593) To Rdr., Thus the penitent findeth the waie, the reformer the vndoubted vnwandring truth. **1740** Cibber *Apol.* v. 92 The Disproportion of his lower Features,..with an unwandering Eye hanging over them. **1791** Cowper *Iliad* XIII. 48 He.. bound their feet With golden tethers.., that unwand'ring they might wait Their Lord's return. *a* **1864** Hawthorne *Amer. Note-bks.* (1879) II. 158 He was a pattern of diligence and unwandering thought. **1867** M. Arnold *Epil. to Lessing's Laocoon* 190 Only a few the life-stream's shore With safe unwandering feet explore.

**Unwa·ning,** *ppl. a.* (Un-¹ 10.) **1807** Coleridge *To Wordsworth* 41 Hope sprang forth like a full-born Deity,.. With light unwaning on her eyes. **1855** Browning *Cleon* 130 That years and days..Follow each other with unwaning powers. *a* **1865** Tennyson *Mystic* 15 Always there stood before him..Dim shadows but unwaning presences.

**Unwa·nted,** *ppl. a.* (Un-¹ 8.)

**1697** Congreve *Mourn. Bride* III. viii, [A] return so unwish'd, unwanted too, it seems. **1731** A. Hill *Advice to Virgins* 10 Yet modest excellence will oft descend To thank unwanted caution in a friend. **1808** Mitford *Hist. Greece* IV. 476 Yet exhortation..seems not to have been unwanted. **1864** 'Annie Thomas' *D. Donne* I. vii. 167 Finding some one located at Donne Place who would prevent his occupying the distressing position of third and unwanted one. **1886** Manning in *Contemp. Rev.* May 693 The duty society owes to the lives of unwanted children.

**Unwa·nton,** *a.* (Un-¹ 7.) **1606** Marston *Parasit.* III. E 3, In heauy sadnes & vnwanton phrase there lies all the braine worke. **1894** E. F. Benson *Dodo* 248 A woman's anger is always much more unwanton than that of a man. **†Unwa·ppered,** *ppl. a. Obs.*⁻¹ [Un-¹ 8 + Wappered, fatigued.] Unexhausted. **1612** *Two Noble K.* v. iv, We come towards the gods Yong, and unwapper'd, not halting under Crymes Many and stale. **†Unwa·rd,** *ppl. a. Obs.*⁻¹ [Un-¹ 8 b + *ward*, ad. ON. *varðr*, p. p. of *verja* to defend.] Unprotected. *c* **1250** *Gen. & Ex.* 480 Lamech droȝe is arwe ner...Caim unwarde it under-feng,..and starf wið-ðan.

**Unwa·rded,** *ppl. a.* [Un-¹ 8.] Unguarded; undefended.

**1382** Wyclif *Gen.* xlii. 12 The vnwardid thingis [L. *immunita*] of this loond. **1553** T. Lever *Serm.* (Arb.) 58 Take heede, that the vncleane spirite of ignoraunce..fynde no place vnwarded, where he may creepe in agayne. **1553** Brende *Q. Curtius* 55 There was one Tiriotes, which.. escaped by a gate that was vnwarded. **1674** Jackson *Recant.* E 3 b, The High-way-man may do what he list, and meet with more Booties than if the Road lay unwarded. **1858** *Household Words* XIX. 64/1, I pass through the strong gates, now unwarded from the Infidel.

**Unwardly,** obs. var. Unwarely *adv.*

**Unwa·re,** *a.*, *sb.*, and *adv.* Now only *arch.* [OE. *unwær* (Un-¹ 7, 12, 11 b), = ON. *úvarr* (MSw. *ovar*). Cf. Unwares.]

**1.** Unwary, incautious; not on one's guard.

*c* **897** K. Ælfred *Gregory's Past. C.* xv. 89 Oft eac ða unwaran lareowas for eȝe ne durron cleopian. **971** *Blickl. Hom.* 61 Þa scinlæcan þa þe galdor-cræftas..begangaþ, & mid þæm unwære men beswicaþ. *c* **1000** Ælfric *Hom.* II. 538 Ȝif ðu unwær bist, þu bist ðe swiðor ȝeswenct. *c* **1200** *Vices & Virtues* 45 Ðe unware mann ðe ðis ȝeherð, ðingþ ðat he seið him god rad. *c* **1205** Lay. 7810 Nu þohte Julius Cezar (ah þer he wes to vnwar), he þohte swa forð teon æfter þere Temese. *a* **1225** *Ancr. R.* 274 Hwonne þeo sunnen þet weren ȝare ibet kumeð eft..& sleað þeo unwarre soule. *c* **1307** Langtoft *Chron.* (Rolls) II. 252 For Scottes Tell i for sottes, And wrecches unwar; Unsele Dintes to dele Tham drohu to Dumbar. **1388** Wyclif *Prov.* xxiii. 28 Sche schal sle hem, whiche sche schal se vnwar. *c* **1450** tr. *De Imitatione* III. xliv. 115 If he miȝt bringe hedily þe unware man into þe gnare of deceite. *Ibid.* I. 121 Fro suche fables & unwar men, lorde, defende me, þat I falle not into her hondes. **1509** Barclay *Shyp of Folys* 37 Suche ar vnware and gyuen to neglygence,..Makynge no prouysyon for the tyme to come. **1557** *Tottel's Misc.* (Arb.) 230 Now vaunt thee loue which ..wounded hast a wight vnwise, vnweaponed and vnware. **1624** H. Mason *Art of Lying* ii. 35 Unware men are ouerreached and caught.

**b.** Of actions: Done incautiously.

*a* **1395** Hylton *Scala Perf.* II. xviii. (Bodl. MS.) fol. 110 An vnware stiringe of himsilf schulde caste him doun aȝen worse þan he was bifore. **1398** Trevisa *Barth. De P. R.* v. xxiv. (Bodl. MS.), Þe þrote is ofte igreued..by vnwise and vnwar taking of mete and of drinke.

**2.** Unaware, ignorant. Const. *of*, *that.*

*c* **1374** Chaucer *Troylus* I. 304 Lo he..was ful vnwar þat loue hadde his dwellynge with-inne þe subtile stremes of here eyen. *c* **1400** *Destr. Troy* 1183 Vnwar of þe weghes þat by the walles lay,..He busket to þe banke with a bolde chere. **1421–2** Hoccleve *Complaint* 375 He that it owght agayne it to hym toke, Me of his haste vnware. **1523** Ld. Berners *Froiss.* I. cvii. 128 We shall entre whyle they be at supper, and vnware of vs. **1563** *Mirr. Mag.* A a iij, O hedeles trust, vnware of harme to cum. **1590** Spenser *F. Q.* II. iv. 17 So me weake wretch,..vnware of such mishap, She brought to mischiefe.

*ellipt.* *c* **1611** Chapman *Iliad* XVI. 109 Ajax seeing..that he shook a headless spear, a little while unware.

**b.** Quasi-*adv.* Without knowing it; in ignorance, innocently.

*c* **1386** Chaucer *Pars. T.* 885 Of this brekynge comth eek ofte tyme that folk vnwar wedden or synnen with hire owene kynrede. **1390** Gower *Conf.* II. 2 Thus bringth he many a meschief inne Unwar, til that he be meschieved. *c* **1450** *Merlin* xxvi. 493 He put vp his goode swerde for doute leste he slough eny man vn-war. **1532** More *Confut. Tindale* Wks. 598/1 After that he..therby made him giue sentence vnware against himselfe. **1533** — *Apol.* 191 b, He playn reproueth his owne processe, & excuseth the clergye hym selfe vnware. *c* **1614** Sir W. Mure *Dido & Æneas* I. 963 Her self, vnwar, thus doth her self betray, And feels the force of this small archer's bowe. **1671** Milton *P. R.* I. 225 The erring Soul Not wilfully mis-doing, but unware Misled.

**3.** Unexpected, unforeseen.

*c* **1374** Chaucer *Boeth.* v. met. i. (1868) 151 It haþ hys propre causes of whiche causes þe cours vnforseyn and vnwar semiþ to han maked happe. *c* **1386** — *Man of Law's T.* 427 Vp on thy glade day haue in thy mynde The vnwar wo or harm þat comth bihynde. *c* **1407** Lydg. *Reson & Sens.* 6181 They turne nat as doth a phane With vnwar wynde. **1430–40** — *Bochas* VIII. 2192 Hih clymbyng vp haþ ofte an vnwar fall. **1509** Hawes *Past. Pleas.* xxxv. (Percy Soc.) 180 At a tyme unware my dette shal be dewe. *a* **1548** Hall *Chron., Edw. IV*, 218 b, Least..the common people hereafter..might..excite an unware rebellion.

**4.** Unknown (*to* one).

**1390** Gower *Conf.* III. 44 Who dar do thing which love ne dar? To love is every lawe unwar. **1529** More *Dyaloge* II. Wks. 190/2 If there came amonge them vnware to you some spies. *a* **1536** Wyatt *Wks.* (1913) I. 130 If I had suffred this to you unware, myn were the fawte, & you nothing to blame.

**5.** As *sb.* **a.** In phr. *on*, *in*, or *at unware*, unawares, unexpectedly.

*c* **1070** *O.E. Chron.* (MS. C) an. 1066, Þa com Harold cyning ..into Tinan on unwaran. *c* **1100** *Ibid.* (MS. D) an. 1043, Man ȝerædde þan cynge þæt he rad..to Wincestre on unwær. **14..** *R. Gloucester's Chron.* 1966 (MS. Digby 205), This prince al in vnware toward hem þan drouȝ. **1561** Norton & Sackv. *Gorboduc* II. ii, Shall I geue leasure by my fonde delayes To Ferrex to oppresse me at vnware?

**b.** Unwariness, carelessness.

**1475** *Bk. Noblesse* (Roxb.) 27 By unware of theire purveiaunce [they] met withe the said Haniballe at certen streightes and narow places.

**6.** *adv.* **a.** Without warning; unexpectedly.

*c* **1100** *O. E. Chron.* (MS. D) an. 1050, Hi comon unwær on heom on ealne ærne merȝen. *Ibid.* an. 1067. *c* **1386** Chaucer *Frankl. T.* 1356 On thee Fortune I pleyne That vnwar wrapped hast me in thy cheyne. **1387** Trevisa *Higden* (Rolls) V. 219 He was bysette..in a harde battaille þat fil uppon hym unwar [L. *inopino*] in þe Ester day. **1426** Lydg. *De Guil. Pilgr.* 13548 They sawh on komen ffaste by, Vnwar, with a gret company. **1454** *Paston Lett.* I. 282 William..and Robert come uppon hem onwarre, and therupon chasid hem. *c* **1510** More *Picus* Wks. 26 Death stealeth on full slily and unware. **1591** Spenser *Virg. Gnat* Ded. 5 If that any Oedipus vnware Shall chaunce..To reade the secrete of this riddle rare. **1613** W. Browne *Brit. Past.* I. iv. 498 Seeking the place of Charitie's resort, Unware I hapned on a Princes Court. **1616** J. Lane *Contn. Sqr.'s T.* VIII. 180 In each quarter, they prepare, to charge the campes sodainlie and vnware. **1875** Morris *Æneid* VI. 104 No face of any care, O maiden, can arise on me in any wise unware.

**b.** Unwarily, incautiously.

**1545** Taverner *Erasm. Prov.* 55 Whiche stones so sone as a man vnware take vp, forthwith he receiueth a wound of the scorpion.

**† Unwa·rely,** *adv. Obs.* [OE. *unwærlíce* (Un-¹ 11), = ON. *úvarliga* (MSw. *ovarlika*, *-ligha*, MDa. *uvarlige*).]

**1.** Incautiously; without taking heed.

*c* **893** K. Ælfred *Oros.* IV. x. § 9 Him com onȝen Hanno se cyning unwærlice, & þær ofslaȝen wearð. **971** *Blickl. Hom.* 57 Swa we þonne þa gastlican lare unwærlice ne sceolan anforlætan. *c* **1100** *O. E. Chron.* (MS. D) an. 1068, Æfter þisum coman Haroldes sunas..into Taw-muðan, & þær unwærlice up-eodon. *a* **1300** *Cursor M.* 8894 Bot vnwarli sco sett hir don Apon þis ilk tre wit chance. **1398** Trevisa *Barth. De P. R.* XII. xiii. (Bodl. MS.), Vnwarliche he falleþ into a candel oþur into fuyre and..brenneþ hym selfe. *a* **1425** tr. *Arderne's Treat. Fistula*, etc. 8 Discouer neuer the leche vnwarly the counsellez of his pacientez. *c* **1480** Henryson *Fables, Cock & Fox* 81 (Bann. MS.), Wnwarlye winkand, [the cock] walkit vp and doun, And syne to chant and craw he maid him boun. **1560** Daus tr. *Sleidane's Comm.* 428 The soldioures of the garrison chaunced than to be some what vnwarely without the gates. **1592** Lyly *Gallathea* I. iii. 20, I shall..vnwarelie blabbe out something by blushing at euery thing.

**2.** Without warning; unexpectedly.

*c* **1200** *Trin. Coll. Hom.* 191 A wiche wise he hem wile bisette þanne þe hem unwarliche his dintes giueð. *c* **1374** Chaucer *Boeth.* I. met. i. (1868) 4 For elde is comen vnwarly vpon me. 1390 Gower *Conf.* III. 252 So mai we knowe bothe tuo Unwarli what oure wyves do. 1412–20 Lydg. *Chron. Troy* iv. 2232 But vp-on hym, vnwarly, or he wende, Cam myȝty Troylus. 1447 Bokenham *Seyntys* (Roxb.) 22 Unwarly, er he wyst what it ment Wyth thy wycchecraft hys lyf was shent. 1514 Pace in Ellis *Orig. Lett.* Ser. iii. I. 176 Thys post departide so hastyly and so unwarly that [etc.]. *a* 1542 Wyatt in *Tottel's Misc.* (Arb.) 65 Vnwarely so was neuer no man caught..as I of late. 1596 Spenser *F. Q.* iv. iii. 8 Yet one [stroke]..Through Cambels shoulder ..vnwarely went.

**Unwa·reness.** Now *arch.* [Un-[1] 12. Cf. OE. *unwærness.*] Unwariness, incautiousness.

1388 Wyclif *Prov.* xiv. 8 The vnwarnesse of foolis errith. *c* 1400 *Destr. Troy* 445 Þis vnwarnes of wit wrixlis hys mynd. 1436 *Pol. Poems* (Rolls) II. 190 Be ware of Walys, Criste Jhesu mutt us kepe, That it make not [us]..to wepe,..if it go his waye By unwarenesse. 1509 Barclay *Shyp of Folys* (1570) 25 But when he had obteyned great honours,..Then his vnwarenes caused him to wayle. 1544 Betham *Precepts War* ii. xliv. L j, The defaulte can not be escaped ne holpen, and al through thyne vnwarenesse. 1899 T. Hardy *Wessex Poems* 97 [She'll think] That my words were not unwareness, but deceit of her.

**Unwa·res,** *adv.*, *sb.*, and *a.* Now *arch.* [Late OE. *unwæres, unwares,* f. *unwær* Unware *a.*]

**A.** *adv.* **1.** Without warning; unexpectedly, suddenly.

*a* 1122 *O. E. Chron.* (Laud MS.) an. 1004, Forþam þe hi unwares comon, & he fyrst næfde þæt he his fyrde ȝegadrian mihte. *Ibid.* an. 1093, Hine þa Rodbeard..unwæres besyrede & ofsloh. *c* 1400 *Found. St. Bartholomew's* 44 Here gladnes was turnyd yn-to waylyng;..vnwarys brake vp an violent tempest. 1512 *Helyas* in Thoms *Prose Rom.* (1828) III. 72 Makaire came wening to smite him al unwars. 1556 Robinson tr. *More's Utopia* To Rdr. (Arb.) 20 Yet haue I in this by chaunce, that on my side vnwares hath fallen, so..behaued myself, that [etc.]. 1615 Chapman *Odyss.* iv. 112 One, murderously, Unwares, unseen, bereft my brother's life. 1642 H. More *Song of Soul* iii. ii. xxvi, Unwares they find a sly still silver light. *c* 1745 A. Skirving *Tranent Muir* v, Menteith the great, where Hersell sate, Un'wares did ding her ower, man. 1805–6 Cary *Dante, Inf.* i. 52 When all unwares is gone, he inwardly Mourns with heart-griping anguish. 1887 Morris *Odyssey* xii. 288 If all unwares upon us a blast of the wind should come.

†**b.** *His unwares,* without his knowledge; unforeseen by him. *Obs.*

1468 *Paston Lett.* II. 328 He hathe promysyd that there schall come non; and if ther do his unwarys, yowr answer may be thys.

†**c.** Const. *of,* or *to* (a person). *Obs.*

*c* 1510 in *Mem. Hen. VII* (Rolls) 286 So came he to the King's secret chamber door unwares of the King. 1532 Tindale *Expos. Matt.* v. 20 Least anie vncleane thyng hadde touched theim unwaeres to all menne. 1625 Bacon *Ps. xc.* ii, As a watch by night, that course doth keepe, And goes and comes vnwares to them that sleepe.

**2.** Unknowingly; without knowledge or intention; unintentionally.

13.. *Cursor M.* 2018 (Gött.), Bitid a day he was for-swonken, And vnwaris of win was dronken. 1526 Tindale *Heb.* xiii. 2 Thereby have dyvers receaved angels into their houses vnwares. 1553 T. Wilson *Rhet.* 54 He did it not willyngly, but vnwares, and by chaunce. 1593 Shaks. *3 Hen. VI,* ii. v. 62 It is my Fathers face, Whom in this Conflict, I (vnwares) haue kill'd. 1610 Holland *Camden's Brit.* i. 260 Tirrell him seeing not Unwares him slew with dint of arrow shot. 1642 H. More *Song of Soul* ii. i. ii. 35 But to return, Lest what we aim'd at we unwares omit.

**B.** *sb.* †**1.** *In unwares,* = A. 2. *Obs.*

*a* 1300 *Cursor M.* 2018 Bitid a day he was for suonken, And in vnwars o wyn was drunken.

†**2.** *At unwares,* = A. 1. *Obs.*

In common use *c* 1575–1610.

*a* 1547 Surrey *Æneis* iv. 90 Like to the..Hinde..which chasing with his dartes Aloofe, the shepheard smiteth at unwares, And leaves unwist in her the thirling head. 1576 Lambarde *Peramb. Kent* 208 The Danes..came freshly vpon the English Mariners at vnwares. 1581 Styward *Mart. Discipl.* i. 28 Hauing aduauntage of such as lie in scowte, who waite their time to assaile them at vnwares. 1606 G. W[oodcocke] *Hist. Ivstine* vi. 32 The Thebanes.. began a new plot of cunning purposing..to set vpon them at vnwares. 1632 Holland *Cyrupædia* 31 They that are skilfull to circumvent their enimies, can..put them first in a good conceit of themselves, and then surprize them at unwares.

**C.** *adj.* †**1.** Unwary, incautious. *Obs.*

1548 Udall, etc. *Erasm. Par. Matt.* vii. 33 b, To the intent he maye poyson with hys heresye, them that be vnwares and negligent. 1565 Stapleton tr. *Bede's Hist. Ch. Eng.* 27 Thinking to steale vppon them and so easely obtaine the victory ouer them, as vnwares and vnarmed.

†**2.** Unexpected, unlooked-for. *Obs.*

1548 Udall, etc. *Erasm. Par. Matt.* xxvi. 26 b, As a thing vnwares & not loked for. *a* 1586 Sidney *Arcadia* iii. x, The most..comfortable ayre, which an unwares sigh might bestow upon them.

†**Unwa·ried,** *ppl. a. Sc. Obs.* [Un-[1] 8.] Not cursed. 1513 Douglas *Æneid* ii. xi. 108 So was I quyte miscareit, That noder god nor man I left wnwareit [*v.r.* unwaryit].

**Unwa·rily,** *adv.* [Un-[1] 11. Cf. Unwary *a.*]

†**1.** = Unwarely *adv.* 2. *Obs.*

1568 Grafton *Chron.* II. 94 King Richard..drue him toward Aubeuyle.., and fell vpon the Frenchmen vnwarily. 1593 Shaks. *John* v. vii. 63 The best part of my powre.. Were in the Washes all vnwarily, Deuoured by the vnexpected flood.

**2.** Incautiously, imprudently; inadvertently.

1580 Hollyband *Treas. Fr. Tong* s.v. *Bric,* When a word vnwarilie spoken, is taken for a confession. 1594 Spenser *Amoretti* xvi, One day as I vnwarily did gaze On those fayre eyes. 1634 Sir T. Herbert *Trav.* 213 One speckled fish the Seamen fed vpon vnwarily. 1670 Clarendon *Contempl. Ps.* Tracts (1727) 382 Being unwarily ensnared by the vanities and levities of the world. 1712 Addison *Spect.* No. 435 ¶ 5 Any little Extravagance into which they are sometimes unwarily fallen. 1758 Johnson *Idler* No. 12 ¶ 1 We all either voluntarily or unwarily at least once an hour confess the truth. 1822 W. Irving *Braceb. Hall* xvi, She had unwarily approached too near the bank. 1891 *Law Times* XCI. 32/1 Pointing out the pitfalls into which they unwarily fall.

**Unwa·riness.** [Un-[1] 12.] The quality of being unwary.

1544 Betham *Precepts War* i. xxiii. C ij, Leste by hys vnwarynesse, some mischaunce & damage do ensue. 1593 *Sidney's Arcadia* iii. (1922) II. 58 Thisbes punishment for my rashe unwarinesse. 1649 J. Taylor *Great Exemplar* ii. 123 He who is angry with a servants vnwarinesse. 1693 Locke *Educ.* 166 The inconsiderate heats and unwariness of Youth. 1711 Addison *Spect.* No. 256 ¶ 3 The same Temper of Mind..betrays us into such Slips and Unwarinesses as are not incident to Men of a contrary Disposition. 1870 Morris *Earthly Par.* III. 95 Thorgerd.. would watch some gesture or some word to catch From his unwariness.

† **Unwarl,** metathetic var. Unwrall *v. Obs.*

1387 Trevisa *Higden* (Rolls) I. 9 As laborintus..haþ many ..wyndynges and wrynkelynges þat wil nouȝt be vnwarled.

**Unwa·rlike,** *a.* (Un-[1] 7 c.)

1590 Spenser *F. Q.* iii. xi. 44 With womanish teares, and with vnwarlike smarts, Priuily moystening his horrid cheek. 1597 Beard *Theatre God's Judgem.* i. vii. 21 Ioshua and his poore people (though vnwarlike and vnacquainted with such actions). *c* 1654 Waller *Panegyric to Ld. Protector* 78 He safely might old troops to battle lead, Against th' unwarlike Persian. 1697 Dryden *Virg. Georg.* ii. 239 Cæsar, whose victorious Arms Avert unwarlike Indians from his Rome. 1739 Glover *London* 473 Thy sons..vainly deem'd that wealth Could..protect Unwarlike freedom. 1841 Elphinstone *Hist. Ind.* I. 525 The inhabitants of the cultivated country were not unwarlike. 1878 Stubbs *Const. Hist.* III. xviii. 73 The only three unwarlike kings who had reigned since the Conquest.

Hence **Unwa·rlikeness.**

1864 Pusey *Lect. Daniel* v. 269 [Babylon's] deliberated unwarlikeness stands in strange contrast to its subsequent energy in rebelling.

**Unwa·rm,** *a.* (Un-[1] 7.) 1694 *Lond. Gaz.* No. 2946/4 He has a Click in his walk when unwarm with one of his hinder Legs. 1824 Coleridge *Lett., Convers.,* etc. II. 170 Induced by the very fine but unwarm day. **Unwa·rm,** *v.* [Un-[2] 6 a.] *intr.* To grow cold. 1826 Hood *Irish Schoolm.* xi, With horrid chill, each little heart unwarms.

**Unwa·rmed,** *ppl. a.* (Un-[1] 8.)

*a* 1625 Fletcher *Hum. Lieut.* iv. iii, What ever may compel..A Heart un-warm'd to melt in Loves desires. 1648 Hexham ii. s.vv. *Ongewermt, Onverwermt.* 1716 Pope *Basset-Table* 76 But of what marble must that breast be form'd, To gaze on Basset, and remain unwarm'd? 1850 Bryant *Journ. Life* 6 Broken gleams of brightness, here and there, Glance through, and leave unwarmed the deathlike air. 1866 Whittier *Snow-Bound* 31 Unwarmed by any sunset light The gray day darkened into night. 1894 Parry *Stud. Gt. Composers, Schubert* 230 The boys suffered..from living and working in unwarmed rooms.

**Unwa·rming,** *ppl. a.* (Un-[1] 10.)

1736 A. Hill *Zara* i. i. 9 Monarchs, Like the Sun, Shine but in vain, unwarming, if unseen. 1794 Burns *Lament* 6 With woe I nightly vigils keep, Beneath thy wan unwarming beam. 1800 Campbell *Beech Tree's Petition* 4 Though bush or floweret never grow My dark unwarming shade below. *a* 1834 Coleridge *Lit. Rem.* (1836) I. 277 The pale unwarming light of hope. 1866 Whittier *Snow-Bound* 152 For such a world and such a night Most fitting that unwarming light.

**Unwa·rn,** *v.* (Un-[2] 3.) 1612 in 10th *Rep. Hist. MSS. Comm.* App. I. 574 The state being advertised of his purpose, thei have sent order to the Retorri of Padoa to unwarne that assembly. 1613 H. Savile in J. Hunter *Deanery of Doncaster* (1828) II. 137, I must unwarne you in halfe a sheete of paper..yt you loose not yr labour to come to me according to my last entreatie.

**Unwa·rned,** *ppl. a.*[1] and *adv.* [OE. *unwarnod* (Un-[1] 8). Cf. MDu. *ongewa(e)rnet,* OHG. *ungiwarnôt* (MHG. *ungewarnet,* G. *ungewarnt*), Sw. *ovarnad.*]

**1.** Not warned or forewarned.

*c* 1000 *Law Northumb. Priests* in Thorpe *Laws* II. 294 Ȝif preost oðerne unwarnode læte þæs, þe he wite, þæt him hearmian wille, ȝebete þæt. 1297 R. Glouc. (Rolls) 1176 He let also arere Vpe þe water stronge hous, þat hii vnwarned nere. 1338 R. Brunne *Chron.* (1810) 13 Scho purueid þat poyson..Brittrik hir lord..Unwarned drank þerof a drauht. 1382 Wyclif *2 Macc.* viii. 6 And he aboue cummynge to castels and cytees, vnwarnyd [L. *improvisas*], brente hem. 1422 Yong tr. *Secreta Secret.* 175 Hit was not y-holde proesse ne chyualry to assayle a man vnwarnyd. 1456 *Cov. Leet Bk.* 295 Because no persones should be greued be these ordenaunces vnwarned, we ordeyn þat þes ordenaunces be radde to euery of þe seid officers. 1693 Locke *Educ.* (1699) 152 As unexperienced young Men are apt to do, if they are unwarn'd. 1715 Ramsay *Great Eclipse* 23 When this strange darkness overshades the plains, 'Twill give an odd surprise t' unwarned swains. 1791 Cowper *Odyssey* i. 48 So now Ægisthus..him at his return Hath foully slain, though not unwarn'd by us, That he would surely perish. 1806 J. Foster *Ess.* (ed. 2) I. 39 Human beings, entering on life, with..unwarned carelessness of heart. 1823 Mrs. Hemans *Vespers Palermo* iii. iv, He must not die unwarn'd. 1877 Mrs. Oliphant *Makers Flor.* ix. 230 Wickedness unwarned and wrong unredressed were rampant.

**b.** Const. *of.*

*c* 1400 *Song of Roland* 314 [They] may..haue vs euyn as they lest, And we vn-warnyd þer-of in this tid. *c* 1425 Wyntoun *Cron.* iii. ii. 330 Vnwarnyt of thare spyise,..[he] went to bed. *c* 1470 Henry *Wallace* viii. 182 Wallace off Beik wnwarnyt than was he. 1513 Douglas *Æneid* xii. x. 8 The Latynis..,Quhilk of hys cumming tho onwarnyt weyr.

†**2.** *adv.* Without warning or announcement.

*c* 1250 *Gen. & Ex.* 2682 Bi a lond weiȝe he wente riȝt, And broȝte vn-warnede on hem fiȝt. *c* 1325 *Song of Yesterday* 170 in *E. E. P.* (1862) 137 Sum men seiþ þat deþ is a þef, And al vnwarned wol on hym stele. 1407 *Exam. W. de Thorpe* (MS. Rawl. C 208) fol. 6 b, Þei ben sodeynli & vnwarned brouȝt forþ to ben apposid of aduersaries. *c* 1450 *Mirk's Festial* 39 Þe kyng hymselfe wold mony a tyme vnwarned come to þe mete.

**3.** Unannounced. Also with *-for.*

*a* 1400 *Minor Poems fr. Vernon MS.* 231/379 Kep vs.. from temptaciun of þe fende, Of sodeyn deþ vnwarned to telle, And also from þe pyne of helle. 1641 Bp. Hall *Serm.* Wks. 1837 V. 455 One..makes sudden embargoes, and unwarned inroads into the adjoining country. 1882 Piazzi Smith in *Nature* XXVI. 552 An interval quite long enough to allow of an unwarned-for cyclone having meanwhile entered the country.

Hence **Unwa·rnedly** *adv.*

15.. *Exam. W. de Thorpe* in Foxe *A. & M.* (1563) 145/2 They be sodeinly and vnwarnedly brought forth to be apposed of their aduersaries.

†**Unwa·rned,** *ppl. a.*[2] [Un-[1] 8 + Warn *v.*[3]] Not guarded or protected. *a* 1240 *Sawles Warde* in *O. E. Hom.* I. 255 For nis his strengðe noht wurð bute hwer se he ifindeð eðeliche ant wake unwarnede of treowe bileaue. **Unwa·rning,** *vbl. sb.* [Un-[1] 13.] Absence of warning; †*of unwarning,* without premeditation. 13.. *Metr. Hom.* (MS. Ashm. 42) fol. 146 b, If wrethe come of vnwarnynge Late it haue in þe no dwellinge. **Unwa·rning,** *ppl. a.* [Un-[1] 10.] †Unguardedly. 1609 Skene *Reg. Maj.* 115 Gif any man rydes vpon ane headstrong horse, and vnwarning runnes in ane water.

†**Unwa·rnished,** *ppl. a. Obs.* [Un-[1] 8.] **a.** Unprepared; unfurnished. **b.** Unwarned.

*c* 1425 Wyntoun *Cron.* ii. xvi. 1532 Vnwarnyst wer þai and vnarrayit. *c* 1430 *Pilgr. Lyf Manhode* ii. cxxxii. (1869) 127 Iudas also was not vnwarnished of hem [*sc.* tools] whan he slowh the kyng jhesu. *Ibid.* iv. lix. 204 My fader, þat was put on þe cros, was not vnwar[ni]shed [F. *desgarny*] of swich a brest al were it nouht neede to shewe it. *c* 1475 *Cath. Angl.* 403/1 (A.), Vnwernyschit, *ex inspirato, ex inprouiso.* 1513 Douglas *Æneid* xi. i. 46 Gif ye vnwarnist beis callit to the fycht. 1535 Stewart *Cron. Scot.* (Rolls) I. 221 Wnwarneist als tha war of ony wicht.

Hence † **Unwa·rnishedly** *adv. Obs.*

1513 Douglas *Æneid* vii. ix. 64 The landwart folkis.. flokkis furth richt fast wnvarnystly. *Ibid.* ix. vi. 87.

**Unwa·rp,** *v.* [Un-[2] 3.] *trans.* **a.** To uncoil, straighten out. **b.** To restore from being warped or prejudiced.

[In the transl. of *Maison Neuve's Gerileon* (1583) i. 64 b, app. a misprint for *vnwrap,* rhyming with *hap.*]

*a* 1659 Osborne *Essex's Death* Wks. 239 This had not been said, but..to unwarp their judgements..that may be drawn aside, by the goodness of Sir Henry Woottons parts. 1670 Evelyn *Sylva* (ed. 2) xxv. 122 When the bark is off, they unwarp it before the fire. 1733 Hervey *Mem. Geo. II.* (1848) I. 257 The Queen herself was enough prejudiced too on this side, till Sir Robert Walpole unwarped her from it. 1802 Leyden *Mermaid* xii, Unwarp, unwind his oozy coils.

**Unwa·rped,** *ppl. a.* [Un-[1] 8.] Not warped (*lit.* and *fig.*).

1744 Thomson *Spring* 925 Honest Zeal unwarp'd by Party-Rage. 1759 Robertson *Hist. Scotl.* iii. Wks. 1813 I. 208 A heart unwarped by political interest. 1836 *Johnsoniana* 205 Totally devoid of all deceit,..and unwarped by any vice. 1855 Kingsley *Glaucus* 53 Long lines of tall elms,..their boughs unwarped by any blast.

**Unwa·rping,** *ppl. a.* (Un-[1] 8.) 1828–32 Webster (citing Dwight). 1902 *How to make Things* 26/2 So as to produce an unwarping flap. **Unwa·rrant.** (Un-[1] 12.) 1876 Mrs. Whitney *Sights & Ins.* II. xi. 100 It would only be to reveal to me by the unwarrant, how strangely sweet the warrant might be. **Unwarrantabi·lity.** (Un-[1] 12.) 1836 G. S. Faber *Prim. Doctr. Election.* i. v. 57 The.. delusive unwarrantability..of preferring any such prayer.

**Unwa·rrantable,** *a.* (Un-[1] 7 b.)

1612 Selden *Illustr. Drayton's Poly-olb.* iv. 215 An unwarrantable report goes, that it was for his martial delivery of the King's daughter from the Dragon. 1642 Fuller *Holy & Prof. St.* iii. xix. 203 If God bolts the doores..against him, he is not..to make his escape by unwarrantable courses. 1757 Smollett *Reprisal* i. vii, An unwarrantable insult. 1783 Burke *Rep. Aff. India* Wks. XI. 16 An unwarrantable extension or application of the municipal Law of England. 1847 H. Rogers *Ess.* (1874) I. v. 218 Alterations of a most unwarrantable description. 1874 H. R. Reynolds *John Bapt.* ii. 83 It is an unwarrantable conjecture that the human intelligence is the highest form of mind.

**b.** *spec.* Of deer: (see quot. 1798).

1798 Hey *Lect. Div.* iv. 337 A Keeper in a King's Forest told me, certain Venison was unwarrantable; that is, could not be sent in return to the Warrants issued by the Officers of the Crown. 1888 *Daily News* 29 Oct. 6/8 Two young unwarrantable deer were shot at a previous hunt.

Hence **Unwa·rrantableness.**

1633 T. Adams *Exp. 2 Peter* ii. 6 The unwarrantablenesse of their designes. *a* 1653 Binning *Usef. Case Consc.* (1693) 7 The Conscience and Conviction of the Unwarrantableness of it for the want of Authority. 1713 E. Calamy *Life Baxter* (ed. 2) xviii. 486 To prove the unwarrantableness of a Nations defending their Rights and Liberties. 1880 Muirhead *Gaius* ii. § 104 *note,* Studemund's revision has also shown the unwarrantableness of the *endo mandatela.*

**Unwa·rrantably,** *adv.* (Un-[1] 11.)

1634 Canne *Necess. Separ.* 70 They found it..unwarrantably to be used for the edifying of the body of Christ. 1682 C. Irvine *Hist. Scott. Nomencl.* Ded. *vj, You,..when they threw away their own Lives unwarrantably, bemoaned their madness. 1734 *Col. Rec. Pennsylv.* III. 561 Unwarrantably confined in a loathsome Goal. 1808 Coleridge *Lett.* (1895) 527 You have been, perhaps rather unwarrantably, severe on my morals. 1830 Mackintosh *Eth. Philos.* Wks. 1846 I. 198 Humility..has of late been unwarrantably used to signify that painful consciousness of inferiority which is the first stage of envy. 1890 *Spectator* 30 Aug. 262/1 His name is unwarrantably dragged into a controversy with which he has nothing to do.

**Unwa·rranted,** *ppl. a.* (UN-[1] 8.)

Also, in recent use (1891-), *unwarrantedly* adv.

**1577** tr. *Bullinger's Decades* 416 It doth sharpely rebuke ..him, for his unwarranted rashenesse. **1587** *Norton's Calvin's Inst.* IV. 490 *margin*, Extreame annointing [is] a forcelesse and vnwarranted ceremonie. **1633** HART *Diet of Diseased* Introd. 8 Ignorant and unwarranted Physitians. **1651** HOBBES *Leviathan* II. xxii. 116 The Assembly cannot Represent any man in things unwarranted by their Letters. **1748** MELMOTH *Fitzosborne Lett.* xlix. (1749) II. 36 Every eminent writer, without indulging any unwarranted licences, has a language which he derives from himself. **1817** JAS. MILL *Brit. India* II. IV. v. 216 The Directors..condemned ..the rapacious and unwarranted proceedings of their servants. **1862** LYTTON *Str. Story* II. 50, I should be utterly unwarranted in supposing that..they were insane.

†**Unwa·rrayed,** *ppl. a.* [UN-[1] 8 + WARRAY *v.*] = next. **1411-12** HOCCLEVE *De Reg. Princ.* 2211 Castelx, by feith, dreden non assailynge, By feith, þe Citees standen vn-werreyed. **Unwa·rred,** *ppl. a.* [UN-[1] 8 + WAR *v.*[1]] Un-assailed, unattacked. **1390** GOWER *Conf.* I. 357 And so thei deden overal,..So that thei leften nothing stonde Unwerred, bot onliche Archade. **Unwa·rren,** *v.* (UN-[2] 6 b.) *a* **1500** in Arnolde *Chron.* (1811) 19 That alle the wareyn of Stanes ..be vnwareyned and vnforested for euermore.

**Unwa·ry,** *a.* [UN-[1] 7.]

**1.** Not wary; unguarded, incautious: **a.** Of persons (or animals).

In Langland's *Piers Pl.* A. IV. 24 two manuscripts have 'vnwary', but the correct reading is doubtful.

**1579** SPENSER *Sheph. Cal.* Dec. 10 O soueraigne Pan.., Which..Doest saue from mischiefe the vnwary sheepe. **1596** — *F. Q.* VI. x. 3 T'entrap vnwary fooles in their eternall bales. **1598** FLORIO, *Disauedere*,..to be vnwarie, not to regard. **1624** GATAKER *Wife in Deed* 63 There is no woman almost so vnwise or vnwarie, that will buy an earthen pitcher,..but she will view it well first. **1651** HOBBES *Leviath.* III. xxxvii. 234 The private actions of an ignorant, unwary man. *a* **1715** BURNET *Own Time* (1766) I. 263 These were his true principles tho' he had disguised them in order to catch un-wary readers. **1759** ROBERTSON *Hist. Scot.* VII. Wks. 1813 I. 513 No wonder pretexts so plausible should impose on the unwary queen. **1820** SCORESBY *Acc. Arctic Reg.* II. 178 The fish were numerous and unwary. **1896** W. K. LEASK *H. Miller* iv. 99 The unwary disputant emerged in a highly battered condition.

*absol.* **1637** EARL MONM. tr. *Malvezzi's Romulus & T.* 177 Tarquin is not to be ranked amongst the unwary. **1707** ATTERBURY *Serm.* (1726) II. 174 Its Emissaries are..very busy in Corners, to seduce the Unwary. **1848** MRS. JAMESON *Sacr. & Leg. Art* I. 70 With..flexile claws..stretched out to seize and entangle the unwary.

**b.** Of actions, conduct, the mind, etc.

**1610** G. FLETCHER *Christ's Vict.* I. lxxxiv, With that the mightie thunder dropt away From Gods unwarie arme. **1643** SIR T. BROWNE *Relig. Med.* I. § 1 Those principles my Parents instilled into my unwary understanding. **1697** DRYDEN *Virg. Georg.* II. 415 Sparkling fire, from hinds' unwary hands. **1703** ROWE *Ulysses* I. i, 'Tis rash, and savours of unwary Youth. **1747** HERVEY *Contempl. Night* (1748) II. 12 How often has an unwary glance, kindled a Fever of irregular Desire in our Hearts? **1803** GOUV. MORRIS in Sparks *Life & Writ.* (1832) III. 180 It is a most unwary step. **1867** LADY HERBERT *Cradle L.* v. 151 An unwary emptying of their..leather water-bottles before half the day was over.

†**2.** Unexpected. *Obs.*[—1]

**1590** SPENSER *F. Q.* I. xii. 25 All in the open hall amazed stood, At suddeinnesse of that vnwarie sight.

**Unwa·shable,** *a.* and *sb.* (UN-[1] 7 b, 12.) **1839** MRS. KIRKLAND *New Home* xxxiv. 231 Those [ladies] who had unwarily sported silks and other unwashables, looked acid and uncomfortable.

**Unwa·shed,** *ppl. a.* [UN-[1] 8, 8 c.]

**1.** Not washed; not cleaned by washing.

?*a* **1390** *Form of Cury* in Warner *Antiq. Culin.* (1791) 21 Take Hares,..and seeþ hem with þe blode unwaisshed in broth. *a* **1400** *Northern Passion* 346 Wasche fote and hand we pray þe, þat nokyn thyng vn wessched be. *c* **1440** *Promp. Parv.* 368/1 On-waschyd, *illotus*. **1543** TRAHERON *Vigo's Chirurg.* II. IV. ii. 66 It is good to laye vppon the place vnwashed woulle. **1605** R. F. *Dedekind's Sch. Slovenrie* (1904) 30 Then with your unwasht knife to cut your meate can breede no hurt. **1675** HAN. WOOLLEY *Gentlew. Comp.* 179 Take Mallows and Mercury unwasht. **1751** AKENSIDE *Ode to T. Edwards* vi, The sophist..With unwashed hands and lips profane. **1815** SCOTT *Guy M.* xliv, She proceeded with unwashed hands to arrange the stipulated bed-linen. **1890** *Anthony's Photogr. Bull.* III. 232 The emulsion is an unwashed one.

*fig.* **1607** B. JONSON *Volpone* Ep. ¶ 2, I..haue loathed the vse of such foule, and vn-wash'd Baudr'y. **1611** — *Catiline* II. i, A slanderous, beastly, vnwash'd tongue. **1849** LEVER *Con Cregan* xv, Wickedness in its most unwashed state.

**2.** *spec.* Of persons: Not having washed; not usually washed or in a clean state.

**1595** SHAKS. *John* IV. ii. 201 Another leane, vnwash'd Artificer, Cuts off his tale, and talkes of Arthurs death. *a* **1727** *Ballad on Quadrille* viii, The King of late..made, of many a Squire and Lord, An unwash'd Knight of Bath. **1781** COWPER *Table-t.* 152 Clubs..To which th' unwash'd artificer repairs. **1822** SCOTT *Nigel* Introd. Ep., All the unwashed artificers connected with literature. **1865** KINGSLEY *Herew.* xviii, Why should not beggars go unwashed? **1868** [T. WRIGHT] *Great Unwashed* Pref., Others who..are by the unwashed workers looked upon as swells.

**b.** *absol.* Those who are not usually in a clean state; the lower orders. Freq. with *great*.

(*a*) **1833** HOOK *Parson's Dau.* II. 119 The 'fat and greasy', and the 'great unwashed,' bowed and smiled their best. **1850** THACKERAY *Pendennis* xxx, Gentlemen, there can be but little doubt that your ancestors were the Great Unwashed. **1868** [T. WRIGHT] *The Great Unwashed* Pref., Whenever..I speak of working men, or the working classes, it is in the 'great-unwashed' sense.

(*b*) **1853** in Thornton *Amer. Gloss.* 920 A great portion of the unwashed, as well as the 'unterrified' left the hall. **1859** F. MAHONY *Rel. Father Prout* 417 The 'waters of instruction' are to be plentifully supplied to the unwashed.

**3.** Not washed *off* or *out*.

**1628** MAY *Virg. Georg.* III. 94 Sweat unwash'd off [will] stick Vpon their new-shorne skins. **1842** MRS. BROWNING *Grk. Chr. Poets* ii. ¶ 6 His happy Athenian associations gave a colour, unwashed out by tears, to his mind and works.

Hence **Unwa·shedness.**

**1893** *Harper's Mag.* Jan. 186/2 Various perfumes of unwashedness and misery.

**Unwa·shen,** *ppl. a.* Now *arch.* [OE. *unwæscen* (UN-[1] 8 b). Cf. (M)Du. *ongewasschen*, MLG., MHG., and G. *ungewaschen*, OHG. *ungiwasgan.*] = UNWASHED *ppl. a.* Also *fig.*

*c* **1000** *Sax. Leechd.* II. 108 Nim sigelhweorfan þa smalan unwæscene. *c* **1200** *Trin. Coll. Hom.* 57 On swinke, on unwasshen weden, on smerte swinginge. *a* **1225** *Ancr. R.* 82 Ful speche is as of lecherie, & of oðre fulðen þet unweaschene muðes spekeð oðer hwule. **13..** *E. E. Allit. P.* B. 34 For-þy hyȝ not to heuen in haterez to-torne, Ne in þe harlotez hod & handez vnwaschen. **1388** WYCLIF *Mark* vii. 2 Whanne thei hadden seen summe of hise disciplis ete breed with vn-waisschen hoondis. **1421-2** HOCCLEVE *Min. Poems* 116/182 Vnwasshen gold shall wasshe a-way that vice. *c* **1430** LYDG. *Min. Poems* (Percy Soc.) 256 Loth to ryse,..With unwassh handys reedy to dyneer. *c* **1450** *M. E. Med. Bk.* (Heinrich) 124 Take vnwasshe loombes wolle. **1526** TINDALE *Matt.* xv. 20 To eate with vnwesshen hondes defyleth nott a man. **1608** BP. HALL *Pharisaism & Christ* (1609) 642 The Pharise [finds fault] with vnwashen hands. **1648** J. BEAUMONT *Psyche* XVI. lxxvi, Prophane unwashen feet farr hence must be, This holy ground belongs to Sanctity. **1832** GEN. P. THOMPSON *Exerc.* (1842) II. 42 Whoever has brains so unwashen as to give up the guidance of himself..to any man. **1856** HAWTHORNE *Eng. Note-bks.* (1870) II. 44 The town..has a very sordid, grimy, shabby, unswept, unwashen aspect. **1870** MORRIS *Earthly Par.* II. III. 435 So from the lower end they came, ill clad, Houseless, unwashen, yet with faces glad.

**Unwa·ssailing,** *ppl. a.* (UN-[1] 10.) **1826** LAMB *Lett.* (1886) II. 238 Old Christmas is a coming. to the confusion of Puritans,..Quakers, and that unwassailing crew. **Unwa·stable,** *a.* (UN-[1] 7 b.) **1575** LANEHAM *Let.* (1871) 44 [Jupiter] seemz too be..in store of municion, vnwastabl. **1623** LISLE *Ælfric on O. & N. Test.* Pref. b 2 b, That vnwastable light,..which they had of old time shining, rather than burning in their sepulchers.

**Unwa·sted,** *ppl. a.* [UN-[1] 8.]

**1.** Not wasted or consumed.

**1340-70** *Alex. & Dind.* 236 Hit scholde nouht lesen his liht..While þe weke & þe waxe vn-wasted lasteþ. *c* **1400** *Found. St. Bartholomew's* 61 What myghte falle to them.. that hastid with a desire to that place of vnwastid pite. **1561** T. NORTON *Calvin's Inst.* IV. xvii. 121 b, The fleshe of Christ is like a riche and vnwasted fountaine. **1625** DONNE *Serm.* 26 Whose meale and oyle God preserved unwasted. **1659** W. CHAMBERLAYNE *Pharon.* I. i. 178 So they preserve his name—A yet unwasted pyramid of fame. **1713** BLACKMORE *Creation* I. 671 Why have those rocks so long unwasted stood? **1826** MILMAN *Anne Boleyn* 35 Unwasted by the pains of earth, Thou didst bring forth the fair immortal birth. **1846** KEBLE *Lyra Innoc.* 73 Through the dim chinks of this decaying earth Gleams, ever and anon, th' unwasted fire.

**2.** Not laid waste; undevastated.

**1570** FOXE *A. & M.* (ed. 2) I. 362 b/1 The kyng might haue had his land vnwasted, and his treasure vnconsumed. **1785** BURKE *Sp. Nabob of Arcot's Debts* Wks. IV. 276 Several of the petty princes of the most southerly of the unwasted provinces. **1836** THIRLWALL *Greece* II. xvi. 331 Tempted by the prospect of saving their still unwasted fields and dwellings.

**3.** Not impaired by waste.

**1758** J. DALRYMPLE *Ess. Feudal Property* (ed. 2) 59 The lord came into the practice of giving a whole year's rent for the king's right of waste, and got the lands safe and unwasted to himself.

**Unwa·steful,** *a.* (UN-[1] 7.) **1570** LEVINS *Manip.* 186 Vn-waystful, *frugalis*. **Unwa·stefully,** *adv.* (UN-[1] 11.) **1618** BACON *Ord. Chancery* (1642) 15, 15 lines in every sheet thereof written orderly and unwastfully.

**Unwa·sting,** *ppl. a.* (UN-[1] 10.)

**1387-8** T. USK *Test. Love* III. iii. (Skeat) l. 127 Wete, I doe brenne; unwasting, I langour and fade. **1722** POPE *Two Chorus's to 'Brutus'* ii. 41 Purest love's unwasting treasure. **1818** MILMAN *Samor* III. 222 Sleets From their unwasting granary barb their darts. **1846** KEBLE *Lyra Innoc.* 143 The Living Fount Of pure unwasting fire. **1868** LYNCH *Rivulet* CXXVIII. iv, 'Seek treasure of unwasting worth,' He said.

**Unwa·tched,** *ppl. a.* (UN-[1] 8.)

*c* **1425** WYNTOUN *Cron.* IV. v. 499 All vnwachit sodanely Thai fell on sleip. **1548** UDALL *Erasm. Par. Luke* iv. 41 b, Of all these dooeth our enemie leaue not one thyng vn-watched, whereby he maie drawe vs to damnacion. **1593** DONNE *Sat.* ii. 98 But when he sells or changes land, he impaires His writings, and (unwatch'd) leaves out *ses heires*. **1602** SHAKS. *Ham.* III. i. 197 Madnesse in great Ones, must not vnwatch'd go. **1795** COLERIDGE *Silver Thimble* 49 And I from unwatch'd needle's erring point Had surely suffer'd on each finger-joint Those wounds. **1812** CRABBE *Tales* xi. 458 Rarely from town, nor then unwatch'd, he goes. **1850** TENNYSON *In Mem.* ci, Unwatch'd, the garden bough shall sway. **1870** BRYANT *Iliad* I. I. 30 Thou ever dost suspect me, Nor can I act unwatched.

**Unwa·tchful,** *a.* (UN-[1] 7.)

**1611** FLORIO, *Inuigilante*, vnuigilant, vnwatchfull. **1651** JER. TAYLOR *Serm. for Year* II. xx. 256 They are..incurious in their walking, unwatchfull in their circumstances. **1720** A. PETRIE *Rules Good Deportm.* (1877) 118 It is not discreet nor just in Ministers..to be unwatchfull over their Flock. *a* **1740** WATTS *Ess. Var. Subj.* (1795) 271 Every christian, even the weak and the unwatchful. *c* **1750** J. NELSON *Jrnl.* (1836) 40 You are more light and unwatchful than you used to be. **1805** WORDSW. *Prelude* II. 300, I..difference Perceived in things, where, to the unwatchful eye, No difference is. **1869** LOWELL *Cathedral* 213 Its once grim bulwarks, tamed to lovers' walks, Look down unwatchful on the sliding Eure.

Hence **Unwa·tchfully** *adv.*, **-fulness.**

**1611** FLORIO, *Inuigilanza*, vnwatchfulnesse. *a* **1658** DURHAM *Comm. Rev.* (1660) 181 There was much..unwatchfulnesse and untendernesse in both these respects before God. **1682** W. ROGERS *Seventh Pt. Chr. Quaker* 78 No wonder if the High as well as the Low come to a Loss through their unwatchfulness. **1787** in *Jrnl. Friends Hist. Soc.* XIX. 92 Through unwatchfulness and the depravity of my heart. **1860** TRENCH *Serm. Westm. Abb.* xxxi. 354 Whether thou wilt be still watchful over thyself, when there is so much to persuade to unwatchfulness. **1867** RUSKIN *Time & Tide* (1872) 75 In summing the observation of past life not un-watchfully spent.

†**Unwa·ter,** *sb. Obs.*[—0] (UN-[1] 12 b. Cf. UNWATERED *ppl. a.* 1 b.) **1611** COTGR., *Camelot plenier*, vnwater Chamlet.

**Unwa·ter,** *v.* [UN-[2] 4.] *trans.* To drain of water, to carry off water from; *spec.* in *Mining* (see b).

The word occurs as a mistranslation in: *a* **1300** *E. E. Psalter* lxxvii. 23 (E., H.), He smot þe stane, and watres outran, And scaldand unwatred [L. *inundaverunt*] þai ilkan.

**a.** **1642** C. VERMUYDEN *Disc. Fennes* 5 By these Out-falls the said Rivers and Lands unwater themselves. **1872** W. F. BUTLER *Gt. Lone Land* iv. (1875) 60 The St. Croix [river] unwatering the great tract of pine land. **1880** HAUGHTON *Phys. Geogr.* x. 192 The rivers of China unwater the whole eastern slope of the table-land.

**b.** **1769** SMEATON in Glynn *Treat. Power Water* (1853) 99 The first complete engine..at work..for draining or un-watering a lead mine. **1778** PRYCE *Min. Cornub.* 146 Many more valuable Lodes have been discovered, than those they were driving to unwater. **1865** J. T. F. TURNER *Slate Quarries* 22 The pits are unwatered by one engine pump. **1883** *Encycl. Brit.* XVI. 458/1 Siphons have been used for unwatering workings in special cases.

Hence **Unwa·tering** *vbl. sb.*

**1778** PRYCE *Min. Cornub.* 152 The innumerable Adits..are of some importance to the unwatering of the Mines.

**Unwa·tered,** *ppl. a.* [UN-[1] 8. Cf. older Flem. *onghewaetert* (Kilian), Du. *ongewatert*, G. *ungewässert*.]

**1.** Not sprinkled, moistened, or artificially supplied with water.

*c* **1440** *Pallad. on Husb.* x. 111 Tyl hit be hard, vnwattred must hit [*sc.* land] be, Lest al the werk corrupte humydite. **1648** HEXHAM II, *Ongewatert*, Vnwatered, or Vnsprinckled. **1731** POPE *Ep. Burlington* 125 Un-watered see the drooping sea-horse mourn. **1899** *Daily News* 12 June 7/5 To facilitate cavalry charges the main thoroughfares remained unwatered.

**b.** Of dress materials: (see WATER *v.* 9).

**1535** in *Archaeol.* IX. 248 A long gowne of unwatered chamblette. **1583** *Rates Custome ho.* B ij, Chamlets watered and vnwatred. **1648** HEXHAM II, *Ongewatert Kamelot*, Vnwatered Chamlot. **1706** *Lond. Gaz.* No. 4189/4 Coarse unwatered Camblets. **1750** LADY JANE COKE *Lett.* (1899) 61 I have given half-a guinea for an unwatered tabby.

†**2.** Not soaked or steeped in water. *Obs.*

**1511** FABYAN *Will* in *Chron.* (1811) p. v, Than I will that the said .xxiiij. peces of fleshe be altered unto saltfyche or stokfyshe, unwatered and unsodeyn. **1570** LEVINS *Manip.* 51 Vnwatred, *immaceratus*. **1648** HEXHAM II, *Ongeweyckt*, Not laid in water, or Vnwatered, as Harberdine, &c.

**3.** Not mixed with water; undiluted.

**1562** TURNER *Herbal* II. 35 b, Entre into a bath, and drynke vnwatered wyne after. **1576** GASCOIGNE *Steele Gl.* 582 Augustus Cæsar..seldome dranke his wine unwatered. **1648** HEXHAM II, *Ongewaterden wijn*, Vnwatered wine, or Vn-mixed with water. **1870** EMERSON *Soc. & Solit.*, *Farming*, The farmer has a great health;..his milk at least, is un-watered. **1887** BOWEN *Æneid* v. 78 Twain huge flagons of wine unwatered.

**b.** *Finance.* (See WATERED *ppl. a.* 4 c.)

**1893** *Westm. Gaz.* 29 June 6/1 The 25 per cent. represents 1,250 per cent. on the original unwatered capital, or over £687,000 on a real capital of £55,000.

**4.** Of land, a district, etc.: Not provided with a natural supply of water; waterless. Also in fig. context.

**1600** SURFLET *Countrie Farm* VI. vii. 740 In hot, drie, and vnwatered places. **1794** A. YOUNG *Trav.* (ed. 2) II. 152 The country (that I saw) is poor and unwatered, in the Milanese. **1794** VANCOUVER *Agric. Cambridge* 55 The grass..is chiefly inferior to that..which grows..upon unwatered ground. **1828** J. MONTGOMERY *Tombs Fathers* Wks. 1841 IV. 178 Kedron's unwater'd brook is dumb. **1860** PUSEY *Min. Proph.* 14 The soul of the sinner is..unfruitful;..for it is.. unwatered by the Fountain of living waters. **1890** 'R. BOLDREWOOD' *Col. Reformer* (1891) 100 The unwatered region away from the river.

**Unwa·tery,** *a.* [OE. *unwæterig* (UN-[1] 7).] Not supplied with or containing water.

*c* **1000** *Ags. Gosp.* Luke xi. 24 He gæð þurh unwæterie stowa, reste secende. *a* **1300** *E. E. Psalter* cvi. 4 Thei erreden in wildernesse, in vnwatri place. **1382** WYCLIF *Ps.* lxxvii. 40 In to wrathe thei to-striden hym in vnwatri place.

**1739** C. WESLEY *Hymns* 222 Divinely led the Favourites pass Th' Unwatry Deep, and emptied Sea. **1872** BROWNING *Fifine* cii, How..The solid surface-shield was outcome..Of simple dew at work to save itself amid The unwatery force around. **1877** BLACKIE *Wise Men* 67 Age to youth May sooner pass than from unwatery crust Be birth of water.

**Unwa·vering,** *ppl. a.* (UN-[1] 10.)

**1570** LEVINS *Manip.* 137 Vnwauering, *immotus*. **1667** H. MORE *Disc. Faith* (1713) 579 Forasmuch as Faith..is nothing but an unwavering assent to some Doctrine [etc.]. **1721** STRYPE *Eccl. Mem.* II. II. i. 253 To shew how unwavering she continued in her formerly declared purpose. **1739** C. & J. WESLEY *Hymns* 12 With Steps unwav'ring, undismay'd Give me in all thy Paths to tread. **1801** COLERIDGE *Triumph Loyalty* I. 330 All objects there will teach me Unwavering Love. **1856** FROUDE *Hist. Eng.* (1858) I. 409 An unwavering pursuit of a single policy. **1884** A. R. PENNINGTON *Wiclif* III. 120 He was as unwavering in his tone as in his reply to the 'motley doctor'.

Hence **Unwa·veringly** *adv.*
**1830** Coleridge *Constit. Ch. & State* I The mark, to which my convictions and wishes have..unwaveringly pointed. **1872** Tennyson *Gareth & Lynette* 139 When the Queen.. Found her son's will unwaveringly one, She answer'd craftily.

**Unwa·ving,** *ppl. a.* (Un-[1] 10.) **1706** J. Weaver *Orchesography* 28 Examples of waving and unwaving Positions, where the Feet turn and return both on the same side. **1818** Milman *Samor* vii. 650 The yellow crown Of the unwaving forest. **1835** Lytton *Rienzi* x. viii, Not a breeze stirred the dark cypress and unwaving pine.

†**Unwa·x,** *v.*[1] *Obs.* [Un-[2] 7.] *intr.* To grow or become less; to decrease. Also *fig.*
**13..** *Coer de L.* 2844 Thus began our folk unwexe, And dyede for hungyr and for woo. *c* **1400** *Pepysian Gosp. Harmony* (1922) 14 For it bihoued nedes þat Jesus wex & þat he vnwex. **14..** in Maskell *Mon. Rit.* (1847) III. 353 Of a man it is seid, the more he wexith the more he unwexith.

**Unwa·x,** *v.*[2] [Un-[2] 4.] *trans.* To deprive of wax; to remove the wax from.
**1817** Kirby & Sp. *Entomol.* II. 148 On the seventh day the part covering the head and trunk of the young female [bee], if I may so speak, is almost entirely unwaxed.

**Unwa·xed,** *ppl. a.* [Un-[1] 8 + Wax *v.*[2]] Not treated with wax. *c* **1410** *Master of Game* (MS. Digby 182) xxi, Oþer meane hornes vnwexed beth goode ynogh for hem [*sc.* woodmen]. [**1775** Ash.] **1832** G. R. Porter *Porcelain & Gl.* xv. 313 The unwaxed under-side of the glass. **1886** *Pall Mall G.* 6 April 1/1 Two rather steep.., uncarpeted and unwaxed, staircases. †**Unway·.** *Obs.* [Un-[1] 4 b. Cf. MDu. *onwech* (Du. *onweg*), MLG. *unwech*, MHG. *unwec* (G. *unweg*), MDa. *uvej.*] A place without ways. *a* **1340** Hampole *Ps.* cvi. 40 He made þaim to erre in vnway [L. *in invio*] & noght in way.

†**Unway·ed,** *a. Obs.* [Un-[1] 9. Cf. MDu. *ongheweget*, MDa. *uvejet.*]
**1.** Not provided with ways or roads.
In both passages rendering L. (*terra*) *invia*.
**1382** Wyclif *Ezek.* xv. 8 Whanne Y shal..ȝyue the loond vnwaied and desolat. — *Hos.* ii. 3 Y shal putte hir as a wildernesse, and ordeyne hir as a lond vnweyed.
**2.** Of horses: Not accustomed to ways or roads; hence, restive, intractable.
**1607** Markham *Cavel.* iv. 15 If the horse be yong and vnwayed. *c* **1640** [? Shirley] *Capt. Underwit* ii. ii, She kicks and flings out like a Colt unwayed. *a* **1642** Suckling *Let.* Wks. (1648) 82 As Colts that are unway'd, and will not go at all.

**Unwea·kened,** *ppl. a.* (Un-[1] 8.)
**1648** Hexham ii, *Ongekrenckt*, vnweakned, or vn-enfeebled. **1662** Boyle *Def. Doct. Air* 74 The unweakned pressure of the outward Air. **1828** Carlyle *Misc.* (1840) I. 201 His heart, though torn, is yet unweakened. **1856** Ruskin *Mod. Paint.* IV. v. xix. § 22 The unweakened and active intellects of Van Eyck and Albert Durer. **1871** Kennedy *Publ. Sch. Lat. Gram.* (1874) 35 Numerous words keep their root-vowel *a* unweakened in the second member of their compounds.

**Unwea·l.** [Un-[1] 12.] Unhappiness; distress.
*a* **1300** *Cursor M.* 5714 To-quils was of israel þe folk ledd wit mikel vn-wel [*v.r.* vn-wele]. *a* **1850** Rossetti *Dante & Circle* I. (1874) 39 Since thou alone hast made my heart to feel This sadness and unweal.

†**Unwea·lful,** *a. Obs.* [Un-[1] 7.] Unhappy; causing misfortune or unhappiness. **1412–20** Lydg. *Chron. Troy* ii. 4234 Vnwelful woman, disturber of oure pes, Þou haste vs brouȝt in meschef & in were. *Ibid.* 8112 To Grekis pleinly þis ryvaille So mortal was & so infortunat, So vnwelful and disconsolat. †**Unwea·lfulness.** *Obs.* [Un-[1] 12. Cf. prec.] = next. *a* **1555** J. Philpot tr. *Curio's Def. Christ's Ch.* (1842) 387, I perceive thou art more happier than all these, Calistus; but it shameth me nothing to be accounted among them, and to be partaker of this unwellfulness with them. †**Unwea·lsomeness.** *Obs.*—[1] [Un-[1] 12.] Unhappiness. **1382** Wyclif *Ps.* xiii. 3 To-brosing and vnwelsumnesse [L. *infelicitas*] in the weies of hem, and the weie of pes thei knewen not.

†**Unwea·lth.** *Obs. rare.* [Un-[1] 12.] Lack of prosperity.
*a* **1300** *Cursor M.* 28697 Þou do him vnder-stand alsua Hu lang þat adam was in wa, And þai þat of his body sprang, Hu þair vnwelth þam lasted lang. *c* **1412** Hoccleve *De Reg. Princ.* (Roxb.) 32 To live..ever after in sorwe & unwelthe.
**Unwea·lthiness.** (Un-[1] 12. Cf. next.) **1886** *Pall Mall G.* 23 Oct. 14/1, I have continued in the same state of unwealthiness as formerly.

**Unwea·lthy,** *a.* (Un-[1] 7).
*c* **1412** Hoccleve *De Reg. Princ.* 1287 He sparith hem that vnwelthy heer ben. **1582** Stanyhurst *Æneis* ii. (Arb.) 46 My father vnwelthy mee sent..hither. **1809–14** Wordsw. *Excurs.* v. 132 An unwealthy mountain Benefice. **1876** Morris *Æneid* viii. 105 The senate poor of that unwealthy folk Cast incense there. **1895** P. White *King's Diary* iii, An unwealthy Tory peer and his pompous belongings.
†**Unwea·ly,** *a. Obs.*—[1] [Un-[1] 7.] Poor; unwealthy. *a* **1300** *E. E. Psalter* lxxviii. 8 (E.), For þat un-weli [*v.r.* poure; L. *pauperes*] for to se Swiþe mikel made are we.

**Unwea·ned,** *ppl. a.* Also 6 -waynde, -wain'd. [Un-[1] 8.] Not weaned; † immature.
**1581** Studley tr. *Seneca, Herc. Œt.* i. 191 b, Coulde I brooke it Toxeus, to see thy death with woe? That wert vnwaynde in yeares, and eake in pits vnpaysde. **1596** Fitz-Geffrey *Sir F. Drake* (1881) 30 Blinde with affection, ignorant of truthe, Vnwain'd from self-love, never at a staye. **1607** Chapman *Bussy d'Ambois* iv. i. 17 Or still-unwean'd sweet Moon-calues with white faces. **1799** Sheridan *Pizarro* i. i. 13 In peace as gentle as the unweaned lamb. **1807** Cogan *Treatise on Passions* (1813) II. 310 An unweaned affection for peculiarities which have no other claim upon us. **1844** H. Stephens *Bk. Farm* III. 1123 The lambs remain unweaned, until they wean themselves. **1871** Whyte-Melville *Sarchedon* I. 3 Like sucking fawn and unweaned child.

**Unwea·pon,** *v.* [Un-[2] 4. Cf. MDu. *ontwapenen, -wapen* (Du. *-wapenen*), MHG. *entwâpenen, -wâpen, -wâfen* (G. *-waffnen*).] *trans.* To deprive of a weapon or weapons.
*a* **1586** Sidney *Arcadia* iii. xxviii, Hee was no more amazed with his being vnweaponed, then with the suddainnesse thereof. **1611** Florio, *Disarmare*, to disarme, to vnweapon. *a* **1646** J. Gregory *Posthuma, Assyrian Mon.* (1650) 248 One night a Plague of Mice came upon him, and unweaponed his souldiers, by devouring their Harness-ties of Leather. **1662** Hibbert *Body Divinity* ii. 106 He beats down our enemies before us, unweaponing them.

**Unwea·poned,** *ppl. a.* [Un-[1] 8. Cf. OE. *ungewǽpnod*, MDu. *ongewapent* (Du. *-wapend*), MHG. *ungewâfent, -wâpent* (G. *ungewaffnet, -wappnet*).] Not equipped with or bearing a weapon or weapons; unarmed.
*c* **1200** *Trin. Coll. Hom.* 191 Ðus fliteð þe fiend wið alle men;..and þo ben alle unwepnede þe ne hauen mid hwan hie hem werien. *c* **1205** Lay. 5654 Þeo cnihtes weoren vnwepned, þa þe wæne heo wes ȝeuede. *c* **1425** *Eng. Conq. Irel.* 22 So as we bene..well y-wepned,..ne dout no man þat such vnwepned rascayll any power haw ows to wythstond. **1513–4** *Act* 5 *Hen. VIII*, c. 6, Wheras they [*sc.* surgeons]..have ben entreatid as Herawdes of Armes aswell in batelles and feldes as other places ther for to stond unharnesed and unwapenned. **1553** Bale *Vocacyon* 28 b, The cruell murtherers..cowardly slewe them all vnarmed & vnweaponed. *a* **1618** Raleigh *Disc. War* (1850) 2 Instruments of much advantage against unweaponed men. **1642** Vicars *God in Mount* 66 Being all unweaponed, and coming onely in a fair and unoffensive manner. **1823** *Monthly Mag.* LV. 409 He hastes his armour off to throw, And stands unweapon'd. **1874** Spurgeon *Treas. Dav.* IV. 371 Not by the aid of others, but by his own unweaponed hand his marvellous conquests have been achieved.
*fig.* **1549** Coverdale, etc. *Erasm. Par. 2 Cor.* 57 b, As lowe and weake as ye thinke vs, yet are we not vnweaponed, nor without strength to suppresse the aduersaries of the gospel. **1594** Marlowe & Nashe *Dido* i. ii, Our hands are not prepar'd to lawles spoyle..: Such force is farre from our vnweaponed thoughts. **1624** Massinger *Bondman* iv. iv, Hee 's more a slaue, then Fortune Or Miserie can make me, that insults Vpon vnweapon'd Innocence. *a* **1628** F. Grevil *Cælica* xx, Since unweaponed care makes men forlorne, Let me first make your Dogge an Vnicorne. **1859** G. Wilson *Mem. E. Forbes* iv. (1861) 131 An accuracy [with the stethoscope]..such as the experience of forty years had often failed to bring to the unweaponed physician.

**Unwea·rable,** *a.* (Un-[1] 7 b.) [**1775** Ash.] **1846** Worcester (citing Grant). **1906** *Daily Chron.* 22 June 4/2 The merry crowd..laughs for the fifteenth time at an unwearable joke.
**Unweariabi·lity.** (Un-[1] 12. Cf. next.) **1853** Hawthorne *Eng. Note-bks.* (1883) I. 464 In instance of Charles Dickens's unweariability.

**Unwea·riable,** *a.* [Un-[1] 7 b.] Incapable of being or becoming wearied or tired; indefatigable, unremitting.
App. disused in the 18th cent., and reintroduced in the 19th, when it came into common use.
**a.** Of persons or things.
**1561** T. Norton *Calvin's Inst.* i. 47 An enemie that is.. in diligence and celeritie vnweriable. **1594** Hooker *Eccl. Pol.* i. iv. § 1 Desire to resemble him in goodnes maketh them vnweariable. **1608** Bp. Hall *Char. Virtues & V.* ii. (1614) 259 If the others eare were as vnweariable as his tongue. **1626** — *Contempl., O. T.* xxi. vi, He is vnweariable with our requests. **1694** in R. H. Story *W. Carstares* (1874) 234 A great fervency in expression, and unweariable lungs, are mistaken by the poor ignorant for zeal and piety. [**1775** Ash.] **1810** Southey *Kehama* xvi. xix, That unweariable foe, With will relentless follows still. **1854** Thoreau *Walden* (1863) 253 So long-winded was he and so unweariable. **1899** Mackail *W. Morris* II. 217 Through all that period, his sister was his..unweariable nurse.
**b.** Of qualities, conditions, or actions.
**1571** Golding *Calvin on Ps.* xxv. 5 He hung uppon God with unweeriable constancie. **1594** Hooker *Eccl. Pol.* Pref. 17 An vnweariable desire of receyuing instruction. **1627** J. Carter *Plain Expos.* 5 It requireth vnweariable labour and paines all our life long. **1651** Gataker in Fuller *Abel Rediv.* (1867) I. 242 An insatiable ardour and unweariable endeavour of continual..hearing or reading.
**1813** Shelley *Q. Mab* vii. 198 Resolved to wage unweariable war With my almighty Tyrant. *a* **1842** Arnold *Hist. Rome* (1845) III. 141 The Numidians..chased them with unweariable speed. **1880** Miss Bird *Japan* II. 260 Their unweariable good nature.
Hence **Unwea·riableness.**
**1647** Trapp *Comm. Acts* vi. 5 Famous for their unweariableness in God's work. **1652** W. Brough *Sacr. Princ.* 64 Why such unweariablnesse to have my will?

**Unwea·riably,** *adv.* [Un-[1] 11. Cf. prec.] Without wearying; indefatigably.
**1612** T. Taylor *Comm. Titus* i. 8 Hereby thou art like God, he sparseth abroad, he vnweariably giveth good, to good and bad. **1643** E. Symmons *Loyal Subjects Belief* 65 Those graces and gifts..which in his service you have..most faithfully and unweariably expended. **1856** Hawthorne *Eng. Note-bks.* (1870) II. 40 A variety of mountain outlines that I could have studied unweariably. **1879** H. W. Warren *Recr. Astron.* xii. 258 Rendered apparent, static, and unweariably operative.

**Unwea·ried,** *ppl. a.* [Un-[1] 8. Cf. OE. *ungewérigod.*] Of persons, things, etc.: Not wearied, tired, or tired out; also, never becoming weary; indefatigable.
*a* **1240** *Sawles Warde* in *O. E. Hom.* I. 261 Þe oðre.. iblescede gastes þe beoð a biuore godd..ant singeð a unwerȝed. *a* **1400–50** *Alexander* 3622 Þe pepill..ware petusly wounded Of Olifauntis..; All at vnweried a-way wynnes in þe stoundis Durst neuir his face to his faes eft on fold bide. *a* **1548** Hall *Chron., Hen. VI*, 141 b, The vnweried chieftain & manly warrior. **1596** Shaks. *Merch. V.* iii. ii. 296 The best condition'd and vnwearied spirit In doing curtesies. **1632** Lithgow *Trav.* i. 27 They intreated me to come vp in the Caroch, but I..would not, replying..my body [was] vnwearied. *a* **1684** Leighton *Comm. 1 Pet.* ii. (1693) 472 The Soul that is most active, and unwearied in Sin. **1707** *Curios. in Husb. & Gard.* 313 We might spend whole Years unwearied in the Examination of them. **1791** Cowper *Iliad* xviii. 293 The sun, Unwearied minister of light. **1816** Wilson *City of Plague* ii. ii. 79 The fairy.. On plumes unwearied ..floateth still. **1818** Milman *Samor* viii. 95 If yet this heart unwearied may bear on. **1871** Jowett *Plato* II. 10 The unwearied and disinterested seeker after truth.
**b.** Of qualities, actions, conditions, etc.: Marked by absence of abatement; unremitting.
**1561** T. Norton *Calvin's Inst.* i. 8 b, He..cesseth not to shewe hys vnweried bountifulnesse vpon miserable sinners. **1594** Hooker *Eccl. Pol.* i. iii. § 2 [The sun] as a Giant doth runne his vnwearied course. **1625** Godwin *Moses & Aaron* (1641) A 2 b, An unwearied assiduity in perusing those sacred Oracles. **1678** Vaughan *Thalia Rediv.* 64 The Wisdom of the Bee, And her unwearied Industry. **1704** J. Trapp *Abra-Mulé* ii. i. 367 Had not my Care, My vigilant, unweary'd Diligence Still balk'd..the Visier's Conduct. **1782** Miss Burney *Cecilia* ii. iii, The ludicrous mixture of groups kept her attention unwearied. **1820** Scott *Monast.* vi, The active and unwearied exercise of his sharp and piercing intellect. **1861** Trench *Comm. Ep. Churches Asia* 69 The unwearied activity of Christ in his Church. **1876** Bancroft *Hist. U. S.* II. xxx. 259 Bond ..languidly thanked him for his faithful and unwearied exertions.

**Unwea·riedly,** *adv.* (f. prec., or Un-[1] 11.)
**1653** Baxter *Chr. Concord* 99 Shall it be said that Separatists will..lay out all their pains unweariedly to divide the Church..? **1673** Hickeringill *Greg. F. Greyb.* 149 The importunities of those..unweariedly troublesome spirits. *a* **1715** Burnet *Own Time* (1766) I. 253 He was..unweariedly active to very little purpose. **1750** Chesterf. *Lett.* (1774) II. 50 Absolute perfection is..unattainable, but..a man of parts may be unweariedly aiming at..it. **1818** Bentham *Ch. Eng.* Introd. 54 The epithet so hardily and unweariedly bestowed upon it. **1860** Froude *Hist. Eng.* VI. 395 He worked unweariedly in the service of the public. **1893** J. Pulsford *Loyalty to Christ* II. 135 Unweariedly intent on bringing Her earth-born children into Her glorious House.

**Unwea·riedness.** (f. as prec., or Un-[1] 12.)
**1617** Hieron *Wks.* II. 101 Yet for largenesse,..for vnweariednesse, the louing kindnesse of the Lord doth farre exceed it. **1642** S. Ashe *Best Refuge* 35 Their frequency and unweariednesse in Prayer. **1702** E. Calamy *Life & Times Baxter* i. 8 He prosecuted all his Studies with Unweariedness and Delight. **1837** Carlyle *Misc. Ess.* (1840) V. 123 Working therein long years, with a filial unweariedness. **1884** Fairbairn *Catholicism* (1899) 42 Unweariedness in well-doing.

**Unwea·rily,** *adv.* [f. Unweary *a.*, or Un-[1] 11.] Unweariedly. **1434** Misyn *Mending Life* 111 If þa forsake seculer occupacions & erandis, & rise vnwerily to þinke & pray. **1435** — *Fire of Love* 82 Vnwerily it byrnys þo þingis to fulfil þat it seys & knawes plesynge to god. **Unwea·riness.** (Un-[1] 12.) **1611** Florio, *Infaticabilita*, vnwearinesse. **1906** *Daily Chron.* 8 May 5/5 A young white kid, symbolical of unweariness. **Unwea·risomeness.** (Un-[1] 12.) **1649** Earl Monm. tr. *Senault's Use Passions* (1671) 312 The Labourer..endeavoreth to overcome the sterility of the soil by the unwearisomeness of his labour.

**Unwea·ry,** *a.* [OE. *unwérig* (Un-[1] 7).] Not weary (*of*); free from weariness; unwearied.
*c* **893** K. Ælfred *Oros.* v. xi. § 4 Þæt mon þæt fæsten bræce, & on fuhte dæȝes & nihtes, simle an legie æfter oþerre unweriȝ. *c* **1000** *Sax. Leechd.* I. 76 Drince þonne on niht nistiȝ, þreo full fulle; þonne bið he sona unweriȝ. *a* **1340** Hampole *Psalter* xvii. 37 Þou has gifen me vnwery brennynge to wirke þe goed and put away slawnes. *c* **1374** Chaucer *Troylus* i. 410 If harme agree me wher-to pleyne I þanne? I not ne whi vnweri þat I feynte. *c* **1425** *Orolog. Sapient.* ii. 20 in *Anglia* X. 339 In to whomme angeles desyrene to loke and beholde with vnwerye felicite. *c* **1475** *Cath. Angl.* 414/2 (A.), Vn Wery, *indefessus*. **1606** Sylvester *Du Bartas* ii. iv. *Magnificence* 168 With unweary limb, Wade thorough Foords, and over Chanels swim. **1659** Eedes *Christ's Exalt.* Ep. Ded., He set himself to the serious study of the Hebrew tongue when he was 40 years old, and such was his unweary industry, that [etc.]. **1818** Milman *Samor* ix. 183 If thine eternal thunderbolts are yet Unweary of their function dire. **1844** Mrs. Browning *Patience taught* 8 Ocean girds Unslackened the dry land, savannah-swards Unweary sweep. **1859** *Habits of Gd. Society* vii. 248 You must not obtrude your unweary mirth at a visit of condolence.

†**Unwea·ry,** *v.* [Un-[2] 4 b.] *trans.* (and *refl.*). To restore from weariness; to refresh or rest.
Chiefly in translations of Fr. (*se*) *delasser*.
**1530** Palsgr. 769/1, I unwerye,..*je delasse.* **1580** Hollyband *Treas. Fr. Tong, Se delasser*, to vnweary himselfe. **1650** Earl Monm. tr. *Senault's Man bec. Guilty* 175 Are not Allegories impertinent? when to un-weary men's minds, they abuse them. **1652** Loveday tr. *Calprenede's Cassandra* i. 43 Having taken a house in the Towne, we there unwearied ourselves for some dayes. **1687** Etheredge *Let.* Wks. (1888) p. xxv, Not being able to prevail with him to stay a day and unweary himself.
*absol.* *a* **1698** Temple *Health & Long Life* Wks. 1720 I. 281 Bathing..unwearies and refreshes more than any thing, after too great Labour and Exercise.
**b.** *refl.* To relieve or ease (oneself) *of* something.
**1633** Earl Manch. *Al Mondo* (1636) 161 A good man..by this surplus of paine, unwearies himselfe of paine.

**Unwea·rying,** *ppl. a.* [Un-[1] 10.]
**1.** That does not grow or become weary; unremitting, untiring.
**1600** J. Melvill *Autob. & Diary* (Wodrow Soc.) 463 An unweireing and constant occupatioun in doctrine, prayer, and praise. **1762** Falconer *Shipwr.* i. 22 She o'er the spacious flood..Unwearying wafted her commercial store. **1824** Miss L. M. Hawkins *Annaline* III. 1 Her unwearying attendant..sought for it. **1843** Carlyle *Past & Pr.* iv. vii, The Heavens, unwearying in their bounty, do send other souls into this world. **1856** Kane *Arct. Expl.* I. xiv. 158 [The dogs] walk in straight and curved lines with anxious and unwearying perseverance.
**2.** Not causing or producing weariness.
**1799** W. Taylor in Robberds *Mem.* (1843) I. 297 The un-

wearied and unwearying eloquence of Mackintosh. **1858** HAWTHORNE *Fr. & It. Note-bks.* (1872) I. 11 Stately edifices prolonging themselves in unwearying magnificence and beauty. **1886** *Athenæum* 24 April 548/3 Success presently waited .. upon the unwearying charms of her person and conversation.

**Unwea·ryingly,** *adv.* (UN-¹ 11, or f. prec.) **1835** BECKFORD *Recoll.* 86 Scientific researches unweary-ingly pursued in calm and studious retirement. **1866** MEREDITH *Vittoria* xxix, The lamp burned unwearyingly. **1889** *Sat. Rev.* 23 March 349/1 The Carlyles themselves were unwearyingly kind to her.

† **Unwea·ther.** *Obs.* [OE. *unweder* (UN-¹ 4 b), = OFris. *unweder* (NFris. *unwedder*), (M)Du. *onweder*, LG. *unweder* (-*wêr*, -*wär*), MHG. *unweter* (G. *unwetter*), ON. *úveðr* (MSw. *ovädher*, Sw. *oväder*, (M)Da. *uvejr*, Norw. dial. *oveer*, etc.).] Bad, rough, or stormy weather.

*c* **950** *Lindisf. Gosp.* Luke viii. 24 He .. ȝeðreade þæt wind & hroeðnise *vel* unweoder ðæs wætres. *c* **1000** *Rule of Chrodegang* vi, Sylle man .. ælcum breðer fif punda ȝewihte wines, ȝif þa unwedru his ne forwyrnað. *c* **1250** *Gen. & Ex.* 3058 Moyses ȝede vt, helde up is hond, And al ðis vnweder ðor atwond. [**1658** PHILLIPS, *Unweather*, (Sax.) a storm or tempest. Hence in Bailey (1721).]

**Unwea·thered,** *ppl. a.* [UN-¹ 8.] Of rocks, etc.: Not exposed to, unaffected by, the action of the weather or atmosphere.

[**1775** ASH.] **1843** PORTLOCK *Geol.* 527 The more compact variety [of rock], where unweathered, is distinctly porphyritic. **1860** TYNDALL *Glac.* II. xx. 338 In no case was he able to discover these fissures in the sound unweathered ice. **1884** *Leisure Hour* Aug. 493/2 Extensive quarries from which fresh, unweathered material could be procured.

**Unwea·ve,** *v.* [UN-² 3, 7. Cf. (M)Du. *ontweven*, OHG. *antwepan* (MHG. and G. *entweben*).]

**1.** *trans.* To take out of a woven, intertwined, or entangled state or condition; esp. to unravel or undo (a woven fabric).

Freq. in fig. context, and in allusion to the story of Penelope (*Odyssey* II. 96–105).

**1542** UDALL *Erasm. Apoph.* 63 b, Then used she this policie, to unweave in the night as much werke, as she had made up in the daye before. **1565** COOPER, *Texta soluere*, to vnweaue that one hath wrought. **1592** SHAKS. *Ven. & Ad.* 991 Now she [*sc.* love] unweaves the web that she has wrought; Adonis lives. *a* **1637** B. JONSON *Celebration of Charis* ix. 50 Nor do wrongs, nor wrongs receive, Nor tie knots, nor knots unweave. **1640** G. SANDYS *Chr. Pass.* I. 81 That I should thus unweave the web of Fate. **1859** TENNYSON *Enid* 1114 She .. pluck'd the grass, .. And into many a listless annulet, Now over, now beneath her marriage ring, Wove and unwove it. **1875** JOWETT *Plato* (ed. 2) I. 461 Weaving instead of unweaving her Penelope's web.

*absol.* **1631** BRATHWAIT *Eng. Gentlew.* 49 Chuse rather with Penelope to weaue and vnweaue, than to giue Idlenesse the least leaue.

*fig.* *a* **1625** FLETCHER *Love's Cure* v. iii, Custom .. You did unweave, and had the power to charm A new creation in me. **1634** HEYWOOD *Witches of Lanc.* IV. G 4 b, Vnweave my age O time, to my first thread. **1820** KEATS *Lamia* II. 237 Philosophy will clip an Angel's wings, .. Empty the haunted air, and gnomed mine—Unweave a rainbow. **1849** DE QUINCEY *Eng. Mail Coach* Wks. 1862 IV. 349 Light unwove the mazes of darkness.

**b.** To untwine (the fingers).

**1863** BARING-GOULD *Iceland* 271 Several of the men came up, and endeavoured to unweave the fingers [from the sword]. **1897** — *Guavas* xviii, She plaited the fingers together and unwove them, to again re-plait them.

† **2.** To make clear by exposition; to expose, disclose. Also *absol.* *Obs.*

**1642** H. MORE *Song of Soul* II. ii. III. xxv, They're mixt, soild and contaminate, But truth doth clear, unweave, and simplifie. **1647** R. STAPYLTON *Juvenal* 48 Dædalus, who flying viewed the whole world (if we believe the poets), or that (if we unweave their fables) made discoveries of the world by sea with his winged sailes.

**3.** *intr.* To become disentangled. In quot. *fig.*

**1798** SOTHEBY tr. *Wieland's Oberon* IV. lviii, How wonderfully strange my fate unweaves!

Hence **Unwea·ving** *vbl. sb.*

**1706** STEVENS *Sp. Dict.*, *Desteximiento*, unweaving. **1847** HELPS *Friends in C.* I. vi. 89 The sleep-inducing weavings and unweavings of political combination. **1893** J. PULSFORD *Loyalty to Christ* II. 112 What unweavings and siftings and cleansings we shall have to undergo!

**Unwe·b,** *v.* [UN-² 3.] *trans.* To unweave. (In quot. *fig.*) **1882** P. HOOD *Cromwell* iii. 98 Eliot was engaged in unwebbing the abominations and the intricacies of the Court.

**Unwe·bbed,** *ppl. a.* (UN-¹ 8.)

**1768** PENNANT *Brit. Zool.* II. 492 The feathers .. long, slender and unwebbed. **1768** — in *Phil. Trans.* LVIII. 92 The shafts [of the feathers are] broad and very thin; the vanes unwebbed. **1804** BEWICK *Brit. Birds* II. 179 Its feathers appear all unwebbed, and look like silky hair. **1872** COUES *N. Amer. Birds* 219 Toes all of the same length, unwebbed at base.

**Unwe·d,** *ppl. a.* [UN-¹ 8 b.] = next.

In quot. 1562 perhaps f. UN-² 8.

**1513** DOUGLAS *Æneid* VI. v. 27 Small childrin, and ȝoung damicellis vnwed. **1562** J. HEYWOOD *Prov. & Epigr.* (1867) 191, We wold wed the sooner .., showyng plaine, That I should the sooner be vnwed againe. **1590** SHAKS. *Com. Err.* II. i. 26 This seruitude makes you to keepe vnwed. **1790** MRS. WHEELER *Westmoreland Dial.* (1821) 47 Be a gud lass, .. en keep the sel unwed en tae can. **1816** BYRON *Ch. Har.* III. lv, Though unwed, That love was pure. **1835** MILMAN *Nala & Damayanti*, etc. 91 Unwed wert thou in virgin bloom. **1873** SYMONDS *Grk. Poets* xi. 353 Timas, whom unwed Persephone locked in her darksome bed.

**Unwe·dded,** *ppl. a.* [UN-¹ 8.]

**1.** Of persons: Not wedded; unmarried. Also *absol.*

*a* **1230** *Hali Meid.* 13 (Titus MS.), Þa ilke sari wrecches, þat i þat ilke fule wurðinge, unweddede, walewið. **1303** R. BRUNNE *Handl. Synne* 7352 Þe fyrst [manner of lechery] ys fornycacyoun, Whan two vnweddyd haue mysdon. **1377** LANGL. *P. Pl.* B. xx. 111 Al manere men wedded & vnwedded. *c* **1430** *Syr Gener.* (Roxb.) 8699 Haue ye noo drede That my ladie vnwedded is? **1484** CAXTON *Fables of Æsop* VI. xvi, To them [*sc.* the aged] is better to be vnwedded than to be euer in trouble with an euyl wyf. **1577** tr. *Bullinger's Decades* 231/2 If a woman play the harlotte with an vnwedded man. *c* **1590** MARLOWE *Faustus* i, So shall the subiects of euery element Be alwaies seruiceable to vs three; .. Sometimes like women, or vnwedded maides. **1718** ROWE tr. *Lucan* IX. 1134 Unwedded Pallas lent a Sister's aid [to Perseus]. **1791** COWPER *Odyssey* XI. 44 Brides, youths unwedded, seniors .., And girls. **1825** SCOTT *Betrothed* xix, A richly-dowered maiden, unwedded, and unlikely to wed. **1877** E. R. CONDER *Basis Faith* v. 225 A large proportion of the .. most vigorous in body and mind die unwedded or childless.

*transf.* *c* **1792** COWPER *Death of Damon* 89 My rambling vines, unwedded to the trees, Bear shrivell'd grapes. **1811** LAMB *Elia* I. *Bachelor's Complaint*, Cerasia .. sent away a dish of Morellas .. to her husband, .. and recommended a plate of less extraordinary gooseberries to my unwedded palate. **1837** LYTTON *Athens* I. 377 Pisistratus conducted himself towards the fair Cæsyra with a chastity .. unwelcome to her affection ... The unwedded wife communicated the mortifying secret to her mother.

**2.** Free from, unattended by, marriage.

**1804** *Europ. Mag.* XLV. 192/2 'Twixt wedded and unwedded loving Great is the difference, they say. **1822** MILMAN *Martyr of Antioch* 101 The saintly quiet of the unwedded state. **1882** FARRAR *Early Chr.* II. 114 Expressions which .. convey no such exaltation of the unwedded life.

Hence **Unwe·ddedness.**

**1830** CARLYLE *Misc.* (1840) II. 368 It is not always our duty to marry; but it is always our duty to abide by right; .. not to avoid unweddedness by untruthfulness.

**Unwe·dge,** *v.* [UN-² 3.] *trans.* (and *refl.*). To free from a wedged condition. Also *fig.*

**1611** FLORIO, *Discugnare*, to vnwedge. **1622** MABBE tr. *Aleman's Guzman d'Alf.* II. 88 He fell off from me by degrees, by a little and a little vnwedging himselfe from mee. **1680** *Exact Jrnl. Siege Tangier* 12 Nine guns .. which he had Unspiked and Unwedged.

**Unwe·dgeable,** *a.* [UN-¹ 7 b.] Incapable of being split by wedges; uncleavable.

In mod. use only in echoes of the Shaks. passage, with a tendency towards the wider meaning 'very hard, stubborn, or difficult to deal with': freq. used by Carlyle.

**1603** SHAKS. *Meas. for M.* II. ii. 116 Mercifull heauen, Thou rather with thy sharpe and sulpherous bolt Splits the vn-wedgable and gnarled Oke, Then the soft Mertill. [**1802–12** BENTHAM *Ration. Judic. Evid.* (1827) V. 521 Men, like oaks, are .. 'gnarled and unwedgeable;' facts, like deals, are fissile.] **1837** CARLYLE *Misc.* (1840) V. 135 He, being unwedgeable, has remained in antiquarian cabinets. **1880** *Spectator* 5 June 722 Propositions which lie buried in these gnarled and unwedgeable periods.

† **Unwe·dset,** *ppl. a.* *Obs.* [UN-¹ 8 b. Cf. WADSET *v.*] Not put in pledge. **1480** *Acta Dom. Conc.* (1839) 70/2 Land .. fre vnset for termes or for male and vnwedset.

**Unwee·ded,** *ppl. a.* [UN-¹ 8. Cf. Du. *ongewied.*]

**1.** Of ground: Not cleared of weeds. Also *fig.*

In later use freq. in fig. context in echoes of quot. 1602.

**1602** SHAKS. *Ham.* I. ii. 135 Oh fie, fie, 'tis an vnweeded Garden That growes to Seed; Things rank, and grosse in Nature Possesse it meerely. **1624** USSHER *Serm.* 48 The field is the same, but weeded now, unweeded then. **1796** MORSE *Amer. Geog.* I. 654 The human mind, like an unweeded garden, has been suffered to shoot up in wild disorder. **1817** COLERIDGE *Lay Serm.* 19 The evils of a rank and unweeded Press. **1824** J. TELFER *Border Ball.* 32 The wood it was dern, unweeded, and wild. **1842** *New Monthly Mag.* I. 400 All the rashness, insolence, and brutality of an unweeded and newly-raised constabulary.

**2.** Not cleared away or rooted up as weeds. In quots. *fig.*

**1626** JACKSON *Creed* VIII. v. § 1 All men by nature (that is from the unweeded relikes of our first parents' pride) are prone to over-value themselves. **1645** HAMMOND *Deathbed Repent.* 29 The .. hospitable soyle, contrary both to the thorny and stony ground, the one when the cares of the world are unweeded, unmortifyed, the other when [etc.].

**Unweel,** Sc. var. of UNWELL *a.*

**Unwee·ned,** *ppl. a.* Now *arch.* [UN-¹ 8. Cf. OE. *unge-*, *unwēned.*] Not thought of or imagined; unexpected.

*c* **1374** CHAUCER *Boeth.* IV. pr. vi. (1868) 139 What so euer þou mayst seen þat is don in þis world vnhoped or vnwened. **1813** HOGG *Queen's Wake* 85 The night unweened had passed away, And dawning ushered in the day. **1894** F. S. ELLIS *Reynard the Fox* 194 When one weens no thing at all, The thing unweened will straight befal.

† **Unwee·ningly,** *adv.* *Sc.* *Obs.* [UN-¹ 11.] Unexpectedly. *c* **1375** *Sc. Leg. Saints* vi. (*Thomas*) 463 Quhen men venis beste þat þai sal lyfe in lykine .., þan cumys ded vnwenandly. **Unwee·ping,** *ppl. a.* (UN-¹ 10.) **1598** DRAYTON *Heroical Ep.* Poems (1605) 55 b, We hold no obijts, no sad exequies Vpon the death-daies of vnweeping eies. **1783** JUSTAMOND tr. *Raynal's Hist. Indies* II. 321 Behold if thou can'st, with an unweeping eye the man who enriches us condemned to perish with misery. † **Unwee·ting,** *vbl. sb.* *Obs.*—¹ [UN-¹ 12.] Ignorance. **14..** *Wycliffite Bible* Acts iii. 17 (New Coll. MS. 67), Now, breþeren, I woot þat bi þe vnwetinge [L. *per ignorantiam*] ȝe diden.

**Unwee·ting,** *ppl. a.* Now *arch.* [UN-¹ 10, 5 d. Cf. MDu. *onwetende* (Du. *onwetend*), MLG. *unwetende*, Sw. *ovetande*, and UNWITTING *ppl. a.*]

**1.** = UNWITTING *ppl. a.* 1.

**1303** R. BRUNNE *Handl. Synne* 11253 Ȝyf þou vnwetyng hyt haue, hyt helpeþ þe nat so moche to saue As ȝyf þou asked hyt by name. **1387–8** T. USK *Test. Love* III. vii. (Skeat) l. 66 Who that .. coveyteth thing unknowe, unweting he shal be quyted. **1590** SPENSER *F. Q.* I. x. 66 She .. in an heaped furrow did thee hyde, Where thee a Ploughman all vnweeting fond. **1634** MILTON *Comus* 539 To inveigle and invite th' unwary sense Of them that pass unweeting by the way. **1667** — *P. L.* x. 335 Hee .. saw his guileful act By Eve, though all unweeting, seconded Upon her Husband. *a* **1718** PARNELL *Fairy Tale* 62 'Twas grief .. Which made my steps unweeting rove Amid the nightly dew. **1768** C. SHAW *Monody* vi, In vain—Perverse, still on th' unweeting head 'Tis thine thy vengeful darts to shed. **1803** W. S. ROSE *Amadis* 82 All who to his bow'rs unweeting came. **1855** SINGLETON *Virgil* I. 42 When Through the unweeting mountains here and there Rove living creatures. **1878** T. HARDY *Ret. Native* II. iv, This unweeting manner of performance is the true ring by which .. a fossilized survival may be known from a spurious reproduction.

**b.** Const. *of.* = UNWITTING *ppl. a.* 1 b.

**1591** SPENSER *Teares Muses* 491 Then wandreth he in error and in doubt, Vnweeting of the danger hee is in. *a* **1592** T. WATSON *Tears of Fancy* xlix, His hounds vnweeting of his sodaine change, Did hale and pull him downe. **1717** E. FENTON *Homer's Odyssey* 91 Me, O King, The Minister of adverse Fate malign'd, Unweeting of Mishap. **1735** SOMERVILLE *Chase* III. 280 Joyous he scents The rich Repast, unweeting of the Death That lurks within. **1793** COLERIDGE *The Rose* 13 When unweeting of the guile Awoke the prisoner sweet. **1812** CARY *Dante*, *Purg.* III. 91 They stopp'd: .. the same did all Who follow'd, though unweeting of the cause. **1870** BRYANT *Iliad* XVIII. II. 225 Two shepherds walked with them, .. all unweeting of the evil nigh.

**c.** With objective clause. = UNWITTING *ppl. a.* 1 c.

**1590** SPENSER *F. Q.* III. x. 22 He .. stood aloofe, vnweeting what to doe. **1621** QUARLES *Div. Poems*, *Esther* Introd., A few from many they extracted forth, .. Vnweeting where the most reward belongs. **1805–6** CARY *Dante*, *Inf.* XXX. 139, I .. all the while Excused me, though unweeting that I did. **1814** WORDSW. *Lines written in copy of Excurs.* 9 He conned the new-born Lay ..; Unweeting that to him the joy was given. **1864** BRYANT *Cloud on Way* 39 Haply, leaning o'er the pilgrim, all unweeting thou art near, Thou mayst whisper words .. of comfort in his ear.

† **2.** In absolute constructions. *Obs.* = UNWITTING *ppl. a.* 2.

*c* **1386** CHAUCER *Can. Yeom. T.* 767 (Camb. MS.), He slyly tok it out, this cursede heyne, Vnwetynge this prest of this false craft. *c* **1400** *Destr. Troy* 8594 Ector .. Went out wightly, vnwetyng his fader. *c* **1400** LOVE *Bonavent. Mirr.* (1908) 74 After that his parens weren gone homwarde, he dwelled stille there in Jerusalem, hem vnwetynge. *c* **1470** HARDING *Chron.* XVIII. vi, He helde Estrylde as his loue and leman, Therof his wife vnwetyng. *c* **1483** *Chron. London* (1827) 123 Oweyn .. hadde iij or iiij^or^ chyldren be here, unwetyng the comoun peple tyl that sche were ded.

*ellipt.* **1398** TREVISA *Barth. De P. R.* XVII. xii. (Bodl. MS.), Wormod .. exciteþ þe smel after slepe ȝif it is ileide vnwetinge vnder þe heed.

**3.** = UNWITTING *ppl. a.* 3.

(*a*) **1387–8** T. USK *Test. Love* I. vii. (Skeat) l. 110 Some of hem token money for thy chambre, .. unwetinge of the renter. *a* **1400** *Partonope* 8931 In-to a chambre .. Vnwetyng of any wight they hym lede. **1454** *Paston Lett.* I. 287 God wote my wif delyvered all, myn unwetyng. *c* **1483** *Chron. London* (1827) 131 The fals contryved evidens that weren sealed be old tyme with the comoun seall, unwetynge of them.

(*b*) **1579** FENTON *Guicciard.* III. 168 From whence, .. vnweeting to the Duke, .. he went to Coma. **1590** SPENSER *F. Q.* III. iii. 57 She resolu'd, vnweeting to her Sire, Aduent'rous knighthood on her selfe to don.

† **4.** Ignorant, uninformed, unlearned. *Obs.*

**1483** CAXTON *Gold. Leg.* 86/2 She said .. he shold abyde wythout and not come in as he that were not worthy but unwetyng. **1706** J. PHILIPS *Cerealia* 70 Have I so long .. my lore Communicated to th' unweeting hind?

**5.** = UNWITTING *ppl. a.* 4. *rare*—¹.

**1793** BURNS '*The last time*' ii, The unweeting groan, the bursting sigh, Betray the guilty lover.

**Unwee·tingly,** *adv.* Now *arch.* [UN-¹ 11. Cf. prec. and UNWITTINGLY *adv.*] Unknowingly; unconsciously; † without it being known.

*a* **1400–50** *Alexander* 134 Furþe .. withouten fole he passis his way, Vn-wetandly to any wee. **14..** *Chaucer's Pardoner's T.* 24 (Corpus MS.), Loth vnkyndely lay by his doughtres tuo vnwetyngly, So drunke he was. *a* **1542** WYATT '*And if*' Wks. 1913 I. 176 To frame all wel, I ame content That it were done unwetingly. **1596** SPENSER *F. Q.* V. viii. 15, I .. found them faring so, As by the way vnweetingly I strayd. **1671** MILTON *Samson* 1680 They only set on sport and play Unweetingly importun'd Thir own destruction to come speedy upon them. **1792** D. LLOYD *Voy. Life* 30 Prone to the lap of lewd Licentiousness The high-flown rabble throngs unweetingly. **1802** J. BAILLIE *1st Pt. Ethwald* IV. iv, Woggarwolfe .. once before unweetingly has served us. *a* **1849** H. COLERIDGE *Ess.* (1851) II. 157 Shakspeare .. assumes the utmost pomp of diction on these occasions, complying, unweetingly, with Aristotle's precepts.

**Unwe·ft,** *ppl. a.* [UN-¹ 8 b. Cf. Sw. *oväfd.*] Unwoven. **1865** MRS. WHITNEY *Gayworthys* xliii, Every filament unweft shall be gathered from .. its entanglement.

**Unwei·ghed,** *ppl. a.* [UN-¹ 8. Cf. Da. *uveiet*, Sw. *ovägd.*]

**1.** Not weighed.

**1481–90** *Howard Househ. Bks.* (Roxb.) 348, lix. bales of Gene wode unweyed. **1535** COVERDALE 1 *Kings* vii. 47 Salomon let all the apparell be vnweyed [**1539** vnwayed, **1611** vnweighed] because the metall was so moch. **1555** *Inv. Ch. Goods* (Surtees) 153, xlv sowes of leade unwaied. **1697** WALSH *Life Virgil* ¶ 17 in *Dryden's Virgil*, Massy Plate, unweigh'd to a great value.

*transf.* **1852** BAILEY *Festus* (ed. 5) 171 Such we hold Thy sanctity of nature, and unweighed Largess of light.

**2.** Not deliberately considered; not pondered before utterance or expression; hasty, inconsiderate.

*a* **1586** SIDNEY *Arcadia* II. xxii, Disgraced with wandring eyes, and vnwaied speeches. **1598** SHAKS. *Merry W.* II. i. 23 What an vnwaied Behauiour hath this Flemish drunkard pickt .. out of my conuersation! **1697** COLLIER *Ess. Mor. Subj.*

I. 111 If an Emperour throws out an unweigh'd Sentence, must we be governed by it? **1725** Pope *Odyss.* I. 84 Daughter! what words have pass'd thy lips unweigh'd? **1828–32** Webster s.v., To leave arguments or testimony unweighed. **1850** J. F. Cooper *Ways of Hour* II. 241 Much unmerited misery is..entailed by such unweighed assertions and opinions.

†**Unwei·ghing,** *ppl. a. Obs.*—[1] [Un-[1] 10. Cf. prec. 2.] Thoughtless; inconsiderate. **1603** Shaks. *Meas. for M.* III. ii. 147 A very superficiall, ignorant, vnweighing fellow. **Unwei·ghted,** *ppl. a.* (Un-[1] 8.) **1883** Annie Thomas *Mod. Housewife* 23 My heart was unweighted, my brow unclouded, by a single household perplexity. **1898** *Daily News* 9 April 6/3 Put to the test of touch, the silks proclaim themselves to be pure and unweighted. **Unwei·ghty,** *a.* (Un-[1] 7. Cf. G. *unwichtig*, Da. *uvigtig*.) **1621** Lady M. Wroth *Urania* 458 Speaking of a friuolous and vnwaighty businesse God knowes. *a* **1674** Clarendon *Surv. Leviath.* (1676) 29 The instances and arguments given by him are very unweighty. †**Unwei·rded,** *ppl. a. Sc. Obs.*—[1] [Un-[1] 4 b, 9.] Subject to adverse fate; ill-fated. *c* **1590** Montgomerie *Sonnets* xlviii. 12 Thou art vnweirdit, I a woful wrech. **Unwe·lcome,** *sb.* [Un-[1] 12.] Unwelcomeness. **1603** Florio *Montaigne* III. iii. 495 Gentlye to beare..the importunitie of yeares, the vnwellcome of wrinckles, and such like minde-troubling accidents. **1654** Whitlock *Zootomia* 33 Since I must quarter the forces of two Garrisons, it will be prudence to dissemble the unwelcome of the one, and silently to welcome the other.

**Unwe·lcome,** *a.* [Un-[1] 7. Cf. med. Du. *onwillecome* (Du. *onwelkom*), G. *unwillkommen*, Da. *uvel-*, Sw. *ovälkommen*.] Not welcome or acceptable; unpleasing.

Rare before *c* 1590. In freq. use from *c* 1665.

*c* **1325** in *Pol. Songs* (Camden) 330 His meyne is unwelcome, comen hii erliche or late. **13..** *E. E. Allit. P.* B. 49 If vnwelcum he were to a worþlych prynce. *a* **1586** Sidney *Arcadia* III. xvi, Unwelcome curtesie is a degree of injury. **1591** Shaks. *Two Gent.* II. iv. 81, I thinke 'tis no vn-welcome newes to you. **1624** Fletcher *Wife for Moneth* II. i, Death is unwelcome never, Unless it be to tortur'd minds..That make their own Hells. **1661** Boyle *Style of Script.* To Rdr. A 7 b, There can as little be an unwelcomer as an unjuster Complement plac'd upon me, than [etc.]. **1670** R. Montagu in *Buccleuch MSS.* (Hist. MSS. Comm.) I. 469 Your Lordship's letter..was much unwelcomer to me than any I yet received from you. **1728** Eliza Heywood tr. *Mme. de Gomez's Belle A.* (1732) II. 174 The Importunities of his unwelcome Tenderness. **1751** Johnson *Rambler* No. 153 ¶ 1 He that has an unwelcome message to deliver. **1817** Scott *Harold* III. vii, He whose daring lay Hath dared unwelcome truths to say. **1840** Barham *Ingol. Leg.* I. *H. Harris* (1905) 126 The unwelcome news of his grandson's dangerous state. **1869** Tozer *Highl. Turkey* II. 171 A name of ridicule..unwelcome to their ears.

**Unwe·lcome,** *v.* [Un-[1] 14.] *trans.* To receive uncordially. **1890** *Atlantic* April 550/2 [The] half-concealed ridicule with which the poor old fellow's sallies are liable to be welcomed—or unwelcomed.

**Unwe·lcomed,** *ppl. a.* (Un-[1] 8.) **1548** W. Patten *Exped. Scotl.* F 1 b, Yf they had kept pointment..they shoulde neyther haue bene vnwelcumed nor vnlooked for. **1590** Spenser *F. Q.* III. vii. 8 At last..She askt..what vnwonted path Had guided her, vnwelcomed, vnsought? **1614** Lithgow *Trav.* P 1 b, The vnwelcomed Arabs inuironed, and inuaded vs with a storme of arrowes. **1651** Vaughan *Olor Iscanus, Boet.* I. met. i. 20 Life adds unwelcom'd length unto my dayes. **1768** Hoole *Cyrus* III. 36 Doom'd again to banishment, Unseen, unwelcom'd, [he] swells this heart with anguish. **1836** Keble *Lyra Apost.* 182 How count we then lost eve and morn, The bell unwelcom'd, prayer unsaid. **1893** *Harper's Mag.* Dec. 26 The Great Love comes to you at last Unwelcomed.

**Unwe·lcomely,** *adv.* (Un-[1] 11.) **1642** Rogers *Naaman* 87 How doth Naaman take it? Surely very ill, and unwelcomly. **1718** Taverner *Artful Wife* v. i. 60 The Thought of him intrudes unwelcomely. **1792** Charlotte Smith *Desmond* III. 23 The task of chiding you..falls on me most unwelcomely. **1833** Sir F. B. Head *Bubbles fr. Brunnen* 121 A calculation which very unwelcomely kept forcing itself into my mind. **1882** C. C. Hopley *Snakes* xxvii. 495 A 'water moccasin'..had been seen..unwelcomely close to a southern residence.

**Unwe·lcomeness.** (Un-[1] 12.) **1682** Boyle *Let.* Wks. 1772 VI. 43 But, together with that unwelcome news, you send me what does much alleviate the unwelcomness of it. **1727** Bailey (vol. II). **1876** Geo. Eliot *Dan. Der.* vii, Her words..had the unwelcomeness which all unfavourable fortune-telling has. **Unwe·lcoming,** *sb.* (Un-[1] 13.) **1838** Mrs. Smythies *Fitzherbert* II. ii. 34 What has sent the young, the brave,..among the cold, the unwelcoming of frigid regions?

**Unwelde,** etc.: see Unwield, etc.

**Unwe·lded,** *ppl. a.* (Un-[1] 8.) [1775 Ash.] **1846** Worcester (citing Turner). **1885** C. G. W. Cooke *Workshop Receipts* Ser. IV. 12/1, (1) unwelded, (2) welded, (rolled) goods. †**Unwe·lewable,** *a. Obs. rare.* [f. Un-[1] 7 b. Cf. Wallow *v.*[2] and Unwallowed *ppl. a.*] That will not fade; unfadable. **1382** Wyclif 1 *Pet.* i. 4 In to heritage vncorruptible, and vndefoulid, and vnwelewable [L. *immarcescibilem*], that shal not fade. *Ibid.* v. 4 The vnwelewable crowne of glory.

**Unwe·ll,** *a.* Also 5 *north.* vnwele; *Sc.* 7 unweal, 9 un-, onweel. [Un-[1] 7. Cf. NFris. (Sylt) *unwel*, WFlem. *onwel*, G. *unwohl*.] Not well or in good health; somewhat ill; indisposed.

Before 1780 almost always north. E., Sc., Anglo-Irish, or U.S. Not in Johnson (edd. 1–4). In very frequent use from *c* 1785. 'Crabbe..told us that Lord Chesterfield was the first person who introduced the word 'unwell' into common use, and..it was forthwith admitted into the vocabulary of fashion' (1825 C. Wordsw. in Overton & W. *Life* (1888) 36).

*c* **1450** *St. Cuthbert* (Surtees) 3649 A man was seke and vnwele. **1653** Urquhart *Rabelais* I. vi. 30 Gargamelle began to be a little unwell in her lower parts. **1666** Mrs. Carstaires in *J. Carstaire's Lett.* (1846) 161 My sister still contanues unwell. The doctour thinks she is in great hazard. *a* **1700** Evelyn *Diary* 10 Oct. 1659, I..tooke lodgings..for all the winter, my son being very unwell. **1737** Berkeley *Let.* Wks. 1871 IV. 248 My three children have been ill... George is still unwell. **1750** C. Gist *Jrnls.* (1893) 34, I was unwell and stayed in this Town to recover myself. **1755** Chesterf. *Let.* 8 Oct., I am what you call in Ireland, and a very good expression I think it is, *unwell*. **1757** Mrs. Griffith *Lett. Henry & Frances* (1767) I. 218, I hope that it is only your spleen, which makes you fancy yourself unwell. **1768** Chesterf. *Let.* 17 Oct., I am, neither well nor ill, but *unwell*. **1788** Anna Seward *Lett.* (1811) II. 117, I have been so unwell with a violent cough. **1826** Scott *Jrnl.* (1890) I. 231, I am well-nigh choked with the sulphurous heat of the weather—or I am unwell. **1856** J. Richardson *Recoll.* I. 61 Morris..suddenly retired as if taken unwell! **1882** Tennyson *Promise of May* III. i, Mr. Steer still continues too unwell to attend to you.

**b.** *euphem.* Having menstrual discharges. **1844** Dunglison *Med. Dict.* (ed. 4) s.v.

Hence **Unwe·llness.**

**1653** Dorothy Osborne *Lett.* (1888) 140 You..never send me any of the new phrases of the town...Pray what is meant by *wellness* and *unwellness*? **1755** Chesterf. *Let.* 8 Oct., This *unwellness* affects the mind as well as the body, and gives them both a disagreeable inertness. **1865** W. M. Punshon in Macdonald *Life* (1887) 250 This chronic 'unwellness' is difficult to understand. **1876** Darwin in *Life* (1887) I. 69 Owing to frequently recurring unwellness, and to one long and serious illness.

**Unwe·mmed,** *ppl. a.* [OE. *unwemmed* (Un-[1] 8). Cf. OE. *ungewemmed*, OHG. *ungawemmit*.]

**1.** Spotless, pure, immaculate. Now *arch.*

**a.** Of persons. Also const. *in, of.*

*c* **950** *Rituale Dunelm.* (Surtees) 104 Ðerh ðone vnwoemmedo drihten..crist. *a* **1175** *Cott. Hom.* 237 Ure halende wes accenned of þam unwemmede mede sante Marie. *c* **1200** Ormin 2877 Jesu Cristess hird Iss clene, & all unnwemmedd Inn hire trowwþe towarrd Godd. *c* **1225** *Ancr. R.* 10 To ancren..þe witeð ou from þe worlde, ouer alle oðre religiuse, clene & unwemmed. *a* **1300** *E. E. Psalter* xviii. 14 Þan vnwemmed be I sal, And I sal be clensed clene Of gilte. **1382** Wyclif *Col.* i. 22 For to haue ȝou hooly, and vnwemmid, and with oute reprof bifore hym. *c* **1400** *Prymer* in Maskell *Mon. Rit.* (1847) II. 40 Thou toke sum tyme the shap of oure bodi, in childynge of the unwemmed vyrgyn. *c* **1500** *Lancelot* 2097 This flour wnwemmyt of hir wirginitee. **1513** Douglas *Æneid* x. Prol. 106 Thou tuke mankynd of ane onwemmyt mayd. **1570** Levins *Manip.* 51 Vnwembed, *immaculatus.* *a* **1643** Cartwright *Ordinary* II. ii, *Moth* [an antiquary]. 'Tis hard to find a Damosel unwenned [*sic*], They being all Coltish and full of Ragery.

*absol.* *a* **1300** *E. E. Psalter* xxxvi. 19 Lauerd daies of vnwemmid knawes he. *a* **1325** *Prose Psalter* xxxvi. 19 Our Lord knew þe dedes of þe vnwemmed. **1382** Wyclif *Song Sol.* v. 2 Opene thou to me,..my culuer, myn vnwemed.

**b.** Of the body, etc.

*c* **1000** Ælfric *Saints' Lives* xxiii. B. 437 Þu wære symle fæmne oncnawen, and þinne lichaman hæbbende clæne and unwemmed. *c* **1200** Ormin 2816 Allmahhtiȝ Drihhtin ..Þatt nu liþ..I þin unnwemmedd wambe. *c* **1375** *Sc. Leg. Saints* iii. (*Andrew*) 442 [The] firste man, þat wes mad of vnwemmyt erd. **1382** Wyclif *Heb.* xiii. 4 Honorable wedding in alle thingis, and bed vnwembid [*v.r.* vnwemyd bed].

**c.** Of qualities, etc.

*c* **1000** *Lambeth Psalter* c. 2 And ic anȝyte weȝe on unwemmed. *a* **1300** *E. E. Psalter* xviii. 8 Lagh of lauerd vnwemmed esse, Tornand saules in to blisse. *c* **1366** Chaucer *A. B. C.* 91 Signe of þin vnwemmed maidenhede. *c* **1375** *Sc. Leg. Saints* xxxvi. (*John Baptist*) 466 Þe firste is of virginite, Þat ay vnuemmyt kepit he. *c* **1449** Pecock *Repr.* v. i. 477 A clene and an vnwemmed religioun. *c* **1872** J. Addis *Eliz. Echoes* (1879) 68 A love unwemmed, guiltless of attaint.

†**2.** Not hurt, injured, or scarred. *Obs.*

*c* **1200** Ormin 14735 All swa summ Ysaac attbrast Unnwundedd & unnwemmedd. *a* **1300** *Cursor M.* 21046 Bot noþer him harmd, hefd ne fott. For als he was o lust vnlame Als was vnwemmed his licam. **1375** Barbour *Bruce* xx. 376 He had gret ferly That sic a knycht..Micht in the face vnwemmyt be.

**3.** Not physically spotted or stained. Now *dial.*

*a* **1300** *Cursor M.* 19504 Godd him geit, þat euer es god, Vn-wemmed his hend in sacles blod. **1876** *Whitby Gloss.* 208/1 *Unwemm'd*, without wrinkle or stain; unblemished.

†**4.** Unblemished; flawless. *Obs. rare.*

*c* **1475** *Partenay* 6569 And so haue I done after my simplesse, Preseruing, I trust, mater and sentence Vnwemmed, vnhurt. **1501** Douglas *Pal. Hon.* II. xxx, Vnwemmit wit deliuerit of all dangeir.

Hence **Unwe·mmedness.** *rare.*

*c* **1200** Ormin 2388 Þatt ȝho mihhte A libbenn i clene maȝȝþhad, & inn unnwemmeddnesse. *Ibid.* 2875, 8220, 10098.

**Unwe·pt,** *ppl. a.* [Un-[1] 8 b.]

**1.** Not wept or mourned for; unlamented.

**1594** Shaks. *Rich. III*, II. ii. 65 Our fatherlesse distresse was left vnmoan'd, Your widdow-dolour, likewise be vnwept. **1633** P. Fletcher *Purple Isl.* I. xx, Had not that great Hart ..piti'd thy wofull plight; There hadst thou lien unwept, unburied. **1637** Milton *Lycidas* 13 He must not flote upon his watry bear Unwept. **1725** Pope *Odyss.* v. 402 A shameful fate now hides my hapless head, Unwept, unnoted, and for ever dead! **1766** Goldsm. *Vicar* xxi, If you fall, though distant, exposed, and unwept by those that love you. **1805** Scott *Last Minstrel* VI. i, The wretch..shall go down To the vile dust, ..Unwept, unhonour'd, and unsung. **1848** Buckley *Iliad* 413 Patroclus lies at the ships, an unwept, unburied corse.

**2.** Of tears: Unshed. *rare*—[1].

**1816** Byron *Parisina* xx, Those tears..in its depth endure, Unseen, unwept, but uncongeal'd.

**Unwe·red,** *ppl. a. rare.* [Un-[1] 8. Cf. OE. *unwered*.] Unwatched, unguarded. *a* **1400** *Pistill of Susan* 124 Þe wif werp of hir wedes vn-werde. †**Unwe·rked,** *ppl. a. Obs.*—[1] [f. Un-[1] 8 + ON. *verka* (MSw. *värka*, Sw., Norw. *verka*, Da. *virke*) to work, fashion.] Unworked, unwrought. *c* **1430** *Chev. Assigne* 175 'Nowe lefte ther ony ouer vn-werkethe ..?' And he recheth her forth haluendele a cheyne.

**Unwerred, -werreyed**: see Unwarred, Unwarrayed *ppl. adjs.*

**Unwe·t,** *a.* [Un-[1] 7.] Not wet or moistened. **1433** *Rolls of Parlt.* IV. 451 Clothes..holdyng xiiii yerdes in lenght, and yerde brode unwette; or elles xii yerdes wette. *c* **1440** *Pallad. on Husb.* XII. 463 Cedur vnwet wol dure. **1585** Jas. VI *Ess. Poesie* (Arb.) 27, I no wais can, vnwet my cheekes, beholde My sisters made..macquerels olde. **1594** Kyd *Cornelia* II. 234 When sand within a Whirl-poole lyes vnwet. **1621** G. Sandys *Ovid's Met.* x. (1626) 212 Their feet, vnwet, the sea might well haue borne. **1683** Moxon *Mech. Exerc., Printing* xxiv. ¶ 9 The un-wet upper part of..the Quire. *c* **1746** Collins *Ode Liberty* 69 He pass'd with unwet feet thro' all our land. **1789** E. Darwin *Bot. Gard.* I. 157 [To] bathe unwet their oily forms, and dwell With feet repulsive on the dimpling well. **1815** Kirby & Sp. *Entomol.* xiii. (1816) I. 425 Their bodies being kept unwet by a coating of air. **1840** N. Hawthorne *Biogr. Sk.* (1879) 178 It was like Gideon's fleece, unwet with dew. **1891** Atkinson *Last of Giant-killers* 234 Emerging from it unwet as well as unharmed.

**b.** Of the eye: Not suffused with tears; tearless. **1601–3** Daniel *Certaine Epistles* 58 He lookes thereon As from the shore of peace with vnwet eie. **1700** Dryden *Sigism. & Guisc.* 673, I meant to meet My Fate with..Eyes unwet. *a* **1743** Ld. Hervey *Epist.* i. 82 Thy breast unruffled, and unwet thy eye. **1823** S. Rogers *Italy, Brides Venice* 135 Eyes not unwet..with grateful tears. **1845** Jerrold *St. Giles* v. (1851) 43 The woman, lifting her apron to her unwet eye.

**Unwe·tted,** *ppl. a.* (Un-[1] 8.) **1664** Boyle *Exp. touching Colours* 56 The Unwetted Parts of the same Bodies. **1815** Kirby & Sp. *Entomol.* i. (1816) I. 16 By means of which she [*sc.* a spider] resides unwetted in the bosom of the water. **1892** Ld. Lytton *King Poppy* Prol. 281 The flash of her unwetted sandal.

†**Unweved,** *pa. pple. Obs.*—[1] [?Un-[2] 9.] Struck off. *c* **1330** *King of Tars* 199 (MS. Vernon), Mony an helm þer was vn-weued, And mony a Bacinet to-cleued.

**Unwex,** variant of Unwax *v.*[1] *Obs.*

**Unwhee·l,** *v.* (Un-[2] 4.) **1632** G. Hughes *Saints Losse*, Ded., Your charet is unwheeled, and your horsemen throwne. **1889** Talmage *Serm.* 28 Apr., God is not dead. The chariots are unwheeled.

**Unwheeme,** var. Unqueme *a. Obs.*

**Unwhe·t,** *v.* (Un-[2] 3.) **1599** T. M[oufet] *Silkwormes* 55 Satiety their stomacks will vnwhet. **1885** R. Bridges *Nero* I. III. v, Come,..be seated. Let not the horrid sight Unwhet your appetites. **Unwhe·tted,** *ppl. a.* (Un-[1] 8.) *a* **1644** Quarles *Sol. Recant.* x. 10 If th' unwhetted edge be blunt, the arm Must give more strength. **1648** Hexham II, *Een ongewet mes*, an Vnwhetted knife.

**Unwhi·g,** *v.* [Un-[2] 6 b + Whig *sb.*] *trans.* To divest of the character or opinions of a Whig.

**1825** Moore *Sheridan* II. 38 Pitt..turned to the person who sat next him, and said, 'I'll *un-Whig* the gentleman for the rest of his life!' **1832** *Q. Rev.* XLVII. 80 Moore did not, indeed, return unwhigged, but he has dealt with American manners not less hardly than Mrs. Trollope. **1892** *Pall Mall G.* 4 May 2 Unwhigging the Duke of Devonshire.

**Unwhi·gged,** *ppl. a.* [Un-[1] 8 + Whig *v.*[2]] Not turned sour. **1756** Home *Bleaching* 79 A piece of cloth..was laid in butter milk unwhigged. **Unwhi·glike,** *a.* (Un-[1] 7 c.) **1808** Syd. Smith in Lady Holland *Mem.* (1855) II. 48 He behaved in an unwhiglike manner. **Unwhi·ning,** *ppl. a.* (Un-[1] 10.) *a* **1750** A. Hill *Poems* Wks. 1753 IV. 119 Bid tears, unwhining, find their source within. **Unwhi·p,** *v* [Un-[2] 3.] *trans.* To cast loose smartly. **1683** Moxon *Mech. Exerc., Printing* xxii. ¶ 7 Before the Cords are unwhipt from the Pages.

**Unwhi·pped, unwhi·pt,** *ppl. a.* [Un-[1] 8, 8 b, c.]

**1.** Not punished (as) by whipping; not flogged or beaten.

**1605** Shaks. *Lear* III. ii. 53 Tremble thou Wretch, Thou hast within thee vndivulged Crimes Vnwhipt of Iustice. **1732** Lady M. W. Montagu & Ld. Hervey *Verses to Pope* 69 If..Unwhipt, unblanketed, unkick'd, unslain, That wretched little carcase you retain. **1737** Pope *Hor. Epist.* II. ii. 18 Once..I caught him in a lie, And then, unwhipp'd, he had the grace to cry. **1863** Holland *Lett. Joneses* xiii. 197 The unwhipped coward rubs his hands over his clever boorishness and brutality. **1889** H. M. Stanley in *Daily News* 4 Dec. 5/2 Numerous peoples..who were as yet unwhipped out of their native arrogance.

*transf.* **1899** *Westm. Gaz.* 27 June 10/1 Time for fishing in unwhipped waters.

**2.** (See Whip *v.* 17.)

**1867** Smyth *Sailor's Word-book* 291 *Feazings*, the fagging out or unravelling of an unwhipped rope.

**Unwhi·rled,** *ppl. a.* (Un-[1] 8.) **1760** Sterne *Tr. Shandy* IV. xxxi, [To] make an example of him, as the first Shandy unwhirled about Europe in a post-chaise. **Unwhi·skered,** *a.* (Un-[1] 9.) **1812** Byron *Waltz* xi. *note*, Buonaparte is unwhiskered, the Regent whiskered. **1828** Hook *Sayings & Doings* I. 105 His neckcloth..was tied lightly round his neck, and his plump unwhiskered cheeks festooned over its upper edge.

**Unwhi·sperable,** *a.* and *sb.* [Un-[1] 7 b.]

**a.** *adj.* Unmentionable even in a whisper.

**1853** Mrs. Gore *Dean's Daughter* II. 193 Turbid waters ..worthy only of the four rivers of an unwhisperable region.

**b.** *sb.* Trousers. *slang.*

**1837** *Knickerbocker Mag.* March 288 How could he..see about procuring himself a new pair of unwhisperables from his host, when [etc.]. **1863** G. A. Sala *Captain Dangerous* I. Pref. p. vi, Unprotected females didn't venture in 'unwhisperables' into the depths of Norwegian forests.

**Unwhi·spered,** *ppl. a.* (Un-[1] 8.) **1821** T. W. Hill *Select. Papers* (1860) 26 An unwhispered *s. Ibid.* 27 The symbols for the unwhispered letters. **1835** Lytton *Rienzi* IV. ii, How many unwhispered and solemn rites hast thou witnessed by thy native Nile! **Unwhi·ted,** *ppl. a.* (Un-[1] 8.) **1621** in Kempe *Losely MSS.* (1836) 458 Mercheants for linin, dyaper, damaske, and of all kynds, but all unwhyted. **1648** Hexham II, *Ongewit*, Vnwhited, or Vnbleached. **Unwhi·tened,** *ppl. a.* (Un-[1] 8.) [1775 Ash.] **1833** Loudon *Encycl. Archit.* § 62 The unwhitened mud and rough stone cottages of England. **Unwhi·tewashed,** *ppl. a.* (Un-[1] 8.) **1846** Worcester (citing Philips). **1866** Augusta Wilson

*St. Elmo* i, A rude unwhitewashed paling. 1893 J. W. Barry *Stud. Corsica* 196 An uninhabited cottage with .. unwhitewashed walls. † **Unwhi·ttle**, *v. Obs.*—1 [Un-2 4 + Whittle *sb.*2] *trans.* To remove a 'whittle' or shawl from. 1654 Gayton *Pleas. Notes* II. i. 34 The Lady lik'd his pregnant fancy, and presently unwhitled, and swathed them [*sc.* babes] to her Paramor.

†**Unwho·le**, *a. Obs.* Forms: α. 1–4 **unhal** (3 *Orm.* **unnhal**), 3–4 **unhale**. β. 3, 5 **unhole** (3 **onhole**), **unhol**, 4 **unholl**, 5 **unhool**. [OE. *unhál* (*un-* Un-1 7 + *hál* Whole *a.*), = OHG. *unheil*, *unhail*, Goth. *unhails* unsound, ON. *úheill* insincere, Norw. dial. *uheil* unhealthy, decayed.]

**1.** Not in good health; unsound, unhealthy; diseased, infirm, sick.

α. c888 K. Ælfred *Boeth.* xi. § 1 Sume habbað bearn ȝenoȝe, ac þa beoþ hwilum unhale oððe yfele & unweorþe. c1000 Ælfric in *O. E. Hom.* I. 296 Unȝemetȝod fæsten, & to mycel forhæfdnyss on æte & on wæte deð þone man unhalne. c1200 Ormin 4778 Hiss bodiȝ toc To rotenn bufenn eorþe All samenn... All þiss wass utenn wiþþ unnhal Þurrh swiþe unnride unnhæle. *Ibid.* 9393 ȝiff þatt tin eȝhe iss all unnhal. c1205 Lay. 17187 Þa men þe beoð un-hal, heo fareð to þan stane. c1325 *Metr. Hom.* 35, I gif the blind..thair siht,..I mac unhale men al hale.

β. a1225 *Ancr. R.* 112 Lo þus þe hole half & te cwike dole drowen þet vuele blod ut frommard þe unhole. c1275 *Sinners Beware* 308 in *O. E. Misc.* 82 He seyþ þenne, Myne Poure vn-hole hyne To eure dure come. 1379 *Glouc. Cath. MS. 19* No. I. I. iv. fol. 12 Ellys the body is vnholl & ther after schewith him the vryn. c1425 *Cursor M.* 5137 (Trin.), Her fadir lay vnhol in bedde.

**b.** Spiritually or morally unsound.

c1000 Ælfric *Hom.* II. 470 Se ðe wenð þæt he hal sy, se is unhal. c1275 *Moral Ode* 114 in *O. E. Misc.* 62 Nis no witnesse al so muchel so monnes owe heorte. For so seyþ þat vnhol is him seolue hwat him smeorteþ. c1325 *Metr. Hom.* 129 Man quaim sinne mad unhale.

**c.** Of unsound mind. *rare*—1.

13.. *E. E. Allit. P.* B. 1681 His hert heldet vnhole, he hoped non oþer Bot a best þat he be, a bol oþer an oxe.

**d.** Unsincere. *rare*—1.

a1352 Minot in *Pol. Poems* (Rolls) I. 74 In hert he was unhale, He come thare moste for mede.

**2.** Of food, etc.: Unwholesome. *rare*—1.

a1225 *Ancr. R.* 370 Ne nomen heo neuer ȝeme hwat was hol, hwat was unhol te eten ne to drincken.

**3.** Imperfect; defective; incomplete. *rare*—1.

a1300 *Cursor M.* 23563 For-þi þat godd has ai wroght al, Of his werkes es noght vnhale [*Trin.* vnhool].

**Unwho·lesome**, *a.* and *sb.* [Un-1 7. Cf. older Flem. *onheylsaem* (Kilian), MHG. (G.) *unheilsam*, ON. *úheilsamr* (MSw. *ohelsamber*).]

**A.** *adj.* **1. a.** Not beneficial, salutary, or conducive to morals, etc.; detrimental or prejudicial to health of mind.

c1200 Ormin 7177 And tatt iss eȝȝþerr himm & hemm Unnhalsumm to þe sawle. 1554 T. Sampson *Let. to Trew Professors* A vi b, Where haue ye your ground in the scripture for this your vnholsome housell. 1657 Hobbes *Absurd Geom.* 16 You..can not expect to publish any unholesome doctrine without some Antidotes from me. 1888 H. M. Stanley in *Standard* (1889) 6 Apr., All unwholesome and evil conjectures. 1889 *Times* 8 Apr. 9/1 A mischievous demagogue who has acquired an unwholesome popularity by discreditable methods. 1900 L. B. Walford *One of Ourselves* xiv, They are keen on doing anything they shouldn't, anything improper and unwholesome.

**b.** Not promoting or conducive to, harmful or prejudicial to, well-being, good condition, soundness, etc.; hurtful, noxious.

a1400-50 *Alexander* 4387 Þe kind of þire customs we kepe euire-mare, Þe quilk, I hope, ser, þe to hald vnhalesom it ware. 1628 May *Virg. Georg.* I. 6 Nor is't unwholesome to subdue the Land By often exercise. 1664 Butler *Hud.* II. i. 794 I'd be loath..To free your heels by any course, That might b' unwholesome to your Spurs. 1787 Winter *Syst. Husb.* 84 When waters remain..on the ground which ..produce rank unwholesome weeds. 1812 Byron *Ch. Har.* I. liii, And must they fall..To swell one bloated Chief's unwholesome reign? 1828 Scott *F. M. Perth* xiii, Perhaps farther stay were unwholesome for my safety.

**2.** Not favourable to or promoting good health; not salubrious, wholesome, or healthful; injurious to health: **a.** Of food, etc.

1297 R. Glouc. (Rolls) 9115 He willede of an lampreye to ete, Ac is leches him vorbode vor it was vnholsom mete. c1380 Wyclif *Wks.* (1880) 475 Þe mynging of þes þingis is vnholsum to man to take. c1440 *Pallad. on Husb.* IX. 187 The water that gooth thorgh the leden penne Is rust corrupt, vnholsum. c1455 Pecock *Folewer* 22 To men is ȝouun þe witt of smellyng, bi which þei schulen knowe sumwhat afer what bodies ben vnholsom to be take vnto her nurischyng. 1482 Caxton *Polycron.* III. xxxi. 152 b, That vnholsomme mete that he hadde eten at soper. 1528 Paynell *Salerne's Regim.* E ij b, Salte meate..is vnholsome for sicke folkes. 1577 Googe *Heresbach's Husb.* 146 A grosse vnholsome kinde of milke. 1622 Peacham *Compl. Gent.* xv. 193 Hauing your..reputation abased, while you sit taking your vnwholesome healthes. 1665 Manley *Grotius' Low C. Wars* 473 Their flesh they found to be unwholsom for food. 1726 Leoni *Alberti's Archit.* I. 65 Its water is unwholsom to drink. 1774 Pennant *Tour Scotl. in 1772*, 305 Fever.. originating from unwholesome food. 1855 Macaulay *Hist. Eng.* xii. III. 233 Leprosies, such as strange and unwholesome diet engenders. 1876 Bancroft *Hist. U.S.* III. viii. 122 Sick at heart, and enfeebled by unwholesome diet.

*transf.* 1855 *Orr's Circ. Sci., Inorg. Nat.* 202 The water cannot be in any other than an unwholesome state, and unfit for general use.

**b.** Of places, conditions, etc.

c1455 Pecock *Folewer* 22 Þe witt of smellyng, bi which þei schulen knowe..what bodies ben vnholsom if with hem þei maken her nyȝ dwellyng. a1533 Berners *Gold. Bk. M. Aurel.* (1546) Q j b, For meate corrupteth in an vnholsome potte. 1579 Stevens in Hakluyt *Voyages* (1589) 160 Raine so vnholesome, that if the water stand a little while, all is full of wormes. 1613 Purchas *Pilgrimage* 486 Alexandria is very vnholesome, as the graue of that Alexandria we before mentioned. 1653 in *Verney Mem.* (1904) I. 551 Unwholesome smells..and most noysome stinks. 1718 Berkeley *Jrnl. Tour Italy* Wks. 1871 IV. 592 A small river seemed to render it marshy and unwholesome. 1779 *Mirror* No. 41 ¶ 5 The vicinity of..the lake..she was sure must be extremely unwholesome. 1847 G. Harris *Life Ld. Hardwicke* I. 207 The walls were not dry, but very damp and unwholesome. 1859 Dickens *T. Two Cities* I. ii, As the waves of an unwholesome sea might do. 1867 Smyth *Sailor's Word-bk.* 707 *Unwholesome ship*,..a sugar ship diverted from her former trade, and not properly cleansed.

**c.** Of climate, air, etc.

1555 Eden *Decades* (Arb.) 87 The great heate and vnholsome ayer. 1592 Breton *Pilgr. Paradise* Wks. (Grosart) I. 14/1 Shee bit her taile, with such vnholsome breath, As ..stung her selfe to death. 1653 W. Ramesey *Astrol. Restored* 267 It shews..unwholsom infectious Mists. c1690 in *10th Rep. Hist. MSS. Comm.* App. I. 139 The air is most unwholesome, and agrees very ill with him. 1726 Leoni *Alberti's Archit.* I. 64 Any very deep Valley reaking with unwholsome Steams. 1796 Morse *Amer. Geog.* I. 750 The atmosphere is very hot, moist and unwholesome. 1825 Scott *Talism.* vi, The alternations of the unwholesome climate. 1859 Landor *Hellenics* 26 Why should we stand beneath This hollow tree's unwholesome breath?

**3. a.** Of persons: Not sound in respect of morals, character, etc.; morally tainted or corrupted.

c1374 Chaucer *Troylus* IV. 330 O olde, vnholsom and mysbyleued man. 1602 Shaks. *Ham.* IV. v. 82 The people muddied, Thicke and vnwholsome in their thoughts and whispers.

**b.** Not sound in health; diseased, infirm, sick.

1656 Osborn *Adv. Son* I. 33 Fly, with Joseph, the Embraces of great Ladyes; lest you..see your leggs rot in the stocks of the Physitian: they being often unwholsome. 1732 Arbuthnot *Rules of Diet* (1736) 415 Children born healthy, often contract the Disease from an unwholsom Nurse. 1848 Thackeray *Van. Fair* lxi, An unwholesome little Miss of seven years of age.

*transf.* 1847 C. Bronte *J. Eyre* i, Large and stout,..with a dingy and unwholesome skin. 1889 Mrs. Oliphant *Poor Gentleman* xliv, Those white, unwholesome, greasy hands.

*Comb.* 1858 *Household Words* XVIII. 519/2 A middling-sized man, with a sharp, unwholesome-looking face.

†**c.** *Naut.* (See quot.) *Obs.*

1627 Capt. Smith *Seaman's Gram.* xi. 52 If she draw little water and be long, she may try and ride well, but neuer hull well, which is called an vnwholsome ship. [1867 Smyth *Sailor's Word-bk.* 707.]

†**4.** *Sc.* Ugly; repulsive. *Obs.*—1

c1480 Henryson *Fables, Paddock & Mouse* 64 Thocht I vnhailsum be to luke vpon.

**5.** Impaired; defective. *rare*—1.

1604 Shaks. *Oth.* IV. i. 124 Prythee beare Some Charitie to my wit, do not thinke it So vnwholesome.

**B.** *sb.* An unwholesome thing.

1858 *Brit. Q. Rev.* LVI. 358 We find him [Lilly]..leaving ..Neve and Wodehouse to provide, as usual, tables of the wholesomes and unwholesomes.

Hence **Unwho·lesomely** *adv.*

c1455 Pecock *Folewer* 51 It is science to knowe..what metis..wole nurische vs vnholsomli. 1563 Foxe *A. & M.* 1712/2 Madam, you were best to come out of the raine. For you sit vnwholesomlye. 1628 Wither *Brit. Rememb.* VIII. 199 Thy Children oft unwholsomly are fed. 1860 Flor. Nightingale *Nursing* 10 The air..unwholesomely close and foul. 1875 Helps *Soc. Press.* xiii. 174 The eyes of an unwholesomely curious world.

**Unwho·lesomeness.** [f. prec. + -ness.]

**1.** Unsound or impaired health; unhealthiness.

c1449 Pecock *Repr.* I. xiii. 68 Thanne thou etist hony aloon. ..And this feding schal turne into thin vnhoolsumnes.

**2.** Unhealthy character (of locality, climate, air, etc.); insalubrity, unhealthfulness.

a1513 Fabyan *Chron.* VII. 377 By reason of ye vnholsomnes of the countre. 1598 Hakluyt *Voy.* I. 396 The vnwholesomnesse of the aire, and corruption of the waters in the hote time of the yeere. 1623 in Foster *Eng. Factories Ind.* (1908) II. 181 The unholsomnes of this clymeatt. 1626 Bacon *Sylva* § 777 The Wholesomenesse or Vnwholesomenesse, as well of Seasons, as of the Seats of Dwellings. 1697 Walsh *Life Virgil* ¶ 2 in Dryden's *Virgil*, The Unwholsomness of his Native Air. 1726 Leoni *Alberti's Archit.* I. 65/1 The damps..will come to you with double..unwholsomness. 1758 in Dodsley *Fug. Pieces* (1761) II. 84 The Unwholesomeness of the Rust and Verdegrease Suffusions. a1843 Southey *Common-pl. Bk.* Ser. II. (1849) 245/2 In the unwholesomeness of this shade the tree..could not possibly flourish. 1879 *Cassell's Techn. Educ.* IV. 42/1 The unwholesomeness of sewage.

**3.** The state or quality of being unwholesome as, or unfit for, food, etc.

1548 *Act 2 & 3 Edw. VI*, c. 10 § 1 The unholsomenes of the drincke..made thereof. 1587 Golding *De Mornay* xiv. 249 Iudging..of the wholsomnes or vnwholsomnes of foode by the taste thereof. 1633 T. Adams *Exp. 2 Peter* ii. 20 The unwholesomenesse of his dyet. 1651 Stanley *Poems* 37 Th' unwholsomenesse of fruit. 1863 *N. & Q.* 3rd Ser. IV. 249 The Scottish objection to eels as an article of food is mainly due to their supposed unwholesomeness.

**4.** Lack of moral wholesomeness; viciousness.

1881 *Sat. Rev.* 15 Jan. 88/2 Happily its unwholesomeness is often lessened by the folly of the language into which the author falls. 1897 *Advance* (Chicago) 25 Mar. 389/1 The absence of [disapprobation of sinners]..is a sure sign of unwholesomeness and decay.

†**Unwi·de**, *a. Obs.* [Un-1 7. Cf. OE. *unwíd*, ON. *úvíðr*.] Narrow, confined. a1300 *Cursor M.* 8667 At ans bath.. we..vr barns bar. In wanes war we stad vn-wide.

†**Unwie·ld**, *sb. Obs. rare.* In 4 **unwelde**, **vnweilde**. [Un-1 12.] Feebleness, weakness, impotence.

13.. *E. E. Psalter* lxx. 9 (V.), Ne for-werpe me in un-welde, In time when I am of elde. c1375 *Cursor M.* 3563 (Gött.), And haue man ben neure so bald, Quen þat he bicomis alde, Til vnweild [he] bigines to falle.

†**Unwie·ld**, *a. Obs.* [Un-1 7.]

**1.** Feeble, weak, impotent; = Unwieldy *a.* 1.

Freq. from c1400 to c1450.

c1220 *Bestiary* 57 Siðen hise limes arn unwelde. c1250 *Gen. & Ex.* 347 Vn-welde woren and in win Here owen limes. ?a1366 Chaucer *Rom. Rose* 359 Al woxen was her body vnwelde, And drie,..for elde. c1386 — *Reeve's Prol.* 32 Oure olde lemes mowe wel been vnweelde. 14.. *Sir Beues* (L.) 34 He..Wexed febull and vn-welde. c1480 *Bk. of Brome* (1886) 106 Hys body gane vax on-wylld.

*absol.* a1300 *Cursor M.* 10539 Sal naman negh þat vnweild.

**2.** Difficult or cumbrous to manipulate or handle; unwieldy. *rare.*

1390 Gower *Conf.* I. 312 The reyni Storm fell doun algates And al here takel made unwelde. a1440 *Sir Eglam.* 309 A clobb of yron..That was mekylle and fulle unwelde.

Hence † **Unwie·ldness.** *Obs.*—1

1437-8 *Rolls of Parlt.* V. 439 In cas that anny of the seide Lordes..fall to suche unweldnesse or impotence.

**Unwie·ldable**, *a. rare*—1. [Un-1 7 b.] Unwieldy. 1500-20 Dunbar *Poems* xxvi. 98 Full mony a waistless wallydrag, With wamis vnweildable. †**Unwie·lded**, *ppl a. Obs.*—1 [Un-2 6, 8.] Made feeble. a1300 *Cursor M.* 23642 Þai [*sc.* the wicked] sal vnweldid be with bale.

**Unwie·ldily**, *adv.* [f. Unwieldy *a.* + -ly 2.] In an unwieldy or awkward manner; cumbrously.

c1610 Chapman *Iliad* To Rdr. A 5, Their long words Shewe in short verse, as in a narrow place, Two opposites should meet, with two-hand swords; Vnwieldily, without or use or grace. 1611 Cotgr., *Inhabilement*,..weakely; vnweldily, vneasily. 1697 Dryden *Virg. Georg.* IV. 623 His finny Flocks about their Shepherd play. .. Unweildily they wallow first in Ooze, Then in the shady Covert seek Repose. 1830 *Fraser's Mag.* I. 24 It slides amain, unwieldily, Into the universal sea. 1848 T. Aird *Summer Day, Noon* 39 The cottar's cow..comes Cantering unwieldily. 1862 Smiles *Engineers* III. 101 Locomotives..dragging themselves unwieldily along at..five or six miles an hour.

**Unwie·ldiness.** [f. Unwieldy *a.*]

**1.** The quality of being incontrollable or unrestrainable; indocility.

1571 Golding *Calvin on Ps.* iii. 5 Such as either blame fortune, or..with vnruly rage power out the vnweeldinesse of their sorow. a1680 Charnock *Attrib. God* (1682) 173 The more unwieldiness there is in our Spirits, the more carnal our affections are in worship, the more evidence there is of the strength of that revolted state.

†**2.** The state or condition of being weak or feeble; weakness, infirmity. *Obs.*

1575 Fenton *Gold. Epist.* (1582) 263 This age of vnweldiness beginnes at fiftie yeares. 1610 Healey *St. Aug. Citie of God* XIX. iv. 757 Strength, beauty, vigour and actiuity, are all subuerted by..sicknesse, faintnesse, and vnweeldinesse. 1698 Fryer *Acc. E. India & P.* 306 The South Wind ..brings Listlessness and an Unweildiness over the whole Body. 1737 Swift *Let. to J. Temple* Feb., She is quite sunk with years and unwieldiness, as well as a very scanty support.

*transf.* 1651 H. More *Enthus. Tri.* (1662) 4 The enormous strength of Imagination (which is yet the Soul's weaknesse or unwieldiness).

**3.** Awkwardness or clumsiness in respect of bulk, build, or movement; *esp.* awkward corpulence; clumsy size or vastness.

1577 B. Googe *Heresbach's Husb.* IV. 163 b, Columella would haue you keepe for euery gander, three geese, thinking by reason of their vnweldynesse, this number to suffise. 1612 T. Taylor *Comm. Titus* iii. 1 Who is he that carrieth flesh about with him, that findeth not the heauinesse and vnweldines of it vnto any thing that is good? 1665 Glanvill *Scepsis Sci.* xi. 62 The supposed unwieldiness of its massie bulk. 1709 Addison *Tatler* No. 116 ¶ 5 The Weight and Unweildiness of the Garment. 1712 — *Spect.* No. 464 ¶ 5 Poverty..preserving them from Gouts, Dropsies, Unwieldiness, and Intemperance. 1794 G. Adams *Nat. & Exp. Philos.* III. 271 If we should suppose animals vastly large,..a heaviness and unwieldiness would arise which [etc.] 1809 *Med. Jrnl.* XXI. 115 An unwieldiness in motion and hurried respiration when walking. 1850 Kingsley *A. Locke* xxxvi, At last, after days of painful crawling, I dragged my unwieldiness to the tree foot. 1879 *Cassell's Techn. Educ.* II. 165/2 In the ordinary descriptions of field-carriages the weight and unwieldiness of the trail alone would be a serious objection to such a method of draught.

*fig.* a1631 Donne *Love's Diet* 1 To what a combersome unweildinesse And burdenous corpulence my love had growne. 1673 Allestree *Lady's Call.* II. iii. § 12. 219 Greatness is now grown to such an unwieldiness, that it cannot stoop tho to the most Christian Offices.

*transf.* a1677 Barrow *Serm.* (1678) 3 Whatever evil.. backwardness, inhability, unwieldiness and confusion of thought beget, Wisdom prevents. 1774 [W. Mitford] *Ess. Harmony Lang.* 132 This line has also been admired for its expressive unwieldiness. Its form is..by no means peculiarly suited to give the idea of unwieldiness. 1866 Dickens *Mugby Junct.* ii, With that absurd sense of unwieldiness of mind and body weighing him down. 1875 Helps *Soc. Press.* iii. 48 The largeness, the unwieldiness, and the temporary nature of habitation in these great centres of population.

**4.** The condition or character of being difficult to guide, direct, or control by reason of extent or size. Also *fig.*

1599 Sandys *Europæ Spec.* (1605) V 1, Since that is great properly which is great in the actions, which one as often impeacheth by vnwildinesse in the bigge, as by weakenesse in the little. 1600 Hakluyt *Voy.* III. 79 Considering the swift course and way of the ships, and the vnwieldinesse of them to stay and turne as a man would wish. 1610 Holland *Camden's Brit.* I. 696 The disordered vnwealdinesse of their owne armie. **1764** Burn *Poor Laws* 226 The objections against county workhouses..seem to require peculiar attention. There is something of unwieldiness in the prospect. **1809** Malkin *Gil Blas* ix. i. ⁋ 7 Noted for the unwieldiness of their ambition. *a* **1873** Lytton *Pausanias* i. v, Armies too large rot by their own unwieldiness into decay. **1898** 'Merriman' *Roden's Corner* ii, The unwieldiness of the empire.

**Unwie·ldly**, *a.* [In early use f. Unwield *sb.* + -ly[1]; later a variant of Unwieldy *a.*

Many quots. for *unwieldly* in reprints from 1681 onwards have, on verification in first edd. or the MSS., proved to be misprints of Unwieldy *a.*, as in quots. 1681–1730. The prevalence of the misprint may be the chief source of the form.]

†**1.** Impotent; weak; = Unwieldy *a.* 1. *Obs.*

*a* **1300** *Cursor M.* 23642 (Edinb.), Þir sal haf weldnes of wale, Þa sal unweldli be wit bale.

**2.** = Unwieldy *a.* 2–4. Also *transf.*

*a* **1513** Fabyan *Chron.* vii. (1516) 153/2 He was vnweldly by reason of ouer ladynge of Flesshe, and myght not well trauayll. *Ibid.* 161 b/2 [They] made them a Mamet of a Fatte and vnwyldely as.

[**1681** *Sanderson's Serm.* 95 As Saul's armour did [sit] upon Davids [back]; unweildly, and sagging about his shoulders. **1730** Bailey, *Inhabile*,..unmeet, unfit, unwieldly, not nimble.] **1763** Churchill *Ghost* i. 261 Horrid, unwieldly, without Form,..in the rear, That Post of Honour, should appear Pomposo. **1858** Faber *Foot of Cross* ii. 93 The interlacings and unfoldings of an unwieldly thunder-cloud. **1881** *Athenæum* 19 March 393/3 Unwieldly though the German language is in conversation and for every-day purposes. **1888** Murie in Kingsley *Riverside Nat. Hist.* IV. 404 Such a great, unwieldly, horned bird as the rhinoceros hornbill.

**Unwie·ldly**, *adv. rare.* [Cf. prec.] In an unwieldy manner. **1793** Wordsw. *Evening Walk* 231 Thence issuing oft, unwieldly as ye stalk, Ye crush..your flow'ry walk.

†**Unwie·ldsome**, *a. Obs.* [Un-[1] 7.]

**1.** Of age: Impotent; = Unwieldy *a.* 1 c. *rare*⁻¹.

**1567** Golding *Ovid's Met.* vii. 85 From dull vnweildsome age to youth he backward drew.

**2.** Unwieldy.

**1579–80** North *Plutarch* (1595) 748 Alexander..perceiuing that his armie was very heauy and vnwildsom to remoue, for the..spoiles they had with them. **1601** Sir W. Cornwallis *Disc. Seneca* (1631) 38 Like prisoners..debarred exercise, fat, and unweildsome. **1674** N. Fairfax *Bulk & Selv.* 138 Body being a stour unweildsom thing,..it cannot stir without asking another bodies leave to crowd by.

**Unwieldy** (ɒnwī·ldi), *a.* Forms: 5–7 **unweldy**, 6 -ye, 6–7 -ie; 5–7 **unweeldy**, 5 -weeldi, 6 -ie; 6–7 **unwealdy**, -ie; 6–8 (9) **unweildy** (6 **-weyldy**, *Sc.* **wnveildy**), 6–7 -ie; 6– **unwieldy**, 7 -ie; 6–7 **unwildy**, 6 -wildie, *Sc.* -wyldy. (Also 5–7 vn-, 5–6 on-.) [Un-[1] 7, 5 b + Wieldy *a.* Cf. the early Unwield *a.* and Unwieldly *a.*]

†**1.** Of persons, the body, etc.: Lacking strength; weak, impotent; feeble, infirm. Also const. with preps., as *for*, *of*, *to* (with inf.). *Obs.*

*c* **1386** Chaucer *Manciple's Prol.* 55 So vnweeldy was this sory palled goost. **1421–2** Hoccleve *Dialog* 248 My lymes sumdell now vnweldy be. **1442** in *Proc. King's Counc. Irel.* (Rolls) App. 274 The said Erlle..is aged, vnweldy and vnlustie. **1513** Douglas *Æneid* viii. v. 71 Furth held the king vnweildy in auld ȝeris. **1584** R. Scot *Discov. Witchcr.* i. vi. (1886) 10 A toothless, old, impotent, and unweldie woman. **1606** G. Woodcocke *Hist. Iustine* xxxiv. 111 Altogither giuen to sloath, and growne so vnweeldy through dayly ryot. **1621** T. Granger *Expos. Eccles.* xii. 321 So doe olde men, because they are vnwealdie, and vnable to auoide dangers. **1659** W. Chamberlayne *Pharon.* i. iii. 72 At that stroke his Limbs Slack their unwieldy Nerves.

*absol.* **1550** Crowley *Way to Wealth* 685 To releue the vnweldy that be not able to labour for theire fode.

(*b*) **1570** Foxe *A. & M.* (ed. 2) I. 80/1 Narcissus..was vnwieldy for his age to gouerne that function alone. **1588** T. Hughes *Misfort. Arthur* i. ii. 13 Any wight vnwildie of herselfe. **1592** Nashe *P. Penilesse* E 2 b, To corrupt the braine, and make it vnapt and vnweldie for anything. **1642** Fuller *Holy & Prof. St.* ii. xix. 128 The weilding of his sword hath not made him unweildie to do any other work.

†**b.** Of age, etc.: Characterized or attended by infirmity, weakness, or impotence. *Obs.*

**1430–40** Lydg. *Bochas* i. 2127 In his vnweeldi age He was compellid to holden his passage Out off Thebes. *c* **1450** — *Secrees* 645 Yif inpotence of his vnweldy age, In his desirs put hym nat abak. **1502** *Will of Wilbey* (Somerset Ho.), Oppressed with gret unweldy age. *a* **1592** Greene *Jas. IV*, iii. iii, Mine age vnweldie and vnmeete for toyle. **1659** W. Chamberlayne *Pharon.* ii. iii. 167 Although unwieldy age allow Not strength to sell my life at such a rate Honour aimes at. **1685** Dryden tr. *Horace, Odes* i. ix. 28 E're with'ring time the taste destroyes, With sickness and unwieldy years!

**2.** Of persons or animals: Moving ungracefully or with difficulty, by reason of corpulence or ponderousness; lacking litheness or flexibility; awkward, clumsy.

**1530** Palsgr. 328/2 Unweldye, boystouse, *lourt.* **1538** Starkey *England* 79 In a dropcy the body ys vnweldy, vnlusty, and slo. **1563** B. Googe *Eglogs*, etc. (Arb.) 69 A bluddy Butcher byg and blunt, a vyle vnweldy knaue,..at hym..let dryue. **1602** *2nd Pt. Return Parnass.* iii. ii. 1257 Then the old vnweldy Camels gin to dance. **1650** R. Stapylton *Strada's Low-C. Wars* x. 11 Others that wore Armes which made them unweldier, not so nimble to avoid a hurt. **1677** Plot *Oxfordsh.* 134 The motion of so unwildy Creatures as Elephants. **1741** J. Wilford *Mem.* App. 41 From the unwieldiest Beast of Land or Deep. **1779** *Mirror* No. 8, I have seen the unwieldy burgess changed into a slender gentleman. **1823** Scott *Quentin D.* xxix, He was, though now somewhat unwieldy, a powerful, athletic man. **1867** E. F. Bowden tr. *Fathers of Desert* 149 An unwieldy Bactrian camel had gone mad.

*transf.* **1553** T. Wilson *Rhet.* 2 b, Nothyng is more nedefull, then..to cherishe these our lompishe and vnweldie natures. **1606** Chapman *Gent. Usher* iii. ii. 174 She shall have an unweldie and dull soule If she be nothing moov'd with my poore tongue. **1635** A. Stafford *Panegyricke* in *Female Glory* e 7, The toylesome burthen of unweldy clay.

**b.** Characterized by clumsy massiveness, awkward shape, or ponderousness.

**1582** Stanyhurst *Æneis* iii. (Arb.) 83 When that..strayts shal be opned neere craggy vnwieldye Pelorus. **1596** Spenser *F. Q.* vi. viii. 28 Th' other Knight, Whom with his weight vnweldy downe he held. **1610** Holland *Camden's Brit.* i. 39 As a ship of exceeding great bulke..endangered through the own unwieldy hugenesse. **1671** Milton *Samson* 54 But what is strength without a double share Of wisdom, vast, unwieldy, burdensom. **1720** Pope *Iliad* xvii. 834 As when two mules..Drag some vast beam, or mast's unwieldy length. **1753** Hogarth *Anal. Beauty* vi. 30 Elephants and whales please us with their unwieldy greatness. **1793** T. Beddoes *Observ.* 101 Two cases of unwieldy corpulence. **1828** Lytton *Pelham* II. xxi, His person..was of no unwieldy obesity. **1856** Kane *Arct. Expl.* I. xx. 260 Of such unwieldy bulk as not unfrequently to be mistaken for the walrus. **1892** *Photogr. Ann.* 374 On account of its unwieldy dimensions.

**c.** Expressed, manifested, or exhibited in a clumsy, awkward, or ungraceful manner; awkwardly performed.

*a* **1635** Corbet *Poems* (1807) 107 What a sting Of lust do their unwildy daunces bring? **1648** J. Beaumont *Psyche* vii. xxxii, O'rpowr'd with most unweildy thanks and praise. **1728** Thomson *Spring* 776 The broad Monsters..flounce, and tumble in unwieldy Joy. **1748** *Anson's Voy.* ii. i. 124 Their motion being the most unweildy that can be conceived. **1789** Cowper *On Queen's Visit to London* 20 [Water] Upspouted by a whale in air, T'express unwieldy joy. **1824** Miss Ferrier *Inher.* lxxviii, The manners of Lady C..made her feel her own as something unwieldy and overgrown. **1850** L. Hunt *Autobiog.* xvii. (1860) 268 Two grampuses..interested us extremely by their unwieldy gambols.

**3. a.** Of weapons: Difficult to handle or wield. Also *transf.*

*a* **1547** Surrey *Æneid* ii. (1557) C ii b, The aged man.. Forceless..cast his weake unweldy dart. **1595** *Locrine* iii. iv. 44 This great vnwildie club. **1646** H. Lawrence *Comm. Angells* 173 The weapon would be too heavy, to unweildy for us to use. **1700** S. L. tr. *Fryke's Voy. E. Ind.* 160 With my unwildy weapon..I struck him into the left side. **1719** De Foe *Crusoe* ii. (Globe) 368 These Swords were strange great unwieldy Things. **1745** P. Thomas *Jrnl. Anson's Voy.* 289 Pole-axes like ours, but somewhat more rough and unweildy.

**b.** Difficult to control, guide, move, manipulate, etc., by virtue of size, shape, or weight; clumsily massive, awkwardly large; unmanageable.

**1552** Elyot s.v. *Inhabilis*, A ship that by reason of the biggenesse is vnwildie. **1644** Milton *Areop.* (Arb.) 71 Untill hee see our small divided maniples cutting through at every angle of his ill united and unweildy brigade. **1663** Cowley *The Complaint* v, The dull work of thy unweildy Plough. **1679** Moxon *Mech. Exerc.* ix. 161 These Doors are commonly un-weildy to lift off and on. **1774** J. Bryant *Mythol.* II. 408 Ships, which were unwieldy, and of great burden. **1814** Ld. J. Russell in S. Walpole *Life* (1889) I. 75 His legs being quite swollen and unwieldy. **1865** Kingsley *Herew.* xxi, A pole..which he dragged after him, like an unwieldy tail. **1879** S. C. Bartlett *Egypt to Pal.* xix. 406 Division-walls,..composed of large and unwieldy stones.

**c.** *fig.*, *transf.*, and in fig. context.

**1538** Starkey *England* iii. 79 We haue ouer-many [priests], wych..make our polytyke body vnweldy and heuy. **1589** *Almond for Parrat* B iij, His..burlibond adiunctes, that so pester his former edition with their vnweldie phrase, as no true syllogisme can haue elbowe roome. **1612** Drayton *Poly-olb.* ix. 139 [To] make us Britains beare Th' unweildy Norman yoke. **1632** Lithgow *Trav.* iv. 144 This vnwealdy body [of the Ottoman dominion in Persia] hauing two heads, began to decline. **1665** Boyle *Occas. Refl.* iv. xix. 125 Though an unwieldy Affluence may afford some empty Pleasure to the Imagination. *a* **1704** T. Brown *Praise Poverty* Wks. 1720 I. 113 Raising their own Fortunes to an unweildy Bulk. **1744** Akenside *Pleas. Imag.* iii. 117 Hints deep-omened with unwieldy schemes, And dark portents of state. **1777** Burke *Let. to Sheriffs of Bristol* Wks. III. 187 The unwieldy haughtiness of a great ruling nation. **1796** Morse *Amer. Geog.* I. p. vi, The second fault of Guthrie's Grammar..is its unwieldy and disproportionate account of Great Britain. **1807** J. Barlow *Columb.* vi. 331 Athenian youths, the unwieldy war to meet, Couch the stiff lance. **1826–7** H. Neele *Lit. Rem.* (1829) 49 The 'Iliad' [of Chapman] is written in the cumbrous and unwieldy old English measure of fourteen syllables.

*absol.* **1702** Steele *Funeral* iii. 44 That strong Masculine thing..pretends to all the Tenderness in the World! and would Fain put the Unwieldy upon us for the Soft, the Languid!

**4.** Indisposed to submit to guidance or command; restive, recalcitrant, indocile. Also const. *to.*

**1513** Douglas *Æneid* xiii. vi. 34 [He] went..the onweldy common pepill ilkane To caus adres eftir thar faculte. **1549** Coverdale, etc. *Erasm. Par. Titus* 28 That nacion beyng rebellious and vnweyldy to be ordered. **1584** Lodge *Alarum* E iv, What praise deserueth he that will proffer..the raine to an unwildie colt? **1611** Speed *Hist. Gt. Brit.* ix. xvi. § 30. 659/2 The Flemings grew vnweildie to his commandements. **1730** T. Boston *Mem.* vi. (1899) 67 In the forenoon I thought my heart was very unwieldy.

*fig.* and *transf.* *c* **1611** Chapman *Iliad* xiv. 13 As when with vnwieldie waues, the great Sea forefeeles winds, That both waies murmure. **1641** Milton *Reform.* i. 13 Exact Reformation is not perfited at the first push, and those unweildy Times of Edward 6. may hold some Plea by this excuse. *a* **1699** J. Beaumont *Psyche* x. ccclxxxvii, He knows the heat of this unweildy Passion, And will allow it brave Immoderation.

†**5.** Inexpert or awkward (*in* doing something); incapable, unpractical. *Obs.*

**1666** J. Davies *Hist. Caribby Isles* 201 They are..so fearful and unwieldy in the handling of Arms, that they are easily reduc'd under subjection. **1709** Steele *Tatler* No. 27 ⁋ 2 A Rake..is a poor unwieldy Wretch, that commits Faults out of the Redundance of his good Qualities.

**Unwi·fed**, *a.* [Un-[1] 9. Cf. Unwived *ppl. a.*] Not made a wife. **1840** Lytton *Pilgr. Rhine* xix, The unwifed mother that..casts her babe upon the river. **Unwi·felike**, *a.* (Un-[1] 7 c.) **1853** Miss Yonge *Heir of Redclyffe* xxxi, I can't be so unwife-like after all; for..nothing makes me feel so small and foolish as that humility of his! **Unwi·fely**, *a.* (Un-[1] 7.) **1864** 'Annie Thomas' *D. Donne* III. 183 His wife's illness came from a most unwifely frame of mind. (Also in recent use.) **Unwi·g**, *v.* [Un-[2] 4.] *trans.* To divest of a wig. **1819** *Metropolis* II. 125 A button.. entangling with her peruque, unmasked, or rather *unwigged* the Virgin of the Sun. **1897** *Westm. Gaz.* 6 Aug. 8/2 A tradition as to Baron Martin having unwigged himself.. at Durham. **Unwi·gged**, *ppl. a.* [Un-[1] 8.] Not covered with a wig. **1845** Ld. Cockburn *Circuit Journeys* (1888) 269 [Lord] Moncrieff..went..and heard his friend..preach. He was unwigged, but perfectly well known in that congregation. **1895** J. C. Snaith *Mistr. D. Marvin* v, His unshaved chin, his unwigged head.

†**Unwi·ght**, *sb. Obs.* [Un-[1] 4 b. Cf. ON. *úvættr* evil spirit.] An evil being or spirit; a fiend or monster; *spec.* the devil.

*a* **1200** *St. Marher.* 3 Ne þole þu neauer þe unwiht þat he weorri mi wit. *c* **1205** Lay. 15734 Nat ic..wha hine biȝate inne weorlde riche, no whaðer hit weore unwiht. *a* **1225** *Ancr. R.* 238 Hwo se..uihteð..aȝan þe unwiht of helle. *Ibid.* 300 Þe sunfule is þe unwihtes lond. *a* **1250** *Owl & Night.* 33 Vnwyht, heo seyde, awey þu fleo. *Ibid.* 218 Hwi dostu þat vnwihtes doþ? Þu singest anyht & nouht aday. *c* **1230** *Hali Meid.* 41 Þu forhores te wið þe unwiht of helle. *c* **1275** *Sinners Beware* 4 in *O.E. Misc.* 72 Þeos holy gostes myhte..wisse vs and theche To wyten vs wyþ þan vnwihte, þat..þencheþ vs to bipeche.

**b.** Used as *adj.* (but the Cotton MS. has *unwrþ* 'unworth', rhyming with *noȝt wrþ*).

*a* **1250** *Owl & Night.* (Jesus MS.) 339 Þu..makest þi song so vnwiht þat me ne telleþ of þe nowiht.

†**Unwi·ght**, *a. Obs.*⁻⁰ (Un-[1] 7.) **1570** Levins *Manip.* 120 Vnwight, *inualidus*. **Unwi·ld**, *a.* [Un-[1] 7. Cf. MDu. *onwilt.*] Not wild; tame. *a* **1400** *Religious Pieces fr. Thornton MS.* 89 Thou was witty and wyse, thi werkes vn-wylde. **1608** Topsell *Serpents* 88 Both these sorts [of wasps], both wilde and vnwilde. †**Unwi·ld**, *v. Obs.*⁻¹ [Un-[2] 6 a.] *trans.* To tame. **1598** Sylvester *Du Bartas* ii. i. *Handy-crafts* 277 Abel desirous still at hand to keep His Milk and Cheese, vnwildes [F. *dessauvage*] the gentle Sheep To make a flock.

**Unwi·lful**, *a.* [Un-[1] 7.]

**1.** Involuntary; unintentional; undesigned.

**1398** Trevisa *Barth. De P. R.* vii. xviii. (Bodl. MS.), Unwilful rennyng of teeres falleþ in þe yȝen somtyme of outeward causes. *c* **1430** *Life St. Kath.* (1884) 38 Þe vnwylfulle confession of fendes ys not to be sette lyght by. *c* **1450** *Myrr. our Ladye* 51 He that leuyth oughte by vnwylfull negly-gence..synneth not deadly. **1577** tr. *Bullinger's Decades* 511/1 Of sinnes some are wilfull and some vnwilfull, or inforced. **1603** H. Chettle *Eng. Mourn. Garment* D 2, How euer wilfull or vnwilfull the acte was, done it was. *a* **1711** Ken *Hymnotheo* Poet. Wks. 1721 III. 128 Few Years will wash away unwilful Taints. **1751** Richardson *Clarissa* (ed. 4) I. 7 To make excuses..for the perhaps not unwilful slights of those whose approbation we wish to engage.

**2.** Not wilful, obstinate, or perverse. *rare.*

**1570** Levins *Manip.* 186 Vnwilfull, *illicentiosus, continens.* **1863** Cowden Clarke *Shaks. Char.* vii. 184 As if, at his years, Lear..could become unwilful, and even pliable.

**Unwi·lfully**, *adv. rare.* [Un-[1] 11. Cf. prec.]

**1.** Unintentionally; involuntarily; undesignedly.

**1382** Wyclif *Prol. Bible* iii. 5 Citees of refuyt..for hem that shedden blood vnwilfully, not of purpos. **1627** Sanderson *Serm.* I. 265 He did it unwittingly, and therefore unwilfully.

†**2.** Against one's wish or will. *Obs.*⁻¹

**1435** Misyn *Fire of Love* 52 Qwho wilfully god despisyd in dedely syn in casting down, vnwilfully after þis lyfe, god demand, sal be dampnyd.

†**Unwi·ll**, *sb.*[1] *Obs.* [OE. *unwilla* (Un-[1] 4 b, 12), = MLG. *unwille*, MDu. *onwille* (Du. *onwil*), OS. **unwillo* (gen. *unwilles*), OHG. *unwillo* (MHG., G. *unwille*), ON. and Icel. *úvili* (Da. *uvilje*, Sw. *ovilja*), displeasure, reluctance.]

**1.** Used adverbially, in genitive (usually with possessive pron.): Against one's will; unwillingly.

The normal OE. genitive *unwillan* is replaced by *unwilles* on the analogy of *willes* (see Will *sb.*[1] 10) and other adverbial genitives. For the adverbial use, cf. OS. *unwilles*, MLG. *unwillens*, older Flem. *onwillens*, MDu. *mijns onwillen*.

*c* **893** K. Ælfred *Oros.* vi. xxxviii, Siþþan sæton þa Gotan þær on lande, sume be þæs caseres willan, sume his unwillan. *c* **1000** in Thorpe *Laws* II. 182 Ȝif he hit dide unwilles. *c* **1000** Ælfric *Saints' Lives* ix. 87 Þeah þu mine hand ahebbe to ðinum hæþenȝilde, And swa þurh me ȝeoffriȝe mines unwilles. *a* **1225** *Juliana* 6 (Roy. MS.), African.. ȝettede him his dohter, & wes sone ihondsald al hire unwilles. *c* **1375** *Sc. Leg. Saints* vii. (*James*) 373 Þe men als þare wnwillis Suld to þe prince be brocht thrillis.

**b.** *At* (or *again*) *one's unwilles*, = prec. *rare*⁻¹. Cf. ON. *at wilja einkvers* against one's will.

*c* **1400** *Anturs of Arth.* 424 (Ireland MS.), Ȝette schalle thou wring thi hondus,..Or any we schild hom weld, atte my unnewilles [*Douce MS.* agayne myne vmwylles].

**2.** Something displeasing or undesired; that which is against a person's will or wish; (one's) dislike or aversion.

*c* **1000** in *Sal. & Saturn* (1848) 262 Nafu ðu to yfel ellen. ðeah ðe sum unwilla on becume. *a* **1023** Wulfstan *Hom.* 12 He dryhð deofles wyllan and godes unwillan. *a* **1200** *St. Marher.* 13 Ich mot nede, ant neoðeles min unwil hit is to don al þat ti wil is. *c* **1200** *Trin. Coll. Hom.* 123 Here [he] wuneð on wanrede and þoleð his unwille. *a* **1225** *Juliana*

(Bodl. MS.) 7 Ha wes him sone ihondsald þah hit hire unwil were. a 1250 *Owl & Night.* 422 Þu farest so doþ þe ille, Euerich blisse him is vnwille. a 1300 *Cursor M.* 25261 Lauerd gif vs to Grace in erth þi wil to do, For to forber all þin vnwil.

**Unwi·ll**, *sb.*2 [Un-1 12 + Will *sb.* Cf. prec.]

1. The fact or condition of being displeased or offended; displeasure.

1872 Whitley Stokes *Goidelica* 182 Great folly, since thou hast proposed (?) to go to death, to be under the unwill of Mary's Son. 1895 K. Meyer *Voy. Bran* i. 14 Woe to him that shall be under His unwill.

2. Lack of will or purpose.

1899 W. S. Blunt *Satan Absolved* 18 Thy Will found counterpart Only in Man's un-Will, Thy Truth in his un-Truth.

**Unwi·ll**, *v.* [Un-2 3.]

1. a. *trans.* To will or resolve the reverse of (something one has willed); = Unresolve *v.*

1650 Howell *Giraffi's Rev. Naples* i. 120 He wold will and unwill a thing at the same instant. 1678 R. L'Estrange *Seneca's Morals* iii. 50 It is the Business of my Age to Unwill one day, that which I Will'd Another. 1849 J. A. Carlyle tr. *Dante's Inf.* 16 One who unwills what he willed. 1870 J. H. Newman *Gram. Assent* i. iv. 69 That which willed it, can unwill it. 1871 Browning *Pr. Hohenst.* 1472 What if the event demonstrate her unwise, If she unwill the thing she willed before?

b. With reference to Will *sb.*1 (= testament).

1660 R. Coke *Power & Subj.* 23 Therefore if a Man make twenty Wills, yet when he will, he may unwill them all. 1854 Warter *Last of Old Squires* xviii. 195 [He saw] that there was a democratic Desire abroad to *unwill* what good Men in former Days had *willed*.

c. To revoke or reverse (one's will or purpose).

1871 Browning *Balaust.* 163 Wouldst thou..Unwill thy will to reign a righteous king?

2. To divest of volition; to deprive (a person) of will-power.

1844 Mrs. Browning *Duchesss May* iii. vi, Now, your will is all unwilled—now, your pulses are all stilled. 1891 Meredith *One of our Conq.* I. xii. 232 The precedent of submission is a charm upon the faint-hearted through love: it unwinds, unwills them.

**Unwille**, *a.*: see Un-1 3.

**Unwi·lled**, *ppl. a.* [Un-1 8 + Will *v.*1]

1. Not willed or intended; not decided by the will; involuntary; unintentional; undesigned.

a 1540 Barnes *Wks.* (1573) 309/1 For our Lord can easely beare and suffer an vnwilled ignoraunce. 1598 Florio, *Inuoluto*, vnwilled, neuer consenting. a 1711 Ken *Hymnarium* Poet. Wks. 1721 II. 133 We..are judg'd by Law innate, And God for unwill'd Failings will abate. ?172. A. Hill *Verses for Mr. Savage* 25 Some secret fate for guilt unwill'd ..Plung'd me thus deep in sorrow's searching flood. 1791 E. Darwin *Bot. Garden* ii. 93 She speaks.. With words unwill'd, and wisdom not her own. 1803 Jane Porter *Thaddeus* vi, This unfortunate event..was completely unwilled on my part. 1854 S. Dobell *Balder* xxiv. 168 At first..[it] Did stir thee with no more than an unwilled Attention. 1857 G. Macdonald *Poems* (1867) 68 My heart with unwilled love grew warm.

2. Undesired. *rare*—0.

1648 Hexham ii, *Ongewilt*, Vnwilled, or not liked off.

3. Left without being willed or purposed.

1868 Ld. Lytton *Ring Amasis* II. 291 Fool, to forget that Will can only be annihilated by Will; that good unwilled is evil willed.

**Unwi·lling**, *ppl. a.* [OE. *unwillende* (Un-1 10), = ON. and Icel. *ú-, óviljandi.* Cf. MLG. *unwillendes.* Re-formed in 16th cent.]

†1. Of persons: Not intending, purposing, or desiring (to do a particular thing). *Obs.*

c 897 K. Ælfred *Gregory's Past C.* xxxiii. 214 Ðæt hie [*sc.* the impatient] ne hliepen unwillende on ðæt scorene clif unðeawa. c 1330 R. Brunne *Chron. Wace* (Rolls) 862 Wyþ þat schote his ffader he slow; Al unwylland þat draught he drow.

2. Of persons, etc.: Not inclined, willing, or ready; averse, reluctant, loath. Also in fig. context.

In quot. 1606 the comparative is used with adverbial force, = more unwillingly.

c 1000 in *Ags. Hom.* (Assmann) 180 Min drihten hit wat, þæt ic hit unwillende do, þæt ic æfre þas dæda ȝefremme.

1538 Elyot, *Inuitus*,..vnwyllynge, or agaynste a mannes wylle. 1586 Marlowe *1st Pt. Tamburl.* ii. i, Marching..with vnwilling souldiers faintly arm'd. 1593 Shaks. *Rich. II*, i. iii. 245 You gaue leaue to my vnwilling tong, Against my will, to do my selfe this wrong. 1606 G. Woodcocke *Hist. Ivstine* ix. 40 To which request Phillip vrged he should of reason so much the vnwillinger condiscend. 1644 Milton *Areop.* (Arb.) 32 The tardiest, and the unwillingest of them that praise yee. 1746 Francis tr. *Horace, Epist.* i. viii. 9 With unwilling Ear The Voice of Comfort, or of Health I hear. 1761 Gray *Descent of Odin* 49 Unwilling I my lips unclose. 1817 Shelley *Rev. Islam* xi. xiv, On each unwilling heart Unusual awe did fall. 1849 James *Woodman* vii, Evidently intended to bring up unwilling eels out of their native mud. 1870 Bryant *Iliad* iv. I. 106. I fully yield me to thy wish Though with unwilling mind. 1897 Nicholson *Golspie* 22 This unwilling workman's curse lay on the family for ever.

*absol.* a 1586 Sidney *Arcadia* ii. xxvii, Thus armed, thus governed, forcing the unwilling,.. they came headlong towarde this lodge. a 1658 Lovelace *Poems* (1904) 193 Fates lead the willing, but unwilling draw. 1765 Blackstone *Comm.* I. 44 Counsel acts only upon the willing, law upon the unwilling also.

b. Const. *to* with inf., or with clause.

In very frequent use from c 1630, usu. with *to* and inf.

1533 Sir T. More *Debell. Salem* Wks. 1030/2, I..shewe my selfe vnwilling that the priestes should doe it neither. 1548 Elyot s.v. *Respuo*, To be vnwillyng to here hym speake. a 1586 Sidney *Arcadia* ii. ix, And so went they away from verie unwilling people to leave them. 1618 Selden *Hist. Tithes* III. vi. 1114 Every man..would have been the unwillinger to have specially endowed the church. 1664 in *Verney Memoirs* (1907) II. 212, I am unwilling you should be soe much alone. 1725 De Foe *Voy. round World* (1840) 115, I was unwilling to run any more risks. 1765 *Museum Rust.* IV. 287 We should be very unwilling to offend him. 1821 Scott *Kenilw.* vi, I own I were unwilling he should learn what nowise concerns him. 1878 Browning *La Saisiaz* 28 Then my fellow takes the tale up, not unwilling to aver..'I knew him best of all'.

c. *transf.* of things.

1592 Shaks. *Ven. & Ad.* 1051 Her eyes,..being open'd, threw unwilling light Upon the wide wound..in his soft flank. 1593 — *Lucr.* 309 As each unwilling portal yields him way. 1692 Dryden *Don Sebastian* iii. i, Why shou'd you pluck the green distasteful Fruit From the unwilling Bough. 1697 — *Virg. Georg.* i. 144 For he, with frequent exercise, commands The unwilling soil, and tames the stubborn lands. 1704 Trapp *Abra-Mulé* ii. i. 416 A stiff unwilling Bow. 1748 Gray *Alliance* 43 There industry and gain their vigils keep, Command the Winds, and tame th' unwilling Deep. 1848 Mrs. Gaskell *M. Barton* iv, She..lighted the unwilling fire, borrowing a pair of bellows to make it burn the faster. 1896 *Idler* March 291/2, I..pushed open the unwilling baize-covered door.

†3. Undesirous *of* something. *Obs. rare.*

a 1575 tr. *Pol. Verg. Eng. Hist.* (Camden, No. 29) 54 Neyther partie was unwilling of peace. 1590 Peele *Polyhemnia* Wks. 1829 II. 210 On lusty horse That, angry with delay,..Would snort,..Unwilling of his master's tarriance.

†4. *Unwilling to* (*unto*), contrary to the will or desire of (a person). *Obs. rare.*

1555 Eden *Decades* (Arb.) 334 They shall not touche any thynge of yowres vnwyllyng vnto yow. 1654 Gayton *Pleas. Notes* iv. 171 Your hair (unwilling to your self) discovers you.

†5. Involuntary; unintentional; unwilled. *Obs.*

1535 *Trevisa's Barth. De P. R.* vii. lv. 105 b/2 Somtyme comyth vnwyllynge pyssynge, and that euyll hyghte.. Diabethica passio. 1587 Golding *De Mornay* 519 This high preest shalbe the..speech of God, cleere from sinne aswel willing as vnwilling. 1596 Shaks. *Tam. Shr.* iv. i. 159 Patience I pray you, 'twas a fault vnwilling. 1687 Dryden *Hind & P.* iii. 842 Good fortune may present some happier time, With means to cancel my unwilling crime.

6. Performed or manifested, expressed or avowed, reluctantly or unwillingly.

1613 in *Sidney's Arcadia* (1629) 343 Then went hee towards Pyrocles..and acquainted him with his vnwilling absenting himselfe. 1659 W. Chamberlayne *Pharon.* iv. v. 403 That soft delays..to an unwilling stay His fierce pursuers would ere long betray. 1665 Bp. Patrick *Parab. Pilgr.* viii. 29 It can [not] be acceptable to God to see men croutch in this fashion to him, and..afford him their unwilling prostrations. 1741 W. Whitehead *Danger Writing Verse* 235 Must the Muse th' unwilling task pursue? 1764 Goldsm. *Trav.* 352 Fictitious bonds, the bonds of wealth and law, Still gather strength, and force unwilling awe. 1822 Milman *Belshazzar* 93 Oh! bear a brief unwilling banishment From thine own home, my heart. 1855 Macaulay *Hist. Eng.* xv. III. 529 That sagacity and energy which had..extorted the unwilling admiration of his enemies.

**Unwi·llingly**, *adv.* [f. prec. + -ly2.]

1. Contrary to one's will; against one's wish or desire; reluctantly.

In frequent use from c 1550.

a 1533 Frith *Disput. Purgat.* Wks. (1572) 19/2 If thou do it for feare or vnwillyngly. a 1568 Ascham *Scholem.* i. (Arb.) 43 What soeuer the mynde doth learne vnwillinglie with feare. 1647 Clarendon *Hist. Reb.* i. (1702) I. 5 The late abuse having..driven his Majesty unwillingly out of that course. 1667 Lilly *Hist. Life & Times* (1715) 88 A new Parliament was called, whereunto I was unwillingly invited by two Messengers. a 1715 Burnet *Own Time* (1897) I. ii. 42 They very unwillingly hearkened to that proposition. 1797 S. & Ht. Lee *Canterb. T.* (1799) I. 141 Not unwillingly, [he] resigned his place to some ladies. 1818 Scott *Br. Lamm.* ix, His was a mind unwillingly roused from contemplative inactivity. 1848 Dickens *Dombey* ii, [He] departed by no means unwillingly. 1883 Miss Broughton *Belinda* iii. ix, She has withdrawn her unwillingly-captured hand.

*transf.* a 1713 in Lady M. W. Montagu *Lett.* (1887) I. 83 In this cold climate where the sun appears Unwillingly.

b. In loose construction.

a 1586 Sidney *Apol. Poetrie* (Arb.) 51 Though a man should graunt their first assumption, it should followe (me thinkes) very unwillingly, that good is not good, because better is better. 1665 J. Webb *Stone-Heng* (1725) 140 The Design of which..follows, the narrowness of the Plate unwillingly depriving you of two of the Entrances at the Trench. 1671 Milton *Samson* 14 This day a solemn Feast the people hold,..unwillingly this rest Thir Superstition yields me.

†2. Involuntarily; unintentionally. *Obs.*

1594 Shaks. *Rich. III*, ii. i. 55 If I vnwillingly, or in my rage, Haue ought committed that is hardly borne. 1644 Nye *Gunnery* (1670) 2 A Monk did unwillingly let fall a spark of fire upon Brimstone and Saltpeter. 1660 Coke *Power & Subj.* 152 If a man slea another not lurking.., or unwillingly, or of necessity.

**Unwi·llingness.** [f. as prec. + -ness.] The state or condition of being unwilling, reluctant, or loath; reluctance; disinclination.

1593 Shaks. *Rich. II*, i. iii. 149 Norfolke: for thee remaines a heauier dombe, Which I with some vnwillingnesse pronounce. c 1600 Chalkhill *Thealma & Cl.* 51 How fain she would have..made Her grief, though with unwillingness, to set Open the floodgates of her speech. 1615 E. S. *Britain's Buss* E 2 b, The difficulties that Vnwillingnes hath obiected. 1694 F. Bragge *Disc. Parables* vii. 248 Unwillingness in doing anything, as if 'twere..forced from one, rather than proceeded from a free inclination. 1720 Wodrow *Corr.* (1843) II. 532 Which made me apprehend his unwillingness was not so great as was talked of. 1796 Mme. D'Arblay *Camilla* V. 52 [He] had..been forced into the party, though with added unwillingness. 1825 Lamb *Elia* ii. *Wedding*, To this unwillingness..may be traced the difference of opinion on this point. 1883 F. M. Peard *Contrad.* I. 34 Leigh went towards it with some unwillingness.

b. Const. *to*, or with *that* and clause.

In very frequent use with *to* from c 1650.

(*a*) 1594 Southwell *M. Magd. Funeral Teares* 6 The vnwillingnesse that his image should die with her. a 1665 J. Goodwin *Filled w. the Spirit* (1670) 313 [These] do not argue any the least degree of unwillingness in God that men should be saved. 1665 Boyle *Occas. Refl.* iv. xii. 80 My Unwillingness that one Theme should detain us any longer. 1884 *Leeds Merc.* 24 Oct. 4/4 His profound unwillingness that the question..should be mooted.

(*b*) 1605 Ld. Mountague in *Facsimiles Nat. MSS.* iv. 10 The unwillingnesse I sawe in her to my goeing downe. 1631 Gouge *God's Arrows* i. § 11. 16 Gods unwillingnesse to plague the righteous with the unrighteous. 1712 Steele *Spect.* No. 427 ¶ 1 The Unwillingness to receive good Tidings. 1855 Macaulay *Hist. Eng.* xxii. IV. 785 An unwillingness to run any great risk. 1882 Besant *All Sorts* xxxiv. (1898) 236 Unwillingness to admit new things..and reluctance to unlearn old things.

†**Unwi·lly**, *a. Obs.* [Un-1 7. Cf. OHG. (G.) *unwillig* (MHG. *unwillic*), (M)Du. *onwillig*, ON. *úviljugr* (Da. *uvillig*, Sw. *ovillig*).]

1. Unwilling (*to do* something); averse.

c 1200 *Trin. Coll. Hom.* 93 Sinne hem is loð to leten, and unwilliche to bete. 1395 Purvey *Remonstr.* (1851) 139 A man vnmyghti othir vnwilli to gouerne it duli. c 1440 *Promp. Parv.* 314 Lothe, or vnwylly, *involuntarius, inspontaneus.* c 1475 *Cath. Angl.* 418/2 (A.), Vn Wylly, *coactus, jnuitus.*

2. Involuntary. *rare*—1.

1398 Trevisa *Barth. De P. R.* vii. lv. (1495) 269 Somtime comyth vnwylly pyssynge. [Cf. Unwilling *ppl. a.* 5.]

**Unwi·ly**, *a.* [Un-1 7.] Not wily, artful, or cunning; † simple, silly.

a 1300 *Cursor M.* 738 He ches a littel best þe quilk es noght vnwiliest. c 1475 *Cath. Angl.* 418/1 (A.), Vn Wyly; *vbi* fonde. 1594 W. Percy in Arber *Garner* (1895) VI. 149 Unwily man! why couldst not keep thee there? 1603 Florio *Montaigne* i. xxiv. 63 The plaine husbandman, or the vnwily shoomaker. 1612 W. Parkes *Curtaine-Dr.* (1876) 12 The skins or cases that the vnwily serpents of our age haue cast. 1846 Worcester (citing *Eclectic Rev.*).

†**Unwi·mple**, *v. Obs.* [Un-2 4. Cf. MDu. *ontwimpelen.*] *trans.* To remove the wimple from.

c 1430 *Syr Gener.* (Roxb.) 9953 She vnwimpled hir..And wipt hir face. 1470–85 Malory *Arthur* x. xxxix. 476 Thenne she vnwympeled her vysage.

†**Unwi·n**, *sb. Obs.* [Un-1 12. Cf. OS. *unwunni*, OHG. *unwunna* (MHG. *unwunne, unwünne*).] Grief, sorrow, distress.

c 1175 *Lamb. Hom.* 71 Kep us..from iwilch heued sunne, þet he ne bringe us in to unwune. a 1200 *Moral Ode* 208 Adam and his of-sprung..Wes fele undret wintre an helle pine and an unwunne. c 1275 *Sayings of Bede* 160 in Horstm. *Alteng. Leg.* (1881) 507 Hy shulen to þere ounwinne. a 1300 in *E. E. P.* (1862) 21 Sinne me hauiþ in care ibroȝt, broȝt in mochil vn-winne. c 1310 in Wright *Lyric P.* xv. 47 Un-wunne haveth myn wonges wet. a 1400 *Northern Passion* 1242 Of me þai hafe gret syn At gaffe me vppe to þis vnvyn. c 1480 *Bk. of Brome* (1886) 96 As they hadyn hym ferder inne Ther he sawe woll mykyll on-wyn. ? a 1500 *Chester Pl.* xxiv. 471 Lord, on this I can not myn,..Thee in mischeif or any vnwyn To shew thee such a will.

†**Unwi·n**, *a. Obs.*—1 [App. f. after prec.] Grievous. c 1320 *Sir Tristr.* 1235 Þe leuedi of heiȝe kenne, His woundes schewe..he lete, To wite his wo vnwinne. **Unwi·ncing**, *ppl. a.* (Un-1 10.) 1802 Wolcot (P. Pindar) *Pitt & Statue, Thief* 21 As soon as Justice had perform'd her part Upon the Rogue's unwincing hide. 1813 *Examiner* 1 Feb. 73/2 A haughty unwincing firmness against every attack.

**Unwind** (ʊnwəi·nd), *v.*1 [Un-2 3. Cf. OE. (rare) *unwindan, onwindan*, = (M)Du. *ontwinden*, OS. *antwindan*, OHG. *intwindan* (MHG. and G. *ent-*), to untwist, disentangle.]

1. *trans.* To wind off, move back, or detach (a wrapping, covering, bandage, etc.); to undo the folds or convolutions of (thread, tape, or the like); to untwine, untwist.

c 1325 *Lai le Freine* 189 Therto he yede and it [*sc.* a furred skin] vnwond, And the..child therin he fond. c 1440 *Promp. Parv.* 368 On-wyndyn, or on-twynyn.., *detorqueo.* 1597 A. M. tr. *Guillemeau's Fr. Chirurg.* 43 b/2 To wind, and agayne vnwinde the same [bandages]. 1599 Shaks. *Hen. V*, i. ii. 101 Gracious Lord, Stand for your owne, vnwind your bloody Flagge. 1605 Bacon *Adv. Learn.* ii. xviii. § 8 Skaynes or Bottomes of thread..bee vnwinded at large, when they come to be vsed. 1713 Blackmore *Creation* vi. 294 Engendering heats these one by one unbind, Stretch their small tubes, and hamper'd nerves unwind. 1759 in *Phil. Trans.* LI. 55 The pod [= cocoon] could not be easily unwinded. 1817 Shelley *Rev. Islam* v. lvii, She did unwind Her veil. 1818 Keats *Endym.* ii. 851 The fair visitant at last unwound Her gentle limbs, and left the youth asleep. 1839 Dickens *Nickleby* xxix, 'Pooh! pooh!' said Mr. Folair, unwinding his comforter.

*refl.* 1740 R. Brookes *Art Angling* 10 As soon as the Pike takes the Bait, .. the Line unwinds itself off the Trimmer. 1831 Scott *Ct. Rob.* xvi, A skein of fine silk.. unwinding itself as it descended.

b. *fig.* and in fig. context.

1387–8 T. Usk *Test. Love* iii. ix. (Skeat) l. 77 In this boke be many privy thinges wimpled and folde; unneth shul leude men the plites unwinde. 1482 Caxton *Polychron.* 5 b, My wytte is full lytil to vnwynde the wrappynges of so wonderful werkes. a 1586 Sidney *Arcadia* ii. xx, That it should have neded a stronger vertue then his, to have unwound so deeply an entred vice. 1591 Shaks. *Two Gent.* iii. ii. 51 As you vnwinde her loue from him; Least it should rauell. a 1613 Overbury *Remedy of Love* 8, I mean not to blot out what I have taught, Nor to unwinde the web that I have wrought. c 1620 Z. Boyd *Zion's Flowers* (1855)

Introd. 13 Thou me unwind that knotty snarled clue. 1669 Glanvill *Catholic Charity* 52 He..hath many prejudices..; and these are not to be torn off all at once, but softly, and by degrees to be unwound. 1820 Shelley *Witch Atl.* lxx, And she unwound the woven imagery Of second childhood's swaddling bands. 1858 O. W. Holmes *Aut. Breakf.-t.* viii, Unwinding the endless tapestry of time. 1908 S. E. White *Riverman* xlvi, There's an awful lot of red-tape to unwind, as there always is in such cases.

*refl.* 1659 W. Chamberlayne *Pharon.* iii. iii. 315 Here his harsh thoughts unwound Themselves in pleasure.

*absol.* 1638 Sir T. Herbert *Trav.* (ed. 2) 1 If my new thoughts have added to your bottom, I know you will unwinde gently for feare of ravelling.

**c.** To cause to uncoil; to free from a coiled state.

1634 Sir T. Herbert *Trav.* 53 These Wormes they vnwinde with a Pinne and come out daintily. 1638 N. Whiting *Albino & Bellama* Author to Bk. 48 Nor beg those niggards' eyes, who grudge to see A watch unwinded in perusing thee. 1810 *Encycl. Brit.* (ed. 4) XX. 532/1 It is indeed difficult to determine the exact extent of the spiral vessels.., for it is by unwinding them alone that they can be known. 1834–6 *Encycl. Metrop.* (1845) VIII. 641/2 At this instant the spring..is now unwound again.

*fig.* a 1613 Overbury *Characters, Melancholy Man*, His imagination..keeps his mind in a continuall motion, as the poise the clocke: he winds up his thoughts often, and as often unwinds them.

**2.** To roll, twist, or turn back the wrapping, bandaging, or covering of (a body, etc.); to unwrap. Also, to untwine thread from (a bobbin); to free (a person) *from* bonds, etc.

1596 Spenser *F. Q.* vi. viii. 27 Then, turning backe vnto that captiue thrall, Who all this while stood..bound,..He from those bands weend him to haue vnwound. 1597 A. M. tr. *Guillemeau's Fr. Chirurg.* 20 b/2 He then vnwyndeth his needle, and openeth the lippes of the wounde. 1608 Sylvester *Du Bartas* ii. iii. *Vocation* 203 Can I thus (alas!) Rudely vnwinde me from the kinde embrace Of their deer arms. 1882 Caulfeild & Saward *Dict. Needlework* 507/2 To unwind a bobbin so that the thread hanging from it is to be longer. 1902 *Munsey's Mag.* XXVI. 585/1 In he [*sc.* a doctor] came,..and unwound and wound me again.

*fig.* and in fig. context. 1609 B. Jonson *Sil. Wom.* ii. iv, I would roule my selfe for this day, in troth, they should not vnwind mee. 1697 Congreve *Mourn. Bride* ii. ix, The conqueror is mine! In chains unseen I hold him by the heart, And can unwind or strain him as I please.

† **b.** *refl.* To free, disengage, or extricate (oneself) from an entanglement, difficulty, etc. *Obs.*

Chiefly employed in figurative contexts.

1561 T. Norton *Calvin's Inst.* ii. 100 Out of these snares we shall easily vnwinde our selues, if we well consider [etc.]. 1597 Hooker *Eccl. Pol.* v. iv. § 2 To vnwinde themselues where the snares of glosing speech doe lye to intangle them. 1601 [? Marston] *Pasquil & Kath.* (1878) ii. 370 Vnwinde thy selfe from out the Labyrinth Of gaping wonder. 1656 W. Montague *Accompl. Wom.* 63 Without the thrid that she gave, how could he [*sc.* Theseus] ever have unwinded himself out of those Mazes? 1691 Norris *Pract. Disc.* 41 The Pythagoreans taught their disciples..that they must unwind themselves even from their very Bodies, if they would be good Philosophers. 1692 Dryden *Don Sebastian* v. i, You could unwind your self from all these dangers. 1701 Norris *Ideal World* i. vi. 412 To unwind ourselves from this intanglement.

**3.** *intr.* To undergo uncoiling or unwinding; to become free from a convoluted state. Also *fig.* and *transf.*

1656 T. Watson *One Thing Necess.* 19 He is like a watch, when he hath been wound up towards heaven, he doth quickly unwinde to earth, and sinne again. 1681 J. Scott *Chr. Life* i. iv. 385 Our holy Fervours will be very apt to cool, our good Purposes to slacken and unwind. 1707 Mortimer *Husb.* 223 Put the Bottoms into clean scalding Water, and..then will they easily unwind. 1818 Byron *Ch. Har.* iv. cxxiii, Who loves, raves—'t is youth's frenzy—but the cure Is bitterer still, as charm by charm unwinds Which robed our idols. 1834–6 *Encycl. Metrop.* (1845) VIII. 635/1 As the spring unwinds and acts with less power. 1839 Bailey *Festus* 334 Would I might die outright! And slip the coil without waiting it unwind. 1860 O. W. Holmes *Elsie V.* x, She danced with a kind of passionate fierceness, ..her round arms wreathing and unwinding.

**4.** *trans.* To open up, to trace or retrace to an issue, outlet, or end. Also in fig. context.

1716 Gay *Trivia* ii. 86 Still the wandring passes forc'd his stay, Till Ariadne's clue unwinds the way. 1744 Young *Nt. Th.* vi. 162 How shall the blessed day of our discharge Unwind, at once, the labyrinths of fate. 1760 Sterne *Tr. Shandy* iv. *Slawkenb. Tale*, The fifth act..terminates in unwinding the labyrinth and bringing the hero..to a state of rest. 1864 Bryant *Little People of Snow* 213 A cloud of twittering swallows..turn and wheel again, Unwinding their swift track.

*fig.* 1821 Bryant *Ages* viii, He whose eye Unwinds the eternal dances of the sky.

Hence **Unwi·nding** *vbl. sb.*

Also, in recent use (1915), *unwinder.*

1648 Hexham ii, *Een ontdraeyinge*,..an Vnwinding. 1708 Watts *Horæ Lyricæ* (1727) 161 The dull unwinding of Life's tedious Thread. 1760–72 H. Brooke *Fool of Qual.* (1809) II. 13 The solution of all knots, and unwinding of all intricacies. 1825 J. Nicholson *Operat. Mechanic* 515 The balance, having now all the velocity it would acquire from the unwinding the spring. 1866 Mrs. Ritchie *Village on Cliff* xiv, The whole thing seemed running through her head like the unwinding of a skein. 1895 *Model Steam Engine* 23 The unwinding of a reel of cotton.

*attrib.* 1889 Sleeman *Torpedoes* (ed. 2) 235 The torpedo is launched, and the engine started which is to work the unwinding reels or drums.

**Unwind** (ʊnwi·nd), *v.*2 [Un-2 4 + Wind *sb.*] *trans.* To deprive (a person) of wind or breath.

1788 *Lond. Mag.* 264 Here, as well as at the pit of the stomach you may unwind him.

**Unwi·nding,** *ppl. a.* [Un-1 10.] Straight; not deviating. 1886 J. Parker *Apost. Life* III. 67 Stopping-places where we may sit down awhile, and then soon be up again to pursue life's unwinding and immeasurable road. **Unwi·ndow,** *v.* (Un-2 3.) 1710 C. Shadwell *Fair Quaker Deal* iii. 38 Shall we ravish all the Women we meet with, and unwindow the Houses? **Unwi·ndowed,** *a.* (Un-1 9.) [1775 Ash.] 1820 Maturin *Melmoth* IV. 52 The low, narrow, and unwindowed rooms. 1897 in W. H. Tomkins *Selborne* (1905) 9 The simple, white-washed, unwindowed gable-side.

† **Unwi·ndowed,** obs. north. var. Unwinnowed.

1578 *Knaresb. Wills* (Surtees) I. 135 Hard corne threshed and unwindowed. 1592 *Wills & Inv. N. C.* (Surtees, 1860) 209, x score bus[h]ells of rye, unwindowed, 20l., Wheat, unwindowed, 4l. 6s. 8d.

**Unwi·ndy,** *a.* (Un-1 7.) 1580 in *Liturg. Serv. Q. Eliz.* (1847) 571 The weather being fair, temperate and unwindy. 1848 Dickens *Haunted Man* iii, His shady corner, where the wind was used to spin with such un-windy constancy.

† **Unwi·ne.** *Obs.* [OE. *unwine* (Un-1 4 b), = ON. and Icel. *ú-, óvinr* (Norw. *uvin*, MSw. *ovin*, Sw. *ovän*, (M)Da. *uven*).] An enemy or foe.

1050 *Will* in Thorpe *Charters* 584 Ȝif ic onȝen ne cume, þat þu it nefre ne let weldon mine unwinan after me. c 1100 *O. E. Chron.* (MS. D) an. 1075, Þæt he mihte..his unwinan unþancas don. c 1175 *Lamb. Hom.* 53 Þos men þe þus todraȝed heore euencristene bi-hinden..beoð cristes unwines. c 1200 Ormin 19838 Þatt time þatt Herode wass Unnwine wiþþ Filippe. a 1225 *Leg. Kath.* 1221 Eð were ure lauerd..to awarpen his unwine.

**b.** *spec.* The Evil One. (So MSw. *ovin.*)

a 1225 *Ancr. R.* 178 Þet te Holi Gost ledde ure Louerd into onliche stude..for to beon itempted of þe unwine, of helle. a 1225 *Juliana* 35 Were me swa wið þen vnwine;..þet þu beo..iheiet eaure in eorðe. a 1240 *Ureison* in *O. E. Hom.* I. 197 Ne þole þu þene unwine þet he me arine.

**Unwi·nged,** *a.* [Un-1 9.] Lacking wings; wingless.

1601 Holland *Pliny* II. 39 The unwinged Locusts called Tryxalides. 1658 Rowland tr. *Moufet's Theat. Ins.* 976 Of these then come the unwinged Glow-worms. a 1711 Ken *Psyche* Poet. Wks. 1721 IV. 216 Our unwing'd Arms shall round each other lie. 1753 *Chambers' Cycl.* Suppl. s.v. *Vine-grub*, Both the winged and the unwinged Vine-grubs. 1848 Mrs. Jameson *Sacr. & Leg. Art* I. 37 Two un-winged colossal-looking angel heads.

*fig.* 1659 W. Chamberlayne *Pharon.* iii. v. 157 He..ends His journey, ere a thought unwinged with love Could lead him forth of 's court. 1818 Milman *Samor* vi. 274 For what thought Unwing'd by inbreath'd Godhead e'er might dream Of glory [etc.].

**Unwi·nged,** *ppl. a.* [Un-2 8.] Deprived of wings. 1613 W. Browne *Brit. Past.* i. iii, And so did she..Conjecture Time unwing'd, he came so slow. 1681 Rycaut tr. *Gracian's Critick* 73 On the other Side was falling the unwinged Icarus..into the Water. †**Unwi·nk,** *v. Obs.*—1 [Un-2 3.] *intr.* Of the eye: To open. c 1440 *Pallad. on Husb.* iv. 25 Whan that their eyen gynneth forto unwynke [L. *aperire*].

**Unwi·nking,** *ppl. a.* [Un-1 10.]

In very frequent use from c 1855.

**1.** Marked by absence of winking; characterized by watchfulness or vigilance.

1782 V. Knox *Ess.* xvii. ⁋9 That unwinking vigilance which a delicate..father will judge necessary in the care of daughters. 1833 Mrs. Browning *Tempest* 88 The open eyes Of that dead man,..With their unwinking, unexpressive stare. 1857 Dickens *Dorrit* ii. xxviii, The attitude..was now expressive of unwinking watchfulness. 1876 Geo. Eliot *Dan. Der.* xxv, No fish could have maintained a more unwinking silence. 1896 A. Morrison *Child Jago* 326 His eyes were red with strained, unwinking attention.

*transf.* a 1873 B. Harte in *Fiddletown*, etc. (1873) 127 The sands had a dreadful unwinking glare.

**2.** Not winking; never closing the eyes.

1811 Lamb *Edax on Appetite* Wks. 1908 I. 153 The broad, unwinking eye of the world. 1863 Cowden Clarke *Shaks. Char.* viii. 201 She watches her prey, lynx-eyed, unwinking upon him. 1880 L. Wallace *Ben-Hur* 227 Such answer as might be looked for from the unwinking sphinx.

*transf.* 1875 Miss Bird *Sandwich Isl.* 5 A white, unwinking, scintillating sun.

Hence **Unwi·nkingly** *adv.* (Freq. from c 1890.)

1849 C. Bronte *Shirley* x, A formidable eye..looked as steadily, as unwinkingly, at you as if it were a steel ball soldered in her head. 1891 J. H. Pearce *Esther Pentreath* iii. viii, She found Aichel..unwinkingly there on the watch.

† **Unwi·nly,** *adv. Obs.* [Un-1 11. Cf. Winly *adv.*] Unpleasantly; sadly, sorrowfully.

13.. *Coer de L.* 6744 Wher be these hethene pawtener, That have the cyte..i-take? Unwynnely I schal yow wake. a 1400 *Sir Degrev.* 823 Sche doys me unwynly to wak, With wongus ful wete. ? a 1400 *Morte Arth.* 955 Thane this wafulle wyfe un-wynly hym gretez. c 1460 *Towneley Myst.* xx. 189 Here is oone of his men that thus vnwynly gars vs wake.

**Unwi·nnable,** *a.* Chiefly *Sc.* [Un-1 7 b.] Not winnable; *esp.* of fortresses: Impregnable.

1536 Bellenden tr. *Boece, Descr. Alb.* ix. (1541) B vi b, This crag is callit the Bas; vnwynnabill be ingyne of man. 1551 Ascham *Let.* Wks. 1865 I. ii. 256 Many castles stand on the tops of these rocks unwinable. 1596 Dalrymple tr. *Leslie's Hist. Scot.* (S.T.S.) II. 289 The place quhilk naturalie was wnwinnable,..was..gyuen ouer on condiciounis. 1621 Lady M. Wroth *Urania* 345 The Castle is impregnable, and she vnwinable, and thus his [= the prisoner's] misfortune fell. a 1670 Spalding *Troub. Chas. I* (1850) I. 291 The assaillantis fynding the place..vn-wynnable without gryte skaith.

*transf.* 1588 A. King tr. *Canisius' Catech.* 23 Giwe me..a valkryffe harte,..a stoute and vnwinnable, that na tribulation may mak veirie.

**Unwi·nning,** *ppl. a. rare.* [Un-1 10.] † **a.** Unconciliatory. *Obs.* **b.** Unattractive.

1655 Fuller *Ch. Hist.* ii. ii. § 7 Pride being an unwinning Quality, rendering the Proud party scorned by his Betters. 1890 'L. Falconer' *Mlle. Ixe* ii, Her affection for this sickly, spoilt, and most unwinning child.

**Unwi·nnowed,** *ppl. a.* (Un-1 8. Cf. Unwindowed.)

1552 Huloet, Vnwinewed wheate, *acerosum frumentum.* 1624 Ussher *Serm.* 48 The graine [is] the same, but winnowed now, unwinnowed then. 1635 Quarles *Embl.* ii. vii. 1 The world's a heap, whose yet unwinnowed grain Is lodg'd with chaff. [1775 Ash.] 1844 H. Stephens *Bk. Farm* II. 273 The unwinnowed heap is becoming less. 1860 Swinburne *Queen-Mother* ii. i, We are the chaff, The gross unwinnowed husks of your fanned wheat. 1884 *Cent. Mag.* Jan. 443/1 The unwinnowed sweepings of English haymows.

**Unwi·nter,** *v.* [Un-2 6 b, 5.]

**1.** *intr.* and *trans.* To lose, or divest of, the qualities of winter.

1611 Florio (citing Dante), *Suernare*, to wax Sommer,..to vnwinter. 1892 C. E. Norton *Dante's Par.* xxvii. 179 Ere January be all un-wintered [It. *sverni*] by that hundredth part which is down there neglected.

† **2.** *trans.* To drive out of winter quarters. *Obs.*

1642 *Let. Student Oxf.* 1 Whatsoever forces shall take up armes to unwinter his Majesty from Oxford.

**Unwi·ntry,** *a.* (Un-1 7.) 1852 M. Arnold *Tristr. & Iseult* i. 63 His closed eye doth sweep O'er some fair unwintry sea, Not this fierce Atlantic deep.

**Unwi·ped,** *ppl. a.* (Un-1 8, 8 c.)

? 1602 in *Donne's Poems* (1912) I. 404 The mind..is like a Table-book, Which, th'old unwipt, new writing never took. 1605 R. F. *Dedekind's Sch. Slovenrie* (1904) 36 Your unwipte knife. 1648 Boyle *Seraph. Love* (1659) 100 A Fatherly Impatience of seeing a Spot unwip'd off in the Face he loves. 1716 Swift *Acc. E. Curll* Wks. 1841 I. 834/2 Recollecting that his own [breech] was unwiped, he abated of his fury. 1797 Coleridge *Osorio* iv. 223 His rosy face besoil'd with unwiped tears. 1852 James *Pequinillo* III. 132 The unwiped noses of the horse-chestnuts. 1855 Browning *Fra Lippo Lippi* 36 The slave that holds..his weapon..yet unwiped.

**Unwi·re,** *v.* (Un-2 4.)

1822 Scott *Peveril* xxvii, I will..unwire this fresh flask, to begin a brimmer. 1851 W. Colton *Ship & Shore* v. 88, I must unwire that cage and liberate the captive.

**Unwi·sdom.** [OE. *unwísdóm* (Un-1 12), = OHG. *unwîstuom, -tuam, -tôm.*]

**1.** Lack or absence of wisdom; ignorance, folly, stupidity.

In very frequent use till c 1390, and (as a new formation) from c 1843, when its currency was due to, or stimulated by, Carlyle. There is lack of evidence from 1612 to 1832.

c 825 *Vesp. Psalter* xxi. 3 God min ic cleopiu..on naeht & nales to unwisdome me. c 897 K. Ælfred *Gregory's Past C.* xlix. 375 Ða ðe unmedome bioð to ðære lare oððe for ȝioȝuðe oððe for unwisdome. c 1205 Lay. 3383 We habbet idon unwisdom Þat we mine fader habbet vnderfon mid þirtti cnihten. a 1225 *Ancr. R.* 278 Bihold i..þine soule, oðer two [things]—sunne & ignorance, þet is, unwisdom & unwitenesse. a 1300 *E. E. Psalter* xxxvii. 5 Stanke and roten mine erres er ma, Fra face of mine vnwisdome swa. 1382 Wyclif *Prov.* xv. 14 The mouth of foolis is fed with vnwisdam. c 1449 Pecock *Repr.* ii. iii. 150 Schamed of her folie and of her vnwisdom and pride. a 1470 H. Parker *Dives & Pauper* (Pynson, 1493) vi. x. s vi/1 Woman lowede hir and knowlegide hir vnwisedom and hir foly. 1509 Fisher *Funeral Serm. C'tess Richmond* Wks. (1876) 301 All we..may saye by lamentable complaynt of our vnwysdome vnto him, Ah domine si fuisses hic. 1535 Stewart *Cron. Scot.* (Rolls) II. 117 For and ȝe do, ȝe ar abill to tak Throw sic wnwisdome..greit skayth. 1612 T. James *Corrupt. Scripture* iii. 13 Forsooth vnwisedome is,..which is plenteous in euill.

1832 *Westm. Rev.* Apr. 321 The unwisdom of persecuting the Saint-Simonians. 1839 Carlyle *Chartism* iv. (1840) 27 The Earth..bountifully sends food and increase; if man's unwisdom did not intervene and forbid. 1873 Spencer *Stud. Sociol.* 170 The unwisdom of officialism is daily illustrated.

**2.** With *a*, etc.: **a.** An instance of folly or ignorance; an unwise act.

1303 R. Brunne *Handl. Synne* 5046 A grete vnwysdom for soþe hyt ys. 1850 Carlyle *Latter-d. Pamph.* vii. 42 Is..the fruit of an unwisdom doubtful? 1855 Kingsley *Misc.* (1859) I. 8 A learned statement of facts in answer to some unwisdom of a Quarterly reviewer. 1869 F. W. Newman *Misc.* 98 It has been pronounced an unwisdom in any one to write in a dramatic form, unless [etc.].

**b.** An unwise Power or Being. *nonce-use.*

1839 Carlyle *Chartism* v. (1858) 27 A world understood always to be made and governed by a Providence and Wisdom, not by an Unwisdom.

**Unwise** (ʊnwəi·z), *a.* [OE. *unwís* (Un-1 7), = NFris. *unwis, -wiss*, (M)Du. *onwijs*, OS. (MLG.) *unwîs*, OHG. *unwîs, unwîsi* (MHG. *unwîse*, G. *unweise*), ON. *úviss* (MSw. and Sw. *ovis*, Da. and Norw. *uvis*), Goth. *unweis.*]

**1.** Lacking or deficient in (practical) wisdom, discretion, or prudence; indiscreet, imprudent, foolish. Also const. *in.*

c 825 *Vesp. Psalter* xci. 7 Wer unwis ne oncnaweð & dysiȝ ne onȝiteð ða. 971 *Blickl. Hom.* 89 Ic wæs..unwisum netenum ȝelic ȝeworden. c 1175 *Lamb. Hom.* 111 Þet is mildheortnesse þet þe wisa mon mid steore þene unwisan irihleche. c 1200 Ormin 16954 Forr unnwis mann iss blunnt. a 1225 *Ancr. R.* 74 Hwose euer wule mei gon in & leden uorð hore asse: þet is, hore unwise soule. c 1290 *S. Eng. Leg.* I. 469/250 Heo was puyrliche vnwys in sawe and in spelle. c 1315 Shoreham iii. 312 Ich wot hy beþ Vn-wyser þane þe wode. c 1325 *Metr. Hom.* 110 Thar mai we graithe ensampel take, Unwise felawschip to forsake, And hald us imang wise men. c 1380 Wyclif *Wks.* (1880) 411 Þis telliþ an opyn blasfemye, þat crist was vnwiss in þis. 1415 Hoccleve *To Sir J. Oldcastle* 77 Thow art vnwys thogh thow thee wys pretende. c 1455 Pecock *Folewer* 38 [They] holden him þerfore in þat neuer þe vnwiser þan creaturis whiche knowen þe same trouþis. 1526 *Pilgr. Perf.* (W. de W. 1531) 86 Saye not as many an unwyse persone sayth. 1573 *New Custom* i. i, Yea, doth! then the more vnwise man you. 1645 Milton *Tetrach.* 42 When as he should bee not unwiser then the Serpent. 1660 — *Way estab. Free Commw.* 6 A nation..unwise in thir counsels. *c* **1700** *Short Acc. Scotland* 56 The younger and unwiser of the Bishops. **1746** FRANCIS tr. *Horace, Epist.* I. v. 22 The grave Disgrace of being thought unwise. **1827** CARLYLE *Misc.* (1840) I. 47 A class of unwise men. **1871** BROWNING *Pr. Hohenst.* 1472 What if the event demonstrate her unwise?

*transf.* **1390** GOWER *Conf.* I. 339 Thus seith the wilde unwise tonge Of hem. **1533** GAU *Richt Vay* 32 Thair onwiz hartis war blyndit. **1831** CARLYLE *Sart. Res.* I. i, That unwise science, which..'By geometric scale Doth take the size of pots of ale'.

**b.** *absol.* as sing. or pl.

*c* **825** *Vesp. Psalter* xiii. 1 Cweð se unwisa in his heortan, nis god. *a* **1300** *Floriz & Bl.* 1016 Ac Floris cleppen hire bigon, And he him also unwise [F. *si fait que fol*]. *c* **1315** SHOREHAM I. 355 Þat fleisch wiþ sleuþe and glotonie.. [acombreþ] þoun-wyse. **1362** LANGL. *P. Pl.* A. IX. 84 Ȝe wyse, soffreþ þe vn-wyse wiþ ow for to libbe. **1484** CAXTON *Fables of Æsop* I. xvii, The vnwyse displeseth there, where as he supposeth to pleȝse. *a* **1542** WYATT in *Tottel's Misc.* (Arb.) 86 For the vnwise Had not ysene such a beast before. **1647** N. WARD *Simp. Cobler* 25 He that instructs a foole, may act th' unwise. **1725** POPE *Odyss.* VIII. 559 Th' unwise prevail,..And by the god's decree proud Ilion falls. **1806** H. K. WHITE *Let.* 25 June, The religion of Jesus Christ is ..wisdom to the unwise. **1871** JOWETT *Plato* I. 367 The opinions of the unwise are evil.

**2.** Not marked, distinguished, or prompted by (practical) wisdom; characterized by lack of sound judgement; injudicious.

**1390** GOWER *Conf.* I. 166 It is an unwys vengance. **1393** LANGL. *P. Pl.* C. I. 49 Pylgrimis & palmers..Wenten forth in hure way with meny vn-wyse tales. *a* **1425** tr. *Arderne's Treat. Fistula*, etc. 44 If þe fynger..haue be long vnheled of vnwise cure. **1513** Q. KATH. in Ellis *Orig. Lett.* Ser. III. I. 153 With my servants unwise demeanur I am noo thing wel contente. **1590** BARROUGH *Meth. Physick* I. xxiv. (1596) 40 There goeth before this euill [*sc.* epilepsy] an vnwise state of the bodie and mind. **1594** SHAKS. *Rich. III*, IV. i. 52 Be not ta'ne tardie by vnwise delay. **1678** BUTLER *Hud.* III. iii. 518 This Gambol thou advisest, Is of all others, the unwisest. **1798** S. & HT. LEE *Canterb. T.* II. 4 Lady Lettingham exacted one compliance, even her brother thought not unwise. *a* **1800** COWPER *Odyss.* (ed. 2) XV. 12 It were a deed unwise, To sojourn longer here. **1809** COLERIDGE *Friend* 158 The conduct..was equally unwise in private life and to individuals. **1846** MRS. A. MARSH *Father Darcy* II. iv. 85 These revolting and most unwise persecutions. **1855** MACAULAY *Hist. Eng.* XX. IV. 522 It would be unwise to bring the prisoners to trial.

†**3.** Out of one's senses; mad. *Obs.*⁻¹

Cf. Flem. *on-wijs* 'demens' (Kilian) and OE. *on unwīs* 'in a mad manner'. Similarly Sc. *no wise* = mad.

*a* **1400** *Morte Arth.* 3817 Schountes he no lengare; Bot alls vnwyse wodewyse he wente at the gayneste. **1481** CAXTON *Reynard* xxviii. (Arb.) 68, I lepe here and there, as an vnwyse [Du. *onvroet*] man.

**Unwi·sely**, *adv.* [OE. *unwīslīce* (UN-¹ 11), = MDu. *onwiselike*, *-lijc* (Du. *onwijslijk*), MLG. *unwīslike*, OHG. *unwīslīhho* (MHG. *-wīslīche*, G. *-weislich*), MSw. *ovislika*, Norw. *uvislege*, Da. *-lig.*] In an unwise, injudicious, or foolish manner; imprudently, foolishly.

*c* **897** K. ÆLFRED *Gregory's Past. C.* xv. 93 Ðæt is ðæt he hie ȝedweleð & unwislice ȝeiecð ða idelnesse. *c* **1000** *Sax. Leechd.* II. 232 Ȝif hio bið unwislice to lange forlæten. *a* **1225** *Ancr. R.* 338 Þauh no mon hit nute, oðer wolde þet ei hit wuste, oðer ȝemeleasliche do hit, oðer to unwisliche, to muchel, oðer to lutel. **1362** LANGL. *P. Pl.* A. XI. 270 Þanne wrouȝte I vnwisly, wiþ alle þe wyt þat I lere. *c* **1375** *Cursor M.* 27047 (Fairf.), Þe þrid letting makis mani mad quen þai vn-wiseli ar drad after rising to falle againe. *c* **1440** *Jacob's Well* 286 Þe hermyte thouȝte þat þis was vnwysely don. *c* **1455** PECOCK *Folewer* 60 Holdyng him silf to seie trewli and wiseli, whanne he seieþ vntrewli and vnwiseli. *a* **1513** FABYAN *Chron.* VII. 309 Kynge Rycharde, walkyng vnwysely about the castell to espye the feblenes therof. *a* **1586** SIDNEY *Arcadia* II. xx, Some unwisely liberall, that more delight to give presentes, then pay debtes. **1605** CHAPMAN *All Fools* III. i. 471 Since you have usd the matter so unwisely. **1647** CLARENDON *Hist. Reb.* II. (1702) I. 112 Every man unwisely thought him whom he found an Enemy to his Enemies, a Friend to all his other affections. **1744** THOMSON *Spring* 136 The skilful Farmer..Nor..The little trooping Birds unwisely scares. **1774** BURKE *Sp. Amer. Tax.* 47 If intemperately, unwisely, fatally, you sophisticate and poison the very source of government. **1805** WORDSW. *Ode to Duty* iii, They..who, not unwisely bold, Live in the spirit of this creed. **1860** FROUDE *Hist. Eng.* V. 389 The same story of authority unwisely caught at and unwisely used. **1899** B. HARRADEN *Fowler* III. i, An unwisely-worded disparagement.

†**Unwiseman.** *Obs.* [f. UNWISE *a.*] A fool or simpleton.

**1400** tr. *Secreta Secret., Gov. Lordsh.* 65 Gyf no fayth to þe sawys of vnwysmen. *a* **1470** TIPTOFT *Orat. G. Flamineus* (Caxton, 1481) 4/2 And thou unwyseman to thy grete shame when thou remembrest thyne owne..simplenesse then [etc.]. *c* **1520** M. NISBET 2 *Pet.* iii. 17 Be nocht desauet be the errour of vnwisemen.

**Unwi·seness.** [UN-¹ 12. Cf. OE. *unwisness* ignorance.] Lack or absence of practical wisdom; foolishness, folly, imprudence.

*a* **1340** HAMPOLE *Psalter* lxviii. 7 God þou wate myn vnwisnes. **1807** *Monthly Mag.* XXIV. 331 An unwiseness, which would not be expected from his sagacity. **1859** T. S. HENDERSON *Life E. Henderson* iv. 200 The wiseness or unwiseness of the means he might employ. **1887** ANNE ELLIOTE *Old Man's Favour* I. II. ii. 208 The worthy merchant admitted the unwiseness of that cheque.

**Unwi·sh**, *v.* [UN-² 3.]

**1.** *trans.* To retract, cancel, or abrogate (a wish, choice, etc.).

**1594** SOUTHWELL *Mary Magd. Funeral Tears* 48 b, If that wish had taken effect, I would now vnwish it again. *a* **1639** W. WHATELEY *Prototypes* II. xxiv. (1640) 12 Had not Job cause to unwish his former wishes. **1651** N. BACON *Disc. Govt. Eng.* II. xxxiv. 267 Who..lived to disdesire and unwish their former choise by late repentance. **1853** MISS YONGE *Heir of Redclyffe* i, 'Never was a more absurd wish,' said Charles..; 'unwish it forthwith'. **1864** MISS SMEDLEY *Linnet's Trial* II. IV. i. 222, I hope you won't un-wish your wish as soon as it is gratified.

*absol.* **1881** MISS YONGE *Lads & Lasses Langley* ii. 110 Frank was left to wish and unwish.

**2.** To make an end of by wishing; to wish away or annihilated. Also *refl.*

**1599** SHAKS. *Hen. V*, IV. iii. 76 Now thou hast vnwisht fiue thousand men: Which likes me better, then to wish vs one. **1658** SIR T. BROWNE *Hydriot.* v. 71 The most tedious being is that which can unwish it self, content to be nothing, or never to have been. **1697** COLLIER *Ess. Mor. Subj.* II. 179 Were I sure never to be pleased, my next Business should be to unwish my self, and pray for Annihilation.

**b.** To wish or desire (a circumstance or thing) not to be.

**1628** QUARLES *Argalus & P.* II. 71 Performe, performe what now it is too late, T' unwish againe, too soone to violate. **1646** SIR T. BROWNE *Pseud. Ep.* I. x. 38 To desire there were no God, were plainly to unwish their owne being. **1709** O. DYKES *Eng. Prov. & Refl.* (ed. 2) 170 Crack'd Maiden-heads cannot be set together again, like broken China,..by unwishing the Misfortune. **1821** BYRON *Sardan.* IV. i. 275 Do not poison all My peace left, by unwishing that thou wert A father. **1876** MISS BROUGHTON *Joan* I. xxviii, What we wish to-day, often we unwish to-morrow.

**c.** *refl.* To seek to remove (oneself) from a particular class or category by wishing; to wish not to be something.

**1615** HALL *Contempl.*, *O. T.* IX. vii, How many shall unwish themselves Christians, when God's revenges have found them out! **1633** T. ADAMS *Exp. 2 Peter* ii. 10 At that dreadfull day how many shall unwish themselves Christians?

Hence **Unwi·shing** *vbl. sb.*

**1699** R. L'ESTRANGE *Fables* II. lxxii. 69 This Levity, of Wishing, and Unwishing, is..the Great Bus'ness and Mistake of Humane Life.

**Unwi·shed**, *ppl. a.* [UN-¹ 8, 8 c.]

**1.** Not wished, desired, or asked for; undesired.

**1583** BABINGTON *Commandm.* To Gentl. of Glam., What proofe this latter hath, and what vnwished matter to furnish out a larger complaint, I spare to speake. **1621** QUARLES *Div. Poems, Esther* i, In lavish Cups..Came wine unwisht. **1626** W. BOSWORTH *Arcadius & Sepha* II. 790 Those griefs.. never ceas'd to move A desp'rate end, for that unwisht mischance Still gnawing on my soul. **1725** POPE *Odyss.* IV. 113 Heaping unwish'd wealth, I distant roam. **1730** THOMSON *Winter* 53 Nor is the night unwish'd; while vital heat,.. and joy, the dubious day forsake. **1757** AKENSIDE *Pleas. Imag.* II. 401 Not poison, nor sharp fire,..Were at that season an unwished exchange. **1855** *Poultry Chron.* III. 338/2 The greatest gain will often, unsought and unwished, attend the first-class.

**b.** Unwanted, unwelcome, unpleasing.

*a* **1586** SIDNEY *Arcadia* I. xiv, Her unwished presence gave my tale a conclusion, before it had a beginning. **1590** SHAKS. *Mids. N.* I. i. 81 His Lordship, whose vnwished yoake, My soule consents not to giue soueraignty. **1697** CONGREVE *Mourn. Bride* III. viii, You seem much surprised At..[a] return so..unexpected!..And so unwish'd, unwanted too, it seems.

**2.** *Unwished-for*, = prec.

**1617** MINSHEU s.v., Un-wished for. **1632** LITHGOW *Trav.* II. 71 Humide vapours..accompany the unwished-for-bed of my repose. **1708** J. PHILIPS *Cyder* II. 155 When..unwish't for Rain Descended. **1807** E. S. BARRETT *Rising Sun* III. 169 Why..do you thus force your unasked—your unwished-for counsels upon me?

**Unwi·shful**, *a.* (UN-¹ 7.) [**1775** ASH.] **1876** *Whitby Gloss.*, *Unwishful*, reluctant; undesirous. **1894** MRS. GAMLIN *G. Romney* 166 Her attire was the most simple, so unwishful was she to attract admiring eyes. **Unwi·shing**, *ppl. a.* (UN-¹ 10.) **1743** FRANCIS tr. *Hor.*, *Odes* III. xvi. 31, I..to th' unwishing Few with Joy A bless'd and bold Deserter fly. **1772** JAS. USHER *Clio* (ed. 3) 131 Without it [*sc.* content] we can never enjoy undisturbed unwishing tranquillity.

**Unwi·st**, *ppl. a.* *Obs.* or *arch.* [UN-¹ 8 b.]

†**1.** Unknown to one; without it being known.

*c* **1374** CHAUCER *Troylus* II. 1294 Hire entent..Was for to loue hym vnwist, if she myghte. **1382** WYCLIF *Gen.* xxxv. 22 Ruben ȝede, and slepte with Bala, the secundarye wijf of his fader, that to hym was not vnwist. **1420–22** LYDG. *Thebes* I. 494 And vttrely remembre, ȝif the lyst, Thy byrth and blood ar bothe two vnwist. *c* **1500** *Lancelot* 219 How he fra that stede In sacret wyss vnwyst away was tak. *a* **1547** SURREY *Æneis* IV. 397 Unfaithfull wight! to cover such a fault Coldest thou hope unwist to leve my land? **1590** SPENSER *F. Q.* III. ii. 26 Of hurt vnwist most daunger doth redound. *Ibid.* ix. 21 Then of them all she plainly was espyde To be a woman wight, vnwist to bee, The fairest woman wight, that euer eye did see.

†**b.** Const. *by*, *of*; *to*, *unto* (or with dat.). *Obs.*

In (*a*) freq. in the 16th c. in the archaic phrase 'unwist of any wight'.

(*a*) *c* **1385** CHAUCER *L. G. W.* 1653 *Hypsipyle*, But on-wist of hire fadyr is she gon To Tessaly. *c* **1500** *Lancelot* 1139 Prevaly, unwist of any wicht. **1587** TURBERV. *Trag. T.* (1837) 153 Unwist of any wight, The murther was unseene. **1590** SPENSER *F. Q.* V. i. 9 It was kept in store In Ioues eternall house, vnwist of wight. **1848** BAILEY *Festus* (ed. 3) 200 There is a secret sign whereby the soul Feels certainty of safety..,public to the universe,..And yet unwist of by a single world.

(*b*) *c* **1412–20** LYDG. *Chron. Troy* I. 3585 Þat sche with hym schal in-to Grece wende.., Vnwist hir fader & euery other wyȝt. **1420–2** — *Thebes* III. 4081 To hym the tyme vnknowen and vnwist. **1476** *Paston Lett.* III. 153, I did it nott onwyst to hyr cowncell. *c* **1500** *Lancelot* 658 For to your folk this mater is wnwist. **1596** SPENSER *F. Q.* IV. iv. 27 The shield and armes..Which Triamond had worne,..to his friend vnwist.

†**2.** Lacking knowledge (*of* something); unknowing; not knowing how. *Obs.*

*c* **1374** CHAUCER *Troylus* II. 1400 Now quod Pandare er owres twyes twelue, He shal þe ese vnwyst of it hym selue. *a* **1547** SURREY *Æneis* IV. 91 The shepheard smiteth at [the hind] unwares, And leaves unwist in her the thirling head. **1596** SPENSER *F. Q.* V. i. 22 When he wak't.., He found him selfe, vnwist, so ill bestad, That lim he could not wag.

**3.** *arch.* Not known or recognized; strange.

**1757** W. THOMPSON *Poems, Nativity* xvi, Three Seers unwist the Captain-Glory led, Of awful Semblance. **1836** MRS. BROWNING *Poet's Vow* II. xxi, Still between the sound and me, White creatures like a mist Did interfloat confusedly,—Mysterious shapes unwist!

**Unwi·stful**, *a.* (UN-¹ 7.) [**1775** ASH.] **1861** LD. LYTTON & FANE *Tannhaüser* 8 So reap'd she honour of unwistful men, Roman, or Greek. **1865** MRS. WHITNEY *Gayworthys* v, What is this space, this circumstance,..that can..keep them so unwistful of each other?

†**Unwi·t**, *sb.* *Obs.* [UN-¹ 12 + WIT *sb.* Cf. ON. *úvit* (MSw. *ovit*, Norw. *uvit*), Goth. *unwiti*; also WANWIT, and OE. *ungewit* stupidity.]

**1.** Lack of wit or practical knowledge; ignorance; stupidity, folly.

*c* **1200** ORMIN 6003 Ȝiff he nohht ne follȝheþþ witt, Acc unnwitt all wiþþ wille Inn all þatt iss onnȝæn Drihhtin. *a* **1225** *Juliana* 22 Hwi destu us ba so wa, þurh þi muchele unwit? *a* **1300** *Cursor M.* 13936 Yee wat quat i am, and mi kin, O yur vn-witt quine wald yee blin? **1340** *Ayenb.* 82 Ȝef wyt of þe wordle ne is bot folye ase zayþ þe wrytinge, and childhede, and onwyt. *c* **1380** WYCLIF *Serm.* Sel. Wks. II. 374 God mai not faile on his side for noun-power or unwitt. *c* **1400** *Pilgr. Sowle* v. xiv. (MS. Bodl. 770) 99/1 It is verey vnwytte to any erthly creature.. to trowen [etc.]. **1468** *Chron. Eng.* in Hearne *R. Glouc.* (1724) 482/1 His hondes..shewethe sumwhat vnwyt and necclygence, for he vtterliche leueth the kepyng of hem.

**2.** An imprudent or foolish act.

*c* **1200** ORMIN 8045 Þatt ifell gast maȝȝ oferr þa þatt follȝhenn barrness þæwess Inn illc unnwitt, inn illc unnitt. *a* **1300** *Cursor M.* 13657 Þou caitif for-lorn In sin was..born, Queþer þou wenis vs nu here O þine vn-wittes for to lere.

Hence † **Unwi·thead**, folly. *Obs.*

**1340** *Ayenb.* 19 Zuych folie is wel y-cleped onwythede.

†**Unwi·t**, *v.*¹ *Obs. rare.* [UN-¹ 14.] *intr.* To know not; to be ignorant *of* something.

*c* **1374** CHAUCER *Boeth.* v. pr. vi. (1868) 175 Whan þat god knoweþ any þinge to be, he ne vnwoot nat [L. *non nesciat*] þat þilke þinge wanteþ necessite to be. **1382** WYCLIF 2 *Cor.* i. 8 We wolen not ȝou for to vnwite of oure tribulacioun.

†**Unwi·t**, *v.*² *Obs.* [UN-² 4.] *trans.* To deprive of wit or wits.

**1604** SHAKS. *Oth.* II. iii. 182 And then..(As if some Planet had vnwitted men) Swords out..In opposition bloody.

**Unwi·tch**, *v.* Now *arch.* [UN-² 3.] *trans.* To free from witchcraft; to uncharm; = UNBEWITCH *v.* Also *refl.*

**1580** HOLLYBAND *Treas. Fr. Tong*, *Desensorceler*, to vnwitch. **1584** R. SCOT *Discov. Witchcr.* III. x. 44 Iesus Christ shall unwitch us. **1601** HOLLAND *Pliny* II. 296 Even the very serpents as they may bee burst by enchauntment, so they can unwitch themselves. **1625** PURCHAS *Pilgrims* II. 1268 Like a..Deuill witching and unwitching the superstitious vulgar. *c* **1640** DEKKER, etc. *Witch Edmonton* II. i, I would have thee so good as to unwitch me. **1764** FOOTE *Mayor of G.* II. Wks. 1799 I. 184, I am unwitch'd, and that you shall know to your cost. **1785** G. A. BELLAMY *Apology* VI. 95 They stopped the play,..ordering all the singers to unwitch themselves. **1884** BLACK *Jud. Shakespeare* xxiv, Come, man, unwitch thee! Collect thy senses.

*absol.* *a* **1656** ROLLE *Abridgment* (1668) I. 45 She is a white Witch, and can witch and unwitch.

†**Unwite**, var. ME. *unweote* (UN-¹ 3).

**Unwithdraw·ing**, *ppl. a.* (UN-¹ 10.) **1634** MILTON *Comus* 711 Wherefore did Nature powre her bounties forth, With such a full and unwithdrawing hand? **1757** MRS. GRIFFITH *Lett. Henry & Frances* (1767) II. 122 Else wherefore, with an unwithdrawing hand, did he create them?

**Unwithdraw·n**, *ppl. a.* (UN-¹ 8 b.) [**1775** ASH.] **1829** SIR W. HAMILTON *Discuss.* (1853) 22 The veil of Isis is thus still unwithdrawn. **1836** JAMES GIBSON in *Lectures on Popery* x. 12/2 A thousand years of ecclesiastical decisions and unwithdrawn claims. **1896** SIR F. LOCKWOOD in *Daily News* 23 Nov. 7/1 The disgraceful charge made against her husband was still unwithdrawn. **Unwi·therable**, *a.* (UN-¹ 7 b.) **1611** COTGR., *Immarcessible*,..vnuadeable, vnwitherable. **1917** SAINTSBURY *Hist. Fr. Novel* I. 382 This reed, which waves..with unwitherable greenness.

**Unwi·thered**, *ppl. a.* (UN-¹ 8.)

**1599** THYNNE *Animadv.* (1875) 48 She..dothe signyfye the oke to be grene and vnseriall, that is..vnwithered, of freshe coolor. **1616** SURFL. & MARKH. *Countrey Farme* 500 Whilest they are in grasse or vnwithered cockes. **1634** HABINGTON *Castara* I. (Arb.) 27 The roses in her cheekes unwithered. **1659** W. CHAMBERLAYNE *Pharon.* I. ii. 211 Whilst youth doth unwithered last. **1745** COLLINS *Epist. to Sir T. Hanmer* 4 She sees her myrtles bloom, Green and unwither'd o'er his honour'd tomb. **1818** MILMAN *Samor* VII. 563 Ye see Mine arm unwither'd, my unbroken sword. **1894** *Outing* XXIV. 307 The poplar branches on top still had unwithered leaves.

*fig.* **1640** FLETCHER, etc. *Coronation* v. i, The yet unwither'd blush That speaks the innocence of mine [*sc.* soul]. **1826** *Literary Souvenir* 349 A nameless charm, By age unwithered. **1842** J. WILSON *Chr. North* I. 248 There is in their unwithered hearts, warm love enough for all [etc.]. **1875** M. G. PEARSE *D. Quorm* p. ix, She has an unwithered faith in the Sword of the Spirit.

**Unwi·thering**, *ppl. a.* (UN-¹ 10.)

**1743** R. BLAIR *Grave* 696 We wish to be where sweets unwithering bloom. **1784** COWPER *Task* III. 570 The spiry myrtle with unwith'ring leaf. **1801** SOUTHEY *Thalaba* v. v, Cypress groves Every where scatter'd in unwithering green. **1839** MOORE *Alciphron* iii. 193 The same unwithering face. **1881** LOWELL *To J. G. Palfrey* 3 As 't were a wreath Unwithering in the adverse popular breath.

**Unwithhe·ld,** *ppl. a.* (UN-[1] 8 b.) **1727** THOMSON *To Mem. Newton* 146 Ye..Who saw him..All unwithheld, indulging to his friends The vast unborrow'd treasures of his mind. **Unwithho·lden,** *ppl. a. arch.* (UN-[1] 8 b.) *a* **1834** COLERIDGE *Lit. Rem.* (1838) III. 192 It is not asserted, that..man unwithholden would not be a Yahoo, morally inferior to the swallow. **Unwithho·lding,** *ppl. a. rare*[−1]. (UN-[1] 10.) **1810** COLERIDGE in *Lit. Rem.* (1838) III. 243 The literary chit-chat and unwithholding frankness of a rich genius. **†Unwithsay·able,** *a. Obs.*[−1] [UN-[1] 7 b.] = UNGAINSAYABLE *a.* *c* **1450** *Mirour Saluacioun* (Roxb.) 129 Be the vnwithsayable prayere of marie oure mediatrice.

**Unwithstoo·d,** *ppl. a.* [UN-[1] 8 b.] Not withstood or hindered; unopposed; also, not successfully opposed.

**1595** DANIEL *Civ. Wars* II. vii, And stately Thames, inricht with many a flood,.. Glides on with pompe of waters vnwithstood. **1708** J. PHILIPS *Cyder* I. 591 Cressy Plains, And Agincourt, deep-ting'd with Blood, confess What the Silures Vigour unwithstood Cou'd do in rigid Fight. **1757** W. WILKIE *Epigon.* I. 18 When the barb'rous tyrant, unwithstood, His hot revenge shall quench in Grecian blood. **1819** SHELLEY *Masque A.* xxxvi, As if their own indignant Earth..Had turned every drop of blood By which her face had been bedewed To an accent unwithstood. **1848** AIRD *Nebuchad.* v. ii, A band..bore the centre of the Persians back...Deep was pushed that column unwithstood.

**†Unwi·tness.** *Obs.*[−1] [f. UNWIT *sb.*] = UNWITTING *vbl. sb.* 2. **1527** ANDREW *Brunswyke's Distyll. Waters* lxviii. L iv b/1 Water [of motherwort] is good agaynste vnwytnes [*other ed.* melancoly], and madnes of the hede.

**Unwi·tnessed,** *ppl. a.* (UN-[1] 8.)

**1407** *Exam. Wm. of Thorpe* (MS. Rawl. C. 208) fol. 33 b, For truþe whanne it is sowen may not ben vnwitnessid. **1592** SHAKS. *Ven. & Ad.* 1023 Trifles, unwitnessed with eye or ear. **1594** HOOKER *Eccl. Pol.* Pref. iii. § 12 Lest their zeale to the cause should any way be unwitnessed. **1615** CHAPMAN *Odyss.* x. 711 Circe..as she came Vanisht againe, vnwitnest by our eyes. **1652** BENLOWES *Theoph.* XIII. xxvi, Th' unwitnest witnes of his love. *a* **1750** A. HILL *Wks.* (1753) II. 66 The unwitnessed reflections of solitude. *a* **1800** COWPER *Odyss.* (ed. 2) x. 583 My friends, who with complaints, By thee unwitness'd, wear my heart away. **1812** CRABBE *Tales* xii. 253, I..share unwitness'd pomp, unenvied power. **1890** 'R. BOLDREWOOD' *Col. Reformer* xiii, The mighty ocean was as yet a wonder unwitnessed by the bold Australian.

**Unwi·tted,** *a. rare*[−1]. [UN-[1] 9.] Witless. **1828** *Lights & Shades* II. 133 Being at the same time unprincipled, unmannered, uncredited, unwitted, undunned. **†Unwi·tted,** *ppl. a. Obs.*[−1] [UN-[1] 8.] Unknown. **1582** STANYHURST *Æneis* I. (Arb.) 34 For to shak hands freendly fear bars, now gladnes on haleth. But the case vnwytted theym lets. **†Unwi·tten,** *ppl. a. Obs.* [UN-[1] 8 b.] = prec. **1456** SIR G. HAY *Gov. Princes* (S.T.S.) II. 112 Men wald purvay thame that thai suld pas with lesse cost and scathe, and save mony mennis lyfis, na it war unwittyn. **†Unwi·tter,** *a. Obs.* [UN-[1] 7. Cf. ON. *úvitr* (MSw. *oviter*).] Unknowing, foolish. *c* **1205** LAY. 16023 Þu ært unwis & vnwiter a ræde. **†Unwi·tterness.** *Obs.* [UN-[1] 12. Cf. prec.] Uncertainty. *a* **1300** *Cursor M.* 26646 Þerof haue we resuns fiue Þat man agh hastili him scriue, Þe first o ded vniwiternes, þat man wat neuer quen it es.

**Unwi·ttily,** *adv.* [f. UNWITTY *a.*, or UN-[1] 11.]

**†1.** In an ignorant, unwise, or foolish manner; unwisely. *Obs.*

**1362** LANGL. *P. Pl.* A. III. 101 Unwittily, ywys, wrouht hastou ofte. **1375** BARBOUR *Bruce* VI. 523 (Edin. MS.), To thaim, and nothyr ellys quhar Had [he] ey, and wrocht unwittily. *?a* **1400** *Morte Arth.* 3802 Þofe we hafe vnwittyly wastede oure selfene. **1548** ELYOT, *Inargute*, vnwittily, without subtilitee. **1560** DAUS tr. *Sleidane's Comm.* 135 Where they condempne the baptisme.., it is vnwittely [L. *inscienter*] done of them.

**2.** In a manner displaying lack of wit or facetious humour.

**1661** COWLEY *Cromwell* Wks. 1906 II. 371 This Man was wanton and merry (unwittily and ungracefully merry) with our Sufferings. **1884** *Imp. Dict.* IV. 524/2.

**†Unwi·tting,** *vbl. sb. Obs.* [UN-[1] 13.]

**1.** Lack of knowledge; ignorance.

**1382** WYCLIF *Acts* iii. 17, I woot that by vnwittinge [L. *ignorantiam*] ȝe diden, as and ȝoure princes. **1620** T. GRANGER *Div. Logike* 34 The involuntarie vnwitting causeth, or effecteth a thing being ignorant thereof.

**2.** Unsoundness of mind; insanity.

**1527** ANDREW *Brunswyke's Distyll. Waters* xvi. B. ij, [Borage-] water..is good agaynst madnes or vnwytyng [G. *unsynnigkeit*] and melancolye.

**Unwi·tting,** *ppl. a.* [OE. *unwitende* (UN-[1] 10, 5 d), = OS. *unwitandi*, OHG. *unwizzanti, -enti*, etc., MHG. *unwizzende* (G. *unwissend*), ON. *úvitandi* (Norw. *uvitande*, MSw. *ovitande*, Sw. *ovetande*, Da. *uvidende*), Goth. *unwitands*. Cf. UNWEETING *ppl. a.*]

Rare after *c* 1600, until revived (perhaps after UNWEETING *ppl. a.*) *c* 1800.

**1.** Having no knowledge or cognizance of a particular fact, thing, etc.; not knowing, unaware, unconscious; hence, unheeding, regardless. Sometimes quasi-*adv.* (= UNWITTINGLY *adv.*).

*pred.* *c* **893** K. ÆLFRED *Oros.* v. xiv. (1883) 248 He eac moniȝ tacen self ȝedyde..þeh he hie unwitende dyde. *Ibid.* v. xv. 250 He oft unwitende sloȝ mid his heafde on þone waȝ. *c* **1375** *Cursor M.* 19100 (Fairf.), [I] vnderstande þat ȝe him slogh vn-witande. **1382** WYCLIF *Joshua* xx. 3 Whoso euer a lijf hath smytn vnwitynge. *c* **1400** *Pilgr. Sowle* I. xiii. (Caxton, 1483) 7 He was weschen vnwiting, and nought willyng hym self..that he myght..discerne to chesen good ne euyl. *a* **1450** *Mirk's Festial* 30 Scho..toke Seynt Steuen's bonys ynstude of hyr maystyrs, vnwyttyng. **1513** DOUGLAS *Æneid* III. ix. 53 My falloschip vnwitting forȝet me heir. *c* **1580** SIDNEY *Ps.* xxxv. vii, Then abiects, while I was unwitting quite, Against me swarme. **1613** FLETCHER, etc. *Hon. Man's Fort.* II. i, I crave your Lordships pardon, your sudden apprehension on my steps made me to frame an answer unwitting and unworthy your respect. **1801** SOUTHEY *Thalaba* VIII. ii, His lean fingers play'd, Unwitting, with the grass that grew beside. **1852** KINGSLEY *Andromeda* 50 No word, once spoken, returneth, Even if uttered unwitting. **1868** MORRIS *Earthly Par.* I. I. 407 From her lips unwitting came a moan.

*attrib.* **1582** STANYHURST *Æneis* II. (Arb.) 53 Thee crack rack crashing the vnwitting pastor amazeth. **1833** H. COLERIDGE *North. Worthies* 5 The danger of which he had been the unwitting cause. **1884** *Chr. Commonwealth* 21 Feb. 439/2 Popular practice..imposes that ceremony [*sc.* baptism] on an unwitting babe.

**b.** Const. *of.*

**1412–20** LYDG. *Chron. Troy* IV. 4863 Þou knewe nouȝt of þat offence, But fully were vnwytinge of þe dede. **1609** HOLLAND *Amm. Marcell.* A j, Both of them.., unwitting of so much themselves, giving place to Christ. **1612** FIELD *Woman a Weathercock* II. i. D 1, This strange shape He altogether is vnwitting of.

**1876** BLACK *Madcap Violet* xxv, Drummond, all unwitting of any change. **1887** BOWEN *Æneid* III. 569 On the Cyclops coast, of the course unwitting, we run.

**c.** With direct object or objective clause.

(*a*) *c* **1400** *Sc. Trojan War* II. 712 It plesed to Pryame þe kyng, As wnwittand þar purposyng. **1869** 'OUIDA' *Tricotrin* xix, 'But?' asked the child,..unwitting the frightful truth that lay in the words.

(*b*) **1810** SCOTT *Lady of L.* III. xx, Children that, unwitting why, Lent the gay shout their shrilly cry. **1814** — *Lord of Isles* v. xv, Unwitting from what source it came. **1866** SALA *Barbary* 229 Quite unwitting that he is to be made king over Israel.

**†2.** In absolute constructions. (Also with *of.*)

*a* **1300** *Cursor M.* 12525 Iesus still him efter stal, Ioseph and mari vnwittand. *c* **1380** WYCLIF *Wks.* (1880) 56 Petir.. wolde haue lettid cristis deþ.., him wnwyttyngge. *c* **1386** CHAUCER *Can. Yeom. T.* 767 (Ellesm. MS.), He slyly tooke it out.., Vnwityng this preest of his false craft. *c* **1400** *Brut* 325 Þe Englissh men..drenchyng al þe men þat were þerin, vnwytyng hem þat þey weren of þat cuntre. *c* **1455** PECOCK *Folewer* 134 Whilis y kepe þe contraries of þo deedis so priueli to me, hem it vnwityng. **1456** SIR G. HAYE *Law Arms* (S.T.S.) 227 Unwittand his ost, he passis fra his company in the woddis. **1500–20** DUNBAR *Poems* ix. 138, I schryve me of all cursit cumpany, All tymes both witting and vnwitting me. **1586** HOOKER *Hist. Irel.* in *Holinshed* II. 130/1 Others of Mounster, who before (and vnwitting the Butlers) had [etc.]. **1598** STOW *Survey* 323 The Lord Gray of Ruthen,..vnwitting the Sergeantes and against their willes (as they said), was first placed. **1622** MABBE tr. *Aleman's Guzman d'Alf.* II. (1623) 189 Which things,..the Captaine unwitting thereof, I clapt up closely within my trunks.

**†3.** Without the knowledge *of* (also with possessive adjs.), unbeknown *to*, a person. *Obs.*

(*a*) *a* **1300** *Cursor M.* 3874 Bisid lya al night he lai, His vnwitand, til it was dai. *c* **1375** *Sc. Leg. Saints* xxix. (*Placidas*) 534 Nere-by, his vnwittand, his sonnis twa ware duelland. **1454** *Paston Lett.* I. 287 My wif delyvered all, myn unwetyng. **1470** *Ibid.* II. 412 He sente to my Lady.., my onwetyng, or wythout eny preyer of me. **1513** DOUGLAS *Æneid* IV. vi. 51 With dissimulance wenyt thow, wnfaithfull wycht, Thow mycht.., myne vnwitting, steill furth of my land?

(*b*) **1340** *Ayenb.* 37 [To] nyme..oþre manne þinges wyþ wrong and onwytinde and wyþ-oute wylle of þe lhorde. *c* **1386** CHAUCER *Frankl. T.* 228 Vnwityng of this Dorigen at al This lusty Squier..Hadde loued hire. **1535** STEWART *Cron. Scot.* (Rolls) I. 531 That samin nycht..[Donald] Come on the king..With greit power wnwittand of this king. *Ibid.* III. 23 Tha dressit thame till go Towart his oist.., Onwittand than of ony Scottis wicht.

(*c*) **1386** *Rolls of Parlt.* III. 226/1 Alle suche wronges hav ben unwytyng to us. **1531** ELYOT *Gov.* III. vi, A gentilman, ..unwyttynge to any persone, dyd cut of his owne eares. **1556** *Chron. Grey Friars* (Camden) 17 The othe that he made un to the kynge of Ynglonde unwyttynge unto the pope. **1630** R. N[ORTON] tr. *Camden's Hist. Eliz.* I. 135 The two Earles.., vnwitting to the rest, presently withdrew themselues. **1633** B. JONSON *Tale Tub* IV. i, Ile marry her to you, Vnwitting to this Turfe.

**4.** Performed unwittingly; unintentional; unpremeditated.

**1818** BENTHAM *Ch. Eng.* Introd. 248 Authors of the unwitting and unwilling transgression. **1856** MISS MULOCK *J. Halifax* xxxvii, The unwitting indication of some crotchets of mine. **1871** FREEMAN *Norm. Conq.* xviii. IV. 268 Whether this sacrilege was designed or unwitting, it was speedily avenged.

**b.** Unconscious.

**1840** LOWELL *Irene* 21 Her large charity (An all unwitting, childlike gift in her).

**5.** *Path.* (See quot.)

**1822–7** GOOD *Study Med.* (1829) I. 159 *Pica..Insulsa*, Unwitting pica. [So called] from want of correct taste or discrimination.

**Unwi·ttingly,** *adv.* [f. prec. + -LY[2], or UN-[1] 11.] Not wittingly, knowingly, or intentionally; unconsciously, inadvertently; ignorantly.

In very frequent use *c* 1380–*c* 1630, and from *c* 1815. For the break in the history, cf. prec.

**1375** BARBOUR *Bruce* XVI. 248 The gude king said..it wes in his awn foly, For he raid sa vnwittandly, So fer befor. **1388** WYCLIF *Joshua* xx. 3 Whoeuer sleeth vnwytyngli a man. *c* **1400** *Cursor M.* 29392 (Cott. Galba), Of him þat dose a light trispase To prest or clerk vnwitandly. **1483** CAXTON *Gold. Leg.* 211/1 The prynce that bete y[e]..did it unwittyngly. **1526** *Pilgr. Perf.* (W. de W. 1531) 163 b, Yf a persone..omyt..agaynst theyr wyll vnwytyngly ony worde or wordes of theyr duty. **1581** HANMER *Jesuites Banner* H 4 b, Yet was it done of ignoraunce, and vnwittingly. **1626** JACKSON *Creed* VIII. xxi. § 3 This acknowledgment was first made (though unwittingly) by the multitude. **1654** BRAMHALL *Just Vind.* ii. 27 Who..if he hold any errours unwittingly and unwillingly, doth implicitely [etc.].

**1794** COLERIDGE *Lett.* (1895) 112, I unwittingly (for I did not know it at the time) borrowed a thought from you. **1808** SCOTT *Marm.* v. xviii, Unwittingly, King James had given, As guard.., The man most dreaded under Heaven By these defenceless maids. **1833** HT. MARTINEAU *Tale of Tyne* ii. 24 He unwittingly spoiled their little arrangements. **1883** WHITELAW *Sophocles, Trachin.* 727 When men have stumbled all unwittingly Anger has pity.

**Unwi·ttingness.** [f. UNWITTING *ppl. a.*]

**†1.** Lack of knowledge; ignorance. *Obs. rare.*

*a* **1300** *E. E. Psalter* xxiv. 7 Giltes of mine youthe in thoghte And mine un-witandnesses [L. *ignorantiæ*] min noght. **1611** FLORIO, *Inscibilita*, ignorance, vnwittingnesse. **1668** J. WILSON tr. *Erasmus' Praise of Folly* (1913) 176 Nor does he cover their crime with any other excuse than that of unwittingnesse—because, saith he, 'they know not what they do'.

**2.** Absence of realization; unconsciousness.

**1873** MRS. WHITNEY *Other Girls* xviii, 'Why don't we preach it ourselves,' said Desire, with inimitable unwittingness. **1876** MEREDITH *Beauch. Career* II. iii. 44 A lovely melting image of her stole over him; all the warmer for her unwittingness in producing it.

**Unwi·tty,** *a.* [OE. *unwittig* (UN-[1] 7), *ungewittig*, = OHG. *unwizzig, -ik* (MHG. *unwitzic*), MSw. *ovitugher*, Norw. *uvitug*, Da. *uvittig*. Cf. WANWITTY *a.*]

**1.** Lacking or deficient in wit, intelligence, or knowledge; ignorant, unwise, witless. Now *rare.*

*c* **1000** ÆLFRIC in Assmann *Ags. Hom.* 29 Ȝe weras, ȝe wif, and ða unwittiȝan cild. *c* **1205** LAY. 786 Þat nan ne beo so wilde, nan swa unwitti þat word talie. **13..** *E. E. Allit. P.* C. 511 Wymmen vnwytte þat wale ne couþe þat on hande fro þat oþer. **1382** WYCLIF *Ecclus.* xvi. 20 In alle these thingus mys felende, or vnwittie, is the herte. *c* **1450** LOVELICH *Grail* xliii. 410 Wel mown they for folis itold be, and vnwitty & madde. *c* **1490** CAXTON *Rule St. Benet* 120 A token of an vnwytty mynde. **1541** R. COPLAND *Guydon's Quest. Chirurg.* B ij, A Cyrurgyen..oughte nat to be a foole, vnwytty, nor of rude vnderstandynge. **1584** HUDSON *Du Bartas' Judith* IV. (1608) 60 [Lot's] wife, that was vnwittie, Cast back her eye. **1617** BP. HALL *Quo Vadis* § 10, I know not wherein Lewis the Eleuenth shewed himselfe vnwitty, but [etc.]. **1670** MILTON *Hist. Eng.* v. 239 One of her waiting Maids; a Maid..not unhansom nor unwitty; who [etc.]. **1859** TENNYSON *Merlin & V.* 344 These unwitty wandering wits of mine.

*absol.* *c* **1000** ÆLFRIC *Hom.* II. 532 Wel deð se ðe unwittiȝum styrð mid swinglum, ȝif [etc.]. *c* **1400** *Apol. Loll.* 25 Wiþ him al þe world schal fiȝt aȝen þe vnwitti.

**†b.** Unexperienced *in* something. *Obs. rare.*

**1594** DANIEL *Cleopatra* 167 Inur'd to warres, in womens wiles vnwitty,..thou fell'st to loue in earnest.

**†2.** Of actions, etc.; Characterized by lack or absence of knowledge; senseless, foolish. *Obs.*

*c* **1200** *St. Marher.* 6 Stute nu and stew þine unwitti wordes. **1435** MISYN *Fire of Love* 54 Qwhilst þou herys of þe wisyst man vnwittiest dede. **1471** RIPLEY *Comp. Alch.* v. xliii. in Ashm. (1652) 158 Therfore ther Warkes provyth unwytty. *a* **1548** HALL *Chron., Hen. V*, 77, I maruell at his vnwitty doyng and rashe enterprise. **1550** *Acts Privy Counc.* III. 73 Those unwitty and superstitiouse vowes. **1587** M. GROVE *Pelops & Hipp.* (1878) 130 Of vnwittie spending.

**3.** Not witty or facetious.

**1637** HEYLIN *Antid. Lincoln.* i. 1 It was an old, but not unwitty application of the Lo: Keeper Lincolns,..that [etc.]. *a* **1763** SHENSTONE *Levities, Simile* 23 He.. Pours forth unwitty jokes, and swears, And bawls. **1849** FROUDE *Nemesis of Fate* ix. 60 He was acute, not unwitty, and with a *savoir faire* about him. **1871** W. ALEXANDER *Johnny Gibb* xviii, A mannie says to me, '..Paul hed naething adee wi' sic plantin';..'t wusna that oonwutty o' the carlie.

**Unwi·ve,** *v.* [UN-[2] 3.] *trans.* To deprive (a person) of a wife. Also *refl.*

**1611** FLORIO, *Dismogliare*, to unwiue. **1633** FORD *Broken H.* II. ii, Had this sincerity beene reall once, My Orgilus had not beene now vn-wiu'd. **1759** SARAH FIELDING *C'tess of Dellwyn* II. 147 He was at once unwived, unhoused, and undone. **1824** MEDWIN *Convers. Byron* I. 95, I began by being jilted, and ended by being unwived. **1851** W. B. MACCABE *Bertha* III. 376, I can do more strange things than unwive myself and wive you.

**Unwi·ved,** *ppl. a.* [UN-[1] 8. Cf. MDu. *onghewijft* wifeless, MHG. *ungewibet* maiden; and UNWIFED *a.*] Not having a wife or wives; wifeless.

**1570** LEVINS *Manip.* 51 Vnwyued, *innxoratus*, *cælebs*. **1611** FLORIO, *Smogliato*, without a wife, unwiued. **1612** SELDON *Illustr. Drayton's Poly-olb.* viii. 357 A competent number of Virgins might be sent ouer to furnish his vnwiu'd Batchelers. [**1775** ASH.] **1827** HOOD *Widow* 63 He look'd so lone, and so unwiv'd, That soon the Widow Cross contriv'd To fall in love. **1866** LYTTON *Lost Tales Miletus* 32 Of his stalwart chiefs [he selected]..all the bravest yet unwived. **1873** E. H. CLARKE *Sex in Educ.* 63 The old story of unwived Rome and the Sabines.

**†Unwi·ving,** *ppl. a. Obs.* [UN-[1] 10.] **a.** Of or pertaining to celibacy. **b.** Celibate.

**1550** BALE *Apol.* Ep. Ded. p. iiii, *Vouere* in that place pertayneth no more to their vnwiuing state, than [etc.]. *Ibid.* 81 b, Wher is now..the vnwyuyng vowe of prestes. **1550** — *Eng. Votaries* II. 33 b, The ordre of prodygyouse buggerers, otherwyse called vnwyuynge masmongers.

**†Unwla·p,** *v. Obs.*[−1] [UN-[2] 3.] *trans.* To free or release from a covering. **1388** WYCLIF *Jer.* li. 25 Y schal vnwlappe [L. *evolvam*] thee fro stoonys. **Unwoe·ful,** *a.* [UN-[1] 7.] †Free from pain. **1570** LEVINS *Manip.* 186 Vnwoful, *indolens.*

**Unwo·man,** *v.* [UN-[2] 6 b.]

**1.** *trans.* To deprive of the qualities or traits of a woman; to remove from the category of women. Occas. *refl.* Also const. *of.*

**1611** FLORIO, *Disdonnare*, to vnwoman. **1614** T. ADAMS *Divells Banket* 5 A degenerate woman, unwomaned..of both modestie and chastitie. **1621** G. SANDYS *Ovid's Met.*

II. (1626) 37 Shee, whose wicked deeds Vnwoman'd her. **1631** BRATHWAIT *Eng. Gentlew.* 123 One weary of her sexe, forbore not to vnwoman her selfe, by assuming not onely a virile habit, but a virago's heart. **1744** ELIZA HEYWOOD *Female Spect.* No. 5 (1748) I. 263 There is nothing..so shocking to the..modesty of our sex,..that we may not..degenerate into, if we proceed to unwoman ourselves. **1839** MRS. BROWNING *Romaunt Page* xxv, My love..shall requite No woman, whether dark or bright, Unwomaned if she be. **1863** MRS. OLIPHANT *Salem Chapel* xxi, Not all her personal wretchedness could unwoman the minister's mother so much as to make her forgive..Phœbe's presumption.

**2.** To unsex (a woman). *rare*$^{-1}$.

**1827** *Lancet* 20 Oct. 71 Taking away the ovaries altogether ..would unwoman her.

**Unwo·manize,** *v.* [UN-[2] 6 c.] *refl.* To render unwomanly. **1744** ELIZA HEYWOOD *Female Spect.* No. 6 (1748) I. 273 When a woman unwomanizes herself, renounces the softness of her nature. **Unwo·manlike,** *a.* (UN-[1] 7 c.) **1635** R. JOHNSON *Hist. Tom a Lincolne* (1828) 108 All these her unwomanlike demeanours. **1786** *Ann. Reg.* II. 29/1 She then cursed and swore in the most unwoman like manner. **Unwo·manliness.** (UN-[1] 12.) **1882** *Society* 4 Nov. 12/2 The heroine..seems to glory in her unwomanliness.

**Unwo·manly,** *a.* [UN-[1] 7.]

**1.** Not befitting or characteristic of a woman; inappropriate to womanly character.

App. disused or rare in the 17th and 18th c.; cf. next.

**1529** MORE *Dyaloge* II. Wks. 198/2 The women folowing the crosse wyth many an vnwomanly songe. **1589** COOPER *Admon.* 39 The vilenesse of her tongue, and other vnwomanly behauiour. **1592** DANIEL *Compl. Rosamond* lxxxiii, Offring me most vnwomanly disgrace. **1608** W. CRASHAW *Newes fr. Italy* xxi. 54 This monstrous vnkindnes and unwomanly answer pierced his heart.

**1821** SCOTT *Kenilw.* xli, She appealed to Foster..not to permit her to be treated with unwomanly violence. **1843** HOOD *Song of Shirt* i, A woman..in unwomanly rags. **1865** 'ANNIE THOMAS' *Theo Leigh* xl, A decrepid old woman.. with hard, bony, unwomanly shoulders, displayed in a hard, bold, unwomanly manner. **1896** 'H. S. MERRIMAN' *Sowers* xix, It was..the face of a womanly woman engaged in unwomanly work.

**2.** Lacking the qualities or traits of a woman.

**1866** G. MACDONALD *Ann. Q. Neighb.* vi, The most hurtful of all beings,..an unwomanly woman. **1886** *Chr. Herald* (N.Y.) IX. 223 The woman of Samaria was hard, impure, and unwomanly.

**Unwo·manly,** *adv.* [UN-[1] 11.] In a manner unbecoming a woman.

App. not used in 18th and early 19th c.; cf. prec.

*c* **1400** *Pilgr. Sowle* IV. xxxviii. (MS. Bodl. 770) 79 b/2 Þis same..helde a parlement ful vnwommanlie befor þe kynges presence. **1565** CALFHILL *Answ. Martiall* 78 b, She most vnwomanly scratched out the eyes of..hir owne sonne. **1684** BUNYAN *Pilgr.* II. 13 For your poor Children's sakes, do not so unwomanly cast away yourself.

**1883** D. C. MURRAY *Hearts* x, An evil story, though.. not..a sad one, and all through most unwomanly womanly. **1891** KIPLING *Light that Failed* xiii, To justify herself, she began, unwomanly, to weigh the evidence.

**Unwo·mb,** *v.* (UN-[1] 5.) **1594** *Zepheria* ix, Like daintie Midwife Flora to vnwoombe Sweet babes of Tellus and Hiperion. **1674** *Jackson's Recant.* A 2, As if both the Globes ..had been unwomb'd from the formless Chaos.

**Unwo·n,** *ppl. a.* [UN-[1] 8 b. Cf. (M)Du. *ongewonnen*, MHG. *ungewunnen*, unconquered.]

**1.** Not won, in various senses. Also const. *by*.

**1593** Q. ELIZ. *Boeth.* I. pr. i. 5 A woman did apeare..of fresche coulor and unwon strengh [L. *inexhausti vigoris*]. *Ibid.* met. iv. 4 Who so quiet in setled life..His chire vnwonne [L. *invictum vultum*] preserues. **1818** MILMAN *Samor* VI. 33 Caswallon..Drives onward, he nought deeming won, while aught Remains unwon. **1855** M. ARNOLD *Haworth Churchyard* 117 She..leaves Half her laurels unwon, Dying too soon. **1874** PUSEY *Lent. Serm.* 14 The soul yet unwon by His grace. **1892** BP. WESTCOTT in *Daily News* 16 March 5/7 The coal remains there to this day unwon.

**2.** *spec.* Of women: Not successfully wooed.

**1601** DANIEL *Cleopatra* I. Wks. F v b, I must die free, And die my selfe vncaptiu'd and vnwonne. **1837** W. MAGINN *Shakesp. Papers* (1859) 287 The anticipation of the lost dinner and unwon lady. **1850** MRS. BROWNING *Sonn. fr. Portuguese* xiii, Seeing that I stand unwon, however wooed.

†**Unwo·nder,** *v. Obs. rare.* [UN-[2] 6 b.] *trans.* To divest of the qualities of a wonder.

**1655** FULLER *Ch. Hist.* II. vi. § 17 Others easily unwonder the same [continency] by imputing it partly to his Impotence. *a* **1661** — *Worthies* I. (1662) 197 But know Reader, that this Wonder is now Unwondred.

**Unwo·ndering,** *ppl. a.* (UN-[1] 10.) **1788** WOLCOT (P. Pindar) *Peter's Prophecy* Wks. 1816 I. 455 Wiser now, th' un-wond'ring world..Gives all poor Herschel's glory to his glass. **1818** MILMAN *Samor* IX. 144 Soft and weak, (Pursued the unwondering Stranger)..There is a strength, that is not of the arm. †**Unwo·ne,** *v. Obs.*$^{-1}$ [UN-[2] 3. Cf. MHG. *entwonen*, G. *-wöhnen*.] *trans.* = UNWONT *v.* a. **1340** *Ayenb.* 32 And zuo he him onwoneþ þe dyeuel wel uor to done.

† **Unwo·ne,** *a. Obs.*$^{-1}$ [UN-[1] 7. Cf. NFris. *unwenn*, OE. *ungewuna*, MDu. *onghewone* (Du. *ongewoon*), OHG. *unga-*, *ungewon* (MHG. *ungewon*) unaccustomed.] Unwonted; unusual.

*a* **1300** *Cursor M.* 10139 It es vncuth and vnwon [*v.r.* vnwone] þe fader to be·cum þe sun.

†**Unwo·ned,** *ppl. a. Obs.*$^{-1}$ [UN-[1] 8.] = UNWONTED *ppl. a.* I. *c* **1455** PECOCK *Folewer* 89 Þis mater is sumwhat straunge and vnwonyd to be talkid.

**Unwo·nt,** *ppl. a.* Now *rare* or *Obs.* [UN-[1] 8 b. Cf. G. *ungewohnt*, *-wöhnt*.]

**1.** Unusual; uncustomary; = UNWONTED *ppl. a.* I.

*c* **1400** *Found. St. Bartholomew's* 46 The man awakid was afrayed of this vnwount vision and..lost his wytte. *c* **1475** *Cath. Angl.* 423/2 (A.), To be vn Wonte, *dessuere*, *dessuescere*. *c* **1520** BARCLAY *Jugurth* (1557) 40 b, The vnwonte and sodayne feare of this treason. **1533–4** *Acts* 25 *Hen. VIII*, c. 21 § 3 Yf it be thought..that dispensacions..in any suche cause unwonte shall passe. **1556** OLDE *Antichrist* 52 b, A fearfull and an unwont blasing starre appeared. *a* **1568** COVERDALE *Bk. Death* III. xii. (1579) 300 If one die an vnwonte death. **1611** COTGR., *Insolite*, strange, vnused, vnaccustomed, vnwont. **1664** BUTLER *Hud.* II. iii. 1185 He..with Activity unwont, Essay'd the lofty Beast to mount. **1816** *Monthly Mag.* XLI. 527 E'en in the chapel watch unwont is kept. **1827** POLLOK *Course T.* I. 114 But what concern hangs on thy countenance, Unwont within this place?

**b.** *poet.* Of persons: Strange *in* manner. *rare*$^{-1}$.

*a* **1843** BAMFORD *Wild Rider* IV, Poems (1864) 76 The knight, from that day, Was altered in look, and unwont in his way.

**2.** Not wont, used, or accustomed *to* do something. Cf. UNWONTED *ppl. a.* 2 (*a*).

**1552** R. MORYSINE in Tytler *England* (1839) II. 136 He hath a face unwont to disclose any hid affection of his heart. **1596** SPENSER *F. Q.* VI. xi. 40 Groomes..Vnwont with heards to watch, or pasture sheepe. **1810** SCOTT *Lady of L.* II. vii, Though [thou art] all unwont to bid in vain. **1823** MRS. HEMANS *Siege Valencia* 171 A stem Unwont to bend or break. **1829** SCOTT *Anne of G.* xiii, I am unwont to press my favours.

Hence **Unwo·ntness.** *rare.*

**1552** HULOET, Vnwontenes, *insolentia*, *dissuetudo*. **1570** T. WILSON tr. *Demosth. Orat.* iv. 35 Beholde what an insolencie and vnwoontnesse the man is growne vnto.

† **Unwo·nt,** *v. Obs. rare.* [UN-[2] 3. Cf. UNWONE *v.*] **a.** *trans.* = DISACCUSTOM *v.* 2. **b.** To disappoint.

**1580** HOLLYBAND *Treas. Fr. Tong*, *Se Desaccoustumer*, to vnwoont. **1629** GAULE *Pract. & The.* 107 If (at any time) his Power and Will shall surprize mine vnwariness, or vnwont mine expectation.

**Unwo·nted,** *ppl. a.* [UN-[1] 8. Cf. UNWONT.]

**1.** Not wonted, usual, or habitual; not commonly heard, seen, practised, etc.; infrequent.

In very frequent use from *c* 1810.

**1553** BRENDE *Q. Curtius* 177 b, They put the Macedones in terrour, troublyng with their vnwonted crye. **1579** E. K. *Ded. to Spenser's Sheph. Cal.* § 1 Old and vnwonted words. **1580** T. WILSON *Rhet.* (ed. 2) 197 His maister marueilyng.. at suche an vnwonted [1553 vnwonte] kindnesse. **1611** B. JONSON *Catiline* I. i, A strange vn-wonted horror doth inuade me. **1668** GLANVILL *Sadducismus* 6 Epocha's made of those unwonted events. **1713** ROWE *Jane Shore* I. ii, Man..Shall pity thee, and with unwonted Goodness, Forget thy Failings. **1743** FRANCIS tr. *Hor.*, *Epodes* v. 88 Soon the Wretch my Wrath shall prove, By Spells unwonted taught to love. **1764** H. WALPOLE *Otranto* ii, It is not seemly for me to hold farther converse with a man at this unwonted hour. **1808** SCOTT *Marm.* III. xxi, His own menials..Beheld..the grisly Sire, In his unwonted hild attire. **1847** C. BRONTE *J. Eyre* vii, Difficulties in habituating myself to new rules and unwonted tasks. **1863** STANLEY *Jew. Ch.* xix. 428 The constant expectation of some new Prophet appearing in the most secluded or unwonted situation. **1876** FREEMAN *Norm. Conq.* (ed. 2) IV. 291 Those who survived kept up life on strange and unwonted food.

**b.** Not wont to appear; rarely seen.

**1784** COWPER *Task* VI. 301 Spring..calls the unwonted villager abroad With all her little ones. **1825** SCOTT *Talism.* xviii, It seemed as if a tear (unwonted guest) were gathering in his dry and glazened eye.

**2.** Not made familiar by practice; unused or unaccustomed to something. Used (*a*) predicatively with *to*, or ellipt., and (*b*) attrib.

(*a*) *a* **1586** SIDNEY *Arcadia* II. xi, Philoclea..tenderly moved her feete, unwonted to feele the naked ground. **1628** MAY *Virg. Georg.* III. 99 The Fishes..Float dead..to the shore: Sea-calves unwonted to fresh rivers fly. **1828–32** WEBSTER s.v., A child unwonted to strangers. **1870** BRYANT *Iliad* II. I. 51 Boys unwonted to the tasks of war.

(*b*) **1791** COWPER *Iliad* I. 735 So He; then Juno,..smiling still, from his unwonted hand Received the goblet. **1822** MILMAN *Martyr Antioch* 108 Are not these chambers thine, That with their splendour load my unwonted eyes?

**3.** Going beyond ordinary limits. *rare*$^{-1}$.

**1642** MILTON *Apol. Smect.* 11 If I shall be large, or unwonted in justifying my selfe to those who know me not.

Hence **Unwo·ntedness.**

**1594** SOUTHWELL *M. Magd. Funeral Teares* 8 b, Let..the vnwontednesse of the miracle plead her pardon. *a* **1652** BROME *Mad Couple* II. i, I confesse it is (by reason of my unwontednesse to it) some difficulty for me. **1698** FRYER *Acc. E. India & P.* 251 We encountred two horrid Shapes both for Grandeur and Unwontedness. **1861** GEO. ELIOT *Silas M.* iv, A too bewildering dreamy sense of unwontedness in his position. **1895** *Daily News* 7 Nov. 5/3 A girdle of rubies which may have given a faint shock of unwontedness to the experience of even a Vanderbilt bride.

**Unwo·ntedly,** *adv.* [f. prec., or UN-[1] 11.] In a strange, unwonted, or unusual manner; unusually; uncommonly.

**1638** R. BAKER tr. *Balzac's Lett.* (vol. II) 140 It must be a very extraordinary vertue that transported him so unwontedly. **1648** HEXHAM II, *Ongewoonlick*, Vnwontedly, or Vn-usually. **1815** SCOTT *Antiq.* xviii, Both his brothers slept unwontedly deep and heavily. **1833** *New Monthly Mag.* XXXVIII. 433 Specimens..are not unwontedly seen invading the snowy surface. **1851** HELPS *Comp. Solit.* vi. 85 The unwontedly sunny pane in December. **1867** 'OUIDA' *C. Castlemaine's Gage* 16 Her heart stirred strangely and unwontedly.

†**Unwo·ntly,** *adv. Obs.*$^{-1}$ [UN-[1] 11.] Contrary to custom. **1540** R. JONAS *Birth of Mankynde* 15 b, If..she haue had dayly and vnwontly her flowres.

**Unwoo·ded,** *ppl. a.* [UN-[1] 8.] Destitute of wood or trees; treeless.

**1628** MAY *Virg. Georg.* IV. 125 Shepheards collect These flowers..On plaine unwooded Valleyes. **1784** *Cook's Voy.* I. 30 That lifeless brown which prevails in countries..that are unwooded. **1816** SOUTHEY *Poet's Pilgr.* I. iii. 83 The unwooded open land. **1860** O. W. HOLMES *Elsie V.* x, A dark, deep dell, unwooded, save for a few..native larches. **1870** MORRIS *Earthly Par.* III. IV. 326 The rugged mountain's bare unwooded feet.

†**Unwoo·dy,** *a. Obs.*$^{-1}$ (UN-[1] 7.) **1635** SWAN *Spec. M.* vi. § 4 The tender and unwoodie branches of shrubs and trees.

**Unwoo·ed,** *ppl. a.* (UN-[1] 8.)

**1570** LEVINS *Manip.* 51 Vnwowed, *impetitus*. *c* **1600** SHAKS. *Sonn.* liv, They liue vnwoo'd and vnrespected fade. **1806** SURR *Winter in Lond.* III. 30 A maiden of the..kindest nature flattered me by an unwooed affection. **1830** TENNYSON *Arabian Nts.* 80 The solemn palms were ranged Above, unwoo'd of summer wind. **1882** MISS BRADDON *Mt. Royal* I. iii. 96 She would have blushed..for her folly in having loved unwooed.

†**Unwoo·lled,** *a. Obs.* [UN-[1] 9.] Lacking wool; shorn. **1538** *Aberdeen Reg.* (MS.) XVI. (Jam.), Small wn-wollit skynnis, sic as hoyg schorlingis. **1648** HEXHAM II, *Ongewolt*, vnwolled, or bare of wool. †**Unwoo·llen,** *a. Obs.* [UN-[1] 7.] **1570** LEVINS *Manip.* 62 Vnwollen, *non laneus*.

† **Unwo·rd,** *v. Obs. rare.* [UN-[2] 4.] *trans.* To deprive of words; to make speechless.

*a* **1625** FLETCHER *Nice Valour* II. i, You should have found my thanks paid in a smile If I had fell unworded. **1654** GAYTON *Pleas. Notes* IV. ix. 230 Uncardinall'd, Unlorded, Outed of all his hopes, but not Unworded; He..Curses Knight-Errants.

**Unwo·rdable,** *a.* [UN-[1] 7 b.] Incapable of being expressed in words; unutterable.

*c* **1660** in *Memoirs of Whiston* (1749) 561 There is but one God the Father,..glorious and unwordable in all his Attributes. *Ibid.* 565 God['s]..Purity and unwordable Holiness. **1877** S. COX *Salv. Mundi* ix. 198 St. Paul..heard what he calls 'unwordable words'. **1882** [LEES & CLUTTERBUCK] *Three in Norway* xxxvi. 337 An unwordable calm, an indescribable tranquillity.

**Unwo·rded,** *ppl. a.* [UN-[1] 8.]

**1.** Not expressed in words.

**1860** MRS. C. CLIVE *Why Paul Ferroll killed his Wife* iii, With all this unworded she accosted him. **1860** [see UNTHOUGHTED]. **1865** MRS. WHITNEY *Gayworthys* xxi, The unworded intercourse between this husband and wife. **1898** MEREDITH *Poems* II. 132 This lone-laid wife was moved to feel Unworded things and old To her pained heart appeal.

**2.** Lacking words; silent. *rare*$^{-1}$.

**1886** R. W. GILDER *Lyrics* 116 So, still unworded, save in memory mute, Rest thou, sweet hour of viol and of lute.

**Unwordily, -wordy,** Sc. varr. UNWORTHILY, UNWORTHY.

**Unwo·rdy,** *a. rare.* [UN-[1] 7.] Not diffuse or verbose; concise.

[**1775** ASH.] **1840** DE QUINCEY *Style* Wks. 1859 XI. 280 The culture of an unwordy diction.

**Unwo·rk,** *sb.* (UN-[1] 12.) **1854** WHITTIER *Yankee Gipsies* Prose Wks. I. 343 That comfortable philosophy..is the real life of this city of unwork.

**Unwo·rk,** *v. rare.* [UN-[2] 3, 5. Cf. OE. *unwyrcan* to undo; also OHG. *intwurchen*, *-wirken*, MHG. *entwürken*, *-wirken* to destroy.]

† **1.** *trans.* To undo or detach (*from* something).

*a* **1548** HALL *Chron. Hen. IV*, 8 But his workyng vnwrought king Richard from his croune.

† **2.** To spoil, mar, or destroy. *Obs.*$^{-1}$

**1587** GOLDING *De Mornay* xvii. 308 The punishments bewray..that wee chastise in vs, not that which God hath made or wrought in vs, but that which wee our selues haue vndone or vnwrought.

**3.** To release from an intertwined condition.

**1634** C. BUTLER *Fem. Mon.* (ed. 2) 92 If they light in..a ded hedg, your best way is, softly to unwoork the hedg til you coom to them.

**4.** To undo by contrary action.

**1726–** [see UNWROUGHT *pa. pple.*]. **1909** W. OGILVIE *Whaup o' the Rede* VII. vii, Thy lady mother..Unwrought the wrong of Wat Harden's hate With her love.

**Unworkabi·lity.** (UN-[1] 12.) **1881** *Nature* XXIV. 371 The then existing laws..were in a state of..confusion and unworkability. **1886** *Times* 7 April 9/1 The unworkability of his plan.

**Unwo·rkable,** *a.* [UN-[1] 7 b.]

**1.** Not workable; not capable of being worked, put into operation or practice, etc.

Freq. from *c* 1880.

**1839** URE *Dict. Arts* 984 The mine is rendered unworkable until..fresh air is introduced. **1861** MILL *Repr. Govt.* vii. 152 Some profess to think the plan unworkable. **1869** A. MACDONALD *Love, Law & Theol.* vi. 102 Lord Aberdeen's Act is quite unworkable. **1887** W. S. S. TYRWHITT *New Chum in Bush* v. 84 To prevent his run being rendered unworkable by having the best parts of it taken from him.

**b.** Of ships: Unmanageable.

**1853** KANE *Grinnell Exp.* xxiii. (1856) 186 She had split her rudder-post so as to make her unworkable. **1885** *Athenæum* 5 Dec. 726/3 The soldiers were untrained..and the ships unworkable.

**c.** Impossible to manage, direct, control, etc., on account of size, numbers, or lack of coherence.

**1862** 'SHIRLEY' (J. Skelton) *Nugæ Crit.* ix. 426 An undisciplined and unworkable rabble. **1874** MORLEY *Compromise* 83 The participation of large numbers of people ..immediately becomes unworkable. **1895** E. OWEN *Wks. G. Edwards* p. xiii, The large and unworkable parish of Wrexham. **1896** BADEN-POWELL *Matabele Campaign* v, We have broken up the original..Force as an unworkable and rather overpaid organization.

**2.** Of materials: Incapable of being worked upon or wrought into shape.

**1854** H. MILLER *Sch. & Schm.* iii. 57 The white stone..is a beautiful though unworkable rock. **1867** W. W. SMYTH *Coal & Coal-mining* 47 Of the measures..the upper half contains only a few unworkable beds. **1879** *Cassell's Techn. Educ.* II. 163/2 Alpaca wool..laid aside..as useless, unworkable material.

*fig.* **1856** R. A. VAUGHAN *Mystics* IX. i. II. 134 Mystics imperfectly subservient—unworkable raw material, and as such flung into the fire.

Hence **Unwo·rkableness.**

**1877** MORLEY *Crit. Misc.* Ser. II. 60 The absolute unworkableness of the new constitution. **1879** *Contemp. Rev.* Oct. 290 The unworkableness of the various systems proposed.

**Unwo·rked,** *ppl. a.* [UN-¹ 8. Cf. OHG. *ungaworaht, ungewurchet* (MHG. *ungeworht*, G. *-wirkt*), MLG. *ungewercht*; also UNWROUGHT and UNWERKED *ppl. adjs.*]

**1.** Not wrought into shape; not worked upon.

**1730** BAILEY (fol.), *Unwrought* (of *un* and *weorcian*, Sax.), unworked. **1862** J. NEWTON in *Trans. Hist. Soc. Lancs. & Chesh.* (N.S.) II. 103 Flint implements..obtained by a few adroit cleavages from the unworked boulders amidst which they lie. **1865** LUBBOCK *Preh. Times* viii. 265 One single unworked flint.

**2.** Not worked in or operated upon. Chiefly *fig.*

**1817** LADY MORGAN *France* (1818) II. 190 Drawing from the unworked mine of fancy and imagination. **1858** GLENNY *Gard. Every-day Bk.* 83/1 This applies to all kinds of unworked subjects. **1874** RAYMOND *Statist. Mines & Mining* 365 Harris Gulch..contains much unworked ground. **1884** *Longm. Mag.* Mar. 486 The ingenuity of inventors..would not allow so fine a field for invention to remain long unworked.

**b.** = UNWROUGHT *ppl. a.* 3 b.

**1883** GRESLEY *Gloss. Coal-m.* 268 *Unwrought* or *Unworked*, coal or other mineral which has not been mined or worked away.

**Unwo·rker.** *rare.* [UN-¹ 12.] = NON-WORKER. **1843** CARLYLE *Past & Pr.* I. ii, Workers, Master Workers, Unworkers, all men, come to a pause.

**Unwo·rking,** *ppl. a.* (UN-¹ 10.)

**1696** LOCKE *Lower. Interest* (ed. 2) 43 Lazy and Unworking Shopkeepers in this being worse than Gamesters. **1724** *Briton* No. 24. 105 Petty includes People of all Professions and Offices..in his unworking Tenth of the Nation. **1830** BOWLES *Life Bp. Ken* I. 201 Obese Bishops, oscitant Deans, and 'unworking' Clergy! **1843** CARLYLE *Past & Pr.* III. ix, The partridge-nets of an Unworking Dilletantism. **1848** MILL *Pol. Econ.* v. x. § 3. II. 495 A practice essentially bad, that of converting the working classes into unworking classes.

**Unwo·rkmanlike,** *a.* [UN-¹ 7 c.] Unlike a workman; unworthy of a good workman; badly executed or finished.

**1647** HEXHAM I, Vnworkemanlike, *niet gelijk een werckmeester.* **1730** BAILEY (fol.), *Inartificial*, artless, unworkmanlike. **1756** C. SMART tr. *Horace, Sat.* II. iii. II. 131 What was carved in an unworkman-like manner. **1820** *Edin. Rev.* XXXIII. 354 He tacks them together in such a clumsy and unworkmanlike style. **1873** HAMERTON *Intell. Life* x. i. 338 The unworkmanlike haste with which it was put together. **1895** *Mod. Stm. Eng.* 64 An unfinished, unworkmanlike appearance is imparted to the whole machine.

**Unwo·rkmanlike,** *adv.* (UN-¹ 11 b.) **1727** BAILEY (vol. II), *Inartificially*, artlesly, unworkmanlike.

**Unwo·rkmanly,** *a.* [UN-¹ 7.] Unworkmanlike.

**1542** BALE *Myst Iniq. P. Pantolabus* (1545) 86 b, For lyke an vnworkemanlye dawber he hath done yt with vntempred claye. **1706** PHILLIPS (ed. Kersey), *Inartificial*, being without Art, Artless, Unworkmanly. **1894** *Season* X. 36/1 The quality of the serge is not fine enough to look 'unworkmanly'. *Ibid.* 58/2 Designed for unworkmanly people.

**Unwo·rkmanly,** *adv.* ? *Obs.* [UN-¹ 11.] In a manner uncharacteristic of a good workman.

**1555** WATREMAN *Fardle Facions* Pref. 7 Clad..with rawe felle and hide, full vnworkemanly patched together. **1555** EDEN *Decades* (Arb.) 94 A golden cheyne vnwoorkmanly wrought.

**Unwo·rld,** *v.* [UN-² 6 b.]

**1.** *trans.* To deprive of the qualities of a world; to undo as a world. Also *refl.*

**1647** N. WARD *Simple Cobler* 20 Take away the least *vericulum* out of the world, and it unworlds all, potentially. **1674** N. FAIRFAX *Bulk & Selv.* 155 The worlds driving up to any thing of Gods being, would as much ungod him, and over and above unworld it self. **1875** BROWNING *Aristoph. Apol.* 106 Such world has, of two courses, one to choose: Unworld itself,—or else [etc.]. *Ibid.* 116 'Unworld the world,' frowns he, my opposite. I cry 'Life!'

**2.** To deprive of a share in worldly activities.

**1868** H. BUSHNELL *Serm. Living Subj.* 404 Why is he [*sc.* a soldier] allowed no more to have any world..? Is he thus unworlded to take the mettle out of him?

**Unwo·rldliness.** [f. next, or UN-¹ 12.] Unworldly character.

**1824** CAMPBELL *Theodric* 217 A wildly sweet unworldliness of thought. **1852** ROBERTSON *Serm.* III. xviii. (1857) 266 Unworldliness is this—..to have the world, and not to let the world have us; to be the world's masters, and not the world's slaves. **1874** MAHAFFY *Soc. Life Greece* v. 161 The gentleness and the unworldliness of the man who loved..the world so keenly.

**Unwo·rldly,** *a.* [UN-¹ 7.]

**1.** Of a type transcending or exceeding what is usually found or experienced in the world.

**1707** G. HICKES *Two Treat. Chr. Priesth.* (1711) II. 5 That pre-eminent unworldly Power..which the Spiritual Governours..have over their Spiritual Subjects. **1817** COLERIDGE *Lay Serm.* 73 The impressive example of their unworldly feelings. **1848** AIRD *Chr. Bride* I. xxiv, Sequestered they in love's unworldly dream. **1863** COWDEN CLARKE *Shaks. Char.* xi. 291 They are in another world, and they revel in unworldly thoughts and unworldly associations.

*Comb.* **1805** WORDSW. *Prelude* IV. 290 A wild, unworldly-minded youth.

**b.** Of persons: Actuated by other than worldly or sordid motives; spiritually-minded.

**1825** T. HOOK *Sayings* Ser. II. III. 180, I know you are guileless, Ma'am, and unworldly. **1844** KINGLAKE *Eothen* xx, This unworldly Sphynx has watched and watched like a Providence. **1855** MILMAN *Lat. Chr.* VII. vi. III. 225 The pious but not unworldly merchants of Venice.

**2.** Not belonging to this world; celestial.

**1765** STERNE *Tr. Shandy* VII. vi, That all-powerful fire which..lights the spirits through unworldly tracts!

**Unwo·rmeaten,** *ppl. a.* (UN-¹ 8 b.) **1653** W. RAMESEY *Astrol. Restored* 12 Wood which we desire to keep..unworm-eaten. **Unwo·rmed,** *a.* [UN-¹ 9.] Not worm-eaten. **1895** *Athenæum* 9 Feb. 178/1 The ordinary reader may see a perfect unwormed copy at the British Museum.

† **Unwo·rmed,** *ppl. a. Obs. rare.* [UN-¹ 8.] Of a dog: Not having the lytta or 'worm' removed from the tongue.

**1618** FLETCHER *Women Pleased* IV. iii, She is mad with Love, As mad as ever unworm'd dog was, Signior. **1817** *Gentl. Mag.* July 40/2 Inflicting a penalty on those who neglected it, and the destruction of the dog unwormed.

†**Unwo·rmwooded,** *a.* [UN-¹ 9 b.] Not bitter or caustic. **1628** FELTHAM *Resolves* II. xx. 66 Vn-wormwooded Iests I like well; but they are fitter for the Tauerne, then the Maiestie of a Temple.

**Unwo·rn,** *ppl. a.* [UN-¹ 8 b, c.]

**1.** Not impaired, decayed, or wasted by use, weather, etc.

*a* **1586** SIDNEY *Ps.* VIII. viii, What things els of waters traceth The unworn pathes, his rule embraceth. **1602** J. DAVIES (Heref.) *Mirum in Modum* Wks. (Grosart) I. 29/2 For in Not-beeings bottome, being fast, Ought would to worse then nought, vnworen wast. **1616** *Extr. Aberd. Reg.* (1848) II. 342 Stanes..[that] abyde baith wind and wather, vnworne or consumeit. *a* **1677** BARROW *Serm.* Wks. 1686 II. 98 This great Machine..unimpaired in its beauty, unworn in its parts. **1757** YOUNG *Paraphr. Job* Wks. I. 215 Will the tall Reem..Submit his unworn shoulder to the yoke. **1771** *Phil. Trans.* LXI. 466 Any two of them, that appeared to be perfect and unworn. **1813** BYRON *Giaour* 1059 There read of Cain the curse and crime, In characters unworn by time. **1818** SHELLEY *Julian* 540 The colours of his mind seemed yet unworn. **1877** MRS. OLIPHANT *Makers Flor.* iv. 102 The beautiful countenance yet unworn with anything worse than the sweet sorrows of a visionary love. **1883** 'OUIDA' *Wanda* I. 41 Those cool, vast, unworn mountain solitudes.

**b.** Not worn or thrown *off.*

**1748** RICHARDSON *Clarissa* VII. lxxviii. 258 The unworn-off effects of the midnight revel.

**c.** Not exhausted or worn out.

**1882** PUSEY *Paroch. & Cathedr. Serm.* vi. 80 A dull heavy temper He will transform into patient unworn endurance for love of Jesus.

**2.** Free from deterioration or weakening; unimpaired, fresh.

**1757** BURKE *Sublime & Beautiful* Introd. ad fin., In the morning of our days, when the senses are unworn and tender. **1831** CARLYLE *Sartor Res.* II. iii, The unworn Spirit is strong. **1846** C. BRONTE in Mrs. Gaskell *Life* (1857) II. 5 While their minds are mostly unemployed, their sensations are all unworn. **1855** BROWNING *In Three Days* i, See how I come, unchanged, unworn!

*absol.* **1851** HELPS *Comp. Solit.* xi. 214 The knowledge to be gained [by travel]..is for the young and the unworn.

**3.** Of dress, etc.: Not hitherto worn; not actually worn.

**1798** S. & HT. LEE *Canterb. T.* II. 226 One who appeared to him to be adorned with the unworn jewels of the Marchioness. **1819** WORDSW. *Misc. Sonn.* I. xxi, [She] Put on fresh raiment—till that hour unworn. **1861** WHYTE MELVILLE *Good for Nothing* I. 140 And yet..the white dress..might have been consigned unworn to its place in the wardrobe. **1894** *Daily News* 7 April 5/3 [In this] painting of Mr. Gladstone..the pince-nez would have been better unworn.

**Unwo·rried,** *ppl. a.* (UN-¹ 8.)

[**1775** ASH.] **1818** KEATS *Endym.* I. 75 Not one fleecy lamb..but pass'd unworried By angry wolf. **1899** SIR E. RUSSELL *That reminds me* 197 All..have lady typewriters constantly at work. They look cool and unworried, and receive a caller [etc.].

† **Unwo·rship,** *sb.*¹ *Obs.* [OE. *unweorþscipe* (UN-¹ 12).]

**1.** Absence of honour, respect, or reverence; dishonour; disgrace.

In frequent use from *c* 1400 to *c* 1450.

*c* **888** K. ÆLFRED *Boeth.* xxvii. § 2 Hwæþer þu nu mæge onȝitan hu micelne unweorðscipe se anwald brengð þam unmedeman ȝif he hine underfehð? *c* **1200** *Vices & Virtues* 53 For ðare unwurscipe ðe me nimð hit al swa unwurðliche swa me nimð ðat bread (of ðæ borde). **13..** *Guy Warw.* (A.) 1857 Unworþschip it wer to me, ȝif y schuld iusti wiþ þe. *a* **1395** HYLTON *Scala Perf.* II. ii. (Bodl. MS.), Þe trespas and þe vnworschip was endeles greet. *c* **1430** *Pilgr. Lyf Manhode* II. xvii. (1869) 81 Wurshipe,..what seyst thou? the unwurshipe is thine. *c* **1440** *Jacob's Well* 165 ȝif þou sodaynly..brekyst out woordys of vnworschype to god. *a* **1470** H. PARKER *Dives & Pauper* (W. de W. 1496) IV. i. 160/2 Thus for scornyng & vnworshyp that the sone dyde to the fader began fyrste boundage.

**2.** An act or instance of disgrace or dishonour; a slight. *rare.*

*c* **1200** *Vices & Virtues* 97 After maniȝe unwurðscipes ðe he for me hier þolede. **1387-8** T. USK *Test. Love* I. v. (Skeat) l. 24 Why, than,..suffre ye such wrong..? Me semeth, to you it is a greet unworship.

**Unwo·rship,** *sb.*² *rare*—¹. [UN-¹ 12 + WORSHIP *sb.*] Lack or absence of divine worship.

**1860** PUSEY *Min. Proph.* 75 All half-belief is unbelief; all half-repentance unrepentance, all half-worship is unworship.

† **Unwo·rship,** *v. Obs.* [UN-² 3.] *trans.* To deprive of honour or dignity; to treat with indignity, disrespect, or irreverence. Also *refl.*

*c* **1380** WYCLIF *Wks.* (1880) 462 Men seyen þat þe pope wole biclippe worldly worchip, & not trewe men for goddis sake, lest he vnworchipe hym silf. **1387-8** T. USK *Test. Love* II. vi. (Skeat) l. 125 Yet is he worthy, for shrewdnesse, to be unworshipped. *a* **1425** tr. *Arderne's Treat. Fistula*, etc. 75 Þerfor it schal noȝt vnworschip [*overlined* ne schame] a lech for to spede profitabily with fewer þings and liȝter. *c* **1450** *Mirk's Festial* I. 87 Þe lest synne þat a man doth, hyt vnworschypyth God. *a* **1470** H. PARKER *Dives & Pauper* (W. de W. 1496) II. i. 110/2 Graunte vs grace no thynge to do..wherby thy name sholde be vnworshyped or ashamed in vs.

Hence † **Unwo·rshipping** *vbl. sb. Obs.*

**1382** WYCLIF *Ecclus* i. 38 Lest parauenture thou falle, and bringe to thi soule vnwrsheping [L. *inhonorationem*]. *c* **1400** LOVE *Bonavent. Mirr.* (1908) 154 The cause was for the gostly fire of his zele,..for the vnworschyppynge of his fader. *c* **1450** *Myrr. our Ladye* 208 The vnworshypynge and offense of god.

**Unwo·rshipful,** *a.* [UN-¹ 7.]

**1.** Unworthy or devoid of esteem or honour.

*c* **1374** CHAUCER *Boeth.* III. met. iv. (1868) 75 Nero..ȝaf somtyme to þe dredeful senatours þe vnworshipful setes of dignites. *c* **1471** FORTESCUE *Wks.* (1869) 456 Indygence in them is not only unworschipfull, but yt may do the most harme. *a* **1664** FRANK *Serm.* (1672) 206 That poor contemptible condition, and unworshipful pickle they found Him in. **1851** CARLYLE *Sterling* I. v, Its high dignitaries..; its worships and worships unworshipful:..a mad world, my masters.

**2.** Characterized by lack of divine worship.

**1862** FABER *Hymn*, '*The Unbelieving World*' i, The wide-spreading world, How lovely..it seems, How full of realities, pure and divine, Yet how bent on unworshipful dreams! **1893** W. A. BARTLETT in *Advance* (Chicago) 21 Dec., So long as the churches are willing to worship in an unworshipful way by proxy.

†**Unwo·rshiply,** *adv.* [UN-¹ 11.] Irreverently.

**1303** R. BRUNNE *Handl. Synne* 981 Ne þou shalt swere vnwurschyply [F. *folement*], By oure lorde.

**Unwo·rshipped,** *ppl. a.* [UN-¹ 8.] Not worshipped or adored; not held in reverence or esteem.

*a* **1395** HYLTON *Scala Perf.* II. xiv. (Bodl. MS.), Vnresonabli he werkiþ þat loueþ not þe souereyn good,..þat is god vnsouȝt and vnloued, vnknowen and vnworschipid. *c* **1430** *Life St. Kath.* (1884) 42 Whom þou byddest be wyth oute worshep hit schal be suffisant to hem to abyde in her owne houses vnworscheped. *a* **1513** FABYAN *Chron.* VII. (1811) 452 The holye seruyce of God [has been] lefte, and holye churche vnworshypped and vnhonouryd. **1587** GOLDING *De Mornay* 595 Had it not bene a cryme to haue left them vnworshipped for Gods? **1667** MILTON *P. L.* v. 667 He resolv'd..to..leave Unworshipt, unobey'd, the Throne supream. **1796** B. S. BARTON *Mem. Fasc. Faculty Rattlesnake* 17 The former [Being]..was merely acknowledged and named, but unworshipped and neglected. **1837** CARLYLE *Fr. Rev.* I. I. i, Thus..had this grand-nephew of the great Richelieu to glide about; unworshipped by the world. **1850** S. DOBELL *The Roman* viii, Oft the unworshipp'd angel passeth While we..adore his footsteps in the sand.

**Unwo·rshipping,** *ppl. a.* (UN-¹ 10.) **1828** WEBSTER (citing J. M. Matthews), *Unworshiping*, a., not worshiping; habitually neglecting the worship of God. **1906** BP. MOULE in *Off. Rep. Church Congress* 411 In this day of unchastened, uncontrite, unworshipping thought upon religion.

**Unwo·rth,** *sb.* [UN-¹ 12. Cf. Du. *onwaarde*, G. *unwerth*, Da. *uværd* worthlessness; also WANWORTH *sb.*]

† **1.** Lack of merit or desert. *Obs. rare.*

**1340** *Ayenb.* 35 Þe þridde manere of gavelinge is ine ham þet habbeþ onworþ to lene of hire hand. *Ibid.* 270 Dyad he [*sc.* Christ] is, þou hest hueruore: and to sterue þou hest onworþ?

**2.** Lack or absence of worth; unworthiness.

**1835** CARLYLE in Froude *Life* (1884) I. 41 Do you reckon..that style (mere dictionary style) has much to do with the worth or unworth of a book? **1872** RUSKIN *Fors Clav.* xiv. 9 Nature and Heaven command you..to discern worth from unworth in everything. **1896** A. AUSTIN *England's Darling* III. i, Why hath the King Laid this great meed on my unworth?

† **Unwo·rth,** *a.*¹ *Obs.* [OE. *unweorþ, unwurþ*, etc. (UN-¹ 7), = OHG. *unwërd* (MHG. *unwërt*, G. *unwerth*), MLG. *unwert*, MDu. *onwert, onwerd*, etc. (Du. *onwaard*), ON. *úverðr*. Cf. WANWORTH *a.*]

**1.** = UNWORTHY *a.* 1-3: **a.** Of persons.

*c* **893** K. ÆLFRED *Oros.* IV. vii. § 4 Æt þæm feorðan cirre hie sendon Hannan heora þone unweorðestan þeȝn, & he hit abæd. *c* **1000** *Rule of Chrodegang* 70 Preost þe bið cypa & of þam arist of wædlan to rican men, & of unwurðum men to wurðfullum. *c* **1200** *Vices & Virtues* 5 Sume oðre forlæteþ ðe world..and sone hem seluen healdeð for hali, and unwurð healdeþ of oðre. *c* **1205** LAY. 3464 He biðe vnworð & lah þe mon þe litul ah. *c* **1230** *Hali Meid.* 33 ȝif þu iwurðest him unwurð, & he ase unwurð þe. *c* **1275** *Prov. Ælfred* 316 (Trin. Coll. MS.), Swo is moni gadeling godelike on horse, wlanc on weiȝe, and unwurþ on wike. **1340** *Ayenb.* 132 Þeruore þe uerþe stape is of þise uirtue: wylni to by y-knawe, and y-healde uor uyl and onworþ. *c* **1425** in *Minor Poems fr. Vernon MS.* 641/143 For þou vnworthe resawes me [= Christ], Þu belewys noȝt þat I suld be he. **1603** M. M. *Ane Godlie Dreame* xviii, O wretch vnworth, my dayes ar vainlie spent.

**b.** Of things.

*c* **960** ÆTHELWOLD *Bened. Rule* (Schröer) 138 Þæt heora heortan furþum mid wacum mettum and unweorþum ne syn ofersymede. *c* **1205** LAY. 24656 And elche untuhtle Heo talden vnwurðe. *a* **1250** *Owl & Night.* 770 Vuel strengþe is lutel wrþ Ac wisdom ne wrþ neuer vnwrþ. *c* **1320** *Cast. Love* 1112 Woldestou þi finger ȝeue.. So vnworth and so vyl chaffare to bugge? **1340** *Ayenb.* 215 Ase þe werm is uoul, and lite, þing onworth.

**c.** With dative, or with preps. (esp. *to*).

*c* **888** K. ÆLFRED *Boeth.* xxviii, Hu ne wes he þeah ælcum witum lað & unweorð? *c* **1000** ÆLFRIC *Saints' Lives* xvi. 367 Se idela ȝylp us beo æfre unwurð. *c* **1175** *Lamb. Hom.* 49 His breowe beoð aweriede and unwurðe gode. *c* **1200** *Trin. Coll. Hom.* 89 Þe alre unwurþeste wig one to riden. *a* **1225** *Leg. Kath.* 1531 Stille þine wordes, for ha beoð me unwurð. *a* 1225 *Ancr. R.* 50 Þe blake cloð bitockneð þæt ȝe beoð blake & unwurðe toward þe worlde wiðuten. *c* 1300 *Beket* 653 Unworth ich am of holi churche wardeyn forto beo. 1340 *Ayenb.* 49 Þis zenne is zuo onworþ to gode, þet he dede rine uer berninde..ope þe cite of sodome.

**2.** Undeserved; = UNWORTHY *a.* 4 a. *rare*[—1].

*a* 1240 *Lofsong* in *O. E. Hom.* I. 207 Bi þe herde hurtes and þe unwurðe wowes ðet he..willeliche þolede.

Hence † **Unwo·rthhead**, contempt. *Obs.*

1340 *Ayenb.* 17 Þe uerste boȝ of prede is ontreuþe, þe oþer onworþhede, þe þridde ouerweninge. *Ibid.* 29 Þe uerþe [sin] is onworþhede of penonce.

**Unwo·rth**, *a.*[2] [UN-[1] 7 + WORTH *a.*] Not worthy of (something); = UNWORTHY *a.* 6. Const. with (*a*) sbs., esp. *while*, or (*b*) vbl. sbs.

(*a*) 1587 TURBERV. *Trag. T.* (1837) 5 Wherein if ought unworth the presse thou finde Unsavorie,..Impute it to the troubles of my minde. 1664 J. WILSON *Projectors* III, Perhaps it may not be unworth your while. 1736 BAILEY *Housh. Dict.* s.v. *Goats*, Which if true or not would not be unworth the while of the curious in anatomy to enquire. 1848 LOWELL *Fable for Critics* 458 You may..deem it not unworth your while to review it. 1903 T. HARDY *Dynasts* I. v. vi, Some poor dolt unworth captivity.

(*b*) 1592 G. HARVEY *Four Lett.* iii. 25 Baggage stuffe, vnwoorth the aunswering, or reading. 1645 MILTON *Tetrach.* 6 Many things might be noted..not ordinary, nor unworth the noting. 1691 J. WILSON *Belphegor* v. iii, He'll tell ye the Story..not unworth your hearing.

† **Unwo·rth**, *v.* *Obs.* [OE. *unweorðian* (f. *unweorþ* UNWORTH *a.*[1]), = MDu. *onwerden*, MLG. *unwerden*, ON. *úvirða*, to slight, etc.; cf. also G. *entwerthen* to deprive of value.]

**1.** *trans.* To treat (a person or thing) disparagingly or with disdain; to slight, despise.

*c* 950 *Lindisf. Gosp.* John viii. 49 Ic diuul ne hafo.., ah ic uorðiȝe faeder min & ȝie un-uorðade mec. *c* 1000 ÆLFRIC in Assmann *Ags. Hom.* 93 Seo cwen..ne unwurðode na þe ænne mid þan, ac ealle þine ealdormenn and eac þine þeȝnas. *c* 1200 *Trin. Coll. Hom.* 181 For we..swo..unwurðeð ure drihten, wurðeð þe deuel. *c* 1200 ORMIN 18285 Hefiȝlike he shameþþ þe & shendeþþ & unnwurrþeþþ. 1340 *Ayenb.* 8 Huo þet onworþeþ his uader and his moder. *Ibid.* 84 Uirtue makeþ wynne heuene, and onworþi þe wordle.

**2.** To dishonour (something).

*c* 1200 *Trin. Coll. Hom.* 213 He sholde..noht shenden godes shafte,..ne swo unwurðin godes handiwerc.

**Unwo·rthily**, *adv.* [f. UNWORTHY *a.*, or UN-[1] 11. Cf. MDu. *onwerdichlike* (Du. *onwaardiglijk*), MLG. *unwerdichliken*, MHG. *unwirdec-*, *unwërdeclîche* (G. *unwürdiglich*); also ON. *uvirðiliga*, *-uliga* scornfully.]

**1.** Without being worthy, fit, or qualified; without having sufficient merit or ability; unmeritedly.

*c* 1290 *Beket* 654 in *S. Eng. Leg.* I. 125 Luytel wuyrth ich am of holi churche wardein for-to beo, And al-so vnwurthþeliche þar-to i-nome. 1303 R. BRUNNE *Handl. Synne* 3037 Vnwrþyly art þou made gentyl ȝyf þou yn wurdys and dedys be yl. *a* 1340 HAMPOLE *Psalter* lxx. 1 As þai sall be [shamed] þat here vnworthily resayfes fals honurs. *c* 1410 *Lanterne of Liȝt* 60 Whanne þei resceyue þe sacramentis, þei gon to hem vnworþili. 1526 TINDALE 1 *Cor.* xi. 27 Whosoevere shall ..drynke off the cuppe vnworthely. *a* 1586 SIDNEY *Arcadia* I. xiii, My name is Basilius, unworthily Lord of this country. 1670 MILTON *Hist. Eng.* III. Wks. 1851 V. 96 So hee..enjoy'd unworthily the rewards of lerning and fidelity. 1849 ROCK *Ch. of Fathers* I. 269 Acknowledging that whatsoever they had, was bestowed unworthily upon each one of them by God.

**2.** In a manner falling short of one's worth, excellence, or merit; without contributory fault or demerit; undeservedly.

Not always clearly distinguishable from sense 3.

*a* 1340 HAMPOLE *Psalter* lxxiii. 23 Rise god,..damyn þat þou ert vnworthily handelde of ill prestis. 1509 BARCLAY *Shyp of Folys* 25 But he and all his were murdred for theyr hyre. And nat vnworthely. 1598 YONG *Diana* 59, I bewailed my great mishap, knowing that he, whom most of al I loued, had so vnwoorthily forgotten me. 1607 E. GRIMSTONE tr. *Goulart's Mem. Hist.* 327 Marryed to an honest Gentlewoman, whom he entreated most unworthily. 1634 SIR T. HERBERT *Trav.* 83 [Nicanor] beginnes with Antiochus, sonne of Alexander, whom vnworthily he slue. 1712 STEELE *Spect.* No. 497 ¶ 4 Can any thing shew your Holiness how unworthily you treat Mankind? 1784 T. TWINING in *Recreat. & Stud.* (1882) 129 The Dean and Chapter..lay all the blame on him for suffering Johnson to be so unworthily interred. 1829 SIR W. NAPIER *Penins. War* II. 263 This arrangement was adopted after a struggle in the cabinet..; nevertheless, sir John Cradock was used unworthily.

**b.** Without sufficient appreciation; in an undervaluing or disparaging manner; derogatorily.

1599 HAKLUYT *Voy.* II. II. 135 Either thinking too worthily of the Spaniards valure,..or too vnworthily of them that vndertooke this iourney against him. 1651 HOBBES *Leviath.* II. xxxi. 190 That those Philosophers, who sayd the World, or the Soule of the World was God, spake unworthily of him. 1725 BROOME *Pope's Odyss.* Notes VII. II. 150 If then we look upon the Odyssey as all fiction, we consider it unworthily. *a* 1768 SECKER *Serm.* (1771) V. 416 Imagining that God can enjoin religious Cruelties,..is thinking..unworthily and absurdly of him.

**3.** In an unworthy, unbecoming, or improper manner; unbecomingly, unfitly, improperly.

1377 LANGL. *P. Pl.* B. xv. 238 And þat conscience and cryst hath yknitte faste, Þei vndon it vnworthily, þo doctours of lawe. 1390 GOWER *Conf.* III. 169 Whan thou to such on as schal deie The worschipe of thi god aweie Hast yoven so unworthely. *c* 1449 PECOCK *Repr.* IV. i. 416 Summe ..vniustli and vnworthili blamen and vndirnymen the clergie. 1456 SIR G. HAYE *Govt. Princes* (S.T.S.) 82 A prince..for.. lusty delytis destroyand his awin gudis unworthily. 1535 COVERDALE 2 *Macc.* v. 16 Them toke he in his hondes vnworthely, & defyled them. 1663 BP. PATRICK *Parab. Pilgr.* xxx, Thou blushest not..to think and do most unworthily, being altogether insensible of thy own Nature. *a* 1677 BARROW *Serm.* Wks. 1686 III. 63 In being discontented we behave our selves very unbeseemingly and unworthily. 1847 TENNYSON *Princ.* v. 177 One loves the soldier, one The silken priest of peace, one this, one that, And some unworthily. 1875 WHITNEY *Life Lang.* viii. 136 The name of Georgium Sidus, with which..it was unworthily sought to flatter a monarch.

† **4.** With indignation or resentment. *Obs. rare.*

In quots. tr. L. *indigne* (*ferens*).

1382 WYCLIF 2 *Macc.* vii. 39 The kyng kyndlid with wrath, ..berynge vnworthily hym self scornyd. — *Mark* xiv. 4 Ther weren summe beringe vnworthily, or heuyli, with ynne hem silf.

**Unwo·rthiness.** [f. as prec., or UN-[1] 12.]

**1.** The character or quality of being unworthy; lack of worth, absence of merit. † Occas. with *to*.

*a* 1340 HAMPOLE *Psalter* ci. 18 Þat knawis þaire frelte & vnworthynes. *c* 1400 LOVE *Bonavent. Mirr.* (1908) 119 With grete drede of hir vnworthinesse that hir teres schulde touche oure lordes feete. 1447 BOKENHAM *Seyntys* (Roxb.) 2 The unwurthynesse Bothe of hys persone and eek hys name. 1485 *Rolls of Parlt.* VI. 274/1 The aforesaid Actes of Atteindre or Forfeiture, disableing, unworthi[n]esse, and unableing. 1526 *Pilgr. Perf.* (W. de W. 1531) 169 b, The vylenesse, vnkyndnesse, & vnworthynesse of man to that loue. 1582 BENTLEY *Mon. Matrones* III. 278 Not remembering, good Lord, mine vnworthinesse..nor frailtie of my passed yeeres. 1631 GOUGE *God's Arrows* III. § 22. 223 Mans unworthinesse and unfitnesse to appeare in Gods sight. 1675 DRYDEN *Aurengz.* IV. i. 1784 You will be kind to my Unworthiness. 1712 STEELE *Spect.* No. 448 ¶ 1 For Men..do not keep up a lively Abhorrence of the least Unworthiness. 1771 *Junius Lett.* xlvi. (1772) II. 173 The people..would probably overlook his immediate unworthiness. 1855 MACAULAY *Hist. Eng.* xvii. IV. 60 It would be absurd to reject, on account of his unworthiness, the inestimable services which it was in his power to render. 1884 A. R. PENNINGTON *Wiclif* viii. 255 The unworthiness of the ministers hinders not the effect of the Sacrament.

**b.** With *an* (and pl.), *that*, *this*.

1533 BELLENDEN *Livy* II. vi. (S.T.S.) I. 149 Traisting to revenge this vnwourthynes be sum..hardy Interprise. 1653 JER. TAYLOR *Serm. for Year* I. xxiii. 304 If it [*sc.* jesting] mingles with any sin, it puts on the nature of that new unworthinesse. 1856 F. W. FABER *Creator & Creature* III. i, The very unworthinesses and short-comings of the creature. 1880 'OUIDA' *Moths* II. 85, I think such a marriage a great unworthiness, a great disgrace.

**c.** With poss. pron., as a fictitious title.

1853 KINGSLEY *Hypatia* I. 239 Pambo asked his name... 'My unworthiness is called Peter the Reader.'

† **2.** Inappropriate or improper action. *Obs.*[—1]

1608 in *Buccleuch MSS.* (Hist. MSS. Comm.) I. 76 It was unworthiness in your Majesty's officers to find him for a Ward.

† **Unwo·rthly**, *a.* *Obs.* [OE. *unweorþlic* (UN-[1] 7).] Of little consequence or worth; base, mean.

*c* 1230 *Hali Meid.* 33 Ȝif þu art unwurðlich & wraðeliche ilatet. 13.. *E. E. Allit. P.* B. 305 With her vn-worþelych werk me wlatez with-inne. 1340 *Ayenb.* 132 Huanne þe man þoleþ in þolemodnesse þet he by uoulliche y-draȝe, and ase persone onworþlych.

† **Unwo·rthly**, *adv.* *Obs.* [OE. *unweorþlice* (UN-[1] 11), = MDu. *onwerdelike* (Du. *onwaardelijk*), MLG. *unwerde-*, *unwertliken*, OHG. *unwerdlîhho* (MHG. *unwertlîche*).] = UNWORTHILY *adv.* 1–3.

*c* 1200 *Trin. Coll. Hom.* 99 Ech þe understandeð þat holi husel unwurðliche. *c* 1200 [see UNWORSHIP *sb.* 1]. *a* 1225 *Ancr. R.* 130 Vor heo witeð unwurðliche ancre nome, & al þet heo euer wurcheð. 13.. R. BRUNNE *Handl. Synne* 981 Ne þou shalt swere vnwurschyply [*Dulwich MS.* vn-wurþly; F. *folement*], By oure lorde. *a* 1400–50 *Alexander* (D.) 869 Vnworthly þou wroght.. When þou was bowne with a brande my body to shende.

† **Unwo·rthness.** *Obs.* [OE. *unweorþnes* (UN-[1] 12) in sense 1, = OHG. *unwerdnissa*.]

**1.** Contempt, scorn.

1340 *Ayenb.* 9 Wreþe oþer onworþnesse þet geþ liȝtliche.. uor to harmi oþren. *Ibid.* 19 Zuo is onworþnesse [*glossed* despit] þet is wel grat zenne.

**2.** Worthlessness.

1587 R. HOVENDEN in *Collect.* (O.H.S.) I. 212 Neyther.. ded [he] respecte..rather the unworthenes of the lease then the..benefitt of the Colledge.

**Unworthy** (*vnwv̄·ɹði*), *a.*, *adv.*, *sb.* [UN-[1] 7. Cf. MDu. *onwerdich* (Du. *onwaardig*), OS. *unwerdig*, MLG. *unwerdich*, OHG. *unwirdîg* (MHG. *unwirdic*, *-ec*, G. *unwürdig*), ON. *úverðugr* (Norw. *uverdug*, Sw. *ovärdig*, Da. *uværdig*), also UNWORTH and WANWORDY *adjs.*]

**A.** *adj.* **I. 1.** Of things: Deficient in worth; having little or no value; worthless.

In later use chiefly ellipt. from 3 b.

*a* 1240 *Wohunge* in *O. E. Hom.* I. 281 Ne was neauer unwurði þing chepet swa deore. 1375 BARBOUR *Bruce* IV. 196 Ane hamelat neir thair-by, A litill toune and vnworthy. 1398 TREVISA *Barth. De P. R.* XVII. cxv. (Bodl. MS.), Barlich ..haþ þe fouleste strawe of alle corne & vnworthieste stobles. *c* 1440 *Gesta Rom.* xiii. 43 Loo! what I haue suffred for the, where as I put non vnworthier thing for the then my owne body. *c* 1445 PECOCK *Donet* 33 Whanne a man..beriþ in his hond sum pore vnworþi sticke. *c* 1532 DU WES *Introd. Fr.* in *Palsgr.* 896 Myn accustomed poore and unworthy servyce. 1599 SHAKS. *Hen. V*, I. ii. 228 France being ours, wee'l bend it to our Awe..Or lay these bones in an vnworthy Vrne. 1618 J. TAYLOR (Water P.) *Penniless Pilgr.* D 2, My poore vnable and vnworthy pen. 1634 BP. HALL *Contempl.*, *N. T.* IV. vi, Our weak and unworthy prayers. 1697 DRYDEN *Virg. Georg.* II. 517 Whose leaves..become the unworthy browse Of buffaloes. 1819 SHELLEY *Cenci* III. i. 129 These limbs, the unworthy temple of Thy spirit. 1854 *Poultry Chron.* II. 78/1 To withhold..prizes in any of the classes in which the specimens are deemed unworthy.

**b.** Not reputable; hurtful or injurious to reputation; discreditable.

1693 DRYDEN *Exam. Poet.* Ded. ¶ 1 A kind of contempt for those who have risen by unworthy ways. 1735 THOMSON *Liberty* III. 376 Unworthy joys! that wasteful leave behind ..No secret ray to glad the conscious soul. 1795–6 WORDSW. *Borderers* I. 255, I suspect unworthy tales Have reached his ear. 1813 SHELLEY *Q. Mab* v. 163 Blunting the keenness of his spiritual sense With narrow schemings and unworthy cares. 1882 BESANT *All Sorts* xxvi, She repressed her indignation at this unworthy suggestion.

**2.** Of persons: Not worthy; lacking worth or merit; undeserving; hence, despicable, contemptible.

*a.* *a* 1240 *Wohunge* in *O. E. Hom.* I. 279 Schomeliche spateling of unwurði ribauz. *a* 1300 *Cursor M.* 23882 Amang þaa hirdes am i an, Sa wreche vnworthi wat i nan. *c* 1375 *Ibid.* 20015 (Fairf.), Al if I be vn-worþi man. *c* 1400 MAUNDEV. (Roxb.) iii. 10 He pryues þaim þat him think vnworthy. 1456 SIR G. HAYE *Law Arms* (S.T.S.) 302 Quhen princis prayis for unworthy personis, God is offendit. 1535 COVERDALE *Ecclus.* xxix. 32 Yet shall he be taken as vnworthy, & heare many bytter rough wordes. 1596 SHAKS. *Merch. V.* II. i. 37 So may I..Misse that which one vnworthier may attaine. 1617 WOODALL *Surg. Mate* Pref., Wks. (1639) B 3, Unworthy impostors under the names of Surgeons. 1686 W. DE BRITAINE *Hum. Prud.* xi. 49 External Fortunes may befal the unworthyest Persons. 1737 E. LEWIS *Let. to Swift* 30 June, [A] family..brought to ruin by that unworthy man lord Kinnoul. 1823 SCOTT *Quentin D.* xv, Campo-basso, the unworthy favourite of Duke Charles, with..his base, treacherous spirit. 1835 JAMES *Gipsy* iii, An unworthy blackguard of that name. 1846 MRS. A. MARSH *Father Darcy* II. viii. 136 The authority confided to me—unworthy—by the church.

*absol.* *c* 1400 tr. *Secreta Secret.*, *Gov. Lordsh.* 52 He þat geuys þe giftys..to vnworthy and to hem þat has non nede. 1555 EDEN *Decades* (Arb.) 59 Fortune..sumtymes fauoureth the vnworthyest. 1602 [see SPURN *sb.*[1] 4]. *a* 1658 LOVELACE *Poems* (1659) 30 'Tis the same wrong th' unworthy to inthrone. 1864 FOX tr. *K. Ælfred's Boeth.* (1895) 97 Canst thou now understand how great dishonour power brings on the unworthy when he receives it?

*β.* *c* 1475 *Cath. Angl.* 424/1 (A.), Vn Wordy, *jndignus*, *jgnobilis*. 1796 R. GALL *Tint Quey* (1819) 29 This is a bonny speech..To come frae your unwordy head. *c* 1820 HOGG *Tales & Sk.* (1837) II. 147 Ah! the unwordy rascal!

**b.** Conventionally or devotionally used as an expression of humility.

*c* 1532 DU WES *Introd. Fr.* in *Palsgr.* 1036 Written by your unworthy servant. 1660 ALLESTRE *Gentl. Calling* 171 O most..bountiful Lord, who..hast in an extraordinary measure abounded to me thy unworthiest Servant. *a* 1700 in *Cath. Rec. Soc. Publ.* IX. 334 S[tr] Agnes of the Jnfant Jesus. Priouresse unworthy. 1754 *Ibid.* VIII. 249 S[iste]r Agnes Howard Abbess unw[orth]y.

**3.** With const. Not of sufficient merit, excellence, or worth. **a.** With *to* (Sc. † *till*) and inf. (Chiefly of persons.)

*a* 1300 *Cursor M.* 14927 Crist and his moder do me to spede! Þat vn-worthi es for to rede. *a* 1310 in Wright *Spec. Lyric P.* 73 Jesu, thah ich be unworthi To love the. *c* 1400 *Destr. Troy* II. 629, I wot me vnworthy þis wirdis to fall. *c* 1449 PECOCK *Repr.* IV. iii. 428 Thanne bi lijk argument..ech gouernaunce and ech thing..weren vnleeful and vnworthi to be had and vsid. *c* 1450 *St. Cuthbert* (Surtees) 2709, I am vnworthy.. Slike hy degre to come toward. 1526 *Pilgr. Perf.* (W. de W. 1531) 84 b, Proclamynge themselfe synners & vnworthy to lyue. 1563 A. NOWELL in *Lett. Lit. Men* (Camden) 21 [To] iudge whether it [= his MS. Catechism] were not unwoorthie..to be maide publike. 1651 HOBBES *Leviath.* II. xxvii. 159 He..is..thought unworthy to have any charge, or preferment in Warre. 1667 MILTON *P. L.* XII. 91 Since hee [*sc.* man] permits Within himself unworthie Powers to reign Over free Reason. 1671 — *P. R.* IV. 346 The rest [are]..unworthy to compare With Sion's songs. 1715 POPE *Iliad* II. 862 His troops in forty ships Podarces led,.. Nor he unworthy to command the host. 1789 COWPER *Queen's Visit* 67 The cumb'rous throng, Not else unworthy to be fear'd. 1827 POLLOK *Course T.* I. 121 Unworthy is your servant To stand in presence of the King. 1865 KINGSLEY *Herew.* xl, His soul, unworthy to be delivered from evil.

**b.** With *of*, † *to*, † *for* (something specified), or clause.

1382 WYCLIF *Tobit* iii. 19 Or I was vnwrthi to hem, or thei parauenture to me weren not wrthi. — *Acts* xiii. 46 Ȝe..han demed vs vnworthi of [1388 to] euere lasting lyf. *c* 1386 CHAUCER *Clerk's T.* 359 Lord, vndigne and vnworthy Am I, to thilke honour. 1565 COOPER *Thesaurus*, *Amicitia indigni*, vnworthy of friendship. 1589 HAKLUYT *Voy.* To Rdr. ¶ 9, I accompt him vnworthy of future fauours. 1608 SHAKS. *Per.* II. v. 40, I am unworthy for her schoolmaster. 1615 SIR W. MURE *Misc. Poems* xiv. 14 Quhich endit ye dayes of this sensuall slaue, Wnwordy the earth sould ȝeild him a graue. 1674 *Jackson's Recant.* A 4, I thought my self unworthy of a forreign Plantation. 1784 COWPER *Task* III. 731 Neglected Nature pines, Abandon'd, as unworthy of our love. 1823 MRS. HEMANS *Siege Valencia* ii. 157 The noble daughter of Pelayo's line Hath nought to ask, unworthy of the name Which is a nation's heritage. 1849 MACAULAY *Hist. Eng.* ii. I. 250 Nor did he appear to the public unworthy of his high fortunes.

**c.** Of superior worth or merit. (Const. *to*.)

1746 FRANCIS tr. *Hor.*, *Sat.* II. ii. 139 Why lives in deep Distress A Man unworthy to be poor?

**4. a.** Of treatment, etc.: Not deserved, warranted, or justified; unmerited.

Chiefly of treatment, fortune, etc., below the deserts or merit of the person or persons concerned.

1382 WYCLIF 2 *Macc.* xiv. 42 Cheesynge for to dye nobly, rather than..aȝeinis his birthis for to be ledd with vnworthi wrongis. *a* 1425 tr. *Arderne's Treat. Fistula* etc. 30 It seemeþ..vnworþi for to vse wele þingis y-giffe þat kan noȝt gette hym mo þingis. 1533 BELLENDEN *Livy* IV. viii, With mony vthir nocht vnwourthy lovingis. 1560 DAUS tr. *Slei-*

*dane's Comm.* 402 b, This vnworthie and lamentable fortune of the Norinbergians. **1596** SPENSER *F. Q.* VI. iv. 34 He inly touched was With tender ruth for her vnworthy griefe. **1603** KNOLLES *Hist. Turks* (1621) 146 [They] ceased not..vntill they had wrought his vnworthie destruction. **1648** T. BEAUMONT *Psyche* VII. cxviii, The holy Travellers through Cold ..And northern Blasts, took their unworthy way. **1700** DRYDEN *Theodore & Hon.* 127 Mov'd with unworthy Usage of the Maid. **1854** TRENCH *Synonyms N. T.* 194 Absolutely unworthy suffering there is none. **1879** FROUDE *Cæsar* xxii. 368 The unworthy treatment of their great enemy.

†**b.** Dishonouring, low, mean. Const. *to*. *Obs.*

**1694** J. COLLIER *Misc. Ess.* I. i. 33 How unworthy and unchristian it is to play upon the Indigence..of another.

**5.** That has not requisite worth or merit; inferior to or below what is merited or deserved; base.

**1533** BELLENDEN *Livy* II. xiv. (S.T.S.) I. 184 Thinkand richt vnworthy þat þare hail sollicitude..was direkkit to na vthir fyne. **1598** YONG *Diana* 130 This villany did the traitor Alfeus work,..for the contempt, which she had of his vnwoorthy affection. **1606** SHAKS. *Ant. & Cl.* III. xiii. 84 Your Cæsars Father oft..Bestow'd his lips on that vnworthy place, As it rain'd kisses. **1662** STILLINGFL. *Orig. Sacræ* III. iii. § 4 Far be such unworthy thoughts from our apprehensions of a Deity. **1760** *Impostors Detected* IV. iii. II. 190, I represented to him how unworthy the profession..was to one of his character. **1820** LAMB *True Story* Wks. 1908 I. 256 A little festival..(though it must bear an unworthier name)..in honour of her guest's recovery.

**b.** Beneath or below, unbecoming or unbefitting, the character, repute, or dignity *of* a person, etc.; not worthy or deserving *of* notice, etc.

**1697** DRYDEN *Æneis* XII. 1156 A wound unworthy of our state to feel. **1700** — *Pref. Fables* ¶ 14 Some people [think] ..these tales..unworthy of my pains. **1733** POPE *Let. to Swift* 2 April, I will take care to suppress things unworthy of him. **1780** *Mirror* No. 73, Some of them are new, and not unworthy of notice. **1869** TOZER *Highl. Turkey* I. 303 A series of domestic tragedies..hardly unworthy of the palace of Atreus at Mycenæ.

**II.** With ellipse of *of*. **6.** Not deserving, meriting, or worthy of. **a.** Of persons. † Also *absol.*

**1382** WYCLIF *Job* xxx. 2 Thei weren trowid vnwrthi that lif [L. *vita ipsa indigni*]. — *Ecclus.* xxv. 11 Blisful..[is he] that seruede not to the vnwrthi hymself [L. *indignis se*]. **1535** *Lett. Suppress. Monast.* (Camden) 103 The poore house which I under God..(though unworthye suche a cure) have hadde mynistration and rule of. *a* **1589** PALFREYMAN *Baldwin's Mor. Philos.* (1600) 64 b, Hee is..much vnworthy honour, that seeketh his owne wealth and oppresseth other. **1600** SHAKS. *Much Ado* II. iii. 216 (Q.), How much he is vnworthy so good a lady. **1634** SIR T. HERBERT *Trav.* 219 Iorwerth..was thought vnworthy the Crowne and dignitie. **1718** POPE *Iliad* IX. 88 Curs'd is the man,.. Unworthy property, unworthy light,..who delights in war. **1794** MRS. RADCLIFFE *Myst. Udolpho* li, She again beheld ..Valancourt unworthy the esteem and tenderness she had once bestowed upon him. **1836** DICKENS *Sk. Boz, New Year*, Until he proves himself unworthy the confidence we repose in him. **1874** DASENT *Half a Life* III. 78 This only shows you are quite unworthy such luck.

**b.** Of things, etc.

**1634** SIR T. HERBERT *Trav.* 207 A place not vnworthy the remembrance. **1661** EARL ORRERY *St. Lett.* (1742) 18 It may not be unworthy your grace's observation, that [etc.]. **1697** DRYDEN *Virg. Georg.* III. 6 All other themes..Are worn with use, unworthy me to write. **1718** PRIOR *Poems* Postscr., A Panegyric, not unworthy the Pen of some future Pliny. **1765** *Museum Rust.* IV. 334 Agriculture..is..not unworthy even the patriot's care. **1809** SYD. SMITH *Serm.* II. 335 Many men..imagine, that this department of medicine is unworthy the name of science. **1832** R. & J. LANDER *Exped. Niger* I. i. 26 Nothing seemed unworthy his acceptance, from fine scarlet cloth to a child's farthing whistle. **1882** *Daily News* 19 Aug. 4/7 Nor is it unworthy notice that [etc.].

**7.** Not befitting or suiting (a person, etc.); derogatory to the dignity, standing, or character of; below the level of.

**1646** H. LAWRENCE *Comm. Angells* 99 Other sins have their aggravations; but this is..the most unworthy a man. **1682** *B. Whitelocke's Mem.* Pref., His posthumous work contains..many things most false, and unworthy so great a name. **1720** POPE *Iliad* XX. 244 Unmanly pride, Unworthy the high race from which we came. **1761** HUME *Hist. Eng.* III. lii. 128 Rigours..unworthy men of their profession. **1798** S. & HT. LEE *Canterb. T., Yng. Lady's T.* II. 394 For her father to expatiate on such baubles, was unworthy both his experience and sex. **1810** SOUTHEY *Kehama* VII. v, The wings of Eagle or of Cherubim Had seem'd unworthy him. **1852** J. H. NEWMAN *Idea of a University* (1873) 53 It would ..have been unworthy a genius..so analytical as Aristotle's, to have laid it down that [etc.]. **1885** 'MRS. ALEXANDER' *At Bay* i, A silly after-glow of boyish folly, unworthy his experience and maturity.

**B.** *adv.* Unworthily; in a manner unworthy *of* (something). Also *ellipt.* (cf. 6–7).

**1661** EARL ORRERY *St. Lett.* (1742) 19 This would engage him to walk not unworthy such an honour. **1708** *Caldwell Papers* (Maitl. Club) I. 217 Our sins in walking unworthy of yᵉ great mercy God hath blest us with. **1740** RICHARDSON *Pamela* (1741) II. 377, I hope I shall not behave unworthy of the good Instructions. **1760–72** H. BROOKE *Fool of Qual.* (1792) V. 43 Letting him know how unworthy he should have acted by his daughter, had he imposed..upon her. **1804** EUGENIA DE ACTON *Tale without Title* III. 7 Let us not act unworthy of beings who have a hope in futurity.

**C.** *sb.* An unworthy person.

Used only in expressed or implied contrast to WORTHY *sb.*

**1616** BRETON *Good & Badde* (title-p.), Descriptions of the Worthies, and Vnworthies of this Age. Where The Best may see their Graces, and the Worst discerne their Basenesse. *a* **1661** FULLER *Worthies* I. (1662) 73 The Worthies of England being your Subject, you have mingled many Unworthies among them. **1886** *Encycl. Brit.* XX. 614/2 John Wilmot..was one of the unworthies of the reign..of Charles II. **1893** E. PEACOCK in *N. & Q.* 22 July 72 Bothwell, Knox,..and other worthies and unworthies of the troubled Marian period.

†**Unwo·rthy**, *v. Obs. rare.* [UN-² 6 a, or f. prec. Cf. UNWORTH *v.*, MHG. *unwirdigen*, and G. *entwürdigen*.]

**1.** *trans.* To dishonour; to do discredit to.

*c* **1230** *Hali Meid.* 35 Þis is sunne, & ec uncunnelicheð þe, & unwurðcheð [*v.r.* unwurdgeð] þi bodi. **1628** FELTHAM *Resolves* II. liii. 156 b, To feed that dispersiue humour, all wayes shall be trodden, though they never so much vnworthy the man.

**2.** To asperse or vilify. Hence **Unwo·rthying** *ppl. a.*

**1654** WHITLOCK *Zootomia* 459 They know not how to raise their slender Merits, but by levelling others that excell them in any thing, with their unworthying Tongues.

**Unwou·nd** (*ʌnwau·nd*), *ppl. a.*¹ [UN-¹ 8 b. Cf. MDu. *onghewonden*, MHG. and older G. *ungewunden*.] Not wound (up).

**1648** HEXHAM II, *Ongewonden*, Vnwound, or Vnwrapped. **1719** J. HUGHES *Morning Apparition* 4 Dumb o'er my pillow hung my watch unwound. **1824** MISS MITFORD *Village* Ser. I. 222 As the hand of an unwound clock stands at one hour of the day. **1897** BRAM STOKER *Dracula* iv, My watch was still unwound.

**Unwou·nd**, *ppl. a.*² [UN-² 8, or f. UNWIND *v.*¹] Released from a coiled or twisted state; untwisted.

**1707** MORTIMER *Husb.* 305 Which Thatching most tie on with Withs, but old pitched Ropes unwound, is much cheaper. **1818** MILMAN *Samor* VIII. 34 The soul, unwound its coarse material chains, Basks in its own divinity.

**Unwou·ndable**, *a.* [UN-¹ 7 b.] Incapable of being wounded.

**1611** COTGR., *Imblessable*, vnhurtable, vnwoundable. **1698** S. CLARKE *Script. Just.* Introd. B 2, In these lie all my strength..and..I hope to be unwoundable. **1731** BAILEY (ed. 2). **1875** TENNYSON *Q. Mary* V. v, Callous with a constant stripe, Unwoundable.

Hence **Unwou·ndableness.** *rare*⁻⁰.

**1660** BLOUNT (ed. 2), *Invulnerability*, unwoundableness.

**Unwou·nded**, *ppl. a.* [OE. *unwundod* (UN-¹ 8), = MDu. *onghewondet* (Du. *ongewond*). Cf. G. *unverwundet*.] Not wounded; unhurt.

*a* **1000** *Genesis* 183 Ne þær ænig com blod of benne, ac him breȝo engla of lice ateah liodende ban, wer unwundod. *c* **1200** ORMIN 14735 All swa summ Ysaac attbrasst Unnwundedd & unnwemmedd. *c* **1350** *Will. Palerne* 1280 Riȝt fewe went a-wey vn-woundet or take. *c* **1400** *Destr. Troy* 10696 Aiax..vnwoundit, i-wis, out of wothe paste. *c* **1450** *St. Cuthbert* (Surtees) 7098 Cuthbert men vnwoundid eschapid. **1502** ATKYNSON tr. *De Imitatione* III. xl. (1893) 229 If thou vse nat on euery hande thy shylde of pacyence, thou shalt nat be longe vnwounded. **1614** TOMKIS *Albumazar* I. vii, With these walk as unwounded as Achilles, Dipp'd by his mother Thetis. **1651** DAVENANT *Gondibert* II. III. xl, Vex'd that the Empire which your wounds did gaine, Was by a young unwounded Army fought! **1700** DRYDEN *Ovid's Met.* XIII. 434 Hector from the Field unwounded went. **1777** POTTER *Æschylus, Choephoræ* 376 [The] envenom'd viper, That poisons with a touch th' unwounded body. **1831** SCOTT *Ct. Rob.* xvi, He covered his eyes with the unwounded hand. **1863** W. C. BALDWIN *Afr. Hunting* vi. 185 An unwounded cow giraffe.

*fig.* and *transf.* **1579** E. K. *Gloss. to Spenser's Sheph. Cal.* Oct. 41 Woundlesse armour, vnwounded in warre, doe rust through long peace. **1622** FLETCHER *Span. Cur.* I. i, We may hear praises when they are deserv'd, Our modesty unwounded. **1624** MASSINGER *Parl. Love* V. i, Provided my fair name Had been unwounded. **1735** POPE *Ep. Lady* 260 She, who can..hear Sighs for a daughter with unwounded ear. **1816** SOUTHEY *Poet's Pilgr.* II. iii. 169 Unwounded here Judæa's balm distill'd Its precious juice. **1818** MILMAN *Samor* IV. 406 The beardless Troilus, Unwounded by soft Cresseide's arrowy eyes.

*absol.* **1768–74** TUCKER *Lt. Nat.* (1834) I. 517, I expect.. that the healed will accompany me as undisturbedly as the unwounded along our future progress.

**Unwo·ven**, *ppl. a.* (UN-¹ 8 b.)

**1429** *Rolls of Parlt.* IV. 360/2 Þe yerne þat leveth unwoven. **1467** *Act 7 Edw. IV*, c. 3 To him or them that espieth or maketh Proof of any such unwoven Yarn. **1566** *Wills & Inv. N. C.* (Surtees, 1835) 260, xv yerds of lining clothe with garne for harden clothe vnwoven. **1648** HEXHAM II, *Ongeweven*, Vnwoven. **1902** *Westm. Gaz.* 1 Oct. 2/3 Death..shakes th' unwoven thread Thridding the shuttle, and the story's told.

†**Unwra·cked**, *ppl. a. Obs.* [UN-¹ 8.] Not wrecked.

**1627** DRAYTON *Elegies, Lady Aston's Depart. Spain* 41 Let them for her sake, Who to thy safeguard doth her selfe betake, Escape vndrown'd, vnwrackt [**1748** unwreck'd].

†**Unwra·ll**, *v. Obs.*⁻¹ [UN-² 3 + WRALL *v.* Cf. UNWARL *v.*] *trans.* To unwind, unroll.

**1387** TREVISA *Higden* (Rolls) I. 9 My witt is ful luyte to unwralle þe wrappynges of so wonder werkes.

**Unwra·p**, *v.* [UN-² 3, 4, 7.]

**1.** *trans.* To remove the wrapping from; to uncover by removing a wrapping or the like. Also *refl.*

Before *c* 1820 somewhat rare; cf. sense 2.

*c* **1386** CHAUCER *Man of Law's Prol.* 5 So soore artow ywoundid That verray nede vnwrappeth al thy wounde hid. **1530** PALSGR. 769/1 Unwrappe this same and looke what is in it. **1580** HOLLYBAND *Treas. Fr. Tong, Dessiller*, to vnwrappe his eies, to restore the sight. *a* **1618** SYLVESTER *Pibrac's Titrastica* lxxxiii, Her spightfull Cords shee can so closely knit, That though at last wee happen to un-wrap us; The print thereof still in our Fames will sit. **1825** J. NEAL *Bro. Jonathan* II. 119 The man-slayer was unwrapping the bundle. **1859** GEO. ELIOT *A. Bede* xxii, He had wrapped the box up in a great many covers, that he might see Hetty unwrapping it with growing curiosity.

*fig.* **1889** R. BRIDGES *Sonn.* xxix, The sun's first rays, That lift the dark west and unwrap the night.

†**b.** *fig.* To unfold, reveal, disclose, explain. *Obs. rare.*

*c* **1374** CHAUCER *Boeth.* IV. pr. vi. (1868) 133 Þou hast ȝeuen ..me to vnwrappen þe hidde causes of þinges. **1593** *Sidney's Arcadia* III. (1629) 366, I will disclose my greatest secret...I will, I say, vnwrap my hidden estate. **1600** FAIRFAX *Tasso* XVII. lxxxvii, That so I could the Catalogue vnwrap Of thy great nephewes, yet vnborne.

**c.** To deliver *out of*, release *from*, free *of*, some envelopment; to liberate or set free. Also *fig.*

**1561** T. NORTON *Calvin's Inst.* I. 12 Like a maze, out of which we can not vnwrapp our selues, vnlesse [etc.]. **1568** EARL OF SUSSEX in E. Lodge *Illustr. Brit. Hist.* (1791) II. 6 And, lastly, to foresee that these Scotts on bothe sydes packe not together, so as to unwrappe..ther mystres owte of all present slaunders, purge her openly [etc.]. **1620** SHELTON *2nd Pt. Don Quix.* xlviii. 321 Vnwrapping him from the Sheet and the Quilt, they pinched him. *c* **1825** BEDDOES *Poems, Torrismond* I. iv, Unwrap me of my years, and hunt me..Into my mother's womb! there unbeget me!

**2.** To open, unwind, or unroll (what is wrapped or wound); † to unfurl (a sail). Also *fig.*

Rare before 19th cent.; cf. sense 1.

**1387** TREVISA *Higden* (MS. Cott. Tib.) fol. 3, Þis matyre.. haþ meny..wyndyngs and wrynkklyngs þat wol noȝt be vnwrappid. *Ibid.*, My wyt ys ful lytel to vnwrappe þe gret hardnes of so wondre werks. **1582** STANYHURST *Æneid* III. (Arb.) 76 Our sayls vnwrapped vphoysing,..thee rough seas deepelye we furrowe. **1807** J. BARLOW *Columb.* III. 821 Where the savage leader lay..[he] directs his eager way, Unwraps the tyger's hide, and strives..To close the wound. **1860** RUSKIN *Unto this Last* ii. (1896) 60 Rags unwrapped from the breasts of goodly soldiers dead. **1894** A. ROBERTSON *Nuggets*, etc. 27 He unwrapped his blankets, [and] spread them on the bed.

**b.** (See quot.)

**1859** T. LUND *Elem. Geom. & Mensuration* III. 316 We may call attention to two cases of curved surfaces, where the surface can be unwrapped, so as to form a plane surface.

**3.** *intr.* To undergo unwrapping or unwinding.

**1833** WHEWELL *Astron.* 218 A stone at the end of a string, when the string is whirled round, and is allowed to wrap round the hand, or to unwrap from it. *c* **1888** YEATS *Poems* (1912) 261 Joy..stirs the young kid's budding horn, And makes the infant ferns unwrap.

**Unwra·pped**, *ppl. a. rare*⁻⁰ [UN-¹ 8.] Not wrapped (up). **1570** LEVINS *Manip.* 51 Vnwrapped, *infasciatus*. **1648** HEXHAM II, *Ongewonden*, Vnwound, or Vnwrapped.

†**Unwra·st**, *a.* (and *sb.*). *Obs.* Forms: 1–3 **unwræst** (3 **-wærste**), **-wreast**, 1, 3–5 **-wrest**, 3–4 **-wreste** (3 *Orm.* **-wresste**); 2–3, 5 **unwraste**, 4–5, *Sc.* 6 **-wrast**. Also 3–4 **on-** (4 **oun-**), 4–5, *Sc.* 6 **vn-**. [OE. *unwrǽst*, *unwrést* (UN-¹ 7).]

**1.** Of a poor, worthless, or vile quality or condition; sorry, miserable; of little account: **a.** Of persons.

*c* **893** K. ÆLFRED *Oros.* III. i. § 5 Hi Læcedemonie..to þon ȝedydon þæt hi hi selfe leton æȝþer ȝe for heane ȝe for unwræste. *c* **1200** *Trin. Coll. Hom.* 29 Vnwreste þu best ȝef þu wreche ne secst hwanne þu time siest. *c* **1205** LAY. 2645 Cuðeð eower kinge, [Bruttus beoþ bolde] ac heo beoð unwræste italde. *a* **1225** *Leg. Kath.* 1260 Hwet nu, unwreste men & wacre þen eni wake! *c* **1350** *Lybeaus Disc.* 2118 The menstrales..Hadde ryche yftes wythalle, And they that weryn unwrest.

**b.** Of things.

*a* **1122** *O. E. Chron.* (Laud MS.) an. 1052, And ȝewendon heom on an to Ealdulfes næse, & wearð him þær on anon unwræste scipe. *c* **1200** *Trin. Coll. Hom.* 29 Ful mai þe þinke, þat forcuðer haueð faire weden and þu unwreste. *c* **1205** LAY. 16307 Þenne þat hæfd is unwræst þe hælp is þæ wurse. *c* **1300** *Havelock* 2821 Him to binden faste Vp-on an asse swiþe un-wraste.

**2. a.** Of persons: Addicted to evil, wickedness, or vice; wicked.

*a* **1225** *Ancr. R.* 124 Þenc hu þe gode holi mon..blescede þe unwreste hond þet hefde ihermed him. *a* **1240** *Wohunge* in *O. E. Hom.* I. 283 And tu..was unwreste folk of world to hoker lahter. **13..** *K. Alis.* (W.) 878 What dostow here, unwrast gome?.. He! fyle ateynte horesone! To misdo was ay thy wone. *c* **1380** *Sir Ferumb.* 2905 Þys schrewede Sarsyns þat wern ounwraste. *c* **1535** M. NISBET *N. T. in Scots* (S.T.S.) III. 349 He..schawis how menn aucht to behaue thaim towart sick as be vnwrast.

*absol.* and as *sb.* *a* **1225** *Ancr. R.* 68 Me ileueð þet vuel sone, & te unwreste bliðeliche lieð on þe gode. *c* **1320** *Castle of Love* 335 Heo him made a-gulte, þulke vn-wreste, And bi-swikide him. *c* **1330** *Arth. & Merl.* 6964 (Kölbing), It were ille, ȝif eueriche vnwrest hadde his wille.

**b.** Of actions, etc.: Characterized by wickedness or evil; iniquitous.

*a* **1122** *O. E. Chron.* (Laud MS.) an. 1131, Ȝif þær wære hure an unwreste wrenc. *a* **1175** *Cott. Hom.* 235 Ac si laȝe sone adiliȝde þurh unwreaste leahtrum. *a* **1250** *Owl & N.* 178 Suche wordes beoþ vnwreste. *c* **1275** LAY. 7033 For þisse onwreste [laȝe] al men him hatede. *c* **1315** SHOREHAM I. 1581 Þanne aȝte..wyues nauȝt aȝens men Non on-wrestnesse werche, Ac þolye, And nauȝt onwrest op-sechen hy. **13..** *Seuyn Sages* (W.) 1917 For mine thre unwrast dede. *c* **1400** *St. Alexius* (Laud 622) 738 Sergeauntz..despised hym fast. Þe wasshyng of her vessel þai cast on hym euerydel, þat was swiþe vnwrast. *c* **1425** *Cursor M.* 9475 (Trin.), Þis foule synne was so vnwrast.

**3.** Untrustworthy, unreliable. Const. *of*. *rare*⁻¹.

**1393** LANGL. *P. Pl.* C. XXI. 313 He were [= would be] vnwrast of hus worde, þat witnesse is of trewþe.

Hence †**Unwra·stness**; also †**Unwra·stship**, wickedness. *Obs.*

*a* **1225** *Ancr. R.* 304 Min owune unwrestschipe hit dude. *c* **1315** [see prec. 2 b]. *c* **1320** *Castle of Love* 1143 For vre vnwrestschupe here þe coroune of þornes on his hed he beere.

†**Unwra·ste**, *adv. Obs.* [UN-¹ 11 b.] = next.

*c* **1205** LAY. 19414 Bruttes..lætten swiðe hokerliche of

Lote..and duden swiðe vnwraste alle his haste. *Ibid.* 2546, 19290, 28415. *a* 1225 *Ancr. R.* 268 Heo beoð to woke, & to unwreste iheorted þet..herdeliche ne uihteð.

† **Unwra·stly,** *adv. Obs.* [OE. *unwrǽstlice*, f. *unwrǽst* UNWRAST *a.*]

**1.** In a weak or feeble manner; weakly, poorly.

*c* 1050 *Byrhtferth's Handboc* in *Anglia* VIII. 334 Þys hiw ealde uðwitan ȝesettan aȝen þam þingum þe zenodotus se eficisca esne unwræstlice ȝesette. *a* 1225 *Ancr. R.* 294 Ȝif þu, þuruh þine ȝemeleaste, werest te erest wocliche [*Trin. MS.* unwreastliche].

**2.** Basely, wickedly.

*c* 1320 *Cast. Love* 1468 Sikerliche vnwrestlyche he deeþ Þat such Fader ne loueþ with al his þouȝt.

**Unwra·thful,** *a.* (UN-¹ 7.) 1542 UDALL *Erasm. Apoph.* Table, Vnwrathfull speakyng. 1548 — *Erasm. Par. Luke* iii. 49 The merciable & vnwrathefull maker of the law euangelicall. 1775 ASH. **Unwra·thfully,** *adv.* (UN-¹ 11.) 1542 UDALL *Erasm. Apoph.* 61 *marg.*, Unwrathfully spoken. *Ibid.* 285 Yᵉ noumbre of thynges unwrathefully & prudentely dooen.

**Unwray,** variant of UNWRY *v. Obs.*

**Unwrea·ked,** *ppl. a.* [UN-¹ 8.] Not revenged or requited; unavenged.

1590 SPENSER *F.Q.* III. xi. 9 How suffrest thou such shamefull cruelty, So long vnwreaked of thine enimy? 1605 *Play of Stucley* in Simpson *Sch. Shaks.* (1878) 208 Who'll let his kinsmans blood unwreaked rest? 1613 CHAPMAN *Rev. Bussy D'Ambois* IV. G 3 b, So wilde, so mad, Shee cannot liue, and this vnwreakt sustaine. 1855 SINGLETON *Virgil* II. 398 Not over me, unwreaked, Nor long, shalt thou..exult, In conquest. 1884 *Macm. Mag.* Nov. 20/1 Unless the accused has an enemy..with an unwreaked grudge against him. 1887 MEREDITH *Ballads & P.* 98 Hoarse for slaughter yet unwreaked.

† **Unwrea·ken,** *ppl. a. Obs.*⁻¹ [UN-¹ 8 b. Cf. OE. *unwrecen.*] = prec. 1592 R. WILMOT *Tancred & Gism.* V. ii. H 1, Shall I then vnwreaken downe descend? Shall I not worke some iust reuenge on him?

**Unwrea·the,** *v.*¹ [UN-² 3. Cf. UNWRITHE *v.*] *trans.* To free from a wreathed or entwined condition; to disentwine, untwist. Also *refl.*

1591 PERCIVALL *Sp. Dict.*, *Destorcer*, to vnwreath, *detorquere.* 1660 BOYLE *New Exp. Phys. Mech.* Digress. 379 The Beards of wilde Oats..continually wreath and unwreath themselves according to the even, light variations of the temperature of the ambient Air. 1731 BAILEY (vol. II), *Unwrithen*, unwreathed, untwisted, straitened. 1810 SOUTHEY *Kehama* XVI. xix, The Beast..Unwreathes his rings and strives to fly. 1822 SHELLEY tr. *Calderon's Mag. Prodig.* III. 75 Leafy Vine, unwreath thy bower.

**Unwrea·the,** *v.*² [UN-² 4.] *trans.* To divest of a wreath or wreaths. (In quot. *absol.*) 1852 GROTE *Greece* II. lxx. IX. 137 Probably the operations of wreathing and unwreathing must here have been performed by the soldiers symbolically. **Unwrea·thed,** *a. rare*⁻⁰. [UN-¹ 9.] Wreathless. 1731 BAILEY (vol. II), *Unwreathed*, ..without a wreath. **Unwre·cked,** *ppl. a.* (UN-¹ 8.) 1748 [see UNWRACKED]. 1775 ASH. 1896 R. BRIDGES *Fair Brass* ii, An effigy of brass..Lieth in the sombre aisle Of this old church unwreckt.

† **Unwree·,** *v. Obs.*⁻¹ [UN-² 3 + WREE *v.*] *trans.* To free (a person) from accusation; to clear.

*a* 1225 *Ancr. R.* 308 Ȝif þu wreiest þe wel her, God wule unwreien [L. *excusat*] þe þer.

† **Unwre·nch,** *sb. Obs.* [OE. *unwrenc* (UN-¹ 4 b, 12).] An evil or base trick, artifice, or turn; a vice or sin.

*c* 897 K. ÆLFRED *Gregory's Past. C.* xxxiii. 215 Ða ȝeðyld ..for ðæm unwrence ðære unȝeðylde..he forlet. *a* 1023 WULFSTAN *Hom.* 54 Mid ðam unwrencan bið Antecrist eal afylled. *c* 1200 *Trin. Coll. Hom.* 79 Ȝif þe unfele man..mid felefolde wiȝeles teð him to unwrenches. *a* 1225 *Ancr. R.* 268 Vor þet is his unwrench..þet holi men mest dredeð. *c* 1250 *Owl & N.* 169 Ne speddestu noȝt mid þine unwrenche, For ich am war.

**Unwre·nch,** *v.* [UN-² 9.] *trans.* To open or detach by wrenching. 1818 MILMAN *Genius* 27 While Rape unwrench'd her wither'd grasp That clung unto the tomb. 1832 J. MONTGOMERY *Cholera Mount* Wks. 1841 IV. 170 The blue pest, whose gripe no art can shun, No force unwrench. **Unwre·nched,** *ppl. a.* [UN-¹ 8.] Not subjected to wrenching. [1775 ASH, *Unranched, Unwrenched.*] 1784 COWPER *Task* IV. 446 Nor will he leave Unwrench'd the door, however well secur'd. 1800 COLERIDGE *Piccolom.* V. vi. 72 To him Nothing on earth remains unwrenched and firm, Who has no faith.

**Unwrest,** variant of UNWRAST *a. Obs.*

† **Unwre·st,** *v. Obs.* Also 5 *pa. t.* and *pa. pple.* vnwrast(e; 7 vnrest. [UN-² 9.] *trans.* To undo, detach, or dislocate, by wresting or wrenching.

*c* 1450 LOVELICH *Merlin* 13942 The ȝate closed aȝen also faste as hit ne hadde neuere ben vnwraste. 1470–85 MALORY *Arthur* VIII. xxxiv. 326 Bothe his handes..were fast bounden vnto two knyghtes;..sodenly he pulled them bothe to hym, and vnwrast his handes. 1509 BARCLAY *Shyp of Folys* 25 Haddest thou leuer se Thy sonnes necke vnwrested wyth a rope, Than [etc.]. 1598 FLORIO, *Distorcere*,..to wriggle, to wrest, to vnwrest. 1613 DANIEL *Coll. Hist. Eng.* II. 139 Their occasions made them somewhat to vnrest [1617 unwrest] the Soueraigntie from that height whereunto hee had strayned it.

**Unwre·sted,** *ppl. a.* [UN-¹ 8.] Not wrested or strained.

1653 *Nissena* 116 Whose wisdom hath always been equal to their unwrested and immaculate Justice. 1712 J. MORTON *Nat. Hist. Northampton.* 7 'Tis..a natural and unwrested observation, that the rivers [etc.]. 1771 WHITAKER *Hist. Manch.* I. 265 The plain unwrested import of the word.

Hence **Unwre·stedly** *adv.*, without forcing.

1615 G. SANDYS *Trav.* 91 Vnto this lamentable subuersion ..may that prophesie of Sibyls be vnwrestedly applied.

**Unwre·sting,** *ppl. a.* (UN-¹ 10.) 1595 DANIEL *Civ. Wars* I. xcix, Let vnwresting charity beleeue That then thy oth with thy intent agreed.

† **Unwri·ed,** *ppl. a. Obs.*⁻¹ [UN-¹ 8.] Not twisted or wrested. 1558 PHAER *Æneid* VI. P iij b, Whan thou duely hast it [*sc.* a bough] spied Lay thou theron thy hand, for willingly with eas, onwried, Itself it shall releas.

**Unwri·nkle,** *v.* [UN-² 3.]

**1.** *trans.* To free (the brow, etc.) from wrinkles; to smooth (a wrinkled surface).

1611 COTGR., *Desplisser*, to..vnwrinkle, vncrumple. *Ibid.* s.v. *Desfroncer*, To cleere, vncloud, or vnwrinckle his visage. 1725 RAMSAY *Gentl. Sheph.* V. iii, See how much joy unwrinkles every brow. 1784 J. POTTER *Virtuous Villagers* II. 185 By unwrinkling the brow of care, [it has] given place to calm contentment. 1822 SCOTT *Nigel* Introd. Epist., To unwrinkle a brow bent with the furrows of daily toil. 1880 MEREDITH *Tragic Com.* x. 181 He unwrinkled the letter carefully for it to be legible.

**2.** *intr.* To become free from wrinkles.

1827 *Perils & Captivity* (Constable's Misc.) 85 Foreheads, lowering and sulky, began to unwrinkle.

**Unwri·nkled,** *ppl. a.* [UN-¹ 8.] Free from wrinkles; smooth.

In freq. use from *c* 1820, esp. with 'brow' or 'forehead'.

1576 NEWTON *Lemnie's Complex.* I. vi. 36 b, The forhead smoth, cheerefull and vnwrynckled. 1592 *Sir T. More* III. i. 172 Mercie, whose maiestick browe Should be vnwrinckled. 1643 DAVENANT *Unfort. Lovers* III. D 4 b, Thy brow Is quite unwrinckled. *a* 1649 CRASHAW *Glorious Epiphany* 28 The world's one, round, Æternall year, Whose full and all-unwrinkled face Nor sinks nor swells with time or place. 1783 MASON *Du Fresnoy's Art Paint.* 283 So the liberal vest In large, distinct, unwrinkled folds should fly. 1784 COWPER *Task* IV. 4 The wintry flood, in which the moon Sees her unwrinkled face reflected bright. 1801 COLERIDGE *Fragm.*, *The Moon* 5 Trees, herbage, snake-like stream, unwrinkled Lake. 1864 BRYANT *Sella* 510 Still she kept her fair Unwrinkled features. 1881 *Longmans' Notes on Bks.* 31 Aug. 83/2 The unwrinkled portrait which Cromwell feared that Lely might draw of himself. 1885 [W. H. WHITE] *Mark Rutherford's Deliverance* vii, Her dress was unwrinkled.

*fig.* 1582 BENTLEY *Mon. Matrones* 74 To leane to..God, and his smooth and vnwrinkled Church. 1648 CRASHAW *Delights Muses*, *Musicks Duell* 39 A Nightingale..Trayles her plaine Ditty in one long-spun note,..A cleare unwrinckled song. 1822 COLERIDGE *Lett., Conv.*, etc. II. 79, I am, with unwrinkled confidence,..Your affectionate friend.

† **Unwri·t,** *ppl. a.* [UN-¹ 8 b.] = UNWRITTEN.

1485 *Waterford Arch.* in *10th Rep. Hist. MSS. Comm.* App. V. 320 The..usages and privieleges..that bene writte and unwritt. 1612 CHAPMAN *Rev. Bussy d'Ambois* II. i. 119 God's unwrit edicts. 1656 in *Verney Mem.* (1907) II. 51 [A letter] that had been better unwritt.

**Unwri·te,** *v.* [UN-² 3.] *trans.* To cancel or abrogate the writing of (something); to annul or rescind (a writing).

1586 J. HOOKER *Hist. Irel.* in *Holinshed* II. 104/2 What he wrote he meant not to vnwrite. 1593 B. BARNES *Poems* (Grosart) 6 Since mercylesse she made that chartyre,.. Sign'd with those hands which neuer can vnwrite it. 1641 MILTON *Animadv.* 65 Yee write them in your closets, and unwrite them in your Courts. 1820 KEATS in Rossetti *Life* (1887) 96 My poor poem, which I would willingly take the trouble to unwrite, if possible. 1861 *Court Life at Naples* II. 269 It is easier to unsay than to unwrite cross words. 1888 GLADSTONE in *Daily News* 6 Nov. 6/3 You cannot unwrite or rewrite the law of time.

**Unwri·teable,** *a.* (UN-¹ 7 b.)

1780 T. TWINING *Recreat. & Stud.* (1882) 76 In gracing, he does the most beautiful, most unassignable, most unwritten and unwriteable things I ever heard. 1801 SOUTHEY *Let. to G. C. Bedford* 19 Aug., These are unwriteable things —the gossip, and the playfulness. 1873 EARLE *Philol. Eng. Tongue* (ed. 2) 110 The first [vowel] we call by an unwriteable name.

† **Unwri·the,** *v. Obs.*⁻⁰ [UN-² 3. Cf. OE. *un-, onwrīþan.*] *trans.* = UNWREATHE *v.*¹ 1611 COTGR., *Destortiller*, to vnwrith, vnwind, open, vnwrap. 1731 BAILEY (vol. II), *Unwrithen*, unwreathed, untwisted, straitened.

**Unwri·ting,** *ppl. a.* (UN-¹ 10.)

1663 COWLEY *Ode upon Verses of Ld. Broghills* i, I wrote, and wrote, but still I wrote in vain,..A rich, unwriting Hand, carry'd the Prize away. 1728 POPE *Dunc.*, *M. Scriblerus*, A deluge of Authors covered the land: Whereby ..the peace of the honest unwriting subject was daily molested. 1828–32 WEBSTER s.v., An unwriting citizen.

**Unwri·tten,** *ppl. a.* Also 4 unwrite. [UN-¹ 8 b. Cf. OE. *unwriten* (*unge-, und-*), ON. *úritinn.*]

**1.** Not committed to writing; left unrecorded.

1362 LANGL. *P. Pl.* A. XI. 255 (MS. Univ. Coll. Oxford), Myn name [was] entred In ye legende of lyf..Or elles vnwrite [B. vnwriten, C. vnwryten] for wiled. *c* 1440 *Jacob's Well* 115 Þat none of here talys schulde be vnwretyn. *c* 1445 PECOCK *Donet* 6 Bettir it is..þan forto leve alle suche þingis vnwritun and vntauȝt. 1533 TINDALE *Supper of Lord* B v, More muste gyve vs leaue to beleue his vnwrytten vanityes (verities I shoulde saye) at leasure. 1577 tr. *Bullinger's Decades* 774/1 An vnwritten tradition of the Apostles. 1635 J. TAYLOR (Water P.) *Very Old Man* C 3, They..might from Sire to Son Haue been unwritten Chronicles, and by Tradition shew Times mutabillity. 1650 BAXTER *Saints' R.* II. iv. § 3. 200 It was a former Record.. delivered to us, and not onely an unwritten Testimony. 1792 S. ROGERS *Pleas. Mem.* II. (1801) 59 High o'er the hearth his forest-trophies hung;..Each vast antler..unwritten records bore, Of gallant feats. 1851 HAWTHORNE *Snow Image, Old News* (1879) 153 Diseases unwritten in medical books. 1878 H. SWEET in *Trans. Philol. Soc.* 404 The characteristic features of a hitherto unwritten dialect.

*absol.* 1880 MEREDITH *Tragic Com.* (1881) 114, I have seen, have seen ahead, seen where all is dark, read the unwritten.

**b.** Of laws, etc.: Not formulated in written codes or documents; not reduced to writing; oral.

1456 SIR G. HAYE *Law Arms* (S.T.S.) 128 Be all lawis wryttin and unwrittin. 1596 SPENSER *State Irel.* P 12 The Brehoone lawe..is a certayne rule of right unwritten, but delivered by tradition from one to another. 1641 MILTON *Ch. Govt.* I. iii. 11 Those unwritten lawes and Ideas which nature hath ingraven in us. *c* 1670 HOBBES *Dial. Com. Laws* (1681) 3 Equity is a certain perfect Reason that interpreteth and amendeth the Law written, it self being unwritten, and consisting in nothing else but right Reason. 1765 BLACKSTONE *Comm.* Introd. I. 63 The municipal law of England..may..be divided into two kinds:..the unwritten, or common law; and..the written, or statute law. 1856 EMERSON *Eng. Traits, Universities* Wks. (Bohn) II. 93 That an unwritten code of honour deals..an even-handed justice. 1888 T. W. REID *Life W. E. Forster* (ed. 2) II. vii. 294 The unwritten law of the Land League.

**c.** Not written *of* or about.

1761 in *Hull Museum Publ.* (No. 102) 13 Which, having been hitherto concealed and unwritten of, is..worthy of a general knowledge.

**2.** Not written upon. Also with *on.*

1542 in T. A. Beck *Ann. Furnes* (1844) App. 87 [He] sealyd therwyth vij. blanckes in perchement then beyng blanckes and unwryttene. 1555 EDEN *Decades* (Arb.) 57 A white paper vnwritten, vpon the which yow may..wryte what yow lyste. 1583 GOLDING *Calvin on Deut.* lxix. 423 This disposednes is as a white vnwritten paper. 1664 SOUTH *Serm.* (1715) II. 46 Like unwritten paper,..it..is white..and fair for an after-Inscription. *a* 1700 EVELYN *Diary* 27 Oct. 1664, He then..ask'd me if I had any paper about me unwritten and a crayon. 1760–2 GOLDSM. *Cit. W.* xlvi, When the large unwritten page presents its snowy spotless bosom to the writer's hand. 1833 T. HOOK *Parson's Dau.* I. xi, So that no possible spot or corner of her letters should escape unwritten on. 1873 B. HARTE *Fiddletown* 26 The unwritten side of one of these squares.

**Unwro·ken,** *ppl. a.* [UN-¹ 8 b. Cf. MDu. *onghewroken* (Du. *ongewroken*), OHG. *ungirohhan, unkirochan* (MHG. and G. *ungerochen*), and UNWREAKEN.] = UNWREAKED *ppl. a.*

*a* 1300 *Cursor M.* 13067 Ouer mikel has þou spoken, And þat sal noght be al vn-wroken. *c* 1400 *Destr. Troy* 4195 Þat any lord of our londe shuld lacche soche a skorne Vnwrokyn with wondis. 1513 DOUGLAS *Æneid* II. x. 197 This day wnwrokin we sall neuir al be slane. *Ibid.* IV. xii. 30, XI. xiv. 19. 1600 FAIRFAX *Tasso* VIII. lxvi. 155 Yet all this season were we willing blinde, Offended, vnreueng'd, wrong'd, but vnwroken.

**Unwro·nged,** *ppl. a.* (UN-¹ 8.)

1598 FLORIO, *Inoffeso*, vnoffended, vntoucht, vnwrongd. 1628 GAULE *Pract. The.* (1629) 352 There lies he now, though by some (perhaps) vnremembred, yet by others not vnwronged. 1789 E. DARWIN *Bot. Gard.* II. 15 Unwrong'd,.. They guard, the Kings of Needwood's wide domains, Their sister-wives. 1841 MRS. BROWNING *Q. Annelida, Complaint* iii, Now is he false—alas, alas!—although Unwronged! 1870 BRYANT *Iliad* I. I. 22 Unwronged and with no cause for tears.

**Unwro·ngful,** *a.* (UN-¹ 7.) 1876 MORRIS *Sigurd* II. 123 Till over a world unwrongful new-born shall Baldur ride. † **Unwro·nging,** *vbl. sb. Obs.*⁻¹ [UN-¹ 13.] Non-committal of a wrong. *c* 1449 PECOCK *Repr.* III. xvi. 382 Experience schewith..how manye..wrongis schulden be..menteyned for riȝtis and vnwrongingis.

**Unwrought** (ʌnrǭ·t), *ppl. a.* [UN-¹ 8 b, c. Cf. OE. *ungeworht*, MLG. *ungewrocht*, MDu. *onghewrocht, -wracht*, Du. *ongewrocht.*]

**1.** Not made, done, formed, performed, etc.; left in an unfinished or incomplete state; uncompleted, unperformed.

*c* 1375 *Sc. Leg. Saints* x. (*Matthew*) 143 Sa þare warke lewit vnwrocht, Fore vndire-stand vthire þai na mocht. *c* 1450 *Myrr. our Ladye* 268 She lefte no verteu vnwroughte in the worlde. *c* 1611 CHAPMAN *Iliad* II. 117 The work that should have wreaked our wrong..lies unwrought. 1819 SHELLEY *Peter Bell 3rd* VII. xx, Love's work was left unwrought—no brood..took wing.

**2.** Not formed or fashioned by being worked on; *esp.* of materials (as fabrics, stone, or metals): Still in a crude, raw, rude, or natural state; not worked into a finished condition; undressed; = RAW *a.* 2 a, ROUGH *a.* 16.

In very frequent use from *c* 1600, esp. with *stone, iron.*

*c* 1400 *Pilgr. Sowle* (Caxton, 1483) V. xiv. 107 God hymself is nature vnformed and vnwrought. 1455 *Rolls of Parlt.* V. 325/1 Never any thing of Silke..in eny wise wrought, but in rawe Silk allone unwrought. 1463–4 *Act* 19 *Hen. VII*, c. 21 All other maner of Sylkes,..rawe or unwrought. 1503 [see RAW *a.* 2 a]. 1545 *Rates of Custom* b i b, Enkyll the pounde vnwrought, iiii d. 1548 COVERDALE, etc. *Erasm. Par.* 1 *Cor.* viii. 23 b, An other vnsquared piece of tymber, or an vnwrought stone. 1571 GOLDING *Calvin on Ps.* lxxiv. 5 The unwrought and rough timber-logs. 1601 [see ROUGH *a.* 16]. 1616 W. BROWNE *Brit. Past.* II. iv. 587 Brests softer farre than tufts of unwrought silke. 1673 TEMPLE *Obs. United Prov.* Wks. 1720 I. 66 We then carry'd out our Wools unwrought. 1719 W. WOOD *Surv. Trade* 85 Every Country which..returns us unwrought Materials to be manufactured here. 1773 HAWKESWORTH *Cook's Voy.* I. v. II. 57 We saw also some pieces of glass and flint among them unwrought. 1799 *Hull Advertiser* 11 May 1/1 A large quantity of unwrought Alum-Rock. 1827 G. HIGGINS *Celtic Druids* 212 Very large unwrought stones. 1841 ELPHINSTONE *Hist. India* I. 371 The cocoa-nut tree and the bamboo furnish all the materials for construction unwrought. 1896 *Daily News* 11 Feb. 2/4 Unwrought steel and cast and wrought iron.

*fig.* 1641 MILTON *Ch. Govt.* II. Concl. 62 Men..whose unchast'ned and unwrought minds [were] never yet..subdu'd under the true lore of religion. 1886 MᶜNEILL *Sir Tristrem* p. xx, After having lain unwrought into any new forms for a couple of centuries, the story [etc.].

**b.** Not developed or worked *out.*

1877 MISS YONGE *Cameos* III. x. 84 He must choose.. whether to continue the art that should diffuse knowledge for good or evil, or leave it unwrought out.

**3. a.** Of a mine, etc.: Not worked. Also in fig. context.

1669 EARL SANDWICH tr. *Barba's Art of Metals* I. (1674) 7 [The mine] lay unwrought for four or five years. 1670

PETTUS *Fodinæ Reg.* 86 Where he findeth a Meer unwrought, he shall score on the Spindle one score. **1796** MORSE *Amer. Geog.* II. 209 This island abounds with iron, lead, and copper mines, though unwrought. **1839** DE LA BECHE *Rep. Geol. Cornwall*, etc. xv. 617 In 1778, also, these iron-lodes still remained unwrought. **1863** N. HAWTHORNE *Our Old Home* II. 15 Treasures of wit and wisdom..still in the unwrought mines of human thought.

**b.** Of coal: Not hewn out, excavated, or won.

**1789** J. WILLIAMS *Min. Kingd.* I. 8 The whole coal wall, that is the unwrought coal. **1883** [see UNWORKED 2 b].

**c.** Of land: Not tilled, laboured, or cultivated.

**1600** FAIRFAX *Tasso* I. lxiv, Or proue at least..Their harts were fertill land, although vnwrought. **1876–** in north. dialect and Sc. use.

**4.** Not employed in, not subjected or inured to, labour. *rare.*

**1550** W. LANE in Froude *Hist. Eng.* (1860) V. 285 Out of the decay of tillage springeth the scarcity of corn and the people unwrought. **1628** MAY *Virg. Georg.* II. 55 Then make strong hedges to keep cattell out, Young beasts especially, and yet unwrought.

**Unwrou·ght,** *pa. pple.* [f. UNWORK *v.*] Put back or restored to a former condition; undone.

**1726** POPE *Odyssey* XIX. 177 The woof unwrought the Suitor-train surprize. **1850** MRS. BROWNING *Sonn. fr. Portuguese* xiv, These things..may Be changed, or change for thee,—and love, so wrought, May be unwrought so.

**Unwru·ng,** *ppl. a.* [UN-[1] 8 b.] Not pinched or galled.

**1604** SHAKS. *Ham.* III. ii. 253 (Q. 2), Your Maiestie, and wee that haue free soules, it touches vs not, let the gauled Iade winch, our withers are vnwrong. [Hence freq. in later echoes of the phrase, or occas. (in recent use) of the word.]

†**Unwry·,** *v. Obs.* [OE. *onwréon, unwréon* (UN-[2] 3). Cf. OHG. *intrîhan, inrîhan* 'revelare'.]

**1.** *trans.* To reveal or expose to sight by the removal of a covering; to uncover, lay bare.

*α.* *c* **825** *Vesp. Psalter* xvii. 16 Onwriȝen werun steaðelas ymbhwyrftes eorðan. *c* **1000** *Ags. Ps.* (Thorpe) cxviii. 18 Onwreoh þu mine eaȝan. *c* **1290** *Beket* 2278 in *S. Eng. Leg.* I. 172 Þe Cardinales nolden nouȝt is bodi al on-wreo [*c* **1300** unwreo]. **1340** *Ayenb.* 58 Hi onwriþ þane pot, and þe uleȝen vlyeþ þerin.

*β.* *c* **975** *Rushw. Gosp.* Mark ii. 4 He..unwreoȝon þæt hus..þær he wæs. *c* **1000** ÆLFRIC *Hom.* II. 334 Ða licmen his neb þærrihte unwruȝon. *a* **1225** *Ancr. R.* 328 Þo he schulde unwrien his wunden. **13..** *K. Alis.* 336 (Laud MS.), His aristable he gan vnwriȝene [*v.r.* vnwreone]. *c* **1374** CHAUCER *Troylus* I. 858 To hym byhoueth first vnwre [*v.rr.* onwrye, vnwry] his wounde. *c* **1430** *Lanfranc's Cirurg.* 85 Unwrey al þe bon, in kuttynge awey al þe flesch. *c* **1440** *Jacob's Well* 197 He ros out of his graue,..& vnwryed þe munkys in here beddys.

**b.** *refl.* To uncover (oneself); to make naked.

*a* **1225** *Ancr. R.* 56 Bersabee..unwreih hire ine Dauies sihðe. *Ibid.* 58 Þurh þet heo unwrien ham ine monne eih sihðe.

**2.** *fig.* To reveal, disclose, make known (some hidden thing or fact, sin, etc.); to communicate or divulge (a matter).

*α.* *c* **825** *Vesp. Psalter* xxxvi. 5 Onwrih dryhtne weȝ ðinne. *c* **1000** *Ags. Gosp.* Luke xvii. 30 Æfter þysum þingum bið on þam dæȝe þe mannes sunu onwriȝen bið. **1340** *Ayenb.* 88 Uor hyer ne zyþ non onwryȝe þe uayrhede of god, bote ase hit by ine ane ssewere. *Ibid.* 174 Þe zike ssel onwri his ziknesse.

*β.* *c* **950** *Lindisf. Gosp.* Matt. x. 26 Nowiht forðon [bið] ȝedeȝled þæt ne se unwriȝen. *c* **1055** *Byrhtferth's Handboc* in *Anglia* VIII. 334 Griphia..byð ȝesett þær þa deopan þing beoð unwroȝene. *a* **1200** *Moral Ode* 160 in *O. E. Hom.* I. 169 Al scal þer bon þanne unwron, þet men wruȝen her. *a* **1225** *Leg. Kath.* 1769 Þer me unwreah me þe wei, þet leadeð to liue. **1297** R. GLOUC. (Rolls) 10457 God wot wuch is herte was, vor he nolde him noȝt vnwre. Þe erchebissop him asoilede. *c* **1330** *Amis & Amil.* 783 When þe douke com in to þat won, Þe steward oȝain him gan gon, Her conseyl for to vnwrain. *c* **1380** *Sir Ferumb.* 1849 Y wil her, as y can, my message to þe ounwrye. *c* **1407** LYDG. *Reson & Sens.* 18 Or [= ere] I do specifye Myn entent for to vnwrie, Or ferther in this boke procede.

Hence †**Unwrye(n)** *ppl. a. Obs.*

*a* **1225** *Ancr. R.* 58 Ȝif eni unwrie put were, & beste feolle þer inne, he hit schulde ȝelden þet þene put unwreih. **1340** *Ayenb.* 88 Hyer ne zyþ non onwryȝe þe uayrhede of god. *Ibid.* 112, 244.

†**Uny,** *v. Obs.* Also 5 vnye. [ad. OF. *uni-er* (1371 in Godef.), or *uni-r* (12th–13th c.; F., Sp., and Pg. *unir*, It. *unire*), a. L. *ūnīre* to UNITE. Cf. UNE *v.*] *trans.* To form, combine, or join into one; to make one; to unite.

Freq. from *c* 1435 to 1535; in later use chiefly *Sc.* The chief types of construction are illustrated by the different groups of quotations.

(*a*) **1433** *Rolls of Parlt.* IV. 441/2 Pretendyng yat all his Auncestres..have had ye Estate, Honour and Dignite, as annexed, unied and appurtenaunt to ye seid Castell, Honour and Lordship. **1483** CAXTON *Gold. Leg.* 435/2 How our lord wold unye or joyne our humanyte to his dyuynytee by grete loue. **1502** *Ord. Crysten Men* (W. de W. 1506) I. iv. D ij b, By the baptem the soule..is incorporat and vnyed with holy chirche. *c* **1510** MORE *Picus* Wks. 13/1 That prayer ..not onelye presenteth the mind to the father: but also vnieth it with hym by vnspeakeable wayes. **1550** J. COKE *Eng. & Fr. Heralds* § 128 Whiche realme..[he] conquered, uniynge it to the Crowne of Espayne.

(*b*) *c* **1450** *Myrr. our Ladye* 294 The prayer of a multytude that is vnyed togyther in charyte. *a* **1513** FABYAN *Chron.* VI. cxciii. 196 He made Dunstanne..bisshop of Worceter, and vnyed and knyt into one the prouynce & lordshyppes of Englande. **1523** LD. BERNERS *Froiss.* I. ccclxxxi. 640 That there be no villayns nor gentylmen, but that we may be all vnyed toguyder. **1541** COPLAND *Galyen's Terap.* A j, Howe Phylosophy and eloquence are..vnyed togyther by offyce and actyon.

(*c*) *c* **1460** FORTESCUE *Abs. & Lim. Mon.* ii. (1885) 112 Euery comunalte vnyed of mony parties must nedis haue an hed. **1482–3** in *Eng. Gilds* (1870) 310 That they..a Gilde or Fraternyte..of the men of the seid Crafte and other, myght make, vnye, founde,..and stablissh. **1509** *Sc. Acts, Jas. IV* (1814) II. 267/1 It sall be lefull till his grace to diuide schirefdomez & create, vny, & annex þe sammyne. **1512** *Helyas* in Thoms *Prose Rom.* (1828) III. 135 In the which time..should be unyed and congregeed the princes of christendom for to passe over the sea.

(*d*) **1562** WINȜET *Wks.* (S.T.S.) II. 41 In Christe Iesus is na commixtioun,..bot bayth the twa naturis vniit in ane persoun. **1596** DALRYMPLE tr. *Leslie's Hist. Scot.* I. 84 At last..the Britanis of Cambrie..war vniit in ane people vndir ane law.

*refl.* *c* **1440** *Gesta Rom.* xli. 26 The Sone of god vnyede hym to mankynde to þe dethe. **1494** *Cov. Leet Bk.* 558 That they..applye them-self to Joyn & vnye themself or to be contributory to other Craft. **1562** WINȜET *Wks.* (S.T.S.) II. 43 The Sone of God..be vniing Him self to man..wes maid man.

Hence †**Unying** *vbl. sb. Obs.*

**1517** *Love's Bonavent. Mirr.* xv. (W. de W.) I iv b, Puttynge a-way occasyon..that myght drawe yᵉ..soule..fro the vnyenge & knyttyng to her spouse Jhesu chryst.

†**Unya·rk,** *v. Obs. rare.* [UN-[2] 3 + YARK *v.* b.] *trans.* To undo or open (a gate).

*a* **1400–50** *Alexander* 2147 Þai vnȝarked him þe ȝatis & ȝald him þe keys. *Ibid.* 3209 Þan ȝode þai furthe & vnȝarkid þe ȝatis of þe cite.

**Unyea·ned,** *ppl. a.* [UN-[1] 8.] **a.** Unborn. **b.** Not having given birth. Also *fig.*

[**1775** ASH.] **1868** GEO. ELIOT *Sp. Gipsy* 148 Trust That men call blind; but..is blind Only as unyeaned reason is. **1884** MISS M. LINSKILL *Betw. Heather & North. Sea* vi, The loss of the ewes, and the unyeaned lambs. **1894** C. VICKERMAN *Woollen Spinning* 46 Sheep..much prized in unyeaned state.

**Unyelde,** var. UNNEALED *ppl. a. Obs.* **Unyement,** obs. f. OINTMENT. **Unyeown,** obs. Sc. f. ONION.

†**Unye·rded,** *ppl. a. Sc. Obs.* [UN-[1] 8 + *ȝerded*: see YIRD *v.*] Not buried. **1596** DALRYMPLE tr. *Leslie's Hist. Scot.* I. 121 Lat him end his lyf vpon ane forke, and [be] kastne by vnȝerdet. **Unyie·lded,** *ppl. a.* [UN-[1] 8.] Not yielded or surrendered. **1640** BP. HALL *Chr. Moder.* II. xi. 101 Here were no tricks of inferences,..no violent deduction of unyeelded sequels. **1700** DRYDEN *Pal. & Arc.* III. 651 O'erpower'd, at length, they force him to the Ground, Unyielded as he was. †**Unyie·lden,** *ppl. a. Obs.*⁻[1] [UN-[1] 8 b.] = prec. **1553** BRENDE *Q. Curtius* VIII. 154 b, Alexander lefte his fotemenne to subdue suche as were yet vnyelden. **Unyie·lding,** *vbl. sb.* (UN-[1] 13.) **1848** DICKENS *Dombey* xl, Looking upon him with neither yielding nor unyielding, liking nor hatred.

**Unyie·lding,** *ppl. a.* [UN-[1] 10.]

**1.** Of substances (or their structure): Not yielding to force or pressure; unpliant, unbending; stiff, hard. Also const. *to.*

**1658** ROWLAND tr. *Moufet's Theat. Ins.* 926 In physicks we see those things that are most stiffe and unyeelding, to be resisted and beaten off with the most soft things. **1736** THOMSON *Liberty* V. 87 How shall this thy mighty Kingdom stand? On what unyielding base? **1744** ARMSTRONG *Art Preserv. Health* II. 537 Hard unyielding unelastic bone. **1768–74** TUCKER *Lt. Nat.* (1834) II. 405 A soil unyielding to pressure. **1805** SOUTHEY *Madoc* II. x. 105 On the unyielding skin the temper'd blade Bent. **1854** OWEN in *Orr's Circ. Sci., Org. Nat.* I. 228 A firm and unyielding support to the large head. **1889** MRS. E. KENNARD *Landing a Prize* vii, An unyielding ledge of wood.

**2.** Of persons, etc.: Not yielding, surrendering, submitting, or giving way; firm, obdurate, obstinate. Also const. *to.*

**1592** SHAKS. *Ven. & Ad.* 423 Remoue your siege from my unyeelding hart. **1724** A. HILL *Prol. to Sir T. Overbury* 15 He swims, unyielding, against Fortune's Stream. **1736** THOMSON *Liberty* IV. 982 His unyielding Son these doctrines drank, With all a Bigot's rage. **1777** POTTER *Æschylus, Seven Chiefs* 191 Ah! what frentic rage possest Each unyielding, ruthless breast! **182.** BRYANT *Hymn to Death* 146 When the earth Received thee, tears were in unyielding eyes And on hard cheeks. **1839** HALLAM *Hist. Lit.* IV. vii. § 19 The unyielding claw of a cold-blooded animal. **1890** 'R. BOLDREWOOD' *Col. Reformer* (1891) 333 Of all people in the wide world,..his cousin was..the most unyielding to argument.

*transf.* **1806** BYRON *Childish Recollections* 6 Unyielding pangs assail the drooping mind. **1850** SCORESBY *Cheever's Whalem. Adv.* i. [An] instance..of what commerce can do against unyielding laws of Nature. **1909** *Daily Chron.* 28 Sept. 5/4 The storm-driven snows had buried and bound the dogs in unyielding frost.

**3.** Characterized by firmness or obstinacy.

**1677** GILPIN *Demonol.* II. ii. 189 A kind of unnatural fury, which hurries Men with violence into an unyielding stifness. **1736** THOMSON *Liberty* V. 370 A zeal unyielding in their country's cause. **1779** *Mirror* No. 8, I..observed an obstinate unyielding silence. *a* **1812** BUCKMINSTER *Serm.* (1827) 60 Unyielding virtue is admired by the corrupt, disinterested goodness by the selfish. **1848** BUCKLEY *Iliad* 227 The Greeks were routed, and an unyielding tumult ensued. **1882** BESANT *All Sorts* xxi, She..sat bolt upright, the picture of unyielding determination.

Hence **Unyie·ldingly** *adv.*

[**1847** WEBSTER.] **1884** PEMBER *Earth's Earliest Ages* i. 14 They hold..opinions of their own, and are unyieldingly tenacious of them. **1889** STANLEY in *Daily News* 25 Nov. 5/8 There is a virtue..even in striving unyieldingly.

**Unyie·ldingness.** (UN-[1] 12, or f. prec.)

**1613** DANIEL *Coll. Hist. Eng.* III. 160 Vpon..the vnyeeldingnesse of King Malcolm,..nothing was effected. **1617** HIERON *Wks.* II. 369 That phrase of a stony heart, a fit terme to note out the stiffenesse and sturdinesse, and vn-yeeldingnesse thereof. *a* **1843** *Encycl. Metrop.* (1845) VII. 263/2 An unyieldingness being imparted to the mass. **1850** L. HUNT *Autobiog.* II. xi. 53 His generalship..came to nothing before the unyieldingness of English, and the advent of Prussian soldiers.

**Unyo·ke,** *v.* [OE. *ungeocian* (UN-[2] 4 b). Cf. older Du. *ontjocken*, Du. *ontjukken*, MHG. and G. *entjochen.*]

**1.** *trans.* To loose (a draught-animal, etc.) from the yoke; to free from harness.

*c* **1000** ÆLFRIC *Gram.* xlvii. (Z.) 277 *Disiungo*, ic ungeocige oððe totwæme. **1398** TREVISA *Barth. De P. R.* XVIII. xiv. (Bodl. MS.), Þan þei vnȝoke hem and bringe hem to þe stalle. **1565** COOPER *Thesaurus*, *Bouem disiunctum curare*, an oxe vnyoked. **1597** SHAKS. 2 *Hen. IV*, IV. ii. 103 Our Army is dispers'd: Like youthfull Steeres, vnyoak'd, they tooke their course East, West, North, South. **1613** HEYWOOD *Brazen Age* II. D 3, My swannes I haue vnyoakt. **1628** MAY *Virg. Georg.* III. 98 The weeping Plowman tother Oxe alone Vnyokes. **1681** D'URFEY *Progr. Honesty* i, The Beasts unyok'd from Teams, Ran lowing to the distant Mead. **1708** J. PHILIPS *Cyder* II. 38 Soon as the Hind, fatigu'd, Unyokes his Team. **1720** POPE *Iliad* XXIII. 596 The chief himself unyokes the panting steeds. **1843** BETHUNE *Sc. Fireside Stor.* 148 While the coachman was preparing to unyoke his cattle. **1870** BRYANT *Iliad* VIII. I. 262 Unyoke the steeds..And set their food before them.

*refl.* **1832** HT. MARTINEAU *Ella of Gar.* ii. 18 The girls of the family unyoked themselves from the harrow which they were drawing over the..sandy soil.

†**b.** (See YOKE *sb.* 2, *v.* 3.) *Obs.*

**1573** [see sense 4 a]. *a* **1589** MASCALL *Govt. Cattle* (1596) 274 Some..vse to ring them [*sc.* hogs] at Michaelmas..; they doe vnyoake them soone after Michaelmas.

**c.** To disconnect (the plough) from a draught-animal. Also in fig. context.

**1821** SCOTT *Pirate* v, It's a finished field with me—I must unyoke the pleugh, and lie down to wait for the deadthraw.

**2.** *fig.* To liberate, release, deliver from oppression, etc. Also *refl.*

**1387** TREVISA *Higden* (Rolls) V. 367 Þo was..Italy unȝoked and delyvered of þe ȝokke of Constantynnoble. **1593** B. BARNES *Poems* (Grosart) 3 So whiles shee sleightly gloas'd, with her new pray, Mine hartes eye..Vnyoak't himselfe, & closely scap't away. **1638** N. WHITING *Albino & Bellama* 5 When British Isles..From sad oppression had unyok'd their necks. **1641** MILTON *Ch. Govt.* II. 61 The property of Truth is,..to unyoke and set free the minds and spirits of a Nation. **1687** MIÈGE *Gt. Fr. Dict.* II. s.v., To unyoke himself out of Bondage, or Slavery. [Hence in Phillips (1706).]

*absol.* (for *refl.*). **1606** WARNER *Alb. Eng.* XV. xcviii. 388 Too aduantagiously from out our Rubrick they vnyoke, And Canons old and new by them are, too securely, broke.

**3.** To disconnect, unlink, disjoin. Also *fig.*

**1595** SHAKS. *John* III. i. 241 And shall these hands,..So newly ioin'd in loue,..Vnyoke this seysure, and this kinde regreete? **1812** H. & J. SMITH *Rej. Addr., Arch. Atoms* 154 The milkman..With sudden sink unyokes the clinking pail. **1862** TROLLOPE *N. America* I. 109 At the rapids the large rafts are, as it were, unyoked, and divided into small portions.

**4. a.** *absol.* To remove the yoke from an animal.

**1573** TUSSER *Husb.* (1878) 32 Let hogs be roong, both old and yoong. No mast vpon oke, no longer vnyoke. **1601** HOLLAND *Pliny* I. 593 When thou [*sc.* the husbandman] doest unyoke and give over thy daies worke. **1612** DRAYTON *Poly-olb.* I. 533 Here I'll unyoke awhile, and turn my steeds to meat. **1794** JAS. DONALDSON *View Agric. Carse of Gowrie* 24 The ploughmen..are in the stable by five o'clock, and unyoking about ten, are employed in cutting grass.

*fig.* **1610** FLETCHER *Faithf. Sheph.* I. i, Ever be thy honour spoke, From that place the morn is broke, To that place Day doth unyoke. **1667** JER. TAYLOR *Gt. Exemp.* (ed. 4) II. 310 It is..but reason such an anger should unyoke, and goe to bed with the Sun.

**b.** *fig.* To cease from labour, etc.; to give over work.

**1594** NASHE *Terrors of Night* C iij b, To nothing more aptly can I compare the working of our braines after we haue vnyoakt and gone to bed. **1602** SHAKS. *Ham.* V. i. 59 Who builds stronger then a Mason, a Shipwright, or a Carpenter? *Clown.* I, tell me that, and vnyoake. **1889** SKRINE *Mem. Thring* 225, I am hastening to unyoke. But I must not do so till I account for something still left unsaid.

Hence **Unyo·king** *vbl. sb.*

**1677** MIÈGE II. s.v., An unyoaking, or Unyoking. **1835** THIRLWALL *Greece* I. 221 The unyoking of the oxen.

**Unyo·ked,** *ppl. a.*[1] [UN-[1] 8.] Not provided with or subjected to a yoke; not wearing a yoke. Also *fig.*

**1573** TUSSER *Husb.* (1878) 93 Now hunt with dog, vnyoked hog. **1596** SHAKS. 1 *Hen. IV*, I. ii. 220, I know you all, and will a-while vphold The vnyoak'd humor of your idlenesse. *c* **1611** CHAPMAN *Iliad* VI. 321 That..we may Twelue vn-yok't Oxen of a yeare, in this thy Temple slaye. **1697** DRYDEN *Æneis* VI. 58 Sev'n Bullocks, yet unyok'd, for Phœbus chuse.

**Unyo·ked,** *ppl. a.*[2] [UN-[2] 4 b, 8, or f. UNYOKE *v.*] Set free from the yoke. Also *fig.*

**1700** A. PHILIPS *Pastorals* II. ad fin., With songs the jovial hinds return from plough; And unyok'd heifers, loitering homeward, lowe. **1751** W. WHITEHEAD *Hymn to Nymph of Bristol Spring* 146 The panting Swain..at evening led His unyok'd heifers to the common stream. **1888** A. H. SMITH *Cat. Gems Brit. Mus.* 191 Rustic with yoke of oxen,..the oxen unyoked from cart and lying down before it.

†**Unyo·lden,** *ppl. a. Obs.* [UN-[1] 8 b.]

**1.** Not yielded or surrendered; †unpaid.

*a* **1325** *MS. Rawl. B.* 520 fol. 29 b, Þe duwe seruices of þulke fees..beth with-drawen ant vn-ȝolde. *c* **1386** CHAUCER *Knt.'s T.* 1784 By the force of twenty is he take Vnyolden, and ydrawe vnto the stake. **1418–20** *Siege of Rouen* in *Archaeol.* XXI. 55 Whyle that Synt Katerynes was unȝolde. *c* **1425** WYNTOUN *Cron.* VIII. xi. 1720 Þaim thocht mare honeste Vnȝoldin to sla þame in melle. **15..** *Christ's Kirk* 177 in *Maitland Folio MS.* 154 For hir saik he wes vnȝoldin Sewin myle quhen he wes chaist. **1575** GASCOIGNE *Weedes, Fruit of Fetters* viii, Whyles the hope of mine unyolden harte..did labor for reliefe.

**2.** Unrequited; unavenged. *rare*—¹.

*c* **1400** *Destr. Troy* 2216 If we, þat are worthy,..Take harme, other hethyng, or hurtys vnȝoldyn, Of any erdyng in erthe.

**Unȝoun, -ȝown(e,** obs. Sc. ff. ONION.

**Unyou·thful,** *a.* (UN-¹ 7.) **1859** J. PAYN *Foster Brothers* xv. 256 His heavy and somewhat unyouthful brows. **1881** M. C. HAY *Missing* II. 80 Her staid, unyouthful guardian.

**Unyou·thfully,** *adv.* (UN-¹ 11.) **1891** H. LYNCH *G. Meredith* 80 Dahlia's lover is legal, sharp, and unyouthfully serious.

**Unzea·lous,** *a.* (UN-¹ 7.)

**1643** PRYNNE *Sov. Power Parl.* App. 217 What then will be our portion, if we be unzealous, negligent, perfidious to it? **1649** MILTON *Eikon.* ix. 84 Those men whose superstition Zealous or unzealous would [etc.]. **1801** *Monthly Rev.* XII. 589 An unzealous tardiness of preparation.

Hence **Unzea·lously** *adv.*, **-ness.**

**1615** HIERON *Wks.* I. 603 Our vnzealousnes, and..our Laodician lukwarmnesse. **1647** TRAPP *Comm. Matt.* v. 45 Is not..our ancient fervour and forwardness [turned] into a general lukewarmness and unzealousness? **1871** *Leisure Hour* 284/2 Some [dancing dervishes]..of the 'earth earthy', shuffled unzealously along.

**Unzo·ned,** *(ppl.) a.* [UN-¹ 8, 9.]

†**1.** (See quot.) *Obs.*—¹

**1662** STANLEY *Hist. Chaldaick Philos.* viii. 24 The unzoned Gods are Sarapis and Bacchus;..they are called unzoned, for that they use their power freely..in the Zones, and are enthroned above the conspicuous Deities.

**2.** Not girt with a zone, belt, or girdle; uncinctured.

**1718** PRIOR *Solomon* II. 167 Full, tho' unzon'd, her Bosom rose. **1799** CORRY *Sat. London* (1803) 58 The Circassian slave, the unzoned waist, the pendent workbag. **1804** ANNA SEWARD *Lett.* (1811) VI. 142 Other bands of lovers..of sultry regions are shewn fanning the unzoned beauty. **1854** S. DOBELL *Balder* iii. 11 One all unzoned in her deep haunts..Hastes not to hide her breast.

**Uo, Uoaman, Uolc, Uoluel, Uor-, Uot,** southern ME. varr. FOE, FOEMAN, FOLK, FULFILL *v.*, FOR-, FOOT *sb.*

**-uous** (iu,əs), a compound suffix, repr. L. *-uōs-us* (*-a, -um*), OF. or AF. *-uous, -uos* (F. *-ueux*), occurring in a number of adoptions from L. (or F.), as *fructuous, halituous, impetuous,* †*monstruous,* †*portentuous, sumptuous, tempestuous, virtuous*; and hence by analogy employed with the sense 'of the nature of, consisting of' in a few E. formations on L. stems, as *ambiguous* (1528–), *strenuous* (1599–), †*subsiduous* (1490), *torrentuous* (1840–).

By assimilation, OE. *rihtwīs* ('righteous') became *rightuous* in the 15–16th c.

**Uox,** southern ME. variant of FOX *sb.*

**Up** (vp), *sb.* [From UP *adv.*¹ and ² or *a.*]

**1.** One who or that which is up, in various senses. *rare.*

**1536** *Rem. Sedition* i b, Say, farewell welth, where lust is lyked, and lawe refused, where uppe is sette downe, and downe sette uppe. **1759** STERNE *Tr. Shandy* I. xi, With us, you see, the case is quite different:—we are all ups and downs in this matter;—you are a great genius;—or..a great dunce. **1890** *Punch* 22 Feb. 85 It's the up-and-down bizness of life, mate, as makes it such fun—for the ups. **1895** M. CORELLI *Sorrows Satan* iv, It implies..that one must choose an up or a down,—genius is the Up, money is the Down.

**b.** A rise or elevation in the ground. Also in fig. context. (Cf. UP AND DOWN *sb.* 1 a.)

**1637** RUTHERFORD *Lett.* (1664) 32 But Oh the windings, the turnings, the up's & the down's, that he hath led me through. **1755** WALPOLE *Let. to Bentley* 18 Sept., The bad choice of the situation in such a country; it is all *ups* that should be *downs.*

**2.** †**a.** The action of arising from bed. *nonce-use.*

**1602** MARSTON *Ant. & Mel.* III. E 3, Here ile sleepe till that the sceane of vp Is past at Court.

**b.** A rise in life; a spell of prosperity; a success. Usu. pl., and contrasted with *down(s).* (Cf. UP AND DOWN *sb.* 2 a.)

**1844** DICKENS *Mart. Chuz.* xvi, And as fraudulent transactions have their downs as well as ups; the major was occasionally under a cloud. **1857** LOCKER *Lond. Life* 20 Life is chequer'd, a patchwork of smiles and of frowns; We valued its ups, let us muse on its downs. **1890** DOYLE *Sign of Four* xii, I've had ups in my life, and I've had downs.

**c.** A rise in price or value.

**1897** *Westm. Gaz.* 19 June 6/3 But there were downs as well as ups, and we find the embryo South-Western..with its £50 shares at 43.

**3.** An 'up' train or coach.

**1884** *Graphic* 15 Nov. 503/2 To spend pleasant quarters of an hour in waiting for the 'ups' and 'downs'.

**Up** (vp), *a.* [f. UP *adv.*¹ and ². Cf. UPSIDE.]

In senses 2 and 4 sometimes hyphened; cf. UP- *prefix* 2 and 2 b.

**1. a.** Dwelling up-country. **b.** Situated on high ground. *rare.*

**13..** *K. Alis.* 7053 (Laud MS.), Þise Sereses als I fynde, Þe vppest folk ben of al ynde. *c* **1710** CELIA FIENNES *Diary* (1888) 128 To persons born in up and dry Countryes.

**2.** Of trains or coaches: Going or running up; up-going. (See UP *adv.*¹ 6 d.)

**1784** J. PALMER *Papers Reform Posts* (1797) App. IV. 40 All the Letters..are sent by the up Coach at night. **1815** *Ann. Reg., Chron.* 57 The up coach, by the way of Cashel, was attacked. **1841** COL. HAWKER *Diary* (1893) II. 216 For an up train to bring it back. **1844** ALB. SMITH *Adv. Mr. Ledbury* I. ii. I. 12 The up-mail-trains of the railway. **1868** M. COLLINS *Sweet Anne Page* II. 160 They caught an up-stage, which landed them in Piccadilly at six. **1890** 'R. BOLDREWOOD' *Col. Reformer* (1891) 131 The up coach leaving and the down one just coming in.

**b.** Belonging to, connected with, up-going trains, coaches, etc.

**1840** *Osborne's London & Birm. Railw. Guide* 67 The rails ..constituting the road used by trains coming up to town and hence..called the up side. **1852** *Mechanic's Mag.* 6 Nov. 369 [He] observed the scarp next the up-line give way. **1885** *Law Times' Rep.* LII. 622/2 The booking-office at Risca is on the up platform. **1895** *Law Times* C. 133/2 A cottage near the up side of the railway line.

**3.** Of fermented liquors: Effervescing, effervescent.

**1815** *Sporting Mag.* XLV. 251 Beer's nothing if not up. **1816, 1828** [see next]. **1840** *Dom. Brewing* 46 The beer is soon what is commonly called *up.*

**b.** *transf.* Sparkling, excited; cheerful, vivacious.

**1815** J. SCOTT *Visit Paris* (ed. 2) 21 Their faces all sparkling and *up,* as we say of soda water. **1828** *Examiner* 806/1 As vain and flippant as a butterfly, and as 'up' as sparkling champagne. **1893** *Sat. Rev.* 7 Jan. 23/2 Mr. Gilfillan was too hurried, too perfervid, 'too much up', if we may borrow an expression from the effervescence of a harmless beverage.

**4.** Directed, inclining or sloping, upwards; ascending.

**1869** [see UP-BEAT *sb.* 1]. **1876** STAINER & BARRETT *Dict. Mus.* 61/2 Alternate bowing will lead to the recurrence of an up-bow on every alternate down-beat. **1901** *Feilden's Mag.* IV. 412/1 If there be long lengths of them horizontal, or with slight up gradient. **1905** ELINOR GLYN *Viciss. Evangeline* 138 He said..that..that up look under the eyelashes was the affair of the devil!

**Up,** *v.* [f. UP *adv.*¹ Cf. OE. *uppian* (once), to mount up, rise. With senses 3 and 4 cf. the uses placed under UP *adv.*¹ 29.]

**I.** *trans.* **1.** To drive up and catch (swans, etc.) so as to provide with the mark of ownership. Cf. UPPING *vbl. sb.*² 1. ? *Obs.*

**1560–1** in W. H. Turner *Select. Rec. Oxford* (1880) 285 For uppyng the ground byrde in porte meade. **1584–5** *Order for Swans,* The Swan-heard..shall vp no Swan nor make any sale of them, without the Maister of the Swannes ..be present. **1602–3** in Willis & Clark *Cambridge* (1886) III. 595 Item yᵉ swanherd for vpping swans, ijˢ.

†**b.** To carry out, perform (the practice of 'upping').

**1593** [see UPPING *vbl. sb.*² 1].

†**2.** To make up, form, or compose *of* something.

*a* **1658** CLEVELAND *London Lady* 102 An Animal together blow'd and made, And up'd of all the shreds of every Trade.

**3.** To raise up (a weapon, etc.), esp. to or upon the shoulder. Cf. sense 7 b.

**1885** RIDER HAGGARD *K. Solomon's Mines* iv, Good.. upped gun, and let drive at..a young cow. **1887** G. R. SIMS *Mary Jane's Mem.* 104 She ups her stick and begins to belabour him across the shoulders.

**4.** *Naut.* **a.** (See sense 7 c.) **b.** To heave or haul up.

**1890** CLARK RUSSELL *Marriage at Sea* vii, There's no English port for her unless she ups hellum and tries back'ards again. **1904** KIPLING *Traffics & Discov.* 133 After us've upped trawl, us'll be glad of a tow.

**II.** *intr.* **5.** To rise to one's feet; to get up from a sitting or recumbent posture; to arise; to rise from bed. Also in fig. context.

**1643** QUARLES *Embl.* II. xiv. 2 The true-bred Gamester ups a fresh, and then, Falls to 't agen. **1647** BP. CORBET *Poems* (1807) 226 Nor can these figures in thy rest endeere, As not to up when chanticleere Speaks the last watch. **1825** JENNINGS *Observ. Dial. W. Eng.* 109 Jerry Nutty..upp'd avaur tha lork. **1913** M. ROBERTS *Salt of Sea* vi. 177 The bloke nods and ups on 'is feet. **1915** C. H. SORLEY *Lett.* (1919) 255 Suddenly the division ups and marches to Aldershot.

**b.** *colloq.* and *dial.* To start up, come forward, begin abruptly or boldly, to say or do something. Usu. followed by *and.* Cf. UP *adv.*¹ 31.

(*a*) **1831** LOVER *Leg.* 82 The bishop ups and he tells him that he must mend his manners. **1865** DICKENS *Mut. Fr.* IV. xiii, Then we both of us ups and says, that minute, 'Prove so!' **1867–** in general dialect use (*Eng. Dial. Dict.*). **1879** R. BROWNING *Ned Bratts* 125 She ups with such a face, Heart sunk inside me: 'Well, pad on my prate-apace!'

(*b*) **1883** STEVENSON *Treas. Isl.* xxix, And you have the Davy Jones's insolence to up and stand for cap'n over me! **1884** 'MARK TWAIN' *Huck. Finn* xxv, All of a sudden the doctor ups and turns on them. He says: [etc.]. **1898** 'H. S. MERRIMAN' *Roden's Corner* xxvii, A gesture that served.. to..invite the Frenchman to up and smite him.

**6.** To move upwards; to rise or ascend. Also with *it.*

**1737** OZELL *Rabelais* II. 103 A Chimney-sweeper *ups* and *downs* it in a Chimney, with his long Broom. *c* **1810** COLERIDGE *Lit. Rem.* (1838) III. 328 He flounders backward and forward, now upping and now downing. **1825** LADY GRANVILLE *Lett.* (1894) I. 360 What an odd thing life is, and how it ups and downs.

**7.** *To up with*: **a.** To come out with (a story, etc.). *rare.*—¹ Cf. OUT *v.* 4 b.

**1715** M. DAVIES *Athen. Brit.* I. 31 Sir Thomas up's with a Story of the Curs baiting of the Butcher's Dog.

**b.** *colloq.* To raise (the arm, etc.); to elevate; to lift or pick up.

**1760** H. BROOKE *Fool of Qual.* (1809) I. 63 She ups with her brawny arm. **1825** T. HOOK *Sayings* Ser. II. II. 356 Mrs. South..'upped with the turbot and popped it into the dish'. **1851** H. NEWLAND *The Erne* 37 Had he upped with his pilgrim-staff, and broken the man's heretical head. **1887** G. R. SIMS *Mary Jane's Mem.* 30 He ups with the spade in a minute.

**c.** *Naut.* To place (the helm or tiller) so as to carry the rudder to leeward.

**1860** W. H. RUSSELL *Diary India* I. 95 And there..stand the four Chinese helmsmen,..upping with the helm and downing with it.

**Up** (vp), *adv.*¹ Forms: 1– up, 4–7 vp, 5–6 *Sc.* wp; 1–7 upp, 4–6 vpp; 3–5 uppe, 3–7 vppe (5 wppe, 6 huppe); 3–5, 9 *dial.* op, 4 ope, 5 oppe, hoppe, hope; 5, 6 *Sc.* vpe, wpe, 6 upe. [OE. *upp, up,* = OFris. *up, op* (WFris. *op,* NFris. *ap*), OLFr. **up* (MDu. *up, op,* Du. *op*), OS. *up* (MLG., LG. *up*), ON. *upp* (Norw. *upp*; MSw. *up, op,* Sw. *upp,* Da. *op*), related to OHG. *ûf* (MHG. *uf, ouf,* G. *auf*) and Goth. *iup.*

There does not appear to be sufficient evidence for the assumption that the normal OE. form was *ūp,* and that *ŭpp, ŭp* are due to the influence of *uppe* UP *adv.*² and *uppan* UP *prep.*¹, unless it is assumed that the same change has taken place in all the related languages except High German.]

**I.** Denoting actual movement or direction in (or in relation to) space.

**1.** To or towards a point or place higher than another and lying directly (or almost directly) above it; so as to raise or bring, come or tend, to or towards a higher position in space.

Freq. denoting the elevating or rising of only part of the thing spoken of.

*c* **888** K. ÆLFRED *Boeth.* xxxiv. § 11 Hwæðer þu nu onȝite forhwy þæt fyr fundiȝe up & sio eorðe ofdune? *a* **1000** *Riddles* lv. [liv.] 4 Hyse..hof his aȝen hræȝl hondum up. *c* **1000** *Sax. Leechd.* III. 252 Æfter heora ȝerepe gæð seo ea up..& ofer flett eall þæt egiptisce land. *a* **1122** *O. E. Chron.* (Laud MS.) an. 1099, Ðises ȝeares..asprang up..sæ-flod. *a* **1225** *Ancr. R.* 280 He iseih hu ueole þe grimme wrastlare of helle breid up on his hupe. *c* **1280** *Vox & Wolf* 75 Wen me shulde þat on op winde, Þat oþer wolde adoun winde. **13..** *Gaw. & Gr. Knt.* 1192 Ho..stel to his bedde, Kest vp þe cortyn [etc.]. **1340–70** *Alex. & Dind.* 483 Whan þe watur wiþ þe wind þe wawus vp casteþ. *a* **1400** *Pistill of Susan* 229 To the ȝate ȝaply þei ȝeoden..And he lift vp þe lach and leop ouer þe lake. *c* **1420** *Anturs of Arth.* 408 He wayned vp his viser fro his ventalle. **1423** JAS. I *King's Q.* clxv, Quhere sum were slungin..vnto the ground, Full sudaynly sche hath [them] vp ythrungin. *c* **1450** *Mirk's Festial* 2 Þe see schall aryse vp yn hyr styd, soo þat þe watyr schall be hear then ayny hyll. **1535** *MS. Rawl.* 777 fol. 86, A smale Rope for the plommers to pull vppe there Irons vnto the leades. **1548** ELYOT, *Scintillatio,*..a sparkelyng vp of fire. **1570** DEE *Math. Pref.* 35 Catchyng hold of their Shyps, and hoysing them vp aboue the water. **1598** SHAKS. *Merry W.* IV. ii. 57 Ile creepe vp into the chimney. **1610** B. JONSON *Alch.* II. iii, Shee'll mount you vp, like quick-siluer, Ouer the helme. **1622** J. TAYLOR (Water P.) *Farew. to Tower-bottles* A 3 b, Thus like Times Football was I often tost In Dock out Nettle, vp downe. **1640** tr. *Verdere's Rom. of Rom.* III. xxx. 129 The Knight of the Eagles presently lift up his Bever. **1667** MILTON *P. L.* III. 574 Thither his course he bends..; but up or downe, ..[it is] hard to tell. **1706** MOTTEUX *Vanbrugh's Mistake* Epil., Nor.., With Glass drawn up, Drive about Covent-Garden. **1766** G. WILLIAMS *Let.* in *G. Selwyn* (1843) II. 42 After he has pulled up his stockings. **1772** HUTTON *Bridges* 99 A large ram of iron..being lift up to the top of them. **1805** *Naval Chron.* XIV. 154 The hatches had bursted up. **1827** FARADAY *Chem. Manip.* iii. (1842) 77 The air..will immediately pass up by the hair or wire.

*transf.* **1843** *Penny Cycl.* XXVI. 419/1 Voices..capable of extending their compass by running up into a falsetto. **1890** *Good Words* Aug. 520/2 The barometer..is going up at a tremendous rate.

**b.** Towards or above the level of the shoulders or head.

*Beowulf* 2575 Hond up abræd Ȝeata dryhten, gryrefahne sloh. *a* **900** *O. E. Martyrol.* 18 April 58 Þonne he hof his hond upp to hiofonum, þonne hofon þa deor heora fotas upp. *c* **1000** ÆLFRIC *Exod.* viii. 17 Aaron ahefde up hys hand. *c* **1250** *Gen. & Ex.* 3057 Moyses..helde up is hond. *a* **1300** *Cursor M.* 4767 Oft he liftud vp his hend To godd, þat he helpe þam wald send. **1387** TREVISA *Higden* (Rolls) VIII. 11 He..haf up his handes and seide, 'I praye [etc.]'. **1455** E. CLARE in *Paston Lett.* I. 315 Than he hild up his hands and thankid God. **1590** LODGE *Euphues Gold. Leg.* (1887) 21 Casting up his hand he felt hair on his face. **1639** E. SPENSER in *Lismore Papers* Ser. II. (1888) IV. 75 He heaved vp his sticke with an intent..to haue strooken me. **1719** DE FOE *Crusoe* I. (Globe) 256, I saw one of the Villains lift up his Arm with a great Cutlash..to strike one of the poor Men. **1853** *Public School Matches* 14 The wicket-keeper puts up his hands. **1887** MRS. PERKS *From Heather Hills* I. vi. 114 Eliza's hands went up in horror.

**c.** So as to raise into a more erect (or level) as well as elevated position.

*c* **897** K. ÆLFRED *Gregory's Past C.* liv. 425 Ne hebbe ȝe to up eowre hornas. Ðonne ahebbað ða synfullan swiðe up hira hornas [etc.]. **971** *Blickl. Hom.* 187 'Rære up þin heafod.'..Þa ahof Paulus up his heafod. *a* **1300**–[see LIFT *v.* 5 c]. **1390** GOWER *Conf.* I. 219 With that he pulleth up his hed, And made riht a glad visage. **1535** COVERDALE *Job.* x. 15 Yf I be rightuous, yet darre I not lift vp my heade. — *Ezek.* viii. 17 Purposly to cast vp their noses vpon me. **1570** *Satir. Poems Reform.* I. 90 Than did sum Lords lyft vp yair hornis on hie. **1607** MARKHAM *Cavel.* II. 208 The horse..dare neyther tosse vp his heade, nor ducke it downe. **1678, 1756** [see TOSS *v.* II]. **1875** WHYTE-MELVILLE *Riding Recoll.* (1878) 48 Up go their heads to avoid the pain.

**d.** So as to raise a thing from the place in which it is lying, placed, or fixed.

For the specific sense 'into a vehicle (boat, etc.)', see TAKE *v.* 90 b e, PICK *v.* 20 e.

*c* **900** *Baeda's Hist.* III. xv. (1890) 200 Þa scipmen þa oncras upp teon, & in þone sæ syndon. *c* **1000** ÆLFRIC *Gen.* vii. 17 Ða wæteru..ahefdon up ðone arc. — *Saints' Lives* viii. 212 Hine ȝelæhte an hors..mid toðum and hefde him upp. *c* **1052** *O. E. Chron.* (MS. C), Hiȝ brudon up ða sona heora ancran. *a* **1300**- [see TAKE *v.* 90 a]. **1382** WYCLIF 2 *Esdr.* ii. 1, I heuede vp the win, and ȝaf to the king. **1387** TREVISA *Higden* (Rolls) VII. 349 A whirlewynd..lefte up sixe rafters of þe cherche. *c* **1430** *Two Cookery Bks.* 5 Þan take hem vp of þe water after þe fyrst boylyng. **1458** in Parker *Dom. Archit.* III. 41 Som oute of her sadels flette to the grounde...Her kyn..caught hem uppe with care. *a* **1533** LD. BERNERS *Huon* lxi. 213 They weyed vp theyr ancres & lyft vp theyr saylles. **1535** COVERDALE 2 *Esdr.* ii. 1, I toke vp the wyne, and gaue it vnto ye kynge. **1602**- [see DIP *v.* 5]. **1662**- [see GET *v.* 72 j]. **1694** *Lond. Gaz.* No. 3023/1 As soon as they could get up their Anchors they sailed away. *a* **1704**- [see PICK *v.* 20 b]. **1725** T. LEWIS *Antiq. Hebr. Rep.* III. 270 When she had lift it [*sc.* a shoe] up. **187**. B. HARTE *High Water Mark* Wks. (1873) 70 She dipped up the water to cool her parched throat.

**e.** So as to invert the relative position of things or surfaces; so as to have a particular surface facing upwards.

*a* **1300** in *E. E. P.* (1862) 21 Turne him uppe, turne him down,..ouer al þou findist him blodi oþer wan. *c* **1340** HAMPOLE *Pr. Consc.* 673 What es man in shap bot a tre Turned up þat es doun. *Ibid.* 1602 Þus es þis world turned up þat es doune. *c* **1375** *Sc. Leg. Saints* xxii. (*Lawrence*) 489 Þe rostit syd turne vpe & ete. **1611**- [see TURN *v.* 80 c, g, h, i]. **1853** DE QUINCEY *Autobiog. Sk.* Wks. I. 189 'We tossed up,' to settle the question...'Heads' came up. **1863** 'CAVENDISH' *Whist* (ed. 5) 37 In trumps, if king or queen is turned up.

**2.** Towards a point overhead, or away from the surface of the earth; into the air.

*Beowulf* 1373 Þonon yðȝeblond up astiȝeð won to wolcnum. *c* **888** K. ÆLFRED *Boeth.* vii. § 3 Þonne ic up ȝefere..swa se earn ðonne he up ȝewit bufan ða wolcnu. **971** *Blickl. Hom.* 143 Þa apostolas tuȝon hie up & hie ȝesetton on..neorxna wange. *c* **1000** ÆLFRIC *Saints' Lives* xxvii. 100 Æfter ðysum wordum ȝewende se engel up. *c* **1220** *Bestiary* 64 Ðer-ouer he fleȝeð, and up he fleȝeð, til ðat he ðe heuene seð. **1382** WYCLIF *Acts* i. 9 He was lift vp, and a cloud receyuede hym. **1526** *Pilgr. Perf.* (1531) 166 As a ball, which yf it be tossed and cast vp streyght, it falleth down [etc.]. **1535** COVERDALE *Job* xxxix. 27 Doth the Aegle mounte vp..at thy commaundement? **1591** RALEIGH *Last Fight Reuenge* B 4 b, Doubting least S. Richard would haue blowne them vp and himselfe. **1599**- [see BLOW *v.* 24]. **1647** N. BACON *Disc. Govt. Eng.* I. lvii. 167 Like a vapour mounted up by the Clergy. **1833** J. HOLLAND *Manuf. Metal* II. vii. 189 The fresh coals..will throw up,..as usual, a body of thick smoke. **1853** *Public School Matches* 16 An appeal to the umpire, and up goes the ball.

**b.** With defining adv. or prep. phrase.

*c* **900** tr. *Baeda's Hist.* III. xvi. (1890) 202 Þa he þa se biscop ȝeseah..þone rec up ofer þære burȝe wallas ahefenne. **971** *Blickl. Hom.* 123 Þes Hælend þe nu up on þysne heofon.. astaȝ. *c* **1000** in *Wulfstan's Hom.* (1883) 100 He stah up to ðam stepele and of ðam stepele hof upp on lyfte. *c* **1200** ORMIN Ded. 234 Þurrh þatt he [*sc.* Christ] stah forr ure god Upp inntill heffness blisse. **1297** R. GLOUC. (Rolls) 168 [To] bloue hom here & þere vp in þe luft anhei. *c* **1340** HAMPOLE *Pr. Consc.* 5027 Alle þat er gude..sal..up in-to þe ayre be ravyste. *c* **1375** *Sc. Leg. Saints* i. (*Peter*) 559 A day he sat þame till, vp in hewine quhen he suld fle. **1482** *Monk of Evesham* (Arb.) 107 Now sche was lyfte vppe an hye. **1539** BIBLE 2 *Sam.* xviii. 9 He was lifte vp betwene heuen & erthe. **1593** SHAKS. *Ven. & Ad.* 853 Here the gentle larke..mounts vp on hie. **1617** MORYSON *Itin.* I. 206 Vines growing up high upon the Elmes. **1680** C. NESSE *Ch. Hist.* 284 Him..whom he hop'd to help up upon the lofty gallows. *a* **1721** SHEFFIELD (Dk. Buckhm.) *Wks.* (1753) I. 12 The sigh ..Up tow'rds the heavens like a bright meteor soar'd. **1824** JAS. TELFER *Border Ball.* 42 They sprang upthrough the welkin high. **1904** SPENCER & GILLEN *Northern Tribes Australia* xv. 487 Then he took him away up into the sky.

**c.** To some height above the ground or other surface; from or off the ground; *spec.* to a seat on horseback; to or towards the mast-head.

*c* **897** K. ÆLFRED *Gregory's Past. C.* 173 Ðonne hi hebbað ..ða earce up. *c* **1200** ORMIN 16705 All swa se Moysæs Hof upp þe neddre i wesste. *c* **1205** LAY. 30607 Heo wunden up seiles to coppe. *c* **1290** *S. Eng. Leg.* I. 41/232 Lupe þou up bi-hynde me. *Ibid.* 134/961 He..a-rerde op is baner. **1377** LANGL. *P. Pl.* B. XVIII. 52 Poysoun on a pole þei put vp to his lippes. **1382** WYCLIF *John* iii. 14 As Moyses reride vp a serpent in desert. *c* **1400** *Destr. Troy* 10858 And pull vp a port, let hom passe furthe. *c* **1440** *Generydes* 2262 Generydes leppe vppe vppon his stede. **1450** *Bk. Hawkyng* in *Rel. Ant.* I. 297 Lete the spanyell flusch up the covey. *c* **1450** *Coventry Myst.* (1922) 301 And he xal make hym to ..gon up on a leddere. **1508** DUNBAR *Gold. Targe* 236 And swyth vp saile vnto the top thai stent. **1582** STANYHURST *Æneis* III. (Arb.) 87 Foorth we take oure passadge, oure sayles ful winged vp hoysting. **1606** SHAKS. *Ant. & Cl.* V. ii. 56 Shall they hoyst me vp, And shew me to the showting Varlotarie Of censuring Rome? **1629**- [see PUT *v.* 53 b]. **1697** DAMPIER *Voy.* 416 Having fine handsome weather, we got up our Yards again. **1738** *Voy. up Thames* 31 Having put up a Sail in one of the small Wherries. **1821** SCOTT *Pirate* xl, Up goes the Jolly Hodge, the old black flag.

**d.** So as to be suspended aloft or on high; into a hanging position.

*c* **1000** ÆLFRIC *Joshua* x. 26 Iosue hi ofsloh ða & siððan up aheng on fif wacum boȝum. *a* **1200** *Vices & Virtues* 49 He ðe weiȝþ upp mid his fingre heuene and ierðe. **1297**- [see HANG *v.* 28 a, b, c]. *c* **1375** *Sc. Leg. Saints* xxxiii. (*George*) 780 Þane gert he men but mare hang hyre hey vpe be þe hare. **1430-40** LYDG. *Bochas* VIII. 1890 How he hymsilfe heng up bi the hals. **1536**- [see TRUSS *v.* 7]. **1711** ADDISON *Spect.* No. 47 ¶ 3 The Dutch..hang up in several of their Streets what they call the Sign of the Gaper.

**3.** From beneath the horizon to the line of vision.

*c* **888** K. ÆLFRED *Boeth.* xxxix. § 13 Þonne hate we hine morȝensteorra, forþam he cymð eastan up. *c* **937** *Brunanburh* 13 Siðþan sunne up..glad ofer grundas. *a* **1000** *Narrat. Angl. Conscr.* (1861) 30 Mid þy ða ærest se mona up eode. *c* **1386** CHAUCER *Sqr.'s T.* 365 Er þat the sonne gan vp glyde. *c* **1400** *Destr. Troy* 755 Whan þe day vp droghe & the dym voidet. *Ibid.* 8455 When the sun vp set with his softe beames. **1508** DUNBAR *Gold. Targe* 4 Wp sprang the goldyn candill matutyne. — *Tua Mariit Wemen* 512 Quhill that the day did vp daw. **1556-1632** [see FETCH *v.* 19 h]. **1655** H. VAUGHAN *Silex Scint.* I. 73 Yet, never sleep the Sun up; Prayer shou'd Dawn with the day. **1698** [see TURN *v.* 80 q]. **1744** THOMSON *Winter* 878 The welcome Sun, just verging up at first, By small Degrees extends the swelling Curve.

*fig.* **1807** J. BARLOW *Columb.* I. 204 The sun's blue ray Topt unknown cliffs and call'd them up to day.

**b.** From below the level of the earth, water, etc., to the surface. With (*a*) intransitive and (*b*) transitive verbs, and freq. with the addition of a prepositional phrase (*of the earth*, etc.).

With *grow*, etc., in reference to plants, passing into sense 4. For further examples with trans. verbs, see DELVE *v.*[4], DIG *v.* 14, GRUB *v.* 3, TURN *v.* 80 r, WEIGH *v.* 6 b.

(*a*) *Beowulf* 1619 Sone wæs [he] on sunde,..wæter up þurhdeaf. *c* **888** K. ÆLFRED *Boeth.* xxxiv. § 6 Þæt wæter..cymð þonne up æt þæm æwelme. *c* **893** — *Oros.* I. i. § 9 Seo ea.. up aspryngð neh þæm clife. *c* **975** *Rushw. Gosp.* Matt. xiii. 5 Hræþe cuomun [hie] upp forþon þe hie næfdon heanisse eorðe. *c* **1000** ÆLFRIC *Gen.* ii. 5 Ælcne telȝor on eorðan, ær ðan ðe he up asprunge.., & eall gærs..ær ðan ðe hi up asprytton. *c* **1220** *Bestiary* 579 Ðe sipes [= ships] sinken .., ne cumen he nummor up. **1297** R. GLOUC. (Rolls) 165 Þe wind þere..Vp of þe erþe ofte comþ. *a* **1300**- [see SPRING *v.*[1] 8 c]. **1303** R. BRUNNE *Handl. Synne* 9767 Vpp of hys graue a fyre vpp smote. **13**.. *E. E. Allit. P.* A. 35 So semly a sede moȝt fayly not, Þat springande spycez vp ne sponne. **1530** PALSGR. 692/1 It is a plesaunt syght to se the water ryse up..out of a spring. **1535** COVERDALE *Job* xiv. 2 He commeth vp, and falleth awaye like a floure. **1667** MILTON *P. L.* VII. 456 Living Creatures..out of the ground up rose. **1835** MARRYAT *J. Faithful* i, My father burst up from the cabin. **1844** DICKENS in *Story of his Life* (1870) 156, I am here—just come up from underground. **1866** SHUCKARD *Brit. Bees* 223 A thick and prodigious quantity of the common mustard plant shot up.

(*b*) *c* **900** *Baeda's Hist.* III. vii. (1890) 168 Hædde biscop heht his lichoman up adon. *a* **1000** *Narrat. Angl. Conscr.* (1861) 35 Hy..delfaþ gold up of eorþan. *c* **1000** ÆLFRIC *Gen.* xxxvii. 28 Hi tuȝon hine up of þam pytte. *c* **1000** — *Saints' Lives* xxi. 136 Eadgar cyning..wolde þæt se halȝa wer wurde up ȝedon. *a* **1122** *O. E. Chron.* (Laud MS.) an. 963, He nam up Sancta Kyneburh & S. Kynesuið. *c* **1375** *Sc. Leg. Saints* xxxvi. (*Baptist*) 561 Sarazenis syne vpe can ta..his banis. **1387** TREVISA *Higden* (Rolls) VII. 77 Hircanus took up þre þowsand talentes of kyng David his grave. *c* **1440** *Promp. Parv.* 118 Delvyn vp owte of the erthe, *effodio.* **1494** *Acc. Ld. High Treas. Scot.* I. 251 Sertane wrychtis..takand wpe the auld schype, that was sunkyne..in the watter. **1548** HALL *Chron.*, *Richard III*, 27 b, Some saye that kynge Richard caused the priest to take them vp,..and to put them in a coffyne. **1563** FULKE *Meteors* (1571) 66 b, When they plowe the grounde [they] turne vp syluer, among the clottes. **1588** SHAKS. *Tit. A.* V. i. 135 Oft haue I dig'd vp dead men from their graues. **1632** MILTON *Penseroso* 109 That thy power Might..call up him that left half told The story of Cambuscan bold. **1660** SHARROCK *Vegetables* 100 This he onely did by casting up their nests. **1748** *Anson's Voy.* II. viii. 219 The taking up oysters from great depths..by Negro slaves. **1821** SCOTT *Pirate* xxxvi, Go down below, my girls,..and send up the rare old man. **1851** MRS. BROWNING *Casa Guidi Wind.* II. 325 Ye called up ghosts, believing they were slack To follow [etc.].

**c.** So as to detach from being fixed in the soil or other surface.

See also GRUB *v.* 3, PLUCK *v.* 8 b, PULL *v.* 31 b, ROOT *v.*[1] 5.

*a* **1100** in Napier *O. E. Glosses* I. 2903 *Euulsum, i. abscisum*, ut alocene, up aliþode. *c* **1200** ORMIN 9285 Illc an treo..Shall bi þe grund beon hæwenn upp. **1297** R. GLOUC. (Rolls) 10264 Ech tre were vp mored þat it ne spronge namore þere. **1362** LANGL. *P. Pl.* A. VII. 104 Summe, to plese perkyn, pykeden vp þe weodes. *a* **1400-50** *Alexander* 409 Þis diuinour..ȝede ..herbis to seche, Reft þam vp be þe rotis. *c* **1440** *Pallad. on Husb.* VIII. 14 Er the Canyculer, the hounde, ascende Haue vp the fern and seggis to be brende. *c* **1550** CHEKE *Matt.* xiii. 29 Leest in weeding ye darnel, ye pluck vp also ye corn. **1573** TUSSER *Husb.* (1878) 37 A pike for to pike them [*sc.* vetches] vp handsom to drie. **1699** DAMPIER *Voy.* II. III. vi. 67 By tearing up the Trees by the Roots. *a* **1701** MAUNDRELL *Journ. Jerus.* (1707) 144 In gathering their Corn,..they pluck'd it up by handfuls from the roots. **1738** *Voy. up Thames* 79 The Humour..of grubbing up every Tree in the Neighbourhood. **1841** *Jrnl. R. Agric. Soc.* II. II. 229 The turnips were taken up and carted.

**d.** From the stomach into, or out at, the mouth; out of the sea on to the shore, etc.

*c* **1000** *Sax. Leechd.* I. 74 Wiþ þon ðe men blod upp wealle þurh his muð. *c* **1315** SHOREHAM *Poems* I. 778 He soffreþ wel to be kest op, And ȝet to be honoured. **13**.. *E. E. Allit. P.* C. 340 Þe whal wendez at his wylle & a warþe fyndez, & þer he brakez vp þe buyrne. **1377** LANGL. *P. Pl.* B. V. 379, I glotoun girt it [*sc.* food] vp, er I hadde gone a myle. **1484**-[see CAST *v.* 83 b, c]. **1541** ELYOT *Image Gov.* 23 He immediately wolde vomit vp colar. **1570** GOOGE *Popish Kingd.* IV. 53 And miserably they reele, till as their stomacke vp they lay. **1599**, **1622** [see FETCH *v.* 19 b]. **1610**, **1648** [see BELCH *v.* 4 b]. **1693**- [see VOMIT *v.* 2 b]. **1733**- [see THROW *v.* 48 b]. **1863** ROBSON *Bards of Tyne* 433 Whey, she had bowk't the sma' beer up.

*fig.* *c* **1205** LAY. 3532 Þa alles vppe abræc, hit wes god þet heo spæc. *a* **1225** *Ancr. R.* 426 Hwon his blowinge ne geineð nout, þeonne bringeð he up some luðer word. **1633** T. ADAMS *Exp. 2 Peter* ii. 22. 1094 Sinne, like *Stibium*, will tarry with no body: up it must.

**4.** So as to extend or rise to a higher point or level, esp. above the surface of the ground. With (*a*) intransitive and (*b*) transitive verbs.

For the use with *run*, etc., in reference to plants, cf. sense 3 b. With *build*, *make* (see MAKE *v.* 96 a, b), etc., restoration is freq. implied (cf. sense 20 b).

(*a*) *a* **900** *O. E. Martyrol.* 21 Dec. 222 On þam wæron þa wealdleðer swa upȝetiȝed, swa swa hiȝ urnon to heofenum up. *c* **1000**- [see sense 26 a]. **1387** TREVISA *Higden* (Rolls) VI. 305 A piler of liȝt þat stood up from his body into hevene. **1390** GOWER *Conf.* I. 173 As the Netle which up renneth The..Roses brenneth. **1530** TINDALE *Exod.* ix. 32 The barly was shott vp [1611 in the eare] & the flaxe was boulled. **1582** STANYHURST *Æneis* IV. (Arb.) 107 If ye be delighted, too see new Carthage vp hoouering. **1610** HOLLAND *Camden's Brit.* I. 288 There riseth up an high mount. **1611** BIBLE *Exod.* ix. 32 The wheat and the rye..were not growen vp. **1699** EVELYN *Kal. Hort.* (ed. 9) 97 If Plants run up to Seed over-hastily. **1726** SWIFT *Gulliver* III. iii, One..plate of adamant, shooting up to the height of about two hundred yards. **1731**- [see RUN *v.* 81 a]. **1840** [see GROW *v.* 13 b]. **1858** LYTTON *What will He do?* I. iv, At the rear of the palace soars up the old Abbey. **1878** SMILES *R. Dick* i. 3 It shoots up into a tall rocky point.

(*b*) **971** *Blickl. Hom.* 127 Þonne is þær..ȝeworht..up oþ mannes breost heah. *c* **1200** ORMIN 9204 Nu sket shall illc an dale beon All heȝhedd upp & filledd. *c* **1205** LAY. 8716 Þa þet work [*sc.* a castle] wes up iset, heom wes alles þa bet. **1297** R. GLOUC. (Rolls) 3023 Þe king..let rere up chirchen. **1338** R. BRUNNE *Chron.* (1810) 88 Whan he was at London, a haule he did vp wright. **1382** WYCLIF 2 *Esdr.* ii. 17 Bilde we vp the wallis of Jerusalem. *Ibid.* iii. 1 Thei bilden vp the ȝatis of the floc. **1390** GOWER *Conf.* I. 53 To him that Thebes ferst on hyh Up sette. *c* **1400** *Destr. Troy* 1535 Priam .. byld vp a bygge towne of þe bare vrthe. *c* **1440** *Pallad. on Husb.* I. 435 When that is drie, vp walle hit euery side In lyke maner. **1479** *Nottingham Rec.* II. 390 That the seid howse be fenysshit, reryd and made upp. **1509** HAWES *Past. Pleas.* XXXV. (Percy Soc.) 182 He stretched hym up and lyft his axe a lofte. **1596** DALRYMPLE tr. *Leslie's Hist. Scot.* (S.T.S.) I. 173 Quhen he had bigit the wal wpe agane. **1687**- [see RUN *v.* 81 j]. **1730** THOMSON *Autumn* 137 On either hand..groves of masts Shot up their spires. **1788** J. MAY *Jrnl. & Lett.* (1873) 86 To-day finished laying up the house, and put on the roof. **1812** L. HUNT in *Examiner* 12 Oct. 642/2 The carpenters that knock up our hustings. **1873** H. SPENCER *Stud. Sociol.* xi. 287 Here are lighthouses we have put up to prevent shipwrecks.

**b.** With indication of a point of measurement.

*c* **1400** *Destr. Troy* 1548 The walle..of marbill was most fro þe myddes vp. **1473-4** *Acc. Ld. High Treas. Scot.* I. 30 Brade clath for ij goonis and ij kirtillis..for the lyning of thaim fra the waist vpe. **1877** RUSKIN *St. Mark's Rest* Suppl. i. 5 All the rest mere flat wall, wainscoted two-thirds up, eight feet or so.

**c.** So as to form a heap or pile, or become more prominent. (Also in fig. expressions.)

See also CAST *v.* 83 e, EARTH *v.* 3, MAKE *v.* 96 b, PUFF *v.* 4, 5, RIDGE *v.* 2, RISE *v.* 10 c, SWELL *v.* 2, THROW *v.*[1] 48 d.

*c* **1310** *Prov. Hendyng* 142 (MS. Harl. 2253), Bynd þine tonge wiþ bonene wal; Let hit don synke, þer hit up swal. **1523** FITZHERB. *Husb.* § 13 In the begynnynge of Marche, rydge it vppe agayne. **1535** COVERDALE *Job* xvi. 4 Then shulde I heape vp wordes agaynst you. — *Zech.* ix. 3 Tyrus shal..heape vp syluer as the sonde. **1576** FLEMING *Panopl. Epist.* 372 Ignoraunce doth..pile them vp one vpon another. **1586** A. DAY *Eng. Secretorie* I. (1595) 140 You must needs heap vp no other but extremities vppon her. **1611** BIBLE *Eccl.* ii. 26 To the sinner hee giueth..to gather and to heape vp. **1664** EVELYN *Sylva* (1679) 10 Your plants beginning now to peep, should be earthed up. **1718** BP. HUTCHINSON *Witchcraft* i. 8 They can huff up their Bellies, that they may seem much swell'd. **1751** JORTIN *Serm.* (1771) II. 37 Some heap up riches. **1776** SEMPLE *Building in Water* 109 To rise or bank up the Bed of the River. **1825** JAMIESON, *Hot*,..a small heap of any kind carelessly put up. **1837** P. KEITH *Bot. Lex.* 37 The vessels become convoluted and swell up into a bunch. **1839** URE *Dict. Arts* 751 The sediment called smitham is taken out, and piled up in heaps.

**5.** So as to raise or rise from a horizontal, relaxed, or drooping posture to an upright or nearly upright position.

*a* **900** *Genesis* 1675 [Hie] to heofnum up hlædræ rærdon. *a* **1240** *Wohunge* in *O. E. Hom.* I. 283 Nu raise þai up þe rode. *a* **1300** *Cursor M.* 22548 (Edinb.), Þe tres forcastin sal þaim payn For to riht þaim op ogayn. **1387** TREVISA *Higden* (Rolls) V. 399 Þey arered up þe baner of þe cros. **1530** TINDALE *Gen.* xxviii. 18 Iacob..toke the stone..and pitched it vp an ende. **1598** MARSTON *Sco. Villanie* II. vi. (1599) 201 Capro reads,..Strokes vp his haire. **1608** TOPSELL *Serpents* 117 The tayle is very long, at the end and turning vp like a Vipers tayle. *a* **1732** T. BOSTON *Crook in Lot* (1805) 152 God will..remove the weight..and let them get up their back long bowed. **1784** J. POTTER *Virtuous Villagers* I. 51 She now and then bridled herself up a little in the..style of an old maid. **1837** MARRYAT *P. Keene* i, The honourable spinster bridled up with indignation. **1850** *Tait's Mag.* XVII. 342/2 The Doctor..drew himself up in offended dignity.

**b.** Upon one's feet from a recumbent or reclining posture; *spec.* out of bed.

Also from a recumbent to a sitting posture: see GET *v.* 72 a, SIT *v.* 25 a, c. With reference to the rising of the dead there may be an admixture of sense 3 b.

(*a*) *c* **900** tr. *Baeda's Hist.* V. xii. (1899) 613/2 On daȝunge he eft acwicode & sæmnunga upp [*v.r.* up heh] asæt. *c* **1200** ORMIN 8363 He ras up & toc þe child,..& for till Israæless land. *c* **1205** LAY. 6495 Þat deor up astod and ræsde o þene stede. *a* **1250** *Owl & Night.* 731 Clerekes, munekes, & canunes..Ariseþ up to middelnyhte. *c* **1325** *Spec. Gy Warw.* 251 Vp he ros þe þridde day. **1382** WYCLIF *Matt.* ii. 13 The aungel of the Lord apperide in sleep to Joseph, sayynge, Ryse vp,..and flee in to Egipt. *a* **1400-50** *Alexander* 5055 Sone as þe day-rawe rase he risis vp belyue. *c* **1400** *Laud Troy Bk.* 5779 Menescen was feld, but op he ros. **1535** COVERDALE 2 *Esdr.* ii. 12, I gat me vp in yᵉ night season. *a* **1550**- [see GET *v.* 72 a]. **1590**- [see RISE *v.* 3 b]. **1629** WADSWORTH *Pilgr.* iii. 14 Euery morning the fift houre summons them vp. **1671** MILTON *P. R.* II. 282 Lightly from his grassy Couch up rose Our Saviour. **1719** DE FOE *Crusoe* II. (Globe) 363 Being thus gotten up, he look'd out. **1803** *Med. Jrnl.* 520 The patients..endeavoured to get up, and to remain out of bed. **1865** L. OLIPHANT *Piccadilly* (1870) 317, I went to bed, and did not get up till the lamps were being lighted in Piccadilly.

(*b*) **971** *Blickl. Hom.* 157 Þa ahof Drihten hie up & hie þa cyste. *c* **1290** *Beket* 85 in *S. Eng. Leg.* I. 109 For Ioye heo ful a-doun i-swowe...þe knaue hire op nam. *a* **1300** *Cursor M.* 25743 Penance..quen we fall vp mai vs lifte. **1470-85** [see HEAVE *v.* 1]. **1537** BIBLE 2 *Sam.* xii. 17 The elders..went to him to take him vp from the erth. 1590 SPENSER *F. Q.* I. viii. 40 He found the meanes that Prisoner vp to reare. 1591–3 [see REAR *v.*[1] 2 b, 2 c]. 1663– [see KNOCK *v.* 16 f]. 1749 FIELDING *Tom Jones* VII. xii, [They] had raised up the body of Jones, but..again let him fall. 1850 TENNYSON *In Mem.* xxxi, Behold a man raised up by Christ!

*fig.* 1642 T. CASE *Gods Rising* (1644) 3 It is the duty of Gods people, to pray him up, when he seems to be down.

**c.** So as to rise from a sitting, stooping, or kneeling posture and assume an erect attitude.

See also GET *v.* 72 a, p, HELP *v.* 6, LEAP *v.* 4, STAND *v.* 103 a. For *up and—*, see sense 31.

*c* 1000 *Ags. Gosp.* John viii. 7 Se hælend abeah nyþer;..þa aras he upp. *c* 1290 *Beket* 1371 in *S. Eng. Leg.* I. 145 Seint thomas wolde op arise: Men beden him sitte a-doun. *c* 1330 R. BRUNNE *Chron. Wace* (Rolls) 1803 Coryneus first vp he stirt, & wyþ a cloþ his body gyrt. 1340 *Ayenb.* 240 Þo ihip op þe mayster and him keste. *a* 1400–50 *Alexander* 82 Artaxenses is..resyn vp with all his rewme to ride vs agayn. *Ibid.* 2074 Þan pullis him vp þe proude kyng. 1503 HAWES *Examp. Virt.* vii. 150 With that dame Iustyce vp arose. 1526 TINDALE *Luke* xiii. 11 [The] woman..was bowed to gether, and coulde nott well lifte vp her silfe. 1535 COVERDALE 1 *Chron.* xxiii. 16 Yet get the vp, and be doynge. — 2 *Esdras* ii. 20 We..are gotten vp, & are buyldinge. 1667 MILTON *P. L.* VIII. 258 Up I sprung...and upright Stood on my feet. 1795 MACNEILL *Scotland's Scaith* v. vii, Up he bang'd; and..Sad and silent took the road. 1802 LEYDEN *Cout of Keeldar* xiv, A wee man..Up started by a cairn. 1877 SPURGEON *Serm.* XXIII. 82 The rebel may stand up in bold defiance.

*fig.* 1656 COWLEY *Chronicle* iii, Till up in Arms my Passions rose, And cast away her yoke.

**6.** So as to mount or rise by gradual ascent, in contact with a surface, to a higher level or altitude; sometimes *spec.* = up-stairs.

*Beowulf* 2893 Heht ðа þæt heaðoweorc to hagan biodan, up ofer ecgclif. *c* 900 tr. *Baeda's Hist.* I. vii. (1890) 38 Þa astah se..Godes andettere mid þa menigeo on þa dune upp. 944 *Charter* in Sweet *A. S. Reader* (1908) 57 Ðonne of ðam þornum up on ða lytlan dune middewearde. 991 in Thorpe *Laws* (1840) I. 286 Þeh..þa menn up ætberstan into þære byriȝ. *c* 1000 ÆLFRIC *Num.* xiv. 40 Sona on ærne merien [hy] astiȝon ȝewæpnode up to ðære dune. *a* 1066 in Kemble *Cod. Dipl.* IV. 221 Ðæt Urk min huskarl habbe his strand..upp of sæ and ut on sæ. *c* 1205 LAY. 25807 Beduer..up a-stæh þene munt. 1382 WYCLIF *Matt.* v. 1 Jhesus forsothe, seynge cumpanyes, wente vp in to an hill. *c* 1386 CHAUCER *Sqr.'s T.* 378 As rody and bright as dooth the yonge sonne That in the Ram is four degrees vp ronne. *c* 1400 *Destr. Troy* 4978 Goand vp by degres þurgh mony gay Alys. 1487–8 *Rec. St. Mary at Hill* (1905) 136 To William paris for amendyng of the floores in the house vppon the steyer, and for beryng vp of ij° sackes sonde. 1531 TINDALE *Exp.* 1 *John* (1538) 76 Yf a rude fellowe shulde breake vp into the kynges priue chambre. 1565 COOPER *Thesaurus* s.v. *Accliuis, Trames accliuis*, a way goyng vp against a hill. 1656 M. BEN ISRAEL *Vind. Jud.* 15 He went up into a belcony in the palace. 1713 SWIFT *Jrnl. to Stella* 10 Feb., Sterne..has been often to see me, he says, but my man has not yet let him up. 1753 *World* 37 There is hardly a chambermaid that will bring me up a bottle of water into my room. 1777 SHERIDAN *Sch. Scand.* I. i, Show him up.—He generally calls about this time. 1798 COLERIDGE *Anc. Mar.* IV. x, The moving Moon went up the sky, And no where did abide: Softly she was going up. 1818 SCOTT *Hrt. Midl.* xx, Widow Butler's bullseg, that I used to see spieling up on my bed. 1844 MRS. BROWNING *Lost Bower* ii, Summer-snow of apple blossoms running up from glade to glade. 1884 *Harper's Mag.* Jan. 211/2 You keep on plunging up and up until you are worn out.

**b.** To a higher point on or within a river, channel, etc., or a point further from the sea. Cf. UP *prep.*[2] 2.

847 in *O. E. Texts* 434 Ðonne up on broc oð heottes dic. *c* 900 *O. E. Chron.* (Parker MS.) an. 893, On þa ea hi tuȝon up hiora scipu oþ þone weald. 935 in Kemble *Cod. Dipl.* V. 220 Upp andlang Ocerburnan to halelan mærscæ.

*a* 1550 LELAND *Itin.* (1711) II. 52 From Mineheved up along the Severne Shore to Stoke Gurcy. 1600 HAKLUYT *Voy.* II. 194 The voyage..vp into the Bay of Saint Laurence..as farre as the Isle of Assumption. 1697 DAMPIER *Voy.* 5 We ..might have gone up into the River, having a strong tyde of flood. 1764 *Pres. St. Navig. Thames* 33 The Price of Carriage thro'..Locks, up even to Wallingford, might also be adjusted. 1790 BRUCE *Source of Nile* I. 48 They border upon another large tribe.., which extends from thence up into Nubia. 1867 SMYTH *Sailor's Word-bk.* 707 *Up along*, sailing from the mouth of the channel upwards. 1881 J. HATTON *New Ceylon* v. 136 The voyage up, with the trade goods, is done in a canoe.

†**c.** On shore; from the sea; at land. *Obs.*

*Beowulf* 224 Þanon up hraðe Wedera leode on wang stiȝon. *Ibid.* 1920 Het þa up beran æþelinga ȝestreon. *c* 893 K. ÆLFRED *Oros.* IV. x. § 10 He..up comon æt Leptan þæm tune. *c* 900 tr. *Baeda's Hist.* I. xxv. (1890) 58 On þyssum ealande com upp..Agustinus. *a* 1122 *O. E. Chron.* (Laud MS.) an. 1014, Cnut..com to Sandwic, & let þær up þa ȝislas þe his fæder ȝesealde wæron. *c* 1175 *Lamb. Hom.* 87 Þa þe heo comen on midden þere se, þa wes þet godes folc up of þere se agan. *c* 1290 *Beket* 1796 in *S. Eng. Leg.* I. 158 At douere were kniȝtes ȝare..Sone ase he come op þere al aredi him to quelle. *Ibid.* 1799. *c* 1350–1483 [see RIVE *v.*[2]]. *c* 1400 *Destr. Troy* 2017 Þai..Past into port,..Lepyn vp to þe lond, leuyn þere ship.

**d.** In conventional uses, esp. in contrast to DOWN *adv.* 2. (See also 26 c.)

[1382 WYCLIF *Matt.* xx. 18 Loo! we gon vp to Jerusalem.] ? 1475 *Stonor Papers* (Camden) I. 156, I com hoppe [= to London]..and grette nede I hadde now of you. 1516– [see COME *v.* 69 a]. 1518 in Leadam *Star Chamber Cases* (Selden) II. 129 The Inhabitauntes..sent vpp the seid John power.. to make further Sute..for Redresse. 1537 *Lett. & Papers Hen. VIII*, XII. I. 10 [They] marvel that..Sir George should ryde huppe at this time. 1610 B. JONSON *Alch.* II. vi, Shee's come vp here, of purpose To learne the fashion. 1667–8 MARVELL *Corr.* Wks. (Grosart) II. 240 Also they have sent for the Lieutenant Governor of Chester; he having writ up news that an apothecary of that town had [etc.]. 1707 *Lond. Gaz.* No. 2306/3 They came out of Ireland,..but met with a violent Storm that put them up as high as Lundy. 1719 DE FOE *Crusoe* II. (Globe) 514 The great..Gulph which goes up to Siam. 1783 LD. PERCY in G. Rose *Diaries* (1860) I. 59, I shall be three days in going up [to London]. 1794 BP. HAY in *Ushaw Mag.* Dec. (1913) 284 He took the opportunity of my company to..go up with me. His business in London [etc.]. 1820 *Examiner* No. 615. 57/2 Pope..resolved to go up to London. 1850 BROWNING *Christmas Eve* iv. 64 The thump-thump..Of the train..up from Manchester. 1853 DICKENS *Bleak Ho.* lvii, Four horses out there for the next stage up! Quick! 1857 HUGHES *Tom Brown* I. iv, Goes through it every day of my life [says the coach-guard]. Twenty minutes afore twelve down—ten o'clock up. 1861 [see GO *v.* 94 a].

**e.** *Naut.* To windward.

1591 RALEIGH *Last Fight Reuenge* B 2, The ships that wer vnder his lee luffing vp, also laid him aborde. 1603 BRETON *Packet Mad Lett.* xii. (1633) 6 My state being so downe the winde,..I know not how to set saile vp in the weather. 1605 SHAKS. *Temp.* III. ii. 2 Beare vp, & boord 'em. 1611 BIBLE *Acts* xxvii. 15 The ship..could not beare vp into the winde. 1633– [see COME *v.* 69 i]. 1669 STURMY *Mariner's Mag.* I. ii. 17 He cannot put up the Helmne. 1720– [see BEAT *v.* 19 b]. 1769 FALCONER *Dict. Marine* (1780) s.v. *Bearing*, We say, up to windward and down to leeward. 1829 MARRYAT *F. Mildmay* v, I..put the helm up. 1830 — *King's Own* xvi, This..brought the ship up in the wind. 1841 R. H. DANA *Seaman's Man.* 78 Put the helm down and bring her up into the wind.

**7.** So as to direct the sight to a higher point or level. (Cf. 26 b.)

See also CAST *v.* 83 d, HEAVE *v.* 1, LIFT *v.* 5, LOOK *v.* 45 a.

*c* 900 tr. *Baeda's Eccl. Hist.* IV. ix. (1890) 290 [He] locade up in heofon. 971 *Blickl. Hom.* 123 Þa hy þa up on þone heofon..locodan. *a* 1000 *Gl.* in Wr.-Wülcker 79 *Ne erigas* [*oculos tuos*], ne ðu up ne arer [ðine eaȝan]. *c* 1000 *Ags. Gosp.* John xi. 41 Se hælend ahof upp his eaȝan. *a* 1300 *Cursor M.* 21393 Constantin..lok up, and in þat sight He sagh þar cristis cros ful bright. 1388 WYCLIF *John* xi. 41 And Jhesus lifte vp hise iȝen, and seide [etc.]. *c* 1420 *Anturs of Arth.* 356 He gliffed vp with his eighen, þat grey were and grete. *c* 1450 *Mankind* 31 (Brandl), Be-holde not þe erthe, but lyfte yowur ey wppe. 1535 COVERDALE *Ps.* xl. 12 My synnes haue taken soch holde vpon me, that I am not able to loke vp. 1621 G. SANDYS *Ovid's Met.* v. (1626) 92 His turn'd-vp eyes. 1719 DE FOE *Crusoe* II. (Globe) 363 He could only look up, and see that it was a clear Starlight Night. 1820 KEATS *Isabella* xxv, Looking up, he saw her features bright. 1854 MRS. JAMESON *Bk. of Th.* (1877) 13 It is good for us to look up, morally and mentally. 1859 SALA *Tw. round Clock* 39 His eyes..cast up to count the peaches on the wall.

**b.** So as to cause sound to ascend, increase, or swell. (Cf. 11 b.)

See also GIVE *v.* 64 f, PIPE *v.*[1] 9, RAISE *v.* 13, 21, SET *v.* 154 c, SPEAK *v.* 20 b.

*Beowulf* 128 Þa wæs æfter wiste wop up ahafen, micel morȝensweȝ. *c* 897 K. ÆLFRED *Gregory's Past C.* xv. 91 Hefe up ðine stefne sua ðes bime. *c* 1205 LAY. 11280 Scottes huuwen up muchelne ræm. *c* 1386 CHAUCER *Merch. T.* 1120 Vp he yaf a roryng and a cry. *a* 1400 *Northern Passion* 257 Ilkone kest vppe a grete cry. 1413– [see LIFT *v.* 5 e]. *c* 1500 *Melusine* xxxvi. 283 He made hys trompettes to blow vp, that euery man shuld be armed. *a* 1548 HALL *Chron., Hen. VIII*, 76 b, Then vp blewe the trumpettes..on bothe sides. 1581 SIDNEY *Apol. Poetrie* (Arb.) 46 Who sometimes rayseth vp his voice to the height of the heauens. 1595 *Locrine* II. vi. 28 Sound drummes & trumpets, sound vp cheerfully. 1611 BIBLE *Job* iii. 8 Let them curse it.., who are ready to raise vp their mourning. 1617 SIR W. MURE *Misc. Poems* xxi. 5 Raise vp thy voice and..proclaime A greater subject. 1869, 1890 [see GO *v.* 94 c].

**II.** In figurative and transferred applications.

Under the following heads are placed only those figurative uses which admit of being classified under some general concept. Further illustration will usually be found under the verbs most commonly occurring in the various phrases, together with many special uses which are confined to one or other of those verbs (see e.g. BRING *v.* 27, CAST *v.* 83, COME *v.* 69, DRAW *v.* 89, etc.). Some uncertainty attaches to the origin and development of many of these uses, the variety of which is so great that the adverb comes to present a number of highly divergent and even directly opposite senses, e.g. *to bind up* (sense 19) in contrast with *to break up* (sense 21 b).

**8.** From a lower to a higher status in respect of position, rank, or affluence. (Cf. SET *v.* 154 j.)

*c* 825 *Vesp. Psalter* xxxvi. 34 Dryhten..hefeð up ðe þæt ðu ineardie eorðan. *c* 888 K. ÆLFRED *Boeth.* xxxix. § 11 Þy læs hi for longum ȝesælðum hi to up ahæbben. *c* 1000 *Ags. Ps.* (Thorpe) xlviii. *heading*, Þæt hy hy upp ne ahofen for heora welum. *c* 1200 ORMIN 10881 Whase shall i Crisstenndom Beon hofenn upp & hadedd Till bisscopp orr till unnderrpreost. *c* 1386 CHAUCER *Monk's T.* 683 From humble bed to roial magestee Vp roos he, Iulius the Conquerour. 1387 TREVISA *Higden* (Rolls) VI. 355 He suffrede no man to stye up to..[that] manere dignitee.., but he were wel i-lettred. *c* 1440– [see LIFT *v.* 2 b]. 1477 EARL RIVERS (Caxton) *Dictes* 142 Yf he see that fortune raise and bring up som other of lower degre. 1530 TINDALE *Practice of Prelates* B vi b, When y^e bishopes office began..to be honorable, then the deacons..clam vp therunto. 1530–1561 [see COME *v.* 69 f]. 1605 CAMDEN *Rem.* 223 This one steppe will not bring you vppe a steppe higher. 1658 *Trad. Mem. K. Jas.* G ij, By what steps the Puritans got up, and the old Clergy degenerated. 1685 W. CLELAND *Poems* (1697) 127 Now down with the confounded Whiggs,..For Hey Boies up go Wee. 1832 HT. MARTINEAU *Life in Wilds* vii. 99 We are getting up in the world.

**b.** Into (greater) repute, credit, or estimation.

1593– [see CRY *v.* 22]. 1641 J. JACKSON *True Evang. T.* I. 65 Oh how doth it cry up Christ, in the world, that he hath such servants. 1711 G. HICKES *Two Treat. Chr. Priesth.* (1847) I. 291 Instead of writing up the other Protestant Churches to the Church of England. 1741 tr. *D'Argens, Chinese Lett.* xx. 137 Men, who preach up nothing but Patience, Humility, Obedience. 1863 GLADSTONE in Morley *Life* II. 99 [Queen Victoria] spoke..of Roundell Palmer; I had a good opportunity of speaking him up. 1871 LOWELL *Study Wind.* (1886) 146 A preacher-up of Nature.

**9. a.** To a higher spiritual or moral level or object.

*c* 888 K. ÆLFRED *Boeth.* xli. § 6 Se mann ana gæþ uprihte; þæt tacnað þæt he sceal ma þencan up þonne nyðer. *c* 1200 ORMIN 2749 Swa þatt hiss herrte iss hofenn upp To follȝhenn Godess wille. *Ibid.* 2754. 1297 R. GLOUC. (Rolls) 9342 Holdeþ vp to god..ȝoure þoȝt. *a* 1340 HAMPOLE *Psalter* xxii. 6 Þou has purged my hert, and liftid vp to haf þe ioy of contemplacioun. *a* 1375 *Lay Folks Mass Bk.* App. iv. 552 Hef vp ȝor hertes in-to heuen. 1526 *Pilgr. Perf.* (1531) 290 It heueth and lyfteth vp the spiryt to god. 1535– [see LIFT *v.* 5 d]. 1589 R. BRUCE *Serm.* (1843) 166 To have..our minds lifted vp to the heavens. *a* 1708 BEVERIDGE *Thes. Theol.* (1711) III. 410 It is a good while before we can get up our hearts from earth to heaven.

**b.** To a state of greater cheerfulness, confidence, resolution, etc.

See also CLEAR *v.* 27, for various senses of *clear up.*

1297 R. GLOUC. (Rolls) 9336 Ȝoure herten hebbeþ vp... Hopieþ al on god. 13..– [see PLUCK *v.* 8 a]. *c* 1430– [see PULL *v.* 31 c]. *c* 1450 *Mirk's Festial* 65 Heue vp þyn hert, and make mery. 1572 tr. *Lauaterus' Ghostes* (1596) 108 Gabriel with comfortable wordes did lift up the blessed Virgin. 1590– [see HEARTEN *v.* 2 b]. 1597– [see CHEER *v.* 10]. *c* 1600 W. FOWLER *Wks.* (S.T.S.) I. 191 O thow..that rayses vp my courage and abaites. 1732, 1875 [see BRIGHTEN *v.* 2 b]. 1894 BARING GOULD *Kitty Alone* II. 116, I really could not pluck up courage to do so.

**c.** Into a state of activity, commotion, excitement, or ferment.

1340– [see STIR *v.* 16]. 1535 COVERDALE *Luke* viii. 24 Then wente they vnto him [*sc.* Christ], and waked him vp. 1596 DALRYMPLE tr. *Leslie's Hist. Scot.* (S.T.S.) I. 76 Sa gret appetite and wil of beiring rule did fyre wpe, and inflame baith the peples. 1689 STILLINGFL. *Serm.* (1698) III. iii. 120 To work up a heated..Imagination to the Fancy of Raptures. 1720 OZELL *Vertot's Rom. Rep.* I. II. 118 Finding the People were blown up again to their former Animosity. 1798–1824 [see FIRE *v.*[1] 5]. 1822 SHELLEY *Chas. I*, I. 123 Their sounds..Rouse up the astonished air. 1869 PHILLIPS *Vesuv.* iii. 59 The mountain, as usual, fired up. 1901 *Scribner's Mag.* April 407/2 Work the crowds up,..but don't get caught yourselves.

**d.** To or at a greater or higher speed, rate, amount, etc.

See also COME *v.* 69 k, GET *v.* 72 d, RUN *v.* 81 g (*d*).

1538 ELYOT, *Equus citatus*, a horse taken vp. 1565 COOPER *Thesaurus* s.v. *Equus*, To fetch vp with the spurre. 1607 MARKHAM *Cavel.* II. (1617) 126 Whose sharpnes and torment ..will so quicken your horse up..that [etc.]. 1664 H. MORE *Myst. Iniq.* 474 They gore and spurre up the Ass. 1677 *Essex Papers* (Camden) II. 130 Upon the late new letting it [*sc.* the Excise], they had..bid up very high upon the present farms. 1839 ALEX. SOMERVILLE *Hist. Brit. Leg.* xi. 236 Flogging the men up, to prevent their falling into the hands of the wandering guerillas. 1883, 1892 [see GO *v.* 94 e]. 1900 ELINOR GLYN *Visits Elizabeth* (1906) 105 Carry had better hurry up and get that house in Park Street.

**10.** To or towards mature age, or proficiency in some art, etc.

*a* 900 *O. E. Martyrol.* 21 Oct. 192 [Hilarion] wæs up cymen in Palestina. *c* 1420 *Chron. Vilod.* 1625 He was norysshut vp in þat place. *c* 1450 *Merlin* vii. 112 And so he..put his owe sone..to be norisshed vp with a-nother woman. 1483– [see BRING *v.* 27 b]. *c* 1530 LD. BERNERS *Arth. Lyt. Bryt.* 505 It semeth wel this people dyd neuer nourysh you up. 1534 in Leadam *Star Chamber Cases* (Selden) II. 207 To take apon hym the Craftes of Bakyng and bruyng where in he was neuer brought vp. 1535– [see GROW *v.* 13 a]. 1597 *Wills & Inv. N. C.* (Surtees, 1835) 172 My mynde is that he shalbe brought up in learnynge. 1611 BIBLE *Prov.* xxii. 6 Traine vp a childe in the way he should goe. 1730 THOMSON *Autumn* 836 Nurse of a people, in misfortune's school Train'd up to hardy deeds. 1796 H. HUNTER tr. *St.-Pierre's Stud. Nat.* (1799) II. 554 We are brought up to sense of fear only, and not of gratitude. 1839 FR. A. KEMBLE *Resid. Georgia* (1863) 11 As soon as they begin to grow up and pass from infancy to youth. 1879 MISS YONGE *Magnum Bonum* I. 290 She 'll be governessed up, and kept to lessons all day. 1894 HALL CAINE *Manxman* 3 He had been brought up to no profession.

**11.** Into existence, prominence, vogue, or currency; so as to appear or prevail.

See also BLAZE *v.*[1] 3 (quot. 1878), GET *v.* 72 r, RISE *v.* 19.

(*a*) *a* 900 *Andreas* 1236 (Gr.), Storm upp aras æfter ceasterhofum. *c* 1000 ÆLFRIC *Saints' Lives* xxx. 61 Ic eom hælende crist þe..ȝedyde þæt leoht up asprang. *c* 1055 *Byrhtferth's Handboc* in *Anglia* VIII. 306 Of þissum syx tidum aspringð up bissextus. *a* 1225 *Ancr. R.* 286 Amidde þe redunge.. þeonne cumeð up a deuociun. *c* 1410 *Lanterne of Liȝt* 28 Liȝt is vp spronngen to þe riȝtwise. *c* 1449– [see COME *v.* 69 e]. 1535 COVERDALE *Wisdom* vi. 22 As for wyszdome, what she is, and how she came vp, I wil tell you. 1556 in W. H. Turner *Select. Rec. Oxford* (1880) 246 The fire got up. 1556– [see START *v.* 13 c]. *a* 1572 KNOX *Hist. Ref.* Wks. 1846 I. 77 Upoun what uther trifeling questionis..the war brak up, we omitt to wryte. 1591 SHAKS. 1 *Hen. VI*, I. iv. 102 A holy Prophetesse, new risen vp. *a* 1679 J. WARD *Diary* (1839) 297 Round knitt capps were the auncient mode before hatts came upp. 1704 SWIFT *T. Tub* ii, Before they were a month in town, great shoulder-knots came up. 1704– [see TURN *v.* 80 v]. 1833 A. CRICHTON *Hist. Arabia* I. 216 Sabellians, Valentinians, and a host of obscurer sects, all rose up. 1844– [see CROP *v.* 10 b]. 1882 A. GRIFFITHS *Chron. Newgate* (1884) I. 13 As usual the difficulty of providing funds cropped up. 1902 T. W. WEBBER *Forests Upper India* xiii. 156 Dinner ready...Smyth, however, had not turned up.

(*b*) *c* 1200 ORMIN 16840 Þeȝȝ..hofenn þurrh hemm sellfenn upp..Settnessess, hu mann birrde..Godess laȝhe follȝhenn. 1393 LANGL. *P. Pl.* C. I. 37 Somme murthes to make,.. And fynde vp foule fantesyes. *a* 1400–50 *Alexander* 829* Nicholas..Had rasyd vp a rode hoste. 1443 *Reg. Mag. Sig. Scot.* 86/2 To the quhilkis we..gert chese upe ane assise of the barony. 1535– [see RAISE *v.* 1 b]. 1560 DAUS tr. *Sleidane's Comm.* 28 b, Suche as eyther Reyse up new customes, or extorte that is forboden. **1568, 1611** [see RAISE *v.* 11]. **1637** HEYWOOD *Royall King* II. iv, Cannot all this stirre his impatience up? **1645** USSHER *Body Div.* 362 That God..would raise up faithfull and painfull Ministers. **1711** ADDISON *Spect.* No. 47 ¶ 5 Stirrers up of Laughter among Men of a gross Taste. **1729** GAY *Polly* I. ix, When Kings by their huffing Have blown up a squabble. **1832** HT. MARTINEAU *Demerara* i. 10 A few..sluggards who had not put up their appearance at the proper hour. **1843** *Blackw. Mag.* LIV. 737 Why couldn't we get up a play? **1867** H. SPENCER *First Princ.* I. (ed. 2) 413 The meteorologic processes eventually set up in the Earth's atmosphere. **1870** H. KINGSLEY *Hillyars & Burtons* lxxvi, It is your grandfather's will. I..drew it up.

**b.** So as to be heard. (Cf. 7 b.)

*a* **1723** [see SPEAK *v.* 20 b]. **1748** THOMSON *Cast. Indol.* I. lxiv, As when..a burnish'd fly..Tunes up amid these airy halls his song. **1802** LEYDEN *Lord Soulis* lii, Then up bespake him, true Thomas. **1853** *Public School Matches* 10 The bell from the Pavilion strikes up.

**12.** To the notice or consideration of a person or body of persons (*spec.* of one in authority).

See also CALL *v.* 35 b, d, SHOW *v.* 4 e.

*a* **1122** *O. E. Chron.* (Laud MS.) an. 1052, Þær bær Godwine eorl up his mal. **1362**– [see PUT *v.* 53 h]. **1414** *Rolls of Parlt.* IV. 22 Or the Petitions biforesaid yeven up yn writing. **1439** *Ibid.* V. 9 In a Petition putte up to the Kyng. **1483**– [see BRING *v.* 27 c]. **1529** in Leadam *Star Chamber Cases* (Selden) II. 34 The byll of compleynt..put vppe to the Kynges highnes. **1559**– [see GIVE *v.* 64 e]. **1585** in *Eng. Hist. Rev.* Jan. (1914) 111 Th' acte..being then sent up by the comens to the lords. **1602** MARSTON *Antonio's Rev.* III. ii, I have a prayer or two to offer up. **1604**– [see CAST *v.* 83 i]. *c* **1633** in *3rd Rep. Hist. MSS. Comm.* 400/2 Ane paper which they send wpe to ȝour Majestie. **1641** [see PUT *v.* 53 h (*b*)]. **1709** T. ROBINSON *Vind. Mosaick Syst.* Introd. 5 It would be Folly for Men to send up Prayers to a God that is not present to hear them. **1820** BYRON *Mar. Fal.* I. ii. 12 The sentence will be sent up to the Doge. **1844** *Fraser's Mag.* XXX. 504 The writ went up to the Lords. **1884** BRIGHT in *Times* 5 Aug. 10/4 When a Bill leaves the House of Commons it has gone up to the House of Lords.

**b.** Before a judge, magistrate, etc.

*c* **1440** *York Myst.* xxxvii. 113 Calle vppe Astrotte and A To giffe þer counsaille in þis case. **1440**– [see PUT *v.* 53 i]. **1749**– [see HAVE *v.* 16 b]. **1753** *World* No. 35, I was unfortunately called up to give evidence against him. **1821** SCOTT *Pirate* xlii, Cleveland and Altamont..were brought up the first of the pirate crew. **1825**– [see PULL *v.* 31 d]. **1865**– [see HAUL *v.* 1 d].

**c.** So as to divulge, reveal, disclose, or let out.

**1593** in *Maitl. Cl. Misc.* (1840) I. 59 That [the names of] all excommunicatis..be gevin wp this daye viij dayes. *a* **1625**– [see GIVE *v.* 64 h]. **1826**– [see SHOW *v.* 27 b]. **1880**– [see OWN *v.* 5 c]. **1884** GILMOUR *Mongols* xxiii. 285 If his two companions in accusation would not own up.

**d.** As a charge or accusation. (Cf. UPBRAID *v.*)

**1604**– [see CAST *v.* 83 i]. **1611** BIBLE *Numb.* xiv. 36 Bringing vp a slander vpon the land. **1889** *N. W. Linc. Gloss.* (ed. 2) 74 *Bring up against* [a person],..to accuse, to charge with. **1890** [see THROW *v.* 48 h].

**13.** Into the hands or possession of another.

See also DELIVER *v.* 7, GIVE *v.* 64 a, b, RESIGN *v.* 1, YIELD *v.* 10 a, 14 b, 16.

**1132** *O. E. Chron.* (Laud MS.), [The king] dide him ȝyuen up ðet abbotrice of Burch. *a* **1225** *Leg. Kath.* 134 Al.. cweðen hire þe meistrie & te menske al up. **13**.. *Cursor M.* 10220 (Gött.), All þair giftes þai ȝeld vp þar [*Trin.* Offerede vp her ȝiftes]. *c* **1375** *Ibid.* 15879 (Fairf.), He deliuered his maister vp. *a* **1400–50** *Alexander* 758 Oþire recouyre me þi rewme or reche vp þe girdill. *c* **1400** *Brut* cl. 162 Here y resyngn op þe crone..of Engeland into þe Popis Hande. *c* **1440** *Jacob's Well* 302 And so, as tretourys, þei ȝeuyn vp þe castel of god. **1568** GRAFTON *Chron.* II. 46 After the geuyng vp of the sayd Citie. **1588–9** *Act 31 Eliz.* c. 6 § 2 For the levinge or resignyng upp of the same. **1604**– [see GIVE *v.* 64 d]. **1613** SHAKS. *Hen. VIII*, II. i. 97 To th' water side I must conduct your Grace: Then giue my Charge vp to Sir Nicholas Vaux. *a* **1690** BP. HOPKINS *Exp. Lord's Prayer* (1692) 47 That his Mediatory Kingdom being fulfilled, it might be delivered up unto the Father. **1713** ATTERBURY *Serm.* (1734) II. 48 Those..who do not surrender themselves up to the Methods it prescribes. **1802** MAR. EDGEWORTH *Moral T., Prussian Vase*, He..yielded himself up a prisoner. **1839** THIRLWALL *Hist. Greece* VI. 281 They were assured that no harm should befal them if they gave up Bessus. **1890** *Spectator* 30 Aug., That rich yield-up of the land that speaks of such abundant future provision.

**b.** So as to relinquish, abandon, or forsake.

*c* **1290**– [see YIELD *v.* 14 c]. **1387** TREVISA *Higden* (Rolls) V. 413 Þanne he awook and ȝalde up þe goost. **1388** WYCLIF *Matt.* xxvii. 50 Jhesus eftsoone..ȝaf vp the goost. *c* **1400** *Laud Troy Bk.* 13252 For thi wyff this werre be-gan, We ȝeue it vp here euery a man. **1457** HARDYNG *Chron.* in *Eng. Hist. Rev.* Oct. (1912) 747 Whan enmye gafe vp pese..As lyon fell he putte hym forth in prese. **1510**– [see GHOST *sb.* 1]. **1530**– [see CAST *v.* 83 h]. **1558**– [see GIVE *v.* 64 b, c, h]. **1596** in *Spalding Club Misc.* I. 88 James Low..said, in his last wordis, befoir he gef wp his braitht [etc.]. **1621–42** [see TURN *v.* 80 p]. **1653** H. MORE *Antid. agst. Ath.* III. ii. (1712) 89 For his unserviceableness he was..turned up loose in the pasture. **1678**– [see THROW *v.* 48 g]. **1885–93** [see THROW *v.* 80 p].

**14.** Into a receptacle or place of storage, as for security, convenience, or use when required.

See also STORE *v.* 4 b, and for special senses, KNOCK *v.* 16 g, LAY *v.*[1] 60 c–g, PUT *v.* 53, SET *v.* 154 00.

*c* **1290** *St. Kenelm* 262 in *S. Eng. Leg.* I. 352 Þis writ was wel nobleliche i-wust and up i-do. **13**.. *Coer de L.* 6770 He..stablede up hys destrers. **1340** *Ayenb.* 232 Þeruore ssel þet tresor by..well y-do op, þet hit ne by uorlore. ? *a* **1366** CHAUCER *Rom. Rose* 184 Gret tresouris vp to leyne. *a* **1368**– [see PUT *v.* 53 n, o, p]. *c* **1470** *Golagros & Gaw.* 1123 Thai.. Put up thair brandis sa braid, burly and bair. **1539** CRANMER *Matt.* vi. 19 Laye not vp for your selues treasure vpon earth. **1567** *Gude & Godlie B.* (S.T.S.) 93 Thy gudnes and beningnitie..; Thow lay thame vp with me in stoir. **1604** SHAKS. *Oth.* I. ii. 59 Keepe vp your bright Swords, for the dew will rust them. **1629** PARKINSON *Parad.* 470 The flowers of Marigolds,..pickled vp against winter. **1631** GOUGE *God's Arrows* II. § 12. 148 God doth sometimes treasure up the sinnes of predecessours. **1692** E. WALKER *Epictetus' Mor.* Praise of Ep. iv, Riches,..Which Knaves hoard up. **1706** PHILLIPS (ed. Kersey), *Rusca Butyri*, a Tub, or Barrel of Butter salted up. **1721** BRADLEY *Philos. Acc. Wks. Nat.* 50 Then they are reckon'd in a right State for Barrelling up for the Markets. **1800**– [see PUT *v.* 53 n (*d*)]. **1867** H. SPENCER *First Princ.* (ed. 2) I. 301 Those highly-compounded nitrogenous molecules in which so much motion is locked up. **1879** H. GEORGE *Progr. & Pov.* I. ii. 36 The heat of the sun is stored up in coal.

*ellipt.* **1760–72** H. BROOKE *Fool of Qual.* (1809) III. 138 May we not order your horses up [= to be stabled]? You must not think of going.

**15.** Into one's possession, charge, custody, etc.

See also GET *v.* 72 o, PICK *v.* 20 c, TAKE *v.* 90 d, l.

*a* **1400–50** *Alexander* 760 Þan set þai þam..a day.., And þar-to tuke vp þaire trouthis. **1479** *Cely Papers* (Camden) 15, I am avysyd to take oppe at London as meche as I schall nede. **1482** *Ibid.* 122 To lette hym [= a horse] ron in a parke tyll Hallowtyd and then take hym wpe. **1659** W. GUTHRIE *Chr. Gt. Interest* viii. (1724) 88 A Man may take up his gracious State by his Faith, and the Acting thereof on Christ. **1674** *Pennsylv. Archives* I. 33 Permission is hereby granted ..for to take vp a certaine peice of land for himself and his heires. **1697** PRIOR *Ep. to Sheppard* 21 Now, as you took me up when little, Gave me my Learning, and my Vittle. **1710** STEELE *Tatler* No. 204 ¶ 6 He has taken up a Resolution. **1711** SWIFT *Jrnl. to Stella* 27 Feb., To get up his debts abroad. **1751** JORTIN *Serm.* (1771) I. iii. 45 His servants ..being employed in gathering up the Tares. **1752–3** A. MURPHY *Gray's Inn Jrnl.* No. 21, After having gleaned up all I could..at School. **1802** MAR. EDGEWORTH *Moral T., Forester* xv, One of his boys was taken up amongst the rioters. **1844, 1876** [see GET *v.* 72 t].

**16.** Into the position or state of being open.

Originally implying the raising of a gate, barrier, etc. For the fig. use of *open up*, see OPEN *v.* 24.

*c* **1205** LAY. 1704 Vp heo duden heora castles ȝaten. *c* **1300** *K. Horn* 1115 (Laud MS.), Horn gan to þe yate turne, And þe wyket op spurne. **1375** BARBOUR *Bruce* XVII. 778 He.. gert all wyde set vp the ȝet. *c* **1386** CHAUCER *Miller's T.* 615 And vp the wyndowe dide he hastily. *a* **1400–50** *Alexander* (Dublin) 783* Þe wy..Brades vppe þe brade ȝate. *c* **1400** *Gamelyn* 311 Gamelyn ȝede to þe ȝate & lete it vp wide. *c* **1450** *Le Morte Arth.* 1839 The chamber dore he sette vp ryght. **1513** DOUGLAS *Æneid* VII. xi. 32 He that.. Thyr ȝettis suld vp oppin and warp wyd. **1523**– [see BREAK *v.* 55 j]. *c* **1600** W. FOWLER *Wks.* (S.T.S.) I. 183 Blist be that houer..that opned vp the wyndowes to disdayne. **1639** SIR E. VERNEY in *V. Papers* (1853) 233, I have broaken upp my packett againe to insert this letter. **1792** A. WILSON *Watty & Meg* xix, Up the door flew—like a fury In came Watty's scawling wife. **1825** JAMIESON *Suppl.* s.v., Set up the door.

**17.** Into an open or loose condition of surface.

See also BREAK *v.* 56 f, g, CUT *v.* 59 e, DIG *v.* 14 c, PLOUGH *v.* 9 e, RIP *v.*[1] 3, TURN *v.* 80 f.

**1377** LANGL. *P. Pl.* B. VI. 109 Dikeres & delueres digged vp þe balkes. *c* **1440** *Pallad. on Husb.* II. 74 The lond vnclene al doluen up mot be. **1577** TUSSER *Husb.* (1878) 83 In January, husband..will breake vp his laie. **1588** SHAKS. *Tit. A.* IV. ii. 87 Sooner this sword shall plough thy bowels vp. **1721** STRYPE *Eccl. Mem.* I. xxviii. 197 To endure the more pain when they should be cut down and ripped up. **1799** J. ROBERTSON *Agric. Perth* 247 He directs the moss to be *delved* or dug up with spades. **1801** *Farmer's Mag.* Nov. 484 An Essay..upon the question of breaking up Grass Land. **1894** *Times* 21 May 4/4 A gang of men was sent.. to pick up and relay the part. **1895** *Ibid.* 5 Feb. 8/2 That would mean taking up all the streets in South London.

**b.** So as to sever or separate, esp. into many parts, fragments, or pieces.

See also BREAK *v.* 2 b, 56 a, CHOP *v.*[1] 3, CUT *v.* 59 b. In OE. a similar use occurs in *upp forlǽtan*, to divide (a river).

**14**.. *Voc.* in Wr.-Wülcker 563 *Anatene*, up cuttynge. **1530** in Leadam *Star Chamber Cases* (Selden) II. 50 To breke vppe or caste downe eny dyche or hedge. **1573** BARET *Alv.* s.v. *Cut*, Cut vp, or winne these partriges. **1611** SHAKS. *Wint. T.* III. ii. 132 Breake vp the Seales, and read. **1827** FARADAY *Chem. Manip.* ii. (1842) 47 The tube itself being broken up and disregarded. **1849** D. CAMPBELL *Inorg. Chem.* 295 Hydrosulphide of ammonium..dissolves it up. **1857** HUGHES *Tom Brown* I. vii, Engaged in tearing up old newspapers..into small pieces.

**18.** To or towards a state of completion or finality. (Frequently serving merely to emphasize the import of the verb.)

**a.** With verbs denoting consuming or destroying.

See also BURN *v.* 8 b, EAT *v.* 18, KILL *v.* 2 b, SLAY *v.* 5 b, SPEND *v.* 13, STIFLE *v.* 1 (quot. 1582).

*a* **1300** *Cursor M.* 6634 Slas vp yon caitefs al bidene! *c* **1374** CHAUCER *Troylus* V. 1470 She made vp frete here corn. **1390** GOWER *Conf.* I. 81 Thei..brenden up the remenant. *c* **1400** *Sowdone Bab.* 414 Destroye vp bothe man and place. **1481** *Cely Papers* (Camden) 80 Schepe dys [= dies] wpe in Englelonde. **1546** BALE *Eng. Votaries* I. (1560) 7 The murthering vp of them whiche hathe done it. *a* **1555** PHILPOT *Apology*, etc. (1555) B 4 b, Lyke humbledories, eating vp the hony of the bees. **1594** NASHE *Unfort. Trav.* Cij b, I heard where they dyde vp all in one Familie, and not a mothers childe escapde. **1609–10** *Act 7 Jas. I*, c. 20 The Sea hath..surrounded and drowned up much hard groundes. **1636** WINTHROP *Hist. New Eng.* (1825) I. 388 The Indians killed up all their swine, so as Capt. Lovell had none. **1647** VICARS *England's Worthies* (1845) 63 The Royalists resolving..to gird up Gloucester..on all sides to tire and starve it up if it might be. **1793** PELLEW in Osler *Life* (1835) 89 We dished her up in fifty minutes, boarded, and struck her colours. **1803**–[see DO *v.* 52 d, e]. **1872** SPURGEON *Treas. Dav.* Ps. lxxix. 7 The oppressor would quite eat up the saints if he could. **1894** HALL CAINE *Manxman* 419 The spendthrift had..sold up the remainder of his furniture.

**b.** With other verbs, denoting progress to or towards an end.

**1307** *York Memo. Bk.* (Surtees) I. 181 Oute taken girdels that er fully wroght upp. *c* **1400** *Laud Troy Bk.* 14614 Thei..heled him vp with medycyns. *c* **1407** LYDG. *Reson & Sens.* 2681 She shal performe vp of ryght Al that euer I haue behight. *c* **1440** *Jacob's Well* 207 Tyl þou haue vp full þi cost & þin expensis. **1480** *Cely Papers* (Camden) 48 Y understond Lombardys has bowght ytt [*sc.* the wool] up yn Ynglond. *c* **1540** in J. R. Boyle *Hedon* (1875) App. 67 Yf any.. offycers die..then the common of burgesis to choise other to occupye upe that yeare. **1560** DAUS tr. *Sleidane's Comm.* 298 He will commaunde the fathers..to finish up their work begon. **1601** R. JOHNSON *Kingd. & Commw.* (1603) 114 By husbandry..they dry vp and drain fenny and vnholsome places. **1639** T. DE GRAY *Compl. Horsem.* 322 Therefore heale him up with sweet butter. **1682** DRYDEN *Medal* Ep. Whigs ¶ 3 Whatever the Verses are, buy 'em up I beseech you. **1726** BERKELEY *Let.* Wks. 1871 IV. 120 It is an infinite shame that the debts are not cleared up and paid. **1771** MRS. HAYWOOD *New Present for Maid* 158 Beat up the yolks of three eggs. **1791** SMEATON *Edystone L.* 121 Lime wetted up in large heaps for use. **1809** MALKIN *Gil Blas* III. ix. ¶ 1 The establishment was paid up and discharged. **1821** BYRON *Juan* III. lxiii, Cloves..were boil'd Up with the coffee. **1873** *Punch* 18 Jan. 21/1 They liquor up despondently. **1882** MISS BRADDON *Mount Royal* III. 195 Could there not be some kind of institution..to force parents to cash up. **1896** *Pall Mall G.* 19 Aug. 5/1 Prices have subsequently firmed up in many instances.

**c.** With vbs. denoting cleaning, putting in order, or fixing in place.

See also CLEAN *v.* 3, CLEAR *v.* 27 c, DECK *v.* 2 b, DO *v.* 52 b, DRESS *v.* 7 d, FIT *v.*[1] 6, GET *v.* 72 l, m, MAKE *v.* 96 i, POLISH *v.* 3, REDD *v.*[2] 6 a, RIG *v.*[2] 1 b, TACKLE *v.* 1, 3, TRIM *v.* 7.

**1419–20** *York Memo. Bk.* (Surtees) I. 199 Pro purgacione (*anglice* clensyng uppe) unius centene [arcuum]. *c* **1440** *Pallad. on Husb.* I. 406 Polish al vp thy werk in goodly tyme. **1500–20** DUNBAR *Poems* xliii. 28 Ȝour ladeis grathit vp gay. **1605** CHAPMAN *All Fools* I. i. 73 Spung'd up, adorn'd, and painted. **1706** POPE *Lett.* (1735) 26 To paint your Shop, and..to brush You up like your Neighbours. **1766** GOLDSM. *Vicar* xi, They can do up small cloaths. **1768** STERNE *Sent. Journ.* (1778) II. 199 The beds..were fixed up..near the fire. **1827** SOUTHEY *Hist. Penins. War* II. 762 The rear-guard of cavalry..remained bridled up all night. **1878** W. S. GILBERT *H. M. S. Pinafore* I, I polished up the handle of the big front door. **1900** *Daily News* 4 June 2/4 We have cleaned up for the month of May,..760 tons.

**19.** By way of summation or enumeration.

See also CAST *v.* 83 j, COUNT *v.* 1 c, MAKE *v.*[1] 96 j, RECKON *v.* 1 b, 2 e, RUN *v.* 81 j (*b*), SUM *v.* 1 (*b*), TOTAL *v.* 2.

**13**.. *E. E. Allit. P.* B. 2 Clannesse who-so kyndly cowþe comende, & rekken vp alle þe resounz þat ho by riȝt askez. *c* **1450** *Bk. Curtasye* 540 in *Babees Bk.*, Tyl countes also þer-on ben cast, And somet vp holy at þo last. **1621** *Stat. Reg.* (Arber) IV. 23 Compendious tables for the speedy casting vp of anie some. **1686** tr. *Chardin's Trav. Persia* 252 Relicks..among which they number up the Veronique. **1727** THOMSON *To Mem. Newton* 132 But who can number up his labours? **1802** MAR. EDGEWORTH *Moral T., Forester* xiii, Hours..spent in casting up and verifying accounts. **1871** R. H. HUTTON *Ess.* (1877) I. 4 If..you numbered up the acts of trust. **1875** JOWETT *Plato* (ed. 2) I. 130 All my years when added up are many.

**b.** To a final or total sum or amount.

*c* **1200** ORMIN 11310 Seofenn siþe sexe gan, ȝiff þatt tu willt hemm sammnenn, Upp inntill fowwerrtiȝ & twa. **1482** *Monk of Evesham* (Arb.) 49 Y addyd..as mony dayes.. as wold make vppe the noumbre of the dayes of lente. **1583** STUBBES *Anat. Abus.* II. (1882) 32 Promising them..that they shall pay no more rent yeerelie, till the same be runne vp. **1601** SHAKS. *Jul. C.* IV. iii. 208 The Enemy, marching along by them, By them shall make a fuller number vp. **1629** J. COLE *Of Death* 195 His deceased children were alive still in heaven; and the ten more given him here, make them up twenty. *a* **1700** [see RUN *v.* 81 g]. **1719** [see MAKE *v.* 96 c *b*]. **1741** in C. F. Jenkins *Tortola* (1923) 86 Next Week we purpose a Monthly Meeting, here being three little Meetings to make it up. **1837**– [see KNOCK *v.* 16 e]. **1895** *Westm. Gaz.* 9 May 5/3 Hearne..had hit up 8 runs when he lost Wright.

**20.** Into a close or compact form or condition; so as to be confined or secured.

See also BIND *v.* 6, 11 b, BUNDLE *v.* 1, 2, COIL *v.*[3] 3 c, DOUBLE *v.* 8 (quot. 1893), FOLD *v.* 1 (quots. 1621, 1712), GATHER *v.* 16 b, ROLL *v.*[2] 8 b, SHUT *v.* 19 f, TIE *v.* 11 a, TRUSS *v.* 1, 6.

*c* **1374** CHAUCER *Troylus* III. 517 There as..al þis heigh matere Towchyng here loue were at þe fulle vp bounde. *c* **1386** — *Prol.* 681 But hood..wered he noon, For it was trussed vp in his walet. *c* **1475** *Golagros & Gaw.* 224 Thai turssit vp tentis and turnit of toun. **1490** CAXTON *Eneydos* li. 144 He made hys thye to be dressed and bounden vp. **1535** COVERDALE *Song Sol.* vii. 5 The hayre of thy heade is like the kynges purple folden vp in plates. **1590** SHAKS. *Mids. N.* III. i. 206 Tye vp my louers tongue, bring him silently. *c* **1600** — *Sonn.* xii, Sommers greene all girded vp in sheaues. **1639** T. DE GREY *Compl. Horsem.* (1656) 373 Rope up all his legges to the body, not suffering him to lie down. **1693** *Humours Town* 44 He is fairly trust up according to his deserts. **1802** MAR. EDGEWORTH *Moral T., Forester* viii, Forester..tied up a small bundle of linen. **1825** LAMB *Elia* II. *Wedding*, Visitors huddled up in corners. **1861** O. W. HOLMES *Elsie V.* xxviii, Old Sophy..bound up her long hair for her sleep. **1876** GROSS *Dis. Bladder*, etc. (ed. 3) 21 The limbs are drawn up as in acute enteritis.

**b.** Into a closed or enclosed state; so as to be shut or restrained.

See also CLOSE *v.* 21 a, DAM *v.*[1] 1, 2, 2 b, PEN *v.*[1] 2, PEND *v.*[2], PENT *ppl. a.* 1 b, TIE *v.* 11 b, d.

*c* **1489**– [see SHUT *v.* 19 c]. **1528** in Leadam *Star Chamber Cases* (Selden) II. 20 Mulso..hath vnlawfully enclosyd vppe ageyn the sayd comon grownde. **1565**– [see LAY *v.* 60 d]. **1568** GRAFTON *Chron.* II. 528 The Englishmen that were shut up in the Castel. **1615** W. LAWSON *Country Housew. Gard.* (1626) 12 Take heede of a doore or window..: yea, though it be nailed vp. **1622** *Reg. Mag. Sig. Scot.* 130/2 The damyng up of the said watter. **1642** *Action before Cyrencester* 4 The streets were barricadoed up with chaines, harrowes and waggons. **1727** THOMSON *Britannia* 244 Her merchants scatter'd wide; Her hollow shops shut up. **1769** MRS. RAFFALD *Eng. Housekpr.* (1778) 323 Mix them all exceedingly well in your cask, close it well up.

**c.** So as to cover or envelop. Also in fig. context.

**13..** *E. E. Allit. P.* A. 434 Knelande to grounde [ho] folde vp hyr face. **1577** HARRISON *England* III. i. (1877) II. 11 Ech peece [of the boar] is wrapped vp..with bulrushes. **1589** [? LYLY] *Pap w. Hatchet* B 4 b, Hee woulde not smoother vp sinne. **1593-** [see FOLD *v.*[2] 8]. **1602-** [see ROLL *v.*[2] 9 b]. **1719** DE FOE *Crusoe* I. (Globe) 56, I..wrapt it up Parcel by Parcel in Pieces of the Sails. **1792** *Munchhausen's Trav.* x. 34 The sentinels were wrapped up in the arms of Morpheus. **1837** P. KEITH *Bot. Lex.* 151 If the wound is covered closely up. **1872-** [see COVER *v.* 20].

**21.** Into a state of union, conjunction, or combination; so as to bring together.

See also GET *v.* 72 o, MAKE *v.* 96 f *e.*

*c* **1450** LOVELICH *Merlin* 6117 Thus thanne was knyt vpe the pes. **1553-** [see GATHER *v.* 16 b, c, d]. **1577** HOLINSHED *Chron.* I. *Descr. Irel.* 7/2 How sagely Ireneus claspeth vp all the whole controuersie. **1599** SHAKS. *Hen. V*, IV. Prol. 13 With busie Hammers closing Riuets vp. **1627** EARL OF MANCHESTER in *Buccleuch MSS.* (Hist. MSS. Comm.) I. 267 Therefore the remain [of the loan] must needs be got up, which is not past 50,000 *l.* **1638** R. BAKER tr. *Balzac's Lett.* (vol. II) 19 If yours were not bound up in one volume with them. **1693** *Humours Town* 16 Those wretched Compounds which make up all your Lives. **1724** WATTS *Logic* II. ii. § 6 A Compound Proposition is made up of two or more Subjects. **1759** STERNE *Tr. Shandy* I. x, That he could draw up..a hole in his breeches. **1820** BYRON *Mar. Fal.* III. i. 43 Your fame, your name, all mingled up in mine. **1846** CARPENTER *Man. Phys.* 8 These substances..being made up of three or four elements. **1869** MRS. WHITNEY *We Girls* v. (1874) 101 She could only stitch up a straight slant.

**b.** So as to supply deficiencies, defects, etc.

*a* **1568-** [see MAKE *v.* 96 c *a*]. **1586-** [see PIECE *v.* 8]. **1589** PUTTENHAM *Eng. Poesie* II. xii. (Arb.) 128 A sillable ouerplus to annexe to the word precedent to helpe peece vp another foote. **1596-** [see FILL *v.* 17]. **1605** B. JONSON *Volpone* III. vi, My dwarf shall dance, My eunuch sing, my fool make up the antic. **1755** JOHNSON, To *Supply*, to fill up as any deficiencies happen. **1774-** [see PATCH *v.* 1].

**22.** To or towards a person or place; so as to approach or arrive.

**1362-** [see COME *v.* 69 b]. *c* **1420** *Anturs of Arth.* 345 Ho raykes vp..bifor þe rialle, And halsed sir Arthur. **1599** HAKLUYT *Voy.* II. 287 Vp comes toward them the other frigat. **1607** SHAKS. *Cor.* I. ii. 29 If they set downe before 's: for the remoue Bring vp your Army. **1659-** [see GET *v.* 72 c]. **1669** in *Buccleuch MSS.* (Hist. MSS. Comm.) I. 429 He rid up to meet him. **1719** DE FOE *Crusoe* I. (Globe) 298 We all mended our Pace, and rid up as fast as the Way.. would give us leave. **1730** THOMSON *Autumn* 439 Hot-steaming, up behind him comes again Th' inhuman rout. **1780** *Mirror* No. 108, The train of Sir Edward brought up their master in the condition I have described. **1797** COLERIDGE *Christabel* I. 22 The Spring comes slowly up this way. **1841** DICKENS *Barn. Rudge* lix, She thought..how he would have rode boldly up, and dashed in among these villains. **1878** T. HARDY *Ret. Native* IV. iii, Leave me before they come up.

**b.** To or towards a particular point or line.

**1513** DOUGLAS *Æneid* XI. xvi. 58 [She] hir hornit bow has bent, Quharin onon the takyll vp is stent; Syne halis vp in ire and felloun haist. **1605-** [see DRAW *v.* 89 f]. **1864-** [see LINE *v.* 8 b]. **1865** BUSHNELL *Vicar. Sacr.* Introd. 16 As if He [*sc.* Christ] were engaged to even up the score of penalty. **1901** *Munsey's Mag.* XXV. 371/1 To even up my account with his people.

**c.** To or into later life.

**1535** COVERDALE *Luke* xviii. 21 All these haue I kepte fro my youth vp. **1596** DALRYMPLE tr. *Leslie's Hist. Scot.* (S.T.S.) I. 235 Frome his barneheid vpp, he was brocht vpp be S. Columba. *c* **1800** WORDSW. *Excurs.* I. 53 We were tried Friends: I from my Childhood up Had known him. **1890** *Review of Rev.* II. 427/2 It has been so from his youth up.

**d.** So as to find, come upon, overtake, or keep on the track of. (Cf. LOOK *v.* 45 g-j.)

*a* **1622-** [see FETCH *v.* 19 g]. **1657-** [see RUN *v.* 81 h]. **1791** W. BARTRAM *Carolina* 488 They enter..with a view of.. hunting up the sturdy bear. **1794-** [see FOLLOW *v.* 21]. **1817** J. BRADBURY *Trav.* 265 It sometimes happens that he is two days in 'hunting them [*sc.* stray hogs] up'. **1868** *Field* 18 July 49/1 Failing to get quite up, [he] was beaten cleverly by three parts of a length. **1879** F. POLLOK *Sport Brit. Burmah* II. 204, I..hit off the tracks of a large herd of bison and followed them up.

**23.** To a stop or halt.

See also BRING *v.* 27 f, g, DRAW *v.* 89 e, FETCH *v.* 19 i, PULL *v.* 31 d, f.

**1623** in Birch *Crt. & Times Jas. I* (1848) II. 392 A man, thinking nothing, pulled up his coach, and so made the horse start a little. **1769** FALCONER *Dict. Marine* (1780), *To Bring-up*, a provincial phrase peculiar to the seamen in the coal-trade, signifying to anchor, &c. **1857** LD. DUFFERIN *Lett. High Lat.* (ed. 3) 14 At Kylakin we were obliged to bring up for the night. **1891** C. ROBERTS *Adrift Amer.* 214 When the river is foggy, the boats have to bring up at night. **1902** *Westm. Gaz.* 26 May 7/3 If all goes well it should fetch up at Sheerness..to-morrow morning.

**III.** With a preposition following.

**24. Up against —.** *To knock* or *run up against*, to come across, to fall in with.

**1886** *Pall Mall G.* 4 Aug. 3/1 Our extradition treaty with the United States has run up against its first snag. **1886** [see RUN *v.* 61 b]. **1887-** [see KNOCK *v.* 16 a].

**25. Up till —.** = *Up to* (in various senses).

*c* **1200** ORMIN 1281 ȝiff þatt tu forrlangedd arrt To cumenn upp till Criste. *Ibid.* 11318. *c* **1250** *Gen. & Ex.* 1606 Iacob ..slep and saȝ,..fro ðe erðe up til heuene bem, A leddre stonden. **1599** SHAKS. *Pass. Pil.* 382 She, poor bird, as all forlorn, Lean'd her breast up-till a thorn.

**1845** R. BUCHANAN in Howie *Scots Worthies* p. xix, Up till that time they had still continued to attend public worship. **1886** *Manch. Exam.* 13 Jan. 4/7 Up till now Greece has altogether disregarded the..admonitions.

**26. Up to —. a.** (*a*) As high or as far as (a specified height or altitude) by ascent or extension.

**944** *Charter* in Sweet *A. S. Reader* (1908) 58 Andlang dic to ðam weȝe þe scytt up to ðam bricgge. *c* **1000** ÆLFRIC *Saints' Lives* xxvi. 183 Heofonlic leoht ofer þæt ȝeteld astreht stod up to heofonum. *a* **1122** *O. E. Chron.* (Laud MS.) an. 1070, Hi..clumben upp to þe stepel. *c* **1200** *Vices & Virtues* 119 He..bar up to heuene ure loac. *a* **1300** *Cursor M.* 22569 (Edinb.), Op to þe lift ris sal þe se. **13..** *Coer de L.* 4171 The pytte..was feld and fordytte, Up to the bank maad al playn. **1390** GOWER *Conf.* I. 137 A tree..Whos heihte straghte up to the hevene. *Ibid.* 273 He styh up to his fader. *c* **1430** HOCCLEVE *New Ploughman's T.* 114 Shee vp to heuene ascendid up and sty. *c* **1450** *Merlin* i. 15 So it was cristened Merlyn, and was delyuered to the women vpe to the wyndowe to the moder. **1526** TINDALE *John* iii. 13 Noo man hath ascended vppe to heven, butt he that cam doune from heven. *a* **1586** SIDNEY *De Mornay* i. ¶ 5 Like as from the Earth wee haue styed up too the Ayre. **1623** GOUGE *Serm. God's Provid.* § 15 A partition..which reached up to the floore of the garret. **1667** MILTON *P. L.* v. 198 Ye Birds, That singing up to Heaven Gate ascend. **1684** BUNYAN *Pilgr.* II. (1900) 173 Let the most blessed be my guide..Up to his Holy Hill. **1799** G. S. CAREY *Balnea* (ed. 2) 178 Whatever way you approach Ludlow, you find an ascent up to the market-place. **1842** LOUDON *Suburban Hort.* 491 When the cuttings get up to the glass,..the outer pot can be changed. **1850** ROSSETTI *Blessed Damozel* vii, The souls, mounting up to God.

(*b*) As high or as far as (a certain part of the body, containing vessel, penetrating weapon, etc.).

For the figurative import of the phrases *up to the ears*, etc., see the sbs. Other figurative phrases denoting completeness or fullness are illustrated under HUB[1] 2, KNOCKER 2 c, NINE *sb.* 6 b, NOTCH *sb.* 1 b.

*c* **950** *Lindisf. Gosp.* John ii. 7 ȝefyldon ða ilca uið to briorde up. *c* **1175** *Lambeth Hom.* 47 Ieremie þe prophete stod..in þe uenne up to his muðe. *a* **1250** *Owl & Night.* 96 Hi fuleþ hit vp to þe chynne. *c* **1305** *Land Cokayne* 181 He mot wade..up to þe chynne So he schal þe londe winne. **13..** *Gaw. & Gr. Knt.* 1594 For þe mon..Hit hym vp to þe hult. *c* **1386** CHAUCER *Knt.'s T.* 802 Vp to the Anclee foghte they in hir blood. **1388** WYCLIF *John* ii. 7 Fille ȝe the pottis with watir. And thei filliden hem, vp to the mouth. *c* **1450** *St. Cuthbert* 1641 With in þe se Vp to þe nek naked stode he. **1470-85** MALORY *Arthur* I. xvii. 61 Her horses went in blood vp to the fytlokys. *a* **1553** [see EAR *sb.*[1] 1 c]. **1590** W. WEBBE *Trav.* (Arb.) 32 She might haue gone vp to the mid leg in..mire. **1599** [see HILT *sb.* 1 b]. **1601** SHAKS. *Jul. C.* III. i. 107 Let vs bathe our hands in Cæsars blood Vp to the Elbowes. **1607** DEKKER & MARSTON *Northw. Hoe* IV. ii, Weele draw all our arrowes of reuenge vp to the head. **1616** [see CHIN *sb.* 1 d]. **1648** HEXHAM II, *Tot den Hecht toe*, up to the Haft. **1662** J. DAVIES tr. *Mandelslo's Trav.* 64 They go bare-breasted, and bare-arm'd up to the Elbows. **1687-** [see HILT *sb.* 3]. **1790** BRUCE *Source of Nile* I. v, The girls..stand up to their knees in the water for a considerable time. **1808** ANDREW SCOTT *Poems* (ed. 2) 101 Up to the haft at ilka stroke Some clash their hooks. **1825** COBBETT *Rur. Rides* (1830) I. 67 With white aprons and bibs..going from the apron up to the bosom. **1883** A. ROBSON *Dead Letter* II. v, Up to our Elbows making Damson Jam. **1884-9** [see EYE *sb.*[1] 2 e].

(*c*) Raised or short so as to leave uncovered.

**1835** LADY DUFFERIN *Charming Woman* 22 Her shoulders are rather too bare, And her gown's nearly up to her knees. **1868** LOUISA M. ALCOTT *Little Women* iv, Sometimes she is so bad, her frock is up to her knees.

**b.** Up towards; aloft in the direction of.

*c* **900** tr. *Baeda's Hist.* I. vii. (1890) 38 Albanus..his eaȝan ahof upp to heofonum. **971** *Blickl. Hom.* 227 He..mid his eaȝum up to heofenum locade. *c* **1000** ÆLFRIC *Gen.* iv. 10 Þines broðor blod clypað up to me of eorðan. *c* **1220** *Bestiary* 187 Deme ðe noȝt wurdi, ðat tu dure loken up to ðe heuene-ward. **1297** R. GLOUC. (Rolls) 9342 Ȝoure riȝt honden holdeþ vp to god. *c* **1375** *Sc. Leg. Saints* v. (*John*) 566 Hevand his handis vpe to þe hevyn. *a* **1425** *Cursor M.* 19468 (Trin.), Vp to heuen he helde his honde. *a* **1626-** [see LOOK *v.* 45 d]. **1719** WATTS *Ps.* cxxi. I Up to the hills I lift mine eyes. **1845** BAILEY *Festus* (ed. 2) 171 Oh! my heart was lift to thee Like a glass up to a star. **1852** MRS. STOWE *Uncle Tom* xxvii, But oh, if mas'r could only look up..—up to the dear Lord Jesus!

**c.** So as to reach or arrive at (a particular place or person).

The precise force of *up* varies in accordance with sense 6.

(*a*) **1516** in E. Lodge *Illustr. Brit. Hist.* (1791) I. 15 If I shulde com up to London the next terme. **1518** in Leadam *Star Chamber Cases* (Selden) II. 150 Oder evill disposed persones..ben commyn vp to hym to maynteyn hym. **1592** *Arden of Feversham* I. i. 531, Ile vp to London straight. **1695** WOODWARD *Nat. Hist. Earth* I. (1723) 41 When I first brought my Collection of these Things up to London. **1774** ABIGAIL ADAMS in *Fam. Lett.* (1876) 48 Mr. Hill's father had some thoughts of removing up to Braintree. **1810** in Milner *Suppl. Mem. Eng. Cath.* (1820) 153 To wait..until Bishop Gibson should come up to town. **1821** J. H. NEWMAN *Lett.* (1891) I. 56 Coming up to Oxford to study. **1889** 'J. S. WINTER' *Mrs. Bob* xxvi, In time to catch the next train up to Town.

(*b*) **1555** R. TOMSON in *Hakluyt's Voy.* (1600) III. 448 Wee did vnbarke our selues and went on lande vp to the citie or head towne. **1599** NASHE *Lenten Stuffe* D j, The three riuers that vagary vp to her. **1659-** [see GET *v.* 72 c]. **1684** BUNYAN *Pilgr.* II. (1900) 173 When Christina came up to the Slough of Dispond. **1694** *Lond. Gaz.* No. 3023/1 He..could not get up again to the Fleet. **1709** *Tatler* No. 114 ¶ 1 When he came up to me, he took me by the Hand. **1726** SWIFT *Gulliver* I. viii, I was forced to swim till I got up to it [*sc.* the boat]. **1806** A. DUNCAN *Nelson* 46 He could not get the bomb vessels up to the point of attack. **1823** SOUTHEY *Hist. Penins. War* I. 171 A carriage with six mules drew up to the guard-house. **1888** F. HUME *Mme. Midas* I. xii, They will never catch up to that horse.

(*b*) As far as (a specified point).

**1832** L. HUNT *Poems* 193 With green up to the door. **1865** EARLE *Sax. Chron.* p. xiii, Back into the mists of high mythology,..and so up to Adam. **1875** *Encycl. Brit.* III. 637/1 Up to the book of Joshua all three [narratives] run side by side. **1881** *Phil. Trans.* CLXXII. 483 The rostrum is very uniform up to near the front end.

(*c*) Till, until (a specified time).

In frequent use from *c* 1835. Cf. UP-TO-DATE.

**1803** M. VENZEE *Fate* 187 Up to the present time. **1834-6** *Encycl. Metrop.* (1845) VIII. 415/2 Up to 1750, he had made about two hundred tons [of zinc]. **1849** ROCK *Ch. of Fathers* I. ii. 125 Up to the present day is still kept..this very rubric. **1864** LEWINS *H. M. Mails* 311 Government letters..may be posted, without extra fee, up to the latest moment. **1891** MEREDITH *One of our Conq.* xxvi, A comprehensible pride ..keeps the forsaken man silent up to death.

*ellipt.* **1851** MRS. BROWNING *Casa Guidi Wind.* I. 993 By councils,—from Nicaea up to Trent.

(*d*) *colloq.* Before (one's face).

**1862** TROLLOPE *Orley F.* II. 111 She told me so, up to my face.

(*e*) As a task or responsibility upon (a person). Cf. UP *adv.*[2] 17 d.

**1908** 'FRANK DANBY' *Heart of Child* xviii, We'll let them know what is going on, and put it up to them to take action.

**d.** So as to reach or attain (a specified point or stage) by action directed to an end.

See also ACT *v.* 9 e, COME *v.* 69 h, KEEP *v.* 57 i, LIVE *v.*[1] 4 f.

**1611** SHAKS. *Wint. T.* IV. iv. 544 Your discontenting Father striue to qualifie And bring him vp to liking. **1629** EARLE *Microcosm.* (Arb.) 81 A verse or some such worke he may sometimes get vp to, but seldome aboue the stature of an Epigram. **1688** DRYDEN tr. *Life Xavier* I. 10 To Exhort them to live up to the Rules of Christianity. **1748** *Biog. Brit.* II. 1305 He was not unacquainted with the antient rules of Poetry, nor was he incapable of writing up to them. **1751** F. COVENTRY *Pompey the Little* II. v. 166 A Country Gentleman, who had lived, as it is called, up to his Income. **1827** FARADAY *Chem. Manip.* iv. (1842) 128 Boiling at different temperatures will, of course, communicate heat up to their boiling points. **1834** J. H. NEWMAN *Par. Serm.* (1837) I. xx. 313 Such men do not practise up to their knowledge. **1855** *Poultry Chron.* II. 538/2 Without it amateurs scarcely know what points to breed up to. **1908** *Animal Managem.* 69 Where horses are called on to work up to their rations.

(*b*) So as to reach by progression or gradual rise,

**17..** RAMSAY *Birth of Drumlanrig* vii, Your Prince, who late Up to the state of manhood run. **1772** *Regul. H.M. Service at Sea* 5 The youngest Officer shall vote first, proceeding in Order up to the President. **1793** JEFFERSON *Writ.* (1830) IV. 482 Money being so flush, the six per cents run up to twenty-one and twenty-two shillings.

(*c*) As many or as much as; including all below (a specified number, etc.).

**1892** *Photogr. Ann.* II. p. cl, The sizes..up to and including 9 inches focus. **1910** T. A. JOYCE *Handbk. Ethnogr. Coll. Brit. Mus.* 259 Good canoes..carrying up to thirty-six men.

**27. Up with —.** (Cf. 30.) **a.** So as to reach.

**1659** *Nicholas Papers* (Camden) IV. 95, 3 Spanish men of warre..who..came vp with vs and fired at vs. **1678-** [see COME *v.* 69 c]. **1719** DE FOE *Crusoe* I. (Globe) 17 Finding the Pirate..would certainly come up with us in a few Hours, we prepar'd to fight. **1761** *Ann. Reg., Chron.* 156/2 At five A.M. we got almost up with the chace. **1795** NELSON in Nicolas *Disp.* (1845) II. 13 As he drew up with the Enemy. **1795** *Ann. Reg.* I. 15 The Russians..came up with his rear.

**b.** *To put up with*: see PUT *v.*[1] 53 p (*b*).

**c.** *To draw* or *take up with*: see DRAW *v.* 89 i, TAKE *v.* 90 z.

**IV.** In elliptic uses.

**28. a.** Used imperatively (with ellipse of verb), as a command or exhortation to action, activity, rising from bed, movement, etc. Cf. UP *v.* 4.

*a* **1300** *Cursor M.* 2819 Vp loth,..þat ȝee ne be tint wit þis cite. **1535** COVERDALE *Judges* iv. 4 Debbora sayde vnto Barak: Vp, this is the daie wherin [etc.]. **1579** SPENSER *Sheph. Cal.* Nov. 47 Then vp I say,..Let not my small demaund be so contempt. **1595** SHAKS. *John* II. i. 295 Vp higher to the plaine, where we'l set forth In best appointment all our Regiments. **1612** DRAYTON *Poly-olb.* iii. 1 Up with the jocund lark (too long we take our rest). **1617** HIERON *Wks.* II. 315 Dauid..was the first which said, 'Vp, let vs flie!' **1625** SANDERSON *Serm.* I. 131 Up then with the zeal of Phinehas, up for the love of God and of His people. **1669** STURMY *Mariner's Mag.* I. ii. 18 Up alaft [*sic*] to the Top-mast-head, and look abroad. **1733** W. ELLIS *Chiltern & Vale Farm.* 5 These with the Thistles, and many others when they get the Dominion, is, up Weed and down Corn. **1798** WORDSW. *Tables Turned* 3 Up! up! my Friend, and quit your books;..Up! up! **1816** SCOTT *Paul's Lett.* 181 'Up, Guards, and at them,' cried the Duke of Wellington. **1827** KEBLE *Chr. Y., Advent Sunday* ii, Awake!..Up from your beds of sloth for shame.

**b.** With auxiliary or other verbs: To go or come up; to rise. Also rarely without verb.

An OE. instance occurs in *Genesis* 497.

**1535** COVERDALE *Ps.* xi[i]. 6, I wil vp (sayeth the Lorde). **1590** SHAKS. *Mids. N.* IV. i. 114 We will..vp to the Mountaines top. *c* **1630** SANDERSON *Serm.* II. 280 He would up therefore to a higher..Judge; and that was the Lord. **1637** R. ASHLEY tr. *Malvezzi's David Persecuted* 205 The great favorites of Princes..fall headlong, they are gone, they cannot up againe. **1647** N. BACON *Disc. Govt. Eng.* I. lix. 184 Perceiving that the Kings spirit would up againe. **1678** LUTTRELL *Brief Rel.* (1857) I. 2 On the 9th the king came.. and sent for the house of commons up. **1727** SWIFT *Imit. Hor.* Wks. 1755 III. ii. 48 Lewis, the dean will be of use; Send for him up, take no excuse. **1816** MUIR *Minstrelsy* 27 (E.D.D.), Up they till't like twa game cocks.

**29.** Followed by a noun in objective relationship to a verb omitted (e.g. *hold, raise, pull*, etc.). Orig. only with imperative force; now freq. in other uses and tending to assume the function of a verb. (Cf. UP *v.* 3-4.)

c 1384 CHAUCER *H. Fame* II. 1021 Now vp the hede for alle ys wele. 1628 RUTHERFORD *Lett.* (1664) 425 Courage, up your heart. a 1751 in A. Whitelaw *Bk. Sc. Song* (1866) 29 She rants up some fule-sang, like, Up your heart, Charlie! 1823 SCOTT *Quentin D.* xxii, Up heart, master, or we are but gone men. 1828 COL. HAWKER *Diary* (1893) I. 343, I 'up gun' and down came a bird. 1853 KANE *Grinnell Exped.* xxx. (1856) 264 When the weather is very cold, I up hood. 1854 F. W. MANT *Midshipman* 88 So that I am free to up stick and away. 1891 KIPLING *Light that Failed* viii, He wants to up-stakes and move out.

*Naut.* 1829 MARRYAT *F. Mildmay* xxiii, We agreed to up helm. 1832 — *N. Forster* x, As soon as the jolly-boat comes on board we'll up anchor. 1834 — *P. Simple* III. 286 She up courses and took in her topgallant sails. 1840, 1859 [see HELM *sb.*² 1 c]. 1859 BARTLETT *Dict. Amer.* (ed. 2), *To up jib*, to be off. A sailor's phrase. 1867 SMYTH *Sailor's Word-bk.* 707–8 Up anchor.. Up boats!.. Up courses!.. Up screw! 1893 MCCARTHY in *Westm. Gaz.* 9 March 5/1 That moment he and his companions would up steam and make for the shores of Gloria.

**30. Up with** (also † *mid*) —. (Cf. 27.) **a.** Denoting the raising of a weapon, the hand, etc., esp. so as to strike. (Cf. UP *v.* 7 b.)

c 1275 LAY. 23931 Arthur vp mid his spere..and pungde vppen Frolle. 1387 TREVISA *Higden* (Rolls) IV. 355 Judas ..up wiþ a stoon and smoot Ruben on þe hede. c 1400 *Gamelyn* 535 Gamelyn vp with his staff..And girt him in þe nek. c 1450 *Knt. de la Tour* xix. 27 Her husbonde up with his fust, and gaue her .ij. or .iij. gret strokes. 1584 in *Cath. Rec. Soc. Publ.* V. 82 The Earle..up with his fiste and gave the poore man a great blow upon the face. 1610 HEALEY *St. Aug. Citie of God* XVIII. xiv. 688 Hercules..one time vp with his harpe and knockt out his maisters braynes. 1689 HICKERINGILL *Ceremony-Monger* Concl. iii, He up with his foot, and kick't it off from the King's Head. 1704 SWIFT *T. Tub* xi, He would down with his knees, up with his eyes, and fall to prayers. 1885 STEVENSON *Pr. Otto* I. ii, Otto.. up with his whip and thrashed him. 1893 *Daily Tel.* 17 July 6/4 She 'up with her fist'.

**b.** Denoting erecting, raising, drawing or pulling up, etc. Chiefly in imperative use. Also *Up with you!* = rise, get up.

c 1377 in *Minor Poems Vernon MS.* 718/99, I ou rede.. þat vch a Mon vp wiþ þe hede, And mayntene him boþe heiȝe and lowe. c 1460 *Towneley Myst.* xxiii. 215 Vp with the tymbre [= cross]. 1594 SHAKS. *Rich. III*, v. iii. 7 Vp with my Tent, heere wil I lye to night! a 1596 *Sir T. More* II. iii. 24 Vpp with the drawbridge, gather som forces To Cornhill. 1645 J. FARY *Gods Severity* 26 Can it..be endured that a tree should stand, yeelding no increase?..No, the good husband-man will up with it. 1816 BYRON *Siege of Cor.* xxii, Alla Hu! Up to the skies with that wild halloo! 1857 HUGHES *Tom Brown* I. vi, 'Let's toss two of them together.' ..'Up with another one.' 1863 A. YOUNG *Naut. Dict.* (ed. 2) 432 Up with the helm.

(*b*) 1809 MALKIN *Gil Blas* VI. i. ¶ 9 Up with you! up with you! was the alarum of..Ambrose. 1846 MRS. A. MARSH *Father Darcy* II. iii. 81 Up, up, with you, my master, and it please you.

**c.** To drink off, consume.

1542 UDALL *Erasm. Apoph.* 30 He demaunded, how that medeicine was to bee taken?..The seruaunte had aunswered, that he must vp with it all at a draught.

**d.** To 'come out' with, to utter or sing (something).

1594 NASHE *Unfort. Trav.* A 3 b, He bad me declare my minde..I vp with a long circumstaunce..and discourst vnto him what [etc.]. 1688 R. L'ESTRANGE *Erasm. Colloq.* 190 Then Fawn up with his story, and tells him [etc.]. 1766 GOLDSM. *Vicar* xvii, 'He has taught that song to our Dick.'..'Then let us have it:..let him up with it boldly.'

**e.** Denoting support or advocacy of a person or thing. † *To be up with*, to commend, praise, laud, extol. *Obs.*

1592 NASHE *P. Pennilesse* D i, They..run their words at random,..and vppe with this man and that man. 1599 — *Lenten Stuffe* D 4 b, One is vp with the excellence of the browne bill and the long bowe: another [etc.]. 1643 TRAPP *Comm. Gen.* xxxi. 44 Laban likewise talks a great deal here; and is up with the more, and down with the less, (as they say). a 1792 in *Statist. Acc. Scotl.* II. 436 That song, 'Up with the souters of Selkirk, and down with the Earl of Hume'. 1815 SCOTT *Guy M.* vi, After some clubs had drunk Up with this statesman, and others Down with him.

*Comb.* 1902 G. K. MENZIES *Prov. Sk.* 105 A 'down-with-the-Lords' young man, An up-with-myself young man.

**31. Up and —,** denoting the act of rising or starting up, accompanied by subsequent action.

13.. *Sir Orfeo* 96 (A.), Ac euer sche held in o cri, And wold vp and owy. c 1374 CHAUCER *Troylus* III. 548 Pandare vp and..straught a morwe vn-to his nece wente. 1542 UDALL *Erasm. Apoph.* 180 b, Achilles..vp and gaue hym suche a cuff on the eare, that he slewe hym. 1682 BUNYAN *Holy War* 240 At the sound of their feet he would up and run, and meet them half way. 1838 DICKENS *O. Twist* xxxi, Why didn't you up, and collar him? 1894 ASTLEY *50 Years Life* II. 258 Refreshed, I up and plod on again.

**b.** With verbs of speaking or saying, implying a sudden or open declaration.

1548 UDALL, etc. *Erasm. Par. Luke* xxiv. 13–24 Thei.. vp & declare at large vnto Jesus the summe of al yᵉ wholle matier. 1562 T. WILSON *Rhet.* (ed. 2) 79 The Italian vp and tolde him all. 1611 MIDDLETON & DEKKER *Roaring Girle* I 1, He forswore all, I vp and opened all. a 1639 W. WHATELEY *Prototypes* II. xxxi. (1640) 111 For the man..up and told them all that had fallen out. 1702 W. J. tr. *Bruyn's Voy. Levant* xlvi. 181 Whereupon she up and told him all that had passed between them. 1836–7 DICKENS *Sk. Boz, Mr. W. Tottle* ii, He seed her several times, and then he up and said he'd keep company with her. 1880 MRS. R. O'REILLY *Sussex Stories* I. 239 She'll up and speak to the gentry themselves. 1891 'R. BOLDREWOOD' *Sydney-side Sax.* Introd., I wonder what he would say if I up and asked him for Miss Cissie.

**Up** (vp), *adv.*² Forms: 1–6 uppe, 3–6 vppe (5 wppe), 3 *Orm.*, 5 upp (7 vpp), 6– up (7 upe, vpe); 4 ope, oppe, 4–5, 9 *dial.* op. [OE. *uppe*, = OFris. *uppa* (*oppa, opa*), OS. *uppa*, MDu. *oppe* (*uppe*), ON. *uppe, uppi* (Icel. *uppi*, Norw. and Sw. *uppe*, Da. *oppe*), f. *upp* UP *adv.*¹

Also in part representing OE. *up, upp* UP *adv.*¹, which is occasionally used in place of *uppe*.]

**I.** In senses denoting position in space.

**1.** At some distance above the ground or earth; high in the air; on high; aloft.

c 897 K. ÆLFRED *Gregory's Past C.* xvi. 101 He ȝeseah ane hlædre standan æt him on eorðan. Oðer ende wæs uppe on hefenum. 975 *O. E. Chron.* (Parker MS.), And þa wearð ætywed uppe on roderum steorra on staðole. c 1000 *Ags. Ps.* (Thorpe) cxiii. 11 Ys ure se halȝa God on heofon-dreame, uppe mid englum. c 1200 ORMIN Ded. 259 Sannt Johan.. sahh upp inn heffne an boc. c 1300 *K. Horn* 1171 (Laud MS.), Ayol was op in toure. c 1375 *Cursor M.* 3148 (Fairf.), Vp hey a-pon ȝone felle sal þou bren þi sone for me. 1593 SHAKS. *Rich. II*, v. v. 112 Mount, mount, my soule, thy seate is vp on high. 1603 — *Meas. for M.* II. ii. 152 True prayers, That shall be vp at heauen, and enter there Ere Sunne rise. 1634 J. LEVETT *Ordering of Bees* 23 The ringing of basons,..which I haue often heard when a swarme is up, or in rising. 1788 DIBDIN *Poor Jack* ii, There's a sweet little cherub that sits up aloft, To keep watch for the life of poor Jack. 1815 SCOTT *Guy M.* v, A flag that's up yonder in the garret. 1842 TENNYSON *Lady Clare* i, The time when ..clouds are highest up in air.

**b.** Of the heavenly bodies: Risen above the horizon; ascended into the sky.

a 1000 in *Narrat. Angl. Conscr.* (1861) 29 Næs se mona þa ȝyt uppe. c 1000 *Sax. Leechd.* III. 272 On winterlicre tide hi [*sc.* the Pleiades] beoð on niht uppe & on dæȝ adune. c 1380 WYCLIF *Sel. Wks.* II. 222 Sunne of riȝtwisnesse is uppe. 1481 CAXTON *Godfrey* lxxii. 116 In the morne whan the sonne was vp. 1526 TINDALE *Matt.* xiii. 6 When the sun was vppe hitt..wyddred awaye. 1599 *Broughton's Let.* v. 15 If the Sunne were vp..he was punished. 1650 B. *Discolliminium* 32 If the Sun be down though the Stars be up. 1719 DE FOE *Crusoe* II. (Globe) 494 Tho' the Moon was up. 1728 CHAMBERS *Cycl.* s.v. *Honey* ¶ 5 The Bees only gather it after the Sun is up. 1812 BYRON *Ch. Har.* II. xxi, The moon is up; by Heaven, a lovely eve! 1844 WILLIS *Contempl.* 1 They are all up—the innumerable stars.

*transf.* 1595 SHAKS. *John* v. v. 21 The day shall not be vp so soone as I.

**2.** On high or (more) elevated ground; more inland; further from the coast or sea.

In OE. also 'on shore; on land; inland'. Cf. UPALAND, UPONLAND.

*Beowulf* 566 Hie..on merȝenne..be yðlafe uppe læȝon. c 897 K. ÆLFRED *Gregory's Past. C.* xxviii. 197 Ða Saul hine wolde secean uppe on ðæm munte. a 900 *Baeda's Hist.* III. xxiii. (1890) 230 Se biscop..him stowe ȝeceas mynster to ȝetimbriȝenne in heawum morum uppe. a 1050 *O. E. Chron.* (MS. D) an. 1016, Ða se kyning ȝeahsade þæt se here uppe wæs, þa ȝesamnade he..ealle Engla þeode.

c 1560 A. SCOTT *Poems* ii. 38 For Sym wes bettir sittin, Nor Will, Vp at the Drum that day. 1697 DAMPIER *Voy.* 218 The City..is 20 mile up in the Country. 1710 *Tatler* No. 254 ¶ 7, I proposed a visit to the Dutch cabbin, which lay about a mile further up in the country. 1825 SCOTT *Betrothed* xxiii, The Red Pool..lies up towards the hills. 1846–8 LOWELL *Biglow P.* I. Poems (1912) 223 Recollect wut fun we hed..Up there to Waltham plain last fall. 1855 BROWNING *Up at a Villa* ii, Up at a villa one lives, I maintain it, no more than a beast.

**3.** In an elevated position; at some distance above a usual or natural level.

c 897 K. ÆLFRED *Gregory's Past C.* xxxiii. 222 Swæ swæ iu ..wæron ða lac forbærndu uppe on ðæm altere. a 1000 *Rood* 8 (Gr.), Ȝimmas..fife wæron uppe on þam eaxleȝespanne. a 1200 *Vices & Virtues* 95 Ðe postes þat sculen beren up ðis weorc. c 1200 ORMIN 1169 All þatt Judewisshe lac þatt ȝuw her uppe iss shæwedd. c 1275 LAY. 17495 He bar þare his croune heȝe vppe on his heued. c 1275 *Doomsday* 51 in *O. E. Misc.* 167 Heo schule iseon þene kyng.. vppe on þe rode myd stronge pyne abouhte. 1377 LANGL. *P. Pl.* B. VII. 91 As wilde bestis with wehe [ȝe] worthen vppe and worchen. a 1400–50 *Alexander* 198 Quen he was semely vp set with septour in hand. *Ibid.* 977 (D.), Alexander hys ayre vppe in hys awne trone. 1526– [see STAY *v.*² 1 c]. 1596 *Edward III*, III. iii. 134 Edwards great linage, .. Fiue hundred yeeres hath helde the scepter vp. 1667 PEPYS *Diary* 22 July, In my Lord's roome,..where all the Judges' pictures hung up. 1669 STURMY *Mariner's Mag.* v. xii. 68 As you hale him out, keep him up that you may bring no Flower out with the Ladle. 1764 FOOTE *Patron* I. Wks. 1799 I. 337 He never brought them..a birth till the christening was over; nor a death till the hatchment was up. 1799 *Hull Advertiser* 13 April 2/1 Cutter-built sloop,.. measures up aloft thirty-two feet. 1819 W. TENNANT *Papistry Storm'd* (1827) 48 At anes the bells baith up and under Begoud to rattle on like thunder. 1855 BAIN *Senses & Int.* II. ii. § 6 An object seems to us to be up or down, according as we raise or lower the pupil of the eye in order to see it. 1899 *Daily News* 6 Nov. 4/5 The accommodation is limited to one room down and two up.

**b.** In fig. phrases or expressions.

c 1386 CHAUCER *Knt.'s T.* 675 As doon thise loueres in hir queynte geres.., Now vp, now doun, as boket in a welle. c 1430 *Pilgr. Lyf Manhode* I. lxxviii. (1869) 46 So michel þow didest, what up what doun, þat to mariage þow haddest hire. 1579 TOMSON *Calvin's Serm. Tim.* 758/1 Wee must ..be readie to forgoe all: wee must alwayes haue one foote vp. 1741 RICHARDSON *Pamela* (ed. 3) I. 199 There I stood, my Heart up at my Mouth. 1749 WALPOLE *Let. to Mann* 23 March, Ned's envy, which was always up at high-water-mark. 1828 *Carr Craven Gloss.* s.v., I can find him nayther up-ner-down; *i.e.* I can find him no where.

**c.** Of an adjustable (esp. sliding) device or part: Raised.

1599 SHAKS. *Hen. V*, II. i. 55 Pistols cocke is vp, and flashing fire will follow. 1600 FAIRFAX *Tasso* VI. xxvi, Her ventall vp so hie, that he descride Her goodly visage. 1610 R. VAUGHAN *Water-workes* P 4 b, Vnlesse..my seruants suffer the Sluces to be vpp when they should be downe. 1708 MRS. CENTLIVRE *Busie Body* IV. ii, He has escap'd out of the Window, for the Sash is up. 1764 MRS. E. CARTER *Let. to Miss Talbot* 3 Feb., The glasses [of the coach] were up and broke to shivers. 1796 SOUTHEY *Joan of Arc* II. 488, I saw him..Riding from rank to rank, his beaver up. 1799 LAMB *Lett.* (1888) I. 112 Travelling with the coach windows sometimes up. 1838 J. F. COOPER *Excurs. Italy* I. 57 We were closely curtained and had the glasses up [in the travelling-carriage]. 1879 MEREDITH *Egoist* i, The visitor carried a bag, and his coat-collar was up. 1892 *Photogr. Ann.* II. 407 It closes itself either way, with the piston up or down.

**d.** *colloq.* On horseback; riding. Also *fig.*

1812 J. H. VAUX *Flash Dict.* s.v., A man who is 'in swell-street', that is, having plenty of money, is said to be 'up in the stirrups'. 1856 H. DIXON *Post & Paddock* vi. 93 His running in a sweepstakes, when Sam [the jockey] was not 'up'. 1857 G. LAWRENCE *Guy Liv.* iii, A match for £50, 10 st. 7 lb. each. Owners up. 1886 in *Fores's Sporting Notes* III. 6 To pace the paddock when Archer's up.

**†4.** Of a gate, door, etc.: Open. *Obs.*

13.. *Cursor M.* 24423 (Gött.), All vp [*Cott.* opind] war þair grauis sene. 1340 *Ayenb.* 255 Yef hi vyndeþ þe gate oppe, hi guoþ in liȝtliche. 1390 GOWER *Conf.* III. 336 The dore is up, and he in wente. c 1480 HENRYSON *Twa Mice* xxi, Bot in he went, and left the dure vp wyde. 1550 CROWLEY *Epigr.* 118 In seruice tyme no dore standeth vp, Where such men are wonte to fyll can and cuppe.

**5. a.** High, in respect of the river-bank or shore.

1387 TREVISA *Higden* (Rolls) II. 51 Seuarne is ofte vppe and passeþ þe brynkes. 1546 *Yorks. Chantry Surv.* (Surtees) 209 At such tyme when the waters be uppe. 1720 DE FOE *Capt. Singleton* xiii. (1840) 221 The tide was up. 1844 W. H. MAXWELL *Wand. Highl.* xxxvii, The sea was up. 1882 'MARK TWAIN' *Roughing It* vii. 35 The Platte was 'up', they said—which made me wish I could see it when it was down.

**b.** Out of the stomach, etc.

1579 GOSSON *Sch. Abuse* (Arb.) 65 If I giue them a Pil to purge their humor, they neuer leaue belking till it bee vp.

**c.** On or above the surface of the ground or water.

1835 *Trans. Zoological Soc.* I. 234 By remaining perfectly quiet when the animal is 'up' the spectator is enabled to attain an excellent view of its movements in the water. 1854 RUSKIN *Let. to Miss Mitford* 7 Aug., The soldanella..is.. distinguished for its hurry to be up in the spring. 1865 G. MACDONALD *A. Forbes* viii, She was as lonely as if she had anticipated the hour of the resurrection, and was the little only one up of the buried millions. 1883 GRESLEY *Gloss. Coal-m.* 268 *Up*, on the bank, or on the surface.

**6. a.** In a standing posture; on one's feet; standing (and delivering a speech).

(*a*) 1297 R. GLOUC. (Rolls) 3828 Is suerd he drou þere Vor to asaile him þerwiþ, ac þe oþer was vp ere. a 1300, 1398 [see BEAR *v.* 18]. c 1440 *Generydes* 44 An hert was fownde .., And vppe vppon his fete he was a non. c 1450 *Mankind* 29 (Brandl), O ȝe souerens, þat sytt, and ȝe brotherne, þat stonde ryghte wppe. 1595 SHAKS. *John* III. iv. 137 He that stands vpon a slipp'ry place, Makes nice of no vilde hold to stay him vp. 1613 WITHERS *Abuses Stript* I. v, They..are so quickly up in a *bravado*. 1682 BUNYAN *Holy War* 164 They were not able without staggering to stand up under it. 1787 'G. GAMBADO' *Acad. Horsem.* (1809) 34 The standing up in your stirrups, whilst trotting.., has a most elegant and genteel effect. 1860– [see HOLD *v.* 44 f]. 1888 J. H. STIRLING in A. H. Stirling *Life* (1912) 310 The student up was just translating in the ordinary slip-slop, unthinking fashion.

(*b*) 1657 *Burton's Diary* (1828) I. 319, I only stood up first, to speak to the orders of the House. But now I am up, I desire [etc.]. 1762 FOOTE *Orator* III. Wks. 1799 I. 220 Silence, gentlemen;..A worthy member is up. 1778 *Ann. Reg., Hist.* 133/2 The Minister concluded a long..speech, which kept him full two hours up. 1835 DICKENS *Sk. Boz, Parl. Sketch*, Members arrive..to report that 'The Chancellor of the Exchequer's up'. 1899 *Daily News* 24 March 2/1 He had a comparatively small audience, augmenting in numbers as news went round that he was up.

**b.** In an upright position.

Also *bolt, right, straight up*: see these words.

1669 PEPYS *Diary* 3 March, My Lord Mayor did retreat out of the Temple by stealth, with his sword up. 1727– [see SIT *v.* 25 c]. 1859 TENNYSON *Geraint & Enid* 546 Bound on a foray..[the earl] Came riding with a hundred lances up. 1884 *Lillywhite's Cricket Ann.* 60 He kept up his wicket until the finish.

**c.** Erected, built.

1613–39 I. JONES in Leoni *Palladio's Archit.* (1742) I. 70 Part of this Building..is finish'd, but the rest have some part of the Basement up only. 1742 LEONI *Ibid.* II. 69 Of the Rings for Races... A third is yet up.., though half-ruined.

**7. a.** Out of bed; risen.

a 1375 *Joseph Arim.* 234 In þe morwe he was vppe and roises þis oþure. c 1400 *Laud Troy Bk.* 16992 The sonne is rysen & schynes bryght, And thei are vppe & redi dyght. 1470–85 MALORY *Arthur* VIII. xxv. 311 Take youre rest and loke that ye be vp by tymes. 1523 FITZHERB. *Husb.* § 149 Go to thy bedde and slepe, and be vppe betyme. 1581 MULCASTER *Positions* 19 Those people..be drousie when they are vp, for want of their sleepe. 1607 DEKKER *Westw. Hoe* II. i, We..must be vp with the lark. 1641 in *10th Rep. Hist. MSS. Comm.* App. I. 78, I vas upe this morninge be two a cloacke. 1693 DRYDEN *Juvenal* III. 218 In vain we rise, and to their Levees run; My Lord himself is up, before, and gone. 1719 DE FOE *Crusoe* II. (Globe) 363 Another..asked, who it was that was up? 1771 MRS. HAYWOOD *New Present for Maid* 255 When the family is up, she should set open the windows of the bed-chambers. 1854 R. S. SURTEES *Handley Cr.* li, Mrs. Jorrocks,..and Benjamin, were up with the lark. a 1873 LYTTON *Ken. Chillingley* xiv, One of the young ladies who attended..to the dairy was already up.

**b.** Not gone to bed; not yet abed.

a 1535 FISHER *Wks.* (1875) 367 Peraduenture he was late vp the night before. 1550– [see SIT *v.* 25 b]. 1622 J. TAYLOR (Water P.) *Shilling* B 5, Whilst all the Drawers must stay vp and waite Vpon these fellowes be it ne're so late. 1763

G. Williams in Jesse *Selwyn & Contemp.* (1843) I. 250 While Lord March and I are up half the night with people of a profligate character. **1779** Warner *Ibid.* (1844) IV. 274, I was in hopes that some of the servants were still up. **1834** Maginn in *Blackw. Mag.* XXXV. 748 My eye caught a light in the window... Seeing that the old fellow was up, I determined to step over. **1852** Dickens *Bleak Ho.* lviii, The corporation of servants are dismissed to bed (not unwilling to go, for they were up all last night). **1855**– [see Wait *v.*[1] 7 f].

**c.** Of game: Roused, started.

**1611** Shaks. *Cymb.* iii. iii. 117 Hearke, the Game is rows'd. ..The Game is vp.

**8. a.** Further away from the mouth towards the source of a river, the inner part of a bay, etc.

**1600** Hakluyt *Voy.* II. 194 Wee..arriued in the Easter-side thereof some ten leagues vp within the Bay. **1697** Dampier *Voy.* 7 We..rowed up to the head of the Creek, being about a mile up, and there we landed. **1766** Goldsm. *Vicar* iii, By taking the current a little farther up, the rest of the family got safely over. **1816** Tuckey *Narr. Exped. R. Zaire* vi. (1818) 223 At day-light sent off all.. the people who had been up with me, to the transport. **1862** Kingsley in *Lett.*, etc. (1877) II. 139, I never saw such a river, though there are very few salmon up.

**b.** Pointing or directed to the stream.

**1821** *Acc. Peculations Coal Trade* 7 Then he recollects there is a punt head up in Mill-hole tier.

**c.** Towards a place or position; forward; advanced in place.

**1613** Shaks. *Hen. VIII*, v. iv. 92 *Porter.* Make way there... *Man.* You great fellow, Stand close vp. **1806** Surr *Winter in London* II. 133 'Is my chariot up?' said the captain. 'Next to the duchess's, sir.' **1867** Smyth *Sailor's Word-Bk.* 368 *Hard up*, the tiller so placed as to carry the rudder close over to leeward of the stern-post. **1868** *Field* 18 July 49/2 Viscount lying second, and the others in close order well up. **1903** Warner in Hutchinson *Cricket* 65 If the ball is a half-volley or well up.

**d.** At or in a place of importance (*spec.* London).

**1845** Carlyle *Cromwell* (1871) III. 126 'Dick Cromwell and his Wife' seem to be up in Town on a visit. **1866** Trollope *Claverings* iv, You'll be up in London by the 10th of next month. **1886** C. E. Pascoe *London of To-day* ii. (ed. 3) 37 Literary parsons 'up' for a week or two's reading at the British Museum.

**e.** *colloq.* At or in school or college.

**1847** Tennyson *Princ.* Prol. 175 We seven stay'd at Christmas up to read. **1866** *Routledge's Ev. Boy's Ann.* 197 The boys were still 'up', that is, in school [=Eton]. **1886** *Law Times' Rep.* LIII. 664/2 The permission to remain up during the vacation.

**9.** In miscellaneous uses: **a.** Facing upward.

**1683** Dryden & Lee *Dk. of Guise* v. i, The world's..better now, 'tis downside up. **1852** Morfit *Tanning & Currying* (1853) 289 The skin is stretched over this, with the grain side up. **1891** *Anthony's Photogr. Bull.* IV. 65 The tissue should be completely immersed, face up.

**b.** Off the ground; in store; in a proper place or receptacle.

*To keep up*: see Keep *v.* 57 a, k. *To lie up* (=in bed, etc.): see Lie *v.*[1] 29.

**1865** Trollope *Belton Est.* iii. 26 Our hay has been all up these three weeks.

**c.** With the surface broken or removed.

**1886** *Daily News* 14 Oct. (Encycl. Dict.), Streets that are up. **1891** C. James *Rom. Rigmarole* 1 A great deal of roadway was 'up'. **1908** *Times* 28 July 2/6 There was a good deal of traffic in the road, part of which was up for repairs.

**II.** In figurative senses.

**10.** In a state of disorder, tumult, revolt, or insurrection; risen in rebellion. Also const. *in* (mutiny, etc.).

**13..** *E. E. Allit. P.* B. 834 Fro þe seggez haden souped.., Er euer þay bosked to bedde þe borȝ was al vp. *c* **1420** *Contin. Brut.* 358 And anon come tydyngez þat Harry of Bolyngbroke was vp with a strong power of pepill. **1487** *Cely Papers* (Camden) 166 The comens of the town..hawe ben upp onys or twyse allredy. *a* **1548** Hall *Chron., Edw. IV*, 208 b, All the Realme was vp, and by open Proclamacion commaunded to make warre against hym. **1593** Marlowe *Edw. II*, i. iv, 'Tis treason to be vp against the king. **1655** *Nicholas Papers* (Camden) II. 298 The Levellers wilbe spedily vpp against Cromwell. **1688** Wood *Life* (O.H.S.) III. 284 Lord de la Mere up in Cheshire with forces and crie 'No bishops!' **1695** C. Hatton in *H. Corr.* (Camden) II. 216 For thes 2 nights a great mob have been up in Holborn and Drury Lane. **1849** Macaulay *Hist. Eng.* ix. II. 529 The eastern counties were up. **1889** C. Doyle *Micah Clarke* 58, I had heard that Monmouth was up, and I knew that you would not lose a night ere starting.

(*b*) **1656** Earl Monm. tr. *Boccalini's Advts. fr. Parnass.* ii. xi. (1674) 150 People that are up in commotion. **1844** P. Harwood *Hist. Irish Rebellion* 137 The British fleet was then up in mutiny.

**b.** *Up in arms*, risen, levied, or marshalled as an armed host. Also *fig.* (see Arm *sb.*[2] 4 b).

*c* **1590** *Sir T. More* i. iii. 77 A number poore artificers are up In arms. *c* **1595** Capt. Wyatt *Dudley's Voy.* (Hakl. Soc.) 47 On a soden yow shall have all quarters up in armes. **1690** C. Nesse *O. & N. Test.* I. 278 All created beings are up in arms to reduce the rebels. **1704** [see Arm *sb.*[2] 4 b]. **1812** Crabbe *Tales* v. 249 Be not a Quixote, ever up in arms To give the guilty and the great alarms. **1879** J. D. Long *Æneid* x. 321 Ascanius, cooped in by wall and ditch, The Latins up in arms, fights hand to hand. **1893** Forbes-Mitchell *Remin. Gt. Mutiny* 108 The public-house keepers ..were up in arms to raise as much opposition as possible.

**c.** Actively stirring or moving about.

*c* **1460** *Wisdom* 518 in *Macro Plays* 52 'Farewell,' quod I; 'þe deuyll ys wppe'. **1611** Beaum. & Fl. *Philaster* i. i, This earth you tread upon..was not left..To your inheritance, and I up and living. **1838** Longf. *Psalm of Life* ix, Let us, then, be up and doing. **1855** Macaulay *Hist. Eng.* xxii. IV. 714 They pursued him: the hue and cry was raised:..the whole country was up. **1872** Spurgeon *Treas. Dav.* Ps. lxxvii. 6 He was up and at it, resolutely resolved that he would not tamely die of despair.

**d.** In a state of agitation, excitement, exaltation, or confidence.

**1470–85** Malory *Arthur* x. lxxv. 546 What,..is your herte vp? yester daye ye ferd as though ye had dremed. **1576** Newton *Lemnie's Complex.* 18 When theyr rage is vp, they will not easily be pacifyed. **1589** R. Harvey *Pl. Perc.* (1590) 7 Now the blood is vp. **1602** Marston *Ant. & Mel.* ii. Wks. 1856 I. 19 My stomack's up...The match of furie is lighted. **1691** Hartcliffe *Virtues* 21 Our Passions,..when they are up, and would hurry us into evil Actions. **1741** Richardson *Pamela* III. 40 It was a nice Part to act; and all his Observations were up, I daresay, on the Occasion. **1766** Goldsm. *Vicar* xvii, Let us have a bottle of the best gooseberry wine, to keep up our spirits. **1805** Wordsw. *Prelude* iii. 18 My spirit was up, my thoughts were full of hope. **1824** Scott *St. Ronan's* xiii, His pluck was up, and finding himself in a fighting humour, he [etc.]. **1859** Dickens *T. Two Cities* ii. v, Up one minute and down the next; now in spirits and now in despondency. **1891** E. Peacock *N. Brendon* I. 111 When his temper is up he might do anything.

**e.** Bound *for* (a place); ready *for* (something). Cf. 17 a (*d*).

**1870** Longf. *John Endicott* ii, On board the Swallow,..Up for Barbadoes. **1894** Blackmore *Perlycross* 131 Christie was quite up for it. She loved a bit of skirmish.

**11. a.** In a state of prevalency, performance, or progress. (In later use mainly with *keep* v.)

*c* **1290** *Beket* 229 in *S. Eng. Leg.* I. 113 Þis Ercedekne.. stifliche heold op hire riȝte. *Ibid.* 404 Þou auȝtest more to holden op þane to with-seggen mi power. **1362** Langl. *P. Pl.* A. iv. 58 Bot ȝif Meede make hit þi Mischef is vppe. **1399** — *Rich. Redeles* i. 29 Þey..cowde no mysse amende whan myscheff was vp. **14..** *Siege Jerusalem* 295 Now is ȝour sorow vppe. **1513**– [see Keep *v.* 57 f]. **1537**– [see Hunt's-up]. **1582**– [see Hold *v.* 44 g]. **1670**– [see Keep *v.* 57 e].

† **b.** In power or force. *Obs.*

**1541** in W. H. Turner *Select. Rec. Oxford* (1880) 163 He shold se er he died friers and monks uppe agayn. **1607** Shaks. *Cor.* iii. i. 109 To know, when two Authorities are vp,..How soone Confusion May enter. **1641** J. Jackson *True Evang. T.* ii. 89 They are such beasts as while the Law was up,..furnished Gods Altar with Sacrifices.

**c.** Much or widely spoken of, whether favourably or (latterly) unfavourably.

Cf. the OE. sense 'disclosed, made known', and ON. and Icel. *uppi*, noted, remembered.

**1618** Bolton *Florus* (1836) 265 The name of Caius Cæsar was up, for eloquence, and spirit. **1680** V. Alsop *Mischief of Imposit.* vii. 41 His name being up, he may lie abed till noon. **1766** G. Williams in Jesse *Selwyn & Contemp.* (1843) II. 33 [He] has again taken to his bed, and now, since his name is up, there he may lie. **1789**, **1809** [see Name *sb.* 5]. **1812** *Sporting Mag.* XXXIX. 283 He observed his name was up there, and he should be suspected. **1824** Mrs. Cameron *Pink Tippet* iii. 16 Your name's up in the town.

**d.** *colloq.* Occurring (as a special, unusual, or undesirable event); taking place, going on. Chiefly with *what*. (Very freq. from *c* 1850.)

**1849** Alb. Smith *Pottleton Legacy* ix. 75 He saw something was 'up'. **1851** Mayhew *Lond. Labour* I. 21 A shout in answer from the other asks 'What's up?' **1908** *Times* 29 May 15/6 We constantly thought that something was going to be up.

**e.** Amiss or wrong *with* a person, etc.

**1887** Rider Haggard *Jess* vii, There's something up with that girl.

**12.** In senses denoting completion.

**a.** Of a period of time, etc.: Completed, ended, expired, over. (Cf. Uphaliday.)

Cf. the same sense of ON. and Icel. *uppi*, LG. *up*, Du. *op*, G. *auf*.

*c* **1400** *Destr. Troy* 7207 When the tyme was ourtyrnyt, and þe tru vp, Agamynon þe grekys gedrit in þe fild. **1596** Dalrymple tr. *Leslie's Hist. Scot.* (S.T.S.) II. 86 The king.. commandis..to lat him pas frie,..or vp trues, against thame he sal proclayme weiris. *Ibid.* 235. **1688** Miège *Gt. Fr. Dict.* ii. s.v., The Quarter is up. **1776** in Sparks *Corr. Am. Rev.* (1853) I. 310 Whose time of enlistment will be up in a few days. **1840** R. H. Dana *Bef. Mast* xxix, He should want a second mate before the voyage was up. **1865** Carlyle *Fredk. Gt.* xix. viii. (1873) VIII. 240 So that the Ball is up; dress-pumps and millineries getting all locked into their drawers again. **1878** H. C. Adams *Wykehamica* xv. 268 As soon as morning school was up, there was a general rush ..to breakfast. **1889** 'J. S. Winter' *Mrs. Bob* xxi, As his leave was nearly up, he..would be off in the morning.

**b.** Of an assembly: Risen; adjourned; over.

**1632** Massinger & Field *Fatal Dowry* i. ii, The court is vp; make way. **1647** Clarendon *Hist. Reb.* iv. § 255 The Duke said..that..all men being upon their feet, and out of their places, he conceiv'd the house had been up. **1711** Swift *Jrnl. to Stella* 7 May, Yet perhaps it may not be till Parliament is up. **1773** Foote *Bankrupt* iii. Wks. 1799 II. 126 As both the Houses are up, I shall adjourn..till their meeting again. **1825** Hone *Every-day Bk.* I. 492 After parliament's up. **1853** Dickens *Bleak Ho.* xxxix, The Chancellor is, within these ten minutes, 'up' for the long vacation. **1881** J. Hatton *New Ceylon* Pref., There was much bustle of departing travellers. Parliament was up.

**c.** (At) the number or limit agreed upon as the score or game.

**1667** Dryden *Sir M. Mar-all* i. i, Which most mads me, I lose all my sets when I want but one of up. **1680** Cotton *Compl. Gamester* (ed. 2) 30 Of Trucks...The Game, because it is sooner up than Billiards, is Nine, and sometimes Fifteen. **1685** Tate *Cuckolds-Haven* ii. ii. 15 Security and his Wife playing at Putt..*Sec.* There's up, Wynny, there's up; Come give me my Winnings. **1740** Richardson *Pamela* II. 259, I had four Honours the first time, and we were up at one Deal. **1873** Bennett & Cavendish *Billiards* 5 The game was twelve up. **1876** *Encycl. Brit.* IV. 180/2 (Bowls), The game..is 'up' or won when the number of casts agreed on have been obtained by the winning side.

**d.** Come to a fruitless or undesired end; 'played out'. Usu. with *game*.

**1787** Jefferson *Writ.* (1859) II. 283 Are we to suppose the game already up? **1800** *Aurora* (Philadelphia) 17 Dec. (Thornton), As the Baltimore paper says, 'The Jigg's up, Paddy'. **1838** Dickens *O. Twist* xix, He feared the game was up. **1848**– [see Jig *sb.* 5]. **1867** Freeman *Norm. Conq.* vi. I. 558 Godwine might well think that the game was up.

**e.** *All up*, completely done or finished; quite over. Also *all* u p (yū pī). (See also U 5.)

**1825** C. M. Westmacott *Eng. Spy* I. 322 That's all up now. **1854** Warter *Last of Old Squires* ix, Now corrupted into the simpler saw, 'It's all U P—up!' **1860** Whyte Melville *Market Harb.* 94 Consequently, when you drop into a run, he goes as long as he can, and it's all u p!

**f.** Const. *with*, in previous sense.

**1833** Disraeli *Cont. Fleming* ii. vi, It is all up with him by this time. **1837** Col. Hawker *Diary* (1893) II. 121 It appears now to be 'all up' with coast gunning. **1854** R. S. Surtees *Handley Cr.* xxxvi Crikey! they're past! and it's U P with old Pug. **1888** McCarthy & Praed *Ladies' Gallery* I. ix. 221 It was all but up with me.

**g.** In other applications.

**1883** Gresley *Gloss. Coal-m.* 268 A stall or heading is said to be *up* when it is driven or worked up to a certain line.., beyond which nothing further is to be worked. **1909** *Cent. Suppl.* s.v., *Up*,..in *printing*, finished; noting completion of a task: as, the chapter is up; the paper is up.

**13. a.** Higher in the ascending scale in respect of position, rank, fortune, etc.; in a position of affluence or influence. Also *fig.* (quot. 1791).

**1509** Barclay *Shyp Folys* 17 b, He that lyeth on hye [is] Nowe vp, nowe downe, vnsure as a Balaunce. **1611** Shaks. *Cymb.* i. v. 39 Which first (perchance) shee'l proue on Cats and Dogs, Then afterward vp higher. **1791** Mme. D'Arblay *Diary* 4 June, I shall be apt to be rather up in the world, as the folks say, if I tope on at this rate! **1877** Tennyson *Harold* i. i, For in our windy world What's up is faith, what's down is heresy. **1905** in *Eng. Dial. Dict.* s.v.

**b.** Increased in power, force, strength, or vigour; actually blowing; ready for action.

**1547** Boorde *Introd. Knowl.* 127 Yf the winde be any thyng vp. **1570** Foxe *A. & M.* (ed. 2) III. 2197/1 The winde was somwhat vp, and it caused the fire to be ye fiercer. **1601** Shaks. *Jul. C.* v. i. 68 The Storme is vp, and all is on the hazard. **1659** Pell *Impr. Sea* 500 His often hushing of the winds, when they are up. **1742** R. Blair *Grave* 32 The wind is up: hark! how it howls! **1833** I. Taylor *Fanat.* i. 16 What shall be the movements of the deep..when the winds are up! **1848** J. Mitchel *Jail Jrnl.* 27 May, A Government steamer..lay in the river, with steam up. **1889** Gunter *That Frenchman* xxi. 298 Steam is up, and the boat is soon ready to leave her dock.

**c.** Advanced, increased, or high in number, value, or price.

**1546** in Ellis *Orig. Lett.* Ser. ii. II. 175 Th' exchaunge is vp agen above xxiiijs. **1722** De Foe *Plague* (1884) 165 The Bill was up at 2785. **1801**– [see Keep *v.* 57 c]. **1855** Bagehot *Lit. Stud.* (1879) I. 3 A head full of sums, an idea that tallow is 'up'. **1887** A. Birrell *Obiter Dicta* Ser. ii. 93 The price of £100 stock was up to £340. **1891** *Science-Gossip* XXVII. 51/1 Six shillings a couple for ducks, and four for teal, as they're up now.

**d.** Advanced *in* years.

*a* **1822** Sir A. Boswell *Old Beau* iii, Though up in life, I'll get a wife. **1834** *Tait's Mag.* I. 417/1 An Irishman, rather up in years. **1884** T. Speedy *Sport Highl.* ii. 13 Gentlemen who are somewhat up in years.

**e.** (So many points, etc.) in advance of a competitor.

**1894** *Times* 19 July 7/2 They were two up at the third hole. **1900** J. Doe *Bridge Man.* 61 When the adversaries are 28 up. **1903** *Times* 6 Feb. 7/6 The former pair winning by three up and two to play.

*fig.* **1919** J. B. Morton *Barber of Putney* vi, It's one up to 'im for stickin' it.

**f.** At a high or lofty pitch.

**1902** O. Wister *Virginian* ix, All the ladies thought the world of her, and McLean had told him she was 'away up in G'. **1905** Elinor Glyn *Viciss. Evangeline* 81 He has a giggle right up in the treble.

**14. a.** Before a magistrate, etc., in court. (Cf. Up *adv.*[1] 16 b.)

**b.** Offered or exposed publicly.

**1921** *Conquest* Sept. 480/1 His business is to set a value on the teas up for sale.

**III.** With a preposition following.

**15. Up against —**, faced or confronted by (difficulties, etc.). *colloq.* (orig. *Amer.*).

**1901** S. Crane *Monster*, etc. 231 All he's up against is a case of grand larceny. **1910** *Chambers's Jrnl.* April 232/1 In Canadian phraseology, we were 'up against it' with a vengeance!

**16. Up in —**, expert or versed, well informed or instructed, in a subject, matter, work, etc. *colloq.*

In frequent use from *c* 1860.

**1838** Dickens *Nich. Nick.* xxiii, 'Intrigue', and 'Ways and Means', you're all up in; so we shall only want one rehearsal. **1856** Miss Yonge *Daisy Chain* i. xxx, As to the examination..the very subjects had been chosen in which he was most up. **1885** 'F. Anstey' *Tinted Venus* 100, I did think Potter was better up in his work.

**17. Up to —. a.** (*a*) Able to perform, do, or undertake; fit or qualified for; capable of.

In frequent use from *c* 1850. For phrases involving this or one of the following senses see also Slum *sb.*[1] 5, Snuff *sb.*[2] 3 a, Thing *sb.*[1] 14 f, Trap *sb.*[1] 5.

**1785** Trusler *Mod. Times* I. 88 He was up almost to any villainy. **1792** Paine *Rights of Man* ii. ii. 17 Man, naturally as he is, with all his faults about him, is not up to the character. **1801** F. Leighton *Let. to J. Boucher* 15 May (MS.), I hope you will have no strangers with you...I am not up to that. **1820** *Examiner* No. 659. 761/2 An old.. hardy Highland Chieftain was up to no such mawkish sentiments. **1856** Mrs. Carlyle *Lett.* (1883) II. 282, I was up to nothing but lying on the sofa all the evening. **1890** 'R. Boldrewood' *Col. Reformer* (1891) 225 The fence..is barely up to the weight of six hundred bullocks..at a high degree of momentum. **1898** 'H. S. Merriman' *Roden's Corner* xvii. 179 To provide situations for elderly men who are no longer up to their work.

(*b*) **1855** Smedley *H. Coverdale* i, Two showy saddle-horses, the best being up to fifteen stone with any hounds. **1861** E. Yates in *Temple Bar* II. 473 A cob 'well up to fourteen stone'.

(*b*) Well aware of and prepared for; competent to deal with; a match for.

**1785** Grose *Dict. Vulgar T.* s.v., Up to their gossip. **1806** Lady S. Lennox *Lett.* (1901) II. 202 To be up to all the wiles and arts used to entrap them. *c* **1830** Mrs. Sherwood *Houlston Tracts* III. lxxxi. 10 To use a vulgar phrase very common with us servants at that time, I was so far up to Anne Simpson, that..I would not be put upon by her. **1864** H. Ainsworth *John Law* v. ix, Sir Patrick and I are both wide awake,..so we shall be up to their tricks. **1890** 'R. Boldrewood' *Col. Reformer* (1891) 321 It takes a smart man to be up to chaps of their sort.

(*c*) Thoroughly acquainted with; expert or versed in; possessing a thorough knowledge of.

In frequent use from *c* 1840.

**1800** Lamb *Let. to Manning* 3 Nov., He does not want explanations..when you make an assertion; up to anything; down to anything. **1823** Mrs. Sherwood *H. Milner* III. v. 88 Sam is not up to many things about a horse. **1853** Kane *Grinnell Exped.* xxii. (1856) 171 They are a..well-educated set of men, thoroughly up to the history of what has been done by others.

(*d*) Ready for. (Cf. 10 e.)

**1849** Thackeray *Pendennis* xxiv, She was up to any party of pleasure by whomsoever proposed. **1893** Miss Yonge *Girl's Little Bk.* 23 Boys fancy they like a jolly girl up to anything,..but they do not respect her.

**b.** Equal in quality or quantity to (something specified); on a level with.

See also Keep *v.* 57 i, and the phrases under Dick *sb.*[5], Knocker 2 c, Nine *sb.* 6 b.

**1809** Windham *Let.* in *Sp.* (1812) I. 114 Though I am considerably above my rate of London health, I am..not quite up to that which residence here ought to have given me. **1821–** [see Mark *sb.*[1] 12 c]. **1826** Disraeli *V. Grey* II. xiv, The Baronet is not up to the nineteenth century. **1862** Thoreau *Excursions* viii, Of course no flavors are thrown away; they are intended for the taste that is up to them. **1883** *Manch. Guard.* 22 Oct. 5/5 The harvest of this year was up to a full average.

(*b*) *Not up to much*, of no great ability, importance, or worth.

**1863** Miss Braddon *Aurora Floyd* xxi, The new chap warn't up to mooch. **1884** Sala *Journ. due South* I. ix, The shoes were not, to use a vulgarism, 'up to much'.

(*c*) *dial.* Even with (a person). Cf. 18 b.

**1853** Mrs. Gaskell *Cranford* xiv, But I'll be up to her... I'll make her a pudding, and a pudding she'll like, too. **1854** Miss Baker *Northampt. Gloss.* 371 'I'll be up to you'; i.e. I'll retaliate.

**c.** Engaged in or bent on (some activity, esp. of a reprehensible nature); occupying or concerning oneself with; doing or planning.

**1837** Dickens *Pickw.* xxvii, What's the old 'un up to, now? **1853** — *Bleak Ho.* xxxix, They are still up to it, sir,..still taking stock, still examining papers. **1875** W. S. Gilbert *Tom Cobb* I, That Whipple 's up to some bedevilment. **1890** R. C. Lehmann *H. Fludyer* 84, I suppose you've been up to some of your games again.

**d.** *colloq.* Obligatory or incumbent upon.

From the game of poker; in common use from *c* 1913.

**1901** S. Crane *Monster*, etc. 212 It's up to us to whirl in an' git some of it. **1902** Greenough & Kittredge *Words* 56 So with the poker terms 'ante up' and 'it is up to you'. **1908** *Westm. Gaz.* 21 Feb. 4/2 It was 'up to him', then, as an American would put it, to say that he had done this thing.

**18. Up with —.** (See also 11 e, 12 f.)

**a.** On a level with (a person, place, etc.).

**1623** Jobson *Golden Trade* 8 When the day appeared we were up with the Iland of Launcerot. *a* **1633**– [see Keep *v.* 57 j]. **1669** Sturmy *Mariner's Mag.* I. ii, We have a Stearn-Chase, but we shall be up with her presently. **1858** Thackeray *Virginians* xxxviii, She makes for the vestry...The two whiskeyfied gentlemen are up with her, however. **1893** Sir G. Chesney *Lesters* II. xxi, Lionel..was the only one quite up with the hounds at the last.

*fig.* **1785** Burns *To W. Simpson* ix, We'll gar our streams an' burnies shine Up wi' the best. **1899** Werner *Capt. of Locusts* 41 But I don't worry myself to keep up with things, as people say.

**b.** Even with; quits with. Now *dial.*

**1741** Richardson *Pamela* III. 308 Let me turn myself about, and I'll be up with you, never fear, Madam. **1778** [W. Marshall] *Minutes Agric.* 3 Feb. 1775, But I will certainly be up with him to-morrow. **1800** Lathom *Dash of Day* IV. i, I'll be up with her for her deceit, I am determined. **1825** Jamieson s.v., I'se be up wi' him for that. **1899** *Cumberland Gloss.* 351.

**IV. 19.** *Comb.* in phrases used attributively, as *up-all-night*, etc.

**1857** Dickens *Dorrit* I. xx, A curious *up-all-night air about it. **1891** S. Mostyn *Curatica* 158 Chimney tops, and *up-all-night-looking window blinds. **1901** *Harper's Mag.* CII. 678/1 She had an *up and coming kind of way with her. **1890** *Advance* (Chicago) 24 April, There is about our Methodist brethren..an *up-and-a-comingness..that [is].. delightful. **1901** *Daily Chron.* 17 Dec. 3/2 She was..the most *up-and-doing woman of all her generation. **1848** Clough *Bothie* II. 59 A sort of unnatural *up-in-the-air balloon-work. **1898** *Westm. Gaz.* 4 June 7/1 The mere *up in the roof ventilation. **1893** K. Sanborn *S. California* 4 In that brilliant and *up-with-the-times city.

**†Up** (*vp*), *prep.*[1] *Obs.* Forms: α. 1–2 uppan, 1–3 uppon (2 huppon), 2–3 uppen, vppen (2 upen, 4 vpen). β. 3–4 vppe, 2–3, 5 uppe (4 oppe), 2–4 upe, 3–6 vpe (4 ope). γ. 3–5 vp (4 op, 5 wp), 3–5 up. [OE. *uppan*, *uppon* (in earlier use *on uppan* Anuppe *prep.*), = OFris. *uppa* (*oppa*), OS. *uppan*, f. *upp* Up *adv.*[1] Cf. OHG. *ûfan*, *ûffan* (MHG. *uffen*).

By gradual loss of the ending (perhaps also by simple assimilation) the prep. finally acquired the same form as the adverbs. A similar reduction (or substitution of the adverbial form) appears in Du. and WFris. *op*, NFris. *üp* (*üb*), LG. *up*, G. *auf*.]

**I.** Denoting motion or direction.

**1.** So as to reach, or be on, by ascension.

*c* **1000** *Ags. Gosp.* Matt. xxvi. 30 Þa ferdon hiȝ uppan Oliuetes dune. *a* **1122** *O. E. Chron.* (Laud MS.) an. 1083, Sume of ðam cnihtan ferdon uppon þone uppflore. *c* **1205** Lay. 26005 Heo..stiȝen up þan hulle. **1297** R. Glouc. (Rolls) 4179 Þo he com vpe þe hul an hey. **1422** Yonge tr. *Secreta Secret.* 166 The Philosofre lepid vp the mule.

**b.** Denoting arrival upon (a coast, etc.) from sea.

*c* **1205** Lay. 13970 Heo droȝen heore scipen uppe þe lond. **1297** R. Glouc. (Rolls) 362 Þo he was iwar þat such folc was arived..vp his londe.

**2.** On or upon. (In various contexts.)

*c* **960** *Rule St. Benet* lviii. (Schröer) 100 Sona swa he þæt ȝewrit uppan ðam altare lecge, beginne þis fers. *c* **1000** *Ags. Gosp.* Matt. xxi. 44 Se þe fylð uppan þysne stan, he byð tobrysed. *c* **1175** *Lamb. Hom.* 35 [Þe] saule..ne mei abeoren alla þa sunne þe þe mon uppon hire deð. *c* **1200** *Trin. Coll. Hom.* 21 Þe holie gast wile cumen uppen þe. *c* **1205** Lay. 6504 And þet deor he smat a-nan uppe þat hæued-bæn. *Ibid.* 13257 Þe crune he nom an honden; he setten heo vppe Costance. *a* **1225** *Ancr. R.* 286 Slep go uppe þe ase þu lokest þeron [*sc.* holy reading]. *c* **1250** *Owl & Night.* 1625 Me may vppe [*v.r.* up one] smale sticke Me sette a wude in þe þikke. **1297** R. Glouc. (Rolls) 3624 Þo þe niȝt vpe hom com. *a* **1325** *Prose Psalter* lii. 3 God loked fram heuen vp mennes sones. *Ibid.* liv. 4 Drede of deþ fel vp me. *Ibid.* cxviii. 135 Liȝt þi face vp þi seruant. **1340** *Ayenb.* 210 Seste þe dore ope þe. **1377** Langl. *P. Pl.* B. XI. 203 For-þi loue we as leue bretheren shal and vche man laughe vp other. *c* **1391** Chaucer *Astrol.* II. § 1 Rekene.. which is the day of thi monthe & ley thi reule vp that same day. **14..** *Cron. Eng.* (Caxton) ccxiii. 222 Thousandes fell to the ground eche vp other in to a hepe.

**b.** Denoting desire: After, for.

*a* **1200** *Vices & Virtues* 51 Alle ȝe Adames children ðe bieð lustfull uppe newe wastmes.

**3. a.** In hostile encounter with or attack on; in active opposition to.

*a* **1122** *O. E. Chron.* (Laud MS.) an. 1086, Þa hæðenan men ..herȝodan uppon þam Xpenan mannan. *c* **1205** Lay. 10563 Carrais..bigon ræuinge uppen Basian þene kinge. **1297** R. Glouc. (Rolls) 5054 Vor naȝt we abbeþ so ofte vpe hom ywonne þat lond. *Ibid.* 8987 Þe erl..bigan to rere worre vpe þe king of france. *c* **1330** *Arth. & Merl.* 6680 (Kölbing), Þe king of þe hundred kniȝtes Com hem vp þo forþ riȝtes.

**b.** Against (as an accusation, penalty, etc.).

*a* **1122** *O. E. Chron.* (Laud MS.) an. 1094, Hi..ealne þone bryce uppon þone cyng tealdon. *c* **1200** *Trin. Coll. Hom.* 51 Þermide [hie] brohten godes wraðe uppen hem. *Ibid.* 105 Werpeð þat gilt uppen ure drihten. *a* **1250** *Owl & Night.* 1683 (Cott.), Schille ich an utest uppen ow grede. *c* **1290** *Beket* 1466 in *S. Eng. Leg.* I. 148 Mo luþere dedene þe king bi-þouȝte ȝeot ope seint thomas. *a* **1325** *MS. Rawl. B.* 520 fol. 54 That..Bissopes ȝeuen þe grete sentense ope alle þulke þat aȝen the foreseide chartres goz. **1393** Langl. *P. Pl.* C. II. 159 Vp man for hus mysdedes þe mercement he taxeþ.

**II.** Denoting rest or location.

**4.** On or upon. (In various contexts.)

α. *c* **1000** Ælfric *Gen.* xlix. 32 He feold his fet uppan his bed. *c* **1000** *Ags. Gosp.* John vi. 19 Þa ȝesawon hiȝ þone Hælend uppan þære sæ gan. *a* **1175** *Cott. Hom.* 243 Cnihtscipe is mannes lif upen eorðe. *c* **1175** *Lamb. Hom.* 147 Þa þe he hefde uppen his hefde þornene helm. *c* **1205** Lay. 23985 Uppen þan gras-bedde his gost he bi-læfde. *a* **1225** *Ancr. R.* 242 Ȝe beoð ouer þisse worldes see, uppen þe brugge of heouene. *c* **1250** *Prov. Ælfred* 262 in *O. E. Misc.* 118 For he schal vppen eorþe dreori i-wurþe.

β. *a* **1175** *Cott. Hom.* 239 Alse fele unþeawes alse [he] hade upe him and sennenn. *c* **1200** *Trin. Coll. Hom.* 93 Ðe asse þe ure helende uppe set. *c* **1250** in *O. E. Misc.* 164 Moni of þisse riche þat..rideþ uppe stede and uppen [*v.r.* uppon] palefrai. **1297** R. Glouc. (Rolls) 6559 Vppe a chaere he sat adoun al vpe þe se sonde. *c* **1315** Shoreham II. 176 Ase þou þoledest, lord, for me Ope caluaryes doune. **1340** *Ayenb.* 180 Þe weddere-cok þet is ope þe steple.

γ. *a* **1250** *Owl & Night.* 494 Euerich vp oþer rideþ. *c* **1275** Lay. 25758 Noht hii ne funde cwic vp þan hulle. **1297** R. Glouc. (Rolls) 6299 King edmond..lenede vp is sseld. *c* **1300** *K. Horn* 1344 (Laud MS.), Op þe scheld was drawe A crowch of ihesu cristes lawe. *a* **1325** *Prose Psalter* xlvi. 8 God shal sitten vp his holy sege. **1377** Langl. *P. Pl.* B. I. 12 Þe toure vp þe toft. *Ibid.* IX. 99 Lesyng of tyme..Is moste yhated vp erthe of hem þat beth in heuene. **1422** Yonge tr. *Secreta Secret.* 184 Thay mete wyth kynge Gurgnynce vp the See. **1470–85** Malory *Arth.* IX. xli. 408 What sygnefyeth this kynge and this quene, and that knyght standynge vp bothe their hedes?

**b.** So as to be suspended from or supported on.

*c* **1175** *Lamb. Hom.* 41 Uppon þan treon he him sceawede þe wrecche saulen a-honge. *c* **1205** Lay. 26475 Alle heo sculleð heongien heȝe uppen treouwe. *c* **1275** *Ibid.* 5863 Of ȝoure hors a-liȝteþ and vp ȝoure feot stondeþ. *c* **1280** *Christ on Cross* 23 in *E. E. P.* (1862) 21 Man bi-hold what ic for þe þolid up þe rode tre. **1297** R. Glouc. (Rolls) 7734 He wolde him sulf vp is fot..Liȝtliche ssete. *c* **1350** *Will. Palerne* 2809 Þe hert & þe hind..ferden ferst on foure fet & seþþe vp tweyne. *c* **1485** *Digby Myst.* (1882) I. 273 This ferdell of gere I ley vp my bakke.

**c.** In transferred or figurative uses.

α, β. *c* **1200** *Vices & Virtues* 31 Ðat liht of his ansiene is ȝemarked riht uppen us. *Ibid.* 71 Bereð min ȝoc uppe ȝeu. **1297** R. Glouc. (Rolls) 5032 Þo vel he in siknesse & sorwe vpen oþer. *a* **1325** *MS. Rawl. B.* 520 fol. 48 b, Þat he..vsurpede some fraunchises ore occupiede ope þe kinge ore his predecessours. *c* **1340** *Ayenb.* 54 Þo þet habbeþ þe lhordssip ope þe bodyes. **1340–70** *Alex. & Dind.* 861 Whan a wolf wanteþ his fode,..he ne fundeþ no flech to feden him vppe.

γ. *c* **1250** *Gen. & Ex.* 2320 Vp quam ðu it findes witterlike. *a* **1325** *Prose Psalter* xl. 3 Our Lord be to hym helpe up þe charge of his sorowe. *Ibid.* xlvi. 8 God shal regne vp men. **1382** Wyclif 2 *Cor.* xi. 21 Vp vnnobley [L. *secundum ignobilitatem*]. **1422** Yonge tr. *Secreta Secret.* 129 Ther-for god ..granted hym mervellous victori vp his enemys..,Namly vp the morthes.

**5. a.** *Up*(*þe*) *land*, = Uponland *adv.*

? *c* **1000** *Ags. Letter* in *Engl. Stud.* VIII. 62 Þu byst uppan lande mid wimmannum oftor þonne ic beo. *a* **1122** *O. E. Chron.* (Laud MS.) an. 1086, To ælcen cyrcean uppe land. *c* **1250** *Owl & Night.* 733 Preostes vpe londe singeþ. *c* **1330** *Arth. & Merl.* 698 (Kölbing), Al þe men..Boþe vp lond & in cite. **1514** Barclay *Cyt. & Uplondyshman* v. Prol. 44 Well he noted the madde enormyte, Enuy,..Whiche reygne in cytes; therfore he ledde his lyfe Up londe in vyllage. **1596** Spenser *F. Q.* v. x. 25 They came vnto a Citie farre vp land.

**b.** On the bank or brink of; close beside.

*c* **1205** Lay. 7 He wonede..at æðelen are chirechen, vppen Seuarne staþe. *Ibid.* 28544 Uppe þere Tambre heo tuhte to-somne. **1340** *Ayenb.* 251 Ope þo welle þe herte resteþ efter þe trauayl of guode workes. *Ibid.*, He him zette and restede ope þe welle. **14..** in *Hist. Coll. Citizen London* (Camden) 96 The kyng made a grete justysse be-syde Kyngys towne uppe Temys.

**6. a.** On or upon, in respect of belief, etc.

*c* **1200** *Trin. Coll. Hom.* 11 Cursed be þe man þe leueð upen hwate. *Ibid.* 93 Þo forsineȝede be hauen al here þonc uppen eorðliche richeise. *a* **1240** in *O. E. Hom.* I. 213 Þu.. lettest me al iwurden wið þeo þet ich truste uppon. *a* **1300** *X Commandments* 23 in *E. E. P.* (1862) 16 Hi..þat liuiþ op goddis mo þan one. *c* **1369** Chaucer *Dethe Blaunche* 922 So frendely, and so wel y-grounded, Vp al resoun so wel y-founded. *c* **1380** Wyclif *Sel. Wks.* III. 88 Up trust of absoluciouun. **1393** Langl. *P. Pl.* C. x. 333 Vp trist of ȝoure tresour tryennels to haue. **1462** *Paston Lett.* II. 114 Up trust that the same John Paston shuld founde there a college.

**b.** According to; in accordance or agreement with; to the extent of.

**1297** R. Glouc. (Rolls) 5137 Ac vpe godes wille it is, wanne it ssal be. *Ibid.* 5657 He..vpe is poer destruede..cristendom. *c* **1300** *K. Horn* 456 (Laud MS.), And helpe þou me to knicte Oppe þine myȝte. **1382** Wyclif *Matt.* ix. 29 Vp ȝour feith be it don to ȝou. **1388** — 2 *Sam.* xxii. 21 The Lord schal ȝelde to me vp my riȝtfulnesse.

**c.** By (chance, guess, etc.).

*c* **1350** *Will. Palerne* 2722 So brod was þe see þat sayle hem bihoued holliche al a niȝt & vp happe wel more. **1377** Langl. *P. Pl.* B. v. 421, I nam nouȝte shryuen..tweies in two ȝere and þanne vp gesse I schryue me. *c* **1380** Wyclif *Wks.* (1880) 375 But vp hap þu art a clerke or a religious man. *a* **1508** *Gest Robyn Hode* 49 Wayte after some vnkuth gest Vp chaunce ye may them mete.

**d.** In comment on or explication of; concerning.

**1340** *Ayenb.* 187 Ase zayþ a glose ope the sautere. **1393** Langl. *P. Pl.* C. xi. 113 Þre daies to-gederes we ȝeoden, Disputynge vp dowel daye after oþere. *c* **1400** *Three Kings Cologne* 39 After þe glose þat is made vp þis tixt. **1422** Yonge tr. *Secreta Secret.* 123 Wp whych matyer, Arystotle answerid in this maner. *Ibid.* 202 Vp this texte Saynte Austyn sayth thus.

**7. a.** On or upon (oath, condition, etc.).

*a* **1122** *O. E. Chron.* (Laud MS.) an. 1095, Forþam se cyng him naþer nolde ne ȝislas syllan, ne uppon trywðan ȝeunnon þæt he..cumon moste. *a* **1200** *Vices & Virtues* 11 Ic habbe..uppe mine lahfulnesse ofte him behet, þat ic næure eft him neȝelæste. **13..** *K. Alis.* (W.) 228 'Dame,' he saide, 'beo thou nought loth, Y am y-come to telle up oth'. *c* **1369** Chaucer *Dethe Blaunche* 750 (Fairf.), I telle hyt the vp a condicioun. *c* **1400** *Gamelyn* 411 Vp suche forward..I wil do þerto alle þat in me is. **1422** Yonge tr. *Secreta Secret.* 175 The tyraunt hit grauntid vp that covnantte.

**b.** Upon pain or under penalty of; on.

Freq. *c* 1380–*c* 1430, esp. with *pain*, *peril*.

(*a*) *c* **1205** Lay. 500 Þat come to hirede,..vppen lif & uppen leomen al þes londes folc. **13..** *Coer de L.* 3875 He ..bad hys folk, up lyff and leme, Noo good off hem for to neme. *c* **1350** *Will. Palerne* 2378 Helpes hastily, hende men i hote, vp ȝour liues! *c* **1425** *Eng. Conq. Ireland* 120 He..,vp mansynge, forbed lered & lewed, that non [etc.]. *c* **1430** Lydg. *Min. Poems* (Percy Soc.) 38 A confortatife And remedye I shal make, up my life.

(*b*) *c* **1205** Lay. 5118 Al comen to Lundene uppe wit of feowerti punden. *c* **1380** Wyclif *Wks.* (1880) 24 Þat þei ben holden to vp peyne of lesynge of here lordischipe. *c* **1386** Chaucer *Sompn. T.* 563 And ye shul seen, vp peril of my lyf,..That [etc.]. **1393** Langl. *P. Pl.* C. v. 128 Neiþer graue ne vngraue of gold ne of suluer, Vp forfeture of þe fee. **14..** *Cron. Eng.* (Caxton) ccxxi. 213 That they shold smyte of syr edmondes heede..vp payne of lyf and lymme. **1474** *Cov. Leet Bk.* 389 Vp þe peyn of vj s. viij d. at euery defalt.

**8.** More than; above.

*a* **1325** *Prose Psalter* l. 8 Y shal be made whyȝte vp snowe. *Ibid.* ii. 3 Þou louedest malice up biisfolhede. **1340** *Ayenb.* 39 Þer byeþ zuo uele oþre maneres.., þet long þing hit were to zigge, ac zome byeþ y-contined, ope þan þet byeþ yzed.

**III.** In respect of time.

**9.** After (a specified time). Cf. Over *prep.* 16.

*c* **1000** *Ags. Gosp.* John x. 11 *marg.*, On sunnan dæȝ feowertyne nyht uppan eastron. *a* **1122** *O. E. Chron.* (Laud MS.) an. 1095, Uppon Eastron on sancte Ambrosius mæsse niht, þæt is .ii. no. Apr. [etc.]. *Ibid.* an. 1103, On morȝen uppon sancte Laurentius mæsse dæȝ. *c* **1205** Lay. 6405 Þa hit wes muchel uppe non, þe king þene duc ouer-com. *Ibid.* 22309 Seouen niht uppen Æstre. *c* **1275** *Ibid.* 2632 Vppen one stunde þe sipes i-maked were. *c* **1290** *Beket* 1123 in *S. Eng. Leg.* I. 138 Þene moruwe ope seint lucus day, tiwesdai it was þo [*sc.* 19 Oct.], he departede fram þe kingus court.

**10.** At; upon (a stated time).
*a* 1200 *Vices & Virtues* 123 ȝif mann ware..uppen his deaðe, and he prest ne mihte habben. *c* 1290 *Beket* 825 in *S. Eng. Leg.* I. 130 Alle..seide þo þat..ope þe pointe he was to beon i-cast In prisone. *c* 1315 SHOREHAM V. 151 Ope þe heȝe eȝtynde day He order-ȝede þe gywen lay. *c* 1374 CHAUCER *Troylus* IV. 1153 Here woful spirit from his propre place, Right with þe word, alwey vp poynt to pace.

**Up** (vp), *prep.*[2] [Elliptical use of UP *adv.*[1], by omission of a preposition, as *against*, *along*, *through*, etc. Cf. the earlier use of *adown* and *down* as prepositions.]

**I.** Denoting or implying movement.

**1.** From a lower to a higher point on or along (an ascent); so as to ascend or mount (a stair, slope, etc.).
1509 HAWES *Past. Pleas.* XXVII. (1555) Q iij, After that they brought me vp a stayre Into a chambre. 1530 PALSGR. 828/1 Up the hyll and downe the vale. 1593 SHAKS. 2 *Hen. VI*, IV. viii. 1 Vp Fish-streete, downe Saint Magnes corner,..throw them into Thames. 1602 — *Ham.* IV. iii. 39 As you go vp the staires into the Lobby. 1607 MARKHAM *Cavel.* VI. 9 Hee may eyther runne..vp hils, or down hils. 1697 DRYDEN *Virg. Georg.* III. 552 The Sun..When up the Skies he shoots his rosie Head. 1730 THOMSON *Autumn* 701 The..exhalations, check'd As up the middle sky unseen they stole. 1786 BURNS *On Dining w. Ld. Daer* i, Sae far I sprackled up the brae. 1807 J. BARLOW *Columb.* I. 190 A heaven-illumined road; That..Reach'd o'er the hills, and lengthen'd up the sky. 1828 LYTTON *Pelham* II. xviii, If your way is up Pall Mall, I have no objection to join you. 1851 *Offic. Catal. Gt. Exhib.* 366 By which the weight on the horse's back is regulated in going up or down hill. 1867 MORRIS *Jason* I. 208 Who, up the temple steps, beneath the weight Of precious things went bending.
*Comb.* 1732 E. ERSKINE *Wks.* (1791) 598/2 This phrase.. implies, that religion is an up-the-hill work and way.
*fig.* 1824 WILSON in *Blackw. Mag.* Aug. 242 Abusing the Germans up-hill and down-dale. 1844 DICKENS *Mart. Chuz.* xxxv, All this time, Martin was cursing Mr. Pecksniff up hill and down dale.

**b.** Extending upwards on.
1574 *Southampton Court Leet Rec.* (1905) I. 101 The Raylles vpe the steares goynge vpe vnto the Wache towere. 1730 THOMSON *Autumn* 679 The vineyard..Spreads o'er the vale; or up the mountain climbs. 1756 *Constat* in *L. T. R. Particulars for Leases* 4974 (P.R.O.), The dimensions up one pair of Stairs are only Thirty one Feet.

**c.** *U.S.* Up into.
1833 [S. SMITH] *Lett. J. Downing* xxiv. (1835) 98, I..walked straight up chamber. *Ibid.* 150 When they undertook to cum up-chamber,..it was time to snub 'em.

**2.** Along (a river, etc.) in a direction from the mouth towards the source.
1513 *Acc. Ld. High Treas. Scotl.* IV. 465 To ane bot [going] wp the watter with cabillis,..xiiij s. 1560 DAUS tr. *Sleidane's Comm.* 360 b, They brought in vitayle both vp the streame and down. 1600 *Reg. Mag. Sig. Scot.* 384/1 Haldand up the said burne to the inver of the burne of Auldclachrie. 1659 *Nicholas Papers* (Camden) IV. 95 Alexandria, from whence I went up the Riuer Nilus to Cairo. 1698 FRYER *Acc. E. India & P.* 38 All the Factories on the Coast..as far as the Bay of Bengala, and up Huygly River. 1738 *Voy. up the Thames* 15 It was propos'd we should take a Voyage up its Banks. 1814 SCOTT *Diary* 3 Sept., in *Lockhart*, With the purpose of running up the loch to see Londonderry. 1849 MACAULAY *Hist. Eng.* ii. I. 191 The Dutch fleet sailed up the Thames. 1877 MISS A. B. EDWARDS (*title*), A Thousand Miles up the Nile.
*Comb.* 1898 *Daily News* 17 Oct. 5/4 There was a nice up Channel breeze.

**3.** Towards the inner or upper end of; into or towards the interior of. Also *transf.*
1596 SPENSER *F. Q.* V. ix. 23 His name was Awe; by whom they passing in Went vp the hall. *a* 1700 in *Orpheus Caledonius* (1725) 28 The wooer he step'd up the House. 1745 P. THOMAS *Jrnl. Anson's Voy.* 63 The Treasure..being sent up the Country..out of our Reach. 1818 *Sketches of Character* (ed. 2) I. 44 Lady Aucherly..sauntered up the room with her three disconsolate nieces. 1849 MACAULAY *Hist. Eng.* ix. II. 482 William's army began to march up the country. 1863 MAYNE REID *Croquet* i. (1865) 25 A ball croque'd beyond the boundaries is sent to 'Hong Kong', or 'up the country'.

**4.** In a direction contrary to; against.
1611 COTGR., *Prendre le vent*, to goe vp, or against, the wind. 1618 BRETON *Court & Country* A 4, For one that goes up the weather a number goe downe the winde. 1674 N. COX *Gentl. Recreat.* (1677) 77 The Huntsman [should]..then draw round apace, first down the Wind, though usually Deer go up the Wind. 1719 D'URFEY *Pills* III. 269 The Fox has broke Covert,..she runs up the Wind. 1816 SCOTT *Bl. Dwarf* ii, I gaed a mile round to get up the wind to them. 1838 [see UP-WIND *adv.*].

**5.** Along (in a horizontal direction or straight course).
*Up street* (dial.), along the street or village.
1669 STURMY *Mariner's Mag.* I. ii. 20 Port, edge towards him [*sc.* a ship]. We will run up his Side. 1683 [see GO *v.* 65]. 1719 DE FOE *Crusoe* I. (Globe) 156, I went up the Shore and down the Shore, but..could see no other Impression. 1758 JOHNSON *Idler* No. 92 ℙ 6 He..walks up a bye-street. 1851 MRS. BROWNING *Casa Guidi Wind.* II. 742 The sun strikes, through the windows, up the floor. 1883 *Harper's Mag.* Oct. 718/1 It is approached up an avenue. 1886 FROUDE *Oceana* 63 After breakfast we went up the town.

**II.** Denoting location.

**6.** In that part of (a place) which is (regarded as) higher than another, or is more remote from the chief centre.
*Up State, up-State* (U.S.), freq. with reference to the State of New York; also *Comb.*
1667 PEPYS *Diary* 8 Sept., Nova Scotia..hath a river 300 miles up the country, with copper mines. 1750 GRAY *Elegy* 112 Nor up the lawn, nor at the wood was he. 1799 *Hull Advertiser* 12 Oct. 1/1 All those five tenements up the yard. 1810 SCOTT *Lady of Lake* II. xxxvi, Far up the lake, 'twere safest land. 1885 JEROME *On the Stage* 43 Mind you all keep well up the stage ('up' the stage means towards the back). 1890 *Cent. Mag.* Aug. 634/1 The man who abandoned a farm up the Hudson. 1901 in *N. Amer. Rev.* Feb. 162 American girls..imported from small towns up-State.
*Comb.* 1815 SCOTT *Guy M.* l, We're just plain up-the-country folk. 1897 *Outing* XXIX. 424 Up-the-creek natives. 1901 *Daily Chron.* 16 Sept. 3/7 All the up-State constituencies. 1904 *Collier's* 16 July 16/1 The crews of the up-State college [Cornell].

**7. a.** At the top of. **b.** At some distance up on or in. (Cf. UPHILL *a.*, UPSTAIRS *adv.* 2.)
For fig. expressions see GUM-TREE 2, TREE *sb.* 7, SLEEVE *sb.* 2 b, SPOUT *sb.* 4 b.
1645 RUTHERFORD *Tryal Faith* xxiii. 261 Heaven.., when sight [of faith] faileth us, [is] toylesome and up the mount. 1714 ARBUTHNOT, etc. *Mem. M. Scribl.* Introd., His lodging was in a small chamber up four pair of stairs. 1833 MOORE *Trav. Ir. Gentl. Search Relig.* I. 1 As I was sitting alone in my chambers, up two pair of stairs, Trinity College. 1846 TENNYSON *Golden Year* 4 We that day had been Up Snowdon. 1860 GEO. ELIOT *Mill on Fl.* I. ii, He'll..sleep up three pair o' stairs—or four, for what I know. 1890 [see SLEEVE *sb.* 2 b].

**U P, U. P.**: see UP *adv.*[2] 12 e and U 5.

**U. P.** (= United Presbyterian): see U 4.

**Up-,** *prefix*, representing OE. *up-*, *upp-* (see below) and corresponding to OFris. *op-*, *up-* (WFris. *op-*, NFris. *üp-*, *ap-*), MDu. and Du. *op-*, OS., MLG., and LG. *up-*, OHG. and MHG. *ûf-* (G. *auf-*), ON., Icel., and Norw. *upp-*, MSw. *up-*, *upp-* (also *op-*, *opp-*), Sw. *upp-*, MDa. and Da. *op-*.
The prefix is identical with the adverb UP[1], from which in OE. it becomes clearly separable only when prefixed to nouns and adjs. In the cognate languages there is much variation in the extent to which it is employed with different parts of speech. In OS. and OFris. it occurs with verbs and nouns, in OHG. with verbs, nouns, and a few adjs., in ON. chiefly with nouns, in MHG., MLG., MDu., MSw. and MDa. with both verbs and nouns, and occasionally adjs. In the later and modern forms of these languages the use of the prefix has increased as in English, and parallel formations are very common; these are cited only when the Eng. compound is important enough to appear as a main word.
Of the numerous formations with *up-* which have been employed in English, only a limited number are of a permanent character. A large proportion consists of forms employed for the nonce, especially for metrical reasons, and the same compound may recur several times without any historical continuity; such isolated occurrences, indeed, are often separated by an interval of several centuries. A number of these are given in the following sections, as illustrations of the various uses of the prefix in the different periods of the language.

**I.** In comb. with sbs. (except as in 7, 8).

**1.** In OE. *up-* occurs freely with sbs. in the sense of 'occupying a higher position', 'upper', 'superior', as *up-eard*, *-ende*, *-engel*, *-flôr*, etc. Some of these, however, are only found in poetry. In ME. this type practically disappears, and in later use is chiefly represented by UPLAND *sb.*[2] and UPSIDE, with an occasional rare formation, as *upwold*.

**b.** With the sense of 'in a supported state', *up-* occurs with nouns in OE. *upheald*, ME. *uphald*, uphold, ME. *uptie* (naut.), and the modern *upkeep*.

**2.** In the sense of 'upwards' OE. had compounds of *up-* with nouns, mainly derived from intransitive verbs, as *up-cyme*, *-færeld*, *-ryne*, *-spring*, *-stige*, rarely from transitive, as *upwearp*. Of these only *upspring* and *upsty* survived in ME., but a number of new formations were added, as the obsolete *uparist*, *-brixle*, *-brud*, *-ras*, *-rist*, and the surviving *upbraid*, *-come*, *-rise*, *-set*. Between 1450 and 1800 new formations are rare, the chief being *upcast* and *upstir* in the 16th cent., with *upskip* and *upstart* (as designations of persons) from the same period; also *upshot* (with variants *-shoot* and *-shut*), in which the force of the *up-* is not clear. After 1800 the type reappears and subsequently becomes common. A considerable number of the examples are of sufficient importance to be entered as main words in their alphabetical places, as *upbeat*, *-break*, *-burst*, *-flow*, *-growth*, *-heaval*, *-lift*, etc. Others of more recent origin or less currency are *upblaze*, *-curl*, *-curve*, *-drift*, *-glance*, *-gush*, *-haul*, *-heave*, *-jet*, *-jump*, *-liftment*, *-slip*, *-sweep*. In *upset*, as in the corresponding verb, the prefix is employed in an unusual sense.
1677 *Sec. Packet of Advices to Men of Shaftesbury* 55 They are better at *Up-cry, and Out-cry, and Down-cry. 1876 MEREDITH *Beauch. Career* xxvi, It suggested an arrow-head in the *up-flight. 1860 HAWTHORNE *Marb. Faun* xvi, The shifting..*up-gush and downfall of water. 1860 VIVIAN *Deb. Coal Clause* (1861) p. xv, The 'Great Lower Veins', varying from 50 feet on the Northern to 100 feet on the Southern outcrop, and upwards of 70 feet on the Central *upheave. 1817 *Sporting Magazine* L. 128 He received some dreadful *up-hits in his throat. 1850 'H. HIEOVER' *Pract. Horsemanship* 189 The moment he does this, give him an *up-pull. 1839 URE *Dict. Arts* 833 The line over s, represents the down-shift, and d' the *up-shift [of a vein]. 1876 *Whitby Gloss.*, **Upshow*,..display.

**b.** More rarely, *up-* is employed in the sense of 'upwards', with other nouns than those of action, e.g. OE. *upweg*, early mod.E. *upway*, and the recent *up-grade*, *-road*, *-shaft*, *-wave*.

**II. 3.** *Up-* is rarely employed in combination with adjs.; *upheaded* (16th cent. and mod. dial.), *upstraight* (17th cent.), *upfingered*, *uphearted*, *upnosed*, and *upsighted* (19th cent.) are unusual types, as also are *upspring* and *upstart* (16th cent.) employed as adjs., but retaining the form of the noun or verb.

**III.** With verbs, participles, verbal substantives, and agent-nouns.

**4.** In OE. the placing of *up* immediately before a verbal form was determined by the syntactical principles which have been explained in the article on OUT-. The number of verbs with which *up* was commonly employed in this way is not large; it includes *âbrecan*, *âhebban*, *âræran*, *ârisan*, etc., *gân*, *hebban*, *ræcan*, *springan*, *spryttan*, *stîgan*, *yrnan*. It is difficult to determine in how many of these the adverb had become a real prefix, but apparently it had attained this function in some forms, as *up-âhebban* and *uphebban*. In ME. the use of the prefix is thoroughly established, though it is not always possible to distinguish between real compounds and simple precedence of the adverb on metrical or rhetorical grounds. A number of these uncertain examples may be found under various senses of UP *adv.*[1] Of those established compounds which require separate entry some occur as early as the 13th century, as *upbraid*, *-break*, *-bring*, *-come*, *-go*, *-nim*, *-stand*, etc., and many more are found from about 1300 onwards, as *upbear*, *-call*, *-cast*, *-draw*, *-give*, *-heave*, *-hold*, *-leap*, etc. Others have been constantly added during the following centuries, so that even with the disappearance of earlier instances the type has been well maintained down to the present day. A considerable proportion, however, occur only in poetry, and are simple substitutions for the verb followed by the adverb, although they are regarded as real compounds and written as one word.

In the OE. collocations or compounds the prefix has regularly the sense of 'upwards'. In ME. it also assumes various transferred or figurative senses of the adverb, and latterly may have any meaning which has attached to this in connexion with a verb, e.g. *upbind* to bind up; *up-pen* to pen up; *upspeed*, to speed up, etc. The same variety of meaning naturally occurs also in combination with participles and verbal nouns.

In addition to those which are entered as main words, the following examples illustrate the tendency to employ the prefix in place of the adverb. The first group contains examples earlier than 1650, the second those of more recent origin (mostly after 1800); where no definition is added, the meaning is that of the simple verb in conjunction with *up*.
The earlier group could be considerably enlarged by the inclusion of examples from Scottish poets of the 16th cent., esp. Douglas, who freely employs such forms as *upblese* (= blaze), *-flow*, *-glide*, *-hese* (= raise), *-kindle*, *-rax* (= stretch), *-rive*, *-sprent*, *-stend*, *-stour*, *-strike*, *-swak*, *-warp*, *-wrele*. Instances from other authors are *upbrace*, *-keek*, *-lese* (= gather), *-sit*, *-skail*, *-spread*, *-sprinkle*, *-win* (= rise).

**a. upari·se** [OE. *up-árisan*], **upbe·nd**, *intr.*; **upbu·rst**, **-ca·ll**, **-de·lve**, *trans.*; **updi·ve**, *intr.*; **upea·t**, *trans.*; **upfi·nd**, *trans.* to invent; **upfly·**, *intr.*; **upfo·**, *trans.* to receive; **upge·t**, *intr.* to rise up; **upgra·ve**, *trans.* to dig up; **upha·rbour**, **-ha·rrow**, *trans.*; **uphea·d**, *trans.* to cover in; **uphea·l**, *intr.*; **uphe·bbe** [OE. *up-hebban*], *trans.* to raise up, exalt; **uphi·lt**, *trans.* to plunge up to the hilt; **upkee·p**, *trans.* to support; **upke·ver**, *intr.* to recover; **upkni·t**, *trans.*; **uplo·pe**, *intr.* to spring up; **uppe·n**, **-pro·p**, *trans.*; **upra·pe**, *intr.* to rise hastily; **upree·k**, *intr.*; **upre·nder**, **-re·nt** (= rend), **-resto·re**, **-ri·d**, *trans.*; **upri·pe**, *trans.* to search out; **upru·n**, *intr.*; **upscrew·**, **-shea·r**, **-shea·th**, **-sho·re**, *trans.*; **upsmi·te**, *intr.*; **upsna·tch**, *trans.*; †**upsou·p**, *trans.* to swallow up; **upspa·r**, **-spea·r**, *trans.* to close up; **upspee·d**, *trans.*; **upspi·re**, *intr.* to shoot up; **upstau·nch**, *trans.*; **upsto·ck**, *trans.* to dig up; **upsu·p**, *trans.*; **upthri·ve**, *intr.*; **uptru·ss**, **-tu·ck**, **-vomit**, *trans.*; **upwa·ff**, *intr.* to begin to blow; **upwa·ll**, *trans.*; **upwa·x**, *intr.*; **upwei·gh**, *trans.* to lift up; **upwei·r**, *trans.* to defend; **upwe·nd**, *intr.* to go up; **upwra·p**, **-wri·ng**, *trans.*
1340 *Ayenb.* 186 Al ase þe oyle *op arist ine þe lompe alle þe oþer woses. 1649 F. ROBERTS *Clavis Bibliorum* 43 Them that against thee up-arose Thou utterly didst overthrow. *c* 1440 *Pallad. on Husb.* I. 1087 First floore it ij feet thicke enclynynge softe The fourneis ward, so that the flaume *vpbende. 1596 SPENSER *F. Q.* VI. xi. 43 But Calidore.. The dores assayled, and the locks *vpbrast.

*c* **1340** HAMPOLE *Pr. Consc.* 4963 Alle men þai sal þan *up-calle And byd þam cum til þe dome alle. *c* **1400** *Northern Passion* (H.) 468 When he saw þai sleped all, Peter first he gan vp call. *c* **1440** *Pallad. on Husb.* IX. 92 Ther as they growe, *vpdelue..v foote into the grounde. **1603** J. DAVIES (Heref.) *Microcosmos* Wks. (Grosart) I. 81/2 Plunge thee ore head and eares in Helicon,..Thence make thy fame *vp-dive. **1630** DRUMM. OF HAWTH. *Shadow of Judgement* 247 In Townes, the liuing doe the dead *vp-eate. *c* **1440** *Pallad. on Husb.* Prohem. 85 What thynge engyne *vpfynde, or reson trie And iustifie. *a* **1542** WYATT *Complaint vpon Love* in *Tottel's Misc.* (Arb.) 49, I gaue him winges, wherwith he might *vpflie To honor, and fame. **1600** FAIRFAX *Tasso* XIX. xviii, But he..Let go his hold, and on his feete vpflew. *a* **1300** *E. E. Psalter* cxvii. 13, I am turned, þat i suld falle; And lauerd *vpfange [*v.r.* onfonge; L. *suscepit*] me with-alle. **1582** STANYHURST *Æneis* I. (Arb.) 27 Æneas..With Phœbus rising *vpgot. *a* **1340** HAMPOLE *Psalter* vii. 16 Þe lake he oppynd and *vp grofe it [L. *effodit*]. *Ibid.*, He vpgraues it when he waitis all þat he may [etc.]. **1563** SACKVILLE in *Mirr. Mag.* 131 b, Such heapes of harmes *upharbard in his brest..my honour to deface. **1582** STANYHURST *Æneis* III. (Arb.) 86 You rest in fre quiet, thee seas you need not *vpharrow. **1519** *Extr. Aberd. Reg.* (1844) I. 96 Alexander Galloway..promittit..to big and *vpheid.. ane chapell and oratour. *c* **1440** *Pallad. on Husb.* XI. 239 Yf a tender tree Me kitte,..in oon yeer *vpheleth hit attonys. **1340** *Ayenb.* 217 Arere we..oure honden to god þet *ophebbeþ oure benes be guode workes. **1582** STANYHURST *Æneis* II. (Arb.) 61 His blad he with thrusting in his old dwynd carcas *vphilted. *c* **1412** HOCCLEVE *De Reg. Princ.* 4930 A bridil, Which þat an hors *vpkepeth fro fallyng. *c* **1350** *Will. Palerne* 2759 For al þat sterne strok stifli he *vp-keuerede, & swam swiftili awei. **1596** SPENSER *F. Q.* IV. vi. 30 Glauce thus gan wisely all *vpknit; Ye gentle Knights [etc.]. *a* **1600** MONTGOMERIE *Misc. Poems* iii. 33 The cadger clims,..And ladds *vploips to lordships all thair lains. **1600** FAIRFAX *Tasso* XVI. xxxiii, What letharge hath in drowsinesse *vppend Thy courage thus? **1601** DONNE *Progr. Soul* 386 Himselfe he *up-props, on himselfe relies. **13..** *Seuyn Sages* (W.) 1620 The wretche stiward ne might nowt slape; Ac in the moreweing he gan *uprape. *c* **1250** *Gen. & Ex.* 3465 Smoke *up-rekeð and munt quakeð. **1551** ROBINSON tr. *More's Utopia* (Arb.) 43 That they..shal..yelde, and *vprender the possession therof. *c* **1620** ROBINSON *Mary Magd.* 48 Blind Cupid seem'd to shoote, and tender hearts *vprent. *a* **1560** PHAER *Æneid* VIII. (1562) Bb iiij b, And seruice left since yesterdaye He gladly *vprestores. **1581–2** *Catal. Anc. Deeds* (1906) V. 484 [They shall] stocke, brushe, *uppe ridde and carie away [all] breers, brembles [etc.]. ? *a* **1400** *Morte Arth.* 3940 The riche kynge ransakes..And *vp-rypes the renkes of alle the Rownde Tabylle. *c* **1440** *Pallad. on Husb.* XII. 598 And next to hem xvj [feet] *vprenneth sone. **1646** G. DANIEL *Poems* Wks. (Grosart) I. 18 Let petty Sphæres their heightned Peggs *vp-Scrue, To rival with the greater. **1430–40** LYDG. *Bochas* III. 5107 So of that lynage he hath the weed *up-shorn. **1614** GORGES *Lucan* II. 47 Let thy vaine rage his sword *vp-sheath. *c* **1557** ABP. PARKER *Ps.* cxix. 364 Yere after yere me then *upshore with thy good helping hand. **1446** LYDG. *Two Nightingale Poems* ii. 39 The bawmy vapour of grassis gan *vp-smyte In-to myn hede. *a* **1566** R. EDWARDS *Damon & Pithias* C iv, Snap yᵉ Tipstaffe.. came and *vpsnatched him. **1382** WYCLIF *Ps.* cxxiii. 4 Per auenture water hadde *vp sopen vs [**1388** sope vs vp; L. *absorbuisset*]. **1630** *Tinker of Turvey* 35 His eyes were.. sparkling like the starres, When the day her light *up sparres. **1538** BALE *Johan Baptystes* ad fin., Adam, by hys pryde, ded paradyse *vp speare. **1338** R. BRUNNE *Chron.* (1810) 77 Saynt Cutberte's clerkes..At Geruans set þer merkes, a hous þei gan *vpspede. **1558** PHAER *Æneid* U j, Whan..stickes are kindled fast, and flame with noyse doth close *vpspyre. *c* **1440** *Pallad. on Husb.* VI. 125 Ek skyn and strynges seryng so tenfire *Vpstauncheth blood. *Ibid.* 46 If ther be treen, *vpstocke hem by the roote. **1537** SURREY in *Tottel's Misc.* (Arb.) 14 The whiche [tears] as sone as sobbyng sighes..*Vpsupped haue, thus I my plaint renewe. *c* **1440** *Pallad. on Husb.* II. 446 The seueth [hour] as v, and eight as iiij *vpthrive. *c* **1340** HAMPOLE *Pr. Consc.* 5567 Silver and gold..Þe whilk þai had in hurde *uptrust. *a* **1529** SKELTON *E. Rummyng* 419 Her kyrtell she did *vptucke. **1582** STANYHURST *Æneis* II. (Arb.) 54 Theire steed hath *vp-vomited from gorge a surfet of armdmen. **13..** *E. E. Allit. P.* B. 949 To wakan wederez so wylde þe wyndez he callez, & þay wroþely *vp-wafte & wrastled togeder. *c* **1440** *Pallad. on Husb.* I. 435 When that is drie, *vpwalle hit euery side. **1340** *Ayenb.* 75 Þer *opwexeþ alle guodes, uayrhede, richesse, worþssipe, blisse. **1513** DOUGLAS *Æneid* VI. vii. 62 The new mone quhen first wpwaxis sche. *a* **1593** MARLOWE *Hero & Leander* I. 450 They..At his..feet the engins layd, Which th' earth from ougly Chaos den *vp-wayd. *a* **1586** MAITLAND *Theivis of Liddisdail* 63 Sum grit men..That..will *vp-weir þair stollin geir. *c* **1200** *Trin. Coll. Hom.* 23 Þo he steah to heuene swo þat his apostles..bihielden hwu he *upwende. *a* **1400** *Isumbras* 510 With wery bones the knyghte up-wenede In to that haythene stede. **1600** FAIRFAX *Tasso* X. lxx. 193 The wilie dame In other foldes our mis-chiefes would *vpwrap. *a* **1560** PHAER *Æneid* IX. (1562) Ff i, The gate..at last he shutts, and bolts *vpwrings.

**b. upbuoy·, -cra·ne, -dra·g, -ha·nd, -ha·rrow, -hee·l, -kni·t, -pri·ck, -re·nd, -shou·lder, -sna·tch, -spee·d, -spew·, -sta·mp, -sti·r, -sway·, -thru·st, -whi·rl,** *trans.*; **upbla·cken, -bla·ze, -blow·, -cree·p, -cu·rve, -fla·me, -flee·, -flow·er, -je·t, -ki·ndle, -kni·t, -mo·ve, -po·p, -rei·n, -rou·se, -ru·n, -spi·re, -stea·m, -ste·p, -te·nd, -we·ll,** *intr.*

**1818** MILMAN *Samor* VIII. 43 The rocks..*Upblacken to the sky. **1839** HOOD *Nocturnal Sketch* ii, The gas *up-blazes with its bright white light. **1798** COLERIDGE *Anc. Mar.* V. xi, The ship mov'd on; Yet never a breeze *up-blew. **1652** BENLOWES *Theoph.* I. lxviii, Pow'rs cannot poets, as they pow'rs *up-buoy. *a* **1850** ROSSETTI *Dante & Circle* II. (1874) 296 Nor even from her did show of love up-buoy This passion **1816** *Monthly Mag.* XLI. 527 To heave aboard the stores, *Upcrane the cannon, roll the water casks. **1874** R. BUCHANAN *Poet. Wks.* III. 234 On thy shore he sinks in death, And thy still tides *upcreep. **1885** B. HARTE *Maruja* iii, Then something like a light ring of smoke *up-curved from the saddle before him. **1847** TENNYSON *Princ.* IV. 347 She..stoop'd to *updrag Melissa. **1826** CARRINGTON *Dartmoor* 87 To Jupiter *upflamed The human hecatomb. **1810** SOUTHEY *Kehama* XVIII. vi, He started,.. and to his head His hands *up-fled. **1803** MRS. A. WEBSTER *Mother & Daughter* (1895) 31 My youth *upflowers with hers. **1865** KINGSLEY *Herew.* iv, To high heaven, all so softly, The angels *uphand him. **1795** MACNEILL *Scotland's Skaith* IV. v, A' thy gentle mind *upharrows—Hate, revenge, and rage uprears. **1877** *The Sea* 1 Dec., The ship was beginning to sink; a sudden breeze springing *upheeled her still more. **1860** TENNYSON *Sea Dreams* 52 With ground-swell, which..*upjetted in spirts of wild sea-smoke. **1857** HEAVYSEGE *Saul* (1869) 189 Why in your eye *upkindles no fierce joy At coming-on of battle? **1889** RIDER HAGGARD *Cleopatra* II. iii, Does the half-death of sleep..thus *upknit the cut thread of human kinship? **1805** *Poet. Register* 178, I reach a cot; the friendly latch *upmoves. **1855** SINGLETON *Virgil* I. 359 So many tongues, Mouths just so many babble, she *uppricks So many ears. **1812** W. TENNANT *Anster F.* I. xxvi, The churlish spirit..*up-popp'd from sea, a tangle-tassel'd shape. **1883** R. W. DIXON *Mano* I. xvii. 57 By his cottage this bold knight *upreined. **1830** TENNYSON *Poems* 126 Music, borne abroad By the loud winds, though they *uprend the sea. **1812** J. BAILLIE *Orra* III. i, *Uprouse ye, then, my merry men! **1791** COWPER *Iliad* XVIII. 543 A son ..[who] like a luxuriant plant *Upran to manhood. **1844** KINGLAKE *Eothen* (1845) 104 A high struggling ridge that *upshouldered itself from out of the wilderness of myrtles. **1844** MRS. BROWNING *Lost Bower* xliv, Mystic Presences of power Had *up-snatch'd me to the Timeless. **1872** J. PAYNE *Songs of Life & Death* 9 In his stead there was *upsped A grisly Death from Hell. **1714** [CROXALL] *Original Canto Spenser* xxi, 'Till from their inly Maw their Loads they did *upspew. **1854** J. D. BURNS *Vision of Prophecy* 165 The temple, like a glorious dream, *upspires Into the lucid air. **1791** COWPER *Iliad* V. 598 A dusty cloud..which steeds ..*Up-stamp'd into the brazen vault of heaven. **1812** CARY *Dante, Parad.* VIII. 75 The vapoury cloud..Bituminous *upsteamed. *a* **1828** *Hynd Horn* xx. in Child *Ballads* I. 207/1 Straight to them ye will *upstep. **1833** MRS. BROWNING *Stanzas Passage Emerson's Jrnl.* vi, As when the war-trump of the wind *Upstirs our dark blue sea. **1811** SCOTT *Don Roderick* II. xvi, That right-hand giant 'gan his club *upsway. *a* **1711** KEN *Christophil* Poet. Wks. 1721 I. 420 She, as to Heav'n each Syllable *uptends, From Syllable to Syllable descends. *a* **1893** CHR. G. ROSSETTI *Poems* (1904) 215/1 As seeds their proper bodies all *upthrust. **1885** R. BRIDGES *Eros & Psyche* X. xix, Out of the topmost stone Of yonder hill *upwells a fountain head. **1845** MANGAN *German Anthol.* I. 40 The maelstrom..*upwhirled and upbore me to daylight at length.

**5.** The use of *up* with past pples., originally syntactical, gave rise to compounds of which several had already so far established themselves in OE. that derivatives in *-nes* and *-líce* were formed from them. Examples are *up(á)hafen, upáhefed, up(á)sprungen, upástigen, upcumen.* In ME. a number of new formations appear; among the earlier of these are *upborne, -drawn, -folden, -hung, -laid, -lifted, -reft, -risen, -set.* In the 16th and 17th cent. there are also frequent examples, and the type is still usual, but at all periods these forms have been mainly employed in verse. When used attributively the stress is normally on the prefix, but metrical instances frequently retain it on the stem.

The following are illustrations of casual examples of earlier and later date; a few others are used by Scottish writers of the 16th cent., esp. Douglas.

(*a*) **†upaheven** [OE. *up-áhafen*], lifted up, uplifted; **†upbounden**, tied up; **upbred, -framed**; **†upgraven**, dug up; **†uphoist**, lifted up; **upled**; **†uplent**, arrived on high; **up-ploughed, -puffed, -pulled, -reft, -rent, -ripped, †upsete(d**, oppressed; **†upshet**, shut up, enclosed; **upshut, -soaked, †-soaken, -stalled; †upstreyht**, upstretched; **upsucked, -trailed, †-whelmed, -wrapped, -wrought.**

*a* **1225** *Juliana* 58 To þonken godd wið honden *upaheuene. *a* **1225** *Leg. Kath.* 2373 Heo biheold upward, wið upaheuen heorte. *c* **1440** *Pallad. on Husb.* III. 514 Now stakid & *vpbounden wol they be. **1590** SPENSER *F. Q.* III. ix. 20 Her golden locks, that were in tramels gay Vpbounden. **1577** HOLINSHED *Chron.* I. *Hist. Scotland* 126 As those that were no Brytaynes borne, but straungers vnto them, being both borne and *vpbred in a forraine countrey. *a* **1560** PHAER *Æneid* VIII. (1562) Bb iij b, A towne there is with aunciaunt stones *vpfraamd. *Ibid.* IX. Ee ij b, A towre..then stood, with skaffolds large of length In place vpframyd fit. *a* **1340** HAMPOLE *Psalter* lxxix. 17 Kyndild at þe fire and *vpgrafen [L. *suffossa*]. *c* **1557** ABP. PARKER *Ps.* ii. G iij b, Lyke dust or chaffe they bee *Uphoyst by winde. **1568** T. HOWELL *Arb. Amitie* (1879) 68 So I vphoyst by wyffling windes.. Doe bide the brunt of bitter blastes. **1667** MILTON *P. L.* VII. 12 *Up led by thee Into the Heav'n of Heav'ns. *c* **1450** *Songs, Carols,* etc. (E.E.T.S.) 71/83 For þat mayst þou joy, man, þat þi cownt is *vplent, Wher God..his body doth present. **1610** G. FLETCHER *Christ's Vict.* I. lxxi, The *up-plowed heart, all..wounded by it selfe. **1573** TUSSER *Husb.* (1878) 147 His looke like a coxcombe, *vp puffed with pride. **1658** A. FOX *Würtz' Surg.* IV. ii. 316 Such wounds, where there appeareth an up-puffed swelling. *c* **1440** *Pallad. on Husb.* X. 166 With roote a plaunte *vppuld & sett, wol springe. *a* **1300** *Cursor M.* 20950 *Vp-reft he [*sc.* Paul] was to thrid heuen. **1584** HUDSON *Du Bartas' Judith* III. (1611) 33 Their Crosbowes were *vprent with yron Racks. **1653** HOLCROFT *Procopius, Goth. Wars* IV. 130 These Barbarians..made a new fashioned Ram, using no timbers *upript, nor lying a crosse. **1390** GOWER *Conf.* III. 283 For of the false Moabites..The poeple of god was ofte *upsete. **1549** LYNNE *Briefe Collection* (title-p.), Yᵉ most blessed.. of them that be vpseted wyth syckness and other visitations of God. *c* **1440** *Pallad. on Husb.* I. 993 [With] water myxt the grount,..*Vpshette aboute, and trampled with catel. *c* **1485** in *E. E. Misc.* (Warton Club) 52 Where are thy bestes, good sone?..They be now up-schete. **1658** A. FOX *Würtz' Surg.* I. viii. 35 That *up-shut moisture will stir at the changing of weathers. **1582** STANYHURST *Æneis* II. (Arb.) 55 Lyke rauening woolfdams *vpsoackt and gaunted in hunger. *Ibid.* III. 77 Theire face wan withred in hunger, With famin *vp-soaken. **1430–40** LYDG. *Bochas* VIII. 208 Domycian..Proudli comaundid, in his estat *up stallid, Of al the world he sholde a god be callid. **1569** E. HAKE *Newes Powles Churchyarde* (1579) F 5 These ranckly feede the pamperd Swyne vpstalled in their nest. *c* **1425** *Orolog. Sapient.* iii. in *Anglia* X. 348/1 To go pruwdelye with an *vp-streyht nekke. **1560** B. GOOGE tr. *Palingenius' Zodiac* II. (1561) D viij, *Vpsuckt the floudes from out the seas, the whyrlwyndes vp doe beare. *c* **1440** *Pallad. on Husb.* I. 290 But vines may ha vices worthy blame: To longe or brode, *vptrailed or extendid. **1568** T. HOWELL *Arb. Amitie* (1879) 38, I rage and rewe.., *Vp-whelmde in woes full sore. **1642** H. MORE *Song of Soul* II. I. i. 2 A Meteor,..Whose inward hidden parts ethereall Ly close *upwrapt in that dull sluggish fime. *c* **1400** *Destr. Troy* 1542 The walles *vp wroght, wonder to se.

(*b*) **upbrightened, -broken, -choked, -conjured, -covered, -cushioned, -flung, -followed, -girt, -hoisted, -led, -lighted, -looped, -mixed, -perched, -pointed, -poised, -propped, -ridged, -shouldered, -shoved, -spouted, -steamed, -swept, -swollen, -swung, -trilled, -wrenched, -wrought, -yoked.**

**1861** *Macm. Mag.* IV. 132/1 Russet and green *upbrightened with white. **1833** MANGAN *Poems* (1903) 124 When the *up-broken dreams of boyhood's span..Come down like night upon the feelings. **1785** BURNS *Winter Night* ii, While burns, wi' snawy wreeths *up-choked, Wild-eddying swirl. **1833** WORDSW. *At Sea off Isle of Man* 5 Suddenly *up-conjured from the Main, Mists rose to hide the Land. **1857** HEAVYSEGE *Saul* (1869) 419 An old man,..*upcovered with a mantle. **1828** CARLYLE *Misc.* (1857) I. 142 The throne's *upcushioned lordliness. **1828** ATHERSTONE *Fall of Nineveh* I. 11 Arms *upflung, and swaying heads. **1903** R. KIPLING *5 Nations, The Destroyers*, Nearer the up-flung beams that spell The council of our foes. **1818** KEATS *Endym.* I. 163 After them appear'd, *Up-follow'd by a multitude,..a fair wrought car. **1890** *Atlantic Monthly* July 35 The braider stands With loin *upgirt. **1768** CHATTERTON *Bristowe Tragedie* 193 Whatte tho', *uphoisted onne a pole, Mye lymbes shalle rotte ynne ayre. **1872** BLACKMORE *Maid of Sker* (1881) 159 Horses.. with their tails uphoisted. **1845** WORDSW. '*Forth from a jutting ridge*' 7 *Up-led with mutual help. **1794** — *Guilt & Sorrow* xlvi, The bag-pipe dinning..In barn *uplighted. **1887** BOWEN *Æneid* I. 320 Bare at the knee, and her fluttering folds *uplooped for the chase. **1821** ATHERSTONE *Poems* 26 In the turbid rain-streams, thick *upmix'd With ashes hot. **1818** KEATS *Endym.* I. 828 The nightingale, *up-perched high. **1830** ATHERSTONE *Fall of Nineveh* II. 102 The threatening spear *Up-pointed, harmless as a wand became. **1864** BRYANT *Constellations* 45 Thine eyes..would see..the Swan *uppoised On gleaming wings. **1784** COWPER *Task* II. 116 Never such a sudden flood, *Uprid'g'd so high.., Possess'd an inland scene. **1879** G. MACDONALD *Sir Gibbie* ix, The..river, flowing..through *upshouldered fields of wheat. **1837** CARLYLE *Fr. Rev.* III. v. vi, The Citoyens, with *upshoved *bonnet rouge*, or with doffed bonnet. **1789** COWPER *Queen's Visit to London* 19 The ocean..*Up-spouted by a whale in air. **1805–6** CARY *Dante, Inf.* XXX. 99 Sharp fever drains the reeky moistness out, In such a cloud *up-steam'd. **1791** COWPER *Iliad* XI. 375 The foam *Upswept by wand'ring gusts fills all the air. **1774** GRAVES *Spir. Quix.* (ed. 2) II. 198 The Rector, in sleek surcingle.., With eyes *up-swoln, and shining double-chin. **1882** G. MACDONALD *Weighed & Wanting* III. xviii. 254 She saw on Amy's neck a frightful upswollen wale. **1868** GEO. ELIOT *Sp. Gipsy* 323 He saw above The form of Father Isidor *upswung. **1799** COLERIDGE *Lines in Concert-room* ii, The long-breathed singer's *uptrill'd strain. **1808** MRS. ILIFF *Poems* (1818) 98 A rocky fragment, from the ground *upwrenched. **1784** COWPER *Task* II. 111 Ocean..,*upwrought To an enormous and o'erbearing height,..invades the shore Resistless. **1837** WHITTOCK *Bk. Trades* (1842) 407 (*Smith*), Afterwards appeared the beer-man with his cans '*up-yoked'.

**6.** The use of *up* before present participles, and forming possible combinations with these, is somewhat rare in OE.; the chief examples which occur are *up(á)stigende, upstandende,* and *upyrnende.* ME. furnishes a few instances, as *uparising, -hanging, -looking, -springing, -tempering*; but this type of formation becomes common only after 1500. In the following illustrations of casual forms the earlier examples are separated from those occurring after 1700.

(*a*) **uparising, -belching, -blowing, -botching, -creeping, -floating, -hasping** (= closing), **-hoising, -leaning, -peaking** (PEAK *v.*²), **-plucking, -riving, -seizing, †-souping** (= swallowing), **†-sparpling** (= scattering), **-steaming, -tempering.**

*c* **1325** *Prose Psalter* xvii. 43 Þou put out þe *vparisand [L. *insurgentes*] oȝaines me. **1576** NEWTON *Lemnie's Complex.* 142 Their Chawes rammishe, And throate *vpbelching fulsome breathes. **1590** SPENSER *F. Q.* III. iv. 13 Till that at last The watry Southwinde from the seabord cost *Vp-blowing, doth disperse the vapour lo'st. **1582** STANYHURST *Æneis*, etc. 95 Theese thre were *vpbotching, not shapte,.. A clapping fyerbolt. **1626** *Parallel Pelag. Error* A 4 b, An euill *vpcreeping since his death. **1582** STANYHURST *Æneis* I. (Arb.) 21 Soom wights *vpfloating on raisd sea wyth armor apeered. *Ibid.* IV. 103 Hee causeth sleeping and bars: bye death eyelyd *vphasping. *Ibid.* 21 Thee northen bluster.. Thee sayls tears tag rag, to the sky thee waues *vphoysing. **1588** SPENSER *Virg. Gnat* 154 Whilst thus his carelesse time This shepheard driues, *vpleaning on his batt. **1590** — *F. Q.* III. ii. 42 With that vpleaning on her elbow weake [etc.]. **1582** STANYHURST *Æneis* III. (Arb.) 76 Thee fourth day..thee shoare, neere setled, apeered And hils *vppeaking. *Ibid.*

II. 52 Hee..sighs *vpplucking from brest ful deepelye, thus aunswerd. 1621 G. SANDYS *Ovid's Met.* IX. (1626) 179 Oft should you see him..solid trees *vp-riuing. *c* 1550 BALE *K. Johan* 1737, I wyll kepe this crowne in myn owne hande, In the Popes behalfe *upseasyng Ynglond. 1582 STANYHURST *Æneis* III. (Arb.) 84 Charybdis On left hand swelleth..In to gut *vpsouping three tymes thee flash water angrye. *a* 1560 PHAER *Æneid* IX. (1562) Ee iiij, A yong stere whyte as snow,..which with his fete *vpsparpling spredes the dust. *a* 1560 *Ibid.* VIII. Bb ij b, An Yle there is..where smoke from stones to starrs *vpsteaming sties. *c* 1440 *Pallad. on Husb.* VII. 243 This flouris smale..*vptempuryng, forsake Noman for hem to make.., As of rosate is taught.

(*b*) **upblazing, -bounding, -bracing, -breaking, -brimming, -bristling, -bubbling, -burning, -charioting, -coiling, -crawling, -flaming, -gaping, -gliding, -heaping, -knelling, -ridging, -rousing, -scaling, -slanting, -snatching, -spearing, -splashing, -stretching, -swarming, -sweeping, -thundering, -tracing, -wafting, -wreathing.**

1801 SOUTHEY *Thalaba* VI. viii, Now its wavy point *Upblazing rose, like a young cypress tree. 1840 MANGAN *Poems* (1903) 136 The startled soul, *upbounding from the mire Of earthliness. *c* 1833 WHITTIER *Randolph of Roanoke* 102 His gaunt frame *upbracing. 1859 TENNYSON *Guinev.* 388 Sheets of hyacinth That seem'd the heavens *upbreaking thro' the earth. *a* 1861 CLOUGH *Ess. Class. Metres, Alcaics* 5 The fury of winds, that all night *Upbrimming, sapping slowly the dyke,..Fall through the breach. 1898 T. HARDY *Wessex Poems* 163 When her dreams were upbrimming with light. 1852 W. WICKENDEN *Hunchback's Chest* 16 Like a wild boar *upbristling for the fight. 1874 R. BUCHANAN *Poet. Wks.* III. 58 The spring *Upbubbling faintly seemeth as a sound. *a* 1865 TENNYSON *Mystic* 45 The last [circle],..with a region of white flame..into a larger air *Upburning. 1812 W. TENNANT *Anster F.* II. ii, The sun, *upcharioting from Capricorn. 1803 WORDSW. *Yew-trees* 18 A growth of intertwisted fibres serpentine *Up-coiling. 1896 KIPLING 7 *Seas, Derelict*, The..weed Folds me and fouls me, strake on strake *upcrawling. 1805 SOUTHEY *Madoc in W.* I. 34 Many a fire *Up-flaming, stream'd..Red lines of lengthening light. 1832 L. HUNT *Dryads* 19 Yellow bills, *up-gaping for their food. 1805–6 CARY *Dante, Inf.* XXV. 7 Another [serpent] to his arms *Upgliding, tied them. 1888 R. BUCHANAN *City of Dream* VIII. 158 And in its inmost shrine the priests of Baal Are not *upheaping gold. 1845 MANGAN *German Anthology* II. 108 Then hear I music sweet *upknelling From many a.. phantom-band. 1791 COWPER *Odyssey* XIX. 555 *Upridging high His bristly back.., he sprang Forth from the shrubs. 1830 ATHERSTONE *Fall of Nineveh* II. 16 With firm tread The thronging echos..*Uprousing as he passed. 1882 ARMSTRONG *Garland fr. Greece* 226 *Upscaling steep and rough to cross the Pass. 1876 C. WELLS *Joseph & Brethren* I. v. 73 The thorns that ye have cast *Upslanting in my path. 1828 ATHERSTONE *Fall of Nineveh* I. 241 The fallen reins *Upsnatching then,..o'er the field The Assyrian looked. 1784 COWPER *Task* V. 23 The bents And coarser grass, *upspearing o'er the rest,..now shine Conspicuous. 1871 R. ELLIS *Catullus* lxiv. 128 She..Now to the brine ran forth, *upsplashing freshly to meet her. 1815 HOGG *Poet. Mirror* Wks. 1866 II. 111 Two long ears *upstretching perpendicularly. 1791 COWPER *Iliad* XII. 541 They..*upswarming show'd On the high battlement their glittering spears. *c* 1873 J. ADDIS *Eliz. Echoes* (1879) 94 Th' uncertain hum Of hosts *upsweeping from the subterrene. 1796 COLERIDGE *Ode Departing Year* viii, Central fires through nether seas *upthundering. 1846 PROWETT *Prometh. Bound* 21 Hollow tones, From Hades' sullen realm upthundering. 1727 THOMSON *Summer* 1100 *Up-tracing, from the vast Inane, The Chain of Causes and Effects to Him. 1757 DYER *Fleece* III. 309 Chimney-tops..*up-wafting to the clouds The incense of thanksgiving. 1849 LONGF. *Building of Ship* 187 Around it columns of smoke, *up-wreathing, Rose.

**b.** In the earlier periods of the language these forms in *-ing* were not employed attributively. Examples of this use begin to appear in the 16th century, but are not common before the 19th. As adjectives, such compounds would normally have the main stress on the prefix, and a secondary stress on the stem (e.g. *u·pbea:ring, u·pcree:ping*), but in verse the full stressing of the stem is frequently retained. The following illustrations of rarer forms are divided into earlier and later instances.

(*a*) **upcreeping, -flinging, -running, -sprouting, -sticking.**

1611 COTGR. s.v. *Eschalas*, A Vine or any other weake-branched, *vp-creeping..Plant. 1566 DRANT *Horace, Sat.* ii. F 2 When with grosse *upflyngyng fumes, your syght is masde and dull. 1527 ANDREW *Brunswyke's Distyll. Waters* H ij, The same is good for the *vpronnyng pymples of the face. 1563 WINȜET *Wks.* (S.T.S.) II. 18 The snairis of the *wpsprouting hæretikis. 1611 COTGR., *Bricot*,..an *vp-sticking stub of a little cut shrub or tree.

(*b*) **upbearing, -bounding, -breaking, -bursting, -cocking, -cropping, -crowding, -flashing, -flowing, -gushing, -pouring, -quivering, -reaching, -sprouting, -stealing, -stretching, -striving, -struggling, -tearing, -tilting.**

1830 TENNYSON *Isabel* iii, A leaning and *upbearing parasite, Clothing the stem. 1845 MANGAN *German Anthology* I. 60 Then *upbounding Life..Unto all that died the Sun shall bring. 1822 J. WILSON *Lights & Shadows* 124 A sort of glimmer, like that of an *upbreaking and disparting storm, gathered about him. 1818 KEATS *Endym.* II. 56 Now he is sitting by a shady spring, And elbow-deep..Stems the *upbursting cold. 1879 STEVENSON *Trav. Cevennes* 159 The roof fell in and the upbursting flames discovered his retreat. 1804 COLLINS *Scripscrap.* 58 A Brainless young Crimp, with an *upcocking snout. 1898 B. GREGORY *Side Lights Confl. Meth.* 249 An occasional *up-cropping consciousness. *c* 1870 M. ARNOLD *Obermann once more* ad fin., The domed Velan, with his snows, Behind the *upcrowding hills. 1813 SHELLEY *Q. Mab* VII. 231 Showers of gore from the *upflashing steel Of safe assassination. 1801 SOUTHEY *Thalaba* II. xxvi, No eye beheld the spring Of that *upflowing Flame. 1845 MANGAN *German Anthology* II. 18 Drink at Life's *upgushing wells! 1858 HAWTHORNE *Fr. & It. Note-bks.* I. 145 An artificial lake with upgushing fountains. 1842 R. FORD in Shorter *Borrow & Circle* (1913) 253 Just dash down the first genuine *uppouring idea and thoughts in the plainest language. 1851 HAWTHORNE *Ho. Sev. Gables* x, One of those *up-quivering flashes of the spirit. 1894 *Outing* (U.S.) XXIV. 151 Where the black *up-reaching ledge Holds high its moss-hung turrets. 1898 CLODD *Tom Tit Tot* iv. 41 Persephone, whom Demeter seeks.., to find her with the *upsprouting corn. 1859 *Roses & Thorns* 254 The *up-stealing shadows of evening. 1827 CARLYLE *Misc. Ess., Richter*, This *upstretching aurora of a morning. 1855 LYNCH *Lett. Scattered* ii. (1872) 26 One *upstriving flame of prayer. 1835 CARLYLE in Froude *Life in London* (1884) I. 46 One glorious *up-struggling ray..which perished,..in a lax, languid, impotent character. 1817 J. SCOTT *Paris Revisit.* (ed. 4) 219 Broad rugged tracks, which seemed as if they had been swept by some fiery *up-tearing stream. 1841 H. MILLER *O. R. Sandst.* vi. 107 The strata..have been unpacked and arranged by the *uptilting agent.

**7.** In OE. the combination of *up-* with a verbal substantive is limited to *uphebbing*, perhaps directly formed from *uphebban*. In ME. a number of instances occur, the earliest being *upastying* (= ascending), *-casting, -coming, -covering* (= recovery), *-nimming, -rising, -stying*, and *-taking*. In the 16th c. the type becomes common, and again in the 19th. Earlier and more recent formations of a casual nature are illustrated in the following groups.

(*a*) **† uparising, †-astying, -bolstering, †-crying, -passing, †-receiving, -sealing, -twinkling, -tying, †-weening.**

1340 *Ayenb.* 213 At yestre [= Easter], his *oparizinge, hou he aros uram dyaþe to liue. *a* 1200 *St. Marher* 1 Efter ure lauerdes..ariste of deað, ant efter his *up astihunge. 1610 J. ROBINSON *Justif. Separation* 258 The Churches vngodly connivency, and *vpboulstring them in their scandalous sinns, makes them nothing the better. 1651 *Burgh Rec. Stirling* (1889) II. 306 To John Wordie for reading the ordoures annent *upcrying the money. 1533 GAU *Richt Vay* (S.T.S.) 49 Ye maner of his [*sc.* Christ's] *vppassing. 1572 *Reg. Privy Council Scot.* II. 145 In thair uppassing and douncuming. 13.. *Castel of Loue* (H.) 1665 The cursede shull in erthe byn.., wyth the *up-receyveng they shulle agryse. 1563 MAN *Musculus' Commonpl.* 281 b, That grace..the token, sacrament and *upsealinge [L. *obsignatio*] whereof is in Baptisme. 1597 *Pilgr. Parnass.* IV. 425 To see A puritane *up-twinckling of his eye. 1614 P. FORBES *Comm. Revelation* 217 Then his *vptying is to bee counted, when..hee is perfectly made fast. 1340 *Ayenb.* 21 Þe þridde boȝ of prede is arrogance þet me clepeþ *opweninge oþer opniminge.

(*b*) **upbubbling, -flickering, -gushing, -lighting, -piling, -ripping, -squatting, -streaming, -summing, -surging, -swelling, -winding, -working.**

1888 *Daily News* 26 May 5/8 To watch the *upbubbling of the flashing..waters. 1881 *Cornh. Mag.* XLIV. 481 The last *up-flickering of his dying intelligence. 1846 HAWTHORNE *Mosses* II. iii. 50 The *upgushings and outpourings of these initiated souls. 1860 J. H. STIRLING *Crit. Ess., Macaulay* (1868) 122 The *up-lighting of the 'age of reason'. 1844 BLACKIE in *Class. Mus.* I. 339 A more cumbrous *up-piling of erudite blunders. 1859 SALA *Tw. round Clock* (1861) 121 The *upripping of his unhappy coat-collar. 1840 BARHAM *Ingol. Leg.* Ser. I. *Ghost*, The Gorgon's head Was but a type of Nick's *up-squatting in the bed. 1880 GEIKIE *Phys. Geog.* (1885) 46 A constant *upstreaming of warm moist air. 1884 J. PARKER *Apost. Life* III. 23 The all but infinite prudence which forecasts totalities and *upsummings. 1883 *Century Mag.* XXVI. 130 The *upsurging..of nobler and better feelings. 1899 *Edin. Rev.* Apr. 317 *Upwellings of molten basalt. 1837 LOCKHART *Scott* IV. i. 22 A better *upwinding of the plot of the Black Dwarf. *a* 1834 COLERIDGE *Notes & Lect.* (1849) I. 230 A wild *up-working of love..is perceptible throughout.

**8.** The use of *up-* with agent-nouns first appears in ME. in the 14th century, the earliest examples being *upstyer* and *uptaker*, with *upbearer, -holder*, and *-raiser* following a little later. Similar forms occur in the 16th cent. (but chiefly Sc.), as *upbigger* (= builder), *-closer, -creeper, -lifter, -looker, -putter, -setter*, and a few in the 17th, as *upbringer, -giver* (Sc.), *-riser*. Later formations are mainly from the 19th cent., as *upbuilder, -climber, -shutter, -stander*.

**U·p-a-daisy,** *interj.* Now *dial.* or *colloq.* Also 8 -dazy, 8–9 -daisey. [f. UP *adv.*[1]: cf. UPSIDAISY and dial. *upaday*. For the ending, cf. *lackadaisy* and (*a*)*lack-a-day*.] An exclamation made to a child on encouraging or assisting it to rise from a fall, etc., or to surmount an obstacle, or when raising it in the arms or jerking it into the air.

1711 SWIFT *Jrnl. to Stella* 5 Feb., Come stand away, let me rise...Is there a good fire?—So—up a-dazy. 1756 TOLDERVY *Hist. 2 Orphans* II. 24 'Up-a-daisey,' said Miss Bella, and then..gave him a push behind. 1854 MISS BAKER *Northampt. Gloss.* 370 *Up-a-daisy*, a fondling expression of a nurse to a child whilst lifting it from the ground, encouraging it to assist itself in rising. 1899 G. FORD *'Postle Farm* ix. 43 'Up-a-daisy!' said Annie, as the fat little legs struggled to mount the steps.

**Upai·thric,** *a.* [f. Gr. ὕπαιθρ-ος + -IC: see HYPÆTHRAL *a.* and cf. HUPAITHRIC *a.*] Open to the air; having no roof; hypæthral.

1819 SHELLEY *Ess. & Lett.* (1852) II. 155 Their temples were mostly upaithric; and..the stars..were seen above. 1851 [J. FANE] *Poems Early Years* 24 A vast upaithric fane.

**† Upaland,** Sc. var. of *upoland* UPONLAND *adv.* (with further reduction of the prep.; cf. ALAND *adv.*). *Obs.*

1500–20 DUNBAR *Poems* l. 19 At feistis and brydallis wpaland, He wan the gre. 1560–1 *1st Bk. Discipl. Ch. Scot.* (1621) 40 If it be upaland where the people convene to the doctrine but once in the week. 1572 *Satir. Poems Reform.* xxxiii. 158 Ȝe do not ȝour office, For vpaland thay haue not dew seruice. *a* 1600 MONTGOMERIE *Sonn.* xxv. 3 This is no lyfe that I live vpaland.

**b.** *Jock upaland*, a rustic. Also allusively.

*a* 1568 *Bannatyne MS.* (Hunter. Club) 268 Thus said Jok vpalland. 1637–50 Row *Hist. Kirk* (Wodrow Soc.) 463 Many are gaping for it [*sc.* a church], and using moyen at Court to gaine it, but it will be Jok up-a-land.

Hence **† Upalands** *a.* = UPLANDS *a.*

1535 LYNDESAY *Satyre* 4040, I leirit ȝow merchants mony ane wyle, Vpalands wyfis for to begyle. 1595 DUNCAN *App. Etym.* (E.D.S.), *Pero*, vpalands shoone.

**Up-a·nchor,** *v.* [UP *adv.*[1] 1 d.] *intr.* To weigh or heave up the anchor.

1897 KIPLING *Capt. Cour.* 185 At last she cleared decks,.. up-anchored and began to move.

**Up and down,** *adv., prep., a.,* and *sb.* [f. UP *adv.*[1] and *adv.*[2] + DOWN *adv.*]

**A.** *adv.* **1.** Alternately on or to a higher and a lower level or plane. Also in fig. context.

*c* 1205 LAY. 14276 He bi-heold þene wal up and dun ouer al. *a* 1300 *Cursor M.* 2238 Þat ai quen we se ani chesun, Freli [we] may climb vp and dun. *c* 1340 *Ayenb.* 246 Þe lheddre ..huerby þe angles..cliue op and doun. *c* 1400 MAUNDEV. (Roxb.) xxxi. 139 Fendez..fliez vp and doune in þe aer with grete thunders. *c* 1485 *Digby Myst.* (1882) III. 1669, I fel ytt ster In my wombe vp and down. 1559 W. CUNNINGHAM *Cosmogr. Glasse* 29 Then rayse vp and downe the ruler.. vnto the sonne. 1583 HOLLYBAND *Campo di Fior* 27 Washe your mouth, and do the water up and downe in your throate. 1633 P. FLETCHER *Purple Isl.* XII. lii, Tost up and down in waves of worldly floud. 1680 in W. Hacke *Coll. Voy.* (1699) III. 7 Which Ebbs and Flows here two Fathom up and down. 1712 J. JAMES tr. *Le Blond's Gardening* 192 The short Cilinder..is moved up and down in the Barrel of the Pump. 1820 BYRON *Juan* V. lxxviii, Wrestling both his arms into a gown, He paused, and took a survey up and down. 1889–91 [see STARE *v.* 2 c]. 1892 *Photogr. Ann.* II. 402 The action is up and down, without vibration.

*fig.* *c* 1374 CHAUCER *Troylus* II. 659 She..gan to casten and rollen vp and down with-inne here þought his excellent prowesse. *c* 1450 *Mirour Saluacioun* (Roxb.) 149 Sekeing oft vp and doune of deth fande thay cause none rightwise. 1513 DOUGLAS *Æneid* x. ii. 100 All the hevynly wychtis dyd quhyspir and roun, In opynyonys full diuers, wp and doun. 1584 D. FENNER *Def. Min.* (1587) 121 Although he knewe.. the meaning of them, yet he turneth them vppe and downe as if they were riddles.

**b.** *fig.* With variation of success or fortune.

1430–40 LYDG. *Bochas* I. 2718 Ay the tribut & seruage off the toun Procedith foorth, thei constreyned wer so sore, Lich as ther lott turned up and doun.

**† c.** *fig.* (In predicative use, passing into adj.) Varying, changeable, unstable. *Obs.*

1643 CARYL *Sacr. Covt.* 36 It is..most unsutable..for us to be up and downe, forward and backward, likeing and disliking, like that Double-minded man. 1645 RUTHERFORD *Tryal & Tri. Faith* 16 Men naturally beleeve, though they be but up and down with Christ, yet Christ doth so bear them at goodwill, as [etc.]. 1650 BAXTER *Saints' R.* iv. 38 His Love to thee will not be as thine was..to him, seldom and cold, up and down.

**2.** Hither and thither; to and fro; backward and forward.

*a* 1200 *Moral Ode* 240 in *O. E. Hom.* I. 175 Ho..walkeð weri up and dun, se water deþ mid winde. 1297 R. GLOUC. (Rolls) 11513 Wiþ him to wende aboute, to sywe him vp & doun. 1303 R. BRUNNE *Handl. Synne* 4034 He ȝede yn hys celle vp and down. *c* 1386 CHAUCER *Nun's Pr. T.* 359 On hise toos he rometh vp and doun. *c* 1440 *Cast. Persev.* 2519 Up & doun þou take þe wey. 1508 DUNBAR *Gold. Targe* 84 There saw I May..Within the gardyng walking vp and doun. 1582 N. LICHEFIELD tr. *Castanheda's Conq. E. Ind.* 93 b, The enymyes were scouring up and downe in the Sea. 1659 PELL *Impr. Sea* 55 Many of you walk up and down in the ships you have command of. 1692 R. L'ESTRANGE *Fables* (1694) 251 You are so..given to squirting up and down, and chattering, that [etc.]. 1713 ADDISON *Cato* III. i, Life wanders up and down Through all her Face, and lights up ev'ry Charm. 1741 RICHARDSON *Pamela* (ed. 3) I. 187 She is up and down so much, that I am afraid of her surprising me. 1811 BYRON *Hints fr. Hor.* 478 And boys shall hunt your bardship up and down. 1872 TENNYSON *Last Tourn.* 647 Pacing moodily up and down.

**3.** Here and there; at various points; *esp.* in several or diverse places throughout a district, country, etc.

In very frequent use from *c* 1635 to 1700.

*a* 1300 *Cursor M.* 11444 Þai..spird him efter vp and dun. *c* 1374 CHAUCER *Compl. Mars* 210 What availeth suche a longe sermon Of auentures of love vp and dovne. 1601 B. JONSON *Poetaster* I. ii. (1905) 18 He..liu'd obscurely vp and downe in boothes, and taphouses. 1680 R. L'ESTRANGE *Citt & Bumpkin* (ed. 3) 3 We had our Agents at all Publick Meetings,..all the Schools up and down. 1712 BUDGELL *Spect.* No. 277 ¶ 3 With several Ribbons stuck up and down in it. 1760 C. JOHNSTON *Chrysal* (1822) III. 37 A few of the eldest..gathered up and down into little sets. 1855 BROWNING *Fra Lippo Lippi* 41 Brother Lippo's doings, up and down, You know them?

**b.** Throughout the works of an author or authors.

1668 H. MORE *Div. Dial.* IV. ix. 31 Intimated up and down in the Gospels by our Blessed Saviour. 1698 T. HEARNE *Duct. Hist.* (1714) I. 35 To relate all the Witticisms scattered up and down in the Books of the Cabalists, about this Word. 1699 BOYER *Fr. Dict., Centon*,..a Poem made up of several Pieces pick'd up and down from the Works of others.

**4.** Upside-down; topsy-turvy. Also *fig.* Now *s.w. dial.*

**1591** PERCIVALL *Sp. Dict., Trastornadura*, ouerthrowing, turning vp and downe. **1600** W. WATSON *Decacordon* Pref. (1602) A 3 b, The Germaines (where the imperiall triple Crowne of Caesar yet remaines vp and downe). **1634** *Malory's Arthur* I. cxiv. Z 4 b, Syre launcelot charged so sore vpon him that his horse reuersed vp and downe. **1888–92** in Somerset and Devon dialect (*Eng. Dial. Dict.* s.v.).

**5.** In or into a vertical position; vertically.

**1669** STURMY *Mariner's Mag.* II. 80 Set the end of the Cross-Staff to the outside of the Eye,..holding it right up and down. **1697** DAMPIER *Voy.* I. x. 298 A long Yard that peeks up and down like a Mizen-yard. **1748** *Anson's Voy.* II. i. 112 We hove the cable right up and down. **1791** SMEATON *Edystone L.* § 132 The..cable..had been hawled in so tight as to keep the swivel from striking the ground, when right up and down. **1867** SMYTH *Sailor's Word-bk.* 574 In anchor work, when the cable is in that condition, the boatswain calls, 'Up and down, sir'. *Ibid.* 707.

**6.** In every respect; entirely, thoroughly, completely. Now *dial.*

**1542** UDALL *Erasm. Apoph.* 291 b, He was even Socrates up and down in this poincte.., yt noman ever sawe hym either laugh or wepe. **1579–80** NORTH *Plutarch* (1595) 170 His eloquent tongue, and ready vtterance,..in those he was Pisistratus vp and downe. **1620** MIDDLETON *Chaste Maid* III. ii, It has the mother's mouth. The mother's mouth up and down. **1649** MILTON *Eikon.* xi, This is the Pharisee up and down, 'I am not as other men are'. **1832** J. BARRINGTON *Personal Sk.* III. 224 God bless him, up and down, wherever he goes, here or hereafter! **1878–89** in dialect glossaries, etc. (Cumbld., Lanc., Linc.).

†**b.** Altogether; in all. *Obs.*—[1]

**1562** J. HEYWOOD *Prov. & Epigr.* (1867) 215 What comth our meate to? foure shyllyngs vp and downe.

**7.** *U.S. colloq.* In a straightforward or blunt manner; acting in this way. (Cf. C. 2 b).

**1869** MRS. STOWE *Oldtown Folks* xx, Talk about coddling! it's little we get o' that, the way the Lord fixes things in this world...He's pretty up and down with us, by all they tell us. **1891** *Cent. Dict.* s.v. *Up*, To handle a matter up and down; to talk up and down.

**B.** *prep.* **1. a.** Backward and forward in; to and fro along or upon.

**1412–20** LYDG. *Chron. Troy* I. 1575 Þe halle in soth sche walkyth vp and down. **1553** T. WILSON *Rhet.* 31 You shall haue a pretie litle boye, runnyng vp and doune youre house. **1568** GRAFTON *Chron.* II. 334 The Lordes counsayled the king..to rowe vp and downe the ryuer. **1645** PAGITT *Heresiogr.* (ed. 2) 32 They wandred up and downe the Countreyes without staves. ?**1676** LADY CHAWORTH in *12th Rep. Hist. MSS. Comm.* App. V. 34 She..is pulled up and down the ponds in them [*sc.* sledges] every day. **1711** STEELE *Spect.* No. 96 ⁋ 3, I was strolling up and down the Walks in the Temple. **1745** P. THOMAS *Jrnl. Anson's Voy.* 230 Every Person of any Account goes up and down them [*sc.* streets] either on Horseback or in a Chair. **1820** SOUTHEY *Wesley* I. 405 Under such feelings he wandered up and down the fields. **1855** MACAULAY *Hist. Eng.* xiii. III. 269 Accompanying James in his last walk, up and down the Mall. **1896** *Law Times Rep.* LXXIII. 615/1 A red light was automatically shown up and down the line.

**b.** Here and there in or upon; in several parts of or diverse places throughout.

**1597** SHAKS. *2 Hen. IV*, II. i. 113 She sayes vp & downe the town, that her eldest son is like you. **1640** H. SPELMAN in *Lett. Lit. Men* (Camden) 164 They that to prevent my election, published up and downe some Colledges that..[I] had declined the choice. **1675** BROOKS *Gold. Key* Wks. 1867 V. 309 They have frequently acknowledged it to be an everlasting covenant, as is evident up and down the Scripture. **1711** STEELE *Spect.* No. 11 ⁋ 4 Sprinkled up and down the Writings of all Ages. **1834** MEDWIN *Angler in Wales* I. 33 The eyes..in some insects amount to six or seven thousand, and spread up and down the body as on the spider. **1849** MACAULAY *Hist. Eng.* ix. II. 444 Early in August hints.. were whispered up and down London. **1894** *Times* 4 June 6/2 To gather into one collected whole statements scattered at present all up and down your columns.

**2.** Alternately on or to a higher and lower plane in or upon.

**1665** HOOKE *Microgr.* 202 A certaine white substance.. may be observ'd to fly up and down the Air. **1726** SHELVOCKE *Voy. round World* 250 The danger..of carrying a load up and down mountains. **1741** RICHARDSON *Pamela* (ed. 3) I. 201 The Maid Nan..asked if any thing was the matter, that I was so often up and down stairs? **1855** [J. R. LEIFCHILD] *Cornwall* 153 Along levels, and up and down winzes (ventilating openings), the air is coursing. **1859** F. E. PAGET *Curate of Cumberworth* 62 The whole herd, tearing up and down the hill side.

**C.** *adj.* (Now usually hyphened.)

**1.** Directed, occurring, or taking place, alternately upward and downward.

**1616** CHAPMAN tr. *Musæus* D 6 b, With vp and down-lookes, whetting his desire. **1795** *Phil. Trans.* LXXXV. 587 The up-and-down motion in walking. **1834** *Encycl. Metrop.* (1845) VIII. 748/2 The up-and-down action is communicated to this machine by chains. **1839** URE *Dict. Arts*, etc. 1110 These faller wires..are guided truly in their up-and-down motions..by a cleaner-plate. **1874** BEDFORD *Sailor's Pocket Bk.* v. 121 To insure getting an 'up and down cast' [of the lead]. **1883** *Black's Guide Devon.* (ed. 11) 175 From here to Brendon Church..is 2½ miles of very up-and-down travelling. *transf.* **1808** VANCOUVER *Agric. Devon* 100 Farming tenantry..rent..from 200 to 300 acres of land, the greater part of which is subject to a system of up-and-down husbandry.

**b.** Adapted or used for hauling up and down.

**1794** *Rigging & Seamanship* II. 281 A chain, called an up-and-down span. **1860** NARES *Seamanship* 37 What tackles are used? A luff and an up-and-down. **1867** SMYTH *Sailor's Word-bk.* 708 Up-and-down tackle.

**c.** Of persons: That hauls, goes, works, etc., up and down.

**1851–61** MAYHEW *Lond. Labour* III. 247/1 'Up-and-down men', or coalwhippers, as they are usually called. **1897** *Westm. Gaz.* 10 April 2/1 A man, a cook-housemaid, an up-and-down girl.

**d.** *fig.* Alternately rising and falling; presenting variations comparable to movement up and down.

**1812** BYRON *Waltz* Ep., A d—d see-saw up-and-down sort of tune. **1819** *Metropolis* I. 104 Uneven measures, sportiveness and fancy must lead them [*sc.* poets]..an up and down dance. **1889** *Spectator* 14 Dec. 839 Even the free-living artist Fra Lippo Lippi talks in Browning's sudden, impatient, up-and-down style.

**2.** Perpendicular; straight up, erect; very steep.

*c* **1710** CELIA FIENNES *Diary* (1888) 232 Its such an Enclosed Country, and such up and down steep hills. **1817** H. T. COLEBROOKE *Algebra*, etc. 15 Repeat the operation till the up and down line contain but two quantities. **1894** C. N. ROBINSON *Brit. Fleet* 278 The *Warrior* and *Defence* classes had plain up and down cutwaters. **1897** *Daily News* 21 Sept. 3/2 With clothes hanging in folds upon her up-and-down figure.

**b.** *U.S.* Direct, straightforward, downright.

**1836** HALIBURTON *Clockm.* Ser. I. xxxvi, No strong-minded, straight-a-head, right up and down man does that. **1869** MRS. H. B. STOWE *Oldtown Folks* xxiv, A well-preserved, up-and-down, positive, cheery, sprightly maiden lady. **1896** *Peterson Mag.* Jan. 94/2 The two women folks..finally had an up-and-down row.

**3.** Having an uneven or irregular surface; consisting of ups and downs.

**1775** S. J. PRATT *Liberal Opin.* cxxiii. (1783) IV. 133 Very few gentlemen..come to such a d—m—d up-and-down place as this. **1830** COLMAN *Random Records* 202 Durham,..a strange up-and-down Episcopal City. **1853** DICKENS *Bleak Ho.* vi, [My room] was of this kind, with an up-and-down roof. **1898** A. AUSTIN *Lamia's Winter Quarters* 49 He lived in an up-and-down hamlet among the hills.

**b.** *fig.* Marked by alternations of success, etc.; changeful, variable.

**1907** A. RANSOME *Bohemia in London* 200 It is an up-and-down-life, my friends.

**4.** Taking place to and fro or backward and forward; spent in moving about.

**1824** MISS MITFORD *Village* Ser. I. I. 111 She has, in the course of an up-and-down life, met with a good many authors. **1876** PREECE & SIVEWRIGHT *Telegraphy* 292 What is called *up* and *down* working; that is,..each station sending alternately one or several messages. **1884** SALA *Journ. due South* II. i, The perpetual up-and-down flowing of the crowd.

**5.** In collocations arising from an ellipse of the sb. after *up*: **a.** *Pugilism.* (See quots.)

**1840** BLAINE *Encycl. Rural Sports* 1218 That species of contest, called up and down fighting, that is, when a man is got down he is kept down and punished till incapable of motion. **1863** KINGSLEY *Water-Bab.* iv, They were fighting; savage, desperate, up-and-down fighting. **1867** [T. WRIGHT] *Some Habits Working Classes* 124 Up-and-down fights, in which..the men fight both up and down.

**b.** Of or pertaining to 'up' and 'down' trains.

**1890** *Daily News* 16 Sept. 6/4 Two complete sets of up and down lines run out of that station. **1898** *Engineering Mag.* XVI. 73 Acting as through stations for the main up-and-down traffic.

**c.** *Watchmaking.* (See quot.)

**1884** F. J. BRITTEN *Watch & Clockm.* 276 [An] up and down Indicator..[is] mechanism for indicating when a watch or chronometer requires winding.

**D.** *sb.*

**I.** Pl. uses (occas. hyphened), **ups and downs.**

**1. a.** Undulations or irregularities on the surface of ground, etc. Also in fig. context.

**1682** *Whitelock's Mem.* Pref., There are flats..as well as ups and downs and precipices. **1687** A. LOVELL tr. *Thevenot's Trav.* I. 159 The Street being full of ups and downs, they make it..smooth from end to end. **1698** T. FROGER *Voy.* 110 The town is nothing throughout but up's and downs and..consequently carriages are very impracticable there. **1717** BERKELEY *Tour in Italy* Wks. 1871 IV. 563 After our ascent through a difficult path, many ups and downs, stony, narrow and uneasy, among shrubby mountains, etc. on foot. **1821** COBBETT *Rur. Rides* (1853) 10 The ups and downs of sea in a heavy swell. **1859** TENNYSON *Marriage of Geraint* 236 Geraint..rode, By ups and downs, thro' many a grassy glade. **1879** HARE *Story of my Life* (1900) V. xx. 169 All the ups and downs of the ground.

**b.** Undulatory motions, tracings, etc. Also *fig.*

**1860** W. H. RUSSELL *Diary India* II. 227, I did not find it easy to sleep in the palkee, with its ups and downs. **1860–70** STUBBS *Lect. Europ. Hist.* (1904) 8 Charles's wars with Francis are a regular seesaw. The Pope is generally the person who pulls the ups and downs. **1888** R. ABERCROMBY *Weather* ii. 30 If we look at the barometer-trace.., the 'ups' and 'downs' suggest the analogy of waves.

**2. a.** Vicissitudes, variations, or alternations in respect of fortune, success, etc. Also const. *of* (life, fortune, etc.).

In frequent use from *c* 1850.

**1659** BUNYAN *Law & Grace Unf.* Wks. 1855 I. 553 The very saints of God have..many ups and downs in this their travel towards heaven. **1680** C. NESSE *Ch. Hist.* 99 The church..continued 450 Y[ears] in its Vps and Downs. **1727** P. WALKER *Remarkable Passages* (1827) I. 293 He..had many Ups and Downs in his Case, warm Blinks and Clouds. **1793–4** AIKIN & MRS. BARBAULD *Even. at Home* (1805) IV. 5, I have had my ups and downs in the world. **1807** SOUTHEY *Espriella's Lett.* II. 178 The ups and downs of commercial Speculation. **1809** MALKIN *Gil Blas* x. ii. ⁋ 7 The ups and downs in the lottery of my own life. **1859** THACKERAY *Virgin.* lxxxi, They had their ups and downs of fortune. **1875** HELPS *Soc. Press.* xx. 297 His life is a life of ups and downs, the ups and downs not being of exceeding magnitude.

**b.** Alternations in respect of condition, quality, etc.; vagaries, variations.

**1855** BRIMLEY *Ess., Westw. Ho!* 301 The ups and downs, the fortunes and emotions, of a passion. **1882** MRS. OLIPHANT *Lit. Hist. Eng.* I. 368 The ups and downs of a mind so precariously balanced. **1899** *Allbutt's Syst. Med.* VI. 897 The ups and downs met with in the course of the disease.

**II.** Singular uses (usually hyphened).

†**3.** A swing-boat. *Obs.*

**1813** *Sporting Mag.* XLII. 20 There were the usual swings, ups-and-downs, and roundabouts. **1816** in Hone *Every-day Bk.* (1825) I. 572 Up-and-downs, merry-go-rounds [at fairs]. **1825** HONE *Ibid.* 1228 There is an 'up and down', or swing, of..woodwork.

**4. a.** Alternate rise and fall, esp. *fig.* in respect of position, fortune, etc.; variation of condition, lot, or circumstances.

**1775** S. J. PRATT *Liberal Opin.* cviii. (1783) IV. 29 [The present world] is in itself one general up-and-down: the human soul abhors sameness. *a* **1838** C. MORRIS *Lyra Urban.* (1840) II. 338 What an up-and-down is this? A shift from palace to cot. **1867** LOWELL *Biglow P.* Ser. II. Introd., Poems (1912) 287/2 The regular up and down of the pentameter churn. **1876** S. LANIER *Clover* 71 Th' incalculable Up-and-Down of Time made plain before my eyes.

**b.** Fluctuation or vacillation *of* passion, etc.

**1905** STOPFORD BROOKE *Ten Plays Shakesp.* 88 The up-and-down of his bewildered passion has passed away.

**5.** An irregularly undulating surface, lineation, etc.

**1856** MRS. BROWNING *Aur. Leigh* I. 1109 Such an up and down Of verdure,—nothing too much up or down, A ripple of land. **1888** *Encycl. Dict.* s.v. *Tonic*, The 'up and down' of pitch is not represented to the eye as on the staff.

Hence **Up-and-dow·nishness; Up-and-dow·ny** *a. nonce-words.*

**1853** R. S. SURTEES *Sponge's Sp. Tour* xliv, The up-and-downy, wavy piece of road. **1873** A. J. ELLIS in *Trans. Philol. Soc.* 130 Such wonderful up-and-downishness does not shew much declamatory taste.

**Upanishad** (*upæ·niʃæd*). [a. Skr. *upa-nishád*, f. *upa* near to + *ni-shad* to sit or lie down.] In Sanskrit literature, one or other of various speculative treatises chiefly dealing with the Deity, creation, and existence, and forming a division of the Vedic literature.

**1805** COLEBROOKE in *Asiatic Researches* VIII. 446, I shall here quote, from this Upanishad, a single dialogue. **1816** R. ROY (*title*), Translation of the Céna Upanishad, one of the chapters of the Sáma Véda. **1861** MAX MÜLLER *Lect. Sci. Lang.* 145 Dárá..became a student of Sanskrit, and translated the Upanishads..into Persian..in the year 1657.

**Upard**, obs. f. UPWARD *adv.*

**Uparise, -arising, -arist**: see UP- 2 b, 4, 6, 7.

‖ **Upas** (yū·păs). Also 9 oopas. [a. Malay اوڤس *ūpas* poison, in the comb. *pōhun* (or *pūhun*) *ūpas* poison-tree.

In senses 1 and 2 correct usage would require the compound *upas-tree*. The full Malay name has been used by some writers in the inexact forms *bohon, bohun, bopon, bon*, and *boa upas*.]

**1.** A fabulous tree alleged to have existed in Java, at some distance from Batavia, with properties so poisonous as to destroy all animal and vegetable life to a distance of fifteen or sixteen miles around it.

The account given in the *London Magazine* of 1783, from which Erasmus Darwin adopted and gave currency to the fiction, professed to be translated from one written in Dutch by Mr. Foersch (who was a surgeon at Samarang in 1773), but was app. the invention of George Steevens. The history of the fable is fully traced in Yule and Burnell's *Hobson-Jobson*, s.v. *Upas*.

*a.* **1783** *London Mag.* 513/1 They are asked.., whether they will go to the Upas tree for a box of poison? **1819** WIFFEN *Aonian Hours* 58 His life was like the Upas-tree, The curse of all his kind! **1841** THACKERAY *Misc. Ess.* (1885) 401 Avoid tobacco as you would the upas plant.

*β.* **1783** *London Mag.* 516/2, I have been convinced, that the gum of the Upas is the..most violent of all vegetable poisons. **1789** E. DARWIN *Loves of Plants* III. 238 Fierce in dread silence on the blasted heath Fell Upas sits, the Hydra-Tree of death. **1815** HELEN M. WILLIAMS *Pres. St. France* iv. 68 Held in as much abhorrence as if they had shed the poisons of the Upas. **1858** SEARS *Athan.* ii. 89 The Upas of the desert, and the nightshade of the jungles.

*attrib.* and *Comb.* **1838** RUSKIN *Scythian Banquet Song* iv, Nor deemed [I] my love, like Upas dew, A plague. **1845** FORD *Handbk. Spain* II. 724 Such is its upas-like atmosphere. **1847** EMERSON *Mithridates* 19 Swing me in the upas boughs, Vampyre-fanned, when I carouse.

**b.** *fig.* A baleful, destructive, or deadly power or influence.

*a.* **1801** SOUTHEY *Thalaba* IX. II. 200 From that accursed venom springs The Upas Tree of Death. **1824** *Westm. Rev.* April 464 That Upas tree, which has since borne all the bitter fruits of Turkish oppression. **1839** FR. A. KEMBLE *Resid. in Georgia* (1863) 90 This tremendous soil. where one grain of knowledge may spring up a gigantic upas-tree. **1885** E. GARRETT *At Any Cost* iv. 64 This failure..lies about the very root of many upas-trees of human life.

*β.* **1818** BYRON *Ch. Har.* IV. cxxvi, This uneradicable taint of sin, This boundless upas, this all-blasting tree. **1865** PARKMAN *Huguenots* viii. (1875) 138 Thus did Spain..crush the upas of heresy in its germ. **1876** FARRAR *Marlb. Serm.* xxxvi. 359 This is the sole resemblance between the tree of life and the upas of evil.

*attrib.* **1832** [R. CATTERMOLE] *Beckett*, etc. 169 Even Despotism's dark upas-root For us a blessing bore. **1853** KINGSLEY *Hypatia* I. p. xi, Was not the Empire trying to extend over the Church itself that upas shadow with which it had withered up every other form of human existence?

**2.** *Bot.* The Javanese tree *Antiaris toxicaria*, yielding a poisonous juice. (Cf. ANTIAR.)

**1814** T. HORSFIELD in *Thomson's Ann. Philos.* IX. 202 An Essay on the Oopas, or Poison Tree of Java. **1834** *Penny Cycl.* II. 98/2 There is such a tree as the upas, and its juice, if mixed with the blood.., is speedily fatal. *Ibid.* 420/2 The Upas tree of Java. **1872** OLIVER *Elem. Bot.* II. 234 The celebrated Upas.. is a native of Java. The juice.. was formerly used by the natives to poison their arrows.

*attrib.* **1857** MILLER *Elem. Chem., Org.* 287 Strychnia.. is one of the active constituents of the upas poison.

**3.** The poison obtained from the upas-tree.

**1783** *London Mag.* 515/2 To suffer death by a lancet poisoned with Upas. *Ibid.* 516/1, I..procured..some grains of Upas. **1814** T. HORSFIELD in *Thomson's Ann. Philos.* IX. 207 One of the experiments..was made with the oopas prepared by myself. **1830** LINDLEY *Nat. Syst. Bot.* 95 An order [of plants] which contains the most deadly poison in the world, the Upas of Java. **1860** MAYNE *Expos. Lex.* s.v.

**Up-ba·nding,** *vbl. sb.* (App. an error for *up-bending*: see UPBEND *pa. pple.*) **1620** QUARLES *Jonah* H 2, 'Tis not your Mimmick mouthes,.. Nor prodigall vp-banding of thine eyes, Whose gashfull balls doe seeme to pelt the skyes.

**U·p-bank,** *adv.* and *a.* [UP *prep.*[2]]

**1.** *adv.* Upwards. *north. dial.*

**1760-** in *Eng. Dial. Dict.* **1808** [see BANK *sb.*[1] 2 b].

**2.** *adj.* (See quot.)

**1883** R. H. SCOTT *Elem. Meteor.* 213 The well-known phenomenon of 'up-bank thaw', when it thaws on the hills, while the frost is unbroken in the valleys below.

**Upbea·r,** *v.* [UP- 4 + BEAR *v.*[1] 18, 21. Cf. MSw. *upbāra* (Sw. *uppbära*), MDa. *upbære*. Freq. in pa. pple. *upborne*: see UP- 5.]

**1.** *trans.* To bear up, support, sustain; also, to lift up, raise.

*a* **1300** *Cursor M.* 7258 Þe post þat al þat huse vpbare Wit bath his handes he it scok. **13..** *K. Alis.* 5163 Swiþe wiȝtlych hij..swymme, Of þe water þat hij were inne Vpberande faire chynne. **1390** GOWER *Conf.* III. 296 He that alle thing mai kepe. broghte him sauf upon a table, Which to the lond him hath upbore. *c* **1440** *Promp. Parv.* 508/1 Vbberyn, or vpberyn, *supporto*. *c* **1470** HENRY *Wallace* IX. 1632 A thourtour bande, that all the drawcht wpbar, He cuttyt it. *a* **1550** LYNDESAY *Syde Taillis* 23 Thocht thare Rob Royallis be vpborne, I think [etc.]. **1582** STANYHURST *Æneis*, etc. (Arb.) 136 Earst the flud, vpbearing thee ship, now the cartwheele vpholdeth. **1590** SPENSER *F. Q.* II. vii. 43 Many great golden pillours did vpbeare The massy roofe. **1667** MILTON *P. L.* II. 408 Who shall..spread his aerie flight Upborn with indefatigable wings Over the vast abrupt. **1725** POPE *Odyssey* V. 542 A monst'rous wave up-bore The Chief. **1784** COWPER *Task* I. 20 Joint-stools were then created; on three legs Upborne they stood. **1831** E. IRVING *Exp. Rev.* I. 60 Upbearing His person as Aaron and Hurr upbore the hands of Moses. **1870** MORRIS *Earthly Par.* II. III. 352 A chief's gold ring his left arm did upbear. **1891** ATKINSON *Moorland Par.* 64 Slabs of stone of sufficient solidity to upbear any loaded vehicle.

**2.** *fig.* To support or sustain; to exalt.

*a* **1300** *E. E. Psalter* lxxvii. 76 He ches Dauyd, hyne hisse; And vp-bare him all with blisse. *Ibid.* cxxx. 1 Vphouen es noght mi hert, Ne vpborn er mine eghen in quert. **1303** R. BRUNNE *Handl. Synne* 7159 He..loueþ alle þat sothfast es; Alle godenes he vp bereþ. *c* **1384** CHAUCER *H. Fame* 818 Euerych ayre other stereth More and more, and speche vpbereth. **1412-20** LYDG. *Chron. Troy* I. 4424, I wil,..vp-born with support of ȝour grace, Forþe a-complische, as I vndertook. *a* **1586** SIDNEY *Ps.* XXX. ii, I..was from ev'l by thee upborne. **1590** SPENSER *F. Q.* II. vii. 65 Food, and sleepe, which two vpbeare, Like mightie pillours, this fraile life of man. **1630** DRUMM. OF HAWTH. *Flowres Sion* viii, A Virgine Maide A weakling did him beare, who all vpbeares. **1829** I. TAYLOR *Enthus.* ix. 248 A..proof of the intrinsic power of Christianity, upbearing so ponderous a mass of error. **1876** LOWELL *Among my Bks.* Ser. II. 325 His own language rarely rises above it, except when it is upborn by the thought.

**†Upbea·rer.** *Obs.* [UP- 8. Cf. prec.] A supporter, sustainer.

**1386** *Rolls of Parlt.* III. 225/1 Nichol Brembre, wyth his upberers. *c* **1400** tr. *Secreta Secret., Gov. Lordsh.* 101 Þe wyt of a kynge ys helpyd by his vpberers. *c* **1440** *Promp. Parv.* 512/2 Vpberere, *supportator*. **1513** DOUGLAS *Æneid* VI. xiii. 89 The wpberar of the hevin, Atlas. **1624** BP. MOUNTAGU *New Gagg* 306 Vasquez himselfe.., that great Upbearer of Roman Idolatry.

**Upbea·ring,** *vbl. sb.* [UP- 7. Cf. UPBEAR *v.*] The action of carrying, raising, taking or holding up; support, sustaining.

*a* **1340** HAMPOLE *Psalter* cxxx. 1 Vpberyng of een withouten is signe of pryde. *a* **1400** *Prymer* (1891) 23 Wonderful been the upberynges of the se. *c* **1440** *Promp. Parv.* 512/2 Vpberynge, *supportacio*. **1501** *Acc. Ld. High Treas. Scot.* II. 114 The chekker..passit to Schir Adam Crechtonis hous, for upbering of the rollis. **1513** JAS. IV *Let.* in Hall *Chron., Hen. VIII* (1548) 30 The greate wronges..quhilk we haue suffred this long time in vpberyng, maynsweryng, nounredressyng of Attemptates. **1878** SPURGEON *Treas. Dav.* V. 48 A most fitting accompaniment to the upbearing of the ark. **1885** *19th Cent.* June 967 The patient upbearing against hardship.

**Upbearing,** *ppl. a.*: see UP- 6 b.

**U·pbeat,** *sb.* [UP- 2.]

**1.** *Mus.* 'The beat of a bar at which the hand is raised; an unaccented beat' (Stainer and Barrett).

**1869** OUSELEY *Counterp.* iii, The up-beat may be either a concord or a discord. **1874** — *Musical Form* 63 The second phrase concludes with the third of the tonic, but at the up-beat.

**2.** *Pros.* **a.** An anacrusis. **b.** An arsis or stressed syllable.

**1883** H. M. KENNEDY tr. *Ten Brink's E. E. Lit.* 194 Orm reproduced the foreign metre with pains-taking accuracy. The up-beat (*auftakt*, *anacrusis*) never fails. **1899** D. HYDE *Lit. Hist. Irel.* xxxviii. 532 If we take it for granted that the syllables in which rhyme or alliteration appear must also bear the accent or up-beat of the voice.

**Upbeild,** obs. Sc. variant of UPBUILD *v.*

**Upbi·gged,** *pa. pple. Sc.* [UP- 5 + BIG *v.* 4.] Built up. Also **Upbi·gger; Upbi·gging** *vbl. sb.*

*c* **1425** WYNTOUN *Cron.* v. vii. 1280 Ierusalem in his tyme gert he Weill agane vpbiggit be. **1514** *Extr. Aberd. Reg.* (1844) I. 91 Dikkis..to be vpbiggit apoun the expensis of the land. **1563** *Reg. Privy Council Scot.* I. 247 Ordanis all paroche kirkis..quhilkis ar decayit..to be reparit and upbiggit. *a* **1837** in R. Murray *Hawick Songs* (ed. 3) 65 Till it seems..A whole fairy city, upbiggit wi' stars. **1562** WINȜET *Wks.* (S.T.S.) II. 3 The..*wpbigare of the wallis of Ierusalem. **1525** *Extr. Aberd. Reg.* (1844) I. 113 The reparat[i]oun and *upbiging of thair portis. **1562** WINȜET *Wks.* (S.T.S.) II. 6 To be a faythful souldiour..in the wpbigging of thir haly wallis.

**Upbi·nd,** *v.* [UP- 4. Cf. Du. *opbinden*, Da. *opbinde*, Sw. *uppbinda*, G. *aufbinden*.] *trans.* To bind up.

**1590** SPENSER *F. Q.* III. iv. 40 His griesly wound:..which hauing well vpbound, They pourd in soueraine balme. **1596** *Ibid.* IV. xi. 52 [They] haue the sea in charge to them assinde,..To bring forth stormes, or fast them to vpbinde. **1650** *Metr. Ps. Ch. Scotl.* cxlvii. 3 Their painfull wounds he tenderly up-bindes. **1746** COLLINS *Ode to Peace* iii, O Peace, thy injur'd robes up-bind.

**Upblaze, -blazing:** see UP- 4, 6.

**†Upblow·ing,** *vbl. sb. Obs.* [UP- 7.] Inflation. **1527** ANDREW *Brunswyke's Distyll. Waters* F ii, In lyke wyse synketh the great..upblowynge of the tongue. **1562** TURNER *Baths* E It is good for them that have..windines or upblowynge of the bellye.

**Upblowing,** *pres. pple.*: see UP- 6.

**Upblow·n,** *pa. pple.* and *ppl. a.* [UP- 5.] Blown up; *esp.* inflated, puffed up.

**1590** SPENSER *F. Q.* I. iv. 21 His belly was vp-blowne with luxury. **1596** *Ibid.* V. i. 17 He, whose spirit was with pride vpblowne. **1810** CRABBE *Borough* xvi. 44 With wine inflated, man is all upblown, And feels a power which he believes his own. **1828** TENNYSON *Lover's T.* II. 175 One morning when the upblown billow ran Shoreward.

**Upboi·l,** *v.* [UP- 4.] **a.** *intr.* To boil up; *fig.* to rise up hotly. **†b.** *trans.* To cause to boil. *Obs.*

**1435** MISYN *Fire of Love* 79 Behald, myn inhir partis has vpbolyd [L. *efferbuerunt*], & þe flawme of charite..has wastyd. *c* **1440** *Pallad. on Husb.* x. 188 Vpboile hit thenne And stere hit vntil honythicke it renne. **1555** *Lydgate's Chron. Troy* II. xiii. I iv/1 She wepeth..With wawes vpboyled from her eyen clere. *a* **1902** E. F. TAYLOR *Æneid* XII. 1099 Then terribly Æneas' wrath upboils.

**Upboi·ling,** *vbl. sb.* (UP- 7. Cf. prec.) **1794** COLERIDGE *Fall Robespierre* I. 88 He feels The dire upboilings of the storm within him. **Upborne:** see UPBEAR *v.* **Upbounden, -bounding, -bracing:** see UP- 5, 6, 7.

**†Upbrai·d,** *sb. Obs.* Forms: α. 3 upbreid, -bræid, 4 -breyd(e, 4–5 -breide; 3– upbraid (5 *Sc.* upbrad), 4–6 upbraide, 5–7 upbrayde (6 -brayed). β. 4 vbbreid(e, obbrayd, 6 obbraid, obrayd, 7 ubbrayd. [f. UP- 2 + BRAID *sb.* 1. Cf. the verb, also UMBRAID *sb.* and UPBRUD.]

**1.** With *a* and pl. A reproach or reproof.

α. *a* **1200** *Vices & Virtues* 41 [Job was assailed] mid maniȝe euele upbreides..of his auene frienden. *a* **1300** *Cursor M.* 5673 Moyses for þis vp-braid Was stonand in his hert. **1338** R. BRUNNE *Chron.* (1810) 219 In ȝow a faute men fynde, & is an ille vpbraid, þat ȝe ere nere blynde. *c* **1449** PECOCK *Repr.* II. xvi. 247 Alle the vpbreidis and alle the reproues which Holi Writ ȝeueth to the worschipers of tho ymagis. **1482** *Monk of Evesham* (Arb.) 106 Vexyd with tormentys and vpbraydys of seche wekyd folke. **1549** COVERDALE, etc. *Erasm. Par.* 1 *Tim.* 11 Not onely any naughtye faulte but also any false feyned vpbrayed. **1575** *Brieff Disc. Troub. Franckford* (1846) 84 They coulde haue nothing with owte bytter upbraids. **1641** *Vind. Smectymnuus* 9 It is no envious upbraid to parallell ours with the former Bishops. **1677** tr. *Groeneveldt's Treat. Stone* 61 Moved at length by the upbraids of the Parents,..he made incision in the groin.

β. **1325** *Metr. Hom.* in *Herrig's Archiv* LVII. 243/1 Of fendes hedde I mony vbbreide. **1575** LANEHAM *Let.* (1907) 17 With spitefull obrayds and vncharitabl chaffings alweiz they freat. *a* **1603** T. CARTWRIGHT *Confut. Rhem. N. T.* (1618) 575 Which..you your selues without the ub-brayd of a lie by your own conscience, cannot deny.

**2.** Without article: Reproach, reproof; evil speaking.

α. *c* **1205** LAY. 26036 Þa nolde Arður on slepen na wiht hine areppen, leste he an uferre daȝe up-bræid iherde. *c* **1275** in *Hist. Holy Rood-tree*, etc. 78 Skoarn, upbraid, and schome speche. *c* **1330** R. BRUNNE *Chron. Wace* (Rolls) 7996 Bytwyxt to þer a stryf þey herde, Of grete vpbreide ilk oþer onswerde. *a* **1400-50** *Alexander* 1800 Lettis neuire it broȝt be on brade for vpbraide of schame. *c* **1460** J. RUSSELL *Bk. Nurture* 395 As it is showed afore, beware of vpbrayde. **1591** SPENSER *M. Hubberd* 2 For disdaine of sinfull worlds vpbraide. **1596** — *F. Q.* IV. ix. 24 Through lewd vpbraide Of Ate and Duessa they fell out.

β. *c* **1325** *Spec. Gy Warw.* 537 Ȝif þi neiheboure misdoþ þe, ..Or in dede, or in vbbreid. *a* **1400** *New Test.* (Paues) Heb. xi. 26 Trowynge þe obbrayd of Crist grettour rychesse þan þe tresour of Egypcyenes. **1548** PATTEN *Exped. Scotl.* Pref. b iv b, So maye the subiect without obbraid of benefites, recount the bcunty of hys Princes larges.

**Upbraid** (ʊpbrēⁱ·d), *v.* Forms: α. 1 upbredan, 3–4 upbreyde (5 -dyn), 4 -breide(n; 4–7 upbrayde (6 wp-), -braide, 4– upbraid (7 -brayd), 5 uppe-, 6 upbrade; *pa. t.* and *pa. pple.* 3, 6 op-, 6–7 upbraid (4 -brayde, 5 -brayd, -brayed), 3–4 upbreide, 4–5 -breyde. β. 5 vbbreydyn, 6 obbrayd, -braid; 5 (*pa. t.*) obreide, 6–7 obrayde, 7 obraid. [OE. *upbregdan*, f. *up-* UP- 4 + *bregdan* BRAID *v.*[1]: cf. MSw. *up-*, *op-*, *o(b)-brygdha*. See also BRAID *v.*[2], ABRAID *v.*[1] and *v.*[2], EMBRAID *v.*[1], IMBRAID *v.*, and UMBRAID *v.*

The orig. strong pa. t. (*upbraid*) gave rise the reduced form UPBRAY *v.*]

**I. †1.** *trans.* To bring forward, adduce, or allege (a matter), as a ground for censure or reproach. Orig. const. with dative of person, later with *to* or *against*. *Obs.*

For the use of *up-* in this connexion cf. the Scottish and northern *to cast up to* (one), CAST *v.* 83 i, the modern *to bring up against* (one), and the dial. *to throw up against*.

α. *c* **1000** WULFSTAN *Hom.* 248 Þæt þu þæt god ȝefylle, þe þu canst, þe læs þe [*v.r.* eow] God upbrede þone godspellican cwide [etc.]. *a* **1225** *Ancr. R.* 426 Þe ancre neuer more þer efter þene ilke gult ne upbreide hire. *a* **1250** *Owl & Night.* 1414 Ne schal no mon wymman bigrede & fleysses lustes hire vpbreyde. *c* **1290** *Beket* 1748 in *S. Eng. Leg.* I. 156 Wel ofte þe king him opbraid þat he dude him er of guode. **1542** UDALL *Erasm. Apoph.* 240 Lest the others might thynke niggardship to bee upbraided unto hym, and cast in his teeth. **1583** GOLDING *Calvin on Deut.* clxxii. 1068 It shall bee vpbraided vs that wee haue turned our heartes backe. **1625** BACON *Ess., Envy* (Arb.) 513 It doth vpbraid vnto them their owne Fortunes; And pointeth at them. **1631** GOUGE *God's Arrows* III. § 60. 294 This is not upbraided to David as a crime. **1672** DRYDEN *Defence of Epilogue* ⁋ 2 It was upbraided to that excellent poet, that he was [etc.]. **1718** PRIOR *Solomon* I. 293 May they not justly to our Climes upbraid Shortness of Night, and Penury of Shade.

β. **1581** J. BELL *Haddon's Answ. Osor.* 343 That we purge ourselves of the cryme of novelty, falsly obbraydid agaynst us by Osorius. **1602** R. T. *Five Godlie Serm.* 143 First reproouing them of errour, and afterwards obraiding against them the cause thereof.

**b.** Without personal const.: To censure, find fault with, carp at.

*c* **1290** *S. Eng. Leg.* I. 61/271 For ȝwane ani Man opbraid is pouerte, he was in gret deliȝt. **1303** R. BRUNNE *Handl. Synne* 672 Þey scorne Ihesu, and vpbreyde hys pyn. **1382** WYCLIF *Ecclus.* xx. 15 Fewe thingus he shal ȝyue, and manye thingus he shal vpbreiden. *a* **1586** SIDNEY *Arcadia* II. x, How much doth thy kindnesse upbraide my wickednesse? **1591** SPENSER *Ruines of Time* 215 His hope is faild,..And euill men, now dead, his deeds vpbraid. **1655** JOHN SERGEANT *Schism Disarm'd* 331 On all occasions you are still up[b]raiding the liberty given to Papists. **1667** MILTON *P. L.* VI. 182 Thy self not free,..Yet leudly dar'st our ministring upbraid. **1719** YOUNG *Busiris* II. i, What far transcends my merit, and for ever Must silently upbraid my little worth. **1741** RICHARDSON *Pamela* IV. 105 Mr. Clerimont then upbraids her Guilt. **1792** WORDSW. *Descrip. Sk.* 251 There doth the maiden watch her lover's sail Approaching, and upbraid the tardy gale. **1821** JOANNA BAILLIE *Metr. Leg., Lady of B.* Introd. 22 For who can these as meaner times upbraid, Who think of Saragossa's valiant maid? **1867** EMERSON *May-day* 621 Who can, like thee, our rags upbraid?

β. **1591** G. FLETCHER *Russe Commw.* 66 The Chrim..sent to the Russe Emperour a knife:..obbraiding this losse, and his desperate case. **1635** HABINGTON *Castara* I. (ed. 2) 58 Why are their rimes So steept in gall? Why so obrayde the times?

**†c.** To insult. *Obs.*[−1]

**1678** SOUTH *Serm.* (1679) 173 The case is so plain, that I shall not upbraid any mans understanding by endeavouring to give it any farther Illustration.

**2.** To reproach, reprove, censure (a person, etc.). Occas. const. *for*, or *that*.

α. *a* **1300** *Cursor M.* 16718 Þe theif þat biside him hang.. him can vp-braid. *a* **1340** HAMPOLE *Psalter* xxxiv. 8 Outrageusly þai vpbraidid my saule. *c* **1374** CHAUCER *Troylus* V. 1710 O Pandarus, that in dremes for to triste Me blamed hast, and wont art ofte vp breyde. *c* **1412** HOCCLEVE *De Reg. Princ.* 3500 A sad wys knyght of his with lokkes greye.. seide Vnto his lord, and þus he hym vp breyde. **1482** *Monk of Evesham* (Arb.) 72 Sche vsyd inpacyently to scolde and vpbrayde hem that dyd her wronge. **1530** PALSGR. 784 Yet to upbrayde hym afore folkes is none honestye. **1590** SHAKS. *Mids. N.* IV. i. 55, I did vpbraid her, and fall out with her. **1600** 1*st Pt. Sir J. Oldcastle* I. ii. 6 Grieuous complaints haue past betweene the lippes Of enuious persons to vpbraide the Cleargy. **1665** MANLEY *Grotius' Low C. Wars* 291 Queen Elizabeth recall'd all her Souldiers,..not without upbraiding the States. **1697** DRYDEN *Virg. Georg.* IV. 507 He sadly stands,..Upbraiding Heav'n from whence his Lineage came. *a* **1721** SHEFFIELD (Dk. Buckhm.) *Wks.* (1753) I. 267 Has she spread wit and learning thro' the world,..And is she now upbraided? **1782** MISS BURNEY *Cecilia* VII. ix, All present were upbraided as if accomplices in the disaster. **1841** LANE *Arab. Nts.* I. 109 On hearing these words, I abstained from upbraiding her. **1872** DARWIN *Emotions* vii. 186 As she upbraided him, her eyebrows became extremely oblique.

*refl.* **1789** BOSWELL *Lett.* (1924) 373, I cried bitterly and upbraided myself for leaving her. **1831** SCOTT *Ct. Rob.* xxxiv, She upbraids herself that..she had also survived Irene.

β. *c* **1412** HOCCLEVE *De Reg. Princ.* (Roxb.) 62 Pharao clept Abraham, & hym obreide [*v.r.* ubreyde]. *c* **1440** *Promp. Parv.* 508/1 Vbbreydyn, or vpbreydyn, *impropero*. **1648** J. HOWELL tr. *Venice Looking-glass* 8 He might well..have obraided her in the same words as Henry the 3. did upbraid Paris.

**b.** Const. †*of* or *with* (the cause of censure).

(*a*) *a* **1250** *Prov. Alfred* 279 in *O. E. Misc.* 118 Heo ne scholde þe forþ vp-breyde of þine baleu-syþes. **1303** R. BRUNNE *Handl. Synne* 724 Þe pyne, he suffred for þy gode, And þou vpbreydyst hym of þe rode. *c* **1330** — *Chron. Wace* (Rolls) 11665 Þey vpbraide vs of our auncessours. *c* **1374** CHAUCER *Anel. & Arc.* 118 Lest he of eny vntrouthe her vpbreyde. **1584** LODGE *Alarum* Wks. (Hunter. Cl.) I. 28 Trust not to straungers, for they will vpbraide you of their benefite.

(*b*) *c* **1440** *Alph. Tales* 318 Þis preste..tolde hur cowncell, & vpbrayed hur þerwith. **1482** *Monk of Evesham* (Arb.) 67 The mynystrys and wykyd angellys of the deuylle vpbraydyn me with the same. **1581** J. BELL *Haddon's Answ. Osor.* 346 This nickname of newe Gospellers (wherewith the Catholickes doe obbrayd us). **1596** WARNER *Alb. Eng.* x. liv. 244 Yeat not her Infancie should be vpbraided with the blood Of many thousand slaughtred Soules. **1640** HABINGTON *Edw. IV*, 150 Obrayding the King with inglorious sloath. **1679** J. GOODMAN *Penit. Pard.* III. iv. 317 It is said..Cæsar's thoughts continually upbraided him with the great exploits

Alexander had effected. 1719 De Foe *Crusoe* II. (Globe) 503, I began to upbraid them with the just Retribution of Heaven in this Case. 1774 J. Bryant *Mythol.* I. 141 Peor, the same with whose rites the Israelites are so often upbraided. 1843 Bethune *Sc. Fireside Stor.* 100 [He] upbraided her with a wish to bring him to an ignominious death.

**c.** *absol.* To speak reproachfully.

*a* 1340 Hampole *Psalter* xli. 14 Whils my banes ere brokyn, [they] vpbrayded til me. 1382 Wyclif *Jas.* i. 5 God, the which ȝiueth to alle men largeli, and vpbraydith not. *c* 1410 *Lanterne of Liȝt* 10 Þanne þis enviouse man sclaundriþ, vpbreidiþ, reproueþ. 1596 Spenser *F. Q.* v. vii. 32 Proud Radigund,..thus vpbrayding, said. *a* 1628 Preston *Mt. Ebal* (1638) 28 He giveth liberally, and obraideth not. 1715 Pope *Iliad* II. 311 Have we not known thee,..The man who acts the least, upbraids the most? 1797 S. & Ht. Lee *Canterb. T.* (1799) I. 185, I come not to upbraid. 1856 O. W. Holmes *Birthday of D. Webster* xvi, In vain the envious tongue upbraids; His name a nation's heart shall keep.

**II. †3.** To cast, pull, or set up. *Obs.*

*c* 1205 Lay. 16519 And seoððe he hine up bræid, swulc he hine to-breken wolde. 13.. *Gaw. & Gr. Knt.* 781 Þe brygge was breme vp-brayde. *c* 1450 Holland *Houlate* 680 The Falcoune..Bad birnis burdis vp braid, with a blyth cheir.

**†4.** *intr.* To come out of a swoon; to start up, spring up. *Obs.*

14.. *Chaucer's Sqr.'s T.* 477 (Petworth MS.), After þat she of swowne gan vpbreide. 1448–9 J. Metham *Wks.* (1916) 69/1869 And with þat word bothe deede bodyis vp-brayd. 1513 Douglas *Æneis* I. iv. 36 Quhill al in flamb the bleis of fyir upbradis.

**†5.** *trans.* To give utterance to. *Obs.*[-1]

1587 Fleming *Contn. Holinshed* III. 1016/2 This woman ..beginneth to vpbraid in the open church verie hard and vnseemelie speeches concerning religion.

**6.** Of food: **a.** To make uneasy with repletion or indigestion. Now *dial.*

1599 Nashe *Lenten Stuffe* F iv b, Because, in the boyling or seathing of it in his maw, he felt it commotion a little and vpbraide him. 1601 B. Jonson *Poetaster, Apol. Dial.* 24 Their spight..who..Haue nothing left, but the vnsau'ry smoake Of their blacke vomit, to vpbrayd themselues. 1664 J. C. *Praxis Lat. Syntax* 118 The fried egge and bacon that I did eat..upbraideth my stomach. 1841 R. W. Hamilton *Nugae Lit.* 340 The grossness of the food..upbraids him. 1866– in dial. glossaries (Yks., Linc.).

**b.** *intr.* To rise in the stomach. Now *dial.*

Cf. earlier quots. s.v. Upbraiding *vbl. sb.* 3.

1604 R. Cawdrey *Table Alph.* 1787 Grose *Provinc. Gloss.* s.v., My dinner upbraids. 1824– in dial. use (Yks., Linc.).

Hence **Upbrai·ded** *ppl. a.*

1700 Dryden *Wife of Bath's T.* 458 If Poverty be my upbraided Crime. — *Ilias* I. 490 His upbraided Mother. 1748 Richardson *Clarissa* II. 305 The upbraider..is in some sense a superior; while the upbraided, if with reason upbraided, must make a figure as spiritless as conscious.

**Upbrai·der.** [f. Upbraid *v.*] One who upbraids; a reprover.

1636 B. Jonson *Discov.* Wks. (1641) 106 The latter hath no upbraiders. 1700 N. Rowe *Amb. Step-Moth.* IV. i. 1718 This Rebel Son! This insolent Upbraider. 1748 [see prec.]. 1751 Smollett *Per. Pic.* xxxi, Assuring the upbraider that he considered her as an object of compassion. 1877 D. M. Wallace *Russia* xxv. 392 'We are quite ready,' they said to their upbraiders, 'to admire your great works as soon as they appear'.

**Upbrai·ding,** *vbl. sb.* [f. as prec.]

**1.** A reproach or reproof.

*c* 1205 Lay. 19117 Þenne nabbeoð ure æfterlinges nane upbreidinges. *a* 1300 *E. E. Psalter* lxxxviii. 49 Mined be, lauerd, of vpbraidinges of þi hine. *c* 1449 Pecock *Repr.* II. xvi. 247 Certis..alle her vpbreidingis mad ben iust. 1590 Shaks. *Com. Err.* v. i. 73 Thou saist his meate was sauc'd with thy vpbraidings. 1611 Speed *Hist. Gt. Brit.* IX. viii. 496/2 When..hee snebs the King for comminatory obraydings, and contumacious malepartnesse. 1627 Sanderson *Serm.* I. 270 The horrors and upbraidings of a condemning heart. 1712 Steele *Spect.* No. 448 ¶6 You your self cannot ..but allow the Justice of the Upbraidings of Your Injured Friend. 1773 Mrs. Chapone *Improv. Mind.* (1774) I. 174 If jealousy is expressed by unkind upbraidings. 1844 Thirlwall *Greece* VIII. 320 He was there received with ..upbraidings, and reproaches. 1894 J. D. Campbell *Life Coleridge* 46 Coleridge then broke out in extravagantly-worded upbraidings.

**2.** The action of reproaching or reproving.

*a* 1300 *E. E. Psalter* cxviii. 22 Bere fra me vpbraidinge and forhoghte. 1303 R. Brunne *Handl. Synne* 766 But ȝe leue ..ȝoure vnkynde vpbreydyng, ȝe shul go a deueyl weye. *a* 1340 Hampole *Psalter* ii. 5 Þat speche sall be vpbraydynge þat þai wild noght doe his biddynge. *c* 1410 *Lanterne of Liȝt* 124 At alle tyme he schal be cursid & worþi vpbreiding. 1526 *Pilgr. Perf.* (W. de W. 1531) 241 b, Without ony exprobracyon, upbraydyng or rebukyng. 1599 Hakluyt *Voy.* I. 562 A thing foolish and vaine,..deuised for the vpbrayding of our nation. 1656 Bramhall *Replie to S. W.* 70 For in my discourse there is nothing either of repining or upbraiding. 1749 Fielding *Tom Jones* VIII. xiv, He received nothing but scorn and upbraiding from me. 1775 Sheridan *Rivals* III. ii, I had come resolved to wear a face of coolness and upbraiding. 1825 Scott *Talism.* xvii, Without a word of upbraiding, she attended upon the Queen. 1878 Miss Braddon *Eleanor's Vict.* iii, No word of upbraiding had ever crossed those tender lips.

**† b.** An object of reproach or censure. *Obs. rare.*

*a* 1300 *E. E. Psalter* xxi. 5, I am worme, and man nathing; Mennes vpbraiding, of folk outkasting. *Ibid.* xxxviii. 12.

**† 3.** Eructation of food; regurgitation. *Obs.*

1533 Elyot *Cast. Helthe* (1541) 73 It tourneth also norishement vnto corrupcion, whiche maketh vpbraidynges fumishe or sharpe. 1561 Hollybush *Hom. Apoth.* 2 The payn of the head commeth..by y^e vpbraything of y^e stomak into the head. 1574 Newton *Health Mag.* 21 When throughe drinkinge of wine there is any upbraidinge and mordication in the stomacke. 1611 Cotgr., *Remors de l'estomac*, the vpbraiding of the stomacke.

**Upbrai·ding,** *ppl. a.* [f. Upbraid *v.* + -ing [2].] Reproachful, reproving.

*a* 1300 *E. E. Psalter* xliii. 18 Steuen of vpbraidand and forspekand. *c* 1449 Pecock *Repr.* II. xvi. 247 Alle tho reprouyng and upbreiding processis vpon ydolatrers ben trewe. 1568 Grafton *Chron.* II. 101 You haue written to vs againe after a threatning sort, and vpbrayding manner. *a* 1618 Sylvester *Epist.* vii. 31 Th' upbraiding blurr of my young Muse's rape. 1625 T. Godwin *Moses & Aaron* I. iii. 12 They vsed no vpbraiding termes towards them. 1663 *Extr. St. Papers Friends* Ser. II. (1911) 183 Mr. Knight returned me this scornfull and vpbraiding answer. 1732 Berkeley *Alciphr.* v. § 30 This being spoke with..an upbraiding air. 1810 Scott *Lady of L.* II. vi, 'Twas thus upbraiding conscience said. 1822 J. Wilson *Lights & Shadows* 143 The Minister looked,..with an upbraiding countenance, on the young man. 1848 Buckley *Iliad* 397 But him..Diana sharply rebuked, and uttered this upbraiding speech.

**Upbrai·dingly,** *adv.* [f. prec.] In an upbraiding manner; with reproach or reproof.

1593 Nashe *Christ's T.* R iij, Any man..that is vpbraidingly dyscontent. 1653 R. Sanders *Physiogn.* 257 Neither should we upbraidingly be accused for our negligence. 1679 Prance *Addit. Narr. Pop. Plot* 9 Upbraidingly telling him, That he should be a Prisoner there. 1748 Richardson *Clarissa* (1768) IV. 173 Afraid, as the women upbraidingly tell me, that I should find it there. 1825 Scott *Talism.* viii, 'I never knew thee before hesitate for fear of life,' said Richard upbraidingly. 1861 Meredith *Evan Harrington* III. ix. 147 Its absence was upbraidingly mentioned.

**† Upbray·,** *sb. Obs.* [Cf. next.] = Upbraid *sb.* I.

1590 Spenser *F. Q.* III. vi. 50 Faire Psyche to him lately reconcyld, After long troubles and vnmeet vpbrayes.

**Upbray·,** *v. Obs.* exc. *dial.* Also 6 ob-, 7 ubbray. [Erroneous back-formation from *upbrayd*, obs. pa. t. of Upbraid *v.*]

**1.** = Upbraid *v.* 1, 2.

1581 J. Bell *Haddon's Answ. Osorius* 337, I my selfe have heard the Jewes obbrayinge us christians with the same faults. 1590 Spenser *F. Q.* II. iv. 45 Vile knight, That knights and knighthood doest with shame vpbray. 1602 W. Basse *Sword & Buckler* lxi. (1893) 25 You needlesly ubbray our haire. 1642 H. More *Song of Soul* I. ii. 27 The hearts do ne're agree But felly one another do upbray. 1898 R. Blakeborough *Wit, etc. N. Riding Yorks.* 466.

**† 2.** = Upbraid *v.* 5. *Obs.*[-1]

*a* 1600 in *Sidney's Arcadia*, etc. (1922) II. 368 Yet not of women judginge as he sayd. But first with rage, his rage on them [he] upbrayde.

**† 3.** = Upbraid *v.* 6. *Obs.*[-1]

1598 Marston *Sco. Villanie* III. x, Vpbray'd by Capons greace, consumed quite By eating stewes, that waste the better spright.

Hence **Upbray·ing** *vbl. sb.*

1585 Parsons *Chr. Exerc.* I. v. 45 Consider the intollerable vpbraying of the wicked infernal spirits.

**U·pbreak,** *sb.* [Up- 2. Cf. next.]

**1.** An eruption or outburst.

1856 Mrs. Browning *Aur. Leigh* VII. 54 Through all The upbreak of the fountains of my heart. 1871 E. F. Burr *Ad Fidem* xiv. 277 A furious upbreak of unbelief.

**2.** A breaking-up or dissolution.

1882 *Macm. Mag.* XLV. 496 The upbreak of the Catholico-Feudal System.

**Upbreak** (vpbrē¹·k), *v.* [Up- 4. Cf. WFris. *opbrekke*, (M)Du. *opbreken*, (M)LG. *upbreken*, LG. *upbräken*, MHG. *ûfbrëchen* (G. *aufbrechen*), Da. *opbrække*.]

**†1.** *intr.* To break out; to begin to speak. *Obs.*

*c* 1205 Lay. 5431 Þeo hit [alles] up bræc, hit wes god þat he spec. *c* 1320 *Castel Love* 457 So þat Pees a-last vp-breek, And þus to hire Fader speek.

**2.** *trans.* To break up; to break open.

1382 Wyclif *Gen.* xix. 9 Now nyȝ it was that thei shulden vp breke [L. *effringerent*] the ȝatis. *a* 1400 *Octouian* 190 The emperour tho..gan vp-breke The dore. *c* 1440 *Pallad. on Husb.* VIII. 1 At Iuyl the lond vpbroken in Aprile Is eft to plowe. 1582 Stanyhurst *Æneis* I. (Arb.) 24 Thee stags vpbreaking they slit to the dulcet or inchepyn. 1855 Lynch *Rivulet* VIII. i, As a field Is by the plough up-broken for the corn. 1885–94 R. Bridges *Eros & Psyche* May iv, The sun..Upbroke the grey dome of the morning sky.

**3.** *intr.* To force or make a way upward or to the surface.

1859 Tennyson *Guinevere* 391 They..rode..over sheets of hyacinth That seem'd the heavens upbreaking thro' the earth. 1887 *Cornhill Mag.* Aug. 214 When from the gloom Of the dark earth upbreaks the tender bloom.

**Upbrea·king,** *vbl. sb.* (Up- 7. Cf. prec.)

1493 *Acta Auditorum* (1839) 171/1 For þe vpbreking of þe said Johnnis Compt burdis. 1578 Lyte *Dodoens* 683 It stoppeth vomitinges, and the vpbreakynges of the stomacke. 1830 Croly *George IV*, 283 The general upbreaking of society. 1876 K. O'Meara *F. Ozanam* xxi. 298 The upbreaking of terrible destructive forces through the calm surface.

**Upbrea·the,** *v.* [Up- 4.] *trans.* To send up as a breath.

1606 Marston *Trag. Sophonisba* III. i, To you corruptlesse hunny, and pure dew, Upbreathes our holy fire. 1844 Mrs. Browning *Rhyme Duchess May* xc, Straight as if the Holy name did upbreathe her as a flame..She upsprang. 1880 S. Lanier *Hymns of Marshes, Sunrise* 5 Up-breathed from the marshes, a message..Came to the gates of sleep.

**† Upbri·ng,** *v. Obs.* [Up- 4. Cf. OFris. *opbringa* (WFris. *opbringe*), (M)Du. *opbrengen*, MLG. *upbringen* (LG. *upbrengen*), MHG. *ûfbringen* (G. *aufbringen*), later Da. *opbringe*, Sw. *uppbringa*.]

**1.** *trans.* To bring up or forth; *fig.* to utter.

*a* 1250 *Owl & Night.* 200 Þo hule one wile hi biþoȝte, & after þan þis word up-broȝte. *c* 1250 *Gen. & Ex.* 3190 Ðor he doluen,..and hauen up-broȝt ðe bones ut of ðe erðe.

**2.** To bring up, to rear. (Cf. Upbrought.)

1297 R. Glouc. (Rolls) 9334 ȝe stalwarde kniȝtes þat þe king henry vp broȝte & honourede. *c* 1375 *Cursor M.* 7924 (Fairf.), [A sheep] þat he had wiþ his siluer boȝt and fra a lambe hit vp-broȝt. 1559 *Mirr. Mag.* (1563) V ij, Beyng one whom earst I had upbrought Euen from his youth.

**3.** To bring forth, produce.

*c* 1440 *Pallad. on Husb.* I. 1005 Right as chaff and donge is profitable On rootis, and vpbryngith breed & wynys. *Ibid.* IV. 681 They oned thus, fruyt of dyuers colour Vpbrynge.

**4.** To raise up, exalt.

1513 Douglas *Æneid* VII. ii. 167 Sic ane air [= heir], Quhilk sall our name abuf the sternis wpbring.

**Upbri·nger.** (Up- 8. Cf. prec. 2.) 1599 Jas. I Βασιλ. Δωρον (1603) 97 Honour also..your gouernours, vp-bringers, and Præceptours.

**U·pbri:nging,** *vbl. sb.* [Up- 7.]

**†1.** The action of building. *Obs.*[-1]

1484 *Extr. Aberd. Reg.* (1844) I. 41 Johne Gray, mason,.. has takin upon him to be..diligent for the vpbringing of the said [St. Nicholas'] wark.

**2.** The action of bringing up young persons; the fact of being brought up while young, or the manner of this; early rearing and training. (Cf. Bringing *vbl. sb.* 3.)

Rare in older Eng. use, but common in Scottish in the second half of the 16th c., and occasionally used by later Scottish writers. In general use only from *c* 1870.

1520 *Calisto & Melib.* C iv b, They can not well labour in dede Be cause in youth of theyr ydyll vpbryngyng. 1568 Fulwell *Like will to Like* E ij, All licenciously was my vp bringing. 1584 Hudson *Du Bartas' Judith* IV. (1611) 45 One of the Captains..discriving, to another, her stock and vpbringing. *a* 1670 Spalding *Troub. Chas. I* (1850) I. 139 The maisteris..of the said college, who cairfullie attendit thair callinges for vpbringing of the youth. 1678 R. Barclay *Apol. Quakers* v. § 23. 173 Men..have the Eye of the Soul darkned or dimmed through Evil up-bringing and Learning. 1822 Carlyle *Let.* in Froude *Life* (1882) I. 171 What have I done to..reward those that had the trouble of my upbringing? 1831 — *Sart. Res.* II. ii, Let me not quarrel with my upbringing! 1864 Burton *Scot Abr.* I. ii. 95 Preserving no traces of the influence of their..hard upbringing. 1873 Morley *Rousseau* II. 197 The theory and art of the upbringing of the young.

**Upbri·stled,** *ppl. a.* (Up- 6 b.) *c* 1611 Chapman *Iliad* II. 126 Zephyr's vehement gusts..make the stiff up-bristled ears [of corn] do homage to his breath. 1885 C. J. Lyall tr. *Anc. Arab. Poet.* 113 A lion with angry mane upbristled.

**† Upbri·xle.** *Obs.*[-1] [Up- 2 (cf. Upbraid *v.*) + ON. *brigzl*, *brigzli* reproach, shame, f. *bregða* (see Braid *v.*[2]). Cf. MSw. *upbrygdhilse*, MDa. *obrygdhilse*, *opbryksel*.] Reproach, scorn.

*c* 1200 Ormin 4871 Icc amm an wurrm, & nohht nan mann, Uppbrixle menn bitwenenn.

**†Upbroi·d,** *v. Obs.*[-1] [Up- 4 + Broid *v.*[1]] *trans.* To entangle. 1387 Trevisa *Higden* (Rolls) VII. 431 Þe kyng maked [them]..appose þe cardinales..and upbroyde [*v.r.* upbreide] hem..wiþ sotil sophyms.

**Upbrou·ght,** *pa. pple.* (Up- 5. Cf. Upbring *v.* 2.)

*c* 1375 *Sc. Leg. Saints* xxxiv. (*Pelagia*) 291 A dekine, þat wes vpe-brocht with bischope veron. ? *c* 1470 G. Ashby *Active Policy* 473 Also chese your servantes.., Remembryng with whom thei haue be vpbraught. 1520 *Calisto & Melib.* C iv b, As long as yong pepyll be euell vpbrought. 1596 Spenser *F. Q.* VI. vi. 9 That same beast was bred of hellish strene, And long in darksome Stygian den vpbrought. *Ibid.* I. ix. 3, etc. 1899 in *Eng. Dial. Dict.* s.v. Up *adv.* I.

**U·p-brow.** *Coal-mining.* [Up- 2 b + Brow *sb.*[1] 8.] (See quots.)

1867 W. W. Smyth *Coal & Coal-mining* 135 The bays..will be connected with the main roads by pairs of drifts (upbrows) carried up the rise of the seam; or sometimes..by down-brows. 1883 Gresley *Gloss. Coal-m.* 268 *Up-brow*, an inclined plane worked to the rise.

**† Upbrud.** *Obs. rare.* [f. Up- 2 (cf. Upbraid *sb.*) + OE. *brȳd*, **brygd*, related to *bregdan* Braid *v.*[1], *v.*[2]] Reproach.

*a* 1225 *Ancr. R.* 108 In his earen he hefde..al þet edwit, & al þet upbrud, & al þe schorn..þet earen muhte iheren. *c* 1230 *Hali Meid.* 33 Hit is..to al his cun schome, vpbrud in uuel muð, tale bimong alle.

**Upbui·ld,** *v.* (Up- 4.) Also **Upbui·lded, -bui·lt; -bui·lder; -bui·lding.**

1513 Douglas *Æneid* VIII. iv. 191 Potitius..Ȝone altar in this cuchill did vpbeild. 1570 *Satir. Poems Reform.* xxii. 43 This baillfull bird richt beinly can vpbeild..hir noysum nest. 1850 Blackie *Æschylus* I. 235, I will upbuild His house who honours thee. 1890 J. Pulsford *Loyalty to Christ* I. 47 We..should be careful to..upbuild our energies, equally from God and from Nature. 1865 J. H. Ingraham *Pillar of Fire* xvi. 188 Each [pyramid], had not the others been *upbuilded, would have been a marvel of grandeur. 1882 *Proc. Soc. Psychical Research* I. II. 149 The science of zoology could not have been upbuilt without it. 1865 E. Burritt *Walk to Land's End* 409 The chief *upbuilders of the place in its industrial enterprise. 1732 E. Erskine *Wks.* (1791) 647/2 A whole Trinity..lay themselves out..for the *upbuilding of this house. 1876 Fairbairn in *Contemp. Rev.* June 138 What he terms its development or upbuilding may be termed its diseased growth. 1898 B. Gregory *Side Lights Confl. Meth.* 379 The impression..was in a high degree..bracing and upbuilding.

**Upbuoy·ance.** (Up- 2.) ?1799 Coleridge *Visit of Gods* 13 Me rather, bright guests! with your wings of upbuoyance Bear aloft to your homes.

**U·pburst.** [Up- 2.] An upward outburst or outbreak.

1843 *Penny Cycl.* XXVI. 424/2 A violent upburst of clouds of scoriæ and ashes. 1872 Bp. Forbes *Kal. Sc. Saints* 290 A scarped upburst of trap-rock out of the surrounding red sandstone. 1876 Mrs. Whitney *Sights & Ins.* II. xxxv. 642 The great upburst of gladness.

**Upbursting,** *ppl. a.*: see Up- 6 b.

**Up-by·,** *adv. Sc.* (and *north. dial.*). Also upbye. [f. Up *adv.*$^2$ 2, 8 d + By *adv.* 2. Cf. In-, Outby.] Up there; up at (or to) a particular place (*spec.* a 'great house' or mansion).

1768 Ross *Helenore* I. 8 Up by the lambie's lying yonder styth. 1816 Scott *Bl. Dwarf* ii, She sits in the neuk yonder, upbye. 1830 J. Wilson *Chr. North* (1856) III. 37 Wha can see the..cairn up-by yonder, when a' the haill heaven is ae coal-cloud? 1871 W. Alexander *Johnny Gibb* xix, Inveetin' the coachman..up bye, aifter Sir Simon gaed awa'.

**Upcall**: see Up- 4.

**U·pcast,** *sb.* Also 9 *dial.* upkest. [Up- 2. Cf. MDa. *opkast* in sense 6.]

1. A chance or accident. *rare.*

1611 Shaks. *Cymb.* ii. i. 2 Was there euer man had such lucke? When I kist the Iacke vpon an vp-cast, to be hit away? 1619 Drayton *Legends, P. Gaveston* cvii, Only some small force..For vs to trust to, Fortune had vs left, On which our Hopes, vpon this Vpcast lay. 1897 Rhoscomyl *White Rose Arno* 131 Pengraig..hoped that he might by some marvellous upcast succeed in overhauling the escaped scoundrel.

2. *Sc.* and *north. dial.* A reproach or taunt; a ground or occasion of reproach.

1681 R. Fleming *Fulfilling of Script.* (ed. 3) 51 This did never occasion bitter reflexions, or was their upcast before the World. 1681 P. Forman in Thomson *Cloud of Witnesses* (1871) 205 Ye are an upcast to poor sufferers. 1825 Brockett *N. C. Gloss.* s.v. 1863 Jean L. Watson *By-gone Days* 124 If she will only come back again, she will never get an upcast frae me nor mine. 1878– in *Eng. Dial. Dict.* (Sc., Cumb., N. Irel.).

3. *Mining* and *Geol.* An upward dislocation or shifting of a seam or stratum; a fault caused by this. (Cf. Upcast *ppl. a.* 3.)

Used in contrast to Downcast or Downthrow.

1793 [Earl Dundonald] *Descr. Estate of Culross* 31 The Proprietors..found their Coals after working to a certain depth, thrown up to the north, by an up-cast, as it is commonly called. 1839 Murchison *Silur. Syst.* i. xxxvii. 510 The upcasts of the various coalfields. 1842 Sedgwick in *Hudson's Guide Lakes* (1843) 200 A great cleft or 'fault'..producing such an enormous 'upcast' towards the N.E., that the carboniferous beds..are on the other side of it. 1872 W. S. Symonds *Rec. Rocks* v. 148 The extraordinary upcast of Silurian rocks in Marloes Bay.

4. *Upcast shaft* (or *pit*), the pit-shaft by which the ventilating air of a mine is returned to the surface.

1816 [see Downcast *sb.* 2]. 1839 Ure *Dict. Arts* 987 The air of the upcast pit being rarefied by the heat. 1867 W. W. Smyth *Coal & Coal-mining* 207 If a really large volume of air be required, we must heat the full height of the column in the upcast shaft.

*ellipt.* 1839 Ure *Dict. Arts* 971 Pit of ventilation or upcast for the smoke. 1864 A. Miller *Rise & Progr. Coatbridge* xxv. 169 The air..is conveyed round the whole of the workings, and guided by air courses to the upcast.

b. A casting or hurling upward; a cast or throw in an upward direction.

1890 *Nature* 6 Nov. 16/1 The 'upcast' to which the air must be subject in a cyclone.

5. *Sc.* An upset.

1824 Scott *St. Ronan's* xxviii, What wi' the upcast and terror..my head is sair eneugh distressed.

6. Material thrown up in digging, etc.

1883 Whitelaw *Sophocles, Antigone* 250 No mattock's stroke indeed, Nor spade's upcast was there. 1891 G. Neilson *Per Lineam Valli* 3 Outside..there lies a vast heap of promiscuous earth, the 'upcast' from the trench.

**Upca·st,** *v.* [Up- 4. Cf. Cast *v.* 83 and MSw. *up-, opkasta*, Sw. *uppkasta*, (M)Da. *opkaste* in sense 3.]

†1. *trans.* To utter loudly. *Obs.*

*Cast up* also occurs in this sense in ME.

13.. *E. E. Allit. P.* B. 1574 Þis cry was vp-caste, & þer comen mony Clerkes out of caldye. a 1400 *Rom. Rose* 7129 The vniuersite..Gan forto braide..at the noys the heed vpcast.

†2. To open or turn up (the eyes). *Obs.*

1390 Gower *Conf.* II. 103 His slombrende yhen he upcaste, And seide [etc.].

3. To cast, throw, or toss up.

c 1386 Chaucer *Man of Law's T.* 808 (Lansd. MS.), Att þe last..Custance and eke hir childe þe see vpkast. 1390 Gower *Conf.* III. 314 At Ephesim the See upcaste The cofre. 1608 Topsell *Serpents* 269 The female..Out of web-breeding-belly..vp-casting twine. 1850 Blackie *Æschylus* II. 180 This brave Capaneus..upcasts Loud billowy boasts in Jove's high face. 1862 Lytton *Str. Story* II. 352 The atoms upcast by the light of the moon. 1875 Morris *Æneid* i. 84 The winds..driving down upon the sea its lowest deeps upcast.

†4. *Sc.* To throw or force open (a gate). *Obs.*

c 1425 Wyntoun *Cron.* viii. xi. 1757 All þe ȝettis þai vpkest [*v.r.* wpcast], To lat þaim entir. 1533 Bellenden *Livy* v. viii. (S.T.S.) II. 176 The portis [war] brokin and vpcassin.

5. *Sc.* and *north. dial.* To bring up against one; to cast in one's teeth; to allege as a fault.

1825 Brockett *N. C. Gloss., Upcast*, to upbraid. 1850 Blackie *Æschylus* II. 186 Thy brother too..He whips with keen reproaches, and upcasts With bitter taunts his evil-omened name. 1865– in *Eng. Dial. Dict.* (Sc., N. Irel., Northumb., etc.).

**U·pcast,** *ppl. a.* [Up- 5. In predicative use *upca·st.*]

1. Of the eye or look: Turned or directed upwards.

c 1402 Lydg. *Compl. Bl. Knt.* 216 Lying in a traunce. With loke up-cast. 1412–20 — *Chron. Troy* iv. 1481 With eye vp-cast in rancour and in Ire. 1676 Dryden *State Innoc.* ii. ii, Beasts with up-cast eyes forsake their Shade. 1715 Addison *To Sir G. Kneller* 61 Old Saturn too with upcast eyes Beheld his abdicated skies. 1816 Keats '*I stood Tip-toe*' 122 Lover of loneliness,..Of upcast eye, and tender pondering! 1887 J. Ker *Serm.* Ser. ii. xiv. 210 With that upcast look to Christ's face.

2. Raised up, prominent. *rare*$^{-1}$.

1658 A. Fox tr. *Wurtz' Surg.* ii. x. 87 Do not stitch [the wound]; ..it would cause an ugly up-cast scarr.

3. *Upcast dyke* (in mining), = Upcast *sb.* 3.

1810 J. Bailey *Agric. Durham* 29 They are denominated up-cast dykes, and down-cast dykes, as the strata are cast up or down, according to the direction in which the colliery is working. 1825 E. Mackenzie *View Northumbld.* (ed. 2) I. 82 When the miner finds the vein he has been working thrown below his feet, he calls it a Downcast Dike; but if it be thrown upwards it is then an Upcast Dike.

4. Cast, thrown, or tossed upwards.

1823 Joanna Baillie *Poems* 260 The mighty Geyser's upcast stream. 1827 Carlyle *Richter, Misc.* (1840) I. 29 Close by their outer churchyards, where crumbled upcast coffin-boards were glimmering. 1892 *Pall Mall G.* 21 Sept. 6/1 The usual upcast spray of water [of a fountain].

**Upca·sting,** *vbl. sb.* [Up- 7.] The action or result of casting or throwing up, in various senses.

[1250–68 *Cockersand Chartul.* (Chetham Soc.) 899 Aliud latus prædictæ terræ jacet ad Houpcastinges terræ meæ.] c 1450 *Mirk's Festial* 172 But when he schuld dye, he myȝt not receue hit [*sc.* the sacrament] for vpcasting. 1808 Jamieson, *Upcasting*, the rising of clouds above the horizon, especially as threatening rain. 1819 W. Tennant *Papistry Storm'd* (1827) 185 A black up-castin' [of clouds], with ane rim o' darkness. 1882 *Proc. Berw. Nat. Club* X. i. 11 Bare ..rounded hills, with..yellow up-castings of soil indicating the retreats of rabbits.

**Upca·tch,** *v.*, **-caught,** *pa. pple.* (Up- 4, 5.)

a 1560 Phaer *Æneid* ix. (1562) Ff 1 b, The wynds vpcaught y$^t$ strocke and Iuno quene ye daunger brake. 1590 Spenser *F. Q.* iii. v. 24 He..His bootelesse bow in feeble hand vpcaught. a 1711 Ken *Psyche* Poet. Wks. 1721 IV. 269 He Psyche, as he Jesus once, upcaught. 1791 Cowper *Odyssey* xii. 118 With ev'ry mouth She bears upcaught a mariner away. 1820 Wordsw. *To Enterprise* 132 Withered leaves, from earth's cold breast Up-caught in whirlwinds, nowhere can find rest.

† **Upchee·r,** *v. Obs. rare.* [Up- 4.] *trans.* To cheer up, to encourage.

c 1586 C'tess Pembroke *Ps.* lv. vi, But, my ore loaden soule, thy selfe upcheare. 1596 Spenser *F. Q.* vi. i. 44 Who comming forth yet full of late affray, Sir Calidore vpcheard.

**Upchoked**: see Up- 5.

**Upcli·mb,** *v.* [Up- 4. Cf. NFris. *upklêm*, MDu. *opclimmen*, *-climmen* (Du. *opklimmen*), MLG. *upklemmen*, MHG. *ûfklimmen* (G. *aufklimmen*).] *intr.* and *trans.* To climb up; to ascend. Also **Upcli·mber, -cli·mbing.**

1546 Joye *Declar.* xcii b, His arrogant vpcliminge and extollinge of him selfe aboue god. 1582 Stanyhurst *Æneis* ii. (Arb.) 54, I run forward.., Wheare shouts vpclymbing most rise. 1600 Fairfax *Tasso* xviii. xci, Farre in the aire vp clombe the fortresse tall, Higher than..church or towre. 1816 *Monthly Mag.* XLI. 527 Some promise to upclimb the light-house spire. 1845 Mangan *German Anthology* II. 133 To the topmost peak upclomb The conquerors in that bloody fray! 1878 T. Sinclair *Mount* 274 To show sincere students and upclimbers some of the footsteps of their predecessors.

**Upclo·se,** *v.* [Up- 4.] *trans.* and *intr.* To close up, in various senses.

c 1440 *Pallad. on Husb.* i. 921 Good is..With affadille vp close her holis alle. c 1590 J. Stewart *Poems* (S.T.S.) II. 63/235 The ring scho did vpclois In till hir mouth. 1603 Bp. Hall *Kings Proph.* xiii, Eliza dyde, and with the closing yeare Her dayes vpclosde. 1868 Arnold *Lines Kensington Gardens* ix, The flowers upclose, the birds are fed. 1898 T. Hardy *Wessex Poems* 173 Now that my page upcloses,..Never to press thy cosy cushions more.

**Upclo·sed,** *pa. pple.*, **Upclo·ser.** (Up- 5, 8.)

c 1450 Lydg. *Secrees* 429, I lakke language breffly for to telle The bawme vpclosyd in your tresourye. a 1566 Glencairn in Knox *Hist. Ref.* (1846) I. 73 The upclosars of Heavins yett; Cankcarit corruptars of the Creid.

**U·p-coast,** *a.* [Up *prep.*$^2$] Situated, extending, etc., further up the coast.

1882 De Windt *Equator* 38 The Resident of one of the up-coast districts. 1900 *Daily News* 16 Jan. 5/2 The column started last night by the up-coast railway line.

**U·pcome,** *sb.* Chiefly *Sc.* [Up- 2.]

1. *Sc.* Way up, ascent. *rare.*

1375 Barbour *Bruce* vi. 167 The vpcom wes then Dittit with slayn hors and men. 1866 Gregor *Banffshire Gloss.* 204.

2. *Sc.* Outward appearance (of a person). ? *Obs.*

Jamieson (1808) suggests that the idea is 'probably borrowed from the first appearance of the..blade after sowing'.

? a 1630 D. Hume *Hist. Ho. Douglas* (1644) 235 A Courtier ..cast in a word of doubting and disparaging: It is true, said he, if all be good that is up-come; meaning if his action and valour were answerable to his personage and body. 1819 [A. Balfour] *Campbell* I. 27, I hae nae doubt o' his abilities, for he promises fair according to his up-come. [1819 Scott *Leg. Montrose* iv, 'A stout fellow,' replied Anderson, 'if all be good that is upcome'. 1823 — *Quentin D.* vii, You should be a right man-at-arms, if all be good that is upcome.]

3. *Sc.* The final or decisive point.

1824 Scott *Redgauntlet* let. iii, My portrait is..scandalously caricatured. *I* fail or quail in spirit at the upcome!

4. The result, yield, or produce.

c 1874 C. Patmore in Champneys *Mem.* (1900) I. 250 The upcome of a year can be reaped in one fine day. 1887 *Sat. Rev.* 11 June 821/1 The positive..upcome of this last of Mr. Gladstone's perambulations.

**Upco·me,** *v. rare.* [Up- 4. Cf. WFris. *opkomme*, MDu. *opcomen* (Du. *opkomen*), MLG. *upkomen*, MHG. *ûfkomen* (G. *aufkommen*), MSw. *up-, opkoma, -komme* (Sw. *uppkomma*), (M)Da. *opkomme.*] *intr.* To come, spring, or rise up.

c 1000 *Ags. Gosp.* Mark iv. 17 Syþþan upcymð deofles costnung. c 1200 Ormin 1267 ȝiff þu..ȝeornesst tatt tu mote sket Uppcumenn inntill heoffne. c 1400 *Master of Game* (MS. Digby 182) xxiv, Of corne and of oþer thynges that vppe commeth of þe londe. 1828 Atherstone *Fall of Nineveh* I. 48 In a moment more, Upcame the monstrous universal shout.

**Upco·ming,** *vbl. sb.* [Up- 7.]

1. The action of coming up, in various senses.

13.. *Guy Warw.* (A.) 7240 Þe best him neyed, & smot him Wiþ his vp-coming so fel & grim [etc.]. a 1340 Hampole *Psalter* lxxii. 19 Þai fal downe þat lang tyme had in vp-comminge. 1387 Trevisa *Higden* (Rolls) V. 229 Me dradde þe arryvynge and upcomynge of straunge men. 1535 Stewart *Cron. Scot.* (Rolls) II. 700 Of the Scrymgeouris and thair Vpcuming. a 1575 *Diurn. Occurr.* (Bann. Cl.) 109 In thair vpcuming my lord of Ergyle bare the croun. 1654 Wariston *Diary* (S.H.S.) II. 292 This checked me in the up-coming out of Leyth. 1746 E. Erskine *Serm.* (1755) 391 The Up-coming of the Breaker is with much awful Majesty. 1862 Carlyle *Fredk. Gt.* xiii. ix. III. 524 In his young time he had a hard upcoming. 1889 *Athenæum* 29 June 831/2 Half-lights reveal on the surface the upcoming of eddies in films from below.

†2. *Sc.* An ascent, an upward path. *Obs.* (Cf. Upcome *sb.* 1.)

1375 Barbour *Bruce* vi. 81 Sua strate wes þe vp-cummyng, Þat twa men mycht nocht sammyn thryng. *Ibid.* 170.

**U·pco·ming,** *ppl. a.* (Up- 6 b.) 1848 T. Aird *Nebuchadnezzar* iii. 12 Upcoming hunters on the hill appear. 1879 McCarthy *Own Times* II. 169 Personal reasons..for particular distrust of the upcoming Emperor.

**U·p-country, up-cou·ntry,** *sb.*, *a.*, and *adv.* [Up *a.* and *prep.*$^2$]

As adv. and adj. the phrase is current in English dialects (cf. quot. 1688), but the general 19th century use originated partly in India and partly in the United States; from c 1875 it has also been employed in, or with reference to, Australia, South Africa, etc.

1. *sb.* † a. An uplying or inland district. *Obs.*

1688 R. Holme *Armoury* iii. 352/2 A Pit Saw in a Frame ..is not in use with us, but in the Up Countreys.

b. The inland part of a country.

Used without article, or with *the.*

(*a*) 1837 [Mrs. Maitland] *Lett. fr. Madras* (1843) 110, I continue to like 'up country', as they call it, far better than the Presidency. 1888 [D'Avigdor] *Antipod. Notes* v. 30 Thousands from up-country make their annual business visit to the capital. 1897 P. Warung *Tales Old Régime* 162 To say good-bye before leaving for up-country.

(*b*) 1872 De Vere *Americanisms* 163 The nearest districts became early known..as the Up Country. 1894 *Cent. Mag.* April 849 Later generations in the up-country have applied the word to the products of corn after cooking.

2. *adj.* Situated in, belonging or relating to, etc., the inland part of a country.

1835 Macaulay in Trevelyan *Life* (1876) I. 406 Any [library] which would be readily accessible at an up-country station [in India]. 1861 Clough *Mari Magno* 29 What racy tales of Yankeeland he had! Up-country girl, up-country farmer lad. 1874 Ranken *Domin. Australia* xiii. 237 The 'up-country store-keeper'..sells everything wholesale or retail. 1884 *Health Exhib. Catal.* p. xliii, Models..of European up-country bungalows, and..of a bazaar in an up-country town.

3. *adv.* In or to the inland part of a country.

1864 Trevelyan *Compet. Wallah* 31 A young couple going to an appointment up-country. 1889 'J. S. Winter' *Mrs. Bob* iii, Whilst we were up-country,..we met Colonel Coles. 1891 Kipling *Light that Failed* ii, I'm going up-country with a column.

†**Upco·vering,** *vbl. sb. Obs.*$^{-1}$ [Up- 7 + Cover *v.*$^2$ 4. Cf. *upkever*, Up- 4.] Recovery. a 1300 *Cursor M.* 25821 Suagat for þair wanhopping þai fall wit-vten vp-couering.

†**Upcree·per.** *Obs.*$^{-1}$ (Up- 8.) c 1534 *Image Hypocr.* i. 531 in *Skelton's Wks.* (1843) II. 429 Thou arte a cursed crekar, a crafty vppcrepar.

**Upcu·rl,** *v.* [Up- 4.] To curl up.

*trans.* 1801 Southey *Thalaba* iv. xxxi, High, high in heaven upcurl'd The dreadful sand-spouts moved. 1852 M. Arnold *Tristr. & Iseult* iii. 118 The..furnace of the world, In whose hot air our spirits are upcurled Until they crumble. 1895 F. Thompson *Sister Songs* 3 Ere..Thou disclose my flower of song upcurled..!

*intr.* 1838 Mary Howitt *Birds & Flowers* 189 Where the branching ferns up-curl. 1845 Mangan *German Anthology* II. 126 A stupendous column of sand..upcurls..in eddies and whirls.

**Upcu·rling,** *vbl. sb.* (Up- 7. Cf. prec.) 1828 *Lights & Shades* II. 185 The up-curling of its widely-dilated nostrils.

**Upcurved,** *pa. pple.* and *ppl. a.* (Up- 5.)

1870 Hooker *Stud. Flora* 183 Bracts upcurved. 1875 Darwin *Insectiv. Pl.* xiv. 328 Covered..near their extremities with upcurved prickles. 1893 *Athenæum* 1 April 399/2 Avocets with up-curved bills.

**Upcyne,** see note to Uptie *sb.*

**Upda·rt,** *v.*, etc. (Up- 4, 5, and 6.)

1722 J. Jones tr. *Oppian's Halieuticks* iii. 143 The Barbel, when encircling Seines inclose,..O'er Battlements of Cork up-darting flies. 1791 Cowper *Iliad* xv. 102 So swift updarted Juno to the skies. 1799 H. Gurney *Cupid & Psyche* 42 High o'er the dragons he will tower Updarting thro' the azure air.

**Updelve, -dive, -drag**: see Up- 4.

†**U·pdraught.** *Obs. rare.* [Up- 2. Cf. Draught *sb.* 23.] = Indraught 3.

14.. *Sailing Direct.* (Hakl. Soc.) 15 A south west mone makith hiest watir by the see coste, and in the updraughtis it dooth not so. *Ibid.* 19.

**Updraw·,** *v.* [Up- 4. Cf. (M)Du. *opdragen*, MLG. *updragen*, *-dregen*, LG. *updragen*, MHG. *ûftragen* (G. *auf-*), MSw. *updragha* (Sw. *uppdraga*), (M)Da. *opdrage.*]

†1. *trans.* To pull out of the ground. Also *fig.*
c 1290 *Holy Rood* 165 in *S. Eng. Leg.* I. 6 He ne miȝte nouȝt aboute þe eorþe swinke, ne þe weodes up drawe. a 1300 *Cursor M.* 6330 Bot moyses..þaa wandes durst he noght vp-drau [*Fairf.* vpdragh]. 13.. *K. Alis.* 2633 (Laud MS.), In þe grounde it stiked fast,..non ne miȝt it vp-drawe. c 1449 Pecock *Repr.* I. ii. 8 Forto meete aȝens the firste bifore spoken opinioun, and forto vnroote and vpdrawe it.

2. To draw up to a height or from a lower place; also, to draw (a bow) to the full.
c 1300 *Havelok* 932 He kam to þe welle, water vp-drow. 13.. *Seuyn Sages* (W.) 2682 Ich wil fol fawe Heghe him honge and vpdrawe. 1390 Gower *Conf.* II. 295 Bardus with his Asse anon Him hath updrawe [*sc.* out of a pit]. c 1440 *Bone Flor.* 532 Ye schoulde..close the yatys, and the brygges up drawe. 1508 Dunbar *Flyting* 90 Thow saw the saill abuif my heid vpdraw. 1600 Fairfax *Tasso* xx. lxiii, Three times her angrie hand the bow vp drew. 1667 Milton *P. L.* II. 874 She..Forthwith the huge Portcullis high up drew. 1791 Cowper *Iliad* I. 597 Their galley they up-drew..From the rude surge remote. 1813 Hogg *Queen's Wake, Glen-Airn* xxviii, Dawning in the air updrew From many a..hill, Her folding robe of fairy blue.

b. *fig.* To bring up before the mind.
1828 Tennyson *Lover's Tale* I. 634 If so be that the echo of that name..had updrawn..a phantasm of the form.

†3. To bring up, to rear. *Obs.*—¹
1390 Gower *Conf.* I. 186 A knyht, whom fro childhode He hadde updrawe into manhode.

**Updraw·n**, *pa. pple.* and *ppl. a.* (Up- 5, 6 b. Cf. prec.)
c 1250 *Gen. & Ex.* 1858 Folc of salem ðor-fore was slaȝen, wiwes, and childre, and aȝte up-draȝen. 1390 Gower *Conf.* II. 238 Fro his lond with sail updrawe Thei wente hem forth. 1582 Stanyhurst *Æneis* III. (Arb.) 79 Oure vessels vpdrawne are grapled at anchor. 1667 Milton *P. L.* IV. 228 The rapid current,..with kindly thirst up drawn. 1762 Falconer *Shipwr.* II. 485 The sounding cord, Updrawn, an undiminish'd depth explor'd. 1866 Lytton *Lost Tales Miletus, Secret Way* 6 As cloud, from purest dews Updrawn, makes sorrowful a star in heaven. 1887 M. Arnold *Ess. Crit.* Ser. II. (1888) 261 Alexis Karénine's updrawn eyebrows. 1901 *Daily Chron.* 26 Aug. 3/5 A tree..has fallen, and the up-drawn roots form a bridge.

**Updre·ss**, *v.* (Up- 4.)
a 1400 *Rom. Rose* 7067 That he wolde vpdresse Engyns bothe more and lesse To cast at vs by euery side. a 1500 *Chaucer's Dreme* 662 Right in his wo he gan to braid, And him vp dresses for to knele. 1600 Fairfax *Tasso* XVI. xxiii, Her curles garland wise she did vpdresse.

**Updrie·d**, *pa. pple.* (Up- 5.) Also **Updry·** *v.*, **Updry·ing** *vbl. sb.*
c 1440 *Pallad. on Husb.* I. 238 Lupyne and ficchis slayn, and on their roote Vpdried, are..londis boote. 1530 Lyndesay *Test. Papyngo* 138 The balmy droppis of dew Tytane vpdryis. c 1586 C'tess Pembroke *Ps.* LXVI. iii, The sea up dried by his hand, Became a field of dusty sand. 1658 A. Fox tr. *Würtz' Surg.* III. xxiii. 290 That updrying..comes from an oppilation of that member, be that caused from what it will.

**Updrinking**, *vbl. sb.* [Up- 7.] (See quot. and cf. Upsitting.) 1819 [A. Balfour] *Campbell* I. 13 At the feast given on my mother's recovery, which in that part of the country was termed the up-drinking. **Upeat**: see Up- 4.
† **Upen**, obs. var. Open *a.* (Cf. Upon *a.*) 13.. *E. E. Allit. P.* A. 1066 Þe ȝates stoken was neuer ȝet Bot euer more vpen at vche a lone.

**Up-e·nd**, *v.* Orig. *dial.* [Up *adv.*¹]
1. *trans.* To set (something) on its end; to turn end upwards; *dial.* to set (also *refl.*, to get) on one's feet.
1823 E. Moor *Suffolk Words* 460 *Upinnd*, to set a cask or any thing on its end. 1868 *Rep. to Govt. U. S. Munitions War* 274 The bursting of a few shells..tearing, up-ending, and setting fire to the planking of the latter [deck]. 1874 Bedford *Sailor's Pocket Bk.* 173 An approaching heavy sea may carry the boat away..and turn it broadside on, or up-end it. 1900 H. Lawson *Over Sliprails* 29 It crawled to the wall, against which it slowly and painfully up-ended itself.
b. In pa. pple.: Sitting up.
1874 E. Waugh *Chimney Corner* (1879) 123, I left him about two minutes sin' up-ended i' bed.
2. *intr.* To rise up on end.
1897 Kipling *Capt. Cour.* 52 They up-eend thet way when they're hungry. 1902 S. E. White *Blazed Trail* xxxii, A log in the advance up-ended; another thrust under it.
Hence **Up-ended** *ppl. a.*
1880 'Mark Twain' *Tramp Abr.* xlvii. 488 Propping them..with her up-ended valise. 1896 C. Allen *Papier Mâché* 121 The up-ended box whereon the student was perched.

**Upfi·ll**, *v.* [Up- 4. Cf. MSw. *upfylla* (Sw. *upp-*), MDa. *upfylle*, Du. *opvullen*.] *trans.* To fill up. Also **Upfi·lled** *pa. pple.*
c 1440 *Pallad. on Husb.* XII. 350 So braunches fewe vpfille a huge londe. 1592 Shaks. *Rom. & Jul.* II. iii. 7, I must vpfill this Osier Cage of ours, With balefull weedes. 1596 Spenser *F. Q.* IV. iii. 42 A cup she hild, The which was with Nepenthe to the brim vpfild. 1861 *Macm. Mag.* June 134 A fine tree..that upfilled a picture with cows or haymakers beneath it.

**Upfi·lling.** [Up- 7. Cf. prec.] Something which serves to fill up.
1822 G. Young *Geol. Surv.* 168 The red sandstone..occupying the valleys in the form of what has been called an upfilling. 1833-4 *Encycl. Metrop.* VI. 705/2 At length the originally rugged chasm is changed by additions and upfillings into the smooth, evenly declining hollow. 1844 H. Stephens *Bk. Farm* III. 810 A gate to be permanent, should be..a simple rectangular frame without upfillings.
†**Upfi·nder.** *Obs.*—¹ [Up- 8.] A deviser. 1430-40 Lydg. *Bochas* IX. 482 Double of hir tunge, vpfyndere of tresoun.

**U·pfloor.** [ad. OE. *upflór*: Up- 1.] A triforium.
This special application is derived from the use of the word with reference to the church at Glastonbury in the *O. E. Chron.* (Laud MS.), an. 1083.
1879 A. Taylor *Guienne* 12 Our ancestors..gave the triforium (then lately devised) the vernacular English name of 'upfloor'. 1912 C. E. Power *Eng. Mediæv. Archit.* I. 20 The 'triforium chamber' or 'up-floor' of monastic writers.

**U·pflow**, *sb.* (Up- 2.) 1871 *Contemp. Rev.* XIX. 40 This incessant out-flow or up-flow (if the physicist will permit the latter word). 1890 *Philos. Mag.* Dec. 501 The final results of the upflow of air limited as to space. *Ibid.*, The strata of air surrounding the upflow. **U·pfold**, *sb. Geol.* [Up- 2.] = Anticline. 1902 Mackinder *Britain & Brit. Seas* vi. 80 The Mendip Range..is a complete upfold of carboniferous limestone.

**Upfo·ld**, *v.* [Up- 4. Cf. LG. *upfolden*, G. *auffalten*.] *trans.* To fold up, fold together; † to raise, push up. Also **Upfo·lded**, †**-fo·lden** *pa. pple.*
13.. *E. E. Allit. P.* B. 643 Abraham, al hodlez with armez vp-folden. a 1460 *Lament. Virgin* in *Chester Plays* (1847) II. 206 The ston owyr hym he can upfolde,..And wente hys wey wherso he wolde. 1600 Fairfax *Tasso* XVI. xiv, The gentle budding rose..her beauties doth vpfold In their deare leaues. 1822 J. Wilson *Lights & Shadows Sc. Life* 342 The leaves yet upfolded might almost be heard budding in the bower. 1878 E. Jones *Sens. & Event* (1879) 200 Come o'er the hills, and pass unto the wold, And all things, as thou passest, in rest upfold.
**Upfollowed, -framed**: see Up- 5.

**Upfu·rled**, *pa. pple.* (Up- 5.)
1818 Keats *Endym.* I. 461 Who, upfurl'd Beneath thy drowsy wing a triple hour, But renovates and lives? 1852 M. Arnold *Parting* 88 Where the white mists, for ever, Are spread and upfurl'd. 1867 G. Macdonald *Disciple*, etc. 32 My roll of ill with theirs upfurled, And flung in deepest hell.

**U·pgang.** Latterly *north. dial.* and *Sc.* [Up- 2. Cf. WFris. *opgong*, Du. *opgang*, OHG. *ûfgang*, *-canc* (MHG. *ûfganc*), ON. *uppgangr* (Norw. *uppgang*, *-gong*); MSw. *up-*, *opgang*, Sw. *uppgång*; MDa. and Da. *opgang*) and *uppganga* (Norw. *uppgonga*).] **a.** The act of ascending; ascension. **b.** An ascent, an upward path or way.
a 900 *Laws Alfred* I. § 25 Ȝif he..æfter sunnan upgonge þis deð, he bið manslеȝes scyldiȝ. 971 *Blickl. Hom.* 201 Hi ne mihton ofer þæt scræf..gongan, ærðon hie ȝerymdon þone upgang. c 1000 *Sax. Leechd.* III. 246 Þas twelf tacna..ȝefyllað twa tida mid hyra upgange oððe nyþergange. 1375 Barbour *Bruce* VI. 141 His hors, that wes born doune, Cummerit thaim the vpgang to ta. *Ibid.* VIII. 38 On the south half, quhar Iames was, Is ane vpgang, ane narrow plas. 1818 Scott *Hrt. Midl.* xxix, Our minny here's rather driegh in the upgang. 1855 [Robinson] *Whitby Gloss.*, *Upgang*,..a track up a hill, as 'Upgang', from the Mulgrave sands to the turnpike on the cliff top.

† **Upganger.** *Obs.* [Up- 8.] (See quot.)
1726 J. Laurence *New Syst. Agric.* 198 Of Brick-Making:..an Up-Ganger, who,..as they become stiff, takes them [*sc.* the new bricks] up, and sets them in Wind-Rows to be dried.

**Upga·ther**, *v.* [Up- 4. Cf. Du. *opgaderen*.] *trans.* To gather up, to collect. Also **U·pgathered** *ppl. a.*, **-ga·thering** *vbl. sb.*
1590 Spenser *Muiopot.* 397 Himselfe he close vpgathered more and more Into his den. 1590 — *F. Q.* III. vi. 19 Soone her garments loose Vpgath'ring, in her bosome she comprized, Well as she might. 1807 Wordsw. *Misc. Sonn.* I. xxxiii, The winds..are up-gathered now like sleeping flowers. 1824 *Examiner* 650/2, I must upgather to the strife the reason that remains. 1851 Longf. *Gold. Leg.* i. ad fin., The stooping sun upgathers his spent shafts. 1883 Ruskin in Collingwood *Life* (1893) I. 223 Any poor little piece of *upgathered silver of my own. 1884 J. Parker *Apost. Life* III. 173 A marvellous *upgathering and focalising of information.

**Upga·ze**, *v.*, etc. (Up- 4, 6, and 7.)
1812 Byron *Ch. Har.* II. liv, Tired of up-gazing still, the wearied eye Reposes gladly [etc.]. 1855 Singleton *Virgil* I. 62 Why, Daphnis, on the ancient risings of the signs Upgaze? 1874 R. Buchanan *Poet. Wks.* III. 122 The shepherds gather'd, Up-gazing dreamily Into the silent air.

† **Upgi·ve**, *v. Sc. Obs.* [Up- 4. Cf. OFris. *op-*, *upieva* (WFris. *opjaen*), (M)Du. *opgeven*, MLG. *upgeven* (LG. *upgäfen*), MHG. *ûfgeben* (G. *auf-*), MSw. *up(p)giva* (Sw. *uppgifva*, *-giva*), Da. *opgive*, Icel. *uppgefa*.]
1. *trans.* To give up, resign, abandon.
1415 *Reg. Mag. Sig. Scot.* (1882) 39/1 Huchon..sal frely delyver and upgif to the sayd Villiam..the sayd landis. 1499 *Munim. de Melros* (Bann. Cl.) 622 Rent..Quhilk..lady Jonet..wpgaif and resignit in our handis. 1513 Douglas *Æneid* XI. iii. 29 Ȝour kyng hes our confiderans vpgeve. 1606 *Munim. de Melros* (Bann. Cl.) 658 To resigne dimit surrander vpgeif and ouergeif..þe maner place of Melrosse. 1652 Z. Boyd in *Zion's Flowers* (1855) App. 26/1 Giveing them full power to upgive the same [*sc.* goods] as if they were given by mine owne mouth. [1840 *Origines Par. Scotiae* I. 440 They upgave to him..the common pasture of Hauden.]
2. To declare, avow. (Cf. Upgiving *vbl. sb.* 2.)
a 1776 *Song Outlaw Murray* lix, And gif you refuse to do that, I freely here upgive with [?*read* to] thee, There will never [etc.].

† **Upgi·ver.** *Sc. Obs.* [Up- 8. Cf. Give *v.* 64 e.] One who furnishes information or particulars (*of* something).
1576 in Balfour *Oppr. Orkney & Shetl.* (1859) 45 Harie Bruce and Thomas Boyne, quha was bayth the upgiffaris of the faltis. 1621 *Sc. Acts Parlt., Jas. VI* (1814) IV. 599/1 [To] caus the pairties vpgevaris of the saidis inventoures everie pairtie subscryve his awin inventar him selff. c 1630 Sir T. Hope *Minor Practicks* (1726) 30 The Caution is holden to be found not by the Minor, but by the Upgiver.

**Upgi·ving**, *vbl. sb. Sc.* [Up- 7.]
1. Surrender; abandonment.
c 1423 *Reg. Mag. Sig. Scot.* (1882) 45/1 For the upgiffin of hys tak of the landdis of Kyrktoun. 1492 *Acta Dom. Conc.* (1839) 246/1 For þe vpgiffing of þe charteris evidentis and all vþer richt þat he haid. 1678 J. Brown *Life of Faith* v. (1726) 121 What could be expected next, but utter upgiving?
† 2. Declaration, presentment. *Obs.*
1574 in C. Rogers *Three Sc. Reformers* (1874) 10 As to my Insprech..I refer to my wifis aith and vpgeving. c 1630 Sir T. Hope *Minor Practicks* (1726) 19 The omitted Benefices, which the Prelates..omitted in the Upgiving of the Rental. a 1670 Spalding *Troub. Chas. I* (1850) I. 338 [He] presentit the subscrivit rollis of the tenthis givin wp be the oath of ilk subscriver, as thay who had commissioun to receave and sie the vpgiveing of the saidis rollis.

**U·pgo**, *sb. dial.* Also *Sc.* **-gae.** [Up- 2.] An ascent; *spec.* a rise in a stratum of rock.
1683 G. Sinclair *Misc. Obs. Hydrost.* 278 Some [strata] again making their rise much more than their course, which they call Up-gaes. 1855 *Whitby Gloss.* 185 *Upgo*, a track up a hill.

**Upgo·**, *v.* [Up- 4. Cf. MDu. *opgaen* (Du. *opgaan*), MLG. *upgân*, MHG. *ûfgân*, *-gen* (G. *aufgehen*), MSw. *up(p)ga*, *op(p)ga*, *-gaa* (Sw. *uppgå*), MDa. and Da. *opgaa*.] *intr.* To go up; to ascend, mount.
c 1250 *Gen. & Ex.* 1608 Iacob..saȝ.., Fro ðe erðe up.., A leddre standen, and ðor-on Angeles dun-cumen and up-gon. c 1440 *Pallad. on Husb.* XI. 139 The tendir plaunte is take anoon & blyue Vpgoth. c 1475 *Golagros & Gaw.* 1151 He gart schir Gawyne vpga. 1513 Douglas *Æneid* VIII. i. 57 Quhill in the ayr vpgois the tuynkilland lycht. 1600 Fairfax *Tasso* XVII. xl, He ceas'd, and then a murmur lowd vp went With noise of ioy. 1791 Cowper *Iliad* XVIII. 1016 Upwent the double roar into the heights Ethereal. 1830 Wordsw. *Egyptian Maid* 183 Then up-went Into the ethereal element The Birds.

**Upgo·ing**, *vbl. sb.* [Up- 7.] The action of going up; *esp.* ascent, ascension.
1555 Watreman *Fardle Facions* App. 315 A faire vp goyng, by a slope bancque of Turfes. 1658 J. Nicoll *Diary* (Bann. Cl.) 211 Upone this accompt..the Scottis Commissioneris, quho wer reddy to pas to Lundoun.., wer stayed from thair upgoing. 1734 E. Erskine *Serm.* Wks. (1791) 697/1, I would speak a little of the solemnity of his [*sc.* Christ's] up-going. 1870 Spurgeon *Treas. Dav.* I. 422 The eye of the psalmist looked..beyond the typical upgoing of the ark to the sublime ascension of the King of glory.

**U·pgo:ing**, *ppl. a.* (Up- 6 b.)
1859 J. Lang *Wand. India* 125 On the down-coming travellers nearing us, the bearers of us—the up-going travellers—called a halt. 1896 *Pop. Sci. Monthly* Feb. 523 The upgoing current..may increase in volume.

**U·p-grade**, *sb.* and *adv.* Orig. *U.S.* [Up- 2 b.]
1. An upward slope or incline.
1888 J. Pennell *Sent. Journey* 236 There were so many long up-grades, and the sign-posts were all wrong. 1893 Kate Sanborn *Truthf. Wom. S. California* 87, I have no taste for overtaking runaway mules on a steep and interminable up-grade.
b. *adv.* Uphill.
1899 *Lutheran* (Phila.) 6 Apr. 327 A railroad train will go for some distance upgrade after the engine is detached.
2. *On the upgrade*, ascending, rising.
1892 *Daily News* 26 Sept. 2/4 In the iron trade..demand seems to be on the up grade.
† **U·pground.** *Obs.*—¹ [Up- 1.] Higher ground; ground above the beach. a 1550 Leland *Itin.* (1768) I. 34 The Shore and upground from Trent Ripe..to Gainesborough is al sandy.

**Upgrow·**, *v.* [Up- 4. Cf. MDa. *opgro*.] *intr.* To grow up, spring up; *fig.* to increase.
c 1430 Lydg. *Min. Poems* (Percy Soc.) 246 In his encrees up-growynge as a flour. c 1440 *Pallad. on Husb.* VII. 77 Yf me wete Her lond, vpgroweth now this herbis sete. 1513 Douglas *Æneid* XI. xi. 14 Ne this luf..of layt in Dyanis breist vpgrew. *Ibid.* XII. viii. 116 Than mair in greif and ire vpgrowis he. 1667 Milton *P. L.* IV. 137 Over head up grew Insuperable highth of loftiest shade. 1791 Cowper *Iliad* II. 810 Tlepolemus spear-famed Had scarce up-grown to manhood's lusty prime. 1848 Clough *Amours de Voy.* III. 90 The cypress-spires..Withering still at the sight which still they upgrow to encounter. 1867 Ld. Houghton *Ess. Reform* 56 Disappointment was not the soil from which a desire for further change upgrew.
**Upgrow·ing**, *vbl. sb.* (Up- 7.) 1430-40 Lydg. *Bochas* II. 2627 The cedre is strong.., In his vpgrowyng riht as any lyne. a 1618 Raleigh *Invent. Shipping* Wks. 1751 II. 87 There are five manifest Causes of the Upgrowing of the Hollanders and Zelanders. **U·pgrow·ing**, *ppl. a.* (Up- 6 b.) 1863 Mrs. Whitney *Faith Gartney's Girlh.* ii. 14 The flower of the upgrowing world. 1895 Clive Holland *Jap. Wife* vii, The responsibilities of a rapidly upgrowing daughter.

**Upgrow·n**, *pa. pple.*, **u·pgrown**, *ppl. a.* [Up- 6, 6 b.] Grown up.
1667 Milton *P. L.* IX. 677 So standing, moving, or to highth upgrown The Tempter all impassiond thus began. 1671 — *P. R.* I. 140 This man born and now up-grown,..henceforth I expose To Satan. 1827 G. Higgins *Celtic Druids* 99 The contests..are only worthy of up-grown babies. 1848 Whewell in Todhunter *Acc. Writ.* (1876) II. 348 A great up-grown body of knowledge. 1895 K. Grahame *Golden Age* 46 To them the inhabited world is composed of..children and upgrown people.

**U·pgrowth.** [Up- 2.]
1. The process or fact of growing up; origination, development.
1844 S. Wilberforce *Hist. Prot. Episc. Ch. Amer.* i. 2 The up-growth of such a body amongst institutions so unlike our own. 1869 A. W. Haddan *Apost. Succession* v. 104 The speedy upgrowth..of contentions and schisms.
2. That which has grown up; a result of growth or development.
1845 Trench *Huls. Lect.* ii. 26 The parts of it being the upgrowth of a single age. 1873 Manning *Serm. Eccl. Subj.* III. p. lxxxiv, The International is a new creation or upgrowth from beneath.
b. *spec.* A raised growth or process.

**1870** ROLLESTON *Anim. Life* 11 The..sixth and seventh [lateral processes] have prominent upgrowths. **1893** BOWER in *Phil. Trans.* B. CLXXXV. 504 Evidence..of the origin of upgrowths (sporangiophores) which would raise the sporangia beyond the surface.

**Upgush, -gushing**: see UP- 2, 6, 7.

† **Uphaˑle,** *v. Obs.* [UP- 4. Cf. (M)Du. *ophalen*, (M)LG. *uphalen*, MHG. *ûfholn* (G. *aufholen*), (M)Da. *ophale*, Sw. *upphala*.] *trans.* To pull or draw up; *fig.* to drink up. Also **Uphaˑled** *pa. pple.*

**14..** in *Pol., Rel., & L. Poems* (1903) 247 The rote of an erbe I sholde vp hale, Men call it chastite. *c* **1540** *Dr. Doubble Ale* 154 in Hazl. *E. P. P.* III. 311 Our Doctour Doubble Ale, Whose countenaunce is neuer pale, So wel good drinke he can vphale. **1582** STANYHURST *Æneis* (Arb.) 19 This Queene.. Downe swasht theyre nauy, thee swelling surges vphaling. *c* **1620** Z. BOYD *Zion's Flowers* (1855) 3 They turn like mist uphaled by the sunne.

**Uˑphaliday.** *Sc. Obs.* exc. *Shetl. dial.* Also 5–6 vphaly (6 -ye) da(y), 6 ouphalliday, uphaldy; 9 vphelly, 9 uphellie, *Shetl.* uphelya, -hellia (day), -helly-a. [f. UP *adv.*[2] 12 a (see quot. 1884) + *haliday* HOLIDAY. Also with omission of *-day* in *uphelly even*, *night*, and in mod. Shetl. forms, in which the final *-a* may stand for *all* adj.]

**1.** The festival of the Epiphany (Jan. 6, Twelfth-day), as the end of the Christmas holidays.

In quot. 1884 the reckoning is by a combination of Old and New Style.

**1478** *Acta Dom. Conc.* (1839) 20/1 Þe lordis continewis þe mater to þe morne efter vphalyday nixt tocum. **1501** *Acc. Ld. High Treas. Scot.* II. 77 The vj day of Januar, Uphalyday, to the Kingis offerand, thre French crounes. **1535** *Burgh Rec. Edinb.* (1871) II. 71 Evin sang in the haly dayes of Yule, New Yeir day, and Vphaly day. **1588** A. KING in *Cath. Tractates* (S.T.S.) 175 Vphaliday when Christ vas reueled first to the gentiles. **1609** SKENE *Reg. Maj., Burrow Lawes* 135 Ane decreit given..vpon Mononday, after Vphaliday. **1884** *Gd. Words* 747 Uphelya, the twenty-fourth day after Yule, and that on which the Holy or holidays are supposed to be 'up'.

**b.** So *Uphalimass* in the same sense.

**1532** *Acc. Ld. High Treas. Scotl.* VI. 39 For the doune putting of thare bassyngis at New ȝear Daye, Uphalymes and Pasche. **1556** *Burgh Rec. Edinb.* (1871) II. 260 The festuall dayis of Yule, New-yeir-mes, and Vphellymes.

**2.** *Uphali(day) even*, the eve of the Epiphany; *uphaly night*, the night of Jan. 6.

**1506** *Acc. Ld. High Treas. Scot.* III. 178 The fift day [of January], Uphaldy evin, to the men that brocht the sensouris. **1582** *Rec. Elgin* (1903) I. 164 That scho in na times to cum sall ring bessingis, brassin nor irn morteris,..within this burgh upon Vphelly ewin. **1881** S. R. MACPHAIL *Relig. Ho. Pluscardyn* xix. 155 The thirteenth night o' Eel [= Yule] was called 'uphellie nicht'.

† **Uphaˑnce,** *v. Obs.* In 4–5 vphauns(e. [UP- 4 + HANCE *v.*] *trans.* To lift up, raise.

*a* **1375** *Joseph Arim.* 515 Þer weoren hedes vn-huled, helmes vphaunset. *c* **1400** *Apol. Loll.* 31 Crie, cese not, vphauns þi vois os a trompe. *c* **1410** *Lanterne of Liȝt* 28 Liȝt ..is vp spronngen, & meke loweli ben vphaunsid.

**Uˑphand,** *a.* [UP- 3.] Operated, or performed, by raising the hand or hands.

**1677** MOXON *Mech. Exerc.* i. 4 The Uphand Sledge, used by under-Workmen when your work is not of the largest;.. they use it with both their hands before them, and seldom lift their Hammer higher than their Head. **1688** HOLME *Armoury* III. 321/2 The third is termed the up-hand Hammer, or up-hand sledge, of some termed the Fore-Hammer. **1835** J. D. CARRICK, etc. *Laird of Logan* 85 (E.D.D.), Girzie..was apt to enforce her commands with uphand emphases.

**Uphaˑng,** *v.* [UP- 4. Cf. (M)Du. *ophangen*, MLG. *uphangen*, G. *aufhangen*, MSw. *up-, op(p)-hängia* (Sw. *upphänga*), MDa. *uphængie* (Da. *ophænge*).] **a.** *intr.* To hang on high. **b.** *trans.* To hang up, suspend. Also **Uphaˑnged** *pa. pple.*, **Uphaˑnging** *vbl. sb.*

*c* **1440** *Ps. Penit.* (1894) 32 Thu were offred uphongyng, For mannes sake on rode tre. **1555** *Lydgate's Chron. Troy* I. 2242 Thus she stode in doubtfull Jeopardy, Of loue and shame.., Full euenly vphanged in balaunce. **1591** SPENSER *Visions Bellay* vi, Soone on a tree vphang'd I saw her spoyle. **1742** SHENSTONE *Schoolmistress* xiv, How Israel's sons.., untuning ev'ry string, Uphung their useless lyres. **1789** T. RUSSELL *Sonn.*, etc. 1 Stern Chivalry her idle spear uphung. **1860** LD. LYTTON *Lucile* II. v. § 4. 10 When soft stars were brightly uphanging the night. **1861** *Macm. Mag.* June 128 To build a stone-pier for the uphanging of great coats or hats.

† **Uphaˑp,** *adv. Obs.* [UP *prep.*[1] 6 c + HAP *sb.*[1] 4 b.] Perhaps, possibly.

*c* **1350**, *c* **1380** [see UP *prep.*[1] 6 c]. **1387–8** T. USK *Test. Love* I. viii. (Skeat) l. 132 Therin thou lesest..uphap thy renome everlasting. *c* **1450** CAPGRAVE *Life St. Aug.* 46 Vphap it semeth a bischop for to were swech on, þouȝ it semeth not ..a pore man.

**Upharbour, -harrow, -hasping**: see UP- 4, 6.

**Upheaˑded,** *a. north. dial.* [UP- 3.] Of cattle: Having upright horns.

**1549** *Knaresb. Wills* (Surtees) I. 55 One whie of foure yeres olde, uppheded. **1582–3** *Durham Wills* (Surtees) III. 99 A browne upheaded stot goinge in the northe feild. **1828** CARR *Craven Gloss.*, *Up-heeaded*, having the horns growing up nearly perpendicularly.

**Upheaˑp,** *v.* [UP- 4. Cf. WFris. *opheapje*, MDu. *ophopen* (Du. *ophoopen*), MLG. *uphupen*, MHG. *ûfhufen* (G. *aufhäufen*).] *trans.* To heap up.

**1469** *Plumpton Corr.* (Camden) 21, I could nott gett it windowd before it went to the ship..therfore I upheaped with a quarter, xxi quarters for xx quarters. **1483** *Cath. Angl.* 404/2 To Vppehepe, *consarcire.., cumulare.* **1641** BEST *Farm. Bks.* (Surtees) 103 First we poore in the meale, and upheap the bushell; then doe wee..thrust it downe.

**Upheaˑped,** *pa. pple.* (UP- 5. Cf. prec.)

*c* **1380** WYCLIF *Wks.* (1880) 370 Þe same malyce in kynde he schal fynde, ȝhe uphepid, in our byschopis. *c* **1440** *Pallad. on Husb.* III. 819 Of peres sowre..yf that they be Ytake & kepte vphepid daies thre. **14..** *W. of Henley's Husb.* (1890) 50 Be wele ware off mesurynge off your bushell þat is vphepide. **1549** COVERDALE, etc. *Erasm. Par. 2 Peter* 16 Let brotherly charitie be augmented and upheaped with love. **1560** B. GOOGE tr. *Palingenius' Zodiac* II. (1561) D v b, Thy barnes vpheaped & hugy mowes of corne. **1596** H. CLAPHAM *Brief of Bible* 95 Their Sinne vpheapt, God sendeth them away To Babylon. **1777** *A. Hunter's Georg. Ess.* I. 416, I..laid on 167 chaldrons of lime, 32 bushels, upheaped, to the chaldron. **1807** CRABBE *Par. Reg.* I. 489 Whose board is high up-heap'd with generous fare. **1828** CARR *Craven Gloss.* II. 228 Excellent measure, not only up-heaped, but pressed down.

*fig.* **1862** [C. C. ROBINSON] *Dial. Leeds* 4 Shoo said he wur a rascal upheaped and downthrussen. [Cf. UPHEAP *v.*, quot. 1641.]

**Uˑpheaped,** *ppl. a.* (UP- 5. Cf. prec.)

**1549** COVERDALE, etc. *Erasm. Par.* 1 *Pet.* iv. 12 God.. shal repaye al with vpheaped mesure. **1565** in Picton *L'pool Munic. Rec.* (1883) I. 86 That the old upheaped mete be.. allowed and none other. *a* **1619** FOTHERBY *Atheom.* I. xi. § 4 (1622) 116 He maketh such vpheaped piles of dishes. **1641** BEST *Farm. Bks.* (Surtees) 103 Wee haue allwayes of a stricken bushell of corne an upheaped bushell of meale. **1821** COLERIDGE *Lett., Convers.*, etc. I. 183 An upheaped love and devotion to her admirable husband. **1850** BLACKIE *Æschylus* II. 159, I alone Must bear the up-heaped murmurings of the whole. **1891** FARRAR *Darkn. & Dawn* lxvi, Amid the upheaped corpses the blood..hissed and bubbled.

**Upheaˑping,** *vbl. sb.* (UP- 7.) *c* **1374** CHAUCER *Boeth.* II. pr. iii. (1868) 37 It delitep me to comen now to þe singuler vphepyng of þi welefulnesse. **Upheaˑping,** *pres. pple.*: see UP- 6. **Up-heaˑrted,** *a.* [UP- 3.] Of good heart; not readily discouraged. **1862** TROLLOPE *Orley F.* xxix, He was cheery and up-hearted, but at the same time gentle.

**Upheaˑval.** [UP- 2.]

**1.** *Geol.* The action of raising, or fact of being raised, above the original level, esp. by volcanic action.

**1838** LYELL *Man. Geol.* v. 96 Very extensive regions..have been undergoing slow and gradual upheaval. **1862** G. P. SCROPE *Volcanoes* 429 The upheaval of the latter strata. **1886** WINCHELL *Walks Geol. Field* 112 This is the general plan of a mountain of upheaval.

**b.** An instance of this; an upward displacement of some part of the earth's crust.

**1849** DANA *Geol.* xvii. (1850) 675 Some of the upheavals the country has experienced, may have opened fissures. **1876** PAGE *Adv. Text-bk. Geol.* ii. 39 Upheavals and subsidences occasioned by..volcanic convulsions. **1897** E. B. NICHOLSON *Golspie* 252 These upheavals took place after..the great Ice Age.

**c.** In general use.

**1890** CLARK RUSSELL *Ocean Trag.* III. xxviii. 74 A volcanic upheaval of flame. **1908** S. E. WHITE *Riverman* iv, Constantly the logs shifted, and..the men shifted also, avoiding the upheavals.

**2.** *fig.* A strong agitation or convulsion of society, etc.; a sudden or violent alteration.

**1850** MCCOSH *Div. Govt.* II. iii. 250 There have been times of upheaval in the moral world, similar to those periods which geologists describe. **1867** C. H. PEARSON *Hist. Eng.* I. 89 It was a general upheaval of peoples. **1887** LOWELL *Democr.* 13 There had also been social upheavals before the Reformation.

Hence **Upheaˑvalist**, an advocate of the theory that geological changes are due to upheaval.

**1862** G. P. SCROPE *Volcanoes* 201 Lyell, in his..examination of this question, decided it against the upheavalists.

**Upheave,** *sb.*: see UP- 2.

**Upheaˑve,** *v.* [UP- 4. Cf. OE. *uphebban*, ME. *uphebbe*, = OFris. *op-, upheva* (WFris. *opheevje*), (M)Du. *opheffen*, MLG. *upheven*, LG. *upheffen*, OHG. *ûfhevan* (MHG. *ûfheben*, G. *aufheben*), MSw. *uphäfia*, *ophävia*, etc. (Sw. *upphäfva*, *-häva*), (M)Da. *ophæve*.]

**1.** *trans.* To heave or lift up; to raise; † to exalt.

*a* **1300** *E. E. Psalter* iii. 3 Lauerd, mi fanger art þou in lande, Mi blisse, and mi heued vpheueande [L. *exaltans*]. *Ibid.* cxliv. 1, I sal vpheue þe, god. *c* **1375** *Sc. Leg. Saints* xliii. (*Cecilia*) 94 Þe ald his handis..Vphewit to þe hewine rycht þare. *c* **1386** CHAUCER *Knt.'s T.* 1570 Arcita anon his hand vp haf. **1513** DOUGLAS *Æneid* XIII. x. 21 The fader Eneas..His handis bayth vphevis towartis hevin. **1563** *Mirr. Mag.* R iv, Vp heauing to the skyes Her wretched handes. **1592** SHAKS. *Ven. & Ad.* 482 Her two blew windowes faintly she vpheaueth. **1620** QUARLES *Feast for Wormes* § 12 No sooner Titan had vp-heau'd his head From off the pillow. **1676** HOBBES *Iliad* I. 429 Chryses pray'd with hands to Heaven upheaved. **1736** GRAY *Statius* I. 15 Another orb upheaved his strong right hand. **1791** COWPER *Iliad* IV. 504 The waves by Zephyrus up-heaved. **1817** *Monthly Mag.* XLIII. 237 Couch'd on the shore his head and shoulders twain, Upheaves a giant shape. **1850** BLACKIE *Æschylus* II. 69 Let the sea upheave her billows! **1855** BROWNING *Saul* xiv, While Hebron upheaves The dawn..on his shoulder.

**b.** *esp.* To toss or throw up with violence; *spec.* in *Geol.*

**1708** J. PHILIPS *Cyder* I. 202 Th' infernal winds..from beneath the solid mass Upheav'd. **1809** WORDSW. *Poems Nat. Indep.* II. xvi, War upheaved The ground beneath thee with volcanic force. **1813** BAKEWELL *Introd. Geol.* (1815) 234 Some great convulsion has upheaved from their foundations ..the whole mass of the chalk rocks. **1867** LADY HERBERT *Cradle L.* vii. 194 There are masses of stone and brick.. lying about as if upheaved and overturned by some tremendous earthquake.

*fig.* **1835** I. TAYLOR *Spir. Despot.* i. 16 Let the infidel and the Dissenter join hands in upheaving the Church. **1854** J. S. C. ABBOTT *Napoleon* (1855) I. i. 23 The portentous rumblings of that approaching earthquake, which soon uphove both altar and throne.

† **2.** = UPLIFT *v.* 4, RAISE *v.*[1] 13. *Obs.*

*a* **1300** *E. E. Psalter* xcii. 4 Þai vphoue, louerd, stremes euen, Vphoued stremes þair steuen. *a* **1593** MARLOWE *Ovid's Elegies* III. v. 52 The bold flood..his hoarse voice vpheau'd, Saying, [etc.].

**3.** *intr.* To rise up.

**1649** LOVELACE *Lucasta* (1904) 99 The July-flow'r.., But for one look of her, upheaves. *a* **1826** J. HYATT in Spurgeon *Treas. Dav.* IV. 108 To represent human nature as upheaving under its load. **1850** B. TAYLOR *Eldorado* I. 170 The surface of the bay..upheaved with a slow, majestic movement. **1893** *Scribner's Mag.* XIII. 92/1 Along the west it upheaves into the fine Valles range.

**4.** *trans.* To support, sustain. *rare*$^{-1}$.

**1729** SAVAGE *Wanderer* IV. 170 Pillars..Which, nodding, just up-heave their crumbling load.

Hence **Uˑpheaved** *ppl. a.*, **Upheaˑvement, Upheaˑver, Upheaˑving** *vbl. sb.* and *ppl. a.*

**1847** EMERSON *Ode to Channing* 30 If earth fire cleave The *upheaved land, and bury the folk. **1859** R. F. BURTON *Centr. Afr.* in *Jrnl. Geog. Soc.* XXIX. 10 The upheaved sea beach..which forms the esplanade. **1866** G. MACDONALD *Ann. Q. Neighb.* xiii, Each like one million-petalled flower of upheaved whiteness. **1841** TRIMMER *Pract. Geol.* 56 It was the agent employed in the *upheavement of chains of mountains. **1864** *Reader* 5 March 301/3 After the last upheavement of the Alps, great fissures or basins of lakes were left there. **1597** A. M. tr. *Guillemeau's Fr. Chirurg.* 7 b/1 An Elevatorium [*marg.* or *vpheaver], to lift vp the bullet and drawe him therout. **1872** SPURGEON *Treas. Dav.* Ps. lxv. 6 Philosophers..too much engrossed with their laws of upheaval to think of the Upheaver. **1892** *Graphic* 18 June 731/3 The pullers up of streets and the upheavers of footways. **1830** LYELL *Princ. Geol.* I. 231 Great *upheavings of the coast. **1856** STANLEY *Sinai & Pal.* i. 23 The traces of igneous action on the granite rocks belong to their first upheaving. **1863** — *Jew. Ch.* xiii. 285 The Conquest was over, but the upheavings of the conquered population still continued. **1880** MCCARTHY *Own Times* xli. III. 226 All over the world there seemed to be an upheaving of old systems. **1821** ATHERSTONE *Poems* 72 Ocean monsters, from their beds..Torn by th' *upheaving billows to the day. **1853** KANE *Grinnell Exp.* xxxii. (1856) 282, I mounted the upheaving ice, and rode upon the fragments. **1881** W. STEPHENS *Chichester* 158 [They] could not foresee what mighty and upheaving changes were at hand.

**Uphebbe**: see UP- 4. **Uˑpheld,** *ppl. a.* (UP- 5.) **1870** MORRIS *Earthly Par.* III. IV. 189 One maiden..Bore in her gleaming upheld skirt Fair silken balls. **1883** JEFFERIES *Story of My Heart* xi. 168 The upheld finger of light.

† **Upheˑlder,** obs. var. UPHOLDER 1.

**1356** in Riley *Mem. London* 282 Stephen Basham, lockyer, and Adam Wayte, upheldere.

**Uphellie, -helly,** dial. ff. UPHALI(DAY).

† **Upheˑnd,** *v. Obs.* [UP- 4. Cf. MDa. *ophente*.] *trans.* To catch or snatch up; to take up, raise.

*a* **1300** *Cursor M.* 12183 Leui..a yeird vp-hint, And gaf him in þe heued a dint. **13..** *Seuyn Sages* (W.) 3133 Vnto the lady the ring he cast...The lady has the ring uphent. *c* **1420** *Sir Amadace* (Camden) lxvii, Then Sir Amadace a squrd vppe-hente. **1513** DOUGLAS *Æneid* v. viii. 63 Acestes ..has vphint in feild His freind Entellus. *Ibid.* XI. i. 49 [Let] the ensenȝeis and baneris be vphynt. **1600** FAIRFAX *Tasso* XII. lxxii, He would not leaue the corses faire in field But in their armes the soldiers both vphent.

**Upher,** variant of UFER (fir-pole).

† **Uphiˑgh,** *v. Obs.* Chiefly *Sc.* [UP- 4. Cf. Du. *ophoogen*, G. *aufhöhen*, MSw. *uphöghia*, *ophöia*, etc. (Sw. *upphöja*), MDa. *uphøge* (Da. *ophøje*), Norw. *upphøgja*.] *trans.* To exalt; to raise up.

**13..** *Prose Psalter* (1891) 190 Heȝe [*v.r.* uphie] him in þe worldel! *c* **1470** HENRYSON *Mor. Fab.* v. *Parl. Beasts* xxi, The lawest heir I can full sone vp hie. **1508** DUNBAR *Poems* vii. 5 Onto the sterris heich vpheyt is thyne honour. **1513** DOUGLAS *Æneid* VIII. i. 72 Tyburinus, furth of the styll river,..hymself vpheis. **1563** WINȜET *Wks.* (S.T.S.) II. 58 Be zeris it mot be strenthit,..and be aige vpheit.

**Uˑphill,** *sb.* and *a.* Also up-hill. [UP *prep.*[2] Cf. next.]

**A.** *sb.* **1.** An ascent; a high or steep rise.

**1548** UDALL *Erasm. Par. Luke* iii. 28 b, That countrey is full of vphilles and downhilles, & almost no parte of it euen, or plain champian ground. **1611** CORYAT *Crudities* 54 [The traveller has] no euen way, but continually high vphils and steepe down-hils til he commeth to Tarare. **1631** A. TOWNSHEND *Albion's Triumph* B, There is no vp-hill in the skyes; Clouds stay not feathered feete. **1671** tr. *Frejus' Voy. Mauritania* 54 Built on very high ground, but..we come insensibly to the Town, without perceiving any up-hill. **1883** C. HOWARD *Roads Eng. & Wales* (ed. 3) 81 From here is a long stiff uphill along the coast.

† **2.** *Gaming.* (See quots.) *Obs.*

*a* **1700** B. E. *Dict. Cant. Crew*, *Uphils*, high Dice. **1785** GROSE *Dict. Vulgar T.*, *Uphills*, false dice that run high. **1824** *Hist. Gaming* 41 To the landlord..he taught the art of..cutting the broads right, and throwing uphills.

**B.** *adj.* **1.** Situated on high ground; elevated.

**1613** PURCHAS *Pilgrimage, India* (1614) 481 Ouer Balaguate, or the vp-hill Countrey (for *Bala* in the Persian Language signifieth the toppe, and *Guate* a Hill). **1701** O. HEYWOOD *Diaries*, etc. (1885) IV. 176 My last and best journey will be to the up-hill city. *a* **1814** *Gonzanga* III. i. in *New Brit. Theatre* III. 121 My passage to the up-hill seat of power. **1853** *Public School Matches* 12 Whatever you do, throw up full from the uphill side.

**b.** Grown on high ground.

**1892** *Daily News* 7 Dec. 6/1 It was a well-known fact that up-hill hay was much the best.

**2.** Leading or directed towards higher ground; going upwards, esp. steeply.

1622 BACON *Hen. VII*, Ep. Ded., And it is with Times, as it is with Wayes. Some are more Up-hill and Down-hill, and some are more Flat and Plaine. 1684 BUNYAN *Pilgr.* II. 65 They love not to take Pains, up-hill way is unpleasant to them. 1728 YOUNG *Love Fame* v. 99 Yet, as immortal, in our up-hill chace We press coy fortune with unslacken'd pace. c 1854 FABER *Hymn*, '*The Light must win*' vi, The Church, the Sacraments, the Faith, Their uphill journey take. 1875 JOWETT *Plato* (ed. 2) III. 234 But before virtue the gods have set toil, and a tedious and uphill road. 1891 T. HARDY *Tess* xxvii, An up-hill and down-dale ride of twenty-odd miles.

**b.** Presenting difficulties; carried on against difficulties or opposition; arduous, hard.

Used esp. with *battle, fight, game, task, work.*

1622 [see prec.]. 1659 TREVOR in *Burton's Diary* (1828) IV. 348, I move not to bring it into question whether it be up-hill or down-hill. 1741 LD. LYTTELTON in *Athenæum* 23 Feb. (1895) 251/3 It was an uphill piece of work considering the difficulties he lies under. 1748 RICHARDSON *Clarissa* (1768) IV. 149 What an up-hill labour! 1849 COBDEN *Speeches* 8 We had an up-hill battle, but we succeeded. 1850 J. H. NEWMAN *Diffic. Anglic.* v. 107 This misfortune is nothing new; we always reckoned on an uphill game. a 1860 ALB. SMITH *Med. Student* (1861) 119 The up-hill struggles..of his laborious future career. 1886 T. FROST *Remin. Country Journalist* xxi. (1888) 245 'It was up-hill work to establish it [*sc.* a newspaper],' he told me.

**c.** Contending against difficulties. *rare.*

1821 HAZLITT *Table-T.* Ser. I. *Indian Jugglers*, He was the best *up-hill* player in the world. 1885 TENNYSON *Ancient Sage* 279 Lay thine uphill shoulder to the wheel, And climb the Mount of Blessing.

**3.** *Uphill and downhill*, alternately cheerful and depressed.

1681 R. CROMWELL *Let.* in *Eng. Hist. Rev.* (1898) 96, I hope shee will find..a better account of the goodness of the Lord then what we meet with by your uphill and downhill letters.

**Uphi·ll**, *adv.* Also up-hill, up hill. [f. UP *prep.*[1] Cf. HILL *sb.* 1 c. In early use unhyphened.]

**1.** Towards the top of the hill or high ground; in an upward direction on a (steep) slope. Also in fig. contexts.

*α.* 1607 TOPSELL *Four-f. Beasts* 311 The Persians..accustome their Horsses to run both down hil, and vp hil. 1687 A. LOVELL tr. *Thevenot's Trav.* I. 10 The Streets..are incommodious, in that one is always going either up hill or down hill. 1737 [S. BERINGTON] *Mem. G. di Lucca* 112 These Men..were approaching to the Line,..and supposing the Structure of..the Earth to be Spheroidal, went up Hill all the way. 1746 in *10th Rep. Hist. MSS. Comm.* App. I. 440 As we march'd, all the way up hill, and over very uneven Ground. 1779 G. KEATE *Sketches fr. Nat.* (ed. 2) I. 67 The successors of Saint Peter..trotted them up hill, and down hill,..just as they pleased to lead the way. 1824 SCOTT *St. Ronan's* iv, Mr. Winterblossom..would gladly have been the personal representative of the company..—but it [*sc.* the walk] was up hill.

*β.* 1712 J. JAMES tr. *Le Blond's Gardening* 118 To be constantly going Up-hill, or Down-hill. 1748 *Anson's Voy.* II. i. 122 The dogs..ran up-hill with great alacrity. 1818 HAZLITT *Eng. Poets* v. 178 Thomson's blank verse..seems always labouring up-hill. 1877 HUXLEY *Physiogr.* 17 To do that the water would have to run up-hill. 1879 F. POLLOK *Sport Brit. Burmah* I. 79 He could only go up-hill backwards.

*fig.* 1682 SIR T. BROWNE *Chr. Mor.* (1716) 109 To offer at iniquities, which have so little foundations in thee, were to be vitious up hill, and strain for thy condemnation. 1876 BANCROFT *Hist. U. S.* VI. 340 We are always working up-hill.

**2.** To or on the upper side *of.*

1922 'CLAXON' *Heather Mixture* xii. 246 The huntsman was riding..on Dicky's left, working to get uphill of the pack.

**Uphi·llward**, *adv.* and *a.* [f. prec.] **a.** *adv.* In an uphill direction. **b.** *adj.* Leading uphill.

c 1655 MILTON *To C. Skinner* Wks. 1738 I. 59 Nor bate a Jot Of Heart or Hope, but still attend to steer Uphillward. 1876 FARRAR *Marlb. Serm.* xii. 112 The path of life is narrow and uphillward. 1877 — *Eternal Hope* (1892) 90 The difficulty of..virtue's uphillward path.

**Uphoa·rd**, *v.* [UP- 4.] *trans.* To hoard or heap up.

1582 STANYHURST *Æneis* III. (Arb.) 72 Thee gould thee traytor vp hurdeth. 1591 SPENSER *Teares Muses* 553 Heapes of huge words vphoorded hideously. 1602 SHAKS. *Ham.* I. i. 134 If thou hast vp-hoorded in thy life Extorted Treasure in the wombe of Earth. 1652 BENLOWES *Theoph.* III. xlv, Eusebia truth for her uphords.

**Uphoising, -hoist, -hoisted**: see UP- 5, 6.

**U·phold**, *sb.* Chiefly *Sc.* and *north. dial.* Also *Sc.* 5–6 vp- (6 wp-, oup-), uphald, 8 **uphad**, 9 **uphadd, -haud, uppal**; 9 *north.* **uphod.** [OE. *uppheald* (f. UP- 1 b + *heald* HOLD *sb.*[1]), = ON. *upphald* (Norw. *upphald*; MSw. *up-, ophald, -hold*, MDa. and Da. *ophold*), MLG. *upholt*, MDu. *ophout*; MHG. *ûfhalt* (G. *aufhalt*) stop, delay; also MSw. *uppe-, oppehald* (Sw. *uppehåll*).]

**1.** A support or stay.

a 1066 in Kemble *Cod. Dipl.* (1846) IV. 232 Ic eom ðæs mynstres mund and upheald. c 1200 ORMIN 9217 Crist, Godess Sune,..Hælennde, & hellpe, & god upphald Till þatt he shall chesenn. 1559 KNOX *First Blast* App. (Arb.) 58 So is the testimonye of a clean conscience to me a stay and vphold. 1596 DALRYMPLE tr. *Leslie's Hist. Scot.* (S.T.S.) II. 45 O cruel creatures, quha dang doune sa strang a stay, piller, and vphald of the Realme! 1791 J. LEARMONT *Poems* 142 Deckit wi' French flutteration, Stap forth the uphads o' the nation. 1825 JAMIESON s.v. *Uppal*, The death o' wives, and the luck o' sheep, are a puir man's uppal. 1894 A. REID *Sangs Heatherland* 16 Wha'll cast the end gin aince ye try To pu' oor uphauds doon?

**2.** The support, sustenance, or maintenance *of* a person, estate, etc. Also without const.

*α.* 1439 *Sc. Acts, Jas. II* (1814) II. 54/2 þe said princesse.. has..assignit..to þe uphald of our said soueryn lord and his sistris..iiij[m] markis. 1456 SIR G. HAY *Govt. Princes* Wks. (S.T.S.) II. 153 The gudis ar the uphald of the lyf. c 1500 *Cartul. St. Nicholai Aberdon.* (New Spald. Cl.) I. 259 Sextene bredir singaris and abill men to ye vphald of devin service. 1552 LYNDESAY *Tragedy* 191, I wes the cause of mekle more myschance, For vphald of my glore and dignitie. 1597 *Sc. Acts, Jas. VI* (1814) IV. 154/2 Oure said souerane Lord..Annexis..to þe same citye..for þe better vphald þerof the foirsaidis liberteis. a 1598 D. FERGUSSON *Coll. Sc. Prov.* (S.T.S.) 84 Pride and sweirnesse wald have meikle uphald. 1808 JAMIESON s.v. *Uphald, Uphadd*, support.

*β.* 1483 in Rymer *Fœdera* (1711) XII. 174/1 To the upholde, maynteyne and encrease of their both Estatis. 1582 in *Archaeologia* (1846) XXX. 166 Those..placed here for the uphold and maintenance of the peace. 1680 in *Proc. Soc. Antiq. Scot.* XLV. 241 The broad curse of God is on ministers and professors, for your joyning for their uphold.

**b.** The maintaining *of* a building, etc., in proper repair.

1471 in *Charters, &c. Edinb.* (1871) 133 For the vphald, reparatioun and bigging of the sammyn [port]. 1527 *Extr. Aberd. Reg.* (1844) I. 116 The biging of the brig of Dee, and ..the gret offeris..be his lordschip, for the vphald of the samyn. 1588 *Exchequer Rolls Scot.* XXI. 403 Payit yeirlie ..for uphald of the brig of Tay.

**c.** *north. dial.* Personal maintenance (in respect of food, etc.).

1855– in dial. glossaries (Cumb., Yks.).

**Upho·ld**, *v.* Forms: *α.* 3–4 **upholden**, 4–6 **vp-**, 5–6 **upholde**, 5–7 **vphold**, 5– **uphold** (6 **upphold**); *north. dial.* 8–9 **uphowd** (8 **upphoud**), 9 **uphod.** *β.* 4 **vp-haldene**; *north.* and *Sc.* 5 **vpp-, uppehalde**, 4, 6 **vp-, uphald**, 9 **uppal**, 8–9 **uphaud**, 9 **uphadd.** [UP- 4. Cf. OFris. *op-, uphalda* (WFris. *ophâlde*), MLG. *upholden* (LG. *upholden, -hollen*), (M)Du. *ophouden*, MSw. *up-, ophalda, -halla, -holda*, etc., Da. *opholde*, MHG. *ûfhalten* (G. *aufhalten*); also MSw. *uppe-, oppehalda* (Sw. *uppehålla*).]

**1.** *trans.* To support or sustain physically; to keep from falling or sinking.

a 1300 *Cursor M.* 538 Hijs fete him bers up fra fall, Als þe erth vp haldes all. 13.. *Gaw. & Gr. Knt.* 2079 þe heuen was vp halt, bot vgly þer vnder. 1390 GOWER *Conf.* I. 75 He hire in hise armes fast Upheld. c 1440 *Pallad. on Husb.* IV. 82 A lighter vyne is with a lesse Stakyng vpholde. 1483 *Cath. Angl.* 404/2 To Vpphalde, *sustentare, supportare.* 1515 BARCLAY *Eclogues* iv. (1570) C vi b/1 With marble pillers the building to vpholde, About be turrets of shape moste excellent. 1590 SPENSER *F. Q.* I. viii. 40 Whose feeble thighes, vnhable to vphold His pined corse, him scarse to light could beare. 1610 HOLLAND *Camden's Brit.* I. 697 An Altar..which I saw there, vpholding now the Staires of an house. 1663 BP. PATRICK *Parab. Pilgr.* xxxvii, The winds that blew, and the rough waves.., were no less subject to that power which upheld him, than [etc.]. 1726 LEONI *Alberti's Archit.* I. 52 Coverings..must..be sufficient for upholding themselves, and their burthens. 1763 MILLS *Pract. Husb.* IV. 359 Poles were extended between them, and these were up-held by props. 1807 CRABBE *Par. Reg.* III. 938 No more his span-girth shanks..Upheld a body of smaller size. 1849 MACAULAY *Hist. Eng.* I. 47 The leading strings, which preserve and uphold the infant. 1880 JEFFERIES *Gt. Estate* 33 The slender stems uphold the cup-like flowers two or three inches above the surface.

**2.** To support, sustain, maintain, by aid or assistance; to preserve unimpaired or intact.

a 1225 *Ancr. R.* 140 Teke þis, heo mot ȝete þuruh hire uorbisne..ȝiuen oðre strenðe, & upholden ham, þet heo ne uallen iðe dunge of sunne. a 1250 *Prov. Alfred* 171 For nys no w[u]rt..þat euer mvwe þas feye furþ vp-holde [*Trin. Coll. MS.* þe lif up helde]. c 1320 *Cast. Love* 609 A child þer is i-boren to vs,..Þat schal vp-holden his kynedome. 1389 in *Eng. Gilds* (1870) 110 The gilde bretherun..that this gilde furst begonne, and lengest sal vp-haldene. 1462–3 *Pol. Poems* (Rolls) II. 268 Falshode, myschyef, secret synne upholdyng, Whiche hathe caused..endelez langoure. 1488 *Act 4 Hen. VII*, c. 12 § 2 The housbondrie..wherby the Chirche of Engleind is upholden. 1542–3 *Act* 34 & 35 *Hen. VIII*, c. 10 § 1 The Citie..hathe been mainteyned and upholden by divers and sundrye handye craftes there used. 1593 SHAKS. 3 *Hen. VI*, III. iii. 106 While Life vpholds this Arme, This Arme vpholds the House of Lancaster. 1647 N. BACON *Disc. Govt. Eng.* I. i. 2 Though great Nations may be upholden by power. 1671 MILTON *Samson* 892 An impious crew Of men conspiring to uphold thir state By worse than hostile deeds. 1725 DE FOE *Voy. round World* (1840) 328 They had..some comforts however which might a little uphold their spirits. 1781 COWPER *Retirem.* 89 Thine, and upheld by thy paternal care, This universal frame. 1838 THIRLWALL *Greece* xxxv. IV. 377 Rather to take the lead in a revolution, than steadily to uphold the established order of things. 1877 FREEMAN *Norm. Conq.* (ed. 3) II. App. 666 Malcolm continued to be powerfully upheld by English help.

*absol.* 1560 BIBLE *Isaiah* lxiii. 5, I loked, & there was none to helpe, & I wondered that there was none to vpholde.

**†b.** To carry out, succeed in. *Obs.*—[1]

c 1450 *Cov. Myst.* (Shaks. Soc.) 214 He wyl us werke ryght mekyl shame, His fals purpos if he upholde.

**c.** To maintain at the same level or standard.

1523 FITZHERB. *Husb.* § 66 That he rere two oxe-calues, and two cowe-calues..to vpholde his flocke. 1832 CHALMERS *Pol. Econ.* (1849) II. 60 Such a high style of husbandry cannot possibly be upholden. 1875 *Economist* 27 Feb. 260/1 Beans and peas..firmly uphold their value. 1883 *Manch. Exam.* 26 Nov. 4/2 The demand for yarns..has been very dull, but quotations have nevertheless been upheld.

**d.** To sustain spiritually.

1820 J. J. GURNEY in Reid *Life W. E. Forster* (1888) I. 33 Both William and his wife were marvellously upheld. 1824 SCOTT *St. Ronan's* xxxvii, God send she may not have been left to hersel'!—God send she may have been upholden!

1864 TENNYSON *En. Ard.* 783 Uphold me, Father, in my loneliness A little longer!

**3.** **†a.** To furnish or provide, to perform or discharge, regularly. *Obs.*

a 1417 *York Memo. Bk.* (Surtees) I. 221 The whilk vj.s. viij.d...sall be keped..to upholde and releve a lyght to be borne..on Corpus Cristy day. 1444 *Extr. Aberd. Reg.* (1844) I. 12 Williame Mathouson..sal vphald the ladymesse with uoce..ilke owke for a yher. 1539 in *Abst. Protocols Town Clerks of Glasgow* (1897) IV. 118 The said maister to uphald and fynd ane pryckat of wax nychtlie byrneand.

**b.** To maintain in good condition or in a proper state of repair.

1511 *Reg. Privy Seal Scotl.* I. 344/2 That the saidis landis salbe uphaldin and keipit unharmit or skaithit. 1535 *Act* 27 *Hen. VIII*, c. 22 § 1 If any Owner..shuld..occupie any suche mese or land..he shulde..uphold and susteyne the same. 1563 *Reg. Privy Council Scot.* I. 246 The Abbottis.. wer accustomat..,upoun thair expenssis, to uphald and big the wallis. 1631 WEEVER *Anc. Funeral Mon.* 333 This Church is vpholden in wondrous good repaire. 1701 in W. O. Blunt *Ch. Chester-le-Street* (1884) 104 Paid Thos. Pearson for upholding y[e] bell wheels for 7 yeare. 1753 *Scots Mag.* Apr. 164/2 Provided that the city be obliged to uphold the..buildings in repair. 1816 SCOTT *Antiq.* i, It's Jamie Martingale that furnishes the naigs on contract, and uphauds them. 1833 *Stat.* 3 & 4 *Wm. IV*, c. 46 § 101 Every person..shall uphold and keep in proper repair the fences aforesaid. 1894 *Westm. Gaz.* 3 May 2/3 He was also bound by a covenant in the lease to 'uphold' the premises.

**c.** To provide with sustenance; to support with food, etc. Now *dial.*

1546 *Reg. Cupar Abbey* II. 36 [He] sall vphald honestlie in meit and claytht..the said Jhone Alane. 1574 *Satir. Poems Reform.* xlii. 380 Rentis sufficient to vphauld Ane gude number of sic Studentis. 1615 MARKHAM *Country Contentm.* I. viii. 101 The best generall foods for the ordinarie vpholding of a dogge in a good state of body. [1684 J. S. *Profit & Pleas. United* 163 The best Food for upholding a dog.] 1863 MRS. TOOGOOD *Spec. Yorks. Dial.* (MS.), I kept my brother some time, but he was so wasteful I couldn't uphod him any longer.

**4.** To support by advocacy or assent; to sustain against objection or criticism.

1485 CAXTON *Paris & V.* (1868) 12 Other knyghtes rise vp that mayntened and vpheld the beaute of Vyenne. 1525 LD. BERNERS *Froiss.* II. xlv. 153 This worde was vpholden and obserued. 1530 PALSGR. 769/1 Sythe he hath sayde it, I wyll upholde it. 1598 R. BERNARD tr. *Terence, Andria* IV. iii, See that thou be readie to answer and vphold my talke. 1753–4 RICHARDSON *Grandison* III. xxvi. 309 He does nothing but hop, skip, and dance about me, grin and make mouths; and every-body upholds him in it. 1781 BURKE *Corr.* (1844) II. 451 Perhaps I have wished to uphold with enthusiasm the honour and dignity of the community I belong to. 1818 CRUISE *Digest* (ed. 2) I. 522 The owner of the inheritance, who was interested in upholding it [*sc.* an arrangement]. 1869 J. MARTINEAU *Ess.* II. 57 This plea..upholds a practice essentially unjust. 1890 *Law Times' Rep.* LXIII. 733/2 He refused to answer that question, and was upheld in his refusal by the learned judge. 1893 *Ibid.* LXVIII. 444/1 On appeal to the County Court Judge..the decision of the registrar was upheld.

**b.** To maintain (a statement), to warrant or guarantee (a fact). Now chiefly *north. dial.* and *Sc.*

Orig. with complementary object or clause. In later usage freq. in loose construction, esp. in dialect forms (see *β* and *Eng. Dial. Dict.* s.v.). Also with indirect personal dative.

*α.* 1530 PALSGR. 769/1, I upholde a ware or marchaundyse to be good. *Ibid.*, I wyll upholde hym for as sounde a horse as any is in Englande. 1583 GOLDING *Calvin on Deut.* Pref. Ep. 2 The other side upholdeth..that it is a vilainous defiling of religion. 1653 BLITHE *English Improver Impr.* 86, I dare uphold one Acre would be as good as divers now are in many parts of it. 1821 SCOTT *Kenilw.* xxix, I know that shall make Varney uphold me sober. 1853 MISS YONGE *Heir of Redclyffe* xli, He always upheld that you acted for his good. 1897 RHOSCOMYL *White Rose Arno* 274 Your names'll do for Chapel, I'll uphold.

*β.* 1787 GROSE *Prov. Gloss.*, *Uphowd*, to warrant. 1793 T. SCOTT *Poems* 357 I'se uphaud ye Owr the lugs i' love to be. 1807 R. ANDERSON *Cumbld. Ball.* 221, I'll uphod ye, we's 'gree. 1820 SCOTT *Monast.* Introd. Ep., 'I'se uphaud him a scholar,' answered David. 1861 WAUGH *Birtle Carter's T.* 8 Yo'd raythar ha' loaf-braide, aw'll uphowd yo. 1891 BARRIE *Little Minister* iii, It was no sport to them, Susy, I'se uphaud.

**5.** To raise or lift up; to direct upwards.

a 1400 *Isumbras* 52 The knyghte felle on his knes..And bothe his handis upehelde. c 1400 *Destr. Troy* 8760 With a noble sword..naked in his hond, Vp holdand on high as he þat wold stryke. c 1450 *Songs, Carols*, etc. (E.E.T.S.) 6/39 Vphold the flowr of gud Jesse, And worship it for ay bewte. c 1480 HENRYSON *Fables, Lion & Mouse* 188 Scho..baith hir handis vnto the heuin vpheld. 1513 DOUGLAS *Æneid* Concl. 8 The bettir part of me sal be vpheild Abuif the starnis perpetualy to ryng. 1618 ROWLANDS *Sacred Mem.* 24 With eyes vpheld To heauen, he did blesse. 1681 DRYDEN *Abs. & Achit.* I. 595 His Hand a Vare of Justice did uphold. 1891 FARRAR *Darkn. & Dawn* xxxix, They upheld their clenched hands..to plead for mercy.

**Upho·ldatory**, *a.* (f. UPHOLD *v.*) 1829 *Moore's Mem.* (1854) VI. 6 Lord L. showed me..a letter..from Lord Anglesey...One word in it rather an odd coinage: 'upholdatory of his government'. **Upho·lden**, *ppl. a.* (UP- 5. Cf. UPHOLD *v.*) 1817 KEATS *Sleep & Poetry* 143 Some with upholden hand and mouth severe. 1838 MRS. BROWNING *Seraphim* II. Wks. (1904) 87 The creature's and the upholden's sacrifice!

**Upho·lder.** Also 4–5 **vpholdere**, 6 **opholder**; 4, 6 *Sc.* **uphalder**, 5 *north.* **uppalder.** (See also UPHELDER.) [f. UPHOLD *v.* (in sense 1 app. in the sense of 'to keep in repair'). Cf. MDa. *op(pe)holdere* in sense 2.]

**1.** **†a.** A dealer in small wares or second-hand articles (of clothing, furniture, etc.); a maker or repairer of such things. *Obs.* **b.** = UPHOLSTERER. Now *rare.*

1333 *Will of Robert de Reppes* 18 June, Quod perquisivi de Thoma Drie upholdere. 1362 LANGL. *P. Pl.* A. v. 168 A Ropere, a Redyng-kyng, and Rose þe disschere,..And of vp-holders an hep. 1377 *Rolls of Parlt.* III. 9 A null Mercer, Coteller, Jualer, Uphalder, ne a nul autre denszein ne forein. 1417 *York Memo. Bk.* (Surtees) I. 183 That na uppalder wyrk in Girdelecrafte. *c* 1440 *Promp. Parv.* 512/2 Vpholdere, þat sellythe smal thyngys, *velaber.* 1495 *Act* 11 *Hen. VII*, c. 19, To the..greate rebuke and disclaunder to the seid Crafte of Upholders. 1598 STOW *Survey* 154 [In] this lane.., in the raigne of Henry the sixt, had ye for the most parte dwelling Fripperers or Upholders, that solde olde apparell and houshold stuffe. 1688 R. HOLME *Armoury* III. 449/2 Such..was of old the Vpholders, or Vpholsterers Arms of Chester. 1711 *Act* 10 *Anne* c. 19 § 84 All..Drapers, Mercers, Upholders,..having..any Stock of..Silks. *a* 1766 MRS. F. SHERIDAN *Sidney Bidulph* (1767) III. 126, I did not like the furniture,..so I..have bespoke new of an upholder. 1807 SOUTHEY *Espriella's Lett.* I. 155 An upholder just now advertises Commodes, Console-tables,..and Chiffoniers. 1812 *Ann. Reg., Chron.* 121 Messrs Wilkinsons, upholders,..having of late been frequently robbed of feathers. 1881 *Instr. Census Clerks* (1885) 53 Upholstery:..Stuffer. Upholder. Upholsterer's Spring Maker. 1910 *Daily Chron.* 9 March 4/7, I have seen 'Carpenter and Upholder' on the signboard of a shop in a Surrey village.

**c.** An undertaker. *Obs.* in general use.

1709 STEELE *Tatler* No. 99 ¶ 4, I..shall give my good Friends the Company of Upholders, full Power to bury all such Dead as they meet with. 1714 GAY *Trivia* II. 347 Th' Upholder, rueful Harbinger of Death, Waits with Impatience for the dying Breath. 1724 SWIFT *Reasons agst. Exam. Drugs* ¶ 5 The company exercising the trade and mistery of upholders. 1903 *Daily Chron.* 8 April 5/2 A large glass sign describing the owners as 'upholders', whereas other evidence shows them to be 'undertakers'.

**2.** A supporter, sustainer, or maintainer (*of* a thing or person).

*c* 1403 LYDG. *Temple of Glas* 468 To ȝov my ladi, vpholder of my life, Mekeli I þanke. 1439 *Coventry Leet Bk.* 191 They ordeyn that..suche maner vpholders..be pursewed as they were persones sole. 1536 *Stories & Proph. Script.* M ij b, The Lorde lyueth, and blessyd be myne opholder. 1547 BALE (*title*), The first Examinacyon of Anne Askewe latelye martyred in Smythfelde, by the Romysh popes vpholders. 1590 NASHE *Pasquil's Apol.* I. B iv b, I wyll not be theyr vpholder which lye sleeping and snorting in their charges. 1642 R. CARPENTER *Experience* III. iii. 12 For God leaveth many things undone,..to preach this doctrine that creatures are not his upholders. 1691 WOOD *Ath. Oxon.* I. 581 The said Duke..was an upholder of him and his unworthy doings. 1710 SWIFT *Poems, Atlas* 22 When the weight of kingdoms lies Too long upon his single shoulders, Sink down he must, or find upholders. 1809 COLERIDGE *Friend* 87 Intellect, and Thought alone can be our Upholder and Judge. 1840 J. H. NEWMAN *Par. Serm.* (ed. 2) V. x. 152 When was the power of the world an upholder of God's truth? 1879 FARRAR *St. Paul* II. 229 A reverence for him far deeper than that of his upholders.

**b.** Of things: A support, stay, or prop.

1398 TREVISA *Barth. De P. R.* v. liv. (Bodl. MS.), It nedeþ to haue so many vndursettinges and vpholders þat suche a beeste may be [more] ablelich..meue and goo. 1571 GOLDING *Calvin on Ps.* lxi. 8 Gentlenesse and faithfulnes are yᵉ trew upholders of kingdomes. 1617 WOODALL *Surg. Mate* Wks. (1639) 80 Wheat flower..is the principall naturall upholder of the life and health of man. 1730 SOUTHALL *Bugs* 40 Two Upholders drove into the Wainscot or Wall. 1884 A. ROSS *Talk upon Hair* 21 A thick Indiarubber ankle upholder, over which is worn the boot and sock.

**Upho·lding,** *vbl. sb.* [UP- 7.]

†**1.** Sustenance; support in necessaries. *Obs.*

*c* 1375 *Sc. Leg. Saints* iii. (*Andrew*) 965 Þu sal hafe þi vphalding with honeste in al thinge In myn doce. 1535 COVERDALE 2 *Macc.* iii. 10 Money layed vp for the vpholdinge of weddowes and fatherlesse children. 1667 *D. Fergusson's Coll. Sc. Prov.* No. 707, Pride and sweerness would have meikle upholding.

**2.** Maintenance in regular use or in proper condition.

*a* 1350 in *Facsimiles Nat. MSS. Scotland* II. (1870) 14 Ad..sustentacionem [*glossed* vphalding] dicti molendini. 1453 *Extr. Aberd. Reg.* (1844) I. 20 For the vphaldyng and eikyng of Godis seruice to be done in the paroche kirk. 1486 in *Exchequer Rolls Scotl.* X. 100 For the uphalding and bering of the..chargis of the said office. 1521 *Lincoln Wills* (1914) 104 To the upholdyng of Notyngham briges. 1522 *Ibid.* 106 To the upholdyng of the forsaid churche. 1543 *Richmond. Wills* (Surtees) 47, I bewhethe the other twenty shelyngs..for the upholdyng of one seirge of waxe yerly. 1613 in *Essex Rev.* XVII. 105 The upholdinge and perfectinge of the companies in good strengh and number. 1631 WEEVER *Anc. Funeral Mon.* To Rdr. 6 For the repairing and vpholding..of that..building. 1842 J. AITON *Clerical Econ.* 112 It must have separate houses, which,..in upholding, must cost disproportionally dear. 1894 C. N. ROBINSON *Brit. Fleet* 62 No sacrifice can therefore be too great for the upholding of our fleet.

**3.** The action of sustaining or supporting by aid or influence.

1599 SANDYS *Europæ Spec.* (1605) 8 The vpholding of their worldly power and glorie of their Order. 1607 HIERON *Wks.* I. 226 The inquirie..how we haue striuen and fought for the vpholding and maintenance of Gods truth. 1637 *Documents agst. Prynne* (Camden) 95 This was my Lord of Lincolne's case in his upholding the creditt of Prydean. 1691 BLOUNT *Law Dict.* (ed. 2), *Maintenance*, signifies the upholding or maintaining of a Cause or Person. 1818 MILMAN *Samor* v. 209 If this life Be worthy thy upholding. 1863 J. COLDSTREAM in Balfour *Biog.* (1865) v. 195 We sensibly felt the 'upholding' graciously vouchsafed. 1872 SPURGEON *Treas. Dav.* III. 10 He asked..for deliverance, and here he returns thanks for upholding.

**4.** The action of maintaining in argument.

1587 GOLDING *De Mornay* ix. 144 What els then is his vpholding of the world to be eternal, than a turning of yᵉ whole world vpside downe?

**5.** The action of raising or holding up.

1574 in *Maitl. Cl. Misc.* (1840) I. 111 He..forder obleist him with uphalding of his hand, that he suld be ane trew sugget. 1598 in J. Ronald *Landmarks Old Stirling* (1899) 338 They promised solemnlie be uphaulding of their hands. 1866 J. G. MURPHY *Comm., Exod.* xvii. 12 Aaron and Hur joining in the upholding of Moses's hands.

**Upho·lding,** *ppl. a.* [UP- 6 b.] Supporting, sustaining.

1553 POYNET *Short Catech.* 43 [The] church, which Paul calleth the piller, and vpholding stay of truth. 1561 T. N[ORTON] tr. *Calvin's Inst.* III. xxi. 239 The vpholdyng stay of sounde affiance. 1674 BOYLE *Excell. Theol.* I. i. 27 Though the soul of man, by the continuance of his ordinary and upholding concourse, may survive the body. 1724 E. ERSKINE *Wks.* (1791) 122/1 His quickening, strengthening, and upholding presence may be withdrawn. 1784 COWPER *Task* III. 658 Flow'rs..expect th' upholding aid Of the smooth-shaven prop. *c* 1830 BRYANT *Forest Hymn* 67 The indwelling Life,..the upholding Love, That are the soul of this wide universe. 1890 'L. FALCONER' *Mlle. Ixe* vi, She..would have fallen, but for the timely aid of two upholding arms.

†**Upho·lster,** *sb. Obs.* Also 5 **upholdester,** 5, 7–8 **upholdster,** 6 *north.* **uphaldster.** [f. UPHOLD *v.* + -STER.] = UPHOLDER 1.

α. 1411 *Close Roll* 12 *Hen. IV* (dorso), Johannes Dryuer, upholdester. 1479 *Paston Lett.* III. 271, iij girdels Staunton. j girdel upholdester. *c* 1481 CAXTON *Dialogues* 2 Of tayllours and vpholdsters. 15.. *York Memo. Bk.* (Surtees) I. 64 Every uphaldster that sellis eny furrez within this citie. 1647 LILLY *Chr. Astrol.* xii. 74 Upholdsters, Limners, Glovers. 1660 PEPYS *Diary* 9 Oct., I found..part of our chambers hung to day by the upholdster. 1722 E. WARD *Parish Gutt'lers* 37 Once on a time he turn'd Upholdster, And slily dealt in Bed and Bolster.

β. 1483–5 *Rec. St. Mary at Hill* 123 Richard Crick, vpholster, for o quarter. 1491 CAXTON *Vitas Patr.* (W. de W. 1495) 144 Whan the chaunger..knewe his gowne that heng at the Vpholsters dore and all redy was there to selle, he was sore wrothe. *c* 1515 *Cocke Lorell's B.* 10 Harpe makers, leches, and upholsters. 1573 in Feuillerat *Revels Q. Eliz.* (1908) 209 Upholster for pendentes of burnished golde for the Maskers garmentes. 1614 in *10th Rep. Hist. MSS. Comm.* App. I. 43 As for a resting chyre.., I did enquyre at an upholster the pryce of itt. 1666 PEPYS *Diary* 22 Aug., My closett is doing by upholsters, which I am pleased with. 1677 WYCHERLEY *Pl. Dealer* III. i, Your Bookseller is properly your Upholster; for he furnishes your Room, rather than your Head. 1725 *Brice's Weekly Jrnl.* 27 Aug. 4 Any Person, having Occasion to imploy an Upholster, may be faithfully serv'd by Ann Hutchins. 1764 H. WALPOLE *Let. to Dalrymple* 31 Jan., Our booksellers..are little more or less than upholsters.

*fig.* 1593 G. HARVEY *Pierce's Super.* 151, I..looue not to be an Vpholster of stuffed, and bombasted malice in other. 1614 J. COOKE *Greene's Tu Quoque* H 1 b, When thou art growne to bee An old Vpholster vnto Venerie. 1660 W. SECKER *Nonsuch Prof.* 156 As for flatterers they may be stiled the Devils Upholsters.

†**b.** Used spec. with reference to the making and selling of beds and bedding. *Obs.*

1554 in W. H. Turner *Select. Rec. Oxford* (1880) 218 George Bedder..to occupy the bedders craft,..to sell upholsters wares wythyn the lybertyes of thys Cytye. 1576 GASCOIGNE *Steele Gl.* (Arb.) 80 When vpholsters sel fethers without dust. 1622 BRETON *Fantastickes* Wks. (Grosart) II. 10/1 The Poulters feathers make toward the Upholster. 1647 TRAPP *Comm.*, 1 *John* iii. 7 These are the devils..upholsters that sow such pillows. 1688 *Secr. Serv. Money Chas. & Jas.* (Camden) 186 To John Poictvin, upholster,..for making two bedds and furniture for the Queen.

**Upho·lster,** *v.* Orig. *U.S.* [Back-formation from UPHOLSTERER or UPHOLSTERY. Cf. next.]

**1.** *intr.* To do upholstery work.

1861 MRS. STOWE *Pearl Orr's Isl.* 21 Miss Roxy and Miss Ruey..could upholster and quilt.

**2.** *trans.* **a.** Of materials: To cover after the manner of upholstery.

1864 LOWELL *Fireside Trav.* 45 The dull weed upholstered the decaying wharves. 1873 J. E. TAYLOR *Half Hours in Green Lanes* x. 292 Several species have already upholstered the rough bark with..delicate shades of velvety green.

**b.** To furnish or trim with, or as with, upholstery. Also *fig.*

1877 'MARK TWAIN' *Mississippi Pilot* 24 The bar keeper had been barbered and upholstered at incredible cost. 1890 C. DIXON *Ann. Bird Life* 85 All [ducks] upholster their nests in the same singular manner. 1891 *Lancet* 24 Jan. 218/1 The whole thorax hollow is now laid bare and upholstered with the skin-muscle flap.

**Upho·lstered,** *ppl. a.* [f. as prec. + -ED.] Furnished or fitted with upholsterer's work.

1837 CARLYLE *Misc.* (1840) V. 167 Farewell, thou old Château, with thy upholstered rooms. 1866 *Lond. Rev.* 6 Jan. 4/1 Sofa-divans, and..arm-chairs all comfortably upholstered with national colours. 1889 MRS. E. KENNARD *Landing a Prize* i, The drawing-room [is] rosewood, upholstered in red damask.

*fig.* 1892 W. H. MALLOCK *Human Document* xviii, Considered by others as an article essential to a decorously upholstered mind.

**Upholsterer** (vpʰᵒ·lstərəɹ). Also 8 **uphoulstarer, upholdsterer.** [f. UPHOLSTER *sb.* + -ER[1] 3.] A tradesman or shopkeeper whose business is the making, finishing, or repairing of articles of furniture and other house-furnishings in which woven or similar fabrics, or materials used for stuffing these, are employed.

1613 MARSTON *Insatiate Countesse* C j b, The fault's in my Vpholsterer, Lady. 1653 W. RAMESEY *Astrol. Restored* 132 If thou makest the childe..a Perfumer,..Glover or Upholsterer. 1677 *Lond. Gaz.* No. 1233/4 Mr. Cooke an Upholsterer next door to the Star. 1722 DE FOE *Plague* (1754) 111 Upholdsterers, Joyners, Cabinet-makers. 1776 ADAM SMITH *W. N.* II. i. I. 334 Upholsterers frequently lett furniture by the month or by the year. 1823 BENTHAM *Not Paul* 85 Tent-making: an art, in which the operations of the architect and the upholsterer are combined. 1875 W. S. HAYWARD *Love agst. World* 6 Painters, decorators, upholsterers,..were immediately set to work.

*fig.* 1642 T. TRESCOT *Zeal. Magist.* 14 Better to meet with sound Reprovers,..than the Devills Vpholsterers. 1779 HERVEY *Nav. Hist.* II. 459 This led the prince of Conti to call Luxembourg 'The Upholsterer of Notre Dame'.

**b.** *transf.* Applied to certain bees and birds. Also *attrib.*

1830 J. RENNIE *Insect Archit.* 53 The leaf-cutting bees..may be denominated more generally 'upholsterer-bees', as there are some of them which use other materials beside leaves. 1840 WESTWOOD *Introd. Mod. Classif. Insects* II. 272 They have been termed..upholsterer bees;..the upholsterers employ in the construction of their cells portions of leaves. 1890 C. DIXON *Ann. Bird Life* 84 Upholsterers.—The birds which come into the present group comprise the Ducks and Geese.

**Upholsteress,** var. of UPHOLSTRESS.

**Upho·lstering,** *vbl. sb.* [f. UPHOLSTER-ER, -Y.] Upholstery. Also *attrib.*

1807 SOUTHEY *Espriella's Lett.* III. 272 The women of the family in which she then worked at the upholstering business. 1896 *Daily News* 15 Dec. 2/2 The velvet upholstering and pile carpets.

**Upho·lstering,** *ppl. a.* [f. as prec.] Serving to upholster.

1828 LYTTON *Pelham* III. xvii, All that especial neatness of upholstering paraphernalia. 1859 SALA *Tw. round Clock* 210 The march of upholstering intellect is there in its entirety.

**Upho·lsterous,** *a.* [f. as prec.] Given to the use of upholstery.

1887 W. CORY *Lett. & Jrnls.* (1897) 523 Since then our educated people have been less happy, though more upholsterous. 1894 T. PINKERTON *Blizzard*, etc. 101 He was not at all upholsterous.

**Upho·lstery.** [f. UPHOLSTER *sb.*] Upholsterer's work or materials; *spec.* the fabrics and materials used in the covering and stuffing of furniture; the collective use of these in a room or house.

1649 J. TAYLOR (Water P.) *Western Voy.* 13 In the Mount I saw a craggy rugged seat, of Rocky Upholstery, which the old fabulous rumour calls St. Michaels Chair. 1653 *Ordin. Contin. Excise* 17 Mar. 111 Linnens fine and course, Upholstery, Haberdashery [etc.]. 1756 W. OWEN *Bk. Fairs* (1788) 62 Hacheston, Suffolk, Nov. 12., for boots, shoes, upholstery, and joiners. 1859 THACKERAY *Virgin.* iv, Mantelpieces, carved cornice-work,..carpets and costly upholstery. 1882 MISS BRADDON *Mt. Royal* I. vi. 147 The bedrooms had been improved by modern upholstery.

*transf.* 1850 LD. OSBORNE *Gleanings W. Irel.* 86 There were drills, and carts, and other farm upholstery.

*fig.* 1862 CARLYLE *Fredk. Gt.* XIV. viii. III. 737 Fantastic Bielfeld..becomes positively wearisome, chanting the upholsteries of Life.

**b.** *attrib.* and *Comb.*

1803 SHERATON *Cabinet Dict.* (title-p.), The Terms used in the Cabinet, Chair and Upholstery Branches. 1844 M. F. OSSOLI *Wom. in 19th C.* (1862) 99 She..is, in short, always spoken and thought of upholstery-wise. 1858 HAWTHORNE *Fr. & It. Note-bks.* II. 123 Their whole charm is..in no degree of the upholstery kind. 1866 *Lond. Rev.* 15 Sept. 287/2 Those upholstery authors..whose books have the run at Mudie's.

Hence **Upho·lsterydom.** *rare*[−1].

1860 SALA in *Cornh. Mag.* I. 572 He went on painting, in spite of all the Morrises in upholsterydom.

**Upho·lstress.** Also **-holsteress.** [f. UPHOLSTER(ER).] A female upholsterer.

1859 *Edin. Rev.* CIX. 321 The London dress-makers..and the upholstresses. 1884 *Pall Mall G.* 2 Aug. 6/1 The Secretary of the Upholsteresses' Society.

†**Upho·ven,** *pa. pple. Obs.* [UP- 5. Cf. UPHEAVE *v.*] Raised up, exalted.

*c* 1200 ORMIN 12148 To beon abufenn alle menn Upphofenn heȝhe & wurrþedd. *Ibid.* 17389. *a* 1300 *E. E. Psalter* lxxiv. 11 Up-hoven ben hornes of rightwys.

**Uphroe,** var. EUPHROE (fir-pole).

**Uphu·ng,** *pa. pple.* Also 4 **uphang,** 6 *Sc.* **-hing.** [UP- 5. Cf. OE. *up-hangen.*] Hung up, suspended.

*a* 1300 *Cursor M.* 20912 Vphang his fette, his hed don, Naild on þe rod he was. *c* 1440 *Pallad. on Husb.* IV. 875 Take brawny bodied [foals],..Smale ballockyng, and euere short vphonge. 1513 DOUGLAS *Æneid* VIII. xii. 116 On the proud pillaris..[he] maid [them] thar be vp hing. 1757 DYER *Fleece* III. 170 Oft the wet web is steep'd..: then uphung On rugged tenters,..Its level surface..it expands. 1805–6 CARY *Dante, Inf.* VIII. 3 Our eyes Its height ascended, where we mark'd uphung Two cressets. 1867 M. ARNOLD *Bacchanalia* ii, Uphung the spear, unbent the bow.

**Uphu·rl,** *v.* [UP- 4.] *trans.* To hurl up, throw aloft. Also **Uphu·rled** *pa. pple.*

1582 STANYHURST *Æneis* II. (Arb.) 63 Thee wals God Neptune, with mace threeforcked, vphurleth. 1845 MANGAN *German Anthology* II. 128 From thousand smoke-enveloped cones, Colossal blocks..Are night by night uphurled in air. 1860 BORROW *Sleeping Bard* 40 For all the ills by hell uphurl'd It has a remedy. 1898 MEREDITH *Poems, Hard Weather* II. 111 Her passion for old giantkind, That scaled the mount, uphurled the rock.

**Upjet, -keep,** *v.*: see UP- 4.

**U·pkeep,** *sb.* [UP- 1 b. Cf. KEEP *v.* 57 d.] Maintenance in good condition or repair; also, the cost of such. (Freq. from *c* 1885.)

1884 *Pall Mall G.* 10 May 10/2 Arrangements..for continuing the up-keep and in-gathering of the crops in Mauritius and Ceylon. 1887 Mrs. Daly *Digging & Squatting* 171 The Northern Territory depends very much upon the gold revenue for the upkeep and support of the settlement. 1893 Dk. Argyll *Unseen Found. Soc.* v. 145 The constant upkeep of innumerable canals.

So **U·pkeeping** *vbl. sb.* (Up- 7.)

1899 *Westm. Gaz.* 26 June 7/1 Premises which took £150 a year for up-keeping. *Ibid.*, The up-keeping of the premises.

**Upkever, -kindle, -knit**: see Up- 4.

**Uplai·d**, *pa. pple.* [Up- 5. Cf. Uplay *v.*]

**1.** Laid up; put away or in place.

*c* 1400 *Northern Passion* (H.) 872 Ilka man said..What þai suld with þe siluer do,..pat it suld sauely be vp laid. *c* 1425 Wyntoun *Cron.* v. vii. 1262 Quhen þe chesabill is vplaid Befor the eleuatioun.

**†2.** Upturned, overthrown. *Obs.*$^{-1}$

1582 Stanyhurst *Æneis* ii. (Arb.) 63 Then dyd I marck playnely thee castel of Ilion vplayd, And Troian buyldings quit topsy turuye remooued.

**†U·pland**, *sb.*[1] and *a.*[1] *Obs.* Also 1, 4 uppe-, 3 upe-, 4 oppe-, 6 uplande. [Subst. and adj. use of the phrase *uppe land*, in the country: see Up *prep.*[1] 5 a, and cf. Uponland *adv.*]

**A.** *sb.* The parts of a country outside the towns; the rural districts.

*a* 1122 *O. E. Chron.* (Laud MS.) an. 1087, Se cyng..bead þæt ælc man..sceolde cuman to him..of porte & of uppelande. 1209 in *Eng. Hist. Rev.* Oct. (1901) 720 Altres gens et numeement cil de upelande. 1303 R. Brunne *Handl. Synne* 1315 Ȝyf þou do any man yn prysun,..Or bynde yn upland or in burgh. 1346 *Little Red Bk. Bristol* (1900) II. 14 Drap qest fulee sur oppelande. *c* 1350 *Cron. London* (Camden) 46 En cele temps fut le vj.me dener de bienz levé en Loundres et en autres cytés en Engletere, et sure upelond le x.me denier. 1377 *Ann. Barber Surgeons* (1890) 36 [Barbers from] uppelande. *c* 1500 *World & Child* 579 Poore men that come from vplande. *c* 1510 Barclay *Mirr. Gd. Manners* (1570) G iv, Forbidding great building sumptuous ..in Countrey or uplande. [1864 Sir F. Palgrave *Norm. & Eng.* IV. 43 Rufus renewed his general summons to his English lieges. From..town and from upland they were called.]

**B.** *adj.*

**1.** Living out in the country; rustic, rural.

14.. in *Sc. Acts Parlt.* (1844) I. 339 Of þe borowyng of uplande mannis pundis. 1598 Hakluyt *Voy.* I. 485 Taking away with him the vpland, or countrey people that should haue tilled the ground. 1599 Nashe *Lenten Stuff* E j b, Other engrating vpland cormorants will grunt out [etc.]. 1615 Chapman *Odyss.* i. 315 Kept alive Within an isle by rude and upland men. 1670 Milton *Hist. Eng.* ii. 48 In peace the Upland Inhabitants besides hunting tended thir flocks and heards.

*Comb.* *c* 1611 Chapman *Odyssey* ix. 308 This heape of fortitude [*sc.* the Cyclops], That so illiterate was, and vpland rude.

**2.** Characteristic of the country; of rustic form or make. *rare*$^{-1}$.

1666 *Despauterius' Gram. Inst.* (1677) C j, *Pero, peronis*, an upland shooe.

**U·pland**, *sb.*[2] and *a.*[2] [f. Up *a.* 1 + Land *sb.*, perhaps partly suggested by prec. Cf. ON. *Upplǫnd* pl., the name of the eastern inland counties of Norway; MSw. *Upland* (Sw. *Uppland*), a district in central Sweden; MDa. *Opland* Sweden, Norw. *uppland*, Da. *opland* the inland country.]

**A.** *sb.* **1.** The part of a country lying away from the sea; the interior or high-lying districts. Also *pl.* Now *arch.*

1579–80 North *Plutarch* (1595) 687 He determined to draw these pirats from the sea into the vpland. 1615 G. Sandys *Trav.* 12 Smal watch-towers, which..do giue knowledge vnto one another (and so to the vpland) of suspected enemies. 1618 Bolton *Florus* iii. vi. (1636) 193 Who transplanted this brood of Mariners..out of the very ken of the sea, and, as it were, teddred them fast in the uplands [L. *mediterraneis agris*]. 1825 Jamieson *Suppl.*, *Upwark*, apparently, labour in the *inland*, or *upland*, as distinguished from employment in fishing. 1857 Hughes *Tom Brown* i. i, Leaving their mark in American forests and Australian uplands.

**2.** An area or stretch of high ground; a piece of high, hilly, or mountainous country. Usually in *pl.*

1566 *Act* 8 *Eliz.* c. 13 § 1 Beakons..in suche Place or Places of the Sea Shores and Uplandes neere the Sea costes. 1589 Fleminge *Virg. Eclogues* vi. 18 You the nymphs of woods, Close in the uplands [L. *claudite saltus*] of your woods. 1617 Brathwait *Law of Drinking* 147 Their Long Acres, Uplands and Downe-lands shall flie in a trice to retaine thee. *a* 1676 Hale *Prim. Orig. Man.* ii. vii. (1677) 192 The Downs or Uplands of Cammington in Huntingdonshire. *Ibid.* 200 The Up-lands in England yield strong, sinewy, hardy Men. 1724 De Foe *Tour Gt. Brit.* (1742) I. 9 They generally chose to leave their own Lasses to their Neighbours out of the Marshes, and went into the Uplands for a Wife. 1764 Goldsm. *Trav.* 107 Its uplands sloping deck the mountain's side. 1787 G. White *Selborne* i, At the foot of this hill, one stage or step from the uplands, lies the village. 1807 J. Barlow *Columb.* i. 298 How slope their uplands to the morning sun! 1825–9 Mrs. Sherwood *Lady of Manor* I. vi. 176 A blue upland in the remotest distance finished this exquisite picture. 1879 Farrar *St. Paul* I. 414 He was working with Paul alone on the wild uplands of Lycaonia.

**b.** In sing. with *the*, or without article.

1699 Dampier *Voy.* II. ii. 111 The whole Country, the Up-land I mean, seems to be much the same [kind of soil]. 1784 Cowper *Task* v. 197 As a shepherd separates his flock, These to the upland, to the valley those. 1813 Scott *Rokeby* v. ii, The eve, that slow on upland fades, Has darker closed on Rokeby's glades. 1856 Merivale *Rom. Emp.* xxxviii. IV 359 They had emerged..from the woods, and had gained the open upland of swamp and moor. 1891 T. Hardy *Tess* viii, Their present speed on the upland being by no means slow.

**3.** High ground, as opposed to meadow or marsh; ground not liable to flooding; a stretch of this. Chiefly *local* and *U. S.*

1572 *Kent & Surrey Sewers Comm.* (1909) 115 Alle the vpp lande betwin Newington and Lambeth Sewinge to the same sluce. 1580 Tusser *Husb.* (1878) 51 New broken vpland..for wheat is not best. 1598 *Archdeaconry of Essex Minutes* (MS.) fol. 49 Being sessed by the acar..at id the acre of vpland and iid the acre for marshe. 1639 in Coffin *Hist. Newberry, Mass.* (1845) 29 All the upland and meadow and marish between us and Ipswich. 1696 Aubrey *Misc.* 11 This Marsh-land..was never worth one Farthing to me, but very often eat into the Rents of the Up-land. 1708 *Lond. Gaz.* No. 4489/3, 46 Acres of Uplands, or Side-hill-Lands. 1763 *Museum Rust.* I. 307 If it was sowed in up-land,..you could not get the timothy-grass out of it. 1774 Goldsm. *Nat. Hist.* I. 159 A large upland, with its houses, its corn, and cattle,..loosened from its place. 1833 Tennyson *Lady of Shalott* i. 34 The reaper weary, Piling sheaves in uplands airy. 1841 N. P. Rogers in *Whittier's Prose Wks.* (1889) II. 227 The Pemigewasset,..meandering from upland to upland through the meadows.

**4.** *ellipt.* in *pl.* Upland cotton. (Cf. B. 2 c.)

1858 Homans *Cycl. Comm.* 448 Cotton..[exported from] Florida. To foreign ports—Uplands, 30,880 bales. 1880 C. R. Markham *Peruv. Bark* 468 Species of cotton...New Orleans or 'Uplands'..'Uplands' grown in India.

**B.** *attrib.* or as *adj.*

**1.** Of districts or places: Lying away from the sea or in the higher parts of a country; inland, remote.

1575 *Russia* (Hakl. Soc. No. 20) 9 The uplande countries of Russia..stretchethe exceding large and long. 1582 Batman *Barth. De P. R.* xviii. lxxxi. 376/2 The want of tillage..decayes villages, hamlets, and vpland townes. 1601 R. Johnson *Kingd. & Commw.* (1603) 14 The vpland townes are fairer and richer, then those that stand nearer the sea. 1632 Milton *L'Allegro* 92 Som times with secure delight The up-land Hamlets will invite. 1829 Scott *Old Mort.* Introd., The little upland village of Balmaclellan, in the Glenkens of Galloway. 1872 A. de Vere *Leg. St. Patrick* 73 Fire takes the little cot beside the mere, And leaps upon the upland village.

**b.** Living inland.

1716 B. Church *Hist. Philip's War* (1865) I. 92 Some.. Narraganset Indians, and some other Upland Indians, in all about 300. 1870 Burton *Hist. Scot.* lxvi. VI. 345 Among the upland folk of Scotland there were strong prejudices against all attempts to settle in distant wilds.

**2.** Lying higher than the surrounding country; forming part of an elevated area; situated on high ground.

1610 Norden *Spec. Brit., Cornw.* (1728) 20 Their haye groweth comonly in the vplande and drye groundes. 1707 Mortimer *Husb.* 12 The worst of Up-land Meadows is that they often need mending or feeding. 1731 Miller *Gard. Dict.* s.v. *Ranunculus*, Take a Quantity of fresh Earth from a rich up-land Pasture. 1795 Southey *Joan of Arc* ix. 292 Dark on the upland bank The hedge-row trees..Rose on the grey horizon. 1843 Lytton *Last Bar.* i. i. 23 The twin green hills..with the upland park and chase. 1879 A. R. Wallace *Australasia* ii. 15 These highlands generally present the appearance of hilly upland plains.

**b.** Living on, or frequenting, high ground. (In modern use freq. in specific names of birds, etc.)

1622 J. Taylor (Water P.) *Farewell to Tower Bottles* A 4, When Vpland Trades-men thus dares take in hand A wat'ry buis'nesse, they not vnderstand. 1695 E. Gibson tr. *Camden's Brit.* 408 Fenmen, a sort of people..of brutish uncivilíz'd tempers, envious of all others whom they term Upland men. *a* 1825 [see Uplander]. 1859 Darwin *Orig. Spec.* vi. 185 There are upland geese with webbed feet which rarely or never go near the water. 1867 Morris *Jason* iv. 2 The upland sheep Must guard themselves..Against the wolf. 1872 Coues *N. Amer. Birds* 260 Upland Plover. Field Plover. 1878 A. Pope (*title*), Upland Game Birds and Water Fowl of the United States.

**c.** Growing upon high ground; belonging to species growing or developed on high ground. *Upland cotton*, a class of short-stapled cotton. Also (of minerals, etc.), found on high ground.

1639 T. de Gray *Expert Farrier* 309 Fine upland hay, which was cut about midsummer. 1759 Miller *Gard. Dict.* (ed. 7) s.v. *Pasture*, The best Sort of Upland Hay Seeds, taken from the cleanest Pastures. 1789 T. Wright *Meth. Watering Meadows* (1790) 43 The hay of watered meadows is by no means equal in value to upland hay. 179. Nemnich *Polyglot Lex.* s.v., Upland willow. The red willow. 1796 Kirwan *Elem. Min.* (ed. 2) II. 173 Upland Argillaceous Iron Ore. 1832 McCulloch *Dict. Commerce* 409 The upland or bowed Georgia cotton forms the..best portion of the short stapled class. 1833 G. B. Wood & Bache *Dispensatory* (1865) 710 *Rhus glabrum*..,called variously smooth sumach, Pennsylvania sumach, and upland sumach. 1858 Homans *Cycl. Comm.* 436/1 The upland cotton is a different species from the sea-island. 1894 *Yellow Book* I. 189 Where the upland hay..stretched thirstily up to the clouds.

**d.** Flowing down from higher ground.

1653 Blithe *Eng. Improver Impr.* 56 Cleer from any Land-floods, or up-land waters running through them. 1707 Mortimer *Husb.* 18 Fenny Lands..drowned by Upland-floods and great Rains.

**†Upland**, *adv.*[1] *Obs.* [Later form of *up land*, *uppe lande*, etc.: see Up *prep.*[1] 5 a.] Out in the country; = Uponland *adv.*

*c* 1380 Wyclif *Wks.* (1880) 176 To..helpe here pore neiȝeboris..& parische chirchis vplond. *c* 1400 *Found. St. Bartholomew's* (1923) 20 Hit ys tolde of a Richemanne vplond dwellyng that come to this Chirche. *c* 1449 Pecock *Repr.* i. vi. 28 Men of the cuntre vplond bringen into Londoun in Mydsomer eue braunchis of trees..and flouris. 1551 Bale *Eng. Votaries* ii. 67 b, In most places they dwelt vplonde.

**b.** *Jack* (*John*) *Upland*, used as a name for a rustic. (Cf. Upaland *adv.* b.)

1402 in Wright *Pol. Poems* (Rolls) II. 16, I, Jacke Upland, make my mone to very God. *Ibid.* 40 A frere..aresoneth Jak Uplonde. 1529 Lyndesay *Compl.* 407 Ihone Upeland bene full blyith, I trow, Because the rysche bus kepis his kow.

**Upland**, *adv.*[2] *rare*$^{-1}$. [f. Up *prep.*[2] 6 + Land *sb.*] In the higher or inner part of a country.

*a* 1674 Milton *Hist. Moscovia* ii. Wks. 1851 VIII. 483 Further up-land they have also built other Cities of Wood.

**U·plander.** [f. Upland *sb.*[2] Cf. Da. *oplænder.*] An inhabitant or native of an upland part or district.

1699 Boyer, Uplander, *montagnard.* 1706 Phillips (ed. Kersey), *Uplander*, one that lives in the High Grounds; an High-lander. 1773 Johnson (ed. 4) s.v. *Upland*, Probably because the uplanders, having less commerce, were less civilised. *a* 1825 Forby *Voc. E. Anglia* II. 365 *Uplander, Uplandman*, an inhabitant of the uplands. 1868 Morris *Earthly Par.* I. i. 14 But fifty knew the shipman's gear, The rest were uplanders. 1888 Oman *Hist. Greece* xi. (1901) 103 These Uplanders occupied the arid hills of the interior.

**Upla·ndish**, *a.* and *sb.* Also 4–5 vplondische, -isshe, -ysche, -ysshe, 6 vplandis(s)he, -ys(s)he, etc. [f. Upland *sb.*[1] and [2] + -ish. Cf. OE. *uplendisc*, MDa. *oplændisk* 'Swedish' (Da. *oplandsk* uplandish), MSw. *upländsker, uplenzsker*, etc. (Sw. *uppländsk*) of Uppland (also = Swedish), Icel. *upplenzkr* of Upplönd in Norway.]

**†1.** Of persons: = Upland *a.*[1] 1. *Obs.*

Very common in the 16th c., freq. in the sense of 'rustic rude, uncultivated, boorish'.

1387 Trevisa *Higden* (Rolls) II. 159 Vplondisshe men [L. *rurales homines*] wil likne hym self to gentil men. 1398 — *Barth. De P. R.* xiv. xlix. (Tollem. MS.), Of þis name *rus* þe uplondische men haue þat name and ben clepid *rustici.* *c* 1440 *Promp. Parv.* 512/2 Vplondysche mann, *villanus.* 1490 Caxton *Eneydos* Prol. A ij, This present booke is not for a rude vplondyssh man to laboure therin.. but onely for a clerke. 1529 More *Dyaloge* iv. Wks. 257/2 Now was thys doctrine in Almaine of the comen vplandishe people..plesauntly harde. 1542 Udall *Erasm. Apoph.* 167 The fair flatte truthe, that the uplandyshe or homely and plain clubbes of ye countree dooen use. 1592 Greene *Upst. Courtier* C 1 b, Shamste thou not vplandish vpstart to heare me discourse thy imperfections? 1603 Knolles *Hist. Turks* (1621) 155 The Grecians.., especially that rusticall and uplandish companie, began to flie. 1647 Ward *Simple Cobler* 76 An uplandish Rusticke [may speak] more in one word than himselfe..understands.

**†b.** Characteristic of, pertaining to, rustics. *Obs.*

1534 Whitinton *Tullyes Offices* ii. (1540) 113 Glory and fame before rychesse: customes..of cyties before uplandisshe customes. 1565 Stapleton tr. *Bede's Hist. Ch. Eng.* 147 The vnsemely dwelling and vplandish rudenesse of the inhabitants.

**†c.** Of bees: Wild. *Obs.*$^{-1}$

1608 Topsell *Serpents* 65 Others [*sc.* bees] againe are altogether wilde, vplandish, and agrestiall.

**2.** Of places: = Upland *a.*[2] 1. Now *rare.*

*c* 1380 Wyclif *Sel. Wks.* I. 197 No drede Crist wente to smale uplondishe touns, as to Bethfage and to Cana. 1513 *Life Hen. V* (1911) 110 All other were lodged in vplandish cots, such as they coulde finde. 1568 Withals *Dict.* 37 b/2 The vplandish house or dwelling place, *villa, tugurium.* 1589 Puttenham *Eng. Poesie* iii. iv. (Arb.) 157 In any vplandish village or corner of a Realme, where is no resort but of poore rusticall or vnciuill people. 1622 Callis *Stat. Sewers* (1647) 66 In Towns and Villages which be in the high uplandish Countries. 1642 *Declar. Lords & Com. Stat.* 5 *Hen. IV*, 4 All such as do lodge strangers in uplandish Towns. [1784 Cullum *Hawsted* 220 *note*, These [districts] used to be called *uplandish*, a term that implied an inferiority in civilization.] 1906 Gasquet *Eng. Mediæval Parish Life* ii. 41 A small, uplandish, remote parish..on the borders of Exmoor.

**†3.** Of ground: = Upland *a.*[2] 2. *Obs.*

1551 Robinson tr. *More's Utopia* ii. (1895) 118, xv. myles space of vplandyshe grounde, where the sea had no passage. 1582 Stanyhurst *Æneis* iii. (Arb.) 88 Then far of vplandish we doe view thee fird Sicil Ætna.

**†b.** = Upland *a.*[2] 2 b, 2 c. *Obs.*

1545 Ascham *Toxoph.* (Arb.) 128 Whether there be any difference, as concernynge the fether of..a fennye goose, or an vplandish goose. 1623 Markham *Cheap Husb.* (ed. 3) 53 For his hay, you shall see that it be dry short vplandish hay.

**†4.** Outlandish, foreign. Also as *sb.*, foreign speech. *Obs.*

1586 Ferne *Blaz. Gentrie* ii. 23 You chop so much vplandish in your tale that by my troth, I scantly vnderstand the halfe of it. 1589 *Rare Tri. Love & Fort.* iv. (Roxb. Cl.) 122 *Bomelio.* You are de runaway from your ma'ter... *Lentulo.* I a runnaway, sirra? goe with your uplandishe, goe. 1607 Heywood *Faire Maide Exch.* E 4, He had..made some scuruy quaint collection Of fustian phrases, and vplandish wordes. 1609 W. M. *Man in Moone* C 3, Natiue apparell will not content him, he flieth for vplandish fashions.

Hence **Upla·ndishness.** *rare*$^{-0}$.

1530 Palsgr. 285/2 Uplandysshnesse, *ruralite.*

**†U·plands**, *a.* *Obs.* Chiefly *Sc.* [f. Upland *sb.* (either possessive sing. or the plur. used attrib.), or Sc. var. of prec.] = Uplandish *a.*

*c* 1330 *Arth. & Merl.* 5077 (Kölbing), The vplondismen, þat hadden ladde Cartes & somers. *Ibid.* 5271, 6776. 14.. in *Sc. Acts Parlt.* (1814) I. 333 Ilke burges may punde ane uplandis man. *c* 1450 Holland *Howlat* 218 Held he na houss; Bot in wplandis townis..Cryand full crowss. 1500–20 Dunbar *Poems* xiii. 1 Ane mvrlandis man of vplandis mak. 1585 Jas. I. *Ess. Poesie* (Arb.) 63 Gif zour purpose be of landwart effairis, [take heed] To vse corruptit and vplandis wordis.

**Uplay·**, *v.* [Up- 4. Cf. Du. *opleggen*, G. *auflegen*, and Uplaid *pa. pple.* 1.] *trans.* To lay up, store up.

1591 SPENSER *Ruins of Time* 212 All is with him dead, Saue what in heauens storehouse he vplaid. *c* 1600 DONNE *To R. Woodward* 32 We..may, If we can..thrive, uplay Much, much deare treasure for the great rent day. 1609 — *Annunc. & Passion* 45 This treasure then, in grosse, my Soule uplay. *a* 1850 ROSSETTI *Dante & Circle* I. (1874) 239 As he who evermore uplays That heavenly wealth which the worm cannot waste.

**U·pleap,** *sb.* [UP- 2.]

**1.** An upward leap or spring.

1876 MISS BROUGHTON *Joan* I. xxxiii, The fire giving one sudden upleap,..plays upon his face. 1885 E. F. BYRRNE *Entangled* III. II. xviii. 140 This upleap of wild regret..was not dependent upon reason.

**2.** *Mining.* (See quot.)

1883 GRESLEY *Gloss. Coal-m.* 268 *Up-leap*, a fault which appears as an up-throw.

**Uplea·p,** *v.* [UP- 4. Cf. OE. *uphléapende* pres. pple. and WFris. *opljeappe*, Du. *oploopen*, MSw. and Sw. *upplöpa*, MDa. and Da. *opløbe*, G. *auflaufen*.] *intr.* To leap or spring up or upwards.

*c* 1205 LAY. 1882 Ofte heo up lupan [*c* 1275 vp leopen], alse heo fleon wolden. *a* 1300 *Cursor M.* 5193 Israel wit þis vp-lepp þat moght noght forwit strid a step. *c* 1350 *Will. Palerne* 3283 þe stede..vp-leped, & faire wiþ his fore fet kneled doun to grounde. *a* 1560 PHAER *Æneid* IX. (1562) Ffi, The wyld seas meeting mixe, and darkning skyes vpleapes yᵉ sands. 1600 FAIRFAX *Tasso* III. xlix, But now Rinaldo from the earth vp lept. 1805 WORDSW. *Prelude* V. 441 And, now and then, a fish up-leaping snapped The breathless stillness. 1888 R. BUCHANAN *City of Dream* VIII. 152 The sable steed upleapt And bounded on.

**Uplea·ping** *vbl. sb.* and *ppl. a.* (UP- 6 and 7.) 1867 'OUIDA' *Idalia* xxxiii, A sudden upleaping of the vivid life within him. 1885–94 R. BRIDGES *Eros & Psyche* Dec. xxvi, Its little rill is an upleaping jet Of cold Cocytus.

**Upled, -lent**: see UP- 5.

**U·plift,** *sb.* [UP- 2. Cf. next.]

**1.** The fact of being raised or elevated.

*a* 1845 WILLIS *David's Grief for Child* 28 His brow Had the inspired up-lift of the king's. 1890 STANLEY *Darkest Africa* I. xvi. 413 There was uniform uplift and subsidence of the constantly twirling spear blades.

**b.** *spec.* An elevation or rise in level, esp. of a portion of the earth's surface.

1853 KANE *Grinnell Exp.* xvii. (1856) 128 The false horizon, which I had selected as an index of the uplift. 1856 — *Arct. Expl.* II. vii. 82 Indicative of secular uplift of coast. 1878 WHITTIER *Seeking Waterfall* xix, The grand uplift of mountain lines. 1882 *U.S. Rep. Prec. Met.* 619 The assumption of an uplift or elevation of the Sierra Nevada.

**2.** *fig.* An elevating effect, result, or influence in the sphere of morality, emotion, physical condition, etc.

In very common use after 1890.

1873 HOLLAND *A. Bonnic.* i. 22 But it is impossible that he could know what an uplift he gave to the life to which he ministered. 1885 E. F. BYRRNE *Entangled* II. II. viii. 255 This uplift of the heart..towards a sterner and more austere allegiance to duty. 1889 *Lancet* 28 Sept. 661/1 The rapidity of the uplift in health in many of the cases. 1893 K. L. BATES *Eng. Relig. Drama* 195 The uplift and the glory of conception melted and were gone.

**Upli·ft,** *v.* [UP- 4. Cf. MSw. *uplypta, -lyfta*, etc. (Sw. *upplyfta*), MDa. *oplyfte* (Da. *opløfte*), and UPLIFT(ED *pa. pples.*]

**1.** *trans.* To elevate in rank, honour, estate, or estimation. Also *absol.* Now *rare.*

1338 R. BRUNNE *Chron.* (1810) 72 þe Londreis..Him for þar kyng vplift, his name was kald Edgar. *a* 1340 HAMPOLE *Psalter*, etc. 501 Lord makis pore and he makis riche: he mekis and he vpliftis. 1390 GOWER *Conf.* I. 27 Alisaundre put hem under,..So that the Monarchie lefte With Grecs, and here astat uplefte. 1554–9 *Songs & Ball. Phil. & Mary* (Roxb.) 3 For of balefull branches and fyere brandes of hel To be members of mersye he hathe us up lyfft. 1611 SHAKS. *Cymb.* v. iv. 103 Your low-laide Sonne, our Godhead will vplift. 1860 PUSEY *Minor Prophets* 593/1 He uplifts ordinary things, that they too should be sacred. 1863 KINGLAKE *Crimea* I. p. x, That which will uplift the repute of the far-famed Russian infantry.

†**b.** To support, assist. *Obs.*⁻¹

1338 R. BRUNNE *Chron.* (1810) 55 þei said he did inouh, þe erle alle vplift, þe kyng forgaf his wraþe.

**c.** *Sc.* To make proud. (Cf. UPLIFTED *ppl. a.* 3.)

1863 JEAN L. WATSON *By-gone Days* 176 Though she was sae bonny, that never seemed to uplift her.

**d.** To elevate morally. (Cf. UPLIFTED *ppl. a.* 2.)

1883 FAIRBAIRN *Stud. Relig. & Theol.* (1910) 94 The regeneration that changes the man and uplifts the life. 1890 J. PULSFORD *Loyalty to Christ* I. 53 That He may be able to uplift and bless men.

**2.** To lift up to a higher level or more erect position; to raise, rear, erect.

*a* 1340 HAMPOLE *Psalter* ci. 11 Vpliftand þou downsmate me. 1390 GOWER *Conf.* I. 48, I uplifte Min hefd with that. *a* 1400–50 *Alexander* 805 þen Alexander in ane ire his arme vp-liftis. *c* 1440 *Ipomydon* 1911 Hys swerd in bothe handis he toke..And hertely he dyd it vplyfte. 1582 STANYHURST *Æneis* IV. (Arb.) 102 Theese woords, vplifting both his hands, he toe Iuppiter vttred. 1590 SPENSER *F. Q.* II. i. 46 The gentle knight her soone with carefull paine Vplifted light, and softly did vphold. 1606 SHAKS. *Ant. & Cl.* v. ii. 211 Slaues..shall Vplift vs to the view. 1667 MILTON *P. L.* VI. 646 They pluckt the seated Hills.., and by the shaggie tops Up lifting bore them in thir hands. 1757 DYER *Fleece* II. 234 Soon..the huge stone Up-lifting to the deck, [they] unmoor'd the bark. 1784 COWPER *Task* IV. 274 The glowing hearth..With faint illumination, that uplifts The shadow to the ceiling. 1820 SHELLEY *Prometh. Unb.* I. 159 At thy voice her pining sons uplifted Their prostrate brows. 1846 HAWTHORNE *Mosses* I. i. 7 The boy uplifted his axe. 1887 *Spectator* 7 May 626/1 Some internal force has uplifted the earth's crust along a certain line.

*fig.* 1594 SPENSER *Amoretti* lxxxii, I..shall all be spent, In setting your immortall prayses forth. Whose lofty argument vplifting me, shall lift you vp vnto an high degree. 1846 MANGAN *Poems* (1903) 24 On thy knees Uplift thy soul to God alone.

**3.** *Sc.* To collect, levy (rents, etc.); to draw (wages).

1508 *Reg. Privy Seal Scot.* I. 256/2 The males, proffitis and dewiteis to rais, uplift and inbring. 1553 *Reg. Privy Council Scot.* I. 139 Under the pane of xl lib., to be uplitit and takin of every Provest. 1617 *Extr. Aberd. Reg.* (1848) II. 354 Vnder the paines following, to be vplifted of the contravenar as oft as they be..convict. 1646 Z. BOYD in *Zion's Flowers* (1855) App. 31/1, I..give the..Colledge full power to uplift the same. 1710 in *Nairne Peerage Evid.* (1874) 44 Since we have uplifted two thousand of the three thousand merks due to him. 1753 *Stewart's Trial* 250 That Glenure..had employed him to uplift the rents from the other tenants. 1869 *Act* 32 & 33 *Vict.* c. 116 § 7 A power ..to enter..the lands disponed in security, and uplift the rents thereof. 1895 CROCKETT *Cleg Kelly* xii, He endeavoured to uplift his week's wage before it was due.

**4.** = RAISE *v.* 13.

1816 SCOTT *Bl. Dwarf* xiii, When he first uplifted the psalm in presence of those persons. 1847 EMERSON *Dæmonic & Celest. Love* 26 New flowerets bring, new prayers uplift. *a* 1850 BRYANT *Earth* 43 Earth Uplifts a general cry for guilt and wrong. 1887 BOWEN *Æneid* VI. 174 All now..uplift their voices in grief.

**Upli·ft,** *pa. pple.* and *ppl. a.* [UP- 5. See LIFT *v.*] = UPLIFTED.

1303 R. BRUNNE *Handl. Synne* 7086 Almes..ys a 3yfte; And for þe 3yuyng, man ys vplyfte. 13.. *E. E. Allit. P.* B. 987 Wyth ly3t louez vplyfte þay loued hym swyþe. 1667 MILTON *P. L.* I. 193 Satan talking to his neerest Mate With Head up-lift above the wave. 1748 RICHARDSON *Clarissa* VI. 63 How many..admirers, with up-lift hands, I should have! *a* 1822 SHELLEY *Fragm. Unf. Drama* 239 O friend, sleep was a veil uplift from Heaven. 1841 KINGSLEY *Palinodia* 2 Torrent-furrowed slopes, And bare and silent brows uplift to heaven. 1868 GEO. ELIOT *Sp. Gipsy* I. 60 A figure lithe, ..now stood With ripened arms uplift and regal head.

**Upli·ftable,** *a.* *Sc. rare*⁻¹. [f. UPLIFT *v.* 3.] Leviable.

1670 in Paterson *Hist. Regality Musselburgh* (1857) 26 An annual rent of 2400 merk upliftable furth of the said toun.

**Uplifted,** *pa. pple.* and *ppl. a.* [UP- 5. Cf. UPLIFT *v.* and *pa. pple.*]

**1.** Raised, elevated, held up; also *fig.*, exalted in estate.

*a* 1300 *E. E. Psalter* xxxvi. 37 Vphouen I saw þe wicked man And lifted [*H.* uplifted; L. *elevatum*] als cedre of Yban. *Ibid.* lxxxvii. 16, I am up-lifted [*L. exaltatus*], I am meked. *c* 1410 *Lanterne of Li3t* 129, I haue sen þe vnpitiouose..enhaunsid & vplifted as þe cedre trees of Liban. 1593 SHAKS. *Rich. II*, II. ii. 50 The banish'd Bullingbrocke ..with vp-lifted Armes is safe arriu'd At Rauenspurg. 1630 MILTON *Solemn Music* 11 Where the bright Seraphim.. Their loud up-lifted Angel trumpets blow. 1667 — *P. L.* I. 347 Th' uplifted Spear Of their great Sultan waving to direct Thir course. 1725 POPE *Odyss.* II. 424 The matron with uplifted eyes Attests th' all-seeing Sovereign of the skies. 1748 RICHARDSON *Clarissa* VII. 125 This dame in effigie, with uplifted head and hand. 1822 SCOTT *Nigel* xiv, 'Now, Heaven bless you, my lord,' said Richie Moniplies, with uplifted eyes. 1868 *Rep. U.S. Commissioner Agric.* (1869) 225 These table-lands..are the uplifted beds of an ancient ocean. 1887 BOWEN *Æneid* IV. 246 The uplifted crest and the proud Slopes of the age-worn Atlas.

*fig.* 1595 SPENSER *Col. Clout* 816 So we him adore With humble hearts to heauen vplifted hie. 1805 WORDSW. *Prelude* V. 226 Yet I..will pour out Thanks with uplifted heart.

**b.** Exalted in fame; renowned.

1596 SPENSER *F. Q.* VI. Prol. vi, Yet so from low to high vplifted is your name. 1885 TENNYSON *Balin & Balan* 491 A name..Which our high Lancelot hath so lifted up, And been thereby uplifted.

**2.** Elevated intellectually, morally, or spiritually.

*c* 1454 PECOCK *Folewer* 15 þe more a man..takiþ into him of kunnyng, þe more is his resoun vp liftid. 1548 GESTE *Pr. Masse* H ij b, With our myndes eleuate and vplifted. 1818 SHELLEY *Eugan. Hills* 360 The winds whose wings rain balm On the uplifted soul. 1839 BAILEY *Festus* 46 Are they not worthy of a deathless state; A boundless scope; a high uplifted life? 1890 J. PULSFORD *Loyalty to Christ* I. 116 Ye gladdened and uplifted ones, come ye aside also awhile with Jesus.

**3.** Elated; rendered proud. Now *Sc.* and *north. dial.*

1606 SHAKS. *Tr. & Cr.* III. ii. 175 Or that perswasion could but thus conuince me,..How were I then vp-lifted. 1747 *Mem. Nutrebian Crt.* II. 82 Maillan, excessively up-lifted with the imagined advancement of his daughter. 1823 SCOTT *Quentin D.* xvi, He said, that..they were uplifted in heart because of their wealth and their privileges. 1897 W. BEATTY *Secretar* xli, Being so uplifted at the part I was like to play.

**4.** Raised in utterance.

1828 ATHERSTONE *Fall of Nineveh* I. 114 Them..with proud uplifted voice, Thus Azareel bespake. 1863 MISS BRADDON *Aurora Floyd* xiii, Did the unlucky speculators ..hide themselves while the uplifted voices were rejoicing?

Hence **Upli·ftedness.**

1893 *Scribner's Mag.* Sept. 387/1, I hate the coldness and upliftedness of religion.

**Upli·fter.** [f. UPLIFT *v.*]

†**1.** *Sc.* A collector (of rents, etc.). *Obs.*

1585–6 *Reg. Privy Council Scot.* IV. 47 The upliftaris of the said taxt. 1641 *Kirkcudbr. War-Comm. Min. Bk.* (1855) 159 He hes constituted the said James Montgomerie uplifter thairof [*sc.* of the king's rents].

**2.** One who raises or elevates.

1650 *Metr. Psalms Ch. Scot.* iii. 3 Yet thou my shield, and glory art, th' uplifter of mine head. 1884 TENNYSON *Becket* I. i, Henry the King hath been..mine uplifter in this world.

1890 J. PULSFORD *Loyalty to Christ* I. 57 Henceforth he should be a man of influence, and a great uplifter of men.

**Upli·fting,** *vbl. sb.* [UP- 7, or f. UPLIFT *v.*]

**1.** The action of raising or lifting up; an instance of this. Also *fig.*

1548 GESTE *Pr. Masse* H iv, Can ther be made to god..an effectual prayer withoute an vplyftinge of oure hartes vnto hym? 1650 *Metr. Psalms Ch. Scot.* cxli. 2 Let..the uplifting of my hands [be] as th' evening sacrifice. 1834 *Tait's Mag.* I. 693/1 An uplifting of the horse's hind heels. 1844 KINGLAKE *Eothen* xv, There was an uplifting of arms, and a repeating of words. 1886 HALL CAINE *Son of Hagar* I. v, With an eloquent uplifting of the hand.

**b.** *Geol.* Elevation in level; an upheaval.

1833–4 J. PHILLIPS *Geol.* in *Encycl. Metrop.* (1845) VI. 685/2 The uplifting of the Western Alps. 1855 *Orr's Circ. Sci., Inorg. Nat.* 51 The uplifting and dislocation of strata. 1881 *Q. Rev.* July 102 Upliftings and downcasts of strata.

**2.** *Sc.* Collection, levying (of rents, etc.).

1594 in *Spalding Club Misc.* I. 9 All receaving vplifting vptacking or intrometting with off ony maillis. 1640 *Kirkcudbr. War-Comm. Min. Bk.* (1855) 128 Unless your lordship caus hasten the uplifting and peyment of all that is dew. 1706 in J. J. Vernon *Parish of Hawick* (1900) 201 Collectors for the uplifting and inbringing of the stent.

**3.** The action of the verb, in various senses.

1824 SCOTT *Redgauntlet* ch. xii, There was heard within the uplifting of a Scottish psalm. 1826 — *Woodst.* v, A crowning mercy—a vouchsafing—an uplifting. 1899 A. C. BENSON *Life E. W. Benson* II. 232 They excluded a source of sacred pleasure and divine uplifting from their lives.

**Upli·fting,** *ppl. a.* [UP- 6 b. Cf. UPLIFT *v.*] That uplifts or elevates. Chiefly *fig.*

1818 SHELLEY *Homer's Hymn Sun* 20 The light vest.. Glows in the stream of the uplifting wind. 1881 [see UP-LOOKING]. 1889 E. W. BENSON in *Life* (1899) II. 290 A friendship..of which every hour was uplifting. 1896 in *Daily News* 24 Feb. 3/3 To-day it [*sc.* the Salvation Army] is one of the greatest uplifting forces in the country.

**Uplo·ck,** *v.* [UP- 4 + LOCK *v.*¹] *trans.* To lock up.

1600 FAIRFAX *Tasso* XIX. xxxix, Come, come,..Thy selfe within this fortresse safe vplocke. 1611 R. BADLEY *Panegyr. Verses* in Coryat *Crudities*, Thy bitter journey..Deserv'd the sweetest wines Piemont up-locks. 1689 in Law *Hampton Court Pal.* (1891) III. 9 Then Benting up-locks His King in a box.

**Uplo·cked,** *ppl. a.* (UP- 5. Cf. prec.) *c* 1600 SHAKS. *Sonn.* lii, So am I as the rich whose blessed key, Can bring him to his sweet vp-locked treasure.

**U·plong,** *prep.*, *sb.*, and *a.* [UP *adv.* + *long* ALONG *prep.* and *adv.*] **A.** *prep.* Up along.

1762 FALCONER *Shipwr.* I. 198 Uplong the slipp'ry Masts the Yards ascend.

**B.** *sb.* A strengthening bar extending along the sail of a windmill.

1819 REES *Cycl.* s.v. *Windmill*, There ought to be three uplongs..to the driving, and two to the leading side,..to strengthen the lattice. 1892 P. H. EMERSON *Son of Fens* xxxii. 356 That uplong have got loose.

**C.** *adj.* Extending upwards.

1875 MORRIS *Æneid* IX. 244 In daily hunt, whereby we learned the river's uplong brim.

**U·plook,** *sb.* [UP- 2.] An upward look or glance.

1869 RUSKIN *Q. of Air* § 135 To all true modesty the necessary business is not inlook, but outlook, and especially *up*look. 1888 FLO. WARDEN *Woman's Face* II. xv. 112 Giving her a very straight uplook into the eyes.

**Uploo·k,** *v.* (UP- 4. Cf. UPLOOKING *pres. pple.*)

*a* 1300 *Cursor M.* 1820 Noe..fined noþeir night ne day For þat caitiue folk to prai,..Bot durst he neuer wel [*Gött.* wid eie] vp-lok. 1596 SPENSER *F. Q.* VI. iii. 11 The morrow next, when day gan to vplooke, He also gan vplooke with drery eye. 1818 MILMAN *Samor* VII. 840 But not as wont, uplooks he to the sky.

**Uploo·ker.** (UP- 8.)

1581 MARBECK *Bk. of Notes* 661 Which thing the Greekes noted by the name of a man, calling him *Anthropos*, an vp-looker. 1895 *Expositor* April 260 Prayers that had long been flashed from the souls of these up-lookers.

**Uploo·king,** *pres. pple.* and *ppl. a.* (UP- 6, 6 b.)

*a* 1340 HAMPOLE *Psalter*, etc. 497 Thynnyd ere myn eghyn..vplokand [L. *suspicientes*] in heghe. 1805 WORDSW. *Prel.* VI. 86 Often have I stood Foot-bound uplooking at this lovely tree. 1838 MRS. BROWNING *Cowper's Grave* vii, Wild timid hares..Uplooking to his human eyes with sylvan tendernesses. 1881 J. MARTINEAU *Ess. & Addr.* (1891) IV. 306 Two minds present with each other in uplooking and uplifting attitude.

†**Uplo·per.** *Obs.* [ad. Du. *oplooper*, f. *oploopen* to leap up: see UPLEAP *v.*] A variety of pigeon resembling a pouter.

1735 J. MOORE *Columbarium* 36 To trip beautifully with his Feet..without Jumping, which is the Quality of an Uploper. 1765 *Treat. Dom. Pigeons* 104 When it approacheth the hen, [it] generally leaps to her with its tail spread, which is the reason of its being called Uploper.

**U·ply·ing,** *ppl. a.* [UP- 6 b.] Situated or lying on elevated ground; upland.

1877 *Scribner's Mag.* Aug. 479/2 The favourite haunt of the wild strawberry is an up-lying meadow. 1884 *Nature* 25 Sept. 530/1 In up-lying situations,..fluxion-structures are seldom detected.

**Upmaist,** Sc. var. UPMOST *a.*

**Upma·ke,** *v. Sc.* [UP- 4 + MAKE *v.*¹ Cf. older Flem. *opmaecken*, Du. *opmaken* to use up, put up, etc., LG. *upmaken*, G. *aufmachen* to put up, etc.]

**1.** *trans.* To make up for (a defect or lack); to supply or fill up where there is a deficiency.

1485 *Sc. Acts Parlt., Jas. III* (1814) II. 172/1 þe werk to be brokin, the werkman to vpmak þe avale to þe finace foresaid. 1526 *Extr. Aberd. Reg.* (1844) I. 114 To cloise the tovnn, and bred the portis of the same, and oupmak all wydis and waistis.

**2.** To construct, build.

**1507** *Extr. Aberd. Reg.* (1844) I. 77 [He] sale..big, oupmak,..and complet the xxxiiij stallis in thar queir.

**U·pma·king,** *vbl. sb.* [UP- 7.]

**1.** *Sc.* The action of making up, in various senses.

**1513** *Extr. Aberd. Reg.* (1844) I. 84 The biggin and vpmakin of thar blokhouse for thair artailzerie. **1681** R. FLEMING *Fulfilling Script.* (ed. 3) 64 When they..compared their gain with their losse, their upmaking with these dayes of trial. *Ibid.* 71 They have therein found a very sensible upmaking. **1856** *Morton's Cycl. Agric.* II. 620/1 The average cost..did not exceed 15*s.* per acre.., with all necessary upmaking. **1897** MRS. OLIPHANT *W. Blackwood* II. xxii. 409 A sheet was often left for him in the 'upmaking' till the last possible moment.

**2.** *Shipbuilding.* (See quot. 1846.)

**1846** A. YOUNG *Naut. Dict.* 357 *Upmaking*,..pieces of plank or timber piled on each other as a filling up; more especially those placed between the bilge-coads and the ship's bottom, preparatory to launching. **1883** *Scotsman* 11 July 5/2 The upmaking never showed any signs of giving way until the vessel was well clear of the standing ways.

**U·pma·king,** *ppl. a. Sc.* [UP- 6 b.]

**1.** That makes up for a defect or lack.

**1682** R. HAMILTON in M. Shields *Faithful Contendings* (1780) 40, I have found my Lord..ay the same up making, (and more than up making portion. **1726** WODROW *Corr.* (1843) III. 269 May he, by his Spirit, be assisting, comforting, and upmaking to you! **1729** E. ERSKINE *Serm.* (1791) 336/1 Rest in him, and upon him, as our upmaking and everlasting all. [**1852** *Chr. Treasury* 405/2 God..is an upmaking portion;..he can supply the place of all things.]

**2.** Seeking acquaintance or intimacy.

**1863** MRS. CARLYLE *Lett.* (1882) III. 166 They were very..'up-making' to me, and pressed me to visit them.

**Upme·t,** *pa. pple.* (UP- 5 + *met* METE *v.* Cf. UPHEAPED *pa. pple.*) **1828** CARR *Craven Gloss.*, *Up-met*, filled above the measure...Hence, the expression 'up-met and down throsten,' excellent measure...Also, 'he's a rogue, up-met and down throsten;' i.e. a complete villain.

**U·pmost,** *a.* Also *Sc.* 6 vpmest, 6–9 upmaist. [f. UP *adv.*² + -MOST.]

**1.** = UPPERMOST *a.* (in various senses).

**1560** BIBLE (Genev.) *Isaiah* xvii. 6 Two or thre beries are in the top of the vpmoste boughs. **1567** DRANT *Horace, Ep.* To Rdr. * iv, He that woulde come to the vpmoste top of an highe hill. **1599** T. M[OUFET] *Silkwormes* 62 That which lies vpmost is of least renowne. **1632** LITHGOW *Trav.* IX. 391 Sulphure streames, which haue burst forth from the vpmost tops of Ætna. *Ibid.* 418 Podalia, the vpmost Countrey of Polland. **1664** EVELYN *Kal. Hort.* 75 Taking away some of the upmost exhausted earth, and stirring up the rest. **1715** LEONI *Palladio's Archit.* (1721) II. 16 The middle of the upmost Wall ought to be perpendicular with the middle of the nethermost. **1808** SCOTT *Let. to Sharpe* 30 Dec. in *Lockhart*, You have..been upmost in my thoughts for some time past. **1859** GULLICK & TIMBS *Paint.* 163 The upmost flat surface is divided into nine compartments. **1875** LIGHTFOOT *Comm. Col.* 411/1 What was the thought upmost in the Apostle's mind..?

**b.** *absol.* or as *sb.*

**1589** FLEMING *Virg. Georg.* III. 43 Let him skarse set his feet vpon th' upmost [*note* The superfie or vppermost part] of the sand.

†**2.** *Sc.* = UMEST *a.* 1. *Obs.*

**1592** *Lyndesay's Wks.* 134–5 The Vicar..will nocht faill to tak ane kow, And vpmaist claith. **1609** SKENE *Reg. Maj.*, *Stat. Will.* 11 The forestar sall take..his vpmaist claith. **1620** *Henry's Wallace* X. i. 229 Wallace in haste gart take their upmost weed.

**Upmou·nt,** *v.* (UP- 4.) *a* **1560** PHAER *Æneid* IX. (1562) Ee iv b, A clamorous noise vpmounts on fortres tops. **Upmou·nted,** *pa. pple.* (UP- 5.) **1616** J. LANE *Contn. Sqr.'s T.* VII. 487 Vpmounted are the greate Artilerie, on owne huge-iron-carriages. **1818** KEATS *Endym.* I. 642, I felt upmounted in that region Where falling stars dart their artillery forth. **Upmou·nting,** *pres. pple.* (UP-6.) **1794** WOLCOT (P. Pindar) *Wks.* III. 221 The Moon..upmounting slow, In solemn stillness. **1820** KEATS *Hyperion* I. 157 Like the mist Which eagles cleave, upmounting from their nest.

**U·pness.** [UP *adv.*²] The quality of being elevated or raised.

**1887** W. JAMES in *Mind* No. 45. 14 Rightness and leftness, upness and downness, are..pure sensation. **1902** *Yorks. Post* 28 Feb., With the..idea of height or up-ness in our minds.

†**Upni·m,** *v. Obs.* [UP- 4. Cf. OFris. *opnima*, *opnema* (WFris. *opnimme*), (M)Du. *opnemen*, MLG. *upnemen* (LG. *upnämen*), MHG. *ûfnemen* (G. *aufnehmen*).] *trans.* To take up.

*c* **1250** *Gen. & Ex.* 3024 It so bi-cam, ðat moyses askes upnam. *c* **1290** *St. Brandan* 11 in *S. Eng. Leg.* I. 220 Bi-twene his armes seint brendan þis holie man op nam. *c* **1320** *Cast. Love* 1488 He þat from heuene com, From louh an heiȝ he vs up-nom. **1340** *Ayenb.* 143 Hi deþ ase deþ þe ilke mayde strongliche opnome of loue.

Hence † **Upni·ming** *vbl. sb. Obs.*

**1340** *Ayenb.* 22 Þe þridde kuead..ys fole opniminge of uals strif. *Ibid.* 83 Fole op-nymynge is huer lite profit liþ, and moche cost.

**Upo'** (vpǭᵘ·), *prep.* Forms: 3, 5, 9 *dial.* uppo, 3, 8 *Sc.* upo (3–4 up-o, 4 opo), 5 vpo; 8– *Sc.* and *dial.* upo' (9 *Sc.* apo'). [f. UP *adv.*² + O, o', *prep.*¹ Cf. UPON *prep.*] = UPON *prep.*, in various senses. (In later use *Sc.* and *north. dial.*)

*c* **1200** ORMIN 11959 Þe deofell brohhte Jesu Crist Wiþþutenn o þe temmple Uppoon an sæte uppo þe rof. *c* **1230** *Hali Meid.* 37 And eauer habben sar care,..& bringe on his moder sorhe up-o sorhe. *c* **1300** *Havelok* 2596 Helpes me and yu-self baþe, And slos up-o þe dogges swiþe. *c* **1310** in Wright *Lyric P.* xlii. 114 Fayrest fode upo loft. *c* **1330** R. BRUNNE *Chron. Wace* (Rolls) 2761 Faste þey fullen opo þem alle. *c* **1400** *Destr. Troy* 7037 The renke vp rose..And foght vpo fote as a freke noble. **1610** B. JONSON *Alchemist* II. ii, Thatch will lie light upo' the rafters, Lungs. **1721** RAMSAY *Ode to the Ph–* vi, If they command the storms to blaw, Then upo' sight the hailstanes thud. **1772** FERGUSSON *To R. Fergusson* xii, [To] hae a charot at the door To wait upo' me. **1773** GOLDSM. *Stoops to Conq.* I. ii, *Landlord.* They have lost their way upo' the forest. **1808** A. SCOTT *Poems* (ed. 2) 101 Upo' the rig she shoor wi' Hab. **1865** G. MACDONALD *A. Forbes* xi, I never kent ony guid come o' bein' ower sair upo' bairns.

**Upon** (ɒpǫ·n), *prep.* Forms: *a.* 3- upon (4–5, 7 up on, 6 *Sc.* uponn), 4–7 vpon (3–5 vp on, 4, 5 *Sc.* vpone, *Sc.* 5–6 wpone, 6–7 wpon), 3–7 uppon, vppon (3 *Orm.* upponn, 4 upp on). *β.* 3–6 opon (4 oupon, opan), 4–5 oppon. *γ.* 3–6, 9 *Sc.* apon (4 apan), 5 *Sc.*, 6apone, 5–6 *Sc.* apoun, 5–7 *Sc.* appon(e, apponne. *δ.* 6 poun, 8–9 'pon. See also UPO'. [Early ME. *upon*, *uppon*, etc., f. UP *adv.*¹ and *adv.*² + ON *prep.*; distinct from late OE. and early ME. *uppon*, var. of OE. *uppan* UP *prep.*¹

The compound may have partly arisen from uses of *upp on* or *uppe on* in OE. (for instances see UP *adv.*¹ and *adv.*²), but the date at which it appears, and the locality of the texts in which it is first prominent, suggest that it was mainly due to the influence of ON. *upp á* (MSw. *up a*, *op a*, *uppa*, *oppa*, etc.; Sw. *på*, Norw. and Da. *paa*), with which it agrees in laying the stress on the preposition and weakening or altogether ignoring the force of *up*. In the mod. Scand. tongues, except Icelandic and Færöese, the reduced form *på*, *paa*, corresponding to Eng. (colloq. or dial.) *'pon*, *'po*, has displaced the simple prep. *á*, *aa* = on.]

Originally denoting elevation as well as contact, the compound has from the earliest period of its occurrence so far lost the former implication, that it has been regularly employed as a simple equivalent of *on*, in all the varieties of meaning which that preposition has developed. The use of the one form or the other has been for the most part a matter of individual choice (on grounds of rhythm, emphasis, etc.) or of simple accident, although in certain contexts and phrases there may be a general tendency to prefer the one to the other. For ease of comparison, the following arrangement of the senses corresponds as closely as possible with that of ON. (See also HERE-, THERE-, WHEREUPON.)

**I.** Of local position outside of, but in contact with or close to, a surface.

**1.** Above and in contact with; in an elevated position on; at rest on the upper surface of; on and supported by; = ON *prep.* 1.

In a few instances in late MSS. (e.g. Hatton Gosp. *Matt.* v. 14) OE. *up on* can be taken in this sense, but appears to be merely a scribal variant or alteration of *uppon* for *uppan* UP *prep.*¹

*c* **1250** *Gen. & Ex.* 2867 Ðat..hise folc..ben ðor ȝare, In ðe deserd an stede up-on, His leue sacrifise to don. *a* **1272** *Luue Ron* 121 in *O. E. Misc.* 97 Hit stont vppon a treowe mote. *c* **1290** *St. Brendan* 368 in *S. Eng. Leg.* I. 229 At ester eue heore procuratour bad heom..heore resurrection opon þe fisches rugge make. *Ibid.* 577 Þe ston þat ich op-on sitte. **13..** *E. E. Allit. P.* A. 1054 The hyȝe trone..Þe hyȝe godez self hit set vpone. *c* **1386** CHAUCER *Miller's T.* 637 Til he cam to þe selle Vpon þe flore. *c* **1440** *Pallad. on Husb.* I. 199 Vynys that vppon the hillis stonde. *c* **1489** CAXTON *Sonnes of Aymon* xxii. 486 Reynawde..was vpon the hyghe gate of Ardeyn. **1508** DUNBAR *Gold. Targe* 20 The birdis sang vpon the tender croppis. *c* **1560** A. SCOTT *Poems* I. 4 Welcum, oure rubent roiss vpoun þe ryce. **1606** SHAKS. *Ant. & Cl.* IV. xiv. 4 A forked Mountaine, or blew Promontorie With Trees vpon't. *a* **1648** DIGBY *Chym. Secr.* II. (1682) 215 Take it upon the point of a knife. **1732** BERKELEY *Alciphr.* IV. § 8 The castle upon yonder hill. **1749** FIELDING *Tom Jones* XIV. ii, She's here, Mrs. Honour is upon the stairs. **1816** J. WILSON *City of Plague* I. i. 191 Wilt thou rest, old man, Upon this traveller's seat? **1825** J. NICHOLSON *Operat. Mechanic* 383 A pair of rollers upon the top of the roving-can. **1903** MRS. DE LA PASTURE *Cornelius* 7 A Crown Derby service was spread forth upon a round table.

**b.** Said with reference to an expanse, as of land, sea, etc.; = ON *prep.* 1 b. (Freq. from *c* 1650.)

*Upon a* († *the*) *level* (*with*): see LEVEL *sb.* 2, 3.

*c* **1250** *Gen. & Ex.* 3273 And moyses stod up-on ðe sond. *c* **1300** *Havelok* 735 Þer sat is ship up-on þe sond. **1340–70** *Alex. & Dind.* 39 Neuere werrede we wiþ wiȝth up-on erþe. *Ibid.* 739 Of swiche bestus..Þei han miht vp-on molde. **1362** LANGL. *P. Pl.* A. IX. 56 Vnder a Lynde, vpon a launde leonede I a stounde. **1390** GOWER *Conf.* I. 53 He syh upon the grene gras The faire freisshe floures springe. *c* **1420** *Chron. Vilod.* 2393 Þis blessud virgyn..Twolfe ȝere..in hurr tombe lay, As saffe, as hole as he vpon vrthe ȝede. *c* **1470** *Gol. & Gaw.* 312 Thai plantit doun ane pailyeoun, vpone ane plane lee. **1526** TINDALE *Mark* vi. 48 When they sawe him walkinge apon the see. **1535** FISHER *Wks.* (1876) 365 He must treade vppon the fallowes. **1568** *Durham Wills* (Surtees) III. 44 Corne..in the barne 58*l.*, Upon the earth at 20*l.* **1609** BIBLE (Douay) *Ezek.* xvi. 5 Thou wast throwen forth upon the face of the earth. **1650** HOWELL *Giraffi's Rev. Naples* I. 15 Benches, Forms,..were burnt all to ashes upon the streets. **1662** J. DAVIES tr. *Olearius' Voy. Ambass.* 203 Wood and Lodging..are very scarce upon that Road. **1711** ADDISON *Spect.* No. 42 ¶ 3 Two or three Shifters of Scenes..make up a complete Body of Guards upon the English Stage. **1812** BYRON *Ch. Har.* I. xiii. 75 Now I'm in the world alone, Upon the wide, wide sea. **1828** LYTTON *Pelham* III. xix, I have no time..to speak of the earlier part of my life. I passed it upon the race-course. **1871** HAWEIS *Music & Morals* (1874) 7 The Painter's art lies upon the surface of the world.

**c.** Denoting the part of the body on which one is supported; = ON *prep.* 1 c.

See also FOOT *sb.* 27, KNEE *sb.* 3 a, TIPTOE *sb.* 1.

**1390** GOWER *Conf.* I. 286 Sche began merci to crie Upon hire bare knes. *c* **1440** *Generydes* 44 Vppe vppon his fete he was a non. **1481** CAXTON *Reynard* (Arb.) 18 He satte vpon his hammes. **1601** SHAKS. *Jul. C.* II. i. 270 Vpon my knees, I charme you,..By all your vowes of Loue. **1661** EARL ORRERY *St. Lett.* (1742) 40 We are now upon our last legs. **1692** tr. *C'tess D'Aunoy's Trav.* 157 Three or four Pages..serve me upon Knee. **1712** STEELE *Spect.* No. 460 ¶ 7 Gallantry strutting upon his Tiptoes. **1784** COWPER *Task* IV. 546 Her tott'ring form Ill propp'd upon French heels. **1800** WORDSW. *Hart-Leap Well* I. xi, Upon his side the Hart was lying stretched. **1843** MACAULAY *Horatius* lxvi, Horatius in his harness, Halting upon one knee.

**d.** Indicating a means of locomotion or conveyance; = ON *prep.* 1 d.

*a* **1300** *Cursor M.* 894 For þou sal slid apon þi brest. *c* **1300** *Havelok* 2041 Yf he mouhte..gangen wel up-on hise fet. **13..** *E. E. Allit. P.* B. 88 Swyerez þat swyftly swyed on blonkez, & also fele vpon fote. **1393** LANGL. *P. Pl.* C. VII. 43 Strengest vp-on stede, and styuest vnder gurdell. *c* **1400** MAUNDEV. (Roxb.) i. 4 It es made sittand apon a hors. *c* **1475** *Rauf Coilȝear* 794 Vpon ane rude Runsy he ruschit out of toun. **1590** SPENSER *F. Q.* I. i. 4 She..heauie sat vpon her palfrey slow. **1648** HEXHAM II, *Een Rijdt-bane*, a Sliding place..to slide upon Schates. **1660** F. BROOKE tr. *Le Blanc's Trav.* 350 The great King, whom they carry upon a *Sindela* of cotton. **1719** DE FOE *Crusoe* II. (Globe) 345 We went on Shore upon the Tide of Flood, near high Water. **1803** SOUTHEY *Queen Orraca* IV. vii, Upon her palfrey she is set, And forward then they go. **1821** SCOTT *Pirate* xxx, She saw him flee forth of the window..upon a dragon. **1853** KANE *Grinnell Exp.* xxxii. (1856) 282, I mounted the upheaving ice, and rode upon the fragments.

**e.** Denoting that on which the hand is placed in taking the oath, or the basis of an oath, etc.; = ON *prep.* 1 f.

See also CONSCIENCE 9, EVANGEL¹ 3, EVANGELY 3, FAITH *sb.* 8, HONOUR *sb.* 9 b, LIFE *sb.* 3 c, REP¹, SOUL *sb.* 10 c, WORD *sb.*

*c* **1290** *Beket* 585 in *S. Eng. Leg.* I. 123 Þat he ne scholde nouȝt swerie op-on þe boke. *c* **1330** R. BRUNNE *Chron. Wace* (Rolls) 10468 He swor hym vpon þe bok, To holde of hym his heritage. **1398** TREVISA *Barth. De P. R.* XV. cxxxvi. (Bodl. MS.), Hoote welles þat..blindeþ þeues ȝif he swereþ vpon þe water and toucheþ heere yȝen þerewiþ. *c* **1400** *Destr. Troy* 642 Yow swiftly shall sweire vppon swete goddes, This couenaunt to kepe. *a* **1460** in *Hist. Coll. Lond. Cit.* (Camden) 119 The for sayde captaynys have sworne a-pon hyr honowre that..they shalle not makyn [etc.]. **1493** *Litt. Red Bk. Bristol* (1900) II. 134 This ys trew apon owre consciens. **1610** SHAKS. *Temp.* II. ii. 130 I'le sweare vpon that Bottle, to be thy true subiect. **1645** *Docq. Lett. Pat. at Oxf.* (1837) 268 Administring of Oathes vpon the Holy Evangelistes. **1710** ADDISON *Tatler* No. 253 ¶ 1 The Assistants..were all sworn upon their Honour. **1722** DE FOE *Col. Jack* (1840) 67 He would come back..and untie him, upon his word. **1776** *Trial Nundocomar* 52/1 You have sworn me upon the waters of the Ganges: how can I tell more than I remember? **1831** JAMES *Phil. Augustus* III. x, I declare that..he himself [is] worthy of death, upon my honour! **1848** DICKENS *Dombey* xxxix, Upon my word and honour,..it would be a charity.

†**f.** Above, more than. *Obs.* Cf. UP *prep.*¹ 8.

**13..** *Guy Warw.* (A.) 359 Opon al oþer y loue þe. *c* **1430** *Syr Gener.* (Roxb.) 969 Son, vpon al thing Doo aftre Nathanaels teching.

†**g.** *fig.* Over (a person, etc.), in respect of rule, authority, or supervision. *Obs.*

See also REIGN *v.* 1 b, RULE *v.* 5 b, RULER 1 (quot. 1382).

*c* **1380** WYCLIF *Wks.* (1880) 383 Þe kyngis of heþen han lordeschip vp-on hem. *c* **1400** MAUNDEV. (Roxb.) iii. 10 Þi powere es grete apon þi subgets. **1422** YONG tr. *Secreta Secret.* 162 Oure Lord god enoyntyd Saule Kynge vppon Israell. **1477** EARL RIVERS (Caxton) *Dictes* 69 He aught to haue lawde That..hath lordship vpon his ennemyes. **1534** WHITINTON *Tullyes Offices* I. (1540) 11 A man that wolde be chefe ruler vpon the commentye.

**h.** Taking part in, forming a member of (an inquest, jury, etc.). Cf. ON *prep.* 1 g.

**1516** *Reg. Privy Seal Scot.* I. 422/2 Thai..being apone the inqueist..in the schiref court. **1609** [see SIT *v.* 26]. **1643** *Docq. Lett. Pat. at Oxf.* (1837) 5 Consociating himselfe with his neighboring Justices in sitting upon an illegal Commission. **1676** *Office Clerk of Assize* a vj, Persons..to serve in or upon the Grand Jury. **1729** JACOB *Law Dict.* s.v. *Jury*, Clergymen, Apothecaries, &c. are exempted by Law from serving upon Juries. **1769** [see JURY *sb.* 2 b].

**i.** Hence in many phrases, originally denoting physical location, of which the sense has become more or less figurative; = ON *prep.* 1 h. See esp. ANVIL *sb.* 2 b, CARPET *sb.* 1 b, HAND *sb.* 32, HIGH *a.* 17 h, 18, LEVEL *sb.* 4, PAR *sb.* 1, SPOT *sb.*¹ 9, TABLE *sb.* 5 b.

**2.** Denoting contact with or location on a surface, etc., whatever its position; = ON *prep.* 2.

(*a*) *c* **1200** ORMIN Ded. 69 Þatt upponn all þiss boc ne be Nan word ȝæn Cristess lare. *a* **1300** *Cursor M.* 23215 Painted fire..Þat apon a wagh war wreght. **1382** WYCLIF *Exod.* xxxiv. 1 Y shal write vpon hem [*sc.* stone tables] the wordes that hadden the tablis. **1535** COVERDALE *Hab.* ii. 2 Wryte the vision planely vpon thy tables. **1552** in J. O. Payne *St. Paul's Cathedral* (1893) 22 A greate clothe of redd silke..with lions of golde upon it. **1566**, **1596** [see INSCULP *v.*]. **1596**– [see RECORD *sb.* 1]. **1605** SHAKS. *Macb.* V. i. 7, I haue seene her..take foorth paper,..write vpon't, read it. *Ibid.* viii. 26 As our rarer Monsters are Painted vpon a pole. **1729** T. INNES *Crit. Essay* (1879) 74 His name is upon it, written with his own hand. **1766** [see ENGRAVE *v.* 3 a]. **1776** *Trial Nundocomar* 97/2 Did you see upon the face of the bond anything to make you suspect it? **1801** *Farmer's Mag.* Apr. 203 Which is very practicable upon paper. **1888** 'J. S. WINTER' *Bootle's Childr.* v, A gold bangle with 'Mignon' upon it..in raised letters.

(*b*) *a* **1225** *Leg. Kath.* 1187 Þe treo Þer he deide upon. *c* **1290** *S. Eng. Leg.* I. 43/300 Þis ȝoungue Man sixe and þritti dawes heng up-on þe galu-treo. **1377** LANGL. *P. Pl.*

B. I. 154 Was neuere leef vpon lynde liȝter þer-after. 14.. LYDG. *Min. Poems* (1911) 252 As he [*sc.* Christ] hangeth vp-on the roode tre. 1536 *Exhort. to North* in Furnivall *Ballads fr. MSS.* I. 307 The gallous apone, prepared for mardoche, hanged he was. 1596 DALRYMPLE tr. *Leslie's Hist. Scot.* I. 121 Lat him end his lyf vpon ane fork. 1605 SHAKS. *Macb.* v. v. 39 Vpon the next Tree shall thou hang. 1867 SMYTH *Sailor's Word-bk.* 411 A sail set upon the flying jib-boom. 1899 *Shetland News* 16 Dec. (*E.D.D.* s.v. *Hing*), I took aff me kjaep, an' hang her apon a nail.

(*c*) *c* 1386 CHAUCER *Prol.* 111 Vp on his arm he baar a gay bracer. *c* 1450 *St. Cuthbert* (Surtees) 813 With broches and golde opon hir arme. 1494 *Act* 11 *Hen. VII*, c. 23 The little Bone that sitteth upon the great Fin. 1523 FITZHERB. *Husb.* § 21 A wedynge-hoke with a socket set vpon a lyttel staffe. 1547 in Feuillerat *Revels Edw. VI* (1914) 10 Th'under sleves of..Satten cut vpon Red Sarcenett. 1655 STANLEY *Hist. Philos.* II. 7 By reflection of the Sunns beams upon a thick cloud, which, not able to pierce it, are refracted upon it. 1774 J. BRYANT *Mythol.* II. 231 Upon the head of the woman is a veil. 1824 T. G. CUMMING *Rail & Tram Roads* 24 Several branches were made..with the flaunche upon the wheel, and not upon the rail. 1847 MARRYAT *Childr. N. Forest* xix, Those clothes would not look so well upon Oswald. 1889 DOYLE *Micah Clarke* 318 Monmouth must fight now, if he ever hopes to feel the gold rim upon his temples.

**b.** Used of immaterial relationships, or in figurative expressions.

*To (be)get..upon* (a woman): see BEGET *v.* 2 b, GET *v.* 26. *a* 1400 *Minor Poems fr. Vernon MS.* xlii. 8 His eȝe is euere þe vppon. 1423 JAS. I *King's Q.* ii, I..toke a boke to rede apon a quhile. *c* 1450 *Mirk's Festial* I. 6 Vnsley old man, goo heþen! for I se apon þe mony meruaysles. 1548–9 (Mar.) *Bk. Com. Prayer* Pref., All thynges must be read vpon the boke. 1591 SHAKS. *Two Gent.* I. i. 20 Vpon some booke I loue, I'le pray for thee. 1662 STILLINGFL. *Orig. Sacræ* II. iii. § 4 That what is spoken hath the impress of Divine authority upon it. *Ibid.* v. § 2 They have a clear and distinct perception of God upon their own minds. 1719 DE FOE *Crusoe* II. (Globe) 498 The Horror which was upon our Minds. 1753–4 RICHARDSON *Grandison* I. xii. 66 Every one's eyes were upon me. 1806 J. BERESFORD *Miseries Hum. Life* (ed. 4) VI. 97 Here am I..with a sort of traveller's lumbago upon me. 1832 L. HUNT *Gentle Armour* I. 142 The page returns with doubt upon his eyes. 1848 BAILEY *Festus* (ed. 3) 230 There was a tale Upon thy tongue he interrupted. 1877 SPURGEON *Serm.* XXIII. 669 It is absurd upon its very face.

**c.** By means of; with. Now *dial.*

*c* 1440 *York Myst.* xix. 212 Þe knyght vppon his knyffe Hath slayne my sone. 1590 SHAKS. *Mids. N.* II. i. 244 To die vpon the hand I loue so well. 1742 *Phil. Trans.* XLII. 266 The Perfection of Smelling in the Inhabitants of the Antibes, who can run a Man upon the Nose like an Hound. 1751 LABELYE *Westm. Bridge* 71 Explaining before them, upon a working Model, the Method I proposed. 1790 BOSWELL *Lett.* (1924) 388, I intended to have printed it upon what is called an English letter. 1865 R. HUNT *Pop. Rom. West Eng.* I. 105 Which eye can you see me upon?

**d.** Used in reference to an axis, pivot, or base; = ON *prep.* 1 e. (Cf. RAISE *v.* 8 b, TURN *v.* 3.)

1570 BILLINGSLEY *Euclid* I. i. 8 A triangle..set or described vpon a line. 1593 FALE *Dialling* 14 Upon E make a halfe circle from H by G. 1679 MOXON *Math. Dict.* s.v. *Circle*, The Circle..is described upon the Centre A. 1728 CHAMBERS *Cycl.* s.v. *Triangle*, A Triangle is equal to a Parallelogram upon the same Base, but half the Altitude. 1796 *Instr. & Reg. Cavalry* (1813) 149 Each describing the portion of a circle upon (P) as a center. 1830 TENNYSON *Mariana* vi, The doors upon their hinges creak'd. 1832 *Prop. Reg. Instr. Cavalry* III. 47 Two contiguous points given as a Base, upon which a body of troops is to march or form. 1877 HUXLEY *Anat. Inv. Anim.* vi. 309 The next four somites..cease to be moveable upon one another.

**3. a.** On the bank of (a river or lake); on the shore of (the sea); on the borders of (a territory, etc.); close by, near to; bordering upon; beside or by; = ON *prep.* 3.

13.. *K. Alis.* 4090 (Laud MS.), A Castel he had vpon þeryue. 1387 TREVISA *Higden* V. 329 He fauȝt..aȝenst þe Saxons ..uppon þe ryver Gleny. *c* 1425 *Eng. Conq. Irel.* 142 The tounes vp-on the see. 1474 *Rental Bk. Cupar-Angus* (1879) I. 197 To mak a myl..othir vpoun the gret watter or vpoun the burn. 1526 *Reg. Privy Seal Scot.* I. 514/1 Theifis and tratouris duelland apoun Levin. 1585 T. WASHINGTON tr. *Nicholay's Voy.* I. viii. 7 b, Alger..is situated vpon the Mediterane Sea. 1601 R. JOHNSON *Kingd. & Commw.* 192 Siras seated vpon the riuer Bindimire. 1662 STILLINGFL. *Orig. Sacræ* III. iv. § 13 The greatest part of the Countries lying upon the Ocean and Mediterranean. 1720 DE FOE *Capt. Singleton* xii. (1840) 226 A tract of land..seated upon some navigable river. 1747 *Col. Rec. Pennsylv.* V. 87 Upon the heads of Joniady River. 1859 TENNYSON *Marriage of Geraint* 145 Arthur..Held court at old Caerleon upon Usk.

† **b.** About; near; close on (a specified number, etc.). *Obs.*

In later use only with CLOSE *adv.* 1 d, NEAR *adv.*[2] 5 c, NIGH *adv.* 12 c.

1451 CAPGRAVE *Life St. Gilbert* 68 He left at his deth swech persones dedicate to God vp-on too þousand too hundred. 1477 CAXTON *Jason* 74 He cessed not to..rowe til he cam nyghe the Ile vpon a bowe shotte. 1478 J. PASTON in *P. Lett.* III. 219 A steppe modyr of hyrs, whyche is upon l. yer of age. 1482 *Cely Papers* (Camden) 102 Ther wylbe in aull with blottes apon xxvij or xxviij sarplers wholl. 1534 TINDALE *Luke* viii. 42 He had but a doughter only, apon a twelve yere of age. *a* 1548 HALL *Chron., Hen. VIII*, 32 b, He had askryed a nomber of horsemen..vppon the poynct of syx thousand. 1600 HOLLAND *Livy* 177 There were upon two thousand & five hundred taken alive. 1660 *Nicholas Papers* (Camden) IV. 226 To pay mee my allowance..as it was regulated upon three years since.

**4.** Denoting collateral position; esp. with *side, hand*, † *half*; *beam* (of a ship), *point* (of the compass); *north, south*, etc.; *right, left*; = ON *prep.* 4.

See also BORDER *v.* 5, TOUCH *v.* 14, VERGE *v.*[1] 2 b.

(*a*) *c* 1330 R. BRUNNE *Chron. Wace* (Rolls) 7929 Southsex ..& Middelsex..marchen vpon Kent. *c* 1400 MAUNDEV. (Roxb.) vi. 22 Mesopotamy also marchez apon þe desertes of Araby. 1568 GRAFTON *Chron.* II. 354 For we [Scots] are so lodged vpon England, that we may..enter which way we lust. 1586– [see NEIGHBOUR *v.* 1, 2]. 1596 DALRYMPLE tr. *Leslie's Hist. Scot.* (S.T.S.) I. 31 Wpon the coste of the Lenox lyes Argyle. 1624 HEYWOOD *Gunaik.* II. 92 That part..which butted upon the west. 1681 DRYDEN *Span. Friar* I. i, Upon the skirts Of Arragon our squandered troops he rallies. 1786 W. THOMSON *Watson's Philip III* (1839) 311 An island bordering upon Istria. 1842 R. I. WILBERFORCE *Rutilius & Lucius* 106 Behind they abutted upon the grounds of Milo. 1873 T. W. HIGGINSON *Oldport Days* v. 115 The house was close upon the water.

(*b*) 13.. *Gaw. & Gr. Knt.* 2069 Þe brode ȝatez [were] Vnbarred, & born open, vpon boþe halue. 1375 BARBOUR *Bruce* XI. 175 Schir Gylys de Argente he set Vpon ane half, his renȝe to get. ? *a* 1400 *Morte Arth.* 3795 We are with Sarazenes be-sett appone sere halfes! *c* 1475 *Rauf Coilȝear* 291 I se the Firmament fair vpon ather syde. 1565 GOLDING *Ovid's Met.* I. 1 b, Twoo Zones do cut the Heauen vpon the righter syde. 1577 B. GOOGE *Heresbach's Husb.* II. (1586) 71 b, A rich grounde, leuell, and lying vpon the Sunne. 1644 in *Eng. Hist. Rev.* Apr. (1913) 341 My Lord Ambassador beinge plac'd..upon his left hand about three Seates distante from him. 1669 STURMY *Mariner's Mag.* I. ii. 4 Upon what Point of the Compass the Object beareth from you. 1739 LABELYE *Piers Westm. Bridge* 5 When the Wind is upon any Point of the Compass between the South and the West. 1791 SMEATON *Edystone L.* § 76 A vessel steering to Foy will have the wind upon her beam. 1823 F. CLISSOLD *Ascent Mt. Blanc* 11 [It] shelved down, upon our right, in one plane of smooth rock.

*transf.* 1656 CROMWELL *Sp.* in Burton *Diary* (1828) I. p. clxix, It was never so upon the thriving hand. 1718 WODROW *Corr.* (1843) II. 362 May the kingdom of our Lord be upon the growing hand. 1852 BAILEY *Festus* (ed. 5) 252 To you, dear ass, upon the sire's side, To you, sir steed, I'm on the dam's allied.

**b.** *transf.* Indicating the side, part, cause, etc., espoused or supported by the agent.

*c* 1430 *Chev. Assigne* 219 'Go we forthe, fader,' quod þe childe, 'vpon goddes halfe!' 1445 in *Anglia* XXVIII. 256 [They] seyen the duke of yorke hath god vpon his side. 1595 SHAKS. *John* I. i. 34 Till she had kindled France and all the world, Vpon the right and party of her sonne. 1611 B. JONSON *Catiline* v. M 2, The least man, that falles vpon our party This day.., Shall walke at pleasure, in the tents of rest. 1821 SHELLEY *Hellas* 440 Famine, and Pestilence, And Panic, shall wage war upon our side!

**c.** Engaged in assailing, or about to attack.

1568 GRAFTON *Chron.* II. 291 The French men were so mingled among their enemies, that some time there was fiue men vpon one Gentleman. *c* 1670 WOOD *Life* (O.H.S.) I. 114 Captain Walter had six rebells upon him, and..fought it out so..gallantly that [etc.]. 1701 W. WOTTON *Hist. Rome* 269 The Senate heard that Severus was just upon them. 1719 DE FOE *Crusoe* I. (Globe) 270 He saw five Men upon him. 1721 — *Mem. Cavalier* (1840) 211 We are all undone, the roundheads are upon us. 1860 *All Year Round* No. 66. 384 Certain manœuvres, which had just time to result.., when the squall was upon us. 1885 *Manch. Exam.* 10 June 4/7 The crisis..is upon us at last.

† **d.** Having a tendency to be; verging towards; bordering on. Freq. with *little*. *Obs.*

Cf. *to run upon* s.v. RUN *v.* 70 b.

1707 LD. RABY in Hearne *Collect.* (O.H.S.) II. 43 He is..a little upon y^e^ dirty as all y^e^ Poles are. 1716 in *Lond. Gaz.* No. 5438/4 Lost.., a large Brilliant.., a little upon the Blue. 1738 SWIFT *Pol. Conversat.* 180, I think he's a little upon the silly, or so. 1740 tr. *De Mouhy's Fort. Country Maid* (1741) I. 35 A Countenance much upon the Wheedler and the Devotee.

**5.** Within the bounds or limits of; in; = ON *prep.* 5. (Cf. UPO' *prep.*, quot 1773.)

13.. *Sir Beues* (A.) 4180 [He] karf..Doun riȝt þe viser wiþ is swerd And half þe her vpon is berd. 1605 SHAKS. *Lear* IV. vi. 256 Seeke him out vpon the English party. 1639 LAUD *Wks.* (1853) V. 364, I find by the bishop's certificate, that he hath constantly resided upon his episcopal houses. 1765 *Museum Rust.* IV. 449 His country seat, possessed and lived upon by his ancestors for several generations. 1824 SCOTT *St. Ronan's* xxii, Miss Clara..just sitting upon the wind of a door [= in a draught].

† **b.** Denoting ratio between two numbers, etc.; = PER *prep.* III. 2, IN *prep.* 4. *Obs. rare.*

1622 MALYNES *Anc. Law-Merch.* 195 In regarde of lecage of tenne or fifteene vpon the hundreth. 1739 LABELYE *Piers Westm. Bridge* 76 The Ascent..not being above one Foot perpendicular upon 20 Feet slope. *Ibid.* 78.

**6.** Denoting the day of an occurrence, regarded as a unit of time. Freq. also with *night, morn, morrow, eve(n, time*, † *tide*, † *hour, occasion*, etc. = ON *prep.* 6.

*Once upon a time*: see ONCE *adv.* 4.

*a* 1300 *Cursor M.* 19810 Apon a dai at þe tid o non An angel com. 1338 R. BRUNNE *Chron.* (1810) 37 Untc Kyngeston.. Com S. Dunstan, opon a Sonenday. 1390 GOWER *Conf.* I. 3 Now upon this tyde Men se the world..so diversed, That [etc.]. ? *a* 1400 *Arthur* 539 And sone after vpon an owr He hurde of Mordred. 1424 *Stonor Papers* (Camden) I. 36 Writen at Sarum apon þe seynt Michell euen. *a* 1470 *Ibid.* 111 My wyf and y welbe with you uppon Ester. 1535 COVERDALE *Job* i. 6 Now vpon a tyme..the seruauntes of God came and stode before the Lorde. 1551 ROBINSON tr. *More's Utopia* (1895) 15 Vpon a tyme, when tidynges came [etc.]. 1631 WEEVER *Anc. Funeral Mon.* 471 Once euery yeare vpon the same day of his Anniuerse. 1663 *Extr. St. Papers Friends* Ser. II. (1911) 183 [They] were all brought before the mayor vpon the 28th of December. 1672 T. GODDEN *Cath. No Idolaters* 35 Would an Impartial Reader (to use Dr. Taylor's expression upon another occasion) say [etc.]? 1711 ADDISON *Spect.* No. 164 ¶ 4 Upon the Day on which..their Marriage was to have been solemnized. 1771 MRS. GRIFFITH *Hist. Lady Barton* III. 285, I wrote upon the instant, but..cannot recollect what I said. *a* 1821 KEATS *Eve St. Mark* 1 Upon a Sabbath-day it fell. 1868 TENNYSON *Lucretius* 24 He..woke upon a morn That mock'd him.

† **b.** In, at, or during (any period of time); in the course of; = ON *prep.* 6 b. *Obs.*

(*a*) 1390 GOWER *Conf.* I. 314 [He] made upon the derke nyht..Gret fyr. *c* 1400 *Destr. Troy* 8684 Wyth myche dole vppon dayes & on derke nightes, Sum walt into wodenes. 1427–9 *Rolls of Parlt.* IV. 364 To make a Toure to be uppon day light a redy Bekyn. 1529 in Leadam *Star Chamb. Cases* (Selden) II. 34 Thomas..directed..the hole recordys ..vppon a yere past or more to vs..to examen the same. 1585 T. WASHINGTON tr. *Nicholay's Voy.* I. xix, Vpon the euening the fire..got into their pouder. 1603 SHAKS. *Meas. for M.* IV. i. 35 Vpon the Heauy midle of the night. 1661 *Act* 13 *Chas. II*, c. 9 § 27 No man in or belonging to the Fleet shall sleep upon his Watch. 1673 in Picton *L'pool Munic. Rec.* (1883) I. 247 Offences committed by them the same day upon the said election. [1820 KEATS *St. Agnes* vi, Upon the honey'd middle of the night.]

(*b*) 1591 UNTON *Corr.* (Roxb.) 103 Upon nowe advertisement is come from the Kinge. 1638 LD. DIGBY *Lett. Conc. Relig.* (1651) 19 To tell you what upon the present..occurreth to me.

† **c.** Within the space of (a specified period of time); = ON *prep.* 6 c. *Obs.*

*c* 1375 *Cursor M.* 510 (Fairf.), Be iournays qua ga hit may, fourty myle a-pon a day. *c* 1386 CHAUCER *Prol.* 704 Vp on a day he gat hym moore moneye Than þat the person gat in Monthes tweye. 1457–8 in *Acta Dom. Conc.* II. Introd. 15 He sall warne thame to pass to the kingis chapell..apone xl dais. 1459 *Rolls of Parlt.* V. 369/2 A commaundement ..to be redy to come..upon a day warnyng. ? *a* 1585 MONTGOMERIE *Misc. Poems* vii. 35 Rome wes not biggit all vpon ane day. 1674 *Reg. Privy Council Scot.* Ser. III. IV. 299 [The lords] ordaines letters of horning upon 48 houres to be direct for that effect.

**d.** At the point of; close on, touching on; = ON *prep.* 6 d.

Usu. with vbl. sb. or gerundive: see group (*a*). *Upon the point of*: see POINT *sb.*[1] D. 5.

(*a*) 1426 AUDELAY *Poems* 6 Have mynd apon ȝoure endyng of the payns of helle. 1491 *Acta Dom. Conc.* (1839) 205/1, I am apone my saling and may nocht lang tary. 1530 PALSGR. 423/1, I am upon my lieng downe, as a woman that is nere her tyme. 1604 DEKKER *Honest Wh.* xii, *Wife.* Comes the Duke this way? *Pio.* Hee's upon comming, mistris. 1611 COTGR., *Emmati*,..faded, vpon withering. 1669–70 MARVELL *Corr.* Wks. (Grosart) II. 310, I intended more, but the post also is upon going. 1707 HEARNE *Collect.* (O.H.S.) II. 10 The King of Prussia is upon sending to the ..Library all the..medals. *a* 1774 GOLDSM. *Hist. Greece* I. 247 The truce..was just upon expiring. 1842 C. WHITEHEAD *R. Savage* I. i, I was just upon commending them to a lower place.

*ellipt.* 1899 *Daily News* 12 Sept. 4/7 The new..recreation garden..is just upon finished.

(*b*) 1585 T. WASHINGTON tr. *Nicholay's Voy.* I. xix. 22 As wee were vpon our departure. 1626 BRETON *Fantasticks* D 3 b, Few that are merry, but..wenches that are vpon the mariage. 1632 MASSINGER *Maid of Hon.* v. i, Signor Adorni is return'd! now upon entrance! 1666 MARVELL *Corr.* Wks. (Grosart) II. 197 The Smyrna fleet..is upon returne. *c* 1680– [see GO *sb.* 8 d]. 1722 POPE *Lett.* (1735) I. 274 I'm told you are all upon Removal very speedily. 1775 S. J. PRATT *Liberal Opin.* cxxxiii. (1783) IV. 206 Our old rector will make a subject by and by;..he's certainly upon the go [= dying]. 1797 MRS. M. ROBINSON *Walsingham* IV. 318 The good fellow is upon the go; his life is not worth six weeks' purchase. 1820 BYRON *Mar. Fal.* IV. ii. 66 *Doge.* How goes the night? *Ber. F.* Almost upon the dawn.

† **e.** By or for (a specified time). *Obs.*

1510 *Brasenose Coll. Doc.* (MS.) A^3^ 43 To make me a Dublett and a Jacket upon Crystmasse next comyng.

† **f.** For the extent or period of. *Obs.*

Cf. *upon a stretch* s.v. STRETCH *sb.* 6 a.

*a* 1548 HALL *Chron., Hen. VII*, 49 b, Which sickenes continued vpon fyue monethes.

**7. a.** On the occasion of; = ON *prep.* 7.

In freq. use *c* 1670–*c* 1825. Group (*b*) illustrates obs. usages. See also OCCASION *sb.* 10 b, SIGHT *sb.* 4 d, 6 b, SUDDEN *sb.* 1 b, SUDDENTY 1 b, VIEW *sb.* 16.

(*a*) *c* 1440 CAPGRAVE *Life St. Kath.* I. 981 Vp-on this hir letter hath she sent. 1492 HEN. VII in G. Griffiths *Hist. Tong* (ed. 2) 224 To thentent that uppon convercacion we may shewe unto you our minde. 1515 in Leadam *Star Chamber Cases* (Selden) II. 79 The saide artificers seyne that by the grauntis made uppon their first corporacion it appereth that [etc.]. 1566 DRANT *Horace, Sat.* I. iii. B v, His maister hangs him straighte upponte. 1596 BACON *Use Com. Law* (1635) 2 If one kill another upon a suddaine quarrell. 1662 CULPEPER in *Extr. St. Papers Friends* Ser. II. (1911) 152 *note*, I haue some Quakers..in prison which I doe intend to let goe upon taking the Oath. 1698 FRYER *Acc. E. India & P.* 74 The Banyans repairing to the Suburbs upon Tattoo. 1705 COLLIER *Ess. Mor. Subj.* III. *Pain* 13 Was ever..any Fencer, worth the naming, heard to groan upon a Hit? 1712 ADDISON *Spect.* No. 369 ¶ 17 They.. were cast into Hell upon their Disobedience. 1774 GOLDSM. *Nat. Hist.* (1776) II. 309 Upon comparing the various animals..with each other, we shall find [etc.]. 1817 MILL *Brit. India* II. 450 They retired upon the brisk advancement of the grenadiers. 1841 LANE *Arab. Nts.* I. 101 Upon which they raised their heads, and answered as before. 1890 LD. ESHER in *Law Times' Rep.* LXIII. 734/1 [He] shall be released from that obligation upon the Director undertaking the case.

(*b*) 1510 *Reg. Privy Seal Scot.* I. 307/1 The slauchter.. committit be him apoun subdante. 1577 HOLINSHED *Chron.* I. 35/1 Cesar..writeth that immediatly vpon knowledge had..he woulde inuade Brytaine. 1646 SIR T. BROWNE *Pseud. Ep.* 269 The Silly-how, that sometimes is found about the heads of children upon their birth. 1707 HEARNE *Collect.* (O.H.S.) II. 63 Y^e^ sneaking Villains, like Worms upon a Rain, crawl'd out. 1726 SWIFT *Gulliver* II. v, Yet often, upon a pinch, I was forced to work like a common mariner. 1736 BUTLER *Anal.* I. iv, Persons may be betrayed into wrong behaviour upon surprise. 1763 JOHNSON in *Boswell* 25 June, He has no tenants..who will follow him to the field upon an emergency.

**b.** Immediately after; following on.

**1390** GOWER *Conf.* II. 71 Whan that he this tale herde, Hou upon that the king ansuerde With Hercules he moste feighte. **1496** *Coventry Leet Bk.* 573 And what persones þat be absent þat day vppon warnyng shall pay xij d. **1523** LD. BERNERS *Froiss.* I. cxlviii. 177 [They] conquered..townes and castels one vpon the other by force. **1562** J. HEYWOOD *Prov. & Epigr.* (1867) 45 So soone vpon supper.., Sleepe maketh yll..digestion. **1596** SHAKS. *Merch. V.* IV. i. 384, I am content..to render it, Vpon his death, vnto the Gentleman. **1614** DAY *Festivals* ix. (1615) 268 Whether the Fault were unawares, or upon advisement. **1645** BP. HALL *Rem. Discontents* 80 After he had upon ten years siege, taken the rich City. **1688** HOLME *Armoury* II. 181/2 The bite or sting of a Scorpion is present Death if..[Swine] drink upon it. **1711** G. HICKES *Two Treat. Chr. Priesth.* (ed. 3) II. 30, I have wrote..not rashly or by chance, but upon thought. **1748** *Anson's Voy.* II. xiii. 276 Immediately upon this fortunate supply they stood to the westward. **1780** *Mirror* No. 95, I left my own house immediately upon the discovery I made. **1814** JANE AUSTEN *Mansf. Park* xi, Coming, as it generally did, upon a week's previous inactivity. **1849** MACAULAY *Hist. Eng.* v. I. 539 This plan had been dropped upon the detection of the Rye House Plot. **1883** HOWELLS in *Harper's Mag.* Dec. 79 The silence which his friend has absent-mindedly let follow upon his last words.

*ellipt.* **1818** COLEBROOKE *Import Colonial Corn* 183 The capital should at first be less productive if,..upon a balance, this become more fruitful.

†**c.** As soon *as*. *Obs.*—1

**1475** *Paston Lett.* III. 128, I woll, uppon as I heer from yow, come to yow in alle hast possible.

†**8.** Denoting physical arrangement, order, etc., = in (masses, a row, etc.). Cf. ON *prep.* 8. *rare.*

*c* **1300** *Havelok* 892 Als he lep þe kok vn-til, He shof hem alle upon an hyl. *c* **1400** *Destr. Troy* 1991 The flode..Rose vppon rockes [=in high masses] as any ranke hylles. *c* **1450** LOVELICH *Merlin* 1474 For thinges that ben past, j knowe, And thinges that ben comeng vppon a rowe. **1665** J. WEBB *Stone-Heng* 68 Nor [could] these have continued upon such a direct line, as still some of them seem to do.

**9.** In (a particular or specified manner, etc.); = ON *prep.* 9.

See also CROSS *sb.* 29, HEAD *sb.* 35 d, LOFT *sb.* 2 a, SLY *sb.* 2 (*a*), SQUARE *a.* 11 a, b.

*c* **1300** *Havelok* 468 Godard..tok þe maydnes bothe samen, Al-so it were up-on hiis gamen. **1338** R. BRUNNE *Chron.* (1810) 25 Bot þat þise lowed men vpon Inglish tellis, Right story can me not ken, þe certeynte what spellis. *a* **1400-50** *Alexander* 3300 Like to þis werke, þat þis coppis opon kellwyse knytt in þe woȝes. *c* **1400** *Destr. Troy.* 7359 There only was ordant of Ectors dethe, With all Soteltie to serche opon sere wise. *c* **1450** HOLLAND *Howlat* 828 The lordis leuch vpoun loft. *c* **1518** SKELTON *Magnyf.* 497 Chanons can not counterfet but vpon thre. **1600** SHAKS. *A. Y. L.* I. i. 2 It was vpon this fashion bequeathed me by will. **1628** FELTHAM *Resolves* II. lxxxii. 233 Though he doth forbeare to call for it, yet I beleeue, vpon the like, thou owest him. **1641** EARL MONM. tr. *Biondi's Civil Wars* III. 146 Charles de Lens..was slaine upon cold bloud.

†**b.** *Upon new*, = ANEW *adv.* 1. *Obs.*—1

**1399** GOWER *Praise of Peace* 315 Every dai it chaungeth uppon newe.

**10. a.** Occupied with; engaged in; employed on; = ON *prep.* 10 b.

For further illustration of group (*b*) see GUARD *sb.* 5 a, PATROL *sb.* 1, SENTRY *sb.* 3, WATCH *sb.* 6 b.

(*a*) **13..** *Seuyn Sages* (W.) 190 He was euer upon his bok, And to his lore tok gret kepe. *c* **1386** CHAUCER *Frankl. T.* 197 Vp on this daunce, amonges othere men, Daunced a squier biforn Dorigen. **1478** *Acta Dom. Conc.* (1839) 19/1 þe lordis..declarit þat þai wald nocht sit apoun na summondis quhil þe said xj day. **1612** in *10th Rep. Hist. MSS. Comm.* App. I. 608 The Electour Palatine is now at the Haghe upon his voyage into England. **1634** W. TIRWHYT tr. *Balzac's Lett.* (vol. I) 154 Those who carve in Brasse or Marble waxe old upon their workes. **1659** VANE in *Burton's Diary* (1828) III. 171 Consider what it is we are upon, a Protector in the office of Chief Magistrate. **1690** LOCKE *Govt.* I. xi. § 146 When Mankind were but one People,..and were upon Building a City together. **1705** HEARNE *Collect.* (O.H.S.) I. 30 He designs to carry on the work, being now upon a IIId volume. **1709** SWIFT *Adv. Relig.* Wks. 1755 II. I. 100 Neither am I at present upon a wild speculative project. **1719** DE FOE *Crusoe* II. (Globe) 563 They seemed to be upon their own affairs. **1741** RICHARDSON *Pamela* I. 163 Well, Jacob, what do you stare at? Pray mind what you're upon. **1784** in B. Ward *Dawn Cath. Revival* (1909) I. iv. 81 That they may be upon the mission all *unius moris in Domino*. **1859** DICKENS *T. Two Cities* II. i, He was never absent..unless upon an errand.

(*b*) **1577-** [see GUARD *sb.* 5 a]. **1647-8** in *Eng. Hist. Rev.* Oct. (1917) 573 There was onely townesmen upon the guarde, and those expressed great joy to see Sir Hugh. **1678** BUTLER *Hud.* III. i. 459 He was upon pursuit, To take you somewhere hereabout. **1681** V'CTESS CAMPDEN in *12th Rep. Hist. MSS. Comm.* App. V. 56 Lady Skidmore..was at Mr. Conisby's house upon a visette. *a* **1716** SOUTH *Serm.* (1717) VI. 378 No Man would spend the Night upon the Sentry, who [etc.].

**b.** Denoting state or condition. Cf. ON *prep.* 10.

See also BEHAVIOUR 3, BY *sb.*2 2 b, CASE *sb.*1 2 b, CONTENT *sb.*2 2, DUTY 5 e, FRET *sb.*2 6, LOAN *sb.*1 3, LOOSE *a.* B. 1, OATH *sb.* 1, PAROLE *sb.* 1, TRIAL *sb.* 12. The uses placed under (*b*) are obsolete.

(*a*) *c* **1290** *S. Eng. Leg.* I. 272/39 Ich am a man opon mi seruiz, and noman serui i-nelle Bote mi louerd. *a* **1400-50** *Alexander* 42 He was wyse enoȝe wirdis to reken..of ledes opon lyfe. **1525** LD. BERNERS *Froiss.* II. lxxvii. [lxxiii.] 229 All suche..were styll in theyr owne houses vpon a redynes. *c* **1580** in *Eng. Hist. Rev.* July (1914) 517 You must kepe good wache by night and be upon your owne kepinge. **1585** T. WASHINGTON tr. *Nicholay's Voy.* I. xi. 13 b, The Caddy..keepeth the town vpon tribute vnder the king of Alger. **1628** FELTHAM *Resolves* II. iv. 7 Their difference is neuer so much vpon the view, as then. **1657** EARL MONM. tr. *Paruta's Pol. Disc.* 35 Large Plains in Italy, wherein he might fight the Romans upon great advantage. **1683** MOXON *Mech. Exerc., Printing* xiii. ¶ 1 It must with the Chissel be split upon a good Blood-Red-Heat in that place. **1706** FARQUHAR *Recruiting Officer* I. i, A Granadeer..absent upon Furlow. **1769** GOLDSM. *Hist. Rome* (1786) II. 373 He never missep hitting..the fleetest animals, though upon full speed. **1788** CLARA REEVE *Exiles* I. 181 Poor Albert..had been upon the fret ever since I left him. **1801** tr. *Gabrielli's Myst. Husb.* III. 86 The kettle was just upon the boil. **1823** SOUTHEY *Hist. Penins. War* I. 686 The fate of the continent was upon the hazard.

(*b*) **1425** *Rolls of Parlt.* IV. 290 For lake of Parsons..children have deghed uncristend..and wymen opon chyld perechyd. **1535** COVERDALE 1 *Chron.* xiii. 17 Yf ye come vpon disceate, and to be mine aduersaries. **1604** SHAKS. *Oth.* I. i. 100 And now in madnesse..Vpon malitious knauerie, dost thou come To start my quiet. **1707** J. STEVENS tr. *Quevedo's Com. Wks.* (1709) 45 Finding a Door upon the jar. *a* **1715** BURNET *Own Time* III. xiv. (1900) II. 357 Lord Russell..was upon all the secret of his [*sc.* Rumsey's] going beyond sea. **1740** tr. *De Mouhy's Fort. Country Maid* (1741) I. 269, I had left the Door upon the Jarr.

**c.** Indicating a sphere of activity or existence.

Partly with implication of locative sense: cf. 1 b.

**1487** *Cely Papers* (Camden) 159 Mony goyth now uppon the bursse at a xjs iiijd ob. the nobull. **1589** NASHE *Pasquil's Ret.* 1, I little thought to meete thee so suddainly upon the Exchange. *c* **1645** HOWELL *Lett.* (1650) I. 26 One may hear 7. or 8. sorts of toungs spoken upon their Bourses. **1709** STEELE *Tatler* No. 48 ¶ 4, I was curious to observe the Reception these Gentlemen met with upon Change. **1712** — *Spect.* No. 266 ¶ 2 This Creature is what they call newly come upon the Town. **1763** JOHNSON in *Boswell* 25 June, A Merchant upon the 'Change of London. **1822** W. IRVING *Braceb. Hall* vii. 59 A dashing young ensign, just come upon the town. **1838** D. JERROLD *Men of Char.* II. 255 Again was John Applejohn upon the world. **1882** PEBODY *Eng. Journalism* xi. 79 He found employment upon the *Morning Post.*

**d.** With sbs. denoting activity or progress.

See also GALLOP *sb.* 1, GOG2, HUNT *sb.*2 1 b, LISTEN *sb.* 2, LONG RUN, SCRAMBLE *sb.* 1, TROT *sb.* 1 d.

**1645** SLINGSBY *Diary* (1836) 176 Our horse, upon a Gallop without once drawing up. **1662** J. WILSON *Cheats* I. i, I was out t'other Night upon the Randan. **1678** in *12th Rep. Hist. MSS. Comm.* App. V. 50 Lord Rochester hath bin att the gates of death, and so penitent that he is upon an amendment. **1728** VANBR. & CIB. *Prov. Husb.* v. i, You will every Day see hundreds as fast upon the Gallop, as she is. **1768** GOLDSM. *Good-n. Man* I. i, Everything upon the waste. **1801** *Farmer's Mag.* Jan. 105 Grain of all kinds continues upon the advance. **1877** SPURGEON *Serm.* XXIII. 505 The leaves are just upon the turn, and the fall of the year is close at hand.

**e.** Denoting situation within a portion of time or space.

**1632** SIR T. HAWKINS tr. *Mathieu's Unhappy Prosperitie* 76 His life was now almost wholly wasted, he is upon the last hour. **1680** R. L'ESTRANGE *20 Sel. Colloq. Erasm.* 258 Observing the Woman to Yawn and just upon her last Stretch, he put [etc.]. **1694-** [see TACK *sb.*1 6]. **1720** DE FOE *Capt. Singleton* xi. (1840) 187 We being then upon our starboard tack.

**11.** Indicating the basis or reason of reliance, trust, etc.

See also COUNT *v.* 9, DEPEND *v.* 5, HANG *v.* 13 b (quot. 1817), RELY *v.* 5, REST *v.* 5 b, STAND *v.* 78 c, STAY *v.*2 2 b, 3 b, SUSPEND *v.* 9, TRIST *v.* 1, TRUST *v.* 1.

*c* **1200** ORMIN 16724 And wha se lefeþþ upponn himm, þatt mann iss all unndemedd. *a* **1225** *Ancr. R.* 280 Uor þet stonding is treowe trust of herdi bileaue uppon Godes strencðe. *c* **1250** *Prayer to Virgin* 18 in *O. E. Misc.* 196 Al min hope is uppon þe. *c* **1315** SHOREHAM V. 51 Four manere ioyen hy hedde here Of hyre sone so lef an dere, Wytnes opan þe godspelle. **1377** LANGL. *P. Pl.* B. I. 117 þei leueden vpon hym þat lyed in þis manere. **1382** WYCLIF *Isaiah* vii. 2 Siria restede vp on Effraym. **1509** *Reg. Privy Seal Scot.* I. 286/2 Ony proclamatioun..anent the intercommonyn and sitting apoun the Inglismenis assouerans. **1574** R. SCOT *Platform Hop Gard.* 2, I, for my part, relye not upon other mens opinions. **1585** T. WASHINGTON tr. *Nicholay's Voy.* I. xx. 24 [He] resolued [=relied] vppon so smal an assuraunce of the Bascha. **1604** SHAKS. *Oth.* I. iii. 295 My life vpon her faith. Honest Iago, My Desdemona must I leaue to thee. **1640** LAUD *Wks.* (1853) III. 279 His Majesty's goodness was confident upon the fidelity of his subjects. **1767** GOOCH *Treat. Wounds* I. 241 It is fallacious, and by no means to be depended upon, as a Criterion. **1796** JANE AUSTEN *Pride & Prej.* i, Depend upon it,..I will visit them all. **1823** SOUTHEY *Hist. Penins. War* I. 715 They counted upon succour from San Juan's troops. **1850** TENNYSON *In Mem.* xxxii. 7 Then one deep love doth supersede All other,..And rests upon the Life indeed.

**b.** According to; in agreement or accordance with; on the model of.

(*a*) **1390** GOWER *Conf.* II. 108, I not if that be Sompnolence, Bot upon youre conscience, Min holi fader, demeth ye. *c* **1400** *Sowdone Bab.* 105 Comaundinge hem vppon her legeaunce To come. *c* **1420** *Avow. Arth.* xxxiii, Quat is thi rawunsun opon ryȝte, The sothe thou me sayn? *c* **1440** *Jacob's Well* 66 To make amendys, fully in trewe restitucyoun, vp-on þi powere. **1516** in *Acta Parlt. Scot.* (1875) XII. 37/1 He..behavis him swa towart..ȝoure brothir..that apon Ressoune na man sall be discontentit of his gyding. **1585** T. WASHINGTON tr. *Nicholay's Voy.* I. xviii. 20 b, The king..was set at libertie, vpon an accord and alliaunce which hee made. **1664** *Extr. St. Papers Friends* III. (1912) 226, I inform'd my Lord..that vpon my certaine knowledge a greate number would meete..att such a house. **1698** FRYER *Acc. E. India & P.* 54 Nothing remaining of it but only what is taken upon Chronicle. **1702** VANBRUGH *False Friend* I. i, I find you much upon my taste in this matter. **1748** RICHARDSON *Clarissa* (1811) VII. 373 Here Mr. Belford gives the substance of it upon his memory. **1867** LOWELL *Fitz Adam's Story* 464 An honest cord [of wood] in Jethro still would fail By a good foot upon the Deacon's scale.

(*b*) *a* **1225** *Leg. Kath.* 994 Hwi schulde he forhohien to wurðen to þet þing þet is iwend [=formed] upon him? **1563** SHUTE *Archit.* B iv, This piller [is]..made by the Ionians, vpon the Simetrie of a strong man. **1776** *Ann. Reg.* 148 A rifle gun upon a new construction. **1790** W. WRIGHTE *Grotesque Archit.* 11 The four minarets at the angles bring the plan upon a square of forty feet. **1791** SMEATON *Edystone L.* § 85 Upon these ideas I drew up..the following plan. **1863** MARY HOWITT tr. *F. Bremer's Greece* I. viii. 264 The new constitution of Greece is formed very much upon that of France. **1882** PEBODY *Eng. Journalism* xxii. 172 The Society papers..are to some extent modelled upon the Reviews.

**c.** Indicating the ground, basis, occasion, or reason of an action, opinion, etc.; = ON *prep.* 11.

In very frequent use from *c* 1525. In group (*b*) with allusion to literal uses (sense 1).

(*a*) **1456** SIR G. HAYE *Law Arms* (S.T.S.) 179 A symple knycht may nocht lede a baroun..apon his sauf condyt. *a* **1500** in C. Trice-Martin *Chanc. Proc.* (1904) 4 Uppon untrue verydyte yoven in London ther lieth none atteynt. **1515** *Reg. Privy Seal Scot.* I. 403/2 The slauchter..committit apoun forthocht felony. **1554-5** in Feuillerat *Revels Q. Mary* (1914) 170 In a redines to serve vpon further warnynge. **1584** R. SCOT *Discov. Witchcr.* x. i. (1886) 143 Those witches that make men beleeve they can prophesie upon dreames. **1602** W. S. *Thomas Ld. Cromwell* v. iv, The great Lord Cromwell arreasted vpon treason! **1647-8** in *Eng. Hist. Rev.* Oct. (1917) 569 How..Cholmeley came first to be imployed in the Parliament service, and upon what grounds hee quitt the same. **1697** WALSH *Life V.* ¶ 26 in Dryden *Virgil*, He has solv'd more Phænomena of Nature upon sound Principles, than Aristotle in his Physics. **1722** DE FOE *Plague* (1754) 14 Upon these Arguments my Brother chang'd my Resolutions again. **1747** W. GOULD *Eng. Ants* Pref., Upon this Reason my Lord Bacon does not approve of the historical Method of writing in Philosophy. **1787** WHITAKER *Mary Q. Scots Vind.* I. 62 They thus condemn the Queen..upon letters unauthenticated by the producers. **1827** SCOTT *Chron. Canongate* Introd., Invernahyle obtained from the Chevalier his prisoner's freedom upon parole. **1846** *Chambers' Jrnl.* VI. 280/2 Upon the most insubstantial of pretexts. **1872** LIDDON *Elem. Relig.* i. 16 The most intellectual Gnostics were Sensualists; Sensualists upon a theory and with deliberation.

(*b*) *a* **1400-** [see FOUND *v.*2 4]. **1565** SIR R. MAITLAND in *Maitland Folio MS.* 23 Grund all thy doing vpon suthfastnes. **1573-** [see BUILD *v.* 6 b]. **1672** T. GODDEN *Catholicks No Idolaters* 23 This is the major Proposition of his Syllogism, and if this fail, the Charge he builds upon it, must needs fall. **1711** ADDISON *Spect.* No. 9 ¶ 8 Our Modern celebrated Clubs are founded upon Eating and Drinking. **1814** JANE AUSTEN *Mansf. Park* xlii, He particularly built upon a very happy..autumn there this year. **1844** BERESF. HOPE *Ess.* 111 This..does give us very different ground to go upon. **1878** HOPPS *Princ. Relig.* iii. 13 Upon this great truth..we base all our hopes.

†**d.** Of (a cause of death or illness). *Obs.*

*c* **1420** *Brut* 344 Mony a worthi man yn þat viage deid vpon þe Flix. **1510** in Leadam *Star Chamber Cases* (Selden) II. 73 Vppon the seid enprisonement the same John..deyed within xij howres. **1600** HOLLAND *Livy* 1264 Upon which fracture he died thirtie daies after. **1645** SLINGSBY *Diary* (1836) 163 Ye Gentlewoman yt had lived in it dead upon Grief. **1696** A. TELFAIR *New Confut. Sadd.* 10 Which frightned him so much, that he fell sick upon it immediately.

**e.** Indicating means of subsistence or existence, or an article of food furnishing sustenance.

Sometimes = 'after having taken or consumed': see (*c*).

(*a*) **1457** HARDING *Chron.* in *Eng. Hist. Rev.* Oct. (1912) 747 His lyfelode exceded noght all clere An hundreth marke to leue vpon in dede. *c* **1489** CAXTON *Sonnes of Aymon* iii. 98 We have loste our store of vytaylles, so that we have noo thynge to lyve upon. **1564** *Child-Marr.* 125 Aspshawe is a very poore man, and liveth apon his neibours. **1583-** [see LIVE *v.*1 2]. **1599** B. JONSON *Ev. Man out of Hum.* Descr. Char., A Thred-bare Sharke. One that..lives upon lendings. **1600** J. PORY tr. *Leo's Africa* v. 249 Monasteries..maintained vpon the common beneuolence of the citie. **1625** BURGES *Pers. Tithes* 45 All liuing vpon Fishing. **1713** [see LIVE *v.*1 3]. **1884** *Pall Mall G.* 9 Sept. 3/1 The lady did not indeed say that she lived *with* her father and mother, but she lived *upon* them. **1885** *Law Times Rep.* LII. 651/1 He earned nothing, and he lived upon some money of mine.

(*b*) *c* **1440** *Pallad. on Husb.* x. 76 Til May hit wol suffice vppon to feede. **1571** DIGGES *Pantom.* Pref. B j, Suche two footed Moules and Todes whom..nature hath ordayned to..suck vpon the muck. **1600** PORY tr. *Leo's Africa* VI. 276 They liue vpon the flesh of Ostriches and camels. **1678** WANLEY *Wond. Lit. World* v. i. § 94. 467/2 'Tis thought he surfeited upon Melons. **1713** STEELE *Guard.* No. 34 He..breakfasted upon toast and ale. **1743** P. FRANCIS tr. *Horace, Sat.* II. iii. 124 While Moths upon his rotting Carpets fed. **1818** G. S. FABER *Horæ Mosaicæ* II. 281 If the Dominical Supper be a feast upon a sacrifice. **1832** HT. MARTINEAU *Life in Wilds* ii. 26 The grass it fed upon. **1885** *Manch. Exam.* 16 June 5/1 M. Henze fed his prize oxen upon silage.

*ellipt.* **1717** PRIOR *Alma* III. 243 Was ever Tartar fierce or cruel, Upon the Strength of Water-Gruel. **1737** BRACKEN *Farriery Impr.* (1757) II. 109 A young Horse may look pretty sleek upon Hay only. **1897** MEREDITH *Amazing Marriage* i, The clergyman,..renouncing strong drinks, because he found that he 'cursed better upon water'.

(*c*) **1663** BOYLE *Usef. Exp. Nat. Philos.* II. vi. 185 Though ..[it] did make her sickish, especially, when she slept upon it. **1829** SCOTT *Jrnl.* 5 July, So to roost upon a crust of bread and a glass of small beer, my usual supper.

†**f.** At (an expense, cost, etc.). *Obs.*

*c* **1400** *R. Gloucester's Chron.* (Rolls) 3799 Al þe bachelerie ..þe nom in is compaynie..vp [*v.rr.* vp on, vppon] is coust. **1476** *Acta Auditorum* (1839) 49/1 þare to remain apoun þare awin expenss. **1513** BRADSHAW *St. Werburge* II. 1157 Many shyps were made vpon the kynges cost. **1563** *Reg. Privy Council Scot.* I. 239 To commande thame to warde, to remane thairin upon thair awne expense. **1577** HANMER *Anc. Eccl. Hist.* 396 He had buylded vpon his owne costes and charges the sepulchres and tumbes. **1674** *Reg. Privy Counc. Scot.* IV. 278 A mudwall rowme..built upon his owne cost. **1711** in *10th Rep. Hist. MSS. Comm.* App. V. 124 Each company..was subsisted upon the cost of every captain for three months.

**g.** Denoting security of a loan, etc.

**1474** CAXTON *Chesse* (1883) 121 The besant..was holden & gaged vpon an ymage. **1562** J. HEYWOOD *Prov. & Epigr.* Bb i b, No man will one peny lende upon it. **1611** BIBLE *Neh.* v. 4 Wee haue borrowed money..vpon our lands and vineyards. **1677** YARRANTON *Eng. Improv.* 7 Moneys lent upon Goods at very easie Interest. **1707** *Lond. Gaz.* No. 4333/8 They will..Lend Money upon Tallies or other good Securities, at 5 l. per Cent. **1742** KAMES *Decis. Crt. Sess.* (1799) 40 The money is secured..upon land. **1791** BOSWELL *Johnson* (1904) I. 328 Security being taken upon the property. **1861** M. PATTISON *Ess.* (1889) I. 36 He assigns 1000 marks..to his son's wife, secured upon the Swiss possessions of his house. **1868** ROGERS *Pol. Econ.* iv. 43 If [a banker].. issues notes upon no property at all, the issue is fraudulent. **1885** *Act* 48–49 *Vict.* c. 54 § 11 Any mortgage or charge duly created..upon the profits of any benefice.

†**h.** On condition of. *Obs.*

**1516** *Reg. Privy Seal Scot.* I. 422/2 The kingis grace dischargis thaim apone thair remaining in ward for the said errour. **1591** SHAKS. *1 Hen. VI*, IV. v. 36 Vpon my Blessing I command thee goe. **1626** in Picton *L'pool Munic. Rec.* (1883) I. 199 Maister Lappage doth..promise that hee will continew his ministry..upon true payment and receivinge the afforesaid allowance. **1662** STILLINGFL. *Orig. Sacræ* III. iii. § 5 If it were suitable to Gods nature to promise life to man upon obedience.

†**i.** Out of; with; by the use of. *Obs. rare.*

**1553** T. WILSON *Rhet.* (1580) 42 He did not make the wife vppon the same claie, whereof he made man. **1683** MOXON *Mech. Exerc., Printing* ii. ¶ 2 That his Letter be Cast upon good Mettal, that it may last the longer.

**j.** In many phrases, as ***upon..accord, account (of), composition, condition, design, distrust, envy, foot, fraud, head, lease, matter, purpose, score, shame, suspicion, trust, whole,*** for which see the sbs.

**12.** At the risk or with the certainty of incurring or suffering (a pain, penalty, etc.); on peril of; = ON *prep.* 12.

See also PAIN *sb.*[1] 1 b, PENALTY *sb.* 2 d.

*c* **1384** CHAUCER *H. Fame* III. 1570 That he shuld fast goon Vpon the peyn to be blynde. *c* **1420** *Contin. Brut* 384 Þe King commaunded to..late hem passe yn pees, vpon deth. *Ibid.* 385 [He] chargyd ham, vpon her lyf, to kepe wel the toun and þe Castell. **1480** CAXTON *Descr. Brit.* 9 Walsshmen shold not passe that dyche with wepen vpon a grete payne. **1540** *Acts Privy Council* (1837) VII. 21 To temperate his tongue hereafter upon adventure of further punishement. **1553** W. CHOLMELEY *Req. & Suite* 19 in *Camden Misc.* (1853) II, Commaundyng..the Aldermen, upon the losse of their auctoritie and office,..to see [etc.]. **1596** *Edward III*, I. i. 70 With threats, Vppon a penaltie, inioynd to come. **1603** PARSONS *2nd Pt. Three Convers. Eng.* xii. 625 The Duke protesteth the contrary (vpon his death). **1656** EARL MONM. tr. *Boccalini's Advts. fr. Parnass.* 126, I have,..upon severe punishment, inhibited the translation of my Alcheron. **1699** BENTLEY *Phal.* 439 He order'd every man upon the pain of death to bring in all the money he had.

**13.** Indicating that which forms the basis of revenue, profit, fines, taxation, lending, etc.; = ON *prep.* 13.

See also RETIRE *v.* 1 e (quot. 1806), TAX *sb.*[1] 1.

**1466** *Acta Auditorum* (1839) 4/2 [He] sall..resaue þe soume of mone aucht till him vppoun þe said annuel. **1495** *Act 11 Hen. VII*, c. 43 *Preamble*, So that the seid Erle upon his seid leasses.., do reserve asmuch rentis..as be nowe usuell. **1535** COVERDALE *Neh.* v. 3 Let vs borowe money of the kinge vpon vsury. **1554** in Leadam *Star Chamber Cases* (Selden) II. 217 They so offending to be payned opon a certen some of money. ?**1677** PETTY *Pol. Arithm.* (1699) 272 Such a part of the full value of their Commodities, as may possibly be lost upon the sale of them. **1719** D'URFEY *Pills* I. 333 Five hundred Pounds upon the brown Bay still. **1798** *Hull Advertiser* 24 Mar. 2/3 Insurance upon..outhouses, and upon unthreshed stock therein. **1845** R. W. HAMILTON *Pop. Education* x. 278 How can the State raise the amount? Is it not to be raised upon the people? **1892** *Law Times* XCIV. 104/1 A commission of over 60 per cent. upon the sums received.

**II.** Of motion or direction towards a position, thing or person, state, etc.

**14.** Upward so as to place or be on a surface, point, etc. Cf. ON *prep.* 14.

*c* **1200** ORMIN 11959 Þe deofell brohhte Jesu Crist Wiþþutenn o þe temmple Uppenn an sæte uppo þe rof. *c* **1250** *Gen. & Ex.* 3899 Moyses ðor made a wirme of bras, And henget heȝe up-on a saft. *c* **1300** *Havelok* 1942 He lep up on a stede lith. **13..** *Seuyn Sages* (W.) 2318 Vpon his palfrai lep Catoun. **1375**, **1470–85** [see START *v.* 1]. **1470–85** MALORY *Arthur* IX. xxx. 384 They came vpon sir launcelot sodenly and vnnethe he myght putte vpon hym his helme. **1535** COVERDALE *Joel* ii. 9 They shal clymme vp vpon the houses. **1627** DRAYTON *Nymphidia* xvii, Flye Cranion her Chariotere, Vpon the Coach-box getting. **1639** S. DU VERGER tr. *Camus' Admir. Events* 130 He leapes upon his Mule. **1725** *Fam. Dict.* s.v. *Pears*, Mount them one upon another Steeplewise. **1847** TENNYSON *Princ.* III. 208 To lift the woman's fall'n divinity Upon an even pedestal with man. **1854** H. MILLER *Sch. & Schm.* xxi. 446 A large loligo..had thrown itself high and dry upon the beach.

**b.** To or towards a position on a surface, etc.; = ON *prep.* 14.

Group (*b*) corresponds to sense 1 c; group (*c*) illustrates non-physical uses.

(*a*) *c* **1200** ORMIN 14667 Sniþ itt, alls itt wære an shep, & leȝȝ itt uppon allterr. *c* **1250** *Gen. & Ex.* 3186 On an gold gad ðe name god Is grauen, and leid up-on ðe flod. *Ibid.* 3949 Vp-on hise ase his sadel he dede. *a* **1300** *Cursor M.* 8894 Vnwarli sco sett hir don Apon þis ilk tre. *c* **1386** CHAUCER *Knt.'s T.* 921 Some drope of pitee..Vp on vs wrecched wommen lat thou falle. *c* **1391** — *Astrol.* II. § 7 Ley thi label vp-on the same degree of the sonne. *c* **1400** *St. Alexius* (Cotton) 257 They hylde water wppon hys hede. *c* **1430** *Two Cookery Bks.* 42 Þan take fayre pecez of Brede..vppe-on þe Eyroun. **1602** MARSTON *Antonio's Rev.* IV. iii, Her head sunk down upon her breast. *a* **1655** SIR T. MAYERNE *Archimag. Anglo-Gall.* No. 84 (1658) 58 Lay this froth upon your sullibub as high as you can. **1697** DRYDEN *Virg. Georg.* IV. 611 The various God..draws a Rock upon his dark Abode. **1728** CHAMBERS *Cycl.* s.v. *Triangle*, If a Perpendicular be let fall upon the Base of an oblique angled Triangle. **1808** SCOTT *Marm.* II. i, Upon the gale she stooped her side. **1844** J. JACK *Hist. of St. Monance* xi. 74 The skipper placed upon the table a large wooden caup or platter. **1870** ANDERSON *Missions Amer. Bd.* IV. xxvi. 63 The mob rushed forward and trampled spitefully upon it.

*ellipt.* *c* **1450** *Mirk's Festial* I. 5 Sle, sle, opon þe broche, rost hote.

(*b*) **1303** R. BRUNNE *Handl. Synne* 952 Syttyþ dowun vppon ȝoure knees. *c* **1400** *26 Pol. Poems* 149/233, I set me doune apon my kne. **1486** *Bk. St. Albans* b iv b, Softe and layserly fall oppon yowre kneys. **1535** COVERDALE *Mark* xv. 19 [They] fell vpon the kne, & worshipped him. *a* **1578** LINDESAY (Pitscottie) *Chron. Scot.* (S.T.S.) I. 209 The said preist..kneillit doune wpoun his knie. **1611** SHAKS. *Cymb.* IV. ii. 288 Come on, away, apart vpon our knees. **1837** SIR F. PALGRAVE *Merch. & Friar* iv. (1844) 176 The Chancellor, dropping off the Woolsack upon his bended knees. **1876** F. K. ROBINSON *Whitby Gloss.* 208, 'Up-end yourself,' get upon your legs.

(*c*) *c* **1325** *Spec. Gy Warw.* 995 And anon god putte his fuisoun Vp-on hire mele. **1382** WYCLIF *Job* xxv. 3 Vp on whom shyneth not the liȝt of hym? **1461** *Rolls of Parlt.* V. 463/2 Takyng upon hym..the Coroune and name of Kyng. **1535** COVERDALE *Num.* vi. 25 The Lorde make his face to shyne vpon the. **1656** EARL MONM. tr. *Boccalini's Advts. fr. Parnass.* II. vi. 210 Whereby they had put themselves.. upon great difficulties. **1697** DRYDEN *Virg. Georg.* IV. 773 The Nymphs, Companions of th' unhappy Maid, This Punishment upon thy Crimes have laid. **1765** STERNE *Tr. Shandy* VIII. xxi, I fell in love all at once..it burst upon me..like a bomb. **1768** BOSWELL *Lett.* (1924) 145, I am thrown upon the wide world again. **1793** T. BEDDOES *Demonstr. Evid.* 79 The magnitudes, being doubled upon themselves, increase so, that [etc.]. **1816** BYRON *Prisoner of Chillon* x, A light broke in upon my brain.

**c.** Denoting incidence, seizure, hold, etc.; = ON *prep.* 14 b.

*c* **1250** *Gen. & Ex.* 2339 Ðo cam iosep swilc rewðe up-on, he dede halle ut ðe toðere gon. **1398** TREVISA *Barth. De P. R.* XVII. cxv. (Bodl. MS.), Ripe & igadered ere corrupcioune oþer rostinge falle vpon whete. **1530** PALSGR. 748/2, I take holde apon one, *jempoygne*. **1535** COVERDALE *Ps.* cxiv. 3 The paynes of hell gat holde vpon me. **1535**– [see LAY *v.*[1] 22]. **1546**– [see SEIZE *v.* 9]. **1632** LITHGOW *Trav.* VII. 303 The Venetian Factor seased vpon all. **1665** *Extr. St. Papers Friends* III. (1912) 240 There was a full congregation of quakers and the like seised vppon by Sir Francis Clarke sunday last. **1880** J. PAYNE *New Poems* 259 A deadly terror got A sudden hold upon her. **1892** H. LANE *Differ. Rheum. Dis.* (ed. 2) 67 It seems to have taken a firm hold upon the public.

**d.** Of the incidence of a blow, stroke, etc.; = ON *prep.* 14 c.

*c* **1300** *Havelok* 2734 He..smot him so up-on þe crune, þat [etc.]. **13..** *Guy Warw.* (A.) 2368 Þan hastiliche þe ost ichon Opon Segyn þat smiten anon. **1470–85** MALORY *Arthur* X. lx. 516 Sir Tristram gaf hym suche a buffet vpon the helme. **1507** in Leadam *Star Chamber Cases* (Selden) 253 He sawe ..Irton being hurt vppon the hed. **1562** *Aberd. Kirk Sess. Rec.* (Spalding Cl.) 6 To be puneist with ane palm vpone the hand for ilk falt. **1594** *Selimus* 1447 Dart Thy smouldring flame Vpon the head of cursed Acomat. **1611** BIBLE *Exod.* vii. 17 Behold, I will smite with the rod..vpon the waters. **1711** ADDISON *Spect.* No. 9 ¶ 11 His Neighbour may give him a Kick upon the Shins. **1737** WHISTON *Josephus, Hist.* I. xxi. 13 Many..have stood amazed..when they saw him.. shoot the arrow upon the mark. **1813** SCOTT *Rokeby* VI. xxv, One stroke, upon the Castle bell, To Oswald rung his dying knell. **1844** MRS. BROWNING *Drama Exile* 64 This is the Eden lost By Lucifer!..this the sword..That smote upon the forehead. **1881** BESANT & RICE *Chapl. of Fleet* I. viii, The cruel cat falling at every step upon their..bleeding shoulders.

**e.** In phrases of the type ***harm upon harm, torment upon torment,*** denoting cumulative addition or repetition; = ON *prep.* 14 d.

*c* **1320** R. BRUNNE *Medit.* 865 Þey wounded here, and heped harm vp on harmes. *c* **1380** WYCLIF *Sel. Wks.* III. 346 And so servauntis upon servantis weren char[g]ious to þis hous. *c* **1485** *Digby Myst.* (1882) IV. 1336 He had torment opon torment. **1529** S. FISH *Supplic. Beggers* (1871) 13 The capteyns of his kingdome..haue heped to him benefice vpon benefice. **1596** SHAKS. *Merch. V.* III. i. 91 Why, thou losse vpon losse! **1599** — *Much Ado* II. i. 252 Hudling iest vpon iest, with..impossible conueiance vpon me. **1613** PURCHAS *Pilgrimage* (1614) 152 Which heaped vpon them Anathema vpon Anathema. **1699** EVELYN *Acetaria* App. P 4, Cover the Bottom of the Jar with some Dill,..then a Bed of Nuts; and so *stratum* upon *stratum*. **1864** KINGSLEY *Roman & T.* 137 Dietrich had had to write letter upon letter. **1882** 'OUIDA' *Maremma* I. 90 Centuries upon centuries of carnage..have laid the land bare. **1884** C. F. WOOLSON in *Harper's Mag.* Feb. 371 Millions upon millions of violets.

**f.** On (a voyage, expedition, mission, etc.); = ON *prep.* 14 e.

**1426** LYDG. *De Guil. Pilgr.* 648 Or I myhte make my passage To gynnen vp-on my pylgrymage. *c* **1430** — *Min. Poems* (Percy Soc.) 12 The kyng procedyng forthe upon his way, kome to the Condyte. **1596** SHAKS. *1 Hen. IV*, I. iii. 150 When the vnhappy King..did set forth Vpon his Irish Expedition. **1711** ADDISON *Spect.* No. 55 ¶ 1 A young Fellow ..sent upon a long Voyage. **1712** W. ROGERS *Voy.* 324 To encourage our South Sea Company..to go upon some Discovery that way. **1817** KIRBY & SP. *Entomol.* xvii. II. 77 The rufescent ants do not leave their nests to go upon these expeditions..till [etc.]. **1839** BAILEY *Festus* 232 As on they sped upon their starward course.

**15.** Into contact or collision with, esp. by way of attack; against; = ON *prep.* 15.

See also COME *v.* 48 b, FALL *v.* 69 b, FLY *v.*[1] 8 b, GO *v.* 66 a, LAY *v.*[1] 32 a, SET *v.* 132 a.

*a* **1300** *Cursor M.* 24461 Me-thoght moght it [*v.r.* i] apon him rine,..I suld ha ben all hale. **13..** *Guy Warw.* (A.) 1996 Þou schalt ȝif þe first asaut Opon þe Almaundes. *c* **1385** CHAUCER *L. G. W.* 1327 *Dido* (Fairf.), On a nyght sleping he let hir lye, And staal a-wey vpon [*v.r.* vnto] his companye. *c* **1400** *Sc. Trojan War* II. 444 Russhande wpone the altare. *c* **1450** *Merlin* iii. 56 Whan Vter saugh..the Danes assembled, he sette vpon hem as vigorously or more. *c* **1500** *Melusine* lix. 348 Go we vpon our enemyes to helpe & socoure our frendes. **1535** COVERDALE *1 Sam.* xvii. 35 And whan he wolde haue bene vpon me, I toke him by his beerde. **1585** T. WASHINGTON tr. *Nicholay's Voy.* I. xix. 22 The Turkes.., vpon whom they of the Castle..gaue an assault. **1622** MABBE tr. *Aleman's Guzman d'Alf.* II. 48, I stumbled..vpon a great dung mixen. **1631** PELLHAM *Gods Power* 2 Wee eight men ..were bound for this Greenland aforesaid, to make a voyage upon Whales or Sea-horse. **1711** ADDISON *Spect.* No. 299 ¶ 2 He drew his Sword upon me before he was nine years old. **1782** COWPER *Royal George* 20 She ran upon no rock. **1801** STRUTT *Sports & Past.* III. i. 130 The two combatants..were thereby prevented from running their horses upon each other. **1857** T. HUGHES *Tom Brown* I. ix, [They] run plump upon one of the masters as they emerge into the High Street.

*ellipt.* *c* **1450** *Merlin* iii. 56 The kynge seide to his peple, 'Now vpon hem in all that we may'. **1535** COVERDALE *2 Sam.* xviii. 14 Not so, I wil vpon him before thy face. **1588** SHAKS. *L. L. L.* IV. iii. 367 Aduance your standards, & vpon them Lords. **1821** BYRON *Sardanap.* IV. i, Upon them! (Trumpet sounds again.)

*fig.* **1535**– [see RUSH *v.*[2] 6 b, 3 a]. **1887** 'L. CARROLL' *Game of Logic* i. 36 Let them Rush upon their Fate!

**16.** In the direction of; towards; = ON *prep.* 16.

**a.** In respect of looking, etc.

See also CAST *v.* 7, FRONT *v.*[1] 1, GAPE *v.* 3, GAZE *v.* 1 b, GLARE *v.* 2, LAUGH *v.* 4, LOOK *v.* 1, PORE *v.* 1, SEE *v.* 21, SMILE *v.* 2 a, SQUINT *v.* 2.

*a* **1225** *Ancr. R.* 56 To kesten kang eien upon ȝunge wummen. *c* **1250** *Gen. & Ex.* 2661 Ðor quiles he seweden [= looked] him up-on, Mani dede bileph un-don. *c* **1340** HAMPOLE *Pr. Consc.* 5024 Þair bodys sal alle unsemely be,..and ugly, opon to se. *c* **1386** CHAUCER *Knt.'s T.* 219 He cast his eye vpon Emelya. **14..** in *E. E. P.* (1862) 144 Dame ypocryte loke vp-on a boke. **1526** TINDALE *1 John* i. 1 That which..we have loked apon, and oure hondes have handled. **1581** [see TURN *v.* 48]. **1632** LITHGOW *Trav.* I. 38 Arthur looked vpon me, and I laughed vpon him. **1710** STRYPE *Life & Acts of E. Grindal* vii. 70 These Unsuccesses were justly looked upon to proceed from the punishing Hand of Heaven. **1790** BRUCE *Source of Nile* I. 5 We pointed our prow directly..upon Alexandria. **1799** WORDSW. *Two April Mornings* 19 Matthew..fixing still his eye Upon the eastern mountain-top. **1845** S. AUSTIN *Ranke's Hist. Ref.* II. 357 The fears of some, the hopes of others, and the attention of all, were now turned upon the young emperor. **1874** FARRAR *Christ* I. 472 He turned His back for a time upon His native land. **1884** MRS. OLIPHANT *Sir Tom* iv, Her gray eyes absolutely flamed upon him.

**b.** In respect of movement, etc.

?*a* **1400** *Morte Arth.* 262 Thow countez no caas, ne castes no forthire, Bot hurles furthe appone heuede, as thi herte thynkes. *c* **1400** *Destr. Troy* 6258 If any stert vpon stray, strike hym to dethe! **1511** *Guylforde's Pylgr.* (Camden) 21 After .viij. dayes..he come vpon [= appeared to] theym ayen. **1634** SIR T. HERBERT *Trav.* 11 [We] were driuen to lee-ward a hundred leagues vpon the Coast of Brazil. **1697** COLLIER *Ess. Mor. Subj.* I. B 1, Unless you point directly upon his Vice. **1716** *Lond. Gaz.* No. 5455/3 Our Fleet..bore down upon them. **1828** in Concanen *Rowe v. Brenton* (1830) 28 To sink a shaft upon the lode. **1829** NAPIER *Penins. War* II. 142 The hospitals..of Salamanca being evacuated upon Lamego, that town was crowded.

**17.** †**a.** In or into (pieces); = ON *prep.* 17 b.

*c* **1400** *Sege Jerusalem* 699 Twey apys.. þat renten þe rawe flesche vpon rede peces.

**b.** Into, as by penetration; = ON *prep.* 17 a.

**1738** HERRING in J. Duncombe *Lett.* (1773) II. 137 The sea, which here indents upon the country.

**18.** Unto, to (a person): in reference to descent or (*Sc.*) marriage; = ON *prep.* 18.

**1492** *Acta Dom. Conc.* (1839) 254/2 His faider..maryit him apoun his sister dochter incontrare his band. **1536** BELLENDEN *Cron. Scot.* (1821) I. 127 The eldest of hir dochteris wes married upon..Marius. **1596** BACON *Use Com. Law* (1635) 32 If this inheritance descend upon a woman. **1667** [see DESCEND *v.* 9]. **1821** GALT *Ann. Parish* i, My marriage upon my own cousin, Miss Betty Lanshaw. **1893** STEVENSON *Catriona* xxi, She was married..upon my Uncle Robin.

**19.** Into, to, or on (some action, occupation, course, or condition); = ON *prep.* 19.

*a* **1300** *Cursor M.* 15580 Alle þe apostels þan bi-gan to fal a-pon a gret. **1390** GOWER *Conf.* I. 30 Thanne upon dissencioun Thei felle. **1435** [see SET *v.* 114]. **1483** in *Acta Dom. Conc.* II. Introd. 103 The said schiref put apone the said inquest..persons quhilk war suspect of the law. *a* **1513** FABYAN *Chron.* 351 A quest of .xii. Knyghtes of Myddlesex, sworne vpon a iurye. **1581**– [see RUN *v.* 70 d]. **1607** T. ROGERS *39 Art.* Pref. § 5 Wee set vpon the building of Gods house. **1625**– [see FALL *v.* 69 d]. **1658** ALLESTREE *Whole Duty Man* XIV. § 22. 300 It puts the child upon shifts, and tricks. **1709** STRYPE *Ann. Ref.* I. xxi. 240 Some while..after the entrance of Queen Elizabeth upon her government. **1750** JOHNSON *Rambler* No. 1 ¶ 1 The perplexity of being forced upon choice. **1764** FOOTE *Mayor of G.* I. Wks. 1799 I. 165 I advised him to pull off his spurs before he went upon action. **1813** *Examiner* 17 May 320/1 It put the Church upon the alert. **1847** WORDSW. in *Mem.* (1851) I. 14 When at school, I..was put upon reading the first six books of Euclid.

**20.** Indicating the person or thing that action, feeling, etc., is directed towards or against, or that is influenced or affected by it; = ON *prep.* 20.

Construed with many verbs, as *attend, await, bear, bespit, bestow, breathe, call, charge*, etc. See also FIE *int.* 1–2, OUT *int.* 2, SHAME *sb.* 16 b.

*c* **1200** ORMIN 1750 Þa bedess, þatt te Laferrd Crist Forr hise þeowwess biddeþþ Uppon hiss faderr heofennking. *Ibid.* 6119 Þe birrþ þin rihhte swinnkess winn Uppenn ȝuw alle nittenn. *a* **1225** *Leg. Kath.* 130 Ah se sone ha..wende hare wiheles, upon ham seoluen. **1297** R. GLOUC. (Rolls) 3167 Þe king ek in is syde is herte up on him caste. *c* **1320** *Cast. Love* 1482 Þat muche wo vs brouȝte vppon. *c* **1400** tr. *Secreta Secret., Gov. Lordsh.* 106 He hadde greuously synned vpon him. **1473** WARKW. *Chron.* (Camden) 8 The

Kynge..losyde his gonnys of his ordynaunce uppone them. *c* **1500** *Melusine* lix. 360 Be ye he that wyl take the trybute vpon my Fortresse? **1533** *Acc. Ld. High Treas. Scot.* VI. 156 To Johne Drummondis childer wirkand upoune the hagbute stokkis. **1585** T. WASHINGTON tr. *Nicholay's Voy.* I. xviii. 21 We will not leaue the following on vpon our purpose. **1633** MARMION *Fine Companion* I. iii. (1875) 114 They can doe no more good upon me, than a young pittifull Lover upon a mistress that has the sullens. **1656** EARL MONM. tr. *Boccalini's Advts. fr. Parnass.* II. v. 206 He..had made their places be conferred upon men void of counsel. **1680** *Laws Nevis* iii. (1740) 6 If the said Offenders are not able to pay..then to be compelled to work it out upon the Forts. **1737** WHISTON *Josephus, Antiq.* XVI. iv. § 3 The father may have a suspicion upon all his sons. **1796** *Ann. Reg., St. Papers* 297 The constitution..is sacredly obligatory upon all. **1805** tr. *Lafontaine's Hermann & Emilia* I. 261 Nothing is more detestable than to offer one's self upon a young man. **1850** ROBERTSON *Serm.* Ser. III. (1857) 7 Persecution is that which affixes penalties upon views held, instead of upon life led. **1896** *Peterson Mag.* Jan. 102/2 The intruded-upon young lady turned her back upon him.

**b.** Denoting the object of regard, desire, etc.; = ON *prep.* 20 b.

See also DOTE *v.*[1] 3, EAGER *a.* 6, KEEN *a.* 6 b, MAD *a.* 4, RUN *v.* 70 b, SET *v.* 37.

*c* **1330** R. BRUNNE *Chron. Wace* (Rolls) 7604 Opon þat meyden he wax al mad. **1382** WYCLIF *Psalm* xxxix. [xl.] 17 Ful out io3e thei, and glade vpon me, alle that sechen thee. *c* **1449** PECOCK *Repr.* II. xx. 267 He schal haue miche gretter affeccioun vpon the seid freend. **1470–85** MALORY *Arthur* x. lvi. 508 Louers..soo mad and soo soted vpon wymmen. *a* **1578** LINDESAY (Pitscottie) *Chron. Scot.* (S.T.S.) I. 169 The king..was covatous wpoun money. **1598** BARCKLEY *Felic. Man* I. 51 A young man..that was..enamoured vpon an Image of marble. **1614** BP. HALL *Recoll. Treat.* 982 In this case, Moses should have beene..cast downe..; yet how hot is hee uppon justice. **1711** ADDISON *Spect.* No. 106 ¶ 3 When he is pleasant upon any of them, all his Family are in good Humour. **1843** *Fraser's Mag.* XXVIII. 619 O'Connell is bent upon the disruption of the British empire.

†**c.** Among (a number of sharers, etc.). *Obs.*

**1492** in *10th Rep. Hist. MSS. Comm.* App. V. 323 Distributers of the same upon the commynes. **1526** TINDALE *Rom.* xv. 26 To make a certayne distribucion apon the poore sanctes. **1598** DALLINGTON *Meth. Trav.* K 3, Hee diuideth the Lands vpon his horsemen, to each his portion.

**d.** Indicating the person by whom a cheque, draft, order, etc., is payable, or the bank on which it is drawn; = ON *prep.* 20 c.

See also CHEQUE *sb.* 3, DRAUGHT *sb.* 35, DRAW *v.* 65.

**1660** *Nicholas Papers* (Camden) IV. 226 Mr. Fox hauing giuen mee a note upon Mr. Shaw to pay me my allowance. *a* **1722** FOUNTAINHALL *Decis.* (1759) I. 12 The bill upon his wife for £200. **1722** DE FOE *Col. Jack* (1840) 216 He shows me a bill upon me, drawn by my wife. **1798** in *Ushaw Mag.* Dec. (1913) 287 An order upon Mr. Wright for £12 as the price of the book sent you. **1843** *Blackw. Mag.* LIV. 736 It may be quite as well..to draw upon the bank.

**21.** Indicating a person or thing towards whom or which hostile or adverse action or language is directed; against; = ON *prep.* 21.

See also (*a*) BLOW *v.* 30, COMPLAIN *v.* 6 b, CRY *v.* 21 b, DESIGN *sb.* 1 b, LIE *v.*[2] 1 b, PEACH *v.* 2, RAGE *v.* 2 b, RAIL *v.*[4] 1 b, STEAL *v.* 5 e; (*b*) GO *v.* 66 a, MAKE *v.* 81, SEEK *v.* 17.

(*a*) *c* **1200** ORMIN 415 Þatt fand mann nan þing uppon hemm To wre3enn, ne to tælenn. *a* **1225** *Leg. Kath.* 2204 Þa Porphire iseh feole, þet me seide hit upon,..dreien to deaðe. *c* **1275** *Passion Our Lord* 241 in *O. E. Misc.* 44 A ueole kunne wise hi lowen him vp-on. *c* **1430** LYDG. *Hors, Shepe & G.* 151 He cryethe affter peasse, compleynnythe vppon þe werres sore. *c* **1440** *Alph. Tales* 12 Þis abbatis..forgaff þaim all þai had saide vppon hur. **1560** DAUS tr. *Sleidane's Comm.* 10 He declareth howe grevously he is complained upon unto the Duke. **1642** LAUD *Diary* 2 Dec., They were sufficiently railed upon in the streets. **1651** H. MORE *Second Lash* in *Enthus. Tri.*, etc. (1656) 253, I now forgive thee heartily for all thy abuses upon me. *a* **1715** BURNET *Own Time* III. (1900) II. 84 The court carried every question.., though with..a protestation made upon every step that was carried. **1737** WHISTON *Josephus, Hist.* v. xiii. § 1 He also jested upon him. **1753** MISS COLLIER *Art Torment.* II. ii. (1811) 130 Nor need you be apprehensive of the others telling tales upon you. **1861** F. TEMPLE *Serm.* 274 The unhappy man who has not courage to tell upon himself. **1891** *Law Times* XC. 441/2 The judges..must accept criticism upon their order.

(*b*) *c* **1200** ORMIN 7155 Forr þatt he wennde þatt tatt follc Upponn himm cumenn wære..for to niþþrenn himm. *c* **1230** *Hali Meid.* 17 Leccherie..secheð earst upon hire, nebbe to nebbe. *c* **1300** *Havelok* 65 Was non so bold..Þat durste upon his menie bringhe Hunger. **13..** *K. Alis.* 4875 (Laud MS.), Euermore hij beþ werrende, And vpon oþer conquerende. *c* **1386** CHAUCER *Monk's T.* 537 The peple roos vp-on hym on a nyght. **1393** LANGL. *P. Pl.* C. VII. 106 Ich am wrathe,..wol gladliche smyte Boþe with ston and with staf, and stele vp-on myn enemy. *c* **1450** *Merlin* ii. 24 The hethen assembled a grete oste vpon hem. **1475** *Bk. Noblesse* (Roxb.) 5 They bring assailours uppon this lande. **1518** in Leadam *Star Chamber Cases* (Selden) II. 137 Afterwardes they sought vpon hym at hys boothe with ij clubbys. **1535** COVERDALE 1 *Esdras* i. 27, I am not sent ..to fight agaynst y^e, for my warre is upon Euphrates. **1608** *Yorksh. Trag.* vii. 17 It shall be my charge To raise the towne vpon him.

(*c*) **1476** *Acta Auditorum* (1839) 55/2 Elene Tulloch..wes marijt þe tim þat þe said det wes recouerit apon hir. **1482** *Cely Papers* (Camden) 85 To see the hurtes and harmes he dyd yow uppon your goodes. **1598** BARRET *Theor. Warres* 28 He is to haue great care that his soldiers grow not licencious vpon their poore hosts. **1647** in *Crawford Proclam.* (1910) II. 55/1 Robberies committed by the tories and rebels upon the protestants. **1678** WANLEY *Wond. Lit. World* v. i. § 98 Encroachments upon his Dominions. **1748** *Anson's Voy.* II. v. 176 The most eligible situation on that coast for cruising upon the enemy. **1754** A. MURPHY *Gray's-Inn Journal* No. 102 ¶ 2 A Design upon one another's Pockets..was introductory of another Crime. **1772** in *Eng. Hist. Rev.* Jan. (1915) 30 He places a number of..sepoys upon them and their families. **1883** *Harper's Mag.* Aug. 448/2 The disadvantages are..unreliability in stays.., hardness upon helms.

**b.** On or against (a person), by way of vengeance or the like.

*a* **1300** *Cursor M.* 5862 Þat suerd apon hus tak na wrak. *c* **1400** *Pilgr. Sowle* (Caxton, 1483) III. viii. 55 They alwey hauen sought vengeaunce.., to be wroken vppon tho that ought haue mysliked them. **1470–85** MALORY *Arthur* x. lv. 506 Soone we shold haue ben reuenged vpon the fals knyghtes. **1526–** [see REVENGE *v.* 1–2]. **1535** COVERDALE *Isaiah* i. 23, I must ease me of myne enemies, and a venge me vpon them. **1595** *Locrine* II. v. 86 Reuenge my death vpon his traiterous head. **1860** HOOK *Lives Abps.* I. vii. 377 Edwy had the power to avenge himself upon Dunstan.

*ellipt. c* **1485** *Digby Myst.* (1882) I. 322 A shamefull deth I aske vpon herowde. **1535** COVERDALE *Ps.* lviii. 10 God letteth me se my desyre vpon myne enemies.

**c.** So as to close in or confine.

**1382** WYCLIF 2 *Kings* iv. 5 The woman wente, and closede the dore vpon hir silf and vpon hir children. **1535** COVERDALE *Num.* xvi. 33 They wente downe quycke in to the hell ..And the earth closed vpon them. — *Ps.* lxix. 15 That.. the pitte shut not hir mouth vpon me. **1633** T. ADAMS *Exp. 2 Pet.* ii. 5 The Lord..himselfe shut the doore of the Arke upon Noah. **1701** PRIDEAUX *Direct. Ch.-wardens* (1712) 10 If they shall meet..with the Doors lock'd, barred, or bolted upon them. **1844** DICKENS *Mart. Chuz.* xlviii, Softly turning the key upon him as they went out.

**22.** With respect or regard to; in reference to; touching, concerning; as to; = ON *prep.* 22.

See also AGREE *v.* 10 b, COMPLIMENT *v.* 3, CONCLUDE *v.* 13, CONSULT *v.* 1, INSIST *v.* 3, LOT *sb.* 1, MATTER *sb.* 25 c, PRIDE *v.* 4, TREAT *v.* 2 a, VALUE *v.* 6.

**1382** WYCLIF *Ecclus.* xxii. 11 A litil weep vp on the deade, for he restede. **1390** GOWER *Conf.* I. 110, I finde upon Surquiderie, How that..Be olde daies was a King [etc.]. *c* **1400** *Contin. Brut* 321 In þe whiche parlement was treted..how he my3te best oppon his wrong be avenged. **1439** *Cases bef. King's Council* (Selden) 105 The Kyngis counsaillours examined the persones..upon the ryot. **1484** *Surtees Misc.* (1888) 43 Surmising none othere upon hyme. **1515** in Leadam *Star Chamber Cases* (Selden) II. 85 Two seuerall Writtes..to theym directed to enquere and examyn vpon certen Interrogatoriez. **1584** COGAN *Haven Health* xc. 81 If you will not be at cost vppon spices, you may make a verie sweete water thus. **1609** BIBLE (Douay) 1 *Kings* xxx. 6 The soule of everie man was bitterly affected upon their sonnes, and daughters. **1680** MOXON *Mech. Exerc.* xiii. 227 Having such good Success upon Brass, I improv'd the Invention so, as to make it serve for Wood also. **1710** STEELE *Tatler* No. 150 ¶ 4, I could name Two, who..fell out and parted Beds upon the boiling of a Leg of Mutton. **1760** *Impostors Detected* III. vii, [She] was not in the least vain or proud upon the encomiums..from every mouth. **1826** *Art of Brewing* (ed. 2) 9 Opinions and practices..completely at variance upon the subject of mashing. **1843** *Blackw. Mag.* LIV. 209, I shall set you at ease..upon that point. **1885** SIR H. C. LOPES in *Law Reports* 14 Q.B.D. 921 This case raises a novel point upon which there is no authority.

**b.** Denoting the object to or towards which mental activity is directed; = ON *prep.* 22 b.

See also CONSIDER *v.* 11 b, MEDITATE *v.* 4 b, MIN *v.*[2] 3 b, MIND *sb.*[1] 7 (quot. 1589), PUT *v.* 27 c, REFLECT *v.* 12, REMEMBER *v.* 4 c, RUN *v.* 70 c, STUDY *v.* 1, 2, THINK *v.*[2] 3 b, TREAT *v.* 2.

*a* **1300** *Sarmun* xxxvi. in *E. E. P.* (1862) 5 And þench þos wordis her ispoke; for-3ite ham no3t ac þench apan. *a* **1300** *Cursor M.* 112 In hir wirschip wald I bigyn A lastand warc apon to myn. **1390** GOWER *Conf.* I. 14 To studie upon the worldes lore Sufficeth now withoute more. *a* **1400** *Isumbras* 427 Sir Ysambrace hym umbithoghte Appone a horse that coles broghte. *c* **1450** *Merlin* iii. 49 The moste remembraunce that I shall haue, shall be vpon yow, and on yowre nedes. **1463** *Bury Wills* (Camden) 34 A remembraunce to thinke vpon me. **1582** N. T. (Rhem.) *Matt.* vii. 28 The multitude were in admiration vpon his doctrine. **1611** BIBLE 1 *Tim.* iv. 15 Meditate vpon these things. **1655** EARL ORRERY *Parthen.* I. VIII. 418 Did you reflect upon it with an vnprejudicate opinion. **1719** DE FOE *Crusoe* I. (Globe) 226, I ask'd him what it was he study'd upon. *Ibid.* II. (Globe) 379 But now the Admiration was turn'd upon another question. **1871** W. ALEXANDER *Johnny Gibb* xlvi, It has a closin'-in heid-piece concern that min's me..upon a mutch that my wife hed ance. **1899** W. J. LOCKE *White Dove* 3 S— was at last able to reflect upon the entire unexpectedness of his presence.

**c.** Denoting the subject of speech or writing; = ON *prep.* 22 c.

Freq. with verbs, as *rave*, *talk*, *write*; AMPLIFY *v.* 7 b, CRITICIZE *v.* 1 b, DISTINGUISH *v.* 8 c, SPEAK *v.* 15.

(*a*) *a* **1390** *Wycliffite Bible* (1850) IV. 303 An other [prologue] vpon Romayns. **1390** GOWER *Conf.* II. 65 Laodomie his lusti wif..Upon a thing wherof sche dradde A lettre ..sende him. **1525** LD. BERNERS *Froiss.* II. Preface, My Preface vpon the fyrst volume of this cronycle. **1533** FRITH *Answ. More* E iij b, The mynde and exposition of the olde Doctours vpon the wordes of Chrystes maundye. **1557** *Tottel's Misc.* (Arb.) 113 Vpon the deceas of W. Ch. **1605** SHAKS. *Macb.* II. i. 23 We would spend it in some words vpon that Businesse. **1697** DE FOE *Ess. Projects* Pref., I wou'd not adventure to appear in Print upon that Subject. **1709** STEELE *Tatler* No. 114 ¶ 1 Our Discourse chanced to be upon the Subject of Death. **1758** BOSWELL *Lett.* (1924) 6 From 1 to 2, [I] attend a college upon Roman Antiquities. **1801** *Farmer's Mag.* Jan. 66 A series of animadversions..published upon it in a provincial paper. **1824** BYRON *Juan* XVI. xlvii, She..Made epigrams..Upon her friends. **1893** STEVENSON *Catriona* xii, He engaged the goodwife..with some compliments upon the rizzoring of our haddocks.

†(*b*) **1483** CAXTON *G. de la Tour* 107 Now I shalle telle yow upon this matere of a good lady. **1528** in Roy *Rede me*, etc. (Arb.) 152 Austyne sayeth vppon the psalter, ye clargy occupyeth the secular lordshyppe secularly. **1574** R. BRISTOW *Treatise* 47 Vpon these two, Christ..and his Church, ronneth al the Scriptures. **1581** FULKE in *Confer.* III. (1583) Q ij b I wil not vouchsafe to replie vpon this answere. **1605** CAMDEN *Rem.* 143 But he repaied him with this re-allusion vppon the name. **1710** STEELE *Tatler* No. 14 ¶ 1 My Design of observing upon Things. **1748** RICHARDSON *Clarissa* (1811) I. 185, I..am the less solicitous..to amplify upon the contents of either.

(*c*) **1481** in Blades *W. Caxton* (1882) 231 The polytyque book..whiche that Tullius wrote vpon the disputacons [etc.]. *c* **1600** W. FOWLER *Wks.* (S.T.S.) 9 A Fvneral Sonet, written vpon the death of..Elizabeth Dowglas. **1709** ADDISON *Tatler* No. 163 ¶ 3 The Sonnet..was written upon a Lady. **1776** JOHNSON in *Boswell* (1904) I. 647 A man who has never been engaged in trade himself may undoubtedly write well upon trade. **1791** 'G. GAMBADO' *Ann. Horsem.* (1809) 55 Had they spent as much time in riding upon turnips, as they have in writing upon them.

**III.** In other senses.

†**23.** From (a person or persons), esp. by means of hostile attack; = ON *prep.* 23. *Obs.* (Cf. 21.)

Const. with verbs, as *make*, *nim*, *recover*, *take*, *win*; also CONQUER *v.* 2 b, GAIN *v.*[2] 4.

**1338** R. BRUNNE *Chron.* (1810) 22 Uppon Saynt Edmunde Northfolk he nam. **1387** TREVISA *Higden* (Rolls) VI. 291 Egbertus..took Chestre uppon þe Britouns. **1412–20** LYDG. *Chron. Troy* III. 3423 Troyens han wonne a-geyn her londe Vp-on Grekis. **1483** in *Acta Dom. Conc.* II. Introd. 114 Quhilk some was recoverit be..Dure apone the said Schir Johne. *a* **1533** LD. BERNERS *Huon* 527 A ryche shyp, the whiche was wonne vpon the sowdans men. **1568** GRAFTON *Chron.* II. 194 They wanne dayly and yerely vpon the sayd Turkes, so that they had..much of the landes. **1643** PRYNNE *Doom Cowardice & Treach.* 6 At last by such forcible assaults the said Towne was taken upon the said Robert. **1654** BRAMHALL *Just Vind.* i. (1661) 2 Whatsoever the Popes of Rome gained upon us. **1660** *Nicholas Papers* (Camden) IV. 187 The prizes made by the Ostenders upon the Kings subjects. **1742** LEONI *Palladio's Archit.* II. 66 The Spoils made upon Pyrrhus King of Epirus.

†**24.** In respect of; = ON *prep.* 24. *Obs.*

*a* **1310** in Wright *Lyric P.* v. 26 He is blosme opon bleo brihtest under bis. **13..** *Cursor M.* 2034 (Gött.), He lis here vte, cum se þu sal, Naked apon his limes all.

**25.** On (a musical instrument).

*c* **1384** CHAUCER *H. Fame* III. 110 Ther herd I pleyen vpon an harpe..Orpheus ful craftely. **1524** *Reg. Privy Seal Scot.* I. 499/1 Playing apoun organis in the Kingis chapell. **1552** in Feuillerat *Revels Edw. VI* (1914) 89, I haue provided one to plaie vppon a kettell drom. **1621** BRATHWAIT *Nat. Embassie* Ded., Able to play vpon an oaten pipe. **1683** KENNETT tr. *Erasm. on Folly* 68 No more skill..than a Pig playing upon the Organs. **1709** MRS. MANLEY *Secret Mem.* I. 149 A great many of 'em..can toot, toot, toot, it upon a Pipe. **1804–6** SYD. SMITH *Mor. Philos.* (1850) 175 Any air..performed upon such an instrument as the bagpipe. **1842** TENNYSON *Locksley Hall* 2 When you want me, sound upon the bugle-horn. **1876** GRANT *Burgh Sch. Scot.* II. 380 Discoursing laments upon the Bagpipes.

**26.** Denoting advance from or improvement on some standard, etc.

See also IMPROVE *v.* 8, IMPROVEMENT 6 b, REFINE *v.* 10.

**1662** EVELYN *Chalcogr.* 50 Which afterwards Sebastian Serli refining upon composed the better part of that excellent book of his. **1711** ADDISON *Spect.* No. 44 ¶ 6 The French have therefore refin'd too much upon Horace's Rule. **1782** PRIESTLEY *Corrupt. Chr.* I. III. 301 An improvement was made upon this doctrine. **1843** *Blackw. Mag.* LIV. 197 Mr. Collins has improved greatly upon his last year's exhibition. **1859** GLADSTONE *Glean.* (1879) II. 171 If he continues to advance upon himself as he has advanced heretofore.

† **Upo·n**, *adv. Obs.* [Ellipt. use of prec.]

**1. a.** On it; on or upon the surface.

**1307** *York Memo. Bk.* (Surtees) I. 181 Lether with the here apon. **1382** WYCLIF *Ecclus.* xxxiii. 6 An hors courser ..vnder eche man vpon sittende ne3eth. **1547** in Feuillerat *Revels Edw. VI* (1914) 13 Changeable Taffita stripyd vpon with blewe golde dornix. **1567** in *Rep. Hist. MSS. Comm.* (1907) IV. 90 A clothe of blacke and redd wroughte with goulde vpon. **1596** SHAKS. *Merch. V.* II. vii. 57 A coyne that beares the figure of an Angell Stampt in gold, but that's insculpt vpon.

**b.** On one's person, as an article of apparel.

*a* **1366** CHAUCER *Rom. Rose* 364 A chapelet, so semly oon, Ne werede neuer mayde vpon. *c* **1386** — *Friar's T.* 84 He [*sc.* a gay yeoman] hadde vp-on a courtepy of grene. **1390** GOWER *Conf.* II. 246 And sche..hir scherte dede upon And caste on hire a mantel clos. **1446** LYDG. *Two Nightingale P.* ii. 123 Whan Crist Ihesu was for mankynd dede And had vpon a garnement ful newe. **1513** BRADSHAW *St. Werburge* I. 1301 His gloues, his gyrdell, the kynge had vpon. **1611** BIBLE 2 *Cor.* v. 2 Desiring to be clothed vpon with our house, which is from heauen. [**1643** CARYL *Expos. Job* 1885 Those bodies of Saints..shall be cloathed upon with a house which is from Heaven.]

**2.** Into or to a position on a surface or object; so as to be put or placed on the thing in question.

**1382** WYCLIF *Num.* xvii. 2 Of echon the name thow shalt vpon write [L. *superscribes*] to his 3erde. *c* **1400** *Lanfranc's Cirurgie* 219 Make it abrood upon a cloob & leie it vpon hoot. *c* **1440** *Pallad. on Husb.* VII. 106 Do donge vppon and vmbe on euery side. **1534** TINDALE *Luke* xx. 18 But on whosoever it faul vpon, it wyll grynde him to powder.

**b.** In a direction towards something indicated or specified.

*c* **1400** *Apol. Loll.* 2 Þer for, if we wil, we mai calle bischoppis, locars up on. **1593–1611** [see LOOK *v.* 46].

**3.** On or upon that (in time or order); thereafter, thereupon. Esp. coupled with *anon*, *near*, *soon*.

See also HEREUPON, THEREUPON, WHEREUPON *advs.*

**14..** *Lydgate's Bochas* v. 2898 Afftir whos deth anon vpon [*MS. Harl.* 1245 vpon anoon] suyng, To Euergetes..She was ageyn ioyned in mariage. *c* **1440** *Generydes* 1926 Thanne came the prince of Cesare sone vppon. *Ibid.* 6632 Kyng auferius fell seke anon vppon. **1523** FITZHERB. *Husb.* § 12 So that they be sowen ere the begynnynge of Marche, or sone vpon. **1602** SHAKS. *Ham.* I. ii. 179 *Ham.* I thinke it was to see my Mothers Wedding. *Hor.* Indeed my Lord, it followed hard vpon. **1603** — *Meas. for M.* IV. vi. 14 The.. Citizens Haue hent the gates, and very neere vpon The Duke is entring. **1606** — *Tr. & Cr.* IV. iii. 3 It is great morning, and the houre prefixt..Comes fast vpon.

**4.** By way of addition, increase, etc.

*a* **1485** FORTESCUE *Wks.* (1869) 487 Why will God put uppon newe turments ovir the travaile of ther labour?

† **Upon**, obs. var. OPEN *a.* (Cf. UPEN *a.*)

**13..** *E. E. Allit. P.* B. 453 Þenne wafte he vpon his wyndowe. **14..** *Sir Beues* (E.) 87/1691 Anon þe gate he vpon look.

† **Uponland**, *adv. Obs.* Also 3–4 **vp o londe**, 5 *Sc.* **upolande**; 5–6 **vp of land**, and UPALAND. [f. *uppe* UP *adv.*[2] + ON *prep.* 1 b (O *prep.*[1]) + LAND *sb.* Cf. UPLAND *adv.*[1]] In the country, as opposed to the town.

α. *a* **900** in Thorpe *Anc. Laws* (1840) I. 118 Be ciepe-monna fore uppe on londe. *c* **1386** CHAUCER *Prol.* 702 A poure person dwellynge vp on lond. **1430–40** LYDG. *Bochas* Prol. 84 Folkis that duellyn vp-on lande. *c* **1480** HENRYSON *Twa Mice* i, The vther [mouse] wynnit vponland. — *Sheep & Dog* xviii, Ane schireff stout, Quhilk .. dytis all the pure men vpon land [**1568** *Bann. MS.* vp of land].

β. *c* **1300** *Havelok* 763 Gode paniers..to beren fish inne, Vp o-londe to selle and fonge. **14..** *Burgh Laws Scotland* xxxiv, It is for to wyt that men upolande may borow thair pundis thryis.

γ. *c* **1440** *Alph. Tales* 173 On a tyme he was lugid on a night in a howse vp of land. **1568** [see α. above].

**b.** *John Uponland*, a rustic. (Cf. UPALAND b.)

*a* **1568** in *Bannatyne MS.* (Hunter. Club) 269/26 This said Johnne vponland.

† **Uponlandis**, obs. Sc. var. UPLANDS *a.*

*c* **1480** HENRYSON *Fables* heading (Harl. MS.), The Taill of the vponlandis Mous and the burges Mous.

† **Uponon(e**, *adv. Obs. rare.* Also uponan. [f. UPON *prep.* + ONE *pron.* 30 f.] = ANON *adv.* 4.

*c* **1400** *Destr. Troy* 2418, I onswaret hym esely euyn vponon. *Ibid.* 6712 Polidamas..can fight, With his Enmeis full egurly, euer vpon-one.

† **Uppe**, *v. Obs.* Forms: 1 **yppan**, 2 **ippen**, 3 **uppen**. [OE. *yppan* (also *geyppan*), f. *upp* UP *adv.*[1], giving southern ME. *üppen*, midland *ippen*. Cf. ON. *yppa* (MDa. *yppe*), and OHG. *ûffan* (MHG. *ûffen*, *ûfen*, obs. G. *aufen*).] *trans.* To display or make manifest; to bring to notice; to make known.

*c* **897** K. ÆLFRED *Gregory's Past. C.* lix. 451 Ðæt we hit ..forðy yppen ðæt mon God herige. *c* **900** tr. *Baeda's Hist.* IV. xxv. (1890) 352 Se Godes mon..ba unrotnesse his heortan ..ypte & cyðde. *a* **1000** *Colloq. Ælfric* in Wr.-Wülcker 102 Ic ne deor yppan þe digla ure. *c* **1200** *Trin. Coll. Hom.* 165 Here wombe is here crist, and all iuele forbisne hie ippen of hem seluen. *a* **1225** *Ancr. R.* 146 Hercneð nu..hu hit is to uppen & ȝelpen of god dede. *Ibid.*, Ancre þet was iwuned ..wel uorte wurchen, & seoððen..uppede hit & scheawede.

Uppen: see UP *prep.*[1]

**U·ppen**, *v. E. Angl.* ? *Obs.* [f. UP *adv.*[1] + -EN[5]. Cf. UPPE *v.*] *trans.* To bring up, mention, disclose.

**1565** GOLDING *Ovid's Met.* III. 344 When that after mickle talke..Joves name was upned. **1567** *Ibid.* XII. 179 Every wyght Delyghts too uppen oftentymes..The perills and the narrow brunts. **1583** — *Calvin on Deut.* xxi. 125/2 It woulde not haue booted at all to haue vppened neuer so many thinges by parcellmeale. **1823** E. MOOR *Suffolk Words* 460 Yeow didnt uppen it did ye?

**Up-pe·nt**, *pa. pple.* (UP- 5.) **1600** FAIRFAX *Tasso* x. xlii, With this siege, if we be long vp pent, Famine I doubt. **1614** GORGES *Lucan* I. 18 A proud Courser..in the stable close vp-pent. **1870** A. O'SHAUGHNESSY *Poems, Neglected Harp* 15 These wondrous melodies up-pent And languishing in me.

**U·pper**, *sb.* [From next.]

**1.** That part of a boot or shoe above the sole and welt. Usu. pl.

**1845** J. COULTER *Adv. in Pacific* ix. 112 My shoes were.. only held together by passing straps of goat-skin under the soles, over the uppers. **1862** *Catal. Internat. Exhib., Brit.* II. No. 4769, Grained leather; machine-closed uppers. **1880** *Times* 21 Sept. 4/4 Forcing the needle through the outer sole, the edge of the upper, and the insole.

*attrib.* **1875** KNIGHT *Dict. Mech.*, *Upper-machines*,..those for cutting out or preparing the uppers of boots or shoes.

**b.** *U.S.* A cloth gaiter for wearing above the shoe over the ankle (*Cent. Dict.* 1891).

**c.** *On one's uppers*, in poor or reduced circumstances; having hard luck. *colloq.* (orig. *U.S.*).

**1891** *Cent. Dict.* s.v. **1901** *Munsey's Mag.* XXV. 432/1 The rumor whirled about the Street that Greener was in difficulties. Financial ghouls..said..'Greener is on his uppers'. **1905** R. MARSH *Spoiler of Men* xxv. 227 'I'm on my uppers...I want money.' 'So do we all.'

**2.** An upper jaw, dental plate, tooth, etc.

**1878** C. HUNTER *Mech. Dentistry* 79 In the case of edentulous or nearly edentulous uppers or lowers. **1900** *Hutchinson's Arch. Surg.* XI. 222 On the backs of both uppers.. there are now peculiar changes. **1904** F. P. DUNNE in *Westm. Gaz.* 14 Oct. 1/3 He [*sc.* a child] has two uppers an' four lowers.

**3.** *U.S.* A log or piece of sawed lumber of superior grade.

**1877** *Lumberman's Gazette* 24 May, The finest stock of uppers to be found in the country.

**Upper** (ʊ·pəɹ), *a.* Also 4–6 **vpper**, 5–7 **vper**; 6 **hoper**. [f. UP *a.* + -ER[3]. Cf. MDu. *upper* (Du. and Flem. *opper*), LG. *upper*, *üpper*, MSw., Norw. *yppare*, older Da. *yppere*, better.] Comparative of UP *a.*, and signifying 'higher', 'over', 'loftier', 'top' (in contrast to *lower*, *nether*, *under*). In some senses replacing the earlier UVER, OVER *adjs.*

**I. 1.** Occupying, comprising or consisting of, rising or more elevated ground (and usu. further in the interior). Freq. in proper names of districts, etc.

**13..** *K. Alis.* 5691 (Laud MS.), Þe kyng þennes went forþ.. in to ynde in þe norþ, Þat is ycleped..þe vpper ynde. **1526** TINDALE *Acts* xix. 1 Paul passed thorow the vpper costes and cam to Ephesus. **1598** GRENEWEY *Tacitus, Ann.* XII. vii. (1622) 163 About the same time vpper Germany quaked with feare. **1601** SHAKS. *Jul. C.* v. i. 3 You said the Enemy would..keepe the Hilles and vpper Regions. *a* **1660** *Contemp. Hist. Irel.* (Ir. Archæol. Soc.) I. 160 Either to Vper Ormond or the countie of Clare. *a* **1676** HALE *Prim. Orig. Man.* (1677) 219 If Inundations prevailed in Greece and those upper Countries, Egypt..could not easily escape them. **1728** CHAMBERS *Cycl.* s.v. *Nimbis*, The Nimbis is seen on the Medals..of the upper Empire. **1791** GEO. III in *Ann. Reg.*, *St. Papers* 124* His majesty thinks..that.. his province of Quebec..should be divided into two separate provinces, to be called the province of Upper Canada, and the province of Lower Canada. **1849** EASTWICK *Dry Leaves* 22 My vessel being an Upper Sindh boat. **1863** LYELL *Antiq. Man* 43 For the river to bring down from the upper country so large a quantity of earthy matter. **1864**– [see WARD *sb.*[2] 20].

**b.** Of peoples: Occupying a higher or more inland district.

**1617** MORYSON in C. L. Falkiner *Illustr. Irish Hist.* (1904) 215 The Iberni, called the upper Irish, inhabiting about Beer-haven and Baltimore. *c* **1790** *Encycl. Brit.* (ed. 3) V. 484/1 The Lower and Upper Cossacks,..and a part of the Don Cossacks.

**c.** Situated in, located on, a higher or loftier position, high ground, etc.; more elevated or lofty; higher in altitude.

Freq. in the proper names of hamlets, villages, etc.

**1467** *Rolls of Parlt.* V. 586/2 Landes and Tenementes in Netherburneham, Upperburneham, West Wode. **1509** HAWES *Past. Pleas.* XXXII. (Percy Soc.) 159 After this, dame Correccion..first..led me to the upper ward. **1611** BIBLE *Joshua* xv. 19 He gaue her the vpper springs, and the nether springs. **1687** MIÉGE *Gt. Fr. Dict.* II. s.v., The Upper Region of the Air. **1708** WATTS *Poems* (1743) II. 160 Around the golden Streets they rove, And bless the Mansions of the upper Skies. **1778** *Encycl. Brit.* (ed. 2) III. 1604/2 The bason [of the lock] being filled with water by an upper sluice to the level of the waters above, a vessel may ascend thro' the upper gate. *Ibid.* 1605/1 So that the water in the lock may rise to a level with the water in the upper canal. **1796** MME. D'ARBLAY *Camilla* V. 296 [She] thought herself in the upper regions, where happiness..consisted of perpetual admiration. **1819** SHELLEY *Peter Bell 3rd* II. vii, Each had an upper stream of thought. **1857** HAWTHORNE *Eng. Note-bks.* (1870) II. 414 Those misty upper-depths seemed almost to be hung with clouds. **1862** J. BROWN *Minchmoor* (1864) 11 You can get a glimpse of the upper woods of Abbotsford. **1873** GEIKIE *Phys. Geog.* § 89 [These] clouds.. are driven along by upper currents of air. **1883** *Good Words* Aug. 529/2 Those plants and animals which live in the 'upper littoral'.

*fig.* **1647** N. BACON *Disc. Govt. Eng.* I. lvii. 166 To make him yet more bold, he had the upper ground of the heire.

**d.** Occupying or forming (part of) the higher or highest portion or division of a building.

**1522–3** *Rec. St. Mary at Hill* 317 A chest in the vpper vestry. **1557** BIBLE (Genev.) *Acts* i. 13 They went vp into an vpper chamber. **1597** J. PAYNE *Royal Exch.* 15 The thrid sort be retaylers in the vpper shopps. **1611** FLORIO, *Soprastanza*, an vpper-lodging. **1665** in *Verney Mem.* (1907) II. 247 A lower and an upper chamber. **1764** HARMER *Observ.* iii. § 1. 89 An upper-story, which is flat on the top. **1779** *Mirror* No. 9, Some of the upper boxes were filled with ladies. **1846** MRS. A. MARSH *Father Darcy* II. xiv. 254 He used to lie..upon the floor of his little upper room.

*fig.* **1647** TRAPP *Comm. 2 Cor.* v. 1 In the wonderful frame of man's body the bones are the timber work, the head the upper-lodging. **1699**– [see STORY *sb.*[2] 1 c]. **1796** [see GARRET *sb.*[1] 3]. **1870** BREWER *Dict. Phrase & Fable* 924/1 'Ill-furnished in the upper story'; a head without brains. **1877** *Holderness Gloss.* 152/1 He's a bit wake (weak) iv his upper-garret.

*Comb.* **1697** DRYDEN *Æneis* Ded. e 3 b, Our Upper-Gallery Audience in a Play-House.

**2.** With partitive terms, esp. *end*, *part*, *side*.

Occas. hyphened or as one word, as †*upperhand*, *upperside*.

**1484** CAXTON *Fables of Æsop* v. vii, He to whome men purposen to doo somme euylle tourn, syth men holden hym at auauntage, men muste putte hym self at the vpper side of hym. *c* **1489** — *Blanchardyn* xlvi. 178 The noble mayden ..ryght fyersli..began to loke vpon hym, drawyng herselfe to the vpperhande of hym. **1526** *Pilgr. Perf.* (W. de W. 1531) 3 b, The vpper parte of this foresayd ymage. **1568** *Freiris Berwik* 22 The tovne,..the castell and the land, The he wallis vpoun the vpper hand. **1570** BILLINGSLEY *Euclid* XI. xxix. 341 Lines..which ioyne together the angles of the vpper and nether bases. *a* **1600** in Child *Ballads* II. 245/2 A grave, a grave,..to put these lovers in; But lay my lady on the upper hand. **1674** HOOKE *Animadv.* 52 The upper side thereof must be plained exactly smooth and flat. **1731** P. MILLER *Gard. Dict.* s.v. *Melo*, The Upperside of the Hot-beds where your early Melons..are planted. **1769** FALCONER *Dict. Marine* (1780), *Down-haul*,..a rope..tied to the upper-corner of the sail. **1778** MISS BURNEY *Evelina* xxi, Driving us to the upper end of Piccadilly. **1805** R. JAMESON *Char. Min.* (1816) 204 When..[the crystal] has upon its upper and under parts, faces that alternate with each other. **1868** *Rep. U.S. Commissioner Agric.* (1869) 360 The well and the opening in the upper side [of the road]. **1886** J. BARROWMAN *Sc. Mining Terms* 69 The upper portion of a [coal] seam.

**b.** Of surfaces. † *Upperface*, = SUPERFICIES.

**1583** STUBBES *Anat. Abus.* II. B 3, Then came there fire.. and consumed them all, from the vpper face of the earth. **1594** BLUNDEVIL *Exerc.* III. (1597) 128 b, Superficies or vpperface, is that which onely hath length and breadth. **1596** *Edward III*, I. ii. 152 Where the vpper turfe of earth doth boast His..party coloured cost, Delue there. **1611** COTGR., *Rez*,..the superficies, or vpper face of a plaine, or leuell peece of ground. **1728** BRADLEY *Dict. Bot.* s.v. *Marrubium*, Leaves..smooth and woolly underneath.., but somewhat.. rugged on the Upperside. **1733** TULL *Horse-hoeing Husb.* 404 The Upper-surface of the Fore-end of the Beam. **1826** KIRBY & SP. *Entomol.* III. 364 *Facies*,..the upper surface of the head. **1884** COUES *Key N. Amer. Birds* 110 The upper and under surfaces of the wing.

**3. a.** That forms the higher of a pair of corresponding things or sets. Also occas. = uppermost.

*Upper-case*, Printing (quots. 1683–): see CASE *sb.*[2] 9.

*c* **1460** [*upper crust*: see 12 a]. **1524** *State Papers Hen. VIII*, II. 117 He shall endevour hymself to cause the Kynges subjectes..to haue the upper berdes to be shaven. **1530** TINDALE *Deut.* xxiv. 6 No man shall take the nether or the vpper milstone to pledge. **1533** *MS. Rawl. D.* 776 fol. 157 b, The vpper flowryng of the same wharffe. **1609** BIBLE (Douay) *Exod.* xii. 22 Sprinkle the uppertransome of the doore therwith. *Ibid.* 23 The bloud on the uppersil, and on both the postes. **1611** COTGR. s.v. *Espée*, The vpper boords of a Vine-presse. **1683** MOXON *Mech. Exerc.*, *Printing* ii. § 3. 19 The Whole Vpper-Case is divided into Ninety eight square Boxes. **1726** SWIFT *Gulliver* II. vii, I first mounted to the upper step of the ladder [= a movable pair of stairs]. **1833** LOUDON *Encycl. Archit.* § 691 The two upper branches or rails of the trunk, or upright piece. **1852** SEIDEL *Organ* 37 A couple of bellows..consist first of an upper and under-board. **1867** SMYTH *Sailor's Word-bk.* 708 *Upper masts*, the top-mast, topgallant-mast, and royal-mast. **1873** *Routledge's Yng. Gentl. Mag.* July 503/1 An upper-iron being screwed on to the lower one to turn the shaving back a little.

*fig.* **1788** *New London Mag.* 264 One blow well told to the upper tire (the head), tells better than three below.

*Comb.* **1738** CHAMBERS *Cycl.* s.v. *Letter*, Printers distinguish their letters into capital..or upper-case letters,..and.. small, or under-case letters. **1771** LUCKOMBE *Hist. Print.* 261 [These letters] are not reckoned..among Upper-case Sorts.

**b.** *spec.* in *Anat.*, etc. (Cf. SUPERIOR *a.* 11.)

**1546** [see 16 a]. **1548** VICARY *Anat.* v. (1577) F ij b, The bones or bony partes, fyrste of the Cheekes be two;..of the vpper Mandibile, two. **1610** HEALEY *St. Aug. Citie of God* 335 [The] crocodile..moueth his vpper chappe. **1646** SIR T. BROWNE *Pseud. Ep.* 108 It conveyeth it into the duodenum or upper gut, thence into the lower bowells. **1728** CHAMBERS *Cycl.* s.v. *Maxillæ*, The..Upper Jaw, is immoveable in Man. **1774** GOLDSM. *Nat. Hist.* V. 274 The upper chap [of the parrot], as well as the lower, are both moveable. **1826** KIRBY & SP. *Entomol.* III. xxxiii. 374 The Upper or Primary Wings. **1838** *Penny Cycl.* X. 141/2 When the upper lid [of the eye] is raised. **1850** J. F. COOPER *Ways of Hour* I. 104 His front upper teeth were all gone. **1884** COUES *N. Amer. Birds* 110 The upper Primary coverts, or coverts of the primaries.

*Comb.* **1879** RUSKIN *St. Mark's Rest* Suppl. ii. 20 The man's thigh and upper-arm bones. **1896** *Godey's Mag.* April 430/1 His upper-limb muscles.

**c.** *Upper bench*, the name during the exile of Charles II of the KING'S BENCH. Now *Hist.*

**1649** *Acts Interregnum* (1911) II. 108 Three or more of the Justices of the upper Bench. **1651** in *Kitchin's Jurisdictions* (1653) 579 The most Vsual Writs which have been used in the Kings Bench, and are most like to continue in that Court, now called the Vpper-Bench. *a* **1675** WHITELOCKE *Mem.* (1682) 375 Voted [on 12 Feb. 1649] that the Kings-Bench Court should be called the Upper Bench.

**d.** *Orange Upperwing*, a European noctuid moth, *Hoporina croceago*.

**1832** RENNIE *Brit. Butterfl. & Moths* 85 The Orange Upperwing..appears in September;..first pair [of wings] golden orange..; second pair white. **1869** E. NEWMAN *Brit. Moths* 373/1.

**4.** †**a.** *Upper-stock*: (see STOCK *sb.*[1] 40). Usu. pl.

**1535** in *Archaeologia* IX. 251 A pair of upper stockis of purple veluette,..also..a newe paire of nether stockis. **1542** *Nottingham Rec.* III. 220 One peyr blacke hoys, the upper stokes blake velvet. *c* **1570** *Pride & Lowl.* (1841) 19 His upper stockes of sylken grogerane. **1606** G. W[OODCOCKE] *Hist. Ivstine* xxxviii. 118 He conueyed a dagger in the vpperstock of his hose. [**1821** SCOTT *Kenilw.* xxxi, His upper stocks of white velvet, lined with cloth of silver.]

**b.** That covers or clothes an upper part of the body, esp. the chest or shoulders. (Cf. 5 a.)

Freq. from 1579 to 1625 in *upper body*.

**1579** *Aldeburgh Rec.* in *N. & Q.* 12th Ser. VII. 328/2 An upper bodye and lyninge and a neckercher for hir. **1587** in *Antiquary* (1896) XXXII. 76 For an upper body and lace, xxiij d. **1625** FLETCHER *Fair Maid* II. ii, Nothing but her vpper bodies. **1871** S. MATEER *Land of Charity* xxi. 278 A cloth or scarf laid over the shoulder, called the 'upper cloth,' as worn by the Súdra women. **1895** C. SILVESTER HORNE *Story of L. M. S.* 298 In 1858, the 'upper cloth' riots broke out again.

**5. a.** Of garments, etc.: Worn above or outside another; outer, exterior; = OVER *a.* 1 b. (Cf. 4 b.)

**1526** TYNDALE *John* xiii. 4 Iesus..layde a syde hys vpper garments. **1547** in Feuillerat *Revels Edw. VI* (1914) 10 Thupper & nether Baces & thunder sleves of clothe of golde. **1598** FLORIO, *Sourafodro*, a false vpper scabbard. **1611** —, *Soprabenda*, an vpper scarfe. **1615** SANDYS *Trav.* 14 Their arme-pits: from whence the skirts flow loosely, fringed below; the vpper shorter than the neather. **1645** RUTHERFORD *Tri. Faith* 305 Christ clothed with love,..and yet his upper garment is vengeance. **1686** *Lond. Gaz.* No. 2193/4 A brown coloured upper Coat. **1759** JOHNSON *Rasselas* xxxviii, When my upper vest was taken off. **1778** CLARA REEVE *Old English Baron* 84 You may take off her upper garments, and any thing of value. **1796** *Grose's Dict. Vulgar T.* (ed. 3), *Upper Benjamin*, a great coat. **1812** J. H. VAUX *Flash Dict.*, *Upper-Ben*, *Upper-Benjamin*, *Upper-Tog*, a great coat. **1819** SCOTT *Ivanhoe* ii, The upper dress of this personage resembled that of his companion in shape. **1850** THACKERAY *Pendennis* iii, A white upper-coat ornamented with cheese-plate buttons.

*fig.* *a* **1634** CHAPMAN *Bussy d'Ambois* v. (1641) 65 Note what he wants? He wants his upper weed, He wants his life, and body.

*Comb.* 1840 THACKERAY *Pict. Rhapsody* Wks. 1899 XIII. 350 A hideous dress, with upper-Benjamin buttons.

**b.** Furthest removed from the door or entrance; innermost. Usually with *end* (cf. 2).

1590 SPENSER *F. Q.* II. ix. 27 Thence she them brought into a stately Hall..At th' upper end there sate..a comely personage. *a* 1613 OVERBURY *Newes* Misc. Wks. (1890) 191 The best company makes the upper end of the table, and not the salt-cellar. 1667 MILTON *P. L.* x. 446 His high Throne..at th' upper end Was plac't in regal lustre. 1711 STEELE *Spect.* No. 109 ⁋ 1 We were now arrived at the Upper-end of the Gallery. 1819 SCOTT *Ivanhoe* iii, The walls of this upper end of the hall.

*fig.* *a* 1672 WILKINS *Nat. Relig.* 331 So only those at the upper end of the world are capable of being counted rich. 1714 R. FIDDES *Pract. Disc.* II. 157 Sometimes the most profligate sinners are seated at the upper end of the world.

**6. a.** Said of the surface of the earth and things upon it, in contrast to the under or nether regions.

1667 MILTON *P. L.* x. 422 For those Appointed to sit there, had left thir charge, Flown to the upper World. 1679 C. NESSE *Antichrist* Ded., You may improve this upper-ground whereon you stand. 1697 DRYDEN *Virg. Georg.* IV. 699 The lovely Bride In safety goes,..Longing the common Light again to share, And draw the vital breath of upper Air. 1815 WORDSW. *Artegal & Elidure* 53 Of Arthur,—who, to upper light restored,..Shall lift his country's fame above the polar star! 1822 BYRON *Vis. Judgem.* xii, He's dead—and upper earth with him has done; He's buried. 1887 BROWNING *Apollo & Fates* 10 *The Fates.* (Below. Darkness.)..We..Deal to each mortal his dole of light On earth—the upper, the glad, the bright.

*Comb.* 1862 SMILES *Engineers* III. 9 The upper-ground workmen employed at the coal-pits.

**b.** Constituting or forming a stratum, layer, bed, etc., lying nearer the earth's surface or formed later in time; *spec.* of stratifications of more recent formation than another of that character and name.

See also 12 b, GREENSAND 1, OOLITE 2–3, SILURIAN *a.* 2 b.

1696 WHISTON *The. Earth* 77 Our upper strata..being generally factitious, or acquir'd at the Universal Deluge. 1733 TULL *Horse-Hoeing Husb.* 251 The..Hills whereof the Upper-Stratum (or Staple) is Mould. *c* 1775 in *Encycl. Brit.* (ed. 2) IV. 2526/1 If a ditch..penetrate through the upper stratum of clay. 1839 MURCHISON *Silur. Syst.* xlv. 605 The Ludlow and Wenlock Formations, or Upper Silurian Rocks. 1852 SEDGWICK in *London Lit. Gazette* 338/3 A part of my Upper Cambrian series. 1873 DAWSON *Earth & Man* iv. 56 The Lower Silurian is the Upper Cambrian of Sedgwick. 1873 E. HULL *Coal-fields Gt. Brit.* (ed. 3) 192 The strata overlying the 'Upper-foot', or 'Bullion-coal'. 1886 J. BARROWMAN *Sc. Mining Terms* 69 *Upper-leaf*, the upper portion of a seam which is separated by a parting into two portions.

*fig.* 1859 G. MEREDITH *R. Feverel* xix, Tossed into the upper stratum of civilized life. 1877, 1890 [see STRATUM 6].

*Comb.* 1865 LUBBOCK *Preh. Times* 299 The height at which the upper-level gravels stand above the present water-line. 1890 *Science-Gossip* XXVI. 146 The upper limestone masses.

**7.** Occurring or taking place in, directed towards, a higher or the highest position. *Upper cut*, in Pugilism (see quot. 1897).

1607 TOPSELL *Four-f. Beasts* 402 An vpper attaint or ouer-reach vpon the backe sinnew of the shanke. 1728 CHAMBERS *Cycl.* s.v. *Attaint*, The Farriers distinguish upper Attaints, given by the Toe of the Hind-foot upon the sinew of the Fore-leg,—And nether Attaints. 1815 J. SMITH *Panorama Sci. & Art* II. 135 The further admission of steam to that side during the upper stroke [of the piston]. 1856 *Sat. Rev.* II. 658/2 Resorting to means of defence against which cross-buttocks and upper-cuts..will do very little good indeed. 1867 SMYTH *Sailor's Word-bk.* 708 *Upper transit*, the passage of a circumpolar star over the meridian above the pole. 1897 *Encycl. Sport* I. 139 *Upper cut*,..a counter, delivered upwards with either hand, when an opponent leads off or rushes in with his head down.

**II. 8.** Occupying a higher (or the highest) position, station, or rank; superior in authority, place, etc.

1477 *Extr. Aberd. Reg.* (1844) I. 36 That Alexander..be continevit vpper and principale maister of wark. 1526 TINDALE *Acts* xxii. 26 The vnder captayne..went to the vpper captayne, and tolde hym. 1561 in *Maitl. Club Misc.* III. 209 We hawe command of ye vppir poweris to put the same in executione. 1647 *Bury Wills* (Camden) 195 At the disposing of..God, whoe is the onely supreme and vpper Lord of all. 1710 STEELE *Tatler* No. 180 ⁋ 4 The Abatement which they suffer when paid, by the Extortion of Upper Servants. 1771 LUCKOMBE *Hist. Print.* 86 He was upper-warden of the Stationer's Company. 1836–9 DICKENS *Sk. Boz, Gt. Winglebury Duel*, I am the upper-boots..; the other man's my man, as..does odd jobs. 1847 C. BRONTË *J. Eyre* v, One of the upper teachers..installed herself at the top of one table. 1862 TROLLOPE *Orley F.* II. 248, 'I was housemaid at Orley Farm.' 'Were you upper or under there?'

**b.** Higher or highest in respect of influence, wealth, office, or dignity; wealthy, aristocratic, influential.

Freq. since *c* 1890, esp. with *class* (cf. CLASS *sb.* 2).

1825 J. WILSON in *Blackw. Mag.* March 373, I wad aiblins introduce the upper ranks intil the wark. 1837 CARLYLE *Fr. Rev.* I. VII. ii, The best-informed Upper-Circles. 1839 — *Chartism* v, The oppressing or neglecting upper classes. 1844– [see 18]. 1856 EMERSON *Eng. Traits, Universities*, These seminaries are finishing schools for the upper classes, and not for the poor.

*Comb.* 1837 CARLYLE *Fr. Rev.* II. v. ix, The riband-cockade, as a symptom of Feuillant Upper-class temper. 1890 *Spectator* 3 May, The upper-class Arabs and Turks. 1897 MARY KINGSLEY *W. Africa* 318 This aristocracy has sub-divisions, the M'pongwe of Gaboon are the upper-circle tribe.

*absol.* 1898 G. MEREDITH *Odes Fr. Hist.* 12 They, the triumphant tonant towering upper, were under; They, violators of home, dared hope an inviolate home.

**9.** Consisting of or including more advanced studies or more proficient students; having a higher place or standing in studies or learning.

1629 WADSWORTH *Pilgr.* iii. 15 The Students of the three vnder schooles, go vp to those of the vpper. 1740 J. CLARKE *Educ. Youth* (ed. 3) 209 The Boys of the upper Classes may be admitted. 1749 FIELDING *Tom Jones* II. iii, His scholars were divided into two classes, in the upper of which was a young gentleman [etc.]. 1857 HUGHES *Tom Brown* I. viii, Three unhappy fellows..whom the Doctor and the master of the form were always endeavouring to hoist into the Upper school. 1897 FLANDRAU *Harvard Episodes* 202 If they happened to be upper classmen.

**10. a.** Of a higher, better, more excellent, or more comprehensive quality; superior.

*a* 1586 SIDNEY *De Mornay* ii. ⁋ 1 We reduce the particulars too an vnderkind, the vnderkinds to an vpperkind, and the vpperkind to a most generall. As for example, we reduce all particular humane persons vnder the terme of man. 1587 GOLDING *Ibid.* x. 163 If the mixture of the Elements cannot make the forme whereby the vpperkyndes differ from one another, as the sencelesse things from the things that haue sence. 1831 CARLYLE *Sart. Res.* II. ix, Here, then, as I lay in that Centre of Indifference; cast, doubtless by benignant upper Influence, into a healing sleep [etc.]. 1895 MARIE CORELLI *Sorrows Satan* iv, [Genius] is..an 'upper' thing, beyond earthly smells and savours.

†**b.** *Upper fortune*, the upper hand (cf. 14).

1613 FLETCHER *Honest Man's Fort.* I. ii, Since You have the upper fortune of him, 'twill Be some dishonor to you to bear your self With any pride or glory over him.

**11.** Constituting or producing a higher tone, note, or notes.

1843 *Penny Cycl.* XXVI. 418/2 The upper or female voice part of the scale. *Ibid.* 419/1 The extreme upper notes of the falsetto. 1880 *Grove's Dict. Music* II. 654/1 The difficulty of hearing the upper partial tones. 1895 *Funk's Stand. Dict.*, *Upper keyboard*, the right-hand side of the keyboard. 1896 A. J. HIPKINS *Pianoforte* 122 *Upper Partial*, any partial or simple division of a compound vibrating string that is above the first, or Fundamental.

**III.** Special collocations.

**12. Upper crust: a.** The top crust of a loaf. Also *transf.* †**b.** The exterior or surface layer of the earth. **c.** *slang.* The human head; a hat. **d.** *dial.* (See quot.) **e.** (See quot. 1848.) Chiefly *U.S. colloq.* (also *attrib.*).

**a.** *c* 1460 J. RUSSELL *Bk. Nurture* 342 Kutt þe vpper crust [of the loaf] for youre souerayne. 1542 BOORDE *Dyetary* xi. (1877) 261 Wherfore chyp the vpper crust of your breade. 1591 A. W. *Bk. Cookrye* 10 b, Put therto a peece of vpper crust of white bread. 1768 W. DONALDSON *Life B. Sapskull* II. 108 The upper-crust of that building [the Mansion-house] is thought too heavy for the simple ingredients of an aldermanic pasty. 1823 J. BADCOCK *Dom. Amusem.* 32 Alum throws up a flowery paleness upon the whole upper crust. 1868 FURNIVALL *Babees Bk.* 271 *margin*, The upper crust of a fine loaf.

**b.** 1555 EDEN *Decades* 234 An other kynde of Rubies..found in the mountaynes in the vpper crust or floure of the earth. 1669 WORLIDGE *Syst. Agric.* (1681) 230 It..doth not bury the upper-crust of the ground so deep as usually is done by digging. 1696 WHISTON *The. Earth* 53 Such an Upper Crust or Shell of Earth on the face of the Abyss. 1762 MILLS *Syst. Pract. Husb.* I. 39 When the upper crust of the earth is removed, all that can be seen, or dug, is marle.

**c.** 1826 *Sporting Mag.* XVIII. 253 Tom completely tinkered his antagonist's upper-crust. 1832 EGAN *Bk. Sports* (Farmer), Sam's nob had been in pepper alley, and his upper crust was rather changed. 1851 *Household Words* II. 320/1 A highly-polished Parisian upper-crust..smashed under the weight of a carter's slouch.

**d.** 1854 MISS BAKER *Northampt. Gloss.* 371 'Mrs. Upper Crust,' a fictitious designation for any female who assumes unauthorised superiority.

**e.** 1836 HALIBURTON *Clockm.* xxviii, It was none o' your skim-milk parties, but superfine uppercrust real jam. 1843 — *Sam Slick in Eng.* xxiv, I want you to see Peel,..Macaulay, old Joe, and so on. These men are all upper crust here. 1848 BARTLETT *Dict. Amer.* 370 *Upper crust*, the aristocracy, the higher circles. 1850 J. F. COOPER *Ways of Hour* vi. I. 186 Those families..are our upper crust—not upper ten thousand, as the newspapers call it, but upper hundred. 1898 *Daily News* 14 Feb. 2/7, 55 magistrates, 46 of whom belonged to what..[is] sometimes called 'the upper crust'.

**13. Upper deck**, the highest continuous deck of a ship. (Orig. the higher of two decks, in contrast to the *lower*.)

1591 RALEIGH *Last Fight Reuenge* B 3, Sir Richard..was neuer so wounded as that hee forsooke the vpper decke. 1598 FLORIO *Dict.* To Rdr. 9, I was but one to sit at sterne, to pricke my carde, to watch vpon the vpper decke. 1626 CAPT. SMITH *Accidence Yng. Seamen* 10 The vpper Decke should be layd with so many beames as arefitting with knees to bind them. *a* 1687 PETTY *Treat. Naval Philos.* I. i, The Hull under the said upper Deck is divided into the Cavity or Hold [etc.]. 1758 J. BLAKE *Plan Mar. Syst.* 2 It is proposed, that..guns run out on the upper deck only. 1769 FALCONER *Dict. Marine* (1780) s.v. *Deep-waisted*, To leave a vacant space, called the waist, on the middle of the upper-deck. 1846 A. YOUNG *Naut. Dict.* 98 That part of the upper-deck which is between the forecastle and poop..is termed the Main-deck. 1889 E. C. STEDMAN in *Life W. Sharp* (1910) ix. 155 You looked down upon its members from the Servia's upper-deck.

*fig.* *a* 1613 OVERBURY *Characters, Saylor* Wks. (1890) 75 Nothing but hunger and hard rockes can convert him, and then but his upper decke neither; for his hold neither feares nor hopes.

*attrib.* 1709 *Lond. Gaz.* No. 4521/2 Upon whom we fired ..our Upper-deck..Guns. 1892 E. REEVES *Homeward Bound* 129 To give third-class passengers a little breathing upper-deck space.

**14. Upper hand: a.** The mastery, control, or advantage (*of*, or *over*, a person, people, etc.); predominance, rule, or dominion. Usu. const. with verbs, as *attain*, *gain*, *get*, *have*, *obtain*. Cf. the earlier OVER-HAND *sb.*, UVER-HAND. (Freq. *c* 1560–*c* 1600.) **b.** A person or party in power or authority. **c.** The place of authority or honour; preference, precedence. (Usu. with *give* or *take*.)

**a.** 1481 TIPTOFT *Tulle of Old Age* (Caxton) g viij b, Marcus Attilius..had the vppirhande and victorye of the men of cartage. 1535 COVERDALE *Ps.* ix. 19 Vp Lorde, let not man haue the vpper hande. 1576 GASCOIGNE *Steele Gl.* (Arb.) 64 Downe goeth al, where they [*sc.* soldiers] get vpper hand. *a* 1616 BEAUM. & FL. *Little Fr. Lawyer* I. i, I have seen fools, and fighters, chain'd together, And the Fighters had the upper hand, and whipt first, The poor Sots laughing at 'em. 1690 SOMERS *Vind. Proc. Late Parlt.* 10 The Jacobites, and the Malecontents..might perhaps get the upper hand, if not prevented in time. 1742 YOUNG *Nt. Th.* III. 479 Where ev'ry ranger of the wilds, perhaps Each reptile, justly claims our upper hand. 1743 POCOCKE *Descr. East* I. 177 When the Greeks got the upper hand,..they treated them with great rigour. 1838 DICKENS *O. Twist* xv, I've got the upper-hand over you. 1861 LD. BROUGHAM *Brit. Const.* xiii. 195 They blindly followed the dictates of the faction which had the upper-hand. 1865 MRS. CARLYLE *Lett.* (1883) III. 303, I decided to take the upper hand with her, and keep it.

*transf.* (of things). 1535 COVERDALE *Wisdom* x. 5 When wickednes had gotten yᵉ vpper-hande, so yᵗ the nacions were puft vp with pryde. 1546 BP. GARDINER *Detect. Devil's Sophistrie* 16 Whiles the bely hath the vpperhande amonge a greate many. 1579 G. HARVEY *Letter-bk.* (Camden) 87 Summer gettith the upperhande of wynter, and wynter agayne of summer. 1622 PEACHAM *Compl. Gent.* xv. 186 Hereby the minde getteth the dominion and vpperhand. 1712 POPE *Spect.* No. 408 ⁋ 3 If a Man suffers them [*sc.* the passions] to get the upper hand. 1796 MME. D'ARBLAY *Camilla* I. 289 Sir Hugh..said it never broke out from him but by accident, which..should never get the upper hand again. 1873 MRS. OLIPHANT *Innocent* III. 160 The natural honesty to which he had appealed gained the upper hand. 1885 *Manch. Exam.* 29 June 5/1 The worst tendencies of the party will gain the upper hand.

**b.** 1548 HALL *Chron., Hen. VI*, 126 The poore inhabitauntes ..were..compelled to yeilde and rendre theimselfes, to the more power, and vpper hande. 1606 *Sir G. Goosecappe* I. iv, One of these painted communities, that are rauisht with Coaches, and vpper hands.

**c.** 1580–3 GREENE *Mamillia* Wks. (Grosart) II. 49 If by chaunce the Vestal virgins walkt abroad, the Senators would giue them the vpper hand. 1598 HAKLUYT *Voy.* I. 68 They ..gaue vs and Duke Ieroslaus the vpper hand, when we were abroad in their companie. 1662 J. DAVIES tr. *Olearius' Voy. Ambass.* 9 The *Priestaf* gave the Ambassadours the upper Hand, and conducted them to the Inn. 1663 PEPYS *Diary* 25 Jan., A late dispute between my Lord Chesterfield ..and Mr. Edward Montagu..who should have the precedence in taking the Queen's upper-hand abroad out of the house. 1715 *Lond. Gaz.* No. 5329/1 The Empress..gave the upper Hand to the [Dowager] Empress Amalia. 1746 FRANCIS tr. *Hor., Sat.* II. v. 26 Yet wait upon him, at his least command, And always bid him take the upper hand. 1809 MALKIN *Gil Blas* VII. ii. ⁋ 9 [At] the second table..the whole household..insisted on giving me the upper hand.

*fig.* 1594 SHAKS. *Rich. III*, IV. iv. 37 If ancient sorrow be most reuerent, Giue mine the benefit of signeurie, And let my greefes frowne on the vpper hand.

**d.** *adv.* (See quots., and cf. UNDERHAND *adv.* 2 c.)

1771 LUCKOMBE *Hist. Print.* 333 The Nut and Spindle, and the Toe of the Spindle, are all to be well oiled; that they may all perform their several offices the easier..; both Upper and Under hand. 1808 STOWER *Printer's Gram.* 530 When the spindle goes soft and easy,..it goes well upper hand or above hand. 1888 JACOBI *Printers' Vocab.* s.v.

**e.** Hence **Upperhandism.** *nonce-word.* [-ISM 2 b.]

1845 E. B. BARRETT *Lett. to R. Browning* (1899) I. 26 The curious thing in this world is not the stupidity, but the upperhandism of the stupidity.

**15. Upper house**, a higher house of deliberation or legislation, esp. the House of Lords.

1532–3 *Act* 24 *Hen. VIII*, c. 12 § 4 The Spirituall Prelatez and other Abbottes and Priours of the upper House assembled..in the Convocacion. *a* 1577 SIR T. SMITH *Commonw. Eng.* II. ii. (1584) 38 Besides the Chauncelor, there is one in the vpper house who is called Clarke of the Parliament. 1640 YORKE *Union Hon.* 66 Which was concluded in the upperhouse of Parliament. *a* 1670 HACKET *Abp. Williams* II. (1693) 180 The Bishops..intended that this Petition.. should be preferred to the King..in the Upper House of Parliament. 1708 J. CHAMBERLAYNE *St. Gt. Brit.* II. (1710) 481 A List of the Members of the Upper-House of Convocation. 1728 CHAMBERS *Cycl.* s.v. *Convocation*, Things are first usually propos'd in the upper House; then communicated to the lower. 1818 BENTHAM *Ch. Eng.* p. x, The Lower House was indeed untaxable. But the Upper House ..taxed themselves. 1849 MACAULAY *Hist. Eng.* iii. I. 325 The abolition of the monasteries deprived the Church..of her predominance in the upper house of parliament. 1859 W. SWAINSON *New Zealand* xi. 289 The Legislative Council, or Upper House. 1885 LOWE *Bismarck* I. 293 The Lower Chamber would not yield an inch to the Crown and the Upper House.

*attrib.* 1610 BOLTON *Elem. Armories* 150 Or should I not doe wrong to Campes, and Parliaments, robbing souldiers, and vpper-house men of their colour?

**16. Upper leather: a.** Leather forming the upper of a boot or shoe; also, = UPPER *sb.* 1. **b.** Sheet-leather suitable or prepared for such.

**a.** 1528 ROY *Rede me* (Arb.) 82 *Ief.* To mangill their good shues so, Me thynketh it but folisshnes. *Wat.* They cutt but the vpper ledder. 1603–4 *Act* 1 *Jas. I*, c. 22 § 23 The upper Leather of any Shooes, Startups, &c. 1708 OCKLEY *Saracens* I. 142 Those who had strong Boots on,..had the Soals torn off from the Upper-Leathers. 1759 *Phil. Trans.* LI. 39 With that shoe struck off, and its upper-leather torn. 1841 *Penny Cycl.* XXI. 410/2 The lasting or tacking of the upper-leather to the in-sole. 1846 THACKERAY *Laman Blanchard* Wks. 1899 XIII. 467 Persons who..polish their upper-leathers as well as they can. **1872** T. HARDY *Under Greenw. Tree* II. ii, The upper-leather of a Wellington-boot. *fig.* **1647** N. WARD *Simple Cobler* (title-p.), Willing to help 'mend his Native Country, lamentably tattered, both in the upper-Leather and sole.

**b.** **1629** *Leather* 12 The..strongest, which might..serue both for sooling leather and vpper leather. *Ibid.* 15 The Market is full of excellent Leather (strong Backes, and good vpper Leathers). **1885** *Harper's Mag.* Jan. 278/1 Upper-leather..is sold by the foot or pound.

**17. Upper lip: a.** The lip on the upper side of the mouth; the superior lip of a person, animal, or insect. **b.** The higher of the two edges of an organ-pipe mouth. **c.** *Bot.* The superior or upper division of a bilabiate corolla or calyx. **d.** *spec.* (See UNDERLIP 1 b.)

**a.** **1546** J. HEYWOOD *Prov.* (1867) 77 He can yll pype, that lacth his vpper lyp. **1596** SPENSER *State Irel.* Wks. (Globe) 635/1 That noe man shall weare his bearde but onely on the upper lipp like muschachoes. **1611** BIBLE *Lev.* xiii. 45 The leper..shall put a couering vpon his vpper lip. **1670** MILTON *Hist. Eng.* VI. 304 The English then useing to let grow on their upper-lip large Mustachio's. **1704** *Dict. Rust.* s.v. *Rules buying Horses*, If his Upper-Lip will not reach his Nether. **1748** RICHARDSON *Clarissa* VI. 387 Which made John's upper-lip..rise to his nose. **1758** J. S. tr. *Le Dran's Observ. Surg.* (1771) 42 It possessed the whole Upper-Lip. **1815** *Massachusetts Spy* 14 June 4/4, I kept a stiff upper lip, and bought license to sell my goods. **1826** KIRBY & SP. *Entomol.* III. xxxiii. 355 *Labrum* (the Upper-lip), a usually moveable organ; which..is situate between the Mandibulæ. **1833–** [see LIP *sb.* 2, STIFF *a.* 11]. **1836** YARRELL *Brit. Fishes* I. 378 [The loach] with four barbules or cirri..on the upper lip in the front. **1849** C. BRONTË *Shirley* xxiii, He had the shorter nose and longer upper-lip of his sister.

**b.** **1728** CHAMBERS *Cycl.* s.v. *Organ*, Over this Aperture is the Mouth..; whose upper Lip.., being level, cuts the Wind as it comes out at the Aperture. **1852** SEIDEL *Organ* 78 The upper lip..forming, together with the under lip, the mouth of the pipe. **1875** KNIGHT *Dict. Mech.* 1709/2 The lower edge of the leaf is termed the upper lip.

**c.** **1731** MILLER *Gard. Dict.*, *Salvia*..hath a labiated Flower, consisting of one Leaf, whose Upper-lip is sometimes arched. **1793** MARTIN *Lang. Bot.*, *Galea* (an helmet), the upper lip of a ringent corolla. **1796** WITHERING *Brit. Plants* (ed. 3) III. 555 *Digitalis purpurea*...Segments of the calyx egg-shaped, acute:..upper lip nearly entire. **1807** J. E. SMITH *Phys. Bot.* 434 *Ajuga* [has] scarcely any upper lip at all.

**18. Upper ten,** the upper classes; the aristocracy. *colloq.* Orig. (U.S.) *upper ten thousand.*

(*a*) **1844** N. P. WILLIS in *Even. Mirror* (N.Y.) 11 Nov. 2/1 At present there is no distinction among the upper ten thousand of the city. **1861** LEVER *One of Them* xix. 149 The Peerage,..the bulky volume that records the alliances and the ages of the 'upper ten thousand'. **1871** *Punch* 15 May 187/2 There was no grievance on the part of the 'upper ten thousand'.

(*b*) **1848** BARTLETT *Dict. Amer.* 370 *The upper ten thousand*, and contracted, *the upper ten*,..the upper circles of our large cities. **1860** W. H. RUSSELL *Diary in India* I. 119 Petty jealousy and 'caste' reigned in the Residency; the 'upper ten' with stoical grandeur would die the 'upper ten'. **1886** C. E. PASCOE *Lond. of To-day* xxxii. (ed. 3) 294 Clubs of some note..patronized by the 'upper ten'. [**1890** RIDER HAGGARD *Beatrice* xi, Plenty of carriages, and other needful things, including of course the *entrée* to the upper celestial ten.]

*transf.* **1879** JEFFERIES *Wild Life* 160 Neither is he [*sc.* the robin] a favourite with the upper class of cottagers—for there is an 'upper ten' even among cottagers.

**b.** Hence **Upper-tendom,** = prec. Chiefly *U.S.*

**1855** *Doesticks* xvi. 131, I did go to a ball for the benefit of the poor—a two-dollar commingling of upper-tendom with lower-twentydom. **1863** N. HAWTHORNE *Our Old Home* II. 199 All the girls, whether daughters of the uppertendom, the mediocrity, the cottage, or the kennel. **1887** [W. F. RAE] *Miss Bayle's Romance* I. 253 This countess belongs to the real upper tendom.

**19. Upper works: a.** That part of a vessel which is above water-level when it is ready or laden for a voyage; = DEAD-WORK 1. (Also †*upper work.*) **b.** The higher portion of a structure. **c.** *slang.* The head; the mental capacity.

**a.** **1591** RALEIGH *Last Fight Reuenge* B 3 b, The mastes all beaten ouer board,..her vpper worke altogither rased. **1627** CAPT. SMITH *Seaman's Gram.* xi. 52 She is brought in narrow to her vpper workes. **1693** *Lond. Gaz.* No. 2865/1 The French Man of War..who fought the Berkeley Castle ..being very leaky,..and all her upper Work torn to pieces. **1745** P. THOMAS *Jrnl. Anson's Voy.* 270 To caulk the Ship's Upper-Works and Decks. **1769** FALCONER *Dict. Marine* (s.v.), Upper-work. **1798** NELSON in Nicolas *Disp.* (1845) III. 106 The Sérieuse was set on fire to burn her upper works which were above water. *c* **1850** *Rudim. Navig.* (Weale) 157 *Upper works*,..all that part which may be considered as separated from the bottom by the main wale. **1898** KIPLING *Fleet in Being* i. 7 The battleships overtook us, their white upperworks showing like icebergs as they topped the sea-line.

*fig.* **1751** SMOLLETT *P. Pickle* vi, I'd have you take care of your upper works; for if once you are made fast to her poop, egad, she'll..make every beam in your body crack with straining.

**b.** **1791** SMEATON *Edystone L.* § 60 The object was to repair or restore the Upper Works.

**c.** **1809** MALKIN *Gil Blas* III. iii. ⁋ 12 Arsenia and Florimonde are not strong in their upper works; but then they have a facility in their vocation which is more than all the wit in the world. **1818** *Sporting Mag.* July 167 Neate gave Oliver..a..hit on his mouth, that his *upper works* were in a complete state of *chaos.* **1860** J. P. KAY-SHUTTLEWORTH *Scarsdale* II. 299 Oi'm i' gradely fettle..i' th' upper warks.

**U·pper,** *adv.* Now *rare.* [f. UP *adv.*[1] or *adv.*[2] + -ER [3].] To or in a loftier place or position; higher, further up.

*c* **1384** CHAUCER *H. Fame* II. 884 With this word, vpper to sore He gan. *c* **1391** — *Astrol.* II. § 12 As the sonne clymbith vppere & vppere. *c* **1550** CHEKE *Matt.* xxiii. 12 Whosoever abaseth himself schal be set vpper. *a* **1552** LELAND *Itin.* (1711) III. 6 A litle Foreland about a Mile upper then Kenor on Severn. **1901** *Punch* 21 Sept. 224/1 We go up, up, up, up, and upper, upper,..skirting..precipices.

†**Upper-bodying,** *vbl.sb. Obs.* (See UPPER *a.* 4 b.) **1502** *Priv. Purse Exp. Eliz. York* (1830) 22 For upper bodyeng sleving and lynyng of a gowne.

**Upper crust:** see UPPER *a.* 12.

**Upper-cut,** *v.* (See UPPER *a.* 7.) **1850** in *Mem. T. Sayers* (1858) 21 Sayers..hit short at Collins with his left, who uppercut him sharply, and slipped down. **1898** A. M. BINSTEAD *Pink 'Un & Pelican* 237 She wouldn't 'old her tongue the other night, an' so..I uppercuts her with the right.

**U·pperest,** *a.* Now *rare.* Also 4 **uppurest,** 4–5 **uppereste,** 5 **-ist;** 6 **upperst.** [A superlative formed on UPPER *a.* Cf. MDu. *upperst* (Du. and Flem. *opperst*), LG. *upperst, üpperst,* Sw. and older Da. *ypperst*, Norw. *ypparst, yppast* best, choicest.] Most high in situation, position, or rank; uppermost, highest, loftiest; † outermost.

In modern use rare for *uppermost.*

**13..** *K. Alis.* 7068 (MS. Linc.), Þeose seresys..Vppurest folk buþ of ynde. *c* **1374** CHAUCER *Boeth.* I. pr. i. 2 (Camb. MS.), By whiche degrees men myhten clymbyn fro the nethereste lettre to the vppereste. **1387–8** T. USK *Test. Love* I. x. (Skeat) l. 32 We men, that..holden the upperest degree, under god, of benigne thinges. **1483** CAXTON *Gold. Leg.* 62 b/1 Moyses..made hym upperist bysshop for his fader Aaron. *Ibid.* 76 b/1 She wente up in the upperist cubicle of the hows. *a* **1548** HALL *Chron., Hen. VIII*, 2 b, His grace ware in his vpperst apparell, a robe of Crimosyn Veluet.

**1874** M. COLLINS *Frances* III. 212 An American of the very upperest five hundred. **1880** W. MORRIS in Mackail *Life* (1899) II. 15 Above the Round House, on what might be called the upperest Thames.

**b.** *absol.* The uppermost or highest point.

**1484** CAXTON *Fables of Æsop* III. iii, He that..is atte vpperest of the whele of fortune, may wel falle doune.

†**U·pperest,** *adv. Obs. rare.* In 5 **up(p)rest.** [f. UPPER *adv.*] In the highest place or position.

**1481** *Cely Papers* (Camden) 71, vij packes..lying be afte the maste, j pack lyeth upprest. *Ibid.* 72 A few broken felles and pesys..lyeth uprest nexte the maste.

**Upper-flapped,** *a.* (UPPER *a.* 3 a.) **1850** 'H. HIEOVER' *Pract. Horsemanship* 107 The Shaftoed upper-flapped, and stuffed lower-flapped saddle.

**Upper hand(ism):** see UPPER *a.* 14 (also 2).

**Upper leather, lip:** see UPPER *a.* 16, 17.

**U·ppermore,** *adv.* and *a.* Now *dial.* Also 5 **vppyr-, vppermare, vpher more,** 6 *Sc.* **vppermair, -mer, vppirmer,** 7 **vppermere,** 9 *north. dial.* **uppermer.** [f. UPPER *adv.* and *a.* + -MORE. Cf. older Da. *yppermere.*]

**A.** *adv.* Higher locally; further up; at or to a greater altitude. (In later use *Sc.*)

*c* **1400** MAUNDEV. (Roxb.) xiv. 63 Vppermare amanges þe mountaynes es a faire citee. *c* **1410** *Master of Game* (MS. Digby 182) xxi, Þat þe flewe be iii. or iiii. fyngres vppermore þanne þe heed. **1435** MISYN *Fire of Love* I. x. 20 Bettyr it is..þat criste..to vs say, 'frende, cum vppyrmare'. **1501** DOUGLAS *Pal. Hon.* III. v, Weil I considderit na vppermair I micht, And to discend sa hiddeous was the hicht, I durst not auenture. **1596** DALRYMPLE tr. *Leslie's Hist. Scot.* (S.T.S.) I. 30 Abone or vppirmer, vpon Leuin, is the toune. **1616** *Barbour's Bruce* (Hart) II. 440 To that word they assented all, And from them walloped vppermere.

**B.** *adj.* That is the more elevated (of two); higher, upper.

*c* **1400** MAUNDEV. (Roxb.) xx. 90 Bathe þe emisperies, þe vppermare and þe nedermare. *a* **1425** tr. *Arderne's Treat. Fistula*, etc. 44 After þat þe vppermore iuncture of þe bone of þe fynger was drawen out. **1869–** in north. dialect use (*Eng. Dial. Dict.*).

**U·ppermost,** *adv., a.,* and *sb.* Also 5 **wpwr-, wppwrmwste,** 6 *Anglo-Ir.* **uppermuste;** 5 **wpwr-,** 6 **vp(p)ermoste** (6 **vppermooste**), 5–7 **vper-,** 6–7 **vppermost.** [f. as prec. + -MOST.]

**A.** *adv.* **1.** In or to the highest, upmost, or most elevated position or place.

**1481** *Cely Papers* (Camden) 74 A packe lyes wpwrmwste apon Dawlttons behynde the maste. *Ibid.* 75 Thay ly behynde the maste wpwrmoste. **1617** J. TAYLOR (Water P.) *Observ. & Trav. fr. London to Hamburgh* E 1 b, A good featherbed vndermost,..and another featherbed vppermost. **1622** SIR R. HAWKINS *Observ. Voy. S. Sea* 3 With a storme ..shee was turned topse-turvie, her Kele vppermost. **1668** BP. HOPKINS *Serm.*, *Vanity* (1685) 76 His hand turns all things here about like so many wheels;..the same part is now uppermost, and anon lowermost. **1712** ADDISON *Spect.* No. 281 ⁋ 11, I..shall therefore only take Notice of what lay first and uppermost. **1747** WESLEY *Prim. Physick* (1762) 55 Lie with that Ear uppermost. **1814** SCOTT *Diary* 7 Aug. in *Lockhart*, This man being uppermost on the cord, ..called out to his brother who was next to him. **1842** LOUDON *Suburban Hort.* 263 Care must be taken that the upper end of the cutting..be kept uppermost. **1860** TYNDALL *Glac.* I. xvi. 118 In making this effort the spike of my axe turned uppermost.

*fig.* **1866** G. MACDONALD *Ann. Q. Neighb.* vii. (1878) 117 If the wine hadn't got uppermost.

**b.** In the first or foremost place in respect of precedence, station, rank, or the like.

**1526** TINDALE *Matt.* xxiii. 6 They..love to sytt vppermooste at feastes. **1530** PALSGR. 713/2, I set hyest, or upper moste in a companye. **15..** *Bk. Precedence* i. 14 All Dukes daughters shall goe all-one with a nother, soe that alwayes the Eldest Dukes Daughter go vpermost. **1628** [see C. 1 b]. **1850** J. F. COOPER *Ways of Hour* I. 317 It is the people to-day;..some prince to-morrow; and by the end of the week we may have..a Robespierre uppermost.

**c.** *fig.* In the chief place or predominancy.

**1805** WORDSW. *Prelude* IX. 389 We..saw..generous love.. Uppermost in the midst of fiercest strife. **1850** ROBERTSON *Serm.* Ser. III. (1857) 125 A mourning in which self is ever uppermost. **1885** 'M. RUTHERFORD' *Deliv.* i. 11 Every now and then, when the subject was uppermost.

**2.** Foremost in, most prominently in or into, the mind, thoughts, conversation, etc.

In frequent use from *c* 1830.

**1693** *Humours Town* 54 Perpetual Chat on whatever comes uppermost. **1719** DE FOE *Crusoe* II. (Globe) 316 It was uppermost in all my Thoughts. **1723** *Pres. St. Russia* II. 151 It was always my Way to say what came uppermost. **1802–12** BENTHAM *Ration. Judic. Evid.* Wks. 1843 VII. 172 Any one word that comes uppermost is sufficient. **1848** THACKERAY *Van. Fair* xli, Ever since she had left them she had not ceased to keep them uppermost in her thoughts. **1860** TROLLOPE *Framley Parsonage* xxvi, To speak out what came uppermost to her tongue.

**B.** *adj.* **1.** Occupying the highest position or place; loftiest, topmost, highest in place; furthest up (on a river, etc.).

*c* **1500** *Melusine* lix. 358 He yede vp to the vpermost stage of the donjon. **1526** TINDALE *Luke* xi. 43 Ye love the vppermost seates in the sinagoges. *a* **1548** HALL *Chron., Hen. VIII*, 226 b, One of the officers demaunded his vpper garment for his fee, meanyng his goune, and he [*sc.* Sir Thomas More]..tooke him his cappe, saiyng it was the vppermoste garment that he had. **1623** BINGHAM *Xenophon* 133 Xenophon..encamped in the vppermost village neere the mountaines. **1657** HOBBES *Absurd. Geom.* 3 Perhaps you mean that the uppermost quantitie o + 1 is equal to the uppermost quantity 1. **1702** *Post Man* 8–11 Aug. 2/1 Inquire at the uppermost House..in the said Buildings. **1764** *Museum Rust.* IV. 19, I preserve only two of the new shoots, the uppermost and its opposite. **1844** KINGLAKE *Eothen* x, The golden juice ascended from..the cellar to the uppermost brains of the friars. **1886** J. A. BROWN in *Q. Jrnl. Geol. Soc.* May 196 There had been a manufactory of Palæolithic implements on this uppermost floor. **1896** A. STERRY *Tale Thames* (1903) 43/1 One the most attractive portions of what may be called the Uppermost Thames.

**b.** Outermost; most external.

*a* **1548** [implied in quot. under 1 above]. **1560** *First Bk. Discipl.* (1621) 48 The uppermost claith, corps-present; clerk maile, the Pasche-offering. **1567** MAPLET *Gr. Forest* 69 The Adder..casteth off yearely his uppermost skin or coate. **1861** J. R. GREENE *Man. Anim. Kingd., Cœlent.* 103 An expanded bulb, above which are disposed..the various appendages... Of these the hydrocysts are uppermost, or external.

†**2.** Maximum, utmost. *Obs.*[−1]

**1579** in *10th Rep. Hist. MSS. Comm.* App. V. 430 If any [person]..steallinge of any..wares, do..restore the thing or thinges so taken or the uppermuste vallue thereof.

**3.** Highest in respect of rank, importance, precedence, etc.; chiefest, first.

**1680** WALTON in Aubrey *Lives* (1898) II. 15 He was in.. the vpermost fforme in Westminster scole. **1699** BENTLEY *Phal.* 188 The Thought [was] so very obvious and uppermost. **1780** WARNER in Jesse *Selwyn & Contemp.* (1844) IV. 398 In the Westminster [election] struggle Rodney is to-day got uppermost. **1876** MISS YONGE *Womankind* xii, This entire seclusion from all means of reaching the poor..is seldom found in the uppermost classes. **1885** *Manch. Exam.* 6 Apr. 5/2 The weather is, in view of the approaching holiday, the uppermost subject of concern.

**b.** Having the chief power, control, or authority; predominant, supreme; most influential.

**1691** WOOD *Ath. Oxon.* I. 887 In the time of the rebellion he sided with those that were uppermost. **1693** *Humours Town* 42 The Violence of those that are uppermost. **1732** BERKELEY *Alciphr.* II. § 21 Where heavy heads are lowest, and men of genius uppermost. **1818** SCOTT *Br. Lamm.* xxvii, Uniform adherents to the party who are uppermost. **1855** MACAULAY *Hist. Eng.* xiv. III. 445 The politician whose practice was always to be on the side which was uppermost.

**C.** *sb.* †**1.** The highest part or portion. *Obs.*

**1484** CAXTON *Fables of Æsop* V. xiii, Yf an Egle were at the vppermost of the heuen. **1613–39** I. JONES in Leoni *Palladio's Archit.* (1742) II. 49 The uppermost of the highest Cornice, is of large Tyles. **1646** J. GREGORY *Notes & Obs.* 11 For so they call Τὰ μετέωρα τῶν οἰκημάτων, the uppermosts of their Houses.

**b.** The highest place or position.

**1628** R. H. *J. Owen's Epigr.* II. liv. 11 Let me set alwayes vppermost at boord, The vppermost in bed I'le you affoord.

†**2.** That which is highest, most predominant, etc. *Obs.*

**1687** *Good Advice* 60 It is certain that two predominant Religions, would be two Uppermosts at once. *a* **1753** BP. BERKELEY in Fraser *Life* (1871) 477 W[t] judgement would he make of uppermost and lowermost who had always seen through an inverting glass?

†**3.** The upper hand; superiority or dominion.

**1718** *Entertainer* No. 43. 302 If ever they get the Uppermost, after their long Struggles for Superiority.

†**Upperplus.** *Obs.*[−1] [f. UPPER *a.*, substituted for *sur-* in *surplus.*] Surplus, balance.

**1578** *Surrey & Kent Sewers Comm.* (1909) 286 To sell the same and satisfye the chardge and make restitucion of the vpperplus.

†**Upper-stocked,** *a. Obs.* (See UPPER *a.* 4 a.) **1535** in *Archaeologia* IX. 250 Two paire of hoose,..the one paire upperstocked with yalowe damaske.

**Upper ten, works:** see UPPER *a.* 18, 19.

**Up-pi·led,** *pa. pple.* and *ppl. a.* (UP- 5.)

**1600** FAIRFAX *Tasso* XIX. xxx. 342 There vnderneath th' vnburied hils vppilde Of bodies dead, the liuing buried lie. **1742** COLLINS *Ode Poet. Char.* 55 High on some cliff, to heav'n up-pil'd. **1796** COLERIDGE *To Yng. Friend* 2 A green mountain variously up-piled. **1818** KEATS *Endym.* II. 288 He cannot see,..up-pil'd, The cloudy rack slow journeying in the west. **1855** SINGLETON *Virgil* I. 88 Thrice the Sire in ruins laid The up-piled mountains with his flash. **1873**

Symonds *Grk. Poets* i. 28 With Homeric games and pyres up-piled to heaven.

†**U·pping**, *vbl. sb.*[1] *Obs.* [OE. *yppińg*, f. *yppan* Uppe *v.*] Manifestation, making known.

*c* 950 *Rit. Durham* 195 *Epiphania, manifestatio*, ypping. *a* 1225 *Ancr. R.* 148 God dede idrawen uorð nis nout one uorloren þuruh þet uppinge, auh þuncheð ȝet atelich biuoren Godes eien.

**U·pping**, *vbl. sb.*[2] [f. Up *v.*]

**1.** The action of catching and marking swans. (See Up *v.* 1, and cf. Swan-hopping, -upping.)

1560–1 in W. H. Turner *Select. Rec. Oxford* (1880) 285 For upping of half game in cowemeade, iiij d. 1570–1 *Ibid.* 338 For upping of swans, viij s. 1593 Buckhurst in Kempe *Losely MSS.* (1836) 306 That the upping of all those swans ..may be upped all in on day wt the upping of the Tems. 1892 *Pall Mall G.* 2 Aug. 2/1 The operation of 'upping' is performed by the Crown and the Companies' swan-masters together.

*attrib.* 1572–3 in W. H. Turner *Select. Rec. Oxford* (1880) 350 Chargys aboute the swanes..at the syttynge tyme and uppynge tyme. 1584–5 *Order for Swans*, His Dinner and Supper free, on the vpping day.

**2.** The action of getting up; only *attrib.* in *upping-block, -stock, -stone*, a horse-block, a mounting-stone. Also in dial. use with *-chock, -steps*.

1796 *Grose's Dict. Vulgar T.* (ed. 3), **Upping block*, steps for mounting a horse. 1826 Cobbett *Rur. Rides* (1830) 529 Houses..with large stone upping-blocks against the walls of them. 1883 *Trans. Amer. Philol. Soc.* 55 *Upping-block*, 'a horse-block,' in common use in West Virginia. *a* 1691 Aubrey *Nat. Hist. Wilts* (1847) 26 At the foot of Shotover-hill, near the *upping-stock. 1820 *Sporting Mag.* VI. 159 An itinerant preacher on the upping-stock at the back of my house. 1856 G. Roberts *Soc. Hist. Eng.* 560 Upping stocks and horse blocks were necessary when double horses were in use. 1809 Hazlitt in *The Hazlitts* (1911) I. 433 A conception of the ladder which I learned from the *upping stone on the down.

**3.** *dial.* The end, issue, or upshot of a matter.

1828– in Yks. and Lanc. glossaries.

**Uppish** (ʊ·piʃ), *a.* Also 8–9 upish. [f. Up *adv.*[2] + -ish.]

†**1. a.** Flush of money. *Obs.*

1678 in Pollock *Popish Plot* (1903) App. B. 382 The one saying to the other that..he would treat him..with wine and oysters, whereupon the other replied..: 'What you are uppish then, are you?' *a* 1700 B. E. *Dict. Cant. Crew*, *Uppish*, rampant, crowing, full of Money. *He is very Uppish*, well lined in the Fob; also brisk.

†**b.** Elevated in station. *Obs.*

1797 *Hubbub* 7 No sooner did he get a little uppish in the world, than [etc.].

**2.** †**a.** Elated; in high spirits; cock-a-hoop.

Common in the early years of the 18th century, freq. const. *upon*. Johnson (1755) defines as 'proud; arrogant' and adds 'A low word'.

α. *a* 1704 T. Brown *Wks.* (1720) I. 173 Half-pay Officers at the Parade very uppish upon the Death of the King of Spain. 1708 T. Cockman in *Ballard MSS.* XXI. 81 Ye Brittish Papists were mighty uppish upon ye attempt made upon Scotland. 1722 Wodrow *Corr.* (1843) II. 643 The Jacobites are uppish, and very big in their hopes. 1746 in *10th Rep. Hist. MSS. Comm.* App. I. 289, I fear the Victory will have very bad consequences, if it render the Ministry uppish and secure.

β. 1710 *Wentworth Papers* (1883) 122 The Torys are very upish and expect all to come in for Places. 1712 Swift *Jrnl. to Stella* 25 Jan., I find Dingley smelled a rat; because the Whigs are upish; but if ever I hear that word again, I'll uppish you. 1802 A. Carlyle *Autobiog.* (1861) 154 He agreed with me that they [*sc.* the Jacobites] had less ground for being so sanguine and upish than they imagined.

†**b.** Elevated with drink. *Obs.*—[1]

1728 Vanbrugh *Journey to London* iii. i, *Lady Head.* Not so drunk, I hope, but that he can drive us? *Serv.* Yes, yes, Madam, he drives best when he's a little upish.

**c.** Ready to take offence; short-tempered, peevish. Now *dial.* or *Obs.*

1778 Miss Burney *Evelina* lv, Miss is so *uppish* this morning, that I think I had better not speak to her again. 1785 Grose *Dict. Vulgar T.*, *Uppish*, testy, apt to take offence. 1823 E. Moor *Suffolk Words* 460 A man prone to take offence is said to be *uppish*:—or *pepperish*; apt to be hot. 1863 Mrs. C. Brock *Margaret's Secret* ii. 31 When I used to find fault he would get uppish with me, and answer back rudely.

**d.** Inclined to be 'stuck up'; putting on airs; aiming at gentility.

1789 O'Keefe *Farmer* i. ii, Must bounce a few, Betty's so upish—likely wou'dn't have me else. 1823 *Blackw. Mag.* XIII. 365 It is according to human nature to feel uppish on preferment. 1858 Trollope *Dr. Thorne* xxxiv, You think he's an uppish sort of fellow, I know, and you don't like to trouble him. 1886 Besant *Childr. Gibeon* ii. xxxii, She's uppish you know,..and he's only a working-man.

**e.** *dial.* (See quots.)

1841 Hartshorne *Salop. Ant.* Gloss. 605 *Uppish*, pert, proud, impudent. 1854 Miss Baker *Northampt. Gloss.*, *Uppish*, captious, pert, self-opinionated, tenacious of opposition.

**3.** Characterized by presumption or affectation of superiority.

*a* 1734 North *Exam.* (1740) 48 It seems [that] daring to rail at Informers..and Officers was not uppish enough, but his Lordship must rise so high as daring to limit the Power.. of the Crown. 1808 Eliz. Hamilton *Cottagers of Glenburnie* ii. 37 Besides, she is getting uppish notions, from sitting up like a lady from morning to night. 1864 J. H. Newman *Apol.* 100 Discouraging and correcting whatever was uppish or extreme in our followers.

**4.** Slightly elevated or directed upwards.

1862 *Morn. Star* 9 June, Hayward sends a long uppish hit. 1887 *Daily News* 1 July 6/4 After two uppish strokes Mr. Scott hit remarkably well. 1895 *Westm. Gaz.* 2 March 5/1 Peel was there to hold the uppish ball.

Hence **U·ppishness**.

1716 N. Hough in Thoresby *Corr.* (1832) II. 341 The uppishness and indiscretion..of some..in the West Riding. *a* 1832 Bentham *Chrestom.* Tab. i, Uppishness a probable result of the distinctions thus obtained. 1867 *Gard. Chron.* 16 Nov. 1180/1 The uppishness, the insolence, and the lawlessness of some of the young men. 1896 J. H. Wylie *Hist. Eng. Hen. IV*, III. 468 The staid authorities resented his uppishness; but his spirit was irrepressible.

**Upplu·cked**, *pa. pple.* (Up- 5. Cf. *upplucking* Up- 6 (*a*), and Du. *opgeplukt*.)

*c* 1440 *Pallad. on Husb.* vii. 61 Now benys,..vpplucked sone, Maad clene, and sette vp. *c* 1449 Pecock *Repr.* i. x. 51 In this wise..is vnrootid and vppluckid..the firste of the iij. opiniouns. 1582 Stanyhurst *Æneis* iii. (Arb.) 71 When an oother wicker is vp pluckt..From that stub.

**Uppon**, var. Up *prep.*[1] *Obs.*; obs. f. Upon *prep.*

**Up-pri·cked**, *pa. pple.* (Up- 5.) 1592 Shaks. *Ven. & Ad.* 271 His eares vp prickt..; His nostrils drinke the aire. 1777 Mason *Eng. Gard.* ii. 343 The coward hare..Will..steal, with ear Up-prick'd, to gnaw the toils.

**U·p-put.** *Sc.* [Up- 1 b, 2.]

**1.** 'The power of secreting' (Jam.).

*a* 1689 Cleland *Poems* (1697) 101 Tho he can swear..And lye, I think he cannot hide...They are not fitt For Stealth, that want a good up-put.

**2.** = Up-putting *vbl. sb.* 2.

1866 Gregor *Banffshire Gloss.* 204. 1893 Stevenson *Catriona* xix, Ye'll can leave your horse here and your bags, for it seems we're to have your up-put.

†**U·p-pu·tter.** *Sc. Obs.* [Up- 8.] One who raises or erects.

*a* 1578 Lindesay (Pitscottie) *Chron. Scot.* (S.T.S.) I. 194 Thair promovearis or vpputaris to that he estait. 1623 *Extr. Aberd. Reg.* (1848) II. 385 The wpputter thairoff,.. that wald hawe the said windo reedifiet,..sall reedifie and put wp the said windo. 1721 in Gordon *Chron. Keith*, etc. (1880) 97 As upputters at the first and proprietors of the sd. loft.

**U·p-pu·tting**, *vbl. sb. Sc.* [Up- 7.]

†**1.** The action of erecting or setting up. *Obs.*

1513 *Extr. Aberd. Reg.* (1844) I. 86 For vpputting of the weddercok of Sanct Nicholace stepill,..v lib. 1597 *Ibid.* II. 158 The perfyting, ending, and vpputting of ane dyell..one the tolbuyith. 1642 in Cramond *Ann. Cullen* (1888) 41 Anent upputting and edifeing the tolbuith. *a* 1670 Spalding *Troub. Chas. I* (1840) I. 313 To tak doun the portrait of our blissid virgyn Marie..that had stand since the vpputting thairof.

**2.** Accommodation, lodging. (Cf. Put *v.* 53 o.)

1815 Scott *Guy M.* ix, You, who have free upputting—bed, board, and washing. 1831 Mrs. Carlyle *Lett. & Mem.* (1903) I. 37 We succeeded in realising a much better up-putting..in the house of a Mrs. Miles. 1895 Crockett *Men of Moss-hags* xxxviii, In the wild country..was no provision for the up-putting of young..maids.

**Uprai·sal.** [Up- 2.] = Upheaval 1.

1865 Jevons *Coal Quest.* ii. 25 The upraisals, the downfalls, the dislocations,..which rocks have suffered.

**U·praise**, *sb. U.S. Mining.* [Up- 2.] A shaft made by working upwards.

1877 Raymond *Statist. Mines & Mining* 158 A drift..has been run through the..ground, and an upraise commenced. 1882 *U.S. Rep. Prec. Met.* 98 At the end of this [tunnel] they are pushing an upraise, finding the rock a little softer as they go up.

**Uprai·se**, *v.* [Up- 4. Cf. MSw. *up-, opresa, -reesa* (Sw. *uppresa*), MDa. *uprese, oprese, opreise* (Da. *oprejse*).]

†**1.** *trans.* To raise from the dead. *Obs.*

*a* 1300 *Cursor M.* 14363 Son oueral þis tiþand ras O lazar þat vpraisid was. *c* 1340 Hampole *Pr. Consc.* 4325 He sal alswa dede men uprays. 1382 Wyclif *Matt.* x. 8 Hele ȝe seke men, vpreyse ȝee dead men. 1533 Gau *Richt Vay* 29 He sal wpraisz agane al thayme to the euerlestand lyff.

**2.** †**a.** To raise by laudation; to extol. *Obs.*

*a* 1300 *Cursor M.* 27584 We agh ilk man upraise, And in vr hert vrself dispraise. 1595 Spenser *Col. Clout* 355 By wondring at thy Cynthiaes praise,..thy selfe thou mak'st vs more to wonder, And her vpraising, doest thy selfe vpraise.

**b.** To raise (or direct) to a higher level; to lift up or elevate; *fig.* to exalt.

In the 19th c. the pa. pple. after the noun is common, as 'with hand upraised'.

*a* 1300 *E. E. Psalter* xxxvi. 37 (E.), I saw þe wicked man.. vpraised als cedre of Yban. *c* 1385 Chaucer *L. G. W.* 1163 *Dido*, Whan that the mone vp reysed hadde his lyght. 1430–40 Lydg. *Bochas* ix. 2351 Lik as Phebus passeth a litil sterre, Hiest vpreised in his mydday speere. 1563 *Mirr. Mag.* V iv, Dead laye his corps,..Tyll swellyng syghes..Upraysde his head. 1748 Thomson *Cast. Indol.* ii. lxvii, The sick up-rais'd their heads, and dropp'd their woes awhile. 1788 Wolcot (P. Pindar) *Brother Peter* Wks. 1816 I. 380 This lord..uprais'd his convert chin. 1791 Cowper *Odyssey* ix. 624 Then pray'd the Cyclops..With hands upraised toward the starry heaven. 1821 Clare *Vill. Minstr.* II. 61 Cowslips,..upraise your loaded stems. 1830 Lyell *Princ. Geol.* I. 458 Both these accounts..agree in expressly stating, that the sea retired, and one mentions that its bottom was upraised. 1874 Spurgeon *Treas. Dav.* Ps. xcv. 5 He bade the isles upraise their heads.

*fig.* 1828 Atherstone *Fall of Nineveh* I. 238 The fire-eyed priest Upraised his voice, and called upon the Gods.

**c.** To raise from a prostrate, low, or dejected state; to assist, encourage, or cheer.

*a* 1340 Hampole *Psalter* cxliv. 15 Lord vpraysis all þat fallis. *c* 1440 *Wycliffite Bible* 1 Sam. ii. 8 (MS. Bodl. 277), He upreisiþ a nedy man fro poudre, and upreisiþ a pore man fro dritt. 1533 Gau *Richt Vay* 105 The vangel or ioiful tithandis..throw the quhilk he wesz wprasit in his hart. 1600 Fairfax *Tasso* i. ii, O heauenly muse,..Inspire life in my wit, my thoughts vpraise. 1610 Fletcher *Faithf. Sheph.* v. i, Once again upraise Her heavy Spirit that near drowned lyes In self consuming care. 1667 Milton *P. L.* x. 946 He.. thus with peaceful words uprais'd her soon. 1723 *Briton* No. 18 (1724) 76 It help'd the Distressed, uprais'd the Heavy-hearted. 1746 Francis tr. *Hor., Sat.* ii. viii. 80 Sure he had wept,..But wise Nomentane thus up-rais'd his Friend. 1809–14 Wordsw. *Excurs.* iv. 574 Furnished thus, How can you droop, if willing to be upraised? 1818 Milman *Samor* vii. 409 Oh, Monarch,..to repentant deeds of mightiest fame Heaven can upraise the farthest sunken. 1850 Blackie *Æschylus* II. 120 They with Mercy's vote upraised us From the prostrate woe.

**d.** To excite, rouse. *rare.*

*a* 1600 *Flodden F.* iv. (1664) 40 Their courage keen now was uprais'd. 1667 Milton *P. L.* ii. 372 This would..our Joy upraise In his disturbance.

**3.** To erect, set up, build.

1338 R. Brunne *Chron.* (1810) 78 Þe kastelle of Bamborgh þe walles he did vpreise. *c* 1400 *Laud Troy Bk.* 4658 Thei ran alle..To sette vp tentis, Pauylons to bylde;..Many a tent was ther vp-reysed. 1513 Douglas *Æneid* xi. vi. 47 That sammyn douchty hand..Quhilk now..Vprasit hes the cite Argyripas. 1582 Stanyhurst *Æneis* i. (Arb.) 26 Romulus..towne wals statelye shal vpraise..Of Rome.

**U·praised**, *ppl. a.* [Up- 5. Cf. prec.]

**1.** Raised or lifted up; elevated.

*c* 1400 tr. *Secreta Secret., Gov. Lordsh.* 117 Vpraysyd shuldren bytoknys sharpe nature. 1785 Wilkins *Bhagvat* xi. 90 The mighty compound..being Haree, having..thus spoken, made evident..his..heavenly form; of many a mouth and eye;..many an up-raised weapon. 1796 Mme. D'Arblay *Camilla* V. 476 The upraised arm of the form before her dropt. 1853 Kane *Grinnell Exp.* xxii. (1856) 173 The thickness of the upraised tables. 1890 'R. Boldrewood' *Col. Reformer* (1891) 204 He saw Hutkeeper leap at him, with upraised tomahawk. 1898 *Allbutt's Syst. Med.* V. 611 Osseous material..beneath the upraised periosteum.

**b.** *spec.* in *Geol.* Raised by upheaval.

1835 Lyell *Princ. Geol.* (ed. 4) II. 342 Near Uddevalla.. we find upraised deposits of shells. 1863 — *Antiq. Man* 45 These upraised strata..form a terrace. 1877 Huxley *Physiogr.* 212 The upraised deposits of silt which skirt the estuary of the Clyde.

**2.** Directed upwards.

1851 D. Jerrold *St. Giles* xii. 124 The big tears that rolled from her upraised eyes.

**3.** Sounded aloud.

1871 S. B. James *Duty & Doctrine* (ed. 3) 173 Penitence.. must mingle with the upraised notes of gladness.

**Uprai·ser.** [Up- 8.] One who raises up.

*c* 1440 *Wycliffite Bible* 2 Sam. xxii. 3 (MS. Bodl. 277), Þe horn of myn helþe, myn upreiser [L. *elevator*], and my refuyt. *c* 1440 *Jacob's Well* 59 Alle comoun baratours, vprayserys of vnryȝtfull batayles. 1533 Gau *Richt Vay* 88 Iesus christus..is..the verray wprayser of al marcie and grace.

**Uprai·sing**, *vbl. sb.* (Up- 7. Cf. ON. *uppreising, -reisning*, MSw. and MDa. *up-, opresning*.)

*c* 1400 Love *Bonavent. Mirr.* (1908) 179 Thou art..Resurreccioun or vpreysynge and lyf. *c* 1454 Pecock *Folewer* 15 His witt schal þerbi take in maner now seid a greet vpreisyng. 1611 Cotgr., *Resource*,..a recouerie, vpraising, rising againe. 1839 Ure *Dict. Arts* 839 The successive upraising of the roof of a gallery.

**Uprai·sing**, *ppl. a.* (Up- 6 b.) 1609 Daniel *Civ. Wars* vii. lxxii, Think whether this poore State..Stands not in need of some vp-raysing hand. 1860 Ellicott *Life Our Lord* v. 229 The upraising hand of the great Healer.

**Uprape**: see Up- 4.

†**Upras**. *Obs.* [a. ON. *upprás*, f. *upp-* Up- 2 + *rás* Race *sb.*[1]] Resurrection.

*a* 1300 *Cursor M.* 17784 Yow thinc selcut..O iesus vp-ras. *Ibid.* 18683 Sant thomas..of his up-ras..was in were.

†**Uprau·ght**, *pa. pple. Obs.* [Up- 5 + Reach *v.* Cf. OHG. *ûfrahta*.] Drawn up, raised.

*c* 1375 *Sc. Leg. Saints* i. (*Peter*) 717 For þu art richt and vpracht [L. *excelsus et altus*], and of our-selfe haf we na maucht. 1563 Sackville *Mirr. for Mag.* 128 These rockes upraught, that threatned most our wreck We seemde to sayle much surer in the streame.

**Uprea·r**, *v.* [Up- 4. Cf. OE. *uprærend* pres. pple.]

**1.** *trans.* To raise up, elevate, erect, etc.

*a* 1300 *E. E. Psalter* cxliv. 14 Lauerd raises alle þat doune falle, And þe hurt he vprers [L. *erigit*] alle. *c* 1400 *R. Gloucester's Chron.* (Rolls) 6509 (MS. α), He..chirchen let vprere þat were arst as uorlore. 1563 *Mirr. Mag.* R ij b, The Percian kyng..With his huge host that..Dismounted hilles, and made the vales vprere. 1596 Spenser *F. Q.* iv. x. 50 Next to her sate goodly Shamefastnesse, Ne euer durst her eyes from ground vpreare. 1597 Beard *Theatre God's Judgem.* (1612) 80 Ieroboam..as he had..vpreared a new kingdome, so..vpreared also a new religion. 1638 Junius *Paint. Ancients* 67 The great Lampe of light up-rearing his flaming head above the earth. 1667 Milton *P. L.* i. 532 Then [he] strait commands that..be upreard His mighty Standard. 1718 Rowe tr. *Lucan* i. 259 So in the field..Uprears some antient Oak his rev'rend head. 1748 Thomson *Cast. Indol.* i. xxxi, Ah! how shall I for this uprear my moulted wing? 1818 Byron *Ch. Har.* iv. xlv, For Time hath..up-rear'd Barbaric dwellings on their shatter'd site. 1842 Borrow *Bible in Spain* xxvi, Millions of maize plants upreared their tall stalks. 1898 Watts-Dunton *Aylwin* v. ii, A cobra uprearing its head to spring at her.

*refl.* 1616 R. C. *Times' Whistle* (1871) 36 When she doth vprear Her selfe vpon her feet.

*fig.* 1840 Mangan *Poems* (1903) 185 See the palace-dome its pride uprearing One fleet hour!

**b.** To raise in dignity; to exalt.

1382 Wyclif *Isaiah* xxxiii. 10 Now I shal ben enhauncid, now I shal ben vp rered [L. *sublevabor*]. *c* 1400 *Cato's Morals* in *Cursor M.* App. iv. 192 Wiþ lernyng & techyng growes graiþ kunnyng, & mani man vp-rered. 1566 Sternhold & H., etc. *Ps.* cxii. 2 His seede on earth God wil vpreare. 1592 Kyd *Sp. Trag.* ii. i, Yet might she loue me to vpreare her state. 1872 Tennyson *Last Tourn.* 122 My realm, uprear'd, By noble deeds at one with noble vows.

**2.** To bring up, tend in growing.

13.. *E. E. Allit. P.* B. 561 Hym rwed þat he hem vprerde & raȝt hem lyflode. *c* 1440 *Pallad. on Husb* III. 303 To thicke vppon the tre do not the vyne, And yf on faile vprere another tre. 1833 HT. MARTINEAU *Fr. Wines & Pol.* iv. 67 Here were..little children upreared by their mothers amidst the fire and smoke.

**3.** To rouse, stir up, excite.

1486 *Bk. St. Albans* e iiij, How many maner beestys as with the lymere Shall be vpreryde in fryth or in felde *a* 1600 *Flodden F.* iv. (1664) 40 His rancor old it was up-rear'd. 1795 MACNEILL *Waes o' War* II. v, Is it nature, vice, or folly,..Hate, revenge, and rage uprears?

**4.** *intr.* To rise up.

1828 ATHERSTONE *Fall of Nineveh* I. 48 Myriads of bright harnessed steeds Were seen uprearing. 1868 MORRIS *Earthly Par.* I. I. 274 A great black fold against him did uprear.

**Upreared,** *pa. pple.* and *ppl. a.* [UP- 5 or f. prec.]

†**1.** Excited in feeling; angry. *Obs.*

1382 WYCLIF *Prov.* xv. 18 A man..who is pacient, swageth the vprered [L. *suscitatas*].

**2.** Raised up, elevated, erected, etc.

1422 YONGE tr. *Secreta Secret.* 222 A grete breste and brode, vprerid and sumwhate fatte. *Ibid.* 223 Shamel[e]s men [have] hey vprerid shuldris. *c* 1430 LYDG. *Min. Poems* (Percy Soc.) 5 His swerd uprерyd, proudly gave manace. *a* 1593 MARLOWE & NASHE *Dido* III. iv, I..vow..Neuer to leaue these newe vpreared walles, Whiles Dido liues. 1597 HALL *Sat.* I. iii. 11 On crowned kings..Or some vpreared, high-aspiring swaine. 1602 MARSTON *Antonio's Rev.* IV. iii, With innocent upreared armes to Heaven. 1798 LANDOR *Gebir* I. 228 The long moon-beam on the hard wet sand Lay like a jaspar column half uprear'd. 1848 A. CLOUGH *Amours de Voy.* III. 14 Where, over fig-tree and orange..,Garden on garden upreared, balconies step to the sky. 1870 MORRIS *Earthly Par.* III. IV. 330 In front of me An upreared changing dark bulk did I see.

**Uprea·ring,** *vbl. sb.* (UP- 7. Cf. UPREAR *v.*)

1551 BALE *Eng. Votaries* II. 54 b, About the ouerthrowe of pryncely autoryte, and vprearynge of Antichristes tyranny. 1853 KANE *Grinnell Exp.* xxvi. (1856) 212 This uprearing of the ice is not a slow work. 1892 *Daily News* 10 March 2/3 The uprearing of the new fabric of British citizenship.

**Upreceiving, -reek, -reft,** etc.: see UP- 4-7.

**Upre·st.** [var. of UPRIST.] Uprising.

1600 W. WATSON *Decacordon* Pref. (1602) A 2 b, Not onely physicall or naturall, but also morall and politicall cadences and vp-rests. 1817 SHELLEY *Rev. Islam* III. xxi, The uprest Of the third sun brought hunger.

**Uprestore, -rid, -ridge, -ridging:** see UP- 4-7.

**Upright** (*ʊ*·prəit, *ʊ*prəi·t), *a.* and *sb.* Forms: 1 upp-, 1, 3-4 upriht, 4-5 vpriht, 4 up-, 5 vp-ryht; 3-5 up-, vpriȝt (4 op-), 4 upriȝte, 5 vpryȝt, vp-ryȝht (upryȝth); *Sc.* 5 vpe-, 6 vp-rycht, vpricht, 6- upricht; 3-7 vpright (4-6 vprighte, 5 vpperight), 4-6 vpryght (4 vppe-ryght, 4-5 vpryghte), 5 upryght (upperyghte, 6 upryghte, upperyght); 4- upright (6 up-righte, 7 uprite). [OE. *up-, uppriht* (f. *up* UP *adv.*[1] + *riht* RIGHT *a.*), = OFris. *upriucht* (WFris. *oprjucht*), MDu. *oprecht, opregt* (Du. *oprecht*), MLG. *uprĕcht, upricht* (LG. *upricht, uprecht, upregt*), OHG. (MHG.) *ûfrëht* (G. *aufrecht, -richt*), ON. *uprēttr* (Da. *opret*, Sw. *upprät*).]

**A.** *adj.* **I.** *pred.* **1.** Erect on the feet or end; in or into a vertical position; perpendicular to the ground or other surface. (Cf. 3.)

**a.** With verbs, as *go, rise, sit, stand, walk.*

In OE. the advb. form *uprihte* is occas. used.

*Beowulf* 2092 Hyt ne mihte swa syððan ic on yrre uppriht astod. *c* 1250 *Gen. & Ex.* 3248 Ðe water up-stod..On twinne half, also a wal up-riȝt. 1297 R. GLOUC. (Rolls) 4306 Þis holi man sat vpriȝt, & ysei is deþes wounde. 1340 *Ayenb.* 56 Huanne þe glotoun geþ in to þe tauerne ha geþ opriȝt. 1388 WYCLIF *Acts* xiv. 9 Rise thou vp riȝt on thi feet. *c* 1400 *Anturs of Arthur* l, The king stode vp righte And commanded pes. 14.. *Sir Beues* (M.) 4184 Sir Beues was wery..That vnnethe he myght sitt vp-right. 1535 COVERDALE *Lev.* xxvi. 13, I haue broken the cepter of youre yocke, and caused you to go vp right. 1582 N. LICHEFIELD tr. *Castanheda's Conq. E. Ind.* I. xxxii. 79 b, Many Noble men..all standing upright uppon theyr feete. 1607 *Merry Devil Edmonton* Induct. 3 My stiffned haire stands vpright on my head. 1697 DRYDEN *Virg. Georg.* III. 121 Upright he walks, on Pasterns firm and straight. 1703 [R. NEVE] *City & C. Purchaser* 278 A Man likewise standing firmest when he stands uprightest. 1782 MISS BURNEY *Cecilia* x. x, Supported by pillows, she sat almost upright. 1821 LAMB *Elia* Ser. I. *My Relations*, He..has a spirit, that would stand upright in the presence of the Cham of Tartary. 1847 MRS. CARLYLE *Lett.* (1883) I. 391, I..can hardly sit upright. 1892 *Photogr. Ann.* II. 419 The films are thick enough to place in racks to wash, or to stand upright to dry.

**b.** With other verbs (or *ellipt.*).

*a* 1300 *Cursor M.* 3804 Þe stan his heued lai on þat night, In takning, he it sett vp right. *c* 1391 CHAUCER *Astrol.* II. § 28 Thise signes arisen more vpriht, & they ben called eke souereyn signes. *a* 1400 *Northern Passion* 143/158 Sodanly þir launces thre..With outt mannys helpe war raysed vppe ryght. *c* 1450 LOVELICH *Merlin* 2698 Bothe dragowns..thanne tornen..hem bothe with gret myht, and meveth al the erthe evene vpryht. 1496 *Cov. Leet Bk.* 575 Maister Meire, hold vp-right your swerde. 1523 FITZHERB. *Husb.* § 24 His forkes and rakes..wolde be..beyked, and sette euen, to lye vpryght in thy hande. 1622 J. TAYLOR (Water P.) *Farew. to Tower-bottles* A 2 b, 'Twas my chance in Bacchus spight, To come into the Tower vnfox'd vpright. 1667 MILTON *P. L.* I. 221 Forthwith upright he rears from off the Pool His mighty stature. 1700 DRYDEN *Theodore & Honoria* 146 Stood Theodore..With chatt'ring Teeth, and bristling Hair upright. 1747 WESLEY *Prim. Physick* (1755) 30 The Apoplexy...Rub the Head,..and let two strong Men carry the Patient upright. 1807 WORDSW. *White Doe* I. 245 A vault where the bodies are buried upright. 1900 L. B. WALFORD *One of Ourselves* xiv, A tall figure reared itself upright at her approach.

**c.** In figurative uses.

*a* 1225 *Ancr. R.* 266 Herdi bileaue makeð ou stonden up-riht. *c* 1340 HAMPOLE *Pr. Consc.* 1298 Þe mare..þat we wax upright In welthe, and in worldly myght. 1390 GOWER *Conf.* I. 8 [They] With good consail on alle sides Be kept upriht in such a wyse, That hate [etc.] 1399 — *Praise of Peace* 6 The worschipe of this lond, which was doun falle, Now stant upriht. *c* 1412 HOCCLEVE *De Reg. Princ.* 537 O engelond! stande vp-ryght on thy feet! *c* 1421 26 *Pol. Poems* xxi. 147 Of erþe ȝe ben cleped 'salt'..; Go vp-riȝt and be not halt. 1551 CROWLEY *Pleas. & Pain* 590 Al men should walk in their callynge vpryght. 1570–6 LAMBARDE *Peramb. Kent* 105 While the honour of the Britons stood vpright. 1609 HOLLAND *Amm. Marcell.* xv. v. 38 Most wished it were to be, that our fortune alwaies continued upright. 1644 MILTON *Divorce* (ed. 2) II. iii. 40 The justice of God stood upright ev'n among heathen disputers. 1670 COTTON *Espernon* III. XII. 601 Yet did he ever keep himself upright from manifesting his sorrow. 1822 LAMB *Elia* Ser. I. *Dream Children*, Pain..could never bend her good spirits, or make them stoop, but they were still upright. 1900 *Westm. Gaz.* 14 June 2/1 To 'keep the country upright' should be..the first aim of the British Government.

†**d.** *Cant.* (See quot.) *Obs.*

*a* 1700 B. E. *Dict. Cant. Crew* s.v., *Go Upright*, said by Taylers and Shoemakers, to their Servants, when any Money is given,..and signifies, bring it all out in Drink, tho' the Donor intended less.

†**2.** Lying or so as to lie at full length, flat or recumbent, on the back and with the face upwards; supine. Usu. with *lie* v. *Obs.*

*a* 1100 in Napier *O. E. Glosses* 58/1 *Supinus*, upriht, astreht. 1297 R. GLOUC. (Rolls) 8635 He pulte him mid is vot & adoun vpriȝt him caste. *c* 1300 *Beket* 93 This maide ful upriȝt iswoȝe tho heo him iseȝ. 13.. *St. Cristofer* 651 in Horstm. *Altengl. Leg.* (1881) 462 In his chayere he welte vpryghte. *c* 1386 CHAUCER *Prioress' T.* 159 Ther he with throte ykoruen lay vpright. *c* 1400 *Pilgr. Sowle* (Caxton, 1483) III. vi. 54 They leyen euen vpright gapyng. *c* 1450 *Mirk's Festial* I. 172 He saue eche tre full of bryddes lying vpryȝt dede. 1539 ELYOT *Cast. Helthe* 48 Lienge vpright on the backe is to be vtterly abhorred. 1555 WATREMAN *Fardle Facions* I. vi. 88 Leaste he should giue vp the ghoste lieng vpright. 1620 VENNER *Via Recta* (1650) 303 Sleeping upright upon the back be not healthfull. 1627 DRAYTON *Nymphidia* vii, And Mab..Brestids young Folks that lye vpright.

**II. 3.** Having the chief axis or distinctive part perpendicular to a surface; set or placed in a vertical position, posture, etc.; pointing or directed upwards; not inclined or leaning over. (Cf. 1 b.)

*pred.* 1398 TREVISA *Barth. De P. R.* v. viii. (Bodl. MS.), An erbe þat growiþ in hard londe is litel and vpright. 1563 GOLDING *Cæsar* (1565) 73 Theyr foredecks wer very streight vpright, and so were also theyr sternes. 1597 GERARDE *Herball* III. 1226 Another kind of *Myrtus*..groweth vpright vnto the height of a man. 1611 BIBLE *Jer.* x. 5 They [*sc.* idols] are vpright as the palme tree. 1666 *Act* 18 & 19 *Chas. II*, c. 8 § 12 That all Lights..made into any of them [*sc.* cellars] be..made upright. 1719 DE FOE *Crusoe* I. (Globe) 128 It cost me a Month to shape it..to something like the Bottom of a Boat, that it might swim upright. 1759 R. BROWN *Compl. Farmer* 112 'Tis a grass that grows very upright. 1787 BEST *Angling* 3 Such [fish] as swim with their backs upright, or at right angles to the horizon.

*attrib.* 1420 *Searchers Verdicts* in *Surtees Misc.* (1890) 16 William of Alne hafes a upperyghte gavell. 1517 in *Archaeologia* (1883) XLVII. 312 For makyng of an upright steyer of assheler. 1570 BILLINGSLEY *Euclid* XII. prop. 18. 382, I call that an vpright cone, whose axe is perpendicular to his base. 1640 PARKINSON *Theat. Bot.* 755 This Violet groweth about a foote high or more, with hard upright stalkes. 1668 R. STEELE *Husbandm. Calling* vii. (1672) 189 No creature upon earth hath an upright countenance as man hath. 1714 YOUNG *Force Relig.* I. 290 When the winds ..descend, The fair and upright stem is forc'd to bend. 1784 COWPER *Task* I. 355 The upright shafts of..[the] tall elms. 1855 *Poultry Chron.* II. 602 Formed of upright bars of stout wire. 1870 LUBBOCK *Orig. Civiliz.* vi. (1875) 294 The custom of marking boundaries by upright stones.

*fig.* 1600 HOLLAND *Livy* 1359 During the upright and flourishing state of Rome.

**b.** In specific names of plants, etc. (see quots.).

1597 GERARDE *Herbal* I. 24 Vpright Dogs grasse or Quich grasse. *Ibid* II. 705 The vpright Pancie. 1597 [see CLAMBERER]. 1640 PARKINSON *Theat. Bot.* 755 *Viola surrecta purpurea*, Vpright Violets. *Ibid.* 1462 Vpright Woodbinde or Hony suckle. 1731 MILLER *Gard. Dict.* s.v. *Malva*, China Upright Mallow, with small white Flowers. 1760 J. LEE *Introd. Bot.* App. 319 Upright Fir Moss, *Lycopodium*. 1822 *Hortus Anglicus* II. 92 *S. Recta.* Upright Stachys. 1830 *Baxter's Libr. Agric. Knowl.* 256 *Nardus stricta*, Upright mat grass. *Ibid.*, *Agrostis stricta*, Upright bent. 1855 MISS PRATT *Flower. Pl.* VI. 105 Upright Brome-grass. 1882 *Garden* 11 March 166/2 The upright Acacia (*fastigiata*), a tree quite as erect in growth as the Lombardy Poplar.

**c.** *spec.* and *techn.* (See quots.)

*Upright pianoforte*: see PIANOFORTE.

1610 GUILLIM *Heraldry* III. xxii. 167 Fishes are borne after a diuers manner, viz. Directly, Vpright, Imbowed [etc.]. 1611 COTGR., *La montée d'vn bastiment*, th' vpper part of a building; or, a representation, or modell thereof, called the vpright plot of a building. 1638 S. FOSTER *Art of Dialling* 12 Of upright declining Plaines. Those Plaines are upright, which point up directly into the Zenith. 1704 J. HARRIS *Lex. Techn.* I. s.v., *Upright South Dyals.* See Prime Verticles. [*Prime Verticals*, or Direct Erect North or South Dyals, are those whose Planes lie parallel to the Prime Vertical Circle.] 1727 BAILEY (vol. II), *Upright* (with Heralds) is a Term used of Shell-fishes, when they stand so in a Coat of Arms. 1795 STODART in *Abridgm. Specif. Patents, Mus.* (1871) 29 An upright grand piano in the form of a bookcase. 1802 LOUD *Ibid.* 44 Improvements in the construction and action of upright pianofortes. 1875 KNIGHT *Dict. Mech.* 2684/1 *Upright*,..a term..applied to a boiler whose hight is greater than its width. *Ibid.*, *Upright*, ..a term applied to a molding-machine whose mandrel is perpendicular. 1884 *Ibid.* Suppl. 915/1 *Upright drill*, a term applied to a drill whose mandril is vertical. *Ibid.*, Upright molding machine. 1887 *Golfing* 96 A club is said to be 'upright' when its head is not at a very obtuse angle to the shaft. 1888 JACOBI *Printers' Vocab.* 150 *Upright flues*, the main flue or shaft which carries the smoke from the furnace beyond the housetop. 1896 A. J. HIPKINS *Pianoforte* 122 *Upright Grand Piano*, accurately a grand piano placed vertically upon a stand;..applied in the present day to the better kinds of the cottage piano. 1898 STAINER & BARRETT *Dict. Mus. Terms* 359/2 The upright spinet and harpsichord.

**d.** Marked by perpendicular position or attitude; characterized by vertical bearing; erect.

An OE. instance occurs in Ælfric's *Hom.* I. 276.

1634 MILTON *Comus* 52 Circe..Whose charmed Cup Whoever tasted, lost his upright shape. 1658 PHILLIPS, *Orthography*,..in Architecture or Fortification,..is taken for the upright erection of any work. 1774 GOLDSM. *Nat. Hist.* (1776) VI. 157 The anal fin..serves to keep the fish in its upright or vertical situation. 1791 MRS. RADCLIFFE *Rom. Forest* ii, It being impossible to preserve it in an upright situation. 1871 W. H. G. KINGSTON *R. Kiffin's Ward* v, Although..more than seventy, he still walked with an upright carriage. 1877 TENNYSON *Har.* III. ii. 39, I have lost Somewhat of upright stature thro' mine oath. 1878 B. TAYLOR *Deukalion* I. ii. 22 His eyes that met the sun, his upright tread.

**4.** Of persons: Erect in carriage. (Chiefly *pred.*)

*c* 1386 CHAUCER *Miller's T.* 78 She was..Long as a Mast and vprighte as a bolt. 1430–40 LYDG. *Bochas* III. 4457 Folk in ther pouerte..Ben..lusti preuid at a neede, Vpriht of lymes ther iournes for to speede. 1588 SHAKS. *L. L. L.* IV. iii. 89 O most diuine Kate,..As vpright as the Cedar. 1597 — 2 *Hen. IV*, II. ii. 91 Away, you horson vpright Rabbet. 1758 JOHNSON *Idler* No. 13 ¶ 11 When these [spinning] wheels are set upon a table.., they will..keep the girls upright. 1840 DICKENS *Barn. Rudge* x, He was..past the prime of life, yet upright in his carriage. 1865 KINGSLEY *Herew.* iii, Hereward, bleeding, but still active and upright, broke away. 1905 'GUY THORNE' *Lost Cause* i, Hibbert was an upright, soldierly-looking man.

†**b.** *Cant.* Of vagrants: Big, strong, or sturdy. Applied spec. to one of the higher classes of vagabonds. Usu. *upright-man*. *Obs.*

1561 AWDELEY *Frat. Vacab.* (1869) 4 An Vpright man is one that goeth wyth the trunchion of a staffe. 1567 HARMAN *Caveat* (1869) 31 A vpright man, the second in secte.. of these rainginge rablement of rascales. 1608 DEKKER *Belman of London* Wks. (Grosart) III. 92 This band of Vpright-men seldome march without fiue or six in a company. 1622 FLETCHER *Beggar's Bush* II. i, Come Princes of the ragged regiment,..Prig my most upright Lord. 1641 BROME *Jov. Crew* II. G 1 You,..That never yet with man did Mell; Of whom no Upright man is taster. *a* 1700 B. E. *Dict. Cant. Crew*, *Dells*,..young bucksome Wenches..[that] have not lost their Virginity, which the 'upright man' pretends to, and seizes. [1815 SCOTT *Guy M.* xxviii, Johnny Faa, the upright man.]

**5. a.** = PERPENDICULAR *a.* 1 b, RIGHT UP *a.* 1.

1596 DANETT tr. *Comines* (1614) 295 We mounted vp such a maruellous steepe and vpright hill. 1599 DALLAM in *Early Voy. Levant* (Hakl. Soc.) 12 This mountayne is verrie upryghte on bothe sides. 1861 WHYTE MELVILLE *Good for Nothing* iii, Another time do not ride so fast at an upright leap.

†**b.** Perpendicular *to* a surface. *Obs.*—[1]

1678 MOXON *Mech. Exerc.* iv. 65 Exactly even and upright to the edges of the Board.

**c.** Of a rectangular superficies: Having the height greater than the breadth.

1888 JACOBI *Printers' Vocab.*, *Upright*, a page or job set or cut to an upright size—the reverse of oblong. 1892 *Photogr. Ann.* II. 523 The remaining portion..permits of upright or oblong pictures being taken.

†**6. a.** Of shoes: That may fit either foot; straight. (Opposed to 'right' and 'left'.) *Obs. rare.*

1608 DAY *Hum. out of Br.* II. ii, A paire of vpright shooes, that gentlemen weare..now of one foote, then of another. 1621 BURTON *Anat. Mel.* II. ii. VI. i, He that weares an vpright shoe, may correct the obliquity. 1642 FULLER *Holy & Prof. St.* IV. v. 262 An upright shoe may fit both feet.

†**b.** Straight in respect of grain. *Obs.*—[1]

1776 G. SEMPLE *Building in Water* 115 The..Braces.. ought to be made of sound hearty upright Oak.

**7.** Taking place in a vertical direction; upward.

1650 ROW *Hist. Kirk* (Wodrow Soc.) 431 Everie christian should be an hawk; his course should be upward and upright, or right up. 1837 P. KEITH *Bot. Lex.* 248 An upright growth of six inches in the year. 1876 STAINER & BARRETT *Dict. Mus. Terms* 352/2 The upright action was invented for the purpose of constructing pianofortes [etc.].

**III.** *fig.* **8.** Of persons: Adhering to or following correct moral principles; of unbending integrity or rectitude; morally just, honest, or honourable.

1530 PALSGR. 328/2 Upright, indifferent bytwene party and party, and nat affectionate, *indifferent,..juste.* 1560 BIBLE 2 *Chron.* xxix. 34 The Leuites were more vpright in heart to sanctifie them selues, then the Priests. *Ibid.*, *Ps.* xi. 2. 1605 CAMDEN *Rem.* 7 That goodly, vpright, provident,..and reasonable creature. 1656 EARL MONM. tr. *Boccalini's Advts. fr. Parnass.* II. xi. (1674) 149 The uprightest and most experienced Senator. 1700 DRYDEN *Pref. Fables* Wks. (Globe) 499, I have..been an upright judge betwixt the parties in competition. *a* 1720 SEWEL *Hist. Quakers* (1795) I. II. 142 They were found upright in their dealing. 1742 POPE *Dunc.* IV. 208 So upright Quakers please both Man and God. 1828 LYTTON *Pelham* III. xiv, I have always thought him the most upright and honourable of men. 1856 FROUDE *Hist. Eng.* (1858) I. ii. 173 [He] bore through England the reputation of an upright and virtuous king. 1904 *Verney Mem.* II. 296 She had been upright in her life.

*absol.* 1560 BIBLE *Prov.* xxviii. 10 The vpright shal inherit good things. — *Ps.* vii. 10 God..preserueth the vpright in heart. **1786** *Paraphrases Ch. Scotland* xxi. 1 Th' upright in heart alone have hope.

**b.** Of the mind, qualities, actions, etc.: Marked or characterized by integrity or probity; having conformity or accordance with moral rectitude.

**1538** STARKEY *England* I. ii. 43 Settyng themselfe in relygyouse housys, ther quyetly to serue God and kepe theyr myndys vpryght. **1549** COVERDALE, etc. *Erasm. Par.* 1 *Cor.* 53 That we both may..haue therwith an vpryght harte to God. **1560** BIBLE *Ps.* xxxvii. 14 To slay suche as be of vpright conuersation. **1579** W. WILKINSON *Confut. Fam. Love* B ij, That we might serve..God..with an vpright righteousnes and holynes. **1623** *Extr. Aberd. Reg.* (1848) II. 388 They sall giwe wnto thame thair trew and upricht counsall whan the same salbe askit. **1667** MILTON *P. L.* I. 18 Thou, O Spirit, that dost prefer..th' upright heart and pure. **1700** T. BROWN *Amusem. Ser. & Com.* 31 Have you any Use in your Country for Upright Honesty? *a* **1721** PRIOR *Vicar of Bray & More* Wks. 1907 II. 259 An upright and unprejudiced Conscience. **1781** COWPER *Conversat.* 682 Those hearts should be reclaim'd, renew'd, upright. **1782** MISS BURNEY *Cecilia* VIII. vi, Now I see the fair promise of his upright youth. **1818** CRUISE *Digest* (ed. 2) II. 458 Fair or upright dealing. **1844** H. H. WILSON *Brit. India* III. 473 The diligent and upright discharge of the duties. **1904** *Verney Mem.* I. 415 His upright chivalrous conduct.

*Comb.* **1654** ALLEN in Thurloe *St. Papers* (1742) II. 214 The honour God hath put uppon him,..I mean that of upright-heartedness to the Lord. **1818** SCOTT *Hrt. Midl.* xliii, The best and most upright-minded men. **1836** [MRS. CHEAP] *Going to Service* xii. 140 An upright-minded girl.

†**9. a.** *Sc.* True; undoubted; rightful; = RIGHT *a.* 16. *Obs.*—[1]

*c* **1480** HENRYSON *Cock & Fox* xi, 3e ar 3our Fatheris Sone and air vpricht.

†**b.** In good condition; in proper order; correct.

**1526** SKELTON *Magnif.* 651 Fansy and I, we twayne,..counterfeted our names we haue, Craftely all thynges vpryght to saue. **1557** TUSSER *Husb.* (1878) 232 Good husbandes that laye, to saue all things vpright: for Tumbrels and cartes, haue a shed redy dight. **1630** SHERLEY in Bradford *Plymouth Plantation* (1856) 270 If it should please God ye one should faile.., yet ye other would keepe both recconings, and things upright.

†**c.** Plain; straightforward; unambiguous. *Obs.*

**1587** HARRISON *Descr. Brit.* I. i. in *Holinshed* I. 2/1 My purpose is to..deliuer such things as I intreat of in distinct and vpright order. **1607** DEKKER *Knt.'s Conjur.* (1842) 56 He had bin in vpright tearmes an vsurer.

**10. a.** Stable, equable. **b.** *dial.* Sound in respect of health.

**1551** ROBINSON tr. *More's Utopia* II. M iij b, The quiete and vpright state of the bodye. **1905** *Eng. Dial. Dict.* VI. 327/2 My horse is quite upright.

**B.** *sb.* †**1.** A vertical front, face, or plane. *Obs.*

**1563** SHUTE *Archit.* C iv b, This is the foundacion through the whiche we knowe and finde all the measures and vprightes belonging to the pillor. **1663** GERBIER *Counsel* 12 Shun too much carved Ornaments on that upright. *Ibid.* 15 Contracting the Balconies within the upright of a Column. **1679** MOXON *Mech. Exerc.* viii. 141 You design the Balcony to project beyond the Upright of the Front. **1703** [R. NEVE] *City & C. Purchaser* 11 The springing of the Arch is skew'd back from the upright of the Jambs. **1726** LEONI *Alberti's Archit.* I. 55 The vacuities..left between the back of the sweep of the Arch, and the upright of the Wall it is turn'd from,..shou'd be fill'd up.

†**b.** = ELEVATION 11, ORTHOGRAPHY 2 b. *Obs.*

**1603** B. JONSON *K. Jas.'s Entertain.* ¶ 1 The scene presented it selfe in a square and flat vpright like to the side of a citty. **1620-50** I. JONES *Stone-Heng* (1655) 56 The groundplot, with the uprights, and profyle of the whole work. *Ibid.* 61 The upright of the work, as when entire. **1712** J. JAMES tr. *Le Blond's Gardening* 216 You may judge by the Upright, of the handsome Effect this Cascade would make. **1782** H. WALPOLE *Vertue's Anecd. Paint.* (ed. 3) I. Suppl. T 1, There are not many uprights, but several ground plans of some of the palaces. **1842** GWILT *Archit.* Gloss. 1049 *Upright*..; a term rarely used.

†**c.** A very steep declivity. Cf. PERPENDICULAR *sb.* 2. *Obs.*—[1]

**1712** HENLEY tr. *Montfaucon's Antiq. Italy* vii. 108 The Lake runs..thro' the Mountain, till it comes to an upright, where there is a mighty Fall.

**2.** An upright or vertical position; the perpendicular.

**1683** MOXON *Mech. Exerc., Printing* xix. 297 So that the Tympan may stand..towards an upright. **1851** LAXTON *Builder's Price Bk.* 133 Plasterer's Work...Dubbing out..not to be allowed unless the work is out of an upright. **1883** in Elworthy *W. Somerset Word-bk.* (1888) 791 Thick there wall's a little bit out of an upright. **1905** *Times* 30 Sept. 8/1 The mullion was much out of upright, and had..an iron stay.

**b.** That which lies immediately above a thing.

**1768** BLACKSTONE *Comm.* III. 217 Every man may do what he pleases upon the upright or perpendicular of his own soil.

**3.** Something set or standing upright, erect, or vertical; a perpendicular stone, post, part, etc.

In frequent use from *c* 1790.

**1742** *De Foe's Tour Gt. Brit.* (ed. 3) I. 259 By which means the Uprights [of Stonehenge] are less liable to fall or swerve. **1776** G. SEMPLE *Building in Water* 131 The upright of c. has a square Hole in the upper End of it. **1786** ABERCROMBIE *Gard. Assist.* 54 Uprights or growing stakes. **1794** *Rigging & Seamanship* 140 Vessels in harbour..have uprights [for awnings]. **1794** BURNS *Caledonia* 46 Rectangle-triangle the figure we'll choose, The upright is Chance, and old Time is the base. **1845** J. SAUNDERS *Cabinet Pict. Eng. Life* 19 A beam laid cross-wise upon two uprights. **1854** AINSWORTH *Flitch of Bacon* IV. iii, A magnificent staircase of many turnings...The uprights on each landing were decorated with rampant nondescripts. **1883** MISS BROUGHTON *Belinda* III. iii, One of the spiked iron uprights of the gate. **1886** FURNIVALL in Shaks. *Ven. & Ad.* (1st Qo. facsimile) p. xix, 'Hooke-nosoe', should be 'hook-nosde'; the upright of the d unluckily failed to print.

**b.** *spec.* One of the vertical members of a framing, etc.

*a* **1700** EVELYN *Diary* 27 Aug. 1666, We plumb'd the uprights in several places. **1791** SMEATON *Edystone L.* § 34 The outside timbers (since called the uprights) were seventy-two in number). **1807** PIKE *Sources Mississ.* I. (1810) App. 46 Part of the houses are framed, and..there are small logs let into mortises made in the uprights. **1851** RUSKIN *Stones Ven.* (1874) I. i. 18 Timbers attached to uprights on the top of the nave pillars. **1870** MORRIS *Earthly Par.* III. IV. 61 The greasy blackened wood Of the hall's uprights.

**c.** (See quots.)

**1856** 'STONEHENGE' *Brit. Rur. Sports* I. x. 82/2 The Spire [has] a brow antler, and half-developed beam, called *uprights*; a Staggart, brow, tray, and uprights. **1878** in Elworthy *W. Somerset Word-bk.* 792 A male deer of one year old has..one straight horn each side only, which we term his *upright*.

**d.** An upright pianoforte (see PIANOFORTE).

**1860** *Builder* 15 Sept. 588/1 The best grands and uprights of the present day. **1894** S. FISKE *Holiday Stories* (1900) 118 The baby grands nestled between the larger instruments. The uprights looked..out of place.

**e.** A kind of fly-hook.

**1878** W. NASH *Oregon* vi. 135 The lawyer put on a 'black palmer' and a 'blue upright'. **1892** *Daily News* 14 April 3/1 The comparatively large uprights and browns are as fatal as ever to the smallest trout.

**4.** An upright stratum; = ARRECT *sb.*

**1811** PINKERTON *Petral.* II. 158 A mountain of a most regular structure; the arrects, or uprights, having their planes parallel to its great axis.

**5.** *slang.* (See quot.)

**1796** *Sporting Mag.* VIII. 107 [They] drank 57 quarts of *upright*, viz. a quart of beer with a quartern of gin in it.

**U·pright,** *adv.* [f. prec. Cf. OE. *uprihte.*]

**1.** = UPRIGHTLY *adv.* 1.

**1509** HAWES *Conv. Swearers* ix, I sende you gretynge..& grace Right wel to gouern vpright your dominion. **1577** B. GOOGE *Heresbach's Husb.* I. (1586) 2 All seeke to lyue, but none to liue upryght. **1591** in *10th Rep. Hist. MSS. Comm.* App. I. 76 That thay may leif togidder in luif, upricht to God. **1624** J. DAVIES *Ps.* xiv, Not one doth good, not one doth well, vpright.

†**b.** In a just manner; correctly. *Obs.*—[1]

**1601** HOLLAND *Pliny* II. 585 In truth, if we will consider this pageant upright, we must needs confesse [etc.].

**2.** In a vertical direction; vertically upwards.

**1590** WEBBE *Trav.* (Arb.) 22 Ye wonderfull..swelling of the water vpright..to ye height of a huge mountaine. **1591** J. DEE *Diary* (Camden) 38 Wownded on his hed by his own wanton throwing of a brik-bat upright, and not well avoyding the fall of it. **1605** SHAKS. *Lear* IV. vi. 27 For all beneath the Moone would I not leape vpright. **1664** BUTLER *Hud.* II. III. 437 That Cannon-Ball,..shot in th' Air point-blank, upright. **1715** DESAGULIERS *Fires Impr.* 12 As for the Rays that go upright, nothing can hinder them from getting out at top of the Chimney. **1736** GRAY *Statius* I. 45 Nor tempts he yet the plain, but hurl'd upright, Emits the mass.

*Comb.* **1842** LOUDON *Suburban Hort.* 352 In the case of upright-grown plants. *Ibid.* 549 The pear is grafted or budded on stocks raised..from any strong upright-growing kind.

**3.** *dial.* Independently; on one's own means.

**1823** E. MOOR *Suffolk Words* 460 A live upright on 'a's forten. **1896** *Westm. Gaz.* 28 April 2/1, I shall be able to retire and 'live upright', as the butler said.

**U·pright,** *v.* Also 5 *Sc.* vp-, wpricht. [f. as prec. Cf. MDu. *uprichten* (Du. *oprigten*), Flem. (Kilian) *oprechten*, OHG. (MHG.) *ûfrihten* (G. *aufrichten*).]

**1.** *trans.* To raise to an upright or vertical position; to erect. Also *fig.* and in fig. context.

*a* **1340** HAMPOLE *Psalter* cxii. 6 He vprightis þe pore out of þe fen of fleyssly lust. *Ibid.* cxlv. 7 Lord vprightys þe smytyn down. **1590** SIR J. SMYTH *Disc. Weapons* 30 They all vpright their piques. **1591** — *Instruct.* (1595) 22 Then are they to saie to the first ranke Vpright your piques. **1609** DANIEL *Civ. Wars* VII. lxxii, It rests within your iudgements, to vp-right..the Land. **1890** *Standard* 5 April 6/3, I..assisted to upright the boat, which was baled out. **1893** *Westm. Gaz.* 16 Sept. 4/1 As soon as he had uprighted his machine [= bicycle].

†**2.** *Sc.* To make reparation to or for; to compensate. *Obs.*

**1463** *Extr. Aberd. Reg.* (1844) I. 26 The forsaide Thomas til sek til his warande gif he hafe ony til vpricht him. **1480** *Ibid.* 411 That the saids persons acht til wpricht and assith him for hir. **1492** *Ibid.* 420 To amende and vpricht the skaitht done.

†**Uprighten,** *v. Obs.* [f. prec. + -EN[5].] *trans.* = prec. 1.

**1617** AINSWORTH *Annot. Ps.* cxlv. 14 Iehovah upholdeth all that fall: and up-righteneth, all that are crooked.

**Upri·ghteously,** *adv. rare*—[1]. [Cf. next.] In an upright manner.

**1603** SHAKS. *Meas. for M.* III. i. 205 You may most vprighteously do a poor wronged Lady a merited benefit.

**Upri·ghteousness.** [Cf. UPRIGHT *a.* and RIGHTEOUSNESS.] The quality of being upright.

**1549** LATIMER *4th Serm. bef. Edw. VI* (Arb.) 110 The vpryghteousnes of hys cause. **1550** THOMAS *Ital. Dict.*, *Dirittura*, vprightwisenesse. **1570** *Satir. Poems Reform.* x. 349 Not only lufit he vprychteousnes, Bot als he hatit vice. **1623** COCKERAM II, *Vprighteousnes*, Sinceritie. **1904** *Daily News* 26 Aug. 6 Respectability and conscious uprighteousness oozing from his every pore.

**U·prighting,** *vbl. sb.* [f. UPRIGHT *v.*] The action of making upright; *spec.* the process of ensuring uprightness of position. Also *attrib.*

**1884** F. J. BRITTEN *Watch & Clockm.* 153 Bad pivots, bad uprighting,..are responsible for much of the trouble experienced in position timing. *Ibid.* 279 An uprighting tool.

**U·prightish,** *a. rare.* [f. UPRIGHT *a.* + -ISH [1].] Somewhat upright.

**1806** J. GALPINE *Brit. Bot.* 112 Stems uprightish:..calyx-teeth setaceous, elongated.

**U·prightly,** *adv.* [f. as prec. + -LY [2].]

**1.** In a just or upright manner; with strict observance of justice, honesty, or rectitude; sincerely, justly. (Freq. *c* 1560–*c* 1590.)

**1549** COVERDALE, etc. *Erasm. Par. Acts* xxiii. 75 Bearyng my selfe vpryghtely and with a good conscience. **1583** STUBBES *Anat. Abus.* II. (1882) 32 In times past when men dealt vprightly, and in the feare of God. **1624** BEDELL *Lett.* x. 129 Iudge now vprightly if this be indifferent dealing. **1649** DAVENANT *Love & Hon.* IV. iii. 27 If you uprightly love her and the prince. **1668** DRYDEN *Dram. Poesy* Ess. (ed. Ker) I. 89 Betwixt the extremes of admiration and malice, 'tis hard to judge uprightly of the living. **1755** JOHNSON, *Honestly*,..uprightly; justly. **1838** ARNOLD *Hist. Rome* I. 296 The first decemvirs..governed uprightly and well. **1847** S. AUSTIN *Ranke's Hist. Ref.* III. 39 A man who would rule uprightly. **1855** MACAULAY *Hist. Eng.* xiv. III. 454 He was sure, he said, that they had acted uprightly.

†**b.** Candidly; straightforwardly. *Obs.*

**1565** *Reg. Privy Council Scot.* I. 340 To declair planelie and uprychtlie the wordis and brute..of the said allegeit conspiracie. **1579** E. K. *Gloss. to Spenser's Sheph. Cal.* Aug. 53 By Perigot who is meant, I can not vprightly say. **1598** J. MELVILL *Diary* (Wodrow Soc.) 439 All sic as stud uprightlie for the established discipline and fredome of the Kirk. **1620** BP. ANDREWES *Serm.* (1629) 130 Besides (to speake vprightly) one might..complaine of the privatenesse of the Angells appearing. **1630** *R. Johnson's Kingd. & Commw.* 13 To speak uprightly, from these Nations..have tortures of more exquisite device taken their originals.

**2.** In an upright position; vertically, perpendicularly. Also *fig.* and in fig. context.

**1601** HOLLAND *Pliny* I. 159 He..shall live in this world uprightly and in even ballance, without enclining more to one side, than unto another. **1639** J. TAYLOR (Water P.) *Part Summers Trav.* 46 You were never known to be drunke, and though you never walke uprightly, yet you never stumbled. *a* **1718** PARNELL *Poems* (1758) 9 The waters were afraid;..In heaps uprightly plac'd they learn to stand. **1751** HARRIS *Hermes* I. v. (1765) 84 These Pronouns..assumed a peculiar Accent of their own, which gave them the name of ὀρθοτονούμεναι, or Pronouns uprightly accented. **1826** in A. C. Hutchinson *Pract. Obs. Surg.* (ed. 2) 173 But I have watched him,—have seen him..walk..as uprightly as you can walk. **1868** LOCKYER *Elem. Astron.* § 168 We found that the Sun was not floating uprightly in our sea, the plane of the ecliptic.

**U·prightness.** [f. as prec. + -NESS.]

**1.** The state or condition of being sincere, honest, or just; equity or justness in respect of principle or practice; upright quality or conduct; moral integrity or rectitude.

**1541** ELYOT *Image Gov.* xii. 22 He loued syncerytie, vulgarly called vprightnesse. **1571** *Act* 13 *Eliz.* c. 11 § 2 Any..Subjectes using uprychtnes and trueth in the barrelling of such Fishe. **1591** SAVILE *Tacitus, Agricola* 242 Agricola..caryed himselfe easily with great vprightnes and iustice. **1628** WITHER *Brit. Rememb.* VII. 1553 They of my uprightnesse judge amisse. **1668** OWEN *Indwelling Sin* vi. 72 Accordingly his design is to walk before God, and his frame is sincerity and uprightness therein. **1736** BUTLER *Anal.* I. v. 92 Those who preserve their Uprightness..raise themselves to a more secure State of Virtue. **1766** AMORY *Buncle* (1770) III. 210 A canted uprightness and seeming piety. **1820** SHELLEY *Liberty* vii, Many a deed of terrible uprightness By thy sweet love was sanctified. **1855** MACAULAY *Hist. Eng.* xi. III. 60 Veracity, uprightness, and manly boldness were then, as now, qualities eminently English. **1879** R. K. DOUGLAS *Confucianism* iii. 72 The Sage..maintains a perfect uprightness and pursues the heavenly way without the slightest deflection.

**b.** Const. *of* (conduct, etc.).

**1560** BIBLE 1 *Kings* iii. 6 He walked..in vprightnes of heart with thee. **1576** FLEMING *Panopl. Epist.* 22 Modestie of life and uprightnesse of manners. **1592** CHETTLE *Kind-harts Dr.* A 4, Diuers of worship haue reported his vprightnes of dealing. **1644** MILTON *Divorce* (ed. 2) II. iv, The uprightnesse of his ways. **1651** HOBBES *Leviath.* II. xxvii. 152 Cleared by the Uprightnesse of his own Intention. **1775** ADAIR *Amer. Ind.* Ded., The uprightness of my intentions as to the information here given. **1795** *Gentl. Mag.* 543/1 Integrity of heart and uprightness of intention. **1831** SIR J. SINCLAIR *Corr.*, etc. II. 393 [He] was distinguished by..great uprightness of conduct.

**2.** The state or character of being erect, vertical, or upright; erect or vertical attitude; erectness.

**1645** WALLER *To Chloris* Poems 180 So the fayre tree..In stormes from that uprightnesse swerves. **1706** STEVENS *Span. Dict.*, *Derechura*, straightness, uprightness. **1782** V. KNOX *Ess.* lxxix. (1819) II. 114 The uprightness of the pilaster. *c* **1815** JANE AUSTEN *Persuasion* vi, Mrs. Croft..had a squareness, uprightness, and vigour of form. **1853** KANE *Grinnell Exp.* xix. (1856) 143 The poor things had lost their uprightness. **1889** *Pall Mall G.* 9 Mar. 7/1 The rigid uprightness of his collars.

†**Uprights,** *adv. Obs.* [f. UPRIGHT *adv.* + -S.]

**1.** In an upright position; perpendicularly.

*c* **1350** *Will. Palerne* 1789 Two white beres..went on alle four.., & whan þei wery were þei went vp-ri3tes. **1390** GOWER *Conf.* I. 140 Than scholde he stonde ayein uprihtes. *c* **1400** MAUNDEV. (Roxb.) xxxi. 143 Þai..gase on fete nerehand vprightes. *c* **1410** *Master of Game* (MS. Digby 182) xii, Men shull take suche an Hounde and holde hym faste and vpreghtes [*v.r.* fast vpry3tes].

**2.** Upon one's back and with the face upwards.

*c* **1420** LYDG. *Sege Thebes* 3911 Many on lay slayen at the gate, Gapyng vprightys. *Ibid.* 4481 Thorgh-girt with many wounde..[they lay] stark vpri3tes.

Upripe, etc.: see UP- 4-7.

**Upri·sal.** [UP- 2.] Uprising.
1871 *Daily News* 7 March, The danger of a sudden uprisal of the north-eastern quarters of Paris. 1889 HERRING & ROSS *Irish Cousin* I. xiv, The sudden uprisal..of an abnormally lengthy dachshund.

**Uprise** (*v*prəi·z, *v*·prəiz), *sb.* [UP- 2. Cf. ON. *upprisa* (MSw. *uprisa*, Sw. *uppresa*), rising up, resurrection.]

†**1.** Resurrection. *Obs.*
*a* 1300 *Cursor M.* 1479 Wit þair vpris fra ded to lijf. *Ibid.* 18571 Þan bigan þai to bede þam hightes For to lei of his vp-rise.

**2. a.** Rising (of the sun, etc.); dawn (of day).
1588 SHAKS. *Tit. A.* III. i. 159 A Larke, That giues sweet tydings of the Sunnes vprise. 1600 S. NICHOLSON *Acolastus' After-witte* A 4, Faire Queene Aurora,..Whose blithsome vp-rise makes Nights prisoners blest. 1635 HEYWOOD *Hierarchy* III. Comm. 183 Because the Sunne in his mornings vprise looketh red and blushing. 1674 J. W[RIGHT] *Seneca's Thyestes* 71 Father of gods and men, at whose Uprise Night doth her beauty loose. 1794 SOUTHEY *Elinor* 11 When in better years poor Elinor Gazed on thy glad uprise with eye undimm'd By guilt. 1818 SHELLEY *Eugan. Hills* 73 The pæan With which the legioned rooks did hail The sun's uprise majestical. *a* 1851 MOIR *Poems, Mine Own* i, Alike at orient day's uprise, And pensive shut of night.

†**b.** The act of rising from bed. *Obs.*
1633 P. FLETCHER *Purple Isl.* XII. iv, Musick and base flattering tongues, Which wait to first-salute my Lords uprise.

**c.** The act of rising to a higher level; ascent.
1690 C. NESSE *O. & N. Test.* I. 126 The dreadful downfal, as well as up-rise, of the waters. 1817 SHELLEY *Rev. Islam* XII. xvi, A blood-red gleam Burst upwards...I heard the mighty sound Of its uprise. 1882 GEIKIE *Text-bk. Geol.* VI. v. 900 An intermittent uprise of the land.

**d.** The beginning of an ascent; an ascending shaft in a mine.
1875 BROWNING *Aristophanes' Apol.* 334 Now bound For Dorion, at the uprise..Of Mount Pangaios. 1877 RAYMOND *Statist. Mines & Mining* 174 Fifty feet in from the mouth of the tunnel an uprise was made.

**3. a.** Ascent to power or dignity; rise to wealth or importance.
1810 JANE PORTER *Scot. Chiefs* x, At the fall of Dunbar.. he again founded his uprise on the ruins of his country. 1877 *N.W. Linc. Gloss.* 265 The uprise o' that family was th' inclosures.

**b.** The act of coming into existence or notice; origination.
1817 SHELLEY *Rev. Islam* VII. ii, Awakened from that dreamy mood By Liberty's uprise. 1844 THACKERAY *Wks.* (1886) XXIII. 205 The young painters..whose uprise this Magazine and this critic were the first to hail. 1862 F. HALL *Hindu Philos. Syst.* 241 The uprise of a new..affection of the internal organ. 1875 WHITNEY *Life Lang.* vi. 107 The uprise of the class of prepositions.

**Uprise** (*v*prəi·z), *v.* [UP- 4. Cf. WFris. *oprize*, MDu. *oprisen* (Du. *oprijzen*), MLG. *uprisen* (LG. *uprîsen*), MHG. *ûfrîsen*.]

**1.** *intr.* To rise to one's feet; to assume a standing posture.
*a* 1300 *Cursor M.* 2733 Quen þai war rest wel vp-ras þai. 13.. *E. E. Allit. P.* C. 378 He radly vp-ros & ran fro his chayer. *c* 1385 CHAUCER *L. G. W.* 1743 *Lucrece*, She anoon vp roos with blysful chere And kyssed hym. 1448–9 METHAM *Amoryus & Cl.* 1867 Hole and sound, with-owte wemme off yowre woundys, Nowe vp-ryse. ? *a* 1550 *Freiris of Berwik* 341 (*Maitland Folio*), Þan the freyr uprais, And tuk his buik and to the flure he gayis. 1590 SPENSER *F. Q.* I. iv. 16 Suddein vpriseth from her stately place The royall Dame. 1715 POPE *Iliad* I. 95 Uprising slow, the venerable sage Thus spoke the prudence and the fears of age. *a* 1800 COWPER *Odyssey* (ed. 2) xxiv. 496 Soon as on full seats The whole assembled senate sat, uprose Eupithes first. 1858 MERIVALE *Rom. Emp.* liii. VI. 216 Then uprose Sabinus to advance his charges. 1870 BRYANT *Iliad* I. I. 14 Now uprose Nestor, the master of persuasive speech.
*fig.* *a* 1300 *E. E. Psalter* xxvi. 6 If vprise ogaine me fight, In þat sal i hope in might. 1812 BYRON *Ch. Har.* I. lxxxi, Ere War uprose in his volcanic rage. 1837 *Mag. Nat. Hist.* I. 134 The whole neighbourhood uprose in arms, till every bird of them was killed.

**b.** To rise from bed.
13.. *Seuyn Sages* (W.) 3181 Opon the morn the knyght vprase. *c* 1386 CHAUCER *Reeve's T.* 329 Aleyn vprist and thoughte, er þat it dawe I wol go crepen In by my felawe. 1503 DUNBAR *Thistle & Rose* 29 Quhairto..sall I vprys at morrow? 1513 BRADSHAW *St. Werburge* I. 2544 She wolde vpryse at an houre conuenyent. 1526–*a* 1628 [see DOWN-LIE *v.*]. 1725 POPE *Odyss.* VI. 59 Uprose the virgin with the morning light. 1878 *Masque Poets* 95 It was a wicked Nephew bold Who uprose in the night.

**2.** Of the sun: To rise.
The Chaucerian *uprist* (= upriseth) has by archaizing writers been taken as a past tense.
*c* 1350 *Will. Palerne* 1791 Al þat long ni͡ȝt, til it dawed to day & sunne to vp-rise. *c* 1374 CHAUCER *Compl. Mars* 4 For when the sunne vprist then wol they sprede. 1471 RIPLEY *Comp. Alch.* II. xii. in Ashm. (1652) 138 For there the Son wyth Day-lyght doth upryse In Somer. 1513 DOUGLAS *Æneid* VII. iii. 56 First as the son wprysis. 1729 T. COOKE *Tales*, etc. 136 The Critic took his Way, Slow pacing, homeward, and uprose the Day. 1798 COLERIDGE *Anc. Mar.* II. iv, Nor dim nor red,..The glorious Sun uprist. 1818 MILMAN *Samor* x. 417 The sun uprising sees the dusk night fled Already from tall Pendle. 1880 W. S. BLUNT *Love Sonn. Proteus* ci, Ere yet the sun uprist.

**3.** To rise from the dead.
*a* 1300 *Cursor M.* 203 How he vprais, how he upstey, Many man on stod and sey. *c* 1340 HAMPOLE *Pr. Consc.* 5026 Alle þat er gude þan and rightwyse, Þat sal be saue, sal first upryse. *c* 1440 *York Myst.* xxxvii. 31, I schall..on the thirde day ryght vprise. 1553 POYNET *Short Catech.* 21 b, The third daye after, he vprose agayne, a lyue in bodye also. 1567 *Gude & Godlie B.* (S.T.S.) 78 Christ maid us Iust quhen he vprais. 1879 ARNOLD *Light of Asia* I. 3 The dead that are to live, the live who die, Uprise, and hear, and hope!

**b.** To come from the underworld.
? *a* 1550 *Freiris Berwik* 524 (Bann. MS.), I coniure the, That thow vprys and sone to me appeir. *a* 1743 SAVAGE *On False Historians* 32 The devil..The sorcerer us'd to raise, the parson lay, When Echard wav'd his pen,..The parson conjur'd, and the fiend uprose. 1816 SHELLEY *Dæmon* II. 21 Erebus With all its banded fiends shall not uprise To overwhelm..The dauntless.

**4.** To rise or ascend to a higher level; to rise into view.
*a* 1300 *Cursor M.* 21074 Þat erth..Men seis vprisand fra þe grund. 13.. *Anticrist* 547 Þe dals [sal] uprise, þe fells dunfalle. *c* 1400 *Secreta Secret., Gov. Lordsh.* 89 For þou seez it [*sc.* an enchanted stone] vprys vpon waterys whenne þay rynne with þe wyndes. 1842 TENNYSON *Vis. Sin* 208 Once more Uprose the mystic mountain range. 1858 LONGF. *M. Standish* v. I As the mists uprose from the meadows. 1867 TENNYSON *Victim* 71 The rites prepared, the victim bared, The knife uprising toward the blow.
*fig.* *a* 1300 *Cursor M.* 17474 All fals sal far þat ilk wise, And euer sal rightwisnes vprise. 1513 DOUGLAS *Æneid* X. ix. 44 Be that gude beleif quhilk thou has eyk Of Ascanyvs vprysyng to estait. 1568 CHARTERIS *Pref. to Lyndesay's Wks.* (1871) 13* Cum, all degreis, in Lurdanerie quha lyis,.. And lerne in vertew how for to vpryis!

**b.** To become erect.
1796 SCOTT *Wild Huntsman* xliv, Uprose the Wildgrave's bristling hair. 1827 PRAED *Red Fisherman* 77 'Twas a sight to make the hair uprise.

**5.** To ascend as a sound.
1503 DUNBAR *Thistle & Rose* 176 The commoun voce vprais of birdis small. 1838 DICKENS *O. Twist* l, The crowd grew light with uncovered heads; and again the shout uprose. 1850 BLACKIE *Æschylus* I. 235 How shall my hymn uprise to bless thee? 1890 [see HALE *sb.*[4] 1].

**6.** To come into existence.
1471 RIPLEY *Comp. Alch.* v. viii. (MS. Ashm. 1445), So ther shulde no frute be vprysinge. 1562 WINȜET *Cert. Tractatis* Wks. (S.T.S.) I. 25, I being drery and dolorus for the schisme..in Godis Kirk, and apperand temporal calamiteis to vpryse tharthrou. 1584 SOUTHWELL *Wks.* (1828) II. 150 So infinite [are] the sects..into which it hath spread, besides new ones daily uprising. 1820 SHELLEY *Prometh. Unb.* I. 82, I had clothed, since Earth uprose, Its wastes in colours not their own. 1880 *Libr. Univ. Knowl.* IX. 300 But now uprise some marvelous phenomena.

**Upri·sen,** *pa. pple.* and *ppl. a.* [UP- 5. Cf. ON. *upprisinn* and prec.] Risen up; arisen.
13.. *Cursor M.* 17384 (Gött.), Fra dede to lijf vp-resen es he. *a* 1400 *Sir Perc.* 977 Up-resyne es a sowdane, Alle hir landes hase he tane. 1446 LYDG. *Nightingale* 401 Hell despoiled, & slayn oure mortall foo, Oure lord vpryse with palme of hye victorie. 1600 FAIRFAX *Tasso* XII. xxxv, These flames vprisen to forestall my way, Perchance more terrour far than danger bring. 1621 BP. MOUNTAGU *Diatribæ* 283 Those new vp-risen brethren *Roseæ Crucis*. 1682 BUNYAN *Holy War* (1905) 345 He is up-risen, and is departed from them. 1849 ROCK *Ch. of Fathers* I. ii. 127 Christ's Body is not only up-risen, but has passed into an incorruptible..state.

**Upri·ser.** (UP- 8.) 1656 [S. HOLLAND] *Don Zara* III. ii. 144 *marg.*, The number of Inhabitants, up-risers and down-lyers in this mighty City. 1823 *Blackw. Mag.* XIV. 692 The uprisers have not mixed wisdom with their cry for freedom.

**Upri·sing,** *vbl. sb.* [UP- 7.]

**1.** The action of rising from death or from the grave; resurrection. Now *rare.*
*c* 1250 *Creed* in Maskell *Mon. Rit.* (1882) III. 251 Hy troue ..forȝifnes of sinnes, uprisinge of fleyes. *c* 1290 *S. Eng. Leg.* I. 416/453 A-sonenday,..Þe day of mine oprisingue. 1297 R. GLOUC. (Rolls) 8530 Bi þe vprisinge of god Robelin me ssal ise..stalwarde kniȝt be. 1340 *Ayenb.* 227 Ine þe oprisinge ne ssel by non spousynge. *c* 1400 *Pepysian Gosp. Harmony* (1922) 73 Þo asked Jesus ȝif þat sche leued it þat he was vprising and lyf. *c* 1440 *Alph. Tales* 195 Ane heresye þat þan began at rise in þaim þat trustid not in vprysyng of flessh. *c* 1450 *Cov. Myst.* (Shaks. Soc.) 371 Of his uprysyng he dede us lere Whan he walkyd with us in fere. *c* 1550 CHEKE *Matt.* xxii. 30 In ye vprising noyer schal men mari nor women be maried. *c* 1555 HARPSFIELD *Divorce Hen. VIII* (Camden) 38 By the death and uprising of Christ. 1648 HERRICK *Hesper.*, '*Here down*' 11 At my up-rising next, I shall..thank ye all. 1852 ROCK *Ch. of Fathers* I. ix. III. 322 The life, the death, the uprising of her divine Son.

**2. a.** The action of rising from bed.
*a* 1300 *K. Horn* 844 Horn..cam to þe kinge At his vprisinge. *c* 1430 *Syr Gener.* (Roxb.) 574 Ful erly in the morning The king made his vprising. 1518 H. WATSON *Hist. Oliver of Castile* (Roxb.) D 4 b, Erly in y^e mornynge his seruauntes came to his chambre for to be at his vprysynge. 1578 H. WOTTON *Courtlie Controv.* 240 Hee..prayed them to goe vnto the kings vprising, and giue hym good morrowe. *a* 1628 PRESTON *New Cov.* (1630) 80 How many there are at vprising and down-lying from day to day. 1675 HAN. WOOLLEY *Gentlew. Comp.* 211 You ought..to..keep due hours for their [*sc.* children's] up-rising and going to bed. 1827 KEBLE *Chr. Y., Morning* vi, New every morning is the love Our wakening and uprising prove. 1863 GEO. ELIOT *Romola* I. Introd. 2 The faint light [of dawn]..fell..on the hasty uprising of the hard-handed labourer.

**b.** The action of rising from a sitting, kneeling, or recumbent posture.
1521 CLERK in Ellis *Orig. Lett.* Ser. III. I. 265 The Master of the ceremonyes..causyd me to kysse his foott, and att myn vprising..his Holynes toke me by the sholders. 1535 COVERDALE *Ps.* cxxxviii. 2 Thou knowest my downe syttinge & my vprisynge. 1865 *Sat. Rev.* 5 Aug. 177 The down-sittings and uprisings of each day. 1893 A. S. ECCLES *Sciatica* 78 Uprising from the couch is performed by the attendant grasping the patient's extended hands.

†**c.** *spec.* The rising of a woman after confinement. *Obs.*
1611 COTGR., *Relevailles d'une femme*, th' vprising, or vp-sitting, also the Churching, of a woman. *a* 1693 URQUHART *Rabelais* III. xli. 336 An uprising or Women Churching Treatment. [1899 *N. & Q.* 9th Ser. III. 212 Child-Bed pew, another name for this was 'uprising seat'.]

**3.** The action of rising after a fall. Also *fig.*
*a* 1300 *Cursor M.* 11363 Þis child..Sal be to fel men in dun fall, And to fell in vprising. *c* 1330 *Arth. & Merl.* 9906 (Kölbing), Often þai made dounfalleing, & when þai mi͡ȝt, vpriseing. *a* 1375 *Cursor M.* 25821 (Fairf.), Squa-gate for þaire wanhoping þai falle wiþ-outin vprising. *a* 1555 LATIMER in Foxe *A. & M.* (1563) 1310/1 For remembraunce of that fal and vprisyng kepeth vs in our fal from dispairing.

**4.** The rising of the sun; †also (quot. 1535), the quarter in which the sun rises.
*c* 1330 *Arth. & Merl.* 3865 (Kölbing), In þe sonnes vpriseing Bigan, certes, þis rideing. *c* 1400 *Three Kings Cologne* (1886) 50 Þei come..in to Ierusalem..in þe vpperisyng of þe sunne. 1412–20 LYDG. *Chron. Troy* IV. 2050 Þe Grekis han, at Phebus vp-rysynge, I-armed hem with gret dilligence. 1471 RIPLEY *Comp. Alch., Rec.* iv. in Ashm. (1652) 187 There is the uprysyng of the Son apperyng whyt and bryght. 1535 COVERDALE 2 *Esdras* xv. 20 All the kynges of y^e earth which are from the vprysinge. 1598 HAKLUYT *Voy.* I. 59 The terrible noise, which the Sunne made at his vprising. 1665 SIR T. HERBERT *Trav.* (1677) 64 Ecbar..gives those Rebels battel at the Suns first up-rising.

**5.** Advancement in place or power; improvement in position or circumstances.
1430–40 LYDG. *Bochas* VIII. 467 Aftir tryumphes and ther uprisinges, What folwith aftir, hir [Fortune's] wheel telle can. 1629 PRYNNE *Anti-Armin.* 52 Who know no other passage to their owne secure vp-rising but by religions downefall. 1868 ATKINSON *Cleveland Gloss.*, *Uprising*, a prosperous rise in one's circumstances and condition; a getting on in the world.

**6.** A rise or ascent; a swelling; a welling-up.
1588 SHAKS. *L. L. L.* IV. i. 2 Was that the King that spurd his horse so hard, Against the steepe vprising of the hill? 1611 COTGR., *Bosse*,..any round swelling, vprising, or puffing vp. 1874 T. HARDY *Far fr. Mad. Crowd* lvi, Something big came into her throat and an uprising to her eyes.

†**b.** *Arch.* Elevation. *Obs.*[−1]
1669 tr. *Scamozzi's Mirr. Archit.* 23 The half of the building on the ground...The other half with the up-rising.

**7.** An insurrection; a popular rising against authority or for some common purpose.
1587 HOLINSHED *Chron.* III. 37/2 It was a greefe to him still to be vexed with such tumults and vprisings as they dailie procured. 1861 M. PATTISON *Ess.* (1889) I. 45 The great communistic uprising under Wat Tyler in 1381. 1871 FREEMAN *Norm. Conq.* xvii. IV. 54 Liable to be driven out whenever the whole nation should join together in one sudden and vigorous uprising.

**8.** The process or fact of coming into existence or notice.
1587 GOLDING *De Mornay* xxxiii. 618 If they judge it by the first vprysing of the Christian Religion. *a* 1591 H. SMITH *Gods Arrow* iv. (1593) I 1 b, The beginning of Mahomets vprising, and of his Sect. 1634 SIR M. SANDYS *Prudence* 251 Death is but..The uprising of Consolation, and the downe-setting of Perturbation. 1657 J. WATTS *Vind. Ch. Eng.* 101 The uprising of bloody Wars, and throwing down of Order. 1851 BRIMLEY *Ess., Wordsw.* 110 The uprising of a new aristocracy of wealth and intellect. 1871 BLACKIE *Four Phases* i. 27 The notable uprising of national spirit and of popular power.

**Upri·sing,** *ppl. a.* [UP- 6 b.] That rises up, in various senses.
*a* 1300 *E. E. Psalter* xxxiv. 13 Vprisand witnes, swikel ware ai. 1585 FOXE *Serm. 2 Cor.* v. 48 Some be repentant and uprysing sinners, some be unrepentant. *a* 1593 MARLOWE *Ovid's Elegies* I. xiii. 28 How oft wisht I, night would not giue thee place, Nor morning starres shunne thy vprising face. 1633 FORD *Love's Sacr.* I. i, My seruice shall pay tribute in my lownesse, To your vprising vertues. 1727 P. WALKER *Life W. Smith* (1827) II. 88 To transmit a tearful Remembrance of them to the up-rising and following Ages. 1819 MRS. BROWNING *Battle of Marathon* III. ad fin., When the uprising morn extends her light. 1884 PROCTOR in *Longm. Mag.* April 597 Uprising streams of aqueous vapour.

†**Upri·st,** *sb. Obs.* [UP- 2 + *-rist* rising: see ARIST *sb.* Cf. OIcel. *uppreist*, MSw. *uprest.*]

**1.** Rising from the dead; resurrection.
*c* 1250 *Song Passion* 79 in *O. E. Misc.* 199 Grante ous, crist, wit þin uprist to gone. *a* 1290 *St. Eustace* 173 in Horstm. *Altengl. Leg.* (1881) 215 Euere he þouhte on Jhesu Crist On his deþ, on his ouprist. *c* 1315 SHOREHAM v. 188 Þe þrydde ioye þat com of cryste Hadde oure leuedy of hys opryste Fram deaþes harde bende. *c* 1400 *Pepysian Gosp. Harmony* (1922) 111 Þe deciples..assembleden hem in a soleer..vpe þe fourtiþe day after his vpryst. *a* 1425 *Cursor M.* 14264 (Trin.), Ihesus seide I am vpriste [*earlier MSS.* vpris, -ras] & lif. *c* 1450 *Mirk's Festial* I. 80 Forto be wyttenes of his [*sc.* Christ's] vprist wyth vs.

**2.** The rising of the sun.
*a* 1300 *K. Horn* 1436 Tofore þe sunne vpriste His schup stod vnder ture. *c* 1386 CHAUCER *Knt.'s T.* 193 In the gardyn at the sonne vpriste She walketh vp and doun. *c* 1430 LYDG. *Min. Poems* (Percy Soc.) 23 When the larke..Salveth the uprist of the sonne shene. ? 1444 *Ibid.* 153 Geyn Phebus uprist syngen wyl the quaylle. 1555 WATREMAN *Fardle Facions* I. iv. 43 Certeine of theim worshippe the Sonne at his vpriјste. 1625 LISLE *Du Bartas, Noe* 132 Both at the suns uprist, and where he goes to bed.

**3.** The act of rising out of bed.
13.. *Seuyn Sages* (W.) 1649 Out of mi lond I rede thou flee, ..For, abide thou min uprist, Thou be honged! 1390 GOWER *Conf.* I. 116 At his upriste Men tolden him how that it ferde.

**Uprist,** *pa. pple.*, archaizing var. UPRISEN.
1579 SPENSER *Sheph. Cal.* Mar. 18 Flora..bids make ready Maias bowre, That newe is vpryst from bedde. 1887 C. MACKAY in *Temple Bar Mag.* June 178, I could trace their pallid features In the moonlight, new up-rist.

†**Upri·ve,** *v. Obs. rare.* [UP- 4 + RIVE *v.*[2]] *intr.* To arrive on shore; to land.
1338 R. BRUNNE *Chron.* (1810) 1 In þe ȝere after..Kom..

Ini & Iuore, In schip out of Irelond, in Wales gan þei vp-ryue. *c* 1425 WYNTOUN *Cron.* VII. x. 3275 Quhare þai mycht wit him till vprif, Thare þai suld meit him þan belif.

**Up-river** (*v*·pri:vəɹ), *a.* and *sb.* [UP *prep.*² 2, 6.]

**1.** *adj.* **a.** Belonging to, situated, etc., farther up, or towards the upper end of, a river.

1877 *Encycl. Brit.* VII. 648/1 The fine 'up-river' quality [of cocoa]. 1886 *Pall Mall G.* 17 April 5/2 The advantages offered by the up-river docks. 1899 KEANE *Man Past & Pres.* 241 The forest and up-river Dyaks.

**b.** Leading or directed towards the source of a river.

1890 'R. BOLDREWOOD' *Col. Reformer* (1891) 319 Wending his way along the 'up-river' road. 1893 D. J. RANKIN *Zambesi Basin* vi. 95 We proceeded on our up-river journey.

**2.** *sb.* The district lying farther up a river.

1902 S. E. WHITE *Blazed Trail* xix, If the men from up-river come by.

**Uproar** (*v*·prōəɹ), *sb.* Also 6 uprour(e, 6–7 uprore (9), -roare. [ad. Du. *oproer* or MLG. *uprôr* (MHG. *ûfruor*, G. *aufruhr*), f. *op-*, *up-* UP- 2 + *roer*, *rôr* ROAR *sb.*² Cf. also WFris. *oproer*, *oproar*, Da. *oprør*, Norw. *upprør*, Sw. *up(p)rör*. In sense 2 associated with ROAR *sb.*¹

First used by Tindale and Coverdale in passages in which Luther's Bible has *aufruhr*. In the same passages the Dutch version of 1563 has *oproer*, which in that of 1531 appears only as a marginal variant to 2 Kings xi. 14.]

**1.** An insurrection or rising of the populace; a serious tumult, commotion, or outbreak of disorder among the people or a body of persons. Also without article. Now *rare*.

*a.* 1526 TINDALE *Acts* xxi. 38 That Ægipcian whych..made an vproure, and ledde out into the wildernes about iiij. thousande men. 1535 COVERDALE 2 *Kings* xi. 14 Athalia rente hir clothes, & sayde vproure, vproure. 1555 WATREMAN *Fardle Facions* II. xi. 247 Among them is no mutinyng, no vproures, no sturres. 1560 DAUS tr. *Sleidane's Comm.* 13 b, Who shall represse the sodayne insurrections and civile vprours [L. *motus*]?

*β.* *a* 1548 HALL *Chron., Hen. VI*, 169 b, The beginning of this temerarious commocion, and sodain vprore. 1561 DAUS tr. *Bullinger on Apoc.* lxxvi. 524 Al wise men haue greuousely condemned seditions, which we are wonte to calle tumultes or vprores. 1595 DANIEL *Civ. Wars* III. xix, Least the realme might chance indure Some new reuolt, or any fresh vprore. 1606 G. W[OODCOCKE] *Hist. Ivstine* XXXIV. 112 That the kingdome should remaine in more safety, and lesse vprore. 1628 COKE *On Litt.* 109 b, Keeping the king's peace in time of sudden uprores.

*γ.* *a*1586 C'TESS PEMBROKE *Ps.* LXV. iv, When stormy uproares tosse the peoples brayn. 1607 DEKKER *Wh. Babylon* C 2 b, Confusion, tyranie, vproares will shake all. 1677 HUBBARD *Narrative* II. 84 These late Uproars amongst the Indians. 1702 CALAMY *Life Baxter* vi. 76 To avoid Uproars of this kind, he was advis'd to withdraw a while from Home. 1748 *Anson's Voy.* III. vi. 347 The officers found it difficult for some time to appease the uproar. 1905 J. H. MCCARTHY *Dryad* 258 There was nothing so wonderful in the crushing of such an uproar as that of the Catalan Grand Company.

**b.** In fig. uses.

1593 SHAKS. *Lucr.* 427 His eye, which late this mutiny restrains, Unto a greater uproar tempts his veins. 1602 MARSTON *Ant. & Mel.* I, The rocks gron'd At the intestine uprore of the maine.

**2.** Loud outcry or vociferation; noise of shouting or tumult.

1544 BETHAM *Precepts War* I. clxiii. H vj, The souldiours ..cannot take anye counsayle of thynges to be doone in suche vprore and wepynges [of women]. 1590 SPENSER *F. Q.* II. ii. 20 That all on vprore..The house was raysd, and all that in did dwell. 1613 PURCHAS *Pilgrimage* (1614) 386 The King was receiued into the house.., where without any vproar he slew seuentie. 1667 MILTON *P. L.* x. 479 Night and Chaos wilde..fiercely oppos'd My journey strange, with clamorous uproare Protesting Fate supreame. 1718 *Free-thinker* No. 63. 52 A Field of War, stained with Blood, and filled with Uproar and Confusion. 1820 KEATS *Hyperion* III. 1 Thus in alternate uproar and sad peace, Amazed were those Titans utterly. 1852 MRS. STOWE *Uncle Tom's C.* xxxv. 317 The sound of wild shrieking,..mingled with the barking of dogs and other symptoms of general uproar.

*transf.* 1726 THOMSON *Winter* 190 Wild Uproar lords it wide; the Clouds commixt, With Stars, swift-gliding, sweep along the Sky. 1820 KEATS *Eve St. Agnes* xl, The arras.. Flutter'd in the besieging wind's uproar.

**b.** With article (*an* or *the*) and in pl.

1572 FORREST *Theophilus* 1057 Although to his shame yt make an uprore Of admyration before the worldes sight. 1623 BINGHAM *Xenophon* 98 We heard vpon the sudden a great vprore and cry, Strike, strike, throw, throw. *a* 1670 HACKET *Abp. Williams* II. (1693) 187 The daily Uproars about his Palace of Whitehall, which did emperil and threaten his Life. 1760 G. COLMAN *Polly Honeycombe* 19 There's always an uproar in the family about marrying the daughter. 1794 MRS. RADCLIFFE *Myst. Udolpho* xxx, It was the wild uproar of riot, not the cheering gaiety of tempered mirth. 1832 DOWNES *Lett. Cont. Countries* I. 291 Hearing..a prodigious uproar in the street, we hastened to the window. 1849 C. BRONTE *Shirley* xv, His uproars are all sound and fury, signifying nothing. 1897 HENTY *On the Irrawaddy* 152 The uproar of the advancing crowd was prodigious. Every man was yelling, at the top of his voice.

**3.** *In (an) uproar*, in a state of tumult, commotion, or excitement.

(*a*) 1548 UDALL, etc. *Erasm. Par. Mark* Pref. C iv b, To haue all the worlde in an vprore, and inquieted with warres. 1596 DANETT tr. *Comines* (1614) 55 Those that escaped put all the country in an vprore as they went. 1635 *Life & Pranks Long Meg of Westm.* viii. 16 The street was in such an uproar. 1778 MISS BURNEY *Evelina* xl, For some minutes the room seemed quite in an uproar [of laughter]. 1831 [HARE] tr. *Tieck's Old Man of Mount.* 40 His head is in an uprore, his heart throbs tumultuously. 1848 L. HUNT *Jar of Honey* 188 Thus it was at Alcamo, where the streets seemed to be in an uproar till after midnight. 1853 KANE *Grinnell Exp.* (1856) 522 Ice in an uproar.

(*b*) 1597 BEARD *Theatre God's Judgem.* (1612) 68 Whereat heauen grieuing, clad it selfe in blacke: But earth in vprore triumpht at their wracke. 1630 *R. Johnson's Kingd. & Commw.* 573 All Persia was in uprore about the election of a new Prince. *a* 1700 EVELYN *Diary* 16 Aug. 1650, As we pass'd St. Denis the people were in uproar.

**U·proar,** *v.* [f. prec.]

**1.** *trans.* To throw into confusion. *rare.*

1605 SHAKS. *Macb.* IV. iii. 99 Nay, had I powre, I should.. Vprore the vniuersall peace, confound All vnity on earth. 1811 W. R. SPENCER *Poems* 48 The demon rage which uproared Europe's peace.

**2.** *intr.* To make an uproar.

1831 CARLYLE *Sart. Res.* III. viii, Do not we..uproar (*poltern*), and revel in our mad Dance of the Dead? 1837 — *Fr. Rev.* III. VI. ii, Danton was not prone..to act or uproar for his own safety. *Ibid.* vii, All men accuse, and uproar, and impetuously acclaim.

† **Uproarer.** *Obs.* [f. UPROAR *sb.*] A creator of uproar; a turbulent person.

1628 GAULE *Pract. The.* (1629) 212 So doe these rude Vproarers snatch and hale Christ..to their High Priests House. 1647 HEXHAM I, An uprorer, or a seditious fellow, *een oproermaker.*

**Uproa·riness.** [f. **uproary*, adj. f. UPROAR *sb.*] = UPROARIOUSNESS.

1806 SURR *Winter in Lond.* II. 112 Like the uproariness of our gallery gods, the rudeness of their boxes must perhaps be tolerated. 1834 M. SCOTT *Cruise Midge* x, The excess of her joy, and the uproariness of her laughter.

**U·proaring,** *vbl. sb.* [f. UPROAR *sb.* or *v.*] A tumult or disturbance.

1827 CARLYLE *Germ. Rom.* III. 285 Every time a conversion happens,..there is an uproaring and a shooting.

**Uproa·rious,** *a.* [f. UPROAR *sb.*]

**1.** Making, or given to making, an uproar.

1819 *Blackw. Mag.* IV. 717 The trio..is altogether so cheerful.., so uproarious, if we may be allowed the expression. 1858 DORAN *Crt. Fools* 101 The bachelor and uproarious Court of William Rufus. 1871 JOWETT *Plato* I. 182 A somewhat uproarious young man.

**2.** Characterized by uproar; noisy.

1849 MRS. CARLYLE *Lett.* (1882) II. 42 We dined. After that, very youthful and uproarious sports till twelve! 1874 GREEN *Short Hist.* viii. § 7. 531 The King..paused..at Oxford, where he was received with uproarious welcome. 1885 *Manch. Exam.* 10 Nov. 4/7 The proceedings were very uproarious.

**3.** *fig.* Disordered, unkempt.

1836 JAS. GRANT *Random Recoll. Ho. Lords* xiv. 316 The uproarious condition of his dark grey hair.

Hence **Uproa·riously** *adv.*, **-ness.**

1838 DICKENS *O. Twist* ix, At which Mr. Charles Bates laughed *uproariously. 1871 L. STEPHEN *Playgr. Eur.* iii. 147 We should..have been uproariously triumphant over our victory. 1847 L. HUNT *Men, Women, & B.* II. xi. 265 His delight at having his head patted by Lord Clarendon, and his honest *uproariousness. 1898 'H. S. MERRIMAN' *Roden's Corner* xxxii. 340 In jail..for intoxication and uproariousness.

† **Uproarish,** *a.* *Obs.* [f. UPROAR *sb.*] Turbulent, unruly. Hence † **Uproarishly** *adv.* *Obs.*

1550 W. LYNNE *Curious Cron.* 180 b, The Poles drew into their faction the vprourysh kynde of men called Thaborites. 1647 HEXHAM I, Vprorish, seditious, or tumultuous. *Ibid.*, Vprorishly or seditiously.

**Upro·ll,** *v.* [UP- 4. Cf. WFris. *oprôlje*, Du. *oprollen*, G. *aufrollen*, Sw. *upprulla*, Da. *oprulle.*]

**1.** *trans.* To impel upwards by rolling.

1513 DOUGLAS *Æneid* VI. ix. 4 Hir rosy chariot the fresche Aurora..Begouth for till wproll and rais on hie. 1743 FRANCIS tr. *Horace, Epodes* xvii. 24 Sisiphus, with many a Groan, Uprolls, with ceaseless Toil, his Stone. 1855 SINGLETON *Virgil* I. 88 Thrice they essayed..on Ossa to uproll Leaf-fraught Olympus.

**2.** To roll or wind up. Also const. *in.*

1613 DRUMM. OF HAWTH. *Cypress Grove* P 7 A swift.. wheele, which twinneth forth and againe vprolleth [1630 vpwindeth] our life. 1623 — *Flowers Sion* xxv, I am that Monarch whom all Monarches feare, Who hath in Dust their farre-stretch'd Pride vproll'd.

**b.** *intr.* To concentrate by rolling; to form a roll.

1805–6 CARY *Dante, Inf.* XXIV. 102 The dust again Uproll'd spontaneous, and the self-same form Instant resumed. 1818 MILMAN *Samor* VI. 17 But far and wide,..Venomous and vast the clouds uproll. 1887 STEVENSON *Mem. & Portraits* xiii. 224 How the congregated clouds themselves uproll, as stiff as bolsters!

**Uprolled,** *pa. pple.* and *ppl. a.* [UP- 5. Cf. prec.] Rolled up; brought together by rolling. Also const. *in.*

1592 WYRLEY *Armorie, Ld. Chandos* 79 Then I call My banner for, vproled I hit bring Vnto my prince. 1600 FAIRFAX *Tasso* IX. lxxxi, The sweat..Seem'd pearles.., The dust therein vprold, adorn'd his haire. 1667 MILTON *P. L.* VII. 291 Thither they Hasted,..uprowld As drops on dust conglobing from the drie. 1762 FALCONER *Shipwr.* III. 406 High o'er the poop th' audacious seas aspire, Uproll'd in hills of fluctuating fire. 1821 SHELLEY *Boat on Serchio* 16 Day had..clothed with light..The mists in their eastern caves uprolled. 1844 EMERSON *Ess., Nat.*, The uprolled clouds and the colours of morning and evening. 1864 E. SARGENT *Peculiar* III. 98 The lids of the eyes hung loosely over the uprolled balls.

**U·proot,** *sb.* [f. next.] An uprooted tree.

1891 E. ROPER *By Track & Trail* iii. 33 Stumps and logs and fallen trees, uproots and old dead weeds.

**Uproo·t,** *v.*¹ [UP- 4 + ROOT *v.*¹: cf. UPROOTED *pa. pple.*] *trans.* To tear up by the roots; to remove from a fixed position.

1695 CONGREVE *Taking of Namur* viii, Uprooting Hills.. To form the High and Dreadful Scale. 1771 BEATTIE *Minstrel* I. xxiv, The river..Down the vale thunders, and.. Uproots the grove. 1796 MORSE *Amer. Geog.* I. 475 Storms and hurricanes sometimes happen, which..uproot trees. 1836–7 DICKENS *Sk. Boz, Tales* iv, Mr. Cymon..uprooted the chairs, and removed them further back. 1860 TYNDALL *Glac.* I. xxv. 185 We were powerfully shaken, but had no fear of being uprooted. 1877 HUXLEY *Physiogr.* 171 The stalks are not uprooted and carried across the field.

**b.** *fig.* To remove as by tearing up; to eradicate, exterminate, destroy.

*a* 1620 J. DYKE *Worthy Commun.* (1640) 193 Before wee can be rooted in Christ, we must be unrooted and uprooted in regard of our natural condition. 1743 FRANCIS tr. *Hor., Odes* III. xxiv. 52 Tear forth, uprooted from the youthful Breast, The Seeds of each deprav'd Desire. 1813 SHELLEY *Q. Mab* IX. 191 [To] uproot The germs of misery from the human heart. 1868 FREEMAN *Norm. Conq.* viii. II. 173 That he acted on any settled scheme of uprooting the nationality, the laws, or the language of England is an exploded fable.

Hence **Uproo·tal**; **Uproo·ter**; **Uproo·ting** *vbl. sb.* and *ppl. a.*

1861 *Macm. Mag.* V. 22 He would have shrieked like a mandrake at *uprootal. 1890 CLARK RUSSELL *Shipmate Louise* II. 285 The sudden uprootal and crash of their one mast and sail. 1828 CAMPBELL *On Battle of Navarino* 10 No! your lofty emprise was to fetter and foil The *uprooter of Greece's domain! 1882 *Blackw. Mag.* CXXXII. 102/2 War..—that remorseless and violent uprooter of ordinary life. 1775 ASH s.v., *Uprooting. 1847 MANGAN *Poems* (1903) 223 But the end of all is Sadness,..Spoliation and Uprooting! 1858 O. W. HOLMES *Aut. Breakf.-t.* x. 95 The uprooting of the ancient gravestones in..our city burial-grounds. 1818 BYRON *Ch. Har.* IV. clxxiii, The *uprooting wind which tears The oak from his foundation. 1880 MEREDITH *Tragic Com.* (1881) 265 Should there come no preternatural uprooting tempest.

**Uproo·t,** *v.*² [UP- 4 + ROOT *v.*²] *trans.* To grub up.

1726 POPE *Odyssey* XVIII. 36 Those teeth.., Like some vile swine's, that..Uproots the bearded corn. 1889 A. R. WALLACE *Darwinism* 16 Some [herbivorous mammals] uproot and devour the buried tubers.

**Uproo·ted,** *pa. pple.* and *ppl. a.* [UP- 5, or f. UPROOT *v.*¹] Rooted up; eradicated. Also *fig.*

*a* 1593 MARLOWE tr. *Lucan* I. 4 We sing..Armies allied, the kingdoms league vprooted. 1667 MILTON *P. L.* VI. 781 At his command the uprooted Hills retir'd. 1737 GLOVER *Leonidas* IX. 294 With prostrate glories lie the stately oak.. And elm uprooted. 1743 FRANCIS tr. *Hor., Odes* III. xxv. 22 The Bacchanalian Maids..Tear from the bursting Glebe th' uprooted Tree. 1809 J. BARLOW *Columb.* x. 257 For him no more..Uprooted mountains sweep the dark profound. 1844 KINGLAKE *Eothen* viii, One man above all others (he is now uprooted from society) she blasted with her wrath. 1861 GEO. ELIOT *Silas M.* iii, Almost as helpless as an uprooted tree.

**Uproused,** *pa. pple.* and *ppl. a.* (UP- 5.)

1592 SHAKS. *Rom. & Jul.* II. iii. 40 Thy earlinesse doth me assure, Thou art vprous'd with some distemprature. 1796 SCOTT *Wild Huntsman* xxii, Again uproused, the timorous prey Scours moss and moor. 1802 J. BAILLIE *2nd Pt. Ethwald* I. ii, What, meanst thou this? Uprous'd again unto this dev'lish pitch? 1848 THACKERAY *Van. Fair* xviii, Cried out this uproused British lion. 1871 HAWTHORNE *Sept. Felton* (1872) 36 To prevent the uproused people from coming..close to the main body.

**U·prush,** *sb.* [UP- 2.] An upward rush or flow. (Common in recent use.)

1873 B. STEWART *Conserv. Force* iv. 108 The up-rush of air through the chimney. 1877 G. F. CHAMBERS *Astron.* (ed. 3) I. i. 5 The uprushes of incandescent gas and metallic vapours.

**Upru·sh,** *v.* [UP- 4.] *intr.* To rush up.

1818 MILMAN *Samor* x. 338 Uprush'd the giant fire, Piercing the dim heavens with its blazing brow. 1826 N. T. CARRINGTON *Dartmoor* 17 Years have flown Sweet Lara, yet thy bank uprushes still With the old charm. 1872 A. DE VERE *Leg. St. Patrick* 119 She knelt, and unto God.. Uprushed the strength of prayer, as when the cloud Uprushes..From billowy deep unseen.

**Upru·shing,** *ppl. a.* (UP- 7.)

1801 SOUTHEY *Thalaba* XII. xvii, But ever the uprushing wind Inflates the wings above. 1869 J. PHILLIPS *Vesuv.* iii. 93 From the source came up continual jets of uprushing incandescent stones. 1895 *Edin. Rev.* Oct. 413 The uprushing, glowing material of sun-flames.

**U·psa·ddle,** *v.* *S. African.* [ad. Du. *opzadelen*, f. *op-* UP- 4 + *zadelen* SADDLE *v.*] *intr.* To saddle a horse.

1863 W. C. BALDWIN *Afr. Hunting* vi. 181 We up-saddled and went in pursuit. 1887 RIDER HAGGARD *Jess* xxx, At midday they offsaddled their horses for an hour...Then they upsaddled and went on.

† **Up-sail.** *Obs.* [UP *adv.*¹] A hoisted sail.

1637 RUTHERFORD *Lett.* (1664) 303 The Devil and the lusts of a deceiving world and sin, are upon horse-back, and follow with up sails. *Ibid.* 346, I wait on..till the Lord send a full sea, that with up-sailes I may lift up Christ.

**Upse-**, var. of UPSY *Obs.* **Upsedoun, -down,** obs. ff. UPSIDE DOWN. † **Upseed.** *Sc. Obs.*⁻¹ [UP *adv.*² 5 c.] *Upseed time*, harvest. 1678 [see STREEKING *vbl. sb.* 2].

† **Upsee·k,** *v.* *Obs.* [UP- 4. Cf. WFris. *opsiikje*, Du. *opzoeken*, MSw. *up-*, *opsökia* (Sw. *uppsöka*), Da. *opsøge.*] *trans.* To seek or search out; to search through.

*c* 1315 SHOREHAM I. 1581 Þanne aȝte..wyues nauȝt aȝens men Non on-wrestnesse werche,..And nauȝt onwrest opsechen hy. *c* 1400 *Destr. Troy* 12010 Grete palis of prise [þai] put into askys,..And all the Cite vp soght to þe sad walles. *a* 1500 *Coventry Corpus Chr. Pl.* i. 809 All the chylder of that age dy the[y] mvst nede; Now with all my myght the[y] schall be vpsoght. 1615–6 BOYS *Wks.* (1630) 462 That we should not expect vntill other vpseeke vs, but that we should seeke and serue them.

†**Upsee·king**, *vbl. sb. Obs.*$^{-1}$ [Up- 7.] A seeking after. **1594** Lyly *Mother Bombie* v. iii, *Accius.* We shall haue good chere these foure dayes. *Lucio.* And be fooles for euer. *Sil.* Thats none of our vpseekings. **Upsee·king**, *ppl. a.* (Up- 6 b.) **1801** Southey *Thalaba* xii. xxxii, Upseeking eyes suffused with tears devout. **1846** Keble *Lyra Innoc.* 58 Or chanced the Thorny Crown her first upseeking glance to win?

**Upsees.** *pseudo-arch.* Also up seyes. (A misuse of *upsee* Upsy.)
**1810** Scott *Lady of L.* vi. v, Off with thy liquor, Drink upsees out, and a fig for the vicar! **1821** — *Kenilw.* xx, Here goes it, up seyes—to Varney and Leicester! **1842** D. Vedder *Poems* 184 And there was wassail in the court, And upsees in the hall.

**U·psend**, *sb.* [Up- 2.] An upward discharge. **1842** *Blackw. Mag.* LII. 409 So soon as the rolling cannonade is over, there is an upsend from the mines beneath.

**Upse·nd**, *v.* [Up- 4. Cf. Du. *opzenden.*] *trans.* To send up; to discharge upwards. **1667** Milton *P. L.* i. 541 At which the universal Host upsent A shout that tore Hells Concave. **1791** Cowper *Iliad* xviii. 257 As when some island..Upsends a smoke to heaven. **1816** *Monthly Mag.* XLI. 144 Huge bonfires first their cones of flame upsend. **1854** S. Dobell *Balder* v. 33 Sudden the universal host upsent Impotent rage.

†**Upserve**, obs. variant of Observe *v.* **1539** in Ellis *Orig. Lett.* Ser. ii. II. 145 Commanding all hys..subjettes to upserve and keype all manner of holly sacrementes.

**U·pset**, *sb.* [Up- 2.]

I. †1. *Sc.* An insurrection, revolt. *Obs.* c **1425** Wyntoun *Cron.* v. xii. 3634 (Cott. MS.), His lufftennandis þai slew þar..In to þat vpset richt fellon. *Ibid.* viii. iv. 699 Þat vpset..Þat Chore agayne Moyses wroucht.

†2. *north.* and *Sc.* The fact of setting up in business as a master, or of becoming a freeman in a particular trade; also, the sum paid to the guild on this occasion. *Obs.* **1463–4** in *York Memo. Bk.* ii. (Surtees) 207 Every foreine walker commyng to this citie..and wil sett up as a maister, ..he shall paie at his upsett xiij*s.* iiij*d.* **1505** in A. Pennecuik *Blue Blanket* (1756) 46 Persons..admitted frie men or master to the saids Crafts,..shall pay at his entrie for his upset, Five pounds. **1598** in J. M. Lambert *2000 Years Gild Life* (1891) 255 The moytie of all Upsettes, incomes, or other receites..accrewinge..to the said Companie. **1639** *Rec. Burgh Lanark* (1893) 133 That nae persone..be admittit..frieman for any les wpsett nor is abone wryttin. **1687** in J. R. Boyle *Hedon* (1875) App. 192 Every apprentice.., his yeares beinge ended, shall pay for his upp sett two shillings to the said Company.

3. †a. A curved part of a bridle-bit, fitting over the tongue of the horse. *Obs.* (Cf. Upset *ppl. a.* 1 b.) **1607** Markham *Cavel.* ii. 64 Others..haue added, from the eye of the byt to the outside of the vpset, a strong trench. *Ibid.*, The fashion of which vpsets..you shall behold in these figures. **1611** Cotgr., *Col d'oye*, the port, or vpset of some Bits. **1611** Florio, *Suenata briglia*, a bit with an open mouth as ports or upsets. c **1720** Gibson *Farrier's Guide* ii. lxii. (1722) 218 The usual Method of Cure is to open the Horse's Mouth with the Upset.

b. *Mining.* (See quots.) **1883** Gresley *Gloss. Coal-m.* 268 *Upset*, a bolt hole or thirl put through between two levels in edge coals. **1886** J. Barrowman *Sc. Mining Terms* 69 *Upset*, a short working place driven to the rise.

4. = Upshot *sb.* 4. **1821** J. W. Croker *Diary* 9 June, The upset, however, is that all is at a stand. **1901** F. E. Taylor *Folk-sp. S. Lancs.*, *Upset*, the upshot.

5. a. A rendering or translation. **1828** T. C. Croker *Fairy Leg. S. Irel.* ii. 71 It would be a thousand pities not to give you his verses; so here's my hand at an upset of them into English.

b. A rough draft. **1841** H. Greeley in *Corr. R. W. Griswold* (1898) 102 Having got the right sort of a letter from Burleigh, I have set right down and written you an upset of it.

II. 6. The overturning of a vehicle or boat; the fact of being overturned. (Cf. Overset *sb.* b.) **1804** Moore *Mem.* (1853) I. 162 Driving through mud and filth,..and risking an upset at every step. **1840** B. Hall *Patchwork* (1841) III. vii. 130 At this..moment, when an upset was obviously inevitable, the horses slackened their pace. **1852** Mansfield *Paraguay*, etc. (1856) 112 The Major..was afraid of the possible consequences of an upset of the canoe. **1880** L. Stephen *Pope* iv. 90 He had good-naturedly lent his own chariot to a lady who had been hurt in an upset.

b. An overturning or overthrow *of* ideas, plans, etc. Also const. *to.* **1822** *Blackw. Mag.* XI. 453 The revolution and the upset of opinions..created a new order of..taste. **1827** Southey in *Corr. W. C. Bowles* (1881) 119 What a strange upset of old principles and old measures! **1886** *Manch. Exam.* 9 June 5/2 The result was a complete upset to all the predictions of the prophets.

c. A physical or (more commonly) mental disturbance or derangement. **1866** Chr. G. Rossetti *Prince's Progr.* xxv, Some old volcanic upset must Have rent..and blackened the crust. **1892** Huxley in *Life* (1900) II. 320 My wife got an awful dose of neuralgia and general upset. **1899** *Allbutt's Syst. Med.* VIII. 301 The poor and hard-working are subject to mental upset..in much larger numbers than the well-off.

d. A quarrel, a misunderstanding. **1887** G. R. Sims *Mary Jane's Mem.* 75 They were always getting at each other and both trying to bring me into their upsets. **1895** *Daily News* 31 Oct. 9/1 We had only one upset there. I happened to hit the defendant.

**Upse·t**, *v.* [Up- 4. Cf. WFris. *opsette*, MDu. *opsetten* (Du. *opzetten*), (M)LG. *upsetten*, MHG. *ûfsetzen* (G. *aufsetzen*), MSw. *upsätia*, *-sättia* (Sw. *uppsätta*), (M)Da. *opsætte* in sense 1. With senses 4–6 cf. Overset *v.* 3–4.]

I. 1. *trans.* †a. To set up, raise up, erect. *Obs.* (Cf. Upset *pa. pple.* 1.) c **1440** *Pallad. on Husb.* i. 395 Bordis of cipresse Playn & direct, vpsette hem in their kynde A foote atwyn. **1513** Douglas *Æneid* xi. i. 15 Ane akin tre..Apone a motys hycht vpset hes he. **1608** Topsell *Serpents* 26 The serpent fierce..rough scales vpsetteth that were deiected.

†b. To establish. *Obs.*$^{-1}$ **1559** in R. Keith *Hist. Ch. & St. Scot.* (1734) 111 To advance the Glory of God, by maintaining and upsetting true Preachers of the Word.

c. *techn.* To force back the end of (a metal bar, etc.) by hammering or beating, esp. when heated. **1677** Moxon *Mech. Exerc.* i. 11 You may Up-set it, that is, take a Flame Heat, and set the heated end upright upon the Anvil, and hammer upon the cold end till the Heated end be beat or up-set into the Body of your Work. **1688** Holme *Armoury* iii. 88/2 *Up-set*, is when at a heat the Iron is beaten back into the Body of the work. **1841** *Penny Cycl.* XX. 156/2 Wire ropes may be..secured at their ends by passing them through the small end of a conical collar, and doubling up, or upsetting, the ends of the wires. **1869** Sandberg tr. *Styffe's Iron & Steel* 11 The author 'upset' or stubbed the bars at the ends. **1884** C. G. W. Lock *Workshop Receipts* Ser. iii. 286/2 A pick should never be 'upset', or hammered endwise.

d. *Agric.* To ridge up. **1764** *Museum Rust.* III. 321 Fifth ploughing, sowing earth, up-set it, and harrowing.

†2. a. *Sc.* To make good, make up for; to get over, recover from (a loss, etc.). *Obs.* **1513** Douglas *Æneid* Direct. 33 God grant I may amend it, With grace and space to vpset this tynsell. **1557** *Extr. Aberd. Reg.* (1844) I. 305 Gif ony dampnage cumis thairthrow,..that the said Gilbert be..obleist to vpsett the same. **1593** *Sc. Acts, Jas. VI* (1816) IV. 26/2 Þe said morowing gift, sa faithfullie..promesit to be vpsett and maid guid. **1606** Rollock *Lect. 2 Thess.* 53 The lose thou getst by deceite wil neuer be vpset. **1806** A. Douglas *Poems* 123 Folk as stout an' clever..Hae gotten skaith they never Upset for mony year.

b. To restore to good or usual condition. *Obs.* exc. *dial.* a **1652** Brome *City Wit* iii. i. (1653) C 8, When she failes by diseases or paine, The Doctor new Vamps and upsets her againe. **1905** in *Eng. Dial. Dict.* s.v., *Cor[nwall].* Two men went up the hill upsetting [=reviving] the fire.

3. *intr.* Of a cylindrical bullet: To become bent. **1859** 'Stonehenge' *Shot-Gun* 306 A pointed cylinder soon 'upsets', as it is termed, and is then at once rendered useless as a projectile. [Cf. Upsetting *vbl. sb.* 1 e.]

II. 4. *intr.* To be overturned or capsized. Said of a vehicle, boat, etc., or of persons in it. **1799** T. Knight *Turnpike-gate* ii. iii, If the horses had not run so fast we should not have upset. **1820** Moore *Mem.* (1853) III. 116 If there came the slightest breath of wind, they would upset with so many on board. **1889** Jerome *Three Men in Boat* iii, The boat..will not be so liable to upset.

5. *trans.* To overturn; to capsize; to knock over. In this or the next sense called 'a low word' by Todd (1818). **1803** Rees *Cycl.*, *Capsize*, in Naval Language, to upset or turn over anything. **1808** Jamieson s.v., To upset a cart, boat, &c. **1813** Southey *Nelson* I. 15 It was with the utmost difficulty that the crew could prevent them from staving or upsetting her. **1852** Mrs. Stowe *Uncle Tom's C.* vii. 45 One luckless wight contrived to upset the gravy. **1871** Jowett *Plato* II. 43 The light active boxer upsetting two stout gentlemen.
*fig.* **1883** *Pall Mall G.* 26 Oct., If the Control had done more it might have upset the apple-cart altogether.

b. To involve (persons) in the accidental overturning of a vehicle or boat. Chiefly in *passive.* **1807** Southey *Espriella's Lett.* II. 192 Had we been..overtaken by storms and upset in the lake. **1819** Moore *Mem.* (1853) II. 345 Very nearly upset by the horse backing down the hill. **1832** A. W. Fonblanque *Eng. under 7 Administr.* (1837) II. 206 'He then built him another [vessel], ..which he succeeded in setting afloat.'..'Aye, and it nearly upset him..at sea.' **1867** P'cess Alice *Mem.* (1884) 176 Mme. d'Usedom..was lately upset with her carriage off the road.

c. *fig.* To overthrow, undo, put out of joint. **1818** Moore *Mem.* (1853) II. 221 Very natural, but very likely to upset the whole concern. **1859** W. Collins *Q. of Hearts* iii, She..upset every one of our calculations on the first day of her arrival. **1884** Sir H. Cotton in *Law Times Rep.* LI. 277/1 A witness who is coming..to assist the plaintiff in upsetting..a fraudulent scheme.

6. a. To throw into mental disorder or discomposure; to trouble or distress. **1805** Blackwood in Nicolas *Nelson's Disp.* (1846) VII. 224, I never was so shocked or so completely upset as..to find that Lord Nelson was even then at the gasp of Death. **1857** Trollope *Barchester T.* III. 116 Eleanor..was a good deal upset, as people say, and could not at the moment collect herself. **1885** *Law Times* 7 Feb. 270/2 Deceased appeared very irritable upon the morning in question, but witness knew of nothing to upset him.

b. To disorder physically. **1845** Budd *Dis. Liver* 261 A young person, delicate, and easily upset by any imprudence in diet. **1889** Mrs. E. Kennard *Landing a Prize* x, The least thing upset his liver.

Hence **Upse·tment**; **Upse·ttable** *a.*; **Upse·ttal.** **1893** *Standard* 10 Mar., For this *upsetment too, nothing would be gained. [Cf. w. Somerset (1888) *upsotment*, 'disturbance, break up'.] **1890** *Sat. Rev.* 4 Oct. 386/1 Persons *upsettable..at their own peril. **1890** *Graphic* 11 Oct. 406/1 Never a little finger did I put to help in his *upsettal.

**Upset**, *pa. pple.* and *ppl. a.* [Up- 5. Cf. prec. and WFris. *opset*, Norw. *uppsett*, Da. *opsat*, Sw. *uppsatt.*]

1. Set up, erected, raised up, etc. **1338** R. Brunne *Chron.* (1810) 70 Now is he in þe see with saile on mast vpsette. **1390** Gower *Conf.* II. 204 Ther scholde be tofore his bed A bord upset and faire spred. c **1400** tr. *Secreta Secret., Gov. Lordsh.* 108 Trees þat hauyn yn hem many braunches and rotes, and þe stoke vpsette. **1430–40** Lydg. *Bochas* ix. 23 Ful of idoles upset on hihe stages. **1513** Douglas *Æneid* ii. iii. 53 Scharslie the statw was in thair temple wpset, Quhen all hir membris bittir teris swet. **1658** A. Fox *Würtz' Surg.* iii. xii. 253 An upset hand is sooner bowed, than a hand which hangeth down, to be set upright. **1824** Mactaggart *Gallovid. Encycl.* 362 Puir Girzey, wi' her upset chin.

†b. *Upset mouth*, = Upset *sb.* 3 a. *Obs.* **1580** Blundevil *Art of Riding* iii. xxvii. 54 The square ports, otherwise called vpset mouthes. **1607** Markham *Cavel.* ii. 52 He..for a more libertie to the tongue, giueth allowance to the cannon, with the vpset mouth. *Ibid.* 64 Others to these vpset mouthes, haue added..a strong trench.

2. Of price: Stated as the lowest sum for which property exposed to auction will be sold; named as the sum from which bidding may start. Orig. *Sc.* and *U.S.* **1814** *Act* 54 *Geo. III*, c. 137 § 42 The Price..shall not be less than the last upset Price at which it had been exposed to public Sale. **1815** Scott *Guy M.* xiv, Mr. Glossin offered the upset price for the lands and barony of Ellangowan. **1834** *Spectator* 8 Nov. 1066/1 The price at which land [in U.S.] is..sold, varies from the upset price to many pounds sterling per acre. **1866** Veness *El Dorado* App. 178 All Crown lands [in S. Australia] are open to purchase at the upset price of £1 per acre. **1884** *Public Opinion* 3 Oct. 434/2 The mansion, park, and home farm..were bought in, the highest bid..being considerably under the upset price.

3. Overturned, capsized. *Upset race* (see quot. 1876). **1842** C. Whitehead *R. Savage* (1845) I. x. 135 He..threw him over the upset table. **1876** *Encycl. Brit.* IV. 812/2 Canoes for 'upset races' (where the canoeist has to jump out, tow his boat while swimming, and then get in). **1882** *Daily News* 3 July 5/2 An upset hansom is a rare thing.

**Up set down**, obs. form of Upside down.

**Upsete**: see Up- 5.

**Upse·tter.** [Up- 8. Cf. Upset *v.*]

†1. *Sc.* One who 'sets up' as a master workman. (Cf. Upset *sb.* 2.) *Obs.*$^{-1}$ **1518** *Perth Hammermen Bk.* (1889) 2 He sall pay..till his upset six markis. And gif the upsetter be ane outman he sall pay sex markis.

2. †a. *Sc.* One who posts up a placard. *Obs.*$^{-1}$ **1567** *Sc. Acts, Mary* (1814) II. 552/1 The first Inventar, writtar, tynar, and vpsettar of the samin.

†b. *Sc.* A founder or establisher. *Obs.* **1581** Hamilton in *Cath. Tractates* (S.T.S.) 84 Thir Caluinian ministers, quha louit so heichlie thair vpsetters. **1581** Burne *Ibid.* 162 The hail hous of the Hamiltonis..vas the cheif vpsettar, and protector of his hæresie.

c. A repairer of stocking-frames. **1839** Ure *Dict. Arts* 653 A set of men employed in this [hosiery] trade, and distinguished by the name of upsetters.

d. Part of a tire-shortening machine. **1875** Knight *Dict. Mech.* 2581/2 A machine for up-setting, cutting, and punching tires. The upper figure shows the upsetter.

†3. *Sc.* A support or prop. *Obs.* **1628** *Maitl. Cl. Misc.* III. 371 For sex knopis to the gairden ȝettis with sevin upsetteris to the ordinance. **1644** *Papers Army Solemn League & Cov.* (S.H.S.) 34 Stanes for upsetters twelve.

4. One who upsets, overturns, disarranges, etc. **1836** Dickens *Sk. Boz, Our Parish* xviii, The volunteer driver of the hackney coach..and the involuntary upsetter of the whole party. **1859** Meredith *R. Feverel* xxix, The upsetter of ordinary calculations. **1886** Macquoid *J. Wentworth* xviii, Willie had upset the upsetter of her peace.

**Upse·tting**, *vbl. sb.* [Up- 7. Cf. Upset *v.*]

I. †1. The action of setting up or erecting. *Obs.* c **1449** Pecock *Repr.* ii. iv. 156 The hauyng, and the vpsetting of ymagis. **1507** *Acc. Ld. High Treas. Scotl.* III. 261 For prenes to the pailȝoun and upsetting of it, x d. **1525** *Reg. Mag. Sig. Scot.* 96 Ilk man of the said craft that settis up ane buth sall pay 40 schillingis at thare buth upsetting.

†b. *Sc.* The action of raising to, or establishing in, position or power. *Obs.* **1470** in Ellis *Orig. Lett.* I. 133 He..confessed that he was cawser of the upsetynge of the Kynge of England that now is. **1560** *Maitl. Cl. Misc.* III. 224 For avancement and upsetting of the Kingdome and glorie of God. **1570** Buchanan *Admon.* Wks. (1892) 27 In doun putting of thevis and upsetting of justice. **1669** R. Fleming *Fulfill. Script.* (1671) I. 151 The Roman empire mouldred down for Antichrist's upsetting. **1748** E. Erskine *Serm.* (1755) 327 What a pleasant Upsetting of Christ, and his Kingdom, would it be, to see him [etc.].

c. *Agric.* (See quot.) **1785** A. Young *Annals Agric.* II. 442, I saw them ploughing their fallows;..they do not ridge up, what is called up-setting in some parts, that is, raising the centers much higher than the furrows.

d. *techn.* (See quots. and Upset *v.* 1 c.) **1815** J. Smith *Panorama Sci. & Art* I. 11 When it is required to thicken any part of a bar of iron without welding, the operation called upsetting must be resorted to. **1831–3** *Encycl. Metrop.* (1845) VIII. 24 Having heated his iron rod, and thickened it by a process..called *upsetting.* **1875** Knight *Dict. Mech.* 2684/1 Shortening [a] tire, to enable it to bind the fellies more firmly, is called upsetting.

e. (See quot. and Upset *v.* 3.) **1859** 'Stonehenge' *Shot-Gun* 306 By upsetting is to be understood the turning sideways of an elongated ball.

f. The action of raising or building up. *nonce-use.* **1882** Besant *All Sorts* xxviii. (1898) 191 The younger men..were quite sure..that with a little more upsetting and downpulling the balance would be set right.

†**2.** = UPSITTING *vbl. sb.* 1. Also *attrib. Obs.*

**1501** *Acc. Ld. High Treas. Scotl.* (1900) II. 41 Giffin to the Maister Cuke that he bocht in Edinburgh to the ladyis upsetting fest,..viij*s*. **1676** COLES, *Up-setting-time*, when the Child-bed woman 'gets up. **1746** *Exmoor Courtship* (E.D.S.) 380 You werent so skittish..up to Darathy Vuzz's Up-setting. **1814** *Monthly Mag.* Sept. 126/2 *Upsetting*, christening...[A word] peculiar to Exmoor.

†**3.** The action of setting up in a trade or occupation. *Obs.*

**1569** *Wills & Inv. N. C.* (Surtees, 1835) 301 Eyther at ye daye of his vpsetting to his science or at the daye of his mariaidge. **1640** [SHIRLEY] *Capt. Underwit* IV. v, The musick at a Convocation of Catts upon a witches upsetting.

**4.** *Sc.* An attempt to set oneself up above others; undue assumption of superiority or superior airs.

**1821** GALT *Ann. Parish* xxix, Partly with upsetting, and partly by the eating rust of family pride. **1823** — *Entail* lxiv, I declare if e'er I heard the like of sic upsetting.

**II. 5.** The action of overturning, or fact of being overturned.

**1819** MOORE *Mem.* (1853) III. 85 Two men on each side of our carriage all the way, to keep it from upsetting. **1820** WORDSW. in C. Wordsw. *Mem.* (1851) II. 103 Of these, one.. was drowned..by the upsetting of a boat in a storm. **1860** *Builder* 14 Jan. 31/2 Brickwork..thrown down by the accidental upsetting of a water-tank. **1873** MRS. BROOKFIELD *Not a Heroine* I. 218 It was an accident—the upsetting of a cart.

**b.** The action of overthrowing, demolishing, etc.

**1827** WORDSW. in C. Wordsw. *Mem.* (1851) II. 21 The upsetting of so diabolical a system as Buonaparte's. **1841** S. WARREN *Ten Thousand a Year* I. vi, The dismal upsetting of his hopes. **1860** GEN. P. THOMPSON *Audi Alt. Part.* III. cxli. 121 All the danger attending the upsetting a nest of thieves.

**c.** A dislocation, disturbance, upset.

**1847** HALLIWELL, *Upsetting*, a disagreement; a quarrel. *South.* **1881, 1887** in Isle of Wight and Kent glossaries. **1884** *Manch. Exam.* 25 Nov. 5/2 We have two or three agitations and upsettings when one would have sufficed.

**Upse·tting,** *ppl. a.* [UP- 6 b. Cf. UPSET *v.*]

**1.** *Sc.* Presumptuous; unduly aspiring, ambitious, or forward.

**1818** SCOTT *Rob Roy* xxxvi, That lang-tongued, conceited, upsetting serving-man o' yours. **1822** GALT *Provost* xlii, He was by nature and inclination one of the upsetting sort. **1854** ['SARAH TYTLER'] *P. Millar* 151 Their poor upsetting attempts at gentility.

*Comb.* **1824** MISS FERRIER *Inher.* lxvi, He's a proud, upsetting-like puppy.

**2.** Overturning, overthrowing, disturbing, etc.

**1872** BAGEHOT *Physics & Pol.* v. 163 A new idea..is, as common people say, so 'upsetting'. **1899** *Westm. Gaz.* 8 June 2/2 A most upsetting amendment to the Service Franchise Bill.

**Upsey-**: see UPSY.

**U·pshoot,** *sb.* [UP- 2.]

**1.** = UPSHOT *sb.* 4. *Obs.* exc. *dial.*

**1588** SHAKS. *L. L. L.* IV. i. 138 Then will shee get the vpshoot by cleauing the pin. **1603** HOLLAND *Plutarch's Mor.* 258 That the chife point of cunning and perfection was in the up-shoot and end of all. **1624** HEYWOOD *Captives* II. i, Hee no questione, That sett mee on to compasse this my will, May when the up-shoote comes assist mee still. **1887** *S. Cheshire Gloss.* 418 Th' upshoot on [= of] it.

**2.** The act of shooting up or the result of this; an upward rush (*of* something).

**1866** ALGER *Solit. Nat. & Man* I. 25 A palm, in its resistless upshoot, cleaving altar and image. **1890** *Nature* 9 Jan. 228/2 If the individual is the mere..upshoot from the continuous root of ancestral plasm. **1898** *Columbus* (Ohio) *Dispatch* 29 Mar. 12/4 The upshoot of flame..was well forward.

**Upshoo·t,** *v.* [UP- 4. Cf. WFris. *opsjitte*, Du. *opschieten*, LG. *upschêten*, G. *aufschiessen*.]

**1.** *intr.* To spring or grow up. Also **Upshoo·ting** *pres. pple.*

**1590** SPENSER *F. Q.* II. xii. 58 The painted flowres, the trees vpshooting hye. **1841** CAMPBELL *Child & Hind* iv, Where Elysian meadows smile, And noble trees upshoot. **1842** TENNYSON *Day-Dream, Sleeping Palace* vi, All round a hedge upshoots. **1876** BLACKIE *Songs Relig. & Life* 4 Like a star in strength upshooting.

**2.** *trans.* and *refl.* To send or raise up.

**1804** W. L. BOWLES *Spir. Discov.* IV. 332 A beauteous tree upshoots amid the glade Its trembling top. **1856** HAWTHORNE *Eng. Note-bks.* (1870) II. 166 A beautiful sheet of water, and a fountain upshooting itself. **1872** BLACKIE *Lays Highl.* 89 Here erect..The Buchail More upshoots his Titan cone.

**U·pshoo·ting,** *ppl. a.* (UP- 6 b. Cf. prec.) **1869** J. PHILLIPS *Vesuv.* ix. 265 The often expanding stream of upshooting stones.

**Upshore**: see UP- 4.

**U·pshot,** *sb.* [UP- 2. Cf. UPSHOOT *sb.* 1, -SHUT.]

†**1.** A final shot in a match at archery; chiefly *fig.*, a closing or parting shot. *Obs.*

**1531** *Privy Purse Exp. Hen. VIII* (1827) 143 Item [paid] to the same Coton for one up shotte that he wanne of the kinges grace, vj s. viij d. **1575** LANEHAM *Let.* (1871) 54 Wel, to this number of biniteez, take ye one mo for an vpshot, & heer an eend. **1589** NASHE *Anat. Absurd.* Ep. Ded. 4 Euery man shotte his bolte, but this was the vpshot, that England afforded many mediocrities. **1597** HOOKER *Eccl. Pol.* v. lxv. § 12 As for their last vpshot of all towards this marke, they are of opinion [etc.]. **1614** JACKSON *Creed* III. i. § 13 As it were for an vp-shot to all the fooles thunderbolts they had let flie before. **1618** BOLTON *Florus* (1636) 56 That event which vertue was about to have given heere, for an upshot, or clozing Victory, fortune gave.

†**2.** A mark or end aimed at. *Obs.*

**1591** SPENSER *M. Hubberd* 770 The onely vpshot whereto he doth ayme. **1595** *Locrine* III. ii. 45 Our regall minde, Which aimes at nothing but a golden crowne, The only vpshot of mine enterprises. **1610** HEALEY *St. Aug. Citie of God* A 3 b, They could not come to the vpshotte of their desires but in the time of warre. **1660** H. MORE *Myst. Godl.* IV. ix. 121 The Ephesians erecting the Image of Hercules.., which is a sign that Pagan Idolatry was the upshot of the plot. **1754** SHERLOCK *Disc.* i. 21 The Upshot of all Religion is to please God.

†**3.** An end, conclusion, or termination. *Obs.*

*c* **1580** STANYHURST *Æneis*, etc. (Arb.) 152 Vertuus he liued, through grace that vertuus eended. What may be then better, than a godly and gratius vpshot? **1595** SOUTHWELL *St. Peter's Compl.*, etc. 55 Death cals her vp, shame driues her out, Despaires her vp-shot make. *a* **1617** BAYNE *On Eph.* (1658) 70 Through fear of death the upshot of evils. **1639** S. DU VERGER tr. *Camus' Admir. Events* 73 To cast him into his grave, and to make a ridiculous upshot of his life. **1662** HIBBERT *Body Divinity* II. 113 They were sung at the departure of the people out of the temple, for an upshot to their divine service.

†**b.** The climax or completion *of* something.

**1586** T. B. *La Primaud. Fr. Acad.* I. 17 For the upshot and perfection of all happines and felicitie in this world.

**c.** The extreme limit. Also *attrib.*

**1699** BOYER *Dict. Royal* II. s.v., A gay Coat and a Grimace is the upshot of what he can pretend to. **1838** DE QUINCEY *Wks.* (1890) XII. 158 We account it frailty that threescore years and ten make the upshot of man's pleasurable existence. **1864** *Field* 23 July 62/1 The odds in this instance were of a more moderate character than those ventured at Liverpool, 4 to 1 being her upshot price.

**4.** The result, issue, or conclusion (*of* some course of action, etc.).

In very frequent use from *c* 1830.

**1604** SHAKS. *Ham.* v. ii. 395 So shall you heare..Of accidentall iudgements,..And in this vpshot, purposes mistooke. **1620** VENNER *Via Recta* iv. 82 You shall commonly see..a dropsey to be the vpshot of all their outragious drinkings. **1649** MILTON *Eikon.* xviii. 166 Hee sought them onely, as by the upshot appeard, to get opportunities. **1680** C. NESSE *Church Hist.* 323 The upshot of all was, our Lord vanquished the devil. **1737** WHISTON *Josephus, Wars* v. xi. 6 The Jews..prevented the upshot of the battle, and retired into the city. **1782** MISS BURNEY *Cecilia* v. xii, Suppose a man was to talk in that manner when he's doing business, what would be the upshot? **1834** PRINGLE *Afr. Sk.* xi. 341 The upshot was, that I found myself overwhelmed with debts. **1856** MERIVALE *Rom. Emp.* xlvi. V. 289 The senators had been growing uneasy, not knowing what upshot to anticipate. **1887** T. A. TROLLOPE *What I remember* I. xvii. 347 A council ..was called, the upshot of which was that our two..allies decided to return to Dover.

**b.** The conclusion resulting from the premises of an argument.

**1639** F. B. tr. *Balzac's Lett.* (vol. IV) 174 This is the upshot of all,..that you must lay a foundation of Bounty. **1677** W. HUGHES *Man of Sin* III. iv. 142 The Upshot..must necessarily come to this, that The Pope is certainly the Man of Sin. **1710** BERKELEY *Princ. Hum. Knowl.* § 75 Yet the upshot of all is—that there are certain unknown Ideas in the mind of God. **1768** FOOTE *Devil* III. Wks. 1799 II. 269 Putting that and t'other together, my notion of the upshot is, that..you must have been born there. **1799** KIRWAN *Geol. Ess.* 496 The upshot of my argument was simply this.

**5.** In phrases: **a.** *In* (rarely *at*, † *upon*) *the upshot*, in the end, at last. † Also const. *of.*

(*a*) **1577** HARRISON *England* III. vii. (1878) II. 28 He..killed them [*sc.* deer] with his hands in the vpshot of that exercise and end of his recreation. **1600** HOLLAND *Livy* XXI. xiv. 401 A cruell commaundement,..but yet needfull, as afterwards it was well seene in the end and upshot of all. **1634** W. TIRWHYT tr. *Balzac's Lett.* (vol. I) 130 We shall in the upshot see them remove mountaines. **1675** ALSOP *Anti-Sozzo* 695 We may be sure that all come to this in the Up shot. **1732** BERKELEY *Alciphr.* VII. § 24 In the upshot, I apprehend you will find it impracticable to destroy all sense of religion. **1768** TUCKER *Lt. Nat.* (1834) I. 37 The service I may do will rise to the same amount in the upshot. **1837** LOCKHART *Scott* I. v. 145 Good for the higher faculties themselves in the upshot. **1854** DE QUINCEY *Wks.* (1889) II. 184 In the upshot, this conclusion *eventuated* (to speak Yankeeishly), that purely on principles of..universal philanthropy could Coleridge have meditated..the upshot.

(*b*) **1617** MORYSON *Itin.* II. 118 It was probable that the King of Spaine would doe something now at the vpshot. *a* **1628** PRESTON *Mt. Ebal* (1638) 48 They shall pay deere for it at the last upshot. **1714** POPE *Let.* 13 July, Wks. 1751 VII. 204 At the upshot, after a life of perpetual application, you reflect [etc.]. **1823** BENTHAM *Not Paul* 81 To apprehend him for the purpose of trying him, and probably at the upshot killing him.

(*c*) **1699** BOYER, Upon the upshot,..*après tout.* **1709** O. DYKES *English Proverbs* 145 Malice, Spite, and Envy, are always Self-Murderers upon the Upshot. **1796** CHARLOTTE SMITH *Marchmont* I. 207 Upon the upshot it appears..that he was deeper in for it than any body thought for.

**b.** *To bring, come*, etc., *to the* (or *an*) *upshot*, to bring to, arrive at, a final or decisive point.

*a* **1600** EDMONDS *Observ. Cæsar's Comm.* (1604) 35 To the end he might bring the matter to a speedy vpshot. **1601** SHAKS. *Twel. N.* IV. ii. 76, I cannot pursue with any safety this sport to the vppeshot. **1646** TRAPP *Comm. John* vii. 50 How far had Judas outstripped Nicodemus till it came to the upshot! **1728** EARL OF AILESBURY *Mem.* (1890) 463 When it came to the upshot he..had all burnt.

†**c.** *At an upshot*, at an end. *Obs.*

**1653** tr. *Stegmann's Brevis Disq.* i. 1 If they once obtain that their Church..is such a Judge..,..the whole businesse is at an upshot.

**6.** †**a.** *slang.* ? A riotous frolic. *Obs.*

**1811** *Lexicon Balatronicum* Pref., They may..abuse their less spirited companions, who prefer a good dinner at home to a glorious up-shot in the highway, without the hazard of a cudgelling.

**b.** *dial.* A merry-making, a feast.

**1837** *Penny Cycl.* VIII. 223/2 Cumbrian peasantry have various festive meetings, called the *kirn*,..sheep-shearing, merry nights, and upshots.

**Upshot,** *ppl. a.* (UP- 5 a.) **1847** SURTEES *Hawbuck Grange* xi. 211 Breaking an upshot column of smoke against his hat brim.

**Upsho·ts,** *adv.* [Cf. UPSHOT *sb.* and UPSIDES *adv.*] (*To be*) *upshots* (*with*), = UPSIDES *adv.* a.

**1877** H. SMART *Bound to Win* I. iii. 61 A rigid resolve to be upshots with Jim Laceby should the opportunity be vouchsafed him.

**U·pshut,** obs. or dial. var. UPSHOT *sb.*

**1620** FORD *Linea V.* 69 This King of men is substitute to his King with this vpshut [etc.]. **1658** A. FOX tr. *Würtz' Surg.* I. ii. 3 In the upshut it proveth meerly an accustomed thing. **1887** *S. Cheshire Gloss.* 418 The form *upshut* is still used in Dorset.

**Upshu·tter.** (UP- 8.) **1809** in *Spirit Pub. Jrnls.* XIII. 81 Thou foe to all fun, thou up-shutter of shops.

**U·psidai·sy,** *int. colloq.* Also **ups(e)y-daisy** (*dial.* **upsa daesy**). [A fanciful variant of the earlier UP-A-DAISY.] (See quot. 1862.)

**1862** [C. C. ROBINSON] *Dial. Leeds* 442 *Upsa daesy!* a common ejaculation when a child, in play, is assisted in a spring-leap from the ground. **1904** *Sat. Rev.* 4 June 713/2 There is little Freddy waiting..to be lifted—'upsidaisy'—into his perambulator.

**U·pside.** Also **up-side.** [UP- 1. Cf. Da. *opside*.]

**1.** The upper side or surface (*of* a thing); the upper half or part.

**1611** COTGR., *Rebourſant*,..turning, or standing inside outward, or the vpside downe. **1654** in E. B. Jupp *Carpenters' Co.* (1887) 316 Two foote 6 inches from the vpside of the trusse to the vpside of the floore. **1678** MOXON *Mech. Ex.* iv. 65 Till the whole upside of the Stuff be Plained. **1706** SWIFT *Baucis & Philemon* 59 With the upside down, to show Its inclination for below. **1833**- [see DOWNSIDE *sb.*]. **1842** J. AITON *Clerical Econ.* 177 It should then be.. put into a dry cloth with the upside down. **1867** MRS. WHITNEY *L. Goldthwaite* v, This glass is in such a horrid light! I don't seem to have but half a face, and I can't tell which is the upside of that!

**2.** *Upside of*, above, beyond.

**1890** *N. & Q.* 26 July 73/1 People whose ages are up-side of forty.

**3.** (See UP *a.* 2 b.) Also *attrib.*

**1880** *Daily News* 13 Dec. 6/7 The upside road [of the railway]..was quite clear. **1898** *Westm. Gaz.* 11 Nov. 7/3 The crowd that thronged the up-side of the station.

**U·pside dow·n,** *adv., sb.*, and *a.* Forms: *α.* 4-5 **up** (5 **upe, uppe**) **so doun** (**don, doune**; 4 *north.* **up swa doune**), 4-6 **up so down** (5-6 **downe**). *β.* 4 **upsa-**, 5 **opsadoun**; 4-6 **upsedoun** (5 **-done**), 5-6 **-downe.** *γ.* 6 **up set doune**; **up** (**uppe**) **set** (**sette**) **downe.** *δ.* 6 **upsyde downe, upside doune** (**downe**), 6- **upside down.** *ε.* 6-7 **vpsidown(e**, 6 **upsidowne**, 6 **upsy(e)downe**, 6 (9) **upsydown.** [Originally *up so* (northern *swa*) *doun*, frequently reduced to *upsa-*, *upse-*, and subsequently altered to *upset* and *upside down*, in the endeavour to make the phrase more intelligible. The use of *so* is peculiar, the only appropriate sense being that of 'as if' (So *adv.* 17 c), and the phrase has no parallel in the cognate languages. It is possible that *up to doun*, occurring in R. Glouc. 6831 (with *up so doun* as a later variant) may be the more original form.]

**A.** *adv.* **1.** So that the upper part or surface becomes the under or lower. Freq. in phr. *to turn upside down*; also in pred. use = inverted, overturned.

*α.* **13..** *Seuyn Sages* (W.) 788 The cradel and the child thai found Up so doun upon the ground. *c* **1340** HAMPOLE *Pr. Consc.* 7230 Þarfor it es ryght and resoune, þat þai be turned up-swa-doune. *c* **1400** *Lanfranc's Cirurg.* 67 Hise iȝen in his heed weren turned vp so doun. *c* **1440** *Pallad. on Husb.* I. 275 The lond aboute a roote is to be moued Al vpsodoun. *c* **1500** *Melusine* v. 25 Raymondyn..wold haue smytte hym betwene the foure legges, For he leye vpsodounne the bely vpward. **1532** HERVET *Xenophon's Househ.* (1534) 48 b, He also must..turne vp so downe and styr the grounde. **1538** ELYOT *Dict.*, *Procello*,..to turn vp so downe.

*β.* **1382** WYCLIF *Matt.* xxi. 12 He turnyde vpsadoun [**1388** vpsedoun] the bordis of chaungeris. *c* **1400** *Brut* I. 253 Wherwiþ þe gode man awoke..and turnede his body opsadoun. *c* **1440** *Promp. Parv.* 512/2 Upsedowne,..*eversus, subversus.* **1523** LD. BERNERS tr. *Froiss.* I. 356 He toke kyng Dampeter by the legge and turned hym vpsedowne.

*γ.* *c* **1520** BARCLAY *Jugurth* (1557) 18 Transuersed or turned vp set downe. **1532** HERVET *Xenophon's Househ.* 55 Lyke this greke lettre, Y, turned vp set downe.

*δ.* *c* **1490** *Liber Pluscardensis* XI. xi. (Bodl. MS.), Iustice makis ryche bath realme & ceteys,..Quhar lak of law bryngis all this vp sid doun [*v.r.* vpsadon]. **1535** COVERDALE *Judg.* vii. 13 Whan it came to the tente, it..ouerthrew it, and turned it vpsyde downe. **1570** FOXE *A. & M.* (ed. 2) 2307/2 The wagon also beyng cast vpsidedowne. **1600** PORY tr. *Leo's Africa* III. 155 Deepely deluing into the earth, they turne vpside downe the foundations of houses. **1669** STURMY *Mariner's Mag.* v.66 Every Fortnight..turn all the Barrels, ..turn them upside down. **1706** LONDON & WISE *Retir'd Gard'ner* I. x. 289 Stick into the Ground a Stake.., put at Top of it a Mug upside down. *c* **1791** *Encycl. Brit.* (1797) VII. 374/1 Others think, that the waters of the sea..turned the whole surface of the earth upside down. **1841** MRS. MOZLEY *Lost Brooch* II. xxi. 154 They will come and search the house, and all our things will be turned upside down. **1889** JEROME *Three Men in Boat* xv, We..decided that the bottom was the top, and set to work to fix it upside-down.

*ε.* **1569** W. HUBBARD *Ceyx & Alcione* A vij, The boisterous windes..our ship on Seas did tosse.., Vntill it was turnd upsidowne. **1590** SPENSER *F. Q.* II. vii. 4 In his lap a masse of coyne he told, And turned vpsidowne, to feede his eye.

**1848** ALB. SMITH *Chr. Tadpole* xiv. 131 [The sand-glass] topples over upsy-down and runs back again.

**2.** *fig.* In, or into, a state of overthrow, reversal, or disorder. Chiefly with *turn*.

*α.* *c* **1327** *Pol. Songs* (Camden) 335 Thus is the ordre of kniht turned up-so-doun. *c* **1374** CHAUCER *Boeth.* v. pr. iii. 156 How fer fro þe soþe and how vp so doun is þis þing þat we seyn. **1390** GOWER *Conf.* I. 282 Al up so doun my joie it casteth. *c* **1430** LYDG. *Min. Poems* (Percy Soc.) 151 The wourld is tournyd almoost up so doun. *a* **1450** *Knt. de la Tour* vi. 9 Atte the yongest doughtres hous it was turned up-so-doun, and alle unthrifti. **1508** FISHER *7 Penit. Ps.* vi. Wks. (1876) 12 The wounde of a mannes conscyence.. stereth vpsodowne the memory. **1559** *Mirr. Mag.* B j, By reason kynge Richarde,..By synister aduyse, had tourned all vpsodowne.

*β.* **13..** *Minor Poems Vernon MS.* lv. 103 For he may turne kuyndes vpsedoun, Þat alle kuyndes made of nouȝt. **1426** LYDG. *De Guil. Pilgr.* 17064, I ha tournd the vp-se-doun..With my trouble and with my wo. ? *a* **1450** in *3rd Rep. Hist. MSS. Comm.* 279/2 Who but antichrist coude turne the treuthe upsedone? **1568** GRAFTON *Chron.* II. 625 To chaunge all things, and tourne the world upsedowne.

*γ.* **1509** BARCLAY *Shyp of Folys* 135 A foole..tournynge the lawes vp set downe By vyle rewardes. **1540** MORYSINE *Vives's Introd. Wysd.* B iij b, Many [things]..have loste their ryghte estimation and are chaunged uppe sette downe. **1569** J. SANFORD tr. *Agrippa's Van. Artes* 89 They disquiet and turne the earth upset downe.

*δ.* **1535** COVERDALE *Ps.* cxlv[i]. 9 As for the waye of yᵉ vngodly, he turneth it vpsyde downe. **1579** KNEWSTUB *Confut.* Ep. Ded. *4 b, H. N. turneth religion vp side downe, and buildeth heauen heere vpon earth. **1627** H. LESLY *Serm. bef. Majesty* 23 Our nature..must be turned up-side-downe, cast into a new mould. **1712** ADDISON *Spect.* No. 305 ⁋ 15 These young Machiavils will, in a little time, turn their College upside-down with Plots and Stratagems. **1817** KEATINGE *Trav.* I. 33 The walls of this town exemplify to us..the world turned upside down. **1855** KINGSLEY *Westw. Ho!* iv, Mr. Frank..would have..turned her poor little flighty brains upside down for ever. **1883** STEVENSON *Treas. Isl.* xxx, Why, your liver, man, is upside down. Did you take that medicine?

*ε.* **1549** LATIMER *Fifth Serm. bef. Edw. VI* (Arb.) 137 Iosias..tourned al vpsydowne, he would suffer no Idolatrye to stand. **1579** G. HARVEY *Letter-bk.* (Camden) 73 Your delicacy would haply have delighted yourself in overturning ye proverbe upsyedowne. **1601** R. JOHNSON *Kingd. & Commw.* (1603) 19 By remaining full of French soldiers all things were turned vpsidowne. **1876** BESANT & RICE *Gold. Butterfly* II. 254 It's a story without an end, it's a story told upsy-down.

†**B.** *sb.* An overturning. *Obs.*

**1593** G. HARVEY *Pierce's Super.* 84 A fewe resolute Aphorismes; that..roundly determine all with an Vpsy-downe. No reformation without an Vpsy-downe.

**C.** *adj.* Turned upside down; inverted.

Written with hyphen (*upside-down*) or as one word.

**1866** G. STEPHENS *Runic Mon.* I. 84 Twisted runes, upside-down runes, and such like. **1882** BESANT *All Sorts* xxviii, The same upsydown, topsy-turvy, one-sided..perverseness. **1883** W. S. GILBERT *Foggerty's Fairy*, etc. (1890) 238 She was..an industrious little girl, and, as far as I could judge by her upside-down reflection, neat in her dress.

Hence **U·pside-dow:nism.**

**1861** F. METCALFE *Oxonian in Iceland* vii. (1867) 106 The Demons of Misrule and Upside-downism.

**U·pside dow·nward(s,** *advs.* [f. prec. + -WARD, -WARDS.] = prec. A.

**1611** COTGR., *Enverser*,..to turne vpside-downeward, or the inside outward. *Ibid.* s.vv. *Rebourssé, Revers.* **1672** BLAKESTON *Lazarillo* II. xiii. T 4 b, She made the peeces of my Cloak to be stiched one to another, and for very hast they put them upside downwards. **1781** C. JOHNSTON *Hist. J. Juniper* II. 131 On his arrival he found the town turned, as we say, upside downwards. **1826** DISRAELI *V. Grey* vi. i, As he tossed, with a careless hand, the great horn upside downwards. **1845** — *Sybil* II. ix, I think the world is turned upside downwards in these parts.

**Upsi·des,** *adv.* [f. UPSIDE *sb.* Cf. MSw. *upsidhis, -es* by the side (of), alongside.]

**1.** *Upsides with*, even, equal, or quits with (a person) by means of retaliation or successful rivalry. *dial.* (orig. *Sc.*) or *colloq.*

**1746** LD. LOVAT in Williams *Hist. Rec. 11th Hussars* (1908) 47, I..am still in good spirits, and hope to be upsides with the barbarous villains who have used me so. **1752** in *Scots Mag.* (1753) Sept. 454/1 He did not care though he should be up-sides with him. **1816** SCOTT *Antiq.* xxi, It's best no to be rash;..I'se be upsides wi' him ae day. **1853** R. S. SURTEES *Sponge's Sp. Tour* xxx, He considered it his duty to be 'upsides' with him, and tell the servants all he knew about him. **1891** ATKINSON *Last of Giant-killers* 65 He did want to be upsides with that insulting little jackanapes.

**2.** *colloq.* On a level *with*; alongside *of*.

**1883** *Standard* 12 Feb. 2/6 Baron Farney must finish at least upsides with his then conqueror. **1894** ASTLEY *50 Years Life* II. 210 Never [to] let any horse get upsides of him if he could help it.

†**Upsie-turvy,** *adv. Obs.* [var. of TOPSY-TURVY, influenced by *upsie-down*. Cf. *upside-turvy* in mod. dial. (s. Linc.).] Topsy-turvy.

*a* **1592** GREENE *Jas. IV*, III. iii, I came to court..There found I all was vpsie turuy turnd.

†**U·psight.** *Obs. rare.* [In sense 1 prob. ad. older Du. and Flem. *opsicht* (mod. *opzicht*); in sense 2 f. UP- 2.]

**1.** View, inspection.

**1515** *St. Papers Hen. VIII* II. 14 Nowe, after the upsyght hereof, he maye pretende no maner ignoraunce. **1648** HEXHAM II, *Opsichtigh*, which hath Regard or Vpsight.

**2.** Height as viewed from below.

*a* **1560** PHAER *Æneid* IX. (1562) Ee ij b, A towre of stepe vpsight [L. *vasto suspectu*] there stood, with skaffolds large of length.

**Upsi·ghted,** *a.* *s.w. dial.* [UP- 3.] Having eyes which cannot readily look downward.

**1847** HALLIWELL. **1903** 'Q' (QUILLER COUCH) *Hetty Wesley* I. viii, An angle which gave an 'up-sighted' expression to his small eyes.

**Upsiloid,** var. HYPSILOID *a.*

**1889** *Buck's Handbk. Med. Sci.* VIII. 156/1 A upsiloid (U-shaped), depressed line with lateral branches.

**Upsilon** (yupsəi·lǫn). [a. Gr. ὖ ψιλόν 'slender u', the adj. having reference to its later sound (*ü*).]

**1.** The Greek letter Υ, υ (originally V, Y) representing the vowel *u* (see U, V, and Y). Also *attrib.*, = having the form of this letter.

**1642** HOWELL *For. Trav.* xi. (Arb.) 56 In some places of the Morea..they confound these three letters η, ι, υ (Eta, Iota, Upsilon). **1693** DRYDEN *Persius, Sat.* iii. 109 *note*, Pithagoras of Samos made the allusion of the Y, or Greek Upsilon, to Vice and Virtue. **1763** *Ann. Reg., Misc.* 194/1 The last notes..(pronounced as the Greek upsilon, or the French u). **1799** TOWNSON *Tracts & Observ. Nat. Hist.* 75 The upsilon Cartilage. **1820** T. S. HUGHES *Trav. Sicily* I. 245 The only people who pronounce the letter *upsilon* like the Italian *u*. **1854** BUSHNAN in *Orr's Circ. Sci., Org. Nat.* I. 121 The hyoid bone is described as having the shape of the Greek upsilon.

**2.** *Ent.* A species of moth (see quot.).

**1832** RENNIE *Brit. Butterfl. & M.* 59 The Upsilon (*Orthosia Upsilon*, Ochsenheimer) appears in July,..the stigmata pale, between which is a black mark resembling a Y or V.

Hence **Upsi·lonism,** tendency to use the letter *u*.

**1879** T. F. SIMMONS *Lay Folks Mass Bk.* Introd. p. lvi, The perpetual upsilonism of our West-Midland text E.

†**U·psitten,** *ppl. a. Sc. Obs.* [UP- 5.] Inactive, indifferent, callous.

**1682** PEDEN *Lord's Trumpet* (1739) 16 The Lord..hath been crying to You in these Lands (and namelie to thee up-sitten Scotland) to watch with him. **1728** P. WALKER *Life Peden* (1827) Pref. 27 These backslidden, upsitten, lukewarm Ministers, Elders and Professors. *Ibid.* 61 The Indulged, Backslidden and Upsitten Ministers of Scotland. [**1896** STEVENSON *Weir of Hermiston* v, The sister of the gardener ..had shown herself 'upsitten'.]

**Upsi·tting,** *vbl. sb.* [UP- 7.]

**1.** The occasion of a woman's first sitting up to receive company after a confinement. *Obs.* exc. *dial.* (Cf. UPSETTING *vbl. sb.* 2.)

**1572** J. JONES *Bathes of Buckstone* 9 b, Some in forme of Cakes, as at weddings; some Rondes of Hogs, as at vp-sittings. **1603** DEKKER *Bachelor's Banquet* C 3, It is your vpsitting, and a fortnight at the least since you were brought to bed. **1641** BROME *Joviall Crew* II. (1652) F 2 b, We will have such..A Christning; such up-sitting and Ghossiping! **1688** R. HOLME *Armoury* III. 12/2 This is a kind of dress which Women in Child-bed usually wear, when they are for Christnings, and up-sittings. **1746** *Exmoor Scolding* (E.D.S.) 24 'Twas thee roil'st upon me up to Daraty Vogwill's Upzitting. **1828**– in dialect glossaries (Yks., Som., Dev.).

†**2.** The fact of sitting up again after an illness.

**1646** FULLER *Wounded Consc.* xix. 140, I must..rejoyce at thy upsitting, whom God hath raised from the bed of despaire. **1742** RICHARDSON *Pamela* IV. 303, I am once more ..enabled to dedicate to you the first Fruits of my Penmanship, on my Upsitting.

†**3.** *Sc.* Inactivity, indifference. *Obs.*

**1680** STEWART in Howie *Cloud of Witnesses* (1778) 74 The Lord hath rubbed shame on all our faces, because of many backslidings and upsitting in duty. **1709** WODROW *Corr.* (1842) I. 55 There is a remarkable upsitting among us in mutual freedom one with another.

**4.** *S. African.* The practice of sitting up during the night as a method of courtship. (After Du. *opzitten*.) Also *attrib.*

**1863** W. C. BALDWIN *Afr. Hunting* vi. 165 When two up-sittings have been going on, at opposite corners of a large room. *Ibid.*, The upsitting business I consider about the best of their old customs. **1896** *Westm. Gaz.* 20 Jan. 1/3 The nocturnal courtship, or 'upsitting'.

**Up-si·tting,** *pres. pple.* (UP- 6.) **1753** G. WEST tr. *Pindar* I. 242 On his Couch up-sitting all Night long. **1776** *Maiden Aunt* II. 148, I..found her up-sitting. †**U·p-skip.** *Obs.* [UP- 2.] An upstart. **1549** LATIMER *2nd Serm. bef. Edw. VI*, E j, Heare menes suetes your selfe..& put it not to the hearing of these veluette cotes, these vp skippes.

**Upsoa·r,** *v.* [UP- 4.] *intr.* To soar upwards. Also **Upsoa·ring** *pres. pple.*

**1582** STANYHURST *Æneis* I. (Arb.) 29 Thow shalt shortlye see townwals, And citty vpsoaring..to skytoppe. **1725** POPE *Odyss.* XV. 565 On the right up-soar'd in air The hawk. **1743** FRANCIS tr. *Hor., Odes* III. iii. 11 Thus to the flamy Towers above, The vagrant Hero..Upsoar'd. **1855** BROWNING *Saul* II. x, As when..upsoareth the cherubim chariot. **1865** TRENCH *Poems* 480 How like a swan..The voice upsoars of thy triumphant song.

**Upsoa·ring,** *vbl. sb.* (UP- 7. Cf. prec.) **1846** HAWTHORNE *Mosses* II. v, Higher upsoarings and baser degradations of the soul. **1876** FAIRBAIRN in *Contemp. Rev.* XXVII. 955 The sudden upsoaring of the revived national spirit. **Upsoa·ring,** *ppl. a.* (UP-¹ 6 b.) **1818** MILMAN *Samor* VII. 259 Mysterious union of upsoaring spirits. †**Upso·lve,** illiterate for ABSOLVE *v.* 6. **1598** B. JONSON *Ev. Man in Hum.* I. iv, You are a scholler, vpsolue me that, now.

**Upspea·k,** *v.* [UP- 4.] *intr.* To speak up; to begin to speak.

**1819** W. TENNANT *Papistry Storm'd* (1827) 103 Let him up-speik as best he may. *a* **1842** W. MAGINN *Homeric Ball.* (1850) 251 They all agreed, and then upspoke the chief of many a wile. **1888** R. BUCHANAN *City of Dreams* VII. 130 But soon the host upspake, and sought to spread A feeble cheer.

**U·pspring,** *sb.* [UP- 2.]

†**1.** Rising *of* the sun; dawn *of* day. *Obs.*

*c* **1000** *Rule of Chrodegang* xviii, Fram þæs dæȝes upspringe to halsungtiman. *c* **1000** *Sax. Leechd.* III. 274 Easterne wind..blæwð fram ðære sunnan upspringe. **1471** RIPLEY *Comp. Alch.* VII. vi. (MS. Ashm. 1486), Thus yᵉ vii gate..In yᵉ vpspryng is of yᵉ soone requyrede. **1562** TURNER *Herbal* II. 50 The..parte of the worlde toward the vpspryng of the son.

**2.** The action of springing up into existence; beginning of growth or development; origin; † generation.

*c* **1000** ÆLFRIC *Gen.* v. 10 Æfter þes upspringe, he leofode .viii. hund ȝeara. **13..** *Cursor M.* 9283 (Gött.), A mayden sal brede, of his hup-spring [*Cott.* ox-spring]. **1554** KNOX *Faythf. Admon.* C 3 b, From the beginning of the late vpspryng of the Gospel in England. **1585** T. WASHINGTON tr. *Nicholay's Voy.* III. iii. 73 Hauing..giuen amply..to vnderstand the vpspring of the Asamoglans. **1651** R. CHILD in *Hartlib's Legacy* (1655) 63 You ought to sow them..in March, April, or May, when frosts are..not so sharp..as to endanger their up-spring. **1825** COLERIDGE *Aids Refl.* 40 A state..favourable to the germination and up-spring of a nobler seed.

†**3.** A kind of dance. *Obs.*⁻¹

For Shaks. *Ham.* I. iv. 9 see note to UPSPRING *a.*

*a* **1634** CHAPMAN *Alphonsus* III. (1654) 33 We Germans have no changes in our dances, An Almain and an upspring, that is all.

†**U·pspring,** *a.* *Obs.* [UP- 3.] Upstart; newly arisen or come in.

In quot. 1602 *upspring* has also been interpreted as sense 3 of the sb., *reels* being taken as a verb with cognate object.

**1591** HORSEY *Trav.* (Hakl. Soc.) 258 The patriarcke,.. bishops and friers, and other the new upspringe nobillitie. **1602** SHAKS. *Ham.* I. iv. 9 The King doth wake to night, and takes his rouse, Keepes wassels and the swaggering vpspring reeles [= revels].

**Upspri·ng,** *v.* [UP- 4. Cf. WFris. *opspringe*, (M)Du. *opspringen*, MLG. *upspringen*; MHG. *ûfspringen* (G. *aufspringen*); MSw. *up-, opspringa* (Sw. *upp-*), (M)Da. *opspringe*.]

**1.** *intr.* Of plants, etc.: To spring up, to grow.

*c* **1000** *Ags. Gosp.* Matt. xiii. 5 Sume feollon on stænihte.. and hrædlice upsprungon. *c* **1200** ORMIN 10543 Allswa summ corn & chaff Uppsprinngenn off an rote. *c* **1374** CHAUCER *Former Age* 10 But corn vp-sprong vnsowe of mannes hond. **1471** RIPLEY *Comp. Alch.* v. viii. (MS. Ashm. 1479), So ther shuld ther of no frute vp spring. **1865** EMERSON *Sphinx* 18 Erect as a sunbeam, Upspringeth the palm. **1876** BLACK *Madcap Violet* ii, Far away..the subtle fire of the earth upsprang in pale primroses.

**b.** *fig.* To arise, come into being.

*c* **1386** CHAUCER *Clerk's T.* 884 Fro Bologne is this Erl of Pavyk come, Of which the fame vp sprang to moore and lesse. *a* **1500** *Ratis Raving* I. 1428 Gud dissert will nocht vp-spring, But hail purpos. **1562** WINȜET *Cert. Tractatis* Wks. (S.T.S.) I. 6 Pryde and auarice, of the quhilkis..hes vp-sprung the electioun of vnqualifeit bischopis. **1596** DALRYMPLE tr. *Leslie's Hist. Scot.* (S.T.S.) I. 325 Frome him the hous and clann of the Cumeinis first vpsprang. **1667** MILTON *P. L.* VII. 462 These [cattle] in flocks Pasturing at once, and in broad Herds upsprung. **1744** THOMSON *Winter* 641 Up-springs the Dance along the lighted Dome. **1821** BYRON *Heav. & Earth* iii. 869 The forests' trees (coeval with the hour When Paradise upsprung). **1842** BORROW *Bible in Spain* xliv, Here upsprang, in Spain's better days, a little city. **1890** J. PULSFORD *Loyalty to Christ* I. 7 The joy of eternity begins to upspring in our bosoms.

**2.** To rise, to ascend; to spring or leap upwards; to start to one's feet.

*c* **1374** CHAUCER *Compl. Mars* 14 Er sunne gan vp sprynge. **14..** in *Anglia* XXVII. 286 We saw his stern in þe est spedily vpspryng. **1500–20** DUNBAR *Poems* xi. 2 Airly as did the day vpspring, Thus sang ane bird. **1563** SACKVILLE *Induct. Mirr. Mag.* lxvi, The flames vpspring, and..crepe From walle to roofe. **1729** SAVAGE *Wanderer* IV. 138 The trout ..Up-springs, and sunward turns its crimson stains. **1760** BEATTIE *Ode to Hope* 22 Startled at the heavenly ray, With speed unwonted Indolence upsprings. **1806** J. GRAHAME *Birds of Scot.* 12 When flush, the game upsprings. **1848** LYTTON *K. Arthur* VI. lv, Upsprung the host, upsprung the guests in ire—Upsprung the gentle dames, and fled affrighted. **1885–94** R. BRIDGES *Eros & Psyche* June vi, Upsprang she then, and kiss'd them and embraced.

**Upspri·nging,** *vbl. sb.* (UP- 7. Cf. prec.)

*c* **1400** tr. *Secreta Secret., Gov. Lordsh.* 92 If þou take seuen graynes..and breke hem yn þe vpsprynggynge of lucyfer and venus. **1851** MRS. BROWNING *Casa Guidi Wind.* I. 5 The upspringing Of such a nimble bird. **1868** MORRIS *Earthly Par.* I. II. 633 The white upspringing of the spurts of spray.

**Upspri·nging,** *ppl. a.* (UP- 6 b. Cf. UPSPRING *v.*)

*c* **1400** tr. *Secreta Secret., Gov. Lordsh.* 112 Stable þou þe mountant, or þe vpspryngand, yn þe tokenynge of þe Lyon. **1551** BALE *Eng. Votaries* II. 95 The vpsprynggynge braunches of Sodome. **1845** HIRST *Com. Mammoth*, etc. 111 The downy wing Of some up-springing bird. **1873** B. HARTE *Fiddletown* 52 By the upspringing light he saw the figure of Kate. **1883** MISS BURNE *Shropsh. Folklore* XXV. 344 Men implored a blessing upon their land and its upspringing crops.

**Upspru·ng,** *pa. pple.* (UP- 5. Cf. UPSPRING *v.*)

*c* **1000** *Ags. Gosp.* Matt. xiii. 6 Soþlice upsprungenre sunnan hiȝ adruwudon. *c* **1250** *Gen. & Ex.* 3050 Trees it for-brac, and gres, and corn, ðat was up-sprungen ðor bi-foren. **1400** tr. *Secreta Secret., Gov. Lordsh.* 99 He hadde no sterre vp-sprongyn þat was euyl no contrary. **1563** WINȜET *Wks.* (S.T.S.) II. 12 Be the negligence..of zour Hienes forebearis ..al this perturbatioun, trible, and hie interpryseis..ar wp-sproung. **1729** SAVAGE *Wanderer* II. 415 Up-sprung, such weed-like Coarseness it [*sc.* the grain] betrays, Flocks on th' abandon'd Blade permissive graze. **1826** E. IRVING *Babylon* I. II. 78 We are not to suppose that the ten..were all up-sprung before the little horn appeared. **1876** F. K. ROBINSON *Whitby Gloss.* 209 *Upsprung*, adj., sprung up in all senses.

†**Upspurner.** *Obs.*⁻¹ [UP- 8 + SPURN *v.*¹ 5 b.] ? One who treats with disdain.

1545 JOYE *Exp. Dan.* iv. 59 b, Howe wretchedly Pompeius that vpspurner of the erth perisshed, Lucanus describeth it.

U·p-sta·ge: see UP *a.* 2.

**U·pstair,** *adv.* and *a.* [UP *prep.*$^2$ 1, 7.]

1. *adv.* = UPSTAIRS *adv.* 1.

1627 DRAYTON *Moon Calf* 165 When vp-stayre one, downe-stayre another hies.

2. *adj.* = UPSTAIRS *a.*

1814 HEYNE *Tracts India* 277, I staid in an upstair room with him for many hours. 1849 ROCK *Ch. of Fathers* I. iii. 230 Many of such upstair-chapels are still to be seen in.. Gloucester cathedral. 1861 FLOR. NIGHTINGALE *Nursing* ii. (ed. 2) 27 But do these people know the up-stair habits of this class [*sc.* young ladies]? 1885 *Fortn. in Waggonette* 18 An upstair sitting-room.

**Upstairs,** *adv., sb.,* and *a.* [UP *prep.*$^2$ 1, 7.]

A. *adv.* (vpstēə·ɪz). 1. So as to ascend a flight of stairs; to the floor at the top of a staircase.

Stressed *u·pstairs* when contrasted with *downstairs*.

1596 SHAKS. *1 Hen. IV*, II. iv. 112 His industry is vp-staires and down-staires, his eloquence the parcell of a reckoning. 1658 E. PHILLIPS *Myst. Love & Eloquence* 75 Up stairs we nimbly creep, And find the Sluts asleep. 1661 in Jamieson *Sc. Dict.* s.v. *Breadberry*, Tripping up stares and down stares with a posset or berry for the laird or lady. 1722 DE FOE *Plague* (1896) 127 Some [running] down stairs and some up stairs. 1767 *Woman of Fashion* I. 244 Shew the Lady up Stairs. 1797 S. & HT. LEE *Canterb. T.* (1799) I. 152 He abruptly walked up stairs, and .. opened the door. 1839 DICKENS *Nickleby* lxii, He made his way up stairs into the room. 1876 T. HARDY *Ethelberta* vii, I think that after the women had gone upstairs the others turned their thoughts upon you again.

b. *fig.* (See KICK *v.* 5 b.)

c1697 BURNET *Orig. Mem.* (1902) 145 He [Halifax] had said he had known many kicked down stairs, but he never knew any kicked up stairs before. 1821 [see KICK *v.* 5 b].

2. At the top of, on a floor or in a room reached by, a flight of stairs; in one of the upper stories of a house.

1781 COWPER *Table T.* 151 To be the Table Talk of clubs up stairs. 1796–7 JANE AUSTEN *Pride & Prej.* lv, Her mother.. was sitting up stairs with Kitty. 1844 KINGLAKE *Eothen* xvi, It is upstairs—on the first floor. 1882 MISS BRADDON *Mt. Royal* III. ii. 28 You would rather dine upstairs, I dare say.

b. quasi-*sb.*

1842 LOVER *Handy Andy* xiv, The ogre's voice from up-stairs. 1898 WATTS-DUNTON *Aylwin* XII. iii, As I spoke I heard a noise...It seemed to come from upstairs.

c. As *sb.* An upper story or floor. Also *transf.*, a person or persons living on an upper floor.

1884 in *Proc. Soc. Psychical Research* Dec. (1885) 329, I was ..present on the day when Mr. Coulomb gave the charge of the upstairs to our party. 1896 *Westm. Gaz.* 23 April 2/3 The magistrate could not discriminate whether upstairs or down-stairs began [the fight].

B. *adj.* (v·pstēəɪz). 1. Situated on an upper story or at the top of a flight of steps.

1782 *Jrnl. Yng. Lady of Virginia* (1871) 46 Nancy had a fire made up in one of the up-stairs rooms. 1850 *Household Words* I. 206/1 In upstairs Infirmary wards. 1879 MRS. A. E. JAMES *Ind. Househ. Managem.* 35 A bungalow has rarely any upstairs rooms.

b. Belonging to, connected with, the upper rooms or parts of a house.

1839 HOOD *On Completing Forty-Seven* iv, I hear the up-stairs bell. 1848 THACKERAY *Van. Fair* xvi, At the usual hour..the upstairs maid knocked at the door of the..bed-chamber. 1894 ELIZ. BANKS *Camp. Curiosity* 10 The up-stairs duties of a first-class lodging-house.

2. Having more than one story.

1840 E. E. NAPIER *Scenes & Sports For. Lands* II. v. 163 Old B— possessed one of the few up-stairs houses in the cantonment, in the lower part of which he had his shop.

Upstalled: see UP- 5.

**U·pstand,** *sb.* [UP- 2.] An upstanding thing; an upright structure or part.

1847 HALLIWELL, *Upstands*, marks for boundaries of parishes, estates, &c., being live trees cut off about breast high. *Kent.* 1880 LOMAS *Alkali Trade* 33 A 14-in. lead up-stand, flanged upon the floor.

**Upsta·nd,** *v.* [UP- 4. Cf. OS. *upstandan*, WFris. *opstean*, MDu. *opstaen* (Du. *opstaan*), MLG. *upstân*, MHG. *ûfstân, -stên* (G. *aufstehen*), MSw. *upstanda, op(p)sta* (Sw. *uppstå*), MDa. *opstande, opsta* (Da. *opstaa*).]

†1. *intr.* To stand erect or upright. *Obs.*

c1205 LAY. 1650 Þa þe castel vp-stod he wes strong & swiðe god. c1250 *Gen. & Ex.* 3247 Ðe water up-stod..On twinne half, also a wal up-riȝt. c1340 HAMPOLE *Pr. Consc.* 4762 Þe se sal ryse,..And in his stede even upstande, Als an heghe hille dus on þe lande. c1440 *Pallad. on Husb.* III. 310 A dight vine in prouyntial manere That lyke a busshe vpstont. 1513 DOUGLAS *Æneid* IX. v. 50 O kyndly goddis..Vndre quhais myghtis all tyme Troy vpstandis. 1552 LYNDESAY *Monarche* 5465 The sey..sall nocht spred ouir the land, Bot, lyke ane wall, ewin straycht vpstand.

2. To rise to one's feet; to stand up. Also *fig.*

a1300 *E. E. Psalter* ii. 2 Vpstode kinges of þe land,.. Ogaine þair lauerd þai come on ane. 13.. *Guy Warw.* (A.) 1599 When he of swoning vp stod, His feren he biheld wiþ drery mod. a1400 *Isumbras* 324 Whenne the wounded knyght myght up-stande,.. Wepande awaye went hee. 1513 DOUGLAS *Æneid* XI. vii. 93 Ane Drances tho vpstud, and speke began. 1596 SPENSER *F. Q.* IV. vi. 23 But die or liue for nought he would vpstand. 1653 MILTON *Psalm* ii. 2 Why do..the Kings of th' earth upstand With power? 1667 — *P. L.* VI. 446 In th' assembly next upstood Nisroc. 1791 COWPER *Yardley Oak* 173 The father of us all,..moulded by his Maker into man At once, upstood intelligent. 1896 in *Westm. Gaz.* 27 May 6/1 With all dignity..Alexandra Feodorovna upstood from her throne.

3. *fig.* To stand up *for* something. *rare*$^{-1}$.

1722 W. HAMILTON *Wallace* IX. i. (1816) 154 In the defence of righteous royal blood, For which thou always loyally up-stood.

**Upsta·nder.** [UP- 8. Cf. Icel. *upp-standari.*] *spec.* One of two upright posts on a sledge.

1856 KANE *Arct. Expl.* II. x. 98 It has two standards, or, as we call them, 'upstanders'. 1903 PEARY in *McClure's Mag.* Feb. 419/2, I had scarcely time to seize the upstanders when my dogs were off.

**Upsta·nding,** *vbl. sb.* [UP- 7.] The action of standing (up), or rising to one's feet; the fact of remaining in place.

Some dialect uses are recorded in the *Eng. Dial. Dict.*

1535 COVERDALE *Isaiah* xxxiii. 3 Graunte..that at thy vpstondinge the Gentiles maye be scatred abrode. 1538 LATIMER in Nichols *Hist. Leics.* (1800) III. 1065/2 He wold be an humble sewter..for the upstandynge of his forsayd howsse. 1861 J. EDMOND *Children's Ch. at Home* xi. 166 There were many feelings expressed in that upstanding and applause. 1886 SPURGEON *Treas. Dav.* Ps. cxxxvi. 6 The original upheaval and perpetual upstanding of the habitable land.

**Upsta·nding,** *pres. pple.* [UP- 6.]

1. Standing up; erect; on one's feet.

c1375 *Lay Folks Mass Bk.* (MS. B.) 261 Saye pater-noster, ȝit vp-standande. c1440 *Pallad. on Husb.* XII. 601 Mydday & ouernoon .. A mydde is noon vpstondyng right. 1596 SPENSER *F. Q.* V. vii. 20 With long locks vp-standing, [he] stifly stared. 1628 MAY *Virg. Georg.* III. 99 The water-snakes, with scales up-standing, dy. 1828 ATHERSTONE *Fall of Nineveh* I. 142 Toward the Median camp, Upstanding in his car, himself looked out. 1861 *Illustr. Lond. News* 1 June 505/1 A white-headed clergyman was called upon to say prayers, which he did upstanding. 1884 LADY BRASSEY *Egypt after War* IV. 17 Feb., In the court outside are two obelisks, one still upstanding.

2. *fig.* Remaining in good estate, intact, or in the same condition. *north. dial.*

c1450 *Lay Folks Mass Bk.* 70 We sall pray..for all lande tyllande, þat god..maynteyn þame so, þat þai may be up-standand. 1649 W. G. *Surv. Newcastle upon Tine* 24 All his stock upstanding, he living all that time of the Profit that his ground yeelded. 1855 [ROBINSON] *Whitby Gloss.*, *Upstanding*, remaining as heretofore.

3. *Mining.* (See quot.)

1883 GRESLEY *Gloss. Coal-m.* 269 *Up-standing*, the condition of a goaf when such portions of the pillars are worked away as still to leave the roof supported.

**Upsta·nding,** *ppl. a.* [UP- 6 b.]

1. Standing up; erect.

c1000 *Sax. Leechd.* I. 332 Aho on upstandende twiȝ. c1000 ÆLFRIC *Gloss.* in Wr.-Wülcker 154 *Pira*, upstandende herebeacn. c1384 CHAUCER *H. Fame* 1389 She Had also fele vpstondyng eres And tonges, as on bestes heres. 1590 SPENSER *F. Q.* II. ix. 13 Staring with hollow eyes, and stiffe vpstanding heares. 1611 COTGR. s.v. *Rasibus*, The top of an open, and vp-standing Hogs-head. 1628–9 in *Maitl. Club Misc.* III. 370 To lay fyre to the upstanding Craig at the greine. 1805 SOUTHEY *Madoc* I. vii. 87 Round the helm A coronal of high upstanding plumes. 1883 *Times* 11 June 4/5 A pigeon is perched upon each of the two upstanding handles. 1898 *St. James's Gaz.* 14 Nov. 13/1 A close round black toque and upstanding feathers.

2. Of animals (esp. horses) or persons: Having an erect carriage; well set up.

(*a*) 1835 SIR G. STEPHEN *Adv. Search Horse* xv. 191 Very superior, well-bred,..up-standing..seasoned horses. 1877 *J. Coleman's Sheep & Pigs* 36 The latter are white and clean in both, and, more, what are generally called *upstanding* sheep. 1883 R. GROOM *Gt. Dane* 13 A large, upstanding dog, of noble presence.

(*b*) 1882 MISS BRADDON *Mt. Royal* III. vi. 106 A well-grown upstanding young woman. 1894 *Strand Mag.* VIII. 156 The Marquis was a tall, upstanding man of spare figure. 1901 *Longm. Mag.* Dec. 147 The Nolans were all fair and big, upstanding men and women.

b. *fig.* Of persons: Of open, honest, or independent bearing; straightforward, downright.

1863 R. S. HAWKER in Byles *Life* (1905) 462 He found the Miners and the Fishermen an upstanding rollicking courageous people. 1889 'R. BOLDREWOOD' *Robbery under Arms* (1890) 2 A lot of game upstanding chaps, that acted like men. 1890 — *Col. Reformer* (1891) 169 As good a specimen of the thoroughbred upstanding pirate as any..in print.

3. *Upstanding wage*, a regular or fixed wage in contrast to one dependent on circumstances.

1888 W. E. NICHOLSON *Coal-Trade Gloss.* 103 *Upstanding Wage*, a certain weekly wage. 1897 *Railway Review* 1 Jan. (E.D.D.), The Company are prepared to arrange a suitable upstanding-wage.

†Upstantial, illiterate var. SUBSTANTIAL *a.* 1589 R. HARVEY *Pl. Perc.* (1590) 16, I will take it vpon the credit of my selfe, an vpstantiall yeoman. Upsta·re, *v.* (UP- 4. Cf. next and Spenser *F. Q.* III. xii. 36.) 1886 DOWDEN *Shelley* I. viii. 372 These wild locks upstared more wildly.

**Upsta·ring,** *pres. pple.* [UP- 6.]

†1. Of hair: Standing on end. *Obs.*

1590 SPENSER *F. Q.* I. ix. 22 They might perceiue his.. curld vncombed heares Vpstaring stiffe. 1610 SHAKS. *Temp.* I. ii. 213 The Kings sonne Ferdinand With haire vp-staring.

2. Gazing upwards.

For 'vp-staring' in Marlowe's *Hero & L.* II. 200 the true reading is prob. 'vp-starting', as in some later edd.

1835 RUSKIN *Tour France* x. Wks. 1903 II. 400, I stood, upstaring at the lofty steeple.

**Upstart** (v·pstaɹt), *sb.* and *a.* [UP- 2, 3.]

A. *sb.* 1. One who has newly or suddenly risen in position or importance; a new-comer in respect of rank or consequence; a parvenu; = START-UP *sb.* 1.

1555 *Instit. Gentl.* C iiij b, These gentlemen are nowe called vpstartes, a terme lately inuented by such as pondered not ye grounde of honest meanes of rising or comming to promocion. 1577 B. GOOGE *Heresbach's Husb.* I. 46 b, The newe vpstart; that takes vpon him the name of a gentleman. 1592 GREENE *Vpst. Courtier* B 4, Mary gyp goodman vp-start, who made your father a gentleman? 1641 MILTON *Reform.* II. 74 Then shall the Nobles possesse all the Dignities..without the improper mixture of Scholastick and pusillanimous upstarts. 1691 HARTCLIFFE *Virtues* 39 An Upstart was to bear himself otherwise in his Petition, than..an ancient Nobleman. 1747 RICHARDSON *Clarissa* (1768) I. xl. 270 None but the prosperous upstart Mush-room'd into rank..was arrogantly proud of it. 1777 J. ADAMS *Fam. Lett.* (1876) 307 There are rascally upstarts in trade, I doubt not, who have made great fortunes in a small period. 1825 MACAULAY *Ess., Milton* ¶ 43 Gods.. compared with whom Jupiter himself was a stripling and an upstart. 1858 FROUDE *Hist. Eng.* III. xiii. 167 The Duke of Norfolk..disdained the dictation of an unknown upstart. 1888 BRYCE *Amer. Commw.* III. lxxxvii. 161 The Greeks thought that the old families ruled their households more gently than upstarts did.

*transf.* 1613 PURCHAS *Pilgrim.* (1614) 319 If it seeme strange, that the Turkish Religion (a newer vpstart) be declared before those former. 1647 N. BACON *Disc. Govt. Eng.* I. xlvii. 123 The Empire perceiving..the youthfull courage of this upstart, was glad to enter mutuall league with it. 1791 COWPER *Yardley Oak* 134 Yonder upstarts of the neighb'ring wood, So much thy juniors. 1834 *Tracts for Times* No. 29. 5 All the meetings [=Dissenting sects] are..in one sense, upstarts.

2. †a. An upward start or spring. *Obs.*$^{-1}$

1645 RUTHERFORD *Tryal & Tri. Faith* vi. 43 The upstarts and boylings of corruption and the flesh that are mixed with our Prayers.

b. *dial.* (See quot.)

a1825 FORBY *Voc. E. Anglia*, *Upstart*, the deep impression of a horse's foot in a clayey soil, soon filled up with water, which, when another horse happens to tread in the very same place, starts upwards and plentifully bespatters the rider.

†3. Upspring, origin. *Obs.*$^{-1}$

1669 PENN *No Cross* xi. (1682) 219 All Men and Families ..have had their Upstarts, that is, their Beginnings.

4. *Sc.* A stick forming a support for a thatched roof. ? *Obs.*

1811 W. AITON *View Agric. Ayrs.* 114 (Jam.), Over these were hung sticks..called cabbers; and smaller ones set on the top of the wall were termed upstarts.

5. The meadow-saffron, *Colchicum Autumnale.*

1852 E. HAMILTON *Flora Homœopath.* I. 199 Common Meadow Saffron, Tuber Root,..Upstart. 1863 PRIOR *Plant-n.* 232 *Upstart*, from its flowers starting up suddenly from the ground without putting out leaves first.

B. *adj.* 1. Of things: Lately come into existence or notice; new-fangled.

1565 STAPLETON *Fortr. Faith* 9 The grounde and foundation of all your vpsterte ghospell. *Ibid.* 94 Their small secret, and late vpstert congregation. 1593 BILSON *Govt. Christ's Ch.* 286 This up-start fansie is far from God's ordinance. 1607 J. NORDEN *Surv. Dial.* I. 18 Surveying..is an upstart arte found out of late. 1654 H. L'ESTRANGE *Chas. I* (1655) 5 Not daring to infuse into so solid a judgement their up-start and erroneous fancies. 1697 J. POTTER *Antiq. Greece* I. iv. 19 All their Laws were repeal'd, and the upstart Form of Government utterly dissolv'd. 1720 SWIFT *Right of Precedence* 23 Physick is as old as the Occasion of it;.. which can by no means be said of the other, in comparison, Upstart Profession. 1772 PRIESTLEY *Inst. Relig.* (1782) II. 62 Christianity was despised as..an upstart thing. 1851 HAWTHORNE *Twice-told T.* i, Now, the old aristocratic edifice hides its time-worn visage behind an upstart modern building. 1878 BOSW. SMITH *Carthage* 365 The upstart naval power of Rome in the West.

b. Characteristic of upstarts.

a1593 MARLOWE *Edw. II*, I. iv. 336 Think you that we can brooke this vpstart pride? 1603 B. JONSON *Sejanus* V. viii, It is a note Of vpstart greatnesse, to..watch For these poore trifles. 1665 MANLEY *Grotius' Low C. Wars* 687 His Death was..rejoyced at by those who envyed his new and upstart Rising. 1727 GAY *Fables* I. xxiv, How insolent is upstart pride! 1788 GIBBON *Decl. & F.* xlvii. IV. 550 He dreaded their upstart ambition. 1817 COBBETT *Pol. Reg.* 25 Jan. 99 The upstart pride of those who call themselves the gentlefolk of Manchester. 1822 HAZLITT *Table-t.* Ser. II. iv. 66, I do not desire to be driven out of my conclusions ..merely to make way for his upstart pretensions.

2. Of persons, families, etc.: Lately or suddenly risen to prominence or dignity.

1566 STAPLETON *Ret. Untr. Jewel* I. 8 Your late vpstert masters of Germany and Geneua. 1586 FERNE *Blaz. Gentrie* 260 He will..passe vp and downe the streates of London in a side gowne, like vnto some newe vp-start Legist. 1615 CROOKE *Body of Man* 88 It is more safe to side with the old Legions led by Galen,..then with new and vpstart Nouices. 1665 MANLEY *Grotius' Low C. Wars* 383 The Covenants..were found fault with by malitious and upstart People. 1687 DRYDEN *Hind & P.* I. 175 Some Authors thus his Pedigree will trace, But others write him of an upstart Race. 1740 RICHARDSON *Pamela* (1824) I. 123 Ours is no upstart family; but is as ancient as the best in the kingdom. 1791 BURKE *App. Whigs* Wks. VI. 19 Scorn and contumely of their upstart masters. 1836 THIRLWALL *Greece* II. xiii. 166 An obscure and upstart race of shepherds. 1879 TOURGEE *Fool's Err.* xxxviii. 271 When reproved..by an upstart superior, he had the boldness [etc.].

†3. Rising on end. *Obs.*$^{-1}$

1590 SPENSER *F. Q.* III. x. 54 He..ran away,..With vp-start haire, and staring eyes dismay.

Hence **U·pstartism, U·pstartness.** *nonce-words.*

1838 *Blackw. Mag.* XLIII. 311 That spirit of upstartness which..characterises all French youth. 1881 *Nat. Rev.* Oct. 406 These latter [ballads] are all broad satires on up-startism.

**Upsta·rt,** *v.* [UP- 4.]

1. *intr.* To start or spring up: *esp.*, of persons, to spring to one's feet. Also *fig.*

With the earlier unhyphened examples, cf. UP *adv.*$^1$ 5 c.

1303 R. BRUNNE *Handl. Synne* 5601 Þys man vp sterte, and toke þe gate. c1386 CHAUCER *Wife's T.* 190 (Lansd. MS.), Wiþ þat worde vpstert [*v.rr.* vp sterte, vp stirte] þis olde wif. c 1400 *Tourn. Tottenham* iv, Upsterte the gadlyngs with thaire lang staues. 1412–20 LYDG. *Chron. Troy* IV. 919 Anoon Dispeir in a rage vp-sterte And cruelly cau3te hym by þe herte. a 1529 SKELTON *Col. Cloute* 646 Sodaynly vpstarte From the dongecarte, The mattocke and the shule, To reygne and to rule. 1554 in Strype *Eccl. Mem.* (1721) III. 139 The suffragan..upstert to the Pulpit. 1590 SPENSER *F. Q.* I. i. 16 Their dam vpstart, out of her den effraide, And rushed forth. 1602 *2nd Pt. Return Parnass.* II. v. 908 At last he [*sc.* the hart] vpstarted at the other side of the water. 1700 DRYDEN *Ovid's Met.* XIII. 3 To these the Master of the sevenfold Shield Upstarted fierce. 1725 POPE *Odyssey* XIV. 569 Upstarted Thoas strait, Andræmon's son. 1816 WORDSW. *Ode Morn. Gen. Thanksgiving* 147 As from a forest-brake Upstarts a glistering snake. 1859 TENNYSON *Merlin & V.* 421 The beauteous beast Scared by the noise upstarted at our feet.

**b.** Of the hair: To rise on end.

1513 DOUGLAS *Æneid* IV. vi. 2 Wpstert his hair, the voce stak in his hals. 1563 *Mirr. Mag.* P iv b, While my heares vpstarted with the sight, The teares out streamde.

**c.** To spring up by growth; to come into existence.

1573 TUSSER *Husb.* (1878) 49 Much wetnes..makes thistles a number foorthwith to vpstart. 1581 J. BELL *Haddon's Answ. Osor.* 363 b, As one errour doth commonly engender another: there upstart another whelpe of the same litter. 1875 MORRIS *Æneid* VIII. 637 There for the sons of Romulus the sudden war upstarts With Tatius.

**d.** To rise suddenly into view.

1874 R. BUCHANAN *Poet. Wks.* I. 4 O wondrous Faces that upstart In this Strange Country. 1880 BROWNING *Pan & Luna* 22 Peak to base, Upstarted mountains.

**2.** *trans.* To cause to start up.

1892 TOWNDROW *Garden* 47 Where the moor-hen shyly pushes Into darkness when upstarted.

**Upsta·rted,** *ppl. a.* (UP- 5. Cf. prec.)

1602 MARSTON *Ant. & Mel.* III. E 2, Gastly amazement, with vpstarted haire, Shall..vsher vs. 1613 CHAPMAN *Rev. Bussy D'Ambois* I. B 3 b, What thoughts the many headed-beast..breathes out concerning me, My ends, and new vpstarted state in Brabant.

Hence **Upsta·rtedness.** *rare.*

1642 HEYLIN *Hist. Episc.* II. 93 Undertaking..to make known the new upstartednesse of their Assemblies.

**Upsta·rting,** *vbl. sb.* (UP- 7.) [1775 ASH.] 1845 S. AUSTIN *Ranke's Hist. Ref.* I. 27 This continual upstarting of refractory powers.

**Upsta·rting,** *pres. pple.* and *ppl. a.* (UP- 6, 6 b. Cf. UPSTART *v.*)

1581 HANMER *Jesuites Banner* B 2 b, This new found order and vpstarting Jesuites. 1592 GREENE *2nd Pt. Conny Catch.* A 2 b, Such vpstarting suckars that consume the sap from the roote of the Tree. 1596 SPENSER *F. Q.* V. v. 13 By this vpstarting from her swoune, she star'd..about her. 1784 COWPER *Task* III. 521 Then rise the tender germs upstarting quick. 1812 J. WILSON *Isle of Palms* II. 70 As to the touch of fairy-hand Upstarting dim the nameless land Extends its mountain line. c 1830 PRAED *Poems* (1864) II. 308 Lo, they will weep.., Upstarting from their broken prayer. 1893 McCARTHY *Dictator* xxvi, She had..slept a little in a fitful, upstarting sort of way.

**Upsta·rtle,** *v.* (UP- 4.) a 1849 POE *Whipple*, etc., Wks. 1864 III. 388 Multitudinous thunders that upstartle aghast the echoes. 1870–4 J. THOMSON *City Dreadf. Nt.* xx. vii, A louder crash upstartled me in dread. **Upsta·rtled,** *ppl. a.* (UP- 5.) 1812 CARY *Dante, Parad.* XXVI. 72 The upstartled wight loathes that he sees. 1846 J. H. STIRLING in A. H. Stirling *Life* (1912) v. 89 Silence, like an upstartled hound, skulked sulkily to its place again.

**Up-State**: see UP *prep.*[2] 6.

**Upstay·,** *v.* [UP- 4.]

**1.** *trans.* To sustain by material support; to prop up.

1590 SPENSER *F. Q.* III. xii. 21 Those two villeins, which her steps vpstayd. 1596 *Ibid.* IV. i. 37 They reared him on horsebacke, and vpstayd. 1642 H. MORE *Song of Soul* I. II. xxvii, An uggly cloven foot this monster doth upstay. 1667 MILTON *P. L.* VI. 195 The tenth on bended knee His massie Spear upstaid. 1793 WORDSW. *Descriptive Sk.* 252 Bare steeps, where Desolation stalks,..by a blasted yew upstay'd. 1814 — *Excurs.* VII. 678 The Child..by some friendly finger's help upstayed. 1873 R. BRIDGES *Elegy on Lady* Poems (1912) 239 Each on high a torch upstaying.

**2.** *fig.* To sustain, support.

1600 FAIRFAX *Tasso* XVII. xliii, For by the sword, the scepter is vpstaid. 1619 DRAYTON *Legends* iv. 338 That Atlas, which the gouernement vpstay'd. 1820 WORDSW. *River Duddon* xxviii. 11 Glad meetings, tender partings, that upstay The drooping mind of absence. 1851 CLOUGH *Relig. Poems* vii. 10 A hand that is not ours upstays our steps. 1883 R. W. DIXON *Mano* I. i. 2 If God..still with life upstay The hand that writes.

**Upsteamed, -steaming**: see UP- 5, 6.. †**Upsteaming,** *pres. pple.* *Obs.*[-1] [UP- 6 + *steam* STEM *v.*[4]] Rising up. 1582 STANYHURST *Æneid* II. 28 Two serpents..Whose brests vpsteaming [L. *arrecta*],..Hygh the sea surmounted.

**Upsteer,** *v.* Now *dial.* [UP- 4.] *trans.* To stir up; to throw into turmoil or disorder.

1557 PHAER *Æneid* VI. (1558) S j, What slaughters wyld shall they vpsteere? 1570 *Satir. Poems Reform.* xi. 38 Wa worth the wit that first began This deir debait for to vpsteir. 1596 DALRYMPLE tr. *Leslie's Hist. Scot.* (S.T.S.) I. 273 His Nobilis..he vpsteiris to take Weapounis. 1889 *N. W. Linc. Gloss.* (ed. 2) 589 All th' rooms was upsteer'd.

Hence **Upstee·rer.** *rare*[-1].

1596 DALRYMPLE tr. *Leslie's Hist. Scot.* (S.T.S.) II. 413 That 3e suld be the..author and vpsteirer of thir tumultes.

**Upstick,** *adv. phr.* (See UP *adv.*[1] 29.) 1904 A. GRIFFITHS *50 Yrs. Pub. Serv.* 81 The Naval Agent..dying to be upstick and away.

**U·pstir.** Now *dial.* Also 6 **upstirre, upsturre.** [UP- 2 + STIR *sb.*[1] Cf. MDa. *opstyr*, Norw. *uppstyr* riot, tumult, disturbance.] A disturbance or commotion.

1549 CHEEKE *Hurt Sedit.* (1569) D j b, Better redresse was entended, then your vpstirres and vnquietnesse coulde obtaine. 1550 HARINGTON tr. *Cicero's Bk. Friendship* (1562) 26 Tiberius Graccus..made an vp stirre in the common wealth. 1847 HALLIWELL. 1849– in general dialect use (*Eng. Dial. Dict.*).

**Upsti·rred,** *pa. pple.* (UP- 5. Cf. next.) 1663 BLAIR *Autobiog.* ii. (1848) 10, I was not a little refreshed and upstirred.

**Upsti·rring,** *vbl. sb.* [UP- 7.] The action of stirring up or arousing; stimulation; incitement, encouragement.

1613 P. FORBES *Comm. Rev.* v. (1614) 30 The singing of the rest should serue the Church for a new vpstirring to insist in his praise. a 1653 BINNING *Serm.* (1735) 634/1 There is no up-stirring to Faith among us. 1671 [R. MACWARD] *True Nonconf.* 393 We are to emulat the grace and principle of zeal..for our upstirring to acts in like manner. 1730 T. BOSTON *Mem.* xi. (1899) 353 The which practice I found useful to my upstirring. 1826 E. IRVING *Babylon* II. 414 The upstirring of infidel principles. a 1861 SIR G. SCOTT *Lect. Archit.* (1878) I. 142 It was a period of deep-seated mental excitement, of a prodigious upstirring of the human intellect.

**Upsti·rring,** *ppl. a.* [UP- 6.] Stimulating, rousing.

1751 R. SHIRRA in *Rem.* (1850) 182 Sacred biography is very upstirring to the godly reader. 1834 D. SMITH *Mem. Rev. John Brown of Whitburn* 57 Only as viewed in promises are they sanctifying and upstirring.

**U·pstoop.** *Mining.* (See quots.)

1883 GRESLEY *Gloss. Coal-mining* 269 When a heading is driven to a point at which another should be put in or meet it at right angles.., the first-named heading is called *up-stoop*. 1886 J. BARROWMAN *Sc. Mining Terms* 69 A working room is *up stoop* or *in stoop* when its length is equal to the side of the pillar to be formed.

† **Upstraight,** *a.* *Obs.* [UP- 3. Cf. ME. *upstreyht* (= upstretched), UP- 5.] Erect, upright.

1598 FLORIO, *Trisciato*, smooth, vp-straight, smug. 1642 H. MORE *Song of Soul* I. III. l, For that old crumpled wight gan go upstraight.

**U·p-stream,** *adv.* (*sb.*) and *a.* Also **up stream, upstream.** [UP *prep.*[2] 2, 6.]

**A.** *adv.* In a direction contrary to the flow of a stream; higher up or along a stream.

Common from c 1890. Properly as two words, with stress on *stream*, except when contrasted with *down stream*. In recent use also const. *of* or *from* (a place).

1681 ROBERTSON *Phraseol. Gen.* 1282 To go up stream, *adverso flumine navigare*. 1839 LONGF. *Hyperion* I. viii. (1844) 58 The rising tide bears against the rushing torrent up stream, and pushes back the hurrying waters. 1849 CUPPLES *Green Hand* xvi, The sound of a loud rush of water up-stream broke upon us. 1889 JEROME *Three Men in Boat* ix. 142 Three or four miles up stream is a trifle, early in the morning.

**b.** quasi-*sb.* A position or place further up a stream.

1891 *Nature* 18 June 152/2 From upstream of it are derived three main trunk canals. 1915 I. H. EVANS in *Man* XV. 25 A spot some two miles to the up-stream of the Tamu ground.

**B.** *adj.* **1.** Situated farther or higher up a stream.

1838 *Civil Eng. & Arch. Jrnl.* I. 150/1 The up-stream angles of the dam. 1843 *Ibid.* VI. 88/1 [A] deposit accumulated largely on the up-stream side. 1875 KNIGHT *Dict. Mech.* 1084/2 The up-stream end of a canal-lock.

**2.** Directed, taking place, up-stream.

1826 J. F. COOPER *Mohicans* iii, They call this up-stream current the tide. 1889 *Science-Gossip* XXV. 209/2 There is an up-stream migration of elvers in the spring. 1894 *Field* 9 June 832/1 Many experienced anglers do not like an up-stream wind for..dun hatchings.

**3.** *U.S.* Difficult, troublesome. *rare*[-1].

1847 J. BROWN in *Boston Public Library Bulletin* May (1900) 177, I do not wish any upstream measure taken to supply funds.

**Upstrea·ming,** *pres. pple.* and *ppl. a.* (UP- 6, 6 b.)

1849 M. ARNOLD *Resignation* 62 There [it] winds, upstreaming slowly still Over the summit of the hill. 1884 GEIKIE *Phys. Geog.* (ed. 2) 87 A zone, in which the currents would meet and ascend as an upstreaming mass of air.

**Upstretched,** *pa. pple.* and *ppl. a.* (UP- 6, 6 b.)

1563 C'TESS HERTFORD in Ellis *Orig. Lett.* Ser. II. II. 278 The Queens..graceous pardon.., wych wyth upstretched hands..most humbly I crave. 1642 H. MORE *Song of Soul* II. II. III. xxii, So must it be upstretch'd unto the skie. 1860 O. W. HOLMES *Elsie V.* v, Two meeting-houses stood on two eminences,..looking..as if they would..crow out of their upstretched steeples.

†**Up-striked,** *pa. pple.* *Obs.*[-1] [UP- 5.] Struck up, arranged. 1677 F. SANDFORD *Genealog. Hist. Kings Eng.* 130 So 'tween Sister and this Prince, The marriage was upstrik'd. †**Up-striker.** *Obs.* [UP- 8.] (See quot.) 1726 J. LAURENCE *New Syst. Agric.* 198 Of Brick-making...An Up-striker, a Boy, that lays the Earth upon the Table, and cuts it out for the Moulder.

**U·p-stroke.** [UP- 2 + STROKE *sb.*[1]]

**1.** *dial.* The upshot, end, or conclusion.

1828– in *Eng. Dial. Dict.* (Yks., Lancs., Derby, Linc.).

**2.** A stroke delivered upwards.

1828 *Gardener's Mag.* III. 30 The air which enters from the valves by the up-stroke of the bellows. 1883 *Encycl. Brit.* XVI. 447/2 When the up-stroke is being made..the piston is forced to make part of a revolution.

**3.** The upward stroke of a pen, etc.

1848 DICKENS *Dombey* lix, [She] clutches the money tight until a receipt..is duly signed, to the last up-stroke. 1856 MRS. BROWNING *Aur. Leigh* I. 847 Some upstroke of an alpha and omega. 1898 *Allbutt's Syst. Med.* V. 822 In the irritable heart of young adults the upstroke in the sphygmogram is brisk and high.

† **Upsty,** *sb.* *Obs.*[-1] [Cf. next and OE. *upstige*, OHG. *ûfstîc*, ON. *upp-stiga.*] Ascension (of Christ).

c 1300 *Cursor M.* 20831 (Edin.), Aftir þe upsteich [*Cott.* vpstei, *Gött.* vpsti] of þat dri3tine.

† **Upsty·,** *v.* *Obs.* Forms: 1 **upsti3an, 3–4 vpstiyhe, 5 up-sti3e, vpsty; 3–4 vpsteghe, vpstei, 4 upstey, 4–5 vpstey.** [OE. *upstîgan* (UP- 4), = WFris. *opstige*, MDu. *opstigen* (Du. *opstijgen*), OHG. *ûfstîgan* (G. *aufsteigen*), ON. *uppstiga* (MSw. *up-*, *opstigha*, Sw. *uppstiga*, Da. *opstige*).] *intr.* To rise or mount up; to ascend.

a 900 CYNEWULF *Crist* 464 Ærþon upsti3e ancenned sunu. c 1000 *Ags. Gosp.* John i. 51 3e 3eseoð..Godes englas upsti3ende & nyþer-sti3ende ofer mannes sunu. a 1300 *E. E. Psalter* ciii. 9 Vpsteghes hilles, and feldes doun gas. a 1300 *Cursor M.* 203 How he [*sc.* Christ] vprais, how he vpstey, Many man on stad and sey. 1382 WYCLIF *Gen.* xxxii. 26 Leeue me, forsothe now vpsteyeth the morewetide. c 1400 LOVE *Bonavent. Mirr.* iii. (Gibbs & Sherard MSS.), Þe syght of hier sone myghtyly to heuene upstyynge.

Hence † **Upsty·ing** *vbl. sb.* *Obs.*

a 1300 *E. E. Psalter* ciii. 3 [He] Þat settes þin vpsteghing kloude [*v.r.* upstiying þine þe kloude]. a 1325 *Prose Psalter* lxxxviii. 18 Our vp-stei3eing ys of our Lord. c 1400 tr. *Secreta Secret., Gov. Lordsh.* 86 After good constellacioun of þe mone, & his remuynge fro nusant sterrys, and his prosperyte of his vpstiyng. c 1450 *Mirk's Festial* I. 152 Yn þys vpsteyng þat ys callet þe assencyon.

† **Upsty·er.** *Obs.*[-1] [UP- 8, or f. prec. Cf. ON. *uppstigari.*] One who mounts; a rider.

c 1340 HAMPOLE *Pr. Consc.* 4180 Þe Dan..sal þe nedder be, ..And sal byte þe hors by þe hufe harde, And mak þe upstegher fal bakwarde.

† **Up-sun,** *adv. phr.* *Obs.* [UP *adv.*[2] 1 b. Cf. SUN-UP.] **a.** *With up-sun*, at sunrise. **b.** *Sc.* Between sunrise and sunset.

a 1400–50 *Wars Alex.* 4067 Þe secund day with vp son he with his sowme ne3es. 1703 FOUNTAINHALL *Decis.* (1761) II. 189 The precise question was, If an ejection may be executed in the night-time,..or if it must be done with up-sun. 1825 JAMIESON, *It was upsun*, the sun was not set. Galloway.

**Upswa·llow,** *v.*, etc. (UP- 4, 5, 6.)

1591 DRAYTON *Harmonie of Church, Song Jonah* 8 Mighty wallowing waves..Have with their power up-swallowed me. 1618 H. AINSWORTH *Ps.* cvii. 27 All their wisdom is upswallowed quight. 1850 BLACKIE *Æschylus* II. 176 And the greedy spear upswallowing, Man by man, its gory food. 1853 F. W. NEWMAN *Odes of Horace* 97 Some, victims to stern-gazing Mars The Furies give: and sailors The greedy sea upswallows.

**Upswa·rm,** *v. trans.* (UP- 4.) 1597 SHAKS. 2 *Hen. IV*, IV. ii. 30 You haue taken vp..The Subiects of Heauens Substitute, my Father, And..Haue here vp-swarmed them.

**Upswarming, -sway**: see UP- 4, 6.

**Upswe·ll,** *v.* [UP- 4 + SWELL *v.* Cf. MDu. *opswellen* (Du. *opzwellen*), MLG. *upswellen*, MHG. *ûfswellen* (G. *aufschwellen*).]

**1.** *intr.* To swell up; to rise up by or as by swelling. Also *fig.*

c 1386 CHAUCER *Prioress' T.* 108 The serpent Sathanas, That hath in Iues herte his waspes nest, Vp swal [*Petworth MS.* vpswall] and seide [etc.]. 1582 STANYHURST *Æneis* II. (Arb.) 52 His feet ar vpswelling with raynes of bridil ybroached. 1740 DYER *Ruins of Rome* 135 The num'rous porticoes and domes upswell, With..columns interpos'd. 1816 WORDSW. *Ode, 1814*, 14 The azure sea upswelled upon the sight. 1828 J. STERLING *Ess.*, etc. (1848) II. 62 The tall ash which..upswells to and waves amid the skies. 1875 MORRIS *Æneid* XII. 666 In his heart upswelled a mighty flood Of..maddening grief.

**2.** *trans.* To increase the volume of (something) by or as by swelling.

1582 STANYHURST *Æneis* II. (Arb.) 56 As a trauayler.. whips backward from woorme, with poysoned anger Vp-sweld. 1793 WORDSW. *Descr. Sk.* 563 Alps overlooking Alps their state upswell. 1845 MANGAN *German Anthology* I. 48 The rain..dashes earthwards in floods, Upswelling the deluging fountains.

**Upswelled,** *ppl. a.* (UP- 5. Cf. prec.) 1878 LE CONTE *Elem. Geol.* 246 These lines of upswelled and folded strata.

**Upswe·lling,** *vbl. sb.* (UP- 7.)

1548 BODRUGAN *Epit. King's Title* 248 In tempestious vp-swellynges of water. 1658 A. FOX *Würtz' Surg.* III. xiv. 260 That water..filleth up that place.., wherby [it]..is enforced to an up-swelling. 1878 LE CONTE *Elem. Geol.* II. v. 253 The amount of upswelling..is fully adequate to account for the upheaval of the greatest mountain-chains.

**Upswe·lling,** *ppl. a.* (UP- 6 b.) 1855 BRIMLEY *Ess.* (1858) 74 The personal unhappiness, the private wrong,..give way before the upswelling sympathy. **Upswollen**: see UP- 5.

† **Upsy,** *prep. phrase.* *Obs.* Forms: 6–7 **vpsy, vpsey, vpse, vpsie,** 7 **vpsee;** 7 **upsy, upsi, upse, upzee,** 7–8 **upsey.** [ad. Du. *op zijn* (= ǫp sei), lit. 'on his (her, or its)', used in such expressions as *op zijn Vriesch*, 'in the Frisian fashion'.] In the..fashion; after the..manner.

**I.** In the phrases *upsy Friese, Dutch, English*, 'after the Frisian, German (or Dutch), English fashion', used originally with reference to modes or habits of drinking.

**A. Upsy Friese. 1.** *adv.* Deeply, heavily, to excess.

The phrase also occurs as the name of a tune (a 1627) in *Historie of Fryer Bacon*. The reason for the addition of *crosse* in quot. 1592 is not clear.

1592 NASHE *P. Penilesse* E iv, He is no body that cannot drinke *super nagulum*, carouse the Hunters hoop, quaffe *vpsey freze crosse*. 1601 [? MARSTON] *Jack Drums Entert.* II. D 4 b, Powre Wine,..Drinke Duch like gallants, lets drinke vpsey freeze. 1606 DEKKER *Sev. Sins* I. (Arb.) 12 They..were drunke, according to all the learned rules of Drunkennes, as Vpsy-Freeze, Crambo, Parmizant, &c. 1635 HEYWOOD *Philocoth.* 65 To drinke Vpse-phreese.

**b.** Thoroughly; entirely; quite.
**1598–9** B. JONSON *Case is Altered* IV. iii, Tut, no more of this surquedry; I am thine own *ad unguem*, upsie freeze, pell mell.

**2.** *sb.* A mode of drinking or carousing.
**1590** LODGE *Euphues Gold. Leg.* D 2, After they had feasted and frolickt it twise or thrise with an vpsey freeze. **1600** NASHE *Summer's Last Will* F j b, *A vous, mounsieur Winter*, a frolick vpsy freese, crosse, ho, *super nagulum*. **1608** DEKKER *Dead Term* A 4 b, At his [*i.e.* the Dutchman's] owne weapon of Vpsie freeze will they dare him.

**b.** Intoxicating liquor. *rare.* (Cf. C.)
**1648** *Canterburie March* B 3 Fill me a cup of upsy-frize To joy our Friends.

**3.** *adj.* Inclined or addicted to carousing. *rare*—¹.
**1631** J. DONE *Polydoron* 105 The Saylor is reasonable at Sea and cannot abide Whistling; but at Land they [*sc.* soldiers and sailors] are both upzeefreeze.

Hence **Upsy-frie·se** *v.*, to drain or empty (a pot of liquor); **Upsy-frie·sy** *a.*, addicted to drinking deeply.
**1617** J. TAYLOR (Water-P.) *Trav. to Hamburgh* B 2, My company and my selfe went to a Dutch drinking-schoole, and..vpsefreez'd foure pots of boone beere. **1622** MASSINGER & DEKKER *Virg. Martyr* II. i, Bacchus..grand patron of rob-pots, upsy-freesy tipplers, and super-naculum takers.

**B. Upsy Dutch. 1.** *adv.* = prec. I.
**1607** DEKKER *Knt.'s Conjur.* (1842) 29 He..swore he could find in his heart to goe presently (hauing drunk vpsy Dutch). **1622** FLETCHER *Beggar's Bush* III. i, Sit downe Lads, And drink me upsey-Dutch. *a* **1634** CHAPMAN *Alphonsus* III. i. (1654) 30 We'l spend this evening lustie upsie Dutch, In honour of this unexpected league. **1670** DAVENANT & DRYDEN *Tempest* IV. 62, I will pledge your Grace Up se Dutch.

**b.** In general use.
*a* **1634** CHAPMAN *Alphonsus* II. ii. (1654) 18 Then kiss your hand three times upsy Dutch. **1721** D'URFEY *Athenian Jilt* Operas, etc. 165 And now do's upsey Dutch endeavour To make himself more valu'd be By bragging of his Family.

**2.** *adj.* Suggestive of having drunk too deeply; heavy.
**1610** B. JONSON *Alch.* IV. vi, I doe not like the dulnesse of your eye: It hath a heauy cast, 'tis vpsee Dutch, And say's you are a lumpish whore-master.

**C. Upsy English** (cf. *Upsy Friese* 2 b).
**1622** FLETCHER *Beggar's Bush* IV. iv, *Prig.* I for the structure, Which is the bowl. *Hig.* Which must be up-sey English, Strong, lusty, London beer.

**II.** In other uses.

**1.** *Upsevant muff* [cf. Du. *want* mitten, and MUFF *sb.*¹, *sb.*²], ?like a fur cap.
**1591** NASHE *Introd. Sidney's Astr. & Stella* A iv b, An Asse is no great stateman in the beastes common-wealth, though he weare his eares *vpseuant muffe*, after the Muscouy fashion.

**2.** As *adj.* or *adv.* Extreme(ly), ultra.
**1650** A. B. *Mutatus Polemo* 10 He that even now was upsie Cavaleer high Royalists. **1694** LOCKE in Ld. King *Life* (1830) I. 383 He that reads this act [for licensing printing] with attention will find it upse ecclesiastical.

**3.** As *prep.* In or after the manner of.
**1663** KILLIGREW *Pars. Wedding* IV. i, Yes, faith, they have treated her upsey Whore, lain with her.

† **U·ptails.** *Obs.* Also **up-tails.** [UP *adv.*¹ + TAIL *sb.*¹ 1, 5.]

**1.** *Up tails all*, the name of an old song and its tune. Also used allusively (see TAIL *sb.*¹ 5, 5 c).
**1598** B. JONSON *Ev. Man in Hum.* I. iii, Hang sorrow, care will kill a cat, vp-tailes all, and a poxe on the hangman. **1607** SHARPHAM *Fleire* (1610) F j b, Shee euerie day sings Iohn for the king, and at Vp-tailes all, shees perfect. **1610** R. VAUGHAN *Water-Workes* K 2, Though I am no Poet yet I can make Ballads, To the tune of vp-tayls-all. **1648** HERRICK *Hesper., Up tailes all*, For love he doth call For his Uptailes all; And that's the part to be acted. **1697** VANBRUGH *Prov. Wife* V. iii, *Mademoiselle.* Why, what be de matter? *Rasor.* The matter? Why, uptails all's the matter..My lady has cuckolded my master.

**2. a.** (With *all.*) A jovial fellow; a reveller.
**1602** DEKKER *Satyrom.* I 2 b, Feele (my light-vptailes all) feele my weapon.

**b.** A woman.
**1671** CROWNE *Juliana* III. 26 How I shall laugh to see the little pretty uptails come to make a home-thrust at a man.

**3.** A card-game.
**1694** *Poor Robin* Dec. B 7 b, Whisk, Uptails, Sant, New-Cut,..With other Games besides, the which I know not.

**U·ptake,** *sb.* Also *Sc.* **uptak'**, *north. dial.* **uptack.** [UP- 2. Cf. ON. and Icel. *upptak* neut., *upptaka* fem.]

**1.** The action of, or capacity for, understanding; comprehension. Usu. *gleg* (*quick, slow*, etc.) *in the uptake.* Orig. (and still chiefly) *Sc.*
**1816** SCOTT *Old Mort.* vii, Everybody's no sae gleg at the uptake as ye are yoursell. **1847** W. E. AYTOUN *Dreepdaily Burghs* iv, 'I really do not understand you, gentlemen.' 'Troth, then, ye're slow at the uptak.' **1871** ALEXANDER *Johnny Gibb* x, I'm nae sayin' 't Benjie hisna a better uptak' nor the like o' him. **1878** A. PAUL *Random Writ.* 112 Children are very quick in the uptake.

**2.** = TAKE-UP *sb.* 4.
**1839** R. S. ROBINSON *Naut. Steam Eng.* 129 The uptake, communicating from each boiler, in the common funnel. **1859** W. RANKINE *Steam-Engine* 451 A chamber called the smoke box, or uptake, in which the various flues terminate. **1887** *Encycl. Brit.* XXII. 499/1 The uptakes from both ends converge to the funnel base above the centre of the boiler's length.

**3.** A ventilating shaft by which foul air ascends.
**1889** WELCH *Text Bk. Naval Archit.* xii. 132 Advantage is taken of the hollow towing bollards..to utilise these also as uptakes. **1908** *Animal Managem.* 248 Permanent air funnels..should be arranged in pairs,..thus furnishing an up-take and down draught (outlet and inlet).

**4.** An upward draught or current of air.
**1887** R. ABERCROMBY *Weather* 79 To assume that the ascensional uptake in front of the main body of the shower is as unsteady as the surface-wind. *Ibid.* 126 Where the uptake is less strong.

**Upta·ke,** *v.* [UP- 4. Cf. TAKE *v.* 90, MSw. *up-, upptaka*, etc. (Sw. *upptaga*), MDa. (and Da.) *optage* in sense 3.]

† **1.** *trans.* To perform or pursue (a flight) upwards. *Obs.*
*c* **1250** *Gen. & Ex.* 277 Min fli3t..ic wile up-taken, Min sete norð on heuene maken. *a* **1711** KEN *Hymnotheo* Poet. Wks. 1721 III. 226 Saints Self-jealous will their Flights uptake, We'll follow of the first the radiant Wake.

† **2.** To deliver up, to surrender. *Obs.*—¹
**1297** R. GLOUC. (Rolls) 7949 Þe king him made þuder wende, mid is owe folc, to make þe folc þat þer inne was þen castel him vp take [*v.r.* optake].

**3.** To pick or take up; to raise from the ground, etc.; to lift. *Obs.* or *arch.*
*a* **1300** *E. E. Psalter* xvii. 19 He sent fra hegh, and vptoke me; Fra many watres me nam he. **13..** *K. Alis.* 7579 (Laud MS.), He was vptaken of gentil men And ysette on hei3e benche. *c* **1340** HAMPOLE *Pr. Consc.* 5142 Ihesu Crist þat here es uptane Fra yhow, til heven. *c* **1420** *Anturs of Arth.* 656 (Douce MS.), Boþe þes trauayled mene þey truly vp take; Vnnethe mi3te þo sturne stonde vp ri3te. *c* **1440** *Pallad. on Husb.* XI. 291 Of see quyete vptaketh they maryne Water purest. **1587** TURBERV. *Trag. T.* 89 b, Then willd he all the Ladies limmes..To be vptaken, peece by peece. **1596** SPENSER *F. Q.* IV. ii. 25 It..befell, That Satyran a girdle did vptake, Well knowne to appertaine to Florimell.
*fig.* **1590** SPENSER *F. Q.* III. ii. 9 The word gone out, she backe againe would call,..But that he it vp-taking ere the fall, Her shortly answered. **1654** GAYTON *Pleas. Notes* II. ii. 37 But Sancho (wise) uptakes That matter, and..Desires with bread and cheese to pacifie His great distemper.

† **b.** *fig.* To raise from distress or straits; to take into one's care or protection. *Obs.*
Only in or after Biblical usage, usually tr. L. *suscipere.*
*a* **1300** *E. E. Psalter* xxvi. 16 Mi fader and mi moder me for-soke þai; Lauerd sothlike vptoke me ai. *a* **1340** HAMPOLE *Psalter* xvii. 38 Þi righthand vptoke me. **1388** WYCLIF *Isaiah* xli. 10 Y coumfortide thee..; and the ri3thond of my iust man vp took thee. *c* **1400** *Prymer* (1895) 84 Uptake þou me bi þi word, & y schal lyue. *c* **1450** *Cov. Myst.* (Shaks. Soc.) 127 Israel for his childe up-toke he to cum. **1551** STERNHOLD & H. *Ps.* vi. 4 Lord turne thee to thy wonted grace, my sely soule vp take [1584 vptake].

† **c.** To raise up, exalt. Also *absol. Obs.*
*c* **1340** HAMPOLE *Pr. Consc.* 8247 Þai salle þan se..Whi ane es uptane tylle a kyngdom, And ane other es putted in-tylle thraldom. *c* **1460** *Towneley Myst.* xxiv. 380 As fortune assyse men wyll she make; hir maners ar nyse, she can downe and vptake.

† **4.** To take possession of; to occupy. *Obs.*
*c* **1425** WYNTOUN *Cron.* IV. ix. 1173 All þe cete þus fand þai With þare fais neire vptane. **1452** *Reg. Mag. Sig. Scot.* 131/2 My gudis..to be frely ressavit, uptakyn, governit and fullely disponit at the will..of the saide Walter. **1513** DOUGLAS *Æneid* III. ii. 108 The lugeingis [were] void and reddy to thair fais, The sete left waist till ony it wptais.

† **5.** To reprove, rebuke. *Obs.*—¹
*c* **1440** *Psalmi Peniten.* (1894) 1 Lord, yn thin anger, uptake [L. *corripias*] me nought.

† **6.** To receive hospitably. *Obs.*—¹
*a* **1470** HARDING *Chron.* IX. i, Winde theim droue..Into Affrique, where..Thei welcomed wer and worthely vptake.

† **7.** *Sc.* To obtain, get, or exact by way of tax, contribution, or payment; to levy; = UPLIFT *v.* 3.
**1493** *Reg. Cupar Abbey* I. 244 Dewiteis of the samyn [lands] to rais and vptak. **1534** *Acc. Ld. High Treas. Scot.* VI. 221 To help the said John Perdovin to uptak the said movable gudis. *c* **1560** A. SCOTT *Poems* i. 133 Teindis ar vptane be testament transgressouris. **1592** *Excheq. Rolls Scot.* XXII. 236 The maillis of the castellandis..intromettit and uptaikin be Johnne, lord Maxwell. **1640–1** *Kirkcudbr. War.Comm. Min. Bk.* (1855) 58 The Committie ordaines him to uptak the pryce according to the feirs of the yeir.

**8.** *Sc.* (and *north. dial.*). To take into the mind; to comprehend, understand.
**1726** *Fleming's Fulfill. Script.* (ed. 5) Table Scots Phr., *Uptake*, to understand a thing. **1829** BROCKETT *N. C. Gloss.* (ed. 2). **1839** R. M. M'CHEYNE in Bonar *Mem.* (1844) 195 Have you really and fully uptaken Christ as the gospel lays him down? **1898** C. SPENCE *From Braes of the Carse* 32 What a pity the Laird is so dull!..For certes he doesna uptak' what I mean.

**Upta·ken,** *pa. pple.* [UP- 5. Cf. prec.] Taken up, captivated, or charmed *with* something.
**1605** in Sylvester *Du Bartas* B 2 b, Hence itching Eares with Toyes and Tales vp-taen. **1876** *Whitby Gloss.* 209/1.

† **Uptaker.** *Obs.* [UP- 8, or f. UPTAKE *v.*]

**1.** One who sustains or supports another; a helper.
*a* **1340** HAMPOLE *Psalter* iii. 3 Þou lord is myn vptakere. [Also xvi. 3, xli. 12, lviii. 10.] **1388** WYCLIF *Ps.* xlv. 8 God of Jacob is oure vptakere. [Also liii. 6, lxxxviii. 27.]

**2.** *Sc.* One who collects or levies taxes, etc.
**1576** *Rec. Sheriff Crt. Aberdeen.* (1904) 242 Uptaker of the multur and knaifschipe of the tounes and lands. **1596** DALRYMPLE tr. *Leslie's Hist. Scot.* (S.T.S) II. 444 Faithful vptakeris of the lyueng and gathereris of the rentis.

**3.** *Sc.* A leader of psalmody; a precentor.
**1620** *Extr. Burgh Rec. Stirling* (1887) 153 Teacher of musik, and uptaker of the psalmes in the kirk. **1662** *Ibid.* 241 The offices of a readder in the kirk,..and uptaker of the psalmes.

**Upta·king,** *vbl. sb.* Chiefly *Sc.* [UP- 7, or f. UPTAKE *v.*]
In Sc. use also with stress *u·pta·king.*

† **1.** The source of a stream. *Obs.*—¹
Probably after ON. *upptaka* in the same sense.
**1241–51** *Cockersand Chartul.* (Chetham Soc. 56) 854 Terram quæ jacet inter Arkelbec et stagnum molendini ad huptaking et est longitudo a le huptaking usque ad terram Margeriæ.

† **2.** The action of sustaining; sustenance, support. *Obs.*
*a* **1300** *E. E. Psalter* lxxxviii. 18 For of lauerd es oure vptakinge [L. *adsumptio*]. **1388** WYCLIF *Ps.* cvii. 9 Effraym is the vptaking [L. *susceptio*] of myn heed. **1447** BOKENHAM *Seyntys* (Roxb.) 46 The uptakyng of oure frele nature Whiche wyth synne was almost schent.

† **3.** *Sc.* **a.** = UPLIFTING *vbl. sb.* 2. *Obs.*
**1471** in *Charters, &c. Edin.* (1871) 134 In the rasing, vptakin and paying of the said custumes. **1512** *Reg. Privy Seal Scot.* I. 374 That 3e ceis fra all intrometting and uptaking of the saidis thre lastis of salmond. *a* **1578** LINDESAY (Pitscottie) *Chron. Scot.* (S.T.S.) I. 164 The rowmes and rentis quhilk they war in wse and possessioun affoir of wptaking thairof. **1594** [see UPLIFTING *vbl. sb.* 2]. *a* **1670** SPALDING *Troub. Chas. I* (1850) I. 78 They fell in sum wordis about the vptaking of this fyne. *Ibid.* 133 Quhilk bred gryte truble in vptaking of the rentall.

† **b.** The levy or raising of forces. *Obs.*—¹
*a* **1578** LINDESAY (Pitscottie) *Chron. Scot.* (S.T.S.) II. 243 The laird..passit..to Dundie..for vptaking of men of weir.

† **c.** (See DITTAY.) *Obs.*—¹
**1609** SKENE *Reg. Maj., Stat. Alex. II*, 15 Vptaking of dittay and pvnissing of malefactours.

† **4.** *Sc.* ? Drawing together, gathering. *Obs.*—¹
**1503** *Acc. Ld. High Treas. Scot.* II. 203 For ane elne lynnyne to the platis uptaking of the crammesy cote, xiiij d.

**5.** *Sc.* A raising, picking, or lifting up.
**1495** *Acta Dom. Conc.* (1839) 394/2 Þe wrangwis..vptaking of þer merchis and stanis. **1503** *Acc. Ld. H. Treas. Scot.* II. 356 For uptaking of certane treis..and carying of thaim to Strivelin. **1513** DOUGLAS *Æneid* IX. vi. 116 Behind thame, for vptakyng quhayr it lay, Mony brycht armour rychly dycht thai left. **1576** in Balfour *Oppr. in Orkney & Shetl.* (1859) 69 The allegeit uptaking of ane pece see-drewin tre. **1613** P. FORBES *Comm. Revelation* xii. (1614) 103 The exalting of the childe, is the deiecting of the Dragon from heauen: and the deiection of the Dragon, is the vptaking of the childe. **1888** C. P. BROWN *Cotton Manuf.* 168 *Uptaking*, Sc. for the take-up motion.

† **6.** *Sc.* The action of leading the psalm; precenting. *Obs.*
**1579** *Burgh Rec. Edin.* (1882) IV. 126 His yeirlie stepend for vptaking of the psalmes in the kirk. **1599** *Extr. Aberd. Reg.* (1848) II. 204 To Patrik Walter for the vptacking of the psalme in the new kirk. **1618** *Extr. Burgh Rec. Stirling* (1887) 150 The soume of ten merkis in feall for uptaking of the psalmes.

**7.** *Sc.* A receiving into or grasping with the mind; comprehension, conception, understanding.
**1614** W. COWPER *Dikailogie* 85 Your errour proceeds from the wrong vptaking of the question. **1663** BLAIR *Autobiog.* ii. (1848) 32, I was thereby much satisfied and confirmed by his uptaking of the nature and notion of faith. **1730** T. BOSTON *Mem.* v. (1899) 59 My preaching..by degrees..ripened into a more clear uptaking of the doctrine of the gospel. *a* **1749** E. ERSKINE *Wks.* (1791) 683/1 It has in it a knowledge and uptaking of a God in Christ. **1811** CHALMERS *Let.* in Hanna *Life* (1851) I. 228 Aunty Jean tries to help out the matter by the uptakings of her quick and confident discernment. **1839** R. M. M'CHEYNE in Bonar *Mem.* (1844) 195 How many that have no uptaking of Christ, and are yet cold-hearted and at ease?

**U·pta·king,** *ppl. a. Sc.* [UP- 6.] **a.** Engrossing, absorbing. **b.** Quick in understanding; intelligent.
**1737** J. WILLISON *Afflicted Man's Comp.* i. (1744) 13 This should be the great and uptaking Business of every Man. **1756** MRS. CALDERWOOD in *Coltness Collect.* (Maitl. Cl.) 148 Though they [the Dutch] have no vivacity, yet I think they are..smarter, a great deall, than the English, that is, more uptaking.

**Uptea·r,** *v.* [UP- 4 + TEAR *v.*¹ Cf. UPTORN.] *trans.* To pull up by the roots or from the foundation; to rend up, tear out.
**1593** *Sidney's Arcadia* Wks. 1922 II. 240 The laborer which cursed earthe upteares With sweatye browes. **1667** MILTON *P. L.* VI. 663 The rest in imitation to like Armes Betook them, and the neighbouring Hills uptore. **1786** BURNS *To Mountain Daisy* v, But now the share uptears thy bed, And low thou lies! **1803** LEYDEN *Scenes Infancy* III. xxii, The forest bull, that..the ground uptore. **1850** BLACKIE *Æschylus* II. 195 He from their socket roots uptore His eyes. **1855** SINGLETON *Virgil* I. 126 Hence it nor storms, nor gusts, nor showers uptear.
*fig.* **1847** C. BRONTE *J. Eyre* xxvii, What good would it do if I bent, if I uptore, if I crushed her? **1850** BLACKIE *Æschylus* II. 61 Such wedlock even now He blindly broods, as shall uptear his kingdom.

**Uptene,** obs. Sc. f. OBTAIN *v.*

**Upthrow** (*v*·pþrōᵘ), *sb.* Also 9 **up-throe.** [UP- 2. Cf. next.]

**1.** *Geol.* and *Mining.* An upward dislocation of a stratum or seam.
**1807** J. HEADRICK *View Arran* 66 A high rock, caused by what is called an up-throe of the metals. *Ibid.*, This up-throe running westward, forms a sort of ridge. **1883** [see UPLEAP *sb.* 2]. **1888** J. PRESTWICH *Geol.* II. 95 An elevation of the strata on one side, and..depression on the other, which are called by the miners the upthrow and the downthrow.
*attrib.* **1839** URE *Dict. Arts* 965 Dikes and faults are denominated upthrow or downthrow, according to the position they are met with in working the mine. **1872** *Proc. Amer. Philos. Soc.* XII. 444 A fine upthrow fault..in East Tennessee. **1882** GEIKIE *Geol. Sk.* 282 A true fault with an upthrow and downthrow side.

**b.** Amount of upward displacement.
**1889** *Hardwicke's Sci. Gossip* XXV. 228/1 A small fault, with five feet upthrow.

**2.** *Geol.* An upheaval of part of the earth's crust or surface; an uplift.

1833 Lyell *Princ. Geol.* III. 338 The sudden upthrow of another system of parallel chains of mountains. 1863 Dana *Man. Geol.* 727 By the upthrow, rocks of the Lower Silurian have been carried up to the level of those of the Subcarboniferous. 1884 Geikie in *Nature* 13 Nov. 31 In the great upthrow, it is this sandstone platform which has been pushed over the limestones.

**3.** An outburst or manifestation.

1855 M. Pattison in *Oxford Ess.* 274 The Wycliff movement,..that last upthrow of Latin philosophy.

**4.** The action of throwing up or casting upwards.

1898 *Daily News* 23 Sept. 2/3 The up-throw with which a marksman jerks his rifle from his shoulder after a successful shot.

**Upthrow** (vpþrōu·), *v.* [Up- 4. Cf. Throw *v.*¹ 48.]

**1.** *trans.* To throw or cast upwards; to toss or fling up.

*c* 1614 Sir W. Mure *Dido & Æneas* II. 276 Both heards of Hart and Hinde..with feet the dust vpthroe. 1748 Thomson *Cast. Indol.* I. xxvii, The fountain..That in the middle of the court up-threw A stream. 1750 Collins *Superstit. Highlands* 144 A Pigmy-folk..Whose bones the delver with his spade upthrows. 1819 Byron *Juan* II. xxix, Fifty tons of water were upthrown By them per hour. 1875 Morris *Æneid* x. 844 [He] both his hands upthrew Toward heaven.

†**b.** To cast up (the eyes). *Obs.*—¹

1600 Fairfax *Tasso* XVII. lxxv, Of Almerike the image.. that vpthrew His eies, like one that vs'd to contemplate.

†**2.** = Uptear *v.* *Obs.*—¹

1627 Drayton *Moon-Calf* 168 The Tempest so outragious grew, That it whole hedgerowes by the roots vp threw.

**Upthrow·ing,** *vbl. sb.* (Up- 7. Cf. prec.) 1825 Jamieson, *Upthrowin*, the vulgar name for puking. 1844 [R. Chambers] *Vestiges Nat. Hist. Creation* 73 An era of local upthrowing of the primitive..matter of our planet.

**U·pthrust,** *sb.* [Up- 2.] The action of thrusting or fact of being thrust upwards, esp. by volcanic action.

1846 *Mem. Geol. Surv. Gt. Britain* I. 228 The upthrust of the Cornish and Devonian granites. 1862 G. P. Scrope *Volcanos* 129 Serpentine and even granite may be..in course of formation and upthrust..at the present day. 1895 *Pop. Sci. Monthly* Mar. 580 A crater of this sort is formed by the upthrust of the masses of lava.

**Upthrust,** *pa. pple.* and *ppl. a.* (Up- 5.)

1845 Browning *Time's Revenges* 36 Some creature..to be down-torn, Upthrust and outward-borne. 1873 Longf. *Wayside Inn* III. *Poet's T.*, *Interl.* 40 Then flash of brazen armour bright,..and spears up-thrust. 1890 *Q. Jrnl. Geol. Soc.* May 216 An upthrust portion of the old crystalline floor.

†**U·ptie,** *sb. Naut. Obs.* Forms: 3–4 upteye, 4 vpteigh, vpteygh, vptieghe, vptihe, 5 vptie (huptie). [Up- 2 + Tie *sb.*] = Tie *sb.* 2.

1295 *Acc. Exch. K. R.* 5/7 In vj. cables et in uno uptey emptis ix. li. xij. s. *Ibid.* 5/12 Pro aliis diversis cordis..que dicuntur listinges upteys et steyes. 1336 *Ibid.* 19/31 m. 4 In xl petris cordis de canabo..pro duobus upteyes inde faciendis. 1359 in *Pipe Roll* 38 *Edw. III*, m. 47 b, iiij. haunsers, .ij. vptieghes, j boterope, j wyndyngrope. ? *a* 1400 *Morte Arth.* 3675 Vptyes [*text* Vpcynes] eghelynge þay ochene þare-aftyre; With þe swynge of þe swerde sweys þe mastys. 1420 in *For. Acc.* 3 *Hen. VI*, H j b, In j. salierd, ij haliers ij. hupties j Cople ȝerderopes. 1424 *Ibid.* 59 m. 22 d j haunser pro upteyes.

**Uptie·,** *v.* [Up- 4 + Tie *v.* II.]

**1.** *trans.* To tie, bind, or fasten up.

1590 Spenser *F. Q.* I. iv. 31 An hatefull Snake, the which his taile vptyes In many folds. *Ibid.* II. ii. 15, VI. iv. 24. 1714 [Croxall] *Orig. Canto Spenser* xx, The Chain, Which did her tender Limbs to th' Rock upty.

*fig.* 1590 Spenser *F. Q.* II. ii. 1 When Sir Guyon with his faithfull guide Had..The end of their sad Tragedie vptyde.

†**2.** To enclose or confine. *Obs.*—¹

1600 Fairfax *Tasso* XIV. x, A narrow roome our glorie vaine vp-ties, A little circle doth our pride containe.

So **Uptie·d** *pa. pple.*, **Upty·ing** *pres. pple.*

*c* 1450 *Cov. Myst.* (Shaks. Soc.) 217 My breche be nott ȝett welle up-teyd, I had such hast to renne away. 1654 Gayton *Pleas. Notes* III. x. 131 (Deny'd accesse, and tongues up ty'd) To Paper Stratagems we turn'd. 1818 Keats *Endym.* II. 803 Every eve saw me my hair uptying With fingers cool as aspen leaves.

**Uptilted,** *pa. pple.* and *ppl. a.* (Up- 5.) 1849 H. Miller *Footpr. Creat.* i. 2 Its various deposits..have been uptilted from the bottom. 1872 W. S. Symonds *Rec. Rocks* ii. 33 Metamorphosed, uptilted, denuded, and formed into a ridge. 1887 Smiles *Life & Labour* 189 The sharp uptilted nose, which has run through the family.

**Up to date, u·p-to-da·te,** *adv. phr.* and *a.* [Up *adv.*¹ 26 c (*c*). See Date *sb.*² 7.]

**A.** *adv. phr.* **1.** Right up to the present time, or the time of writing.

1868 W. M. Baker *New Timothy* xiii, So of Solomon in reference to Rehoboam, and of every father in reference to his son, up to date. 1882 *Imperial Dict.* s.v. *Post* v., To make the requisite entries on [a book] up to date. 1899 Plummer *Saxon Chronicles* II. p. xxvii, But up to 1001 the Winchester monks kept it up to date.

**2.** In a condition abreast of the times in respect of qualities, style, knowledge, presentation of facts, etc.

1889 Sims & Pettitt (*title*), Faust Up to Date. Burlesque Opera. 1890– [see Date *sb.*² 7]. 1892 *Photogr. Ann.* II. 293 The improvements for this season render this camera quite 'up to date'. 1892 *Bookseller* 8/2 The..information seems.. to be as accurate and as well up to date as ever. 1894 *Daily News* 9 June 5/2 Why, then, should Lord Salisbury sharpen his faculties and keep them, as the odious modern phrase is, up to date?

**B.** *adj.* **1.** Extending to the present time; presenting or inclusive of the latest facts, details, etc.; employing or involving the latest methods or devices.

1888 *Academy* 4 Feb. 73/2 In the absence of a good up-to-date English work on the islands. 1890 *Sat. Rev.* 16 Aug. 209/2 A complete and up-to-date summary of Demosthenic scholarship. 1892 *Pall Mall G.* 8 Feb. 2/1 Providing Malta dockyard with proper and up-to-date salvage and pumping apparatus. 1894 Sala *London up to Date* 30 Juvenility of appearance and general up-to-date smartness.

**2. a.** *pred.* Of persons: Having or employing the latest information, facts, or methods; keeping or being abreast of the times.

1889 W. S. Gilbert *Gondoliers* I, A Grand Inquisitor is always up to date. 1892 *Spectator* 5 March 339/1 The young farmer is thoroughly up to date, to use the modern catch-word. 1896 *Pall Mall Mag.* March 397 Jimmy is up to date, and much too clever for me.

**b.** *attrib.* Having tastes, style, manners, etc., regarded as prevailing at or characteristic of the present time.

1891 *Star* 16 Dec. 3/4 Up-to-date damsels, and eighteenth century belles. 1897 McCarthy *Own Times* V. v. 99 The 'up-to-date' reader, to use a vile slang phrase of the present day, does not much care about classics.

Hence **Up-to-da·teness** (freq. in recent use); **Up-to-da·tish(ness; Up-to-da·tism.**

1891 *Bicycling News* 21 Feb. 113/2 Their list..suggests cheapness and up-to-dateness. 1893 *Educat. Rev.* May 423 His up-to-dateness..in the right view of handling history in class. 1893 *Pall Mall Mag.* I. 75 The terrible well-informedness and alarming up-to-datism. 1902 *Westm. Gaz.* 14 July 2/3 And this, they keep saying, is 'up-to-datishness'. 1903 *Chr. Endeavour Times* 5 Nov.; *The Academy*, under its new editor, is decidedly more up-to-datish.

**Uptorn,** *pa. pple.* and *ppl. a.* (Up- 5. Cf. Uptear *v.*)

*a* 1586 Sidney *Certaine Sonets* Wks. 1922 II. 303 Time haste my dying hower: Place see my grave uptorne. 1729 Savage *Wanderer* v. 192 Her Tombs wide-shatter'd, and her Dead up-torn. 1784 Cowper *Task* IV. 438 The gardener's pale, the farmer's hedge..Uptorn by strength,.. he bundles up the spoil. 1818 Keats *Endym.* III. 499 [She was] seated upon an uptorn forest root. 1841 *Dublin Rev.* May 344 The broken window and uptorn brass. 1877 L. Morris *Epic Hades* II. 121 The humble homes uptorn To gain one poor fair face.

**Upto·ss,** *v. intr.* and *trans.* (Up- 4.)

1828 Campbell *Death-boat of Heligoland* 22 Now surf-sunk for minutes, again they uptossed. *a* 1851 Moir *Graves of Dead* iv, When..the groaning Tempest uptosses the forests. 1890 *St. Nicholas* Aug. 866/1 The noble steed uptossed his head.

**Uptow·er,** *v. intr.* and *trans.* (Up- 4.)

1848 B. D. Walsh *Aristoph.*, *Clouds* I. iv, There uptowers the Holy Temple. 1850 Blackie *Æschylus* I. 224 They their tents Against these high-towered infant walls uptowered. 1872 A. de Vere *Leg. St. Patrick* 102 The mitred brow Uptowered sublime.

**Up-tow·n,** *adv.*, **u·p-town,** *a.* (Also without hyphen.) [Up *prep.*²]

**1.** *adv.* In, to, or into the higher or upper part of a town, or (*U.S.*) the residential portion of a town or city.

1855 Clarke, *Uptown*, up the town. 1861 Dickens *Gt. Expect.* vii, I had heard of Miss Havisham up town. 1883 *Century Mag.* Oct. 856/2 The current of domestic life..then flowed onward up-town. 1899 J. L. Williams *Stolen Story*, etc. 30 Two..told me about it uptown at dinner.

**2.** *adj.* Situated or dwelling up-town; of or pertaining to the upper (also, *U.S.*, residential) part of a town.

1838 J. L. Stephens *Trav. Greece* I. 83 Even I,..a quondam speculator in 'up-town lots'. 1859 *Habits of Gd. Society* v. 192 So universal is insolence in America,..even in what is called good society—the 'up-town' sets. 1883 *Century Mag.* Oct. 857/2 The course of the up-town movement at first included Broadway.

**Up train:** see Up *a.* 2.

**Uptrai·ned,** *pa. pple.* (Up- 5.)

1569 Preston *Cambyses* D j b, The King himselfe was godly vp trained. 1590 Spenser *F. Q.* II. x. 27 Three faire daughters, which were well vptraind. *a* 1711 Ken *Hymns Festiv.* Poet. Wks. 1721 I. 282 In Jesus Love the Saint up-train'd, Wou'd humble Deacon be ordain'd.

†**Up tro,** *adv. phr. Obs.*—¹ [a. LG. *up troe* (Du. *op trouw*). Cf. Trow *sb.*¹] In good faith; really.

1654 Gayton *Pleas. Notes* IV. xxv. 282 To gather up the arms Came Sancho up tro, or revenge Don's harmes?

**U·pturn,** *sb.* [Up- 2.]

**1.** An upturned or upthrown part.

1868 Kinglake *Crimea* IV. v. 90 A little upturn of the soil with a few Turks standing behind it.

**2.** *fig.* = Upheaval 2.

1864 *Gd. Words* 231/1 The upturns and the overthrows of war. 1873 Symonds *Grk. Poets* viii. 239 That idea of world-destruction, of that total upturn and Titanic revolution in the universe. 1883 *19th Cent.* May 796 There has been no greater revolution and upturn of all preconceived notions.

**Uptu·rn,** *v.* [Up- 4. Cf. Turn *v.* 80.]

†**1.** *trans.* To overthrow, subvert, or cause to fall.

*a* 1340 Hampole *Psalter* cxvii. 13, I am put and vpturnyd [*L. eversus sum*], þat i had fallyn: and þe lord resayued me. *a* 1400 *Wycliffite Bible* Titus i. 11 Ther ben manye..the whiche subuerten [*v.r.* vpturnen; L. *subvertunt*] alle housis.

**2.** To turn, throw, or tear up; to cast or turn over.

1567 Drant *Horace, Ep.* xiv. E v, The countrye clownes when they see me vnfitte Vpturning cloddes,..theill stande, and lawghe at it. 1667 Milton *P. L.* x. 700 Boreas and Cæcias..rend the Woods and Seas upturn. 1725 Pope *Odyss.* VIII. 218 Fierce from his arm th' enormous load he flings;..Down rushing, it up-turns a hill of ground. 1762 Falconer *Shipwr.* II. 156 Th' approaching squall..Upturns the whitening surface of the deep. 1855 Singleton *Virgil* I. 74 Come then, the soil Of earth..Let straight upturn stout bullocks. 1881 *Fortn. Rev.* Feb. 209 He..then with a backward heave upturns the whole.

†**3.** To turn upside down. *Obs.*—¹

1610 Holland *Camden's Brit.* I. 3 Where Driver, hight Arctophylax, doth his drie waine up-turn [L. *resupinat*].

**4.** To direct or cast (the eye, face, etc.) upwards.

1667 Milton *P. L.* x. 279 The grim Feature..upturn'd His Nostril wide into the murkie Air. 1744 Thomson *Winter* 131 With broaden'd Nostrils to the Sky upturn'd, The conscious Heifer snuffs the stormy Gale. 1789 E. Darwin *Bot. Gard.* (1791) II. 33 Vallisner sits, up-turns her tearful eyes. 1828 Atherstone *Fall of Nineveh* I. 32 With brazen throats upturned,..ten thousand [trumpets] spake again. 1838 Mrs. Browning *To Bettine* i, Upturning worship and delight With such a loving duty To his grand face, as women will.

**5.** *intr.* To turn or move up or upwards.

1805 Wordsw. *Prelude* IV. 448 Up-turning, then, along an open field, We reached a cottage. 1818 Byron *Ch. Har.* IV. li, Laid on thy lap, his eyes to thee upturn.

**U·pturned,** *ppl. a.* [Up- 5. Cf. prec.]

**1.** Turned or directed upwards: **a.** Of the eye, face, etc.

1592 Shaks. *Rom. & Jul.* II. ii. 29 The white vpturned wondring eyes, Of mortalls that fall backe to gaze on him. 1797 Mrs. Radcliffe *Italian* i, The thousand upturned faces of the gazing crowd. 1835 Longf. in *Life* (1891) I. 213 How strange looked the upturned faces..in that glare! 1837 Carlyle *Fr. Rev.* I. I. ii, With upturned awestruck eye. 1863 Geo. Eliot *Romola* Proem *ad fin.*, Upturned living faces, and lips moving to the old prayers for help.

**b.** In general use.

1839 De la Beche *Rep. Geol. Cornwall*, etc. v. 140 It may ..even rest upon the edges of upturned strata. 1865 Tylor *Early Hist. Man.* 48 The upturned hands seem to expect some desired object to be thrown down.

**2.** Turned upside-down; inverted, overturned, capsized; turned up by digging, etc.

1816 Wordsw. *Ode, 1815*, 31 The upturned soil receives the hopeful seed. 1849 C. Bronte *Shirley* xxvii, You knelt on the floor with..your upturned box before you. 1895 *Daily News* 14 May 2/5 The body of a young man had been found, together with an upturned canoe.

**3.** Turned upwards at the point, extremity, or end; curved.

1843 Lytton *Last Bar.* I. iv, Solomon in pointed upturned shoes. 1847 W. C. L. Martin *The Ox* 73/2 A fine and somewhat up-turned muzzle. 1876 Bristowe *Th. & Pract. Med.* 571 The nose..broad at the root, and upturned. 1885 J. E. Taylor *Brit. Fossils* 225 A perforation in the upturned beak.

**Uptu·rner.** (Up- 8. Cf. Upturn *v.* 2.) 1870 *Contemp. Rev.* XIV. 618 A field..that would repay with interest an intelligent upturner and cultivator.

**Uptu·rning,** *vbl. sb.* [Up- 7. Cf. Upturn *v.*] The action of turning or causing to turn upwards; an instance of this.

[1775 Ash.] 1846 Dana *Zooph.* (1848) 131 An upturning of the margin. 1855 J. Phillips *Man. Geol.* 388 The upturning of the strata through an arc of 90°. 1869 E. A. Parkes *Pract. Hygiene* (ed. 3) 583 There has been much upturning of the soil. 1873 Black *Pr. Thule* vii, A quick upturning of the face.

*fig.* 1864 Trevelyan *Compet. Wallah* ix. 309 The general up-turning of society occasioned by the rebellion.

**Uptu·rning,** *ppl. a.* (Up- 6 b.) 1762 Falconer *Shipwr.* II. 81 Th' upturning points his ponderous bulk sustain.

**Upwa·fted,** *pa. pple.* (Up- 5.)

1791 Cowper *Iliad* VIII. 635 From the plain, Upwafted by the winds the smoke aspired. 1817 Moore *Lalla R., Par. & Peri* 85 Ev'ry breath Upwafted from the innocent flow'rs. 1874 R. Buchanan *Poet. Wks.* I. 242 Unto your dim distance My soul upwafted is on wings.

**Upwafting:** see Up- 6.

**Upwa·ke,** *v. rare.* [Up- 4. Cf. MDu. *opwaken*, (M)LG. *upwaken*, Da. *opvaage*, G. *aufwachen*.] *intr.* and *trans.* To wake up.

*c* 1250 *Gen. & Ex.* 3466 Slep ðor non ðe ða ne up-wakeð. 1535 *Goodly Primer, Evensong* Ps. iii, I myself shall upwake me. 1842 Mangan *Poems* (1859) 121 Mine inner sense upwakes to see The Ghostworld's..wondrous Deep. 1845 — *German Anthology* I. 105 An earthquake shout upwakes the North: Forward!

**Upwall:** see Up- 4.

**Upward** (vpwə̆ɹd), *adv.*, *prep.*, *a.*, and *sb.* Forms: *α.* 1 upweard (2 uppweard), 2– upward (3 *Orm.* uppwarrd), 3–7 vpward (4–5 opward), 4–6 vp-, 6 vpp(e)warde; 3 (9 *Sc.*) upwart, 5, *Sc.* 6 vpwart (5 *Sc.* wp-). *β.* 3–4, *dial.* 9 uppard, 4 vppard, 3–4 vpard, 4 opard; 3 uppart, 5 *Sc.* vpart. [OE. *upweard*, f. *up* Up *adv.*¹ + *weard* -ward. Cf. MLG. *upwart*, *-wort*, MDu. *opwaert*, *-wert*, *-werd*, etc. (Du. *opwaart*), MHG. *ufwart*, *-wert*. See also Upwards.]

**A.** *adv.* **I. 1.** To or towards a higher position or plane; from a lower to a loftier level or object; in an ascending course or direction: **a.** In reference to movement or extension through space.

Occas. *upward and downward*, = Up and down *adv.* I.

*α. a* 900 Cynewulf *Elene* 805 (Gr.), He mid bæm handum.. upweard plegade. *c* 1000 Ælfric *Hom.* II. 548 Ða ȝewende eal se sang upweard to heofenum. *c* 1200 Ormin 12826 ȝe shulenn sen..Godess enngless Uppwarrd & dunnwarrd baþe upponn þe manness Sune stiȝhenn. *a* 1225 *Ancr. R.* 72 Ase ȝe muwen iseon þe water, hwon me punt hit,..þeonne is hit ined aȝein uor to climben upward. 1297 R. Glouc. (Rolls) 6564 þe water uaste wax vpward hei & wide. 1303 R. Brunne *Handl. Synne* 5272 þe fendys þat were yn þe pytte Smote vpwarde. *c* 1374 Chaucer *H. Fame* II. 236 Fire or sovne Or smoke..Alwey..seke vpwarde on hight. *c* 1400 *Pilgr. Sowle* (Caxton, 1483) v. i. 69 Now..fle we vpward, as fast as we may! **1481** Caxton *Reynard* (Arb.) 33, I will helpe that the ladder be sette vp, that he may goo vpwart theron. **1500–20** Dunbar *Poems* x. 42 Now spring vp flouris fra the rute, Reuert ȝow vpwart naturaly. **1598** B. Jonson *Ev. Man in Hum.* iii. v, He voided a bushell of soot yesterday, upward and downeward. **1620** Venner *Via Recta* i. 21 Because it fumeth vpward, it causeth drowsinesse. **1697** Dryden *Virg. Georg.* i. 499 Watchful Herons,..mounting upward with erected Flight,..soar above the Sight. **1706** Prior *Ode to Queen* v, Upward the Noble Bird directs his Wing. **1771** J. S. *Le Dran's Observ. Surg.* (ed. 4) 172 Mr. Morand..dilated the Part upward and downward. **1823** Byron *Island* iii. i, Sulphury vapours upward driven Had left the earth. **1876** Tennyson *Harold* i. i, Like a spirit in Hell who..cannot scape the flame..Steam'd upward from the undescendible Abysm.

*fig.* and *transf.* **1297** R. Glouc. (Rolls) 2957 As sone as eldol him ysey is herte vpward drou. **1766** Goldsm. *Vicar* xxviii, Thus to..fling those curses upward that must soon descend to crush thy own grey head..! **1850–1** Longf. *Golden Leg.* iv. Cloisters 15 Upward steals the life of man, As the sunshine from the wall.

*β.* *c* **1200** *Trin. Coll. Hom.* 105 Ech god ȝiue..cumeð of heuene dunward, and ech idel, and unnit and iuel, neðen uppard. *a* **1225** *Leg. Kath.* 1964 (Bodl. MS. 17), Hwenne þe twa walden keasten uppart þing þet ha chahten. **13..** *R. Gloucester's Chron.* (1724) 321 So þat þe water vaste waxe vppard hey & wyde. ?**13..** *Geburt Jesu* 181 in Horstm. *Altengl. Leg.* (1875) 75 Heo ne bi heold after fader ne moder, þo heo vppard steiȝ.

**b.** In reference to aspect, attitude, or direction.

*a* **1000** *Boeth. Metr.* xxxi. 23 Nis þæt ȝedafenlic þæt se modsefa monna æniȝes niðerheald wese, & þæt neb upweard. *c* **1175** *Lamb. Hom.* 59 Þene Mon he lufede and welbiþohte, and for-þi his neb upward he wrohte. *a* **1225** *Leg. Kath.* 2372 Heo biheold upward, wið upaheuen heorte. **1303** R. Brunne *Handl. Synne* 6664 He loked vpwarde with hys yne. **1362** Langl. *Piers Pl.* A. v. 262 A þousent of Men..Criȝinge vpward to Crist..To haue grace [etc.]. **1390** Gower *Conf.* I. 64 Upon his brest..he leith His hond, and cast upward his yhe. **1484** Caxton *Fables of Æsop* v. x, He loked and byheld vpward to the heuen. **1565** Cooper s.v. *Resupinus*, He standeth vpright with his clawes or nayles vpwarde to heauen. *a* **1586** Sidney tr. *De Mornay* i, If yee looke upward, yee see there infinite bodies. **1646** Sir T. Browne *Pseud. Ep.* iv. i. 181 To gape or looke upward with the eye. **1697** Dryden *Æneis* v. 687 Acestes,..shooting upward, sends his shaft. **1703** Pope *Thebais* 644 His sad companions upward gaze. **1789** Wordsw. *Evening Walk* 25 Impatience, pointing upward, showed, Through passes yet unreached, a brighter road. **1812** J. Wilson *Isle of Palms* ii. 79 Upward when he turns his sight. **1818** Shelley *Rosal. & Helen* 1155 His countenance Raised upward, burned with radiance. **1850** *Household Words* I. 229/1, I saw him looking upward.

*fig.* *a* **1670** Hacket *Abp. Williams* ii. (1693) 194 They.. look't downward upon those dishonourable Actions, not upward upon his Vertues. **1836** W. Irving *Astoria* I. 29 To these were added an aspiring spirit that always looked upward; a genius [etc.].

**c.** *fig.* To or towards a loftier stage, level, or standard, in respect of thought, feeling, life, distinction, excellence, etc.

*c* **1200** Ormin 6014 God mann riseþþ aȝȝ uppwarrd In alle gode dedess. *a* **1225** *Ancr. R.* 132 [They] þencheð uppard, of þe blisse of heouene. *c* **1449** Pecock *Repr.* iii. x. 337 The chirche grewe vpward bothe in kunnyng and in lyuyng. *c* **1510** More *Picus* Wks. 2/2 Whose mind should alway as the fyre aspire vpward to heauenlye thinges. *a* **1535** — *Rich. III*, Ibid. 68/1 Sir James Tyrell..had an high heart and sore longed vpwarde. **1605** Shaks. *Macb.* iv. ii. 24 *Rosse.* Things at the worst will cease, or else climbe vpward, To what they were before. **1692** Dryden *Eleonora* 152 Now 'tis Faith ascends, Now Hope, now Charity, that upward tends. **1732** Pope *Ess. Man* i. 173 What would this Man? Now upward will he soar, And little less than Angel, would be more. **1849** Thirlwall *Rem.* (1878) III. 352 Upward hearts—upward, above all paltry, sordid, grovelling aims and desires. **1898** Illingworth *Divine Immanence* i. 9 Every form of conscious life, from the lowest sensitive organism upward.

**d.** Higher in respect of price or value, etc.

**1874** *Times* 12 Jan. 6/5 The trade was very firm, with a strong inclination upward in price. *Ibid.*, There appears to be a strong tendency upward [in the price of corn].

**2.** Up along the course of a stream, etc.; further into the interior of a country; to or towards a centre, metropolis, source, etc. Also in fig. context.

*a* **1122** *O. E. Chron.* (Laud MS.) an. 1013, Sweȝen cyning mid his flotan..wende..in to Humbran muðan, & swa upp weard andlang Trentan. *c* **1205** Lay. 9298 Hamun arnde upward & oðer while adunward. **1387** Trevisa *Higden* (Rolls) II. 73 Þanne vpward aboue þat is þe ilond Farne. *c* **1450** Capgrave *Life St. Aug.* 3 In þis same Numedie stant ..Tagatenses..sumwhat upward mor on-to Cartage. **1505** in Leadam *Star Chamber Cases* (Selden) 223 Euery Trow or Cobull passing vpward vndre the seide Brugge. **1568** Grafton *Chron.* II. 765 The yong kyng..he conueyed vpwarde towarde the Citie of London. **1697** Dryden *Virg. Georg.* iv. 408 An ancient Legend I prepare to sing, And upward follow Fame's immortal Spring. **1709** Pope *Ess. Crit.* 127 Be Homer's works your study,..And trace the Muses upward to their spring.

**b.** Towards the body or head. (Cf. 3 b, 5.)

**1600** Shaks. *Hen. V*, ii. iii. 19 (Q. 1), I felt to them [*sc.* his feet],..And to his knees,..and so vpward, and vpward. **1647** N. Bacon *Disc. Govt. Eng.* i. xlvii. 123 The vast body of the Roman Empire like a body wasting with age, died upward.

**3.** In, occupying, or so as to occupy a higher or the highest position or place.

*a* **1300** *Cursor M.* 23316 Þai sal be sett in þair prisun, Vpward þair fete, þair hefdes dun. *c* **1375** *Sc. Leg. Saints* i. (*Peter*) 688 It is myn will one þe croice to be festnyt swa, myn fet vp-wart. *c* **1440** *Pallad. on Husb.* iii. 787 Vpwarde The bottom, do this vessel closid so. *c* **1450** *Two Cookery-bks.* 101 Ley the pike in a charger, the wombe side vpward. **1523** Fitzherb. *Husb.* § 16 The plough..tourneth the roote vpwarde, that it maye not growe. *a* **1548** Hall *Chron.*, *Hen. VIII*, 40 They make of hym an Image paynted reuersed with his heles vpwarde. **1601** Shaks. *Jul. C.* v. iii. 93 *Messa[la].* Titinius face is vpward. *Cato.* He is slaine. **1613**, **1641** [see Invert *v.* 1]. **1667** Milton *P. L.* vi. 649 Coming towards them..they saw The bottom of the Mountains upward turn'd. **1755** Johnson, *Supination*, the act of lying with the face upward. **1809** in *Naval Chron.* XXI. 369 Puncheons..were placed end-upward. **1849** Ainsworth *Lanc. Witches* ii. iii, [He has nailed] a horse-shoe..to t' threshold.., heel uppard.

**b.** In respect of the upper part or parts, esp. of the body.

*c* **1400** Maundev. (1919) xxx. 178 Sum men seyn þat þei [*sc.* griffins] han the body vpward as an Egle, and benethe as a Lyoun. **1426** Lydg. *De Guil. Pilgr.* 1704 Tak exaumple off thy staff Wych Grace Dieu vn-to the gaff: Thogh the poynt be sharp & kene, Yt ys vpward pleyn, smothe & clene. **1575** Laneham *Let.* (1907) 54 Fyrst, oour too feet, too legs, too kneez, so vpward: and abooue, too shoolderz [etc.]. **1607** *Puritan* i. iv. 75 Hee lookes like a Monkey vpward, and a Crane downe-ward. **1667** Milton *P. L.* i. 463 Dagon his Name, Sea Monster, upward Man And downward Fish.

**†4.** Upright; erectly. *Obs. rare.*

*c* **1290** *S. Eng. Leg.* I. 82/11 A wei þer was of scharpe stones: and opward stoden echon. **1297** R. Glouc. (Rolls) 7186 He sat him vpward vp is bed.

**5.** With (vertical) extension *from* a point or part (esp. of the body) to another expressed or implied.

**1387** Trevisa *Higden* (Rolls) V. 209 A child..þat hadde tweie bodyes from þe navel upward. *c* **1400** Maundev. (Roxb.) ii. 5 Þai made þat peece þat went fra [*ed.* 1839 from] þe erthe vpward..of cypresse. *Ibid.* vii. 24 It had..fra þeine vpward þe schappe of a gayte. *c* **1440** *Wycliffite Bible* 1 Sam. ix. 2 (MS. Bodl. 277), Fro þe schuldre and upward he appeeride ouer þe peple. *c* **1450** *Mirk's Festial* i. 97 Fendes token vp þe body, and beten hyt wyth brennyng scorgys from þe nauell vpward. *c* **1511** *1st Eng. Bk. Amer.* (Arb.) p. xxxiii/2 The whyche ben fro the myddel vpward lyke men. **1539** Bible *Ezek.* i. 27 As it had bene all of fyre within from hys loynes vpward. **1592** *Soliman & Pers.* iv. ii. 41 His skin is but pistol profe from the girdle vpward. **1600** Shaks. *Much Ado* iii. ii. 36 (Q. 1), A Spaniard from the hip vpward. **1642** Howell *For. Trav.* (Arb.) 57 It is well known the Habassines are Jacobites and Christians from the girdle upward.

**6.** *Comb.*, as (sense 1) *upward-gazing, -rushing, -shooting, -stirring, -striving*; *upward pointed*; (sense 2) *upward-bound.*

**1710** *Lond. Gaz.* No. 4681/3 The *upward-bound Ships for the Eastward. **1800** *Hull Advertiser* 18 Oct. 3/2 The upward-bound..are at anchor. **1871** Palgrave *Lyr. Poems* 64 As some still *upward-gazing lake. **1821** Atherstone *Poems* 6 With *upward pointed hands, these pray'd aloud. **1871** Tennyson *Last Tournament* 440 An ever *upward-rushing storm and cloud Of shriek and plume. **1857** Dufferin *Lett. High Lat.* (ed. 3) 328 The *upward shooting fluff of seas. **1844** Emerson *Ess.* ii. viii, In countless *upward-striving waves The moon-drawn tide-wave strives.

**II. 7.** Backward in order of time; continuously into the past.

*c* **1055** *Byrhtferth's Handboc* in *Anglia* VIII. 327 Swa fela daga tell þu fram martius monðes ende upweard. *c* **1175** *Twelfth Cent. Hom.* 34 Lucas tealde þanon..upweard to Adame seofen & hund-seofentiȝ mæȝða. *c* **1200** Ormin 2056 Cristess kinn Onn eorþe, o moderr hallfe, Bi weppmann shollde reccnedd ben Uppwarrd & dunnwarrd baþe. **1611** Bible *Haggai* ii. 18 Consider now from this day, and vpward, ..euen from the day that the foundation of the Lords Temple was laid, consider it. *Ibid.* 15.

**8. a.** To or into later life. Cf. Up *adv.*[1] 22 c.

*c* **1530** Tindale *Num.* viii. 24 From .xxv. yere vppwarde they shall goo in to wayte [etc.]. **1531** Elyot *Gov.* i. xvi, Children ..from the age of xiiii. yeres upwarde. **1711** Steele *Spect.* No. 136 ⁋ 2, I am, and ever have been from my Youth upward, one of the greatest Liars. **1875** Jowett *Plato* (ed. 2) V. 54 He was a soldier from his youth upward. **1890** J. Pulsford *Loyalty to Christ* I. 123 From childhood and upward, our ears have been..thronged with the jargon of idolaters.

**b.** *And* (also *or*) *upward*, = Upwards *adv.* 6 b.

(*a*) **1555** Eden *Decades* (Arb.) 369 Children of th[e] age of .xii. or .xiii. yeares or vppewarde. **1595** Platt *Discov. Eng. Wants* A 3, Seacoale..at the rate of 8s the chawdren or vpwarde. **1596** Harington *Anat. Metam. Ajax* L iij b, A Cesterne containing a barrell [of water] or vpward. **1708** *Lond. Gaz.* No. 4479/8 A black Cart Gelding, about 15 hands high, or upward.

(*b*) **1560** Daus tr. *Sleidane's Comm.* 422 He was xxxii. yeares olde and vpwarde. **1608** *Relat. Trav. W. Bush* E j b, To the number of two thousand people and vp-ward. **1796** H. Hunter tr. *St.-Pierre's Stud. Nat.* (1799) I. 162 A series of a hundred and fifty leagues in length, and upward.

**c.** To a higher number or amount. *rare*[−1].

**1575** Laneham *Let.* (1907) 54 So az all..numbrings from too vntoo three, and so vpward, may well be counted numberz.

**9.** *Upward of*, = Upwards *adv.* 8.

**1613** Shaks. *Hen. VIII*, ii. iv. 36, I haue beene your Wife, in this Obedience, Vpward of twenty yeares. *a* **1628** F. Grevil *Sidney* (1652) 199 The builders of any ships upward of so many hundred Tuns. **1864** *Intellectual Observer* VI. 282 A good swarm..containing at the lowest estimate upward of 40,000.

**† B.** *prep.* Up; along the line of ascent of. *rare.*

*c* **1485** *Digby Myst.* (1882) v. 388, I se hym now com vpward the hill. **1818** Keats *Endym.* i. 266 Whether to surprise The squatted hare..; Or upward ragged precipices flit To save poor lambkins.

**C.** *adj.* (Cf. OE. *upweard* adj.)

**†1.** Facing upwards; lying on the back; supine; = Upright *a.* 2. *Obs.*

A few examples occur in OE.

**1607** Topsell *Four-f. Beasts* 465 A certaine herbe..which ..maketh him to fall presently vpon his backe & lye vpward without stirring. **1615** Crooke *Body of Man* 268 The position or manner of lying of the sickeman, eyther prone that is downeward, or supine that is vpward. **1646** Sir T. Browne *Pseud. Ep.* 194 Women drowned float prone,.. but men supine or upward, is an assertion wherein the..point it selfe is dubious.

**2.** Directed towards a higher or loftier point, place, or plane; having a vertical or ascensional course or direction; taking place or inclined upwards; ascending.

**1607** Shaks. *Timon* iv. iii. 190 Common Mother [= the earth],..Teeme with new Monsters, whom thy vpward face Hath to the Marbled Mansion all aboue Neuer presented. **1634** Milton *Comus* 98 The slope Sun his upward beam Shoots against the dusky Pole. **1700** Dryden *Theodore & Hon.* 315 So spread upon a Lake, with upward Eye, A plump of Fowl behold their Foe on high. **1704** Prior *Let. to Boileau* 174 The Eagle..directs her upward Flight. **1718** — *Solomon* iii. 875 The Angel said; With upward Speed His agile Wings He spread. **1784** Cowper *Tiroc.* 383 The exalted prize demands an upward look. **1839** Bailey *Festus* 334 The last high upward slant of sun on the trees. *a* **1842** Wordsw. *Misc. Sonn.* iii. xxxi, She stands.., One upward hand..lying softly on her breast. **1890** J. Pulsford *Loyalty to Christ* I. 104 The upward slopes of the new life are delightful, and the prospects enrapturing. **1899** *Allbutt's Syst. Med.* VIII. 81 The movement and discomfort in the hands may be relieved..by very gentle upward rubbing.

*transf.* **1843** *Penny Cycl.* XXVI. 419/1 The speech-note on the word 'pale' will consist of an upward movement of the voice.

*Spec.* **1875** Knight *Dict. Mech.* 2684/1 *Upward filter*, a filter in which the flow of the liquid is upward.

**b.** Having a trend, course, drift, etc., which indicates advance, progress, or increase.

**1596** Shaks. 3 *Hen. VI*, v. iii. 1 Thus farre our fortune keepes an vpward course. **1852** *Lawson's Merchant's Mag.* July 236 A change..in the weather..has checked the upward tendency in quotations [of grain]. **1870** *Pall Mall G.* 23 Sept. 9/2 Where there is any change [in the Stock Markets] it is in the upward direction. **1914** *Eng. Hist. Rev.* Jan. 135 The upward movement which raised the lower labouring classes.

**c.** Having lofty aims or purpose.

**1850** Tennyson *In Mem.* xli. vi, Tho' following with an upward mind The wonders that have come to thee.

**3.** Situated or lying aloft or above; higher in place or position; lofty.

**1622** Boys *Wks.* 957 Troubles in this world (quoth Austin) are an vpward hell. **1815** Shelley *Alastor* 278 A swan.. with strong wings Scaling the upward sky. **1819** W. Tennant *Papistry Storm'd* (1827) 79 Barns spy'd, frae his upwart place,..George's face.

**4. †a.** (See quot.) *Obs.*

**1729** Boyer *Dict. Royal* ii. s.v., Upward Goods, or Merchandize, (so inland Traders call Goods designed for London).

**b.** Directed, moving, etc., up along a stream or river; taking place up-stream.

**1731** in *Extr. Navig. Rolls Thames* (1772) 22 The Master or chief Boatman of any upward Boat or Barge. **1816** Tuckey *Narr. Exped. R. Zaire* iv. (1818) 134 Running directly on the rocks, and forming a strong upward eddy on its west side. *Ibid.* 144 Our upward view of the river. **1818** M. Birkbeck *Notes Journ. Amer.* (ed. 4) 80 The upward navigation of these streams. **1887** *Field* 31 Dec. 985/3 In regard to other migratory fish..the same weirs have the effect..of ..arresting their upward migration.

**†5.** Going backward in time. *Obs.*[−1]

**1603** B. Jonson *Panegyre* 90 She then remembred to his thought..the vpward race Of kings, præceding him in that high court.

**D.** *sb.* **†1.** The top part; the crown or summit.

**1605** Shaks. *Lear* v. iii. 136 From th' extremest vpward of thy head, To the discent and dust below thy foote.

**2.** Upward movement. Also *fig.*

**1898** Meredith *Odes Fr. Hist.* 30 Not singing the spirally upward of rapture, the downward of pain Rather, the drop sheer downward from pressure of merciless weight.

**U·pwardly,** *adv.* [f. prec. + -ly [2].] In an upward direction; upwards.

**1816** L. Hunt *Rimini* iv. 387 There lay she praying, upwardly intent. **1835** Browning *Paracelsus* v. 883 All tend upwardly though weak, Like plants in mines which never saw the sun. **1844** Mrs. Browning *Brown Rosary* iii. xxii, She glanced upwardly mute. **1875** Knight *Dict. Mech.* 2706/1 The pistons..were fitted with upwardly opening valves.

**U·pwardness.** [f. Upward *a.* + -ness.]

**1.** Tendency or proclivity to rise or mount upwards; the quality of suggesting upward movement.

**1614** Latham *Falconry* 21, I haue reclaimed an outragious, vnstaied hawke;..shee hath falne cleane from her vpwardnesse and high flying. **1618** *Ibid.* ii. 117 If by nature there were euer any vpwardnesse or high flying in her. **1860** W. J. C. Muir *Pagan or Christian* 62 The lancet-headed windows, arches, niches, all are in harmony of upwardness. *Ibid.* 88 This entire upwardness of composition [in Gothic architecture]. **1877** Blackie *Wise Men* 305 They by natural upwardness Remount to earth.

**2.** The quality of being upward; relative altitude.

**1896** Dk. Argyll *Philos. Belief* 122 We cannot shake off the conception of high and low, of upwardness and downwardness.

**Upwards** (*ɒ*·pwǫ̈ɹdz), *adv.* and *prep.* Forms: 1 up-, uppweardes, 2, 5–6 upwardes (6 upp-), 5, 6 vpwardes, 6–7 vp-, 7– upwards (7 upp-); 6 *Sc.* vpwartis, 9 *dial.* up-, uppards, etc. [OE. *up-, uppweardes*, f. *upweard* Upward *adv.* + *-es* of adv. genitive: see -wards. Cf. OS. *upwardas*, MLG. *upwordes*, MDu. *op-, upwaerts, -werdes*, etc. (Du. *opwaarts*), MHG. *ufwertes* (G. *aufwärts*).]

**A.** *adv.* **I. 1. a.** = Upward *adv.* 1 a.

† *To make upwards* (quot. 1575): see Make *v.*[1] 45.

*c* **888** K. Ælfred *Boeth.* xxxiv. § 10 Þæt he onȝinð of þæm wyrtrumum & swa upweardes grewð oð ðone stemn. *c* **1000** *Boeth. Metr.* xiii. 62 Sio sunne..stihð a upweardes, oð hio eft cymeð þær hire yfemesð bið eard ȝecynde. *c* **1410** *Master* *of Game* (MS. Digby 182) xiii, þe tayle..streight and a litell crompynge vpward [*MS. Reg.* vpwardes]. **1575** TURBERVILE *Faulconrie* 158 To make a high fleeing Hawke vpwards. *Ibid.*, It hapneth oftentimes that a hawke..wil yet be long before she be made upwards. **1578** BANISTER *Hist. Man* v. 76 The vretarie vessels..also prohibite that vpwardes none [*sc.* urine] may returne agayne. **1613** BIBLE *Gen.* vii. 20 Fifteene cubits vpwards [**1611** vpward], did the waters preuaile. **1647** COWLEY *Mistr.*, *My Fate* i, Go bid the Stones a journey upwards make. **1711** ADDISON *Spect.* No. 62 ¶ 5 His ambitious Love is a Fire that naturally mounts upwards. **1786** PINKERTON *Anc. Sc. Poems* I. p. lxvii, Their shoulders are moved upwards and downwards. **1815** J. SMITH *Panorama Sci. & Art* II. 189 A dry glass rod or tube, rubbed..upwards and downwards with a dry hand. **1827** FARADAY *Chem. Manip.* iv. (1842) 89 Another..mode..is to continue the furnace upwards by a deep ring. **1858** GLENNY *Gard. Every-day Bk.* 230/2 These..trailing plants ..are more frequently trained upwards.

*fig.* **1828** LYTTON *Pelham* II. xvi, Men..who join ignorance of every principle of legislation to indifference for every benefit to the people:..who level upwards, and trample downwards. **1905** FORSYTH in *Contemp. Rev.* Oct. 581 The Christ needs the apostle, the preacher. The Mediator upwards needs mediators downwards.

*transf.* **1907** J. H. PATTERSON *Man-Eaters of Tsavo* viii. 87 Lions always begin at the tail of their prey and eat upwards towards the head.

*Comb.* **1844** NOAD *Electricity* (ed. 2) 272 The upwards bent platinum wire.

**b.** = UPWARD *adv.* 1 b.

*c* **890** WÆRFERTH tr. *Gregory's Dial.* 286 Þa færinga locode heo uppweardes,..& ȝeseah þone hælend þider cuman to hire. *c* **1000** *Sax. Leechd.* III. 38 Nim mid þinum twam handum uppeweardes. *c* **1175** *Lamb. Hom.* 59 Neb upwardes he him [*sc.* man] wrohte. *c* **1400** *Pepysian Gosp. Harmony* (1922) 70 Jesus..wiþstoode and biheld hym vpwardes. **1648** HEXHAM II, *Opwaerts sien*, to See upwards, or to Looke on high. **1709** T. ROBINSON *Vind. Mosaick Syst.* 112 Man..hath his Head upwards towards Heaven. **1795–6** WORDSW. *Borderers* II. 988 Upwards I cast my eyes. **1805** — *Prelude* VII. 200 Behold, turned upwards, a face hard and strong In lineaments. **1817** SHELLEY *Rev. Islam* v. xlix, She paused, and pointed upwards. **1860** TYNDALL *Glac.* I. ii. 21 Looking upwards we saw a series of coloured rings.

**c.** *fig.* = UPWARD *adv.* 1 c.

**1557** in Lodge *Illustr. Brit. Hist.* (1791) I. 274 Prisoners ..of the degree of a Baron, or uppewardes. **1605** in *Archaeologia* (1800) XIII. 321 The lorde who beeinge an earle or upwardes,..is to have..a cloathe of estate. **1732** BERKELEY *Alciphr.* v. § 33 The army; wherein the tendency is always upwards from lower posts to higher. **1855** *Poultry Chron.* II. 423 The character of the..fowls proves that their progress is upwards in quality.

*attrib.* **1849** ROBERTSON *Serm.* (1863) 160 Not mere change, but true, ever upwards progress.

**d.** = UPWARD *adv.* 1 d.

**1874** *Times* 1 Jan. 7/6 Coffee.—A strong demand prevails, with few sellers, and the market still tends upwards. **1875** *Economist* 2 Jan. 5/2 Straits tin..after a moderate reaction upwards fell to 92*l* 5*s* in August.

**2.** = UPWARD *adv.* 2.

**1513** DOUGLAS *Æneid* VIII. ii. 65 Bayth nycht and day ilk man..Can spend in routh..Our slidand fast vpwartis the river. **1538** in *Lett. Suppress. Monast.* (Camden) 245, I am cumyng upwardes [=to London] as fast as my sekenes will suffre me. **1598** W. PHILLIP tr. *Linschoten* I. x. 19 First Daman, from thence fifteene miles vpwardes..the towne of Basaim. **1601** HAKLUYT *Galvano* 90 From thence vpwards ..he went along the coast of the Abassins. **1662** R. VENABLES *Exper. Angler* x. 99 In small Brooks you may angle upwards. **1801** *Rusher's Reading Guide* 7 The Mail Coaches to and from Bath, Bristol, &c. pass upwards and downwards every night. **1859** TOZER *Highl. Turkey* I. 184 We followed this stream upwards. **1893** *Field* 17 June 904/3 For years the labourers have been in the habit of going 'upwards'—that is, up round London—for mowing and haymaking.

*fig.* **1805** WORDSW. *Prelude* XI. 177 This..Soured and corrupted, upwards to the source, My sentiments.

**3.** = UPWARD *adv.* 3.

**1548** VICARY *Anat.* vii. (1577) I i, The brode end..[of the heart] is vpwardes, and the sharpe ende is downewardes. **1599** SHAKS. *Much Ado* III. ii. 71 Shee shall be buried with her face vpwards. **1658** ROWLAND tr. *Moufet's Theat. Ins.* 928 The mouthes or passages of their cells are..altogether downward; and they very providently place the bottom of their cels upwards, that [etc.]. **1668** MOXON *Mech. Dyalling* 18 Holding the Center A upwards, so as the Plumb-line play free in the Grove. *Ibid.* 31 If this Dyal were turned with its Center upwards. **1733** TULL *Horse-Hoeing Husb.* 304 The Share, turn'd Bottom upwards. **1839** TIMPERLEY *Dict. Printers* 104 He..then puts a quantity of the worked off sheets on it, taking care to have the printed side upwards. **1848** BAILEY *Festus* (ed. 3) 228 For the Infinite is upwards, and above The highest thing created—upwards aye. **1875** SIR T. SEATON *Fret-Cutting* 91 Take a set of gouges, stand the largest of the set edge upwards.

**b.** = UPWARD *adv.* 3 b. *rare*[−1].

*c* **1400** MAUNDEV. (1919) xix. 110 Þerfore make þei the halfondel of ydole of a man vpwardes, & the toþer half of an ox dounwardes.

**4.** = UPWARD *adv.* 5.

**1599** HAKLUYT *Voy.* II. I. 224 These men goe naked from the girdle vpwardes. **1634** SIR T. HERBERT *Trav.* 187 They ..goe naked from the waste vpwards. **1855** *Orr's Circ. Sci.*, *Inorg. Nat.* 106 One genus (*Belemnites*), very common.. among all the secondary rocks, from the lias upwards.

**5.** *Upwards of*, at or to a higher level than; above.

**1853** G. JOHNSTON *Nat. Hist. E. Bord.* I. 140 Upwards of this, the hill is well-covered with..turf and heather.

**II. 6. a.** To a higher aggregate, figure, or the like.

**1523** in Ellis *Orig. Lett.* Ser. I. I. 221 The goods to paye j^e of the li. from xx^li upwards. **1617** *Eastland Co.* (Camden) 21 Deales from Eighteene foote longe uppwards. *Ibid.*, Greate masts from fifteene hand upwards the peece. **1910** *Stage Year Bk.* 47 First-class hotel accommodation..for two and a half or three guineas a week, upwards.

**b.** Usu. *and upwards, or upwards.* Freq. = somewhat more or rather above a specified age, number, value, size, etc. = UPWARD *adv.* 8 b.

(*a*) **1570** FOXE *A. & M.* (ed. 2) 2268/2 *Hussy.* How old art thou? *Eliz.* Forty and vpwardes. **1612** SIR D. CARLETON in *10th Rep. Hist. MSS. Comm.* App. I. 572 Diverse companies to the number of 700 men and upwards. **1693** R. LYDE *Acc. Retaking of The Friend's Adventure* Title-p., Their Majesties Customs of the said ship amounted to 1,000 l. and upwards. **1717** in *Nairne Peerage Evidence* (1874) 31 Robert Robertson..aged fiifty years and upwards. **1729** T. INNES *Crit. Essay* (1879) 315 Within these last hundred years and upwards. **1818** [S. WESTON] *La Scava* 25 Eighty whetstones and upwards..have been found. **1839** TIMPERLEY *Dict. Printers* 105 All above 52 Pica ems, upon Small Pica and upwards. **1887** *Daily Chron.* 17 Jan. (Encycl. Dict.), Some of them worth as much as £30 and upwards.

(*b*) **1593** *Tell-Troth's N. Y. Gift* A 3, Ioyning..their daughters of twentye yeares olde or vnder, to rich cormorants of threescore or vpwards. **1687** MIÉGE *Gt. Fr. Dict.* II. s.v., It amounts to ten Pounds, or upwards. **1709** *Lond. Gaz.* No. 4502/1/2 A Ship of 70 Guns, or upwards. **1857** MILLER *Elem. Chem.*, *Org.* 74 A solution of soda..which contains two per cent. or upwards of alkali. **1861** *Brit. Postal Guide* 1 Jan. 28 Messengers, whose weekly wages..are..8*s*. or upwards.

**c.** To later life; = UPWARD *adv.* 8 a.

**1805** WORDSW. *Prelude* VIII. 348 Even then, And upwards through late youth, until not less Than two-and-twenty summers had been told. **1851** DIXON *W. Penn* 252 The great idea which he had nursed from his youth upwards. **1874** FARRAR *Christ* xv. 166 Might they not have understood that, from childhood upwards, He had not lived by bread alone?

**7.** Backwards in time; into the past.

*a* **1654** SELDEN *Table-T.* (Arb.) 69 Some of them are asham'd upwards, because their Ancestors were too great. **1729** T. INNES *Crit. Essay* (1879) 142 [He] pronounced this genealogy..from Fergus, son of Erch, to Fergus, son of Ferchar, and upwards. **1887** SKEAT *Princ. Eng. Etym.* I. 52 English should be traced downwards as well as upwards. **1890** GRINDLESTONE *Foundations of Bible* 19 History of the art of writing, from the days of Nehemiah upwards [to the time of Moses].

**8.** *Upwards of*, (rather) more than; = UPWARD *adv.* 9.

In frequent use from *c* 1760.

**1721** PERRY *Daggenh. Breach* 17 A large Chest or Machine, upwards of eighty Foot long. **1753–4** RICHARDSON *Grandison* III. xvi. 227 He..kept his word till he was upwards of seventy. **1841** BORROW *Zincali* II. xi. III. 109 Considerably upwards of a century. **1885** *Law Rep.* 29 Chanc. Div. 538 The estate.. was found liable for upwards of £5,000. **1893** J. PULSFORD *Loyalty to Christ* II. 321 Upwards of three thousand years ago.

**b.** Used erron. for: Somewhat less than (a specified amount); nearly, not quite. Chiefly *dial.*

**1902** *Yorks. Post* 28 Feb., Thus 'upwards of a hundred' would mean nearly, or well on to a hundred. **1902–** in colloquial use, Linc. to Devon (*Eng. Dial. Dict.*).

†**B.** *prep.* Up along the course of; = UP *prep.*[2] 2. *Obs.*

**1601** HAKLUYT *Galvano* 72 He went into Arabia, Persia, and vpwards the riuer Euphrates.

† **U·pwark.** *Sc. Obs.* [UP *adv.*[2] 12 a + *wark* WORK *sb.*] Cessation of work.

**15..** *Aberdeen Reg.* XXI. (Jam.), Upwark, quhen the fysching wes done. **1570** *Rec. Inverness* (New Spalding Club) I. 197 [He] alse protestis for ane sufficient oxe of sex yeiris auld at vpwark.

**Upwax**: see UP- 4.

**U·pway.** *rare*[−1]. [UP- 2 b. Cf. OE. *upweg*, WFris. *opwei*, Du. *opweg*, LG. *upweg*.] Ascent.

**1616** CHAPMAN tr. *Musæus* D 8 b, Hopelesse, dangerous The bar'd vp-way is to a Virgins bed.

**Upways,** *adv. rare*[−1]. [f. UP *prep.*[2]] In an upward direction; upwards (*from*).

**1890** *Telegr. Jrnl.* 28 Nov. 653/1 Distance measured upways from OA indicates roughly the degree of hardness.

**Upweening, -weigh**: see UP- 4, 7.

**Upwe·lling,** *ppl. a.* (UP- 6 b.)

**1854** WHITTIER *Hermit of Thebaid* 1 O strong, upwelling prayers of faith. **1875** HELPS *Social Pressure* i. 4, I foresee a source of enjoyment,..a very constant and up-welling source. **1884** *Century Mag.* XXIX. 108 Blushing deeply with upwelling patriotism and bashfulness.

**Upwent,** pa. t. of UPGO *v.* **Upwhelmed**: see UP- 5.

**Upwhi·rled,** *pa. pple.* (UP- 5.) **1667** MILTON *P. L.* III. 493 All these upwhirld aloft Fly..Into a Limbo large and broad. **1821** WORDSW. *Eccles. Sonn.* II. *Reflect.* 8 The 'trumpery' that ascends in bare display..Upwhirled, and flying o'er the ethereal plain. **Upwhi·rling,** *vbl. sb.* (UP- 7.) **1877** G. F. CHAMBERS *Astron.* (ed. 3) x. ii. 828 The up-whirling of the glowing gases. **Upwhi·rling,** *ppl. a.* (UP-[1]6.) **1801** SOUTHEY *Thalaba* v. xl, The upwhirling flood received Mohareb, then..Engulph'd him in the abyss.

**Upwind** (ʊpwəi·nd), *v.* [UP- 4. Cf. UPWOUND *pa. pple.*, and (M)Du. *opwinden*, MLG. *upwinden*, MHG. *ûfwinden* (G. *aufwinden*), MSw. *op-*, *upvinda* (Sw. *uppvinda*), Da. *opvinde*.]

†**1. a.** *intr.* To fly up. *Obs.*[−1]

*c* **1250** *Gen. & Ex.* 2988 He smot..on ðe lond, And gnattes bird ðor ðicke up-wond.

†**b.** *trans.* = UPTAKE *v.* 1. *Obs.*[−1]

*c* **1250** *Gen. & Ex.* 3084 A suðen wind is fliȝt up-wond, And blew ðat day and al ðat niȝt.

†**2.** To finish up; to complete. *Obs.*[−1]

*c* **1440** *Pallad. on Husb.* VII. 47 Thus shal an ox in dayes fewe vpwynde An heruest al.

**3.** To wind, coil, or roll up (something).

**1560** *Nice Wanton* 51 *Barn.* Learne..to spyn and sowe... *Ism.* Spyn, quod ha? Yea, by the masse, and with youre heles vp-wynd. **1613** DRUMM. OF HAWTH. *Cypress Grove* Wks. (S.T.S.) II. 71 The motion of a swift & euer-whirling wheele, which twinneth forth and againe vp-windeth our life?

**b.** To raise or hoist by winding.

**1600** FAIRFAX *Tasso* XV. vii, Her anchors she vpwound, And lanched foorth to sea her pinnese flit.

**4.** *intr.* To become coiled up.

**1616** J. LANE *Contn. Sqr.'s T.* XI. 256 Speckd snakes.. which turninge round, out sprange at length, and in againe vpwound.

**5.** To wind upwards.

**1880** LANIER *Sunrise* 103 Low multitudinous stirring Upwinds through the woods.

**Up-wind** (ʊ·pwi·nd), *adv.* [UP- *prep.*[2] 4.] Contrary to the course of, against, the wind.

**1838** SCROPE *Deer-stalking* 17 Deer..always run up wind. **1861** WHYTE MELVILLE *Market Harb.* 7 Here their fox had made his point good up-wind. **1897** HINDE *Congo Arabs* 202 They always started up-wind from our quarters.

**U·pwith,** *adv., prep., sb.*, and *a.* Chiefly *Sc.* (ʊ·pwiþ) and now *rare*. [UP *adv.*[1] + WITH.]

**A.** *adv.* In an upward course or direction; upwards. Also *fig.*

**1513** *Acc. Ld. High Treas. Scot.* IV. 515 Tua drawyn towis to keip hir [*sc.* a cannon] at upwith and dounewith. **1535** STEWART *Cron. Scot.* (Rolls) II. 548 The Danis..Traistand the Scottis vpwith to the hill, Suld tyre ilkone than or tha come thame till. *a* **1598** D. FERGUSON *Prov.* (S.T.S.) 10 As meikle upwith, as meikle down with. **1858** M. PORTEOUS *Souter Johnny* 30 Ye'll wi' a braindge Jirk aff the mune, an' upwith whud Far furth to range. **1864** LATTO *Tam. Bodkin* xxiii, They..durstna mount upwith to the riggin'.

**B.** *prep.* Up along the course of.

**1504** in *Reg. Mag. Sig. Scot.* (1888) 239/2 Ascendand upwith the said swaill quhill it cum to the littill stane calsay.

**C.** *sb.* Upward course. Also *fig.*

**1508** DUNBAR *Tua Mariit Wemen* 401 All is bot frutlese his effeir, and falȝeis at the vp-with. **1607** MARKHAM *Cavel.* VI. 9 If the fierce horse haue in his skelping course, either vpwithes..or downewithes, which is, that hee may eyther runne..vp hils, or down hils. **1808** JAMIESON s.v., *To the upwith*, taking a direction upwards.

**b.** An ascent or rising ground. *rare*[−1].

**1819** *St. Patrick* II. 91 Will ye see how the[y]'re spankin' along the side o' that green upwith?

**D.** *adj.* Having an upward inclination, tendency, or slope; rising.

**1864** A. WALLACE *Sc. Tales*, *M. Lauder* 37 It was a good bit upwith gate, so she would give her a tankard of ale to make her climb the brae the better. **1875** W. ALEXANDER *Ain Folk* 99 They'll be an upwith market shortly, or it chates me.

**U·pwold.** (UP- 1.) **1875** KINGLAKE *Crimea* V. vi. 90 The upwold, or high level part of the neck [of the isthmus]. *Ibid.* 92 The spine of the upwold.

**Upwound** (ʊpwau·nd), *pa. pple.* (UP- 5. Cf. UPWIND *v.*)

**1590** SPENSER *F. Q.* I. i. 15 Her huge long taile..was in knots and many boughtes vpwound. **1610** G. FLETCHER *Christ's Vict.* I. xii, Pale Sicknes, with his kercher'd head upwound. **1642** H. MORE *Song of Soul* II. III. ii. 6 The lowest is not awake, Therefore the midst lies close in sleep upwound.

**Upwrap, -wrapt, -wreathing**, etc.: see UP- 4, 5, 6.

† **Up-yie·ld,** *v. Obs.* [UP- 4.] *trans.* To yield or deliver up; to resign.

**1297** R. GLOUC. (Rolls) 7406 Þat lond þat him was iȝiue, þat he ssolde him vp ȝelde. *c* **1315** SHOREHAM II. 114 Þe soule he gan op-ȝelde. *c* **1350** *Lybeaus Disc.* 517 To syr Lybeaus they gon up-yelde..har sperys. *c* **1380** *Sir Ferumb.* 4016 Fayne y wolde þe croune op-ȝelde. **1502** in *Antiq. Rep.* (1808) II. *321 Our King Henry..to..Arthure hadde the seid londs remysed and uppyelden.

**Ur** (ɒ̄ɪ). Also **urh.** [Echoic. Cf. HURR *v.*] An inarticulate sound, uttered instead of a word that the speaker is unable to remember or bring out.

**1846** O. W. HOLMES *Rhymed Lesson* Poems (1896) 50/2 When you stick on conversation's burs, Don't strew your pathway with those dreadful urs. **1891** *Pall Mall G.* 13 June 2/1 The only pauses are the pauses of rhetoric, and the hesitating 'urh, urh' is never heard.

**Ur,** obs. or dial. var. OUR *pron.*

‖ **Ur-** (ūᵊr), *prefix*, repr. G. (also MHG., OHG.) *ur-*, denoting 'primitive, original, earliest,' and occurring in a few terms, as *ur-Hamlet*, *-origin*, *-stock*.

G. *ursprache* (= primitive language) has been freq. used in recent English philological works.

[**1864** MAX MÜLLER *Lect. Sci. Lang.* (1871) II. 133 The most troublesome of all vowels, the neutral vowel, sometimes called *Urvocal*, better *Unvocal*.] **1889** JACOBS *Caxton's Aesop* I. 37 Any light he can throw on the Ur-origin of the Fables. **1901** BOAS *Kyd's Wks.* p. xlv, The *Ur-Hamlet* may have contained a number of these borrowings.

**Uracan, -ano,** obs. varr. HURRICANE.

**U·rachal,** *a.* [f. URACH-US + -AL.] Of or pertaining to, affecting or found on, the urachus.

**1890** BILLINGS *Med. Dict.* **1905** H. D. ROLLESTON *Dis. Liver* 251 Various abdominal cysts, such as pancreatic, omental, chylous, urachal, mesenteric cysts.

‖ **Urachus** (yūᵊ·răkɒ̆s). *Anat.* [mod. L., ad. Gr. οὐραχός urinary canal of a fœtus.] A fibrous cord binding the apex of the bladder to the anterior abdominal wall and the peritoneal folds.

[**1578** BANISTER *Hist. Man* v. 83 b, Out of the higher part and middest of the bottome of the bleddar a way springeth ..called Vrachos.] **1615** CROOKE *Body of Man* (1631) 213 The ligament of the bladder cald Vrachus. **1646** [see ALLANTOIS]. **1661** LOVELL *Hist. Anim. & Min.* Introd. b 5 b, To the urachus the umbilicall arteries are joyned. **1728** CHAMBERS *Cycl.* s.v. *Umbilical*, The Urachus is only plainly found in Brutes. **1788** *Encycl. Brit.* (ed. 3) I. 742 These fibres have been considered as the urachus, though without having been ever found pervious. **1804** *Med. Jrnl.*

XII. 14 From their uniting part arose the umbilical vessels, meeting as usual the urachus. **1890** *Retrospect Med.* CII. 336 An enormously dilated urachus.

**Uraconite** (yūᵊ·rǟkǫnəit). *Min.* [f. URA-NIUM + Gr. κον-ία dust, etc.: see -ITE[1] 2 b.] 'Sulphate of uranium, found as a lemon-yellow powder' (Chester).

**1868** DANA *Min.* 668 Uraconite. Uranochre. **1888** *Cassell's Encycl. Dict.*, *Uraconite*,..a mineral..occurring in exceedingly minute scales, or earthy, on uraninite..at Joachimsthal, Bohemia.

‖ **Uræmia** (yurī·miă). *Path.* Also **uremia.** [mod.L., f. Gr. οὖρ-ον urine + αἷμα blood. Cf. It. *uremia*, F. *urémie*.] A morbid condition resulting from the presence in the blood of urinary constituents, which are normally eliminated by the kidneys.

**1857** DUNGLISON *Med. Lex.*, *Uræmia*.., a condition of the blood in which it contains urine or urea. **1867** A. FLINT *Princ. Med.* 84 An excess of uric acid..in the blood constituting a condition differing from uræmia. **1886** *Buck's Handbk. Med. Sci.* II. 253/1 The respirations..are slow in the coma of compression and uræmia.

**Uræmic** (yurī·mik), *a.* *Path.* Also **uremic.** [f. UREM-IA + -IC. Cf. F. *urémique*.]

**1.** Of or pertaining to, marked or characterized by, uræmia.

**1855** W. D. MOORE tr. *Heller's Chem. Urine* 85 Uremic vomitus occurs in connexion with other uremic phenomena. **1871** A. MEADOWS *Man. Midwifery* (ed. 2) 367 The influence of the uræmic poisoning on the central nervous system. **1886** *Buck's Handbk. Med. Sci.* II. 535/1 In chronic uræmic dropsies. **1890** CAGNEY tr. *Jaksch's Clin. Diag.* 51 Uræmic blood shows an increased quantity of urea and extractives.

**2.** Of persons: Affected by uræmia.

**1890** BILLINGS *Med. Dict.* **1905** H. D. ROLLESTON *Dis. Liv.* 226 The patient becomes more drowsy and uræmic.

‖ **Uræus** (yurī·ŏs). *Egyptian Antiq.* Pl. **uræi** (yurī·əi). [A modern Latinization of οὐραῖος, given by Horapollo as the Egyptian name for the cobra (now transliterated as *i'r·t*), perhaps influenced in form by the Gr. adj. οὐραῖος, f. οὐρά tail.] A representation of the sacred asp, snake, or serpent, or of its head and neck, employed as an emblem of supreme power, sometimes *spec.* as worn on the head-dress of ancient Egyptian divinities and sovereigns.

**1832** G. LONG *Egypt. Antiq.* I. xi. 254 The snake called Chnuphis or Uræus, the symbol of royalty found so often on the monuments of Egypt. **1847** LEITCH *C. O. Müller's Anc. Art* § 232. 205 The Sun-god..with the head of a hawk ..with the sun's disc, upon it an uræus. **1890** RIDER HAGGARD & A. LANG *World's Desire* I. vi, I will..stake the sacred circlet upon my brow, against the Royal uraeus on thine. **1904** BUDGE *3rd & 4th Egypt. Rooms Brit. Mus.* 116 A canopy of a bier..ornamented with a row of uræi wearing disks.

*attrib.* **1858** BIRCH *Anc. Pottery* I. 20 Figures of vultures, of the uræus serpent, and a scarabæus. *Ibid* 89 The crocodiles of Sabak, uræi or cobra-capella snakes, emblems of the gods. **1889** RIDER HAGGARD *Cleopatra* II. ix, The sceptre in her hand, and on her brow the uræus diadem of gold.

**Ural**[1] (yūᵊ·răl). [See def.] The name (more freq. *Urals*, *Ural mountains*) of a mountain-chain forming the north-eastern boundary of Europe with Asia, used attrib. in various specific appellations of birds, animals, etc., native to or found in that region, as *Ural duck*, *lizard*, etc. (see quots.).

**1785** LATHAM *Gen. Synop. Birds* VI. 514 *Ural Duck, *anas mersa*,..is a trifle bigger than the common Teal. **1881** LYELL *Pigeons* 81 The smooth-legged chequered or spangled ones are known in this country as *Ural ice[-pigeons]. **1802** SHAW *Gen. Zool.* III. 252 *Ural Lizard, *Lacerta Uralensis*, ..moves with great swiftness. **1781** LATHAM *Gen. Synop. Birds* I. 148 *Ural Owl, *Stryx Uralensis*,..is very full of feathers. **1824** STEPHENS *Shaw's Gen. Zool.* XII. II. 218 *Ural Scoter (*Oidemia Leucocephala*),..Ural Duck [of Latham],..is particularly abundant in Russia, Livonia, and Fionia.

**b.** *Ural-Altaic*, pertaining or belonging to the region including the Ural range and the Altaic mountains (in central Asia), its inhabitants, or their speech. Also *absol.*, the family of agglutinative languages spoken in eastern Europe and northern Asia; Turanian; Finno-Tartar.

**1855** MAX MÜLLER *Lang. Seat of War* 96 The third or Turkic branch of the Ural-Altaic division. **1880** SAYCE *Introd. Sci. Lang.* viii. II. 194 It seems to have been a possession of the undivided Ural-Altaic community. **1888** A. H. KEANE in *Encycl. Brit.* XXIV. 1/2 Hence it is that the roots..in Ural-Altaic are always in evidence.

**Ural**[2] (yūᵊ·răl). *Med.* [Irreg. f. UR-ETHANE.] A preparation of chloral hydrate and urethane, used as a hypnotic; chloral-urethane; = URALIUM.

**1891** *Cent. Dict.* **1895** *Buck's Handbk. Med. Sci.* IX. 922/2 Ural has no advantage over chloral, and has the inconvenience of being soluble in water.

‖ **Urali** (urā·li). [var. of OORALI. Cf. WOORALI.] The urari-plant (*Strychnos toxifera*), or the poison obtained from this. Also *attrib.*

**1862** in Veness *El Dorado* (1867) 131 The well-known Urali Poison is prepared from the bark of the Urali (*Strychnos toxifera?*). **1883** IM THURN *Among Indians Guiana* 311 In Europe it is variously called..urari, urali, and ourali.

**Uralian** (yurēⁱ·liăn), *a.* [f. URAL[1] + -IAN. Cf. F. *ouralien*.] Of or pertaining to, dwelling in or near, the Ural mountains; also, Ural-Altaic.

[**1797** *Encycl. Brit.* XVIII. 691 Urallian Chain..of mountains.] **1801** *Ibid.* Suppl. II. 757/1 The Uralian Cossacs are all enthusiasts for the ancient ritual. **1866** *Chamb. Jrnl.* 28 Apr. 257/1 Some malachite specimens of doors, vases, and clocks, contributed by the emperor of Russia. These were for the most part Uralian, I believe. **1875** MAINE *Hist. Inst.* 65 That portion of..mankind which has lately been called Uralian, the Turks, Hungarians, and Finns.

**Uralic** (yuræ·lik), *a.* [f. as prec. + -IC.] Of or belonging to the Ural mountains, or the peoples living in or near them.

**1861** MAX MÜLLER *Lect. Sci. Lang.* 302 It is generally supposed that the original seat of the Finnic tribes was in the Ural mountains, and their languages have been therefore called Uralic. **1880** SAYCE *Introd. Sci. Lang.* viii. II. 191 The Finno-Ugric or Uralic dialects. *Ibid.* 192 The civilization and migrations of the primitive Uralic tribes.

**Uralite** (yūᵊ·rǟləit). *Min.* [ad. G. *uralit* (1831), f. *Ural* (mountains) + -ITE[1] 2 b. Cf. F. *ouralite*.] 'Pyroxene altered to amphibole' (Chester).

**1835** *Penny Cycl.* III. 85/2 The uralites of [Professor G.] Rose appear to be its natural consequence. **1849** MURCHISON *Siluria* App. C. 538 Hypersthene and diallage are partly changed into uralite. **1888** RUTLEY *Rock-Forming Min.* 180 The well-known paramorphic conversion [of augite] into hornblende, the result being termed Uralite.

**b.** *Uralite-porphyry*, *-syenite*: (see quots.).

**1868** *Watts' Dict. Chem.* V. 940 *Uralite-porphyry*, an aphanite-porphyry occurring in the Ural, containing uralite, and sometimes also crystals of labradorite. **1888** *Cassell's Encycl. Dict.* VII. 382 *Uralite-syenite*, a variety of syenite ..which contains uralite.

**Uralitic** (yūᵊrăli·tik), *a.* *Min.* [f. prec. + -IC.] Of or pertaining to, containing or consisting of, uralite.

**1845** tr. *Humboldt's Cosmos* I. 268 Melaphyre, Augitic, Uralitic, and Oligoglassic [*sic*] Porphyry. **1879** RUTLEY *Stud. Rocks* xii. 218 A little hornblende occurs, which..is generally of a uralitic character.

**Uralium** (yurēⁱ·liŏm). *Med.* [See URAL[2] and -IUM.] = URAL[2].

**1889** *Brit. Med. Jrnl.* 16 March 609/1 Gustavo Poppi, a medical student of Bologna, recently described..the effects of a new hypnotic, which he proposes to call 'uralium'. *Ibid.*, Uralium induces sleep more quickly..than any other known hypnotic. **1891** *Lancet* 3 Jan. 46/1 Uralium or chloral-urethane..has recently been carefully tested.

**Uralo-** (yurēⁱ·lo), combining form of URAL[1], occurring in a few terms, as *Uralo-Altaic* (= URAL[1] b); *Uralo-Caspian*, pertaining to or situated near the Ural river and the Caspian sea; *Uralo-Finnic*, of or pertaining to the ethnically-allied Ural-Altaic and Finnic peoples.

**1867** *Chambers' Encycl.* IX. 670/1 The Uralo-Caspian deserts. **1876** J. B. MITCHELL *Dates & Data* 76 The Uralo-Finnic dialects of the present day. *Ibid.* 77 The Uralo-Finnic speaking people. **1879** *Encycl. Brit.* IX. 219/2 It is maintained by some that the Finnic languages represent the oldest forms among the Uralo-Altaic groups.

**Uramil** (yuræ·mil). *Chem.* [G. *uramil*, f. UR-EA or UR-IC *a.* + AM-MONIA (or -IUM) + *-il* -YL.] Dialuramide; amido-barbituric acid; murexan.

**1839** R. D. THOMSON in *British Ann.* 378 Uramil. **1841** BRANDE *Chem.* (ed. 5) 1381 Uramil..a product of the decomposition of thionuric acid. *Ibid.*, Uramil is soluble in sulphuric acid. **1878** C. M. TIDY *Handbk. Mod. Chem.* 717 Boiling uramil and mercuric oxide in a weak solution of ammonia.

**Ura·mile.** *rare.* [-ILE.] = prec.

**1843** T. THOMSON *Chem. Animal Bodies* 118 Uramile is soluble in potash ley. *Ibid.*, The constituents of uramile. **1866** ODLING *Anim. Chem.* 137 Mesoxalic Mon-ureides [include] Uramile.

**Uramilic** (yūᵊrămi·lik), *a.* *Chem.* [f. URAMIL + -IC 1 b.] Obtained or derived from uramil. Usu. *uramilic acid*.

**1839** R. D. THOMSON in *British Ann.* 382 Uramilic acid. **1841** BRANDE *Chem.* (ed. 5) 1383 Uramilic acid forms soluble crystallizable salts with ammonia, and with the fixed alkalis. **1856** WATTS tr. *Gmelin's Handbk. Chem.* X. 191 Uramilic acid dissolves in cold nitric acid without evolution of gas.

**Uran-** (yūᵊ·răn), combining form of URANITE, URANIUM, occurring in a few terms, as *uranatemnite*, etc. (see quots.).

Cf. G. *Uran-ocher*, *-oxyd*, *-vitriol*; F. *uranochre*.

**1843** E. J. CHAPMAN *Min.* 104 *Uranatemnite. (Pitchblende.)..Sk. black; no cleavage. **1843** *Penny Cycl.* XXVI. 40/1 Carbonate of Uranium, *Uran Bloom. **1805** *Phil. Trans.* XCV. 348 If this mineral be the *Uran-glimmer [= uran-mica]. **1837** DANA *Min.* 246 Uranite. *Uranalus Quadratus*...Chalcolite-Uranglimmer. **1816** JAMESON *Syst. Min.* (ed. 2) III. 553 Uranium. This Order contains three species, viz. Pitch-ore, *Uran-mica, and Uran-ochre. **1855** *Orr's Circ. Sci.*, *Geol.*, etc. 548 *Autunite*.—Yellow Uranite, Uran-mica, Phosphate of Uranium. **1812** SIR H. DAVY *Chem. Philos.* 424 Uranium..may be procured from the ores called Pechblende, and *Uranochre. **1855** *Orr's Circ. Sci.*, *Geol.*, etc. 506 *Pechuran*.—Pitch Blende, Uran Ochre, ..Oxide of Uranium. *c* **1840** *Encycl. Metrop.* (1845) VI. 518/2 Pitchblende. *Uran-pitch-ore. **1850** ANSTED *Elem. Geol.*, *Min.*, etc. § 492 Johannite, *Uran vitriol, sulphate of uranium.

**Urana·lysis.** *Med.* [f. UR-INE *sb.* + ANALYSIS. Cf. URINALYSIS.] Chemical analysis or examination of urine.

**1894** C. W. PURDY (*title*), Practical Uranalysis and Urinary Diagnosis.

**Uranate** (yūᵊ·rănĕt). *Chem.* [f. URAN-IC + -ATE[1] 1 c. Cf. F. *uranate*.] A salt produced by the action of uranic oxide upon a base.

**1842** T. GRAHAM *Elem. Chem.* 644 The alkaline and earthy uranates. **1868** *Watts' Dict. Chem.* V. 947 Uranate of Ammonium...Uranate of Barium. *Ibid.* 948 Uranate of Zinc. **1878** C. M. TIDY *Handbk. Mod. Chem.* 337 Uranic oxide can act both as base and acid, forming in the latter case the compounds called uranates.

**Urang-utang**, var. ORANG-OUTANG.

‖ **Urania** (yurēⁱ·niă). [L. *Urania* (the muse of astronomy), ad. Gr. Οὐρανία 'the Heavenly One', fem. of οὐράνιος heavenly, f. οὐρανός heaven. Cf. F. *Uranie* (Du Bartas) in sense 1.]

**1.** As the title of a book or poem dealing with celestial or astronomical themes, etc.

? **1614** DRUMMOND OF HAWTH. *Poems* 66 b, Vrania, or Spirituall Poems. **1615** J. TAYLOR (Water P.) *title*, Vrania, or His Heauenly Muse. **1621** LADY M. WROTH (*title*), The Countesse of Mountgomeries Urania. **1754** J. HILL (*title*), Urania: or, a compleat view of the Heavens. **1880–** (*title*), Urania: a Monthly Journal of Astrology, Meteorology, and Physical Science.

**2.** *Astr.* One of the planetoids or asteroids.

**1865** *Chambers' Encycl.* VII. 577.

**Uranian** (yurēⁱ·niăn), *a.*[1] [f. URANI-A + -AN.]

**1.** Pertaining to or befitting heaven; celestial, heavenly. (Freq. from *c* 1890.)

**1600** TOURNEUR *Transf. Metam.* lxxv, He bent his mind to pure Vranian vses. **1619** A. GARDEN *Bp. Elphinston* (Hunt. Cl.) 680 That concord, loue, and peace,..Ar suirlie.. Uranian and Diuine. **1818** SHELLEY *Prose Wks.* (1880) III. 21 Surrounded by sculptures of divine workmanship, he sees the earthly image of Uranian Love. **1854** S. DOBELL *Balder* xxiii. 90 That old Italian whose Uranian pride, When his great prince had forfeited the skies, Built him another heaven. **1893** F. THOMPSON *Poems* 21 And parting from her, in me linger on Vague snatches of Uranian antiphon.

**b.** As a distinctive epithet of Venus (or Aphrodite): Heavenly, spiritual. (Cf. the etym. note to PANDEMIC.)

**1768** TUCKER *Lt. Nat.* III. 301 Genuine Liberty, offspring of all-protecting Jove, and sister of Uranian Venus. **1847** TENNYSON *Princ.* I. 239 O'er his [*sc.* Cupid's] head Uranian Venus hung. **1904** L. TRACY *Rainbow Island* viii, One might almost fancy her ladyship the Moon appearing on the scene as a Uranian Venus.

**2.** Pertaining, belonging, or dedicated to Urania.

**1656** EARL MONM. tr. *Boccalini's Advts. fr. Parnass.* II. iii. (1674) 136 Euclide..was set upon by some under the Uranian Porch. **1820** SHELLEY *Milton's Spirit* 2, I dreamed that Milton's spirit rose, and took From life's green tree his Uranian lute. **1885** BLACKIE *Lett. to Wife* (1909) 333, I paid worship to the Uranian muse.

**3.** Of or pertaining to astronomy; astronomical.

**1761** *Ann. Reg.*, *Chron.* 194/2 Crabtree, whom Horrox had, by letter, invited to this Uranian banquet [= observing the transit of Venus, 1639]. **1832** FROST (*title*), Uranian Guide; or, Outline Celestial Atlas. **1839** (*Broadside title-p.*), Uranian Society is established for the advancement of Astronomical Science.

**Uranian** (yurēⁱ·niăn), *a.*[2] and *sb.* [f. URAN-US + -IAN.]

**A.** *adj.* Of or pertaining to the planet Uranus.

**1844** SMYTH *Cycle Celestial Objects* I. 205 The Uranian astronomer must be well stationed for watching comets. **1866** LOCKYER *Guillemin's Heavens* 263 The simultaneous presence or absence of these bodies from the Uranian sky. **1870** PROCTOR *Other Worlds than Ours* vii. 167 During the long Uranian year. **1885** AGNES CLERKE *Pop. Hist. Astron.* 114 No further Neptunian or Uranian satellites can be perceived.

**B.** *sb.* An inhabitant of Uranus.

**1870** PROCTOR *Other Worlds than Ours* vii. 168 For upwards of 20 years..the Uranians—if there are any—never see the small Uranian sun. *Ibid.*, The year of the Uranians lasts 84 of our years.

† **Ura·niate.** *Chem.* *Obs. rare.* [f. URANI-UM + -ATE[1] 1 c.] A salt produced by the action of uranium trioxide on a base.

**1825** T. THOMSON *First Princ. Chem.* II. 30 The uraniate of potash. *Ibid.* 37 The uraniate of barytes, when pure, is a sesqui-uraniate. **1826** HENRY *Elem. Chem.* II. 81 The decomposition of uraniate of lead by exposing the anhydrous salt, ignited, to hydrogen gas.

**Ura·nic**, *a.*[1] Also **ouranik.** [f. L. *ūran-us*, Gr. οὐραν-ός heaven, + -IC 1. Cf. med.L. *ūranic-us*.] Astronomical, celestial.

? *c* **1860** CARLYLE (Webster), Drawing accurately his meridian line, on I know not what telluric or uranic principles. **1883** R. BROWN *Eridanus* 44 There is another ouranik and doubtless preconstellational stream, namely the *Via Lactea*.

**Uranic** (yuræ·nik), *a.*[2] *Chem.* [f. URAN-IUM + -IC 1 b. Cf. F. *uranique*.] Formed from, or related to, the higher oxide of uranium.

**1837** DANA *Min.* 246 Uranic Ochre, *Uranalus Ochraceus*. **1842** FRANCIS *Dict. Arts* s.v., Uranic acid, peroxyde of uranium, or the sesquioxyde of uranium. **1866** ROSCOE *Elem. Chem.* 203 The uranous salts are green, whilst the uranic compounds are yellow. **1868** *Watts' Dict. Chem.* V. 942 Uranic nitrate, or Nitrate of Uranyl. *Ibid.*, Uranic sulphate, or Sulphate of Uranyl. **1873** RALFE *Phys. Chem.* 196, 1 C.C. of the uranic oxide solution.

**Ura·nic**, *a.*[3] *Anthropol.* [f. Gr. οὐραν-ός palate (sky, etc.: see URANO-[1]) + -IC 1.] Pertaining or relating to the palate. Freq. *uranic index*.

**1901** F. RUSSELL in *Amer. Anthrop.* III. 38.

† **Ura·nical**, *a.* *Obs.* [f. med. L. *ūranic-us* celestial (cf. URANIC *a.*[1]) + -AL.] **a.** Astronomical. **b.** Astrological.

**a.** **1595** J. BLAGRAVE *Astrol. Uran.* (title-p.), An Instrument or generall Astrolabe..called the Vranicall Astrolabe. **1619** J. BAINBRIDGE *Descr. Late Comet* 3 Tycho Brahe, of whose admirable Vranicall instruments many honourable witnesses are still suruiuing. **1716** M. DAVIES *Athen. Brit.* II. 341

Captain Hally, whose method of taking Uranical Observations had been..question'd. **b.** **1671** SALMON *Syn. Med.* To Rdr. *4 The Uranical Precepts are more subtile and pure; whose Sublimity is Heaven it self. *Ibid.* *5 In our Uranical Disquisitions, even through all the three Books.

**Uranice·ntric,** *a. rare*—1. [f. URAN-US.] Having Uranus as the centre.

**1867** G. F. CHAMBERS *Astron.* 152 Their [*sc.* Uranus' satellites] Uranicentric motion is retrograde.

†**Ura·nics,** *sb. pl. Obs.*—1 [See URANIC *a.*1 and -IC 2.] Astrological matters; astrology.

**1671** SALMON *Syn. Med.* To Rdr. *4b, So much as Spiritual and Heavenly things exceed Natural and Earthy, so much do the Uranicks exceed the Physicks.

**Urani·diform,** *a.* [f. mod.L. *Uraniidæ* (see def.).] Having the form characteristic of the *Uraniidæ*, a family of lepidopterous insects.

**1859** *Ann. Rep. Smithsonian Instit. 1858*, 186 Uranidiform larvæ will be found possibly..in Florida.

**U·ranile,** obs. var. URANYL. (Cf. -ILE.)

**1855** J. SCOFFERN in *Orr's Circ. Sci., Chem.* 484 Some chemists regard sesquioxide of uranium as really the protoxide of a radical termed uranile.

**Uraninite** (yuræ·ninəit). *Min.* [f. URANIUM + -IN1: see -ITE1 2 b.] Pitchblende.

**1879** *Amer. Jrnl. Sci.* Ser. III. XVIII. 153 The masses contain in many cases, a nucleus of uraninite. **1897** L. FLETCHER *Introd. Study Min.* 89 Uraninite, or Pitchblende, consists almost entirely of oxygen and uranium.

**Ura·nious,** var. URANOUS *a.*

**1912** *Archæol.* LXIII. 107 The uranious sand employed by the ancient glass-maker.

**Urani·sco-,** comb. form of mod.L. *uraniscus* (ad. Gr. οὐρανίσκος 'roof of the mouth'), occurring in a few medical and surgical terms, as *uraniscонitis*, *-plastic*, *-plasty* [cf. F. *uraniscoplastie*], *-rraphy*. (1848– in medical dicts., etc.)

**Uranite** (yūᵊ·rănəit). [a. G. *uranit* (Klaproth, 1789), or F. *uranite*, f. URAN-IUM + -ITE1 2 b, 4.]

†**1.** *Chem.* = URANIUM 1. *Obs.*

**1794** G. PEARSON *Table Chem. Nomencl.* 20 One new Metal, the Uranite, was discovered by Klaproth in 1790 [*sic*]. **1796** KIRWAN *Elem. Min.* (ed. 2) II. 301 Uranite..is soluble in the nitrous acid. **1821** URE *Dict. Chem. & Min.*, *Uranite* or *Uranium*, a new metallic substance, discovered by the celebrated Klaproth in the mineral called Pechblende.

**2.** *Min.* An ore or mineral composed largely of uranium, and consisting of the two varieties autunite and torbernite.

**1802** *Paris as it was* II. lxix. 385 A collection of tin ore, cobalt, uranite, &c. from Saxony. **1815** A. AIKIN *Mineralogy* (ed. 2) 138 Uranite, Uran glimmer *W.*,..occurs crystallized in rectangular prisms and tables. **1839** URE *Dict. Arts* 1263 A double phosphate of uranium and copper, called green uranite, and uran mica, occurs in Cornwall. **1866** ROSCOE *Elem. Chem.* 203 Uranium..existing combined in two somewhat rare minerals, pitchblende and uranite.

**Urani·tic,** *a.* [f. prec. + -IC.] Of, pertaining to, or containing uranite (or uranium).

**1796** KIRWAN *Elem. Min.* (ed. 2) II. 302 Uranitic Calx is insoluble in alkalis. *Ibid.* 469 Crystals of uranitic vitriol. **1819** BRANDE *Man. Chem.* 265 The uranitic ore, called by the Germans *uran glimmer*, is a hydrate of the yellow oxide. **1836** *Ibid.* (ed. 4) 733 The mineral called uranitic ochre is generally considered as a hydrated peroxide.

**Uranium** (yurēi·niŏm). [mod.L. (Klaproth, c 1790), f. the name of the planet URAN-US + -IUM.]

**1.** A rare, heavy, grayish metallic element, found esp. in pitchblende and uranite.

In first quot. erron. identified with *pitchblende*.

**1797** *Encycl. Brit.* (ed. 3) XVIII. 691 *Uranium*, a fossil found..in Saxony, and..in Bohemia, and is, by the miners, called *Pechblend*. **1805** *Phil. Trans.* XCV. 348 The solution ..contained oxide of uranium. **1842** E. A. PARNELL *Chem. Anal.* 169 Both the peroxide and protoxide of uranium are precipitated from their solutions by ammonia. **1843** *Penny Cycl.* XXVI. 39/2 Uranium is very combustible;..it burns with a remarkably white and shining light. **1857** MILLER *Elem. Chem.*, *Org.* x. § 1. 592 Salts of uranium. **1868** WATTS *Dict. Chem.* V. 940 Péligot, in 1840, showed that the body previously regarded as metallic uranium was really the protoxide (UO); he likewise obtained the true metal. **1875** VOGEL *Chem. Light* xvi. 267 Uranium itself is a rare metal whose combinations play a great part in colouring materials.

**b.** *attrib.*, esp. in the names of salts, ores, etc., as ***uranium acetate, nitrate, -ore, oxide, phosphate, vitriol***; also *Comb.*, as ***uranium-bearing, -prepared***.

Various other examples appear in special or recent Dicts., as *uranium-bloom, -green, -ochre, -orange, -yellow* (1868 *Watts' Dict. Chem.* s.v.).

**1837** DANA *Min.* 372 Pitchblende. *Uranius amorphus*. Uncleavable Uranium-Ore. **1850** WATTS tr. *Gmelin's Handbk. Chem.* IV. 175 Monosulphate. Found native as Uranium-vitriol. **1862** *Catal. Internat. Exhib., Brit.* II. No. 3054, Developments of uranium-prepared papers. **1873** RALFE *Phys. Chem.* 237 The solution of Uranium Nitrate. **1890** CAGNEY tr. *Jaksch's Clin. Diagn.* 269 Uranium acetate or nitrate is added in solution. *Ibid.*, A solution of uranium oxide.

**2.** *ellipt.* A solution of a salt or nitrate of uranium. Chiefly *attrib.* and *Comb.*

**1878** ABNEY *Photogr.* 155 Printing with iron and uranium compounds. **1890** *Anthony's Photogr. Bull.* III. 361 The uranium intensifier..in my own practice has proved the simplest and best of all intensifiers. **1892** *Photogr. Ann.* II. 422 Carbutt's Positive Films..are amenable to uranium toning. **1900** J. A. HODGES *Pract. Enlarging* xiii. (ed. 4) 98 The appearance of a uranium-toned print.

**Urano-1** (yūᵊ·rănŏ), combining form of Gr. οὐρανός sky, heaven(s), roof of the mouth, occurring in: **a.** †**urano·gnosy** (see quot.); **urano·latry,** worship of the heavenly bodies; **uranoma·nia, -pathy, -photo·graphy, -photo·meter, -sco·pian** (a fish of the family *Uranoscopidæ*), **-theism** (see quots). **b. uranostomato·scopy,** examination of the hard palate and back of the mouth; also URANOPLASTIC *a.*, -PLASTY.

**a.** *a* **1831** BENTHAM *Logic* App., Wks. 1843 VIII. 286/2 By *Uranognosy, rather than Astronomy, may that branch of Topography, taken in its largest sense, which remains after the substraction of Geography be designated. **1877** W. H. RULE *Oriental Rec., Mon.* 6 *Uranolatry was grown into a system, and the Chaldean or Babylonian astronomy had become a science. **1890** BILLINGS *Med. Dict.* II. 723 **Uranomania*, monomania involving the idea of a divine or celestial origin or connection; a species of megalomania. **1868** W. CORY *Lett. & Jrnls.* (1897) 246 That crenopathy and *uranopathy, that yielding of ourselves to running water and to still clouds. *a* **1909** WOODBURY *Encycl. Photogr.* 304 **Urano-photography*, the photography of celestial spaces. **1876** *Nature* 21 Dec. 170/1 The diffuse light of the sky.. has recently been a subject of study by M. Wild,..who has endeavoured to measure it with a somewhat complicated instrument devised by him and named a '*uranophotometer'. *c* **185** . *Sir J. Richardson's Mus. Nat. Sci.* II. 120/1 *Uranoscopians, or Sky-gazers. **1801** *Monthly Mag.* XI. 646 *Uranotheism, or the worship of sun, moon, thunder, and meteors.

**b.** *a* **1891** *Medical News* XLIX. 559 (Cent.), Phrenopathic uranostomatoscopy. (Recent Dicts. give *uranoplegia, -rrhaphy, -schisis, -staphyloplasty, -staphylorraphy*.)

**U·rano-2,** combining form of URAN-IUM, occurring, usu. in the sense 'containing, composed or having the structure of, uranium', in various (chiefly mineralogical) terms (some of which have little or no real currency in the language, but are mere borrowings from German sources), as *urano-ammonic, -chalcite, -circite, -niobate, -phane, -phyllite, -pilite, -pissite, -sphærite, -spinite, -tantal(ite, -thallite, -thorite, -til(e.*

**1850** WATTS tr. *Gmelin's Handbk. Chem.* IV. 184–5 Urano-ammonic Carbonate, .. Urano-ammonic Sulphate. **1850** ANSTED *Geol. & Min.* 220. **1855** *Orr's Circle Sci., Geol.* 531. **1867** BRANDE & COX *Dict. Sci.* III. 905. **1868** DANA *Min.* **1868** *Watts' Dict. Chem.* V. 186, 949. **1883** *Encycl. Brit.* XVI. 407, 425, 427. **1896** CHESTER *Dict. Min.* 278–9.

**Uranography** (yūᵊrănǫ·grăfi). Also 7–8 (9) ourano-. [ad. Gr. οὐρανογραφία: see URANO-1 and -GRAPHY. Cf. F. (1762) *uranographie*, Sp. and Pg. *uranografia*.]

†**1.** A description of heaven. *Obs. rare.*

**1650** FULLER *Pisgah* II. v. i. 189, I found the Canaan by him described no Geography, but Ouranography, no earthly truth, but mysticall prediction. **1710** B. JENKS (*title*), Ouranography; or, Heaven opened. The Substance of Cardinal Bellarmine's Five Books concerning the Eternal Felicity of the Saints.

**2.** The science of describing or delineating the sidereal heavens; a description or delineation of the stars. Also *transf.*

**α.** **1675** SHERBURNE *Manilius' Sphere* a ii, Constellations ..are distinguished into prophane and Sacred Figures or Morphoses, according to the different Uranography of the Antient Ethnicks. **1699** HOWE *Redeemer's Dominion* Wks. 1724 II. 85 When our Lord is said to have ascended far above all Heavens,..whose Uranography [will suffice] to describe how far that is? **1715** tr. *Gregory's Astron.* I. 310 From hence did he [*sc.* Hevelius] deduce his Uranography or Tables of all the Stars. **1833** HERSCHEL *Astron.* 159 So in uranography, any conspicuous star may be selected as an initial point. **1890** *Science-Gossip* XXVI. 102/1 An Uranography, or brief description of the constellations visible in the Northern Hemisphere..illustrated by star maps.

**β.** **1684** in Birch *Hist. Royal Soc.* (1757) IV. 272 The ingenious Mr. Hooke, in his animadversions on Hevelius's ouranography. **1881** tr. *Verne's Fur Country* 17 He had rendered great services to ouranography.

Hence **Urano·grapher,** one who practises or studies uranography; **Uranogra·phic(al** *adjs.*, of or pertaining to uranography; **Urano·graphist,** = URANOGRAPHER.

**1686** GOAD *Celest. Bodies* II. xi. 316 He is as great as the Greatest *Uranographer can make him. **1861** G. F. CHAMBERS *Astron.* 313 Many of the above smaller constellations are.. rejected by modern uranographers. **1715** tr. *Gregory's Astron.* I. 310 These *Uranographic Schemes of the Constellations are delineated in *Plano*. **1855** *Tallis's Crystal Palace* II. 245 Detouche and Houdin (France) exhibited a uranographic apparatus. **1882** R. BROWN *Law Kosmic Order* 52 A remarkable conical black Babylonian Stone.., which, though not strictly zodiacal, is certainly uranographic in character. **1833** HERSCHEL *Astron.* 179 The *uranographical effect of aberration. **1844** *N. Brit. Rev.* I. 394 His whole stores of ouranographical and astronomical knowledge. **1861** G. F. CHAMBERS *Astron.* 273 The determination of the exact uranographical position of a star. **1731** BAILEY (vol. II), **Ouranographist*,..an astronomer, or one who describes the heavens. **1812** SOUTHEY *Omniana* II. 142 The great Swedish Ouranographist [*sc.* Swedenborg], whose discoveries were not always confined to heaven.

**Ura·nolite.** *rare.* [See URANO-1 a and -LITE.] An aerolite or meteoric stone.

**1815** *Monthly Mag.* XXXIX 299 The name of *uranolite* has long appeared to me to be better suited to bodies.. which tend towards the earth through that boundless space in which the stars move. **1860** WORCESTER (citing Hutton).

So **Ura·nolith.** [-LITH.]

**1889** C. A. YOUNG *Gen. Astron.* xviii. 430 The pieces which fall from it are called..uranoliths (heaven-stones), or simply meteoric stones.

**Urano·logy.** Also 9 ouran-. [See URANO-1 a and -(O)LOGY. Cf. Pg. *uranologia*.]

**1.** The study of the sidereal heavens; astronomy.

**1735** B. MARTIN *Philos. Gram.* 10 Cosmology or Uranology ..treats of..the Universe in general, and particularly of our solar System. *Ibid.* 107 Of Uranology, or the Doctrine of the heavenly Bodies. **1740** — *Bibl. Techn.* xvii. 325 Uranology..may be considered under the following branches: Heliography;..Astrography. **1792** SIBLY *Occult Sci.* I. 53 Uranology is a science which treats of the natural body of Heaven. **1816** BENTHAM *Chrestom.* Table, Wks. 1843 VIII. 13/1 Acquaintance with Uranology, more frequently termed Astronomy.

**b.** A treatise or discourse on the sidereal heavens; a system of astronomy.

**1736** BAILEY (folio) Pref., 41. *Uranology*,..a Treatise or Discourse of the..celestial Regions and the Bodies in them contained. **1854** OWEN in *Orr's Circ. Sci., Org. Nat.* I. 261 One must not strive to make an ouranology out of a system of metaphysics.

**2.** Doctrine as to heaven. *rare*—1.

**1866** *Reader* No. 170. 317/1 Angelology and uranology.

So †**Urano·loger,** an astronomer; **U:ranolo·gical** *a.*, of or pertaining to uranology.

**1686** GOAD *Celest. Bodies* II. i. 129 The Words of that great Uranologer John Kepler. **1816** BENTHAM *Chrestom.* 55 Uranological Geography. **1851** tr. *Humboldt's Cosmos* III. 29 The uranological portion of the physical description of the world. *Ibid.*, The uranological..domain of the Cosmos.

†**Uranomancy.** *Obs.*—1 [See URANO-1 a and -MANCY.] Divination by the stars; astrology.

**1657** G. STARKEY *Helmont's Vind.* 16 All other natural practical Arts, as Geometry, Astronomy, Uranomancy, Geography, Arithmetick, and the like.

‖**U:ranome·tria.** [mod.L. *uranometria* (Bayer, 1603).] = URANOMETRY.

**1882** *Pop. Sci. Monthly* XX. 700 Uranometria of the Southern Heavens. **1885** *Encycl. Brit.* XVIII. 841/1 Sir John [Herschel]..did not go on to the formation of a complete 'uranometria'.

**U:ranome·trical,** *a. rare*—1. [See next and -ICAL.] Relating or pertaining to uranometry.

**1652** CHARLETON *Darkn. Atheism Dispelled* 327 The simple and demonstrable Uranometrical observations and Axioms of Antiquity.

**Urano·metry.** [ad. mod.L. *uranometria* URANOMETRIA: see URANO-1 a and -METRY. Cf. F. (1776) *uranométrie*, Sp. and It. *-metria*.]

**1.** A work descriptive of the heavens and esp. the fixed stars, showing or recording their magnitudes, relative positions, etc.

**1715** tr. *Gregory's Astron.* I. 310 He says that Bayer, who, in his Uranometry, attempted the contrary, thoughtlessly inverted all the Stars. **1879** NEWCOMB & HOLDEN *Astron.* 435 The uranometries of..Heis and Gould give the lucid stars..laid down on maps. **1898** W. PECK *Observer's Atlas* Pref., Thanks to the various modern Uranometries,..accurate maps of the star sphere can now be produced.

**2.** The measurement of the real or apparent distances of heavenly bodies.

**1792** SIBLY *Occult Sci.* I. 53 Uranometry..is a science that points out the magnitude, measure, and motion of the heavens. **1849** HERSCHEL *Outl. Astron.* 71 The problems of uranometry..consist in the solution of a variety of spherical triangles. **1883** C. PRITCHARD in *Mem. R. Astron. Soc.* XLVII. 367 The aims of these observers have not been especially directed to Uranometry.

**U:ranopla·stic,** *sb.* and *a.* [f. URANOPLASTY + -IC 2.] **a.** *sb. pl.* = URANOPLASTY. **b.** *adj.* Of or pertaining to uranoplasty.

**a.** **1861** *Medical Times* 20 July 70/1 He had the opportunity of performing uranoplastics on a patient. **b.** **1890** BILLINGS *Med. Dict.* s.v. **1903** *Med. Record* 30 May 884 (Cent. Suppl.).

**U·ranopla:sty.** *Surg.* [a. F. *uranoplastie*: see URANO-1 b and -PLASTY.] Plastic surgery of the hard palate.

**1846** BRITTAN tr. *Malgaigne's Man. Oper. Surg.* 370 Uranoplasty...The ligatures being placed as in Staphyloplasty,.. the operator detaches..the layer of soft parts. **1862** *N. Syd. Soc. Year-Bk. Med.* 248 Uranoplasty by detachment of the Mucous-peritoneal Covering of the Palate. **1872** COHEN *Dis. Throat* 200 [An] operation of uranoplasty for cleft of the hard palate.

†**Ura·noscope.** *Obs.* [a. F. (16th c.) *urano-*, *ouranoscope*: see URANOSCOPUS.] = URANOSCOPUS.

**1591** SYLVESTER *Du Bartas* (1605) I. v. 232 Th' Vranno-scope [*margin* Vrano-Scopus], so, hid in mud, doth put Out of his gullet a long limber gut. **1753** *Chambers' Cycl.* Suppl. s.v. *Trachinus*, This is the uranoscope, or *Trachinus* of authors, called also *callionymus*. Artedi.

**U:ranosco·pic,** *a. rare.* [f. Gr. οὐρανοσκόπ-ος observing the heavens.] **a.** Pertaining to the study of the heavens. **b.** Directed towards the heavens.

**1816** BENTHAM *Chrestom.* Wks. 1843 VIII. 86 Uranoscopic Physiurgics has for its single-worded synonym the adequately expressive appelative Astronomy. **1854** *Fraser's Mag.* L. 203 Till his uranoscopic eyes warn him that the..fishes.. are within gulp of his open sepulchre of a throat.

‖**Urano·scopus.** *Ichth.* Also 6 -ascapos, -oscopos. [L. *ūranoscopus*, or ad. Gr. οὐρανοσκόπος: see prec.] = STAR-GAZER 2.

**α.** **1584–7** GREENE *Carde of Fancie* Wks. (Grosart) IV. 143 The Fish called Vranascapos. **1594** T. B. *La Primaud. Fr. Acad.* II. 552 One fish..hath the eyes set in the top of the head, and therefore it is called by the Græcians *vranoscopos*.

**β.** **1591** [see URANOSCOPE]. [**1623** COCKERAM *Eng. Dict.* III. Hence in PHILLIPS.] **1753** *Chambers' Cycl.* Suppl. s.v., The situation of the eyes of the *Uranoscopus*. **1774** GOLDSM. *Nat. Hist.* VI. 306 The *Uranoscopus*,..the mouth flat; the eyes on the top of the head;..an inhabitant of the Mediterranean Sea. **1803** SHAW *Gen. Zool.* IV. I. 130 The Weever was by Artedi considered as not generically distinct from the Uranoscopus. **1854** BADHAM *Halieut.* 127 The name of this fish, *uranoscopus*, or 'sky-gazer', is derived from the position of the eyes, which are singularly planted on the crown of the head.

**Uranoscopy.** *rare.* Also **ourano-** [ad. mod. Gr. οὐρανοσκοπία: see prec. and -Y³. Cf. It. *uranoscopia.*] (See quots.)

**1656** BLOUNT *Glossogr.*, *Uranoscopy*, (Gr.) a speculation or view of the Heavens. [**1658**– Phillips, Bailey, and later Dicts.] **1681** R. WITTIE Οὐρανοσκοπία, etc. 73 Of which I have been discoursing more at large in my *Ouranoscopy*, or *Survey of the Heavens.*

**Urano·so-**, combining form of URANOUS *a.*, occurring in a few chemical terms, as **uranoso-ammonic, -potassic, -uranic.**

**1850** WATTS tr. *Gmelin's Handbk. Chem.* IV. 181–7 Uranoso-uranic oxide, .. uranoso-ammonic Carbonate, .. uranoso-ammonic sulphate, .. uranoso-potassic Sulphate. **1868** — *Dict. Chem.* V. 941 Pitchblende .. consists of impure uranoso-uranic oxide. *Ibid.* 946.

**Uranous** (yūᵊ·rănəs), *a.* *Chem.* [f. URAN-IUM + -OUS c. Cf. F. *uraneux.*]

**1.** Formed from or related to the lower oxide of uranium.

**1842** T. GRAHAM *Elem. Chem.* 643 The uranous sulphate yields, by evaporation, green prismatic crystals. **1866** ROSCOE *Elem. Chem.* 203 There are two oxides which form salts, viz., uranous oxide, UO, and uranic oxide, $U_2O_3$. **1868** *Watts' Dict. Chem.* V. 942 Uranous Bromide. *Ibid.*, Uranous chloride. **1894** G. S. NEWTH *Inorg. Chem.* 617 Uranium dioxide .. yielding the unstable uranous salts, such as uranous sulphate.

**2.** Of or pertaining to, typical of, uranium.

**1878** ABNEY *Photogr.* 159 This is reduced to the uranous state by the action of light in the presence of organic matter.

**Uran-outang**, obs. f. ORANG-OUTANG.

**1853** J. CUMMING *Scripture Reading Genesis* ii. 18 The absurdity of supposing such a similarity between .. an uran-outang and man.

**Uranus** (yūᵊ·rănŏs). *Astr.* [a. L. *Ūranus*, a. Gr Οὐρανός husband of Gæa (Earth) and father of Cronos (Saturn).] The most remote but one of the planets, situated between Saturn and Neptune.

Discovered in 1781 by Sir Wm. Herschel, who named it 'the Georgium sidus', 'the Georgian planet'. The name *Uranus* was first proposed by Bode, in conformity with other planetary names from classical mythology.

**1802** O. GREGORY *Treat. Astron.* 128 By some astronomers it is called *Herschel*, in honour of the discoverer; though among almost all foreigners, it has acquired the name of *uranius* [sic], which it is likely to retain. **1822** *Encycl. Metrop.* (1845) III. 498/1 Both these appellations are, however, now nearly become extinct, that of *Uranus* being almost universally adopted. **1860** OLMSTED *Mech. Heavens* 267 Uranus was the remotest known planet.., until the discovery of .. Neptune.

**Uranyl** (yūᵊ·rănil). *Chem.* [f. URAN-IUM + -YL.] A radical ($UO_2$) held to exist in many compounds of uranium.

**1850** WATTS tr. *Gmelin's Handbk. Chem.* IV. 181 Chloride of uranyl. **1863** — *Dict. Chem.* I. 797 Carbonate of Uranyl and Ammonium. *Ibid.*, Uranyl, $U^2O^2$, is a diatomic radicle which may be supposed to exist in the uranic salts, e.g. uranic nitrate. **1884** FRANKLAND & JAPP *Inorg. Chem.* 708 Salts in which the dyad radical uranyl ($U^{vi}O_2$) plays the part of a dyad metal.

**b.** *Uranyl chloride, oxide, phosphate, salts*: (see quots.).

**1865** MANSFIELD *Salts* 285 The so-called 'Uranyl' Salts of Peligot, supposed to be of the form $U_2O_2$. **1878** C. M. TIDY *Handbk. Mod. Chem.* 337 Uranic oxide (sesquioxide) or Uranyl oxide. **1888** *Encycl. Brit.* XXIV. 7/2 Solutions of uranyl salts (nitrate, &c.). **1888** *Cassell's Encycl. Dict.* VII. 384 *Uranyl-chloride*, Uranic-oxychloride. **1903** *Amer. Jrnl. Sci.* Ser. IV. XVI. 237 The filtering of a precipitate of ammonium uranyl phosphate through a Gooch crucible.

Hence **Urany·lic** *a.* (See -IC 1 b.)

**1884** FRANKLAND & JAPP *Inorg. Chem.* 708–711 Uranylic chloride, .. bromide, .. fluoride, .. nitrate, .. sulphate, .. pyrosulphate, .. sulphide.

‖ **Urao** (urā·o). *Min.* [Native name. So F. *urao.*] = TRONA.

**1839** URE *Dict. Arts* 1263 Urao, is the native name of a sesquicarbonate of soda found at the bottom of certain lakes in Mexico. **1863** *Watts' Dict. Chem.* I. 796 Tetrasodic Carbonate or Sesquicarbonate of Sodium .. occurs .. as *urao* at the bottom of a lake in Maracaibo, South America. **1889** *Amer. Nat.* XXIII. 814 The composition of urao, a mineral .. from Venezuela.

‖ **Urari** (urā·ri). Also **urary, urare; ourari, oorara.** [See CURARE, and cf. URALI, OORALI, WOORALI.] (See quots. 1859, 1866.)

α. **1838** in *Annals Nat. Hist.* (1841) VII. 417 The whole of the Urary is poured by degrees through the small funnel. **1876** *Daily News* 21 June 2 The prohibition of the use of urari as an anæsthetic.

β. **1859** A. S. TAYLOR *On Poisons* (ed. 2) 771 The poison known under the name of .. Woorali, Oorara, and Curara. **1866** *Treas. Bot.* 1106 *Strychnos toxifera* also yields a frightful poison called Ourari .., employed by the natives of Guiana.

**b.** *attrib.* and *Comb.*, as *urari-house, -maker, poison*; **urari bark**, bark of the **urari plant**, *Strychnos toxifera.*

**1838** in *Annals Nat. Hist.* (1841) VII. 416, I was fortunate enough in purchasing a quake or basket of Urary bark. *Ibid.*, The much-famed Urary poison. *Ibid.* 417 Other fire than that made by the Urary-maker is not allowed to come under the roof of the Urary-house. **1841** *Ibid.* 415 The pure bark of the Urari plant, *Strychnos toxifera.* **1862** MILLER *Elem. Chem., Org.* (ed. 2) 502 The Urari or woorara poison of South America.

‖ **Ura·ster.** [a. mod.L. *uraster* (Agassiz).] The common star-fish, *Asterias rubens.*

**1863** *Intell. Observer* Nov. 251 The commoner Urasters, found everywhere between tide-marks, are examples of the five-rayed form.

‖ **Uratæ·mia.** *Path.* [mod.L., f. URATE + Gr. αἷμα blood.] A morbid condition due to accumulation of urates in the blood. Cf. URÆMIA.

**1897** *Allbutt's Syst. Med.* III. 162 A condition which may be termed uratæmia prevails.

**Urate** (yūᵊ·rĕt). *Chem.* Also **urat.** [a. F. *urate*: see UR-IC *a.* and -ATE¹ 1 c.] A salt produced by the action of uric acid on a base.

**1800** tr. *Lagrange's Chem.* II. 404 The urate of potash may be decomposed by the muriatic acid. **1811** HENRY in *Manchester Soc. Mem.* (1813) II. 403, I have examined the properties of each individual urate. **1826** — *Elem. Chem.* II. 462 Uric acid, urate of ammonia, and phosphate of lime. **1844** G. BIRD *Urin. Deposits* 88 Uric acid and urates may occur in great abundance in the urine. **1869** TANNER *Clin. Med.* (ed. 2) 330 Being made up of urates of lime, magnesia, soda.

*attrib.* **1877** HUXLEY *Anat. Inv. Anim.* vii. 441 The granules .. probably consist of urate of ammonia (Kölliker). Hence the cells of the layer which contain them are termed by Schulze the 'urate cells'. **1886** *Buck's Handbk. Med. Sci.* II. 258/2 Urate concretions .. are especially common as renal calculi in children. **1890** F. TAYLOR *Man. Pract. Med.* (1891) 924 Urate deposits in gout.

**Uratic** (yuræ·tik), *a.* [f. prec. + -IC 1 b.] Of or pertaining to, containing or consisting of, a urate or urates. *Uratic diathesis*: (see quot. 1885).

**1876** BRISTOWE *Th. & Pract. Med.* 618 Scanty urine with abundant uratic deposit. *Ibid.* 885 These results being due .. to uratic infiltration. **1885** *Encycl. Brit.* XVIII. 388/2 The peculiar liability from uric acid is sometimes called the uric-acid or uratic diathesis or constitution. **1897** *Brit. Med. Jrnl.* 27 March 769 Uratic crystals forming only in necrosed and never in healthy tissues.

‖ **Urato·sis.** *Path.* [f. as prec. + -OSIS.] A morbid condition of health resulting from the deposit of urates in the tissues or fluids of the body.

**1890** SIR W. ROBERTS in *Lancet* 29 Nov. 1162/1 He ventured to suggest that uratic precipitation .. should be known by the name of 'uratosis'. **1897** *Allbutt's Syst. Med.* II. 981 He [Sir Wm. Roberts] believes that both the gouty diathesis and lead poisoning have the same tendency (for which he has coined the word 'uratosis') to precipitate crystalline urates in the tissues or fluids of the body. *Ibid.* III. 167 Uratosis cannot occur, so far as is known, without co-existing uratæmia.

† **Uraught.** *Anglo-Irish. Obs.* Also **uriaght.** [a. Irish *oireacht* faction, party, clan.] An Irish petty chief.

**1586** *Treaty[se] of Ireland* in *MS. Bodl.* Add. c 39 fol. 49 b, McGuyer is one of Oneills Uraughts. *Ibid.*, Ochan is chefe of Oneylls Uraughts. **1601** Q. ELIZ. *Let.* in Moryson *Itin.* (1617) II. 201 If our Armes must be accompanied with any .. mercy, rather to imploy the same in receiuing the secondary members and Vriaghts from him. **1603** *Ibid.* 280, I doe absolutely renounce all challenge or intermedling with the Vriaghts .. or exacting any blacke rents of any Vriaghts (or bordering Lords).

**Urban** (ɒ̄·ɹbăn), *a.* and *sb.* [ad. L. *urbān-us* (whence It., Sp., Pg. *urbano*), f. *urb-s* city. Rare before the 19th cent.; cf. next.]

**A.** *adj.* **1.** Pertaining to or characteristic of, occurring or taking place in, a city or town.

**1619** A. GARDEN *Bp. Elphinston* (Hunt. Cl.) 2239 Vrban and tunishe [=townish] turns, Or for the land's effairs, .. his wit Him fit for all declairs. *c* **1770** ERSKINE in *Encycl. Brit.* II. 912 Predial servitudes are divided into rural servitudes, or of lands; and urban servitudes, or of houses. **1821** LAMB *Elia* I. *Valentine's Day*, I include all urban and all rural sounds. **1845** R. W. HAMILTON *Pop. Educ.* iii. 42 It is contended that urban labour is engrossing, unhealthy, and demoralising. **1867** W. L. NEWMAN in *Quest. Reformed Parl.* 121 The progressive forces of urban and agricultural life. **1877** GLADSTONE *Glean.* (1879) I. 157 We .. are apt to say that the influence of money .. is a considerable element in the strength of urban Toryism.

**b.** Constituting, forming, or including a city, town, or burgh, or part of such.

**1841** W. SPALDING *Italy & It. Isl.* II. 309 One uniform system of municipal government, embracing all districts, rural as well as urban. **1867** A. O. RUTSON *Ess. Reform* 297 The activity of mind and the zeal for improvement which belong to urban constituencies. **1872** *Act* 35–36 *Vict.* c. 79 § 3 Such urban and rural sanitary districts. **1888** BRYCE *Amer. Commw.* II. lxi. 433 A 'town' in New England .. is a rural and not an urban area. **1894** *Act* 56–57 *Vict.* c. 73 § 21 Urban sanitary authorities shall be called urban district councils, and their districts shall be called urban districts.

**2.** Exercising authority, control, supervision, etc., in or over a city or town.

Used by Howell in place of his usual *urbane.*

**1651** HOWELL *Venice* 16 All Magistrats are either Urban or Forren, viz. of Town or Countrey. *a* **1704** T. BROWN *Walk Lond. & Westm.* Wks. 1720 III. 317 The pathetick Harangue of that Urban Magistrate a R—r. **1815** J. C. HOBHOUSE *Substance Lett.* (1816) II. 17 The national guard of Paris, .. that urban guard whose patriotism and approved zeal [etc.]. **1872** *Act* 35–36 *Vict.* c. 79 § 4 Urban sanitary authorities shall be the several bodies of persons specified [etc.]. **1886** *Encycl. Brit.* XX. 145/2 The Urban Quæstors.

**b.** Residing, dwelling, or having property in a city or town.

**1837** C. LOFFT *Self-formation* I. 40 His urban, or sub-urban brother, the man of the multitude, the unit of the mob. **1849** ALISON *Hist. Eur.* I. ii. 225 Government has .. found a counterpoise to the vehemence of urban democracy. **1873** MORLEY *Struggle Nat. Educ.* 95 The brutalising lives that are led by the rural and urban poor in their crowded hovels. **1889** *Spectator* 14 Dec. 834 How do they justify the absorption of the increment of value from urban landholders alone?

**B.** *sb.* One who belongs to or lives in a town or city.

**1891** *Cent. Dict.* Also in recent use (1922).

Hence **U·rbanism**, urban character. [Cf. F. *urbanisme.*]

**1889** *Universal Rev.* Oct. 210 The local colour or detail, the sentiment or the social life, the provincialism or urbanism of the story.

**Urbane** (ɒɹbē¹·n), *a.* [ad. F. *urbain* (14th c.), or L. *urbān-us* URBAN *a.* For the difference, in form and stress, between *urban* and *urbane*, cf. *human* and *humane.*]

**1.** Of or pertaining to, characteristic of or peculiar to, a town or city. Now *arch.* or *Obs.*

**1533** BELLENDEN *Livy* I. xx. (S.T.S.) I. 114 Siclike vrbane & civil laubouris. *Ibid.* v. v. II. 161 Thus had al þe romane tentis almaist bene replete of seditioun vrbane. **1570** LEVINS *Manip.* 19 Vrbane, *vrbanus.* **1607** R. C[AREW] tr. *Estienne's World Wond.* 233 They see greater cunning and dexteritie, and a more ciuill and vrbane kind of life. **1681** STAIR *Inst. Law Scot.* XVII. 343 Negative Urbane Servitudes, do chiefly concern the light view or prospect of Tenements. **1788** *Trifler* No. 26. 344 In the simple beauty of the country the once wealthy merchant of Bassora lost the recollection of urbane magnificence. **1809–14** WORDSW. *Excurs.* VIII. 71 A poor brotherhood who walk the earth, .. Raising .. savage life To rustic, and the rustic to urbane.

†**b.** Exercising jurisdiction over, dwelling or residing in, a town or city. *Obs.*

**1651** HOWELL *Venice* 16 Among the Urbane or Cittie Magistrats the Judges are rankd. **1652** GAULE *Magastrom.* 373 M. Æmilius, the urbane prætor. **1658** J. HARRINGTON *Oceana* Introd. B j b, The Urbane Tribes of Rome consisting of the Turbaforensis [etc.]. **1681** H. NEVILE *Plato Rediv.* 61 The Rustik Tribes being twenty seven, and the Vrbane nine.

**c.** Following the pursuits, having the ideas or sentiments, characteristic of town or city life.

**1698** FRYER *Acc. E. Ind. & P.* 54 The Citizens are urbane, being trained up to Commerce. **1870** LOWELL *Study Wind.* (1871) 177 The same combination of circumstances produced Béranger, an urbane or city poet.

**2.** Having the manners, refinement, or polish regarded as characteristic of a town; courteous, civil; also, blandly polite, suave.

**1623** COCKERAM I, *Vrbane*, ciuill, courteous. **1656** BLOUNT *Glossogr.*, *Urbane*, .. civil in curtesie, .. pleasant in behaviour and talk. **1796** T. HOLCROFT tr. *Stolberg's Trav.* lxii. I. 483 The urbane youth .. gave due praise to the country of Menelaus. **1827** LYTTON *Pelham* xv, We took advantage of our acquaintance with the urbane Frenchman to join his party. **1873** DIXON *Two Queens* IV. 139 In Eustace Chapuys, master of requests, he had a man of law, .. urbane, alert, unscrupulous. **1882** STEVENSON *Mem. & Portr.* xi. (1887) 170, I feel never quite sure of your urbane and smiling coteries.

**b.** Characterized by urbanity, courtesy, or politeness.

**1679** MARG. MASON *Tickler Tickled* 2 To treat a Lady of Mrs. Ellen Rigby's Quality, with the name of Bitch-Fox, .. is not at all Urbane. **1800** W. TOOKE *Cath. II*, III. 105 *n.*, A man remarkable for his talents and urbane manners. **1832** W. IRVING *Alhambra* II. 289 His manners were gentle, affable, and urbane. **1860** W. COLLINS *Wom. in White* II. 279 Stepping forward in the most urbane manner. **1871** BROWNING *Balaust.* 1839 To guests, a servant should not sour-faced be, But do the honours with a mind urbane.

**3.** Refined in expression; politely expressed.

**1806** W. L. BOWLES *Pope's Wks.* I. 298 The latter part of it [*sc.* an epistle] is certainly urbane, elegant, and unaffected. **1876** LOWELL *Among my Bks.* Ser. II. 139 We miss the point, the compactness, and above all the urbane tone of the original.

Hence **Urba·nely** *adv.*; **Urba·neness** (Bailey, 1727).

**1822** *Monthly Rev.* XCVII. 540 This taste is so finely polished and so urbanely expressive. **1881** 'RITA' *My Lady Coquette* xiii, 'I am going to the wood,' he answers urbanely.

**U·rbanist.** [f. the Papal name *Urban* (see defs.) + -IST. Cf. F. *Urbaniste* in sense 2.]

**1.** An adherent of Pope Urban VI (1378–89), the opponent of anti-pope Clement VII. *rare.*

**1523** LD. BERNERS *Froiss.* I. ccccxxx. 305 b, All the flemynges be as good Urbanystes as we be. **1855** MILMAN *Lat. Chr.* VI. 17 As Clement's party drew back, the Urbanists took up the cry.

**2.** A nun of a branch of the Poor Clares, following the rule as mitigated by Pope Urban IV in 1264.

**1687** MIÈGE *Gt. Fr. Dict.*, *Urbanistes*, .. Vrbanists, a sort of Nuns. **1756–9** A. BUTLER *Lives Saints, B. Colette*, She .. took the habit of .. the mitigated Clares, or Urbanists. **1806** *Archaeol.* XV. 93 They were also called Urbanists, from Pope Urban IV, who mitigated the rigour of their rules as originally drawn up by St. Francis. **1884** *Catholic Dict.* 667/1 The order [of nuns of St. Clare] was thus divided into two branches, the larger being known by the name of Urbanists, the latter by that of Clarisses.

**Urbanity** (ɒɹbæ·nĭti). [a. F. *urbanité* (13–14th c.), or ad. L. *urbānitāt-*, *urbānitās*, f. *urbān-us* URBAN *a.* Cf. It. *urbanità*, Sp. *urbanidad*, Pg. *urbanidade.*]

**1.** The character or quality of being urbane; courtesy, refinement, or elegance of manner; refined or bland politeness or civility.

In frequent use since *c* 1825.

**1535** STEWART *Cron. Scot.* (Rolls) II. 328 Ane man he wes of greit vrbanitie. **1547** BOORDE *Brev. Health* (1557) Prol., Egregious doctours, .. of your Urbanitie exasperate not youre selfe agaynst me. *a* **1566** R. EDWARDS *Damon & Pithias* (1906) 46 A right courtier is virtuous, gentle and full of urbanity. **1606** BRYSKETT *Civ. Life* 245 The meane which teacheth the tempering of those excesses, called the vertue of Vrbanitie, a Latine name, which in English we cannot better. 1693 DRYDEN *Juvenal* (1697) p. lxii, His Urbanity, that is, his Good Manners, are to be commended. 1713 *Guardian* No. 36 ¶ 11 The Virtue called Urbanity by the Moralists, or a Courtly Behaviour. 1746 *Gentl. Mag.* 7/2 Urbanity is a certain impression of politeness and goodness, which appears in the mind, conversation and sentiments of a person. 1777 W. DALRYMPLE *Trav. Sp. & Port.* vii, He was all urbanity and good humour. 1814 SCOTT *Wav.* xi, If you have no respect for the laws of urbanity. 1849 MACAULAY *Hist. Eng.* iv. I. 439 That exquisite urbanity, so often found potent to charm away the resentment of a justly incensed nation. 1878 PATER *Child in House* (1894) 15 A kind of comeliness and dignity, an *urbanity* literally, in modes of life, which he connected with the pale people of towns.

*transf.* 1616 J. LANE *Contn. Sqr.'s T.* IX. 152 Cambuscan ..eyenge Giant Horbills iollite, rann at his tassant plumes vrbanitie.

**b.** Const. *of* (manners, etc.)

1793 V. KNOX *Let. Yng. Nobleman* v, Wks. 1824 V. 10 You cannot read and taste his beauties, without improving your urbanity of manners. 1798 S. & HT. LEE *Canterb. T.* II. 129 From the moment they quitted France, urbanity of manners vanished. 1808 *Med. Jrnl.* XIX. 258 The late Dr. Purcell, ..whose urbanity of manners..will long be remembered. 1816 SCOTT *Old Mort.* xxxv, The gentleness and urbanity of his general manners.

**c.** *pl.* Civilities, courtesies.

1646 SIR T. BROWNE *Pseud. Ep.* I. vi. 23 The passages of societie and daily urbanities of our times. 1822 GALT *Provost* xlii, There is a surprising difference, in regard to the urbanities in use among those who have not yet come to authority. 1866 FELTON *Anc. & Mod. Gr.* II. v. 71 In the urbanities of social life,..Athens was without an equal, without a second.

† **2.** Conversation characteristic of well-bred townspeople; cheerful, witty, or pleasant talk; polished wit or humour. *Obs.*

*a* 1566 R. EDWARDS *Damon & Pithias* (1571) B i b, Then grudge not at all, if in my behauiour, I make the Kinge mery, with pleasant vrbanitie. 1640 BP. REYNOLDS *Passions* xxi. 214 Men are delighted..with Elegancies,Tests,Vrbanity, and Flowers of wit. 1656 E. REYNER *Rules Govt.Tongue* 223 Use Recreational speeches;..this is urbanity,or pleasantness of speech. 1693 DRYDEN *Juvenal* (1697) p. liv, Moral Doctrine, says he, and Urbanity, or well-manner'd Wit,..constitute the Roman Satire.

**3.** The state, condition, or character of a town or city; life in a city; town-life.

In freq. use from *c* 1898.

1549 *Compl. Scotl.* vi. 43 Tha detestit vrbanite, and desirit to lyue in villagis. 1789 BELSHAM *Ess.* I. xvii. 328 The serenity, the elegance and urbanity of Paris. 1877 R. MARTINEAU tr. *Goldziher's Mythol. Heb.* iv. 83 This trait of glorification of the old-fashioned Beduin-life, to the disparagement of the free urbanity of the townsmen. 1898 MAITLAND *Township & Borough* 13 A difference between.. urbanity and rusticity. 1900 A. JESSOPP in *Birm. Weekly Post* 14 April 5/3 A glimpse of the world of streets and the docks and the seamy side of 'urbanity'.

**Urbaniza·tion.** [f. next + -ATION.] The process of investing with an urban character; the condition of being urbanized.

Freq., esp. in journalistic use, since 1904.

1888 *Advance* (Chicago) 8 Mar. 152 One of the most remarkable characteristics of the time is 'the urbanization of the country'. 1904 *Parl. Rep. Comm. Phys. Degeneration* 16 The 'urbanization' of the population cannot have been unattended by consequences prejudicial to the health of the people.

**Urbanize** (ɒ·ɹbănəiz), *v.* [f. URBANE or URBAN *a.* + -IZE, or (in sense 2) ad. F. *urbaniser* (1873). Cf. Pg. *urbanisar* in sense 1.]

**1.** *trans.* To render urbane or civil; to make more refined or polished.

1642 HOWELL *For. Trav.* (Arb.) 14 Those more refined Nations, whom Learning and Knowledge did first Vrbanize and polish. 1785 *Hist. & Antiq. York* II. 2 In order to cultivate a better Understanding of human Nature amongst them, and urbanize their savage Disposition.

**2.** To make of an urban character; to convert or transform into a city.

Freq. in journalistic use since *c* 1900.

1884 [see the *ppl. a.*]. 1888 *Boston* (Mass.) *Jrnl.* 4 Feb. 2/3 It is impossible to urbanize the country.

Hence **U·rbanized** *ppl. a.*

Also, in recent use (1923), *urbanizing* ppl. a.

1884 *Western Morn. News* 17 July 4/5 The Government will..then appeal to the urbanised counties.

**Urba·rial,** *a. rare.* [f. G. *urbari-um* register of landed property, f. MHG. *urbar* (revenue from) landed property.] Of or pertaining to, based or founded on, the register of landed property.

1849 *Blackw. Mag.* LXV. 622 The projected reform of the Urbarial code [in Hungary]. *Ibid.* 629 The lands held by urbarial tenure. 1852 *Times* 26 June 6/4 The draught of indemnification for the loss of urbarial [*printed* urbanal] rights in Hungary has been completed.

**U·rbian,** *a. rare*⁻¹. [f. L. *urbi-s*, *urbs* a city + -AN. Cf. SUBURBIAN *a.*] Of or pertaining to a city.

1710 *Brit. Apollo* No. 85. 3/1 Urbian Piles advanc'd their tow'ring head.

**U·rbic,** *a. rare.* [ad. L. *urbic-us*, f. *urbs* a city.] † **a.** = URBICARY *a.* **b.** Of or pertaining to a city.

1664 OWEN *Vind. Animad. Fiat Lux* iv. 67 She failed under the just hand of God, when the persons of that Vrbick Church were extirpated..by Totilas. 1855 *Fraser's Mag.* LI. 261 Nor, if sufficiently opulent to have maintained a mint, would some urbic, or other district coin, have failed [etc.].

† **Urbica·rian,** *a. Obs.* [f. L. *urbicāri-us* (see next) + -AN.] Of or belonging to a city, esp. the City of Rome.

1654 H. HAMMOND *Answ. Animadv. Ignat.* v. § 1. 121 Rome the Metropolis of the Roman Province, or Urbicarian region. 1656 BLOUNT *Glossogr.*, *Urbicarian*, belonging to a City.

† **U·rbicary,** *a. Obs.* [ad. L. *urbicāri-us*, f. *urbicus* URBIC *a.*] (See quots. and SUBURBICARY *a.*)

1683 CAVE *Govt. Anc. Ch.* 261 The Roman Bishop began to extend his jurisdiction commensurate to the urbicary diocess, within which his metropolitical was swallowed up. 1725 tr. *Dupin's Eccl. Hist. 17th C.* I. v. 151 They gave the Name of Urbicary or Suburbicary, to all the Provinces which depended upon the Jurisdiction of the Vicar of Rome. 1728 CHAMBERS *Cycl.* (1738) s.v. *Suburbicary*, Those provinces of Italy, &c., which composed the antient diocese, or patriarchate, of Rome, .. were also sometimes called urbicary provinces.

**U·rceiform,** *a.* [f. L. *urce-us* water-pot + -(I)FORM. Cf. Sp. *urceiforme.*] Having the form of a vase or goblet.

1840 *Penny Cycl.* XVIII. 366/1 *Polypiaria dubia.* Animals urceiform, provided with long .. tentacula. 1860 MAYNE *Expos. Lex.* 1321.

† **U·rcelle.** *Obs.*⁻¹ [a. OF. *urcel* (12th c.), or med. L. *urcell-us* (Dief.), = L. *urceolus* URCEOLUS.] A little pitcher.

1483 CAXTON *Gold. Leg.* 247 b/2 Thenne Romayne brouȝt an urcelle or a cruse with water..and receyued baptysme of hym.

**Urce·olar,** *a. Bot.* [ad. L. *urceolāris*, f. *urceolus* URCEOLUS.] = URCEOLATE *a.* 1.

1860 R. FOWLER *Med. Vocab.* s.v.; and in later Dicts.

**Urceolate** (ɒ·ɹsiŏlět), *a.* [ad. mod.L. *urceolat-us*, f. L. *urceolus* URCEOLUS.]

**1.** Having the shape of an urn or pitcher; *esp.* in *Bot.*, *Anat.*, etc.

**a.** 1760 J. LEE *Introd. Bot.* III. xxii. (1765) 229 The Corolla is *Urceolate*, Pitcher-shaped, when it is inflate and gibbous on all Sides, after the Manner of that Vessel. 1776 MARTYN *Lett.* xxvi. (1785) 408 An urceolate or pitcher-shaped stigma. 1821 W. P. C. BARTON *Flora N. Amer.* I. 14 Calix regularly urceolate. 1832 LINDLEY *Introd. Bot.* 104 They thus form a single urceolate body. 1887 W. PHILLIPS *Brit. Discomycetes* 216 Hymenium urceolate, black; stem short.

**b.** 1826 KIRBY & SP. *Entomol.* III. 423 In the *Rutelidæ*, the *labium* is urceolate. 1847 *Todd's Cycl. Anat.* IV. 4/1 Capsule Animalcules..; body..covered with a univalve urceolate or scutellate shell. 1867 MURCHISON *Siluria* ix. (ed. 4) 203 The glabella has only two pairs of furrows and is long and urceolate.

**c.** 1823 *Christie's Catal. Grk. Vases of Englefield* 18 A small Vase (urceolate) with triply-scalloped lip. 1833 *Christie & Manson's Catal. Grk. Pottery*, etc. 8 A one-handled urceolate vase.

**2.** 'Provided with or contained in an urceolus, as a rotifer' (*Cent. Dict.*, 1891).

**U·rceolated,** *a. Zool.* [f. as prec. + -ED¹ 2.] = URCEOLATE *a.* 1.

1752 HILL *Hist. Anim.* 107 The extremity of the body is terminated by a kind of rattle, formed of a series of urceolated articulations. 1822 J. PARKINSON *Outl. Oryctol.* 64 The cells, rather membranous, urceolated, ventricose [etc.]. 1840 *Penny Cycl.* XVIII. 366/1 *Polypiaria membranacea.* Animals very short, urceolated.

**U·rceole.** *Eccl. rare.* [ad. L. *urceolus* URCEOLUS. Cf. obs. F. *urceolle.*] = CRUET 2.

After Fuller (*Ch. Hist.* IV. 157), who thus uses *urceolum.*

1824 SOUTHEY *Bk. of Ch.* I. 353 The candlestick, taper, and urceole were taken from him as acolyte. [1865 BONAR *Last Days Martyrs* (ed. 2) v. 125 The alb and maniple were next removed; then the candlestick, taper, and urceole.]

‖ **Urceolus** (ɒɹsī·ŏlɒs). [L., dim. of *urceus* pitcher.] (See quots. 1866–86.)

1832 LINDLEY *Introd. Bot.* 104 The true nature of the urceolus. 1845 *Encycl. Metrop.* XXV. 1006/1 Corolla [of *Vahia*] urceolate; ovarium girded by an entire urceolus. 1866 *Treas. Bot.* 1193/2 *Urceolus*, the two confluent bracts of *Carex*; any flask-shaped or cup-shaped anomalous organ. 1886 *Encycl. Brit.* XXI. 4/2 Several genera [of *Rotifera*] present an external casing or sheath or tube which is termed an 'urceolus'. *Ibid.* 5/1 The urceolus serves as a defence.

**Urchin** (ɒ·ɹtʃin). Forms: *α.* 4 vrchun, 4–5 vrchon (5 nurchon, norchon), 4–6 urchone, 5 vrchone, vrchoun(e, 6–7, 8–9 *dial.* urchon, 7 urchan. *β.* 5–7 urchen, 6 vrchen, vrchyn, 6–7 vrchin (7 -ine, urching), 7– urchin; 5 norchen, 6, 9 *dial.* orchen. *γ.* 5 vrchion (9 *dial.* urchion), 6 vrcheon, 5, 7, 9 *dial.* urcheon. *δ.* 7 orchant, ourchant, 9 *dial.* urchint, -ont, -ant, -unt. [var. of HURCHEON and IRCHIN, agreeing in vowel with the former, and with the latter in the dropping of *h*.]

**A.** *sb.* **1.** = HEDGEHOG 1.

*α.* *a* 1340 HAMPOLE *Psalter* ciii. 19 The stone fleyng til vrchuns [L. *petra refugium herenacijs*]. 1382 WYCLIF *Lev.* xi. 5 An vrchon, that chewith kude,..is vnclene. *c* 1400 *Rom. Rose* 3135 Like sharp vrchouns his here was growe. 1480 CAXTON *Chron. England* 53 b, Till that his body Stykked as full of arewes as an vrchone is full of prikkes. *a* 1500 in *Rel. Ant.* I. 81 A norchon by tho fyre rostyng a greyhownde. 1530 PALSGR. 285/2 Urchone a beest, *herysson.* 1676 GREW *Musæum, Anat. Stomach & Guts* ii. 8 The Gulet of an Urchan enters the Stomach towards the middle. 1683 in W. S. Banks *Walks Yorks.* (1871) 43 To March lad for one urchon, [£]o o 2. 1750 J. COLLIER (Tim Bobbin) *Lanc. Dial.* Wks. (1862) p. xxxvii, Od rottle the; whot seys to? Hes to foryeat'n th' Tealier finding th' Urchon; an th' Rimes? 1876– in Westm., Yks., and Lancs. dialect use (*Eng. Dial. Dict.*).

*β.* *c* 1425 *St. Christina* x. in *Anglia* VIII. 123/28 In þe maner of an vrchyn þe lumped body 3ode to þe owne shappe. 14.. *Nom.* in Wr.-Wülcker 700 *Hic urunacius*,..a urchen. 1556 J. HEYWOOD *Spider & Fly* iii. 32 To grounde be shranke Like an vrchyn vnder an aple tree. 1591 SYLVESTER *Du Bartas* I. vii. 683 Thou Sluggard,..Go learn the Emmet's and the Urchin's Art. 1624 BURTON *Anat. Mel.* (ed. 2) II. iii. VII. 291 As a Tortoise in his shell,..or an Vrchin round,.. I decline their fury and am safe. *a* 1653 G. DANIEL *Idyll* v. 98 Stript Porcupine May to an Vrchin, of his wants complaine; Well-thatcht, gainst Winter's Stormes. 1698 FRYER *Acc. E. India & P.* 290 However here are Salmon..., and the Urchin..under the Hedges and Trees of an Orchard. 1779 *Gentl. Mag.* 350 The poor persecuted creature to which I allude is the Hedge-hog or Urchin. 1813 BINGLEY *Anim. Biog.* (ed. 4) I. 349 Urchins..feed, for the most part, on roots, worms, and the larvæ of insects. 1863 ATKINSON *Stanton Grange* 218 Sae, I reckon, it is with the urchin. 1867 EMERSON *May-day* 306 The pebble loosened from the frost Asks of the urchin to be tost.

*γ.* 14.. in *Rel. Ant.* I. 51 Tak the grees of an urcheon, and the fatte of a bare. *c* 1475 *Cath. Angl.* 404/2 Vrchion, *erecius, erinacius.* 1522 SKELTON *Why not to Court* 163 They are..Lyke vrcheons in a stone wall. 1895 J. K. SNOWDEN *Web of Weaver* x, We had no more to liven us than an urcheon has in winter-time.

*δ.* 1665–6 *Ormskirk Churchw. Acc.* (Lanc. & Chesh. Hist. Soc.) Ser. III. VI. 174 Paid Thos. Mawdsley for one orchant and one kyde [= kite], oolb. 01s. 06d. 1682 in W. S. Banks *Walks Yorksh.* (1871) 43 Paid for 21 ourchants and 7 fylomots, [£]o 5 10. 1883 *Almondbury Gloss.*, *Urchint*, a hedgehog. 1891 *Sheffield Gloss.* Suppl. 62 *Urchont*, a hedgehog.

**b.** Applied allusively to persons (see quots.).

1593 G. HARVEY *Pierce's Super.* 12 But Agrippa was an urcheon, Copernicus a shrimpe, Cardan a puppy,..Cuiacius a bable to this Termagant. 1594 *Selimus* K 1, Enter Selimus..at one door, and Acomat.., Vizier, and their soldiers at another. *Sel.* What are the vrchins crept out of their dens, Vnder the conduct of this porcupine? 1632 HEYWOOD *2nd Pt. Iron Age* I. i. B 2 b, *Ther*[*sites*]. By the gods Wee haue two meeting soules: be my sweete Vrchin. *Syn*[*on*]. I will, And thou shalt bee mine vgly Toade.

† **c.** A goblin or elf. (From the supposition that they occas. assumed the form of a hedgehog.)

1584 R. SCOT *Discov. Witchcr.* VII. xv. 122 They have so fraied us with bull beggers, spirits, witches, urchens, elves, ..that [etc.]. 1592 NASHE *Four Lett. Confut.* K j b, The Fairies and night Vrchins. 1594 — *Terrors of Night* H j b, An old wiues tale of diuells and vrchins. 1598 SHAKS. *Merry W.* IV. iv. 49. 1614 *Hawking*, etc. 7 in T. Ravenscroft *Briefe Disc.*, By the moone we sport and play;..Trip it, little Vrchins all, Lightly as the little little bee.

**2.** *transf.* † **a.** Applied to the porcupine. *Obs.*

*c* 1400 MAUNDEV. (Roxb.) xxxi. 143 Þere ben also vrchounes als grete as wylde swyn here; wee clepen hem *Porcz de Spyne.*

**b.** A sea-urchin or sea-hedgehog; = ECHINUS 1.

1601 HOLLAND *Pliny* I. 253 Of the same sort that the Crabs be, are the Vrchins of the sea called Echini. 1661 LOVELL *Hist. Anim. & Min.* 230 *Urchin*...The ashes of the shells help sordid ulcers. 1796 H. HUNTER tr. *St.-Pierre's Stud. Nat.* II. 381 The violet-coloured urchins, armed with points and spears. 1845 GOSSE *Ocean* vi. (1849) 277 The irregular movements of the spined urchins. 1853 ANNE PRATT *Common Things Sea-Coast* v. 308 The Purple-tipped Urchin (*Echinus miliaris*). *Ibid.*, Heart urchins, and Fiddle-heart urchins, and Cake urchins; names all expressive of the shape.

† **c.** *U.S.* = URSON. *Obs. rare.*

1796 MORSE *Amer. Geog.* I. 201 The Urchin, or Urson,.. is commonly called Hedgehog or Porcupine, but differs from both those animals.

**3.** One who is deformed in body; a hunchback. Now *dial.*

1528 ROY *Rede me*, etc. (Arb.) 43, I trowe the vrchyn will clyme To some promocion hastely. 1607 TOPSELL *Four-f. Beasts* 278 In English, a Hedghog, or an vrchine: by which name also we call a man that holdeth his Necke in his bosome. 1706 PHILLIPS (ed. Kersey), *Urchin*,..a Dwarf. 1821 SCOTT *Kenilw.* ix, A queer, shambling, ill-made urchin, who, by his stunted growth, seemed about twelve or thirteen years old. 1824 BYRON *Def. Transf.* I. i, *Bert.* Out, hunchback! *Arn.* I was born so, mother!.. *Bert.* Out, urchin, out! 1891 *Sheffield Gloss.* Suppl. 62 *Urchont*, a humpbacked person.

**4.** A pert, mischievous, or roguish youngster; a brat.

*c* 1530 *Calisto & Melib.* B i, Come hydyr, thou lytyll fole let me see the:..What lytyll vrchyn hast forgotyn me? 1599 BRETON *Miseries Mauillia* Wks. (Grosart) II. 37/1 Come on, you urchen, you will never come to good. 1726 SWIFT *Gulliver* II. iii. 125, I could not tell to what extremity such a malicious urchin might have carried his resentment. 1828 CARR *Craven Gloss.* s.v., Thou lile urchin thou!

**b.** *poet.* Applied to Cupid.

1709 PRIOR *Venus Mistaken* ii, Who's blind now Mamma? the Urchin cry'd. 1713 SWIFT *Cadenus & Vanessa* 515 The urchin..Took aim, and shot with all his strength A dart. 1799 SOUTHEY *Love Elegies* III. v, From you, sweet locks! he wove the subtile line Wherewith the urchin angled for my Heart. 1805 ANDREW SCOTT *Poems* 184 Cupid, blind urchin.

**5.** A little fellow; a boy or youngster; † a child or infant.

In frequent use from *c* 1780. Often applied with commiserative force to children poorly, raggedly, or untidily clothed.

1556 J. HEYWOOD *Spider & Fly* C ij, Will ye have this urchin, of eyght weekes olde? It is a babling brat above all other. 1600 NASHE *Summers Last Will* E ij, Learne of him, you deminitiue vrchins, howe to behaue your selues in your vocation. 1648 J. BEAUMONT *Psyche* IX. cxlv, As for thy Lord, He term'd him Josephs Brat, The silly Carpenter's poor Urcheon. 1683 KENNETT *Erasm. on Folly* 82 Looking big upon the trembling Urchins. 1790 COWPER *Let. to Mrs. Throckmorton* 10 May, He sent an urchin (I do not mean a hedgehog,..but a boy, commonly so called). 1799 SHERIDAN *Pizarro* II. i, The little darling urchin robs me, I doubt, of some portion of thy love, my Cora. 1812 BYRON *Ch. Har.* II. xviii, And well the docile crew that skilful urchin guides. 1839 FR. A. KEMBLE *Resid. in Georgia* (1863) 11 The tone of insolent superiority assumed by even the gutter urchins over their dusky companions. 1892 STEVENSON & L. OSBOURNE *Wrecker* iii. 42 [He] took a fancy to the urchin [and] carried him on with him in his wandering life.

† b. Applied to a literary production. *Obs. rare.*

1589 [? Lyly] *Pappe w. Hatchet* E ij, This is the Epistle which he woonders at himselfe, and like an olde Ape hugges the Vrchin so in his conceit, as [etc.]. 1813 H. & J. Smith *Horace in London* 89 Then may new Drury's widely yawning pit O'erwhelm thy urchin, and engulph thy muse.

† c. *transf.* An offspring *of* hell, etc. *Obs. rare.*

1584 Harsnet *Serm. Ezek.* (1658) 129 How can he but hate him?..the childe of Darkness,..the Urchin of Hel? 1648 J. Beaumont *Psyche* x. xxix, Unhappy Saturninus, how hast thou Prov'd thine own selfe an urcheon of Damnation!

† 6. An ugly or uncomely woman; a hag. *rare.*

1657 Thornley tr. *Longus' Daphnis & Chloe* 203 It is incredible that of such an old Churle, and such an Urchin as his Wife, there should come a child so fair.

† b. A girl or young woman, esp. of an ill-tempered or roguish disposition. *Obs.*

1534 More *Comf. agst. Trib.* ii. Wks. 1182/2 What eyleth this gyrle? that eluish vrchin weneth I wer a diuell I trow. 1768 Goldsm. *Good-n. Man* ii. i, You did indeed dissemble, you urchin you; but where's the girl that won't dissemble for a husband? *a* 1777 — *Epilogue to 'The Sisters'* 23 The little urchin smiles, and spreads her lure, And tries to kill, ere she's got power to cure.

7. *techn.* (See later quots.)

1835 Ure *Philos. Manuf.* 167 By this repeated transfer from one cylinder-card or urchin to another..the filaments become separated and expanded. 1839 — *Dict. Arts* 348 Some cards consist entirely of cylinders, the central main cylinder being surrounded by a series of smaller ones called urchins or squirrels. 1875 Knight *Dict. Mech.* 2684/1 *Urchin*, one of a pair of rapidly revolving small card cylinders, arranged around the periphery of a large card drum.

8. *attrib.* and *Comb.*, as (sense 1 c) †*urchin blast*, †*show*; (sense 7) *urchin card, cylinder*; *urchin-like* adj., *-snouted* ppl. a.; † **urchin cockle** (see quot.); † **urchin crowfoot**, the ranunculus, *R. arvensis*; **urchin fish**, (*a*) the sea-urchin; (*b*) the porcupine-fish or sea-porcupine; **urchin-form**, the form or form-type of an echinus; † **urchin lump-fish**, † **mushroom**, † **rind**, † **star-fish**, † **-worm** (see quots.).

1634 Milton *Comus* 845 Helping all *urchin blasts, and ill luck signes That the shrewd medling Elfe delights to make. 1851 Gordon *Art Jrnl. Illustr. Catal.* p. iv**/2 The large card-drum is generally surmounted by *urchin or squirrel cards instead of tops. 1688 Holme *Armoury* ii. 339/1 *Concha Echinata*,..a Cockle covered or set with pricks. An *Urchin Cockle. 1578 Lyte *Dodoens* 420 White Crowfoote, or *Urchin Crowfoote. 1835 Ure *Philos. Manuf.* 168 When the fibres have been thus thoroughly teazed out by..*urchin cylinders. 1566 Drant *Horace, Sat.* iv. G 8 b, Whence purple coloure flowes..from Micen *vrchen fishe. 1688 Holme *Armoury* ii. 343/2 The Globe Star fish ..is by some Authors termed the *Urchin fish, or Sea Urchin. 1773 *Gentl. Mag.* 220 The Urchin or Hedgehog Fish. 1863 Wood *Illustr. Nat. Hist.* III. 337 The Urchin-Fish or Sea Hedgehog is a good example of the genus Diodon, or Two-toothed fishes. 1878 F. J. Bell *Gegenbaur's Comp. Anat.* 198 The decrease in size of the antambulacral surface..will give us the *Urchin-form. 1708 Kersey, **Urchin-like Rind*, the outward Husk of the Chesnut. 1855 Gosse *Man. Marine Zool.* i. 63 Round depressed urchin-like disks. 1688 Holme *Armoury* ii. 337 The *Urchin, or Hedghog Lump fish, hath its skin set with more sharper and longer pricks. *c* 1711 Petiver *Gazophyl.* x. xcii, *Urchin Mushroom:..From its roughness underneath. 1688 R. Holme *Armoury* ii. 85/1 The *urchin rind, is the cover of the Chestnut. [Cf. *urchin-like*.] 1610 Shaks. *Temp.* ii. ii. 5 But they [*sc.* spirits] 'll nor pinch, Fright me with *Vrchyn-shewes, pitch me i' th mire [etc.]. 1592 — *Ven. & Ad.* 1105 This foule, grim, and *vrchin-snowted Boare. 1688 Holme *Armoury* ii. 349/2 An *Urchin Star-fish; this is a Star-fish of five long and slender Rays. 1668 Charleton *Onom.* 53 *Echini*,..*Vrchin-Worms.

b. Appositive or as adj., as *urchin article, bitch, deity, messenger, prince.*

1534 More *Comf. agst. Trib.* iii. xxiv. (1553) T vij, I feare me when I here once that vrchin bitche bark, I shal..forgeat altogether. *a* 1670 Hacket *Abp. Williams* ii. (1693) 91 Our Bishop..made himself merry with the Conceit, how easie it was to stride over such Urchin Articles. No man would find leisure to read the whole 36, they are so frivolous. 1818 Hazlitt *Eng. Poets* ii. (1870) 53 The triumph of Cupid at the mischief he has made is worthy of the malicious urchin deity. 1826 Scott *Woodst.* xxxii, The urchin messenger entered the hall, making several odd bows. 1830 Ld. Lyttelton in *Lady L.'s Corr.* (1912) 259 The two urchin Princes..in little Hussar dresses.

Hence **U·rchiness**, a female urchin (= prec. 4); **U·rchinly** *a.*, of the nature of, resembling, an urchin.

1852 *Househ. Words* V. 378/2 Many were the names of urchins and *urchinesses..which decked the plaster walls of Broad-Bumble school. 1654 *New Brawle* 11 Like a feeble *Vrchinly Rascall as thou art. 1834 *Fraser's Mag.* IX. 741 Applying a foot to the part of his urchinly person corresponding with that particular department of Sir John Doyle.

**Urdee**, *a.* *Her.* Also 7 urde, 9 urdé. [Of obscure origin: possibly due to a misreading and misunderstanding of F. *vidée* in the phrase *croix aiguisée et vidée*.]

1. Of a cross: Having the extremities drawn to a sharp point instead of being cut at right angles to the beam; pointed.

1562 Legh *Armory* 61 b, He beareth Tenne, a crosse vrdee, Or. 1572 Bossewell *Armorie* 26 Crosses enuecked, entrayled,..Batune, formye, vrdee, pomelle. 1688 Holme *Armoury* i. 49/1 He beareth Gules, a Cross Urdee (or champain) Or. *Ibid.* iv. xii. (Roxb.) 509/1 Charged with a crosse vrdee voided at each point a pommell. *c* 1828 Berry *Encycl. Her.* I. s.v., A cross, urdée, is the same as that which French heralds call clechée. 1882 Cussans *Handbk. Her.* viii. (1893) 126 *Aiguisé*, or *Urdé*: used by French and the early English Heralds to signify pointed.

2. Of a bend, etc.: Having the margin or containing line broken into a series of parallel pointed projections. Also of a line broken in this fashion.

1688 Holme *Armoury* i. 32/1 He beareth Argent, a Bend Urdee, or Champaine, Vert. *Ibid.* 75/1 He beareth party per Bend Urde, Gules and Or. *Ibid.* 93 He beareth party per Pale, Barry of six contrary Urdee...Some term it..Barry of 6 Urdee at the ends, or contrary champion at the sides. 1722 A. Nisbet *Syst. Her.* I. 23 The other Line is blazoned Urdee or Champagne by Ferne. Upton calls it Vere; because its Points are formed like Pieces of Vair.

**Urdeur**, obs. f. Ordure.

**U·rdite.** *Min.* [a. Da. *urdit* (1855), f. the local Norwegian place-name *Urd-a* (= 'the scree'): see -ite[1] 2 b.] = Monazite.

1868 *Watts' Dict. Chem.* V. 949 *Urdite*, a mineral of unknown composition, occurring in the orthoclase of Notteröe in Norway. 1908 *Athenæum* 16 May 609/2 The rare element scandium..only occurs terrestrially in a few uncommon minerals, such as urdite.

**Urdu** (ūə·ɹdū), *sb.* and *a.* Also 8–9 **Oordoo.** [a. Hindustani (Pers.) اردو *urdū* camp (ad. Turkī *ordu*, etc.: see Horde *sb.*), ellipt. for *zabān-i-urdū* 'language of the camp'.]

A. *sb.* = Hindustani *sb.* 2.

1796 J. B. Gilchrist *Gram. Hindoostanee Lang.* 261 The Rekhtu,..that mixed Dialect, also called Oordoo..or the polished language of the Court. 1813 J. Shakespear *Gram. Hindustani Lang.* 1 The dialect most generally used in India, especially among the Muhammadan inhabitants, .. is called *Urdū* (camp) or *Urdū zabān* (camp-language). 1824 Heber *Jrnl.* 6 Sept., The boys read Oordoo, Persian, and English. 1847 W. Yates *Hindustani Dict.* Pref., The Hindustaní or Urdú is peculiarly the language of the Muhammadan population of Hindústán. 1872 Beames *Comp. Gram. Aryan Lang.* I. 39 By a curious caprice, Hindi, when it uses Arabic words, is assumed to become a new language, and is called by a new name—Urdu. 1878 [see Hindustani *sb.* 2].

*Comb.* 1880 *Encycl. Brit.* XI. 849/2 A collection of stories ..in mixed Urdū-Hindi.

B. *adj.* Of or pertaining to, printed, written, or composed in, the Hindustani language.

1845 J. T. Thompson (*title*), An English and Oordoo, and Oordoo and English Dictionary. 1847 W. Yates *Hindustani Dict.* Pref., In good Urdú writing or conversation. 1880 *Encycl. Brit.* XI. 847/2 The origin of Urdū literature. *Ibid* 848/1 The earliest Urdū authors.

**Urdy**, Anglicized form of Urdee *a.* 2.

1688 Holme *Armoury* i. 75/1 He beareth party per Bend Urde, Gules and Or. *Ibid.*, There is a difference between Urde, and Urdee or Urdy; the first being of a single number, the other signifies many. 1831 *Encycl. Metrop.* (1845) V. 600/2 *Palissy*, or *Urdy*, is an imitation of the palisading of a trench.

† **Ure**, *sb.*[1] *Obs.* [a. AF. **eure*, = OF. *uevre, euvre, evre* (13th cent.; F. *œuvre*):—L. *opera* Opera *sb.*]

I. **In ure**: 1. a. In or into use, practice, or performance. Often with vbs., as *bring, come, have*, and esp. *put* (freq. *c* 1510–*c* 1630). Also rarely with *into*.

(*a*) *c* 1420 Lydg. *Assembly of Gods* 1448 Whom folowyd Dethe, whych wold nat tary Hys feruent power there to put in vre. *c* 1440 *Pallad. on Husb.* i. 215 And elder than oon yeer, no grayn in vre Thou putte, in drede hit die. *c* 1500 Medwall *Nature* (Brandl) 815 He hath shewed me a praty whyle [= wile], If I may put yt in vre. 1522 More *De Quat. Noviss.* Wks. 76/2 Yt this only lesson wel learned & busily putte in vre, must nedes leade vs to heauen. 1591 Sylvester *Du Bartas* i. vi. 1031 Even as a Surgeon..before in ure he put His violent Engins on the vicious member. 1627 Hakewill *Apol.* (1630) 287 Would God men would be pleas'd to put this course in ure. 1682 *New News fr. Bedlam* Postscr., You have put his jealous Pen in Ure. 1702 R. L'Estrange *Josephus, Antiq.* xvi. i. 444 That was the Course therefore, they resolved to put in Ure.

(*b*) 1563 Shute *Archit.* F i, They maye be practised and brought in vre to diuers vses. 1581 Pettie tr. *Guazzo's Civ. Conv.* i. (1586) 26 b, Perchaunce they haue brought in ure both publikelie and priuatlie vices far more pernitious than this. *a* 1604 Hanmer *Chron. Ireland* (1633) 175 If hee dyed seised during that time, his wife shall not be indowed of the same land as came late in ure. 1606 Holland *Sueton.* 97 Martiall discipline he required most sharply, bringing again into ure and execution certaine..chastisements.

(*c*) *c* 1475 *Partenay* 3722 My goddoughter I may calle hir in vre. 1494 in *Househ. Ord.* (1790) 112 The sitting of all Dukes, Earles, and Barons sonnes.., such things hathe beene well had in ure. *c* 1530 *Remedy of Love* xxiii, But this am I sure, Moche lyke thyng I haue had in vre. *a* 1542 Wyatt *Poet. Wks.* (1913) I. 11 Trouth is tryed where craft is in ure. 1545 Ascham *Toxoph.* (Arb.) 57 What thing a man in tender age hath most in vre. 1577 Hanmer *Anc. Eccl. Hist.* 128 Neither had it any agreement with that which is in vre among vs. 1613 W. Browne *Brit. Past.* i. v, The staires of rugged stone, seldome in ure.

b. With dependent infinitive.

*a* 1530 Heywood *Love* (Brandl) 33 No tonge can attayne to put in vre Her to discryue. 1575 Gascoigne *Glasse of Govt.* ii. vi, Greate the paines which teachers put in ure, To trade them still, in verteous qualities. 1598 Marston *Sco. Villanie* ii. (1599) 175 [To] dare put in ure To make Jehoua but a couverture To shade ranck filth.

c. With reference to statutes, etc.: In or into effect, force, or operation. Chiefly with vbs., esp. *put*.

1454–5 in Bolton *Stat. Irel.* (1621) 23 All the Statutes.. against Escheators shall be put in ure, and be of force. *a* 1513 Fabyan *Chron.* vii. 505 To the entente that they shulde see ye sayde proclamacyon put in vre. 1539 *St. Papers Hen. VIII*, I. 597 My letters to the said Depute shall not nede to be put in ure. 1581 Lambarde *Eiren.* i. xviii. 165 Ye statute of Northampton..is now..put in vre for the punishment of Forcible Entries. 1610 Holland *Camden's Brit.* i. 420 They ment to bring..S. Edwards lawes and liberties againe In ure. 1614 Bacon *Draft of King's Speech* Wks. 1869 V. 30 His Majesty could wish the ancient statutes were put in ure. *c* 1670 Hobbes *Dial. Com. Laws* (1681) 141 That the Diocesan hath Jurisdiction of Heresie, and that so it was put in ure in all Queen Elizabeths reign. 1701 Atterbury *Add. to 1st Ed. Rights Convocation* 48 They would not Enact, put in Ure, Promulge, or Execute any New Canons. 1711 G. Hickes *Two Treat. Chr. Priesth.* (ed. 3) II. 79 Without any retrospection to old Principles, the King's Ecclesiastical Supremacy in Virtue of these Laws, was put in Ure.

d. In remembrance or recollection. Only *to have..in ure.*

1432–50 tr. *Higden* (Rolls) I. 347 The peple..sayethe.. Gurmunde..to have made those dyches, hauenge not Turgesius in vre or in remembraunce. *c* 1450 *Harl. Contin. Higden* (Rolls) VIII. 452 The kynge havynge not in ure of the seide promisse.

e. In or into a state of prevalence or existence. Chiefly with vbs., as *come, draw, put.*

1470 in Ellis *Orig. Lett.* Ser. ii. I. 134 Towchinge the tyme whene the Mariage shalbe put in ure. 1477 *Paston Lett.* III. 191 For th'enconvenyence that I have knowe let in ur in case lyke, and yit enduryth in Kente. *a* 1547 Surrey in *Tottel's Misc.* (Arb.) 15 Like as when, rough winter spent, The pleasant spring straight draweth in vre. 1548 Udall *Erasm. Par. Luke* xxii. 167 b, What thyng Petur did, the same would the other disciples also haue dooen, if lyke necessitee had cum in vre. 1549 Proctor *Fall of late Arrian* R iij b, Touchynge the dispensacion of the flesh, and the misterye nowe in force and vre, Christ shalbe subiected vnto the father. 1638 Farley *Emblems* H 3, This waxen torch is able to endure The winds, when Æolus puts them in ure.

2. Of persons, their faculties, etc.: In or into the regular exercise or practice of a particular pursuit. Usu. with verbs, as *fall, put,* and chiefly (esp. *c* 1580–*c* 1685) *keep.*

(*a*) *c* 1460 J. Russell *Bk. Nurture* 1173 Y haue shewed the, & brought þe in vre, to know þe Curtesie of court. 1513 More *Rich. III* (1883) 18 Himself had bene al his dayes in ure therwith. *a* 1548 Hall *Chron., Edw. IV*, 217 To put his people in vre, that thei might bee the more ready to fight. 1571 Campion *Hist. Irel.* ii. i. (1633) 69 Sundry times came Lacy to quicken his labourers, full glad to see them fall in ure with any such exercise. 1594 Plat *Jewell-ho.* 42 Till they have brought their hande in ure with the shape and fashion of the Letters. 1677 Miège *Gt. Fr. Dict.* s.v., To put himself in ure, *s'accoûtumer.*

(*b*) 1539 Latimer *Serm. & Rem.* (Parker Soc.) 416, I pray you, keep your hand in ure. 1577 tr. *Bullinger's Decades* 84 Hee..by the Crosse doth keepe our patience in vre. 1611 Speed *Hist. Gt. Brit.* ix. xxiv. 351 To keepe in vre and exercise, the skill and valour of her English. 1627 Bp. Hall *Epist.* iii. viii. 329 To keepe the heart in vre with God is the highest taske of a Christian. 1627 — *Art. Divine Medit.* xxxi, The minde is by turnes depressed and lifted vp:..which order doth best hold it in vre, and just temper. 1690 W. Walker *Idiomat. Anglo-Lat.* 254 He lies to keep his tongue in ure. 1692 R. L'Estrange *Fables* 92 Keeping his hand in Ure with somewhat of Greater Value.

II. 3. *Out of ure*: a. Out of use; disused; obsolete.

1553 Brende *Q. Curtius* Q vi, Oure naturall toungue throughe the conversation of straunge nacions is gone out of ure. 1567 Jewel *Def. Apol. Ch. Eng.* v. v. § 1. 524 Al these thinges are woorne nowe out of vre, and nighe deade. *a* 1600 Hooker *Eccl. Pol.* vii. xiv. § 2 The mention of contrary orders worn so many ages since quite and clean out of ure.

b. Out of practice. *rare*—[1].

1625 Bacon *Ess., Simulation* (Arb.) 509 Which..maketh him practise Simulation in other things, lest his Hand should be out of vre.

III. 4. Custom or habit on the part of persons; wont *to* do something. *rare.*

*c* 1425 *Cast. Persev.* 3629 in *Macro Plays* 185 Þe vij dedis of mercy, who-so hadde vre to Fylle. 1506 *Kalender of Sheph.* A iv b, I Nouembre wyll not abyde behynde, To shewe my kyndly worthynes and vre. 1556 Abp. Parker *Ps.* cvii. 316 Ryght oft is hys vre by loue to allure. 1557 F. Seager *Sch. Virt.* 716 in *Babees Bk.* (1868) 344 And sure it is taken by custome and vre, whyle yonge you be there is helpe and cure. *c* 1600 Sylvester *Miracle of Peace* xxv, Or (if you cannot leave your wonted ure) Leave (at the least) all mutinous alarmes.

5. *Sc.* Work; labour. *rare*—[1].

*a* 1510 Douglas *K. Hart* i. 2 King Hart, into his cumlie castell strang Closit about with craft and meikill vre.

† **Ure**, *sb.*[2] *Sc. Obs.*—[1] [App. repr. OE. *ór* beginning, front, van, taken in the sense of *ord* point, front, beginning.] The point of a weapon.

1432 *Sc. Acts Parlt., Jas. I* (1814) II. 21 Gif he hurtis or defoulis with fellon assailȝeing with ege or vre, he sal remayn in preson.

† **Ure**, *sb.*[3] *Obs.* Also 7 **owre.** [a. OF. *ure* (16th c.), or ad. L. *ūrus* Urus. Cf. OE. *úr*, OHG. (MHG.) *ûr*, ON. *úrr*.] = Urus, Aurochs.

1563 Golding *Cæsar* (1565) 163 Ures..are of bignes somwhat lesse than Elephantes, in kind and color and shape like a Bull. 1577 Harrison *England* iii. iv. (1878) ii. 29 As for the plowing with vres (which I suppose to be vnlikelie) and alkes. 1600 Fairfax *Tasso* iii. xxxii, The swift Vre by Volgaes rolling flood. 1668 Charleton *Onomasticon* 6 *Urus Jubatus*, the Owre. [1706 Phillips (ed. Kersey), *Owre*, a kind of wild Bull. (Hence in Bailey and some later Dicts.)]

**Ure** (ōr), *sb.*[4] *Orkney* and *Shetland.* Forms: 6–7 uris-, 6 wyris-, uyerris-, 7 vrs-, 8 urs-, erys-, 9 eris-; 8– ure (9 eure). [ad. ONorw. *øyrir* (Norw. *øyre, øre*), = MSw. and Sw. *öre*, MDa. and Da. *øre*, Icel. *eyrir*, ounce of silver (also denoting a standard of value and latterly a coin), ad. L.

*aureus* a gold solidus (taken at its value in silver); the original vowel remains unmutated in the ON. pl. *aurar*. Cf. ORA[1] and ORE[4].]

**1.** In genitive combinations (ON. *øyris-, eyris-*). **a.** *Uris-land* [ON. *øyrisland*, MSw. *örisland*], land giving the rent of one-eighth of a mark; an ounce-land. (From the feu-duty formerly paid to the superior.) *Obs.* exc. *Hist.*

1534 in *Orkney & Shetl. Rec.* (1907) 64 Quhatsumevir that pertenis..to ws..wythin the half wyris land of Sabbaye. 1589 in *Reg. Mag. Sig. Scot.* (1890) 460/1 The landis of Trosnes extending to ane urisland. 1592 *Ibid.* (1892) 117/2 My 6 merk land and 2 uyerris land of Kildabuster. 1627 in Peterkin *Rentals of Orkney* (1820) III. 94 Lying in the vrs-lands off Brabister. 1772 G. GIFFORD in Low *Orkney* (1879) 144 Our Ure or Ursland..contains 18 Pennylands. 1795 *Statist. Acc. Scot.* XIV. 323 Every Erysland of 18 penny land had one [chapel] for matins and vespers. 1805 BARRY *Orkney* 220 The entries are first by islands and parishes,.. and lastly by marklands, erislands [*printed* erls-] or ounce-lands.

**b.** *Uris-cop* [ON. *øyris-, eyris-kaup*], = prec.

1609 *Reg. Mag. Sig. Scot.* 128/2, 6 lie uriscoppis in Glenna, cum lie quoyis. *Ibid.*, 9 lie uriscoppis de Mo.

† **c.** *Uris-thift*, stolen goods to the value of an ounce of silver. *Obs.*⁻¹

1602 *Shetland Law Rep.* in *Scotsman* (1886) 29 Jan. 7/1 Gif he beis apprehendit with the walor of an uristhift.

**2.** *Ure of land*, = 1 a. [So MSw. *öre*.]

[1624 *Reg. Mag. Sig. Scot.* (1894) 212/1, 2 merc. 5 lie uris terrarum de Brabister.] 1799 *Statist. Acc. Scotl.* XXI. 278 In these parishes there are 1618 merks 4 ures of land. 1821 SCOTT *Pirate* i, Scarce a merk—scarce even an ure of land. 1884 *Scotsman* 26 July 3/1 (Shetland advt.), Three Merks, One Ure and One-Third of an Ure of Land.

*ellipt.* 1774 G. GIFFORD in Low *Orkney* (1879) 145, 8 Ures make 1 Mark [of Land]. 1799 *Statist. Acc. Scotl.* XXI. 278 An ure is the eighth part of a merk. 1822 HIBBERT *Descr. Shetl. Isl.* 179 *note*, The division of a mark of land into Ures, appears to have been first introduced..in the year 1263.

*attrib.* 1814 SHIRREF *Agric. Surv. Orkn.* 31 The lands in Orkney had been early divided into ure or ounce lands. 1822 HIBBERT *Descr. Shetl. Isl.* 179 *note*, [Hacon] divided the islands into Eurelands or Ouncelands.

**Ure,** *sb.*[5] *local Sc.* [a. ON. *úr* drizzling rain.]

**1.** A damp mist.

1818 *Edinburgh Mag.* Sept. 155/1 The mune be this was shinan clearly abune a' the ure. *a* 1824 in Mactaggart *Gallovid. Encycl.* 333 Glowring at the azure sky, And loomy oceans ure.

**2.** An atmospheric haze, esp. of a coloured nature. Freq. *dry ure*.

*a* 1824 in Mactaggart *Gallovid. Encycl.* 455 The east was blae, dry ure bespread the hills. 1824 MACTAGGART *Ibid.* 455 *Ure*, a kind of coloured haze, which the sun-beams make in the summer time. 1875 J. VEITCH *Tweed & other Poems* 49 The dry ure glow of sky-enkindled flame.

**Ure,** var. EURE *sb.* and *v. Obs.*; obs. f. EWER[2] (pitcher, etc.); var. EWER[3], YURE (udder) *dial.*; obs. f. HOUR; obs. var. ORE[2].

† **Ure,** *v.*[1] *Obs.*⁻¹ [ad. OF. *urer, ourer, orer*:— L. *ōrāre* to pray.] *intr.* To pray.

*a* 1225 *Ancr. R.* 286 Ofte, leoue sustren, ȝe schulen vren [*v.r.* preyen] lesse uorte reden more.

† **Ure,** *v.*[2] *Obs.*⁻¹ [var. of EURE *v.*] *intr.* To have good fortune.

*c* 1440 *Pallad. on Husb.* III. 845 In hillis is to cure To sette hem on the south, yf they schal vre.

† **Ure,** *v.*[3] *Obs.* [f. URE *sb.*[1]] *trans.* = INURE *v.* 1.

*a* 1500 *Chaucer's Dreme* C.'s Wks. (1598) 356/1 And in my selfe I me assured, That in my body I was vred. 1530 PALSGR. 769/2 And he be ones ured to it, he wyll do well ynoughe. 1551 ROBINSON tr. *More's Utopia* I. (1895) 49 The Frenche souldiours..haue byne practysed and vrede in feates of armes. 1596 *Edward III*, I. i. 159 Thou must begin Now to..vre thy shoulders to an Armors weight.

**Ure,** obs. var. OUR *pron.*

**-ure** (iŭr), a suffix, repr. F. *-ure*, L. *-ūra* (hence It., Sp., Pg. *-ura*), occurring in many words of F. or L. origin. In L. *-ūra* primarily denoted action or process, hence result of this, office, etc.; after further development in F., the use was extended in Eng., and denoted action or process, the result or product of this (e.g. *enclosure, figure, picture, scripture*), function, state, rank, dignity, or office (e.g. *judicature, prefecture, prelature*), a collective body (e.g. *legislature*), that by which the action is effected (e.g. *clausure, closure, ligature, nouriture*), etc. Many words were adopted from F. at an early date, as *figure* (*a* 1225–), *scripture* (*a* 1300–), *nouriture* (*c* 1374–), *censure, closure, investiture, juncture, pressure, tonsure* (1380–), *fissure, scissure* (*c* 1400–), etc.; while a few others, as *clausure* (1398), *plicature* (1578), *mercature* (*a* 1620), *aperture* (1649–), were directly adapted from L. The suffix was also added to Eng. stems of L. origin, giving *composure* (1599–), *disposure* (1569–), *exposure* (1605–), or to true L. stems, whence *vomiture* (1598), † *beneplaciture* (1662), *ructure* (1657–69), *unigeniture* (1659–); and was further used with stems of Romance origin, as in † *bankrupture* (1617–22), † *disembogure* (1653), † *praisure* (1622), and with native or other bases, as in † *clefture* (1545, 1596), † *raisure* (1613, 1677), and *wafture* (1601–).

To this form various F. suffixes (as *-eure, -ir, -or, -our*) have been assimilated in Eng., as in *pleasure, soilure*, † *trappure* (TRAPPER *sb.*[1]), *treasure, velure*.

‖ **Urea** (yūᵊrī·ă). *Chem.* [ad. (with Latinized ending) F. *urée* (1803), f. Gr. οὖρον urine, or the verb οὐρέω. Cf. It., Sp., Pg. *urea*.]

**1.** A soluble crystalline compound, forming an organic constituent of the urine in mammalia, birds, and some reptiles, and also found in the blood, milk, etc.; carbamide, $CO(NH_2)_2$.

1806 *Phil. Trans.* XCVI. 374 A decomposition of a portion of urea. 1819 BRANDE *Chem.* 446 Urea is the principle which confers upon urine its chief peculiarities. 1862 HUXLEY *Lect. Working Men* 72 Urea..forms one of the waste products of animal structures. 1878 KINGZETT *Anim. Chem.* 190 Urea was discovered by Boerhaave before 1720, and was called by him the essential salt of urine.

**2.** *attrib.* and *Comb.*, as *urea excretion, -formation, -residue*; **urea nitrate, oxalate** (see quots. 1873).

1866 ODLING *Anim. Chem.* 129 The assumption of pre-existent urea-residues in uric acid. 1873 RALFE *Phys. Chem.* 83 Urea oxalate ($2CN_2H_4O,C_2H_2O_4$): the crystals form long, transparent, tufted laminæ. *Ibid.*, Urea nitrate ($CN_2H_4O,HNO_3$): the crystals form shining, rhombic plates. 1897 *Allbutt's Syst. Med.* IV. 292 Observations on the urea excretion. *Ibid.* 72 Pointing to the liver as the chief seat of urea-formation.

**Urea-,** combining form of UREA, occurring in a few terms, as **urea·meter, -metry** (see quots. and cf. UREO-).

1890 CRUISE in *Lancet* 22 March 643/2 The importance of ureametry is far greater than testing for albumen. *Ibid.* 644/2, I venture to draw attention to this very simple ureameter. 1895 C. J. MAYHEW *Ibid.* 10 Aug. 334/1 A new ureameter which I have designed.

**Ureal** (yūᵊrī·ăl), *a.* [f. URE-A + -AL.] Of or pertaining to, of the nature of, urea; characterized by excessive urea.

1848 DUNGLISON *Med. Lex.* (ed. 7) 266/1 D[iabetes] Ureal. 1864 E. A. PARKES *Pract. Hygiene* 154 With no excess of ureal excretion. 1869 *Ibid.* (ed. 3) 340 The formation of ammonium carbonate from ureal decomposition. 1891 *Cent. Dict.* s.v., A ureal solution.

**Urech,** obs. southern var. FRECK *a.* (greedy).

**Uredine** (yurī·dəin), *sb.* and *a. Bot.* [f. the pl. UREDINES (in place of the correct sing. UREDO), or mod.L. *Uredine-æ*, f. L. *ūrēdin-is, ūrēdo*.]

**1.** *sb.* A fungus of the N.O. *Uredineæ* of minute ascomycetal fungi (including mildew, rust, smut, etc.), parasitic upon and frequently injurious to living plants.

1889 PLOWRIGHT *Brit. Uredineæ* i. 2 According to the nature of the Uredine under examination. *Ibid.* ii. 7 The mycelium of a Uredine. 1895 [see UREDOSPOROUS *a.*].

**2.** *adj.* Pertaining or belonging to the Uredines.

1889 PLOWRIGHT *Brit. Uredineæ* iii. 15 The Uredine yeast-spore falls to the bottom of the fluid. *Ibid.*, Uredine spermatial cultures. 1902 *Nature* 20 Nov. 72/2 The Uredine Fungus *Pucciniæ dispersa*.

**Uredi·neous,** *a.* [f. mod.L. *Uredine-æ* (see prec.) + -OUS.] Pertaining or belonging to the Uredines; affected by uredo; uredinous. (1891– in Dicts.)

‖ **Uredines** (yurī·dinīz). *Bot.* [L.: see UREDO. Cf. F. *urédinés*.] Species of fungi parasitic upon and injurious to plants, etc. Cf. UREDO.

1753 *Chambers' Cycl.* Suppl. s.v. *Blast*, That species called *uredines*, or fire-blasts. 1836 BERKELEY *Fungi* in *Smith's Eng. Flora* V. II. 6* Many entophytal parasites, such as *Uredines*, &c. 1843 *Penny Cycl.* XXVI. 47/2 The whole three plants were branded with myriads of Uredines. 1858 IRVING *Handbk. Brit. Pl.* 156 One of these [sub-orders] contains the *Uredines* (Cornbrands). 1860 BERKELEY *Outl. Brit. Fungology* xiii. 87 In the same way the relations of *Tremellini* to *Uredines* are clear, if [etc.].

**Uredinous** (yurī·dinǝs), *a.* [f. L. *ūrēdin-* (see next and UREDINE) + -OUS.]

**1.** *Bot.* Of the nature of a uredine; belonging to the *Uredines*.

1865 M. C. COOKE *Microscopic Fungi* 122 One of the most showy of uredinous fungi. 1889 *Athenæum* 20 April 509/3 Affected with a parasitic disease due to a uredinous fungus.

**2.** *Path.* Affected with, of the nature of, nettle-rash. (1891– in Dicts.)

‖ **Uredo** (yurī·do). *Bot.* [L. *ūrēdo* (pl. *ūrēdinēs*) blight, blast, itch, f. L. *ūrĕre* to burn.]

**1.** A form of blight, = BRAND *sb.* 7. *rare.*

1706 PHILLIPS (ed. Kersey), *Uredo*, the blasting of Trees or Herbs. 1728 CHAMBERS *Cycl.* s.v. *Disease*, Diseases of Plants...9. Uredo, or Scorching, of which there are two Kinds. 1832 LINDLEY *Introd. Bot.* 299 *Albigo, ferrugo*, and *uredo*, commonly called mildew, smut, rust, brand, and other names, are diseases caused by the presence of myriads of minute fungi.

**2.** A name for various fungi (popularly called *rust, smut, mildew*, etc.) parasitic on grain and certain other plants; formerly regarded as a distinct genus, but now known to be only the intermediate stage of the *Uredineæ* or rust fungi (cf. UREDOSPORE). Usu. with capital.

1836 M. J. BERKELEY *Fungi* 369 The specimens are referred by Klotzsch to *Uredo*. 1843 *Penny Cycl.* XXVI. 47/1 The wheat became attacked with Uredo. 1889 PLOWRIGHT *Brit. Uredineæ* 125 The Uredo and Uromyces frequently attack the petioles.

**b.** A species or plant of this.

1836 M. J. BERKELEY *Fungi* 375 Elongated Uredo... Parallel Uredo. 1843 *Penny Cycl.* XXVI. 47/1 He diffused the granules of a Uredo in water. 1849 *Lancet* 17 Nov. 531/2 The uredo is studded all over with sharp points. 1889 *Berwick. Nat. Club's Proc.* XII. 488 A brown *Uredo* or *Puccinia* of the Common Mallow.

**c.** A receptacle or hymenium in which uredospores are formed. *rare*⁻¹.

1879 *Encycl. Brit.* IX. 831/2 Again, in a few days, this mycelium forms a new kind of receptacle, the uredo.

**3.** *attrib.*, as *uredo-form, -patch*; **uredo-fruit,** a group of uredospores; **uredo stage,** the summer stage of certain rust fungi.

1875 BENNETT & DYER tr. *Sachs's Bot.* 248 While the Fungus is multiplying..during the summer in its *uredo-form, the production of a new form of spores begins in the older *uredo-fruits. 1887 BENTLEY *Man. Bot.* (ed. 5) 380 These uredo-fruits consist of a dense mycelium [etc.]. 1887 HILLHOUSE tr. *Strasburger's Pract. Bot.* 265 The haulm of an oat which is infected with rusty *uredo-patches. 1880 BESSEY *Bot.* 316 Later in the season..the *uredo stage begins to make its appearance..upon the leaves. 1895 M. C. COOKE *Study Fungi* xx. 246 In this group [sc. *Pucciniopsis*] of species the uredo stage is deficient.

**Ure·dospore.** *Bot.* [f. prec. + SPORE.] One or other of the peculiar summer spores developed during the uredo stage in rust fungi.

1875 BENNETT & DYER tr. *Sachs's Bot.* 248 These uredospores are dispersed after the rupture of the epidermis. 1882 BENTLEY *Man. Bot.* (ed. 4) 372 From which vertical branches shoot upwards bearing at their extremities oval granular spores, the uredospores.

Hence **Ure:dospo·ric** *a.*, 'of or pertaining to a uredospore' (*Cent. Dict.*, 1891); **Ure:dospori·ferous** *a.*, bearing uredospores; **Ure:dospo·rous** *a.*, characterized by uredospores.

1895 M. C. COOKE *Study Fungi* xx. 242 The uredosporiferous sori are variously coloured. *Ibid.* xx. 248 Species of uredosporous Uredines.

**Ureide** (yūᵊrī·iəid). *Chem.* Also **ureid.** [f. URE-A + -IDE, -ID[4].] A derivative of urea containing acid radicles.

1857 MILLER *Elem. Chem.*, *Org.* 617 Urea likewise gives rise to the formation of a class of compounds analogous to the amides, forming substances which have been called ureides. 1867 BLOXAM *Chem.* 620 They are, therefore, sometimes styled ureides, and sometimes compound ureas. 1884 *Encycl. Brit.* XVII. 519/2 Ureids are a class of bodies which are related to urea as amido-bodies are to ammonia.

**Ureisun,** obs. f. ORISON.

**Ureit,** obs. Sc. var. WRIT *sb.*, WRITE *v.*

**Uremia, -ic,** varr. URÆMIA, URÆMIC.

**U·rent,** *a. rare.* [a. L. *ūrent-, ūrens*, pres. pple. of *ūrĕre* to burn. Cf. It. and Sp. *urente*.] Burning; causing a burning sensation.

1656 BLOUNT *Glossogr.* 1777 S. ROBSON *Brit. Flora* 6 *Urent*, beset with venomous stings, as in Nettles. 1863 J. G. WOOD *Illustr. Nat. Hist.* III. 741 The cables retain their urent property long after they have been detached from the animal.

**Ureo-** (yūᵊrī·o), combining form of URE-A, occurring in a few words, as **ureo-carbonate, -carbonic, ureometer, ureometry**: (see quots. and cf. UREA-, URO-[1]).

1852 WATTS tr. *Gmelin's Handbk. Chem.* VII. 377 It is resolved into alcohol and a *ureo-carbonate of the alkali. *Ibid.*, The constituents of vinic ether and of hypothetically anhydrous *ureo-carbonic acid. 1876 J. G. BLACKLEY in *Jrnl. Chem. Soc.* II. 467 A modification of Russell and West's *ureometer. 1884 KNIGHT *Dict. Mech.* Suppl. 915/1 In Hüfner's new ureometer, .. the exact methods for the determination of urea in organic liquids are..complex and tedious. 1901 *Lancet* 9 March 697/1, I have examined the urine with Martindale's ureometer. 1876 J. G. BLACKLEY in *Jrnl. Chem. Soc.* II. 447 The operation of *ureometry.

**Ure-ox** (yūᵊ·rǫks). [ad. MHG. *ūr-ochse* (G. *urochs* UROCHS, *auerochs* AUROCHS), or f. URE *sb.*[3] + OX.] = URUS.

1607 TOPSELL *Four-f. Beasts* 722 Their large bodies and manes..it is not vnfit to attribute..also to the Vre-Oxe. *Ibid.* 723 In Malonia neer Lituania..those Vre-oxen are kept as it were in parkes and chases. 1611 COTGR., *Ure*, the huge-bodied, bulch-backed, short-horned, and red-eyed wild Oxe, called the Vre-oxe. 1661 LOVELL *Hist. Anim. & Min.* 23 Bull, *Taurus*... Hereto may be referred the Bison; and Vre-oxe.

1887 tr. *Hahn's Wand. Plants & Anim.* 495 The ure-ox and wisent of the German forests. 1888 E. GERARD *Land beyond Forest*: *Transylvania* II. 11 Whoever..let himself be lured into quaffing mead from her ure-ox drinking horn, was doomed.

**Urerythrine** (yūᵊreri·þrəin). *Chem.* [f. UR-INE + ERYTHRIN.] (See quots.)

1858 THUDICHUM *Urine* 321 Urerythrine occurs in fresh urine generally in a dissolved state. 1878 KINGZETT *Animal Chem.* 238 Urerythrine is a substance first described by Proust under the name of rosacic acid.

**Ures,** obs. f. OURS.

**Ureson, Uresun,** obs. ff. ORISON.

**-uret** (iŭret), *Chem.*, a suffix, ad. mod.L. *-urētum, -orētum*, added to a stem or truncated word to form names of simple compounds of an element with another element or a radical. First used (after F. words in *-ure*) about 1790 in *azoturet, hydruret, phosphuret, sulphuret* (from *azote, hydr-ogen, phosph-ure, sulph-ure*), it was extended to other terms, as *carburet, nitruret* (1794), *ioduret* (1816), *seleniuret* (1818), and (more recently) *arseniuret, bromuret, chloruret, cyanuret, floruret,* *hydroguret*, *telluret*, etc. It is now largely replaced by -IDE, q.v.

The French school of chemists in 1787 proposed the suffix *-urētum*, *-orētum*, in mod.L. terms (as *phosphorētum*, *sulphurētum*); but in F. words they preferred the suffix *-ure* (1787 De Morveau, etc. *Méthode de Nomenclature Chimique* 207, 231, etc.).

† **U·retary**, *a.* and *sb.* *Obs. rare.* Also 7 **uritary.** [ad. F. *uretaire* (16th c.), f. *uretère*: see next.] **a.** *adj.* Of, pertaining to, or constituting the ureters. **b.** *sb.* = URETER.

**1578** BANISTER *Hist. Man* v. 75 b, The extreme endes of the vretarie vessels, which both giue passage to the vrine discendyng into the bleddar. **1650** EARL MONM. tr. *Senault's Man bec. Guilty* IV. v. 213 That which Divine Justice shews in the sicknesses of the earthly Monarches when by a grain of sand he stops the uritaries [F. *vretaires*].

**Ureter** (yurī·təɹ). *Anat.* Also 6–7 **vretere, vreter,** 7 **uriter.** [a. medical L. *ūrētēr*, a. Gr. οὐρητήρ, f. οὐρεῖν to make water. Cf. F. *uretère* (1541), It. and Pg. *uretere*, Sp. *uréter.*] Either of the fibro-muscular tubes or vessels which convey the urine from the pelvis of the kidney to the bladder; a urinary duct.

**1578** BANISTER *Hist. Man* v. 78 b, From this veyne springeth a vessell called *Vreter*. **1591** JAS. I *Poet. Exerc., Furies* 862 A Stone, which stops..The sliddrie vreter, carier of Salt vrine. **1615** CROOKE *Body of Man* (1631) 190 The paine of the Stone is..acute when it mooueth into or toward the Vreter. **1725** *Fam. Dict.* s.v. *Stone*, To make use of his Probe, and to thrust it [*sc.* the stone] thro' the Ureter into the Bladder. **1800** *Med. Jrnl.* IV. 392 On the left side of the bladder, near the termination of the ureter. **1835–6** *Todd's Cycl. Anat.* I. 348/1 The ureter [in birds]..has the same structure as in the mammalia. **1875** HUXLEY & MARTIN *Elem. Biol.* 198 The duct [of the frog]—ureter (female) or genito-urinary canal (male)—running..to the cloaca. **1893** *Brit. Med. Jrnl.* 7 Jan. 11/2 A calculus impacted in the lower end of the ureter.

*attrib.* **1601** HOLLAND *Pliny* II. 72 The juice of Mallows ..enlargeth the Vretere conduits. **1898** *Brit. Med. Jrnl.* 5 Nov. 1412/2 The ureter catheters..must be used with aseptic precautions.

**b.** More usually in pl.

**1578** BANISTER *Hist. Man* v. 83 b, Two other passages.. deducyng Urine from the reynes, and called Vreteres. **1594** T. B. *La Primaud. Fr. Acad.* II. 372 Two other passages, called vreteres or vrine pipes. **1625** HART *Anat. Ur.* I. ii. 30 They shew forth the disposition..of the kidneyes, vreters, or vrine-pipes, and the bladder. **1653** H. MORE *Conject. Cabbal.* 156 Fishes, and..birds,..are both also destitute of Vreters. **1707** FLOYER *Physic. Pulse-Watch* 346 This shews the Constitution of the Veins and Ureters, by which we may understand the phlegmatic Temper. **1755** *Gentl. Mag.* XXV. 416 The ureters..are situated near the seminal vessels on each side of the spine. **1808** BARCLAY *Muscular Motions* 556 The urine..is propelled by the successive muscular action of the ureters into the bladder. **1848** CARPENTER *Anim. Phys.* 282 In all Mammalia, and in others, we find the ureters..dilated at their lower extremity into a bladder. **1876** *Clin. Soc. Trans.* IX. 26 Both ureters were full of thick yellow pus.

**Ure·teral**, *a.* *Anat.* [f. prec. + -AL.] Of or pertaining to, affecting or connected with, a ureter.

**1883** DUNCAN *Clin. Lect. Dis. Women* (ed. 2) x. 76 The similar condition of the urine in hysteria..and in ureteral fistula. **1894** *Ann. Surgery* Sept. 267 The treatment of the ureteral wound.

**Ure:tere·ctomy.** *Surg.* [f. as prec. + Gr. ἐκτομή: see -TOMY.] Surgical removal of a ureter.

**1893** *Brit. Med. Jrnl. Epit.* 1 Apr. 49/3 Ureterectomy. Reynier..reports a case in which he removed the whole of one ureter. **1897** *Allbutt's Syst. Med.* IV. 437 Ureterectomy for diseases of Ureter.

**Ureteric** (yūᵊrīte·rik), *a.* [f. as prec. + -IC. Cf. F. *urétérique.*] Pertaining to, affecting, or occurring in a ureter or the ureters.

**1822** GOOD *Study Med.* IV. 444 Ureteric stoppage of urine. **1890** BILLINGS *Med. Dict.* s.v., Superior,..middle,..and inferior ureteric arteries. *Ibid.*, Ureteric calculus,..Ureteric fold.

**Ureteritis** (yurītĕrəi·tis). *Path.* [f. as prec. + -ITIS. Cf. F. *urétérite*, It. *ureterite.*] Inflammation of a ureter.

**1823** CRABB *Dict. Technol.* II. s.v. *c* **1840** *Encycl. Metrop.* VII. 653/2 Ureteritis and cystitis rarely co-exist with diseases of other parts. **1889** *Buck's Handbk. Med. Sci.* VIII. 560/2 A simple uncomplicated ureteritis probably never occurs. **1898** *Lancet* 1 Jan. 17/2 If the ureter is found to be..in a condition of tuberculous ureteritis.

**Uretero-** (yurī·tĕro), combining form of URETER, occurring in various surgical and medical terms, as **uretero-cystoneostomy, -cystostomy, -enterostomy, -lithotomy, -stomy, -tomy** *sbs.*; **uretero-genital, -uterine, -vaginal, -vesical** *adjs.*

Many other instances occur in recent Dicts., etc., as *ureterodialysis, -lith, -lithic, -lysis, -nephrectomy, -plasty, -pyelitis, -pyosis, -rrhaphy, -stenosis, -ureteral.*

**1893** *Medical Press* 15 Nov. 503/2 *Uretero-Cystoneostomy,..that [operation] of placing a severed ureter in communication direct with the bladder. **1903** *Med. Record* 13 June 958 (Cent. Suppl.), *Ureterocystostomy. **1893** *Brit. Med. Jrnl. Epit.* 4 Mar. 34/1 Any attempt at *ureteroenterostomy would..be contraindicated in cases of atonic or relaxed condition of the lower orifice of the ureter. **1887** *Lancet* 3 Sept. 496/1 (*heading*), *Uretero-genital fistulæ. **1893** *Brit. Med. Jrnl.* 7 Jan. 11/2 Case III. *Uretero-Lithotomy...The patient was placed in the lithotomy position [etc.]. **1901** *Lancet* 6 April 1034/1 The operations of ureterotomy and lumbar *ureterostomy. **1885** *Ibid.* 14 Feb. 296/2 Removal of the calculus impacted in the ureter by intra-peritoneal *ureterotomy is feasible. **1894** *Ann. Surgery* Sept. 289 This case was one in which *ureteroureterostomy might have been performed with advantage. **1887** *Lancet* 3 Sept. 496/2 Conditions similar to those which give rise to *uretero-uterine fistulæ. *Ibid.*, *Uretero-vaginal fistulæ. **1893** *Brit. Med. Jrnl. Epit.* 4 March 34/1 The *uretero-vesicle [*sic*] sphincter..is only relaxed to give issue from time to time to a jet of urine.

**Urethane** (yure·þēⁱn). *Chem.* Also **-an.** [a. F. *uréthane*: see UR-EA and ETHANE.] Ethyl carbamate; valued as an anæsthetic.

**1838** T. THOMSON *Chem. Org. Bodies* 600 The specific gravity of the vapour of urethan. **1844** FOWNES *Man. Chem.* 386 Urethane is a white, solid, crystallizable body, fusible below 212°. **1885** *Lancet* 19 Dec. 1167/2 He had slept comfortably by the aid of urethan.

**Urethra** (yurī·þră). *Anat.* [a. late L. *ūrēthra* (whence F. *urèthre*, *urètre*, It., Sp., Pg. *uretra*, Pg. *urethra*), a. Gr. οὐρήθρα, f. οὐρεῖν to urinate.] The membranous tube or canal through which the urine is discharged from the bladder.

**1634** JOHNSON tr. *Paré's Wks.* XIX. i. 723 There bee some who have the Urethra or passage of the yard obstructed by budding caruncles. **1638** A. REID *Anat. Body of Man* 215 There is no conspicuous passage, by the which the seed passeth into the urethra. **1682** T. GIBSON *Anat.* xix. (1684) 127 In Men it [*sc.* the neck of the bladder] is longer and narrower, and..opens into the Urethra. **1732** ARBUTHNOT *Rules of Diet* iv. (1736) 428 In the Urethra, or Passage of the Urine from the Bladder. *c* **1790** *Encycl. Brit.* (ed. 3) V. 271/2 The urethra..terminates in the podex. **1840** G. V. ELLIS *Anat.* 584 The urethra..reaches from the bladder to the extremity of the penis in the male, or to the vulva in the female. **1880** *Lancet* 24 Jan. 119/1 The urethræ of men differ in calibre. **1884** W. PYE *Surg. Handicraft* 465 Normal urethras differ greatly in their calibre.

*attrib.* and *Comb.* **1875** KNIGHT *Dict. Mech.* 2684/2 *Urethra-cutter*.., an instrument for enlarging the urethral canal..in case of stricture. *Ibid.*, *Urethra-syringe*,..a syringe with a long nozzle.

**Urethra-**, combining form of URETHRA (cf. URETHRO-), occurring in a few terms, as **ure·thragraph, -tome, urethra·meter** (see quots.).

**1875** KNIGHT *Dict. Mech.* 2684/2 *Urethratome*,..a knife for dividing strictures of the urethra. **1883** G. HERSCHEL in *Lancet* 2 June 943/2 The instrument which I have devised, and to which I propose to give the name of *urethragraph. *Ibid.*, Every surgeon who..habitually makes use of the *urethrameter. **1885** *Brit. Med. Jrnl.* 11 July 54/2 Having found out the number, situations, and sizes of the contractions [of the urethra]..by the urethrameter.

**Urethral** (yurī·þrăl), *a.* [ad. mod.L. *ūrēthrāl-is*, or f. URETHR-A + -AL. Cf. F. *uréthral*, Pg. *urethral*, *uretral.*]

**1.** *Anat.* Of or pertaining to the urethra; constituting the urethra.

**1835–6** OWEN in *Todd's Cycl. Anat.* I. 354/1 There is no true urethral canal [in birds]. *Ibid.* 355/2 Prostatic or other urethral glands. **1857** SIR H. THOMPSON *Dis. Prostate* (1861) 16 The urethral mucous membrane. **1884** — *Tumours of Bladder* 25 For which purpose the small urethral incision suffices.

**2.** *Path.* Affecting or occurring in the urethra; resulting from operating on the urethra.

In frequent use since *c* 1875.

**1843** R. J. GRAVES *Syst. Clin. Med.* xxv. 309 The running and urethral inflammation. **1845** *Encycl. Metrop.* VII. 600/2 Urethral hæmorrhage is a flux of blood from the urethra. **1884** W. PYE *Surg. Handicraft* 466 This urethral fever, or urethral shivering,..is generally transient.

**3.** Adapted for, used in, operating on the urethra.

**1852** *Lancet* 7 Feb. 144/1 The prompt removal of strictures of the urinary canal with the urethral guide and tubes. **1861** ERICHSEN *Surg.* (ed. 3) 1028 Urethral lithotrite. **1884** KNIGHT *Dict. Mech.* Suppl. 263/2 The urethral divulsor for obliterating strictures. *Ibid.* 551/2 Urethral forceps... Urethral scoop.

**Urethra·lgia.** *Path.* [f. URETHR-A + Gr. ἄλγος pain.] A painful affection of the uretha.

**1859** *New Syd. Soc. Yearbk.* 193 A case of urethralgia.. yielded to frictions of chloroform liniment.

**Urethre·ctomy.** *Surg.* [f. URETHR-A + Gr. ἐκτομή: see -TOMY.] Surgical removal of the urethra or part of it.

**1893** *Medical Press* 29 March 324/1 Urethrectomy as a method for radical treatment of rupture of the urethra, fistula, or organic stricture. **1898** *Brit. Med. Jrnl.* 11 June 1556/1 A case of urethrectomy for impermeable stricture with retention of urine.

**Urethritis** (yūᵊrīþrəi·tis). *Path.* [f. URETHR-A + -ITIS. Cf. F. *uréthrite.*] Inflammation of the urethra.

**1823** CRABB *Dict. Technol.* II. s.v. **1843** R. J. GRAVES *Syst. Clin. Med.* xxvii. 347 The extension of urethritis sympathetically or by metastasis. **1888** *Lancet* 14 Jan. 58/1 The condition commonly known as chronic granular urethritis.

Hence **Urethri·tic** (-i·tik), *a.* **a.** Arising from, due to, urethritis. **b.** Affected with urethritis.

**a.** **1860** MAYNE *Expos. Lex.* 1313 Urethritic or gonorrhœal prostatitis. **b.** **1891** *Cent. Dict.*

**Urethro-** (yurī·þro), combining form of URETHRA, occurring in various surgical and pathological terms, as **urethrocele, -gram, -graph, -meter, -plasty, -rrhaphy, -scope, -scopy, -stenosis, -stomy, -tome, -tomy** *sbs.*; **urethrogenital, -metric, -plastic, -rectal, -scopic, -sexual, -vaginal, -vesical** *adjs.*

Various other terms appear in recent or special Dicts., as *urethrobulbar, -cystitis, -penile, -perineal, -phraxis, -plastic, -scopical, -spasm, -tomic*, etc. (Cf. F. *uréthroplastie*, *-rrhagie*, *-rrhaphie*, *-rrhée*, *-scope*, *-scopie*, *-tome*, *-tomie.*)

**1873** *Lancet* 7 June 811/2 Such a *urethrocele proved extremely inconvenient to a married lady. **1885** *Buck's Handbk. Med. Sci.* I. 519/1 Urethrocele..affects the posterior wall a few millimetres above the orifice. **1840** G. V. ELLIS *Anat.* 452 The *urethro-genital portion of the perinæal space. **1893** *Medical Press* 8 Feb. 144/1 The Urethrometer.—B shows the mechanism which takes a *urethrogram by the pencil points A writing on a sliding slip of paper. **1884** G. HERSCHEL in *Lancet* 5 April 608/1 A technical description of my *urethrograph. **1884** ERICHSEN *Surg.* (ed. 8) II. 1092 For the purpose of measuring these slight strictures, Otis, of New York, has invented an instrument which he calls the '*urethrometer'. **1895** *Arnold & Sons' Surg. Instrument Catal.* 572 Urethrometer (Mac Munn's), automatic. **1884** KNIGHT *Dict. Mech.* Suppl. 916/2 **Urethrometric Sound*, an olivary sound in a canula. **1856** *Lancet* 4 Oct. 378/2 Delpech ..performed a *urethroplastic operation. **1845** *Ibid.* 25 Jan. 83/2 (*heading*), *Urethro-plasty. **1861** ERICHSEN *Surg.* (ed. 3) 1095 Urethroplasty may in such cases be advantageously practised. **1857** *Lancet* 5 Sept. 247/2 Followed by the formation of a *urethro-rectal fistula. **1883** *Holmes' Syst. Surg.* (ed. 3) III. 682 *Urethroraphy is performed by refreshing the edges of the fistula [etc.]. **1893** *Lancet* 13 May 1135/2 The above cases of circular urethrorraphy. **1868** *Ibid.* 12 Dec. 768/2 A very simple *urethroscope. **1886** *Buck's Handbk. Med. Sci.* II. 659 The Urethroscope in position. **1895** *Arnold & Sons' Surg. Instrument Catal.* 573 *Urethroscopic Tube (Otis's). **1899** *Brit. Med. Jrnl.* 2 Dec. 1544 Urethroscopic examination showed the presence of a simple gonorrhœa. **1890** BILLINGS *Med. Dict.* II. 725 *Urethroscopy. **1901** *Lancet* 31 Aug. 599/1 The illumination..by a source of light from the outside, reflected into the tube, is as old as urethroscopy itself. **1835–6** OWEN in *Todd's Cycl. Anat.* I. 348/1 The same segment of the cloaca..is therefore termed the *urethro-sexual cavity. **1841** *Penny Cycl.* XXI. 161/1 The urethro-sexual canal. **1848** DUNGLISON *Med. Dict.* (ed. 7) 874 **Urethrostenosis*, stricture of the urethra. **1900** R. HARRISON *Vasectomy* 44 Remote results of structural lesions in urethro-stenosis. **1900** *Brit. Med. Jrnl. Epit.* 28 April 66/2 Perineal *Urethrostomy:..In this operation, the first stage of which is an ordinary external urethrotomy, the exposed urethra is cut across. **1849** CRAIG s.v., *Urethrotome. **1860** *Lancet* 21 July 58/2 Two cases of stricture of the urethra successfully treated by the urethrotome dilator. **1874** *Ibid.* 13 June 830/2 Along this the tunneled eye of the urethrotome is threaded. **1848** DUNGLISON *Med. Dict.* (ed. 7) 874 *Urethrotomy. **1852** *Lancet* 28 Aug. 204/2 Who invented urethrotomy on a grooved staff as a cure for stricture? **1867** *Biennial Retrospect* (New Syd. Soc. XXXII) 321 Internal urethrotomy is more prompt in execution. **1853** ERICHSEN *Surg.* 864 *Urethro-vaginal fistulæ are..of most common occurrence. **1885** *Buck's Handbk. Med. Sci.* I. 519/1 The whole thickness of the urethro-vaginal wall. **1873** *Lancet* 15 Nov. 699/2 *Urethrovesical calculus.

**Urethylane** (yure·þilēⁱn). *Chem.* [f. UR-EA: see ETHYL and -ANE 2 b.] Methyl-urethane; methyl carbamate.

**1844** FOWNES *Man. Chem.* 417 It yields with dry ammonia a solid crystallizable substance, called urethylane. **1852** WATTS tr. *Gmelin's Handbk. Chem.* VII. 292 Urethylane crystallizes in tables derived from an oblique rhombic prism. **1863** *Watts' Dict. Chem.* I. 751 Carbamate of Methyl. Urethylane.

**Ure·tic**, *a.* (and *sb.*). [ad. late L. *ūrētic-us*, a. Gr. οὐρητικός, f. οὐρεῖν to urinate. Cf. obs. F. *uretique* (1581), *ourétique.*] † **a.** *Uretic acid*, phosphoric acid (1857 Mayne *Expos. Lex.* 847/1). *Obs.* **b.** Diuretic (1849 Craig; hence in later Dicts.).

**Ure·tte.** [f. UR-INE *sb.* + -ETTE.] (See quot.)

**1840** J. BUEL *Farmer's Comp.* 72 Urette is animal urine, absorbed and rendered dry by mixture with calcareous earth.

**Urge** (ɒ̄ɹdʒ), *sb.* [f. next.] The action of urging or fact of being urged or prompted; an impelling motive, force, pressure, etc.

In frequent use from *c* 1910.

*a* **1618** SYLVESTER *Forgive us our Trespasses* xxvii, O may it please thy heavenly grace,..That we may pray without all urge; Forgive us, Lord, our debts. **1884** WHITMAN *Leaves of Grass* 324 O I am sure they really came from Thee, The urge, the ardor, the unconquerable will. **1886** R. W. GILDER *Lyrics, Recognition* i, Creation,..With swift, concentric, never-ceasing urge, Resolving gradual to one disk of fire. **1914** J. L. PATON *J. B. Paton* xviii. 317 Every good deed is bound to grow. There is an inward urge that forces it upwards.

**Urge** (ɒ̄·ɹdʒ), *v.* Also 6 **urdge.** [ad. L. *urgē-re* to press, drive, compel, etc. (whence It. *urgere*, Sp. and Pg. *urgir*).]

**I. 1.** *trans.* To bring forward, present, or press upon the attention (a fact, reason, argument, etc.) in an earnest or urgent manner; to plead with or by way of argument or excuse; to allege, affirm, or state, esp. in justification, extenuation, or defence.

In frequent use from *c* 1685.

**1560** DAUS tr. *Sleidane's Comm.* 315 b, The Emperour.. aunswered him plainly that he could not..praise the same decree, and still vrged his promesse and couenaunt. **1565** CALFHILL *Answ. Martiall* 155 Ye vrge a miracle, for euery ..splinter of the Crosse, inasmuch as a Church..was preserued from burning by it. **1596** *Edw. III*, II. i. 447, A spatious field of reasons could I vrge. **1655** FULLER *Ch. Hist.* I. 8 This..were an argument (as K. James did once pleasantly urge it) to prove our Old stile before the New. *a* **1695** J. SCOTT *Chr. Life* II. Wks. 1718 I. 419 The Apostle urges our having a compassionate High Priest in Heaven to intercede for us. **1713** BERKELEY *Hylas & Phil.* II. Wks. 1871 I. 314, I am at a loss what more to urge. **1784** COWPER *Task* VI. 56 The few.., seeking grace t'improve the prize they hold, Would urge a wiser suit than asking more. **1798** S. & HT. LEE *Canterb. T.* II. 164 [He] urged his weak health, as rendering it necessary he should travel very leisurely. **1816** J. SCOTT *Paris Revisit.* (ed. 3) 321 Canova appeared as a claimant in behalf of Rome, which had only her venerable name to urge. **1855** *Poultry Chron.* III. 242/2

The most fastidious can urge no objection. **1864** D. G. MITCHELL *Sev. Stor.* 279 The Count urged the scandal which would grow out of such a measure.

**b.** Const. *on, upon*; *to*, etc.; also *against*.

**1593** SHAKS. *Rich. II*, II. i. 299 Vrge doubts to them yt feare. **1607** — *Cor.* IV. vii. 19 He knowes not What I can vrge against him. **1654** BRAMHALL *Just Vind.* iii. 35 Yet three things are urged against it. **1667** MILTON *P. L.* VI. 622 The terms we sent were terms of weight,..and full of force urg'd home. **1749** FIELDING *Tom Jones* VII. xv, So far from being an Advocate for the present Prisoner, she urged his Guilt to his Officer. **1841** A. COMBE *Physiol. Digestion* (ed. 3) 304, I shall..urge upon him the necessity of rendering our knowledge more complete. **1872** TENNYSON *Gareth & Lynette* 1313 Lancelot on him urged All the devisings of their chivalry.

**c.** With clause as object, either introduced by *that* or directly quoted.

(*a*) **1560** DAUS tr. *Sleidane's Comm.* 227 The French men ..especially vrged that the Scotes myght be comprised in the peace. **1596** DRAYTON *Legends* i. 352 Further to urge what she before had said. **1638** JUNIUS *Paint. Ancients* 2 Wee doe therein urge somewhat further, that [etc.]. **1672** H. STUBBE *Justif. Dutch War* 24 The Queen urged, that ..she was to be Arbitress. **1817** JAS. MILL *Brit. India* II. IV. v. 217 It was urged..that the servants..ought not to be deprived of such precious advantages. **1885** 'MRS. ALEXANDER' *At Bay* ix, I urged that the disappearance of the.. money..would tell against him.

(*b*) **1689** PRIOR *Epistle to Fleetwood Shephard* 78 So Atoms dancing round the Center, They urge, made all Things at a Venture. *a* **1743** OZELL tr. *Brantome's Sp. Rhodom.* (1744) 67 M. de Lansac urged, It was absolutely necessary. *a* **1792** SIR J. REYNOLDS *Journ. Flanders & Holland* Wks. 1797 II. 124 There is lightness, airiness, and facility in Rubens, his advocates will urge. **1838** DICKENS *Nickleby* vi, 'Father,' urged the maiden [to the monk],.. 'our daily alms have been distributed.' **1865** — *Mut. Fr.* III. i, 'Don't break out, Lammle,' urged Fledgeby, in a submissive tone. **1884** tr. *Lotze's Logic* 424 We are left after all, it will be urged,..walled in within the all-embracing delusions of those ideas.

**2.** To advocate or advise earnestly (some course of action, etc.); to press with importunity, claim or demand pressingly.

**1595** SHAKS. *John* IV. ii. 204 Why vrgest thou so oft yong Arthurs death? **1596** WARNER *Alb. Eng.* IX. xlvi. (1602) 217 Then proudly pricke the mounted Sers, the Harrolds..vrging fees to gentellize their name. **1601** SHAKS. *Jul. C.* IV. iii. 261, I should not vrge thy duty past thy might. **1661** *Reg. Privy Council Scot.* I. 5 The Lord Chancellour..is to urge of them the oath of supremacie. **1682** DRYDEN *Medal* 187 What vengeance will they urge, Whose Ordures neither Plague nor Fire can purge. **1805** *Med. Jrnl.* XIV. 206, I thought it my duty to urge the operation. **1816** SCOTT *Old Mort.* xxxiii, He hath ever urged peace with the malignants. **1831** JAMES *Phil. Augustus* II. v, The many, which were all eager to urge a course that..he would have been the first to follow, but [etc.].

**b.** With impersonal subject.

**1592** KYD *Sp. Trag.* III. i. 61 Embassadour, What news hath vrg'd this sodain entrance? *Ibid.* IV. iv. 87, I see your lookes vrge instance of these wordes. **1605** SHAKS. *Lear* V. i. 52 The Enemy's in view, draw vp your powers;..your hast Is now vrg'd on you. **1667** MILTON *P. L.* IX. 250 For solitude somtimes is best societie, And short retirement urges sweet returne. **1872** GEO. ELIOT *Middlem.* lxxxvi, A past error may urge a grand retrieval.

**II. 3.** To entreat or plead with (a person) pertinaciously; to importune, press, or ply with arguments or strong persuasion; to prompt, solicit, or request earnestly. Also, with impersonal subject: To incite or impel strongly.

**1568** BIBLE (Bishops') *Luke* xi. 53 The lawyers and the pharisees began to vrge hym vehemently, and to prouoke hym to speake many thynges. **1586** DAY *Eng. Secretorie* II. (1625) 25 To vrge me as you doe, may but breed that which neither of vs may returne pleasing. **1595** SHAKS. *John* II. i. 475, I see a yeelding in the lookes of France;..vrge them while their soules Are capeable of this ambition. **1640** HABINGTON *Queen of Arragon* II. 366, I urg'd Them with the memory of their former deedes. **1667** MILTON *P. L.* IX. 588 Hunger and thirst at once,..quick'nd at the scent Of that alluring fruit, urg'd me so keene. **1692** DRYDEN *St. Euremont's Ess.* 24 Urged with an apprehension of their ruine, [they] abandoned themselves to the Conduct of Xantippus. **1717** POPE *Iliad* X. 135 Strong necessity our toils demands,..and urges all our hands. **1814** J. AUSTEN *Mansf. Park* xv, Do not urge her, madam...It is not fair to urge her in this manner. **1847** HELPS *Friends in C.* I. v. 83 Men ..cannot be moved in masses as of old. At one time chivalry urged all men—then the Church. **1853** J. H. NEWMAN *Hist. Sk.* (1873) I. 183 The barbarian..moves when he is urged by appetite.

**b.** Const. *to* with inf.; also with advs. (as *on, onward*) and preps.

(*a*) **1565** COOPER *Thesaurus* s.v. *Insto*, Vrge me not, or presse me not to iudge. **1613** SHAKS. *Hen. VIII*, IV. ii. 157 Vrge the King To do me this last right. **1671** MILTON *Samson* 1677 A spirit of phrenzie..Who..urg'd them on with mad desire To call in hast for their destroyer. **1753–4** RICHARDSON *Grandison* II. xxiii. 167 Should she engage without waiting for his consent; as she was urged to do, by Letters. **1816** SCOTT *Bl. Dwarf* xviii, His patriotism urged him to serve his country abroad. **1891** FARRAR *Darkn. & Dawn* xxix, Seneca..urged the Emperor to summon him into his presence.

(*b*) **1600** *1st Pt. Sir J. Oldcastle* IV. ii. 9 Pardon, my Lord; my conscience vrg'd me to it. **1776** PAINE *Com. Sense* 9 Hunger in the mean time would urge him from his work. **1791** COWPER *Iliad* V. 904 Venus..and the Archer..have urged, themselves, to this The frantic Mars. **1832** LYTTON *Eugene A.* I. v, They urge us onward, yet present no limit to our progress. **1846** MRS. A. MARSH *Father Darcy* II. iv. 98 He was not urging others to a course in which he never intended to venture himself. **1871** *Leisure Hour* 480/1 Two guineas paid to..his clerk, to urge him on with the works.

†**c.** To charge strongly *with* something. Also with *that* and clause. *Obs.*

**1599** THYNNE *Animadv.* (1875) 54 Speakinge to his wyfe, he urgethe her that she cannott denye yt. **1628** SIR W. MURE *Spir. Hymne* 144 Thou of our innocence the ground, for vs, with guilt was vrgde. **1689** WOOD *Life* (O.H.S.) III. 310 Speed's daughter told the bishop of it and the bishop urg'd him with it. **1703** ROWE *Fair Penit.* V. i, Thou com'st to urge me with the wrongs I ha' done thee.

**4. a.** To serve or act as a constraining influence on (something); to bear pressingly on; to spur, actuate, or constrain.

**1576** FLEMING *Panopl. Epist.* 62 More I may say to you, then any mans mynde is urged to accomplishe. **1592** KYD *Sp. Trag.* III. iv. 14 A guiltie conscience, vrged with the thought Of former euils, easily cannot erre. *Ibid.* IV. iv. 145 But loue of him..Did vrge her resolution to be such. **1633** BP. HALL *Hard Texts, O.T.* 620 Yee have extreamely urged the patience of the Lord. **1823** SCOTT *Quentin D.* ii, I..will pay fitting respect to your age, if you do not urge my patience with mockery. **1843** NEALE *Hymns for Sick* 23 Give me when those last trials urge Thy Very Flesh and Blood. **1878** *Masque Poets* 42, I was wrong to urge your will And wrong to mar your life.

†**b.** To treat (a mineral, etc.) with great heat.

**1758** REID tr. *Macquer's Chym.* I. 69 If the calx of Tin be urged by a strong fire. **1828–32** WEBSTER s.v., To urge an ore with intense heat.

**III. 5.** To hasten or press forward (a proceeding, enterprise, etc.); to prosecute with effort, energy, or vigour; to push forward.

**1565** COOPER *Thesaurus* s.v. *Insto, Instabit huic loco*,..He shall vrge this, or be earnest in this. **1583** STUBBES *Anat. Abus.* I. H 4, [It] bringeth death before nature vrge it,..or age require it. **1598** HAKLUYT *Voy.* I. 145 Swandepolcus.. affirming that himselfe neuer prospered so long as he vrged warre against them. **1667** BOYLE *Orig. Formes & Qual.* 430 This Substance..will..(if the Distillation have been urg'd far enough) [be] brittle. **1684** EARL ROSCOM. *Ess. Transl. Verse* 238 Urge your Success, deserve a lasting Name. **1697** DRYDEN *Æneis* V. 273 The Crew of Mnestheus,..with elated Minds, Urge their Success. *Ibid.* VII. 660 While Turnus urges thus his Enterprise. **1713** ADDISON *Cato* III. v, Why wilt thou urge the fate Of wretched men? **1781** COWPER *Table-T.* 214 The peasants urge their harvest. **1789** E. DARWIN *Bot. Gard.* II. 79 When..wither'd Famine urged the work of death. **1855** PRESCOTT *Philip II*, I. viii. I. 239 Henry obstinately urged his fate, and compelled the count ..to take the saddle. **1855** MACAULAY *Hist. Eng.* xii. III. 213 The bills which the Commons were urging forward. **1885** *Daily Tel.* 11 Sept. (Encycl. Dict.), Urging the carnage, and eyeing with pleasure all the horrors of war.

*transf.* **1857** RUSKIN *Pol. Econ. Art* 110 Every kind deed ..in relieving distress..would..open and urge, in a thousand unforeseen directions, the sluices of commerce and the springs of industry.

**6.** To press forcibly in some direction; to force or impel forward or onward; to drive. Also with preps. or advs., as *against, away, down, through*.

**1594** KYD *Cornelia* V. 188 Now we of our side vrge them to retreate, And nowe before them we retyre as fast. **1634** SIR T. HERBERT *Trav.* 87 The first walke is set with pipes of Lead and Brasse, through which the water is vrged. **1693** T. CREECH *Juvenal* XIII. 93 Rivers chang'd to Blood Roul wond'rous Waves, or urge a Milky Flood. **1742** POPE *Dunc.* IV. 592 From Stage to Stage the licens'd Earl may run,..The Senator at Cricket urge the Ball. **1791** COWPER *Iliad* V. 70 For Menelaus..the spear urged through his breast. **1813** BYRON *Corsair* III. xv, The blue waves sport around the stern they urge. **1827** FARADAY *Chem. Manip.* xvi. 395 The latter [*sc.* air] being urged away from the tube by a force proportionate [etc.]. **1862** CALVERLEY *Verses & Tr.* 16 Still I see you..Urge, towards the table's centre,..the squail.

*transf.* **1737** POPE *Imit. Hor., Ep.* II. ii. 253 Heir urges heir, like wave impelling wave. **1821** SHELLEY *Adonais* xxi, As long as skies are blue,..Evening must usher night, night urge the morrow.

*fig.* **1870** BRYANT *Iliad* II. I. 77 The fates Decreed their early death and urged them on.

**b.** To cause to move, hasten, or gather speed; to accelerate the pace of; to speed up. Usu. with advs. (as *forward, on*) or preps.

*a* **1721** PRIOR *Journey to Copt-Hall* 12, I mount, and..With unarm'd kick urge on my horse. **1760** FAWKES tr. *Anacreon, Ode* lix. 8 With tighten'd Rein, I'll urge thee round the dusty Plain. **1821** SHELLEY *Epithalamion* 20 Nay, return, Vesper! urge thy lazy car! **1846** MRS. A. MARSH *Father Darcy* II. xix. 317 Their wearied horses..gave evidence of the fierce desperation with which they had been urged forward. **1902** VIOLET JACOB *Sheep-Stealers* x, Coachmen were urging their horses up to the door.

*refl.* **1805** BINGLEY *Anim. Biog.* (ed. 2) II. 159 [Birds] urge themselves forward in the air by means of wings.

**c.** To press or pursue (one's flight, way, the chase); to hasten or accelerate (one's pace, etc.).

**1697** DRYDEN *Virg. Georg.* III. 75 High Epidaurus urges on my speed, Fam'd for his hills, and for his horses' breed. **1703** POPE *Thebais* 558 Hapless Tydeus..Thro' the thick deserts headlong urg'd his flight. **1735** SOMERVILLE *Chase* III. 543 He..up the Breeze Urges his Course with eager Violence. *a* **1763** SHENSTONE *Elegies* xvi. 94 Led by their beams I urg'd the pleasing chase. **1801** M. G. LEWIS *Tales of Wonder, Sir Hengist* ii, Sir Hengist urged his courser's pace. **1804** W. L. BOWLES *Spir. Discov.* IV. 579 With De Quiros to the South Still urge thy way. **1840** THIRLWALL *Greece* VII. 61 He had several motives to urge his progress. **1854** H. MILLER *Sch. & Schm.* xvi. 340, I should have to urge my way through the works of our best writers.

**7. a.** To stimulate to expression or action; to provoke or excite; to increase or intensify.

**1594** *1st Pt. Contention* (1843) 24 Forbeare ambitious Prelate to vrge my griefe. **1594** KYD *Cornelia* I. 166 The wrath of heauen (though vrg'd) we see is slow In punishing the euils we haue done. **1616** W. BROWNE *Brit. Past.* II. iv. 516 Anger and pitty, in his manly brest, Urge, yet restraine his teares. **1800** tr. *Lagrange's Chem.* I. 401 Then urge the fire gradually, bring the crucible to a white heat. **1820** SHELLEY *Prometh. Unb.* I. 42 While from their loud abysses howling throng The genii of the storm, urging the rage Of whirlwind. **1839** URE *Dict. Arts* 1124 The heat having been briskly urged for a short time. **1865** J. M. NEALE *Hymns on Paradise* 28 All his spite my Tempter urges.

**b.** To provoke to anger; to irritate or annoy. Also with clause (quot. 1593). Now *dial.*

**1593** LODGE *Will. Longbeard* E 3 This is it that urgeth me that I fall into his hands. **1655** [see URGING *ppl. a.* 1 b]. **1876–** in dialect use (*Eng. Dial. Dict.* s.v. *Urge v.*[1] 2).

**8.** To ply vigorously; to use, work, or employ briskly or diligently.

**1697** DRYDEN *Æneis* V. 301 Both urge their Oars. *a* **1760** I. H. BROWNE *Fireside Poems* (1768) 126, I urge the gay flask With a set of old friends. **1820** SHELLEY *Fragm. Satire on Sat.* 25 Follow his flight with winged words, and urge The strokes of the inexorable scourge.

**IV.** *intr.* **9.** To press by inquiry or statement; to adduce or bring forward arguments, allegations, etc. Also const. *to* with inf.

**1592** *Soliman & Pers.* III. i. 73 Erastus, ile not yet vrge to know the cause That brought thee hether. **1613** SHAKS. *Hen. VIII*, V. iii. 48, I doe beseech your Lordships, That.. my Accusers..may stand forth face to face, And freely vrge against me. **1804** *Something Odd* I. 130 When she had no company at home, he would urge to go and seek it abroad. **1818** SHELLEY *Julian* 616, I urged and questioned still, she told me how All happened.

**b.** To press solicitously, make a strong claim, *for* something.

**1607** SHAKS. *Timon* III. ii. 13 One of his men..vrg'd extreamly for't [*sc.* money], and shewed what necessity belong'd too't. **1660** SHARROCK *Vegetables* 67 Infinite storyes of strange conjunctions which urge earnestly for credit. **1726** SWIFT *Serm. Martyrd. K. Chas.* Wks. 1765 XV. 134 That wicked faction.., not content with all those marks of his justice.., urged still for more. **1753–4** RICHARDSON *Grandison* II. ix. 60 He again urged for her hand, and for a private marriage. **1769** GOLDSM. *Hist. Rome* I. 183 The tribunes..began once more to urge for the removal.

†**c.** To strive *for* (mastery). *Obs.*[−1]

**1691** tr. *Emilianne's Frauds Rom. Monks* (ed. 3) 302 His lovely Countenance, where the Lilly and the Rose did urge for Mastery.

**10.** To press, push, or hasten on. Esp. with advs., as *along, on, onward, upward*.

**1605–8** DONNE *To Sir H. Goodyere* 8 A Palace..decayes: But hee which dwels there, is not so; for hee Strives to urge upward, and his fortune raise. **1653** MILTON *Psalm* vii. 21 Rise Jehovah in thine ire, Rouze thy self amidst the rage Of my foes that urge like fire. **1692** PRIOR *Ode, Imit. Horace* V. 31 Darius flies, young Ammon urges on. **1712** STEELE *Spect.* No. 374 ¶ 1 Those behind him, if he does not urge on, will tread him down. **1821** CLARE *Vill. Minstr.* II. 27 Thou hast heard the thorn's in flower, And childhood's bliss is urging on. **1857** SUSANNA WINKWORTH tr. *Life Tauler* ix. 247 Through all this he shall urge onward, till [etc.]. **1907** *Westm. Gaz.* 19 Oct. 3/1 A woman.., moaning inarticulately, urges wearily along.

**11.** To act as an impelling or prompting motive, stimulus, or force; to incite or stimulate; to exercise pressure or constraint.

**1645** WALLER *Poems* 142 Let Brutes..that cannot thinke, So far as drought and Nature urges, drinke. **1656** SMITH *Pract. Physick* 147 Since two things do urge, either Malignity or the Feaver; if that urge, most Antidotes are necessary. *a* **1660** *Contemp. Hist. Irel.* (Ir. Archæol. Soc.) I. 157 Therefore thriued your precept may vrge, but your example is not souldierlike. **1667** MILTON *P. L.* I. 66 Hope never comes That comes to all; but torture without end Still urges. **1698** FRYER *Acc. E. India & P.* 172 The present Occasions urging, and [they] being willing to blind themselves. **1716** POPE *Iliad* VI. 453 The combat urges, and my soul's on fire. **1752** HUME *Pol. Disc.* viii. 138 Necessity calls, fear urges, reason exhorts. **1791** COWPER *Iliad* V. 848 The time Urges, and need appears that we ourselves Now call to mind the fury of our might. **1805–6** CARY *Dante's Inf.* IV. 21 Our length of way Urges to haste.

†**b.** To be of weight or importance. *Obs.*

**1654** Z. COKE *Logick* 145 A Syllogism leading to absurdity, much urgeth in disputing.

Hence **Urged** (ɒ̄ɹdʒd) *ppl. a.*

**1595** DANIEL *Civ. Wars* IV. lxxxiv, Whilst looking onely on the vrged crime Vnto the farther drift they take no heed. *c* **1611** CHAPMAN *Iliad* XVI. 264 Remember you expresse Your late-urged virtue. **1628** FELTHAM *Resolves* II. lxv. 186 Gifts are the greatest Vsurie; because a two-fold retribution is an vrged effect, that a Noble nature prompts vs to. **1786** BURNS *On W. Chalmers* ii, I am nae stranger to..his warm-urged wishes. **1883** DUNCAN *Clin. Lect. Dis. Women* (ed. 2) ii. 8 And such urged passing [of uterine bougie] induces spasms.

**Urgence** (ɒ̄·ɹdʒĕns). [a. F. *urgence* (1572), or f. URGENT *a.*: see -ENCE.]

**1.** Earnest or pressing solicitation; importunity; = URGENCY 2.

*c* **1592** MARLOWE *Jew of Malta* Prol., This all that he intends, (And that too, at the vrgence of some friends). **1624** HEYWOOD *Gunaik.* II. 100 His urgence overcame the silence of the Oracle. **1634** — *Maidenh. well lost* I. C 2, At my vrgence He promis't you a parley. **1879** HOWELLS *L. Aroostook* 166 She tried to remember at his urgence, something of her childhood. *Ibid.* 219 'Oh I give you the right,' he cried with passionate urgence. **1893** F. ADAMS *Egypt* 255 At the united urgence of France and England.., [he] resigned.

**2.** Urgent need; pressing necessity or importance; = URGENCY 1.

*c* **1605** BODLEY in *Trecentale Bodleianum* (1913) 44 The Keeper may sometimes, vpon Vrgence of buisnesse,..desire a dispensation for his personal absence from his charge. **1610** HEYWOOD *Gold. Age* IV. i, Urgence calls me hence To an enforced absence. **1639** DAVENPORT *New Trick* I. i, His businesse craves dispatch, And is of serious urgence.

**3.** Quickness, expedition, haste.
**1612** J. COTTA *Dang. Pract. Physic* I. viii. 60 Drunkennesse, whose ordinarily knowne effects are..in some imaginations..quicke and readie, in some with as apparent vrgence, yet senselesse. **1868** GEO. ELIOT *Sp. Gipsy* 72 Late despatches sent With urgence by the Count of Bavien. **1869** BLACKMORE *Lorna D.* x, We found good reason for the urgence and melancholy of the duck-birds.

**4.** Impelling force; = URGENCY 5.
**1874** S. LANIER *Poems, Corn* 13 Expirations strong Throb from young hickories..With stress and urgence bold of prisoned spring. **1876** GEO. ELIOT *Dan. Der.* v. xxxvi, A shrinking finally overcome by the urgence of poverty. **1876** DOWDEN *Poems* 2 The lapsing waters tell The urgence uncontrollable Which makes the trouble of their breast.

**Urgency** (ɜ̄·ɹdʒĕnsi). [f. next (see -ENCY), or ad. late L. *urgentia*. Cf. It. *urgenza*, Sp. and Pg. *urgencia*, and prec.]

**I. 1.** The state, condition, or fact of being urgent; pressing importance; imperativeness.
**1540** *Act* 32 *Hen. VIII*, c. 48 § 6 If the importaunce or urgency of the cause..so require. **1594** HOOKER *Eccl. Pol.* I. viii. § 8 Only in case of so great vrgency. **1624** *Impeachm. Dk. Buckhm.* (Camden) 129 Alleadgeing the urgency of the present service. **1686** tr. *Chardin's Trav. Persia* 63, I told him the Urgency of my Occasions. **1793** JEFFERSON *Writ.* (1859) IV. 96 The ascertaining of this point becomes a matter of present urgency. **1797** MRS. RADCLIFFE *Italian* xi, The urgency of your circumstances. **1833** I. TAYLOR *Fanat.* i. 7 There are..motives..of far greater force, and these..have a peculiar urgency in reference to the present moment. **1866** GEO. ELIOT *F. Holt* xxv, I will not wait for the urgency of necessity. **1877** ERICHSEN *Surg.* I. 13 The four cases of extreme surgical urgency.

**b.** *spec.* (See quot. 1884.)
**1883** MAY *Treat. Parlt.* (ed. 9) 383 By the aid of these rules of urgency, a serious political crisis had been overcome. **1884** *Imp. Dict.* IV. 529 In parliament, *urgency* is when, by a vote of three to one in a house of not less than 300 members, a measure is declared urgent in the interest of the state.

**2.** Pressure by importunity or entreaty; urgent solicitation; insistence.
**1611** COTGR., *Importunite*, importunitie, vrgencie, earnestnesse. **1735** SWIFT *Gulliver's Let. to Simpson* ¶ 1 By your great and frequent urgency, you prevailed on me to [etc.]. **1782** MISS BURNEY *Cecilia* VII. iv, This confession..was torn from her by..[Delville's] impetuous urgency. **1828** LYTTON *Pelham* III. x, In spite of all the urgency and entreaties of my letters for a reply. **1882** T. MOZLEY *Remin. Oriel College*, etc. I. Introd. 4 At his encouragement and urgency I stood for a Fellowship.

**3.** Stress *of* wind, weather, etc.
**1660** BURNEY Κέρδ. Δῶρον (1661) 12 There was never any tender nightingale so preserved in the urgencie of the weather. **1859** W. M. THOMSON *Land & Book* I. 66 Neither heavy weights.., nor the importunate urgency of the wind, can sway it [*sc.* a palm-tree] aside from perfect uprightness.

**4.** Persistence, eagerness. *rare*⁻¹.
*a* **1677** BARROW *Serm.* xvi. Wks. 1686 III. 184 And why with less expedition or urgency should we persue the certain means of our present security?

**5.** Impelling or prompting force or quality.
**1816** SCOTT *Antiq.* xxxvi, What she has told you..from no apparent impulse but the urgency of conscience. **1858** J. MARTINEAU *Stud. Chr.* 281 The urgency of desire and devotion. **1863** GEO. ELIOT *Romola* II. xxx, The new urgency of this habitual thought brought a new suggestion.

**II. 6.** An urgent need or situation.
**1647** MAY *Hist. Parl.* II. i. 11 Collections through the Kingdom being too slow for such an urgency. **1695** LOCKE *Further Consid. Value Money* 58 The accidental difference ..is sometimes (but rarely) two pence in five shillings, or somewhat more in great urgencies. **1820** KEATS *Isabella* xxix, With sudden speed,..Because of some great urgency and need In their affairs. **1832** *Rolls of Parlt.* Index 467/2 Agrees to respite the Levy..for Two Years,..unless any Urgency should arise.

**7.** A driving or constraining impulse or motive.
**1664** H. MORE *Myst. Iniq.* xx. 76 Pinched betwixt the sense of poverty and quick urgencies of Devotion. **1822** GOOD *Study Med.* I. 343 The patient..will still perhaps be tormented with..a perpetual urgency to expulsion. *c* **1830** CHALMERS *Lect. Romans* lxix. (1840) 346 Evil might ensue from unbridled and unreasonable urgencies of talk upon this subject. **1883** D. C. MURRAY *Hearts* viii, A superstitious reverence for his guest's genius, and its various urgencies.

**8.** *pl.* Earnest representations or entreaties; importunities.
**1823** JEFFERSON *Writ.* (1830) IV. 376 We..met, and after the urgencies of each on the other, I consented to undertake the task. **1877** 'H. A. PAGE' *De Quincey* xvii. II. 40 Books ..to be returned, in answer to the urgencies of librarians. **1883** MISS BROUGHTON *Belinda* III. v, Belinda,..despite the warm urgencies of the..strangers, retires in favour of her visitors.

**III. 9.** *attrib.*, as *urgency order*, *pledge*, *rate*.
**1883** MAY *Treat. Parlt.* (ed. 9) 383 It became necessary to revive the urgency resolution of the 3rd February 1881. **1890** *Lunacy Act* § 11 In cases of urgency where it is expedient..that the alleged lunatic should be forthwith placed under care and treatment, he may be received and detained ..upon an urgency order. **1891** *Pall Mall G.* 7 April 5/2 It is said Mrs. Cathcart is confined under an urgency order. **1898** MORLEY in *Daily News* 14 Feb. 3/7 The Press agencies ..paid what is called an urgency rate—that is about, I think, twenty or thirty times higher than the ordinary Press rate. **1906** R. WHITEING *Ring in the New* 47 Taking in urgency pledges after the closing of the pawn-shops.

**Urgent** (ɜ̄·ɹdʒĕnt), *a.* [a. F. *urgent* (14th c.), a. L. *urgent-*, *urgens*, pres. pple. of *urgēre* to URGE. Cf. It., Sp., Pg. *urgente*.]

**I. 1.** Pressing, impelling; demanding or calling for prompt action; marked or characterized by urgency. (Freq. from *c* 1800.)
In earliest use with *cause* or *necessity*.
**1496** *Rolls of Parlt.* VI. 515/1 Towarde the..mayntenaunce of the Armye aforsaid, and urgent causes concernyng the same. **1526** *Pilgr. Perf.* (W. de W. 1531) 162 b, But onely whan cause vrgent, & very necessite compelleth. **1558** BP. WATSON *Sev. Sacram.* xix. 119 Where the Sacrament is excluded by vrgent necessitye. *a* **1586** SIDNEY *Arcadia* III. iv, The more I stirre about urgent affaires. **1604** THORNBOROUGH *Discovrse* (title-p.), The euident vtilitie and vrgent necessitie of the desired happie Vnion. **1660** MILTON *Free Commw.* Wks. 1851 V. 451 To the retarding..oft times of thir Counsels or urgentest occasions. **1676–7** MARVELL *Corr.* Wks. (Grosart) II. 521 The true remedy of the urgent condition of this poore Nation. **1712** SWIFT *Jrnl. to Stella* 25 Feb., I have no urgent business upon my hands. **1755** YOUNG *Centaur* vi. Wks. 1757 IV. 282 With only this additional, and still more urgent,..motive for reformation. **1772** W. BUCHAN *Dom. Med.* (ed. 2) 278 Unless these symptoms are urgent, it is safer to let it alone. **1816** J. SCOTT *Paris Revisit.* (ed. 3) 117 They were soon forced to separate to attend to their respective urgent duties. **1843** R. J. GRAVES *Syst. Clin. Med.* xx. 239 What may be done by simple means in relieving an urgent disease. **1866** ROGERS *Agric. & Prices* I. xxi. 528 The necessity not being so urgent as it is now.

**b.** Of commands, messages, etc., by which a matter is strongly pressed upon a person's attention.
**1611** BIBLE *Dan.* iii. 22 The Kings commandement was vrgent. **1779** *Mirror* No. 32, The remonstrances of his man of business, aided by very urgent requests from me. **1816** BENTHAM *Chrestom.* 262 Other objects, for the illustration of which the demand..is accordingly still more urgent. **1856** STANLEY *Sinai & Pal.* iv. 205 This summons was as urgent as words can describe. **1883** O. W. HOLMES *Pages fr. Old Vol. Life* 63 A second telegraphic message..so direct and urgent that I should be sure of an answer to it. **1886** BARING-GOULD *Court Royal* xxxviii, 'Papa,' said Lady Grace in urgent tones.

**2.** Of a feeling, etc.: That constrains, impels, or prompts. Also const. *of*.
**1559** *Reg. St. Andrews Kirk Session* (S.H.S.) I. 18 Giue thei be vexed and urnet with ustioun and urgent appetites of the flesche. **1566** DRANT *Hor., Sat.* II. i. E vij b, Yf I haue suche vrgent luste, and lykyng to indite. **1641** MILTON *Ch. Govt.* I. vii, The miseries of Ireland are urgent of a speedy redress. **1748** G. WHITE *Serm.* (MS.), If people will not follow nature in her most urgent affections, and importunate Requests. **1873** MORLEY *Rousseau* (1905) II. 34 When men are beginning to feel the urgent spirit of a new time.

**3.** Of persons: Pressingly solicitous; importunate, insistent. Also with preps., as *for*, *in*, *on*, † *unto*.
**1548** ELYOT, *Premo*,..*premere*,..to be vrgent or instante vpon. **1565** COOPER *Thesaurus* s.v. *Premo*, I was not more vrgent or instant on any pointe, then, &c. *a* **1593** MARLOWE & NASHE *Dido* III. i, All these..Haue been most vrgent suiters for my loue. **1611** BIBLE *Exod.* xii. 33 The Egyptians were vrgent vpon the people that they might send them out of the land in haste. **1698** COLLIER *Immor. Stage* 107 Oedipus is..Urgent for an account of Particulars. **1732** LEDIARD *Sethos* II. x. 355 The officers of his fleet were urgent in offering their services. **1778** MISS BURNEY *Evelina* ii, The advice and entreaties of all his friends, among whom I was myself the most urgent. **1820** W. IRVING *Sketch Bk.* II. 149 His family have been very urgent for him to make an expedition to Margate. **1883** *Law Times* 20 Oct. 408/1 The public and the Profession were alike urgent in calling for sweeping reforms.

**b.** Eagerly desirous *to* do something.
**1753–4** RICHARDSON *Grandison* II. xxviii. 227, I never knew him to be so very urgent to know my heart. **1798** S. & HT. LEE *Canterb. T.* II. 181 [It] made him..urgent to set out for England. **1826** GALT *Last of Lairds* xxxiv. 302 Mr. Loopy..had been calling, urgent to see me. **1846** MRS. A. MARSH *Father Darcy* II. 243 He is very urgent to see him.

**II. 4.** Impelling, pressing, or bearing onwards.
**1546** *Yorks. Chantry Surv.* (Surtees) 209 When as the waters of Rothere and Downe are so urgent, that the curate of Rotherham cannot to them repayre. **1876** R. BRIDGES *Growth of Love* v, Her launched passion when she sings Wins on the hearing like a shapen prow Borne by the mastery of its urgent wings. **1879** — *A Passer-by* i, Whither, O splendid ship, thy white sails crowding, Leaning across the bosom of the urgent West.

**†5.** Oppressive; severe; heavy. *Obs.*
**1545** BRINKLOW *Compl.* ii. 10 b, An vrgent dammage to the common welth. **1600** HAKLUYT *Voy.* III. 49 During the two houres of those two dayes the heat is very vrgent. **1606** SHAKS. *Ant. & Cl.* I. ii. 187 Not alone The death of Fuluia, with more vrgent touches, Do strongly speake to vs. *a* **1699** J. BEAUMONT *Psyche* III. 147 Which Jesus seeing, He upon him threw The urgent yoak of an express Injunction.

**†6.** Of time: Pressing; passing quickly. *Obs.*
**1611** SHAKS. *Wint. T.* I. ii. 465 Please your Highnesse To take the vrgent houre. **1791** COWPER *Iliad* I. 74 But time is urgent; haste we to consult Priest, prophet, or interpreter of dreams.

Hence **U·rgentness**, urgency. *rare.*
**1598** BARRET *Theor. Warres* II. i. 25 The vrgentnesse of the cause doeth deepely require it. **1727** BAILEY (vol. II), *Pressingness*, Urgentness.

**U·rgently**, *adv.* [-LY².] In an urgent manner.
**1548** UDALL, etc. *Erasm. Par. John* xix. 108 b, Therfore the Jewes called more vrgentely vpon the matter. **1611** COTGR., *Importunément*, importunately, vrgently, earnestly. **1789** in C. F. Jenkins *Tortola* (1923) 90, I thank thee for thy kind advice thou hast so urgently given me. **1840** THIRLWALL *Greece* VII. 303 His attention..was urgently claimed by the danger which now threatened him. **1871** A. MEADOWS *Man. Midwifery* iii. (ed. 2) 361 Prompt action is urgently necessary.

**Urger** (ɜ̄·ɹdʒəɹ). [f. URGE *v.* + -ER¹.]

**1.** One who urges or incites. Also with *on*.
**1598** FLORIO, *Scongiuratore*, a conspirer, a coniurer, an vrger. **1605** W. BRADSHAW *Eng. Puritanism* v. 29 They hould that such an ooth (on the vrgers part) is most damnable. **1659** F. OSBORN *Misc. Ess.*, etc. 149, I confesse Necessity cannot onely abate the Edge of these Reasons; but turne their Poynts against the Urger. **1704** D'URFEY *Heir Adopted* lxx, 'Twas past all Bounds before, And needed not an urger on. **1753** RICHARDSON *Grandison* (1781) II. xxix. 276 If the urger suspects not the fitness of his addresses. **1837** B. D. WALSH *Aristoph., Knights* IV. i, The urgers-on of nimble steeds. **1892** *Temple Bar Mag.* Dec. 496 Scott..was the tempter and urger in a ruinous policy. **1903** T. HARDY *Dynasts* I. VI. iii, The Eternal Urger, pressing change on change.

**2.** An instigator or advocate, an earnest supporter or presenter, *of* something. Now *rare.*
In frequent use *c* 1620–*c* 1670.
**1575** *Brieff Disc. Troub. Franckford* 215 From whose.. pennes, the vrgers of theis [letters] receiued first the light off the gospell. **1632** LE GRYS tr. *Velleius Paterc.* 39 Marcus Cato, the perpetuall urger of the destruction thereof. **1640** in Rushw. *Hist. Coll.* (1692) I. 114 The Author and Urger of some Particular Changes. **1678** CUDWORTH *Intell. Syst.* 209 The Urgers of the forementioned Objection. **1847** COVENTRY DICK in Brown *Horæ Subs.* (1882) 406 Nought detains the urger of these pleas, But dinners.

**U·rging**, *vbl. sb.* [f. as prec. + -ING¹.] The action of the verb; an instance of this.
**1590** SHAKS. *Com. Err.* v. i. 359 Her vrging of her wracke at sea. **1615** HIERON *Wks.* I. 606 It is by such vrgings as this, which..it pleaseth Him to make effectuall. **1651** HOBBES *Leviath.* II. xxv. 133 [It] is manifest enough, by the long and vehement urging. **1721** BAILEY, *Importunity*, an eager pressing or urging. **1838** LYTTON *Alice* x. iv, After repeated conferences and urgings. **1876** GEO. ELIOT *Dan. Der.* xlv, A painful urging of something vague and difficult. **1897** RHOSCOMYL *White Rose Arno* 82 One whose vigorous urgings to immediate action had [etc.].

**U·rging**, *ppl. a.* [f. as prec. + -ING².]

**1.** That serves as a motive or impelling cause; that constrains, or actuates; inciting, spurring, stimulating, strongly prompting; compelling.
**1612** SELDEN *Illustr. Drayton's Poly-olb.* VI. 106 If it be the same with *Lyra*, as some think, although urging reason and authority are to the contrary. **1668** OWEN *Indwell. Sin* ii. 16 It is..an inbred, working, impelling, urging Law. **1678** DRYDEN *Limberham* I. i, How stand thy Affections to her, thou lusty Rogue? *Wood.* All o'fire: A most urging Creature! **1723** *Pres. St. Russia* II. 273 Causes..weighty and urging enough for Russia to begin a War. **1728** SWIFT *Let. to Abp. of Dublin* ¶ 22 We shall..sacrifice all honesty to the present urging advantage. **1802** WOLCOT (P. Pindar) *Isl. Innocence* 63 The sportive fry,..leaping oft as urging hunger calls, Meet the dropp'd crumb. **1870** TYNDALL *Fragm. Sci.* (1871) 322 It is a useful urging force.

**b.** *dial.* Of words: Taunting, irritating.
**1655** *N. Riding Rec.* (1887) V. 191 A Sumersides yeoman [tried] for giving scandallous, urginge and provoking words.

**c.** Strongly operative or active.
**1658** SIR T. BROWNE *Hydriot.* iii. 43 How slender a masse will remain upon an open and urging Fire of the carnall composition.

**†2.** Characterized by urgency; urgent. *Obs.*
**1647** COTTERELL *Davila's Hist. Fr.* I. 49 It would be very easie, this urging necessity once past, to moderate..the.. power of the Duke of Guise. **1683** HOWE *Union among Prot.* Wks. 1863 IV. 261 The case was at that time urging and important. **1683** KENNETT *Erasm. on Folly* 150 If at any time some urging occasions require them to become entangled in secular affairs.

Hence **U·rgingly** *adv.*
**1893** *Temple Bar* XCVII. 524 She instinctively and urgingly clapped her hands to a faster tune.

**Urgo·nian**, *a.* *Geol.* [ad. F. *Urgonien* (D'Orbigny, 1852), f. *Orgon* (see def.).] Forming or belonging to a series of massive limestones of the Lower Cretaceous system as developed at Orgon in the Durance valley.
**1856** *Quart. Jrnl. Geol. Soc.* XII. 69 M. d'Orbigny's Urgonian series, or upper division of the Neocomian group. **1888** DAWSON *Geol. Hist. Plants* 282 These beds are regarded as Lower Cretaceous (Urgonian).

**-uria** (yūə·riă), a second element in Latin form (cf. DYSURIA, ISCHURIA), derived from Gr. -ουρία, employed in various pathological terms denoting morbid conditions of the urine, as *albuminuria*, *glycosuria*, *hæmatinuria*, *hæmaturia*, *hæmoglobinuria*, *oxaluria*, *planuria*, *polyuria*, *pyuria*.

**Urial**, variant of OORIAL.

**Uric** (yūə·rik), *a.* *Chem.* Also 8–9 ouric. [a. F. *urique*, f. *ur-ine* URINE *sb.*¹: see -IC 1 b.]

**1.** *Uric oxide*: (see quot. 1860).
**1797** PEARSON in *Phil. Trans.* LXXXVIII. 37 It will be necessary to give a name to this urinary animal oxide...I trust that philological critics will find the name ouric or uric oxide perfectly appropriate. **1803** FESSENDEN *Poet. Petition* 12 Such a man..May view this uric oxyd's basis, And tell exactly what the case is. **1844** *Lancet* 19 Oct. 129/1 It is clear that uric oxide differs from uric acid simply in containing two atoms less of oxygen. **1860** MAYNE *Expos. Lex.* 1314 *Uric Oxide*,..a substance constituting a very rare ingredient in vesical calculi, and otherwise termed urous oxide, and xanthic oxide.

**2.** *Uric acid*, a crystallizable acid, $C_5H_4N_4O_3$, found in the urine of man, certain animals, reptiles, and birds, being produced in the metabolism of nitrogenous bodies, and excreted by the kidneys.
**1800** tr. *Lagrange's Chem.* II. 404 To separate the uric acid from the latter salts. **1803**– [see LITHIC *a.* 1]. **1826** HENRY *Elem. Chem.* II. 467 It is in those organs..that a new acid, the uric, is generated. **1872** HUXLEY *Physiol.* v. 106 Urea and uric acid are both composed of the elements carbon, hydrogen, oxygen, and nitrogen.
*ellipt.* (and *attrib.*). **1822** GOOD *Study Med.* IV. 508 The uric calculi..are of a yellowish or reddish-brown colour. **1846** G. E. DAY tr. *Simon's Anim. Chem.* II. 460 One minute calculus passed at the same time with others of pure uric, had a nucleus of oxalate of lime.

b. *attrib.* and *Comb.*, as *uric acid calculus, diathesis, -excreting, -excretion, gravel*, etc.

1819 *Rees' Cycl.* XXXVII. 3 X/2 Lithic or Uric Acid Calculus. 1843 *Penny Cycl.* XXVI. 52/1 Uric Acid Crystals. 1845 *Encycl. Metrop.* VII. 552 A gouty or rheumatic state of the constitution, or uric acid diathesis. 1864 GARROD *Mat. Med.* (ed. 2) 108 In cases of uric acid gravel. 1866 ODLING *Anim. Chem.* 128 The uric acid group of compounds. 1880 *Encycl. Brit.* XI. 7/2 The uric-acid-excreting function of the kidneys.

c. **Uric-acidæmia**, = URICÆMIA; **uric-acidity**, the condition of containing an excess of uric acid.

1893 *Brit. Med. Jrnl.* Suppl. 26 Aug. 33 Nervous conditions depending upon *uric acidæmia. 1897 *Lancet* 15 May 1338/2 Symptoms .. which would seem to depend upon uricacidæmia. 1893 A. S. ECCLES *Sciatica* 30 The *uric-acidity of the blood and tissues.

**Uricæmia** (yūərisī·miă). *Path.* Also **uric-hæmia.** [mod.L., f. *uric-us* URIC *a.* + Gr. *αἷμ-α* blood.] = LITHÆMIA.

1867 A. FLINT *Princ. Med.* 84 An excess of uric acid (in the form of urates) in the blood constituting a condition differing from uræmia; it is desirable to distinguish it by a name... I would propose *uricæmia.* 1900 *Lancet* 25 Aug. 572/1 The relation of urichæmia to the different symptoms of the malady.

Hence **Uricæ·mic** *a.*, = LITHÆMIC *a.*

1900 *Lancet* 25 Aug. 571/2 These urichæmic states in no degree determine gout, renal function being adequate.

**Uriconian** (yūərikōu·niăn), *a. Geol.* [f. *Uriconi-um*, name of Roman town at Wroxeter, + -AN.] Consisting of, pertaining to, a series of volcanic rocks such as constitute the Wrekin in Shropshire.

1886 C. CALLAWAY in *Q. Jrnl. Geol. Soc.* XLII. 481 In the Uriconian series itself I had found conglomerates full of rounded pieces of granitoid and gneissic rocks. *Ibid.* 483 The Charlton conglomerates are of Uriconian age. 1893 GEIKIE *Text Bk. Geol.* (ed. 3) 710 The Uriconian volcanic group .. is probably pre-Cambrian.

**U·ride.** *Chem.* [f. UR-IC *a.* + -IDE.] A compound of uric acid with another element, or with a radical. Also *attrib.*

1887 A. M. BROWN *Anim. Alkaloids* 68 A body apparently of the uride family. *Ibid.* 90 He had obtained from normal urines a uride, allantoine.

**Uridro·sis.** *Path.* [mod.L., f. Gr. *οὖρ-ον* URINE *sb.*[1] + *ἱδρόω* I sweat: see -OSIS.] A morbid excretion of certain urinary constituents in the perspiration; urinous sweating.

1857 DUNGLISON *Med. Dict.* 947. 1860 MAYNE s.v. 1899 *Allbutt's Syst. Med.* VIII. 736 Uridrosis. A minute amount of urea is normally present in sweat.

**-urient** (yūə·riĕnt), *suffix*, ad. L. *-urient-*, pres. pple. stem of desiderative verbs, occurring first in a few direct adoptions from L., as *parturient* (1592), † *micturient* (1654), *esurient* (*a* 1672), and hence occas. added to L. stems to form adjs. with the meaning 'desiring, characterized by a desire, (to do something)', as in † *novaturient* (1679), *nupturient*, † *vomiturient* (1666).

1878 *Eagle Mag.* (St. John's Coll. Camb.) X. 81 The vapid concourse of dangling men and nupturient maids.

‖ **Urim** (yūə·rim). [a. Heb. אוּרִים *ūrīm*, pl. intens., referred to אוֹר *ōr* 'light', pl. אוֹרִים *ōrīm*, and by some taken as = lights, *φωτισμοὶ* 'illuminations' (Symmachus).]

1. Certain objects, the nature of which is not known, worn in or upon the 'breast-plate' of the Jewish high-priest, by means of which the will of Jehovah was held to be declared.

Used chiefly in the collocation *Urim and Thummim* (once *Thummim and Urim*), occurring five times in the O. T. In the earlier English versions rendered after the Vulgate *doctrina et veritas* (from the LXX *δήλωσις καὶ ἀλήθεια*), whence Wyclif 'doctryne [l.v. techyng] and trewthe'; Coverdale has 'light and perfectnesse', following Luther's *licht und recht*, but in the 'Great' Bible of 1539 and in later versions the words are left untranslated.

(*a*) 1537 BIBLE (Matthew's) *Num.* xxvii. 21 Eleazar yᵉ preast..shal aske councell for him after the iudgement of Urim before the Lorde. *Ibid.* 1 *Sam.* xxviii. 6 Nether by dreame nor by Urim nor yet by prophetes. 1598 SYLVESTER *Du Bartas* II. ii. *Babylon* 400 That never Vrim, Dream, or Vision sung Their Oracles, but all in Isaak's tongue. 1641 MILTON *Ch. Govt.* I. v, The Priests..had the Oracle of Urim to consult with. 1659 J. HARRINGTON *Lawgiving* II. ii. 38 When God was enquired of by Urim, he gave his Oracle by the shining of certain stones or jewels in the breastplate of the high priest. 1737 WHISTON *Josephus, Antiq.* III. viii. § 9 *note*, The very last instance of any thing like the prophetic Urim among the Jewish nation.

(*b*) 1537 BIBLE (Matthew's) *Exod.* xxviii. 30 Thou shalt put in the brestlappe of iudgement vrim and Thumin. 1560 BIBLE (Genev.) *Deut.* xxxiii. 8 Let thy Thummim and thine Vrim be wᵗ thine holy one. 1595 W. CLERKE *Polimanteia* I 4, Concerning the reuelation done by Vrim and Thummim. 1613 PURCHAS *Pilgrimage* (1614) 198 Lord, doe it for [Aaron] the Priest, with Vrim and Thummim. 1671 MILTON *P. R.* III. 14 Thy Counsel would be as the Oracle Urim and Thummim, those oraculous gems On Aaron's breast. *a* 1763 SHENSTONE *Ess. Men & Mann.* Wks. 1768 II. 229 An illiterate stupid preacher discoursing upon Urim and Thummim, and beating the pulpit cushion. 1768–74 TUCKER *Lt. Nat.* (1834) II. 343 In the course of the Levitical law,..answers by urim and thummim..gradually ceased. 1874 GEO. ELIOT *Coll. Breakf.-P.* 144 An oracular gem in price beyond Urim and Thummim lost to Israel. 1877 C. GEIKIE *Christ* I. 393 'The..prophet', who should bring back the lost Urim and Thummim.

b. *transf.* and *fig.*

1618 BP. HALL *Contempl., N. T.* I. i. How little were the Jews better for this, when they had lost the Urim and Thummim, sincerity of doctrine and manners! *a* 1652 J. SMITH *Sel. Disc.* v. 134 Whenever we look upon our own soul.., we shall find an Urim and Thummim there, by which we may ask counsel of God himself. *a* 1670 HACKET *Abp. Williams* I. (1693) 164 Conscience and Honour, the Urim and Thummim, with which the Noblest..should consult in all things. 1760–72 H. BROOKE *Fool of Qual.* (1792) III. 19 Every mechanic professed, like Aaron, to carry a Urim and Thummim about him. 1825 J. NEAL *Bro. Jonathan* II. 193 He stood and spoke..like one to whom old age is..the sign of wisdom and power—the urim and thumim of survivorship. 1851 KINGSLEY *Yeast* x, The heart..enshrines the priceless pearl of womanhood,..the 'Urim and Thummim', before which gross man can only inquire and adore. *a* 1886 W. B. ROBERTSON *Dream Foolish Virgin* (1898) 17 And stars repeat it.., The Urim and the Thummim on the breastplate of the night.

2. *Mormon Ch.* (See quots.)

1843 H. CASWALL *Proph. of 19th Cent.* v. 77 The mystic Urim and Thummim, which appeared in the form of two transparent stones, set in the rim of a bow, like a pair of spectacles, and fastened to a golden breastplate. 1864 *Chambers's Encycl.* VI. 569/2 Along with the records was found a curious instrument, called by Smith 'Urim and Thummin'... By means of these stone spectacles [etc.].

**U·rinable,** *a. rare*⁻¹. [f. URINE *v.* + -ABLE.] Capable of being excreted in the urine.

*c* 1900 *Buck's Handbk. Med. Sci.* III. 543 (*Cent. Suppl.*).

**Urinæ·mia.** *U.S. Path.* Also -emia. [mod.L.: see URINE *sb.* and cf. URÆMIA.] A morbid condition due to retention in the blood of certain constituents normally eliminated in the urine.

1860 R. FOWLER *Med. Voc.* s.v. 1871 HAMMOND *Dis. Nervous Syst.* 46 Epilepsy, urinæmia, stomachal vertigo.

**Urinal** (yūə·rinăl), *sb.* Forms: 3–7 **vrinal**, 4–6 **-all(e**, 4–5 **vrynal**, 4–6 **-all(e**, 6–7 **urinall** (6 **-alle**, 7 **-ell**), 7– **urinal**; 5 **orinal**, **orynal**; also 3 **vrnal**, 6 **vrnall**. [a. OF. *urinal* (12th c.; also *orinal*, pl. *orignaulx*), a. L. *ūrīnal*, f. *ūrīna* URINE *sb.*[1] Cf. Pr. *urinal*, Pg. *ur-, ourinol*, It. *orinale*, Pr. and Sp. *orinal*.]

† 1. A glass vessel or phial employed to receive urine for medical examination or inspection. *Obs.*

*c* 1275 LAY. 17724 He nam his vrinal [*c* 1205 glæs-fat] anon, an þe king meh þar on; one wile after þan þe vrnal an honde he nam. 13.. *Seuyn Sages* (W.) 1049 The yonge man..taketh an vrinal for to sen. *c* 1386 CHAUCER *Pard. Prol.* 19 Thyne vrynals and thy Iurdones. *c* 1440 *Promp. Parv.* 370/1 Orynal, or vrynal, *urinale.* 1495 *Nottingham Rec.* III. 284, ij vrinalles, price iiij d. 1548 RECORDE *Urin. Physick* iv. 14 b, The Vrinall..shulde be of pure clere glasse, not thyck, nor greene in colour. 1596 NASHE *Saffron Walden* R 3 b, Then shee neuer need to haue her water cast in an vrinall for the greene sicknes. 1642 FULLER *Holy & Prof. St.* II. ii. 53 Reasons drawn from the urine alone are as brittle as the urinall. 1685 BOYLE *Effects of Motion* Suppl. 142 Thin Vessels of Glass, especially Urinals, to be diligently made clean with Sand. 1737 *Phil. Trans.* XLI. 707 The *Capillamenta*, whilst in the Urinal, and till the Urine was decanted. 1757 *Keysler's Trav.* IV. 19 While her maid is stirring a medicine in a spoon, and the physician looking into the urinal. 1858 THUDICHUM *Urine* 19 In some hospitals the ancient urinal is still in use.

*fig.* *c* 1645 HOWELL *Lett.* (1650) II. 2 When I found those letters..which he sends as urinals up and down the world, to look into his water for discovery of the crazie condition of his body. 1663 SIR G. MACKENZIE *Religious Stoic* 19 There ye shall know by the Urinal of his eyes, and the water standing therein, what convulsion-fits his soul suffers.

*transf.* 1688 HOLME *Armoury* III. xiv. (Roxb.) 10/2 He beareth Argent, a vrinall Azure.

† 2. *Alchemy.* (See quot. 1738.) *Obs.*

*c* 1386 CHAUCER *Can. Yeom. T.* 73 Sondry vessels maad of erthe and glas, Oure vrynals and our descensories. 1559 MORWYNG *Evonym.* 1 Men call it a receiver or a urinall. *Ibid.* 212 If ij urinals be set together. 1584 R. SCOT *Discov. Witchcr.* XII. xvii. (1886) 212 Take a glasse viall full of holie water... On the mouth of the viall or urinall, two olive leaves must be laid. 1667 BOYLE *Orig. Forms & Qual.* 298, I took two parcels of Gold,..and having cast each of these in a distinct Urinal,..I caus'd [etc.]. 1738 CHAMBERS *Cycl.*, *Urinal*, in chemistry, is an oblong glass vessel, used for making solutions.

3. A chamber-pot.

*c* 1475 *Cath. Angl.* 405/1 (A.), An Vrynalle, *vrinaria,..vbi* Jordane. 1519 HORMAN *Vulg.* 168 b, Se that I lacke nat by my beddis syde a chayer of easement:..and an vrnall bye. 1542 UDALL *Erasm. Apoph.* 212 b, His groome whose dayly office it was to geve unto hym his urinall in his chaumbre. 1622 MABBE tr. *Aleman's Guzman d'Alf.* I. 232 Not finding any of his Pages there, he..tooke the Vrinall himselfe, which stood at his beds head. 1642 MILTON *Apol. Smect.* 13 Some Politicians..lyable to a night-walking cudgeller, or the emptying of a Urinall. 1695 CONGREVE *Love for L.* II. iii, [To] warm your Bed, and..set the Candle and your Tobacco-Box, and your Urinal by you. 1739 R. BULL tr. *Dedekindus' Grobianus* p. viii, He finds Occasion to inspect the Urinal and the Bed-pan. *a* 1774 GOLDSM. tr. *Scarron's Com. Romance* (1775) I. 35 Pray reach me the chamber-pot, quoth Rancour... The other..took up the urinal, and gave it to Rancour. 1822 GOOD *Study Med.* IV. 540 Forming red sand on the surface, as it probably would otherwise have done in the bladder or the urinal. 1875 H. C. WOOD *Therap.* (1879) 342 The use of chloral to keep free from odor the urinals of paraplegics.

*transf.* *a* 1700 B. E. *Dict. Cant. Crew*, *Urinal of the Planets*, Ireland,..because of its frequent and great Rains.

4. A vessel or reservoir with conductor worn on the person for incontinence of urine.

1855 OGILVIE *Suppl.* 1895 *Arnold & Sons' Catal. Surg. Instrum.* 707 Urinals for Invalids, Travellers, etc. The best quality of Urinals are all made of specially prepared Ætherized India-rubber. 1899 *Allbutt's Syst. Med.* VIII. 244 The wearing of indiarubber urinals, and other means of avoiding 'accidents'.

5. A building, erection, or enclosure for accommodating persons when requiring to pass urine.

1851 J. H. STIRLING in A. H. Stirling *Life* (1912) vi. 106, I had put my back to one of the urinals. 1869 E. A. PARKES *Pract. Hygiene* (ed. 3) 319 Earthen-ware or slate urinals should be used, with water running through them. 1898 G. B. SHAW *Plays* II. *Candida* 29 A vast district..well served with ugly iron urinals.

6. *attrib.* and *Comb.*, as *urinal-glass* (= sense 1), *-like, metal*; † **urinal cherry** (see quot. 1629); † **urinal monger**, † **quack**, † **shaker**, a quack doctor who diagnoses by inspecting the urine.

1611 COTGR., *Vrinaire*, .. vrinall-like. 1629 PARKINSON *Parad.* 572 The Vrinall Cherrie..is long and round, like vnto an Vrinall. 1641 COWLEY *Guardian* II. v, That damn'd Urinal-monger..has not so much physick as would cure the toothach. 1651 FRENCH *Distill.* i. 37 Put upon it another urinall-glasse inverted. *a* 1652 BROME *Queenes Exch.* IV. E 4 b/2 He thinks my skull's made but of urinal mettal. 1663 COWLEY *Cutter Coleman St.* II. viii, *Wor.* He's a kind of Grave-maker, *Cut.* A Urinal Shaker. 1763 J. CLUBBE *Physiognomy* 7 How came this art into reputation?..By the same means that Urinal Quacks and Conjurors have had a run here. 1881 *Instr. Census Clerks* (1885) 99 Urinal Cleaner, Attendant, &c.

**Urinal,** *a.* ? *Obs.* [a. F. *urinal* (16th c.), ad. late L. *ūrīnāl-is*, f. *ūrīna* URINE *sb.*[1]]

1. a. Of or pertaining to, consisting or characteristic of, urine.

1541 R. COPLAND *Guydon's Quest. Chirurg.* I iv, Wherby receyueth the bladder the superfluite vrynal of the kydnees? 1653 URQUHART *Rabelais* I. xxxvi, The pisse of that Urinal flood ran glib away. 1703 T. H. (*title*), Compleat Treatises of Urines, shewing the right Method of Urinal Prognostication. 1743 *Lond. & Country Brew.* IV. (ed. 2) 285 Though it be of an Urinal Taste.

b. Marked by immoderate discharge of urine.

1822 GOOD *Study Med.* IV. 459 Both [kinds of diabetes] were named indifferently diabetes,..urinary diarrhœa, urinal dropsy, and..water-flux.

2. = URINARY *a.* 1.

1615 CROOKE *Body of Man* (1631) 212 The Pipe or Canale of the yarde which in greeke they call *οὐρήθρα*, the vrinal pipe. 1620 VENNER *Via Recta* vii. 154 They..purge the reines, and vrinall passages. *a* 1651 *Recorde's Urin. Physick* To Rdr. A 2 b, The Urine..returneth back again in the veines, to the liver and urinall vessels. 1803 *Med. Jrnl.* X. 512 The effects of..cantharides to the urinal system.

† **U·rinalist.** *Obs.* [f. URINAL *sb.*] A urinologist.

1631 DEKKER *Match me in London* III, I..bid him..To keepe my health from falling, which I felt Tottering.., but my Vrinalist..left no Artery Vnstretcht vpon the Tenters.

**Urina·lysis.** *U.S. Med.* [Irreg. f. L. *ūrīn-a* URINE *sb.*[1] + ANALYSIS.] = URANALYSIS.

1889 *Buck's Handbk. Med. Sci.* VII. 416/1 Processes to be found in large works on urinalysis. 1897 *Columbus* (Ohio) *Dispatch* 18 June 5/2 He..was familiar with the term urinalysis.

**U·rinant,** *a. Her.* [ad. L. *ūrīnant-, ūrīnans*, pres. pple. of *ūrīnārī* to dive.] Borne with the head downward, and the tail erect.

1688 HOLME *Armoury* II. xiv. 327/1 He beareth Gules, a Dolphin reversed, Argent; (or else a Dolphin with the tail erected;) but more properly a Dolphin Urinant. *c* 1828 BERRY *Encycl. Her.* I. Gloss., *Diving*, or *Urinant*, is said of a dolphin or other fish, borne with the head downwards. 1863 BOUTELL *Her. Hist. & Pop.* xi. 67 A fish is..urinant when its head is in base.

**U·rinary,** *sb.* ? *Obs.* [ad. med.L. *ūrīnāri-um*, f. L. *ūrīnāre* to URINE. Cf. F. *urinoir.*] † a. (See first quot.) *Obs.*⁻⁰ b. = URINAL *sb.* 5.

1828–32 WEBSTER, *Urinary, Urinarium*,..a reservoir or place for the reception of urine, &c., for manure. 1836 J. M. GULLY *Magendie's Formul.* (ed. 2) 135 The chloruret of lime may also be..used in the disinfection of water-closets, urinaries,..hospital-wards, &c.

**Urinary** (yūə·rinări), *a.* [ad. med.L. **ūrīnāri-us* (whence It., Sp., Pg. *urinario*, It. *orinario*, F. *urinaire*), f. *ūrīna* URINE *sb.*[1]]

1. Affording passage to, effecting or assisting in the secretion and discharge of, urine.

1578 BANISTER *Hist. Man* v. 83 The begynnyng of the Urinarie passage. 1600 SURFLET *Countrie Farme* II. xxvi. 235 The decoction..casteth out grauell contained in the vrinarie vessels. 1625 HART *Anat. Ur.* II. i. 52 A stoppage of the Liuer, kidneyes, and the vrinarie vessels. 1688 [see 3 a]. 1728 CHAMBERS *Cycl.* s.v. *Bladder*, From whence it takes various Denominations, as Urinary-Bladder, Gall-Bladder, &c. 1732 ARBUTHNOT *Rules of Diet* in *Aliments*, etc. I. 358 Everything which drives the Blood into the Urinary Canals. 1794 G. ADAMS *Nat. & Exp. Philos.* I. xi. 488 The alkaline solution..is apt..to prove irritating to the urinary passages. 1843 *Penny Cycl.* XXVI. 50/1 Indicating..the state of the urinary system. 1864 GARROD *Mat. Med.* (ed. 2) 93 It is desirable to keep uric acid in solution during its transit through the urinary organs. 1877 ROSENTHAL *Muscles & Nerves* (1881) 98 The urinary duct, in which each drop of urine leaving the kidneys produces a wave which propagates itself..to the urinary bladder.

2. Of the nature of urine; excreted as urine.

1646 SIR T. BROWNE *Pseud. Ep.* v. v. 239 Whereby it [*sc.* the bladder] dischargeth the waterish and urinary part of its aliment. 1822 GOOD *Study Med.* IV. 500 The urinary secretion in a state of health is one of the most compound fluids of the animal system. 1872 HUXLEY *Physiol.* v. 105 The urinary fluid flows..into the bladder. 1874 GARROD & BAXTER *Mat. Med.* (ed. 4) 129 Citrate of potash sits easily upon the stomach, and..slightly increases the urinary water.

† b. = URINOUS *a.* 1. *Obs.*⁻¹

1819 *Rees' Cycl.* XXXVII. s.v., Some urinary salts crystallize when precipitated.

**3. a.** Adapted for using on the urinary passage.
1688 HOLME *Armoury* III. xx. (Roxb.) 237/2 The Lapidillum..is a spoon..; with it the stone is taken out of the Urinary passages. Some call it the Urinary Probe.

**b.** Adapted for receiving or containing urine.
1822 GOOD *Study Med.* IV. 494 In incontinence of urine.., the patient will find it very convenient to be provided with a light urinary receptacle.

**4. a.** Lodged or formed in the urinary organs or bladder; excreted in the urine.
*c* 1793 *Encycl. Brit.* (ed. 3) XI. 91/2 Urinary calculi. 1797 WOLLASTON in *Phil. Trans.* LXXXVII. 386 On Gouty and Urinary Concretions. 1808 *Nicholson's Jrnl.* XX. 317 Analysis of a Urinary Calculus. 1845 *Encycl. Metrop.* VII. 580 Of Urinary Deposits. *Ibid.*, Precipitable substances.. which..form urinary sediments. 1857 DUNGLISON *Med. Lex.* 427/2 Diabetic, Urinary, and Hepatic sugar. 1887 A. M. BROWN *Anim. Alkaloids* 65 The urinary alkaloid obtained by Pouchet.

**b.** Of or pertaining to, affecting or occurring in, the urinary system or organs.
1822 [see URINAL *a.* 1 b]. 1828–32 WEBSTER s.v., Urinary abscesses. 1845 G. E. DAY tr. *Simon's Anim. Chem.* I. 59 Laws of much importance in urinary pathology. 1874 VAN BUREN *Dis. Genit. Org.* 1 Its urinary function is purely secondary. 1875 H. C. WOOD *Therap.* (1879) 478 When lessened urinary excretion is purely functional in its origin. 1890 *Lancet* 14 June 1295/1 Urinary fever is believed by some to be neurotic in its origin.

**Urinate** (yūᵊ·rineᶦt), *v.*[1] [f. med.L. *ūrīnāt-*, ppl. stem of *ūrīnāre* to pass water, f. L. *ūrīna* URINE *sb.*[1]]

**1.** *intr.* To discharge urine; to make water; to micturate.
1599 A. M. tr. *Gabelhouer's Bk. Physicke* 170/2 When the Patient vrinateth in the bath. 1831 J. DAVIES *Mat. Med.* 208 Diuretics (διουρεω, I urinate), act upon the general system in the same manner as stimulants. 1845 *Lancet* 25 Jan. 83/2 The patient now urinates very freely. 1879 DUNCAN *Clin. Lect. Dis. Wom.* x. 110 A hysterical woman, when she is under the influence of that condition, urinates frequently.

**2.** *trans.* **a.** To wet or saturate with urine.
1768 [see URINATED *ppl. a.*]. 1885 H. O. FORBES *Nat. Wand. E. Archip.* 116 The adjags first urinate all the grass.

**b.** To pass as or after the manner of urine.
1915 *Evid. before Bryce's Committee German Outrages* 142 During this journey..about 20 of the men..urinated blood.

Hence **U·rinated** *ppl. a.*
1768 [W. DONALDSON] *Life Sir B. Sapskull* II. ix. 74, I was swaddled in my urinated blankets.

**† Urinate,** *v.*[2] *Obs.*⁻⁰ [f. L. *ūrīnāt-*, ppl. stem of *ūrīnārī* (ante-class. *ūrīnāre*).] *intr.* (See quot.)
1623 COCKERAM I [following Cooper], *Vrinate*, to diue or swimme vnder water.

**Urination**[1] (yūᵊrinēⁱ·ʃən). [a. med.L. **ūrīnātiōn-*, **ūrīnātio*, noun of action f. *ūrīnāre* to URINATE. Cf. F. *urination.*] The action of passing water; micturition.
1599 A. M. tr. *Gabelhouer's Bk. Physicke* 176/1 The Milte of a yonge Goate..causeth gentle, and easye vrinatione. 1699 G. HARVEY *Van. Philos. & Physick* xi. 93 Infrequent Urination, or making of Water. 1857 DUNGLISON *Med. Dict.* 948/1 *Urination*, micturition. 1868 T. G. THOMAS *Dis. Women* (1869) 100 If the effusion reaches the urethra, there is obstruction to urination. 1897 *Allbutt's Syst. Med.* III. 545 The patients..complain only of increased thirst and increased urination.

**† Urina·tion**[2]. *Obs.*⁻¹ [f. L. **ūrīnātiōn-*, **ūrīnātio*, noun of action f. *ūrīnārī* URINATE *v.*[2]] The action of diving.
1697 EVELYN *Numism.* viii. 281 Those also who have perfected the way of Diving and Urination.

**† U·rinative,** *a. Obs.*⁻¹ [ad. med.L. type **ūrīnātīv-us* (cf. It. *ur-, orinativo*), f. *ūrīnāre* to URINATE.] Provoking or stimulating urination.
1626 BACON *Sylva* § 43 Medecines Urinative do not work by Rejection and Indigestion, as Solutive do.

**† U·rinator.** *Obs.* [a. L. *ūrīnātor*, agent-noun f. *ūrīnārī* to dive.] One who dives under water; = DIVER 1.
In frequent use from *c* 1655 to *c* 1685.
1648 WILKINS *Math. Magic* II. v. 183 It is observed, that a barrell or cap..will not serve a Urinator or Diver for respiration. 1682 BEALE *Let.* in *Boyle's Wks.* (1772) VI. 446 His majesty's urinator, Mr. Curtis, published in the Gazette, how he had practised. *Ibid.*, Which minds me how easy it were..for our merchants, in all their voyages, to be furnished with such urinators. 1691 RAY *Creation* I. (1692) 73 All those Relations of Urinators belong only to those places where they have dived.

**Urine** (yūᵊ·rin, yūᵊ·rəin), *sb.*[1] Forms: *α.* 4–5 **vryne**, 4–6 **uryne**, 4–7 **vrine**, 4– **urine**; 4–5 **ureyne**, 5 **vreyne**. *β.* 4–6 **vryn**, 4–7 **vrin**, 7 **urin**; 5 **uren**. [a. OF. *urine* (12th c.), ad. L. *ūrīna* (whence It., Pr., Pg. *urina*, Pg. *ourina*, It. and Sp. *orina*, OF. *orine*, Du. *urine*, G., Da., Sw. *urin*), related to Gr. οὖρον.]

**1.** The excrementitious fluid secreted from the blood by the kidneys in man and the higher animals, stored in the bladder, and voided at intervals through the urethra; = WATER *sb.* 18.
Also freq. in *Path.* with qualifying terms, denoting morbid condition.
*α.* *c* 1325 in *Pol. Songs* (Camden) 333 He wole wagge his urine in a vessel of glaz. 13.. *Seuyn Sages* (W.) 1571 In vrine he segh he mighte libbe. *c* 1400 *Lanfranc's Cirurg.* 60 Vreyne of a ȝong man wiþ nitre. 14.. LYDG. *Daunce of Machabree* 417 Maister of Phisike, which on your vryne So looke and gase and stare agaynst the sunne. 1484 CAXTON *Fables of Alfonce* i, Whan the medecyns had sene..his vryne also, they sayd that he had no bodyly sekeness. 1509 HAWES *Past. Pleas.* xvi. (Percy Soc.) 67 A physycyen, truely, can lyttel descerne Ony maner sekenes wythout syght of uryne. 1584 B. R. tr. *Herodotus* I. 34 Mandâne: whom hyr father on a night dreamed to haue let her vryne in..great aboundance. 1601 HOLLAND *Pliny* I. 217 Their urine (after it is made) congealeth into a certain ycie substance. 1662 H. NEWCOME *Diary* (Chetham Soc.) 74 My urine gave mee some alarm, & so yᵉ Dʳ seeinge it [etc.]. 1732 ARBUTHNOT *Rules of Diet* in *Aliments*, etc. I. 248 Cucumbers are useful in bloody Urine. 1787 WINTER *Syst. Husb.* 58 Human and animal urine are composed of water, oil, and salt. 1803 FESSENDEN *Poet. Petition* 10 For bottled urine has, no doubt, In public mails, been frank'd about. 1819 J. G. CHILDREN *Chem. Anal.* 308 The sugar of diabetic urine. 1873 RALFE *Phys. Chem.* 188 Healthy human urine is a clear, transparent, amber-coloured fluid. 1897 *Allbutt's Syst. Med.* II. 1075 If chylous urine is passed into a urine glass. 1897 [see SMOKY *a.* 6].
*β.* *c* 1330 R. BRUNNE *Chron. Wace* (Rolls) 9011 He tasted his pous, saw his vryn. 13.. *Coer de L.* 3030 Rychard bad his men seche For some wys clerk..For to loke hys uryn. *a* 1400–50 *Alexander* 3826 Sum of his awen vryn & sum on Iren lickid. *c* 1440 *Pallad. on Husb.* I. 950 Oil dregges and oxe uren. 1548 VICARY *Anat.* (1888) 76 The more that the bladder is filled with vrin. 1663 BOYLE *Usef. Exp. Nat. Philos.* II. App. 324 Vrin is a Body, which, as homely and despis'd as 'tis wont to be, may [etc.]. 1691 RAY *N. Co. Words* (ed. 2) 52 *Netting*, Chamber-Lee, Urin.

**b.** With *an*, etc., and pl.
1483 *Cath. Angl.* 404/2 An Vryn, *vrina*..; *vbi* pissynge. 1525 R. BANKES *Seynge of Vryns* (title-p.), Here begynneth the seynge of vryns,..with medycynes annexed to euery vryne. 1541 ELYOT *Castel of Helth* IV. ix. 82 The most common iudgement in sicknes is by vrines. 1625 HART *Anat. Ur.* I. iv. 39 The vrines of women with child alter almost euery day. 1656 R. SHORT *Drinking Water* 95 They..that will not vought-safe to look upon an urine. 1707 FLOYER *Physic. Pulse-Watch* 312 Black Vomits, Spits, or black Urines or Stools. 1728 CHAMBERS *Cycl.* s.v., The Author establishes two kinds of Urines. 1840 *Cat. MSS. Brit. Mus.* I. 10/1 Receipts..; with rules for the discerning of urines. 1887 A. M. BROWN *Anim. Alkaloids* 64 The existence of kreatinine in urines.

**† 2.** [Partly f. the vb.] The action of passing urine; urination. *Obs. rare.*
1561 in H. B. Wilson *Hist. Merchant-Taylors' Sch.* (1814) 17 Unto their uryne the schollers shall goe to the places appointed them. 1638 RAWLEY tr. *Bacon's Life & Death* (1650) 54 The quantity of..drink, which a man..receiveth into his body, is..much more than he voideth again..by urine, or by sweating. 1662 R. MATHEW *Unl. Alch.* 43 It drank with White-wine..oft-times at urine sends forth like jags of cloath. *Ibid.* 57 Losing his blood at Urine. *Ibid.* [He] meets with my Pills..and..quite stopt his Urine of Blood.

**3.** *attrib.* and *Comb.*, as *urine analysis*, †*-bladder*, *-cistern*, *drainage*, *expulsor*, *-gutter*, *-monging*, *pigment*, *-provoking*, *-soaked*, etc.; **urine battery** (see quot.); **urine-cart**, one for conveying urine; **urine fever** (see quot.); **urine-glass**, = URINAL *sb.* 1; †**urine-lake**, *poet.* the contents of the bladder; †**urine leader**, †**urine-pipe**, a ureter; †**urine probe** (see quot. and cf. URINARY *a.* 3 a); †**urine-river**, *poet.* urine passing through a ureter; **urine-salts**, salts of urine; **urine sugar**, urinary sugar.
1884 THOMPSON *Tumours of Bladder* 6 The whole subject of *urine analysis. 1884 KNIGHT *Dict. Mech.* Suppl. 916/2 **Urine battery*, (Electricity). The plates are immersed in a trough through which urine flows. 1738 CHAMBERS *Cycl.* s.v. *Bladder*, From whence it takes various denominations, as *urine-bladder, gall-bladder, &c. 1837 *Flemish Husb.* 92 in *Husb.* (L.U.K.) III, The carrots,..by the help of the *urine-cart, soon swell to a good size. *Ibid.* 90 His *urine-cistern is twenty feet square, and seven feet deep. 1888 R. HARRISON in *Lancet* 14 Jan. 57/2 Cases where it was impossible to obtain perfect *urine drainage. 1597 A. M. tr. *Guillemeau's Fr. Chirurg.* 48 b/2 The *urine expulsors, or urine-provoking remedyes. 1888 R. HARRISON in *Lancet* 14 Jan. 57/2 An aguish form of pyrexia, which I shall speak of henceforth as *urine fever. 1880 *Ibid.* 15 May 771/1 *Urine-glasses with glass or vulcanite stop-cocks at the bottom to draw off the sediment have been made. 1844 H. STEPHENS *Bk. Farm* II. 443 Have every particle of filth removed daily from..the *urine-gutters. 1633 P. FLETCHER *Purple Isl.* II. xxv, The *Urine-lake..By little swells, and fills his stretching sides. 1615 H. CROOKE *Body of Man* (1631) 149 The Vreters or *vrine leaders or vessels of Vrine. 1623 HART *Arraignm. Ur.* (title-p.), The manifold errors and abuses of ignorant *Vrine-monging Empirickes. 1625 — *Anat. Ur.* I. ii. 15 The ordinarie sort of vrine-monging Physitians. 1860 P. MUNK in *New Syd. Soc. Year-bk.* 108 On *Urine Pigment. 1863 W. O. MARKHAM tr. *Anal. Urine*, etc. 371 The quantity of urine pigment is considerably increased in all acute febrile diseases. 1594 T. B. *La Primaud. Fr. Acad.* II. 372 Two other passages, called vreteres or *vrine pipes. 1625 HART *Anat. Ur.* II. ix. 107 This suppression is..procured by the obstruction..of the Kidneys and Vrine-pipes. 1688 HOLME *Armoury* III. 429/2 The Catheter, or *Urine probe,..is a long pipe with some few holes at one end. 1597 A. M. tr. *Guillemeau's Fr. Chirurg.* 48 b/2 *Vrine-prouoking remedyes. 1633 P. FLETCHER *Purple Isl.* II. xxiv, Into a lake the *Urine-river falls. 1846 G. E. DAY tr. *Simon's Anim. Chem.* II. 141 If the *urine-salts froth very much upon being treated with an acid. 1876 ROBERTS *Urinary Dis.* 485 Marked symptoms of deranged *urine-secretion. 1908 *Animal Managem.* 77 A dirty, damp, *urine-soaked mass. 1876 *Clin. Soc. Trans.* IX. 37 The *urine sugar still continuing to be very copious. 1837 *Flemish Husb.* 83 in *Husb.* (L.U.K.) III, The whole being swept into the *urine-tank below. 1873 T. H. GREEN *Introd. Pathol.* (ed. 2) 319 The interstitial growth..produces.., in the kidney, compression of the *urine-tubes. 1839 URE *Dict. Arts* 675 The *urine vat is prepared by digestion of the ground indigo in warmed stale urine.

**b. Urine †-caster, -doctor, -inspector, †-monger, †-prophet,** one who diagnoses diseases by inspection of the urine.
1625 HART *Anat. Ur.* I. iv. 38 Who told these *vrine-mongers that the wombe daunced attendance on the bladder? 1654 WHITLOCK *Zootomia* 82 Admirers of Urine-prophets. [Cf. PISS-PROPHET.] 1763 *Brit. Mag.* IV. 116 Tenant, an urine caster. 1815 KIRBY & SP. *Entomol.* iv. (1816) I. 141 The prescription of a famous urine-doctor. 1843 *Penny Cycl.* XXVI. 50/1 In former times, the Uromantes, or Urine-casters, pretended [etc.]. 1863 W. O. MARKHAM tr. *Anal. Urine*, etc. 281 Dozens of specimens of urine were sent daily..to a female urine-inspector.

**† Urine,** *sb.*[2] *Obs. rare.* [Of obscure origin; perh. an error for *grine* GRIN *sb.*[1] 1.] In *Hawking*: (see quots.).
1486 *Bk. St. Albans* a ij b, Who so will take hawkes he must haue nettis wich ben kalled vrines and tho must be made of good small threde. [1621 MARKHAM *Hunger's Prevent.* xii. 150 You shall take a paire of those Nettes which Faulkoners commonly doe call Vrines or Vrnes.]

**Urine** (yūᵊ·rin, yūᵊ·rəin), *v.* ? *Obs.* [f. URINE *sb.*[1], or ad. F. *uriner* (16th c.), ad. med.L. *ūrīnāre* (whence It. *urinare*, *orinare*, Pr. and Pg. *urinar*, Pg. *ourinar*, Sp. *orinar*, OF. *oriner*) to URINATE.]

**1.** *intr.* To pass or make water; to urinate.
In freq. use from *c* 1645 to *c* 1700.
1605 B. JONSON *Volpone* IV. i, By the way, I cheapend sprats: and at Sᵗ Markes, I vrin'd. 1629 MASSINGER *Roman Actor* II. i, This hopefull youth Vrines vpon your monument. 1638 FORD *Fancies* I. ii, I will..urine in thy bason. 1705 *Phil. Trans.* XXV. 2111, I ask'd him..whether he found any ease when he did either Vomit, Sweat or Urined. 1757 *Gentl. Mag.* Aug. 364/2 [He] felt for the first time a difficulty in urining. 1796 'A. PASQUIN' *New Brighton Guide* 18 As to grinning when jobbernowls urin'd upon me, 'Tis false. 1817 JAS. MILL *Brit. India* I. II. iv. 154 When a man spits on another, when he urines on him. 1828 FLEMING *Hist. Brit. Anim.* 11 [The dog] urines sidewise, lifting his hind leg.

**2.** *trans.* To cause to pass *out*, as urine.
1662 R. MATHEW *Unl. Alch.* 44 This man..did drink without measure, but could not urine it out.

Hence **U·rining** *vbl. sb.* Also *attrib.*
1668 WILKINS *Real Char.* 241 Urining,..make water. *Ibid.* Alph. Dict., *Ureter*,..Urining Vein.

**Urini·ferous,** *a. Anat.* [ad. mod.L. *ūrīniferus*: see URINE *sb.*[1] and -(I)FEROUS, and cf. F. *urinifère.*] Conveying urine. Usu. with *duct*, *tubule*, or (most freq.) *tube*.
1744 tr. *Boerhaave's Inst.* III. 151, I therefore concluded ..that the Blood..had dilated the uriniferous Ducts of the Kidneys. 1831 R. KNOX *Cloquet's Anat.* 799 The inner [membrane]..even introduces itself into the uriniferous tubes. 1857 G. BIRD *Urin. Deposits* (ed. 5) 142 A uriniferous tubule. 1880 BRADY *Copepoda* III. 18 The hinder portion of the alimentary canal is perhaps also uriniferous.

**Urini·parous,** *a. Anat.* [f. as prec. + -PAROUS. Cf. F. *urinipare.*] Secreting urine.
1857 DUNGLISON, *Uriniparous*,..an epithet for tubes in the cortical portion of the kidney, which prepare the urine. [Hence in Webster (1864), and later Dicts.]

**Urino-** (yūᵊ·rino), combining form of L. *ūrīn-a* URINE *sb.*[1], occurring in various terms, as **u:rino-ge·nitary**, = URINOGENITAL *a.* 1; **urino·logist**, a urologist; **urino·logy** (see quot. and cf. UROLOGY b); **u·rinomancy**, diagnosis of diseases by examination of the urine; **u:rinopykno·meter** (see quot.); **u:rinosco·pic**, of or pertaining to the inspection of urine as a means of diagnosing diseases (*Cent. Dict.*, 1891); **urino·scopist, -scopy,** = UROSCOPIST, -SCOPY.
1878 F. J. BELL *Gegenbaur's Comp. Anat.* 523 The vascular system, and *urino-genitary organs. 1897 *Columbus* (Ohio) *Dispatch* 18 June 5/2 The doctor was again summoned to.. produce urine in the presence of the *urinologist. 1900 *Nature* 17 May 53/2 The book should be of value to urinologists. 1860 R. FOWLER *Med. Voc.*, **Urinology*, the branch of Medicine which treats of the urine. [Hence in various Dicts.] 1904 G. S. HALL *Adolescence* I. 116 The many centuries when *urinomancy and urinoscopy vied with astrology. 1905 *Brit. Med. Jrnl.* 1 July 27 The *urino pyknometer..is serviceable for making a rough clinical estimate of the specific gravity of small quantities of urine. 1836 R. FURNESS *Astrologer* II. Poet. Wks. (1858) 146 Let some one..Take Thor's first morning water in a phial, And give the *Urinoscopist a trial. *Ibid.* 150 Volumes of *Urinoscopy. 1839 SPILLAN tr. *Schill's Outl. Pathol. Semeiology* 7 With that exception, ignorance and superstition prevailed in this half of the second period. Urinoscopy occupied the place of semeiology. 1904 [see *urinomancy* above].

**U:rinoge·nital,** *a.* [f. prec. + GENITAL *a.*]
**1.** = UROGENITAL *a.*
1836 *Penny Cycl.* VI. 249/1 A specific effect will be exerted on the urino-genital organs. 1879 E. P. WRIGHT *Anim. Life* 12 The urino-genital opening. 1881 F. BALFOUR *Compar. Embryol.* II. 599 The urethra and vagina open independently into the common urinogenital sinus.

**2.** Affecting or occurring in the urogenital organs.
1846 G. FRANKS *Urino-genital Diseases* 45 It is a fruitful source of stricture, impotence, and general deranged state of the urino-genital functions.

**Urino·meter.** [f. as prec. + -METER. Cf. F. *urinomètre.*] An instrument for determining the specific gravity or weight of urine.
Also, in recent Dicts. (1891–), *urinome·tric*, *-o·metry*.
1843 *Penny Cycl.* XXVI. 55/1 [The] Urinometer..is constructed on the principle of a common hydrometer. 1858 THUDICHUM *Urine* 34 Which, when destined to be used for the urine only, should be called urogravimeter, but has been wrongly styled urinometer. 1898 *Allbutt's Syst. Med.* V.

426 A urinometer possessing a somewhat extensive scale of graduations.
*attrib.* 1898 *Allbutt's Syst. Med.* V. 426 Chloroform and benzol are mixed in an ordinary urinometer glass.

† **Urino·se**, *a. Obs.*—[1] [ad. mod.L. *ūrīnōs-us*: see next.] Of the nature of urine.
1692 RAY *Creation* II. 64 In the Kidneys there should be such innumerable..Tubes conveying the Urinose Particles to the Pelvis and Ureters.

**Urinous** (yūə·rinəs), *a.* [ad. mod.L. *ūrīnōs-us* (whence It. and Pg. *urinoso*, It. and Sp. *orinoso*), f. L. *ūrīna* URINE *sb.*[1] Cf. prec., F. *urineux* (1611), and the earlier MERDURINOUS *a.*]

1. Possessing or partaking of the essential properties of urine.
In frequent use from *c* 1670 to *c* 1700.
1644 G. PLATTES in *Hartlib's Legacy* (1655) 217, 1. Nitrous Salt, 2. Urinous Salt, in which are comprehended, 3. all Dungs, Horns, Shreads, and the like. 1663 BOYLE *Usef. Exper. Nat. Philos.* II. 200 What an Acid Menstruum dissolves, an Alcalizate, or an Urinous will precipitate. *Ibid.* 201 Volatile and Urinous Spirits, as Spirits of Urine it self. 1698 W. KING tr. *Sorbière's Journ. Lond.* 33 As Meat rots, it becomes more Urinous and Salt. 1708 J. KEILL *Anim. Secretion* 74 Lime does strongly attract Urinous Salts. 1763 W. LEWIS *Comm. Phil.-Techn.* 95 A mixture of the vitriolic acid with the same urinous spirit. 1819 *Rees' Cycl.* XXXVII. s.v., Urinous Salts are the same with what we otherwise call alkaline salts, or alkalies.

b. Characteristic or suggestive of that of urine.
In frequent use from *c* 1800.
1670 H. STUBBE *Plus Ultra* 135 The former in that mixture lost its urinous smell. 1677 PLOT *Oxfordsh.* 38 A salt of a urinous tast. 1742 *Lond. & Country Brew.* III. (ed. 2) 235 It will certainly give the Beer..an urinous Taste. 1758 *Ann. Reg., Extraord. Adv.* 280/2 A urinous volatile effluvia came from the prison. 1786 *Phil. Trans.* LXXVI. 136 An exceeding sharp urinous smell. 1813 J. THOMSON *Lect. Inflam.* 355 The urinous smell of the perspiration. 1837 WHITTOCK *Bk. Trades* (1842) 179 Soap..would give the liquor a 'urinous' taste. 1863 W. O. MARKHAM tr. *Anal. Urine*, etc. 291 The 'urinous-odour' (as it is called) of patients, depending chiefly upon the presence of this salt.

c. Obtained or derived from urine. *rare*—[1].
1663 BOYLE *Usef. Exp. Nat. Philos.* II. v. vii. 180 By tempering the Urinous extract with a convenient quantity of good Wood Ashes.

2. Of fluids, etc.: Of the nature of urine.
1669 W. SIMPSON *Hydrol. Chym.* 74 Which should separate from the blood an urinous latex. 1728 CHAMBERS *Cycl.* s.v. *Urine*, The serous or urinous Parts [are there] secreted [from the blood]. 1753 N. TORRIANO *Midwifry* 22 Which second Evacuation some have supposed..to have been urinous. 1788 tr. *Swedenborg's Wisd. Angels* § 341 Excrementitious and stercoraceous, rancid and urinous matters. 1847–9 *Todd's Cycl. Anat.* IV. 462/1 A urinous fluid was passed off from the stomach by vomiting. 1860 MAYNE *Expos. Lex.*, *Uridrosis*,..urinous sweat. 1876 W. ROBERTS *Urin. & Renal Dis.* III. viii. (ed. 3) 487 Sometimes the organic urinous matters only exist in traces.

3. Marked by the presence or prevalence of urine.
1788 tr. *Swedenborg's Wisd. Angels* § 341 Wherefore those Hells have their Names from thence, and some are called ..stercoraceous, some urinous, and so on. 1851 S. NOBLE tr. *Swedenborg's Heaven & Hell* § 488 Those who have applied divine truths to promote their own loves,..love urinous substances and places.

Hence **U·rinousness**, 'urinous quality'.
1727 BAILEY (vol. II).

**Uris**, obs. var. OURS.

**Urisk** (ūə·risk). Also ‖ uruisg. [a. Gaelic *ùruisg, uirisg*.] In the Highlands of Scotland: A supernatural being supposed to frequent lonely places; a brownie.
1806 P. GRAHAM *Scenery Perthshire* 19 The Urisks were a sort of lubberly supernaturals, who..could be gained over by kind attentions, to perform the drudgery of the farm. 1853 C. ROGERS *Week at Bridge of Allan* (ed. 3) 330 The Urisks, a species of beings of which the existence was long credited in the upland and secluded districts of Scotland. 1885 *Chamb. Jrnl.* 371 The urisks..acted the part ascribed to the brownies of England.

**Urison, -soun, -sun**, obs. ff. ORISON.

**Uritary**, var. URETARY *Obs.*

† **Urith**, = *vrith*, s. dial. var. FRITH *sb.*[2] 3.
1671 SKINNER, *Urith*, vox in Com. Wilts usitatissima. [Hence in Bailey (1721), etc.]

† **Uritive**, *a. Obs.*—[1] [f. L. *ūr-ĕre* to burn: see -IVE.] Dry, parching.
*a* 1425 tr. *Arderne's Treat. Fistula*, etc. 82 Vertegrese is ful mich penetratife, dissolutiue, pungityue, vrityue, and liquefactyue.

† **Uritory**, variant of URETARY *a. Obs.*
1657 W. COLES *Adam in Eden* cxcix, To wash the Reines and Uritory parts from Gravell or Stones gathered therein.

† **Uriture**, obs. variant of URETER.
1662 R. MATHEW *Unl. Alch.* 4 If the defect be amongst the Uritures, Kidneys, Reins or Bladder.

**Urke**, obs. var. IRK *a.*
1460 *Paston Lett.* Suppl. (1901) 64, I am urke of variaunces.

**Url(e**, obs. ff. EARL. **Urle**, obs. var. ORLE.

† **Urle.** *Obs.*—[1] [Of obscure origin.] A tare.
1659 C. HOOLE tr. *Comenius Visible World* xvii. 37 Pease, Beans, Vetches, and those that are lesse than these, Lentils and Urles (or Tares) [L. *lentes et cicera*].

† **Urle**, *v.*[1] *Obs. rare.* [ad. OF. *ourle-r* (13th c.), or med.L. *url-are*, f. OF. *ourle, urle*: see ORLE.] *trans.* To provide with a border; to border or trim *with* something.
*c* 1330 R. BRUNNE *Chron. Wace* (Rolls) 12463 [Ryton ordered Arthur to] flowe of his owen berd,..For he wolde vrle his pane wyþ-al Aboute wiþ a ffylet smal. *Ibid.* 12472. 1599 THYNNE *Animadv.* (1875) 35 The kinges dalmaticall garmente of the same samitte..vrled or bordrede..withe orfreyes.

**Urle**, *v.*[2] *north. dial.* [See URLING[2].] *intr.* (See quots.)
1683 G. MERITON *Yorksh. Dial.* (1684) 48 What ails our Tibb, that she urles seay ith Neauke? 1684 — *Yorksh. Ale* Gloss. 112 To *Vrle*, is to draw ones self up on a heap. 1781 W. HUTTON *Tour to Caves* (ed. 2) Gloss., *Url*, to look sickly, or to go back in health. 1828 [CARR] *Craven Gloss.*, *Url*, to be pinched with cold.

**Urled**, *ppl. a. north. dial.* [f. prec. + -ED[1].] Stunted in growth; dwarfed, dwarfish, ill-thriven.
1691 RAY *N. Co. Words* 78. *a* 1800 PEGGE *Suppl. Grose* s.v. 1828– in dialect glossaries (n. Cy., Cumbld., Westm., Yks., Lancs.).

† **U·rling**[1]. *Obs.*—[1] [See URLE *v.*[1] and -ING[1]; cf. ORLE.] The border, hem, or edge of a garment.
*a* 1300 *E. E. Psalter* cxxxii. 2 Als þe smerle..Þat doune falles in vrlinge [L. *in ora*] Of him, þat es þe klethinge.

**U·rling**[2], north. dial. variant of WIRLING.
1691 RAY *N. C. Words* 78 An *Urling*, a little dwarfish person. 1807 J. STAGG *Poems* 91 Thou's a menceless urlin ista. 1824– in Yks. dial. glossaries, etc. 1881 SARGISSON *Joe Scoap's Jurneh* 107 He turnt on t'urlin noo at ah still held be t'neck.

**Urn** (ɜ̄ɹn), *sb.* Also 5 vrn (6 *Sc.* wrn), 4–7 vrne, 5 uryn, 7 urne. [ad. L. *urna* (whence It., Sp., Pg. *urna*, F. *urne*), f. *ūrĕre* to burn.]

1. An earthenware or metal vessel or vase of a rounded or ovaloid form and with a circular base, used by various peoples esp. in former times (notably by the Romans and Greeks) to preserve the ashes of the dead. Hence vaguely used (esp. *poet.*) for 'a tomb or sepulchre, the grave'.
In frequent use from *c* 1640.
1374 CHAUCER *Troylus* v. 311 The poudre..prey I þe þow take and it conserue In a vessel, þat men clepeþ an vrne, Of gold. 14.. LYDG. *Bk. Lyfe of our Lady* (Caxton) i. vi b, The pyece..Was by an aungel in an vrne of golde To charlis brought. 1420–2 — *Thebes* III. 4575 Some of hem with vrnes made of gold, whan the asshes fully weren made cold, Tenclosyn hem. 1591 SHAKS. 1 *Hen. VI*, I. vi. 24 When she is dead, Her Ashes, in an Vrne..Transported, shall be at high Festiuals. 1595 — *Hen. V*, I. ii. 228 Lay these bones in an vnworthy Vrne, Tomblesse, with no remembrance ouer them. 1607 DEKKER *Hist. Sir T. Wyatt* A 3, Alasse, how small an Vrne containes a King! 1658 SIR T. BROWNE (*title*), Hydriotaphia, Urne-Buriall, or, a Discourse of the Sepulchrall Urnes lately found in Norfolk. 1685 DRYDEN *Thren. August.* xiii, So, rising from his Fathers Urn, So Glorious did our Charles return. 1702 ECHARD *Eccl. Hist.* III. iv. 376 Ordering his Urn to be brought,..[Severus] said 'Little Urn, thou shalt now contain what the whole World could not before'. 1750 GRAY *Elegy* xi, Can storied urn or animated bust Back to its mansion call the fleeting breath? 1824 BYRON *Juan* XVI. xviii, As you turn Backward and forward.., voices from the urn Appear to wake. 1838 [J. MURRAY] *Econ. Vegetation* iii. 76 The capsule of the poppy ..seems to have been adopted as the pattern of the cinerary urn. 1875 W. EASSIE *Cremation* 16 In both ancient Greece and Rome the dwelling-house was made the repository of the funeral urns. *Ibid.* 123 Urns of gold and silver were not uncommon in ancient times, and are even yet used in Siam.

2. A vessel for holding voting-tablets, lots, or balls, in casting lots, voting, etc. Chiefly *Roman Antiq.*
1513 DOUGLAS *Æneid* VI. i. 46 The deidlie vrne.., Out of the quhilk the lottis warrin draw. *Ibid.* vii. 18 The fatale wrn and ballance. 1601 B. JONSON *Poetaster* v. iii, Come, We of the bench Let's rise to the vrne, and condemne 'hem. 1658 J. HARRINGTON *Oceana* 72 The number of the Ballottants at either Urn. 1703 PRIOR *Ode Memory G. Villiers* 92 When th' Infernal Judges dismal Pow'r From the dark Urn shall throw Thy destin'd Hour. 1720 OZELL *Vertot's Rom. Rep.* II. xii. 235 To draw out of the Urn none but the Names of such Tribes. 1781 J. MOORE *View Soc. Italy* I. xi. 121 Each elector..throws a little billet into an urn...On this billet is inscribed the person's name. 1825 FOSBROKE *Encycl. Antiq.* 201 Urns for the Ballot...These urns were of two kinds. 1838 DE MORGAN *Ess. Probab.* 54 A white ball has been drawn, and from one or other of the two following urns. 1884 tr. *Lotze's Logic* 368 Suppose we put in an urn..3 white balls, in a second urn.. 4 white balls.

† b. *In the urn*, not yet discovered; unknown.
1658 SIR T. BROWNE *Hydriot.* i. 2 That great Antiquity America lay buried for a thousand years, and a large part of the earth is still in the Urne unto us.

c. A ballot-box.
1888 *Times* (weekly ed.) 21 Dec. 6/1 Nearly 75 per cent. of the..voters appeared at the urns. 1892 *Nation* (N.Y.) 8 Dec. 428/1 Since the extension of the suffrage [in Italy], the attendance at the urns has considerably fallen off.

3. A hollow (esp. earthenware) vessel or pot of an oviform or rounded shape, and having a circular base; used for various purposes. Also in fig. context.
*a* 1639 CAREW *Poems* (1651) 8 Vesta is not displeas'd if her chast urn Doe with repayred fuell ever burn. 1648 WILKINS *Math. Magick* II. x. 234 As a rustick was digging the ground ..he found an Urne..in which there was another urne, and in this lesser, a lamp clearly burning. 1656 COWLEY *Mistr.*, *Dialogue* iv, Like Tapers shut in ancient Urns. 1754 GRAY *Progr. Poetry* 109 Bright-eyed Fancy..Scatters from her pictured urn Thoughts, that breathe. 1827 POLLOK *Course T.* VIII. 633 He put A penny in the urn of poverty. 1851 NEALE *Med. Hymns* 102 Here the urn of manna standeth.
*transf.* 1857 HEAVYSEGE *Saul* (1869) 234 [A] song..Falling as faintly and as dewlike down Into the urn of my night-opened ear.
*fig. a* 1854 H. REED *Lect. Brit. Poets* xiv. (1857) II. 171 The steady orb of a planet, its golden urn filled at the fountain of the sun. 1857 EMERSON *Ode sung in Town Hall* 2, O tenderly the haughty day Fills his blue urn with fire. 1860 SANGSTER *Hesperus* 26 Morn on the mountains lights his urn of fire.

b. A sculptured ornament resembling or shaped like a vase, water-pot, or cinerary urn.
1653 in *Verney Mem.* (1907) I. 530 Her statue..set uppon an Urne or Pedestall. 1658 SIR T. BROWNE *Hydriot.* Ep. Ded., Theatrical Vessels, and great Hippodrome Urns in Rome. 1728 CHAMBERS *Cycl.*, *Urn*,..a kind of Vase,..used ..as Ornaments over Chimney-pieces, a-top of Buildings, Funeral Monuments, &c. 1767 JAGO *Edge-hill* I. 472 Nor the lone Hermit's Cell, or mournful Urn Build on the sprightly Lawn. 1842 TENNYSON *Day-Dream* 29 Soft lustre bathes the range of urns On every slanting terrace-lawn. 1849 C. BRONTE *Shirley* xi, The cedar on the lawn,..and the granite urns on the garden wall. 1885 J. B. FLEMING *Let. to Dr. W. G. Blackie* 20 March (MS.), The Draped Urn of Monumental Sculpture. *Ibid.*, Draped or Monumental Urns.

4. An oviform pitcher or vessel for holding water, etc.; a water-pitcher, water-pot.
1613 R. CAWDREY *Table Alph.* (ed. 3), *Vrne*, a pot or pitcher. 1649 OGILBY *Æneis* VII. (1684) 286 There Argus watch'd, lest to her shape she [*sc.* Io] turn, By Inachus pouring from a graven Urn. 1688 HOLME *Armoury* III. 205/2 Temperance hath a Cup in the one hand, and a Bottle Urn in the other, pouring Wine thereout. 1725 POPE *Odyssey* II. 398 But by thy care twelve urns of wine be fill'd. 1747 SPENCE *Polymetis* 172 Aquarius..holds the cup or little urn in his hand, inclined downwards. 1796 H. HUNTER tr. *St.-Pierre's Stud. Nat.* I. 252 Some very ancient medals, in which rivers were represented by figures leaning on an urn. 1821 SHELLEY *Adonais* xi, One from a lucid urn of starry dew Washed his light limbs. 1846 KEBLE *Lyra Innoc.* (ed. 3) 280 The wedding guests are met, The urns are duly set. 1867 MORRIS *Jason* IV. 460 To turn the mill, and carry forth the urn Unto the stream.
*fig.* and *transf.* 1720 POPE *Iliad* XXIV. 663 Two urns by Jove's high throne have ever stood;..From thence the cup of mortal man he fills, Blessings to these, to those distributes ills. 1781 COWPER *Charity* 436 When one, that holds communion with the skies, Has fill'd his urn where these pure waters rise. 1838 LYTTON *Alice* I. iii, Her simplicity of thought was daily filled, from the urns of invisible spirits. *a* 1866 B. TAYLOR *Summer Camp* 13 Shadelike dew Poured from the urns of twilight.

b. The source of a stream, river, etc.; a spring or fountain. Also, the course of a stream.
From the practice of representing river gods or nymphs in sculpture or painting as holding, leaning upon, or pouring water from, an urn.
[1692 PRIOR *Ode Imit. Hor.* x, Where-e'er old Rhine his fruitful Water turns, Or fills his Vassals Tributary Urns.] 1728 YOUNG *Love Fame* VII. 207 From the rich store one fruitful urn supplies, Whole kingdoms smile, a thousand harvests rise. 1767 JAGO *Edge-hill* I. 209 From many a subterraneous Reservoir,..the rocky Urns..their liquid Stores discharge. 1781 COWPER *Retirem.* 76 Ten thousand rivers poured..From urns that never fail. 1810 T. L. PEACOCK *Genius of Thames* 10 The streams roll on, nor e'er return To fill again their parent urn. 1824 LONGF. *Woods in Winter* iv, From their frozen urns, mute springs Pour out the river's gradual tide. 1830 TENNYSON *Ode to Mem.* 61 The brook.. Drawing into his narrow earthen urn..The filter'd tribute of the rough woodland.

c. A bottle or vase for holding tears (freq. with *lachrymal*). Also *transf.*
1753 *Chambers' Cycl.* Suppl. s.v., Another kind of Urns were those which they called *lachrymales*, or the tear-Urns. These were contrived to receive the tears of the friends of the deceased. 1771 MRS. GRIFFITH *History of Lady Barton* III. 46, I opened the little trunk,..which may properly be called the lachrymal urn of the unfortunate Maria. 1837 *Popular Encycl.* VI. 764 Little vessels have occasionally been found in ancient tombs, denominated lachrymal urns.

d. *Astr.* The constellation of Aquarius.
1633 P. FLETCHER *Pisc. Ecl.*, etc. *To W. R.* iv, The sunne, which yet in fishes hasks, Or wat'ry urn, impounds his fainting head. 1697 CREECH *Manilius* II. 65 The Fish oppose the Maid, the watry Urn With adverse Fires sees raging Leo burn. 1770 AKENSIDE *Odes* I. xvi. 1 With sordid floods the wintry Urn Hath stained fair Richmond's level green.

5. Short for *tea-urn*, TEA *sb.* 9 c.
1781 W. HAYLEY *Tri. Temper* IV. 120 No smoke arises from the silver urn, And the blank tea-board..Only supplied the paper of the day. 1784 COWPER *Task* IV. 38 The bubbling and loud-hissing urn. 1834 DICKENS *Sk. Boz, Boarding-ho.* ii, James brought up the urn, and received an unlimited order for dry toast and bacon. 1880 MISS BRADDON *Just as I am* xxi, Miss Blake presided over the urn and teapots.

6. a. *Bot.* The spore-case or capsule of urn-mosses.
1840 *Penny Cycl.* XVI. 9/2 The urn (*sporangium*, or *theca*) in which the spores, or seed-like bodies, are generated. 1858 CARPENTER *Veg. Phys.* § 736 The fructification of Mosses.. consists of a capsule or urn, borne at the top of a long footstalk, which grows out from the centre of a cluster of leaves. 1890 *Nature* 20 Feb. 379 The mosses unfold the delicate lacework of their dainty urns.

b. *Biol.* An urn-shaped process or part.
1877 HUXLEY *Anat. Inv. Anim.* xi. 655 An infusoriform, bilaterally symmetrical embryo, which consists of an urn, a ciliated body, and two refractive bodies. 1883 H. DRUMMOND *Nat. Law in Spir. W.* 370 No power on earth can make these little urns of the *Polycystinæ* except Life.

7. *attrib.* and *Comb.*, as (sense 1) *urn-burial, -field, -graveyard, -niche*; (sense 5) *urn-room, -stand*; (sense 2 c) *urn-system*; *urn-burying, -cornered, -like, -maker, -shaped*, etc.; **urn animalcule, -flower, -moss** (see quots.).
1847 T. R. JONES in *Todd's Cycl. Anat.* IV. I. 11 The Trichodinæ, or *Urn animalcules,..are provided with a fasciculus or circlet of cilia situated in front of their bodies,

which are disc-shaped, bowl-shaped, or conical. 1658 *Urn-burial [see sense 1]. *a* 1796 in *Gentl. Mag.* LXVI. I. 41/1 The latter [*sc.* Danish] people used urn-burial, and burnt their dead. 1836 *Archaeol.* XXVI. 370 Evidence..that urn burial had been disused at length by the Romans. *a* 1682 SIR T. BROWNE *Tracts* (1683) 154 They might be erected..before the term of *Urn-burying or custom of burning the dead expired. 1895 K. GRAHAME *Golden Age* 45 Terrace after terrace of shaven sward, stone-edged, *urn-cornered. 1889 *Soc. Antiquaries, Notice of Meeting* 5 Dec., Celtic Pottery from an ancient British *urn-field. 1891 *Cent. Dict.*, *Urceolina pendula* and *U. latifolia* are border plants from Peru, known in cultivation as *urn-flower*. 1888 R. BROWN *Our Earth & its Story* II. 264/1 A separate kind of burial-place are the *urn-graveyards. *a* 1661 HOLYDAY *Persius* (1673) 295 The hollow womb Of his..*urn-inclosing tomb. 1826 GALT *Last of Lairds* xxxii. 281 A tall *urn-like china-pot. 1830 LINDLEY *Nat. Syst. Bot.* (1836) 407 *Thecæ*, hollow urn-like cases seated upon a seta or stalk. 1881 *Instr. Census Clerks* (1885) 46 Tray Maker. *Urn Maker. 1846 LINDLEY *Veg. Kingd.* 66 *Urnmosses are found in all parts of the world where the atmosphere is humid. 1866 *Treas. Bot.* 1194/2 *Urn-Mosses*,..the *Bryaceæ* or true Mosses. 1848 J. GRANT *Adv. of Aide-de-camp* xii, The dismal aspect of the place—its dark walls and darker *urn-niches. 1901 *Guinness Trust, Fulham P. Rd.* 6 The *urn room..is fitted with a series of copper kettles. 1857 in W. Eassie *Cremation* (1875) 127 Burning the Dead, or *Urn-Sepulture..generally considered. 1796 WITHERING *Brit. Plants* (ed. 3) I. 211 Nectary concave, *urn-shaped. 1875 BENNETT & DYER tr. *Sachs' Bot.* 246 The spermogonia..are urn-shaped receptacles. 1862 *Catal. Internat. Exhib., Brit.* No. 5773, Marble chess-table and *urn-stand. 1901 *Westm. Gaz.* 7 Mar. 6/1 The *urn system existing in the French Chamber. 1839 BAILEY *Festus* 54 An *urn-topped column.

† **Urn**, *v.*[1] *Sc. Obs.* Also 7 uren, 9 ern. [Of obscure origin.]

**1.** *trans.* To cause pain or anguish to (a person); to pain, irritate. Also *absol.*

*c* 1470 HENRY *Wallace* v. 384 So bett I am with strakis sad and sar; The cheyle wattir vrned me mekill mar. 1559 *Reg. St. Andrews Kirk Session* (S.H.S.) I. 18 Give thei be vexed and urnet with ustioun and urgent appetites of the flesche. *a* 1600 MONTGOMERIE *Misc. Poems* xl. 58 Let furious Faits be fearce; Let absence vrne; let Cupids arrou peirce. *a* 1614 J. MELVILL *Autob. & Diary* (Wodrow Soc.) 270 When he died, I mervelit at my awin hart that was so urened and moved with it. 1808 JAMIESON, *To urn the ee*, to pain the eye, as a mote or a grain of sand does. 1825 — *Suppl.* s.v. *Ern*, Nae sae muckle as would ern your ee.

**2.** *intr.* To feel or suffer pain. *rare*⁻¹.

*a* 1600 MONTGOMERIE *Sonn.* xxxvi. 4, I vrne for anger, ȝit I haif no yre.

**Urn** (ɜ̄ɹn), *v.*[2] [f. URN *sb.* Cf. INURN *v.*] *trans.* To deposit (ashes, or bones) in a cinerary urn; to enclose in or as in an urn. Also *transf.*

1612 *Two Noble K.* I. i. 47 He will not suffer us..To urne their ashes. 1651 W. BARKER in Cartwright *Poems* b 7, Their scatter'd Ashes are rak't up and Urn'd. 1744 YOUNG *Nt. Th.* VII. 830 When horror universal shall descend, And heav'n's dark concave urn all human race. 1849 J. WILSON in *Blackw. Mag.* LXVI. 380 Nature has, during a season, cased and urned its torpid and death-like repose. 1855 SINGLETON *Virgil* II. 87 The gathered bones In a bronze casket Corinæus urned.

† **b.** To place in a tomb; to bury. *Obs.*⁻¹

1649 G. DANIEL *Trinarch., Hen. V*, xli, Richard, whose Bones..Slept in a Cottage; Harry doth remove To better lodging; vrnes him, like a King.

**Urn**, obs. f. EARN *v.*; s.w. dial. var. RUN *v.*

**U·rnal**, *a.* ? *Obs.* [f. URN *sb.* + -AL. Cf. L. *urnāl-is* containing an urn (of liquid measure).]

**1.** Of the nature of a cinerary urn; also, sepulchral.

1573 TWYNE *Æneid* XI. H hj b, The Ashes heapes which there confused lay, In urnal pottes they put. 1631 in Habington *Surv. Worcs.* (Worcs. Hist. Soc.) I. 376 Baynham still longes to wayte uppon her to thys nocturnall urnall den.

**2.** Effected in a sepulchral urn.

1658 SIR T. BROWNE *Hydriot.* iii. 48 Urnall enterrments and burnt Reliques lye not in fear of worms. 1761 *Ann. Reg.* II. 154/2 The reduction of the body to ashes, the urnal inclosure of those ashes.

† **Urnal, urnell**, varr. ORNEL *Obs.*

1348 *Acc. Exch. K. R.* 471/1 m. 3 Pro iiij$^{xx}$. xj. pedibus de Asshelere emptis pro predicta posterna;..pro .ij$^{c}$. pedibus de Vrnal emptis pro eodem. 1365 in Brayley & Britton *Hist. Anc. Pal. Westm.* (1836) 187 [5675 feet of stone called] urnell.

**Urnare**, obs. var. RUNNER.

† **Urnary.** *nonce-use.* [f. URN *sb.*: cf. -ERY 2.] The designing or making of urns.

1750 LADY LUXBOROUGH *Let. to Shenstone* 14 Feb., I do not yet know what to say about the inscription to the urn. Mr. Alley is vastly against its being in English...I find it is against rule, if rules there be in *Urnary*.

**Urne**, dial. var. OURN *poss. pron.*

**Urne**, s.w. dial. var. RUN *v.*

**Urned** (ɜ̄ɹnd), *a.* [f. URN *sb.* + -ED[1].]

**1.** Deposited or buried in an urn. Also *fig.*

1631 EARL MANCH. *Al Mondo* 25 Many times..the vrned bones doe meete with foule hands. 1849 CARLYLE in Reid *Life Houghton* (1890) I. 435, I know no more urned books than his. It is like the writing of a ghost.

**2.** Of the nature of, effected in, a cinerary urn.

1909 A. REID *Regality Kirriemuir* i. 3 Urned cists, a crannog, and canoes, are among the recorded 'finds'. 1911 J. WARD *Rom. Era Brit.* viii. 138 Cremation was supplanted by inhumation, but not suddenly, the skeleton followed by an urned interment implying an overlap.

**Urnement**, obs. var. ORNAMENT.

**Urnest**, obs. f. EARNEST *sb.*[1]

**U·rnful.** [-FUL.] The fill of an urn.

1820 *Monthly Rev.* XCIII. 539 Here is another such urnful of posthumous remains. 1864 WEBSTER.

**Uro-**[1] (yūᵊro), combining form of Gr. οὖρο-ν urine, used in many terms of physiological chemistry, etc., which denote esp. (*a*) pigments present in or derived from urine, as *urocy·anin, -cya·nogen, -me·lanin, -phæ·in(e, -pi·ttin(e, -rho·din, -theobro·min(e*; (*b*) a morbid condition of the urine (or urinary organs), as *urocysti·tis, -pla·nia*; (*c*) instruments for investigating the urine, as *urogravi·meter, uro·meter*, = URINOMETER; also used in various adjs., as *uroleu·cic (acid)*; *uropha·nic*, appearing in the urine; *uro·phanous*, passing into the urine; *urose·xual*, urogenital; etc. The more important or earlier examples will be found below, as UROBENZOATE, -CHROME, -GENITAL, etc.

Also (in medical or some recent Dicts.) *urocele, -cyst(ic, -genous, -lith, -lithic, -lithology, -phthisis, -rrhagy, -rrhœa, urosis*, etc. (Cf. F. *urocyanine, -cystite, -mètre, -planie.*)

1820 GOOD *Nosology* 451 *Paruria erratica*..has often been described under the name of uroplania. 1852 *Todd's Cycl. Anat.* IV. II. 1244/1 The urethra, or uro-sexual canal. 1855 W. D. MOORE tr. *Heller's Chem. Urine* 15 Heller's urometer. *Ibid.* 25 Kreatin and kreatinin..occur in the flesh of muscle, and are urophanous. 1858 COPLAND *Dict. Pract. Med.* III. 1196 Chronic uro-cystitis is often..a consequence of stricture of the urethra. 1858 THUDICHUM *Urine* 34 Urogravimeters..made of..glass or metal. *Ibid.* 131 This denomination may be considered as corresponding to Heller's urophæine. *Ibid.* 380 Urophanic Organic Acids. 1868 *Watts' Dict. Chem.* V. 963 Urorhodin,..uromelanin,..uropittin. 1883 C. A. MCMUNN in *Brit. Med. Jrnl.* 1 Dec. 1060/2 The various colouring matters which I have met with in urine..are normal and febrile—urobilin, urohæmatin, urolutein,..urohodin, and others without names. 1888 KIRK in *Brit. Med. Jrnl.* 4 Aug. 233/1 The finest specimens have been of an opaque, almost milk-white, hue; and from this circumstance we would propose to call this body 'uroleucic acid'. 1900 *Lancet* 6 Jan. 36/1 Urotropine..appears to be a compound produced by the action of formaldehyde on ammonia and is known shortly as formin.

**Uro-**[2] (yūᵊro), combining form of Gr. οὐρ-ά tail, occurring in many terms of comparative anatomy, etc. (of which the more important are entered in their places below), designating or relating to a posterior, caudal, or tail-like part, region, segment, or process, as *urogaster, -mere, -pod, -pteran, -some, -somite, -steon, sternite* sbs.; *urochordal, -gastric, -podal, -pyloric, -sacral, -stylar* adjs.

Various other examples are entered in some recent or special Dicts., as *uromeric, -platoid, -somatic, -stegal, -stege, -stegite, -sthene, -sthenic*, etc.

1825 *Encycl. Metrop.* XVII. 595/1 *Decapoda*. The hinder part of the body, which Latreille calls the post-abdomen, or *Urogaster*, but which is usually though erroneously called the tail. [Hence in Mayne, etc.] 1842 BRANDE *Dict. Sci.*, etc. 1278 Uropterans, *Uroptera*,..a family of Amphipodous Crustaceans, including those in which the tail is terminated by enlarged appendages in the shape of fins. 1877 HUXLEY *Anat. Inv. Anim.* vi. 319 A strong calcified urocardiac process. 1884 COUES *N. Amer. Birds* 114 Urosacral or false tail-bones. 1896 CALMAN *Deep-Sea Crustacea* 19 The outer plate of the uropod. 1898 A. S. PACKARD *Text-book of Entomology* 163 We have designated the abdomen, as the urosome; the abdominal segments of insects..as uromeres, and the sternal sclerites as urosternites.

**Urobe·nzoate.** *Chem.* [a. F. *urobenzoate*: see next and -ATE[1] 1 c.] = HIPPURATE.

*c* 1845 MILLER in *Todd's Cycl. Anat.* III. 800/2 Solutions of the urobenzoates furnish a cinnamon brown precipitate. 1860 MAYNE *Expos. Lex.* 1315 *Urobenzoate*,..a combination of urobenzoic acid with a salifiable base.

**Urobenzo·ic**, *a. Chem.* [ad. mod.L. *urobenzoicus*: see URO-[1] and BENZOIC *a.*] *Urobenzoic acid*, hippuric acid.

1836 BRANDE *Chem.* (ed. 4) 1179 The urine of the rhinoceros: ..the clear portion,..on the addition of muriatic acid, deposits urobenzoic acid. 1858 COPLAND *Dict. Pract. Med.* III. 1204 Urobenzoic acid exists chiefly in the urine of herbivorous animals.

**Urobilin** (yūᵊrobəi·lin). *Chem.* Also -ine. [f. URO-[1] + L. *bīl-is* bile: see -IN[1], and cf. F. *urobiline.*] A brownish resinous pigment found in the urine, and occas. in the blood.

1876 tr. *Wagner's Gen. Path.* (ed. 6) 638 The urine of man constantly contains a red pigment—urobilin. 1887 *Brit. Med. Jrnl.* 17 Sept. 645/2 Urobiline exists in the urine either alone, or associated with bilary pigments.

**U:robilinu·ria.** *Path.* [f. prec. + Gr. οὖρ-ον urine: see -IA[1].] A morbid condition characterized by excess of urobilin in the urine.

1887 *Brit. Med. Jrnl.* 17 Sept. 645/2 Urobilinuria is always met with in the period of asystolia, in cardiac diseases. 1897 *Lancet* 27 March 884/1 That trional would give rise to excessive urobilinuria.

**Urochord** (yūᵊ·rŏkǭɹd). *Zool.* [f. URO-[2] + CHORD *sb.*]

**1.** The notochord of ascidians and tunicates, regarded as corresponding to the primordial spinal column in vertebrates.

1877 HUXLEY *Anat. Inv. Anim.* x. 595 The appendage.. may be termed the *urochord*. *Ibid.* 598 A ganglion..passes along one side of the urochord to its extremity. 1880 A. WILSON in *Gentl. Mag.* Jan. 46 Among the sea-squirts, the 'urochord' persists throughout life.

**2.** One of the *Urochorda*, a branch consisting of ascidians or tunicates.

1885 F. J. BELL *Comp. Anat.* 313 Amphioxus has no external skeleton, nor have those Urochords that are tailed throughout life.

**U·rochrome** (-krōᵘm). *Chem.* [f. URO-[1] + Gr. χρῶμα CHROME. Hence F. *urochrome.*] A yellow, amorphous pigment found in the urine.

1864 THUDICHUM in *Brit. Med. Jrnl.* 5 Nov. 513/1, I consider that there is one colouring matter in the urine, to which I appropriate the name of Urochrome. 1900 *Lancet* 10 Nov. 1329/2 To urochrome itself a place must be assigned among the derivatives of hæmoglobin.

‖ **Urochs** (ūᵊ·r-, yūᵊ·rǫks). [G., var. of *auerochs* AUROCHS. Cf. URE-OX.] (See quots.)

1839 *Penny Cycl.* XIV. 54/2 An animal peculiar to Lithuania is the urochs, or bison. 1864 J. HUNT tr. *Vogt's Lect. Man* xii. 335 The bones found belonged to..the now extinct 'urochs' (*Bos primigenius*);..the Lithuanian Bison, or Auerochs (*Bos urus*, or *Bison Europæus*)..is a distinct species. 1881 *Nature* XXIII. 296 Post-tertiary animals (such as mammoth, rhinoceros, urochs).

**Urode·lan**, *sb. Zool.* [f. next + -AN.] = next.

1872 HUMPHRY *Myology* 3 In Urodelans..the movements of the bony pieces are restricted, or nearly so, to one plane. 1879 NICHOLSON *Palæont.* (ed. 2) II. 175 The *Palæosiren* of Geinitz..is from the Lower Permian, and is believed by its discoverer to be a Urodelan.

**Urodele** (yūᵊ·rŏdīl), *sb.* and *a. Zool.* [a. F. *urodèle*, usu. pl. *urodèles* (Duméril), or ad. mod.L. *Urodēla*, neuter pl. of *ūrodēlus, f. Gr. οὐρ-ά URO-[2] + δῆλος evident.]

**A.** *sb.* A member of the order *Urodela* of amphibians, in which the larval tail persists in adult life; a Urodelan.

1842 BRANDE *Dict. Sci.*, etc. 1278 Urodeles, *Urodelæ*,.. that tribe of Caducibranchiate Batracian reptiles which preserve the tail through all stages of their existence. *c* 1850 *Todd's Cycl. Anat.* IV. II. 1254 The amphibious *Urodeles*. 1874 MIVART *Frog* 42 The largest existing Urodele—the gigantic Salamander (*Cryptobranchus*)—is found in Japan.

**B.** *adj.* Belonging to the *Urodela* (see prec.).

1874 MIVART *Common Frog* 49 The world's surface may be divided according to its Urodele population into three legions. 1875 HUXLEY in *Encycl. Brit.* I. 762/1 No urodele amphibian has more than four digits in the manus.

Hence **Urode·lous** *a.*, pertaining to, having the characteristics of, the *Urodela*.

*c* 1844 *Todd's Cycl. Anat.* III. 448/2 The urodelous kinds of Caducibranchiates. 1861 R. E. GRANT *Tabular View Rec. Zool.* 14 Noctilionida...With distinct tail (urodelous). 1881 A. S. PACKARD *Zool.* 479 A step higher in the Urodelous scale is the *Menopoma*.

**Uro,ery·thric**, *a. Chem.* [f. next: see -IC 1 b.] Derived from uroerythrin.

1871 WATTS tr. *Gmelin's Handbk. Chem.* XVIII. 408 Uro-erythric acid [is obtained] by mixing urine with half its volume of hydrochloric acid.

**Uro,ery·thrin.** *Chem.* Also -ine. [f. URO-[1] + ERYTHRIN.] A reddish pigment found in the urine of persons suffering from fevers, esp. rheumatic fever.

1845 G. E. DAY tr. *Simon's Anim. Chem.* I. 216 Uroerythrin, in all probability, owes its origin to the hæmatin of the blood-corpuscles. 1863 W. O. MARKHAM tr. *Anal. Urine*, etc. 49 Uroerythrine is the pigment which gives to sediments of uric acid and urate of soda their brick or rosy red colour. 1889 *Buck's Handbk. Med. Sci.* VII. 416 Its oxidation [*i. e.* of urochrome] gives rise to a red pigment called uroerythrin.

**Uroge·nital**, *a.* (and *sb.*). *Comp. Anat.* [f. URO-[1] + GENITAL *a.* Cf. F. *urogenital* and URINOGENITAL *a.*]

**1.** *adj.* Pertaining or belonging to the urinary and genital products or organs; genito-urinary.

1848 *Quain's Elem. Anat.* II. 1278 Transformation of the uro-genital sinus. 1870 ROLLESTON *Anim. Life* p. xlvii, All Mammalia have a urogenital canal independent..of the termination of the intestine. 1883 E. R. LANKESTER in *Encycl. Brit.* XVI. 693/2 In the *Ostrea edulis* fertilization of the eggs is effected at the moment of their escape from the uro-genital groove.

**2.** *sb.* A urogenital organ. Usu. *pl.*

1891– in various Dicts.

So **Uroge·nitary** *a.*

1883 *Lancet* 19 May 875/2 Co-existent defects of urogenitary organs.

**Uroglaucin** (-glǭ·sin). *Chem.* Also -ine. [a. G. *uroglaucin*: see URO-[1] and -IN[1], and cf. GLAUCOUS *a.*] A blue pigment found in the human urine during certain diseases, as scarlet fever.

1846 G. E. DAY tr. *Simon's Anim. Chem.* II. 523 The existence of a large quantity of uroxanthin in urine is indicated..by the presence of the products of its oxidation, uroglaucin and urrhodin. 1863 W. O. MARKHAM tr. *Anal. Urine*, etc. 45 Uroglaucine presents itself in the form of a blue powder. 1889 *Buck's Handbk. Med. Sci.* VII. 417/1 Uroglaucin (blue) and urrhodin (red) are closely related to indigo blue and indigo red.

**Urohæmatin** (yūᵊrohī·mătin). *Chem.* Also -hematin(e. [f. URO-[1] + HÆMATIN.] A variety of hæmatin forming the colouring matter or pigments of the urine.

1863 W. O. MARKHAM tr. *Anal. Urine*, etc. 43 Dr. Harley calls this body urohæmatine. 1865 *N. Syd. Soc. Year-bk. Med.* 161 An excessive excretion of uro-hæmatin. 1878 KINGZETT *Anim. Chem.* 239 Under the name of Urohæmatine, Proust, Scherer, Harley, Heller, Marcet, constituted the colouring principles of urine.

**Urohyal** (-həi·ăl), *a.* and *sb. Comp. Anat.* [f. URO-[2]: see HY-OID *a.* and -AL 1.] **a.** *adj.* Forming or relating to a median posterior process or part of the hyoid arch in fishes or birds. **b.** *sb.* The bone forming this.

1835-6 Owen in *Todd's Cycl. Anat.* I. 345/1 The superior larynx [in birds]..rests upon the uro-hyal element of the os hyoides. 1848 — *Archetype & Homol. Vertebr. Skel.* 69 In most others [*sc.* fishes] there is..another..bone, which expands vertically as it extends backwards, in the middle line, from the basihyals; this is the 'urohyal'. 1888 Rolleston & Jackson *Anim. Life* 93 A thin median bone, the basi-branchiostegal (= urohyal of Huxley).

**Urology** (yurǫ·lŏdʒi). Also 8 (9) **ourology.** [f. Uro-¹ + -logy. Cf. F. *urologie* (1877) and Urinology.] †**a.** A treatise or discourse on urines. *Obs.* **b.** The scientific study of urine, its secretion and constituents.

1753 *Chambers' Cycl.* Suppl. s.v., The chemists have given us treatises on the analysis of urine, and the preparations of it, such as the phosphorus, &c. under the name of *ourologies.* 1855 Day in *British & For. Medico-Chirurg. Jrnl.* July 71 Contributions to Urology. 1895 *Lancet* 12 Jan. 99/2 Now there are many works on urology.

Hence **Urolo·gical** *a.*, pertaining to or dealing with urology; **Uro·logist,** one versed or skilled in urology.

1855 Day in *Brit. & For. Medico-Chirurg. Jrnl.* July 89 The various causes..are discussed..by Beneke in his Urological Studies. 1889 *Lancet* 15 June 1216/1 Professor Heller..had a high reputation as a urologist. 1913 *Times* 9 Aug. 4/1 The Surgical and Urological Sections [of the Congress of Medicine].

† **U·romancy.** *Obs.* [ad. mod.L. *uromantia*: see Uro-¹ and -mancy, and cf. F. *uromancie*, Sp. *uromancia.*] = Urinomancy.

1569 J. Sanford tr. *Agrippa's Van. Artes* lxxxiii. 145 b, For this cause Scatomancie, Oromancie [*sic*], Drymimancie, be called the diuinations or Prognostications of Phisitians, gathered by ordures and vrines. 1625 Hart *Anat. Ur.* I. v. 47 This Parson being..reputed famous in vromancie. [1721 Bailey. 1823 Crabb.]

† **Uroma·ntical,** *a. Obs.*—¹ [f. mod.L. *uromant-ia* (see prec.) + -ical.] Of or pertaining to urinomancy.

1623 Hart *Arraignm. Ur.* v. 70 A certaine Physitian of no small account and fame for his supposed uromanticall skill.

‖ **Uroma·stix.** *Zool.* [mod.L.: see Uro-² and -mastix.] One or other species of a genus (*Uromastix*) of thorn-tailed, agamoid ground-lizards, native to parts of the Old World and Australia.

In earlier use only as the generic name.

[1681 Grew *Musæum* 46. 1753 *Chambers' Cycl.* Suppl. s.v. *Cordylus.* 1838 *Penny Cycl.* XII. 441. 1840 *Cuvier's Anim. Kingd.* 275.] 1860 Tristram *Gt. Sahara* 406 *Uromastix Spinipes*, Geoff.; the dabb (common uromastyx).

**Uroo** (yūᵊru). *Austr.* Also **yuro.** [Native name (also *euro*, *waroo*).] A species of kangaroo. Also *attrib.*

186. Waterhouse in R. P. Whitworth *Bailliere's S. Austral. Gazetteer* (1866) 165 The uroo kangaroo was occasionally seen in the same localities. 1876 — in Harcus *S. Austral.* 284 *Osphranta crebescens.* Uroo kangaroo. 1885 Mrs. Praed *Head Station* II. 256 Cliffs, with ledges and crannies that afforded foothold only to yuros and rock-wallabies.

**Uropoietic** (yūᵊropoi,e·tik), *a.* Also 8 **-poetic.** [ad. mod.L. *uropoietic-us*: see Uro-¹ and Poietic *a.*, and cf. F. *uropoëtique.*] Concerned with, of or pertaining to, the secretion of urine; secreting or excreting urine.

1783 H. Watson in *Med. Commun.* I. 234 The uropoetic viscera were not..diseased. 1793 T. Beddoes *Calculus* 37 Such an action of the uropoietic organs. 1839-47 *Todd's Cycl. Anat.* III. 366/1 The uropoietic system..communicates with the respiratory cavity. 1877 Huxley *Anat. Inv. Anim.* i. 62 Uropoietic organs..are probably represented by the water-vascular system and segmental organs of the worms.

**Uropygial** (-pi·dʒiăl), *a.* and *sb. Ornith.* [a. F. *uropygial*: see Uropygi-um and -al.]

**1.** *adj.* Situated on, belonging to, the rump or uropygium. Usu. *uropygial gland.*

1870 Rolleston *Anim. Life* 16 The crop and the uropygial gland are peculiar to, though not universally found in Birds. 1884 Coues *N. Amer. Birds* 86 This is a two-lobed..gland, saddled upon the 'pope's nose', at the root of the tail, and hence sometimes called the uropygial or rump gland. 1891 *Cent. Dict.* s.v., Uropygial feathers.

**2.** *sb.* A rump-feather.

1886 Newton in *Encycl. Brit.* XX. 180/2 The middle feathers of the tail, ordinarily concealed..by the uropygials, are black.

‖ **Uropygium** (-pi·dʒiŏm). *Ornith.* [med.L. *ūropygium* (Diefenb.), ad. Gr. οὐροπύγιον. Cf. It. and Pg. *uropigio.*] The rump in birds.

1813 Bingley *Anim. Biog.* (ed. 4) II. 235 The brilliant train of the Peacock..not growing from the *uropygium* (or rump,) but upon the back. 1835-6 Owen in *Todd's Cycl. Anat.* I. 349/1 A gland which is situated above the coccyx or uropygium. 1886 P. L. Sclater *Catal. Birds Brit. Mus.* XI. 17 Cap, uropygium, and upper wing-coverts shining blue.

**Uroscopy** (yurǫ·skŏpi). Also 7 **ouroscopie,** 9 **-scopy.** [ad. mod.L. *uroscopia*: see Uro-¹ and -scopy, and cf. Sp. *uroscopia*, F. *uroscopie.*]

**1.** The scientific examination of urine, esp. as a means of diagnosing diseases; = Urinoscopy.

1646 Sir T. Browne *Pseud. Ep.* To Rdr. A 4, Composed by snatches of time, as medicall vacations and the fruitlesse importunity of Vroscopy would permit us. [1656 Blount. 1658 Phillips.] 1804 *Edin. Rev.* III. 415 Uroscopy has, in some measure, given way to cranioscopy. 1863 W. O. Markham tr. *Anal. Urine*, etc. 281 The progress of Organic Chemistry, and the general study of the microscope, first gave its scientific value to uroscopy. 1888 *Libr. Mag.* (N.Y.) Mar. 252 As a physician he was skilful in dietetics and uroscopy.

†**2.** Divination by inspection of the urine; = Uromancy. *Obs. rare.*

1650 H. Brooke *Conserv. Health* 209 The Vanities and Deceits of Vroscopy, or Devination by Vrin. 1651 Wittie *Primrose's Pop. Err.* To Rdr., Many of them doe by Ouroscopie or Chiromancie undertake to tell Fortunes. 1857 Mayne *Expos. Lex.* 847 *Ouroscopia*,..ouroscopy.

Hence **Urosco·pic** *a.* [F. *uroscopique*], = Urinoscopic *a.* (*Cent. Dict.*, 1891); **U·roscopist,** one skilled or versed in uroscopy.

1889 *Buck's Handbk. Med. Sci.* VII. 403/2 Actuarius, the 'Uroscopist' of the Byzantine court, described in the minutest detail the visible changes of urine in health and in disease.

**Uroste·alith.** *Chem.* [ad. G. *urostealit* (Heller, 1845), f. *uro-* Uro-¹ + Gr. στέαρ fat + *-lit* -lith.] A peculiar fatty substance found in certain urinary calculi.

1846 G. Bird *Urin. Deposits* (ed. 2) 314 The urine, in the only case in which urostealith has been hitherto found. 1858 Thudichum *Urine* 415 Urostealith was found dissolved in the urine.

*attrib.* 1872 Bryant *Pract. Surg.* 523 The uro-stealith, and the siliceous formations. 1883 *Holmes' Syst. Surg.* (ed. 3) III. 250 The uro-stealith calculus is another of the pseudo-forms.

So **Uroste·alite.** [Cf. -lite.]

1854 R. D. Thomson *Cycl. Chem.* 511/2 *Urostealite*, an urinary calculus insoluble in water. 1868 *Watts' Dict. Chem.* V. 968.

**U·rostyle.** *Biol.* [f. Uro-² + Gr. στῦλος pillar.] The posterior unsegmented portion of the vertebral column in certain fishes and amphibians.

1875 Huxley & Martin *Elem. Biol.* 183 The commencement of the canal of the urostyle. *Ibid.* 204-6. 1878 F. J. Bell *Gegenbaur's Comp. Anat.* 433 A long dagger-shaped bony piece..ordinarily known as the urostyle. 1888 Rolleston & Jackson *Anim. Life* 94 The last or terminal caudal vertebra..has the centrum prolonged into the urostyle.

**Uroto·xic,** *a.* [See Uro-¹ and Toxic *a.*] Of or pertaining to the toxicity or toxic materials of the urine.

1890 Billings *Med. Dict.* s.v. 1897 *Allbutt's Syst. Med.* IV. 330 By comparing the amount of urine injected with the weight of the animal he established what he [*sc.* Bouchard] called urotoxic equivalents. 1898 [see next].

**U·rotoxy.** [Cf. prec. The fuller form *urotoxicity* is sometimes used.] The toxic quality or substance of the urine; a unit of urine in respect of its toxicity.

1890 G. M. Gould *Med. Dict.* 452/2 *Urotoxy*, a term invented by Bouchard to denote the standard of toxicity of urine necessary to kill a kilogramme of living substance. 1898 V. C. Vaughan *Ptomains*, etc. 125 The term urotoxy has been employed to designate the relative toxicity of the urine in various conditions. *Ibid.* 127 The urotoxic coefficient is the number of urotoxies which 1 kgm. of man forms in twenty-four hours.

**Urouer, Urour**(e, south. var. Frover *sb. Obs.*

†**U·rous,** *a. Chem. Obs.* [f. Ur-ine *sb.*¹ + -ous c.] *Urous acid, oxide*: (see quots.).

1855 Dunglison *Med. Dict.*, *Urous acid*, uric oxide. 1860 Mayne *Expos. Lex.* 1314 *Uric Oxide*,..otherwise termed urous oxide, and xanthic oxide. 1878 Kingzett *Anim. Chem.* 206 Xanthine..is known in old publications also as uric oxide and urous acid.

**Urous,** var. Eurous *a. Obs.*

**Urox,** anglicized f. Urochs. (Cf. Ure-ox.)

1879 J. Todhunter *Alcestis* 19 Uroxen from the mountains..Lashing their lazy tails. [1879- in various Dicts.]

**Uro·xanate.** *Chem. rare*—¹. [f. Uroxan-ic *a.* + -ate¹ 1 c.] A salt of uroxanic acid.

1868 Watts *Dict. Chem.* V. 969 After several weeks or months, tabular crystals of potassic uroxanate are formed.

**Uroxanic** (yūᵊrǫksæ·nik), *a. Chem.* [f. Uroxan-thin + -ic 1 b.] Of an acid: Obtained by oxidation of uric acid in alkaline solution.

1854 R. D. Thomson *Cycl. Chem.* 512/1 Uroxanic Acid..; obtained by allowing a solution of uric acid in excess of potash to stand, when this acid is deposited along with urate of potash. 1858 *Watts' Dict. Chem.* V. 969 A yellowish hygroscopic substance is left,..having the composition of uroxanic anhydride, $C^5N^4H^8O^5$ (which is also that of dialurate of ammonium). 1884 Roscoe & Schorlemmer *Treat. Chem.* III. II. 297 Uroxanic Acid, $C_5H_8N_4O_6$, is formed when a solution of uric acid in caustic potash is exposed for some months to the action of air free from carbon dioxide.

**Uroxa·nthin** (yūᵊrǫzæ·nþin). *Chem.* Also **-ine.** [a. G. *uroxanthin* (Heller): see Uro-¹ and Xanthin(e. Cf. F. *uroxanthine.*] = Indican.

1846 G. Bird *Urin. Deposits* (ed. 2) 73 Heller has lately given the name of uroxanthin to the reputed pigment, but which he has not succeeded in separating. 1858 Thudichum *Urine* 4 The lemon-yellow colour, sometimes met with in cholera, or in spinal disease, is due to the presence of an excess of uroxanthine. 1889 *Buck's Handbk. Med. Sci.* VII. 416/2 Urine indican (Heller's uroxanthin and the indogen of Thudichum) is not a pigment.

‖**Urraca.** Also **uraca.** [Sp. *urraca* magpie.] (See quots.)

1882 E. W. White in *Proc. Zool. Soc.* 619 *Guira piririgua* (Vieill.)..The native name of this noisy bird is 'Uraca'; and it is found abundantly all over the [Argentine] Republic. *Ibid.*, The Uracas are sometimes tamed and kept in houses to rid them of insects. 1894-5 Lydekker *Roy. Nat. Hist.* III. 321 The urraca jay (*Cyanocorax chrysops*) is a well-known Brazilian species.

**Urre,** var. Irre *sb. Obs.*

**Urrhodin** (yūᵊrǫ·din). *Chem.* Also **-ine.** [ad. G. *urorhodin* (Heller), f. *uro-* Uro-¹ + Gr. ῥόδ-ον the rose + -in¹.] A red colouring matter or pigment found in the urine in certain morbid conditions.

1846 G. E. Day tr. *Simon's Anim. Chem.* II. 522 Uroglaucin and urrhodin occur in diseases..similar in one [character]—the presence of an excess of urea in the blood. 1863 W. O. Markham tr. *Anal. Urine*, etc. 45 In an amorphous state, urrhodine forms rosy-red granules. 1889 [see Uroglaucin].

Hence **Urrhodinic** (-i·nik) *a.*, pertaining to or derived from urrhodin.

1886 R. Kirk in *Brit. Med. Jrnl.* 27 Nov. 1018/2 We would propose to call it, from its source and from its colour, Urrhodinic acid. *Ibid.*, The crystals of urrhodinic acid.

†**Urring tanye,** obs. var. Orange-tawny *sb.*

1575 G. Harvey *Letter-bk.* (Camden) 143 Yᵉ small inamled ring with a ribben of urring tanye.

**Urry.** *dial.* ? *Obs.* [Of obscure origin.] (See quots.)

1669 Worlidge *Syst. Agric.* 24, I have seen much of the blew Clay which they call Urry that's digged out of Coalmines, and lyes neer the Coal, laid on Meadow, and Pasture-lands, to a very considerable advantage. [Hence in *Dict. Rust.*, Kersey, *Fam. Dict.*, etc.] 1712 J. Morton *Nat. Hist. Northampt.* 119 The black Earth call'd Urry.

**Urrysone, Urs,** obs. ff. Orison, Ours.

‖ **Ursa** (ǖ·ısă). [L. *ursa* bear (esp. she-bear), Great Bear constellation. Cf. Urse, and Pr. and Pg. *ursa*, It. *orsa*, Sp. *oso.*]

**1.** *Astr.* = sense 2.

*c* 888 K. Ælfred *Boeth.* xxxix. § 13 Ne se steorra þe we hatað Ursa ne cymð næfre on þam westdæle. *c* 1374 Chaucer *Boeth.* IV. met. vi. (1868) 143 Þe sterre ycleped þe bere...Þe same sterre vrsa. 1791 Cowper *Iliad* XVIII. 606 The might Of huge Orion, with Him Ursa call'd, Known also by his popular name, the Wain, That spins around the pole.

**2.** *Ursa Major*: **a.** *Astr.* The northern constellation also called the Great Bear.

1398 Trevisa *Barth. De P. R.* VIII. xxiii. (Bodl. MS.), Þe taille of þe figure that hatte vrsa maior. 1412-20 Lydg. *Chron. Troy* I. 710 Amongis sterrys..sche is stallyd, And Vrsa Maior is of clerkys callyd. 1553 Eden *Treat. Newe Ind.* (Arb.) 22 Being not farre from *Vrsa maior*, called charles wayne. 1605 Shaks. *Lear* I. ii. 141 My Natiuity was vnder *Vrsa Maior*, so that it followes, I am rough and Leacherous. 1728 Chambers *Cycl.* s.v. *Constellation*, Thus, Hevelius, *v.g.* between Leo and Ursa Major, makes Leo Minor;..under the Tail of Ursa Major, Canes Venatici, &c. 1843 Carlyle *Past & Pr.* III. xi, The huge Winds, that sweep from Ursa Major to the Tropics. 1868 Lockyer *Elem. Astron.* § 341 One of the most striking circumpolar constellations is Ursa Major,..the Plough, or Charles' Wain, as it is otherwise called

**b.** †(*a*) One whose sign or symbol is a bear (see first quot.). *Obs.* (*b*) A person (regarded as) having a very bearish disposition or appearance.

*a* 1635 Naunton *Fragm. Reg.* (Arb.) 31 There were others that steered and stood at the Helm besides himself [Burleigh], and more Starres in the Firmament of her grace [Q. Eliz.] than *Vrsa major*, or the Bear with the ragged staffe. 1773 Boswell *Tour Hebrides* 6 Nov., My father's opinion of Dr. Johnson may be conjectured from the name he afterwards gave him, which was *Ursa Major.* 1788 Burns *Fête Champetre* i, Or him [*sc.* Jas. Boswell] wha led o'er Scotland a' The meikle Ursa-Major. 1893 Crockett *Stickit Min.* 273 Strong, stalwart, unkemp, John Bradford,..Minister of the Queen, strode over the Galloway heather in his rough homespun. 'Ursa Major' they called him in the House.

**3.** *Ursa Minor*, the Little Bear constellation.

[1597 G. Harvey *Trim. Nashe* G 2 b, At last louing like..the two sisters *Vrsa maior* and *Vrsa minor*, wee may bee carried vp to heauen together, and there translated into two starres. 1638 Chilmead *Treat. Globes* iii. (Hakl. Soc.) 50 The first [northern constellation] is called in Latine Ursa Minor,..that is to say, the lesser Beare.] 1728 Chambers *Cycl.* s.v. *Septentrio*, A Northern Constellation, more usually call'd *Ursa minor*, or the little Bear. 1843 *Penny Cycl.* XXVI. 55/1 Ursa major and Ursa Minor..[are] two of the most remarkable constellations of the northern hemisphere. 1868 Lockyer *Elem. Astron.* § 341 The northern celestial pole lies in Ursa Minor.

**U·rsal,** *a.* [f. L. *urs-a* or *urs-us* bear + -al.] Resembling a bear in disposition or characteristic features; hence *fig.*, bearish. (Cf. Ursine *a.* 3.)

1837 *Fraser's Mag.* XVI. 201 The subsequent encouragement of these ursal authorities was generally referable to military commanders. 1840 tr. *Cuvier's Anim. Kingd.* 100 The Otaries [include]..The Ursal..(*Arctocephalus ursinus*..)—Eight feet long, no mane, varying from brown to whitish. 1848 Maunder *Treas. Nat. Hist.* 718/2 *Ursal*, [applied to] a species of Seal,..It is said to be..most pugnacious and ferocious.

† **Urse.** *Sc. Obs. rare.* [ad. L. *urs-a* or *urs-us* bear. Cf. Ursa.]

**1.** *pl.* The Great and Little Bear constellations.

1513 Douglas *Æneid* XIII. Prol. 67, I se the poill, and eik the Ursis brycht. 1536 Bellenden *Cron. Scot.* (1541) A i b, Abone our heid wes the vrsis twane.

**2.** A bear.

1600 Colville *Palinod* (1604) A 5, As the wounded Vrse or wyldegoat seeking his Origane.

**Ur-seluen,** obs. f. Ourselves.

**U·rsicidal,** *a.* [f. L. *ursi*, *ursus* bear: see -cide 2 and -al.] Of or pertaining to the killing of bears.

1857 *Fraser's Mag.* LVI. 146/2 Various ursacidal [*sic*] schemes to be put in practice at Jan Mayen. 1901 *Daily News* 8 March 4/7 It greatly disturbed the mental balance of the brown bear. Ursicidal mania was his complaint.

**U·rsicide.** [f. as prec. + -cide 1.] One who kills a bear.

*a* 1861 T. Winthrop *Life in Open Air* x. (1863) 75 Vain hope! I was not to be an ursicide.

**U·rsiform,** *a.* [f. L. *ursi-* (see URSICIDAL *a.*) + -FORM. Cf. Pg. *ursiforme.*] Having the form or appearance of a bear.

*c* 1793 SHAW *Naturalist's Misc.* III. C c, The Ursine Bradypus, or Ursiform Sloth. 1798 [PENNANT] *View Hindoostan* II. 258 A new and most singular animal, the Ursiform Sloth.

**Ursine** (ɒ·ɹsəin, -in), *a.* [ad. L. *ursīn-us* (whence Sp. and Pg. *ursino*, It. *orsino*, Pr. *orsin*, Fr. *oursin*), f. *ursus* bear.]

**1.** Of or pertaining to, characteristic of, due to, a bear or bears.

*c* 1550 *Clariodus* IV. 1063 Full corpolent he was with breist ursyne,..and sperit leonine. 1656 BLOUNT *Glossogr.*, *Ursine*, ..of or belonging to a Bear. 1841 HOR. SMITH *Moneyed Man* I. x. 290 Quotations from Scripture as to the ursine fate of prophet-mockers. 1851 KINGSLEY *Yeast* xiii, The ursine howls of the new-comer. 1880 HARTING *Brit. Anim. Extinct* I. 14 Portions of ursine skeletons.

**2.** Of the nature of, resembling or having the essential characteristics of, a bear; consisting of bears.

1833–4 J. PHILLIPS *Geol.* in *Encycl. Metrop.* (1845) VI. 695/2 Bones of ursine..animals..are rare. 1859 SALA *Tw. round Clock* 132 Any fierce or ancient member of the ursine tribe. 1870 FREEMAN *Norm. Conq.* (ed. 2) I. App. 768 The bear.. had also, it would seem, known ursine descendants.

**b.** In specific names of animals: (see quots.).

1802 BINGLEY *Anim. Biog.* (1805) I. 64 The *Ursine Baboon. These animals..are found in great numbers among the mountains at the Cape. 1834 PRINGLE *Afr. Sk.* viii. 274 The ursine or dog-faced baboon..is covered with shaggy hair, of a greenish brown colour. *c* 1793 SHAW *Naturalist's Misc.* III. Cc. pl. 58, The *Ursine Bradypus, or Ursiform Sloth. *c* 1842 *Todd's Cycl. Anat.* III. 259/1 *Dasyurus* [*ursinus*]..The *Ursine Dasyure or Devil of the Tasmanian Colonists. 1884 *Imp. Dict.* IV. 530 *Ursine howler, the *Mycetes ursinus.* 1800 SHAW *Gen. Zool.* I. II. 504 *Ursine Opossum. *Didelphis Ursina*...The largest of all the Opossums:..Native of New Holland. 1839 *Penny Cycl.* XIV. 454/2 The Ursine Opossum utters a kind of hollow barking. *c* 1842 *Todd's Cycl. Anat.* III. 262/2 The *Ursine and other Phalangers. 1778 COOK *Voy. Pac. Ocean* IV. v. (1784) II. 377 From the colour and shagginess of the hair,..we judged it might probably be..the large male *ursine seal, or sea-bear. 1802 BINGLEY *Anim. Biog.* (1805) I. 193 The Ursine Seals live in families. Every male is surrounded by a seraglio of from eight to fifty mistresses. 1849 *Sk. Nat. Hist.*, *Mammalia* III. 195 The skin of the ursine seal is very thick. 1800 SHAW *Gen. Zool.* I. I. 159 *Ursine Sloth. *Bradypus Ursinus*... Black Sloth, with very long shaggy hair. 1867 BRANDE & COX *Dict. Sci.*, etc. III. 910/1 The labiated bear, commonly called the ursine sloth.

**3.** Suggestive of that or those of a bear; bear-like. Also *transf.* (cf. BEARISH *a.* 2).

1837 SOUTHEY *Lett.* (1856) IV. 522 Whatever remarkable persons have been noted for ursine manners. 1858 CARLYLE *Fredk. Gt.* IV. v. (1872) I. 307 An ursine man-of-genius. 1899 *Westm. Gaz.* 13 Dec. 11/1 To the joy of all, from the Governor of the Bank of England down to the gambler in mining shares—always excepting the ursine fraternity.

Hence †**U·rsinal** *a. Obs.*—[1]

*a* 1693 *Urquhart's Rabelais* III. xlii. 344 His Dam..put his Members into that..shape which Nature had provided for those of an..Ursinal kind.

**Urson** (ɒ·ɹsən). *Zool.* [a. F. *ourson* (1549), dim. of *ours* m., bear. Cf. It. *ursone*, Pg. *ursão.*] The Canada porcupine, *Erethizon dorsatus.*

1774 GOLDSM. *Nat. Hist.* IV. 114 The urson..is a native of Hudson's Bay...Several of the trading Americans depend on them for food, at some seasons of the year. 1833 *Penny Cycl.* I. 443/2 The urson..is the only species of porcupine..which appears to have the power of climbing trees. 1891 E. ROPER *By Track & Trail* xvii. 253 There are several kinds of grouse,..wolves, ursons.

**Ursone** (ɒ·ɹsoun). *Chem.* [f. L. (*ūva*) *urs-i* (see UVA) + -ONE.] A crystalline principle obtained esp. from the leaves of the bearberry.

1866 WATTS tr. *Gmelin's Handbk. Chem.* XVII. 361 Ursone burns with a yellow smoky flame. 1885 *Buck's Handbk. Med. Sci.* I. 482/1 Ericolin..is an amorphous, yellowish glucoside, yielding with diluted acids sugar, and an essential oil—ursone. 1892 C. E. A. SEMPLE *Mat. Med.* 318 Two crystallisable principles, Ursone ($C_{20}H_{32}O_2$) and Arbutin ($C_{12}H_{16}O_7$).

**Ursuline** (ɒ·ɹsiuləin, -in, -īn), *sb.* and *a.* [f. St. *Ursul-a*, name of a legendary early British virgin-martyr, + -INE.]

**A.** *sb. pl.* A religious order of nuns, established under the rule of St. Augustine in 1572 from a company founded at Brescia in 1537, for the teaching of girls, nursing of the sick, and the sanctification of the lives of its members.

1693 *Emilianne's Hist. Monast. Orders* 248 They are called Urselines, from a holy Virgin called Ursula..who suffered Martyrdom..near Colen. 1701 in *Cath. Rec. Soc. Publ.* VII. 88 We were..afterwards at ye Grand Ursulines. 1797 MRS. RADCLIFFE *Italian* xiii, A convent of Ursulines, remarkable for their hospitality to strangers. 1823 SCOTT *Quentin D.* xxxv, These it is my purpose to dedicate to Heaven in the convent of the Ursulines. 1884 ADDIS & ARNOLD *Cath. Dict.* (1897) 912 The Ursulines do not now increase so rapidly as in former times.

**B.** *adj.* Pertaining or belonging to the Ursulines.

1739 GRAY *Lett.* (1900) I. 17 We went also to the chapels of the Jesuits and Ursuline Nuns. 1804 MARY LAMB *Lines Picture Two Females* 2 The Lady Blanch..To the Urs'line convent hastens. 1815 MILMAN *Fazio* 45 Our convent gates are rude,..Our Ursuline veils of such a jealous woof [etc.]. 1894 T. C. UPHAM *Life Mme. Guyon* i. 2 She was placed at the Ursuline Seminary.

**Urter,** dial. form of HURTER [2] I.

1616 *Vestry Bks.* (Surtees) 72 For thre gudgions and thre vrters and a windband.

**Urth(e,** obs. varr. EARTH *sb.*

‖**Urtica** (ɒ·ɹtikă, ɒɹtəi·kă). [L. *urtīca* nettle (whence It. *ortica*, Sp. *ortiga*, Pg. *urtiga*):—*ūrĕre* to burn.]

†**1.** = SEA-NETTLE. *Obs. rare.*

*a* 1682 SIR T. BROWNE *Norf. Fishes* Wks. 1835 IV. 333 Sea stars in great plenty,..whether they be bred out of the urticas [*printed* urticus], squalders, or sea jellies, as many report, we cannot confirm. 1753 *Chambers' Cycl.* Suppl. s.v., The *Urtica*..is obliged to throw out the shell fish alive again.

**2.** A genus of apetalous plants, typical of the Nat. Order *Urticaceæ*, including the true nettles; also, a plant of this, a stinging-nettle.

The original stressing *urti·ca* (cf. quots. 1764–89) is retained in some modern dictionaries. Ash (1775), however, gives *u·rtica*, and this is usual in Dicts. from 1888–.

1706 PHILLIPS (ed. Kersey), *Urtica*, the Nettle, an Herb so call'd because it raises Blisters. 1764 GRAINGER *Sugar Cane* II. 505 The fring'd urtica spreads her purple form To catch the gale. 1789 E. DARWIN *Bot. Gard.* II. 103 Wide o'er the mad'ning throng Urtica flings Her barbed shafts. 1840 *Penny Cycl.* XVI. 163/1 The Nettle-trees..having leaves resembling those of some kinds of Urtica. 1899 *Allbutt's Syst. Med.* VIII. 489 Certain species of urtica or nettle.

**Urticaceous** (ɒɹtikē^i·ʃəs), *a. Bot.* [f. mod.L. *Urticace-æ* (see prec.) + -OUS.] Belonging to, consisting of, the *Urticaceæ*; resembling that of, having the character of, a nettle.

1836 LINDLEY *Nat. Syst. Bot.* (ed. 2) 175 Batis has a common Urticaceous fruit. 1842 BRANDE *Dict. Sci.*, etc. 1273/1 *Ulmaceæ*..are apetalous Exogens, nearly allied to the Urticaceous order. 1846 LINDLEY *Veg. Kingd.* 261 The old Urticaceous Order.

**Urtical** (ɒ·ɹtikăl, ɒɹtəi·kăl), *a.* and *sb. Bot.* [f. L. *urtic-a* URTICA + -AL.]

**1.** *adj.* Typified by the genus *Urtica* of stinging-nettles; pertaining or belonging to the sting-nettles.

1846 LINDLEY *Veg. Kingd.* 258 The plants of the Urtical Alliance. *Ibid.* 259 Urtical Exogens, with 2-lobed anthers splitting vertically.

**2.** *sb.* An exogenous plant belonging to the genus *Urtica.*

1846 LINDLEY *Veg. Kingd.* 258 Natural Orders of Urticals. *Ibid.* 273 Euphorbials may be regarded then as a higher form of Urticals.

**U·rticant,** *a.* [a. med.L. *urtīcant-*, ppl. stem of *urtīcāre* to URTICATE. Cf. F. *urticant.*] Adapted for stinging; producing an itching sensation.

1870 J. H. BENNET *Winter Medit.* (ed. 4) I. vi. 151 A crowd of polyps armed with urticant filaments.

‖**Urticaria** (ɒɹtikē^ə·riă). *Path.* [mod.L., f. L. *urtīca* URTICA.] = NETTLE-RASH.

1771 *Encycl. Brit.* III. 59/1 *Exanthemata*, or eruptive fevers; comprehending..7. Scarlatina; 8. Urticaria. 1800 *Med. Jrnl.* IV. 201 Diseases admitted under the Care of the Physicians..[included] Urticaria, 1 [case]. 1842 T. H. BURGESS *Man. Dis. Skin* 52 Urticaria is one of the few cutaneous eruptions which can be traced distinctly to its source. 1880 *Lancet* 4 Sept. 406/1 The urine shortly becomes scanty and of a deep orange tint, and the urticaria then appears. 1899 *Allbutt's Syst. Med.* VIII. 484 The name urticaria was applied to this affection because a process of wheal-formation..is often a conspicuous clinical feature.

*attrib.* and *Comb.* 1881 *Lancet* 18 June 990/2 Evanescent urticaria wheals and tubercles. 1899 *Allbutt's Syst. Med.* VIII. 609 Every prurigo papule has an urticaria-like basis.

**Urtica·rial,** *a. Path.* [f. prec. + -AL.] Of or pertaining to, appearing in, or characteristic of urticaria. Also *Comb.*

1883 *Lancet* 16 June 1044/2 The lesion is of an urticarial nature. 1886 *Ibid.* 22 May 968 An urticarial rash. *Ibid.*, Urticarial asthma. 1899 *Allbutt's Syst. Med.* VIII. 559 Even urticarial-like rashes may appear.

**Urtica·rious,** *a. Path.* [f. as prec. + -OUS.]

**1.** Appearing in, characteristic of, urticaria.

1849–52 *Todd's Cycl. Anat.* IV. 1154/2 An individual, licking an urticarious eruption. 1897 *Allbutt's Syst. Med.* III. 50 The erythemas occur chiefly in children, in marginate, papular, or urticarious forms.

**2.** Resembling, or showing the symptoms of, urticaria.

1899 *Hutchinson's Arch. Surg.* X. 176 A peculiar form of persistent Urticarious Dermatitis.

**Urticate** (ɒ·ɹtikē^i t), *v.* [a. med.L. *urtīcāt-*, ppl. stem of *urtīcāre* (Dief.), f. L. *urtīca* URTICA.]

**1.** *intr.* To sting, as or like a nettle; to affect with a tingling pain or stinging sensation.

1843 [see URTICATING *ppl. a.*]. 1855 OWEN *Lect. Compar. Anat.* (ed. 2) ix. 167 An oval capsule from which a stiff bristle-like spine protrudes: these do not urticate. 1882 SALA *Amer. Revis.* I. xix. 271 The Brush-fiend..not only urticates, he hurts. 1899 *Allbutt's Syst. Med.* VIII. 469 Various 'rashes'..which may urticate or vesicate.

**2.** *trans.* To flog with fresh stinging-nettles; also *gen.*, to flagellate, whip.

1861 *Illustr. Lond. News* 5 Jan. 10/1 Those who are partial ..to being urticated with laurel rods. 1873 M. COLLINS *Miranda* III. 206 The one at the end of it shall be urticated. ..I mean that..the worst man on the list shall be flogged with sting-nettles.

**b.** To produce urtication in or on (a part of the body, etc.); to affect with a stinging pain.

1862 *Temple Bar Mag.* VI. 335 Do I urticate my back hair with two brushes? 1882 SALA *Amer. Revis.* I. xix. 270 With an ordinary implement made of bristles..he brushes you 'off'; and while he urticates you he utters a low crooning murmur. 1899 *Allbutt's Syst. Med.* VIII. 480 That scratching urticates the lesions is undoubted.

**3.** To irritate *to* indignation, etc.; to goad, nettle.

1873 M. COLLINS *Squire Silchester* II. xvi. 195 Urticated to unwonted indignation, it is thought he swore—slightly.

Hence **U·rticating** *ppl. a.*, causing or producing urtication.

1843 OWEN *Lect. Compar. Anat.* ix. 102 This stinging or urticating property..procured for the 'Radiares Mollasses' of Lamarck the name of Acalephæ. 1855 *Ibid.* (ed. 2) 176 The urticating tentacles. 1861 HULME tr. *Moquin-Tandon* II. IV. i. 235 The ancients employed urticating caterpillars in the formation of Sinapisms. 1877 *Nature* 4 Oct. 475/1 Urticating Organs of Planarian Worms.

**U·rticate,** *a.* [ad. med.L. *urtīcāt-us*: see prec.] Presenting the appearance characteristic of urticaria.

1899 *Allbutt's Syst. Med.* VIII. 469 The macular, urticate, centrifugally enlarging, and figured eruptions so commonly seen after poisoning by tinned food.

**Urtication** (ɒɹtikē^i·ʃən). [a. med.L. *urtīcātiōn-*, *urtīcātio*, n. of action f. *urtīcāre* to URTICATE. Cf. F. *urtication*, It. *orticazione*, Pg. *urtic-*, *urtigação.*]

**1.** The action or function of urticating or stinging like or as a nettle; a stinging operation.

1655 JER. TAYLOR *Unum Necess.* v. § 3. 253 A body may be said to be lustful though it be asleep, or eating, without the sense of actual urtications and violence, by reason of its constitution. 1858 LEWES *Sea-side Stud.* 146 Certain minute organs found in all Polypes, and variously styled 'thread-capsules', 'filiferous capsules', or urticating cells, are organs of urtication or stinging. *Ibid.* 148 Here, then, we have the organ, without any corresponding function; 'urticating cells', but no urtication!

**b.** A burning or pricking sensation suggestive of stinging with nettles.

1859 HUXLEY *Oceanic Hydrozoa* 94 The mucus which produces the well-known urtication of the human skin. 1899 *Allbutt's Syst. Med.* VIII. 483 So that..urtication.. may be excited in them [i. e. elements of a certain eruption] by mechanical irritation or heat.

**2.** The flogging or pricking of a benumbed part or paralytic limb with green nettles, so as to restore sensation, etc.

1837 J. G. MILLINGEN *Curios. Med. Exper.* II. 55 A case of obstinate lethargy was cured..by repeated urtication of the whole body. 1870 J. G. BERTRAM *Flagellation* xxii. 207 Elidœus Paduanus recommends whipping with nettles, or urtication,..for assisting the development of the eruption in exanthematic diseases. 1873 M. COLLINS *Miranda* III. 206 Urtication is the best cure for rheumatism.

**Urtico·se,** *a.* ? *Obs.* [ad. mod.L. *urticōs-us*, f. L. *urtīca* URTICA.]

**1.** 'Full of nettles' (Bailey, 1721).

**2.** *Path.* Marked or characterized by minute red, itching pimples.

1822 GOOD *Study Med.* IV. 553 Most of these remarks apply equally to the urticose variety [of lichenous rash].

‖**Urubu** (ūrubū·). [a. Brazilian (Tupi) *urubú.*] The black vulture *Cathartes foetens* or *atrata*, native to the southern United States and South America.

*a* 1672 WILLUGHBY *Ornith.* (1676) 68 The Brasil Vulture called Urubu. 1753 *Chambers' Cycl.* Suppl. *App.* s.v. *Vultur*, The Brasilian, white-legged vultur, called by some authors *urubu* and *aura.* In size it is equal to the common kite. 1834 MCMURTRIE *Cuvier's Anim. Kingd.* 119 The Urubu or carrion crow of the south. 1870 GILLMORE tr. *Figuier's Reptiles & Birds* 604 In these countries the Urubus perform the whole duty of cleansing the public streets from all kinds of filth and garbage. 1884 F. WHYMPER in *Girl's Own Paper* 28 June 613/1 Note..hard by, the sociable vulture,..the urubu of South America.

‖**Urucu** (ūrukū·). Also 8 uruca, 9 uruku. [a. Brazilian (Tupi) *urucú* anatta. Cf. ROUCOU.] †**a.** Anatta; = ROUCOU 2. *Obs.* **b.** The anatta-tree, *Bixa orellana*; = ROUCOU I.

1613 PURCHAS *Pilgrimage* (1614) 840 The women..are well faced, painted red with Vrucu, which growes in a cod like a beane. 1666 J. DAVIES tr. *Rochefort's Caribby Isles* 43 The Roucou is the same tree which the Brasilians call Urucu. 1681 GREW *Musæum* II. § ii. i. 217 The Fruit of the Urucu. 1753 *Chambers' Cycl.* Suppl., *Orleana*, in the materia medica, the name of the arnotto, or uruca. 1863 BATES *Nat. Amazon* I. 222 The red [tints are made] with the seeds of the Urucú, or anatto plant.

*attrib.* 1894 *Nation* (N.Y.) 14 June 451/3 A red oil made of the uruku-plant.

‖**Urucuri** (ūrukū·ri). [a. Brazilian (Tupi) *urucurí* palm.] The Brazilian palm-tree, *Attalea excelsa* (also *A. funifera*); rarely (collect.), the nuts obtained from this.

1863 BATES *Nat. Amazon* I. 342 The broad-leaved Murumuru and Urucuri, the slender Assai. 1880 C. R. MARKHAM *Peruv. Bark* 457 The milk is subjected to the smoke of the *urucuy* [sic] or nuts of the *Atholea excelsa* palm.

*attrib.* 1863 BATES *Nat. Amazon* II. 168 A quantity of the Urucuri plums. 1866 *Treas. Bot.* 1063/2 Burning the nuts of the Urucuri palms. 1882 BENTLEY *Man. Bot.* (ed. 4) 705 The Coquilla nuts of commerce..are also termed urucuri nuts.

‖**Urus** (yū^ə·rɒs). *Zool.* Pl. ‖uri (uruses). [a. L. *ūrus*, = Gr. οὖρος, OTeut. *ūrus: see AUROCHS. Cf. URE *sb.*3, URE-OX.]

**1.** = AUROCHS, URE-OX.

1601 HOLLAND *Pliny* II. 323 Those Neat or Buffles called Vri and Bisontes. 1688 HOLME *Armoury* II. 130/2 Such as have Horns, and chew the Cud, as..Goat, Elk, Urus, Bison, etc. 1752 J. HILL *Hist. Anim.* 583 The bull, in it's wild state;..Authors have called it..Urus, as if of a different species. 1766– [see AUROCHS]. 1791 SMELLIE tr. *Buffon* VI. 171 The urus, or aurochs, is the same animal with the common bull in its natural and wild state. 1829 SCOTT *Anne of G.* ii, One of those huge horns made out of the spoils of the urus, or wild bull. 1841 *Penny Cycl.* XX. 237/1 The forest of Bialoviza..is the only place where the *urus* is still found. **1888** E. GERARD *Land beyond Forest* II. 176 The ibex and urus have completely died out, the last urus known of in Transylvania having been killed..in 1775.

**2.** Applied to species of fossil or prehistoric oxen.

**1823** BUCKLAND *Reliq. Diluvianæ* 63 The horn of a very large urus..found at a considerable depth in digging away the diluvium. **1869** LUBBOCK *Preh. Times* (ed. 2) vi. 198 The urus, or great fossil ox, is now altogether extinct. **1874** J. GEIKIE *Gt. Ice Age* 405 Associated with this ancient peat-moss are found the bones of the Asiatic elephant,..the urus or great ox.

**Urycan**, obs. f. HURRICANE.

†**Uryn**, obs. var. ARAIN (spider).

*c* **1450** *Mirk's Festial* I. 181 An adyrcope þat somme men callyn an vryn.

**Urysone, Urysoun**, obs. ff. ORISON.

**Us** (*vs*), *pers.* and *refl. pron.* Forms: *α.* 1–2 ús, 3–5 (9 *dial.*) ous, 4–5 ows; 3– us (3 *Orm.*, 7 uss, 4 os, 6 *Sc.* usz), 3–7 vs (5 vsse, 7 vss), 4 vus, 4–6, *Sc.* 7 ws (6 *Sc.* wsz), 9 *north. dial.* uz. *β.* 2–5, 9 *north. dial.* hus (5 huse), 9 *north. dial.* and *Sc.* huz. See also 's 3. [Common Teutonic: OE. *ús*, = OFris. *ûs* (WFris. *ús*, NFris. *üüs*), OS. (MLG.) *ûs* (LG. *ûs*, *üs*), ON. and Icel. *oss* (Norw., Sw., Da. *os*); these forms have lost an *n* which appears in MDu. (and Du.) *ons*, OHG. (MHG. and G.) *uns*, Goth. *uns* (and *unsis*); the stem represents the weak grade of Indo-Eur. **nes*, retained in Skr. *nas*.] The objective case of the pronoun WE, repr. the OE. accusative and dative.

**I.** With reference to two or more persons.

**1. a.** Accusative, as direct object of a verb.

*c* **825** *Vesp. Ps.* xliii. 26 Aris dryhten ȝefultume us & ȝefrea us. *c* **975** *Rushw. Gosp.* Matt. vi. 13 Ne ȝelaet us ȝelaede in costnungae ah ȝelese us of yfle. *c* **1175** *Lamb. Hom.* 53 Þe feder, and þe sune,..iscilde us þer wið. *c* **1205** LAY. 26490 Nimeð heom, slæh heom: Iscend heo us habbeoð. **1297** R. GLOUC. (Rolls) 1886 Vor godes loue bring us of þis wrechede. *a* **1300** *Cursor M.* 12622 Leue sun, qui has þou gloppend hus? *c* **1315** SHOREHAM I. 711 Hys blod he let os drynke. *c* **1330** R. BRUNNE *Chron. Wace* (Rolls) 11785 Auaunce now boþe þy self & ous. *c* **1386** CHAUCER *Prol.* 748 To the soper sette he vs anon And serued vs with vitaille. *c* **1460** *Towneley Myst.* xx. 189 Here is oone of his men That thus vnwynly gars vs wake. **1480** *Cely Papers* (Camden) 43 Jhesu kepe you and huse. **1526** *Pilgr. Perf.* (W. de W. 1531) 6 Vnto the tyme it hath brought vs to our iourneys ende. **1581** CAMPION in R. Simpson *Life* (1907) 435 In condemning us you condemn all your own ancestors. **1632** MILTON *L'Allegro* 117 Towred Cities please us then. **1665** SIR T. HERBERT *Trav.* (1677) 174 The Sultan..ushered us to our lodging. **1712** STEELE *Spect.* No. 374 ¶ 1 If our past Actions reproach us. **1766** GOLDSM. *Vicar* iv, These rufflings..will only make us hated. **1802** WORDSW. *Milton* 7 We are selfish men; Oh! raise us up. **1877** LOWELL *Bankside* 7 The same shadows on the water lean, Outlasting us.

**b.** Dative, as indirect object, = To us.

*α.* *c* **825** *Vesp. Ps.* iv. 6 Hwelc oteaweð us god? *c* **888** K. ÆLFRED *Boeth.* xix. § 1 Behealde he..hu neara þære eorðan stede is, þeah heo us rum þince. *c* **1000** ÆLFRIC *Hom.* II. 124 Us ȝedafenað þæt we Godes swingle..ondrædan. *c* **1055** *Byrhtferth's Handboc* in *Anglia* VIII. 306 Us com nu to mode hu se arwurða abbud [etc.]. *c* **1200** ORMIN Ded. 175 Off all þiss god uss brinngeþþ word. *c* **1205** LAY. 25577 Lauer sæi us þi sweuen. *c* **1275** *Ibid.* 902 Þis vs þincheþ wel idon. **1297** R. GLOUC. (Rolls) 1081 Gret vilte þou askest ous. *a* **1310** in Wright *Lyric P.* xxv. 73 Jesu, my soule bidde y the, Everemore wel us be. **1340–70** *Alex. & Dind.* 447 Þanne is vs grayþed no graue in þe grounde doluen. *c* **1386** CHAUCER *Prol.* 785 Vs thoughte it was noght worth to make it wys. *c* **1386** — *Can. Yeom. Prol. & T.* 393 Vs moste putte oure good in auenture. **1393** LANGL. *P. Pl.* C. I. 175 We myȝte be lordes aloft and lyue as vs luste. *c* **1440** *Pallad. on Husb.* I. 8 Tilynge is vs to write of euery londe. *c* **1450** *Mirk's Festial* I. 1 God..ȝif vs all his blessyng. **1508** DUNBAR *Tua Mariit Wemen* 153 Confese ws the treuth. **1535** COVERDALE 1 *Chron.* xiii. 19 It mighte cost vs oure neckes. **1611** DONNE *Anat. World* 21 Enough is us to praise them. **1659** MRQ. NEWCASTLE in *Nicholas Papers* (Camden) IV. 125 God sende vss a good meetinge att Whit Hall. **1668** MARVELL *Corr.* Wks. (Grosart) II. 258 Lord Bellasis writ the letter..and red us it over. *a* **1700** in *Cath. Rec. Soc. Publ.* VIII. 25 This year the widdow Belt gave us 12 Gennis. **1743** BULKELEY & CUMMINS *Voy. S. Seas* 20 It had almost cost us our Lives. **1819** SHELLEY *Cenci* III. i. 328 Give us clothes, father! Give us better food! **1847** TENNYSON *Princess* IV. 396 Unless you send us back Our son, on the instant, whole.

*β.* *a* **1175** *Cott. Hom.* 223 God hus for-bead þes trowes westm. *a* **1300** *Cursor M.* 114 For to do man knaw hir kyn, Þat hus scli wirschip cum to wyn. *c* **1300** *Havelok* 1217 Wel is hus we sen þe on lyue. *a* **1400–50** *Wars Alexander* 3528 So sall I gete hus ay þe gree. *c* **1460** *Towneley Myst.* iii. 46 Oyle of mercy he hus hight. **1828** CARR *Craven Gloss.* s.v. *Huz*, Shoe gavv huz ten words for yan.

**c.** As object of a prep. (or other governing word or phrase).

*c* **825** *Vesp. Ps.* iv. 7 Ȝetacnad is ofer us leht ondwlitan ðines dryhten. **971** *Blickling Hom.* 115 And æȝhwonon þes middanȝeard flyhþ from us mid mycelre biternesse. *c* **1100** *O. E. Chron.* (MS. D) an. 1052, Betwyx us sylfum to mycclum forwyrde. *a* **1175** *Cott. Hom.* 229 He com to us, þat he wolde for hus deað þrowian. *c* **1205** LAY. 25288 Þu art hæxt ouer us. *a* **1300** *Cursor M.* 4533 Aiþer of hus a drem we sau. *c* **1315** SHOREHAM IV. 124 No longeþ noþyng to ous. **1390** GOWER *Conf.* I. 1 Good is that we also..among ous hiere Do wryte of newe som matiere. **1405** *Lay Folks Mass Bk.*, *Bid. Prayer* ii. 66 At sche pray for hus. *c* **1475** *Golagros & Gaw.* 323, I rede we cast ws betuene, How best is to done. **1508** DUNBAR *Gold. Targe* 197 The batail broucht on bordour hard vs by. **1584** ALLEN in *Cath. Rec. Soc. Publ.* V. 116 The whole worlde did runne from Christe ..after Edwarde the vj[th] with us into Zwynglianisme. **1659** *Nicholas Papers* (Camden) IV. 95, 3 Spanish men of warre ..came vp with vs and fired at vs. **1712** STEELE *Spect.* No. 374 ¶ 1 So most of us take Occasion to sit still. **1748** RICHARDSON *Clarissa* (1768) I. 173 We have but one mind between us. **1815** SCOTT *Antiq.* xv, He hasna settled his account.. wi' huz for sax months. **1845** J. COULTER *Adv. in Pacific* xiii. 184 Our enemy numbers three times us. **1880** TENNYSON tr. *Battle Brunanburh* v, Fiercely we hack'd at the flyers before us.

**d.** With participles in absolute construction.

**1549** COVERDALE, etc. *Erasm. Par. Acts* 24 b, Vntill he ascended vp (all vs beholdyng hym) to heauen. **1667** MILTON *P. L.* VII. 142 This inaccessible high strength,..us dispossest, He trusted to have seis'd.

**e.** In ethical dative. *Obs.* exc. *arch.*

**1685** TRAVESTIN *Siege Newheusel* 48 They also killed us Captain Feluck. **1711** *Lond. Gaz.* No. 4864/1 They wounded us only one Man.

**2.** Reflexive, = Ourselves. (Also †*us selven*: see SELF A. 3.) †**a.** Accusative, as direct object of a verb. *Obs.*

**971** *Blickl. Hom.* 37 Ȝeþencean we ȝeornlice þæt we us healdan on þas tid, & on ælce, wiþ þa heafodlican leahtras. *c* **1175** *Lamb. Hom.* 69 And halde we us from uniwil. *c* **1200** ORMIN 7542 Ȝiff we wolldenn shunenn azȝ To fillenn uss wiþþ esstess. *a* **1300** *E. E. Psalter* xcix. 3 And he vs made, and our-self noght vs. *c* **1386** CHAUCER *Merch. T.* 597 For we han leue to pleye vs by the lawe. *c* **1430** *Hymns Virgin* (1867) 19 For we may not hide us from þin iȝe. **1526** *Pilgr. Perf.* (1531) 26 We may lerne how to prepare vs towarde our iourney. **1594** KYD *Cornelia* IV. i. 160 Shall we..Submit vs to vnurged slauerie. **1625** PURCHAS *Pilgrims* I. II. 1133 We made vs fast to the stones of them. **1719** DE FOE *Crusoe* II. (Globe) 552 We stopp'd..to refresh us. **1729** LAW *Serious C.* xvi. 289 We must not let this hour pass, without presenting us to him.

†**b.** Dative, as indirect object, or as object of a prep. *Obs.*

*c* **1000** *Ags. Gosp.* Luke iii. 8 We habbað us to fæder abraham. *c* **1175** *Lamb. Hom.* 65 Her is swiþe ufel bone, ȝif we hetieð us bitwene. *c* **1500** *Yng. Children's Bk.* 27 in *Babees Bk.* 19 Fore oure mete, & drynke, & vs, Thanke we owre lord Ihesus. **1596** SHAKS. *Merch. V.* II. iv. 5 We haue not spoke vs yet of Torch-bearers. **1600** — *A. Y. L.* II. i. 21 Come, shall we goe and kill vs venison? **1605** — *Macb.* IV. iii. 214 Let's make vs Med'cines of our great Reuenge.

**c.** After some verbs of motion or posture. Now *arch.* or *dial.*

*c* **1350** *Will. Palerne* 4594 Þus sped we vs out of spayne. **1526** *Pilgr. Perf.* (W. de W. 1531) 72 b, These thynges.. we shall spede vs..to declare. **1587** [see HIE *v.* 3]. **1599** *George a Greene* B 2 b, Let vs hye vs to Wakefield. **1641** [see HIE *v.* 3]. **1781** COWPER *Expost.* 289 The cry..is still the same—Speed us away to battle and to fame. **1892** in *Eng. Dial. Dict.* s.v., We sat us dahn on a wall top.

†**3.** Each other. *Obs. rare.*

**13..** *Guy Warw.* (A.) 4575 Ouer alle oþer we loueden ous. *c* **1400** T. CHESTRE *Launfal* 108 But, syr meyr,..May y take with the sojour? Som tyme we knewe us yore.

**4.** In restricted use with defining term added.

*c* **1400** *Brut* I. lxxx. 81 To maken oppen werr and contak aȝeyns vs of Rome. *a* **1547** SURREY *Æneid* II. 252 Us caitifes then a far more dredful chaunce Befell. **1596** SHAKS. 1 *Hen. IV*, II. ii. 89 Bacon-fed Knaues, they hate vs youth. **1612** R. CH. *Olde Thrift newly revived* 38 The true state and dislike of vs Husband-men and Farmers. **1641** in A. H. Matthew *Convers. Sir T. Matthew* (1904) 176 Concerning the loyalty of us Catholics. *a* **1680** T. GOODWIN *Wks.* (1861) I. 152 None of us creatures had ever come into this after-account. *a* **1718** PRIOR *Epilogue to Phædra* 5 To let Us Moderns know How Women lov'd two thousand years ago. **1814** *Spaniards* II. ii, Thou 'rt..fond to pass The inventions..As real facts upon us simple men. **1825** SCOTT *Talism.* xxv, Thou art ever prompt to pleasure us poor women. *c* **1850** LOWELL *Interview M. Standish* x, They understand us Pilgrims! **1871** JOWETT *Plato* I. 154 None of us unskilled individuals can..become physicians.

**5.** Used as a nominative, in place of WE. Now *dial.*

**1607** DEKKER & WEBSTER *Sir T. Wyat* B j, Come my Lords, shall vs march? **1699** O. HAIG in J. Russell *Haigs* xi. (1881) 339 May us and all our posterity be thankful to Heaven. **1737** DYCHE *Dict.*, *We*, ourselves, us that are present. *a* **1775** *Dick o' the Cow* ii. in Child *Ball.* III. 464 England and us has been long at a feed. **1846–** in general dialect use (*Eng. Dial. Dict.*). **1880** MRS. PARR *Adam & Eve* II. 25 Us'll have down the big Bible and read chapters verse by verse. **1904** [see UP *v.* 4].

**b.** With sb. or adj. numeral in apposition.

*c* **1489** CAXTON *Sonnes of Aymon* ix. 212 None other shall knowe the same, but oonly we, vs thre. **1611** SHAKS. *Cymb.* V. iv. 70 For this..we came, our Parents, and vs twaine. **1663** PEPYS *Diary* 8 June, Mr. Coventry and us two did discourse with the Duke. **1814** MOORE *Mem.* (1853) II. 36 A thing us men ought..to bless God for. **1840** THACKERAY *Barber Cox* May, What enjoyments us aristocracy used to have! **1853** DICKENS *Bleak Ho.* vii, Us London lawyers don't often get an out. **1889** 'R. BOLDREWOOD' *Robbery under Arms* xxxv, Only us five were in possession of the secret.

**c.** In continuative or exclamatory clauses introduced by *and.*

**1848** DICKENS *Dombey* xlvi, And him so rich..And us so poor!

**d.** In the predicate after the verb *to be.*

Common in dialect and colloquial use, and occasionally employed in writing.

**1883** STEVENSON *Treas. Isl.* xxx, It's us must break the treaty when the times come. **1890** W. JAMES *Princ. Psychol.* I. 291 Our bodies themselves, are they simply ours, or are they *us*? **1897** *Westm. Gaz.* 25 Sept. 8/2 That is one of the things we all take for granted—because the Empire is Us.

**6.** The word *us.*

**1748** RICHARDSON *Clarissa* (1768) VII. 18 If by thy *We's* and *Us's* thou meanest thyself or me.

**7.** *Naut.* = Our vessel.

**1622** R. HAWKINS *Voy S. Sea* 66 We had taken the Vice-admirall, the first time shee bourded with vs. **1719** DE FOE *Crusoe* II. (Globe) 519 They crowded after us, and endeavoured to come under our Stern, so as to board us. *c* **1800** in *N. & Q.* 12th Ser. XI. 42 Gen[era]l Bowls..happened to be on board of us, taking his passage..to Jamaica.

**II.** With reference to a single person.

**8.** Used by a sovereign or other potentate or magnate. Cf. WE *pron.* 2 a. Also quasi-*sb.* (quot. 1863).

In older Sc. also used for *we* before the name of a person.

**1258** HENRY III *Proclam.* 4 And we hoaten alle vre treowe in þe treowþe þæt heo vs oȝen. **1425** *Reg. Mag. Sigilli Scot.* 11/1 Be it kend tel al men throwch thir present letteris ws Archibald Erle of Douglas [etc.]. **1436** K. HENRY VI in *Rep. Hist. MSS. Comm.*, *Var. Coll.* IV. 200 That he may wythoute delay certefie Us of the same. **1477** JAS. III in *Excheq. Rolls Scotl.* VIII. 403 *note*, Landis..the quhilkis umquhile Cuthbert Colvile had of ws of before. **1579** Q. ELIZ. in Nicolas *Hatton* (1847) 106 Such Princes as..have sought us in way of marriage. **1585** JAS. VI in *Spalding Club Misc.* I. 3 Send the samen extract attentiklie subscriuit be the shireff clerk to ws. **1601** Q. ELIZ. in Moryson *Itin.* II. (1617) 151 Tell Our Army from Vs, that [etc.]. **1708** *Royal Proclam.* 18 Jan., in *Lond. Gaz.*, They shall be liable to be Imprest, except the Watermen belonging to Us. **1710** in *Nairne Peerage Evidence* (1874) 151 Be it kend to all men by thir present letters Us William lord Nairne..Forasmuch as we considering it [etc.]. **1823** SCOTT *Quentin D.* xxvii, Should our host murder us on this spot—us, his King and his kinsman. **1850** CDL. WISEMAN *Pastoral* 7 Oct., His Holiness was pleased to raise us..to the rank of Cardinal Priest of the Holy Roman Church. **1863** 'OUIDA' *Held in Bondage* i, I did know his family—the royal-sounding 'Us'.

**b.** In editorial or authorial use.

**1835** J. POOLE *Sk. & Recoll.* I. 87 Respecting the subscriptions..to his weekly balls, it is not for *us* to speak. **1895** *Westm. Gaz.* 9 May 2/2 The man chosen to do it was the one public man who is supposed never to read Us.

**9.** *dial.* and *colloq.* Me; to me.

**1828** CARR *Craven Gloss.* s.v., 'Give us some bread,' i.e. give me some bread. **1854–** in dialect use (*Eng. Dial. Dict.*). **1857** HUGHES *Tom Brown* I. iv, Tell us something more about the pea-shooting.

**Us**, obs. f. USE *sb.*

†**-us**, phonetic var. *as*, *es* HIS *pers. pron.*[2] ('them').

*c* **1420** *Chron. Vilod.* 1916 Bot whethen he cometh & houdere he wolle þou shaltus not knawe.

**Usable** (yū·zăb'l), *a.* Also useable. [a. OF. *usable* (1311), f. *user*: see USE *v.* and -ABLE. Cf. It. *usabile*, Pr. *uzable*.] That may or can be used; capable of use.

Somewhat rare *a* 1800 (not in Johnson). Freq. from *c* 1840.

**1382** WYCLIF *Exod.* xxxix. 36 Thei offerden vp..the candelstik, lanterns, and the vsable thingis of it. — *Ps.* cxlviii. 10 Bestis, and alle vsable bestis. *c* **1449** PECOCK *Repr.* II. xviii. 259 Forwhi no vntrewe speche..is alloweable and vsable. *c* **1454** — *Folewer* 26 Þe werk and office..not resonable to be excercible and vseable bi eny of þe wittis bifore seid. **1619** *Time's Storehouse* 756/1 If it be neither vse-able, nor beneficiall. **1666** J. SMITH *Old Age* 82 How much service they [*sc.* the grinders] do to man while usable. **1768–74** TUCKER *Lt. Nat.* (1834) II. 636 Every wood is usable for some good purpose. **1801** *Monthly Mag.* II. 289 There is a difference..between words used and words useable. **1832** COLERIDGE *Lett.* (1895) 761 This tract is a very treasure, and never more usable as a medicine for our clergy. **1848** MILL *Pol. Econ.* I. 53 The books, or other useable or saleable articles. **1893** *Cosmopolitan* XIV. 462/2 The synonym is shorter, more usable.

Hence **Usabi·lity, U·sableness.**

**1842** *Blackw. Mag.* LII. 730 It is not the utility, but the useability of a thing which is in question. **1872** H. W. BEECHER *Pop. Lect. Preaching* iv. 110, I do not know anything that can compare in facility of usableness with phrenology. **1888** *Standard* 26 Jan. 2/4 They had a right to half the 'usability', if he might use the term, of the line.

**Usage** (yū·zėdʒ), *sb.* Forms: 3–7 vsage, 4– usage (5 osage, 6 uzag, yousage, usaige); 6 vsadge, 6–7 usadge (7 usadg, usidge, 9 *dial.* yousetch). [a. AF., OF. *usage* (OF. also *usaige*), = Pr. *uzatge*, Sp. *usage*, It. *usaggio*, med.L. *ūsāticum*, f. L. *ūs-us* USE *sb.*]

**1.** Habitual use, established custom or practice, customary mode of action, on the part of a number of persons; long-continued use or procedure; custom, habit. (= USE *sb.* 7, 9.) In group (*b*), coupled with cognate terms, esp. *custom.*

**13..** *K. Alis.* 1286 (Laud MS.), Comeþ messagers..And asken of Philipp trovage, Of wood, & water, & londe, by vsage. **1387–8** T. USK *Test. Love* III. i. (Skeat) l. 111 Custome is of commen usage by length of tyme used; and custome nat writte is usage. *c* **1440** *Partonope* 332 He brente hys bonus in grette haste, That was the vsage of that contre. **1456** SIR G. HAYE *Law Arms* (S.T.S.) 73 The usage was that thai suld enter in barras. *c* **1530** LD. BERNERS *Arth. Lyt. Bryt.* (1814) 422 According to the vsage y[t] was than in y[t] country. **1581** PETTIE *Guazzo's Civ. Conv.* II. (1586) 65 Yet they are content in speaking to followe the common usage. **1680** PRIDEAUX *Lett.* (Camden) 78 The liberty of printeing by long usage, and..granted by charter till the time of K. Charles y[e] 1[st], whose grant recites the sayd usage. **1697** W. WALSH *Life Vergil* in *Dryden's V.* (1721) I. 44 Every one should serve the Gods after the Usage of his own Country. **1709** PRIOR *Henry & Emma* 67 Usage confirm'd what Fancy had begun. **1768** BLACKSTONE *Comm.* III. 108 Laws..corrected, altered, and amended by acts of parliament and common usage. **1785** PALEY *Mor. Philos.* VI. xii. 642 The greater part [of the rules] have grown insensibly into usage. **1809** COLERIDGE *Friend* 225 Reasoners, who argue for a change in our government from former usage and from Statutes still in force. **1849** MACAULAY *Hist. Eng.* v. I. 573 The custom house officers..had gone on board according to usage. **1888** BRYCE *Amer. Commw.* II. xl. 83

The charter contained a sort of skeleton constitution, which usage had clothed with nerves.

(*b*) *c* 1400 MAUNDEV. (Roxb.) xiii. 58 Thurgh comoun custom and vsage þat þai er wont vnto. *c* 1444 PECOCK *Donet* 176 Þe peple schulen be brouȝt into vsage and custom..forto attende into þe doctryne. *a* 1548 HALL *Chron., Hen. VIII*, 189 Ther awne lawes and constitucions..the spiritualitie sore defended..by prescription and vsage. 1558 in *10th Rep. Hist. MSS. Comm.* App. V. 417 The costome and usadge of the contry beinge evidently knouin. 1728 CHAMBERS *Cycl.* (1738) s.v. *Usance*, The usage and custom of the places whereon they [*sc.* bills of exchange] are drawn. 1759 FRANKLIN *Ess.* Wks. 1840 III. 378 They alleged, usage and custom against reason and justice ought to have but little weight.

† **b.** In predicative use without article. *Obs.*

*c* 1330 *Arth. & Merl.* 727 In þis lond was þo vsage, Who so [etc.]. 13.. *Sir Beues* (A.) 3470 Ase hit was lawe & riȝt vsage. 1390 GOWER *Conf.* II. 386 To bidde..unto thymage Of Venus, as was thanne usage.

† **c.** *By usage*, customarily; usually. *Obs.*

*c* 1374 CHAUCER *Former Age* 4 The fructes..Whiche þat the feldes yaue hem by vsage.

**2.** With *a* and pl.: An established or recognized mode of procedure, action, or conduct; a custom or practice; *spec.* one which has force in law.

1297 R. GLOUC. (Rolls) 3945 Vor hii hulde þe olde vsages, þat men wiþ men were Bi hom sulue & wymmen bi hom sulue. 13.. *E. E. Allit. P.* B. 710 Now haf þay skyfted my skyl & scorned nature, & henttez hem in heþyng an vsage vn-clene. *a* 1400 in *Eng. Gilds* (1870) 349 Þese ben þe olde vsages of þe Cite of Wynchestre. *c* 1450 *Mirk's Festial* I. 241 Wherefor ȝeet yn the lond of Surry ys an vsage þat when þe gospell schall be red, anon yche knyght ..draweth out his sword. 1473 *Rolls of Parlt.* VI. 66/1 Dyvers Privileges, Liberties and free Usages. *a* 1568 GRAFTON *Chron.* II. 330 There was and is an vsage in England in many places, that the noble men..hauing Fraunchises ought to haue seruices of the commons. 1630 *R. Johnson's Kingd. & Commw.* 29 Three other usages have we had in England, which have kept our people in spirit and valour. 1680 [see CUSTOM *sb.* 2]. 1724 S. KNIGHT *Life J. Colet* 60 Colet thought some Usages in the Church were intolerable. 1734 tr. *Rollin's Anc. Hist.* I. Pref. p. xxxi, All I have here related was a receiv'd usage. 1766 BLACKSTONE *Comm.* II. 263 If there be a usage..that all the inhabitants of that parish may dance on a certain close, at all times,..(which is held to be a lawful usage) this is strictly a custom. 1811 *Regul. & Orders Army* 25 Well versed in the Usages and Customs of the Service. 1867 SMYTH *Sailor's Word-bk.* 708 Besides the general laws of merchants, there are certain commercial and seafaring usages which prevail in particular countries with the force of law. Underwriters are bound by usages. 1883 VILLARI *Machiavelli* IV. 117 Recommending every usage of the Romans. 1884 A. R. PENNINGTON *Wiclif* ix. 285 Every ecclesiastical usage should rest on Scriptural grounds.

**b.** *The Usages*, in *Ch. Hist.* (see quot. 1855).

1718 SPINCKES *No Sufficient Reason* 2 The Pleas brought for the Essentiality of the Usages now contended for. 1788 SKINNER *Eccl. Hist.* II. [623 Many of the ejected clergy..wished to revive these ancient usages..in the eucharistic service. *Ibid.*] 633 On the 9th. of July 1724, there was a general meeting of them all at Edinburgh, where, after much communing and reasoning about the Usages, the following stipulations were agreed to. *Ibid.* 634 On the commencement of the dispute about the Usages. 1855 PROCTER *Hist. Bk. Com. Pr.* 145 The ceremonies revived in the new Communion Office were, The mixing of Water with the Wine, Prayer for the Dead, Prayer for the descent of the Holy Spirit on the elements, and the Prayer of Oblation. These were called The Usages, and those who practised them were called Usagers. 1887 ABBEY *Eng. Ch. & Bps.* I. 191 A little before Hickes's death, in 1715, they were hotly at variance among themselves on the subject of the 'usages'.

**c.** *local.* A right-of-way.

1829 T. FAULKNER *Chelsea* (ed. 2) I. 40 Charles Street,.. Crooked Usage,..Chapel Row. 1884 *N. & Q.* 23 Feb. 148/1 Crooked Usage is a narrow lane..[in] Chelsea. 1902 *Academy* 12 July 56/1 The straight strips of ground between the various holdings of land were known as usages.

**3.** The body of rules or principles followed by a particular set of persons, or recognized in a particular craft, occupation, etc. Const. *of.*

*c* 1340 HAMPOLE *Pr. Consc.* 3790 For þe lovyng of God principaly And for usage of haly kyrk. *c* 1386 CHAUCER *Prol.* 110 Of woodecraft wel koude he al the vsage. 1489 CAXTON *Faytes of A.* IV. vii, More ought men to obey therunto, than to the vsage of armes. 1548-9 (Mar.) *Bk. Com. Prayer, Confirm.* Pref., It is agreeable with the vsage of the churche. 1585 T. WASHINGTON tr. *Nicholay's Voy.* III. xv. 99 b, Sonnets, compounded after the vsage of their rime. 1787 J. A. PARK *Law Marine Insur.* 13 Provided the usage of the trade..sanctions it. 1827 JARMAN *Powell's Devises* II. 357 If she had been married to him according to the usage of the church of England. 1878 MACLEAR *Celts* x. 163 Adamnan was won over from the Celtic to the Catholic usage.

**4.** Manner of (ordinarily) bearing or comporting oneself; usual conduct or behaviour.

*a* 1300 *Cursor M.* 28456, I..has hade it in myn vsage, O mete and drinke to do vtrage. *c* 1386 CHAUCER *Clerk's T.* 729 Among al this after his wikke vsage This Markys yet his wyf to tempte moore..haþ [etc.]. *c* 1400 *St. Alexius* (Laud 622) 86 Men þat ȝeden in pilerinage..was his vsage Often forto fede. *c* 1440 *Jacob's Well* 31 Þey hadde leuere fulfyllen here malyce,..þan for to leue þat malyce,..& here fals vsage, for to gon to heuene. 1548 COVERDALE, etc. *Erasm. Par. Rom.* vii. 17 b, My synful vsage was not onely not restrayned, but also seemed quyckened. 1574 WHITGIFT *Def. Aunsw.* i. 71 What opinion they had of their vsage in their offices. 1606 *Arraignem. & Execution of Late Traitors* 3 (Hindley II), The little shew of their sorrow, their usage in prison, and their obstinacy to their end. 1848 DICKENS *Dombey* viii, Mrs. Wickam, agreeably to the usage of some ladies in her condition, pursued..the subject without any compunction.

**b.** A practice or habit on the part of a person or persons.

1303 R. BRUNNE *Handl. Synne* 7669 Comunly, þat men done yn ȝenkþe, Yn age haunte þey hyt on lenkþe; And mowe nat leue þat foule vsage þat þey toke yn ȝouþe. 14.. *Chaucer's Rom. Rose* (Thynne) 293 Enuye..ne loked but awrie Or ouertharte al baggyngly And she had a foule vsage. *c* 1440 *Ipomydon* 1498 To the tayle was turnyd his visage; They bad hym lerne a new vsage. 1523 LD. BERNERS tr. *Froiss.* I. xiv. 14 They put in wrytynge all the dedis of the kyng..and all his vsages, and euyll behauyngis. 1587 A. DAY *Daphnis & Chloe* (1890) 16 Of these [they] found diuers pastimes wherewith to occupie them selues togethers. Their vsages were holie. 1655 JER. TAYLOR *Golden Grove* 88 O let us never..by unworthy usages profane thy holy Name.

† **c.** *Of usage*, as a habit or custom; regularly. *Obs. rare.*

*c* 1381 CHAUCER *Parl. Foules* 15 Of vsage what for lust & what for lore On bokis rede I ofte. 1525 LD. BERNERS *Froiss.* II. cxvi. [cxii.] 333 And of usage his bedde was wont to be chafed with a bason with hote coles.

† **5.** The fact of accustoming or being accustomed to do or employ something. *Obs.*

*c* 1374 CHAUCER *Boeth.* I. pr. i. (1868) 6 Þei holden þe hertes of men in usage, but þei ne delyuere not folk fro maladye. 1456 SIR G. HAYE *Law Arms* (S.T.S.) 84 A knycht is usit in harnes.., the quhilk usage makis him hardy and expert. 1585 T. WASHINGTON tr. *Nicholay's Voy.* IV. xvi. 130 b, They haue also the commoditie & vsage to speake and vnderstand all other sortes of languages.

**6.** The action of using something; the fact of being used; use, employment.

*c* 1374 CHAUCER *Boeth.* IV. pr. vi. (1868) 140 Þe vsage & exercitacioun of pacience. *c* 1385 — *L. G. W.* 2337 *Philomene*, He..kepte hire to his vsage & his store. *c* 1400 *Cato's Morals* 315 in *Cursor M.* App. iv. 1673 If þou haue carlis boȝt to serue þe in þi þoȝt, to þine vsage. 1490 CAXTON *How to Die* 18 Thou haste the vsage of reason. 1509 HAWES *Past. Pleas.* I. (Percy Soc.) 5, I myght not slake Of my great musyng..of these two wayes so muche in usage. 1548 UDALL, etc. *Erasm. Par. Mark* i. 6 The world had far swarued from the right vsage of the law of nature. 1574 in Feuillerat *Revels Q. Eliz.* (1908) 242 Paper for patternes ..& such other necessary uzag in thoffice. 1609 *Manch. Crt. Leet Rec.* (1886) II. 248 A doore which Pluermitie did open and leade vnto the vsage of a barne. 1617 WOODALL *Surg. Mate* (1639) 8 Incision sheeres..are..scarce once in a mans life worth the usage. 1688 HOLME *Armoury* III. 317/2 The Coopers Axe..is contrary to all other Workmens Axes both for shape and usage. 1782 PRIESTLEY *Corrupt. Chr.* I. I. 94 The constant usage of the form of baptism. 1844 *Fraser's Mag.* XXX. 429/1 The usage of hops was entirely unknown to the ancient Gauls. 1870 F. R. WILSON *Ch. Lindisf.* 127 The parish register..has suffered from time, damp, and usage. 1885 TENNYSON *Anc. Sage* 270 Nor thou be rageful, like a handled bee, And lose thy life by usage of thy sting.

† **b.** The use *of* something as an article of food or drink. *Obs.*

1542 BOORDE *Dyetary* xxix. (1870) 292 Beware of the vsage of fruytes. 1585 T. WASHINGTON tr. *Nicholay's Voy.* IV. xxvii. 146 They forbade him the vsage of any kind of meat. *Ibid.* xxix. 150 [He] taught the Thebans to plant the vines and the vsage of wine.

**7.** Action, behaviour, or conduct towards a person, etc.; manner of using or being used; treatment. Also const. *of*, † *to* (= of). **a.** With qualifying adjs.

In freq. use (esp. during 17th c.) from *c* 1600.

1563-4 CLOUGH in Burgon *Life Gresham* (1839) II. 48 Here is suche talke of the ill yousage of owre offysers. 1582 STANYHURST *Æneis* III. (Arb.) 87 This loa..bringeth firme hoape for peaceable vsadge. 1588 SIR E. RADCLYFFE in Ellis *Orig. Lett.* Ser. II. III. 142 Her Majestie hath..comforted many of us with her most gratious usage. 1621 in Foster *Eng. Factories Ind.* (1906) 233 For kinde usadge ore refreshinge for sick men. 1687 A. LOVELL tr. *Thevenot's Trav.* I. 229 Another Saycot seeing this..came..and surrendred of her own accord, in hopes of better usage. 1706 E. WARD *Wooden World Diss.* (1708) 95 Bad Usage makes him as dull and useless as an old Razor. 1784 P. WRIGHT *New Bk. Martyrs* 794/2 The barbarous usage of those poor people. 1840 R. H. DANA *Bef. Mast* xxiii, On the whole, there was good usage on board. 1892 *Photogr. Ann.* II. 563 Without fear of their being injured by the roughest usage during transit.

*transf.* 1675 T. HOWARD in Lady Newdegate *Cavalier & Puritan* (1901) 74 The severe usage of the gout making me unfit to appear in any company.

**b.** Without adj.

1605 SHAKS. *Lear* II. iv. 26 Resolue me..which way Thou might'st deserue, or they impose this vsage, Comming from vs. 1614 LATHAM *Falconry* II. iv. 88 When you haue a Hawke.., you must be very carefull in her vsage. 1666 EARL ORRERY *St. Lett.* (1742) 197 Our usage in England amazes me. They will not only wound our estates, but our titles. *a* 1700 EVELYN *Diary* Sept. 1646, He..was..displeas'd at the usage we received. 1717-8 HEARNE *Collect.* (O.H.S.) VI. 153 She justifyeth her Usage to [= of] the Queen of Scots. 1766 GOLDSM. *Vicar* xxvi, To try how you may like the usage of another master. 1799 S. FREEMAN *Town Officer* 75 To inquire into the usage of children legally bound out. 1849 J. J. G. WILKINSON *Swedenborg* II. 191 He complained that he had met with usage the like of which had been offered to none since the establishment of Christianity in Sweden.

**8.** Established or customary use or employment of language, words, expressions, etc.

1697 DE FOE *Ess. Projects* 236 The Voice of this Society should be sufficient Authority for the Usage of Words. 1785 PALEY *Mor. Philos.* III. 158 All senses of all words are founded upon usage, and nothing else. 1818 CRUISE *Digest* (ed. 2) VI. 384 To make words stand for ideas, in opposition to the sense which usage had put upon them. 1845 *Encycl. Metrop.* I. 132/1 When we speak of nouns and verbs, we only conform to the established usage. 1875 WHITNEY *Life Lang.* xii. 231 As to the common name by which they shall be called, usage is very diverse.

† **9.** Interest on money lent; rate of interest; = USANCE 4 b. *Obs.*

1822 SCOTT *Nigel* v, The money, meanwhile, lying at the ordinary usage. 1824 — *St. Ronan's* xxxix, Some debts.. have been paid up by Mr. Touchwood, who contented himself with more moderate usage.

† **Usage**, *v.* *Obs. rare*$^{-1}$. [a. OF. *usager* (15th c.), *usagier* (1289), f. *usage* USAGE *sb.*] *trans.* To habituate or accustom (a person).

1530 PALSGR. 769/2 Whan a man is nat usaged in a thyng, it is no marvayle though he can nat do it.

**Usager** (yū·zėdʒəɹ). [f. USAGE *sb.* In sense 1 perh. a. F. *usager.*]

† **1.** One who has the usufruct of something. *Obs.*$^{-1}$

1596 DANIEL *Civ. Wars* III. lxxxviii, He consum'd the common Treasurie: Whereof he being the simple vsager.. Did alien at his pleasure.

**2.** *Ch. Hist.* A member of that section of nonjurors which observed 'the usages' in celebrating Holy Communion. See USAGE *sb.* 2 b.

1788 J. SKINNER *Eccl. Hist.* II. 623 Bishop Jeremy Collier, the laborious Church-historian,..appeared keenly at the head of the Usagers, as we shall now call them. 1845 LATHBURY *Nonjurors* 291 Mr. Peck went to Scotland in 1718, on behalf of..the Usagers, as they were designated. 1877 A. J. ROSS *Mem. A. Ewing* xiii. 179 'Usagers' was the designation of a certain party in the Scottish Episcopal Church.

**Usance** (yū·zăns). Also 4-7 vsance (6 *Sc.* vsans), 5-6 vsaunce (5 hew-, 6 ewsaunce). [a. OF. *usance* (1271 in Godef.), = Pr. *uzansa*, Sp. and It. *usanza*, Pg. *usança*, med.L. *ūsancia*, *-zia*, f. *ūsant-*, *ūsans*, pres. pple. of *ūsāre* to use.]

**1.** Habit, custom, wont; = USAGE *sb.* 1.

*c* 1380 *Sir Ferumb.* 2217 Wat doþ ȝour men of fraunce; Of hure disport & ek hure play, what is ȝour mest vsaunce? *c* 1385 CHAUCER *L. G. W.* 586 *Cleopatra*, For to conqueren regnes and honour Vnto the tovne of Rome, as was vsaunce. 1456 SIR G. HAYE *Law Arms* (S.T.S.) 159 Efter the custum of the contree, and the usaunce of the weris. 1489 CAXTON *Faytes of A.* IV. vii, To doo suche a thinge, it is vsaunce of armes. 1513-4 *Act* 5 *Hen. VIII*, c. 7 Accordyng to the olde usance and custome. 1568 GRAFTON *Chron.* II. 134 By meane of which Proclamation, nothing was taken..but it were streight payed for.., which vsance continued but a while. 1620 E. BLOUNT *Horæ Subs.* 49 That must bee referred to publike vsance, not to Cæsars power. 1656 EARL MONM. tr. *Boccalini's Advts. fr. Parnass.* I. lxxii. (1674) 90 Obsolete Proclamations and Edicts, which have lost their validity by contrary usance. 1715 M. DAVIES *Athen. Brit.* I. 224 The same different Martyrologe usance obtain'd here in England. 1825 *New Monthly Mag.* XIII. 19 Ruffs.. were confined by special usance to the fair sex. *a* 1839 PRAED *Poems* (1864) II. 194 By established usance, Miss Gravity is quite amiss [etc.]. 1878 J. J. AUBERTIN tr. *Camoens' Lusiad* IX. l, The Nereids' beauteous choir.. grouped together move, In graceful dances, as of usance old.

**b.** With *a*, *this*, or plural.

*c* 1475 *Pol. Poems* (Rolls) II. 285 In thyse dayes ther is a hewsaunce, That puttyth the pore pepylle to grett hynderaunce. 1583 STOCKER *Civ. Warres Lowe C.* IV. 40 Laudable and auncient Customes, Usances, and..particuler Rightes. 1606 DANIEL *Queen's Arcadia* 2568 Custome..inchaines our iudgements and discourse Vnto the present vsances. 1658 OSBORNE *Q. Eliz.* Ep. A 3 b, Strangers to the Usances of the Ancients. 1673 RAY *Journ. Low C., Venice* 197 In our time this usance is not observed. 1860 BUCKLE in Huth *Life* (1880) II. 33, I have in this way heard something of the prospects and usances of teachers.

**c.** Habit or custom on the part of the individual. Also with *a*, = USAGE *sb.* 4 b.

1470-85 MALORY *Arthur* x. xvii. 440 This is a shameful custumme and a vylaynous vsaunce for a Quene to vse. *a* 1568 in *Bannatyne MS.* (Hunterian Club) 195/42 In yowtheid vse the to temprance, And so begin the with vsance. 1862 SALA *Acc. Addresses* 226, I tried to recollect the things to which we have grown so accustomed.., that usance has begotten familiarity.

**2.** = USAGE *sb.* 6. Now *arch.*

*c* 1460 *Wisdom* 658 in *Macro Plays* 57 Lust ys in so grett vsance. *Ibid.* 1031 Lo, wakynge ys a holy thynge! Þer yt ys hade with goode vsance, Many gracys of yt doth sprynge. *a* 1470 HARDING *Chron.* CXII. i, He a nonne had rauyshed to his vsaunce. *c* 1489 CAXTON *Blanchardyn* vii. 30 She fell doune dyuerse tymes in a swoune..or euer thusaunce of speche was in her restored. 1502 *Ord. Crysten Men* I. iv. (W. de W. 1506) E i, As sone as he cometh to haue dyscrecyon & vsaunce of vnderstandinge. 1591 SPENSER *Daphn.* 503 Riches, beautie,..nought of them is yours, but th' onely vsance Of a small time. 1615 T. ADAMS *Mystical Bedlam* 59 But why doe you call this benefit made of our money, vsurie..? It is but vsance, and husbandring [*sic*] of our stocke. 1659 FULLER *App. Inj. Innoc.* I. 50 What was wanting..hath since sufficiently been supplyed..by usance thereof to Gods Service only. 1869 LD. LYTTON *Poems* (1894) 128 Life is good;..so is beauty. Mere stuff Are all these for Love's usance.

† **3.** Enjoyment by use. *Obs.*$^{-1}$

1483 CAXTON *Gold. Leg.* 306/1 Therto ben thre thynges necessarye:..Souerayne loue,..parfyght knowlege,..and perpetuel fruycion or usaunce.

† **4.** The practice or fact of lending or borrowing money at interest. Cf. USE *sb.* 5. *Obs. rare.*

1570 FOXE *A. & M.* (ed. 2) I. 356/1 To borrow vppon vsance, to make the money which was required. 1585 SIDNEY *Let. to Walsingham* 1 Dec., I have takne up three hundred powndes of Hans Barnard at usance. 1596 SHAKS. *Merch. V.* I. iii. 109 Many a time and oft In the Ryalto you haue rated me About my monies and my vsances. 1611 R. FENTON *Usury* I. ii. 4 They will not call it Vsurie...But it shall be termed Vse or Vsance in exchange.

**b.** = INTEREST *sb.* 10, USE *sb.* 5 b. Also *fig.*

The use in the 19th cent. is a literary revival.

1584 LODGE *Alarm agst. Usurers* D ij, My stocke might lye without vsaunce to my vtter vndooing. 1592 G. HARVEY *Four Lett.* iii. 48 Vse heauenly Eloquence indeede: and employ thy golden talent with amounting vsance indeede. 1596 SHAKS. *Merch. V.* I. iii. 46 He .. brings downe The rate of vsance here. 1615 MELLIS *Recorde's Gr. Arts* 221 Sir, this is yet within the compasse of some reasonable vsance. 1823 BYRON *Let. to Kinnaird* 18 Jan., Make an investment of any spare monies as may render some usance to the owner. 1862 T. A. TROLLOPE *Marietta* I. 30 The old Catholic doctrine that no usance whatever could be unsinfully received for the use of money. 1890 HATTON *By Order of Czar* I. iv, He..had made money by dint of saving his profits and lending them at fair usance.

**c.** A document acknowledging a loan of money.

1843 CARLYLE *Past & Pr.* II. iv, One almost hopes he..had his [*sc.* a Jew's] usances and quittances and horseleech papers summarily set fire to!

**5.** The time or period (varying in respect of different countries) allowed by commercial usage or law for the payment of a bill of exchange, etc., esp. as drawn in a foreign or distant land.

Orig. in the phrase *at usance*: see below.

1617 MORYSON *Itin.* I. 278 Touching the exchange from London to Venice farther distant, by the word vsance three moneths are signified, and by double vsance six moneths. 1651 MARIUS *Advice Bills of Exchange* 20 You must not count every 30 Days a Usance,..but a moneth by denomination. 1682 SCARLETT *Exchanges* 101 Sometimes Usance is taken for some certain time after the date of the Bill, sometimes for some certain time after sight. 1728 CHAMBERS *Cycl.* (1738) s.v., At London, usance is a calendar month; and double usance, two months. 1732 *De Foe's Eng. Tradesman* (ed. 3) I. 361 Usance from Antwerp or Amsterdam, payable at Venice, is two Months, payable in bank. 1759 CHESTERF. *Let.* 2 Feb., The Specie, the Banco, Usances, Agio, and a thousand other particulars. 1834 MCCULLOCH *Dict. Commerce* (ed. 2) 560 The usance and days of grace for bills drawn upon some of the principal commercial cities. 1875 JEVONS *Money* 246 Government bonds..differ..in the fact that they have very long, or even interminable, usance.

**b.** In the phr. *at usance*; *at..usance(s)*.

1487 *Cely Papers* (Camden) 159, I hawe made yow ower be exchaunge..an ciiij$^{xx}$ nobulles ster: payabull at usuance [*sic*]. 1572 T. WILSON *Disc. Usury* 120 b, It shal go at vsance, which is a moneths time, at xxiiii.s. iiii.d. and at double vsance, which is ij. moneths time, at xxiiii.s. viii.d. 1617 MORYSON *Itin.* I. 278 Our Merchants write their bils of exchange..to bee paid, at sight, at vsance, at halfe vsance, and at double vsance. 1682 SCARLETT *Exchanges* 25 At Usance, Pay this my first Bill of Exchange..to Mr. N.W. or his Order. 1704 *Lond. Gaz.* No. 4070/8 A Bill of Exchange of 50l..., drawn at double Usance, on Monsieur Kesterman. 1716 *Ibid.* No. 5472/4 A First Foreign Bill of Exchange.., payable to Tho. Ellis at two Usance. 1849 FREESE *Comm. Class-bk.* 73 A bill drawn in London upon Hamburg at usance, signifies..one month after it is dated; if at two usances, two months after date. 1878 *Encycl. Brit.* VIII. 795/1 No bills are now drawn in London at usance, and the practice is being gradually dropped in other countries.

**†Usant**, *a.* *Obs.* Also vsant(e, vsaunt. [a. OF. *usant*, pr. pple. of *user* to USE.] Accustomed or wont *to* do something; addicted *to* some practice.

c 1380 *Sir Ferumb.* 3296 In þat sche may sche ys vsaunt to do þe yule to spede. c 1386 CHAUCER *Pars. T.* ⁋ 821 He that is vsant to this synne of Glotonye. 1412–20 LYDG. *Chron. Troy* IV. 1629 His 3onge kny3tes..Swyche as he was vsant for to lede. a 1470 H. PARKER *Dives & Pauper* (W. de W. 1496) II. iv. 113/2 Be not vsaunt in swerynge to medle the with saynetes names.

**b.** Habitual. *rare*$^{-1}$.

a 1470 H. PARKER *Dives & Pauper* (W. de W. 1496) II. vi. 115/2 Comonly grete swerers & vsaunt swerers ben full false.

Hence **†Usantly** *adv.*, habitually. *Obs.*$^{-1}$

a 1470 H. PARKER *Dives & Pauper* (W. de W. 1496) II. x. 119/2 Yf he do it [*i.e.* swear] with auysement or vsauntly it is dedely synne.

**†Usation.** *Obs.*$^{-1}$ [ad. med.L. *ūsātiōn-, ūsātio, noun of action f. ūsāre to USE. Cf. Sp. *usacion.*] Customary action; established usage.

1556 J. HEYWOOD *Spider & Fly* xxxvii. 25 If..the flies do here pike That quarell to spiders, in customes vsacion. That is tit for tat.

**Uschaw, Uschay**, obs. Sc. variants of ISSUE *sb.*
**Usche**, var. USH *v.*$^1$ *Sc. Obs.* **Uschew, -u**, obs. north. varr. ISSUE *sb.* and *v.*

**†Uscova**, obs. variant of USQUEBAUGH.

1632 LITHGOW *Trav.* x. 431 Gentlemen..reserue euer in their houses, Spanish Sack, and Irish Vscoua.

**Use** (yūs), *sb.* Forms: α. 3–5 vs (4–5 vss), 4, 7 *Sc.* us (3–4 hus, 4–5 uss), 5 ws (5 owse, 5–6 *Sc.* wss), 5–7 vse (5 vce, *Sc.* 5–6 wse), 4– use (5 uce, 6 usse). β. *Sc.* and *north.* 4 oise, 4–5 oys, oyse, 5 oysse, ois, 6 oiss; 4 vice, 5 vys, 5–6 vyss. [a. AF. and OF. *us, uus, hus* m. (also *use* f.):—L. *ūsus*, f. the ppl. stem of *ūtī* to use.]

I. Act of using, or fact of being used.

**1.** The act of employing a thing for any (esp. a profitable) purpose; the fact, state, or condition of being so employed; utilization or employment for or with some aim or purpose, application or conversion to some (esp. good or useful) end.

α. a 1225 *Ancr. R.* 16 Þis word habbeð muchel on vs & i muðe euch time þet 3e muwen. 1297 R. GLOUC. (Rolls) 2211 Ne conne 3e no3t lerni þing þat 3e ne dude neuer er; Change 3oure hond & to þe vs of suerd & lance is [? *read* it] do. 1340 *Ayenb.* 55 Ine þe greate bysihede þet hy habbeþ, to porchaci...Efterward, mid grat lost þet hy habbeþ ine þe us. 1382 WYCLIF *Coloss.* ii. 22 Nether 3e schulen touche, nether taste, nether trete with hondis tho thingis, the which alle ben into deeth by the ilke vss. c 1440 *Promp. Parv.* 335/1 Mesure, in vse of..nedefulle thyngys, ..*frugalitas*. 1558 in Feuillerat *Revels Q. Mary* (1914) 251 To lend me the vse of one of your maskes. 1599 B. JONSON *Cynthia's Rev.* v. i, Denying to the world the precious vse Of hoorded wealth. 1605 VERSTEGAN *Dec. Intell.* i. (1628) 23 The Picards..are said first to haue gotten that name of their great and most accustomed use of pikes. 1646 SIR T. BROWNE *Pseud. Ep.* I. vii. 26 In..Law and History, there is ..a frequent and allowable use of testimony. 1690 LOCKE *Hum. Und.* III. x. § 1 The obscurity and confusion that is so hard to be avoided in the Use of Words. 1729 T. INNES *Crit. Essay* 444 The ancient use of letters among the Irish. 1753 CHALLONER *Cath. Chr. Instr.* Pref. p. vi, What the Doctor has alledged against the Use of Incense. 1782 MISS BURNEY *Cecilia* VIII. viii, Is the gift of speech only granted us to pervert the use of understanding? 1831 SCOTT *Ct. Rob.* xi, His excellence in the use of the French language. 1860 WARTER *Sea-board* II. 436 Certainly use and abuse are very different things. 1891 SIR A. WILLS in *Law Times* XCI. 232/2 Massey..lent the use of his name to Kensington in order to oblige him.

β. 1375 BARBOUR *Bruce* XVII. 252 For in Scotland..The oys of thame [*sc.* cannon] had nocht beyn sene. c 1425 WYNTOUN *Cron.* I. 1310 As þe makaris had daynte Off þa bestis and delyte Be freyte or oysse, or be profyte.

**b.** In legal phr., coupled with *occupation* (or *occupancy*).

1738 *Act* 11 *Geo. II*, c. 19 § 14 In an Action on the case, for the Use and Occupation of what was so held or enjoyed. 1772 BULLER *Introd. Law Nisi Prius* (1775) 139 In Case for Use and Occupation of an House by Permission of the Plaintiff. 1808 W. SELWYN *Law Nisi Prius* II. 1180 Chap. xxxvii.—Use and Occupation. 1918 *Nation* (N.Y.) 7 Feb. 165/1 A percentage..will be paid on a pro-rata basis for each day of lost use and occupancy.

**c.** Freq. *to make* or *take* (..) *use of.*

1591 SHAKS. *Two Gent.* II. iv. 67 Sir Protheus..Made vse, and faire aduantage of his daies. 1606 CHAPMAN *M. D'Olive* I. i, At my chamber, where we may take free use of our selves, that is, drinke sack, and talke Satyre. 1663 GERBIER *Counsel* 55 Those that mind the making use of Chalk in their walls. 1711 ADDISON *Spect.* No. 62 ⁋ 5 The Words Fire and Flame are made use of to signify Love. 1774 GOLDSM. *Nat. Hist.* (1776) V. 264 This bird's making use of the bed or nest of another to deposit its own brood in. 1823 P. NICHOLSON *Pract. Build.* 420 Plate-glass is the most beautiful glass made use of. 1862 TYNDALL *Mountaineer.* ii. 16 We made use of all our strength. 1897 T. HARDY *Well-Beloved* I. vi, Perhaps she had only made use of him as a convenient aid to her intentions.

**†d.** *Your* (*their*, etc.) *use*, = use of you (them, etc.). *Obs.*

1596 SHAKS. 1 *Hen. IV*, I. iii. 21 When we need Your vse and counsell, we shall send for you. 1667 MILTON *P. L.* IX. 750 Thy praise hee also who forbids thy use, Conceales not from us. 1691 T. H[ALE] *Acc. New Invent.* 37 The Ingredients..being Forraign, such has sometimes been the scarcity thereof here, (even when their use has been most wanted).

**2. a.** In various prepositional phrases (with *in*, *to*, *into*, *out of*, *for*, *of*).

(*a*) a 1340 HAMPOLE *Psalter* cxviii. 48 For of mykil thynkynge of þe comandmentis cumys in oyse goed werke. c 1400 *Lanfranc's Chirurg.* 306 Þe .i. instrument þat is comoun & moost in vss, is clepid nodulum. 1558–9 *Act* 1 *Eliz.* c. 2 § 13 That suche Ornamentes of the Churche and of the Ministers therof shall bee reteyned and bee in use as was in this Church of Englande. 1568 GRAFTON *Chron.* II. 345 Gonnes were first in vse, which were inuented by one of Germany. 1631 GOUGE *God's Arrows* IV. Ded. p. v, I remember a Proverbiall speech in use among the Iewes. 1691 T. H[ALE] *Acc. New Invent.* 5 To apply themselves forthwith to the putting in use this Invention upon some of his own Ships. 1711 STEELE *Spect.* No. 36 ⁋ 8 All the fashionable Phrases and Compliments now in use. 1755 JOHNSON, *To Quarry*,..to prey upon. A low word not in use. 1801 *Med. Jrnl.* XXI. 83 Every plan of cure at present in use. 1885 *Manch. Exam.* 10 July 5/2 Those [lamps] now in use. 1890 SIR N. LINDLEY in *Law Times Rep.* LXIII. 690 These two forms of order..are in constant use in the Chancery Division.

(*b*) 1388 WYCLIF *Neh.* x. 31 The puplis..that bryngen in thingis set to sale, and alle thingis to vss. a 1425 tr. *Arderne's Treat. Fistula*, etc. 89 Be it kept to vse in ane erþen potte. c 1460 FORTESCUE *Abs. & Lim. Mon.* vi. (1885) 120 It nedith þat ther be lyvelode asseigned ffor the payment therof; wich lyvelode be in no wyse putte to no other vse. 1552–3 in Feuillerat *Revels Edw. VI* (1914) 112 By him bought and prouided and spent to the vse aforesaid. 1570 BILLINGSLEY *Euclid* II. prop. ii. 63 Which oftentimes serueth to great vse in working. 1590 SHAKS. *Com. Err.* III. ii. 97, I know not what vse to put her too. 1628–a 1700 [see PUT *v.*$^1$ 18]. 1748 CHESTERF. *Let.* 16 Feb., Every moment may be put to some use. 1893 *Nat. Observer* 7 Oct. 536/1 The gallows were put to real use.

(*c*) c 1444 PECOCK *Donet* 51 Or ellis he takiþ into vse alle kyndis of hem [*sc.* goods]. 1688 MIÉGE *Gt. Fr. Dict.* II. s.v., To put a Thing into Use. 1728 NORTH *Mem. Music* (1846) 55 Instruments..invented, and brought into common use. 1835 *Penny Cycl.* IV. 398/1 At what time..bills of exchange were first brought into use is a matter..not..satisfactorily ascertained. 1879 M. J. GUEST *Lect. Hist. Eng.* l. 508 Two wonderful instruments had lately come into use. 1890 *Sat. Rev.* 8 Feb. 175/2 This word came into use to express [etc.].

(*d*) 1538 ELYOT, *Exoletus*, he that is passed growynge.. olde, or out of vse. 1579 E. K. *Spenser's Sheph. Cal.* Epist., Such good and naturall English words, as haue ben long time out of vse. 1603 G. OWEN *Pembrokeshire* iii. (1891) 36 And soe was the English growne out of use..and used only amonge the basest sorte of people. a 1700 EVELYN *Diary* 18 March 1649, The blessed Sacrament, now wholly out of use in the Parish Churches. 1710 STEELE *Tatler* No. 174 ⁋ 3 A broken Limb will recover its Strength by the sole Benefit of being out of Use. 1892 *Monthly Packet* Oct. 430 The name..had in some way gone out of use.

(*e*) 1548 ELYOT, *Vsualis*,..vsuall, that serueth for our vse. a 1648 DIGBY *Chym. Secr.* II. (1684) 195 Make it up into Balls..and keep them for Use. 1697 DRYDEN *Virg. Georg.* III. 480 The Fleece, when drunk with Tyrian Juice, Is dearly sold; but not for needful use. 1742 YOUNG *Nt. Th.* II. 154 Since Time was giv'n for use, not waste. 1807 CRABBE *Par. Reg.* I. 81 There pious works for Sunday's use are found. 1896 LUCAS *Cyclealities* 117 A small Hold-all for use with handle-bar carriers.

(*f*) 1611 BIBLE *Transl. Pref.* ⁋ 1 Thus it is apparent, that these things..are of most necessary vse. 1648 SANDERSON *Serm.* (1653) 6 Words..of very frequent use in the New Testament. 1833 HOLLAND *Manuf. Metal* II. 285 Articles of such universal use and importance. 1839 FR. A. KEMBLE *Resid. in Georgia* (1863) 18 Implements..of household use. 1880 J. BRITTEN *Old Words* p. xiv, Others [*sc.* words] apparently of general use.

**†b.** *In the use of*, making use of. *Obs.*

1594 *Southampton Court Leet Rec.* (1906) II. 296 Robert Russell, william cortney, John grant nowe in the vse of Thomas heths brewary.

**†c.** *Of use*, used, employed. *Obs.*$^{-1}$

1634 SIR T. HERBERT *Trav.* 183 [The jacks] boyld giue food no lesse pleasant..then doe the Date-stones of vse in Persia.

**3.** In special senses: **a.** The act of using or fact of being used as food, etc.; consumption.

1586 DAY *Eng. Secretorie* I. (1595) 27 A kind of graine growing in great cods, whereby we sometimes obtaine (though not the naturall) yet some vse of bread. 1588 KYD *Househ. Philos.* Wks. (1901) 259 The Nurses shoulde not be so narrowly forbidde the often vse of wynes. 1697 DRYDEN *Virg. Georg.* IV. 231 They..hoard, for Winter's Use, the Summer's Gain. 1708 OCKLEY *Saracens* I. Table, *Sawik*, a sort of Food in Use among the Arabians. 1725 N. ROBINSON *Th. Physick* 290 The Patient should be exhorted not to leave off the Use of the Bark too soon. 1772 W. BUCHAN *Dom. Med.* (ed. 2) 255 Wholesome food, and a moderate use of generous liquors. 1836 A. COMBE *Physiol. Digestion* (ed. 2) 319 Many persons imagine that spirits..cannot be injurious, because they feel no immediate bad effects from their use. 1862 *Chambers's Encycl.* III. 552/2 Certain substances [*i.e.* tobacco, tea, and coffee] which..may fairly be considered, from the universality of their use, to exert a definite influence on the organism.

**b.** Employment or maintenance for sexual purposes. (See also quot. 1841.) Cf. USE *v.* 10 b.

1565 COOPER *Thes.* s. v. *Fruor*, He hath the vse of hir, &c. 1607 TOURNEUR *Rev. Trag.* II. ii, I cannot honor her [*ante* my mother],..Her tongue has turnd my sister into vse. 1647 A. ROSS *Mystag. Poet.* viii. (1675) 176 His step-mother desired the use of his body. *Ibid.* ix. 225 [Ixion] began to fall in love with Juno, desiring the use of her body. 1676 R. DIXON *Two Testaments* 551 A wife, not a Concubine, might be taken by use; for a whole un-interrupted year without usurpation. 1748 *Earthquake Peru* iii. 247 Two ancient Ways of marrying still subsist in this Country; that of keeping a Mistress is very answerable to that which was call'd by Use. 1841 HARTSHORNE *Salop. Ant.* Gloss. 606 A mare is said to be 'in use' when she is under the influence of certain appetites or affections. 1894 *Nature's Method in Evol. Life* iii. 45 The bulls [are] put to use about twelve months old. *Ibid.*, Stallions are commonly in use long before they are full grown.

**4.** *Law.* The act or fact of using, holding, or possessing land or other property so as to derive revenue, profit, or other benefit from such.

1535–6 *Act* 27 *Hen. VIII*, c. 10 § 6 Concernyng such right, title, use, interest, or possession as they..have clayme or pretende to have. 1579 RASTELL *Termes de la Ley* 183 b/2 The stat. of An. 27. H. 8. c. 10 prouided..that who hath the vse of the lande, the same hath y$^e$ possession therof by vertue of that estatute. 1596 BACON *Max. & Use Com. Law* II. (1635) 57 They conveyed their full estates of their lands in their good health, to friends in trust,..and this trust was called, the use of the land. 1642 tr. *Perkins' Prof. Bk.* viii. § 528. 231 Before the statute of West. 3,..there was no use of lands or of houses if not that it were expressed upon the delivery of the estate. 1681 STAIR *Institut.* xvi. 327 Usufruct is the power of disposal of the use and fruits, saving the Substance of the thing. 1706 STANHOPE *Paraphr.* III. 334 The longest Inheritance and Descent, is in truth but the longest Use, but not so much as a Lease or Tenant-right. 1734 POPE *Hor. Sat.* II. ii. 165 'Pity! to build, without a son or wife:'..Well, if the use be mine, can it concern one, Whether the name belong to Pope or Vernon? 1766 BLACKSTONE *Comm.* II. 137 The property or possession of the soil being vested in one man, and the use, or profit thereof, in another. 1818 CRUISE *Digest* (ed. 2) I. 474 No use would have resulted to the father, because blood was a sufficient consideration to have vested the use in the son. 1888 *Encycl. Brit.* XXIII. 596/1 The conveyance of an estate to a friend on the understanding that they should retain the use, *i.e.*, the actual profit and enjoyment of the estate.

**b.** A trust or confidence reposed in a person for the holding of property, etc., of which another receives or is entitled to the profits or benefits.

1535 *Act* 27 *Hen. VIII*, c. 10 § 1 Fraudulent feoffementes, fynes, recoveryes, and other assurances craftely made to secrete uses, intentes, and trustes. *Ibid.* § 12 Any person.. seasid of or in any Landes, Ten[emen]tes, or Hereditamentes to any use, trust, or confydence. 1579 RASTELL *Termes de la Ley* 183 b/2 Vses of Land had beginning after that the custome of propertie began among men. 1628 COKE *On Litt.* 272 b, An Vse is a Trust or Confidence reposed in some other. 1759 STERNE *Tr. Shandy* I. xv, By force and virtue of the statute for transferring of uses into possession. 1765 BLACKSTONE *Comm.* II. 335 This is sometimes called a secondary, sometimes a shifting, use. 1766– [see SPRINGING *ppl. a.* 8]. 1845 WILLIAMS *Law Real Prop.* 124 A doctrine was laid down, that there could not be a use upon a use. 1882 F. POLLOCK in *Macm. Mag.* XLVI. 365 The Statute of Uses (A.D. 1535) was passed in order to prevent the severance of legal from beneficial ownership. 1888 *Encycl. Brit.* XXIII. 596/1 The feoffee to uses, as he was called, or the person seised to the use of another.

**c.** In the phrase *in use* or *to* (..) *use.*

1491 *Act* 7 *Hen. VII*, c. 2 § 5 They and their feoffes to the use of every of theym. 1535 *Act* 27 *Hen. VIII*, c. 10 § 1 Any Honoures, Castelles,..Remaynders or other Hereditamentes, to the use, confidence or trust of any other..parsones or of anye bodie polytike. *Ibid.*, In suche lyke estates as they had or shall have in use, trust, or confidence of or in the same. 1596 SHAKS. *Merch. V.* IV. i. 383 So he will let me haue The other halfe in vse, to render it Vpon his death, vnto the Gentleman. 1606 — *Ant. & Cl.* I. iii. 44 But my full heart Remaines in vse with you. 1720 T. WOOD *Inst. Laws Eng.* 436 Where no Uses are Declared, the Feoffment, Fine or Recovery shall enure to the Use of the Feoffor,

Cognizor, etc. **1818** Cruise *Digest* (ed. 2) V. 525 Supposing the Earl of Derby a feoffee to use,..still the grant..was free and gratuitous. **1888** *Encycl. Brit.* XXIII. 596/1 This alienation of land in use was looked upon with great disfavour by the common law courts.

**5.** The fact of using money borrowed or lent at a premium.

**1603** Holland *Plutarch's Mor.* 283 [They] choose..to pawn them for to borrow money thereupon & pay for use. **1607** Harington *Nugæ Ant.* (1804) II. 232 Sending some present, enough perhaps to pay for the use of 1000 li. **1641** *Aldeburgh Rec.* in *N. & Q.* 12th Ser. IX. 146/2 Rec[ei]vd of Mr. John Blowers for one yeeres use of 40 li., 2 [li.] 16. 00. **1729** Jacob *Law Dict.* s.v. *Usury*, Reasonable Interest may be taken for the Use of Money at this Day. **1767** Blackstone *Comm.* II. 454 When money is lent on a contract to receive..an increase by way of compensation for the use. **1862** [see Usance 4 b].

**b.** Premium on money lent to another; interest, usury. Now *dial.* or *arch.* Freq. *to* † *take* or *pay use.*

In frequent use from *c* 1612 to *c* 1690.

**1611** Rich *Honest. Age* (Percy Soc.) 60 Therefore, (sayth the Vsurer), we may take vse of him that is rich. **1655** Stanley *Hist. Philos.* III. (1687) 104/2 If the Moon Ne'r rise again, I'me bound to pay no use..'Cause use you know is paid by th' Month. **1690** Child *Disc. Trade* 207 With them ..there is not any Use for Money tollerated, above the rate of Six in the Hundred. **1728** T. Sheridan tr. *Persius* vi. 93 Do not you..advise me, to live upon the Use of my Money. **1747** *Mem. Nutrebian Crt.* I. 55 On whom he settled the use of 20,000 crowns for her life. **1825** Jamieson. **1869–** in dialect use (*Eng. Dial. Dict.*). **1872** Tennyson *Foresters* iv, 'Here be one thousand marks.'..'Ay, ay, but there is use, four hundred marks.'

*fig.* **1599** Shaks. *Much Ado* ii. i. 286 Hee lent it [*sc.* his heart] me a while, and I gaue him vse for it, a double heart. **1628** Earle *Microcosm., Vniuersitie Dunne* (Arb.) 74 The sole place to supply him is the Butterie, where hee takes grieuous vse vpon your Name. **1648** J. Beaumont *Psyche* vi. ccxxiii, The Serpent, whose illustrious skin Plaid with the Sunne and sent him back his beams With glorious Use. **1784** Cowper *Task* iii. 364 Human life Is but a loan to be repaid with use. **1874** Hardy *Far fr. Mad. Crowd* xli, You'll never see Fanny Robin no more—use nor principal—ma'am.

*transf.* **1637** in *Verney Mem.* (1907) I. 104 He threatens to make him pay use for his barn.

**c.** In the phr. *at, to,* † *upon* (..) *use.* Now *dial.*

(*a*) **1598** E. Guilpin *Skial.* (1878) 21 As heresie he shuns all merriment, And turn'd good husband, puts forth sighs to vse. **1631** Massinger *Emperor East* i. ii, I, alas! Lend out my labouring brains to use, and sometimes For a drachma in the pound. **1642** D. Rogers *Naaman* 158, I would not put my mony to use; but that it is against a Common wealth to keepe it. **1680** R. L'Estrange *Erasm. Colloq.* (1725) 248 They Buy, they Sell, they take to Use, they put to Use. **1700** Astry tr. *Saavedra-Faxardo* II. 149 We read, that Pompey put out his Money to Use. **1738** tr. *Guazzo's Art Convers.* 43 Two Florentine Brethren, who let out their Money to Use. **1785** Cumberland *Natural Son* v. (ed. 2) 82 You are my own son;—you have put my money out to use already.

(*b*) **1618** *Barnevelt's Apol.* C 4 *b*, Our last borrowed money is..at vse at sixteene. **1656** Earl Monm. tr. *Boccalini's Advts. fr. Parnass.* 95 One Menalcas..took up money at use. **1727** Swift *To Earl of Oxford* Wks. 1755 III. ii. 47 Is your money out at use? **1784** R. Bage *Barham Downs* I. 172, I had three hundred pounds at use. **1814** Scott *Wav.* xlii, If his honour had mair ready siller..he could put it out at use..at great profit. **1841** Hartshorne *Salop Ant.* Gloss. 606 Money out at use. **1849–** in dialect use (*Eng. Dial. Dict.* s.v.).

(*c*) **1622** Mabbe tr. *Aleman's Guzman d'Alf.* ii. 251 Let him but take vp so much vpon Vse. **1630** *R. Johnson's Kingd. & Commw.* 353 Some doe give voluntarily, others doe lend frankly, or upon light use. **1667** Duchess of Newcastle *Life Duke of N.* (1886) II. 146 The loss of my Lord's estate, in plain rents, as also upon ordinary use.

† **d.** *Use upon* (also *on*) *use*, compound interest; excessive interest. Also *fig. Obs.*

[**1591** Sylvester *Du Bartas* i. iii. 521 You City-Vipers, that (incestious) joyn Use vpon use, begetting Coyn of Coyn!] **1620** Sanderson *Serm.* (1632) 111 Your vse vpon vse, that doubleth the principall in seven yeares, is nothing to it. **1651** Cleveland *Smectymnuus* 70 No Eccho can improve the Author more, Whose lungs paies use on use to half a score. **1682** Sir T. Browne *Chr. Mor.* (1756) 15 To famish in plenty, and live poorly to die rich, were multiplying improvement in madness, and use upon use in folly.

**6.** Employment or usage resulting in, or such as to cause, impairment, wear, etc.

*c* **1440** *Promp. Parv.* 522/2 Weryn or wax olde and febyl by vse,..*veterasco, vetero, invetero.* **1670** Sir Sackville Crow in *12th Rep. Hist. MSS. Comm.* App. V. 15 Theire ordnary designes [in tapestry]..with a whiles use will soone loose theire luster. **1697** Dryden *Virg. Georg.* iii. 6 All other Themes that careless Minds invite, Are worn with Use. **1755** Johnson, *To wear*,..to waste with use or time. **1840** Dickens *Old C. Shop* xvii, Everything told of long use and quiet slow decay. **1848** Mill *Pol. Econ.* I. 44 Although deteriorated in some small degree by each use, it does not do its work by being deteriorated. **1904** *Verney Memoirs* I. 68 The wear and tear of even holiday use.

**II.** Habit of using.

**7.** With *the.* The habitual, usual, or common practice; continual, repeated, or accustomed employment or exercise; habit, custom. (Cf. 9.)

**1297** R. Glouc. (Rolls) 9402 Þe wone & hus [*v.r.* vse] þat ȝe abbeþ euere ibe aboue þat aȝte make ȝou abbe to fiȝte þe betere loue. *a* **1400–50** *Alexander* 2950 Sen þe vse is here vn-honorable here I þam lefe. *c* **1480** Henryson *Sheep & Dog* ii, By the vse, and cours, and commoun style On this maner [he] maid his Citatioun. **1565** Cooper *Thesaurus* s.v. *Usus*, To suche a one as was nowe paste the vse and custome of lewde doeynge. **1577** B. Googe *Heresbach's Husb.* ii. 66 The vse of sowing of them is best. **1594** Marlowe & Nashe *Dido* i. i, It is the vse for Turen maides to weare Their bowe and quiuer in this modest sort. **1604** Jas. I *Counterbl. to Tobacco* To Rdr., The vile vse (or other abuse) of taking Tobacco. **1637** Earl Monm tr. *Malvezzi's Romulus & Tarquin* 209 The use of seeing dead men takes mercy totally away. **1656** — tr. *Boccalini's Advts. fr. Parnassus* ii. xxviii. 271 The use of being drunk, being rather a piece of publick cunning amongst the Dutch, then [etc.]. **1720** Ozell *Vertot's Rom. Rep.* (1740) II. xi. 170 Metellus Pius commanded them, as a Proconsul, according to the Use of those Days. **1725** Pope *Odyssey* x. 551 The cause remov'd, habitual griefs remain, And the soul saddens by the use of pain. **1825** Scott *Betrothed* xxi, One not in the use to speak before his purpose was fixed. **1854** C. Wordsw. *Misc.* (1879) I. 104 The use is inveterate, and it would be difficult to reform it. **1877** Mrs. Oliphant *Makers Flor.* iv. 112 The painter followed the religious use and wont of his time.

**b.** In the phr. *as the use is*, etc. Cf. 9 b.

**1432** in *15th Rep. Hist. MSS. Comm.* App. VIII. 44 The saidis Jone and Elisabeth sall be handfast, as the oys is, in haly Kirk. *c* **1475** *Harl. Contin. Higden* (Rolls) VIII. 441 That men electe to be bischoppes..may..be confermede of theire metropolitans as the use was afore. **1535** Coverdale *Judith* xvi. 20 The people was ioyfull, as the vse is. **1611** Bible 2 *Macc.* xii. 39 Vpon the day following as the vse had bene,..his company came to take vp the bodies. **1633** P. Fletcher *Purple Isl.* i. v, Wake thy..Muse, And thank them with a song, as is the use. **1871** W. Alexander *Johnny Gibb* xxxv, They fixed it [*sc.* the settlement of the minister], as the use and wont is, for a week day.

**c.** With limiting genitive or possessive pron.

**1390** Gower *Conf.* I. 15 Upon the hond to were a Schoo.. Acordeth noght to the behove Of resonable mannes us. *c* **1400** *Destr. Troy* 6426 Nay, warloghe wolfe,..Þat neuer of forray art full, with þi foule vse. *c* **1425** *Cast. Persev.* 774 in *Macro Plays* 100 Messenger, do now þyne vse! *Ibid.* 949 Do now wel ȝoure olde owse whanne ȝe com to Mankynde! **1432** *Rolls of Parlt.* IV. 404/1 Eny clothis..made aftre the use of the Countrey. **1535** Coverdale 2 *Macc.* xi. 25 That they maye lyue acordinge to the vse & custome of their forefathers. **1568** Grafton *Chron.* II. 89 His vse was to ride with a thousande horses continually. *c* **1600** Shaks. *Sonn.* lxxviii, So oft haue I inuok'd thee for my Muse,..As euery Alien pen hath got my vse. **1609** Dekker *Gull's Horn-bk.* v. 22 Let it be your vse to repaire thither some halfe houre after eleuen. **1612** Shelton *Quix.* i. iv. (1620) 24 It is the vse of Cowards to doe that which thou dost. **1670** Walton *Lives* ii. 126 After his customary publick Devotions, his use was to retire into his Study. **1800** Wordsw. *Michael* 155 Not alone For pastime and delight, as is the use Of fathers. **1836** Husenbeth *Faberism Exposed* v. 528 The use and practice of the Catholic Church..of reordaining clerical converts from the Anglican Church. **1864** Tennyson *Aylmer's F.* 566 The gentle creature shut from all Her charitable use,..slowly lost..her hold on life.

**8.** A custom, habit, or practice.

*c* **1350** *Lybeaus Disc.* 752 In fyghtyng he hath an us Knyghtes to begyle. *c* **1425** Wyntoun *Cron.* ii. v. 376 In till Egipt..That vys is kepit to þis day. *c* **1450** *Mirk's Festial* i. 113 Þou marterys me by a foule vse and custom of sweryng. *c* **1489** Caxton *Sonnes of Aymon* ix. 200 Be not dismayed for no thynge, for this is but an vse of werre; suche a thyng befalleth often to many one. **1542** Boorde *Dyetary* (1870) 252 Englande hath an euyll vse in syttynge longe at dyner. **1587** R. Hovenden in *Collect.* (O.H.S.) I. 217 We never let our woods but once and that by great oversight: this one tyme we trust your Lordship will not count an use. **1601** Hakluyt *Galvano's Discov. World* 15 It was a vse also..to passe to India by land. **1613** Purchas *Pilgrimage* (1614) 749 They haue a filthy and detestable vse in marrying their Maidens. **1721** Kelly *Scot. Prov.* 272 An ill Use ought to be early broken off. **1728** Chambers *Cycl.* (1738) s.v., Uses and Customs of the sea. **1819** Shelley *Cenci* iv. iv. 177 She knows not yet the uses of the world. **1875** Gladstone *Glean.* (1879) VI. 124 When such an use came in, it was thought to be like a sign of the double superlative in High Churchmanship.

**9.** Without article. Accustomed practice or procedure; habit, usage, custom, wont. (Cf. 7.) Also (*b*) coupled with synonymous term, esp. *wont.*

(*a*) *c* **1340** Hampole *Pr. Consc.* 7634 Planetes..styk noght fast, als smale sternes dose, Ilk ane his course mase thurgh use. **1340–70** *Alex. & Dind.* 720 ȝe schullen bi ordre of vse offren to venus A ful derworþe douue. **1390** Gower *Conf.* I. 133 The which to comun us is strange. *c* **1440** *Alph. Tales* 273 Opon þe day of his translacion it was vse to bere his bonys furth of þe kurk. *c* **1480** Henryson *Fox & Wolf* 173 Use drawis Nature swa in propertie Of beist and man, that neidlingis thay man do As thay of lang tyme hes bene hantit to. **1565** Cooper *Thesaurus* s.v. *Usus*, Vse, the inuentour of woordes. **1585** Fetherstone tr. *Calvin on Acts* vi. 2 Vse is the father of wisedome. **1651** Hobbes *Leviath.* ii. xxvi. 138 Long Use obtaineth the authority of a Law. **1697** Dryden *Virg. Georg.* ii. 366 So strong is Custom; such Effects can Use In tender Souls of pliant Plants produce. **1733** Swift *Apology* Wks. 1755 IV. i. 212 Madam, the mighty pow'r of use Now strangely pleads in my excuse. **1781** Cowper *Convers.* 189 To rush into a fixt eternal state,..Whatever use may urge, or honour plead, On reason's verdict is a madman's deed. **1812** Cary *Dante, Parad.* xxvi. 135 In mortals, use Is as the leaf upon the bough: that goes, And other comes instead.

(*b*) **1526** *Pilgr. Perf.* (W. de W. 1531) 162 b, Let vs not come to yͤ chirche by vse and custome, as the oxe to his stall. **1609** Skene *Reg. Maj.* 44 He craues onelie na other service, bot vse and wont. **1689** in *Acts Parlt. Scot.* (1875) XII. 58/2 Þat the maltmen þer be lyable for the excyse according to use and wont. **1728** Chambers *Cycl.* s.v. *Language*, 'Tis Use and Custom is the Rule of a Language. **1762** in *Nairne Peerage Evidence* (1874) 95 Priviledges belonging to the said lands conform to use and wont. **1805** Wordsw. *Prelude* xiv. 158 The tendency..Of use and custom to bow down the soul Under a growing weight of vulgar sense. **1825** R. Wilson *Sk. Hist. Hawick* 190 This tax,..by the law of 'use and wont',..has become part and parcel of the system. **1850** Tennyson *In Mem.* xxix. 11 Make one wreath more for Use and Wont, That guard the portals of the house.

*attrib.* **1845** Carlyle *Cromwell* (1871) IV. 42 Constitutional Presbyterian persons, Use-and-wont Neuters. **1885** Pater *Marius* I. 131 A careless, half-conscious, 'use-and-wont' reception of our experience.

**b.** *Sc.* In the phr. *as use is*, etc. Cf. 7 b.

*c* **1375** *Sc. Leg. Saints* xviii. (*Egipciane*) 126 Syne, as oyse was, Þai entryt in þare oratore. **1423** in *Charters, &c. of Edinburgh* (1871) 55 Payand of the chaldre as vse and custume is and as thai war wont to pay [etc.]. **1549** *Reg. Aberdon.* (Maitl. Cl.) I. 434 As vse euer hes beyne in tyme bygane. **1557** *Reg. Cupar Abbey* II. 140 Payand ȝerle..ten merkis money.., as vse and wont wes. **1697** *Jedburgh Fleshers' Book* (MS.), [He] has payed all dewes as use is.

**c.** Freq. in the phr. *in* (..) *use.* Also (chiefly *Sc.*), *to be in use of*, or *to* (do something).

(*a*) *c* **1450** *Mirk's Festial* i. 45 Mony fals opynyons of wychecraft..þe whech ben noght to telle among crysten men, lest þay wer drawen yn vse. **1565** Cooper *Thesaurus, Increbuit consuetudo*, the custome did grow in vse. **1579** Spenser *Let. to Harvey* Poet. Wks. (1912) 635/2 As for the twoo worthy Gentlemen,..they haue me..in some vse of familiarity. **1662** Stillingfl. *Orig. Sacr.* ii. vii. § 9 The reason of the ceremoniall precepts did respect the customs in use when they were given.

(*b*) **1504** *Munim. de Melros* (Bann. Cl.) 601 That the said schirref was in vse of calling of the said landis..in thare courtis. **1574** *Reg. Privy Council Scot.* II. 389 He has bene in use of pament of the soume of fourtie pundis yeirlie. **1581** *Ibid.* III. 399 They wer nevir in use of setting of new takkis befoir the expyring of the auld. **1800** A. Carlyle *Autobiog.* (1860) 44, I was in use of going to my father's on Saturdays.

(*c*) **1566** *Reg. Privy Council Scot.* I. 492 The Personis of Glasgow hes alwayis bene in use to furneis breid. *c* **1630** Sir T. Hope *Minor Practicks* (1726) 26 The Executors..are in Use..to protest that [etc.]. **1759** Robertson *Hist. Scot.* (1761) II. 77 The respect, with which the Scots were in use to receive her ministers. **1780** *Mirror* No. 101, He too had been in use to talk of feeling and of sentiment. **1829** Bentham *Justice & Cod. Petit.* 82 A multitude of distinguishable sources, out of which complexity is in use to arise. **1862** *Chambers's Encycl.* III. 608/2 The emperors were in use expressly to confer upon the universities the right of appointing doctors of laws.

† **d.** Ordinary or usual experience. *Obs.*—1

**1588** Kyd *Househ. Phil.* Wks. (1901) 266 One should so helpe another as wee see by vse in our owne bodies; when the one leg is weary we can rest it on the other [etc.]. **1601** Sir W. Cornwallis *Ess.* ii. xxxii, But to my vse, we leaue our women ignorant, and so leaue them fearefull.

**10.** Const. *of.* **a.** Opportunity, occasion, habit, or practice of using. Chiefly *to have the use of.*

*a* **1340** Hampole *Psalter* lii. 2 Thai ere brokyn fra oyse and strenght of reson. *c* **1380** Wyclif *Wks.* (1880) 453 As seyntes þat ben in heuene han vss of alle þes worldly godis. *Ibid.*, Þis is þe freest vss þat men han off worldly godis. **1565** Cooper *Thesaurus, Ususfructuarius*,..he that hath the vse and fruite of a thyng, but not the proprietie. **1577** Holinshed *Chron.* I. *Hist. Scotl.* xiv. 21/2 The Pict (saith Herodian) hath generally no vse of apparell. **1590** Sir J. Smyth *Disc. Weapons* 42 b, The weapon of all others that God hath put into the hearts of men, to deuise and vse ..to chasten..other such Nations, as..had the perfect vse of the same. **1656** H. Phillips *Purch. Patt.* (1676) 137 Men, who have daily use hereof, have tables and lines upon their Rulers. **1698** T. Froger *Voy.* 75 Not having the use or knowledge of iron. **1715** Leoni *Palladio's Archit.* (1742) I. 82 The Ancients not having had the Use of Stirrups. **1774** J. Bryant *Mythol.* I. 341 They had the use of the sphere, and were acquainted with the zodiac. **1780** *Mirror* No. 81, I was never allowed the use of my limbs, because I could afford a coach. **1814** Wordsw. *Excurs.* v. 849 Nature's..higher creatures born and trained To use of reason. **1826** Galt *Last of Lairds* ix. 85 Considering the use ye have had of his money.

**b.** The power of using some faculty, etc.; ability to use or employ.

**1483** Caxton *Gold. Leg.* 432/1 Fyue wymmen..recouerd the use of goyng whiche they had loste by dyuers sekenesse. **1539** Elyot *Cast. Helth* (1541) 64 Passions of the mynde.. bryng a man from the vse of reason, and somtime in the displeasure of almightye God. **1585** T. Washington tr. *Nicholay's Voy.* Ep. Ded., He had the exquisite vse of two and twenty sundry tongues. **1592** in J. Morris *Troubles Cath. Forefathers* (1877) 30 Another Catholic, that had but the use of one of his hands. **1610** Shaks. *Temp.* iii. iii. 38 People..expressing (Although they want the vse of tongue) a kinde Of excellent dumbe discourse. *a* **1654** Gataker *Antid. Errour* Ep. Ded. (1670) A 3 b, If God had granted him a little longer use of light [= life]. **1711** Steele *Spect.* No. 36 ⁋ 8 How hard a thing it is for those to keep Silence who have the Use of Speech. **1753** Challoner *Cath. Chr. Instr.* 23 Till a Person is come to the Use of Reason. **1859** Tennyson *Merlin & V.* 495 She lay as dead, And lost all use of life. **1860** Mrs. Carlyle *Lett.* (1883) III. 51 'Little darling' has lost the use of an arm and hand by paralysis.

**11.** The act of accustoming or fact of being accustomed by repeated exercise, employment, application, etc.; habituation, practice.

**1382** Wyclif 1 *Sam.* xvii. 39 Thanne Dauid..began to asaye if armyd he myȝte goo...And Dauid seide to Saul, I may not thus goo, for and vse I haue not. *c* **1440** *Promp. Parv.* 508/1 Vse, oftyne tymys, þat ys callyd excersyse,.. *exercicium.* *c* **1470** Henry *Wallace* viii. 1259 Lang ws in wer gert thaim desyr thair will. **1529** More *Dyaloge* i. Wks. 144/2 Howe far so euer his people fal from the vse of vertue. **1551** T. Wilson *Logike* C viii, When men can by muche vse, leape, wrastle, or cast the barre, better then any other. *a* **1586** Sidney *Astroph. & Stella* cvii, Giue thy lieuetenancie To this great cause, which needes both use and art. **1680** Moxon *Mech. Exerc.* xii. 203 Use has made the Mawl more handy for them. *a* **1774** Goldsm. tr. *Scarron's Com. Romance* (1775) I. 154, I frequented all the fencing-schools to keep my hand in vse. **1788** Gibbon *Decl. & F.* xli. IV. 130 The infantry..yielded to the more prevailing use and reputation of the cavalry. **1805** Wordsw. *Prelude* vii. 332 Ere we have learnt by use to slight the crimes And sorrows of the world. **1819** Shelley *Cenci* iii. i. 173 Should the offender live?..and make, by use, His crime Thine.. element.

**12.** *Eccl.* The distinctive ritual and liturgy, form of service or public worship, that prevailed or obtained in a particular church, province, diocese, community, etc. Now *Hist.*

*c* **1380** WYCLIF *Sel. Wks.* III. 202 To seie matynes and masse and evensong bi Salisbury uss. *Ibid.* 482. *c* **1430** *St. Cuthbert* (Surtees) 7549 Of monkys vse þai saide þair houres. *c* **1470** HENRY *Wallace* x. 1006 Salysbery oyss our clerkis than has tan. **1527** *Prymer* (title-p.), This prymer of Salysbury vse. **1548–9** (*title*), The Booke of the Common Prayer.. after the vse of the Churche of England. *Ibid.* Pref., Some folowyng Salsbury vse, some Herford vse, some the vse of Bangor, some of Yorke, and some of Lincolne. *Ibid.*, From hencefurth, all the whole realme shall haue but one vse. **1590** in Fuller *Ch. Hist.* (1655) IX. 198 The said Thomas Cartwright..conformed himself in both to the use and form of some other forraign Churches. **1636** PAGITT *Christianogr.* III. 95 The Popes Legates..brought in the Roman use or service into Ireland. **1643** BAKER *Chron., Hen. V*, 58 In his third yeare, the order of Church Service.. was changed from the use of Pauls to the use of Salisbury. **1849** ROCK *Ch. of Fathers* I. v. (1903) I. 321 Almost the whole of the Salisbury Use had been printed while this country was still Catholic. **1878** SIMMONS *Lay Folks Mass Bk.* 89 The Order of Mass for Trinity Sunday, according to the use of York. *Ibid.* 354 A comparative calendar and index of fixed feasts, so necessary in the identification of uses.

**b.** Religious rite or ceremony observed in particular services of the church; a customary form of religious observance or service.

**1382** WYCLIF *Exod.* xxvii. 19 Alle the vessels of the tabernacle, into alle vsis and serymonyes,..thow shalt make of brasse. *c* **1425** WYNTOUN *Cron.* II. 715 His body..Was put in honest sepulture, Wiþ swylk oysse and solempnyte As þat tyme was in þat cuntre. **1560** DAUS tr. *Sleidane's Comm.* 34 He him selfe..cannot tell what time this accustomed vse of masse..came vp. **1877** A. J. ROSS *Mem. A. Ewing* 180 Some very remarkable 'uses'.., such as mixing water with the wine in the Holy Communion. **1889** PATER *G. de Latour* (1896) 39 This mother of churches, which had also its own picturesque peculiarities of 'use'. **1897** *Daily News* 12 April 6/7 The revived 'use' of the Victorian era in the Anglican Church.

**13.** The custom, usage, or practice obtaining or prevailing in a particular country, community, etc.

**1432–50** tr. *Higden* (Rolls) I. 401 The vse of that cuntre differrethe from the rite of Englonde in clothenge,..and in mony other thynges. *c* **1450** CAPGRAVE *Life St. Augustine* 47, I trowe þat he had þe vse of Itaile whilles he studied þere, and coude not litly out of þe same vse, for þei ete not mech at onys. *c* **1500** *Melusine* xxvi. 207 The halle was hanged nobly with ryche clothes after the vse of the land. **1582** N. LICHEFIELD tr. *Castanheda's Conq. E. Ind.* I. lxxvi. 155 His night gowne was..after the French use laced about, with lase of golde. **1885** DUNCKLEY in *Manch. Weekly Times* 23 May 5/6 The proper pronunciation..was handed down by oral tradition and by the use of the synagogue.

†**b.** *Sc.* Accustomed manner of life. *Obs.*

*c* **1425** WYNTOUN *Cron.* VII. 1218 His awyn oysse to lif wertual, May mirroure and ensampil be Til alkyn statis. *c* **1470** HENRY *Wallace* VII. 1279 In wtlaw oys he lewit thar but let.

**III.** Manner of using.

**14.** Manner or mode of employing, applying, turning to account, etc.: **a.** With qualifying adjs.

*c* **1325** *Metr. Hom.* 3 That wisdom..That God hauis giuen us for to spend, In god oys til our liues end. *a* **1340** HAMPOLE *Psalter* lxxvii. 14 He gifis þaim..riches, and þai disperd þaim in ill oyse. *c* **1340** — *Prose Tr.* 11 All maner of wilfull pollusyone procurede one any maner agaynes kyndly oys. **1390** GOWER *Conf.* III. 136 Loke wel that he ne schifte Hise wordes to no wicked us. **1526** TINDALE *Romans* i. 27 Lyke wyse also the men lefte the naturall vse of the woman. **1563** *Homilies* II. *Use of Ch.* II. Cc iij, Concernyng the right vse of the temple of god. **1592** WYRLEY (*title*), The True Vse of Armorie, shewed by Historie. **1667** MILTON *P. L.* IV. 204 [He] perverts best things To worst abuse, or to thir meanest use. **1781** COWPER *Retirem.* 170 Nor these alone prefer a life recluse, Who seek retirement for its proper use. **1804** *Med. Jrnl.* XII. 433 The result of the advantageous use of that remedy.

**b.** Without qualification.

**1624** E. GUNTER (*title*), The Description and vse of the Sector. The Crosse-staffe and other instruments. **1669** STURMY *Mariner's Mag.* I. ii. 5 So have you made the Mariner's Sea-Compass. The Use shall be shew'd in its place. **1703** MOXON *Mech. Exerc.* 348 The use of the Line of Chords. As its use is very easie, so its convenience is very great.

**15.** With *a* and pl. A manner or method of using, utilizing, or employing; an instance of this. *To make a ... use of*: cf. 1 c.

**1386** *Rolls of Parlt.* III. 226/1 The whiche comune wronge uses [of the king's power], and many other if it lyke to yow mowe be shewed. **1611** BIBLE *Transl. Pref.* ¶ 4 But what mention wee three or foure vses of the Scripture? **1634** SIR T. HERBERT *Trav.* 154 If they casually finde a piece of paper that has his [*sc.* Jesus'] name in it, they preserue it from all bad uses. **1651** J. READING *Guide to Holy City* xxxv. 428 To make a more thankfull, prudent, and holy use thereof [*sc.* of health]. **1725** WATTS *Logic* (1736) 359 There is a proper Use to be made of large Paraphrases. *Ibid.*, There is also a Use of shorter Hints. **1774** GOLDSM. *Nat. Hist.* (1776) VI. 250 With respect to their [*sc.* animals] uses indeed,..they differ much. **1819** SHELLEY *Cenci* IV. iii. 55 Thou wert a weapon in the hand of God To a just use. **1825** SCOTT *Talism.* xii, A use of the weapon, sometimes..resorted to, when a missile was necessary. **1849** MACAULAY *Hist. Eng.* vi. II. 64 He..made so dexterous an use of the influence of that cabal that [etc.]. **1875** JOWETT *Plato* (ed. 2) IV. 157 Some of these uses of the word are confusing.

**IV.** Purpose served by the thing used.

**16.** A purpose, object, or end, esp. of a useful or advantageous nature.

*c* **1340** HAMPOLE *Pr. Consc.* 3674 Yhit may it availle to a gude use. **1382** WYCLIF *Titus* iii. 14 Forsothe and oure men lerne for to be bifore in good werkis, to necessarie vses, that thei be not vnfruytouse. *c* **1425** WYNTOUN *Cron.* II. 246 He ordaynyt þe iugis set [=seat] To be for þat oysse þe market. **1495** GLANVIL *Trevisa's Barth. De P. R.* v. lxiv. (W. de W.) 182 Skynnes of beestes been graunted to men for ryght many maners and dyuerse vses. **1552–3** in Feuillerat *Revels Edw. VI* (1914) 104 Prouided for lynyng of..his officers garmentes and like vses. **1597** HOOKER *Eccl. Pol.* v. lxxix. § 1 If we..convert some small contemptible portion thereof to charitable uses. **1623** J. TAYLOR (Water P.) *Discov. by Sea* B 8 b, At his death perhaps..he will giue.. a little money to Pious vses. **1669** STURMY *Mariner's Mag.* II. vi. 67 This is sufficient for that Use, to shew you the difference between the true Compass and the Steering Compass. **1726** SWIFT *Gulliver* I. viii, I had the tallow.. for greasing my boat, and other uses. **1736** *Act* 9 *Geo. II*, c. 36 Many large..Alienations or Dispositions made by.. Persons, to Uses called Charitable Uses. **1818** SHELLEY *Julian & Maddalo* 100, I..saw..A building on an island; such a one As age to age might add, for uses vile. **1842** TENNYSON *Day-Dream* 201 To what uses shall we put The wildweed-flower that simply blows?

**b.** With limiting genitive phr. or poss. pron.

**1382** WYCLIF *Exod.* xxx. 37 Siche a makynge ȝe shulen not make into ȝoure owne vses. **1535** COVERDALE *Baruch* vi. 10 The prestes..take the golde and syluer from them, and put it to their owne vses. **1550** *Extr. Aberd. Reg.* (1844) I. 277 That tha may caus mak inuintour thairof to be keipit to the vsis of the altaragis thairof in tymes cuming. **1600** SHAKS. 2 *Hen. IV*, II. i. 127 (Q. 1), You haue..made her serue your vses both in purse and in person. **1654** *Nicholas Papers* (Camden) II. 43 There is some oweing to me, that I have layd out for his Highnes uses. **1673** RAY *Journ. Low C.* 36 To cast the Rain Water..into a large Cistern, where it is kept for the uses of the House.

†**c.** The provision, supplying, or maintenance *of* something. *Obs. rare.*

**1382** WYCLIF 2 *Sam.* xxiv. 22 Hast thou..a wayn, and ȝockis of oxen into the vse of trees [1388 in to vss of wode]. **1427** *Cov. Leet Bk.* 110 Dyuers somes..to go to þe vce of vestments of þe Trinite chirche. **1496** *Ibid.* 572 Euery other person [to pay]..xx d. to þe vse of þe Cundith. **1497** *Ibid.* 587.

†**d.** A part of a sermon or homily devoted to the practical application of doctrine. *Obs.*

**1631** MASSINGER *Emperor East* III. ii, I am so tir'd With your tedious exhortations, doctrines, vses, Of your religious morality. **1641** BROME *Joviall Crew* Ded., I will winde up all, with a Use of Exhortation. **1679** SOUTH *Serm.* 43, I proceed now to the Uses which may be drawn from the Truths delivered. **1734** WATTS *Relig. Juv.* (1789) 81 In his last sermon he had an use of reproof, for some vices which were practised..in his parish. **1816** SCOTT *Old Mort.* xvii, A..devout, Christian woman, whom many thought as good as himself at extracting a doctrine or an use. *Ibid.* xviii, The discourse..was divided into fifteen heads, each of which was garnished with seven uses of application.

*fig.* **1632** MASSINGER *Maid of Hon.* I. i, When you had been Cudgell'd well twice or thrice, and from the doctrine Made profitable uses.

**e.** *Forging.* (See quots. 1861 and 1875.)

**1783** H. CORT in *Patents Manuf. Iron* (1858) 10 Peculiar method..of preparing, welding, and working various sorts of iron, and of reducing the same into uses by machinery. **1861** SIR W. FAIRBAIRN *Iron* 102 The forging of 'uses,' that is,..those peculiar forms so extensively in demand for steam-engines, steam-boats, railway carriages, and other works. **1863** *Appleby's Handbk. Mach. & Iron Work* 49 Forgings... Boss Uses. **1875** KNIGHT *Dict. Mech.* 2685 *Use*,..a slab of iron welded to the side of a bar near the end, to be drawn down by the hammer in prolongation of the length of the bar.

**17.** The fact or quality of serving the needs or ends *of* a person or persons.

*a* **1340** HAMPOLE *Psalter* iv. 8 Whet, wyne and oile..ere mast nedful til mannys oise. **1375** BARBOUR *Bruce* XIX. 196 [They] distroyit the men ilkane, And till thar oys thar gude has tane. *c* **1400** MAUNDEV. (Roxb.) xviii. 84 Of þe whyte peper sell þai bot lytill,..bot kepez it till þair awen vse. *c* **1450** LOVELICH *Merlin* 946 (Kölbing), God to his ws hath taken it, trewly. *c* **1480** HENRYSON *Pract. Medecyne* 47 This vntment is rycht ganand for ȝour awin vs. **1522** in *Ripon Ch. Acts* (Surtees) 357 To the usse and behowe of Cecill my wiffe. **1560** BIBLE *Judith* xii. 15 Her maide..spred for her skinnes..which she had receiued of Bagoes for her daily vse. — *Wisdom* xv. 7 The potter..facioneth euerie vessel with labour to our vse. **1617** J. TAYLOR (Water P.) *Observ. & Trav. fr. London to Hamburgh* F 2, Hares..killed..and carried to the markets by cart-loads, and sold for the vse of the honourable owners. **1657** MILTON *Lett. State* Wks. 1851 VIII. 387 Rice, Sugar, and Coffee..for the use of the Grand Seignior. **1713** BERKELEY *Hylas & Phil.* I. Wks. 1871 I. 273 Common language..is framed by and for the use of the vulgar. **1774** GOLDSM. *Nat. Hist.* (1776) I. 230 We shall never know whether the things of this world have been made for our use. **1821** SCOTT *Pirate* ii, A bargain of rock-cod, purchased..for the use of the family. **1895** SCULLY *Kafir Stories* 106 Food for the use of the Zulus on the journey would be provided.

**18.** *Law.* The advantage *of* a specified person or persons in respect of profit or benefit derived from lands or tenements, etc.

In AF. the original *us* (also *use*) was later replaced by the unrelated forms *oes, eus, eups, ops, oeps*: see OEPS.

**1393** in *Collect. Topogr.* (1836) III. 256 A rente charge paiable to the vs and profit of his chanterie there. **1429** *Rolls of Parlt.* IV. 344/1 Any of the seide Lordes shal,..to thair use or behove, receyve or take any astate, feffement, or possession of landys..that standith..in debate. **1442** *Ibid.* V. 57/1 The said Feffees haue no title ner interest therynne, but only upon trust, and to his use, to execute his will. **1487** *Act* 3 *Hen. VII*, c. 4 All dedes of gyfte of goodes and catalles..made of trust to thuse of that persone or persones that made the same dede of gyfte. **1535–6** *Act* 27 *Hen. VIII*, c. 10 § 4 Where..purchase of any Landes.. shalbe made..to any other person or persones..to the use and behove of the seid Husbond and Wife or to the use of the wife. **1599** in *Roxb. Ball.* (1886) VI. p. xxvi, The somme of sixteene poundes of myne Restinge in the handes and keepinge for me and to my use of Richard Oringe. **1729** JACOB *Law Dict.*, *Cestui que Use*..signifies him to whose Use any other Man is enfeoffed of any Lands or Tenements. **1766** BLACKSTONE *Comm.* II. 271 The lands were granted.. to nominal feoffees to the use of the religious houses. **1818** CRUISE *Digest* (ed. 2) I. 338 If the heir refuses to come in.., the Lord..may seize the estate to his own use. **1843** *Penny Cycl.* XXVI. 65 If a feoffment had been made to A for life to his own use, with remainder to B in fee for the use of C.

**19.** Office; function; service.

**1509** HAWES *Past. Pleas.* xxiv. (Percy Soc.) 108 This is the use of the eyene intere, To se all thynges. **1560** BIBLE (Genev.) 1 *Chron.* xxviii. 15 For the candlestickes of siluer, ..and the lampes thereof, according to the vse of euerie candlesticke. *a* **1718** PRIOR *Alma* ii. 398 Observe but in these Neighb'ring Lands, The diff'rent Use of Mouths and Hands. **1729** LAW *Serious C.* iv. 47 Things may, and must differ in their use. **1811** A. T. THOMSON *Lond. Disp.* (1818) 442 The use of the sand in these processes is to prevent the amber.. from passing over into the receiver. **1858** SEARS *Athan.* xviii. 161 It performs its use in the grand economy.

**20.** The character, property, or quality which makes a thing useful or suitable for some purpose; capability for securing some end; usefulness, utility; advantage, benefit.

**1598** MANWOOD *Lawes Forest* To Rdr., The necessarie vse and common good, that may arise..by the publishing of this Treatise. **1628** PRYNNE *Cens. Cozens* 40, I would willingly learne but this much..: what vse there is of these Deuotions ..in our Church or State? **1667** MILTON *P. L.* VII. 346 God made two great Lights, great for thir use To Man. **1700** LOCKE *Hum. Und.* (ed. 4) IV. vii. § 14, I may have reason to think their use is not answerable to the great Stress which seems to be laid on them. **1712** STEELE *Spect.* No. 492 ¶ 2 Here's a little Country Girl that's very cunning, that makes her use of being young and unbred. **1759** JOHNSON *Rasselas* xxxi, He that has built for use, till use is supplied, must begin to build for vanity. **1780** BENTHAM *Princ. Legisl.* (1789) p. ccxcv, A few words, for the purpose of giving a general view of the method of division here pursued,..may have their use. **1853** KANE *Grinnell Exp.* xxix. (1856) 248 Her position changes so constantly that there is little use of recording it. **1878** T. HARDY *Ret. Native* II. ii, Is there any use in saying what can do no good, aunt? **1880** MRS. FORRESTER *Roy & V.* I. 3 What is the use of making up my mind.

**b.** In the phr. *to* or *of* (*no, little*, etc.) *use.*

(*a*) **1382** WYCLIF *Wisdom* xiii. 13 To noon vse, a crokid tree..he maketh. **1542** UDALL tr. *Erasm. Apoph.* 157 b, Denying the arte of geometrie..to bee to veraye litle use or purpose. **1611** BIBLE *Tobit* vi. 6 To what vse is..the gall of the fish? **1643** CROMWELL *Lett. & Sp.* (1871) II. 288 It is to no use any man's saying he will do this or that. **1868–** in Yks. and Oxford dialect use (*Eng. Dial. Dict.*).

(*b*) **1627** J. TAYLOR (Water P.) *Armado, or Navy of Land Ships* C 1, The Snarle, a small dogged Pinnace, of more vse then profit. **1634** SIR T. HERBERT *Trav.* 35 A Castle planted with great Ordnance and Ammunition, but of small vse. **1663** BP. PATRICK *Parab. Pilgr.* xxxvi, It is a thing of great Use, and great Value. **1711** ADDISON *Spect.* No. 121 ¶ 2 Beasts and Birds..that are of Assistance and Use to Man. **1735** JOHNSON *Lobo's Abyssinia* Voy. iv. 27 Some pieces of Callicoe, which were of the same Use as Money. **1810** CRABBE *Borough* xx. 322 To be of use Would pleasant thoughts and heavenly hopes produce. **1859** F. E. PAGET *Curate Cumbersworth* 354, I had good reason to hope that I was being of use at Roost. **1880** GEIKIE *Phys. Geog.* ii. 83 Snow is of great use in winter, as it protects vegetation from being nipped by severe frost.

**c.** With ellipse of prep.

**1820** SHELLEY *Let. to Maria Gisborne* 222 Alas! it is no use to say, 'I'm poor!' **1837** J. H. NEWMAN *Lett.* (1891) II. 230 From their thinking it no use doing good, unless it is talked about. **1874** DASENT *Half a Life* III. 46 Fifty years before it might have been some use to him. **1886** 'H. CONWAY' *Living or Dead* xxv, Rothwell [tried]..to look as much at his ease as possible. But it was no use.

**21.** Need or occasion for using or employing; necessity, demand, exigency. Freq. *to have use for* (or † *of*).

**1604** SHAKS. *Oth.* III. iii. 319 Giue it [*sc.* a handkerchief] me...I haue vse for it. **1607** NORDEN *Surv. Dial.* 213 For there is no Country..but hath vse of timber. **1633** BP. HALL *Hard Texts, N. T.* 95 Not out of any necessity or use of nature..he took that fish. **1672** *Mede's Wks.* (ed. 3) *Life* p. xxxvi, A Book of Mathematicks which he had great use of, and had long thirsted after. **1695** DRYDEN *Parallel Poetry & Paint.* Ess. (ed. Ker) II. 140 Our author calls them figures to be let; because the picture has no use of them. **1826** ANDREW SCOTT *Poems* 39 The warld will still have use for you and me. **1854** H. MILLER *Sch. & Schm.* vii, There was no use, they said, for being in the Devil's Cave so late.

**b.** In the phr. *to have no use for*, to be set against; to wish to have nothing to do with; to dislike. Orig. *U.S.*

**1887** *Trans. Amer. Philol. Assoc.* XVII. 46, I have no use for him—don't like him. **1896** *Harper's Mag.* XCII. 771/1 Bülow..spoke his mind freely to his adjutant. 'I have no use for Bernadotte,' said he. **1903** 'H. S. MERRIMAN' *Last Hope* xl, The Marquis had..spoken in French, and the Captain had no use for that language.

**V. 22.** *attrib.* and *Comb.*, as **use-value**; *use-established*, *-making*, *-trampler*; **use-forge** (see 16 e and FORGE *sb.*); **use-inheritance** (see quot. 1890). Also USE-MAN, -MONEY.

**1608** DOD & CLEAVER *Expos. Prov.* ix–x. 15 A profitable use-making of the undeserued favour..shewed unto them. **1617** HIERON *Wks.* (1620) II. 290 The well vnderstanding and right vse-making of these. **1873** *Iron* 5 Apr. 356/1 A use forge with a 45-cwt. double-acting Nasmyth's steam hammer. **1887** BROWNING *Parleyings, Apollo & Fates* 61 What if we granted—law flouter, use-trampler—His life at the suit of an upstart? **1887** tr. *Marx' Capital* I. 2 The utility of a thing makes it a use-value. *Ibid.*, Use-values become a reality only by use or consumption. **1890** W. P. BALL *Effects Use & Disuse* 23 The increasing difficulty of complex evolution by natural selection is no proof whatever of use-inheritance. [*Note.*] I venture to coin this concise term to signify the direct inheritance of the effects of use and disuse in kind. **1897** *Month* April 364 'Mass,' in the honest, use-established sense, means the Roman Mass.

**Use** (yūz), *v.* Forms: *α.* 3–4, 7 vsen (5 vsyn, vson), 3–4 usen (5 usyn), 4–7 vse (3–4 vsi, 4 vsy, 4–5 vsie, *Sc.* 5–6 wse, 6 ws, vsz), 4– use (4 usy, 8 ues); 5 ouse, yowese, 6 (9 *dial.*) youse, 9 *dial.* yuse, 5 (9 *dial.*) hewse, 6 euse (9 *dial.* ewse). *β. north.* and *Sc.* 4 oise, 4–6 oys, oyse, 5–6 oyss (5 oysse, os, ose), 6 oiss; 4 wyse, 5 vyse, 6 vise. [ad. OF. *user* (also F.), *useir, usser, uiser*, etc. (= Sp. and Pg. *usar*, It. *usare*, med.L. *ūsāre*), f. L. *ūs-*, ppl. stem of *ūtī*: see prec.]

**I. 1.** *trans.* To celebrate, keep, or observe (a rite, custom, etc.); to pursue or follow as a custom or usage.

*a* **1240** *Lofsong* in *O. E. Hom.* I. 207 Þurh alle þe oðre sacremenz þet holi chirche foluweð and useð. *c* **1290** *Beket* 518 in *S. Eng. Leg.* I. 121 Customes here weren bi-fore i-vsed, ich onder-stonde. **1340** *Ayenb.* 48 Vor alle þe sacremens of holi cherche me ssel vsi clenliche. **1387** Trevisa *Higden* (Rolls) IV. 351 Þat manere is ȝit i-used in the chirche of Rome. *c* **1400** *Destr. Troy* 9097 Þen ordant was..a fynerall fest, þat frekes þen vset. ? *a* **1450** *Compend. Treat.* in Roy *Rede me*, etc. (Arb.) 183 The lettre of the ceremonies of ye olde lawe sleyth the Iewes and them that nowe vsen them. *c* **1450** *St. Cuthbert* (Surtees) 2076 Þai vsed customes vnstabill. **1504** in Leadam *Star Chamber Cases* (Selden Soc. 1911) II. 286 Contrare to ther costomez out of tyme of mynde vsed. *c* **1592** Marlowe *Jew of Malta* iv. ii, *Bar.* No, 'tis an order which the Fryars vse. **1622** J. Taylor (Water P.) *Farew. Tower-bottles* A 2 b, So..did Customes change: The Ancient vse, vs'd many yeares before, Was solde. **1625** Purchas *Pilgrims* II. 1132 The like custom is vsed throughout the Dominions of Mutezuma. *a* **1648** Ld. Herbert *Hen. VIII* (1683) 7 That the Crown might be put on the King's Head with that Solemnity, which in former times was used. **1889** Meiklejohn *New Hist. Eng.* i. 11 Many noble Britons assumed and used the Roman toga,.. and the customs and manners of their conquerors.

†**b.** (*To be*) *used*, to constitute a use, usage, or custom; to be usual or customary. Also (*b*) with *to* (and inf.), or *that* (and clause). *Obs.*

**13..** *Gosp. Nicodemus* (G.) 122 Of Emperoures þat are had bene þis was used in þat land. **1387** Trevisa *Higden* (Rolls) V. 145 It was i-ordeyned þe Lente fastynge of Crist..schulde bygynne and dure as it is now i-used. **1422** Yonge tr. *Secreta Secret.* 247 Aftyr the..houre of the day y-custumet or vset. **1550** Crowley *Last Trumpet* 1231 Thou shalt not fynd that thou maiest..leauy a great fine More then hath bene vsed alwayes. **1582** Stanyhurst *Æneis* i. (Arb.) 28 Of Tyrian virgins too weare thus a quiuer is vsed [L. *mos est*]. **1648** Gage *West Ind.* 88, I thought..of Indians turned into the shape of beasts (which amongst some hath been used). **1650** in W. S. Perry *Hist. Coll. Amer. Col. Ch.* (1860) I. 2 It shall be lawful, as it hath been used heretofore, to make Probates of wills..in the Colony.

(*b*) **1377** Langl. *P. Pl.* B. xviii. 377 It is nouȝt vsed in erthe to hangen a feloun Ofter þan ones. *c* **1450** in *Surtees Misc.* (1890) 62 It is usyd that the sayd Burgese schall chese..two ale tastars. **1487** *Sc. Acts, Jas. III* (1814) II. 182/2 Ane vthir to..haue thare feis as wes vsit to be gevin to..changeoures in ald tymes. **1523** Fitzherb. *Husb.* § 15 It is vsed in many countreys, the husbandes to haue an oxe-harowe..made of sixe smal peces of timbre. **1548** Hall *Chron., Hen. VII*, 50 b, It was also vsed that he..shoulde likewise..be..committed to the Bishoppes pryson. **1577** Fulke *Answ. True Christian* 42 From the beginning it was not vsed to praye for the deade. **1621** Bp. Mountagu *Diatribæ* 531 It was in old times vsed..for men to shaue themselues. **1642** tr. *Perkins' Prof. Bk.* ii. § 119. 53 Forasmuch as it is commonly used to write a deede before it be sealed.

†**2.** To observe or comply with (a law, rule, etc.); to enforce or put into practice. *Obs.*

*a* **1300** *Cursor M.* 9478 Þis es bot lagh..Vsed in curth þis ilk dai. *c* **1320** *Cast. Love* 240 In þe kynges court ȝit vche day Me vseþ þulke selue lay. *c* **1350** *Will. Palerne* 5240 Alle luþer lawes þat long hadde ben vsed. **1440** *Paston Lett.* I. 40 The Duk..hath made his oath upon the Sacrement, and usyd it, never for to bere armes ayenst Englond. *c* **1450** *St. Cuthbert* (Surtees) 2076 To vse þair reule þai [*sc.* monks] had na wille. *Ibid.* 3706 Our haly faders statutes,..Vyse ȝe þaim besyly as ȝow aghte. **1526** Tindale 1 *Tim.* i. 8 We knowe that the lawe is god, yf a man vse it lawfully. **1609** Skene *Reg. Maj.* 3 Al Barons sall receaue, and vse the lawes, as they are vsed in the Kings court.

**3.** To prosecute or pursue (some course of action); to do, perform, carry on. Now *rare.*

*α.* *a* **1352** Minot *Poems* (ed. Hall) ii. 30 Þe Skotte..vses all threting with gaudes and gile. **1444** *Rolls of Parlt.* V. 121 The seid Co[mun]alte..may use accion of the somes of money accorded to be payd to the seid Co[mun]alte, ayeinst him. **1454** *Ibid.* 255 That all manere of persones..use thaire continuel abood uppon thaire said Office. **1547** Boorde *Introd. Knowl.* 217 They be lyght fyngerd and vse pyking. **1573** Tusser *Husb.* (1878) 113 Use now in thy rie, little raking or none. **1648** Gage *West Ind.* x. 35 The chiefest Market place, where all the buying and selling was used. **1670** Narborough *Jrnl.* in *Acc. Sev. Late Voy.* i. (1694) 52 They use bathing and stuping those places. **1765–8** Erskine *Inst. Law Scot.* ii. ix. § 4 The superior's consent is presumed, from his not using acts of interruption. **1873** W. Stokes *Rapid Writing* 100 The Art of using writing should be ..inculcated by all teachers.

*β.* **1375** Barbour *Bruce* x. 565, I oysit lang that travalling, So that I can that rod ga richt. *c* **1425** Wyntoun *Cron.* vii. x. 3528 In Ingilwode and Bernnysdaile Þai oyssit al þis tyme þar trawale. *c* **1450** *St. Cuthbert* (Surtees) 7008 At his graue he vysit praying. **1513** Douglas *Æneid* xii. xiv. 110 Oys furth thy chance: quhat nedis proces mar?

†**4.** To ply or carry on (an occupation, profession, etc.); to follow or exercise; to discharge the functions of (an office). *Obs.*

**1375** Barbour *Bruce* xii. 414 Men that oysis thai mysterls. **1382** Wyclif 1 *Chron.* xxiv. 2 Eleasar vsede presthode, and Ythamar. *c* **1440** *Generydes* 1176 Wherefore they calle vs noo good lauenders, And we haue vsid it thus many yerez. **1495** *Acta Dom. Conc.* (1839) 415/1 In caise..Alexander haid remanit..nocht within þe said toune nor vsand þe Course of merchandise þerintill. **1542** *Reg. Cupar Abbey* II. 22 We will at nane hant nor vs the office of brewing, bakin, selling of wyne [etc.]. **1556** *Rec. Inverness* (New Spald. Cl.) I. 2 Aganis the law the sayd Thom..dispresit him wsand his office. **1585** T. Washington tr. *Nicholay's Voy.* ii. viii. 42 [If] she will continue in that occupation, she..may vse it at her pleasure. **1611** Bible 1 *Tim.* iii. 10 Then let them vse the office of a Deacon, being found blamelesse. **1652** Needham tr. *Selden's Mare Cl.* 197 Merchants..using Commerce in the very Sea with the Inhabitants. **1665** in De Foe *Plague* (1754) 48 That no Searcher..be permitted to use any public Work or Employment. **1721** Perry *Daggenh. Breach* 115 Commanders of Ships, particularly those who use the Southern Trade. **1773** *Life N. Frowde* 75 An Implement Mr. M'Namara had worn ever since he used the Mediterranean Trade.

*transf.* **1730** *Lett. to Strickland rel. Coal Trade* 16 A Number of Ships crouded into the [Coal] Trade, that did not use it before.

†**b.** To follow or pursue (a manner or course of life). *Obs.*

*c* **1340** Hampole *Prose Tr.* 25 Our Lorde forto stere som forto vse this medlid liffe toke [etc.]. *a* **1450** *Knt. de la Tour* (1868) 12 [She] used the blessed lyf that any woman might. **1483** Caxton *Gold. Leg.* 195 b/1 Whan she had lyued and usyd thys lyf fyfty yere. **1578** *Scot. Poems 16th C.* (1801) II. 125 The wicked life that I did vse. **1821** Scott *Pirate* xxxi, I am determined to turn honest man, and use this life [*sc.* piracy] no longer.

**c.** To spend or pass (a period of time) in a certain way. (Now only as implying sense 7.)

**1477** Earl Rivers (Caxton) *Dictes* 5 He is happy that usith his dayes in doyng couenable thinges. *a* **1533** Ld. Berners *Huon* lxxxii. 256 In grete doloure & payne I haue vsyd my youth. **1538** Starkey *England* i. i. 24 So now also vse your tyme..to the mayntenance..of the same. **1607** Shaks. *Timon* iii. i. 39, I haue obserued thee alwayes for.. one that knowes what belongs to reason; and canst vse the time wel. **1613** *Sidney's Arcadia* iii. 390 Now me thinks it time To goe vnto the Bride, and vse this day. **1873** W. Stokes *Rapid Writing* 43 Use your spare moments in practising Writing.

†**d.** To frequent (another's company). *Obs.*

**1547** Boorde *Brev. Health* cccxxxix. C vij, Fyrste lyue out of syn..and than vse honest myrth and honest company. **1564** *Child-Marriages* (1897) 101 As report is, she hath vsid the evill Companie of William Gallimour. **1599** Shaks., etc. *Pass. Pilgr.* 422 They that fawn'd on him before Use his company no more.

**5.** To engage in, practise (a game, etc.).

**1320–30** *Horn Ch.* 42 To harpe wele, and play at ches, And al gamen that used is. *c* **1380** *Sir Ferumb.* 2225 Summe þay vseþ a maner of play to caste wel a spere. **1557** North *Gueuara's Diall Pr.* i. ii. (1568) 163 They agree to their scollers to vse some pastyme. **1581** *Southampton Court Leet Rec.* (1906) ii. 221 Dennys Edwardes..comenly vssethe vnlawffull games. **1626** Bacon *Sylva* § 299 Use not Exercise and a Spare Diet;..if much Exercise, then a Plentifull Diet. *c* **1636** A. Stafford *Just Apol.* (1860) p. xxxix, To shoote in ..Cross-Bowes, and to vse diverse other Recreations. **1764** in Willis & Clark *Cambridge* (1886) III. 539 A..corpulent Man, who lived freely and used no Exercise. ? **1770** T. Bridges *Homer* 11 Let discord cease, Use War abroad, at home use Peace. **1794** S. Williams *Vermont* 83 In such a situation, he uses no exercise. **1801** Strutt *Sports & Past.* ii. ii. 74 In old time,..wrestling was more used than it has been of later years.

†**b.** To have experience, or be engaged, in (war).

*c* **1440** *Alph. Tales* 76 Alde knyghtis þat..vsyd batels & cuthe gyff gude cowncell. **1474** Caxton *Chesse* ii. iv. (1883) 44 He had longe tyme vsid the warre. **1523** Ld. Berners *Froissart* I. cclxxv. 167 b/2 He had long tyme vsed the warre, and sene great experience therin.

**6.** To put into practice or operation; to carry into action or effect.

In very freq. use, with a variety of objects, *c* 1340–*c* 1610.

*α.* **13..** *Gaw. & Gr. Knt.* 2106 He is a mon methles, & mercy non vses. **13..** *Coer de L.* 4670 Yiff thou it [*sc.* clemency] use, Thou dedest nought as I the bad. *c* **1400** *Ywaine & Gaw.* 36 For trowth and luf es al bylaft, Men uses now another craft. *c* **1440** *Alph. Tales* 353 He vsid robborie, avowtrie, inceste. **1483** Caxton *G. de la Tour* e vj b, He ..vsed all euyl dedes whiche he couthe ymagyne to doo. **1542** Brinklow *Lament.* 1 Certayne greate vyces vsed therin [*sc.* in London]. **1550** Baldwin *Mor. Philos.* N vi, To vse vertue is perfecte blessednesse. **1589** Greene *Menaphon* (Arb.) 88 Twas a good world when such simplicitie was vsed, sayes the old women of our time. **1616** R. C. *Times' Whistle* (1871) 50 All lawyers I cannot heerof accuse, For some there are that doe a conscience vse. **1644** Milton *Areop.* (Arb.) 37 The like severity no doubt was us'd. *a* **1680** Butler *Rem.* (1759) I. 15 She [Nature] affects so much to use Variety, in all she does. **1710** W. King *Heathen Gods & Heroes* 41 Her other Brother Neptune used the same Freedom with her. **1758** S. Hayward *Serm.* p. xiv, It is certainly a minister's duty..to use plainness and faithfulness. **1839** Fr. A. Kemble *Resid. in Georgia* (1863) 76 They consider it the lowest degradation in a white to use any exertion. **1898** *Scribner's Mag.* Dec. 690 It was her regular smile, the one she used every evening.

*β.* *a* **1340** Hampole *Psalter*, etc. 497 Oysand sorow for my syn. *c* **1375** *Sc. Leg. Saints* xii. (*Matthias*) 108 Quhen na man mycht se, Þane wald he oyse sic cruelte. **1447** Bokenham *Seyntys* (Roxb.) 167 For þe facundye wych she oysyd þere. *c* **1500** *Lancelot* 1699 To mych to oys familiaritee Contempnyng bryngith one to hir dugre.

**b.** To practise or exercise towards, against, or upon others.

**1387** Trevisa *Higden* (Rolls) VII. 17 He wolde have i-used þe strengþe of religioun, but þe cruelte of Gascoyns wolde nouȝt suffre it. **1388** Wyclif *Matt.* xx. 25 Thei that ben gretter, vsen power on hem. *c* **1460** Fortescue *Abs. & Lim. Mon.* ii. (1885) 111 Vsing vppon thaim the lordshippe that is callid *dominium regale tantum*. **1470** Henry *Wallace* vi. 895 Sic salusyng I oyss till Inglis men. **1542** Udall in *Lett. Lit. Men* (Camden) 4 It maye please your maistership to use towardes me sum moderacion. **1598** R. Bernard tr. *Terence, Andria* Prol., I pray you..use not parcialitie, and diligently weigh the matter. **1632** Massinger & Field *Fatal Dowry* v. i, Therefore use a conscience..To me. **1653** Holcroft *Procopius, Goth. Wars* i. 6 The Goths..had used hostility upon Gratiana. **1656** Earl Monm. tr. *Boccalini's Advts. fr. Parnass.* i. xv, Ingratitude which moral Philosophers were daily seen to use towards their benefactors. **1702** *Eng. Theophrast.* 124 The violences we commit upon our selves are oftentimes more painful, than those which other people use towards us. **1737** Whiston *Josephus, Antiq.* vi. iii. § 4 The ungrateful conduct they have used towards me. **1822** Shelley tr. *Calderon* iii. 78 Tell me all, what poisonous Power Ye use against me.

**II. 7.** To make use of (some immaterial thing) as a means or instrument; to employ for a certain end or purpose.

*α.* *c* **1315** Shoreham i. 532 Wel bet may god to oure prou Dyuerse formes vsy. *c* **1340** Hampole *Pr. Consc.* 3503, I rede ilk man..Þat he use þa ten thinges sere Þat fordus..Alle veniel syns. *c* **1375** *Sc. Leg. Saints* iii. (*Andrew*) 946 Vndir ȝour proteccione to luf in contemplacione, and warldly thingis to refuse and hewinly thing sine to wse. *c* **1400** *St. Alexius* (Laud 622) 672, I graunt wel þat it be so, Þine bedes ȝif þou wilt ouse. *c* **1410** *Lantern of Liȝt* 132 Þat helpe may cum of vsing Goddis word. **1464** *Rolls of Parlt.* V. 561/2 The preferment of labour and occupacion, such as hath been used by the makyng of the seid Cloth. **1537** Cromwell in Merriman *Life & Lett.* (1902) II. 107 That vising your effortes ernestly..in other pointes of your charche & comission you schalbe playne with the said depute. **1568** Grafton *Chron.* II. 52 He so vsed the matter with Adrian the fourth., that he was by him dispensed of his aforesayde othe. **1592** *Arden of Feversham* i. i. 256 As sharpe witted Poets..Vse humble promise to their sacred Muse. **1614** T. Davies (Heref.) *Eclogue* 198, I nill vsen any skill so mytch ..as this so nice, and free. **1671** Milton *P. R.* ii. 380 And who withholds my pow'r that right to use? **1732** Bp. Berkeley *Alciphr.* v. § 35 Freedom is either a blessing or a curse as men use it. **1766** Goldsm. *Vicar* xxi, His generous patron..judged it highly expedient to use dispatch, lest [etc.]. **1819** Shelley *Cenci* i. i. 127 The third of my possessions! I must use Close husbandry, or gold..Falls from my withered hand. **1877** Sparrow *Serm.* xiv. 183 The blessings of this life generally, he says, the good man uses but does not serve. **1884** tr. *Lotze's Metaph.* 433 Using the images of processes which themselves spring from it in a way we cannot explain.

*β.* *a* **1340** Hampole *Psalter* Prol. (1884) 4 He spekis of crist..in þat at he oises þe voice of his seruantes. *c* **1375** *Sc. Leg. Saints* xxvi. (*Nicholas*) 730, I pray ȝou þat ȝe wil oys it [*sc.* the legend] dewotly. *a* **1400** in *Hampole's Wks.* (Horstm.) I. 261 Þan awe it maste of alle othire Orysouns to be Oysede in all-haly kyrke.

**b.** With *to* (and inf., or sb. denoting purpose).

*c* **1275** Lay. 24293 Moche hii vsede þat craft [= astronomy] to lokie in þan lufte. **1377** Langl. *P. Pl.* B. x. 129 Þo þat vseth þis hauelounes to blende mennes wittes. **14..** *Lydgate's Horse, Shepe & G.* 507 in *Pol., Rel., & L. Poems* (1903) 36 Vse her yiftes & her prerogatives To that same eende. **1486** *Bk. St. Albans* c v, That an hauke use hir craft all the seson to flye or lefe. **1551** in Feuillerat *Revels Edw. VI* (1914) 56 In the meane tyme to vse soche dilligence to his furnyture, as shall seme to you expedyent. **1578** Timme *Calvin on Gen.* 109 Sacrifices were used of the holy fathers, to celebrate the benefits of God. **1644** *Direct. Publique Worship* 32 Endeavours ought to be used to convince him. **1728** Veneer *Sincere Penitent* Pref. p. x, The emperor was obliged to use all his authority to make him leave Antioch. **1798** S. & Ht. Lee *Canterb. T.* II. 3 The arguments used by Lady Lettingham to detain her brother. **1821** Scott *Kenilw.* xxxviii, Until she had used her own efforts to have her rights acknowledged by him. **1874** Green *Short Hist.* vii. 409 Elizabeth used the daring blow to back her negotiations for peace.

**c.** To employ (a standard, type, etc.).

*a* **1300** *Cursor M.* 27274 Vsand oþer weght or mette Again þe lagh in land es sett. *Ibid.* 28437 Again þe lagh..Haf i wysed fals weght and mette. **1387** Trevisa *Higden* (Rolls) I. 37 Þey haueþ a ȝere of apperynge þat þey vseþ in calculynge and in cronicle. **1563** Shute *Archit.* B j b, Afterwardes vsing then the measures of the forsayde Pillours. **1662** Stillingfl. *Orig. Sacræ* i. i. § 20 They might use the form of the Phœnician Letters. **1706** *Act 6 Anne* c. 11 § 17 That..the same Weights and Measures shall be used throughout the United Kingdom. **1826** Jas. Veitch *Tables*, etc. 7 The weight used for Hay..contains 22 pounds..in the Stone.

**8.** To employ or make use of (an article, etc.), esp. for a profitable end or purpose; to utilize, turn to account.

**1303** R. Brunne *Handl. Synne* 2391 Ȝif þe be leyde a borde to wedde,..Ȝif þou hit vse aȝens hys wylle, holy cherche seyþ þat þou dost ylle. *a* **1340** Hampole *Psalter* Prol. (1884) 4 Þis boke of all haly writ is mast oysed in halykyrke seruys. *c* **1400** *Cato's Morals* 152 in *Cursor M.*, Þat þou has gitin to þe, vse hit in honeste, & be noȝt calde niþing. *c* **1450** *St. Cuthbert* (Surtees) 1098 In swete mylk sethe floure of wheete, And vyse it whils it hase þe heete. **1486** *Bk. St. Albans* e iv b, At holyrode day he gooth to Ryde, And vsith the bit When he may gete hit. **1556** *Rec. Inverness* (New Spald. Cl.) I. 2 The serwandis quha wes wyrkand and wssand the bot on the loch. **1585** T. Washington tr. *Nicholay's Voy.* i. xviii. 21 Vpon high places they vse cesternes, but vppon the plaine..they haue many welles. **1680** Moxon *Mech. Exerc.* x. 187 When the Wheel is used, its Edge stands athwart the Cheeks of the Lathe. **1736** Bailey *Housh. Dict.* s.v. *Acorns*, Both the Acorn and husk, are us'd in many astringent medicines. *a* **1815** in A. T. Thomson *Lond. Disp.* 524 It is necessary that all the vessels,..which are used, be of glass. **1833** J. Holland *Manuf. Metal* II. 36 In the manufacture of surgeons' instruments.., the very best steel..should be exclusively used. **1900** *Longm. Mag.* March 435, I received for answer that the first flower used felt cooler than the second one.

**b.** To wear as an article of apparel.

*c* 1375 *Cursor M.* 2048 (Fairf.), Na breke was vsed þan in lande. *c* 1375 *Sc. Leg. Saints* vii. (*James Minor*) 59 Na claþs of sylk he wald nocht were, bot lenyne clath he oysit ay. *a* 1450 MYRC *Par. Pr.* 1032 Hast þou ben prowde of any gyse Of any þynge þat þou dedust vse, Of party hosen, of pykede schone. 1593 MARLOWE *Hero & Leander* I. 31 Buskins of shels all siluered vsed she. *a* 1660 *Contemp. Hist. Irel.* (Ir. Archæol. Soc.) I. 183 How the Councell ussed vizards. 1857 R. M. BALLANTYNE *Coral Island* iv, As they [*sc.* boots] fitted his large limbs and feet, he consented at last to use them. 1885 DILLON *Fairholt's Costume* II. 302 A cloak with a hood, used when travelling 1889 [see 1].

**c.** To make use of (land, ground, etc.) by working, tilling, or occupying.

1573 TUSSER *Husb.* (1878) 17 To get good plot to occupie, and store and vse it husbandlie. 1604 E. G[RIMSTONE] *D'Acosta's Hist. Indies* IV. 209 Although there be.. many mines..as at the Indies, yet they vse none but those of gold and silver. 1641 *Aldeburgh Rec.* in *N. & Q.* 12th Ser. IX. 146/2 Of Robt. Fowler for a yeeres fearme for the shopp he useth. *Ibid.*, Rec'd: of Henry Lawrence for usinge the Towne ground. 1736 PEGGE *Kenticisms* (E.D.S.) 54 He uses it [*sc.* land for farming] himself. *Ibid.*, Who uses this or that farm?

**9.** To work, employ, or manage (an implement, instrument, etc.); to manipulate, operate, or handle, esp. to some useful or desired end.

13.. *K. Alis.* 5256 The glevmen useden her tunge; The wode aqueightte so hy sunge. 1340-70 *Alex. & Dind.* 439 Vs ne likeþ no lome in oure land vse. 1446 LYDG. *2 Nightingale Poems* i. 305 The fende.. Leying hys lynes and with mony a bayte Wsynge his hokes. 1474 CAXTON *Chesse* II. iv. (1883) 44 That he had longe tyme vsid..armes. 1539 BIBLE (Great) *Numb.* x. 2 That thou mayst vse them [*sc.* trumpets] to call ye congregacion together. 1582 N. LICHEFIELD tr. *Castanheda's Conq. E. Ind.* I. iii. 8 b, The people..using the selfe same sorte of darts. 1596 SHAKS. *Merch. V.* II. ii. 5 Good Launcelot Iobbo, vse your legs,.. run awaie. 1611 BIBLE *Jer.* xxiii. 31, I am against the prophets..that vse their tongues. 1613 PURCHAS *Pilgrimage* (1614) 62 In their festiuals they vsed..musical instruments. 1733 TULL *Horse-Hoeing Husb.* 295 A Farmer who uses this Plow, may Till in all Weathers. 1765 A. DICKSON *Treat. Agric.* (ed. 2) 154 Of the instruments used in tillage. 1828 SCOTT *F. M. Perth* ii, While I form armour and weapons for others, I cannot myself withstand the temptation of using them. 1859 TENNYSON *Geraint & Enid* 900 [I have] wrought too long with delegated hands, Not used mine own. 1880 *Encycl. Brit.* XI. 504/2 In these investigations he..used a *perspicillum* or simple lens.

**10.** To employ (a person, animal, etc.) in some function or capacity, esp. for an advantageous end.

1382 WYCLIF *2 Macc.* iv. 40 The cumpanyes aȝein rysynge,.. Lysymacus almest three thousand aarmyd wickid hondis bygan for to vse, [by] sum tyraunt duyk. *c* 1470 HENRY *Wallace* v. 27 In Gyllisland thar was that brachell brede, Sekyr off sent to folow thaim at flede. So was scho vsyt on Esk. 1526 *Pilgr. Perf.* (W. de W. 1531) 299 Vpon the asse, whiche of no man before had ben vsed ne exercised. 1541 WYATT *Declar.* Wks. 1816 II. 281, I used Weldon and Sworder..to be spies over Brauncetour. 1598 FLORIO s.v. *Mulatiere*, The carriers..driue mules, and vse them to carrie. 1600 W. WATSON *Decacordon* (1602) 214 He had better haue vsed his friend in another matter. 16.. MIDDLETON, etc. *Old Law* I. i, If you want money, to-morrow use me. 1671 MILTON *Samson* 1499 Were not his purpose To use him further yet in some great service. 1706 *Act 6 Anne* c. 16 § 6 If any Person..shall keep or use any Greyhounds ..to kill and destroy the Game. 1802 JAMES *Milit. Dict.* s.v., He used his choicest troops on that decisive day. 1875 JOWETT *Plato* (ed. 2) V. 54 They used and honoured all the talent which they could find. 1897 A. LILLIE *Croquet* 170 In making your break use your partner in preference to your adversary.

*transf.* *c* 1600 BRETON *Daffodils & Primroses* Wks. (Grosart) I. 20/1 Some will saie (that many muses vse) There are but nyne, that euer vsde to wryte.

**b.** To have sexual intercourse with. *Obs.* exc. *dial.* (Cf. USE *sb.* 3 b.)

13.. *Gaw. & Gr. Knt.* 2426 Alle þay were biwyled With wymmen þat þay vsed. 1382 WYCLIF *Prol. Bible* iii. 6 Thei that han..newly weddid a wyf, and not vsid hir. 1411–2 HOCCLEVE *De Reg. Princ.* 1583 For þise causes thow hire vse muste, And for non othir. 1541 *Act* 33 *Hen. VIII*, c. 21 If the queene or wife of the prince..stirre any person..to vse or haue carnal knowledge with them. 1565 *Child-Marriages* (1897) 201 Hit hath bene told this deponent, that they have vsid either other at bed and board, as man and wief. 1584 R. SCOT *Discov. Witchcr.* IV. v. (1886) 63 Manie are so bewitched that they cannot use their owne wives. 1611 COTGR., *Accommoder vne femme*, to vse a woman. 1650 BULWER *Anthropomet.* 197 Bels of gold,.. which they put in when they are of age to use Women. 1889 *N. W. Linc. Gloss.* (ed. 2) 590 *To use women*, to commit fornication or adultery.

**11.** To take or partake of as food, drink, etc.; to consume by eating or drinking. Also *fig.*

13.. *E. E. Allit. P.* B. 11 Þay teen vnto his temmple & temen to hym seluen,..Þay hondel þer his aune body & vsen hit boþe. 1382 WYCLIF *Exod.* xxx. 38 Eche man that doth lyik thing, that he ful vse [L. *perfruatur*] the smel [1388 odour] of it, he shal peryshe fro his puplis. 1390 GOWER *Conf.* III. 23 For who that useth that [food] he knoweth Ful selden seknesse on him groweth. *a* 1450 MYRC *Par. Pr.* 1940 ȝef any flye, gnat, or coppe Doun in-to þe chalys droppe, ..Vse hyt hol alle i-fere. *c* 1480 HENRYSON *Lion & Mouse* xiii, Quhilk vsis daylie meittis delitious. 1542 BOORDE *Dyetary* xxvi. (1870) 289 And vse these thynges, Cowe mylke, Almon mylke, yolkes of rere egges. 1585 T. WASHINGTON tr. *Nicholay's Voy.* IV. xix. 134 [In] Lent they doe fast.., vsing none other food, then..hearbs, frutes, and certaine leane pottages. 1613 PURCHAS *Pilgrimage* (1614) 483 They drinke not wine, nor vse vinegar, but onely water. 1632 LITHGOW *Trav.* III. 102 Lemmons..the Turkes vse at their meate, as we doe the Verges. 1859 TENNYSON *Merlin & V.* 462 Yea! Love..carves A portion from the solid present, eats And uses, careless of the rest.

†**b.** To partake of (the sacrament); to take or receive (the eucharist). *Obs.* (Chiefly *absol.*)

*c* 1450 *St. Cuthbert* (Surtees) 7074 Þe sacrement..At þe last he..vsed and toke. 1567 *Gude & Godlie B.* (S.T.S.) 17 Quha vsis it vnworthilie Ressauis deide eternallie.

*absol.* *a* 1375 *Joseph Arim.* 660 Þenne com Ihesu crist..; He vsede of Goddes bord & a writ brouhte. 1389 in *Eng. Gilds* (1870) 14 From þe leuacioun of cristis body sacrid in til þat þe preest haue vsed. 14.. *Pol., Rel., & L. Poems* (1906) 122 When þe preste hath don his masse, Vsed, & his hondes wasche. *c* 1450 *St. Cuthbert* (Surtees) 7058 When he [*sc.* a priest] suld vse, In to þe chalys lokes he.

**12.** To expend or consume (a commodity, etc.) by use; to exhaust by employment.

*c* 1440 *Promp. Parv.* 522/2 Weryn, or vson, as clothys and other thyngys.., *vetero*.

1699 BOYER *Fr. Dict.* s. v. *User*, They use, waste or burn a great deal of Wood in that House. 1747 MRS. GLASSE *Cookery* p. ii, A Cook that used six Pounds of Butter to fry twelve Eggs. 1791 R. MYLNE *2nd Rep. Thames Navig.* 11 The Millers..were using all the Water as fast as possible. 1849 SOYER *Mod. Housewife* 557 [As] the cream..rises in a froth,..place it on the sieve; continue till all is used.

**13.** *To use up*: **a.** To consume (a commodity or stock) by use; to exhaust the supply of.

1785 GROSE *Dict. Vulgar T.*, *Used up*, killed; a military saying, originating from a message sent by the late general Guise, on the expedition to Carthagena [etc.]. 1811 LD. BROUGHAM in Bentham *Wks.* (1843) X. 462, I cannot possibly better use up (as the housewives say) this little credit. 1847 *Illustr. Lond. News* 10 July 27/3 To see if there were anything there that had not yet been used up. 1875 MERIVALE *Gen. Hist. Rome* li. 406 The genuine Roman race must have been almost used up in the desperate warfare.

**b.** To dispose or 'make an end' of (a person). Orig. *U.S. colloq.*

1833 JAS. HALL *Leg. West* 38 It's a mercy, Miss, that the cowardly varments hadn't used you up body-aciously. 1863 in *Southern Hist. Soc. Papers* XII. 220 If you advance ..on them in front while I attack them in flank I think we can use them up.

**c.** *colloq.* To exhaust with fatigue, overwork, etc.; to overtire, wear out.

1850 SMEDLEY *F. Fairlegh* x, I saw you were getting used up. 1882 BESANT *All Sorts* xxviii. (1898) 199 The girls grow up narrow-chested, stooping, consumptive. They are used up wholesale. 1884 'EDNA LYALL' *We Two* v, Even if it should use me up, what then? 1887 *Daily Tel.* 5 March (Encycl. Dict.), We have used up no fewer than six Irish Secretaries in little more than as many years.

**14.** *To use off* or *out*, = sense 13 a.

1812 SOUTHEY *Omniana* II. 2 An obscure..periodical publication, which has long since been used off as 'winding sheets for herrings'. 1849 FROUDE *Nemesis of Faith* 109 The heart will have used out its power, and thoughts..will be unreal still.

**III. 15.** To speak or converse in (a language); to write or talk.

*c* 1275 LAY. 10068 Folk gan to vsi Yrlondes speche. *c* 1330 *Arth. & Merl.* 23 Freynsche vse þis gentilman, Ac euerich Inglische Inglische can. *c* 1500 *Droichis Part of Play* 111 For never in land quhair Eriche was vsit, To dwell had I dellyte. 1547 BOORDE *Introd. Knowl.* i. (1870) 120 In England is vsed all maner of languages and speches of alyens in diuers Cities. *Ibid.* xxxv. 210 Where Laten is most vsed. 1628 MILTON *Vac. Exerc.* 8 Hail native Language,..Here I salute thee and thy pardon ask, That now I use thee in my latter task. 1668 WILKINS *Real Char.* 3 The Language used in Denmark. 1819 SCOTT *Ivanhoe* ii, The Prior..using the lingua Franca, or mixed language, in which [etc.]. 1821 — *Kenilw.* xxxvi, Can falsehood use thus boldly the language of truth? 1888 JESSOPP *Visit. Norwich* p. xxxix, [He] should be able to use Latin, not merely to understand it.

**b.** To employ or give utterance to (words, phrases, etc.); to say, utter.

*a* 1340 HAMPOLE *Psalter* lxxiii. 23 Na wise man oysis gret athis, in þe whilke werid men vpbraydis god of his mercy. *c* 1374 CHAUCER *Boeth.* II. pr. ii. (1868) 33, I wolde plete wiþ þee a fewe þinges, vsynge þe wordes of fortune. *a* 1425 *Cursor M.* 12050 (Trin.), Teche him..Blessyng to vse & not to ban. 1484 CAXTON *Fables of Æsop* I. Pref., Esope.. techeth also to be humble and for to vse wordes. *a* 1500 in *Ratis Raving*, etc. 98 Oys fare langage in alkyne thinge. 1539 BIBLE (Great) *Ecclus.* xxiii. 11 A man yᵗ vseth moch swearing. 1596 HARINGTON *Metam. Ajax* (1814) 24 [When] such phrases..are used to ribaldry. 1621 BP. MOUNTAGU *Diatribæ* 14 Euery where, either directly, or indirectly, you doe, to use your owne phrase, Cry downe that right. 1655 STANLEY *Hist. Philos.* I. (1687) 27/2 Using speeches, the effect whereof, he afterwards thus exprest in Verse. 1728 CHAMBERS *Cycl.* s.v. *Viscera*, This Word is also frequently used singularly, *Viscus*, to express some particular part of the Entrails. 1729 T. INNES *Crit. Essay* (1879) 295 Nennius ..uses promiscuously the names of Scythæ and Scoti for the same people. 1793 MARTYN *Lang. Bot.* s.v. *Leaflets*, For the same reason, if we use *leaf*, we must not use *foliole*. 1820 SHELLEY *Orpheus* 100 Nature must lend me words ne'er used before. 1838 LYTTON *Leila* II. i, Thou usest plain language, my friend. 1875 JEVONS *Money* (1878) 250 We use a great many words with a total disregard of logical precision.

**16.** To resort to (a place) frequently or habitually; to frequent or haunt; also, to dwell in. Now *rare*.

*c* 1400 MAUNDEV. (1839) xxxi. 307 ȝif the Merchauntes useden als moche that Contre as thei don Cathay. *c* 1440 *Promp. Parv.* 512/2 Vsyn, or hawntyn, *frequento*. 1528 in Leadam *Star Chamber Cases* (Selden) II. 175 All iiij [have] eusyd & occupyd the market and inhaunsyd the pryse of grayne. 1535 COVERDALE *Jer.* ii. 23 Like a wilde Asse, that vseth the wildernesse. 1603 SHAKS. *Meas. for M.* III. ii. 231 [I am] Not of this Countrie, though my chance is now To vse it for my time. 1611 in B. Camm *Benedictine Martyr in Eng.* (1897) 268 The other was Mr. Somers, alias Wilson, who used London altogether. 1658 COKAINE *Obstinate Lady* I. i, Poems (1874) 55 Use the Tavern once or twice a day. 1686 tr. *Chardin's Coronat. Solyman* 143 Forty large Barques, such as use the Caspian Sea. 1708 *Lond. Gaz.* No. 4427/16 He useth the Queen's-head Ale-house. 1725 SLOANE *Jamaica* II. 320 It uses more the low sandy inland parts than the plovers, snipes, &c. 1848 THACKERAY *Van. Fair* xxxviii, He did not fail to tell everybody who 'used the room'. 1867 *Cornh. Mag.* Apr. 449 Doubtless also in his sojourn here..he used this house, as our expressive phrase has it. 1884 *Good Words* June 399/2 Your ordinary thief.. may..lord it in the public-houses he 'uses'.

**b.** *To use the sea* († *seas*), to practise the calling of a sailor. Cf. FOLLOW *v.* 9.

*a* 1634 ISAACSON *Andrewes* in Fuller *Abel Rediv.* (1867) II. 156 His father, having most part of his life used the seas. 1681 R. KNOX *Hist. Ceylon* 124 These many years..have I used the seas. 1728 MORGAN *Algiers* II. ii. 223 Rais was then about thirty, and had used the Sea full ten years. 1773 *Life N. Frowde* 24 His Name was George White,..who had used the Seas from my own Age. 1791 SMEATON *Edystone L.* § 314 John..continued for some time to use the sea. 1894 *Pall Mall Mag.* Sept. 4 He had used the sea for above thirty years, had built, owned and commanded ships.

†**c.** To associate with (a person). *Obs.*⁻¹

1594 in *Cath. Rec. Soc. Publ.* V. 262 At my being there I could not heare or perceyue he used any Inglishman much.

**17. a.** To treat or deal with (a person or thing) in a specified manner; to behave or act towards (another) in a particular way.

In frequent use from *c* 1550 to *c* 1730.

1483 CAXTON *G. de la Tour* g v, They wold use her of an enorme and ouer foule faytte. 1542 UDALL *Erasm. Apoph.* 171 Many noble menne vsen their frendes none other wyse. 1568 GRAFTON *Chron.* II. 804 Then he that tolde him the tale vsed him with good wordes. 1590 MARLOWE *Edw. II*, v. ii, Vse Edmund friendly, as if all were well. 1639 in *Verney Mem.* (1907) I. 106 My Collonel useth me with very greate courtesy. 1680 OTWAY *Orphan* II. iv, But use me gently like a loving Brother. 1709 STEELE *Tatler* No. 11 ¶ 4, I am used by some People as if Isaac Bickerstaff..was no Body. 1756 C. SMART tr. *Hor., Sat.* II. ii, When years shall approach, and feeble age require to be used more tenderly. 1768 STERNE *Sent. Journ.*, *Translation*, 'Tis.. using him worse than a German. 1859 TENNYSON *Merlin & V.* 534 So used as I, My daily wonder is, I love at all. 1863 KINGLAKE *Crimea* I. 311 They won France. They used her hard. 1888 'J. S. WINTER' *Bootle's Childr.* iv, I didn't use poor Bill any too well.

**b.** *refl.* To conduct or comport (oneself). †Also, to resort or repair (cf. sense 22).

Freq. from *c* 1530 to *c* 1590.

*c* 1470 HENRY *Wallace* XI. 1031 Yhe haiff so lang her oysyt yow allane, Quhill witt tharoff is in till Ingland gane 1496–7 12 *Hen. VII*, c. 6 § 1 Every persone frely to use theym self to his moost avauntage, without exaccion. 1513 BRADSHAW *St. Werburge* I. 2354 He folowed saynt Werburge counsell, Vsynge hym after her swete ghostly doctryne. 1547 BOORDE *Brev. Health* ccvii, Thus vsynge my selfe, I thanke God I dyd make my selfe whole. 1590 *Southampton Court Leet Rec.* (1906) II. 285 Being called before vs, [they] vsed themselves contemtuously. 1621 LADY M. WROTH *Urania* 307 Who comming to my fathers house, vsed himselfe..insolently. *a* 1648 LD. HERBERT *Hen. VIII* (1683) 295 He used himself more like a Fellow to your Highness, than like a Subject. 1653 *Nissena* 108 Excusing himself for that he had not before used himself with such obsequiousness towards them as he ought. 1860 MISS YONGE *Hopes & Fears* I. 387 Her eyes were on the alert to judge how he had been using himself in the last half-year.

**IV. 18.** To make (a person, etc.) familiar or accustomed by habit or practice; to habituate, accustom; to inure. Freq. const. † *in* or *with* (something).

In later use *Sc.*, and chiefly in pa. pple.; cf. c below.

*c* 1305 *St. Edmund Conf.* 78 in *E.E.P.* (1862) 73 In penance he was so wel yused & þeron ȝung ibroȝt þat..hit ne greuede him riȝt noȝt. *a* 1340 HAMPOLE *Psalter* cxviii. 71 It is profetabil till me, þat þou oysid me in sere temptacиouns. 1387 TREVISA *Higden* (Rolls) VI. 289 He þat was idel..meoveþ hym to batayle þat is i-used in dedes of armes. *c* 1425 *Eng. Conq. Ireland* 22 Throgh kynd of Fraunce, we ben vsed in wepene. 1489 CAXTON *Faytes of A.* I. viii. Bij b, To see his men vsed & wel taught in the said art and fait of armes. *a* 1500 *Ratis Raving* 32 With wordis of lawte vs thi twnge. *c* 1586 C'TESS PEMBROKE *Ps.* LXXVII. xii, A path whereon thy crew As shepherds use their sheep. 1587 HOLINSHED *Chron.* (ed. 2) II. *Hist. Scotl.* 391 This man had accesse unto the queene to plaie at cards, and to use hir with other courtlie pastimes. 1606 CHAPMAN *Gentl. Usher* v. ii, Using thy husband in those vertuous gifts For which thou first didst choose him. 1711 *Countrey-Man's Lett. Curat* 85 Many..had been used with the English Liturgie..at London. 1815 SCOTT *Guy M.* lv, The like o' them's used wi' graves and ghaists. *a* 1826 in Child *Ball.* IV. 98/1 She took my gay lord frae my side, And used him in her company. 1835 D. WEBSTER *Orig. Sc. Rhymes* 115, I had little been used wi' sic resolute foes.

*refl.* 1534 in Leadam *Star Chamber Cases* (Selden) II. 211 Compleynaunt hathe vseyd hymselfe in exercysyng the fete of bakyng. 1560 BECON *New Catech.* Wks. 1564 I. 320 This verye selfe same bodye..whiche vseth it selfe here with the soule in all maner of good workes.

**b.** Freq. with *to* (and sb. or inf.).

*c* 1386 CHAUCER *Pars. P.* ¶ 245 For to vsen a man to doon goode werkes. 1535 COVERDALE *Ecclus.* xxiii. 13 Vse not thy mouth to vnhonest and fylthye talkynge. 1560 DAUS tr. *Sleidane's Comm.* 231 b, That they do eschew all..idle talke, and vse their familie to do lykewyse. 1585 T. WASHINGTON tr. *Nicholay's Voy.* IV. i. 114 b, [Hunting being] an argument & occasion to vse men to ryse betimes. *c* 1643 LD. HERBERT *Autobiog.* (1824) 70 You shall do well also to use your Horse to Swimming. 1688 SHADWELL *Sqr. Alsatia* II. i, Some moderate skill in it will use a man to reason closely. 1740 CHESTERF. *Lett.* Oct., To use your ear a little to English verse. 1769 GOLDSM. *Hist. Rome* (1786) I. 402 Having used his body much to antidotes, the poison had but little effect. 1783 JUSTAMOND tr. *Raynal's Hist. Indies* VII. 91 It is not..surprising that the seal..should use her little ones to live under water. 1814 SCOTT *Wav.* liv, He wanted to use her by degrees to live without meat. **1873**– in dialect use (*Eng. Dial. Dict.*). **1877** MRS. LEAR tr. *Fenelon's Spiritual Lett.* 240 So as to wean you like a child, and use you to dry bread instead of milk.

*refl.* *c* **1305** *St. Edmund Conf.* 44 in *E. E. P.* (1862) 72 So longe hi hem vsede þerto. *a* **1450** *Knt. de la Tour* (1868) 9 For suche lyff as ye wille contynue, use you to in youre youthe. *a* **1568** ASCHAM *Scholem.* II. (Arb.) 88 For translating, vse you your selfe..to chose out some Epistle..of Tullie. *a* **1568** in *Bannatyne MS.* (Hunter. Cl.) 195 In yowtheid vse the to temprance. **1615** tr. *De Montfort's Surv. E. Indies* 39 Those who have us'd themselves to Tobacco. **1697** DRYDEN *Virg. Georg.* I. 63 Use thyself betimes to hear and grant our Pray'rs. **1719** DE FOE *Crusoe* I. (Globe) 211 Using himself to them [*sc.* garments], at length he took to them very well. **1753** L. M. *Accompl. Woman* II. 213 We may use ourselves to fear as well as to be bold. *a* **1818** M. G. LEWIS *Jrnl. W. Ind.* (1834) 296 Mithridates used himself to poisons. *a* **1850** KEBLE *Lett.* (1870) 104 Using themselves when they wake in the night to rise and say the fifty-first Psalm.

**c.** More usu. in pa. pple. (Const. *to* or † *of*.)

*c* **1480** HENRYSON *Fables, Two Mice* 58 To tender meit my stomok is ay vsit. **1483** CAXTON *G. de la Tour* e iv b, So were the seuen Cytees brenned..by cause that they were moche vsed of the fylthe and ordure of lechery. **1526** *Pilgr. Perf.* (W. de W. 1531) 94 b, Wherby man..be accustomed & vsed to chose..yᵉ thynge that is of lesse goodnes. **1555** EDEN *Decades* I. x. (Arb.) 104 Such as haue byn vsed to owr breade made of wheate. **1607** TOPSELL *Four-f. Beasts* 80 It is requisite that they bee alwaie vsed to hand. *c* **1645** HOWELL *Lett.* (1678) 48 This City was us'd to fetch all those Spices. **1682** LISTER *Godartius Of Insects* 54 The Catterpillar..as soon as it perceives any thing it is not us't to. **1720** MANDEVILLE *Free Thoughts* (1729) 276 St. Poinct..was used to ask, whether the farce..was ready to be acted. **1796** MME. D'ARBLAY *Camilla* IV. 329 I'm not used to be used in this manner! **1833** DISRAELI *Cont. Fleming* VI. vi, The friar smiled, and was evidently used to this raillery. **1850** THACKERAY *Pendennis* li, A person..used to making sacrifices. **1888** 'J. S. WINTER' *Bootle's Childr.* xi, Which..had stirred Terry's heart just as it had been used to stir it years and years ago.

**V.** *intr.* **19.** To do a thing customarily; to be in the habit of so acting or doing; to be wont to do. (Chiefly in clauses introduced by *as*, and now only literary.) **a.** Of persons.

*c* **1380** WYCLIF *Sel. Wks.* III. 434 And so shulde perish makyng of prests and doyng of sacraments, as holy Chirche usiþ. *c* **1400** MAUNDEV. (1839) v. 40 Clothed in..the Sarazines guyse, and as the Sarazines usen. **1473** *Reg. Cupar Abbey* I. 182 Tha sal tak iijˣˣ of fuderis of petis quhar thai oysit befor. **1533** in Leadam *Star Chamber Cases* (Selden) II. 205 The boucher..grevyd shall signifie..the name..of any such person..that so vsith. **1596** SPENSER *State Irel.* Wks. (Globe) 645/1 To manure and husband it as good farmors use. **1616** J. LANE *Contn. Sqr.'s T.* x. 388 This familiar Dove twixt yond twoe kinges went boldlie to and fro, as vsen frendes. **1663** BUTLER *Hud.* I. i. 632 We should, as learned Poets use, Invoke the Assistance of some Muse. **1720** OZELL *Vertot's Rom. Rep.* (1740) II. XII. 237 In the sight of all the Citizens, as the Censors use, when they [etc.]. **1748** *Earthquake Peru* ii. 161 To kill animals in the same Manner as they always had used. **1791** SMEATON *Edystone L.* § 267 We had got up our stones..as we had used from the beginning. **1816** WORDSW. '*A little onward*' 30 To push forth His arms, as swimmers use, and plunge..into the 'abrupt abyss'. **1852** T. L. PEACOCK *Misc.* Wks. 1875 III. 364 First, as the truly pious always use, Approach with prayer. **1875** BROWNING *Aristoph. Apol.* 365 Die at good old age as grand men use.

† **b.** Of things. *Obs. rare.*

**1656** tr. *T. White's Peripat. Inst.* 152 It varies its figure with every motion as fire uses. **1676** *Phil. Trans.* XI. 773 In the same manner as the trunk of the lymphaticks uses.

**20.** With *to* and inf.: To be accustomed or wont *to* do something.

In very frequent use from *c* 1400, but now only in pa. t. *used to*, with pronunc. (yūst tu, yū·stŭ).

*α.* **1303** R. BRUNNE *Handl. Synne* 691 For ryche men vse comunly Sweryn [*v.r.* to swere] grete oþys grysly. *Ibid.* 2661. *c* **1385** CHAUCER *L. G. W.* 787 *Thisbe*, For olde payenys that Idolys heryed Vsedyn tho in feldys to ben beryed. *c* **1386** — *Reeve's T.* 20 A theef he was,..a sly, and vsaunt [*v.r.* usand] for to stele. *c* **1440** *Gesta Rom.* v. 12 His modir vsith euery day gretly to sorowe. **1464** *Rolls of Parlt.* V. 563/2 Dyvers persones have gretely used to shippe woll.. oute of this Reame. **1542** UDALL *Erasm. Apoph.* 43 Such as the beggerye philosophiers..usen to weare. **1550** *Southampton Court Leet Rec.* (1905) I. 14 Thomas Casberd hathe vsid to sett his carte in the streate. **1596** SPENSER *F. Q.* v. viii. 17 Her name Mercilla most men vse to call. **1612** WEBSTER *White Devil* I. ii. 202 Your silke-worme useth to fast every third day. **1625** J. KING *David's Strait* 15 As we vse to maligne a Bayliue. **1670** MILTON *Hist. Eng.* VI. 304 The English then useing to let grow on their upper-lip large Mustachio's. **1728** GAY *Begg. Op.* II. iv, You are not so fond of me, Jenny, as you use [*sic*] to be. **1767** *Woman of Fashion* II. 26 How did we all use to admire her! **1837** LOCKHART *Scott* I. iv. 122 He used to get all the copies of these ballads he could. **1884** W. C. SMITH *Kildrostan* 53 You used to be a leal, true-hearted girl.

*Comb.* **1883** J. W. RILEY *Poems Here at Home* (1893) 21 There lies a land, long lost to me, The land of Used-to-be.

*β.* *c* **1375** *Lay-Folks Mass-Bk.* (MS. B) 401 A litel belle men oyse to ryng. *c* **1425** WYNTOUN *Cron.* I. 1265 Tebany þai oysse to calle In to Grece þe Thebis all. *c* **1470** HENRY *Wallace* v. 760 Now thow sall feyll how I oys to lat blude.

**b.** Predicated of things.

In frequent use from *c* 1620 to *c* 1675.

**1445** in *Anglia* XXVIII. 267 Al goddesses..Haue ioyned her dauncys within thi breste, which vsid hem to receive. **1547** *Homilies* I. *Salvation* III. ¶ 7 Therfore scripture vseth to saie, that faithe without woorkes dooth iustifie. **1586** J. CHILTON in Hakluyt *Voy.* (1589) 588 Where the ships vse to ride, made fast to ye said wal, with their cables. **1609** HOLLAND *Amm. Marcell.* 333 What time folkes minds.. use to be dull and dead. **1662** STILLINGFL. *Orig. Sacræ* I. i. § 6 Jewels do not use to lie upon the surface of the earth. **1684** *Contempl. St. Man* II. ix. (1699) 231 Temporal Felicity uses often to end in Eternal Misery. **1726** LEONI *Designs* 5 b, In that Season of the Year when the Water uses to be lowest. **1778** *Hist. Eliza Warwick* I. 260 Alas! his absence ..did not use thus to affect me! **1810** SCOTT *Lady L.* I. xxi, Yet seemed that tone..Less used to sue than to command. **1839** FR. A. KEMBLE *Resid. in Georgia* (1863) 245 It is now ..the rule, though it used not to be so formerly. **1884** F. M. CRAWFORD *Rom. Singer* I. 35 They used to be only a baiocco apiece.

† **c.** In passive construction. *Obs.*

**1523** FITZHERB. *Husb.* § 132 If a tree be heeded, and vsed to be lopped and cropped. **1607** SHAKS. *Cor.* III. iii. 25 He hath bene vs'd Euer to conquer. *a* **1648** LD. HERBERT *Hen. VIII* (1683) 399 As concerning Annates used to be paid. *a* **1706** EVELYN *Hist. Relig.* (1850) I. 402 Nor were they used of old to be read in churches. **1737** WATERLAND *Eucharist* 393 Prayer was then used to be offered up for that Purpose. **1788** *London Mag.* 399 The Tuilleries, where boats were used to be found.

**21.** † **a.** To act, conduct oneself or one's affairs, in a particular or specified manner. *Obs. rare.*

*a* **1325** *Prose Psalter* lxxvi. 12 Y shal þenchen in alle þyne werkes, and y shal vse [L. *exercebor*] in alle þy fundynges. *c* **1375** *Cursor M.* 24931 (Fairf.), Bot now men vsis on oþer wise, þer is mare of hir seruise. **1523** LD. BERNERS *Froiss.* I. xv. 15 Kyng Edward..and yᵉ quene his mother..vsed moche after yᵉ counsell of syr Thomas Wage. **1579** TOMSON *Calvin's Serm. Tim.* 181/1 And therfore we haue to vse of our selues modestly.

**b.** *Sc.* To accustom oneself, become accustomed or habituated, get used, *to* something.

**1836** CARLYLE *Let.* in *Atlantic Monthly* Sept. (1898) 295/1 'You will use, you will use,' and get hefted to the place, as all creatures do. **1842** MRS. CARLYLE *Lett.* (1883) I. 158 If I do not use to the noise. **1894** CROCKETT *Raiders* 284 So soon does one use to the sight.

**22.** To go frequently, to resort or repair customarily, to a place or person; to frequent or haunt a place. Freq. with advs. (as *thither*, *where*), or with preps. (esp. in earlier use with *to*). Latterly *dial.* (Eng. Dial. Dict. s.v.) and *U.S.*

(*a*) *c* **1470** HENRY *Wallace* I. 209 Into the toun he wsyt everilk day. *Ibid.* II. 290 He wsyt offt to that religious place. **1590** in *Cath. Rec. Soc. Publ.* V. 181 [They] be good witnesses ..howe many severall persons have vsed to the saienge of masses. **1599** SIR R. WROTHE in Ellis *Orig. Lett.* Ser. II. III. 181 Sertaine lewde fellowes..doe frequente and use aboute Layton heath. **1602** BRETON *Mother's Blessing* Wks. (Grosart) I. 6/1 Presumptuous fooles, and irreligious Iewes, Emong the Nobler sort should neuer vse. *a* **1613** OVERBURY *Characters, Ord. Widdow*, Shee uses to cunning women to know how many husbands she shall have. **1653** HOLCROFT *Procopius, Pers. Wars* II. 51 Then shall you by our Countrey have the conveniencie of using to Roman Seas. **1663** *Extr. St. Papers Friends* Ser. II. (1911) 168 When he is in London he vseth frequently at Mr. Lawries howse. **1834** J. HALL *Kentucky* II. 40 'But you seem acquainted with these woods.' 'Yes, I use about here some.' **1884** 'M. TWAIN' *Huckleberry Finn* vi, If he didn't quit using around there she would make trouble for him.

(*b*) **1470–85** MALORY *Arthur* XVIII. xxii. 765, I am a gentilwoman that vseth here in this forest huntynge. **1592** in J. Morris *Troub. Cath. Forefathers* Ser. II. (1875) 54 Cotton did use thither divers times. **1596** SPENSER *F. Q.* VI. Prol. ii, Conduct me well In these strange waies, where neuer foote did vse. *a* **1700** B. E. *Dict. Cant. Crew, Flash-ken*, a House where Thieves use. **1848** BARTLETT *Dict. Amer.* 372, I can see where the deer used. **1851** MAYHEW *Lond. Labour* II. 475/2 The master of the hotel or the gents that uses there.

*transf.* **1591** SYLVESTER *Ivry* 370 Even as a Galley, in smooth Sea subdues The tallest Ship that in the Streights doth use. **1637** MILTON *Lycidas* 136 Ye valleys low where the milde whispers use, Of shades and wanton winds.

† **b.** To inhabit, reside, or dwell in or at a place.

*a* **1585** MONTGOMERIE *Cherrie & Slae* 97 Musis that vsis At fountaine Helicon. **1610** FLETCHER *Faithf. Sheph.* III. i, I will give thee for thy food, No Fish that useth in the mud. **1628** MAY *Virg. Georg.* III. 93 Snakes that use within the house for shade, Securely lurk. **1707** SLOANE *Jamaica* I. p. xviii, This is known by the places where they [*sc.* fish] use.

† **c.** To associate (or cohabit) *with* a person. *Obs.*

**1382** WYCLIF *John* iv. 9 Jewis vsen not with Samaritans. **1559** BERCHER *Nobylytye Wymen* (Roxb.) 141 The daughters of Lot, which vsed carnallye with their ffather. **1566** STERNHOLD & H. *Ps.* xxvi. 4, I do not lust to haunt or vse, with men whose deeds are vayne.

† **23.** To make use *of* some thing. *Obs.*

*c* **1500** *Melusine* xx. 110 As long that ye shall vse of feythfulnes. **1542** UDALL *Erasm. Apoph.* 44 For in the same solemnitees men usen of a custom. **1704** N. N. tr. *Boccalini's Advts. fr. Parnass.* II. 171 He us'd of all the Rhetorick he had, to praise that Vice.

† **b.** Similarly with *with*. *Obs. rare.*

*a* **1400–50** *Alexander* 3594 Olyfauntis.., As ilkane vsyd with in ynde vmquile with to fiȝte. **1502** *Ord. Crysten Men* (W. de W. 1506) IV. xxi. Xvj, He ought iustely to vse with his puyssaunce and not in abusynge.

**Used** (yūzd), *ppl. a.* [f. USE *v.* + -ED ¹.]

**I.** † **1.** Customarily employed, experienced, or met with; accustomed, usual, wonted. *Obs.*

*c* **1374** CHAUCER *Boeth.* I. met. v. (1868) 22 Þe euesterre esperus ..comeþ eft aȝeynes hir vsed cours. *c* **1440** CAPGRAVE *St. Kath.* IV. 1719 These too natures in oure lord ihesu were.. coupled to-geder ageyn vsed kynde. **1445** in Willis & Clark *Cambridge* (1886) I. 343 Thei shall ocupye with all maner of cariagez..the vsed way within the ground. **1449** PECOCK *Repr.* v. ii. 489 These now had and vsid religiouns in the chirche. **1480** *Wardr. Acc. Edw. IV.* (1830) 150 A pane of scarlet furrid with used ermyns. **1579** E. K. *Spenser's Sheph. Cal.* Gen. Argt. ¶ 2 To call them by the vsed and best knowen name. **1650** HOWELL *Giraffi's Rev. Naples* I. 2 Forcing him [*sc.* Gensericus] to bid a us'd farewell to fair Italie. **1655** MOUFET & BENNET *Health's Improv.* xxix. 272, I perswade strong and indifferent stomachs to continue their used Diet.

**b.** That is or has been made use of; utilized.

**1594**– [see WELL-USED]. **1758** B. FRANKLIN *Poor Richard* (1890) 270 The used Key is always bright. **1864** E. A. PARKES *Pract. Hygiene* 157 The used surfaces of the teeth begin to bear a square mark. **1885** J. W. PALMER *Bric-à-Brac* 27 Papering a room with used stamps.

**2.** † **a.** Established by usage; customary. *Obs.*

*c* **1450** tr. *De Imitatione* III. xiii. 81 The olde used custom wol wiþstonde, but it shal be ouercomen by a better custom. **1603** FLORIO *Montaigne* II. xv. 358 An auncient custome, and vsed cerimony.

**b.** *Used and wont*, that is usual or customary; according to use and custom. *Sc.*

**1510** *Reg. Privy Seal Scotl.* I. 315/2 Payand thairfor ȝerelie four pundis thre s. usuale money,..with all maner of dewiteis usit and wount. **1562** *Reg. Cupar Abbey* I. 362 Item, to the convent..for ane part of thair sustentatioun vsit and wont. **1609** SKENE *Reg. Maj.* II. Table 63 Bot the four heire sall make service vsed and wont. **1718** in *Nairne Peerage Evidence* (1874) 34 With the rights rents and services..used and wont. **1814** SCOTT *Wav.* l, [He] claimed permission to perform..the service used and wont. **1864** *Jedburgh Council Rec.* 31 Oct. (MS.), With all ceremonies used and wont.

**3.** Experienced (*in* something); expert. Latterly *Sc.*

*c* **1425** *Eng. Conq. Ireland* 23 Throgh kynde of Fraunce, we ben wsyd in wepyn. *c* **1470** HENRY *Wallace* III. 379 For thai war wicht, and weill wsyt in wer. **1786** BURNS *Epist. to J. Rankine* ix, Some auld us'd hands had taen a note, That [etc.]. **1824** SCOTT *St. Ronan's* iii, Dick..was an auld used hand.

**II. Used up. 4.** *U. S.* Discussed thoroughly; talked of, or written about, critically.

**1839** MRS. KIRKLAND *A New Home* xxxv. 237 After tea the poor Brents were completely 'used up', to borrow a phrase much in vogue with us, and the next day I was.. asked..if I had heard that Mr. and Mrs. Brent were going to 'part'. **1848** POE *J. R. Lowell* Wks. 1895 VIII. 5 The various criticisms, in which we have been amused (rather ill-naturedly) at seeing Mr. Lowell 'used up'.

**5.** *slang* or *colloq.* Thoroughly exhausted by physical exertion or hardship; tired out, 'done up'.

**1840** R. H. DANA *Bef. Mast* xxviii, [He was] barefooted..; 'clean out' to the last real, and completely 'used up'. **1850** SMEDLEY *F. Fairlegh* xlvii, Why, the perspiration is pouring down your face,—you look regularly used-up. **1888** J. C. HARRIS *Free Joe*, etc. 226 It was a five-mile excursion; and he returned, as Mrs. Haley expressed it, 'a used-up man'.

**b.** Knocked up by excess.

**1890** GUNTER *Miss Nobody* xiii, My heavens! what a head I have accumulated over night!..I wonder if Avonmere is used up likewise?

**6.** Worn out, debilitated, rendered useless, as with hard work, age, dissipation, etc.

**1848** DICKENS *Dombey* x, A smoke-dried, sunburnt, used-up, invalided old dog of a Major, Sir. **1862** CALVERLEY *Poems* 57 What is coffee, but a noxious berry, Born to keep used-up Londoners awake? **1863** W. C. BALDWIN *Afr. Hunting* vi. 214 An old used-up brute [*sc.* horse]. **1871** ELEANOR GROVE tr. *Ebers' Egypt. Princess* I. Preface (Tauchn.) p. xv, In days when a used-up man of the world, like Antony, could desire in his will that [etc.].

*transf.* **1852** C. B. MANSFIELD *Paraguay*, etc. (1856) 369 The more respectable people here..have a sort of used-up look, which is not inviting. **1853** DICKENS *Bleak Ho.* liii, The cousin..yawns, 'Vayli'—being the used-up for 'very likely'. **1871** EARLE *Philol. English Tongue* I 106 The extreme oddity of our sound of *U* comes out under a used-up or languid utterance. **1875** J. GRANT *One of the '600'* iii, The used-up bearing of those..who affect to act as if.. life itself was a bore.

**b.** Emotionally exhausted; blasé.

**1845** C. J. MATHEWS *Used Up* I. i. 8 Here I am, at thirty-three, completely blazé—a man literally 'used up'! **1853** MRS. GASKELL *Ruth* xxiii, He was pleased to feel jealous again. He had been really afraid he was too much 'used-up' for such sensations.

**7.** Reduced, exhausted, or consumed by using; rendered unserviceable by use.

**1855** DELAMER *Kitchen Garden* 179 In short, make a general clearance of used-up things [in a garden]. **1881** SHAIRP *Asp. Poetry* 132 The accumulations of used-up verbiage, which had so long choked the sources of inspiration. **1896** *Allbutt's Syst. Med.* I. 312 The contaminated or used-up air.

Hence † **U·sedly** *adv.*, commonly; **U·sedness.** Also **Used-upness.** *nonce-use.*

**1561** T. NORTON *Calvin's Inst.* IV. 81 But it was..vsedly the custome..to shorten their journey. **1680** BAXTER *Answ. Stillingfl.* xxxiii. 48 If Usefulness and Usedness..may afford us a Prognostick. **1871** MRS. WHITNEY *Real Folks* xiii, You would notice instantly the consummate usedness to the world. **1891** 'L. KEITH' *Halletts* II. 220 There was a good deal of used-upness about Spenceley, though..the world had still certain points open to his combativeness.

**Usee·.** *U. S.* [f. USE *v.* + -EE ¹.] 'A person for whose use a suit is brought in the name of another' (*Cent. Dict.*, 1891).

**Use-fruyt**, Sc. var. USUFRUIT *Obs.*

**Useful** (yū·sfŭl), *a.* and *sb.* [f. USE *sb.* + -FUL.]

Implied in the one early instance (1483) of *usefulness*, but app. not current till *c* 1600; cf. USELESS *a.*

**1.** Of persons: Having the ability or qualities to bring about good, advantage, benefit, etc.; helpful for any purpose; serviceable. Also of animals (cf. 2).

**1595** SHAKS. *John* v. ii. 81, I am too high-borne to be propertied,..Or [a] vsefull seruing-man. **1646** *Verney Mem.* (1907) I. 343 Women were never soe usefull as now. **1671** MILTON *Samson* 564 Now blind, disheartn'd,..quell'd, To what can I be useful? ?*a* 1700 *Tak your Auld Cloak about ye* ii. in Ramsay *Evergreen*, My Cromie is a useful cow. **1708** J. C. *Compl. Collier* (1845) 19 Especially when such an Adventurer is so useful to the Publick. **1776** GIBBON *Decl. & F.* ii. (1782) I. 49 If he had any opportunity of rendering himself either useful or agreeable. **1831** SIR J. SINCLAIR *Corr.* II. 349 Baron Itzenplitz..wishes [to see] his children.. useful for their country. **1861** WHYTE MELVILLE *Market Harb.* ix, Useful horses;..and seem pretty fit to go. *Ibid.*, Very like hunters: remarkably useful horses indeed! **1887** RUSKIN *Præterita* II. 422 [He] was benevolently useful, as a landlord should be, in his county.

**b.** *Theatr.* (See quot.)

**1824** W. IRVING *T. Trav.* II. (1848) 187, I was enrolled among the number of what are called *useful men*; those who enact soldiers, senators, and Banquo's shadowy line.

**2.** Of things, actions, etc.: Having the character or quality to be of use or utility; suitable for use; advantageous, profitable, beneficial.

**1606** SHAKS. *Ant. & Cl.* IV. xiv. 80 With a wound I must be cur'd. Draw that thy honest Sword, which thou hast worne Most vsefull for thy Country. **1634** SIR T. HERBERT *Trav.* 183 Food no lesse pleasant and vsefull to Kine. **1644** MILTON *Educ.* 99 The usefullest points of grammar. **1669** STURMY *Mariner's Mag.* II. x. 76 How to make a most useful Instrument of the Stars. *c* **1737** SWIFT *Corr.* (1913) V. 435, I cannot doubt of your being willing to encourage all useful inventions. **1752** HUME *Pol. Disc.* iv. 67 Every thing useful to the life of man, arises from the ground. **1780** *Mirror* No. 80, They..publish useful information to mankind. **1846** LANDOR *Imag. Conv.* Wks. I. 197/2 We are not always to consider in our disquisitions what is pleasantest, but sometimes what is usefullest. **1871** JOWETT *Plato* IV. 309 Exercises..useful both in peace and war. **1875** R. F. MARTIN tr. *Havrez's Winding Mach.* 8 We thus see that.. the useful load exceeds the half of the total load. **1890** 'R. BOLDREWOOD' *Col. Reformer* (1891) 337 A steady reader in her own line, which she denominated 'useful'.

*absol.* **1802** C. FINDLATER *View Agric. Peebles* 55 Admirers of the curious, as much as of the useful, in farming. **1818** J. FOSTER *Contrib. Eclectic Rev.* (1844) I. 482 The useful was to him the *summum bonum*. **1836–8** [see USELESS 1]. **1892** ZANGWILL *Bow Mystery* 157 A man who has always preached the Useful day and night.

**b.** *sb.* A useful article. *rare*⁻¹.

**1662** PETTY *Taxes* 21 Metals, cloth, linen, leather, and other usefuls.

Hence **U·sefullish** *a.*, somewhat useful. *rare*⁻¹.

**1848** CARLYLE in Froude *Life in London* (1884) I. 421, I seem to them a desperate half mad, if usefullish fireman.

**U·sefully,** *adv.* [f. prec. + -LY [2].] In a useful manner; so as to be of use; to a useful end; beneficially, profitably, serviceably.

**1634** MASSINGER *Very Woman* III. ii, Serve usefully, Serve all with diligence. **1656** COWLEY *Davideis* III. 281 How the kind Sun usefully comes and goes. **1711** STEELE *Spect.* No. 145 ⁋ 2 You cannot employ yourself more usefully. **1781** GIBBON *Decl. & F.* xxx. III. 175 Whose arms would have been more usefully employed to maintain the Roman limits. **1807** G. CHALMERS *Caledonia* I. III. v. § 3. 357 The notices of topography come in here, usefully, to illustrate the obscurity of history. **1868** KINGLAKE *Crimea* III. 144 It was hardly one which could be usefully submitted to a numerous assembly.

**U·sefulness.** [f. as prec. + -NESS.]

†**1.** The advantage or benefit *of* (a place). *Obs.*⁻¹

**1483** DUKE GLOUCS. in R. Davies *Extr. Munic. Rec. York* (1843) 147 For the wele and usefullnes of þe realme.

**2.** The state or condition of being useful or serviceable; utility, serviceableness.

**1617** WOODALL *Surg. Mate* (1639) B 3 b, The goodnesse and usefulnesse thereof, for the preserving of mens lives. **1662** STILLINGFL. *Orig. Sacræ* III. i. § 16 The peculiar usefulness of the several parts of mans body. **1749** BERKELEY *Word to Wise* Wks. 1871 III. 437 We are all agreed about the usefulness of meat, drink, and clothes. **1760** 'PORTIA' *Polite Lady* x. 28 The usefulness and importance of all the different parts of education. **1835** *Penny Cycl.* IV. 398/1 *Bill of Exchange*, a well-known mercantile instrument, of great and extensive usefulness. **1860** RUSKIN *Unto this Last* (1862) 125 In accurate terms, usefulness is value in the hands of the valiant. **1871** JOWETT *Plato* IV. 19 The preliminary sciences..are to be studied partly with a view to their practical usefulness.

**b.** With pl.: A good, benefit, or advantage. *rare.*

**1664** H. MORE *Exp. 7 Epist.* Pref. c iv b, And these..are main Usefulnesses discoverable in the Interpretation. **1668** — *Div. Dial.* I. To Rdr. a j b, The particular Vsefulnesses of the Creation.

**Usel,** obs. variant of ISEL (ashes, etc.).

**Useless** (yū·slės), *a.* [f. USE *sb.* + -LESS.]

**1.** Of things, actions, etc.: Destitute of useful qualities; serving no good end or profitable purpose; not answering or promoting the proposed or desired end; unserviceable, ineffectual, inutile.

In frequent use from *c* 1650.

**1593** SHAKS. *Lucr.* 859 The aged man..like still-pining Tantalus..sits, And useless barns the harvest of his wits. *a* **1623** FLETCHER *Love's Cure* I. i, Let your deeds Make answer to me: useless are all words Till you have writ performance with your swords. **1645** STAPYLTON tr. *Musæus* C 3 b, The giddy Seas their uselesse drinke bestow'd. **1697** DRYDEN *Virg. Georg.* III. 833 Useless to the Currier were their Hides. **1729** T. INNES *Crit. Essay* (1879) 56 An useless as well as an endless discussion. *Ibid.* 206 It became quite useless towards supporting Buchanan's schemes. **1776** GIBBON *Decl. & F.* ii. (1782) I. 55 According to the useless rhetoric of that age. **1825** SCOTT *Betrothed* xvii, He..fell.. ere Raoul could afford him his support, useless as that might have proved. **1855** MACAULAY *Hist. Eng.* xix. IV. 271 The six thousand waggons which had accompanied the French army were useless. **1890** *Retrospect Med.* CII. 177 Physicians, almost without exception, give nearly useless doses of arsenic.

*absol.* **1836–7** SIR W. HAMILTON *Metaph.* i. (1859) I. 4 What is a utilitarian? Simply one who prefers the Useful to the Useless. **1838** *Penny Cycl.* XI. 345/2 To distinguish good from evil, the useful from the useless.

**b.** For which there is no present use.

**1745** *Transl. & Paraphr.* 50 They'll lay the useless Trumpet by, and study War no more.

**2.** Of persons: Destitute of competence or capacity; of inadequate or insufficient ability; inefficient.

**1670** COVEL in *Early Voy. Levant* (Hakl. Soc.) 135 With great courage..[he] turn'd upon the Rogues, who were uselesse, and thought they had him safe. **1710** W. KING *Heathen Gods & Heroes* vi. (1722) 12 [Prometheus] brought Men out from the Caves where they liv'd useless, and like Beasts. **1783** BURKE *Rep. Aff. India* Wks. 1842 II. 52 That Mr. Hastings..had recalled a useless officer. **1810** CRABBE *Borough* xx. 331, I lost my sight, and my employment gone, Useless I live. **1840** THIRLWALL *Greece* VII. 180 He..sent the baggage and all his useless people to Melitæ. **1855** LONGF. *Hiaw.* x. 29 Bring not here a useless woman.

**U·selessly,** *adv.* [f. prec. + -LY [2].] In a useless or fruitless manner; ineffectually; † so as to become of no use.

**1615** G. SANDYS *Trav.* III. 151 The grasse wast-high, vnmowed, vneaten, and vselessly withering. **1690** LOCKE *Hum. Und.* II. i. § 15 To be so idlely and uselesly employ'd. **1765** *Museum Rust.* IV. 371, I would not so uselesly misapply ..your time. **1774** PENNANT *Tour Scotl. in 1772*, 272 My money had been so uselessly laid out. **1831** SCOTT *Cast. Dang.* vi, You have been long, and I hope not uselessly, my pupil. **1880** McCARTHY *Own Times* lxvi. IV. 506 He had thrown away his life uselessly in a quarrel.

**U·selessness.** [f. as prec. + -NESS.] The quality of being useless; futility, inutility.

**1690** LOCKE *Hum. Und.* III. iv. § 10 Another Peripatetick definition..which..betrays its Uselesness and Insignificancy. **1733–4** BP. BERKELEY in Fraser *Life* (1871) vi. 217 The impropriety and uselessness of..going to Cloyne. *a* **1768** SECKER *Serm.* (1771) VI. 69 The Revelation of St. John is accused of Obscurity, and consequently of Uselessness. **1845** JAMES *Arrah Neil* v, The uselessness of remonstrance or opposition. **1889** S. LANGDON *Appeal to Serpent* i. 23 These vast monuments of laborious uselessness.

†**U·sell,** *a.* *Obs.* [a. ON. *ú-sæll* unhappy (MSw. *usal*, Sw. *usel*, Da. *ussel*, miserable, pitiful), f. *ú-* UN-[1] + *sæll* happy.] Wretched, miserable. Hence †**U·selldom,** wretchedness. *Obs.*⁻¹

*c* **1200** ORMIN 891 Forr baþe leddenn usell lif I metess & i claþess. *Ibid.* 3668 Unnorne & wrecche & usell child Inn ure mennisscnesse. *Ibid.* 3708 To libbenn her onn eorþe Full wrecchelike inn uselldom Off metess & off claþess.

†**Use-man.** *Obs. rare.* [f. USE *sb.* 5, 16 d.]

**1.** A usurer.

**1633** HEYWOOD *Eng. Trav.* III. i, If I can aswell put off my Vse-man This day, I shall be maister of the field.

**2.** (See quot. and USE *sb.* 16 d.)

*a* **1716** SOUTH *Serm.* (1717) V. 34 To give those Doctrine and Vse-men, those Pulpit-Engineers their due.

**U·se-money.** Now *dial.* [f. USE *sb.* 5 b.] = INTEREST *sb.* 10. Also *fig.*

**1616** HEALEY *Theophrastus* 66 When he coms to his debtors for his vsemony. **1626** MIDDLETON *Anything for Quiet Life* I. i, Never did any man thrive that purchased with use-money. **1656** TRAPP *Comm.* (ed. 2) *Matt.* v. 26 All that wicked men suffer here is but a paying the use-money required for that dreadful debt, that must be paid at last. **1700** T. BROWN *Amusem. Ser. & Com.* 29 There sneaks a Hunger-starv'd Usurer in quest of a Crasie Citizen for Use and Continuance-Money. **1849–** in dialect use (Durham, Cumbld., Yks., Lincs., Somerset). **1874** T. HARDY *Far fr. Mad. Crowd* viii, When the use-money is gied away to the second-best poor folk.

**User** [1] (yū·zəɹ). Also 6 *Sc.* usar. [f. USE *v.* + -ER [1]. Cf. OF. *useur.*]

**1.** One who has or makes use of a thing; one who uses or employs anything.

*c* **1400** LOVE *Bonavent. Mirr.* (1908) 70 So ofte þe maker and þe vsere offendeth god. *a* **1425** tr. *Arderne's Treat. Fistula*, etc. 8 Þe forseid [counsels]..shal giffe a gracious going to þe vser to þe hiȝte of worship. **1467** in *Eng. Gilds* (1870) 387 That it be so stopped by the doers or vsers therof. **1579** NORTHBROOKE *Dicing* (1843) 177 God graunt that..the magistrates..may..set sharpe punishment for the vsers and teachers thereof. *c* **1600** SHAKS. *Sonn.* ix, But beauties waste hath in the world an end, And kept vnvsde the vser so destroyes it. **1626** DONNE *Serm.* (1640) 675 As he [*sc.* God] sees him a good or bad user of his graces. **1683** TRYON *Way to Health* 223 These Superfluities..are become as it were Essential to the Nature of the Users. **1711** *Countrey-Man's Lett. Curat.* 58 What tho' all our Reformers had been users and readers of the English Service? **1738** WARBURTON *Div. Legat.* I. 84 The utmost Consumption may be made..without Injury to the User. **1846** GREENER *Sci. Gunnery* p. vii, The safety of the user of guns. **1846** MOZLEY *Ess.* (1878) I. 251 He is a user of Puritanism. **1862** *Cornh. Mag.* VI. 608 A moderate user of tobacco. **1876** WHITNEY *Language & its Study* iii. 74 It seeks..to save time and labour to the users of language.

†**2.** *Sc.* One who puts a writ, etc., in force or execution. *Obs.*

**1576** in *Excheq. Rolls Scotl.* XX. 504 David Fowlar,.. usar of the said precept, declarit that he deliverit [it]..to John Kellie. **1609** SKENE *Reg. Maj.*, *Forme of Proces* 122 The wreit or evident is declared to be fals:..And the vser thereof, is punished capitallie. *c* **1630** SIR T. HOPE *Minor Practicks* (1734) 242 If the King..give a Letter of Regress; ..when the Order of Redemption is used and declared, the User of the Redemption is immediately seased, upon the Sight of the Regress.

†**3.** A usurer. *Obs.*⁻¹

**1566** DRANT *Horace, Sat.* I. ii. A viij b, What soeuer cums by vsers skylle, to get, and gender more.

**4.** *north. dial.* A useful animal.

**1828** CARR *Craven Gloss.* s.v., A cow is said to be a good *user*, when she yields abundance of milk, &c. **1863** MRS. TOOGOOD *Yorks. Dial.* (MS.).

**U·ser** [2]. *Law.* [a. F. *user* to USE, or inferred from NON-USER. Cf. the earlier ABUSER [2], DISUSER.] Continued use, exercise, or enjoyment of a right, etc.; presumptive right arising from use.

**1835** CROMPTON, MEESON & ROSCOE *Rep. Cases* I. 418 *marg.*, No right having been acquired by user or length of possession. **1858** LD. ST. LEONARDS *Handy-bk. Prop. Law* xxv. 191 That there should be an user proved every year during the period. **1888** *Pall Mall G.* 29 Feb. 1/1 An open space in which the public has an uninterrupted right of user for purposes of public meeting.

*transf.* **1875** BLACKMORE *Alice Lorraine* II. xvi. 207 A crust of mud, as if some underground duct were anxious to maintain user of its right of way.

*attrib.* **1897** *Westm. Gaz.* 16 June 4/2 In which [judgement] there was only one slight reference to the user question.

**Userer, -y,** etc., obs. varr. USURER, USURY.

**Ush,** *sb. Sc.* Also 5–6 vsche, 5 wsche. [See next and ISH *sb.*]

†**1.** = ISH *sb.* 1, EGRESS *sb.* 1. *Obs.*

**1429** *15th Rep. Hist. MSS. Comm.* App. VIII. 10 [He] sall haf fre vsche and entre in to the said castell. **1534** *Munim. de Melros* (Bann. Cl.) 628 To be haldin..in houssis, ..pastouris, lesouris, fre vsche and entray.

†**2.** = ISH *sb.* 2, ISSUE *sb.* 2.

**1463** *Extr. Aberd. Reg.* (1844) I. 23 To fynd the childe of the brok of his gudis to the vsche of fyue yeris. **1472** *Rental Bk. Cupar-Angus* (1879) I. 164 The sade John Sperk entrand at the vsche of his [*sc.* Cant's] tak. **1489** *Sc. Acts, Jas. IV* (1814) II. 215 Þat a proclamacioune be maid at the vsche of this parliament.

†**3.** A fine or amerciament; = ISSUE *sb.* 7 b. *Obs.*

**1417** *Reg. Aberdon.* (Maitland Cl.) I. 215 Þe kyrk..is in possession of þe tend penny of all wardis, relefis, and mariagis, vscheis of courtis, eschetis.

**4.** = ISSUE *sb.* 9. *rare.*

*a* **1900** *Caithness Words* (E.D.D.), *Ush*, the entrails of a slaughtered animal.

**Ush,** *v.*[1] *Sc.* (†and *north.*). Also 5 vssh(e, 5–6 wsch, 6 vsche, 7, 9 ushe. [var. of ISH *v.*[1]]

†**1.** *intr.* To issue, come *out* (or *forth*). *Obs.*

*c* **1420** *Avow. Arth.* lxiv, On a day we vsshet oute. *c* **1470** HENRY *Wallace* v. 1050 Thai..wsched furth upon the secund day. *Ibid.* VIII. 116 Erll Patrik wschyt, for bid him wald he nocht. ?**1550** *Freiris Berwik* 130 (*Maitland MS.*), He had ane preuie postroun..That he micht vsche [*Bann.* ische] quhen [that] him list vnknawin. *a* **1578** LINDESAY (Pitscottie) *Chron. Scot.* (S.T.S.) II. 11 Certaine of the castell men wschit out. *a* **1614** J. MELVILL *Diary* (Wodrow Soc.) 273 Hendrie Hamilton ushes out of a hous, where he lay in wait for bloode.

†**b.** To go or come *in*; = ENTER *v.* 1. *Obs.*

*a* **1400** *Sir Degrev.* 1078 (1062), Þey vschen in with banere, v. hunderyd knyȝtus.

†**2.** *trans.* To clear (a place) of people; to expel or drive out (occupants). *Obs.*

*a* **1578** LINDESAY (Pitscottie) *Chron. Scot.* (S.T.S.) II. 83 [They] dang out the portar ffrome the ȝett and wschit all the rest of the place. *a* **1614** J. MELVILL *Diary* (Wodrow Soc.) 317 The King, taking me asyde, caussit ushe the Cabinet. *a* **1639** SPOTTISWOOD *Hist. Ch. Scot.* VI. (1655) 374 Presently the roomes were ushed, and the Earl with his company went forth. **1685** *Acts of Sederunt* (1790) 163 The Lords..recommends to the Ordinary..to order the house to be ushed and cleared.

**b.** To empty, cleanse.

**1887** *Suppl. Jamieson* 257/1 To ushe the belly.

**Ush,** *v.*[2] *dial.* or *colloq.* [Back-formation from USHER *sb.*]

**1.** *trans.* To guide, escort, or lead.

*a* **1824** in C. K. Sharpe *Ballad Bk.* (1824) 11 Three valets,.. To beir my tail up frae the dirt, And ush me throw the toun.

**2.** *intr.* To act the usher. (USHER *sb.* 1 d.) *U.S.*

**1910** *Harper's Mag.* Mar. 613/1 Man alive, you've crossed half a continent to 'ush' at that wedding!

**Usher** (ʌ·ʃəɹ), *sb.* Forms: 4–5 vsscher, usscher, uscher, 5 vschere, vshure, 6 vscher; 4–5 vssher (5 -ere), 4–6 ussher (5 -ere), 6 vsher, 5– usher (7 ushier); 4 oyschere, 5 oischer; *Sc.* 5 isscheare, 5–6 ischar, 6 ischair, -ear, 7 isher. [a. AF. *usser* (12th c.), OF. *ussier, uissier, uscier*, var. of *huisier*, etc., HUISHER *sb.* Cf. OSTIAR(Y.]

**1.** An official or servant who has charge of the door and admits people to a hall, chamber, etc.; a door-keeper; in later use esp. an officer in a court of justice, or an attendant who conducts people to seats in a church, public hall, or place of amusement.

*c* **1386** CHAUCER *Sqr.'s T.* 293 The vsshers and the squiers been ygoon, The spices and the wyn is come anoon. *a* **1400–50** *Boke of Curtasye* 30 in *Babees Bk.* 300 Whille marshalle or vssher come fro þe dore, And bydde the sitte, or to borde the lede. *c* **1400** *Northern Passion* (H.) 617 Saint iohn spak to vsscher þan. *c* **1410** *Sir Cleges* 287 The vsscher at the hall dore was Wyth a staffe stondynge. *a* **1470** H. PARKER *Dives & Pauper* (W. de W. 1496) VI. xi. 249/1 She dyd hyr offyce, for she was usshere and keper at the dore. **1525** LD. BERNERS *Froiss.* II. xcvi. 110 b/1 Than the squyer..called the vssher to open the dore. *c* **1610** in [T. Maude] *Verbeia or Wharfdale* (1782) App. 43 The Usher's Wordes of Directions. First,..he must go before them thro' the hall [etc.]. **1677** *Govt. Venice* 121 He disposes of the little Offices about the Palace, as the Ushers and others. **1694** E. CHAMBERLAYNE *Pres. St. England* I. III. 681 Chelsea College...There are several other..Servants, as..Sexton, Usher, Porters [etc.]. **1728** CHAMBERS *Cycl.* (1738) s.v., The ushers of the inquisition ..think themselves highly honoured, by only looking to the doors of the sacred tribunal. **1799** *Report Comm. Courts of Justice* 29 Usher of the Court. *Ibid.* 31 The Court of

King's Bench..[Officers include] Usher and Cryer. Deputy Cryers. Deputy Ushers. **1868** DICKENS *Let.* 3 Jan., He met one of the 'ushers' (who show people to their seats) coming in with Kelly. **1898** A. M. BINSTEAD *Pink 'Un & Pelican* 181 Like the legal gent.., asked to define the duties of the ushers in the law courts.

**b.** *fig.*, *transf.*, and in fig. context.

*c* **1380** WYCLIF *Sel. Wks.* II. 163 Crist..haþ resoun of many þingis; for he is dore, he is ussher. **1387** TREVISA *Higden* v. xvii. (MS. Cott. Tib. D. VII.) fol. 188 Seþþe..so meny..priueleges..were ygrauntet to petur y dare noȝt wiþ-sygge [so] grete and soche an oyschere and porter. **1573** TUSSER *Husb.* (1878) 20 Make eie to be vsher, good vsage to haue, make bolt to be porter. **1594** *Zepheria* v. B 3, Feare, Centinell of sad discretion,..Cares Vsher, Tenant to his owne oppression. **1630** PRYNNE *Anti-Armin.* 258 Arminianisme is but a Bridge, an Vsher vnto grosse Popery. **1638** T. WHITAKER *Blood of Grape* 4 As if Satiation were the Usher of diseases. **1709** STEELE & SWIFT *Tatler* No. 67 ⁋ 10 In this chamber of Fame..no historians are to be admitted at any of these tables; because they..are to be made use of as ushers to the assemblies. **1878** STEWART & TAIT *Unseen Univ.* i. § 5. 27 Being the usher of souls in their passage to the future state.

**c.** Const. *of* (the hall, chamber, etc.).

*a* **1400–50** *Bk. Curtasye* 432 in *Babees Bk.*, Speke I wylle a lytulle qwyle Of vssher of chambur, with-outen gyle. [Description of his duties follows.] ? **1436** *Pol., Rel., & L. Poems* (1903) 13, I was put to þe Soudenys house & was made vssher of halle. **1480** *Acta Dom. Conc.* (1839) 49/1 Sir Johne of Culquhone..vschare in þe tyme of oure souerane lordis chawmer durre. **1503** *Acc. Ld. High Treas. Scot.* II. 311 John Knox ischar of the hall. **1538** ELYOT, *Admissionales*, vshers of the chambre. **1623** COCKERAM II, An Vsher of a Hall, *atrict.* **1728** CHAMBERS *Cycl.* (1738) s.v., In the French Court there are two ushers of the ante-chamber, or hall where the king dines in public.

*fig.* *a* **1500** *Assemb. Ladies* in Skeat *Chaucerian Pieces* (1897) 383, I am..Of her [*sc.* Loyalty's] chambre her ussher. **1501** DOUGLAS *Pal. Hon.* III. lviii, Humanitie and trew Relatioun Bene ischaris of his chalmer.

**d.** *U. S.* One who performs the functions of an usher (sense 1) at a wedding.

**1895** *Outing* (U.S.) XXVII. 181 He sent the young lady a beautiful Colport cup and saucer,..at the same time breathing a prayer that Elliott would not ask him to be usher.

**2.** An officer at court, in a dignitary's household, etc., whose duty it is on occasion to walk or go before a person of high rank; also, a chamberlain. *Usher of the Black Rod, Green Rod*: (see BLACK ROD, and quot. 1869).

**1518** H. WATSON *Hist. Oliver of Castile* (Roxb.) N 2 b, There came dyuers kynges and herauldes of armes, and after came the Vsshers. **1553** *Rutland Papers* (Camden) 118 The Duke of Northfolke..claymethe to be highe vssher the daye of the coronacion. **1641** *Sc. Acts Chas. I* (1870) V. 332/1 Commandit..to goe befoir the king as Ischear with ane rod in his hand. **1678** PHILLIPS (ed. 4) s.v., Usher of the Black-rod. **1689** *Breviate St. Scot.* 10 The Second Great Heritable Offices in the Kingdom, are The Lord High Constable,..The Heritable Usher. **1718** ECHARD *Hist. Eng.* III. 622 The Usher of the Black-Rod commanded their Attendance in the House of Lords. **1721** RAMSAY *Poems* I. List of Subscribers, Usher of the Green Rod, and daily Waiter to his Majesty. **1850** MARSDEN *Early Purit.* 402 The king sent down the usher of the House of Lords with a message. **1869** CUSSANS *Her.* 235 The Officers attached to this Noble Order [of the Knights of the Thistle] are: The Dean;..and the Usher of the Green Rod.

*fig.* **1641** MILTON *Reformation* 2 Faith needing not..the Senses, to be either the Vshers, or Interpreters, of heavenly Mysteries. **1673** A. WALKER *Leez Lachrymans* 18 When he is pleased to send this usher of the Black-Rod, Death,..a white-staffe is too weak to make Resistance.

*transf.* **1577** B. GOOGE *Heresbach's Husbandry* III. 116 A Colt..passeth bridges, not tarriing for an vsher, nor fearing the Ise. **1606** SHAKS. *Ant. & Cl.* III. vi. 44 The wife of Anttony Should haue an Army for an Vsher. **1626** T. H[AWKINS] *Caussin's Holy Crt.* 37 Anciently Pearles were called Vshers, because they made way for Ladyes, who were attyred with them. **1726** POPE *Odyssey* XVII. 251 The good old proverb how this pair fulfill! One rogue is usher to another still. **1763** CHURCHILL *The Ghost* IV. 37 A downright Usher to admit New-Comers to the Court of Wit.

†**b.** A male attendant on a lady. *Obs.*

**1621** FLETCHER *Wild-G. Chase* III. i, If she want an Usher; such an implement; One that is throughly pac'd; a clean made Gentleman; Can hold a hanging up. **1649** DAVENANT *Love & Honour* I. i, Consumptive Ushers that are decay'd In their Ladies service. **1664** BUTLER *Hud.* II. i. 96 She call'd for Hood And Usher, Implements abroad Which Ladies wear. **1749** SMOLLETT *Gil Blas* I. xvi, A lady who..was squired by an old usher [F. *écuyer*], and a little black moor carried her train. **1809** MALKIN *Gil Blas* I. xvi. ⁋ 2 She released her sweet hand from the custody of the usher [F. *écuyer*].

**3.** One who precedes or arrives before another, esp. a higher dignitary or personage; a precursor. Also *transf.* Cf. HARBINGER *sb.* 3.

**1548** UDALL *Erasm. Par. Matt.* iii. 28 By his ussher and messenger John. *c* **1550** N. SMYTH tr. *Herodian* III. 40 b, He had certayne Usshers going before him, whiche commaunded eueryе man to auoyde the stretes. **1641** J. JACKSON *True Evang. T.* II. 151 That other lesson..[Christ] suffered his Ushers that went before him to teach. **1847** EMERSON *Initial Love* 75 Heralds high before him [*sc.* Cupid] run, He has ushers many a one.

**b.** *transf.* That which precedes or gives intimation of the approach or advent of a person or thing.

*c* **1586** C'TESS PEMBROKE *Ps.* L. i, God comes,..His guarde huge stormes, hot flames his ushers goe. **1599** SIR J. DAVIES *Hymns of Astræa* 5 Early, chearfull, mounting Larke, Lights gentle Vsher. **1633** P. FLETCHER *Elisa* I. xxviii, Ah death!..Thou one meals fast, usher to endlesse feasting. **1640** J. GOWER *Ovid's Festiv.* II. 32 In comes the Lecher bold;..His groping hands his warie ushers were. **1645** STAPYLTON tr. *Musæus* C j b, Leander..Expecting the sad Torch, and to be led By that bright Vsher to his private bed.

*fig.* *a* **1586** SIDNEY *Arcadia* II. xxvii, Stretching out his hand, and making vehement countenances the ushers to his speches. **1597** HOOKER *Eccl. Pol.* v. lxxii. § 18 Fasts haue beene set as Vshers of festiuall dayes. **1607** SHAKS. *Cor.* II. i. 173 [Stage direction] A showt, and flourish. *Volum.* These are the Vshers of Martius. **1632** tr. *Bruel's Praxis Med.* 58 Troublesome dreames are vshers to this disease. *c* **1670** M. BRUCE *Gd. News in Evil Times*, etc. (1708) 26 They make the Sabbath, as it were, Mr. Usher to their Visiting of Christ.

**c.** *Ent.* A species of moth.

**1819** SAMOUELLE *Entomol. Compend.* 360 *Geometra leucophearia*, The Spring Usher. *Ibid.*, [*G.*] *nigricaria*, The dark-bordered Usher. **1832** RENNIE *Brit. Butterfl. & Moths* 102 The Spring Usher (*Anisopteryx leucophearia*, Stephens) appears in oak woods the end of February. *Ibid.*, The Wall Usher (*A. Æscularia*).

**4.** An assistant to a schoolmaster or head-teacher; an under-master, assistant-master. Now *rare.* Also in fig. context.

**1512** *Nottingham Rec.* (1885) III. 453 To..establisshe one free schole of one Schole Maister and one Vssher. **1561** in H. B. Wilson *Hist. Merchant-Taylors' Sch.* (1814) 15 Yff both the maister and the usshers be sick at once (as God defend) then let the schoole cease for that while. **1581** J. BELL *Haddon's Answ. to Osorius* 259 b, Who hath made you usher I pray you, or prepositour of Ciceroes schoole? **1632** D. LUPTON *London & Countrey carbonadoed* 119 Country Vshers..are vnder the Head-maister, equall with the chiefe Schollers, and aboue the lesser boyes. **1653** BAXTER *Worc. Petit. Def.* 6 We are but Ushers, and Christ is the ..chief Master of the School. **1669** E. CHAMBERLAYNE *Pres. St. Eng.* II. 483 This Colledge consists of a Master.., a Chaplain,..a Master and Usher to instruct 44 Scholars. **1687** WOOD *Life* (O.H.S.) III. 247 His being usher to a Presbyterian scholemaster. **1711** HEARNE *Collect.* (O.H.S.) III. 205 Tollet is made IId Master, he being before a chief Usher. **1791** BOSWELL *Johnson* an. 1732, He accepted of an offer.. as usher in the school of Market-Bosworth. **1818** SCOTT *Hrt. Midl.* xxvii, Conning over a few pages of Horace or Juvenal with his usher. *c* **1868** in Hughes *Tom Brown* (ed. 6) Pref., Persecution..he can't stop; no more could all the ushers in the world. **1876** *Scheme C.C. 8 governing Foundation Thetford School Hosp.* 6 From the same date..the present usher of the said School shall cease to hold his office as such Usher.

†**b.** *transf.* A teacher or preceptor acting under another. *Obs.*

**1533** MORE *Confut. Tindale* Wks. 585/2 Oure sauiour.. sent him [*sc.* Judas] forth..for one of hys vsshers to teache in his owne time. **1577** HANMER *Anc. Eccl. Hist.* VI. xiv. 105 He ordained Heraclas..his fellowe helper, and Usher,.. committing vnto him the instruction of the inferiour sort. **1613** PURCHAS *Pilgrimage* I. iv. 16 Nature was his Schoole master; or if you will rather, Gods Usher.

**c.** = PROVOST *sb.* 8.

**1545** [see PROVOST *sb.* 8]. **1699** BOYER I, *Prevost de sale d'armes*, the Provost, or Usher of a Fencing-School. **1765** ANGELO *Sch. Fencing* 52 When an usher..has finished his apprenticeship under an able master,..he is obliged to fence with several masters.

†**5.** *Usher of the coins*, *Change*, or *Exchange*, an officer of the Mint. *Obs.*

**1485** *Cal. Patent Rolls* (1914) 49 [The] countroller,.. clerk and ussher of the coynes. **1485** *Rolls of Parlt.* VI. 365/2 The Office of Usher of the Exchaunge of oure said Soveraigne Lord, within his Towre [of London].

**6.** *attrib.* and *Comb.*, as *usher life*, *-like.*

**1580** FULKE *Martiall Confut.* iv. 164 An other foolish brable and vsherlike construing, he maketh of Cyprians words. **1873** W. CORY *Lett. & Jrnls.* (1897) 341 The eight years I had then gone through of usher life.

Hence **U·sherdom**, the office or status of an usher; **U·sheress**, a female usher; **Ushe·rian**, of or pertaining to an usher or ushers; **U·sherism**, conduct or comportment characteristic of ushers.

**1846** WORCESTER (citing *Qu. Rev.*), **Usherdom.* **1905** A. C. BENSON *Upton Lett.* 106 The ugly slough of usherdom. **1879** *Ch. Times* 5 Sept., An appointment..as an '*usheress' in a big establishment. **1826** DISRAELI *V. Grey* I. iv, Certain powers were..delegated to..beings called Ushers...The *usherian rule had, however, always been comparatively light at Burnsley Vicarage. **1869** ELLIS *E. E. Pronunc.* I. vi. 625 That kind of pedantic self-sufficiency which is the true growth of half-enlightened ignorance, and may be termed '*usherism'.

**Usher** (*v·ʃəɹ*), *v.* [f. prec. Cf. HUISHER *v.*]

**1.** *trans.* To act as usher to (a person or persons); to admit ceremoniously; to conduct, attend, or introduce with ceremony *from*, *to* or *unto* or esp. *into* (a place), etc.; to announce, introduce, or bring *in* as an usher.

In frequent use from *c* 1820. In group (*b*) with advs.

(*a*) **1596** WARNER *Alb. Eng.* XII. lxxv. 312 Vnto their Lodging Stafford did the Ladies Vsher then. **1632** J. HAYWARD tr. *Biondi's Eromena* A 3 b, Excuse my boldnesse in ushering her Excellencie..into so excellent a presence. **1725** POPE *Odyss.* XVII. 447 My Lords! this stranger..The good Eumæus usher'd to your court. **1773** *Cook's Voy S. Pole* II. ii. (1777) I. 202 An old gentleman came along-side, who..was some king or great man. He was accordingly, ushered on board. **1821** SCOTT *Kenilw.* xiv, The hall..to which Tressilian was ushered by one of the Earl's attendants. **1844** DISRAELI *Coningsby* III. iii, Whose gracious lot it was to usher them from the apartment. **1891** FARRAR *Darkn. & Dawn* xxv, The tribune ushered her into the Emperor's chamber.

(*b*) **1749** FIELDING *Tom Jones* XIV. x, He..ushered his visitant up stairs. **1760** in Doran *Mann. & Manners* (1876) II. 63 For which purpose I set forth in a Coach and Six, and ushered him in. **1835** DICKENS *Sk. Boz, Parish* i, Simmons bows assent, and ushers the woman out. **1853** C. BRONTE *Villette* xli, Ushering me in, he shut the door behind us.

**b.** Predicated of things. Also *transf.*

**1623** T. SCOT *Tongve-Combat* 63 This brauerie..vshers them into the company of best princes. **1697** LUTTRELL *Brief Rel.* (1857) IV. 311 Boats having mett them with divers sorts of musick to usher them into that harbour. **1807–8** W. IRVING *Salmag.* (1824) 169 The piece opens with a gentle *andante affetuoso*, which ushers you into the Assembly-room.

**c.** *fig.*, *transf.*, and in fig. context.

**1594** [SOUTHWELL] *Mary Magd. Funeral Tears* 69 b, As desire is euer vshered by hope, and waited on by feare. **1612** DRAYTON *Poly-olb.* iii. 3 Yet the blushing dawn out of the chearfull east Is ushering forth the day. **1623** COCKERAM III, *Nusculus*, a friendly fish to the Whale, it vshers him from rocks, shelues, and shores. *a* **1661** FULLER *Worthies, Leic.* II. (1662) 130 Sir Tho. Lake may be said to have ushered him [*sc.* Villiers] to the English Court. **1715** ROWE *Lady Jane Gray* IV. i, As if his traitor father's haggard ghost, And Somerset,.., had usher'd him to ruin. **1749** FIELDING *Tom Jones* IV. i, [The hero] is generally ushered on the Stage by a large Troop of..Scene-shifters. **1790** BURKE *Fr. Rev.* 6 That mode of signature to which you have thrown open the folding-doors of your presence chamber, and have ushered into your National Assembly. **1806** J. BERESFORD *Miseries Hum. Life* (ed. 4) II. xiii, A furious wind which ushers the dust into your eyes. **1867** H. MACMILLAN *Bible Teach.* vi. 109 A new class of objects is now ushered upon the scene. **1891** FARRAR *Darkn. & Dawn* lxvi, Those whom we ushered into the reader's presence at the beginning of this book.

*refl.* **1812** *Ann. Reg., Chron.* 47 This singular person ushered himself into public notice in London, by [etc.].

**d.** *absol.* To act as or after the manner of an usher. Also *fig.*

**1612** DONNE *Progresse of Soule, 2nd Anniversary* 156 Yet Death must usher, and unlocke the doore. Thinke further on thy selfe, my Soule. **1657** F. COCKIN *Div. Blossomes* 4 For to insinuate into his will, And usher, thorough his Judgment to 's Affection..That he may give to Thee all due subjection.

**2.** To precede, escort, or go before (a dignitary) ceremonially as an usher.

**1612** in *10th Rep. Hist. MSS. Comm.* App. I. 599 All his equippage was ushered by certaine officers in ritche coates. **1665** BRATHWAIT *Comment Two Tales* (1900) 47 If I at any time use him for the Squire of my Body, or to Usher me in the streets. **1676** *Office Clerk of Assize* E vij, His Bayliffs, with their white wands in their hands, do usher the Justices from the Court, to the place where they dine. *a* **1700** EVELYN *Diary* 23 April 1667, His Majesty went to Chappell with the Knights of the Garter.., usher'd by the Heraulds.

†**b.** To precede (a person, esp. of higher rank) as a forerunner or harbinger. Also in fig. context.

**1629** GAULE *Pract. The.* A 5, You shall see your Sauiour at once Vshered, Afforded, Humbled, and Exalted: Vshered by his Prophets, afforded in his Person. **1639** FULLER *Holy War* III. vi. 118 [Richard I] set forth [to the Crusade] with many of our nation, which either ushered or followed him. **1646** G. H[ILS] *Odes of Casimire* Pref., Juno and Venus ushered by chaste love Through..Flora's banks here move.

**c.** *fig.* and *transf.*

**1599** T. STORER *Life & D. Wolsey* H j b, Who follow'd me, but Fortune was at hand, To follow him? or, if she went before, To vsher him? **1602** MARSTON *Ant. & Mel.* III. E 2, Gastly amazement..Shall hurry on before, and vsher vs. **1609** B. JONSON *Sil. Wom.* IV. i, Nor will it bee out of your gaine to make loue to her too, so shee follow, not vsher, her ladies pleasure. **1621** BRATHWAIT *Nat. Embassie*, etc. (1877) 203 My friends..Wish'd that all good successe might vsher mee. *a* **1668** DAVENANT *Play House to let* III. i, Wilt thou now guided be By that bright Star which ushers me.

**d.** To precede, come or happen immediately before, in order of time; to lead up to. (Cf. 7 c.)

**1607** *Merry Devil Edmonton* I. ii. 55 In and feed, And let that vsher a more serious deed. *c* **1611** CHAPMAN *Iliad* V. 864 Pitchy tempests threat, Usher'd with horrid gusts of wind. **1616** B. JONSON *Epigrams* ci, Some better sallade Vshring the mutton. **1647** CLARENDON *Hist. Reb.* VII. § 282 Such an application to Court as usually ushered those promotions. **1821** SHELLEY *Adonais* xxi, Evening must usher night, night urge the morrow. **1821** BYRON *Sardanap.* V. i, The day at last has broken. What a night Hath usher'd it!

†**3.** To wait at (a banquet) as an usher. *Obs.*[−1]

**1602** DEKKER *Satirom.* K 3 b, Euen thus the Mercury of Heauen Vshers th' ambrosiate banquet of the Gods.

**4.** To introduce (something uttered); to preface. (Cf. 7 e.)

**1635** A. STAFFORD *Fem. Glory* 55 She made two pawses usher her answer. **1637** C. DOW *Answ. to H. Burton* 159 Divine offices..must not bee curtall'd..by..any new-devised formes of praier, either ushering, or following them. **1717** POPE *Eloisa to Abelard* 32 Oh name for ever sad!..Still breath'd in sighs, still ushered with a tear.

†**5.** To lead, conduct, or direct (a thing) to some point. *Obs. rare.*

**1668** CULPEPPER & COLE tr. *Barthol. Anatomy* II. x. 120 The External [membrane]..sticks close to the intermediate Ligaments.., and ushers along the recurrent Nerves. **1791** COWPER *Iliad* II. 649 Skill In ushering to its mark the rapid lance.

**6.** To introduce or bring *into* the world.

**1679** C. NESSE *Antichrist* 6 Harbingers..to usher him into the world. **1713** STEELE *Englishm.* No. 1. 5 The Jest ..is ushered into the World by the loudest Laughter. **1756** H. JOHNSON in J. Duncombe *Lett.* (1773) III. 38 You have done a great favour to the world in ushering so noble..a work into it. **1835** MARRYAT *J. Faithful* i, It was about a year after the loss.., that I was ushered into the world. **1855** BREWSTER *Newton* II. xviii. 172 The theory he ushered into the world.

*transf.* **1835** MARRYAT *J. Faithful* v, I am very nearly ushered into the next World.

**7. To usher in**: (see also 1). **a.** To bring in (a banquet, meat, etc.) with ceremony.

**1613** HEYWOOD *Silver Age* II. i, Vsher me in a costly banquet straight To entertaine my Lord. **1706** E. WARD *Wooden World Diss.* (1708) 94 The Captain's Bell calls him to usher in the Apple-dumplins. **1829** S. H. CASSAN *Lives Bps. Bath & Wells* 262 The meat was ushered in.

**b.** To inaugurate or bring in (a period of time).

*c* **1600** SHAKS. *Sonn.* cxxxii, That full Starre that vshers in the Eauen. 1656 S. Winter *Serm.* 147 That so he might usher in the eternitie of the world. 1698 Fryer *Acc. E. India & P.* 276 The Morning being ushered in with..Music. 1781 Cowper *Hope* 717 If chance..A tempest usher in the dreaded morn. 1791 Smeaton *Edystone L.* § 306 The year 1762 was ushered in with stormy weather. 1827 Longf. *Life* (1891) I. viii. 121 The day was 'ushered in', as the newspapers say, by the firing of cannon. 1850 Tennyson *In Mem.* lxxii, Dim dawn,..Who usherest in the dolorous hour With thy quick tears. 1872 Yeats *Techn. Hist. Comm.* 298 The French Revolution ushered in a new era of taste.

**c.** = sense 2 d.

1641 Maisterton *Serm.* 18 An anteambulo to usher in a thousand pains. 1663 South *Serm.* (1717) V. 89 Every Fast portended some Villany, as still a Famine ushers in a Plague. 1695 J. Edwards *Perfect. Script.* 414 The Lord, who was to be usher'd in by Elijah the prophet. 1707 *Curios. in Husb. & Gard.* 44 Flowers..appear only to usher in the Fruit, or the Seed; afterwards they fade. 1712 Addison *Spect.* No. 363 ⁋ 18 That vision of Lewdness and Luxury which usher in the Flood. *a* 1721 Prior *Many Daughters have done well* 10 How welcome did that light appear Which usher'd in a form all Heav'nly fair.

**d.** To mark the introduction, beginning, or occurrence of (an event, etc.); to introduce.

1646 J. Hall *Horæ Vac.* 8 They generally usher in uproares in the State. 1650 R. Stapylton *Strada's Low C. Wars* vii. 49 These punishments seemed only to usher in the Death of the two Counts. 1697 Dampier *Voy.* (1729) I. 394 A convenient place to usher in a Commerce with the neighbouring country. 1784 Cowper *Task* iv. 23 But oh th' important budget! usher'd in With..heart-shaking music. 1801 *Med. Jrnl.* V. 231 Increased heats..already described as ushering in the hæmorrhage. 1843 R. J. Graves *Syst. Clin. Med.* x. 106 The symptoms..bear a very strong analogy to those which usher in typhus. 1870 Freeman *Norm. Conq.* (ed. 2) I. 738 The event of 1018..was ushered in by a comet.

**e.** = sense 4.

1662 Stillingfl. *Orig. Sacr.* ii. vi. § 5 Their deliverance by Cyrus..he ushers..in with this preface that [etc.]. 1673 *True Worship of God* 8 These Sacrifices not only accompanying their Confessions..; but their Hymns and Doxologies also,..to usher them in with more acceptance. 1699 Bentley *Phal.* 222 He would have usher'd the Word in with some kind of introduction. 1757 Gray *Let.* Poems (1775) 252 All that ushers in the incantation from 'Try we yet..', I am delighted with. *a* 1763 W. King *Lit. & Polit. Anecd.* (1819) 154 He was..so unfortunate as to usher in his criticisms with [etc.]. 1814 Chalmers *Evid. Chr. Revel.* ii. ii, The quotation is..ushered in by the general words, 'As it is written'.

Hence **U·shering** *ppl. a.*

1628 [A. Leighton] *Appeal to Parliament* 145 Why breaketh out the fearfull wrath of God..among us, but because of Baal-peor his ushering Ceremonies..? 1634 Milton *Comus* 279 Could that [*sc.* darkness] divide you from neer-ushering guides? 1820 Clare *Rural Life* (ed. 3) 32 That rural call..All noises now to silence lulls, In soft and ushering sounds.

† **U·sherage.** *Obs. rare.* [f. prec. + -age.] The act of ushering or introducing; insertion.

1661 Hickeringill *Jamaica* 28 [An interstice] admitting not so much as the intermedium or usherage of a twig. 1662 — *Apol. Distressed Innoc.* Wks. 1716 I. 298 If the usherage of Sanctity cannot hand in their black deformities of Rapine.

† **U·sherance.** *Obs.* [f. as prec. + -ance.] The action of introducing or bringing in; introduction.

1711 Shaftesb. *Charac.* III. 190 Our Author's First Letter ..occasion'd the revival of this abortive Piece, and gave Usherance to its Companions.

**U·sherer.** [f. Usher *v.* + -er¹.] One who or that which ushers in; an usher or harbinger. Also with *in.* Occas. *fig.*

1598 Marston *Scourge of Villanie* ii. v. E 4 b, Codrus my well-fac'd Ladies taile-bearer, (He that some-times play'th Flauias usherer). 1640 Reynolds *Passions* xxxv. 424 The Usherers in, or Attendants and followers on the Grave, Age, Infirmity, Sicknesse. *c* 1645 Howell *Lett.* iv. xxix. (1890) 607 True spiritual Pride, the usherer-in of all Confusions. 1824 Galt *Rothelan* II. iii. ii. 16 The Past is usherer to the Future. 1892 Walt Whitman in *Harper's Mag.* April 709/2 Thee [*sc.* Death], envoy, usherer, guide at last of all.

**U·shering,** *vbl. sb.* [f. as prec. + -ing¹.] The action of the verb, in various senses. Also with *in.*

1588 Shaks. *L. L. L.* v. ii. 328 Nay he can sing A meane most meanly, and in Vshering Mend him who can. *a* 1613 Overbury *Characters, A Fine Gentleman,* Afterwards he maintaines himselfe an implement of houshold, by carving and ushering. *a* 1693 *Urquhart's Rabelais* iii. xxx. 247 At the ushering in [F. *l'apport*] of the Second Service, Panurge..[made] a low Reverence. 1850 O. Winslow *Inner Life* x. 273 The ushering in of that great event. 1851 Gallenga *Italy* i. 21 The ushering in of a new political phasis. 1866 Trollope *Claverings* ii, Even though he had earned that money by 'ushering' for the last two years.

**U·sherless,** *a.* [f. Usher *sb.* + -less.] Lacking an usher, herald, or harbinger. In earlier use *fig.*

1598 Sylvester *Du Bartas* ii. i. iv. *Handy-crafts* 88 Where Usher-lesse, both day and night, the..windes enter and goe forth. 1604 Marston *Malcontent* iv. v. G j, There Vsherlesse the ayre comes in and out. 1815 Milman *Fazio* 80 Who art thou thus usherless and unbidden Scarest my privacy? 1883 J. Payn *Thicker than Water* II. xxix. 217 On the great staircase he met Mrs. Sotheran coming up usherless.

**U·sherment.** *rare*⁻¹. [f. Usher *v.* + -ment.] The fact of being prefaced, introduced, or ushered in.

1887 Saintsbury *Hist. Elizab. Lit.* ii. 46 These last..do not come in with the somewhat ostentatious usherment and harbingery, which for instance laid the even more splendid bursts of Jeremy Taylor open to the sharp sarcasm of South.

**U·shership.** [f. Usher *sb.* + -ship.]

**1.** The office or functions of an usher.

1580 Fulke *Martiall Confut.* iv. 165 Yᵉ Priestes are appointed to vse those signes, which if Martials Vshership will not admit, [etc.]. 1631 T. Powell *Tom of all Trades* 44 To leape into instantly, and imediately out of a Ladies vshership. 1740 Ld. Harrington in *10th Rep. Hist. MSS. Comm.* App. I. 275 The Ushership of the Exchequer. 1788 Cowper *Let.* Wks. 1836 VI. 201 When I was under his ushership at Westminster. 1825 T. Hook *Sayings* Ser. ii. III. 93 To assume the ushership of the black rod at Montgomery Place. 1881 *Daily News* 1 Aug. 5/3 In Algeria.. his years of ushership had been the most wretched of his life.

**2.** A post or position as a (school-) usher.

1825 Hone *Every-day Bk.* I. 79 The son..being put to school, obtained successive userships. 1880 R. K. Dent *Old & New Birmingham* 79 Johnson having found the drudgery of an ushership..too irksome for him.

**Ushewe,** obs. f. Issue *sb.*

† **Ushing,** var. Ishing *vbl. sb. Obs.* (Cf. Ush *v.*¹)

1375 Barbour *Bruce* vi. 363 (E.), Hys wyt schawyt hym the strait entre off the furd, and the uschyng alsua.

‖ **Usine** (*üzīn, yuzī·n*). [F. *usine* factory, (in early use) water-mill.] A factory; esp. in later use, a West Indian sugar factory.

In first quot. the word is misapplied.

1798 W. Eton *Turk. Empire* 216 Their furnaces are of *usine*, which is particularly adapted to the casting of iron. 1858 Simmonds *Dict. Trade* 396 *Usine*, a glass-house; an iron-work. 1878 *Times* 10 May 4/3 Furnaces and vast usines. 1888 *Daily News* 13 April 5/4 Of these usines, or crushing factories, there are already several in Trinidad, St. Lucia, and British Guiana.

**Using** (*yū·ziŋ*), *vbl. sb.* [f. Use *v.* + -ing¹.]

**1.** The action of making use of something, or the fact of being used.

*a* 1340 Hampole *Psalter* liv. 2, I am made sary in myn vsynge. 1387–8 T. Usk *Test. Love* iii. vi. l. 60 They han as wel dyvers aptes and dyvers maner usinges. *c* 1400 *Cursor M.* 29369 (Cott. Galba), Þat oþer [case] es of..portere, in vsyng of þaire awin mistere. 1422 Yonge tr. *Secreta Secret.* 247 Vsynge of honementys aftyr the tyme and complexcione. *c* 1445 Pecock *Donet* 50 Mesurable and resonable vsing of worldly goodis. 1526 *Pilgr. Perf.* (W. de W. 1531) 45 In iust commutacion & vsyng of these thynges. 1560 Bible (Genev.) *Col.* ii. 22 Which all perishe with the vsyng of them. 1656 Earl Monm. tr. *Boccalini's Advts. fr. Parnass.* ii. li. (1674) 202 The using of the same severities which Augustus.. practised. 1690 Locke *Hum. Und.* iii. x. § 2 The using of Words, without clear and distinct Ideas. 1705 *Lond. Gaz.* No. 4114/4 A fine Coach lined with Velvet, little the worse for using. 1774 Goldsm. *Nat. Hist.* III. 315 His teeth wear, like those of most other animals, by using. 1826 *Art of Brewing* (ed. 2) 94 The twelve principal houses have..disclaimed the using of any material in their Beer, except malt and hops. 1893 C. C. King in *Social Eng.* I. 43 Of..arrowheads as missile weapons there are none that seem worth the using.

† **b.** The celebration of the Eucharist. *Obs.*

1452 *Paston Lett.* I. 237 The seid servaunts..knelyng to see the usyng of the Masse. 1454 *Ibid.* 280. *c* 1500 *Langforde's Meditacyons* in Wickham Legg *Tracts on Mass* (1904) 28 From the sacryng vnto the vsing be done, you may remember..the Passyon and deith of our sauyour.

**c.** The action of accustoming *to* something.

1702 *Eng. Theophrast.* 212 It goes a great way towards Felicity, the using of our selves to other Peoples Follies.

**2.** Manner of usage or employment.

1388 Wyclif *Rom.* Prol., Thei weren brouȝt in to the lawe and profetis, that is, in to cerymonyes..acordynge with tho cerymonyes, which vsyng is contrarie now to the treuthe.. of Cristis gospel. 1553 T. Wilson *Rhet.* 114 b, iii. The placing of these Images, is like vnto wordes written. iiii. The vtteraunce and vsing of them, is like vnto readynge. 1669 in *Buccleuch MSS.* (Hist. MSS. Comm.) I. 32 Extolling the King of England's using of people. 1726 Leoni *Alberti's Archit.* I. 62 b/2 For the right using of these benefits, the Fathers may provide by Laws and Statutes. 1827 Keble *Chr. Y., Palm Sunday* v, As in this bad world below Noblest things find vilest using.

**3.** *Using-up*, consumption or exhaustion *of* a commodity, etc.

1863 Jas. Sanderson *Agric. Berw. & Roxb.* 32 The using-up of the manure is the preferable mode. 1889 Hamerton *French & English* i. i. 14 The decline caused by industrialism and the rapid using-up of life in large cities.

**4.** Special Comb.: **using-file**, a file affixed to the work-bench (instead of being held in the hand), for having the work rubbed upon it; **using-ground** *U.S.*, the haunt of wild-fowl; † **using stone** (see quot. 1688).

1683 Moxon *Mech. Exerc., Printing* xii. ⁋ 2 The Using-File..is about nine or ten Inches long, and three or four Inches broad..The two broad sides must be exactly flat and straight. 1688 Holme *Armoury* iii. 303/1 The using File..; the teeth not half so rough as the common File. *Ibid.* 382/1 The Using Stone [of jewellers]..is a flat smooth Stone shooting out into two angles or points on each side. 1893 *Harper's Mag.* Oct. 681/2 The 'using-grounds' of the coveys are generally known or suspected by the farmer.

**U·sitate,** *a.* [ad. L. *ūsitāt-us*, pa. pple. of *ūsitārī* to use often.] **a.** Customary, usual. **b.** Much used *of* (= by).

1885 Dixon *Hist. Ch. Eng.* xx. III. 462 The usitate dignities of rural deans and archdeacons. 1890 *Sat. Rev.* 27 Sept. 383/1 A form of punishment usitate of French novelists.

**U·sitative,** *a. rare*⁻¹. [f. as prec. + -ive.] That denotes customary action.

1849 Alford *Gk. Testament* I. 19 Not the usitative aorist, but declarative of the definite past εὐδοκία of the Father in Him.

† **Usker.** *Obs. rare*⁻¹. [a. Irish *usgar.*] An ornament or jewel. In quot. *collect.*

1536–7 *Act 28 Hen. VIII*, in Bolton *Stat. Irel.* (1621) 130 That also no woman vse or weare any kyrtell, or cote.. couched ne layd with vsker, after the Irish fashion.

**Usle,** obs. var. Isel (ashes, etc.).

**U·snate.** *Chem.* [f. Usn-ic + -ate¹ 1 c.] A salt produced by a combination of usnic acid with a base.

1866 Watts tr. *Gmelin's Handbk. Chem.* XVII. 50–51 Usnate of Ammonia,..Usnate of Potash,..Usnate of Soda, ..Usnate of Baryta,..Usnate of Copper. 1868 *Watts' Dict. Chem.* V. 970 The usnates of the alkali-metals are soluble in water.

‖ **Usnea** (*v·snĭ,ă*). Pl. usneas, usneæ. [med.L. (12th cent.), ad. Arab. and Pers. أشنة *ushnah* moss. Hence F. *usnée* (1530).] A genus of gymnocarpous lichens, typical of the family *Usneidæ*; a species or plant of this.

1597 Gerarde *Herbal* iii. clvi. 1369 *Muscus quernus*;..the Arabians and the Apothecaries call it *Vsnea.* 1693 tr. *Blancard's Phys. Dict.* (ed. 2), *Usnea*, Moss which grows upon Bones or Trees. 1706 Phillips (ed. Kersey), *Usnea*, a kind of green Moss..which is us'd in Physick. 1753 *Chambers' Cycl.* Suppl., *Usnea*,..of this genus of plants there are nineteen known species: 1. The stringy-tree moss, or common *Usnea* of the shops. *Ibid.*, 19. The smallest of all the *Usneas*..grows on the barks of old trees. 1857 M. J. Berkeley *Introd. Crypt. Bot.* 417 *Usneæ*, finally, when well-grown, are perhaps the most beautiful of Lichens. 1857 Thoreau *Maine W.* ii. (1867) 155 The spruce still grows shaggy with usnea. 1861 H. Macmillan *Footn. fr. Page Nat.* 109 So late as the seventeenth century, some of the filamentous lichens were sold in the shops of barbers and perfumers under the name of Usnea.

*attrib.* 1878 H. M. Stanley *Dark Cont.* II. vii. 204 From many of the branches depended the Usneæ moss in graceful and delicate fringes.

**U·snic,** *a. Chem.* Also usneic. [f. Usn-ea + -ic 1 b.] *Usnic acid*, carbusnic acid; usnin.

1847 W. Gregory *Handbk. Org. Chem.* (ed. 2) 502 Usnic Acid..is found in many lichens,..and in many species of *Usnea* [etc.]. 1848 Fownes *Elem. Chem.* (ed. 2) 514 The *Usnea barbata* and several other lichens contain usneic acid. 1861–7 [see Usnin].

**Usnin** (*v·snin*). *Chem.* Also -ine. [f. Usn-ea + -in¹.] Usnic acid.

1861 H. Macmillan *Footn. fr. Page Nat.* 82 Alpine lichens generally are more or less of a brown or black colour. This peculiarity seems to be owing to the presence of usnine or usnic acid. 1867 Brande & Cox *Dict. Sci.*, etc. III. 912/2 Usnin or Usnic Acid..forms yellow crystals, which with great difficulty are fused like a resin.

‖ **Uso.** *Obs.* [It. or Sp. *uso.*] = Usance 5, 5 b.

1704 *Lond. Gaz.* No. 3992/4 Two first Bills of Exchange, ..payable to Jean Voordagh or Order, at 2 uso 8 days. 1740 W. Douglass *Disc. Curr. Brit. Plant. Amer.* 4, Notes of Hand payable in Silver at certain Uso's or Periods.

† **U·sque.** *Sc. Obs.* Also 8 usquæ, husque, usky (cf. Whisky *sb.*¹). Short for next.

1728 Ramsay *Friends in Ireland* 10 Drinking roundly rum and claret, Ale and usquæ. *c* 1730 Burt *Lett. N. Scotl.* (1754) I. 188 This drink [common ale] is of itself apt to give a Diarrhea, and therefore..they interlace it with Brandy or Usky. 1739 A. Nicol *Poems* 76 Good ale and Usque ga'd about In Healths.

*attrib.* *c* 1730 Burt *Lett. N. Scotl.* (1754) II. 83 My Merchants..mov'd the Usky Vessels before 'em. *Ibid.* 84 The Usky Men were my Companions.

**Usquebaugh** (*v·skwĭbǭ*). Forms: *α.* 6 vskebeaghe, 7 vsque-ba'he, vskebah (uskkiba), 7–9 usquebah (7 usquabah), 7 vsquebach; 7 vsque-, 7– usquebagh, 7 vsce-, usce-, uskabagh; 6 vscough-, 7– usquebaugh. *β.* 7 vsque-, usque-, husquo-, uskebath. *γ.* (Chiefly *Sc.*) 6 iskie-bae, 7 usquebay, 8–9 usquebae (8 usquabae). [a. Irish and Sc. Gaelic *uisge beatha* (*uisci-betha* in Ann. Loch Cé, an. 1405), lit. 'water of life' (cf. Aqua-vitæ), f. *uisge* water, and *beatha* life. The latter word is differently pronounced in Irish and Scottish Gaelic, approximately (bā) and (bē). Cf. Whisky (bae.)] = Whisky *sb.*¹

With *α*-forms, in very freq. use from *c* 1610.

*α.* 1581 Derricke *Image Ireland* F ij, She filles them then with Vskebeaghe. 1600 Sir R. Cecil *Lett.* (Camden) 33 Remember..the Lord Threasurer with a couple of pugges or some vscough baugh. 1610 Beaum. & Fl. *Scornf. Lady* ii. i, A bottle of Usquebaugh. 1658 Rowland tr. *Moufet's Theat. Ins.* 913 The Irish prepare a distilled Oenomeli made with Honey, Wine and some herbs, which they cal Vsquebach. 1682 *Lond. Gaz.* No. 1776/4 There is right Irish Usquebagh to be sold..at the Rein-Deer in Tuttle-street,.. By one from Ireland. 1706–7 Farquhar *Beaux' Strat.* i. i, An honest Gentleman that came this way from Ireland, made her a Present of a dozen bottles of Usquebaugh. 1762 Foote *Orators* iii. 61 Usquebaugh..is an exhilirator of the bowels, and a stomatic to the head. 1818 Hazlitt *English Poets* vii. 260 The last long precious draught of his favourite usquebaugh. 1882 Miss Braddon *Mt.-Royal* I. iv. 118, I wonder whether she had a strong brogue, and a sneaking fondness for usquebaugh.

*attrib.* 1630 Randolph *Aristippus* 24 Are you there you Vsquebaugh Rascall, with your Metheglin iuyce?

*β.* 1621 S. Ward *Life of Faith* 33 Vsing it [*sc.* faith] as Vsquebath and strong Waters for swones and heart qualmes onely. 1681 T. Dineley *Jrnl. Tour Irel.* in *Trans. Kilkenny Archaeol. Soc.* Ser. ii. II. 25 As thou did not want Usquebath Oat cakes,..How is it then that thou diedst? 1713 Tyldesley *Diary* (1873) 117 Hee gave us two drames of uskebath.

*γ.* 1583 *Leg. Bp. St. Androis* 1062 And George Gipsones iskie bae Had all the wyte he womit sae. *a* 1689 W. Cleland *Poems* (1697) 12 A Tupe Horn fill'd with Vsquebay. 1715 Ramsay *Christ's Kirk Gr.* ii. viii, Another gill Of usquebae. 1791 Burns *Tam O'Shanter* 108 Wi' usquabae, we'll face the devil! 1819 Scott *Leg. Montrose* iv, A flask of usquebæ, designed for the refreshment of Lord Menteith. 1840 R. Bremner *Excurs. Denmark*, etc. II. 211 Morning drinkers of usquebae.

**Ussay, usscha, usscho, usse,** obs. Sc. varr. ISSUE *sb.* **Us self,** etc.: see SELF A. 3–4. **Ussell,** obs. or dial. var. OUZEL. **Usshe,** obs. form of USH *v. Sc.* **Usshew, Ussu,** etc., obs. varr. ISSUE *sb.* **Uste,** obs. Sc. var. HOST *sb.*[4] 2. **Ustel-, Ustilement,** etc., obs. ff. HUSTLEMENT.

† **Usterosis,** obs. var. HYSTEROSIS.

*a* 1661 FULLER *Worthies, Bedford.* I. (1662) 121 Mean time we take notice of an *Usterosis*, beholding R. Basset (though first named) as his Under-Sheriff.

**Ustilagi·neous** (*v*stilēdʒi·nĭ,əs), *a. Bot.* [f. mod.L. *Ustilagine-æ* (see def.) + -OUS.] Of or pertaining to the *Ustilagineæ* (brand fungi).

1889 PLOWRIGHT *Brit. Uredineæ* x. 60 One peculiarity of most of the Ustilagineous mycelia. 1900 B. D. JACKSON *Gloss. Bot. Terms* 283 *Usterophyte*,.. Berkeley's name for one of the Ustilagineous Fungi.

**Ustila·ginous** (*v*stilæ·dʒinəs), *a. Bot.* [f. mod.L. *Ustilagin-*, USTILAGO + -OUS.]

1. Resembling, belonging or allied to, *Ustilago*.

1857 M. J. BERKELEY *Introd. Crypt. Bot.* 323 Besides the Ustilagineous species, there are others. 1900 B. D. JACKSON *Gloss. Bot. Terms* 283.

2. 'Affected with ustilago; smutty' (*Cent. Dict.*).

‖ **Ustilago** (*v*stilē·go). Pl. **ustilagines** (-ē·dʒinīz). *Bot.* [Late L. *ūstilāgo*, app. a kind of thistle; in mod.L. applied to smut on account of its burned or blackened appearance: cf. next.] Smut on oats, barley, or other grain, etc.; also *spec.*, a genus of parasitic fungi, typical of the N.O. *Ustilagineæ* (brand fungi).

1578 LYTE *Dodoens* 471 *Vstilago* is a certayne disease, or infirmitie, that happeneth vnto..ebare eares, but especially vnto Otes. *Ibid.*, This barren and vnfruitefull herbe is nowe called *Vstilago*, that is to say, Burned, or Blighted. *a* 1722 LISLE *Husb.* (1757) 130, I could find little ustilago in my oats. *Ibid.*, The ustilago is common to the ears of grass as well as of corn. 1822–7 GOOD *Study Med.* (1829) II. 118 Wheat which is.. infested with albigo (mildew), ustilago (smut), and clavus (ergot or spur). 1857 M. J. BERKELEY *Introd. Crypt. Bot.* 323 Scarcely ever so much as to make them disagreeable objects like the Ustilagos. 1866 *Treas. Bot.* 1197/2 *Ustilago*, smut, a disease in which the natural tissue is replaced by black powder. 1895 M. C. COOKE *Study Fungi* xxi. 251 It was..customary to associate the Ustilagines with the Uredines.

† **U·stion.** *Obs.* [a. OF. *ustion* (13th c., =Sp. *ustion*, It. *ustione*, Pg. *ustão*), ad. L. *ūstiōn-em*, noun of action f. *ūst-us*, pa. pple. of *ūrĕre* to burn. Cf. ADUSTION, INUSTION.]

1. The action of burning, or fact of being burnt.

1567 MAPLET *Gr. Forest* 10 Likewise Incision..kepeth the place of vstion, free and cleare from yll smelling and rancoring. 1617 WOODALL *Surg. Mate* (1639) 274 Vstion is a preparation of things..by burning them in a crucible, or in the fire. 1673 *Phil. Trans.* VIII. 6132 All these to be further examined by..Arefaction, Assation, Ustion, Calcination. 1728 CHAMBERS *Cycl.* s.v., The Ustion of Minerals, is a more imperfect kind of Calcination. 1778 PRYCE *Min. Cornub.* 241 It may be worth enquiry, whether..Ores..may not be advanced in value by a previous ustion. 1802 *Trans. Soc. Arts* XX. 209 Another [cause of the fetid smell]..is ustion or burning the [fish-] oil.

2. The action of searing; cauterization.

1588 J. READ tr. *Arcæus' Meth. curing Woundes* 60 That imperfection..cannot bee holpen without vstion or burning. 1638 A. READ *Chirurg.* ii. 14 Wee ought not, but upon great necessitie, to have recourse to ustion. 1651 BIGGS *New Disp.* ⁋ 256 They..have stoutly played the Vulcans, and have appointed also Arabick ustions..for the sciatica. 1684 tr. *Bonet's Merc. Compit.* xix. 712 The ustion of the Ioynts that was grown out of use, has been restored. 1737 BRACKEN *Farriery Impr.* (1756) I. 319 Ustion or Burning was the Remedy most used.

b. A place or surface presenting the appearance of being seared or cauterized.

1607 TOPSELL *Four-f. Beasts* 255 The roote of the greater Siler..cureth those cold vstions in the flesh or belly, when the place looketh blacke or looseth sence.

3. *fig.* Concupiscence; libidinous desire. *rare.*

1559 [see URN *v.*[1] 1]. 1624 SANDERSON *Serm.* I. 228 Marriage,..the sole allowed remedy against..burning lusts; by the apostle..commanded in case of ustion to all men.

† **U·stive,** *a. Obs. rare.* [f. L. *ūst-us* (see prec.) + -IVE.] a. Caustic. b. Adapted for a burn.

1597 A. M. tr. *Guillemeau's Fr. Chirurg.* 22 b/2 Causticke or vstive medicamentes, as Aqva fortis. 1599 — tr. *Gabelhouer's Bk. Physicke* 332/1 Linteseede-oyle..is an excellent ustive oyntment.

† **Usto·rious,** *a. Obs.*—[1] [See prec. and -ORIOUS.] Characterized by the faculty or power of burning.

1724 WATTS *Logic* I. vi. § 3 It is by an ustorious Quality in the Mirrour or Glass,..arising from a certain unknown substantial Form in them.

† **U·stulate,** *v. Obs.*—[0] [ad. L. *ūstulāt-*, ppl. stem of *ūstulāre* to burn.] *trans.* (See quots.)

1623 COCKERAM, *Vstulate*, to curle or burne. 1656 BLOUNT *Glossogr.*, *Ustulate*, to burn or sear a thing [so Cooper s.v. *Vstulo*]; also to frizel or curle. 1775 ASH, *Unustulated*,.. not ustulated; not burnt.

**Ustulate** (*v*·stiŭlĕt), *a.* [a. L. *ūstulāt-us*, pa. pple.: see prec.] (See quots.)

1826 KIRBY & SP. *Entomol.* IV. xlvi. 289 *Ustulate*,..so marked with brown as to have the appearance of being scorched. 1840 PAXTON *Bot. Dict.* 325/2 *Ustulate*, blackened. [Hence in later works.]

**Ustulation** (*v*stiŭlē·ʃən). [ad. med.L. *ūstulātiōn-*, *ūstulātio*, noun of action f. L. *ūstulāre* to burn.]

1. The action of burning or fact of being burnt; *spec.* in later use, torrification, roasting.

1658 tr. *Porta's Nat. Magic* x. xii. 267 To extract Oyl by Descent..is common and vulgar to all; for it is done by Ustulation. 1667 SPRAT *Hist. R. Soc.* 296 The ustulation or affriction between the Nave and the Axel-tree. 1753 *Chambers' Cycl.* Suppl., *Ustulation*,..the roasting or torrefying of humid or moist substances over a gentle fire, so as to render them fit for powdering. 1780 J. T. DILLON *Trav. Spain* (1781) 262 Melting and ustulation of the mercurial ores. 1811 *Self Instructor* 534 Blacking lies in the iron, and particularly in its ustulation. 1839 URE *Dict. Arts* 820 The combustion must be so conducted as..to prolong the ustulation, and let the whole mass be equably penetrated with heat.

† 2. *fig.* = USTION 3. *Obs. rare.*

1660 JER. TAYLOR *Ductor* III. iv. rule 20 § 13 A state of cœlibate exposes us to a perpetual ustulation. *Ibid.* § 16 It is not certain that they took the better part when they chose ustulation before marriage.

**Ustyl(l)ment,** obs. varr. HUSTLEMENT.

† **Usuable,** obs. var. USABLE *a.*

1544 in Leadam *Sel. Cases Crt. Requests* (Selden) 112 By the olde vsuable custome of the seyd manoyr.

† **Usuage,** obs. var. USAGE *sb.*

1641 in *Verney Mem.* (1904) I. 203 Contrary to the custom & usuage of Parliment. 1708 *Brit. Apollo* No. 50. 1/1 So customary an Usuage. *a* 1744 T. INNES in *Spalding Club Misc.* (1842) II. 365 These usuages of Sarum were..confirmed by the rescripts..of popes.

**Usual** (yū·ʒuăl, -iuăl), *a.* Forms: 4–7 vsual, -all (6 vsial, wsuall), 6– usual (6–7 -all, 7 usewal); 4–7 vsu-, usuale; 4–5 vsu-, usuell. [a. OF. *usual* (1298 in Godef.), *usuel* (F. *usuel*), or ad. L. (post-class.) *ūsuāl-is* (whence It. *usuale*, Sp. and Pg. *usual*, Pr. *uzual*), f. *ūsus* USE *sb.*].

1. That is in ordinary use or observance; having general currency, validity, or force; commonly observed or practised; current, prevalent.

1396 in *Scottish Antiq.* XIV. 218, xix. marcis of vsuale moneth. 1396–7 in *Eng. Hist. Rev.* (1907) XXII. 296 Oure usuel presthod þe qwich began in Rome. *c* 1450 *Godstow Reg.* 553 Robert yaf to him xij. shillings of vsuall money. 1495 *Act 11 Hen. VII*, c. 43 *Preamble*, Noe gretter fees.. but such [as] at this tyme be usuell. 1523 FITZHERB. *Surv.* 36 b, F. G...payeth vnto the lordes at the termes their vsuels sixtene shillynges. 1575 *Extr. Aberd. Reg.* (1848) II. 24 Fortie markis wsuall money of Scotland. *a* 1577 SIR T. SMITH *Commw. Eng.* II. xii. (1589) 67 In this court [of Chancery] the vsuall and proper forme of pleading of England is not vsed. 1620 *Extr. Aberd. Reg.* (1848) II. 368 Tua vsuall termis in the yeir, Witsonday and Martimes. 1687 A. LOVELL tr. *Thevenot's Trav.* I. 278 He never goes up thither but at the usual hours, unless it be [etc.]. 1747 BERKELEY *Lett.* Wks. 1871 IV. 315 Pray give him the usual fee for the best lawyer. 1848 WHARTON *Law Lex.*, *Usual terms*, a phrase in the common law practice, which means pleading issuably, rejoining gratis, and taking short notice of trial. 1855 *Poultry Chron.* II. 580/2 At half the usual rates of charge. 1897 *Daily News* 10 April 7/2 Stay of execution for a fortnight upon 'the usual terms'.

† 2. a. Of a year: Solar. *Obs. rare.*

1387 TREVISA *Higden* (Rolls) I. 37 For þe Iewes in tretys and couenauntes haueþ a ȝere vsual, and bygineþ in Ianuarie. 1398 — *Barth. De P. R.* IX. iii. (Tollem. MS.), Some ȝere is clepid usuale, as is þe ȝere of þe sonne.

† b. Of a month: Calendar. *Obs.*—[1]

1594 BLUNDEVIL *Exerc.* III. I. xlv. (1597) 172 b, The vsuall month is that number of daies which are set downe in our common Kalenders.

3. Ordinarily used; constantly or customarily employed; in common use; ordinary, customary.

*c* 1444 PECOCK *Donet* 34 He must take þe eukarist, not as oþire comoun or vsual meete and drynk. *a* 1479 CAXTON *Epil. Boeth.* 92 b, Maister Geffry Chaucer hath translated this sayd werke oute of latyn in to oure vsual and moder tonge. 1532 MORE *Confut. Tindale* Wks. 621/1 He turned the vsuall englyshe woordes of churche, priest, and penaunce, to congregacyon, senior, and repentaunce. 1550 BALE *Eng. Votaries* II. 40 A Consuetudynary or vsuall boke of the churche. 1579 FULKE *Refut. Rastel* 781, Thou perhaps wilt say, my bread is common and vsual bread. 1610 HOLLAND *Camden's Brit.* I. 673 From whence there is an usuall passage over into Ireland. 1641 J. JACKSON *True Evang. T.* I. 37 Earth-quakes, which (according to the usuall scandall)..were ascribed as a punishment to the Christians. 1671 MILTON *P. R.* IV. 316 They..Rather accuse him [*sc.* God] under usual names, Fortune and Fate. 1729 T. INNES *Crit. Essay* (1879) 236 He reforms the bard Forchern's story of it (according to the usual custom of posterior bards). 1776 *Trial Nundocomar* 24/2 What was Selabut's usual method of attesting papers as a witness? 1797 *Monthly Mag.* III. 549 The sheriff shall make..proclamations..at or near to the most usual door of the church, or chapel. 1836 W. IRVING *Astoria* II. 31 He began by the usual expressions of friendship. 1860 TYNDALL *Glac.* I. ix. 61 We reached the place by the usual route. 1883 *Manch. Exam.* 30 Oct. 8/4 Beer in the usual stately German flagons with pewter covers.

† b. Habitually done or made. *Obs. rare.*

1576 FLEMING *Panopl. Epist.* A ij b, Often reading, and usual marking the epistles of Tullie. *Ibid.* 2 Sundry Gentlemen, that haue usual resort to my house. 1577 HARRISON *England* II. iii. (1877) I. 81 One thing onlie I mislike in them, and that is their vsuall going into Italie.

c. Of persons: Commonly employed or serving in a particular capacity.

1590 SHAKS. *Mids. N.* V. i. 35 Where is our vsuall manager of mirth? *Mod.* He sent the money by his usual messenger. Our usual postman did not come to-day.

4. That ordinarily happens, occurs, or is to be found; such as is commonly met with or observed in ordinary practice or experience; common, wonted.

1577 *Misogonus* IV. i, Gods providence in shewinge mercye to his servauntes is alwayes vsiall. 1579 TOMSON *Calvin's Serm. Tim.* 248 It was a verie vsuall thing in the East countrie, for a man to haue two or three wiues. 1638 JUNIUS *Paint. Anc.* 8 So is it likewise an usuall thing in..our life, that we..study alwayes to [etc.]. 1651 HOBBES *Leviath.* II. xxii. 122 The usuall meeting of men at Church, or at a publique Shew, in usuall numbers. 1759 R. BROWN *Compl. Farmer* 91 The usual signs that precede their swarming. 1784 COWPER *Task* II. 61 And th' old..earth has had her shaking fits More frequent, and forgone her usual rest. 1831 JAMES *Phil. Augustus* III. v, A table groaning under a repast not very usual on the boards of a prison. 1855 J. PHILLIPS *Man. Geol.* 204 The usual hardening of sandstone and shale, carbonization of coal, &c., occur.

b. Customary on the part of a person or persons *to* do something.

1605 VERSTEGAN *Dec. Intell.* ix. 310 It hath..grown somwhat vsuallin England, to giue vnto children..the surnames of their Godfathers. 1630 *R. Johnson's Kingd. & Commw.* 183 It is usuall with all the Gauls..to constraine Travellers (though unwilling) to stay. 1716 ADDISON *Freeholder* No. 10 ⁋ 5 It was usual for him to shew the Delicacy of his Taste by [etc.]. 1719 LONDON & WISE *Compl. Gard.* 312 It is very usual to meet with those. 1825 *Encycl. Metrop.* (1845) XVII. 36/1 In most Pigeon-houses it is usual to have a Saltcat. 1839 HALLAM *Hist. Lit.* IV. vii. 506 *note*, It is not usual for..[a] woman to turn it into drollery.

c. Common or habitual *to* a person or thing.

1655 MRQ. WORCESTER *Cent. Inv.* § 18 Several shapes and effects usual to Fountains of pleasure. 1693 CONGREVE *Old Bach.* I. i, Why truth on't is, these early Sallies are not usual to me.

d. *As* (or *than*) *usual*, as (or than) is or was customary or habitual. (Cf. USUALLY *adv.* 1 b.) *As per usual*: see PER *prep.* III. 1.

[1617 MORYSON *Itin.* I. 114 Liuing things cast into that caue, and held there for longer time then is vsuall.] 1716 ADDISON *Freeholder* No. 22 ⁋ 2 Our Conversation opened, as usual, upon the Weather. 1725 *Fam. Dict.* s.v. *Pulse*, When the Strokes are much smaller than usual. 1795 *Gentl. Mag.* 539/2 The blights were this year..more destructive than usual. 1854 *Poultry Chron.* II. 348/2 The poultry department was, as usual, the principal attraction. 1865 DICKENS *Mut. Fr.* I. xiv, The huddled buildings looked lower than usual. 1876 [see USUALNESS].

† 5. *Usual fruit*, = USUFRUIT, USUFRUCT. *Sc.*

1558 KNOX *First Blast* (Arb.) 46 God wold not suffer that the commoditie and vsuall frute..shulde passe to an other [tribe].

† 6. Of persons: Customary, regular. *Obs.*

1579 *Southampton Crt. Leet Rec.* (1906) II. 167 Owen symons is a vsuall convayor of wood beyond the seas.

† b. Habitually resorting. *Obs.*—[1]

1597 J. PAYNE *Royal Exch.* 27 The devill perswades sum carnall and vicioluse parsons that there tyme ys well spent, beinge vsuall in the taverne.

7. *absol.* a. *The* (*his*, etc.) *usual*, what is usual, customary, or frequent (esp. with a person or persons).

1876 GEO. ELIOT *Dan. Deronda* v. xxxv. III. 22 To be an unusual young man means for the most part to get a difficult mastery over the usual. 1892 E. REEVES *Homeward Bound* 189 Nothing in Naples is so clean as the horses' harness, and to-day the drivers outdid their usual. 1897 *Daily News* 23 Dec. 3/5 Coroner: How much whisky did he drink?—Witness: Eighteen half quarterns a night..was his usual.

b. *colloq.* Customary state of health.

1887 ANNIE S. SWAN *Gates of Eden* xx, Aunt Susan is in her usual, I know.

Hence **U·sualness.**

1653 H. MORE *Antid. Ath.* I. x. 30 The usualnesse of such dangers have made them loose the sense of the danger. 1705 CLARKE *Evid. Nat. & Rev. Relig.* xiv. (1716) 297 'Tis only usualness or unusualness that makes the distinction. 1727 BAILEY (vol. II), *Frequentness*, oftenness; usualness. 1876 MRS. WHITNEY *Sights & Ins.* II. ix. 405 They had been two days together, as usual; and usualness is a great power.

**Usually** (yū·ʒuăli, -iuăli), *adv.* [f. prec. + -LY[2].]

1. In a usual or wonted manner; according to customary, established, or frequent usage; commonly, customarily, ordinarily; as a rule.

In frequent use from *c* 1600.

1477 *Rolls of Parlt.* VI. 191/2 All the Membres usuelly called to the forseid Parlementes. 1485 *Yorks. Archaeol. Soc., Record Ser.* XLI. 1 [He] awaytid vpon hym thyder according as he vsually dyde. 1526 *Pilgr. Perf.* (W. de W. 1531) 17 The moost vyle meet that is vsually ordeyned for beestes. 1587 *Southampton Crt. Leet Rec.* (1906) II. 262 Emery lake doth vsually delyver his key of the lynnen hawle to straungers at all dayes. 1613 PURCHAS *Pilgrimage* (1614) 331 b, Through their excellencie in horsemanship they vsually made the victorie..to be certaine. 1634 W. TIRWHYT tr. *Balzac's Lett.* (vol. I) 203 If thy letters be so short, as usually they are. 1682 NORRIS *Hierocles* 10 The Keeper of this observation was usually call'd..by the mystical Name Oath. 1709 STEELE *Tatler* No. 17 ⁋ 2 The Ornaments which are usually given to the Actions of the Great. 1766 GOLDSM. *Vicar* xii, One of those observations I usually made to impress my wife. 1825 SCOTT *Betrothed* xv, The blessings which are usually bestowed on a departing kinswoman. 1840 *Penny Cycl.* XVII. 174/1 Palms are woody plants, usually trees, with simple stems. 1878 JEVONS *Prim. Pol. Econ.* 66 Even a successful strike usually occasions loss.

b. In the phr. *than usually* (now only as in quot. 1875), † *as usually*. Cf. USUAL *a.* 4 d.

*a* 1700 EVELYN *Diary* 18 Jan. 1645, A very large payr of stayres, round, without any stepps as usualy. 1713 DERHAM *Phys. Theol.* I. iii. 22 The Summer of 1708, part of which.. was much colder than usually. 1749 FIELDING *Tom Jones* xv. iii, The Company behaved as usually on these Occasions. 1805 *Med. Jrnl.* XIII. 107 It absorbs this substance more eagerly from the surface of the body than usually. 1875 JOWETT *Plato* (ed. 2) IV. 38 The mind of man has been more than usually active in thinking about man.

†**2.** In a regular manner; regularly. *Obs. rare.*
**1573** TUSSER *Husb.* (1878) 17 To walke thy pastures vsuallie To spie ill neighbours subtiltie. **1605** CAMDEN *Rem.* 233 He would not have so weighty a matter tumultuously and rashly done, but vsually and orderly.

**Usuary** (yū·ziuˌări). *Roman Law.* [ad. late L. *ūsuāri-us* sb., f. *ūsuārius* a., f. L. *ūsus* USE *sb.*] One who has the use but not the ownership of a thing.
**1871** POSTE *Gaius* IV. 507 As the usufructuary has no possession, it follows a fortiori that the usuary has no possession.

**Usuca·pient.** *Roman Law.* [ad. L. *ūsū-capient-*, pres. pple. stem of *ūsū-capĕre*: see USUCAPION.] One who has acquired, or claims title to, property by usucapion.
**1875** POSTE *Gaius* (ed. 2) II. 192 The possession of the usucapient must be based on a justa causa or titulus. **1880** MUIRHEAD *Gaius* Dig. 457 A thing delivered to the usucapient by one who was not its owner.

**Usucapion** (yūziukēⁱ·piǫn). [a. L. *ūsū-capiōn-*, *ūsū-capio* (whence F. and Sp. *usucapion*, It. *usucapione*, Pg. *-capião*), f. *ūsū-capĕre* to acquire ownership by prescription. Cf. USUCAPTION.] In *Roman* and *Civil Law*, the acquisition of ownership by long use or enjoyment; prescription in virtue of continuous undisturbed possession. Also *fig.*
**1606** BIRNIE *Kirkburial* xix, The vnion is so indissoluble, that neyther prescription of tyme, vsucapion of person, nor boutgate of circumstance can giue a regresse. **1617** COLLINS *Defence Bp. of Ely* II. x. 471 The name Catholike appertaining thereunto, by vsucapion forsooth, by plaine prescription, as Campian dreameth. **1681** STAIR *Instit.* xxii. I. 433 Prescription which is short in Moveables, is commonly called Usucapion. **1765–8** ERSKINE *Inst. Law Scot.* III. vii. § 14 Thus things sacred or public could not by the Roman law be acquired by usucapion. **1841** *Penny Cycl.* XX. 117/2 Without affecting to give him ownership, which the law alone could give him by virtue of usucapion. **1855** LORENZ tr. *Van der Keessel's Select Theses* ccvii, By no means opposed to the usucapion of a movable thing in three years. **1871** POSTE *Gaius* II. 153/2 The Senate..decreed that such usucapions are revocable.
*attrib.* **1875** POSTE *Gaius* (ed. 2) IV. 641 Possession..is transformed by a certain lapse of time into dominion; and is called Usucapion-possession.

Hence **Usuca·pionary** *a.*, in virtue of usucapion.
**1880** MUIRHEAD *Gaius* Dig. 585 By completing his usucapionary possession, he cured the defect.

**Usucapt** (yū·ziukæpt), *v. Roman Law.* [ad. L. *ūsū-capt-*, past pple. stem of *ūsū-capere*: see USUCAPION.] *trans.* To acquire ownership of or title to (a property, etc.) by usucaption. Also *absol.*
**1880** MUIRHEAD *Gaius* II. § 93 A usufructuary cannot usucapt. **1886** — in *Encycl. Brit.* XX. 692/2 Upon him who had usucapted by possession the greater part of a deceased person's estate.

Hence **Usuca·ptable, -ible** *adjs.*, capable of being held by usucaption; **Usuca·ptor**, = USUCAPIENT.
**1880** MUIRHEAD *Gaius* Dig. 582 The land was not usucaptable. *Ibid.* II. § 57 Such usucapions may be revoked, and the heir recover from the usucaptor. **1886** — in *Encycl. Brit.* XX. 690/2 Any citizen..holding movables as his own, provided they were usucaptible.

**Usuca·ption** (yūziukæ·pʃən). *Roman Law.* [a. OF. *usucaption*, *-cion*, or med.L. *ūsūcaptiōn-*, ad. L. *ūsū-capiōn-* USUCAPION.] = USUCAPION.
**1656** BLOUNT, *Usucaption* (*usucaptio*), prescription or long possession or the attaining a thing thereby. **1728** CHAMBERS *Cycl.* s.v., Some make a Difference between Prescription and Usucaption, maintaining that the latter is only used with regard to Moveables, and the former with regard to Immoveables. **1760** tr. *Vattel's Law of Nations* II. xi. 166 Usucaption is the acquisition of domain founded on a long possession, uninterrupted and undisputed. **1826** G. SPENCE *Orig. Laws Mod. Europe* p. xvii, Modes of acquiring property or ownership in individual things: Of usucaption and prescription. **1853** WHEWELL *Grotius* I. 276 The right of usucaption, by which a thing long used becomes the property of the possessor. **1874** MOTLEY *Barneveld* I. 283 Rather by usucaption than usurpation, Holland had..come to consider herself..the Republic itself.
*attrib.* **1871** POSTE *Gaius* IV. 501 Possession,..which we will call usucaption-possession.

**Usufruct** (yū·ziufrʋkt), *sb.* [a. late L. *ūsūfruct-us* (whence Sp. and Pg. *usufructo*, It. *usu-*, *usofrutto*, Pr. *usufrug*), ad. L. *ūsus-fructus* (abl. *ūsū-fructū*). Cf. USUFRUIT.]
**1.** *Law.* The right of temporary possession, use, or enjoyment of the advantages of property belonging to another, so far as may be had without causing damage or prejudice to this. Also *transf.*
*c* **1630** SIR T. HOPE *Minor Practicks* (1734) 252 After the Usu-fruct is once lawfully constitute by a Seasin. **1681** STAIR *Instit.* xvi. 327 Usufruct is the power of disposal of the use and fruits, saving the Substance of the thing. **1710** J. HARRIS *Lex. Techn.* II. s.v. *Services*, Services Personal, are those due from a Thing to a Person, and of these they account..Usufruct, Use and Habitation. **1766** BLACKSTONE *Comm.* II. 105 A subject therefore hath only the usufruct, and not the absolute property of the soil. **1839** CARLYLE *Chartism* x. 176 Lawsuits in chancery for some short usufruct of a bit of land. **1853** J. H. NEWMAN *Hist. Sk.* (1873) I. I. ii. 74 They held it [*sc.* Sogdiana] in possession..for 90 or 100 years; they came into the usufruct and enjoyment of it. **1868** BROWNING *Ring & Bk.* II. 211 He owned some usufruct, had moneys' use Lifelong.
*fig.* **1863** PATMORE *Angel in Ho.* I. II. ii, Could eternal life afford That tyranny should thus deduct From this fair land ..A year of the sweet usufruct.

**b.** An office of which one is usufructuary. *rare.*
**1848** HALLAM *Suppl. Notes Hist. Mid. Ages* 116 M. Guérard ..is of opinion that, though benefices were ultimately fiefs, in the first stage of the monarchy they were only usufructs.

**2.** *gen.* Use, enjoyment, or profitable possession (*of* something).
**1811** LAMB *Elia* I. *Bachelor's Compl.*, In the rich man's houses and pictures..I have a temporary usufruct at least. **1835** GRESWELL *Parables* IV. 490 No more than preliminary to the usufruct of the Kingdom itself. **1863** KINGLAKE *Crimea* I. 41 Which of the rival Churches should have the control and usufruct of every holy shrine.

**b.** *esp.* Beneficial use or enjoyment of land. Also *fig.* and *transf.*
**1864** MARSH *Man & Nat.* 35 Man has too long forgotten that the earth was given to him for usufruct alone, not for consumption. **1870** HUXLEY *Lay Serm.* xii. 313 Depriving man of the usufruct of one of the most fertile fields of his great patrimony, Nature. **1898** HARCOURT in *Times* 30 March 8/2 The 'usufruct' of Port Arthur and Ta-lien-wan had been granted to Russia. 'Usufruct' appears to be a new word [in this connection].

**3.** *attrib.*, as *usufruct discipline*, *right.*
**1845** R. W. HAMILTON *Pop. Educ.* iv. 69 A sordid, utilitarian, usufruct, discipline of the youthful mind. **1881** 'H. H.' *Century of Dishonor* 115 The usufruct right of the Indians to the lands occupied by them.

Hence **Usufru·ction**, = sense 2 b.
**1846** *Congressional Globe* 27 May 862/3 They saw..that they could..get the whole [boundary-line], at least for a long time, under our own delusive project of joint usufruction.

**U·sufruct**, *v.* [f. prec. Cf. med.L. *ūsūfructāre*, *-uāre*, It. *usufruttare*, *-uare*, Sp. *usufructuar.*] *trans.* To hold (property) as a usufructuary; to possess in or subject to usufruct. Also *absol.*
**1880** MUIRHEAD *Gaius* II. § 14 It is..the right of usufructing, and the right under the obligation that is incorporeal. **1886** — in *Encycl. Brit.* XX. 709/2 Property usufructed should revert unimpaired to the owner.

Hence **U·sufructed** *ppl. a.*
**1880** MUIRHEAD *Gaius* II. § 94 Whether we can possess and usucapt through a usufructed slave.

†**Usufructuar**, obs. Sc. variant of next.
**1531** *Dunfermline Reg.* (Bann. Cl.) 362 Legat of scotland and vsufructuar of þe abbay of dunfermeling.

**Usufructuary** (yūziufrʋ·ktiuˌări), *sb.* [ad. late L. *ūsūfructuāri-us*, f. *ūsūfructu-s* USUFRUCT *sb.* Cf. Pg. *usufructuario*, It. *usufruttuario.*]
**1.** *Law.* One who has the temporary use and reaps the fruits or profits of an estate, benefice, office, etc., legally belonging to another or others; one who enjoys the usufruct of a property, etc.
*a* **1618** RALEIGH in Gutch *Coll. Cur.* I. 72 The ordinary *ususfructus* is determined by the death of the usufructuary. **1658** BRAMHALL *Consecr. Bps.* viii. 186 He held all these Bishopricks..as an Vsufructuary not as a true owner. **1692** WASHINGTON tr. *Milton's Def. Pop.* vi. 158 He, that has but the Crown, and the Revenues that belong to it, as an Usufructuary. **1710** PRIDEAUX *Draught of a Bill*, *Reasons* 2 The Ministers are only the usufructuaries to receive the annual income. **1726** AYLIFFE *Parergon* 86 The Parsons of Parishes are not in Law accounted Proprietors, but only Usufructuaries. **1790** FRANCIS in Burke *Corr.* (1844) III. 166 The Church..whose property its usufructuaries very wisely said it would be sacrilege to invade. **1820** *Ann. Reg.* II. 718 The land-tax is not taken into account except for the proprietor or usufructary [*sic*]. **1868** BROWNING *Ring & Bk.* III. 159 A certain yearly sum,—our Pietro being,..an usufructuary,— Dropped in the common bag as interest Of money, his till death. **1881** DISRAELI in *Daily Tel.* 27 April, That all books ..[be] properly preserved by..the usufructuary thereof for the time being.

**b.** *transf.* and *fig.*
*a* **1638** MEDE *Wks.* (1672) 121 Because the whole land was holy, and God's land, and they but Usufructuaries. **1648** SANDERSON *Serm.* II. 24 God hath entrusted us with the..culture of our own hearts..: the fruits wholly accrue to us, as usufructuaries. **1652** NEEDHAM *Selden's Mare Cl.* 483 What advantages..are made by others, who of Usufructuaries [of the sea] by permission, have in design now to make themselvs absolute Lords of the Fee. **1702** J. HOWE *Self Ded.* 27 God indeed is the only Proprietor, Men are but usufructuaries. **1768–74** TUCKER *Lt. Nat.* (1834) II. 150 We do not possess in property but only as usufructuaries, and we know the lading will be taken off our backs..at the end of our journey through life. **1866** ALGER *Solit. Nat. & Man* IV. 370 [To conform] to the will of God..as its grateful executives and usufructuaries.

**2.** In general use: One who has the use or enjoyment *of* something.
**1621** BACON in Spedding *Lett.*, etc. (1874) VII. 226, I have ..ever..counted myself but an usufructuary of myself, the property being yours. **1622** MABBE tr. *Aleman's Guzman d'Alf.* I. 125 The Vsufructuarie, and free inioyer of thy life. **1652–3** LEICESTER in Collins *Lett. & Mem. State* (1746) II. 680 If the Gift be of your self..you shall be but an Usufructuary of yourself. **1794** J. GIFFORD *Reign Louis XVI*, 425 We are but usufructuaries of life. **1839** HALLAM *Hist. Lit.* III. iv. 359 That the supreme power or sovereignty..does not reside in the chief magistrate, but in the people themselves, and that no other is proprietor or usufructuary of it. **1886** W. GRAHAM *Soc. Problem* 458 The present usufructuaries of the blessings of civilisation.

**Usufru·ctuary**, *a.* [ad. late L. *ūsūfructuāri-us* (whence Sp. and Pg. *usufructuario*, It. *usufruttuario*, F. *usufructuaire*): see prec.]
**1.** Pertaining or relating to usufruct; of the nature of usufruct.
**1710** PRIDEAUX *Orig. Tithes* i. 17 To receive and enjoy them in a usustructuary [*sic*; **1736** usufructuary] tenure under him. **1810** COLERIDGE *Jer. Taylor* Wks. 1838 III. 245 The ordinary graces bequeathed by Christ to his Church as the usufructuary property of all its members. **1880** MUIRHEAD *Gaius* II. § 30 So that the cessionary shall have the usufructuary right, he himself retaining the bare property.

†**2.** Holding or enjoying an office, etc., by usufruct. *Obs.*⁻¹
**1728** CHAMBERS *Cycl.* s.v. *Usufruit*, The Incumbents of Benefices are only Usufructuary.

†**Usufruictor, -uor**, obs. varr. USUFRUCTUARY.
**1689** *Def. Liberty agst. Tyrants* 107 At the least we may esteem him [*sc.* the king] Usufruictuor of the Kingdom, and of the Demean; nay, truly we can allow him to have the Usufruit for being Usufrictor [*sic*].

†**U·sufruit.** *Obs.* Also 5 *Sc.* vse-fruyt, 7 usufrute. [a. OF. (and F.) *usufruit* (13th c.), ad. late L. *ūsū-fructus* USUFRUCT *sb.*] = USUFRUCT *sb.* 1.
**1478** *Acta Dom. Conc.* (1839) 13/1 Robert nor nane vþeris ..has þe vse fruyt of þer wifis propir landis for þer life tyme. **1547** *Bk. of Marchauntes* d iiij, Possession was..adiugged to hym in herytage wyth yᵉ vsufruits of the tres growing ther. *a* **1577** SIR T. SMITH *Commw. Eng.* III. viii. (1589) 134 The husband shal haue the vsufruite of her landes. **1604** E. G[RIMSTONE] *D'Acosta's Hist. Indies* IV. xi. 240 The vsufruite was adiudged to him by sentence as the discoverer [of the mine]. **1689** [see prec.]. **1728** CHAMBERS *Cycl.* s.v. *Substitution*, Certain Persons, who are likewise to have the Usu-fruit in their Times, but never the Property.

†**Usura·rious**, *a. Obs. rare.* [f. L. *ūsūrāri-us* (see USURARY *a.*) + -OUS.] Usurious.
**1623** R. CARPENTER *Conscionable Christian* 14 Usurarious extorting State-spoyling money-mongers. **1646** J. BENBRIGGE *Vsura Accom.* 4 Such lending ought to be praised.. and in no case conceived to be Usurarious. **1660** JER. TAYLOR *Ductor* I. v. rule vi. § 1 All usurarious contracts. *Ibid.* II. ii. rule vii. § 7 If a common-wealth permits an usurarious exchange or contract.

†**U·surary**, *sb. Obs. rare.* [ad. med.L. *ūsūrāri-us* (Diefenb.): see next.] A money-lender.
*c* **1440** *Alph. Tales* 524 Som tyme in Colayn þer was ane vsurarie. *Ibid.* 526 All þies vsuraries rase and went oute confusid.

†**U·surary**, *a. Obs. rare.* [ad. L. *ūsūrāri-us* (whence It., Sp., Pg. *usurario*, F. *usuraire*), f. *ūsūra* USURY *sb.*] Marked by the payment of interest; on which excessive interest is paid.
**1649** BP. HALL *Cases Consc.* i. 7 How odious..usurary contracts have been in all times. *Ibid.* 13 Every increase by loan of money is not usurarie. **1678** SIR G. MACKENZIE *Crim. Laws Scot.* I. xxiv. § 7 (1699) 124 That the Usurary Bond or Contract shall be reduced. **1693** STAIR *Instit.* (ed. 2) II. x. 331 That if it [*sc.* a lease] were in the Terms of the old Act, Parl. 1449. cap. 19. far within the true Avail, it were usurary and null.

†**Usure**, *sb. Obs.* Also 4–5 vsere, 5 vsur, usur. [a. OF. *useure* (13th c.), *usure* (also AF. and F.), ad. L. *ūsūra* (whence It., Sp., Pg. *usura*, Pr. *uzura*), n. of action f. *ūs-us*: see USURY *sb.*]
**1.** The fact or practice of lending money at interest. Cf. USURY *sb.* 1.
*a* **1325** *Prose Psalter* liv. 11 Usure [L. *usura*] and trecherie ne failed nouȝt in his waies. [**1382**, **1388** WYCLIF *Ibid.*] *c* **1380** WYCLIF *Wks.* (1880) 277 Þat þe sotil vsure of riche clerkis & marchaundes be hurled out of lond. *c* **1400** MAUNDEV. (1919) iii. 12 Men of Grece..sey also þat vsure is no dedly synne. **1436** *Pol. Poems* (Rolls) II. 176 Thus they lyve..wyth suche chevesaunce That men calle usure, to oure losse and hinderaunce. **1456** SIR G. HAYE *Law Arms* (S.T.S.) 70 Thair digniteis, that thai have gottyn wrangwisly throu usur, scisme, or symony. *c* **1530** *Pol., Rel. & L. Poems* (1903) 60 What is vsure, but..a lawfulle thefe that tellyth ys entent. **1533** BELLENDEN *Livy* II. xi. (S.T.S.) I. 167 Þis dett ..was ay duplyit on him be vsure and okkir. **1605** B. JONSON *Volpone* I. i, I turne no moneys, in the publike bank; Nor vsure priuate.
*Personif.* **1362** LANGL. *P. Pl.* A. II. 66 Hit witen..þat I, Fauuel, feffe Fals to þat mayden Meede,..With þe Yle of vsure And Auarice þe False. **1390** GOWER *Conf.* II. 274 Upon the bench sittende on hih With Avarice Usure I sih.

**b.** A usurious act or practice.
*a* **1325** *Prose Psalter* lxxi. 14 He shal raunsoun her soules fram vsures and wickednes. **1382** WYCLIF *Ibid.* *c* **1440** *Alph. Tales* 472 With myne vsuris I grevud God bothe day & nyght. **1456** SIR G. HAYE *Law Arms* (S.T.S.) 188 Usuris and barat, subtilitee and trechery.

**2.** = INTEREST *sb.* 10, USURY *sb.* 2. Also occas. *at*, *to usure.*
Freq. in Wyclif (1382), occas. in plural, tr. L. *usuræ*.
**1338** R. BRUNNE *Chron.* (1810) 224 Þe chartres & þe scris þat noied Cristen men, þat lay for vsure in pris elleuen als for ten. ? *a* **1366** CHAUCER *Rom. Rose* 185 That is that for vsure Leneth to many a creature. **1377** LANGL. *P. Pl.* B. VII. 83 For beggeres borwen euermo and her borghe is god almyȝti, To ȝelden hem þat ȝiueth hem and ȝet vsure more. **1382** WYCLIF *Lev.* xxv. 37 Thi money thow shalt not ȝyue to him to vsure. *c* **1400** *Rom. Rose* 7026 If a wight, out of mesure, Wolde lene his gold, and take vsure. **1483** CAXTON *Gold. Leg.* 431 b/1 That no Justycer shold..constrayne them that were bounden to the Jewes..to paye or yelde to them theyr vsure or growyng. *a* **1513** FABYAN *Chron.* VII. 353 As a Iewe wolde haue forced a Cristen man to haue gyuen to hym more than .ii.d. for the vsure of .xx.s. for a weke.

†**Usure**, *v. Obs.* [ad. OF. *usurer* (13th c.), ad. med.L. *ūsūrāre* (whence Sp. and Pg. *usurar*), f. L. *ūsūra*: see prec.]
**1.** *intr.* To practise usury; to lend at interest. Also *fig.*
*c* **1380** WYCLIF *Sel. Wks.* II. 207 Þus God usuriþ for oure prow, for alle þingis..he ȝyveþ us for þis eende. **1382** — *Prov.* xix. 17 He vsureth to the Lord, that hath reuthe of the pore. — *Jer.* xv. 10. **1530** PALSGR. 769/2 If our charyte were utterly parfyte, one christenned man shulde nat usure with an other.

**2.** *trans.* To lend (money) at a premium. *rare*⁻¹.
**1620** BRATHWAIT *Five Senses* ii. 24 Oppresse I cannot, when I heare the Orphans teare...Vse my money, but vsure it I will not.

**Usurer** (yū·ziŭrəɹ). Forms: *α.* 3–7 vsurer, 4–5 -ere, 5, *Sc.* 6 -ar; 5 usurere, 6– usurer. *β.* 4–6 vserer, 5 -ere, 6–7 userer (6 uss-). [a. AF. *usurer*, *userer*, = OF. *usureor*, ad. med.L. *ūsūrārius* USURARY *sb.* Cf. USURIER, and Sp. *usurero*, Pg. *usurario*, It. *usurajo.*] One who practises usury or lends money at interest; a money-lender, esp. in later use one who charges an excessive rate of interest.

*α.* *c* **1290** *St. Magdalena* 117 in *S. Eng. Leg.* I. 465 An vsurer was ȝwilene, þat hadde dettores tweyne. **1303** R. BRUNNE *Handl. Synne* 2611 Whan any vsurere was dede, þe chercheȝerde þey hym forbede. **1377** LANGL. *P. Pl.* B. XI. 275 If prestes weren parfyt þei wolde..nouȝte [take] her mete of vsureres. *c* **1410** *Lantern of Light* 132 In þis chirche ben vsureris, okureris, iourours. *a* **1450** *Knt. de la Tour* (1906) 53 Other..ben bawdes and theues, usureres, bariters. **1551** T. WILSON *Logike* G ij, No Christian is an vsurer. **1584** LODGE *Alarum agst. Usurers* B iij, The Broker in this matter, getteth..thousand thankes of this diuellish Vsurer. **1606** DEKKER *Sev. Sins* VI. (Arb.) 39 These are Vsurers: who for a little money..bring yong Nouices into a fooles Paradice till they haue sealed the Morgage of their landes. **1677** WOOD *Life* (O.H.S.) II. 395 Mr Deane, the old usurer. **1742** YOUNG *Nt. Th.* II. 270 As all-rapacious usurers conceal Their doomsday-book from all-consuming heirs. **1781** GIBBON *Decl. & F.* xvii. II. 70 The usurer, who derived from the interest of money a silent and ignominious profit. **1839** DICKENS *Nickleby* i, This promising lad commenced usurer on a limited scale at school. **1874** RUSKIN *Fors Clav.* xliv. 129, I know myself to be an usurer as long as I take interest on any money.

*β.* **1303** R. BRUNNE *Handl. Synne* 2453 Cauuarsyns and vserers, þys are, Lucyfer, þy peres. *c* **1440** *Promp. Parv.* 206/2 Gowlare, or vserere, *usurarius.* *c* **1450** *Merlin* xxiii. 434 The riche vserer that deliteth in his richesse. **1581** *Southampton Crt. Leet Rec.* (1906) II. 221 Edwardes..is an extreme usserer. **1588** *Marprel. Epist.* (Arb.) 32 He beareth ..to vserer Haruies good chear and money bags. **1616** R. COCKS *Diary* (Hakl. Soc.) I. 198 This man is a greate userer; and the King of Firando oweth hym much money. **1699** in E. W. Dunbar *Soc. Life Moray* (1865) 31 Under the certificating of being pursued as Occurrers or Userers.

**b.** *attrib.* and *Comb.*, as *usurer class*, *-like.*

**1729** BOYER *Dict. Royal* I, *Usurairement*, usurer-like. **1892** *Pall Mall G.* 23 April 7/1 The usurer-ridden peasantry and overworked operatives. **1902** *Fabian News* May 20/1 The landlord and usurer classes of India.

**U·suress.** *rare.* [f. USUR-ER + -ESS.] A female usurer.

**1641** BRATHWAIT *Eng. Gentlew.* 300 A religious divine comming to a certaine usuresse,..told her [etc.]. **1648** HEXHAM II, *Een Woeckeresse*, an Usuresse, or a woman Usurer. **1898** *Daily Tel.* 28 May 7/3 The defendants.. evinced no little hostility to the usuress.

†**Usurier.** *Obs.*⁻¹ [a. OF. (F.) *usurier*, ad. med.L. *ūsūrārius* USURARY *sb.*] A usurer.

*c* **1481** CAXTON *Dialogues* 2 Of paintours and vsuriers.

†**U·suring,** *ppl. a.* *Obs.* Also 6 usering. [f. USURE *sb.* or *v.* + -ING ².]

**1.** Of persons: Practising or given to usury; usurious.

**1593** MUNDAY *Def. Contraries* 37, I shall see no more.. the vsuring Geneway, nor the boasting Modenan. **1622** MABBE tr. *Aleman's Guzman d'Alf.* I. 178 My Vsuring Merchant had hanging at his girdle a paire of kniues. **1681** COLVIL *Whigs Supplic.* (1751) 22 The fatherless and widows portion, Which usuring fathers lent to lairds. **1710** *Brit. Apollo* II. No. 105. 3/1 Straight to a Usuring Dog I hurry'd.

*fig.* and *transf.* **1598** MARLOWE & CHAPMAN *Hero & Leander* VI. 266 Filthie vsering Rocks that would haue blood, Though they could get of him no other good. *a* **1640** J. DAY *Parl. Bees* x. (1881) 60 Fenerator, Or the Vsuring Bee.

**2.** Looking for ample return or increase; causing cost without return. *rare.*

**1607** SHAKS. *Timon* IV. iii. 516 Is not thy kindnesse subtle, couetous, If not a Vsuring kindnesse, and..Expecting in returne twenty for one? **1609** HEYWOOD *Brit. Troy* VII. viii, The barraine fieldes deceive the Plow-mans trust, The usuring seede is molded unto dust.

**Usurious** (yuziū·riəs), *a.* [f. USURY *sb.* + -OUS. Cf. next.]

**1.** Characterized by, of the nature of or involving, usury or excessive interest.

**1610** HOLLAND *Camden's Brit.* 748 Vsurious contracts, voluptuous and vicious life. **1611** FENTON *Vsurie* 21 If it be a gaine couenanted meerely in respect of loane, it is condemned as vsurious. **1678** R. L'ESTRANGE *Seneca's Mor.* II. xii. 154 We have found out wayes,..by Bloody Usurious Contracts, to undoe one another. **1729** JACOB *Law Dict.* s.v. *Usury*, A Bond..shall not be avoided by a corrupt usurious Agreement between others. **1784** COWPER *Task* III. 798 An usurious loan To be refunded duely, when his vote..shall have earn'd its worthy price. **1840** HOOD *Kilmansegg, Marriage* xxix, Fruits obtained before they were due At a discount most usurious. **1855** MILMAN *Lat. Chr.* IX. vii. IV. 125 The Jews were especially to be compelled..to abandon all their usurious claims. **1869** SPURGEON *Treas. Dav.* I. 209 To lend money even at the lowest interest to their fellow farmers [*sc.* Jews] in times of poverty would have been usurious.

**b.** Of interest, etc.: Charged by way of, acquired by virtue of, usury; exorbitant, excessive. Freq. with *interest.*

**1611** COTGR., *Vsuraire*, vsurious; taken, or giuen for interest or vse. **1729** JACOB *Law Dict.* s.v. *Usury*, It is not material, whether the Payment of the Principal and the usurious Interest, be secured by the same, or by different Conveyances. **1776** ADAM SMITH *W. N.* I. ix, The same usurious interest which is usually required from bankrupts. **1812** CRABBE *Tales* xiv. 160 If thus he grasp'd at such usurious gains. **1847** C. BRONTË *J. Eyre* iv, A usurious rate of interest—fifty or sixty per cent. **1880** L. OLIPHANT *Gilead* x. 291 To lend money on mortgage..at a reasonable rate, instead of at the usurious percentage at present charged.

*transf.* **1634** RAINBOW *Labour* (1635) 41 Pile up thine house with obligatory parchment,..farme out th' usurious time..and let each day redouble thine hundreds.

**2. a.** Practising usury; taking or charging excessive interest on loaned money; exacting in respect of interest. Also *transf.*

*a* **1631** DONNE *Love's Usury* 2 For every houre that thou wilt spare mee now, I will allow, Usurious God of Love, twenty to thee. **1635** QUARLES *Embl.* III. xv. 183 Plead not; Vsurious Nature will have all, As well the Int'rest, as the Principall. **1836** J. ABBOT *Way to do Good* iii. 96 The most hard-hearted usurious creditor. **1870** MACDUFF *Mem. Patmos* x. 136 The usurious vendors dealing out a stinted pennyworth to the famishing. **1870** H. SMART *Race for Wife* iv, Even a usurious solicitor is possessed of pride of some kind.

**b.** Characteristic of a usurer.

**1727** BAILEY (vol. II), *Usuriousness*, usurious or extortioning Quality or Disposition. **1832** *Rolls of Parlt.* Index 958 The usurious Conduct of Peter de Appelby. **1862** J. SMALL *Eng. Metr. Hom.* p. vii, The knight, whose usurious feelings suddenly returned, proposed to the beggar to leave the grain.

†**3.** Liberal, abundant. *Obs.*⁻¹

**1780** BURKE *Sp. at Bristol* Wks. III. 376, I shall..pay ample atonement and usurious amends to..humanity for my unhappy lapse.

Hence **Usu·riously** *adv.*

Also *usuriousness* (see 2 b, quot. 1727). *rare*⁻⁰.

**1670** SIR T. CULPEPER *Necess. Abating Usury* 38 Finding ..nothing sweet but summes usuriously improved. **1798** COLERIDGE in Cottle *Early Recoll.* (1837) I. 311 To make the present moment act fraudulently and usuriously towards the future time. **1808** HAN. MORE *Cœlebs* xii. I. 152 She flatters egregiously and universally, on the principle of being paid back usuriously in the same coin.

†**U·surous,** *a.* *Obs. rare.* [f. USURE *sb.* + -OUS.] = USURIOUS *a.*

**1605** CHAPMAN, etc. *Eastw. Hoe* II. B 4, I am now loose, to get more children of perdition into my vsurous bonds. **1616** B. JONSON *Ev. Man out of Hum.* V. v. Wks. 165, I referre mee to your vsurous Cannibals, or such like. *c* **1624** CHAPMAN *Batrach.* 270, I can by no means th' usurous darner move To let me have the mantle to restore. **1738** tr. *Guazzo's Art Convers.* 53 The usurous Contracts he made with certain poor Men. **1794** W. BLAKE *Songs of Exper., Holy Thursday* i, Babes. Fed with cold and usurous hand.

†**Usu·rp,** *sb.* *Obs.*⁻¹ [f. next.] Usurpation.

*a* **1647** HABINGTON *Surv. Worcs.* (Worcs. Hist. Soc.) I. 540 The Normans, who overcame them with the vsurp of the Crowne.

**Usurp** (yuzɔ̄·ɹp), *v.* [ad. OF. *usurper* (14th c.), ad. L. *ūsūrpāre* (whence It. *usurpare*, Pr., Sp., Pg. *usurpar*) to seize for use, to use, employ.]

**I. 1.** *trans.* To appropriate wrongfully to oneself (a right, prerogative, etc.). †Also const. *against*, *upon.*

*a* **1325** *MS. Rawl. B.* 520 fol. 56 b, ȝif þe Eir mid wronge vsurped þe seisine of Eldere þoru deseisine. **1399** LANGL. *Rich. Redeles* III. 257 To vsurpe þe service þat to sages bilongith, To be-come conselleris er þey kunne rede. **1569** J. SANFORD tr. *Agrippa's Van. Artes* 154 b, Apicius more then all others haue vsurped ye glory and fame of this arte. *a* **1578** LINDESAY (Pitscottie) *Chron. Scot.* (S.T.S.) I. 18 [He] sould have usurpat all honour riches and authoritie. **1596** *Edward III*, I. i. 80 Tell him, the Crowne that hee vsurpes is myne. **1607** COWELL *Interpr., Quo Warranto*, is a writ that lyeth against him, which vsurpeth any Frawnchis or libertie against the king. **1656** EARL MONM. tr. *Boccalini's Pol. Touchstone* (1674) 277 That pretence of Right, which the violence of the Sword hath usurp'd upon other mens Estates. *a* **1680** BUTLER *Rem.* (1759) I. 346 They were fain to usurp the Right of his Cause, to justify their own. **1709** STRYPE *Ann. Ref.* I. xiv. 187 The people by a great consent usurped them [*sc.* favours] to themselves. **1791** COWPER *Iliad* I. 624 Him with shame The King of men hath overwhelm'd, by force Usurping his just meed. **1813** SHELLEY *Q. Mab* VI. 223 The almighty Fiend Whose name usurps thy honours. **1838** LYTTON *Leila* I. ii, My uncle usurped my birthright.

*fig.* and *transf.* *a* **1586** SIDNEY *Arcadia* II. vii, So ougly a darkenesse..usurped the dayes right. **1634** FORD *Perk. Warbeck* II. iii, Tis our pleasure To giue our Cosen Yorke for wife our kinswoman the ladie Katherine: Instinct of soveraigntie Designes the honor, though her peevish Father Vsurps our Resolution.

**b.** *esp.* To intrude forcibly, illegally, or without just cause into (some dignified or important office, position, etc.); to assume or arrogate to oneself (political power, rule, authority, etc.) by force; to claim unjustly.

**1440** *Jacob's Well* 28 Þo þat vsurpyn of newe tyme þe kepyng or þe amonicyoun of ony cherch in tyme of voydaunce. **1447** BOKENHAM *Seyntys* (Roxb.) 28 Andronicus..be tyranny Usurpyd the pryncehood of that plas. *a* **1513** FABYAN *Chron.* IV. xx. 49 He..vsurpyd the Rule and domynyon of the lande. **1538** TONSTALL *Serm. Palm Sund.* (1823) 5 Wherfore he [*sc.* Christ] dyd not vsurpe equalitie vnto god, but [etc.]. **1598** BARRET *Theor. Warres* IV. i. 103 To vsurpe the preheminence, which onely is due to the Camp-Master. **1651** HOBBES *Leviath.* II. xxviii. 162 The acts of power usurped,..are not acts of publique Authority. **1681** H. NEVILE *Plato Rediv.* 34 Either to usurp Tyranny over his own Country, or to lead men forth to..subdue another. **1729** T. INNES *Crit. Essay* (1879) 32 Carausius..usurped the empire in Britain towards the end of the third century. **1751** JOHNSON *Rambler* No. 166 ¶ 5 Eager to usurp the station to which he has no right. **1836** THIRLWALL *Greece* III. 245 Cleon..did not wish to usurp the functions of Nicias. **1844** H. H. WILSON *Brit. India* III. 280 To set aside the local government, and usurp an independent and paramount authority. **1891** *Pall Mall G.* 9 Oct. 2/1 Mr. Parnell repeated...—'You attempted to put the resolution and usurp my authority as chairman'.

*fig.* and *transf.* **1603** SHAKS. *Meas. for M.* III. ii. 99 To.. vsurpe the beggerie hee was neuer borne to. **1667** MILTON *P. L.* XII. 421 So he dies, But soon revives, Death over him no power Shall long usurp. **1722** WOLLASTON *Relig. Nat.* 24 The bridle will be usurped by those appetites which it is a principal part of all religion..to curb. **1781** COWPER *Conversat.* 745 The world grown old,..Usurps God's office, lays his bosom bare. **1799** SICKELMORE *Agnes & L.* II. 195 In the silent hours of retirement reflection usurped the empire of the leaden god. **1839** SIGOURNEY *Lett. to Mothers* xv, The worldly and common trains of thought, which usurp dominion over us. **1857** TOULMIN SMITH *Parish* 119 Too much intermeddling from the Home Office has been allowed to be gradually usurped.

**2.** To seize or obtain possession of (territory, land, etc.) in an unjust or illegal manner; to assume unjust rule, dominion, or authority over, to appropriate wrongfully. Also const. *on*, *upon* (= against), *over.*

*c* **1400** MAUNDEV. (1839) 145 He..usurped the Lond, and helde it to himself, and cleped him Emperour of Trapazond. **1432–50** tr. *Higden* (Rolls) II. 103 The Danes vsurpede the realme of Estenglonde. **1483** CAXTON *Gold. Leg.* 224 b/1 By cause that he wold usurpe to hym self hys heritage. **1507** *Reg. Privy Seal Scotl.* I. 208/2 Gif ony of thaim occupiis and usurpis ony part of the kingis propir lands. **1579** FENTON *Guicciard.* 358 To reconquer to the sea Apostolike, all those places..that had bene vsurped vpon the Church. **1598** HAKLUYT *Voy.* I. 147 The cities adhearing vnto the king vsurped diuers Castles belonging to the Master, tooke certain..knightes. **1653** H. COGAN tr. *Pinto's Trav.* iv. 11 Having usurped the town of Goa upon him. **1687** A. LOVELL tr. *Thevenot's Trav.* I. 223 That Church..was usurped by the Turks, and serves them..for their chief Mosque. *a* **1721** PRIOR *Dial. Dead, Cromwell & Porter* Wks. 1907 II. 267 The three Kingdoms You Usurped. **1809** BAWDWEN *Domesday Bk.* 2 Walden usurped two houses of Ketel the priest.

*fig.* and *transf.* **1592** SHAKS. *Ven. & Ad.* 591 Whereat a sudden pale..Usurps her cheek. **1592** *Arden of Feversham* I. 99 Sweete Mosbie is the man that hath my hart: And he vsurpes it. **1633** G. HERBERT *Temple, Bunch of Grapes* i, One aire of thoughts usurps my brain. *a* **1700** EVELYN *Diary* 3 Aug. 1656, Blasphemous and ignorant mechanics usurping the pulpets every where. **1726** POPE *Odyssey* XX. 430 Universal night usurps the pole! **1807** J. BARLOW *Columb.* II. 210 Ere..Memphian pyramids usurp'd the skies. **1841** EMERSON *Ess., Love* ¶ 4 The proportion which this topic of personal relations usurps in the conversation of society.

**b.** *transf.* To occupy or take the place of, physically; to encroach or trench upon.

**1635** QUARLES *Embl.* I. ii. 10 The white-mouth'd Water now usurpes the Shore. **1687** DRYDEN *Hind & P.* III. 863 A just Reprise would only be Of what the Land usurped upon the Sea. **1764** GOLDSM. *Trav.* 290 The firm connected bulwark [= dyke of Holland] seems to grow; Spreads its long arms amidst the watery roar,..and usurps the shore. **1817** BYRON *Manfred* III. iv, Ivy usurps the laurel's place of growth. **1841** T. R. JONES *Anim. Kingd.* 730 The placenta completely usurps the place of the allantois.

**c.** Of feelings, passions, etc.: To take possession of, occupy, or assume predominance in (the mind, bosom, etc.).

**1749** SMOLLETT *Regicide* V. viii, Distemper'd passion.. Usurped my troubled bosom. **1798** FERRIAR *Illustr. Sterne*, etc., *Genius* 282 When frenzy and imposture usurp the regard. **1824** CAMPBELL *Theodric* 490 Alarm..now usurp'd his brain. **1853** KANE *Grinnell Exp.* xviii. (1856) 138 The object which seemed to usurp the undivided attention of our party.

**d.** *To usurp the place of*, in fig. uses.

**1573** BARET *Alv.* K k i, Concerning I consonant, which oftentimes vniustly vsurpeth the sounde and place of g. **1739** BUTLER *Serm.* Wks. 1874 II. 229 True religion takes up that place in the mind, which superstition would usurp. **1781** COWPER *Table-t.* 320 When tumult..usurp'd authority's just place. **1863** HOLLAND *Lett. Joneses* xix. 271 The love of party has always usurped the place of the love of Country. **1879** H. PHILLIPS *Notes Coins* 5 Copper began to usurp the place of other metals.

†**3.** To take or hold possession of (something belonging to another or others) by sleight or force; to appropriate by ruse or violence; to steal.

*c* **1412–20** LYDG. *Chron. Troy* V. 73 Þat he þis relik reioisshe shulde of riȝt, Be sleiȝte wonne.., And vsurpeth, be maner of avaunt. **1484** CAXTON *Fables of Æsop* II. xviii, I beleue wel that thow hast vsurped and robbed som thynge. **1560** DAUS tr. *Sleidane's Comm.* 242 b, The reuenewes of some they haue vsurped already. **1620** BRENT tr. *Soave's Hist. Counc. Trent.* I. 100 The Ecclesiasticall goods should not be vsurped. **1643** BURROUGHES *Exp. Hosea* vii. 375 As a man that hath his goods taken away from him usurped.

*fig.* and *transf.* *a* **1425** tr. *Arderne's Treat. Fistula*, etc. 30 Any oþer witty man perceyuyng his werk mow vsurpe it to hymself. **1602** SHAKS. *Ham.* I. i. 46 What art thou that vsurp'st this time of night? **1605** — *Lear* IV. ii. 28 To thee a Womans seruices are due, My Foole vsurpes my body. *a* **1637** B. JONSON *Discov.* Wks. (Rtldg.) 747/2 Their own fox-like thefts..are so rank, as a man may find whole pages together usurped from one author.

**4.** To make use of (something not properly belonging to one or one's estate); to use or employ wrongfully.

*c* **1412** HOCCLEVE *De Reg. Princ.* 440 Certes to blame ben þe lordes grete,..þat hir men lete Vsurpe swiche a lordly apparaille. *a* **1548** HALL *Chron., Hen. VI*, 114 Beside this, she vsurped a cote of arms. **1578** LYTE *Dodoens* 727 The barke of..Sorbus..is in some places wrongfully vsurped..for the diseases of the milte. **1601** SHAKS. *All's Well* IV. iii. 119 His heeles haue deseru'd it, in vsurping his spurres so long. **1661** SPARROW *Bk. Com. Prayer* (ed. 2) A 6, Learned Jews from that time, usurp the same partition of Chapters on the Old Testament. **1713** ADDISON *Cato* IV. i, Who's this that dares usurp The Guards and Habits of Numidia's Prince? **1831** SCOTT *Ct. Rob.* iii, A portrait of Alexander, in executing which, some inferior dauber has usurped the pencil of Apelles.

*fig.* and *transf.* **1598** B. JONSON *Ev. Man in Hum.* (Q.) V. i. 307 Which suit..I put on, and vsurping your mans phrase and action, caried a message to Signior Thorello in your name. **1744** *Harl. Misc.* I. 66 To Prince and People, that usurp unlawful Methods to accomplish their unjust Intentions. **1781** COWPER *Table-T.* 637 [To] claim the palm for purity of song, That lewdness had usurp'd and worn so long. **1813** SHELLEY *Q. Mab.* IX. 100 The old thorn .. Usurped the royal ensign's grandeur.

**b.** To assume or claim (a name or title) unduly as one's own; to arrogate or take to oneself. Also simply, to assume, bear.

**1549** W. THOMAS *Hist. Italie* 15 b, Theyr owne priuate capitaines enterprised many tymes not onely to rebell, but also to vsurpe the name of emperours. **1577** HOLINSHED *Chron., Hist. Eng.* I. 202/1 Euery one..sought..to vsurp yᵉ title of King. **1592** SHAKS. *Ven. & Ad.* 794 Call it not love, for Love to heaven is fled, Since sweating Lust on earth usurp'd his name. **1610** HEYWOOD *Gold. Age* F 4, Let that Clime henceforth be cal'd Arcadia, and vsurpe thy name. **1675** DRYDEN *Aurengz.* V. (1676) 81 The noble Arimant usurp'd my name. **1776** GIBBON *Decl. & F.* I. 58 The name .. of Orator was usurped by the sophists. **1781** COWPER *Retirem.* 319 He that has not usurp'd the name of man. **1883** F. POLLOCK in *Proc. Roy. Instit.* X. 381 The name of claymore (commonly usurped by the much later basket-hilted pattern).

**c.** To take (a word or words) into use; to borrow or appropriate from another language, source, etc.; to employ, use.

**1531** ELYOT *Gov.* I. xxii, Of them two [*sc.* 'celeritie' and 'slownesse'] springeth an excellent vertue where unto we lacke a name in englisshe. Wherfore I am constrained to usurpe a latine worde, callyng it *Maturitie.* **1559** W. CUNNINGHAM *Cosmogr. Glasse* 56 [The word] stadium..is vsurped, for a place where men exercise ther horse, ronnyng a rase. **1573** DAUS tr. *Bullinger on Apoc.* (ed. 2) 254 b, And these wordes haue more grace in ours and other straunge languages, vsurped than translated. So haue remayned in the Church, Osanna, Amen [etc.]. **1601** B. JONSON *Poetaster* III. i, 'White' is there vsurpt for her brow. **1649** MILTON *Eikon.* 126 He usurps a common saying, That it is kingly to doe well and heare ill. **1690** LEYBOURN *Curs. Math.* 347 *ddd* is..there usurped for *ggc.* **1859** SIR W. HAMILTON *Lect.* (1877) I. xi. 197 The[se] Latin terms..were very rarely usurped in their present psychological meaning.

†**5.** To exercise, practise, or inflict (injury, cruelty, etc.); to put into act, impose. Occas. const. *on, towards.* Also *transf. Obs. rare.*

**1456** SIR G. HAYE *Law Arms* (S.T.S.) 134 It is..honest to oppos..all injure or violence unlauchfully usurpit. **1583** STOCKER *Civ. Warres Lowe C.* III. 103 b, Usurping on them all kinde of crueltie, and warlike licence. **1625** [? SKINNER] tr. *Montanus Inquis.* 89 Certaine penalties and punishments vsurped towards offenders. *a* **1700** DRYDEN *Sigism. & Guisc.* 419 [State laws] are usurp'd on helpless Woman-kind, Made without our Consent, and wanting Pow'r to bind.

**6.** To supplant, oust, or turn out (a person); † to deprive (one) *of* possessions. Also *refl. rare.*

*a* **1325** *MS. Rawl. B.* 520 fol. 56 Þoru þat he him vsurpede bi-þoute iugement þoru his oune propre auctorite. **1512** *Helyas* in Thoms *Prose Rom.* (1828) III. 91 The erle .. wyllynge to usurpe her of her duchy. **1601** SHAKS. *Twel. N.* I. v. 198 *Vio.* Are you the Ladie of the house? *Ol.* If I do not vsurpe my selfe, I am. **1622** MABBE tr. *Aleman's Guzman d'Alf.* I. 194 No man shall dare or presume, to vsurpe or defraud one another in this kinde. **1890** *Pall Mall G.* 9 Oct. (1891) 2/1 'How dare you, sir, attempt to usurp me in the chair?' he [*sc.* Mr. Parnell] exclaimed.

*transf.* **1821** SHELLEY *Hellas* 260 O miserable dawn, after a night More glorious than the day which it usurped!

**II.** †**7.** *intr.* To claim or make pretensions, to assume or attempt arrogantly, *to* be or do something. *Obs.*

*c* **1391** CHAUCER *Astrol.* Prol., I ne vsurpe nat to haue fownde this werk of my labour. **1430–40** LYDG. *Bochas* VIII. 772 This Karansynvs..Proudli vsurped to be the gouernour. *Ibid.* IX. 125 He gadred peeple, gan wexe a werreiour, Ageyn Heraclius...And vsurped to ride in tho cuntres. **1483** CAXTON *Gold. Leg.* 204/4 To be crucyfyed upryght I haue not usurped. **1521** in Ellis *Orig. Lett.* Ser. II. I. 282 The said Dukes fader tooke upon hym and usurped to be king ageinst his elder broder.

**8.** To act or play the usurper; to rule or exercise authority as a usurper. Also const. *over, against.* Now *rare.*

*c* **1425** WYNTOUN *Cron.* V. x. 2476 He..hald him of his part content, Vsurpand nocht oure his extent. **1477** NORTON *Ord. Alch.* V. in Ashm. (1652) 67 When he usurpeth above equality. *a* **1513** FABYAN *Chron.* IV. lxxiv. 51 Whenne he had reygned, or more verely vsurped, by the terme of iiii. yeres. *c* **1585** [R. BROWNE] *Answ. Cartwright* 83 If any do usurpe, as traitors, against her maiesty. **1592** KYD *Sol. & Pers.* III. iv, Your Lord vsurps in all that he possesseth. **1596** [see USURPATION 4]. **1640** HABINGTON *Edw. IV*, 224 The house of Lancaster usurping against Edward. **1653** HOLCROFT *Procopius, Vandal Wars* I. 9 Basiliscus..attempted to usurp, and prevailed...And Basiliscus usurped a year and eight months. *a* **1733** RAYMOND *Reports* (1743) 954 Though he afterwards usurp and die, and the advowson descend to his heir.

*fig.* **1667** MILTON *P. L.* IX. 1132 Sensual Appetite .. Usurping over sovran Reason claimd Superior sway. *Ibid.* XI. 823 All fountaines of the Deep Broke up, shall heave the Ocean to usurp Beyond all bounds. **1827** KEBLE *Chr. Year*, *Sexagesima Sunday* vi, Chaining to earth..Hearts that would highest else aspire, And o'er the tenderer sex usurping ever most.

**9.** *To usurp on* or *upon*: **a.** To practise usurpation upon, to commit illegal seizure or action against (a person or persons).

**1470–85** MALORY *Arthur* I. iii. 39 Kyng Vther felle seke.., And in the meane whyle hys enemyes Vsurpped vpon hym. **1530** PALSGR. 769/2 Howe longe it is sythe he began first to usurpe upon you. **1576** *Southampton Court Leet Rec.* (1905) I. 138 His breethren doo vssurpe vppon the Comers vnto of this towne. **1640** HABINGTON *Edw. IV*, 21 Women who usurpe on their husbands. **1677** *Govt. Venice* 250 Popes..have usurped upon Seculars in the very power of suppressing of Heretical Books. **1701** WATSON *Clergyman's Law* 85 If any other Person..doth usurp upon the Lessee. **1760–72** H. BROOKE *Fool of Qual.* (1809) III. 36 When any of the three estates have usurped upon the others. **1889** LOWELL *Latest Lit. Ess., Walton* (1891) 77 When he speaks of himself he never seems to usurp on other people.

*fig.* **1603** FLORIO *Montaigne* III. x. 606 The motions of love, which I felt to vsurpe vpon me. **1608** SHAKS. *Per.* III. ii. 82 (Q. 1), Death may vsurpe on Nature many howers, and yet The fire of life kindle againe the ore-prest spirits.

**b.** To encroach or infringe upon (a right, privilege, etc.); to arrogate to oneself unjustly.

**1493** *Acta Dom. Conc.* (1839) 287/1 Vsurping apon þe fredomez & priuilegis of þe said burghe. **1531** *Dialogues on Laws Eng.* xxvi. 58 That they vsurpe vpon the popes auctorite. **1594** O. B. *Quest. Profit. Concern.* 31 *b, Such destroying fathers vsurped vpon the right. **1598** DALLINGTON *Meth. Trav.* L 2 b, The Noblesse of Athens hauing vsurped vpon the Democratie of that City. **1643** S. MARSHALL *Copy of Let.* 25 It is most apparent that they have not usurped upon His Majesties Prerogative. **1684** T. BURNET *Theory Earth* I. Ep. to King, Those that would usurp upon the fundamental priviledge and birth-right of mankind. **1720** GORDON & TRENCHARD *Independ. Whig* (1728) 153 It is..the highest Sacrilege to usurp upon this great Authority. **1771** GOLDSM. *Hist. Eng.* II. 141 The commission..had usurped upon his authority. **1822** *Monthly Mag.* LIII. 333 This would.. suffer Sweden and Prussia gradually to usurp on its Baltic ascendancy. **1868** MANNING in *Ess. Relig. & Lit.* Ser. III. (1874) 12 The Saxon and the Norman kings gradually usurped upon the freedom of the Church by customs. **1879** M. PATTISON *Milton* 123 Many matters, in which the old prelatic church had usurped upon the domain of the state.

*transf.* **1599** B. JONSON *Ev. Man out of Hum.* Charac. Persons, Shift, a thread-bare shark:..He vsurps vpon cheats, quarrels, and robberies which he neuer did. **1654** G. GODDARD in *Burton's Diary* (1828) I. 83 Whensoever any advantage offers itself, the one will usurp on the other, and.. strive totally to subvert it. **1670** H. STUBBE *Plus Ultra* 137 To prevent the Virtuosi from usurping upon my discoveries and intendments. **1840** DE QUINCEY *Style* Wks. 1859 XI. 175 This tendency in political journals to usurp upon the practice of books. **1870** LOWELL *Study Wind.* 212 The unclean rites of Baal..usurp on the worship of the one only True and Pure.

**c.** To seize, intrude or lay hold upon (land, property, etc.) without right or just cause; to assume authority or domination over, to become superior to.

**1630** *R. Johnson's Kingd. & Commw.* 576 The Moores or Arabians,..usurping upon the maritime coasts of the Country, have built them places and Cities. *a* **1674** CLARENDON *Surv. Leviath.* (1676) 160 When he usurp'd upon France with equal Tyranny. *a* **1700** EVELYN *Diary* 18 March 1649, The parish churches, on which the Presbyterians and fanatics had usurp'd.

*fig.* and *transf.* **1588** SHAKS. *Titus A.* III. i. 268 This sorrow is an enemy, And would vsurpe vpon my watry eyes. *a* **1613** BREREWOOD *Lang. & Relig.* (1614) 10 At this day, the Greek tongue is very much decayed:..in..the west, the natural languages of the countries have usurped upon it. **1622** WALLER *On Danger his Majesty escaped* 86 The loud winds usurping on the main. **1633** MARMION *Antiquary* I. i, Usurp then on the proffer'd means, Show yourself forward in an action. **1709** MRS. MANLEY *Secret Mem.* (1720) II. 263 Her killing Eyes now seem'd to lay aside their Darts: Languishments usurp'd upon the Fire. *a* **1859** DE QUINCEY *Posth. Wks.* (1893) II. 42 The heart of stone had usurped upon the heart of flesh.

**d.** To encroach upon physically. (Cf. 2 b.)

**1658** CLEVELAND *Rustick Rampant* (1687) 447 The honest Husbandmen..repairs the Banks, but does not usurp upon the Stream.

†**10.** To take possession *of* a thing by usurpation; to become participator *of. Obs.*

*a* **1513** FABYAN *Chron.* VII. (1811) 429 He had vsurpyd of the comon grounde of yᵉ cytie, in settynge of the said towre. **1609** BIBLE (Douay) *Joshua* vii. 1 The children of Israel transgressed the commandment, and usurped of the anathema.

† **Usu·rpant**, *a. Obs. rare.* [a. L. *ūsūrpānt-*, pple. stem of *ūsūrpāre*: see USURP *v.*] That usurps; guilty of or inclined to usurpation.

**1461** in Halliwell *Lett. Kings Eng.* (1846) I. 126 Harry late usurpant king of our said realm. **1473** *Rolls of Parlt.* VI. 92/2 For takyng of Henry late usurpant uppon our magistee Roiall. **1659** GAUDEN *Tears Ch.* 473 Some factious..Presbyters ventured to be extravagant and usurpant.

† **Usurpate**, *v. Obs.*⁻¹ [ad. L. *ūsūrpāt-*, pa. pple. stem of *ūsūrpāre.*] *trans.* = USURP *v.* 1 b.

**1542** in Halliwell *Lett. Kings Eng.* (1846) I. 382 The princes of Christendom, whose powers he euer practiseth to usurpate.

† **Usurpate**, *a. Obs.* [ad. L. *ūsūrpāt-us*: see prec.] Characterized by, based upon, usurpation or unwarranted encroachment.

**1560** ABP. PARKER in J. Ware *Hunt. Romish Fox* (1683) 116 By our Reformation, and denying of unlawful Demands, which be proud and usurpal [*sic*] of the Bishops of Rome. **1598** W. WATSON in *Archpriest Controv.* (Camden) I. 96 Their malice..towards priests is in nothing more plaine, then managing oute yᵗ vsurpate archpriest. **1600** — *Decacordon* (1602) 15 The vsurpate pretend of Iesuiticall esteeme. *Ibid.* 32, 168, 360. **1612** T. JAMES *Jesuits' Downef.* 44 The most egregious, tyrannicall, vsurpate, intrusiue auctoritie of the Iesuits.

Hence † **Usurpately** *adv. Obs.*⁻¹

**1536–7** *Ir. Act* 28 *Hen. VIII*, c. 12 (1621) 113 The said Proctors..doe..vsurpitly take vpon themselues to be parcell of the body. **1537** *Orig. & Sprynge of Sectes* 1 The Byshop of Rome (that vsurpatly called hymselfe Pope).

**Usurpation** (yūzəɹpēⁱ·ʃən). [a. OF. and AF. *usurpacion* (F. *usurpation*), ad. L. *ūsūrpātiōn-*, *ūsūrpātio*, n. of action f. *ūsūrpāre*: see USURP *v.* Cf. It. *usurpazione*, Sp. *usurpacion*, Pr. *-cioun*, Pg. *usurpação.*]

**I. 1.** Claim or assertion that is unwarranted or unauthorized; unjustified assumption, arrogation, or pretension.

**1387–8** T. USK *Test. Love* I. ix. (Skeat) l. 117 Their name of godliheed, they [*sc.* devils] han by usurpacion, as the prophete sayth [etc.]. **1426** LYDG. *De Guil. Pilgr.* 17716 Fyrst, ageynes al resoun, I wolde, by vsurpacioun, Fro poynt to poynt in ech degre, The zodyak sholde obeye me. **1622** MALYNES *Anc. Law-Merch.* 4 The Customes of Merchants concerning trafficke,..when they are not truely obserued in some places, by some errour or misprision,..loose their names, and are called Vsurpation. **1650** BULWER *Anthropomet.* 203 She might the better conceal her usurpation and counterfeit manhood. **1727** DE FOE *Syst. Magic* I. i. (1840) 20 As he usurped divine honours, so he made a figure suitable to his usurpation. *a* **1854** H. REED *Lect. Brit. Poets* i. (1857) 18 The sovereignty of even Homer or Shakspeare could hold no exclusive usurpation.

**2.** The action of usurping, illegally seizing, or wrongfully occupying some place or property belonging to a person or persons; unlawful encroachment upon or intrusion into the office, right, etc., of another or others; unjust or illegal possession. Also *personif.*

*c* **1420** LYDG. *Assembly of Gods* 661 Vsurpacion, with Horryble Vengeaunce, Came alther last of that company. **1480** *Acta Dom. Conc.* (1839) 74/2 Þe vsurpacion and purprisioun done in þe takin vp of þe malis of þe samyn landis. **1573** *Extr. Aberd. Reg.* (1848) II. 10 The usurpatioune of the preuilegeis of the burght. **1597** HOOKER *Eccl. Pol.* V. lxii. § 22 Considering that the worke of externall ministerie in Baptisme is only a preeminence of honor, which they that take to themselues..doe,..by meanes of such vsurpation, incurre the iust blame of disobedience to the Law of God. **1654** BRAMHALL *Just Vind.* i. (1661) 2 Whatsoeuer the Popes of Rome gained upon us..was meer tyranny and usurpation. **1692** DRYDEN *Disc. Satire* Ess. (ed. Ker) II. 88 The usurpation of that prince upon their freedom. **1766** J. Z. HOLWELL *Orig. Princ. Anc. Bramins* II. iv, [Men] do, by the force of their tyrannic usurpation, labor to make their [*sc.* the animals'] state more miserable. **1784** COWPER *Task* V. 760 Ye will not find..A liberty like his, who, unimpeach'd Of usurpation, and to no man's wrong, Appropriates nature as his father's work. **1817** JAS. MILL *Brit. India* II. IV. v. 199 The servants of the Company were now vested with a right to that plentiful source of gain, in which they had hitherto participated only by usurpation. **1819** SCOTT *Ivanhoe* xliv, I will appeal to Rome against thee..for usurpation on the immunities and privileges of our Order. **1837** HT. MARTINEAU *Soc. Amer.* II. 80 The United States having furnished the means by which the usurpation of Texas had been achieved.

*fig.* and *transf.* **1655** in *Verney Mem.* (1907) II. 24 There is a soveranity in honour which noe usurpation can depose. **1900** 'J. DOE' *Bridge Man.* 18 If the usurpation of your right to double make no difference to the original lead.

**b.** *esp.* The unlawful or forcible seizure or occupation of a throne, sovereign power, etc.; wrongful assumption of supreme authority.

**1470** *Rolls of Parlt.* V. 456/2 Edward.., late by usurpacion Kyng of England. **1485** *Ibid.* VI. 276/1 Callinge and nameinge hymself, by usurpacion, Kinge Richard the IIIᵈ. **1578** T. N. tr. *Conq. W. India* 77 Those Princes began their usurpation by way and colour of Religion. **1595** SHAKS. *John* II. i. 9 To rebuke the vsurpation Of thy vnnaturall Vncle, English Iohn. **1610** HOLLAND *Camden's Brit.* I. 725 The violent usurpation of Henry the Fourth. **1683** *Brit. Spec.* 64 This Power he got by Usurpation, and not by any Election of..the People. **1729** T. INNES *Crit. Essay* (1879) 402 This leaves no room for his expedition.., either before or after his usurpation. **1776** GIBBON *Decl. & F.* xii. I. 330 Florianus shewed himself unworthy to reign, by the hasty usurpation of the purple, without expecting the approbation of the senate. **1791** BURKE *Corr.* (1844) III. 282 The assembly cannot annihilate the constitutional states. It is itself an usurpation, and its acts are void. **1844** H. H. WILSON *Brit. India* III. 189 He also calculated upon..the cooperation of a strong party inimical to the usurpation. **1856** *N. Brit. Rev.* XXVI. 289 This government of generals, successively ruling..by forcible usurpation. **1877** FROUDE *Short Stud.* (1883) IV. I. ii. 19 The usurpation of Stephen had left behind it a legacy of disorder.

**c.** With *a* and pl.: An act of usurping another's rights, privileges, etc.; an instance of encroachment *on* or *upon* (liberty, etc.).

**16..** ROWLEY *Birth Merl.* IV. iii 14 *Vort.* The Saxons which thou broughtst To back thy usurpations, are grown great. **1638** R. BAKER tr. *Balzac's Lett.* (vol. II) 3 This so tyrannical an usurpation upon the liberty of mens spirits. **1679** C. NESSE *Antichrist* 213 The corruptions and usurpations of Antichrist. **1721** BOLINGBROKE in *Swift's Lett.* (1766) II. 41 Exercising an insolent and cruel usurpation over their brethren. **1757** in *10th Rep. Hist. MSS. Comm.* App. I. 217 What he called Our Usurpations in America. **1771** GOLDSM. *Hist. Eng.* III. 250 The depression of the nobility as a necessary consequence of the popular usurpations on the crown. **1823** *Tonstall's Serm. Palm Sund.* Pref. 2 The bondage of a baneful and preposterous usurpation on the liberties of mankind. **1863** H. COX *Instit.* I. vii. 82 Usurpations of unconstitutional powers by the House of Commons.

**d.** *transf.* Physical encroachment on sea or land. *rare.*

**1553** BRENDE *Q. Curtius* 41 b, The Tyrians deuined that Neptune reuenging the vsurpacion that the Macedons had made vpon the sea, would shortely destroy the worcke. **1597** SHAKS. *Hen. IV*, I. i. 63 So lookes the Strond, when the Imperious Flood Hath left a witnest Vsurpation.

**3.** *Eccl. Law.* The action on the part of a stranger of dispossessing a lawful patron of the right of presenting a cleric to a benefice.

1596 Bacon *Max. Com. Law* (1630) 2 So if I be seised of an advouson in gross, and an vsurpation bee had against mee, and at the next avoidance I vsurpe arere, I shall be remitted. 1628 Coke *On Litt.* 277 b, When an estranger that no right hath presenteth to a Church, and his Clarke is admitted and instituted, hee is said to bee an vsurper, and the wrongfull act..is called an Usurpation. 1701 W. Watson *Clergyman's Law* 89 By Usurpation the rightful Patron may be divested of the possession of his Advowson. *a* 1733 Raymond *Reports* (1743) 953 If a purchaser of an advowson in fee-simple, before any presentment, suffer an usurpation. 1768 Blackstone *Comm.* III. 242 Another species of injury, called usurpation; which is an absolute ouster or dispossession of the patron. 1877 F. G. Lee *Gloss. Liturg. & Eccl. Terms* 432 No usurpation can displace the estate or interest of any patron, nor turn it to a mere right.

†**4.** Usurpatory rule or power. *Obs. rare.*

1654 tr. *Scudery's Curia Pol.* 125 To re-conquer Amuraths Usurpation, and attain to the King my Fathers Throne. 1667 Milton *P. L.* II. 983 If I that Region lost, All usurpation thence expell'd, reduce To her original darkness and your sway. 1761 Hume *Hist. Eng.* II. xxiii. 67 The duke ..attempted to overthrow that usurpation which he himself had so zealously contributed to establish.

**b.** *The usurpation*, the period of the Commonwealth (Commonwealth 4).

[1664 G. Fell in *Extr. St. Papers Friends* Ser. III. (1912) 227 Seduced into that Phanatique opinion of the Quakers in the late time of Vsurpation.] 1682 in *Scottish Antiq.* July (1901) 4 The tyme of the late rebellione and wsurpatione. 1727 Swift *Lett. Eng. Tongue* Wks. 1755 II. I. 187 During the usurpation, such an infusion of enthusiastic jargon prevailed in every writing, as [etc.]. 1782 Pennant *Journ. Chester to Lond.* 235 On the usurpation, he had the meanness to sit in Cromwell's mock parlement. 1829 Scott *Hrt. Midl.* Note R, He afterwards advanced £20,000 for the service of King Charles, during the usurpation.

†**5.** *Roman Law.* Interruption of usucapion.

1675 R. Dixon *Two Testaments* 551 A wife: not a Concubine, might be taken by use; for a whole un-interrupted year without usurpation.

**II. 6.** The action of taking into use or making use of a thing; acceptance or agreement in the use of anything; usage, employment.

1583 Fulke *Def. Tr. Script.* 160 Which worde [*sc.* priests] is taken vp by common vsurpation, to signifie sacrificers. 1589 Puttenham *Eng. Poesie* III. xix. (Arb.) 250 By common vsurpation, nothing is wiser then the Serpent, more couragious then the Lion, more bewtifull then the Angell. 1611 Guillim *Heraldry* VI. v. 269 No man had his Badge set on a Wreath vnder the degree of a Knight: But..time and vsurpation concurring with prescription, hath so much preuailed, as that [etc.]. 1659 Pearson *Creed* 252 There can be no kind of certainty in any such observations of the Articles, because the Greeks promiscuously often use them, or omit them, without any reason of their usurpation or omission.

†**b.** A special use of a word or expression. *Obs.*

1644 Bulwer *Chirol.* To Rdr. A 6 b, Humane literature, wherein..I shall lay claime to all metaphors, proverbiall translations or usurpations.

Hence **Usurpa·tionist**, one who advocates usurpation. Also *attrib.*

1899 R. Wallace *G. Buchanan* iii. 58 A principle..subversive of the despotic doctrine of the Divine right of Kings, so prevalent in usurpationist quarters in that day.

**Usurpative** (yuzɒ·ɹpătiv), *a.* [ad. late L. *ūsurpātīv-us*, f. L. *ūsurpāre*: see Usurp *v.*] Of the nature of, marked or characterized by, usurpation; arbitrary.

1797 J. Pinkerton *Hist. Scot.* I. 10 Pretensions, which now strike as vague or usurpative. 1811 *Monthly Rev.* LXVI. 470 Laurence was of a less usurpative and more tolerant disposition. 1827 G. S. Faber *Sacr. Calend. Prophecy* (1844) II. 64 A clear usurpative invasion of the..coequal independence of all the other Patriarchs. 1879 Tourgee *Fool's Err.* xx. 115 The foolish usurpative acts of the President. 1908 *Amer. Naturalist* XLII. 16 The usurpative control of their nutrition by the fungus suggests [etc.].

Hence **Usu·rpatively** *adv. rare*$^{-1}$.

1838 G. S. Faber *Inquiry* 334 Let him not dare usurpatively to administer any divine sacrament, until [etc.].

†**Usurpator.** *Obs.* Also 6 -our. [ad. OF. (F.) *usurpateur* (14th c.), or a. late L. *ūsurpātor*, agent-n. f. L. *ūsurp-āre*: see Usurp *v.* Cf. It. *usurpatore*, Pr., Sp., Pg. *usurpador*.] A usurper.

1529 Rastell *Pastyme* (1811) 63 Tirantis and usurpatours of the empyre. 1549 *Compl. Scot.* ix. 79 The inglismen var violent vsurpatours of al scotland. 1654 Howell *Parthenop.* II. 37 Under the Iron yoak of Usurpators.

**Usurpatory** (yuzɒ·ɹpătəri), *a.* [ad. late L. *ūsurpātōri-us*, f. *ūsurpātor* Usurpator. Cf. F. *usurpatoire.*] Marked or characterized by usurpation; usurping.

1847 Webster. 1864 *Daily Tel.* 16 July, To let it [= an assembly] alone while harmless, to prorogue it when mischievous, and to bring it to book when usurpatory. 1906 *Times* 26 Dec. 7/3 A usurpatory claim that can no longer be admitted.

†**Usurpatrix.** *rare*$^{-0}$. [a. late L. *ūsurpātrix*, fem. of *ūsurpātor* Usurpator.] = Usurpress.

1611 Cotgr., *Vsurpatrice*, an usurpatrix.

**Usurpature** (yū·zɒɹpēⁱtiŭɹ). *poet.* [f. L. *ūsurpāt-*, ppl. stem of *ūsurpāre* to usurp, + -ure.] Usurpation. Also *transf.*

The stressing (*usu·rpature*) given in various Dicts. from 1884 is not borne out by the quots.

1845 Browning *Flight of Duchess* xiv, Her step kept pace with mine nor faltered, As if age had foregone its usurpature. 1860 Ld. Lytton *Lucile* II. iv. § 7. 65 Something superior;..from my innermost nature Not wholly expell'd by the world's usurpature. 1869 Browning *Ring & Bk.* XII. 5 Up and up roared and soared A rocket, till the key o' the vault was reached, And wide heaven held..In brilliant usurpature.

**Usurped,** *ppl. a.* [f. Usurp *v.* + -ed¹.]

**1.** Seized, obtained, held, etc., by usurpation or force; possessed unjustly or illegally; arrogated wrongfully.

*c* 1375 *Sc. Leg. Saints* xxi. (*Eugenia*) 135 Sen vsurpyt pouste has mad me ȝoure lady be. *c* 1430 Lydg. *Min. Poems* (Percy Soc.) 158 No vengable herte shal..Extort power nor fals usurpyd myhte. 1477 *Rolls of Parlt.* VI. 191/1 A pretensed Parlement..by usurped auctorite summoned..by your Rebell and Enemye. 1504 Atkynson tr. *De Imitatione* I. xxiv. 175 Than shalbe more allowable a constaunt pacience than all vsurped power. *a* 1548 Hall *Chron., Hen. V*, 34 b, Gregory..did put doune hymself of his owne propre mocion from his foolishe usurped name and Popishe dignitee. 1569 T. Knell *Epit. Boner* A iiij, Sus taught *Mineruam* there to long, Which held vsurped place. 1590 Spenser *F. Q.* III. iii. 47 That from the Danishe Tyrants head shall rend Th' vsurped crowne. 1629 Milton *Hymn Nativity* xviii, Th' old Dragon under ground..Not half so far casts his usurped sway. 1672 South *Serm.* (1717) V. 294 A Nation under an usurped Government. 1746 Ld. Hardwicke in Harris *Life* (1847) II. 305 This usurped power was audaciously made use of. 1759 Sterne *Tr. Shandy* I. xviii, The many other usurped rights which..the constitution was hourly establishing. 1831 James *Phil. Augustus* I. xi, The resistance he meditated to the usurped authority of the pope. 1861 Paley *Aeschylus, Agam.* (ed. 2) 1447 *note*, That the.. usurped female authority over them, is intolerable to bear. *fig.* 1781 Cowper *Conversat.* 462 Yet fashion, leader of a chatt'ring train,..Holds an usurp'd dominion o'er his tongue.

**b.** Marked or characterized by usurpation.

1430–40 Lydg. *Bochas* I. 2990 In ther fals vsurped tirannye To holde peeplis in long subieccioun. 1461 *Rolls of Parlt.* V. 467/2 The usurped reigne of the same Henry. 1464 *Ibid.* 511/2 The same Humfrey..traiterously adhered unto the seid Henry.., and..in his fals and usurped quarell,..toke hoole and full parte. 1597 Hooker *Eccl. Pol.* v. lxii. § 13 His vsurped actions haue in him the same nature. 1771 Goldsm. *Hist. Eng.* I. 216 Henry was now resolved..to dispute..Stephen's usurped pretensions. *c* 1850 *Fullarton's Gaz. Scotl.* I. 135/1 During the usurped and military possession of Scotland by Edward I of England.

†**2.** Of persons: Holding office, exercising authority, by virtue of usurpation. *Obs.*

1569 L. Avale (*title*), A Commemoration or Dirige of Bastarde Edmonde Boner,..vsurped Bisshoppe of London. 1790 Burke *Fr. Rev.* 84 Another revolution, to get rid of this illegitimate and usurped government.

†**3.** Used or employed without due justification or warrant; appropriated, borrowed. *Obs. rare.*

*a* 1548 Hall *Chron., Hen. V*, 34 b, Gregory the .xij...did put doune hymself..from his foolishe usurped name. 1611 Shaks. *Twel. N.* v. i. 257 *Vio*[*la*]. This my masculine vsurp'd attyre. 1673 J. Faldo *Quakerism* Title-p., A Key, for the understanding their sense of their many usurped and unintelligible words and phrases.

†**b.** False, counterfeit. *Obs. rare*$^{-1}$.

1604 Shaks. *Oth.* I. iii. 346 Come, be a man:..follow thou the Warres, defeate thy fauour, with an vsurp'd Beard.

Hence **Usu·rpedly** *adv.*

1545 Brinklow *Compl.* 47 b, His accustomyd pollagys, which vsurpedly he had out of this reame. 1556 J. Heywood *Spider & Fly* lxv. Ee ij, This spider hath vsurpedlie growne To potentate state. 1647 Lilburne & Overton *Out-cryes Oppr. Commons* 1 The Lords..now sitting at Westminster, who have usurpedly..assumed..a power in criminall causes.

**Usurper** (yuzɒ·ɹpəɹ), *sb.* Also 5 usurpur, 6 *Sc.* -ar. [a. OF. *usurpeur* (1321), or f. Usurp *v.* + -er¹. Cf. Usurpor, and Pr. *usurpaire.*]

**1.** One who usurps a crown or throne; one who seizes or arrogates supreme power or authority without right or just cause.

In frequent use from *c* 1700.

1414 Earl of Cambridge in Ellis *Orig. Lett.* Ser. II. I. 45 Harry of Lancastre usurpur of Yngland. 1477 *Rolls of Parlt.* VI. 193/2 His enemies mortall, the usurpers, laboryng..to exclude hym..from the Regalie. 1520 *Caxton's Chron. Eng.* v. 62 b/1 He..slewe Leo the vsurper of his realme. 1574 *Homilies* II. *Rebellion* VI. 609 That forraigne false vsurper the Bishop of Rome. 1587 *Mirr. Mag., Porrex* x, Vsurpers may perswade themselues a while There is no God, no lawes of sacred crowne. 1627 P. Fletcher *Locusts* I. xxi, They crowne Usurpers with a wreath of lead. 1663 South *Serm.* (1717) V. 95 They sounded the first Trumpet to Rebellion,..courting and recognizing an Usurper [*sc.* Cromwell]. 1727 De Foe *Syst. Magic* I. iii. (1840) 68 If the Devil, the ancient usurper of his throne, had not been at work again to step up in his room. 1790 Burke *Fr. Rev.* 32 But King James was a bad king with a good title, and not an usurper. 1831 James *Phil. Augustus* II. ii, The barons of England adhered to an usurper..rather than to their legitimate prince. 1869 J. Baldwin Brown *Misread Passages* ix. 124 Who would recognise an usurper because he occupies the palace and assumes the signet of the rightful king? 1882 J. Rhys *Celtic Britain* v. 189 Macbeth was not a mere usurper.

*attrib.* and *Comb.* 1670 Dryden *1st Pt. Conq. Granada* III. i, Too well I know her blandishments to gain, Usurper-like, till settled in her reign. 1877 W. R. Cooper *Egypt. Obelisks* xii. 66 The power of the half usurper king of Egypt.

**b.** One who illegally or unjustly seizes, appropriates, or intrudes into any office, property, rights, etc. Also const. *upon.*

*c* 1425 Lydg. *Assembly of Gods* 682 There were bosters, braggars, & brybores,..Wrong vsurpers, with great extorcioners. 1567 *Reg. Privy Council Scot.* I. 547 Gif he [*sc.* a discharged custom-house officer] forder intromettis, he salbe repute ane usurpar to our Soverane Lordis authoritie. 1599 T. Storer *Life & D. Wolsey* D 4, Victorious Iosuah that in armes subdued Prophane vsurpers of their hallowed things, And smote their leaders. 1628 [see Usurpation 3]. 1697 Dryden *Virg., Past.* VIII. 62 In Desarts thou wert bred; And at the Dugs of Salvage Tygers fed: Alien of Birth, Usurper of the Plains. 1713 Gibson *Codex* 782/2 If the Incumbency be by Usurpation, and the Usurper and Ordinary Confirm the Parson's Lease. 1769 Robertson *Chas. V*, x. Wks. 1813 III. 214 Compelled..to submit to the jurisdiction of magistrates whom they destested as usurpers. 1771 Goldsm. *Hist. Eng.* III. 19 They represented him as..an unjust usurper upon the privileges of the council. 1818 Cobbett *Pol. Reg.* XXXIII. 237 The tyrant usurpers of our rights. 1840 Hood *Up Rhine* 47 'The end was, I got my bed.' 'And what excuse..did the usurper offer for his intrusion?'

**c.** *fig.* and *transf.*

*a* 1628 F. Grevil *Cœlica* xcvi. (1633) 244 Pleasure is chosen as a Goddesse fit, The wealth of Nature freely to impart; ..Which faire Vsurper runnes a Rebel's way. 1632 Lithgow *Trav.* v. 186 The vsurpers of Gods word..maintaine..that famous Kingdome, being but one thousand and fifty Turkes in all. 1847 Emerson *Repr. Men, Napoleon* P 4 [He] becomes..actually a monopolizer and usurper of other minds. 1898 Talmage *Serm.* in *Chrn. Herald* (N.Y.) 12 Jan. 24/3 That man has made that which might be a healthful recreation an usurper of his affections. 1900 'J. Doe' *Bridge Man.* 9 If a player deals out of turn he may be stopped.., but if he completes his deal, the deal holds good, and the usurpers make the declaration.

†**2.** A conqueror or vanquisher *of* something.

1509 *Parl. Devylles* lxiv, I [*sc.* Christ] am lorde and kynge of blysse, Usurper of dethe, myghty in fyght.

Hence **Usu·rpership.** *rare*$^{-1}$.

1781 Bp. Watson in Farquhar *Bps. of Dunkeld* (1915) iii. 18 As if the Lord's Day had been equally the institution of his [George III's] present usurpership.

†**Usu·rper,** *v. Obs.*$^{-1}$ [f. prec.] *intr.* (with *it*). To play the usurper.

1656 S. H. *Gold. Law* 57 He invades, and evades Law, and..yet neither Usurpers nor Arbytraters it.

**Usu·rping,** *vbl. sb.* [f. Usurp *v.* + -ing¹.] The action of the verb; usurpation; an instance of this. Also in fig. context.

1521 Ld. Dacre in Ellis *Orig. Lett.* Ser. II. I. 282 The Dukes fader..in the tyme of his usurping made diverse knightes. 1550 Crowley *Inform. & Petit.* 1 The vsurpyng of tenthes to priuate commoditie. 1595 Shaks. *John* II. i. 119 Excuse it is to beat vsurping downe. 1649 Lovelace *Lucasta* Poems (1904) 37 Dropping December shall come weeping in, Bewayle th' usurping of his Raigne. 1656 Earl Monm. tr. *Boccalini's Advts. fr. Parnass.* I. lxxi. (1674) 89 The injurious usurping the Countries liberty. *a* 1667 Jer. Taylor *Pol. Disc.* (1674) b 4, To secure the inclosures of the Clerical orders from the usurpings and invasions of..unhallowed spirits.

**Usu·rping,** *ppl. a.* [f. as prec. + -ing².]

**1.** That usurps, in various senses. Also in fig. context.

1574 *Homilies* II. *Rebellion* VI. 611 [To] blesse the cursynges of suche wicked vsurpyng bishops and tyrantes. 1586 Marlowe *1st Pt. Tamburl.* IV. iii, That such a base vsurping vagabond Should..weare a princely crowne. 1596 *Edward III*, III. iii. 35 The vsurping King of Fraunce. *a* 1642 Godolphin in *Caroline Poets* II. (1906) 247 Hear an usurping soule doth dwell. 1659 *Nicholas Papers* (Camden) IV. 164 'Tis a reasonable..demaunde, specially as to new and vsurpinge lords. 1707 Norris *Treat. Humility* vii. 313 God is jealous of his glory;..he makes war against the proud man, as an usurping invader of it. 1715 Pope *Iliad* II. 242 That worst of tyrants, an usurping crowd. 1818 Byron *Ch. Har.* IV. cliii, I have..survey'd Its [*sc.* St. Sophia's] sanctuary the while the usurping Moslem pray'd. 1833 J. H. Newman *Arians* II. i. 160 To expel an usurping idol from the house of God. 1901 Glover *Life & Lett. in 4th Cent.* Introd. 9 Usurping and suspicious Emperors.

**b.** *transf.* Of things.

1588 Shaks. *L. L. L.* IV. iii. 259 It mournes, that painting vsurping [= false] haire Should rauish doters with a false aspect. 1590 — *Com. Err.* II. ii. 180 If ought possesse thee from me, it is drosse, Vsurping Iuie, Brier, or idle Mosse. 1634 Milton *Comus* 337 If your influence be quite damm'd up With black usurping mists. *a* 1661 Fuller *Worthies* III. (1662) 226 It follows not that the Usurping Tulip is better then the Rose.

**c.** *fig.* Of emotions, qualities, etc.

1633 G. Herbert *Temple, Love* II. iii, Thou shalt recover all thy gods in kinde, Who wert disseized by usurping lust. 1659 W. Chamberlayne *Pharon.* I. III. 319 By that flood To wash usurping grief from off that part Where most she reigned. 1698 W. Chilcot *Evil Thoughts* vi. 165 There are none more apt to grow usurping and ungovernable..than these [thoughts]. 1747 Johnson *Winter* ii, The ling'ring hours prolong the night, Usurping Darkness shares the day.

**2.** Characterized by usurpation.

1809 Wordsw. '*O'er the wide earth*' 8 In these usurping times of fear and pain.

Hence **Usu·rpingly** *adv.*

1589 *Hay any Work* 25 Many other causes, which you bishops..do usurpingly take from the ciuill magistrate. 1621 T. Williamson tr. *Goulart's Wise Vieillard* 76 Either for that their children misgouerne themselues, or their wiues behaue themselues vsurpingly. 1661 *Sir H. Vane's Politicks* 3 It skills not much whether lineally descended, or usurpingly advanced. 1827 Poe *Tamerlane* 32 The fever'd diadem on my brow I claim'd and won usurpingly.

†**Usu·rpious,** *a. Obs.*$^{-1}$ [See Usurp *v.* and -ious.] Exercising or practising usurpation.

1606 Warner *Albion's Eng.* xv. xcvii. 387 From Rome vsurpious, bloodie, proud, hereticall then seuer Ye Creatures of Hers.

†**Usu·rpment.** *Obs. rare.* [f. Usurp *v.* + -ment.] Usurpation. Also *attrib.*

*a* 1470 Harding *Chron.* ccx. *heading*, The kynge sayde at hys deathe..nought of repentaunce of [his] vsurpement of the realme. 1660 *Extr. St. Papers Friends* Ser. II. (1911) 123 Ashfeild..took no oath or covenant under the late usurpment powers.

†**Usu·rpor.** *Obs. rare.* Also 5–6 -our. [a. AF. *usurpor*: see Usurp *v.* and -or 2.] = Usurper.

1474 *Rolls of Parlt.* VI. 119/2 Harry the sext late usurpour. 1563 *Mirr. Mag., Hastings* xciii, The vsurpour Boare, that hellyshe freak. 1586 FERNE *Blaz. Gentrie* 303 If the Vsurpor haue enemies that compasse his death.

† **Usu·rpously**, *adv.* *Obs.*$^{-1}$ [f. USURP *v.*: see -OUS and -LY [2].] By usurpation; usurpingly.

1461 *Rolls of Parlt.* V. 463/2 Takyng upon hym usurpously the coroune and name of kyng.

**Usurpress** (yuzɒ̄·ɹprės). [f. USURPER + -ESS [1].] A female usurper.

1640 HOWELL *Dodona's Gr.* 26 She is a double Vsurpresse, in detaining not only Elaiana from her right, but [etc.]. *c* 1650 *Don Bellianis* 210 Faint not, Usurpress of anothers heart, but animate yourself. 1658 CLEVELAND *Rustic Rampant* 122 She had seized the Kingdome as an Usurpresse by Tyrannie. 1805 *Pennant's London* 245 An innocent usurpress [*sc.* Lady Jane Gray] succeeded to her apartments in 1553. 1873 DIXON *Two Queens* I. viii. I. 56 The Austrians ..detested Isabel as a usurpress.

**Usury** (yū·ziŭri), *sb.* Forms: α. 4–6 **vsurye**, 5–6 **usurye**, 7 **-ie**, 5–7 **vsury**, **-ie**, 6 **-ee**, 5– **usury**. β. 4–5 **vsery(e**, 4, 6 **vserie**, 6–7 **usery**. [a. AF. **usurie*, ad. med.L. *ūsūria*, f. L. *ūs-us*, pa. pple. of *ūtī* to use. Cf. USURE *sb.*]

**1.** The fact or practice of lending money at interest; esp. in later use, the practice of charging, taking, or contracting to receive, excessive or illegal rates of interest for money on loan.

1303 R. BRUNNE *Handl. Synne* 2417 To whom þat vsery ys lefe, Gostely he ys a þefe. 1377 LANGL. *P. Pl.* B. II. 175 Lat sadel hem with siluer owre synne to suffre, As auoutrie..and derne vsurye. *c* 1445 PECOCK *Donet* 68 Siþen in vseri þe leener..compelliþ þe borewer to..paie a summe of his owne good bisidis þe summe borewid. 1487 *Act 3 Hen. VI*, c. 6 That all unlefull Chevysaunces and Usurye be dampned, and none to be used, upon payne [etc.]. 1514 BARCLAY *Cyt. & Uplondyshman* (Percy Soc.) 23 Some lyve by rapyne,..and some in usury. 1595 MOSSE (*title*), Arraignment and Conuiction of Vsurie. That is, the Iniquitie, and Vnlawfulnes of Vsurie, displayed in sixe Sermons. 1643 MILTON *Divorce* 33 The Christian Magistrate permits usury. 1663 in *Verney Mem.* (1907) II. 195, I hate this rack-renting; 'tis worse than usury. 1711 STEELE *Spect.* No. 114 ⁋1 His Estate is dipped, and is eating out with Usury. 1754 ERSKINE *Princ. Sc. Law* (1809) 520 The crime of usury, before the Reformation, consisted in the taking of *any* interest for the use of money; and now in taking an higher rate of interest than is authorised by law. 1787 BENTHAM *Def. Usury* ii. 7, I know of but two definitions that can possibly be given of usury: one is, the taking of a greater interest than the law allows of... The other is the taking of a greater interest than it is usual for men to give and take. 1801 *Farmer's Mag.* Aug. 338 The criminality of usury.. [consists] in exacting more than the usual rate of the market. 1858 LD. ST. LEONARDS *Handy-bk. Prop. Law* xiv. 87 The statutes against usury..are repealed, so that you may take for your money whatever amount of interest you can get.

*Personif.* *c* 1420 LYDG. *Assembly of Gods* 644 Pety capteyns.., As..Vsury, Periury, Ly, and Adulacion. *c* 1430 — *Min. Poems* (Percy Soc.) 172 Usurye lyethe fetrede in dystresse. 1606 DEKKER *Sev. Sins* II. (Arb.) 22 Thou doest likewise Lye with Vsury. 1615 BRATHWAIT *Strappado* (1878) 28 O vsurie.., how much haue we Occasion to proscribe thee from our land.

*attrib.* 1813 (*title*), A Treatise on the Usury Laws with Disquisitions on the Arguments adduced against them by Bentham.

**2.** Premium or interest on money (or goods) given or received on loan; †gain made by lending money. Now *arch.*

*c* 1440 *Alph. Tales* 472 Þer was ane vsurar þat wolde neuer restore his vsurie agayn. 1555 EDEN *Decades* (Arb.) 365 With increase of dowble vsurie. 1567 *Termes Laws* (1579) 184/1 *Vsurie* is a gayne of any thing aboue the principal, or that which was lent, exacted onely in consideration of the loane, whether it be of corne, meat,..or such like, as money. 1600 HOLLAND *Livy* 262 Albeit the Vsurie was well eased by bringing it downe from twelve to one. 1621 CULPEPPER *Tract agst. Usury* 8 For Vsury going at ten in the hundred, if a man borrow fiue pounds [etc.]. 1690 CHILD *Disc. Trade* 209 The rate of Usury is the measure by which all men Trade,..or any other ways bargain. 1729 FRANKLIN *Ess.* Wks. 1840 II. 273 This may bring down the common usury to the pitch it is determined at by law. 1746 P. FRANCIS tr. *Horace, Sat.* I. ii. 14 *note*, The Laws allowed an Usury..which doubled the capital Sum in an hundred Months.

**b.** *fig.* and in fig. context. Freq. *with usury.*

1549 COVERDALE, etc. *Erasm. Par.* 1 *Pet.* 2 That you may waxe riche in the encreasing vsury of good workes, more and more. 1590 SPENSER *F. Q.* I. viii. 27 Behold what ye this day haue done for mee, And what I cannot quite, requite with vsuree. 1595 — *Col. Clout* 39 Of good passed newly to discus, By dubble vsurie doth twise renew it. 1606 B. JONSON *Hymenæi* C 4 Haste, therefore,..and call, Away: The gentle Night is prest to pay The vsurie of long delights, She owes to these protracted rites. 1661 RUST *Origen's Opin.* 66 What is it then..which they may not have with usury and advantage in a body of purer Consistence? 1695 PEPYS in *Academy* 9 Aug. (1890) 111/1, I repay you with usury yo^r kinde Wishes. 1732 LEDIARD *Sethos* II. IX. 342 The motive of taking Siga has been accomplish'd with usury. 1750 JOHNSON *Rambler* No. 48 ⁋10 [He] must not only pay back the hours but pay them back with usury. 1790 BURKE *Fr. Rev.* 117 Learning paid back what it received..with usury. 1813 SHELLEY *Q. Mab* IV. 209 They have three words:—well tyrants know their use, Well pay them for the loan, with usury. 1842 TENNYSON *Talking Oak* 196, I would have paid her kiss for kiss, With usury thereto.

**c.** In the phrases *at, to, on, upon usury.*

13.. *Prose Psalter* xiv. 6 (Dublin MS.), He þat ȝaf mony to vsurye ne toke noȝt ȝiftes vp on innocentes. 1535 COVERDALE *Deut.* xxiii. 20 Vnto a straunger thou maiest lende vpon vsury. 1579 G. HARVEY *Letter-bk.* (Camden) 62 Lett me borrow them both upon tolerable usurye. 1603 HOLLAND *Plutarch's Mor.* 283 That it might not be lawfull for those to borrow upon usurie. 1651 HOBBES *Leviath.* I. viii. 35 Taking mony at usurie, for the present payment of interest. 1702 *Eng. Theophrastus* 332 'Tis lending on Usury, under the pretence of giving freely. 1844 tr. *M. T. Asmar's Mem. Babylonian Princess* II. 105 If I put it [*sc.* corn] at usury, shall not my bones howl from my grave. 1888 *Encycl. Brit.* XXIV. 17 The man who does not..lend his capital upon 'usury' is..lacking in his duty to himself or his family.

†**3.** *pl.* Instances or kinds of usury. *Obs.*

1603 HOLLAND *Plutarch's Mor.* 284 Their rootes of debts ..bring foorth infinite troubles and intolerable usuries. 1603 SHAKS. *Meas. for M.* III. ii. 7 Since of two vsuries the merriest was put downe, and the worser allow'd by order of Law. 1611 — *Cymb.* III. iii. 45 Did you but know the Citties Vsuries, And felt them knowingly.

†**4.** *transf.* Increase, augmentation; advantage.

1576 FLEMING *Panopl. Epist.* 352 Howe bountifull a seruitour is the earthe, to the husbandeman? what vsurie doeth it pay for that which it borroweth? 1599 T. M[OUFET] *Silkwormes* 71 Diuine we hence, or rather reckon right, What vsury and proffit doth arise, By keeping well these ..creatures white. 1613 HEYWOOD *Silver Age* III. G 3, With full sickles You shall receiue the vsury of their seeds. 1624 — *Gunaik.* 31 The profitable usurie arising from agriculture.

†**5.** The use or employment of anything. *rare.*

1607 TOURNEUR *Rev. Trag.* IV. ii, To prostitute my brest to the Dukes sonne: And put my selfe to common vsury. 1625 GILL *Sacr. Philos.* II. 127 That thou mightest inioy the usury of this aire but for the time.

Hence † **U·sury** *v. trans.*, to give *out* (favours), with a view to advantageous return. *Obs.*

1654 WHITLOCK *Zootomia* 368 We usury out, not bestow our Favours, each Curtesie being a Designe not so much of doing, as receiving good, with unconscionable Advantage.

**Usward** (ɒ·swəɹd), *adv.* Now *arch.* [f. US. See -WARD, TOWARD, and cf. HER-, HIM-, ME-WARD.] Orig. (and chiefly) *to usward*, =toward us. Also *from usward.*

(*a*) *c* 1391 CHAUCER *Astrol.* I. § 17 Thanne bygynnyth the sonne to come agayn to vs-ward. 1420 in Rymer *Fœdera* (1709) IX. 907/1 The Letters..enseled undir the Grete Seel of our said Fader to usward, and under Ours to hymward. 1451 *Paston Lett.* I. 202 The baly..knewe not..what myn unkyll was to us ward. 1529 FRITH *Pistle to Chr. Reader* 4 b, In kindnes to vsward thorow Christ Jesus. 1611 BIBLE *Ps.* xl. 5 Many..are..thy thoughts, which are to vs ward. 1642 J. EATON *Honey-comb Free Justif.* 344 Mystically to us-ward, and inwardly and spiritually to God-ward. 1650 *Metr. Psalms Ch. Scotl.* cxvii. 2 For great to us-ward ever are his loving kindnesses. 1779 J. BROWN in R. Mackenzie *Life* (1918) 220 How kind His thoughts to usward! 1809 COBBETT *Pol. Reg.* 22 April 618 To us-ward, both Parties are as much alike as two peas. 1881 SWINBURNE *Mary Stuart* I. ii, From France our friends Lift up their heads to usward.

(*b*) 1603 J. DAVIES *Microcosm.* 37 Sol..makes vs heavie going from vs-ward. 1902 *Westm. Gaz.* 8 Aug. 1/3 She went her way from usward.

**b.** With ellipse of prep.

1871 SWINBURNE *Songs bef. Sunrise, Eve Revolution* 70 Thy vesture wrought of ages legendary Hides usward thine impenetrable sleep.

**Ut** (ut, ɒt), *sb. Mus.* [L. *ut* 'that': see note on GAMUT. Cf. F., Sp., Pg., and It. *ut.*] The first note in Guido's hexachords, and of the octave in modern solmization, now commonly Do *sb.*[2]; the note C in the natural scale of C major.

Cf. also EFFAUT, GAMUT, G-SOL-RE-UT.

*c* 1325 in *Rel. Ant.* I. 292 Sol and ut and la. *c* 1550 *Armonye of Byrdes* 185 in Hazl. *E. P. P.* III. 194 Chaungyng their key From ut to rey. ?1596 BATHE *Brief Introd.* A v b, The next thing necessary to be knowne for the right naming of notes, is the place where that note standeth which is named Ut. 1645- [see MI]. *c* 1656 LOVELACE *To T. S.* iv, Poems (1904) 172 But yet the Spoaks by which they scal'd so high, Gamble hath wisely laid of Ut Re Mi. 1754- [see Do *sb.*[2]]. 1797 *Encycl. Brit.* (ed. 3) XII. 547/2 From the adjuncts of the mode, that is to say, the modes of its two fifths, which for *ut* are *fa* and *sol.* 1801 BUSBY *Dict. Mus.* s. v., Ut and do are always the tonic, or key-note, of the major-mode, and the..third of the minor mode. 1890 [see FA].

**b.** *Ut, re,* etc.: the notes of the gamut; also *transf.*, the 'gamut' or elements *of* something.

1588 SHAKS. *L. L. L.* IV. ii. 102 Olde Mantuan, Who vnderstandeth thee not loues thee not, *vt re sol la mi fa.* 1599 B. JONSON *Cynthia's Rev.* II. i, Your courtier elementary, is ..as it were in the alphabet, or *ut-re-mi-fa-sol-la* of courtship. 1728 CHAMBERS *Cycl.* s. v. *Note*, Of the seven musical Notes, ut, re, mi, fa, sol, la, si, the first six are ascribed to Aretine.

**Ut, Utal**, obs. ff. OUT *adv.*, UDAL.

**Utas**[1] (yū·tæs). Now *Hist.* Also 5 **vtaus**, **vtauce**, **vtase** (*Sc.* **wtast**, **wtes**), 5–7 **vtas** (7 **outas**), 6 **utais**, 7 **vtis**. [Reduced form of the pl. *utaves*: see OCTAVE *sb.*] **a**, **b.** = OCTAVE *sb.* 1 a, b.

1387, *c* 1420 [see OCTAVE *sb.* 1]. *c* 1430 *Pilgr. Lyf Manhode* III. xx. (1869) 146, I selle it by dayes, and bi wookes, bi vtases and bi quinsimes, bi monethes, and bi yeeres. 1463–93 [see OCTAVE *sb.* 1]. 1563 BECON *Reliques* 175 b, For..euery day of the Vtas an hundred days of pardon in remission of al their sinnes. 1599, 1610 [see OCTAVE *sb.* 1]. 1657 SPARROW *Bk. Comm. Prayer* 178 It was the custome of our fore-fathers to observe the Octave or Vtas of their high and principall Feasts. 1672 MANLEY *Cowell's Interpr.*, *Utas*,..is the eighth day following any Term or Feast,..and any day between the Feast and the Octave, is said to be within *the utas.* 1701 HODY *Hist. Councils* 368 The Octaves or..the Utas of S. Martin. 1762 *Gentl. Mag.* 567 These Octaves or Uta's [*sic*], as they are often called. 1810 *Stat. Realm* I. 390/1 This present Parliament holden..at the Utas of the Holy Trinity [1369]. 1833 NICOLAS *Chronol. Hist.* (1838) 102 The Octave or Utas of each Feast..is always the seventh day after it occurs; or the eighth day, if the day of the Festival be included.

*attrib.* 1453 *Paston Lett.* I. 257 Wretyn at Norwych, on the Utas day of Peter and Powll.

**c.** *transf.* A period of festivity; = OCTAVE 1 c.

1597–1602 [see OCTAVE 1 c].

**U·tas**[2]. Also 9 *dial.* **utis.** [Later var. OUTAS.]

†**1.** = OUTAS. *Obs.*$^{-1}$

1600 HOLLAND *Livy* 134 The Romanes were in dread of your *utas* and outcries.

**2.** *dial.* Clamour, din.

1875 A. PORSON *Quaint Words* 26 The hounds were here this marning and kicked up a deuce of a utis. 1910 *19th Cent.* May 901 She complains of a *utis* after the village club-feast or merrymaking—a loud, riotous noise.

**Ut-borewe**, etc., obs. ff. OUTBORROW.

**Ut-draȝen**, ME. var. OUTDRAW *v.*

† **Ute**, *v.* *Obs.* Forms: 1 **utun**, 1–2 **uton**, **utan**, 2–3 **uten**, **ute**, **vte** (3 **oute**). [Later form of OE. *witon, wuton*, originally subj. (= 'let us go') of OE. *gewitan* I-WITE *v.*[2]] An interjectional form used with an infinitive verb, having the force of a subjunctive, with the sense 'Let us —'.

*c* 888 K. ÆLFRED *Boeth.* xxxiv. § 7 Uton lætan þonne bion þa spræce. *c* 1000 *Ags. Gosp.* Matt. xvii. 4 Ȝyf þu wylt, uton wyrcean her þreo eardung-stowa. *a* 1175 *Cott. Hom.* 241 Ute we nu isi wice bioð ure ifo. *a* 1200 *Moral Ode* 333 Vte we us bi-werien wid þes wrecches worldes luue. *c* 1205 LAY. 20635 Uten we heom to liðe. *c* 1275 *Passion of our Lord* 173 in *O. E. Misc.* 42 Riseþ vp..and vte we heonne go.

**Ute**, var. OUTE *adv.* *Obs.* **Utebrast**, etc.: see OUTBURST *v.*, etc. **Utemest**, etc., obs. ff. UTMOST *a.* **Utenn wiþþ**, obs. var. OUTWITH.

**Utensil** (yute·nsil), *sb.* Forms: α. 5 **vtensele**, **utensyle**, 6 **-cyle**, **vtensyle**, 6–7 **-sile**, 7 **utensile.** β. 5 **vtensyl**, 6 **-sylle**, **utensille**, 7 **vtensil**, 7–8 **utensill**, 7– **utensil**; 5–6 *Sc.* **vtensel**, 6 **-cell**, **utencell**, 7 **vtensell(e.** [a. OF. *utensile*, etc. (14th c.; F. *ustensile*), a. med.L. *ūtēnsile* sb., f. L. *ūtēnsil-is* adj., fit for use, useful. Cf. It. *utensile*, Sp. and Pg. *utensilio.*

The stressing *u·tensil*, evidenced by metrical examples down to *c* 1800, is corroborated by Johnson and some later Dicts. down to 1835; but the present stressing appears in Bailey's Dict. (1730), and is supported by Ash, Todd, etc.]

†**1.** *collective sing.* Vessels or instruments for various domestic uses. Chiefly *Sc.* *Obs.*

*c* 1375 *Sc. Leg. Saints* xlvi. (*Anastasia*) 170 In it [*sc.* the prison] for to kepe vmquhile Of þe kechine ves vtensel [L. *coquinæ utensilia*]. 1411 *E. E. Wills* (1882) 18 Y be-qweythe to lucye my wyfe..alle þe vtensyl of myn hows, þat ys to say, in halle, in Chambre, in Pantrie and Botrie, in larder and Kechyn. 1428 *Reg. de Aberbrothoc* (Bann. Club) II. 58 Hal chawmyr kechyng and butre with swilk vtensele as the said John Vernour vsis. 1535 STEWART *Cron. Scot.* (Rolls) III. 222 Mony come him till,..With wyffe and barne, and all thair vtencell, As tha in Scotland euir mair sould duell.

**2.** Any article useful or necessary in a household; a domestic implement, vessel, or article of furniture; now *esp.*, an instrument or vessel in common use in a kitchen, dairy, etc.; † freq. *pl.*, = household goods.

α. 1484 CAXTON *Fables of Poge* i, He gaf to her all new utensyles to kepe houshold. *c* 1510 MORE *Picus* Wks. 6/1 Much siluer vessel and plate, with other..costly vtensiles of houshold. 1575 LANEHAM *Let.* (1871) 48 Kenelwoorth Castl..so fully furnisht of rich apparell, & vtensilez apted in all pointes to the best. 1611 COTGR., *Vtensile*, an vtensile; any implement,..or houshold stuffe. 1648 MASY in *Nightingale Ejected of 1662* (1911) 922 The enemie hath..spoyled my house, windowes, dores & all utinseles [*sic*].

β. 1542 *Test. Ebor.* (Surtees) VI. 160 All the utensilles nowe beinge at Snape. 1546 in *Eng. Gilds* (1870) 199 Certen other plate..with diuerse vtensylles. 1610 SHAKS. *Temp.* III. ii. 104 He ha's braue Vtensils..Which when he ha's a house, hee'l decke withall. *a* 1661 FULLER *Worthies, Yorks.* III. (1662) 186 Small utensils, as Salt-cellars, and the like. *c* 1710 CELIA FIENNES *Diary* (1888) 141 Ye stands, table, and fire utensills. 1767 A. YOUNG *Farmer's Lett. to People* 218 No expences are calculated for the dairy, such as wood, utensils, &c. 1771 SMOLLETT *Humph. Cl.* To Lewis 11 Oct., There was no furniture but the utensils of the kitchen. 1836 W. IRVING *Astoria* III. 47 The culinary utensils of the party. 1865 DICKENS *Mut. Fr.* I. vi, The tap and parlour..were provided with comfortable fireside tin utensils. 1904 *Verney Mem.* I. 550 Household utensils were apt to run short in the families of the English planters.

**b.** Any vessel († article, implement, etc.) serving a useful end or purpose.

1502 *Ord. Crysten Men* IV. (W. de W. 1506) X iij b, Vtensyles as lynnen cloth or wollen, flesshe, corne, & wyne. 1551 in Feuillerat *Revels Edw. VI* (1914) 62 Instrumentes vtensiles and other furniture..appertaynynge to the Lorde of Mysrule. 1554–5 — *Revels Q. Mary* (1914) 173 Hedpeces wepons and other vtensiles for maskes. 1660 WATERHOUSE *Arms & Arm.* 11 Coat-armours and other portable utensiles which we call *Insignia*. 1671 MILTON *P. R.* III. 336 Waggons fraught with Utensils of war. 1689 'PHILOPOLITES' *Grumble. Crew* p. ii, Gibbets you know, are Utensils of State. 1705 W. DERHAM in *Lett. Lit. Men* (Camden) 316 The utensils for observing the Quantities of Rain which fall. 1751 ELIZA HEYWOOD *Betsy Thoughtless* IV. 227 She..made her wearing apparel be also disposed of in proper utensils. 1805 *Act 45 Geo. III*, c. 30 § 10 By melting any metal..in any pot, crucible, or other utensil. 1858 HAWTHORNE *Fr. & It. Note-bks.* (1871) I. 2 A foot-warmer (a long, flat tin utensil, full of hot water) was put into the carriage.

*transf.* 1657 W. RAND tr. *Gassendi's Life Pieresc* II. 246 A large Library, and other literary utensils. 1691 RAY *Creation* I. (1692) 62 Fire..is..a Subject or Utensil of..various and inexplicable use. 1705 HEARNE *Duct. Hist.* (ed. 2) I. 190 The Reader will find plenty of necessary Utensils for the improvement of his Manners.

**c.** *esp.* An implement or tool useful to or used by an artisan, mechanic, farmer, etc.

**1604** R. CAWDREY *Table Alph.*, *Vtensils*, things necessary for our use..in a trade. **1659** W. CHAMBERLAYNE *Pharon.* IV. v. 337 The straitened 'prentice..Changes the baser utensils of trade For burnished arms. **1669** WORLIDGE *Syst. Agric.* 277 *Utensils*, Instruments used in any Art, especially Husbandry. **1693** EVELYN *De la Quint. Compl. Gard.* II. 178 If we find the Walks..kept neat and clean, and no Garden Tools or Utensils any where neglected. **1708** J. C. *Compl. Collier* (1845) 15 [In] sinking a Coal-Pit, what Utensils are requisite? **1774** *Act* 14 *Geo. III*, c. 71 § 1 The exportation of the several tools or utensils made use of in preparing..the Cotton and Linen Manufactures. **1791** SMEATON *Edystone L.* § 212 *note*, The tools and utensils contrived or adapted to the Edystone works. **1841** W. SPALDING *Italy & It. Isl.* III. 378 Agricultural implements, and utensils of trade. **1848** LYTTON *Harold* I. i, That tablinum..was now filled with..faggots, and farming utensils.

† **d.** *Mil.* In *pl.* = FREE-QUARTER. *Obs.*⁻⁰

**1702** *Milit. & Sea Dict.* (1711), *Utensils*, the Necessaries due to every Soldier, and to be furnish'd by his Host where he is quarter'd. They are, a Bed with Sheets, a Pot, a Glass or Cup to drink out of, a Dish, a Place at the Fire, and a Candle. [Hence in Phillips (1706) and James (1802).]

**3.** † **a.** A part of the human frame serving a special purpose. *Obs. rare.*

**1601** SHAKS. *Twel. N.* I. v. 264, I will giue out diuers scedules of my beautie. It shalbe Inuentoried and euery particle and vtensile labell'd to my will. **1664** POWER *Exp. Philos.* I. 67 The whole Body, and all the Organs and Utensils therein. **1675** BAXTER *Cath. Theol.* II. VIII. 156 Is not the whole frame of Humane Nature (and our Utensils) put into the hand and power of Christ the Redeemer.

**b.** One who is made use of; a useful person. *rare.*

**1678** OTWAY *Friendship in F.* v. i, A Sot, a Beetle, a Droan of a Husband, a mere Utensil. **1692** E. WALKER tr. *Epictetus' Mor.* xxx, I thus shall useless grow To those I love,.. Nor raise them to be Utensils of State. [**1794** WOLCOT (P. Pindar) *Remonstrance* 69 Yet is a King a utensil much wanted—A screw..to keep together The ship's old leaky sides in stormy weather.] **1896** T. HEALY in *Daily News* 14 Feb. 2/4 The first use the Unionist Government made of their Viceregal utensil.

**4.** A sacred vessel, furnishing, etc., belonging to, and esp. used in the services of, a church, temple, or other place of worship.

**1650** HOBBES *De Corp. Pol.* 150 All the Utensils of sacrifice and other holy Things, were ordered by Moses. **1660** JER. TAYLOR *Ductor* III. iv. rule vi. § 20 The Rulers office..may extend to sumptuousness, to ornaments of churches, to rich utensils, to splendor, to majesty. **1701** PRIDEAUX *Direct. Ch.-wardens* (1712) 30 What are not fixed to the Freehold of the Church, but are of the moveable Goods belonging thereto, are called the Utensils of the Church. **1751** *Affect. Narr. of Wager* 155 The Jesuits Church.., the Utensils of which are exceedingly valuable. **1805** FOSTER *Ess.* IV. iv. 164 Consecrated utensils stolen out of a temple. **1836** THIRLWALL *Greece* II. 52 In certain solemn processions..they were compelled to bear a part of the sacred utensils. **1877** J. D. CHAMBERS *Div. Worship* 249 The forms for Benediction of the Sacramental Utensils.

**5.** A stool for evacuation; a chamber-pot. Spec. *chamber utensil.*

**1699** GARTH *Dispens.* II. 24 The Springs of Life their former Vigour feel, Such Zeal he had for that vile Utensil. **1731** SWIFT *Strephon & Chloe* 173 The nymph..brings a vessel into bed: Fair utensil, as smooth and white As Chloe's skin. **1768–74** A. TUCKER *Lt. Nat.* (1834) II. 147 If Alexander and Cæsar could never be easy off the stool, I would not deny them that needful utensil. **1834** *Westm. Rev.* XX. 494 On being waked by her house on fire, [she] laid hold of the chamber utensil and rushed out. **1851** FLOR. NIGHTINGALE *Nursing* (ed. 2) 16 Any chamber utensil without a lid.

† **Utensil,** *a. Obs.* In 6 vtensel, -sile, 7 utensile. [ad. L. *ūtensil-is*: see prec.] Necessary for use, esp. in a household.

**1490** *Acta Dom. Conc.* (1839) 148/2 Johne..sall restore.. certane gudis vtensill and domicill. **1549** *Compl. Scot.* xvii. 145 Mettellis var meltit to mak vtensel veschel necessair to serue ane houshald. **1552** HULOET, Vtensile or necessarye to be vsed, *vtensilis*. **1617** MORYSON *Itin.* III. 219 The gift of vtensile goods made to the husband. *Ibid.*, In Misen the wife hath not the vtensile goods, which [etc.].

† **Utensilies,** *sb. pl. Obs.* [ad. L. *ūtensilia* things for use.] Utensils, esp. of a household.

**1496–7** *Act* 12 *Hen. VII*, c. 13 § 12 Implementis of Houshold..and utensilies of the same. **1509** *Bury Wills* (Camden) 109 All my ostylmentys, vtensiliez, and joell that to my hows bylonge. **1531** MORE *Dyaloge* (ed. 2) I. 8 b, Christ was serued with syluer & gold in the vessels vtensylys and ornamentes of his chyrche. **1602** *2nd Pt. Return Parnass.* I. ii. 128 If my kitchen want the vtensilies of viands.

† **Utensilment.** *Obs.*⁻¹ [-MENT; after *ustil-*, HUSTLEMENT.] = UTENSIL *sb.* 2.

**1428** *E. E. Wills* (1882) 78 All the vtensilmentes longyng to my kechyn.

**Uter, -ast,** obs. ff. UTTER, UTTEREST *adjs.*

**Ut-rage,** obs. form of OUTRAGE *sb.*

† **Uterine,** *sb.*¹ *Obs.*⁻¹ [ad. med.L. *uterīnus*, f. late L. *uterīnus* adj.: see next.] *pl.* Children or offspring of the same mother.

**1432–50** tr. *Higden* (Rolls) V. 29 Thei were [not] uterynes or childer of oon woman.

**Uterine** (yū·tĕrəin, -in), *a.* and *sb.*² Also 5–6 uteryne, 7 uterin. [a. OF. *uterin*, *-ine* (F. *utérin*, *-ine*), or ad. late L. *uterīnus* (whence It., Sp., Pg. *uterino*), f. L. *uterus* UTERUS.]

**A.** *adj.* **1.** Having the same mother, but not the same father. Also in fig. context.

**1432–50** tr. *Higden* (Rolls) V. 295 Medardus..and Gildardus, ..bothe breþer uteryne, borne in oon day. **1447** BOKENHAM *Seyntys* (Roxb.) 45 Melchy..Pantars brother.. Weddyd iacobes modyr & gat ely. So iacob & ely wer bretherne vteryne. *c* **1555** HARPSFIELD *Divorce Hen. VIII* (Camden) 174 To be taken not only of the brother by father and mother but of the uterine and half brother also. **1600** W. WATSON *Decacordon* (1602) 359 Saint Peter was the onely vterine, and germane brother to saint Andrew. *c* **1629** DONNE *Serm.* (1640) 621 If Sodome and Jerusalem were Sisters, Babylon and we may be so too; uterin sisters of one wombe. *a* **1695** WOOD *Ath. Oxon.* (1721) II. 1094/2 Walter Pope, uterine Brother to Dr. Joh. Wilkins. **1703** QUICK *Dec. Wife's Sister* 19 His uterine Sister. **1765–8** ERSKINE *Inst. Law Scot.* III. viii. § 8 Brothers or sisters of the deceased by the mother only, who are called *uterine*. **1844** W. K. KELLY tr. *Michelet's Hist. France* I. 561 The uterine sister of Henry III. **1860** EMERSON *Cond. Life* i. 11 People are born with the moral ..bias—uterine brothers with this diverging destination.

**b.** Related by blood through the mother. *rare.*

**1632** LITHGOW *Trav.* x. 503 Whose Vterine blood he is, and present Brother..sprung from one Mother. **1816** TUCKEY *Narr. Exped. R. Zaire* iv. (1818) 161 The property.. devolves to his brothers or uterine uncles. **1888** *N. & Q.* 7th Ser. V. 493/2 The direct lineal ancestress in the female line, or what is sometimes termed umbilical or uterine ancestress.

**c.** (See quot.) *rare*⁻¹.

**1882** A. MACFARLANE *Consanguinity* 11 The uterine system, that is, the system resulting from tracing kinship through females only.

**2.** *Surg.* Adapted for using or operating on or in the uterus or womb.

**1615** CROOKE *Body of Man* 239 Wee must proceede by the guide of a vterine probe. **1849** *Lancet* 29 Dec. 699/2 Dr. Routh exhibited to the Society three uterine scarificators. **1857** DUNGLISON *Dict. Med. Sci.* 851/2 *Sound, Uterine*, Uterine bougie. **1865** *Lancet* 29 April 465/1 The uterine tents made from dried stem of sea-tangle. **1875** KNIGHT *Dict. Mech.* 2685 Uterine dilator,..elevator, redressor, scarificator, speculum.

**3.** Of, pertaining or belonging to, the uterus; situated in, connected with, the womb.

**1646** SIR T. BROWNE *Pseud. Ep.* VII. vii. 352 In hot climates and where the uterine parts exceed in heat. **1728** CHAMBERS *Cycl.* s.v., From a Turgescency or Inflation of the Uterine Vessels. **1788** *Encycl. Brit.* (ed. 3) I. 744/2 The Fallopian or uterine tubes, which open into the cavity of the uterus. **1800** *Med. Jrnl.* IV. 191 In the fœtus, we note several contrivances for the uterine state. **1834** J. FORBES tr. *Laennec's Dis. Chest* (ed. 4) 665 The only arteries in which it can be supposed to be produced are the hypogastric, iliac, and uterine. **1838** *Lancet* 7 July 497/2 The diseases of the uterine organs. **1877** W. TURNER *Hum. Anat.* II. 519 A uterine venous plexus is arranged on and in the wall of the uterus.

**b.** Affecting, occurring or taking place in, the uterus.

*Uterine souffle*: see SOUFFLE, and cf. PLACENTAL 1.

*a* **1661** FULLER *Worthies*, *Somerset.* III. (1662) 20 Our Bath-waters..are good for uterine effects, proceeding from cold and windy Humours. **1669** W. SIMPSON *Hydrol. Chym.* 77 This exotick acidity coagulating the blood..is the author of most of their uterine infirmities. **1728** CHAMBERS *Cycl.* s.v., Maids that were..seiz'd with the Uterine Fury. **1752** SMELLIE *Midwifery* 142 Vomiting,..in a few,..prevails during the whole time of uterine gestation. **1771** *Encycl. Brit.* III. 163/1 Of the Immoderate Flux of the Menses, or Uterine Hæmorrhage. **1838** *Penny Cycl.* X. 333/2 The embryo..during the rest of its uterine life has been denominated the fœtus. **1839** C. WEST tr. *Naegele's Auscultation* 13 The uterine sound varies in its intensity..within a very short time. **1851** E. HAMILTON *Flora Homœop.* I. 111 Boerhaave..employed it in uterine diseases. **1889** *Buck's Handbk. Med. Sci.* VII. 448/1 This congestion causes..painful uterine contractions.

**c.** Suitable or adapted for remedying or aiding the uterus.

**1771** *Encycl. Brit.* III. 163/1 Uterine cathartics are aloes, myrrh, bryony, colocynthus [etc.]. **1849** *Lancet* 22 Dec. 661/2 A new uterine supporter. **1875** KNIGHT *Dict. Mech.* 2685/1 *Uterine douche*, a form of irrigator for the uterus.

**4.** Of the nature of a uterus.

**1841** T. R. JONES *Anim. Kingd.* 201 The exact nature of the uterine sacculus..is imperfectly understood.

**5.** Of vellum: Prepared from the skin of a fœtal or abortive calf or lamb.

**1870** ROCK *Text. Fabr.* p. cxxxv, That now rare kind of vellum called, among manuscript collectors, 'uterine'.

† **B.** *sb.* A medicine or herb remedial in uterine affections. *Obs.* Cf. UTERINE *a.* 3 c.

**1661** LOVELL *Hist. Anim. & Min.* 460 Uterines, in..flux, inflammation, scirrhus and ulcers of the womb. **1697** FLOYER *Eng. Baths* i. 18 In the *Mola Uteri*, let Women swim in salt Water, or apply the Steam of it in which Uterines are boyl'd. **1718** QUINCY *Compl. Disp.* 81 Some commend it as a good Uterine.

‖ **Uteritis** (yūtĕrəi·tis). *Path.* [mod.L., f. UTER-US + -ITIS.] Inflammation of the womb; metritis.

*c* **1840** *Encycl. Metrop.* (1845) VII. 771/1 Parts secondarily ..affected in the female [in gonorrhœa]. Inguinal glands producing Bubo. Uterus producing Uteritis.

**Utero-** (yū·tĕro), comb. form of L. *uter-us* UTERUS, occurring in various medical and surgical terms esp. with the sense 'of or pertaining to the womb and —', as **U:tero-abdo·minal** *a.*, relating to, suitable for, the uterus and the abdomen. **U:tero-inte·stinal** *a.*, affecting or occurring in the uterus and the intestines. **U:tero-ova·rian** *a.*, of or pertaining to the uterus and the ovary. **U:tero-peritone·al** *a.*, pertaining to, connecting, the uterus and the peritoneum. **U:tero-place·ntal** *a.*, pertaining to the uterus and the placenta. **U:tero-sa·cral** *a.*, pertaining to, connecting, the uterus and the sacrum. **U·terotome**, an instrument for incising the uterus. **Utero·tomy**, surgical incision of the uterus; hysterotomy. **U:tero-tra·ctor** *U.S.*, a kind of 'tractor' or forceps used in operating for vaginal hysterectomy. **U:tero-va·ginal, -vagi·nal**, *a.*, pertaining to, connected with, the uterus and the vagina. **U:tero-ve·sical** *a.*, of or pertaining to the uterus and the bladder.

Various other terms are given in recent American or medical Dicts., as *uterocervical*, *-copulatory*, *-deferent*, *-fixation*, *-lith*, *-mania*, *-pelvic*, *-pexy*, *-tubal*.

**1838** *Lancet* 21 April 125/2 The *utero-abdominal supporter. **1896** *Nomencl. Diseases* 199 Fistula. *a.* Utero-vesical. *b.* *Utero-intestinal. **1896** *Lancet* 4 Jan. 33/1 Rheumatoid arthritis was neither the cause nor the effect of *utero-ovarian disturbance. **1872** *Ibid.* 18 May 680/1 Case of *utero-peritoneal fistula. **1857** DUNGLISON *Med. Dict.* 721 The *utero-placental veins. **1859** *Todd's Cycl. Anat.* V. 707/1 As high up as the level of the *utero-sacral ligaments. **1863** WEISS *Catal. Surg. Instr.* Pl. xxix, Sim's *Uterotome..and Caustic Holder. **1846** BRITTAN tr. *Malgaigne's Man Oper. Surg.* 559 Incision of the Neck of the Uterus, or Vaginal *Uterotomy. **1890** *Retrospect Med.* CII. 111 A small, but important, detail is not to introduce the *utero-tractor into the uterine cavity. **1856** *Lancet* 2 Feb. 129/1 New *utero-vaginal plug. **1897** *Allbutt's Syst. Med.* II. 1092 The long combined utero-vaginal passage. **1822** GOOD *Study Med.* IV. 153 *Utero-vesical Prolapse. **1891** MOUILLIN *Surg.* 1346 The uterovesical pouch of peritoneum.

**U:tero-gesta·tion.** [See prec. and GESTATION.] The progressive development of the embryo in the womb from conception till birth.

**1775** A. HAMILTON *Pract. Midwifery* 70 During the whole term of Utero-Gestation. **1836–9** *Todd's Cycl. Anat.* II. 436/1 Utero-gestation in the Mammalia is terminated by parturition or the birth of the young. **1888** *Brit. Med. Jrnl.* 14 April 800/1 Acute intestinal obstruction complicating utero-gestation.

‖ **Uterus** (yū·tĕrŏs). Pl. ‖ uteri (yū·tĕrəi). [L.; whence F. *utérus* (Paré). Cf. It., Sp., Pg. *utero.*]

**1.** In the primates: The organ in which the young are conceived, developed, and protected till birth; the female organ of gestation; the womb.

**1615** CROOKE *Body of Man* IV. xiii. (1631) 222 It is called *Vterus* properly in women. **1638** A. READ *Man. Anat. Body of Man* 239 The hypogastricall veins,..as soone as they come to be implanted into the substance of the uterus, ..lose their owne coats. **1702** DRAKE in *Phil. Trans.* XXIII. 1236 The Observation and Experiment being made on the Uterus of a Cow. **1728** CHAMBERS *Cycl.* s.v. *Matrix*, The Cavity of the Uterus. **1770** *Med. Observ.* (1772) IV. 388 The History of a fatal Inversion of the Uterus. **1834** OWEN in *Phil. Trans.* CXXIV. 333 A Description of the Impregnated Uterus of the Kangaroo. **1837** BALY tr. *Müller's Physiol.* 1580 An examination of recently impregnated uteri. **1871** DARWIN *Desc. Man* I. iv. 123 In all mammals the uterus is developed from two simple primitive tubes.

*transf.* **1728** CHAMBERS *Cycl.* s.v. *Generation*, Every Herb and Tree bears its Seed..; which being thrown into the Earth, as into its Uterus, spreads forth its Roots.

**b.** In the lower female animals, fishes, or birds: The matrix; the ovary.

**1753** *Chambers' Cycl.* Suppl. s.v., Uterus of Fishes. **1839** *Penny Cycl.* XIII. 383/2 Leeches are oviparous. The ova remain in the uterus for some time. **1877** HUXLEY *Anat. Inv. Anim.* 178 The outer, or vaginal, end of the uterus [in *Turbellaria*]. **1878** F. J. BELL tr. *Gegenbaur's Comp. Anat.* 182 Special portions of the oviduct [in *Vermes*] function as a Uterus, by which name parts, very different morphologically, are known. **1880** GÜNTHER *Fishes* 166 The ends of the uteri open..into the cloaca.

**c.** (See quot.)

**1841** T. R. JONES *Anim. Kingd.* 200 The vulva [in leeches] ..leads into a pear-shaped membranous bag, which is usually, but improperly, named the uterus.

**2.** *Bot.* **a.** = PERICARP.

**1676** GREW *Anat. Flowers* vii. *heading*, The Time, in which the Uterus or Fruit and Seed-Case are formed. **1677** — *Anat. Fruits* III. v. § 1 The Fruit, strictly so called, is, A Fleshy Uterus, which grows more moist and Pulpy, as the Seed ripens. But the Seed-Case..is, A Membraneous Uterus.

† **b.** (See quot.) *Obs. rare*⁻¹.

**1776** J. LEE *Introd. Bot.* 396 *Stygma*, the female Uterus, at the Top of the Pistil, furnished with a moist Humour.

**c.** In Fungi: (see later quots.).

**1829** LOUDON *Encycl. Plants* 981 *Angiogastres.* Uterus finally bursting forth, separate from the receptacle. **1836** M. J. BERKELEY *Fungi* in *Smith's Eng. Flora* V. II. 19 *Uterus* sessile, bursting irregularly, marbled internally with anastomosing veins. **1866** *Treas. Bot.* 1197/2 *Uterus*, the volva or receptacle of certain fungals. **1895** M. C. COOKE *Study Fungi* 356/2 *Peridium*, the enveloping coat of a sporophore, or receptacle in which the spores are developed in a closed cavity. In Gastromycetes sometimes called the uterus, the contents being the gleba.

† **3.** A hollow or cavity. *Obs.*⁻¹

**1693** RAY *Three Disc.* 137 The *Tophus* it self must have vegetated, containing a cavity or *uterus* of the shape of the Tooth, into which an osseous humour,..filling the cavity of the *Uterus*, must there have coagulated.

**Ute-tan,** etc., obs. ff. OUT-TAKEN, etc. **Utface,** var. OUTFACE (surface) *Obs.* **Utfangthef(e, -theif,** etc., varr. OUTFANGTHIEF. *Obs.* **Uth,** obs. f. YOUTH. **Uthail, -ale, -all,** obs. ff. UDALL.

† **Uthe.** *Sc. Obs.*⁻¹ [For earlier **ōth*, a. ON. *óð-r* poetry, melody.] Harmony.

*c* **1465** *Liber Pluscardensis* XI. xi, Rycht as [all] stringis ar reulit in a harp In ane accord, and tunyt al be an uth. [Rhyming with *suth* 'sooth' and *muth* dull = MOTHE *a.*]

**Uthe,** obs. f. YOUTH. **Uþe:** see UNNE *Obs.* **Uðe,** var. YTHE (wave) *Obs.* **Uthel(ler,** obs. ff. UDAL(LER. **Uther,** etc., obs. f. OTHER, etc.; obs. or dial. f. UDDER. **Uthes,** var. OUTAS *sb. Obs.*

† **Uþwite.** *Obs.* [OE. *úþwita*, f. *úþ-* (Goth.

*unþa-*) away, beyond + *wita* one who knows, WITE *sb.*] A wise man; a sage.

*c*888 K. ÆLFRED *Boeth.* xxxiii. § 4 Swa swa ure uðwita sæde, Plato. *c* 1000 *Menologium* 166 in *O. E. Chron.* (1892) I. 278 Swa hit foregleawe ealde uþwitan ærer fundan. *c* 1200 ORMIN 7083 Þa þatt sohhtenn Jesu Crist Wæren Mægy ȝehatenn,..Upwitess swiþe wise.

† **U·tible,** *a.* [ad. L. *ūtibilis*, f. *ūtor* to use, employ.] That may be used; useful, serviceable.

**1623** COCKERAM, *Vtible*, profitable. **1656** BLOUNT *Glossogr.* ? **1711** (*title*), Proposals by the Utible Society, for the Insurance on Marriages, by a weekly Dividend.

**Utile** (yū·təil), *a.* Now *rare*. Also 5–6 **vtyle**, 6 **vtyll, utyle, utille.** [a. OF. (F.) *utile* (13th c.), ad. L. *ūtilis*, f. *ūtī* to use. Cf. It. *utile*, and OF., Pr., Sp., Pg. *util*.] Useful, profitable, advantageous. Also const. *to, unto*.

**1484** CAXTON *Fables of Æsop* I. x, Theyre felauship [*sc.* of evil folk] is not good ne vtyle. **1518** H. WATSON *Hist. Oliver of Castile* (Roxb.) B 4, To whome it semeth good and vtyll for the prosperyte of bothe partyes. *c* **1532** DU WES *Introd. Fr.* in *Palsgr.* 1072 Of all meates the best and most utille to the body of man is of capons. **1578** BANISTER *Hist. Man* v. 74 The most pure and vtile substaunce. **1653** H. COGAN tr. *Pinto's Trav.* lxx. 284 To shew that the conquest thereof would have been far more utile unto us. **1678** GALE *Crt. Gentiles* IV. III. 5 Means utile and conducible to the promoting of Divine glorie. **1839** J. ROGERS *Antipopopr.* i. 69 An order that He has given..to employ our energy in the utile pursuit of following. **1894** *Advance* (Chicago) 24 May, There is the cost value...There is the productive or utile value.

*absol.* **1685** COTTON tr. *Montaigne* (1711) III. 2 Wherein he quitted the utile for the honest.

† **Uti·lious,** *a. Obs.*⁻¹ [f. L. *ūtili-s* UTILE *a.* + -OUS.] Useful.

**1652** F. KIRKMAN *Clerio & Lozia* 190 This Treason was so utilious to this Barbarian, and so prejudicial to ours, that he ..retook the Towns.

**Utilitarian** (yutilitēə·riăn), *sb.* and *a.* [f. UTILIT-Y, after sbs. and adjs. in *-arian*. Hence Pg. and It. *utilitario*, F. *utilitaire*.]

**A.** *sb.* One who holds, advocates, or supports the doctrine of utilitarianism; one who considers utility the standard of whatever is good for man; also, a person devoted to mere utility or material interests.

**1781** BENTHAM *Let.* Wks. 1843 X. 92/1 He is a utilitarian, a naturalist, a chemist, a physician. **1821** GALT *Ann. Parish* xxxv, I thought they had more sense than to secede from Christianity to become Utilitarians. **1835** WORDSW. *Yarrow Revisited*, etc. 326 A right in the people (not to be gainsaid by utilitarians and economists) to public support when [etc.]. **1860** MAURY *Phys. Geog.* (Low) iv. 268 The utilitarian who compares the water-power that the falls of Niagara would afford if applied to machinery. **1875** JOWETT *Plato* (ed. 2) IV. 29 We are therefore justified in calling Socrates the first utilitarian.

**B. 1.** *adj.* Of philosophy, principles, etc.: Consisting in or based upon utility; *spec.* that regards the greatest good or happiness of the greatest number as the chief consideration or rule of morality.

**1802** BENTHAM *Let.* Wks. 1843 X. 390 A new religion would be an odd sort of a thing without a name: accordingly there ought to be one for it—at least for the professors of it. Utilitarian..would be the more *propre*. **1814** *New Brit. Theatre* I. 50 The sublime ideas of the utilitarian philosophy. *Ibid.* 227 The philanthropy of the true utilitarian principles. **1841** GLADSTONE *State in Relat. Ch.* (ed. 4) I. 107 A reason quite irreconcilable with the utilitarian theories. **1861** MILL *Utilit.* iv. (1863) 51 The utilitarian doctrine is, that happiness is..the only thing desirable, as an end. **1869** LECKY *Europ. Mor.* I. 18 They were at once profoundly antipathetical to Utilitarian morals.

**b.** Of or pertaining to utility; relating to mere material interests.

**1830** *Westm. Rev.* Jan. 3 So far from its being proscribed by Utilitarian notions, they demand its existence. **1853** KANE *Grinnell Exp.* x. (1856) 77 Their application to the fishing grounds..would be a matter of large utilitarian interest. **1859** W. S. COLEMAN *Woodlands* 58 Turning from the picturesque or romantic, to the utilitarian view of this tree. **1873** MRS. BROOKFIELD *Not a Heroine* I. 23 From a utilitarian point of view.

**c.** In quasi-depreciative use: Having regard to mere utility rather than beauty, amenity, etc.

**1847** H. MILLER *First Impr. Eng.* xvi. 294 For the hill-top cottage..I found a modern hard-cast farm-house, with a square of offices attached, all exceedingly utilitarian, well kept, stiff, and disagreeable. **1876** MISS BRADDON *J. Haggard's Dau.* I. 29 A good garden of the old-fashioned utilitarian type.

**2.** Of persons: Holding or advocating utilitarian views, principles, etc.; aiming at, supporting, or advancing utilitarianism; also, preferring mere utility to beauty or amenity.

**1802** [see 1]. **1828** BENTHAM *Let.* Wks. 1843 XI. 2/2 The accomplished utilitarian statesman. **1834** K. H. DIGBY *Mores Cath.* v. x. 360 The favour of utilitarian philosophers, or of self-interested reformers. **1862** SIR B. BRODIE *Psychol. Inq.* II. i. 32 The mere utilitarian philosopher, having his views limited to some immediate practical result. **1873** MILL *Autobiog.* 79 [In the winter 1822–3] the name I gave to the society I had planned was the Utilitarian Society. It was the first time that any one had taken the title of Utilitarian; and the term made its way into the language from this humble source.

**3.** Of times: Marked or characterized by prevalence of utilitarian doctrine, principles, or views. (Freq. with *age*.)

**1828** CARLYLE *Goethe* P 16 In these hard, unbelieving utilitarian days. **1839** *Morn. Herald* 3 Sept., The cold 'philosophy' of a money-getting utilitarian age. **1854** *Poultry Chron.* II. 251/1 In these utilitarian days, every thing seems to..play its proper part.

Hence **Utilita·rianly** *adv. rare*⁻¹.

**1878** *Fraser's Mag.* XVII. 665 A new tower..built, utilitarianly, of common yellow brick.

**Utilita·rianism.** [f. prec. + -ISM. Hence F. *utilitarianisme* (1885).] Utilitarian doctrine, principles, theories, or practices; *spec.* in *Philos.*, the doctrine that the greatest happiness of the greatest number should be the guiding principle of conduct.

**1827** G. S. FABER *Sacr. Cal. Prophecy* (1844) I. 202 Intent only upon the present,..men will..devote themselves..to a life..of sordid godless Utilitarianism. **1839** DICKENS *Nickleby* xxxvi, But knockers may be muffled for other purposes than those of mere utilitarianism. **1861** MILL *Utilit.* ii. (1863) 16 Utilitarianism, therefore, could only attain its end by the general cultivation of nobleness of character. **1878** W. H. DALL *Later Preh. Man* 31 The growth of sentiment (as opposed to savage utilitarianism), which is characteristic of the human mind in all ages.

**Utilita·rianist.** *rare*⁻¹. [f. as prec. + -IST.] A utilitarian.

**1882** H. J. GAMBLE *W. Dalton* 20 A distinguished utilitarianist of the present day.

**Utilita·rianize,** *v. rare.* [f. as prec. + -IZE.] *trans.* To turn to a utilitarian end or purpose; to invest with a utilitarian character.

**1852** MRS. C. MEREDITH *Home in Tasmania* I. 143 The colonists, sad matter-of-fact people that they are! who utilitarianize everything. **1907** *Jrnl. Educ.* Oct. 671/1 Utilitarianize your secondary education.

**Utility** (yuti·lĭti), *sb.* Also 5–6 **vtilite** (6 -ie), 6 **utillitie** (7 *Sc.* **vtillatie**), **utilite**, 7 **-ie.** [a. OF. *utilitei*, *utelite* (1291), *utilitet* (12th c.), etc. (F. *utilité*), ad. L. *ūtilitāt-*, *ūtilitās*, f. *ūtili-s* UTILE *a.* Cf. Sp. *utilidad*, Pg. *-idade*, It. *utilità*.]

**1.** The fact, character, or quality of being useful or serviceable; fitness for some desirable purpose or valuable end; usefulness, serviceableness.

In frequent use *c* 1540–*c* 1650, and from *c* 1755. The constructions in the two earliest quots. are obsolete.

*c* **1391** CHAUCER *Astrol.* II. § 26 The vtilite to knowe the Assenciouns in the rihte cercle. *a* **1425** tr. *Arderne's Treat. Fistula* 55 Maners of curacions..to be noted vnder compendiousnez to þe vtilite of helyng. *c* **1440** *Gesta Rom.* xciv. 424 (Add. MS.), I clad my seruaunte, that is, my manhode, nought but to vtterly vtilite and necessite. **1528** R. THORNE in Hakl. *Voy.* (1589) 251 The commoditie and vtilitie of this Nauigation. *c* **1566** J. ALDAY tr. *Boaystuau's Theat. World* S ij, The wonderfull Invention, Utilitie and Dignitie of Printing. **1603** HOLLAND *Plutarch's Mor.* 19 Where..the attractive pleasure and sweetenesse of speech, is not without some fruit nor void of utilitie. **1651** HOBBES *Leviathan* IV. xliv. 349 The utility of Prayer for the Dead. **1758** JOHNSON *Idler* No. 93 P 1 He discussed the utility..of the Islington turnpike. **1762–71** H. WALPOLE *Vertue's Anecd. Paint.* (1786) II. 266 The circular court is a picturesque thought, but without meaning or utility. **1801** S. & HT. LEE *Canterb. T.* IV. 418 A cottage..more calculated for utility than ornament. **1841** ELPHINSTONE *Hist. Ind.* II. 71 The extent and utility of his public works. **1871** MOZLEY *Univ. Serm.* vi. (1876) 124 The older poetical view brought in more the utility and active force of nature. **1878** JEVONS *Prim. Pol. Econ.* 15 Everything which forms a part of wealth must be useful, or have utility.

**b.** In the phrase *of* (..) *utility*.

*c* **1440** *Pallad. on Husb.* III. 524 Rootys smale of noon vtilite Cutte of. **1514** BARCLAY *Cyt. & Uplondyshman* (Percy Soc.) 5 Fayre warkes of grete utylyte. **1598** BARRET *Theor. Warres* v. i. 139 Which thinke you to be of most vtilitie in the warres? **1759** ROBERTSON *Hist. Scot.* II. P 32 This victory..was of no real utility. **1778** *Learning at a Loss* II. 11 Five thousand other Instruments of Equestrian Utility. **1801** S. & HT. LEE *Canterb. T.* IV. 424 Those in whose hands..[life] is an engine of either private or public utility. **1831** D. E. WILLIAMS *Life & Corr. Sir T. Lawrence* II. 42 The habit..is of the greatest utility. **1857** RUSKIN *Pol. Econ. Art* 11 The two great objects of utility and splendour.

**c.** *Philos.* The ability, capacity, or power of a person, action, or thing to satisfy the needs or gratify the desires of the majority, or of the human race as a whole.

**1751** HUME *Princ. Mor.* v. 73 In common Life..the Circumstance of Utility is always appeal'd to. **1780** BENTHAM *Princ. Legisl.* i. (1789) p. iii, An action then may be said to be conformable to the principle of utility..when the tendency it has to augment the happiness of the community is greater than any it has to diminish it. **1785** PALEY *Moral & Pol. Philos.* I. vi, Or must we give up our principle, that the criterion of right is utility? **1830** MACKINTOSH *Progr. Eth. Philos.* vi. Wks. 1846 I. 194 A theory founded on Utility.. requires that we should cultivate..those other habitual dispositions which we know..to be generally the source of actions beneficial to ourselves and our fellows. **1861** MILL *Utilit.* ii. (1863) 9 The creed which accepts as the foundation of morals, Utility, or the Greatest Happiness Principle. **1883** H. SIDGWICK *Pol. Econ.* I. iii. 77 There is another difficulty lurking in the conception of Utility as a measure of wealth.

† **2.** The quality of being advantageous or profitable, profit, advantage, use. Freq. const. *of* (a person, etc.). *Obs.*

In frequent use *c* 1535–*c* 1580, esp. coupled with *profit*.

*c* **1440** *Pallad. on Husb.* III. 485 This wey is light and more vtilite. **1455** *Paston Lett.* I. 365 Charges born and payd.. for the avauncement of his conquest, the good and utilite of hym, of his seyd royaume and duchie forseid. **1471** CAXTON *Recuyell* (Sommer) 120 This is ayenst your prosperite and utilite. **1509** HAWES *Past. Pleas.* VI. (Percy Soc.) 25 You shall, quod she, my scyence wel lerne, In tyme and space, to your gret utilite. **1533–4** *Act 25 Hen. VIII*, c. 9 § 1 To the greate profete and vtilitie of a greate number of the Kynges Subjectes. **1576** LAMBARDE *Peramb. Kent* Ded. ¶ iii b, What vtilitie foloweth the studie of Hystories. **1657** *Rec. Old Aberd.* (New Spalding Club) I. 94 The hundreth merkis ..left in legacie be..George Clerk..for the vse and vtillatie of the said cittie. **1698** KEILL *Exam. Th. Earth* 63 Choosing such..positions of things as bring with them the greatest good and utility to the Universe. **1752** J. LOUTHIAN *Form of Process* (ed. 2) 238 Circuit Courts was [*sic*] introduced for the manifest Utility of the Lieges.

**3.** A useful, advantageous, or profitable thing, feature, etc.; a use. Chiefly in pl.

**1483** CAXTON *Cato* a viij b, By the comyn wele of a londe is saued all synguler prouffytes and utylyties. **1489** — *Faytes of A.* I. vi. 14 For the regarde of somme particuler vtilite. **1502** ARNOLDE *Chron.* Index (1811) 6 That money ..to be chosen..for necessites and vtylites of the same cite. **1541** COPLAND *Guydon's Quest. Chirurg.* B iij b, The scyence of the Nathomy is..nedefull to the Cyrurgyen for .iiij. vtylyties. **1586** A. DAY *Eng. Secretorie* I. (1595) 142 Iudge by your owne decernment..howe greatlie you are ledde awrie, in thus careleslie roaming vpon others vtilities. **1604** E. G[RIMSTONE] *D'Acosta's Hist. Indies* VII. i. 496 If therefore there were no other fruite in the Historie..of the Indians, but this common vtilitie. **1659** PEARSON *Creed* i. 34 Which no man who considereth the uses and utilities of every species can deny. **1688** BOYLE *Final Causes Nat. Things* iii. 82 Of several of his creatures, whereof men.. make some uses, they shall hereafter discover other utilities. **1775** HARRIS *Philos. Arrangem.* ix. 196 The Knowledge of Nature, and the Utilities of common Life. **1800** W. TAYLOR in Robberds *Mem.* (1843) I. 355 Genius never was remarkable for teaching the practical utilities. **1876** HOLLAND *Seven Oaks* xii. 169 It had lifted him above the bare utilities of a house, so that he could see the use of beauty. **1908** S. E. WHITE *Riverman* xxviii, Heinzman wanted the improvements..sold as a public utility to the highest bidder.

**b.** *Pol. Econ.* (See quots., and cf. 1 c.)

**1848** MILL *Pol. Econ.* I. iii. I. 56 What we produce..is always..an utility. Labour is not creative of objects, but of utilities. **1904** R. T. ELY & WICKER *Elem. Princ. Economics* 81 A good or utility is anything which can satisfy a human want.

**4.** Short for *utility actor* (sense 5 a).

**1885** JEROME *On the Stage* 80 A 'lead' may get three pounds..., and a young 'utility' thinks himself very well off indeed on a guinea. **1889** H. B. BAKER *London Stage* II. 168 She was playing utility, that is to say, going on for anything, at the Park Theatre.

**5.** *attrib.* passing into *adj.*: **a. Utility actor**, an actor of the smallest speaking-parts in a play; so *utility-business*; **utility man**, (*a*) a utility actor; (*b*) *U.S.* a substitute capable of taking any position in a baseball team (*Webster's Dict.*, 1911).

**1851** MAYHEW *Lond. Labour* I. 383/1 At one of the theatres,..I eventually rose to a 'general utility man', at 12*s.* per week. **1860** *Cornh. Mag.* II. 748 Known respectively as 'eccentric comedian' and 'utility actor'. *Ibid.*, The leading lady..and the utility man will all act in the same way. **1879** *Era Almanack* 46 The drudgery of 'utility' business.

**b.** Of a dog, fowl, etc.: That is bred, reared, or kept to serve a useful end or object as distinct from purposes of beauty, display, show, etc.

**1877** STABLES *Pract. Kennel Guide* 96 The Points of Utility Dogs, including the Newfoundland, the Collie [etc.]. **1903** H. FRANCKLIN (*title*), Incubating and Rearing Utility Fowls. **1904** *Daily Chron.* 10 Feb. 3/2 The utility poultry keeper. **1908** *Westm. Gaz.* 29 Sept. 4/2 A utility vehicle.. good for ten or even fifteen years' hard service.

**U·tilizable,** *a.* Also **-isable.** [a. F. *utilisable*, or f. UTILIZE *v.* + -ABLE.] Capable of being utilized.

**1881** 'FORTIOR' *Fair Trade Cry* 13 The utilizable lands of America. **1889** J. A. BERLY tr. *Reynier's Voltaic Accumulator* 138 The mean utilisable fall of potential in normal discharge.

**Utilization** (yūtiləizē·ʃən). Also **-isation.** [a. F. *utilisation* (1812): see next and -ATION.] The action of utilizing; the fact of being utilized.

**1847** WEBSTER. **1864** LOWELL *Fireside Trav.* (1909) 57 A man of genius, but of genius that evaded utilization. **1881** SIR W. THOMSON in *Nature* XXIV. 434 The utilisation of tidal energy. **1894** GRANT ALLEN in *Westm. Gaz.* 12 June 2/1 The whole history of the human race on earth is a continuous history of successive utilisations.

**Utilize** (yū·tiləiz), *v.* Also **-ise.** [ad. F. *utiliser* (1792), ad. It. *utilizzare* (1760), f. *utile* UTILE *a.*: see -IZE, and cf. Sp. *utilizar*, Pg. *-isar*.]

**1.** *trans.* To make or render useful; to convert to use, turn to account.

Rare before 1858. '*Utilize* is fast antiquating *improve*, in the sense of "turn to account"' (1873 F. Hall *Mod. Eng.* 167).

**1807** J. BARLOW *Columbiad* IX. 683 [To] Improve and utilise each opening birth, And aid the labors of this nurturing earth. **1824** *Westm. Rev.* April 454 Izmail and Kilia.. are respectively able to nullify or to utilize the northern mouth of the Danube. **1860** RUSKIN *Mod. Paint.* V. IX. xi. § 22 Let all physical exertion..be utilized. **1882** PITMAN *Mission Life in Greece & Pal.* 123 Her services could not be utilised for missions.

**2.** *intr.* To make oneself of use. *rare*⁻¹.

**1883** HOWELLS *Register* i, Come in here and sympathize a little!..*Miss S.* No; you come out here and utilize a little.

Hence **U·tilized** *ppl. a.*, **U·tilizing** *vbl. sb.*

**1859** in *N. & Q.* 3rd Ser. VI. 306/1 Odd proposals for the utilising of power. **1881** P. GEDDES in *Nature* XXIV. 524 The application of the utilised matter and energy by the given society.

**U·tilizer.** Also **-iser.** [f. prec. + -ER¹.] One who or that which utilizes.

**1873** DAWSON *Earth & Man* xv. 380 Man was..to be..a care-taker and utiliser..of the things given to him. **1883** *Standard* 21 Nov. 5/3 Not a man of science, but only a utiliser of scientific results. **1884** *Health Exhib. Catal.* 66/1 Register Stove fitted with the Oxford Heat Utilizers.

‖**U·tinam.** *Obs.* [L. *utinam* oh that! would that!, f. *uti* (*ut* conj.) + *nam* indeed.] An earnest wish or fervent desire.

**1643** SIR T. BROWNE *Relig. Med.* § 24 'Tis not a melancholy *Utinam* of mine owne, but the desires of better heads. **1646** — *Pseud. Ep.* I. x. 38 Nor can the will which hath a power to runne into velleities..have any *utinam* of this. **1718** *Entertainer* No. 9. 56 Our Religion is pure and undefiled... A Glance or a *Utinam*, in Christianity, are Criminal.

†**U·ting,** *vbl. sb. Obs.* [Later var. of *yowting, veoting*, YOTING *vbl. sb.*] The action of steeping grain in the process of brewing. Only attrib. in *uting-fat, -room, -vat*.

**1610** R. VAUGHAN *Water-Workes* E 4, Vting-rooms, Garnars, Matting-roomes [etc.]. *Ibid.* K 3, The water from my Vting-vats will doe the like. **1702** *Act* 1 *Anne* Stat. 2, c. 3 § 3 All Cisterns Uting-Fats Utensils and other Vessels. **1720** *Lond. Gaz.* No. 5864/3 Corn..steeped in any Cistern or Uting-Fat. **1800** *Act* 41 *Geo. III*, c. 6, Every Maltster..should wet or steep his Barley..in the Cistern, [or] Uting-fat.

**Utis,** variant of UTAS.

†**U·tlagary.** *Obs.* [a. AF. *utlagarie, -erie*: see OUTLAWRY.] = OUTLAWRY I.

**1440** *Paston Lett.* I. 41 As the seide utlagare was certyfyed. **1567** *Lanc. Wills* (Chetham Soc.) II. 82, I have byn divers tymes wrongfullye sued and brought to the poynt of utlagari. **1642** tr. *Perkins Prof. Bk.* i. § 27. 12 Attainder of Felony..by utlagery, by verdict and by confession. **1660** *Act 12 Chas. II*, c. 12 ¶ 12 Any person..whose Conviction, Utlagary or Attainder is by this Act discharged.

**Utlagh(e, -laȝe, -lahe, -law(e,** obs. ff. OUTLAW. **Utlarie, -y(e, -lawry(e,** obs. ff. OUTLAWRY. **Utleden,** var. OUTLEAD *v. Obs.*

†**Utlega·tion.** *Obs.*⁻¹ [ad. med.L. *utlagātion-*, n. of action f. *utlagāre*: see OUTLAW *v.*] The legal process by which a person was outlawed. (Cf. OUTLAWRY I.)

**1678** BUTLER *Hud.* III. i. 1521 When to a Legal Utlegation You turn your Excommunication.

**Utlepe, -leph, -lete,** obs. ff. OUTLEAP *sb.*, etc.

†**Utmer, utmore,** *a. Obs. rare.* [f. *utm-est* UTMOST *a.*, with comparative ending: see -MORE, and cf. OUTMER *a.*] = OUTER *a.* I.

**1382** WYCLIF *Ezek.* xlvi. 21 That thei bere not out in to the vtmer house [1388 to the outermere halle]. — *Matt.* xxii. 13 Sende ȝee hym into vttermore [*v.r.* vtmore, vtmer] derknessis. *Ibid.* viii. 12.

**Utmost** (*ʌ·tmōᵘst, ʌ·tmǒst*), *a.* and *sb.* Forms: α. 1 ute-, utmest (*Northumb.* wut-), 3 ute-, 4 ut-, 5, 6 *Sc.* vtmest; 5 *north.* and *Sc.* vtmast, *Sc.* 6 vt-, 9 utmaist; 4–7 vt-, 5–6 vtte-, 7– utmost (6 vtmoste, vtmoost). β. 3–4 otemost, 4–5 ottemoste; 4 ot-, ottemeste. [OE. *ūtemest, ūtmest* (rare, and chiefly northern, variants of the usual *ȳte-, ȳtmest*), a double superlative (cf. FOREMOST, INMOST) from *ūte* or *ūt* OUTE, OUT *advs.* + *-m-est*: see -MOST. Cf. the later OUTMOST *a.*

In Layamon 11023 *utemæste* prob. represents OE. *ȳtemeste*. The ME. forms with *ote-, otte-, ot-* seem to imply an earlier *ŭte-* with shortened vowel (as in Icel. *útan* from *ūt*). The shortening in *utmost* may be partly due to the double consonant, and partly to the influence of UTTER *a.*]

**I. 1. a.** Situated farthest from the centre; occupying, lying at, or dwelling in the extreme bound or bounds; most external or remote in position or location; outermost, uttermost; OUTMOST *a.* I.

α. *c* **950** *Lindisf. Gosp.* Matt. xxii. 13 Sendas hine in ðiostrum ðæm utmestum. *c* **1100** *Ælfred's Boeth.* xix. (Bodl. MS.), Þeah hit nu ȝebyriȝe þæt ða utemestan ðioda eowerne naman up ahebban. *c* **1320** *Sir Orfeo* 357 (Auchinleck MS.), Al þe vtmast wal Was..schine as cristal. *c* **1400** *Destr. Troy* 5487 Beyten is out in the orient the vtmast syde. *c* **1425** WYNTOUN *Cron.* III. i. 8 Ane of his tais with The vtmast endis be þe lith Quyt wes smyttyn of þaim. *c* **1450** *Godstow Reg.* 106 His ende vttemost toward the tenement of the forsaid Vincente Menge. **1526** TINDALE *Matt.* viii. 12 The children of the Kingdom shalbe cast out in to the vtmoost dercknes. **1590** SPENSER *F. Q.* II. x. 12 Corineus had that Prouince vtmost west To him assigned. **1618** LAWSON *New Orchard* (1623) 46 We admit without the fence, of Walnuts in most plaine places, Trees middle-most, and..Elmes vtmost. **1660** BARROW *Euclid* I. prop. 21 The utmost points of one side of a triangle. **1697** DRYDEN *Æneis* IX. 221 Where the foes their utmost guards advance. **1729** T. INNES *Crit. Ess.* (1879) 63 The utmost extremities of the north of Britain. **1798** S. & HT. LEE *Canterb. T.* II. 326 The utmost limit of creation! **1820** SHELLEY *Prometh. Unb.* IV. 372 It..doth pass Into the utmost leaves and delicatest flowers. **1859** TENNYSON *Elaine* 525 Knights of utmost North and West. **1877** RUSKIN *St. Mark's Rest* iv. (1894) 50 The entire tablet varied to its utmost edge.

*fig.* **1667** SOUTH *Serm.* (1715) II. 24 Which surely must reach the utmost Thoughts of any Atheist whatsoever.

β. **1297** R. GLOUC. (Rolls) 11433 Þe castel hii asailede,..& brake þe otemoste wal. **1387** TREVISA *Higden* (Rolls) I. 303 In þe vttermeste (MS. α. otmeste) ende of all þe erþe. *a* **1390** *Wycliffite Bible* Num. xxii 36 (MS. Bodl. 959), [A] toun..sette in ye otmest coostys of Arnon. **1398** TREVISA *Barth. De P. R.* xv. clv. (Bodl. MS.), Þe ottemoste norþe..of Germania. *c* **1450** *M. E. Med. Bk.* (Heinrich) 93 Pile þe barke þe ottemoste [*v.r.* ottemoste rynde] awey.

†**b.** Of garments: Outermost; exterior. *Obs.*

**1553** *Respublica* 1774 Doe of your vtmoste robes eche one. **1584** T. HUDSON *Du Bartas' Judith* IV. (1611) 47 Her vtmost robe was colour blew Cœlest.

**c.** Furthest extended; greatest in extent, length, measure, etc.

**1709** FELTON *Diss. Classics* (1718) 12 To put forth Your Hand to the utmost Stretch, and reach whatever You aspire at. **1746** FRANCIS tr. *Horace, Epist.* I. xvi. 108 Death is..That utmost Course, where human Sorrow ends. **1791** COWPER *Odyss.* XI. 454 A night of utmost length. **1844** KINGLAKE *Eothen* xvii, All the whole earth that I could reach with my utmost sight and keenest listening was still.

**2.** That is of the greatest or highest degree; of the largest amount, number, etc.; extreme.

Somewhat rare before 1590; in freq. use since 1710.

*a* **1325** *Prose Psalter* lvii. 6 God shal defoulen her teþe..; our Lord shal breke þe uttemast [*Dublin MS.* ottermast] tuels of þe wicked. *c* **1375** *Sc. Leg. Saints* xii. (*Mathias*) 113 Scho let hym wyt þe vtmast thinge, þat he wes but a fundlynge. **1482** *Monk of Evesham* xxli. (Arb.) 53 He was takyn..to the vtmest peynys and ponissement of dethe. **1526** *Pilgr. Perf.* (W. de W. 1531) 2 b, The vttemost perfeccyon that man may attayne to. **1586** MARLOWE *1st Pt. Tamburl.* II. iii, With amitie we yeeld Our vtmost seruice to the faire Cosroe. **1610** *Chester's Triumph* B 4, What e're our more then strained vtmost-All Can possibly performe, performe we shall. **1628** MAY *Virg. Georg.* III. 84 Her temptations make Two stubborne Bulls..with their Hornes to try their utmost deedes. **1667** MILTON *P. L.* I. 103 His utmost power with adverse power oppos'd In dubious Battel. **1704** EVELYN *Diary* 7 Sept., This day was celebrated the thanksgiving..with the utmost pomp and splendour. **1782** MISS BURNEY *Cecilia* v. iv, Her mind was now in a state of the utmost confusion. **1805** WORDSW. *Waggoner* II. 73 The utmost anger of the sky. **1833** HT. MARTINEAU *Brooke Farm* iii. 35 The utmost profit of a cow. **1876** GEO. ELIOT *Dan. Der.* I. vii, His antigropelos, the utmost approach he possessed to a hunting equipment.

**3.** Latest in order or time; last, final. Now *rare.*

*c* **1460** *Towneley Myst.* xxv. 248 Mary, me mynnys, thi moder hight, the vtmast ende of all thy kyn. **1526** TINDALE *Matt.* v. 26 Till thou have payed the vtmost [1611 vttermost] farthing. **1590** SPENSER *F. Q.* II. i. 49 In these sad words she spent her vtmost breath. **1591** — *Ruins of Time* 45 From their first vntill their vtmost date. **1642** MILTON *Apol. Smect.* 41 Many wise men have miscarried in praising great designe before the utmost event. **1670–1** MARVELL *Corr.* Wks. (Grosart) II. 367 Censure..against those who, after an utmost day set, shall persist to absent themselves. **1672** DRYDEN *Conq. Granada* II. i, 'Till I have found the last and utmost Foe. **1691** SWIFT *Ode Athenian Society* xi, When the sad melancholy muse Stays but to catch his utmost breath. **1772** PRIESTLEY *Inst. Relig.* (1782) I. 82 They prolong life to the utmost term of nature. **1809–12** MAR. EDGEWORTH *Absentee* iv, He would use it [*sc.* the power] to obtain the utmost penny of his debt. **1818** BYRON *Juan* I. lxxx, I..hear these freedoms form the utmost list Of all o'er which such love may be a ranger. **1856** KANE *Arct. Expl.* I. xv. 171 Grating it down nicely,..and adding the utmost oil as a lubricant.

**II.** *absol.* and as *sb.*

In *Lindisf. Gosp.* Mark v. 23 *in utmestum* is used to render the L. *in extremis* (= at the point of death).

**4.** That which is most outward, distant, or remote; the farthest part, district, limit, etc., *of* an extent or area. Now only *arch.*

*c* **825** *Vesp. Psalter* cxxxviii. 9 In ðem utmestan sæs. *a* **950** *Ritual Dunelm.* (Surtees) 55 Oð to vtmeste earðes. **1382** WYCLIF *Job* xxxvi. 30 The vtmost of the se he shal couere. **1382** — *Acts* i. 8 ȝe schulen be witnessis to me..to the vtmeste [*v.r.* vtermest] of erthe. **1614** W. B. *Philosopher's Banquet* (ed. 2) 43 The vtmost of the taile is poyson. **1615** G. SANDYS *Trav.* 177 A City..on the utmost of the ridge of a hill. **1887** MORRIS *Odyssey* XI. 13 At last unto the utmost of the Ocean-stream we came.

†**b.** *sb. pl.* Remotest parts *of* the earth, etc. *rare.*

**1382** WYCLIF *Ps.* cxxxiv. 7 Bringende out cloudis fro the vtmostis [*v. r.* vttermostis] of the erthe. **1382** — *Isaiah* vii. 18 The fleȝe, that is in the vtmostes [*v.r.* vttermostis] of the flodus of Egipt.

**5.** That which is greatest or of the highest degree; the most or greatest possible or attainable in respect *of* force, skill, etc.; the utmost point, extreme limit or degree, *of* something.

**1472** *Cov. Leet Bk.* 377 Thei..seid thei wold abyde with the Maire..to the vtmost of herr goodes in that mater. **1526** TINDALE *Acts* xxiv. 22 When Lisias..is come, I will know the vtmost of youre matters. **1594** *1st Pt. Contention* C 4, To morrow we will ride to London, And trie the vtmost of these Treasons forth. **1596** SPENSER *F. Q.* VI. i. 38 Thinking the vtmost of their force to trie. **1622** MABBE tr. *Aleman's Guzman d'Alf.* II. 346 The Painter..shew'd therein the vtmost of his skill. **1667** EARL ORRERY *St. Lett.* (1742) 331 The utmost I aimed at..was to tell your grace what others told me. **1752** HUME *Ess. & Treat.* (1777) I. 95 The utmost we have to boast of are a few essays. **1764** REID *Inquiry* i. 75 The utmost which the human faculties can attain. **1805** J. SPAULDING *Universalism* 129 That the damned suffer the utmost of their desert. **1838** THIRLWALL *Greece* V. 153 Thebes had accomplished the utmost she could now reasonably aim at. **1855** BAIN *Senses & Int.* I. ii. § 23 The utmost that can be said in the present state of our knowledge.

**b.** With possessive adjs.: The highest, greatest, or best of one's ability, power, etc.; the very most. Freq. with *do.*

*c* **1611** CHAPMAN *Iliad* II. 119 Comethen,..and fly to our loved home; for now, nor ever, shall Our utmost take in broad-wayed Troy. **1646** GAULE *Cases Consc.* 118 Their utmost is but to produce a..false species of things. **1660** SOUTH *Serm.* (1715) IV. 23 Nor will it suffice..to rally up all one's little Utmost into one Discourse. **1690** LOCKE *Hum. Und.* IV. xix. § 15 A Man, having..done his utmost to inform himself in all Particulars,..may [etc.]. **1708** ADDISON *Pres. State of War* 26 Let us perform our utmost,..and we shall overwhelm 'em. **1785** BURNS *To Rev. John M'Math* xvi, [One who] to his utmost would befriend Ought that belang'd ye. **1818** COBBETT *Pol. Reg.* XXXIII. 633 Will you do your utmost to obtain justice? **1856** MISS YONGE *Daisy Chain* I. xviii, His work, after he goes to Oxford, will be doing his very utmost—and you know what an utmost that is. **1887** P. MᶜNEILL *Blawearie* 136 It taxed to its utmost the ingenuity of the rival wooers.

**c.** As *sb.* An extreme amount, degree, or limit.

**1856** [see prec. sense]. **1863** JEAN INGELOW *Poems* 24 Forever yawns before our eyes An utmost—that is veiled.

**6.** The end, finish, or issue *of* something.

**1603** SHAKS. *Meas. for M.* II. i. 36 See that Claudio Be executed;..let him be prepar'd, For that's the vtmost of his pilgrimage. **1666** BOYLE *Orig. Forms & Qual.* 264 An Accident robb'd me of my Glasse, before I could see the utmost of the Event. **1674** [see UTTERMOST *a.* 6].

**7.** *To the utmost,* to the extreme or uttermost degree, extent, capacity, or limit. Also const. *of* (one's power, etc.).

*c* **1450** *Mirk's Festial* I. 91 Gracyously he woll þat a man be demed wyth mercy and not to þe vtmast here. **1526** TINDALE *1 Thess.* ii. 16 For the wrath off God is come on them, even to the vtmost. **1613** SHAKS. *Hen. VIII*, v. iii. 146 Some of ye..Would trye him to the vtmost, had ye meane. **1685** BOYLE *Enq. Notion Nat.* vii. 266, I grew weary before I had prosecuted it to the utmost. **1738** WESLEY *Ps.* v. vi, Thy wrath on the rebellious Race Shall to the utmost come. **1756** C. LUCAS *Ess. Waters* III. 307 Let us pursue our enquiries to the utmost. **1834** HT. MARTINEAU *Demerara* iv. 46 He was sure to..torment the animal to the utmost. **1860** MOTLEY *Netherl.* ii. I. 59 He would keep his pledge to the utmost. **1873** F. HALL in *Scribner's Monthly* VI. 465 The sages..have certainly consulted his comfort to the utmost.

(*b*) **1596** *Edward III*, IV. v. 86 That same man..keepes it [*sc.* his word] to the vtmost of his power. **1659** *Nicholas Papers* (Camden) IV. 147, I shall to the vttmost of my power constantly endeauour to doe him right. **1729** LAW *Serious C.* vi. 90 So sure is it, that we are to do them to the utmost of our power. **1802** MRS. E. PARSONS *Myst. Visit* II. 245 The good woman..fortunately succeeded to the utmost of her wish. **1875** MANNING *Mission H. Ghost* xii. 346 Let us to the utmost of our power, submit our will to the will of God.

**8.** *At the utmost* († *at utmost*), at the very most in respect of time, quantity, etc. Cf. MOST *a.* 6.

**1619** in Foster *Eng. Factories India* (1906) I. 143, 15 dayes stay there, or 20 at utmost. **1643** TRAPP *Comm. Gen.* xi. 7 [He] beautified it, or, at utmost, inlarged it. **1722** WHISTON *The. Earth* III. iii. 247 The Modern Age of Men at the utmost is not 80. **1753** *Chambers' Cycl.* Suppl. *App.* s.v. *Vultur*, The head..has, at the utmost, only a downy matter on it. **1818** CRUISE *Digest* (ed. 2) II. 418 At the utmost it was in the discretion of the Court.

Hence †**U·tmostness.** *nonce-use.*

**1674** N. FAIRFAX *Bulk & Selv.* 7 With all that earnestness of threatning, that may beget in man the utmostness of dread.

**Utnemis:** see OUTNEME *a.* and *adv.*

**Utnume(nn, -liȝ:** see OUTNUMEN(LY.

†**Utole,** var. OUT-TOLL *Sc. Obs.* (Cf. OUT-PENNY.)

**1742** in Kilkerran *Decisions Crt. Sessions 1738–52* (1775) 504 The resignation of an annual-rent out of a tenement in Aberdeen in the year 1720, being made with the symbol of a penny utole.

**Utopia** (*yutōᵘ·piă*). [mod.L. (More, 1516), f. Gr. οὐ not + τόπ-ος a place: see -IA¹, and cf. EUTOPIA. Hence It., Sp., Pg. *Utopia*, F. *Utopie*.]

**1.** An imaginary island, depicted by Sir Thomas More as enjoying a perfect social, legal, and political system.

**1551** (*title*), A fruteful and pleasaunt Worke of the beste state of a publyque weale, and of the newe yle called Utopia; written in Latine by Syr Thomas More knyght [publ. 1516], and translated into Englyshe by Raphe Robynson. **1570** FOXE *Bk. Martyrs* (ed. 2) 1156/2, I do not..thinke, that..there is any such fourth place of Purgatory at all (vnles it be in M. Mores Vtopia). **1607** A. BREWER *Lingua* II. vi, I remember in the Country of Utopia, they use no other kind of artillery. **1625** BACON *Ess., Usury* (Arb.) 544 So as that Opinion must be sent to Vtopia. **1685** CROWNE *Sir C. Nice* I. Dram. Wks. 1874 III. 270 He will find it is a dream fit for nothing but Utopia. **1692** BENTLEY *Boyle Lect.* 66 Once upon a time,..in the land of Utopia, there was a dialogue between an oak and a cedar. **1725** [MRS. E. HAYWOOD] (*title*), Memoirs of a certain Island adjacent to the Kingdom of Utopia. **1751** J. BROWN *Shaftesb. Charac.* 65 But of this infallible race I know none, except the inhabitants of Utopia. **1818** [see CACOTOPIA]. **1837** MACAULAY *Ess., Lord Bacon* (1897) 402 An acre in Middlesex is better than a principality in Utopia. **1895** LUPTON *More's Utopia* 115 Plate, Reduced facsimile of the woodcut of the Island of Utopia.

*transf.* **1802–12** BENTHAM *Ration. Judic. Evid.* Wks. 1843 VI. 206 The law is an Utopia—a country that receives no visits, but [etc.].

**b.** *transf.* Any imaginary, indefinitely-remote region, country, or locality.

**1610** TH. TH[ORPE] *Healey's St. Augustine's City of God* Ded., Then [in translating Hall's *Mundus Alter et Idem*, he treated] of a deuised Country scarse on earth, now of a desired Citie sure in heauen; then of Vtopia, now of Eutopia. **1646** SIR T. BROWNE *Pseud. Ep.* III. xii. 132 Some say it liveth in Æthiopia, others in Arabia, some..in Utopia, for such must that be which is described by Lactantius. **1684** J. P. tr. *J. Ludolphus' Hist. Ethiopia* (ed. 2) 46 Ignorant where this River rises,..whether in Asia, in Africa, or in Utopia. *a* **1779** WARBURTON *Div. Legat.* II. § 4 Wks. 1788 I. 206 A fabulous relation of a voyage to the imaginary island of Panchæa, a kind of ancient Utopia.

**2.** A place, state, or condition ideally perfect in respect of politics, laws, customs, and conditions.

**1613** PURCHAS *Pilgrimage* (1614) 708 The reports of this his voyage savour more of an Vtopia, and Plato's Commonwealth, then of true Historie. **1642** CHAS. I in Rushw. *Hist. Coll.* (1692) I. 727 That new Vtopia of Religion and Government into which they endeavour to transform this Kingdom. **1691** NORRIS *Pract. Disc.* 177 To contemplate all this not..as an uncertain Reversion, or imaginary Vtopia, but as a state that will shortly and certainly be. **1738**

WARBURTON *Div. Legat.* I. 272 No romantic impracticable Utopia. **1760–72** H. BROOKE *Fool of Qual.* (1792) II. 213 But the law-suits..will not permit me to go in search of my Utopia. **1818** SHELLEY *Julian* 179 'Aye, if we were not weak—and we aspire How vainly to be strong!' said Maddalo: 'You talk Utopia.' **1871** MORLEY *Condorcet* in *Crit. Misc.* Ser. I. 78 To find adequate gratification in the artificial construction of hypothetical utopias. **1883** *Manch. Exam.* 22 Nov. 5/2 Ingenious speculators who hope to reach Utopia by the nationalisation of the land.

**b.** An impossibly ideal scheme, esp. for social improvement.

*a* **1734** NORTH *Lives* II. 364 Young men, for want of experience,..create Utopias in their own imagination, and calculate according to their present fancy. **1843** MARRYAT *M. Violet* xliii, These are not the wild utopias of a heated imagination. **1869** LECKY *Europ. Mor.* I. 180 Averse to all enthusiasm, mysticism, utopias, and superstition.

**3.** *Comb.*, as *Utopia-maker*, *-monger*.

**1821** *Edin. Rev.* XXXV. 320 The fantastic brain of some Utopia-monger. **1901** GLOVER *Life & Lett. in 4th C.* 362 The general satire,..no doubt a fling at the Utopia-makers.

Hence **Uto·pia-ize** *v. intr.*, to conceive or form impossibly ideal schemes. *nonce-word.*

**1853** MRS. GORE *Dean's Daughter* III. 57 A Virginia Hargreave, born to Utopia-ise over a Bostonian tea-table, concerning triumphs to be achieved.

**Utopian** (yutōu·piăn), *a.* and *sb.* [ad. mod.L. *Utopian-us* (More, 1516): see prec. and -AN.]

**A.** *adj.* **1.** Of or belonging to the imaginary island of Utopia or its people.

**1551** ROBINSON *More's Utopia* Ep. (1895) 1 This boke of the vtopian commen wealth. **1556** *More's Utopia* Printer to Rdr. (Arb.) 168 The Vtopian Alphabete. **1622** J. TAYLOR (Water P.) *Sir G. Nonsence* Wks. (1630) Aa j b, He..began to declare in the Vtopian speech, what I haue here..Translated. **1633** ROWLEY *Match at Midn.* v. I 1 b, Two Vtopian Trunks, full of gold and Iewels. **1681** (*title*), A Pleasant Battle between two Lap-dogs of the Utopian Court. **1808** CAYLEY tr. *More's Utopia* II. 7 That I should anticipate him in what belongs to the Utopian Commonwealth. **1895** LUPTON *More's Utopia* 117 On this and other repellent features of the Utopian character, as drawn by More.

†**b.** Having no known location; existing nowhere. *Obs. rare.*

**1609** in Capt. Smith *Wks.* (Arb.) 637 It hath beene to the Spaniards more fearefull then an Vtopian Purgatory. **1678** CUDWORTH *Intell. Syst.* 60 They must be imagined to subsist in certain intermundane spaces and Utopian regions without the world. **1689** SWIFT *Ode to Sir W. Temple* i, Search out this Utopian ground, Virtue's *terra incognita*.

†**c.** Having no assigned diocese or sphere of work. *Obs.*⁻¹

**1709** BINGHAM *Antiq.* IV. vi, The Nullatenenses of latter Ages, as Panormitan calls Titular and Utopian Bishops.

**2.** Possessing or regarded as having impossibly or extravagantly ideal conditions in respect of politics, customs, social organization, etc.

In this and next sense occas. with small letter.

**1613** PURCHAS *Pilgrimage* (1614) 520 Yea, no Vtopian State comparable to theirs. **1647** *Mercurius Anti-pragmaticus* No. 6. 4 They are like to wander forty yeeres..ere they arrive in their Utopian Paradise. **1651** C. WALKER *Hist.* III. 14 To these..they entrust the Administration of this Utopian Commonwealth. **1768** TUCKER *Lt. Nat.* (1834) II. 302 The introduction of an Utopian state. **1782** H. WALPOLE *Vertue's Anecd. Paint.* IV. 284 When he was laying out so magnificent, charitable, and philosophic an Utopian villa. **1855** KINGSLEY *Westw. Ho!* xix, When we have babbled together of Utopian governments in days which are now dreams to me. **1856** H. ROGERS *Ess.* II. viii. 380 Considered as a possible political structure..Plato's 'Republic' deserves to be considered the most Utopian that ever entered the mind of man.

**b.** Involving, based or founded on, imaginary or chimerical perfection; impossibly ideal, visionary.

**1621** BURTON *Anat. Mel.* To Rdr. 58 Vtopian parity is a thing to be wished for rather then effected. **1643** PRYNNE *Sov. Power Parl.* App. 1 A new Utopian absolute Royall Prerogative..not bottomed on the Lawes of God or the Realm. **1646** J. COOK *Vind. Law* 28 Thats but a Vtopian consideration, a possibility which never comes into Act. **1659** BP. WALTON *Consid. Considered* 72 This, I doubt, will prove an Utopian conceit. **1762** KAIMES *Elem. Crit.* ii. (1774) I. 35 For confuting such Utopian systems without the fatigue of reasoning. **1798** FERRIAR *Illustr. Sterne* iii. 59 He indulges himself in an Utopian sketch of a perfect government. **1806** H. SIDDONS *Maid, Wife, & W.* III. 6 The sentiments which inspired me may be laughed at as Utopian. **1849** C. BRONTË *Shirley* ix, Marriage! I cannot bear the word: it sounds so silly and utopian. **1877** BURROUGHS *Taxation* 22 They have regarded any attempt to practise absolute equality as Utopian.

**3.** Of persons: That belongs to or dwells in a Utopia. *rare*⁻¹.

**1620** J. TAYLOR (Water P.) *Jack a Lent* Wks. (1630) 113/2 As Nymshag an ancient Vtopian Philosopher declares.

**b.** That conceives, proposes, or advocates impracticably ideal projects or schemes for social welfare, etc.; believing in or aiming at the perfecting of polity or social conditions.

**1597–8** DONNE *Let. to Sir H. Wotton* 46 If men..Durst looke for themselves..They would like strangers greet themselves, seeing than Utopian youth, growne old Italian. **1661** COWLEY *Cromwell* Wks. 1906 II. 373 You are..a Theoretical Common-wealths-man, an Utopian Dreamer. **1680** BUTLER *Characters* (1908) 24 A Republican is a civil Fanatic, an Utopian Senator. **1691** BAXTER *Nat. Ch.* xii. 52 As capable of Governing one Kingdom, as an Utopian College of Bishops (that some dream of). **1857** W. SMITH *Thorndale* v. iii. (1858) 427 An Eclectic and Utopian Philosopher. **1868** PEARD *Water-farm.* xi. 114 We are not so Utopian as to assert that [etc.].

**B.** *sb.* **1.** A native or inhabitant of Utopia; a dweller in some Utopia. Also *Comb.*

**1551** ROBINSON tr. *More's Utopia* II. (1895) 218 The wyttes therefore of the Vtopians..be maruelous quycke. **1597** HOOKER *Eccl. Pol.* v. xxxvi. § 4 Such suttle opinions as few but Vtopians are likely to fall into. **1614** RALEIGH *Hist. World* III. viii. § 1 They liued Vtopian-like, saue that they vsed no other occupation than Warre. **1684** BURNET tr. *More's Utopia* Pref. A 7 The precaution used in Marriages among the Utopians. **1771** J. ADAMS *Diary* 10 Nov., The good humor,..and wisdom of the Utopians, is charming. **1857** W. SMITH *Thorndale* IV. v. (1858) 312, I know not precisely how his Utopians intend to deal with war. **1905** *Edin. Rev.* Oct. 426 The admiration of the Utopians..was by no means confined to the strictly classical authors.

**2.** One who conceives, proposes, or introduces schemes supposed or intended to bring about improved or perfect social and political conditions, etc.; an advocate of social reform.

*a* **1873** LYTTON in *Life* (1883) I. 101 My grandfather..in youth..was a Utopian, and remained to the last much more than a 'Whig'. **1878** SEELEY *Stein* II. 363 Stein..was never the utopian here described. **1887** J. C. MORISON *Serv. Man* p. xxiv, He looks with coldness on Utopians who are equally ignorant of capital, labour, or hard work.

Hence **Uto·pianist**, = UTOPIAN *sb.* 2.

**1854** J. S. C. ABBOTT *Napoleon* (1855) II. xxix. 556 What seemed a crime to the eyes of Utopianists. **1876** *Contemp. Rev.* xxviii. 447 Neither abandoned nor disregarded by a few devoted Utopianists.

**Utopianism** (yutōu·piăniz'm). [f. prec. + -ISM.]

†**1.** A Utopian idea or condition. *Obs.*⁻¹

*a* **1661** HOLYDAY *Juvenal* (1673) 194 Plato indeed would have his cittizens ambidexters:..this was but one of his vtopianismes.

**2.** The body of views, aims, or tenets of Utopians; impossibly ideal schemes for the amelioration or perfection of social conditions, etc.

**1802–12** BENTHAM *Ration. Judic. Evid.* (1827) IV. 69 Such an improvement that the stamp of Utopianism..threatens to render the acceptance of it next to hopeless. **1833** CHALMERS *Const. Man* (1835) I. vi. 237 The abortive enterprises of wild yet benevolent Utopianism. **1879** KAUFMANN *Utopias* 258 The superiority of the most recent forms of Utopianism over previous schemes of social improvement.

**Uto·pianize** (yutōu·piănəiz), *v.* [f. as prec. + -IZE. Cf. UTOPIA-IZE *v.*] *trans.* To render Utopian; to form a Utopia of.

**1834** [implied in next]. **1913** *Public Opinion* 26 Dec. 715/1 The international aspect of Utopianising the modern world.

Hence **Uto·pianizer**, one who projects or conceives a Utopian state or polity.

**1834** SOUTHEY *Doctor* ccxli, Like most Utopianisers the legislator of this Columbia had placed his Absolute King and his free People under..strict laws.

**Uto·piast.** [f. UTOPIA + -(I)ST.] = UTOPIAN *sb.* 2.

**1854** tr. *Lamartine's Celebr. Char.* II. 384 The visionary Utopiasts, who advocate a purely metaphysical form of government. **1887** *Westm. Rev.* Jan. 130 It is the weakness of Utopiasts..to place themselves outside the pale of their own system.

†**Uto·pical,** *a. Obs. rare.* [f. UTOP-IA + -ICAL.] Impracticable; chimerical.

**1620** BP. HALL *Hon. Marr. Clergy* III. xiii. 805 King Edgars Vtopicall decree. *c* **1628** — *Beauty & Unity of Ch.* (1634) II. 368 Let no idle Donatist..dreame hence of an Utopicall perfection. **1628** — *Rem. Wks.* (1660) 20 There is no freedom with these unquiet dispositions, but in..their own utopical prescriptions.

**Utopism** (yū·tŏpiz'm). [f. as prec. + -ISM.] = UTOPIANISM 2.

**1888** *Cycl. Political Sci. & U. S. Hist.* III. 258/2 It is utopism to believe that the state will have more unity, more harmony,..because [etc.]. **1901** *Field* 19 Oct. 606/2 What remains of impracticable Utopism that may cling to this new project.

**Utopist** (yū·tŏpist). [f. as prec. + -IST. Cf. F. *utopiste* (1857), It., Sp., Pg. *Utopista*, and UTOPIANIST.] = UTOPIAN *sb.* 2.

**1845** LEWES *Hist. Philos.* I. 100 Like the Utopists of modern days, he [*sc.* Plato] has developed an *à priori* theory of what the State should be. **1881** MORLEY *Cobden* xxix. II. 268 Men..who..thought that the existing government..was better than the anarchy of utopists, anarchists, and talkers. **1898** *Salesian Bulletin* 15 Feb. 404 The indefatigable utopist of abandoned youth.

†**U·touth,** *prep.* and *adv. Sc. Obs.* Forms: 4–6 ututh, -outh, 5 -owth, 6 utoth; 4–6 vt-, wtouth (5 vttouth), 5 vtouthe, 6 vtowth; 4–5 otouth (5 otow, otowth, outhouth), 5 oututh, 6 -outh; 5 vteuthe, 6 uteucht, utewcht (6 wtew). [Sc. var. of OUTWITH.]

**A.** *prep.* **1.** Without, outside of, in respect of position.

*c* **1375** *Sc. Leg. Saints* xxviii. (*Margaret*) 68 Scho..gefine wes to fostir & fede wtouth the towne. **14..** *Burgh Laws* vii. in *Sc. Acts Parlt.* I. (1844) 334/2 He sall noch mote ututh þe burgh. **1478** *Acta Auditorum* (1839) 59/2 [He] nocht being lauchfully warnit to his defenss and seruit vteuthe þe schire. **1536** [see OUTWITH *prep.* 1]. **1557** *Peebles Burgh Rec.* (1872) 237 Vnfremen that duellis..vtouth the burgh.

**2.** Out of, out or away from, throughout, in respect of motion.

**1375**, *c* **1375** [see OUTWITH *prep.* 1 b]. **1530** *Burgh Rec. Edinb.* (1871) II. 37 The said seiknes..spreddis vtouth the toun in diuers placis. **1534** BELLENDEN *Livy* II. vi. (S.T.S.) I. 147 Þai durst put na thing vtouth þe wallis.

**B.** *adv.* Without; on the outside; outwardly.

**1375** BARBOUR *Bruce* II. 299 Till thaim wtouth send thai sone, And bad thaim herbery thaim that nycht. *c* **1375** *Sc. Leg. Saints* xxxii. (*Justin*) 170 A lytil vngument he hym tacht, & bad hyme ga..& þe wallis oututh ennoynt. **1398** *Munim. de Melros* (Bann. Cl.) 489 My demaynis..with al þe appourtenaunce vtouth and enovth. **1455** in *Charters* &c. *Edinb.* (1871) 80 Baith in the watter and vtouth. **1491** *Cartular. St. Nicholai Aberdon.* (New Spald. Cl.) I. 255 Nay chaplane of the College nor vtouthe. **1512** *Acc. Ld. High Treas. Scot.* IV. 348 Ane coup..nettit with gold of florising utewcht. **1532** *Reg. Privy Seal Scot.* II. 190/2 Assemblies to be had within our realme or utouth.

*transf.* **1453** *Dunfermline Reg.* (Bann. Cl.) 341 Þe quhilkis ..I will all vtrali be excludit and neuer to be herd in jugement na vtouth. **1496** *Acta Dom. Conc.* II. 23 Decerning the sammyn to be of nane availe..in tyme tocum in jugment nor utouth.

**Utrack**, etc.: see OUTRAKE, etc.

†**Utra·lity.** *nonce-word.* [f. L. *uter, utr-*, which (of two), after NEUTRALITY.] Tendency to favour both sides; inclination towards either party.

**1642** W. PRICE *Serm.* 2 Apostacy and neutrality, or rather utrality (if you will pardon the word).

**Utraly**, obs. Sc. var. UTTERLY.

**Utraquism** (yū·trăkwiz'm). *Hist.* [f. as next + -ISM.]

**1.** The doctrine or tenets of the Utraquists.

**1861** LD. ACTON *Lett.* (1906) 186 In Bohemia Utraquism was the national faith. **1892** *Athenæum* 2 Jan. 10/1 From the dawn of Utraquism to its eclipse..in the disaster of the White Mountain in 1620.

**2.** The use or employment of two languages on an equal footing. *rare*⁻¹.

**1897** *Speaker* 10 April 392/2 The [Austrian] concession..[*sc.* of officially recognising Czech] is spoken of as sanctioning 'the *utraquism* of German and Czech'.

**Utraquist** (yū·trăkwist), *sb.* and *a.* [ad. mod. L. *Utraquista*, f. L. *utraque* each, both (in the phrase *sub utrāque speciē* 'under each kind': see SPECIES *sb.* 2, KIND *sb.* 13 b). Cf. -IST, and F. *Utraquiste.*]

**A.** *sb.* **1.** *Hist.* = CALIXTIN 1.

**1836** *Pop. Encycl.* I. 814/1 *Utraquists*, a sect of Hussites in Bohemia. **1855** MILMAN *Lat. Chr.* VI. 248 They were called the Utraquists, as insisting on the Eucharist in both elements. **1881** STANLEY *Chr. Instit.* v. 95 When the Bohemian Utraquists fought with desperate energy to recover the use of the cup.

**2.** 'One who composes in both Latin and the vernacular' (Webster, 1911).

**B.** *adj.* **1.** *Hist.* Belonging to the Utraquists; demanding, insisting on, or advocating the receiving the Communion in both kinds.

**1894** F. I. ANTROBUS tr. *Pastor's Hist. Popes* III. 214 The Utraquist Clergy. **1900** *Pilot* 27 Oct. 539/1 The Hussites..were pre-eminently utraquist.

**2.** Speaking or using both or two languages.

**1867** *Chambers's Encycl.* IX. 686/1 The name Utraquist is still applied to certain districts or villages in Bohemia and Moravia..to convey that..*both languages*, Bohemian and German, are spoken.

Hence **U·traquistic** *a.*

**1894** F. I. ANTROBUS tr. *Pastor's Hist. Popes* III. 216 This oath was thoroughly Catholic, and left no room for any Utraquistic interpretation.

**Utrecht** (yū·trekt, ü·trext). Also *Sc.* 5 **Vtt-, Out-, Owtrecht, Outrech, -rik, 7 Utrik.** The name of a town and province in Holland, used attrib. in the sense 'coined, made, etc., at Utrecht', as †*Utrecht gulden, noble.*

**1494** *Halyburton's Ledger* (1867) 52 An Vttrecht gudlyn and a Gentis gudlyn. **1497** *Ibid.* 125 Item lent hym..7 Outrecht guldynis. **1604** *Extr. Burgh Rec. Stirling* (1887) 108 Aucht haill Utrik nobles.

†**b.** *ellipt.* or as *sb.* A Utrecht gulden. *Obs.*

**1493** *Halyburton's Ledger* (1867) 31 Item resauit fra him..3 Outrikis, price 4s. **1498** *Ibid.* 249 Gyffyn the Archden..at his partyn, 10 Outrech...Som of thir Owtrechtis, 2 li. 1s. 8.

**c.** **Utrecht velvet**, a strong, thick kind of plush made of worsted, mohair, or mohair and cotton, used in upholstering furniture, carriages, etc.; furniture plush.

**1848** H. R. FORSTER *Stowe Catal.* 252 Armchairs, covered with Utrecht velvet. **1897** *Daily News* 14 June 6/6 Green Utrecht velvet upholstered oak furniture.

†**U·trechted,** *pa. pple. Obs.*⁻¹ [f. prec. + -ED.] Having its seaward defences destroyed, as stipulated in the Treaty of Utrecht (1713).

**1748** H. WALPOLE *Lett.* (1846) II. 217 Dunkirk to remain as it is, on the land side; but to be Utrecht'd again to the sea.

**Utrely**, obs. Sc. f. UTTERLY *adv.*

†**U·tricide.** *Obs.*⁻¹ [ad. L. *ūtricīda*, f. *ūtri-s*, *ūter* leathern bottle, vessel of skin: see -CIDE 1.] One who stabs an inflated vessel of skin.

**1566** ADLINGTON *Apuleius* 30 That I, after the slaughter of so many enemies,..might embrace..not an homicide but an utricide. [**1879** LEWIS & SHORT, *Utricida*, one who cuts skins or bags in pieces, a skin-slayer, utricide.]

**Utricle** [1] (yū·trik'l). [ad. F. *utricule* (18th c.), or L. *ūtriculus* UTRICULUS [1].]

**1.** *Bot.* A small sac or bladder-shaped body; a bottle-shaped part or structure.

*Primordial utricle*: see PRIMORDIAL *a.* 4 b.

**a.** **1731** MILLER *Gard. Dict.* s.v. *Sap*, All Male Flowers that have Utricles at the Bottom of the Petala. **1793** MARTYN *Lang. Bot.* s.v. *Vessels*, Utricles, or little Bags; usually full of a green pulp. **1816** KEITH *Phys. Bot.* I. 349 The structure of the utricles of the tree is also said to be different from that of the utricles of the herb. **1875** DARWIN *Insectiv. Pl.* xvii.

419 The spherical glands were still white but their utricles were broken up. **b.** 1826–34 *Encycl. Metrop.* (1845) VII. 50/1 An utricle is a membranous, elastic pericarp. 1861 BENTLEY *Man. Bot.* 314 The Utricle is a superior, one-celled, one or few-seeded fruit. **c.** 1849 [see PRIMORDIAL *a.* 4 b]. 1857 HENFREY *Elem. Course Bot.* 495 The primordial utricle is a layer of substance of a dense mucilaginous consistence.., applied intimately to the inner surface of the cell-membrane of young cells [etc.]. 1875 BENNETT & DYER *Sach's Bot.* 62 The hydrostatic pressure which the vacuole-fluid exercises on the protoplasm [1882 primordial] utricle. **d.** 1858 IRVINE *British Pl.* 240 The Carex Tribe...Fruit without hairs at the base, enclosed in a peculiar envelope (utricle). 1897 WILLIS *Flower. Pl.* II. 126 The axil of a second glume (the utricle) which closely enwraps it. **e.** 1874 COOKE *Fungi* 49 After the spores have become ripe, the free point of the utricle bursts. **f.** 1875 DARWIN *Insectiv. Plants* xviii. 451 Found within the utricle or neck of one leaf.

**2.** *Anat.* and *Biol.* A small cell, sac, or bladder-like process.

1822 GOOD *Study Med.* IV. 603 Those utricles, or minute bladders of the cuticle containing a watery fluid. 1836–9 TODD *Cycl. Anat.* II. 413/2 Utricles floating loosely in the abdominal cavity. 1899 *Allbutt's Syst. Med.* VIII. 905 Microbacillus of the 'peladic utricle'.

**b.** The larger of the two sacs in the membranous labyrinth of the ear.

1837 *Penny Cycl.* IX. 239/1 The utricle, or sinus of the vestibule [in birds]. 1857 HOLDEN *Hum. Osteol.* (ed. 2) 252 The utricle occupies the upper half of the vestibule. 1886 *Buck's Handbk. Med. Sci.* II. 563/2 The vestibular membranous labyrinth is divided into sacs: (1) the oblong utricle or..common sinus [etc.].

**3.** *gen.* A small bladder-like body; a globule.

1858 GRAHAM & WATTS *Elem. Chem.* (ed. 2) II. 681 Vapour of sulphur, when it comes in contact with cold bodies, condenses in the form of *utricles*, that is to say, of globules composed of a soft external pellicle filled with liquid sulphur. ..This utricular condition has also been observed in selenium.

**U·tricle**[2]. *Anat.* [ad. F. *utricule*, or L. *utriculus* UTRICULUS[2].] A small cul-de-sac in the prostatic portion of the urethra in man; the prostatic vesicle.

1861 SIR H. THOMPSON *Dis. Prostate* (ed. 2) 28 The Utricle..is a small sac..opening on the anterior aspect of the verumontanum. 1888 *Cassell's Encycl. Dict.* s.v., There is a utricle of the male urethra.

**b.** In the cat: (see quot.).

1881 MIVART *Cat* 242 A small, ridge-like prominence, called the *verum montanum*, in the midst of which is a narrow, slit-like depression, named the utricle.

**Utricular** (yutri·kiŭlăɹ), *a.*[1] [f. L. *ūtricul-us* small leathern bag, UTRICULUS[1] + -AR[1]. Cf. F. *utriculaire*.]

**1.** Of the nature of, resembling or like, a utricle.

1760 J. LEE *Introd. Bot.* III. xviii. (1765) 211 *Utricular*, like little Bottles. 1775 ELLIS in *Phil. Trans.* LXVI. 8 The Gorgonia .. has no series of utricular vessels, as the transverse vessels of wood are called by Malpighi. 1822 J. PARKINSON *Outl. Oryctol.* 92 The bottle encrinite, possessing a utricular form. 1856 W. CLARK *Van der Hoeven's Zool.* I. 184 Body utricular, roundish, marked with transverse rugæ. 1858 [see UTRICLE[1] 3]. 1881 BENTHAM in *Jrnl. Linn. Soc.* XVIII. 367 A single utricular glume enclosing the flower.

**2.** Composed of utricles or small bladders.

1835 LINDLEY *Introd. Bot.* (ed. 2) 5 Cellular, Utricular, or Vesicular tissue, generally, consists of little bladders..adhering together in masses. 1849 HENFREY in *Rep. & Papers Bot.* (Ray Soc.) 163 In such cases the cavities appear like utricles. This utricular structure [etc.].

**Utri·cular,** *a.*[2] [f. L. *utricul-us* little womb, etc. (UTRICULUS[2]) + -AR[1]. Cf. F. *utriculaire*.] Of or pertaining to the uterus or abdomen; uterine.

1827 J. FORBES tr. *Laennec's Dis. Chest* (ed. 2) 58 The entrance and escape of the air through the wound gave rise to an extremely distinct utricular buzzing. 1857 BULLOCK *Cazeaux' Midwif.* 180 The utricular glands also become visibly enlarged. 1871 A. MEADOWS *Man. Midwifery* (ed. 2) 21 The lining membrane of the uterus..appears to be made up of a countless number of small tubes, the utricular glands or follicles.

‖**Utricularia** (yutrikiŭlē·riă). Pl. -ariæ. [mod.L. (1737), f. L. *ūtricul-us* UTRICULUS[1].] A genus of scrophulariaceous plants, characterized by bearing small bladders at the margins of their leaves; bladderwort, hooded (water) milfoil; a species or plant of this.

1753 *Chambers' Cycl.* Suppl., *Utricularia*,..the name of a plant used by Linnæus for..hooded water milfoil. 1793 MARTYN *Lang. Bot.* s.v. *Folliculus*, Follicles..are vessels distended with air: as at the root in *Utricularia*. 1819 *Rees' Cycl.* XXXVII. 4 F 2/2 Almost every morning's walk afforded them a new Utricularia. *Ibid.*, Twenty-four Utriculariæ, natives of New Holland alone. 1863 T. W. HIGGINSON *Out-Door Papers* 278 The slender Utricularia, a dainty maiden whose light feet scarce touch the water.

**Utriculate** (yutri·kiŭlĕt), *a. rare.* [ad. mod. L. *ūtriculāt-us*, f. L. *ūtriculus* UTRICULUS[1].] (See quots.)

1860 MAYNE *Expos. Lex.* 1318/1 *Utriculatus*, Bot. having the form of a small leathern bottle..: utriculate. 1864 DANA in *Webster's Dict.* 1457/2 *Utriculate*, a., swollen like a bladder; inflated; utricular.

**U·tricule.** *Bot. rare*[−1]. [a. F. *utricule*: see UTRICLE[1].] A small bladder-like sac or body.

1830 LINDLEY *Nat. Syst. Bot.* 240 The reservoirs of oil in the leaves of Labiatæ..are little utricules having an open orifice.

**Utri·culoid,** *a. rare*[−0]. [f. L. *ūtricul-us* UTRICULUS[1] + -OID.] Resembling a bladder; utricular.

1864 DANA in *Webster's Dict.* 1457. [Hence in later Dicts.]

‖**Utriculus**[1] (yutri·kiŭlɒs). [L., dim. of *ūter* leathern bag or bottle: see -CULUS. Cf. Pg. *utriculo*.]

**1.** *Bot.* (See quots. and UTRICLE[1] 1.)

1753 *Chambers' Cycl.* Suppl. s.v., The leaves of trees, whose cuticle has been eat off on one side by small insects, sometimes afford views of these *Utriculi*. 1793 MARTYN *Lang. Bot.*, *Utriculi*,..utricles; reservoirs to secrete and receive the sap. 1838 *Penny Cycl.* XI. 346/1 Fruit [of grasses]..occasionally an utriculus. 1857 HENFREY *Bot.* 428 (Sedges), A single erect anatropous ovule, forming in fruit an utriculus. 1866 *Treas. Bot.* 1197/2 *Utriculus*,.. the two confluent glumes of *Carex*. 1885 GOODALE *Physiol. Bot.* 346 Utricularia, a genus named from the utriculi or little bladders found on the dissected leaves of some of its species.

**2.** *Anat.* Of the ear; = UTRICLE[1] 2 b.

1847 TODD & BOWMAN *Phys. Anat.* II. 82 As the osseous canals open into the vestibule, so the membranous ones open at both ends into the utriculus. 1878 F. J. BELL *Gegenbaur's Comp. Anat.* 535 The sacculus and utriculus contain otoliths.

‖**Utri·culus**[2]. *Anat.* [L., dim. of *uterus* UTERUS: see -CULUS.] = UTRICLE[2].

1848 *Brit. & For. Med.-Chirurgical Rev.* I. 271 A canal, originating by the usual opening on the utriculus. *c* 1848 *Todd's Cycl. Anat.* IV. 152/1 That the utriculus is a male uterus. 1893 D. J. CUNNINGHAM *Man. Pract. Anat.* I. 609 This [small recess] is the *sinus pocularis* or the *utriculus*.

**Utriform** (yū·trifɔ̨ɹm), *a. rare.* [ad. mod.L. *ūtriform-is* (whence F. *utriforme*), f. L. *ūtri-s*, *ūter* bag, bottle, etc.: see -FORM.] Having the shape of a leathern bottle.

1860 MAYNE *Expos. Lex.* 1318/2 *Utriformis*,..swoln out and without apparent pedicle, as in the *Lycoperdon utriforme*: utriform. 1889 *Quart. Jrnl. Geol. Soc.* XLV. 566 The zoœcia..have the exsert parts conical, or, again, they may be leathern-bottle-shaped (utriform).

**Utrique(ing,** varr. OUTREIK(ING *Sc. Obs.*

‖**U·trum.** *Obs.* or *Hist.* [L. *utrum*, neut sing. of *uter* which, whether.] A writ authorizing the holding of an assize to decide the status of a property (see quot. 1728). Usu. in *assize of utrum*.

*c* 1290 BRITTON (1865) II. 206 La quarte assise est de *Utrum*. *Ibid.* 207 Le bref de *Utrum* pur le clerc.

1592 RASTELL *Law Terms*, *Vtrum* is a writ and it lyeth when the right of any Church is aliened and holden in lay fee. 1728 CHAMBERS *Cycl.* [following Cowell s.v. *Assise de utrum*], *Assize of Utrum*, lies for a Parson against a Layman, or a Layman against a Parson, for Land or Tenement, doubtful whether it be in Lay-fee, or Free-alms. 1865 NICHOLS *Britton* II. 207 *margin*, *Utrum*, the parson's writ of right. *Ibid.* 208 *margin*, No assize of *Utrum* for land belonging to cathedral or convent. 1881 TWISS *Bracton* (Rolls) IV. 622 [Assise] of Utrum may not be brought by a vicar for a small pension paid to a religious house. *Ibid.*, Assise of utrum can never be taken upon a previous assise of utrum.

**Utt, Utter,** obs. ff. OUT, UDDER.

**U·tter,** *sb. Mech.* [See quot. 1879.] *pl.* Indentations or marks made on a surface by the vibration or too great pressure of a tool.

1853 O. BYRNE *Artisan's Handbk.* 351 Excessive pressure ..only fills the work with furrows, or produces an irregular indented surface, which by workmen is said to be full of utters. 1879 HOLTZAPFFEL *Turning* IV. 342 Fine lines or striæ, also called 'utters',..from the sound emitted by the work when in vibration against the tool.

**Utter** (ʋ·təɹ), *a.* Forms: α. 1 utera, uterra, utra, 4–6 vter, *Sc.* 6 vtir, utyr, 6, 9 uter. β. 2 uttera, uttra, 3, 6 uttre, 4–6 vttre, 4– utter (4–6 uttir, 5 uttere); 4–7 vtter (4 otter, 5 outter, vttere, 6–7 *Sc.* wtter), 4–6 vttur, 5 vtture, vttir, 4 vttyr. [OE. *ūtera*, *ūterra*, *ūttera*, *ūttra*, etc. (also *ȳtera*, *ȳtra*, *ȳttra*) adj. (comparative formed on *ūt* OUT *adv.*), = OFris. *ūtera*, *uttera*, *uttra*, MLG. *utere*, *uter* (LG. *ûter*, *üter*), MDu. *utere* (Du. *uiter-*), OHG. *ûȥero*, *ûȥaro* (MHG. *ûȥer*, G. *äusser*), also ON. *ytri*, MSw. *ytre*, etc. (Sw. *yttre*), Norw. *ytre*, Da. *ydre*. Cf. OUTER *a.*

Shortening of the original *ū* of the stem is normal before the group *ttr*, which in OE. was regularly developed from *tr*.]

**I. 1.** That is farther out than another (implied or distinguished as *inner*); forming the exterior part or outlying portion; relatively far out, outward, external, exterior; also, indefinitely remote. Cf. OUTER *a.* 1. Now only *poet.*

In very frequent use from *c* 1400 to *c* 1620. App. in disuse *c* 1670–*c* 1825, except in *utter bar*, *barrister* (see BAR *sb.*[1] 24, BARRISTER).

α. *a* 901 ÆLFRED *Laws* c. 44 § 1 Ȝif ðæt uterre [*v.rr.* utre, uttere] ban bið þyrel. 13.. [see 1 b]. 1507 *Acc. Ld. High Treas. Scot.* III. 292 The Kingis offerandis in the utir kyrk. 1535 STEWART *Cron. Scot.* (Rolls) III. 48 Suppois than of that toun The vter wallis win war and put doun. 1592 *Reg. Mag. Sig. Scot.* 753/1 Lie uter port de Halyrudhous. 1887 *Jamieson's Suppl.* 257/2 The uter door.

β. *c* 1125 [see α]. *c* 1374 CHAUCER *Troylus* III. 664 (Camb. MS.), In þis vttir [*v.rr.* vtter, outter] hous. *a* 1400–50 *Bk. Curtasye* 444 in *Babees Bk.* 313 For lordys two beddys schalle be made, Bothe vtter and inner. *c* 1435 *Chron. London* (Kingsford, 1905) 40 By the hemme off the kyngis cote, vndir his vttir garnement. 1471 *Paston Lett.* III. 20 Opyn the cofyr that standyth in the utter chambyr. 1526 TINDALE *Matt.* xxv. 30 Cast that vnprophetable servaunt into vtter dercknes. 1542 BOORDE *Dyetary* iv. (1870) 239 If there be an vtter courte made. 1578 LYTE *Dodoens* 752 An ounce of the utter barke taken with wine. 1614 SYLVESTER *Little Bartas* 432 Earth's but a Point, compar'd to th' upper Globe; Yet, who hath seen but half her utter Robe? 1661 P. GORDON *Diary* (Spalding Club) 49 Whilst my servants were cleansing the inner room, he breake downe the oven in the utter roome. 1667 MILTON *P. L.* VI. 716 Drive them out From all Heav'ns bounds into the utter Deep. 1827 POLLOK *Course T.* IX. 1180 They heard, Afar to left, among the utter dark, Hell rolling o'er his waves of burning fire. 1848 BAILEY *Festus* (ed. 3) 107 From Time's last orb which eyes The inner and the utter infinite. 1870 J. PAYNE *Masque of Shadows* Ded., Whoso is fain To enter in this shadow-land of mine, He must forget the utter summer's shine.

*fig.* 1608 B. JONSON *Masques* Wks. (1616) 934 I,.. who haue neuer touch'd so much as to the barke, or vtter shell of any knowledge. 1877 L. MORRIS *Epic Hades* II. 147 So high a strain arose As trembled on the utter verge of being.

**b.** Freq. with partitive terms, as †*deal*, *end*, *part*, †*party*, and esp. *side*. Also *fig.* Now *rare*.

*a* 1300 *Cursor M.* 9912 Þis castell..es painted a-bute þe vtter [*Gött.* vter] side. *c* 1340 HAMPOLE *Pr. Consc.* 4815 Þe world sal bryn on ilk syde,..Until þe utter end of alle helle. 1387 TREVISA *Higden* (Rolls) I. 59 For betynge of veynes is bettre i-knowe in þe vttre parties of bodies þan ynward. *Ibid.* VI. 251 Þe utter deel of his oost. *c* 1400 *Beryn* 3928 [He] had a mantell..; The vttir part of purpill. 1457 *Cov. Leet. Bk.* 298 The newe Crosse vppon the heth at the vtter syde of theyre fraunchice. 1508 *Bk. Keruynge* A iv, The vtter ende of the clothe on the vtter syde of the table. 1526 TINDALE *Matt.* xxiii. 25 Ye make clene the vtter side off the cuppe, and off the platter. 1577 B. GOOGE *Heresbach's Husb.* I. 21 b, A little rayne falling, hath but wette the vtter part, and not gone deepe. 1629 SIR W. MURE *True Crucifixe* 485 Like painted Tombs who clense the vtter side, [Cf. Matt. xxiii. 27]. 1637 RUTHERFORD *Lett.* (1671) 183 For two feathers or two straws of the devil's painted pleasures, onely lustred in the utter side. 1848 BAILEY *Festus* (ed. 3) 59, I have looked down upon the utter side Of such thoughts from the leeming room of reason.

†**2.** = OUTER *a.* 2. *Obs.*

*c* 900 tr. *Baeda's Hist.* IV. xiii. (1890) 304 Þæt heo seolfe wæron ȝe on þæm nearran [*v.r.* inneran] godum, ȝe on þæm utteran [*v.r.* uttran] mid heofonlice ȝife ȝewelȝade. *c* 1000 *Ags. Ps.* (Thorpe) xv. 7 Þeah he me þara uterrena ȝewinna ȝefreode, þeah winnað wið me þa inran unrihtlustas. *a* 1225 *Ancr. R.* 92 Hwo se ȝemeleasliche witeð hire uttre eien,.. heo ablindeð in þe inre eien. 1357 *Lay Folks' Catech.* (L.) 330 The be-houys to know þy fyue wyttys þe vttyr and þe ynnyr. *c* 1386 CHAUCER *Sec. Nun's T.* 498 (Camb. MS.), Teere lakkyth no thyng to thyn vtter Iyen. 1398 TREVISA *Barth. De P. R.* III. ix. (1495) 54 The vtter wytte conteyneth the syghte,.. taastynge and towchynge. *c* 1450 tr. *De Imitatione* III. xiv. 82 For þe utter enemy is sonner ouercomen, if þe ynner be destroied.

†**b.** *Utter man*, = OUTWARD *a.* 2 c. (Cf. OUTER *a.* 2 b.) *Obs.*

*a* 1050 *Liber Scintill.* x. (1889) 53 Þæt ys fullfremed & ȝesceadwislic fæsten þænne ure mann uttra fæst, se inra ȝebitt. *a* 1340 HAMPOLE *Psalter* ix. 20 Þat..þe utter man haf noght maistry of þe inere. *c* 1380 WYCLIF *Sel. Wks.* I. 53 Þis is bifore spiritual joy, as utter man is bifore spiritual. 1388 — 2 *Cor.* iv. 16 Thouȝ oure vtter man be corruptid. 1565 JEWEL *Reply Harding* 430 Simple folke, beinge not hable to discerne, what thinges they be in the Holy Scriptures, that are to be applied to the Inner Man, and what to the Vtter.

†**3.** = OUTWARD *a.* 4. *Obs.*

*a* 1225 *Ancr. R.* 4 Ye schullen alles weis..wel witen þe inre & þe uttre [*sc.* riwle] vor hire sake. *a* 1275 *Ibid.* 420 *note* (Cotton MS.), Understondeð þet of alle þeose þinges nis nan hest ne forbot; for alle ha beoð of þe uttere riwle, þet is lute strencðe of. 1526 TINDALE *John* vii. 24 Judge not after the vtter aperaunce. 1548 HOBY in Strype *Eccl. Mem.* (1721) II. App. Y. 80 He..is even now..as content to the utter shew, as he was at any time of his most prosperity. 1558 BP. WHITE *Ibid.* III. App. lxxxi. 279 You in time of divine service, do..both in heart and utter gesture..adore the same flesh. 1563 *Homilies* II. *Place & Time of Prayer* 282 Strayghtly to obserue and kepe the vtter ceremonyes of the Saboth-day. 1593 NASHE *Christ's T.* R 4 b, Lyke the Geometritians, they square about poynts and lynes, and the vtter shew of things.

**II. 4.** Going to the utmost point; extreme, absolute, complete, entire, total.

In very frequent use from *c* 1515.

*c* 1430 *Generides* (Roxb.) 3040 This wer to vs..an vttir shame for euermore. 14.. *Lydgate's Thebes* 4122 (MS. Laud Misc. 557, fol. 58), It were to hem a perpetuall shame, An vtter [*v.r.* outre] hyndryng vnto Grekes name. *a* 1512 FABYAN *Chron.* VI. clxxxix. 191 To the..vtter displeasure of the Kynge. 1550 CROWLEY *Epigr.* 1241 Ambition was punished wyth vtter exile. 1562 WINȜET *Cert. Tract.* Wks. (S.T.S.) I. 7 Ane manifest confusion and vter extermination of this realme. 1606 DEKKER *Newsfr. Hell* Wks. (Grosart) II. 143 Burning Riuers In which..are [*sic*] no vtter danger. 1662 STILLINGFL. *Orig. Sacræ* I. ii. § 1 We have seen already an utter impossibility of having any ancient Records among them. 1718 PRIOR *Poems* Dedication b j, Two Things which were his utter Aversion. 1778 MISS BURNEY *Evelina* xxi, I saw they were in utter amazement. 1812 J. WILSON *Isle of Palms* III. 535 A graceful calm is seen All foreign to this utter solitude. 1849 RUSKIN *Sev. Lamps* vii. § 11. 184 Restraint, utter and unrelaxing, can never be comely. 1871 TYLOR *Prim. Cult.* I. 277 Her utter belief that in her vision she had really seen this bright being. 1889 CLARK RUSSELL *Marooned* xii, The arrest of his movements could not have been more spasmodic and utter.

**b.** Freq. said of destruction, ruin, loss, etc.

1412–20 LYDG. *Chron. Troy* IV. 2443 He him [Agamemnon] had brouȝt in gret distresse, To outter meschef and confusioun. ? 1456– [see UNDOING *vbl. sb.*[1] 3 c]. 1523 *Act* 14 & 15 *Hen. VIII*, c. 1 § 1 The utter ruyne, decaye, impoverysshyng and undoyng of a great nombre of the Kynges owne naturall Subjectes. 1560 DAUS tr. *Sleidane's Comm.* 40 To the vtter destruction of the common wealthe. 1591 SHAKS. 1 *Hen. VI*, v. iv. 112 The vtter losse of all the Realme. 1667 MILTON *P. L.* III. 308 Thou hast..quitted all to save A World from utter loss. 1674 *Jackson's Recant.* B 1 b, Turn'd out of Doors, to their utter ruin and destruction. 1772 PRIESTLEY *Inst. Relig.* (1782) I. 408 The utter ruin of their city..was foretold. 1827 KEBLE *Chr. Y.*, *11th Sunday after Trinity* v, Full many a soul..To utter death that hour shall sweep.

**1841** Miss Mitford in L'Estrange *Life* (1870) III. viii. 125 Dark depression and utter failure of intellect. **1846** Mrs. A. Marsh *Father Darcy* II. xxi. 359 The utter destruction of all reverence for the unseen.

**c.** Of answers, decisions, etc.: Given without reserve or qualification; unmodified, decisive, definite. In early use chiefly *Sc.*

**1456** Sir G. Haye *Law Arms* (S.T.S.) 173 As for utter ansuere to this questioun,..lawe and gude faith avidis that ..he is behaldin [etc.]. **1472** *Stonor Papers* (Camden) I. 126 But and [=if] ye..conceyve þat shee hath yoven ycu an utter nay. **1515** Q. Marg. in Ellis *Orig. Lett.* Ser. I. I. 127 Send me ȝour uter mynd and ansuer in all thyng. **1560** Rolland *Seven Sages* 33 This is my vter minde and will, That ȝe prepair [etc.]. *a* **1600** Montgomerie *Misc. Poems* xxxii. 86 ȝour vter ansueir courteously I crave. **1647** Clarendon *Hist. Reb.* VIII. § 15 The utter refusal of the auxiliary regiments of London and Kent to march farther. **1828–32** Webster s.v., An utter refusal or denial.

**d.** Of darkness, etc: Complete, absolute.

**1596** Shaks. 1 *Hen. IV*, III. iii. 42 But thou..wert indeede, but for the Light in thy Face, the Sunne of vtter Darkenesse. **1814** Wordsw. *Excurs.* VII. 357 Then, shall the slowly-gathering twilight close In utter night. **1825** Scott *Talism.* v, They blew out their lights at once, and left the knight in utter darkness. **1830** Tennyson *Confess. Sens. Mind* 95 What if Thou..seest me drive Through utter dark a full-sailed skiff Unpiloted. **1868** — *Lucretius* 70 Then, from utter gloom stood out the breasts..of Helen.

**e.** Pure; unalloyed. *rare*[—1].

**1875** Morris *Æneis* IX. 262 Two cups of utter silver wrought.

**5.** Of persons: That is such to an absolute degree; out-and-out, complete, 'perfect'.

In early use, usu. with 'enemy'; in 19th c., freq. with 'stranger'.

*c* **1420** Lydg. *Assembly of Gods* 594 He hathe be euer myn vtter enemy. **1555** J. Bradford in Strype *Eccl. Mem.* (1721) III. App. xlv. 131 That he shoulde be..the Kinges utter enemye. **1560** Daus tr. *Sleidane's Comm.* 82 b, Their moste vtter and mortall ennemie. **1633** G. Herbert *Temple, Method* vii, Those Who heare not him, but quickly heare His utter foes? **1662** Trenchfield *Chr. Chym.* 39 Julius Cæsar having taken..the Cabinets of Pompey and Scypio his utter enemies. **1678** Bunyan *Pilgr.* I. 163 Ye be utter strangers to me; I know you not. **1828** Scott *F. M. Perth* xiii, Some of them are yet utter heathens. *a* **1845** Hood *Lamia* vi. 80 And thou wilt..say the outer woman is utter woman, And not a whit a snake! **1849** Lever *Con Cregan* xviii, To win some acknowledgment of confidence from an utter stranger. **1875** Jowett *Plato* (ed. 2) III. 70 The persons..are utter rogues.

**b.** *ellipt.* (in affected use).

**1881** W. S. Gilbert *Patience* II, (The Officers have some difficulty in maintaining their constrained [æsthetic] attitudes.)..*Ang.* Oh, Saphir, are they not quite too all-but? *Saph.* They are indeed jolly utter. **1882** H. S. Leigh *Strains fr. Strand* 5 You and I have been together Dining up at Eaton Square. Pretty creature, tell me whether All was not 'quite utter' there. *Ibid.* 131 My wife has gone 'utterly utter'.

†**6.** Uttermost, utmost. *Obs.*

Freq. in Sc. use in 16th cent., with *power*.

**1513** Douglas *Æneis* IX. ix. 16 Quham to assailȝe,..all the Italianis At vtir power ombeset atanis. **1533** Bellenden *Livy* I. iv. (S.T.S.) I. 30 Þare husbandis wald gif þare vter besines..to recovir baith [etc.]. **1576** Fleming *Panopl. Epist.* 59 My request, which yt you wold accomplish to my utter expectation, we..beseech you most earnestly. **1590** *Hecuba's Mishaps* in T. Fenne *Frutes* Ff 2 b, When that I had..shewed my utter might.

†**b.** Ultimate, original. *Obs.*[—1]

**1634** Sir T. Herbert *Trav.* 144 They haue neuer altered the Dialect [of Persia] from its vtter sence, at this day being cald *Pharsee.*

†**7.** Final; last. *Obs.*[—1]

**1558** Phaer *Æneid* II. D iii b, Our vtter houre is comen alas, fell destinies death hath brought.

**8.** *The utter*, that which is utter or extreme; = Uttermost *a.* 7, Utmost *a.* 5, 5 b. *rare.*

**1584** Raleigh *Let.* in Aubrey *Lives* (1898) II. 192 Readie to countervaile all your courtesies to the utter of my power. **1894** *Athenæum* 29 Sept. 418/1 Nothing suits him but the utter. His heroine is 'beautifully modelled' [etc.].

**III.** †**9.** *Combs.* (hyphened, or as one word): *utter-bark, -brass, -court, -deal* (Deal *sb.*[1] 1 d), *-end, -gate, -room, -shape* (see sense 3), *-side*; **utter-ward** (see Ward *sb.*[2] 14 c); also *fig.* (quot. *c* 1440); **utter-wit**, knowledge of things external to one.

**1398** Trevisa *Barth. De P. R.* v. xxx. (Bodl. MS.), Þe vtterdele þereof is clene and bright. *c* **1440** *Jacob's Well* 222 As þou hast v. watyrgatys in þe vttere-warde, owtward in þe pytt of þi body. *c* **1450** *Brut* II. 545 The vtterward of the castell of Chestre. **1483** Caxton *Gold. Leg.* 309/2 The towne..in the utterende of Dalmace. **1485** *Rolls of Parlt.* VI. 353 The Uttergate of the Castell of Flynte. **1495** *Trevisa's Barth. de P. R.* III. vi. c viij/1 Felynge, bodyly wytte and Ymagynacyon arne sytuate in the soule that he is onid to the body, and yeue it lyfe, & Innerwytte & vtterwytt to perfeccion of the body. *c* **1530** Ld. Berners *Arth. Lyt. Bryt.* (1814) 139 One [bed]..yᵉ vtterbrass therof were of grene jasper. **1530** Palsgr. 286/1 Utterbarke of a tree, *escorche*. *Ibid.*, Uttercourt, *basse court*. *a* **1550** Leland *Itin.* (1769) VII. 118 Estward to the utterward of the Chyrch. **1567** Drant *Horace, Sat.* iii. G 4 To folow showes, and uttershapes,..Is folie leude. **1577** Harrison *England* II. xii. (1877) I. 236 The vtterside of their mansions. **1603** Daniel *Def. Rhime* H 6, When we heare musicke, we must be in our eare, in the vtter-roome of sense. **1675** Hobbes *Odyssey* XXI. 258 [He] shut the utter-Gate.

†**Utter**, *adv. Obs.* Forms: 1 utor, 6 *Sc.* uter; 1 uttor, 2, 7, 9, utter, 3–5 uttere (6 *Sc.* uttir), 4–7 vtter (5 vttir, vttyr), 4–5 vttere. [OE. *útor*, *úttor*, *útter* (compar. of *út* Out *adv.*), = MLG. *uter*, G. *ausser*, ON. *útarr*.]

**1.** Farther out, away, or apart; out, outside, without.

*c* **888** Ælfred *Boeth.* xxxiv. § 12 Nabbað hi nan god ofer þæt to secanne, ne hi nanwuht ne maȝonne ufor ne utor findan. *c* **1000** *Ags. Gosp.* Matt. xx. 28 Þonne byþ ðe arwurðlicor þonne þe man uttor scufe. *c* **1200** *Trin. Coll. Hom.* 73 [He] ne dar his sinnes seien þe prest leste hit uttere cume þat hie tweien witen. **13..** *E. E. Allit. P.* B. 42 He schulde be halden vtter, With mony blame ful bygge,.. Hurled to þe halle dore. **13..** *Gaw. & Gr. Knt.* 1565 Þer he..made hym, maw-gref his hed, forto mwe vtter. **1399** Langl. *Rich. Redeles* III. 232 Þe portir with his pikis þo put him vttere. *c* **1440** *Pallad. on Husb.* v. 112 In wynter to his codde an heep of stonys Is good, that in the somer vtter don is. *c* **1450** *Mirk's Festial* I. 258 Þys man..set to þe roches his schuldyr, and bade hom..sterte vttyr. *c* **1500** *World & Child* 527 Stonde vtter, felowe! Where doest thou thy curtesy preue. *a* **1529** Skelton *E. Rummyng* 535 A strawe, sayde Bele, stande vtter.

**2.** From among others; = Out *adv.* 1 e. Cf. Out-try *v.* 1. *rare*[—1]

*c* **1440** *Pallad. on Husb.* II. 294 In Nouember kitte of the bowes drie, Superfluent & thicke ek vtter trie.

**3.** To an utter degree; quite, altogether.

**1611** Beaum. & Fl. *King & No K.* IV. i, I know they will deny me gracious Madam, Being..So utter empty of those excellencies That tame Authority. **1652** G. Sandys *Trav.* (ed. 5) 47 It utter [*earlier edd.* utterly] excludes his former excuse of an allegory. **1816** Accum *Chem. Tests* (1818) 139 Exposed in an utter dark place, to a brisk current of air.

**4.** *Utter-fine*: **a.** Of metals: Superfine. *Sc.*

**1562–3** *Reg. Privy Council Scot.* I. 232 Fourtie five unce of uter fyne silvir. **1641** in Cochran-Patrick *Rec. Coinage Scot.* (1876) I. Introd. 31 Vtter fynne gold. **1641** *Reg. Mag. Sig. Scot.* 366/2 Per ferramenta trium petrarum purissimi lie utter fyne argenti.

**b.** *ellipt.* A superfine make or quality of cloth. *Sc.* (Freq. *c* 1537–50.)

**1529** *Acc. Ld. High Treas. Scot.* V. 365 Ane eln tua quarteris, and ane half of uterfyne to be tua pair of hois. **1537** *Ibid.* VI. 351 Ten elnis uter fyne to be ane goun. **1564** *Reg. Privy Council Scot.* I. 309 Sevintene cairsayis and fyve stekis of uttir fyne.

**Utter** (*v*·təɹ), *v.*[1] Forms: *α.* 5 outer, outre (ottre, *Sc.* vtre), 6 vter, outter. *β.* 5 utterne, uttren, 5–7 vtter (6–7 *Sc.* wtter), vttre, 5 vttyr, 6 vttar; 5– utter, 6–7 uttre. [Partly from Out *adv.* or *v.* (with shortening of the vowel as in Utter *adv.*), partly ad. MDu. *uteren* (also *uyteren*, Du. *uiteren*, WFris. *uterje*) to drive away, announce, speak, show, make known, or MLG. *üteren*, *ütern* to turn out, sell, speak, demonstrate, etc. (LG. *ütern*), = MHG. *ûzeren*, *ûzern*, *iuzern* (G. *äussern* to speak, declare, † bring forth); Da. *ytre*, *yttre*, Sw. *yttra*, Norw. *ytra*, are from LG. The AF. *uttrer* (1463), Anglo-L. *utterare* (1551) are obviously from the English word.

For the earlier *oute(n*, *owten*, in Chaucer *Wife's Prol.* 521 and *Canon Yeom. Prol. & T.* 281, two later readings are respectively *outer*, *vttren*.]

**I.** †**1.** To put (goods, wares, etc.) forth or upon the market; to issue, offer, or expose for sale or barter; to dispose of by way of trade; to vend, sell. *Obs.*

In very frequent use from *c* 1540 to *c* 1655.

*α.* ?*c* **1400** *Chaucer's Wife's Prol.* 521 (Petw. MS.), With daungere outer [*v.rr.* oute, outen, owten] we al oure chaffare. **1423** *Rolls of Parlt.* IV. 255/1 Swiche warkes..[they] kepen and senden unto the fayres.., and ther thei outre hem. **1483** in J. H. Glover *Kingsthorpiana* (1883) 43 Yf any man brewe for the avayle of the Churche, that all other brewers cesse for the tyme uppon lefulle warnynge tyll that be outred.

*β.* **1425** *Rolls of Parlt.* IV. 307/2 Þat your said Commens may utter and sende her Corn, Bestus and Merchaundise over the see, into the parties abovesaid. **1436** *Pol. Poems* (Rolls) II. 175 At Venice of them men wol it bye, Then utterne [*v.r.* Thei utter] there the chaffare be the payse. *c* **1450** *Harl. Contin. Higden* (Rolls) VIII. 450 These men of Flaundres commynge to londe to utter theire merchandyse. **1523** *Act* 14 & 15 *Hen. VIII*, c. 1 § 1 Yf any person..doo nat ther or elles where bargayne utter and sell the sayed Clothe. **1570** Foxe *A. & M.* (ed. 2) 1206/1 Seeing good wyne nedeth no tauerne bushe to vtter it. **1607** Middleton *Michaelmas Term* IV. ii. 13 Do they [*sc.* traders] not thrive best when they utter most? **1649** Bp. Hall *Cases Consc.* III. vii. 296 When they gathered their Frankincense, none of it might be uttered till the Priest had the tithe of it. *a* **1668** Lassels *Voy. Italy* (1698) I. 68 Besides they utter a world of Taffataes, Velvets,.. and other things of value. **1735** Berkeley *Querist* § 544 Whether she [*sc.* Lyons] doth not receive and utter all those commodities. **1764** Burn *Poor Laws* 243 To keep a common ale-house.., and to utter and sell therein victuals. **1825** Scott *Betrothed* xxiii, Where other men are admitted that have wares to utter. [**1863** H. Cox *Instit.* I. xi. 279 Booksellers were, by statute.., prohibited from uttering Tindal's translation of the Bible.]

*fig.* and in fig. context. *c* **1430** Lydg. *Poems* (Percy Soc.) 150 Uttre nevir no darnel with good corn, Begyn no trouble whan men trete of pees. **1588** Shaks. *L. L. L.* II. i. 16 Beauty is bought by iudgement of the eye, Not vttred by base sale of chapmens tongues. **1613** J. Taylor (Water P.) *Watermen's Suit* Wks. (1630) 174/1 [The waterman's] worke and ware is seene and knowne, and hee vtters it with the sweat of his browes. **1624** Quarles *Job* v. 60 Earth's black babbling Daughter (she that heares, And vents alike, both Truth and Forgeries, And vtters, often, cheaper then she buyes). **1828** Scott *F. M. Perth* vi, The devil has factors enough to utter his wares.

*absol.* **1600** Cornwallis *Ess.* ii. C 5, Let vs receiue, and vtter, be capable, and returne increase of this fruite.

**b.** To announce for sale; = Cry *v.* 5 b. *rare.*

**1806–7** J. Beresford *Miseries Hum. Life* (1826) IV. i, The infernal dialects in which their goods are *uttered*.

†**c.** *intr.* Of goods: To find purchasers; = Sell *v.* 6. *Obs.*[—1]

**1611** Cotgr., *Marchandise d'emploicte*, ware that sells well, that vtters quickly.

**2.** To give currency to (money, coin, notes, etc.); to put into circulation; *esp.* to pass or circulate (base coin, forged notes, etc.) as legal tender.

*c* **1483** *Chron. London* (1827) 110 Every man, because of the said newe exchange, outred gold, and kept sylver. *c* **1550** *Disc. Common Weal Eng.* (1893) 78 Strangers haue conterfeted oure coine,..and heare vttered it, as well for oure gold and silver, as for oure chefe commoditie. **1554–5** *Act* 1–2 *Philip & Mary* c. 1 To the intent to utter or make paiment withe the same [*sc.* counterfeit foreign coin] within this Realme. **1602** Fulbecke *1st Pt. Parall.* 86 To utter or cause to be uttered false mony knowing it to be false. **1697** Evelyn *Numism.* i. 16 Tokens which every Tavern.. presumed to stamp and utter. **1718** S. Sewall *Diary* 21 Sept., Found Guilty of uttering Counterfeit Bills of Credit. *c* **1740** Fielding *Ess. Char. Men* Wks. 1784 IX. 417 Uttering great number of promissory notes. **1780** H. Walpole in Jesse *Selwyn & Contemp.* (1844) IV. 317 Last night I saw a proof-piece of seven-shilling pieces...I know they were not uttered, but could you get me one from the Mint? **1825** W. O. Russell & Ryan *Crown Cases* 455 The prisoner was ..convicted..of the offence of uttering and publishing, as true, a forged promissory note. **1848** Akerman *Introd. Study Anc. & Mod. Coins* i. 2 The earliest coins..bearing the symbol of the state by which they were uttered. **1861** *Act* 24–25 *Vict.* c. 99 § 9 Whosoever shall tender, utter, or put off any false or counterfeit Coin.

*absol.* **1863** Stephen *Blackstone's Comm.* (ed. 5) IV. 227 The punishment of forging, uttering, and the like at common law. **1905** *Daily Chron.* 22 May 5/7 Charged with being in the possession of counterfeit coins and plant for making them, and..accused also of 'uttering'.

**b.** *fig.* and *transf.* Also *absol.*

**1588** Kyd *Househ. Philos.* Wks. (1901) 274 Memory,..imprinting in it selfe al the Images and formes of visible.. things, could not vtter them in time conuenient..vnlesse it had so ordered. **1609** B. Jonson *Sil. Wom.* IV. vi, Mavis was more deceiu'd then we; 'twas her commendation vtter'd 'hem [*ante* 'these adulterate knights'] in the colledge. **1800** Addison *Amer. Law Rep.* 44 Misner was indicted..for uttering this assignment. **1839** Bailey *Festus* 145 The great bards Of Greece, of Rome,..Men who have forged gods—uttered—made them pass.

†**c.** To issue by way of publication; to publish. *Obs.*

**1561** in Haynes *Cecil Papers* (1740) 368 Sondry Booke-bynders and Stationers do utter certen Papers, wherein be prynted the Face of hir Majesty. *c* **1567** Stowe in *Surv.* (1908) I. p. li, Ye same [book] was well vtteryd by ye printar. **1584** *Star Chamb. Decree Printers & Stationers* (1863) 9 Bokes printed in England are uttered no where els.

**3.** † **a.** To send out; *esp.* to issue or give out from or as from a store. *Obs. rare.*

**1529** More *Dyaloge* III. Wks. 213/2 To by [= buy] many of the same suyte.., whiche were by them vttred to diuers yonge scolers such as thei founde properly witted. **1578** in *Househ. Ord.* (1790) 272 All those [pieces] that have beene uttered out of the store.., for the supplie of the fortes. **1617** Moryson *Itin.* II. 243 Such victuals as are..vnfit to be vttered to the souldier.

**b.** To put or thrust forth, shoot or urge out; to discharge, emit, eject, exhale. Also with *forth, out.* Now *dial.*

**1536** Latimer in Strype *Eccl. Mem.* (1721) I. 260 God prosper you, to the uttering all hollow harts of England. **1565** Cooper *Thesaurus, Tortuosa vrina*, vrine vttered with payne. **1579** Spenser *Sheph. Cal.* March 15 Thilke same Hawthorne studde..beginnes to budde, And vtter his tender head. **1607** Breton *Murmurer* Wks. (Grosart) II. 10/1 His Tongue like the sting of a Serpent, which vttereth nothing but poison. **1673** R. Head *Canting Acad.* 168 He that utters his Stomach in his next fellows Boots. **1820** W. Irving *Sketch Bk.* (1821) I. 69 The sage Nicholas Vedder, with his..fair long pipe, uttering clouds of tobacco smoke. **1821** Lamb *Elia* I. *Old Benchers*, The little cool playful streams those exploded Cherubs uttered [*sc.* from Lincoln's Inn Square fountain]. **1905** *Eng. Dial. Dict.* s. v., The spouts couldn't utter the water.

*transf.* **1881** P. Brooks *Candle of Lord* 14 Every candle of the Lord must utter its peculiar light.

*fig.* *a* **1586** Sidney *Arcadia* II. iv, Shee might give passage to her thoughts, and so as it were utter out some smoke of those flames. **1588** Shaks. *Tit. A.* v. iii. 12 My tongue may vtter forth The Venemous Mallice of my swelling heart.

†**c.** To produce or yield; to send out, supply, or furnish. Also in fig. context. *Obs.*

**1547** *Homilies* I. *Faith* B iiij b, They that..doe lyue in sinne.., not vttering the frutes that do belong to suche an high profession. **1603** Owen *Pembrokeshire* (1892) 54 The cheeffest and greatest comoditie that this sheere vttereth. *Ibid.* 57 It also vttereth yerelie great store of oysters. **1620** Markham *Farw. Husb.* 8 The mixt Earth, which vtters Whynnes, Bryars [etc.].

†**4.** *intr.* Of a horse: To go out of the lists or course at a tournament. *Sc. Obs. rare.*

**1550** Lyndesay *Sqr. Meldrum* 506 Bot Talbartis Hors, with ane mischance, He outterit, and to ryn was laith. *a* **1578** Lindesay (Pitscottie) *Chron. Scot.* (S.T.S.) I. 234 Schir Patrickis horse wtterit witht him and wald on nowayis reconter his marrow.

**II. 5.** *trans.* To send forth as a sound; to give out in an audible voice; to give vent or expression to (joy, etc.); to burst out with (a cry, yell, etc.).

*c* **1400** [see Uttering *vbl. sb.*]. **1530** Palsgr. 769/2, I utter ..my voyce, *je profere.* **1560** Daus tr. *Sleidane's Comm.* 215 b, He vttereth great gladness. **1611** Shaks. *Wint. T.* IV. iv. 185 Hee singes seuerall Tunes, faster then you'l tell money: hee vtters them [etc.]. **1612** Brinsley *Lud. Lit.* iii. 15 They [*sc.* vowels] being rightly vttered. **1621** J. Taylor (Water P.) *Sir G. Nonsence* Wks. (1630) Aa 1 b, Three sighs, smilingly vttered in the Hebrew Character. **1667** Milton

*P. L.* III. 347 A shout..sweet As from blest voices, uttering joy. **1712** STEELE *Spect.* No. 468 ¶ 1 Dictating to a Set of young Players, in what Manner to speak this Sentence, and utter t'other Passion. **1786** tr. *Beckford's Vathek* 209 She uttered a tremendous yell. **1800** WORDSW. *Michael* 347 When I heard thee.. First uttering, without words, a natural tune. **1815** STEPHENS in *Shaw's Gen. Zool.* IX. I. 18 The male has a very melancholy note..which is..uttered..while the female is sitting. **1833** COLERIDGE *Table Talk* (1884) 253 Man only can utter consonants. **1863** W. C. BALDWIN *Afr. Hunting* ii. 49 One lion..uttered a fierce roar.

*fig.* and *transf.* **1590** SHAKS. *Mids. N.* IV. ii. 44 And most deare Actors, eate no Onions, nor Garlicke; for wee are to vtter sweete breath. **1874** R. BUCHANAN *Poet. Wks.* III. 106 Unto me all seasons utter'd pleasure.

**b.** With advs., esp. *forth.* Also *transf.*

**1594** SPENSER *Amoretti* xlviii. 10 To vtter forth the anguish of his hart. **1603** SHAKS. *Meas. for M.* III. i. 87 There my fathers graue Did vtter forth a voice. **1728** ADDISON *'The Spacious firmament'* iii, In reason's ear they [*sc.* stars] all rejoice, And utter forth a glorious voice. **1827** POLLOCK *Course T.* VI. 86 What harp of..exhaustless woe, Shall utter forth the groanings of the damned? **1872** TENNYSON *Gareth & Lynette* 1053 [When] birds..utter forth May-music growing with the growing light.

**6.** To give utterance to (words, speech, a sentence, etc.); to speak, say, or pronounce. Occas. with advs., as *forth, out.*

In frequent use from *c* 1840.

*c* **1400** *Destr. Troy* 12215 Then answard Vlixes, & vtterit his speche. *c* **1444** LYDG. in *Pol. Poems* (Rolls) II. 215 Yiff thow art feerffulle to ottre thy language. *c* **1475** *Partenay* 3570 For that heuy word he was ther outring. **1509** HAWES *Past. Pleas.* XII. (Percy Soc.) 48 Utterynge the sentence Wythout..intellygence. **1587** in Feuillerat *Revels Q. Eliz.* (1908) 392 For them that are to utter certeine speches. **1598** *Mucedorus* Induct. 48 Giue me the leaue to vtter out my play. *c* **1614** SIR W. MURE *Dido & Æneas* II. 832 Her latest words scarce heard, nor vtt'red right. **1651** HOBBES *Leviath.* III. xlii. 298 While he was uttering the words of Consecration. **1711** ADDISON *Spect.* No. 1 ¶ 3, I scarce uttered the Quantity of an hundred Words. **1793** COWPER *To Mary* 22 Like language utter'd in a dream. **1796** H. HUNTER tr. *St.-Pierre's Stud. Nat.* IV. 197 She began to sob and weep without uttering a single word. **1816** SCOTT *Bl. Dwarf* xiv, The phrase which..she had compelled herself to utter. **1890** *Retrospect Med.* CII. 137 Voices of different qualities uttering sentences.

**b.** To give expression to (a subject, theme, one's thoughts, etc.); to express, describe, or report in words; to speak of or about.

In very frequent use *c* 1560–*c* 1600, and from *c* 1820.

*To utter one's stomach*, etc.: see STOMACH *sb.* 6 b.

*a.* *c* **1449** PECOCK *Repr.* IV. ix. 471 This thing..Crist expressith and outrith in a larger and generaler fourme. *c* **1475** *Partenay* 1233 All is trouth that I outre you or say.

*β.* *c* **1445** PECOCK *Donet* 6 It is honest ynou3 a man to speke and write aftir oon of þo opynyouns, and an oþire tyme to vttre þe oþire opinioun. **1526** *Pilgr. Perf.* (W. de W. 1531) 216 b, In vttrynge his malycyous mynde. **1565** HARDING *Answer Jewell's Chalenge* 169 The wordes of Hilarius the Pope vtter the same doctrine. **1590** WEBBE *Trav.* Ep. to Rdr., I haue undertaken in this short discourse, to vtter vnto thee ye most part of such things. **1611** BIBLE *Isaiah* xxxii. 6 His heart will worke iniquitie,..to vtter errour against the Lord. **1616** SIR W. MURE *Misc. Poems* xvii. 6 A mourning mynd, Quhich fain wold wtter.. Thir latest dutyes of a dulefull hert. **1667** MILTON *P. L.* I. 626 Th' event was dire, As this place testifies, and this dire change Hateful to utter. **1710** STEELE *Tatler* No. 2 ¶ 3, I must not prostitute the Liberal Sciences so far, as not to utter the Truth in cases which [etc.]. **1755** YOUNG *Centaur* iii. Wks. 1757 IV. 181 His terrified imagination uttered horrors not to be repeated. **1816** J. WILSON *City of Plague* II. i. 115, I have many a heavy thought to utter. **1841** LANE *Arab. Nts.* I. 110 If, at my grave, you utter my name. **1888** A. K. GREEN (Mrs. Rohlfs) *Behind Closed Doors* ii, This acknowledgment was uttered with emphasis.

*fig.* **1560** BIBLE *Ps.* xix. 2 Daie vnto daie vttereth the same [**1611** speech]. **1850** L. HUNT *Autobiog.* III. xxiii. 205 Flowers utter their beauty and their fragrance, as much as birds utter their songs.

**c.** With clause as object, introduced by *what, how*, etc., or with words directly quoted.

*c* **1449** PECOCK *Repr.* I. xvi. 90 And therfore..for drede of God..y write and outre what y now haue outrid. **1530** TINDALE *Answ. More* Wks. (1573) 293/2 He vttereth how fleshly mynded he is. **1539** BIBLE 2 *Macc.* iii (ch. heading), Symon vttereth what treasure is in the temple. **1582** STANYHURST *Æneis* I. (Arb.) 32 O wights most blessed, whose wals be thus happelye touring, Æneas vttred. **1611** SHAKS. *Wint. T.* I. ii. 104 Then didst thou vtter, I am yours for euer. **1781** COWPER *Conversat.* 381 Yes ma'am, and no ma'am, utter'd softly. **1818** SCOTT *Hrt. Midl.* xv, 'The new-born infant was barbarously murdered,' he uttered in a low ..voice. **1859** TENNYSON *Elaine* 1173 Lancelot kneeling utter'd 'Queen, Lady, my liege'.

†**7.** To disclose or reveal (something unknown, secret, or hidden); to make manifest; to declare, divulge. *Obs.*

In frequent use from *c* 1525 to *c* 1590.

**1444** *Rolls of Parlt.* V. 74/1 He nethir uttered ne communed of the specialite of the matiers concernyng..the said Tretie of peas. **1477** EARL RIVERS (Caxton) *Dictes* 11 Uttre not the secretes of thy hert but to them that thou hast preued. **1530** PALSGR. 769/2 He that uttereth my counsayle ones, I wyll never truste hym whyle I lyve. **1548** UDALL, etc. *Erasm. Par. Mark* 33 Jesus..woulde not vtter her by name, lest [etc.]. **1575** *Record's Gr. Artes* Ee viij b, As my erroure hath vttered my follye, so it hath procured mee better vnderstanding. **1614** RALEIGH *Hist. World* III. x. 125 Silanus the Sooth-sayer, who had vttered Xenophons purpose. **1670** WALTON *Lives* III. 209 With what gravity..his Tongue and Pen uttered Heavenly Mysteries. **1677** TEMPLE *Let. to Sir J. Temple* Wks. 1720 II. 459 The Prince,..uttering his whole Heart, told me [etc.].

†**b.** To show, display; to bring to light.

**1542** HEN. VIII *Declar. Scots* in *Compl. Scot.* App. i. 200 After this homage done the Scottis vttered some piece of their naturall disposition. **1548** UDALL *Erasm. Par. Matt.* xiii. 59 b, At length the cockelles growynge vp together (their vnlykenes vtteryng or shewyng them,) began to appere. **1575** LANEHAM *Let.* (1871) 12 Dauncing of Lordes and Ladiez..vttered with..liuely agilitee & commendabl grace. **1582** STANYHURST *Æneis* I. (Arb.) 32 The Princesse Theare the pate, in digging, of an horse intractabil vttred.

*refl.* **1548** UDALL, etc. *Erasm. Par. Luke* xvii. 132 Yet did he hyde within hym a secrete power of the nature of the godhed, whiche than & neuer before vttred it self. **1574** WHITGIFT *Def. Answ. to the Admonition* 135 When doe.. sinister affections more vtter themselues, then when an election is committed to many?

†**8.** To declare, reveal, make known, or set forth the character or identity of (a person or thing). *Obs.*

**1526** TINDALE *Mark* iii. 12 He streyghtly charged them that they shulde not vtter him. — 2 *Thess.* ii. 6, 8. **1534** MORE *Treat. Passion* Wks. 1305/2 John, whome Christe so tenderly loued, that..to hym secretely he vttred the false dissimuled traytour. **1548** GESTE *Pr. Masse* A vi, Yf they wold, [they] could handle and vtter hyr [*ante* 'this pryvate masse'] accordingly.

*refl.* *c* **1530** TINDALE *Gen.* xlv. 1 Ioseph..commaunded.. that there shuld be no man with him, whyle he vttred him selfe vnto his brethern. **1565** STAPLETON tr. *Bede's Hist. Ch. Eng.* 137 If he wold playing utter and shewe himselfe, what he was. **1587** GOLDING *De Mornay* v. 54 God hath voutsafed to vtter himselfe vnto vs in his Scriptures.

†**b.** Const. *to* (be or do something). *Obs. rare.*

**1548** UDALL *Erasm. Par. Matt.* xxvi. 104 Thy speche doth vtter the to be a Galilean. **1560** DAUS tr. *Sleidane's Comm.* 134 The kyng..stroke of her heade, and whan she was dead, vttered her to haue played the whore. **1562** LEGH *Armorie* 205 He vtterith him self yͤ better to be yͭ officer, whose name he beareth.

**9.** *refl.* To express (oneself) in words.

**1600** HOLLAND *Livy* 35 The Consul was..so much surprised..that he had no power to speak. But, soon after, when he began to utter himself [etc.]. **1655** tr. *Sorel's Com. Hist. Francion* VIII. 18 He beheld a Man upon the Bed, who..uttered himself in a thousand contumelious words to a Woman. **1711** ADDISON *Spect.* No. 119 ¶ 5 Several..utter themselves often in such a manner as a Clown would blush to hear. **1845** T. W. COIT *Puritanism* 129 His only refuge is to utter himself to One who is never prejudiced. **1860** HAWTHORNE *Marble Faun* xliii, Straying with Hilda.., he meant, at last, to utter himself upon that theme. **1881** SHAIRP *Asp. Poetry* 132 Each [English] poet..uttered himself in his own way,..as native passion prompted.

*fig.* **1824** W. IRVING *T. Trav.* II. 9 My feelings refused to utter themselves in rhyme.

*transf.* *a* **1648** *Ess. on Death* in *Bacon's Remaines* 9 An excellent Musician..cannot utter himself upon a defective instrument. **1878** FR. A. KEMBLE *Rec. Girlhood* II. 18 She [*sc.* an actress] remained to utter herself in Juliet to the English public. **1913** JANE E. HARRISON *Anc. Art & Ritual* iv. 91 So this intense desire uttered itself in the..[rite] of his resurrection.

**10.** *intr.* To exercise the faculty of speech; to speak. Also (rarely) const. *of, on.*

In the first quot. app. with indirect object.

? *a* **1400** *Morte Arth.* 418 The kyng in his concelle, curtaise and noblee, Vtters þe alienes, and ansuers hyme seluene. *c* **1440** *Alph. Tales* 532 When þai come aforn hym..he was compellid to vttyr. *c* **1475** *Partenay* 1024 To whome ful suetly outred she and sayd, 'Now vnderstandith' [etc.]. *Ibid.* 3156 Of Gaffray..I shall you outre and say. **1576** G. BAKER *Gesner's Jewell of Health* 101 b, Bellonius, uttering and wryting of those medycines.., affirmeth [etc.]. **1587** GOLDING *De Mornay* vi. 94 The highest God commaundeth, the second ordereth, and the third vttereth or publisheth. **1774** *Francis Lett.* (1901) I. 236 My trembling was so great for a few minutes that I could not utter. **1820** CREEVEY in *C. Papers* (1904) I. 338 Western..is close by my side, but has not uttered yet—such is his surprise. **1867** BP. WILBERFORCE in *Life* (1882) III. 226, I think it probable we shall utter now on the Vestments of the Minister. **1870** MISS BROUGHTON *Red as Rose* I. 141 You may sit by a person for hours and never utter to them! **1898** *Westm. Gaz.* 27 Aug. 2/1 Not a word was, of course, spoken by the men save *àpropos* of golf.., and as for the women.., they never uttered at all.

*transf.* **1873** MISS THACKERAY *Old Kensington* ii, Sacred voices that will utter to her through life.

**b.** Of words, etc.: To be spoken; to undergo utterance.

**1792** CHARLOTTE SMITH *Desmond* II. 36 Could you have seen the countenance of Geraldine, while this speech was uttering! **1850** WORDSW. *Prelude* v. 110 While this was uttering,..I wondered not. **1857** J. HAMILTON *Lessons fr. Gt. Biog.* 314 Wishes that cannot be understood, and words that will not utter.

Hence **U·ttering** *ppl. a.*

**1818** KEATS *Endym.* III. 475 That my words not burn These uttering lips, while I in calm speech tell [etc.].

†**Utter**, *v.*² *Obs. rare.* [a. OF. *utrer, outrer, oultrer*, etc. (AF. *ultrer*), to cross, traverse, excel, vanquish, f. *outre* prep., ad. L. *ultrā* beyond.]

**1.** *trans.* To vanquish, conquer, or overcome.

*c* **1400** *Destr. Troy* 5819 Philmene.., with a fell dynt, Vttrid Vlixes vne in the place;..And he gird to þe ground. *Ibid.* 7076 Honerable Ector..That holly the herhond hade at his wille, And haue vttred his Enmyes angur þat tyme. *c* **1532** DU WES *Introd. Fr.* in *Palsgr.* 951 To hurte, *oultrager*; to utter, *oultrer*.

**2.** *refl.* To exclude *from* some privilege, etc.

*a* **1450** *Knt. de la Tour* (1868) 162 They lyue in blame.. and outre hem self from the grace of God [F. *en oultre l'amour et la grace de Dieu*].

**Utterable** (*v*·tərăb'l), *a.* [f. UTTER *v.*¹ + -ABLE.]

†**1.** That may be disposed of by sale. *Obs.*

**1581** MULCASTER *Positions* xxxix. 210 Some gainefull commoditie verie vtterable abroade. **1611** COTGR., *Marchandise Latine*,..the best, or most vtterable commodities.

**2.** Capable of being uttered or expressed in words.

**1648** SALTMARSH *Spark. Glory* 168 That is, the speakings or manifestations of the Spirit of God are not so utterable by the flesh or voice of man. **1735** DYCHE & PARDON *Eng. Dict.* s.v. *Effable*, Whatever is utterable, or capable of being expressed. **1782** MISS BURNEY *Cecilia* x. viii, When his woe became utterable, he wrung his hands. **1826** *Q. Rev.* XXXIII. 397 And then she touches in utterable words upon unutterable things. **1846** DE QUINCEY in 'H. A. Page' *Life* (1877) I. xv. 326 All this wretchedness, not utterable to any human ear. **1893** *Nat. Observer* 15 April 534/1 Dividing all things utterable into things which are, and things which are not.

*absol.* **1873** CARLYLE *Lett.* (1913) I. 497 While he was discoursin' the utterable concernin' all sorts o' high topics. **1896** *Edin. Rev.* Oct. 302 The vision of the utterable passes into the vision of the unutterable.

Hence **Utterabi·lity**, capability of being uttered; also *pl.*, things that may be uttered.

**1851** CARLYLE *Sterling* II. vi, He flashed..into a subject; gathered it up into organic utterability, with truly wonderful dispatch. **1858** — *Fredk. Gt.* IV. i. I. 389 He learned also to clothe his bits of notions, emotions, and garrulous utterabilities, in the French dialect.

**Utterance**¹ (*v*·tərăns). Forms: 5– **utterance** (5–6 **-aunce**), 5–7 **vtterance** (5–6 **-aunce**, 6 **-ans**), 5 **vttrawnce** (6 **-ance**), **vttr-**, 8 **utt'rance**; 5 **ottyrance**, **oterauns**, **uter-**, 6 **vteraunce**. [f. UTTER *v.*¹ + -ANCE.]

**I.** †**1.** The disposal of goods, commodities, etc., by sale or barter. *Obs.*

**1436** *Rolls of Parlt.* IV. 499/1 If it seme come to, that utterance and sale of the seid Wolle..be so escarse. **1461** in *10th Rep. Hist. MSS. Comm.* App. V. 300 If ony citsaine ..wil gyve the utterance of ony marchandise..unto a strangere. *a* **1513** FABYAN *Chron.* VII. 630 Theyr vtteraunce of clothe of golde and sylkys to the..lordes of the realme. **1579** *Southampton Court Leet Rec.* (1906) II. 176 The fishemongers should have shoppes..built in the ffishe marcket for the..vtterance of the same. *c* **1630** T. MUN *Eng. Treas.* (1664) 18 We must..sell as cheap as possible..rather than to lose the utterance of such wares. **1632** in *10th Rep. Hist. MSS. Comm.* App. V. 478 The greate losse which husbandmen receive for want of utterance for their corne.

†**b.** In the phr. *to have* or *make* (...) *utterance.*

**1502** ARNOLDE *Chron.* (1811) 129 The said peper is so musty ..your said suppliant as yet can haue non vttraunce therof. *Ibid.*, He is neuer lyke to haue ani vttiraunce of the said peper heraftir. **1577** HARRISON *England* II. v. (1877) I. 136 By ridding their worke to make speedie vtterance of their wares. **1600** HAKLUYT *Voy.* (1810) III. 594 There hee had reasonable vtterance of his English commodities. **1622** MABBE tr. *Aleman's Guzman d'Alf.* II. 313 Having no such vtterance of her Ware. **1675** *Machiavelli's Prince* Wks. 258 Towards the Sea-side they have no utterance for any thing.

†**2.** The action of giving out of a store; issue. *Obs. rare.*

*a* **1483** *Liber Niger* in *Househ. Ord.* (1790) 57 That ye take ..suche oversightes of all..stuffe, comprised within your charge,..that the utterance of it be guyded to the King's most worship and profitt. **1603** BRETON *Packet Mad Lett.* xliii, Usurers are halfe mad, for lacke of vtterance of their mony. **1757** JOS. HARRIS *Coins* 86 Coining only ascertains the quantity of metal contained in the several pieces, at their utterance out of the mint.

*fig.* *c* **1585** *Fair Em* I. iv. 24 Nature vniust, in vtterance of thy arte, To grace a pesant with a Princes fame!

**3.** The action of uttering with the voice; vocal expression of something; speaking, speech. Also with *of.*

Also freq. from *c* 1667 in the phrase *to give utterance* (*to* something).

*c* **1456** PECOCK *Bk. of Faith* (1909) 130 A publisching or a nakid uttraunce, telling, or denouncing. **1474** CAXTON *Chesse* II. iii. (1883) 38 Oftetymes they selle as welle theyr scilence as theyr vtterance. **1489** *Cov. Leet Bk.* 536 For disclosure & vtteraunce of certain seducious langage. **1553** T. WILSON *Rhet.* 4 Utterance therefore is a framyng of the voyce, countenaunce, and gesture, after a comely maner. *a* **1589** PALFREYMAN *Baldwin's Mor. Philos.* (1600) 156 The holinesse and cleannesse of the mouth, standeth in the utterance of rightnesse and truth. **1589** GREENE *Menaphon* (Arb.) 51 Samela..seeing his vtterance full of broken sighes. **1642** MILTON *Apol. Smect.* 47 In vaine therefore do they pretend to want utterance in prayer, who can finde utterance to preach. **1648** WILKINS *Math. Magic* II. iv. 176 The utterance of articulate sounds. **1667** MILTON *P. L.* X. 1066 Adam..At length gave utterance to these words constraind. **1703** ROWE *Fair Penit.* I. i, Utterance all is vile; since I can only Swear you reign here, but never tell how much. **1784** COWPER *Task* VI. 339 The total herd..resolv'd..To give such act and utt'rance as they may To ecstasy. **1794** MRS. RADCLIFFE *Myst. Udolpho* xxix, Her courage failed as often as she attempted utterance. **1839** DICKENS *Nickleby* xii, With such energy of utterance as might have been..mistaken for rapture. **1847** MRS. S. AUSTIN *Ranke's Hist. Ref.* III. 141 These protests were only the utterance of the feeling that France yielded to force. **1861** GEO. ELIOT *Silas M.* ix, The Squire was purple with anger.., and found utterance difficult.

*transf.* **1602** SHAKS. *Ham.* III. ii. 378 These [*sc.* recorder stops] cannot I command to any vtterance of hermony, I haue not the skill. **1842** TENNYSON *Love & Duty* 61 We..to the want..Gave utterance by the yearning of an eye. *a* **1854** H. REED *Lect. Brit. Poets* i. (1857) 14 The souls of mighty poets finding utterance in the music of English words.

**b.** The action of expelling breath.

**1844** W. UPTON *Physioglyphics* 186 This primary reference ..of *a r*, to the utterance of the breath with earnestness.

**4.** The faculty or power of speech; manner of speaking.

**1474** CAXTON *Chesse* III. v. (1883) 119 The gracious speche and vtterance of rethorique. **1480** — *Trevisa's Higden* (1482) 140 He..was connyng in crafte of fayre vtteraunce.

1526 *Pilgr. Perf.* (W. de W. 1531) 30 To some persones is gyuen syngular good vtteraunce of eloquence. 1553 WILSON *Rhet.* 116 b, Hauing a good tongue,..he shall be thought to passe all other, that haue the like vtteraunce. 1602 *2nd Pt. Return Parnass.* III. i. 1151 It remaines to try whether you bee a man of good vtterance. 1667 MILTON *P. L.* III. 62 All the Sanctities of Heaven .. from his sight receiv'd Beatitude past utterance. 1676 DRYDEN *Aureng Z.* Ep. Ded. A 2 b, 'Tis onely because God has not bestow'd on them the gift of utterance. 1709 STEELE *Tatler* No. 27 ⁋ 5 She has naturally a very agreeable Voice and Utterance. 1782 MISS BURNEY *Cecilia* v. iv, All utterance seemed denied her. 1828 D'ISRAELI *Chas. I*, I. ii. 21 The King's difficult utterance rendered his addresses..painful to himself and the Parliament. 1848 DICKENS *Dombey* xxiii, A deep, gruff, husky utterance. 1871 TYLOR *Prim. Cult.* I. 45 A kind of Singhalese patois, peculiar in dialect and utterance.
*fig.* 1702 STEELE *Grief à-la-Mode* III. i. 43 Her Charms are Dumb, they want utterance.

**5.** That which is uttered or expressed in words; a spoken (or written) statement or expression; an articulated sound.

Freq. from *c* 1865, esp. with *an* and pl.

*c* 1454 PECOCK *Folewer* 103 Suche wordis, countenauncis, gesturis and vttrauncis. 1596 *Edw. III*, II. i, I might perceiue ..His eare to drinke her sweet tongues vtterance. 1667 MILTON *P. L.* IV. 410 Eve..turnd him all eare to heare new utterance flow. 1817 SHELLEY *Rev. Islam* VII. xxxii, Sweet melodies Of love..I caught,..when thy dear eyes Shone through my sleep, and did that utterance harmonize. 1831 CARLYLE *Sart. Res.* I. iii, To hear a whole series and river of the most memorable utterances. 1860 GEO. ELIOT in Cross *Life* (1884) II. 131 The 'Mill on the Floss' be it then!..The title is rather a laborious utterance. 1871 BLACKIE *Four Phases* i. 97 Let us attempt to analyse this utterance. 1887 BOWEN *Æneid* IV. 280 Horror bristles his locks, on his lips all utterance dies.

**II.** †**6.** A place of egress; an outlet. *Obs.*

1662 CHANDLER *Van Helmont's Oriat.* 222 In what part the Stomach layeth open at top,..is called its Orifice or mouth: But its utterance beneath [L. *infernus vero ejus exitus*], is named the *Pylorus* or Porter.

**Utterance²**. Now *lit.* or *arch.* Forms: 5-7, 9 **utterance**, 6 **-aunce**, 5 **vtterauns(e, -ans**, 5-6 **-aunce**, 6-7 **-ance**, 5 **uttraunce**, 6-7 **-ance**, 5-7 **vttraunce**, 5-6 **-anse**; 5 **vtraunce**, 6 **vterance**, **-aunce**, *Sc.* **vtyrrans**, **wterance**. [ad. OF. *oultrance*, *outrance*: see OUTRANCE.]

†**1.** A degree which surpasses bounds or goes beyond measure in respect of severity, vehemence, etc.; immoderate force or violence; excess, the uttermost. *Obs.*

*c* 1400 *Destr. Troy* 5130 Þen Vlixes, with vtterans vne vpponone, The derfe wordis of Diamede dullit with speche. *Ibid.* 5808 Vlixes with vtteraunse vnder his shild Mony stithe in stoure stroke on þere helmes. 1430-40 LYDG. *Bochas* IX. 3221 In tokne that God his quarel wolde auaunce, Disconfiture was maad on that partie, Vpon King Iohn be violent vttraunce. 1470-85 MALORY *Arthur* VII. v. 218 It doth me good to fele your myght and yet my lord I shewed not the vtteraunce. *a* 1513 FABYAN *Chron.* I. xv. (1811) 15 The Circumstaunce of the vtterans of yᵉ vnkyndnesse of his .ii. doughters. 1590 GREENE *Royal Exch.* B 1 b, Anie..that had [not] doone some exployte before in some battaile of vtterance.

**2. a.** *To* (*unto*, *into*) *the* (*such*, etc.) *utterance*, to an extreme degree; to the bitter end; to the last or utmost extremity. Freq. (*b*) with *fight*, etc. Now *lit.* or *arch.* (revived in 19th cent.).

*c* 1400 *Destr. Troy* 7981 Þat all the deire of the ded be done on vs two, To vttranse & yssue vne at this tyme. *c* 1450 LOVELICH *Merlin* 10088 So that they sworen..there-on to ben avenged jnto þe vttrawnce. 1470-85 MALORY *Arthur* VII. xii. 230 Thenne will I haue adoo with hym to the vtteraunce. 1525 LD. BERNERS *Froiss.* II. xlviii. 163 No frensshmen wolde vndertake to kepe it [*sc.* a town] to the vtteraunce, for it was not stronge ynoughe. 1567 PAYNELL tr. *Treas. Amadis of Gaule* 239, I must take the sword by the way of armes betwene you and me onely unto the utterance of your life or mine. 1587 GREENE *Euphues* Wks. (Grosart) VI. 158 To make a counterpoyse of discourtesie to the vtteraunce. 1601 HOLLAND *Pliny* I. 428 Corne steeped in water, whereof they will drinke to the utterance, and be drunke. 1605 SHAKS. *Macb.* III. i. 72 Come Fate into the Lyst, And champion me to th' vtterance.

1860 MOTLEY *Netherl.* iv. I. 130 The champion to the utterance against Spain, stood there with lance in rest. 1907 McCARTHY *Needles & Pins* xi, She had loved him well and proved it to the utterance.

(*b*) 1475 *Bk. Noblesse* 77 To doo armes in liestis to the utteraunce. 1512 *Helyas* in Thoms *Prose Rom.* (1828) III. 93 Here is my gauge to sustain it to the utteraunce. 1550 J. COKE *Eng. & Fr. Heralds* § 59 Heralde the usurper fought the battayle to th' utteraunce. 1578 H. WOTTON *Courtlie Controv.* 7 Thus the Gentlemen..skirmished to the vtterance. 1600 HOLLAND *Livy* 1126 He prepared warre with all his power to the utterance. 1606 — *Sueton.* 16 At the saide solemnity of sword-plaiers, there fought to the uttrance..Fvrivs Leptinvs..and A. Calpenvs.

1821 SOUTHEY *Exped. Orsua* 56, I will fight him to the utterance upon this quarrel. 1834 SIR H. TAYLOR *Artevelde* II. v. ii, The Lower Lis They to the utterance will dispute. 1837 BROWNING *Strafford* v. ii, I fought her [*sc.* England] to the utterance, I fell, I am hers now, and I will die.

†**b.** *To bring* or *put to* (or *unto*) *utterance*, to overcome completely, vanquish thoroughly; to bring to ruin or subjection, put to death. *Obs.*

1430 LYDG. *St. Margaret* 324 Thou hast me brought shortly to vttraunce, I am venquysshed. *c* 1430 — *Min. Poems* (Percy Soc.) 135 Whan Amelech was brouhte unto uttraunce. *c* 1477 CAXTON *Jason* 138 Whan his complices apperceyued that he was put to vtteraunce. 1509 BARCLAY *Shyp of Folys* 185 If thy iustyce sholde put vs to vttraunce, We sholde be damnyd for our mysgouernaunce. *a* 1533 LD. BERNERS *Huon* xvii. 47 He hath brought his enemy to vttranse, and slayne hym. 1596 Z. J. tr. *Lavardin's Hist. Scanderbeg* 92 The Christians increasing still in fury..did on all parts put them to utterance.
*fig.* 1509 BARCLAY *Shyp Folys* 226 Assaynge for to put our fayth to harde vttraunce.

†**3.** *At* (*the*) *utterance*: **a.** With the highest degree of energy or vigour; with the utmost force or violence; to the last or uttermost degree. Freq. with verbs, esp. *fight*. (Cf. 2 a.)

1480 CAXTON *Chron. Eng.* ccxlii. 148 b, Than thees two worthy lordes comen..and weren redy in the place for to fight at vtteraunce. 1485 — *Chas. Gt.* 62 They lete theyr horses renne wyth a grete courage for to Iuste at vtteraunce. *Ibid.* 142 Þe pylers of marble & other stones bygonnen to brenne & make fyre at vtteraunce. *a* 1548 HALL *Chron., Rich. III*, 26 He woulde fighte with hym at the vtteraunce. 1600 HOLLAND *Livy* 684 Corbis and Orsua made profession to trie the title at the utterance by dint of sword. 1611 SHAKS. *Cymb.* III. i. 73 Of him, I gather'd Honour, Which he, to seeke of me againe, perforce, Behooues me keepe at vtterance. *a* 1630 D. HUME *Hist. Ho. Douglas & Angus* (1644) 30 Hee used them so gently, which he would not have done if he had taken it [*sc.* the castle] at utterance.

†**b.** To the utmost *of* (one's power). *Obs.*

1513 DOUGLAS *Æneid* XII. ix. 124 Euery man..At the vtyrrans of all his fors gan fycht.

†**c.** At the last extremity. *Obs. rare*⁻¹.

1525 LD. BERNERS *Froiss.* II. xxiv. 26/1 A varlet..stode by and sawe the batayle...And whan he sawe his maister almost at vttraunce, he was sorie.

**U·tterancy.** *rare*⁻¹. [f. UTTER *v.*¹ + -ANCY. Cf. UTTERANCE¹.] The action of uttering or expressing.

1827 COLERIDGE *Improvisatore* Poems (1907) 356 A constitutional communicativeness and *utterancy* of heart and soul.

**Uttered** (ʌ·təɹd), *ppl. a.* [f. as prec. + -ED¹.] To which utterance has been given; expressed by the voice.

*a* 1586 SIDNEY *Apol. for Poetry* (Arb.) 27 The faulte is.. not in the sweet foode of sweetly vttered knowledge. 1593 *Sidney's Arcadia* IV. (1922) II. 112 Overwayed with her so wisely uttred affection. 1594 HOOKER *Eccl. Pol.* II. iv. § 1 The name of faith..must needs haue reference vnto some vttered word. 1801 SOUTHEY *Thalaba* IX. x, She wakes as from a dream, She asks the utter'd voice. 1820 KEATS *Eve St. Agnes* xxiii, No utter'd syllable, or, woe betide! 1858 CARLYLE *Fredk. Gt.* IX. i, Uttered intellect is not what permanently makes way, but unuttered.

**Utterer** (ʌ·tərəɹ), *sb.* Also 6 *Sc.* **-ar**. [f. as prec. + -ER¹.]

†**1.** One who sells; a seller, vendor. *Obs.*

1542-3 *Act* 34 & 35 *Hen. VIII*, c. 6 The Penaltie..shall oonelie extende to the Utterer and Seller of the saide Pynnes. 1593 *Brief Note Obs. Fish-Days* ⁋ 6 Net-makers, Saile-makers,..and Vtterers of Fish, maintained chiefly by fishing. 1653 *Ordin. Contin. Excise* 17 Mar. 110 For all Spirits..,upon every Gallon, to bee paid by the Utterer and Seller thereof, one shilling.

**b.** One who utters counterfeit coin, forged notes, etc.

1731 *Flying Post* 24 June 2/1 The Utterer of the forged Bank-notes. 1796 COLQUHOUN *Police Metropolis* 107 This sort of counterfeit coinage is..the least profitable to the Dealer; who..disposes of it to the utterers, vulgarly called Smashers. 1859 H. KINGSLEY *G. Hamlyn* xiii, We could lay our hands on the utterer of the [forged] cheques at any moment. 1862 H. MARRYAT *Year in Sweden* II. 241 Coiners and utterers of base money. 1887 *Pall Mall G.* 19 March 3/2 The coiners manufacture, and the utterers buy and distribute.

**2.** One who utters, speaks, or expresses in language.

1509 HAWES *Past. Pleas.* XII. (Percy Soc.) 47 Whan the utterer, wythout impediment,..Dothe his tale unto them tretably. 1567 DRANT *Horace, Ep.* To Rdr. *iiij, To be able vtterers of the gospell. 1594 HOOKER *Eccl. Pol.* II. iv. § 1 Things are made credible, either by the knowne Condition and qualitie of the Vtterer, or [etc.]. 1613 W. BROWNE *Brit. Past.* I. ii. 35 Barre I those lips? fit to be th' vttrers, when The heauens would parly with the chiefe of men. 1672 DRYDEN *Assignation* III. i, For Beatrix, she's a meer Utterer of Yes and No. 1785 HOLCROFT *Tales of Castle* (ed. 2) I. 69 Falsehood..sooner or later..brings dishonour on its utterer. 1841 S. WARREN *Ten Thousand a Year* II. iv, A single successful speech..opens before its utterer the shining doors of fashion. 1846 MAURICE *Relig. World* II. ii. (1861) 170 He feels and confesses himself to be only a reflection of the divine Light, an utterer of the divine Voice. 1893 LIDDON *Life Pusey* I. iv. 84 The utterer of maxims..useful to bear in mind.

†**b.** One who discloses, reveals, declares, or publishes. *Obs.*

1549 COVERDALE, etc. *Erasm. Par. Rom.* 18 The lawe is not authour of synne, but the vtterer and apeacher therof. 1560 DAUS tr. *Sleidane's Comm.* 101 That holy spyrit (vtterer of all truthe). 1587 HOLINSHED *Chron.* (ed. 2) III. 1132/1 The vtterer of which conspiracie was one White. 1590 SPENSER *F. Q.* II. ix. 25 Vtterers of secrets he from thence debard.

†**U·tterer**, *a. Obs. rare.* [A double comparative, f. UTTER *a.* + -ER³.] Situated farther out.

*c* 1410 *Lantern of Light* 73 Crist seide..sende him in to þe vttirar dercknes.

**Utterest** (ʌ·tərest), *a.* (*sb.*). Also 3 **uttrest**, 5 **otter(e)st**, **vttyreste**, **vterrest(e**, **vttrest(e**, **-ist**, **utteres**, *Sc.* **uterast**. [f. UTTER *a.* + -EST. Cf. OFris. *ûterst*, *utterst*, *utrest*, etc., OLG. *ûtrist*, MDu. *uterst* (Du. *uiterst*), OHG. *ûzar-*, *ûzzar-*, *ûzprosto*, etc. (MHG. *ûzzer-*, *-ûzereste*, G. *äusserst*), ON. *útarst* adv. (Da. *yderst*, Norw. *ytrast*, *yttarst*), MSw. *yterst(e*, *ytärsta*, etc. (Sw. *ytterst*), a superl. formed on a comparative: cf. OUTEREST *a.*]

Now rare, the usual form being *uttermost*.

**I.** †**1.** Most outward; = UTMOST *a.* 1. *Obs.*

*c* 1200 *Vices & Virtues* 17 Ðanne clepeð he his pineres, & hat hem me nemen,..& werpen me in ðe uttreste þiesternesse. *Ibid.*, Þe uttreste is se þiesternesse of hellě. *c* 1350 *Leg. Rood* 69 Þai fell In-to þe vtterest end of hell. *c* 1374 CHAUCER *Boeth.* I. pr. i. (1868) 7 Þo come sche nere and sette hir doun vpon þe vterreste corner of my bedde. 14.. *M. E. Med. Bk.* (Heinrich) 93 Doo away the vttrest barke. 1464 *Rolls of Parlt.* V. 568/2 Your seid Town is sette in the utterest place of this youre Reame. 1491 CAXTON *Vitas Patr.* (W. de W. 1495) I. xvi. 19 b/1 He had dwellyd in thutterest or last desertes of Heracleos.

**2. a.** Extreme; = UTMOST *a.* 2. Now *rare*.

*c* 1386 CHAUCER *Clerk's T.* 787 (Camb. MS.), His wif to tempte more To the vttyreste priue of hire corage. *c* 1400 *Pilgr. Sowle* III. iv. (Caxton, 1483) 53 Doyng yow to wite, that ye ben now wretchid poure Caitifs at the vtterest meschyef. *c* 1444 PECOCK *Donet* 90 Gloriose benefetis of god..ben in her vtterist goodnes and felicite. *a* 1470 H. PARKER *Dives & Pauper* (W. de W. 1496) II. ii. 120/2 Punysshed with the uttrest payne & torment. 1481 *Cely Papers* (Camden) 67, I schall do my best in sayelles [*sc.* sales] to my otterst poyer. 1530 BAYNTON in *Palsgr.* p. xii, He..may..in a brefe tyme attayne to his utterest desyre. 1883 J. PARKER *Tyne Ch.* 89 The utterest darkness of the wintriest night.

**b.** Of persons: That is such to a superlative degree; greatest.

1593 NASHE *Christ's T.* 8 If you should denie it,..the diuill (my vttrest enemy) would confirme it. 1873 'OUIDA' *Pascarèl* II. 140 The utterest fool..in all the universe.

†**3.** Last, final; = UTMOST *a.* 3. *Obs.*

*c* 1400 LOVE *Bonavent. Mirr.* xxxvi. (1908) 184 He wolde ..myȝtily suffre the malice of his pursueres in to the vtterest ende. *c* 1440 *Promp. Parv.* 513/1 Vttrest, and laste of alle,..*extremus*, *novissimus*. 1456 SIR G. HAYE *Law Arms* (S.T.S.) 272 Till all gude resoun of uterast conclusioun of understanding of this poynt. *c* 1470 G. ASHBY *Active Policy* 371 Thaugh your wytt excelle & be more hable To discerne the vtterest Iugement In any case to you appurtenent.

**II.** *absol.* or as *sb.*

†**4.** Extreme limit, part, etc.; = UTMOST *a.* 4.

*a* 1300 *E. E. Psalter* cxxxiv. 7 Fra vttrest of erthe kloudes ledand. *Ibid.* cxxxviii. 8 If i..eerde in vtrest of þe se. *a* 1325 *Prose Psalter* cxxxviii. 8 Ȝif þat y take my liȝtynges ..and wonne in þe vtterest [*Dublin MS.* vttermast] of þe see.

†**5.** The very most; = UTMOST *a.* 5, 5 b. *Obs.*

*c* 1410 *Lantern of Light* 122 We must do oure vttirest to conforme oure wille to þis. 1450 *Paston Lett.* I. 156 That wyll sette hym verely to do the utterest ayens yow. 1481 CAXTON *Reynard* (Arb.) 109, I haue not yet shewde the vtterist of my myght on yow. 1571 FORTESCUE *Forest* 145 b, Defending theim selues to their vtterest, from the force of any other. 1577 HELLOWES *Gueuara's Chron.* 41 Traiane did vtter and expend the vtterest of his skill, deuice, and policie, to take him.

**6.** *To the utterest*, = UTMOST *a.* 7.

*c* 1400 MAUNDEV. (Roxb.) xxiv. 111 Þe emperour..destruyd þam to þe vtterest. ? *c* 1430 *Brut* II. 437 Thei two ffoughten togederis, armyd at all poyntis, to the vtterist. 1474 *Stonor Papers* (Camden) I. 150 He seith hit..wolbe sued to the utterest accordyng to your title. 1481 CAXTON *Reynard* xlii. (Arb.) 115 Neuer for noman wold I torne fro yow, But abyde by yow to the utterist. 1571 FORTESCUE *Forest* 129 Paulus Emilius..did his paine to the vttereste, that his children should be like hym. 1884 J. PAYNE *Tales fr. Arabic* I. 302 She was distinguished to the utterest for chastity.

(*b*) 1513 W. SABYN in *Lett. & Papers War France* (1897) 142, I do yt to the utterest off my power. 1540 CROMWELL in Merriman *Life & Lett.* (1902) II. 272 To the utterest of my Remembraunce. 1549 COVERDALE, etc. *Erasm. Par. Rom.* 41 Jesus Christe, whose worke I labour in, to the vtterest of my power.

†**7.** *At* (*the*) *utterest*: **a.** = sense 6. *Obs.*

*c* 1420 *Brut* II. 355 Þeze ij worthi lordez comyn yn to þe ffelde, clene armed.., and were yn the place redy to fiȝt at þe vttrest. *c* 1449 PECOCK *Repr.* I. xvii. 99 If eny man dare not..suffre his feith and hise othere opinions be brouȝt into liȝt..to be at uttrist examyned.

†**b.** At the utmost limit or latest period of time. *Obs.*

*c* 1425 *Orolog. Sapient.* v. in *Anglia* X. 361/24 To-morowe or atte þe vtterist with-in þis seuen-nyȝte. 1487 *Cely Papers* (Camden) 169 Wythyn viij or x days wee schall knowe at the uttrest.

**U·ttering**, *vbl. sb.* [f. UTTER *v.*¹ + -ING¹.] The action of the verb, in various senses.

*c* 1400 *Found. St. Bartholomews* 45 For defawtynge of his hert, the vtteryng of his voice begane to breke. 1428 in *Surtees Misc.* (1890) 3 He gart forge yt in shapp of osmundes for uttering of his iren so into Iseland. *c* 1449 PECOCK *Repr.* I. xvi. 89 Bi greet kunnyng of preching and bi sauory vttring therof. 1530 PALSGR. 286/1 Uttryng or sellyng of ware, *uente*. 1579 SPENSER *Let. to Harvey* Wks. (1912) 635/1, I was minded for a while to haue intermitted the vttering of my writings. *a* 1586 SIDNEY *Arcadia* I. ii, An eloquence as sweete in the uttering, as slowe to come to the uttering. 1616 R. C. *Times' Whistle* (1871) 43 Daily each one, in vttering of his wares, Cosens his chapmen. 1633 T. STAFFORD *Pac. Hib.* II. iv. 157 Monies of this new Standard of Ireland, after their first uttering. 1648 in Rushw. *Hist. Coll.* III. (1692) I. 221 The Proclamation for the sole composition and uttering of Tabaco. 1742 *Act* 15 *Geo. II*, c. 28 The uttering of false Money, knowing it to be false, is a Crime. *a* 1777 in Evans *Old Ballads* I. 59 Nor fears [he] the blasting of his iron, Nor uttering of his wares. 1835 *Penny Cycl.* IV. 404/1 The uttering of any such forged bill or indorsement with a knowledge of the forgery, is a felony. 1887 *Pall Mall G.* 19 March 3/2 The coining and the uttering are generally two distinct branches.

**Utterless** (ʌ·təɹlės), *a.* [f. as prec. + -LESS.]

**1.** Incapable of being uttered; unutterable.

1643 MILTON *Divorce* 45 To endure a clamouring debate of utterles things. 1820 KEATS *Hyperion* II. 120 How he means to load His tongue with the full weight of utterless thought. **1840** LOWELL *The Moon* 12 Its only voice a vast dumb moan, Of utterless anguish speaking. *a* **1893** CHR. G. ROSSETTI *Poems* (1904) 271/2 Pangs of utterless desire.

**b.** Incapable of being expressed or described; inexpressible.

**1832** MOIR in *Blackw. Mag.* XXXI. 238 Cold were the heart, and bigoted indeed, Which..Could destine all that differ'd from his creed To utterless perdition. **1850** S. DOBELL *Roman* i. 14 By thine eternal youth, And coeternal utterless dishonour.

**2.** Incapable of utterance; speechless. *rare*—1.

**1854** S. DOBELL *Balder* xxiii. 100 As a trusting maid who waits Her far false lover,..Chilled with the bitter day where love is not, Blighted and mute,..Stands utterless.

†**U·tterlike,** *adv. Obs.*—1 [f. UTTER *a.* + -LIKE 2 b. Cf. UTTERLY *adv.*] = OUTWARDLY *adv.* 2.

*c* **1200** ORMIN 16510 Fele..Bigunnenn sone ann onn himm To lefenn..Acc nohht wiþþ innwarrd herrte ȝet, Ne nohht wiþþ fulle trowwþe, Acc utterlike.

†**U·tterly,** *a. Obs. rare.* Also 3 -liche. [f. UTTER *a.* + -LY1. Cf. MHG. *ûterlîk*, MDu. *ûterlic* (Du. *uiterlijk*), MHG. *ûzerlîch* (G. *äusserlich*), Da. *yderlig*, Sw. *ytterlig*, extreme, excessive.]

**1.** Open, manifest; = OPENLY *a.*

**12..** *Ancr. R.* 344 To eueriche preoste mei ancre schriuen hire of swuche openliche [*v.r.* utterliche] sunnen.

**2.** Absolute, extreme; final.

*c* **1440** *Gesta Rom.* xciv. 424, I clad my seruaunte, that is, my manhode, nought but to vtterly vtilite and necessite. **1553** GRESHAM *Let.* in *S. P. For. Edw. VI*, XII. fol. 37 (P.R.O.), Plenttye of merchauntes wythe-owght exsperyence and substaunce ys the vttyerly [*sic*] distruccioune of anny Realme.

**Utterly** (*v*·təɪli), *adv.* Forms: *α.* 3– utter-, 3–6 vtter- (5 *Sc.* wtter-), 4–6 vttir-, 4–5 uttir-, 5–6 uttur-, 6 ottorly; also 3–5 -liche, 4–5 -lich, -li (5 -le), 6–7 -lie, -lye. *β.* 4–5 vterliche, 4 uter-, 4–5 vterly (6 -lie), 4 vtyrly (*Sc.* wtirly), 6 vtirlie, -ly, vturlie; 4–5 vtrely, -li, *Sc.* wtrely, 5 wttrely, 4–5 wtraly, 5 vtraly, vtt-, wtt-, uttraly. [f. UTTER *a.* + -LY2. Cf. MLG. *uterlike*, *-liken*, MDu. *uterlike*, *-lijc*, *-lic* (Du. *uiterlijk*), MHG. *ûzerliche*, *-lich* (externally, etc.), ON. *útarliga* (far out); also ALL-UTTERLY, OUTERLY *advs.*]

†**1.** Without reserve or extenuation; sincerely, truly, plainly; straight out, straightway. *Obs.*

*a* **1225** *Ancr. R.* 206 Ine ȝuweðe me deð wundres: gulche hit ut ine schrifte, utterliche. *Ibid.* 314 Ȝif he nefde iseid utterliche þet ilke þing þet he dude ine childhode, he were idemed among þe uorlorene. *c* **1330** *Arth. & Merl.* 8615 (Kölbing), Ich ȝou sigge vterliche, Þei in þis warld war non oþer swiche [etc.]. *c* **1380** WYCLIF *Wks.* (1880) 213 Whanne it is reserued to þe holy gost to ȝeue vtterly conseil in special poyntis. **1450** FASTOLF in *Paston Lett.* I. 155 Yff the wydow wolle sylle it.., sendyth me utterly word, for I wolle not melle of it ellys thus avysed. **1539** BIBLE *Luke* iv. 23 Ye wyll utterly saye unto me this proverbe. **1558–9** *Act 1 Eliz.* c. 1 § 9, I A. B. doo utterly testifie and declare in my Conscience, that the Quenes Highnes is [etc.].

†**b.** Truly, verily, indeed. *Obs. rare.*

*c* **1400** *Beryn* 848 For vtterlich to have a child was al hir delite. **1526** TINDALE *1 Cor.* vi. 5 Ys there vtterly no wyse man amonge you? *Ibid.* 7.

**2.** In a complete or utter manner; to an absolute or extreme degree; altogether, entirely, absolutely; fully, thoroughly, out and out.

In very frequent use from *c* 1400 with *α*-form.

*α.* *c* **1374** CHAUCER *Troylus* II. 710 If I wolde vttirly his sight fle. *c* **1380** WYCLIF *Wks.* (1880) 280 Þat is vterly aȝenst goddis biddynge. *a* **1400–50** *Alexander* 1472 We er vtterly vndone. *c* **1430** *Syr Tryam.* 271 Marrok thoght utturly To do the quene a velanye. *c* **1489** CAXTON *Sonnes of Aymon* xxiv. 514 The persans shall be now vttirli discomfyted. **1528** ROY *Rede me* c ij, Par case they will not admitt But vtterly make resistence. **1568** GRAFTON *Chron.* II. 283 They with in the Towne perceauing they were vtterly without reliefe. **1593** *Sidney's Arcadia* IV. (1922) II 117 Ah of all sides utterly ruined Philoclea, said she. **1615** G. SANDYS *Trav.* 92 The suburbes..are vtterly razed. **1651** HOBBES *Leviath.* II. xxvi. 150 The Common-wealth faileth, and is Utterly dissolved; as a building whose Foundation is destroyed. *a* **1700** EVELYN *Diary* 23 March 1688, The French Tyrant..utterly taking away their estates, and their children. **1706** POPE *Let. to Wycherley* 10 April, Pray let me know your mind in this, for I am utterly at a loss. **1766** GOLDSM. *Vicar* xxviii, They will not be utterly forsaken. **1844** KINGLAKE *Eothen* v, The lowly grave..has closed over all his rich fancies... He is utterly married! **1865** KINGSLEY *Herew.* xxxvi, Torfrida turned herself utterly to serve the Lady Godiva. **1871** TYLOR *Prim. Cult.* I. 370 Men who so utterly believe that [etc.]. **1883** WHITELAW *Sophocles, Ajax* 519 My life hangs utterly on thee.

*β.* **1375** BARBOUR *Bruce* III. 196 Then wtraly wencusyt is he. *c* **1375** *Sc. Leg. Saints* xii. (*Mathias*) 115 Quhene he vyst wtrely, Þat it wes swa. *c* **1425** WYNTOUN *Cron.* I. xvi. 1556 (Cott. MS.), Men may trow ful werraly, And mystrow þis ful vttraly. *c* **1470** HENRY *Wallace* XI. 1377 So wttraly it suld beyn at his will. *c* **1520** M. NISBET *N. Test. in Scots* (S.T.S.) III. 269 And vtralie the fire tuichet nocht thame. **1596** DALRYMPLE tr. *Leslie's Hist. Scot.* (S.T.S.) I. 51 The fatt syde..hes throuch leinnes bene vtirlie deformet.

**b.** Freq. with verbs of perishing, refusal, etc.

(*a*) *c* **1375** *Sc. Leg. Saints* iii. (*Andreas*) 430 Þat thinge restoryt is but wene, Þat utterly periste has bene. *c* **1380** WYCLIF *Last Age Ch.* (1840) 29 Petir þe Apostle..myȝte not uttirly distrie Symoun Magus, but bi helpe of Poul. *a* **1400** *Chast. Goddes Chyld.* 20 They falle in to perylle of deth or elles utterly they lityll and deye. **1456** SIR G. HAYE *Law Arms* (S.T.S.) 175 That he be in perile to be maid outhir crepill,..or to dee utterly. **1538** STARKEY *England* 19 Ther be men wych..affyrme..euery one in hys secte to be sauyd, and non to perysch vtturly. **1577** B. GOOGE *Heresbach's Husb.* II. (1586) 69 b, It vtterlie destroyeth them. **1611** BIBLE *2 Peter* ii. 12 They..shall vtterly perish in their owne corruption. **1631** GOUGE *God's Arrows* III. § 1. 181 Gods purpose against Amalek..was utterly to root him out. **1711** ADDISON *Spect.* No. 124 ⁋ 2 Millions of Volumes, that would be utterly annihilated. **1816** SHELLEY *Dæmon* 562 For what thou art shall perish utterly. **1860** TYNDALL *Glaciers* I. 98 It would be utterly destroyed before reaching the bottom. **1874** GREEN *Short Hist.* vi. § 3. 287 Literature indeed seemed..to have died as utterly as freedom itself.

(*b*) **1422** YONGE tr. *Secreta Secret.* 188 Thou shalt wythstonde a losengeoure vtreli. *c* **1450** tr. *De Imitatione* III. xxxvii. 107 Sonne, þou maist not haue parfit liberte, but þou denye þiself utterly. **1477** EARL RIVERS (Caxton) *Dictes* 66 He refused hit utterly. *a* **1513** FABYAN *Chron.* VII. (1811) 370 But peas was to theym vtterly denyed. **1558–9** *Act 1 Eliz.* c. 1 § 9 Therfore I doo utterly renounce and forsake all forraine Jurisdiccions. **1655** FULLER *Ch. Hist.* IX. 163 Whitgift..in the presence of the Queen utterly refused it. **1695** LD. PRESTON *Boeth.* III. 145 Fire doth utterly refuse any such Division. **1801** *Med. Jrnl.* V. 571 By utterly denying their origin from dentition, he has equally departed from truth. **1855** KINGSLEY *Westw. Ho!* xxvii, She refused utterly to sing anything but the songs and psalms.

**c.** Qualifying adjs. (Freq. from *c* 1660, esp. with words implying negation, defect, or opposition).

**1395** PURVEY *Remonstr.* (1851) 24 [It] is vttirli vnleful. **14..** in *Hist. Coll. Citizen London* (Camden) 123 Every subgett..shall be utterly fre. *c* **1489** CAXTON *Blanchardyn* 138 His suster..was vttyrly fayre. **1553** EDEN *Treat. New Ind.* (Arb.) 5 One not vtterlye ignoraunt hereof. *a* **1586** SIDNEY *Arcadia* III. xviii, The one [knight] was utterly unable to defend himselfe. **1641** J. JACKSON *True Evang. T.* III. 206 That all warres were utterly unlawfull. **1662** STILLINGFL. *Orig. Sacr.* II. ii. § 1 It was utterly impossible. **1728** MORGAN *Algiers* II. iv. 274 That of which he was utterly ignorant. **1777** R. WATSON *Philip II* (1793) II. XIV. 23 The limitations..were utterly repugnant to Philip's temper. **1815** SHELLEY *Alastor* 660 When heaven remained utterly black. **1844** THIRLWALL *Greece* VIII. lxii. 173 An utterly hollow pretext. **1871** B. TAYLOR *Faust* (1875) I. I. v. 69 There the utterly deepest bottom is. **1879** F. HARRISON *Choice of Bks.* i, It is..of utterly no importance.

†**Uttermore,** *a.* and *adv. Obs.* Forms: 4–5 vtter-, etc., vtirmere (6 *Sc.* -maire), 5–6 -mer; 4–7 -more, 5 vttermor. [f. UTTER *a.* + -MORE. Cf. ON. *útar meirr*, MSw. *yttermere* (Sw. *-mera*, Da. *ydermere*), and OUTERMORE *a.*]

**A.** *adj.* **1.** More outward, remoter, farther removed; exterior, outer (opp. to *inner*).

**1382** WYCLIF *Matt.* xxii. 13 His hondis and feet bounden, sende ȝee hym into vttermore derknessis. **14..** *Wycliffite Bible* Ezek. xlvi. 21 Wher thei shuln say sacrifice, that thei bere not out in to the vtmer [*v.r.* vttermore] house. *c* **1520** M. NISBET *Matt.* viii. 12 [They] salbe castin out into vttirmaire mirknessis. **1565** *Raynald's Byrth Mankynde* p. li, The seconde or vttermer infolder of the bottome of the matrix. *a* **1608** DEE *Relat. Spirits* I. (1659) 249 The foresaid letter,..and moreover..the Copy of the Emperour's letter, all in one uttermore paper closed (Letter like). **1610** HOLLAND *Camden's Brit.* I. 701 The two Pyramides in the middest..did almost touch one another: the uttermore stand not far off.

**2.** Very great; utmost. *rare*—1.

**1382** WYCLIF *Exod.* xx. 18 Al the puple..ferde and smitun togidere with vttermore drede.

**3.** External; secular; lay. *rare*—1.

**1395** PURVEY *Remonstr.* (1851) 138 It were bettere to him that ertheli dedes constreyniden him to deth, vndir vttirmore other worldli abide.

**4.** = OUTWARD *a.* 4. *rare*—1.

*a* **1420** *Wycliffite Bible* Prov. iii. 3 *margin*, Temperaunce and oneste in vtirmere conuersacioun.

**B.** *adv.* Farther outward. *rare*—1.

**1414** *26 Pol. Poems* 58 Whanne ȝe han made pes wiþ-ynne All ȝoure reme in vnyte, Vttere-more ȝe mot bygynne.

**Uttermost** (*v*·təɪmǒst), *a.* (*sb.*). Forms: see UTTER *a.*; also 4– -most, 5–7 -moste, 6 -moost; 4–5 -mest, -meste, 4–6 -mast, 5–6 -maste, 6 *Sc.* -maist; 4–5 vttre-, 5 vttrmest, 6 uttirmuste, *Sc.* utermost(e, vtermast. [f. UTTER *a.* + -MOST. Cf. OUTERMOST *a.*]

**I. 1.** Outermost; farthest out or off; remotest; = UTMOST *a.* 1 a, OUTMOST *a.* 1.

In frequent use *c* 1385–*c* 1630. Now somewhat *rare*.

**13..** *Coer de L.* 2911 [He swore] But yff it were i-brought adoun Be noon, the uttermeste wall, He scholde hym hew to peses small. **13..** *Prose Psalter* cxxxiv. 7 (Dublin MS.), Þe ottermast endes of þerþe. **1398** TREVISA *Barth. De P. R.* III. xx. (1495) 67 The vttermest sydes and partyes of the tongue. **1486** *Bk. St. Albans* a viij, The vttermest Clees ye shall call the Pety Sengles. **1585** LUPTON *Thous. Notable Th.* (1660) 37 The uttermost or last joint of the tail. **1632** LITHGOW *Trav.* I. 23 It reacheth..to the vttermost bounds of the Dutchy of Ferrara. **1651** HOBBES *Leviath.* III. xxxviii. 248 From the uttermost parts of the Earth. **1667** MILTON *P. L.* VII. 266 To the uttermost convex Of this great Round. **1819** SHELLEY *Mask of Anarchy* lxvii, From the corners uttermost Of the bounds of English coast. **1872** BLACKIE *Lays Highl.* Introd. 49 To indulge in the flight to uttermost Unst.

†**b.** Of garments or other coverings: = UTMOST *a.* 1 b. *Obs. rare.*

*c* **1471** FORTESCUE *Wks.* (1869) 452 If it be a pore Cote under their uttermost Garment. **1532–3** *Act 24 Hen. VIII*, c. 13 Their Gownes, Cootes with Sleves or other uttermost Garmentes. **1545** RAYNALD *Byrth Mankynde* I. ii. (1552) 1 b, Of the which [coats] the first and vttermost is called the skyn.

**c.** Greatest in extent; longest. *rare.*

*a* **1586** SIDNEY *Apol. Poetrie* (Arb.) 63 The vttermost time presupposed in it, should be..but one day. *a* **1586** — *Arcadia* III. xviii, [He] stood..with..his shield at the uttermost length of his arme.

**2.** Extreme; = UTMOST *a.* 2.

**13..** [see UTMOST *a.* 2]. **1429** *Rolls of Parlt.* IV. 352/1 To the uttermast distruction and anientisment of the said Merchantz. **1468** SIR J. PASTON in *Paston Lett.* II. 329 The uttermost pryse had not passyd v. mark. **1544** in Leadam *Star Chamber Cases* (Selden) II. 306 As they will answere ..for the same att their uttermost perilles. **1556** OLDE *Antichrist* 59 The best..that shoulde lye in his uttermost possible power to doo. **1607** NORDEN *Surv. Dial.* III. 88 You that haue bene here presently sworn to performe your uttermost duties. **1676** HALE *Contempl.* II. 212 Thou.. may'st most justly expect from the children of Men our uttermost Love, and Fear. **1702** H. DODWELL *Apol.* § 1 in S. Parker *Cicero's De Finibus*, The time wherein Philosophy ..received its uttermost Perfection. *a* **1796** in Morse *Amer. Geog.* I. 91 His friendships are.. faithful to the uttermost extremity. **1807** WORDSW. *White Doe* III. 91 A voice of uttermost joy. **1856** RUSKIN *Mod. Paint.* IV. 74 To speak with uttermost truth of expression. **1890** HALLETT *Thous. Miles on Elephant* 430 It is in the uttermost degree unlikely.

†**b.** Of persons: = UTTEREST *a.* 2 b. *Obs.*

**1572** FORREST *Theophilus* 743 Howe happened thee to goe ..Vnto his enemye moste vttermoste..? **1606** G. W[OODCOCKE] *Hist. Ivstine* XXII. 82 They were solde..to the vttermost enemy of their estate.

†**3.** Last in time; final. Cf. UTMOST *a.* 3. *Obs.*

*c* **1440** *York Myst.* xxxvii. 232 And Marie me menys þi modir hight, Þe vttiremeste ende of all þi kynne. **1463** *Paston Lett.* II. 133 For..the Sunday was the uttermest day. **1470–85** MALORY *Arthur* x. lxxxvi. 567 To the vttermest dayes of my lyf. **1549** COVERDALE, etc. *Erasm. Par.* 2 *Tim.* 20 He..is hable ynoughe to kepe vnto the vttermost daye, the thing that [etc.]. **1593** *Sidney's Arcadia* IV. (1922) II. 111 The uttermost instant is scope enough for him, to revoke every thing. **1600** HOLLAND *Livy* V. xxii. 195 b, The finall end and fall of Veij,..which even in this last and uttermost [L. *ultimus*] calamitie shewed her mightinesse.

**b.** Last of a series, store, etc. Chiefly in *uttermost farthing*.

**1553** LATIMER *Sermon on Lord's Prayer* (1562) 51 b, The lord..caste him into prison, there to lye till he had paied the vttermost farthing. **1611** BIBLE *Matt.* v. 26 Thou shalt by no meanes come out thence, till thou hast payd the vttermost farthing. **1622** BACON *Hen. VII*, 183 Vowing not to leaue him, till the vttermost drop of their bloud were spilt. **1630** *R. Johnson's Kingd. & Commw.* 446 The first borne is heire to all, even to the uttermost farthing. **1821–2** SHELLEY *Chas. I*, II. 77 The uttermost Farthing exact from those. **1837** CARLYLE *Fr. Rev.* III. II. viii, His accounts lie all ready, correct in black-on-white, to the uttermost farthing.

**II.** *absol.* or as *sb.*

**4.** External limit, part, etc.; = UTMOST *a.* 4.

**13..** [see UTTEREST *a.* 4]. **1382** WYCLIF *Deut.* vi. 15 Lest eny tyme the woodnes of the Lord..doo thee awey fro the vttermoost of the erthe. *c* **1520** M. NISBET *Acts* i. 8 In al Judee,..and into the vtermast of the erd. **1563** SHUTE *Archit.* D iv, From the vttermost of the Abacus. **1851** LONGF. *Gold. Leg.* III. *Nativity* iii. 43 The Angel of the uttermost Of all the shining, heavenly host.

**b.** *sb. pl.* = UTMOST *a.* 4 b. *Obs. rare.*

*a* **1390** *Wycliffite Bible* Isaiah xlii. 10 (MS. Douce 369), Singiþ..his praisynge fro þe vttermostis of þe erþ [L. *ab extremis terræ*]. (See also UTMOST *a.* 4 b.)

†**5.** The very most; = UTMOST *a.* 5, 5 b. *Obs.*

*a* **1425** tr. *Arderne's Treat. Fistula*, etc. 83 For þe vertu of þam aboute fire is þe vttermoste of strenght. ? **1477** *Stonor Papers* (Camden) II. 34 You schalle vnderstonde the vttermeste of my stomake. *a* **1513** FABYAN *Chron.* VII. (1811) 645 For the encrece & augmentacion thereof, to the vttermoost of theyr powers. **1526** *Pilgr. Perf.* (W. de W. 1531) 37 He wolde haue done his vttermost. **1578** H. WOTTON *Courtlie Controv.* 40 In doing wherof, you shall bynde me with the vttermoste of my seruice to acknowledge the honoure. *c* **1590** MARLOWE *Faustus* iii, But be resolute, And trie the vttermost magicke can performe. **1604** SHAKS. *Oth.* III. iv. 167 Ile moue your suite, And seeke to effect it to my vttermost. **1610** R. FIELD *Fifth Bk. Ch.* lvii. 466 The vttermost therefore that our Aduersaries can say, is [etc.]. **1638** JUNIUS *Paint. Ancients* 228 The uttermost on either side is vicious. **1668** SANDERSON *Cases* 75 Let the Daughters disobedience deserve all this uttermost of punishment, from the offended Father.

†**6. a.** End; issue; = UTMOST *a.* 6. *Obs. rare.*

**1470–85** MALORY *Arthur* VII. vii. 223 Aweye wille I not tyl I see the vttermest of this Iourneye. **1593** *Sidney's Arcadia* III. (1922) II. 4 Zelmane..had now looked to the uttermoste [*ed.* 1674 utmost] of it, and established her minde upon an assured determination.

**b.** The extreme or furthest limit (in time). *Obs.*—1

**1601** SHAKS *Jul. C.* II. i. 213 *Bru.* By the eight houre, is that the vttermost? *Cin.* Be that the vttermost, and faile not then.

**7.** *To the uttermost*, = UTMOST *a.* 7. Now *rare* or *Obs.*

*c* **1400** *Pilgr. Sowle* (Caxton, 1483) IV. xxix. 61 Ne he ne shalle nought ben of power..for to descryuen to the uttermost, be it good or badde. **1470–85** MALORY *Arthur* IV. vii. 128 To doo the bataille to the vttermest. **1526** *Pilgr. Perf.* 13 b, All the appetites of man shalbe replenysshed with all goodnes, and saciat with glory, to the vttermoste. **1588** A. KING tr. *Canisius' Catech.* 51 The sonne of god.. hes sufferit all things to the vttermaist. **1598** R BERNARD tr. *Terence* (1607) *Andria* IV. i, To labour to the vttermost with might and maine. **1605** *London Prodigal* III. ii, Her loue will then be tried to the vttermost. **1622** R. HAWKINS *Voy. S. Sea* 120 The cause that every man forceth himselfe to the vttermost, to doe the labour of two men. **1772** COOK *First Voyage* III. i. (1773) III. 493 They..seemed resolved to defend their coast to the uttermost. **1844** MRS. BROWNING *Lost Bower* lxxiii, The prayer preserves it greenly, to the last and uttermost. **1846** TRENCH *Mirac.* xxvii. 359 Now the Scribes were pressing the advantage which they had gained..to the uttermost. **1871** FREEMAN *Norm. Conq.* xviii. IV. 139 To withstand the stranger to the uttermost.

(*b*) **1489** *Rolls of Parlt.* VI. 424 True and faithfull service to the uttermost of his power. **1557** *Order of Hospitalls* E 4 b, To the best and uttermost of your wits and powers.

1593 *Sidney's Arcadia* v. (1922) II. 158 To the uttermost of my skill. 1594 HOOKER *Eccl. Pol.* II. i. § 1 That..we defend, to the vttermost of that habilitie which he hath giuen. 1611 BIBLE *Translators to Rdr.* ¶ 3 To haue care of Religion,..yea to promote it to the vttermost of their power. 1638 *Hamilton Papers* (Camden) 32 The Couenanters haue ..labored to the uttermost of ther pouer to procure the rescinding. 1725 DE FOE *Voy. round World* (1840) 183 The natives..will generally be..kind also to the uttermost of their power.

8. † a. *At the uttermost* (also *at uttermost*), = UTMOST *a.* 8. *Obs.*

1530 in W. H. Turner *Select. Rec. Oxford* (1880) 87 For every pott iij$^{s}$, or at the uttermuste iiij$^{s}$. 1535 LAYTON in *Lett. Suppress. Monast.* (Camden) 72 On Wedinsday by nyght, at utermoste. 1577 B. GOOGE *Heresbach's Husb.* I. 30 b, Within three monethes, or foure at the vttermost after they are sowen. 1582 N. LICHEFIELD tr. *Castanheda's Conq. E. Ind.* I. ii. 6 b, Not aboue thirtie leagues distaunt from thence at the vttermost.

b. *At one's uttermost*, at the utmost point of test or danger. *rare*$^{-1}$.

1859 TENNYSON *Marr. Geraint* 502 But if I live, So aid me Heaven when at mine uttermost, As I will make her truly my true wife.

**U·tterness.** [f. UTTER *a.* + -NESS.] The condition or quality of being utter, absolute, or complete; absoluteness.

1827 LYTTON *Falkland* II. 113, I have started to find the utterness of my desolation! 1871 *Daily News* 1 Mar., The utterness of her collapse. 1904 *Westm. Gaz.* 9 Nov. 2/1 He tried it on Catherine—with a resulting utterness of failure.

**Utterquidaunce**, var. OUTRECUIDANCE *Obs.*

† **U·tterward**, *adv.* and *a.* *Obs. rare.* [f. UTTER *a.* or *adv.* + -WARD.]

A. *adv.* Outside; outwardly, externally.

1436 *Pol. Poems* (Rolls) II. 157 The trewe processe of Englysh polycye, Of utterwarde to kepe thys regne in rest Of oure England. 1538 in *Lett. Suppress. Monast.* (Camden) 228 The state of the howse bothe inwardely and utterward.

B. *adj.* Of confession: Made to a member of a religious house by a non-member.

c 1535 T. BEDYLL in G. J. Aungier *Syon Mon.* (1840) 88 To know his pleasire..towching the muring up of the howses of utterward confessions. [Cf. UTTWARD (quots. c 1535).]

**Utteward, utward**, obs. varr. (with shortened vowel) of OUTWARD *adv.*

a 1425 tr. *Arderne's Treat. Fistula*, etc. 12 Vpon þe aposteme, forsoþe, vtward be putte a gode emplastre. 1428 in *Surtees Misc.* (1888) 9 For other occupacions that he had to doo utteward.

**Uttrage(ouss**, obs. ff. OUTRAGE(OUS.

**Uttward, utward**, etc., obs. varr. (with shortened vowel) of OUTWARD *a.*

1503-4 *Act* 19 *Hen. VII*, c. 4 Preamble, Honour & Victorie..goten ageyne utwarde enymyes. 1526 TINDALE 2 *Cor.* iv. 16 Though oure vttward man perisshe. c 1535 T. BEDYLL in G. J. Aungier *Syon Mon.* (1840) 87 The place where thes frires haue beene wont to hire uttward confessiouns of all commers. *Ibid.*, Hering of utward confessions hath beene the cause of muche evyl. [Cf. UTTERWARD *a.*]

‖ **Utu** (ū·tū). *New Zealand.* [a. Maori *utu* return for anything, satisfaction, reward, reply.] Recompense, satisfaction, return or price paid for injuries received.

1840 J. S. POLACK *Manners & Customs N. Zealand* II. 63 Utu or payment is invariably expected for any injustice committed [by the Maoris]. 1852 MUNDY *Antipodes* x. II. 89 'Utu', (which may be freely translated,) 'blood for blood', is with him [*sc.* the Maori] a sacred necessity. 1890 J. M. MOORE *N. Zealand* iii. 49 The utu, or satisfaction for murder (*lex talionis*), theft, or any other crime, .. was rigorously carried out among the Maoris.

b. *transf.* (See quot.)

1902 *Webster's Suppl.* 226/3 *Utu*,..any compensation, as for services rendered; reward, payment, wages; often corrupted to *hoot*.

**Utward(e**, ME. varr. OUTWARD *adv.* **Utwit, utwith**, obs. forms of OUTWITH. **Uuen** (in on uuen): see ANOVEN *adv.* **Uuenan, -en, -on**, varr. OVENON, -AN *Obs.* **Uut-yede**, obs. pa. t. of OUTGO.

**Uva** (yū·vă). Pl. **uvæ** (yū·vī). [L. *ūva* grape, uvula, etc. (whence It., Pr., Sp., Pg. *uva*, F. *uve*).]

† 1. (See quot.) *Obs. rare*$^{-1}$.

App. an error for, and misunderstanding of, UVEA.

1562 TURNER *Herbal* II. 67 Oliue..is good for the diseases of the ey called vua, and for wheles. [Hence in Langham *Garden of Health* (1579) 439.]

2. *Bot.* A grape or raisin; a grape-like fruit.

1670 EVELYN *Sylva* (ed. 2) 25 Nor may we here omit to mention the Galls, Misletoe, Polypod, Agaric (us'd in Antidots) Vuæ, Fungus's to make Tinder. [Hence in Mortimer *Husb.* (1707) 327.] 1753 *Chambers' Cycl.* Suppl., *Uva*, Grape. See the article *Grape*. 1862 M. C. COOKE *Man. Bot. Terms* 87 *Uva*, (Lat. a grape), applied to such succulent indehiscent fruits as have a central placenta. [Hence in *Imp. Dict.* (1884), and later Dicts.] 1892 C. E. ARMAND SEMPLE *Elem. Mat. Med.* 225 *Uvæ*—Raisins.—The ripe fruit of Vitis Vinifera.

3. *Uva ursi* (yū·vă₁ɔ·ɹsəi), the bearberry, *Arctostaphylos Uva-ursi*, a trailing plant valued as furnishing an astringent tonic.

1753 *Chambers' Cycl.* Suppl. s.v., There is only one known species of the *Uva Ursi*, which is the plant called..the whortle-berry. 1786 ABERCROMBIE *Arrangem.* 39 in *Gard. Assist.*, Evergreen Trees and Shrubs [include]..Uva ursi, or bearberry. 1820 GOOD *Nosology* 454 The powder of the uva *ursi*,..recommended by Linnéus as [a] valuable lithontriptic. 1822 *Encycl. Metrop.* (1845) XIV. 742 As a remedy the Uva-Ursi was used by the ancients. 1873 BENTLEY *Man. Bot.* (ed. 3) 562 Trailing Arbutus.—The leaves and stems possess similar properties to Uva-Ursi.

b. *Med.* The leaves of the bearberry, or an infusion of these.

1805 *Med. Jrnl.* 465 A combination of such medicines with the uva-ursi, was..administered. 1842 BRANDE *Dict. Sci.*, etc. 138 The leaves of this plant, under the name *uva ursi*, are used as an astringent and tonic in medicine. 1892 C. E. ARMAND SEMPLE *Mat. Med.* 318 Uva ursi may also be used for gleets.

Hence † **U·val** *a.*, = UVEAL *a.* 1. [Cf. F. *uval.*]

1656 BLOUNT *Glossogr.*, *Uval*,..pertaining to a Grape or Vine.

**Uvarovite** (uvæ·rŏvəit). *Min.* Also ouw-, uwarowite; ouw-, ouvarovite. [Named in 1832 by G. H. Hess, after Count S. S. *Uvarov*, President of St. Petersburg Academy: see -ITE$^{1}$ 2 b.] An emerald-green variety of garnet.

1837 DANA *System Mineralogy* 353 Ouwarowite..occurs in transparent emerald-green dodecahedrons. 1855 *Orr's Circ. Sci., Geol.*, etc. 526 Uwarowite.—Chrome and Lime Garnet...Translucent;..infusible. Found in the Ural. 1897 L. FLETCHER *Introd. Study Min.* 102 Uvarovite is a green chrome-garnet.

† **Uve.** *Obs.* [ad. L. *ūva* UVA.] = UVULA 1.

c 1530 *Judic. Urines* II. vii. 29 b, Epiglotum is moost parte all waye calleth in Phisike & in gramer also, vua or vuula, *anglice* y$^{e}$ vue, or y$^{e}$ vuule.

‖ **Uvea** (yū·vĭă). *Anat.* [med.L. *uvea* (whence It., Sp., Pg. *uvea*, F. *uvée*), f. L. *ūva* UVA.]

† 1. The posterior coloured surface or choroid coat of the eye. *Obs.*

1525 tr. *Jerome of Brunswick's Surg.* B j b/2 The vtter most [part of the coat]..is named vuea, & hath the hole of the ball of the iye. 1543 TRAHERON *Vigo's Chirurg.* Interpr. Words s.v., One of the skynnes of the eye is called vuea bycause it is lyke the stone of a grape. 1615 CROOKE *Body of Man* (1631) 555 Figure 4 sheweth the Vuea or Grapy coate with a portion of the Opticke Nerue. 1676 *Phil. Trans.* II. 746 Where he considers, why the Uvea or Choroides is black in Men, but of divers colours in Brutes. 1685 [see PUPIL *sb.*$^{2}$ 1 β]. 1728 CHAMBERS *Cycl.* (1738) s.v. *Eye*, The crystalline [humour], situate immediately under the aqueous, behind the uvea, opposite to the pupil. 1797 MRS. M. BRYAN *Syst. Astron.* 156 The uvea commences where the choroides divides from the sclerotica, from which part..the pupil is called the iris.

2. A layer of pigmented cells forming the posterior covering of the iris; the middle coat or vascular tunic of the eye, composed of the choroid, iris, and ciliary body; the uveal tract.

1745 R. JAMES *Med. Dict.* s.v. *Iris*, The generality of Anatomists call that Membrane, which I have spoke of under the Name of Iris, the Uvea. c 1760 A. MONRO *Anat. Nerves* Wks. (1781) 349 Small fibres..running along the choroid coat on the outside of the retina in their course to the uvea or iris. 1771 *Encycl. Brit.* I. 289/2 This portion [of the coat of the eye] goes commonly by the particular name of uvea..and..has likewise got the name of iris. 1838 *Penny Cycl.* X. 139/2 A vertical section of the globe, showing the ciliary body and processes with the uvea.

**Uveal** (yū·vĭăl), *a.* [f. UVE-A + -AL.]

† 1. (See quot. and cf. UVAL *a.*) *Obs. rare*$^{-0}$.

1658 PHILLIPS, *Uveal*, belonging to a Grape, like a Grape.

2. Pertaining or belonging to, constituting or consisting of, the uvea.

*Uveal tract*, = UVEA 2.

1658 PHILLIPS s.v. *Tunicle*, The Uveal, the Vitreal or glassy, and the Christalline [tunicles of the eye]. 1869 J. S. WELLS *Dis. Eye* iii. 144 The whole forming, in reality, one tissue, the uveal tract. 1891 *Lancet* 21 March 678/1 A glandular apparatus by which the aqueous humour is secreted. Dr. Nicati names it the 'uveal gland'. 1894 D. J. CUNNINGHAM *Man. Pract. Anat.* II. 624 The portion on the deep surface of the iris forms its posterior uveal pigmentary layer.

b. Affecting or occurring in the uvea.

1896 *Lancet* 15 Feb. 422/2 A case of Uveal Cysts in the Iris in a man aged forty-seven.

‖ **Uveitis** (yūvĭ₁əi·tis). *Path.* [mod.L., f. med. L. *uve-a* UVEA + -ITIS. Cf. F. *uvéite.*] Inflammation of the uvea.

1848 DUNGLISON *Med. Dict.* s.v. [Hence in later Dicts.] 1889 WALSHAM *The. & Pract. Surg.* (ed. 2) 499 Plastic uveitis is characterized by a great tendency to deposition of lymph.

**Uvel(e**, obs. ff. EVIL *a.* and *sb.*

**Uvelien**, ME. var. EVIL *v.* *Obs.*

**U·velloid**, *a.* [f. mod.L. *ūvell-a*, dim. of L. *ūva* UVA, + -OID.] Like or resembling a small cluster of grapes.

1880 W. SAVILLE-KENT *Man. Infusoria* I. 190 Similar, but detached, uvelloid clusters. *Ibid.* 191 The propagation of the species by the detachment of entire uvelloid masses.

† **U·vemest**, *a.* *Obs.* Forms: 1 ufemest, -myst, 3 ufenmeste; 3 uue- (huue-), uvemest, vuemest(e, uuemaste. [Late OE. *ufemest*, *-myst* (rare for *yfemest*, *yfemyst*), superl. of *ufera* (comparative, UVER *a.*), f. root *uf-*: see OVEMEST *a.*, and cf. UMEST *a.*] Uppermost; topmost; highest.

c 1000 ÆLFRIC *Hom.* II. 76 On midne dæg bið seo sunne on ðam ufemestum ryne stiȝende. c 1000 — *Genesis* xl. 17 (Laud MS.), On þam ufemystan windle wære maneȝra cynna ȝebæc. c 1200 [see OVEMEST *a.* a]. c 1205 LAY. 6085 Vp heo hine duden heȝe an ufenmeste þan turre. c 1220 *Bestiary* 775 Vp he ris..and steȝ to heuene uvemest. a 1225 *Ancr. R.* 328 Heo hudet eke hore ihole cloðes, & doð an alre vuemeste [*a* 1275 *Cotton MS.* ueward] on viterokes al to torene.

† **U·veous**, *a.* *Obs.* [a. late or med.L. *ūveus* (Quicherat): see UVE-A and -OUS.] = UVEAL *a.* 2.

1691 RAY *Creation* ii. (1692) 25 The Uveous Coat or Iris of the Eye. 1696 J. EDWARDS *Demonstr. Exist. God* II. 31 A round hole in the middle and forepart of this uveous membrane. 1710 J. CLARKE tr. *Rohault's Nat. Philos.* (1729) I. 281 The Rays..are hindred from going any further by the Uveous Tunick.

**U·ver**, *a.* Now *dial.* Forms: 1 uferra, ufera, ufara, 2–3 ufere, 3 uferre, vfere, vuere, uuere; *Sc.* 4, 6 uvyr, 6 uuir, 5 wuyr, vuir, 5–6 vuer, 6, 9 uver, uvir, 9 iver, ever; *dial.* 8–9 uvver, 9 uvvor. [OE. *uferra*, *ufera*, *ufara* (also *yferra*, *yfera*), = OS. *oƀarro*, MLG. *overe*, OHG. *obaro*, *obero*, etc. (MHG. and G. *obere*, *ober*); cf. ON. *øfri* (Icel. *efri*), MSw. *öfre*, *öffre* (Sw. *öfre*), Da. *øvre* (Norw.), *øver*. See also OVER *a.*]

1. a. That is higher or loftier in position; upper; = OVER *a.* 1.

c 825 *Vesp. Psalter* ciii. 3 Ðu biðeces in wetrum ða uferran his. c 897–c 1275 [see OVER *a.* 1 a]. 1372 *Reg. Mag. Sig. Scot.* 151 Baronia de Uvyrcrelyne. 1424 in *Antiq. Aberd. & Banff* (1862) IV. 388 Terras de..Nethirbulgny, Wuirbulgny, Midilmast Bulgny. 1495 *Ibid.* 439 Terrarum de Vuer Towiis, Nethir Towiis. 1511 *Reg. Privy Seal Scotl.* I. 342/2 Litera..super terris de le Uver part de Lany. 1550 *Abstr. Protocols Town Clerks of Glasgow* (1894) I. 18 The foir uvyr hows, viz., hall, chalmer and wairdrop, with the peis waist. 1596 DALRYMPLE tr. *Leslie's Hist. Scot.* I. 14 In vuir Clydisdale and in nethir Clidisdale. 1703 THORESBY *Let. to Ray*, *Uvver*, for *upper*, or *over*. 1808 JAMIESON s.v. *Ouer*. 1824 [CARR] *Craven Gloss.* 8 Th' uvver side o' th' Gill. 1828– in Yks., Derby, Leics., Northampt., and Shropsh. dialect use (*Eng. Dial. Dict.* s.v. OVER *a.* 21).

b. *Uver lip*, the upper lip; = OVER-LIP.

1027–34 *Laws of Cnut* in *Liebermann* 334 Þonne do man ut his eaȝan, & ceorfan of .. his earan & þa uferan lippan. 1788 [see OVER-LIP]. 1854 MISS BAKER *Northampt. Gloss.* 373. 1864 B. PRESTON *Poems* 10 (E.D.D.), His hair..spraated abt fro' t' uvvor lip. 1876 *Whitby Gloss.* 209.

c. *Uver hand*, the 'upper hand'; the superiority or mastery; = OVER-HAND *sb.*

c 1205 LAY. 18325 Þa wes hit swa ufel idon, þæt þat hæðene uolc þa ufere hond hafeden. 1562 WINȜET *Wks.* (S.T.S.) I. 50 *margin*, The wicket hes the vuir hand. 1808 JAMIESON s.v. *Ouer*, *The uvir hand*, the upper hand. 1828 *Craven Gloss.* II. 25 To have the..uvver-hand. 1891 *Sheffield Gloss.* Suppl. 42 He's got t' uvver hand of him.

† 2. Later; after; future; = OVER *a.* 5. *Obs.*

*Beowulf* 2200 Eft þæt ȝe-iode ufaran dogrum. c 1000, c 1205 [see OVER *a.* 5]. c 1205 LAY. 26035 Þa nolde Arður on slepen na wiht hine areppen, leste he an uferre daȝe up-bræid iherde.

† **U·ver-mar**, *adv.* *Obs.*$^{-1}$ In 3 uferr-mar. [f. OE. *ufor* higher, highest + *-mar* -MORE. Cf. ON. *ofar meir*, MSw. *öwermeer*, *öffuermere*.] Higher up; above.

c 1200 ORMIN 1715 All þiss icc seȝȝde ȝuw littlær Her uferr mar a litell.

**U·vermost**, *a.* Now *dial.* In 6 *Sc.* uvirmest, 9 *dial.* uvvermost, -must. [f. UVER *a.* + -MOST.] Uppermost; highest.

1549 *Burgh Rec. Stirling* (1887) 55 Anent the tua uvirmest lychtis. 1841 C. H. HARTSHORNE *Salopia Antiqua* 606 Gwon to th' uvvermost leasow. 1880 MISS JACKSON *Shropshire Word-bk.* 463 Keep the Maister's collars uvvermost.

† **U·veward**, *a.* *Obs.* In 1 ufeweard, ufawærd, ufweard, 3 uueward. [OE. *ufe-*, *ufeweard*, etc., f. root *uf-* (see OVEMEST *a.*) + *-weard* -WARD 2. Cf. OE. *ufanweard*, ON. *ofan-verðr*.] Upper, higher; forming the upper part. Also *absol.*

c 897 K. ÆLFRED *Gregory's Past. C.* i. 28 Forðon ða eaȝan bioð on ðæm lichoman foreweardum & ufeweardum. c 950 *Lindisf. Gosp.* Matt. xxvii. 51 And heonu waȝhrahel temples ..tosliten wæs..from ufawærd wið to nioðaweard. a 1000–c 1200 [see NETHEWARD *a.*]. a 1275 [see UVEMEST *a.*].

† **U·vid**, *a.* *Obs. rare.* [ad. L. *ūvid-us* damp, etc.] Moist, wet.

1656 BLOUNT *Glossogr.*, *Uvid*, moist, or wet. [Hence in PHILLIPS (1658).] 1762 *Gentl. Mag.* 544 On land, their uvid locks new grace acquire.

† **U·viferous**, *a.* *Obs.*$^{-0}$ [f. L. *ūvifer-us* bearing grapes (f. *ūv-a* UVA) + -OUS.] (See quot.)

1656 BLOUNT *Glossogr.*, *Uviferous*,..that bears Grapes or Vines.

**Uvrou, -ow**: see EUPHROE, YUFFROUW.

‖ **Uvula** (yū·viŭlă). Forms: 5–7 vuula, 6 uuula, 6–7 vvula, 7– uvula; 6 euuela, uuila, vuola, vuala. [a. med.L. *ūvula* (whence Sp. and Pg. *uvula*, It. *uvola*, *ugola*, OF. *uvule*, *uvele*, *huvele* UVULE), dim. of L. *ūva* UVA.]

1. *Anat.* The conical fleshy prolongation hanging from the middle of the pendent margin of the soft palate in man and some other primates.

c 1400 *Lanfranc's Cirurg.* 261 Aboue þis instrument is vuula þat is þe palet of þe mouþ & helpiþ for to make soun. *Ibid.*, Sumtyme vuula wexiþ to long. 1525 tr. *Jerome of Brunswick's Surg.* B ii/2 Tonge, rowfe, and vuula, y$^{e}$ whiche is a lytell deme hangynge in y$^{e}$ throte lyke the spynne. 1569 ANDROSE *Alexis' Bk. Med.* III. 33 Against the falling of the Vuola, and swelling of the Pallate. 1607 TOPSELL *Four-f. Beasts* 495 Good and ready helpes for the sorenes of the vuula which is in the Horses mouthes. c 1645 HOWELL *Lett.* II. i. (1650) 1 The same defluxion..fell..into my throat in Oxford, and distilling upon the uvula impeached my utterance a little. 1676 WISEMAN *Surg.* IV. vii. 333 An Elongation of the Uvula through the abundance of salivous Humour flowing upon it. 1705 *Phil. Trans.* XXV. 1984 The Uvula..is moved by three pair of Muscles. 1724 RAMSAY *Health* 183 When th' uvula has got its mortal wound. 1753 TORRIANO *Gangr. Sore Throat* 4 After having examin'd her, they found the Uvula much lengthened. **1805** *Med. Jrnl.* XIV. 150 On inspecting the throat, the tonsils and uvula were not observably altered. **1831** R. KNOX *Cloquet's Anat.* 597 The uvula..forms the inferior edge of the velum palati into a double arch. **1866** HUXLEY *Physiol.* vi. 146 The soft palate, or velum—the middle of which is produced into a prolongation, the uvula. **1902** HUGHES & KEITH *Man. Pract. Anat.* III. 368 The uvula is connected with each tonsil by the furrowed band, to be seen when the uvula is pulled gently aside.

**b.** A small eminence forming the apex of the trigone, and projecting into the urethral orifice.

**1835-6** *Todd's Cycl. Anat.* I. 386/1 The uvula in the child is the most depending part of the bladder. **1861** SIR. H. THOMPSON *Dis. Prostate* (ed. 2) 7 The mucous membrane and submucous tissues around the internal meatus, particularly those forming the uvula or luette vesicale. *Ibid.* 26 A faint whitish line directly in front of the uvula.

**c.** A lobe or triangular elevation situated between the two tonsils of the cerebellum.

**1848** DUNGLISON *Med. Lex.* (ed. 7) 887 The inferior vermiform process..consisting of three portions—the pyramid, the uvula, and the nodulus.

†**2.** *ellipt.* Inflammation of the uvula; uvulitis.

**1539** ELYOT *Cast. Helthe* (1541) 69 b, Whereby are ingendred Catarres or reumes, the uuula, the cough, and the stytche. **1570** T. WILSON *Demosth. Orat., Life* 133 Troubled with the Vvula being a swelling in the throte.

**3.** *attrib.* and *Comb.*, esp. in the names of surgical instruments for operating on the uvula, as *uvula elevator, scissors, spoon*, etc.; also **uvula-cushion** (see quot. 1884); **uvula trill** (see quot. 1908); † **uvula-wort**, the nettle-leaved bell-flower, *Campanula Trachelium.*

**1597** GERARDE *Herbal* II. ii. 366 [It] is called .. in English ..Throtewoort or *Vuula* woort, of the vertue it hath against the paine and swelling thereof. **1678** PHILLIPS (ed. 4), *Uvula-spoon*.. is an Instrument to be held right under the Uvula. **1710** [see UVULAR *a.* 1]. **1728** BRADLEY *Dict. Bot.* s.v., Uvula Wort; see Throat-wort. **1869** ELLIS *E. E. Pronunc.* I. 8 *R r* uvula trill, F. *r* provençal or grasseyé. *Ibid.* 198 A sharp uvula rattle without any moisture. **1875** KNIGHT *Dict. Mech.* 2685/2 Uvula-scissors with claws. **1876** tr. *Ziemssen's Cycl. Pract. Med.* IV. 43 The instrument.. called the uvula-holder. *Ibid.* 67 A uvula elevator. **1884** M. MACKENZIE *Dis. Throat & Nose* II. 253 Beneath the septum the base of the uvula containing the azygos muscle forms a slight projection, called the 'uvula-cushion'. **1895** *Arnold & Sons' Catal. Surg. Instrum.* p. xlv, Uvula Hook, Scissors, Twitch. **1908** SWEET *Sounds of English* 40 The 'burred *r*' is a uvula-trill; the uvula..is driven upwards by the force of the outgoing air [etc.].

**Uvular** (yū·viŭlăɹ), *a.* (*sb.*). [ad. mod.L. *ūvulār-is* (whence also F. *uvulaire*), f. med.L. *ūvula* UVULA.]

**1.** Used in disorders of the uvula. *rare*—¹.

**1710** T. FULLER *Pharm. Extemp.* (1719) 480 Uvular Powder..Let the Powder be blown upon the Uvula with a Pipe or Uvula Spoon.

**2.** Pertaining or belonging to the uvula.

**1843** WILKINSON *Swedenborg's Anim. Kingd.* I. ii. 67 The palatine and uvular glands. **1848** DUNGLISON *Dict. Med. Sci.* (ed. 7) 878 *Uvular glands*, are small follicles, belonging to the mucous membrane covering the uvula. **1891** *Cent. Dict.* s.v., Uvular muscle.

**3.** Produced by vibration of the uvula.

**1873** MURRAY *Dialect So. Counties* 241 The uvular trill in French Paris. **1884** *Schaff's Encycl. Relig. Knowl.* III. 2155 The Semitic alphabet is..characterized by fulness of guttural, uvular, and spirant consonants. **1889** ELLIS *E. E. Pronunc.* v. 642 The German uvular *r*.

**b.** As *sb.* A uvular consonant.

**1884** *Schaff's Encycl. Relig. Knowl.* III. 2155 In the several [Semitic] dialects, the movement has been towards a diminution of the number of gutturals and uvulars.

Hence **U·vularly** *adv.*, with a thick obstructed utterance, as when the uvula is unduly long.

**1860** DICKENS *Uncomm. Trav.* iii, Number Two laughed (very uvularly), and the skirmishers followed suit.

‖ **Uvularia** (yūviŭlē·riă). *Bot.* [early mod.L. *ūvulāria*, f. med.L. *ūvula* UVULA.]

†**1.** The S. European shrub *Ruscus Hypoglossum.*

**1706** PHILLIPS (ed. Kersey), *Uvularia*, the Herb Horse-tongue.

**2.** One or other species of *Uvularia*, a small liliaceous genus typical of the tribe *Uvulareæ* of melanthaceous plants.

**1829** LOUDON *Encycl. Plants* 271 A plant like an Uvularia in habit. **1846** LINDLEY *Veg. Kingd.* 199 Uvularias are said to be simply astringent. **1850** MISS WARNER *Wide World* xl, Wild columbine, the delicate corydalis, and more uvularias, which she called yellow bells.

**Uvulatome** (yū·viŭlătōum). [f. UVULA + Gr. τομ-ός cutting. Cf. UVULOTOME.] An instrument for cutting or removing the uvula.

**1872** COHEN *Dis. Throat* 145 An uvulatome..renders the operation very easy of performance. **1880** M. MACKENZIE *Dis. Throat & Nose* I. 13 The uvulatomes..in use in this country at the end of the eighteenth century were of very rough construction.

**Uvulatomy** (yūviŭlæ·tŏmi). [See prec. and -TOMY. Cf. UVULOTOMY.] The operation of cutting or excising the uvula.

**1887** *Lancet* 7 May 935/2 Uvulatomy gives very various results in the subsequent degree of discomfort during cicatrisation. **1890** BILLINGS *Nat. Med. Dict.* II. 731. [Hence in recent Dicts.]

† **Uvule.** Also 6 **vuels.** *Obs.* [a. older F. *uvule* (also OF. *uvele, huvele*), or ad. med.L. *ūvula* UVULA.]

**1.** *Anat.* = UVULA 1.

*c* **1530** *Judic. Urines* II. vii. 30 A sekenes yᵗ is called.. casus vuule, yᵗ is no more for to say but sekenes of vuule. **1547** BOORDE *Brev. Health* xxvi. 16 Metyng with reume at the vuels in the rough [= roof] of the mouth. *Ibid.* ccclxxviii. 121 In Englyshe it is named vuels the whiche doth lye in the roufe of the mouthe lyke lytle longe teetes.

**2.** (See quot.) *rare*—¹.

**1589** J. BANISTER *Antidotary* (1633) 87 A Gargarisme for them that be roofe-fallen, commonly called the Vvule.

‖ **Uvulitis** (yūviŭləi·tis). *Path.* [mod.L., f. med.L. *ūvul-a* UVULA + -ITIS. Cf. F. *uvulite.*] Inflammation of the uvula.

**1848** DUNGLISON *Med. Dict.* (ed. 7) 187 *Cionitis*, inflammation of the uvula; uvulitis. **1880** M. MACKENZIE *Dis. Throat & Nose* I. 18 [In] Uvulitis..the uvula..becomes intensely red, swollen, and elongated. **1897** *Allbutt's Syst. Med.* IV. 733 Chronic uvulitis is usually associated with chronic pharyngitis.

**Uvulotome** (yū·viŭlŏtōum). [f. *uvulo-*, used as comb. form of UVULA, + Gr. τομ-ός cutting.] = UVULATOME.

**1897** *Allbutt's Syst. Med.* IV. 734 In performing uvulotomy ..the tip of the uvula—unless the uvulotome be used—should be..gently drawn forward.

**Uvulo·tomy.** [See prec. and -TOMY.] = UVULATOMY.

**1889** *Buck's Handbk. Med. Sci.* VII. 505/2 At the present day uvulotomy is practised with an increasing degree of discretion. **1897** [see prec.].

**Uwing**, obs. Sc. f. OWING *ppl. a.*

**Uxorial** (ɒksōə·riăl), *a.* [f. L. *ūxōri-us* UXORIOUS *a.* + -AL.]

**1.** Of or pertaining to a wife or wives.

**1800** A. GEDDES *Crit. Rem. Script.* 172 The speech [of Zipporah (Exodus iv. 25)] is not a speech of reproach or indignation, but of uxorial endearment. **1837** BP. WILBERFORCE *Let.* in Ashwell *Life* (1880) I. 105 All your uxorial connections living in the neighbourhood. **1853** LYTTON *My Novel* IV. i, The beauty of wives—the uxorial beauty. **1896** *Parl. Papers, Turkey* No. 3 (1897) CI. 23 The rather generous uxorial laws of Islam.

**2.** = UXORIOUS *a.* 2.

**1853** LYTTON *My Novel* VIII. xii, Riccabocca..melted into absolute uxorial imbecility at the sight of that mute distress. **1872** F. W. ROBINSON *Bridge of Glass* II. xx, 'Waiting for your wife!' exclaimed Lady Coedstown. 'Uxorial, is it not?' he asked.

Hence **Uxoria·lity**, the condition of being a wife; wifehood. *rare*—¹.

*a* **1832** BENTHAM *Deontol.* (1834) I. 235 Maritality, uxoriality, paternity, maternity, filiality.

**Uxoricide**¹ (ɒksōə·risəid). [ad. mod.L. **ūxōricīd-a*, f. L. *ūxor* wife: see -CIDE 1.] One who murders his wife.

**1860** WORCESTER. **1889** *Macm. Mag.* Jan. 237/2 Henry.. the tyrant and uxoricide. **1894** *Columbus* (Ohio) *Dispatch* 13 Oct. 6/5 To-day the uxoricide was arrested.

**Uxo·ricide**². [ad. med.L. *ūxōricīd-ium*: see prec. and -CIDE 2.] The murder of one's wife.

**1854** *Fraser's Mag.* xlix. 307 Such a detail of premeditated murders, suicides,..uxoricides, and fratricides. **1861** GOLDW. SMITH *Doctr. Hist. Progress* 39 They can embrace..the butcherly vagrancy laws of a Tudor King, his brutal uxoricides, his persecutions. **1887** *Fortn. Rev.* Nov. 659 Adultery, incest, uxoricide, usually by poison, prostitution, are terribly frequent [in Sicily].

Hence **Uxo·ricidal** *a.*, of, pertaining or tending to, uxoricide.

**1891** *Cent. Dict.* (citing *Cornhill Mag.*).

**Uxorious** (ɒksōə·riəs). [f. L. *ūxōri-us* (f. *ūxor* wife): see -OUS.]

**1.** Of persons: Dotingly or submissively fond of a wife; devotedly attached to a wife.

**1598** BP. HALL *Sat.* IV. vi, Whose mannish housewives.. make a drudge of their uxorius mate. **1609** B. JONSON *Sil. Wom.* IV. i, Hee's an asse that will be so vxorious, to tie his affections to one circle. **1649** MILTON *Eikon.* 64 Effeminate and Uxorious Magistrates, govern'd and overswaid at home under a Feminine usurpation. **1680** C. NESSE *Ch. Hist.* 178 Whom, being an uxorious man, Jezabel his wife stirred up. **1730** FIELDING *Rape upon Rape* Wks. 1775 II. 39 You are not the only wife who would give her husband this advice...Were all men so uxorious to take it, Tyburn [etc.]. **1782** W. F. MARTYN *Geog. Mag.* I. 218 The uxorious monarch [*sc.* Solomon]. **1822** T. ATTWOOD in C. M. Wakefield *Life* (1885) vii. 89, I am a little what vulgar folks call uxorious, and am never truly eloquent upon any subject but my wife and children. **1836-7** DICKENS *Sk. Boz, Charac.* vii, A living warning to all uxorious old boys. **1899** *Allbutt's Syst. Med.* VIII. 150, I have found that uxorious men..may bring themselves into a somewhat similar state of debility.

*transf.* **1708** PRIOR *Turtle & Sparrow* 417 Uxorious Inmate, Bird obscene, Dar'st thou defile..These silent Seats of faithful Loves?

**b.** *fig.* (of inanimate objects, etc.).

**1634** CARTWRIGHT *Ordinary* I. iv, We have got One that will doe more good with 's tongue that way Than that uxorious showre that came from Heaven. **1719** D'URFEY *Pills* (1872) VI. 196 Weary Ploughmen cursed the Stay Of the too Uxorious Day. **1743** FRANCIS tr. *Hor., Odes* I. ii. 19 Th' uxorious River glides away,..smooth-winding to the Sea. **1813** H. & J. SMITH *Horace in London* 19 Sir Francis ..To father Thames commits his fate. In secret the uxorious tide Safe bears him to the Surrey side. **1863** CONINGTON tr. *Horace, Odes* I. ii. 20 Old Tiber,..spite of Jove, his banks o'erflows, Uxorious flood.

**2.** Of actions, etc.: Marked or characterized by excessive affection for one's wife.

**1623** B. JONSON *Time Vind.* ad fin., The Boy..hath plots upon you all. A Pensioner unto your wives, To keepe you in uxorious gives. **1631** WEEVER *Anc. Fun. Mon.* 13 Husbands ..were wont to straw..vpon the graues..of their deceased deare wiues,..diuers purple flowers: by which vxorious office, they did..lessen the griefe of their hearts. *a* **1704** T. BROWN *Dial. Dead* Wks. 1711 IV. 29 My dotage on her Charms had bred in me..a fond, blind, uxorious Vice. **1739** EARL ORRERY in *O. Papers* (1903) I. 269 My Hours..at Caledon.. slide away in uxorious happiness, and rustic Joys. **1813** *Edin. Rev.* XXI. 199 The..uxorious propensities of the dynasty. **1835** DICKENS *Sk. Boz, Mr. Watkins Tottle* i, A rather uncommon compound of strong uxorious inclinations, and an unparalleled degree of anti-connubial timidity. **1879** F W. FARRAR *St. Paul* I. 309 Claudius..with all his pedantic and uxorious eccentricity was not devoid..of kindness.

Hence **Uxo·riously** *adv.*

**1647** STAPYLTON *Juvenal* 87 If thou'lt uxoriously to one adhere, Submit thy willing necke the yoke to beare. **1693** DRYDEN tr. *Juvenal, Sat.* VI. 292 If thou art thus Uxoriously inclin'd, To bear thy Bondage. *a* **1721** SHEFFIELD (Dk. Buckhm.) *Wks.* (1753) II. 152 Uxoriously led by the nose all your life. **1827** SOUTHEY *Lett.* (1856) IV. 70 A foolish wife, of whom he was uxoriously fond. **1903** *Sat. Rev.* 28 Feb. 261/1 She is quite worthy to have plays written uxoriously round her.

**Uxo·riousness.** [f. prec. + -NESS.] The character or quality of being uxorious; doting or submissive fondness of one's wife.

**1626** DONNE *Serm.* 24 Feb. 12 If he satisfied her, and his owne Vxoriousnesse, any satisfaction is not nothing. **1688** PENTON *Guardian's Instruction* 26 You may manage your uxoriousness more warily than I have done. **1775** H. DOWNMAN *Infancy* II. 308 Courage may be changed To brutal force;..and tender Nuptial Love To mean Uxoriousness. **1830** D'ISRAELI *Chas. I*, III. vii. 120 Charles..is accused by all parties of..spiritless uxoriousness and subserviency to his Queen. **1859** TENNYSON *Marriage of Geraint* 60 A prince whose manhood was all gone, And molten down in mere uxoriousness.

**Uxtar**, obs. Sc. form of HUCKSTER *sb.* **Uȝten**, variant of UGHTEN *Obs.* **Uylie**, Sc. var. OIL *sb.*¹

† **Uyre**, obs. northern var. ORE².

**1530-1** *Durham Househ. Bk.* (Surtees) 47 In every lode 60 stone of uyre and 12 lb. of leyde to yᵉ ston.

**Uz**, dial. f. US *pron.*

**Uzzard**, variant (now dial.) of IZZARD.

*a* **1697** (*Bodl.*) *MS. Eng. Bib. c. 3* fol. 37 Uzzard, Z.

**Uzzle**, dial. var. OUZEL.